Merriam-Webster's Geographical Dictionary

THIRD EDITION

Merriam-Webster's Geographical Dictionary

THIRD EDITION

MERRIAM-WEBSTER, INCORPORATED, *Publishers*
Springfield, Massachusetts, U.S.A.

Library of Congress Cataloging in Publication Data
Main entry under title:

Merriam-Webster's geographical dictionary. — 3rd ed.
p. cm.
Rev. ed. of: Webster's new geographical dictionary. 1972.
ISBN 0-87779-546-0 (alk. paper)
1. Gazetteers. I. Merriam-Webster, Inc. II. Webster's new geographical dictionary.
G103.5.W42 1997
910′.3—dc21 96-52365
CIP

Made in the United States of America

8HC04

Contents

Preface

Merriam-Webster's Geographical Dictionary, Third Edition, is a completely new edition of a book that first appeared in 1949 as *Webster's Geographical Dictionary* and was reedited to appear in 1972 as *Webster's New Geographical Dictionary*. During the more than four decades that have passed since the book was introduced, the world has experienced many significant historical events and economic and political developments, and a sound geographical dictionary must reflect the place-name changes attendant on them. Many of those changes were recorded in successive revisions of the first two editions, but the limitations of revisions and the magnitude of change have now made it essential to review critically the entire work and recompose the book in a new edition.

In creating this work, the Merriam-Webster editiorial staff was faced with a formidable challenge. In addition to accommodating new names and information and checking for accuracy all the details provided within the entries, the varied stylings of place-names had to be studied in an attempt to provide as many variants as the reader might be likely to encounter. In choosing variants to include, the editors made decisions wherever possible on the basis of accumulated evidence. Current population figures worldwide were obtained where these were available, information on economic activity and points of interest was confirmed or corrected, and an extensive review of historical data was undertaken.

For many aspects of this project, Merriam-Webster's unique collection of citations of place-names and place-name pronunciations, which was begun prior to publication of the first edition of this book, proved an invaluable source. The editors were also very fortunate to be able to draw upon the staff and resources of Encyclopædia Britannica.

Merriam-Webster's Geographical Dictionary, Third Edition, is a comprehensive desk-sized guide to the places of the world. Its objective is to provide, in text and maps, essential information on spelling, pronunciation, type of feature, location, and depending on the nature of the entry, population, size (as area, height, depth, or length), economy, history, and other matters of importance. Entries have been selected on the basis of their usefulness and interest to the general reader and include the world's independent states, dependencies, major administrative subdivisions, largest cities, and significant natural and artificial physical features. In addition, a large number of entries of historical interest have been included. Inasmuch as this book will have its widest distribution in the United States and Canada, entries for those two countries, and to a lesser extent for other English-speaking states, have been included on a scale considerably broader than that used for other parts of the world. In the United States, for example, nearly all incorporated places with a population of 2500 or more have been included, and all county seats have been included without regard to population size. All incorporated places in Canada with a population of 4500 or more are included. Examples of minimum figures for other countries are as follows: Algeria 30,000, Bangladesh 100,000, Belgium 22,500, Brazil 50,000, China 100,000, Denmark 30,000, Egypt 50,000, El Salvador 40,000, Greece 75,000, India 50,000, Indonesia 50,000, Iran 75,000, Italy 30,000, Japan 75,000, Mexico 30,000, Nigeria 50,000, Norway 23,000, Pakistan 50,000, Portugal 25,000, Russia 40,000, Slovakia 25,000, South Africa 8000, South Korea 125,000, Spain 28,000, Sweden 32,000, Tanzania 15,000, Turkey 30,000, United Kingdom 10,000, and Venezuela 75,000. It is important to note that these figures were only general guidelines for the editors. A large number of communities with populations below the minima indicated above have been included because of their regional importance or historical interest.

The expanded front matter of this edition contains information that students of place-name usage will find especially interesting. Paragraphs on transliteration, variants, apostrophes, capitalization, and use of the definite article *the* with place-names have been added to give the reader an idea of the nuances of this usage and the number of variables that had to be considered in determining the entries. The tables of foreign-language geographical terms have been transferred to the back matter and enlarged to include more than a hundred additional terms, most of which appear in the boldface main entries of this dictionary as well. Joining these tables in the back matter is a section new for this edition—a glossary of terms used in the book that readers may find unfamiliar.

Merriam-Webster's Geographical Dictionary, Third Edition, is the result of a collective effort by the editorial staff of Merriam-Webster, Incorporated. Kathleen M. Doherty coordinated revision of historical information, assisted by Michael D. Roundy, Susan L. Brady, Rebecca R. Bryer, Deanna Chiasson, Michael G. Guzzi, Thomas F. Pitoniak, and Karen L. Wilkinson. The highly detailed job of cross-reference was handled by Adrienne M. Scholz with assistance from Donna L. Rickerby, Maria A. Sansalone, and editors Chiasson and Guzzi. Brian M. Sietsema reviewed and updated the pronunciations and end-of-line division points. James G. Lowe copyedited the manuscript. Miscellaneous editorial jobs were handled by Paul F. Cappellano, Jennifer N. Cislo, Jill J. Cooney, Jennifer S. Goss, Brett P. Palmer, Jennifer B. Tufts, and editors Guzzi, Roundy, and Sansalone. Special tasks were completed by editor Chiasson (Russian transliterations), editor Doherty (reference acquisition), and James L. Rader (foreign geographical terms and place-name origins). In addition to editors named above, proofreading was done by staff members Michael G. Belanger, Peter D. Haraty, Joan I. Narmontas, Stephen J. Perrault, Amy K. Van Vranken, Amy West, and Linda Picard Wood, and by freelance editors Cynthia S. Ashby, Margaret Bain, Mary W. Cornog, John Fiscella, and Karen P. Singson. Carol A. Fugiel provided clerical assistance. Scheduling and production were painstakingly directed by Madeline L. Novak, who in the latter job was assisted by editor Roundy. The maps in this book were provided by the Cartography Department of Encyclopædia Britannica, Incorporated. Members of that group who made important contributions to this project are Barbra A. Vogel, Brian L. Cantwell, Gregory P. Babiak, Steven Bogdan, John E. Nelson, and Antonio R. Perez. Special thanks are due editors Doherty and Novak, who made an extraordinary effort to see this project through, and Senior Vice President John M. Morse, whose advice and encouragement made this edition possible.

Daniel J. Hopkins
Editor

Explanatory Notes

In preparing *Merriam-Webster's Geographical Dictionary, Third Edition,* the objective has been clarity of presentation rather than absolute uniformity or rigid consistency in the arrangement of information. Thus the basic patterns of arrangement that are used in general throughout the book have been modified to suit the needs of particular entries. The basic patterns of the entries and the principal details of arrangement are described herein.

Alphabetical Arrangement of Entries

1. For entries in this dictionary, the ordinary rules of alphabetical sequence govern: (1) the single name; (2) this name with a preceding modifier—necessarily represented for alphabetical purposes with the modifier, preceded by a comma, following the name; (3) this name followed by another word or words. Thus:

George

George, Cape

George, Lake

George V Coast

George Land

A name containing a numeral, such as **George V Coast**, above, is alphabetized as if the numeral were spelled out. Likewise, the mountain peak **K2** is alphabetized as if it were "Ktwo."

A name spelled as a solid word or a hyphenated word precedes the same name when spelled as an open compound; thus **Georgetown** precedes **George Town**.

2. Names beginning with the prefix *Mc* or *M'* are all alphabetized as if spelled with the full form of this prefix, *Mac*. In alphabetizing, no distinction is made between these and other names (such as *Macclesfield*) in which the initial letters *M a c* are not a prefix.

3. Names of natural features, such as capes, lakes, points, and straits, are generally entered at the specific part of the full name; thus, Cape Malea is entered at **Malea, Cape**; Point Barrow is entered at **Barrow, Point**; Lake Michigan is at **Michigan, Lake**; Strait of Malacca is at **Malacca, Strait of**; Paso del Inca is at **Inca, Paso del**.

4. In many cases, the words *Bay, Island, Lake, Mount,* etc., have been included as part of the boldfaced vocabulary entry. With rare exceptions, the word *River* has been omitted, so, for example, the consultant looking for the Amazon River should look at **Amazon**.

5. In most cases, names beginning with *Al, El, De, Du, Des, L', La, Le, Les,* etc., are alphabetized at **Al**, **El**, **De**, etc., respectively. Names containing *The* are at the main word; thus, *The Everglades* is at **Everglades, The**.

6. Two or more names identical in spelling and pronunciation usually are combined in a single entry. Thus:

Thebes \'thēbz\. **1.** … Ancient ruined city, Egypt ….
2. Commune, E Central Greece region, Greece ….

7. Names with identical spelling that differ in pronunciation or etymology are often entered separately, as at **Acre**, **Bayonne**, and **Tigre**.

Guide Words

A pair of guide words is printed at the top of each page. The entries that fall alphabetically between the guide words are found on that page.

It is important to remember that alphabetical order rather than position of an entry on the page determines the selection of guide words. The first guide word is the alphabetically first boldfaced entry on the page and the second guide word is the alphabetically last boldfaced entry on the page (except as indicated below):

Dokkum	**Dominica**

The entry need not be a main entry. Another boldface word—a variant or a boldface word in the middle of a definition—may be selected as a guide word. For this reason the first or last main entry on a page is not always one of the guide words:

Duffel	**Dumfriesshire**

On page 334, where these guide words are used, **Dumfries and Galloway** is the last printed entry, but **Dumfriesshire**, a variant at sense 2 of **Dumfries**, is alphabetically later and so has been chosen as the second guide word. The boldface variant **Isola Lunga**, which appears on page 334 in the entry for **Dugi Otok**, was not chosen as a guide word because the guide words must be in alphabetical order from page to page. The first guide word on a page cannot precede alphabetically the last main entry on the previous page, and the second guide word on a page cannot follow alphabetically the first main entry on the next page.

Variants and Their Labels

Many of the entries in this dictionary show one or more boldfaced variant names. These variants fall into two major categories: acceptable alternatives and former names. When a former name is shown, the main entry is usually the current name, and the variant is preceded by one of the following labels:

formerly	indicates a simple name change
anc. (ancient)	indicates that the name following the label has been out of use for a long period
mostly formerly	indicates that there is still some use of the former name

When a name has reverted to a former name after a period during which a different name was used, the intervening name is simply preceded by the dates of use:

Ry•binsk …; *1946–57* **Shcher•ba•kov** …; *1984–89* **An•dro•pov**

Sometimes it is the ancient name that merits the definition, with a less important present-day name shown as a variant and labeled *mod.* (modern):

Daph•nae … *or mod.* **Tall al–Da•fa•na**

Acceptable alternative names may be spelling or styling variants, language variants, national names (as in the case of rivers that form or cross international boundaries), or names that serve some specific function (such as administrative names which differ from the names used by locals, or official names which are usually longer, more formal versions of widely used names):

Oder … *or Czech and Polish* **Odra** … River, cen. Europe; rises in the mountains of E Czech Republic; flows N through W Poland to join the Neisse 21 mi. (34 km.) SSE of Frankfurt, Germany, where it forms the boundary bet. Poland and Germany, thence N into the Baltic Sea …

Wu•xing …; *locally* **Hu•zhou**

San•tia•go …
4. *or in full* **Re•gión Met•ro•po•li•ta•na de Santiago**

In general, names that are separated by *or* are equally common variants. Both are acceptable and either one may be used according to personal preference. A name following the word *also* is a secondary variant and is used less frequently than the name or names that precede it. Nevertheless, it is an acceptable alternative. Once *also* is used to indicate a secondary variant, all following variants, which are also secondary, are preceded by *or*.

The labels *Eng.* (in the English language) and *angl.* (anglicized version) should be clearly distinguished. *Eng.* usually indicates translation or transliteration of the native name:

Campagna di Ro•ma … *or Eng. often* **Roman Campagna**

The label *angl.* usually indicates alteration to a form that native English speakers are more familiar with:

Ni•caea … **1.** *angl.* **Nice**

The inclusion of many variant names is not for the purpose of confusing the dictionary user, but to cover those spellings that are likely to be encountered in other sources and to make it clear that there is not always a single correct way to style a place-name.

Composite Entries

Names that are closely related to each other or that form parts of a whole are sometimes treated together in a single entry in order to give the consultant a more complete geographical and historical picture of their relationship. Such names are printed in boldfaced type. Thus, at **Gaul** are included the early divisions of the ancient country, at **Nile** are described the several sections of the river, at **Taymyr Peninsula** are included the similarly named **Taymyra River**, **Taymyr Lake**, **Taymyr Bay**, and **Taymyr Island**.

Transliteration

There is considerable variation in the methods that are used in English for transliterating place-names from languages not using the Roman alphabet. This dictionary includes transliterations that are judged to be reasonable and useful to the dictionary consultant.

Because the Pinyin method of transliterating Chinese is now prevalent, entries for Chinese place-names can be found under the Pinyin spelling. Wades-Giles transliterations, as well as older and more traditional stylings, are treated as variants at the main entry:

Bei•jing … *or W.-G.* **Pe•king** …; *or from 1928 to 1949* **Pei•ping**

For Russian names in the Cyrillic alphabet, the system of transliteration used by the United States Board on Geographic Names is followed in most cases for determining the place of entry:

Gus'–Khru•stal'•nyy *or* **Gus–Khru•stal•ny**

Exceptions are usually instances where an English spelling is far more prevalent than the strictly transliterated form:

Mos•cow … *or Russ.* **Mos•kva**

Ukrainian names are entered, wherever possible, as a transliteration from their Ukrainian spelling, with transliteration from the Russian spelling given as a variant:

Kry•vyy Rih … *or* **Kri•voy Rog** *also* **Kri•voi Rog**

Placement of definitions for places with names from other languages using Cyrillic (such as Belorussian and Bulgarian) is based on the spelling the dictionary user seems most likely to encounter:

Ho•myel' … *or* **Go•mel** … *or* **Ho•mel**

So•fia *also* **So•phia** … *or Bulg.* **So•fi•ya**

Great variation in methods of transliteration occurs with Arabic names. A survey of English-language sources shows a wide range of stylings with regard to spelling, hyphenation, capitalization, and use of diacritics. No single method is given preference in this dictionary. Entries for Arabic place-names can be found at the stylings that, according to available evidence, are the ones most likely to be encountered by the dictionary user, with less common stylings shown as variants:

El Faiyûm … *or* **Al Fay•yūm**

Al Qa•ţīf … *or* **Qa•tif** …; *mostly formerly* **El–Ka•tif**

Capitalization

Most entries in this dictionary begin with a capital letter. Foreign-language geographical terms, which are entered in the dictionary proper to direct users to the specific parts of names, are entered in capitalized form for consistency:

Ras … Arabic word meaning "cape"; for many names beginning with it, see the distinguishing element.

Gu•nung … *or* **Gu•nong** … Indonesian and Malaysian terms respectively, meaning "mountain," as in **Gunung Awu**, **Gunong Ta•han.** See 2d element of the name.

Such terms, however, should only be capitalized when they are being used as part of specific place-names, not when they occur in running text as ordinary words.

There is solid evidence for both capitalized and lowercased stylings of words that are sometimes considered general vocabulary terms. Thus, names such as *Equator/equator, North Pole/north pole, Outback/outback, Western Hemisphere/western hemisphere* can be styled according to user preference.

Foreign-language articles (such as *le* and *Das*) that begin place-names are capitalized or lowercased according to evidence, but likewise can be styled according to preference.

End-of-Line Division

The end-of-line division shown for a boldfaced name indicates those points at which the name may be broken at the end of a line. A name may be divided wherever a centered period or a hyphen appears in a boldfaced name. Thus, the place-name *Pe·tro·kre·post'* may be broken:

Pe-

Petro-

Petrokre-

and continued on the next line with:

trokrepost'

krepost'

post'

The rules for such division, established for each language by long and widespread practice, are in some respects more or less arbitrary; accordingly, the division of a name sometimes differs from that of its respelled pronunciation, which attempts to show how the word is syllabified when spoken.

A slanted double hyphen at the end of a line in this dictionary (as in the entry **Bandra**) stands for a hyphen that belongs at that point in a hyphenated word and that is retained when the word is written as a unit on one line.

Apostrophes in Place-names

Some place-names include words that look like possessives but that may or may not contain apostrophes. The presence or absence of apostrophes in such place-names in this dictionary is based on evidence. In many instances, names that originally contained apostrophes (such as *Harpers Ferry* and *Pikes Peak*) have lost them over time.

In entries that show forms containing and lacking an apostrophe as variants, the more commonly used styling is shown first:

Saint George's *or* **Saint Georges**

Generic Terms

Some boldfaced entry words and variants contain generic geographical terms (such as *shan* in **Tian Shan** and *peak* in **Nacimiento Peak**). Many of these terms are explained in the back matter: English language terms are defined in the glossary; foreign-language terms are shown in two lists that give their English equivalents.

In addition, there are several foreign-language generic terms entered in the dictionary proper. Such entries are included whenever a foreign generic term that is unfamiliar to most native English speakers appears as the first element in several place-names entered in this book. In such cases, the entry for the generic term instructs the consultant to check the alphabetical location of the distinguishing element, since that is where the definition is located:

Rio ... For most names of rivers beginning with Rio (Span. *Río,* Port. *Rio,* "river"), see the distinguishing element.

Wa·di ... In the Near East and North Africa Arabic word used in place names, meaning "valley, river, dry river bed." For names beginning with this term, see the 2d element (e.g., for Wadi al-Mawjib, see MAWJIB, WADI AL-).

Use of *The*

Certain types of place-names are frequently preceded by the capitalized or lowercased article *the:*

1. Names of rivers (*the Susquehanna, the Nile*), mountain ranges (*the White Mountains, the Alps*), island groups (*the Aleutian Islands, the Malay Archipelago*), and regions (*the Midwest, the Arctic*).
2. Place-names that are plural in form (*the Great Plains, The Netherlands*).
3. Place-names that are also general vocabulary terms (*the South, the Continent*).
4. Place-names that are adjective/noun compounds (*the Western Hemisphere, the Red Sea*).

Some place-names fall into more than one of these categories, while others, such as *The Bronx* and *the Ukraine,* occur with the article for obscure, usually historically-rooted reasons. Arguments for use or omission of the article with certain place-names are varied and complex. Factors that should be considered in such cases include whether the name will be used alone or in context, orally or in print (in text or on a map), formally or informally, and whether the name seems overly awkward without the article. To a lesser extent, the same usage considerations apply to capitalization of the article. However, the final determination should be user preference.

In most cases initial *the* is omitted from boldfaced place-names in this dictionary. Exceptions are made for a few entries for which evidence of usage with *the* is particularly strong. Examples include **Commonwealth, the** and **Continent, the**, where the article appears as part of the main entry word, and **Bahamas** and **Sudan**, where variants containing the article are shown.

Absence of the article from an entry does not preclude its use by the consultant and should not discourage such use when it is deemed appropriate. Considerable liberty is afforded in this regard. However, a cautionary remark is warranted here: for country names that are not plural in form (Gambia, Sudan, Ukraine), some people find use of the article inappropriate or offensive, despite its widespread occurrence.

Pronunciation

Pronunciation is indicated between a pair of reversed virgules \ \ immediately following a boldfaced place-name. A full key to pronunciation is given on page 26a, and a guide key appears at the bottom of each odd-numbered text page in the dictionary.

Effort has been made to secure accurate information on the pronunciation of all names included in the dictionary, and the pronunciations included are in large measure based on information supplied by native speakers and by consulting specialists. Where usage has established an anglicized pronunciation in addition to the local pronunciation, both are given.

Where there is more than one entry in which the same boldfaced name occurs, the pronunciation and syllabication usually appear only at the first entry:

Alas·ka \ə-'las-kə\
Alaska, Gulf of
Alaska Highway

If an entry word has two or more forms that are spelled differently but pronounced the same, the single pronunciation usually appears after all forms are given:

Abu Qir *also* **Abu·kir** *or* **Abou·kir** \ˌá-bü-'kēr\

In entries in which no syllabication and pronunciation are given, the syllabication and pronunciation are those of the nearest preceding entry. When there are preceding entries showing differing syllabications and pronunciations for the same term, those of the appropriate language apply. For the entries **Florida Bay** and **Florida City**, for example, the appropriate syllabication and pronunciation are found at the first entry for **Florida**, showing its use as a place-name in English, rather than at the second entry, which shows its use as a place-name in Spanish.

A hyphen that precedes or follows a pronunciation indicates an element that is given a pronunciation respelling in a previous entry or earlier in the same entry:

Al·föld, Great \'öl-ˌfœld\. ... The **Little Alföld** *also* **Kis–Alföld** \'kish-\ is a plain ...

To·wa·da \tō-'wä-dä\.

Towada–Ha·chi·man·tai National Park \-ˌhä-chē-'män-ˌtī\.

Pronunciations for generic terms such as *Island* in **Deception Island** or *Plateau* in **Kaibito Plateau** may be found in *Merriam-Webster's Collegiate Dictionary, Tenth Edition.*

Sense Order

For numbered parts within an entry, the order described below has been followed:

1. Senses are ordered alphabetically by country, except that places in the United States precede all others. For this purpose, territories and dependencies of the United States and dependencies of other countries are treated as if independent countries.

When, however, the entry name applies to a country, this sense is generally listed first, followed by the remaining senses in the order described above:

Denmark ... **1.** ... Kingdom, NW Europe ...
2. Town, Bamburg co., SW South Carolina ...

2. If more than one sense pertains to a particular country, natural features are listed before political entities, which are arranged in descending order, as in:

1. State or province ...
2. County ...
3. City (or town or village) ...

Definitional Material

1. The principal details of each entry (or each numbered part of an entry) treating a political division are given usually in the following order: the entry word in boldfaced type with end-of-line division points plainly indicated; pronunciation (where not given in a preceding entry); alternative forms and names in boldfaced type (with end-of-line division points and pronunciation); identification; location; area and population; geographical and physical features; economic data; and items of general interest, such as names of colleges and universities and historical information. If the information given on a particular topic (as history) is long enough, it is placed in a separate paragraph introduced by an italicized subject label.

Not all of the details of the basic pattern described above are included at each entry, since in some entries certain details are not applicable or are not of sufficient importance to warrant inclusion.

2. In entries treating natural features, besides the identifying description and the location, the following kinds of information are included: size, such as lengths of rivers, heights of mountains, lengths and areas of islands and of lakes; economic data, such as navigability of rivers, mineral wealth of mountains, agricultural and industrial products of islands; and historical information, such as date of discovery, colonization, or acquisition.

3. Details of information concerning U.S. states usually follow a definite basic pattern: the entry word with its end-of-line division points and pronunciation; identification; geographical location; rank in area and the area figure; rank in population and the population figure; capital; and date of admission to the Union. Then, in separate labeled paragraphs, come: nickname; state flower; motto; rivers; mountains; chief products; chief cities; counties or equivalent subdivisions listed in tabular form; and history.

4. The treatment of long entries of major countries, major administrative subdivisions, etc., follows more or less closely the general arrangement used for U.S. states (see paragraph 3., above).

5. Many administrative subdivisions, such as departments, provinces, and counties, are entered with only a cross-reference to a table at the main entry at which information about the mininstrative subdivision can be found. (See the section entitled *Cross-Reference* for a sample entry.) Others are described briefly at their own entries, following the general arrangement of information (see paragraph 1., above). Similar treatment is accorded to U.S. dams, national parks, national monuments, and other such entries.

6. Population data are presented in one of three ways: as estimates (e); as projected or preliminary census figures (p); as final census figures (c). The abbreviation immediately follows the year to which it applies (1990c, 1985e, etc.). In entries containing more than one population figure for the same year, the year is given only once.

Cross-Reference

Two general formats are used in this dictionary for cross-references, which direct the reader to look elsewhere for information. In one format, the name to which the consultant is directed is set in special type (SMALL CAPITALS) and preceded by the word "see." Such cross-references may stand alone as the only definitional matter for an entry or sense, or they may supplement the information in a definition. In the other type of cross-reference, the name to which the consultant is directed is set in regular roman type and is followed by the letters *q.v.* (for Latin *quod vide,* meaning "which see") or, if reference is to more than the one name, *qq.v.* (for Latin *quae vide,* meaning "which [plural] see"). Thus:

Eger … **1.** River, Germany and Czech Republic. See OHŘE. **2.** City, Czech Republic. See CHEB.

Euxine Sea. See BLACK SEA.

Fau•quier. County in Virginia. See table at VIRGINIA.

Federation of Malaya. See MALAYA, FEDERATION OF.

Fin•ger Lakes … incl. notably Lakes Seneca, Cayuga, Keuka, Canandaigua, Owasco, and Skaneateles (*qq.v.*).

Go•me•ra … One of the Canary Is. (*q.v.*)

Grand Coulee Dam. See UNITED STATES, *Dams and Reservoirs.*

Throughout this dictionary, the words UNITED STATES are used only in cross-entries and cross-references that refer to the entry **United States of America**.

Abbreviations and Symbols

Abbreviations are used throughout the book, in vocabulary entries, tables, and maps, wherever it is felt that their use saves space without jeopardizing clarity of meaning. Abbreviated points of the compass indicate direction and are not part of a place-name. They are set in sans serif type with no following period (thus: "SW Maine," meaning "southwestern Maine," and "SW of Hartford," meaning "southwest of Hartford"). A complete list of the abbreviations used in this book is given on pages 14a–15a.

The symbol ✻ used in definitions denotes a capital, and the symbol ⊗ denotes a county seat.

Tables

1. To make the information provided more usable, entries of certain classes of names are given in the form of tables, and each name in a table is also shown as a cross-entry at its own alphabetical place in the dictionary. For example, the counties of the state of California are listed in a table at **California**, and each county name is entered at its own alphabetical place, where a cross-reference directs the reader to the table; the metropolitan boroughs of London are given in tabular form at **London**, and each name is likewise cross-entered to the table at **London**. Other examples are the tables of ranges at **Alps** and dams at **Tennessee Valley Authority** and the several tables at **United States of America**.

2. The United States National Park System contains more than 350 units having approximately a dozen and a half different designations. In general, the designations used for the more prominent, earlier established, larger, and more numerous units of the park system are the ones presented in tables of information as part of the **United States** entry. Brief descriptions of the pertinent designations—national battlefield, national historical park, national military park, national monument, and national park—can be found in the glossary at the back of the book.

Biographical Names

The styling of biographical names used in entries is consistent with that of *Merriam-Webster's Collegiate Dictionary, Tenth Edition,* and *Merriam-Webster's Biographical Dictionary*.

With very few exceptions, we have glossed biographical names with descriptive identifiers (as in "religious reformer Girolamo Savonarola").

Abbreviations and Symbols

ab. about
abbr. abbreviated, abbreviation
A.D. Anno Domini (*Latin,* in the year of our Lord)
Adm. Admiral
A.F.B. Air Force Base
Ala. Alabama
Alb. Albania, Albanian
alt. altitude
Amer. America, American
anc. ancient
angl. anglicized
ANZUS Australia-New Zealand-United States Treaty
approx. approximate, approximately
Apr. April
Arab. Arabic
Ariz. Arizona
Ark. Arkansas
A.S.S.R. Autonomous Soviet Socialist Republic
Aug. August
Aust. Austria
Austl. Australia
Auton. Autonomous
av. average
A.V. Authorized Version
Ave. Avenue
Azer. Azerbaijan
B.C. Before Christ
Belg. Belgian, Belgium
bet. between
bib. biblical
Blvd. Boulevard
Bos. and Herz. Bosnia and Herzegovina
Braz. Brazilian
Brit. British
Bulg. Bulgaria, Bulgarian
c census (after a date)
c. circa (before a date; *Latin,* about)
C Centigrade
C. Cape
C.&D. Chesapeake and Delaware
Calif. California
Can. Canada, Canadian
Capt. Captain
cen. center, central
cent(s). century (centuries)
Chin. Chinese
Chron. Chronicles
co. county
Col. Colonel, Colossians
Coll. College, Collège
Colo. Colorado
COMECON Council for Mutual Economic Assistance
Conn. Connecticut
Cor. Corinthians
cos. counties
Cr. Creek
Croat. Croatian
cu. cubic
d. died
Dak. Dakota
Dan. Daniel, Danish
D.C. District of Columbia
Dec. December
Del. Delaware
Depr. Depression
dept(s). department(s)
Deut. Deuteronomy
dist(s). district(s)
div. division
Dr. Doctor
Du. Dutch
e estimate (after a date)
E east, eastern
EC European Community
Eccles. Ecclesiastes
EEC European Economic Community
EFTA European Free Trade Association
e.g. exempli gratia (*Latin,* for example)
elev. elevation
Eng. England, English
Eph., Ephes. Ephesians
esp. especially
est. estimate, estimated
Est. Estonia, Estonian
estab. established
Esth. Esther
etc. et cetera (*Latin,* and so forth)
EU European Union
Exod. Exodus
Ez., Ezr. Ezra
Ezek. Ezekiel
F Fahrenheit
Feb. February
Fed. Federation
ff. following
Finn. Finnish
fl. flourished
Fla. Florida
Flem. Flemish
form. former, formerly
fr. from
Fr. French, France
ft. foot, feet
Ft. Fort
Ga. Georgia
Gal. Galatians
Gen. General, Genesis
Gens. Generals
Ger. German, Germany
Gk. Greek
Gov. Governor
Hab. Habakkuk
Hag. Haggai
Heb. Hebrew(s)
Hist. Historic, Historical
Hos. Hosea
Hts. Heights
Hung. Hungarian, Hungary
I. Island
Icel. Icelandic
i.e. id est (*Latin,* that is)
Ill. Illinois
in. inch(es)
incl. including
incorp. incorporated
Ind. Indian, Indiana
Inst. Institute, Institution
Ir. Irish
Ire. Ireland
Is. Islands
Isa. Isaiah
Ital. Italian, Italy
Jan. January
Jas. James
Jer. Jeremiah
Josh. Joshua
Jp. Japan, Japanese
Jr. Junior
Judg. Judges
Kans. Kansas
km. kilometer(s)
Ky. Kentucky
La. Louisiana
Lam. Lamentations
lat. latitude
Lat. Latin
Lev. Leviticus
Lieut. Lieutenant
Lith. Lithuania, Lithuanian
long. longitude
Lt. Lieutenant
m. meter(s)
Mal. Malachi
Mar. March
Mass. Massachusetts
Matt. Matthew
max. maximum
Md. Maryland
Me. Maine
Mem. Memorial
met. metropolitan
Mex. Mexican, Mexico
mi. mile(s)
Mic. Micah
Mich. Michigan
Mil. Military
Minn. Minnesota
Miss. Mississippi

Mo.	Missouri
mod.	modern
Mon.	Monument
Mongol.	Mongolian
Mont.	Montana
Mt(s).	Mount(s), Mountain(s)
mtn.	mountain
munic.	municipal, municipality
N	north, northern
Nah.	Nahum
N.A.S.A.	National Aeronautics and Space Administration
Nat.	National
Nat'l	National
NATO	North Atlantic Treaty Organization
Naut.	Nautical
naut. mi.	nautical mile(s)
N.C.	North Carolina
NE	northeast, northeastern
Nebr.	Nebraska
Neh.	Nehemiah
Neth.	Netherlands
Nev.	Nevada
N.H.	New Hampshire
N.H.S.	National Historic Site
N.J.	New Jersey
N.M.	National Monument
N. Mex.	New Mexico
Norw.	Norway, Norwegian
Nov.	November
N.P.	National Park
N.T.	New Testament
Num.	Numbers
NW	northwest, northwestern
N.W. Terr.	Northwest Territories
N.Y.	New York
N.Z.	New Zealand
Ob.	Obadiah
occas.	occasional, occasionally
Oct.	October
O.E.	Old English
Okla.	Oklahoma
Ont.	Ontario
opp.	opposite
Ore.	Oregon
org.	organized
orig.	original, originally
O.T.	Old Testament
p	preliminary census (after a date)
p.	page
Pa.	Pennsylvania
Penin.	Peninsula
Pers.	Persian
Pet.	Peter
Phil.	Philippines
Pk.	Park
Pkwy.	Parkway
P.O.	Post Office
Pol.	Poland, Polish
pop.	population
Port.	Portugal, Portuguese
pp.	pages
P.R.	Puerto Rico
pron.	pronounced, pronunciation
prov(s).	province(s)
Prov.	Proverbs
Ps., Psa.	Psalms
pub.	published
qq.v.	quae vide (*Latin,* which [plural] see)
Que.	Quebec
q.v.	quod vide (*Latin,* which see)
R.	Río, Rio, River
Rd.	Road
Rec.	Recreational
Rep.	Republic
Res.	Reservation, Reservoir
Rev.	Revelation
R.I.	Rhode Island
Rom.	Romania, Romanian
R.R.	Railroad
Russ.	Russian
S	south, southern
Sam.	Samuel
S.C.	South Carolina
Sch.	School
Scot.	Scotland, Scottish
SE	southeast, southeastern
sep.	separate, separated
Sept.	September
Serb.	Serbian
S.F.S.R.	Soviet Federated Socialist Republic
Sol.	Solomon
Somal.	Somaliland
Span.	Spanish
sq.	square
sq. mi.	square mile(s)
Sr.	Senior
S.R.	Socialist Republic
S.S.R.	Soviet Socialist Republic
St.	Saint, Sankt, Sint, Street
Ste.	Sainte
Sts.	Saints
SW	southwest, southwestern
Swed.	Swedish
Switz.	Switzerland
Tenn.	Tennessee
Terr.	Territory
Tex.	Texas
Theo.	Theodore
Thess.	Thessalonians
Tim.	Timothy
U.K.	United Kingdom
Ukrain.	Ukrainian
UN	United Nations
unincorp.	unincorporated
Univ.	University
U.S.	United States
U.S.A.	United States of America
U.S.S.R.	Union of Soviet Socialist Republics
usu.	usual, usually
Va.	Virginia
var(s).	variant(s)
Vt.	Vermont
W	west, western
Wash.	Washington
W.-G.	Wade-Giles
Wis.	Wisconsin
W. Va.	West Virginia
WWI	World War I
WWII	World War II
Wyo.	Wyoming
yd(s).	yard(s)
Yorks.	Yorkshire
Zech.	Zechariah
Zeph.	Zephaniah

❋	capital
⊗	county seat, parish seat, district seat (Ontario)
°	degree(s)
′	minute(s)
″	second(s)
&	and
%	percent

Map Projections

The Globe

Technically, the earth is not round but is flattened at the poles and takes a shape most accurately described as an ellipsoid. The deviation from a perfect sphere is relatively minor, and although the distinction is of critical importance in surveying and geodesy, for most purposes it can be assumed that the earth is spherical.

A globe is the only true means of representing the surface of the earth and maintaining accurate relationships of location, direction, and distance, but it is often more desirable to have a flat map for reference. However, in order for a round globe to be portrayed as a flat map, various parts of the globe's surface must stretch or shrink, thereby altering the geometric qualities associated with it. To control this distortion, a systematic transformation of the sphere's surface must be made. The transformation and resultant new surface is usually derived mathematically and is referred to as the map projection.

An infinite number of map projections can be conceived, but the only ones which are effective are those projections which ensure that the spatial relationships between true (known) locations on the three-dimensional sphere are preserved on the two-dimensional flat map.

The four basic spatial properties of location are area, angle, distance, and direction. No map projection can preserve all four of these basic properties simultaneously. In fact, every map will possess some level of distortion in one or more of these dimensions. The map surface can be developed such that individual properties are preserved to a certain extent, or that certain combinations of properties are preserved to some extent, but every projection is, in some way, a compromise and must distort some properties in order to portray others accurately.

Before discussing the ways in which the sphere can be transformed, it is important to understand some basic characteristics of the globe and properties of scale.

The Graticule

By its nature a sphere has no natural starting or stopping point, but because the earth rotates and revolves in an ordered and regular way, ancient scientists and scholars were able to develop a reference system which could be fixed to its surface.

This spherical referencing system is anchored at the poles and is described in the north-south direction by a series of parallel circles (parallels) which vary in length as one moves toward the poles, and in the east-west direction by a series of circles (meridians) which are of equal length and converge at the poles.

The distance measures along these lines are known as latitude in the north-south direction, and longitude in the east-west direction. It is important to note that meridians are equal in length, meet at the poles, and are evenly spaced on the parallels, and that the distance between them decreases as they converge. Parallels decrease in length as they get closer to the poles, and are evenly spaced on the meridians, but the distance between them remains constant.

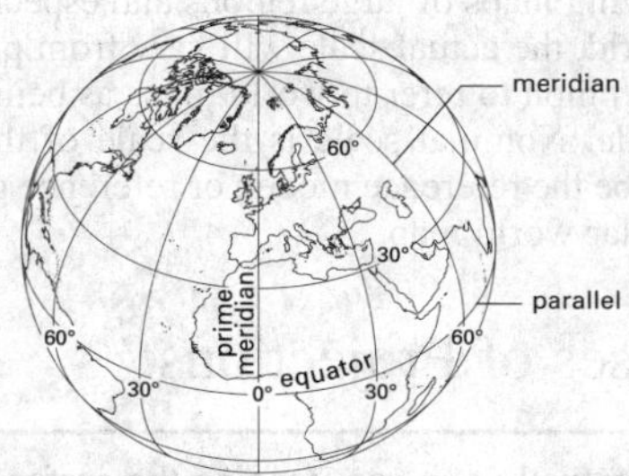

Figure 1. The globe reference grid is a network of parallels and meridians.

The reference grid system made up of parallels of latitude and meridians of longitude is often referred to as the graticule. It is by the systematic transformation of the graticule that the spatial relationships found on the globe are controlled and maintained.

Scale

Map scale is an expression of the relationship between some distance on the earth's surface and the corresponding representation on the map. Statements to indicate the nature of this relationship typically take several forms, the most common of which in modern mapping is the fraction or ratio. This is referred to as the "representative fraction" and is stated, for example, as 1:250,000.

$$\text{scale factor} = \frac{\text{distance on map}}{\text{distance on globe}}$$

Figure 2. The scale will vary from point to point on any map, but will be equal to 1.0 along the line or point on which the map is centered.

It is useful to think of maps as being either large or small scale. Large scale maps represent small areas of the earth's surface. Small scale maps represent large areas. A map with a representative fraction of 1:24,000 will be larger in scale and thus be capable of showing more detail than a map with a representative fraction of 1:250,000.

The exact point at which a specific scale is differentiated as being small or large is not formally defined, but in general, maps of regions, countries, or continents are referred to as being small in scale. This distinction is important because as the area to be mapped becomes larger, the error introduced by the curvature of the earth becomes more of a factor in controlling and understanding the nature of scale variations within any particular map. As stated earlier, it is not possible to flatten, or transform, the surface of a globe to a map without altering the spherical surface in some uneven manner. This means that the scale of the flat map will vary in different parts of the map, depending on the amount of flattening that has occurred. It is important to note that in the case of viewing maps of large regions and especially maps of the world, the actual scale will vary from point to point. It is common to refer to world maps as being of a nominal scale. Nominal scale is the scale of the globe that would be the reference model, or reference globe for that particular world map.

Classes of Projections

Conceptually one can imagine the surface of a sphere projected onto a sheet of paper that has been formed into a simple geometric shape of either a cylinder (wrapped around it), a cone (sitting on top of it), or a plane (tangential to it).

These simple geometric forms are then flattened into a two-dimensional surface to produce three basic classes of projections, characterized by the pattern of the grid formed by plotting the parallels and meridians on the flat map. These three classes of projections are referred to as either cylindrical, conic, or azimuthal (planar) in construction. As the illustrations show, the patterns of distortion are distinct for each class. In addition to these three basic shapes, discussed below, there is an oval class of projections, which includes many of the most optimal projections for portraying the world, and a fairly large class of unrelated and miscellaneous projections.

Cylindrical

Cylindrical projections are also referred to as rectangular projections, because their characteristic grid pattern is formed by lines of longitude that are parallel to each other and are crossed at right angles by the lines of latitude. While projections of this class are often used for world maps, forcing the globe onto this shape results in extreme shape distortion in many areas.

Perhaps because it produces maps that easily fit onto a page or wall, the cylindrical projection has become one of the most widely used and recognized classes of projections. Another reason for its popularity may be that it has been in use as the base for nautical charts for well over 300 years. It is for this use, in fact, that certain cylindrical projections are best suited. A straight line plotted on a cylindrical grid, having specific placement of the parallels in relation to the meridians, will represent a line of constant direction.

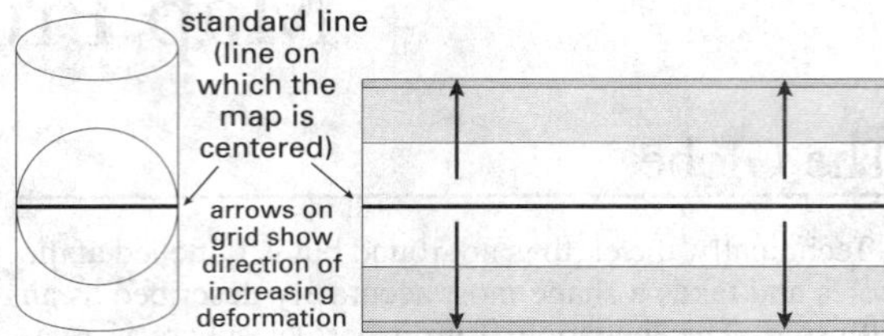

Figure 3. Tangential cylindrical grid and resulting pattern of deformation.

Conic

In general, a projection that is based on a cone where the axis of the cone is aligned with the axis of the globe will result in a pattern, when the cone is laid open, in which the meridians converge as they approach the poles and diverge as they move away.

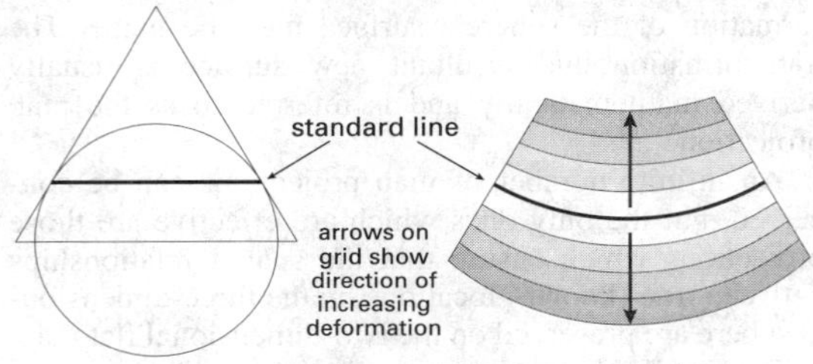

Figure 4. Tangential conic grid and resulting pattern of deformation.

Conic projections are typically not well suited for showing the world, but they are highly useful for plotting maps of areas that extend over large areas in an east-west orientation.

Azimuthal

Azimuthal projections are based on a plane, and one of their most significant attributes is that all directions from their center are correct. If the central point of the projection corresponds to one of the poles, then the parallels are shown as concentric circles and the meridians are straight lines radiating out from the center.

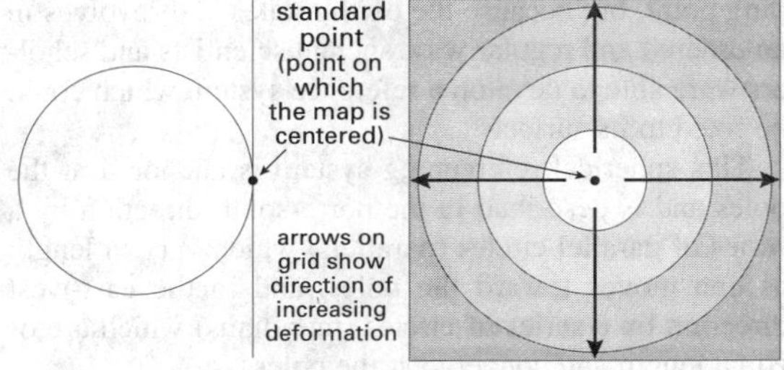

Figure 5. Tangential azimuthal grid and resulting pattern of deformation.

Most azimuthal projections are not useful for showing the whole globe, as the level of distortion becomes too great at the outer margins, and the outer boundary line of the map will be equivalent to the point opposite the point used as the center of the projection.

Attributes

We assume that the globe accurately represents certain characteristics of the earth's surface. These assumptions are: that areas are correctly shown, that distances are correctly represented, that the shape of any area is portrayed correctly, and that direction is true. Because no map can maintain all of these basic spatial properties, it is useful to further classify map projections based on the extent to which the map preserves a particular attribute.

Area

Often it is desirable to be able to represent areas in their correct proportions. This is especially true when comparing particular geographies or regions of similar geography. Projections that maintain correct proportions are known as equal-area projections. In this case, the relative size of features is maintained. The area is preserved but shape is distorted. For example, a circle drawn on the globe will appear as an ellipse when projected onto the map's flat surface.

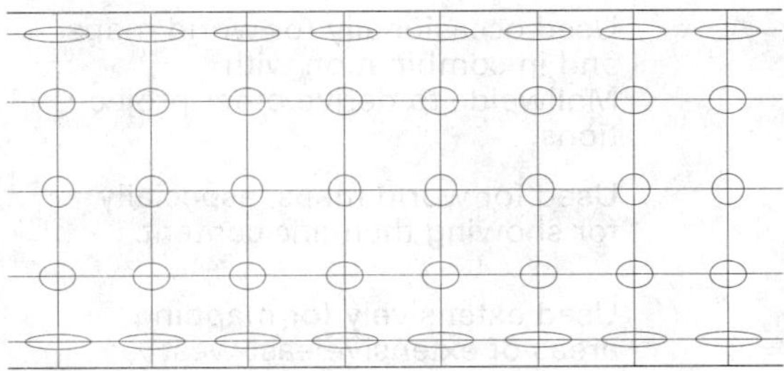

Figure 6. Cylindrical equal-area projection centered on 0°.

Angle (Shape)

When issues of navigation or movement from one place to another are of primary concern, it is important to have a map in which the angular distance between points is preserved. This attribute is referred to as conformality, and projections that preserve it are called conformal projections. The shapes of small features are preserved in such projections but area can become greatly distorted. A circle drawn on the globe becomes a larger or smaller circle depending on its location on the flat map.

Although the term *conformal* implies shape, it is only in a relative sense that those shapes can be preserved. The angular relationships at each point on the map are correct, but there will be a systematic change in scale when moving from point to point. Therefore, depending on the area to be covered, noticeable distortions can be observed in a map produced on a conformal projection.

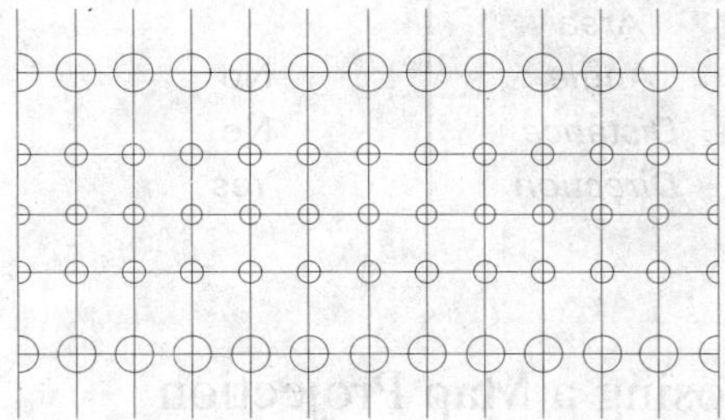

Figure 7. Cylindrical conformal projection centered on 0°.

Distance

No map can be uniform in scale, but when it is uniform in one direction, the projection is said to be equidistant. The property of equidistance can be achieved only in a limited sense, in that "true" distance on the map will only lie between points along the line that is of the same length at the nominal scale of the reference globe, and that scale can be maintained in all directions from only one or two points.

Direction

Direction is preserved, and direction to all points (relative to a central point) is true on projections called azimuthal projections.

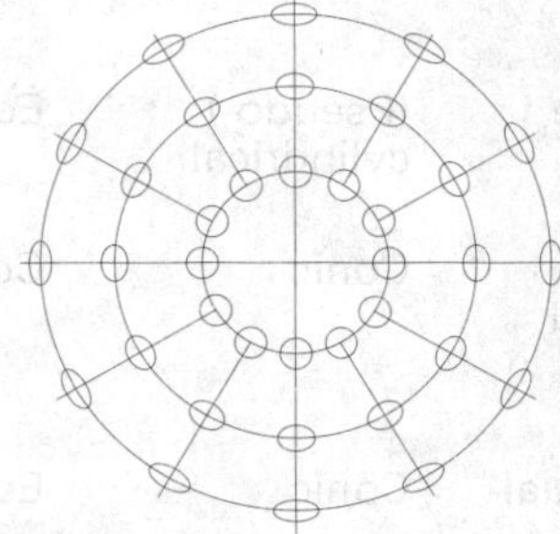

Figure 8. Azimuthal equal-area projection centered on tangent point and having 30° grid.

Combining of Attributes

Map projections can be developed such that certain combinations of properties are preserved. For example, a projection can have both true direction and true area, in which case it is called an azimuthal equal-area projection, or it can have both true direction and true distance, in which case it is called an azimuthal equidistant projection. However, as equivalence of area and conformality are mutually exclusive, no map can be both equal-area and conformal. The following table illustrates which properties can and cannot be combined into one projection.

Attribute	Area	Angle	Distance	Direction
Area	-	No	No	Yes
Angle	No	-	No	Yes
Distance	No	No	-	Yes
Direction	Yes	Yes	Yes	-

Choosing a Map Projection

The question of which map projection is best might be better stated as which map projection is most appropriate for the intended purpose of the map. For example, navigation demands correct direction, while road atlases will be concerned with preserving distance. Another important consideration is the extent and area of the region to be mapped.

Some common guidelines include the use of cylindrical projections for low latitudes, conic projections for middle latitudes, and azimuthal projections for polar views. World maps are rather special cases and are commonly shown on a class of projection that may be neither equal-area nor conformal, referred to as compromise projections, typically on an oval grid.

Common Map Projections

Name	Class	Attribute	Common Uses
Mercator	Cylindrical	Conformal	Best suited for navigation uses, but often used inappropriately for world maps.
Sinusoidal	(Pseudo-) cylindrical	Equal-area	Used occasionally for world maps and in combination with Mollweide to derive other projections.
Mollweide	(Pseudo-) cylindrical	Equal-area	Used for world maps, especially for showing thematic content.
Lambert Conformal Conic	Conic	Conformal	Used extensively for mapping areas of extensive east-west extent in the mid-latitudes (such as the U.S.).
Albers Equal-area	Conic	Equal-area	Similar to Lambert Conformal Conic in use.
Polyconic	Polyconic	Neither Equal-area nor Conformal	Used by U.S. Geological Survey in mapping topographic quadrangles and was used for early coastal charts and some military mapping.
Bonne	(Pseudo-) conic	Equal-area	Frequently used in atlases for showing continents.
Gnomonic	Azimuthal	Equal-area	Used most frequently in navigation.
Stereographic	Azimuthal	Conformal	Most often used for topographic maps of polar regions and for navigation.
Orthographic	Azimuthal	Neither Equal-area nor Conformal	Most popular use is for pictorial views of earth, especially as seen from space.

Map Symbols

Cities and towns

City symbol
(corresponding populations shown in map legend)

National capital

Second level political capital

Urban area (on insets)

Other Features

Lava flow

Dikes

Canal

Aqueduct

Falls

Rapids

Dam

Historical site

Point of interest

Historic wall

Continental divide

Boundaries

International

Disputed

Line of control

Disputed defacto

Regional

Political subdivision

Intermittent lake and stream

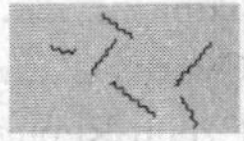
Reefs

Glacier

Tunnel

Pass (named)

Bridge (named)

Indian reservation

National park or reserve

National park site

Spot elevation:

above sea level

below sea level

List of Maps

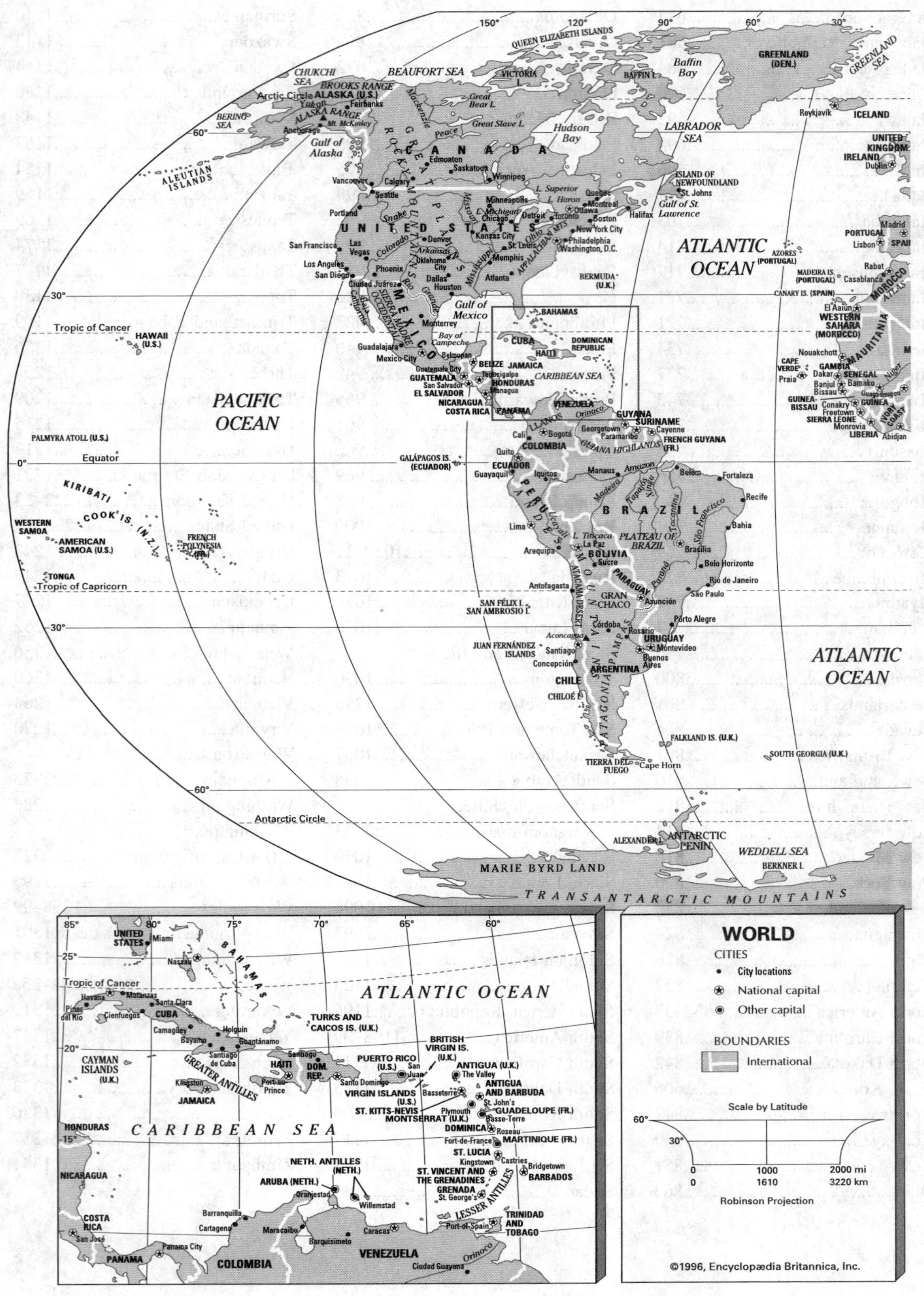

150°
120°
90°
60°
30°
QUEEN ELIZABETH ISLANDS
GREENLAND (DEN.)
GREENLAND SEA
Baffin Bay
BAFFIN I.
VICTORIA I.
BEAUFORT SEA
CHUKCHI SEA
BROOKS RANGE
ALASKA (U.S.)
Arctic Circle
Yukon
ALASKA RANGE
Fairbanks
Mt. McKinley
BERING SEA
Anchorage
Mackenzie
Great Bear L.
Great Slave L.
Peace
Hudson Bay
LABRADOR SEA
Reykjavík
ICELAND
UNITED KINGDOM
IRELAND
Dublin
Gulf of Alaska
ALEUTIAN ISLANDS
60°
CANADA
ROCKY MOUNTAINS
GREAT PLAINS
Edmonton
Saskatoon
Winnipeg
Vancouver
Calgary
Seattle
ISLAND OF NEWFOUNDLAND
St. Johns
L. Superior
Quebec
L. Huron
Montreal
Ottawa
Minneapolis
L. Michigan
Chicago
Detroit
Toronto
Boston
Halifax
Gulf of St. Lawrence
Portland
Snake
Missouri
New York City
Philadelphia
Washington, D.C.
UNITED STATES
APPALACHIAN MTS.
Ohio
Denver
Kansas City
St. Louis
Memphis
San Francisco
Las Vegas
Colorado
Arkansas
Oklahoma City
Mississippi
Los Angeles
San Diego
Phoenix
Dallas
Atlanta
Ciudad Juárez
Houston
Rio Grande
SIERRA MADRE OCCIDENTAL
Baja California
BERMUDA (U.K.)
ATLANTIC OCEAN
AZORES (PORTUGAL)
PORTUGAL
Lisbon
Madrid
SPAIN
Rabat
MADEIRA IS. (PORTUGAL)
Casablanca
MOROCCO
CANARY IS. (SPAIN)
El Aaiún
WESTERN SAHARA (MOROCCO)
MAURITANIA
Nouakchott
CAPE VERDE
Praia
GAMBIA
SENEGAL
Dakar
Banjul
Bamako
Bissau
GUINEA-BISSAU
Conakry
GUINEA
Freetown
SIERRA LEONE
Monrovia
LIBERIA
IVORY COAST
Abidjan
Niger
30°
Gulf of Mexico
MEXICO
SIERRA MADRE
Monterrey
Bay of Campeche
Tropic of Cancer
HAWAII (U.S.)
BAHAMAS
CUBA
DOMINICAN REPUBLIC
HAITI
JAMAICA
CARIBBEAN SEA
Guadalajara
Mexico City
Belmopan
BELIZE
Guatemala City
GUATEMALA
Tegucigalpa
HONDURAS
San Salvador
EL SALVADOR
Managua
NICARAGUA
COSTA RICA
PANAMA
PACIFIC OCEAN
VENEZUELA
Orinoco
GUYANA
SURINAME
Georgetown
Paramaribo
Cayenne
FRENCH GUYANA (FR.)
GUIANA HIGHLANDS
LLANOS
Cali
Bogotá
COLOMBIA
PALMYRA ATOLL (U.S.)
Equator
0°
GALÁPAGOS IS. (ECUADOR)
Quito
ECUADOR
Guayaquil
Iquitos
Manaus
Amazon
Belém
Fortaleza
Recife
KIRIBATI
COOK IS. (N.Z.)
WESTERN SAMOA
AMERICAN SAMOA (U.S.)
FRENCH POLYNESIA (FR.)
TONGA
Tropic of Capricorn
PERU
ANDES
Madeira
Tapajós
Xingu
Tocantins
BRAZIL
São Francisco
Lima
Ucayali
L. Titicaca
La Paz
PLATEAU OF BRAZIL
Bahia
Brasília
Arequipa
BOLIVIA
Sucre
Belo Horizonte
Antofagasta
ATACAMA DESERT
PARAGUAY
Paraná
Rio de Janeiro
São Paulo
GRAN CHACO
Asunción
SAN FÉLIX I.
SAN AMBROSIO I.
-30°
Pôrto Alegre
Córdoba
Rosario
Aconcagua
URUGUAY
Montevideo
JUAN FERNÁNDEZ ISLANDS
Santiago
Buenos Aires
PAMPAS
ATLANTIC OCEAN
Concepción
ARGENTINA
CHILE
CHILOÉ I.
PATAGONIA
FALKLAND IS. (U.K.)
SOUTH GEORGIA (U.K.)
TIERRA DEL FUEGO
Cape Horn
-60°
Antarctic Circle
ALEXANDER I.
ANTARCTIC PENIN.
WEDDELL SEA
BERKNER I.
MARIE BYRD LAND
TRANSANTARCTIC MOUNTAINS
85°
80°
75°
70°
65°
60°
UNITED STATES
Miami
Nassau
BAHAMAS
25°
Tropic of Cancer
ATLANTIC OCEAN
Havana
Matanzas
Santa Clara
Pinar del Río
Cienfuegos
CUBA
Camagüey
Holguín
TURKS AND CAICOS IS. (U.K.)
Bayamo
Guantánamo
20°
Santiago de Cuba
BRITISH VIRGIN IS. (U.K.)
CAYMAN ISLANDS (U.K.)
Santiago
HAITI
DOM. REP.
PUERTO RICO (U.S.)
San Juan
ANTIGUA (U.K.)
The Valley
GREATER ANTILLES
Kingston
JAMAICA
Port-au-Prince
Santo Domingo
ANTIGUA AND BARBUDA
VIRGIN ISLANDS (U.S.)
Basseterre
St. John's
ST. KITTS-NEVIS
Plymouth
GUADELOUPE (FR.)
MONTSERRAT (U.K.)
Basse-Terre
DOMINICA
HONDURAS
15°
CARIBBEAN SEA
Roseau
Fort-de-France
MARTINIQUE (FR.)
ST. LUCIA
Kingstown
Castries
Bridgetown
BARBADOS
NETH. ANTILLES (NETH.)
NICARAGUA
ST. VINCENT AND THE GRENADINES
ARUBA (NETH.)
Oranjestad
Willemstad
GRENADA
St. George's
LESSER ANTILLES
Barranquilla
COSTA RICA
Cartagena
Maracaibo
Caracas
Port-of-Spain
TRINIDAD AND TOBAGO
San José
Barquisimeto
Panama City
PANAMA
COLOMBIA
VENEZUELA
Orinoco
Ciudad Guayana
WORLD
CITIES
City locations
National capital
Other capital
BOUNDARIES
International
Scale by Latitude
60°
30°
0
1000
2000 mi
0
1610
3220 km
Robinson Projection

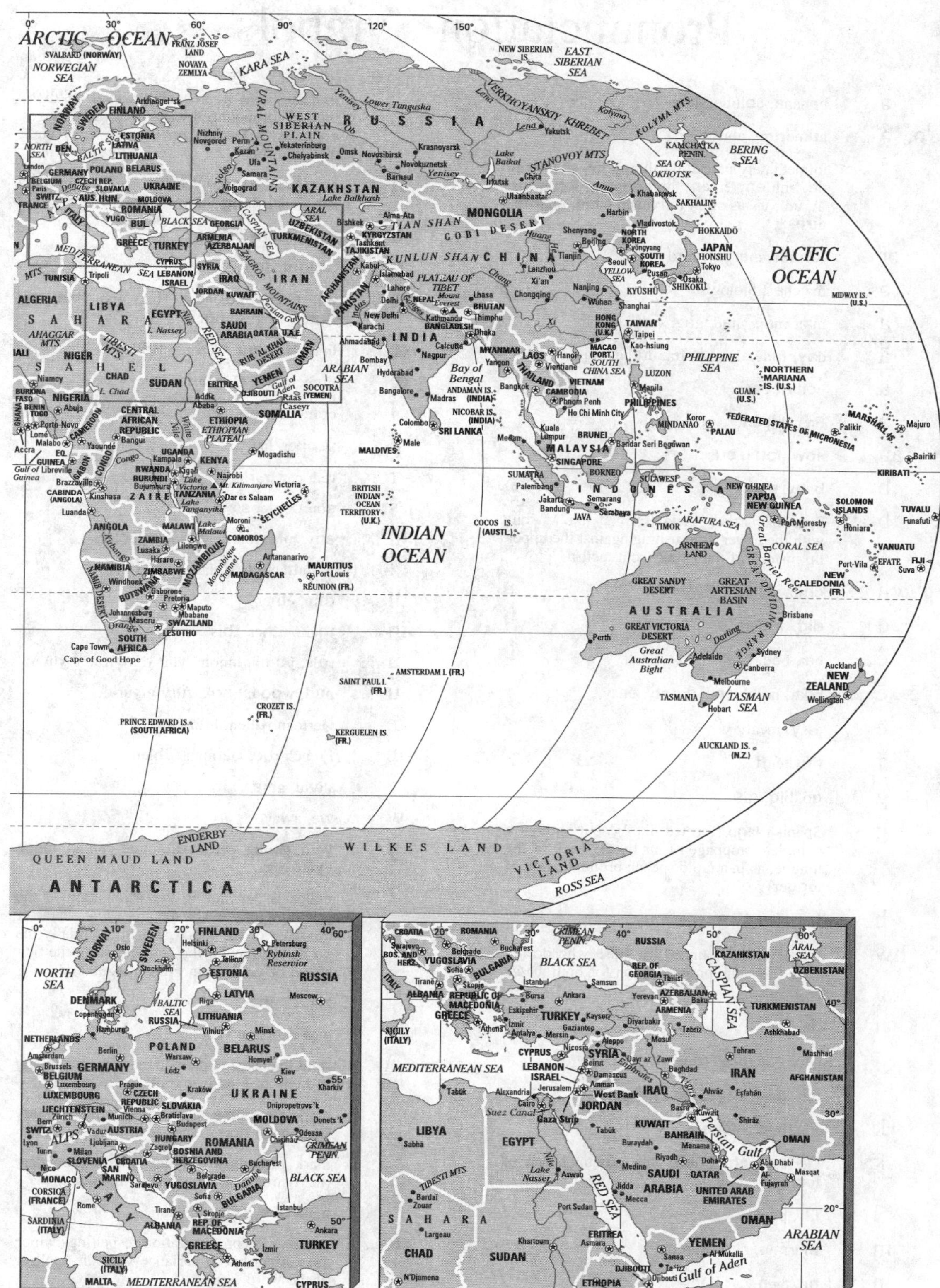
ARCTIC OCEAN
NORWEGIAN SEA
KARA SEA
EAST SIBERIAN SEA
RUSSIA
WEST SIBERIAN PLAIN
URAL MOUNTAINS
KAZAKHSTAN
MONGOLIA
CHINA
GOBI DESERT
TIAN SHAN
KUNLUN SHAN
PLATEAU OF TIBET
JAPAN
PACIFIC OCEAN
INDIA
IRAN
SAUDI ARABIA
EGYPT
LIBYA
ALGERIA
SAHARA
SAHEL
NIGER
CHAD
SUDAN
ETHIOPIA
SOMALIA
NIGERIA
ZAIRE
ANGOLA
NAMIBIA
BOTSWANA
SOUTH AFRICA
MADAGASCAR
INDIAN OCEAN
ARABIAN SEA
Bay of Bengal
SOUTH CHINA SEA
PHILIPPINE SEA
INDONESIA
PAPUA NEW GUINEA
AUSTRALIA
GREAT SANDY DESERT
GREAT VICTORIA DESERT
GREAT ARTESIAN BASIN
CORAL SEA
TASMAN SEA
NEW ZEALAND
ANTARCTICA
QUEEN MAUD LAND
ENDERBY LAND
WILKES LAND
VICTORIA LAND
ROSS SEA
NORTH SEA
BALTIC SEA
FINLAND
SWEDEN
NORWAY
DENMARK
POLAND
GERMANY
UKRAINE
ROMANIA
ITALY
TURKEY
BLACK SEA
MEDITERRANEAN SEA
CASPIAN SEA
Persian Gulf
RED SEA
Gulf of Aden
YEMEN
OMAN

Pronunciation Symbols

ə ... b**a**nan**a**, c**o**llide, **a**but

ˈə, ˌə ... h**u**mdr**u**m, ab**u**t

ə ... immediately preceding \l\ and \n\, as in bat**tle**, mitt**en**, eat**en**; immediately following \l\, \m\, \r\, as often in French tab**le**, pris**me**, tit**re**

ər ... f**ur**th**er**, m**er**g**er**, b**ir**d

ə̇ ... match**e**s, biolog**i**st

a ... m**a**t, m**a**p, m**a**d, g**a**g, sn**a**p, p**a**tch

ā ... d**ay**, f**a**de, d**a**te, **a**orta, dr**a**pe, c**a**pe

ä ... b**o**ther, c**o**t

ȧ ... French p**a**tte

au̇ ... n**ow**, l**ou**d, **ou**t

b ... **b**a**b**y, ri**b**

b̲ ... Spanish ha**b**lar, A**v**ila (formed like \v\ but with the lower lip brushing against the upper lip instead of the upper front teeth)

ch ... **ch**in, nature \ˈnā-chər\

d ... **d**i**d**, a**dd**er

e ... b**e**t, b**e**d, p**e**ck

ˈē, ˌē ... b**ea**t, nosebl**ee**d, **e**venly, **ea**sy

ē ... eas**y**, meal**y**

f ... **f**i**f**ty, cu**ff**

g ... **g**o, bi**g**, **g**ift

g̅ ... Spanish la**g**o (formed like \g\ but without a complete stoppage of air by the back of the tongue, as in a rapid speech pronunciation of lo**gg**er)

h ... **h**at, a**h**ead

hw ... **wh**ale as pronounced by those who do not have the same pronunciation for both *whale* and *wail*

i ... t**i**p, b**i**g

ī ... s**i**te, s**i**de, b**uy**, tr**i**pe

j ... **j**ob, **g**em, e**dge**, **j**oin, **j**u**dge**

k ... **k**in, **c**oo**k**, a**che**

k̲ ... German i**ch**, Bu**ch**; one pronunciation of lo**ch**

l ... **l**i**l**y, poo**l**

m ... **m**ur**m**ur, di**m**, ny**m**ph

n ... **n**o, ow**n**

^{n} ... indicates that a preceding vowel or diphthong is pronounced with the nasal passages open, as in French *un bon vin blanc* \ˌœ^{n}-ˌbō^{n}-ˌva^{n}-ˈblä^{n}\

ŋ ... si**ng** \ˈsiŋ\, si**ng**er \ˈsiŋ-ər\, fi**n**ger \ˈfiŋ-gər\, i**n**k \ˈiŋk\, thi**ng** \ˈthiŋ\

ō ... b**o**ne, kn**ow**, b**eau**

ȯ ... c**augh**t, d**o**g

ö ... **a**ll, Greek k**o**sm**o**s, Hungarian M**a**gy**a**r, British English b**o**nd

œ ... French b**oeu**f, German H**ö**lle

œ̅ ... French f**eu**, German H**öh**le

ȯi ... c**oi**n, destr**oy**

p ... **p**e**pp**er, li**p**

r ... **r**ed, ca**r**, **r**a**r**ity

s ... **s**our**ce**, le**ss**

sh ... **sh**y, mi**ss**ion, ma**ch**ine, spe**ci**al

t ... **t**ie, a**tt**ack, la**te**, la**t**er, la**tt**er

th ... **th**in, e**th**er

t̲h̲ ... **th**en, ei**th**er, **th**is

ü ... r**u**le, y**ou**th, union \ˈyün-yən\, few \ˈfyü\

u̇ ... p**u**ll, w**oo**d, b**oo**k, f**u**ry \ˈfyu̇r-ē\

ue ... German f**ü**llen, h**ü**bsch

u̅e̅ ... French r**ue**, German f**üh**len

v ... **v**i**v**id, gi**ve**

w ... **w**e, a**w**ay

y ... **y**ard, **y**oung, cue \ˈkyü\, mute \ˈmyüt\, union \ˈyün-yən\

^{y} ... indicates that during the articulation of the sound represented by the preceding character the front of the tongue has substantially the position it has for the articulation of the first sound of *yard*, as in French *digne* \ˈdēn^{y}\

z ... **z**one, rai**se**

zh ... vi**si**on, azure \ˈazh-ər\

\ ... slant line used in pairs to mark the beginning and end of a transcription: \ˈpen\

ˈ ... mark preceding a syllable with primary (strongest) stress: \ˈpen-mən-ˌship\

ˌ ... mark preceding a syllable with secondary (next-strongest) stress: \ˈpen-mən-ˌship\

\- ... mark of syllable division

sic ... notation for pronunciation respellings which are correct but at variance with the spelling of the word

A Dictionary of Place-Names

Aa \'ä\. **1.** Small river, N France; rises in Pas-de-Calais dept., flows into North Sea at Grand-Fort-Philippe.

2. *or* **Sar·ner–Aa** \'zär-nər-'ä\. River, Unterwalden, cen. Switzerland; flows N through Lakes Lungern and Sarnen into Lake of Lucerne.

3. River, N cen. Switzerland; rises in Lucerne canton, flows N into Aargau canton, expanding into Lakes Baldegg and Hallwil, and continues into Aare River.

4. Two rivers, Latvia. See GAUJA and LIELUPE.

Aabenraa. See ÅBENRÅ.

Aa·chen \'ä-k̲ən\. **1.** Administrative district, North Rhine-Westphalia, Germany; 1208 sq. mi. (3129 sq. km.); formerly part of Prussia.

2. *or Fr.* **Aix–la–Cha·pelle** \ˌeks-lȧ-shȧ-'pel\; *anc.* **Aquae Gra·ni** \ˌa-kwē-'grā-ˌnī, ä-kwī-'grä-ˌnē\ *or* **Aquis·gra·num** \ˌa-kwəs-'grā-nəm, ˌä-kwis-'grä-nu̇m\. City, its ✻, 40 mi. (64 km.) WSW of Cologne; pop. (1991e) 241,861; glass, textiles; railroad junction; tourist resort; mineral springs and baths; town hall built 1333–70 on ruins of Holy Roman Emperor Charlemagne's palace; cathedral founded by Charlemagne c. 800; technical university (1870).

History: Site of Roman baths first cent. A.D.; 2d ✻ of empire of Charlemagne, who was probably born there; favorite residence of Charlemagne after 768; center of Carolingian culture and site of Charlemagne's great palace (practically destroyed by Norsemen 881 but restored 983); given rights of an imperial city 1166 and 1215; coronation city of Holy Roman Empire 813–1531; treaties of Aix-la-Chapelle drawn up here to provide for peace terminating War of Devolution 1668 and War of Austrian Succession 1748; given to France by Peace of Lunéville 1801; returned to Prussia 1815; scene of Conference of Holy Alliance (also called Congress of Aix-la-Chapelle) 1818; Prussian military base in Franco-Prussian War 1870–71; air base in WWI; captured by Allied armies Oct. 1944; over half the city was destroyed during WWII, but has since been rebuilt.

Aa·iún, El \ˌel-ä-'yün\ *or* **Laa·youne** *or* **La'youn** \lä-'yün\. Town, ✻ of Western Sahara, NW Africa; near Atlantic coast; pop. (1982c) 93,875.

Aalborg. See ÅLBORG.

Aa·len \'ä-lən\. City, Baden-Württemberg, Germany, 44 mi. (71 km.) E of Stuttgart; pop. (1991e) 64,781; free imperial city 1360–c. 1803.

Aalesund. See ÅLESUND.

Aals·meer \'äls-ˌmār\. Commune, North Holland prov., Netherlands, 8 mi. (13 km.) SW of Amsterdam; pop. (1992e) 22,118; horticultural center.

Aalst \'älst\ *or Fr.* **Alost** \ȧ-'lȯst\. City, East Flanders prov., Belgium, 14 mi. (22 km.) NW of Brussels; pop. (1991c) 76,382; beer, textiles, textile machinery; a former ✻ of the counts of Flanders; held by France 1667–1706; under German control during both World Wars.

Aa·rau \'är-ˌau̇\. Commune, ✻ of Aargau canton, N Switzerland, on Aare River 23 mi. (37 km.) W of Zürich; pop. (1989c) 15,836; founded in 13th cent.; taken from Hapsburgs by Bern 1415; became ✻ of Helvetic Republic 1798 (see SWITZERLAND), ✻ of Aargau canton 1803.

Aa·re \'är-ə\ *or* **Aar** \'är\; *anc.* **Obrin·ga** \ō-'briŋ-gə\. River, cen. and N Switzerland; flows NW from Bernese Alps, traversing Hasli Tal (valley) and passing through the Gorge of the Aare (**Aa·re·schlucht** \'är-ə-ˌshlu̇kt\) then through Brienzersee and Thunersee, past Bern, thence NE past Solothurn and Aarau to Rhine; 183 mi. (294 km.) long; navigable to Thun; connected by canal with Bielersee.

Aar·gau \'är-ˌgau̇\ *or Fr.* **Ar·go·vie** \ȧr-gō-'vē\. Canton, N Switzerland; ✻ Aarau; dairy products, fruit; precision instruments; tourism. See table at SWITZERLAND.

History: Anciently part of Helvetia; conquered by Franks in 6th cent.; under Hapsburgs 1264–1415; taken by Cantonal League and divided bet. Bern and Lucerne; in part to Helvetic Republic 1798; member of Swiss Confederation 1803; constitution fixed by Congress of Vienna 1815, replaced 1831.

Aarhus. See ÅRHUS.

Aa·si·aat \'ä-sē-ˌät\ *or* **Ege·des·min·de** \'ā-gə-t̲h̲əs-ˌmi-nə\. Settlement on S Qeqertarsuup Tunua Bay, W Greenland.

Aath. See ATH.

Aba \'ä-bä\. Town, Imo State, Nigeria, ab. 40 mi. (64 km.) NE of Port Harcourt; pop. (1991e) 263,800; furniture, soap, textiles.

Ab·a·co \'a-bə-ˌkō\. Two islands, **Great Abaco** and **Little Abaco,** of Bahamas in Atlantic Ocean E of S Florida; 776 sq. mi. (2010 sq. km.).

Ābā·dān \ˌä-bə-'dän, ˌa-bə-'dan\. **1.** Island, Khūzestān prov., W Iran, on the Shatt al Arab; 42 mi. (68 km.) long, from 2 to 12 mi. (3.2 to 19 km.) wide; probably settled before time of Greek historian Herodotus; long disputed bet. Persia and Turkey, but assigned to Persia by treaty 1847.

2. Town on Ābādān I., on the Shatt al Arab, 33 mi. (53 km.) from Persian Gulf; large oil refineries; destroyed and depopulated during 1980s war with Iraq.

Abae \'ā-ˌbē\. Ancient town, Phocis, cen. Greece, on Boeotian border 10 mi. (16 km.) SE of Elateia; famous for oracle of Apollo; pillaged by Persians, partially restored through Roman Emperor Hadrian.

Abae·te·tu·ba \ȧ-ˌbī-te-'tü-bə\. Municipality, Pará state, N Brazil; pop. (1980c) 74,630.

Abai. See NILE.

Abai·ang \ə-'bī-ˌäŋ\. Island (atoll), NW Kiribati, W Pacific Ocean, just N of the Equator; 16 mi. (26 km.) long by 5 mi. (8 km.) wide; first residence of American missionaries 1857, under Hiram Bingham.

Aba·kan \ˌə-bə-'kän\. **1.** River, Khakassia, S Russia in Asia, rises at W end of Sayan Mts. and flows NE to Yenisey River; 350 mi. (563 km.) long.

2. Town, ✻ of Khakassia, S Russia in Asia, on the Yenisey at confluence of the Abakan; pop. (1992e) 158,000.

Aba·los Point \ä-'b̲ä-lōs, *angl.* ə-'bä-ləs\. Cape, W coast of Cuba, N of Guadiana Bay.

\ə\ abut \ə̇\ matches \ᵊ\ kitten, Fr table \ər\ further \a\ ash \ā\ ace
\ä\ cot, cart \ȧ\ Fr bac \au̇\ out \b̲\ Span Avila \ch\ chin \e\ bet \ē\ easy
\g\ go \i\ hit \ī\ ice \j\ job \k̲\ Ger ich, Buch \ⁿ\ Fr vin
\ŋ\ sing \ō\ go \ö\ all \ȯ\ law \œ\ Fr bœuf \œ̄\ Fr feu \ȯi\ boy
\th\ thin \t̲h̲\ this \ü\ loot \u̇\ foot \ue\ Ger füllen \ue̅\ Fr rue
\y\ yet \ʸ\ Fr digne \'dēnʸ\, nuit \'nwʸē\ \yü\ few \yu̇\ fury \zh\ vision

Abana *or* **Abanah.** See BARADA.

Aban·cay \ˌä-bäŋ-ˈkī, *angl.* -bäŋ-\. Town, Peru, 80 mi. (129 km.) W of Cuzco in valley of Andes; pop. (1981p) 19,807; alt. 7200 ft. (2194 m.).

Aba·no Ter·me \ˈä-bä-nō-ˈter-mā\. Commune, Padova prov., Veneto, N Italy, 5 mi. (8 km.) SW of Padua; resort; hot springs and mud baths.

Ab·a·rim Mountains \ˈa-bə-rim\. Ancient name (*Num.* xxxiii. 47, 48) of low mountain range or bluffs overlooking Dead Sea from NE, now in Jordan; highest point Mt. Nebo (see PISGAH, MOUNT 2) 2644 ft. (806 m.).

Aba·shi·ri \ˌä-ˈbä-shē-rē\. Town, Hokkaidō prefecture, Japan, NE coast of Hokkaidō I.; pop. (1990p) 44,416; railroad terminus on **Abashiri Bay;** fishing.

Abay *or* **Abbai.** See NILE.

Aba·ya, Lake \ä-ˈbī-ä\. Lake, SW Ethiopia, E Africa; 485 sq. mi. (1256 sq. km.).

Ab·be·ville \ˈa-bē-ˌvil\. **1.** County in W South Carolina. See table at SOUTH CAROLINA.
2. City, ⊗ of Henry co., SE Alabama; pop. (1990c) 3173.
3. City, ⊗ of Wilcox co., S cen. Georgia, on Ocmulgee River; pop. (1990c) 907.
4. Town, ⊗ of Vermilion parish, S Louisiana, in rice-growing region; pop. (1990c) 11,187.
5. City, ⊗ of Abbeville co., W South Carolina, 14 mi. (22 km.) W of Greenwood; pop. (1990c) 5778; in manufacturing region; settled by Huguenots in 18th cent.; scene of last cabinet meeting of Confederate President Jefferson Davis 1865.

Abbeville \àb-ˈvēl\; *anc.* **Ab·ba·tis Vil·la** \ə-ˌbā-təs-ˈvi-lə\. Commune, Somme dept., N France, on Somme River 25 mi. (40 km.) NW of Amiens; pop. (1990c) 24,588; late-Gothic church of St. Wulfran begun 1488. Dependent upon St.-Riquier abbey 9th cent. A.D.; ✻ of Ponthieu (*q.v.*); received charter as a commune 1184; under English rule from 1272 to 1369. Church survived bombardment during WWII.

Ab·bots·ford \ˈa-bəts-fərd\. **1.** City, British Columbia, Canada, 45 mi. (72 km.) ESE of Vancouver; pop. (1991c) 86,928.
2. Estate, Roxburgh co., SE Scotland, on Tweed River 2.5 mi. (4 km.) W of Melrose; residence 1812–32 of poet and novelist Sir Walter Scott.

Ab·bott·abad \ˈa-bə-tə-ˌbäd\. Town and military cantonment, Pakistan, 35 mi. (56 km.) N of Islamabad; pop. (1981p) 96,000; alt. 4120 ft. (1256 m.); hill resort; founded 1853.

Abd al–Ku·ri \ˌàbd-àl-ˈkůr-ē\. Rock and coral reef in Arabian Sea, halfway between Cape Asir, Somalia, and the island of Socotra; ab. 1 mi. (1.6 km.) long; belongs to Yemen.

Ab·de·ra \ab-ˈdir-ə\. **1.** *or Gk.* **Av·di·ra** \äv-ˈthē-rä\. City of ancient Thrace, on Aegean Sea E of the mouth of the Mesta, nearly opp. Thásos; now in ruins. First settled 7th cent. B.C.; colonized 2d time by inhabitants of Teos in Ionia c. 544 B.C.; birthplace of several famous Greeks, esp. philosophers Democritus (c. 460 B.C.) and Protagoras (c. 580 B.C.). Its inhabitants gained reputation for foolishness, whence the term *Abderite* became one of reproach.
2. Seaport, Spain. See ADRA.

Abé·ché \à-bā-ˈshā\. Town, E cen. Chad, 400 mi. (644 km.) NE of Fort-Lamy; pop. (1992e) 95,800.

Abela. See ÁVILA 2.

Abellinum. See AVELLINO 2.

Abel–Me·ho·lah \ˌā-bəl-mə-ˈhō-lə\. Ancient town, now an archaeological site, Jordan, 35 mi. (56 km.) NNW of Amman; birthplace of Hebrew prophet Elisha (*1 Kings* xix. 16).

Abel Tas·man National Park \ˈā-bəl-ˈtaz-mən\. National park on Tasman Bay, N coast of South I., New Zealand.

Ab·e·ma·ma \ˌä-bā-ˈmä-mä\. Island (atoll), cen. Gilbert Is., Kiribati, W Pacific Ocean, 0°21′N, 173°51′E; pop. (1990c) 3218; 12 mi. (19 km.) long by 5 mi. (8 km.) wide; good anchorage; occupied by Japanese 1942; seized by U.S. marines after bitter battle Nov. 1943.

Åben·rå *or* **Aa·ben·raa** \ˌó-bən-ˈró\ *or Ger.* **Apen·ra·de** \ˌä-pən-ˈrä-də\. Town, ⊗ of Sønderjylland co., Denmark, at head of fjord opening on Little Belt, 15 mi. (24 km.) S of Haderslev; pop. (1989e) 21,349; received civic rights 1335; formerly German, passed to Denmark by plebiscite 1920.

Abens·berg \ˈä-bəns-ˌberk\. City, Bavaria, Germany, 18 mi. (29 km.) SW of Regensburg; pop. (1980c) 8755; founded ab. 1040; scene of Austrian defeat by French Emperor Napoléon 1809.

Abe·o·ku·ta \ä-ˈbā-ō-ˌkü-tä\. Town, ✻ of Ogun state, SW Nigeria, on railroad line ab. 60 mi. (96 km.) N of Lagos; pop. (1991e) 377,100; center of palm kernel and cocoa-producing region; estab. ab. 1830 as refuge from slave hunters; chief town of the Egbas, who made treaty with the British 1893.

Aberbrothock. See ARBROATH.

Ab·er·carn \ˌa-bər-ˈkärn\; *formerly* **New·bridge** \ˈnyü-brij, ˈnü-\. Town, Gwent co., SE Wales, in coal-mining region 26 mi. (42 km.) WNW of Bristol; pop. (1981p) 17,604.

Abercorn. See MBALA.

Ab·er·crom·bie, Mount \ˈa-bər-ˌkräm-bē, -ˌkrəm-\. Peak, Stevens co., NE Washington; 7308 ft. (2227 m.).

Ab·er·dare \ˌa-bər-ˈdar\. Town, Mid Glamorgan co., S Wales, 20 mi. (32 km.) NNW of Cardiff; pop. (1981p) 36,621.

Aberdare Range *also* **Aberdare Mountains.** Mountain range, W Kenya; av. height 11,000 ft. (3350 m.); S part estab. as **Aberdare National Park.**

Aberdaugleddyf. See MILFORD HAVEN.

Ab·er·deen \ˈa-bər-ˌdēn\. **1.** Residential town, Harford co., NE Maryland, 29 mi. (47 km.) ENE of Baltimore; pop. (1990c) 13,087. Nearby is **Aberdeen Proving Ground,** a military testing ground comprising 35,000 acres (14,175 hectares) along W side of upper Chesapeake Bay.
2. City, ⊗ of Monroe co., NE Mississippi, 24 mi. (39 km.) N of Columbus; pop. (1990c) 6837.
3. Town, Moore co., North Carolina; pop. (1990c) 2700.
4. City, ⊗ of Brown co., NE South Dakota, ab. 90 mi. (145 km.) W of Big Stone Lake; pop. (1990c) 24,927; railroad and wholesale distributing center in agricultural region; flourmills, grain elevators, stockyards and packing plants; dairy products; Northern State Coll. (1901); Preservation Coll. (1922); settled 1880.
5. City and port of entry, Grays Harbor co., W Washington, at E end of Grays Harbor 46 mi. (74 km.) W of Olympia; pop. (1990c) 16,565; Grays Harbor Coll. (1930); founded 1867; incorp. 1890.
6. Lake, S Nunavut, Canada; 475 sq. mi. (1230 sq. km.).

Aberdeen \ˌa-bər-ˈdēn\. **1.** *or* **Ab·er·deen·shire** \-shər, -ˌshir\. Former county, NE Scotland; Rivers Dee, Don, Ythan; Grampian Hills in SW.
2. *anc.* **De·va·na** \di-ˈvā-nə\. Burgh and commercial center, ⊗ of Grampian region, E Scotland, on the North Sea; part in Kincardine co.; pop. (1991e) 211,080; base for North Sea gas and oil operations; Univ. of Aberdeen (1860).

History: Royal burgh and seat of a bishopric from 12th cent.; a Scottish royal residence 12th–14th cents.; supported King Robert the Bruce in wars for Scottish independence, captured and for a time made headquarters of English King Edward I; burned by his grandson Edward III 1336; welcomed Charles II 1650; occupied by Gen. George Monck and Cromwellians 1651; garrisoned by English until 1659; declared for Stuarts 1715 and 1745.

Ab·er·fel·dy \ˌa-bər-ˈfel-dē\. Burgh, W cen. Tayside region, Scotland, on Tay River 25 mi. (40 km.) NW of Perth; pop. (1981p) 1627; supposed scene of poet Robert Burns's *Birks of Aberfeldy;* Black Watch regiment raised here 1725.

Ab·er·foyle \ˌa-bər-ˈfȯil\. Parish and village, Central region, Scotland, ab. 6 mi. (10 km.) SE of Loch Katrine; parish pop. (1981p) 546; immortalized by author Sir Walter Scott's *Rob Roy;* summer resort for residents of Glasgow.

Ab·er·ga·ven·ny \ˌa-bər-gə-ˈve-nē\; *anc.* **Go·ban·ni·um** \gō-ˈba-nē-əm\. Municipal borough, Monmouthshire, SE Wales, at confluence of Gavenny and Usk rivers; pop. (1981p) 9390.

Abergwaun. See FISHGUARD.

Aberhonddu. See BRECON 2.

Ab·er·nathy \ˈa-bər-ˌna-thē\. City, Hale and Lubbock cos., NW Texas, 21 mi. (34 km.) N of the city of Lubbock; pop. (1990c) 2720.

Abert, Lake \ˈā-bərt\. Lake, cen. Lake co., S Oregon; ab. 20 mi. (32 km.) long and 5 mi. (8 km.) wide; has no outlet and is sometimes dry; to the E is the N to S trending **Abert Rim,** a large fault scarp.

Abertawe. See SWANSEA 3.

Aberteifi. See CARDIGAN 2.

Ab·er·til·lery \ˌa-bər-tə-ˈler-ē\. Town, Gwent co., SE Wales, ab. 30 mi. (48 km.) NW of Bristol, England; pop. (1981p) 19,319.

Ab·er·yst·wyth \ˌa-bə-ˈris-ˌtwith, -ˈrəs-\. Municipal borough, Dyfed, W Wales, on Cardigan Bay; pop. (1981p) 8666; seaside resort; Univ. Coll. of Wales (1872), Welsh National Library (completed 1955). Town built around 13th cent. fortress.

a–Bhuird, Ben–. See BEN-A-BHUIRD.

Abia \ä-ˈbī-ä\. State of Nigeria. See table at NIGERIA.

Abi·a·thar Peak \ə-ˈbī-ə-ˌthär\. Mountain, Yellowstone National Park, NW Wyoming; 10,928 ft. (3331 m.).

Ab–i–Diz. See DEZ.

Ab·i·djan \ˌä-bē-ˈjän, ˌa-bi-\. City, seat of government and former official ✻ of Ivory Coast, W Africa; pop. (1988c) 1,934,342; beer, soap; exports bananas, cocoa, coffee; university (1963); port facilities estab. 1951.

Abi·ko \ä-ˈbē-kō\. City, Chiba prefecture, SE Honshū, Japan; pop. (1990p) 120,629.

Abila. See MUSA, JEBEL.

Ab·i·lene \ˈa-bə-ˌlēn\. **1.** City, ⊗ of Dickinson co., E cen. Kansas, on Smoky Hill River 25 mi. (40 km.) E of Salina; pop. (1990c) 6242; distribution center; Eisenhower Center; former frontier town, railhead 1867–71 for cattle-raising region to SW.
2. City, ⊗ of Taylor co., NW cen. Texas, 145 mi. (233 km.) WSW of Fort Worth; pop. (1990c) 106,654; food products, oil refining; Hardin-Simmons Univ. (1891), Abilene Christian Univ. (1906), McMurry Coll. (1923).

Ab·i·le·ne \ˌa-bi-ˈlē-nē\. Region in Syria, E of Anti-Lebanon Mts.; c. 29 A.D. comprised Tetrarchy of Lysanias (*Luke* iii. 1).

Abindonia. See ABINGDON 3.

Ab·ing·don \ˈa-biŋ-dən\. **1.** City, Knox co., W Illinois, 11 mi. (18 km.) S of Galesburg; pop. (1990c) 3597.
2. Town, ⊗ of Washington co., SW Virginia, in Blue Ridge Mts. 15 mi. (24 km.) NE of Bristol; pop. (1990c) 5660; site of Black's Fort 1776; settled c. 1770.
3. *anc.* **Ab·in·do·nia** \ˌa-bin-ˈdō-nē-ə, -nyə\. Town, Oxfordshire, S England, on the Thames 6 mi. (10 km.) S of Oxford; pop. (1981p) 22,686; has many interesting antiquities; site of a Benedictine abbey founded 675; received charter 1556.

Abingdon Island. See PINTA ISLAND.

Ab·ing·ton \ˈa-biŋ-tən\. Township, Montgomery co., SE Pennsylvania, N of Philadelphia; pop. (1990c) 56,322; Ogontz Campus of Pennsylvania State Univ. (1950).

Ab·i·shim \ä-bi-ˈshēm\. Mountain, West Azerbaijan prov., NW Iran, SW of Daryācheh-ye Orūmīyeh; 8392 ft. (2558 m.).

Abi·sko National Park \ˈä-bēs-ˌkü\. National park, N Sweden, bordering on Torne Träsk (lake).

Ab·i·tibi \ˌa-bi-ˈti-bē\. County, SW Quebec, Canada. See table at QUEBEC.

Abitibi, Lake. Lake on E boundary of Ontario, Canada; 369 sq. mi. (956 sq. km.) mostly in Ontario; source of **Abitibi River** (340 mi. or 547 km. long), E Ontario, flowing N to Moose River near James Bay.

Abi·ti·bi–Ouest \ˌa-bə-ˈti-bē-ˈwest\. County, Quebec, Canada. See table at QUEBEC.

Ab·khaz Republic \ab-ˈkaz, əb-ˈkäs\ *also* **Ab·kha·zia** \ab-ˈkā-zhə, -ˈka-, -zhē-ə\ *or* **Ab·khaz·ska·ya Republic** \ˌəb-ˈkä-skī-ə\. Autonomous republic, NW Republic of Georgia, on Black Sea coast at W end of Caucasus Mts.; 3320 sq. mi. (8599 sq. km.); pop. (1991e) 533,800; ✻ Sukhumi; became Christian under Byzantine Emperor Justinian in 6th cent.; Russian protectorate formally estab. 1810; annexed by Russia 1864; created an autonomous republic 1919; proclamation of sovereignty (1992) rejected by Georgia.

Ablain–Saint–Na·zaire \ä-ˈblaⁿ-saⁿ-nä-ˈzer\. Commune, Pas-de-Calais dept., N France, near Vimy Ridge 7 mi. (11 km.) N of Arras; completely destroyed during WWI.

Åbo. See TURKU.

Ab·o·mey \ˌa-bō-ˈmā, ə-ˈbō-mē\. Town, S Benin, 65 mi. (104 km.) NNW of Porto-Novo; pop. (1982e) 54,418; 19th cent. palace ruins; museum; former slave center; ✻ of former native kingdom of Dahomey (*q.v.*); fired and abandoned to French 1892; rebuilt by French and connected with coast by rail 1905.

Abo·ny \ˈö-ˌbónʸ, *angl.* ˈó-ˌbō-nyə\. Commune, Pest co., cen. Hungary, 10 mi. (16 km.) E of Cegléd.

Aboukir. See ABŪ QĪR.

Abra \ˈä-brə\. **1.** River, NW Luzon, Philippines; rises in S cen. part of Mountain Prov. in Cordillera Central, flows N then W to South China Sea; ab. 100 mi. (160 km.) long; 3d longest river on the island.
2. Inland mountainous province, NW Luzon, Philippines; chief town and ✻ Bangued; traversed by middle course of Abra River and its many tributaries N and E; greatly broken by mountain ranges and groups of the Cordillera Central, and by hills; highest point Mt. Manmanoc 6634 ft. (2022 m.) on E border. Under nominal Spanish rule late 16th cent.–late 19th cent.; under American control first part of 20th cent. See table at PHILIPPINES.

Abra·ham, Mount \ˈā-brə-ˌham\. **1.** Mountain, Franklin co., W Maine; 4049 ft. (1234 m.).
2. Peak, Addison co., W Vermont; 4052 ft. (1235 m.).

Abraham, Plains of *or Fr.* **Plaines d'·Abra·ham** \ˌplen-dá-brá-ˈám\. Plateau, SW of old city of Quebec, Canada; battlefield Sept. 13, 1759 where the British under Gen. James Wolfe defeated the French under the Marquis de Montcalm de St.-Véran, decisive battle of the French and Indian War; during American Revolution held by U.S. forces in their siege of Quebec 1775–76; now a park within the city limits.

Abran·tes \ə-ˈbräⁿn-tish\; *anc.* **Au·ran·tes** \ó-ˈran-tēz\. Commune, Santarém dist., W cen. Portugal, on Tagus River 32 mi. (51 km.) ENE of the commune of Santarém; founded c. 300 B.C.; captured Nov. 24, 1807 by French Emperor Napoléon's Gen. Andoche Junot, who assumed title of duc d'Abrantès.

Abre·us \ä-ˈbrā-üs\. Town and municipality, Las Villas prov., W cen. Cuba, 12 mi. (19 km.) NW of Cienfuegos.

Abro·lhos \á-ˈbrōl-yüs\. Group of pointed rocky islands off Caravelas, S Bahia state, Brazil, bet. 17° and 18°S lat.; comprise **Abrolhos Marine National Park** (estab. 1983).

Abrotonum. See SABRATA.

Abruz·zi \ä-ˈbrüt-sē\. Autonomous region, cen. Italy; 4168 sq. mi. (10,795 sq. km.); pop. (1991p) 1,249,388; ✻ L'Aquila; grapes, sugar beets, wheat, livestock; formerly part of Abruzzi e Molise. See table at ITALY.

Abruzzi Apennines *or* **Abruzzese, Appennino.** See table at APENNINES.

Abruzzi e Mo·li·se \ā-mō-ˈlē-ˌzā\. Former administrative region, cen. Italy, bet. Adriatic Sea and Apennines (which attain their greatest height here) and Tronto and Sangro rivers; now divided into Abruzzi and Molise.
History: District formed part of duchy of Spoleto in Lombard times and of Puglia under Normans; in 1240 made a single province by Holy Roman Emperor Frederick II, who founded L'Aquila; province of Angevin kingdom of Naples, to which it was of strategic importance; incorp. in kingdom of Italy as part of Naples 1860; administrative region estab. 1948, dissolved 1965.

Ab·sa·ro·ka Range \ab-ˈsär-ə-kə, -ˈsór-kē, -ˈzór-\. Range of Rocky Mts., from S Montana across NE corner of Yellowstone Park into NW Wyoming; ab. 175 mi. (282 km.) long; highest point Franks Peak 13,140 ft. (4005 m.); others Mt. Crosby 12,435 ft. (3790 m.) and Dead Indian Peak 12,216 ft. (3723 m.).

Ab·se·con \ab-ˈsē-kən\. City, Atlantic co., SE New Jersey, 6 mi. (10 km.) NW of Atlantic City; pop. (1990c) 7298.

Absecon Inlet. Narrow strait leading from Atlantic Ocean through barrier islands in Atlantic co., SE New Jersey; its S

---

shore is the N end of **Absecon Island** (10 mi. or 16 km. long) on which Atlantic City is situated.

Abu, Mount \ˈə-ˌbü\ *or* **Gu·ru Peak** \ˈgu̇r-ü\. **1.** Hill, Aravalli Range, Rajasthan, NW India; 5650 ft. (1722 m.).
2. Hill station, on Mt. Abu, Rajasthan, NW India, 115 mi. (185 km.) N of Ahmadabad; pop. (1991p) 15,547; site of Dilwara Jain temples (11th–13th cents.) and Achalgarh temples (15th cent.); was administrative center of former Rajputana Agency.

Abuam. See TAFILALT.

Abu·cay \ä-ˈbü-ˌkī, ˌȧ-bü-ˈkī\. Municipality near E coast of Bataan prov., Luzon, Philippines, N of Balanga.

Abu Dha·bi \ˌä-bü-ˈdä-bē, *Arab.* ˌȧ-bü-ˈt͟hä-bē\ *also* **Abū Za·bī** *or* **Abū Za·by** \-ˈthä-bē\. **1.** Emirate. See table at UNITED ARAB EMIRATES.
2. Town, its ✱, and ✱ of the United Arab Emirates; pop. (1989c) 363,432; settled 1761.

Abu Do·khān, Ge·bel \ˈje-bəl-ˌȧ-bü-dō-ˈkän\. Mountain, E Egypt, near coast at N end of Red Sea; 5492 ft. (1674 m.); porphyry deposits, source of the red building stone used by the Romans.

Abu·ja \ä-ˈbü-jä\. City, ✱ of Nigeria, in cen. part of the country; replaced Lagos as official ✱ 1991.

Abukir *or* **Aboukir.** See ABŪ QĪR.

Abu Klea \ˌȧ-bü-ˈklā\. Locality, N Sudan, W of the Nile, 63 mi. (101 km.) SW of Ed Damer; scene of battle Jan. 17, 1885 in which large force of Mahdists was repulsed by British.

Abu·ku·ma \ä-ˈbü-kü-mä\. River, N Honshū, Japan; flows NNE into Pacific Ocean ab. 15 mi. (24 km.) S of Sendai; 122 mi. (196 km.) long.

Abu Kurkas. See ABU QURQĀS.

Abulliont. See APULYONT.

Abū Mū·sá \ˌȧ-bü-ˈmü-sə\. Small island, Persian Gulf, 25°52′N, 55°03′E; administered by Sharjah until 1971 agreement with Iran permitting stationing of Iranian troops on island; takeover by Iran 1992.

Abu·ná \ˌä-bü-ˈnä\. River, N Bolivia; flows NE forming a section of Brazil-Bolivia boundary and empties into Madeira River at N point of Bolivia; ab. 200 mi. (320 km.) long.

Abū Qīr *also* **Abu·kir** *or* **Abou·kir** \ˌȧ-bü-ˈkēr\. **1.** Bay, Egypt, bet. Rosetta mouth of Nile and Alexandria.
2. Village, 13 mi. (21 km.) NNE of Alexandria, Egypt, on Abū Qīr Bay; approx. site of ancient Canopus (*q.v.*). In the bay was fought the "Battle of the Nile" Aug. 1–2, 1798, in which British Adm. Horatio Nelson completely defeated French fleet under Adm. F. P. Brueys; near the village French Emperor Napoléon defeated Turks 1799 and British General Sir Ralph Abercromby landed and defeated French 1801.

Abu Qur·qās *or* **Abu Kur·kas** \ˌȧ-bü-ku̇r-ˈkäs\. Town on Nile River, Egypt, 13 mi. (21 km.) SSW of El Minya.

Abury. See AVEBURY.

Abus. See HUMBER 2.

Abu Sim·bel \ˌȧ-bü-ˈsim-bel\ *also* **Abu Sun·bul** \ˌȧ-bü-ˈsu̇n-bu̇l\ *or* **Ip·sam·bul** \ˌip-sȧm-ˈbül\. Locality, Egypt, 22°22′N, 31°38′E; site of two rock temples of Ramses II (c. 1250 B.C.), discovered early 19th cent.; larger temple had four colossi of the king more than 65 ft. (20 m.) high; colossi cut apart and reassembled on higher ground due to flooding of area 1966.

Abu·ye Me·da *or* **Abu·ya Mye·da** \ˈä-bü-yə-ˈmyā-də\. Peak, cen. Ethiopia, ab. 130 mi. (209 km.) NE of Addis Ababa; 13,120 ft. (3999 m.).

Abu·yog \ä-ˈbü-ˌyōg\. Municipality on E coast of Leyte, Philippines, 34 mi. (55 km.) S of Tacloban.

Abū Zabī *or* **Abū Zaby.** See ABU DHABI.

Aby·dos \ə-ˈbī-dəs\. **1.** Ancient town, Mysia (*q.v.*), on the Hellespont; site of town NE of modern Çanakkale, NW Turkey; scene of crossing of Persian King Xerxes' army when he invaded Greece 480 B.C.; resisted Philip V of Macedon 200 B.C.; scene of story of Hero and Leander; toll station until late Byzantine times.
2. Town, ancient Egypt, on left bank of Nile ab. 100 mi. (160 km.) below Thebes; one of oldest Egyptian cities, mentioned in early inscriptions; site of ruins from Ist to XXVth dynasties; esp. prosperous in XIXth dynasty when temples dedicated to Osiris were built by Seti I and Ramses II; has many tombs of rulers; site near modern Araba al-Madfuna.

Abyla. **1.** Mountain, Morocco. See MUSA, JEBEL.
2. City, Spain. See ÁVILA 2.

Abyssinia. See ETHIOPIA.

Aca·dia \ə-ˈkā-dē-ə\. **1.** Parish in S Louisiana. See table at LOUISIANA.
2. *or Fr.* **Aca·die** \ȧ-kȧ-ˈdē\. Original name, of Micmac origin, of Nova Scotia (*q.v.*), first used 1603 in commission to French colonizer Sieur de Monts (Pierre du Gua), who made first settlement 1604; in early 17th cent. region extended to include all territory bet. St. Lawrence River and Gulf of St. Lawrence and Atlantic Ocean, with indefinite W boundary, but included New Brunswick and E Maine. Settled 1632–1713 by French, who formed farming community in the Grand Pré district; fought over by England and France in colonial wars of 18th cent.; its inhabitants (ab. 10,000 Acadians) deported by English 1755 and scattered from Maine to Louisiana (see ACADIAN COAST).

Acadia National Park. See UNITED STATES, *National Parks*.

Aca·di·an Coast \ə-ˈkā-dē-ən\. District, S Louisiana, W of lower Mississippi River and WNW of New Orleans; settled 1760 and later by exiled Acadians from Nova Scotia; now chiefly in St. James parish.

Aca·je·te \ˌä-kä-ˈhā-tē\. Municipality, Puebla state, Mexico, 80 mi. (129 km.) SE of Mexico City.

Aca·jut·la \ˌä-kä-ˈhüt-lä\. Seaport town, Sonsonate dept., SW El Salvador; pop. (1986e) 39,492; breakwaters and new port facilities constructed 1956–61.

Acám·ba·ro \ä-ˈkäm-bä-ˌrō\. Municipality, Guanajuato state, cen. Mexico, 90 mi. (145 km.) NW of Mexico City; pop. (1990p) 112,734; railroad junction.

Acan·thus \ə-ˈkan-thəs\. Ancient town, N Greece, on E coast at base of Acte Penin., Chalcidice, ab. 4 mi. (6.4 km.) W of site of Persian King Xerxes' canal cut across the Isthmus of Acte 480 B.C.

Aca·po·ne·ta \ˌä-kä-pō-ˈnā-tä\. Municipality, Nayarit state, W Mexico, on **Acaponeta River.**

Aca·pul·co \ˌä-kä-ˈpu̇l-(ˌ)kō, *angl.* ˌa-, -ˈpül-\ *or in full* **Acapulco de Juá·rez** \t͟hā-ˈhwär-ˌes\. Seaport, Guerrero state, Mexico, on Pacific Ocean, 190 mi. (306 km.) SSW of Mexico City; munic. pop. (1990p) 592,187; international resort; shipping point. For 250 years (1565–1815) chief port for Spanish trade with Philippines (the "Manila galleons" making yearly voyages across the Pacific to and from Manila) and for transshipment across Mexico.

Acarahy, Serra. See SERRA ACARAÍ.

Acaraí, Serra. See SERRA ACARAÍ.

Aca·raú \ˌȧ-kə-rȧ-ˈü\. Municipality, Ceará state, NE Brazil, on north coast, 130 mi. (209 km.) NW of Fortaleza; pop. (1980c) 72,112.

Aca·ri·gua \ˌä-kä-ˈrē-gwä\. Town, Portuguesa state, W cen. Venezuela, 165 mi. (265 km.) WSW of Caracas; pop. (1990c) 116,551.

Ac·ar·na·nia \ˌa-kər-ˈnā-nē-ə\ *also* **Akar·na·nía** \ä-ˌkär-nä-ˈnē-ä\. Mountainous country of ancient Greece, in W part, W of Aetolia and on Ionian Sea, separated from Aetolia by the Achelous River; chief town Stratus. Loosely organized into Acarnanian League; dominated by Sparta c. 391 B.C. and by Thebes c. 371 B.C.; allied with King Philip V of Macedon against Rome; required to give up federal ✱ and submit to Rome 167 A.D.

Acate \ä-ˈkä-tē\; *formerly* **Bis·ca·ri** \bēs-ˈkär-ē\. Village, Ragusa prov., SE Sicily, Italy, 15 mi. (24 km.) E of Gela; pop. (1981p) 6736; in WWII its airfield captured by U.S. army 1943.

Aca·te·nan·go \ˌä-kä-tā-ˈnän-gō\. Volcano, Guatemala, ab. 31 mi. (50 km.) SW of the city of Guatemala; 13,044 ft. (3976 m.).

Aca·tlán de Oso·rio \ˌä-kä-ˈtlän-dā-ō-ˈsōr-ē-ō\. Municipality, Puebla state, SE cen. Mexico, 58 mi. (93 km.) S of the city of Puebla.

Aca·yu·cán \ˌä-kä-yü-ˈkän\. Municipality, SE Veracruz state, E Mexico, 37 mi. (60 km.) SE of San Andrés Tuxtla; pop. (1990p) 69,756.

Accad. See AKKAD.
Accho. Seaport city, Israel. See ACRE.
Ac·co·mac \ˈa-kə-ˌmak\. **1.** *or officially* **Ac·co·mack** \ˈa-kə-ˌmak\. Coastal county in N part of E peninsula of Virginia. See table at VIRGINIA.
2. Town, its ⊗, on N part of Delmarva Penin.; pop. (1990c) 466; twice a refuge of Gov. Sir William Berkeley during Bacon's Rebellion 1675–76.
Ac·cra \ˈä-krə, ˈa-; ə-ˈkrä\. Seaport city, ✱ of Ghana; pop. (1984c) 867,459; food products; has anchorage with breakwater and wharves; terminus of railroad to Kumasi; Univ. of Ghana.
History: Site of trading forts, James and Crèvecœur, founded by English and Dutch 17th century, and of Danish Fort Christiansborg; Fort Crèvecœur ceded to British 1850, Fort Christiansborg ceded 1871; became ✱ of Gold Coast Colony 1876, ✱ of Ghana 1957.
Ac·cring·ton \ˈa-kriŋ-tən\. Town, Lancashire, NW England, 20 mi. (32 km.) N of Manchester.
Acelum. See ASOLO.
Acer·ra \ä-ˈcher-rä\. Commune, Napoli prov., Campania, S Italy, 9 mi. (14 km.) NE of Naples; pop. (1989c) 40,523; site of ancient city, **Acer·rae** \ə-ˈser-(ˌ)ē, ä-ˈker-ˌī\, which received Latin rights 332 B.C.; destroyed by Carthaginian Gen. Hannibal 216 B.C.; restored 210 B.C.; Roman headquarters in Social War 90 B.C.
Acesines. See CHENAB.
Achaea \ə-ˈkē-ə\ *or* **Acha·ia** *or Gk.* **Akhaïa** \ə-ˈkī-ə, *angl.* -ˈkā-ə\. **1.** Region, ancient Greece, N part of the Peloponnese, bordering on Gulfs of Corinth and Patras on N and bounded by Elis, Arcadia, and Sicyonia on SW, S, and SE respectively; chief towns Patrae, Helice, and Aigion.
History: Region presumably settled by the Achaeans, an early Greek people; first given loose political unity by the formation of the Achaean League of 12 Achaean cities, which allied with Athens against Sparta 362 B.C.; aided Greek efforts to stop invasions by Kings Philip II and Alexander the Great of Macedon 4th cent. B.C.; renewed 280 B.C. the Achaean League, which supported the wars against Macedon until the Roman defeat of Philip V 197 B.C. and was dissolved by Rome 146 B.C. for assisting Macedon. As a Roman imperial province 146 B.C.–c. 4th cent. A.D. included all of Greece S of Thessaly; a province of the Eastern Roman (Byzantine) Empire until made a Latin principality 1204; overrun by Turks 1460; to Greece 1828.
2. Department of Greece; approx. coextensive with historical region. See table at GREECE.
Achaea Phthi·o·tis \thī-ˈō-təs\. Region, S part of ancient Thessaly, Greece, N of Mt. Othrys, extending E to the Pagasikós Kólpos.
Achal·pur \ä-chəl-ˌpu̇r\; *formerly* **El·lich·pur** *or* **El·ich·pur** \ˈe-lich-ˌpu̇r\. Town, N Maharashtra, cen. India, 110 mi. (177 km.) W of Nagpur; pop. (1991p) 96,216. May have been founded 11th cent.; became seat of Imad Shāh dynasty of Berar 1484; hereditary ruler in 1803 received the title of nabob; family died out in 19th cent.
Achard Point \ä-ˈshär\. Cape, W San Cristóbal I., SE Solomon Is., W Pacific Ocean.
Achar·nae \ə-ˈkär-ˌnē\ *or Gk.* **Akhar·naí** \ˌä-k̲är-ˈnā\. Village, Attica, Greece, N of Athens; charcoal burners of the village gave their name to a play of Aristophanes, *The Acharnians,* performed 425 B.C.
Acheen. See ATJEH.
Ach·e·lo·us \ˌa-kə-ˈlō-əs\ *or Gk.* **Akhe·ló·os** \ˌä-k̲e-ˈlō-ōs\ *also* **As·pro·pot·a·mos** \ˌas-prō-ˈpä-tə-məs\. River, W Greece; rises in Pindus Mts., NW Thessaly, and flows S to Ionian Sea; 137 mi. (220 km.) long; longest river in Greece.
Acherusia, Palus. See FUSARO.
Achi Ba·ba \ä-ˈchē-bä-ˈbä\ *or Turk.* **Al·çı Te·pe** \äl-ˈchē-te-ˈpe\. Height dominating tip of Gallipoli Penin., Turkey in Europe; main position of Turkish defense in Gallipoli fighting of 1915.
Ach·ill \ˈa-kil\. Island, W coast of Ireland, NW of Clew Bay; ab. 15 mi. (24 km.) long; 56 sq. mi. (145 sq. km.); at W end is cape, **Achill Head.**

Achin. See ATJEH.
Achinsk \ˈä-chinsk, ə-ˈchinsk\. Town, SW Krasnoyarsk Kray, SW cen. Russia in Asia, on Chulym River and on Trans-Siberian R.R. 90 mi. (145 km.) W of the town of Krasnoyarsk; pop. (1991e) 122,000.
Achmetha. See HAMADĀN 2.
Achray, Loch \ˈlōk̲-ə-ˈk̲rā, ˈläk-ə-ˈkrā\. Lake, Central region, Scotland; 1.25 mi. (2 km.) long; max. depth 97 ft. (30 m.); connects with Loch Katrine.
Acht·kar·spe·len \ˈäk̲t-ˌkär-spə-lən, ˈäkt-\. Commune, Friesland prov., N Netherlands; pop. (1981e) 26,984.
Aci·re·a·le \ˌä-chē-rā-ˈä-lē\. Seaport, Catania prov., E Sicily, Italy, on E coast 10 mi. (16 km.) N of the commune of Catania; pop. (1989p) 47,294; resort with sulfur baths; earthquake 1693.
Ack·er·man \ˈa-kər-mən\. Town, ⊗ of Choctaw co., cen. Mississippi, 44 mi. (71 km.) WSW of Columbus; pop. (1990c) 1573.
Ack·er Peak \ˈa-kər\. Mountain in the Sierra Nevada, E Tuolumne co., cen. California; 10,918 ft. (3328 m.).
Ack·lins Island \ˈa-klinz\. One of the Bahamas in Atlantic Ocean, adjoining Crooked Island and W of Mayaguana I.; 120 sq. mi. (311 sq. km.).
Ac·o·ma \ˈa-kō-mə, ˈä-\. Pueblo of Acoma Indians, Cibola co., New Mexico; on reservation 60 mi. (96 km.) W of Albuquerque, pop. (1990c) 2590; situated on rock mesa (**Acoma Rock**) 357 ft. (109 m.) high with steep sides and difficult trail. Discovered by Spanish explorer Francisco Coronado's men 1540; captured by Juan de Oñate 1599; joined in Pueblo revolts against Spanish 1680, 1696; subdued 1692, 1699.
Acon·ca·gua \ˌä-kōn-ˈkä-gwä\. **1.** Mountain, W Argentina, near Chilean border at Uspallata Pass; 22,834 ft. (6960 m.); highest peak of Andes and of Western Hemisphere; first climbed 1897.
2. River, cen. Chile; rises on slopes of Aconcagua Mt.; flows W into Pacific Ocean 12 mi. (19 km.) N of Valparaíso; ab. 120 mi. (193 km.) long.
3. Former province of cen. Chile.
4. See VALPARAÍSO 2.
Acon·qui·ja \ˌä-kōn-ˈkē-ä\. Peak in the Andes, Tucumán prov., N Argentina; ab. 16,400 ft. (5000 m.).
Açores. See AZORES.
Ac·qui Ter·me \ˈä-kwē-ˈter-mā\; *anc.* **Aq·uae** \ˈa-ˌkwē, ˈä-ˌkwī\ *or* **Aquae Sta·ti·el·lae** \ˌstā-shē-ˈe-lē, ˌstä-tē-ˈe-ˌlī\. Commune, Alessandria prov., Piedmont, NW Italy, 17 mi. (27 km.) SSW of the commune Alessandria; pop. (1989c) 20,960; sulfurous waters and mud baths, known in Roman times.
Ac·rae \ˈa-ˌkrē\. Ancient town, SE Sicily, Italy, near present-day commune of Palazzolo Acreide; ancient Greek theater and necropolis. Founded 664 B.C. by Siracusans; suffered earthquake 1693.
Acragas. See AGRIGENTO 2.
Acre \ˈä-krə, -kər, *chiefly Brit* ˈā-kər\ *or* **ʻAk·ko** \ˈä-kō\ *or Fr.* **Saint–Jean–d'Acre** \san^{n}-zhä^{n}-ˈdȧkr^{ə}\; *Old Testament* **Ac·cho** \ˈä-kō, ˈa-\ *or New Testament* **Ptol·e·ma·ïs** \ˌtä-lə-ˈmā-is\. Seaport city, Israel, on promontory 13 mi. (21 km.) N of Mt. Carmel; pop. (1990e) 37,400; fishing.
History: As a city of Phoenicia, known as Ptolemaïs; captured by Arabs 638 A.D.; a Syrian town under the Seljuq Turks when attacked by Crusaders 12th cent.; as St.-Jean-d'Acre, included in the Kingdom of Jerusalem set up by Crusaders 1104–87, 1191–1291; conquered by Muslim Sultan Saladin 1187, reconquered by French King Philip Augustus 1191; residence of Knights of St. John 13th cent.; became Muslim again at fall of Jerusalem 1291; captured by Turks 1517; declined until 18th cent.; besieged by French Emperor Napoléon 1799; as part of Syria captured by Egyptian Viceroy Muḥammad ʻAlī Pasha 1832; taken by British 1840 and

restored to Ottoman Empire; again taken by British Sept. 23, 1918; part of Israel 1948.

Acre \'ä-krē, -ˌkrā\; *formerly* **Aqui·ry** \ˌä-kē-'rē\. **1.** River, W cen. South America; ab. 400 mi. (644 km.) long; chief tributary of Purus; forms part of boundary bet. Brazil and Bolivia, and bet. Brazil and Peru.

2. State, W Brazil; ✻ Rio Branco; rubber production (esp. important 1895–1910); formerly territory of Bolivia; encroachment of Brazilian traders led to trouble with Bolivia; revolt 1899 and independence declared; annexed by Brazil by treaty (1903), with payment of about $10,000,000 to Bolivia. See table at BRAZIL.

Acro·ce·rau·nia \ˌa-krō-sə-'rò-nē-ə\. Promontory, NW Epirus, ancient Greece, opp. SE point of Italy. To S along coast and inland heights sometimes called **Ac·ro·ce·rau·ni·an Mts.** \-nē-ən, -nyən\ *also* **Ka·na·lit Mts.** \kä-'nä-lēt\. Promontory now known as Cape Gjuhëzës in SW Albania.

Ac·ro·co·rin·thus \ˌa-krō-kə-'rin-thəs\. Acropolis of Corinth, Greece, a rock 1887 ft. (575 m.) high on which was anciently a citadel, also a temple of Aphrodite; at its foot the Pirene spring; in Middle Ages site of Byzantine fortifications.

Acro·ï·num \ə-'krō-i-nəm\ *or* **Akro·i·non** \ə-'krō-i-ˌnän\. Ancient town, S Phrygia, Asia Minor, near the modern Afyon, W cen. Turkey; battle 739 A.D. in which Byzantine Emperor Leo III defeated the Muslims.

Ac·te \'ak-tē\ *or Gk.* **Ak·tí** \äk-'tē\. Most easterly of the three peninsulas of Chalcidice, Macedonia, NE Greece, extends SE into Aegean Sea bet. Strymonic Gulf on the N and Singitic Gulf on the S; ab. 35 mi. (56 km.) long; at its tip is Mt. Athos (see ATHOS). Its narrow isthmus, where it joins the mainland near Acanthus, was cut by a canal by orders of Persian King Xerxes 480 B.C.

Ac·ti·um \'ak-shē-əm, 'ak-tē-\. Promontory and ancient town, W cen. Greece, on S side of entrance to Amvrakitós Kólpos; scene of naval battle 434 B.C. preliminary to Peloponnesian War and of famous naval victory of Roman leader Octavius over rival Marcus Antonius and Egyptian Queen Cleopatra 31 B.C. by which Octavius became emperor of Rome as Augustus.

Ac·ton \'ak-tən\. **1.** Town, Middlesex co., NE Massachusetts, 13 mi. (21 km.) SSE of Lowell; pop. (1990c) 17,872.

2. County, Quebec, Canada. See table at QUEBEC.

3. Former municipal borough, SE England; now part of London borough of Ealing; known as a center of Puritanism during the Commonwealth.

Acton Vale. Town, S Quebec, Canada, 36 mi. (58 km.) NW of Sherbrooke; pop. (1991c) 4468.

Açúcar, Pão de. See PÃO DE AÇÚCAR.

Acunum Acusio. See MONTÉLIMAR.

Acush·net \ə-'kùsh-nət\. Town, Bristol co., SE Massachusetts, on inlet of Buzzards Bay 3 mi. (4.8 km.) N of New Bedford; pop. (1990c) 9554; settled c. 1659; devastated during King Philip's War; scene of battle Sept. 1776 bet. minutemen and British troops.

Ac·worth \'ak-wərth\. City, Cobb co., NW Georgia; pop. (1990c) 4519.

Ada \'ā-də\. **1.** Mountain, E side of Baranof I., Alaska; 4536 ft. (1382 m.).

2. County in SW Idaho. See table at IDAHO.

3. City, ⊗ of Norman co., NW Minnesota, 32 mi. (51 km.) NNE of Moorhead; pop. (1990c) 1708.

4. Village, Hardin co., NW cen. Ohio, 15 mi. (24 km.) E of Lima; pop. (1990c) 5413; manufacture of footballs; Ohio Northern Univ. (1871).

5. City, ⊗ of Pontotoc co., S cen. Oklahoma, 65 mi. (104 km.) SE of Oklahoma City; pop. (1990c) 15,820; East Central Univ. (1909); settled 1889; incorp. 1910.

Adabazar. See ADAPAZARI.

Adai Khokh. See UILPATA.

Adair \ə-'dar\. **1.** Name of counties in four states of the U.S. See tables at IOWA, KENTUCKY, MISSOURI, OKLAHOMA.

2. Bay at NE end of Gulf of California, extending into NW Sonora state, Mexico.

Adak \'ā-ˌdak, 'ä-ˌdäk\. Island, cen. Andreanof Is., Aleutian Is., SW Alaska; 289 sq. mi. (748 sq. km.); treeless and barren but has several good harbors.

Ada·lar \ä-dä-'lär\. District, comprising group of small islands, E Sea of Marmara, İstanbul prov., Turkey in Asia; pop. (1990p) 19,353.

Adalia. See ANTALYA 2.

Adalia, Gulf of. See ANTALYA, GULF OF.

Adam \'á-dám\. Inland town, E Oman, SE Arabian Penin., W of Sur.

Ad·am, Mount \'a-dəm\. Peak, N West Falkland, Falkland Is.; 2297 ft. (700 m.).

Ad·a·mana \ˌa-də-'ma-nə\. Village, Apache co., Arizona, 20 mi. (32 km.) E of Holbrook; gateway to Petrified Forest National Park.

Ad·a·ma·wa \ˌä-dä-'mä-wä\. **1.** Region in W Africa, bet. Bight of Biafra and Lake Chad; ab. 50,000 sq. mi. (129,500 sq. km.); largely a plateau (1500 to 2000 ft. or 460 to 610 m.) with highest point about 6000 ft. (1830 m.); crossed by Benue River and tributaries; inhabited by Fulani and Hausa peoples, among others. First explored by Germans, then by French. From about 1900 divided by France, Germany, and Great Britain. German sector (former Kamerun) divided 1919 into British and French mandates: French mandate now part of Cameroon, British mandate as of 1961 vote split bet. Cameroon and Nigeria.

2. State of E Nigeria. See table at NIGERIA.

Ada·mel·lo, Mon·te \'mōn-tā-ˌä-dä-'mel-lō\. Mountain, Rhaetian Alps, N Italy, 27 mi. (43 km.) WNW of Trento and N of Lake Garda; 11,657 ft. (3553 m.).

Ad·ams \'a-dəmz\. **1.** Name of counties in 12 states of the U.S. See tables at COLORADO, IDAHO, ILLINOIS, INDIANA, IOWA, MISSISSIPPI, NEBRASKA, NORTH DAKOTA, OHIO, PENNSYLVANIA, WASHINGTON, WISCONSIN.

2. Town, N Berkshire co., W Massachusetts, 14 mi. (22 km.) NNE of Pittsfield; pop. (1990c) 9445. Settled 1762; incorp. as town 1778.

Adams, Mount. **1.** Peak in White Mts., Coos co., New Hampshire, in Presidential Range N of Mt. Washington; 5798 ft. (1767 m.), 2d highest peak of White Mts.

2. Peak, Essex co., NE New York; 3584 ft. (1092 m.).

3. Peak in Cascade Range, SW Yakima co., Washington, S of Mt. Rainier; 12,307 ft. (3751 m.).

Adams, Point. Cape at mouth of Columbia River, NW Oregon.

Adam's Bridge. Chain of shoals bet. Sri Lanka and SE coast of India (Tamil Nadu); ab. 30 mi. (48 km.) long; traditionally, the remains of a causeway built by Rama, hero of the *Ramayana,* to allow the passage of his army from India to Ceylon (now Sri Lanka) in order to rescue his wife Sita.

Adam's Peak *or Singhalese* **Sa·ma·na·la** \'sə-mə-nə-lə\. Mountain, S cen. Sri Lanka; 7360 ft. (2243 m.); sacred as place of pilgrimage for Hindus, Buddhists, and Muslims — named, according to the Muslim legend, after a large hollow (5 ft. or 1.5 m. long), resembling a footprint, in rock on its summit, said to have been made by Adam, Buddha, or Siva, standing there on one foot as an act of penance.

Ad·ams·town \'a-dəmz-ˌtaùn\. Village on Pitcairn I. (*q.v.*).

Adana. See ADEN.

Ada·na \ˌä-dä-'nä, *angl.* ə-'dä-nə, 'ä-də-ˌnä\; *formerly* **Sey·han** \sā-'hän\. **1.** Province of Turkey in Asia. See table at TURKEY.

2. City, its ✻, on left bank of Seyhan River about 30 mi. (48 km.) from its mouth; met. area pop. (1990p) 916,150; textiles.

History: Roman military station; after decline, restored by Caliph Hārūn ar-Rashīd c. 782 A.D.; held by Egyptians 1832–40; scene of Armenian massacres of 1909; occupied by French army 1919–21; scene of conference Jan. 30–31, 1943 bet. British Prime Minister Winston Churchill for Allies and Turkish officials.

Ada·pa·za·rı \ˌä-dä-ˌpä-zä-'rə, *angl.* -'rē\; *formerly* **Ada·ba·zar** \ˌä-dä-bä-'zär\. Town, ✻ of Sakarya prov., NW Turkey in Asia, ab. 80 mi. (130 km.) E of İstanbul; pop. (1990p) 171,225; tobacco products; has rail connections with Üsküdar.

Adare \ə-ˈdar\. Cape, NE Victoria Land, Antarctica, in Ross Dependency, 71°17′S, 170°14′E.

Ad·da \ˈäd-dä\. River, Lombardy, N Italy; flows S through Lake Como into Po River 7 mi. (11 km.) W of Cremona; 194 mi. (312 km.) long.

Ad Da·bah \ȧd-ˈdȧ-bə\ *or* **El Dab'a** \ȧl-\. Village on coastal road, NW Egypt, 30 mi. (48 km.) W of El Alamein; seized by Germans June 1942 in their advance to El Alamein.

Ad Dabbah. See ED DEBBA.

Ad Dah·nā' \ˌȧd-dȧk̲-ˈnä\ *or* **Dah·na** \dȧk̲-ˈnä, dä-\ *also* **Da·ha·na** \ˌdȧ-hə-ˈnä\. Desert region, NE Nejd, Saudi Arabia; links the deserts of An Nafūd to the N and Rub' al-Khali to the S.

Ad Dāmir. See ED DAMER.

Ad Dam·mām \ˌȧd-dȧm-ˈmäm, *angl.* ˌad-də-ˈmam\ *or* **Dam·mam.** City and oil center E Saudi Arabia, near coast of Persian Gulf opp. Bahrain; pop. (1980e) 200,000; has an international airport.

Ad–Dawhah. See DOHA.

Ad·ding·ton \ˈa-diŋ-tən\. See *Lennox and Addington* in table at ONTARIO.

Ad Dir'īyah \ˌȧd-der-ˈē-ə\ *also* **De·rai·yeh** *or* **Di·ri·yah** \de-ˈrē-ə\. Town, cen. Saudi Arabia, just W of Riyadh; formerly ✻ of the Wahhabis; captured and sacked by Egyptian commander Ibrāhīm Pasha 1818.

Ad·dis Ab·a·ba *or Ital.* **Addis Abe·ba** \ˈäd-dis-ˈä-bä-ˌbä, ˈa-dəs-ˈa-bə-bə\. City, ✻ of Ethiopia, in cen. part; pop. (1989e) 1,732,080; alt. over 8000 ft. (2438 m.); footwear, textiles; food processing; university (1961); site of headquarters of Organization of African Unity. Scene of peace treaty by which Italy recognized the independence of Ethiopia 1896; ✻ of Ethiopia since 1896; occupied by Italians May 5, 1936 signaling end of Ethiopian resistance to invasion; restored by British April 1941.

Ad·di·son \ˈa-də-sən\. **1.** County in W Vermont, bordering on Lake Champlain. See table at VERMONT.
2. Village, Du Page co., NE Illinois, W of Chicago; pop. (1990c) 32,058; residential.
3. City, Dallas co., NE Texas, N of the city of Dallas; pop. (1990c) 8783.
4. Town, Washington co., SE Wisconsin; pop. (1990c) 3051.

Ad Dī·wā·nī·yah \ˌȧd-ˌdē-ˌwä-ˈnē-yə\. Town, S cen. Iraq, on the Euphrates 40 mi. (64 km.) SE of Al Ḩillah; on the Baghdad-Basra railroad line; in an agricultural region.

Ad·do Elephant National Park \ˈa-dō\. National park, S Eastern Cape prov., Rep. of South Africa; 26.5 sq. mi. (69 sq. km.); habitat for rare Addo elephant and Cape buffalo; estab. 1931.

Ad Duwaym. See ED DUEIM.

Adel \ā-ˈdel\. **1.** City, ⊗ of Cook co., S Georgia; pop. (1990c) 5093.
2. Town, ⊗ of Dallas co., S cen. Iowa, 24 mi. (39 km.) W of Des Moines; pop. (1990c) 3304.

Ad·e·laide \ˈa-də-ˌlād\. City, ✻ of South Australia, Australia, in SE part on Torrens River and 7 mi. (11 km.) by rail from its port, Port Adelaide; met. area pop. (1989e) 1,036,700; large export trade; Univ. of Adelaide (1874), Flinders Univ. of South Australia (1966), two cathedrals; founded 1837; first municipality in Australia to be incorp. (1840).

Adelaide Island. Island, W of Antarctic Penin., British Antarctic Terr., Antarctica; ab. 68 mi. (109 km.) long, 20 mi. (32 km.) wide.

Adelaide Peninsula. Peninsula, Nunavut, Canada, 68°09′N, 97°45′W, opp. King William I.

Adé·lie Coast *also* **Adé·lie Land** \ˈa-də-lē\ *or Fr.* **Terre Adé·lie** \ˌter-ȧ-dā-ˈlē\. Part of Antarctica, bet. 66° and 67°S, 136° and 142°E; estimated area ab. 150,000 sq. mi. (388,500 sq. km.). First sighted by Capt. d'Urville of French navy 1840; explored by Australian explorer Douglas Mawson in his expeditions of 1911–14, 1929–31; placed under French sovereignty by decree 1938; part of French Southern and Antarctic Territories. See WILKES LAND.

Adelsberg. See POSTOJNA.

Aden \ˈä-dən, ˈā-\; *anc.* **Ad·a·na** \ˈȧ-dȧ-nə\. **1.** Former British colony on coast of SW Arabian Penin., now part of Yemen; 75 sq. mi. (194 sq. km.), with Perim I. 80 sq. mi. (207 sq. km.).
2. Seaport, S Yemen, on Gulf of Aden; pop. (1984e) 318,000; formerly ✻ of the People's Democratic Republic of Yemen, and before that ✻ of Aden Protectorate.

History: Trading port in Roman times; chief port on medieval Arab trade route between the Red Sea and the Persian Gulf and India; unsuccessfully attacked by Portuguese under Afonso de Albuquerque 1513; captured by Turks 1538; ruled by sultans of San'a from 17th century; held by British and governed as part of India 1839–1937; increased greatly in importance as coaling station and transshipment point after opening of Suez Canal 1869; separated from India and made crown colony 1937; a fortified naval base during WWII; member of Federation of South Arabia 1963–67; ✻ of independent republic 1968 until moved to San'a 1990.

Aden, Gulf of. Arm of Indian Ocean bet. S coast of Arabian Penin. and Somalia, E Africa; ab. 550 mi. (885 km.) long; connecting on W through Bab el Mandeb with the Red Sea. Controlled by British after their occupation of Aden 1839, Perim 1857, and Socotra 1876 (*qq.v.*).

Aden Protectorate. Former British protectorate, S coast of Arabian Penin., extending from Aden to border of Oman; 112,000 sq. mi. (290,080 sq. km.); consisted of a number of states whose rulers had entered into treaty relations with Great Britain 1882–1914; states in W region formed Federation of South Arabia Feb. 1959, joined by other states 1959–65; became part of independent People's Democratic Rep. of Yemen 1967.

Adernò. See ADRANO.

Ad·i·a·be·ne \ˌa-dē-ə-ˈbē-nē\. Region of ancient Assyria in N part, E of the Tigris River and bet. the Great Zab and the Little Zab; later much extended.

Adi·ge \ˈä-dē-ˌjā, -də-\ *or Lat.* **Ath·e·sis** \ˈa-thə-səs\ *or Ger.* **Etsch** \ˈech\. River, NE Italy; rises in Rhaetian Alps, flows SE and S past Merano, Trento, and Verona to Adriatic Sea bet. Venice and mouths of Po; 255 mi. (410 km.) long; navigable for 170 mi. (274 km.). Changed its course 587 A.D.; scene of many battles, the best known of which occurred 1799, when French Gen. Barthélemy Schérer defeated the Austrians, and in the Austrian-Italian campaign of 1916 during WWI.

Adigey Autonomous Oblast. See ADYGEA..

Ad·i·ron·dack Mountains \ˌa-də-ˈrän-ˌdak\. Mountain group, chiefly in Clinton, Essex, Hamilton, and Franklin cos., NE New York; highest Mt. Marcy 5344 ft. (1629 m.); others Algonquin Peak 5114 ft. (1559 m.), Skylight 4926 ft. (1501 m.), and Haystack 4960 ft. (1512 m.); includes many lakes, as Saranac, Placid, Tupper, Long, and Raquette; source of Hudson and Ausable rivers; noted for fine scenery; has many resorts, esp. for winter sports. In center of mountain region is the **Adirondack Park,** area over 5,000,000 acres (2,025,000 hectares), set aside by state with camp sites for public recreation and to conserve forests and water supply.

Adı·ya·man \ä-ˌdə-yä-ˈmän\. **1.** Province of Turkey in Asia. See table at TURKEY.
2. Town, its ✻; pop. (1990p) 100,045.

Adjar·i·an Autonomous Republic \ə-ˈjär-ē-ən\ *or* **Adzhar** \ˈä-ˌjär, ə-ˈjär\ *or* **Adzhar·ia** *or* **Ajar·ia** \ə-ˈjär-ē-ə\. Subdivision, SW Republic of Georgia, on Black Sea coast, bordering Turkey to the S; 1158 sq. mi. (2999 sq. km.); pop. (1991e) 381,500; ✻ Batumi; mountainous with dense forests; has heavy rainfall; watered in SW by lower course of Çoruh (Chorokh) River; plain along Black Sea has subtropical vegetation; avocados, citrus fruits, tea, tobacco; livestock rearing; oil refining. Controlled 17th and 18th cents. by Turks who introduced Islamic influences; greater part of region annexed by Russia middle of 19th cent. and Batumi acquired 1877–78; after Bolshevik Revolution of 1917 held by Turks

---

\ə\ **abut** \ᵊ\ matches \ᵊ\ kitten, Fr table \ər\ **further** \a\ **ash** \ā\ **ace** \ä\ cot, **cart** \ȧ\ Fr bac \au̇\ **out** \b\ Span Avila \ch\ **chin** \e\ **bet** \ē\ **easy** \g\ **go** \i\ **hit** \ī\ **ice** \j\ **job** \k̲\ Ger **ich, Buch** \ⁿ\ Fr **vin** \ŋ\ **sing** \ō\ **go** \ȯ\ **all** \ȯ\ **law** \œ\ Fr **bœuf** \œ̄\ Fr **feu** \ȯi\ **boy** \th\ **thin** \t͟h\ **this** \ü\ **loot** \u̇\ **foot** \ue\ Ger **füllen** \u̇e\ Fr **rue** \y\ **yet** \ʸ\ Fr digne \ˈdēnʸ\, nuit \ˈnwʸē\ \yü\ **few** \yu̇\ **fury** \zh\ **vision**

for a time but restored to Russia 1921; an autonomous republic of the U.S.S.R. before 1991.

Ad·jun·tas \äth-ˈkün-täs\. Town and municipality, W cen. Puerto Rico; munic. pop. (1990c) 19,451; summer resort.

Ad·mi·ral·ty Bay \ˈad-mrəl-tē, -mə-rəl-\. See SOUTH SHETLAND ISLANDS.

Admiralty Inlet. **1.** Branch of Puget Sound, NW Washington, bet. Whidbey I. and mainland (Island and Jefferson cos.). **2.** Fjord, NW Baffin I., Nunavut, Canada, opening into Lancaster Sound; 180 mi. (290 km.) long; cuts off Brodeur Peninsula to the W.

Admiralty Island. **1.** Island, N Alexander Archipelago, SE Alaska, bet. mainland on E and Chichagof and Baranof islands on W; ab. 90 mi. (145 km.) long; 1650 sq. mi. (4724 sq. km.). **2.** See MANUS 2.

Admiralty Islands *or often* **Ad·mi·ral·ties** \ˈad-mrəl-tēz, -mə-rəl-\. Island group, W Pacific Ocean, N of the island of New Guinea and ab. 260 mi. (418 km.) W of New Hanover I.; 800 sq. mi. (2072 sq. km.); pop. (1989e) 29,700; comprises Manus, the only large island, Rambutyo, and ab. 16 small islands; part of Bismarck Archipelago, constituting with Northwestern Is. the Manus dist. of Papua New Guinea; ⁕ Lorengau; copra; fishing. First seen by Dutch explorers Willem Schouten and Jakob Le Maire 1616; became part of German protectorate 1884; occupied by Australian forces 1914; mandated to Australia 1920. Seized by Japanese 1942; liberated by Allied forces 1944.

Admiralty Mountains. Mountains on coast, N part of Victoria Land, Antarctica.

Admiralty Sound. Deep inlet, SW coast of Tierra del Fuego, Chile.

Ado·na·ra \ˌä-dō-ˈnä-rä\ *also* **Adu·na·ra** *or* **Adoe·na·ra** \ˌä-dü-\. Island, Lesser Sunda Is., Indonesia; bet. E end of Flores and Lomblen islands; ab. 23 mi. (37 km.) long by 11 mi. (18 km.) wide; 224 sq. mi. (580 sq. km.); main settlement Sagu on N coast.

Ado·ni \ə-ˈdō-nē\. Town, W Andhra Pradesh, S India, 142 mi. (228 km.) SW of Hyderabad; pop. (1991p) 135,718.

Adour \ə-ˈdür\; *anc.* **At·u·rus** \ˈa-tyů-rəs, -chů-\. River, SW France; flows NW and W from Pyrenees to Bay of Biscay near Biarritz; 208 mi. (335 km.) long.

Adra \ˈä-thrä\; *anc.* **Ab·de·ra** \ab-ˈdir-ə\. Seaport, Almería prov., SE Spain, 30 mi. (48 km.) W of the seaport of Almería; pop. (1991c) 20,104. Ancient town, Abdera, in Baetica, S Hispania, at foot of hill below present town; a maritime city founded by Carthaginians, taken by Romans.

Adramyttium. See EDREMİT.

Adramyttium, Gulf of. See EDREMİT, GULF OF.

Adra·no \ä-ˈdrä-nō\; *formerly* **Ader·nò** \ˌä-der-ˈnō\; *anc.* **Ha·dra·num** \hə-ˈdrā-nəm\. Commune, Catania prov., E Sicily, Italy, at foot of Mt. Etna and 24 mi. (39 km.) NW of the commune of Catania; pop. (1989c) 35,045; founded c. 400 B.C. by Syracusan ruler Dionysius the Elder; parts of ancient walls still standing; has Norman castle built in 1157.

Adranos. See ATRANOS.

Adrar \ä-ˈdrär\. Name of several mountainous regions in Sahara Desert region of NW Africa: (1) Region, W Mauritania, bordering on SE Western Sahara; (2) *or in full* **Adrar des Ifo·ras** \dā-ˌzē-fō-ˈrä\. Region, cen. Sahara, NE of Tombouctou, Mali.

Adria. See ADRIATIC SEA.

Adria \ˈä-drē-ä\; *anc.* **Ha·dria** \ˈhā-drē-ə\ *also* **Ha·tria** \ˈhā-trē-a\ *or* **Atria** \ˈā-trē-ə\. Commune, Rovigo prov., Veneto, NE Italy, 15 mi. (24 km.) E of the commune of Rovigo; pop. (1989c) 21,288; orig. on Adriatic Sea but now 13 mi. (21 km.) inland. Ancient Etruscan settlement which gave its name to Adriatic Sea; in Roman times, a port and naval station.

Adri·an \ˈā-drē-ən\. City, ⊗ of Lenawee co., SE Michigan, on Raisin River 59 mi. (95 km.) SW of Detroit; pop. (1990c) 22,097; Adrian Coll. (1845), Siena Heights Coll. (1919); settled 1825; incorp. as city 1853.

Adrianople. See EDİRNE.

Adrianopolis. See EDİRNE 2.

Adri·at·ic Sea \ˌā-drē-ˈa-tik-, ˌa-\ *or Ital.* **Ma·re Adri·a·ti·co** \ˈmä-rā-ˌä-drē-ˈä-tē-ˌkō\; *anc.* **Adria** \ˈā-drē-ə\ *or* **Mare Adri·at·i·cum** \ˈmar-ē-ˌā-drē-ˈa-ti-kəm, ˌa-drē-\. Arm of Mediterranean Sea bet. Italy and Balkan Penin.; ab. 500 mi. (804 km.) long, av. width ab. 110 mi. (177 km.).

Adua. See ADWA.

Adu·la \ˈä-dü-ˌlä\. Mountain group, Lepontine Alps, SE Switzerland; highest peak Rheinwaldhorn 11,158 ft. (3401 m.).

Adul·lam \ə-ˈdə-ləm\. Ancient village, Israel, 15 mi. (24 km.) SW of Jerusalem; now an archaeological site; a cave in its vicinity was from early times a place of refuge (mentioned several times in Bible).

Adunara. See ADONARA.

Aduwa. See ADWA.

Ad·vent Bay \ˈad-ˌvent\. Bay in Ice Fjord, Spitsbergen, Svalbard, Norway; settlements at Longyearbyen and Advent City.

Advent City. Mining settlement on Advent Bay, Spitsbergen, Norway.

Ad·wa \ˈä-dwä, ˈa-\ *also* **Adu·wa** *or Ital.* **Adua** \ˈä-dü-ä\. Town, N Ethiopia, ab. 80 mi. (129 km.) S of Asmara, Eritrea; pop. (1989e) 17,476; scene of disastrous defeat of Italians March 1, 1896 by Emperor Menelik II, because of which Ethiopia secured recognition of its independence; captured by Italians soon after invasion of Ethiopia Oct. 1935; included in Eritrea 1935–41; retaken by British 1941.

Ad·wick le Street \ˈa-dwik-lə-ˈstrēt, -dik-\. Town, West Riding, Yorkshire, England, 20 mi. (32 km.) NE of Sheffield.

Ady·gea *or* **Ady·ge·ya** \ˌä-di-ˈgā-ə\. Republic, S Russia in Europe, NE of Black Sea, entirely surrounded by Krasnodar Kray; 2934 sq. mi. (7599 sq. km.); pop. (1991e) 437,400; Kuban' River marks N border; land partly river basin, partly hilly; corn, potatoes, tobacco, wheat; livestock raising; lumber, petroleum. Part of former Kuban' administrative unit, inhabited in part by a Circassian people who had been Christianized in 6th cent. and converted to Islam 17th cent.; created an autonomous area 1922 and a region 1936. In WWII occupied by Germany Aug. 1942–Jan. 1943; declared itself a republic within Russia 1991; subsequently became member of Russian Federation; an autonomous oblast (**Ady·gei** *or* **Adi·gey** \ˌə-di-ˈgyā\) of the U.S.S.R. before 1991.

Adzhar. See ADJARIAN AUTONOMOUS REPUBLIC.

Adzhar Autonomous Soviet Socialist Republic *or* **Adzhar·ska·ya Autonomous Soviet Socialist Republic** \ə-ˈjär-skə-yə\. Autonomous republic of Georgian S.S.R., U.S.S.R. See ADJARIAN AUTONOMOUS REPUBLIC.

Adzharia. See ADJARIAN AUTONOMOUS REPUBLIC.

Aea. See KUTAISI.

Aeaea. See CIRCEO, MONTE.

Ædua. See AUTUN.

Aegadian Islands. See EGADI, ISOLE.

Ae·ga·le·os, Mount \ˌe-ˈgä-lā-ˌōs, *angl.* ē-ˈgā-lē-ˌōs\. Mountain, W Attica, Greece, just W of Athens; overlooks the Bay of Eleusis and the island of Salamis; 1573 ft. (479 m.); on it sat Persian King Xerxes watching the defeat of his fleet by the Greeks in the battle of Salamis 480 B.C.

Aegates. See EGADI, ISOLE.

Ae·ge·an Islands \ē-ˈjē-ən\. **1.** Islands of the Aegean Sea, incl. the Cyclades, Sporades, and Dodecanese, among others.

History: Cyclades and S islands probably part of Aegean civilization 2d millennium B.C. (see AEGEAN SEA); colonized by Aeolian, Dorian, and Ionian Greeks from mainland c. 1000–700 B.C.; during Greek wars with Persia, islands in Thracian Sea helped Persia, but E islands were under influence of revolting Ionian cities; allied with or dependent upon Athens, the leader of the Delian League (see ATHENS 10), 5th cent. B.C.; except for Cyclades, chiefly controlled by Macedonian empire until they were conquered by Rome 2d cent. B.C.; ruled by Byzantine Empire 5th–13th cents.; ravaged and seized by Roger II of Sicily during Second Crusade 1147; Naxos became center of duchy of Naxos which was established 1207 by Venice from its acquisitions in the Fourth Crusade; in 13th cent., politically controlled by leading Venetian families and commercially dominated by Venetian traders; Imbros, Samothrace, Lesbos recovered by Byzantine Empire 1261; W islands remained under Venetian

Duchy of the Archipelago; Chios held by Genoese 1261–1329; Rhodes belonged to Knights of St. John of Jerusalem (Hospitalers) 1310–1522; in a series of Venetian wars with Ottoman Turks during 15th and 16th cents., gradually conquered by Turks; part of Ottoman Empire from death of Sultan Süleyman the Magnificent 1566 until joined Greek revolt 1821; most of islands became part of independent Greece by Treaty of Adrianople 1829.

2. *or Ital.* **Iso·le Ita·li·a·ne dell'·Egeo** \ˈē-zō-ˌlā-ē-ˌtä-lē-ˈä-nā-ˌdel-ā-ˈjā-ō\. The Italian Aegean Is. (Dodecanese, Rhodes, and Castelrosso) 1923–47.

Aegean Sea *or Gk.* **Ai·gai·on Pé·la·gos** \ˈe-ye-ˌön-ˈpā-lä-ˌgōs\. Arm of Mediterranean Sea bet. Greece and Turkey; ab. 400 mi. (644 km.) long by 200 mi. (322 km.) wide. It was the center of earliest European civilization, formerly called Mycenean or Minoan but in broader aspects now termed Aegean (c. 3000–1100 B.C.).

Ae·ge·ri, Lake of \ˈā-gə-rē\ *or Ger.* **Äge·ri·see** \ˈā-gə-rē-ˈzā\. Lake, Zug canton, Switzerland, E of Lake of Zug; ab. 3 sq. mi. (8 sq. km.).

Ægidia. See KOPER.

Ae·gi·na \ē-ˈjī-nə\ *or Gk.* **Aí·yi·na** \ˈe-yē-nä\. **1.** Island in the Saronic Gulf, attached to Attica dept., Greece; off SE coast of Greece; 9 mi. (14 km.) long.

2. Commune, Attica dept., Greece, on W coast of Aegina I.; pop. (1991p) 5440.

History: Greek state of maritime importance even in pre-Dorian times; first state in European Greece to coin money in the standard which came to prevail in ancient times; a leading commercial state at the beginning of 5th cent. B.C., but gradually eclipsed by Athens; ravaged Attica on behalf of Thebes; gave submission to Persia 491 B.C.; scene of battle in the so-called First Peloponnesian War in which Aeginetans, allies of Sparta, were defeated by Athens 457 B.C.; lost its greatness after Athens expelled its people 431 B.C.; taken by the Romans 133 B.C. Center of the rebel Greek government after its defeat by the Turks at Mesolóngion 1826.

Aegina, Gulf of. See SARONIC GULF.

Aegium. See AÍYION.

Ae·gos·pot·a·mi \ˌē-gə-ˈspä-tə-ˌmī\ *or* **Ae·gos·pot·a·mos** \-məs\. Small river and town, ancient Thrace, in the Chersonese. Mouth of river on the Dardanelles scene of Spartan victory under Lysander over Athenian fleet 405 B.C., the last battle of the Peloponnesian War.

Aegusa. See LINOSA.

Aegyptus. See EGYPT.

Aelana. See AQABA.

Aelaniticus, Sinus. See AQABA, GULF OF.

Aelia Capitolina. See JERUSALEM 3.

Æmilia. See EMILIA-ROMAGNA.

Æmilianum. See MILLAU.

Aeminium. See COIMBRA 2.

Aenaria. See ISCHIA.

Aenos. See ENEZ.

Aenus. See INN.

Aeoliae Insulae. See LIPARI ISLANDS.

Ae·o·lis \ˈē-ō-lis\ *or* **Ae·o·lia** \ē-ˈō-lē-ə, -lyə\. Ancient country, NW Asia Minor; included island of Lesbos; settled by Aeolian Greeks, a Thessalian people, who founded a number of cities along the coast before 1000 B.C. Later formed a district of Mysia and Lydia, overcome by Lydian King Croesus.

Aequum Tuticum. See ARIANO IRPINO.

A–erh–chin Shan. See ALTUN SHAN.

Ærø \ˈer-œ, -ə\. Island in the Baltic, Fyn co., Denmark, S of Fyn I.; ab. 15 mi. (24 km.) long; 34 sq. mi. (88 sq. km.); pop. (1989e) 7940.

Æsernia. See ISÉRNIA.

Æsis. See IESI.

A Es·tra·da \ˌä-es-ˈträ-t͟hä\ *or* **La Es·tra·da** \ˌlä-\. City, Pontevedra prov., NW Spain, 20 mi. (32 km.) NNE of the commune of Pontevedra; pop. (1991c) 22,391.

Aethalia. See ELBA 2.

Ae·thi·o·pia \ˌē-thē-ˈō-pē-ə\. Ancient name for the region of NE Africa, including all or part of modern Egypt, Sudan, Eritrea, Ethiopia, Djibouti, and as far S as the knowledge of the ancients extended.

Ae·to·lia \ē-ˈtō-lē-ə, -lyə\ *also* **Ai·to·lia** \ˌe-tō-ˈlē-ä\. Ancient district, cen. Greece, N of Gulf of Patras and Locris, and E of Acarnania, now part of Aetolia and Acarnania dept. from which it is separated by the Achelous River.

History: In early times home of a group of tribes; first given unity by the formation of the Aetolian League 4th cent. B.C., a military confederation which at its height included most of cen. Greece and separated Sparta from the Achaean League (see ACHAEA); driven out of area of Peloponneses by Achaeans and Philip V of Macedon 3d cent. B.C.; helped Rome defeat Macedonians at Cynoscephalae 197 B.C.; punished by Rome for aiding Antiochus III of Syria 189 B.C.; subsequently incorporated into the Roman province of Achaea; became part of Byzantine (Greek) Empire 1204 A.D.; under Scanderbeg (see ALBANIA), Venetians, and Turks in the course of 15th cent.

Aetolia and Ac·ar·na·nia \ˌa-kər-ˈnā-nē-ə, -nyə\ *or Gk.* **Ai·to·lía kai Akar·na·nía** \ˌe-tō-ˈlē-ə-ˌke-ˌä-ˌkär-nä-ˈnē-ə\. Department of Greece. See table at GREECE.

Afars and Is·sas, French Territory of the \ä-ˈfär, ə-ˈfärz ... ē-ˈsä, i-ˈsäz\. Former overseas territory of France; became (1977) independent republic of Djibouti (*q.v.*).

Af·ghan·i·stan \af-ˈga-nə-ˌstan\. Islamic state, cen. Asia, bounded on N by Turkmenistan, Uzbekistan, and Tajikistan, on NE by China, on E and S by Pakistan, and on W by Iran; 250,775 sq. mi. (649,507 sq. km.); pop. (1992e) 18,052,000; ✱ Kabul.

Physical features: Has Helmand River in center and SW, flowing into Lake Helmand, Harī in NW, Amu Dar'ya on NE boundary, and Kabul in E, flowing to Indus; very mountainous in cen. and N sections, Hindu Kush ranges 15,000 to 25,000 ft. (4572 to 7620 m.); many fertile plains and valleys; desert regions in S; Khyber Pass on E border to Pakistan.

Chief products: Before the economy was devastated by the 1980s civil war, products included: Barley, corn, rice, wheat, fruits; cotton, wool; livestock; iron ore, natural gas, coal, copper; cement, textiles; carpets.

Chief cities: Kabul, Qandahār, Herat, Mazār-i-Sharīf.

History: In early times formed part of Persian and Alexander the Great's empires; Turkoman dynasty set up at Ghaznī (*q.v.*) in 10th century; conquered by Turkic ruler Ṭimur c. 1400; part, incl. Kabul, added to the Mogul Empire of India by its founder, Bābur (Ẓahīr-ud-Dīn Muḥammad) (1483–1530); Qandahār became independent 1709; with W India, seized by Persian King Nāder Shāh 1737; consolidated as a separate unit by Aḥmad Shāh Durrāni, at whose death (1773) the Afghan empire included E Persia, Afghanistan, Baluchistan, Kashmir, and the Punjab; under successive rulers soon lost Punjab and other territory; in 1809 entered first agreement with the British against the Persians and Russians; invaded by British in First Afghan War 1839–42; later fought Second Afghan War 1878–79; maintained a degree of independence under 'Abdorraḥmān Khān (1880–1901) who confirmed the cession of the Khyber Pass (*q.v.*) to the British; settled boundaries with India 1893, with Russia 1895. Neutral in WWI; recognized as independent by the British in the Treaty of Rawalpindi 1919; entered treaties with Persia, Turkey, and U.S.S.R., 1921; under the modernizing influence of Amānolāh Khān (1919–29), adopted constitution 1923; at the overthrow of Amānolāh, established new line of rulers under Nāder Khān (1929–33) whose son joined Turkey, Iraq, and Iran in forming an Oriental Entente 1937. Neutral in WWII; first Afghan minister to U.S. sent to Washington 1943; initiated its first five-year economic plan 1956; adopted new constitution 1964; monarchy overthrown and republic proclaimed July 17, 1973; bloody coup April 1978; invasion by Soviet troops Dec. 1979 to shore up a pro-Soviet

government; 10-year civil war ensued bet. guerrillas and Soviet and Afghan government troops; Soviet troops withdrew early 1989; Islamic republic proclaimed April 1992.

Af·ghan Turkistan \ˈaf-ˌgan, -gən\. Region, part of Turkistan (*q.v.*), NE Afghanistan, about coextensive with the district around Mazār-i-Sharīf. Some include also the prov. of Badakhshān to the E. Long under Uzbek influence and claimed by Russia; settled in favor of Afghanistan by Anglo-Russian Agreement 1859.

Afog·nak \ə-ˈfòg-ˌnak, -ˈfäg-\. Island, W side of Gulf of Alaska, N of Kodiak I. and separated from mainland by Shelikof Strait; 47 mi. (76 km.) long; 721 sq. mi. (1867 sq. km.).

Afon·so Cláu·dio \ə-ˈfōⁿ-(ˌ)sü-ˈklaù-dē-ˌü\. Municipality, Espírito Santo state, E Brazil, ab. 50 mi. (80 km.) WNW of Vitória.

Afra·go·la \ˌä-frä-ˈgō-lä\. Commune, Napoli prov., Campania, S Italy; pop. (1989c) 62,359.

Af·ri·ca \ˈa-fri-kə, ˈä-\. Second largest continent on the globe, in both Northern and Southern hemispheres with greater part N of the Equator; 4970 mi. (7997 km.) long, 4600 mi. (7401 km.) broad (max. E to W extent); 11,677,239 sq. mi. (30,244,049 sq. km. incl. offshore islands); coastline ab. 16,100 mi. (25,905 km.) long; pop. (1992e) 657,658,000.

Boundaries: On N, Mediterranean Sea; most northerly point Ras ben Sekka, 37°21′N; on NW separated from Europe by Strait of Gibraltar; joined on NE to Asia at Sinai Penin. On E, Red Sea and Indian Ocean (chief subdivisions Gulf of Aden and Mozambique Channel); chief island Madagascar, and several small groups; most easterly point Ras Hafun, 51°26′E. On S, Indian and Atlantic oceans (with arbitrary separation line at 20th meridian E long.); most southerly point Cape Agulhas, 34°52′S. On W, Atlantic Ocean (subdivision Gulf of Guinea); chief islands St. Helena and Ascension in South Atlantic and Cape Verde, Canary, and Madeira Is. groups in North Atlantic; most westerly point Cape Almadies, 17°32′W.

Mountains: Atlas Mts. in NW (highest peak 13,671 ft. or 4167 m.); high plateau region of Ethiopia in NE, Mts. Kenya and Kilimanjaro (its peak Mt. Kibo, highest in Africa, 19,340 ft. or 5895 m.) and Ruwenzori in E, and the Drakensberg in E part of Rep. of South Africa. Other notable physical features are the great desert of the Sahara in the N, partly desert region of the Sudan, the smaller Libyan and Nubian deserts of Egypt bordering the Nile Valley, and the Kalahari Desert in the S; nearly all the S third of the continent is plateau region.

Rivers: Nile in NE, Niger and Senegal in W, Congo in cen. part, and Zambezi, Orange, and Limpopo in S.

Lakes: Victoria, Tanganyika, Albert, and Rudolf in E, sources of the Nile or Congo, and Malawi in SE with outlet to the Zambezi; in cen. Sudan (region) is Chad, with area much reduced in dry season.

Political divisions: (1) Mainland: Algeria, Angola, Benin, Botswana, Burkina Faso, Burundi, Cameroon, Central African Rep., Chad, Democratic Rep. of the Congo, Rep. of the Congo, Djibouti, Egypt, Equatorial Guinea, Eritrea, Ethiopia, Gabon, Gambia, Ghana, Guinea, Guinea-Bissau, Ivory Coast, Kenya, Lesotho, Liberia, Libya, Malawi, Mali,

Mauritania, Morocco, Mozambique, Namibia, Niger, Nigeria, Rwanda, Senegal, Sierra Leone, Somalia, Rep. of South Africa, Sudan, Swaziland, Tanzania, Togo, Tunisia, Uganda, Western Sahara, Zambia, Zimbabwe. (2) Offshore islands: British Indian Ocean Territory, Canary Is., Cape Verde Is., Comoros, Madagascar, Madeira Is., Mauritius, Réunion, St. Helena and dependencies, São Tomé and Príncipe, Seychelles. Most of these states achieved independence bet. 1957 and 1968; see their individual entries for description and history.

Africa, Roman. Proconsular Roman province (*Lat.* **Africa Pro·con·su·la·ris** \ˌprō-ˌkän-sə-ˈlar-is\ formed after 146 B.C. from territory around Carthage, extended to include Numidia and N part of modern Libya. Later (bet. 30 B.C. and 180 A.D.) Egypt, Cyrenaica, Marmarica, and Mauretania became parts of Roman Empire; lost to Vandals in 5th cent. except for Egypt which was part of Byzantine Empire, later (641) conquered by Muslims.

Africa Orientale Italiana. See ITALIAN EAST AFRICA.

Afrine \ä-ˈfrēn\. River, S Turkey and NW Syria; rises in Gaziantep prov., S Turkey, flows S and SW through swamp region to join the Orontes at Antakya; 100 mi. (161 km.) long.

Afrique, Cape \å-ˈfrēk\. Cape, E Tunisia.

Af·ton \ˈaf-tən\. **1.** City, Washington co., Minnesota, on the St. Croix River; pop. (1990c) 2645.

2. River, SE Ayrshire, Scotland, flowing N to the Nith; 9 mi. (14 km.) long.

ʻAfu·la \ä-ˈfü-lə\. Town, N Israel, 6 mi. (10 km.) S of Nazareth; pop. (1990e) 25,000; railway junction; built 1925.

Af·yon \ä-ˈfyōn\ *or* **Af·yon·ka·ra·hi·sar** \ä-ˈfyōn-ˌkä-rä-hē-ˈsär\. City, ✻ of Afyonkarahisar prov., Turkey in Asia, on railroad line 128 mi. (206 km.) NW of Konya; pop. (1990p) 98,618; captured by Greeks Mar. 1921, and retaken by Turks Aug. 1921 during Greco-Turkish War.

Afyonkarahisar. Province of Turkey in Asia. See table at TURKEY.

Agade. See AKKAD 2.

Aga·dez \ä-gä-ˈdez\ *or* **Aga·dès** \-ˈdes\. City, W cen. Niger; pop. (1988p) 50,164.

Aga·dir \ˌä-gä-ˈdir, ˌa-\. Seaport, SW Morocco, ab. 123 mi. (198 km.) SW of Marrakech; pop. (1982c) 110,479.

History: Occupied in early 16th cent. by Portuguese; later became important port of Morocco; 2d crisis bet. France and Germany over authority in Morocco precipitated by arrival of German gunboat *Panther* 1911, but resolved peacefully (see MOROCCO); opened to commerce as a projected port Jan. 1, 1930. Destroyed by earthquakes 1960, since largely rebuilt.

Aga·le·ga Islands \ˌä-gä-ˈlā-gä\. Group of small islands in Indian Ocean, 540 mi. (869 km.) ENE of Madagascar; dependency of Mauritius.

Ag·a·men·ti·cus, Mount \ˌa-gə-ˈmen-ti-kəs\. Elevation, S York co., SW Maine, ab. 5 mi. (8 km.) from coast, 43°13′N lat.; 692 ft. (211 m.); a sailors' landmark.

Aga·na \ä-ˈgän-yä\. Town, ✻ of Guam, on W coast of island, on **Agana Bay** ab. 8 mi. (13 km.) NE of Apra Harbor, Mariana Islands, W Pacific Ocean; pop. (1990c) 1139.

Agar·ta·la \ə-ˈgər-tə-lə\. Town, ✻ of Tripura state, NE India, 125 mi. (201 km.) SSW of Shillong; pop. (1991p) 157,636.

Ag·as·siz, Mount \ˈa-gə-ˌsē\. Peak, Duchesne co., NE cen. Utah; 12,433 ft. (3790 m.).

Agassiz Needle. Peak in the Sierra Nevada, E Fresno co., S cen. California; 13,882 ft. (4231 m.).

Agassiz Peak. See SAN FRANCISCO PEAKS.

Agate Fossil Beds National Monument. See UNITED STATES, *National Monuments.*

Agatha. See AGDE.

Ag·at·tu \ˌä-gə-ˈtü\. Island, Near Is. group at W end of Aleutian Is., SW Alaska, SE of Attu; 85 sq. mi. (220 sq. km.); highest point 3089 ft. (942 m.); temporarily occupied by Japanese during WWII.

Ag·a·wam \ˈa-gə-ˌwäm\. **1.** Indian village on site of Ipswich, Essex co., Massachusetts; sold to white settlers 1638. Cultural center in 17th cent.; residence of poet Anne Bradstreet and of religious leader Nathaniel Ward.

2. Town, Hampden co., Massachusetts, SW of Springfield; pop. (1990c) 27,323; amusement park; settled 1636; incorp. 1885.

Agbatana. See HAMADĀN 2.

Agde \ˈägd\; *anc.* **Ag·a·tha** \ˈa-gə-thə\. Commune, Hérault dept., S France, 30 mi. (48 km.) SW of Montpellier; settled 6th cent. B.C. by Phocaeans; held by Visigoths; episcopal see 400–1790; 12th cent. medieval fortress cathedral (St.-Étienne).

Agedabia. See AJDĀBIYAH.

Agedincum. See SENS.

Agen \å-ˈzhe^{n}\; *anc.* **Agin·num** \ə-ˈji-nəm\. City, ✻ of Lot-et-Garonne dept., SW France, on Garonne River 74 mi. (119 km.) SE of Bordeaux; pop. (1990c) 32,233; noted for production of prunes. Was ✻ of Agenais (*q.v.*); a bishopric since 4th cent. A.D.; at end of Albigensian Crusade, location of an inquisition tribunal; joined Catholic League against Huguenots 1589.

Age·nais \åzh-ˈne, å-zhə-ˈnā\ *or* **Age·nois** \å-zhe-ˈnwä\. Historical region, SW France; part of ancient Guienne; ✻ Agen; approx. coextensive with Lot-et-Garonne dept.

History: Home of Nitiobriges, an ancient people of Gaul; in 4th cent. A.D. *Civitas Agennensium* which formed diocese of Agen (*q.v.*); part of Aquitaine (*q.v.*); acquired by dukes of Aquitaine as a hereditary countship c. 1038; passed to England 1152; given by Richard I as part of dowry of his sister Joan who married Count Raymond VI of Toulouse 1196; to French crown, but restored to England 1279; changed hands frequently in Hundred Years' War, but French after 1444; reunited to French crown 1615.

Agen·cy Lake \ˈā-jən-sē\. Inlet, Klamath co., S Oregon, at N end of Upper Klamath Lake.

Agenois. See AGENAIS.

Ageo \ˈä-gā-ˌō\. City, Saitama prefecture, Honshū, Japan, 25 mi. (40 km.) NNW of Tokyo; pop. (1990p) 194,952.

Ägerisee. See AEGERI, LAKE OF.

Aggershus. See AKERSHUS.

Agg·te·lek \ˈög-te-ˌlek\. Village, N Hungary, 25 mi. (40 km.) NNW of Miskolc; site of great limestone grotto with stalactites, underground stream, and many passages, of archaeological interest.

Agheila, Al– *or* **Agheila, El.** See AL ʻUQAYLAH.

Aghri Dagh. See ARARAT 2.

Aghrim. See AUGHRIM.

Agía Triáda. See HAGIA TRIADA.

Agin–Bur·yat Autonomous Okrug \ə-ˈgēn-bu̇r-ˈyät … ˈō-ˌkrük, -ˌbu̇r-ē-ˈät\. Administrative district, S Russia in Asia; 7336 sq. mi. (19,000 sq. km.); pop. (1991e) 77,800; ✻ Aginskoye; formed 1937.

Ag·in·court \ˈa-jin-ˌkōrt, ˈä-zhən-ˌku̇r\ *or Fr.* **Azin·court** \å-za^{n}-ˈkür\. Village, Pas-de-Calais dept., N France, 33 mi. (53 km.) WNW of Arras; scene of victory of Henry V of England over a larger force of French, demonstrating effectiveness of warfare by archers against heavily armed feudal array Oct. 25, 1415.

Aginnum. See AGEN.

Agin·sko·ye \ə-ˈgēn-skə-yə\. Town, ✻ of Agin-Buryat Autonomous Okrug, Russia, ab. 70 mi. (113 km.) SE of Chita; pop. (1991e) 9200.

Ágios Nikólaos. See ÁYIOS NIKÓLAOS.

Agi·ra \ä-ˈjē-rä\; *anc.* **Agyr·i·um** \ə-ˈjir-ē-əm\. Commune, Enna prov., cen. Sicily, Italy, 15 mi. (24 km.) ENE of the commune of Enna; ancient Siculian city colonized with Greeks by Greek Gen. Timoleon 339 B.C.

Aglar. See AQUILEIA.

Agna·del·lo \ˌä-nyä-ˈdel-lō\. Village, Cremona prov., N Italy; scene of defeat of Venetians by the French (as members of League of Cambrai) May 14, 1509.

\ə\ **abut** \ˈə\ matches \$^{ə}$\ kitten, Fr table \ər\ **further** \a\ **ash** \ā\ **ace** \ä\ **cot, cart** \å\ Fr bac \au̇\ **out** \b̲\ Span Avila \ch\ **chin** \e\ **bet** \ē\ **easy** \g\ **go** \i\ **hit** \ī\ **ice** \j\ **job** \k̲\ Ger **ich, Buch** \$^{n}$\ Fr vin \ŋ\ **sing** \ō\ **go** \ȯ\ **all** \ȯ\ **law** \œ\ Fr **bœuf** \œ̄\ Fr **feu** \ȯi\ **boy** \th\ **thin** \t̲h̲\ **this** \ü\ **loot** \u̇\ **foot** \ue\ Ger **füllen** \ue̅\ Fr **rue** \y\ **yet** \$^{y}$\ Fr digne \ˈdēn^{y}\, nuit \ˈnw^{y}ē\ \yü\ **few** \yu̇\ **fury** \zh\ **vision**

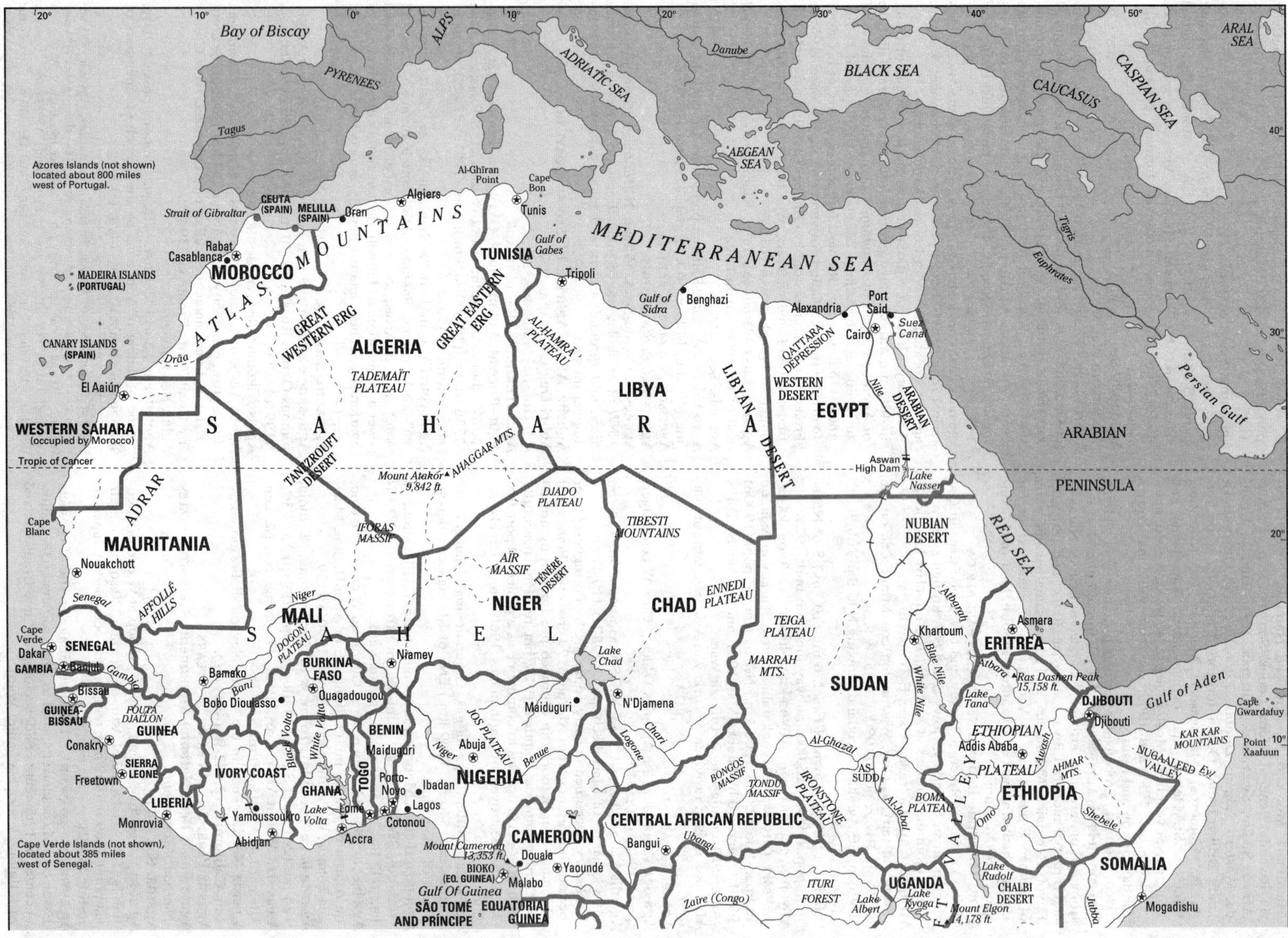

Bay of Biscay
PYRENEES
Tagus
ALPS
ADRIATIC SEA
Danube
BLACK SEA
AEGEAN SEA
CAUCASUS
CASPIAN SEA
ARAL SEA
Azores Islands (not shown) located about 800 miles west of Portugal.
Strait of Gibraltar
CEUTA (SPAIN)
MELILLA (SPAIN)
Oran
Algiers
Al-Ghīran Point
Cape Bon
Tunis
MEDITERRANEAN SEA
Tigris
Euphrates
Rabat
Casablanca
MOROCCO
ATLAS MOUNTAINS
MADEIRA ISLANDS (PORTUGAL)
CANARY ISLANDS (SPAIN)
Drâa
El Aaiún
GREAT WESTERN ERG
ALGERIA
TADEMAÏT PLATEAU
GREAT EASTERN ERG
TUNISIA
Gulf of Gabes
Tripoli
AL-HAMRĀ PLATEAU
Gulf of Sidra
Benghazi
LIBYA
LIBYAN DESERT
Alexandria
Port Said
Suez Canal
Cairo
QATTARA DEPRESSION
WESTERN DESERT
EGYPT
Nile
ARABIAN DESERT
Persian Gulf
ARABIAN
PENINSULA
WESTERN SAHARA (occupied by Morocco)
SAHARA
Tropic of Cancer
TANEZROUFT DESERT
Mount Atakor 9,842 ft.
AHAGGAR MTS.
Aswan High Dam
Lake Nasser
ADRAR
Cape Blanc
DJADO PLATEAU
TIBESTI MOUNTAINS
NUBIAN DESERT
RED SEA
MAURITANIA
IFORAS MASSIF
Nouakchott
AÏR MASSIF
TÉNÉRÉ DESERT
Senegal
AFFOLLÉ HILLS
Niger
MALI
NIGER
CHAD
ENNEDI PLATEAU
Atbarah
Asmara
SAHEL
DOGON PLATEAU
Cape Verde
Dakar
SENEGAL
GAMBIA
Banjul
Gambia
Niamey
Lake Chad
TEIGA PLATEAU
Khartoum
ERITREA
Bamako
Bani
BURKINA FASO
Ouagadougou
MARRAH MTS.
Blue Nile
White Nile
Atbara
Ras Dashen Peak 15,158 ft.
Bissau
GUINEA-BISSAU
Bobo Dioulasso
Maiduguri
N'Djamena
SUDAN
Lake Tana
DJIBOUTI
Djibouti
Gulf of Aden
Cape Gwardafuy
FOUTA DJALLON
GUINEA
Conakry
Black Volta
White Volta
BENIN
JOS PLATEAU
Chari
Logone
Al-Ghazāl
ETHIOPIAN PLATEAU
Addis Ababa
Awash
KAR KAR MOUNTAINS
Point Xaafuun
NUGAALEED VALLEY
SIERRA LEONE
Freetown
IVORY COAST
TOGO
Porto-Novo
Abuja
Benue
NIGERIA
Ibadan
Lagos
BONGOS MASSIF
TONDOU MASSIF
IRONSTONE PLATEAU
AS SUDD
AHMAR MTS.
ETHIOPIA
RIFT VALLEY
LIBERIA
Monrovia
Yamoussoukro
GHANA
Lake Volta
Lomé
Cotonou
Accra
Abidjan
CENTRAL AFRICAN REPUBLIC
Al-Jabal
BOMA PLATEAU
Omo
Shebele
Cape Verde Islands (not shown), located about 385 miles west of Senegal.
Mount Cameroon 13,353 ft.
CAMEROON
Douala
Yaoundé
Bangui
Ubangi
BIOKO (EQ. GUINEA)
Malabo
Gulf Of Guinea
SÃO TOMÉ AND PRÍNCIPE
EQUATORIAL GUINEA
Zaire (Congo)
ITURI FOREST
Lake Albert
UGANDA
Lake Kyoga
Mount Elgon 14,178 ft.
Lake Rudolf
CHALBI DESERT
Jubba
SOMALIA
Mogadishu
20°
10°
0°
10°
20°
30°
40°
50°
40°
30°
20°
10°

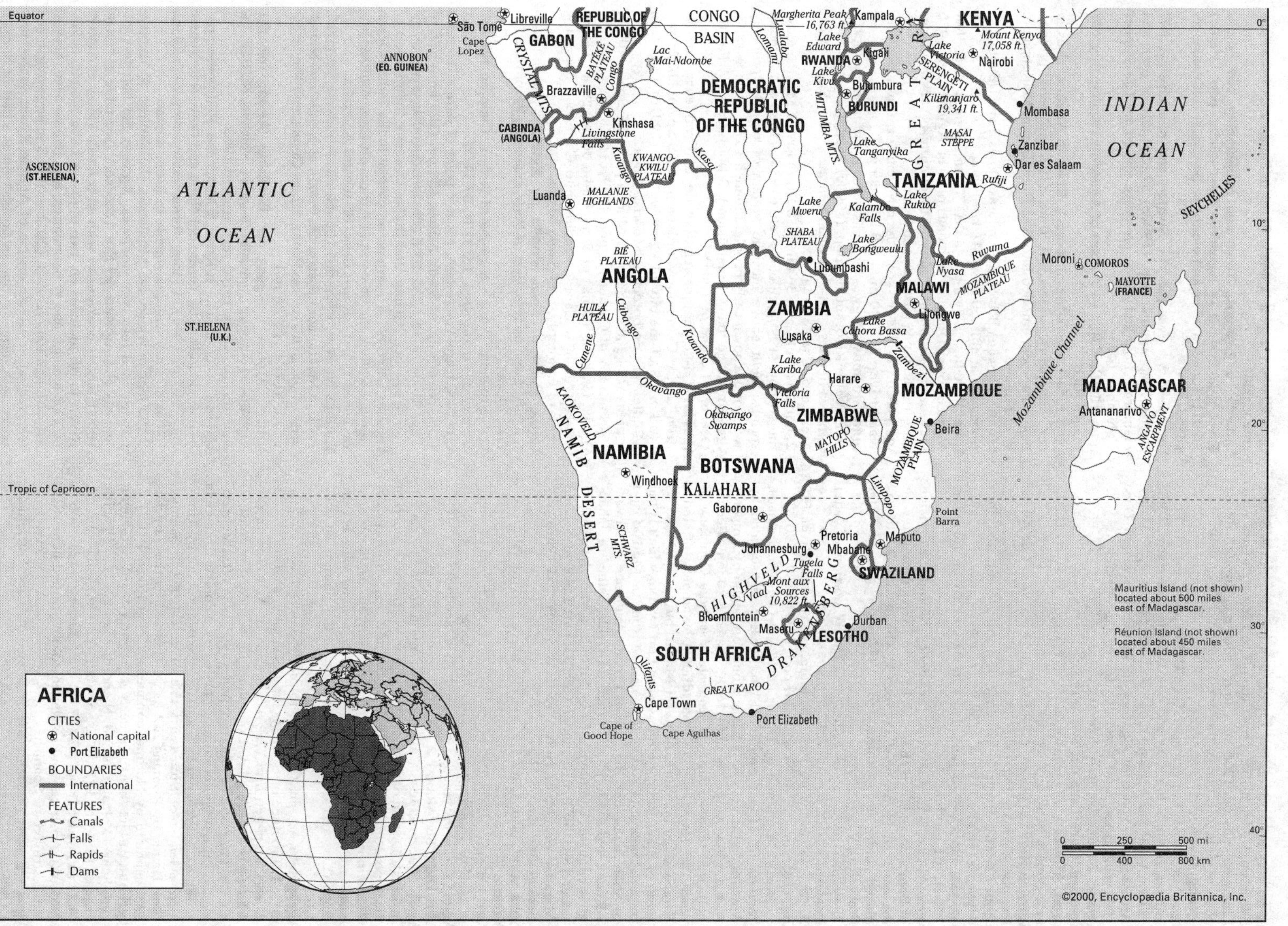

AFRICA
CITIES
National capital
Port Elizabeth
BOUNDARIES
International
FEATURES
Canals
Falls
Rapids
Dams
Equator
Tropic of Capricorn
ATLANTIC OCEAN
INDIAN OCEAN
ASCENSION (ST.HELENA)
ANNOBON (EQ. GUINEA)
ST.HELENA (U.K.)
São Tomé
Cape Lopez
Libreville
GABON
CRYSTAL MTS.
REPUBLIC OF THE CONGO
BATÉKÉ PLATEAU
Congo
Brazzaville
CABINDA (ANGOLA)
Kinshasa
Livingstone Falls
CONGO BASIN
Lac Mai-Ndombe
DEMOCRATIC REPUBLIC OF THE CONGO
Lomami
Lualaba
Kasai
Kwango
KWANGO-KWILU PLATEAU
Luanda
MALANJE HIGHLANDS
BIÉ PLATEAU
ANGOLA
HUILA PLATEAU
Cubango
Cunene
Kwando
Margherita Peak 16,763 ft.
Kampala
Lake Edward
RWANDA
Kigali
Lake Kivu
Bujumbura
BURUNDI
MITUMBA MTS.
Lake Tanganyika
Lake Mweru
SHABA PLATEAU
Kalambo Falls
Lake Bangweulu
Lubumbashi
KENYA
Mount Kenya 17,058 ft.
Lake Victoria
Nairobi
SERENGETI PLAIN
Kilimanjaro 19,341 ft.
GREAT R
MASAI STEPPE
Mombasa
Zanzibar
Dar es Salaam
TANZANIA
Rufiji
Lake Rukwa
Ruvuma
Lake Nyasa
MOZAMBIQUE PLATEAU
MALAWI
Lilongwe
ZAMBIA
Lusaka
Lake Cahora Bassa
Zambezi
Lake Kariba
Harare
Victoria Falls
ZIMBABWE
MATOPO HILLS
MOZAMBIQUE
Beira
MOZAMBIQUE PLAIN
Limpopo
Okavango
Okavango Swamps
KAOKOVELD
NAMIB DESERT
NAMIBIA
Windhoek
BOTSWANA
KALAHARI
Gaborone
SCHWARZ MTS.
Pretoria
Johannesburg
Mbabane
Maputo
SWAZILAND
Point Barra
HIGHVELD
Vaal
Tugela Falls
Mont aux Sources 10,822 ft.
DRAKENSBERG
Bloemfontein
Maseru
LESOTHO
Durban
SOUTH AFRICA
Olifants
GREAT KAROO
Cape Town
Port Elizabeth
Cape of Good Hope
Cape Agulhas
Moroni
COMOROS
MAYOTTE (FRANCE)
SEYCHELLES
Mozambique Channel
MADAGASCAR
Antananarivo
ANGAVO ESCARPMENT
Mauritius Island (not shown) located about 500 miles east of Madagascar.
Réunion Island (not shown) located about 450 miles east of Madagascar.
0°
10°
20°
30°
40°
0 250 500 mi
0 400 800 km

Ag·no \ˈäg-nō\. River, NW Luzon, Philippines; flows S and SW through Pangasinan prov., then N to Lingayen Gulf near Lingayen; 128 mi. (206 km.) long; course is through floodplain of rich soil; one of the important rivers of Luzon.

Agoeng, Goenoeng. See AGUNG, MOUNT.

Agoo \ˌä-gō-ˈō\. Municipality, S La Union prov., Luzon, Philippines, on main highway and railroad line near coast 21 mi. (34 km.) S of San Fernando; one of oldest towns in the Malay Archipelago. Scene of fighting in Japanese invasion Dec. 1941 and on return of American forces Jan. 1945.

Agosta. Commune, Italy. See AUGUSTA.

Agostini, Cordillera de. See ANDES.

Agou, Mount \ˈä-gü\. Mountain, SW Togo; 3937 ft. (1200 m.); highest peak in Togo.

Agou·ra Hills \ə-ˈgu̇r-ə\. City, SW California, W of Los Angeles; pop. (1990c) 20,390.

Agout \ȧ-ˈgü\. River, S tributary of Tarn, Hérault and Tarn depts., S France; 112 mi. (180 km.) long.

Ago·yan Falls \ä-ˈgō-yän\. Falls in Pastaza River, Ecuador; 200 ft. (61 m.) high.

Agra \ˈä-grə, ˈə-\. **1.** Former presidency, NE India; a division of Bengal Presidency 1833–35; became 1835 a province with the name of North-West Provinces, which with Oudh was placed under one administrator 1877; now part of Uttar Pradesh (*q.v.*).

2. Former province of India; now the W portion of Uttar Pradesh; 82,176 sq. mi. (212,836 sq. km.).

3. City, W cen. Uttar Pradesh, India, on Yamuna River 115 mi. (185 km.) SE of New Delhi; pop. (1991p) 891,790.

History: Captured by Bābur (Zahīr-ud-Dīn Muḥammad), founder of Mogul Empire, 1526; present city created by Muslim conquerors of N India; stone fort begun by Emperor Akbar 1564; Mogul ✻ until 1658; visited by John Miedenhall, first representative of English East India Company to reach ✻ 1603; site of magnificent examples of Indo-Saracenic architecture, incl. Taj Mahal, built c. 1631–45 as tomb of Shāh Jahān's empress, the Fort (within which is the imperial palace of Akbar, the Pearl Mosque or Moti Masjid of Shāh Jahān, and the Hall of Private Audience or Diwan-i-Khas), and the tomb of Itimad ud-Daula, father of Jahāngīr's empress; captured 1784 by Sindhia, a Maratha dynasty; taken 1803 by British under Gen. Gerard Lake in Second Maratha War; ✻ of North-West Provinces mid-19th cent.; besieged by sepoys 1857.

Agra and Oudh, United Provinces of. See UTTAR PRADESH.

Agram. See ZAGREB.

Agri \ˈä-grē\. River, Basilicata, S Italy; flows E into the head of Gulf of Taranto; 68 mi. (109 km.) long.

Ağrı \ä-ˈrə\. Province of Turkey in Asia. See table at TURKEY.

Ağrı Dağı. See ARARAT 2.

Ag·ri Dec·u·ma·tes \ˈa-grī-ˌde-kyu̇-ˈmā-tēz, ˈä-grē-ˌde-kü-ˈmä-tās\. District of the Roman Empire, W Europe, E and N of the upper Rhine and N of the Danube (now lies within Baden-Württemberg, Germany); taken from Germans as they retired eastward; later given to Gauls and to Roman veterans as tithe lands (Lat. *agri decumates*); incorp. in the Empire 2d cent. A.D.

Agri·gen·to \ˌä-grē-ˈjen-tō\; *formerly* **Gir·gen·ti** \jēr-ˈjen-tē\. **1.** Province of S Sicily, Italy. See table at ITALY.

2. *anc.* **Ag·ri·gen·tum** \ˌa-gri-ˈjen-təm\ *or* **Ac·ra·gas** *or Gk.* **Ak·ra·gas** \ˈä-krä-ḡäs\. Commune, its ✻, near SW coast 60 mi. (96 km.) SSE of Palermo; pop. (1991p) 54,603; archaeological ruins; exports sulfur. Founded by colonists from Gela c. 580 B.C.; destroyed by Carthage 406 B.C.; rebuilt by Timoleon, a leader of Siracusa; scene of defeat of Carthaginian Gen. Hanno by Romans 262 B.C. Colonized by the Saracens 828; captured by Norman conqueror Count Roger I 1087.

Agri·han \ˌä-grē-ˈhän\; *formerly* **Agri·gan** \-ˈgän\ *or* **Gri·gan** \grē-ˈgän\. Volcanic island, N end of Mariana Is., W Pacific Ocean, 18°46′N, 145°40′E; ab. 6 mi. (10 km.) long by 2 mi. (3.2 km.) wide; 18 sq. mi. (47 sq. km.); highest point 3166 ft. (965 m.). American and Hawaiian colony formed here 1810, but destroyed by Spanish.

Agua \ˈä-ḡwä\. Volcano, SW of Guatemala City, Guatemala; 12,388 ft. (3776 m.).

Agua Cla·ra \ˈä-ḡwä-ˈklä-rä\. River in Panama E of the Panama Canal.

Agua·da \ä-ˈḡwä-t͟hä\. Town and municipality, NW Puerto Rico, near S shore of Aguadilla Bay; munic. pop. (1990c) 35,911; founded 1511 and claims to be oldest settlement on island.

Agua·di·lla \ˌä-ḡwä-ˈt͟hē-yä\. Seaport and municipality, NW Puerto Rico; munic. pop. (1990c) 59,355; site of park and memorial. Founded 1775; probably visited by Christopher Columbus 1493.

Aguadilla Bay. Bay on W coast of Aguadilla municipality, NW Puerto Rico.

Agua Fria \ˈä-gwə-ˈfrē-ə, ˈä-wə-\. River in Arizona; rises in cen. Yavapai co., flows S; 120 mi. (193 km.) long; prior to being dammed, emptied into Gila River in cen. Maricopa co. W of Phoenix.

Aguán \ä-ˈḡwän\. River, N Honduras; flows E and NE into Caribbean Sea; ab. 150 mi. (241 km.) long.

Agua Pri·e·ta \ˈä-ḡwä-prē-ˈā-tä\. Town, Sonora state, NW Mexico, opp. Douglas, Arizona; plan of Agua Prieta 1920 was formal statement of aims of revolutionists seeking to depose President Venustiano Carranza.

Agua·ri·co \ˈä-ḡwä-ˈrē-kō\. River, N Ecuador; flows ESE into Napo River; ab. 240 mi. (386 km.) long.

Aguas Bue·nas \ˈä-ḡwä-ˈbwā-näs\. Town and municipality, E cen. Puerto Rico; munic. pop. (1990c) 25,424.

Aguas·ca·lien·tes \ˌä-ḡwä-ˌskäl-ˈyen-ˌtās\. **1.** State, cen. Mexico. See table at MEXICO.

2. City, its ✻, by rail 364 mi. (586 km.) NW of Mexico City; munic. pop. (1990p) 506,384; alt. 6193 ft. (1888 m.); mineral springs; built above intricate system of tunnels, probably work of unknown early people; founded 1575; made ✻ 1835.

Agui·jan \ˌä-gē-ˈhän\. Small island, S Mariana Is., W Pacific Ocean, off S end of Tinian I.

Agui·lar \ˌä-ḡē-ˈlär\ *or* **Aguilar de la Fron·te·ra** \ˌdā-lä-ˌfrōn-ˈtā-rä\. Commune, Córdoba prov., S Spain, ab. 25 mi. (40 km.) S of the city of Córdoba; pop. (1991c) 13,114; in Middle Ages on border of Moorish lands.

Agui·las \ˈä-ḡē-ˌläs\. Seaport, Murcia prov., SE Spain, 40 mi. (64 km.) SW of Cartagena; pop. (1991c) 24,894.

Agu·ja, Cape \ä-ˈgü-hä\ *or Span.* **Ca·bo de la Aguja** \ˈkä-bō-t͟hā-lä-ä-ˈḡü-hä\. Cape extending into Caribbean Sea on N coast of Colombia, E of Santa Marta.

Aguja, Point *or Span.* **Pun·ta de Agu·ja** \ˈpün-tä-t͟hā-ä-ˈgü-hä\. Cape on NW coast of Peru, extending W into the Pacific Ocean.

Agu·je·re·a·da, Point \ˌä-gü-ˌhā-rā-ˈä-thä\. Cape on NW extremity of Puerto Rico, 18°31′N, 67°08′W.

Agul·has, Cape \ə-ˈgə-ləs\. Most S point of Africa, Western Cape prov., Rep. of South Africa, 120 mi. (193 km.) ESE of Cape Town, at 34°52′S, 20°E (the meridian that serves as dividing line bet. Atlantic and Indian Oceans); lighthouse.

Agulhas Current. A warm ocean current in the Indian Ocean flowing S along the SE coast of Africa; off Cape Agulhas it is deflected to the left and flows SE toward Australia.

Agulhas Ne·gras, Pi·co das \ˈpē-kü-däs-ä-ˈgül-yəs-ˈnā-grəs\. Peak in Mantiqueira Range, SE Brazil, at junction of boundaries of the states of São Paulo, Minas Gerais, and Rio de Janeiro; 9141 ft. (2786 m.).

Agung, Mount \ˈä-güŋ\ *or* **Gu·nung Agung** *or Du.* **Goe·noeng Agoeng** \ˈgü-ˌnüŋ-ˈä-ˌgüŋ\. Volcano, NE Bali, Indonesia; 10,308 ft. (3142 m.); erupted 1963.

Agu·san \ä-ˈgü-ˌsän\. **1.** River, E Mindanao, Philippines; rises in highlands of SE Davao del Norte and flows N to Butuan Bay; 240 mi. (386 km.) long; forms fertile valley 40 to 50 mi. (64 to 80 km.) wide; navigable in lower course.

2. Former province, NE Mindanao, Philippines; ✻ Butuan; now divided into two provinces, **Agusan del Nor·te** \del-ˈnȯr-tā\ and **Agusan del Sur** \del-ˈsür\ (see table at PHILIPPINES); largely coextensive with wide fertile valley of Agusan River; in NE includes ab. two thirds of Lake Mainit; mountainous along E and W boundaries, esp. Diuata Mts., highest Mt. Hilonghilong 6599 ft. (2011 m.); in S is large marsh and lake region in middle course of Agusan River; timber produced in Agusan del Sur. In Spanish times a part of Surigao prov.; estab. as separate province by Americans 1914; divided into two provinces 1970.

Agu·ta·ya \ˌä-gü-ˈtä-yä\. Island in Cuyo group, Palawan prov., Philippines, N of Cuyo I.; 6 sq. mi. (16 sq. km.).

Agylla. See CAERE.

Agyrium. See AGIRA.

Ahag·gar Mountains \ə-ˈhä-gər, ˌä-hə-ˈgär\ *or* **Hog·gar Mountains** \ˈhäg-ər, ȯ-ˈgär\. High plateau region in cen. Sahara, S Algeria; highest peak 9842 ft. (3000 m.).

Ahi·pa·ra Bay \ī-ˈpär-ə\. Bay on extreme NW coast of N extension of North I., New Zealand.

Ah·len \ˈä-lən\. City, North Rhine-Westphalia, Germany, 17 mi. (27 km.) SE of Münster; pop. (1991e) 54,169.

Ah·mad·a·bad *also* **Ah·med·a·bad** \ˈä-mə-də-ˌbäd, -ˌbad\. City, Gujarat, NW India, on left bank of Sabarmati River 290 mi. (467 km.) N of Bombay; pop. (1991p) 2,954,526; cotton processing; university (1949); many well-known monuments and buildings, incl. Jama Masjid (Great Mosque) and tomb of Aḥmad Shāh of Gujarat, Hathi Singh Jain temple (built 1848).

History: Founded in 1411 by Ottoman Sultan Aḥmad Shāh of Gujarat on site of previous Hindu cities; built 1411–42; at height in 15th cent. as ✱ of Gujarat kingdom; declined 1512–72 with Gujarat dynasty; revived under Mogul emperors 1572–1707; reverted to British with other holdings of Peshwa 1818; became modern manufacturing and trading center, esp. noted for cotton textiles; associated with Indian nationalist cause as scene of an anti-British rebellion 1918 and of beginning of nationalist leader Mohandas Gandhi's efforts 1930 and his arrest 1933.

Ahmadi, Al–. See AL-AHMADI.

Ah·mad·na·gar *also* **Ah·med·na·gar** \ˌä-məd-ˈnə-gər\. City, Maharashtra, W cen. India, 130 mi. (209 km.) E of Bombay; pop. (1991p) 181,015.

History: Founded 1490 as one of the five Muslim kingdoms of the Deccan (*q.v.*); conquered by Shāh Jahan 1636 when it became part of Mogul Empire; exchanged several times bet. British and Marathas in wars of 18th cent.; seized by Gen. Richard Wellesley 1803; ceded to British by Treaty of Poona 1817; has fort and cantonment.

Aho·me \ä-ˈō-mā\. Municipality, Sinaloa state, W Mexico; munic. pop. (1990p) 305,507.

Ahos·kie \ə-ˈhäs-kē\. Town, Hertford co., NE North Carolina, 44 mi. (71 km.) W of Elizabeth City; pop. (1990c) 4391.

Ah·rens·burg \ˈär-ənz-ˌbu̇rk\. City, Schleswig-Holstein, Germany, 22 mi. (35 km.) SW of Lübeck; founded in 13th cent.

Ahua·cha·pán \ˌä-wä-chä-ˈpän\. **1.** Department of SW El Salvador. See table at EL SALVADOR.
2. Town, its ✱, near Guatemalan border; pop. (1986e) 81,210; alt. 2470 ft. (753 m.); hot mineral waters nearby.

Ahu·ri·ri \ä-ˈhü-rē-rē\. River, S cen. South I., New Zealand; one of the headstreams of the Waitaki.

Ah·vāz \ä-ˈväz\ *or* **Ah·waz** \ä-ˈwäz\. Town, ✱ of Khūzestān prov., SW Iran, on the Kārūn River ab. 70 mi. (113 km.) NNE of Khorramshahr; pop. (1986c) 579,826; connected by rail with Persian Gulf port of Bandar-e Khomeyni; has oil pipelines; important commercially, esp. in oil business. Under the Arabs in 12th and 13th cents. was a trade center for sugar, rice, and silk; modern town laid out on extensive ruined area of ancient Persian city.

Ahvenanmaa See ÅLAND.

Ahwaz. See AHVĀZ.

Ai \ˈā-ˌī\. Town in mountains of E Canaan, ancient Palestine, SE of Bethel; destroyed by Israelite leader Joshua (*Josh.* vii–viii).

Ai·bo·ni·to \ˌī-bō-ˈnē-tō\. Town and municipality, SE cen. Puerto Rico, 30 mi. (48 km.) NW of Guayama; munic. pop. (1990c) 24,971.

Ai·chi \ˈī-ˌchē\. Prefecture, Honshū, Japan. See table at JAPAN.

Aidin. See AYDIN.

Ai·ea \ī-ˈā-ə\. Unincorporated settlement, Honolulu co., S Oahu, Hawaii, on E shore of Pearl Harbor; pop. (1990c) 8906.

Aigai. See VERGHINA.

Aigaion Pelagos. See AEGEAN SEA.

Aigues–Mortes \eg-ˈmȯrt\; *anc.* **Aq·uae Mor·tu·ae** \ˌa-kwē-ˈmȯr-chü-ˌē, ˌä-kwī-ˈmōr-tü-ˌī\. Commune, Gard dept., S France, in Rhone estuary 25 mi. (40 km.) SSW of Nîmes. Founded by King Louis IX (St. Louis), who connected it by canal with Gulf of Lion and used it as embarkation point for Sixth Crusade 1248 and Seventh Crusade 1270; fortified 1272 by Philip the Bold, duke of Burgundy; of little importance today except for Tour de Constance and fine medieval military ramparts.

Aiguille d'Argentière. See ARGENTIÈRE, AIGUILLE D'.

Aiguille de Chambeyron. See CHAMBEYRON, AIGUILLE DE.

Aiguille des Glaciers. See GLACIERS, AIGUILLE DES.

Ai·gun \ˈī-ˈgün\ *also* **Ai·hun** \ˈī-ˈhün\. Locality, NE Heilongjiang prov., NE China, on the Amur River 20 mi. (32 km.) S of Blagoveshchensk, Russia. By treaty signed here 1858 China ceded left bank of Amur and right bank below the Ussuri to Russia; destruction by fire 1900 followed by decline in trade.

Aihui \ˈī-ˈhwē\ *or* **Hei·he** \ˈhā-ˈhə\ *also* **Ta·hei·ho** \ˈtä-ˈhā-ˈhə\ *or Jp.* **Hei·ho** \ˈhā-ˈhə\. Town, NE Heilongjiang prov., NE China, on the Amur River; ✱ of former Heiho prov.

Ai·ja·lon \ˈā-jə-ˌlän, ˈī-\ *or* **Aj·a·lon** \ˈa-jə-\. Town in valley of Aijalon, ancient Palestine, 13 mi. (21 km.) NW of Jerusalem. On frontier of kingdoms of Ephraim and Judah; valley scene of biblical episode in which Israelite leader Joshua commanded the sun and moon to stand still (*Josh.* x. 12); assigned to tribe of Dan.

Ai·ken \ˈā-kən\. **1.** County in W South Carolina. See table at SOUTH CAROLINA.
2. City, its ⊗, 52 mi. (84 km.) SW of Columbia; pop. (1990c) 19,872; winter resort; fiberglass manufacture; in farming region; Univ. of South Carolina-Aiken (1961). Scene of battle bet. Union and Confederate troops Feb. 1865.

Ai·lette \ā-ˈlet\. River, Aisne dept., N France, tributary of Oise from SE near Laon; ab. 40 mi. (64 km.) long.

Ail·sa Craig \ˌāl-sə-ˈkrāg, ˌāl-zə-\. Rocky island at mouth of Firth of Clyde, 10 mi. (16 km.) off coast of SW Scotland.

Aimorés, Serra dos. See SERRA DOS AIMORÉS.

Ain \ˈe^{n}\. **1.** River, E France; rises in Jura Mts. and flows S into Rhone River; ab. 120 mi. (195 km.) long.
2. Department of E France. See table at FRANCE.

Aïn Beï·da \ˈīn-ˈbā-dä, ˈān-\. Commune, NE Algeria, 50 mi. (80 km.) SE of Constantine; pop. (1987p) 61,997; founded 1848.

Ain Ja·lut *or Arab.* **'Ayn Jā·lūt** \ˈīn-jä-ˈlüt, ˈān-\. Locality near Nazareth, N Israel; here in 1260 the Mamlūks of Egypt destroyed the Mongol army of Hülegü and recovered Syria.

Aïn Se·fra \ˈīn-se-ˈfrä, ˈān-\. Commune in Atlas Mts., NW Algeria, 200 mi. (322 km.) S of Oran; pop. (1987p) 23,799.

Ains·worth \ˈānz-ˌwərth\. City, ⊗ of Brown co., N cen. Nebraska; pop. (1990c) 1870; trade center.

Aintab. See GAZİANTEP 2.

Aïn Té·mou·chent \ˈīn-ˌtā-mü-ˈshent\. Commune, NW Algeria, ab. 45 mi. (72 km.) SW of Oran; pop. (1987p) 47,479.

Ain·tree \ˈān-trē\. Locality, N of Liverpool, Lancashire, England; racecourse where Grand National steeplechase is run every March.

Ai–pi. See EBINUR.

Aïr \ä-ˈir, ˈīr\ *also* **Az·bine** \äz-ˈbē-nā, -ˈbēn\ *or* **As·ben** \az-ˈben\. Mountainous region, N cen. Niger; ab. 30,000 sq. mi. (77,700 sq. km.); highest peaks ab. 5000 ft. (1524 m.); former native kingdom; main products dates, millet, and senna. Inhabited by Tuaregs; a native kingdom, called Asben, until conquered by Berbers.

Air, Point of \ˈar\. Point at mouth of Dee River, Clwyd, NE Wales.

Aira Force \ˈar-ē-ˈfōrs\ *also* **Air·ey Force** \ˈar-ē\. Waterfall (Scot. *force*), Cumbria, NW England; 80 ft. (24 m.) high; in

\ə\ abut \ˈə\ matches \$^{ə}$\ kitten, Fr table \ər\ **further** \a\ ash \ā\ ace \ä\ cot, cart \ȧ\ Fr bac \au̇\ **out** \b̲\ Span Avila \ch\ **chin** \e\ bet \ē\ easy \g\ go \i\ hit \ī\ ice \j\ job \k̲\ Ger **ich,** Buch \$^{n}$\ Fr vin \ŋ\ sing \ō\ go \ȯ\ all \ȯ\ law \œ\ Fr bœuf \œ̄\ Fr feu \ȯi\ boy \th\ **thin** \th̲\ **this** \ü\ loot \u̇\ foot \ue\ Ger füllen \ue̅\ Fr rue \y\ yet \$^{y}$\ Fr digne \ˈdēn^{y}\, nuit \ˈnw^{y}ē\ \yü\ **few** \yu̇\ fury \zh\ vision

small stream flowing into Ullswater Lake, in the Lake District.

Air·drie \ˈar-drē\. Burgh, Strathclyde region, S cen. Scotland, 11 mi. (18 km.) E of Glasgow; deposits of coal and iron nearby.

Aire \ˈar\. **1.** River, W Yorkshire, England; flows SE and E through Leeds to Ouse River; 70 mi. (113 km.) long; navigable to Leeds. **Aire·dale** \-dāl\, valley of the Aire, original home of the Airedale terrier.

2. River, Meuse and Ardennes depts., NE France; flows NW through the Argonne to Aisne River near Vouziers; ab. 80 mi. (129 km.) long; severe fighting on its banks in WWI.

3. *anc.* **Vi·cus Ju·lii** \ˈvī-kəs-ˈjü-lē-ˌī, ˈwē-ˌku̇s-ˈyü-lē-ˌē\; *later* **Atu·ra** \ə-ˈtu̇r-ə\. Commune, Landes dept., SW France, on left bank of Adour ab. 20 mi. (32 km.) SE of Mont-de-Marsan; residence of the kings of the Visigoths; bishopric in 5th cent., later an episcopal town.

Aire·bor·ough \ˈar-ˌbər-ə, -ō\. Town, West Yorkshire, N England; pop. (1981p) 31,414.

Airey Force. See AIRA FORCE.

Ai·ro·lo \ī-ˈrō-lō, -ˈrò-\. Commune, Ticino canton, SE cen. Switzerland, at S end of St. Gotthard Tunnel in valley of Ticino River.

Ai·sén del Ge·ne·ral Car·los Ibá·ñez del Cam·po \ī-ˈsān-ˌdel-ˌgā-nā-ˈräl-ˈkär-lōs-ē-ˈbän-yāth-ˌdel-ˈkäm-pō\. Region of S Chile. See table at CHILE.

Ai·shi·hik \ˈā-shi-ˌhik\. Lake, SW Yukon, Canada; 107 sq. mi. (277 sq. km.); outlet through Alsek River to the Pacific.

Aisne \ˈen\; *anc.* **Ax·o·na** \ˈak-sō-nə\. **1.** River, N France; rises in Meuse dept., flows NW and W from Argonne Forest to Oise near Compiègne; 165 mi. (265 km.) long. Four major battles in valley in WWI: (1) Defeat of Germans Sept. 15–18, 1914 in their retreat from the Marne; (2) French seizure Apr.–July 1917 of heights (Chemin des Dames) N of Aisne; (3) German capture of heights May–June 1918; (4) Final defeat of Germans by French and Americans Sept.–Oct. 1918. In WWII crossed Aug. 1944 by American troops in pursuit of Germans.

2. Department of N France. See table at FRANCE.

Ai·ta·pe *also* **Ei·ta·pe** \ˌī-tä-ˈpā, ī-ˈtä-pā\. Seaport town, Papua New Guinea, on N coast of New Guinea; govt. station. American forces landed here and at Hollandia April 1944; airfields taken; large Japanese force cut off.

Ait·kin \ˈā-kin\. **1.** County, E cen. Minnesota. See table at MINNESOTA.

2. Village, its ⊗, on Mississippi River 26 mi. (42 km.) ENE of Brainerd; pop. (1990c) 1698.

Aitolia. See AETOLIA.

Aitolía kai Akarnanía. See AETOLIA AND ACARNANIA.

Ai·tu·ta·ki \ˌī-tü-ˈtä-kē\. Island in S group of Cook Islands (*q.v.*), S Pacific Ocean, NW of Rarotonga; 18°52′S, 159°45′W; 7 sq. mi. (18 sq. km.); pop. (1986c) 2390; has wide surrounding reef and large lagoon (5 mi. or 8 km. across); 2d to Rarotonga in importance. Sighted by the *Bounty* 1789.

Aiud \ä-ˈyüd\ *or Hung.* **Nag·yen·yed** \ˈnö-dye-ned\ *or Ger.* **Strass·burg** \ˈshträs-ˌbu̇rk\. Town, Alba co., Romania, on Mureşul River 20 mi. (32 km.) NNE of Alba Iulia; pop. (1989c) 30,055; college; natural science museum; citadel (13th–16th cents.).

Aivali. See AYVALIK.

Aix–en–Pro·vence \ˌeks-äⁿ-prō-ˈväⁿs\ *also* **Aix** \ˈeks\; *anc.* **Aquae Sex·ti·ae** \ˌa-ˌkwē-ˈsek-stē-ˌē, ˌä-ˌkwī-ˈseks-tē-ˌī\. City, Bouches-du-Rhône dept., SE France, 19 mi. (31 km.) N of Marseille; pop. (1990c) 126,854; tourism; cathedral; palace; university (1413, reconstituted 1896).

History: Founded as military colony by Romans 123 B.C.; scene of defeat 102 B.C. of the Teutones by Roman Gen. Marius; chief city of E Narbonensis (4th cent.); occupied by Visigoths 477, by Saracens 731; in Middle Ages as ✱ of Provence reached high cultural levels; became part of France c. 1487.

Aix–la–Chapelle. See AACHEN 2.

Aix–les–Bains \ˌeks-lā-ˈbeⁿ\; *anc.* **Aquae Gra·ti·a·nae** \ˈa-ˌkwē-ˌgrā-shē-ˈa-ˌnē, ˈä-ˌkwī-ˌgrä-tē-ˈä-ˌnī\. Commune, Savoie dept., E France, on SE shore of Lake Bourget 9 mi. (14 km.) N of Chambéry; pop. (1990c) 24,826; resort; its sulfur baths famous in Roman times.

Aíyina. See AEGINA.

Aí·yi·on \ˈē-yē-ˌòn, -gē-\ *or* **Ae·gi·um** \ˈē-jē-əm\. Seaport town, Achaea dept., NW Peloponnese, Greece, on Gulf of Corinth.

Ai·zawl \ī-ˈzau̇l\. Town, ✱ of Mizoram, E India; pop. (1991p) 154,343.

Ai·zu·wa·ka·mat·su \ä-ˈē-ˌzü-ˌwä-kä-ˈmät-ˌsü\. City, cen. Fukushima prefecture, Honshū, Japan; pop. (1990p) 119,084.

Ajac·cio \ä-ˈyä-chō, à-zhàk-ˈsyō\. Seaport commune, ✱ of Corse-du-Sud dept., France, on N side of **Gulf of Ajaccio** on W coast of Corsica; pop. (1990c) 59,318; tourist center; episcopal see; founded 15th cent.; became French 1768 (see CORSICA); birthplace of French Emperor Napoléon 1769; ✱ of Corsica 1810–1975.

Ajai·garh \ə-ˈjī-gər\. Former state, cen. India; 788 sq. mi. (2041 sq. km.); now part of Madhya Pradesh.

Ajalon. See AIJALON.

Ajan·ta \ə-ˈjən-tə\. Village in hills of cen. Maharashtra, S cen. India, NNE of Aurangabad; nearby are ab. 30 remarkable caves, the earliest dating from 200 B.C. to 200 A.D. and the latest from 7th cent. A.D., comprising halls and dormitories with walls covered with fresco paintings; caves excavated by Buddhists; discovered early 19th cent.

Ajanta Range. Range of hills, cen. India, extending across N cen. Maharashtra; watershed for tributaries of Tapti and Godavari rivers.

Ajaria. See ADJARIAN AUTONOMOUS REPUBLIC.

Ajax \ˈā-ˌjaks\. Town, Durham municipal region, SE Ontario, Canada, on Lake Erie 27 mi. (43 km.) NE of Toronto; pop. (1991c) 57,350.

Ajax Mountain. Peak in Bitterroot Range on Montana-Idaho state boundary; 10,900 ft. (3322 m.).

Aj·dā·bi·yah \aj-ˈdä-bē-ə\ *also* **Ag·e·da·bia** \ˌä-je-ˈdä-bē-ə\. Town, near E coast of Gulf of Sidra, N Libya; caravan stop during early Middle Ages; headquarters for British in the area during WWII.

Aj·dir, Cape \aj-ˈdēr\ *or Arab.* **Ras Ajdīr** \ˌräs\. Cape extending into the Mediterranean Sea, on border bet. Tunisia and Libya.

Aji·ka·wa \ˌä-jē-ˈkä-wä\. See YODO 2.

Aj·ka \ˈòi-kö\. Town, Veszprem co., W Hungary; pop. (1991e) 33,900.

ʻAj·mān \aj-ˈman\. **1.** Emirate. See table at UNITED ARAB EMIRATES.

2. Coastal town, its ✱; pop. (1980c) 33,651.

Aj·mer \ˌəj-ˈmir, ˌaj-, -ˈmer\ *also* **Aj·mere** \-ˈmir\. City, Rajasthan, NW India, 84 mi. (135 km.) SW of Jaipur; pop. (1991c) 402,700; situated at base of rocky hill Taragarh (3000 ft. or 914 m.); conducts large trade in salt; manufactures oils and cotton cloths, and is noted for its dyeing of the latter.

History: Founded c. 145 A.D.; stronghold of Chauhan Rajputs until 12th cent.; conquered 1193 by the Muslim dynasty at Delhi (*q.v.*); feudal state dependent upon Delhi until 1365; ruled by Udaipur (*q.v.*) until captured by Mogul Emperor Akbar 1556; in 1770 given to Marathas under whom it was scene of violent upheavals until ceded to British 1818 by Maratha ruler of Gwalior after the Pindari War; has notable ruins, esp. dargah (tomb) of famous Muslim saint.

Aj·na·da·in \ˌaj-na-ˈdä-in\ *or* **Jan·na·ba·ta·in** \ˌja-na-ba-ˈtä-in\. Village, ancient Palestine, just SW of Jerusalem; scene of victory 634 A.D. by Arabs over Theodorus, brother of Byzantine Emperor Heraclius, which opened way for Muslim conquest of Syria.

Ajo \ˈä-ˌhō\. Unincorporated settlement, Pima co., S Arizona; pop. (1990c) 2919; an early copper-mining center.

Ajodh·ya \ə-ˈjōd-yə\ *also* **Ayodh·ya** \-ˈyōd-\. Former town, United Provinces, N India, on right bank of Ghaghara River E of Faizābād; now part of that city (now in Uttar Pradesh). In ancient times one of the greatest of Indian cities; ✱ of kingdom of Kosala, as described in the *Ramayana;* a revived Brahmanism under King Vikramaditya restored it c. 57 B.C., and ab. 400 A.D. it became ✱ of Chandragupta II; birthplace of founder of Jainism and center of pilgrimages. From it modern Oudh derives its name.

Ajus·co \ä-'hüs-kō\. Volcanic mountain, Federal District, Mexico, S of Mexico City and just N of Cuernavaca; 12,887 ft. (3928 m.).

Akaba. See AQABA.

Aka·gi \ä-'kä-gē\ *or Jp.* **Aka·gi·san** \-'sän\. Group of peaks, cen. Honshū, Japan; highest point 5996 ft. (1828 m.); surrounds a volcanic crater, **Lake Akagi.**

Akai·shi \ä-'kī-shē\. Peak, N part of Shizuoka prefecture, cen. Honshū, Japan; 10,234 ft. (3119 m.).

Aka·koa Point \ˌä-kä-'kō-ä\. Cape on N coast of Hawaii I., Hawaii.

Akal·kot \'ə-kəl-ˌkōt, ə-'kəl-\. **1.** Former state, W India; 473 sq. mi. (1225 sq. km.); now part of Maharashtra.
2. Town, India; 25 mi. (40 km.) SE of Sholapur, Maharashtra.

Akamagaseki. See SHIMONOSEKI.

Aká·mas, Cape \ä-'kä-mäs\. Cape, most westerly part of Cyprus.

Akarnanía. See ACARNANIA.

Aka·roa \ˌä-kə-'rō-ə\. Borough and administrative co., E South I., New Zealand, 30 mi. (48 km.) SSE of Christchurch on **Akaroa Harbor,** an inlet in Banks Penin.; borough pop. (1986c) 722; claimed by British 1840 a few days before arrival of French; some of French immigrants remained and descendants still live here.

Aka·shi \ä-'kä-shē\. City, Hyōgo prefecture, W Honshū, Japan, on coast 12 mi. (19 km.) W of Kōbe; pop. (1992e) 278,458; separated from N end of Awaji I. by **Akashi Strait,** E end of Inland Sea; its meridian 135°E is standard time meridian for Japan.

Akas·sa \ä-'käs-sä\. Village, East-Central State, Nigeria, at mouth of Niger. See BRASS.

Ak·dağ *or* **Ak Dağ** \'äk-'dä\. Name of several mountains in Turkey in Asia, esp.: (1) Range in cen. part W of Sıvas, highest point 8860 ft. (2701 m.); (2) Peak 10,125 ft. (3086 m.), SW of Antalya near coast; (3) Peak 9350 ft. (2850 m.), in Taurus Mts. E of Cilician Gates; (4) Peak 8186 ft. (2495 m.), SSW of Afyon.

Ak·dar, Je·bel \'je-bel-'ák-ˌdȧr\. Mountain range, Oman, SE Arabian Penin.; highest peak Jebel Sham, 9927 ft. (2495 m.).

Akers·hus *also* **Ag·gers·hus** \'ä-kərs-ˌhüs\. County of E Norway. See table at NORWAY.

Akesu. See AKSU 2.

Ak Göl \'äk-'gœl\. Salt lake (*göl*), S cen. Turkey in Asia, N of Taurus Mts.

Akhaïa. See ACHAEA.

Akhal·tsi·khe \ə-ˌkəlt-'sē-kyə\. Town, S Republic of Georgia, near left bank of upper Kura River 65 mi. (104 km.) E of Batumi; ✻ of Turkish Armenia 1579–1828; chief town of a pashalik of Ottoman Empire and center of slave trade; district ceded to Russia by Treaty of Adrianople 1829.

Akharnaí. See ACHARNAE.

Akhelóos. See ACHELOUS.

Ak·hi·sar \ˌäk-hi-'sär\; *anc.* **Thy·a·ti·ra** \ˌthī-ə-'tī-rə\. Town, N Manisa prov., W Turkey in Asia, 52 mi. (84 km.) NE of İzmir; pop. (1990p) 151,957; exports cotton and tobacco. Ancient Greek city of Thyatira in Lydia was colonized and named 280 B.C. by Seleucid ruler Seleucus I Nicator; its inhabitants famous for skill in dyeing purple; one of the Seven Churches of Asia Minor (*Rev.* i. 11, ii. 18–24).

Akh·mīm *also* **Ekh·mīm** \ˌek-'mēm\; *anc.* **Chem·mis** \'kemis\; *later* **Pa·nop·o·lis** \pə-'nä-pə-lis\. Town on right bank of Nile River, Sohâg governorate, Egypt, 66 mi. (106 km.) S of Asyūt. Chemmis an important city of the Thebais; famous for its manufacture of linen and its limestone quarries; religious center, with temple of Pan.

Akh·tyr·ka \ək-'tir-kə\. Town, Sumy subdivision, N Ukraine, ab. 65 mi. (104 km.) WNW of Kharkiv; cathedral (1753).

Aki \'ä-kē\. Former province, SW Honshū, Japan; now part of Hiroshima prefecture.

Ak·i·mis·ki Island \ˌa-ki-'mis-kē\. Island in James Bay, Northwest Terr., Canada, opp. mouth of Attawapiskat River, S Hudson Bay; 1137 sq. mi. (2945 sq. km.).

Aki·shi·ma \ˌä-kē-'shē-mä, ä-'kē-shē-mä\. City, Tokyo prefecture, Honshū, Japan, 23 mi. (37 km.) WNW of Tokyo; pop. (1990p) 105,375.

Aki·ta \ä-'kē-tä, 'ä-kē-ˌtä\. **1.** Prefecture, Honshū, Japan. See table at JAPAN.
2. City, its ✻, on right bank of Omono River near its mouth; pop. (1990p) 302,359; university (1949); petroleum products.

Ak·kad *also* **Ac·cad** \'a-ˌkad, 'ä-ˌkäd\. **1.** The N division of ancient Babylonia. From about 4th millennium B.C., inhabited by a leading Semitic people called the Akkadians; after a period of Sumerian rule (see SUMER) under kings Sargon and Naram-Sin, developed empire which included Sumer, Elam, the upper Tigris, and N Syria to the Mediterranean 24th–23rd cents. B.C.; adopted Sumerian culture and developed great art (relief of Naram-Sin); lost supremacy c. 22d cent. B.C.; united with Sumer under latter's leadership; invaded by Amorites (see BABYLON 2).
2. *anc.* **Aga·de** \ə-'gä-dā, -'gā-dē\. Ancient city, its ✻, in cen. Mesopotamia, placed by some near Sippar.

Akkerman. See BELGOROD-DNESTROVSKI.

'Akko. See ACRE.

Aklan \ä-'klän\. Province, Panay I., Philippines (see table at PHILIPPINES); rice; formed 1957.

Akla·vik \ə-'klä-vik\. Community on left bank of Mackenzie River near its mouth, NW Northwest Terr., Canada; pop. (1991c) 801.

Ak Mechet. See SIMFEROPOL.

Akmola. See ASTANA.

Akmolinsk. See ASTANA.

Ako·bo \ä-'kō-(ˌ)bō\. **1.** River on border bet. Ethiopia and SE Sudan, E cen. Africa; flows NW into Pibor River; 270 mi. (434 km.) long.
2. Town, SE Sudan, at confluence of Akobo and Pibor rivers on border of Ethiopia.

Ako·la \ə-'kō-lə\. City, India, in Maharashtra, 140 mi. (225 km.) WSW of Nagpur; pop. (1991p) 327,946; center of cotton trade.

A–k'o–su. See AKSU 2.

Ak·pa·tok Island \'ak-pə-ˌtäk\. Island at mouth of Ungava Bay, E Northwest Terr., Canada; 296 sq. mi. (767 sq. km.).

Ák·ra \'ä-krä\. Greek word meaning "cape, point"; often used in place names. For names containing this word, see the 2d element.

Ákra Akrítas. See GALLO, CAPE.

Akragas. See AGRIGENTO 2.

Ákra Sidhirókastron. See SIDEROKASTRON.

Ákra Voúxa. See BUSA, CAPE.

Akroïnon. See ACROÏNUM.

Ak·ron \'a-krən\. **1.** Town, ⊗ of Washington co., NE Colorado; pop. (1990c) 1599.
2. Village, Erie co., W New York, ab. 22 mi. (35 km.) ENE of Buffalo; pop. (1990c) 2906.
3. City, ⊗ of Summit co., NE Ohio, 35 mi. (56 km.) SE of Cleveland on Little Cuyahoga River; pop. (1990c) 223,019; on old Indian Portage Trail bet. Cuyahoga and Tuscarawas rivers; notable rubber industry; trucking center; Univ. of Akron (founded as Buchtel Coll. 1870); settled ab. 1825; incorp. as village 1836; made county seat 1842; granted charter as city 1865; first rubber factory estab. 1870 by Dr. B. F. Goodrich; after 1910 began phenomenal growth due to demand for tires and other rubber goods.
4. Borough, Lancaster co., SE Pennsylvania, 11 mi. (18 km.) NE of Lancaster; pop. (1990c) 3869.

Akro·te·ri Peninsula \ˌä-krō-'ter-ē\. Peninsula, on N coast of Crete near W end, Greece; Canea is at its base on the W and Suda Bay enclosed by it on SE; ab. 10 mi. (16 km.) long.

Akro·ti·ri Bay \ˌä-krō-'tē-rē\. Inlet of Mediterranean Sea on S coast of Cyprus; Limassol is on it.

\ə\ **abut** \ə\ matches \$^{ə}$\ kitten, Fr table \ər\ **further** \a\ **ash** \ā\ **ace** \ä\ cot, cart \ȧ\ Fr bac \au̇\ **out** \b\ Span Avila \ch\ **chin** \e\ **bet** \ē\ **easy** \g\ **go** \i\ **hit** \ī\ **ice** \j\ **job** \k\ Ger **ich**, Buch \$^{n}$\ Fr vin \ŋ\ **sing** \ō\ **go** \ȯ\ **all** \ȯ\ **law** \œ\ Fr bœuf \œ̄\ Fr **feu** \ȯi\ **boy** \th\ **thin** \th\ **this** \ü\ **loot** \u̇\ **foot** \ue\ Ger füllen \ue̅\ Fr **rue** \y\ yet \$^{y}$\ Fr digne \'dēn^{y}\, nuit \'nw^{y}ē\ \yü\ **few** \yu̇\ **fury** \zh\ **vision**

Ak·sa·ray \ˌäk-sä-ˈrī\. **1.** Province of Turkey in Asia. See table at TURKEY.

2. Town, N Niğde prov., S cen. Turkey in Asia, 85 mi. (137 km.) NE of Konya; highway junction point SE of Tuz Lake.

Ak·şe·hir \ˌäk-shä-ˈhēr\; *formerly* **Ak·shehr** \äk-ˈsher\; *anc.* **Phil·o·me·li·on** \ˌfi-lō-ˈmē-lē-ən\. Town, Konya prov., SW cen. Turkey, on railroad line 70 mi. (113 km.) NW of Konya; on ancient highway in fertile plain S of Akşehir Gölü; known to Roman statesman Cicero and important as frontier town under Byzantine emperors; became a Seljuq town ab. 1400.

Akşehir Gö·lü \gœ-ˈlue\. Lake, W cen. Turkey in Asia, E of Afyon.

Ak·su \äk-ˈsü\. **1.** River, SW Turkey; flows S into Gulf of Antalya; ab. 80 mi. (129 km.) long.

2. *also* **Ake·su** *or W.-G.* **A–k'o–su** \ˈä-ˈkə-ˈsü\. Town, Xinjiang Uygur, W China, at foot of Tian Shan Range; Mongol ✱ in 14th cent.; with establishment of new town 10 mi. (16 km.) to the S, old Aksu renamed Wensu.

Ak·sum *also* **Ax·um** \ˈäk-ˌsüm\. Town, N Ethiopia, 5 mi. (8 km.) WSW of Adwa; pop. (1989e) 21,857.

History: The ✱ of an ancient Ethiopian kingdom known as the Axumite empire which was ruled by Himyaritic emigrants from Arabia; flourished esp. 3d–6th cents. A.D.; religious center which contained, according to tradition, the Ark of the Covenant brought from Jerusalem by descendant of Solomon, King of Israel, and Queen of Sheba.

Aktí. See ACTE.

Ak·tyu·binsk \ək-ˈtyü-binsk\ **1.** Subdivision of Kazakhstan, in W cen. part; 115,753 sq. mi. (299,800 sq. km.); pop. (1991e) 752,900; chromium; steppe region traversed by Emba and Irgiz rivers, by the Orenburg-Tashkent R.R. and by oil pipelines; an oblast of the U.S.S.R. before 1991.

2. *or* **Aq·tö·be** \ək-ˈtœ-be\. Town, its ✱; pop. (1991e) 266,600; founded 1869.

Akun \ä-ˈkün\. Island, Aleutian Is., Alaska, just NE of Akutan I.; 63 sq. mi. (163 sq. km.); separated on NE from Unimak I. by Unimak Pass.

Aku·re \ä-ˈkü-rā\. Town, ✱ of Ondo state, SW Nigeria, ab. 130 mi. (209 km.) NE of Lagos; pop. (1991e) 143,200; agricultural school, teacher-training college.

Akur·ey·ri \ˈä-kœr-ˌā-rē\. Town on Eyja Fjord, N Iceland; pop. (1990c) 14,189; incorp. 1786.

Aku·tan \ˌä-kü-ˈtan\. One of the Fox Is., Aleutian Is., Alaska; 127 sq. mi. (329 sq. km.); an active volcano 4275 ft. (1303 m.); separated on SW from Unalaska I. by **Akutan Pass.**

Akwa Ibom \ˈä-kwä-ˈē-ˌbōm\. State of SE Nigeria, carved from Cross River state 1988. See table at NIGERIA.

Akyab. See SITTWE.

Al·a·bama \ˌa-lə-ˈba-mə\. **1.** Navigable river, Alabama; formed by confluence of Tallapoosa and Coosa rivers, flows SW from cen. Alabama to join the Tombigbee and form the Mobile and Tensaw rivers flowing into Mobile Bay at Mobile; 315 mi. (507 km.) long.

2. A southern state of U.S.A., bounded on N by Tennessee, on E by Georgia, on S by Florida and the Gulf of Mexico, and on W by Mississippi; 29th state in area, 51,705 sq. mi. or 133,916 sq. km. (land area 50,851 sq. mi. or 131,704 sq. km.); 22d state in population, (1990c) 4,040,587; ✱ Montgomery; 22d state admitted to Union (1819). See table of states at UNITED STATES.

Nickname: Heart of Dixie.

State flower: Camellia.

Motto: We Dare Defend Our Rights.

Rivers: Mobile, formed by Alabama and Tombigbee; Alabama (see ALABAMA 1); Tombigbee, formed by junction of E and W forks in NE Mississippi; Tennessee, flowing W across N counties (for great dams, see TENNESSEE 1 and TENNESSEE VALLEY AUTHORITY); Chattahoochee forming SE boundary with Georgia; Conecuh and Pea, in S and SE part. Mobile and Tensaw (part of its estuary) flow into Mobile Bay, arm of Gulf of Mexico. Lake Martin in E is expansion of Tallapoosa River.

Mountains: S end of Appalachian Mts. (chief ranges Raccoon and Lookout) in NE corner extending as far as Birmingham. Highest point Cheaha Mt. 2407 ft. (734 m.), in Cleburne co.

Chief products: Corn, soybeans, peanuts; livestock; coal, iron ore, limestone, petroleum; manufacturing: iron and steel, chemicals, textiles; historically notable cotton production.

Chief cities: Birmingham, Mobile, Montgomery, Huntsville.

Political divisions: Divided into the following 67 counties (for pronunciation of their names, see their individual entries):

NAME	AREA[1] (sq. mi.)	AREA[1] (sq. km.)	POP. (1990c)	CO. SEAT
Autauga	599	1,551	34,222	Prattville
Baldwin	1,758	4,553	98,280	Bay Minette
Barbour	899	2,328	25,417	Clayton
Bibb	625	1,619	16,576	Centerville
Blount	640	1,658	39,248	Oneonta
Bullock	615	1,593	11,042	Union Springs
Butler	773	2,002	21,892	Greenville
Calhoun	611	1,582	116,034	Anniston
Chambers	599	1,551	36,876	Lafayette
Cherokee	600	1,554	19,543	Centre
Chilton	699	1,810	32,458	Clanton
Choctaw	918	2,378	16,018	Butler
Clarke	1,238	3,206	27,240	Grove Hill
Clay	603	1,562	13,252	Ashland
Cleburne	574	1,487	12,730	Heflin
Coffee	677	1,753	40,240	Elba
Colbert	596	1,544	51,666	Tuscumbia
Conecuh	850	2,202	14,054	Evergreen
Coosa	650	1,684	11,063	Rockford
Covington	984	2,548	36,478	Andalusia
Crenshaw	611	1,582	13,635	Luverne
Cullman	743	1,924	67,613	Cullman
Dale	559	1,448	49,633	Ozark
Dallas	976	2,528	48,130	Selma
De Kalb	778	2,015	54,651	Fort Payne
Elmore	624	1,616	49,210	Wetumpka
Escambia	962	2,492	35,518	Brewton
Etowah	555	1,437	99,840	Gadsden
Fayette	627	1,624	17,962	Fayette
Franklin	644	1,668	27,814	Russellville
Geneva	577	1,494	23,647	Geneva
Greene	640	1,658	10,153	Eutaw
Hale	662	1,714	15,498	Greensboro
Henry	565	1,463	15,374	Abbeville
Houston	577	1,494	81,331	Dothan
Jackson	1,079	2,795	47,796	Scottsboro
Jefferson	1,116	2,890	651,525	Birmingham
Lamar	605	1,567	15,715	Vernon
Lauderdale[2]	662	1,714	79,661	Florence
Lawrence	685	1,774	31,513	Moulton
Lee	612	1,585	87,146	Opelika
Limestone	545	1,412	54,135	Athens
Lowndes	715	1,852	12,658	Hayneville
Macon	616	1,595	24,928	Tuskegee
Madison	803	2,080	238,912	Huntsville
Marengo	978	2,533	23,084	Linden
Marion	743	1,924	29,830	Hamilton
Marshall	571	1,479	70,832	Guntersville
Mobile	1,240	3,212	378,643	Mobile
Monroe	1,032	2,673	23,968	Monroeville
Montgomery	790	2,046	209,085	Montgomery
Morgan	570	1,476	100,043	Decatur
Perry	734	1,901	12,759	Marion
Pickens	887	2,297	20,699	Carrollton
Pike	673	1,743	27,595	Troy
Randolph	581	1,505	19,881	Wedowee
Russell	639	1,655	46,860	Phenix City
Saint Clair	640	1,658	50,009	Pell City
Shelby	798	2,067	99,358	Columbiana
Sumter	915	2,370	16,174	Livingston
Talladega	750	1,942	74,107	Talladega
Tallapoosa	705	1,826	38,826	Dadeville
Tuscaloosa	1,338	3,465	150,522	Tuscaloosa
Walker	808	2,093	67,670	Jasper
Washington	1,066	2,761	16,694	Chatom
Wilcox	899	2,328	13,568	Camden
Winston	633	1,639	22,053	Double Springs

[1] Area = land area.
[2] Bounded by Tennessee River, including Wilson Dam.

History: Original inhabitants were American Indians whose settlement sites and burial mounds are in evidence; the major groups were Cherokees, Chickasaws, Choctaws, and Creeks when area first explored by Spaniards, notably by Hernando de Soto 1539–40; first permanent settlement estab. 1711 by French at site of Mobile on Mobile Bay; be-

88°
87°
86°
85°
35°
34°
33°
32°
31°
30°
TENNESSEE
ALABAMA
CITIES
State capital
County seat
City
BOUNDARIES
State
County
FEATURES
Dams
0 20 40 mi
0 30 60 km
Elk R.
CUMBERLAND PLATEAU
Tennessee R.
Pickwick Lake
Cloverdale
LAUDERDALE
Wilson Dam
Wheeler Dam
Anderson
LIMESTONE
Ardmore
New Market
Bridgeport
Stevenson
Meridianville
MADISON
Huntsville
JACKSON
Cherokee
Florence
Muscle Shoals
Athens
Flat Rock
Allsboro
Sheffield
Tuscumbia
Leighton
Wheeler Lake
Madison
Owens Cross Roads
Scottsboro
Henagar
Section
SAND MTN.
Valley Head
COLBERT
Littleville
Hatton
Decatur
New Hope
Guntersville Lake
Fort Payne
Russellville
LAWRENCE
Hartselle
Guntersville Dam
Rainsville
Red Bay
FRANKLIN
Moulton
MORGAN
MARSHALL
DE KALB
LOOKOUT MTN.
Phil Campbell
Sipsey Fork
Falkville
Arab
Guntersville
Tombigbee R.
Hackleburg
Haleyville
Vinemont
Albertville
Collinsville
Cedar Bluff
WINSTON
Addison
Cullman
Boaz
MARION
Double Springs
CULLMAN
ETOWAH
Centre
Weiss Lake
Hamilton
Blountsville
CHEROKEE
Brilliant
Lynn
Hanceville
Altoona
Attalla
Gadsden
Hokes Bluff
Guin
Lewis Smith Lake
Garden City
BLOUNT
Gallant
Rainbow City
Glencoe
Sulligent
Winfield
Carbon Hill
Oneonta
Piedmont
Jasper
Warrior
Ashville
CALHOUN
Jacksonville
LAMAR
FAYETTE
WALKER
Sumiton
Springville
Ragland
Atlanta
Vernon
Fayette
Cordova
JEFFERSON
Pinson
SAINT CLAIR
Weaver
Dora
Parrish
Graysville
Gardendale
Anniston
Heflin
Sipsey R.
Berry
Bankhead Lake
Adamsville
Tarrant City
Pell City
Eastaboga
CLEBURNE
Millport
Birmingham
Leeds
Oxford
Ranburne
Logan Martin Lake
Moores Bridge
Fairfield
Mtn. Brook
Cheaha Mtn. 2,408 ft.
Hueytown
Homewood
Lake Tuscaloosa
Bessemer
Midfield
Talladega
Woodland
Reform
Gordo
Bluff Park
Vincent
TALLADEGA
Lineville
RANDOLPH
TUSCALOOSA
PICKENS
Northport
Peterson
Green Pond
SHELBY
Childersburg
Wedowee
West Point Lake
Carrollton
Holt
Alabaster
Coosa R.
Ashland
Tallapoosa R.
Aliceville Dam
Tuscaloosa
Mignon
Sylacauga
CLAY
Rock Mills
Black Warrior R.
Calera
Columbiana
Wadley
Roanoke
Aliceville
West Blocton
Cahaba R.
Montevallo
New Site
Standing Rock
Goodwater
TALLAPOOSA
CHAMBERS
Panola
Moundville
BIBB
Jemison
Mitchell Lake
COOSA
Alexander City
Lafayette
Lanett
GREENE
Brent
Centreville
Thorsby
Rockford
Shawmut
Langdale
Eutaw
Akron
CHILTON
Dadeville
Gainesville Dam
HALE
Maplesville
Clanton
Camp Hill
Fairfax
Cooper
Lake Harding
MISSISSIPPI
Greensboro
PERRY
Stanton
Verbena
Epes
Forkland
Eclectic
Lake Martin
Opelika
SUMTER
Marion
Plantersville
ELMORE
Auburn
LEE
GEORGIA
Newbern
Lake Jordan
Claud
Notasulga
Livingston
Lake Demopolis
Suttle
AUTAUGA
Smiths
Demopolis
Wetumpka
Tallassee
Carrville
York
Uniontown
Autaugaville
Prattville
Tuskegee
Phenix City
Bellamy
Browns
Selma
Shorter
Fort Mitchell
Whitfield
Jefferson
DALLAS
Alabama R.
Montgomery
MACON
Seale
Linden
Thomaston
Orrville
Sardis
Lowndesboro
MONTGOMERY
Fort Davis
Hurtsboro
RUSSELL
Holy Trinity
Choctaw
MARENGO
Alberta
Pleasant Hill
Hayneville
Snowdoun
Union Springs
Pittsview
Lisman
Nanafalia
Dannelly Reservoir
Millers Ferry
Minter
LOWNDES
Fleta
Sellers
BULLOCK
Sweet Water
Braggs
Calhoun
Midway
Butler
Furman
Ramer
CHOCTAW
Camden
Fort Deposit
BARBOUR
Lower Peach Tree
WILCOX
Lapine
Shady Grove
Eufaula
Walter F. George Reservoir
Thomasville
Coy
Pine Apple
Honoraville
PIKE
Clayton
Coffeeville Dam
Fulton
Vredenburgh
Greenville
Troy
Louisville
Baker Hill
Silas
Grove Hill
Beatrice
BUTLER
Luverne
Brundidge
Pea R.
Clio
Walter F. George Dam
Frankville
Tombigbee R.
CLARKE
Finchburg
Chapman
CRENSHAW
Glenwood
Abbeville
Millry
Whatley
MONROE
Sepulga R.
Georgiana
Brantley
Choctawhatchee R.
Shorterville
Chatom
Jackson
Monroeville
McKenzie
Ariton
HENRY
Alma
Evergreen
Red Level
DALE
Ozark
WASHINGTON
Frisco City
Escambia R.
Elba
New Brockton
Newville
Fruitdale
Alabama R.
CONECUH
River Falls
Andalusia
COFFEE
Newton
Headland
Uriah
Conecuh R.
Enterprise
Daleville
Columbia
McIntosh
Castleberry
Opp
Dothan
Chattahoochee R.
McCullough
ESCAMBIA
COVINGTON
Kinston
Ashford
Mt. Vernon
Brewton
East Brewton
Samson
GENEVA
Slocomb
Citronelle
Mobile R.
Tensaw R.
Hartford
HOUSTON
Atmore
Canoe
Flomaton
Lockhart
Florala
Geneva
Cottonwood
MOBILE
Stockton
Chunchula
Satsuma
Bay Minette
Perdido R.
Escambia R.
Saraland
Chickasaw
Lake Seminole
Prichard
Stapleton
FLORIDA
Mobile
BALDWIN
Loxley
Choctawhatchee R.
Escatawpa R.
Daphne
Pensacola Bay
Choctawhatchee Bay
St. Elmo
Mobile Bay
Fairhope
Robertsdale
Point Clear
Lillian
Bayou La Batre
Foley
Mississippi Sound
Grants Pass
Bon Secour
Dauphin Island
Gulf Shores
Perdido Bay
Gulf of Mexico
©1996, Encyclopædia Britannica, Inc.

came English 1763; S part included in West Florida, retroceded to Spain in 1783 and claimed by U.S. as part of Louisiana Purchase 1803; rest of Alabama became part of U.S. 1783, with dividing line under dispute until 1795 when Spain ceded claim north of 31°; parts included in Terr. South of the Ohio River 1790 and Mississippi Terr. 1798 ff. (*qq.v.*); organized as a territory 1817; S tip formally ceded to U.S. 1819; first constitutional convention July 1819; admitted to Union Dec. 14, 1819; 2d constitutional convention Jan. 7–Mar. 20, 1861 passed ordinance of secession Jan. 11, 1861; government of Confederate States of America organized at Montgomery Feb. 4, 1861; 3d constitutional convention Sept. 12–30, 1865 declared secession null and void, and abolished slavery; readmitted to Union 1868; present constitution, formulated by 6th constitutional convention, adopted 1901 (see BIRMINGHAM 1).

Al·a·bas·ter \ˈa-lə-ˌbas-tər\. Town, Shelby co., cen. Alabama, 20 mi. (32 km.) S of Birmingham; pop. (1990c) 14,732.

Ala·bat \ˌä-lä-ˈbät\. Long narrow island, at S end of Lamon Bay off Luzon, Philippines; 74 sq. mi. (192 sq. km.); ab. 15 mi. (24 km.) long; pop. (1980c) 11,385.

al–Abyad, Bahr. See NILE.

Ala·ca·hö·yük \ˌä-lä-ˈjä-hœ-ˌyu̇ēk\; *formerly* **Ue·yuk** *or* **Uyuk** \ūē-ˈyu̇ēk\. Ruins, Çorum prov., N cen. Turkey in Asia, ab. 100 mi. (160 km.) ENE of Ankara; ancient Hittite site, ruins include carved sphinx gate, building remains, and royal tombs.

Ala·chua \ə-ˈla-chə-wə, *by some residents also* ə-ˈlä-chə-ˌwā\. **1.** County in N peninsula of Florida. See table at FLORIDA.

2. City, Alachua co., N Florida; pop. (1990c) 4529.

Ala·dağ *or* **Ala Dağ** \ˌä-lä-ˈdä, -ˈdäg\. Name of several mountains in Turkey, esp.: (1) Mountain 60 mi. (96 km.) N of Adana, 11,066 ft. (3373 m.); (2) Mountain N of Lake Van, 10,994 ft. (3351 m.); (3) Mountain ab. 60 mi. (96 km.) SSW of Kars, 10,282 ft. (3134 m.).

Al–Agheila. See AL ʽUQAYLAH.

Ala·go·as \ˌȧ-lə-ˈgō-əs\. State of E Brazil; ✻ Maceió; cotton, sugar. See table at BRAZIL.

Ala·goi·nhas \ˌȧ-lə-ˈgȯi-nyəs\. City, Bahia state, E Brazil, 70 mi. (113 km.) N of Salvador; munic. pop. (1980c) 101,939.

Ala·gón \ˌä-lä-ˈgōn\. River, W Spain; flows SW into Tagus River 2 mi. (3.2 km.) NE of Alcántara; ab. 120 mi. (193 km.) long.

Al–Ah·madi \ˌȧl-ˈȧ-mȧ-dē\. Town, Kuwait, ab. 22 mi. (35 km.) SSE of the seaport of Kuwait; pop. (1985c) 26,899.

Alai \ˈä-ˌlī\. **1.** Mountain range in SW Kyrgyzstan, running E and W; av. height 16,000 ft. (4877 m.); highest peak 19,554 ft. (5960 m.). See TRANS ALAI.

2. Valley of Kyzyl-Su (a N tributary of the Amu Dar'ya), S of Alai Mts.

Alais. See ALÈS.

Ala·jue·la \ˌä-lä-ˈhwā-lä\. **1.** Province, cen. Costa Rica (see table at COSTA RICA); plateau region.

2. Town, its ✻, 14 mi. (22 km.) W of San José; pop. (1991e) 44,890; center of sugar industry.

Ala·kol' *also* **Ala Kul** \ˌä-ˌlä-ˈkül\. Lake, E Kazakhstan, E of Lake Balkhash; 803 sq. mi. (2080 sq. km.).

Ala·la·kei·ki \ˌä-ˌlä-lä-ˈkā-kē\. Channel bet. SW Maui and Kahoolawe, Hawaii; 6 mi. (10 km.) wide.

Alalia. See ALERIA.

Al·a·ma·gan \ˌä-lä-mä-ˈgän\. One of the Mariana Is. (*q.v.*), W Pacific Ocean, 165 mi. (265 km.) N of Saipan, 17°36′N, 145°50′E; included in Japanese mandate 1919; taken by U.S. Aug. 1945.

Al·a·mance \ˈa-lə-ˌmans\. **1.** Small stream (**Alamance Creek,** a headstream of Cape Fear River), N cen. North Carolina; on its banks ab. 20 mi. (32 km.) W of Hillsboro colonial forces of British Governor William Tryon decisively defeated Regulators May 16, 1771.

2. County in N cen. North Carolina. See table at NORTH CAROLINA.

Al·a·man·nia \ˌa-lə-ˈma-nē-ə\. Region, on both sides of Upper Rhine (modern E France and SW Germany), W Europe; home of the Alamanni; in time of Frankish King Clovis, a Frankish province; later (c. 1000) a duchy.

Al ʽA·mā·rah \ˌal-ha-ˈmä-rə\ *also* **Ama·ra** \ə-ˈmä-rə\. Town, Iraq, on E bank of the Tigris 100 mi. (161 km.) NW of Basra; pop. (1985e) 131,758; taken by Gen. Charles Townshend as part of Mesopotamian campaign of British advance to Baghdad June 1915. See AL KŪT.

Al·a·me·da \ˌa-lə-ˈmē-də\. **1.** County in W California. See table at CALIFORNIA.

2. City, Alameda co., W California, on island near E shore of San Francisco Bay, 6 mi. (10 km.) E of San Francisco, separated from Oakland by estuary; pop. (1990c) 76,459; port of entry; commercial airports, starting point for first China Clipper flight Nov 22, 1935; shipping center; shipbuilding yards; incorp. 1854.

3. Former city, Bannock co., SE Idaho; now part of Pocatello.

Alameda–Oakland Tunnel. Vehicular tunnel under an inlet of San Francisco Bay, California, connecting Alameda with Oakland; 4500 ft. (1372 m.) long.

Alamein *or* **Alamein, El.** See EL ALAMEIN.

Ala·mi·nos \ˌä-lä-ˈmē-nōs\. Municipality, NW Pangasinan prov., Luzon, Philippines, near W shore of Lingayen Gulf; pop. (1980c) 47,715.

Al·a·mo \ˈa-lə-ˌmō\. **1.** Town, ⊗ of Wheeler co., SE cen. Georgia; pop. (1990c) 855.

2. Town, ⊗ of Crockett co., W Tennessee; pop. (1990c) 2426.

3. City, Hidalgo co., S Texas, 10 mi. (16 km.) E of McAllen; pop. (1990c) 8210.

Alamo, The. Fort in San Antonio, Texas; Spanish Franciscan mission (Mission San Antonio de Valero) estab. at present location 1724; converted to a fort 1793; renamed The Alamo 1801; in the Texan war of independence from Mexico, besieged by the Mexicans under Gen. Antonio López de Santa Anna Feb. 23–Mar. 6, 1836; defended to the last man of the Texan garrison of 187; became a symbol of Texan fortitude as used in Gen. Samuel Houston's cry "Remember the Alamo!" at the battle of San Jacinto 46 days later.

Al·a·mo·gor·do \ˌa-lə-mə-ˈgȯr-dō\. City, ⊗ of Otero co., S New Mexico, W of Sacramento Mts. 60 mi. (96 km.) NE of Las Cruces; pop. (1990c) 27,596; alt. 4350 ft. (1326 m.); to the SW are White Sands National Monument and **Hol·lo·man Air Force Base** \ˈhäl-ə-mən\; *formerly* **Alamogordo Air Base;** ab. 55 mi. (88 km.) to the NW at N end of the desert which extends between the Rio Grande and the San Andres Mts. is site of the first man-made atomic explosion July 16, 1945.

Alamogordo Dam. Dam, N De Baca co., New Mexico, across Pecos River; height 148 ft. (45 m.); completed 1938; impounds water, Sumner Lake, for irrigation.

Alamogordo Reservoir. See SUMNER LAKE.

Alamo Heights \ˈa-lə-ˌmō\. City, Bexar co., S cen. Texas, lying within boundaries of San Antonio; pop. (1990c) 6502.

Alamos, Los. See LOS ALAMOS.

Al·a·mo·sa \ˌa-lə-ˈmō-sə\. **1.** County in S Colorado. See table at COLORADO.

2. City, its ⊗, on Rio Grande 84 mi. (135 km.) WNW of Trinidad; pop. (1990c) 7579; Adams State Coll. (1921); founded 1878.

Ala·mut, Rock of \ˌä-lä-ˈmüt\. Elevation, N Iran, W end of Elburz Mts., ab. 70 mi. (113 km.) NW of Tehran; stronghold of the Assassins, a secret order of the Ismailians, in the Middle Ages.

Åland \ˈō-ˌlän\ *or* **Ahv·e·nan·maa** \ˈäh-ve-nän-ˌmä\. Archipelago in S Gulf of Bothnia bet. Sweden and Finland, constituting a province of Finland (see table at FINLAND); ✻ Mariehamn; of ab. 300 total islands and rocky islets, ab. 80 inhabited; chief island **Åland** *or* **Ahvenanmaa.**

History: Colonized early (12th cent.) by Swedes; Swedish fleet defeated and islands seized by Russian Czar Peter the Great 1714; restored by Russia to Sweden 1721; ceded with Finland by Sweden to Russia 1809; subject of international disputes and treaties in 19th cent.; part of independent Finland 1917; tried to secede from Finland; League of Nations arbitrated and while archipelago is still part of Finland, it has a singular autonomy in its governing system.

Åland Sea. Body of water bet. Åland archipelago at the entrance to the Gulf of Bothnia and the mainland of Sweden.

Alang·a·lang \ˈä-ˌläŋ-ˈä-ˌläŋ\. Municipality, N Leyte prov., Philippines, 12 mi. (19 km.) W of Palo; pop. (1980c) 29,453.

Ala·nia \ä-ˈlän-yä\ *or* **North Os·se·tia** \ä-ˈsē-shə, -shē-ə\ *or* **North Os·se·ti·ya** \ä-ˈse-tē-yə\. Republic, S Russia in Europe, on N slopes of cen. Caucasus Mts., bounded on N by Stavropol Kray, on E by Ingushetia, on S by Republic of Georgia, and on W and NW by Kabardino-Balkaria; 3089 sq. mi. (8001 sq. km.); pop. (1992e) 695,000; ✻ Vladikavkaz. Mountainous region watered by unnavigable Terek and tributaries; on its SE border is Mt. Kazbek, one of the highest peaks of the Caucasus; in SW Ossetian Military Road leads over mountains through Mamison Pass to Republic of Georgia. Mineral resources include lead and zinc; chief occupations fruitgrowing, lumbering, cattle raising. Chief nationalities Ossetian and Russian. Ossets are descended from the Alans, a division of the early Scythian tribes of the region and speak an Indo-Iranian language; came successively under nominal control of Khazars (see KHAZARIA), Mongols of the Golden Horde, and Russians; came in conflict with Russians 18th cent. and were conquered and annexed early 19th cent.; after Bolshevik Revolution became part of the Mountain Republic until 1924, then it became an autonomous region; became autonomous republic 1936; comprised **North Os·se·ti·an A.S.S.R.** \ä-ˈsē-shən, -shē-ən\ of the U.S.S.R. until 1991; became republic within Russia 1991; subsequently became member of Russian Federation.

Ala·o·tra \ˌä-lä-ˈō-trə\. Lake, NE cen. Madagascar; 70 sq. mi. (181 sq. km.); the republic's largest lake.

Ala·pa·yevsk \ˌə-lə-ˈpī-əfsk\. Town, Sverdlovsk Oblast, W Russia in Asia NNE of Yekaterinburg; pop. (1991e) 50,300.

Ala·pii Point \ˌä-lä-ˈpē\. Cape on W coast of Kauai I., Hawaii.

Al–ʻAqabah. See AQABA.

Al–Aq·qa·qir *or* **El Aqqaqir** \ˌal-ˈak-ka-ˌkēr, ˌel-\. Village, N Egypt, near El Alamein; scene of tank battle Nov. 2–3, 1942 in which Germans were severely beaten; closing phase of battle of El Alamein.

Al–Aqsur. See LUXOR.

al–ʻArab, Bahr. See BAHR EL ARAB.

Al–Araish. See LARACHE.

Alar·cos \ä-ˈlär-kōs\. Hill and former village, Ciudad Real prov., S cen. Spain, 7 mi. (11 km.) W of the commune of Ciudad Real; scene of battle 1195 in which the Almohads under Muslim ruler Abū Yūsef Yaʻqūb al–Manṣūr defeated Alfonso VIII of Castile.

Al ʻArīsh *or* **El ʻArîsh** \ˌal-a-ˈrēsh, ˌel-\; *anc.* **Rhi·no·co·lu·ra** \ˌrī-(ˌ)nō-kə-ˈlu̇(ə)r-ə\. Town, ✻ of Shamāl Sīnā' governorate, NE Egypt on Mediterranean Sea in N Sinai Penin.; in WWI important point in advance of British toward Palestine, taken Dec. 20, 1916; occupied by Israel 1967–79.

Al Ar·ṭā·wī·yah \ˌal-ar-ˌtä-ˈwē-yə\ *or* **Ar·ta·wi·ya** \ˌär-tə-ˈwē-yə\. Town, NE Nejd, N Saudi Arabia; founded since 1912 as first Ikhwan colony in Wahhabi revival.

Ala·şe·hir \ä-ˌlä-she-ˈhēr\; *formerly* **Ala·shehr** \-ˈsher\; *anc.* **Phil·a·del·phia** \ˌfi-lə-ˈdel-fē-ə, -fyə\. City, Manisa prov., W Turkey in Asia, on Alaşehir River (tributary of Gediz) and on railroad line 75 mi. (121 km.) E of İzmir; pop. (1990p) 36,535.

History: Site of ancient city of Philadelphia founded c. 150 B.C. by Attalus II (Philadelphus) of Pergamum; one of the Seven Churches of Asia Minor (*Rev.* i–iii); after a long period of resistance, the last city of Asia Minor to fall to the Turks 1390; said to have been conquered by Turkic ruler Timur 1402; largely destroyed by the Greeks 1922.

A–la Shan **1.** Mountain range, China. See HELAN SHAN. **2.** Desert region, China. See TENGGER SHAM.

A–la Shan–k'ou. See DZUNGARIAN GATE.

Al–Ash·mū·nein *or* **El Ashmūnein** \ˌal-ˌash-ˌmü-ˈnān, -ˈnīn, ˌel-\. Village, Egypt, near W bank of the Nile; site of **Her·mop·o·lis Mag·na** \hər-ˈmä-pə-lis-ˈmag-nə\, in ancient times center of the worship of Anubis or Thoth.

Al–ʻĀṣī, Nahr. See ORONTES 2.

Alas·ka \ə-ˈlas-kə\ *or when claimed by Russia (to 1867)* **Russian America.** A state of U.S.A., the NW part of North America, bounded on N by Arctic Ocean, on E by Canada, on SW by Pacific Ocean, and on W by Bering Sea and Arctic Ocean; first state in area, 591,004 sq. mi. or 1,530,700 sq. km. (land area 571,065 sq. mi. or 1,479,058 sq. km.); 49th state in population, (1990c) 550,043; ✻ Juneau; 49th state admitted to Union (1959). See table of states at UNITED STATES.

Nickname: The Last Frontier.

State flower: The forget-me-not.

Motto (unofficial): North to the Future.

Capes and Islands: Most northerly point is Point Barrow 71°23′N; Cape Prince of Wales, W point of Seward Penin., separated by Bering Strait (53 mi. or 85 km. wide) from Asia; Alaska Penin. and Aleutian Is. in SW extend 1200 mi. (1931 km.) toward Asia enclosing Bering Sea on S (furthest point W Attu I. 172°30′E); many other islands off coast: St. Lawrence, Nunivak, and Pribilof in Bering Sea, Kodiak and Afognak E of Alaska Penin., and islands of Alexander Archipelago off narrow strip of mainland in SE bordering British Columbia.

Rivers: Yukon (lower course) crosses from E to W (tributaries: Porcupine, Tanana, Koyukuk), Noatak in N, Kuskokwim in SW, Susitna and Copper in S.

Mountains: Wrangell Mts. in SE extending to Yukon border, Chugach Mts. along S coast, Alaska Range in S cen. part, Brooks Range in N, and Aleutian Range on Alaska Penin. Highest point Mt. McKinley 20,320 ft. (6194 m.). Has eight national parks, four national monuments, and two national historical parks.

Chief industries: Oil extraction, quarrying (sand and gravel); fishing; timber, tourism.

Chief cities: Anchorage, Fairbanks, Juneau.

Political divisions: Divided into the following 25 divisions (for pronunciation of their names, see their individual entries):

NAME	LOCATION	AREA[1] (sq. mi.)	AREA[1] (sq. km.)	POP. (1990c)
Aleutians East[2]	SW	6,985	18,091	2,464
Aleutians West[3]	SW	4,402	11,401	9,478
Anchorage[2]	S	1,698	4,398	226,338
Bethel[3]	W	41,087	106,415	13,656
Bristol Bay[2]	SW	519	1,344	1,410
Dillingham[3]	SW	18,467	47,830	4,012
Fairbanks North Star[2]	cen.	7,362	19,068	77,720
Haines[2]	SE	2,357	6,105	2,117
Juneau[2]	SE	2,594	6,718	26,751
Kenai Peninsula[2]	S	16,079	41,645	40,802
Ketchikan Gateway[2]	SE	1,220	3,160	13,828
Kodiak Island[2]	S	6,463	16,739	13,309
Lake and Peninsula[2]	S	23,632	61,207	1,668
Matanuska-Susitna[2]	S cen.	24,694	63,957	39,683
Nome[3]	W	23,013	59,604	8,288
North Slope[2]	N	87,860	227,557	5,979
Northwest Arctic[2]	NW	35,862	92,882	6,113
Prince of Wales-Outer Ketchikan[3]	SE	7,324	18,969	6,278
Sitka[2]	SE	2,882	7,464	8,588
Skagway-Yakutat-Angoon[3]	SE	12,881	33,362	4,385
Southeast Fairbanks[3]	cen.	25,994	67,324	5,913
Valdez-Cordova[3]	S	36,945	95,688	9,952
Wade Hampton[3]	SW	17,124	44,351	5,791
Wrangell-Petersburg[3]	SE	5,808	15,043	7,042
Yukon-Koyukuk[3]	W	157,121	406,943	8,478

[1] Area = land area.
[2] Equivalent to a county.
[3] Census area.

History: Original inhabitants (American Indians and Inuits) thought to have immigrated over Beringia as well as from the Arctic area. Explored by Russian voyages, esp. of Vitus Bering 1741; their first permanent settlement on Kodiak I. 1792; visited by British explorers James Cook, George

\ə\ **abut** \ˈə\ matches \ᵊ\ kitten, Fr table \ər\ **further** \a\ **ash** \ā\ **ace** \ä\ **cot, cart** \ȧ\ Fr bac \au̇\ **out** \ḇ\ Span Avila \ch\ **chin** \e\ **bet** \ē\ **easy** \g\ **go** \i\ **hit** \ī\ **ice** \j\ **job** \k̲\ Ger **ich, Buch** \ⁿ\ Fr vin \ŋ\ **sing** \ō\ **go** \ȯ\ **all** \ȯ\ **law** \œ\ Fr bœuf \œ̄\ Fr feu \ȯi\ **boy** \th\ **thin** \t͟h\ **this** \ü\ **loot** \u̇\ **foot** \ue\ Ger füllen \ūē\ Fr rue \y\ **yet** \ʸ\ Fr digne \dēnʸ\, nuit \nwʸē\ \yü\ **few** \yu̇\ **fury** \zh\ **vision**

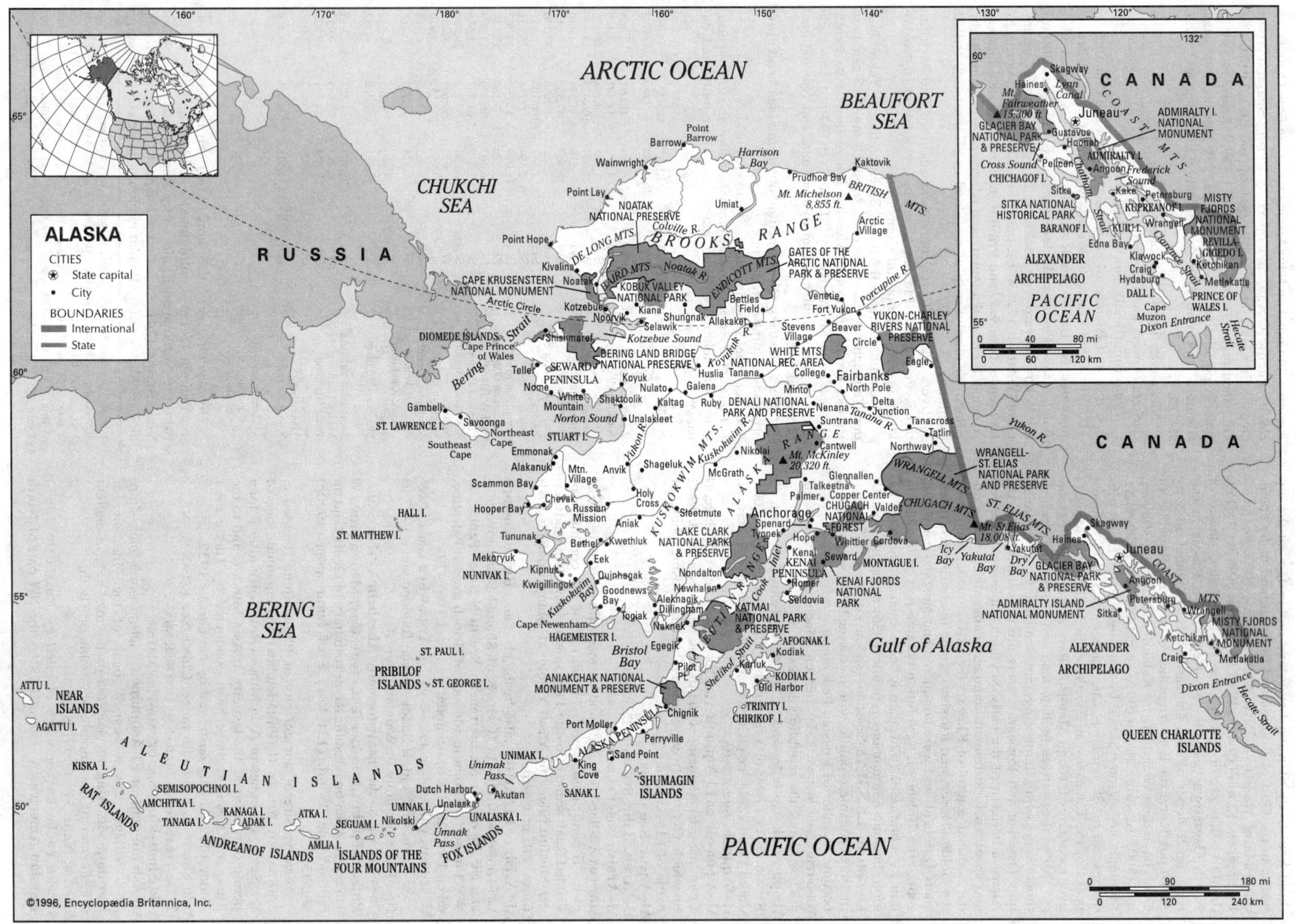
ALASKA
CITIES
State capital
City
BOUNDARIES
International
State
ARCTIC OCEAN
BEAUFORT SEA
CHUKCHI SEA
BERING SEA
PACIFIC OCEAN
Gulf of Alaska
R U S S I A
C A N A D A
BROOKS RANGE
ALASKA RANGE
ALEUTIAN ISLANDS
Arctic Circle
Mt. McKinley 20,320 ft.
Mt. Michelson 8,855 ft.
Mt. St. Elias 18,008 ft.
Anchorage
Fairbanks
Juneau
Nome
Barrow
Kodiak
Ketchikan
Sitka
Skagway
ALEXANDER ARCHIPELAGO
QUEEN CHARLOTTE ISLANDS
PRIBILOF ISLANDS
SHUMAGIN ISLANDS
NEAR ISLANDS
RAT ISLANDS
ANDREANOF ISLANDS
ISLANDS OF THE FOUR MOUNTAINS
FOX ISLANDS
ST. LAWRENCE I.
NUNIVAK I.
KODIAK I.
SEWARD PENINSULA
KENAI PENINSULA
ALASKA PENINSULA
Bristol Bay
Norton Sound
Kotzebue Sound
Bering Strait
Yukon R.
DENALI NATIONAL PARK AND PRESERVE
GATES OF THE ARCTIC NATIONAL PARK & PRESERVE
WRANGELL-ST. ELIAS NATIONAL PARK AND PRESERVE
GLACIER BAY NATIONAL PARK & PRESERVE
KATMAI NATIONAL PARK & PRESERVE
0 90 180 mi
0 120 240 km
©1996, Encyclopædia Britannica, Inc.

Vancouver, and Sir Alexander Mackenzie and by Hudson Bay traders 1778–1847; under trade monopoly of Russian-American Fur Company 1799–1861, first managed by Aleksandr Baranov; ownership claimed by Russia; region S to 54°40′ ceded by Russia to U.S. for $7,200,000 by treaty of 1867 negotiated by Secretary of State William H. Seward (hence early nickname of Alaska, "Seward's Folly"); organized 1884; received final U.S. territorial status 1912; gold discoveries, incl. Klondike 1896; disputed boundary with British Columbia arbitrated in favor of U.S. 1903; restriction of seal fisheries by treaties with Great Britain, Russia, and Japan 1911; in WWII Aleutian islands of Attu and Kiska occupied by Japanese June 1942–Aug. 1943; present constitution adopted 1956; was granted statehood 1959; suffered severe earthquake damage 1964; large oil reserves discovered 1968; crude-oil pipeline S from North Slope to Valdez begun 1975, opened 1977.

Alaska, Gulf of. Gulf, S Alaska, bet. Alaska Penin. and Alexander Archipelago.

Alaska Current. A warm ocean current formed as a division of the west-wind drift of the North Pacific Ocean and directed counterclockwise in the Gulf of Alaska.

Alaska Highway. Military and commercial road, extending from Dawson Creek, E British Columbia, Canada, NW across N British Columbia; 1519 mi. (2444 km.) long; built as **Al·can Highway** \ˈal-ˌkan\ (*Al*aska and *Can*ada) by U.S. Army engineers Mar.–Nov. 1942; later, improved and partly relocated; passes through Fort St. John, Fort Nelson, and Lower Post, then through Teslin, Whitehorse, and Kluane in SW Yukon, and Tanacross, Big Delta (where it meets the Richardson Highway, *q.v.*), and Richardson in E Alaska, to Fairbanks.

Alaska Panhandle; *sometimes shortened to* **the Panhandle.** The SE projection of land in Alaska.

Alaska Peninsula. Peninsula, SW Alaska, extending from Iliamna Lake to Unimak I.; ab. 475 mi. (764 km.) long.

Alaska Pipeline. See TRANS-ALASKA PIPELINE.

Alaska Range. Mountain range, S Alaska, extending in a semicircle from Alaska Penin. to Yukon boundary; highest Mt. McKinley. See MCKINLEY, MOUNT.

Al–As·nam. See ECH-CHELIFF.

Alas Strait \ä-ˈläs\. Channel bet. Lombok and Sumbawa islands, Lesser Sunda Is., Indonesia, connecting W Flores Sea with Indian Ocean; 10 to 15 mi. (16 to 24 km.) wide.

A–la–t'ao Shan. See DZUNGARIAN ALA TAU.

Ala Tau \ä-lä-ˈtau̇\. Several ranges of the Tian Shan mountain system, E Kazakhstan and Kyrgyzstan, around and NE of Issyk-Kul; max. elev. ab. 18,000 ft. (5486 m.).

Ala·taw Shan \ˈä-lä-ˌtau̇-ˈshän\. Mountain range, cen. Asia. See DZUNGARIAN ALA TAU.

Alataw Shan·kou \ˈshäŋ-kau̇\. Pass in Tian Shan. See DZUNGARIAN GATE.

Ala·tri \ä-ˈlä-trē\; *anc.* **Ale·tri·um** \ə-ˈlē-trē-əm\. Commune, Frosinone prov., Lazio, cen. Italy, 6 mi. (10 km.) N of the commune of Frosinone; pop. (1989c) 25,014; remains of pre-Roman wall of cyclopean masonry.

Ala·tyr \ˌə-lə-ˈtir\. Town, SW Chuvash Rep., on left bank of the Sura River 120 mi. (193 km.) SW of Kazan; thermal power station.

Ála·va \ˈä-lä-bä\. Province of N Spain. See table at SPAIN.

Al·a·va, Cape \ˈa-lə-və\. Cape, Clallam co., NW Washington, just S of Cape Flattery, 124°44′W, 48°10′N; most westerly point of U.S. mainland excl. Alaska.

Al–'Ay·zar·ī·yah \ˌa̍l-ˌī-zä-ˈrē-yə\; *formerly* **Beth·a·ny** \ˈbe-thə-nē\. Village, Jordan, on Mt. of Olives ab. 2 mi. (3.2 km.) E of Jerusalem; in area occupied by Israel 1967.

Al–'Azī·zī·yah \ˌa̍l-ä-ˈzē-zē-yə\. Town on Tigris River, Iraq, ab. 50 mi. (80 km.) downstream from Baghdad.

al–Azraq, Bahr. See NILE.

Al·ba. **1.** \ˈäl-bä\; *anc.* **Alba Pom·pe·ia** \ˈal-bə-päm-ˈpē-ə, ˈäl-bä-pōm-ˈpā-ä\. Commune, Cuneo prov., Piedmont, NW Italy, on Tanaro River 33 mi. (53 km.) NE of the commune of Cuneo; pop. (1989c) 30,363.

2. \ˈäl-bə\. County, W cen. Romania. See table at ROMANIA.

Al·ba·ce·te \ˌäl-bä-ˈsā-tā\. **1.** Province of SE Spain. See table at SPAIN.

2. Commune, its ✻, 138 mi. (222 km.) SE of Madrid; pop. (1989c) 130,023; produces wine; well-known for cutlery manufacture; founded 1365; development followed draining of nearby malarial swamps in 19th cent.

Al–Bahnasā. See OXYRHYNCHUS.

Al–Bahr. See NILE.

Alba Iu·lia \ˈäl-bə-ˈyül-yə\ *or Lat.* **Apu·lum** \ə-ˈpyü-ləm\ *or Hung.* **Gyu·la·fe·hér·vár** \ˈjü-ˌlö-ˌfā-her-ˌvär\ *or Ger.* **Karls·burg** \ˈkärlz-ˌbu̇rk\. Town, ⊗ of Alba co., Romania, on Mureşul River; pop. (1989c) 72,331; food processing.

History: Site of Roman colony; bishopric since 11th cent.; contains tomb of Hungarian national hero, János Hunyadi; 16th cent. residence of princes of Transylvania (*q.v.*); while under Austria, upper citadel built 1716–35 by Emperor Charles VI; as traditional center of Romanian nationalism, scene of proclamation of union of Transylvania with Romania 1918 and of coronation of King Ferdinand I and Queen Marie 1922.

Alba Lon·ga \ˈal-bə-ˈlȯŋ-gə\. Ancient city, the oldest in Latium, Italy, 12 mi. (19 km.) SE of Rome, extending in long line in Alban Hills to E shore of Albanus Lacus. Traditionally founded by Ascanius, son of Aeneas; legendary birthplace of Romulus and Remus, the founders of Rome; razed by early Roman King Tullus Hostilius c. 650–600 B.C.

Albana. See DERBENT.

Al·ban Hills \ˈȯl-bən-, ˈal-\ *or Ital.* **Mon·ti Al·ba·ni** \ˈmȯn-tē-äl-ˈbä-nē\; *anc.* **Al·ba·nus Mons** \äl-ˈbä-ˈnəs-ˈmȯns\. Mountain group near Albano Laziale, Italy, SE of Rome; a part of the Lower Apennines; comprised of extinct volcanoes; summer resort.

Al·ba·nia \al-ˈbā-nē-ə, -nyə, ȯl-\. **1.** Ancient country of E Caucasus region on W side of Caspian Sea, extending N from Cyrus and Araxes rivers and corresponding largely to NE Azerbaijan and S Dagestan Rep., Russia. Inhabited by fierce Scythian tribe who fought under Mithradates VI of Pontus against Roman Gen. Pompey the Great.

2. *or officially* **Republic of Albania;** *Albanian* **Shqip·ni** \shkip-ˈnē\ *or* **Shqip·ri** \shkē-ˈprē\ *or* **Shqi·pë·ri** \ˌshkyē-pə-ˈrē\. Republic, W Balkan Penin., bet. Yugoslavia, the Rep. of Macedonia, and Greece, on E coast of Adriatic; 11,100 sq. mi. (28,749 sq. km.); pop. (1992e) 3,357,000; ✻ Tiranë.

Physical features: Very mountainous country; North Albanian Alps in N (highest peak 9026 ft. or 2751 m.).

Rivers: Drin in N, Shkumbin and Seman in center, Vijosë in S; SE part of Lake Scutari on N border, outlet Buenë River; parts of Lake Ohrid and Lake Prespa in SE.

Chief products: Corn, potatoes, sugar beets, cotton, tobacco, wheat; deposits of coal, chrome, copper, oil; manufacturing: chemicals, textiles; hydroelectric power production; one of Europe's least developed economies.

Chief towns: Tiranë, Durrës, Shkodër, Vlorë, Korçë.

Political divisions: Divided into the following districts (for pronunciation of their names, see their individual entries):

NAME	AREA (sq. mi.)	AREA (sq. km.)	POP. (1990e)	CAPITAL
Berat	396	1,026	180,489	Berat
Dibër	606	1,570	153,775	Peshkopi
Durrës	327	847	251,029	Durrës
Elbasan	572	1,481	248,676	Elbasan
Fier	460	1,191	251,115	Fier
Gjirokastër	439	1,137	67,392	Gjirokastër
Gramsh	268	694	44,791	Gramsh
Kolonjë (formerly Ersekë)	311	805	25,291	Ersekë
Korçë	842	2,181	218,219	Korçë
Krujë	234	606	109,876	Krujë

NAME	AREA (sq. mi.)	AREA (sq. km.)	POP. (1990e)	CAPITAL
Kukës	604	1,564	104,731	Kukës
Lezhë	185	479	63,505	Lezhë
Librazhd	391	1,013	73,871	Librazhd
Lushenjë	275	712	137,830	Lushenjë
Mat	397	1,028	78,754	Burrel
Mirditë	269	697	51,701	Rrëshen
Përmet	359	930	40,419	Përmet
Pogradec	280	725	73,333	Pogradec
Pukë	374	969	50,286	Pukë
Sarandë	424	1,098	89,456	Sarandë
Shkodër	976	2,528	241,549	Shkodër
Skrapar	299	774	47,605	Çorovodë
Tepelenë	315	816	51,022	Tepelenë
Tiranë	478	1,238	374,483	Tiranë
Tropojë	403	1,044	45,965	Bajram Curri
Vlorë	621	1,608	180,725	Vlorë

History: Home of ancient Mediterranean people, divided into Ghegs in the N, Tosks in S; later became Muslims converted from Christianity; as a race little affected by Greco-Roman or Slavonic penetration; held by Goths 4th and 5th cents., Byzantine Empire 6th–13th cents., and Serbs in 14th cent.; despite resistance 1443–68 of national hero, George Castriota (Scanderbeg), overcome by Turks; part of Ottoman Empire until 1912; independence proclaimed as a principality 1912; invaded for brief time 1913 by Serbs; independence again proclaimed 1917 and confirmed 1920 by treaty with Italy and admission into League of Nations; boundary dispute with Yugoslavia settled by League 1921; republic 1925–28; guaranteed territorial integrity and defensive alliance by Italy 1927; monarchy 1928 with Ahmed Bey Zogu as king (Zog I); attacked and overrun April 1939 by Italian troops and placed under rule of king of Italy; invaded in S 1941 by Greek army, which was later driven out by German conquest of Greece. German forces finally driven out Nov. 1944 and again independent; estab. a people's (Communist) republic Jan. 1946; became a member of the Warsaw Pact 1955 (withdrew 1968); formed political relationship with China 1961–77; political unrest followed antigovernment demonstrations 1990; non-Communist government elected 1992.

3. Commune, France. See AUBAGNE.

4. Ancient name of Scotland, N of the Clyde.

Albaniae Pylae. See CASPIAN GATES 2.

Al·ba·no, Lake \al-ˈbä-nō, äl-\ *or Ital.* **La·go di Albano** \ˈlä-gō-dē-äl-ˈbä-nō\; *anc.* **Al·ba·nus La·cus** \al-ˈbā-nəs-ˈlā-kəs\. Lake, in crater of extinct volcano near Albano Laziale, Italy; 3 sq. mi. (8 sq. km.); max. depth 558 ft. (170 m.); its outlet a rock-hewn tunnel ab. 1 mi. (1.6 km.) long made 398–397 B.C., on advice of Delphic Oracle, still in use. Castel Gandolfo and many beautiful villas on its shores.

Albano La·zia·le \al-ˈbä-nō-lä-ˈtsyä-lā\. Commune, Roma prov., Lazio, cen. Italy, 14 mi. (22.5 km.) SE of Rome on Lake Albano and Appian Way; pop. (1989c) 31,460; summer resort; Roman ruins. Near early town of Alba Longa, estab. by Roman Emperor Septimius Severus c. 195 A.D.

Albanus Lacus. See ALBANO, LAKE.

Albanus Mons. See ALBAN HILLS.

Al·ba·ny \ˈȯl-bə-nē\. **1.** Name of counties in two states of the U.S. See tables at NEW YORK and WYOMING.

2. Residential city, Alameda co., W California, N of Oakland on San Francisco Bay; pop. (1990c) 16,327; incorp. 1908.

3. \ˈȯl-bə-nē, -ˌbe-; al-ˈbā-nē\. Commercial city, ⊗ of Dougherty co., SW Georgia, on Flint River 65 mi. (104 km.) N of Florida border; pop. (1990c) 78,122; radium springs nearby; Albany State Coll. (1903), Albany Junior Coll. (1966).

4. City, ⊗ of Clinton co., S Kentucky; pop. (1990c) 2062.

5. City, ⊗ of Gentry co., NW Missouri, 45 mi. (72 km.) NE of St. Joseph; pop. (1990c) 1958.

6. City, ✻ of New York state and ⊗ of Albany co., on W bank of Hudson River 145 mi. (233 km.) N of New York; pop. (1990c) 101,082; Albany Medical Coll. (1839), State Univ. of New York at Albany (1844), Albany Coll. of Pharmacy (1881), Coll. of St. Rose (1920), state capitol (1871), Schuyler Mansion (1761).

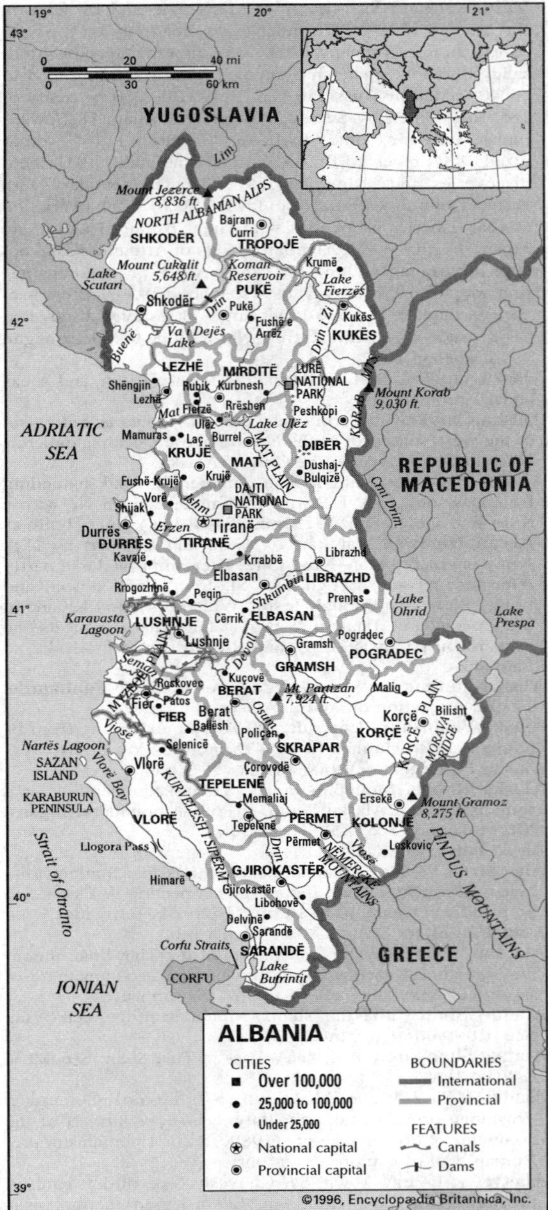

History: Second oldest permanent European settlement within 13 colonies, begun 1614 by establishment of Dutch trading post; actual colonization 1624 when Fort Orange was founded by Dutch West India Company; village, granted independence from the patroon, became Beverwyck 1652; after surrender of Fort Orange to English 1664, Beverwyck became Albany; received charter 1686; long a center for fur trade and contact with Indians; scene of the Albany Congress of the seven English colonies and the Iroquois 1754 when Albany Plan of Union was drafted; seriously menaced by British attack during Revolutionary War, esp. in 1777; became ✻ of state of New York 1797; expanded as a commercial center after opening of Erie Canal 1825 and of Albany-Schenectady R.R. 1831.

7. City, ⊗ of Linn co., W Oregon, on Willamette River 10 mi. (16 km.) NE of Corvallis; pop. (1990c) 29,462; estab. 1848.
8. City, ⊗ of Shackelford co., N cen. Texas, 30 mi. (48 km.) NE of Abilene; pop. (1990c) 1962.
9. Seaport municipality, on King George Sound, SW Western Australia, Australia, ab. 260 mi. (418 km.) SE of Perth; pop. (1991p) 13,599; estab. as a military settlement called Frederickstown 1826; renamed 1832. Possesses good harbor, but lost much of its importance with improvements at Fremantle 1901; popular vacation and health resort.
10. River, N cen. Ontario, Canada; rises in chain of lakes (largest St. Joseph) in W Ontario and flows E and NE into W James Bay at Fort Albany; 610 mi. (981 km.) long; chief tributaries the Kenogami and Ogoki rivers.

Alba Pompeia. See ALBA 1.

Al–Basrah. See BASRA.

Al·ba·tross Point \ˈal-bə-ˌtrȯs, -ˌträs\. Cape on NW cen. coast of North I., New Zealand, at S entrance to Kawhia Harbor.

Al·bay \äl-ˈbī\. **1.** Province, SE Luzon, Philippines (see table at PHILIPPINES); includes the islands of Batan, Cagraray, Rapu-Rapu, and San Miguel; very mountainous, includes among other peaks the perfect cone of Mayon Volcano; watered by many small streams; very fertile, esp. well adapted to hemp (abacá) and rice. Under nominal Spanish rule late 16th cent.–late 19th cent.; suffered from great eruption of Mayon 1815; under American control first part 20th cent.
2. Municipality on Albay Gulf, now part of Legazpi (*q.v.*).

Al Bay·ḍā' \ˌȧl-ˌbī-ˈdä\. Town, NE Libya, NE of Benghazi; elev. ab. 2000 ft. (610 m.).

Albay Gulf. Inlet of Pacific Ocean in SE Luzon, Philippines, on E coast of Albay prov.; ab. 30 mi. (48 km.) long by 8 to 12 mi. (13 to 19 km.) wide; its N shore formed by islands of Cagraray, Batan, and Rapu-Rapu. Port of Legazpi is at its head.

Al·be·marle \ˈal-bə-ˌmärl\. **1.** County in cen. Virginia. See table at VIRGINIA.
2. Town, ⊗ of Stanly co., S cen. North Carolina, 42 mi. (68 km.) NE of Charlotte; pop. (1990c) 14,939.

Albemarle Island. See ISABELA ISLAND.

Albemarle Sound. Inlet of Atlantic Ocean, in NE North Carolina; 52 mi. (84 km.) long; forms parts of Currituck, Camden, Pasquotank, Perquimans, and Chowan cos. on the N, Bertie co. on W, and Washington, Tyrrell, and Dare cos. on S; receives the Chowan River in the NW.

Al·ben·ga \äl-ˈbeŋ-gə\; *anc.* **Al·bum In·gau·num** \ˈal-bəm-iŋ-ˈgȯ-nəm\ *or* **Al·bin·gau·num** \ˌal-bəŋ-ˈgȯ-nəm\. Seaport, Savona prov., Liguria, NW Italy, on Ligurian Sea 22 mi. (35 km.) SW of the seaport of Savona; pop. (1989c) 22,578; Gothic cathedral; museum; remains of Roman bridge.

Al·ber·che \äl-ˈber-ˌchā\. River, cen. Spain; 113 mi. (182 km.) long.

Al·bères, Monts \ˌmō^{n}-zȧl-ˈber\. Easternmost section of the Pyrenees, bet. SW France and NE Spain; highest peak Pic Noulos 4128 ft. (1258 m.).

Al·ber·ga \al-ˈbər-gə\. Intermittent river, N South Australia; flows E from Musgrave Range and in rainy season joins with Finke River; ab. 350 mi. (563 km.) long.

Al·ber·ni Canal \al-ˈbər-nē\. Narrow fjord, S cen. Vancouver I., SW British Columbia, Canada; ab. 30 mi. (48 km.) long; an inlet of the Pacific opening into Barkley Sound. Port Alberni is at its head.

Al·bert \ˈal-bərt\. County in SE New Brunswick, Canada. See table at NEW BRUNSWICK.

Albert \ȧl-ˈber\; *formerly* **An·cre** \ˈä^{n}kr^{ə}\. Commune, Somme dept., N France, ab. 17 mi. (27 km.) NE of Amiens; on edge of battle of the Somme 1916, almost completely destroyed in battles of 1918.

Al·bert, Lake \ˈal-bərt\ *or* **Lake Mo·bu·tu Se·se Se·ko** \mō-ˈbü-tü-ˈsā-sā-ˈsā-kō\. Lake bet. Uganda and Democratic Rep. of the Congo, cen. Africa, ab. 135 mi. (217 km.) NW of Lake Victoria; 100 mi. (161 km.) long by 20 mi. (32 km.) wide; 2075 sq. mi. (5374 sq. km.); max. depth 168 ft. (51 m.); elev. 2030 ft. (619 m.). It receives at SW end the Semliki; outlet of Lake Edward; at NE corner just below Murchison Falls it receives Victoria Nile from Lake Victoria. Its outlet at N end is Albert Nile section of Nile. Discovered by Sir Samuel Baker 1864; circumnavigated by Italian explorer Romolo Gessi (Gessi Pasha) 1876 and by German explorer Emin Paşa 1884; initially part of Uganda (*q.v.*); now part of international border.

Al·ber·ta \al-ˈbər-tə\. **1.** Province, W Canada, most westerly Prairie Province, bounded on N by Northwest Territories, on E by Saskatchewan, on S by U.S. (Montana), and on W by British Columbia; ✱ Edmonton.

Physical features: An extensive plateau with higher portion in S; main range of the Canadian Rockies along its SW border; many peaks 8000 to 11,000 ft. (2440 to 3350 m.); its E slopes have been in large part set aside for their scenery (see *Jasper, Banff,* and *Waterton Lakes National Parks* in table at CANADA); in N is the S half of Wood Buffalo National Park; in SE cen. part of province is Elk Island National Park; contains also ab. 50 provincial parks. Prairie lands well watered, in N by Athabaska and Peace river systems, in center by the North Saskatchewan, and in S by the South Saskatchewan. In NE corner is Lake Claire and W end of Lake Athabaska; in cen. part is Lesser Slave Lake.

Chief products: Wheat, barley; livestock; petroleum, natural gas, coal; chemicals, paper; tourism.

Chief cities: Calgary, Edmonton. See table at CANADA.

History: Orig. long inhabited by various Indian peoples; part of territory ruled by Hudson's Bay Company until 1870; as part of Northwest Territories, under the Dominion of Canada 1870–82; S part set up as a district, bet. Rocky Mts. and 112°W and S of 55°N, 105,300 sq. mi. (272,727 sq. km.), with ✱ at Calgary; developed by an increasing number of "homesteaders" after completion of Canadian Pacific R.R. 1886; dominated by ranching until ab. 1900; became famed for its wheat and mineral production; received provincial status 1905; important oil reserves discovered 1947.
2. Mountain, Rocky Mt. Range, SW Alberta, at S end of Jasper National Park; 11,874 ft. (3619 m.).

Al·bert Canal \ˈal-bərt\. Canal, NE Belgium, from Liége to Antwerp; 80 mi. (129 km.) long, 140 ft. (43 m.) wide; crossed by Germans May 1940; retaken by British Sept. 1944.

Al·bert Ed·ward \ˈal-bərt-ˈed-wərd\. Peak in the Owen Stanley Range, Papua New Guinea, SE New Guinea, N of Port Moresby; 13,097 ft. (3992 m.).

Albert Edward Nyanza. See EDWARD, LAKE.

Al·bert Lea \ˈal-bərt-ˈlē\. City, ⊗ of Freeborn co., S Minnesota; pop. (1990c) 18,310.

Al·bert Mark·ham, Mount \ˈal-bərt-ˈmär-kəm\. Peak in Victoria Land, Antarctica, 81°23′S, 158°12′E, N of Mt. Markham; 10,460 ft. (3188 m.).

Al·bert Mountains \ˈal-bərt\. Mountain range, Papua New Guinea; has several peaks over 10,000 ft. (3000 m.), highest ab. 13,600 ft. (4145 m.); connects with Owen Stanley Range on SE.

Albert Nile. See NILE.

Al·ber·ton \ˈal-bər-tən\. Town, NE cen. Rep. of South Africa, SE of Johannesburg.

Al·bert·ville \ˈal-bərt-ˌvil\. City, Marshall co., NE Alabama, 20 mi. (32 km.) NW of Gadsden; pop. (1990c) 14,507.

Albertville \ˌȧl-ber-ˈvēl\. Town, Savoie dept., SE France; site of Winter Olympic Games 1992.

Albertville. See KALEMIE.

Al·bi \ȧl-ˈbē\ *or anc.* **Al·bi·ga** \al-ˈbī-gə\. Commune, ✱ of Tarn dept., S France, on Tarn River 42 mi. (68 km.) NE of Toulouse; pop. (1990c) 48,707; 13th cent. Gothic cathedral; archbishop's palace; ✱ of Romano-Gallic Albigenses and of medieval viscounty of Albigeois, which later became part of Toulouse; from it, the Albigensian movement of the 12th and 13th cents. took its name.

Al·bia \ˈal-bē-ə\. City, ⊗ of Monroe co., S Iowa, 22 mi. (35 km.) W of Ottumwa; pop. (1990c) 3870.

Albiga. See ALBI.

\ə\ **abut** \ə\ **matches** \$^{ə}$\ **kitten, Fr table** \ər\ **further** \a\ **ash** \ā\ **ace** \ä\ **cot, cart** \ȧ\ **Fr bac** \au̇\ **out** \b̲\ **Span Avila** \ch\ **chin** \e\ **bet** \ē\ **easy** \g\ **go** \i\ **hit** \ī\ **ice** \j\ **job** \k̲\ **Ger ich, Buch** \$^{n}$\ **Fr vin** \ŋ\ **sing** \ō\ **go** \ȯ\ **all** \ȯ\ **law** \œ\ **Fr bœuf** \œ̄\ **Fr feu** \ȯi\ **boy** \th\ **thin** \th̲\ **this** \ü\ **loot** \u̇\ **foot** \ue\ **Ger füllen** \u̅e\ **Fr rue** \y\ **yet** \$^{y}$\ **Fr digne** \ˈdēn^{y}\, **nuit** \ˈnw^{y}ē\ \yü\ **few** \yu̇\ **fury** \zh\ **vision**

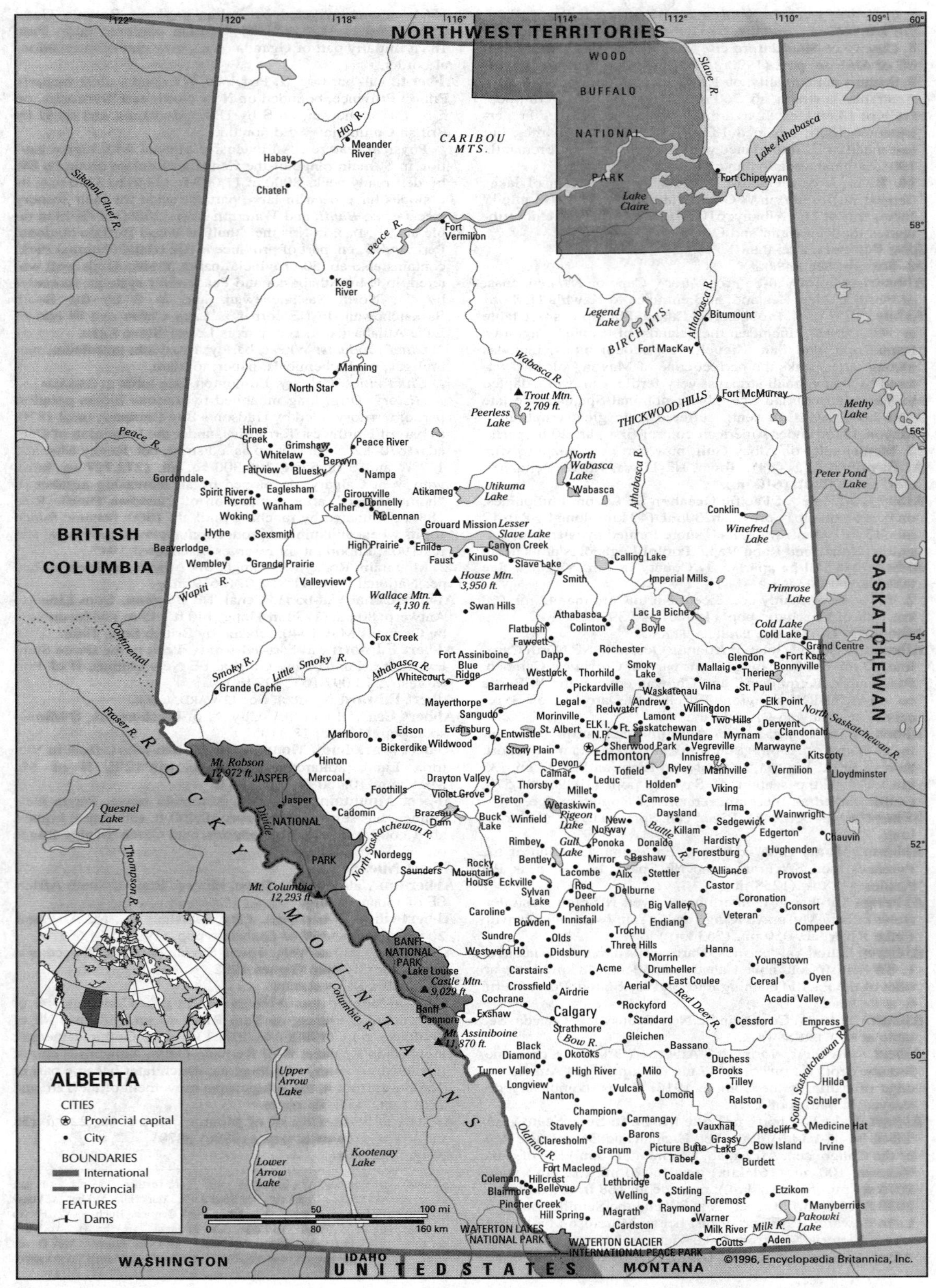

NORTHWEST TERRITORIES
WOOD BUFFALO NATIONAL PARK
Slave R.
Lake Athabasca
Fort Chipewyan
Lake Claire
CARIBOU MTS.
Hay R.
Meander River
Habay
Chateh
Sikanni Chief R.
Peace R.
Fort Vermilion
Keg River
Legend Lake
BIRCH MTS.
Athabasca R.
Bitumount
Fort MacKay
Wabasca R.
Manning
North Star
Trout Mtn. 2,709 ft.
Peerless Lake
THICKWOOD HILLS
Fort McMurray
Methy Lake
Hines Creek
Grimshaw
Peace River
Whitelaw
Berwyn
Fairview
Bluesky
Nampa
Gordondale
North Wabasca Lake
Wabasca
Peter Pond Lake
Spirit River
Eaglesham
Rycroft
Wanham
Girouxville
Falher
Donnelly
McLennan
Atikameg
Utikuma Lake
Woking
Conklin
Winefred Lake
BRITISH COLUMBIA
Hythe
Sexsmith
Grouard Mission
Lesser Slave Lake
Beaverlodge
High Prairie
Enilda
Canyon Creek
Wembley
Grande Prairie
Faust
Kinuso
Slave Lake
Calling Lake
Valleyview
Smith
Imperial Mills
Wapiti R.
House Mtn. 3,950 ft.
Wallace Mtn. 4,130 ft.
Swan Hills
Primrose Lake
SASKATCHEWAN
Athabasca
Colinton
Lac La Biche
Cold Lake
Cold Lake
Flatbush
Fawcett
Boyle
Grand Centre
Continental
Fox Creek
Dapp
Rochester
Glendon
Fort Kent
Bonnyville
Smoky R.
Little Smoky R.
Athabasca R.
Fort Assiniboine
Blue Ridge
Smoky Lake
Mallaig
Therien
Whitecourt
Westlock
Thorhild
Vilna
St. Paul
Grande Cache
Barrhead
Pickardville
Waskatenau
Elk Point
Mayerthorpe
Legal
Redwater
Andrew
Willingdon
North Saskatchewan R.
Fraser R.
Sangudo
Morinville
Lamont
Two Hills
Derwent
Clandonald
Evansburg
Entwistle
St. Albert
ELK I. N.P.
Ft. Saskatchewan
Mundare
Myrnam
Marlboro
Edson
Bickerdike
Wildwood
Stony Plain
Sherwood Park
Vegreville
Marwayne
Kitscoty
Edmonton
Innisfree
Devon
Tofield
Ryley
Mannville
Vermilion
Lloydminster
Mt. Robson 12,972 ft.
JASPER
Hinton
Mercoal
Drayton Valley
Calmar
Leduc
Thorsby
Holden
Viking
Foothills
Millet
Violet Grove
Breton
Camrose
Irma
Jasper
NATIONAL
Cadomin
Brazeau Dam
Wetaskiwin
Daysland
Wainwright
Quesnel Lake
Divide
Buck Lake
Winfield
Pigeon Lake
New Norway
Sedgewick
Killam
Edgerton
North Saskatchewan R.
Rimbey
Ponoka
Donalda
Hardisty
Chauvin
PARK
Gull Lake
Bashaw
Forestburg
Hughenden
Thompson R.
Nordegg
Saunders
Rocky Mountain House
Bentley
Mirror
Battle R.
Alliance
Provost
Lacombe
Alix
Stettler
Eckville
Mt. Columbia 12,293 ft.
Sylvan Lake
Red Deer
Delburne
Castor
Coronation
Penhold
Big Valley
Consort
Caroline
Veteran
Innisfail
Endiang
Bowden
Compeer
Sundre
Olds
Trochu
Westward Ho
Three Hills
Hanna
Didsbury
Morrin
BANFF NATIONAL PARK
Carstairs
Acme
Drumheller
Youngstown
Lake Louise
Castle Mtn. 9,029 ft.
Crossfield
Aerial
East Coulee
Cereal
Oyen
Airdrie
Columbia R.
Cochrane
Rockyford
Red Deer R.
Acadia Valley
Banff
Canmore
Exshaw
Calgary
Standard
Cessford
Empress
Strathmore
Mt. Assiniboine 11,870 ft.
Gleichen
Bow R.
Bassano
Black Diamond
Okotoks
Duchess
Turner Valley
High River
Brooks
Milo
Longview
Tilley
Hilda
Upper Arrow Lake
Nanton
Vulcan
Lomond
Ralston
Schuler
Champion
South Saskatchewan R.
Stavely
Carmangay
Vauxhall
Redcliff
Medicine Hat
Claresholm
Barons
Grassy Lake
Bow Island
Irvine
Granum
Picture Butte
Taber
Burdett
Oldman R.
Kootenay Lake
Fort Macleod
Lower Arrow Lake
Coleman
Hillcrest
Bellevue
Lethbridge
Coaldale
Blairmore
Welling
Stirling
Etzikom
Pincher Creek
Foremost
Manyberries
Hill Spring
Magrath
Raymond
Warner
Pakowki Lake
Cardston
Milk River
Milk R.
Coutts
Aden
WATERTON LAKES NATIONAL PARK
WATERTON GLACIER INTERNATIONAL PEACE PARK
ROCKY MOUNTAINS
WASHINGTON
IDAHO
UNITED STATES
MONTANA
©1996, Encyclopædia Britannica, Inc.
ALBERTA
CITIES
Provincial capital
City
BOUNDARIES
International
Provincial
FEATURES
Dams
0 50 100 mi
0 80 160 km
122° 120° 118° 116° 114° 112° 110° 109°
60° 58° 56° 54° 52° 50°

Al·bi·geois \ˌal-bē-ˈzhwä\. Former region, S France, around Albi, viscounty of Languedoc, now entirely in Tarn dept.; joined to France 1247.

Al·bi·na \äl-ˈbē-nä\. Seaport town, NE Suriname, on W bank of Maroni River opp. St. Laurent, French Guiana.

Albina, Point *or Port.* **Pon·ta Albina** \ˌpō^{n}n-tə-ˌal-ˈbē-nə\. Cape on SW coast of Angola; 15°51′S, 11°44′E.

Albingaunum. See ALBENGA.

Al·bi·on \ˈal-bē-ən\. **1.** City, ⊗ of Edwards co., SE Illinois; pop. (1990c) 2116.
2. Town, ⊗ of Noble co., NE Indiana; pop. (1990c) 1823.
3. City, Calhoun co., S Michigan, 23 mi. (37 km.) ESE of Battle Creek; pop. (1990c) 10,066; Albion Coll. (1835).
4. City, ⊗ of Boone co., E cen. Nebraska, 40 mi. (64 km.) WSW of Norfolk; pop. (1990c) 1916.
5. Village, ⊗ of Orleans co., W New York, ab. 10 mi. (16 km.) S of Lake Ontario and 32 mi. (51 km.) W of Rochester; pop. (1990c) 5863.
6. Oldest name of Great Britain; retained as poetical name of England.

Al Biqā'. See BEKÁA VALLEY.

Al Bīrah \ˌal-ˈbē-rə\; *bib.* **Be·e·roth** \bē-ˈir-ˌōth, ˈbir-\; *anc.* **Be·roea** \bə-ˈrē-ə\. Town in West Bank, 9 mi. (15 km.) N of Jerusalem on a rocky hilltop; in region occupied by Israel 1967.

Albis. See ELBE.

Albona. See LABIN.

Al·bo·rán \ˌäl-bō-ˈrän\. Island in W Mediterranean Sea, part of Almería prov., Spain, N of Melilla and 45 mi. (72 km.) off coast of Spain.

Ål·borg *or* **Aal·borg** \ˈȯl-ˌbȯr\; *anc.* **Al·burg·um** \al-ˈbər-gəm\. Commercial seaport, ⊗ of Nordjylland co., Denmark; pop. (1991e) 155,664; cement, textiles, shipbuilding; castle (1539); founded 1342.

Albuera, La. See LA ALBUERA.

Al·bu·fe·ra \ˌäl-bü-ˈfā-rä\. Lagoon, E coast of Spain, 7 mi. (11 km.) S of Valencia; 11 mi. (18 km.) long and 4 mi. (6.4 km.) wide.

Al–Buhayrah al–Murrah al–Kubrā. See BITTER LAKES.

Al–Buhayrah al–Murrah as–Sughrā. See BITTER LAKES.

Al·bu·la \ˈäl-bü-lä\. Mountain pass over Rhaetian Alps, Graubünden canton, SE Switzerland; extends from valley of **Albula River** (upper tributary of Rhine) to Upper Engadine Valley; alt. 7583 ft. (2311 m.); railroad passes through **Albula Tunnel** (3.67 mi. or 6 km. long, alt. 5970 ft. or 1820 m.) just S of the pass.

Album Ingaunum. See ALBENGA.

Al·bu·quer·que \ˈal-bə-ˌkər-kē, -byü-\. City and health resort, ⊗ of Bernalillo co., cen. New Mexico, on the Rio Grande 55 mi. (88 km.) SW of Santa Fe; pop. (1990c) 384,736; largest city in the state; research and development; defense-related services; tourism; site of annual state fair; ski area at nearby Sandia Mts.; Univ. of New Mexico (1889). Old town founded 1706; military post during Spanish and Mexican regimes; outpost of U.S. Military Dept. after Mexican War 1846–70; alternately occupied by Union and Confederate forces during Civil War; new town platted 1880; incorp. as city 1890.

Alburgum. See ÅLBORG.

Al·bury \ˈȯl-bə-rē\. Town, S New South Wales, SE Australia, 170 mi. (274 km.) NE of Melbourne; pop. (1991p) 40,154; on Murray River at head of navigation and on main railroad line bet. Melbourne and Sydney; regional center; became municipality 1859.

Al·cá·cer do Sal \äl-ˈkä-sār-dü-ˈsäl\. Village, Setúbal dist., Portugal, ab. 25 mi. (40 km.) SE of the seaport of Setúbal; battle 1217 in which King Alfonso II of Portugal defeated the Moors.

Al·ca·ço·vas \ál-ˈkä-sü-vəsh\. Town, Évora dist., S cen. Portugal, ab. 19 mi. (31 km.) SW of the commune of Évora; treaty signed here bet. Spain and Portugal Mar. 6, 1480 in which possession of regions in West Africa, Guinea, and Atlantic islands was settled.

Al·ca·lá de Gua·dai·ra \ˌäl-kä-ˈlä-thā-gwä-ˈthī-rä\. Commune, Sevilla prov., SW Spain, 10 mi. (16 km.) SE of Seville on left bank of Guadaira River; pop. (1991c) 52,257; Moorish remains, esp. the castle (surrendered to Ferdinand III of Castile 1244).

Alcalá de He·na·res \thā-ā-ˈnär-ās\; *anc.* **Com·plu·tum** \kəm-ˈplü-təm\. Commune, Madrid prov., cen. Spain, ab. 20 mi. (32 km.) ENE of the city of Madrid; pop. (1991c) 159,355; after reconquest frequently royal residence of Castilian kings; birthplace of English King Henry VIII's first queen, Catherine of Aragon (1485), writer Miguel de Cervantes (1547), and explorer Juan Diaz de Solis (c. 1470); university, 2d only to Salamanca, founded by Cardinal Francisco Jiménez de Cisneros 1508 (moved to Madrid 1836); noted for production (1513–17) of Complutensian Polyglot Bible, so called from ancient name of city.

Alcalá la Re·al \lä-rā-ˈäl\. Commune, Jaén prov., S Spain; pop. (1991c) 21,090; scene of French victory of Count Sebastiani over Spanish 1810.

Al·ca·mo \ˈäl-kä-ˌmō\. Commune, Trapani prov., NW Sicily, Italy, 25 mi. (40 km.) ESE of the seaport of Trapani; pop. (1989c) 43,231; agricultural trade; near site of ancient Segesta; founded by Saracens 828 A.D.; site moved by Holy Roman Emperor Frederick II 1233.

Alcan Highway. See ALASKA HIGHWAY.

Al·cán·ta·ra \äl-ˈkän-tä-rä, *angl.* al-ˈkan-tə-rə\. Commune, Cáceres prov., W Spain, on Tagus River near Portuguese border; pop. (1991c) 2076. Named from the bridge built here by Roman Emperor Hadrian 105 A.D. (total length 670 ft. or 204 m.; its two main arches 110 ft. or 34 m. wide and 210 ft. or 64 m. above normal level of river), one of finest Roman monuments in existence; home of knightly order (organized 1156, as the Knights of St. Julian, to drive the Moors from Spanish territory) which changed its name to Order of Alcántara when the town was given it 1217 by Alfonso IX of León.

Alcaraz, Sierra de. See SIERRA DE ALCARAZ.

Al·ca·traz \ˈal-kə-ˌtraz\. Rocky island, San Francisco Bay, California, ab. 4 mi. (6.4 km.) NW of San Francisco, opp. the Golden Gate; U.S. fortification and penitentiary, estab. 1868 for military prisoners and 1934 for federal prisoners, closed 1963.

Al·cá·zar de San Juan \äl-ˈkä-thär-thā-ˌsän-ˈkwän\. Commune, Ciudad Real prov., S cen. Spain, 80 mi. (129 km.) SE of Madrid; pop. (1991c) 25,996; center of wine trade; railroad shops; called **Al·ce** \ˈal-sē\ by Romans; captured by Roman statesman Tiberius Sempronius Gracchus 180 B.C.; ruled by Knights of St. John 1186–1292.

Alcazarquivir. See KSAR EL KEBIR.

Al·chevsk \ál-ˈchefsk\ *or* **Kom·mu·narsk** \kə-mü-ˈnärsk\; *1931–61* **Vo·ro·shi·lovsk** \ˌvə-rə-ˈshē-ləfsk\. City, Luhans'k subdivision, E Ukraine; pop. (1991e) 126,000; industrial city in Donets Basin.

Al·ci·ra \äl-ˈthē-rä\ *or* **Al·zi·ra** \-ˈthē-, -ˈsē-\; *anc.* **Su·cro** \ˈsü-ˌkrō\. Commune, Valencia prov., E Spain, 23 mi. (37 km.) S of the commune of Valencia on Júcar River; pop. (1991c) 40,309; produces oranges and rice.

Al·çı·te·pe \ˌäl-chə-ˈtā-pā\ *or* **Kir·te** \ˈkir-te\ *also* **Krith·ia** \ˈkri-thē-ə\. Village near tip of Gallipoli Penin., Turkey in Europe; early objective of Anzac troops in Gallipoli campaign 1915.

Alçı Tepe. See ACHI BABA.

Al·coa \al-ˈkō-ə\. City, Blount co., E Tennessee, 15 mi. (24 km.) S of Knoxville; pop. (1990c) 6400.

Al·co·ba·ça \ˌál-kō-ˈbä-sə\. Town, Leiria dist., W cen. Portugal, 18 mi. (29 km.) SSW of the commune of Leiria; pop. (1991p) 5159; famous Cistercian abbey founded c. 1150 by Alfonso I; tombs of Portuguese kings and Spanish noblewoman Inés de Castro.

Al·co·lea \ˌäl-kō-ˈlā-ä\. Village, Spain, ab. 5 mi. (8 km.) NE of Córdoba on the Guadalquivir River; scene of defeat Sept. 28,

1868 of Spanish royal forces by Marshal Francisco Serrano y Domínguez during revolution which deposed Isabella II.

Al·co·na \al-'kō-nə\. County in NE Michigan. See table at MICHIGAN.

Al·co·ra \äl-'kō-rä\. Commune, Castellón de la Plana prov., E Spain, ab. 10 mi. (16 km.) WNW of the city of Castellón de la Plana; pop. (1991c) 8367; noted in 18th cent. for its manufacture of Alcora porcelain, a rich faïence.

Al·corn \'ȯl-,kȯrn\. County in NE Mississippi. See table at MISSISSIPPI.

Al·co·va Dam \al-'kō-və\. Dam across North Platte River below Pathfinder Dam, S cen. Natrona co., cen. Wyoming; height 265 ft. (81 m.); completed 1938; impounds water, **Alcova Reservoir,** for irrigation.

Al·coy \äl-'kȯi\. Commune, Alicante prov., SE Spain; pop. (1991c) 65,514.

Al·cu·dia, Bay of \äl-'kü-t͟hē-ä\. Bay on N coast of island of Majorca.

Al·dab·ra \äl-'dä-brə\. **1.** Uninhabited island group belonging to Seychelles in Indian Ocean N of Madagascar, formerly part of British Indian Ocean Terr.; includes Aldabra and Assumption; constitutes a nature preserve featuring unusual flora and fauna; visited by Portuguese 1511; French dependency in 17th cent.; became British 1810; returned to Seychelles 1976.

2. Chief island in group; 20 mi. (32 km.) long; 60 sq. mi. (155 sq. km.); an oval atoll enclosing a lagoon.

Al·dan \'ȯl-dən\. Borough, Delaware co., SE Pennsylvania, 7 mi. (11 km.) W of Philadelphia; pop. (1990c) 4549.

Al·dan \əl-'dän\. **1.** River, SE Sakha Rep., Russia in Asia; rises in Aldan Mts. and flows into Lena River at Batamay, forming its 2d major tributary; 1393 mi. (2241 km.) long; navigable for 800 mi. (1287 km.).

2. Town, SE Sakha Rep., Russia in Asia, in Aldan valley S of the river and on S-to-N highway from the Trans-Siberian R.R. to Yakutsk; gold deposits.

Aldan Mountains. NW spur of Stanovoi Mts., S Sakha Rep., Russia in Asia, forming watershed bet. upper Aldan and Olekma rivers.

Al·den \'ȯl-dən\. Village, Erie co., W New York, 20 mi. (32 km.) E of Buffalo; pop. (1990c) 2457; summer resort.

Aldenville. See CHICOPEE 2.

Alder, Ben *or* **Mount Alder.** See BEN ALDER.

Al·der·ney \'ȯl-dər-nē\ *or Fr.* **Au·ri·gny** \ȯ-rē-'nyē\; *anc.* **Ri·du·na** \ri-'dü-nə, -'dyü-\. Northernmost of Channel Is., in Guernsey bailiwick, United Kingdom; 4.5 mi. (7 km.) long; 3 sq. mi. (8 sq. km.); pop. (1986c) 2130; ✻ St. Anne; separated from France by dangerous 8 mi. (13 km.) wide tidal channel, **Race of Alderney.**

Al·der·shot \'ȯl-dər-,shät\. Town, Hampshire, S England, 32 mi. (51 km.) SW of London; pop. (1981p) 32,654; its permanent military camp (estab. 1855) became 1904–14 center for English military training. See BISLEY.

Al·dridge \'ȯl-drij\. Town, Staffordshire, England, N of Birmingham.

Ale·do \ə-'lē-,dō\. City, ⊗ of Mercer co., NW Illinois, 25 mi. (40 km.) SSW of Rock Island; pop. (1990c) 3681.

Ale·gre \ȧ-'lā-grē\. Municipality, Espírito Santo state, E Brazil, 90 mi. (145 km.) SW of Vitória; pop. (1980c) 33,544.

Ale·gre·te \,ȧ-le-'grā-tē\. Municipality, Rio Grande do Sul state, S Brazil, 260 mi. (418 km.) W of Pôrto Alegre; pop. (1991p) 78,740.

Alejandro Selkirk. See MÁS AFUERA.

Ale·ksan·dra Land \,ä-lek-'sän-drə; ,a-lik-'san-drə, -lig-'zan-\. See FRANZ JOSEF LAND.

Alek·san·dri·ya \,ə-lyik-sən-'drē-yə\. Town, Kirovohrad region, cen. Ukraine, ab. 45 mi. (72 km.) ENE of the city of Kirovohrad; pop. (1991e) 105,000; coal deposits.

Aleksandropol. See GYUMRI.

Alek·san·drov \,ə-lyik-'sän-drəf\. Town, Vladimir Oblast, W cen. Russia in Europe, WNW of the city of Vladimir; founded by Czar Ivan the Terrible 1564.

Aleksandrovka. See BELOGORSK 1.

Ale·ksan·drovsk \,ə-lyik-'sän-drəfsk\. **1.** *or* **Aleksandrovsk–Grushevskiy.** City, Russia. See SHAKHTY.

2. City, Ukraine. See ZAPORIZHZHYA 2.

Aleksandrovsk–Grushevskiy. See SHAKHTY.

Aleksandr Range. See KYRGYZ RANGE.

Alek·sin \ə-'lyek-sin\. Town, Tula Oblast, W Russia in Europe, NW of the city of Tula; pop. (1991e) 74,200.

Alek·si·nac \ä-'lek-sē-,näts\. Town, E cen. Yugoslavia, on Morava River, 18 mi. (29 km.) NNW of Niš; battle 1876 in which Serbs and Russians were defeated by Turks.

Alemtejo. See ALENTEJO.

Alen·çon \,ȧ-läⁿ-'sōⁿ\. City, ✻ of Orne dept., NW France, on Sarthe River 28 mi. (45 km.) N of Le Mans; known for lacemaking.

History: Town, center of medieval territory of Alençon, successively a lordship, county, and duchy, the title to which usually belonged to member of royal house 13th–16th cents.; after 1525 seat of court of Margaret of Navarre, sister of Francis I; lace introduced by Minister of Finance Jean-Baptiste Colbert as part of effort to develop French industry (in 2d half of 17th cent.).

Alen·te·jo; *formerly* **Alem·te·jo** \ȧ-lāⁿn-'tā-zhü\. Region of SE Portugal; 9083 sq. mi. (23,525 sq. km.); consists of Beja, Évora, and Portalegre dists.; drained by Tagus, Sado, and Guadiana rivers; an historical province of Portugal with ✻ at Évora.

Ale·nu·i·ha·ha \,ä-lā-,nü-ē-'hä-,hä\. Channel, Hawaiian Is., bet. Hawaii and Maui; 26 mi. (42 km.) wide.

Alep·po \ə-'le-pō\ *also* **Alep** \ä-'lep\; *Arab.* **Ha·leb** *or* **Ha·lab** \'ha-lab\. **1.** Former Turkish province, now largely in N Syria.

2. *anc.* **Be·roea** \bə-'rē-ə\. City, NW Syria; pop. (1992e) 1,445,000; textiles; fruits and nuts; university (1960).

History: Ancient city, ✻ of a kingdom, first taken by Hittites as early as 2000 B.C.; scene of conflict between Hittites and Egyptians, esp. in 15th century B.C.; an independent Hittite principality until conquered by Assyrian king 853 B.C.; enlarged by Seleucid King Seleucus Nicator (306–280 B.C.) and named Beroea; see SYRIA for events of significance up to Muslim conquest; taken by Muslim Arabs 638 A.D.; temporarily recovered by Greeks under Byzantine Emperor Nicephorus Phocas 969; held by Seljuqs 1090–1117; unsuccessfully besieged by Crusaders 1118, 1124; sacked by Mongols 1260 and by Turkic ruler Timur 1401; after capture by Ottoman Turks 1517, experienced revival of trade with East; a flourishing trade center in 16th cent., gradually declined because of use of sea route to India and later opening of Suez Canal (1869); largely destroyed by earthquakes 1822, 1830; taken by Egyptian Gen. Ibrāhīm Pasha 1832; in 1918 captured by British and Arabs under British Field Marshal Edmund Allenby as part of WWI campaign against Turkey; organized as state of French mandate of Syria 1920; united with Damascus to form state of Syria 1925.

Ale·ria \ə-'lir-ē-ə\ *or* **Ala·lia** \ə-'lā-lē-ə\. One of the chief cities of ancient Corsica, near E coast; modern commune is **Alé·ria** \ä-'lā-rē-ä\.

Alert Bay \ə-'lərt\. Village and port on island off NE coast of Vancouver I., British Columbia, Canada, at S end of Charlotte Strait; pop. (1991c) 628.

Alès \ȧ-'les\; *formerly* **Alais** \ȧ-'les\. City, Gard dept., S France, 27 mi. (43 km.) NNW of Nîmes; pop. (1990c) 42,296; tourism.

Ale·sia \ə-'lē-zhə, -zhē-ə\. Town, NE Celtic Gaul, on a hill, near source of Sequana; site of successful siege of Gallic chief Vercingetorix by which Roman Gen. Julius Caesar put down Gallic revolt 52 B.C.

Ales·san·dria \,ä-les-'sän-drē-ä\. **1.** Province of Piedmont, NW Italy. See table at ITALY.

2. Commune, its ✻, on the Tanaro River 35 mi. (56 km.) ESE of Turin; pop. (1991p) 90,475; railroad and commercial center.

History: Founded 1168; became member of the Lombard League; besieged unsuccessfully by Holy Roman Emperor Frederick Barbarossa 1174; seized by Francesco Sforza, duke of Milan, 1522; attacked by French 1657; captured by Austrian Gen. Prince Eugene of Savoy 1707; ceded to Savoy 1713; citadel built 1728; occupied by French 1800–14.

Alessio. See LEZHË 2.

Åle·sund *or* **Aa·le·sund** \'ȯ-lə-ˌsu̇n\. Seaport city, Møre og Romsdal co., W Norway, on an island bet. Bergen and Trondheim; pop. (1990c) 35,751; trading center, esp. for Norwegian W coast cod and herring fisheries; headquarters for Arctic sealing fleet.

Aletrium. See ALATRI.

Aletsch·horn \'ä-lech-ˌhȯrn\. Mountain, Bernese Alps, Valais canton, Switzerland, ab. 5 mi. (8 km.) SSE of the Jungfrau; 13,763 ft. (4195 m.).

Aleu·tian Islands \ə-'lü-shən\ *or commonly* **Aleu·tians** \-shənz\; *formerly* **Cath·er·ine Archipelago** \'ka-thrin, -thə-rin\. Chain of volcanic islands, Alaska, extending 1700 mi. (2735 km.) W from Alaska Penin. 163°W to 172°30′E (but E of International Date Line); 6821 sq. mi. (17,666 sq. km.); islands separate Bering Sea from North Pacific Ocean; chief islands and groups from E to W are Fox Is. (incl. Unimak and Unalaska), Islands of the Four Mountains, Andreanof Is., Rat Is., and Near Is. (incl. Attu, only 500 mi. or 804 km. E of Kamchatka); chief town Dutch Harbor on Unalaska; several volcanoes still active (highest Shishaldin, on Unimak, 9370 ft. or 2856 m.); even climate but much fog and rain; fertile soil; industries fishing, raising fur-bearing animals, and some agriculture.

History: Inhabited orig. by the native Aleuts, islands first came to the notice of Westerners during explorations by Danish navigator Vitus Bering and Russian Aleksey Chirikov 1741 (see ALASKA); exploited by Siberian fur traders; served as approach for Russian expansion to mainland of Alaska; purchased with Alaska by U.S. from Russia 1867; basis of U.S. claim with Great Britain in controversy over right to pelagic fishing in Bering Sea (*q.v.*); W islands (Attu and Kiska) occupied by Japanese June 1942; Attu retaken by U.S. forces May 1943; Kiska abandoned by Japanese Aug. 1943; site of U.S. airfields and radar stations.

Aleutian Range. Mountain range along E coast of N Alaska Penin.; includes Mt. Katmai (6715 ft. or 2047 m.) and Katmai National Monument.

Aleutians East. Division in Alaska. See table at ALASKA.

Aleutians West. Division in Alaska. See table at ALASKA.

Aleutian Trench. Ocean trench, North Pacific Ocean S of Aleutian Is., extending in a generally E to W arc from E of Kodiak I. to S of the Komandorskiye Ostrova; subduction zone according to theory of plate tectonics.

Al·ex·an·der \ˌa-lig-'zan-dər, ˌe-\. Name of counties in two states of the U.S. See tables at ILLINOIS and NORTH CAROLINA.

Alexander, Cape. Cape, NW Choiseul I., Solomon Is., W Pacific Ocean, 6°35′S, 156°30′E.

Alexander Archipelago. Group of ab. 1100 islands, SE Alaska, made up of tops of submerged mountains, with irregular coastlines and deep channels bet. them; from N to S chief islands are Chichagof, Admiralty, Baranof, Kupreanof, Prince of Wales, and Revillagigedo; chief towns Sitka and Ketchikan.

Alexander Bay. Bay on extreme NW coast of Western Cape prov., Rep. of South Africa, at the mouth of the Orange River.

Alexander City. City, Tallapoosa co., E Alabama, 5 mi. (8 km.) N of Lake Martin; pop. (1990c) 14,917; Central Alabama Community Coll. (1965); incorp. 1873.

Alexander Graham Bell National Historic Park. Reservation, Cape Breton I., Nova Scotia, Canada.

Alexander Island; *formerly* **Alexander I Island.** Island in Antarctica, W of base of Antarctic Penin., British Antarctic Terr.; ab. 235 mi. (378 km.) long; 16,700 sq. mi. (43,253 sq. km.); formerly considered part of Antarctic continent; discovered and named by Russian Adm. Fabian Gottlieb von Bellingshausen on expedition 1819–21.

Alexander Range. See KYRGYZ RANGE.

Alexandra, Mount. See RUWENZORI, MOUNT.

Al·ex·an·dra Land \ˌə-lyik-'sän-drə, *angl.* ˌa-lig-'zan-drə-, ˌe-\. Island, W part of Franz Josef Land, Russia, 80°45′N, 46°E.

Al·ex·an·dret·ta \ˌa-lig-(ˌ)zan-'dre-tə, ˌe-\ *or Turk.* **İs·ken·de·run** \ˌis-ken-de-'rün\. **1.** Formerly a sanjak (district) of Turkey; after WWI (1920) a semiautonomous region of NW Syria extending ab. 100 mi. (160 km.) along Gulf of İskenderun and E Mediterranean; ab. 5000 sq. mi. (12,950 sq. km.). Set up as a state with limited autonomy 1925; incorp. in Turkish republic by agreement bet. France and Turkey 1939. Contains Nur Mts., with Musa Dagh at its S end, Orontes and Afrine rivers, and the port of Süveydiye, N of mouth of Orontes.

2. *or Fr.* **Alex·an·drette** \á-lek-sä^n-'dret\. City. See İSKENDERUN.

Alexandretta, Gulf of. See İSKENDERUN, GULF OF.

Al·ex·an·dria \ˌa-lig-'zan-drē-ə, ˌe-\. **1.** City, Madison co., cen. Indiana, 17 mi. (27 km.) WNW of Muncie; pop. (1990c) 5709.

2. City, ⊗ of Campbell co., N Kentucky; pop. (1990c) 5592.

3. City, ⊗ of Rapides parish, cen. Louisiana, 100 mi. (161 km.) NW of Baton Rouge; pop. (1990c) 49,188; Louisiana State Univ. at Alexandria (1960).

4. City, ⊗ of Douglas co., W cen. Minnesota, 60 mi. (96 km.) WNW of St. Cloud; pop. (1990c) 7838; resort center in lake region.

5. City, ⊗ of Hanson co., SE South Dakota; pop. (1990c) 518.

6. Independent city, Virginia, on Potomac River 6 mi. (10 km.) S of Washington, D.C.; 15 sq. mi. (39 sq. km.); pop. (1990c) 111,183; residential; port of entry; home of George Washington, first U.S. president; founded 1749; ⊗ of Fairfax co. 1752; incorp. as town 1779; became part of District of Columbia 1791, but was returned to Virginia as free city 1847; ⊗ of Alexandria (now Arlington) co. 1847–98; became city 1852; occupied by Union forces during Civil War; seat of Unionist Alexandria government 1863–65.

7. Commune, ⊗ of Teleorman co., S Romania, on lower Vedea River; pop. (1989c) 58,384; site of Dacian excavations.

Alexandria *or Arab.* **Al–Is·kan·da·rī·yah** \ˌal-(ˌ)is-ˌkan-dá-'rē-yə\. **1.** Governorate of N Egypt. See table at EGYPT.

2. Seaport, its ✱, on strip of land bet. the Mediterranean and Lake Mareotis; pop. (1990e) 3,170,000; approx. coextensive with Alexandria governorate; cotton is chief export; car assembly, oil refinery, food processing nearby; university (1942). Ancient island (Pharos) on which was famous lighthouse considered one of the Seven Wonders of the Ancient World, now a peninsula connected with mainland by sandy isthmus filled in around ancient mole; modern harbor is W of peninsula and formed partly by a breakwater.

History: Founded by Macedonian King Alexander the Great after his capture of Egypt 332 B.C.; a trading center, also became a center of Hellenistic culture, famed as meeting ground of Greek, Arab, and Jewish ideas; site of greatest library of ancient times which was founded by Ptolemy I (323–285 B.C.) and was alleged to have contained 700,000 papyri; library partly lost in a conflagration which occurred when Roman Gen. Julius Caesar captured city 48 B.C. and was gone by 4th cent. A.D.; captured by Arabs 640 A.D. and by Turks 1517; occupied by French 1798–1801 during French Emperor Napoléon's Egyptian campaign (see ABŪ QĪR); after a long period of decline in its significance because of rise of Cairo and neglect to dredge the silted harbor, revived commercially when Egyptian ruler Muḥammad ʽAlī Pasha joined it by a canal to the Nile early 19th century; bombarded and occupied by British 1882, after a series of nationalist riots against foreign domination of Egypt; temporarily taken over by British troops because of riots 1921. British naval base in WWII; saved from capture by German Field Marshal Erwin Rommel by battle of El Alamein Oct.–Nov. 1942; evacuated by British forces 1946.

Alexandria Arachosiorum. See QANDAHĀR.

Alexandria Bay. Village, Jefferson co., N New York, on St. Lawrence River 25 mi. (40 km.) N of Watertown; pop.

\ə\ abut	\ə\ matches	\$^ə$\ kitten, Fr table	\ər\ further	\a\ ash	\ā\ ace
\ä\ cot, cart	\á\ Fr bac	\au̇\ out	\b̲\ Span Avila	\ch\ chin	\e\ bet
\ē\ easy	\g\ go	\i\ hit	\ī\ ice	\j\ job	\k̲\ Ger ich, Buch
\$^n$\ Fr vin	\ŋ\ sing	\ō\ go	\ȯ\ all	\ȯi\ law	\œ\ Fr bœuf
\œ̄\ Fr feu	\ȯi\ boy	\th\ thin	\th̲\ this	\ü\ loot	\u̇\ foot
\ue\ Ger füllen	\ūe\ Fr rue	\y\ yet	\$^y$\ Fr digne \'dēn^y\, nuit \'nw^{y}ē\	\yü\ few	\yu̇\ fury
\zh\ vision					

(1990c) 1194; summer resort and tourist center for Thousand Is. region.

Alexandria Troas. See TROAS 2.

Al·ex·an·dri·na, Lake \ˌa-lig-(ˌ)zan-ˈdrē-nə, ˌe-\. Lake, SE South Australia, Australia, at mouth of Murray River; 220 sq. mi. (570 sq. km.); actually a lagoon with shallow outlet, a fact that hinders navigation of the Murray; its S arm is the Coorong (*q.v.*).

Alexandropol. See GYUMRI.

Ale·xan·droú·po·lis \ˌä-lek-sän-ˈthrü-pō-lēs\ *or Turk.* **De·de Ag·ach** \de-ˈde-ä-ˈgäch\. Seaport city, ✻ of Evros dept., West Thrace, Greece, on Aegean 10 mi. (16 km.) NW of mouth of Maritsa River; pop. (1991p) 39,283; episcopal see; a trading town. Annexed by Bulgaria 1915–18; by treaty after WWI returned to Greece. Occupied by Bulgaria 1941–44; subsequently restored to Greece.

Al·fal·fa \al-ˈfal-fə\. County in N Oklahoma. See table at OKLAHOMA.

Al Fal·lū·jah *also* **Al–Fal·lu·ja** \ˌȧl-fȧl-ˈlü-jə\. Town, cen. Iraq, on left bank of Euphrates 35 mi. (56 km.) W of Baghdad and E of Hawr Al Habbānīyah.

Al·fa·ro \äl-ˈfä-rō\; *formerly* **Du·rán** \dü-ˈrän\. Railroad center, Guayas prov., W Ecuador, on Guayas River opp. Guayaquil; starting point of Guayaquil-Quito railroad, completed 1908.

Al–Fashir. See EL FASHER.

Al Fāw \al-ˈfaů\ *or* **Fao** \ˈfaů\. Port, SE Iraq, near Persian Gulf at mouth of the Shatt al Arab, which is 1 mi. (1.6 km.) wide here but obstructed by bar across channel; captured by Iran Feb. 12, 1986.

Al Fayyūm. See EL FAIYÛM.

Alfiós. See ALPHEUS.

Al·föld, Great \ˈȯl-ˌfœld\. Great central plain of Hungary, traversed by Danube and Tisza rivers. The **Little Alföld** *also* **Kis–Alföld** \ˈkish-\ is a plain in NW Hungary and SW Slovakia, near Bratislava.

Al·fort·ville \ˌȧl-fȯr-ˈvēl\. Commune, Val-de-Marne dept., N France, on Seine and Marne rivers 4 mi. (6.4 km.) SE of Paris; separated from Maisons-Alfort 1885.

Al·fred \ˈal-frəd\. **1.** Town, ⊗ of York co., SW Maine; pop. (1990c) 2238.

2. Village, Allegany co., SW New York; pop. (1990c) 4559; Alfred Univ. (1836), State Univ. of New York Coll. of Technology at Alfred (1908).

Alfred, Mount. Peak, Coast Mts., SW British Columbia, Canada, 80 mi. (129 km.) NE of Vancouver; 8450 ft. (2576 m.).

Al·fre·ton \ˈȯl-frit-ᵊn\. Town, Derbyshire, N cen. England, 14 mi. (22.5 km.) NNE of Derby; pop. (1981p) 23,124; foundation traditionally ascribed to King Alfred the Great.

Alfsborg. See ÄLVSBORG.

Al Fu·jay·rah \ȧl-fü-ˈjī-rə\ *or* **Fu·jai·rah** \-ˈjī-rə\. **1.** Emirate. See table at UNITED ARAB EMIRATES.

2. Coastal town, its ✻; pop. (1980c) 12,659.

Al–Fung *or* **El Fung** \ˌȧl-ˈfüŋ, ˌel-\. Former province, E Anglo-Egyptian Sudan, now part of Blue Nile prov., Sudan.

Al–Furāt. See EUPHRATES.

Al–Fustāt. See CAIRO (Egypt).

Al·gar·ro·bo, Point \ˌäl-gär-ˈrō-bō\. Cape on W coast of Puerto Rico.

Algarrobo Bay. Inlet of Pacific Ocean on W cen. coast of Chile below Valparaíso.

Al·gar·ve \ȧl-ˈgär-vē\. Ancient kingdom, S Portugal; ✻ Faro; forms modern district of Faro; Serra do Monchique (highest point 2959 ft. or 902 m.) in N; fish, fruit; mining. Medieval Moorish kingdom (✻ Silves) conquered 1253 by Alfonso III and title king of Algarve added to Portuguese crown 1253; later reduced to a province.

Al·gäu *or* **All·gäu** \ˈäl-ˌgȯi\. Region, SW Bavaria, Germany; noted for dairy products. In its widest sense, the territory extending N to the Danube, S to the Inn, and W to the Lech.

Algäu Alps *or* **All·gäu·er Alps;** *Ger.* **Alg·äu·er Al·pen** *or* **All·gäu·er Al·pen** \ˈäl-ˌgȯi-ər-ˈäl-pən\. Mountains extending E from Lake of Constance forming W section of Bavarian Alps, bet. Bavaria, Germany, and Tirol, Austria. They include such peaks as Hohes Licht (8706 ft. or 2654 m.), Mädelegabel (8689 ft. or 2648 m.), Hochvogel (8505 ft. or 2592 m.) and contain sources of the Lech and Iller rivers. See ALPS.

Al–Ga·za·la *or* **El Gazala** \ˌȧl-gȧ-ˈzȧ-lə, ˌel-\. Village, NE Libya, on coast W of Tobruk; in WWII an Axis supply port; in early part of 1942 part of British defense line, evacuated in June.

Al·ge·ci·ras \ˌäl-k̲ā-ˈthē-räs, ˌal-jə-ˈsir-əs\. Seaport, Cádiz prov., SW Spain, 6 mi. (10 km.) W of Gibraltar; pop. (1991c) 101,256; cork is a chief export.

History: Held by Moors 711–1344; after famous siege conquered by Alfonso XI of Castile; Moorish city destroyed and site reoccupied by Spanish 1704 who erected the modern town 1760; station for Spanish fleet during siege of Gibraltar 1780–82; scene of conference of the European Powers 1906 called to settle crisis with Germany over authority in Morocco; gave name to Act of Algeciras which, in substance, gave France and Spain control of Morocco (*q.v.*).

Algeciras, Bay of. See GIBRALTAR, BAY OF.

Al·ge·me·sí \ˌäl-hā-mā-ˈsē\. Commune, Valencia prov., E Spain, ab. 6 mi. (10 km.) N of Alcira; pop. (1991c) 25,375.

Al·ger \ˈal-jər\. County in N Upper Penin. of Michigan. See table at MICHIGAN.

Alger. See ALGIERS.

Al·ge·ria \al-ˈjir-ē-ə\ *or officially* **Democratic and Popular Republic of Algeria;** *Fr.* **Al·gé·rie** \ȧl-zhā-ˈrē\. Republic, N Africa, bounded on N by the Mediterranean Sea, on E by Tunisia and Libya, on S by Niger and Mali, and on W by Mauritania, Western Sahara, and Morocco; 918,497 sq. mi. (2,378,907 sq. km.); pop. (1987c) 22,971,000; ✻ Algiers.

Physical features: N part traversed by Atlas Mts. and Saharan Atlas; highest peak is Djebel Chélia 7648 ft. (2331 m.), in NE; cen. and S parts occupy a large section of N Sahara Desert, incl. the Ahaggar massif and part of the Adrar des Iforas; coastline has few inlets and rivers are small.

Chief products: Wheat, barley, grapes, olives, dates, citrus fruit; livestock; oil, natural gas, iron ore, phosphates, lead, zinc; manufacturing: cement, fertilizers, steel, transportation equipment; food products.

Chief cities: Algiers, Oran, Constantine, Annaba.

History: Territory known to Romans as Numidia; conquered by Vandals 430–31 A.D., by Eastern Roman (Byzantine) Empire 531–34, and by Arabs in 7th century; nominally under rule of Ottoman Empire until 1705; repudiated Turkish rule and controlled by tribal organizations under dey of Algiers until occupied by French 1830; hinterland not subjugated until 1847 after a series of intermittent wars by French against Arab leader Abdelkader; placed under military rule by French Emperor Napoléon III; in 1863 given a land law which helped break up tribal organization; after 1879 under civil rule as a part of France; scene of an uprising during French difficulties with Tunis 1881; under a reorganized government after 1898. In WWII under Vichy control until Nov. 1942; occupied by Allied forces Nov. 8–12, 1942; nationalist revolt against French rule 1954–61; granted independence following referendum of July 1, 1962; government overthrown in *coup d'état* 1965; subsequent rule by military; new constitution approved 1989; elections 1991 provoked political unrest.

Al·ghe·ro \äl-ˈger-ō\. Seaport, Sassari prov., NW Sardinia, Italy, 17 mi. (27 km.) SSW of the commune of Sassari; pop. (1989c) 40,858; founded by Doria family (Genoese) ab. 1102; settled by Catalonians 14th cent.; under house of Aragon 1354–1720 and subsequently under house of Savoy.

Al Ghur·da·qah \ˌȧl-ˈg̅ür-dȧ-kə\ *or* **Hur·gha·da** \ˈhür-g̅ä-də\. Town, ✻ of Red Sea governorate, Egypt.

Al·giers \al-ˈjirz\. **1.** *or Fr.* **Al·ger** \ȧl-ˈzhā\ *or Arab.* **Al–Ja·zā'·ir** \ˌȧl-jȧ-ˈzä-ir\. Former Barbary state, N Africa, now Algeria.

2. *also Fr.* **Alger** *anc.* **Ico·si·um** \ī-ˈkō-sē-əm\. Seaport city, ✻ of Algeria, on W side of **Bay of Algiers;** pop. (1987p) 1,507,241; wine is a chief export; university (1859, reorganized 1909); cathedral; national library; astronomical observatory.

History: Founded in the 10th cent. on site of a Roman town; held by Spain 1509–17; invaded disastrously by Holy

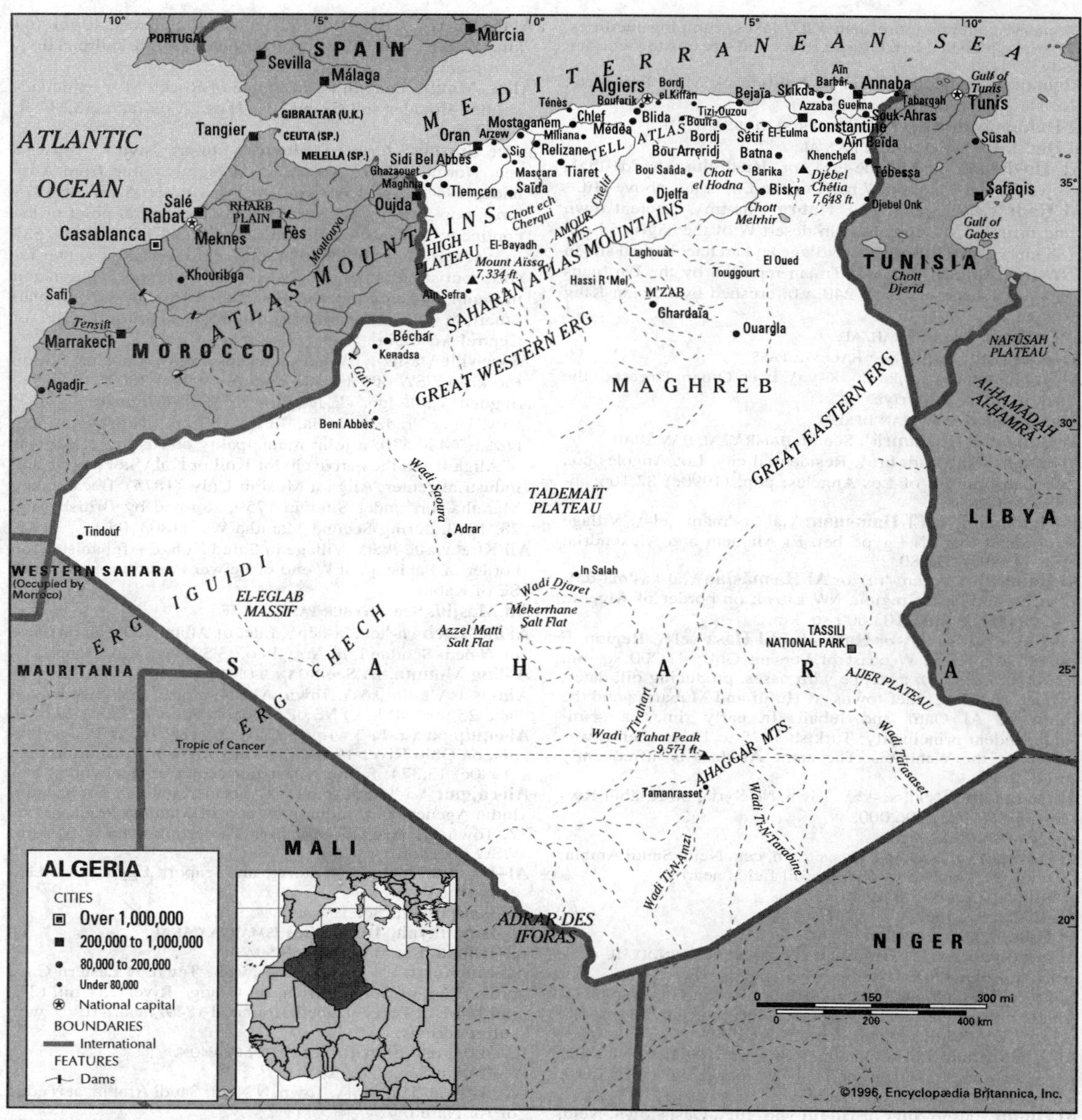

Roman Emperor Charles V 1541; chief among the Barbary States which exacted tribute from European shipping; included in U.S. wars against the Barbary States 1801–05, 1815; encouraged by the absence of U.S. naval vessels to attack American shipping in the Mediterranean, finally forced to cease exaction of tribute after defeated by American naval officer Stephen Decatur's punitive expedition 1815; bombarded by British 1816 in effort to force the dey to end Christian slavery; dey deposed by French 1830; became an important trading center as ✱ of the French colony of Algeria (*q.v.*); became Allied headquarters for North Africa during WWII; important during nationalist revolt against French rule during 1950s.

Al·goa Bay \al-ˈgō-ə\. Bay on coast of Eastern Cape prov., Rep. of South Africa, ab. 420 mi. (676 km.) E of Cape Town; discovered by Portuguese 15th cent.; Port Elizabeth (*q.v.*) founded by British on its shores 1820.

Al·go·ma \al-ˈgō-mə\. **1.** City, Kewaunee co., E Wisconsin, on Lake Michigan 28 mi. (45 km.) NE of Green Bay (city); pop. (1990c) 3353.
2. District in S Ontario, Canada. See table at ONTARIO.

Al·go·na \al-ˈgō-nə\. City, ⊗ of Kossuth co., N Iowa, 38 mi. (61 km.) N of Fort Dodge; pop. (1990c) 6015.

Al·go·nac \ˈal-gə-ˌnak\. Village, St. Clair co., SE Michigan, on St. Clair River 24 mi. (39 km.) S of Port Huron; pop. (1990c) 4551; summer resort.

Al·gon·quin \al-ˈgän-kwən, -ˈgäŋ-\. Village, McHenry co., N Illinois, 40 mi. (64 km.) NW of Chicago; pop. (1990c) 11,663.

Algonquin Park. Canadian provincial park in SE Ontario, 180 mi. (290 km.) N of Toronto; 2910 sq. mi. (7537 sq. km.); game preserve; noted for its fishing waters and beautiful

\ə\ abut \ə\ matches \ᵊ\ kitten, Fr table \ər\ further \a\ ash \ā\ ace
\ä\ cot, cart \á\ Fr bac \aù\ out \b̲\ Span Avila \ch\ chin \e\ bet \ē\ easy
\g\ go \i\ hit \ī\ ice \j\ job \k̲\ Ger ich, Buch \ⁿ\ Fr vin
\ŋ\ sing \ō\ go \ȯ\ all \ȯ\ law \œ\ Fr bœuf \œ̄\ Fr feu \ȯi\ boy
\th\ thin \th̲\ this \ü\ loot \u̇\ foot \ue\ Ger füllen \ue̅\ Fr rue
\y\ yet \ʸ\ Fr digne \ˈdēnʸ\, nuit \ˈnwʸē\ \yü\ few \yu̇\ fury \zh\ vision

scenery; contains more than 1200 lakes; camping facilities. Covers watershed bet. Ottawa River and streams to Georgian Bay.

Algonquin Peak. Mountain in Adirondack Mts., Essex co., NE New York; 5114 ft. (1559 m.).

al Habbānīyah, Hawr. See HAWR AL HABBĀNĪYAH.

al Ḥadd, Ra's. See ḤADD, RA'S AL.

Al Ha·dī·thah \ˌal-ha-ˈdē-thə\ *or* **Ha·di·tha** \hə-ˈdē-thə\. Town, W cen. Iraq, on W bank of the Euphrates above Hīt.

Al Ḥaḍr \ˌal-ˈhä-dər\; *anc.* **Hat·ra** \ˈha-trə\. Ancient town and fortress, Mesopotamia, in desert W of the Tigris 55 mi. (88 km.) SW of Mosul; now village and archaeological site in NW Iraq; Roman Emperor Trajan repulsed by the Parthians 117 A.D.; scene of revolt 240 A.D. crushed by Persian King Shāpūr I.

al Ḥajārah. See ḤIJĀRAH, AL.

Al–Halfāyah, Nagb. See HALFAYA PASS.

Al Ḥal·lā·nī·yah \ˌal-ˌka-lä-ˈnē-yə\. Islet, Oman; largest of the Jazā'ir Khurīyā Murīya.

Al–Hamad. See SYRIAN DESERT.

Al Ḥamādah Al Ḥamrā'. See AL ḤAMRĀ', AL ḤAMĀDAH.

Al·ham·bra \al-ˈham-brə\. Residential city, Los Angeles co., SW California, E of Los Angeles; pop. (1990c) 82,106; incorp. 1903.

al–Ḥam·mām *or* **El Ḥam·mâm** \ˌal-ha-ˈmäm, ˌel-\. Village on coastal road, N Egypt, bet. El Alamein and Alexandria; pop. (1989e) 58,180.

Al Ḥam·rā' \ˌal-ˌkam-ˈrä\ *or* **Al Ḥa·mā·dah** \ˌal-ka-ˈmä-də\. Plateau and desert region, NW Libya, on border of Algeria; ab. 40,000 sq. mi. (103,600 sq. km.).

Al–Ha·sa \al-ˈha-sə\ *or* **Hasa** *also* **El Hasa** \el-\. Region, E Saudi Arabia, on W coast of Persian Gulf; 41,200 sq. mi. (106,708 sq. km.); a steppe with oases, producing oil, dates, wheat, and rice; chief towns Al Hufūf and Mubarraz and the ports of Al Qaṭīf and Jubail. In early times a semi-independent principality; Turkish 1875 to 1914 when it was taken by the Wahhabis. The name Al-Hasa is infrequently used now.

Al Ḥa·sa·kah \al-ˈkä-sə-kə\. Town, NE Syria, on Khābūr River; pop. (1992e) 106,000.

al–Hawtah. See LAḤIJ.

Al Ḥaw·ṭah \al-ˈkau̇-tə\. Oasis town, cen. Nejd, Saudi Arabia, 80 mi. (129 km.) S of Riyadh; oil fields nearby.

al Ḥijārah. See ḤIJĀRAH, AL.

Al–Hijaz. See HEJAZ.

Al Ḥillah. See ḤILLAH, AL.

Al Hindīyah *and* **Al Hindīyah Barrage.** See HINDĪYAH, AL.

al–Hīrah. See HIRA.

Al·hu·ce·mas \ˌäl-ü-ˈsā-mäs\. Name of bay and three small islands on Mediterranean coast of Morocco, ab. 50 mi. (80 km.) W of Melilla; islands administered by Spain since 1673.

Al Ḥu·day·dah \ˌal-hō-ˈdā-də, -ˈdī-\ *or* **Ho·dei·da** \hō-ˈdā-də\. Seaport, W Yemen, on Red Sea; pop. (1986c) 155,110; the port for Sanaa; exports coffee.

Al Hu·fūf \ˌal-hō-ˈfüf\ *or* **Ho·fuf** \hō-ˈfüf\. Oasis town, Nejd, Saudi Arabia, in S part on route from Riyadh to the United Arab Emirates; 19th cent. mosque; active market.

Alia·ga \äl-ˈyä-gə\. Municipality, W Nueva Ecija prov., Luzon, Philippines; pop. (1980c) 32,349.

Ali·ák·mon \äl-ˈyäk-ˌmōn\ *also* **Vi·strit·sa** \vē-ˈstrēt-sä\; *anc.* **Hal·i·ac·mon** \ˌha-lē-ˈak-ˌmän\. River, W Macedonia, N Greece; rises near Florina and flows SE and NE into head of Gulf of Salonika; 195 mi. (314 km.) long.

Al·i·ba·tes Flint Quarries National Monument \ˌa-lə-ˈbä-tēz\. See UNITED STATES, *National Monuments.*

Ali·can·te \ˌä-lē-ˈkän-tā\. **1.** Province of SE Spain. See table at SPAIN. **2.** Seaport city, its ✻, 77 mi. (124 km.) S of Valencia; pop. (1991c) 265,473; commercial port of Madrid; wine and produce are chief exports; tourism. Said to be ancient Roman city of **Lu·cen·tum** \lü-ˈsent-əm\ and previous to that a Greek colony; captured by Moors early 8th cent.; recaptured 1265 by James I of Aragon; besieged by French 1709 and 1812 and by federalists of Cartagena 1873.

Al·ice \ˈa-lis\. City, ⊗ of Jim Wells co., S Texas, 40 mi. (64 km.) W of Corpus Christi; pop. (1990c) 19,788; railroad division point.

Alice, Mount. Peak in Front Range of Rocky Mts. on boundary bet. Boulder and Grand cos., N cen. Colorado; 13,310 ft. (4057 m.).

Alice Springs; *formerly* **Stu·art** \ˈstü-ərt, ˈstyü-\. Town, S cen. Northern Terr., Australia, on highway line from Adelaide (994 mi. or 1599 km.) to Darwin (1105 mi. or 1778 km.); pop. (1991p) 25,586; virtually the central point of the continent; in Macdonnell Ranges with alt. of 1926 ft. (587 m.); center of pastoral and mining region; popular winter resort; tourist attractions include an historic park, an aviation museum, and a casino. Site discovered 1860 by J. McDouall Stuart; ✻ (1927–31, under the name Stuart) of former Terr. of Central Australia.

Al·ice·ville \ˈa-lis-ˌvil\. City, Pickens co., W Alabama, 35 mi. (56 km.) WSW of Tuscaloosa; pop. (1990c) 3009.

Ali·garh \ˌa-lē-ˈgər, ˈa-lē-ˌgär\ *or* **Koil–Aligarh** \ˈkō-il-\. City, Uttar Pradesh, India, 43 mi. (69 km.) N of Agra; pop. (1991c) 480,520; a joint municipality consisting of fortress of Aligarh and the native city of **Koil** *or* **Kol** \ˈkōl\; trade and industrial center; Aligarh Muslim Univ. (1875). Became key Maratha fort under Sindhia 1759; stormed by British Aug. 28, 1803, during Second Maratha War (1803–05).

Ali Khel \ˌa-lē-ˈkel\. Village in Safed Koh, E Afghanistan, on border of Pakistan, at W end of Peiwar Pass 50 mi. (80 km.) SE of Kabul.

Ali Masjid. See KHYBER PASS.

Al·ine, Loch \a-ˈlēn, ˈa-ˌlēn\. Inlet of Atlantic Ocean on coast of W cen. Scotland, in Argyll co.; 3.5 mi. (6 km.) long.

A–ling Mountains. See NGANGLONG KANGRI.

Alings·ås \ˈä-liŋ-ˌsōs\. Town, Älvsborg prov., SW Sweden, on lake 25 mi. (40 km.) NE of Göteborg; pop. (1980p) 29,637.

Al·i·quip·pa \ˌa-lə-ˈkwi-pə\. City, Beaver co., W Pennsylvania, on Ohio River 19 mi. (31 km.) WNW of Pittsburgh; pop. (1990c) 13,374; formerly a major center of steelworks.

Ali·raj·pur \ə-ˈlē-ˌräj-ˌpu̇r\. **1.** Former state in SW Central India Agency, cen. India; now part of Madhya Pradesh. **2.** Town, its ✻, in SW Madhya Pradesh 100 mi. (161 km.) WSW of Indore.

Al–Iskandarīyah. Governorate and seaport, Egypt. See ALEXANDRIA.

Al–Ismā'īlīyah. See ISMAILIA.

Al–Ismā'īlīyah, Tur'at. See ISMAILIA CANAL.

Al–Ittihad. See MADINAT ASH SHA'B.

Ali·wal North \ˈä-lē-ˌväl, ˈa-lē-ˌwȯl\. Town, N Eastern Cape prov., Rep. of South Africa, on Orange River 231 mi. (372 km.) NNE of Port Elizabeth; founded 1849; health resort with sulfur springs.

Al–Jabal ash Sharqī. See ANTI-LEBANON.

Al–Jadida See EL JADIDA.

Al Jawf \al-ˈjau̇f, ˈjȯf\. Town, N Nejd, Saudi Arabia, at N edge of An Nafūd.

Al Jawlān. See GOLAN HEIGHTS.

Al–Jazā'ir. See ALGIERS 1.

Al Jazīrah. See BLUE NILE 2.

Al–Jazīrah. See JAZĪRAH, AL.

Al Jīzah. See GIZA.

Al·ju·bar·ro·ta \ˌäl-zhü-bə-ˈrō-tə\. Village, Leiria dist., W cen. Portugal, in Valley of the Liz 16 mi. (26 km.) SSW of the commune of Leiria. Scene of most important battle in Portuguese history in which invading Castilian forces under John I were defeated 1385 by John I of Portugal; battle estab. Portuguese independence. See BATALHA.

Al Jubayl. See JUBAIL.

Al–Juf See EL DJOUF.

Al Ju·frah \ˌal-ˈju̇-frə\ *or* **Gio·fra** \ˈjȯ-frə\. Oasis, NW cen. Libya.

Al–Jumhūrīyah al–'Arabīyah as–Sūrīyah. See SYRIA 3.

Al Ju·nay·nah \ˌal-jü-ˈnī-nə\ *or* **Ge·nei·na** \je-ˈnā-nə\ *or* **El Ge·nei·na** \ˌel-\. Town, W Darfur region, W Sudan, on border W of El Fasher.

Al–Kan·ta·ra. See EL KANTARA.

Al Ka·rak \ˌal-ˈka-rak\ *also* **Ka·rak;** *anc.* **Kir Mo·ab** *or* **Kir of Moab** \ˈkər … ˈmō-ˌab\. Town, W Jordan, E of S end of Dead Sea; munic. area pop. (1990e) 49,770; fortified mid-12th cent. by Crusaders who called it **Le Crac** \lə-ˈkrak\; taken by Muslims under Sultan Saladin 1188; taken by Turks 13th cent.

Al–Kasr. See AL-QASR.

Al Kā·ẓi·mī·yah \ˌal-ˌkä-zē-ˈmē-yə\. City, cen. Iraq, a N suburb of Baghdad; one of the three Shiite holy cities of Iraq.

Al–Kef. See LE KEF.

Al–Khābūrah. See KHABURA.

Al–Khalīl. See HEBRON 4.

Al Khā·ri·jah \ˌal-ˈkä-rē-jə\ *or* **El Khâr·ga** \ˌel-ˈkär-gə\. Town, ✻ of New Valley governorate, Lower Egypt, in Khārga oasis.

Al Kharj \ˌal-ˈkärj\. Oasis, cen. Saudi Arabia, SE of Riyadh.

Al Khums \al-ˈkoms\; *mostly formerly* **Homs** \ˈhoms\ *or* **Khoms** \ˈkoms\. Seaport, Libya, 65 mi. (105 km.) ESE of Tripoli; ruins of ancient Leptis Magna (*q.v.*) ab. 2 mi. (3.2 km.) to the E.

Alk·maar \ˈälk-ˌmär\. Commune, North Holland prov., W Netherlands, on North Holland canal 20 mi. (32 km.) NNW of Amsterdam, intersected by canals; pop. (1992e) 91,817; specially noted for its cheese market; buildings include the town hall, church (Groote Kerk, built 1470–98), and a weighhouse (1582). First Dutch city successfully to resist Spanish 1573; duke of York forced to capitulate by French under Marshal Guillaume Brune 1799 and permitted to evacuate Russian-English forces.

Al–Ku·fa \ˌal-ˈkü-fə\. Town on W bank of the Euphrates, S cen. Iraq, ab. 90 mi. (145 km.) S of Baghdad.

History: Founded 638 A.D. by Caliph ʻUmar I at the same time as Basra, became one of the two Islamic centers of the early Umayyad caliphs; in 7th and 8th cents. A.D. prosperous ✻ of perhaps 200,000 population, a Muslim literary, theological, and political center. Overwhelmed by Qarmatians early 10th cent. Developed the Kufic angular script of Arabic used almost exclusively for the Koran and on monuments and coins.

Al–Ku·frah \ˌal-ˈkü-frə\ *or* **Ku·fra** \ˈkü-frə\. Group of five oases in cen. Libyan Desert, Libya; ab. 7000 sq. mi. (18,130 sq. km.); stronghold of the Senusi, overcome by Italians 1930–31.

Al–Kuneitrah. See AL QUNAYTIRAH.

Al Kūt \al-ˈküt\ *also* **Kut** \ˈküt\. City, Iraq, on the Tigris 100 mi. (161 km.) SE of Baghdad; pop. (1985e) 73,022. In WWI captured by British after battle of Sept. 1915; besieged by Turks from Dec. 1915 until they finally forced British surrender Apr. 1916; recaptured by new British expeditionary force under Gen. Sir Frederick Stanley Maude Feb. 1917.

Al–Ku·wait \ˌal-kü-ˈwāt\ *or* **Al Kuwayt.** See KUWAIT 2.

Al·la·da \ˌä-lä-ˈdä\. Town, Benin, about 25 mi. (40 km.) N of Ouidah; in 17th and 18th cents. chief town of an extensive kingdom of same name.

Al·la·gash \ˈa-lə-ˌgash\. River, in Piscataquis and Aroostook cos., N Maine; flows N into St. John River; outlet of many lakes incl. **Allagash Lake** in N Piscataquis co.

Al·lah·a·bad \ˈä-lä-hä-ˌbäd, ˈa-lə-hə-ˌbad\. City, SE Uttar Pradesh, N India, on the Ganges at its junction with the Yamuna; pop. (1991c) 806,486; administrative, legal, and transportation center; trades in cotton and sugar. Has historic Jama Masjid (Great Mosque), various public buildings, and Univ. of Allahabad (1887).

History: Ancient city, a holy city of India, long sacred to Hindu pilgrims; under Muslim rule 1194–1801; a residence of Mogul Emperor Akbar, who built fort there late 16th cent.; taken by British under Robert Clive 1765; restored to ruler of Oudh 1771 in political bargains arranged by English colonial administrator Warren Hastings; finally ceded to British 1801; scene of a serious outbreak in Indian mutiny 1857; site of Pillar of Aśoka (erected 240 B.C.).

Al·laire \ə-ˈlar\. Deserted iron-industry village, Monmouth co., E cen. New Jersey, ab. 8 mi. (13 km.) SW of Asbury Park; once owned by newspaper editor Arthur Brisbane.

Al–Lajā \ˌal-ˈla-jä\. Region of lava wilderness, containing many caves, on W frontier of Jebel ed Druz, SW Syria.

Al·la·lin·horn \ˌä-lä-ˈlēn-ˌhorn\. Mountain, Pennine Alps, Valais canton, Switzerland, 8 mi. (13 km.) NNE of Monte Rosa and 8 mi. (13 km.) ENE of Zermatt; 13,213 ft. (4027 m.).

Al·la·ma·kee \ˌa-lə-mə-ˈkē\. County in NE corner of Iowa. See table at IOWA.

All–American Canal. See IMPERIAL VALLEY.

Al·lan Mountain \ˈa-lən\. Peak in Bitterroot Range, NE Lemhi co., E cen. Idaho; 9154 ft. (2790 m.).

Al·lan·myo \ˈa-lən-ˌmyō, ˈä-län-\. Town, Myanmar, on Irrawaddy River opp. Thayetmyo.

Al·lan·ridge \ˈa-lən-rij\. Town, Free State, cen. Rep. of South Africa.

Al·la·too·na \ˌa-lə-ˈtü-nə\. Hamlet and creek, SE Bartow co., Georgia; battle (**Allatoona Pass**) at creek 12 mi. (19 km.) NW of Marietta Oct. 5, 1864 following Union Gen. William T. Sherman's Atlanta campaign.

Alle. See LAVA.

Al·le·gan \ˈa-li-gən\. **1.** County in SW Michigan. See table at MICHIGAN.

2. City, its ⊗, 22 mi. (35 km.) NNW of Kalamazoo; pop. (1990c) 4547.

Al·le·ga·ny \ˌa-lə-ˈgā-nē, -ˈge-\. **1.** Name of counties in two states of the U.S. See tables at MARYLAND and NEW YORK.

2. Village, Cattaraugus co., SW New York, on Allegheny River 4 mi. (6 km.) W of Olean; pop. (1990c) 1980. St. Bonaventure Univ. (1859) in nearby **Saint Bon·a·ven·ture** \ˌbä-nə-ˈven-chər\. Nearby is **Allegany State Park,** 60,400 acres (24,462 hectares).

Al·le·gha·ny \ˌa-lə-ˈgā-nē, -ˈge-\. Name of counties in two states of the U.S. See tables at NORTH CAROLINA and VIRGINIA.

Alleghany Mountains. See ALLEGHENY MOUNTAINS.

Al·le·ghe·ny \ˌa-lə-ˈgā-nē, -ˈge-\. **1.** River, Pennsylvania and New York; rises in Potter co., Pennsylvania, loops NW into SW New York state, turns S across Pennsylvania border in Warren co., flows S through W Pennsylvania, and unites with Monongahela River to form Ohio River at Pittsburgh; 325 mi. (523 km.) long; navigable for ab. 200 mi. (320 km.); chief tributaries: the Clarion, French Creek, and the Kiskiminetas.

2. County in SW Pennsylvania. See table at PENNSYLVANIA.

Allegheny Heights. Elevation, Garrett co., NW corner of Maryland; 3187 ft. (971 m.).

Allegheny Mountain. Peak, Pendleton co., E West Virginia; 4017 ft. (1224 m.).

Allegheny Mountains *also* **Alleghany Mountains** *or* **Al·le·ghe·nies** \-nēz\. Ranges of Appalachian system in Pennsylvania, Maryland, Virginia, and West Virginia, W of and generally parallel with the Blue Ridge; varying in height from 2000 to over 4800 ft. (610 to over 1460 m.); E slope sometimes called **Allegheny Front** and the entire upland area from Cumberland Plateau on S to Mohawk Valley in New York is known as the **Allegheny Plateau.**

Allegheny Reservoir. See KINZUA DAM.

Al·len \ˈa-lən\. **1.** Name of a parish in SW Louisiana and of counties in four states of the U.S. See tables at INDIANA, KANSAS, KENTUCKY, LOUISIANA, OHIO.

2. City, Collin co., NE Texas; a N suburb of Dallas; pop. (1990c) 18,309.

Allen, Bog of. Series of peat bogs, cen. Ireland, from ab. 17 mi. (27 km.) W of Dublin almost to the Shannon; ab. 370 sq. mi. (958 sq. km.); in cos. Kildare, Offaly, Laoighis, and Westmeath; source of the Brosna, Boyne, and Barrow rivers; cut by Grand and Royal canals.

Allen, Lough \ˈläk, ˈlōk\. Lake (*lough*), Ireland, 8.5 mi. (14 km.) N of Carrick; ab. 14 sq. mi. (36 sq. km.); the Shannon River flows through it.

\ə\ abut \ˈə\ matches \ᵊ\ kitten, Fr table \ər\ further \a\ ash \ā\ ace \ä\ cot, cart \a\ Fr bac \au̇\ out \b̲\ Span Avila \ch\ chin \e\ bet \ē\ easy \g\ go \i\ hit \ī\ ice \j\ job \k̲\ Ger ich, Buch \ⁿ\ Fr vin \ŋ\ sing \ō\ go \ȯ\ all \ó\ law \œ\ Fr bœuf \œ̄\ Fr feu \ȯi\ boy \th\ thin \t͟h\ this \ü\ loot \u̇\ foot \ue\ Ger füllen \ue̅\ Fr rue \y\ yet \ʸ\ Fr digne \ˈdēnʸ\, nuit \ˈnwʸē\ \yü\ few \yu̇\ fury \zh\ vision

Allen, Mount. Peak in Adirondack Mts., Essex co., NE New York; 4345 ft. (1324 m.).

Al·len·dale \ˈa-lən-ˌdāl\. **1.** County in SW South Carolina. See table at SOUTH CAROLINA.

2. Township, Ottawa co., W Michigan; pop. (1990c) 8022; Grand Valley State Univ. (1960).

3. Borough, Bergen co., NE corner of New Jersey, 8 mi. (13 km.) N of Paterson; pop. (1990c) 5900.

4. Town, ⊗ of Allendale co., SW South Carolina, SW of Orangeburg; pop. (1990c) 4410; settled in mid-18th cent.

Allende. See SAN MIGUEL DE ALLENDE.

Al·len Park \ˈa-lən\. City, Wayne co., SE Michigan, 10 mi. (16 km.) WSW of Detroit; pop. (1990c) 4649.

Allenstein. See OLSZTYN 2.

Al·lens·town \ˈa-lənz-ˌtau̇n\. Town, Merrimack co., S cen. New Hampshire, E of Concord; pop. (1990c) 4649.

Al·len·town \ˈa-lən-ˌtau̇n\. City, ⊗ of Lehigh co., E Pennsylvania, on Lehigh River 48 mi. (77 km.) N of Philadelphia; pop. (1990c) 105,090; mineral deposits nearby; manufactures electronic equipment; Muhlenberg Coll. (1848), Cedar Crest Coll. (1867), United Wesleyan Coll. (1921), Lehigh County Community Coll. (1966); first platted 1762; sheltered Liberty Bell during Revolution; incorp. as borough 1811 and made ⊗; incorp. as city 1867.

Al·lep·pey *also* **Al·lep·pi** \ə-ˈle-pē\. Town, cen. Kerala, S India, on Malabar Coast 130 mi. (209 km.) S of Calicut; pop. (1991p) 174,606; coconut oil, carpets; good harbor.

Al·ler \ˈä-lər\. River, N and cen. Germany, rises near Magdeburg, flows NW into Weser River SE of Bremen; 131 mi. (211 km.) long.

Aller \äl-ˈyer\. Commune, Asturias, NW Spain, 20 mi. (32 km.) SE of Oviedo; pop. (1991c) 17,538.

Allgäu. See ALGÄU.

Allgäuer Alpen *or* **Allgäuer Alps.** See ALGÄU ALPS.

Al·lia \ˈä-lē-ä\. Small river of ancient Italy ab. 11 mi. (18 km.) N of Rome, flowing into the Tiber on the left bank. According to Roman historian Livy, scene of battle in which Romans were defeated by Gauls under Brennus 390 B.C. and the way opened for sack of Rome.

Al·li·ance \ə-ˈlī-əns\. **1.** City, ⊗ of Box Butte co., NW Nebraska, 45 mi. (72 km.) ENE of Scottsbluff; pop. (1990c) 9765; regional trade center.

2. City, Stark co., NE Ohio, on Mahoning River 16 mi. (26 km.) ENE of Canton; pop. (1990c) 23,376; Mount Union Coll. (1846); settled by Quakers 1805; incorp. as village 1854, as city 1889.

Al·lier \ål-ˈyā\. **1.** *or anc.* **Ela·ver** \i-ˈlā-vər\. Navigable river, S cen. France; ab. 4 mi. (6 km.) W of Nevers; 255 mi. (410 km.) long; flows NNW into Loire River.

2. Department of cen. France. See table at FRANCE.

Al·li·ga·tor Lake \ˈa-lə-ˌgā-tər\. Lake in Alligator Swamp, NW Hyde co., E North Carolina.

Alligator Point. Point on E coast of Orleans parish, SE Louisiana, extending into Lake Borgne.

Alligator Swamp. Great swamp, E North Carolina, extending bet. Albemarle Sound and Pamlico Sound and surrounding **Alligator River,** inlet of Albemarle Sound.

Al·li·son \ˈa-li-sən\. Town, ⊗ of Butler co., NE cen. Iowa; pop. (1990c) 1000.

Al·lis·ton \ˈa-lis-tən\. Town, Simcoe co., SE Ontario, Canada, 20 mi. (32 km.) SSW of Barrie.

Al–Līṭanī, Nahr. See LITANI.

Al·loa \ˈa-lō-ə\. Seaport burgh, Central region, Scotland, 25 mi. (40 km.) NE of Glasgow near mouth of Forth River; pop. (1981p) 26,390; seat of the Erskine family, holders of the earldom of Mar.

Al·lou·ez \ˈa-lü-ˌwā\. Village, Brown co., Wisconsin, just S of the city of Green Bay; pop. (1990c) 14,431.

Al·lo·way \ˈa-lə-ˌwā\. Hamlet, Strathclyde region, Scotland, S of Ayr near mouth of the Doon; birthplace of poet Robert Burns 1759 and the scene of his *Tam O'Shanter.*

All Saints Bay *or Port.* **Ba·ía de To·dos os San·tos** \bä-ˈē-ə-dē-ˈtō-düs-üs-ˈsäⁿn-tüs\. Bay on E coast of Bahia state, E Brazil; ab. 100 mi. (160 km.) in circumference; at its E entrance is the city of Salvador.

Al Lu·ḩay·yah \ˌål-lu̇-ˈkī-yə\; *mostly formerly* **Lo·heia** \lu̇-ˈhā-yə, -kā-\. Seaport, W Yemen, on Red Sea coast ab. 100 mi. (160 km.) NW of Sanaa.

Al·lu·mette \ˌa-lyü-ˈmet\. Island in Ottawa River, SW Quebec, Canada, opp. Pembroke, Ontario; 70 sq. mi. (181 sq. km.); the expansion of Ottawa River SW of island sometimes known as **Allumette Lake.**

Al·ma \ˈal-mə\. **1.** City, Crawford co., W Arkansas, NE of Fort Smith; pop. (1990c) 2959.

2. City, ⊗ of Bacon co., SE Georgia; pop. (1990c) 3663.

3. City, ⊗ of Wabaunsee co., E Kansas, 35 mi. (56 km.) W of Topeka; pop. (1990c) 871.

4. City, Gratiot co., cen. Michigan, 17 mi. (27 km.) S of Mount Pleasant; pop. (1990c) 9034; Alma Coll. (1886).

5. City, ⊗ of Harlan co., S Nebraska; pop. (1990c) 1226.

6. City, ⊗ of Buffalo co., W Wisconsin; pop. (1990c) 790.

7. Island, S Quebec, Canada, bet. the outlets of Lac St.-Jean.

8. City, Quebec, Canada. See SAINT-JOSEPH-D'ALMA.

9. Small river, SW Crimea; enters Black Sea 17 mi. (27 km.) N of Sevastopol'. Scene of defeat of Russians under Prince Aleksandr Sergeyevich Menshikov by English and French Sept. 20, 1854, one of earliest battles of Crimean War.

Al·ma–Ata \əl-ˈmä-ə-ˈtä; ˌal-mə-ˈä-tə, -ə-ˈtä\. **1.** Subdivision, of Kazakhstan, bounded on N by Lake Balkhash, on NE by Taldy-Kurgan subdivision, on SE by Xinjiang Uygur, China, on S by Kyrgyzstan, and on W by Zhambyl subdivision; 40,425 sq. mi. (104,701 sq. km.); pop. (1991e) 2,149,500; ✻ Alma-Ata; largely desert, traversed by the Ili River, except in S along N slope of Ala Tau Mts.; sugar beets, tobacco, wheat; before 1991 constituted an oblast of the U.S.S.R.

2. *or now usu.* **Al·maty** \əl-ˈmä-tē\; *formerly* **Ver·nyi** \ˈvern-yē\ *also* **Vyer·nyi** \ˈvyern-yē\. City, its ✻ and formerly ✻ of Kazakhstan, in SE part N of Issyk-Kul; pop. (1991e) 1,156,200; university (1934); founded by Russians as a fort 1854; developed as trading center, esp. after building of Turkistan-Siberian R.R.

Al·ma·da \ål-ˈmä-də\. City, Setúbal dist., W Portugal, on Tagus estuary, opp. Lisbon; pop. (1981p) 142,980.

Alma Dağ. See NUR MOUNTAINS.

Al·ma·dén \ˌäl-mä-ˈthān\; *anc.* **Sis·a·pon** \ˈsi-sə-ˌpän\. Commune, Ciudad Real prov., S cen. Spain, 50 mi. (80 km.) WSW of the commune of Ciudad Real; pop. (1991c) 8012; bet. two mountains of the Sierra Morena; site of mercury deposits, hence the name **Almadén del Azo·gue** \ˌthel-ä-ˈthō-gā\ [Span. *azogue,* "mercury"]. Mercury mines known to Romans and Moors, leased to Fugger family of Augsburg in 16th cent.; from 1645 worked by royal exchequer; leased to London branch of the Rothschild family in 19th cent.

Al·ma·di·es, Cape \äl-ˈmä-dyes\. The extreme tip of the peninsula forming Cap Vert (*q.v.*), Senegal, near Dakar, 17°32′W; the westernmost point of Africa.

Al–Madīnah. See MEDINA 7.

Al–Madrakah, Ras. See MADRAKA, CAPE.

al Malik, Wadi. See MILK, WADI EL.

Al·ma·lyk *also* **Ol·ma·liq** \əl-ˌmə-ˈlik\. Town, Tashkent subdivision, E Uzbekistan, 40 mi. (64 km.) SE of the city of Tashkent; pop. (1991e) 116,400; copper, zinc, molybdenum.

Al–Mamlakah al–ʻArabīyah as–Saʻūdīyah. See SAUDI ARABIA.

Al–Mamlakah al–Maghribīyah. See MOROCCO 1.

Al–Manamah. See MANAMA.

Al·ma·nor, Lake. \ˈal-mə-ˌnȯr\. Reservoir, NW Plumas co., NE California; created by damming of N fork of Feather River for waterpower.

Al·man·sa \äl-ˈmän-sə\ *or formerly* **Al·man·za** \-ˈmän-thə\. Commune, Albacete prov., SE Spain, 43 mi. (69 km.) ESE of the commune of Albacete; pop. (1991c) 22,599. Scene of decisive victory 1707 by French under James Fitzjames, duke of Berwick, over English and Portuguese under Henri de Massue, earl of Galway (War of the Spanish Succession).

Al Manṣūrah. See EL MANSÛRA.

Al Manzilah, Buḩayrat. See MANZALA LAKE.

Al·man·zor, Pi·co de \ˈpē-kō-thā-ˌäl-män-ˈthȯr\. Highest peak in the Sierra de Gredos, W cen. Spain; 8501 ft. (2591 m.).

Al·man·zo·ra \ˌäl-män-ˈthō-rä\. River, SE Spain; 65 mi. (104 km.) long; flows E through cen. Almería prov. into Mediterranean Sea.

Al Marj \äl-ˈmärj\ *or Ital.* **Bar·ce** \ˈbär-chā\. Town, N Libya, ab. 60 mi. (97 km.) NE of Benghazi. Ancient Barka, a member of the Pentapolis in Cyrenaica, was founded ab. 550 B.C.; became center for Greek refugees; plundered by Persians 512 B.C.; declined under the Ptolemies; again important under Muslims.

Al–Ma·ta·rī·ya *or* **El Matarīya** \ˌäl-ˌmä-tä-ˈrē-yə, ˌel-\. Town, Daqahlīya governorate, Lower Egypt, a NE suburb of Cairo; pop. (1986p) 74,554; near ruins of Heliopolis.

Almaty. See ALMA-ATA 2.

Al–Mawṣil. See MOSUL.

Al–Me·chi·li \ˌäl-me-ˈkē-lē\ *or* **Me·ki·li** \me-ˈkē-lē\ *or* **Al Mu·khay·lá** \ˌäl-mü-ˈkī-lä\ *or* **Al Mu·khay·lī** \-ˌlē\. Town, Libya, ab. 50 mi. (80 km.) SSW of Darnah on road connecting Salūm, Egypt and Benghazi, Libya; set up as a gasoline depot by the British Dec. 1940; taken by Germans in advance on Egypt but retaken Nov. 1942.

Al·mei·da \äl-ˈmā-də\. Fortified commune, Guarda dist., NE Portugal; pop. (1981p) 10,677; sulfur waters; formerly one of chief strongholds against Spain; captured 1762 by Spain, but shortly afterward reverted to Portuguese; in Peninsular War captured by French 1810, recaptured by British and Portuguese 1811.

Al·me·lo \ˈäl-mə-ˌlō\. Commune, Overijssel prov., E Netherlands, 9 mi. (14 km.) NW of Hengelo; pop. (1992e) 63,383; seat of the barons van Rechteren 1350 ff. and counts Limpurg 1711 ff.

Al·me·nar \ˌäl-mā-ˈnär\. Commune, Lérida prov., NE Spain, ab. 11 mi. (18 km.) NNE of the commune of Lérida; pop. (1991c) 3573; scene of defeat of Spanish ruler Philip V by Austrians 1710 during War of Spanish Succession.

Al·me·na·ra \ˌäl-mā-ˈnär-ä\. Commune, S Castellón de la Plana prov., Spain, 20 mi. (32 km.) NNE of Valencia; pop. (1991c) 5030; scene of defeat of Moors 1238 by James I.

Al·men·dra·le·jo \ˌäl-ˌmen-drä-ˈlā-kō\. Commune, Badajoz prov., SW Spain, 27 mi. (43 km.) ESE of the city of Badajoz; pop. (1991c) 24,268.

Al·me·ría \ˌäl-mä-ˈrē-ä\. **1.** Province of S Spain. See table at SPAIN.

2. *anc.* **Un·ci** \ˈən-ˌsī, ˈün-ˌsē\ *also* **Por·tus Mag·nus** \ˈpōr-təs-ˈmag-nəs\. Seaport, its ✻, 65 mi. (104 km.) ESE of Granada at head of Gulf of Almería; pop. (1991c) 155,120; chemicals; metalworking.

History: One of chief Roman harbors after 19 A.D.; after fall of Umayyad as rulers of Spain, became head of small independent Moorish state, then a petty kingdom dependent on Granada; a leading seaport and source of piracy for Moors; captured by Alfonso VII of Castile 1147, but retaken and held by Moors until 1489.

Almería, Gulf of. Inlet of Mediterranean Sea in S Almería prov., Spain; one of leading harbors in Spain.

Almesbury. See AMESBURY 2.

Al·me·tyevsk \əl-mi-ˈtyefsk\. Town, Tatarstan (republic), E cen. Russia in Europe, ab. 140 mi. (225 km.) ESE of Kazan'; pop. (1992e) 133,000; oil refinery; founded 1950.

Al·mi·na, Point \äl-ˈmē-nä\. Point of land extending into the Mediterranean Sea at extremity of peninsula on which Ceuta is situated, NE Morocco; at SE entrance to Strait of Gibraltar.

Al Minya See EL MINYA.

Al·mi·ran·te \ˌäl-mē-ˈrän-tā\. Port on NW side of Chiriquí Lagoon, NW Panama; pop. (1980p) 4664.

Almirante Brown \ˈbrau̇n\. City, S suburb of Buenos Aires, Argentina; pop. (1991p) 449,105.

Almissa. See OMIŠ.

Al·mo·dó·var del Cam·po \ˌäl-mä-ˈthō-vär-thel-ˈkäm-pō\. Commune, Ciudad Real prov., S cen. Spain, 22 mi. (35 km.) SW of the commune of Ciudad Real; pop. (1991c) 7723; old Moorish fortress.

Al·mond \ˈä-mənd\. River, Tayside region, SE Scotland; flows E and NE to Firth of Forth; 24 mi. (39 km.) long.

Al·monte \ˈal-ˌmänt\. Town, Lanark co., SE Ontario, Canada, on Mississippi River 32 mi. (51 km.) WSW of Ottawa; pop. (1991c) 4382.

Al·mo·ra \äl-ˈmōr-ə, əl-\. Town, in Uttar Pradesh, N India, 160 mi. (257 km.) NE of Delhi; pop. (1991p) 26,080; alt. 5494 ft. (1674 m.).

Al Mu·har·raq \ˌäl-mo-ˈhä-rək\ *also* **Muharraq** *or* **Mo·ha·rek** \mo-ˈhä-rək\. **1.** Island of Bahrain, Persian Gulf, ab. 1.5 mi. (2.4 km.) NE of Bahrain I.; 4 mi. (6 km.) long by 1 mi. (1.6 km.) wide.

2. Town on Al Muharraq I.; pop. (1991c) 74,245; connected by causeway with Manama, Bahrain I.

Al Mu·kal·lā \ˌäl-mu̇-ˈkä-ˌlä\ *or* **Mu·kal·la** \mu̇-ˈka-lə\. Seaport and chief town of Ḥaḍramawt, Yemen, 320 mi. (515 km.) NE of Aden.

Al Mukhā. See MOCHA.

Al Mukhaylá *or* **Al Mukhaylī.** See AL-MECHILI.

al–Munastīr. See MONASTIR 1.

Al·mu·ñé·car \ˌäl-mü-ˈnyā-ˌkär\; *anc.* **Sexi** \ˈsek-ˌsī\. Mediterranean seaport, Granada prov., S Spain, ab. 32 mi. (51 km.) S of the city of Granada; pop. (1991c) 20,408; landing place 756 of ʻAbd ar-Raḥmān I, founder of the emirate of Córdoba.

Aln *or* **Alne** \ˈo̊n, ˈo̊ln, ˈaln\. River, N Northumberland, N England; flows E into North Sea at Alnmouth; 16 mi. (26 km.) long.

Aln·wick \ˈa-nik\. Town, Northumberland, N England, on Aln River 37 mi. (60 km.) N of Newcastle upon Tyne; pop. (1981p) 7191; feudal fortress (Alnwick Castle, seat of dukes of Northumberland) stands at N entrance of town; besieged by Scots several times bet. 11th and 15th cents.

Alo·fi \ä-ˈlō-fē\. **1.** One of the Futuna Is. (*q.v.*).

2. Chief village of Niue I., Cook Is., on W coast; pop. (1989c) 706.

Alón·ni·sos *or* **Aló·nis·sos** \ä-ˈlō-nē-ˌsös\ *also* **Ili·o·dhró·mia** \ē-ˌlē-ō-ˈthrō-mē-ä\. Island of the Northern Sporades, NW Aegean Sea, part of Magnesia dept., Greece, NE of Skopelos.

Alor \ˈa-ˌlo̊r, ˈä-\; *formerly* **Om·bai** \ˈo̊m-ˌbī\. Island, E end of Lesser Sunda Is., Indonesia, 20 mi. (32 km.) N of Timor and WSW of Wetar; ab. 60 mi. (96 km.) long; 810 sq. mi. (2098 sq. km.); chief town Kalabahi; very mountainous, highest point 6033 ft. (1839 m.) at E end; has harbor (Kalabahi Bay) at W end. With Pantar forms the **Alor Islands** group (1126 sq. mi. or 2916 sq. km.).

Álo·ra \ˈä-lō-rä\. Commune, Málaga prov., S Spain, 18 mi. (29 km.) WNW of the city of Málaga; pop. (1991c) 13,168; mineral springs.

Alor Se·tar \ˈa-ˌlo̊r-sə-ˈtär, ˈä-\ *also* **Alor Star** \ˈstär\. Town, ✻ of Kedah state, Malaysia, near coast 50 mi. (80 km.) N of George Town; on highway and railroad N to Thailand.

Alor Strait. Channel bet. Lomblen and Pantar islands in the Lesser Sundas, Indonesia; ab. 10 mi. (16 km.) wide; connects Flores Sea with Savu Sea.

Alor·ton \ə-ˈlo̊rt-ᵊn\. Village, St. Clair co., SW Illinois; pop. (1990c) 2960.

Alost. See AALST.

Al–Oued. See EL OUED.

Al·pen \ˈäl-pən\. German form of *Alps.* See table at ALPS.

Al·pe·na \al-ˈpē-nə\. **1.** County in NE Michigan. See table at MICHIGAN.

2. City, its ⊗, on Thunder Bay, Lake Huron, at mouth of Thunder Bay River 50 mi. (80 km.) N of mouth of Saginaw Bay; pop. (1990c) 11,354; summer resort; Alpena Community Coll. (1952).

Al·pes \ˈal-(ˌ)pēz\. Latin form of *Alps.* See table at ALPS.

Alpes \ˈälp\. French form of *Alps.* See table at ALPS.

Alpesa. See ELVAS.

Alpes–de–Haute–Pro·vence \ˌälp-də-ˌōt-prȯ-ˈvä^n s\; *formerly* **Basses–Alpes** \bȧz-ˈzälp\. Department of SE France. See table at FRANCE.

Alpes–Mar·i·times \ˌȧlp-ˌmä-rē-ˈtēm\. Department, France. See table at FRANCE.

Al·pha \ˈal-fə\. Borough, Warren co., NW New Jersey, 3 mi. (5 km.) SSE of Phillipsburg; pop. (1990c) 2530.

Al·pha·ret·ta \ˌal-fə-ˈre-tə\. City, Fulton co., NW cen. Georgia, 20 mi. (32 km.) NNE of Atlanta; pop. (1990c) 13,002.

Al·phen \ˈäl-fən\ *or in full* **Alphen aan den Rijn** \ˌän-dən-ˈrīn\. Commune, South Holland prov., Netherlands, ab. 19 mi. (30 km.) NE of Rotterdam; pop. (1981e) 53,556.

Al·phe·us \al-ˈfē-əs\ *or Gk.* **Al·fi·ós** \äl-ˈfyȯs\ *also* **Rou·fi·ás** \rü-ˈfyäs\. River, W Peloponnese, S Greece; rises in Arcadia, flows NW through S Elis into Ionian Sea near Pyrgos; ab. 75 mi. (121 km.) long; Olympia is on its N bank.

Alp·hu·bel \ˈälp-ˌhü-bəl\. Mountain and pass in the Alps, Valais canton, SW cen. Switzerland, ab. 6 mi. (10 km.) NE of Zermatt; 13,799 ft. (4206 m.).

Al·pi \ˈäl-pē\. Italian form of *Alps.* See table at ALPS.

Alpi Apuane. See table at APENNINES.

Al·pine \ˈal-ˌpīn\. **1.** County in E California. See table at CALIFORNIA.
2. Town, ⊗ of Brewster co., W Texas, 130 mi. (209 km.) SE of El Paso; pop. (1990c) 5637; in mountainous region; granite and mineral deposits nearby; Sul Ross State Univ. (1920).

Alportel, São Brás de. See SÃO BRÁS DE ALPORTEL.

Alps \ˈalps\; *anc.* **Al·pes** \ˈal-(ˌ)pēz\. Mountain system of S cen. Europe, extending in crescent shape ab. 660 mi. (1060 km.) from Mediterranean coast bet. France and Italy into Switzerland and along N boundary of Italy, through SW Austria, Slovenia, S and W Croatia, Bosnia and Herzegovina, and into Yugoslavia and Albania; area occupied estimated at ab. 80,000 sq. mi. (207,200 sq. km.); highest point Mont Blanc (*q.v.*) 15,771 ft. (4807 m.); geologically of many rock types and varied folds and thrusts; noted for magnificent scenery with many glaciers, valleys (Chamonix, Interlaken, Engadine, Lauterbrunnen, Grindelwald, Zermatt) and lakes (Geneva, Thun, Lucerne, Brienzerzee, Zug, Zürich, Constance, Maggiore, Como, Garda, Iseo); source of major rivers or their tributaries (Danube, Rhine, Rhone, Po). See also NORTH ALBANIAN ALPS, AUSTRALIAN ALPS. The principal ranges (all of which have offshoot ranges and subsidiary groups), famous passes, and tunnels are shown in the tables on pages 37 and 38.

Al·pu·jar·ras, Las \ˌläs-ˌäl-pü-ˈḵär-räs\. Mountainous region, Granada and Almería provs., S Spain, S of the Sierra Nevada and parallel to it, bet. Motril and Almería; extremely fertile valleys; populated by colonists, esp. from Extremadura, and descendants of Moors who took refuge there after fall of Granada; scene of Moorish uprisings throughout much of 16th cent.

Al–Qaḏārif. See GEDAREF.

al–Qādisīyah. See KADISIYA.

Al–Qāhirah. See CAIRO 2 (Egypt).

Al Qā·mish·lī \ˌȧl-ˌkä-ˈmish-ˌlē\ Town, NE Syria, on border with Turkey; pop. (1992e) 151,000.

Al Qan·ṭa·rah *or* **El Qan·ta·ra** \ˌȧl-ˈkȧn-tə-rə, ˌel-\ *or* **Qantara.** Village on E bank of Suez Canal, Sinai governorate, NE Egypt, bet. Port Said and Ismailia; occupied by Israel 1967; forces withdrawn 1982 following Camp David accords.

Al–Qāsh. See MAREB.

Al–Qasr *or* **El Qasr** *also* **Al–Kasr** \ˌȧl-ˈkȧ-sər, ˌel-\ *or Lat.* **Cas·trum** \ˈkas-trəm\. Chief town of Dakhla oasis, New Valley governorate, Egypt.

Al–Qaṣ·rayn \ˌȧl-kȧs-ˈrīn\ *or* **Kas·ser·ine** \ˌka-sə-ˈrēn\. Village, N cen. Tunisia, ab. 135 mi. (217 km.) SW of Tunis; pop. (1989e) 59,767; nearby **Kasserine Pass** was scene of heavy fighting bet. Germans and Americans in WWII before U.S. achieved a decisive victory 1943.

Al Qa·ṭīf \ˌȧl-kä-ˈtēf\ *or* **Qa·tif** \kä-ˈtēf\; *mostly formerly* **El–Ka·tif** \ˌel-kä-ˈtēf\ Seaport of E Nejd, Saudi Arabia, on Persian Gulf 37 mi. (60 km.) NW of Bahrain I. Taken by Wahhabis from Turks 1914.

Al–Qa·trā·nah *or* **El Qa·tra·na** \ˌȧl-kȧ-ˈträ-nə, ˌel-\ *or* **Qatrana.** Town, W cen. Jordan, on railroad line ab. 50 mi. (80 km.) S of Amman.

al–Qayrawān. See KAIROUAN.

Al–Quds. See JERUSALEM 3.

Al Qu·nay·ti·rah \ˌȧl-kü-ˈnī-tə-rə, -ˈnā-\ *or* **El Qu·nay·ti·rah** \ˌel-\ *or* **El Quneitra;** *mostly formerly* **El Ku·nei·trah** \ˌel-kü-ˈnā-trə\. Town, SW Syria, ab. 40 mi. (64 km.) SW of Damascus; captured by Israel and subsequently abandoned during 1967 war.

Al Qur·nah \ˌȧl-ˈkür-nə\ *also* **Kur·na** \ˈkür-nə\. Town, SE Iraq, on the lower Tigris River where it joins the Euphrates to form the Shatt al Arab, ab. 45 mi. (72 km.) NNW of Basra.

Al Quṣayr. See QUSEIR.

Al–Qusur. See LUXOR.

Als \ˈäls\ *or Ger.* **Al·sen** \ˈäl-zən\. Island off E coast of S Jutland, Sønderjylland co., Denmark; 124 sq. mi. (321 sq. km.); pop. (1991e) 50,804; in the Little Belt, separated from mainland by Sound of Alsen (**Al·sen·sund** \-ˌzu̇nt\); fertile soil, pleasant beaches. Under Danish government to 1864, Prussian 1864–1919, Danish (by plebiscite) from 1920.

Al·sace \ȧl-ˈzȧs, *angl.* al-ˈsas, -ˈsās, ˈal-ˌ\ *or Ger.* **El·sass** \ˈel-ˌzäs\; *anc.* **Al·sa·tia** \al-ˈsā-shə, -shē-ə\. Region, NE France, bet. Rhine River and Vosges Mts.

History: Ruled by Rome (see STRASBOURG); gradually penetrated by Germanic peoples; created a Frankish duchy; part of Middle Kingdom (see LORRAINE) assigned to Holy Roman Emperor Lothair I by Treaty of Verdun 843 A.D.; belonged to Holy Roman Empire 870–1648; broken up into feudal principalities controlled chiefly by bishop of Strasbourg and Hapsburg family in 14th cent.; Upper Alsace given to Burgundy 1469, but soon broke free; a center of the Peasants' Revolt of 1525; occupied by French in Thirty Years' War; linked with France by means of Louis XIV's "Chambers of Reunion" 1680; consolidated into provs. of Bas-Rhin and Haut-Rhin after 1789 and under Napoléon; ceded to Germany by Treaty of Frankfurt 1871. For recent history, see ALSACE-LORRAINE.

Al·sace–Lor·raine \-lȯ-ˈren, *angl.* -ˈrān\ *or Ger.* **El·sass–Lo·thring·en** \ˈel-ˌzäs-ˈlō-triŋ-ən\. Frontier region of NE France; except for Rhine on E has indefinite boundaries; now usu. considered to comprise the French depts. of Moselle, Bas-Rhin, and Haut-Rhin.

History: Formed from French prov. of Alsace, French dept. of Moselle, and some subdivisions (*arrondissements*) of the former dept. of Meurthe which were ceded to Germany by Treaty of Frankfurt 1871; administered in three divisions, **Upper Alsace** (*Ger.* **Ober·el·sass** \ˈō-bər-ˌel-ˌzäs\), **Lower Alsace** (**Un·ter·el·sass** \ˈu̇n-tər-ˌel-ˌzäs\), and **Lorraine** (**Lothringen**), under the German Empire 1871–1918; subject to unsuccessful attempts to Germanize 1880–1910; restored to France by Treaty of Versailles 1919. In WWII held by Germany 1940–44; retaken by French and American armies and again restored to France.

Al·sa·ger \ˈȯl-si-jər, ȯl-ˈsā-\. Town, Cheshire, NW England; pop. (1981p) 11,203.

Alsatia. See ALSACE.

Als·dorf \ˈäls-ˌdȯrf\. City, North Rhine-Westphalia, Germany, 8 mi. (13 km) NNE of Aachen; pop. (1980c) 46,373.

Al·sek \ˈal-ˌsek\. River, SW Yukon and SE Alaska; rises in Aishihik Lake and flows S through E end of St. Elias Mts. and Alaska to the Pacific; 260 mi. (418 km.) long.

Alsen *and* **Alsensund.** See ALS.

Al·sip \ˈal-səp\. Village, Cook co., NE Illinois, bordering SW Chicago; pop. (1990c) 18,227.

Al·ta \ˈal-tə\. Town, Salt Lake co., N Utah, in Wasatch Range SE of Salt Lake City; pop. (1990c) 397; center of a winter-sports area.

Alta. See ALTEELVA.

Alta California \ˈäl-tä\ *or Eng.* **Upper California.** Name used to differentiate former Spanish possessions in what is now the U.S. from those in Baja California, (*q.v.*) Mexico.

Al·ta·de·na \ˌal-tə-ˈdē-nə\. Unincorporated settlement, Los Angeles co., SW California; pop. (1990c) 42,658.

Alta Fjord. See ALTEELVA.

ALPS—PRINCIPAL RANGES

NAME: English	NAME: Classical[1]	NAME: Native	LOCATION	HIGHEST POINT
WESTERN				
Maritime Alps	**Al·pes Ma·ri·ti·mae** \'al-'pēz-mə-'ri-tə-ˌmē\	*Fr.* **Alpes Ma·ri·times** \ˌȧlp-ˌmȧ-rē-'tēm\; *Ital.* **Al·pi Ma·rit·ti·me** \'äl-pē-mä-'rēt-tē-ˌmā\	In S bet. France and Italy	Punta Argentera 10,817 ft. (3297 m.)
Li·gu·ri·an Alps \lə-'gyu̇r-ē-ən\		*Ital.* **Al·pi Li·gu·ri** \'äl-pē-'lē-gü-re\	E extension of Maritime Alps along coast of NW Italy	Saccarello 7216 ft. (2199 m.)
Cot·ti·an Alps \'kä-tē-ən\	**Alpes Cot·ti·ae** \'al-ˌpēz-'kä-tē-ˌē\	*Fr.* **Alpes Cot·ti·ennes** \ˌȧlp-kȯ-'tyen\; *Ital.* **Al·pi Co·zie** \'äl-pē-'kȯts-yā\	N of Maritime Alps bet. Alpes-de-Haute prov. and Hautes-Alpes depts., France, and Torino prov., Italy	Mount Viso 12,602 ft. (3841 m.)
Gra·ian Alps \'grā-yən, 'grī-\	**Alpes Gra·iae** \'al-ˌpēz-'grā-ˌē, -'grī-\	*Fr.* **Alpes Graies** \ˌȧlp-'grā\; *Ital.* **Alpi Graie** \ˌäl-pē-'grä-yā\	Savoie dept., France, and NW Piedmont, Italy	Gran Paradiso 13,323 ft. (4061 m.)
Dau·phi·né Alps \ˌdō-fi-'nā\		*Fr.* **Alpes du Dau·phi·né** \ˌȧlp-dᵫ-ˌdō-fē-'nā\	In old prov. of Dauphiné (*q.v.*), France, W of Cottian Alps	Barre des Écrins 13,461 ft. (4103 m.)
Sa·voy Alps \sə-'vȯi\		*Fr.* **Alpes de Sa·voie** \ˌȧlp-də-sȧ-'vwȧ\	In Haute-Savoie dept., France	Mont Blanc 15,771 ft. (4807 m.)
CENTRAL: *Southern*				
Pen·nine Alps \'pe-ˌnīn\	**Alpes Pen·ni·nae** \'al-ˌpēz-pə-'nī-nē\	*Fr.* **Alpes Pen·nines** \ˌȧlp-pe-'nēn\; *Ital.* **Al·pi Pen·ni·ne** \'äl-pē-pān-'nē-nā\	In Valais canton, SW cen. Switzerland, and N Piedmont, Italy, NE of Graian Alps	Dufourspitze 15,203 ft. (4634 m.)
Le·pon·tine Alps \li-'pän-ˌtīn, 'le-pən-\		*Fr.* **Alpes Lé·pon·ti·ennes** \ˌȧlp-lā-pōⁿ-'tyen\; *Ital.* **Al·pi Le·pon·ti·ne** \'äl-pē-ˌlā-pōn-'tē-nā\	On boundary bet. Switzerland and Italy and in Ticino and Graubünden cantons, Switzerland	Monte Leone 11,654 ft. (3552 m.)
Rhae·tian Alps \'rē-shē-ən\	**Alpes Rae·ti·cae** \'al-ˌpēz-'rē-tə-ˌsē\	*Fr.* **Alpes Rhé·tiques** \ˌȧlp-rā-'tēk\; *Ital.* **Al·pi Re·ti** \'äl-pē-'rā-tē\; *Ger.* **Rä·ti·sche Al·pen** \'rā-ti-shə-'äl-pən\	E Graubünden canton, Switzerland	Piz Bernina 13,284 ft. (4049 m.)
CENTRAL: *Northern*				
Bern·ese Alps \ˌbər-'nēz, 'bər-ˌ\		*Fr.* **Alpes Ber·noises** \ˌȧlp-ber-'nwȧz\; *Ger.* **Ber·ner Ober·land** \'ber-nər-'ō-bər-ˌlänt\ or **Berner Al·pen** \'äl-pən\	S cen. Switzerland—Bern, Valais, and Uri cantons	Finsteraarhorn 14,022 ft. (4274 m.)
EASTERN				
Nor·ic Alps \'nȯr-ik, 'när-\	**Alpes No·ri·cae** \'al-ˌpēz-'nȯr-ə-ˌsē, 'när-\	*Ger.* **No·ri·sche Al·pen** \'nō-ri-shə-'äl-pən\	Austria, bet. valleys of Mur and Drava	Eisenhut 8006 ft. (2440 m.)
Ho·he Tau·ern \ˌhō-ə-'tau̇-ərn\		*Ger.* **Hohe Tauern**	Bet. Carinthia and Tirol, W Austria	Grossglockner 12,470 ft. (3801 m.)
Car·nic Alps \'kär-nik\	**Alpes Car·ni·cae** \'al-ˌpēz-'kär-nə-ˌsē\	*Ger.* **Kar·ni·sche Al·pen** \'kär-ni-shə-'äl-pən\; *Ital.* **Al·pi Car·ni·che** \'äl-pē-'kär-nē-kā\	Bet. S Austria and NE Italy and in Carniola	Kellerwand 9217 ft. (2809 m.)
Do·lo·mites \'dō-lə-ˌmīts, 'dä-\ (**Tri·den·tine Alps** \trī-'den-tīn, 'trīd-ᵊn-\)	**Alpes Ve·ne·tae** \'al-ˌpēz-'ve-nə-ˌtē\	*Ital.* **Do·lo·mi·ti** \ˌdō-lō-'mē-tē\	NE Italy, bet. valleys of Adige and Piave	Marmolada 10,965 ft. (3342 m.)
Ju·lian Alps \'jül-yən\	**Alpes Ju·li·ae** \'al-ˌpēz-'jü-lē-ˌē\	*Ital.* **Al·pi Giu·lie** \'äl-pē-'jül-yā\; *Ger.* **Ju·li·sche Al·pen** \'yü-li-shə-'äl-pən\	In NW Slovenia	Triglav 9395 ft. (2864 m.)
Ka·ra·wan·ken \ˌkär-ə-'väŋ-kən\	**Ca·ra·van·ca Mons** \ˌkar-ə-ˌvaŋ-kə-'mänz\	*Ital.* **Ca·ra·van·che** \ˌkä-rä-'väŋ-kā\	S of the valley of the Drava bet. S Austria and N Slovenia	Hochstuhl 7341 ft. (2238 m.)
Di·nar·ic Alps \də-'nar-ik\	**Alpes Di·nar·i·cae** \'al-ˌpēz-də-'nar-ə-ˌsē\	*Ital.* **Al·pi Di·na·ri·che** \'äl-pē-dē-'nä-rē-kā\; *Serbo–Croat.* **Di·na·ra Pla·ni·na** \'dē-nä-rä-plä-'nē-nä\	Parallel to Adriatic coast in Slovenia, Croatia, Bosnia and Herzegovina, and Montenegro, S to Albania	Bobotov Kuk 8274 ft. (2522 m.)

[1] Latin names given of those ranges known by name to the ancients.

ALPS—NOTABLE PASSES AND TUNNELS[1]

NAME	DESCRIPTION AND LOCATION
Arl·berg \'ärl-ˌberk, -ˌbərg\	Pass, SW Austria; alt. 5881 ft. (1792 m.); connects Vorarlberg and Tirol; railroad tunnel beneath pass 6.25 mi. (10 km.) long, on road from Bludenz to Landeck, opened 1884; road tunnel 8.7 mi. (14 km.) opened 1979.
Bren·ner \'bre-nər\ *or Ital.* **Bren·ne·ro** \'bre-ne-ˌrō\	Pass bet. Austria and Italy; 59 mi. (95 km.) long; highest point at Brenner, alt. 4497 ft. (1371 m.); the lowest of any of the important Alpine passes; much frequented from earliest times; crossed by Teutonic invaders of Italy; carriage road built 1772 and railroad completed 1867; highway built early 1970s.
Great Saint Ber·nard \ˌsānt-bər-'närd \ *or Fr.* **Grand–Saint–Bernard** \ˌgräⁿ-ˌseⁿ-ber-'när\	Pass bet. Valais, SW cen. Switzerland and Aosta prov., Piedmont, N Italy; modern road (built 1823) partly superseded by 3.5 mi. (5.6 km.) tunnel beneath the pass 1964; alt. 8090 ft. (2468 m.); known since Roman times (*Lat.* **Mons Jo·vis** \mänz-'jō-vəs\); much frequented by pilgrims and clerics on visits to Rome and later often crossed by medieval armies; used 1800 by French Emperor Napoléon for his 40,000 troops for campaign in N Italy; named after the hospice at the summit of the pass, founded in the 11th cent. by St. Bernard of Menthon; hospice is a stone building dating from 16th cent. kept by Augustinian monks who, with their St. Bernard dogs, are historically noted for aiding travelers.
Little Saint Bernard \ˌsānt-ber-'närd\ *or Fr.* **Pe·tit–Saint–Bernard** \pə-ˌtē-ˌseⁿ-ber-'när\	Pass from Bourg-St.-Maurice, Savoie dept., France, over Savoy Alps 39 mi. (63 km.) to La Thuile, Aosta prov., Piedmont, Italy; alt. 7178 ft. (2188 m.); known in Roman times, has hospice founded in 11th cent.
Mont Ce·nis \ˌmōⁿ-sə-'nē\ *or Ital.* **Mon·te Ce·ni·sio** \'mòn-tā-chā-'nē-zyō\	Pass bet. Modane, Savoie dept., France, and Susa, Torino prov., Piedmont, Italy; alt. 6831 ft. (2082 m.); ab. 46 mi. (74 km.) over the Mont Cenis Massif in Graian Alps; an ancient invasion route; carriage road constructed 1803–10 by order of French Emperor Napoléon. **Mont Cenis Tunnel** \ˌmōⁿ-sə-'nē\ or **Fré·jus Tunnel** \frā-'zhᵫs\, railroad tunnel 8.5 mi. (14 km.) long, is 16 mi. (26 km.) SW of Mont Cenis Pass, near Fréjus Pass; highest point 4246 ft. (1294 m.); opened 1871, first of the great tunnels through the Alps; road tunnel opened 1980.
Saint Gott·hard *or* **Saint Got·hard** \'sānt-'gä-tərd\ *or Fr.* **Saint–Go·thard** \ˌseⁿ-gò-'tär\	Pass bet. Altdorf in Uri canton and Bellinzona in Ticino canton, Switzerland; actual pass ab. 19 mi. (30 km.) over St. Gotthard group of Lepontine Alps, Göschenen to Airolo; alt. 6916 ft. (2108 m.); road over pass open since Middle Ages; named after the pass hospice dedicated to St. Gotthard, bishop of Hildesheim (d. 1038), built in 14th cent.; carriage road built 1820–30 and **Saint Gotthard Tunnel**, railroad tunnel 9.5 mi. (15 km.) long, highest point 3788 ft. (1154 m.), opened 1882; road tunnel 10 mi. (16.3 km.) long opened 1980.
Sim·plon \'sim-ˌplän\ *or Ital.* **Sem·pio·ne** \sem-'pyō-nā\	Pass bet. Brig, Valais canton, SW cen. Switzerland, and Iselle, NE Piedmont, Italy; 29 mi. (47 km.) over Alps; alt. 6590 ft. (2009 m.); marks dividing line bet. Pennine and Lepontine Alps; named from village of Simpeln or Simplon in the pass; hospice at summit; carriage road built by French Emperor Napoléon 1800–07; pass less used since completion 1906 of first **Simplon Tunnel**, railroad tunnel 12.5 mi. (20 km.) long, from Brig to Iselle under Monte Leone at W end of Lepontine Alps, alt. at highest point 2313 ft. (705 m.).
Splü·gen \'shplᵫ-gən\ *or Ital.* **Splu·ga** \'splü-gä\	Pass bet. Splügen, Graubünden canton, E Switzerland, and Chiavenna, Lombardy, Italy, near head of Lake Como, 25 mi. (40 km.) over Rhaetian Alps; alt. 6946 ft. (2117 m.); road built by Austrian government (completed 1822).

[1] See also Mont Blanc Tunnel at BLANC, MONT.

Al·ta·gra·cia \ˌäl-tä-'grä-sē-ä\. Town, Zulia state, NW Venezuela, on NE shore of Lake Maracaibo and opp. Maracaibo.

Al·ta Gra·cia \'äl-tä-'grä-sē-ä\. Mountain resort, W Córdoba prov., N cen. Argentina, ab. 30 mi. (48 km.) SSW of the city of Córdoba; pop. (1980p) 30,628.

Altai. See GORNO-ALTAY.

Altai Kray. See ALTAY KRAY.

Altai Shan. See ALTAY SHAN.

Al·ta·ma·ha \'òl-tə-mə-ˌhò\. River, SE Georgia; formed by junction of Ocmulgee and Oconee rivers at SE tip of Wheeler co.; flows SE to **Altamaha Sound**, inlet of the Atlantic ab. 12 mi. (19 km.) N of Brunswick; 137 mi. (220 km.) long.

Al·ta·mi·ra \ˌäl-tä-'mē-rä\. Caverns (*cuevas*) in Cantabria prov., N Spain, ab. 13 mi. (21 km.) WSW of Santander; prehistoric drawings and paintings of animals, assigned to Upper Magdalenian age, discovered 1879.

Al·ta·mont \'al-tə-ˌmänt\. Town, ⊗ of Grundy co., S cen. Tennessee; pop. (1990c) 679.

Al·ta·monte Springs \'al-tə-ˌmänt\. City, Seminole co., cen. Florida, 6 mi. (10 km.) N of Orlando; pop. (1990c) 34,879; grew rapidly in 1970s.

Al·ta·mu·ra \ˌäl-tä-'mü-rä\; *anc.* **Lu·pa·tia** \lü-'pā-shə, -shē-ə\. Commune, Bari prov., Puglia, SE Italy, at foot of the Apennines 28 mi. (45 km.) SW of the seaport Bari; pop. (1989c) 56,631; wine; walled city rebuilt 1232 by Holy Roman Emperor Frederick II.

Al·tan·bu·lag *also* **Al·tan Bu·lak** \'äl-tän-'bü-läk\; *formerly* **Mai·ma·chin** \ˌmī-ˌmä-'chēn\. Commercial town, N Mongolia, opp. Kyakhta in Buryatia, S Russia in Asia, and just E of Orhon River; on caravan route and highway 150 mi. (241 km.) N of Ulaanbaatar.

Altan–Nor. See ELTON, LAKE.

Alta Peak \'al-tə\. Mountain in the Sierra Nevada, NE Tulare co., S cen. California; 11,204 ft. (3415 m.).

Al·tar \äl-'tär\; *formerly* **Ca·pac–Ur·cu** \kä-'päk-'ür-ˌkü\. Volcano in the Andes, cen. Ecuador, E of Riobamba; 17,725 ft. (5402 m.).

Alta Ve·ra·paz \'äl-tä-ˌvā-rä-'päs\. Department of cen. Guatemala. See table at GUATEMALA.

Al·ta·vis·ta \ˌal-tə-'vis-tə\. Town, Campbell co., S cen. Virginia, on Roanoke River 23 mi. (37 km.) S of Lynchburg; pop. (1990c) 3686.

Altay. See GORNO-ALTAY.

Al·tay Kray *or* **Al·tai Kray** \al-'tī-'krī\. Administrative subdivision of S Russia in Asia; 101,042 sq. mi. (261,699 sq. km.); pop. (1992e) 2,666,000; ✱ Barnaul; formerly included at its E end the Gorno-Altay Autonomous Oblast; traversed by the upper Ob', flowing generally N into Novosibirsk Oblast; corn, oats, wheat; barium, copper, lead, zinc.

Al·tay Shan *or* **Al·tai Shan** \al-'tī-'shän, 'al-ˌtī, 'äl-ˌtī, əl-'tī\. Mountain system bet. W Mongolia and NE Xinjiang Uygur, W China and bet. Kazakhstan and Gorno-Altay Rep., S Russia in Asia; highest peak ab. 15,000 ft. (4570 m.); source of Irtysh and Ob' rivers.

Altbreisach. See BREISACH AM RHEIN.

Alt·dorf \'ält-ˌdòrf\ *also* **Al·torf** \'äl-ˌtòrf\. Commune, ✱ of Uri canton, cen. Switzerland, near SE tip of Lake of Lucerne 20 mi. (32 km.) SE of Lucerne; pop. (1989c) 8249; connected with William Tell legend, having a colossal statue of Tell (by Richard Kissling) on the supposed site of the apple-shooting episode, and a theater for the annual production of Friedrich von Schiller's drama *Wilhelm Tell;* site of oldest Capuchin monastery (1581) in Switzerland.

Al·te·el·va \ˌäl-tə-ˈel-və\; *formerly* **Al·ta** \ˈäl-tə\. River, N Norway; flows N in Finnmark co. into **Alta Fjord** *or* **Alten Fjord** \ˈält-ᵊn\, inlet of Arctic Ocean at 70°N, hiding place of German fleet in WWII.

Al·te·na \ˈäl-tə-ˌnä\. City, North Rhine-Westphalia, Germany, 47 mi. (76 km.) S of Münster; pop. (1980c) 24,571.

Al·ten·burg \ˈäl-tən-ˌbu̇rk\. **1.** City, Thuringia, E Germany, in valley of the Pleisse 49 mi. (79 km.) E of Weimar; pop. (1991e) 48,926.

History: One of oldest German cities E of Saale River (mentioned as early as 976); seat of a burgrave from 12th cent.; given to Wettin family as fief of Holy Roman Empire 1329; burned by Hussites 1430; held by Ernestine branch of family 1485–1547 and from 1554; scene 1568–69 of conference bet. Lutherans and Philippists, two groups of German Protestants; from 1603–72 and 1826–1918 ✱ of independent duchy of Saxe-Altenburg.

2. Town, Hungary. See MOSONMAGYARÓVÁR.

Alten Fjord. See ALTEELVA.

Al·ten·kir·chen im Wes·ter·wald \ˈäl-tən-ˌkir-k̲ən-im-ˈves-tər-ˌvält\. Town, Rhineland-Palatinate, Germany, 22 mi. (35 km.) N of Koblenz; scene of two battles bet. Austrians and French during War of the First Coalition 1796.

Al–Tih *or* **El Tih** \ˌál-ˈtē, ˌel-\ *also* **Ja·bal at Tīh** \ˈje-bel-ˌát-ˈtē\. Plateau, cen. Sinai Penin., NE Egypt, just N of the Egma Plateau; alt. ab. 1800 to 3600 ft. (550 to 1100 m.).

Altin Tagh. See ALTUN SHAN.

Al·ti·pla·no \ˌäl-tē-ˈplä-nō\. Region, W Bolivia, extending into SE Peru; comprises a series of high plains in the area of Lake Titicaca and La Paz, Bolivia.

Alt·mühl \ˈält-ˌmu̅e̅l, -ˌmyül\. River, S Germany; flows E in Bavaria to join the Danube River at Kelheim; 137 mi. (220 km.) long.

Al·to, Pi·co \ˈpē-kü-ˈäl-tü\. Volcanic peak on Pico I. in the Azores; 7713 ft. (2351 m.); highest point in the Azores.

Alto Adi·ge \ˈäl-tō-ˈä-dē-ˌjā\ *or* **South Ti·rol** \tē-ˈrōl, ˈtir-ˌōl\. Former administrative district, now N part of Trentino-Alto Adige, N Italy; language rights of its German-speaking residents object of pact bet. Austria and Italy approved 1969.

Al·ton \ˈȯlt-ᵊn\. **1.** City, Madison co., SW Illinois, on Mississippi River 22 mi. (35 km.) N of East St. Louis; pop. (1990c) 32,905; shipping point; oil refineries, limestone.

2. City, ⊗ of Oregon co., S Missouri; pop. (1990c) 692.

3. Town, Hampshire, England, on the Wey River ab. 24 mi. (39 km.) NE of Southampton; pop. (1981p) 14,646.

Al·to·na \ˈäl-tə-ˌnä\. Former city, now part of Hamburg, Germany.

History: Fishing village when passed to Denmark 1640; granted customs privileges with intention of making it rival Hamburg, its neighbor; burned by Swedes 1713; despite Napoleonic Wars, prospered until 1853 when it lost privileges; occupied 1864 in name of North German Confederation; became Prussian 1866; with Hamburg joined *Zollverein* (German customs union) 1888; became part of Hamburg 1937. See HAMBURG 4.

Al·to·na \al-ˈtō-nə\. City, S Victoria, Australia, a SW suburb of Melbourne; pop. (1991c) 34,492.

Al·too·na \al-ˈtü-nə\. **1.** City, Polk co., S cen. Iowa; an ENE suburb of Des Moines; pop. (1990c) 7191.

2. City, Blair co., S cen. Pennsylvania, near source of Juniata River in bituminous-coal region 90 mi. (145 km.) E of Pittsburgh; pop. (1990c) 51,881; 5 mi. (8 km.) W is scenic Horseshoe Curve of railroad; settled 1849; incorp. as city 1868.

3. City, Eau Claire co., W Wisconsin, 5 mi. (8 km.) E of Eau Claire; pop. (1990c) 5889.

Al·to Par·a·guay \ˈäl-tō-ˌpä-rä-ˈgwī, -ˈgwā\. Department of N Paraguay. See table at PARAGUAY.

Alto Pa·ra·ná \ˈäl-tō-ˌpä-rä-ˈnä\. **1.** River. See PARANÁ 1.

2. Department of E Paraguay. See table at PARAGUAY.

Altorf. See ALTDORF.

Alto Son·go \ˈäl-tō-ˈsōŋ-gō\. Town and municipality, E Cuba, NE of Santiago.

Alt·ran·städt \ˈält-ˌrän-ˌshtet\. Village, E Germany, ab. 15 mi. (24 km.) W of Leipzig. Gave name to two treaties: (1) treaty of 1706, during Great Northern War, by which Augustus II, king of Poland and elector of Saxony, was forced by Charles XII of Sweden to renounce claim to Polish crown in favor of Stanisłas I Leszczyński; (2) treaty of 1707, in which Austrian Emperor Joseph I guaranteed to Charles XII religious toleration and freedom for Protestants in Silesia.

Al·trinc·ham \ˈȯl-triŋ-əm\. Town, Greater Manchester, NW England, 8 mi. (13 km.) SW of Manchester; pop. (1981p) 39,641.

Altsohl. See ZVOLEN.

Alt·stät·ten \ˈält-ˌshtet-ᵊn\. Commune, St. Gall canton, NE Switzerland, in fertile Rhine Valley; pop. (1980c) 9260; rebuilt after 1410 fire.

Al·tun Shan \ˌäl-ˈtün-ˈshän\ *or* **Al·tyn Tagh** *also* **Al·tin Tagh** \ˌäl-ˈtün-ˈtäg\ *or W.-G.* **A–erh–chin Shan** \ˌä-ˌər-ˈjin-ˈshän\. Mountain range, N Tibet and S Xinjiang Uygur, W China; highest peak ab. 25,000 ft. (7620 m.); branch of the Kunlun Shan.

Al·tu·ras \al-ˈtu̇r-əs\. City, ⊗ of Modoc co., NE corner of California, on Pit River 138 mi. (222 km.) NE of Chico; pop. (1990c) 3231; settled 1869; called **Dor·ris Bridge** \ˈdȯr-is\ until 1874.

Al·tus \ˈal-təs\. City, ⊗ of Jackson co., SW Oklahoma, 58 mi. (93 km.) W of Lawton; pop. (1990c) 21,910; Western Oklahoma State Coll. (1926); founded 1891.

Altyn Tagh. See ALTUN SHAN.

Al Ubayyid. See EL OBEID.

Al·u·la \ä-ˈlü-lä\. Small port on Gulf of Aden, NE Somalia, W of Ras (cape) Asir.

Al ʻU·qay·lah \ˌál-u̇-ˈkī-lə\ *also* **Al–Agheila** *or* **El Agheila** \ˌál-á-ˈgā-lə, ˌel-\. Town, on coastal road, N Libya, near SE end of the Gulf of Sidra; starting point for caravans S; scene of several battles of WWII; site of first blow of German Field Marshal Erwin Rommel's offensive against British Jan. 1942; captured by Allies Dec. 1942.

Al–ʻUqayr. See OQAIR.

Al–Uqsor. See LUXOR.

Al·va \ˈal-və\. City, ⊗ of Woods co., NW Oklahoma, 53 mi. (85 km.) WNW of Enid; pop. (1990c) 5495; business center; Northwestern Oklahoma State Univ. (1897).

Al·va·ra·do \ˌäl-vä-ˈrä-dō\. Seaside resort, Argentina. See MIRAMAR.

Alvarado, Pa·so de \ˈpä-sō-t͟hā-\. Andean mountain pass on Argentina-Chile border, bet. W Mendoza prov., Argentina and E Santiago prov., Chile; alt. 12,484 ft. (3805 m.).

Álvaro Obregón. See FRONTERA.

Al·ver·stone, Mount \ˈal-vər-ˌstōn\. Mountain, St. Elias Mts., Yukon, Canada; 14,500 ft. (4420 m.).

Al·vin \ˈal-vin\. City, Brazoria co., SE Texas, 25 mi. (40 km.) S of Houston; pop. (1990c) 19,220; Alvin Community Coll. (1949).

Älvs·borg *also* **Alfs·borg** *or* **Elfs·borg** \ˈelfs-ˌbȯrʸ, *angl.* -ˌbȯr-ē\. Province of SW Sweden. See table at SWEDEN.

Al Wajh \ál-ˈwáj\ *also* **Wejh** \ˈwej\ Port on the Red Sea, W Saudi Arabia, 260 mi. (418 km.) NW of Medina.

Al–Wak·rah \ˌál-ˈwá-krə\. Town, Qatar, S of Doha; pop. (1986c) 23,682.

Al·wand, Mount \ˈäl-ˌwänd\ *or* **Mount El·vend** \ˈel-ˌvend\ *or Pers.* **Kuh–i–Alwand** \ˈkü-hē-\; *anc.* **Oron·tes** \ō-ˈrän-ˌtēz\. Mountain, W Iran, just SW of Hamadān; 11,640 ft. (3548 m.).

Al·war *also* **Al·wur** \ˈəl-wər, -vər\. **1.** Former Indian state, now part of Rajasthan, NW India; 3158 sq. mi. (8179 sq. km.); founded by Rajput chieftain Pratap Singh in 1771; joined British against Marathas 1803.

\ə\ **abut** \ə\ matches \ᵊ\ kitten, Fr table \ər\ **further** \a\ **ash** \ā\ **ace** \ä\ **cot, cart** \á\ Fr bac \au̇\ **out** \b̲\ Span Avila \ch\ **chin** \e\ **bet** \ē\ **easy** \g\ **go** \i\ **hit** \ī\ **ice** \j\ **job** \k̲\ **Ger ich, Buch** \ⁿ\ Fr vin \ŋ\ **sing** \ō\ **go** \ȯ\ **all** \ȯ\ **law** \œ\ Fr bœuf \œ̄\ Fr feu \ȯi\ **boy** \th\ **thin** \t͟h\ **this** \ü\ **loot** \u̇\ **foot** \ue\ Ger füllen \u̅e̅\ Fr rue \y\ **yet** \ʸ\ Fr digne \ˈdēnʸ\, nuit \ˈnwʸē\ \yü\ **few** \yu̇\ **fury** \zh\ **vision**

2. City, its ✻, ab. 80 mi. (130 km.) SW of Delhi; pop. (1991p) 206,107; surrounded by wall and moat; has several palaces and temples.

Al–Zallāqah. See ZALLAKA.

Al·zette \äl-ˈzet\. River, cen. Luxembourg; flows N into Sûre River; 43 mi. (69 km.) long.

Alzira. See ALCIRA.

Ama·cu·ro \ˌä-mä-ˈkü-rō\ *also* **Ama·ku·ra** \-ˈkü-rä\. Small river, NE Venezuela, flowing NE then NW to Orinoco delta; along its middle course forms short section of Venezuela-Guyana boundary (as surveyed 1841–43 by British explorer Sir Robert Hermann Schomburgk but not accepted by Venezuela until confirmation of British claims by arbitration 1899).

Am·a·de·us, Lake \ə-ˈma-dē-əs\. Large lake, cen. Australia, in SW corner of Northern Terr., S of Macdonnell Ranges; E to W extent ab. 90 mi. (145 km.); very shallow.

Amadj·uak Lake \ə-ˈma-jü-ˌak\. Lake in S Baffin I., E Nunavut, Canada.

Am·a·dor \ˈa-mə-ˌdȯr\. County in cen. California. See table at CALIFORNIA.

Amador, Fort. American-built fort at the Pacific terminus of the Panama Canal.

Ama·do·ra \ˌá-mə-ˈdō-rə\. City, Lisbon dist., W Portugal, ab. 6 mi. (10 km.) NW of the city of Lisbon; munic. pop. (1981p) 160,410.

Ama·ga·sa·ki \ˌä-mä-gä-ˈsä-kē, -ˈgä-sä-\. City, Hyōgo prefecture, W Honshū, Japan, on NE shore of Ōsaka Bay; pop. (1992e) 497,333; a suburb of Ōsaka and an important chemical and iron and steel center in the Ōsaka-Kōbe industrial area; connected with Ōsaka by Ōsaka Port Bridge (cantilever; main span 1673 ft. or 510 m.; completed 1974).

Ama·ger \ˈä-ma-yər\. Island forming a part of Denmark, lying in Øresund off the NE cen. coast of the island of Sjælland and separated from Sjælland by the harbor of Copenhagen; 25 sq. mi. (65 sq. km.); pop. (1989e) 149,476; includes a section of the city of Copenhagen; inhabitants are largely descendants of 16th cent. Dutch colonists.

Amak·nak \ə-ˈmak-ˌnak\. Small island, Unalaska Bay, Unalaska I., E Aleutian Is.; ab. 4 mi. (6 km.) long; highest point 1640 ft. (500 m.).

Amakura. See AMACURO.

Ama·ku·sa \ä-ˈmä-kü-ˌsä\. Island group off W coast of Kyūshū, Japan, E of **Amakusa Sea** and S of Nagasaki; 342 sq. mi. (886 sq. km.); in Kumamoto prefecture; comprises two large islands and ab. 65 small islands.

Amal·fi \ä-ˈmäl-fē\. Town, Salerno prov., Campania, Italy, on N coast of Gulf of Salerno, ab. 22 mi. (35 km.) SE of Naples; pop. (1991p) 5585; built on mountain slope; resort; archiepiscopal see; cathedral of Sant'Andrea (11th cent.) with bronze doors cast at Constantinople before 1066.

History: Orig. a Byzantine settlement, became important commercial port in 9th cent. equal to Venice and Genoa; by 839 succeeded in freeing itself from Naples and Benevento; as a leading naval power, helped Pope Leo IV against Saracens mid-9th cent.; one of first Italian cities to become independent republic (under rule of doges) near beginning of 11th cent.; captured by Normans under Roger II of Sicily 1131; sacked by Pisans 1135, 1137; declined gradually until inundation of 1373 destroyed much of town and harbor. Notable particularly for the *Tabulae Amalphitanae,* its maritime code, recognized on the Mediterranean until 1570.

Amal·ner \ə-ˈməl-nər, -ˈmäl-\. Town, Gujarat, India, on tributary of Tapti River 145 mi. (233 km.) E of Surat; pop. (1991p) 76,406.

Amambaí, Serra de. See SERRA DE AMAMBAÍ.

Amam·bay \ä-ˌmäm-bä-ˈē\. Department of E Paraguay. See table at PARAGUAY.

Amambay, Cordillera de. See SERRA DE AMAMBAÍ.

Ama·mi \ä-ˈmä-mē\ *also, officially* **Oshi·ma** \ˈō-shē-mä, ō-ˈshē-\. Island group N Ryukyu Is., Japan, NE of Okinawa; 498 sq. mi. (1290 sq. km.); includes Amami-Ō-shima, or Ō-shima (largest), Tokuno-Shima, Okierabu, Kikai Shima, and others.

Amana \ə-ˈma-nə\. Village, Iowa co., Iowa, 18 mi. (29 km.) SW of Cedar Rapids; oldest of seven villages in Iowa co. collectively known as **Amana Colonies** and founded by a religious communal society under Christian Metz, originating in a German Pietist sect, which became established near Buffalo, New York 1842–54 and migrated to Iowa in 1855. Communities incorp. as Amana Society 1859.

Ama·na \ˌä-mä-ˈnä\. Peak, S French Guiana, in the Tumuc-Humac Mts.; 1950 ft. (594 m.).

Amanus. See NUR MOUNTAINS.

Aman·zim·to·ti \ä-ˌmän-zēm-ˈtō-tē\. Coastal town, Kwazulu-Natal, Rep. of South Africa.

Ama·pá \ˌá-mə-ˈpä\. **1.** State of N Brazil; ✻ Macapá; timber, nuts; fishing; formed as a territory 1943; became a state 1990. See table at BRAZIL.

2. *formerly* **Mon·te·ne·gro** \ˌmōⁿn-tē-ˈne-grü\. Municipality, Rio Grande do Sul, S Brazil, 60 mi. (96 km.) NW of Porto Alegre; pop. (1991p) 289,050.

Ama·pa·la \ˌä-mä-ˈpä-lä\. Seaport on Tigre I., Gulf of Fonseca, Honduras, ab. 70 mi. (113 km.) SSW of Tegucigalpa; only good anchorage on Pacific coast of Honduras.

ʻAma·ra, Al *also* **Amara.** See AL ʻAMĀRAH.

Ama·ran·te \ˌá-mə-ˈräⁿn-tē\. Town, Piauí state, Brazil, on Parnaíba River 240 mi. (386 km.) SSW of Parnaíba; munic. pop. (1980c) 14,545; trade center.

Ama·ra·pu·ra \ˌä-mä-ˌrä-ˈpü-rä\. Town on E bank of Irrawaddy River, Mandalay div., Myanmar; a S suburb of Mandalay. Founded 1783 as new ✻ of kingdom of Burma; destroyed by fire 1810; declined after removal of native court to Ava 1823; ✻ again 1837–60, when it was abandoned for Mandalay; suffered from earthquake 1839.

Ama·ra·va·ti \ˌə-mə-ˈrä-və-tē, ˌäm-\. Ruined city, cen. Andhra Pradesh, E India, on S bank of Krishna River ab. 60 mi. (96 km.) from its mouth; ancient Buddhist center of the Andhras; has stupa with elaborate carvings of life of Buddha.

Am·ar·go·sa \ˌa-mär-ˈgō-sə\. River, S Nevada and E California; flows into Death Valley, E California.

Amargosa Range. Mountains in SE California, E of Death Valley; highest point 6384 ft. (1946 m.).

Am·a·ril·lo \ˌa-mə-ˈri-lō\. City, Potter and Randall cos., NW Texas, ⊗ of Potter co., 65 mi. (104 km.) E of New Mexico border; pop. (1990c) 157,615; alt. 3658 ft. (1115 m.); commercial center of Texas Panhandle; supply center for oil and helium gas (helium plant); zinc smelters, grain elevators, oil refineries; Amarillo Coll. (1929).

ʻAmârna, Tell el–. See TELL EL-ʻAMÂRNA.

Ama·ro \ä-ˈmä-rō\. Peak in the Apennines, Abruzzi, SE cen. Italy; 9170 ft. (2795 m.).

Ama·roú·sion \ˌä-mä-ˈrü-sē-ˌȯn\. City, Greece, NE of Athens.

Ama·sya \ˌä-mä-ˈsyä\. **1.** Province of Turkey in Asia. See table at TURKEY.

2. *anc.* **Am·a·sia** \ˌa-mə-ˈsī-ə, -ˈsē-\. Commercial city, its ✻, 50 mi. (80 km.) SSW of Samsun; pop. (1990c) 55,602.

History: Ancient town ✻ of kingdom of Pontus (*q.v.*); site of rock-cut tombs of Pontine kings; base of King Mithradates the Great's operations against Romans first cent. B.C.; made free city by Roman Gen. Pompey 65 B.C.; one of chief cities of Greek empire of Trebizond (see TRABZON) and of the Seljuqs; withstood siege by Turkic ruler Timur; an early residence of Ottoman (Turkish) sultans; birthplace of the Greek geographer Strabo c. 64 B.C.

Am·a·tig·nak \ˌa-mə-ˈtig-ˌnak\. Small island, most southwesterly of the Andreanof Is., Aleutian Is., Alaska.

Ama·ti·que Bay \ˌä-mä-ˈtē-kā\ *or Sp.* **Bahía de Amatique** \bä-ˈē-ä-ˌthä-\. Arm of Gulf of Honduras, NE Guatemala and SE Belize.

Ama·ti·tlán \ˌä-mä-tē-ˈtlän\. **1.** Lake in mountains of SE Guatemala; ab. 8 mi. (13 km.) long and 3 mi. (5 km.) broad; a tourist resort noted for beautiful scenery.

2. Town on the lake, ab. 12 mi. (19 km.) SW of Guatemala City; munic. pop. (1981p) 32,784; coffee and sugar plantations.

Amatongaland. See TONGALAND.

Amay \á-ˈmā\. Commune, Liège prov., Belgium, on the Meuse ab. 12 mi. (19 km.) SW of the city of Liège; pop. (1991c) 12,786.

Am·a·zon \ˈa-mə-ˌzän, -zən\ *or Port.* **Rio Ama·zo·nas** \ˈrē-ü-ˌȧ-mə-ˈzō-nəs\ *or Span.* **Río de las Amazonas** \ˈrē-ō-t͟hā-läs-ˌä-mä-ˈzō-näs\; *orig.* **Orel·la·na** \ˌō-rā-ˈyä-nä\. Largest river in the world by volume (exceeded in length by the Nile River), South America; flows N in the Peruvian Andes, then E through N Brazil to Atlantic Ocean; length of Amazon incl. Marañón, which rises ab. 100 mi. (160 km.) from Pacific Ocean and is usu. considered the Amazon proper, 4000 mi. (6436 km.); length incl. Ucayali and its headstream, the Apurímac, 3915 mi. (6299 km.); its basin ab. 2,053,318 sq. mi. or 5,318,094 sq. km. (incl. Tocantins, ab. 2,722,000 sq. mi. or 7,049,980 sq. km.) extends through 25° of latitude from source of Rio Branco near Mt. Roraima (5°N) to source of a headstream of the Madeira in S Bolivia (ab. 20°S); formed in Peru by union of its two headstreams, the Marañón and Ucayali, just above Iquitos; in Brazil called Solimões from Peruvian border to mouth of Negro.

Chief tributaries: On N receives the Napo from N Ecuador and Peru and the Içá (Putumayo), Japurá, Negro, Trombetas, Paru, and Jari in Brazil; on S the Huallaga in N Peru, Javarí forming part of boundary bet. Peru and Brazil, Jutaí, Juruá, Purus, Maderia, Tapojós, Xingu, and Tocantins (strictly not a tributary). At its mouth has two branches around island of Marajó (*q.v.*); N branch (at the Equator) has Caviana and many smaller islands in it; S and E branch, known as Pará, receives Tocantins; has tidal phenomenon, known as bore, reaching far upstream and at times 16 ft. (5 m.) in height; discharge at its mouth averages 7,000,000 cu. ft. (198,000 cu. m.) per second; volume of river so great that its discharge can be detected 200 mi. (320 km.) out in ocean; navigable for ocean vessels 2300 mi. (3701 km.) up to Iquitos; its most important port Manaus, at mouth of Negro, 1000 mi. (1609 km.) from mouth; its high water floods occur in June causing width to vary from 5 to 400 mi. (8 to 644 km.); has extremely low gradient, alt. 35 ft. (11 m.) at 2000 mi. (3218 km.) from the sea. In S Venezuela confluence of Negro and Casiquiare unites Amazon and Orinoco systems.

History: Discovered by Spanish adventurer Vicente Yáñez Pinzón 1500; first descended (from Andes) by Spanish soldier and explorer Francisco de Orellana 1541 and ascended by Portuguese soldier Pedro Teixeira 1637–39; except for occasional ascents in search of slaves, little explored until mid-19th cent.; steam navigation authorized by Emperor Pedro II of Brazil 1850, and a company, formed 1852, began to operate vessels 1853; opened to world shipping by decree 1866; valley of Amazon and its tributaries center of crude-rubber industry which reached height in 1910–11 but declined by 1915 after shift of market to East Indies rubber; explored by scientific expeditions of Theodore Roosevelt and Brazilian Col. Cândido Rondon 1913–14, Hamilton Rice 1910–24, American Geographical Society, and others; perpetual free navigation of Amazon guaranteed by treaty bet. Colombia and Brazil (ratified by Colombia 1929).

Ama·zo·nas \ˌȧ-mə-ˈzō-nəs\. **1.** State of NW Brazil; ✻ Manaus; rubber, jute, timber; made a province 1852, a state 1889. See table at BRAZIL.

2. Department of SE Colombia. See table at COLOMBIA.

3. Territory of S Venezuela. See table at VENEZUELA.

Am·a·zo·nia \ˌa-mə-ˈzō-nē-ə\. The regions about the Amazon River in South America, incl. the greater part of Brazil and parts of bordering countries, esp. Colombia, Ecuador, Peru, and Bolivia; so called because Francisco de Orellana and other early Spanish explorers thought they saw female warriors on its banks.

Ama·zô·nia National Park \ˌȧ-mə-ˈzō-nyə\. National park, Amazonia, cen. N Brazil, along the Tapajós River; diverse flora and fauna; estab. 1974.

Ambacia. See AMBOISE.

Am·ba·la \əm-ˈbä-lə\. City, in Haryana, N India, 115 mi. (185 km.) NNW of Delhi; pop. (1991p) 119,535; cotton, flour, food products; trades in grain and sugar.

Am·ba·to \äm-ˈbä-tō\. City, ✻ of Tungurahua prov., cen. Ecuador, ab. 70 mi. (113 km.) S of Quito and near N base of Mt. Chimborazo; pop. (1990c) 124,166; alt. 8435 ft. (2571 m.); known as "garden city" of Ecuador; raises much fruit; tanneries; food products, textiles.

Am·ber \ˈəm-bər, ˈäm-\. Ruined city, ancient ✻ of Jaipur state, now in E Rajasthan, NW India, 5 mi. (8 km.) N of Jaipur, picturesquely situated at mouth of a mountain gorge by lake; made famous by Rajput structures incl. the old palace (begun 1600) and the Diwan-i-ʻAm, richly decorated with sculpture; seized by Rajputs 1037; supplanted by Jaipur 1728.

Amber, Cape \ˈam-bər\ *or Fr.* **Cap d'Am·bre** \kȧp-dä^{n}br^ə\. N point of Madagascar, 11°57′S, 49°17′E.

Am·berg \ˈäm-ˌberk\. City, Bavaria, Germany, 35 mi. (56 km.) E of Nürnberg; pop. (1980c) 44,264; formerly ✻ of Upper Palatinate; enamels, glass, earthenware; blast furnaces, breweries; iron mined in the vicinity. Scene of defeat of French 1796 by Archduke Charles (of Austria) during War of the First Coalition (1792–97).

Am·ber·gris Cay \ˈam-bər-ˌgris-ˈkē, -ˌgrēs-, -ˈkā\. Island, Belize, in Caribbean Sea, off NE coast; encloses S part of Chetumal Bay.

Ambergris Cays. Group of islets (cays) in Caicos Is., West Indies.

Am·ber·ley \ˈam-bər-lē\. Village, Hamilton co., SW Ohio, ENE of Cincinnati; pop. (1990c) 3108.

Ambianum. See AMIENS.

Am·bler \ˈam-blər\. Borough, Montgomery co., SE Pennsylvania, N of Philadelphia; pop. (1990c) 6609.

Am·blève \ä^n-ˈblev\. River, E Belgium; flows NW into Ourthe River a few miles S of Liège; ab. 53 mi. (85 km.) long; Stavelot is on it.

Am·bo·di·fo·to·tra \ˌȧm-ˌbō-dē-fō-ˈtō-trȧ\. Town, Nosy Boraha, off NE coast of Madagascar.

Am·boi·na \am-ˈbȯi-nə\. **1.** Island, Indonesia. See AMBON 1.

2. District, Indonesia. See CENTRAL MALUKU.

3. Town, Indonesia. See AMBON 3.

Am·boise \ä^n-ˈbwäz\ *or Lat.* **Am·ba·cia** \am-ˈbā-shə, -shē-ə\. Commune, Indre-et-Loire dept., NW cen. France, on left bank of Loire River 15 mi. (24 km.) E of Tours; notable particularly for its castle.

History: Lordship under counts of Anjou in 11th cent., united to royal domain by Charles VII 1431; castle, rebuilt and beautified by Charles VIII and successors, became a residence of French kings and later a state prison, Arab leader Abdelkader having been confined there 1848–52; said to be burial place of Italian painter Leonardo da Vinci; gave name to conspiracy of Amboise 1560, an unsuccessful plot of Huguenots to remove Francis II from influence of Guise family, and to Edict of Amboise 1563, a pacification, concluded by Queen Catherine de Médicis with Huguenots, which guaranteed liberty of worship to Protestant nobility and gentry; castle, confiscated in French Revolution, finally restored to house of Orléans 1872.

Amboland. See OVAMBOLAND.

Am·bon \äm-ˈbȯn, ˈam-ˌbän\ *also* **Am·boi·na** *or* **Am·boy·na** \am-ˈbȯi-nə\. **1.** Island of the Moluccas, Indonesia, Malay Archipelago, off SW coast of Ceram I.; 31 mi. (50 km.) long by 10 mi. (16 km.) wide; 314 sq. mi. (813 sq. km.); formed by two long strips of land connected by narrow isthmus; has high peaks that are active volcanoes (highest Salhutu 3360 ft. or 1024 m.); main products tropical fruits and spices.

2. District, Indonesia. See CENTRAL MALUKU.

3. Seaport, its chief town and ✻ of Maluku prov., on harbor (**Ambon Bay**); by air 1150 mi. (1850 km.) ENE of Surabaya and 425 mi. (684 km.) SE of Manado; pop. (1990c) 276,955; university (1962).

History (town and island): Portuguese settled 1521; source of Portuguese clove monopoly until Portuguese were ousted by Dutch East India Company 1605; settlement made on the island by English traders 1615; scene of incident known as "Massacre of Amboina" 1623 when Dutch killed English on pretext of latter's treachery (until 1654, a bitter issue of Anglo-Dutch relations); entire island claimed by Dutch when they took over suzerainty of Moluccas (1683); captured by British 1796, 1810, but finally restored to Dutch 1814; a separate residency until united with Ternate to form Government of the Moluccas 1927; in 1930 census a division of Moluccas residency; under Japanese control 1942–45; inhabitants proclaimed short-lived republic 1950; movement subsequently suppressed.

Am·bo·ró National Park \ˌäm-bō-ˈrō\. National park, cen. Bolivia; contains wildlife incl. some endangered species.

Am·bos Ca·ma·ri·nes \ˈäm-ˌbōs-ˌkä-mä-ˈrē-nes\. Former province, Philippines, now divided into the provs. Camarines Norte and Camarines Sur.

Am·bo·si·tra \ˌȧm-bü-ˈsē-trə\. Inland town, S cen. Madagascar, S of Antsirabe; road junction.

Amboyna. See AMBON.

Ambracia. City, Greece. See ARTA 3.

Ambracian Gulf. See AMVRAKIKÓS KÓLPOS.

Ambre, Cap d'. See AMBER, CAPE.

Am·bridge \ˈam-brij\. Borough, Beaver co., W Pennsylvania, on Ohio River 17 mi. (27 km.) WNW of Pittsburgh; pop. (1990c) 8133; built on site of German communal settlement called Economy (estab. 1825).

Am·brim *or* **Am·brym** \ˈam-ˌbrim, -ˌbrēm\. Island, NE part of Vanuatu, SW Pacific Ocean, E of Malekula I.; 24 mi. (39 km.) long by 16 mi. (26 km.) wide; pop. (1991e) 7189; has active volcano that has erupted several times during 20th cent.

Am·briz \ä^{n}m-ˈbrēsh\. Seaport, NW Angola, 75 mi. (121 km.) N of Luanda.

Am·brose Channel \ˈam-ˌbrōz\. Channel forming entrance to New York harbor SSE of the Narrows; 7.5 mi. (12 km.) long, 40 ft. (12 m.) deep, and from 1850 to 2000 ft. (564 to 610 m.) wide; dredged 1899–1913. **Ambrose Channel Lightship,** marking its entrance, is ab. 9 mi. (14 km.) E of Sandy Hook.

Ambrym. See AMBRIM.

Am·bur \əm-ˈbür\. Town, Tamil Nadu, S India, ab. 107 mi. (172 km.) WSW of Madras on Palar River; pop. (1991p) 75,728; commands pass into the Carnatic; scene of battle 1749.

Am·bu·ra·yan \ˌäm-bü-ˈrä-ˌyän\. **1.** River, Luzon, Philippines; rises in the Cordillera Central, flows W then NW through S Ilocos Sur to South China Sea near Tagudin; ab. 60 mi. (96 km.) long.

2. Region, NW Luzon; former Spanish military district (*comandancia*); became a subprovince of Mountain Prov., joined with Lepanto to form Lepanto-Amburayan subprovince, and was later divided bet. Ilocos Sur, La Union, and Mountain Prov.

Am·chit·ka \am-ˈchit-kə\. Island in the Aleutian Is., at E end of Rat Is. group 69 mi. (111 km.) SE of Kiska; ab. 15 mi. (24 km.) long and 5 mi. (8 km.) wide; 121 sq. mi. (313 sq. km.); occupied 1942 by U.S. task force and air base set up for operations against Japanese on Kiska and Attu Jan.–May 1943.

Ame·ca \ä-ˈmā-kä\. **1.** River, W cen. Mexico; flows W into Banderas Bay; ab. 140 mi. (225 km.) long.

2. Town, Jalisco state, W cen. Mexico, on Ameca River 45 mi. (72 km.) W of Guadalajara; munic. pop. (1990p) 54,438.

Ame·ca·me·ca \ä-ˌmā-kä-ˈmā-kä\ *or in full* **Amecameca de Juá·rez** \thä-ˈkwä-rās\. Town, México state, cen. Mexico, 36 mi. (58 km.) SE of Mexico City; alt. 7600 ft. (2316 m.). Important center of pre-Spanish civilization; has shrine Sacro Monte, hill built over a cave where one of earliest Christian missionaries in Mexico lived, which is visited by thousands of pilgrims during Holy Week. Starting point for ascents of Popocatépetl and Iztaccíhuatl.

Ame·land \ˈä-mə-ˌlänt\. Island, Friesland prov., Netherlands, in North Sea, belongs to West Frisian Is.; ab. 13 mi. (21 km.) long and 2 mi. (3.2 km.) wide.

Ame·lia \ə-ˈmēl-yə\. County in SE cen. Virginia. See table at VIRGINIA.

Amelia \ə-ˈmāl-yə\; *anc.* **Ame·ria** \ə-ˈmir-ē-ə\. Commune, Terni prov., Umbria, cen. Italy, 12 mi. (19 km.) W of the commune of Terni; pop. (1981p) 10,977.

Amelia Courthouse \ə-ˈmēl-yə\. Village, ⊗ of Amelia co., SE cen. Virginia.

Amelia Island. Island, Nassau co., NE Florida, in Atlantic Ocean; ab. 15 mi. (24 km.) long and 4 mi. (6 km.) wide; 24 sq. mi. (62 sq. km.); chief city Fernandina Beach.

History: Part of Spanish, later of American, Florida; resort of smugglers during U.S. embargo on trade with Europe 1807; scene of incident known as "Amelia Island Affair" in which U.S. sent naval expedition to remove forces of Luis Aury, a South American adventurer, who had set up a government on the island and invited Florida to throw off Spanish rule 1817; captured by U.S. Union forces from Confederates during Civil War 1862.

Ameria. See AMELIA.

Amer·i·ca \ə-ˈmer-ə-kə\ *or Span. or Port.* **Amé·ri·ca** \ä-ˈmā-rē-kä\. A name derived from *Americus* Vespucius, Latinized form of name of Amerigo Vespucci (1451–1512), Italian navigator, and first used in a popular account of his travels in the New World published 1507 by the German geographer Martin Waldseemüller. Orig. (as applied by Waldseemüller), the lands discovered by Christopher Columbus, *i.e.* South America and the West Indies; later (as used 1538 by Flemish cartographer Gerardus Mercator), the New World, *i.e.* the lands of the Western Hemisphere. In current use: either continent of the Western Hemisphere (North America or South America); often, specifically, the United States of America (*q.v.*); also, although in this application the plural form **the Americas** is the usual one, all the lands of the Western Hemisphere incl. North America, South America, and the West Indies.

History: Orig. inhabited by Native American peoples believed to have migrated from Asia during the late Pleistocene epoch; earliest European discovery of any part of the Americas was of NE coast of North America by the Norse (Leif Ericsson 1000, Thorfinn Karlsefni 1004–06); general European knowledge of the Americas dates from the voyages of Columbus, whose first landfall was at San Salvador (island in the Bahamas) Oct. 12, 1492, and who later (voyages of 1495, 1498, 1502) touched coasts of Central and South America; in Europe until 16th and 17th cents. known as *the Indies, West Indies,* or *New World;* separation of North America from Asia established by voyage of Portuguese navigator Ferdinand Magellan 1519–21. For more detailed information, see NORTH AMERICA, SOUTH AMERICA, CENTRAL AMERICA, and WEST INDIES.

America Islands. Name sometimes applied to a group of islands in N part of the Line Is. (*q.v.*), 5°50′N to 2°N, incl. Palmyra, Teraina (Washington), Tabuaeran (Fanning), and Kiritimati (Christmas Islands) (*qq.v.*).

Amer·i·can \ə-ˈmer-ə-kən\. River, N cen. California; formed by three forks, flows SW into Sacramento River at Sacramento; ab. 30 mi. (48 km.) long.

Ame·ri·ca·na \ȧ-ˌmir-ē-ˈkä-nə\. City, E cen. São Paulo state, Brazil; pop. (1991p) 153,592; settled by people from the U.S. Confederate states after losing the Civil War.

American Falls. 1. Falls, Niagara River. See NIAGARA FALLS 1.

2. City, ⊗ of Power co., SE Idaho; pop. (1990c) 3757; shipping point.

American Falls Reservoir. Reservoir, SE Idaho, formed in Snake River 1927 by **American Falls Dam.**

American Fork. City, Utah co., N cen. Utah, on Utah Lake 14 mi. (22.5 km.) NNW of Provo; pop. (1990c) 15,696.

American Samoa *also* **Eastern Samoa.** Group of islands of Samoa (*q.v.*), SW cen. Pacific Ocean, E of 171°W and ab. 14°S; 76 sq. mi. (197 sq. km.); pop. (1992e) 49,600; ✻ Pago Pago; includes islands of Tutuila, Manua Is. (Tau, Olosega, Ofu), Aunuu, Rose, and Swains; chief economic activities: government, fishing. See WESTERN SAMOA.

History: Ruled by native chiefs until ab. 1860; object of American interest since expedition of Commodore Charles Wilkes 1839; visited by Commander Richard W. Meade, U.S.N., 1872; Pago Pago naval station rights and trading and extraterritorial rights granted to U.S. 1878; under joint administration of U.S., Germany, and England 1889–99 and by treaty of 1899 granted to U.S.; Swains I. annexed 1925. Administered by U.S. Dept. of the Navy before 1951 and by U.S. Dept. of the Interior since then. Constitution, setting up a local legislature, adopted Apr. 1960; Constitution revised 1967; first elected governor 1978.

American Samoa National Park. See UNITED STATES, *National Parks.*

American Virgin Islands. See VIRGIN ISLANDS.

Amer·i·cus \ə-ˈmer-i-kəs\. City, ⊗ of Sumter co., SW cen. Georgia; pop. (1990c) 16,512; Georgia Southwestern Coll. (1906).

Ame·rong·en \ˈä-mə-ˌròŋ-ən\. Commune, Utrecht prov., cen. Netherlands, near the Lower Rhine 23 mi. (37 km.) SE of the city of Utrecht; pop. (1981e) 6527; its castle of Count William Bentinck was first refuge of Kaiser William II of Germany 1918.

Amers·foort \ˈä-mərs-ˌfōrt\. Commune, Utrecht prov., cen. Netherlands, 12 mi. (19 km.) NE of the city of Utrecht; pop. (1992e) 104,390; railroad junction; has 13th cent. church, Jansenist college, and 312-foot (95-meter) Gothic tower built c. 1450.

Amery Ice Shelf \ˈā-mə-rē\. Area of shelf ice bet. Lars Christensen Coast and Ingrid Christensen Coast, Antarctica, S of Indian Ocean, extending inland ab. 250 mi. (400 km.).

Ames \ˈāmz\. City, Story co., cen. Iowa, 28 mi. (45 km.) N of Des Moines; pop. (1990c) 47,198; Iowa State Univ. (1858); incorp. 1870.

Ames·bury \ˈāmz-ˌber-ē, -bə-rē\. **1.** Town, Essex co., NE Massachusetts, on Merrimack River 24 mi. (39 km.) NE of Lowell; pop. (1990c) 14,997.

2. *formerly* **Almes·bury** \ˈāmz-bə-rē\. Town, Wiltshire, England, 8 mi. (13 km.) N of Salisbury on Avon River; market and fair; known particularly for Stonehenge (1.5 mi. or 2.4 km. W), principal surviving megalithic structure in British Isles (see AVEBURY). Scene of a witenagemot (Anglo-Saxon advisory council to the king) 932; site of nunnery built ab. 980.

Amestratus. See MISTRETTA.

Am·ga \əm-ˈgä\. River, SE Sakha Rep., Russia in Asia; rises in Aldan Mts. and flows NE to Aldan River ab. 175 mi. (282 km.) E of the town of Yakutsk; ab. 800 mi. (1290 km.) long.

Am·gun \əm-ˈgünʸ, -ˈgün-yə\. River, Khabarovsk Kray, E Russia in Asia; rises in mountains NW of Khabarovsk and flows NE to the Amur near its mouth above Nikolayevsk-na-Amure; 490 mi. (788 km.) long.

Am·hara \am-ˈhar-ə, äm-ˈhär-ə\. Former kingdom, NW Ethiopia; 76,235 sq. mi. (197,449 sq. km.); ✻ Gonder; a province (1936–41) of Italian East Africa; gave name (*Amharic*) to official and court language of Ethiopia.

Am·herst \ˈa-mərst, ˈam-ˌhərst\. **1.** County in cen. Virginia. See table at VIRGINIA.

2. Town, Hampshire co., W Massachusetts, 19 mi. (30.5 km.) N of Springfield; pop. (1990c) 35,228; Amherst Coll. (1821), Univ. of Massachusetts–Amherst (1863), Hampshire Coll. (1965).

3. Town, Hillsborough co., S New Hampshire, 11 mi. (18 km.) SW of Manchester; pop. (1990c) 9068; settled 1733.

4. Town, Erie co., W New York, NE of Buffalo; pop. (1990c) 111,711; Daemen Coll. (1947).

5. Village, Lorain co., N Ohio, 27 mi. (43 km.) WSW of Cleveland; pop. (1990c) 10,332.

6. Town, ⊗ of Amherst co., cen. Virginia; pop. (1990c) 1060.

7. Seaport, Myanmar. See KYAIKKAMI.

8. Town, ⊗ of Cumberland co., N Nova Scotia, Canada, 5 mi. (8 km.) E of NE end of Chignecto Bay; pop. (1991c) 9742. A thriving Acadian village was located here prior to being refounded as English town 1760 and named after Jeffrey, Lord Amherst. The inland gateway to Nova Scotia; noted as geographical center of Maritime Provinces; ruins of Forts Lawrence and Beauséjour nearby.

Am·herst·burg \ˈa-mərst-ˌbərg\. Town, Essex co., SE Ontario, Canada, on Detroit River in fertile agricultural section 14 mi. (22.5 km.) S of Windsor; pop. (1991c) 8921. Founded 1796 on site of old French settlement, visited by French explorer Sieur de La Salle 1679; contains Fort Malden National Historical Park.

Amherst Island. **1.** Island at NE end of Lake Ontario, Ontario, Canada, SW of Kingston.

2. Chief island of the Magdalen Is. in the Gulf of St. Lawrence, Quebec, E Canada.

Amherst Mountain. Peak, La Plata co., SW Colorado; 13,100 ft. (3993 m.).

Amida. See DİYARBAKIR 2.

Am·i·don \ˈa-mi-ˌdän\. Village, ⊗ of Slope co., SW North Dakota; pop. (1990c) 24.

Amiens \ȧm-ˈyeⁿ\; *anc.* **Sam·a·ro·bri·va** \ˌsa-mə-rō-ˈbrī-və\; *later* **Am·bi·a·num** \ˌam-bē-ˈā-nəm\. City, ✻ of Somme dept., N France, on Somme River 72 mi. (116 km.) N of Paris; pop. (1990c) 136,234; rail junction; a major center of the French textile industry (since 16th cent.), machinery, tires; trades in agricultural products; university (1965); site of world-famous cathedral of Notre Dame, largest church in France and one of leading representatives of Gothic architecture in Europe.

History: Was ✻ (as Samarobriva) of the Ambiani; became Roman stronghold; chief city of medieval county **Amié·nois** \ˌam-(ˌ)yān-ˈwä\, which became crown land 1185; passed to Burgundy by Peace of Arras 1435, but returned to France at death of Duke Charles the Bold 1477; captured by Spanish 1597 and recovered by Henry IV; ✻ of Picardy to 1790; scene of signing 1802 of Peace of Amiens bet. France and Britain; captured by Prussians 1870; held by Germans for a short time in 1914; gave name to WWI battle (Aug. 1918) which was part of successful Allied counteroffensive against Germany. In WWII occupied by Germans May 1940–Aug. 1944. Thought to be the birthplace of Peter the Hermit, who preached the First Crusade 1095.

Amindivi Islands. See LACCADIVE ISLANDS.

Am·i·rante Islands \ˈa-mi-ˌrant\ *or* **Am·i·rantes** \-ˌrants\. Island group in Indian Ocean E of Tanzania 6°00′S, 53°10′E; pop. (1987c) 113; administratively a dependency of Seychelles Is.

Amisia. See EMS 1.

Amisus. See SAMSUN 2.

Amite \ə-ˈmēt\. County in SW Mississippi. See table at MISSISSIPPI.

Amite City \ā-ˈmēt\. Town, ⊗ of Tangipahoa parish, SE Louisiana, 45 mi. (72 km.) ENE of Baton Rouge; pop. (1990c) 4236.

Am·i·ter·num \ˌa-mi-ˈtər-nəm\. Ancient town, Italy, ab. 58 mi. (93 km.) NE of Rome, 5 mi. (8 km.) N of modern L'Aquila in valley of Aterno River; birthplace c. 86 B.C. of historian and politician Sallust; ruins of imperial Roman structures; Christian catacombs in vicinity.

Am·i·ty·ville \ˈa-mə-tē-ˌvil\. Village, Suffolk co., SE New York, on dividing line bet. Nassau and Suffolk cos., on Great South Bay on Long Island 32 mi. (51 km.) E of New York City; pop. (1990c) 9286; residential suburb and formerly a seaside summer resort.

Am·lia \ˈam-lē-ə\. Island at E end of Andreanof Is., Aleutian Is., SW Alaska; 169 sq. mi. (438 sq. km.).

Am·man \a-ˈmän, -ˈman\ *bib.* **Rab·bah Am·mon** \ˈra-bə-ˈa-mən\ *or* **Rab·bath Ammon** \ˈra-bəth\; *anc.* **Phil·a·del·phia** \ˌfi-lə-ˈdel-fyə, -fē-ə\. Town, ✻ of Jordan, 25 mi. (40 km.) NE of the Dead Sea; munic. area pop. (1990e) 1,213,300; administrative, financial, and commercial center; university (1962).

History: Chief city of the Ammonites; besieged and captured by Hebrew soldier Joab and King David (2 *Sam.* xi–xii); improved by Egyptian King Ptolemy II Philadelphus (285–246 B.C.) and named Philadelphia after him; was most southerly of 10 cities of the Decapolis; attained greatest prosperity under Eastern Roman (Byzantine) Empire; made

✻ 1921 of Transjordan (now Jordan); parts of city damaged in Jordanian civil war 1970.

Am·man·ford \ˈa-mən-fərd\. Town, Carmarthenshire, S Wales, 17 mi. (27 km.) ESE of Carmarthen; pop. (1981p) 5711; coal deposits.

Ammassalik. See ANGMAGSSALIK.

Ammer Lake \ˈä-mər\ *or Ger.* **Am·mer·see** \ˈä-mər-ˌzā\. Lake, Bavaria, Germany, 21 mi. (34 km.) WSW of Munich; 10 mi. (16 km.) long; 18 sq. mi. (47 sq. km.); in glacial region characterized by irregular moraine.

Ammin. See ANMYŎN.

Ammoedara. See HAÏDRA.

Ammonium. See SIWA.

Am·mo·noo·suc \ˌa-mə-ˈnü-sək, -sik\. River, Coos and Grafton cos., New Hampshire; flows W and SW from White Mts. to Connecticut River; ab. 100 mi. (160 km.) long.

Amne Machin Mountains. See A'NYÊMAQÊN SHAN.

Amne Machin Shan. See MAQÊN GANGRI.

Amnok. See YALU.

Amo. See BLACK 9.

Āmol *also* **Amul** \ˈō-mōl\. City, Māzanderān prov., N Iran, 23 mi. (37 km.) W of Bābol; pop. (1986c) 118,242.

Amor·gos \ə-ˈmȯr-gəs\ *or Gk.* **Amor·gós** \ˌä-mör-ˈgōs\. Island of the Cyclades, S Aegean Sea, 18 mi. (29 km.) SE of Naxos; 47 sq. mi. (122 sq. km.); part of Cyclades dept., Greece.

Amo·ry \ˈā-mə-rē\. City, Monroe co., NE Mississippi, 22 mi. (35 km.) SSE of Tupelo; pop. (1990c) 7093; shipping point.

Amos \ˈā-məs\. Town, ⊗ of Abitibi co., SW Quebec, Canada, on Harricanaw River NE of Rouyn-Noranda; pop. (1991c) 13,783.

Amour Mountains \ä-ˈmu̇r\. Range of the Atlas Mts., N Algeria; highest point ab. 5800 ft. (1768 m.).

Amoy See XIAMEN.

Am·pa·to \äm-ˈpä-tō\. Peak, S Peru; 20,702 ft. (6310 m.).

Am·per \ˈäm-pər\. River, Bavaria, Germany; rises in Tirol near Oberammergau and flows through Ammer Lake into Isar River 2 mi. (3.2 km.) N of Moosburg; 104 mi. (167 km.) long.

Am·phip·o·lis \am-ˈfi-pə-ləs\. Ancient city, E Macedonia, on Struma River ab. 3 mi. (5 km.) above its mouth; colonized by Athens 437 B.C.; in 424 captured by Spartans during Peloponnesian War; became independent after Peace of Nicias 421; captured by King Philip II of Macedon 358 B.C. setting off 10-year war with Athens; headquarters of Roman governor of Macedonia.

Am·phis·sa \am-ˈfi-sə\ *or* **Sa·lo·nae** \sə-ˈlō-nē\. Town, Phocis dept., Greece, at foot of W slope of Mt. Parnassus, 85 mi. (137 km.) NNW of Athens; chief town of ancient Western Locris (see LOCRIS).

Am·qui \äⁿ-ˈkē\. Town, on Gaspé Penin., SE Quebec, Canada, on Matapédia River 25 mi. (40 km.) S of Matane; pop. (1991c) 4339.

ʻAm·rān \am-ˈrän\. Town, W cen. Yemen, 38 mi. (61 km.) NW of Sanʻa.

Am·ra·va·ti \ˌəm-ˈrä-və-tē, äm-\; *formerly* **Am·rao·ti** \-ˈrau̇-tē\. Town, NE Maharashtra state, cen. India, on branch of Purna River 85 mi. (137 km.) WSW of Nagpur; pop. (1991c) 421,576; important cotton center. Has a fine stupa dating from 2d cent. A.D., whose rich relief decorations are preserved in British Museum (London) and in Madras.

Am·re·li \əm-ˈrā-lē\. Town, SW Gujarat, 135 mi. (217 km.) SW of Baroda; pop. (1991p) 67,740.

ʻAm·rit \am-ˈrēt\; *anc.* **Mar·a·thus** \ˈmar-ə-thəs\. Town on coast, SW Latakia, Syria, 45 mi. (72 km.) S of the seaport of Latakia and opp. Arwad I.

Am·rit·sar \ˌəm-ˈrit-sər, äm-\. City, in Punjab, N India; pop. (1991p) 709,456; tanning; textiles.

History: Founded by Sikh leader Rām Dās 1577 on site granted by Mogul Emperor Akbar; site of Golden Temple, center of worship of Sikhs; part of Sikh confederacy under Ranjit Singh (d. 1839); as part of Punjab (*q.v.*), annexed by British 1849; scene of incident known as Amritsar Massacre Apr. 13, 1919 when British, under Gen. Reginald E. H. Dyer, fired on and killed about 400 and wounded many others in a riot caused by Rowlatt Acts (antisedition laws); scene of violent confrontation 1984 bet. the Indian army and Sikh extremists.

Am·ro·ha \əm-ˈrō-hə\. Town, Uttar Pradesh, India, 78 mi. (126 km.) E of Delhi; pop. (1991p) 136,893; site of tomb of Muslim saint, Sheikh Saddu, the object of pilgrimages.

Am·rum \ˈäm-ˌru̇m\. Island, Germany, in North Frisian Is., SW of Föhr; 8 sq. mi. (21 sq. km.).

Am·stel·veen \ˈäm-stəl-ˌvān\. Commune, North Holland prov., Netherlands; pop. (1992e) 71,939; suburb of Amsterdam.

Am·ster·dam \ˈäm-stər-ˌdäm, ˈam-stər-ˌdam\. **1.** City, Montgomery co., E New York, on New York State Barge Canal and Mohawk River 28 mi. (45 km.) NW of Albany; pop. (1990c) 20,714. Settled 1783, named Veedersburg; renamed Amsterdam 1804; incorp. as city 1885.

2. City, ✻ of the Netherlands, North Holland prov., on S side of IJ (or Y) River, connected with North Sea by ship canal; pop. (1992e) 713,407; a major port; chemicals, foodstuffs, textiles; diamond cutting, metalworking; engineering; Univ. of Amsterdam (1632), Free Reformed Univ. (1880); Royal Palace (1648–55); Rembrandt House.

History: Orig. a fishing hamlet, developed by Giesebrecht II and III of Amstel, who built a castle nearby and dammed up the sea (early 13th cent.); received charter as town 1300; joined Hanseatic League 1369; grew steadily in 14th and 15th cents. as evidenced by extent of its walls erected in 1482; received an influx of wealthy merchants from Brabant, and a stream of Portuguese Jews, esp. after decline of Antwerp 1585; with vastly increased population and wealth, became source of the growing Dutch commercial and naval power in 17th cent.; center of Dutch East India and West India Companies (founded in 1602 and 1621) and of Bank of Amsterdam (1609); became leading financial and trade metropolis of Europe, esp. after closure of the Schelde by Treaty of Westphalia (1648) had sealed the fate of its rival Antwerp; opened its dikes against French King Louis XIV 1672; attracted French Huguenots after revocation 1685 of the Edict of Nantes; after a partial commercial decline in 18th cent., increased its prosperity when connected with North Sea by a canal 1875; ✻ of the Batavian Republic erected by French Emperor Napoléon, later of the kingdom of Holland; became part of French First Empire 1810; as part of Holland, entered kingdom of the Netherlands 1815; site of Summer Olympic Games 1928; under German occupation 1940–45; Amsterdam-Rhine Canal officially opened 1952.

3. *or* **New Amsterdam.** Volcanic island, S Indian Ocean, 37°52′S, 77°32′E, near St. Paul I.; 18 sq. mi. (47 sq. km.); part of French Southern and Antarctic Territories.

Amsterdam Ship Canal. See NORTH SEA CANAL.

Am·stet·ten \äm-ˈshtet-ᵊn\. Town, N cen. Austria, NE of Steyr; pop. (1991c) 21,972.

Amu Dar'·ya \ˌä-ˌmü-ˈdär-yə, ə-ˈmü-dər-ˈyä\; *anc.* **Ox·us** \ˈäk-səs\ *or Arab.* **Jay·hun** \jī-ˈhün\; *in Tajikistan* **Dar·"yoi Amu** \ˈdär-ˌyō-ˈä-ˌmü\; *in Uzbekistan* **Amu·dar·yo** \ˈä-ˌmü-ˈdär-ˌyō\; *in Turkmenistan* **Amy·der·ya** \ˈä-mē-ˈder-yä\. River, cen. and W Asia, from Pamirs plateau to the Aral Sea; rises in lakes and mountains of high Pamirs in two headstreams: Vakhsh and Pandj; flows NW down Hindu Kush slope, forming boundary bet. Tajikistan and NE Afghanistan, then generally W and NW through E Turkmenistan and W of Uzbekistan into marshes on S shore of Aral Sea in Karakalpak Autonomous Rep., where it forms delta 100 mi. (161 km.) long; total length ab. 1578 mi. (2539 km.); area of basin ab. 180,000 sq. mi. (466,200 sq. km.); chief tributaries on N are Vakhsh, Kafirnigan, and Surkhab, on S Kundūz; in middle course a source of wide irrigation systems (Karakumskiy Kanal system); navigable for ab. 900 mi. (1450 km.); in lower course flows through great expanse of sandy desert. In mid-19th cent., part of course came to be recognized as boundary bet. Afghanistan and Russia. For its history as site of campaigns by Macedonian King Alexander the Great, see SOGDIANA and BACTRIA.

Amuk·ta \ä-'mu̇k-tə\. Volcanic island in Aleutian Is., W of the Islands of the Four Mountains; separated by **Amukta Pass** from Seguam I. on W; 36 sq. mi. (93 sq. km.).

Amul. See ĀMOL.

Amund Ring·nes Island \'ä-mən-'riŋ-,nās\. One of the Sverdrup Is. (*q.v.*), SW of Axel Heiberg I.; 2515 sq. mi. (6514 sq. km.).

Amund·sen Bay \'ä-mən-sən, 'a-\; *formerly* **Ice Bay.** Inlet of Indian Ocean, Antarctica, bet. Enderby Land on E and Queen Maud Land on W, ab. 66°55′S and 50°E; ab. 30 mi. (48 km.) wide.

Amundsen Gulf. Body of water, a SE extension of Beaufort Sea, bet. the NW coast of mainland Northwest Territories, Canada, the S coast of Banks I., and the W coast of Victoria I.; ab. 250 mi. (400 km.) long.

Amundsen Sea. Arm of South Pacific Ocean off Marie Byrd Land, Antarctica, bet. Thurston I. on E and Cape Dart on W; 72°S and bet. 123°W and 98°W; explored 1928–29.

Amur \ä-'mu̇r\ *or Chin.* **Hei·long** \'hā-'lȯŋ\ *or W.-G.* **Hei–lung** \-'lu̇ŋ\. River, NE Asia; formed by junction of Shilka and Argun rivers (*qq.v.*) at ab. 53°20′N, 121°28′E; forms boundary bet. N Manchuria and two subdivisions of Russia (Chita Oblast and Khabarovsk Kray); flows E, SE, and NE to N end of Tatar Strait bet. mainland and Sakhalin I.; below Khabarovsk wholly in Russian territory; length with Argun and Kerulen ab. 2705 mi. (4352 km.), from junction ab. 1786 mi. (2874 km.); est. area of basin 770,000 sq. mi. (1,994,300 sq. km.); below junction receives N tributaries Zeya and Bureya, and on S Kumara, Songhua, and Ussuri; chief cities on it: Blagoveshchensk, Khabarovsk, Komsomolsk-na-Amure, and Nikolayevsk-na-Amure (near mouth); navigable for ab. 2000 mi. (3220 km.) up to Sretensk on the Shilka.

History: Peoples S of the Amur (including Chinese) in contact with peoples N of the Amur (including Russians) from 17th cent.; Russia compelled by China to withdraw from valley in Treaty of Nerchinsk (*q.v.*) 1689; settled by Russians from 1847; by treaty signed at Aihun (see AIGUN) 1858, left bank of Amur yielded by China to Russia, and Ussuri region by Treaty of Peking 1860; occupied by Russians and developed economically, esp. after building of Trans-Siberian R.R.; Blagoveshchensk (*q.v.*) became chief cultural and commercial center; after Japanese occupation of Manchuria, scene of Soviet-Japanese clashes 1937; also scene of Sino-Soviet border clashes during the late 1960s. See also JEWISH AUTONOMOUS OBLAST.

Amur Bay; *Russ.* **Amur·skiy Za·liv** *also* **Amur·ski Zaliv** \ə-'mu̇r-skē-zə-'lyēf\. NW arm of Peter the Great Bay, SE Russia in Asia; ab. 42 mi. (68 km.) long; Vladivostok is on inlet of its E shore.

Amur Oblast \'ȯ-bləst, -,blast\. Administrative subdivision, SE Russia in Asia; 140,425 sq. mi. (363,701 sq. km.); pop. (1992e) 1,075,000; ✱ Blagoveshchensk; grain, timber; formed 1932 from Khabarovsk Kray; region incorp. into Russia 1858.

Amurskiy Zaliv *also* **Amurski Zaliv.** See AMUR BAY.

Am·vra·ki·kós Kól·pos \äm-,vrä-kē-'kös-'köl-,pös\ *or* **Am·bra·cian Gulf** \am-'brā-shən\ *or* **Gulf of Ar·ta** \'är-tä\. Inlet of Ionian Sea, S Epirus, on W coast of Greece; 25 mi. (40 km.) long and from 4 to 10 mi. (6 to 16 km.) wide; on its shores are ruins of several cities important in ancient Greece; battle of Actium (*q.v.*) fought near its entrance 31 B.C.

Amy·clae \ə-'mī-(,)klē\. Ancient town, Laconia, SE Peloponneses, S Greece, ab. 3 mi. (5 km.) S of Sparta; chief city of Laconia under the Achaeans and before rise of Dorian Sparta; ultimately conquered by Sparta.

Amyderya. See AMU DAR'YA.

'Ana \'ä-nə\. Town, W Iraq, on W bank of Euphrates ab. 75 mi. (121 km.) NW of Hit; pop. (1985e) 6197. An old town, dating from before 1000 B.C.; in medieval period controlled transport on the river and was starting point for caravan routes across the desert to Syrian cities.

Anaa Island \,ä-'nä\ *or* **Chain Island** \'chān\. Atoll in the Tuamotu Archipelago, French Polynesia, S Pacific Ocean; 17°25′S, 145°30′W; 10 sq. mi. (26 sq. km.); pop. (1988c) 648; has 11 islets around a lagoon; called Chain I. by Capt. James Cook, who visited it 1769.

An·a·capa Islands \,a-nə-'ka-pə\. Small group of islands in cen. Channel Island group, Pacific Ocean; part of Ventura co., SW California; part of group included in Channel Islands National Park (see UNITED STATES, *National Parks*).

Anacapa Pass. Strait SW California; off NW Los Angeles co., bet. Anacapa Is. and Santa Cruz I.

Ana·co \ä-'nä-kō\. Town, Anzoátegui state, N Venezuela, ab. 50 mi. (80 km.) SSE of Puerto La Cruz.

An·a·con·da \,a-nə-'kän-də\. City, ⊗ of Deer Lodge co., SW Montana, 23 mi. (37 km.) WNW of Butte; county pop. (1990c) 10,278. City started growing with the building of a copper-smelting plant in 1884 by Anaconda Copper Mining Company of Butte, later expanded to contain one of the largest nonferrous production plants in world; the city's government was consolidated with that of Deer Lodge co. 1977.

Anaconda Mountain. Peak in Glacier National Park, NW Montana; 8300 ft. (2530 m.).

An·a·cor·tes \,a-nə-'kȯr-təs\. City, Skagit co., NW Washington, on island in Puget Sound 19 mi. (30.5 km.) S of Bellingham; pop. (1990c) 11,451; commercial fisheries, oil refineries; incorp. 1889.

An·a·cos·tia \,a-nə-'kȯs-tē-ə, -'käs-\. **1.** River in the District of Columbia; flows into Potomac River immediately S of the city of Washington; 12 mi. (19 km.) long.

2. A neighborhood of S Washington, D.C., on left bank of Anacostia River.

An·a·dar·ko \,a-nə-'där-(,)kō\. City, ⊗ of Caddo co., W cen. Oklahoma, on Washita River 65 mi. (104 km.) SW of Oklahoma City; pop. (1990c) 6586; trading center; founded 1901.

Anadir Range. See CHUKOTSHOYE NAGOR'YE.

Anadolu. See ANATOLIA.

Ana·dyr \ə-,nə-'dir\. **1.** River, Chukchi Autonomous Okrug, NE Russia in Asia; rises in mountains S of Chukotshoye Nagor'ye and flows S and E to Gulf of Anadyr; 694 mi. (1117 km.) long; area of drainage basin 57,915 sq. mi. (150,000 sq. km.).

2. Town, ✱ of Chukchi Autonomous Okrug, NE Russia in Asia.

Anadyr, Gulf of *or* **Gulf of Anadir.** Inlet of N Bering Sea, S of Chukchi Penin., Chukchi Autonomous Okrug, NE Russia in Asia.

Anadyr Range *or* **Anadyrskiy Khrebet.** See CHUKOTSKOYE NAGOR'YE.

Ana·far·ta Bay \ä-,nä-fär-,tä\ *also* **Su·vla Bay** \sü-'vlä\. Small bay, W coast of Gallipoli Penin., Turkey in Europe; landing of Anzacs and battle Aug. 1915.

Anafarta Heights. Group of hills, W Gallipoli Penin., Turkey in Europe, ab. 4 mi. (6 km.) E of Anafarta Bay; highest 882 ft. (269 m.); scene of British attacks 1915 during battle of Suvla Bay.

Aná·fi *also* **An·a·phe** \ä-'nä-fē\. Island, SE Cyclades, S Aegean Sea, 85 mi. (137 km.) N of Crete; 7 mi. (11 km.) long by 2 mi. (3.2 km.) wide; has no harbor.

Ana·gni \ä-'nän-yē\; *anc.* **Anag·nia** \ə-'nag-nē-ə\. Commune, Frosinone prov., Lazio, cen. Italy, 12 mi. (19 km.) NW of the commune of Frosinone; pop. (1991p) 19,304; episcopal see since 487; sulfur deposits and springs. Principal town of the Hernici; conquered by Rome 306 B.C.; besieged by Saracens 877 A.D.; scene of the imprisonment of Pope Boniface VIII by the French 1303.

An·a·heim \'a-nə-,hīm\. City, Orange co., SW California, E of Long Beach; pop. (1990c) 266,406; site of Disneyland amusement park. Founded 1857 on communal basis by 50 German families.

Ana·ho Bay \ä-'nä-hō\. Bay, N coast of Nuku Hiva I., Marquesas Is., S Pacific Ocean.

An·a·huac \ˈa-nə-ˌwak\. City, ⊗ of Chambers co., Texas, 35 mi. (56 km.) NE of Galveston on NE shore of Galveston Bay; pop. (1990c) 1993; formerly a Mexican military post, attacked 1832 by American settlers in Texas in effort to release William B. Travis and others, thus furnishing issue preliminary to Texan War of Independence.

Aná·huac \ä-ˈnä-ˌwäk\. Valley, S cen. Mexico, in Mexican Plateau; site of Mexico City.

Analostan Island. See THEODORE ROOSEVELT ISLAND.

Anam. See ANNAM.

Ana Ma·ría, Gulf of \ˈä-nä-mä-ˈrē-ä\. Gulf in SW coast of Camagüey prov., E cen. Cuba.

Anam·bas Islands \ä-ˈnäm-bäs\. Group of islands of Indonesia, 200 mi. (322 km.) NE of Singapore in the South China Sea, bet. SE Malay Penin. and W Borneo; 260 sq. mi. (673 sq. km.); administratively a part of Riau prov., Sumatra; chief islands Djemadja and Siantan.

Anam·bra \ä-ˈnäm-brä\. State of S Nigeria. See table at NIGERIA.

An·a·mo·sa \ˌa-nə-ˈmō-sə\. City, ⊗ of Jones co., E Iowa, 23 mi. (37 km.) ENE of Cedar Rapids; pop. (1990c) 5100.

Ana·mur, Cape \ˌä-nä-ˈmür\ *or Turk.* **Anamur Bur·nu** \bür-ˈnü\. Cape on S coast of Turkey in Asia, projecting into Mediterranean Sea opp. Cape Kormakiti on N coast of island of Cyprus.

Anan·ta·pur \ə-ˈnən-tə-ˌpu̇r\. Town, Andhra Pradesh, S India; pop. (1991p) 174,792.

Ana·pa \ə-ˈnä-pə\. Seaport town, W Krasnodar Kray, S Russia in Europe; pop. (1991e) 55,900. Turkish fortress founded to maintain Turkish relations with Caucasus region 1781; twice captured and restored by Russia, finally remained Russian by terms of Treaty of Adrianople 1829.

An·a·phe. See ANÁFI.

An·á·po·lis \ä-ˈnä-pü-lēs\. City, Goiás state, cen. Brazil, at end of railroad line N from São Paulo; munic. pop. (1980c) 179,973; grains, coffee, livestock.

Anapurna. See ANNAPURNA.

Anas. See GUADIANA.

Añas·co \ä-ˈnyäs-kō\. Town and municipality, W Puerto Rico, 6 mi. (10 km.) N of Mayagüez.

Añasco, Grande. See GRANDE AÑASCO.

Anasquam. See ANNISQUAM.

An·as·ta·sia Island \ˌa-nə-ˌstā-zhə, -zhē-ə\. Island, NE Florida, off coast of St. Johns co., S of St. Augustine, bet. Matanzas River (*q.v.*) and the Atlantic; ab. 14 mi. (22.5 km.) long and 3 mi. (5 km.) wide; 13 sq. mi. (34 sq. km.).

Ana·ta·han \ˈä-nä-tä-ˈhän\. Small island, cen. Northern Mariana Is., 80 mi. (129 km.) N of Saipan, 16°22′N, 145°40′E; highest point 2585 ft. (788 m.).

An·a·to·lia \ˌa-nə-ˈtō-lē-ə, -lyə\ *or Turk.* **Ana·do·lu** \ˌä-nä-dō-ˈlü\. The part of Turkey in Asia equivalent to the peninsula of Asia Minor (*q.v.*) up to indefinite line on E from Gulf of İskenderun to Black Sea, comprising ab. three fifths of Turkey's provinces.

Ana·yac·si \ˌä-nä-ˈyäk-sē\. Peak, Oruro dept., W Bolivia; 18,380 ft. (5602 m.).

An·cas·ter \ˈan-ˌkas-tər\. Town, SE Ontario, Canada, W of Hamilton; pop. (1991c) 21,988.

An–ch'ing. See ANQING.

An·chor·age \ˈaŋ-kə-rij\. Seaport city, S Alaska, at head of Cook Inlet near base of Kenai Penin.; comprises an administrative division of Alaska; pop. (1990c) 226,338; connected by railroad with Fairbanks 470 mi. (756 km.) to N and with Seward 114 mi. (183 km.) to S; salmon canneries; state's most important port and supply center for its oil industry; Univ. of Alaska, Anchorage (1954); Alaska Pacific Univ. (1957); founded as construction camp for railroad; now important army post and airport; headquarters of Alaska Defense Command during WWII; severely damaged in 1964 earthquake; grew rapidly in 1970s. See table at ALASKA.

An·co·hu·ma \ˌäŋ-kō-ˈü-mä\. The higher peak of Mt. Sorata, Bolivia; 20,958 ft. (6388 m.). See ILLAMPU.

An·con \ˈaŋ-kən\ *or Span.* **An·cón** \äŋ-ˈkōn\. Town, Panama, NW suburb of Panama City; administrative area pop. (1990p) 11,327; site of Gorgas Hospital.

An·cón \äŋ-ˈkōn\. **1.** Town, S coast of Santa Elena Penin., Ecuador; ab. 60 mi. (96 km.) SSW of Guayaquil; oil fields. **2.** Town and oceanside resort, cen. Peru, 22 mi. (35 km.) N of Lima; as a port, superseded by Callao; has Inca remains.

History: Scene of treaty which terminated War of Pacific (1879–83) bet. Chile and Peru Oct. 1883 (for treaty bet. Bolivia and Chile see VALPARAÍSO 2) and by which Peru ceded Tarapacá and Chile was to remain in occupation of Tacna and Arica (*qq.v.*) for 10 years until plebiscite should determine final ownership. Failure to carry out plebiscite provision caused Tacna-Arica dispute.

An·co·na \äŋ-ˈkō-nä\. **1.** Province of Marche, Italy. See table at ITALY.

2. Seaport, its ✻ and ✻ of Marche, cen. Italy, on Adriatic coast ab. 125 mi. (200 km.) ESE of Florence; pop. (1991p) 101,179; pharmaceuticals; shipbuilding; transportation center. Ancient mole designed by Roman Emperor Trajan topped by triumphal arch by Greek architect Apollodorus (erected 115 A.D.); modern mole by Pope Clement II has lighthouse and triumphal arch by Luigi Vanvitelli.

History: Founded by Greek refugees from Siracusa c. 390 B.C.; after improvement of harbor by Emperor Trajan who departed from it on second expedition to Moesia and Dacia 105 A.D., became important seaport and naval station; one of the Pentapolis (*q.v.*) under exarchate of Ravenna; chief town of **March of Ancona** (in extent about equivalent to modern Marche region), attached to Holy Roman Empire 1138–1254; later a municipal republic under papal protection until taken by Federigo Gonzaga, duke of Mantua, for Clement VII 1532; captured by Italian troops soon after Castelfidardo (*q.v.*) victory over papal forces 1860; bombed by Austrian fleet 1915. In WWII captured by Polish forces 1944.

An·cre \ˈäⁿkrᵊ\. **1.** River, Somme dept., France; from NE flows into Somme River near Corbie ab. 9 mi. (14 km.) E of Amiens; 25 mi. (40 km.) long; scene of several battles 1916–18, esp. of successful Allied advance against Germans Nov. 1916, in which tanks were first used.

2. Commune, France. See ALBERT.

An·cud \äŋ-ˈküth\ *or in full* **San Car·los de Ancud** \ˌsän-ˈkär-lōs-ˌthā-\. Seaport, Los Lagos region, S cen. Chile, on N Chiloé I. 60 mi. (96 km.) SW of Puerto Montt; formerly ✻ of Chiloé prov.; pop. (1990e) 33,434.

Ancud, Gulf of. Inlet of Pacific Ocean on S cen. coast of Chile, E of N Chiloé I.

Ancyra. See ANKARA 2.

Ån·dals·nes \ˈȯn-dȧls-ˌnās\. Village and railhead port, Møre og Romsdal co., W Norway, at head of Romsdalsfjord, in mountain-resort region ab. 55 mi. (88 km.) E of Ålesund; occupied for a very short time by Allied forces Apr. 1940; forced by Germans to evacuate May 1940.

An·da·lu·sia \ˌan-də-ˈlü-zhə\. **1.** City, ⊗ of Covington co., S Alabama, 65 mi. (104 km.) W of Dothan; pop. (1990c) 9269; Lurleen B. Wallace State Junior Coll. (1969).

2. *or Span.* **An·da·lu·cía** \ˌän-thä-lü-ˈthē-ä\. Region, S Spain; comprises an autonomous community consisting of the modern provs. of Almería, Granada, Jaén, Málaga, Cádiz, Córdoba, Huelva, and Sevilla; traversed by mountain ranges, among them the Sierra Morena (forming the N boundary) and the Sierra Nevada, and incl. the Mulhacén (11,407 ft. or 3477 m.) and Picacho de Veleta (11,125 ft. or 3391 m.) peaks; watered by the Guadalquivir and its principal affluents, the Guadalimar, Guadiato, and Genil rivers; wide range of difference in climate, vegetation, and people; divided into **Upper Andalusia,** valley of upper Guadalquivir, and **Lower Andalusia,** valley of lower Guadalquivir; celebrated for its fertility (often called the "granary" of Spain) and for its picturesque beauty; mountainous regions abound in mineral wealth, esp. copper and coal; agricultural products include wine, sugarcane, fruit, cotton, and grapes. See table at SPAIN.

History: As kingdom of Tartessus (the biblical Tarshish, *q.v.*), served as outlet for Spanish minerals and tin from the N in latter half of 2d millennium B.C.; colony of Gadir (see CÁDIZ 2) estab. by Phoenicians c. 1100 B.C.; settled by Carthaginians who destroyed the Tartessian kingdom 480 B.C.; under Romans its W part comprised most of prov. of

Baetica; invaded by Vandals and Visigoths 5th cent. A.D.; subjugated by Moors 711–1492; under Muslim Umayyad dynasty of Spain (756–1031), resident at Córdoba (*q.v.*), became intellectual and political center of the peninsula; Lower Andalusia reconquered by Christians 1212; Upper Andalusia, the ancient Moorish kingdom of Granada, reconquered by King Ferdinand and Queen Isabella 1492; declined with subjugation of Moors; restored to some importance through discovery of New World and consequent commercial rise of Seville and Cádiz; remained a Spanish province until divided 1833 into eight modern provinces.

An·da·man and Nic·o·bar Islands \ˈan-də-mən, -ˌman … ˌni-kō-ˈbär, ˈni-kō-ˌbär\ *also* **Andamans and Nicobars.** Union territory of India, comprising two groups of islands in the Bay of Bengal, ab. 400 mi. (644 km.) directly W of coastal Myanmar; ✻ Port Blair; copra, timber, rubber, fruit, rice. United for administrative purposes 1872. See ANDAMAN ISLANDS, NICOBAR ISLANDS, and table at INDIA.

Andaman Islands *also* **Andamans.** North group of islands in E part of Bay of Bengal; 2461 sq. mi. (6374 sq. km.); part of territory of Andaman and Nicobar Is., India. Chief islands North Andaman, Middle Andaman, and South Andaman, close together in a group (known as Great Andaman) and separated from Little Andaman on the S by Duncan Passage; separated from SW Myanmar by Preparis Channels and from the Nicobars by Ten Degree Channel.

History: British first settled 1789; settlement transferred to Port Cornwallis 1791 but abandoned 1796; Port Blair estab. as Indian penal settlement by Government of India 1858; scene of murder of Viceroy Richard Southwell Bourke, earl of Mayo 1872; joined to Nicobar group to form administrative division of Andaman and Nicobar Is. (*q.v.*); under Japanese control 1942–45; became part of India 1947.

Andaman Sea. That part of the Bay of Bengal E of the Andaman and Nicobar Is.; bounded on N and E by coast of Myanmar, on E and SE by Malay Penin., and on S by Strait of Malacca and Sumatra; 218,000 sq. mi. (564,620 sq. km.).

An·da·va·ka, Cape \ˌän-dä-ˈvä-kä, -vä-ˈkä\. Cape on SE coast of Madagascar extending into Indian Ocean S of Fort-Dauphin.

An·de·an Community \ˈan-dē-ən, an-ˈdē-\ *or* **Andean Group** *or* **Andean Pact.** Economic organization, consisting of Bolivia, Colombia, Ecuador, Peru, Venezuela, and formerly Chile; has proposed adoption of a common external tariff and establishment of other common market institutions; formed 1969; Chile withdrew 1976.

Andelys, Les. See LES ANDELYS.

Andematunnum. See LANGRES.

An·denne \äⁿ-ˈden\. Commune, Namur prov., Belgium, on right bank of Meuse River, ab. 22 mi. (35 km.) SW of Liége; pop. (1991c) 23,075; in region abounding in lead, iron, zinc, coal, marble, and clay. Grew up around abbey founded by St. Bregga; taken and burned by inhabitants of Liége ab. 1159.

An·der·lecht \ˈän-dər-ˌlekt\. Commune, WSW suburb of Brussels, Brabant prov., Belgium, on Senne River; pop. (1991c) 87,884; 15th cent. Gothic church.

An·der·lues \ˌäⁿ-der-ˈlue̅, ˌän-dər-ˈlü\. Commune, Hainaut prov., Belgium, ab. 30 mi. (48 km.) S of Brussels; pop. (1991c) 11,421; coal deposits.

An·der·matt \ˈän-dər-ˌmät\ *also* **Ur·se·ren** \ˈu̇r-zə-rən\ *or Ital.* **Or·se·ra** \ōr-ˈsā-rä\. Commune, Uri canton, cen. Switzerland, 17 mi. (27 km.) S of Altdorf; on route over St. Gotthard Pass; pop. (1980c) 1375; tourist resort, particularly for winter sports; church (1695).

An·der·nach \ˈän-dər-ˌnäk\; *anc.* **An·tun·na·cum** \ˌan-tə-ˈnā-kəm\. City, Rhineland-Palatinate, Germany, on the left bank of the Rhine 10 mi. (16 km.) NW of Koblenz; has 12th cent. watchtower, 13th cent. late-Romanesque parish church.

History: Founded as a castle by Roman Gen. Drusus Senior 12 B.C.; scene of defeat 876 of Holy Roman Emperor Charles the Bald by Louis III, son of Louis the German; member of Hanseatic League 1253; burned by the French 1689; to France 1795; ceded to Prussia 1815. In WWII taken by Allies Mar. 1945.

An·der·son \ˈan-dər-sən\. **1.** Name of counties in five states of the U.S. See tables at KANSAS, KENTUCKY, SOUTH CAROLINA, TENNESSEE, TEXAS.

2. City, Shasta co., N California, 10 mi. (16 km.) S of Redding; pop. (1990c) 8299.

3. City, ⊗ of Madison co., cen. Indiana; pop. (1990c) 59,459; prehistoric Indian mounds. Anderson Univ. (1917); founded 1823; incorp. as town 1838, as city 1865.

4. City, ⊗ of Anderson co., NW South Carolina, 28 mi. (45 km.) SSW of Greenville; pop. (1990c) 26,184; commercial and shipping center; Anderson Coll. (1911); site of branch of Confederate treasury 1864–65.

5. Town, ⊗ of Grimes co., E cen. Texas.

6. River, NW mainland portion of Northwest Territories, Canada; rises in lakes N of Great Bear Lake and flows W and N into Beaufort Sea; 430 mi. (692 km.) long.

Anderson, Mount. Mountain, Antarctica, 78°09′S, 86°13′W; 13,957 ft. (4254 m.).

Anderson Ranch Dam. See UNITED STATES, *Dams and Reservoirs.*

An·der·son·ville \ˈan-dər-sən-ˌvil\. Village, Sumter co., Georgia, ab. 55 mi. (88 km.) SW of Macon; pop. (1990c) 277; large national cemetery; site of large Confederate military prison 1864–65, where conditions were so bad that many Union soldiers died.

Andes. See VIRGILIO.

An·des \ˈan-dēz\; *Span.* **Los Andes** \ˌlōs-ˈän-ˌdās\ *or less correctly* **Cor·dil·le·ra de los Andes** \ˌkōr-t͟hē-ˈyä-rä-t͟hā-, -t͟hēl-\. Great mountain system of South America; extends entire length along W coast from Tierra del Fuego to Panama, 4500 mi. (7240 km.); has many volcanoes; source of Cauca, Magdalena, Orinoco, Amazon (Marañón and Ucayali), Pilcomayo, and all large rivers of Argentina except Paraná; in places, esp. N Argentina, Bolivia, Peru, and Colombia, spreads out over high plateaus in several parallel ranges (cordilleras).

Divisions: (1) Range in Tierra del Fuego runs E and W along S shore (highest ab. 7600 ft. or 2316 m.). (2) Range from S point of Chile runs due N bet. Chile and Patagonia, Argentina, (**Cordillera de Agos·ti·ni** \t͟hā-ˌä-gō-ˈstē-nē\) with many lakes and peaks bet. 6000 and 12,000 ft. (1830 and 3660 m.). (3) Range from ab. 42°S lat. N to Bolivia, bet. Chile and Argentina, contains highest peaks of system (many bet. 17,000 and 23,000 ft. or 5180 and 7010 m.); entirely in Chile: Pular 20,423 ft. (6225 m.) and Pili 19,849 ft. (6050 m.); entirely in Argentina: Aconcagua 22,834 ft. or 6960 m. (highest in system), Mercedario 22,211 ft. (6770 m.), Bonete 22,546 ft. (6872 m.), Nevada 20,023 ft. (6103 m.); on boundary line bet. Chile and Argentina: Ojos del Salado 22,539 ft. (6870 m.), Tupungato 22,310 ft. (6800 m.), Incahuasi 21,720 ft. (6620 m.), Tres Cruces 20,853 ft. (6356 m.); many beautiful lakes (resorts) at S end on both sides bet. 39° and 42°S (incl. Nahuel Huapí, Llanquihue, Ranco, Todos los Santos); passes (*pasos*) at intervals, esp. Uspallata or La Cumbre bet. Mendoza, Argentina, and Santiago, Chile (with the scenic Puente del Inca and the Transandine R.R., tunnel nearly 2 mi. (3.2 km.) long at highest point 10,469 ft. or 3191 m.); in N (ab. 23° to 28°S) is Puna de Atacama, desolate plateau region with av. height of 11,000 to 13,000 ft. (3350 to 3960 m.), flanked on W in Chile by **Cordillera Do·mey·ko** \dō-ˈmā-kō\. (4) Cen. part in Bolivia covers nearly two fifths of country in elevated plateau (altiplano) 10,000 to 12,000 ft. (3050 to 3660 m.) and encloses Lakes Poopó and Titicaca (part in Peru); main range is **Cordillera Re·al** \rā-ˈäl\ with highest peaks Ancohuma 20,958 ft. (6388 m.), Illimani 21,201 ft. (6462 m.), Illampu 20,867 ft. (6360 m.). (5) From Bolivian Andes direction turns NW extending full length of Peru in many ranges covering territory from 200 to 300 mi.

(320 to 480 km.) wide; includes **Cordillera Orien·tal** \ˌō-rē-ˌān-ˈtäl\ (in SE Peru), **Cordillera Oc·ci·den·tal** \ˌȯk-sē-ˌt͟hān-ˈtäl\ (along the coast), **Cordillera de Ca·ra·ba·ya** \t͟hā-ˌkä-rä-bī-ä\ (extension of Cordillera Real in SE Peru), **Cordillera Huay·huash** \ˈwī-ˌwäsh\ (cen. Peru, N of Lima, watershed bet. Marañón and Pacific streams); highest peaks: Coropuna 21,079 ft. (6425 m.), Huascarán 22,205 ft. (6768 m.), Solimana 20,068 ft. (6117 m.), Salcantay 20,574 ft. (6271 m.). (6) In Ecuador, system (**Cordillera Real**) narrows and runs nearly due N; highest peaks: Chimborazo 20,561 ft. (6267 m.), Cotopaxi 19,347 ft. (5897 m.), Cayambe 18,996 ft. (5790 m.), Antisana 18,228 ft. (5556 m.). (7) In Colombia, system spreads out into three great ranges: **Cordillera Occidental** near coast; **Cordillera Cen·tral** \sān-ˈträl\ bet. valleys of Cauca and Magdalena rivers; **Cordillera Oriental** in interior (extending as **Cordillera Mé·ri·da** \ˈmā-rē-t͟hā\ into W Venezuela); highest peaks: Tolima 18,425 ft. (5616 m.), Nevado del Huila 18,865 ft. (5750 m.), Puracé 15,604 ft. (4756 m.); connecting range in E Panama and NW Colombia, Serranía del Darién.

Andes, Lake \ˈan-dēz\. Lake, Charles Mix co., S South Dakota.

Andes, Los. See LOS ANDES.

An·de·vo·ran·to \ˌän-dē-vō-ˈrän-tō, -rän-ˈtō\. Coastal town, E cen. Madagascar; ab. 100 mi. (160 km.) E of Antananarivo.

An·dhra Pra·desh \ˌän-drə-prə-ˈdāsh, -ˈdesh\. State, SE India, bordering on Bay of Bengal; ✻ Hyderabad; rice; textiles, chemicals; shipbuilding; largest cities: Hyderabad, Vishakhapatnam, Vijayawada. Formed 1953 from part of Madras state; enlarged 1956 by addition of part of abolished Hyderabad state. See table at INDIA.

Andíparos. See ANTIPAROS.

Andípaxoi. See ANTIPAXOS.

An·di·zhan \ˌan-di-ˈzhan, ˌən-dyi-ˈzhän\ *or* **An·di·jon** \ˌan-di-ˈjōn\ *also* **An·di·jan** \ˌan-di-ˈjan, ˌən-dyi-ˈjän\. **1.** Administrative subdivision, E Uzbekistan; 1660 sq. mi. (4299 sq. km.); pop. (1991e) 1,795,100; ✻ Andizhan; oil and natural gas deposits; before 1991 comprised an oblast of the U.S.S.R.

2. City, ✻ of Andizhan subdivision, Uzbekistan, 155 mi. (249 km.) ESE of Tashkent on upper Syr Dar'ya; pop. (1991e) 298,300.

And·khüi \ənd-ˈkü-ē\. Town, N Afghanistan, ab. 100 mi. (160 km.) W of Balkh near Turkmenistan border; chief town of former khanate.

An·dor·ra \an-ˈdȯr-ə\ *or in full* **Principality of Andorra.** Independent principality on S slope of E Pyrenees, bet. Ariège dept., France, and Lérida prov., Spain; 180 sq. mi. (482 sq. km.); pop. (1992e) 57,100; ✻ Andorra la Vella; consists of gorges, narrow valleys, and many high peaks; contains seven parishes and has good highway connections with both France and Spain; has excellent pastureland (cattle and sheep raising); tobacco; tourism. Language spoken is Catalan. Of Carolingian origin; placed under joint suzerainty of French counts of Foix and Spanish bishops of La Seu d'Urgell 1278; French rights passed to ruler, Henry IV, 1589, and ultimately to president of France; with adoption of constitution 1993 became an independent parliamentary democracy.

Andorra la Vel·la \-lä-ˈvel-yä\ *also* **Andorra.** Town, ✻ of Andorra; pop. (1990e) 20,437.

An·do·ver \ˈan-ˌdō-vər\. **1.** Town, Essex co., NE Massachusetts, 9 mi. (14 km.) E of Lowell; pop. (1990c) 29,151; site of Phillips Academy (preparatory school estab. 1778, oldest incorporated school in U.S.).

2. City, Anoka co., E Minnesota, 15 mi. (24 km.) N of Minneapolis; pop. (1990c) 15,216.

3. Parish, ⊗ of Victoria co., New Brunswick, Canada; pop. (1991c) 1094.

4. Town, Hampshire, S England, on the Anton 22 mi. (35 km.) N of Southampton; pop. (1981p) 31,006.

And·ø·ya \ˈä-nœ-yə\. Northernmost island of the Vesterålen, Norway, in the Norwegian Sea, off NW coast; 188 sq. mi. (487 sq. km.); hilly and marshy; has coal beds; fishing.

An·dre·a·nof Islands \ˌan-drē-ˈa-nȯf, ˌän-drā-ˈä-nəf\. One of main groups of Aleutian Is., Alaska, extending from 172°W (Seguam I.) to 179°E (Amchitka I. in Rat Is.); chief islands: Atka, Tanaga, Adak, Kanaga. Several military bases developed, esp. on Adak I. during WWII.

An·dre·as, Cape \än-ˈthrā-äs\. Cape at end of long narrow peninsula of NE Cyprus, 35°40′N, 34°35′E.

An·drew \ˈan-ˌdrü\. County in NW Missouri. See table at MISSOURI.

Andrew Jackson, Mount. See JACKSON, MOUNT 4.

An·drews \ˈan-ˌdrüz\. **1.** County in NW Texas. See table at TEXAS.

2. Town, Cherokee co., W tip of North Carolina, 78 mi. (126 km.) WSW of Asheville; pop. (1990c) 2551.

3. Town, Georgetown and Williamsburg cos., E South Carolina, 17 mi. (27 km.) W of Georgetown; pop. (1990c) 3050.

4. City, ⊗ of Andrews co., NW Texas; pop. (1990c) 10,678.

An·dria \ˈän-drē-ä\. Commune, Bari prov., Puglia, SE Italy, 31 mi. (50 km.) WNW of the seaport of Bari; pop. (1989c) 89,762; old Gothic cathedral; trades in olives, grain, and almonds. Founded by Peter, first Norman count of Andria, 1046; favorite residence of Holy Roman Emperor Frederick II, who built Castel del Monte (9 mi. or 14 km. S).

Andropov. See RYBINSK.

An·dros \ˈan-drəs\. Chief island of a W group of Bahamas; 1600 sq. mi. (4144 sq. km.); largest island of Bahamas; with other islands constitutes an electoral district (2300 sq. mi. or 5957 sq. km.).

Án·dros \ˈän-ˌthrös, ˈan-drəs\. **1.** Island, part of Cyclades dept., Greece, S Aegean Sea; separated from SE Euboea by narrow strait; ab. 25 mi. (40 km.) long; 147 sq. mi. (381 sq. km.). Populated chiefly by Ionian Greeks; in mid-7th cent. B.C. sent colonies to Chalcidice; revolted from Athens ab. 411 B.C.; important as naval post, conquered by Macedonian, Ptolemaic, and Pergamene rulers; annexed to Rome as part of Pergamum 133 B.C.; became part of Greece 1829.

2. Town, its ✻, on E coast.

An·dros·cog·gin \ˌan-drə-ˈskä-gin\. **1.** River, NE New Hampshire and SW Maine; rises in Umbagog Lake on Maine-New Hampshire boundary, flows S in New Hampshire, turns E across Maine border and SE into Kennebec River near Bath, S Maine; ab. 157 mi. (253 km.) long.

2. County in SW Maine. See table at MAINE.

An·dru·so·vo \ən-ˈdrü-sə-və\. Locale, W Russia in Europe, a few miles S of Smolensk. Scene of treaty 1667 terminating war bet. Poland and Russia (1654–67) and by which Smolensk and E Ukraine, incl. Kiev, were ceded to Russia.

An·dú·jar \än-ˈdü-ˌkär\; *anc.* **Il·li·tur·gis** \ˌi-lə-ˈtər-jəs\. Commune, Jaén prov., S Spain, on right bank of Guadalquivir 24 mi. (39 km.) NW of the commune of Jaén; pop. (1991c) 36,661; known esp. for its mineral springs and for the production of pottery.

Anécho. See ANÉHO.

Ane·cón Gran·de \ˌä-nä-ˈkōn-ˈgrän-dā\. Peak, SW Río Negro prov., S cen. Argentina; 6593 ft. (2010 m.).

An·e·ga·da \ˌa-nə-ˈgä-də\. Island, British Virgin Is., West Indies; ab. 10 mi. (16 km.) long.

Anegada Bay \ˌä-nā-ˈgä-thä\. Inlet of Atlantic Ocean on SE coast of Buenos Aires prov., E Argentina, S of Bahía Blanca.

Anegada Passage \ˌa-nə-ˈgä-də\. Channel in the British Virgin Is., West Indies, E of Anegada I. and Virgin Gorda I.; ab. 40 mi. (64 km.) wide.

Ané·ho \ä-ˈnā-hō\ *or* **Ané·cho** \-chō\. Town, S Togo, W Africa, near border with Benin and 30 mi. (48 km.) E of Lomé.

Anei·tyum \ä-ˈnā-ˌtyüm\. Most southerly island of Vanuatu, SW Pacific Ocean, 20°12′S, 169°45′E; ab. 55 sq. mi. (142 sq. km.); pop. (1980p) 464; cen. peak 2788 ft. (850 m.).

Ane·to, Pi·co de \ˈpē-kō-ˌt͟hā-ä-ˈnā-tō\ *or Fr.* **Pic de Né·thou** \ˌpēk-də-nā-ˈtü\. Peak in the Maladeta Range, Lérida prov., NE Spain, just S of French border; 11,168 ft. (3404 m.); highest in the Pyrenees.

Anfa. See CASABLANCA.

An·ga \ˈəŋ-gə, ˈäŋ-\. Ancient name of E Bihar, NE India.

An·ga·da·nan \ˌäŋ-gä-ˈdä-nän\. Municipality, SW Isabela prov., Luzon, Philippines, on left bank of Cagayan River 28 mi. (45 km.) S of Ilagan; pop. (1980c) 27,706.

An·ga·mos, Point \än-'gä-mōs\. Cape extending into Pacific Ocean from W cen. Antofagasta region, N Chile, S of Bay of Mejillones del Sur.

An·ga·ra \ən-ˌgə-'rä, ˌäŋ-gə-'rä\. **1.** Navigable river, S Russia in Asia; flows from SW corner of Lake Baikal N past Irkutsk and then W to Yenisey River, Irkutsk Oblast; 1151 mi. (1852 km.) long; area of its drainage basin ab. 400,000 sq. mi. (1,036,000 sq. km.); formerly called Upper (Verkhnyaya) Tunguska in its lower course in Krasnoyarsk Kray; chief tributaries Oka and Ilim.

2. *or Russ.* **Verkh·nya·ya Angara** \'verk-nyə-yə\ *or* **Upper Angara.** River, N Buryat Rep., S Russia in Asia; flows SW into N end of Lake Baikal; ab. 200 mi. (320 km.) long.

An·garsk \ən-'gärsk\. Town, Irkutsk Oblast, S Russia in Asia; ab. 25 mi. (40 km.) NW of the city of Irkutsk; pop. (1992e) 269,000.

An·gat \äŋ-'gät\. River, Bulacan prov., Luzon, Philippines; rises in mountains on Quezon border; utilized for production of hydroelectric power.

An·ga·tho·ní·si \ˌäŋ-gä-thō-'nē-sē\; *formerly* **Gai·da·ro** \'gī-də-ˌrō\. Small island in the E Aegean Sea, S of Sámos, Greece; included in the Dodecanese group.

Ang·aur \äŋ-'au̇r\. Small island at S end of Palau, W Pacific Ocean, 6°54′N, 134°09′E; phosphate deposits; chief village Saipan, on W coast.

An·ge·di·va \ˌan-zhə-'dē-və, ˌan-jə-\ *or* **An·ji·div** \'ən-ji-ˌdēv, 'än-\ *or* **An·ji·di·va** \ˌən-ji-'dē-və, ˌän-\. Island off W coast of India, S of Goa; near Karwar in Karnataka state; formerly Portuguese.

Án·gel de la Guar·da \'äŋ-ˌgel-thā-lä-'gwär-dä\. Island off NE cen. Baja California, in upper Gulf of California; ab. 43 mi. (69 km.) long.

An·ge·les \'äŋ-gā-ˌlās\. Chartered city, NW cen. Pampanga prov., Luzon, Philippines, on Manila-Dagupan railroad line 10 mi. (16 km.) NW of San Fernando; pop. (1990p) 236,000.

Angeles, Mount \'an-jə-ləs\. Peak, Clallam co., NW Washington; 6454 ft. (1967 m.).

An·gel Falls \'ān-jəl\. Waterfall, SE Venezuela, on side of large (ab. 20 mi. or 32 km. long) flat-topped mountain E of Caroní River; 3212 ft. (979 m.) high; world's highest waterfall.

An·ge·li·na \ˌan-jə-'lē-nə\. **1.** River, E Texas; flows from Smith co. SSE to Neches River on E boundary of Tyler co.; 119 mi. (191 km.) long.

2. County in E Texas. See table at TEXAS.

Angel Island \'ān-jəl\. Island in San Francisco Bay, California, 2 mi. (3.2 km.) E of Sausalito; ab. 1 sq. mi. (2.6 sq. km.); belongs to Marin co.; contains former immigration detention center.

Ang·eln \'äŋ-əln\. Region, NE Schleswig-Holstein, Germany; area 320 sq. mi. (829 sq. km.); bounded on the N by the Flensburger Förde, on E by Kiel Bay, and on S by Schlei Inlet; ground moraine; fertile farmlands; cattle and pig raising; traditionally home of Angles, a people who are supposed to have migrated in 5th cent. A.D. to E, cen., and N parts of England (see EAST ANGLIA).

Angerapp. See WEGORAPA.

Angerburg. See WĘGORZEWO.

Ång·er·man \'ȯŋ-ər-mən\. River, cen. Sweden; rises on W boundary of Sweden, flows SE and S into Gulf of Bothnia just N of Härnösand; 279 mi. (449 km.) long; navigable for ab. 31 mi. (50 km.); course marked by cataracts and waterfalls; noted for beauty of landscape; hydroelectric power.

Ång·er·man·land \'ȯŋ-ər-mən-ˌland\. Region, formerly a province of E Sweden, on Gulf of Bothnia, ab. coextensive with modern Västernorrland and Västerbotten provs.

Ang·er·mün·de \'äŋ-ər-ˌmœn-də\. City, Brandenburg, E Germany, ab. 45 mi. (72 km.) NNE of Berlin; 13th cent. Gothic church; scene of defeat of Pomeranians by Elector Frederick I of Brandenburg 1420.

An·gers \än-'zhā\; *anc.* **Ju·li·om·a·gus** \ˌjü-lē-'ä-mə-gəs\. City, ✻ of Maine-et-Loire dept., W France, on Maine River 48 mi. (77 km.) ENE of Nantes; pop. (1990c) 146,163; distilling; textiles, machinery; episcopal see from 3d cent.; 13th cent. Gothic cathedral of St. Maurice; university (closed by French Revolution, reorganized 1875); important slate quarries—whence its sobriquet "Black Angers" or the "Black City."

History: Ancient ✻ of the Andecavi tribe; invaded by Norsemen in 9th cent. and by English in 12th and 15th cents.; became seat of counts of Anjou in 9th cent. and later the ✻ of the duchy (see ANJOU 2); scene of defeat of Vendean royalists 1793.

Ang·kor \'aŋ-ˌkȯr, 'äŋ-\; *orig.* **Angkor Thom** \'tōm\. Ruined ancient city, Cambodia, SE Asia, NW of Tonle Sap ab. 4 mi. (6 km.) from Siem Reap; old ✻ of the Khmers. Founded first cent. A.D. by Khmers from NE Burma who transplanted Indian civilization and flourished for several centuries; Angkor Thom built 12th–13th cents. A.D., a city of 5 sq. mi. (13 sq. km.) having moat and walls, and within, palaces, temples, and a great tower, richly carved, esp. with four faces of the god Siva. About 1 mi. (1.6 km.) S is **Angkor Wat** *or* **Vat** \'wät\, built early 12th cent., rectangular temple of three stories, with towers, porticoes, galleries, and stairways, the entire structure covered with exquisite bas-reliefs. After Siamese conquest of the Khmers in 15th cent. city and temples in ruins and buried in jungle; discovered by French botanist c. 1860 who brought it to world's attention; later cleared and partially restored by government. See CAMBODIA.

An·glem, Mount \'aŋ-gləm\. Peak, N Stewart I., New Zealand; 3208 ft. (978 m.).

An·gle·sey *or* **An·gle·sea** \'aŋ-gəl-sē\ *or Welsh* **Môn** \'mōn\. **1.** *anc.* **Mo·na** \'mō-nə\. Island, NW Wales, separated from mainland by Menai Strait; 276 sq. mi. (715 sq. km.); pop. (1991p) 67,800; most of land given over to sheep pastures; agriculture; tourism; copper formerly an important export. Notable druidic ruins, esp. dolmens; subdued by Romans under Suetonius Paulinus 61 A.D. who demolished sacred groves of the druids; ruled by princes of North Wales 9th–13th cents.; conquered by English King Edward I 1282.

2. Former county in Wales, incl. Anglesey I. and Holyhead I; ⊗ Beaumaris. See GWYNEDD 2.

An·glet \ä^{n}-'glā\. Commune, Pyrénées-Atlantiques dept., SW France, W suburb of Bayonne.

An·gle·ton \'aŋ-gəl-tən\. City, ⊗ of Brazoria co., SE Texas, 36 mi. (58 km.) W of Galveston; pop. (1990c) 17,140; oil wells.

An·gleur \ä^{n}-'glœr\. Commune, Liège prov., Belgium, 2.5 mi. (4 km.) SE of the city of Liège near Meuse and Ourthe rivers; coal deposits.

Anglia. See ENGLAND 1.

Anglo–Egyptian Sudan. See SUDAN 2.

Ang–lung–kang–jih. See NGANGLONG KANGRI.

Ang·mags·sa·lik \ä-'mä-sə-ˌlik, äŋ-, -'mäk-\ *or* **Am·mas·sa·lik** \ä-'mä-\. Settlement and trading post on island of same name off E coast of Greenland, just below Arctic Circle; pop. (1991e) 1512.

An·gol \äŋ-'gōl\. City, La Araucanía region, S cen. Chile, in agricultural and fruit-growing district 325 mi. (523 km.) S of Santiago; formerly ✻ of Malleco prov.

An·go·la \aŋ-'gō-lə, an-\. **1.** *formerly* **Portuguese West Africa.** Independent state, SW Africa, bounded on N and NE by Democratic Rep. of the Congo, on SE by Zambia, on S by Namibia, and on W by the Atlantic Ocean; 481,351 sq. mi. (1,246,699 sq. km.); pop. (1992e) 10,609,000; includes prov. of Cabinda (*q.v.*), N of the Congo River; ✻ Luanda.

Physical features: Interior forms part of Central African Plateau, alt. 4000 to 6000 ft. (1220 to 1830 m.); coastal plain ab. 1000 mi. (1610 km.) long, varies in width from 30 to 100 mi. (48 to 160 km.); highest point Mt. Moco 8397 ft. (2559 m.), in W.

Chief rivers: Congo, which for nearly 100 mi. (160 km.) forms part of N boundary; many S tributaries of Kasai, notably the Kwango, which have their source in NE; Cuanza in

\ə\ abut \ᵊ\ matches \ᵊ\ kitten, Fr table \ər\ further \a\ ash \ā\ ace \ä\ cot, cart \ȧ\ Fr bac \au̇\ out \b\ Span Avila \ch\ chin \e\ bet \ē\ easy \g\ go \i\ hit \ī\ ice \j\ job \k\ Ger ich, Buch \$^{n}$\ Fr vin \ŋ\ sing \ō\ go \ȯ\ all \ȯ\ law \œ\ Fr bœuf \œ̄\ Fr feu \ȯi\ boy \th\ thin \t͟h\ this \ü\ loot \u̇\ foot \u̇e\ Ger füllen \ūe\ Fr rue \y\ yet \$^{y}$\ Fr digne \'dēn^{y}\, nuit \'nw^{y}ē\ \yü\ few \yu̇\ fury \zh\ vision

cen. part, flowing NW to Atlantic; Cunene in S, in part forming boundary with Namibia; Cubango (Okavango) and Cuíto in SE, flowing into the Okavango Basin; Kwando (or Cuando), an upper tributary of the Zambezi, in SE.

Chief products: Coffee, corn, sisal, peanuts, cotton, sugarcane, palm oil; iron ore, oil, diamonds.

Chief towns: Luanda, Huambo, Benguela, Lubango.

Political divisions: Divided into the following 18 provinces (for pronunciation of their names, see their individual entries):

NAME	AREA (sq. mi.)	AREA (sq. km.)	POP. (1992e)	CAPITAL
Bengo	12,112	31,371	171,000	Caxito
Benguela	12,273	31,788	660,000	Benguela
Bié	27,148	70,314	1,153,000	Kuito
Cabinda	2,807	7,270	168,000	Cabinda
Cuando-Cubango	76,853	199,049	134,000	Menongue
Cuanza Norte	9,340	24,190	385,000	Ndalatando
Cuanza Sul	21,490	55,660	660,000	Sumbe
Cunene	34,495	89,342	235,000	Ondjiva
Huambo	13,233	34,274	1,562,000	Huambo
Huíla	28,958	75,002	887,000	Lubango
Luanda	934	2,418	1,717,000	Luanda
Lunda Norte	39,684	102,783	297,000	Lucapa
Lunda Sul	17,625	45,649	156,000	Saurimo
Malanje	37,684	97,602	911,000	Malanje
Moxico	86,109	223,023	325,000	Luena
Namibe	22,447	58,137	120,000	Namibe
Uíge	22,663	58,698	863,000	Uíge
Zaire	15,494	40,130	205,000	M'Banza Congo

History: Influx of Bantu-speaking peoples during first millennium ultimately led to their dominance of area c. 1500; coast reached by Portuguese sailors 1483; São Paulo de Loanda (now Luanda) settled by Portuguese late 16th cent.; Portuguese rule estab. over coastal area bet. 1575 and 1680, extended S to Moçâmedes 1840; given Cabinda exclave by agreement with Belgian Congo 1886; frontiers largely determined by Portuguese treaties with other European nations late 19th cent.; native uprisings 1902, 1907; settled boundary with South-West Africa (now Namibia) 1926; status changed from colony to overseas province 1951; outbreak of fighting between Portuguese forces and anti-Portuguese nationalists 1961; received independence Nov. 1975; fighting ensued bet. rival factions; peace agreement reached 1991; elections held 1992 prompted fighting bet. factions to resume.

2. City, ⊗ of Steuben co., NE Indiana, 40 mi. (64 km.) N of Fort Wayne; pop. (1990c) 5824; Tri-State Univ. (1884).

Angora. See ANKARA 2.

An·gos·tu·ra \ˌäŋ-gō-ˈstü-rä, ˌaŋ-gə-ˈstu̇r-ə\. River port, Venezuela. See CIUDAD BOLÍVAR.

An·gou·lême \ˌäⁿ-gü-ˈlām, -ˈlem\; *anc.* **Ic·u·lis·ma** \ˌi-kyü-ˈliz-mə\. City, ✻ of Charente dept., W France, on Charente River 64 mi. (103 km.) NNE of Bordeaux; pop. (1990c) 46,194; noted for papermaking; episcopal see from 379; Byzantine Romanesque cathedral of St. Pierre (c. 12th cent.).

History: Taken from Visigoths by Clovis, king of Franks, 507 A.D. in which year he built its first cathedral; from 9th cent. center of countship, held by Lusignan family from 1220; ceded to England by Peace of Bretigny 1360 but restored to France by Charles V 1373; passed to house of Orléans 1394; center of duchy (1515–1844) created by Francis I; united to crown 1714; ✻ of pre-Revolutionary prov. of Angoumois (*q.v.*).

An·gou·mois \ˌäⁿ-gü-ˈmwä\. Historical region of W cen. France, bounded on N by Poitou, on E by Limousin, on SE by Guienne, on SW by Gironde estuary, and on NW by Aunis; ✻ Angoulême; watered by Charente River. Medieval county ceded to England by Peace of Bretigny 1360 and restored

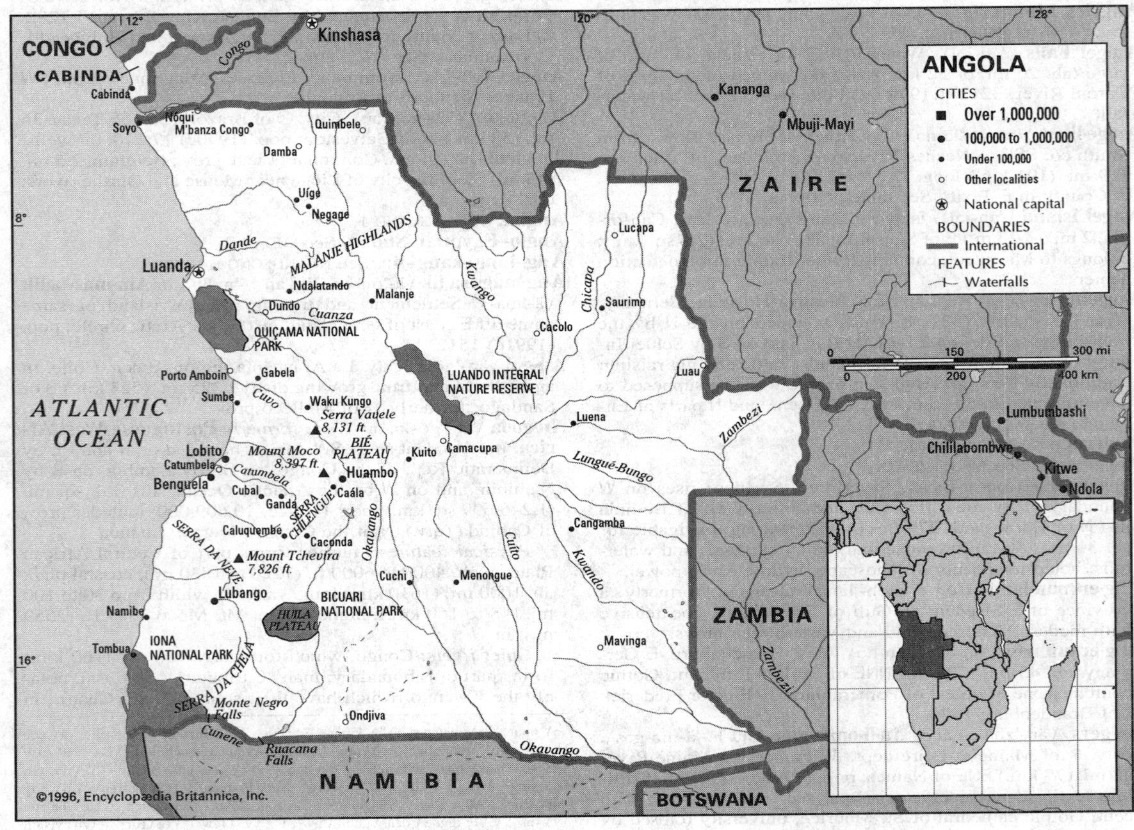

1373 to France by Charles V; appanage of royal crown to 1515; raised to rank of duchy by Francis I 1515.

An·gra do He·ro·ís·mo \ˈäŋ-grə-dü-ˌer-ü-ˈēzh-mü\. **1.** Former district of Portugal comprised of Terceira, São Jorge, and Graciosa islands, Azores.

2. Seaport, Azores, at head of deep bay on S coast of Terceira I.; pop. (1991p) 11,672; episcopal see; harbor protected by promontory; NATO airbase nearby; exports wine, fruit (esp. pineapples), grain, flax. Founded 1534; until 1832 ✻ of Azores.

Angrapa. See WEGORAPA.

Angra Pequena. See LÜDERITZ.

An·gren \əŋ-ˈgryen\. Town, Tashkent subdivision, E Uzbekistan, ab. 50 mi. (80 km.) ESE of Tashkent; pop. (1991e) 132,600.

An·gri \ˈäŋ-grē\. Commune, Salerno prov., Campania S Italy, 11 mi. (18 km.) WNW of the seaport of Salerno; pop. (1989c) 29,848. Ancient Mons Lactarius (S of Angri) scene of defeat of Ostrogoths 553 by Byzantine Gen. Narses.

Ang Thong *or* **Ang·thong** \äŋ-ˈtȯŋ\. **1.** Province, S Thailand; 379 sq. mi. (982 sq. km.); pop. (1991e) 280,550.

2. Town, its ✻, on the Chao Phraya River; pop. (1991e) 9270.

An·guil·la \aŋ-ˈgwil-ə, an-\. Island, Leeward Is., West Indies, ab. 60 mi. (96 km.) NW of St. Kitts; 35 sq. mi. (91 sq. km.); pop. (1992e) 8700; salt; fishing, tourism; a British dependency; formerly administratively linked with St. Kitts-Nevis, rebelling against union 1967, 1969 (union dissolved 1971); British dependency status formally confirmed 1980; new constitution in effect 1982.

Anguilla Cays. Group of cays or islets of Bahamas, N of Cuba, bet. Santaren Channel and Nicholas Channel.

An·guille, Cape \aŋ-ˈgwil, -ˈgil; ˈaŋ-ˌgwīl\. Cape, SW Newfoundland, Canada, S of entrance to St. George's Bay.

An·gus \ˈaŋ-gəs\; *formerly* **For·far** \ˈfȯr-fər\ *or* **For·far·shire** \-ˌshir, -shər\. Former county, E Scotland, bounded on the N by Aberdeen and Kincardine cos., on E by North Sea, on S by Firth of Tay, and on W by Perth co.; ⊗ Forfar; irregular, hilly land; cut by North Esk, South Esk, and Isla rivers; chief towns: Dundee, Forfar, Montrose, Arbroath.

An·gwin \ˈaŋ-gwin\. Unincorporated settlement, Napa co., California, ab. 20 mi. (32 km.) NNW of the city of Napa; pop. (1990c) 3503; Pacific Union Coll. (1882).

An·halt \ˈän-ˌhält\. Former German state, now located in cen. Germany; 893 sq. mi. (2313 sq. km.); ✻ Dessau; included part of Harz Mts.; watered by Elbe, Mulde, and Saale rivers.

History: Named from castle of Anhalt built c. 1100; began separate territorial status when inherited as part of Saxony by Duke Henry I of Anhalt (1214–44); subdivided and reunited continuously until reconstituted as duchy of Anhalt by Leopold IV 1863; joined North German Confederation 1866; became part of German Empire 1871; ducal status ended on becoming state of Weimar Republic 1919; reconstituted Saxony-Anhalt after WWII under Soviet occupation; became part of East Germany 1949, reunified Germany 1990.

Anhilwara. See PATAN 1.

An·holt \ˈän-ˌhȯlt, -ˌhōlt\. Island, Århus co., Denmark, in middle of Kattegat ab. 45 mi. (72 km.) E of Jutland; 8 sq. mi. (21 sq. km.); lighthouse.

An·hui *or W.-G.* **An·hwei** \ˈän-ˈhwā\. Province, E China, bounded on N by Jiangsu and Shandong, on E by Jiangsu and Zhejiang, on S by Jiangxi, and on W by Hubei and Henan; ✻ Hefei; crossed by lower course of Chang (ab. one third of province S of river) and in N by Huai; contains Chao Hu; lowland in N and in valley of Chang, mountainous in S. Under Ming dynasty (14th–17th cents.), part of prov. of Kiangnan (Kiangsu the other part). See table at CHINA.

Chief products: cotton, tea, rice, wheat, millet, soybeans; coal; iron and steel; hydroelectric power.

Chief towns: Hefei, Huainan, Bengbu, Wuhu.

An·i·ak·chak Crater \ˌa-nē-ˈak-ˌchak\. Crater, Alaska Penin., SW Alaska; 6 mi. (10 km.) in diameter; one of the largest known explosion craters.

Aniakchak National Monument. See UNITED STATES, *National Monuments.*

Aniche \á-ˈnēsh\. Commune, Nord dept., N France, 8 mi. (13 km.) ESE of Douai; coal beds.

Anicium. See LE PUY.

Anie·ne \än-ˈyā-nā\ *also* **Te·ve·ro·ne** \ˌtā-vā-ˈrō-nā\; *anc.* **An·io** \ˈan-yō\. River, cen. Italy; flows into the Tiber River just above Rome. 67 mi. (108 km.) long.

A–ni–ma–ch'ing Shan. See A'NYÊMAQÊN SHAN.

Ani·va, Cape \ə-ˈnyē-və\. Cape, SE extremity of Sakhalin I., E Russia in Asia.

Aniva Bay *or Jp.* **Ani·wa Wan** \ˌä-ˈnē-ˌwä-ˈwän\. Bay, E Russia in Asia, at S end of Sakhalin I.

An·jen·go \ˌən-ˈjeŋ-gō\. Village on coast of Kerala, SW India, ab. 20 mi. (32 km.) NW of Trivandrum; one of the earliest (1684) English settlements in India.

Anjidiv *or* **Anjidiva.** See ANGEDIVA.

An·jō \än-ˈjō\. City, Aichi prefecture, Honshū, Japan, 22 mi. (35 km.) SE of Nagoya; pop. (1992e) 146,770.

An·jou \ˈan-ˌjü, äⁿ-ˈzhü\. **1.** Town, Montreal co., S Quebec, Canada, a N suburb of Montreal; pop. (1991c) 37,210.

2. Historical region of NW France, bounded on N by Maine, on E by Touraine, on SE by Saumurois, on S by Poitou, and on W by Brittany; ✻ Angers; watered by Loire River.

History: County erected as a fief by the Capetian kings; under Fulk III Nerra (987–1040) and his successors, Angevin house acquired Touraine 1044 and later, Maine; became English 1154 at accession of Henry II (who had inherited it 1151 from his father, Duke Geoffrey of Anjou); returned to French crown when taken from King John 1204; inherited in 1246 by Prince Charles, known as Charles of Anjou, who became king of Naples and Sicily; raised to a duchy 1297, returned to royal domain through accession of Philip VI 1328; from 1350 to 1480 under 3d house of Anjou, founded by Louis I (count of Provence 1339–84 and duke of Anjou 1360–84), 2d son of John II (1350–64); became duchy 1360; annexed to French crown by Louis XI 1480.

An·jouan \äⁿ-ˈzhwäⁿ\ *or* **Nzwa·ni** \ən-ˈzwä-nē\. One of Comoros, 80 mi. (129 km.) SE of Grande Comore, 12°15′S, 44°25′E; 89 sq. mi. (231 sq. km.); pop. (1990e) 186,077.

An·ju \ˈän-ˈjü\; *formerly* **An·shu** \ˈän-ˈshü\. Town, North Korea, ab. 38 mi. (61 km.) N of P'yŏngyang; pop. (1987e) 186,000; coal deposits.

An·ka·ra \ˈäŋ-kə-rə, ˈaŋ-\. **1.** Province of W cen. Turkey in Asia. See table at TURKEY.

2. *formerly* **An·go·ra** \aŋ-ˈgōr-ə, an-\; *anc.* **An·cy·ra** \an-ˈsī-rə\. City, ✻ of Turkey and of Ankara prov., ab. 220 mi. (354 km.) ESE of İstanbul; pop. (1990c) 2,559,471; built on a hill 500 ft. (152 m.) above a plain and on **Ankara River** (ab. 115 mi. or 185 km. long), a tributary of Sakarya River; commercial center; building materials, foodstuffs, textiles; Univ. of Ankara (1946), Middle East Technical Univ. (1956), Hacettepe Univ. (reorganized 1967).

History: Important commercial center (Ancyra) from early times; ✻ of Celtic kingdom of Galatia (*q.v.*) in 3d cent. B.C., of Roman prov. of Galatia after 25 B.C.; conquered in succession by Persians, Arabs, Seljuq Turks, Latin Crusaders, and finally 1360 by Ottoman Turks; nearby occurred victory of Turkic ruler Timur over Sultan Bayezid I 1402; part of Ottoman Empire after recovery by Turks 1431; center in which Turkish Nationalists set up provisional government 1920 which in 1923 proclaimed the republic of Turkey (*q.v.*); made ✻ of Turkey 1923; name officially changed from Angora to Ankara 1930; scene of treaty by which Turkey and Greece recognized territorial status quo and agreed to naval equality in Mediterranean 1930.

An·ka·ra·tra \ˌäŋ-kä-ˈrä-trä\. Mountain group, cen. Madagascar; highest peak 8674 ft. (2644 m.).

An·ke·ny \ˈaŋ-kə-nē\. City, Polk co., cen. Iowa, N of Des Moines; pop. (1990c) 18,482; Faith Baptist Bible Coll. and Seminary (1921).

Anking. See ANQING.

An·klam \ˈäŋ-ˌkläm\. City, Mecklenburg-West Pomerania, NE Germany, on right bank of Peene River, 40 mi. (64 km.) SE of Greifswald; pop. (1981c) 20,356. Settled in 11th cent.; joined Hanseatic League 1283; sacked during Thirty Years' War and Seven Years' War; acquired by Prussia 1720.

An·ko·bra \äŋ-ˈkō-brä\. River, W Ghana; enters Gulf of Guinea just W of Axim; 130 mi. (209 km.) long; navigable for 50 mi. (80 km.).

An·ko·le \äŋ-ˈkō-lā\. Plateau region in SW Uganda, bet. Lake Victoria and Lake Edward; formerly a native kingdom.

An·myŏn \ˈän-ˈmyȯn\ *formerly* **Am·min** \ˈäm-ˈmin\. Island in the Yellow Sea off W coast of South Ch'ungch'ŏng prov., South Korea.

Ann, Cape \ˈan\. **1.** Eastern peninsula of Essex co., Massachusetts, N of Massachusetts Bay.

2. Cape on coast of Enderby Land, Antarctica, extending into Indian Ocean, 66°10′S, 51°22′E.

An·na \ˈa-nə\. City, Union co., SW Illinois, 28 mi. (45 km.) SW of Marion; pop. (1990c) 4805.

An·na·ba \ȧn-ˈnä-bə\; *formerly* **Bône** \ˈbōn\; *until French occupation known as* **Bo·na** \ˈbō-nə\. Seaport, NE Algeria, 70 mi. (113 km.) NE of Constantine; pop. (1987p) 305,526; large trade in phosphates and iron ore; steel; railway workshops, chemical works.

History: Identified with **Aph·ro·di·si·um** \ˌa-frə-ˈdi-zē-əm, -zhē-əm, -zhəm\, the port of ancient **Hip·po** *or* **Hippo Re·gi·us** \ˈhi-pō-ˈrē-jē-əs\, whose ruins are 1 mi. (1.6 km.) to the S, a rich city of Roman Africa to c. 300 A.D. and the bishopric and home 396–430 of St. Augustine. Hippo and its port severely damaged by Vandals 431 and Arabs and Bona built on latter site by Arabs in 7th cent. Held in medieval times by Italians, Spaniards, Genoese, Algerines; occupied by French 1832.

An Na·ba·ṭī·yah at Taḩ·tā \ȧn-ˌnȧ-bȧ-ˈtē-yə-ȧt-ˈtȧk̲-ˌtä\. Town, cen. S Lebanon; pop. (1985e) 100,000.

An·na·berg–Buch·holz \ˈä-nə-ˌberk-ˈbük̲-ˌhōlts\; *formerly* **Annaberg.** City, Saxony, E Germany, near Czech border in Erzgebirge 18 mi. (29 km.) S of Chemnitz; pop. (1991e) 25,010; former center of German lace, braid, and ribbon industry 16th cent.; gained first importance through the mining of silver, tin, bismuth, and cobalt; marble.

An Na·fūd \ˌȧn-nȧ-ˈfüd\ *or* **Nafud** *also* **Ne·fud** \ne-ˈfüd\. A desert of red sand in N Saudi Arabia; 140 mi. (225 km.) wide at max. extent.

An Na·jaf \ȧn-ˈnȧ-jȧf\. Town, S cen. Iraq, on lake W of the Euphrates; pop. (1985e) 242,603; contains shrine of ʻAlī, son-in-law of Muḥammad, a pilgrimage destination, and is starting point of pilgrimage route to Mecca.

An·nam \a-ˈnam, ˈa-ˌnam\ *or* **Anam** \ˈa-ˌnam\. Historic kingdom situated on E coast of Indochina, now a region in Vietnam; 56,974 sq. mi. (147,563 sq. km.); ✻ Hue; coastline ab. 850 mi. (1370 km.) long; mountain range extending entire length with max. elev. ab. 7900 ft. (2410 m.).

History: Conquered c. 200 B.C. by Chinese who gave the area its name which has not been used by indigenous inhabitants; became independent 1428; came under French influence in late 18th cent., but ruled by emperor of Annam at beginning of 19th cent.; French control extended by various treaties until estab. as protectorate 1883; partitioned bet. North and South Vietnam 1954; its last emperor was deposed 1955. See INDOCHINA 2.

An·nan \ˈa-nən\. **1.** River, S Scotland; flows S in Dumfries and Galloway region into Solway Firth; 49 mi. (79 km.) long.

2. Burgh, Dumfries and Galloway region S Scotland, on Annan River 2 mi. (3.2 km.) from its mouth; pop. (1981p) 8285; nearby are several atomic reactors.

An·nan·dale–on–Hud·son \ˈa-nən-ˌdāl- … -ˈhəd-sən\. Village, Dutchess co., New York, on E bank of Hudson River 21 mi. (34 km.) N of Poughkeepsie; Bard Coll. (1860).

An·nap·o·lis \ə-ˈna-pə-ləs\. **1.** Seaport, ✻ of Maryland and ⊗ of Anne Arundel co., on S bank of Severn River near its mouth at Chesapeake Bay, 22 mi. (35 km.) SSE of Baltimore; pop. (1990c) 33,187; boatyards; site of U.S. Naval Academy (founded 1845 by George Bancroft) and of St. John's Coll. (1696).

History: Settled as town of **Prov·i·dence** \ˈprä-və-dəns\ by Puritans from Virginia 1649, later known as **Anne Arundel Town** \ˈan-ə-ˈrənd-ᵊl\; became ✻ of Maryland and renamed Annapolis in honor of Princess (later Queen) Anne 1694; received city charter 1708; scene of meeting of Continental Congress Nov. 26, 1783–June 3, 1784; seat of the Annapolis Convention 1786 in which delegates from five states met to resolve problems with Articles of Confederation but took no action (precursor of Constitutional Convention of 1787).

2. County, in W Nova Scotia, Canada. See table at NOVA SCOTIA.

Annapolis Basin. Inlet of Bay of Fundy on W coast of Annapolis co., W Nova Scotia, Canada; receives **Annapolis River** (75 mi. or 121 km. long) from NE.

Annapolis Roy·al \ˈrȯi-əl\. Town, ⊗ of Annapolis co., W Nova Scotia, Canada, on S shore of Annapolis Basin 70 mi. (113 km.) N of Yarmouth; pop. (1991c) 633; site of first tidal power-generating plant in North America, began operating 1984.

History: One of the oldest European settlements in North America N of the Gulf of Mexico; founded as **Port Royal** 1605 by French explorers Pierre du Gua (Sieur de Monts) and Samuel de Champlain; several times captured by English in 17th cent. and restored to France; became seat of French government in Acadia 1684; finally seized 1710 and became permanently British 1713 by Treaty of Utrecht; name changed in honor of Queen Anne; until 1749 was ✻ of Nova Scotia.

An·na·pur·na *or* **Ana·pur·na** \ˌa-nə-ˈpu̇r-nə\. Mountain range in the Himalayas, Nepal; highest peak 26,504 ft. (8078 m.); first climbed 1950 by French expedition.

An Nāqūrah. See EN NAQURA.

Ann Ar·bor \ˈan-ˈär-bər\. City, ⊗ of Washtenaw co., SE Michigan, 36 mi. (58 km.) W of Detroit; pop. (1990c) 109,592; medical and research center; scientific and photographic equipment; Univ. of Michigan (1817), Concordia Coll. (1962), Washtenaw Community Coll. (1965); settled 1824.

An Nā·si·rī·yah *or* **An Na·si·ri·ya** \ˌȧn-ˌnȧ-si-ˈrē-yə\. Town, SE Iraq, on left bank of Euphrates River, ab. 100 mi. (161 km.) NW of Basra; pop. (1985e) 138,842; in WWI taken by British July 1915.

Anne, Mount \ˈan\. Mountain, Antarctica, 83°48′S, 168°30′E; 12,703 ft. (3872 m.).

Anne Arun·del \ˌan-ə-ˈrənd-ᵊl\. County in cen. Maryland. See table at MARYLAND.

Anne Arundel Town. See ANNAPOLIS 1.

An·ne·cy \ȧn-ˈsē\ *or Lat.* **An·ne·ci·a·cum** \ˌa-nə-ˈsī-ə-kəm\. City, ✻ of Haute-Savoie dept., E France, at NW end of Lake Annecy 63 mi. (101 km.) ENE of Lyon; pop. (1990c) 51,143; tourism; noted bell foundry in vicinity, **Annecy–le–Vieux** \-lə-ˈvyœ\ *anc.* **Anneciacum Ve·tus** \ˈvē-təs\, 1.5 mi. (2.4 km.) N; ancient castle, cathedral, and church of St. Francis. Ruled by counts of the Genevois; under dukes of Savoy 1401–1860.

Annecy, Lake. Lake in the Alps, Haute-Savoie dept., E France, 22 mi. (35 km.) S of Geneva; 9 mi. (14 km.) long, 2 mi. (3.2 km.) wide, 10 sq. mi. (26 sq. km.); connected with Fier River by Thiou Canal which runs through Annecy; surrounded by steep, scenic mountains.

Annesley Bay. See ZULA, GULF OF.

An·nette \a-ˈnet, ə-\. Small island S of Revillagigedo I., SE Alaska; 132 sq. mi. (342 sq. km.); American Indian reservation; salmon fishing.

An Nhon \ˈän-ˈnōn\; *formerly* **Binh Dinh** \ˈbin-ˈdin\. Town near coast, Vietnam, ab. 152 mi. (244 km.) SSE of Da Nang; its port is Qui Nhon.

An·nis·quam; *earlier* **An·as·quam** \ˈa-ni-ˌskwäm\. Village and summer resort, E Essex co., NE Massachusetts, on Annisquam Harbor.

Annisquam Harbor. Inlet of Atlantic Ocean on N shore of Cape Ann, E Essex co., NE Massachusetts.

An·nis·ton \'a-ni-stən\. City, ⊗ of Calhoun co., NE Alabama, 28 mi. (45 km.) SE of Gadsden; pop. (1990c) 26,623; iron ore mines; founded as private industrial village; incorp. as city 1879; opened to public 1883.

Annobón. See PAGALU.

An·no·nay \,à-nò-'nā\; *anc.* **An·no·ni·a·cum** \,a-nə-'nī-ə-kəm\. Commune, Ardèche dept., SE France, on Cance River 36 mi. (58 km.) N of Privas; 14th cent. Gothic church; birthplace of Montgolfier brothers who built balloon in which first manned ascent was made 1783.

An Nuhūd. See EN NAHUD.

Ann·ville \'an-,vil\. Unincorporated settlement in Annville township, Lebanon co., SE cen. Pennsylvania, ab. 4 mi. (6.4 km.) W of Lebanon; limestone; Lebanon Valley Coll. (1866); platted 1762.

Ano·ka \ə-'nō-kə\. **1.** County in E Minnesota. See table at MINNESOTA.
2. City, its ⊗, on Mississippi River 17 mi. (27 km.) NNW of Minneapolis; pop. (1990c) 17,192; trade center.

An Pass \'än, 'an\. Mountain pass in cen. part of Arakan Yoma, W Myanmar; alt. ab. 5000 ft. (1525 m.); leads from Sittwe and coast towns to Magwe and Minbu on the Irrawaddy.

An·qing *or W.-G.* **An–ch'ing** \'än-'chiŋ\ *or* **An·king** \-'kiŋ\; *formerly* **Ngan–king** \'ŋän-'kiŋ\ *or* **Huai–ning** \'hwī-'niŋ\. City, Anhui prov., E China, on N bank of Chang; pop. (1990c) 250,718; ravaged by Taipings 1853; occupied by Japanese 1938.

Ans \'ä^{n}s\. Commune, Liège prov., E Belgium, NW suburb of the city of Liège; pop. (1991c) 27,554; coal deposits.

An·sa·ri·ya, Dje·bel \,je-bel-,àn-sà-'rē-yə\. Mountain range, Syria, running N and S ab. 70 mi. (113 km.) along W bank of the Orontes River; highest point ab. 5100 ft. (1555 m.); N extension of Lebanon Mts.

Ans·bach \'äns-,bäk\. **1.** Former principality, now part of Bavaria, Germany; ruled by Franconian branch of Hohenzollern family of Brandenburg until its transference to Prussia 1791–92; with Bayreuth (forming margravate of Ansbach-Bayreuth), ceded to Bavaria by Prussia 1806, confirmed by Congress of Vienna 1815.
2. City, Bavaria, Germany, 25 mi. (40 km.) SW of Nürnberg; pop. (1991e) 37,893; built around Benedictine monastery founded in 8th cent. by St. Gumbertus; ✻ of former Ansbach principality.

An·se·ba \än-'se-bə\. River, W Eritrea; rises E of the Baraka, flows N and joins the Baraka S of Sudanese border.

An·shan *or* **An–shan** \'än-'shän\. City, Liaoning prov., NE China, on railroad line 55 mi. (88 km.) SSW of Shenyang; pop. (1990c) 1,203,986; one of China's most important steelmaking centers; also produces cement, chemicals. Occupied 1930s by Japanese who advanced steelmaking capacity; bombed by U.S. aircraft WWII 1944; looted by Soviets following WWII; subsequently redeveloped by Chinese as important industrial center.

An·shan \'an-,shan\ *or* **An·zan** \'an-,zan\. Region of ancient Persia, NE of Babylonia; a small kingdom, probably in S Elam (*q.v.*), closely connected with or inclusive of Susa; seat of authority of early Achaemenian kings, predecessors of Cyrus the Great who founded Persian Empire 6th cent. B.C.

Anshu. See ANJU.

An·shun *or* **An–shun** \'än-'shün\. City, Guizhou prov., S China, WSW of Guiyang; pop. (1990c) 174,142.

An·son \'an-sən\. **1.** County in S North Carolina. See table at NORTH CAROLINA.
2. City, ⊗ of Jones co., NW cen. Texas, 25 mi. (40 km.) NNW of Abilene; pop. (1990c) 2644.

Anson Bay. Inlet of Joseph Bonaparte Gulf of Timor Sea on NW coast of Northern Terr., Australia; receives Daly River.

An·son·go \än-'sòŋ-gō\. Town on left bank of Niger, SE Mali, 50 mi. (80 km.) SE of Gao; pop. (1987p) 7188; above this point Niger is navigable for 1000 mi. (1609 km.).

An·so·nia \an-'sō-nē-ə, -nyə\. City, New Haven co., S Connecticut, on Naugatuck River 8 mi. (13 km.) WNW of New Haven; pop. (1990c) 18,403; settled 1651 as part of Derby, independently organized mid-19th cent., became borough 1864, city 1893; the town (incorp. 1889) is coextensive with the city.

An·ta·kya \,än-tä-'kyä\ *or* **An·ta·ki·yah** \-'kē-yə\; *anc.* **An·ti·och** \'an-tē-,äk\ *or Lat.* **An·ti·o·chia** \,an-tē-ō-'kī-ə\ *or Gk.* **An·ti·o·chea** \-'kē-ə\. City, Hatay prov., S Turkey in Asia, 27 mi. (43 km.) S of İskenderun; pop. (1990c) 123,871; olives and tobacco grown nearby.
History: Antioch founded by Macedonian Gen. Seleucus I Nicator 300 B.C.; became commercial rival of Alexandria; ✻ of Syria (see SYRIA 1) until 64 B.C. when Roman Gen. Pompey conquered the province; a mission center for early Christianity; ancient city destroyed by earthquake 526 A.D.; conquered by Arabs c. 638; captured by Byzantine Empire under Nicephorus Phocas 969; taken by the Seljuq Turks c. 1085, regained by the Crusaders 1097–98, and as a principality given to Norman Crusader Bohemond; subject of dispute bet. Normans and Byzantine emperor whose suzerainty Bohemond agreed to recognize 1099; Latin Christian principality destroyed by Baybars I, Mamlūk sultan of Egypt and Syria, 1268. For later history, see SYRIA 3.

An·tal·ya \,än-täl-'yä\. **1.** Province of SW Turkey in Asia. See table at TURKEY.
2. *formerly* **Ada·lia** \ə-'dä-lē-ə\ *anc.* **At·ta·leia** \,a-tə-'lī-ə\ *bib.* **At·ta·lia** \-'lī-ə\. Seaport, its ✻, on Gulf of Antalya; pop. (1990c) 378,208; food processing; timber export. Ancient city founded c. 150 B.C. on seacoast of Pamphylia by Attalus II Philadelphus, king of Pergamum; from this port St. Paul sailed with St. Barnabas to Antioch on his first missionary journey (*Acts* xiv. 25).

Antalya, Gulf of *or* **Gulf of Adalia** *or Turk.* **Antalya Kör·fe·zi** \,kœr-fe-'zē\. Inlet of Mediterranean Sea, SW coast of Turkey in Asia; ab. 130 mi. (209 km.) wide.

An·ta·na·na·ri·vo \,än-tä-,nä-nä-'rē-vō, -rē-'vō\ *or Malagasy* **Ta·na·na·ri·vo** \tä-,nä-nä-'rē-vō, -rē-'vō\ *formerly* **Ta·na·na·rive** \tä-,nä-nä-'rēv\. City, ✻ of Madagascar, in E cen. part; met. area pop. (1990e) 802,390; built on basaltic ridge at elev. of 4094 ft. (1248 m.); university (1955, university status 1961).

Ant·arc·ti·ca \ant-'ärk-ti-kə, -'är-\ *also* **Ant·arc·tic Continent** \-tik\. A continent lying around the South Pole.
Physical features: About 5,500,000 sq. mi. (14,245,000 sq. km.); covered by ice cap having av. thickness of 1 mi. (1.6 km.); divided into **West Antarctica** (includes Antarctic Penin.) and **East Antarctica** by the **Transantarctic Mountains** \,trans-,ant-, ,tranz-\, a mountain range running from Victoria Land (*q.v.*) to Coats Land (*q.v.*); max. ice thickness in West Antarctica over 15,000 ft. (4500 m.), in East Antarctica ab. 9000 ft. (2740 m.); highest of the continents, with av. elev. of ab. 8000 ft. (2440 m.); highest peak Vinson Massif 16,860 ft. (5139 m.); existence of coal indicative of warmer climate in earlier age.
Ownership: Claims advanced by several nations: Norway (Queen Maud Land) from 20°W to 45°E; Australia (Enderby Land, Wilkes Land, George V Coast, part of Oates Coast) from 45°E to 136°E and from 142°E to 160°E; France (Adélie Coast) from 136°E to 142°E; New Zealand from 160°E to 150°W; Chile from 90°W to 53°W; Great Britain from 80°W to 20°W; Argentina from 74°W to 25°W; claims not recognized by U.S.
History: Reference to large S continent found in writings of ancient Greeks, incl. geographer Ptolemy; its presumed area considerably reduced through voyages of Portuguese explorers Vasco da Gama 1497 and Ferdinand Magellan 1520, English navigator Francis Drake 1579, and Dutch explorer Abel Tasman 1642; significant exploration of region begun with voyages of Capt. James Cook who proved 1768 that New Zealand was not part of the S continent, and who

---

first crossed Antarctic Circle in circumnavigation of continent 1772–75; region visited by British and American whalers 1778–1839; first land within Antarctic Circle sighted by Russian Adm. Fabian Gottlieb von Bellingshausen 1819–21; Weddell Sea, Graham Coast, Enderby Land, Adélie Coast discovered during period 1823–40; Ross Sea and Ross Ice Shelf discovered 1841 by Scottish Capt. James Ross, who estab. 1842 record of 78°9′S, not surpassed until 1902; discovery of region and scientific study of mainland carried on by successive German, Norwegian, Belgian, and British expeditions, esp. after 6th International Geographical Congress of 1895; first landing on continent made by member of Norwegian expedition 1895; Ross Ice Shelf to 82°17′S crossed by Robert F. Scott 1902–04; S end of Ross Ice Shelf passed by Sir Ernest Shackleton's expedition 1908, and South Magnetic Pole reached by other members of his group 1909; South Pole discovered by Capt. Roald Amundsen Dec. 14, 1911; continuity of coast from George V Coast to Enderby Land demonstrated by land explorations of Sir Douglas Mawson's expeditions 1911–14, 1929–31; explored and mapped from air by Sir Hubert Wilkins 1928–29 and by Commander Richard Byrd 1928–30, 1933–35; part of Pacific coast explored by Byrd's 3d expedition 1939–40 and 4th 1946–47; Ronne (U.S.) expedition 1947–48 determined Antarctica to be a single continent; Fuchs (British) expedition 1957–58 made first land crossing of the continent; establishment of continent as demilitarized zone by treaty 1959; creation of several areas for conservation of flora and fauna 1966–67.

Antarctic Archipelago. See PALMER ARCHIPELAGO.

Antarctic Circle. The parallel of latitude that is approx. 66.5° S of the Equator and that circumscribes the S frigid zone.

Antarctic Peninsula *formerly* **Palm·er Peninsula** \ˈpäl-mər, ˈpä-\. Peninsula, Antarctica, extending ab. 700 mi. (1126 km.) from 73°S to approx. 63°S, and lying between 59°W and 67°W; claimed by Britain, Argentina, and Chile; N part known as Graham Land, S part as Palmer Land; separated from South Shetland Is. by Bransfield Strait; near its base on W are Alexander I. and Charcot I. and further N on the W lies the Palmer Archipelago; British and Chilean scientific stations destroyed by volcanic activity 1969.

Antarctic Regions. Antarctica (*q.v.*) and the S waters of the Atlantic, Pacific, and Indian oceans (66°58′S, 176°14′W) greatest depth recorded in these southern waters is 21,043 ft. or 6414 m.; subpolar conditions extend to 55°S and reach 45°S in area S of Africa; (sometimes inappropriately termed **Antarctic Ocean**). See POLAR REGIONS; ARCTIC, THE.

An·te·lope \ˈan-tə-ˌlōp\. **1.** County in NE Nebraska. See table at NEBRASKA.

2. Island, SE Great Salt Lake, Utah; forms part of Davis co.; 15.5 mi. (25 km.) long.

Antelope Peak. 1. Mountain in the Sierra Nevada on boundary bet. Mono and Alpine cos., E cen. California; 10,200 ft. (3109 m.).

2. Mountain, SW Eureka co., cen. Nevada; 10,220 ft. (3115 m.).

Antelope Range. Range in White Pine and Elko cos., NE Nevada.

An·te·que·ra \ˌän-tā-ˈkā-rä\; *anc.* **An·ti·quar·ia** \ˌan-tə-ˈkwer-ē-ə\. Commune, Málaga prov., S Spain, 22 mi. (35 km.) NNW of Málaga; pop. (1991c) 38,765; captured from Moors 1410. Caves in vicinity.

An·tero, Mount \-an-ˈter-ō\. Peak in Sawatch Range, Chaffee co., cen. Colorado; 14,269 ft. (4349 m.).

Antero Peak. Mountain in Sawatch Range, Saguache co., S cen. Colorado; 13,245 ft. (4037 m.).

An·tho·ny \ˈan-thə-nē\. **1.** City, ⊗ of Harper co., S Kansas, 62 mi. (100 km.) S of Hutchinson; pop. (1990c) 2516.

2. Town, El Paso co., Texas, near New Mexico border; pop. (1990c) 3328.

Anthony Peak. Mountain in the Sierra Nevada, SE Alpine co., E cen. California; 10,200 ft. (3109 m.).

An·tho·nys Nose \ˈan-thə-nēz\. **1.** Promontory, E side of Hudson River, New York, in Putnam co. near Peekskill; 900 ft. (274 m.).

2. Peak, Washington co., E New York; 1048 ft. (319 m.).

Anti–Atlas. See ATLAS MOUNTAINS.

An·tibes \äⁿ-ˈtēb\; *anc.* **An·tip·o·lis** \an-ˈti-pə-ləs\. Seaport, Alpes-Maritimes dept., SE France, on Mediterranean 11 mi. (18 km.) SW of Nice; pop. (1990c) 70,688; winter resort. Founded c. 340 B.C. by the Phocaeans; became Roman municipium, Roman remains still being extant; episcopal see 400–1244. The **Cap d'Antibes** \ˌkȧp-däⁿ-ˈtēb\, 3 mi. (4.8 km.) SSW, is also a noted winter resort.

Anticithera. See ANTIKÝTHĒRA.

An·ti·cos·ti Island \ˌan-tə-ˈkȯs-tē\. Island in St. Lawrence estuary and Gulf of St. Lawrence, Quebec, E Canada; ab. 130 mi. (209 km.) long; 3043 sq. mi. (7881 sq. km.); has well-developed fisheries and extensive forests. Sighted 1534 by French explorer Jacques Cartier; purchased 1895 by Henri Menier, French chocolate manufacturer; ownership transferred to Consolidated Paper Corporation 1926; now primarily a recreation area.

An·tie·tam Creek \an-ˈtē-təm\. Creek in N Maryland, rising in Franklin co., S Pennsylvania, and flowing S through Washington co., Maryland, to empty into Potomac River 7 mi. (11 km.) N of Harpers Ferry. Near its confluence with Potomac is village of **Antietam,** 3 mi. (4.8 km.) N of which, at Sharpsburg, was fought 1862 the battle of Antietam. See SHARPSBURG and UNITED STATES, *National Historical Parks.*

An·ti·fer, Cape \ˌan-ti-ˈfer\ *or Fr.* **Cap d'Antifer** \ˈkȧp-däⁿ-tē-ˈfer\. Cape, Normandy, N coast of France, 15 mi. (24 km.) NNE of Le Havre; marks W terminus of chalk cliffs of French coast stretching WSW from the Somme and also the NE point of the Bay of the Seine.

An·ti·go \ˈan-ti-ˌgō\. City, ⊗ of Langlade co., NE Wisconsin, 25 mi. (40 km.) NE of Wausau; pop. (1990c) 8276; founded after the Civil War.

An·ti·go·nish \ˌan-ti-gō-ˈnish\. **1.** County, N Nova Scotia, Canada. See table at NOVA SCOTIA.

2. Town, its ⊗, on St. Georges Bay 35 mi. (56 km.) E of New Glasgow; pop. (1991c) 4924; St. Francis Xavier Univ. (1853), Mount St. Bernard Coll. (1883); first British settlement made 1785 by disbanded officers and men of Nova Scotian regiment.

An·ti·gua \an-ˈtē-gə, -gwə\. Island, E part of Leeward Is., E West Indies, 260 mi. (418 km.) SE of Puerto Rico; 108 sq. mi. (280 sq. km.); a constituent part of Antigua and Barbuda (*q.v.*). Mountainous, partly volcanic and partly of coral formation; many natural harbors, esp. St. John's on NW, 2 mi. (3.2 km.) long by .75 mi. (1.2 km.) wide; cotton, fruit, and vegetables; tourism.

History: Discovered by Christopher Columbus 1493; settled by English from St. Kitts 1632; occupied by French troops in 1666; returned to England by Treaty of Breda 1667; became self-governing 1967, independent 1981. Two areas (Parham Harbour on N coast, 430 acres or 174 hectares, and shoreline strip on Judge's Bay, 1.4 sq. mi. or 3.6 sq. km.) leased to U.S. for seaplane base Mar. 27, 1941; 900 acres (364 hectares) released 1960.

Antigua and Barbuda. Independent state, comprising the islands of Antigua, Barbuda, and Redonda; area 171 sq. mi. (443 sq. km.); pop. (1992e) 83,000; ✱ St. Johns; tourism is chief industry; sugar formerly important.

Antigua Guatemala *or* **Antigua.** City, ✱ of Sacatepéquez dept., S cen. Guatemala; munic. pop. (1990e) 20,715; former ✱ of Guatemala; founded mid-16th cent.; once an important city in Spain's colonial American empire; destroyed by earthquake 1773.

An·ti·ký·thē·ra \ˌän-dē-ˈkē-thē-rä\; *formerly* **An·ti·ci·the·ra** \ˌan-tə-ˈsi-thə-rə\. Small island, midway in passage from Sea of Crete to Mediterranean, Greece, SE of Kíthira and NW of the NW point of Crete (Cape Busa).

An·ti–Leb·a·non \ˌan-ti-ˈle-bə-nən, -ˌnän\ *or* **Anti–Li·ban** \ˌäⁿ-tē-lē-ˈbäⁿ\; *anc.* **An·ti·lib·a·nus** \ˌan-ti-ˈli-bə-nəs\ *or Arab.* **Al–Ja·bal ash Shar·qī** \ȧl-ˌjȧ-bȧl-ȧsh-ˈshär-kē\. Mountain range, running N and S bet. Lebanon and Syria; highest point Mt. Hermon 9232 ft. (2814 m.).

An·ti·lla \än-ˈtē-yä\. Coastal town and municipality, E Cuba; munic. pop. (1981p) 11,979; sugar.

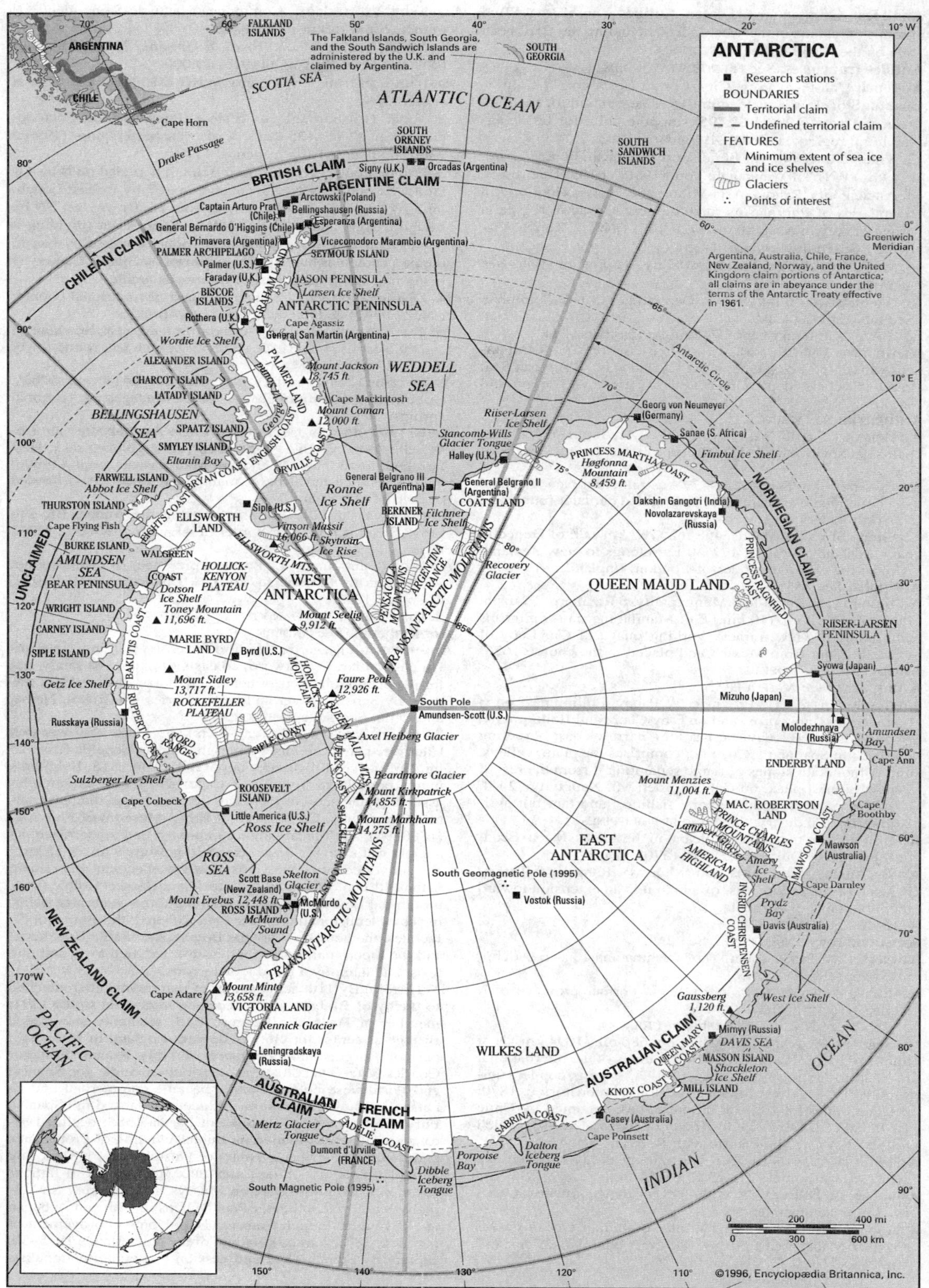
ANTARCTICA
Research stations
BOUNDARIES
Territorial claim
Undefined territorial claim
FEATURES
Minimum extent of sea ice and ice shelves
Glaciers
Points of interest
The Falkland Islands, South Georgia, and the South Sandwich Islands are administered by the U.K. and claimed by Argentina.
Argentina, Australia, Chile, France, New Zealand, Norway, and the United Kingdom claim portions of Antarctica; all claims are in abeyance under the terms of the Antarctic Treaty effective in 1961.
ATLANTIC OCEAN
SCOTIA SEA
WEDDELL SEA
BELLINGSHAUSEN SEA
AMUNDSEN SEA
ROSS SEA
PACIFIC OCEAN
INDIAN OCEAN
DAVIS SEA
BRITISH CLAIM
ARGENTINE CLAIM
CHILEAN CLAIM
NORWEGIAN CLAIM
AUSTRALIAN CLAIM
FRENCH CLAIM
NEW ZEALAND CLAIM
UNCLAIMED
South Pole
Amundsen-Scott (U.S.)
WEST ANTARCTICA
EAST ANTARCTICA
QUEEN MAUD LAND
WILKES LAND
ANTARCTIC PENINSULA
TRANSANTARCTIC MOUNTAINS
South Geomagnetic Pole (1995)
South Magnetic Pole (1995)
Vostok (Russia)
Greenwich Meridian
©1996, Encyclopædia Britannica, Inc.

An·til·les, Greater *and* **Lesser Antilles** \an-ˈti-lēz\. Two groups of islands in the West Indies, bounding the Caribbean Sea on the N and E. See WEST INDIES.

Antilles françaises. See FRENCH WEST INDIES.

An·ti·och \ˈan-tē-ˌäk\. **1.** City, Contra Costa co., W California, on S bank of San Joaquin River near mouth of the Sacramento; pop. (1990c) 62,195; shipping point for fertile agricultural region; settled 1849; incorp. 1890.

2. Village, Lake co., NE Illinois, on Wisconsin border 15 mi. (24 km.) WNW of Waukegan; pop. (1990c) 6105; lake resort.

3. Ancient city, Pisidia, Asia Minor; at certain periods within boundaries of Phrygia; its ruins lie near Yalvaç in N İsparta prov., Turkey in Asia, 80 mi. (129 km.) WNW of Konya. Visited by St. Paul (*Acts* xiii. 14–52).

4. *or* **Antiochea** *or* **Antiochia.** City, Turkey in Asia. See ANTAKYA.

An·ti·o·quia \än-ˈtyō-kyä\. **1.** Department of NW Colombia. See table at COLOMBIA.

2. Town, Antioquia dept., Colombia; founded 1541.

An·tip·a·ros \an-ˈti-pə-ˌräs, ˌan-ti-ˈpar-ˌäs\ *or Gk.* **An·dí·pa·ros** \än-ˈdē-pä-ˌrös\. One of the Cyclades Is., S Aegean Sea; part of Cyclades dept., Greece; SW of Paros I.; 13 sq. mi. (34 sq. km.).

Antipatria. See BERAT 2.

An·ti·pax·os \ˌan-ti-ˈpak-ˌsäs\ *or Gk.* **An·dí·pax·oi** \än-ˈdē-päk-sē\. Small island, NW Greece, in the Ionian Sea, S of Paxos.

An·tip·o·des \an-ˈti-pə-ˌdēz\. **1.** Australia and New Zealand —a colloquial use originating in England but later found also in North America.

2. Group of rocky islands, 458 mi. (737 km.) SE of Dunedin, New Zealand, 49°30′S, 177°30′E; belongs to New Zealand. Almost the exact antipodes of London, England.

Antipolis. See ANTIBES.

An·ti·po·lo \ˌän-tē-ˈpō-lō\. Municipality, S Rizal prov., Luzon, Philippines, 12 mi. (19 km.) E of Manila; mecca for pilgrims who come to view miracle-working image of Our Lady of Peace brought from Mexico and placed in the church 1626.

Antipyrgos. See TOBRUK.

Antiquaria. See ANTEQUERA.

An·ti·que \än-ˈtē-kā\. Province, W Panay, Philippines; on N bounded by Capiz prov. and on E by Capiz and Iloilo provs.; ✱ San Jose de Buenavista; has long narrow coast bordering on NE Sulu Sea facing Cuyo Is.; comprises the plain, valleys, and W mountain slopes of range separating it from the rest of Panay; highest peak, on Capiz border, Mt. Nangtud 6724 ft. (2049 m.). Lacks good harbors; fishing important but agriculture main industry. See table at PHILIPPINES.

An·ti·sa·na \ˌän-tē-ˈsä-nä\. Volcano in the Andes, N cen. Ecuador, just SE of Quito; 18,714 ft. (5704 m.).

An·ti–Tau·rus Mountains \ˌan-ti-ˈtȯr-əs\. Range in E Turkey in Asia, NE of Taurus Mts. of which it is an extension toward the mountains of Armenia.

Antium. See ANZIO.

Antivari. Town, Yugoslavia. See BAR.

Ant·lers \ˈant-lərz\. Town, ⊗ of Pushmataha co., SE Oklahoma; pop. (1990c) 2524.

An·to·fa·gas·ta \ˌän-tō-fä-ˈgäs-tä\. **1.** Former province of N Chile.

2. Region of N Chile. See table at CHILE.

3. Seaport, ✱ of Antofagasta region, 680 mi. (1094 km.) N of Santiago; pop. (1992p) 218,754; terminus of the international railroad to Oruro and La Paz, Bolivia; exports copper; university (1956). Town founded on Bolivian territory c. 1870; became outlet for Chilean nitrate mines; occupied by Chile 1879 and ceded to Chile by Treaty of Valparaíso 1884 which followed War of the Pacific with Bolivia.

An·to·fal·la \ˌän-tō-ˈfä-yä\. Volcanic peak, NW Argentina, near Chilean border; 21,129 ft. (6440 m.).

An·toine–La·belle \äⁿ-ˈtwän-lȧ-ˈbel\. County, Quebec, Canada. See table at QUEBEC.

An·ton·gil Bay \äⁿ-tōⁿ-ˈzhēl\. Inlet of Indian Ocean on NE coast of Madagascar; 50 mi. (80 km.) long and 25 mi. (40 km.) wide.

An·to·ny \ˌäⁿ-tō-ˈnē\. Commune, Hauts-de-Seine dept., N France, 5 mi. (8 km.) S of Paris.

An·tra·tsit \ˌän-trət-ˈsit\. Town, E Ukraine, 33 mi. (53 km.) SSW of Luhans'k; pop. (1991e) 73,000.

An·trim \ˈan-trim\. **1.** County in NW Michigan. See table at MICHIGAN.

2. Town, Hillsborough co., S New Hampshire, on Contoocook River 22 mi. (35 km.) W of Manchester; pop. (1990c) 2360; first settled 1741; incorp. 1777.

3. Former county, NE Northern Ireland; bounded on N by Atlantic, NE and E by North Channel, on SE by Belfast Lough, on S by Lagan River (dividing it from co. Down), on SW by Lough Neagh, and on W and NW by Bann River (dividing it from Derry district); coastal area widely covered by basalt, the perpendicular basalt column known as Giant's Causeway being notable; greater part of interior is arable.

4. District, Northern Ireland, in S part of traditional county; estab. 1974. See table at IRELAND, NORTHERN.

5. Town, Antrim district, Northern Ireland, near NE shore of Lough Neagh; pop. (1981c) 22,342; has ancient round tower 93 ft. (28 m.) high.

Ant·si·ra·be \ˌänt-si-ˈrä-bā\ *or Fr.* **Ant·si·ra·bé** \äⁿt-sē-rȧ-ˈbā\. Commune, Ankaratra Mts., cen. Madagascar; thermal springs.

An·tsi·ra·na·na \ˌän-tsē-ˈrä-nə-nə\ *also* **An·tsi·ra·ne** \ˌän-tsē-ˈrä-nē\; *formerly* **Di·é·go–Sua·rez** \dē-ˈā-gō-ˈswä-res\. Harbor and town near N end of Madagascar; pop. (1990e) 54,418; French naval base (maintained since 1901) handed over to Madagascar 1975.

An·tu·co \än-ˈtü-kō\. Volcanic peak in the Andes, Bío-Bío prov., S cen. Chile, near border of Argentina; 9060 ft. (2761 m.).

An·tung \ˈän-ˈdu̇ŋ\. **1.** Former province, S Manchukuo; 16,202 sq. mi. (41,963 sq. km.); ✱ Dandong; formed 1932, dissolved 1945.

2. City, China. See DANDONG.

Antunnacum. See ANDERNACH.

Ant·werp \ˈant-ˌwərp\. **1.** Province, N Belgium, adjoins Dutch frontier; ✱ Antwerp; consists of extensive sandy, but fertile, plain with tracts of heath and morass in N and NE; watered by Schelde River and its tributaries, the Rupel, Nèthe, and Dijle. See table at BELGIUM.

2. *or Fr.* **An·vers** \äⁿ-ˈver, -ˈvers\ *or Flem.* **Ant·wer·pen** \ˈänt-ˌver-pən\. City, its ✱, on right bank of Schelde River 23 mi. (37 km.) N of Brussels; pop. (1991c) 467,518; Belgium's major port; large volume of trade; shipyards, automobile-assembly plants, oil refineries; food processing, diamond cutting; State Univ. Center (1965), Royal Museum of Fine Arts (1880–90), zoological garden; improved and modernized, its ancient walls having been extended (now ab. 8 mi. or 13 km.) and converted into boulevards; vestiges of ancient city remain in the 14th cent. cathedral of Notre Dame (largest Gothic structure in the Low Countries, containing three celebrated paintings by Flemish painter Peter Paul Rubens), the church of St. Jacques, the hôtel de ville, the Bourse, the Vieille Boucherie, and the Steen (part of ancient castle); fortified by 8 outlying forts, and later, by a 2d row of 15 forts.

History: By 11th cent., center of margravate later attached to duchy of Brabant (*q.v.*); received municipal rights 1291; member of Hanseatic League 1315; gradually superseded Brugge as center for cloth trade with England in 15th cent.; part of Burgundian inheritance of Holy Roman Emperor Charles V (see BELGIUM); as distribution center for Spanish and Portuguese colonial trade, became commercial and financial capital of Europe in 16th cent.; attacked in "Spanish Fury" 1576; captured by duke of Parma 1585; declined because of these destructive invasions, eviction of Protestants, and finally, provision in Treaty of Westphalia (1648) closing Schelde to navigation (see AMSTERDAM 2); center of famous schools of painting (Quentin Massys in 16th cent., Sir Anthony Van Dyck and Peter Paul Rubens in 17th cent.); began to revive after French Emperor Napoléon's improvement of harbor c. 1803; part of kingdom of the Netherlands 1815–30; capture by French 1832 and cession to Belgian nationalists meant success of Belgian revolt from Netherlands; with expanded harbor and dock facilities and aided by free navigation of Schelde 1863, became one of world's leading ports; site of Olympic Games (1920); besieged and taken by Germans during both World Wars; city and port rebounded each time.

Antwerp Island. See ANVERS ISLAND.

An Uaimh. See NAVAN.

Anu·da Island \ä-ˈnü-dä\ *or* **Cher·ry Island** \ˈcher-ē\. One of the Santa Cruz Is., SW Pacific Ocean, in E part of group on 170°E long.

Anu·ra·dha·pu·ra \ə-ˈnu̇r-ə-də-ˌpu̇r-ə\. Town, ✻ of N Central Prov., Sri Lanka, 106 mi. (170 km.) NNE of Colombo; pop. (1990e) 37,000.

History: Ancient ✻ of Singhalese kings of Ceylon; traditionally founded in 5th cent. B.C.; sacred to Buddhists as site of conversion to Buddhism of Ceylonese ruler by Mahinda, son of Indian King Aśoka, who visited the island ab. 251–246 B.C.; contains sacred Bo Tree, oldest existing historical tree, grown from a slip of the original sacred tree at Bodh Gayā (*q.v.*); abandoned as ✻ of Singhalese line late 10th or early 11th cent. A.D. in order to escape Tamil invasions; discovered in ruins and reopened by British in 19th cent.

Anvers. See ANTWERP 2.

An·vers Island \äⁿ-ˈver, -ˈvers\; *formerly* **Ant·werp Island** \ˈant-ˌwərp\. Largest island of the Palmer Archipelago, off W coast of Antarctic Penin., Antarctica, 64°33′S, 63°35′W. Visited and named 1898 by a Belgian expedition.

Anxur. See TERRACINA.

An·yang *or* **An–yang** \ˈän-ˈyäŋ\. **1.** Town, NE Henan prov., E cen. China, 90 mi. (145 km.) N of Kaifeng; pop. (1990p) 480,668; archaeological site and an ancient ✻ of Shang dynasty 2d millennium B.C.

2. City, NW South Korea, pop. (1985c) 361,577.

A'·nyê·ma·qên Shan \ˈä-ˌnyä-ˌmä-ˈchen-ˈshän\ *or W.-G.* **A–ni–ma–ch'ing Shan** \ˈä-nē-ˌmä-ˈchiŋ-ˈshän\ *or Eng.* **Am·ne Ma·chin Mountains** \ˈäm-nē-mä-ˈchin\. Range of the Kunlun Shan in E cen. Qinghai, W cen. China; highest peak, Maqên Gangri (*q.v.*).

Anyui \ə-ˈnyü-ē\. River, N Khabarovsk Kray, SE Russia in Asia; rises in Chukoshoye Nagor'ye and flows in two branches W to lower Kolyma River; ab. 420 mi. (675 km.) long.

An·zac Cove \ˈan-ˌzak\. Small bay, an inlet of the Aegean Sea, on Gallipoli Penin. S of Anafarta Bay, Turkey in Europe, 14 mi. (22.5 km.) from its S tip. Anzacs (Australian and New Zealand troops) landed here Apr. 25, 1915, and engaged in actions up to June 30 to retain hold; battle of Sari Bair followed Aug. 6–10, 1915 with heavy loss of lives; all troops withdrawn by Jan. 1916.

Anzali, Bandar–e. See ENZELI.

Anzan. See ANSHAN (Persia).

An·zhe·ro–Sud·zhensk \ən-ˈzher-ə-sü-ˈjensk\. Town, Kemerovo Oblast, S Russia in Asia, in the Kuznetsk Basin 50 mi. (80 km.) E of Tomsk on Trans-Siberian R.R.; pop. (1992e) 106,000; coal, limestone.

An·zin \äⁿ-ˈzeⁿ\. Commune, Nord dept., N France, on Schelde River 26 mi. (42 km.) SE of Lille; center of richest coal-bearing area in France. Destroyed in large part by Germans 1914–18.

An·zio \ˈänt-sē-ˌō, ˈan-zē-ˌō\; *formerly* **Por·to d'Anzio** \ˈpōr-tō-ˈdänt-sē-ˌō\; *anc.* **An·ti·um** \ˈan-shē-əm\. Mediterranean seaport, Roma prov., Lazio, Italy, 33 mi. (53 km.) SSE of Rome; pop. (1989c) 33,523; fishing; seaside resort, with **Net·tu·no** \net-ˈtü-nō\ (1.5 mi. or 2.4 km. E), the favorite of the Romans.

History: In ancient times, a pirate stronghold under the Volscians; lost independence after rising with Latium against Rome 341 B.C.; colonized by Emperor Nero who also improved harbor; sacked by Saracens in 9th and 10th cents.; modern town dates from restoration of harbor 1698 by Pope Innocent XII; site of discovery of ancient artifacts; birthplace of Nero 37 A.D. and probably of Emperor Caligula 12 A.D. In WW II site of amphibious landing Jan. 22, 1944 of U.S. and British troops, with purpose of disrupting rear communications of Germans at Cassino; after much severe fighting Allied drive on Rome begun May 25, 1944.

An·zo·á·te·gui \ˌän-sō-ˈä-tā-gē\. State of N Venezuela. See table at VENEZUELA.

ANZUS. See AUSTRALIA-NEW ZEALAND-UNITED STATES TREATY.

Ao·ba \ä-ˈō-bä\ *also* **Oba** \ˈō-bä\. Island, Vanuatu, SW Pacific Ocean, ab. 30 mi. (48 km.) E of Espíritu Santo; 26 mi. (42 km.) long and 9 mi. (14 km.) wide; 152 sq. mi. (394 sq. km.); pop. (1991e) 8583; copra.

Ao·la \ä-ˈō-lə\. Village, Solomon Is., W Pacific Ocean; on N coast of Guadalcanal, at mouth of **Aola River,** a short stream flowing N.

Ao·mo·ri \ä-ˈō-mō-rē\. **1.** Prefecture, Honshū, Japan. See table at JAPAN.

2. Seaport city, its ✻, on Mutsu Bay; pop. (1992e) 287,354; has most important harbor and trading center of N Honshū; important transportation center; S terminus of Seikan Tunnel; ships fish.

Aonia \ā-ˈō-nē-ə, -nyə\. A district of Boeotia, E cen. Greece; contains the mountains Helicon and Cithaeron considered sacred to the Muses.

Aóös. See VIJOSË.

Ao·raï, Mount \ˈau̇-ˌrī\. Peak in center of Tahiti I., Society Is., French Polynesia, near Mt. Orohena; 6788 ft. (2069 m.).

Aorangi. See COOK, MOUNT 2.

Aor·nos \ā-ˈȯr-nəs\. **1.** Town, Afghanistan. See TASHKURGHĀN.

2. A great rock, Pakistan, thought to be W of the Indus River and NE of Peshawar; successfully stormed by Macedonian King Alexander the Great 326 B.C.

Ao·sta \ä-ˈȯs-tä\; *anc.* **Au·gus·ta Prae·to·ria** \ȯ-ˈgəs-tə-pri-ˈtōr-ē-ə\. Commune, its ✻, also ✻ of Valle d'Aosta, NW Italy, 48 mi. (77 km.) NNW of Turin, at junction of Great and Little St. Bernard passes; pop. (1989c) 36,339; tourism; cathedral said to have been founded by St. Eusebius; Roman remains, incl. triumphal arch of Emperor Augustus, city walls, ruins of amphitheater. Erected c. 24 B.C. as Roman military post by Augustus to celebrate Gen. Terentius Varro Murena's victory over the Salassi (25 B.C.).

Apa \ˈä-pä\. River forming part of E boundary of Paraguay; flows W into Paraguay River; 125 mi. (201 km.) long.

Apache \ə-ˈpa-chē\. County in NE corner of Arizona. See table at ARIZONA.

Apache Junction. City, Pinal co., S cen. Arizona, E of Phoenix; pop. (1990c) 18,100.

Apache Lake. See HORSE MESA DAM.

Apache Mountains. Mountain group S of Guadalupe Mts., W Texas, bet. Pecos River and the Rio Grande; highest peak 5657 ft. (1724 m.).

Ap·a·lach·ee Bay \ˌa-pə-ˈla-chē\. Inlet of Gulf of Mexico, N Florida, on S coast of Wakulla and Jefferson cos., receiving the Aucilla River on the NE.

Ap·a·lach·ia Dam \ˌa-pə-ˈla-chə, -ˈlā-, -chē-ə\. See table at TENNESSEE VALLEY AUTHORITY.

Ap·a·lach·i·co·la \ˌa-pə-ˌla-chi-ˈkō-lə\. **1.** Navigable river, NW Florida; flows S into Apalachicola Bay (Gulf of Mexico); 90 mi. (145 km.) long. Former boundary bet. East and West Florida (see *History* at FLORIDA). E terminus of Gulf Intracoastal Waterway (*q.v.*) is near its mouth.

2. Seaport city, ⊗ of Franklin co., NW Florida, on Apalachicola Bay at mouth of Apalachicola River; pop. (1990c) 2602; sportfishing center; founded c. 1821 as West Point; incorp. 1827; renamed 1831.

Apalachicola Bay. Inlet of Gulf of Mexico, NW Florida, on S coast of Franklin co., receiving the Apalachicola River on the N.

Apa·lit \ä-ˈpä-lēt\. Municipality, SE Pampanga prov., Luzon, Philippines, on right bank of Pampanga River ab. 7 mi. (11 km.) SE of San Fernando; near the Manila-Dagupan railroad line at SW corner of Candaba swamp; pop. (1980c) 48,253.

Apam \ä-ˈpäm\. Town, SE Hidalgo state, E Mexico, N of Tlaxcala; in center of finest maguey region of Mexico and noted for its pulque.

Ap·a·mea \ˌa-pə-ˈmē-ə\. Name of several ancient cities, esp.: (1) City, NW Mesopotamia, on left bank of Euphrates River W of Edessa; (2) **Apamea ad Oron·tem** \ad-ə-ˈrän-təm\, city of W Syria on Orontes River, built by Seleucid King Seleucus Nicator; destroyed by Khosrow II of Persia 7th cent. A.D.; rebuilt, but completely ruined by earthquake 1152; (3) **Apamea Ci·bo·tus** \si-ˈbō-təs\, city on the Maeander (Menderes) River near its source and adjoining Celaenae, S Phrygia, built by Syrian King Antiochus Soter 3d cent. B.C.; conquered 133 B.C. by Rome which kept control only after Mithradatic Wars (first century B.C.); declined with rise of Constantinople as trade center; taken by Turks 1070.

Apa·pa \ä-ˈpä-pä\. Town, Lagos state, SW Nigeria, across channel W of Lagos; has good anchorage for large vessels.

Apa·po·ris \ˌä-pə-ˈpōr-ēs\. River, S Colombia; flows SE to Brazilian border and empties into Japurá River on Colombia-Brazil boundary of which it forms a small section; ab. 550 mi. (885 km.) long.

Apa·ra·dos da Ser·ra National Park \ˌä-pä-ˈrä-düs-də-ˈser-rə\. National park, S Brazil, in Rio Grande do Sul; chief feature is a deep canyon.

Apar·ri \ä-ˈpä-rē\. Municipality on N coast of Cagayan prov., Luzon, Philippines, on E side of Cagayan River near its mouth; pop. (1980c) 45,070; has best harbor on N coast of Luzon with active coast and river trade; fishing; first visited by Spaniards 1572; under Japanese control during WWII.

Apa·seo el Gran·de \ˌä-pä-ˈsā-ō-el-ˈgrän-dā\. Town, Guanajuato state, cen. Mexico, 20 mi. (32 km.) WSW of Queretaro; munic. pop. (1990p) 64,385.

Apa·ta·ki \ä-pä-ˈtä-kē\. Atoll, Tuamotu Archipelago, French Polynesia, S Pacific Ocean, ab. 65 mi. (104 km.) NW of Fakarava Atoll; 6 sq. mi. (15.5 sq. km.); has lagoon 18 mi. (29 km.) long by 15 mi. (24 km.) wide.

Apat·zin·gan \ä-ˌpät-sēŋ-ˈgän\. Town, Michoacán state, SW Mexico, 30 mi. (48 km.) SW of Uruapan; munic. pop. (1990p) 101,173.

Apa·yao \ä-ˈpä-ˌyaů\. Former subprovince, N Luzon, Philippines; now part of Kalinga-Apayao (*q.v.*).

Apel·doorn \ˈä-pəl-ˌdōrn\. Commune, Gelderland prov., Netherlands, ab. 17 mi. (27 km.) N of Arnhem; pop. (1992e) 148,745; railroad junction; connected by canals with Zwolle and Zutphen; garden city; noted papermills; chemicals; nearby is the Loo (Du. *Het Loo*), summer residence of royal family, orig. a hunting lodge of the dukes of Gelder.

Ap·en·nines \ˈa-pə-ˌnīnz\ *or Ital.* **Ap·pen·ni·no** \ˌä-pe-ˈnē-nō\ *or Lat.* **Ap·en·ni·nus Mons** \ˌa-pə-ˈnī-nəs-ˈmänz\. Mountain range, cen. Italy, arbitrarily divided from the Ligurian Alps in the NW, extending the full length of the peninsula in a bow-shaped range from near Savona in the NW to Reggio di Calabria in the S; ab. 838 mi. (1350 km.) long, 25 to 80 mi. (40 to 129 km.) wide; highest peak Monte Corno 9560 ft. (2914 m.). Source of most of the rivers of Italy—many short streams on steep slopes of E side and of longer rivers (Arno, Tiber, Volturno, Garigliano) on W. Crossed by many passes, ab. 13 of main importance. Climate severe in higher areas; vegetation includes (to 1500 ft. or 457 m.) olives, garden plants, and winter pasturage, (to 3000 ft. or 914 m.) chestnut and oak trees and agricultural products, (to 6000 ft. or 1829 m.) beech and coniferous trees, and (above 6000 ft. or 1829 m.) shrubs, alpine plants, and summer pasturage; resemble Alps in geological structure. Famous for hill towns incl. Pistoia, Florence, Arezzo, L'Aquila, and Benevento. See LOWER APENNINES. For the principal ranges and notable passes and tunnels, see table on page 59.

Apenrade. See ÅBENRÅ.

Apeú \ˌä-pā-ˈü\. Island in Atlantic Ocean off NE coast of Pará state, Brazil.

Apex \ˈā-ˌpeks\. Town, Wake co., E cen. North Carolina, 10 mi. (16 km.) WSW of Raleigh; pop. (1990c) 4968.

Aph·ro·dis·i·as \ˌa-frə-ˈdi-zē-əs\. Ancient town, NE Caria, Asia Minor, S of the Maeander (Menderes) River and ab. 50 mi. (80 km.) ESE of modern Aydın; important archaeological discoveries esp. since 1960s; important in Roman times; home of Alexander of Aphrodisias, Greek philosopher, c. 200 A.D.

Aphrodisium. See ANNABA.

Api \ˈä-pē\. Peak in the Himalayas, NW corner of Nepal, near source of Kali River; 23,399 ft. (7132 m.).

Api. See EPI.

Apia \ä-ˈpē-ä\. Seaport, ✱ of Samoa, SW cen. Pacific Ocean, on N coast of island of Upolu; pop. (1991p) 32,859; Scottish writer Robert Louis Stevenson buried nearby; scene 1889 of naval disaster (see SAMOA).

Api·ku·ni *or* **Ap·pe·kun·ny** \ə-ˈpē-kə-nē\. Mountain peak in Glacier National Park, NW Montana; 9053 ft. (2759 m.).

Ap Iwan \äp-ˈē-wän\. Peak in NW tip of Santa Cruz prov., S Argentina, on Chilean border; 7600 ft. (2316 m.).

Apo, Mount \ˈä-pō\. Highest mountain in the Philippines, SE Mindanao, ab. 24 mi. (39 km.) WSW of City of Davao; 9692 ft. (2954 m.); an active volcano with three peaks on its summit; its slopes and immediate vicinity have been estab. as **Mount Apo National Park,** in Cotabato and Davao del Sur provs.

Apol·da \ä-ˈpȯl-də\. City, Thuringia, cen. Germany, 81 mi. (130 km.) ENE of Weimar; pop. (1981c) 28,863.

Apo·li·ma \ˌä-pō-ˈlē-mä\. Small island, Samoa, SW cen. Pacific Ocean, in middle of **Apolima Strait** (10 mi. or 16 km. wide) bet. E Savai'i I. and W Upolu I.

Apol·lo \ə-ˈpä-lō\. Borough, Armstrong co., W Pennsylvania, 25 mi. (40 km.) ENE of Pittsburgh; pop. (1990c) 1895; coal, gas, limestone deposits.

Ap·ol·lo·nia \ˌa-pə-ˈlō-nē-ə\. **1.** Lake, Turkey. See APULYONT. **2.** Name of numerous ancient towns, esp.: (1) Town on N coast of Cyrenaica, E of Cyrene and its port; belonged to the Pentapolis; (2) Town, Illyria, near coast of Adriatic S of Dyrrhachium; a Greek colony important commercially and culturally; Octavius (later Emperor Augustus) studied here; (3) Town, E Macedonia, 30 mi. (48 km.) SW of Amphipolis; visited by St. Paul (*Acts* xvii. 1); (4) Town, NE Thrace, on Pontus Euxinus coast; *mod.* **So·zo·pol** \sȯ-ˈzȯ-pəl\, village on Black Sea SSE of Burgas, Bulgaria.

Apop·ka \ə-ˈpäp-kə\. City, Orange co., cen. Florida Penin., 10 mi. (16 km.) NNW of Orlando; pop. (1990c) 13,512. Settled 1856 on site of Seminole Indian village; incorp. 1929.

Apopka, Lake. Lake on W boundary of Orange co., cen. Florida Penin.

Apos·tle Islands \ə-ˈpä-səl\. Group of islands in SW Lake Superior, off NW coast of Wisconsin; known also as the **Twelve Apostles,** but there are ab. 20 islands; they include the islands of Madeline (with only settlement, La Pointe), Outer, Stockton, Oak, Michigan, Long, and Sand; maintained by the federal government as part of the national park system.

Apostolic See. See VATICAN CITY.

Ap·pa·la·chia \ˌa-pə-ˈlā-chə, -ˈla-, -chē-ə\ *also* **Ap·pa·la·chian America** \-chən\. Region of E United States incl. the various ranges of the Appalachian Mts., with no definite boundaries but generally comprising the S tier of New York, most of Pennsylvania, and the mountainous parts of Virginia, West Virginia, Kentucky, Tennessee, North Carolina, South Carolina, Georgia, and Alabama; historically (c. 1690–1756) included also early settlements beyond the colonies of the Atlantic seaboard.

Ap·pa·la·chian Mountains \-chən\ *or* **Ap·pa·la·chians** \-chənz\. Mountain system of E North America, extending from the Canadian provs. of Newfoundland, Quebec, and New Brunswick SW to cen. Alabama; highest peak Mt. Mitchell (6684 ft. or 2037 m.) in Yancey co., North Carolina. Includes the White Mts. in New Hampshire, the Green Mts. in Vermont, the Catskills in New York, the Alleghenies in Pennsylvania, the Blue Ridge in Virginia and North Carolina, and the Cumberland Mts. in Tennessee.

Appalachian National Scenic Trail. Footpath extending from Mt. Katahdin in Maine to Springer Mt. in N Georgia; over 2000 mi. (3218 km.) long; traverses mountains of the

APENNINES

PRINCIPAL RANGES

NAME English	NAME Italian	LOCATION AND DESCRIPTION	HIGHEST POINT
NORTHERN			
Li·gu·ri·an Apennines \lə-'gyu̇r-ē-ən\	**Appennino Li·gu·re** \'lē-gü-rā\	From upper Bormida River near Savona SE to La Cisa Pass above La Spezia; along coast of Ligurian Sea; many hydraulic plants	Maggiorasca 5840 ft. (1780 m.); on N border of Liguria
Tus·can Apennines \'təs-kən\	**Appennino Tos·ca·no** \tȯs-'kä-nō\ *or* **Tos·co–E·mil·ia·no** \'tȯs-kō-ˌā-mēl-'yä-nō\	From La Cisa Pass SE to sources of the Tiber, 43°50′N; detached range to SW, the **Ap·u·an Alps** \'a-pyu̇-wən\ (*Ital.* **Al·pi Apua·ne** \ˌäl-pē-ä-'pwä-nā\), W of the valley of the Serchio and containing marble quarries of Carrara	Monte Cimone 7103 ft. (2165 m.); in S Emilia-Romagna, SW of Bologna
Um·bri·an Apennines \'əm-brē-ən\	**Appennino Um·bro** \'üm-brō\	From sources of the Tiber SSE to Scheggia Pass above Gubbio and near Cagli	Monte Nerone 5007 ft. (1526 m.); in NW Marche
CENTRAL			
Roman Apennines	**Appennino Um·bro–Mar·chi·gia·no** \'üm-brō-mär-kē-'jä-nō\	From near Cagli SSE to Tronto River, 42°50′N; comprise many parallel ranges with low passes	Monte Vettore 8130 ft. (2478 m.); on SW border of Marche
Abruz·zi Apennines \ä-'brüt-sē\	**Appennino Abruz·ze·se** \ˌä-brüt-'sā-sā\	From the Tronto River SSE to the Sangro; consist of three parallel chains and include mountain knot of Gran Sasso d'Italia	Monte Corno 9560 ft. (2914 m.); NNE of L' Aquila in Abruzzi
SOUTHERN			
Neapolitan Apennines	**Appennino Na·po·le·ta·no** \ˌnä-pō-lā-'tä-nō\	From the Sangro and Volturno valleys S to the Ofanto River; include the **Ma·te·se Mts.** \mä-'tā-sā\	Monte Miletto 6726 ft. (2050 m.); on N border of Campania
Lu·ca·ni·an Apennines \lü-'kā-nē-ən\	**Appennino Lu·ca·no** \lü-'kä-nō\	From the Ofanto River S to the Crati; mark roughly S limit of limestone Apennines	Monte Pollino 7375 ft. (2248 m.); on border bet. Calabria and Basilicata
Ca·la·bri·an Apennines \kə-'lā-brē-ən, -'lä-\	**Appennino Ca·la·bre·se** \ˌkä-lä-'brā-sā\	From the Crati River to S tip of toe of peninsula; include granite plateau of **La Si·la** \lä-'sē-lä\ (**Si·la·gi·an Mts.** \sə-'lā-jē-ən\)	Montalto Peak in Aspromonte Ridge 6417 ft. (1956 m.); S Calabria, E of Reggio di Calabria

NOTABLE PASSES AND TUNNELS

NAME	DESCRIPTION AND LOCATION
Boc·chet·ta \bō-'ke-tä\	Pass, Liguria, NW Ligurian Apennines, N of Genoa, 2532 ft. (772 m.); through it passes highway from Genoa to Alessandria; old Roman road, Genua (Genoa) to Dertona (Tortona)
Ci·sa *or* **La Cisa** \lä-'chē-zä\	Pass, marking division bet. Ligurian and Tuscan Apennines, N Tuscany near source of Magra River, 3414 ft. (1040 m.); railroad from La Spezia to Parma passes under it through tunnel
Fu·ta *or* **La Futa** \lä-'fü-tä\	Pass, S Emilia-Romagna, in Tuscan Apennines, 2962 ft. (903 m.); in valley of the Reno; highway and railroad, Florence to Bologna
Gio·vi \'jō-vē\	Pass and railroad tunnel (5 mi. 250 ft. or 1686 m. long, alt. 1080 ft. or 329 m.), NW Ligurian Apennines, N of Genoa; railroad, Genoa to Turin and Milan
Pe·sca·ra \pe-'skä-rä\	Pass through Abruzzi Apennines along Pescara River, S of Gran Sasso d'Italia; railroad, Pescara to Rome, passes through several tunnels; old Roman road (Valerian Way)
Scheg·gia \'ske-jä\	Pass, N Umbria, marking division bet. Northern and Central Apennines, 1886 ft. (575 m.); lies bet. Gubbio and Cagli

Appalachian Range; highest point on the trail Clingmans Dome (6643 ft. or 2025 mi.) in Great Smoky Mts.; completed 1937.

Ap·pa·noose \'a-pə-ˌnüs\. County in S Iowa. See table at IOWA.

Appekunny. See APIKUNI.

Appennino. Italian form of *Apennines*. See APENNINES.

Ap·pen·zell \'ä-pən-ˌtsel, 'a-pən-ˌzel\. **1.** Former canton, Switzerland, now subdivided into demicantons: **Appenzell Inner Rhodes** \'rōdz, rȯd\ *or Ger.* **Appenzell Inner Rho·den** \'rō-dən\; 67 sq. mi. (174 sq. km.); pop (1989c) 13,656; ✻ Appenzell, almost wholly Catholic, and **Appenzell Outer Rhodes** *or Ger.* **Appenzell Aus·ser Rhoden** \'au̇-sər\; 94 sq. mi. (243 sq. km.); pop (1989c) 51,167; ✻ Herisau, almost wholly Protestant. Agricultural and manufacturing canton, notable for scenic beauty; highest point the Säntis 8205 ft. (2501 m.). Orig. part of dominions of princely abbots of St. Gall; formed alliance with Swabian imperial cities and adopted own constitution 1377; under protection of Swiss Confederation 1411, becoming a member 1513; divided 1597 into demicantons because of religious differences; assumed present status 1803; known for its institution of the Landsgemeinde, a cantonal legislative meeting of concerned citizens. See table at SWITZERLAND.

2. Commune, ✻ of Appenzell Inner Rhodes demicanton, NE Switzerland, 7 mi. (11 km.) S of St. Gall; pop. (1989c) 5270;

\ə\ **abut** \ə\ matches \ᵊ\ kitten, Fr table \ər\ **further** \a\ **ash** \ā\ **ace** \ä\ cot, cart \à\ Fr bac \au̇\ **out** \ḇ\ Span Avila \ch\ **chin** \e\ **bet** \ē\ **easy** \g\ **go** \i\ **hit** \ī\ **ice** \j\ **job** \k\ Ger **ich, Buch** \ⁿ\ Fr vin \ŋ\ **sing** \ō\ **go** \ȯ\ **all** \ȯ\ **law** \œ\ Fr bœuf \œ̄\ Fr feu \ȯi\ **boy** \th\ **thin** \th\ **this** \ü\ **loot** \u̇\ **foot** \ue\ Ger füllen \ue̅\ Fr rue \y\ **yet** \ʸ\ Fr digne \'dēnʸ\, nuit \'nwʸē\ \yü\ **few** \yu̇\ **fury** \zh\ **vision**

resort; ancient chapel of abbots of St. Gall, who made summer home here; Capuchin convent and monastery; 2 mi. (3.2 km.) to the SE is **Weiss·bad** \ˈvīs-ˌbät\, a summer resort.

Ap·pi·an Way \ˈa-pē-ən\ *or Lat.* **Via Ap·pia** \ˈvī-ə-ˈa-pē-ə, ˈvē-ə\. First paved Roman road; extended 132 mi. (212 km.) straight SE from Rome past Lake Albanus to Tarracina, thence along the coast and inland to Capua; built 312 B.C. by Appius Claudius Caecus, censor; later extended through Beneventum to Brundusium, total of 366 mi. (589 km.); near Rome lined with tombs and monuments.

Ap·pi·sto·ki Peak \ˌa-pə-ˈstō-kē\. Mountain in Glacier National Park, NW Montana; 8135 ft. (2480 m.).

Ap·ple·by \ˈa-pəl-bē\. Town, ⊗ of former Westmorland co., NW England, on the Eden 26 mi. (42 km.) SE of Carlisle; pop. (1981p) 2384; trade center; baronial castle (rebuilt in 17th cent.).

Ap·ple·gate Peak \ˈa-pəl-ˌgāt\. Mountain, W Klamath co., SW Oregon, on S rim of Crater Lake; 8135 ft. (2480 m.).

Ap·ple·ton \ˈa-pəl-tən\. City, ⊗ of Outagamie co., E Wisconsin, on Fox River 17 mi. (27 km.) N of Oshkosh; pop. (1990c) 65,695; Lawrence Univ. (1847), Fox Valley Technical Coll. (1967); incorp. 1857; first hydroelectric power plant in U.S. opened 1882.

Ap·ple Valley \ˈa-pəl\. **1.** Town, SE California, N of San Bernardino; pop. (1990c) 46,079; bet. 1980 and 1990 it became incorporated while the population more than tripled.
2. Village, Dakota co., SE Minnesota; pop. (1990c) 34,598; residential suburb 10 mi. (16 km.) S of St. Paul; Twin Cities metropolitan area zoo.

Ap·ple·wood \ˈa-pəl-ˌwu̇d\. Unincorporated settlement, Jefferson co., N cen. Colorado; pop. (1990c) 11,069.

Ap·pling \ˈa-pliŋ\. **1.** County in SE Georgia. See table at GEORGIA.
2. Town, ⊗ of Columbia co., E Georgia.

Ap·po·mat·tox \ˌa-pə-ˈma-təks\. **1.** River, SE cen. Virginia; rises in Appomattox co., flows E into James River at Hopewell; 137 mi. (220 km.) long; navigable to Petersburg.
2. County in cen. Virginia. See table at VIRGINIA.
3. Town, its ⊗, 18 mi. (29 km.) E of Lynchburg; pop. (1990c) 1707; estab. as ⊗ 1892 after fire struck **Appomattox Courthouse** (old county town) 3 mi. (5 km.) NE, the site where on Apr. 9, 1865 Confederates under Gen. Robert E. Lee had surrendered to Union army under Gen. Ulysses S. Grant to end the Civil War; site now a national historical park. See *Appomattox Court House* at UNITED STATES, *National Historical Parks*.

Apra Harbor \ˈä-prä\ *also* **Port Apra;** *formerly (Span.)* **San Lu·is d'Apra** \ˈsän-lü-ˈēs-ˈdä-prä\. Harbor on W coast of island of Guam, W Pacific Ocean; best anchorage in the island, protected on S by Orote Penin. and on N by Cabras I. and reefs; Piti, the port of entry, is on its NE shore.

Apre·mont \ˌá-prā-ˈmōⁿ, ˈa-prə-ˌmänt\. Village, Ardennes dept., NE France, on Aire River ab. 20 mi. (32 km.) NW of Verdun; scene of advance of U.S. division Sept.–Oct. 1918 in battle of the Argonne.

Apri·lia \ä-ˈprēl-yä\. Commune, Latina prov., SW Lazio, W Italy, near Anzio and ab. 22 mi. (35 km.) S of Rome; pop. (1989c) 45,888; founded on reclaimed land of Agro Pontino 1937.

Ap·she·ron \ˌəp-shi-ˈrȯn\. Peninsula, E Azerbaijan projecting into the Caspian Sea; 400 sq. mi. (1036 sq. km.); contains hills that are an E extension of the Caucasus and salt lakes; extensive oil fields; Baku is on SW coast.

Apt \ˈäpt\; *anc.* **Ap·ta Ju·lia** \ˌap-tə-ˈjül-yə\. Commune, Vaucluse dept., SE France, 29 mi. (47 km.) E of Avignon; ocher and sulfur deposits; episcopal see 3d–18th cents.; 12th cent. church (former cathedral); Roman remains. Rebuilt by Julius Caesar (who added to its name the epithet *Julia*).

Apuan Alps. See table at APENNINES.

Apuania. **1.** Province, Italy. See MASSA-CARRARA.
2. Commune, Italy. See CARRARA.

Apu·ca·ra·na \á-pü-ká-ˈrä-nə\. Municipality, Paraná state, S Brazil, 300 mi. (483 km.) W of São Paulo; pop. (1980c) 80,124.

Apu·lia \ə-ˈpül-yə, -ˈpü-lē-ə\. **1.** Historical region, SE Italy. Home of ancient Apulians, a people allied to Rome in Second Samnite War (322–304 B.C.), but unfriendly during Punic Wars (see CANNAE); came under rule of republican Rome by end of 3d cent. B.C.; united with Calabria to form administrative unit of Roman Empire; ruled in Middle Ages variously by Lombards, Byzantines, Normans; invaded by papal forces c. 1228 in struggle bet. Holy Roman Emperor Frederick II and Pope Gregory IX. For later history, see NAPLES 4.
2. Autonomous region, Italy. See PUGLIA.

Apulum. See ALBA IULIA.

Apul·yont \ˌä-ˌpu̇l-ˈyȯnt\ *also* **Abul·liont** \ˌä-ˌbu̇l-ˈyȯnt\ *or Lat.* **Ap·ol·lo·nia** \ˌa-pə-ˈlō-nē-ə\. Lake, NW Turkey in Asia, W of Bursa and S of Sea of Marmara; 18 mi. (29 km.) long, 12 mi. (19 km.) wide; traversed by Atranos River.

Apu·re \ä-ˈpü-rā\. **1.** River, W Venezuela; rises on E slopes of N Andes, flows E into Orinoco River; 509 mi. (819 km.) long; navigable for over 300 mi. (483 km.).
2. State of W Venezuela. See table at VENEZUELA.

Apu·rí·mac \ˌä-pü-ˈrē-ˌmäk\. River, S and cen. Peru; rises in Lake Villafro in Andes, less than 100 mi. (161 km.) from the Pacific, flows N to unite with Urubamba River and form Ucayali River, an upper tributary of the Amazon; 428 mi. (689 km.) long; its lower course for short stretches called the Perené and Tambo.

Aqa·ba \ˈá-ká-bə\ *or* **Al–ʻAqa·bah** \ˌál-\; *also* **Aka·ba** \ˈä-kə-bə, ˈa-\; *anc.* **Elath** \ˈē-ˌlath\; *later* **Ae·la·na** \ē-ˈlā-nə\. Seaport town, SW Jordan, at head of the Gulf of Aqaba and on highway S from Maʻan, at S end of great valley of the Wadi al-ʻArabah; pop. (1990e) 46,090; Jordan's only seaport.

History: As ancient Elath was on the caravan route from Egypt to Arabia and just E of Ezion-geber; a chief city of the Edomites. Called Aelana by the Romans and made a strong military post. In medieval times an important port of Palestine; later held by Egypt, then by Turkey; part of Hejaz 1917–25 and in 1925 taken over by Jordan; occupied by Israel Nov. 1956–Jan. 1957; served as important supply transit point for Iraq during its war with Iran 1980s.

Aqaba, Gulf of; *anc.* **Si·nus Ae·la·nit·i·cus** \ˈsī-nəs-ˌē-lə-ˈni-ti-kəs\. NE extension of the Red Sea, bet. NW Saudi Arabia and the Sinai Penin., Egypt; 100 mi. (161 km.) long.

Aqmola *or* **Akmola.** See ASTANA.

Aqqaqir, Al– *or* **Aqqaqir, El.** See AL-AQQAQIR.

Aqsur, Al–. See LUXOR.

Aq·taū \ˈäk-ˌtau̇\; *formerly* **Shev·chen·ko** \shəv-ˈcheŋ-kō\. Town, SW Kazakhstan, on E coast of the Caspian Sea; pop. (1991e) 169,000; its founding and growth result from development of oil extraction facilities.

Aqtöbe. See AKTYUBINSK 2.

Aquae. See ACQUI TERME.

Aquae Augustae. See DAX.

Aquae Calidae. See BATH 6.

Aquae Flaviae. See CHAVES.

Aquae Grani. See AACHEN 2.

Aquae Gratianae. See AIX-LES-BAINS.

Aquae Mortuae. See AIGUES-MORTES.

Aquae Panoniae. See BADEN 1.

Aquae Sextiae. See AIX-EN-PROVENCE.

Aquae Solis. See BATH 6.

Aquae Statiellae. See ACQUI TERME.

Aquae Tarbellicae. See DAX.

Aqui·da·ban *or Span.* **Aqui·da·bán** \ˌä-kē-t͟hä-ˈbän\. River, N cen. Paraguay; flows W to Paraguay River; ab. 150 mi. (240 km.) long. Scene of battle ending war (1865–70) of Paraguay with Argentina, Brazil, and Uruguay, in which Paraguayan forces were completely crushed and their president, Francisco Solano López, was killed 1870.

Aquidneck Island. See RHODE ISLAND 1.

Aquila. See L'AQUILA.

Aquila degli Abruzzi. See L'AQUILA.

Aqui·le·ia *or* **Aqui·le·ja** \ˌä-kwē-ˈlā-yä\; *anc.* **Aqui·le·ia** \ˌa-kwə-ˈlē-ə\; *medieval* **Aglar** \ə-ˈglär\. Town, Udine prov., Friuli-Venezia Giulia, Italy, 6 mi. (10 km.) inland at head of Adriatic and 22 mi. (35 km.) WNW of Trieste; pop. (1991p) 3359; ancient cathedral; formerly in Austria.

History: Founded by Romans as strongly fortified outpost against Illyrian peoples 181 B.C.; became most flourishing commercial city of northern Italy; ravaged by Attila and Huns 452 A.D., whereupon inhabitants fled to lagoons (see VENICE 4); seat of patriarch who refused allegiance to Roman see 6th cent.; belonged to Carolingian march of the Friuli in 9th line and to march of Verona and Aquileia (fief of Holy Roman Empire); came under authority of Venice in 15th cent.

Aquin·cum \ə-'kwiŋ-kəm\. Ancient town, Pannonia, on the Danube; the modern Buda (see BUDAPEST).

Aquiry. See ACRE.

Aquisgranum. See AACHEN 2.

Aq·ui·taine \'a-kwə-ˌtān\. **1.** Historical region of SW France; orig. roughly equivalent in extent to Roman Aquitania at time of its conquest by Frankish King Clovis, later shrinking in size; ✻ Toulouse.

History: For earlier history, see AQUITANIA. After Frankish conquest 507 A.D., became semiautonomous duchy until subjugated by Frankish King Pépin the Short 768; made subkingdom by Holy Roman Emperor Charlemagne and given to his son Louis I (called the Pious) 781; reunited to French crown 877; after Carolingian decline, became powerful feudal duchy which by 11th cent. controlled most of France south of Loire; passed to Capetian line when Duchess Eleanor of Aquitaine married French King Louis VII 1137, and later to English Plantagenets on Eleanor's second marriage to Henry II, king of England, 1152; from about 10th cent. called Guienne, a corruption of Aquitaine. For later history, see GUIENNE and GASCONY.

2. Region of SW France. See table at FRANCE.

Aq·ui·ta·nia \ˌa-kwə-'tā-nyə, -nē-ə\. A Roman division of SW Gaul; under Roman Gen. Julius Caesar consisted of country bet. Pyrenees Mts. and Garonne River peopled by an Iberic race or races, the Aquitani, whom he conquered 56 B.C.; under Emperor Augustus made one of five divisions of Gaul and expanded to include all of Gaul S and W of the Loire (Liger) and Allier (Elaver) rivers; in 3d cent. A.D. subdivided into: **Aquitania Pri·ma** \'prī-mə\, E part of district bet. Loire and Garonne rivers, with ✻ at Bourges; **Aquitania Se·cun·da** \sə-'kən-də\, W part of district, with ✻ at Bordeaux; became the Guienne of medieval France; **Aquitania Ter·tia** \'tər-shē-ə, -shə\ *or* **No·vem·pop·u·la·na** \'nō-vəm-ˌpä-pyə-'lā-nə\, the original Aquitania bet. the Pyrenees and the Garonne, with ✻ at Éauze. Conquered by Visigoths c. 419; became part of Frankish kingdom on defeat of Visigoth King Alaric II by Clovis, king of the Franks, in battle near Poitiers 507. For later history, see AQUITAINE and GUIENNE.

Aquitanicus Sinus. See BISCAY, BAY OF.

Ara *or* **Ar·rah** \'ər-ə\. Town, W Bihar, NE India, 35 mi. (56 km.) W of Patna; pop. (1991p) 156,871; oilseed processing; scene of defense against overwhelming odds by small body of British troops during Indian mutiny 1857.

Ar·ab \'ā-ˌrab\. Town, Marshall co., NE Alabama, 28 mi. (45 km.) S of Huntsville; pop. (1990c) 6321.

Arab, Shatt al. See SHATT AL ARAB.

'Ara·bah, Wa·di \'wȧ-dē-'ȧr-ȧ-bə\ *or* **Wadi al–'Arabah** *or* **Wadi el–'Arabah** \ˌel-\. Large valley extending S from the Dead Sea to the Gulf of Aqaba, on the border bet. SE Israel and SW Jordan.

Ara·ba al–Mad·fu·na \'ȧr-ȧ-bə-ˌȧl-mȧd-'fü-nə\. Village, Egypt; site of ancient Abydos. See ABYDOS 2.

Ara·bat Spit \ˌər-ə-'bät, ˌär-\ *or* **Tongue of Arabat** *or Russ.* **Ara·bat·ska·ya Strel·ka** \ˌər-ə-'bät-skə-yə-'strel-kə\. Narrow sandy peninsula, Ukraine, on W side of Sea of Azov; part of NE Crimea; ab. 70 mi. (113 km.) long.

Arabia. See ARABIAN PENINSULA.

Arabia Deserta *and* **Arabia Felix.** See ARABIAN PENINSULA.

Ara·bi·an Desert \ə-'rā-bē-ən\ *or* **Eastern Desert.** Desert area, E Egypt, E of Nile and bordering Gulf of Suez and N Red Sea; from ab. 22°N to the Mediterranean; 86,000 sq. mi. (222,740 sq. km.).

Arabian Gulf. See PERSIAN GULF 1.

Arabian Peninsula *or* **Ara·bia** \ə-'rā-bē-ə\ *or Turk.* **Ara·bi·stan** \ˌär-ə-bi-'stän, ə-'rä-bi-ˌ\. Great peninsula of SW Asia, extending N and S bet. 12° and 32°N and 35° and 60°E; length (along Red Sea) ab. 1200 mi. (1930 km.), max. breadth (from S Yemen to NE Oman) 1300 mi. (2092 km.); ab. 1,000,000 sq. mi. (2,590,000 sq. km.). In early times divided into: **Arabia Pe·traea** \pə-'trē-ə\, the NW part incl. Sinai Penin. (not part of modern Arabian Penin.), the only part ever conquered, which became a Roman province; **Arabia De·ser·ta** \di-'zər-tə\, the N part bet. Syria and Mesopotamia; **Arabia Fe·lix** \'fē-liks\ the main part of the peninsula, but by some geographers restricted to that part of Yemen formerly comprising the Yemen Arab Republic. Bounded on N by Jordan and Iraq, on E by Persian Gulf and Gulf of Oman, on SE by Arabian Sea, on S by Gulf of Aden, on W by Red Sea; fertile in some coastal regions, but arid plateau in its central part; no rivers, but many short wadis; important oil-producing region.

Political divisions: Bahrain (islands in Persian Gulf), Kuwait, Oman, Qatar, Saudi Arabia, United Arab Emirates, Yemen.

History: Seat of little-known southern Minaean and Sabaean kingdoms in first millennium B.C.; invaded or crossed by Assyrians, Hebrews, and at different times by Romans; part held by Persians 575 A.D.; before Muḥammad, occupied by Semitic tribes; consolidation begun by Muḥammad and extended after his death 632; center of orthodox caliphate 632–661; under Umayyad caliphate, ruled from Damascus 661–750; lapsed into tribal warfare following Muslim disintegration in 8th cent.; dominated by Karmathians in 10th cent.; in general dominated by Mamlūks and after 1517 by the Ottoman Turks but subdivisions of Al-Hasa, Oman, Yemen, and Nejd were practically independent; influenced by rise of Wahhabi movement centered in Nejd which organized resistance against the Turks (18th–19th cents.); reconquered for Turks by Egyptian Muḥammad 'Alī Pasha 1811–20; Wahhabi empire reestablished 1843–65; internally divided bet. tribes and sects (see HEJAZ and NEJD); in revolt against Turks 1916; resistance directed by British Col. T.E. Lawrence (Lawrence of Arabia) 1917; gradual consolidation by 1932 of Saudi Arabia under its founder Ibn Sa'ūd; for recent history, see individual states.

Arabian Sea. The section of the Indian Ocean lying bet. India on the E and Arabian Penin. on the W.

Arabia Petraea. See ARABIAN PENINSULA.

Arabistan. 1. Peninsula, Asia. See ARABIAN PENINSULA. **2.** Province, Iran. See KHŪZESTĀN.

Arab League \'ar-əb\ *or officially* **League of Arab States.** Political organization, consisting of Algeria, Bahrain, Comoros, Djibouti, Egypt, Iraq, Jordan, Kuwait, Lebanon, Libya, Mauritania, Morocco, Oman, the Palestine Liberation Organization, Qatar, Saudi Arabia, Somalia, Sudan, Syria, Tunisia, United Arab Emirates, Yemen; headquarters at Cairo, Egypt. Formed 1945; boycotted by Egypt 1962–63 and by Tunisia after 1965; Egypt suspended from membership 1979 and headquarters moved to Tunis, Tunisia 1979–90; Egypt readmitted 1989; has coordinated members' policies with regard to economic boycott of Israel and oil deliveries to the West.

Arab Magh·reb Union. \'mä-greb\. Political organization, consisting of Algeria, Libya, Mauritania, Morocco, Tunisia. Formed 1989.

Arab Republic of Egypt. See EGYPT.

Arab Republics, Federation of. Short-lived confederation of Egypt, Libya, and Syria; formed 1971 to effect a united policy against Israel.

Ar·abs Gulf \'ar-əbz\. Inlet of Mediterranean Sea, W of Alexandria, N Egypt.

Ar·a·by \'ar-ə-bē\. Archaic, poetic, or informal name for Arabian Peninsula. See ARABIAN PENINSULA.

\ə\ **abut** \ə̇\ matches \ᵊ\ kitten, Fr table \ər\ **fur**ther \a\ **a**sh \ā\ **a**ce
\ä\ **co**t, **ca**rt \ȧ\ Fr b**a**c \au̇\ **ou**t \b̲\ Span A**v**ila \ch\ **ch**in \e\ b**e**t \ē\ **ea**sy
\g\ **g**o \i\ h**i**t \ī\ **i**ce \j\ **j**ob \k̲\ Ger i**ch**, Bu**ch** \ⁿ\ Fr v**in**
\ŋ\ si**ng** \ō\ g**o** \ȯ\ **a**ll \ȯ\ l**aw** \œ\ Fr b**œu**f \œ̄\ Fr f**eu** \ȯi\ b**oy**
\th\ **th**in \t͟h\ **th**is \ü\ l**oo**t \u̇\ f**oo**t \ue\ Ger f**ü**llen \ue̅\ Fr r**ue**
\y\ **y**et \ʸ\ Fr digne \'dēnʸ\, nuit \'nwʸē\ \yü\ **few** \yu̇\ **fu**ry \zh\ vi**si**on

Ara·ca·ju \ˌȧr-ə-kə-ˈzhü\. City, ✻ of Sergipe state, E Brazil, on the right bank at the mouth of the Cotinguiba River; munic. pop. (1980c) 293,285; in region producing cotton and sugar; university (1967).

Ara·ca·ti \ˌȧr-ə-kə-ˈtē\. Seaport, Ceará state, NE Brazil, at mouth of Jaguaribe River; munic. pop. (1991p) 60,708.

Ara·ça·tu·ba \ˌȧr-ə-sə-ˈtü-bə\. City, São Paulo state, SE Brazil; munic. pop. (1991p) 159,499.

Ar·a·cho·sia \ˌar-ə-ˈkō-zhə, -zhē-ə\. Ancient province, E part of Persian Empire and of the empire of Macedonian King Alexander the Great; ab. equivalent to S part of modern Afghanistan.

Árachthos. See ÁRAKHTHOS.

Arad \ä-ˈräd\. **1.** County, W Romania. See table at ROMANIA. **2.** City, W Romania, on Mureş River; pop. (1989c) 191,428; transportation and commercial center; lathes, textiles, railway cars. A Turkish fort in 17th cent.; belonged to Austria after 1685 and figured prominently in Hungarian struggle for independence 1848–49; passed to Romania 1919 after WWI.

Ara·duey \ˌä-rä-ˈdwā\ *also* **Val·de·ra·duey** \ˌväl-dä-rä-ˈdwā\. River, NW cen. Spain; ab. 100 mi. (161 km.) long; tributary of Duero River.

Aradus. See ARWAD.

Ara·fat \ˌȧ-rȧ-ˈfät\. Granite hill Saudi Arabia; 15 mi. (24 km.) SE of Mecca; object of pilgrimages.

Ar·a·fu·ra Sea \ˌä-rä-ˈfü-rä\. Sea bet. N Australia and Indonesia; 800 mi. (1287 km.) long by ab. 350 mi. (560 km.) wide; W New Guinea touches it on NE and several groups of islands (Tanimbar, Kai, and Aru) lie along its N border.

Ar·a·gats \ˌər-ə-ˈgäts, ˌar-ə-ˈgats\. Mountain, Armenia, NW of Yerevan; 13,418 ft. (4090 m.).

Ar·a·gon \ˈar-ə-ˌgän, -gən\ *or Span.* **Ara·gón** \ˌä-rä-ˈgōn\. **1.** River, N Spain; rises in the Pyrenees and flows SW into Ebro River in Navarra prov.; ab. 80 mi. (129 km.) long. **2.** Autonomous community and ancient kingdom, NE Spain; bounded on N by the Pyrenees, on E by Catalonia, on SE by Valencia, on SW by New Castile, on W by Old Castile, and on NW by Navarre; comprises an autonomous community consisting of the modern provs. of Huesca, Zaragoza, and Teruel; mountainous in N and S portions. See table at SPAIN.

History: After overthrow of Carthaginian power in Spain, became part of Roman prov. of Hispania Tarraconensis; conquered by Visigoths in 5th cent. A.D. and by Moors in 8th cent.; became Carolingian county, emerging from Navarrese rule as independent kingdom 1035; ruled Navarre 1076–1134, Saragossa 1118; united with Catalonia 1137 and 1164, with Barcelona 1150; lost Provence 1196; conquered Balearic Is. 1229–35, Valencia 1238; ruler of Aragon obtained kingdom of the Two Sicilies (1282–85) which he later surrendered for Sardinia and Corsica; held duchy of Athens 1311–88; conquest of Naples initiated c. 1435; united with Castile 1479. See SPAIN.

Ara·go·na \ˌä-rä-ˈgō-nä\. Commune, Agrigento prov., SW Sicily, Italy, 7 mi. (11 km.) N of the commune of Agrigento; pop. (1981p) 10,216; sulfur; near mud volcano **Mac·ca·lu·ba** \ˌmä-kä-ˈlü-bä\, 135 ft. (41 m.) high, 860 ft. (262 m.) above sea level.

Ara·gua \ä-ˈrä-gwä\. State of N Venezuela. See table at VENEZUELA.

Ara·guaia *or* **Ara·guaya** \ˌȧr-ȧ-ˈgwī-ə\. River, cen. Brazil; rises in S cen. Mato Grosso state and flows N into Tocantins River; 1366 mi. (2198 km.) long.

Ara·gua·ri \ˌȧr-ȧ-gwȧ-ˈrē\. **1.** River, NE Brazil; flows into Atlantic N of Amazon River; ab. 240 mi. (385 km.) long. **2.** Municipality, W Minas Gerais state, E Brazil, 290 mi. (467 km.) WNW of Belo Horizonte; pop. (1980c) 83,530.

Araish, Al–. See LARACHE.

Araito. See ATLASOVA.

Ara Jovis. See ARANJUEZ.

Arāk \ȧ-ˈräk\; *formerly* **Sul·tan·a·bad** \sul-ˌtä-nə-ˈbäd\. City; ✻ of Markazi prov., W cen. Iran; on highway N from Ahvāz, junction point ab. equally distant (80 mi. or 129 km.) from Hamadān to NW and Qom to NE; pop. (1986c) 265,349; pottery; known for carpet manufacture.

Ara·ka·ka \ˌär-ə-ˈkä-kə\. Town, W Guyana, on Barima River 140 mi. (225 km.) NW of Georgetown; goldfields.

Arakan. See RAKHINE.

Ara·kan Hill Tracts. \ˌä-rä-ˈkän, ˌar-ə-ˈkan\. Former district of Burma (Myanmar); 1901 sq. mi. (4924 sq. km.); now part of Chin state.

Arakan Yo·ma \ˈyō-mə\. Mountain range in W cen. Myanmar, extending from Manipur state, NE India, S to Cape Negrais; highest peak Saramati 12,663 ft. (3860 m.); includes the Naga Hills, Chin Hills, and Mizo Hills and forms barrier between Myanmar and India.

Árakh·thos \ˈä-räk-ˌthös\ *also* **Árachthos** *mostly formerly* **Ar·ta** \ˈär-tə\. River, W Greece; flows S to Amvrakitós Kólpos; ab. 80 mi. (130 km.) long; chief river of Epirus; navigable to Arta.

Araks \ä-ˈräks\ *in Turkey and Iran* **Aras** \ä-ˈräs\; *anc.* **Arax·es** \ə-ˈrak-(ˌ)sēz\. River, Turkey in Asia, Armenia, and Azerbaijan; rises in mountains of Turkish Armenia S of Erzurum, flows E to join the Kura, about 60 mi. (96 km.) from its mouth, and also since 1897 flows by its own mouth into the Caspian Sea; 568 mi. (914 km.) long; for about half its course, 43°45′E to 48°E, forms the boundary bet. Armenia and Azerbaijan on the N and Turkey and NW Iran on the S; has a very rapid current; chief tributaries Hrazdan from the N and Qareh from the S.

Ar·al Sea \ˈar-əl\ *or Russ.* **Aral·sko·ye Mo·re** \ə-ˈral-skə-yə-ˈmȯr-yə\; *formerly* **Lake Aral;** *anc.* **Ox·i·a·nus La·cus** \ˌäk-sē-ˈā-nəs-ˈlā-kəs, -ˈa-\. Inland sea, bet. Kazakhstan and Uzbekistan; salinity 10.7 percent; previously covered 25,659 sq. mi. (66,457 sq. km.) and was 4th largest inland body of water in the world; diversion of water for irrigation since 1960 has resulted in shrinkage of nearly half; except on S its shores are steppe or desert and uninhabited; on NE receives the Syr Dar'ya and on S the Amu Dar'ya; historically its level has varied greatly over a period of years.

Ar·am \ˈar-əm\. Ancient country in SW Asia extending from the Lebanon Mts. to beyond the Euphrates River; the Hebrew name of ancient Syria; named from a northern Semitic people, the Aramaeans, who emerged from Syrian Desert to invade Syria and Upper Mesopotamia (c. 14th cent. B.C.–1100 B.C.) and who (esp. in 10th cent. B.C.) built up numerous highly civilized city-kingdoms, best known of which was Damascus (*q.v.*); gave its name to Aramaic language. See SYRIA 1.

Ar·an \ˈar-ən\. Island, co. Donegal, Ireland, in Atlantic Ocean off NW coast of Ireland; 7 sq. mi. (18 sq. km.).

Aran·das \ä-ˈrän-däs\. Town, Jalisco state, W cen. Mexico, 70 mi. (113 km.) E of Guadalajara; munic. pop. (1990p) 63,164.

Aran Islands \ˈar-ən\ *or Irish* **Arana Naomh** \ˈar-ə-nə-ˈnyüv\. Group of small islands, co. Galway, W Ireland, off W coast at entrance to Galway Bay; 18 sq. mi. (47 sq. km.); comprises Inishmore or Aranmore (the largest), Inishmaan, and Inisheer; oats, potatoes, fish; chief town Kilronan, on Inishmore; pre-Christian remains. Irish name Arana Naomh literally means "Aran of the Saints."

Aran·juez \ˌä-ˌräŋ-ˈkwāth\; *anc.* **Ara Jo·vis** \ˈar-ə-ˈjō-vis\. Commune, Madrid prov., cen. Spain, 26 mi. (42 km.) SSE of the city of Madrid; pop. (1991c) 36,162; planned and built by Ferdinand VI; known chiefly as site of royal summer palace built by Philip II, rebuilt and expanded by Ferdinand VII and Charles III; abdication of Charles IV 1808.

Aran Mawdd·wy *or* **Aran Mowdd·wy** \ˈar-ən-ˈmau̇th-wē\. Peak, Merionethshire, W Wales, ab. 30 mi. (48 km.) NE of Aberystwyth; 2970 ft. (905 m.); highest in Cambrian Mts.

Aranmore. See INISHMORE and ARAN ISLANDS.

Aran·sas \ə-ˈran-səs\. Coastal county in Texas. See table at TEXAS.

Aransas Bay. Inlet of Gulf of Mexico NE of Corpus Christi Bay, S Texas, bet. mainland and St. Joseph I.

Aransas Pass. **1.** Channel between the Gulf of Mexico and the inlets Aransas Bay and Corpus Christi Bay, S Texas. **2.** City, Aransas, Nueces, and San Patricio cos., S Texas, on a peninsula in Aransas Bay, 21 mi. (34 km.) NE of Corpus Christi; pop. (1990c) 7180; fishing, esp. for shrimp. **Port Aransas** is a fishing resort on nearby Mustang I.

Arap·a·ho \ə-ˈra-pə-ˌhō\. Town, ⊗ of Custer co., W Oklahoma; pop. (1990c) 802.

Arap·a·hoe \ə-ˈra-pə-ˌhō\. County in NE cen. Colorado. See table at COLORADO.

Arapahoe Peak. Mountain in Front Range of Rocky Mts., Grand and Boulder cos., N cen. Colorado; 13,506 ft. (4117 m.).

Ara·pi·les \ˌä-rä-ˈpē-lās\. Village, Salamanca prov., W Spain, 4 mi. (6.4 km.) SE of the commune of Salamanca; pop. (1991c) 488; site of battle of Salamanca 1812 in which allied troops under the Arthur Wellesley, duke of Wellington defeated French under Viesse de Marmont.

Ara·pi·ra·ca \ˌȧr-ə-pē-ˈrȧ-kə\. Municipality, Alagoas state, E Brazil, 60 mi. (96 km.) WSW of Maceió; pop. (1980c) 136,418.

Ara·pon·gas \ˌȧr-ə-ˈpȯŋ-gəs\. Municipality, Paraná state, S Brazil, 300 mi. (483 km.) W of São Paulo; munic. pop. (1991p) 64,528.

Arar. See SAÔNE.

Ara·ra \ä-ˈrär-ä\. Village on N coast of Irian Jaya, Indonesia, nearly opp. Wakde Is. and ab. 125 mi. (200 km.) W of Jayapura; scene of landing of Allied troops 1944 during WWII.

Ara·ra·qua·ra \ˌȧr-ə-rə-ˈkwär-ə\. City, cen. São Paulo state, SE Brazil, 150 mi. (241 km.) NE of São Paulo; munic. pop. (1980c) 128,130.

Ar·a·rat \ˈar-ə-ˌrat\. **1.** Ancient kingdom. See URARTU.
2. *or Armenian* **Ma·sis** \mä-ˈsēs\; *Turk.* **Ağ·rı Da·ğı** *or* **Agh·ri Dagh** \äg-ˈrē-dä-ˈgē, ä-ˈrē-dä-ˈē\; *Pers.* **Koh–i–nuh** \ˈkō-ē-ˈnü\. Isolated mountain in Ağri prov., in E extremity of Turkey, near Iranian border; has two peaks, Great Ararat (16,945 ft. or 5165 m.) and Little Ararat (12,877 ft. or 3925 m.); legendary landing place of Noah's Ark (*Gen.* viii. 4); first climbed in modern times 1829.

Aras. See ARAKS.

Arau·ca \ä-ˈrau̇-kä\. **1.** Department of E Colombia. See table at COLOMBIA.
2. Town, its ✻, on Arauca River.
3. River, W Venezuela; flows E forming a part of Venezuela-Colombia boundary; empties into Orinoco; ab. 430 mi. (690 km.) long.

Ar·au·ca·nía \ˌä-rau̇-ˈkä-nyä\. Region of S cen. Chile, S of Bío-Bío River; home of the Araucanian Indians.

Arau·co \ä-ˈrau̇-kō\. **1.** Former province of S cen. Chile.
2. Commune on coast of Arauco prov., S cen. Chile, 35 mi. (56 km.) S of Concepción.

Arauco, Gulf of. Inlet of Pacific Ocean in coast of S cen. Chile, S of Concepción.

Arausio. See ORANGE (France).

Ara·val·li Range *or* **Aravalli Hills** \ə-ˈrä-vä-lē\. Mountain range, in cen. and S Rajasthan, NW India; ab. 300 mi. (480 km.) long; av. height 1000 to 3000 ft. (305 to 914 m.), highest Mt. Abu 5650 ft. (1722 m.); generally bare and thinly inhabited.

Ara·wa Harbour \ä-ˈrä-wä\; *formerly* **Ra·wa Harbour** \ˈrä-wä\. Anchorage on E coast of Bougainville I., NW Solomon Is.

Ara·we \ä-ˈrä-wā\. Village and peninsula (ending in Cape Merkus) on S coast at W end of New Britain I., Papua New Guinea; first point of Allied invasion of island Dec. 20, 1943.

Ara·xá \ˌȧr-ə-ˈshä\. Town, Minas Gerais state, E Brazil, 65 mi. (104 km.) E of Uberaba; munic. pop. (1980c) 53,436.

Araxes. See ARAKS.

Araxus. See PAPAS.

Ara·yat \ä-ˈrī-ät\. **1.** Isolated extinct volcano, NE Pampanga prov., Luzon, Philippines; 3867 ft. (1179 m.).
2. Municipality, NE Pampanga prov., Luzon, Philippines, at S foot of Mt. Arayat 11 mi. (18 km.) N of San Fernando; pop. (1980c) 56,742.

Ar·ba Minch \ˌär-bä-ˈminch\. Town, SW Ethiopia; pop. (1989e) 24,724.

Arbe. See RAB.

Arbela. See ARBĪL.

Ar·ber \ˈär-bər\. Highest peak in Bohemian Forest, Bavaria, Germany, E of Regensburg; 4780 ft. (1457 m.).

Ar·bīl \ˈar-ˌbēl, ˈär-, -ˌbil\ *or* **Er·bīl** \ˈer-\ *or* **Ir·bīl** \ˈir-, ˈər-\ *also* **Ar·be·la** \är-ˈbē-lə\. City, N Iraq, 50 mi. (80 km.) E of Mosul and S of the Great Zab; in rich agricultural region; a very old city, probably a Sumerian settlement that came to be one of chief places of Assyria; still has important trade; not scene of battle of Arbela, which was really fought at Gaugamela (*q.v.*) 331 B.C.; neighborhood overrun and conquered by Mongols 1236 A.D.

Ar·bo·ga \är-ˈbü-gə, -ˈbō-\. Town, Västmanland prov., E Sweden, 8 mi. (13 km.) N of Lake Hjälmaren on **Arboga River** 9 mi. (14 km.) W of its mouth in Lake Mälaren; pop. (1980p) 14,944; site of first diet in Sweden 1435 and of diet of 1561 at which Arboga Articles were adopted enabling Eric XIV to curb power of nobility.

Ar·bon \är-ˈbōⁿ\; *anc.* **Ar·bor Fe·lix** \ˈär-bər-ˈfē-liks\. Commune, Thurgau canton, NE Switzerland, on SW coast of Lake Constance 16 mi. (26 km.) SE of Konstanz; pop. (1980c) 11,333; Neolithic pile dwellings.

Ar·broath \är-ˈbrōth\; *anc.* **Ab·er·bro·thock** \ˌa-bər-ˈbrȯ-thək\. Seaport, Tayside region, E Scotland, 45 mi. (72 km.) SSW of Aberdeen; pop. (1981p) 24,093; site of meeting of Scottish King Robert the Bruce with Scottish nobles to resist claims of English King Edward II 1320.

Ar·buck·le Mountains \ˈär-ˌbə-kəl\. Low mountain region, centered in W Murray co., S cen. Oklahoma.

Ar·ca·chon \ˌär-kȧ-ˈshōⁿ\. Commune, Gironde dept., SW France, on S coast of the **Bas·sin d'Ar·ca·chon** \ˌbȧ-ˈseⁿ-ˌdȧr-\ (inlet of Bay of Biscay), 32 mi. (51 km.) WSW of Bordeaux; resort.

Ar·cade \är-ˈkād\. Village, Wyoming co., W New York, 33 mi. (53 km.) SE of Buffalo; pop. (1990c) 3938.

Ar·ca·dia \är-ˈkā-dē-ə\. **1.** Residential city, Los Angeles co., SW California, 13 mi. (21 km.) E of Los Angeles; pop. (1990c) 48,290.
2. City, ⊗ of De Soto co., SW cen. Florida Penin., 43 mi. (69 km.) ESE of Sarasota; pop. (1990c) 6488; winter resort.
3. Town, ⊗ of Bienville parish, NW Louisiana, 52 mi. (84 km.) E of Shreveport; pop. (1990c) 3079; salt deposits.
4. *or Gk.* **Ar·ka·dhía** \ˌär-kä-ˈthē-ä\. Ancient country in cen. Peloponnese, Greece; mountainous, highest peak ab. 8000 ft. (2440 m.).
Chief cities: Tegea, Mantinea, Orchomenus, and Megalópolis.
History: Home of Arcadians, an ancient Greek people who never attained full political unity; Tegea fought against Sparta c. 800 B.C. but c. 560 B.C. became its subject ally; Arcadian cities later allied with Árgos, but were forced to return to Sparta 469 B.C.; formed leagues against Sparta 420 B.C. and 370 B.C.; Megalópolis founded 370 B.C. as federal ✻. Suffered in medieval period under Frankish barons, recovered under Turkish rule, again devastated during War of Independence 1821–29.
5. *or Gk.* **Arkadhía.** Department of Greece, nearly coextensive with ancient country. See table at GREECE.

Ar·ca·dy \ˈär-kə-dē\. Archaic and poetic name for Arcadia. See ARCADIA 4.

Ar·ca·ta \är-ˈkā-tə\. City, Humboldt co., NW California, on N end of Humboldt Bay 8 mi. (13 km.) NE of Eureka; pop. (1990c) 15,197; Humboldt State Univ. (1913).

Arc Dome \ˈärk\. Peak, Nye co., cen. Nevada; 11,775 ft. (3589 m.).

Ar·ce·tri \är-ˈchā-trē\. Village, Firenze prov., Tuscany, cen. Italy, near Florence; home of astronomer Galileo Galilei 1633–42.

Archangel. See ARKHANGEL'SK.

Archangel, Gulf of. See DVINA GULF.

Archangel Oblast. See ARKHANGEL'SK OBLAST.

Arch·bald \ˈärch-ˌbȯld\. Borough, Lackawanna co., NE Pennsylvania; pop. (1990c) 6291; anthracite coal.

Arch·bold \'ärch-ˌbōld\. Village, Fulton co., NW Ohio, 42 mi. (68 km.) WSW of Toledo; pop. (1990c) 3440.

Arch·dale \'ärch-ˌdāl\. Town, Randolph co., cen. North Carolina, 19 mi. (30 km.) SW of Greensboro; pop. (1990c) 6913.

Ar·cher \'är-chər\. County in N Texas. See table at TEXAS.

Archer City. City, ⊗ of Archer co., N Texas, 25 mi. (40 km.) S of Wichita Falls; pop. (1990c) 1748.

Arch·es National Park \'är-chəz\. See UNITED STATES, *National Parks.*

Ar·chi·pel·a·go \ˌär-ki-'pe-lə-ˌgō, ˌär-chi-\ *or Turk.* **Je·za·iri–Bahri–Se·fid** \ˌje-zä-ē-'rē-bä-rē-se-'fēd\. Former Turkish province in Asia Minor, composed of islands off W coast; 2660 sq. mi. (6889 sq. km.); now mostly Greek.

Archipel de la Société. See SOCIETY ISLANDS.

Archipiélago de Colón. See GALÁPAGOS ISLANDS.

Archipiélago de los Chonos. See CHONOS ARCHIPELAGO.

Ar·chu·leta \ˌär-chə-'le-tə\. County in S Colorado. See table at COLORADO.

Ar·cis–sur–Aube \är-'sē-suer-'ōb\. Commune, Aube dept., NE France, 17 mi. (27 km.) N of Troyes; battle Mar. 20–26, 1814 in which allied forces under Field Marshal Karl Philipp zu Schwarzenberg defeated French Emperor Napoléon.

Ar·co \'är-kō\. **1.** Village, ⊗ of Butte co., Idaho; pop. (1990c) 1016.

2. Commune, Trentino-Alto Adige, NE Italy, 4 mi. (6.4 km.) N of Lake Garda; pop. (1981p) 11,562.

Arcobriga. See ARCOS DE LA FRONTERA.

Ar·co·la \är-'kō-lə\. City, Douglas co., E cen. Illinois, 37 mi. (60 km.) ESE of Decatur; pop. (1990c) 2678.

Ar·co·le \'är-kō-ˌlā\. Village, Verona prov., N Italy, 15 mi. (24 km.) SE of the commune of Verona; pop. (1981p) 4428; critical battle in French Emperor Napoléon's early career in which he defeated the Austrians 1796.

Ar·cos de la Fron·te·ra \'är-ˌkōs-thā-lä-frōn-'tā-rä\ *or Lat.* **Ar·co·bri·ga** \ˌär-kə-'brī-gə\. Commune, Cádiz prov., SW Spain, 31 mi. (50 km.) NE of the city of Cádiz; pop. (1991c) 26,946; Gothic church; ancient fortifications; ruled by Moors under name of **Me·di·na–Ar·kosh** \mə-ˌdē-nə-'är-ˌkȯsh, -ˌkůsh\; captured by Alfonso X (el Sabio), king of Castile and Léon, in 13th cent.

Ar·cot \'är-ˌkät\. Town, E Tamil Nadu, S India, on Palar River 65 mi. (104 km.) W of Madras; pop. (1991p) 45,193; ✻ of the nabobs of the Carnatic (*q.v.*) from 1712; seized by British soldier and colonialist Robert Clive 1751 during struggle of English against French domination of Carnatic; control fluctuated until formally passed to British with Carnatic 1801.

Arc·tic, the \'ärk-tik, 'är-\ *also* **Arctic Regions.** The Arctic Ocean and lands in it and adjacent to it, about to 70°N; incl. Point Barrow in Alaska, the Arctic Archipelago of Canada, two thirds of Greenland, Svalbard, Franz Josef Land, Novaya Zemlya, N Siberia. See POLAR REGIONS.

History: Areas within Arctic Circle first explored 9th–12th cents. A.D. by Norse, who discovered White Sea, Iceland, Greenland, NE North America, and probably Spitsbergen; exploration advanced 16th and 17th cents. by English and Dutch as by-product of search for Northeast Passage or Northwest Passage (*qq.v.*) to China; S part of Baffin I. discovered and Hudson Strait entered by English mariner Sir Martin Frobisher 1576–78; Davis Strait explored by John Davis 1585–87; W coast of Novaya Zemlya, Yamal Penin., and Spitsbergen discovered by Dutch navigator Willem Barents 1594–97; Hudson Strait and E coast of Hudson Bay navigated by English navigator Henry Hudson 1610–11; knowledge of N Canadian coast advanced by workers of Hudson's Bay Company and of Siberian coast by Russian merchant expeditions and government expeditions (from 18th cent.); area near Spitsbergen and Greenland frequented by whaling expeditions; in 19th cent. its exploration became scientific rather than commercial; as result of loss of Sir John Franklin, who had proved route of Northwest Passage 1845–47, more than 7000 mi. (11,300 km.) explored by 40 relief expeditions 1848–59; Franz Josef Land discovered by Austrians 1871–74, carefully explored by Russian scientists, annexed by U.S.S.R. 1928; Northeast Passage first made by Swedish explorer Nils Nordenskjöld 1878–79 and Northwest Passage by Norwegian explorer Roald Amundsen 1903–06; drift across Polar Basin accomplished by Norwegian explorer Fridtjof Nansen 1893–96; North Pole reached by American explorer Robert Peary 1909; Canadian Arctic explored by extensive sledge expeditions (MacMillan, Stefansson, Rasmussen); first explored from air by Americans Richard Byrd and Floyd Bennett 1926; traversed from Spitsbergen to Alaska in flight of Roald Amundsen, Umberto Nobile, and Lincoln Ellsworth 1926; floating scientific station (Soviet) first utilized 1937; first submerged transit of North Pole (*USS Nautilus* and *Skate*) 1958; exploration and development of natural resources spurred esp. by discovery of oil in Alaska late 1960s; virtually all of the Arctic has now been mapped and modern technology has made much of it accessible.

Arctic Archipelago *also* **Canadian Arctic Islands.** Large group of islands in Arctic Ocean; area ab. 550,000 sq. mi. (1,424,500 sq. km.); nearly coextensive with former Franklin dist., Northwest Territories, Canada; includes the large islands of Baffin, Ellesmere, Victoria, Banks, Prince of Wales, Devon, Somerset, the Parry and Sverdrup groups, and many smaller islands.

Arctic Circle. The parallel of latitude that is approx. 66.5°N of the Equator and that circumscribes the N frigid zone.

Arctic Current. See LABRADOR CURRENT.

Arctic Ocean. The ocean N of the Arctic Circle; 5,427,000 sq. mi. (14,055,930 sq. km.); max. depth 17,880 ft. or 5450 m. (82°23′N, 19°31′E), av. depth ab. 4300 ft. (1311 m.); various sections are known by specific names, as Barents Sea, Beaufort Sea, Chukchi Sea, East Siberian Sea, Greenland Sea, Kara Sea, Laptev Sea, Lincoln Sea, Norwegian Sea.

Arctic Red. River, NW Northwest Territories, Canada; flows NW to the Mackenzie at **Arctic Red River,** post on the Mackenzie SE of Aklavik; 310 mi. (499 km.) long.

Arctic Slope. See NORTH SLOPE 1.

Ar·cueil \ȧr-'kœi\ *or Lat.* **Ar·cu·li** \'är-kyü-ˌlī\. Commune, Val-de-Marne dept., N France, 4 mi. (6.4 km.) S of Paris; notable for its aqueducts, the first (Arcus Julianus, now in ruins) built by Roman Emperor Julian in 4th cent., the 2d by Queen Marie de Médicis 1613–24, the 3d, superimposed on the 2d, 1868–72.

Ard, Loch \'ärd\. Small lake, Central region, cen. Scotland, 2 mi. (3.2 km.) W of Aberfoyle; max. depth 107 ft. (33 m.).

Ar·da \'är-dä\. River, S Bulgaria and Turkey in Europe; rises on S slopes of Rhodope Mts. and flows E joining Maritsa opp. Edirne in NW Turkey; 180 mi. (290 km.) long.

Ar·da·bīl *or* **Ar·de·bil** \ˌär-də-'bēl\. City, East Azerbaijan prov., NW Iran, on the Qareh Sū 30 mi. (48 km.) W of the Caspian Sea; pop. (1986c) 281,973; carpets and rugs; formerly a favorite residence of the Persian court. Home and shrine of Persian saint, Ṣafī od-Dīn (1252–1334).

Ar·da·han \ˌär-dä-'hän\ *or Russ.* **Ar·da·gan** \ˌär-də-'gän\. Fortified town, Kars prov., NE Turkey, 45 mi. (72 km.) N of the city of Kars; stormed by Russians 1877 in Russo-Turkish War; ceded to Russia 1878 but with Kars returned to Turkey c. 1921.

Ar·dea \'är-dē-ə\. Ancient town, Lazio, Italy, near coast; chief town of the Rutuli; conquered and colonized by the Romans 442 B.C. In caves to the N (**Ar·de·a·tine Caves** \'är-dē-ə-ˌtīn\) 336 Italians were massacred by Germans Mar. 24, 1944 as a reprisal measure.

Ardebil. See ARDABĪL.

Ar·dèche \ȧr-'desh\. **1.** River, Ardèche dept., SE France; rises in Cévennes Mts., empties into Rhone; 69 mi. (111 km.) long.

2. Department of SE France. See table at FRANCE.

Ar·den, Forest of \'är-dən\. Wooded region, SW Warwickshire, cen. England, W of Stratford-upon-Avon; 17 mi. (27 km.) by 12 mi. (19 km.); orig. part of a tract supposed to have covered much of cen. and E England; probably the original of William Shakespeare's Forest of Arden in *As You Like It.*

Arden Hills. Village, Ramsey co., E Minnesota, 5 mi. (8 km.) N of St. Paul; pop. (1990c) 9199.

Ar·dennes \är-'den\ **1.** *or* **Forest of Ardennes;** *anc.* **Ar·du·en·na Sil·va** \ˌär-dyů-'we-nə-'sil-və\. Wooded plateau

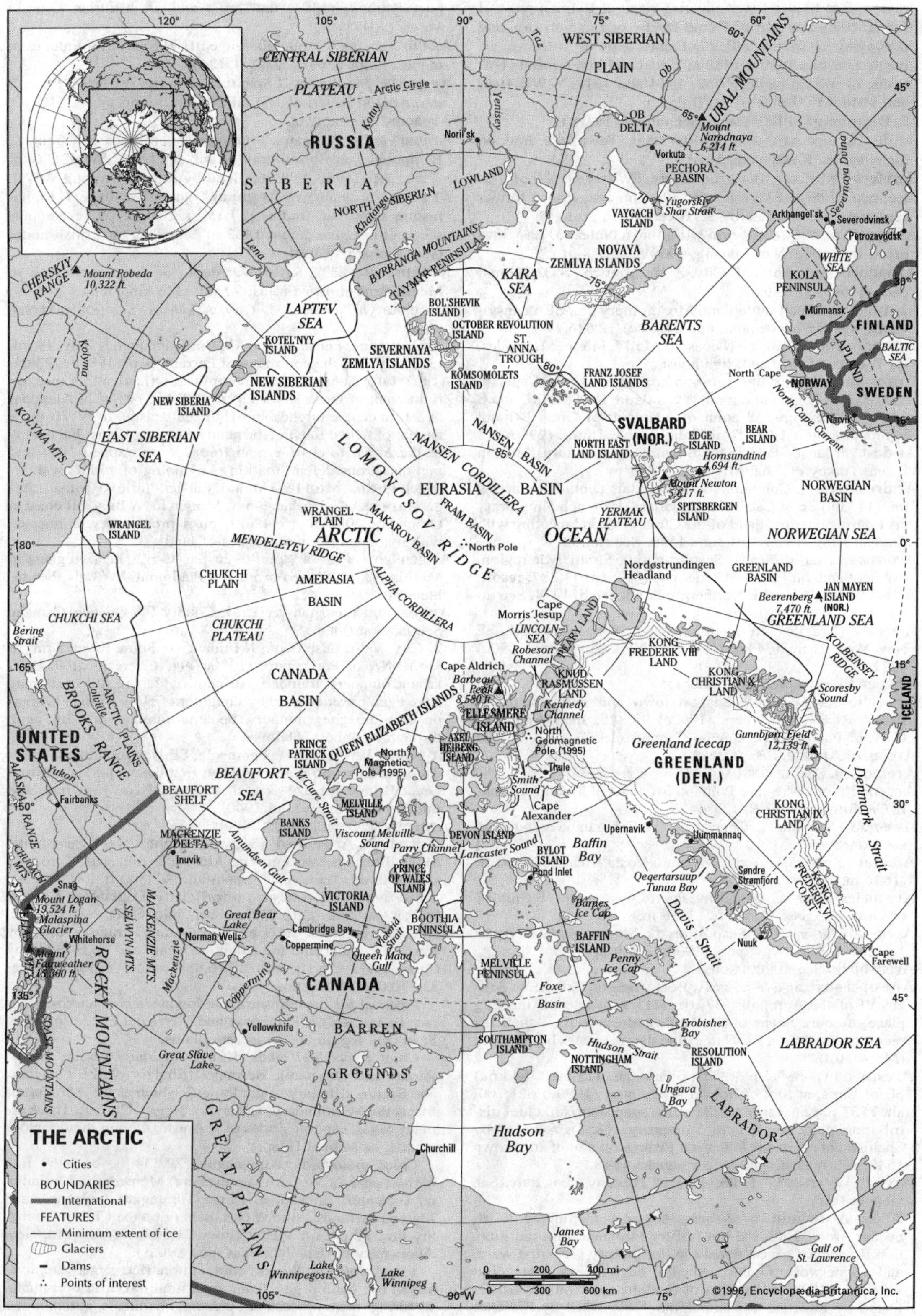
THE ARCTIC
Cities
BOUNDARIES
International
FEATURES
Minimum extent of ice
Glaciers
Dams
Points of interest
CENTRAL SIBERIAN PLATEAU
Arctic Circle
WEST SIBERIAN PLAIN
URAL MOUNTAINS
Mount Narodnaya 6,214 ft.
OB DELTA
Vorkuta
PECHORA BASIN
RUSSIA
SIBERIA
NORTH SIBERIAN LOWLAND
Noril'sk
Kotuy
Yenisey
Taz
Ob
Khatanga
Lena
Kolyma
Severnaya Dvina
Yugorskiy Shar Strait
VAYGACH ISLAND
Arkhangel'sk
Severodvinsk
Petrozavodsk
WHITE SEA
KOLA PENINSULA
Murmansk
FINLAND
LAPLAND
BALTIC SEA
SWEDEN
NORWAY
North Cape
Narvik
North Cape Current
BYRRANGA MOUNTAINS
TAYMYR PENINSULA
NOVAYA ZEMLYA ISLANDS
KARA SEA
BARENTS SEA
CHERSKIY RANGE
Mount Pobeda 10,322 ft.
LAPTEV SEA
BOL'SHEVIK ISLAND
OCTOBER REVOLUTION ISLAND
ST. ANNA TROUGH
KOTEL'NYY ISLAND
SEVERNAYA ZEMLYA ISLANDS
KOMSOMOLETS ISLAND
FRANZ JOSEF LAND ISLANDS
NEW SIBERIAN ISLANDS
NEW SIBERIA ISLAND
KOLYMA MTS.
EAST SIBERIAN SEA
LOMONOSOV RIDGE
NANSEN CORDILLERA
NANSEN BASIN
EURASIA BASIN
SVALBARD (NOR.)
NORTH EAST LAND ISLAND
EDGE ISLAND
BEAR ISLAND
Hornsundtind 4,694 ft.
Mount Newton 5,617 ft.
SPITSBERGEN ISLAND
NORWEGIAN BASIN
YERMAK PLATEAU
WRANGEL PLAIN
WRANGEL ISLAND
FRAM BASIN
MAKAROV BASIN
ARCTIC OCEAN
North Pole
NORWEGIAN SEA
MENDELEYEV RIDGE
CHUKCHI PLAIN
AMERASIA BASIN
ALPHA CORDILLERA
Nordøstrundingen Headland
GREENLAND BASIN
JAN MAYEN ISLAND (NOR.)
Beerenberg 7,470 ft.
GREENLAND SEA
CHUKCHI SEA
Bering Strait
CHUKCHI PLATEAU
Cape Morris Jesup
LINCOLN SEA
PEARY LAND
Robeson Channel
KONG FREDERIK VIII LAND
KOLBEINSEY RIDGE
ICELAND
Cape Aldrich
Barbeau Peak 8,580 ft.
KNUD RASMUSSEN LAND
KONG CHRISTIAN X LAND
Scoresby Sound
CANADA BASIN
ELLESMERE ISLAND
Kennedy Channel
QUEEN ELIZABETH ISLANDS
North Geomagnetic Pole (1995)
Greenland Icecap
Gunnbjørn Fjeld 12,139 ft.
BROOKS RANGE
ARCTIC PLAINS
Colville
UNITED STATES
PRINCE PATRICK ISLAND
North Magnetic Pole (1995)
AXEL HEIBERG ISLAND
GREENLAND (DEN.)
Yukon
ALASKA RANGE
BEAUFORT SEA
BEAUFORT SHELF
M'Clure Strait
Smith Sound
Thule
Cape Alexander
Fairbanks
MELVILLE ISLAND
KONG CHRISTIAN IX LAND
Denmark Strait
BANKS ISLAND
Viscount Melville Sound
DEVON ISLAND
Upernavik
Uummannaq
Baffin Bay
MACKENZIE DELTA
Inuvik
Amundsen Gulf
Parry Channel
Lancaster Sound
BYLOT ISLAND
Pond Inlet
CHUGACH MTS.
Snag
ST. ELIAS MTS.
Mount Logan 19,524 ft.
Malaspina Glacier
PRINCE OF WALES ISLAND
Qeqertarsuup Tunua Bay
Søndre Strømfjord
KONG FREDERIK VI COAST
VICTORIA ISLAND
Barnes Ice Cap
Davis Strait
Great Bear Lake
Cambridge Bay
BOOTHIA PENINSULA
Victoria Strait
BAFFIN ISLAND
Whitehorse
Mount Fairweather 15,300 ft.
Norman Wells
Coppermine
Queen Maud Gulf
Nuuk
Cape Farewell
MACKENZIE MTS.
SELWYN MTS.
Mackenzie
MELVILLE PENINSULA
Penny Ice Cap
Foxe Basin
Coppermine
CANADA
ROCKY MOUNTAINS
COAST MOUNTAINS
Yellowknife
BARREN GROUNDS
SOUTHAMPTON ISLAND
Frobisher Bay
Hudson Strait
RESOLUTION ISLAND
LABRADOR SEA
Great Slave Lake
NOTTINGHAM ISLAND
Ungava Bay
LABRADOR
GREAT PLAINS
Hudson Bay
Churchill
James Bay
Gulf of St. Lawrence
Lake Winnipegosis
Lake Winnipeg
0 200 400 mi
0 300 600 km
120°
105°
90°
75°
60°
45°
30°
15°
0°
180°
165°
150°
135°
90°W
65°
70°
75°
80°
85°
©1996, Encyclopædia Britannica, Inc.

region, E of Meuse River covering most of Belgian prov. of Luxembourg and part of Grand Duchy of Luxembourg, and occupying the Meuse Valley in French dept. of Ardennes; av. height less than 1600 ft. (488 m.); coal and iron mines in NW. Scene of several battles, WWI 1914 and 1918; WWII 1940 and 1944–45 ("Battle of the Bulge").

2. Department of NE France. See table at FRANCE.

Ar·de·stān *also* **Ar·di·stan** \ˌär-de-ˈstän\. Town, cen. Iran, on highway bet. Kāshān and Yazd.

Ard·fert \ˈärd-fərt\. Town, co. Kerry, SW Ireland NW of Tralee; pop. (1986c) 622; ruins of 13th cent. cathedral; a former espiscopal see founded by St. Brendan 6th cent.

Ar·dju·no *or Du.* **Ar·djoe·no** \är-ˈjü-nō\. Volcano, East Java prov., Indonesia, N of Malang; 9968 ft. (3038 m.).

Ard·more \ˈärd-ˌmōr\. **1.** City, ⊗ of Carter co., S Oklahoma; pop. (1990c) 23,079.

2. Unincorporated settlement, Montgomery co., SE Pennsylvania, NW of Philadelphia; pop. (1990c) 12,646.

Ardmore Point. Cape on N coast of Mull I. in Inner Hebrides, off W coast of Scotland; lighthouse.

Ard·na·mur·chan Point \ˌärd-nə-ˈmər-kən, -kən\. Cape on NW coast of Highland region, W Scotland, N of Mull I. and S of Eigg I.; extreme W point of mainland of Great Britain; lighthouse, built 1849, fixed light, visible 18 mi. (29 km.).

Ar·dost \är-ˈdȯst\. Peak in the Bulgar Dağları, Taurus Mts., in S cen. Turkey in Asia; 11,444 ft. (3488 m.).

Ar·dres \ˈȧdrᵊ\. Commune, Pas-de-Calais dept., N France, 9 mi. (14 km.) SE of Calais; headquarters of French King Francis I during nearby "Field of the Cloth of Gold" meeting with English King Henry VIII June 1520. See GUÎNES.

Ard·ros·san \är-ˈdrȯ-sən\. Seaport burgh, Strathclyde region, SW Scotland, on Firth of Clyde; pop. (1981p) 11,337; resort.

Ards \ˈärdz\. District E Northern Ireland; estab. 1974. See table at IRELAND, NORTHERN.

Ards·ley \ˈärdz-lē\. Residential village, Westchester co., SE New York, 21 mi. (34 km.) N of New York City; pop. (1990c) 4272.

Arduenna Silva. See ARDENNES 1.

Are·ci·bo \ˌä-rä-ˈsē-bō\. Seaport town and municipality, N Puerto Rico; munic. pop. (1990c) 93,385; Inter American Univ. of Puerto Rico, Arecibo Campus (1957).

Arelas *or* **Arelate.** See ARLES 2.

Aremorica. See ARMORICA.

Are·na, Point \ə-ˈrē-nə\. Point on SW coast of Mendocino co., W California, 38°57′N, 123°44′W.

Ar·e·nac \ˈar-ə-ˌnak\. County in E Michigan. See table at MICHIGAN.

Are·nal \ˌä-rä-ˈnäl\. Active volcano, Costa Rica; ab. 5360 ft. (1634 m.).

Are·na·les \ˌä-rä-ˈnä-lās\. Peak, Puerto Aysén prov., S Chile, E of Gulf of Penas; 11,273 ft. (3436 m.).

Aren·dal \ˈär-ən-ˌdäl\. Seaport on the Skagerrak, ⊗ of Aust-Agder co., S Norway; pop. (1990c) 12,305.

Arensburg. See KURESSAARE.

Ar·e·op·a·gus \ˌar-ē-ˈä-pə-gəs\. Rocky height, Greece, in Athens W of the Acropolis; 377 ft. (115 m.); ancient meeting place of court. Scene of St. Paul's address to the Athenians recorded in *Acts* xvii. Name literally means "Hill of Ares (Mars' Hill)."

Are·qui·pa \ˌä-rä-ˈkē-pä\. City, S Peru, ab. 475 mi. (764 km.) SE of Lima, at foot of Volcān Misti; pop. (1990e) 621,700; alt. 7557 ft. (2303 m.); textile mills; soap; tourism; chief distributing point for S Peru; university (1828); founded by Spanish conquistador Francisco Pizarro on site of Inca town 1540; nearly destroyed by earthquake 1868.

Arez·zo \ä-ˈret-sō\. **1.** Province of Tuscany, cen. Italy. See table at ITALY.

2. *anc.* **Ar·re·tium** \ə-ˈrē-shəm, -shē-əm\. Commune, its ✱, on the Arno 39 mi. (63 km.) SE of Florence; railroad junction. In ancient times, noted esp. for pottery (Arretine ware) and copperwork. Gothic cathedral begun 13th cent.; city-state from 1098; in struggles of Guelphs and Ghibellines, defeated by Florence at Campaldino 1289; ruled by Florence from 16th cent. until unification of Italy 1860. Birthplace of poet Petrarch (1304) and artist and art historian Giorgio Vasari (1511).

Ar·fak \ˈär-ˌfäk\. Mountain range in NW Irian Jaya, Indonesia; highest point Kwoka 8042 ft. (2451 m.).

Ar·ga \ˈär-gä\. River, N Spain; rises in the Pyrenees, flows S into Aragón River; ab. 60 mi. (96 km.) long.

Argaeus. See ERCİYAS.

Ar·gao \är-ˈgä-ō, -ˈgau̇\. Municipality on E coast of Cebu I., Philippines, on Bohol Strait 36 mi. (58 km.) SSW of City of Cebu; pop. (1980c) 44,060; held by Japanese during WWII.

Ar·gaon \ˈär-ˌgau̇n\ *or* **Ar·gaum** \-ˌgau̇m\. Village, N Maharashtra state, cen. India, 137 mi. (220 km.) W of Nagpur; scene of decisive defeat 1803 of Marathas by British under Gen. Richard Wellesley.

Ar·gens \ȧr-ˈzhäⁿ\. River, Var dept., SE France; flows E to Mediterranean near Fréjus; 72 mi. (116 km.) long.

Ar·gen·ta \är-ˈjen-tə\. **1.** City, Arkansas. See NORTH LITTLE ROCK.

2. Commune, Ferrara prov., Emilia-Romagna, N Italy, 19 mi. (30 km.) SE of the commune of Ferrara; pop. (1989c) 22,801.

Ar·gen·tan \ˌȧr-ˌzhäⁿ-ˈtäⁿ\. Commune, Orne dept., France, on right bank of Orne River 23 mi. (37 km.) NNW of Alençon; two 15th cent. churches and 15th cent. castle. In WWII the S anchor of Allied line in Normandy campaign, opp. Falaise; W of these two towns German forces were trapped 1944 and met disastrous defeat, marking beginning of withdrawal.

Ar·gen·ta·rio, Mon·te \ˈmȯn-tā-ˌär-jen-ˈtär-ē-ˌō\; *anc.* **Ar·gen·tar·i·us** \ˌär-jən-ˈtar-ē-əs\. Mountain, W Italy, off coast at Orbetello; 2081 ft. (634 m.); on a promontory, connected with mainland by two tongues of land.

Ar·gen·te·ra, Pun·ta \ˈpün-tä-ˌär-jen-ˈtā-rä\. Peak, highest in Maritime Alps, Cuneo prov., SW Piedmont, NW Italy. See table at ALPS.

Ar·gen·teuil \ˌȧr-zhən-ˈtœi\. **1.** County, SW Quebec, Canada. See table at QUEBEC.

2. City, Val-d'Oise dept., N France, on Seine River 5 mi. (8 km.) NNW of Paris; pop. (1990c) 94,162; residential. Built around nunnery founded 7th cent. which in 8th cent. may have been presided over by daughter of Holy Roman Emperor Charlemagne; nunnery became famous in 12th cent. through its abbess, Héloïse.

Ar·gen·tia \är-ˈjen-chə\. Peninsula, SE Newfoundland, Canada, extending into Placentia Bay; first base lend-leased from Great Britain for use as U.S. Army and Navy air base and military training ground 1940.

Argentiera. See CIMOLUS.

Ar·gen·tière, Ai·guille d' \ā-ˈgwē-ˌdȧr-zhäⁿ-ˈtyer\. Peak in the Mont Blanc massif, Pennine Alps, E France, ab. 8 mi. (13 km.) ENE of Chamonix-Mont-Blanc; 12,800 ft. (3901 m.).

Ar·gen·ti·na \ˌär-jən-ˈtē-nə\ *or officially* **Ar·gen·tine Repub·lic** \ˌär-jən-ˌtēn, -ˌtīn\. Federal republic, S cen. and S South America, bounded on N by Bolivia and Paraguay, on E by Brazil, Uruguay, and the Atlantic Ocean, and on S and W by Chile; 1,072,156 sq. mi. (2,776,884 sq. km.); pop. (1992e) 33,070,000; ✱ Buenos Aires.

Physical features: Subtropical lowlands characterize the N (see GRAN CHACO); Patagonia and Tierra del Fuego (*qq.v.*) in S; in cen. region are temperate plains.

Chief rivers and lakes: Río de la Plata (estuary of the Paraná and Uruguay); Bermejo, tributary of the Paraguay, and Salado, tributary of the Paraná, which as the Alto Paraná forms the NE boundary; Colorado, Negro, Chubut. There are many lakes, esp. on slopes of S Andes; among them famous resorts, as Nahuel Huapí.

Chief mountains: Aconcagua (22,834 ft. or 6960 m.), highest peak of Western Hemisphere, Mercedario, Llullaillaco (volcano), Incahuasi, Cerro Tupungato (volcano), and Maipo (volcano), all in W part, near or on the Chilean boundary line, all except Maipo above 21,000 ft. (6400 m.). Near Aconcagua is Uspallata Pass (see ANDES).

Chief products: Wheat, corn, cotton, rice, sugarcane; livestock; oil, natural gas, lead, zinc, uranium, iron ore; manufacturing: meat processing; cement, chemicals, automobiles, steel, textiles.

ARGENTINA
CITIES
Over 350,000
50,000 to 350,000
Under 50,000
National capital
Provincial capital
BOUNDARIES
International
Provincial
FEATURES
Canals
Waterfalls
Dams
Points of interest
BOLIVIA
PARAGUAY
BRAZIL
URUGUAY
CHILE
PACIFIC OCEAN
ATLANTIC OCEAN
Tropic of Capricorn
Antofagasta
Llullaillaco Volcano 22,103 ft.
Mount Chañi 20,336 ft.
Mount Palermo 20,073 ft.
Antofalla Salt Flat
ATACAMA PLATEAU
Mount Pissis 22,235 ft.
JUJUY
San Salvador de Jujuy
SALTA
Salta
Campo Durán
Tartagal
San Ramón de la Nueva Orán
Libertador General San Martín
San Pedro de Jujuy
General Martín Miguel de Güemes
Metán
GRAN CHACO
Pilcomayo
Bermejo
Bermejito
FORMOSA
Formosa
Clorinda
Ibarreta
Pirané
Asunción
Iguazú Falls
Iguazú
Tancredo Neves International Bridge
IGUAZÚ NATIONAL PARK
Eldorado
MISIONES
Posadas
Oberá
San Ignacio Miní
Paraná
Paraguay
Uruguay
TUCUMÁN
San Miguel de Tucumán
Tafí Viejo
Monteros
Concepción
Aguilares
CATAMARCA
Catamarca
Andalgalá
Belén
La Cocha
Tinogasta
SANTIAGO DEL ESTERO
Santiago del Estero
La Banda
Añatuya
Frías
Ambargasta Salt Flat
CHACO
Castelli
El Colorado
Presidencia Roque Sáenz Peña
Campo del Cielo
Resistencia
Villa Ángela
General José de San Martín
CORRIENTES
Corrientes
Bella Vista
Goya
Santo Tomé
Yapeyú
Paso de los Libres
Curuzú Cuatiá
Monte Caseros
MESOPOTAMIA
Avellaneda
Reconquista
SIERRA DE FAMATINA
PAMPEAN SIERRAS
NORTHWEST ANDES
Chilecito
La Rioja
LA RIOJA
Grande Salt Flat
Salado
Dulce
SANTA FE
Lake Mar Chiquita
Rafaela
Esperanza
Santa Fe
La Paz
ENTRE RÍOS
Salto Grande Reservoir
Concordia
Paraná
Villaguay
Nogoyá
Concepción del Uruguay
Gualeguaychú
Fray Bentos Bridge
Gualeguay
Rosario
San Nicolás de los Arroyos
Largo Brazo Bridge
SAN JUAN
San Juan
Jáchal
Bermejo
Caucete
Mount Mercedario 22,205 ft.
Mount Aconcagua 22,825 ft.
Puente del Inca
Valparaíso
Santiago
Mendoza
San Martín
Mount Tupungato 21,549 ft.
Desaguadero
Deán Funes
Jesús María
Cruz del Eje
Córdoba
Primero
Segundo
Villa Carlos Paz
Villa Dolores
Alta Gracia
Río Tercero
Mount Champaquí 9,157 ft.
Villa María
CÓRDOBA
Bell Ville
San Francisco
Marcos Juárez
Carcarañá
Río Cuarto
San Luis
Mercedes
San Martín Monument
Quinto
Laboulaye
Casilda
Venado Tuerto
Baradero
Zárate
Pergamino
Rufino
Junín
Tigre
FEDERAL DISTRICT
Buenos Aires
Río de la Plata
Montevideo
La Plata
Luján
Cañuelas
Chacabuco
Lincoln
General Villegas
Bragado
Lobos
Chascomús
Pehuajó
Bolívar
Las Flores
Dolores
Samborombón Bay
Point Sur del Cabo San Antonio
San Rafael
Diamante
General Alvear
MENDOZA
Atuel
SAN LUIS
PAMPAS
General Pico
Eduardo Castex
Trenque Lauquen
Santa Rosa
LA PAMPA
General Acha
BUENOS AIRES
Daireaux
Olavarría
Azul
Rauch
Tandil
Ayacucho
General Juan Madariaga
SIERRA DEL TANDIL
Pigüé
Coronel Suárez
Coronel Pringles
Juárez
Balcarce
Mar del Plata
Miramar
Tres Arroyos
Necochea
Coronel Dorrego
SIERRA DE LA VENTANA
SIERRA LIHUEL-CALEL
Bahía Blanca
Blanca Bay
Domuyo Volcano 15,445 ft.
Concepción
Neuquén
Cerros Colorados Reservoir
NEUQUÉN
Neuquén
Zapala
Cipolletti
General Roca
Colorado
LANÍN NATIONAL PARK
Ezequiel Ramos Mexia Reservoir
Limay
Negro
Gualicho Salt Flat
Carmen de Patagones
Viedma
NAHUEL HUAPÍ NATIONAL PARK
Lake Nahuel Huapí
Mount Tronador 11,450 ft.
San Carlos de Bariloche
RÍO NEGRO
SOMUNCURÁ PLATEAU
San Matías Gulf
PATAGONIA
ANDES
VALDÉS PENINSULA
Puerto Madryn
Trelew
Point Ninfas
Rawson
LOS ALERCES NATIONAL PARK
Esquel
Chubut
CHUBUT
Lake Colhué Huapí
CASTILLO PLAIN
Comodoro Rivadavia
San Jorge Gulf
Caleta Olivia
Deseado
Cape Tres Puntas
Lake Buenos Aires
PERITO MORENO NATIONAL PARK
SANTA CRUZ
Lake San Martín
Chico
LOS GLACIARES NATIONAL PARK
Lake Viedma
Santa Cruz
Lake Argentino
Grande Bay
FALKLAND ISLANDS (ISLAS MALVINAS)
(Administered by U.K.; claimed by Argentina)
Stanley
Río Turbio
Gallegos
Río Gallegos
Strait of Magellan
TIERRA DEL FUEGO
Río Grande
TIERRA DEL FUEGO
Strait of Le Maire
Ushuaia
ISLA DE LOS ESTADOS
Beagle Channel
Cape Horn
Argentina also claims a portion of Antarctica; all claims in Antarctica are in abeyance under the terms of the Antarctic Treaty effective in 1961.
0 150 300 mi
0 200 400 km
76° 72° 68° 64° 60° 56°
22° 26° 30° 34° 38° 42° 46° 50°
©1996, Encyclopædia Britannica, Inc.

Chief cities: Buenos Aires, Córdoba, Rosario, La Plata, San Miguel de Tucumán, Santa Fe, Mar del Plata, and Salta; large suburbs of Buenos Aires include: La Matanza, Morón, Quilmes, and Avellaneda.

Political divisions: Divided into a Federal District and 22 provinces (for pronunciation of their names, see their individual entries):

NAME	AREA (sq. mi.)	AREA (sq. km.)	POP. (1991p)
Federal District[1]	77	199	2,960,976
Provinces			
Buenos Aires	118,843	307,803	12,538,007
Catamarca	38,540	99,819	264,940
Chaco	38,468	99,632	799,302
Chubut	86,751	224,685	356,445
Córdoba	65,161	168,767	2,764,176
Corrientes	34,054	88,200	780,778
Entre Ríos	29,428	76,218	1,021,042
Formosa	27,825	72,067	363,035
Jujuy	20,548	53,219	513,213
La Pampa	55,382	143,439	260,041
La Rioja	35,649	92,331	220,910
Mendoza	58,239	150,839	1,400,142
Misiones	11,506	29,800	787,514
Neuquén	36,324	94,079	385,606
Río Negro	78,383	203,012	506,314
Salta	59,759	154,776	863,688
San Juan	34,614	89,650	526,263
San Luis	29,632	76,747	286,379
Santa Cruz	94,186	243,942	159,726
Santa Fe	51,354	133,007	2,782,809
Santiago del Estero	52,222	135,255	670,388
Tierra del Fuego	8,210	21,264	69,450
Tucumán	8,697	22,525	1,142,321

[1] Comprises capital city of Buenos Aires.

History: Little is known of indigenous population before coming of Europeans. Río de la Plata discovered by Spanish navigator Juan Díaz de Solís 1516; explored for Spain by English navigator Sebastian Cabot 1526–30; permanent colonization undertaken by Pedro de Mendoza at Buenos Aires (*q.v.*) 1536; Asunción, Santa Fe, Buenos Aires settled by 1580; attached to viceroyalty of Peru 1620; included with regions of modern Uruguay, Paraguay, and Bolivia in viceroyalty of La Plata or Buenos Aires 1776; Buenos Aires attacked by British 1806–07; with setting up of United Provinces of the Plate River 1816, accomplished its independence from Spain; recognized as independent by U.S. 1823, Great Britain 1825; with its recognition of an independent Uruguay, settled dispute with Brazil 1828; torn by warfare bet. Federalists and Unitarians; after dictatorship of Juan Manuel de Rosas (1835–52), set up federal constitution 1853; allied with Brazil and Uruguay in war against Paraguay 1865–70; finally resolved struggle bet. Buenos Aires and provinces 1880; represented at first Pan-American Congress 1890; settled boundaries with Brazil by arbitration 1895, with Chile 1899, 1902; participated in ABC (Argentina, Brazil, and Chile) mediation of U.S. dispute with Mexico 1914; neutral in WWI; among first to join League of Nations 1920; withdrew 1921 at failure of its proposals for compulsory arbitration; returned to League 1933; participant in all Pan-American conferences; neutral in WWII; government overthrown by army 1943; army leader, Juan Perón, elected president 1946; Perón overthrown by army 1955 and civilian rule restored; military government reestablished 1966; return of Perón and his reelection as president 1973; his wife Isabel became president upon his death 1974; military coup 1976 followed by military government; war with United Kingdom over Falkland Is. 1982; defeat of Argentines resulted in return to civilian government 1983; suffered political and economic difficulties during 1980s.

Argentine Republic. See ARGENTINA.

Ar·gen·ti·no, Lake \ˌär-jen-ˈtē-(ˌ)nō\. Lake, W Santa Cruz prov., S Argentina; 546 sq. mi. (1414 sq. km.).

Argentoratum. See STRASBOURG.

Ar·geş \ˈär-ˌjesh\. **1.** River, S Romania; flows S into Danube River at Olteniţa; utilized for hydroelectric power production; battle Dec. 1–5, 1916 in which Austro-German army defeated the Romanians.

2. County of S cen. Romania. See table at ROMANIA.

Ar·gi·nu·sae \ˌär-jə-ˈnü-ˌsē, -ˈnyü-\. Group of small islands off SE coast of island of Lesbos in E Aegean Sea; naval battle in Peloponnesian War 406 B.C., last victory of Athens over Sparta in the war.

Argirocastro. See GJIROKASTËR.

Ar·go \ˈär-gō\. **1.** Island in Nile River, N cen. Sudan; 25 mi. (40 km.) long, 5 mi. (8 km.) wide.

2. Town on the Nile opp. N end of Argo I.

Ar·go·lis \ˈär-gə-lis\. **1.** A district of E Peloponnese, ancient Greece, forming a peninsula; under Mycenaean influence until invaded by Dorians; dominated, although never completely united, by Árgos.

2. Department of Pelopónnisos, Greece. See table at GREECE.

Argolis, Gulf of *also* **Gulf of Nau·plia** \ˈnäf-plē-ä, ˈnȯ-plē-ə\. Inlet of Aegean Sea on E coast of Peloponnese, S Greece, SE of Árgos; Nauplia is at its N end.

Argolis and Cor·inth \ˈkȯr-ənth\ *or Gk.* **Argolis kai Ko·rin·thia** \ˌär-gō-ˈlēs-ke-ˌkō-rēn-ˈthē-ä\. Former department of Greece, now divided into Argolis and Corinth depts.

Ar·gonne \är-ˈgȯn, är-ˈgän, ˈär-ˌgän\ *or* **Argonne Forest.** Wooded plateau, NE France, in Meuse, Ardennes, and Marne depts. near Belgian border S of Ardennes, lying bet. the Meuse, and the Aisne, with Verdun at its S end; ab. 25 mi. (40 km.) long and 10 mi. (16 km.) wide, alt. ab. 1150 ft. (350 m.). Scene of campaign of French Gen. Charles-François Dumouriez against Prussians before battle of Valmy 1792; also scene of Allied offensive in WWI Sept.–Nov. 1918, often known as the Meuse-Argonne offensive; in WWII overrun by German armies June 1940; crossed by Americans Aug. 1944.

Ár·gos \ˈär-ˌgōs, -ˌgäs, -gəs\. City, Argolis dept., NE Peloponnese, Greece, 7 mi. (11 km.) NNW of Nauplia; pop. (1991p) 22,256; railroad junction.

History: As a city-state under King Pheidon c. 680 B.C., claimed hegemony over Peloponnese, a weak state in continual conflict with Sparta after latter's rise; entered alliances with enemies of Sparta, esp. the Quadruple Alliance (Corinth, Mantinea, Elis, and Árgos) against Sparta c. 420 B.C. and the alliance with Corinth, Athens, and Thebes in Corinthian War 395–387 B.C.; joined Achaean League 229 B.C.; headquarters of Achaean power under Rome; remained under Byzantine Empire until captured by Franks early 13th cent.; held in fief to Athens 1246–61; successively part of Byzantine Empire and then of Ottoman Empire; seat of national assembly in movement for Greek independence 1822; destroyed by Ottoman Gen. Ibrāhīm Pasha 1825.

Ar·go·stó·lion \ˌär-gō-ˈstōl-ˌyōn\ *or sometimes* **Ar·go·sto·li** \-ˈstō-lē\. Seaport city, ✱ of Cephalonia dept., Ionian Is., Greece, on SW coast of Cephalonia I.; pop. (1981p) 7294; good harbor; episcopal see.

Argovie. See AARGAU.

Ar·guel·lo, Point \ˌär-ˈgwe-lō\. Cape, SW Santa Barbara co., SW California; site of missile-testing center.

Ar·guin \är-ˈgwēn\. Island in **Arguin Bay,** N coast of Mauritania, ab. 50 mi. (80 km.) SE of Cape Blanc; discovered by Portuguese 15th cent.

Ar·gun *or Chin.* **Er·gun** \ˈär-ˈgün\ *or W.-G.* **O–erh–ku–na** \ˈō-ˈär-ˈgü-ˈnä\. Navigable river, NE Asia; rises in Da Hinggan Ling, forming part of boundary bet. NE China and Russia, and unites with Shilka River on extreme N boundary to form Amur River; ab. 450 mi. (724 km.) long; called Hailar (*q.v.*) in its upper course.

Ar·gyle, Lake \ˈär-ˌgīl\. Lake, N Australia, in NE Western Australia; formed 1971 as a result of damming of Ord River for irrigation; largest body of freshwater in Australia.

Ar·gyll \är-ˈgīl, ˈär-ˌgīl\ *or* **Ar·gyll·shire** \-ˌshir, -shər\. Former county, W Scotland; ⊗ Lochgilphead; other towns Campbeltown, Dunoon, Oban; mountainous region; coast indented by many lochs and includes many islands (Mull, Islay, Jura, Coll, Tiree, and others) and the Kintyre Penin.

Argyrokastron. See GJIROKASTËR.

År·hus *or* **Aar·hus** \ˈȯr-ˌhüs\. **1.** County, E Jutland, Denmark. See table at DENMARK.

2. Seaport city, its ⊗, on **Århus Bay;** pop. (1989e) 259,493; machinery, textiles; transportation center; university (1928); one of the oldest cities in Denmark, first mentioned 948 A.D.

Ar·ia \ˈar-ē-ə, ə-ˈrī-ə\. **1.** An E province of ancient Persian Empire, now in NW Afghanistan and E Iran.

2. City, Afghanistan. See HERĀT.

Ari·a·ke Bay \ˌä-ˈrē-ä-ke\ *or Jp.* **Ariake Wan** \ˈwän\. Inlet of Pacific Ocean on SE coast of Kyūshū I., Japan.

Ar·i·a·na \ˌar-ē-ˈā-nə, -ˈa-\. An extensive region of ancient Persian Empire incl. the E provs. of Aria, Arachosia, Carmania, Drangiana, Gedrosia and Parthia; named from Aria.

Ar·i·a·na \ˌär-yä-ˈnä\. City, NE Tunisia, N of Tunis; pop. (1989c) 131,403.

Aria·no Ir·pi·no \ˌä-rē-ˈä-nō-ēr-ˈpē-nō\; *formerly* **Ariano di Pu·glia** \dē-ˈpül-yä\. Commune, Avellino prov., Campania, S Italy, 23 mi. (37 km.) NE of the commune of Avellino; pop. (1989c) 23,569; built on rocky height in Apennines; subject to earthquakes; episcopal see; many old churches. Occupies supposed site of ancient Samnite town **Ae·quum Tu·ti·cum** \ˈē-kwəm-ˈtü-ti-kəm, -ˈtyü-\.

Aria Palus. See HAMUN-I-MASHKEL.

Ari·ca \ä-ˈrē-kə\ *or in full* **San Mar·cos de Arica** \ˌsän-ˈmär-kōs-ˌthā-\. Seaport city, Tarapacá region, extreme N Chile; pop. (1992p) 177,330; northernmost port of the republic; located on Pan-American Highway; terminus of railroad line from La Paz, Bolivia (285 mi. or 458 km.).

History: Peruvian seaport in colonial times; occupied by Chile 1880 after boundary disputes resulting in War of the Pacific 1879–84; by Treaty of Ancón (*q.v.*) 1883, which followed Chilean victory, awarded to Chile for 10 years with provision for plebiscite; claimed by Peru and Chile in dispute which long embittered Chilean-Peruvian relations and came to head 1921–29; access to sea through Arica claimed by Bolivia through League of Nations 1920; by settlement of 1929 awarded to Chile but guaranteed as free port for Peru and outlet for Bolivia via Arica-La Paz railroad; with its vicinity made a department of Tarapacá prov. 1930; modern port facilities completed 1965.

Aric·cia \ä-ˈrē-chä\; *formerly* **Ari·cia** \ə-ˈri-shə, -shē-ə\. Town, Lazio, cen. Italy, at foot of Alban Hills on the Appian Way 16 mi. (26 km.) SE of Rome; pop. (1981p) 14,007; resort. One of the oldest towns of Italy; subdued by Romans 338 B.C.; famous for its temple and grove of Diana.

Ar·i·chat \ˈar-i-ˌshat\. Unincorporated village, ⊗ of Richmond co., on Madame I. off S coast of Cape Breton I., Nova Scotia, Canada; first settled early 18th cent.

Ari·chu·na \ˌä-rē-ˈchü-nä\. River, W Venezuela; flows E and joins Arauca River in Apure state; 240 mi. (386 km.) long.

Aricia. See ARICCIA.

Ariège \ȧr-ˈyezh\. **1.** River, S France; rises in E Pyrenees Mts. forming border bet. Pyrénées-Orientales dept. and Andorra; flows NNW through wide alluvial valley into Garonne River 5 mi. (8 km.) S of Toulouse; 106 mi. (170 km.) long; navigable for ab. 26 mi. (42 km.).

2. Department of S France. See table at FRANCE.

Arīhā. See JERICHO 2.

Ari·ma \ə-ˈrē-mə\. Borough, N cen. Trinidad, West Indies, 16 mi. (26 km.) E of Port of Spain; pop. (1990c) 29,695.

Ar·i·ma·thea *also* **Ar·i·ma·thaea** \ˌar-i-mə-ˈthē-ə\. Greek form of Ramah; town, probably in Samaria but not definitely identified, whence came the councillor Joseph who placed the body of Jesus in his own tomb (*Matt.* xxvii. 57 ff.).

Ariminum. See RIMINI.

Ari·nos \ə-ˈrē-nüs\. River, W cen. Brazil; rises in cen. Mato Grosso state, flows N into Juruena River; ab.400 mi. (644 km.) long.

Ari·pua·nã \ˌȧr-ē-pwə-ˈnä^n\. River, W cen. Brazil; rises in N Mato Grosso state, flows N to the Madeira River; ab. 400 mi. (644 km.) long; in SE Amazonas state it is joined by the Rio Roosevelt; by some the lower course is named the Roosevelt. See ROOSEVELT, RIO.

ʻArīsh, Al *or* **ʻArīsh, El.** See AL ʻARĪSH.

Ar·is·taz·a·bal Island \ˌar-ə-ˈstaz-ə-ˌbal\. Island, E side of Hecate Strait, off W British Columbia, Canada, W of Princess Royal I.; 27 mi. (43 km.) long.

Ari·tao \ˌä-rē-ˈtaů\. Municipality, Nueva Vizcaya prov., cen. Luzon, Philippines; pop. (1980c) 22,004.

Arius. See HARĪ.

Ar·i·zo·na \ˌar-i-ˈzō-nə\. A southwestern state of U.S.A., bounded on N by Utah, on E by New Mexico, on S by Mexico, and on W by California and Nevada with the Colorado River separating it from California and in part from Nevada; 6th state in area, 114,000 sq. mi. or 295,260 sq. km. (land area, 113,563 sq. mi. or 294,128 sq. km.); 24th state in population, (1990c) 3,665,228; ✻ Phoenix; 48th state admitted to Union (1912). See table of states at UNITED STATES.

Nickname: Grand Canyon State, formerly the Copper State.

State flower: Saguaro cactus.

Motto: Ditat Deus (God Enriches).

Rivers: Colorado on W border, widened at N by Hoover Dam to form Lake Mead; Verde in cen. part flowing SE into Salt; Salt, rising in E region, flowing W into Gila and widened by Roosevelt Dam to form Roosevelt Lake in cen. Arizona; Gila, flowing SW into Colorado River; Little Colorado, rising in E region and flowing NW into the Colorado.

Highest point: Humphreys Peak, 12,633 ft. (3850 m.), in Coconino co.

Scenic features: Grand Canyon National Park in N; Petrified Forest National Park in E.

Chief products: Cotton, citrus fruit; copper, molybdenum, gold; manufacturing: electronic equipment; food processing, tourism.

Chief cities: Phoenix, Tucson, Mesa, Glendale, Tempe, Scottsdale.

Political divisions: Divided into the following 15 counties (for pronunciation of their names, see their individual entries):

NAME	AREA[1] (sq. mi.)	AREA[1] (sq. km.)	POP. (1990c)	CO. SEAT
Apache[2]	11,171	28,933	61,591	St. Johns
Cochise	6,256	16,203	97,624	Bisbee
Coconino	18,562	48,076	96,591	Flagstaff
Gila	4,748	12,297	40,216	Globe
Graham	4,618	11,961	26,554	Safford
Greenlee	1,879	4,867	8,008	Clifton
La Paz[3]	4,430	11,474	13,844	Parker
Maricopa	9,238	23,926	2,122,101	Phoenix
Mohave	13,227	34,258	93,497	Kingman
Navajo	9,910	25,667	77,658	Holbrook
Pima	9,240	23,932	666,880	Tucson
Pinal	5,386	13,950	116,379	Florence
Santa Cruz	1,246	3,227	29,676	Nogales
Yavapai	8,091	20,956	107,714	Prescott
Yuma	5,561	14,403	106,895	Yuma

[1] Area = land area.
[2] Its NE point, the only point in U.S. common to four states (Ariz., N. Mex., Colo., and Utah).
[3] Carved from Yuma 1983.

History: Inhabited probably from 25,000 B.C. Notable early cultures Hohokum 300 B.C.–1400 A.D. and Anasazi after 100 A.D. Apache and Navajo came later c. 1300. Spanish exploration began with expedition of Franciscan friar Marcos de Niza 1539; Coronado followed 1540; ruled by Spain as part of New Spain 1598–1821; inauguration of Spanish missions to Hopis 1638; region acquired by U.S. by Treaty of Guadalupe Hidalgo 1848 and Gadsden Purchase (*q.v.*) 1853; included in New Mexico Terr. 1850; organized as territory of Arizona 1863; Apache wars continued up to latter part of 19th cent. until Geronimo finally surrendered 1886; with New Mexico refused statehood 1906; submitted a constitution for congressional approval 1911; congressional resolution accepting this constitution vetoed by President William Howard Taft chiefly because of provision allowing recall of judges by popular vote; after objectionable matter withdrawn from constitution, admitted to Union Feb. 14, 1912; by state

\ə\ **abut** \ˈə\ matches \ᵊ\ kitten, Fr table \ər\ **further** \a\ **ash** \ā\ **ace** \ä\ **cot, cart** \ȧ\ Fr bac \aů\ **out** \b̲\ Span Avila \ch\ **chin** \e\ **bet** \ē\ **easy** \g\ **go** \i\ **hit** \ī\ **ice** \j\ **job** \k̲\ Ger **ich, Buch** \$^n$\ Fr **vin** \ŋ\ **sing** \ō\ **go** \ȯ\ **all** \ȯ\ **law** \œ\ Fr **bœuf** \œ̄\ Fr **feu** \ȯi\ **boy** \th\ **thin** \t̲h̲\ **this** \ü\ **loot** \ů\ **foot** \ue\ Ger **füllen** \üe\ Fr **rue** \y\ **yet** \$^y$\ Fr digne \ˈdēn^y\, nuit \ˈnw^{y}ē\ \yü\ **few** \yů\ **fury** \zh\ **vision**

ARIZONA
UTAH
NEVADA
COLORADO
NEW MEXICO
CALIFORNIA
MEXICO
MOHAVE
COCONINO
NAVAJO
APACHE
YAVAPAI
LAPAZ
MARICOPA
GILA
YUMA
PINAL
GRAHAM
GREENLEE
PIMA
SANTA CRUZ
COCHISE
COLORADO PLATEAU
PAINTED DESERT
MOGOLLON PLATEAU
GLEN CANYON NATIONAL REC. AREA
Lake Powell
Four Corners: Only point in the United States common to four states
Pastora Peak 9,412 ft.
Humphreys Peak 12,633 ft.
Hualapai Peak 8,417 ft.
Baker Butte 8,077 ft.
Mazatzal Peak 7,894 ft.
Mt. Graham 10,713 ft.
LAKE MEAD NATIONAL REC. AREA
GRAND CANYON NATIONAL PARK
PETRIFIED FOREST NATIONAL PARK
GREAT DESERT
Phoenix
Tucson
Flagstaff
Yuma
CITIES
State capital
County seat
City
BOUNDARIES
International
State
County
FEATURES
Dams
Points of interest
0 50 100 mi
0 70 140 km
©1996, Encyclopædia Britannica, Inc.

constitutional amendment restored the provision allowing recall of judges Nov. 1912.

Ar·jo·na \är-ˈk̲ō-nə\. **1.** Town, Bolívar dept., N Colombia, just SE of Cartagena.
2. Commune, Jaén prov., S Spain, 19 mi. (30 km.) WNW of the commune of Jaén; pop. (1991c) 5492.

Ar·ka·del·phia \ˌär-kə-ˈdel-fē-ə\. City, ⊗ of Clark co., SW Arkansas, on Ouachita River 28 mi. (45 km.) S of Hot Springs; pop. (1990c) 10,014; Ouachita Baptist Univ. (1886), Henderson State Univ. (1929); founded 1839.

Ar·ka·dhía \ˌär-kä-ˈt̲h̲ē-ä\. See *Arcadia* in table at GREECE.

Ar·kaig, Loch \är-ˈkāg\. Lake, S Highland region, NW Scotland, 10 mi. (16 km.) N of Fort William; 12 mi. (19 km.) long; 6 sq. mi. (15 sq. km.); trout fishing.

Ar·kan·sas. 1. \är-ˈkan-zəs *is usual in Kansas and frequent in Colorado,* ˈär-kən-ˌsȯ *is usual elsewhere*\. River, rising in Lake co., cen. Colorado, and flowing E through S Kansas and SE across NE corner of Oklahoma; bisects Arkansas and empties into Mississippi River in Desha co., SE Arkansas; 1450 mi. (2333 km.) long; navigable 650 mi. (1046 km.); its largest tributaries are the Canadian and Cimarron rivers. See ROYAL GORGE.
2. \ˈär-kən-ˌsȯ\. A south central state of U.S.A., bounded on N by Missouri, on E by Mississippi River separating it from Tennessee and Mississippi, on S by Louisiana, on W by Texas and Oklahoma; 27th state in area, 53,187 sq. mi. or 137,754 sq. km. (land area 52,175 sq. mi. or 135,133 sq. km.); 33d state in population, (1990c) 2,350,725; ✻ Little Rock; 25th state admitted to Union (1836). See table of states at UNITED STATES.

Nickname: Land of Opportunity.

State flower: Apple blossom.

Motto: Regnat Populus (The People Rule).

Rivers: Arkansas, bisecting state from W to E and flowing into the Mississippi; Red, flowing E and S in extreme SW area, forming part of boundary with Texas; Ouachita rising in W area and flowing E and then S; White, flowing from N to SE into Arkansas River near confluence with Mississippi.

Highest point: Magazine Mt. in Logan co., 2753 ft. (839 m.).

Chief products: Soybeans, cotton, rice; livestock (esp. poultry); bauxite; machinery; food processing.

Chief cities: Little Rock, Fort Smith, North Little Rock, Pine Bluff.

Political divisions: Divided into the following 75 counties (for pronunciation of their names, see their individual entries):

NAME	AREA[1] (sq. mi.)	AREA[1] (sq. km.)	POP. (1990c)	CO. SEAT(S)
Arkansas	1,015	2,629	21,653	DeWitt, Stuttgart
Ashley	928	2,404	24,319	Hamburg
Baxter	537	1,391	31,186	Mountain Home
Benton	886	2,295	97,499	Bentonville
Boone	593	1,536	28,297	Harrison
Bradley	651	1,686	11,793	Warren
Calhoun	629	1,629	5,826	Hampton
Carroll	634	1,642	18,654	Berryville, Eureka Springs
Chicot	643	1,665	15,713	Lake Village
Clark	878	2,274	21,437	Arkadelphia
Clay	639	1,655	18,107	Corning, Piggott
Cleburne	539	1,396	19,411	Heber Springs
Cleveland	601	1,556	7,781	Rison
Columbia	768	1,989	25,691	Magnolia
Conway	561	1,453	19,151	Morrilton
Craighead	716	1,854	68,956	Jonesboro, Lake City
Crawford	596	1,544	42,493	Van Buren
Crittenden	608	1,575	49,939	Marion
Cross	625	1,619	19,225	Wynne
Dallas	672	1,740	9,614	Fordyce
Desha	736	1,906	16,798	Arkansas City
Drew	832	2,155	17,369	Monticello
Faulkner	641	1,660	60,006	Conway
Franklin	613	1,588	14,897	Charleston, Ozark
Fulton	608	1,575	10,037	Salem
Garland	658	1,704	73,397	Hot Springs
Grant	631	1,634	13,948	Sheridan
Greene	579	1,500	31,804	Paragould
Hempstead	736	1,906	21,621	Hope
Hot Spring	621	1,608	26,115	Malvern
Howard	600	1,554	13,569	Nashville
Independence	752	1,948	31,192	Batesville
Izard	574	1,487	11,364	Melbourne
Jackson	629	1,629	18,944	Newport
Jefferson	873	2,261	85,487	Pine Bluff
Johnson	673	1,743	18,221	Clarksville
Lafayette	523	1,354	9,643	Lewisville
Lawrence	590	1,528	17,457	Walnut Ridge
Lee	608	1,575	13,053	Marianna
Lincoln	563	1,458	13,690	Star City
Little River	541	1,401	13,966	Ashdown
Logan	718	1,860	20,557	Booneville, Paris
Lonoke	796	2,062	39,268	Lonoke
Madison	832	2,155	11,618	Huntsville
Marion	584	1,512	12,001	Yellville
Miller	623	1,614	38,467	Texarkana
Mississippi	904	2,341	57,525	Blythville, Osceola
Monroe	607	1,572	11,333	Clarendon
Montgomery	775	2,007	7,841	Mount Ida
Nevada	616	1,595	10,101	Prescott
Newton	822	2,129	7,666	Jasper
Ouachita	736	1,906	30,574	Camden
Perry	551	1,427	7,969	Perryville
Phillips	686	1,777	28,838	Helena
Pike	600	1,554	10,086	Murfreesboro
Poinsett	760	1,968	24,664	Harrisburg
Polk	860	2,274	17,347	Mena
Pope	812	2,103	45,883	Russellville
Prairie	661	1,712	9,518	Des Arc, De Valls Bluff
Pulaski	765	1,981	349,660	Little Rock
Randolph	647	1,676	16,558	Pocahontas
Saint Francis	635	1,645	28,497	Forrest City
Saline	724	1,875	64,183	Benton
Scott	898	2,326	10,205	Waldron
Searcy	664	1,720	7,841	Marshall
Sebastian	527	1,365	99,590	Fort Smith, Greenwood
Sevier	585	1,515	13,637	De Queen
Sharp	598	1,549	14,109	Ash Flat
Stone	608	1,575	9,775	Mountain View
Union	1,050	2,720	46,719	El Dorado
Van Buren	619	1,603	14,008	Clinton
Washington	962	2,492	113,409	Fayetteville
White	1,041	2,696	54,676	Searcy
Woodruff	591	1,531	9,520	Augusta
Yell	929	2,406	17,759	Danville, Dardanelle

[1] Area = land area.

History: Early inhabitants, American Indians c. 500 A.D.; among first European explorers, Hernando de Soto 1541, Jacques Marquette and Louis Joliet 1673, Sieur de La Salle and Henry de Tonti 1682; Arkansas Post first permanent settlement (1686); in region claimed by France and yielded to Spain 1762; retroceded to France 1800; included in Louisiana Purchase (*q.v.*) 1803, Louisiana Terr. 1805, and Missouri Terr. 1812; **Arkansas Territory** organized 1819, which included current state plus most of what is now Oklahoma (except a strip along the N boundary), and which was reduced to the current state's boundaries by 1828; adopted first constitution 1836 and admitted to Union June 15 of same year; seceded 1861; capture of Arkansas Post from Confederates 1863; readmitted into Union 1868; implementation of strict Jim Crow laws ensued; federal troops sent to Little Rock 1957 to enforce school desegregation laws.
3. \ˈär-kən-ˌsȯ\. County in E Arkansas. See table at ARKANSAS.

Ar·kan·sas City. 1. \ˈär-kən-ˌsȯ\. Town, ⊗ of Desha co., SE Arkansas, on Mississippi River; pop. (1990c) 523.
2. \är-ˈkan-zəs\. City, Cowley co., S Kansas, at confluence of Arkansas and Walnut rivers 47 mi. (76 km.) S of Wichita; pop. (1990c) 12,762; flour; oil refineries; Cowley County Community Coll. (1922).

Arkansas Post National Memorial. Site of oldest white settlement (1686) in Arkansas and in lower Mississippi valley, on N bank of Arkansas River just above its junction with the

\ə\ **abut** \ˊə\ matches \ᵊ\ kitten, Fr table \ər\ **further** \a\ **ash** \ā\ **ace** \ä\ **cot, cart** \á\ Fr **bac** \au̇\ **out** \b\ Span Avila \ch\ **chin** \e\ **bet** \ē\ **easy** \g\ **go** \i\ **hit** \ī\ **ice** \j\ **job** \k̲\ Ger **ich, Buch** \ⁿ\ Fr **vin** \ŋ\ **sing** \ō\ **go** \ö\ **all** \ȯ\ **law** \œ\ Fr **bœuf** \œ̄\ Fr **feu** \ȯi\ **boy** \th\ **thin** \t̲h̲\ **this** \ü\ **loot** \u̇\ **foot** \ue\ Ger **füllen** \ue̅\ Fr **rue** \y\ **yet** \ʸ\ Fr **digne** \ˈdēnʸ\, **nuit** \ˈnwʸē\ \yü\ **few** \yu̇\ **fury** \zh\ **vision**

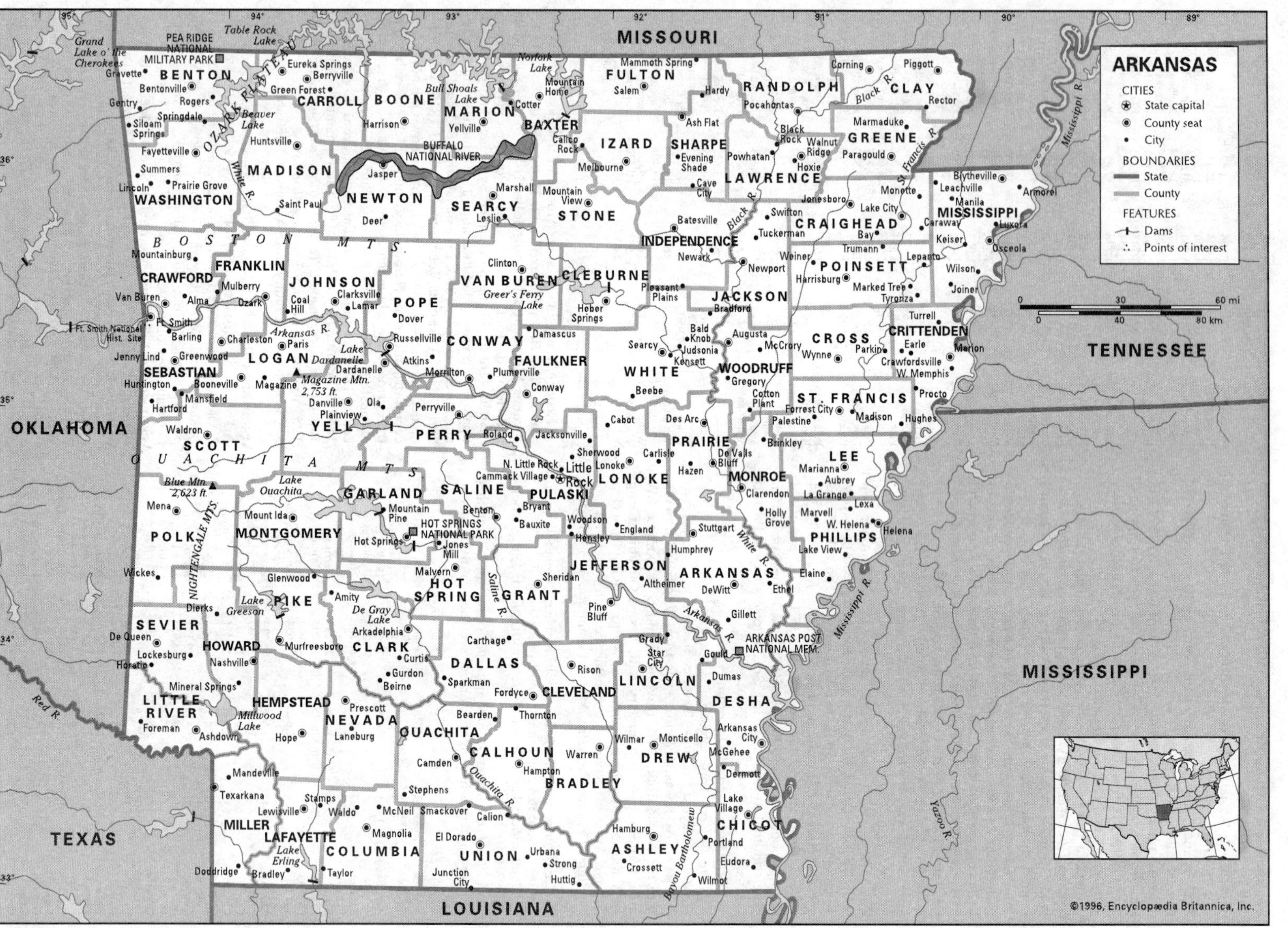
ARKANSAS
CITIES
State capital
County seat
City
BOUNDARIES
State
County
FEATURES
Dams
Points of interest
0 30 60 mi
0 40 80 km
MISSOURI
TENNESSEE
MISSISSIPPI
LOUISIANA
TEXAS
OKLAHOMA
BENTON
CARROLL
BOONE
MARION
BAXTER
FULTON
RANDOLPH
CLAY
SHARPE
IZARD
GREENE
LAWRENCE
MADISON
WASHINGTON
NEWTON
SEARCY
STONE
INDEPENDENCE
CRAIGHEAD
MISSISSIPPI
POINSETT
JACKSON
CRAWFORD
FRANKLIN
JOHNSON
POPE
VAN BUREN
CLEBURNE
CONWAY
FAULKNER
WHITE
WOODRUFF
CROSS
CRITTENDEN
LOGAN
SEBASTIAN
ST. FRANCIS
SCOTT
YELL
PERRY
PRAIRIE
LEE
PULASKI
LONOKE
MONROE
GARLAND
SALINE
POLK
MONTGOMERY
PHILLIPS
JEFFERSON
ARKANSAS
HOT SPRING
GRANT
PIKE
SEVIER
HOWARD
CLARK
DALLAS
LINCOLN
CLEVELAND
DESHA
LITTLE RIVER
HEMPSTEAD
NEVADA
OUACHITA
CALHOUN
DREW
BRADLEY
MILLER
LAFAYETTE
COLUMBIA
UNION
ASHLEY
CHICOT
PEA RIDGE NATIONAL MILITARY PARK
BUFFALO NATIONAL RIVER
OZARK PLATEAU
BOSTON MTS
OUACHITA MTS
NIGHTENGALE MTS
HOT SPRINGS NATIONAL PARK
ARKANSAS POST NATIONAL MEM.
Ft. Smith National Hist. Site
Magazine Mtn. 2,753 ft.
Blue Mtn. 2,623 ft.
Grand Lake o' the Cherokees
Table Rock Lake
Beaver Lake
Bull Shoals Lake
Norfork Lake
Greer's Ferry Lake
Lake Dardanelle
Lake Ouachita
Lake Greeson
De Gray Lake
Millwood Lake
Lake Erling
Mississippi R.
Arkansas R.
White R.
Black R.
St. Francis R.
Saline R.
Ouachita R.
Red R.
Yazoo R.
Bayou Bartholomew
Little Rock
North Little Rock
Fayetteville
Fort Smith
Jonesboro
Pine Bluff
Hot Springs
Texarkana
El Dorado
Helena
©1996, Encyclopædia Britannica, Inc.

Mississippi; estab. by Henry de Tonti, one of Sieur de La Salle's expedition; colonized by John Law 1717–1720; became part of Louisiana Terr. 1763; ✱ of Arkansas Terr. 1819–21; captured by Union troops Jan. 12, 1863; declined after Civil War; park created 1960.

Arkansas River Navigation System. See MCCLELLAN-KERR ARKANSAS RIVER NAVIGATION SYSTEM.

Ar·khan·gel'sk *or* **Ar·khan·gelsk** \ˌər-'kän-gilsk, är-'kan-ˌgelsk\ *or Eng.* **Arch·an·gel** \'är-ˌkān-jəl\. City, ✱ of Arkhangel'sk Oblast, Russia, on right bank of Northern Dvina near its mouth ab. 460 mi. (740 km.) NE of St. Petersburg; pop. (1992e) 414,000; major export is timber; shipbuilding, paper and pulp making. At head of Dvina Gulf with very large harbor, closed by ice sometimes as much as 190 days in a year, but this handicap now much reduced by icebreakers; has much river and canal traffic and is terminus of rail lines to Moscow and St. Petersburg; has a monastery dedicated to the Archangel Michael, from which it received its name.

History: Vicinity settled by Norsemen 10th cent. A.D.; harbor discovered by English trading expedition under Richard Chancellor who had been sent to discover Northeast Passage 1553; town began with establishment there of first factory (trading station) of Muscovy Company; opened to trade of other European nations by Czar Boris Godunov (1598–1605); flourished as sole Russian seaport until building of St. Petersburg 1703; a scene of Allied (British, French, and American) support of N Russian government which resisted Bolshevik government of Russia 1918–19; of great importance in WWII, receiving convoys of lend-lease goods from England and U.S. 1941–45.

Arkhangel'sk Oblast *or* **Arkhangelsk Oblast** \'ó-bləst, -ˌblast\ *or* **Ar·khan·gel'·ska·ya Oblast'** \ˌər-'kän-gil-skə-yə\ *or Eng.* **Archangel Oblast.** Subdivision of Russia in Europe, bordering on Barents Sea; its W coast extends along the White Sea; 226,795 sq. mi. (587,399 sq. km.); pop. (1992e) 1,571,000; ✱ Arkhangel'sk. Includes also two large island groups in the Arctic, Novaya Zemlya and Franz Josef Land. Chief rivers: Northern Dvina, Onega, and lower course of Mezen. Climate is severe and coastal waters are frozen from late October for an av. of 140 days; lumbering, fishing; chief settlements: Arkhangel'sk, Onega, Severodvinsk, Mezen, Kotlas; formed 1937.

Ark·low \'är-ˌklō\. Market town and seaport, co. Wicklow, SE Ireland, on E coast at mouth of Avoca River 37 mi. (60 km.) S of Dublin; pop. (1986c) 8388; fisheries; ancient castle of the Ormondes captured and demolished by English Parliamentarian commander Oliver Cromwell 1649; Irish insurgents defeated by British 1798.

Ar·ko·na \är-'kō-nə\. Promontory on N coast of Rügen I., NE Germany, in Baltic Sea, 148 ft. (45 m.) above sea level; remains of foundation of ancient temple, destroyed 1168 by Danes and Pomeranians, found 1921.

Arl·berg \'ärl-ˌberk\. Alpine valley, pass, and tunnel in the Tirol, W Austria. In the valley the "Arlberg technique" in skiing was perfected. See table at ALPS.

Arles \'årl, 'ärlz\. **1.** Medieval kingdom, also called kingdom of Burgundy (*q.v.*), formed from union by Rudolf II, king of Burgundy, in 933 of kingdoms of Cisjurane Burgundy and Transjurane Burgundy; attached to Holy Roman Empire under Emperor Conrad II 1033–34; kingdom had only nominal unity in 11th and 12th cents., although title king of Arles was assumed by German emperors, notably by Frederick Barbarossa 1178; gradually split up, Provence passing to house of Anjou 1246 and to French crown 1481, and Dauphiné 1349, Franche-Comté 1678, and Savoy 1860 being annexed to France.

2. *anc.* **Ar·e·las** \'ar-ə-ləs\ *or* **Ar·e·la·te** \ˌar-ə-'lā-tē\. City, Bouches-du-Rhône dept., SE France, on left bank of Rhone 45 mi. (72 km.) NW of Marseille; pop. (1990c) 52,593; olive trees; connected with Mediterranean by canal; medieval Romanesque cathedral; ancient remains, incl. Roman burial place and ruins of palace of Emperor Constantine the Great. Vincent van Gogh painted here.

History: Began to prosper as trading center after the Roman consul Marius had built canal connecting it with sea 103 B.C., and some of Gen. Julius Caesar's legions had settled there; as outlet for commerce of Gaul, surpassed Massilia and became, next to Rome, wealthiest city of early Roman Empire; episcopal see from first cent. A.D.; residence of Emperor Constantine; seat of Council of Arles which decided Donatist controversy 314 A.D. and of several later ones; in 5th and 6th cents. captured by Visigoths, besieged by Franks, and taken by Ostrogoths; sacked by Saracens in 8th cent.; ✱ of kingdom of Arles 933–1246; besieged by Holy Roman Emperor Charles V 1526; archiepiscopal see suppressed by 1790.

Ar·ling·ton \'är-liŋ-tən\. **1.** County in N Virginia. See table at VIRGINIA.

2. Locality, Riverside co., SE California, SW part of city of Riverside.

3. Town, Middlesex co., NE Massachusetts, 6 mi. (10 km.) NW of Boston; pop. (1990c) 44,630; residential suburb of Boston.

4. Unincorporated settlement, Hudson co., NE New Jersey, on Passaic River ab. 3 mi. (5 km.) NNE of Newark; part of Kearny.

5. Unincorporated settlement, Dutchess co., New York, E of Poughkeepsie; pop. (1990c) 11,948.

6. City, Tarrant co., N Texas, E of Fort Worth; pop. (1990c) 261,721; Univ. of Texas at Arlington (1895), Arlington Baptist Coll. (1939).

7. Unincorporated settlement, ⊗ of Arlington co., Virginia, across the Potomac from Washington, D.C.; comprises entire county except for the independent city of Alexandria; pop. (1990c) 170,936; site of Arlington National Cemetery (on former estate of Confederate Gen. Robert E. Lee), containing memorial amphitheater (dedicated 1920) and Tomb of the Unknown Soldier; Marymount Univ. (1950); Pentagon building, headquarters of U.S. Dept. of Defense; Fort Myer nearby.

8. Town, Snohomish co., Washington; pop. (1990c) 4037.

Arlington Heights. **1.** Village, Cook and Lake cos., NE Illinois, 25 mi. (40 km.) NW of Chicago; pop. (1990c) 75,460; horse racing.

2. Village, Hamilton co., SW Ohio; pop. (1990c) 1084; N suburb of Cincinnati.

Ar·lon \år-'lō^{n}\; *anc.* **Or·o·lau·num** \ˌór-ə-'lō-nəm\. Commune, ✱ of Luxembourg prov., SE Belgium, near border of Grand Duchy of Luxembourg; pop. (1991c) 23,422; museum of Roman antiquities. Fortified by Romans 4th cent.; occupied by French 1684–97; victories of Jean-Baptiste Jourdan over Imperial forces 1793, 1794; Belgian since 1831.

Ar·ma·ged·don \ˌär-mə-'ged-^{ə}n\. Greek form of Hebrew name of place, probably Megiddo (*q.v.*), where, according to *Revelation* xvi. 16, a great battle of prophecy is fought.

Ar·magh \är-'mä, 'är-ˌmä\. **1.** Former county, S Northern Ireland, touched S shore of Lough Neagh; major towns included Armagh, Portadown, Lurgan.

2. District, Northern Ireland comprising N part of traditional county; estab. 1974. See table at IRELAND, NORTHERN.

3. Town, its ⊗, 33 mi. (53 km.) SW of Belfast; pop. (1990e) 49,100; linen; seat of Roman Catholic and Protestant archbishops. According to tradition, founded by St. Patrick; seat of famous medieval school of theology; metropolis of Ireland and a leading intellectual center of the Western world from 5th to 9th cents.

Ar·ma·gnac \ˌär-må-'nyåk\. Small territory in the old province of Gascony, SW France, now in dept. of Gers; capitals successively Auch and Lectoure. Known for viticulture, producing famous Armagnac brandy.

History: Region near Auch (*q.v.*) part of Roman prov. of Aquitania; became separate countship of Armagnac c. 960; in 15th cent. countship extended from the Garonne to the

---

\ə\ **abut** \$^{ə}$\ **kitten**, Fr **table** \ər\ **further** \a\ **ash** \ā\ **ace** \ä\ **cot, cart** \å\ Fr **bac** \aů\ **out** \b\ Span **Avila** \ch\ **chin** \e\ **bet** \ē\ **easy** \g\ **go** \i\ **hit** \ī\ **ice** \j\ **job** \k\ Ger **ich**, **Buch** \$^{n}$\ Fr **vin** \ŋ\ **sing** \ō\ **go** \ö\ **all** \ó\ **law** \œ\ Fr **bœuf** \œ̄\ Fr **feu** \ói\ **boy** \th\ **thin** \th\ **this** \ü\ **loot** \ů\ **foot** \ue\ Ger **füllen** \ue̅\ Fr **rue** \y\ **yet** \$^{y}$\ Fr **digne** \'dēn^{y}\, **nuit** \'nw^{y}ē\ \yü\ **few** \yů\ **fury** \zh\ **vision**

Adour; first annexed to French crown 1497, but returned finally by descent through Navarre family 1607; countship granted 1645 by Louis XIV to Henry of Lorraine, count of Harcourt, by whose family it was held until 1789.

Ar·ma·vir \ər-ˌmə-ˈvēr\. City, Krasnodar Kray, S Russia in Europe, 100 mi. (161 km.) E of the city of Krasnodar, NE of Maykop oil fields; pop. (1992e) 163,000; center of fertile agricultural region; food processing; founded 1839; in WWII under German control 1942.

Ar·me·nia \är-ˈmē-nē-ə, -nyə.\ **1.** *bib.* **Min·ni** \ˈmiˌnī\. Ancient country in W Asia, now divided bet. the independent country of Armenia, Turkey, and Iran. It centered in the mountainous region (highest point Mt. Ararat) SE of Black Sea and SW of Caspian Sea; included sources of Euphrates and Araks rivers and Lakes Van and Sevan.

History: Equivalent to ancient kingdom of Van c. 1270–850 B.C. bet. Caucasus and Lake Van; residence of Vannic peoples, repeatedly attacked by Assyrians who called it Urartu (*q.v.*); conquered by Medes 612 B.C.; occupied by Armenian peoples and under kings of Media 612–549 B.C.; administered as a Persian satrapy 549–331 B.C.; under Macedonian King Alexander the Great and successors 331–317 B.C.; following independence and division into two, reunited with Artaxata as ✻ by Tigranes the Great (95–55 B.C.), most powerful ruler of Asia; after defeat by Roman Gen. Lucius Lucullus 69 B.C., became allied to Rome; first to adopt Christianity as national religion 303 A.D.; persecution of Christians 4th–5th cents.; separated from Greek rite c. 491; changed hands frequently in wars bet. Neo-Persian and Roman empires 3d–7th cents.; under caliphates, scene of strife bet. Arabs, Seljuqs, Byzantines, and Mongols; ruled by Ottoman Turks from 1514; E part ceded to Persia 1620; its N boundary contiguous with Russia 1802 after latter's occupation of Georgia; two districts ceded to Russia 1828, 1829; rise of Armenian nationalism among its scattered peoples 19th cent.; subject of "Armenian question" which plagued European powers after Ottoman Empire failed to carry out reforms first promised in Treaty of Berlin 1878; part ceded to Russia by Turkey by Treaty of San Stefano 1878; scene of a series of massacres which began 1893–94 and continued spasmodically throughout WWI; suffering aggravated as scene of Russo-Turkish hostility during war; after Turkish defeat, Russian part set up as Soviet republic 1921, rest remaining under Turkey (see ARMENIA, TURKISH).

2. *or Armenian* **Ha·yas·dan** \ˌhī-ə-ˈstän, ˌhä-yəs-ˈdän\. Republic, SW Asia, in S Transcaucasia, bounded on N by Republic of Georgia, on S and E by Azerbaijan, on S by Iran, and on W by Turkey; 11,506 sq. mi. (29,800 sq. km.); pop. (1992e) 3,426,000; ✻ Yerevan. Mountainous, with many peaks above 10,000 ft. (3048 m.), highest Aragats 13,418 ft. (4090 m.). Contains Lake Sevan with its outlet the Hrazdan River, a tributary of the Araks which forms boundary with Turkish Armenia on SW; products include copper, grapes and wine, processed food.

Chief cities: Yerevan, Gyumri, Vanadzor.

History: Set up as Soviet republic 1921; joined Georgian S.S.R. and Azerbaijan S.S.R. 1922 to form the Transcaucasian S.F.S.R. which soon became part of the U.S.S.R.; following abolition of the Transcaucasian S.F.S.R. 1936, comprised Armenian Soviet Socialist Rep., a constituent republic of U.S.S.R., 1936–91; suffered devastating earthquake 1988; in late 1980s because of dissolution of U.S.S.R. and subsequent Armenian independence has experienced renewed ethnic fighting.

Ar·me·nia \är-ˈmān-yä\. City, ✻ of Quindío dept., W cen. Colombia, W of Ibagué; pop. (1992e) 212,300; university (1960); in rich coffee district.

Armenia, Greater. See GREATER ARMENIA 2.

Armenia, Lesser. See CILICIA.

Armenia, Turkish. The NE part of Turkey in Asia, comprising the whole or parts of nine provinces; ab. 57,000 sq. mi. (147,630 sq. km.); chief towns: Kars, Erzurum, Erzincan. For history, see ARMENIA 1.

Armenia Maj·or \ˈmā-jər\. See GREATER ARMENIA 1.

Armenia Minor *or* **Lesser Armenia.** In Roman times, an E district of prov. of Pontus, bordering W Armenia.

Armenian Soviet Socialist Republic. See ARMENIA 2.

Ar·men·tières \ˌär-mä^{n}-ˈtyer, ˌär-mən-ˈtirz\. Commune, Nord dept., N France, 8 mi. (13 km.) WNW of Lille; pop. (1990c) 26,240; WWI-era song "Mademoiselle from Armentières" associated with it; commune destroyed by Germans WWI; rebuilt after war.

Ar·me·ro \är-ˈmer-ō\. Town, Tolima dept., W cen. Colombia; devastated by volcanic eruption Nov. 1985.

Ar·mi·dale \ˈär-mi-ˌdāl\. Town, NE New South Wales, SE Australia, 240 mi. (386 km.) N of Sydney; pop. (1991c) 21,605; Univ. of New England (1954).

Ar·mor·i·ca \är-ˈmȯr-i-kə\; *older* **Ar·e·mor·i·ca** \ˌar-ə-\. Ancient name for region in NW France comprising the coast of Gaul bet. Seine and Loire rivers. Inhabited by Cymric Celts; with Julius Caesar's subjugation of Veneti 56 B.C., came under Roman rule; organized as Roman prov. of Lugdunensis; extreme NW part invaded in 5th cent. A.D. by Britons (Celtic peoples from Britain) and thereafter called Brittany (*q.v.*); E part became Normandy.

Ar·mour \ˈär-mər\. City, ⊗ of Douglas co., S South Dakota; pop. (1990c) 854; grain fields nearby.

Arm·strong \ˈärm-ˌstrȯŋ\. **1.** Name of counties in two states of the U.S. See tables at PENNSYLVANIA, TEXAS.

2. Former county in South Dakota; annexed to Dewey co. 1954.

Ar·nett \är-ˈnet\. Town, ⊗ of Ellis co., NW Oklahoma; pop. (1990c) 547.

Arn·hem \ˈärn-ˌhem, ˈär-nəm\. Commune, ✻ of Gelderland prov., E Netherlands, on right bank of Rhine near confluence with IJssel 33 mi. (53 km.) ESE of Utrecht; pop. (1992e) 132,928; textile fibers, chemicals; 16th cent. town hall; Groote Kerk; museum.

History: First mentioned 893 A.D.; home of the dukes of Gelderland 13th–16th cents.; formerly member of the Hanseatic League. Conquered 1473 by Charles the Bold, duke of Burgundy; came under States-General 1585; taken by French 1672 and 1795 and by Prussians 1813. In WWII captured by Germans 1940; scene of heroic fight Sept. 17–25, 1944 by British First Airborne Division encircled by Germans in unsuccessful attempt to secure Rhine bridges; finally taken by Allies Apr. 13, 1945.

Arn·hem, Cape \ˈär-nəm\. Point, NE Arnhem Land, Australia, on NW coast of Gulf of Carpentaria.

Arn·hem Land *also* **Arn·hem·land** \ˈär-nəm-ˌland\. Region on N coast of Northern Terr., Australia; bauxite, manganese; occupied by aborigines long before visited in 1623 by expedition of Jan Carstensz. Much of the area now a reservation for aborigines.

Ar·no \ˈär-nō\; *anc.* **Ar·nus** \ˈär-nəs\. River, Tuscany, cen. Italy; rises in Monte Falterona, flows W from the Apennines through Florence into Ligurian Sea 7 mi. (11 km.) below (W of) Pisa; 150 mi. (241 km.) long; navigable up to Florence; near Arezzo connected with Tiber by its canalized tributary, the Chiani; subject to sudden rises and disastrous floods.

Ar·nold \ˈär-nəld\. **1.** City, Jefferson co., E Missouri, ab. 12 mi. (19 km.) SSW of St. Louis; pop. (1990c) 18,828.
2. City, Westmoreland co., SW Pennsylvania, on Allegheny River 16 mi. (26 km.) NE of Pittsburgh; pop. (1990c) 6113.
3. Town, Nottinghamshire, N cen. England, 5.5 mi. (8.8 km.) NE of Nottingham; pop. (1981p) 37,242.

Arnon. See MAWJIB, WADI AL-.

Arn·øya \ˈär-nœ-yə\. Island in Arctic Ocean off N coast of Norway, ab. 50 mi. (80 km.) NE of Tromsø.

Arn·pri·or \ˈärn-ˌprī-ər\. Town, Renfrew co., SE Ontario, Canada, at confluence of Madawaska and Ottawa rivers 37 mi. (60 km.) W of Ottawa; pop. (1991e) 75,864.

Arns·berg \ˈärns-ˌberk, ˈärnz-ˌbərg\. City, North Rhine-Westphalia, W cen. Germany, on Ruhr River 42 mi. (68 km.) SSE of Münster; pop. (1991e) 75,864; ancient ✻ of Westphalia; founded 1077; received munic. charter c. 1237; joined Hanseatic League; became Prussian 1815.

Arn·stadt \ˈärn-ˌshtät\. City, Thuringia, cen. Germany, S of Erfurt; pop. (1991e) 28,743; ancient ✻ of principality of Schwarzburg-Sondershausen; first mentioned 704 A.D.; received munic. rights 1266; bought by counts of Schwarzburg 1306 whose seat it was until 1716.

Arnswalde. See CHOSZCZNO.

Arnus. See ARNO.

Aro \ˈä-rō\. River, cen. Venezuela; flows N into the Orinoco; ab. 100 mi. (160 km.) long.

Aroe Islands. See ARU ISLANDS.

Arol·sen \ˈä-ròl-zən\. Town, ✻ of former Waldeck principality, now in Hesse, cen. Germany; pop. (1980c) 16,356.

Aromata. See CASEYR, RAAS.

Aroos·took \ə-ˈrüs-tu̇k, -ˈru̇s-, -tik\. **1.** River, N Maine; rises in NE Piscataquis co., flows NE across New Brunswick (Canada) border and into St. John River; 140 mi. (225 km.) long. This region was scene of "Aroostook War" 1839, a clash bet. authority of Maine and New Brunswick over territory near the river, a preliminary to determining the boundary of Maine in Webster-Ashburton Treaty 1842.
2. County in N Maine. See table at MAINE.

Aro·roy \ˌä-rä-ˈròi\. Municipality, port on N coast of Masbate I., Masbate prov., Philippines; pop. (1980c) 38,618.

Arpachiya. See TELL ARPACHIYA.

Ar·pi·no \är-ˈpē-nō\; *anc.* **Ar·pi·num** \är-ˈpī-nəm\. Commune, Frosinone prov., Lazio, cen. Italy, 13 mi. (21 km.) E of the commune of Frosinone; pop. (1981p) 7734; marble deposits. Ancient town of the Volsci and, later, of the Samnites; conquered by Romans 305 B.C.; given Roman civic privileges 188 B.C. Birthplace of Roman Gen. Marius c. 157 B.C., statesman and orator Cicero 106 B.C., and naval commander Marcus Vipsanius Agrippa c. 63 B.C.

Ar·qua Pe·trar·ca \är-ˈkwä-pe-ˈträr-kä\. Village, Veneto, NE Italy, on SE slope of Euganean Hills ab. 15 mi. (24 km.) SW of Padua; the poet Petrarch died here 1374.

Arques \ˈärk\ *or in full* **Arques–la–Ba·taille** \-ˌlä-bə-ˈtī\. Village and castle, Seine-Maritime dept., France, just S of Dieppe, Normandy; scene of battle 1589 in which Henry IV defeated forces of the Holy League under duc de Mayenne.

Arquipélago dos Bijagós. See BIJAGÓS, ARQUIPÉLAGO DOS.

Arrah See ARA.

Ar Rahad. See RAHAD, AR.

Ar·rai·ján \ˌär-rī-ˈkän\. Town, Panama, on Pan-American Highway W of Balboa; pop. (1990p) 24,711.

Ar Ramādī \ˌar-rä-ˈmä-dē\ *also* **Ra·ma·di** \rə-ˈmädē, -ˈma-\. Town, cen. Iraq, on right bank of Euphrates River 60 mi. (97 km.) W of Baghdad; pop. (1985e) 137,388; starting point of highway across the desert to Mediterranean towns. Founded 1869; in WWI scene of battle 1917 in which British forces defeated the Turks.

Ar Ramal. See RAMLEH.

Ar·ran \ˈar-ən\. Island, Strathclyde region, in Firth of Clyde, off SW coast of Scotland; 166 sq. mi. (430 sq. km.); harbors at Brodick and Lamlash; prehistoric and Danish relics; hideout for Scottish King Robert the Bruce (King's Caves); seat of the dukes of Hamilton (Brodick Castle).

Ar Raq·qah \ȧr-ˈrȧk-kə\ *also* **Rak·ka** \ˈrä-kə\; *anc.* **Ni·ce·pho·ri·um** \ˌnī-si-ˈfōr-ē-əm\. Town, N cen. Syria, on the left bank of the Euphrates River 100 mi. (161 km.) SE of Aleppo; near the confluence of the Balikh with the Euphrates. Prominent under the Abbasid caliphs, esp. Hārūn ar-Rashīd, who estab. residence there; the home of the Arab astronomer al-Battānī (d. 929).

Ar·ras \ȧ-ˈrȧs, ˈar-əs\; *anc.* **Nem·e·to·cen·na** \ˌne-mə-tə-ˈse-nə\. City, ✻ of Pas-de-Calais dept., N France, 25 mi. (40 km.) SW of Lille; pop. (1990c) 42,715; administrative and trading center; episcopal see from 390; famous cathedral, abbey of St. Vaast, and city hall.

History: Principal town of the Atrebates; destroyed by Attila, king of the Huns, 451 A.D. and by Norsemen 800; ruled by county of Flanders; noted as medieval center for manufacture of tapestries; scene of two treaties: (1) bet. Burgundians and Armagnacs 1435, and (2) terminating war bet. Maximilian I of Austria and Louis XI of France 1482; ceded to France by latter treaty and its name changed (temporarily) by Louis XI to **Fran·chise** \fräⁿ-ˈshēz\; ceded to Maximilian of Austria 1493 and held by Spanish branch of Hapsburgs to 1640; gave name to league of Catholic provinces of Netherlands which were loyal to Spain 1579; taken by Louis XIII of France 1640, and, as part of Artois (*q.v.*), ceded to France 1659; scene of fierce battles WWI and WWII; historical buildings heavily damaged; largely rebuilt.

Ar Ray·yān \ˌȧr-rī-ˈyän\. Town, Qatar, W of Doha; pop. (1986c) 91,996.

Ar·re·ci·fe \ˌä-rā-ˈsē-fā\ *or* **Puer·to Arrecife** \ˈpwer-tō\. Seaport, Las Palmas prov. (E Canary Is.), Spain, on SE coast of Lanzarote I. 129 mi. (208 km.) NE of the city of Las Palmas; pop. (1991c) 33,906.

Arretium. See AREZZO 2.

Arriaca. See GUADALAJARA 2.

ar–Ri·fāʻ \ˌär-rē-ˈfä\. Municipality, N cen. Bahrain, SSW of Manama; pop. (1991c) 45,956.

Ar Rimal. See RUBʻ AL-KHALI.

Arroe Islands. See ARU ISLANDS.

Ar·ro·manches–les–Bains \ˌȧ-rō-ˈmäⁿsh-lā-ˈbeⁿ\. Coast village, Calvados dept., N France, 5 mi. (8 km.) NNE of Bayeux; site of one of the two portable harbor installations used by Allies June 1944 in invasion of Normandy.

Ar·row, Lough \ˈläk-ˈar-ō\. Lake, SE co. Sligo, Ireland; 4 mi. (6 km.) long, 2.5 mi. (4 km.) wide; its outlet flows ab. 12 mi. (19 km.) NW into Owenboy River S of Sligo.

Arrow Lakes *or* **Arrow Lake** \ˈar-ō\. Reservoir, a widening of Columbia River in SE British Columbia, Canada; ab. 93 mi. (150 km.) long; 199 sq. mi. (515 sq. km.); usu. divided into **Upper Arrow Lake** (to the N) ab. 36 mi. (58 km.) long, and **Lower Arrow Lake** (to the S) ab. 51 mi. (82 km.) long.

Arrow Peak. Mountain in San Juan Mts., San Juan co., SW Colorado; 13,810 ft. (4209 m.).

Ar·row Rock Dam \'ar-ō-'räk\. Dam across Boise River, E of Boise, Idaho; height 350 ft. (107 m.); completed 1915; impounds water in **Arrow Rock Reservoir.**

Ar·royo \ə-'rȯi-ō\. Town and municipality, on the coast, SE Puerto Rico; munic. pop. (1990c) 18,910.

Arroyo Gran·de \'gran-dē\. City, San Luis Obispo co., SW California, 11 mi. (18 km.) SSE of the city of San Luis Obispo; pop. (1990c) 14,378.

Ar Ruṭ·bah \är-'rüt-bə\ *or* **Rut·ba** \'rüt-bə\ *also* **Rut·bah Wells** \'rüt-bə\. Town, W Iraq, on Wadi Ḩawrān in the Syrian Desert; a junction of highways from the Euphrates River to the Mediterranean coast.

Arsanias. See MURAT NEHRI.

Arsenaria. See ARZEW.

Ar·sen'·yev \ər-'sye-nyif\; *before 1952* **Se·me·nov·ka** \səm-'yō-ˌnəf-kə\. Town, Primorskiy Kray, Russia in Asia; ab. 100 mi. (160 km.) NE of Vladivostok.

Ar·sie·ro \är-'syā-rō\. Commune, Vicenza prov., Veneto, NE Italy, 20 mi. (32 km.) NNW of the commune of Vicenza; pop. (1981p) 3555; marble deposits; burned by Austrians 1916.

Ar·sin·oë \är-'si-nō-ē\. **1.** Ancient town, one of the Pentapolis of Cyrenaica, on the coast NE of Berenice (*mod.* Benghazi, Libya).

2. *older* **Croc·o·di·lop·o·lis** \ˌkrä-kə-də-'lä-pə-lis\. City of ancient Egypt, on Birket (lake) Qārūn near the site of modern El Faiyûm; said to have been founded c. late 3d millennium B.C.; chief seat of early Egyptian worship of the crocodile; received its later name from sister and wife of Ptolemy II Philadelphus.

Arta \'är-tə\. **1.** River, Greece. See ÁRAKHTHOS.

2. Department of Greece. See table at GREECE.

3. *anc.* **Am·bra·cia** \am-'brā-shə, -shē-ə\. City, its ✻, S Epirus, NW Greece, on Árakhthos River N of Amvrakikós Kólpos; pop. (1991p) 20,451; episcopal see.

History: Ambracia founded by Corinthians 7th cent. B.C.; became ✻ of Pyrrhus, king of Epirus, 295 B.C.; after its decline, new town of Arta founded on its site and became important fortification in Byzantine times; seat of despot of Epirus in 13th and 14th cents.; taken 1449 by Turks, by Turkish brigand Ali Paşa 1798, by Turkish statesman Reşid Paşa 1822; to Greece 1881.

Arta, Gulf of. See AMVRAKIKÓS KÓLPOS.

Artawiya. See AL ARṬĀWĪYAH.

Ar·tax·a·ta \är-'tak-sə-tə\. Ruined city, ancient ✻ of Armenia, on left bank of Araks River 17 mi. (27 km.) S of Yerevan; destroyed 58 A.D. by Roman Gen. Corbulo.

Ar·tei·jo \är-'tā-k̲ō\ *or* **Ar·te·xio** \är-'tek-sē-ō\. Commune, La Coruña prov., Spain, 6 mi. (10 km.) SW of the commune of La Coruña; pop. (1991c) 17,931.

Ar·tem *or* **Ar·tyom** \ər-'tyȯm\. Town, Primorskiy Kray, SE Russia in Asia, ab. 20 mi. (32 km.) NE of Vladivostok; thermal power station.

Ar·te·mi·sa \ˌär-tā-'mē-sä\. Town and municipality, E Pinar del Río prov., W Cuba; town pop. (1989e) 51,841.

Ar·te·mi·sium \ˌär-tə-'mi-zhē-əm, -zē-əm, -zhəm\ *or Gk.* **Ar·te·mí·si·on** \ˌär-te-'mē-sē-ˌȯn\. Promontory forming NE point of Greek island of Euboea, Aegean Sea; scene of naval battle bet. the Greeks and the Persians 480 B.C.

Ar·te·movsk \ər-'tyȯ-məfsk\; *formerly* **Bakh·mut** \'bäk̲-müt\. City, E Ukraine, 45 mi. (72 km.) N of Donets'k in the Donets Basin; pop. (1991e) 91,000; railroad junction; extensive salt deposits; also coal and mercury.

Ar·te·sia \är-'tē-zhə\. **1.** City, Los Angeles co., California, NE of Long Beach; pop. (1990c) 15,464.

2. City, Eddy co., SE New Mexico, 38 mi. (61 km.) S of Roswell; pop. (1990c) 10,610.

Artesium. See ARTOIS.

Artexio. See ARTEIJO.

Ar·tha·bas·ka \ˌär-thə-'bas-kə\. **1.** County, S Quebec, Canada. See table at QUEBEC.

2. Town, its ⊗, 38 mi. (61 km.) SE of Trois-Rivières; pop. (1991c) 7584.

Ar·thing·ton \'är-thiŋ-tən\. Town, W Liberia, 30 mi. (48 km.) NNE of Monrovia.

Ar·thur \'är-thər\. **1.** County in W Nebraska. See table at NEBRASKA.

2. Village, its ⊗; pop. (1990c) 128.

3. River, NW Tasmania, Australia; rises in NW part of cen. highland and flows WNW to Indian Ocean S of Cape Grim; ab. 100 mi. (160 km.) long.

Arthur Kill \'kil\. Channel, NE New Jersey, bet. New Jersey and Staten I., New York; connects Newark Bay with Raritan Bay.

Arthur Peak. **1.** Mountain, E boundary of Yellowstone National Park, NW Wyoming; 10,426 ft. (3178 m.).

2. Peak, N South I., New Zealand; 8800 ft. (2682 m.).

Ar·thur's Pass \'är-thərz\. Mountain pass through Otira Gorge in Southern Alps, cen. South I., New Zealand.

Arthur's Pass National Park. National Park, N cen. South I., New Zealand; contains several peaks of the Southern Alps.

Arthur's Seat. Hill in Edinburgh, Scotland, overlooking SE section of city; elev. 823 ft. (251 m.); from it King Arthur is said to have watched the defeat of the Picts by his army.

Ar·ti·bo·nite \ˌär-tē-bȯ-'nēt\. River, Hispaniola, flowing W from Cordillera Central, Dominican Rep. through Haiti into Golfe de la Gonâve.

Ar·ti·gas \är-'tē-gäs\. **1.** Department of NW Uruguay. See table at URUGUAY.

2. *or* **San Eu·ge·nio** \ˌsän-eü-'zhā-nyü\ *also* **San Eugenio del Cua·reim** \ˌdel-kwä-'rām\. Town, its ✻, near Brazilian border, ab. 304 mi. (489 km.) N of Montevideo; pop. (1985c) 35,119.

Ar·tois \är-'twä\ *or Lat.* **Ar·te·sium** \är-'tē-zhē-əm, -zē-əm, -zhəm\ *or Flemish* **Atrecht** \'ä-ˌtrek̲t\. Historical region of N France, bounded on N by the Strait of Dover, on E by Flanders, on S and on W by Picardy; ✻ Arras.

History: Western part of county of Flanders, given as dowry to Isabella of Hainaut on her marriage to King Philip Augustus of France 1180; inherited by Louis VIII who made it part of royal domain 1222; returned to count of Flanders 1382; passed to dukes of Burgundy who held it 1384–1477; with marriage 1477 of Mary, duchess of Burgundy, to Hapsburg Maximilian I, passed to Austria, ultimately to Philip IV of Spain 1640; France received final sovereignty over it by Treaties of the Pyrenees 1659 and of Nijmegen 1678; scene of extensive fighting during WWI.

Art·vin \ärt-'vēn\. **1.** Province of NE Turkey in Asia. See table at TURKEY.

2. Town, its ✻; pop. (1990p) 20,238.

Artyom. See ARTEM.

Aru·ba; *formerly also* **Oru·ba** \ə-'rü-bə\. Island off coast of NW Venezuela; an internally self-governing integral part of the Netherlands realm; 19 mi. (30 km.) long by ab. 5 mi. (8 km.) wide; 69 sq. mi. (179 sq. km.); pop. (1992e) 69,000; chief town Oranjestad; barren; oil refining was the chief economic activity prior to 1985; tourism. In WWII the refineries were shelled by German submarines 1942; separated constitutionally from Netherlands Antilles Jan. 1986.

Aru·cas \ä-'rü-käs\. Commune, Las Palmas prov. (E Canary Is.), Spain, on Grand Canary I. 6 mi. (10 km.) W of the city of Las Palmas; pop. (1991c) 26,974; sugarcane.

Aru Islands; *mostly formerly* **Aroe Islands** *also* **Ar·roe Islands** \'ä-ˌrü\. Group of islands off SW coast of New Guinea, Maluku prov., Indonesia; 3305 sq. mi. (8560 sq. km.). Chief island ab. 122 mi. (196 km.) long by 58 mi. (93 km.) wide, divided into six sections by narrow channels.

Ar·un \'ar-ən\. River, Sussex, S England; flows S into the English Channel at Littlehampton; 37 mi. (60 km.) long.

Aru·na·chal Pra·desh \'är-ü-ˌnä-chəl-prə-'desh, -'dāsh\; *formerly* **North East Frontier Agency.** State, NE India; ✻ Itanagar; estab. as a union territory 1972; became a state 1986. See table at INDIA.

Ar·un·del \'ar-ən-dəl\. **1.** Town, West Sussex, England, on Arun River 5 mi. (8 km.) from its mouth; pop. (1981p) 2235; formerly a flourishing seaport connected 1813 by canal with

London; now small market town; site of Arundel Castle, seat of dukes of Norfolk.

2. Small island of the New Georgia Is., cen. Solomon Is., off NW tip of New Georgia and at SW end of Kula Gulf.

Aru·sha \ä-ˈrü-shä\. **1.** Region of NE Tanzania. See table at TANZANIA.

2. Town, its ✻, in NE part of region.

Aru·sha National Park \ä-ˈrü-shä\. National Park, N Tanzania; contains Mt. Meru and Ngurdoto Crater; park estab. 1960.

Aru·tanga \ˌä-rä-ˈtäŋ-gä\. Chief village of Aitutaki, Cook Is., S Pacific Ocean, on W coast.

Aru·wi·mi \ˌä-rü-ˈwē-mē\. River, cen. Africa; rises in NE Democratic Rep. of the Congo near Lake Albert, flows SW and W across N part of the country into Congo River; 620 mi. (998 km.) long; called the Ituri in its upper course.

Arva. See ORAVA.

Arvad. See ARWAD.

Ar·vada \är-ˈva-də\. Town, Adams and Jefferson cos., Colorado, W of Denver; pop. (1990c) 89,235.

Ar·vi·ka \är-ˈvē-kə\. Town, Värmland prov., W Sweden, ab. 30 mi. (48 km.) NW of Lake Vänern; pop. (1980p) 26,891.

Ar·vin \ˈär-vən\. City, Kern co., S California, 16 mi. (26 km.) SE of Bakersfield; pop. (1990c) 9286.

Ar·wad *or* **Ar·wād** \är-ˈwad, -ˈwäd\ *or Fr.* **Île Rou·ad** \ēl-rů-ˈäd\; *bib.* **Ar·vad** \ˈär-ˌvad\; *anc.* **Ar·a·dus** \ˈar-ə-dəs\. Island ab. 2 mi. (3.2 km.) off the coast of Syria, near Tartūs; seaport of ancient Phoenicia (*Ezek.* xxvii. 8) and a flourishing city during Phoenician ascendancy (see TRIPOLI 3). In WWI first point on Syrian coast occupied by French; made postal station 1916; at end of war became part of French mandate of Latakia.

Ar·za·mas \ər-ˌzə-ˈmäs\. Town, S Nizhegorod Oblast, Russia in Europe, ab. 60 mi. (96 km.) S of Nizhniy Novgorod; pop. (1992e) 112,000; a junction point on railroad bet. Moscow and Kazan'.

Ar·za·no \är-ˈdzä-nō\. Commune, Napoli prov., Campania, S Italy, 3 mi. (5 km.) N of Naples; pop. (1989c) 39,627.

Ar·zew *or* **Ar·zeu** \är-ˈzœ̄\; *anc.* **Ar·se·nar·ia** \ˌär-sə-ˈnar-ē-ə\. Seaport, NW Algeria, 22 mi. (35 km.) NE of Oran near Cape Ferrat; pop. (1987p) 35,784.

Aš *or Ger.* **Asch** \ˈäsh\. Town, extreme W Czech Republic; pop. (1980p) 13,551; textile mills. One of the first towns occupied by Germans in their seizure of Sudetenland Oct. 1938.

Asa·ba \ˌä-sä-ˈbä\. City, S Nigeria, on Niger River; pop. (1991e) 52,380; ✻ of Delta state.

Asa·han \ˌä-sə-ˈhän\. River, N Sumatra, Indonesia; outlet of Lake Toba flowing ENE into cen. Strait of Malacca; ab. 75 mi. (120 km.) long.

Asa·hi Da·ke \ä-ˈsä-hē-ˈdä-ke\; *formerly* **Ishi·ka·ri Dake** \ˌē-shē-ˈkä-rē\. Mountain, cen. Hokkaidō I., Japan; 7513 ft. (2290 m.).

Asa·hi·ka·wa \ä-ˌsä-ˈhē-kä-wə\ *or* **Asa·hi·ga·wa** \-gä-\. City, cen. Hokkaidō I., Japan; pop. (1992e) 361,736; textiles, wood products, brewing.

Asa·ka \ä-ˈsä-kä\. City, Saitama prefecture, Honshū, Japan; pop. (1990p) 103,621.

Asa·ma \ä-ˈsä-mä\ *or* **Asa·ma·ya·ma** \ä-ˌsä-mä-ˈyä-mä\. Active volcano on W border of Gumma prefecture, cen. Honshū, Japan, 85 mi. (137 km.) NW of Tokyo; ab. 8300 ft. (2530 m.); one of the largest active volcanoes in Japan; had disastrous explosion 1783.

Asan·sol \ˌə-sən-ˈsōl\. City, West Bengal, NE India, 120 mi. (193 km.) NW of Calcutta; pop. (1991p) 261,836; rail junction; coal deposits nearby.

Asben. See AÏR.

As·best \əz-ˈbyest\. Town, Sverdlovsk Oblast, W Russia in Asia, ab. 40 mi. (64 km.) ENE of Yekaterinburg; pop. (1991e) 84,900; asbestos deposits.

As·bes·tos \as-ˈbes-təs, az-; ˌáz-bes-ˈtōs\. **1.** County, Quebec, Canada. See table at QUEBEC.

2. Town, S Quebec, Canada, 26 mi. (42 km.) N of Sherbrooke; pop. (1991c) 6487; site of asbestos mines.

As·bury Park \ˈaz-ˌber-ē, -bə-rē\. City and summer resort, Monmouth co., E cen. New Jersey, on Atlantic Ocean 24 mi. (39 km.) SSE of Perth Amboy; pop. (1990c) 16,799; orig. developed as summering place chiefly for temperance advocates 1870; became city 1897; once known for its oceanside auditorium, convention hall, pier, and boardwalk; summer-theater center.

Ascalon. See ASHQELON 1.

Ascania. See İZNİK LAKE.

As·cen·sion \ə-ˈsen-chən\. **1.** Parish in SE Louisiana. See table at LOUISIANA.

2. British island in S Atlantic Ocean, 7°57′S, 14°22′W, 700 mi. (1126 km.) NW of St. Helena; 9 mi. (14 km.) long, 6 mi. (10 km.) wide; 34 sq. mi. (88 sq. km.); pop. (1987e) 1400; since 1922 administratively a part of British colony of St. Helena; only settlement Georgetown. Of volcanic origin, its extinct crater (Green Mt.) 2817 ft. (859 m.); important turtle breeding ground; transmission relay station. Discovered by Portuguese navigator João da Nova on Ascension Day 1501; visited by English navigator William Dampier 1701; used as refueling base by Americans in WWII and by British in their conflict with Argentina over Falkland Is. 1982; U.S. maintains a satellite-tracking station here.

Asch. See AŠ.

Aschaf·fen·burg \ä-ˈshä-fən-ˌbůrk\. City, Bavaria, S Germany, on right bank of Main River 21 mi. (34 km.) ESE of Frankfurt am Main; pop. (1991e) 64,098. Castle built on site of Roman castrum; scene of imperial diet 1447; taken several times in Thirty Years' War; part of grand duchy of Frankfurt 1806; ceded with Lower Franconia to Bavaria 1814.

Aschers·le·ben \ˈä-shərs-ˌlā-bən\. City, Saxony-Anhalt, cen. Germany, 26 mi. (42 km.) SSW of Magdeburg; pop. (1991e) 32,545; potash, coal, and salt deposits. Founded probably in 11th cent.; under episcopal see of Halberstadt 1315 and of Brandenburg 1648; to Prussia 1813.

Asco·li Pi·ce·no \ˈäs-kō-lē-pē-ˈchā-nō\. **1.** Province of Marche, cen. Italy. See table at ITALY.

2. *or Lat.* **As·cu·lum Pi·ce·num** \ˈas-kyə-ləm-pī-ˈsē-nəm\. Commune, its ✻, 87 mi. (140 km.) NE of Rome; pop. (1991p) 52,371; in rich agricultural region; episcopal see; Roman and medieval remains, incl. bridges still in use.

History: One of most ancient cities of Italy; ✻ of ancient Picenum; taken 268 B.C. by Rome; all Roman citizens within its walls massacred 90 B.C. during Social War; recaptured by Rome 89 B.C.; occupied by Roman Gen. Julius Caesar, after crossing the Rubicon 49 B.C.; taken by Totila, king of Ostrogoths in Italy, 545 A.D.; ruled by bishops from 8th cent., became free republic in 12th cent., and joined papal possessions in 15th cent.

Ascoli Sa·tria·no \ˌsä-trē-ˈä-nō\; *anc.* **Aus·cu·lum Ap·u·lum** \ˈós-kyə-ləm-ˈa-pyə-ləm\ *or* **As·cu·lum** \ˈas-kyə-ləm\. Commune, Foggia prov., Puglia, SE Italy, on E slope of Apennines 18 mi. (29 km.) S of the commune of Foggia; pop. (1981p) 7524; episcopal see; site of Roman defeat by Pyrrhus, king of Epirus, 279 B.C. when Pyrrhus lost a large part of his army, a situation which often happened in his military campaigns, thus the term "Pyrrhic victory," a victory achieved at excessive cost.

As·co·na \äs-ˈkō-nə\. Commune, Ticino canton, S Switzerland, on N shore of Lake Maggiore; a resort.

As·cot \ˈas-kət\. Village, Berkshire, England, 6 mi. (10 km.) SSW of New Windsor, 29 mi. (47 km.) SW of London by rail; fashionable two-mile race track (at **Ascot Heath**) estab. 1711 by Queen Anne.

Asculum. See ASCOLI SATRIANO.

Asculum Picenum. See ASCOLI PICENO 2.

As·cut·ney, Mount \ə-ˈskət-nē\. Peak, SE Windsor co., E Vermont; 3320 ft. (1012 m.).

\ə\ **abut** \ə̇\ **matches** \ᵊ\ **kitten, Fr table** \ər\ **further** \a\ **ash** \ā\ **ace** \ä\ **cot, cart** \ȧ\ Fr **bac** \aů\ **out** \b̲\ Span **Avila** \ch\ **chin** \e\ **bet** \ē\ **easy** \g\ **go** \i\ **hit** \ī\ **ice** \j\ **job** \k̲\ Ger **ich, Buch** \ⁿ\ Fr **vin** \ŋ\ **sing** \ō\ **go** \ö\ **all** \ȯ\ **law** \œ\ Fr **bœuf** \œ̄\ Fr **feu** \ȯi\ **boy** \th\ **thin** \th̲\ **this** \ü\ **loot** \ů\ **foot** \ue\ Ger **füllen** \ue̅\ Fr **rue** \y\ **yet** \ʸ\ Fr **digne** \ˈdēnʸ\, **nuit** \ˈnwʸē\ \yü\ **few** \yů\ **fury** \zh\ **vision**

Aseb *also* **As·sab** \'ä-səb\. Seaport, Eritrea; pop. (1989e) 39,569; acquired by Italian government 1882, becoming its first African colonial possession; was important to Ethiopian shipping before Eritrea gained independence 1993.

Ase·la \ä-'sā-lə\. Town, cen. Ethiopia; pop. (1989e) 40,175.

Ase·nov·grad \ä-'se-nəf-,gräd\; *before 1934* **Sta·ni·ma·ka** \,stä-ni-'mä-kə\. Town, S Bulgaria, 10 mi. (16 km.) SE of Plovdiv; pop. (1991e) 60,804.

Ashan·ti \ə-'shan-tē, -'shän-\. Region, cen. Ghana; ✱ Kumasi. See table at GHANA.

History: Orig. an African kingdom with ✱ at Kumasi (*q.v.*); expanded towards Gold Coast and came into conflict with British from early 19th cent.; waged several wars with British during 19th cent.; claimed as British protectorate 1894; after capture of Kumasi by Sir Francis Scott 1896 again declared protectorate; rose against British 1900 and besieged Kumasi but repressed; annexed to British Gold Coast Colony 1901; administration reorganized 1934; became an administrative region of Ghana 1957; greatly reduced in area 1959.

Ash·bourne \'ash-,bōrn\. Town, Derbyshire, England, on a branch of the Dove 11 mi. (18 km.) NW of Derby; pop. (1981p) 5960.

Ash·burn \'ash-bərn\. City, ⊗ of Turner co., S Georgia, 30 mi. (48 km.) ENE of Albany; pop. (1990c) 3139.

Ash·burn·ham \'ash-bərn-,ham\. Town, Worcester co., cen. Massachusetts, 7 mi. (11 km.) WNW of Fitchburg; pop. (1990c) 5433.

Ash·bur·ton \'ash-,bərt-ᵊn\. **1.** River, NW Western Australia, Australia, flows NW to Indian Ocean near Exmouth Gulf; ab. 400 mi. (644 km.) long.
2. Town, Devon, England, 19 mi. (30 km.) NE of Plymouth; pop. (1981p) 3564; market town; tourism; 15th cent. church.
3. River, E cen. South I., New Zealand; flows SE into Canterbury Bight; 56 mi. (90 km.) long.

Ash·by–de–la–Zouch \'ash-bē-də-lä-'züsh\. Town, Leicestershire, England, 15 mi. (24 km.) NW of Leicester; pop. (1981p) 11,518; coal; castle, known through Scottish writer Sir Walter Scott's *Ivanhoe* and as prison for Mary, Queen of Scots, lies S of town; fine late-perpendicular church.

Ash·dod \'ash-,däd\; *anc. Gk.* **Azo·tos** \ə-'zō-təs\ *or Lat.* **Azo·tus** \ə-'zō-təs\. City, Israel, ab. 3 mi. (5 km.) inland from the Mediterranean, 35 mi. (56 km.) W of Jerusalem; pop. (1990e) 76,600; important harbor facilities constructed on coast; at a location nearby, historical Ashdod was one of five Philistine city-kingdoms and a center of worship of Dagon (*1 Sam.* v). Besieged for 29 years by Psamtik I of Egypt.

Ash·down \'ash-,daün\. City, ⊗ of Little River co., SW Arkansas, 18 mi. (29 km.) NNW of Texarkana; pop. (1990c) 5150.

Ashe \'ash\. County in NW North Carolina. See table at NORTH CAROLINA.

Ashe·boro \'ash-,bər-ə, -,bə-rə\. Town, ⊗ of Randolph co., cen. North Carolina, 25 mi. (40 km.) S of Greensboro; pop. (1990c) 16,362.

Ashe·ville \'ash-,vil, -vəl\. City, ⊗ of Buncombe co., W North Carolina, near E entrance to Great Smoky Mountains National Park; pop. (1990c) 61,607; alt. 1985 ft. (605 m.); health and tourist resort; Biltmore estate founded by George Vanderbilt; birthplace of novelist Thomas Wolfe 1900; tobacco; feldspar, copper, and mica deposits. Univ. of North Carolina at Asheville (1927), Asheville-Buncombe Technical Community Coll. (1959); founded 1794; incorp. 1797; chartered as city 1835.

Ash·field \'ash-,fēld\. Municipality, E New South Wales, Australia, WSW of Sydney; pop. (1991c) 40,558.

Ash Flat \'ash-'flat\. Town, ⊗ of Sharp co., N Arkansas; pop. (1990c) 667.

Ash·ford \'ash-fərd\. Town, Kent, SE England, on Great Stour River 20 mi. (32 km.) W of Dover; pop. (1991p) 90,900.

Ashgabat. See ASHKHABAD.

Ashi·ka·ga \,ä-shē-'kä-gä\. Commercial city, cen. Honshū, Japan, in Tochigi prefecture 50 mi. (80 km.) N of Tokyo; pop. (1992e) 167,696; center of weaving industry, probably estab. several centuries ago; nylon. As the ancestral home of Ashikaga shoguns, gave its name to a Japanese dynasty (1338–1573).

Ash·ing·ton \'a-shiŋ-tən\. Town, Northumberland, N England, 13 mi. (21 km.) N of Newcastle upon Tyne; pop. (1981p) 23,658; coal deposits.

Ashi·ya \'ä-shē-,yä\. City, Hyōgo prefecture, Honshū, Japan, 13 mi. (21 km.) NW of Ōsaka; pop. (1990c) 87,528; one of Japan's wealthiest cities.

Ashi·zu·ri, Cape \ä-'shē-zü-rē\; *formerly* **Cape Sa·da** \'sä-dä\. Cape, W extremity of Shikoku I., Japan, at N end of Bungo Strait, 32°44′N, 133°01′E.

Ashkelon. See ASHQELON.

Ashkh·a·bad \'ash-kə-,bad, -,bäd\ *or* **Ash·ga·bat** \'äsh-gä-,bät\; *formerly* **Pol·to·ratsk** \,päl-tə-'rätsk\. City, ✱ of Turkmenistan, in S part on Iranian border; pop. (1991e) 412,200; situated in fertile oasis; food processing; textiles; university (1950); founded 1881; rebuilt after earthquake 1948.

Ash·land \'ash-lənd\. **1.** Name of counties in two states of the U.S. See tables at OHIO, WISCONSIN.
2. Town, ⊗ of Clay co., E Alabama; pop. (1990c) 2034.
3. City, ⊗ of Clark co., S Kansas; pop. (1990c) 1032.
4. City, Boyd co., NE Kentucky, on Ohio River; pop. (1990c) 23,622.
5. Town, Aroostook co., N Maine, on Aroostook River 20 mi. (32 km.) W of Presque Isle; pop. (1990c) 1542; shipping center.
6. Town, Middlesex co., NE Massachusetts, 20 mi. (32 km.) E of Worcester; pop. (1990c) 12,066.
7. Village, ⊗ of Benton co., N Mississippi; pop. (1990c) 490.
8. City, ⊗ of Ashland co., N cen. Ohio, 13 mi. (21 km.) NE of Mansfield; pop. (1990c) 20,079; Ashland Coll. (1878); platted 1815, became city 1844, ⊗ 1846.
9. City, Jackson co., SW Oregon, 8 mi. (13 km.) SSE of Medford; pop. (1990c) 16,234; site of annual Shakespeare festival; gold and granite deposits; ski resort nearby; Southern Oregon State Coll. (1926).
10. Borough, Schuylkill and Columbia cos., E cen. Pennsylvania, 11 mi. (18 km.) NE of Pottsville; pop. (1990c) 3859; coal; platted 1847.
11. Town, Hanover co., E cen. Virginia, 16 mi. (26 km.) N of Richmond; pop. (1990c) 5864; began as health resort 1848. Randolph-Macon Coll. (1830; moved from Boydton 1868).
12. City and port of entry, ⊗ of Ashland co., N Wisconsin, on Lake Superior 58 mi. (93 km.) E of Superior; pop. (1990c) 8695; granite; Northland Coll. (1892).

Ashland City. Town, ⊗ of Cheatham co., NW cen. Tennessee; pop. (1990c) 2552.

Ash·ley \'ash-lē\. **1.** River, SE South Carolina; rises in Berkeley co. and flows SE into Charleston harbor where it joins the Cooper River; ab. 40 mi. (64 km.) long.
2. County in SE Arkansas. See table at ARKANSAS.
3. City, ⊗ of McIntosh co., S North Dakota; pop. (1990c) 1052.
4. Borough, Luzerne co., E Pennsylvania, 3 mi. (5 km.) SW of Wilkes-Barre; pop. (1990c) 3291; settled 1810; coal.

Ash·more Islands *or* **Ashmore Reef** \'ash-,mōr\. Uninhabited islands, constituting an external territory of Australia, ab. 200 mi. (320 km.) N of N Western Australia; ab. 2 sq. mi. (5 sq. km.); formerly administratively part of Northern Terr.; in 1978 became federally administrated.

Ash·mūn \ash-'mün\. Town, Minūfīya governorate, Egypt, on railroad line in Nile delta 25 mi. (40 km.) NW of Cairo; pop. (1986p) 54,450.

Ashmūnein, Al– *or* **Ashmunein, El.** See AL-ASHMŪNEIN.

Asho·kan Dam \ə-'shō-kən\ *or* **Ol·ive Bridge Dam** \'ä-liv\. Dam across Esopus Creek, N Ulster co., SE New York; height 252 ft. (77 m.); completed 1912; forms **Ashokan Reservoir,** 12 mi. (19 km.) long, ab. 13 sq. mi. (34 sq. km.), estimated capacity 130 billion gallons, which supplies water for New York City.

Ash·qe·lon *also* **Ash·ke·lon** \'ash-kə-,län\. **1.** *also* **As·ca·lon** \'as-kə-,län\. Archaeological site, Israel, on coast 41 mi. (66 km.) WSW of Jerusalem; formerly a city-state.

History: Under Egyptian control 13th cent. B.C.; one of five city-kingdoms of Philistines who occupied it c. 1200–900 B.C.; conquered by successive ancient empires (see PALESTINE) but never by Israelites and Jews; conquered by Arabs 636 A.D.; scene of victory of Crusaders under Godfrey of Bouillon, duke of Lower Lorraine, and Norman hero Tancred over sultan of Egypt 1099; captured by Baldwin III 1153; retaken by Muslim Sultan Saladin 1187 and demolished 1191; finally destroyed by Sultan Baybars I 1270.

2. City, Israel, ab. 38 mi. (61 km.) WSW of Jerusalem; cement; founded 1949.

Ash Shām. **1.** Ancient country. See SYRIA 1.

2. City, Syria. See DAMASCUS.

Ash–Shaqrā. See SHAQRA.

Ash Shā·ri·qah \ˌash-ˈshä-rē-kə\ *or* **Shar·jah** \ˈshär-jə\. **1.** Emirate. See table at UNITED ARAB EMIRATES.

2. Town, its ✻, on Persian Gulf; pop. (1981p) 125,149.

Ash Shar·qāṭ \ˌash-shar-ˈkät\. Village, N Iraq, on right bank of the Tigris 60 mi. (97 km.) S of Mosul at site of ancient Ashur (*q.v.*).

Ash·ta·bu·la \ˌash-tə-ˈbyü-lə\. **1.** River, NE Ohio; rises in E Ashtabula co., and flows N and W into Lake Erie at city of Ashtabula.

2. County in NE corner of Ohio. See table at OHIO.

3. City, Ashtabula co., NE Ohio, on Lake Erie 55 mi. (88 km.) NE of Cleveland; pop. (1990c) 21,633; important transshipment point; settled 1803, incorp. 1831, chartered as city 1892.

Ash·ta·roth \ˈash-tə-ˌrȯth\. Ancient city of Bashan, in the Decapolis region, SW Syria, ab. 32°50′N, 36°E; a seat of worship of the Phoenician goddess Astarte. Now ruins at a village 22 mi. (35 km.) E of Sea of Galilee.

Ash·ton \ˈash-tən\ *or in full* **Ashton–under–Lyne** \ˈlīn\. Town, Lancashire, NW England, on Tame River 6 mi. (10 km.) E of Manchester; coal deposits.

Ashton–in–Ma·ker·field \ˈmā-kər-ˌfēld\. Town, Greater Manchester, England, 15 mi. (24 km.) W of Manchester; pop. (1981p) 29,341; coal.

Ash·ua·nipi \ˌash-wə-ˈni-pē\. Lake, SW Labrador, Newfoundland, Canada; 319 sq. mi. (826 sq. km.); source of the Churchill River (see CHURCHILL 4), called **Ashuanipi River** in its upper course.

Ashuapmuchuan *or* **Ashuapmushuan.** See CHAMOUCHOUANE.

Ash·ue·lot \ash-ˈwē-lət\. River, SW New Hampshire; rises in SE Sullivan co., flows SW into Connecticut River near Massachusetts border; 75 mi. (121 km.) long; provides power at Keene and other towns in its course.

Ashur \ˈa-shər, ˈä-ˌshu̇r\. **1.** Ancient empire, Asia. See ASSYRIA.

2. Ancient Sumerian settlement; now the village of Ash Sharqāṭ (*q.v.*), Iraq, on Tigris River S of Mosul.

Ash·wau·be·non \ash-ˈwä-bə-ˌnän, -nən\. Village, Brown co., E Wisconsin, S of Green Bay (city); pop. (1990c) 16,376.

ʽĀsī, Nahr Al–. See ORONTES 2.

Asia \ˈā-zhə, -shə\. **1.** Largest continent on the globe; 17,139,445 sq. mi. (44,391,162 sq. km.); pop. (1990e, excl. Russia in Asia, and the countries comprising the former Soviet Central Asia) 3,108,000,000.

Boundaries: (1) On N, Arctic Ocean (chief subdivisions Kara Sea, Laptev Sea, and East Siberian Sea); most northerly point Cape Chelyuskin 77°45′N; chief islands: Severnaya Zemlya, New Siberian Is., and Wrangel I. (2) On E, Pacific Ocean (chief subdivisions Bering Sea, Sea of Okhotsk, Sea of Japan, Yellow Sea, East China Sea, and South China Sea); marked by peninsulas of Kamchatka and Korea and by Malay Penin.; most easterly point Mys Dezhneva 169°40′W; chief islands: Sakhalin, Japan (four large islands), Taiwan, Luzon. (3) On S, Indian Ocean (chief subdivisions Bay of Bengal, Arabian Sea, Persian Gulf, and Gulf of Aden); most southerly point on mainland Cape Piai (Malaysia), 1°15′N; chief island in S Sri Lanka, in SE Borneo and Sumatra. (4) On W, Red Sea, Isthmus of Suez, Mediterranean Sea, Aegean Sea, and Black Sea, Caucasus Mts., NW Caspian Sea, steppe lands of W Kazakhstan (E of Volga River) and Ural Mts., the latter having long been conventional boundary bet. Europe and Asia; most westerly point Cape Baba, NW Turkey, 26°04′E; chief island Cyprus.

Mountains: The Himalayas in S containing highest peak in the world Mt. Everest 29,028 ft. (8848 m.), with branches of Hindu Kush to W, Pamirs and Tian Shan to NW, and on the N the great Plateau of Tibet, China, (av. height above 15,000 ft. or 4572 m.) with Kunlun Shan on N side; Altay Shan in W Mongolia, Da Hinggan Ling in NE China, and Verkhoyansk, Stanovoy, Cherski, and Kolyma ranges in E Siberia; many high volcanic peaks in Kamchatka and Japan; in SW the Elburz Mts. of N Iran (highest 18,934 ft. or 5771 m.) and the ranges of W and NW Iran.

Other notable physical features: Gobi Desert of Mongolia, Taklimakan Desert of Xinjiang Uygur, China, the Deccan plateau of S India, the plateau of Iran, the great deserts of Syria and Arabian Penin., and the Kirgiz Steppe of Kazakhstan.

Rivers: Ob', Yenisey, Lena in the N, Amur in NE, Huang, Chang, and Xi in the E (the three great rivers of China), Mekong, Salween, and Irrawaddy in SE, Brahmaputra, Ganges, and Indus in S (in Tibet [China] and India), Euphrates and Tigris in SW (in Turkey and Iraq), and Ural in W.

Lakes: Caspian Sea (inland sea) and Aral Sea in SW, Baikal in N, Balkhash in W cen. part, the smaller Dongting Hu and Poyang Hu in China, and many other comparatively large lakes in Turkey, Iran, and China.

Political divisions: Afghanistan, Armenia, Azerbaijan, Bahrain, Bangladesh, Bhutan, Brunei, Cambodia, China, Cyprus, Egypt (part), India, Indonesia, Iran, Iraq, Israel, Japan, Jordan, Kazakhstan, North Korea, South Korea, Kuwait, Kyrgyzstan, Laos, Lebanon, Malaysia, Maldives, Mongolia, Myanmar, Nepal, Oman, Pakistan, Philippines, Qatar, Republic of Georgia, Russia (part), Saudi Arabia, Singapore, Sri Lanka, Syria, Taiwan, Tajikistan, Thailand, Turkey (part), Turkmenistan, United Arab Emirates, Uzbekistan, Vietnam, and Yemen.

2. A province of ancient Rome, W part of Asia Minor; ✻ Pergamum, and later Ephesus; formed 133 B.C. out of the kingdom of Pergamum and included Mysia, Lydia, Caria, Phrygia, and smaller districts; reorganized by politician Sulla 84 B.C.; made a senatorial province 27 B.C.; broken up by Emperor Diocletian.

Asia·go \äz-ˈyä-gō\. Commune, Vicenza prov., Veneto, NE Italy, on plateau at foot of the Dolomites 24 mi. (39 km.) N of the commune of Vicenza; pop. (1981p) 6760; chief town of the Altipiano dei Sette Comuni; scene of famous battle with Austrians 1916.

Asia Islands. Group of three small islands, Indonesia, ab. 130 mi. (209 km.) NW of the Doberai Penin., Irian Jaya; in WWII a Japanese observation post; captured by U.S. forces 1944.

Asia Mi·nor \ˈmī-nər\ *or* **An·a·to·lia** \ˌa-nə-ˈtō-lē-ə, -lyə\. The peninsula forming W extremity of Asia, bet. Black Sea on N and Mediterranean Sea on S and bordering on Aegean Sea on W; forms the greater part of Turkey.

History: Original location of kingdom of Hittites c. 1900–1200 B.C.; W part center of Phrygian kingdom 1000–750 B.C.; W coast settled by Greeks (Aeolians, Dorians, and Ionians) c. 1000 B.C.; W part under kingdom of Lydia (*q.v.*) 670–546 B.C.; conquered by Persian ruler Cyrus the Great 546 B.C.; despite temporary alliance of coastal (Greek) cities with Athens, remained under Persian rule until 4th cent. B.C.; conquered by Macedonian King Alexander the Great c. 333 B.C. who was followed by Antigonus, founder of a separate kingdom which included most of Asia Minor; under Alexander's successors (Diadochi), divided into small kingdoms (see PERGAMUM, CAPPADOCIA, BITHYNIA, and PONTUS) 3d–1st cents. B.C.; coast and S part contested by Seleucids and Ptolemies; gradually conquered by Rome, W coast

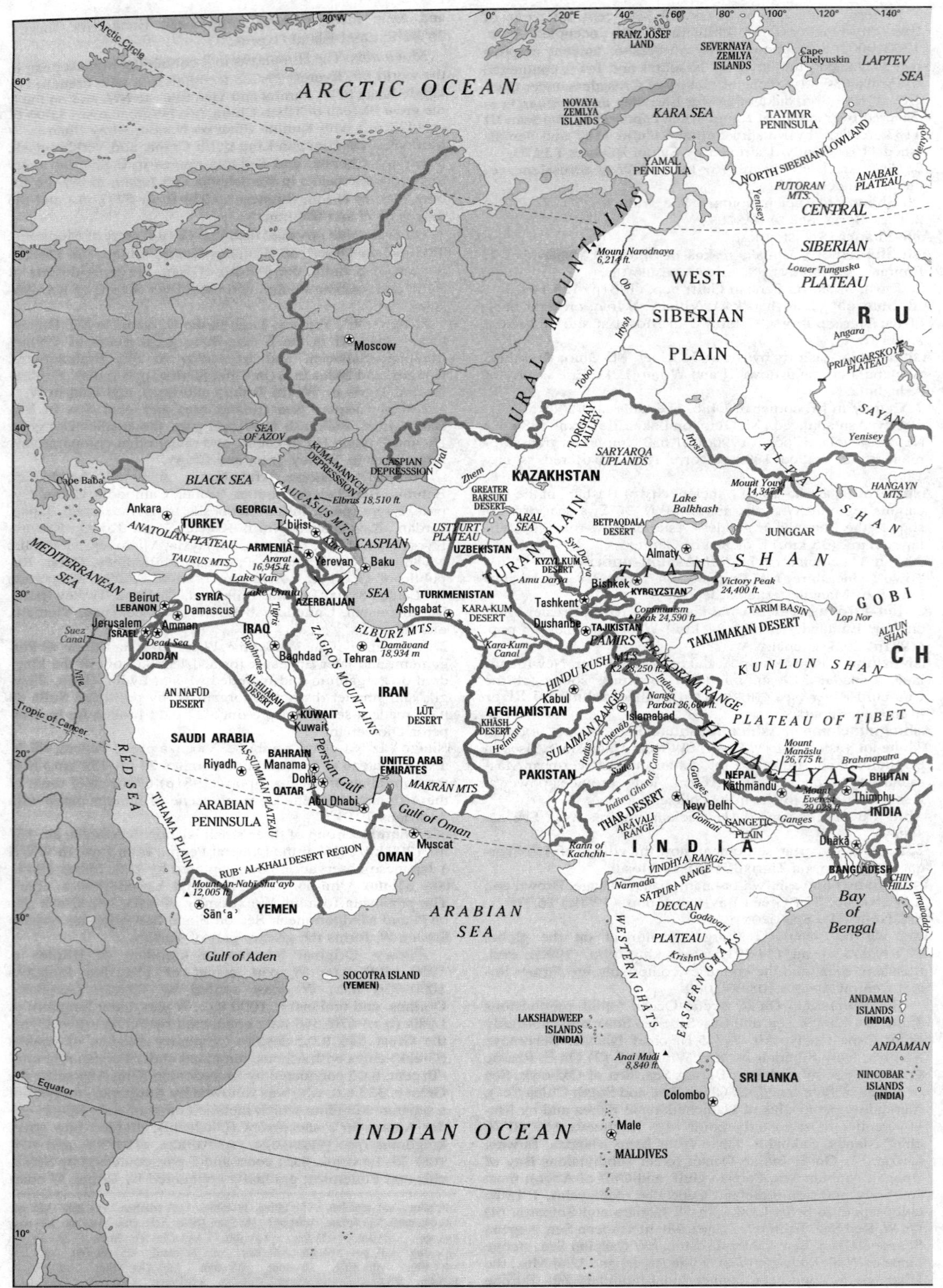
ARCTIC OCEAN
Arctic Circle
20°W
0°
20°E
40°
60°
80°
100°
120°
140°
60°
50°
40°
30°
20°
10°
0°
10°
FRANZ JOSEF LAND
SEVERNAYA ZEMLYA ISLANDS
Cape Chelyuskin
LAPTEV SEA
NOVAYA ZEMLYA ISLANDS
KARA SEA
TAYMYR PENINSULA
YAMAL PENINSULA
NORTH SIBERIAN LOWLAND
Olenyok
PUTORAN MTS.
ANABAR PLATEAU
Yenisey
CENTRAL
SIBERIAN
PLATEAU
Lower Tunguska
URAL MOUNTAINS
Mount Narodnaya 6,214 ft.
Ob
WEST
SIBERIAN
PLAIN
Irtysh
Tobol
R U
Angara
PRIANGARSKOYE PLATEAU
Moscow
SAYAN
Yenisey
ALTAY
Irtysh
TORGHAY VALLEY
SARYARQA UPLANDS
SEA OF AZOV
KUMA-MANYCH DEPRESSION
CASPIAN DEPRESSSION
Ural
Zhem
KAZAKHSTAN
Mount Youyi 14,347 ft.
HANGAYN MTS.
Cape Baba
BLACK SEA
CAUCASUS MTS.
Elbrus 18,510 ft.
GREATER BARSUKI DESERT
ARAL SEA
Lake Balkhash
SHAN
Ankara
TURKEY
GEORGIA
T'bilisi
USTYURT PLATEAU
TURAN PLAIN
BETPAQDALA DESERT
JUNGGAR
ANATOLIAN PLATEAU
ARMENIA
Kura
CASPIAN
UZBEKISTAN
Syr Dar'ya
KYZYLKUM DESERT
Almaty
TIAN SHAN
MEDITERRANEAN SEA
TAURUS MTS.
Ararat 16,945 ft.
Yerevan
Baku
Amu Darya
Bishkek
KYRGYZSTAN
Victory Peak 24,400 ft.
Lake Van
Lake Urmia
SEA
AZERBAIJAN
TURKMENISTAN
Tashkent
GOBI
Beirut
LEBANON
SYRIA
Damascus
Ashgabat
KARA-KUM DESERT
Communism Peak 24,590 ft.
TAJIKISTAN
TARIM BASIN
Lop Nor
Jerusalem
ISRAEL
Amman
Suez Canal
Dead Sea
JORDAN
Tigris
IRAQ
Euphrates
Baghdad
ELBURZ MTS.
Damāvand 18,934 m
Tehran
Dushanbe
PAMIRS
KARAKORAM RANGE
TAKLIMAKAN DESERT
ALTUN SHAN
CH
Kara-Kum Canal
K2 28,250 ft.
KUNLUN SHAN
Nile
ZAGROS MOUNTAINS
IRAN
HINDU KUSH MTS.
Kabul
AFGHANISTAN
Indus
Nanga Parbat 26,660 ft.
AN NAFŪD DESERT
AL-HIJĀRAH DESERT
KUWAIT
Kuwait
LŪT DESERT
Islamabad
PLATEAU OF TIBET
Tropic of Cancer
SAUDI ARABIA
ASSUMMĀN PLATEAU
KHĀSH DESERT
Helmand
SULAIMAN RANGE
Chenāb
HIMALAYAS
Mount Manāslu 26,775 ft.
Brahmaputra
BAHRAIN
Manama
Persian Gulf
UNITED ARAB EMIRATES
Indus
Sutlej
Indira Ghandi Canal
BHUTAN
RED SEA
Riyadh
Doha
QATAR
MAKRĀN MTS.
PAKISTAN
Ganges
NEPAL
Kāthmāndu
Mount Everest 29,028 ft.
Thimphu
TIHAMA PLAIN
ARABIAN PENINSULA
Abu Dhabi
THAR DESERT
New Delhi
INDIA
Gulf of Oman
Gomati
GANGETIC PLAIN
Ganges
ARĀVALI RANGE
Muscat
Dhākā
Rann of Kachchh
INDIA
RUB' AL-KHALI DESERT REGION
OMAN
VINDHYA RANGE
Mount An-Nabi Shu'ayb 12,005 ft.
Narmada
SĀTPURA RANGE
BANGLADESH
CHIN HILLS
Bay of Bengal
Irrawaddy
Sān'a'
YEMEN
ARABIAN SEA
DECCAN
Godāvari
PLATEAU
Krishna
WESTERN GHĀTS
EASTERN GHĀTS
Gulf of Aden
SOCOTRA ISLAND (YEMEN)
ANDAMAN ISLANDS (INDIA)
LAKSHADWEEP ISLANDS (INDIA)
ANDAMAN
Anai Mudi 8,840 ft.
SRI LANKA
NINCOBAR ISLANDS (INDIA)
Colombo
Equator
INDIAN OCEAN
Male
MALDIVES

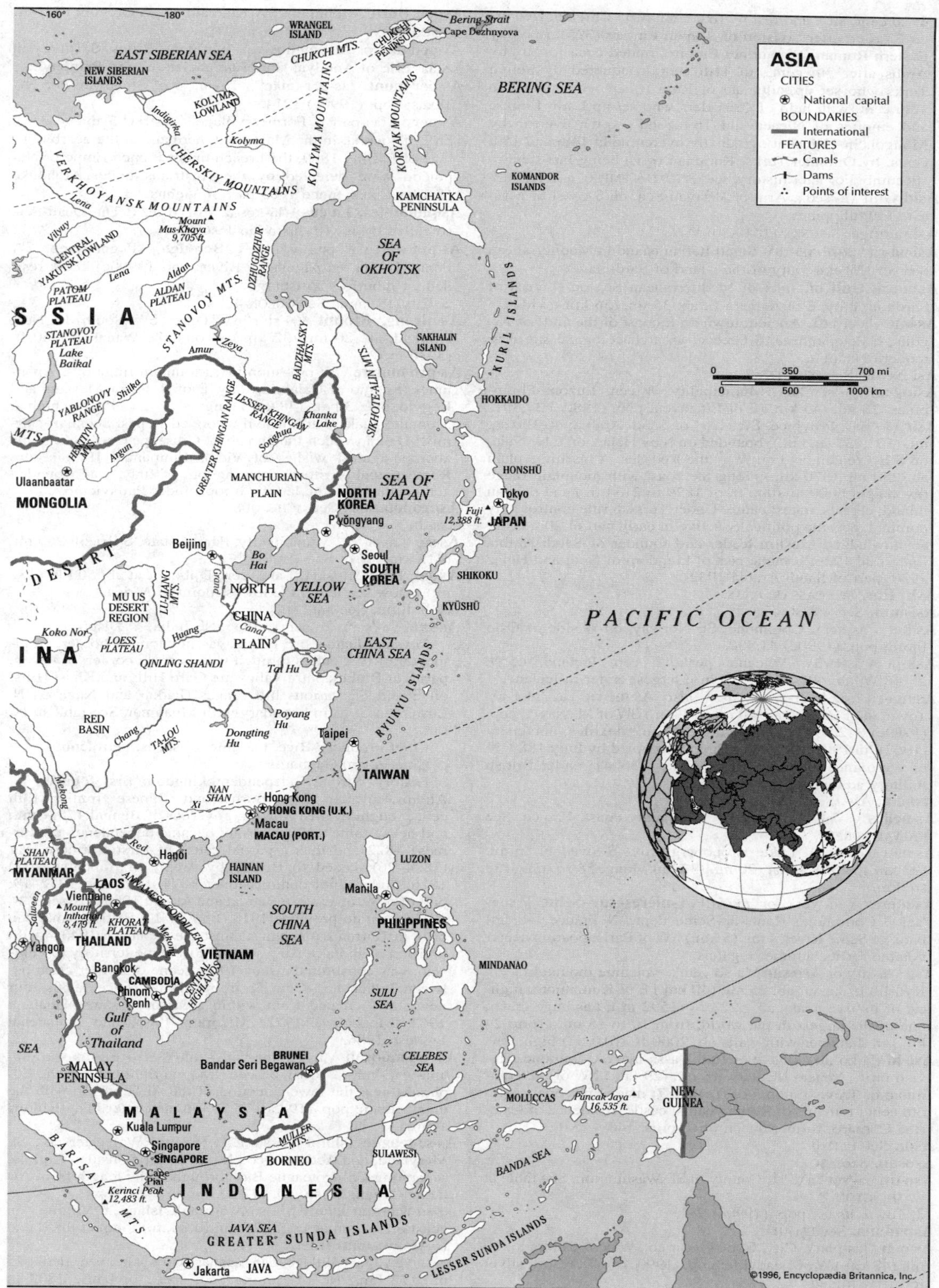
ASIA
CITIES
National capital
BOUNDARIES
International
FEATURES
Canals
Dams
Points of interest
0 350 700 mi
0 500 1000 km
160°
180°
WRANGEL ISLAND
CHUKCHI MTS.
CHUKCHI PENINSULA
Bering Strait
Cape Dezhnyova
EAST SIBERIAN SEA
NEW SIBERIAN ISLANDS
BERING SEA
KOLYMA LOWLAND
Indigirka
Kolyma
KOLYMA MOUNTAINS
KORYAK MOUNTAINS
CHERSKIY MOUNTAINS
VERKHOYANSK MOUNTAINS
KOMANDOR ISLANDS
KAMCHATKA PENINSULA
Lena
Mount Mus-Khaya 9,705 ft.
Vilyuy
CENTRAL YAKUTSK LOWLAND
Aldan
DZHUGDZHUR RANGE
SEA OF OKHOTSK
PATOM PLATEAU
ALDAN PLATEAU
STANOVOY MTS.
KURIL ISLANDS
SSIA
STANOVOY PLATEAU
Lake Baikal
Zeya
Amur
BADZHALSKY MTS.
SAKHALIN ISLAND
SIKHOTE-ALIN MTS.
YABLONOVY RANGE
Shilka
LESSER KHINGAN RANGE
HOKKAIDO
MTS.
HENTIYN MTS.
Argun
GREATER KHINGAN RANGE
Songhua
Khanka Lake
Ulaanbaatar
MONGOLIA
MANCHURIAN PLAIN
SEA OF JAPAN
HONSHŪ
NORTH KOREA
Tokyo
Fuji 12,388 ft.
JAPAN
P'yŏngyang
Beijing
Seoul
SOUTH KOREA
DESERT
Bo Hai
Grand
NORTH CHINA PLAIN
YELLOW SEA
SHIKOKU
LU-LIANG MTS.
MU US DESERT REGION
KYŪSHŪ
PACIFIC OCEAN
Koko Nor
Huang
Canal
LOESS PLATEAU
INA
EAST CHINA SEA
QINLING SHANDI
Tai Hu
RYUKYU ISLANDS
RED BASIN
Poyang Hu
Chang
TA-LOU MTS.
Dongting Hu
Taipei
TAIWAN
Mekong
NAN SHAN
Xi
Hong Kong
HONG KONG (U.K.)
Macau
MACAU (PORT.)
SHAN PLATEAU
Red
Hanoi
MYANMAR
LAOS
HAINAN ISLAND
LUZON
Vientiane
ANNAMESE CORDILLERA
Mount Inthanon 8,479 ft.
Manila
Salween
KHORAT PLATEAU
Mekong
SOUTH CHINA SEA
PHILIPPINES
Yangon
THAILAND
VIETNAM
Bangkok
CAMBODIA
CENTRAL HIGHLANDS
MINDANAO
Phnom Penh
SULU SEA
Gulf of Thailand
SEA
BRUNEI
Bandar Seri Begawan
CELEBES SEA
MALAY PENINSULA
MOLUCCAS
Puncak Jaya 16,535 ft.
NEW GUINEA
MALAYSIA
Kuala Lumpur
MULLER MTS.
Singapore
SINGAPORE
BORNEO
SULAWESI
BANDA SEA
Cape Piai
BARISAN MTS.
Kerinci Peak 12,483 ft.
INDONESIA
JAVA SEA
GREATER SUNDA ISLANDS
LESSER SUNDA ISLANDS
Jakarta
JAVA
©1996, Encyclopædia Britannica, Inc.

in 2d cent. B.C., and rest by first cent. A.D.; Christianized after 33 A.D.; after division of Roman Empire (395), ruled by Eastern Roman (Byzantine) Empire; raided occasionally by Arabs after 7th cent.; in 11th cent. conquered by Seljuq Turks who set up sultanate of Rum (*q.v.*); reconquered in 12th cent. with help of Crusaders who set up Latin Empire and empires of Nicaea and Trebizond (*qq.v.*); overrun by Mongols in 13th cent.; gradually overcome in 14th and 15th cents. by Ottoman Turks, Karaman (*q.v.*) being last state to succumb. For later history, see OTTOMAN EMPIRE and TURKEY.

Asid Gulf \ä-'sēd\. Arm of Visayan Sea, on S coast of Masbate I., Philippines.

Asinalunga. See SINALUNGA.

Asi·na·ra \ˌä-sē-'nä-rä\. Small Italian island in Mediterranean Sea off NW extremity of the island of Sardinia.

Asinara, Gulf of. Inlet of Mediterranean Sea on N coast of Sardinia, Italy, E of Asinara I.; ab. 35 mi. (56 km.) wide.

As·i·ne \'a-si-nē\. Ancient town on E coast of the Gulf of Argolis, E Peloponnese, S Greece; an archaeological site near modern Nauplia.

Asi Nehri. See ORONTES 2.

Asing·an \ä-'sēŋ-än\. Municipality, W cen. Luzon, Philippines, 28 mi. (45 km.) E of Lingayen; pop. (1980c) 37,301.

Asir \ȧ-'sir\. Province, SW coast of Saudi Arabia; 40,130 sq. mi. (103,937 sq. km.); bounded on N by Hejaz, on E by Nejd, on S by Yemen, and on W by the Red Sea. A maritime plain ab. 230 mi. (370 km.) along the coast with mountain range (av. height 6000 to 7000 ft. or 1829 to 2134 m.) and plateau inland; cereals, dates; cattle. Under Turkish rule control only nominal; became politically active in early part of 20th cent.; acknowledged Muslim leader and founder of Saudi Arabia Ibn Sa'ūd 1926; became part of kingdom of Nedj and Hejaz 1930; part of Saudi Arabia 1932.

Asir, Ras. See CASEYR, RAAS.

Asisium. See ASSISI.

As·ker \'ȧs-kər\. Commune, SE Norway, on W side of Oslo Fjord; pop. (1990c) 41,430.

Ask·ja \'äs-kyä\. Volcanic peak, E cen. Iceland, 65°N, 16°48'W; ab. 4954 ft. (1510 m.); largest crater in Iceland.

As·ma·ra \az-'mär-ə, -'mar-ə\ *also* **As·me·ra** \az-'mer-ə\. Town, ✻ of Eritrea, ab. 40 mi. (64 km.) SW of Massawa; pop. (1989e) 342,706; alt. 7765 ft. (2367 m.); textiles; university (1967); in 19th cent. under Egypt; occupied by Italy 1889; ✻ of a province of Italian East Africa 1936–41; under British military administration 1941–52.

Asnam, Al–. See ECH-CHELIFF.

As·nelles \ä-'nel\. Village on Normandy coast, France. See CALVADOS REEF.

Ås·nen \'ös-nen\. Lake, Kronoberg prov., S Sweden, 56 mi. (90 km.) W of Kalmar; 20 mi. (32 km.) long; 58 sq. mi. (158 sq. km.).

As·nières \ȧn-'yer\ *or in full* **Asnières–sur–Seine** \-sœr-'sen\. Commune, Hauts-de-Seine dept., N France, on left bank of Seine River 3 mi. (5 km.) NW of Paris; boating center notable for its summer regattas.

Aso \'ä-sō\ *or* **Aso·san** \'ä-sō-ˌsän\. Volcanic mountain, cen. Kyūshū I., Japan, ab. 25 mi. (40 km.) E of Kumamoto; highest of its five peaks ab. 5223 ft. (1592 m.); has huge crater, one of the largest in the world, from 10 to 15 mi. (16 to 24 km.) in diameter with walls ab. 2000 ft. (610 m.) high.

Aso·lo \'ä-zȯ-ˌlō\; *anc.* **Ac·e·lum** \'a-sə-ləm\. Commune, Treviso prov., Veneto NE Italy, 18 mi. (29 km.) NW of the commune of Treviso; pop. (1981p) 6387; made episcopal see in 6th cent.; remains of Roman baths; castle; residence of Caterina Cornaro, former queen of Cyprus, 1489–1510.

Asor. See ULITHI.

Asosan. See ASO.

Aso·tin \ə-'sōt-ᵊn\. **1.** County in SE Washington. See table at WASHINGTON.
2. Town, its ⊗; pop. (1990c) 981.

Aspadana. See EŞFAHĀN 2.

As·pen \'as-pən\. City, ⊗ of Pitkin co., W cen. Colorado, 30 mi. (48 km.) W of Leadville; pop. (1990c) 5049; resort; silver formerly mined.

Aspen Butte. Mountain, SW Klamath co., S Oregon; 8210 ft. (2502 m.).

As·pen·dus *or* **As·pen·dos** \as-'pen-dəs\. Ruins, S Turkey in Asia, ENE of Antalya; site of an ancient city of Pamphylia.

As·per·mont \'as-pər-ˌmänt\. Town, ⊗ of Stonewall co., NW Texas; pop. (1990c) 1214.

As·pern \'äs-pərn\. Former village, Austria, 5 mi. (8 km.) ENE of Vienna, in the Marchfeld; here and at the nearby village of Essling 1809, the French under French Emperor Napoléon were defeated by the Austrians under Archduke Charles Louis; since 1905 part of Vienna.

As·phal·ti·tes, La·cus \'lā-kəs-ˌas-fȯl-'tī-tēz\. The Dead Sea, so called by Jewish historian Josephus.

As·pin·wall \'as-pən-ˌwȯl\. **1.** Borough, Allegheny co., SW Pennsylvania, on Allegheny River; pop. (1990c) 2880; residential suburb of Pittsburgh.
2. City, Panama. See COLÓN 4.

As·pir·ing, Mount \ə-'spīr-iŋ\. Peak, SW South I., New Zealand, ab. 20 mi. (32 km.) W of Lake Wanaka; 9960 ft. (3036 m.).

As·pro·mon·te \ˌäs-prō-'mȯn-tā\. Mountain ridge of S Apennines, Reggio di Calabria, Italy, E of Strait of Messina and Reggio; over 30 mi. (48 km.) long; 6417 ft. (1956 m.) high at Montalto peak; sharp, heavily wooded slopes. Scene of skirmish 1862 in which Italian patriot Giuseppe Garibaldi, in his attempt against wishes of Victor Emmanuel II to secure Rome (papal territory) for kingdom of Italy, was wounded and captured by the latter's troops under Pallavicino.

Aspropotamos. See ACHELOUS.

Assab. See ASEB.

As·saí \ˌa-sä-'ē\. Municipality, Paraná state, S Brazil, 260 mi. (418 km.) W of São Paulo.

As·sal, Lake \ä-'säl\. Lake, cen. Djibouti; at ab. 500 ft. (152 m.) below sea level; the lowest point in Africa.

As–Sallūm. See SALŪM.

As·sam \a-'sam, 'a-ˌsam\. State, NE India; ✻ Dispur.

Physical features: E Himalayas lie along N border; Brahmaputra River enters through gorges at NE corner; in W cen. part S of Brahmaputra Valley are Garo Hills and Khasi Hills; on E and SE various hill ranges (Patkai and Naga on N, Lushai on S) form boundary with Myanmar. See table at INDIA.

Chief products: Rice, tea, jute, oilseeds; petroleum.

Chief town: Gauhati.

History: Strong independent kingdom first founded by Ahoms, invaders from Burma and Chinese frontier, 13th cent.; fought against Muslim governor of Bengal 17th cent., and never came under his rule; became dependency of Burmese 1822 and thus a partial cause of First Burmese War (1824–26); ceded to British by Treaty of Yandabu (*q.v.*) 1826; under chief commissioner 1874–1905 and 1912–19; part of prov. of Eastern Bengal and Assam 1905–12 (see BENGAL), separate province 1919. In WWII a British-American base in Burma campaign against the Japanese 1943–45. In division of India in August 1947 lost some territory to Pakistan; was constituted a state 1950; scene of border clash between Indian and Chinese troops 1962. Since 1960s four new states created from within areas of Assam: Nagaland 1963, Meghalaya 1972, Mizoram 1986, and Arunachal Pradesh 1986.

As Sa·mā·wah \ˌas-sə-'ma-wə, -'mä-\ *also* **Sa·ma·wa** \sə-'ma-wə, -'mä-\. Town, SE cen. Iraq, on right bank of the Euphrates near the lower junction of the Al Hindīyah with the main stream; pop. (1985e) 75,293; trade center in agricultural area.

As·sa·teague Island \'a-sə-ˌtēg\. Island, Worcester co., SE Maryland, and Accomac co., N part of E peninsula, Virginia, separating Chincoteague Bay throughout its length from Atlantic Ocean; 28 sq. mi. (72 sq. km.).

As·sa·wa·man Island \'a-sə-ˌwä-mən\. Island, E Virginia, on coast off Accomac co.; 4.25 mi. (6.8 km.) long; at the N end is **Assawaman Inlet.**

As·sa·ye \ä-'sī\ Village, cen. Maharashtra state, cen. India, 45 mi. (72 km.) NE of Aurangabad; scene of battle 1803 in which British Gen. Arthur Wellesley completely defeated Sindhia and Nagpur branches of Marathas.

As·sen \ˈäs-ᵊn\. Commune, ✻ of Drenthe prov., Netherlands, 16 mi. (26 km.) S of Groningen; pop. (1992e) 50,880; connected by canal with Groningen and Meppel and the Waddenzee; built around old nunnery now serving as public buildings; in vicinity are the "Giants' Caves" mentioned by Roman historian Tacitus, and prehistoric stone monuments resembling those at Stonehenge; founded 1257.

Asshur. See ASSYRIA.

As·sin·i·boia \ə-ˌsi-nə-ˈbȯi-ə\. **1.** Early region of W Canada, c. 1811–70, with indefinite boundaries; controlled by Hudson's Bay Company with headquarters at Fort Garry; included Red River Settlement.

2. Former district, formed 1882 out of Northwest Terr., Canada, W of Manitoba and S of Saskatchewan dist.; 89,000 sq. mi. (230,510 sq. km.); ✻ Regina. Greater part of it united Sept. 1, 1905 with Saskatchewan dist. and E part of Athabaska dist. to form Saskatchewan prov.

As·sin·i·boine \ə-ˈsi-nə-ˌbȯin\. River, S Canada; rises in SE Saskatchewan, flows S and E across S Manitoba into the Red River of the North at Winnipeg; 590 mi. (949 km.) long; navigable for ab. 300 mi. (483 km.). Explored by Sieur de La Vérendrye 1736; its valley was route to the plains by colonists from Red River Settlement.

Assiniboine, Mount. Mountain in Rocky Mts., Canada, on border bet. SE British Columbia and SW Alberta, ab. 25 mi. (40 km.) SW of Banff; 11,870 ft. (3618 m.).

Assiout. See ASYŪT.

As·si·si \ə-ˈsē-sē, -ˈsē-zē\; *anc.* **Asi·sium** \ə-ˈsi-zhē-əm, -zē-əm, -zhəm\. Commune, Perugia prov., Umbria cen. Italy, on S slope of Monte Subasio; pop. (1988c) 24,669; episcopal see; famous as place of birth and death of St. Francis of Assisi (1182–1226); Gothic Franciscan monastery and upper and lower church of St. Francis, containing paintings by old masters, esp. Giotto.

Assiut. See ASYŪT.

As·siz \ə-ˈsēs, -ˈsēz\. City, São Paulo state, SE Brazil, ab. 240 mi. (386 km.) WNW of São Paulo; munic. pop. (1980c) 67,403.

Association of Southeast Asian Nations *or abbr.* **ASEAN** \ˈä- sē-ˌän, ˈa-, -ən\. Political organization, consisting of Brunei, Cambodia, Indonesia, Laos, Malaysia, Myanmar, Philippines, Singapore, Thailand, Vietnam; headquarters Jakarta, Indonesia; purpose is to stimulate economic growth and maintain regional stability; estab. 1967.

Assomption, L'. See L'ASSOMPTION.

As·sos *or Lat.* **As·sus** \ˈa-səs\. Ancient city of S Troas, in Aeolis, on coast of Gulf of Adramyttium (Edremit) W of Mt. Ida and opp. N shore of Lesbos; founded c. 900 B.C. and long an important city and port. Greek philosopher Aristotle taught here 348–345 B.C. Its ruins now an archaeological site and part of village of **Beh·ram·köy** \ˌber-äm-ˈkœi\, Çanakkale prov., NW Turkey.

Assouan *or* **Assuan.** See ASWĀN.

As·suad, Cape \ə-ˈswäd\. Cape extending into Indian Ocean, cen. part of E coast of Somalia.

as–Sudd. See SUDD.

as–Sulaymānīyah. See SULAYMĀNĪYAH, AS-.

As·sump·tion \ə-ˈsəmp-shən\. **1.** Parish in SE Louisiana. See table at LOUISIANA.

2. Island, Indian Ocean. See ALDABRA.

Assur. See ASSYRIA.

Assus. See ASSOS.

As Su·way·dā \ˌȧs-sü-ˈwī-də\ *also* **Es Su·wei·da** \ˌes-sü-ˈwā-də\ *or* **Es Su·wei·di·ya** \-dē-yə\ *or Fr.* **Souei·da** \swā-ˈdä\. Town, ✻ of former Druze territory of Jebel ed Druz, now a part of Syria, railroad terminus ab. 56 mi. (90 km.) S of Damascus; on site of an ancient Roman settlement.

As–Suways. See SUEZ.

As·synt, Loch \ˈa-sint\. Lake, Highland region, N Scotland, draining W into Enard Bay; 6.5 mi. (10 km.) long.

As·syr·ia \ə-ˈsir-ē-ə\; *anc.* **As·sur** \ä-ˈsu̇r, ˈä-ˌsu̇r\ *or* **Ashur** *or* **As·shur** \ˈä-shu̇r, -shər\. One of the great ancient empires, holding dominion in W Asia; early ✻ Nimrud, later ✻ Nineveh; extended along E bank of middle Tigris and over foothills to the E. May have originated in 3d millennium B.C. in Sumerian settlement of Ashur but later became part of Akkadian empire; in 2d millennium B.C. was involved with Babylonians, Hittites, and Hurrians. Slowly gained control of trade routes under Tiglath-pileser I during late 12th and early 11th cents. B.C. but was esp. powerful in c. 884 to c. 782 B.C. when it reached Mediterranean in conquests under Ashurnasirpal II and Shalmaneser III and their successors, and in c. 745 to c. 626 B.C. when it conquered Israel, Damascus, Babylon, and Samaria, and conducted successful campaigns against Egypt; its greatest rulers then were Tiglath-pileser III, Sargon II, Sennacherib, Esarhaddon, and Ashurbanipal. Lost power rapidly and completely 626–612 B.C. when Nineveh was destroyed by kings of Media and Babylonia. For later history of the region, see MESOPOTAMIA.

Astaboras. See ATBARA.

Asta Colonia. See ASTI 2.

Astacus. See İZMİT.

As·ta·na \ä-stä-ˈnä\; *before 1961* **Ak·mo·linsk** \ȧk-ˈmȯ-linsk\ *or* **Ak·mo·la** \ȧk-ˈmȯ-lə\; *1961-90* **Tse·lin·o·grad** \tsi-ˈlē-nə-ˌgrät, -ˌgrad\; *1991-98* **Akmola** *or* **Aq·mo·la** \ȧk-ˈmȯ-lə\. **1.** Administrative subdivision of Kazakhstan; 35,560 sq. mi. (92,100 sq. km.); pop. (1991e) 885,400; ✻ Astana; traversed by Ishim River and by two trunk railroads; Lake Tengiz in S.

2. Town, its ✻ and since 1997 ✻ of Kazakhstan, on bank of Ishim River near its source; in center of a mineral-rich steppe region.

Asta Pompeia. See ASTI 2.

As·ta·ra \ˌəs-tə-ˈrä\. Seaport, SE Azerbaijan, on W coast of Caspian Sea, on border of Iran.

Astarabad *or* **Asterabad.** See GORGĀN.

Asti \ˈäs-tē\. **1.** Province of Piedmont, NW Italy. See table at ITALY.

2. *anc.* **As·ta Pom·pe·ia** \ˈas-tə-päm-ˈpē-ə\ *or* **Has·ta Pompeia** \ˈhas-tə\ *or* **Asta Co·lo·nia** *or* **Hasta Colonia** \kō-ˈlō-nē-ə\. Commune, its ✻, on left bank of Tanaro River 20 mi. (32 km.) W of Alessandria; pop. (1989c) 74,649; known for the sparkling wine Asti spumante; Gothic cathedral built early 14th cent.; many medieval structures. Powerful medieval republic; burned by Holy Roman Emperor Frederick Barbarossa 1155; captured by the Visconti of Milan c. 1348; ceded to France c. 1387 as part of a dowry of daughter of Gian Galeazzo Visconti; given to dukes of Savoy 16th cent.

Astigi. See ÉCIJA.

Asti·pá·laia \ˌäs-tē-ˈpä-lā-ˌä\ *also* **Asty·pa·laea** \ˌas-ti-pə-ˈlē-ə\ *or* **Asty·pa·laia** \-ˈlā-ə\ *or Ital.* **Stam·pa·lia** \stäm-ˈpäl-yä\. One of the Dodecanese Is. (*q.v.*), Greece; 37 sq. mi. (96 sq. km.).

As·ton \ˈas-tən\. **1.** Residential township, Delaware co., Pennsylvania, SW of Philadelphia; pop. (1990c) 15,080; Neumann Coll. (1965).

2. Ward, Birmingham borough, South Yorkshire, W cen. England.

As·tor, Mount \ˈas-tər\. Peak, Antarctica, 86°01′S, 155°30′W; 12,175 ft. (3711 m.).

As·tor·ga \ä-ˈstȯr-gə\; *anc.* **As·tu·ri·ca Au·gus·ta** \as-ˈtu̇r-i-kə-ȯ-ˈgəs-tə, -ˈtyu̇r-\. Commune, León prov., NW Spain, 28 mi. (45 km.) WSW of the city of León; pop. (1991c) 12,500; episcopal see; medieval fortifications; Gothic 15th cent. cathedral. Ancient Roman ✻ of Asturias and military center; a famous center of Spanish resistance against Moors in 8th cent.; captured by French 1810 and retaken by Spaniards 1812 (Peninsular War).

As·to·ria \a-ˈstōr-ē-ə, ə-\. **1.** Former village, Queens co., SE New York, on Long Island, on East River, now section of Long Island City (*q.v.*) in Queens, New York City.

2. City and port of entry, ⊗ of Clatsop co., NW Oregon, on S bank and near mouth of Columbia River; pop. (1990c)

\ə\ abut \ᵊ\ matches \ᵊ\ kitten, Fr table \ər\ further \a\ ash \ā\ ace \ä\ cot, cart \ȧ\ Fr bac \au̇\ out \b\ Span Avila \ch\ chin \e\ bet \ē\ easy \g\ go \i\ hit \ī\ ice \j\ job \k\ Ger ich, Buch \ⁿ\ Fr vin \ŋ\ sing \ō\ go \ȯ\ all \ȯ\ law \œ\ Fr bœuf \œ̄\ Fr feu \ȯi\ boy \th\ thin \t͟h\ this \ü\ loot \u̇\ foot \ue\ Ger füllen \ue̅\ Fr rue \y\ yet \ʸ\ Fr digne \ˈdēnʸ\, nuit \ˈnwʸē\ \yü\ few \yu̇\ fury \zh\ vision

10,069; site of Astoria Bridge, world's longest continuous truss bridge (main span 1232 ft. or 376 m.; completed 1966), spanning Columbia River; fisheries; Clatsop Community Coll. (1958); near site of Fort Clatsop, estab. by Lewis and Clark expedition 1805. Founded as trading post by fur trader and financier John Jacob Astor 1811; taken by British 1813; restored to U.S. 1818.

Astrabad. See GORGĀN.

As·tra·khan \ˈas-trə-ˌkan, -kən\. City, ✱ of Astrakhan Oblast, Russia in Europe, on left bank of the Volga at head of its delta ab. 235 mi. (378 km.) SE of Volgograd; pop. (1992e) 512,000; alt. 50 ft. (15 m.) below sea level; port frozen for about one third of the year; fish processing; wood products, textiles; transshipment point esp. for grain; has fortress, or *kreml* (built late 16th cent. on a hill); university (1919).

History: The ✱ of a Tatar khanate on lower Volga, which became independent of former Kipchak (Golden Horde) empire (1237–1486; see MONGOLIA and RUSSIA 3); conquered 1554–56 by Russian Czar Ivan IV who thus gained control for Russia of entire course of Volga, an important route for eastward expansion; town burned by Turks 1569; center of Czar Peter the Great's campaign against Persia; given special trade privileges by Empress Catherine II.

Astrakhan Oblast \ˈȯ-bləst, -ˌblast\. Subdivision, S Russia in Asia, W and SW of the lower Volga with narrow strip along its E bank; 17,027 sq. mi. (44,100 sq. km.); pop. (1992e) 1,010,000; ✱ Astrakhan; formed 1945.

As·tro·labe, Cape \ˈas-trə-ˌlāb\. Cape, NW point of Malaita I., E Solomon Is., W Pacific Ocean.

Astrolabe Bay. Inlet of Bismarck Sea on NE cen. coast of New Guinea I., Papua New Guinea, at W end of Vitiaz Strait.

As·tu·ra *Lat.* ˈas-chu̇r-ə, *Ital.* ä-ˈstü-rä\. Village, Roma prov., Lazio, Italy, 36 mi. (58 km.) SSE of Rome and near Anzio; formerly an islet, now a peninsula; site of a favorite villa of statesman and orator Cicero from which he embarked on the flight that ended with his murder at Formiae 43 B.C.; site of medieval castle of the Frangipani family where Prince Conradin, the last of the Hohenstaufen family of German sovereigns, unsuccessfully sought refuge after battle of Tagliacozzo 1268.

As·tu·ri·as \ä-ˈstür-yäs; as-ˈtu̇r-ē-əs, -ˈtyu̇r-\. **1.** Municipality on W coast of Cebu I., Philippines, 22 mi. (35 km.) NW of City of Cebu; pop. (1980c) 28,655.

2. Autonomous community, province, and ancient kingdom, NW Spain, bounded on N by Bay of Biscay, on E by Cantabria, on S by Castilla y León and the Cantabrian Mts., and on W by Galicia; ✱ Oviedo; comprises an autonomous community of modern Spain (see table at SPAIN); picturesque mountain woodlands, steep chasms, fertile valleys; rich pasturage, producing an excellent breed of horses and cattle; deposits of coal, iron, and other minerals; excellent fisheries; corn.

History: Conquered by Romans under Emperor Augustus 25 B.C.; refuge for Goths from Saracen onslaught in 8th cent.; kingdom created by Pelayo (718–737), successor to Visigoth ruler, and successfully defended by him against Moors; became part of kingdom of León on accession of Alfonso III 866, and later of kingdom of León and Castile; made principality 1388, held until 1931 by heir apparent to the Spanish throne with title Prince of the Asturias; from 1838 officially a province; from 1981 also an autonomous community.

3. City, NW Spain. See OVIEDO 2.

Asturica Augusta. See ASTORGA.

Asty·pa·laea *or* **Astypalaia.** See ASTIPÁLAIA.

Asun·cion \ä-ˌsün-ˈsyōn\. Small island, N end of Mariana Is., W Pacific Ocean, 19°40′N, 145°24′E.

Asun·ción \ä-ˌsün-ˈsyōn\ *or* **Nues·tra Se·ño·ra de la Asunción** \ˈnwās-trä-sā-ˈnyō-rä-ˌthā-lä-ä-ˌsün-ˈsyōn\. City, ✱ of Central dept., and of Paraguay, on E bank of Paraguay River at the confluence of the Pilcomayo; pop. (1992p) 502,426; commercial center; food products, footwear, textiles; National Univ. (1890), Catholic Univ. (1960).

History: Founded 1537 by expedition under Spanish conquistador Domingo Martínez de Irala sent inland from coast by Spanish explorer Pedro de Mendoza; first permanent settlement in La Plata region; ✱ of region until Buenos Aires refounded 1580 and developed; seat of revolutionary junta which threw off rule of Buenos Aires 1811 (see PARAGUAY); occupied 1868 by forces of Brazil, Argentina, and Uruguay in war for Greater Paraguay; under Brazilian control 1868–76.

Asunción, La. See LA ASUNCIÓN.

Asunción Mi·ta \ˈmē-tä\. Town, Jutiapa dept., SE Guatemala; munic. pop. (1981c) 30,366.

As·wān *or* **As·wan** *also* **As·souan** *or* **As·suan** \a-ˈswän, ä-\. **1.** Governorate of SE Egypt. See table at EGYPT.

2. *anc.* **Sy·e·ne** \sī-ˈē-nē\. City, its ✱, on right bank of the Nile, ab. 10 mi. (16 km.) N of Lake Nasser; pop. (1986p) 191,461; steel, textiles; popular winter resort; has Egyptian and Roman ruins; ancient Syene an important town in first millennium B.C. Ab. 3.5 mi. (6 km.) to the S of the city at the beginning of the first of several cataracts is the great **Aswān Dam,** 6400 ft. (1951 m.) long, built 1898–1902 to replace 19th cent. barrage; above it is the **Aswān High Dam** (364 ft. or 111 m. in height), dedicated 1971, impounding water (Lake Nasser) which is utilized for irrigation and power production.

As·yūṭ *also* **As·siout** *or* **As·siut** \ȧs-ˈyüt\ *or* **Siut** \ˈsyüt\. **1.** Governorate of E cen. Egypt. See table at EGYPT.

2. *anc.* **Ly·cop·o·lis** \lī-ˈkä-pə-lis\. City, its ✱, on left bank of the Nile, roughly half way bet. Cairo and Aswān; pop. (1986p) 273,191; noted for its pottery and ornamental wood and ivory work; university (1957).

Ata·ba·po \ˌä-tä-ˈbä-pō\. River, S Venezuela; flows N to Orinoco River and forms section of boundary bet. Colombia and Venezuela; 140 mi. (225 km.) long.

Ata·ca·ma \ˌä-tä-ˈkä-mä\. **1.** Former province of N cen. Chile.

History: While under Bolivian administration, its valuable nitrate deposits were developed by Chilean capital; subject of disagreement bet. Chile and Bolivia which led to War of Pacific (1879–84); control transferred to victorious Chile by Treaty of Valparaíso 1884 (see also ANTOFAGASTA); awarded permanently to Chile 1905.

2. Region of N cen Chile. See table at CHILE.

Atacama, Pu·na de \ˈpü-nä-t͟hā\. Highland region in NW Argentina and adjacent region of Chile, with av. alt. of 11,000 to 13,000 ft. (3350 to 3960 m.).

Atacama Desert. Arid area in N cen. Chile, extending N from Copiapó, covering most of Antofagasta region and N part of Atacama region; completely barren, with borax lakes and saline deposits and large nitrate deposits; for years a chief source of the world's nitrates.

Ata·fu \ˌä-tä-ˈfü\ *or* **Duke of York Island.** Island (atoll) in Tokelau group (*q.v.*), cen. Pacific Ocean, bet. Phoenix Is. and Samoa; pop. (1980p) 577; consists of a reef ab. 1 sq. mi. (2.6 sq. km.) with 62 islets; orig. inhabited prob. by Samoans; first visited by Europeans 1765.

Atak·pa·mé \ˌä-täk-ˈpä-ˌmā\. Town, Togo, 103 mi. (166 km.) N of Lomé.

At·a·lan·te \ˌat-ᵊl-ˈan-tē\ *or Gk.* **Ata·lán·tē** \ˌä-tä-ˈlän-dē\. Channel extending bet. the island of Euboea, Aegean Sea, and Greece, N of Evripos Strait.

Ata·lé·ia \ˌȧ-tə-ˈlā-ə\. Municipality, E Minas Gerais state, E Brazil.

Ata·mi \ä-ˈtä-mē\. City on Sagami Sea, on E coast of Izu Penin., Shizuoka prefecture, Honshū, Japan, ab. 55 mi. (88 km.) SW of Tokyo; pop. (1990c) 47,290.

Atar \ä-ˈtär\. Town, W Mauritania; pop. (1988c) 21,366.

Atas·ca·dero \ə-ˌtas-kə-ˈder-ō\. City, W cen. San Luis Obispo co., California; pop. (1990c) 23,138.

At·a·sco·sa \ˌa-tə-ˈskō-sə\. County in S Texas. See table at TEXAS.

At·a·turk Dam \ˌä-tä-ˈtu̇rk\. Dam across the Euphrates in SE Turkey in Asia; one of world's largest earth and rock fill dams; put into use 1990.

Atáviros. See ATTAIRO.

Atax. See AUDE 1.

At·ba·ra *or* **'At·ba·rah** \ 'at-bə-rə, 'ät-\; *anc.* **As·tab·o·ras** \ as-'ta-bə-rəs\. **1.** River, NE Africa; flows NW through E Sudan into the Nile at Atbara; ab. 500 mi. (800 km.) long; last tributary of the Nile; its headstream, the Tekeze, rises in N Ethiopia.

2. Town, NE Sudan, at the junction of Atbara and Nile rivers; pop. (1983c) 73,009; victory of Anglo-Egyptian army over forces of Sudanese religious and nationalist leader Muḥammad Aḥmad (known as "al Mahdī") April 8, 1898.

Atchaf·a·laya \ ə-ˌcha-fə-'lī-ə\. River, S Louisiana; rises in Avoyelles parish, cen. Louisiana, flows S into Atchafalaya Bay; ab. 225 mi. (362 km.) long; an additional outlet for Red and Mississippi rivers during periods of high water.

Atchafalaya Bay. Inlet of Gulf of Mexico on S boundary bet. St. Mary and Terrebonne parishes, SE Louisiana; receiving (through Grand Lake) the Atchafalaya River on the N.

Atchin. See ATJEH.

Atch·i·son \ 'a-chi-sən\. **1.** Name of counties in two states of the U.S. See tables at KANSAS and MISSOURI.

2. City, ⊗ of Atchison co., NE Kansas, on Missouri River 20 mi. (32 km.) N of Leavenworth; pop. (1990c) 10,656; incorp. 1855; stopping place of westbound caravans in the gold rush and later; Benedictine Coll. (1971).

Ater·no \ ä-'ter-nō\; *anc.* **Ater·nus** \ ə-'tər-nəs\. River, SE cen. Italy; flows out of the Apennines SE and then NE into Adriatic Sea at Pescara; ab. 80 mi. (129 km.) long; in its lower course known as the **Pe·sca·ra** \ pes-'kär-ä\.

Aternum. See PESCARA 3.

Ateste. See ESTE.

Ath *or* **Aath** \ 'ät\. Commune, Hainaut prov., SW Belgium, on left bank of Dender River 55 mi. (88 km.) SW of Brussels; pop. (1991c) 24,080; medieval tower sole remains of ancient town; railroad junction.

Ath·a·bas·ca *also* **Ath·a·bas·ka** \ ˌa-thə-'bas-kə\. **1.** River, S tributary of the Mackenzie, in Alberta, W cen. Canada; rises in Rocky Mts. in Jasper National Park, flows NE and N into Lake Athabaska; 765 mi. (1231 km.) long; chief tributaries Pembina, Lesser Slave, and La Biche; important because of oil sands along its course, believed one of largest oil reservoirs in world.

2. Former district, cen. Canada, formed 1882 out of Northwest Territories bet. 60°N and 55°N, approx. the N part of present Alberta; extended 1885 to include N part of present Saskatchewan. Both parts absorbed 1905 by the modern provinces.

Athabasca, Lake. Lake, W cen. Canada, extending across N section of the Alberta-Saskatchewan boundary; 208 mi. (335 km.) long; 3120 sq. mi. (8081 sq. km.); on SW receives Athabaska River and on NW discharges into Slave River; connected at its E end by Fond du Lac River with Lake Cree.

Ath·a·ma·nia \ ˌa-thə-'mā-nē-ə\. A district of ancient Epirus, NW Greece, W of Pindus Mts.

Ath·el·ney \ 'a-thəl-nē\. Locality in Somersetshire, SW England, ab. 8 mi. (13 km.) ENE of Taunton; in King Alfred's time an isle in W cen. Wessex, surrounded by marshes; Alfred's refuge from the Danes 878–879. Site of monastery founded by Alfred.

Athenae. See ATHENS 10.

Ath·ens \ 'a-thənz\. **1.** County in SE Ohio. See table at OHIO.

2. City, ⊗ of Limestone co., N Alabama, 12 mi. (19 km.) N of Decatur; pop. (1990c) 16,901; Athens State Coll. (1822); occupied by Union troops on and off during Civil War; under Gen. Nathan Bedford Forrest, Confederates retook the city.

3. City, ⊗ of Clarke co., NE Georgia, 60 mi. (96 km.) ENE of Atlanta; pop. (1990c) 45,734; Univ. of Georgia (chartered 1785, estab. 1801), oldest state university

4. \ *also* 'ā-\. Town, Greene co., SE New York, on Hudson River near Catskill Mts. 26 mi. (42 km.) S of Albany; pop. (1990c) 3561; settled 1686; incorp. 1805.

5. Commercial city, ⊗ of Athens co., SE Ohio, 32 mi. (51 km.) W of Marietta; pop. (1990c) 21,265; Ohio Univ. (1804); settled c. 1797; became ⊗ 1805.

6. Borough, Bradford co., N Pennsylvania, on Susquehanna River 3 mi. (5 km.) S of New York border; pop. (1990c) 3468; settled 1778.

7. City, ⊗ of McMinn co., SE Tennessee, 27 mi. (43 km.) NNE of Cleveland; pop. (1990c) 12,054; Tennessee Wesleyan Coll. (1857); founded 1823; incorp. 1868.

8. City, ⊗ of Henderson co., NE Texas, 30 mi. (48 km.) WSW of Tyler; pop. (1990c) 10,967; oil wells nearby; settled 1848.

9. Town, Mercer co., S West Virginia, ab. 6 mi. (10 km.) NE of Princeton; pop. (1990c) 741; Concord Coll. (1872).

10. *or Gk.* **Athí·nai** \ ä-'thē-ne\; *anc.* **Athe·nae** \ ə-'thē-nē\. City, ✱ of Greece and ✱ of Attica region, E Greece, near the Saronic Gulf, on Attic plain enclosed on three sides by hills; pop. (1991p) 748,110; commercial and transportation center; chemicals, textiles; food processing, oil refining; tourism; national library; national museum; numerous schools of archaeology, technical university (1836), university (1837). Formerly connected with its harbor Piraeus by the Long Walls; contains the Acropolis, the Areopagus (on which hill St. Paul preached) and the excavated ancient marketplace Agora; among the principal ancient structures on and around the Acropolis (112 ft. or 34 m. above the city) were the Odeum, Parthenon, Erechtheum, Propylaea, and Dionysiac theater.

History: Ancient Greek city-state which by the beginning of the 7th cent. B.C. included the territory known as Attica; under statesman Solon's law code of 594 B.C., freed from the Draconian code (published c. 621 B.C.); ruled by tyrants, the most famous of whom was Peisistratus (560–527 B.C.); largely a democracy after the reforms of statesman Cleisthenes of Athens 508 B.C.; under Themistocles, first chosen archon in 493–492 B.C., began building strong fleet in anticipation of Persian invasion; defeated Persia at battle of Marathon (*q.v.*) 490 B.C.; destroyed by Persian King Xerxes 480 B.C. in campaign in which Persians were finally defeated by the Peloponnesian League; began fortification of city and Piraeus 479 B.C.; headed the Delian League which was founded in 478 B.C., with headquarters on the island of Delos, as a confederacy against Persia but became the instrument of Athenian empire after subjugation of Naxos and of Thásos c. 460s B.C.; at height of its commercial prosperity, leadership in architecture and culture, and of political democracy under statesman Pericles c. 450s–429 B.C.; after a long period of opposition to Sparta, withdrew from Peloponnesian League and entered so-called First Peloponnesian War 460–445 B.C.; transferred treasury of Delian League from Delos c. 454 B.C.; at height of empire (c. 450 B.C.) allied to Thessaly, Achaea, Árgos, Samos, Chios, and Lesbos, and had as dependents Euboea, Ándros, Naxos, and the remaining Cyclades, most of the extreme W coast of Asia Minor, the entrances to the Propontis and to the Euxine Sea, the coast and islands of the Thracian Sea, and Chalcidice; built Parthenon 447–432 B.C.; lost supremacy in Greece after being defeated in the renewed (Second) Peloponnesian War 431–404 B.C.; sentenced philosopher Socrates to death 399 B.C.; allied against Sparta in Corinthian War 395–c. 387 B.C. and again in 377 B.C.; opposed by former allies in the Social War 357–355 B.C.; anti-Macedonian under orator and statesman Demosthenes, defeated by King Philip II of Macedon 338 B.C.; under Macedonian hegemony after 322 B.C. Established friendly relations with Rome 228 B.C. and was aided by Rome against Macedonians, who were finally defeated at Cynoscephalae 197 B.C., with Roman destruction of the Achaean League 146 B.C., as part of Greece, became subject to Rome; part of Roman prov. of Achaea (*q.v.*); visited by St. Paul c. 50 A.D.; taken by the Heruli 267 A.D.; surrendered to Alaric and the Goths 395; became a duchy after the Latin conquest of Greece 1204; conquered by the Ottoman Empire 1456; Parthenon destroyed during siege by Venetians 1687–88; city soon reverted to Turks; became the ✱ of modern Greece in early 1830s; site of first modern Olympic Games 1896. In

WWII occupied by Germans April 1941 to Oct. 1944, but historical monuments were spared.

Ath·er·ton \ˈa-thər-tən\. **1.** Town, San Mateo co., W California, suburb of Redwood City, 22 mi. (35 km.) SE of San Francisco; pop. (1990c) 7163; Menlo Coll. (1915); incorp. 1923.

2. \ *also* ˈa-t͟hər-\. Town, Lancashire, NW England, 13 mi. (21 km.) WNW of Manchester; pop. (1991c) 5206.

Atherton Plateau *or* **Atherton Tableland.** Plateau region, NE coast of Queensland, NE Australia, at N end of Great Dividing Range; ab. 15,000 sq. mi. (38,850 sq.km.); highest point Mt. Bartle Frere 5287 ft. (1611 m.).

Athesis. See ADIGE.

Ath·garh \ˈət-ˌgär, ˈät-\. Former Indian state, now part of Orissa, E India, on Mahanadi River; 163 sq. mi. (422 sq. km.); chief town Athgarh 15 mi. (24 km.) NW of Cuttack.

Athi \ˈä-tē\. River, Kenya; rises near Nairobi and flows SE through **Athi Plain,** noted for its wild game, to the Sabaki River; ab. 200 mi. (320 km.) long. See SABAKI.

Athínai. See ATHENS 10.

Athis–Mons \à-tēs-ˈmō^{n}s\. Commune, Essonne dept., N France, on Seine River 8 mi. (13 km.) SSE of Paris.

ʻAthlit. See ʻATLIT.

Ath·lone \ath-ˈlōn\. Town, W co. Westmeath, N cen. Ireland, on the Shannon River; pop. (1986c) 8815; successfully stormed 1691 by Dutch Gen. Godard van Reede-Ginkel, in the service of William of Orange, after withstanding siege by William.

Ath·mal·lik \ˌət-ˈmə-lik, ät-ˈmä-\. Former Indian state, now part of Orissa, E India, on N bank of Mahanadi River.

Ath·ol \ˈa-ˌthȯl\. Town, Worcester co., cen. Massachusetts, 21 mi. (34 km.) W of Fitchburg; pop. (1990c) 11,451.

Ath·oll *or* **Ath·ole** \ˈa-thəl\. Mountainous district, Tayside region, Scotland, at S base of Grampian Mts.; ab. 450 sq. mi. (1166 sq. km.); includes Tay River and Loch Rannoch; land generally uncultivable; extensive hunting tracts.

Ath·os, Mount \ˈä-ˌthös, ˈa-ˌthäs, ˈā-\. *or* **Áyi·on Óros** \ˈä-yē-ön-ˈö-ˌrös\ *also* **Ha·gi·on Oros** \ˈhä-gē-ən-ˈȯr-əs\. Mountain occupying E end of Acte Penin., Chalcidice, NE Greece; 6667 ft. (2032 m.); inhabited since 10th cent. A.D. by monastic communities of Greek Rule of St. Basil; the "Holy Mountain" of the Greek Church; declared a theocratic republic 1927.

Athy \ə-ˈthī\. Town, SW co. Kildare, E Ireland, 37 mi. (60 km.) SW of Dublin; pop. (1986c) 4734; has two ancient castles; as site of a ford of the Barrow River, strategically important in historic time and scene of many battles.

Ati·mo·nan \ˌä-tē-ˈmō-ˌnän\. Municipality, S Quezon prov., Luzon, Philippines, on SW shore of Lamon Bay 21 mi. (34 km.) E of Lucena; pop. (1980c) 39,894; harbor.

Ati·tlán \ˌä-tē-ˈtlän\. **1.** Lake, SW Guatemala, 12 mi. (19 km.) long, 6 mi. (10 km.) wide; alt. 4700 ft. (1432 m.); occupies a crater 1000 ft. (305 m.) deep.

2. Volcano, S of the lake; ab. 11,650 ft. (3551 m.).

3. Town, Guatemala. See SANTIAGO ATITLÁN.

Atiu \ˌä-tē-ˈü\ *also* **Va·tiu** \ˌvä-tē-ˈü\. Island in S group of Cook Is., S Pacific Ocean, 116 mi. (187 km.) NE of Rarotonga, 20° S, and 158° W; 10 sq. mi. (26 sq. km.); pop. (1986c) 957.

Atjeh \ˈä-chā\ *also* **Achin** *or* **Acheen** *or* **Atchin** \ä-ˈchēn\. Autonomous district of Indonesia, N Sumatra. See table at INDONESIA.

History: Former sultanate; visited by member of Portuguese navigator Tristão da Cunha's fleet 1506; destination of first ventures of Dutch and English East India companies 1599 and 1602; sultanate, at height of power 1607–37, controlled entire W tip of Sumatra; unsuccessfully attacked Portuguese at Melaka 1615; declined after 17th cent.; treaty with British 1819 to exclude other Europeans lapsed after British ceded Sumatran claims to Dutch; region never brought under total Dutch control; rebelled against central government 1953; given status equivalent to that of a province 1956; unrest continued.

At·ka \ˈät-kə, ˈat-\. Island, largest of the Andreanof group, Aleutian Is., SW Alaska; 422 sq. mi. (1093 sq. km.); chief settlement Atka city (pop. [1990c] 73). In N is Korovin volcano. Most inhabitants are native Aleuts.

At·kin·son \ˈat-kin-sən\. **1.** County in S Georgia. See table at GEORGIA.

2. Town, Rockingham co., New Hampshire; pop. (1990c) 5188.

At·lan·ta \ət-ˈlan-tə, at-\. **1.** City, ✱ of Georgia and ⊗ of Fulton co., located in De Kalb and Fulton cos., NW cen. Georgia, 55 mi. (88 km.) E of Alabama border; pop. (1990c) 394,017; largest city in the state; alt. 1050 ft. (320 m.); important center of commerce, finance, transportation, government, and services for the SE section of U.S. Site of Summer Olympic Games 1996. Georgia Institute of Technology (1885), Morehouse Coll. (1867), Morris Brown Coll. (1881), and Spelman Coll. (1881); in nearby suburbs are Oglethorpe Univ. (1835), Emory Univ. (1836), Georgia State Univ. (1913), Atlanta Coll. of Art (1928), Mercer Univ. Atlanta (1968), Clark Atlanta Univ. (1988).

History: Region around Atlanta ceded to Georgia by Creek Indians 1821; selected 1836 by railroad as end of line and named **Ter·mi·nus** \ˈtər-mi-nəs\; incorp. 1843 as town of **Mar·thas·ville** \ˈmär-thəz-ˌvil\; name changed to Atlanta 1845; reincorporated as city 1847; made ⊗ of newly-created Fulton co. 1853; became market center for its area; Confederate supply depot in Civil War; burned by Union Gen. William T. Sherman Nov. 15, 1864; scene of constitutional convention 1867–68; temporary ✱ of Georgia 1868, permanent ✱ from 1887. Site of several expositions during late 19th cent., the last, 1895, at which educator Booker T. Washington delivered the influential speech "Atlanta Compromise"; continued to grow in national importance throughout 20th cent. Birthplace and burial site of clergyman and civil rights leader Martin Luther King, Jr. (1929–1968). First major Southern city to elect a black mayor 1973.

2. Village, ⊗ of Montmorency co., NE Michigan.

3. City, Cass co., NE Texas, on Arkansas border 20 mi. (32 km.) S of Texarkana; pop. (1990c) 6118; oil wells.

At·lan·tic \ət-ˈlan-tik, at-\. **1.** County in SE New Jersey. See table at NEW JERSEY.

2. City, ⊗ of Cass co., SW Iowa, 47 mi. (76 km.) ENE of Council Bluffs; pop. (1990c) 7432; livestock feed; engine bearings; sports apparel.

3. Seaside resort, Accomac co., N part of E peninsula, Virginia, 8 mi. (13 km.) SW of Chincoteague.

Atlantic Beach. City, Duval co., NE Florida, bordering on Jacksonville; pop. (1990c) 11,636.

Atlantic City. City, Atlantic co., SE New Jersey, on Atlantic Ocean ab. 60 mi. (96 km.) SE of Philadelphia; pop. (1990c) 37,986; noted seaside resort; built 1852 on Absecon I.; incorp. as city 1854; railroad terminus; 4-mile (6.4-kilometer) boardwalk of steel and concrete (built 1896); amusement and recreation piers; casino gambling since 1978.

Atlantic Highlands. Borough and summer resort, Monmouth co., E cen. New Jersey, on S shore of Sandy Hook 14 mi. (22 km.) ESE of Perth Amboy; pop. (1990c) 4629.

Atlantic–Indian Ridge. Ridge, S Atlantic Ocean floor, extending from E of Bouvet I. to SW of the Prince Edward Is. in a general E to W direction; a center of oceanic crust formation according to theory of plate tectonics.

Atlantic In·tra·coast·al Waterway \ˌin-trə-ˈkōs-təl\. A system of inland waterways incl. rivers, bays, and canals along the Atlantic coast of the U.S.A. from Cape Cod to Florida Bay; includes the Cape Cod Canal, the Chesapeake and Delaware Canal, and the Dismal Swamp Canal; main points on the system are Trenton, New Jersey; Norfolk, Virginia; Beaufort, North Carolina; Jacksonville and Miami, Florida.

At·lán·ti·co \ät-ˈlän-tē-ˌkō\. Department of N Colombia. See table at COLOMBIA.

Atlantic Ocean \ət-ˌlan-tik-, at-\; *anc.* **Oce·anus At·lan·ti·cus** \ō-ˈsē-ə-nəs-ət-ˈlan-ti-kəs\. Body of water separating North and South America from Europe and Africa; 31,814,640 sq. mi. or 82,399,918 sq. km. (with its branches 41,081,040 sq. mi. or 106,399,894 sq. km.); av. depth 12,257 ft. (3736 m.). Often divided into **North Atlantic Ocean** (max. depth 28,374 ft. or 8648 m. in Puerto Rico Trench at 19°35′N, 68°17′W) and **South Atlantic Ocean** (max. depth 27,113 ft.

or 8264 m. in South Sandwich Trench at 55°07′S, 26°46′W). Merges with Arctic Ocean N of 60° N; S of South America connects with Pacific Ocean by Drake Passage; S of Africa arbitrarily separated from Indian Ocean by meridian 20°E. See SARGASSO SEA.

Atlantic Peak. Mountain, SW Fremont co., cen. Wyoming; ab. 12,730 ft. (3880 m.).

Atlantic Provinces. The Canadian provinces of Newfoundland, New Brunswick, Nova Scotia, and Prince Edward I.

At·lán·ti·da \ät-'län-tē-thä\. Department of N Honduras. See table at HONDURAS.

At·las Mountains \'at-ləs\. Mountain system, NW and N Africa, extending from Cape Dra on SW Morocco coast to Cape Bon on NE Tunisia coast; highest peak Toubkal in W Morocco 13,671 ft. (4167 m.). In ancient times the name Atlas Mts. was restricted to the Grand Atlas Range on the S border of Mauritania. Comprises several ranges: **Grand Atlas** *or* **High Atlas** in W and S Morocco containing highest peaks; **An·ti–At·las** \'an-tē-, 'an-,tī-\ to the S and parallel with it, highest point ab. 6750 ft. (2057 m.); **Middle Atlas** *or Fr.* **Moy·en At·las** \mwȧ-,ye-nȧt-'läs\ in N cen. Morocco, highest ab. 11,000 ft. (3350 m.); **Mar·i·time Atlas** \'mar-ə-,tīm\ *or* **Little Atlas** *also* **Tell Atlas** \'tel\, coastal ranges, generally lower (averaging 5000 ft. or 1525 m.) from Ceuta eastward in Morocco and Algeria to Cape Bon in Tunisia; and **Sa·har·an Atlas** \sə-'har-ən, -'här-\ *or Fr.* **Atlas Sa·ha·rien** \ȧt-,läs-sȧ-ȧ-'ryeⁿ\ incl. the Aurès Range in E Algeria, highest Djebel Chélia 7648 ft. (2331 m.). Not explored extensively until 19th cent.

At·la·so·va \ət-'lä-sə-və\ *or Jp.* **Arai·to** \ə-'rī-tō\. Small island off NW coast of Paramushir I. at N end of Kuril Is., Sakhalin Oblast, Russia in Asia; its peak 7674 ft. (2339 m.) highest point in the Kuril chain.

At·lin Lake \'at-lin\. Long, narrow lake, NW British Columbia and SW Yukon, Canada; 299 sq. mi. (774 sq. km.); connects with Tagish Lake to the W. Town of **Atlin** is on E shore.

'At·lit \'ät-,lēt\ *also* **'Ath·lit** \'ät-\. Ancient town and present-day archaeological site, on coast of Israel, ab. 8 mi. (13 km.) SSW of Haifa; noted for discovery of remarkable fossil specimens. Last place in Holy Land held by Crusaders 1291.

Atlix·co \ä-'tlēs-kō\. Town, Puebla state, SE cen. Mexico, 58 mi. (93 km.) SE of Mexico City; munic. pop. (1990p) 104,186.

At·more \'at-,mōr\. City, Escambia co., Alabama, 35 mi. (56 km.) NE of Mobile Bay; pop. (1990c) 8046.

Ato·ka \ə-'tō-kə\. **1.** County in S Oklahoma. See table at OKLAHOMA.
2. City, its ⊗, 43 mi. (69 km.) SE of Ada; pop. (1990c) 3298; founded 1867.

Ato·yac, Río \'rē-ō-,ä-tō-'yäk\. River, headstream of the Balsas, cen. Mexico; rises in Tlaxcala and flows S and SW into Guerrero; ab. 150 mi. (241 km.) long; unnavigable.

Atoyac de Al·va·rez \,ä-tō-'yäk-thā-äl-'bä-res\. Town, Guerrero state, S Mexico, ab. 43 mi. (69 km.) WNW of Acapulco; munic. pop. (1990p) 59,482.

Atrak. See ATREK.

Atra·nos \,ä-trä-'nòs\ *also* **Adra·nos** \-drä-\; *anc.* **Rhyn·da·cus** \'rin-də-kəs\. River, NW Turkey in Asia; flows NW from beyond Kütahya and through Lake Apulyont to the Susıgırlık near the Sea of Marmara; ab. 150 mi. (240 km.) long.

Atra·to \ä-'trä-tō\. River, NW Colombia; flows N into Gulf of Darien; ab. 350 mi. (563 km.) long. See TRUANDO.

Atrecht. See ARTOIS.

Atrek \ȧ-'trek\ *or* **Atrak** \-'trak\. River, NE Iran; flows W forming section of boundary bet. Iran and Turkmenistan and empties into SE Caspian Sea in Turkmenistan; ab. 300 mi. (480 km.) long.

Atri \'ä-trē\; *anc.* **Ha·tria Pi·ce·na** \'hā-trē-ə-pī-'sē-nə\ *or* **Ha·dria Picena** \'hā-drē-ə\. Commune, Teramo prov., Abruzzi, cen. Italy, near Adriatic coast 14 mi. (22 km.) ESE of the commune of Teramo; pop. (1981p) 11,215; agricultural products; Romanesque-Gothic cathedral; remains of ancient town; became Roman colony in early 3d cent. B.C.

Atria. See ADRIA.

Atropatene. See AZERBAIJAN 1.

Atsu·gi \ät-'sü-gē, 'ät-sù-\. Town, Kanagawa prefecture, SE Honshū, Japan, 15 mi. (24 km.) W of Yokohama; pop. (1992e) 203,775; commercial center; manufactures automobile parts, communications equipment.

Atsu·ta \'ät-sù-,tä\. Former town, Aichi prefecture, S Japan, at head of Ise Bay; now part of Nagoya, in S part of city.

Aṭ Ṭā'if. See TAIF.

At·tai·ro \ə-'tī-rō\ *or Gk.* **Atá·vi·ros** \ä-'tä-vē-,rös\. Mountain, highest on Rhodes I., Greece; 3986 ft. (1215 m.).

At·tala \ə-'ta-lə\. County in cen. Mississippi. See table at MISSISSIPPI.

Attaleia *or* **Attalia.** See ANTALYA 2.

At·tal·la \ə-'ta-lə\. City, Etowah co., NE Alabama, 5 mi. (8 km.) W of Gadsden; pop. (1990c) 6859.

At·ta·wa·pis·kat \,a-tə-wə-'pis-kət\. River, NE Ontario, Canada; rises in chain of lakes in NW Ontario, flows E and NE into James Bay; at 88°W flows through **Attawapiskat Lake**; 465 mi. (748 km.) long.

At·ter, Lake \'ä-tər, 'a-\ *or* **Lake Kam·mer** \'kä-mər\; *Ger.* **At·ter·see** \'ä-tər-,zā\ *or* **Kam·mer·see** \'käm-ər-,zā\. Lake, Upper Austria, Austria; 40 mi. (64 km.) SW of Linz; 12 mi. (19 km.) long; 17 sq. mi. (44 sq. km.); its shores form a summer-resort region.

At·ti·ca \'a-ti-kə\. **1.** City, Fountain co., W Indiana, on Wabash River 22 mi. (35 km.) WSW of Lafayette; pop. (1990c) 3457; sandstone deposits nearby.
2. Village, Genesee and Wyoming cos., W New York, 31 mi. (50 km.) E of Buffalo; pop. (1990c) 2630; state penitentiary.
3. Ancient division and state of E Greece, forming the territory of Athens; bounded on N by Boeotia, on E by Aegean Sea, on S by Saronic Gulf, and on W by Megaris; included the island of Salamis; chief towns were Athens, Piraeus, and Eleusis.
History: Orig. inhabited by Pelasgians; a center of Mycenaean culture 2d millennium B.C.; invaded by Ionian Greeks by c. 1300 B.C.; territory without political unity until gradually unified under Athens by 700 B.C. (traditionally accomplished by King Theseus). For later history, see ATHENS 10.
4. *or Gk.* **At·ti·kí** \,ä-tē-'kē\. Region of Greece; 1470 sq. mi. (3807 sq. km.); pop. (1991c) 3,522,769.

Attinianum. See VODNJAN.

At·tle·boro \'at-ᵊl-,bər-ō, -,bər-ə\. City, Bristol co., SE Massachusetts; pop. (1990c) 38,383.

Attock. See CAMPBELLPORE.

At·tu \'a-tü\. Rocky island in Near I. group and most westerly of the Aleutian Is., SW Alaska, 52°55′N, 172°30′E; 338 sq. mi. (875 sq. km.); highest point more than 3000 ft. (914 m.); formerly a prosperous Aleut settlement. Occupied by Japanese June 1942; retaken by U.S. forces May–June 1943.

Atuel \ä-'twel\. River, W Argentina; rises in the Andes, flows E and SSE in Mendoza prov. to unite with the Salado in N La Pampa prov.; ab. 300 mi. (480 km.) long.

Atu·o·na \,ä-tü-'ō-nä\ *or* **Atu·a·na** \-'ä-nä\. Village, Hiva Oa I., French Polynesia; formerly ⁕ of Marquesas Is.

Atura. See AIRE 3.

Aturus. See ADOUR.

At·wa·ter \'at-,wò-tər, -,wä-\. City, Merced co., California, NW of Merced; pop. (1990c) 22,282.

At·wood \'at-,wùd\. City, ⊗ of Rawlins co., NW Kansas; pop. (1990c) 1388.

Atwood Cay. See SAMANA CAY.

Aty·raū \'ä-tē-,raù\; *formerly* **Gur·yev** *or* **Gur·ev** \'gür-yif\. **1.** Subdivision of Kazakhstan, bounded on S by Turkmenistan and on W by Caspian Sea and Astrakhan Oblast, Russia; 107,567 sq. mi. (278,598 sq. km.); pop. (1991e) 447,100; an oblast of the U.S.S.R. before 1991; ⁕ Atyraū; largely marsh and desert; has long coastline on the Caspian, incl. Buzachi Penin. and Mangyshlak Penin. crossed by lower courses of Ural and Emba rivers; oil; livestock raising, fishing.

2. Seaport town, ✻ of Atyraū subdivision, SW Kazakhstan, at N end of Caspian Sea at mouth of Ural River; pop. (1991e) 156,700; terminus of oil pipeline NE to Aktyubinsk and Orsk.

Au·au Channel \ˈaù-ˌaù\. Strait bet. NW Maui I. and Lanai I., Hawaii; 7 mi. (11 km.) wide. See LAHAINA.

Au·bagne \ō-ˈbànʸ, -ˈban-yə\; *anc.* **Al·ba·nia** \al-ˈbā-nē-ə, -nyə, òl-\. Commune, Bouches-du-Rhône dept., SE France, 8 mi. (13 km.) E of Marseille; pop. (1990c) 41,187.

Aube \ˈōb\. **1.** River, N cen. France; rises in Haute-Marne dept., flows NW and W into Seine River 23 mi. (37 km.) NNW of Troyes; 154 mi. (248 km.) long.

2. Department of NE France. See table at FRANCE.

Au·be·nas \ˌō-bə-ˈnä\. Commune, Ardèche dept., SE France, on Ardèche River at foot of Cévennes Mts.; near several extinct volcanoes.

Au·ber·vil·liers \ˌō-bər-(ˌ)vēl-ˈyā\; *formerly* **No·tre Dame des Ver·tus** \ˌnò-trə-dàm-dā-ver-tü\. Commune, Seine-St.-Denis dept., N France, NNE suburb of Paris 2 mi. (3 km.) from right bank of Seine River.

Aubigny. See LÉVIS-LAUZON.

Au·burn \ˈò-bərn\. **1.** City, Lee co., E Alabama, 8 mi. (13 km.) W of Opelika; pop. (1990c) 33,830; Auburn Univ. (1856).

2. City, ⊗ of Placer co., E California, 36 mi. (58 km.) NE of Sacramento; pop. (1990c) 10,592; founded as gold-mining camp 1848; incorp. as city 1888.

3. City, Sangamon co., cen. Illinois, 17 mi. (27 km.) S of Springfield; pop. (1990c) 3724; coal deposits.

4. City, ⊗ of De Kalb co., NE Indiana, 22 mi. (35 km.) NNE of Fort Wayne; pop. (1990c) 9379.

5. City, ⊗ of Androscoggin co., SW Maine, on Androscoggin River opp. Lewiston 30 mi. (48 km.) N of Portland; pop. (1990c) 24,309; health care; diversified industries.

6. Town, Worcester co., cen. Massachusetts, 5 mi. (8 km.) SSW of Worcester; pop. (1990c) 15,005; residential suburb of Worcester.

7. City, ⊗ of Nemaha co., SE Nebraska, 55 mi. (88 km.) SE of Lincoln; pop. (1990c) 3443.

8. City, ⊗ of Cayuga co., cen. New York, on outlet of Lake Owasco 25 mi. (40 km.) WSW of Syracuse; pop. (1990c) 31,258; Cayuga County Community Coll. (1953), state prison (1816); founded 1793; became ⊗ 1805; chartered as city 1848.

9. City, King co., W cen. Washington, 11 mi. (18 km.) ENE of Tacoma; pop. (1990c) 33,102.

10. Municipality, E New South Wales, SE Australia, W suburb of Sydney; pop. (1991c) 48,566.

Auburn, Lake. Lake, SW Maine, N of Auburn.

Au·burn·dale \ˈò-bərn-ˌdāl\. Residential city, Polk co., cen. Florida Penin., 10 mi. (16 km.) E of Lakeland; pop. (1990c) 8858.

Au·burn Hills. City, Oakland co., SE Michigan, to the E and N of Pontiac; pop. (1990c) 17,076.

Au·bus·son \ˌō-bü-ˈsōⁿ\. Commune, Creuse dept., cen. France, on Creuse River 20 mi. (32 km.) SE of Guéret; long celebrated for its carpets and tapestries; a school of decorative arts founded in 19th cent. still hand looms the articles.

Au·by \ō-ˈbē\. Commune, Nord dept., N France, 3 mi. (5 km.) NNW of Douai; coal deposits.

Auch \ˈōsh\; *anc.* **El·im·ber·rum** \ˌe-lim-ˈber-əm\; *later* **Au·gus·ta Aus·co·rum** \ò-ˈgəs-tə-ós-ˈkōr-əm\. City, ✻ of Gers dept., SW France, on Gers River 42 mi. (68 km.) W of Toulouse; pop. (1990c) 24,728; tiles, tobacco; late-Gothic cathedral (begun 1489) famous for its stained-glass windows and handworked choir stalls; museum and library. Chief town of the Ausci, a Celtiberian people; medieval ✻ of Armagnac; became ✻ of the generality of Gascony in the 17th cent.

Au·chel \ō-ˈshel\. Commune, Pas-de-Calais dept., N France, 20 mi. (32 km.) NW of Arras.

Au·chin·leck \ˌò-kən-ˈlek, -kən-\. Parish, Strathclyde region, SW Scotland; family home of biographer James Boswell.

Auchterhouse Hill. See SIDLAW HILLS.

Au·cil·la \ò-ˈsi-lə\ *also* **Ocil·la** \ō-\. River, N Florida; flows S from S Georgia into Apalachee Bay; ab. 70 mi. (113 km.) long.

Auck·land \ˈò-klənd\. Seaport city, on Waitemata and Manukau Harbors, North I., New Zealand; pop. (1991c) 315,668, met. area 953,980; New Zealand's principal port; chemicals; food processing; nearby production of textiles, footwear, clothing; motor-vehicle assembly. Univ. of Auckland (1882, reorganized 1957), City Art Gallery (1888), Museum of Transport and Technology (1964); founded 1840 as ✻ of New Zealand, but replaced by Wellington 1865.

Auckland Islands. Uninhabited group of islands, New Zealand, 200 mi. (322 km.) S of South I., 50°32′S, 166°13′E; 234 sq. mi. (606 sq. km.); discovered 1806; mountainous; several good harbors.

Aude \ˈōd\. **1.** *anc.* **Atax** \ˈa-ˌtaks\. River, S France; rises on the slopes of the Pyrenees, flows N and E into Mediterranean Sea near Narbonne; 130 mi. (209 km.) long.

2. Department of S France. See table at FRANCE.

Au·de·narde. See OUDENAARDE.

Au·den·shaw \ˈò-dən-ˌshò\. Town, Lancashire, NW England, 5 mi. (8 km.) E of Manchester; pop. (1981p) 10,744.

Au·der·ghem \ˌō-dər-ˈgem\ *or Flem.* **Ou·der·gem** \ˈaù-dər-gəm\. Commune, Brabant prov., cen. Belgium, SE suburb of Brussels (1.5 mi. or 2.4 km.); pop. (1991c) 29,224.

Audh. See OUDH.

Au·drain \ò-ˈdrān, ˈò-ˌdrān\. County in NE cen. Missouri. See table at MISSOURI.

Au·du·bon \ˈò-də-bən, -ˌbän\. **1.** County in W Iowa. See table at IOWA.

2. City, its ⊗, W Iowa, 59 mi. (95 km.) NE of Council Bluffs; pop. (1990c) 2524.

3. Borough, Camden co., SW New Jersey, 4 mi. (6 km.) SSE of the city of Camden; pop. (1990c) 9205; suburb of Camden.

Audubon, Lake *or* **Audubon Lake.** The easternmost part of Lake Sakakawea in W cen. North Dakota.

Audubon, Mount. Peak in Front Range of the Rocky Mts., Boulder co., N cen. Colorado; 13,223 ft. (4030 m.).

Aue \ˈaù-ə\. City, Saxony, E Germany, in the Erzgebirge 13 mi. (21 km.) SE of Zwickau; pop. (1991e) 24,447; received city charter 1629.

Au·er·bach \ˈaù-ər-ˌbäk, -ˌbäk\. City, SW Saxony, Germany, 55 mi. (88 km.) S of Leipzig; founded c. 1144.

Au·er·stedt *or* **Au·er·städt** \ˈaù-ər-ˌshtet\. Village, cen. Germany, 14 mi. (22 km.) NE of Weimar; scene of defeat of Prussians under duke of Brunswick by French under Louis-Nicolas Davout Oct. 14, 1806, simultaneously with French Emperor Napoléon's victory over main Prussian army at Jena.

Aufidus. See OFANTO.

Aughrabies Falls. See AUGRABIES FALLS.

Augh·rim *or* **Agh·rim** \ˈò-grim\. Parish and town, co. Galway, Ireland, 30 mi. (48 km.) E of Galway; scene of decisive victory of William III, prince of Orange over British King James II July 12, 1691, which, together with battle of the Boyne (July 1, 1690), is commemorated in Northern Ireland on Orangemen's Day (July 12).

Augila. See AWJIDAH.

Au·glaize \ò-ˈglāz\. **1.** River, W Ohio; rises in Auglaize co. and flows W and N to the Maumee River at Defiance; ab. 100 mi. (160 km.) long.

2. County in W Ohio. See table at OHIO.

Au·gra·bies Falls *also* **Au·ghra·bies Falls** \ō-ˈkrä-bēs, -ˈgrä-bēz\. Falls in the Orange River, NW Northern Cape prov., Rep. of South Africa, ab. 35 mi. (56 km.) E of Namibian border; 480 ft. (146 m.) high.

Au Gres, Point \ò-ˈgrā\. Point on SE coast of Arenac co., E Michigan, at N entrance to Saginaw Bay.

Augs·burg \ˈaùks-ˌbùrk, ˈògz-ˌbərg\; *anc.* **Au·gus·ta Vin·del·i·co·rum** \ò-ˈgəs-tə-vin-ˌde-lə-ˈkōr-əm\. Commercial city, Bavaria, S Germany, on the Lech River 30 mi. (48 km.)

WNW of Munich; pop. (1991e) 256,877; machinery, chemicals, textiles, aircraft; university (1970); notable buildings include the cathedral, the town hall, and the episcopal palace.

History: Roman colony founded by Emperor Augustus c. 14 B.C.; received municipal rights from Emperor Hadrian; scene of defeat of Hungarians by Holy Roman Emperor Otto I 955 A.D.; recognized as free imperial city 1276; because of location and undertakings of Fugger and Welser families, became center for trade bet. N and S Europe in 15th and 16th cents.; scene of diet to which German religious reformer Philipp Melanchthon presented Confession of Augsburg 1530, and of drafting of Religious Peace of Augsburg 1555; League of Augsburg against France 1686; lost municipal freedom and became part of Bavaria 1806. In WWII frequently bombed 1940–45 and suffered heavy damage; some restoration has taken place.

Au·gus·ta \ȯ-ˈgəs-tə\. **1.** County in N cen. Virginia. See table at VIRGINIA.

2. City, ⊗ of Woodruff co., NE cen. Arkansas, on White River 56 mi. (90 km.) SW of Jonesboro; pop. (1990c) 2759.

3. City, ⊗ of Richmond co., E Georgia, on Savannah River 105 mi. (169 km.) ENE of Macon; pop. (1990c) 44,639; kaolin deposits; Medical Coll. of Georgia (1828), Paine Coll. (1882), Augusta Coll. (1925); settled in 1735 by English soldier and philanthropist James Oglethorpe; captured by British 1778, but retaken by Americans under "Lighthorse Harry" Lee 1781; ✱ of Georgia 1786–95; incorp. as city 1798.

4. City, Butler co., S Kansas, 20 mi. (32 km.) E of Wichita; pop. (1990c) 7876; oil wells.

5. City, ✱ of Maine and ⊗ of Kennebec co., SW Maine, on Kennebec River 25 mi. (40 km.) NE of Lewiston; pop. (1990c) 21,325; alt. 120 ft. (36 m.); summer resort; Univ. of Maine at Augusta (1965); at head of navigation on Kennebec River; trading post in 17th cent.; site of Fort Western 1754; incorp. as town 1797, as city 1849; made ✱ of Maine 1832.

Au·gu·sta \au̇-ˈgü-stä\ *or* **Ago·sta** \ä-ˈgō-stä\. Commune, Siracusa prov., SE Sicily, Italy, 12 mi. (19 km.) N of the seaport of Siracusa; pop. (1989c) 39,904; on small island, formerly the peninsula of Xiphonia, connected by bridge with Sicilian mainland; exports wine, cheese, fruits, sardines. Founded by Holy Roman Emperor Frederick II 1232; near site of ancient Megara Hyblaea (*q.v.*); almost completely destroyed by earthquake 1693. In WWII was a beachhead for Allied invasion 1943.

Au·gus·ta, Cape \au̇-ˈgü-stä\. Cape extending into Caribbean Sea on N coast of Colombia at Barranquilla.

Augusta Auscorum. See AUCH.

Augusta Bay. See EMPRESS AUGUSTA BAY.

Augusta Praetoria. See AOSTA 2.

Augusta Suessionum. See SOISSONS.

Augusta Taurinorum. See TURIN.

Augusta Treverorum. See TRIER.

Augusta Vangionum. See WORMS 2.

Augusta Vindelicorum. See AUGSBURG.

Au·gus·tine \ˈȯ-gə-ˌstēn\. Island, SW part of Cook Inlet, Alaska; 41 sq. mi. (106 sq. km.); highest point 3999 ft. (1219 m.); volcano, eruptions 1883, 1976, 1986.

Augustobona Tricassium. See TROYES.

Augustodunum. See AUTUN.

Augustodurum. See BAYEUX.

Augustonemetum. See CLERMONT-FERRAND.

Augustoritum Lemovicensium. See LIMOGES.

Au·gus·tów \au̇-ˈgü-stüf, -stəf\ *or Russ.* **Av·gus·tov** \äf-ˈgü-stəf\. Town, NE Suwałki prov., NE Poland, 50 mi. (80 km.) N of Białystok; pop. (1989e) 28,207; founded 1650 by Sigismund II Augustus of Poland. Battle in WWI in which Russians defeated Germans 1914; during WWII held by Germans; taken by Soviet troops 1944; part of Byelorussian S.S.R. 1945–46.

Au-ké·na \ˌō-kā-ˈnä\. Small island of Gambier Is., French Polynesia, S Pacific Ocean.

Au·ki \ˈau̇-kē\. Chief village, on W coast of Malaita I., Solomon Is., W Pacific Ocean.

Auld·earn \ȯl-ˈdərn\. Village, Highland region, NE Scotland, E of Nairn; scene of victory of James Graham, marquess of Montrose over the Covenanters under Sir John Urry 1645.

Aulie Ata. See ZHAMBYL 2.

Au·lis \ˈȯ-ləs\. Harbor in Boeotia on Evripos Strait, E cen. Greece; according to tradition, starting place of Greek fleet sailing against Troy at beginning of the Trojan War, and scene of the sacrifice of Iphigenia, daughter of Agamemnon.

Aullagas, Lake. See POOPÓ, LAKE.

Aul·nay–sous–Bois \ō-ˌnā-sü-ˈbwä\. Commune, Seine-St.-Denis dept., N France, 6 mi. (10 km.) NE of Paris.

Aulon. See VLORË 2.

Aundh \ˈau̇nd\. **1.** Former Indian state, now part of Maharashtra state, India.

2. Town, its ✱, 27 mi. (43 km.) SE of Satara.

Au·nis \ō-ˈnēs\. Historical region of W cen. France; bounded on N by Poitou, on E by Angoumois, on S by Gironde estuary, and on W by Bay of Biscay; ✱ La Rochelle. Early became a feudal dependency of Poitou.

Aunus. See OLONETS 1.

Auob \ˈüb\. River bed, SW Africa, extending from S cen. Namibia to the Molopo; ab. 300 mi. (480 km.) long.

Au·rang·abad *also* **Au·rung·abad** \au̇-ˈrəŋ-gä-ˌbäd\. City, N Maharashtra, W cen. India, 207 mi. (333 km.) ENE of Bombay; pop. (1991c) 573,272; tourism; university (1958). Founded 1610 by Malik Ambar; Mogul Emperor Aurangzeb's ('Ālamgīr's) ✱ in 17th cent. campaign against S Indian Muslim states; here he erected to his wife a beautiful mausoleum sometimes compared with the Taj Mahal; later the ✱ of independent Nizams before it was removed to Hyderabad.

Au·ra·ni·tis \ˌȯr-ə-ˈnī-təs\. That part of Hawrān in the time of Herod the Great, king of Judea (37–4 B.C.), forming NE section of his kingdom, E of the Sea of Galilee.

Aurantes. See ABRANTES.

Au·rar·ia \ȯ-ˈrar-ē-ə\. First settlement in Colorado, estab. 1858; soon united (1860) with two other villages to become Denver.

Au·ray \ō-ˈre\. Commune, Morbihan dept., NW France, on Auray River 11 mi. (18 km.) W of Vannes; famed church of Ste. Anne d'Auray 3 mi. (4.8 km.) NW; pilgrimage resort.

Aurelia Aquensis. See BADEN-BADEN.

Aurelianum. See ORLÉANS.

Au·re·lian Way \ȯ-ˈrēl-yən\ *or Lat.* **Via Au·re·lia** \ˈvī-ə-ȯ-ˈrēl-yə, ˈvē-ə\. Roman highway, called the "Great Coast Road," running NW along the coast of Etruria, at first to Pisae (Pisa), but later extended to Genua (Genoa) in Liguria; near Luna (W of Apuania) it was joined by the Cassian Way.

Au·rès Mountains \ō-ˈres\. Mountain massif in the Saharan Atlas, NE Algeria; highest peak Djebel Chélia 7648 ft. (2331 m.).

Au·ri·gnac \ˌō-rēn-ˈyak\. Commune, Haute-Garonne dept., S France, 37 mi. (60 km.) SW of Toulouse; caves with significant Paleolithic remains, the appropriate subdivision of the Stone Age now being called the Aurignacian period.

Aurigny. See ALDERNEY.

Au·ril·lac \ˌō-rē-ˈyak\. City, ✱ of Cantal dept., S cen. France, 105 mi. (169 km.) NNE of Toulouse; pop. (1990c) 32,654; 11th cent. castle. Developed around 9th cent. abbey of St. Géraud; famous seat of medieval learning.

Au·ro·ra \ə-ˈrōr-ə, ȯ-\. **1.** County in SE cen. South Dakota. See table at SOUTH DAKOTA.

2. Suburban residential city, Adams and Arapahoe cos., NE cen. Colorado, 5 mi. (8 km.) E of Denver; pop. (1990c) 222,103; military facilities.

3. City, Kane co., NE Illinois, 37 mi. (60 km.) W of Chicago; pop. (1990c) 99,581; tourism; Aurora Univ. (1893); incorp. as a city 1857.

4. City, Dearborn co., SE Indiana, on Ohio River 54 mi. (87 km.) SE of Shelbyville; pop. (1990c) 3825.

5. Village, St. Louis co., NE Minnesota, 13 mi. (21 km.) E of Virginia; pop. (1990c) 1965; trade center for region.
6. City, Lawrence co., SW Missouri, 30 mi. (48 km.) SW of Springfield; pop. (1990c) 6459; trade center; zinc and lead deposits nearby.
7. City, ⊗ of Hamilton co., SE cen. Nebraska, 18 mi. (29 km.) E of Grand Island; pop. (1990c) 3810.
8. Village, Cayuga co., cen. New York, on E shore of Cayuga Lake ab. 12 mi. (19 km.) SSW of Auburn; pop. (1990c) 687; Wells Coll. (1868); settled 1789.
9. Town, Erie co., New York; pop. (1990c) 13,433; includes East Aurora village (*q.v.*).
10. Town, York municipal region, SE Ontario, Canada, 25 mi. (40 km.) N of Toronto; pop. (1991c) 29,454.
11. Province, E Luzon, Philippines. See table at PHILIPPINES.
12. Island of Vanuatu. See MAÉWO.

Aur·sund·en \'au̇r-ˌsu̇n-ən\. Lake in cen. Norway, N of Femund Lake; drains into headwaters of Glåma River.

Aurungabad. See AURANGABAD.

Ausa. See VICH.

Au Sa·ble \ȯ-'sā-bəl\. River, N cen. Michigan; flowing from Crawford co. E into Lake Huron in NE Iosco co; 80 mi. (129 km.) long.

Au Sable Point. **1.** Point on NE coast of Alger co., N Upper Penin. of Michigan, extending into Lake Superior.
2. Point on E coast of Iosco co., NE Michigan, extending into Lake Huron.

Au·san·ga·te, Ne·va·do \nā-'vä-t͟hō-ˌau̇-säŋ-'gä-tā\ *or Eng.* **Ausangate Knot.** Mountain, SE Peru; 20,945 ft. (6384 m.); highest point in the Cordillera de Carabaya.

Auschwitz. See OŚWIĘCIM.

Ausculum Apulum. See ASCOLI SATRIANO.

Aussig. See ÚSTÍ NAD LABEM.

Aust–Ag·der \'au̇st-ˌäg-dər\. County of S Norway. See table at NORWAY.

Aus·tell \ȯ-'stel\. City, Cobb and Douglas cos., NW Georgia, 15 mi. (24 km.) NW of Atlanta; pop. (1990c) 4173.

Aus·ten, Mount \'ȯs-tən, 'äs-\. Hill and landmark ab. 4 mi. (6 km.) S of Henderson Field, cen. Guadalcanal, Solomon Is.; in WWII held by Japanese during early part of campaign for the island; taken by U.S. marines Dec. 1942.

Austerlitz. See SLAVKOV U BRNA.

Aus·tin \'ȯs-tən, 'äs-\. **1.** County in SE cen. Texas. See table at TEXAS.
2. Town, Scott co., SE Indiana, 30 mi. (48 km.) N of New Albany; pop. (1990c) 4310.
3. City, ⊗ of Mower co., S Minnesota, 34 mi. (55 km.) SW of Rochester; pop. (1990c) 21,907; meatpacking; Austin Community Coll. (1940).
4. Village and former ⊗ of Lander co., cen. Nevada; founded 1862; important mining and trading center and post station during early gold-rush period in Nevada.
5. City, ✻ of Texas and ⊗ of Travis co., cen. Texas, on Colorado River 75 mi. (121 km.) NE of San Antonio; pop. (1990c) 465,622; commercial and research center; electronic equipment. Huston-Tillotson Coll. (1875), Univ. of Texas at Austin (1881), St. Edward's Univ. (1885), Austin Presbyterian Theological Seminary (1902), Concordia Lutheran Coll. (1926), Episcopal Theological Seminary of the Southwest (1951), Austin Community Coll. (1972). Site first settled as Waterloo 1835; chosen as ✻ of Republic of Texas 1839, incorp., and renamed Austin; government returned to Houston 1842–45 because of conflicts with Mexicans and Indians; ✻ of state of Texas from 1845.

Austin, Lake. Lake, Western Australia, Australia, 310 mi. (499 km.) NNE of Perth; 320 sq. mi. (829 sq. km.).

Aus·tral·asia \ˌȯs-trə-'lā-zhə, ˌäs-, -'lā-shə\. Variably and now infrequently used term for a region of the Southern Hemisphere usu. thought to include Australia, New Zealand, and their dependencies; sometimes expanded to include other nearby South Pacific islands.

Australes, Îles. See AUSTRAL ISLANDS.

Aus·tra·lia \ȯ-'strāl-yə, ä-\ *or in full* **Commonwealth of Australia.** Independent state, smallest continent on the globe, bounded on N by Timor and Arafura seas, on NE by Coral Sea, on E by South Pacific Ocean, and on S and W by Indian Ocean; 2,967,909 sq. mi. (7,686,884 sq. km.); pop. (1992e) 17,562,000; ✻ Canberra.

Physical features: Entirely in Southern Hemisphere; largely desert; many salt lakes, esp. in S (lowest Lake Eyre) and W; low Artesian Basin in E cen. part. Mountain range (Great Dividing Range), parallel with E coast from N Queensland around to cen. Victoria, highest point Mt. Kosciusko (*q.v.*); also plateau uplands in E New South Wales. Coast indented with extensive Gulf of Carpentaria in NE (Cape York Peninsula on E) and Great Australian Bight and Spencer Gulf in S; coastline rugged with few good harbors, but some excellent: Port Jackson (harbor of Sydney), Newcastle (mouth of Hunter River), Brisbane (Moreton Bay), Darwin (Port Darwin), Fremantle (estuary of Swan River), Port Adelaide, Port Pirie, and Port Lincoln in South Australia, and Melbourne (on Port Phillip Bay). Many islands and reefs along coast, esp. Great Barrier Reef on NE, Thursday I. and others in Torres Strait, Melville I. N of Darwin, Kangaroo I. off South Australia, and Fraser I. off SE Queensland; Tasmania, constituting a state, is separated from mainland by Bass Strait.

Chief rivers: Murray-Darling system; others Fitzroy, Burdekin, Flinders, Swan, Cooper Creek.

Chief products: Wheat, barley, oats, fruit, sugarcane; livestock, wool, lamb, mutton, beef; bauxite and alumina, gold, silver, lead, zinc, copper, iron, tungsten, coal, natural gas, uranium, tin, diamonds, oil; manufacturing: iron and steel, machinery, chemical products, textiles; tourism.

Chief urban centers: Sydney, Brisbane, Perth, Adelaide.

Political divisions: Divided into the following six states and two territories (for pronunciation of their names, see their individual entries). Exercises control over these external territories: Ashmore Is., Australian Antarctic Terr., Christmas I., Cocos Is., Coral Sea Islands Terr., Heard and McDonald Is., and Norfolk I.

NAME	AREA (sq. mi.)	AREA (sq. km.)	POP. (1993e)	CAPITAL
States				
New South Wales	309,433	801,431	5,732,032[1]	Sydney
Queensland	667,000	1,727,530	3,116,200	Brisbane
South Australia	380,070	984,381	1,462,900	Adelaide
Tasmania	26,383	68,332	471,400	Hobart
Victoria	87,884	227,620	4,244,221[1]	Melbourne
Western Australia	975,920	2,527,633	1,676,400	Perth
Territories				
Australian Capital Terr.	939	2,432	229,000	Canberra
Northern Terr.	520,280	1,347,525	169,300	Darwin

[1]Pop. (1991c).

History: Orig. populated for perhaps 40,000 years by aborigines who probably came from Asia; may have been visited by various Oceanic people before arrival of Europeans; first sighted by Spanish in early 17th cent.; missed by navigator Luis Vaez de Torres, who sailed up Torres Strait (*q.v.*) 1606; not reached by Europeans until landing of Dutch ship *Duyfken* on E coast of Gulf of Carpentaria 1606; in first half of 17th cent. N and W coasts explored by Dutch, who named it New Holland (see also TASMANIA and NEW ZEALAND, both first European visits by Dutch mariner Abel Tasman c. 1642); W coast navigated by William Dampier 1688; E part claimed for Britain 1770 by Capt. James Cook, who went ashore several times, incl. at Botany Bay (*q.v.*) and named the land New South Wales; first English settlement 1788, by mainly convicts and seamen at Port Jackson (see SYDNEY); circumnavigated by Matthew Flinders 1801–03, who thus proved continental unity of New South Wales and New Holland; came to be called Australia in 19th cent.; entire continent claimed by Britain by 1829; colonies, except for Western Australia, given limited self-government by the time of passage of Australian Colonies Government Act 1850; developed rapidly after gold rush of 1851; crossed from E to W by J. McDouall Stuart 1862; opened transcontinental telegraph lines 1872; completed railroad from Sydney to Melbourne 1883; carried out federalization 1885–1901; act federating separate colonies into commonwealth passed by

British Parliament 1900 and put into force 1901; passsed Immigration Restriction Act 1901 effectively working toward a "white Australia"; adopted federal tariff and woman suffrage 1902; administered Terr. of Papua (*q.v.*) after 1906 and Northern Terr. after 1910; maintained Royal Australian Navy after 1911; participated in WWI; esp. noted for ANZAC (Australia and New Zealand Army Corps) campaign at Gallipoli; represented at Peace Conference 1919; received mandate of certain German possessions in Pacific (see NEW GUINEA, TRUST TERRITORY OF); occupied new ✻ Canberra (*q.v.*), 1927; received authority over one third of Antarctica 1933; joined Great Britain in WWII 1939; Darwin and its N coast threatened by Japanese 1941–42 but battle of Coral Sea and campaigns in the Solomon Is. and New Guinea prevented invasion. Placed Terr. of Papua and Trust Terr. of New Guinea under single administration 1949; signed a Pacific defense pact with the U.S. and New Zealand (ANZUS treaty) 1951; took part on side of U.S. in Korean War, Vietnam War; became a member of the Southeast Asia Treaty Organization 1954; since 1960s, partly as a result of political pressure, has sought to deal with aborigines more fairly; also, loosening of enforcement of Immigration Restriction Act has led to more heterogeneous population; Papua New Guinea granted independence 1975; constitutional links allowing British intervention in government formally abolished 1986.

Australia Fe·lix \ˈfē-liks\. A name given to the fertile river valleys of cen. Victoria, SE Australia c. 1836.

Aus·tra·lian Alps \ȯ-ˈstrāl-yən, ä-\. Mountain range, E Victoria and SE New South Wales, SE Australia, forming the S end of the Great Dividing Range and the watershed bet. the headstreams of the Murrumbidgee River and the short streams flowing S to the Pacific Ocean; av. height 2500 to 5000 ft. (760 to 1525 m.); highest Mt. Kosciusko 7316 ft. (2230 m.); other peaks are Mt. Jagungul 6754 ft. (2059 m.), Mt. Bogong 6508 ft. (1984 m.), Mt. Feathertop 6307 ft. (1922 m.), Mt. Hotham 6108 ft. (1862 m.); site of important hydroelectric-power project.

Australian Antarctic Territory. External territory of Australia lying S of 60°S and bet. 160°E and 45°E; ab. 2,360,000 sq. mi. (6,112,400 sq. km.); does not include Adélie Coast.

Australian Capital Territory; *formerly* **Federal Capital Territory.** Territory of Australia; consists of enclaves: (1) area surrounding Canberra (ceded by New South Wales 1911), 911 sq. mi. (2359 sq. km.), and (2) area at Jervis Bay (ceded 1917), 28 sq. mi. (72 sq. km.). Parliament opened at Canberra by duke of York 1927. See table at AUSTRALIA.

Australia–New Zealand–United States Treaty; *abbr.* **ANZUS.** Military alliance, consisting of Australia, New Zealand, U.S.; purpose is to coordinate defense planning; formed 1951; the U.S. suspended its defense obligations to New Zealand 1986 in protest of New Zealand's ban on nuclear vessels in its ports.

Aus·tral Islands \ˈȯs-trəl, ˈäs-\ *or Fr.* **Îles Au·strales** \ˌēl-ō-ˈstrȧl\ *also* **Tu·bu·ai Islands** \tü-bwä-ē\. Group of small volcanic islands, S French Polynesia, S Pacific Ocean, S of Society Is. and SW of Tuamotu Archipelago; form a chain ab. 850 mi. (1370 km.) long bet. lat. 21°50′ to 27°41′S and long. 144°22′ to 155°W; 54 sq. mi. (140 sq. km.); pop. (1988c) 6509. The inhabited islands of the group, from NW to SE, are Rimatara, Rurutu, Tubuai, Raevavae, Rapa (*q.v.*). Islands are well-watered and fertile. Sighted by English explorer Capt. James Cook 1769 and 1777 and by English navigator George Vancouver 1791; taken over by French late 19th cent.

Aus·tra·sia \ȯ-ˈstrā-zhə, ä-, -shə\ *or* **Os·tra·sia** \ä-\. The E dominions of the Merovingian Franks, extending from the Meuse River to the Bohemian Forest.

History: Emerged as E part of kingdom of Franks after division of lands which followed death of King Clovis I (511 A.D.); ruled by Merovingian kings, alternately as separate kingdom and as kingdom in conjunction with rule of Neustria (*q.v.*), 6th cent.; original seat of authority of mayors of palace of house of Pépin III (the Short) who founded Carolingian line of Frankish kings in 8th cent.; although recognized as territorial division in partitions of land which were customary at ruler's death, ceased to exist in Frankish empire as it was consolidated by Holy Roman Emperor Charlemagne (768–814).

Aus·tria \ˈȯs-trē-ə, ˈäs-\ *or Ger.* **Öster·reich** \ˈœ̄-stər-ˌrīk̲\. Republic, cen. Europe, bounded on N by Germany and Czech Republic, on E by Slovakia and Hungary, on S by Slovenia and Italy, and on W by Liechtenstein, Switzerland, and Germany; 32,375 sq. mi. (83,851 sq. km.); pop. (1991c) 7,812,100; ✻ Vienna.

Physical features: A mountainous country, N of the Alps, containing many of its spurs and branches; bordered on S by Karawanken, Carnic, and Ötztaler Alps and on S Bavarian border by Bavarian Alps; highest point Grossglockner in the Hohe Tauern 12,470 ft. (3801 m.). Chief passes to Italy are the Brenner and Plöcken, and to Slovenia the Loibl. Chief river is the Danube (*or Ger.* Donau) crossing in N from Bavaria, Germany, to Hungary with many tributaries, esp. the Inn, Traun, and Enns; in the S are the Mur and Drava. Neusiedler Lake on E border is largest lake; in W and S are many other lakes, many of them health and resort centers.

Chief products: Wheat, rye, fruit, potatoes, timber; cattle; iron ore, magnesite, coal, lead, salt, petroleum, natural gas; manufacturing: iron and steel, pulp, chemicals, textiles, transportation equipment, ski equipment; tourism.

Chief cities: Vienna, Graz, Linz, Salzburg, Innsbruck, and Klagenfurt.

Political divisions: Divided into eight states and the city of Vienna (for pronunciation of their names, see their individual entries):

NAME	AREA (sq. mi.)	AREA (sq. km.)	POP. (1991c)	CAPITAL
Burgenland	1,531	3,965	273,541	Eisenstadt
Carinthia	3,681	9,534	552,421	Klagenfurt
Lower Austria[1]	7,402	19,171	1,480,927	Sankt Pölten
Salzburg	2,762	7,154	483,880	Salzburg
Styria	6,327	16,387	1,184,593	Graz
Tirol	4,883	12,647	630,358	Innsbruck
Upper Austria	4,625	11,979	1,340,076	Linz
Vienna	160	414	1,533,176	Vienna
Vorarlberg	1,004	2,600	333,128	Bregenz

[1] Excluding Vienna.

History: Territory inhabited by Celtic tribes, conquered by Rome c. 14 B.C.; included Roman settlement of Vindobona (see VIENNA); invaded by Marcomanni and Quadi 2d cent. A.D., by Huns 5th cent.; settled 590 by Slovenes who later formed kingdom of the Avars; erected by Holy Roman Emperor Charlemagne into a border state, East Mark (*or Ger.* Österreich); became part of Holy Roman Empire under Saxon line; after defeat of Magyars 955, reestablished as East Mark by Holy Roman Emperor Otto the Great; as an independent duchy 1156, granted to Henry of Austria in return for Bavaria; claimed by Otakar II, ruler of the Slavic kingdom of Bohemia (1253–78); after defeat of Ottokar by Rudolf of Hapsburg 1278, remained Hapsburg until 1918; failed in effort to enforce control over Swiss cantons; as archduchy, center of imperial authority which also ruled adjacent duchies of Styria, Carinthia, Carniola, and county of Tirol; one of 10 circles of empire 1512 organized under first great emperor, Maximilian I (1493–1519); with other cen. European lands of Hapsburgs, passed to Spanish King Charles I (Holy Roman Emperor Charles V 1519–56); continued to be separate from holdings of Spanish Hapsburgs after it was inherited by Ferdinand I c. 1556; E European bulwark against the Turks who besieged Vienna 1529; lost Alsace and more than nominal authority over Holy Roman Empire 1648; saved from Turks by Poles under John III Sobieski 1683; by Peace of Karlowitz 1699, received Slavonia, Transylvania, and most of Hungary; awarded Spanish Netherlands (see BELGIUM), Sardinia, and Naples 1713; entered

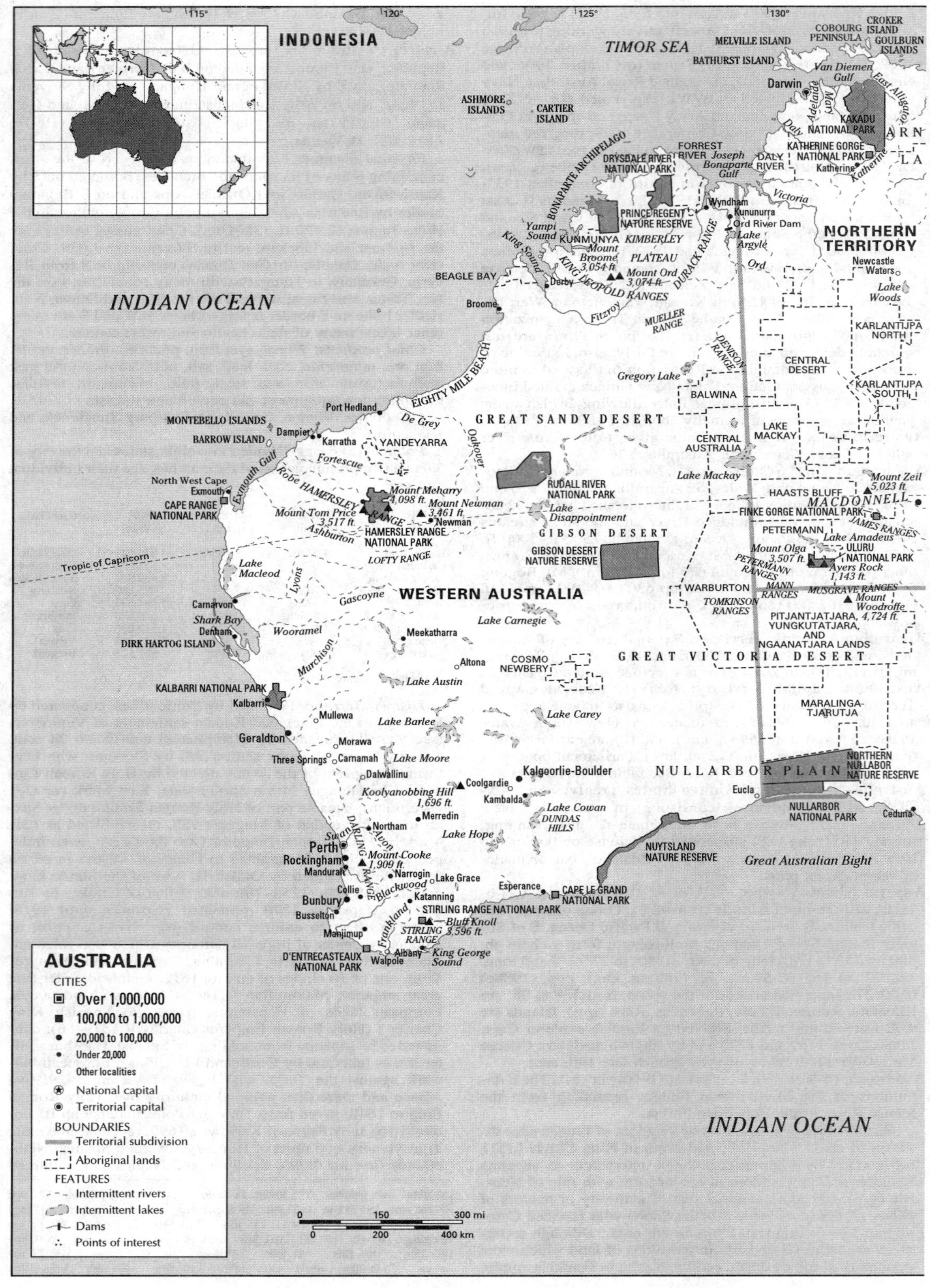

115°
120°
125°
130°
INDONESIA
TIMOR SEA
MELVILLE ISLAND
BATHURST ISLAND
COBOURG PENINSULA
CROKER ISLAND
GOULBURN ISLANDS
Van Diemen Gulf
East Alligator
Darwin
Adelaide
Mary
Daly
KAKADU NATIONAL PARK
KATHERINE GORGE NATIONAL PARK
Katherine
ASHMORE ISLANDS
CARTIER ISLAND
BONAPARTE ARCHIPELAGO
DRYSDALE RIVER NATIONAL PARK
FORREST RIVER
Joseph Bonaparte Gulf
DALY RIVER
Victoria
PRINCE REGENT NATURE RESERVE
Wyndham
Kununurra
Ord River Dam
Lake Argyle
Ord
Yampi Sound
KUNMUNYA
KIMBERLEY PLATEAU
Mount Broome 3,054 ft.
Mount Ord 3,074 ft.
KING LEOPOLD RANGES
DURACK RANGE
King Sound
Derby
BEAGLE BAY
NORTHERN TERRITORY
Newcastle Waters
Lake Woods
INDIAN OCEAN
Broome
Fitzroy
MUELLER RANGE
KARLANTIJPA NORTH
DENISON RANGE
CENTRAL DESERT
KARLANTIJPA SOUTH
Gregory Lake
BALWINA
EIGHTY MILE BEACH
Port Hedland
De Grey
GREAT SANDY DESERT
LAKE MACKAY
CENTRAL AUSTRALIA
MONTEBELLO ISLANDS
BARROW ISLAND
Dampier
Karratha
YANDEYARRA
Oakover
Fortescue
Exmouth Gulf
Robe
HAMERSLEY RANGE
Lake Mackay
Mount Zeil 5,023 ft.
North West Cape
Exmouth
CAPE RANGE NATIONAL PARK
Mount Meharry 4,098 ft.
Mount Newman 3,461 ft.
Mount Tom Price 3,517 ft.
Newman
RUDALL RIVER NATIONAL PARK
Lake Disappointment
HAASTS BLUFF
MACDONNELL
FINKE GORGE NATIONAL PARK
JAMES RANGES
Ashburton
HAMERSLEY RANGE NATIONAL PARK
GIBSON DESERT
PETERMANN
Lake Amadeus
Tropic of Capricorn
LOFTY RANGE
GIBSON DESERT NATURE RESERVE
Mount Olga 3,507 ft.
ULURU NATIONAL PARK
Ayers Rock 1,143 ft.
PETERMANN RANGES
Lake Macleod
Lyons
WARBURTON
MANN RANGES
MUSGRAVE RANGES
Gascoyne
WESTERN AUSTRALIA
Mount Woodroffe
TOMKINSON RANGES
PITJANTJATJARA, 4,724 ft.
YUNGKUTATJARA, AND NGAANATJARA LANDS
Carnarvon
Shark Bay
Denham
DIRK HARTOG ISLAND
Wooramel
Meekatharra
Lake Carnegie
Murchison
Altona
COSMO NEWBERY
GREAT VICTORIA DESERT
KALBARRI NATIONAL PARK
Kalbarri
Lake Austin
MARALINGA-TJARUTJA
Mullewa
Lake Barlee
Lake Carey
Geraldton
Morawa
Three Springs
Carnamah
Lake Moore
Dalwallinu
NULLARBOR PLAIN
NORTHERN NULLABOR NATURE RESERVE
Kalgoorlie-Boulder
Koolyanobbing Hill 1,696 ft.
Coolgardie
Kambalda
Eucla
Lake Cowan
DUNDAS HILLS
NULLARBOR NATIONAL PARK
Ceduna
Merredin
Swan
Avon
Northam
Lake Hope
Perth
DARLING RANGE
Rockingham
Mount Cooke 1,909 ft.
Mandurah
NUYTSLAND NATURE RESERVE
Great Australian Bight
Narrogin
Lake Grace
Blackwood
Collie
Bunbury
Katanning
Esperance
CAPE LE GRAND NATIONAL PARK
Busselton
STIRLING RANGE NATIONAL PARK
Bluff Knoll 3,596 ft.
Frankland
STIRLING RANGE
Manjimup
Albany
King George Sound
D'ENTRECASTEAUX NATIONAL PARK
Walpole
AUSTRALIA
CITIES
Over 1,000,000
100,000 to 1,000,000
20,000 to 100,000
Under 20,000
Other localities
National capital
Territorial capital
BOUNDARIES
Territorial subdivision
Aboriginal lands
FEATURES
Intermittent rivers
Intermittent lakes
Dams
Points of interest
INDIAN OCEAN
0
150
300 mi
0
200
400 km

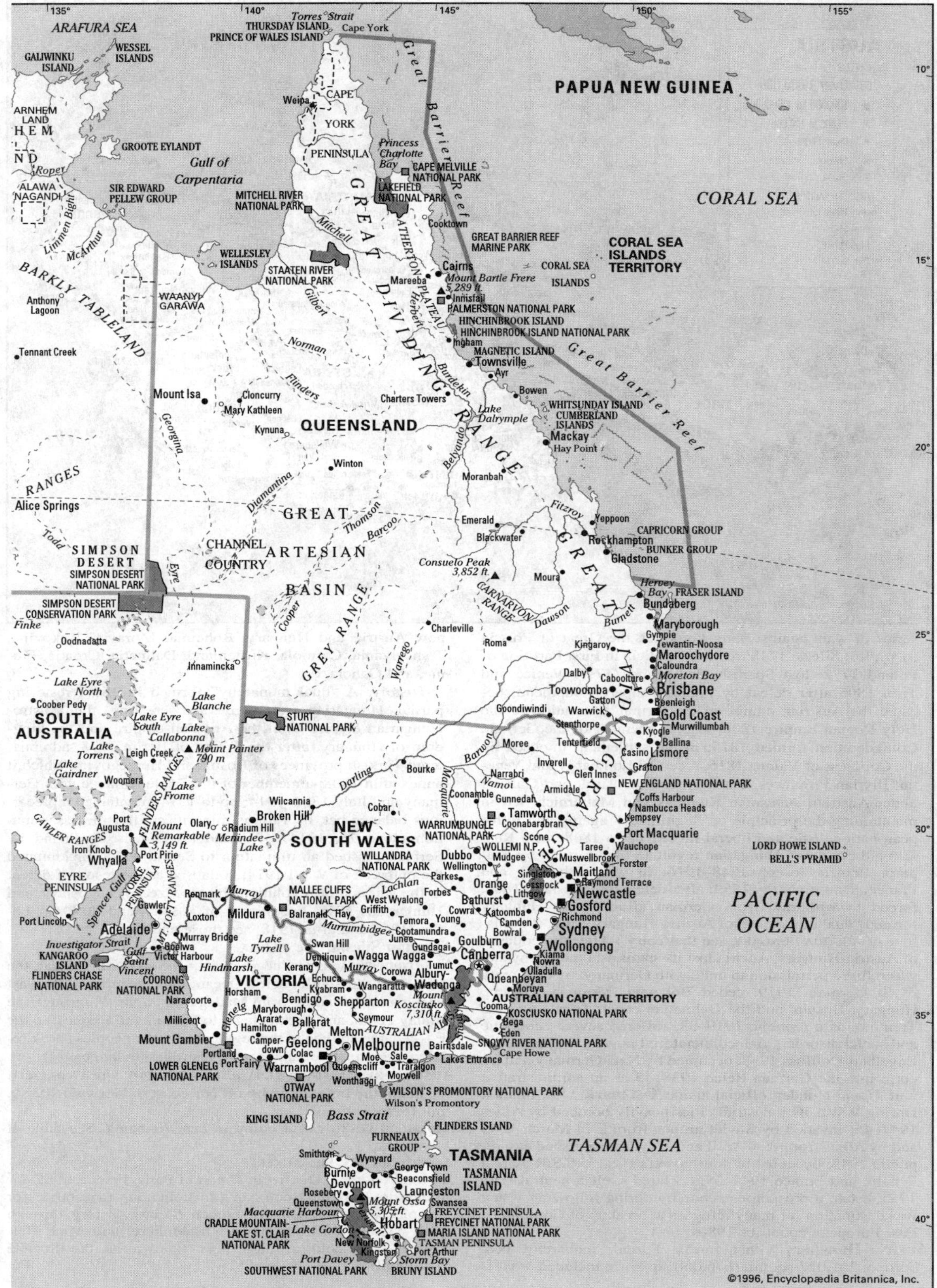

135°
140°
145°
150°
155°
10°
15°
20°
25°
30°
35°
40°
ARAFURA SEA
Torres Strait
THURSDAY ISLAND
PRINCE OF WALES ISLAND
Cape York
WESSEL ISLANDS
GALIWINKU ISLAND
PAPUA NEW GUINEA
ARNHEM LAND
H E M
N D
Weipa
CAPE
YORK
PENINSULA
Great Barrier Reef
GROOTE EYLANDT
Gulf of Carpentaria
Ropei
ALAWA
NAGANDI
Princess Charlotte Bay
CAPE MELVILLE NATIONAL PARK
LAKEFIELD NATIONAL PARK
SIR EDWARD PELLEW GROUP
MITCHELL RIVER NATIONAL PARK
CORAL SEA
Limmen Bight
McArthur
Mitchell
GREAT DIVIDING RANGE
ATHERTON PLATEAU
Cooktown
GREAT BARRIER REEF MARINE PARK
CORAL SEA ISLANDS TERRITORY
WELLESLEY ISLANDS
BARKLY TABLELAND
STAATEN RIVER NATIONAL PARK
Cairns
Mareeba
Mount Bartle Frere 5,289 ft.
Innisfail
CORAL SEA ISLANDS
Anthony Lagoon
WAANYI GARAWA
Gilbert
Herbert
PALMERSTON NATIONAL PARK
HINCHINBROOK ISLAND
HINCHINBROOK ISLAND NATIONAL PARK
Tennant Creek
Norman
Ingham
MAGNETIC ISLAND
Townsville
Ayr
Burdekin
Mount Isa
Cloncurry
Mary Kathleen
Flinders
Charters Towers
Bowen
WHITSUNDAY ISLAND
CUMBERLAND ISLANDS
Lake Dalrymple
Georgina
QUEENSLAND
Kynuna
Mackay
Hay Point
Belyando
Winton
Moranbah
RANGES
Alice Springs
Diamantina
GREAT
Thomson
Emerald
Fitzroy
Yeppoon
Blackwater
Rockhampton
CAPRICORN GROUP
BUNKER GROUP
Gladstone
Todd
SIMPSON DESERT
SIMPSON DESERT NATIONAL PARK
CHANNEL COUNTRY
ARTESIAN
BASIN
Barcoo
Consuelo Peak 3,852 ft.
CARNARVON RANGE
Moura
Eyre
Hervey Bay
FRASER ISLAND
Bundaberg
SIMPSON DESERT CONSERVATION PARK
Finke
Cooper
GREY RANGE
Charleville
Dawson
Burnett
Maryborough
Gympie
Tewantin-Noosa
Maroochydore
Caloundra
Moreton Bay
Oodnadatta
Roma
Kingaroy
Innamincka
Warrego
Dalby
Caboolture
Brisbane
Lake Eyre North
Coober Pedy
Lake Blanche
Toowoomba
Gatton
Beenleigh
Warwick
Gold Coast
SOUTH AUSTRALIA
Lake Eyre South
Lake Callabonna
STURT NATIONAL PARK
Goondiwindi
Stanthorpe
Murwillumbah
Kyogle
Lake Torrens
Leigh Creek
Mount Painter 790 m
Moree
Tenterfield
Ballina
Casino
Lismore
Lake Gairdner
FLINDERS RANGES
Barwon
Inverell
Grafton
Woomera
Darling
Bourke
Macquarie
Narrabri
Namoi
Glen Innes
NEW ENGLAND NATIONAL PARK
Lake Frome
Armidale
Coffs Harbour
Nambucca Heads
Wilcannia
Coonamble
Gunnedah
Broken Hill
Cobar
Tamworth
Kempsey
GAWLER RANGES
Port Augusta
Mount Remarkable 3,149 ft.
Olary
Radium Hill
Menindee Lake
NEW SOUTH WALES
WARRUMBUNGLE NATIONAL PARK
Coonabarabran
Port Macquarie
Iron Knob
Whyalla
Port Pirie
Scone
WOLLEMI N.P.
Taree
Wauchope
LORD HOWE ISLAND
BELL'S PYRAMID
WILLANDRA NATIONAL PARK
Dubbo
Wellington
Mudgee
Muswellbrook
Forster
EYRE PENINSULA
Spencer Gulf
YORKE PENINSULA
MT. LOFTY RANGES
Parkes
Orange
Singleton
Cessnock
Maitland
Raymond Terrace
Newcastle
Renmark
Murray
MALLEE CLIFFS NATIONAL PARK
Lachlan
Forbes
Gawler
West Wyalong
Bathurst
Lithgow
Gosford
PACIFIC OCEAN
Port Lincoln
Loxton
Mildura
Balranald
Hay
Griffith
Cowra
Katoomba
Richmond
Adelaide
Murrumbidgee
Temora
Young
Camden
Sydney
Investigator Strait
Murray Bridge
Lake Tyrrell
Cootamundra
Junee
Bowral
Swan Hill
Gundagai
Goulburn
Wollongong
KANGAROO ISLAND
Gulf Saint Vincent
Goolwa
Victor Harbour
Deniliquin
Wagga Wagga
Canberra
Kiama
Nowra
Ulladulla
Tumut
FLINDERS CHASE NATIONAL PARK
COORONG NATIONAL PARK
Lake Hindmarsh
Kerang
VICTORIA
Echuca
Corowa
Albury-Wodonga
Queanbeyan
Moruya
Horsham
Kyabram
Wangaratta
Mount Kosciusko 7,310 ft.
AUSTRALIAN CAPITAL TERRITORY
Bendigo
Shepparton
Naracoorte
Maryborough
Cooma
KOSCIUSKO NATIONAL PARK
Ararat
Seymour
Millicent
Glenelg
Hamilton
Ballarat
AUSTRALIAN ALPS
Snowy
Bega
Eden
Mount Gambier
Melton
Camperdown
Geelong
Melbourne
Bairnsdale
SNOWY RIVER NATIONAL PARK
Portland
Colac
Moe
Sale
Cape Howe
LOWER GLENELG NATIONAL PARK
Port Fairy
Warrnambool
Queenscliff
Traralgon
Lakes Entrance
Morwell
Wonthaggi
OTWAY NATIONAL PARK
WILSON'S PROMONTORY NATIONAL PARK
Wilson's Promontory
KING ISLAND
Bass Strait
FLINDERS ISLAND
FURNEAUX GROUP
TASMAN SEA
Smithton
Wynyard
TASMANIA
George Town
Burnie
Beaconsfield
TASMANIA ISLAND
Devonport
Launceston
Rosebery
Queenstown
Mount Ossa 5,305 ft.
Swansea
Macquarie Harbour
FREYCINET PENINSULA
FREYCINET NATIONAL PARK
CRADLE MOUNTAIN-LAKE ST. CLAIR NATIONAL PARK
Lake Gordon
Derwent
Hobart
MARIA ISLAND NATIONAL PARK
New Norfolk
TASMAN PENINSULA
Kingston
Port Arthur
Port Davey
Storm Bay
SOUTHWEST NATIONAL PARK
BRUNY ISLAND
©1996, Encyclopædia Britannica, Inc.

series of wars against King Frederick the Great of Prussia (*q.v.*); lost Silesia 1748; received Galicia in First Partition of Poland 1772; lost Spanish Netherlands 1797, Venice and Tirol 1805 after defeat by French Emperor Napoléon; became the Austrian empire at the formal dissolution of the Holy Roman Empire 1806; leading member of the German Confederation formed 1815; in the settlement imposed by the Congress of Vienna 1815, received Lombardy and Venetia, Illyrian Provinces, Salzburg and the Tirol, and Galicia; under Austrian statesman Klemens von Metternich, led in maintaining the principle of "legitimacy" against the European nationalistic and liberal revolts up to 1848; with Russian aid put down Hungarian revolt 1848–49; ruled by Emperor Francis Joseph 1848–1916; in war with Italy and France, lost Lombardy 1859; after defeat by Prussia in 1866, forced to withdraw from German affairs; with Hungary formed "dual monarchy" of Austria-Hungary 1867. (For history of AUSTRIA-HUNGARY, see that entry.) After the collapse of Austria-Hungary, Austria lost its status as a monarchy and was refused permission to unite with Germany; by the Treaty of St.-Germain 1919, ceded Bohemia, Moravia, Galicia, Hungary, Bosnia, and the Dalmatian coast, Trieste and the Trentino; as a republic 1919–33, suffered severe economic and social disorder; yielded dictatorial powers to Chancellor Engelbert Dollfuss 1933; occupied by Nazi Germany and incorp. into the German Reich 1938–45 as an administrative unit (*Land*) under official name **Ost·mark** \ˈȯst-ˌmärk\. During WWII its industrial cities heavily bombed by Allies 1944–45; invaded by Soviet armies from E in March 1945 and by Allies from W in April and May; reestablished as a republic 1945; occupied by four powers U.S., U.S.S.R., Great Britain, and France 1945–55; declared itself a neutral state 1955; estab. a prosperous economy during following years; was destination for many refugees at breakup of Communist East European countries 1980s.

Austria–Hun·ga·ry \-ˈhəŋ-gə-rē\. Former monarchy, cen. Europe; 261,027 sq. mi. (676,060 sq. km.); included what is now Austria and Hungary, Bohemia, Moravia, Bukovina, Transylvania, Carniola, Kustenland, Dalmatia, Croatia, Fiume, and Galicia.

History: A "dual monarchy" formed in 1867, restoring partial Hungarian autonomy and creating the Austro-Hungarian empire from the Austrian empire and the kingdom of Hungary; after the Treaty of Berlin 1878, administered Turkish provinces of Bosnia and Herzegovina which it annexed in 1908; a member of the Triple Alliance with Germany and Italy 1882–1914; up to 1914 maintained a precarious balance bet. its various minorities; after the assassination (June 28, 1914) of Archduke Francis Ferdinand by Serbians, issued an ultimatum to Serbia which precipitated the outbreak of WWI 1914; collapsed as the result of defeat in the war and of revolutions by the Czechs, Yugoslavs, and Hungarians 1918. For history of AUSTRIA and HUNGARY before 1867 and after 1918, see those entries.

Austrian Silesia. See SILESIA.

Aus·tro·ne·sia \ˌȯs-trə-ˈnē-zhə, ˌäs-, -ˈnē-shə\. In general, the islands of the South Pacific Ocean; more accurately, the vast island area extending from Madagascar in the W, through the Malay Penin. and Archipelago, to Hawaii and Easter I. in the E —a name applied to the region where the peoples speak related agglutinative languages (Austronesian languages).

Aust·våg·øy \ˈau̇st-ˌvȯ-gœi\ *also* **Öst·våg·öy** \ˈœst-vȯ-ˌgœi\. Island in the Lofoten group off NW coast of Norway; 203 sq. mi. (526 sq. km.).

Au·tau·ga \ȯ-ˈtȯ-gə\. County in cen. Alabama. See table at ALABAMA.

Autesiodorum. See AUXERRE.

Au·teuil \ō-ˈtœi\. District in W part of Paris, France, at SE entrance to Bois de Boulogne (*q.v.*); famous racecourse for steeplechasing; notable in French literary history through poet Nicolas Boileau, playwright Molière, and Mme Helvétius, who held a salon here (known as the Société d'Auteuil).

Au·tlán *or* **Autlán de Na·var·ro** \aù-ˈtlän-ˌt͟hā-nä-ˈvä-rō\. Town, SW Jalisco state, W cen. Mexico, 80 mi. (129 km.) SW of Guadalajara; munic. pop. (1990p) 46,624.

Autricum. See CHARTRES.

Au·tun \ō-ˈtœ^{n}, -ˈte^{n}, -ˈtən\; *anc.* **Æd·ua** \ˈē-dyù-wə, ˈe-\; *later* **Au·gus·to·du·num** \ò-ˌgəs-tə-ˈdü-nəm, -ˈdyü-\. Commune, Saône-et-Loire dept., E cen. France, 51 mi. (82 km.) NNW of Mâcon; 12th cent. Gothic cathedral; 12th cent. castle; Roman remains; residence of Roman prefects of Gaul; economic and educational center under Romans; ruined by barbaric invasions 406–895; under dukes of Burgundy.

Au·vergne \ō-ˈvern^{y}, -ˈver-nyə\. **1.** Historical region of S cen. France; bounded on N by Bourbonnais, on NE by Lyonnais, on SE by Languedoc, on SW by Guienne, on W by Limousin, and on NW by Marche; ✻ Clermont (now Clermont-Ferrand); mountains of volcanic origin; medicinal springs.

History: Inhabited by Arverni, Gallic people led by Vercingetorix and defeated by Roman Gen. Julius Caesar; yielded to Visigoths 475 A.D.; conquered by Franks under Clovis I 507; part of Aquitaine; became countship 8th cent.; divided into four lordships, one of which, Terre d'Auvergne, became duchy 1360 (✻ Riom), passed to Bourbons 1416, to France c. 1530.

2. Region of S cen. France, incl. the historical region of Auvergne. See table at FRANCE.

Auvergne Mountains. Mountain range in cen. France; highest peak Puy de Sancy 6188 ft. (1886 m.).

Aux Barques, Pointe \ˌpòint-ō-ˈbärk\. Point, Michigan's Lower Peninsula, extending into Lake Huron.

Aux Cayes. See CAYES.

Au·xerre \ō-ˈser\; *anc.* **Au·te·si·o·do·rum** \ò-ˌtē-zē-ə-ˈdōr-əm, -ˌtē-sē-\. Commercial city, ✻ of Yonne dept., NE cen. France, on Yonne River 96 mi. (154 km.) SE of Paris; pop. (1990c) 40,597; wine; 13th cent. cathedral; old abbey; flourished in pre-Roman and Roman days; taken by Franks under Clovis I; part of kingdom of Burgundy; captured by English 1359; united to France by Louis XI; bombarded by Germans 1870.

Au·xonne \ō-ˈsòn\. Commune, Côte-d'Or dept., E France, on left bank of Saône River 18 mi. (29 km.) ESE of Dijon. Chartered 1229; under dukes of Burgundy from 13th cent.; surrendered to Austrians 1815.

Aux Sources, Mont \ˌmō^{n}-tō-ˈsùrs\. Peak in Drakensberg, N Lesotho, on the border with Kwazulu-Natal; 10,822 ft. (3298 m.).

Au·yán–te·puí \aù-ˈyän-tā-ˈpwē\ *or* **Dev·il Mountain** \ˈdevil\. Plateau, SE Venezuela, E of the Caroní River; 20 mi. (32 km.) long.

Au·yu·it·tuq National Park \aù-ˈyü-i-tək\. See CANADA, *National Parks.*

Ava \ˈā-və\. City, ⊗ of Douglas co., S Missouri; pop. (1990c) 2938.

Ava \ˈä-vä, ə-ˈwä\. Ruined city on Irrawaddy River, Sagaing div., Myanmar, 6 mi. (10 km.) SW of Mandalay; founded in 14th cent.; on and off for 400 years ✻ of Burma; replaced by Amarapura in 1783; again ✻ 1823–37.

Av·a·lanche Peak \ˈa-və-ˌlanch\. Mountain, E boundary of Yellowstone National Park, NW Wyoming; 10,566 ft. (3220 m.).

Aval·lon \ˌá-vá-ˈlō^{n}\. Commune, Yonne dept., NE cen. France, on Cousin River 27 mi. (43 km.) SE of Auxerre; on hill of red granite; 12th cent. church. Celtic in origin; sacked by Saracens and by Normans; viscounty in medieval duchy of Burgundy; joined to French crown 1477.

Av·a·lon \ˈa-və-ˌlän\. **1.** Resort city, Los Angeles co., SW California, at E end of Santa Catalina I. 50 mi. (80 km.) S of Los Angeles; pop. (1990c) 2918; recreation center; incorp. 1913.

2. Residential borough, Allegheny co., SW Pennsylvania, on Ohio River 6 mi. (10 km.) NW of Pittsburgh; pop. (1990c) 5784.

3. Large peninsula of SE Newfoundland, Canada, bet. Trinity and Placentia bays.

Avalon Dam *and* **Avalon Lake.** See CARLSBAD 2.

Avan·ti \ə-ˈvən-tē, -ˈvän-\. Early kingdom of N India 6th–4th cents. B.C., about coextensive with Malwa; ✻ Ujjain.

Avarau. See PALMERSTON.

Avaricum. See BOURGES.

Avar·is \ə-ˈvar-əs\. City of ancient Egypt in E part of Nile delta, the Hyksos ✻; completely destroyed, but has been identified with Tanis.

Ava·rua \ˌä-vä-ˈrü-ä\. Village, ✻ of the Cook Is., on N coast of the island of Rarotonga, S Pacific Ocean.

Avdira. See ABDERA 1.

Ave·bury \ˈāv-bə-rē\ *or* **Abury** \ˈā-bə-rē\. Village, Wiltshire, England, 29 mi. (47 km.) E of Bristol; vast megalithic remains of uncertain date and origin.

Avei·ro \ə-ˈvā-rü\. **1.** Salt lagoon on NW coast of Portugal, S of Pôrto.

2. District of NW Portugal. See table at PORTUGAL.

3. Seaport, its ✻, on Aveiro lagoon 135 mi. (217 km.) N by E of Lisbon, connected by canal with Atlantic Ocean; pop. (1991p) 35,246; episcopal see; produces sea salt; fisheries (esp. sardines); seaweed; ceramics. Once said to be Roman **Tal·a·bri·ga** \ˌta-lə-ˈbrī-gə\; well known through João Afonso's exploitation of Newfoundland dried codfish trade in 16th cent.

Avel·la·ne·da \ˌä-vā-zhä-ˈnā-dä\. City, Buenos Aires prov., E Argentina, a suburb of Buenos Aires (city); pop. (1991p) 346,620.

Avel·li·no \ˌä-vā-ˈlē-nō\. **1.** Province of Campania, S Italy. See table at ITALY.

2. *anc.* **Ab·el·li·num** \ˌa-bə-ˈlī-nəm\. Commune, its ✻, 29 mi. (47 km.) ENE of Naples; pop. (1989c) 55,886; has suffered many earthquakes; ruins of ancient town nearby; convent of Monte Vergine (founded 1119) pilgrim resort.

Avenches \a-ˈvä^{n}sh\; *anc.* **Aven·ti·cum** \ə-ˈven-ti-kəm\. Commune, Vaud canton, W Switzerland, near Lake of Morat 8 mi. (13 km.) NW of Fribourg; pop. (1980c) 2177; one of oldest cities of Switzerland; ✻ of ancient Helvetia; made Roman colony by Emperors Vespasian and Titus; destroyed c. 260 A.D.; refounded 12th cent. by Burkhardt, bishop of Lausanne. Roman antiquities, incl. ruins of city walls.

Avenio. See AVIGNON 2.

Av·en·tine \ˈa-vən-ˌtīn, -ˌtēn\. One of the Seven Hills of Rome. See SEVEN HILLS.

Aver·nus, Lake \ə-ˈvər-nəs\ *or Ital.* **La·go d'Aver·no** \ˈlä-gō-dä-ˈver-nō\; *anc.* **La·cus Aver·nus** \ˈlā-kəs-ə-ˈvər-nəs\. Lake, Napoli prov., Campania, Italy, in crater of extinct volcano 8 mi. (13 km.) W of Naples; ab. 2 mi. (3 km.) in circumference; because of its sulfurous vapors, considered by ancient Romans (as Roman poet Virgil) as entrance to underworld; grove of Hecate, grotto of the Cumaean Sibyl, and home of the Cimmerii placed nearby in ancient legend; transformed by Roman Gen. Marcus Vipsanius Agrippa into naval base (**Por·tus Iu·li·us** \ˈpōr-təs-ˈyü-lē-əs\), and connected with Lacus Lucrinus.

Aver·sa \ä-ˈver-sä\. Commercial commune, Caserta prov., Campania, S Italy, 8 mi. (13 km.) NNW of Naples; pop. (1989c) 57,817; known for its sparkling white wine (Asprino); built near site of ancient Atella by Normans 1030, being the first settlement in Italy granted them.

Avery \ˈā-və-rē\. County in W North Carolina. See table at NORTH CAROLINA.

Aves, Is·las de \ˈēs-läs-t͟hā-ˈä-b͟äs\ *or* **Islas Las Aves** \läs-ˈä-b͟äs\. Group of small Venezuelan islands in Caribbean Sea E of Bonaire.

Aves Island \ˈä-ˌvās\ *or* **Is·la de Aves** \ˈēs-lä-t͟hā\ *also* **Bird Island** \ˈbərd\. Uninhabited islet in E Caribbean Sea W of N Dominica; belongs to Venezuela, but was the subject of a dispute with Dominica in the 1970s and was at earlier times claimed by a number of different countries.

Avesnes \ä-ˈven\. City, Nord dept., N France, 25 mi. (40 km.) SE of Valenciennes; built around 11th cent. castle; held by

\ə\ abut \ə\ matches \ᵊ\ kitten, Fr table \ər\ further \a\ ash \ā\ ace \ä\ cot, cart \á\ Fr bac \aù\ out \b\ Span Avila \ch\ chin \e\ bet \ē\ easy \g\ go \i\ hit \ī\ ice \j\ job \k͟\ Ger ich, Buch \$^{n}$\ Fr vin \ŋ\ sing \ō\ go \ò\ all \ȯ\ law \œ\ Fr bœuf \œ̄\ Fr feu \òi\ boy \th\ thin \t͟h\ this \ü\ loot \ù\ foot \ue\ Ger füllen \ue̅\ Fr rue \y\ yet \$^{y}$\ Fr digne \ˈdēn^{y}\, nuit \ˈnw^{y}ē\ \yü\ few \yù\ fury \zh\ vision

Spain 1559–1659; captured by Prussians 1815; occupied by Germans in WWI.

Aves·ta \'ä-və-,stä\. Town, Kopparberg prov., Sweden, 92 mi. (148 km.) NW of Stockholm; pop. (1993e) 24,538.

Avey·ron \,ȧ-vā-'rōⁿ\. **1.** River, S France; flows W into Tarn River 7 mi. (11 km.) NW of Montauban; ab. 150 mi. (240 km.) long.

2. Department of S France. See table at FRANCE.

Avez·za·no \,ä-vet-'sä-nō\. Commune, L'Aquila prov., Abruzzi, cen. Italy, 22 mi. (35 km.) S of the commune of L'Aquila; pop. (1991p) 37,076; episcopal see; 15th cent. castle ruins; suffered from earthquake 1915; subsequently rebuilt; heavily damaged in WWII.

Avgustov. See AUGUSTÓW.

Avi·glia·no \,ä-vēl-'yä-nō\. Commune, Potenza prov., Basilicata, S Italy, 7 mi. (11 km.) NNW of the commune of Potenza; pop. (1981p) 11,342; marble deposits and mineral springs.

Avi·gnon \,ȧ-vē-'nyōⁿ\. **1.** County, Quebec, Canada. See table at QUEBEC.

2. *anc.* **Ave·nio** \ə-'vē-nē-,ō\. City, ✻ of Vaucluse dept., SE France, near confluence of Rhone and Durance rivers 50 mi. (80 km.) NNW of Marseille; pop. (1990c) 89,440; ancient cathedral; papal palace; bridge, familiar through popular song "Sur le Pont d'Avignon."

History: Founded as Phocaean colony; conquered by Romans, Goths, Burgundians, Ostrogoths, finally Franks; part of kingdom of Arles (*q.v.*); republic 1135–46; part of Venaissin (see COMTAT VENAISSIN); sold by Joanna I of Naples to Pope Clement VI 1348; seat of Papacy 1309–77 and of Avignonese popes during Western Schism 1378–1417; united to France 1791.

Ávi·la \'ä-bē-lä\. **1.** Province of cen. Spain. See table at SPAIN.

2. *anc.* **Ab·y·la** *or* **Ab·e·la** \'a-bə-lə\. City, its ✻, 53 mi. (85 km.) WNW of Madrid; pop. (1991c) 45,977; founded as walled city in late 11th cent.; cathedral; site of university (1455–1807) founded by Ferdinand II of Aragon and Isabella I of Castile; birthplace of St. Teresa (1515).

Avi·lés \,ä-bē-'lās\. Seaport, Asturias prov., NW Spain, 14 mi. (22 km.) NNW of Oviedo on an inlet of the Bay of Biscay; pop. (1991c) 85,351; coal deposits; fishing.

Avion \ȧv-'yōⁿ\. Commune, Pas-de-Calais dept., N France, 9 mi. (14 km.) NNE of Arras; severe fighting in WWI 1917; taken by Canadians.

Aviz \ə-'vēzh\. Commune, Portalegre dist., E cen. Portugal, 30 mi. (48 km.) SW of the commune of Portalegre; gives name to Portuguese and Brazilian Order of Aviz (founded orig. as Order of Evora late 12th cent.); in early 14th cent. head of the order became king of Portugal inaugurating Aviz dynasty; house ruled to 1850.

Avlona. See VLORË 2.

Avo·ca \ə-'vō-kə\. **1.** Borough, Luzerne co., E Pennsylvania, 7 mi. (11 km.) SW of Scranton; pop. (1990c) 2897; coal deposits.

2. *or* **Ovo·ca** \ə-'vō-kə\. Valley and river in co. Wicklow, E Ireland; celebrated in one of Thomas Moore's songs.

Avo·court \,ȧ-vō-'kür\. Commune, Meuse dept., NE France, 11 mi. (18 km.) NW of Verdun; battles 1916–18, the forest **Bois d'Avocourt** \,bwä-,dȧ-\ being taken by Germans Mar. 1916 and retaken by American forces Sept. 1918.

Avo·la \'ä-vō-lä\. Seaport, Siracusa prov., SE Sicily, Italy, 14 mi. (22 km.) SW of seaport of Siracusa; pop. (1989c) 32,198.

Avon. **1.** \'ā-,vän\. Town, W cen. Hartford co., N Connecticut; pop. (1990c) 13,937; incorp. 1830.

2. \'ā-,vän\. Town, Norfolk co., E Massachusetts, 4 mi. (6.4 km.) N of Brockton; pop. (1990c) 4558; residential suburb of Brockton.

3. \'a-vən\. Village, Livingston co., W New York, on Genesee River 18 mi. (29 km.) S of Rochester; pop. (1990c) 2995.

4. \'ā-,vän\. City, Lorain co., N Ohio, 17 mi. (27 km.) W of Cleveland; pop. (1990c) 7337.

5. \'ā-vən\. Upper course of the Swan River (*q.v.*), Western Australia, Australia; ab. 200 mi. (320 km.) long.

6. \'ā-vən\. Administrative county, SW England; estab. 1974. See table at ENGLAND.

7. *or* **East Avon** \'ā-vən\. River, S England; rises near Devizes in Wiltshire, flows S into English Channel; 48 mi. (77 km.) long.

8. *or* **Lower Avon** \'ā-vən\. River, SW England; rises in Gloucestershire, flows S and W through the city of Bristol into Bristol Channel at Avonmouth; 75 mi. (121 km.) long.

9. *or* **Upper Avon** \'ā-vən\. River, cen. England; rises in Northamptonshire, flows WSW into the Severn at Tewkesbury; 96 mi. (154 km.) long; the "Shakespeare" Avon.

10. \'än, 'ā-vən, 'a-vən\. River, cen. Scotland; flows E into Firth of Forth; 18 mi. (29 km.) long.

Avon, Ben. See BEN AVON.

Av·on–by–the–Sea \'a-vən\. Borough, Monmouth co., E cen. New Jersey; pop. (1990c) 2165; seaside resort.

Av·on·dale \'a-vən-,dāl\. City, Maricopa co., Arizona, W of Phoenix; pop. (1990c) 16,169.

Avon Lake \'ā-,vän\. Village, Lorain co., N Ohio, on Lake Erie 18 mi. (29 km.) W of Cleveland; pop. (1990c) 15,066.

Avon·mouth \'ā-vən-,mau̇th\. Suburb of Bristol, Gloucestershire, SW cen. England, at mouth of the Avon; deep-sea docks of port of Bristol.

Avon Park \'ā-,vän\. City, Highlands co., cen. Florida Penin., 43 mi. (69 km.) SE of Lakeland; pop. (1990c) 8042; South Florida Community Coll. (1965).

Avoy·elles \ə-'vȯi-əlz, ,a-vwä-'yel\. Parish in cen. Louisiana. See table at LOUISIANA.

Avranches \ə-'vräⁿsh\. Commune, Manche dept., NW France, on inlet 32 mi. (51 km.) E of St.-Malo; resort. Once the site of a Roman city; important center of learning in medieval times; site of English King Henry II's reconciliation (1172) with the pope after Archbishop Thomas Becket's murder; in WWII 1944 scene of decisive Allied breakthrough by Gen. George Patton.

Avre \'ävrᵊ\. River, Somme dept., N France; flowing into Somme River near Amiens; 36 mi. (58 km.) long.

Av·şa \äv-'shä\. Island, SW Sea of Marmara, W of Kapudağ Penin., Çanakkale prov., Turkey in Asia.

Awaj \'a-waj, 'ä-\. See PHARPAR.

Awa·ji \ä-'wä-jē\. Island, Japan, in Hyōgo prefecture, E of Harima Sea, S of Honshū, and NE of Shikoku I.; area 230 sq. mi. (596 sq. km.); chief town Sumoto.

Awa·sa \'ä-wä-sä\. Town, S cen. Ethiopia; pop. (1982e) 29,448.

Awash \'ä-wäsh\ *or* **Ha·wash** \'hä-\. River, E Ethiopia; flows NE into the Danakil Desert; ab. 500 mi. (800 km.) long.

Awe, Loch \'ȯ\. Lake, Strathclyde region, cen. Scotland; 24 mi. (39 km.) long; 16 sq. mi. (41 sq. km.); max. depth 307 ft. (94 m.); extends NNE to base of Ben Cruachan; empties by means of **Awe River** into Loch Etive.

Aw·ji·dah \ȯ-'jē-də\; *formerly* **Au·gi·la** \au̇-'jē-lə\. Oasis and town, Libya, ab. 200 mi. (320 km.) SSE of Benghazi.

Aw·ka \'ȯ-kä\. City, ✻ of Anambra state, S Nigeria; pop. (1993e) 103,100.

Awu, Gu·nung *or Du.* **Goe·noeng Awoe** \'gü-,nu̇ŋ-'ä-wü\. Volcanic peak on Sangihe I., Sangihe Is. (*q.v.*), Indonesia; major eruptions 1856, 1892.

Ax. See DAX.

Ax·ar Fjord \'äk-,sär\. Inlet of the Arctic Ocean on N coast of Iceland, E of Eyja Fjord.

Axel Hei·berg \'äk-səl-'hī-,bərg\. One of the Sverdrup Is. (*q.v.*), N Canada, W of Ellesmere I.; 15,779 sq. mi. (40,868 sq. km.).

Ax·im \ä-'shēm, 'ak-sim\. Coast town, SW Ghana, at mouth of Ankobra River ab. 30 mi. (48 km.) W of Takoradi.

Axiós, Axius. See VARDAR.

Ax·min·ster \'ak-,smin-stər\. Town, Devon, England, on Axe River 23 mi. (37 km.) ENE of Exeter; formerly (1755–1835) famous for its carpets.

Axona. See AISNE.

Axum. See AKSUM.

Aya·cu·cho \,ī-ä-'kü-chō\. Town, S Peru, 200 mi. (322 km.) SE of Lima; pop. (1990e) 101,600; alt. above 9025 ft. (2750 m.); textiles, pottery; tourism; university (1677); founded 1539 by Spanish conquistador Francisco Pizarro and known as Guamanga or Huamanga until 1825; decisive battle on small plain of Ayacucho, near the village of La Quinua, Dec. 9, 1824, in which the Spanish viceroy José de La Serna y Hinojosa was defeated by Gen. Antonio José de Sucre, won independence for Peru.

Aya·guz \ˌä-yə-ˈgüs\. **1.** River, E Kazakhstan; flows generally SW into NE end of Lake Balkhash; ab. 240 mi. (386 km.) long.
2. *formerly* **Ser·gi·o·pol** \ˌsər-gē-ˈō-pəl\. Town, E Kazakhstan, on Ayaguz River 185 mi. (298 km.) S of Semey; on Turkistan-Siberian R.R.

Aya·mon·te \ˌä-yä-ˈmōn-tā\. Seaport, Huelva prov., SW Spain, on left bank of Guadiana River near its mouth, 23 mi. (37 km.) W of Huelva; pop. (1991c) 15,082.

Aya·se \ä-ˈyä-sā\. City, Kanagawa prefecture, Honshū, Japan; pop. (1990p) 77,926.

Aya Soluk. See SELÇUK.

ʻAybāl, Jabal. See EBAL, MOUNT.

Ay·den \ˈā-dən\. Town, Pitt co., E North Carolina, 35 mi. (56 km.) E of Goldsboro; pop. (1990c) 4740.

Ay·dın *or* **Ai·din** \ī-ˈdən\. **1.** Province of Turkey in Asia. See table at TURKEY.
2. *anc.* **Tral·les** \ˈtra-lēz\. Town, its ✱, on Menderes River 55 mi. (88 km.) SE of İzmir; pop. (1990c) 107,011; railroad and trading town. In ancient times Tralles was a flourishing city of Lydia.

Ayer \ˈar\. Town, Middlesex co., NE Massachusetts, 10 mi. (16 km.) E of Fitchburg; pop. (1990c) 6871; WWII WAC training center nearby.

Ayer's Cliff \ˈarz\. Village, S Quebec, Canada, 18 mi. (29 km.) S of Sherbrooke; pop. (1991c) 821.

Ayers Rock \ˈarz\ *or aboriginal* **Ulu·ru** \ü-ˈlü-rü\. Outcrop, cen. Australia, in SW Northern Terr.; 1143 ft. (348 m.) high; ownership returned to aborigines 1985.

Áyion Óros. See ATHOS, MOUNT.

Áyios Dhi·mí·tri·os \ˈä-yē-ōs-t͟hē-ˈmē-trē-ōs\. City, Greece, a S suburb of Athens.

Áyios Evstrátios. See HAGIOS EVSTRÁTIOS.

Áyiosilías, Mount. See HAGIOS ELIAS, MOUNT.

Áyi·os Ni·kó·la·os \ˈä-yē-ˌōs-nē-ˈkō-lä-ˌōs\ *or* **Ági·os Ni·kólaos** \ˈä-gē-\ *also* **Ha·gi·os Nikólaos** \ˈhä-gē-ˌōs-ni-ˈkō-lə-ˌōs\. Seaport town, ✱ of Lasithion dept., E Crete, Greece; on W shore of Mirabello Gulf; pop. (1981p) 8194.

Ayles·bury \ˈālz-bə-rē, -ˌber-ē\. Town, ⊗ of Buckinghamshire, SE cen. England, 32 mi. (51 km.) NW of London; in Thames valley (**Vale of Aylesbury**); engineering, food processing; historically notable lace industry.

Ayl·mer \ˈāl-mər\. **1.** Town, Elgin co., SE Ontario, Canada, 11 mi. (18 km.) E of St. Thomas; pop. (1991c) 6244.
2. Resort town, SW Quebec, Canada, on Ottawa River 7 mi. (11 km.) W of Hull; pop. (1991c) 32,244.

Aylmer, Lake. Lake, E cen. mainland portion of Northwest Territories, Canada; 340 sq. mi. (881 sq. km.).

ʻAyn Jālūt. See AIN JALUT.

Ayodhya. See AJODHYA.

Ay·ot Saint Law·rence \ˈā-ət-sānt-ˈlȯr-əns, sənt-, ˈlär-\. Village, cen. Hertfordshire, England, NW of Welwyn Garden City; home of author George Bernard Shaw.

Ayr \ˈar\. **1.** Coastal town, Queensland, Australia; pop. (1991c) 8637.
2. *or* **Ayr·shire** \-ˌshir, -shər\. Former county, SW Scotland; chief towns: Ayr, Kilmarnock, Prestwick, Irvine, Girvan, Troon; rivers Ayr and Doon.
3. Seaport, its ⊗; pop. (1981p) 49,481; machinery, metal goods.

Ayre, Point of \ˈar\. N extremity of the Isle of Man, Irish Sea; lighthouse.

Ayuthaya *or* **Ayuthia.** See PHRA NAKHON SI AYUTTHAYA.

Ayu·tla \ä-ˈyüt-lä\ *or in full* **Ayutla de los Li·bres** \ˌt͟hā-lōs-ˈlē-b͟rās\. Town, Guerrero state, S Mexico, 45 mi. (72 km.) E of Acapulco; plan of Ayutla (1854), demanding President Antonio López de Santa Anna's removal, framing of new constitution, and establishment of representative government, was program of revolution led by Juan Álvarez 1855.

Ayutthaya. See PHRA NAKHON SI AYUTTHAYA.

Ay·va·lık \ˌī-vä-ˈlək\ *also* **Ai·va·li** \ˌī-vä-ˈlē\; *anc.* **Her·a·clea** \ˌher-ə-ˈklē-ə\. Coastal town, NW Turkey in Asia, on strait opp. Lesbos I.

ʻAyzarīyah, Al–. See AL-ʻAYZARĪYAH.

Azam·garh \ˈə-zəm-gər, ˈä-\. Town, in Uttar Pradesh, N India; pop. (1991c) 78,382.

Azamor. See AZEMMOUR.

Aza·na·que \ˌä-sä-ˈnä-kā\. Peak, W Bolivia, on SE shore of Lake Poopó; 16,840 ft. (5133 m.).

Azbine. See AÏR.

Az·ca·po·tzal·co \ˌäs-kə-pət-ˈsäl-kō\. City, Federal District, cen. Mexico, NW of Mexico City.

Azem·mour *also* **Aza·mor** \ˌa-zə-ˈmür\. Seaport, NW Morocco.

Azer·bai·jan \ˌa-zər-bī-ˈjän, ˌä-, -ˈzhän\. **1.** *anc.* **At·ro·pa·te·ne** \ˌa-trō-pə-ˈtē-nē\ *or* **Me·dia Atropatene** \ˈmēd-ē-ə\. Former province, NW Iran, now divided into **East Azerbaijan** and **West Azerbaijan** (see table at IRAN); mountainous country that includes Orūmīyeh Lake, and one of the most fertile regions of Iran; occupied by Soviet forces WWII; returned to Iranian control 1946–47. Ancient Media Atropatene (see MEDIA) nearly coincided with the former province; it was the N part of Media and for some time after the death of Macedonian King Alexander the Great was an independent kingdom.
2. *officially* **Republic of Azerbaijan.** Country, SW Asia, in E Transcaucasia, bounded on N by Republic of Georgia and Dagestan Rep. (of Russia), on E by the Caspian Sea, on S by Iran, and on W by Armenia; 33,436 sq. mi. (86,599 sq. km.); pop. (1992e) 7,237,000; ✱ Baku. It includes Naxçıvan and Nagorno-Karabakh. Central part is a plain through which flow the Kura River and its tributaries, esp. the Araks whose upper course forms part of boundary with Iran; N of the plain is E end of Caucasus Mts.
Chief products: Barley, corn, cotton, rice, tea, fruit, tobacco; oil, copper.
Chief towns: Baku, Gäncä, Sumqayit.
History: In ancient times home of Scythian tribes and part of Roman Empire; in medieval times overrun by Turks in 11th cent.; after fall of Turkic ruler Timur site of several Tatar khanates, esp. Shirvan; again under Persians in 17th cent.; larger part conquered by Russia early 19th cent.; scene of fighting in WWI; with part of Azerbaijan prov. of Persia set up as a republic 1918; invaded by Soviet troops 1920; established a Soviet government 1920; as member of Transcaucasian Federation (*q.v.*) joined U.S.S.R. 1922; comprised **Azerbaijan Soviet Socialist Republic** 1936–91; ethnic rivalry created political instability in late 1980s; Soviet army intervened 1990; the republic declared its independence 1991; declined to join Commonwealth of Independent States 1992.

Azil, Le Mas d'. See LE MAS D'AZIL.

Azincourt. See AGINCOURT.

ʻAzīzīyah, Al. See AL ʻAZĪZĪYAH.

Azle \ˈā-zəl\. City, Parker and Tarrant cos., N Texas, 15 mi. (24 km.) NW of Fort Worth; pop. (1990c) 8868.

Azof. See AZOV.

Azo·gues \ä-ˈsō-ges\. City, ✱ of Cañar prov., W cen. Ecuador, 80 mi. (129 km.) ESE of Guayaquil; pop. (1990c) 21,060.

Azores \ə-ˈzōrz, ˈā-ˌzōrz\ *or Port.* **Aço·res** \ə-ˈsō-rish\. Group of nine islands and several islets constituting an autonomous region of Portugal in the N Atlantic Ocean, bet. lat. 36°50′ and 39°44′N and long. 25° and 31°16′W; ab. 800 mi. (1290 km.) off the coast of Portugal; 905 sq. mi (2344 sq. km.).; pop. (1991p) 241,592; chief islands: Flores, Corvo, Terceira, São Jorge, Pico, Faial, Graciosa, São Miguel, and Santa Maria; highest point Pico Alto 7713 ft. (2351 m.). See table at PORTUGAL.

Chief town: Ponta Delgada. Other towns Horta and Angra do Heroísmo.

Chief exports: Fruits, grain, fish, and wines.

History: Date of discovery uncertain, but existence known in Europe in 14th cent.; visited by Portuguese navigator Diogo de Sevilha 1427–31; known for a time as Flemish Is. owing to Flemish settlement which followed gift of Faial to Isabella of Burgundy 1466; assigned to Portugal by Treaty of Alcatçovas 1480; subject to Spain 1580–1640; famous sea fight off Flores 1591 bet. *Revenge* under British naval commander Sir Richard Grenville and Spanish fleet; contested by rival claimants of Portuguese crown 1830–31. In WWII naval and air bases granted Great Britain 1943. In agreement with Portugal became site for American NATO base 1951.

Azotos *or* **Azotus.** See ASHDOD.

Azov *or* **Azof** \ə-ˈzȯf; ˈä-ˌzȯf, ˈa-\. Town, SW Rostov Oblast, S Russia in Europe, near mouth of Don River on S shore of E end of Gulf of Taganrog; pop. (1991e) 80,700; fishing. It is near site of ancient Tanais, a Greek colony. Captured by Vladimir I, grand prince of Kiev, in 10th cent. and by Genoese in 13th cent., who fortified it and made it a trading port for Oriental goods; sacked by Turkic ruler Timur 1395; held alternately by Russians and Turks until 1739 when it was secured to Russia under Empress Anna.

Azov, Sea of *or* **Sea of Azof** *or Russ.* **Azov·sko·ye Mo·re** \ə-ˈzȯf-skə-yə-ˈmȯr-yə\; *anc.* **Pa·lus Mae·o·tis** \ˈpā-ləs-mē-ˈō-tis\. Sea, bet. Crimea, Ukraine and Rostov Oblast and Krasnodar Kray, Russia in Europe; ab. 200 mi. (320 km.) long; 14,517 sq. mi. (37,599 sq. km.); connected with Black Sea on S by Kerch Strait; shallow, sandy shores (see ARABAT SPIT); its NE arm, the Gulf of Taganrog, receives the Don River.

Az·pei·tia \äs-ˈpāt-ē-ä\. Commune, Guipúzcoa prov., N Spain, 17 mi. (27 km.) SW of San Sebastián; pop. (1991c) 13,427; mineral springs; site nearby (on road to W) of the Santa Casa, said to be birthplace of St. Ignatius of Loyola.

Azraq, Bahr al–. See NILE.

Az·tec \ˈaz-ˌtek\. City, ⊗ of San Juan co., NW corner of New Mexico; pop. (1990c) 5479.

Aztec Mountain. Peak, La Plata co., SW Colorado; 13,200 ft. (4023 m.).

Aztec Ruins National Monument. See UNITED STATES, *National Monuments.*

Azua \ˈäs-wä\. **1.** Province, S Dominican Republic. See table at DOMINICAN REPUBLIC.

2. *or* **Azua de Com·pos·te·la** \thā-ˌkōm-pō-ˈstā-lä\. Town, its ✻, on S coast; pop. (1981p) 63,556.

Azua·ga \ä-ˈswä-gä\. Commune, Badajoz prov., SW Spain, NW of Córdoba; pop. (1991c) 9935.

Azuay \ä-ˈswī\. Province of S Ecuador. See table at ECUADOR.

Azúcar, Pan de. See PAN DE AZÚCAR.

Azue·ro Peninsula \ä-ˈswā-rō\. Peninsula on S Panama coast, W of Gulf of Panama.

Azu·fre \ä-ˈsü-frā\. Volcanic peak, SE corner of Antofagasta prov., N Chile, near Argentina border; 18,635 ft. (5680 m.).

Azufre, Pa·so del \ˈpä-sō-thel-\. Andean mountain pass bet. W cen. Argentina and E cen. Chile.

Azul \ä-ˈsül\. **1.** Peak, S Los Andes prov., NW Argentina; 16,600 ft. (5060 m.).

2. City, Buenos Aires prov., E Argentina, 170 mi. (274 km.) SW of Buenos Aires; pop. (1980p) 43,582.

Azu·ma \ˈä-zü-ˌmä\. Volcano, one of a group of peaks on S boundary of Yamagata prefecture, N Honshū, Japan, W of Fukushima; ab. 6775 ft. (2065 m.); major eruption 1900.

Azu·sa \ə-ˈzü-sə\. City, Los Angeles co., SW California, 18 mi. (29 km.) E of the city of Los Angeles; pop. (1990c) 41,333; citrus fruit grown nearby; Azusa Pacific Univ. (1899); settled 1887.

Aẓ Ẓahrān. See DHAHRAN.

Az–Zaqāzīq. See ZAGAZIG.

Az–Zarqā'. See ZARQA 2.

Az–Zā·wi·yah \ˌaz-ˈzä-wē-yə\ *also* **Zā·wia** \ˈzä-wē-ə\. Coastal town, NW Libya, ab. 30 mi. (48 km.) WSW of Tripoli.

Az Zuqar. See ZUQAR.

Az Zuwaytīnah. See QARYAT AZ ZUWAYTĪNAH.

B

Ba. See MBA.

Ba·al·bek \'bä-əl-ˌbek, 'bäl-ˌbek\ *or* **Ba·'al·bek** \'bä-ˌäl-, 'bal-\ *or* **Ba'·la·bakk** \'bä-lə-ˌbäk\; *anc.* **He·li·op·o·lis** \ˌhē-lē-'ä-pə-lis\. Village, E Lebanon, 35 mi. (56 km.) N of Damascus and on railroad and highway from Beirut to Aleppo; in ancient times a city of great size and importance, built on the lower W slope of the Anti-Lebanon Mts.; its identification with the worship of Baal as a Semitic sun-god gave rise to its Greek name Heliopolis, "City of the Sun"; made a Roman colony by Gen. Julius Caesar. Its ruins cover a great area; most of the buildings erected under the Romans, esp. during reign of Antoninus Pius (138–161).

Baar·le–Her·tog \'bär-lə-'her-ˌtȯk\. Belgian exclave in Netherlands, ab. 22 mi. (35 km.) W of Eindhoven; 3 sq. mi. (7.8 sq. km.); pop. (1991c) 2126.

Baarn \'bärn\. Commune, Utrecht prov., cen. Netherlands, 11 mi. (18 km.) NE of the city of Utrecht; resort.

Ba·ba, Cape \bä-'bä\ *or Turk.* **Baba Bur·nu** \bu̇r-'nü\; *anc.* **Lec·tum** \'lek-təm\. Cape on W coast of Turkey in Asia, 39°29′N, 26°04′E, N of entrance to Gulf of Edremit; most westerly point of Asia.

Bā·bā Mountains \bä-'bä\ *or* **Koh–i–Baba** \'kō-hē-\. Mountain range, E cen. Afghanistan; a SW extension of the Hindu Kush; highest peak Shah Fulādi 16,872 ft. (5143 m.).

Ba·ba·ho·yo \ˌbäb-ə-'hō-ˌyō\; *formerly* **Bo·de·gas** \bō-'t͟hā-gäs\. **1.** River, W cen. Ecuador; its estuary known as the Guayas River (*q.v.*); navigable for ab. 200 mi. (322 km.).
2. Town, ✻ of Los Ríos prov., W cen. Ecuador, 40 mi. (64 km.) NE of Guayaquil; pop. (1990c) 50,285.

Bab al–Zakak. See GIBRALTAR, STRAIT OF.

Ba·bar Islands \'bä-ˌbär\. Island group of Maluku prov., Indonesia, on S side of Banda Sea ENE of Timor I. and W of Tanimbar Is.; 314 sq. mi. (813 sq. km.); comprises **Babar Island** (the only large island, 220 sq. mi. or 570 sq. km.) and five small islands; densely forested.

Ba·bel \'bā-bəl, 'ba-\. Biblical city in the plain of Shinar (*Gen.* x. 10; xi. 1–9).

Babeldoab. See BABELTHUAP.

Bab el Man·deb \'bȧb-äl-'mȧn-deb\ *or* **Bab al–Man·dab** \-ˌdȧb\. Strait bet. SW Arabian Penin. and the African coast, uniting Red Sea and Gulf of Aden (Indian Ocean); 20 mi. (32 km.) wide.

Ba·bels·berg \'bä-bəls-ˌberk\; *formerly* **No·wa·wes** \ˌnō-vä-'väs\. Former city, now part of Potsdam, E Germany; 18th cent. palace; founded by Prussian King Frederick the Great 1751.

Ba·bel·thu·ap \ˌbä-bəl-'tü-ˌäp\ *also* **Ba·bel·doab** \-'dō-ˌäb\. Largest island of Palau group in W Pacific Ocean, ab. 27 mi. (43 km.) long and bet. 1 and 8 mi. (2 and 13 km.) wide; 143 sq. mi. (370 sq. km.); mountainous, well-wooded, and fertile.

Ba·bia Gó·ra \'bäb-yə-'gü-rə\. Peak, highest of the Beskids, W Carpathian Mts., in West Beskids on border bet. Slovakia and Poland; 5659 ft. (1725 m.).

Ba·bine Lake \ba-'bēn\. Long narrow lake, cen. British Columbia, Canada; 194 sq. mi. (503 sq. km.); drains N through **Babine River** (ab. 55 mi. or 89 km. long) into Skeena River.

Babine Mountains. Range of the Coast Mts. in W cen. British Columbia, Canada; highest point ab. 8000 ft. (2438 m.).

Bā·bol \bä-'bōl\ *also* **Ba·bul** \bä-'bül\; *formerly* **Bar·fu·rush** \ˌbär-fü-'rüsh\ *or* **Bal·frush** \bäl-'früsh\. City, N Iran, 15 mi. (24 km.) S of the Caspian Sea, in Māzandarān prov.; pop. (1986c) 115,320; trading center; nearby is resort of **Bābol Sar** \'sär\.

Ba·bo·qui·va·ri Mountains \ˌbä-bō-ki-'vär-ē\. Small range in S Pima co., S Arizona; highest point 7730 ft. (2356 m.).

Ba·bor Mountains \bä-'bȯr\. Range of Little Atlas Mts., N Algeria; highest point ab. 6560 ft. (2000 m.).

Babruysk. See BOBRUYSK.

Ba·bu·na \'bä-bü-ˌnä\. Mountain range, cen. Republic of Macedonia, N of Bitola.

Ba·bush·kin \'bä-bu̇sh-ˌkin\; *formerly* **Lo·si·no·os·trovsk** \ˌləs-yi-nə-ə-'strȯfsk\. Former city, Moscow Oblast, U.S.S.R.; incorp. into the city of Moscow 1960.

Ba·bu·yan \ˌbä-bu̇-'yän\. Island in Babuyan group, N of Luzon, Philippines; 28 sq. mi. (73 sq. km.).

Babuyan Channel. Passage bet. Babuyan Is. and N Luzon, Philippines; ab. 135 mi. (217 km.) long and 25 mi. (40 km.) wide.

Babuyan Cla·ro \'klä-rō\. Active volcano, Babuyan I., Philippines; 3569 ft. (1088 m.).

Babuyan Islands *or* **Ba·bu·ya·nes** \bä-bü-'yä-nās\. Island group, N Philippines, N of Luzon; belongs to Cagayan prov.; contains 24 islands; ab. 225 sq. mi. (583 sq. km.); of volcanic origin; chief islands: Babuyan, Camiguin, Calayan, Fuga, and Dalupiri.

Bab·y·lon \'ba-bə-lən, -ˌlän\. **1.** Village, Suffolk co., SE New York, on Great South Bay on Long Island, 37 mi. (56 km.) E of New York City; pop. (1990c) 12,249.
2. Ancient city, now in ruins, on Euphrates River ab. 55 mi. (89 km.) S of Baghdad, Iraq, near modern Al Ḩillah; ✻ of Babylonia.

History: Ancient town probably in existence from 3d millennium B.C.; one of a number of small city-kingdoms of Babylonia, it was seized by Semitic Amorites around the turn of the 2d millennium B.C.; under Amoritic line of kings (c. 2050–1750 B.C.) of which Hammurabi was greatest, became ✻ of Old Empire of Babylonia and chief commercial city of Tigris-Euphrates Valley; ruled by Kassites and Assyrians (see BABYLONIA); destroyed by Assyrian King Sennacherib 689 B.C. but rebuilt; ✻ of Neo-Babylonian Empire (see CHALDEA) 625–538 B.C.; attained greatest glory under Nebuchadrezzar II 605–562 B.C.; captured by Persian King Cyrus the Great c. 538 B.C. and in 331 B.C. by Macedonian King Alexander the Great who died there 323 B.C.; gradual commercial decline accelerated by removal of ✻ to Seleucia (*q.v.*) by Seleucus I Nicator (312–280 B.C.).

Bab·y·lo·nia \ˌba-bə-'lō-nyə, -nē-ə\. Ancient country in the lower Euphrates Valley, SW Asia, coinciding with the plain bet. Baghdad, Iraq, and the Persian Gulf. See 'IRAQ 'ARABI.

History: For earliest historic period, see SUMER and AKKAD. City-kingdom of Babylon attained hegemony under first dynasty (Amoritic) 2050–1750 B.C.; led by Hammurabi (c. 1790–1750 B.C.), 6th and greatest ruler of first dynasty, conquered all of Mesopotamia and spread its administration (Code of Hammurabi) and civilization over entire area; raided by Hittites; conquered and ruled by Kassites, a non-Semitic people, c. 1570–1180 B.C.; invaded by Arameans in 11th and 10th cents. B.C.; devastated by wars with Assyria (*q.v.*) which ruled Babylon 722–626 B.C.; ruled 625–538 B.C. by Chaldea (*q.v.*); under Chaldean (Neo-Babylonian) Empire controlled Mesopotamia and Syria, captured Jerusalem c. 588 B.C. thus initiating the Babylonian captivity of the Jews; empire broke up at fall of Babylon c. 538 B.C.; ruled by Persia 538–331 B.C. when Macedonian King Alexander the Great captured Babylon, by Seleucids 312–171 B.C., by Parthians 171 B.C.–226 A.D., and by Sassanids 226–641 A.D. (see IRAN).

Ba·ca \'bā-kə\. County in SE corner of Colorado. See table at COLORADO.

\ə\ abut \ˈə\ matches \$^{ə}$\ kitten, Fr table \ər\ further \a\ ash \ā\ ace \ä\ cot, cart \ȧ\ Fr bac \au̇\ out \b̲\ Span Avila \ch\ chin \e\ bet \ē\ easy \g\ go \i\ hit \ī\ ice \j\ job \k̲\ Ger ich, Buch \$^{n}$\ Fr vin \ŋ\ sing \ō\ go \ȯ\ all \ȯ\ law \œ\ Fr bœuf \œ̄\ Fr feu \ȯi\ boy \th\ thin \t͟h\ this \ü\ loot \u̇\ foot \ue\ Ger füllen \ue̅\ Fr rue \y\ yet \$^{y}$\ Fr digne \'dēn^{y}\, nuit \'nw^{y}ē\ \yü\ few \yu̇\ fury \zh\ vision

Ba·ca·bal \ˌbə-kə-ˈbäl\. Municipality, Maranhão state, NE Brazil, ab. 125 mi. (201 km.) SSW of São Luís; pop. (1991p) 98,817.

Ba·ca·cay \ˌbä-kä-ˈkī\. Municipality on E coast of Albay prov., Luzon, Philippines, on Tabaco Bay, ab. 10 mi. (16 km.) N of Legazpi.

Ba·can *also* **Ba·tjan** *or* **Ba·chian** \ˈbä-ˌchän\. Largest island of a group in Moluccas, Indonesia, Malay Archipelago, just SW of Halmarhera; 50 mi. (81 km.) long by ab. 27 mi. (43 km.) wide; 914 sq. mi. (2367 sq. km.); irregular in shape, mountainous and volcanic; highest point 6926 ft. (2111 m.); remarkable for its fauna and flora. Formerly a sultanate; seized by Dutch 1609 and put under control of sultan of Ternate. The group (2268 sq. mi. or 5874 sq. km.) includes the smaller islands of Kasiruta and Mandioli to the W and the large group of Obi Is. (*q.v.*) to the S.

Ba·cău \bə-ˈkau̇\. **1.** County of E cen. Romania. See table at ROMANIA.
2. City, its ⊗, on Bistriţa River; pop. (1989c) 193,269; paper, textiles, chemicals, aircraft, woodworking products, pulp, leather, building materials, foodstuffs.

Bachian. See BACAN.

Bachi Channel. See BASHI CHANNEL.

Bač·ka *or* **Bach·ka** \ˈbäch-kȧ\. Former subprovince in N Yugoslavia; now represented approx. by W part of Vojvodina autonomous region.

Back Alleghany Mountains. Ridge running N and S in Pocahontas co., E cen. West Virginia.

Back Bay \ˌbak-ˈbā\. Fashionable residential neighborhood of Boston, Massachusetts.

Back·bone Mountain \ˈbak-ˌbōn\. Mountain, Garrett co., W extremity of Maryland; 3360 ft. (1024 m.); highest point in the state; extends SW into N West Virginia.

Backergunge. See BAKARGANJ.

Back·nang \ˈbäk-ˌnäŋ\. City, Baden-Württemberg, S Germany, 18 mi. (29 km.) NE of Stuttgart; became city 1245.

Back River; *formerly* **Great Fish River.** River, N Canada; rises in lakes along Northwest Territories-Nunavut border, flows NE through Lake Pelly and Garry Lake into Chantrey Inlet; 605 mi. (974 km.) long.

Back·stairs Passage \ˈbak-ˌstarz\. Channel bet. E end of Kangaroo I. and mainland of South Australia, Australia; ab. 7 mi. (11 km.) wide; forms SE entrance to Gulf St. Vincent.

Bac Ninh \ˈbäk-ˈnin\. Town, N Vietnam, on railroad line 16 mi. (26 km.) NE of Hanoi.

Ba·co, Mount \ˈbä-kō\. Mountain, cen. Mindoro I., Philippines; 8163 ft. (2488 m.).

Ba·co·lod \bä-ˈkō-ˌlōd\. Chartered city, ✻ of Negros Occidental, Negros, Philippines, on Guimaras Strait opp. Guimaras I.; pop. (1990p) 364,000; university (1957).

Ba·co·lor \ˌbä-kō-ˈlōr\. Municipality, Luzon, Philippines, 3 mi. (5 km.) SW of San Fernando; former ✻ of Pampanga prov.

Ba·con \ˈbā-kən\. County in SE Georgia. See table at GEORGIA.

Ba·co·or \ˌbä-kō-ˈōr\. Municipality, NE Cavite prov., Luzon, Philippines, on shore of Bacoor Bay SE of City of Cavite and ab. 9 mi. (15 km.) SSW of Manila.

Bacoor Bay. Large inlet of SE Manila Bay, Philippines, on Cavite shore S of Cavite Penin.; inner anchorage of Cavite naval base.

Bács–Kis·kun \ˈbäch-ˈkēsh-kün\. County of S cen. Hungary. See table at HUNGARY.

Bactra. See BALKH 2.

Bac·tria \ˈbak-trē-ə\ *also* **Bac·tri·a·na** \ˌbak-trē-ˈa-nə, -ˈä-, -ˈā-\. Ancient country of SW Asia; ab. 250 mi. (402 km.) long by 120 mi. (193 km.) wide, bet. Hindu Kush and Oxus River; ✻ Bactra; partly desert; home of nomadic people, the Bactrians; made part of the Persian Empire by Cyrus the Great (550–529 B.C.); conquered by Macedonian King Alexander the Great 328 B.C.; from 302 B.C. ruled as province of Seleucid empire; under its Greek satrap, Diodotus, revolted and became independent kingdom c. 250 B.C.; expanded to include part of Afghanistan and of Punjab; after 135 B.C., kingdom destroyed by invasion of possibly Sacae, mixed Scythian, Tatar, and Chinese tribes. Region later became known as Balkh (*q.v.*); conquered by Muslims 7th cent. A.D.

Ba·cup \ˈbā-kəp\. Town, Lancashire, NW England, on the Irwell River 21 mi. (34 km.) N of Manchester; coal deposits.

Bad \ˈbad\. River, S cen. South Dakota; rises in E Pennington co., flows E into Missouri River opp. Pierre; ab. 110 mi. (177 km.) long.

Ba·da·csony \ˈbö-dö-ˌchōnʸ\. Plateau region, Hungary, NW of Lake Balaton; produces white wine.

Ba·da·joz \ˌbä-t͟hä-ˈhōs\. **1.** Province of SW Spain. See table at SPAIN.
2. *anc.* **Pax Au·gus·ta** \ˈpaks-ȯ-ˈgəs-tə\. City, its ✻, 52 mi. (84 km.) SW of Cáceres near Portuguese border, on left bank of Guadiana River; pop. (1991c) 122,225; food processing; 13th cent. cathedral. Center of 11th cent. Moorish kingdom; captured c. 1227 by Alfonso IX of León; besieged by Portuguese 1660 and by allies 1705 (War of the Spanish Succession); besieged and taken by French during Peninsular War, retaken by British Gen. Sir Arthur Wellesley, (later first duke of Wellington) 1812; besieged during Spanish Civil War (1936–39).

Ba·dakh·shān \ˌbä-däk-ˈshän\. Mountainous region, NE Afghanistan bet. the upper Amu Dar'ya on the N and the Hindu Kush Range on the S, with the Kundūz River as its W boundary; wheat, barley, corn, cotton; livestock; in ancient times a part of the Greek Bactria.

Badakhshan. See GORNO-BADAKHSHAN.

Ba·da·lo·na \ˌbä-dä-ˈlō-nä\; *anc.* **Bae·tu·lo** \ˈbē-chu̇-ˌlō\. Seaport, Barcelona prov., NE Spain; a N industrial suburb of the city of Barcelona; pop. (1991c) 218,725.

Ba·dâ·ri, El. See EL BADÂRI.

Bad Axe \ˈbad-ˌaks\. City, ⊗ of Huron co., E Michigan, 15 mi. (24 km.) S of mouth of Saginaw Bay; pop. (1990c) 3484.

Bad Cann·statt \ˈbät-ˈkän-ˌshtät\ *also* **Cannstatt.** N suburb of Stuttgart, Baden-Württemberg, S Germany; mineral springs; received munic. charter 1330; site of discovery 1700 of human skull (the Cannstatt skull) thought to be representative of a Neolithic race.

Bad·deck \bə-ˈdek\. Village (unincorporated), ⊗ of Victoria co., NE Nova Scotia, Canada, on N arm of Bras d'Or Lake 30 mi. (48 km.) W of Sydney; pop. (1991c) 1064; scene of first airplane flight in British Empire Feb. 23, 1909.

Bad Do·be·ran \ˌbät-ˌdō-bə-ˈrän\. Town, Mecklenburg-West Pomerania, N Germany, ab. 2 mi. (3 km.) from shore of Mecklenburg Bay 7 mi. (11 km.) W of Rostock; resort; ruins of 12th cent. Cistercian abbey; 14th cent. Gothic church.

Bad Dürk·heim \bät-ˈdu̇rk-ˌhīm\ *also* **Dürkheim.** Town, Rhineland-Palatinate, W Germany, 15 mi. (24 km.) NW of Speyer; pop. (1992e) 17,566; mineral springs; health resort; in 11th cent. associated with a Benedictine abbey.

Bad Ems \bät-ˈems, bäd-ˈemz\ *or* **Ems.** Town, Rhineland-Palatinate, W Germany, on the Lahn River 11 mi. (18 km.) SE of Koblenz; health resort; here on Aug. 25, 1786 the four Roman Catholic archbishops of Cologne, Trier, Mainz, and Salzburg prepared the Punctuation of Ems asserting episcopal rights against the pope; also scene of interview bet. the king of Prussia and the French ambassador July 13, 1870 resulting in the sending by Prussian statesman Otto von Bismarck of the famous Ems dispatch, a direct cause of the Franco-Prussian War 1870–71.

Ba·den \ˈbād-ᵊn\. Residential borough, Beaver co., W Pennsylvania, 19 mi. (31 km.) NW of Pittsburgh; pop. (1990c) 5074.

Baden \ˈbäd-ᵊn\. **1.** *or* **Baden bei Wien** \bī-ˈvēn\; *anc.* **Aq·uae Pa·no·ni·ae** \ˈa-kwē-pə-ˈnō-nē-ˌē, ˈä-\. Commune, Lower Austria, Austria, 14 mi. (23 km.) S of Vienna; pop. (1991c) 23,998; famous for warm mineral springs frequented since Roman times.
2. Former German state, now part of Baden-Württemberg state, S Germany; 5817 sq. mi. (15,066 sq. km.); ✻ Karlsruhe.

History: Became political unit when Frederick, son of margrave of Verona, took title of margrave of Baden 1112; split up and reunited many times before final reunion of all territories under Margrave Charles Frederick 1771; became new electorate 1803; supported French Emperor Napoléon against Austria in War of Third Coalition and received rest of Hapsburg territory in W Germany and rank of grand duchy 1805 (Treaty of Pressburg: see BRATISLAVA); member of Confederation of Rhine until joining allies against Napoléon 1813; member of German Confederation 1815; received constitution 1818; joined Zollverein 1835; became a leader of German liberal movement and center of action in revolution 1848–49; supported Austria against Prussia 1866; forced to pay indemnity and become military ally of Prussia; joined North German Confederation 1870 and German Empire 1871; proclaimed republic 1918; under new constitution became part of Weimar Republic 1919; S part became a state of West Germany 1949, N part incorp. in Württemberg-Baden state; following a referendum (1951) both states merged to form Baden-Württemberg state (1952).

3. City, S Germany. See BADEN-BADEN.

4. Commune, Aargau canton, N cen. Switzerland, 13 mi. (21 km.) ENE of Aarau; old castle; its sulfur springs and baths known since Roman times.

Baden–Baden \ˈbäd-ᵊn-ˈbäd-ᵊn\ *or* **Baden;** *anc.* **Au·re·lia Aquen·sis** \ȯ-ˈrēl-yə-ə-ˈkwen-sis\. City, Baden-Württemberg, S Germany, 18 mi. (29 km.) SSW of Karlsruhe; pop. (1992e) 52,524; tourist resort; its thermal baths frequented since Roman times.

Ba·den·wei·ler \ˌbäd-ᵊn-ˈvī-lər\. Village, Baden-Württemberg, SW Germany, 28 mi. (45 km.) NE of Basel, Switzerland; mineral springs; Roman baths.

Baden–Würt·tem·berg \ˌbäd-ᵊn-ˈvu̇rt-əm-ˌberk\. A state of Germany and formerly of West Germany; ✱ Stuttgart; textiles; engineering industries; established 1952. See table at GERMANY. For history, see BADEN 2 and WÜRTTEMBERG.

Bad Frei·en·wal·de \ˌbät-ˈfrī-ən-ˌväl-də\ *or* **Freienwalde an der Oder** \ˌän-dər-ˈō-dər\ *also* **Freienwalde.** City, Brandenburg, E Germany, near Oder River and Polish border; health resort; warm mineral springs.

Bad·ga·stein \ˌbät-gä-ˈstīn\ *or* **Ga·stein** \gä-ˈstīn\. Village, Salzburg, Austria, 47 mi. (76 km.) S of Salzburg in N foothills of Hohe Tauern on the Gasteiner Ache; pop. (1981c) 5600; health resort. By Convention of Gastein 1865, Holstein came under Austrian control and Schleswig came under Prussian control.

Bad·ger Pass \ˈba-jər\. Mountain pass, cen. California; alt. 7100 ft. (2164 m.); in Yosemite National Park; skiing.

Bad Go·des·berg \ˌbät-ˈgō-dəs-ˌberk\ *also* **Godesberg.** Former city, North Rhine-Westphalia, W Germany, on left bank of the Rhine 4 mi. (6 km.) S of Bonn; mineral springs; ruins of castle (called the Godesburg, founded c. 1210, destroyed 1583 by Bavarians) nearby; scene of conference 1938 bet. British Prime Minister Neville Chamberlain and German Chancellor Adolf Hitler, prior to that at Munich, in regard to Czechoslovakia; site of a number of foreign legations; became part of Bonn 1969.

Bad Harz·burg \ˌbät-ˈhärts-ˌbu̇rk\ *also* **Harzburg.** Town, Lower Saxony, cen. Germany, N of the Harz Mts.; pop. (1992e) 23,975; mineral springs; resort.

Bad Hers·feld \ˌbät-ˈhers-ˌfelt\ *also* **Hersfeld.** City, Hesse, cen. Germany, 32 mi. (52 km.) SSE of Kassel; ruins of 11th cent. abbey church.

Bad Hom·burg \ˌbät-ˈhȯm-ˌbu̇rk\ *also* **Homburg** *or in full* **Bad Homburg vor der Hö·he** \ˌfōr-dər-ˈhœ̄-ə\. City, SW Hesse, Germany, 18 mi. (29 km.) ENE of Wiesbaden; pop. (1992e) 51,663; mineral baths; health and tourist resort; 17th cent. castle with fine tower; historically noted for manufacture of hats (first Homburg hats made here). Ruled by landgraves of Hesse-Homburg 1622–1866.

Ba·di·an \ˌbä-dē-ˈän\. Municipality on W coast of Cebu I., Philippines, at S end of Tanon Strait.

Badin Lake. See NARROWS DAM.

Bad Ischl \ˌbät-ˈish-ᵊl\ *also* **Ischl.** Commune, Upper Austria, Austria, on Traun River S of Lake Traun 51 mi. (82 km.) SW of Linz; pop. (1991c) 13,887; trade center; tourist and health resort; mineral springs.

Bad Kis·sing·en \ˌbät-ˈki-siŋ-ən\ *also* **Kissingen.** Town, Bavaria, Germany, on Fränkische Saale River ab. 62 mi. (100 km.) E of Frankfurt; mineral waters.

Bad Kreuz·nach \ˌbät-ˈkrȯits-ˌnäk\ *also* **Kreuznach.** City, Rhineland–Palatinate, Germany, on Nahe River; pop. (1992e) 41,458; mineral springs; health resort; trades in wine.

Bad·lands \ˈbad-ˌlandz\; *orig. Fr.* **Mau·vaises Terres** \ˌmō-vāz-ˈter\ *or* **Terres Mauvaises** \ˌter-mō-ˈvāz\. Barren region with eroded surface in SW South Dakota E of the Black Hills and in NW Nebraska; contains extensive fossil deposits; marked by steep hills, deep gullies, and other features of geological interest.

Badlands National Park. See UNITED STATES, *National Parks.*

Bad Nau·heim \ˌbät-ˈnau̇-ˌhīm\ *also* **Nauheim.** Town, Hesse, Germany, ab. 24 mi. (39 km.) N of Frankfurt am Main; saline thermal waters.

Bad Neu·en·ahr–Ahr·weil·er \ˌbät-ˈnoi-ə-ˌnär-ˈär-ˌvī-lər\. City, Rhineland-Palatinate, W Germany, 13 mi. (21 km.) S of Bonn.

Badnur. See BETUL.

Badoeng Strait. See BADUNG STRAIT.

Bad Reich·en·hall \ˌbät-ˈrī-kən-ˌhäl\ *also* **Reichenhall.** Town, Bavaria, Germany; pop. (1992e) 16,891; baths; health resort since 19th cent.

Ba·dri·a·gua·to \ˌbä-thrē-ä-ˈgwä-ˌtō\. Municipality, Sinaloa state, Mexico, 50 mi. (81 km.) N of Culiacan.

Ba·dri·nath \ˌbə-dri-ˈnät, ˌbä-\. Peak in the Himalayas, Uttar Pradesh, N India; 23,420 ft. (7138 m.); village and temple on its slope at 10,291 ft. (3137 m.).

Bad River. See BAD.

Bad Salz·uf·len \bät-ˈzält-sü-flən\. City, North Rhine-Westphalia, W cen. Germany, 45 mi. (72 km.) SW of Hanover; pop. (1992e) 53,998; thermal springs; health resort. Founded 1048; became city 1488.

Ba·dul·la \bə-ˈdə-lə\. Town, SE Sri Lanka, 85 mi. (137 km.) E of Colombo; pop. (1990e) 32,000; in tea-growing region.

Ba·dung Strait *or* **Ba·doeng Strait** \ˈbä-ˌdu̇ŋ\. Channel bet. SE Bali and the island of Nusa Besar, Indonesia; ab. 9 mi. (15 km.) wide; connects with Lombok Strait (*q.v.*).

Bad·wa·ter \ˈbad-ˌwȯ-tər, -ˌwä-\. Small salt pool, Death Valley, California; 282 ft. (86 m.) below sea level; lowest point in North America.

Ba·e·na \bä-ˈā-nä\. Commune, Córdoba prov., S Spain, 32 mi. (52 km.) SE of the city of Córdoba; pop. (1991c) 20,423; Roman ruins.

Bær·um \ˈbar-əm\. Municipality, Akershus co., suburb of Oslo, SE Norway; pop. (1990c) 89,221.

Baeterrae. See BÉZIERS.

Bæ·ti·ca \ˈbē-ti-kə\. A province of the Roman Empire in S Spain, roughly equivalent to W Andalusia.

Baetis. See GUADALQUIVIR.

Baetulo. See BADALONA.

Ba·e·za \bä-ˈā-thä\. Commune, Jaén prov., S Spain, ab. 24 mi. (39 km.) NE of the commune of Jaén; pop. (1991c) 15,064; as medieval Moorish city, fell to Ferdinand III of Castile 13th cent.

Ba·fa, Lake \bä-ˈfä\ *or Turk.* **Bafa Gö·lü** \gœ̄-ˈlue̅\. Lake in W Turkey in Asia at the mouth of the Menderes River; 22 sq. mi. (57 sq. km.); remains of sites of ancient Priene and Miletus in the vicinity.

Baf·fin \ˈba-fən\. Region, NE Canada, a former administrative subdivision of Northwest Territories, consisting of the E part of the earlier dist. of Franklin; area 393,007 sq. mi. (1,017,889 sq. km.).

Baffin Bay. **1.** Inlet of Laguna Madre, S Texas.

2. Large inlet of Atlantic Ocean bet. W Greenland and E Baffin I.; connected with Atlantic Ocean by Davis Strait; first

---

\ə\ abut \ᵊ\ matches \ᵊ\ kitten, Fr table \ər\ further \a\ ash \ā\ ace \ä\ cot, cart \á\ Fr bac \au̇\ out \b̲\ Span Avila \ch\ chin \e\ bet \ē\ easy \g\ go \i\ hit \ī\ ice \j\ job \k̲\ Ger ich, Buch \ⁿ\ Fr vin \ŋ\ sing \ō\ go \ȯ\ all \ȯ\ law \œ\ Fr bœuf \œ̄\ Fr feu \ȯi\ boy \th\ thin \th̲\ this \ü\ loot \u̇\ foot \ue\ Ger füllen \ue̅\ Fr rue \y\ yet \ʸ\ Fr digne \ˈdēnʸ\, nuit \ˈnwʸē\ \yü\ few \yu̇\ fury \zh\ vision

European visitor probably was John Davis 1586–87 expedition; visited later and explored by expedition led by Robert Bylot which included William Baffin c. 1615.

Baffin Island; *formerly* **Baffin Land.** Largest island of Arctic Archipelago, E Nunavut, Canada, W of Baffin Bay and Davis Strait; 183,810 sq. mi. (476,068 sq. km.); 5th largest island in the world; separated from Quebec on the S by Hudson Strait; in NW is Admiralty Inlet, in S part two lakes, Amadjuak and Nettilling, and on SE coast two large inlets, Cumberland Sound and Frobisher Bay; coal, iron ore; may have been visited by Norse 11th cent.; visited by English mariner Martin Frobisher 1576–78. Named for Arctic explorer William Baffin.

Baffin Island National Park. See *Auyuittuq* at CANADA, *National Parks.*

Ba·fing \bə-ˈfiŋ, -ˈfeⁿ\. The upper course of the Senegal River in Guinea and Mali; rises in the Fouta Djallon Highlands and flows NE and N to join the Bakoye at Bafoulabé; ab. 350 mi. (563 km.) long.

Ba·fou·la·bé *or* **Ba·fu·la·bé** \ˌbȧ-fü-lȧ-ˈbā\. Town on Senegal River at confluence of its headstreams, Bafing and Bakoye, W Mali, 13°48′N, 10°50′W.

Ba·fra \bä-ˈfrä\. Town, Samsun prov., N Turkey in Asia, on Kızıl Irmak near its mouth.

Ba·gac \bä-ˈgäk\. Municipality on W coast of Bataan prov., Luzon, Philippines, ab. halfway bet. Subic Bay and Mariveles.

Ba·ga·mo·yo \ˌbä-gä-ˈmō-yō\. Seaport town, E Tanzania, NW of Dar es Salaam.

Ba·ga·na \bä-ˈgä-nä\. Volcano, S cen. Bougainville I., Papua New Guinea; 6558 ft. (1999 m.).

Bagaria. See BAGHERIA.

Bagdad. See BAGHDAD.

Ba·gé \bə-ˈzhā\. City, S Rio Grande do Sul state, S Brazil.

Bagh·dad *or* **Bag·dad** \ˈbag-ˌdad, bäg-ˈdäd\. City, ✻ of Iraq, on both sides of the Tigris; pop. (1987c) 3,841,268; commercial and transportation center; cement, textiles, tobacco products; Univ. of Baghdad (1957).

History: Settlement on site of Baghdad from ancient times; sacked by Muslim Arabs c. 635 A.D.; rose to importance after its choice 762 A.D. by Caliph al-Manṣūr as ✻ of ʻAbbāsid caliphate; as center of Islam, especially under Caliph al-Maʼmūn (813–833), second only to Constantinople as trade and cultural center (estimated pop. of ab. 2,000,000); though power of Baghdad caliphate declined from about middle of 9th cent., city remained commercially important and continued to rule area corresponding roughly to modern Iraq; almost destroyed when Hülegü, grandson of Genghis Khan (see MONGOLIA), overthrew ʻAbbāsid caliphate 1258 and began rule of Il-Khans of Persia (c. 1260–1340); conquered by Turkic ruler Timur 1401; though captured by Süleyman the Magnificent 1534, did not become part of Ottoman Empire until 1638; objective of British Mesopotamian campaign 1915–17, it was finally captured 1917; became ✻ of kingdom of Iraq (*q.v.*) 1921; scene of *coup d'état* against monarchy 1958; economic prosperity increased 1970s; prosperity interrupted during several years of war bet. Iraq and Iran 1980s; severely damaged by bombing during Persian Gulf War 1991.

Baghdadi, Khan. See KHAN BAGHDADI.

Ba·ghel·khand \ˈbə-gəl-ˌkənd, ˈbä-gəl-ˌkänd\. Former agency, E division of British Central India Agency, India; 14,706 sq. mi. (38,089 sq. km.).

Ba·ghe·ria; *formerly* **Ba·ga·ria** \ˌbä-gä-ˈrē-ä\. Commune, Palermo prov., NW cen. Sicily, Italy, near Bay of Palermo 8 mi. (13 km.) SE of the seaport of Palermo; pop. (1989c) 45,615.

Bagh·lān \ˈbä-ˌglän\. Town, NE Afghanistan; pop. (1988e) 46,300.

Bagirmi. See BAGUIRMI.

Ba·ğır·pa·şa Dağ \bä-ˌgər-pä-ˈshä-ˈdäg, -ˈdä\. Peak, E Turkey in Asia, 70 mi. (113 km.) SW of Erzurum; 10,768 ft. (3282 m.).

Bag·ley \ˈba-glē\. City, ⊗ of Clearwater co., NW Minnesota; pop. (1990c) 1388; lake resort.

Ba·gna·ca·val·lo \ˌbä-nyä-kä-ˈväl-lō\. Commune, Ravenna prov., Emilia-Romagna, N Italy, 12 mi. (19 km.) W of the commune of Ravenna; birthplace of the painter Il Bagnacavallo (Bartolommeo Ramenghi) 1484.

Bag·nell Dam \bag-ˈnel\. Dam on Osage River, in Miller co., S cen. Missouri; completed 1931 forming Lake of the Ozarks.

Ba·gnères–de–Bi·gorre \bȧ-ˈnyer-də-bē-ˈgȯr\. Commune, Hautes-Pyrénées dept., SW France, 13 mi. (21 km.) SSE of Tarbes; health resort, known since Roman times; historically noted for production of barège, a gauzelike fabric containing wool, first made at Barèges ab. 25 mi. (40 km.) SSW.

Ba·gneux \bȧ-ˈnyœ\. Commune, Hauts-de-Seine dept., N France, S suburb of Paris; battle during siege of Paris, 1870.

Ba·gni di Luc·ca \ˈbä-nyē-dē-ˈlük-kä\. Commune, Lucca prov., Tuscany, cen. Italy, 13 mi. (21 km.) NNE of the commune of Lucca; thermal mineral springs.

Bagni San Giuliano. See SAN GIULIANO TERME.

Ba·gno a Ri·po·li \ˈbä-nyō-ä-ˈrē-pō-lē\. Commune, Firenze prov., Tuscany, cen. Italy, 4 mi. (6 km.) SE of Florence; pop. (1989c) 27,548; remains of ancient Roman bath.

Bagno di Ro·ma·gna \dē-rō-ˈmä-nyä\. Commune, Forlì prov., Emilia-Romagna, N Italy, ENE of Florence; summer resort; thermal springs.

Ba·gno·let \ˌbȧ-nyō-ˈlā\. Commune, Seine-St.-Denis dept., N France, E suburb of Paris.

Ba·go \ˈbä-gō\. Chartered city, W Negros Occidental, Negros, Philippines, on Guimaras Strait ab. 12 mi. (19 km.) SSW of City of Bacolod; pop. (1990p) 124,000.

Bagradas. See MEDJERDA.

Ba·gra·ti·o·novsk \bə-ˌgrȧ-tē-ˈȯ-nəfsk\; *formerly* **Preus·sisch Ey·lau** \ˈprȯi-sish-ˈī-ˌlau̇\ *or* **Eylau.** Town, Kaliningrad Oblast, Russia, 23 mi. (37 km.) S of the seaport of Kaliningrad; formerly in East Prussia, Germany; scene of indecisive battle Feb. 8, 1807 bet. the allied Russians and Prussians and the French under Emperor Napoléon.

Ba·guio \ˈbä-gē-ˌō\. Chartered city, W cen. Benguet prov., NW Luzon, Philippines, ab. 130 mi. (209 km.) N of Manila; pop. (1990c) 183,000; elev. 4500 ft. (1372 m.); summer resort and until 1976 summer ✻ of the Philippines; visited by Spaniards 1829 but until 20th cent. of less importance than La Trinidad (*q.v.*) to the N; incorp. as City of Baguio 1909; occupied by Japanese Dec. 1941; retaken by Americans Apr. 29, 1945.

Ba·guir·mi *or* **Ba·gir·mi** \bȧ-gēr-ˈmē\. Former sultanate, now part of SW Chad, SE of Lake Chad; ✻ before 1898 Massénya; level area ab. 1000 ft. (305 m.) above sea level, traversed by tributaries of the Chari River which forms its W and SW boundary; N'Djamena is in NW corner. Explored by English soldier Dixon Denham 1823, German geographer Heinrich Barth 1855, and German explorer Gustav Nachtigal 1872; came under French protection late 19th cent.

Ba·ha·ma Banks \bə-ˈhä-mə\. Two areas of shoal water in Bahamas: **Little Bahama Bank,** N of Grand Bahama I. and bet. it and Abaco on E; **Great Bahama Bank,** covering a large curved area some 330 mi. (531 km.) long with Andros on its E rim, separated from Cuba on S by Old Bahama Channel and from Florida on W and NW by Straits of Florida.

Ba·ha·mas \bə-ˈhä-məz\ *or officially* **Commonwealth of the Bahamas** *or esp. in text* **the Bahamas** *or* **The Bahamas.** Independent state comprising a chain of islands, cays, and reefs lying SE of Florida and N of Cuba; total area 5386 sq. mi. (13,950 sq. km.), area of inhabited islands ab. 4404 sq. mi. (11,406 sq. km.); pop. (1993e) 268,000; ✻ Nassau (on island of New Providence). A major tourist resort.

Chief islands (from N to S): Grand Bahama, Abaco, Eleuthera, New Providence, Andros, Cat I., San Salvador (or Watling), Exuma, Long I., Crooked I., Acklins I., Mayaguana, Inagua; chain of islands terminates in Turks and Caicos Is. (*q.v.*).

Chief products: shellfish, lumber, aragonite, salt, vegetables, pharmaceuticals, rum, fruit.

History: Islands inhabited by Lucayan Indians at time of sighting by explorer Christopher Columbus Oct. 12, 1492 (see SAN SALVADOR 1); assigned to Spain by papal grant but

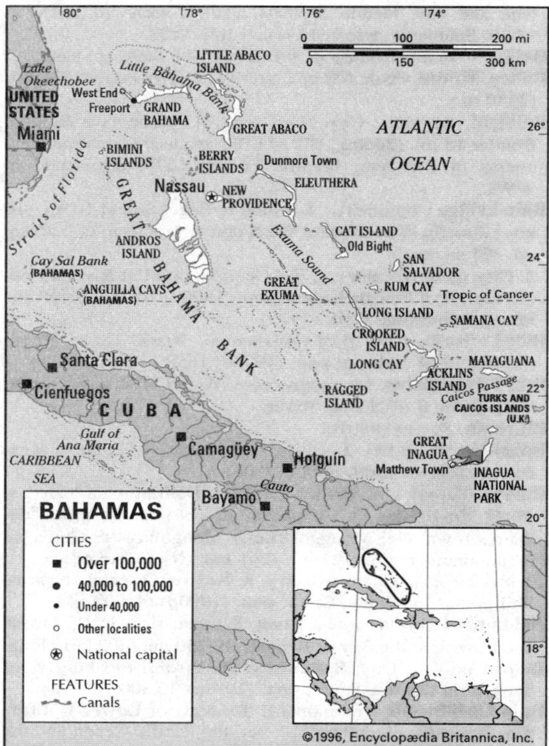

visited only by slave raiders and buccaneers; granted by British crown 1629 to Sir Robert Heath, suffered from Spanish attacks during 17th and 18th cents. and from use as pirates' base; settlement of islands by company of Eleutherian Adventurers (incorp. 1647) composed of disaffected Bermudians; settlements probably made on Eleuthera and on New Providence; islands granted to lords proprietors of Carolina 1670 but civil and military government assumed by crown 1717; piracy in islands ended by Capt. Woodes Rogers, first royal governor, 1718; first meeting of general assembly in Nassau 1729; Nassau seized and disarmed by American force 1776; islands capitulated to Spain 1782 but restored to Great Britain by Treaty of Versailles 1783; influx of American Loyalists as settlers 1783–84; proprietary rights of lords proprietors surrendered to crown 1787; Turks Is. under administration of colony c. 1800–48; abolished slavery 1834; base for blockade-running to Confederate States during American Civil War 1861–65; site on Mayaguana leased to U.S. for naval base 1940; British air base maintained on New Providence during WWII; received internal self-government 1964; became independent July 10, 1973.

Ba·ha·ram·pur \ˈbä-hə-rəm-ˌpu̇r\ *also* **Ber·ham·pore** \ˈbər-həm-ˌpu̇r\. Town, cen. West Bengal, NE India, on left bank of Bhagirathi River 110 mi. (177 km.) N of Calcutta; founded as British military station 1757; early involvement in Indian mutiny 1857. Includes remnant of **Cos·sim·ba·zar** \ˈkäs-əm-ˌbäz-ˌär\, a city formerly important.

Ba·ha·rī·ya *also* **Be·ha·ri·eh** *or* **Ba·ha·ri·eh** \ˌbȧ-hȧ-ˈrē-yə\. Oasis in the Libyan Desert, Matrūh governorate, Egypt, ab. 28°15′N, 28°57′E.

Ba·ha·wal·pur \bə-ˈhä-wəl-ˌpu̇r\ *or* **Bha·wal·pur** \ˈbä-wəl-\. **1.** Former Indian state, SW Punjab, now part of Pakistan; 17,494 sq. mi. (45,310 sq. km.); region stretches more than 300 mi. (483 km.) along the Sutlej, Panjnad, and Indus rivers with practically all of its territory in the Thar Desert. Its rulers became independent of Afghans in early 19th cent.; made treaty with British 1838; joined Pakistan 1947; reconstituted into an administrative division 1955.

2. City, its ✻, near Sutlej River ab. 225 mi. (362 km.) SW of Lahore; cotton, goods, soap.

Ba·hia \bä-ˈē-ə\. **1.** State, E Brazil; ✻ Salvador; sugar, cigar tobacco. See table at BRAZIL.

2. City, Brazil. See SALVADOR.

Ba·hía \bä-ˈē-ä\. Spanish word meaning "bay". For names containing this word, see the distinguishing element.

Ba·hía, Is·las de la \ˈēz-ˌläs-ˌt͟hā-lä-bä-ˈē-ä\ *also* **Bay Islands** \ˈbā-\. Group of islands in Caribbean Sea off N Honduras coast, incl. Roatán, largest of the group, and Guanaja; a department of Honduras. See table at HONDURAS.

Bahía Blan·ca \bä-ˈē-ä-ˈbläŋ-kä\. **1.** Large bay in SE Buenos Aires prov., E Argentina.

2. City, Buenos Aires prov., E Argentina, at head of this bay; pop. (1991p) 271,467; naval port; shipping point for La Pampa, Neuquén, and Río Negro provs.; exports cattle, wheat, wool; university (1956); dates from military and trading post 1828.

Bahía de Campeche. See CAMPECHE, BANK OF.

Bahía de Cochinos. See PIGS, BAY OF.

Bahnasā, Al–. See OXYRHYNCHUS.

Ba·ho·ru·co \bä-ō-ˈrü-kō\. **1.** Mountain range, SW Dominican Republic; highest peak 5346 ft. (1630 m.)

2. Province, SW Dominican Republic. See table at DOMINICAN REPUBLIC.

Bahr, Al–. See NILE.

Bah·raich \bə-ˈrīk\. Town, E Uttar Pradesh, N India, on affluent of Ghāghara River 65 mi. (105 km.) NE of Lucknow; pop. (1991p) 135,352; contains tomb of Masud, a champion of Islam, a place of pilgrimage for both Hindus and Muslims.

Bah·rain *also* **Bah·rein** \bä-ˈrān\; *anc.* **Ty·los** \ˈtī-ˌlȯs\ *or* **Ty·ros** \-ˌräs\. Independent state, an archipelago in W Persian Gulf, 20 mi. (32 km.) off the coastal region of Al-Hasa on the Arabian Penin., NW of Qatar; 255 sq. mi. (661 sq. km.); pop. (1993e) 485,600; ✻ Manama; comprises low-lying islands of **Bahrain** (the largest, 27 mi. or 43 km. long by 10 mi. or 16 km. wide and connected to Saudi Arabia by King Fahd Causeway 15.5 mi. or 25 km. long, completed 1986), Al Muharraq, Sitrah, and several islets; extensive oil fields, natural

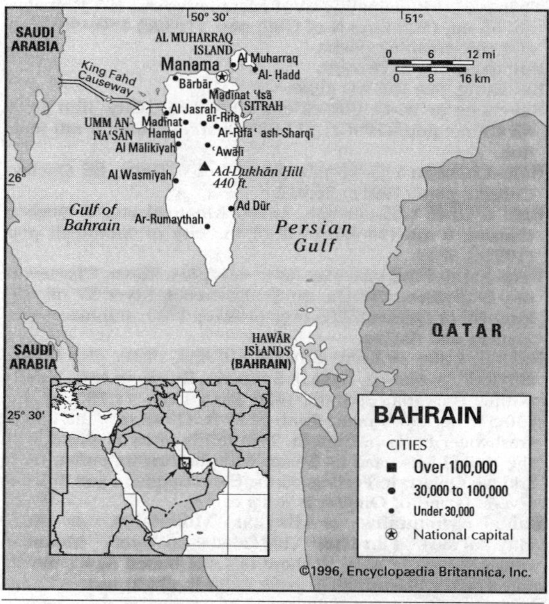

\ə\ abut \ᵊ\ matches \ᵊ\ kitten, Fr table \ər\ further \a\ ash \ā\ ace \ä\ cot, cart \a̐\ Fr bac \au̇\ out \b\ Span Avila \ch\ chin \e\ bet \ē\ easy \g\ go \i\ hit \ī\ ice \j\ job \k\ Ger ich, Buch \ⁿ\ Fr vin \ŋ\ sing \ō\ go \ȯ\ all \ó\ law \œ\ Fr bœuf \œ̄\ Fr feu \ȯi\ boy \th\ thin \t͟h\ this \ü\ loot \u̇\ foot \ue\ Ger füllen \ue̅\ Fr rue \y\ yet \ʸ\ Fr digne \ˈdēnʸ\, nuit \ˈnwʸē\ \yü\ few \yu̇\ fury \zh\ vision

gas; aluminum; shipbuilding, ship repair; dates, fish, vegetables.

History: Known as important trading center for a long time; mentioned in Persian, Greek, and Roman references; ruled by Arabs from 7th cent. A.D.; occupied by Portuguese 1521–1602, by Arab subjects of Persia to 1783; ruled since then by a member of the Khalifah family; its defense a British responsibility 1820–1971; Persian ownership denied by British 1928; oil discovered 1932; established a Council of State 1970; became a member of the UN 1971; with five other Arab states joined Gulf Cooperation Council 1981.

Bahr al–Abyad. The White Nile. See NILE.

Bahr al–Azraq. The Blue Nile. See NILE.

Bahr al–Gha·zal \ˌbär-ȧl-gȧ-ˈzȧl\. **1.** River, SW Sudan; 445 mi. (716 km.) long; formed by confluence of Bahr el Arab and Jur rivers in a swampy area of the S cen. part of Sudan; flows E to unite at Lake No with the Bahr el Jebel and form the White Nile (see NILE).

2. Former province of SW Sudan; ✻ Wau.

Bahr el Arab \ˌbär-ȧl-ˈä-rəb\ *or* **Baḥr al–ʻArab** \ˌbä-hər-ȧl-ˈä-rəb\. River, S Sudan, NE Africa; flows E to join with the Jur and form the Bahr al-Ghazal.

Bahr el Je·bel \el-ˈje-bel\ *or* **Baḥr al Ja·bal** \ˌbä-hər-ȧl-ˈjȧ-bȧl\. Section of the Nile in S Sudan. See BAHR AL-GHAZAL.

Bahrein. See BAHRAIN.

Bahr en Nīl. See NILE.

Bahret Lut. See DEAD SEA.

Bahr·gan, Cape \bär-ˈgän\. Cape on W coast of Iran, projecting into NE corner of the Persian Gulf.

Bahri, Deir el–. See DEIR EL-BAHRI.

Bahr Tabariya. See GALILEE, SEA OF.

Bahr Yûsef. See YÛSEF, BAHR.

Bai *or W.-G.* **Pai** \ˈbī\ *or* **Pei** \ˈbā\. River, NE China; rises beyond the Great Wall in Hebei prov. and flows SE through Beijing munic. and through Tianjin munic. where it becomes known as the Hai from its junction with the Grand Canal (Da Yunhe) to its mouth on Bo Hai at Dagu; ab. 300 mi. (483 km.) long; navigable for ab. 100 mi. (160 km.).

Baía de Todos os Santos. See ALL SAINTS BAY.

Ba·ia Ma·re \ˌbä-yä-ˈmä-rā\ *or Hung.* **Nagy·bá·nya** \ˈnȯj-ˈbän-ˌyȯ\. Municipality, ⊗ of Maramureş co., NW Romania, ab. 65 mi. (105 km.) N of Cluj; pop. (1989c) 150,456; lead- and zinc-smelting plants.

Baibazar. See BEYPAZARI.

Bai Bung. See MUI BAI BUNG.

Bai·cheng *or W.-G.* **Pai–ch'eng** \ˈbī-ˈchəŋ\. City, Jilin prov., NE China; pop. (1990c) 217,987; market center at rail junction.

Baie–Co·meau \bā-ˈkō-mō, ˌbā-kō-ˈmō\. Town, SE Quebec, Canada; pop. (1991c) 26,012.

Baie d'Ur·fé \ˌbā-dür-ˈfā\. Town, Montreal co., S Quebec, Canada, 9 mi. (14 km.) SW of the city of Montreal; pop. (1991c) 3849.

Baie–Saint–Paul \ˌbā-sānt-ˈpȯl, -seⁿ-ˈpȯl\. Town, Charlevoix co., S Quebec, Canada, on St. Lawrence River 57 mi. (92 km.) NE of Quebec City; pop. (1991c) 3733; summer resort; hunting and fishing.

Bai·kal, Lake *or* **Lake Bay·kal** \bī-ˈkäl, -ˈkal\ *also* **Oze·ro Baykal** \ˈō-zyer-ə\. Lake in S Siberia, Russia in Asia, chiefly within Buryatia; 395 mi. (636 km.) long; 11,780 sq. mi. (30,510 sq. km.); max. depth 5715 ft. (1742 m.); the largest freshwater basin in Eurasia. Two thirds of its W shore, with the Baikal Mts., and its S end, with the Angara outlet, lie in Irkutsk Oblast; it receives on the E the Barguzin and Selenga rivers. Island of Olkhon is in its center.

Baikal Mountains *or* **Baykal Mountains.** *or Russ.* **Bay·kal'skiy Khre·bet** \bī-ˈkäl-skē-kri-ˈbyet\ Mountain range, Russia in Asia, W shore of Lake Baikal (*q.v.*), mostly in Irkutsk Oblast; highest peak 6890 ft. (2100 m.).

Bai·ko·nur. See BAYKONUR.

Bai·lan. See BELEN.

Bail·don \ˈbāl-dən\. Town, West Riding, Yorkshire, N England, 7 mi. (11 km.) N of Bradford.

Baile Atha Cliath. See DUBLIN 7.

Bai·lén \bī-ˈlān, -ˈlen\. Commune, Jaén prov., S Spain, 20 mi. (32 km.) N of the commune of Jaén; pop. (1991c) 16,865; galena and zinc blende deposits nearby; scene of battle in which Spaniards defeated French July 1808.

Bai·ley \ˈba-lē\. County in NW Texas. See table at TEXAS.

Bailey, Mount. Peak, NW of Crater Lake, SW Oregon; 8363 ft. (2549 m.).

Bail·leul \bȧ-ˈyœl\. City, Nord dept., N France, near Belgian frontier 15 mi. (24 km.) NW of Lille; made free commune by counts of Flanders; became French 1678; devastated in WWI.

Bain·bridge \ˈbān-brij\. **1.** Island in Puget Sound 10 mi. (16 km.) directly W of Seattle, Washington, in Kitsap co.; 26 sq. mi. (67 sq. km.).

2. City, ⊗ of Decatur co., SW Georgia, on Flint River 13 mi. (21 km.) N of Florida border; pop. (1990c) 10,712; barge terminal; Bainbridge Coll. (1970).

Baird \ˈbard\. City, ⊗ of Callahan co., N cen. Texas, 20 mi. (32 km.) E of Abilene; pop. (1990c) 1658.

Baird Mountains. Mountain range, W end of Brooks Range, NW Alaska, S of Noatak River.

Baireuth. See BAYREUTH.

Bai·ri·ki \ˈbī-ˌrē-kē\. Locality, administrative center of Kiribati on Tarawa Atoll; pop. (1990c) 2226.

Bai·rin You·qi \ˈbī-ˈrin-ˈyō-ˈchē\ *or* **Da·ban** \ˈdä-ˈbän\ *or W.-G.* **Pa–lin–yu–ch'i** \ˈbä-ˈlin-ˈyü-ˈchē\ *or* **Ta–pan** \ˈdä-ˈbän\. Town, Nei Monggol (Inner Mongolia), NE China; in mountainous region 125 mi. (201 km.) N of Chengde.

Ba·is \ˈbä-ˌēs\. Chartered city, E Negros Oriental, Negros, Philippines, on Tanon Strait; pop. (1990p) 60,000.

Bai·ta·ra·ni \bī-ˈtär-ə-nē\. River, E India; rises in NE Orissa and flows into the Bay of Bengal; ab. 250 mi. (402 km.) long.

Ba·ja \ˈbȯ-yȯ\. City, S Hungary, ab. 60 mi. (96 km.) W of Szeged on Danube River; pop. (1991e) 40,300.

Baja Ca·li·for·nia \ˈbä-hä-ˌka-li-ˈfȯr-nyə\ *or* **Lower California.** Peninsula extending SSE bet. the Pacific Ocean and the Gulf of California, NW Mexico; divided into two states: **Baja California** (*also called* **Baja California Nor·te** \ˈnȯr-tā\), to the N, and **Baja California Sur** \ˈsu̇r\ (until 1974 a territory), to the S (see table at MEXICO). Inhabited by Indians for perhaps 9,000 years before the coming of the Spanish 1533–34; successfully settled by Jesuit missions (from late 17th cent.); separated from what is now the U.S. state of California in treaty 1848 following the Mexican War.

Bajada de Santa Fe. See PARANÁ 2.

Bājah. See BÉJA.

Baja Ve·ra·paz \ˈbä-hä-ˌvā-rä-ˈpäs\. Department of cen. Guatemala. See table at GUATEMALA.

Ba·jos de Ha·i·na \ˈbä-hōs-thā-ä-ˈē-nä\. City, S Dominican Republic, SW of Santo Domingo.

Baj·ram Cur·ri \bī-ˈräm-ˈku̇r-ē\. Town, ✻ of Tropojë dist., N Albania.

Ba·jur Bay \ˈba-jər\; *formerly* **Ko·ning·in·ne Bay** \ˈkō-niŋ-ˈi-nə\. Inlet of Indian Ocean, W coast of Sumatra, Indonesia; on its NW shore is Telukbajur, port of Padang.

Bakan. See SHIMONOSEKI.

Ba·kar·ganj *or* **Back·er·gunge** \ˈbäk-ər-ˌgənj\. Former district, Bengal prov., British India; now part of Bangladesh.

Ba·ker \ˈbā-kər\. **1.** Name of counties in three states of the U.S. See tables at FLORIDA, GEORGIA, OREGON.

2. City, E Baton Rouge parish, SE cen. Louisiana, 10 mi. (16 km.) N of the city of Baton Rouge; pop. (1990c) 13,233.

3. City, ⊗ of Fallon co., E Montana; pop. (1990c) 1818.

Baker, Mount. Peak in Cascade Range, cen. Whatcom co., NW Washington; 10,778 ft. (3285 m.).

Baker Butte. Butte in cen. Arizona, at S border of the Mogollon Rim; 8077 ft. (2462 m.) high.

Baker City; *formerly* **Baker.** City, ⊗ of Baker co., E Oregon, on fork of Powder River; pop. (1990c) 9140; gold, silver, copper deposits nearby; agriculture; tourism; settled in 1863; became ⊗ 1868; incorp. 1874.

Baker Island. Atoll in cen. Pacific Ocean near the Equator at 176°31′W; less than 1 sq. mi. (2.6 sq. km.). Visited for guano 1850 to 1890; claimed by U.S. and Great Britain; occupied by colonists (Hawaiians) for U.S. 1935 and formally proclaimed U.S. territory 1936. See HOWLAND ISLAND.

Baker Lake. Lake, the expansion of upper (W) Chesterfield Inlet, Nunavut, Canada; 975 sq. mi. (2525 sq. km.); receives outlet of Aberdeen Lake at NW and Kazan River in S.

Ba·kers·field \ˈbā-kərz-ˌfēld\. City, ⊗ of Kern co., S California, on Kern River at S end of San Joaquin Valley; pop. (1990c) 174,820; shipping center for cotton and other agricultural products; Bakersfield Coll. (1913), California State Univ., Bakersfield (1965); city laid out 1869.

Ba·kers·ville \ˈbā-kərz-ˌvil\. Town, ⊗ of Mitchell co., W North Carolina; pop. (1990c) 332; mica deposits.

Bakh·chi·sa·ray *or* **Bakh·chy·sa·ray** \ˌbäk-chi-sə-ˈrī\. Town, S Crimea, Ukraine, on railroad line 15 mi. (24 km.) SSW of Simferopol; from 15th cent. to 1783 ✻ of Tatar khanate.

Bakhmut. See ARTEMOVSK.

Bākh·ta·rān \ˌbäk-tä-ˈrän\. **1.** *formerly* **Ker·mān·shāh·an** \ˌker-män-shä-ˈhän\. Province of W Iran. See table at IRAN. **2.** *formerly* **Ker·mān·shāh** \ˌker-män-ˈshä\ *also* **Kir·man·shah** \ˌkir-\. City, its ✻; pop. (1986c) 560,514; trade center for agricultural region; oil refining.

Bakh·te·gān \ˌbȧk-ti-ˈgän\ *or* **Ni·riz** \ni-ˈrēz\. Salt lake, N cen. Fārs prov., SW Iran; 10 mi. (16 km.) long; formerly 60 mi. (97 km.) long.

Bakh·tī·a·rī \bäk-ˈtē-ə-rē\. Mountainous region in W Iran; highest peaks above 12,000 ft. (3658 m.).

Bakhtīarī va Chahār Mahāll. See CHAHĀR MAHĀLL VA BAKHTĪARĪ.

Ba·kır·köy \ˌbä-kər-ˈkœi\. Suburban district, İstanbul prov., Turkey in Europe; 112 sq. mi. (290 sq. km.); its chief town, Bakırköy, is SW of İstanbul near coast of Sea of Marmara.

Ba·kony Forest \ˈbȯ-ˌkōnʸ\ *or Ger.* **Ba·ko·nyer·wald** \bä-ˈkōn-yər-ˌvält\. Mountain range bet. the Rába (Raab) River and Lake Balaton, Hungary; av. alt. 2000 ft. (610 m.).

Ba·koye *or* **Ba·koy** \bä-ˈkȯi\. River, W Mali, ab. 300 mi. (483 km.) long; a headstream uniting with the Bafing to form the Senegal; chief tributary the Baoulé.

Ba·ku \bä-ˈkü\. City, ✻ of Azerbaijan, a port on SW shore of the Apsheron Penin. on the W coast of the Caspian Sea; pop. (1989p) 1,150,000; center of an extensive oil-producing region (formerly one of the most productive in the U.S.S.R.); oil refineries; cement, chemicals, textiles; shipbuilding; university (1920).

History: Old part of city dates back to 9th cent.; has Arabic and 11th cent. Persian architectural remains; Persian town when seized by Russians 1723 but restored 1735; finally incorp. into Russia 1806; suffered from disastrous fires and riots 1901, 1904–05, and during the Russian Civil War of 1917–21; made ✻ of Bolshevik government 1917; became ✻ of new republic of Azerbaijan 1920.

Bakwanga. See MBUJI-MAYI.

Ba·la·bac \bä-ˈlä-ˌbäk\. Island, SW Philippines, SW of Palawan I.; 125 sq. mi. (324 sq. km.); part of Palawan prov.; Balabac town on E coast has good harbor.

Balabac Strait. Passage connecting Sulu Sea with South China Sea, bet. S end of Balabac I., Philippines, and islands off N coast of Sabah, Borneo; 34 mi. (55 km.) wide.

Ba'labakk. See BAALBEK.

Ba·la·ba·la·gan Islands \ˌbä-lä-ˈbä-lä-gän\; *mostly formerly* **Little Pa·ter·nos·ters** \ˈpa-tər-ˌnäs-tərz, ˈpä-\. Group of about 30 low coral islets in W cen. Makassar Strait, bet. Borneo and Sulawesi, Indonesia.

Ba·la·ghat \ˈbä-lə-ˌgät\. Town, Madhya Pradesh, S cen. India, on Wainganga River NE of Nagpur.

Ba·lah Lakes \ˈba-lə\. Contiguous lakes, N Egypt, on W side of Suez Canal at its N end; contain several islands; connected with Lake Manzala.

Ba·lakh·na \bə-ˈläk-nə\. Town, Nizhegorod, cen. Russia in Europe, ab. 25 mi. (40 km.) NW of Nizhniy Novgorod.

Ba·la·kla·va \bə-lə-ˈklä-və, ˌbä-\. Seaport village, SW Crimea, Ukraine, SE of Sevastopol'; scene Oct. 25, 1854 of indecisive battle of Crimean War memorable for charge of Light Brigade.

Ba·la·ko·vo \bə-lə-ˈkȯ-və\. Town, Saratov Oblast, Russia in Europe, ab. 85 mi. (137 km.) WNW of the city of Saratov.

Bala Lake \ˈba-lə\. Lake, E Gwynedd, Wales; ab. 4 mi. (6 km.) long; source of Dee River; largest natural lake in Wales but smaller than the artificial Lake Vyrnwy (*q.v.*).

Ba·lam·ban \ˌbä-läm-ˈbän\. Municipality, W coast of Cebu I., Philippines, on Tanon Strait; pop. (1980c) 41,498.

Ba·lam·bang·an \ˌbä-läm-ˈbäŋ-gän\. Island, N Sabah, Malaysia, just S of main channel of Balabac Strait.

Ba·lan·ga \bä-ˈläŋ-gä\. Municipality, ✻ of Bataan prov., Luzon, Philippines, near E coast in cen. part.

Ba·lan·guin·gui \ˌbä-län-ˈgēŋ-gē\. **1.** Former name of Samales (*q.v.*) group of islands, Sulu Archipelago, Philippines. **2.** Most important island of the group, ab. 18 mi. (29 km.) E of E tip of Jolo I.; 1 sq. mi. (2.6 sq. km.).

Ba·la·shi·kha \ˌbȧ-lə-ˈshē-kə\. Town, Moscow Oblast, W cen. Russia in Europe, ab. 14 mi. (23 km.) ENE of the city of Moscow; pop. (1992e) 138,000.

Ba·la·shov \ˌbȧ-lə-ˈshȯf\. Town, SW Saratov Oblast, S cen. Russia in Europe, 110 mi. (177 km.) W of the city of Saratov; pop. (1991e) 97,300.

Ba·la·si·nor \ˌbä-lə-si-ˈnȯr\. **1.** Former Indian state, now part of Gujarat state, W India; 195 sq. mi. (505 sq. km.). **2.** Town, its ✻, 45 mi. (72 km.) E of Ahmadabad.

Balasore. See BĀLESHWAR.

Ba·las·sa·gyar·mat \ˈbȯ-lȯ-shȯ-ˈjȯr-ˌmȯt\. City, N Hungary, 42 mi. (68 km.) N of Budapest; pop. (1980p) 18,534.

Bal·a·ton, Lake \-ˈbȯ-lȯ-ˌtōn\ *or Ger.* **Plat·ten·see** \ˈplät-ᵊn-ˌzā\. Lake, W Hungary, 55 mi. (89 km.) SW of Budapest; 232 sq. mi. (601 sq. km.); max. depth 35 ft. (11 m.); largest lake in cen. Europe; has many resorts on its shores.

Ba·la·yan \ˌbä-lä-ˈyän\. Municipality on SW coast of Batangas prov., Luzon, Philippines, on NW shore of Balayan Bay 26 mi. (42 km.) NW of the municipality of Batangas; pop. (1980c) 43,486.

Balayan Bay. Large inlet of South China Sea in SW Batangas prov., Philippines; from 14 to 16 mi. (23 to 28 km.) wide; Cape Santiago is its SW point and Maricaban I. lies to SE.

Bal·bi \ˈbäl-bē\. Active volcano in Emperor Range, NW Bougainville I., Papua New Guinea; 8999 ft. (2743 m.); highest point on the island.

Bal·boa \bal-ˈbō-ə\. **1.** District occupying SE part of Panama Canal area; 222 sq. mi. (575 sq. km.). **2.** Town, Panama at Pacific entrance to Panama Canal; pop. (1990c) 1179.

Balboa Heights. Suburb of Balboa; former location of U.S. administrative center for the Canal Zone.

Bal·brig·gan \bal-ˈbri-gən\. Seaport, NE coast of co. Dublin, E Ireland, 19 mi. (31 km.) NNE of the city of Dublin.

Bal·car·ce \bäl-ˈkär-sā\. Town, Buenos Aires prov., E cen. Argentina; pop. (1980p) 28,985.

Balch Springs \ˈbȯlch\. City, Dallas co., Texas, E suburb of the city of Dallas; pop. (1990c) 17,406.

Bal·clu·tha \bal-ˈklü-thə\. Borough near mouth of Clutha River, SE South I., New Zealand; pop. (1981c) 4495.

Bal·co·nes Escarpment \bal-ˈkō-nis\. Escarpment, S cen. Texas, running from near Mexican border to Dallas area and separating Texas coastal plain from Edwards Plateau.

Balcones Heights. City, Bexar co., S cen. Texas, entirely within city limits of San Antonio; pop. (1990c) 3,022.

Balda, Atraf–i–. See ATRAF-I-BALDA.

Bal·degg \ˈbäl-ˌdek\. Lake, N cen. Switzerland, in N Lucerne canton; 3.5 mi. (5.6 km.) long; 2 sq. mi. (5 sq. km.); formed by expansion of Aa River.

Bald·face Mountain \ˈbȯld-ˌfās\. Peak in the Adirondack Mts., Essex co., NE New York; 3903 ft. (1190 m.).

Bald Hills \ˈbȯld\. Range in Pennington co., SW South Dakota; alt. 5000 ft. (1524 m.).

Bald Mountain. **1.** Peak, Summit co., cen. Colorado; 13,694 ft. (4174 m.). **2.** Peak, cen. Custer co., cen. Idaho; 10,313 ft. (3143 m.).

3. Peak, NW Elmore co., SW cen. Idaho; 9389 ft. (2862 m.).
4. Peak, Grant co., E cen. Oregon; 8330 ft. (2539 m.).
5. Peak, Lawrence co., W South Dakota; 7000 ft. (2134 m.).
6. Peak, S Summit co., NE Utah; 11,947 ft. (3641 m.).
7. Peak, Big Horn co., N Wyoming; 10,029 ft. (3057 m.).
8. Peak, in Wind River Range, W cen. Wyoming; 10,760 ft. (3280 m.).

Bald Mountains. Range of the Appalachian Mts. along the Tennessee-North Carolina boundary, NE of Great Smoky Mts.; highest point ab. 5560 ft. (1695 m.).

Bal·dwin \ˈbȯld-win\. **1.** Name of counties in two states of the U.S. See tables at ALABAMA and GEORGIA.
2. Township, ⊗ of Lake co., W Michigan; pop. (1990c) 726.
3. Unincorporated settlement, Nassau co., SE New York, S shore of Long Island 23 mi. (37 km.) E of Brooklyn; pop. (1990c) 22,719.
4. Borough, Allegheny co., Pennsylvania, on Monongahela River S of Pittsburgh; pop. (1990c) 21,923.

Baldwin City. City, Douglas co., E Kansas; pop. (1990c) 2961; Baker Univ. (1858).

Baldwin Park. City, Los Angeles co., California, SE of Monrovia; pop. (1990c) 69,330.

Baldwin Peninsula. See KOTZEBUE.

Bal·dwins·ville \ˈbȯld-winz-ˌvil\. Village, Onondaga co., cen. New York, on New York State Barge Canal 14 mi. (23 km.) NW of Syracuse; pop. (1990c) 6591; natural-gas deposits nearby.

Baldy, Mount \ˈbȯl-dē\. Mountain, California. See SAN ANTONIO PEAK 1.

Baldy Mountain. Mountain, Manitoba, Canada, ab. 120 mi. (193 km.) NNW of Brandon; 2729 ft. (832 m.); highest peak in Manitoba.

Baldy Peak. **1.** *also* **Thom·as Peak** \ˈtä-məs\. Mountain, S Apache co., E Arizona; 11,590 ft. (3533 m.).
2. Mountain, New Mexico. See SANTA FE BALDY.
3. Mountain, W Texas. See LIVERMORE, MOUNT.
4. Peak, E Beaver co., SW Utah; 12,000 ft. (3658 m.).

Bâle. See BASEL.

Ba·le·a·res \ˌbä-lā-ˈä-rās\. Autonomous community and province of Spain. See table at SPAIN.

Bal·e·ar·ic Islands \ˌba-lē-ˈar-ik\ *or Span.* **Is·las Ba·le·a·res** \ˈēs-ˌläs-ˌbä-lā-ˈä-rās\. Island group in W Mediterranean Sea near E coast of Spain; 1936 sq. mi. (5014 sq. km.); pop. (1991p) 702,770; ✱ Palma; forms Spanish autonomous community and province of Baleares; comprises the islands of Majorca, Minorca, Ibiza, Formentera, Cabrera (*qq.v.*), and 11 smaller islands; popular resort, noted esp. for its picturesque scenery and mild climate; produces fruits, wine, grain, cattle; fishing.

History: Became part of Carthaginian empire 5th cent. B.C.; conquered by Rome c. 120 B.C.; overrun by Vandals middle of the 5th cent. A.D.; reconquered for Byzantine Empire by Gen. Belisarius 534; raided by Arabs in 9th cent. but not permanently conquered until early 10th cent. by Umayyad line at Córdoba (*q.v.*); kingdom of Mallorca taken by James I of Aragon 1229–35 and made a separate kingdom for his son, united to kingdom of Aragon by Pedro IV 1344; fought over during 18th cent. among Spanish, British, and French; became Spanish 1802.

Balearis Major. See MAJORCA.

Ba·ler Bay \bä-ˈler\. Inlet of Pacific Ocean on E coast of Luzon, Philippines, 15°50′N, 121°37′E. Near its head on short stream is municipality of **Baler** which has one of best harbors on Pacific coast of Luzon.

Balesh. See ELVAS.

Bā·lesh·war \ˈbə-lish-ˌwär, ˈbä-\ *or* **Ba·la·sore** \ˈbə-lə-ˌsōr, ˈbä\. Town, E Orissa, E India, SW of Calcutta; pop. (1991p) 86,116.

Baleswar. See GANGES DELTA.

Ba·le·te Pass \bä-ˈlā-tā\. Pass in Caraballo Mts., SW Nueva Vizcaya prov., Luzon, Philippines, on main highway bet. cen. Luzon and valley of the Cagayan River in the N.

Bal·frin \bäl-ˈfrēn\. Peak in the Pennine Alps, in Valais canton, SW cen. Switzerland; 12,454 ft. (3796 m.).

Balfrush. See BĀBOL.

Ba·li \ˈbä-lē, ˈba-\. Island, Indonesia, off E end of Java and bet. Bali Sea and Indian Ocean, westernmost of the Lesser Sunda Is.; constitutes with minor adjacent islands, a province (see table at INDONESIA); mountainous, with highest peaks in E (Mt. Agung 10,308 ft. or 3142 m.) and N cen. part; at S end has low hook-shaped peninsula; lacks good harbors; its rivers are mostly unnavigable and generally run S from the N plateau; has luxuriant vegetation and grows a great variety of tropical products: rice, sweet potatoes, cassava; copra; meat processing; tourism.

History: Colonized direct from India in early times, its civilization is Hindu; many fine old temples; little contact with Dutch before 19th cent., when Balinese princes recognized Dutch supremacy but retained local autonomy; native piracy overcome by Dutch expedition 1846; bet. 1882 and 1908 came definitely under Dutch government; naval battle Feb. 19, 1942 off SE coast in Badung Strait, won by Allied Nations, did not prevent occupation of island by Japanese, who later surrendered to Allies 1945; became part of Indonesia 1950.

Bali and Lom·bok \ˈlȯm-ˌbȯk\. Residency of the former Netherlands Indies, comprising the islands of Bali and Lombok; now part of the Indonesian provs. of Bali and West Nusa Tenggara.

Ba·lı·ke·sir \ˌbä-lə-ke-ˈsir\. **1.** Province of Turkey in Asia. See table at TURKEY.
2. City, its ✱, on tributary of the Simav 50 mi. (80 km.) S of Sea of Marmara; pop. (1990c) 170,589; textiles.

Ba·līkh \bä-ˈlēk\. River, W Asia; rises in S Turkey N of Urfa and flows S to the Euphrates in N Syria near Ar Raqqah; ab. 120 mi. (193 km.) long.

Ba·lik·pa·pan \ˌbä-lik-ˈpä-ˌpän\. Seaport town, SE Borneo, Indonesia, on **Balikpapan Bay** 225 mi. (362 km.) NE of Banjarmasin; pop. (1990c) 309,492; has become one of the major oil centers of Borneo. Naval engagement off the bay 1942 bet. U.S. destroyers and Japanese warships; occupied by Japanese 1942–45 and severely damaged; rebuilt after WWII.

Ba·lin·ga·sag \ˌbä-liŋ-gä-ˈsäg\. Municipality, Mindanao, Philippines, on E shore of Macajalar Bay; pop. (1980c) 38,364.

Ba·lin·tang Channel \ˈbä-lin-ˌtäŋ\. Strait bet. Batan Is. on the N and Babuyan Is. on the S, N Philippines; connects Philippine Sea and South China Sea; 50 mi. (80 km.) wide.

Bali Sea. Body of water bet. Kangean Is. on the N and Bali on the S, Indonesia; forms SW part of Flores Sea; Madura Strait opens into it from the W.

Bali Strait. Channel bet. E end of Java and W end of Bali, Indonesia, connecting Bali Sea with the Indian Ocean; only 1 mi. (1.7 km.) wide at narrowest point just N of Banyuwangi, Java.

Ba·li·uag \bä-ˈlē-wäg\. Municipality, W Bulacan prov., Luzon, Philippines, on right bank of Angat River 10 mi. (16 km.) NE of Malolos; pop. (1980c) 70,555; rice market. Taken by American forces May 2, 1899 during Philippine rebellion; lost to Japanese Dec. 1941; retaken Jan. 1945.

Bal·kan Mountains \ˈbȯl-kən\ *or Bulg.* **Sta·ra Pla·ni·na** \ˈstä-rä-ˌplä-nē-ˈnä\; *anc.* **Hae·mus** \ˈhē-məs\. Range of mountains extending E and W across cen. Bulgaria from Yugoslav border to the Black Sea; highest point Botev Peak 7793 ft. (2375 m.); crossed by Shipka Pass, N of Kazanlŭk.

Balkan Peninsula. Peninsula in SE Europe bet. the Adriatic and Ionian seas on the W, the Mediterranean Sea on the S, and the Aegean and Black seas on the E.

Bal·kans \ˈbȯl-kənz\ *also* **Balkan States.** Countries occupying the Balkan Peninsula: Slovenia, Croatia, Bosnia and Herzegovina, Macedonia, Yugoslavia, Romania, Bulgaria, Albania, Greece, and Turkey in Europe.

History: For earlier history, see GREECE and MACEDONIA. Incorp. as Roman provinces 168 B.C.–107 A.D. (see EPIRUS, ACHAEA, MACEDONIA, DALMATIA, MOESIA, PANNONIA, THRACE, DACIA, and ILLYRIA); settled by Slavic invaders, Serbs, Croats, Slovenes, and Slavonized Bulgars, who were pushed into Balkan region in 6th cent.; gradually organized into kingdoms (see BULGARIA, CROATIA, SERBIA, and BOSNIA); except for Montenegro, conquered by Ottoman Turks 14th and 15th cents.; aroused by nationalism and encouraged by decline of

Turkish authority, began series of revolts against Turkish rule 1804 (see SERBIA); independence of region, alternately supported and opposed by the Great Powers, was part of issue of European politics known as "Eastern Question"; by 1912, Greece (1829), Serbia, Montenegro, and Romania (all in 1878), and Bulgaria (1908) were recognized as independent states, Croatia, Dalmatia, Bosnia, and Herzegovina belonged to Austria-Hungary, and Macedonia remained in Turkish hands; in First Balkan War 1912–13, Bulgaria, Serbia, Montenegro, and Greece took Macedonia from Turkey, and the independence of Albania (*q.v.*) was proclaimed; in Second Balkan War 1913, former allies and Romania united against Bulgaria; in WWI which was precipitated by Austrian demands on Serbia, only Bulgaria joined Central Powers; Romania, Yugoslavia, Greece, and Turkey signed Balkan Pact 1934, Bulgaria not joining because of desire for revision of boundaries received by peace treaties of WWI; in WWII, Albania became Italian 1939, Bulgaria joined Axis, Greece was conquered by Germany, and Yugoslavia and Romania were occupied by Axis forces 1941. Yugoslavia 1945, Albania and Bulgaria 1946 proclaimed republics; peace treaties with Bulgaria and Romania signed by UN Feb. 10, 1947. Following WWII, Albania, Bulgaria, Romania, and Yugoslavia came under U.S.S.R. influence; Yugoslavia broke with U.S.S.R. and maintained its own Communist system 1948; Greece and Turkey joined NATO; Albania broke with U.S.S.R. 1961; in late 1980s with break up of U.S.S.R. individual Balkan countries reexerted independence; Yugoslavia split into Slovenia, Croatia, Bosnia and Herzegovina, Macedonia, Yugoslavia (Serbia and Montenegro), with extensive ethnic fighting ensuing; Romania overthrew existing government; Albania and Bulgaria replaced existing rulers; much political and ethnic unrest existed throughout the peninsula.

Balkaria. See KABARDINO-BALKARIA.

Balkh \ˈbälk̲\. **1.** Historical region, N Afghanistan; approx. coextensive with ancient Bactria (*q.v.*); in medieval times on trade route bet. India and Europe.

2. *anc.* **Bac·tra** \ˈbak-trə\. Ancient city, ✻ of Bactria; once a center of Zoroastrianism; destroyed by Mongul conqueror Genghis Khan 13th cent.; rebuilt by Turkic ruler Timur 15th cent.; in 19th cent. reduced to village (Wazīrābād) near Mazār-i-Sharīf.

3. Village, N Afghanistan, just N of Wazīrābād (site of ancient Balkh).

Bal·khash *or* **Bal·qash** \bäl-ˈkäsh, bal-ˈkash\. Town on N shore of Lake Balkhash, E Kazakhstan; pop. (1991e) 87,600.

Balkhash, Lake *or Kazakh* **Balqash.** Freshwater lake in SE Kazakhstan, 600 mi. (965 km.) E of the Aral Sea; 376 mi. (605 km.) long; 7115 sq. mi. (18,428 sq. km.); max. depth 85 ft. (26 m.); frozen Nov.–March; its chief feeder is the Ili entering at SE in a wide delta.

Ball, Mount \ˈbȯl\. Peak in SW Canada, on border bet. Alberta and British Columbia; 10,865 ft. (3312 m.).

Bal·la·rat \ˈba-lə-ˌrat\. City, S cen. Victoria, SE Australia, 70 mi. (113 km.) WNW of Melbourne; pop. (1991c) 34,501; school of mines; a former gold-mining town; settled when gold was discovered c. 1850.

Bal·lard \ˈba-lərd\. County in W Kentucky. See table at KENTUCKY.

Ballari. See BELLARY.

Bal·la·ter \ˈba-lə-tər\. Village, Grampian region, NE Scotland, on the Dee E of Balmoral; pop. (1981p) 1238; medicinal springs nearby.

Bal·le·ny Islands \ˈba-lə-nē\. Group of volcanic islands in Ross Dependency, Antarctica, ab. 66°S, 163°E.

Bal·le·rup \ˈbä-lə-ˌrōb\. Commune, Sjælland I., Denmark; pop. (1989e) 45,197.

Bal·lia \ˈbä-lē-ə\. Town, E Uttar Pradesh, India, near N bank of Ganges; pop. (1991p) 84,758.

Bal·li·na \ˈba-lə-nə\. Town, N co. Mayo, NW Ireland, on Moy River; pop. (1991p) 6563; trade center; fishing.

Bal·li·na·muck \ˌba-lə-nə-ˈmək\. Village, N co. Longford, N cen. Ireland; scene of surrender 1798 of Irish insurrectionary forces.

Bal·li·na·sloe \ˌba-lə-nə-ˈslō\. Town, E co. Galway, W Ireland; pop. (1991p) 5793; annual cattle fair.

Bal·lin·ger \ˈba-lin-jər\. City, ⊗ of Runnels co., W cen. Texas, 32 mi. (51 km.) NE of San Angelo; pop. (1990c) 3975.

Bal·lin·skel·ligs Bay \ˌba-lin-ˈske-ligz\. Inlet of Atlantic Ocean on SW coast of Ireland, N of Kenmare River.

Ball's Bluff \ˈbȯlz\. Locality in Loudoun co., NE Virginia, on the Potomac 33 mi. (53 km.) NW of Washington; battle Oct. 21, 1861 in which Union force was severely defeated, a conflict of no military importance but one which aroused much criticism in the North.

Ball·ston Spa \ˈbȯl-stən-ˈspä, ˈspȯ\. Village, ⊗ of Saratoga co., E New York, ab. 6 mi. (10 km.) SW of Saratoga Springs; pop. (1990c) 4937; resort; mineral springs; founded c. 1787.

Ball·win \ˈbȯl-wən\. City, St. Louis co., Missouri, W of St. Louis; pop. (1990c) 21,816.

Bal·ly \ˈbä-lē\. Town, West Bengal, India, on Hugli River across from Calcutta; pop. (1991p) 181,978.

Bal·ly·cas·tle \ˌba-lē-ˈka-səl\. Town, ⊗ of Moyle dist., N Northern Ireland.

Bal·ly·me·na \ˌba-lē-ˈmē-nə\. **1.** District, Northern Ireland in cen. part of traditional co. Antrim; See table at IRELAND, NORTHERN.

2. Town, its ⊗.

Bal·ly·mon·ey \ˌba-lē-ˈmə-nē\. **1.** District, NE Northern Ireland. See table at IRELAND, NORTHERN.

2. Town, its ⊗.

Bal·ly·na·hinch \ˌba-lə-nə-ˈhinch\. Town, Down dist., SE Northern Ireland, 14 mi. (23 km.) S of Belfast; battle 1798 in which United Irishmen were defeated by the yeomanry.

Bal·maz·új·vá·ros \ˈbȯl-ˌmȯz-ˌü-ē-ˈvär-ōsh\. Commune, E cen. Hungary, W of Debrecen; pop. (1980p) 17,371.

Bal·mor·al \bal-ˈmȯr-əl, -ˈmär-\. Castle in SW Grampian region, Scotland, on the Dee River E of Braemar; Scottish residence of British sovereigns since 1852.

Balochistan. See BALUCHISTAN 2.

Balqash. See BALKHASH.

Bal·quhid·der \bal-ˈhwi-dər\. Village and parish, Central region, Scotland, ab. 28 mi. (45 km.) NW of Stirling; district won by Macgregor clan 1558.

Bal·sam Lake \ˈbȯl-səm\. Town, ⊗ of Polk co., NW Wisconsin; pop. (1990c) 1067.

Balsad. See VALSAD.

Bal·sas \bäl-säs\ *also* **Mex·ca·la** \mäs-ˈkä-lä\. River, cen. Mexico; rises in Tlaxcala state, flows S and then W through Guerrero into Petacalco Bay; 426 mi. (685 km.) long; its lower course forms boundary bet. Michoacán and Guerrero.

Bal·ta \ˈbäl-tə, ˈbȯl-\. Town, Odessa subdivision, Ukraine, on a tributary of the Bug River ab. 112 mi. (180 km.) NNW of the city of Odessa; center of an agricultural region raising especially grain and cattle; a Turkish town, formerly in Podolia; became Russian by treaty 1792; ✻ of Moldavian A.S.S.R. 1924–29.

Bălţi \ˈbəlts\ *or* **Bel·tsy** \ˈbyelt-sē\. Town, N cen. Moldova, on a W tributary of the Dniester; pop. (1991e) 164,900; formerly in Romania.

Bal·ti·ca \ˈbȯl-ti-kə\. Former landmass roughly comprising present-day Europe, and believed to have merged with Laurentia to form Laurussia (*qq.v.*) in mid-Paleozoic era; by subsequent merger and separation, believed to have successively formed part of Pangaea, Laurasia, and Eurasia (*qq.v.*).

Baltic Port. See PALDISKI.

Bal·tic Provinces \ˈbȯl-tik\. The former Russian administrative units of Estonia, Livonia, and Courland, which in 1918 were formed into the independent republics of Estonia and Latvia. See BALTIC STATES.

Baltic Sea *or Ger.* **Ost·see** \ˈȯst-ˌzā\ *or Russ.* **Bal·ti·sko·ye Mo·re** \bəl-ˈtyē-skə-yə-ˈmȯr-yə\; *anc.* **Ma·re Sue·vi·cum** \ˈmā-rē-ˈswē-vi-kəm, ˈmä-rā\. Sea in N Europe, an arm of the

Atlantic Ocean connecting with the North Sea through the Skaggerak, Kattegat, and Øresund, and extending roughly NE to SW bet. 54° and 66°N lat. and 9° and 30°E long.; 1056 mi. (1699 km.) long; 163,050 sq. mi. (422,300 sq. km.); max. depth 1539 ft. (469 m.); enclosed by Denmark, Sweden, Finland, Estonia, Latvia, Lithuania, Poland, and Germany. Has two large arms: Gulf of Bothnia bet. Sweden and Finland, and Gulf of Finland bet. Finland and Estonia.

Baltic States. The republics of Estonia, Latvia, and Lithuania on the E shore of the Baltic Sea, which were estab. as independent states in 1917 out of the Baltic Provinces (*q.v.*) of Russia and the government of Kovno and part of Wilno (later Lithuania); aided by German and Allied forces in forcing out Bolshevik invasion 1919; incorp. in the U.S.S.R. Aug. 3, 1940; overrun by German forces 1941; recovered by Soviet troops in summer and fall of 1944; regained independence 1991. Name has sometimes been applied to include Finland and Poland as well.

Bal·tīm \bal-'tēm\. Town, Egypt, near coast in Nile Delta midway bet. Rosetta and Damietta mouths and at E end of Lake Burullus.

Bal·ti·more \'bȯl-tə-ˌmōr, 'bȯlt-mər, 'bȯl-mər\. **1.** County in N Maryland. See table at MARYLAND.

2. City, Maryland, on Patapsco River at upper end of Chesapeake Bay ab. 40 mi. (64 km.) NE of Washington, D.C.; pop. (1990c) 736,014; geographically in S Baltimore co. but administratively independent (see table at MARYLAND); important seaport; site of Francis Scott Key Bridge (continuous truss; main span 1200 ft. or 366 m.; completed 1977) spanning Patapsco River estuary; manufactures aerospace equipment, chemicals, steel; copper refining; St. Mary's Seminary and Univ. (1791), Univ. of Maryland at Baltimore (1807), Maryland Institute Coll. of Art (1826), Loyola Coll. (1852), Peabody Institute of Johns Hopkins Univ. (1857), Towson State Univ. (1866), Morgan State Univ. (1867), Coll. of Notre Dame of Maryland (1873), Johns Hopkins Univ. (1876), Goucher Coll. (1885), Coppin State Coll. (1900), Baltimore Hebrew Coll. (1919), Univ. of Baltimore (1925).

History: Purchased by Maryland legislature 1729 and made a shipbuilding and export center; during American Revolution, meeting place for American Congress during the British occupation of Philadelphia; incorp. as city 1797; first U.S. Roman Catholic diocese 1789; bombardment of its Fort McHenry by British Sept. 12–13, 1814 inspired American lawyer and poet Francis Scott Key to write *The Star Spangled Banner* adopted as the U.S. national anthem in 1931; in 1827 local merchants organized Baltimore and Ohio R.R. to retain share in trans-Allegheny trade which the Erie Canal threatened to draw entirely to New York; during Civil War, sympathy with the South occasioned riots when Union troops marched through Apr. 19, 1861; suffered from a destructive fire Feb. 7, 1904; burial place of writer Edgar Allan Poe.

Baltiski. See PALDISKI.

Baltiskoye More. See BALTIC SEA.

Bal·ti·stan \ˌbȯl-tə-'stan, ˌbəl-\ *or* **Little Ti·bet** \tə-'bet\. Part of Ladakh region in Pakistani-controlled sector of Jammu and Kashmir state, bet. 34° and 36°N lat. and 75° and 77°E long.; contains some of highest peaks of W Himalayas; inhabited by Baltis, Tibetan-speaking Muslims.

Bal·tiysk *or* **Bal·tisk** \bəl-'tēsk\ *or Ger.* **Pil·lau** \'pi-ˌlau̇\. Town, on sandspit at entrance of the Vislinski Zaliv, Kaliningrad Oblast, Russia in Europe, formerly in East Prussia, Germany; fishing. Site of landing of Swedish King Gustavus II Adolph 1626. Assigned to U.S.S.R. at Potsdam Conference 1945.

Baltiyskaya Kosa. See VISLINSKI ZALIV.

Bal·to·ro \bȯl-'tōr-ō, bäl-\. Glacier, Karakoram Range, bet. K2, Gasherbrum, and Masherbrum peaks, in region administered by Pakistan; 35 mi. (56 km.) long, ab. 2 mi. (3 km.) wide near its terminus.

Balūchestān va Sīstān. See SĪSTĀN VA BALŪCHESTĀN.

Ba·lu·chi·stan \bə-ˌlü-chi-'stan, -'stän\. **1.** *also* **Be·lu·chi·stan** \bə-\. Region, W Asia, encompassing territory lying in E Iran and SW Pakistan. Iranian sector (formerly called **Persian Baluchistan**) part of Kermān prov. until it united with Sīstān (1959) forming Balūchestān va Sīstān prov. For Pakistani sector, see BALUCHISTAN 2.

2. *or* **Ba·lo·chi·stan** \bə-ˌlȯ-\. Province, SW Pakistan, bounded on N by Afghanistan, on E by provs. of North-West Frontier, Punjab, and Sind, on S by the Arabian Sea, and on W by Iran; mountainous, esp. in NE; Sulaiman Range on NE border, Kirthar Range on SE; ranges of 5000 ft. (1524 m.) in cen. part; Hamuni-Mashkel marsh and desert in NW; much of land is barren with irregular and scant water supply, but with some fertile valleys. See table at PAKISTAN.

Rivers: Mashkel, Dasht, Hingol, Hab.

History: In ancient times, part of Gedrosia; traversed by Macedonian King Alexander the Great 325 B.C.; part of Bactrian kingdom (see BALKH 2); ruled from 7th–10th cents. A.D. by Arabs who overthrew Persia; except for period when part of Mogul Empire 1594–1638, returned to moderate form of Persian rule; under Nasir Khan of Kalat (1739–95), most able of its princes, included several districts of Sind; by treaty of 1876 made virtually a British dependency; districts, assigned at close of Afghan War (1878–79), enlarged; made British province of India 1887; boundaries with Afghanistan and Persia settled 1885 and 1896; its subdivisions (1) **British Baluchistan** (9084 sq. mi. or 23,528 sq. km.; ✻ Quetta), (2) Agency territories (43,613 sq. mi. or 112,958 sq. km.; ✻ Quetta), (3) Kalat (in cen. part; 59,068 sq. mi. or 152, 986 sq. km.; ✻ Kalat), (4) Kharan (in NW part; 14,210 sq. mi. or 36,804 sq. km.), and (5) Las Bela (in SE part; 7132 sq. mi. or 18,472 sq. km.) became part of Pakistan 1947–48; **Baluchistan States** (a union of Kalat, Kharan, and Las Bela, formed 1952) lost most of its administrative functions 1955; reconstituted as a separate province 1970.

Baluchistan, Persian. See BALUCHISTAN 1.

Ba·lut \bä-'lüt\. Island, larger and westernmost of the Sarangani Is., SW Davao del Sur prov., Mindanao, Philippines; 22 sq. mi. (57 sq. km.); has volcano 3110 ft. (948 m.).

Bal·zar \bal-'sär\. Town, Guayas prov., W Ecuador, 55 mi. (88 km.) N of Guayaquil.

Bam \'bam, 'bäm\. Town, Kermān prov., SE Iran, on caravan route SE of Kermān; pop. (1986c) 50,709; its trade more important in Middle Ages than in modern times; has citadel held by Afghans 1719–1801.

Ba·ma·ko \'bä-mä-ˌkō\. Town, ✻ of Mali, on Niger River ab. 90 mi. (145 km.) NE of the Guinea border; met. area pop. (1992e) 745,787; commercial center; terminus of railroad line from Dakar in Senegal.

Bam·ba·ri \ˌbäm-bä-'rē\. Town, S cen. Central African Rep.; pop. (1988e) 52,100.

Bam·ba·ta·na \ˌbäm-bä-'tä-nä\. Chief settlement, on cen. part of W coast of Choiseul I., Solomon Is., W Pacific Ocean.

Bam·berg \'bam-ˌbərg\. **1.** County in SW South Carolina. See table at SOUTH CAROLINA.

2. Town, its ⊗, 18 mi. (29 km.) SW of Orangeburg; pop. (1990c) 3843.

Bamberg \'bäm-ˌberk\. City, Bavaria, S cen. Germany, on Regnitz River near its confluence with the Main 30 mi. (48 km.) W of Bayreuth; pop. (1992e) 70,689; cathedral (Romanesque-Gothic transition); 16th cent. bishop's palace; seminary; observatory; first mentioned in 902.

Bam·burgh; *earlier* **Bam·bor·ough** \'bam-bə-rə\. Village, E Northumberland co., N England, on coast 17 mi. (27 km.) SE of Berwick-upon-Tweed; as Bamborough was ✻ of ancient Bernicia and for a time ✻ of Northumbria.

Bā·mi·ān \ˌbä-mē-'än\. **1.** Valley and pass in W Hindu Kush Mts., NE Afghanistan, ab. 60 mi. (97 km.) NNW of Kabul; alt. 12,500 ft. (3810 m.).

2. City, cen. Afghanistan, in Bāmiān Valley, N of the Koh-i-Baba; pop. (1988e) 8,700; ruins of great towers and numerous cave dwellings in the walls of the valley, also two colossal images of Buddhist figures, described 630 A.D. by Chinese traveler Hsüan-tsang. Its early history obscure, but it flourished in 12th cent. under Ghūrid dynasty; besieged and destroyed 1221 by Mongol conqueror Genghis Khan.

Bam·pūr \bäm-ˈpu̇r\. Town, Balūchestān va Sīstān prov., SE Iran; in a fertile valley; chief town of former Persian Baluchistan.

Bam·ra \ˈbäm-rə\. Former Indian state, now part of Orissa, E India; 1974 sq. mi. (5113 sq. km.); ✻ Deogarh.

Ba·mu \ˈbä-mü\. Island in Pool Malebo (*q.v.*) in Congo River, W Africa; belongs to Rep. of the Congo.

Ba·na·ba \bä-ˈnä-bä\ *or* **Ocean Island.** Island, Kiribati, in W Pacific Ocean ab. 55 mi. (90 km.) S of the Equator; ab. 2.5 sq. mi. (6 sq. km.); pop. (1990c) 284; former ✻ of colony of Gilbert and Ellice Is.; formerly contained large phosphate deposits. Claimed by British 1900 and made part of Gilbert and Ellice Islands Colony 1916; occupied by Japanese 1942–45; part of independent Kiribati from 1979.

Ba·na·hao, Mount \bä-ˈnä-ˌhau̇\. Extinct volcano, SW Quezon prov., Luzon, Philippines, on Laguna border NW of Lucena; 7103 ft. (2165 m.); last major eruption 1730.

Ba·nam \bə-ˈnam\ *or* **Phu·mi Banam** \ˈpü-mē\. Town, Cambodia, on left bank of the Mekong 30 mi. (48 km.) SE of Phnom Penh.

Ba·nana \bə-ˈna-nə\. **1.** River, actually a wide part of the lagoon bet. Canaveral Penin. and Merritt I., Brevard co., E Florida.

2. Seaport town, W Bas-Zaïre administrative region, W Democratic Rep. of the Congo, on N side of the mouth of Congo River; pop. (1991e) 3165.

Banana Islands. Group of small islands in Atlantic Ocean off S point of Sierra Leone Penin., Sierra Leone, once a station for English slave traders.

Ba·na·nal \ˌbȧ-nə-ˈnäl\. Island in Araguaia River, NW Goiás state, Brazil; over 200 mi. (322 km.) long.

Banaras. See VARANASI 1.

Ba·nas \ˈbə-ˌnäs, ˈbä-\. River, S Rajasthan, N cen. India; rises at S end of Aravalli Range in Udaipur, flows NE to the Chambal; 330 mi. (531 km.) long.

Banâs, Ras \ˈba-nəs\ *also* **Ras Be·nas** \räs-ˈbe-nəs\; *Eng.* **Cape Banas.** Cape (*ras*) on E coast of Egypt, projecting into Red Sea N of Foul Bay; 23°54′N, 35°48′E.

Ba·nat \ˈbä-ˌnät\. **1.** Agricultural region (also known as the Vojvodina, *q.v.*) formerly in S Hungary E of Tisza River, S of the Mures, N of the Danube, and W of the Transylvanian Alps; divided bet. Romania and Yugoslavia, except a small strip near Szeged. In Middle Ages, 9th–14th cents., settled chiefly by Magyars and Serbs; fell into neglect under rule of Turks 1552–1718; reclaimed by Austrian Empress Maria Theresa (after 1740), incorp. into Hungary 1779, made an Austrian crown land 1849, and reverted to Hungary 1860. After WWI divided mostly bet. Yugoslavia and Romania 1919; in WWII its W part (in Yugoslavia) seized by Hungary 1944–45.

2. Region, W Romania; 7224 sq. mi. (18,710 sq. km.); formerly part of the Banat region of Hungary, later a province of Romania.

3. Former subprovince in N Yugoslavia; ✻ Veliki Bečkerek (Petrovgrad); later (1929–45) a part of Dunavska co.; since 1945 forms the autonomous region Vojvodina in Yugoslavia.

Ba·na·ue \bä-ˈnä-ˌwä\. Municipality, NW Ifugao prov., Luzon, Philippines; pop. (1980c) 22,900.

Ban·bridge \ban-ˈbrij\. **1.** District, SE Northern Ireland. See table at IRELAND, NORTHERN.

2. Town, its ⊗, SE Northern Ireland, on the Bann River; pop. (1981c) 9650.

Ban·bury \ˈban-ˌber-ē, -bə-rē\. Town, Oxfordshire, cen. England, on the Cherwell 38 mi. (61 km.) SE of Birmingham; pop. (1981p) 35,796; famous for its Banbury cakes.

Banco, El. See EL BANCO.

Ban·da \ˈbän-də, ˈban-\. Town, S Uttar Pradesh, India, on Ken River 95 mi. (153 km.) W of Allahabad; pop. (1991p) 97,227.

Banda, La. See LA BANDA.

Ban·da At·jeh \ˈbän-dä-ˈä-chē\; *formerly* **Koe·ta·ra·dja** *or* **Ku·ta·ra·ja** \ˌkü-tä-ˈrä-jä\. Town, ✻ of Atjeh prov., Sumatra, Indonesia; pop. (1990c) 184,699.

Ban·da Be·sar \ˈbän-dä-bä-ˈsär\ *or* **Great Banda** *or* **Ban·da·lon·tor** \-ˌlōn-ˌtȯr\. Largest of the Banda Is., Indonesia; 7.5 mi. (12 km.) long; volcanic in origin; with Bandanaira and Gunungapi encloses a small inland sea that forms the harbor of Bandanaira, one of best in the Malay Archipelago.

Ban·dai \ˈbän-ˌdī\. Volcano in a national park in Fukushima prefecture, N cen. Honshū, Japan, N of Lake Inawashiro; 5968 ft. (1819 m.); had four peaks, one of which was blown off in a destructive eruption July 1888.

Ban·da Islands \ˈbän-dä, ˈban-\. Island group of the S cen. Moluccas, Indonesia, Malay Archipelago, 66 mi. (106 km.) S of E Ceram; 72 sq. mi. (186 sq. km.); ✻ Bandanaira; comprises three large islands Banda Besar, Bandanaira, and Gunungapi, and seven small islands, all of volcanic origin. For centuries important in the spice trade; nutmegs, and other spices, coconuts, fruits. Annexed by Portuguese 1512; conquered by Dutch 1621; settlement and interference of English led to Amboina Massacre 1623; held by British 1796–1800 and during Napoleonic Wars; restored to Dutch 1814; under Japanese control during WWII; became part of independent Indonesia following WWII.

Bandalontor. See BANDA BESAR.

Ban·da·ma \bän-ˈdä-mä\. River, cen. Ivory Coast, flows S into Atlantic; 497 mi. (800 km.) long.

Ban·da·nai·ra *or* **Ban·da Nei·ra** \ˌbän-dä-ˈnī-rä\. **1.** Small island, most important of the Banda Is., Indonesia.

2. Town on the island, ✻ of the Banda Is.; its harbor is formed by close juxtaposition of Banda Besar and Gunungapi (*qq.v.*); from 16th to 19th cents., an important trade center for spices.

Ban·da Ori·en·tal \ˈbän-dä-ˌȯr-ē-en-ˈtäl\. Former name of Uruguay (*q.v.*).

Bandar. See MACHILIPATNAM.

Ban·dar ʻAb·bās \ˈbȧn-dȧr-ȧ-ˈbäs\ *or* **Ban·dar–e–Ab·bas** \ˈbȧn-dȧr-ē-\; *formerly* **Gom·broon** \gäm-ˈbrün\. Seaport, ✻ of Hormozgān prov., S Iran, on the Strait of Hormuz; pop. (1986c) 201,642; founded 1623 by Shāh ʻAbbās I; has long been one of the chief ports of Iran, English and Dutch factories having been estab. for trade in 17th cent.

Ban·dar–e An·za·li \ˈbən-dər-ē-ˈan-zə-lē\ *also* **En·ze·li** \ˈen-zə-lē\; *formerly* **Bandar–e Pah·la·vī** \ˈpä-lə-ˌvē\. Town on Caspian Sea; NW Iran; pop. (1986c) 87,063.

Bandar–e–Bushehr. See BŪSHEHR 2.

Ban·dar–e Kho·mey·ni *or* **Bandar Kho·mey·nī** \k̲ō-ˈmā-nē\; *formerly* **Bandar–e Shāh·pūr** \shä-ˈpu̇r\. Town, SW Iran, 55 mi. (88 km.) ENE of Ābādān; pop. (1986c) 49,355; S terminus of Trans-Iranian R.R. and port at head of Persian Gulf; oil storage and shipping disrupted by war with Iraq in 1980s.

Ban·dar–e Len·geh \ˈbȧn-dȧr-ē-leŋ-ˈgā\; *formerly* **Lin·geh.** Seaport town, Persian Gulf prov., S Iran, on the Persian Gulf, opp. W end of Qeshm I. and ab. 100 mi. (161 km.) SW of Bandar ʻAbbās. Old trading port, formerly a center for export of pearls and later carpets, fruits, tobacco, hides. Held by Arabia from latter part of 18th cent. to 1887.

Bandar–e Pahlavī. See BANDAR–E ANZALI.

Ban·dar–e Tor·ke·man \ˈbȧn-dȧr-ē-ˌtȯr-ke-ˈmän\; *formerly* **Bandar–e Shāh** \ˈshä, ˈshȯ\. Port, N Iran, at SE corner of Caspian Sea; N terminus of Trans-Iranian R.R. from Bandar-e Khomeyni.

Bandar Lampung. See TANJUNGKARANG.

Bandar Maharani. See MUAR 2.

Bandar Penggaram. See BATU PAHAT.

Ban·dar Se·ri Be·ga·wan \ˈbȧn-dȧr-ˈser-ē-be-ˈgä-wȧn\; *formerly* **Bru·nei** \ˈbrü-ˌnī, -ˌnā\ *or* **Brunei Town.** Town, ✻ of Brunei; pop. (1991c) 21,484; urban area pop. (1988e) 52,300; royal palace; mosque.

Ban·da Sea \ˈbän-də, ˈban-\. Body of water in E Malay Archipelago, SE of Sulawesi, S of Buru I. and Ceram I., W of Kai Is. and Aru Is., NW of the Tanimbar group, and NE of Timor I.; 285,000 sq. mi. (738,150 sq. km.); max. depth ab. 21,000 ft. (6401 m.).

Ban·dei·ra, Pi·co da \ˈpē-kü-ˌdä-bän-ˈdā-rə\. Mountain, E Brazil, on border between Espírito Santo and Minas Gerais; 9495 ft. (2894 m.).

Ban·dei·ran·tes \ˌbäⁿ-dā-ˈraⁿ-tēs\. Municipality, Paraná state, S Brazil, ab. 215 mi. (346 km.) WNW of São Paulo.

Ban·de·lier National Monument \ˌban-də-ˈlir\. See UNITED STATES, *National Monuments.*

Ban·de·ra \ban-ˈder-ə\. **1.** County in SW cen. Texas. See table at TEXAS.

2. City, its ⊗; pop. (1990c) 877; alt. ab. 1260 ft. (384 m.); resort.

Ban·de·ras Bay \bän-ˈdā-räs\. Inlet of the Pacific Ocean on W cen. coast of Mexico, chiefly in NW Jalisco state.

Ban·dır·ma \ˌbän-dər-ˈmä\; *formerly* **Pan·der·ma** \ˈpän-dər-ˌmä\. Town on S shore of Sea of Marmara, NW Turkey in Asia; pop. (1990p) 77,211.

Bandjarmasin. See BANJARMASIN.

Bandoeng. See BANDUNG.

Ban·don \ˈban-dən\. Town on **Bandon River,** S co. Cork, SW Ireland; pop. (1986c) 1943; a noted stronghold of Protestantism in the 17th cent.

Ban·dra \ˈbän-drə\. Suburb of Bombay, Maharashtra, W India, at S end of Salsette I.; population includes many native-born Christians who date their religious affiliations back to 16th cent. and 17th cent. Portuguese missionaries.

Ban·dun·du \bän-ˈdün-dü\. **1.** Administrative region of W Democratic Rep. of the Congo. See table at ZAIRE 1.

2. Town, its ✻, on Kasai River; pop. (1991e) 77,345.

Ban·dung *or Du.* **Ban·doeng** \ˈbän-ˌdůŋ\. City, ✻ of West Java prov., Indonesia, on railroad line 75 mi. (121 km.) SE of Jakarta; pop. (1990c) 2,057,442; alt. 2346 ft. (715 m.); textiles; surrounded by volcanoes and high mountains; center of Sundanese cultural life; several universities and colleges; nuclear research center (1964). In WWII was main defense position of Dutch government and Allied headquarters but was captured by Japanese Mar. 7, 1942; site of Asian-African Conference 1955; founded 1810.

Ba·nes \ˈbä-nās\. Seaport and municipality, E Cuba; munic. pop. (1981p) 84,731.

Banff \ˈbamf\. **1.** Resort town near Lake Louise (*q.v.*) in Banff National Park, SW Alberta, Canada; pop. (1991c) 5668; alt. ab. 4535 ft. (1382 m.).

2. *or* **Banff·shire** \-ˌshir, -shər\. Former county, NE Scotland; ⊗ Banff; other large town Buckie; rivers Spey and Deveron.

3. Burgh, N Grampian region, Scotland; pop. (1981p) 3929; seaside resort; fishing.

Banff National Park. See CANADA, *National Parks.*

Ban·ga·lore \ˈbaŋ-gə-ˌlōr\. City, S India, ✻ of Karnataka, 183 mi. (294 km.) W of Madras; pop. (1991c) 3,302,296; alt. 3113 ft. (949 m.); transportation equipment, pharmaceuticals, textiles, agricultural implements; Bangalore Univ. (1964), Univ. of Agricultural Sciences (1964), National Aeronautical Research Laboratory (1960). Founded in 16th cent.; later a possession of the Marathas; became a fief of Indian ruler and soldier Hyder Ali 1758; taken 1791 by British under Lord Charles Cornwallis; except for civil and military station restored to raja of Mysore (now Karnataka) 1881.

Ban·ga·na·pal·le \ˌbəŋ-gə-nə-ˈpə-le\. **1.** Former Indian state, now part of Tamil Nadu, S India, 210 mi. (338 km.) NW of Madras; 259 sq. mi. (671 sq. km.); once under Hyderabad, control ceded to Madras government 1800.

2. Town, its ✻.

Ban·gas·sou \ˌbäŋ-gä-ˈsü\. Town, S Central African Rep., on N bank of Bomu River.

Bang·gai Archipelago \ˈbäŋ-ˌgī\. Group of islands off E coast of Sulawesi, Indonesia, Malay Archipelago; 1221 sq. mi. (3162 sq. km.); islands include **Banggai Island,** Peleng (*q.v.*), and many small islands and islets.

Bang·gi \ˈbäŋ-gē\. Island, N Sabah, E Malaysia, S of the main channel of Balabac Strait.

Bangi. See BANGUI.

Bang·il \ˈbaŋ-ˌil\. Town, East Java prov., Indonesia, near SW coast of Madura Strait; on railroad line ab. 20 mi. (32 km.) S of Surabaya.

Bang·ka \ˈbaŋ-kä\. **1.** *or* **Ban·ka** \ˈbaŋ-\. An island of Indonesia, at NW corner of the Java Sea off SE Sumatra; 136 mi. (219 km.) long by 69 mi. (111 km.) wide; 4609 sq. mi. (11,937 sq. km.); separated from Sumatra by the narrow **Bangka Strait** (ab. 10 mi. or 16 km. wide); chief town Pangkalpinang; formed greater part of former Bangka residency; an important tin-producing area; chief port Muntok at N end of Bangka Strait. Formerly belonged to ruler of Palembang; ceded to British 1812; became Dutch by exchange in 1814 for Cochin in India; under Japanese control 1942–45; part of independent Indonesia 1949.

2. *or officially* **Bangka and Dependencies.** Former residency, SE Sumatra, Netherlands Indies, now part of the Indonesian prov. of South Sumatra; ✻ Pangkalpinang; comprised the islands of Bangka (see BANGKA 1) and Belitung.

Bang·ka·lan \ˌbäŋ-kä-ˈlän\. Town, W coast of Madura I., East Java prov., Indonesia.

Bang·kok \ˈbaŋ-ˌkäk, baŋ-ˈ\ *or Thai* **Krung Thep** \ˈkrůŋ-ˈtep\. City, ✻ of Thailand, on the Chao Phraya 25 mi. (40 km.) above its mouth; munic. pop. (1991e) 5,620,591; transportation center; port facilities; cement, paper, textiles; food processing; several universities and colleges, several hundred Buddhist temples; old section of city built on pontoons or piles with many canals. Only an agricultural village and a fort before 1767 when it became a stronghold against the Burmese; became the ✻ 1782. Seized by Japanese Dec. 8, 1941; frequently bombed by Allied planes 1944–45; city incorporated outlying areas 1971–72; from 1955 to 1977 site of headquarters of Southeast Asia Treaty Organization; site of headquarters of the UN Economic Commission for Asia and the Far East.

Ban·gla·desh \ˌbäŋ-glə-ˈdesh, ˌbaŋ-, -ˈdāsh\; *before independence* **East Pakistan.** Republic, S Asia, bounded on N and E by India, on SE by India and Myanmar, on S by the Bay of Bengal, and on W by India; 55,126 sq. mi. (142,776 sq. km.); pop. (1993e) 115,075,000; ✻ Dhaka.

Physical features: Generally flat, with max. elev. ab. 660 ft. (200 m.); characterized by alluvial plains, which are dissected by numerous connecting rivers and streams; S part consists of E sector of Ganges-Brahmaputra Delta; chief rivers Ganges and Brahmaputra (here known as Jamuna), uniting to form Padma; much of area subject to extreme flooding (mean annual rainfall in excess of 60 in. or 152 cm.) often causing great loss of life.

Chief products: Rice, jute, tea, natural gas, wheat, fertilizer, newsprint.

Chief towns: Dhaka, Chittagong, Khulna. For history of region, see BENGAL; was part of Pakistan 1947–71; scene of defeat (1971) of Pakistani forces by Bengali nationalists (supported by Indians), following Pakistani attempt to suppress Bengali autonomy movement; subsequently became independent 1971; political unrest has continued.

Bangong Co. See PANGONG TSO.

Ban·gor \ˈbaŋ-ˌgȯr, ˈban-ˌgȯr, ˈbaŋ-gər\. **1.** City, ⊗ of Penobscot co., E cen. Maine, at head of navigation on Penobscot River 60 mi. (97 km.) NE of Augusta; pop. (1990c) 33,181; Bangor Theological Seminary (1814), Husson Coll. (1898); incorp. 1791.

2. Borough, Northampton co., E Pennsylvania, 23 mi. (37 km.) NE of Allentown; pop. (1990c) 5383; founded 1773.

3. \ˈbaŋ-gər\. Town, ⊗ of North Down dist., SE Northern Ireland, on S side of entrance to Belfast Lough 12 mi. (19 km.) ENE of Belfast; pop. (1981c) 46,585; seaside resort.

4. \ˈbaŋ-gər, -gȯr\. City, Gwynedd co., NW Wales; pop. (1981p) 12,174; slate deposits nearby; Univ. College of North Wales (1884).

Bang Pla Soi. See CHON BURI.

Ban·gued \bäŋ-ˈged\. Municipality, ✻ of Abra prov., NW Luzon, Philippines, on Abra River; pop. (1980c) 28,666.

Ban·gui *also* **Ban·gi** \bäŋ-ˈgē, ˈbäŋ-ˌ\. City, ✻ of Central African Rep., on Ubangi River; pop. (1988p) 451,690.

Bangui \ˈbäŋ-gē\. Municipality, N Ilocos Norte, Luzon, Philippines, on Bangui Bay 25 mi. (40 km.) NNE of Laoag; pop. (1980c) 11,122.

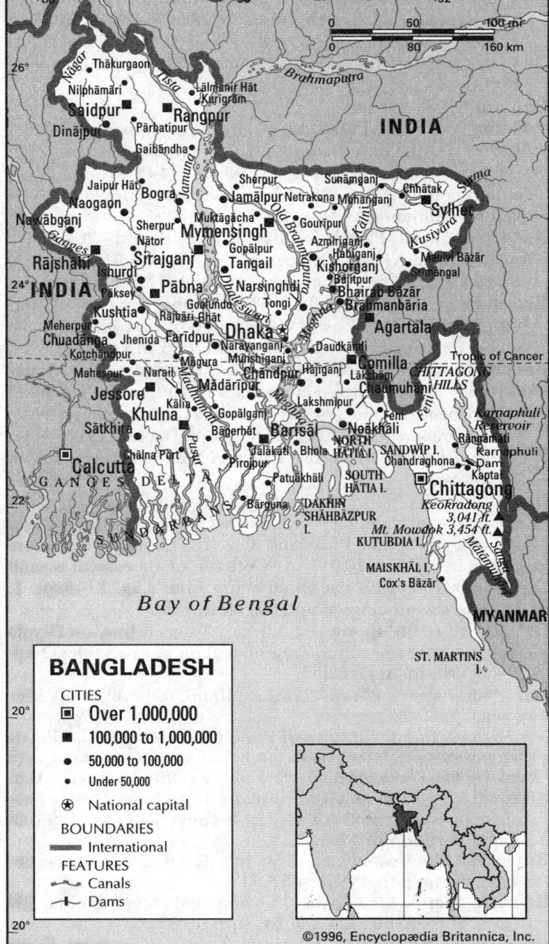

©1996, Encyclopædia Britannica, Inc.

Bangui Bay. Inlet of South China Sea on N coast of Ilocos Norte prov., Luzon, Philippines, extending from Dialao Point on NE to Negra Point on SW; ab. 10 mi. (16 km.) wide.

Bang·we·u·lu, Lake \ˌbäŋ-gwā-ˈü-lü\ *or* **Lake Bang·we·o·lo** \-ˈō-lō\. Lake, N Zambia, SSE of Lake Mweru and SSW of Lake Tanganyika; 45 mi. (72 km.) long; 3800 sq. mi. (9842 sq. km.) (incl. swamps); its outlet is the Luapula, a headstream of the Congo. First visited by Scottish missionary and explorer Dr. David Livingstone 1868; circumnavigated 1896.

Ba·ní \bä-ˈnē\. City, ✻ of Peravia prov., S Dominican Republic, SW of Santo Domingo; pop. (1981p) 95,008.

Banī Suwayf. See BENI SUEF.

Bā·ni·yās *also* **Ba·ni·as** \ˈbȧ-nē-yȧs\. **1.** Town on coast of Syria, 25 mi. (40 km.) S of Latakia.

2. *or* **Pa·ne·as** \pə-ˈnē-əs\ *anc.* **Cae·sa·rae Phi·lip·pi** \ˌsē-zə-ˈrē-ə-ˈfi-lə-ˌpī, ˌse-sə-, ˌse-zə-, fə-ˈli-ˌpī\. Village, SW Syria, in region occupied by Israel 1967; ancient city; has temple built by Herod the Great and enlarged by Philip the Tetrarch; important in Roman times.

Ban·jak Islands *or* **Ban·yak Islands** \ˈbän-ˌyäk\. Island group, Atjeh autonomous dist., Indonesia, in the Indian Ocean off NW Sumatra; 123 sq. mi. (319 sq. km.); comprises about 65 islands, most of them very small, **Great Banjak,** the largest, being ab. 20 mi. (32 km.) by 7 mi. (11 km.).

Ba·nja Lu·ka \ˈbän-yä-ˈlü-kä\. Town, N Bosnia and Herzegovina on Vrbas River; pop. (1991p) 195,139; thermal springs. Probably dates back to a Roman fort; esp. important 16th–18th cents. when it was several times a battlefield bet. Austrians and Turks. In 1992 became ✻ of Serbian Rep. of Bosnia and Herzegovina, an autonomous region within Bosnia and Herzegovina.

Ban·jar·ma·sin *also* **Ban·djar·ma·sin** \ˈbän-jär-ˌmä-sin\. Town, ✻ of South Kalimantan prov., Indonesia, on Martapura River near its junction with the Barito, SE Borneo; pop. (1990c) 481,371; ab. 24 mi. (39 km.) from the sea and a port of call for large vessels; trade center for Barito River basin, exporting timber, pepper, rubber; university (1961). In early times under Hindu influences; became Muslim ab. 1500 under Javanese; settled by Dutch 1711; held by English 1811–17; bombed by Japanese and seized by them Feb. 13, 1942; retaken by Allies Aug. 1945.

Ban·jul \ˈbän-ˌjül\; *until 1973* **Bath·urst** \ˈba-ˌthərst\. Seaport, ✻ of Gambia, on Island of St. Mary in Gambia River; pop. (1983c) 44,188; important commercial center.

Ban·ju·mas *also* **Ban·yu·mas** *or Du.* **Ban·joe·mas** \ˈbän-yü-ˌmäs\. **1.** Former residency, Java, Netherlands Indies, now part of the Indonesian prov. of Central Java; 2472 sq. mi. (6402 sq. km.). First came under Dutch 1705.

2. Town, its ✻.

Banjuwangi. See BANYUWANGI.

Banka. See BANGKA 1.

Banks \ˈbaŋks\. County in NE Georgia. See table at GEORGIA.

Banks, Cape. Point on coast of New South Wales, SE Australia, on N shore of entrance to Botany Bay.

Banks Island. 1. Small island in Torres Strait, N of Cape York, Queensland, NE Australia.

2. Island off W cen. British Columbia, Canada, on E side of Hecate Strait; 50 mi. (80 km.) long; 400 sq. mi. (1036 sq. km.).

3. Island, W Northwest Territories, Canada, NW of Victoria I.; ab. 250 mi. (400 km.) long; 27,038 sq. mi. (70,028 sq. km.); separated from mainland by Amundsen Gulf.

Banks Islands. Group of five small islands and a number of islets, SW Pacific Ocean, N of Vanuatu; pop. (1991e) 5521; administered as part of Vanuatu; chief islands Vanua Lava and Santa María; volcanic and fertile, with luxuriant vegetation; visited by English naval officer Capt. William Bligh 1793; named for his patron, naturalist Joseph Banks.

Banks Peninsula. Peninsula projecting from E cen. coast of South I., New Zealand; ab. 35 mi. (56 km.) long and 25 mi. (40 km.) wide; Christchurch is at its base on N side, Akaroa Harbor at its SE extremity.

Banks Strait. Passage separating the Furneaux Group of islands from NE Tasmania (*q.v.*); ab. 13 mi. (21 km.) wide.

Banks·town \ˈbaŋks-ˌtau̇n\. City, E New South Wales, Australia, WSW of Sydney; pop. (1991c) 153,904.

Ban·ku·ra \ˈbäŋ-ku̇-ˌrä\. Town, West Bengal, NE India, 95 mi. (153 km.) WNW of Calcutta; pop. (1991p) 114,927; four colleges.

Ban Mak Khaeng. See UDON THANI.

Ban·me·thu·ot \ˈbän-mā-ˈtüt\. Town, Vietnam, 160 mi. (257 km.) NNE of Ho Chi Minh City.

Bann \ˈban\. Name of two rivers in Northern Ireland: the **Upper Bann** 25 mi. (40 km.) long, rising in Newry and Mourne dist. and flowing NW into Lough Neagh; the **Lower Bann** 33 mi. (53 km.) long, flowing N out of Lough Neagh into the Atlantic.

Ban·nack \ˈba-nək\. Mountain in Yellowstone National Park, NW Wyoming; 10,300 ft. (3139 m.).

Ban·ner \ˈba-nər\. County in W Nebraska. See table at NEBRASKA.

Banner Peak. Mountain in the Sierra Nevada, in NE Madera co., cen. California; 12,957 ft. (3949 m.).

Ban·ning \ˈba-niŋ\. City, Riverside co., SE California, 25 mi. (40 km.) ESE of San Bernardino; pop. (1990c) 20,570; founded 1883.

\ə\ **abut** \ˈə\ matches \ᵊ\ kitten, Fr table \ər\ **further** \a\ **ash** \ā\ **ace** \ä\ cot, cart \ȧ\ Fr bac \au̇\ **out** \b̲\ Span Avila \ch\ **chin** \e\ **bet** \ē\ **easy** \g\ **go** \i\ **hit** \ī\ **ice** \j\ **job** \k̲\ Ger **ich, Buch** \ⁿ\ Fr vin \ŋ\ **sing** \ō\ **go** \ö\ **all** \ȯ\ **law** \œ\ Fr **bœuf** \ᴂ\ Fr **feu** \ȯi\ **boy** \th\ **thin** \th̲\ **this** \ü\ **loot** \u̇\ **foot** \ue\ Ger **füllen** \ᵫ\ Fr **rue** \y\ yet \ʸ\ Fr digne \ˈdēnʸ\, nuit \ˈnwʸē\ \yü\ **few** \yu̇\ **fury** \zh\ **vision**

Ban·nock \ˈba-nək\. County in SE Idaho. See table at IDAHO.

Ban·nock·burn \ˈba-nək-ˌbərn, ˌba-nək-ˈ\. Town, Central region, cen. Scotland, 2.5 mi. (4 km.) SSE of Stirling; battle June 1314 in which Scottish King Robert the Bruce routed the English under Edward II and took Stirling Castle.

Bannock Peak. Mountain, W of Bannock Range, cen. Power co., SE Idaho; 8321 ft. (2536 m.).

Bannock Range. Mountains on W border of Bannock co., SE Idaho.

Ban·nu \ˈbə-nü, ˈbä-\; *formerly* **Ed·war·des·abad** \ed-ˈwär-də-sə-ˌbäd\. Town, S cen. North-West Frontier prov., Pakistan, on Kurram River 100 mi. (161 km.) SSW of Peshawar; pop. (1981c) 43,000; military station.

Ba·ño·las *or* **Ban·yo·les** \bä-ˈnyō-läs\. Town, Gerona prov., NE Spain, 10 mi. (16 km.) N of the commune of Gerona; skull found here 1887 has been classified as Neanderthal type.

Baños, Los. See LOS BAÑOS.

Bans·da \ˈbänz-də\. **1.** Former Indian state, now part of Gujarat, W India; 212 sq. mi. (549 sq. km.).
2. Town, its ✻, S Gujarat.

Ban·ská Bys·tri·ca \ˈbän-ˌskä-ˈbis-tri-ˌtsä\ *or Hung.* **Besz·ter·cze·bá·nya** \ˈbes-tər-tsə-ˈbän-yȯ\ *or Ger.* **Neu·sohl** \ˈnȯi-ˌzōl\. Commune, cen. Slovakia, on Hron River 100 mi. (161 km.) NE of Bratislava; pop. (1991p) 85,007.

Ban·stead \ˈban-ˌsted, -stəd\. Town, Surrey, S England; pop. (1981p) 43,163; Epsom racecourse borders on **Banstead Downs**.

Bans·wa·ra \bänz-ˈwär-ə\. **1.** Former Indian state, now part of Rajasthan, NW India; 1606 sq. mi. (4160 sq. km.).
2. Town, its ✻; pop. (1991p) 67,952.

Ban·tam \ˈban-təm, ˈbän-ˌtäm\. **1.** Former residency, Java, Netherlands Indies; 3067 sq. mi. (7944 sq. km.); now part of the Indonesian prov. of West Java; ✻ Serang; comprised W end of Java bet. Java Sea and Indian Ocean, with W coast on Sunda Strait; region mountainous in S, contains Mt. Karang in midst of N plain; well developed agriculturally.
History: In early 16th cent. became powerful Muslim sultanate which extended its control over parts of Sumatra and Borneo; invaded by Dutch, Portuguese, and English; recognized Dutch sovereigns 1684, annexed by Dutch 1809; scene of several revolts in 19th cent.; suffered severely from volcanic eruption of Krakatau (*q.v.*) 1883.
2. Town, Indonesia. See BANTEN.

Bantam Bay. See BANTEN BAY.

Bantam Lake \ˈban-təm\. Lake, Litchfield co., NW Connecticut; 25 sq. mi. (65 sq. km.); its outlet is **Bantam River,** a tributary of the Shepaug.

Ban·ta·yan \ˌbän-tä-ˈyän\. **1.** Island, cen. Philippines, 9 mi. (14 km.) W of N tip of Cebu I. and 20 mi. (32 km.) NE of Negros; 45 sq. mi. (117 km.); part of Cebu prov.
2. Municipality on SW coast of Bantayan I.; pop. (1980c) 47,711.

Ban·ten \ˈbän-ˌten\; *formerly* **Ban·tam** \ˈban-təm, ˈbän-ˌtäm\. Former town on Banten Bay, N coast of West Java prov., Indonesia; now in ruins. ✻ of Muslim sultanate; Portuguese trading station after 1545; site of first Dutch settlement 1596 and of British factory 1603, bet. which great rivalry developed until expulsion of British 1683; under British control 1811–14; reverted to Dutch.

Banten Bay; *formerly* **Bantam Bay.** Inlet of Java Sea on NW coast of Java, Indonesia, E of Sunda Strait.

Ban·ton \bän-ˈtȯn\. Small island, Romblon prov., Philippines, NNW of Romblon I. and N of Simara I.; 11 sq. mi. (28 sq. km.); pop. (1980c) 7362.

Ban·try \ˈban-trē\. Town at head of Bantry Bay, SW co. Cork, SW Ireland; pop. (1986c) 2811; fishing center.

Bantry Bay. Bay, SW co. Cork, SW Ireland; ab. 25 mi. (40 km.) long; site of unsuccessful French attempts at landing 1689 and 1796 to help Irish insurrections.

Banyak Islands. See BANJAK ISLANDS.

Banyoles. See BAÑOLAS.

Ban·yu·mas. See BANJUMAS.

Ban·yu·wan·gi *also* **Ban·ju·wan·gi** *or Du.* **Ban·joe·wan·gi** \ˌbän-yü-ˈwäŋ-gē\. Seaport on Bali Strait, East Java prov., Indonesia; port for Bali I.

Ban·zare Coast \ˈban-ˌzar\. Section of coast of Wilkes Land, Antarctica, extending along Indian Ocean from ab. 121°E to 126°E.

Bao \ˈbau̇\. Short stream in NW Leyte I., Philippines, flowing S into Ormoc Bay.

Bao'an. See SHENZHEN.

Bao·ding *or W.-G.* **Pao–ting** \ˈbau̇-ˈdiŋ\; *formerly* **Ch'ing–yüan** *or* **Tsing·yüan** \ˈchiŋ-ˈywen\. City, cen. Hebei prov., NE China, on railroad line ab. 90 mi. (145 km.) SSW of Beijing; pop. (1990c) 483,155. In civil war following WWII taken by Communists Nov. 1948.

Bao·ji *or W.-G.* **Pao–chi** \ˈbau̇-ˈjē\ *or* **Pao·ki** \ˈbau̇-ˈkē\. Town, W Shaanxi prov., NE cen. China, on Wei River ab. 100 mi. (160 km.) W of Xi'an; pop. (1990c) 337,765.

Bao·shan *or W.-G.* **Pao–shan** \ˈbau̇-ˈshän\; *formerly* **Yung-chang** \ˈyu̇ŋ-ˈchäŋ\. Town, W Yunnan prov., S China, bet. the Nu and Lancang rivers; alt. 5500 ft. (1676 m.).

Bao·tou *or W.-G.* **Pao–t'ou** \ˈbau̇-ˈtō\. Town, cen. Nei Mong-gol (Inner Mongolia), N China, on left bank of the Huang at its great bend 90 mi. (145 km.) W of Hohhot; pop. (1990c) 983,508; trade center; steel; occupied by Japanese 1937–45.

Ba·ou·lé *or* **Ba·u·le** \ˌbau̇-ˈlā\. River, W Mali; chief tributary of the Bakoye.

Ba·paume \bä-ˈpōm\. Commune, Pas-de-Calais dept., N France; scene of victory of French Gen. Louis-Léon-César Faidherbe over the Prussians Jan. 1871; scene of severe fighting in 1916 and 1917 in WWI and of successful assault by British forces on the Hindenburg Line Aug. 21–Sept. 1, 1918, the town being completely destroyed.

Ba'·qū·bah *or* **Ba'·qu·ba** \bä-ˈkü-bə\. Town, E Iraq, on Diyala River in fertile agricultural region and on railroad line 32 mi. (51 km.) NE of Baghdad.

Bar \ˈbär\. Town, W cen. Ukraine, 40 mi. (64 km.) W of Vinnytsya.
History: Important town of Podolia, in 16th cent. a Lithuanian possession, later Polish but held for a short time in 17th cent. by the Turks; headquarters of the Confederation of Bar, formed here 1768 as a Polish patriotic and anti-Russian association, suppressed 1770–72; became Russian 1793 in Second Partition of Poland.

Bar *or Ital.* **An·ti·va·ri** \än-ˈtē-və-rē\. Town, SW Montenegro, S Yugoslavia; pop. (1991p) 37,520.

Ba·ra·ba Steppe \ˈbär-ə-ˌbä\. Swamp and steppe region, SW Siberia, Russia, bet. Ob and Irtysh rivers.

Bar·a·boo \ˈbar-ə-ˌbü\. **1.** River, S cen. Wisconsin; flows from Juneau co. SE into Wisconsin River below Portage, Columbia co.; ab. 90 mi. (145 km.) long.
2. City, ⊗ of Saulk co., S cen. Wisconsin, 15 mi. (24 km.) WSW of Portage; pop. (1990c) 9203.

Ba·ra·cal·do \ˌbä-rä-ˈkäl-dō\. Commune, Vizcaya prov., N Spain, just NW of Bilbao; pop. (1991p) 104,883; iron and steel works.

Ba·ra·coa \ˌbä-rä-ˈkō-ä\. Seaport and municipality on N coast of E Cuba; munic. pop. (1981p) 76,873; oldest town in Cuba, settled 1512 by Spanish soldier and administrator Diego Velásquez.

Ba·ra·da \ˈbär-ə-də\; *bib.* **Ab·a·na** *or* [*2 Kings* v. 12] **Ab·a·nah** \ˈa-bə-nə\; *classical* **Chry·sor·rho·as** \kri-ˈsȯr-ə-wəs, -ˈsär-\. One of the chief rivers of Damascus, W Syria, flowing SE ab. 45 mi. (72 km.) from Anti-Lebanon Mts. past Damascus to swamps at edge of desert.

Bar·a·ga \ˈbar-ə-gə\. County in NW Michigan. See table at MICHIGAN.

Ba·ra·gan Steppe \ˈbär-ə-ˌgän\. Level open tract on the lower Danube River, E Walachia, Romania.

Ba·ra·ho·na \ˌbä-rä-ˈō-nä\. **1.** Province, SW Dominican Republic. See table at DOMINICAN REPUBLIC.
2. City, its ✻; pop. (1983e) 51,000; sugar, coffee.

Ba·rail Range \bə-ˈrīl\. Mountain range, NE India, along boundary bet. Assam and Manipur; the S continuation of the Naga Hills; highest peak Mt. Japvo 9890 ft. (3014 m.).

Ba·rak \bə-ˈräk\. Upper course of the Surma River in Manipur, NE India. See SURMA.

Ba·ra·ka \bä-ˈrä-kä\. River in NE Africa; rises in cen. Eritrea flows N, receives the Anseba from E; crosses into Sudan; empties into Red Sea; ab. 400 mi. (645 km.) long.

Ba·ra·kī Ba·rak \ˈbȧ-rə-kē-ˈbä-rək\. Town, E Afghanistan.

Ba·ram *or* **Bar·ram** \ˈbär-ˌäm\. River, N Sarawak, East Malaysia; flows NW into South China Sea at Baram Point; ab. 250 mi. (400 km.) long.

Baram Point *or Malay* **Tan·jong Baram** \ˈtän-ˌjȯŋ-ˈbär-ˌäm\. Cape on N coast of Sarawak, East Malaysia; projects into South China Sea, ab. 4°36′N, 113°58′E.

Ba·ra·mu·la *or* **Ba·ra·mul·la** \ˌbär-ə-ˈmu̇-lə\. Town, Jammu and Kashmir, N India, ab. 30 mi. (48 km.) WNW of Srinagar.

Ba·ra·na·gar \bə-ˈrä-nə-gər\. Town, West Bengal, India, N suburb of Calcutta on Hugli River; pop. (1991p) 223,770.

Ba·ra·noa \ˌbä-rä-ˈnō-ä\. Town, Atlántico dept., N Colombia, near Barranquilla.

Bar·a·nof \ˈbar-ə-ˌnȯf, -ˌnäf, bə-ˈrä-nəf\. Island, W Alexander Archipelago, SE Alaska, S of Chichagof I.; ab. 100 mi. (160 km.) long; 1597 sq. mi. (4136 sq. km.); Sitka is on its W coast.

Ba·ra·no·vi·chi \bə-ˈrä-nə-ˌvē-chē\ *or Pol.* **Ba·ra·no·wi·cze** \ˌbär-ə-nȯ-ˈvē-che\. City, Brest subdivision, W cen. Belarus, 85 mi. (137 km.) SW of Minsk; pop. (1991e) 166,700; important railroad junction; was Polish frontier station to Russia; became Russian 1939 although held by Germans during WWII 1941–44.

Ba·ra·nya \ˈbȯ-rȯn-ˌyȯ\. County of S Hungary. See table at HUNGARY.

Ba·raque Mi·chel \bə-ˌräk-mē-ˈshel\. Peak in Hohe Venn Mts., near Spa, E Belgium; 2211 ft. (674 m.).

Bar·a·tar·ia Bay \ˌbär-ə-ˈtar-ē-ə\. Inlet of Gulf of Mexico on boundary bet. Jefferson and Plaquemines parishes, SE Louisiana.

Barataria, Bayou. Bayou, SE Louisiana, W of the mouth of the Mississippi; region connected with legends and activities early 19th cent. of Jean and Pierre Lafitte, who led a band of privateers and smugglers.

Barataria Pass; *formerly* **Grand Pass.** Narrow strait connecting Barataria Bay, SE Louisiana, with Gulf of Mexico.

Ba·rat Da·ya, Ke·pu·lau·an \ˌkā-pü-ˈlau̇-än-ˈbä-rät-ˈdä-yä\ *or Eng.* **South West Islands.** Group of islands, SE part of Indonesia, on S edge of Banda Sea and NE of Timor; includes the islands of Wetar, Kisar, Damar, Moa, and Sermata.

Ba·raun·dha \bə-ˈrau̇n-də\. Former Indian state, now part of Madhya Pradesh, cen. India; 228 sq. mi. (591 sq. km.).

Bar·ba \ˈbär-bä\. Volcano, cen. Costa Rica, N of San José; 9534 ft. (2906 m.).

Bar·ba·ce·na \ˌbär-bä-ˈsā-nä\. City, S Minas Gerais state, E Brazil, 125 mi. (201 km.) N of Rio de Janeiro; munic. pop. (1991p) 100,038; alt. 3500 ft. (1067 m.).

Bar·ba·co·as \ˌbär-bä-ˈkō-äs\. Municipality and river port, Nariño dept., SW Colombia, 45 mi. (72 km.) ESE of Tumaco.

Bar·ba·dos \bär-ˈbā-dəs, -dōz, -dōs\. Island in the Lesser Antilles, West Indies, E of cen. Windward Is.; 166 sq. mi. (430 sq. km.); pop. (1993e) 260,000; ✻ Bridgetown. Chiefly of coral formation with no good harbors and only small streams; generally level but with hills in cen. part, highest point Mt. Hillaby 1104 ft. (336 m.); exports sugar, molasses, and rum; tourism.

History: Probably orig. inhabited by Arawaks; first visited by Europeans 16th cent.; claimed for England early 17th cent.; first settled under auspices of William Courteen c. 1625; included in grant to earl of Carlisle 1627 whose settlers overcame those of Courteen 1629; leased by Lord Francis Willoughby, a Royalist, who governed until forced to yield to Commonwealth 1652; taken over by crown 1663; became prosperous as sugar producer, esp. in 17th and 18th cents.; suffered from wars of England with France, Spain, and later with U.S.; slaves freed 1838; seat of government for Windward Is. 1833 to 1885, when made separate administration; member of West Indies (Federation) 1958–62; achieved independence within the Commonwealth 1966; joined Caribbean Free Trade Area 1968 (which became Caribbean Community and Common Market 1973); also member of United Nations and Organization of American States.

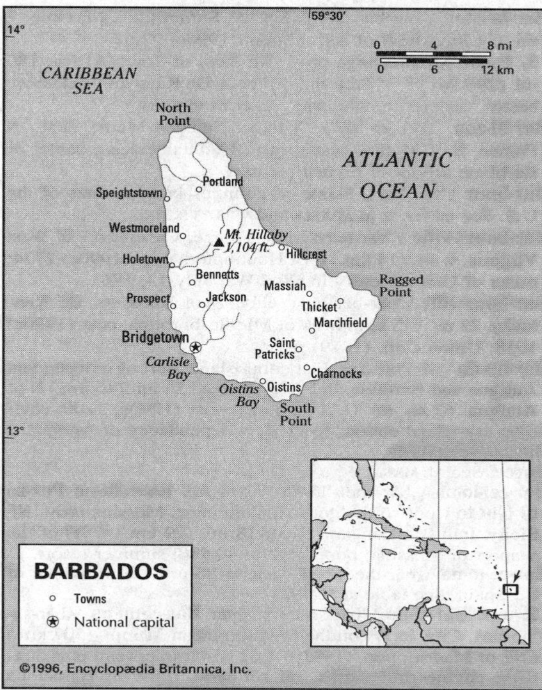

Bar·ba·ry \ˈbär-bə-rē\. Coastal region in N Africa, extending from Egypt to the Atlantic Ocean.

History: For early history, see MAURETANIA, NUMIDIA, and CYRENAICA. Overrun by Vandals under King Genseric 5th cent. A.D.; conquered by Gen. Belisarius for Byzantine Empire 533–534; gradually overcome by Islam 7th cent.; broken up into independent Muslim states known as **Barbary States** (see MOROCCO, ALGIERS, TUNIS, and TRIPOLI); European penetration begun by occupation of Ceuta by Portuguese 1415; Oran, Bejaïa, and Tripoli conquered by Spanish 1509–11; dominion of corsair Barbarossa reduced by victory 1535 of expedition of Holy Roman Emperor Charles V under Genoese Adm. Andrea Doria, but Algiers held out; Barbarossa helped establish Algiers as base for piracy actions for next 300 years; Tripoli lost to Turks 1551; carried on piracy against European commerce and collected tribute from leading European states; after U.S. war with Tripoli 1801–05, U.S. expedition to Algiers 1815, and bombardment of Algiers by British 1816, ceased exaction of tribute and Christian slavery. For later history, see under separate states.

Bar·bas, Cape \ˈbär-bəs\. Cape on SW coast of Western Sahara; 22°18′N, 16°41′W.

Bar·bas·tro \bär-ˈbäs-trō\. Commune, Huesca prov., Spain; pop. (1991c) 14,778; old city, known in Roman times; 16th cent. cathedral.

Bar·ba·te, Río \ˈrē-ō-bär-ˈb̠ä-tä\. Short stream in Cadiz prov., SW Spain, flowing SW to the Atlantic Ocean just E of Cape Trafalgar; on its banks in 711 A.D. is supposed to have been fought the battle in which Roderick, last king of the Visigoths, was defeated and probably slain by the Muslims under Gen. Tāriqibn Ziyād.

Bar·ber \ˈbär-bər\. County in S Kansas. See table at KANSAS.

Bar·bers Point \ˈbär-bərz\ *also* **Ka·la·e·loa Point** \kä-ˌlä-ā-ˈlō-ä\. Cape on SW corner of Oahu I., Hawaii, W of Pearl Harbor, 21°18′N, 158°07′W.

Bar·ber·ton \ˈbär-bər-tən\. **1.** City, Summit co., NE Ohio, 7 mi. (11 km.) SSW of Akron; pop. (1990c) 27,623.
2. Town, Mpumalanga prov., NE Rep. of South Africa, 180 mi. (290 km.) E of Pretoria; center of De Kaap goldfields; asbestos, magnesite, talc, and nickel in vicinity.

Bar·bi·zon \ˌbär-bə-ˈzōⁿ\. Village, Seine-et-Marne dept., N France, S of Melun, near forest of Fontainebleau; center of Barbizon school of French painters.

Bar·bour \ˈbär-bər\. Name of counties in two states of the U.S. See tables at ALABAMA and WEST VIRGINIA.

Bar·bours·ville \ˈbär-bərz-ˌvil\. Village, Cabell co., W West Virginia, 9 mi. (14 km.) E of Huntington; pop. (1990c) 2774; scene of Union victory in Civil War July 13, 1861.

Bar·bour·ville \ˈbär-bər-ˌvil\. City, ⊗ of Knox co., SE Kentucky, 22 mi. (35 km.) NNW of Middlesborough; pop. (1990c) 3658; Union Coll. (1879).

Bar·bu·da \bär-ˈbü-də\. Flat coral island, part of independent Antigua and Barbuda, in E West Indies, 25 mi. (40 km.) N of Antigua; 62 sq. mi. (161 sq. km.); pop. (1990e) 1100; chief crop sea-island cotton; formerly a dependency of Antigua.

Barca. See BARKA.

Barce. See AL MARJ.

Bar·cel·lo·na \ˌbär-chel-ˈlō-nä\ *or in full* **Barcellona Poz·zo di Got·to** \ˈpȯt-sō-dē-ˈgȯt-tō\. Commune, Messina prov., NE Sicily, Italy, on Longano River 18 mi. (29 km.) WSW of the seaport of Messina; pop. (1989c) 39,980; summer resort.

Bar·ce·lo·na \ˌbär-the-ˈlō-nä, ˌbär-sə-ˈlō-nə\. **1.** Province of NE Spain. See table at SPAIN.
2. *anc.* **Bar·ci·no** \ˈbär-sə-ˌnō\; *later* **Bar·ci·no·na** \ˌbär-sə-ˈnō-nə\. City, its ✻, on the Mediterranean 315 mi. (507 km.) ENE of Madrid; pop. (1991p) 1,623,542; important port; textiles; engineering works, oil refinery; Univ. of Barcelona (15th cent.), Autonomous Univ. of Barcelona (1968); 13th cent. Spanish-Gothic cathedral; ancient ruins; old Roman wall fortifications destroyed 1868.
History: Traditionally, city founded 3d cent. B.C. by Gen. Hamilcar Barca of Carthage; ruled by Romans, Visigoths; taken by Moors c. 715 A.D.; retaken by Franks for Holy Roman Emperor Charlemagne 801 and made ✻ of Spanish March (see CATALONIA); Frankish county of Barcelona became almost independent in 9th cent.; after Catalonia united with Aragon 1137, city became flourishing commercial center, an originator of deposit banking, and the rival of Italian ports; captured in 1652 as center of resistance in great Catalonian rebellion; abandoned by Allies 1714; in 19th cent. became center of radical social movements and of movement for Catalonian separatism; seized in military coup of Gen. Miguel Primo de Rivera y Orbaneja 1923; Loyalist ✻ 1937–39; its capture in 1939 brought collapse of Catalonian resistance; site of Summer Olympic Games 1992.
3. Town, ✻ of Anzoátegui state, N Venezuela, 150 mi. (241 km.) ESE of Caracas; pop. (1990p) 109,061; coal nearby; founded 1634.

Bar·ce·lo·ne·ta \ˌbär-se-lō-ˈnā-tä\. Town and municipality, N Puerto Rico, on the Manatí River and on railroad line 28 mi. (45 km.) W of San Juan; munic. pop. (1990c) 20,947.

Barcino *or* **Barcinona.** See BARCELONA 2.

Barcoo River. See COOPER CREEK.

Bard·dha·man \ˈbär-də-mən, ˈbər-\; *formerly* **Bar·dwan** \ˈbär-dwən\ *or* **Bur·dwan** \ˈbər-\. Town, West Bengal, NE India, on Damodar River 73 mi. (117 km.) NW of Calcutta; pop. (1991p) 244,789; temple; palace; university (1960).

Bar·de·jov \ˈbär-də-yȯf\ *or Hung.* **Bárt·fa** \ˈbärt-ˌfȯ\ *or Ger.* **Bart·feld** \ˈbärt-ˌfelt\. Town, NW Slovakia, in S foothills of Carpathian Mts. 20 mi. (32 km.) N of Prešov; pop. (1989c) 30,801; hot springs.

Bar·de·ra \bär-ˈder-ə\. Town, S Somalia, on the Jubba River ab. 250 mi. (400 km.) W of Mogadishu.

Bar·dī·yah *or* **Bar·dia** \ˈbär-dē-ə, bär-ˈdē-ə\; *formerly* **Por·to Bardia** \ˈpōr-tō\. Town on coastal road, NE Libya, near Egyptian border. Several times captured in WWII: starting point of Italian attack Sept. 1940; taken by British Dec. 1940–Jan. 1941; lost to German Field Marshal Erwin Rommel's forces Apr. 1941; finally recaptured Nov. 1942.

Bard·sey \ˈbärd-zē\. Island, Gwynedd co., Wales, in the Irish Sea off the W Welsh coast N of entrance to Cardigan Bay; 2 mi. (3 km.) long; fishing, farming; ruins of 13th cent. abbey on foundation thought to date from 6th cent.; in medieval times a place of religious pilgrimage.

Bards·town \ˈbärdz-ˌtau̇n\. City, ⊗ of Nelson co., cen. Kentucky, 36 mi. (58 km.) SSE of Louisville; pop. (1990c) 6801.

Barduli. See BARLETTA.

Bardwan. See BARDDHAMAN.

Bard·well \ˈbärd-ˌwel, -wəl\. City, ⊗ of Carlisle co., SW Kentucky; pop. (1990c) 819.

Ba·règes \bä-ˈrezh, -ˈrāzh\. Village, Hautes-Pyrénées dept., SW France, in the Pyrenees Mts.; alt. ab. 4070 ft. (1240 m.); health resort. See BAGNÈRES-DE-BIGORRE.

Ba·reil·ly *or* **Ba·re·li** \bə-ˈrā-lē\. **1.** Region, Uttar Pradesh, India. See ROHILKHAND.
2. City, Uttar Pradesh, N India, on Ramganga River 130 mi. (209 km.) ESE of Delhi; pop. (1991c) 590,661; sugar, furniture; site of a military cantonment; college (1837); important railroad junction. Founded 1537.

Ba·rents Island \ˈbar-ənts, ˈbär-\. Island, E Spitsbergen Archipelago, Arctic Ocean, N of Edge I., 78°27′N, 21°15′E; 37 mi. (60 km.) long; 514 sq. mi. (1331 sq. km.).

Barents Sea. Part of Arctic Ocean N of Norway and Russia and bet. Spitsbergen and Novaya Zemlya; 529,096 sq. mi. (1,370,359 sq. km.).

Bar·fleur \bär-ˈflœr\. Town, Manche dept., NW France, on NE point of Cotentin Penin. 2 mi. (3 km.) S of **Point Barfleur** which marks the NW point of the Bay of the Seine; resort; fishing; in Middle Ages an important port.

Barfurush. See BĀBOL.

Bar·ga \ˈbär-gä\. **1.** Commune, Lucca prov., Tuscany, cen. Italy, 17 mi. (27 km.) N of the commune of Lucca.
2. Region, NE China. See HULUN BUIR.

Bar·gu·zin \ˌbär-gə-ˈzēn\. **1.** *or* **Bar·gu·zin·skiy** \-skē\. Mountain range, W Buryatia, Russia in Asia; parallel with the Barguzin River and bet. it and Lake Baikal; highest point 8862 ft. (2701 m.).
2. River, W Buryatia, Russia in Asia; flows SW to Lake Baikal; 437 mi. (703 km.) long.
3. Town on right bank near mouth of the river.

Bar Harbor \ˈbär\. Town, Hancock co., SE Maine, on Mt. Desert I. on Frenchman Bay; pop. (1990c) 4443; Coll. of the Atlantic (1969); first permanent English settlement 1763; summer resort; greatly damaged by fire 1947.

Ba·ri \ˈbä-rē\ *or in full* **Bari del·le Pu·glie** \ˌdel-le-ˈpül-yā\. **1.** Province of Puglia, Italy. See table at ITALY.
2. *anc.* **Bar·i·um** \ˈbar-ē-əm\. Commercial seaport, its ✻ and ✻ of Puglia, SE Italy, on Adriatic Sea; pop. (1991p) 341,273; oil refining, boatbuilding, textiles, wine; 11th cent. cathedral and church; pilgrim resort; university (1924).
History: Leading commercial center of Puglia since 2d cent. B.C.; successively dominated by Goths, Greeks, Saracens, Byzantines, Normans, Germans, and Venetians; became part of kingdom of Naples c. 1557. Heavily damaged in WWII.

Ba·ria *or* **Ba·ri·ya** \ˈbär-ē-ə\. Former Indian state, now part of Gujarat, W India; 810 sq. mi. (2098 sq. km.).

Baria. River in S Venezuela; rises in mountains on border, Serra Curupira, in extreme S tip of Venezuela, flows N into Casiquiare River.

Ba·ri Do·ab \ˈbä-rē-dō-ˈäb\. Plain region, mostly in Punjab, Pakistan, with NE section in India, lying bet. Sutlej and Ravi rivers.

Ba·ri·li \bə-ˈrē-lē\. Municipality near W coast of Cebu I., Cebu prov., Philippines, 30 mi. (48 km.) SW of City of Cebu; pop. (1980c) 39,560.

Ba·ri·lo·che \ˌbä-rē-ˈlō-chā\ *or* **San Car·los de Bariloche** \sän-ˈkär-lōs-thā-\. Town, SW Río Negro prov., S cen. Argentina, on S shore of Lake Nahuel Huapí; resort.

Barīm. See PERIM.

Ba·ri·ma \bä-ˈrē-mä\. River, NW Guyana; flows SE, then curves to the NW, crosses the Venezuelan border and empties into Atlantic Ocean at the S Orinoco delta; ab. 250 mi. (400 km.) long; navigable for 52 mi. (84 km.).

Ba·ri·nas \bä-ˈrē-näs\. **1.** *formerly* **Za·mo·ra** \sä-ˈmō-rä\. State of W cen. Venezuela. See table at VENEZUELA.
2. Town, its ✻, 260 mi. (418 km.) SW of Caracas; pop. (1990p) 152,853; cattle-trading center.

Ba·rin·go, Lake \bä-ˈriŋ-gō\. Lake, Kenya, NE of Lake Victoria; ab. 50 sq. mi. (130 sq. km.).

Ba·ri·pa·da \ˌbär-ə-ˈpä-də\. Town, Orissa, E India, 115 mi. (185 km.) SW of Calcutta; pop. (1991p) 49,569; ✻ of former Mayurbhanj state.

Ba·ri·sāl \ˈbar-ə-ˌsäl\. City, Bangladesh, near Tetulia mouth of Ganges River, 73 mi. (117 km.) S of Dhaka; pop. (1991p) 180,014; river port with active trade; rice market; exports fish; three colleges; noted for natural phenomenon known as "Barisal guns," noises like distant thunder or cannon fire, thought to be of seismic origin.

Ba·ri·san Mountains \ˈbär-i-ˌsän\. Mountain system extending the length of the island of Sumatra, Indonesia, chiefly along the W coast; ab. 1000 mi. (1610 km.) long, containing many volcanic peaks from 6000 ft. (1829m.) to more than 12,400 ft. (3780 m.); highest peak Kerinci 12,483 ft. (3805 m.); for the most part made up of two parallel chains with a series of mountain lakes in the high valley bet. them, largest of which is Toba (*q.v.*).

Ba·ri·to \bä-ˈrē-tō\. River, SE Borneo, Indonesia; rises in E ranges of Muller Mts., flows S into Java Sea; ab. 550 mi. (885 km.) long; its lower course flows through wide marshy region in which cross branches connect with other streams; one of the largest rivers of Borneo, navigable for boats of moderate size for ab. 250 mi. (400 km.).

Barium. See BARI 2.

Bariya. See BARIA.

Bar·ka *also* **Bar·ca** \ˈbär-kə\. **1.** Region, NE Libya, esp. the height of land (**Barka Plateau,** highest point ab. 2340 ft. or 715 m.) surrounding the ancient town of Barca (see AL MARJ); part of the Pashalik of Tripoli under the Ottoman Turks.
2. Town in Libya. See AL MARJ.

Bar·king and Dag·en·ham \ˈbär-kiŋ … ˈdag-ᵊn-əm\. Borough of Greater London, SE England. See table at LONDON 4.

Bark·ley Sound \ˈbär-klē\. Inlet of Pacific Ocean, in SW Vancouver I., SW British Columbia, Canada.

Bark·ly Tableland \ˈbär-klē\. Plateau region, Australia, mostly in E Northern Terr., but its SE end in Queensland; alt. ab. 1000 ft. (305 m.); cattle raising.

Barkly West. Town, Northern Cape prov., Rep. of South Africa, on N bank of Vaal River; formerly an important town in Griqualand.

Bar·kol \ˈbär-ˈkȯl\ *or W.-G.* **Pa–li–k'un** \ˈbä-li-ˈkün\; *formerly* **Bar·kul** \ˈbär-ˈkül\. Town, NE Xinjiang Uygur, W China, in mountain region on SE shore of **Barkol Hu** \ˈhü\ (lake), off main highway ab. 60 mi. (96 km.) NW of Hami.

Bârlad. See BÎRLAD.

Bar–le–Duc \ˌbär-lə-ˈdu̅e̅k\ *or unofficially* **Bar–sur–Or·nain** \ˈbär-ˌsu̅e̅r-ȯr-ˈneⁿ\. Commune, ✻ of Meuse dept., NE France, 128 mi. (206 km.) E of Paris; pop. (1990c) 18,577; 14th cent. church; old Roman gate.

Bar·lee, Lake \ˈbär-lē\. Large salt lake, W Western Australia, Australia.

Bar·let·ta \bär-ˈle-tə\; *anc.* **Bar·du·li** \ˈbär-du̇-ˌlī, -ju̇-, -ˌlō\. Seaport, Bari prov., Puglia, SE Italy, on Adriatic coast near mouth of Ofanto River 34 mi. (55 km.) WNW of the seaport of Bari; pop. (1989c) 88,074; 12th cent. Romanesque cathedral and 13th cent. Gothic church; college founded by Ferdinand IV.

Bar·lin \bär-ˈleⁿ\. Commune, Pas-de-Calais dept., N France, NW of Arras; coal deposits.

Bar·mouth \ˈbär-məth\. Town, Gwynedd co., N Wales, on coast of Cardigan Bay; pop. (1981p) 2138; resort nearby is first property acquired by the National Trust (1895).

Bar·nard, Mount \ˈbär-nərd\. Peak in the Sierra Nevada, near Mt. Whitney, SE cen. California; 13,990 ft. (4264 m.).

Barnard Castle. Town, Durham, N England, on Tees River 17 mi. (27 km.) W of Darlington; pop. (1981p) 5016; castle begun 12th cent. figures in Sir Walter Scott's poem *Rokeby.*

Bar·na·ul \ˌbər-nə-ˈül\. Town, ✻ of Altay Kray, S Russia in Asia, on the Ob River 110 mi. (177 km.) S of Novosibirsk; pop. (1992e) 606,000; engineering works; diesel motors, textiles, timber; located on Turkistan-Siberian railroad line; in rich mining region; meteorological observatory (founded 1841); mining school; museums; founded 1738.

Bar·ne·gat Bay \ˈbär-ni-ˌgat, -gət\. Inlet of Atlantic Ocean, extending N to S in Ocean co., New Jersey; ab. 30 mi. (48 km.) long.

Barnegat Inlet. Strait bet. Long Beach I. and Island Beach leading from Atlantic Ocean into Barnegat Bay.

Barnegat Light; *before 1948* **Barnegat City.** Borough, New Jersey, at N tip of Long Beach I. on Barnegat Inlet; pop. (1990c) 675; site of lighthouse built 1855, abandoned 1930.

Barnes \ˈbärnz\. County in E North Dakota. See table at NORTH DAKOTA.

Barnes·boro \ˈbärnz-ˌbər-ə\. Borough, Cambria co., SW cen. Pennsylvania, 24 mi. (39 km.) WNW of Altoona; pop. (1990c) 2530; coal deposits.

Barnes·ville \ˈbärnz-ˌvil, -vəl\. **1.** City, ⊗ of Lamar co., W cen. Georgia, 35 mi. (56 km.) WNW of Macon; pop. (1990c) 4747; Gordon Coll. (1852).
2. Village, Belmont co., E Ohio, 38 mi. (61 km.) SW of Steubenville; pop. (1990c) 4326; coal and natural-gas deposits nearby.

Bar·net \ˈbär-nət\. A borough of Greater London, SE England; pop. (1991p) 283,000; scene of decisive Yorkist victory Apr. 14, 1471, in the Wars of the Roses, in which Richard Neville, earl of Warwick (called "the Kingmaker"), was killed. See table at LONDON 4.

Bar·ne·veld \ˈbär-nə-ˌvelt\. Commune, Gelderland prov., E Netherlands, 10 mi. (16 km.) E of Amersfoort; pop. (1992e) 43,353.

Barne·ville–Car·te·ret \ˌbȧr-nə-ˈvēl-ˌkȧrt-ˈre\. Town, Manche dept., NW France. See CARTERET.

Bar·nolds·wick \bär-ˈnōldz-ˌwik, *locally* ˈbär-lik\. Town, Lancashire, N England, 9 mi. (15 km.) N of Burnley; pop. (1981p) 10,141.

Barns·ley \ˈbärnz-lē\. Town, ⊗ of South Yorkshire, N England, on the Dearne 30 mi. (48 km.) ENE of Manchester; pop. (1991p) 217,300; coal deposits nearby.

Barn·sta·ble \ˈbärn-stə-bəl\. **1.** County in SE Massachusetts. See table at MASSACHUSETTS.
2. Town, its ⊗, on S shore of Cape Cod Bay; pop. (1990c) 40,949; summer resort.

Barn·sta·ple \ˈbärn-stə-pəl, -stə-bəl\. Market town, Devon, SW England, on the Taw estuary 50 mi. (81 km.) N of Plymouth; pop. (1981p) 19,025; tourism; one of the oldest royal boroughs; site of Cluniac priory of 11th cent.; incorp. 1557.

Barnstaple Bay. Bay on NW coast of Devon, SW England; receives the Taw River from the E.

Barn·well \ˈbärn-ˌwel, -wəl\. **1.** County in SW South Carolina. See table at SOUTH CAROLINA.
2. City, its ⊗, 36 mi. (58 km.) SW of Orangeburg; pop. (1990c) 5255.

Ba·ro \ˈbär-ō\. River, W Ethiopia; 190 mi. (306 km.) long; unites with Pibor River on border of SE Sudan to form Sobat River.

Ba·ro·da \bə-ˈrō-də\. **1.** Former Indian state, W India; 8176 sq. mi. (21,176 sq. km.); had four divisions, three in Gujarat and one in peninsula of Kathiawar. Once a part of Mogul Empire; in 18th cent. its princes belonged to Maratha Confederacy; c. 1721 secured part of Gujarat; in 19th cent. subject to British administrative control until 1881; became part of Bombay state 1948 and of Gujarat state 1960.
2. Division of former Baroda state, E of Surat; 1922 sq. mi. (4978 sq. km.).
3. City, Gujarat, India. See VADODARA.

Baroda and Gu·ja·rat States Agency \ˌgü-jə-ˈrät, ˌgu̇-\. A political agency of W India (1937–47), consisting of the state of Baroda and a number of smaller states; now part of Gujarat, W India.

Ba·ro·ghil Pass \bə-rō-ˈgēl, bə-ˈrō-ˌgil\. Pass over the Hindu Kush bet. Chitral, N Pakistan, and the Vākhān Valley; alt. 12,457 ft. (3797 m.).

Ba·ro·tac Nue·vo \bä-rō-ˈtäk-ˈnwā-b̲ō\. Municipality, SE Iloilo prov., Panay, Philippines, 16 mi. (26 km.) NNE of City of Iloilo; pop. (1980c) 34,276.

Ba·rot·se \bä-ˈrō-tsā\. Province, W Zambia; 48,798 sq. mi. (126,387 sq. km.); pop. (1980p) 487,988; ✻ Mongu; crossed by Zambezi River; approx. coextensive with **Ba·rot·se·land** \-ˌland\, region inhabited by the Barotse people.

Bar·que·ri·zo Mo·re·no \ˌbär-kā-ˈrē-sō-mō-ˈrā-nō\. Town, ✻ of Galápagos prov., Ecuador; on San Cristóbal I.

Bar·qui·si·me·to \ˌbär-kē-sē-ˈmā-tō\. City, ✻ of Lara state, NW Venezuela, 170 mi. (274 km.) WSW of Caracas; pop. (1990p) 602,622; at N end of Cordillera Mérida at alt. of 1856 ft. (566 m.); center of agricultural region; cement; university (1968); founded 1552.

Bar·ra \ˈbar-ə\. Chief island of S group in the Outer Hebrides, off NW coast of Scotland; ab. 8 mi. (13 km.) long and bet. 2 and 3 mi. (3 and 5 km.) wide; chief village Castlebay, with ruins of Kisamul Castle, seat of the ancient clan Macneil; with ab. 20 smaller islands (incl. Vatersay, Sandray, Mingulay, Berneray) constitutes parish of **Barra** or **Barra Islands;** administratively a part of Western Isles region; fishing; many Norse and Celtic remains.

Barra, Sound of. Channel bet. South Uist I. and Barra I. in the Outer Hebrides, off NW coast of Scotland.

Bar·rack·pore \ˈbar-ək-ˌpōr\ *also* **Bar·rack·pur** \-ˌpu̇r\. Town, West Bengal, NE India, 15 mi. (24 km.) N of Calcutta on left bank of Hugli River; pop. (1991p) 133,429; station for troops since 1772; scene of mutiny 1824 which was suppressed; scene of disbandment of first Indian (sepoy) regiment to mutiny Mar. 1857.

Bar·ra de São Fran·cis·co \ˈbär-ə-də-ˌsau̇ⁿ-frən-ˈsis-kü\. Municipality, Espírito Santo state, E Brazil; pop. (1980c) 51,611.

Barra do Pi·raí \ˈbär-ə-dü-ˌpē-rȧ-ˈē\. City, Rio de Janeiro state, SE Brazil; munic. pop. (1991p) 78,437; railroad junction point ab. 45 mi. (72 km.) NW of Rio de Janeiro.

Bar·ra·fran·ca \ˌbär-rä-ˈfräŋ-kä\. Commune, Enna prov., cen. Sicily, Italy, 14 mi. (23 km.) SSW of the commune of Enna; pop. (1981p) 15,144; sulfur deposits.

Barra Head. Cape on Berneray I., the S point of Barra Is., Outer Hebrides, off W coast of Scotland; lighthouse.

Barram. See BARAM.

Bar·ra Man·sa \ˈbȧr-ə-ˈmäⁿ-sə\. City, Rio de Janeiro state, SE Brazil, NW of the city of Rio de Janeiro; munic. pop. (1991p) 167,124.

Bar·ran·ca·ber·me·ja *or* **Bar·ran·ca Ber·me·ja** \bär-ˈräŋ-kä-ber-ˈmā-hä\. River port, Santander dept., NW cen. Colombia, on the Magdalena River ab. 50 mi. (81 km.) W of Bucaramanga; pop. (1985c) 136,012; oil refinery.

Bar·ran·cas \bär-ˈräŋ-käs\. River, SW cen. Argentina; rises near Chilean border, flows SE to unite with Río Grande and form Colorado River.

Bar·ran·co \bär-ˈräŋ-kō\. Town, S suburb of Lima, Peru, on the coast; pop. (1990e) 53,500.

Bar·ran·que·ras \ˌbär-rän-ˈkā-räs\. River port, Chaco prov., N Argentina, on Paraná River near Corrientes.

Bar·ran·qui·lla \ˌbär-rän-ˈkē-yä\. City and port, ✻ of Atlántico dept., N Colombia, on Magdalena River 10 mi. (16 km.) from its mouth; pop. (1992e) 1,018,800; textiles; Atlántico Univ. (1941); river channel dredged regularly for oceangoing vessels; founded 1629.

Bar·ran·qui·tas \ˌbär-rän-ˈkē-täs\. Town and municipality, cen. Puerto Rico; munic. pop. (1990c) 25,605.

Bar·re \ˈbar-ē\. **1.** Town, Worcester co., cen. Massachusetts, 19 mi. (31 km.) WNW of the city of Worcester; pop. (1990c) 4546.

2. City, Washington co., N cen. Vermont, 7 mi. (11 km.) SSE of Montpelier; pop. (1990c) 9482; extensive granite deposits and works; settled c. 1788; organized as town 1793, as city 1894.

Barre des Écrins \ˌbär-dā-zā-ˈkreⁿ\. Highest peak in the Dauphiné Alps and in the Pelvoux group of that range, SE France. See table at ALPS.

Bar·rei·ro \bä-ˈrā-rü\. City, Setúbal dist., W Portugal, on Tagus estuary, opp. Lisbon; pop. (1981p) 86,974.

Bar·ren \ˈbar-ən\. **1.** River, S Kentucky; flows NW out of Monroe co. into Green River; 130 mi. (209 km.) long.

2. County in S Kentucky. See table at KENTUCKY.

Barren Grounds *or* **Barren Lands.** Low level treeless plains of N Canada, chiefly E of the Mackenzie basin and NW of Hudson Bay; marked by many lakes, swamps, thin soil; sparsely inhabited by Inuit.

Bar·re·tos \bə-ˈrā-tüs\. City, N São Paulo state, SE Brazil; munic. pop. (1991p) 95,414.

Bar·rett Dam \ˈbar-ət\. Dam across Cottonwood Creek, S San Diego co., SW California; height 213 ft. (65 m.); completed 1922.

Barr·head \ˈbär-ˌhed\. Town, Alberta, Canada, 54 mi. (87 km.) NW of Edmonton; pop. (1991c) 4160.

Barrhead \bär-ˈhed\. Burgh, Strathclyde region, SW Scotland, on Levern River; pop. (1981p) 18,411.

Bar·rie \ˈbar-ē\. City, ⊗ of Simcoe co., SE Ontario, Canada, on W extremity of Lake Simcoe; pop. (1991c) 62,728; alt. ab. 726 ft. (220 m.); resort.

Bar·ri·er, Cape \ˈbar-ē-ər\. Cape on S end of Great Barrier I., off NE North I., New Zealand.

Barrier Range. See MAIN BARRIER RANGE.

Barrier Reef. See GREAT BARRIER REEF.

Bar·ri·ga·da, Mount \ˌbä-rē-ˈgä-dä, ˌbar-ə-\. Elevation in E cen. Guam, Mariana Is., 5 mi. (8 km.) E of Agana; 674 ft. (205 m.).

Bar·ring·ton \ˈbar-iŋ-tən\. **1.** Village, Cook and Lake cos., NE Illinois, NW of Chicago; pop. (1990c) 9504.

2. Borough, Camden co., SW New Jersey, 6 mi. (10 km.) SSE of the city of Camden; pop. (1990c) 6774.

3. Town, Bristol co., E Rhode Island, E of Narragansett Bay and 8 mi. (13 km.) ESE of Providence; pop. (1990c) 15,849; residential and resort center; incorp. by Massachusetts 1717; became part of Rhode Island 1746–47; incorp. by Rhode Island 1770.

Barrington Hills. Village, Cook, Kane, Lake, and McHenry cos., N Illinois, NW of Chicago; pop. (1990c) 4202.

Bar·ro Col·o·ra·do \ˈbär-rō-ˌkō-lō-ˈrä-t͟hō\. Island in Gatun Lake, Panama, in former Canal Zone; 6 sq. mi. (16 sq. km.); biological station; wildlife preserve.

Bar·ron \ˈbar-ən\. **1.** County in NW Wisconsin. See table at WISCONSIN.

2. City, its ⊗, 8 mi. (13 km.) SW of Rice Lake (city); pop. (1990c) 2986.

Bar·ro·sa \bä-ˈrō-sə\. Village, Cádiz prov., Spain, SE of the seaport of Cádiz; British victory over French nearby 1811.

Bar·row \ˈbar-ō\. **1.** County in N Georgia. See table at GEORGIA.

2. City, Alaska. See BARROW, POINT.

3. Island off NW coast of Western Australia, Australia, NE of North West Cape; produces oil.

4. River, SE Ireland; flows S from SE co. Offaly to Waterford Harbour; 119 mi. (192 km.) long.

Barrow, Point. Most northerly point of Alaska, 71°23′N, 156°30′W, on Arctic Ocean ab. 550 mi. (885 km.) NE of Nome and an equal distance NW of Fairbanks; has small Inuit settlement. City, **Barrow** (pop. [1990c] 3469) ab. 12 mi. (19 km.) S, is government station with post office and radio and weather bureau stations; has been important in explorations and aviation; extensive oil and gas deposits in area. Barrow Arctic Science Station opened by U.S. Navy 1947.

Barrow Creek. Communications station in desert region of cen. Northern Terr., Australia.

Bar·row·ford \ˈbar-ō-fərd, -ə-\. Town, Lancashire, NW England, on Leeds and Liverpool Canal 27 mi. (43 km.) N of Manchester; pop. (1981p) 5132.

Bar·row–in–Fur·ness \ˈbar-ō-in-ˈfər-nəs\. Port, Cumbria, NW England, on Furness Penin. opp. Isle of Walney 52 mi. (84 km.) N of Liverpool; pop. (1991p) 71,900.

Barrow Strait. Channel bet. Bathurst and Cornwallis Is. on the N and Prince of Wales and Somerset Is. on the S, Nunavut, Canada; from 40 to 70 mi. (64 to 113 km.) wide; ab. 150 mi. (241 km.) long.

Bar·ry \ˈbar-ē\. **1.** Name of counties in two states of the U.S. See tables at MICHIGAN and MISSOURI.

2. Seaport, South Glamorgan co., SE Wales; pop. (1981p) 43,828; shipping point for coal; resort.

Bar·sac \bär-ˈsak\. Commune, Gironde dept., SW France, near the Garonne; sauterne wine (see SAUTERNES).

Bar·si \ˈbär-sē\. Town, S Maharashtra, W India, 200 mi. (322 km.) ESE of Bombay; active trade center.

Bar·sing·haus·en \ˌbär-ziŋ-ˈhau̇z-ᵊn\. City, Lower Saxony, Germany, 12 mi. (19 km.) WSW of Hannover; pop. (1980c) 32,962; residential; first mentioned 991.

Bar·stow \ˈbär-ˌstō\. City, San Bernardino co., California; pop. (1990c) 21,472; Barstow Coll. (1960).

Bar–sur–Aube \ˌbȧr-su̅e̅r-ˈōb\. Commune, Aube dept., NE France; evidences of Roman occupation found nearby; destroyed by Huns 5th cent.; rebuilt, gained commercial importance; now market center for region producing wine, grain. Scene of battle 1814 in which allies defeated the French.

Bar–sur–Ornain. See BAR-LE-DUC.

Bartenstein. See BARTOSZYCE.

Bártfa *or* **Bartfeld.** See BARDEJOV.

Bar·thol·o·mew \bär-ˈthä-lə-ˌmyü\. County in S cen. Indiana. See table at INDIANA.

Bartholomew Bayou. River, SE Arkansas and NE Louisiana; rises in Jefferson co., SE cen. Arkansas, winds SE and S across Louisiana border into the Ouachita River in NE Louisiana; 275 mi. (443 km.) long; navigable 150 mi. (241 km.).

Bar·ti·ca \bär-ˈtē-kə\. Town, N Guyana, at confluence of Essequibo, Mazaruni, and Cuyuni rivers 45 mi. (72 km.) SW of Georgetown; point of departure for gold and diamond fields.

Bar·tle Frere, Mount \ˈbär-təl-ˌfrir\. Mountain in Atherton Plateau, S of Cairns, NE Queensland, Australia; 5289 ft. (1612 m.); highest peak in Queensland.

Bar·tles·ville \ˈbär-təlz-ˌvil\. City, ⊗ of Washington co., NE Oklahoma, 41 mi. (66 km.) N of Tulsa; pop. (1990c) 34,256; oil and gas wells; oil research; oil-field equipment; Bartlesville Wesleyan Coll. (1910); founded 1877.

Bart·lett \ˈbärt-lət\. **1.** Village, Cook and Du Page cos., NE Illinois, W of Chicago; pop. (1990c) 19,373; hardware, vacuum cleaners, electronic equipment.

2. Village, ⊗ of Wheeler co., NE cen. Nebraska; pop. (1990c) 131.

3. Town, Carroll co., E New Hampshire, on Saco River 11 mi. (18 km.) NW of Conway; pop. (1990c) 2290; alt. ab. 680 ft. (207 m.); resort in White Mts.

4. Town, Shelby co., SW Tennessee; a suburb of Memphis; pop. (1990c) 26,989.

Bartlett Dam. Dam across Verde River in Salt River Indian Reservation, E Maricopa co., S cen. Arizona; height 287 ft. (88 m.); completed 1939; impounds water for irrigation.

Bart·lett's Ferry Dam \ˈbärt-ləts\. Dam across Chattahoochee River, on Georgia-Alabama border, ab. 18 mi. (29 km.) N of Columbus, Ga.; height 145 ft. (44 m.); completed 1926; impounds water for power.

Bar·ton \ˈbärt-ᵊn\. **1.** Name of counties in two states of the U.S. See tables at KANSAS and MISSOURI.

2. Town, Orleans co., N Vermont; pop. (1990c) 2967.

3. Town, Washington co., SE Wisconsin; pop. (1990c) 2637.

Barton–upon–Hum·ber \-ˈhəm-bər\. Town, Parts of Lindsey, Humberside, E England, 8 mi. (13 km.) SW of Hull; pop. (1981p) 8498; important port in 14th cent.

Bar·ton·ville \ˈbärt-ᵊn-ˌvil\. Village, Peoria co., NW cen. Illinois, 7 mi. (11 km.) SW of the city of Peoria; pop. (1990c) 5643.

Bar·to·szy·ce \ˌbär-tȯ-ˈshit-se\ *or Ger.* **Bar·ten·stein** \ˈbärt-ᵊn-ˌshtīn\. Town, N Olsztyn prov., N Poland, N of the city of Olsztyn; pop. (1989e) 25,078; founded c. 1325.

Bar·tow \ˈbär-tō\. **1.** County in NW Georgia. See table at GEORGIA.

2. City, ⊗ of Polk co., cen. Florida Penin., 15 mi. (24 km.) SSE of Lakeland; pop. (1990c) 14,716.

Ba·rú \bä-ˈrü\; *formerly* **Chi·ri·quí** \ˌchē-rē-ˈkē\. Volcanic peak, W Panama, near the border of Costa Rica; 11,400 ft. (3475 m.).

Bar·wa·ni \bər-ˈwä-nē\. **1.** Former Indian state, now part of Madhya Pradesh, cen. India, in Satpura Range S of Narmada River; 1189 sq. mi. (3080 sq. km.).

2. Town, its ✻; pop. (1991p) 33,669.

Bar·won \ˈbär-wən\. Upper course of Darling River in NE New South Wales, SE Australia; rises in SE Queensland and flows SW ab. 400 mi. (644 km.); forms part of boundary bet. Queensland and New South Wales.

Barygaza. See BROACH.

Ba·ry·saw *or* **Bo·ri·sov** \bə-ˈrē-səf\. Town, N cen. Belarus, on left bank of Berezina River 50 mi. (81 km.) NE of Minsk; pop. (1991e) 150,200; glassworks. Held by Germans July 1941 to July 1944. See BEREZINA.

Basăk. See BASSAC.

Basarabia. See BESSARABIA 2.

Bas·co \ˈbäs-kō\ *or in full* **San·to Do·min·go de Basco** \ˈsän-tō-dō-ˈmiŋ-gō-thā-\. Municipality, ✻ of Batanes prov., N Philippines, on W shore of Batan I. ab. 150 mi. (241 km.) N of Aparri; pop. (1980c) 4341.

Bas·cu·ñán, Cape \ˌbäs-kü-ˈnyän\. Cape on SW coast of Atacama prov., N cen. Chile.

Ba·sel \ˈbäz-ᵊl\ *or older* **Basle** \ˈbäl\ *or Fr.* **Bâle** \ˈbȧl\. **1.** Former canton, Switzerland; now subdivided into demicantons: **Basel–Land** \-ˈlänt\ *also* **Ba·sel·land** \-ˈlänt\ *or* **Basel (Land);** 165 sq. mi. (427 sq. km.); pop. (1991e) 230,112; ✻ Liestal; and **Basel–Stadt** \-ˈshtät\ *also* **Ba·sel·stadt** \-ˌshtät\ *or* **Basel (Stadt);** 14 sq. mi; (36 sq. km.); pop. (1991e) 191,787; ✻ Basel. See table at SWITZERLAND.

2. City, ✻ of Basel-Stadt demicanton and of Basel canton, NW Switzerland, on both sides of Rhine 43 mi. (69 km.) N of Bern; pop. (1989c) 171,465; transport center; chemicals, textiles; 11th cent. church; university (1460).

History: Scene of famous (Roman Catholic) church council which lasted from 1431 for several years; became member of Swiss Confederation 1501; Confession of Basel adopted by Protestants 1534; peace treaties signed here Apr. 5, July 22, and Aug. 28, 1795, bet. Prussia, Spain, and France; burial site of Dutch scholar Erasmus.

Ba·sey \bä-ˈsā\. Municipality, S Samar, Philippines, on N shore of San Pedro Bay; pop. (1980c) 36,760.

Ba·shahr \ˈbə-shər\ *also* **Bus·sa·hir** \ˈbu̇-sə-ˌhir\. Former Indian state, now part of Punjab, N India; 3439 sq. mi. (8907 sq. km.).

Ba·shan \ˈbā-shən\. Northernmost of E Palestine's three ancient divisions; region now in S part of Syria.

Ba·shi Channel \ˈbä-shē\; *formerly* **Ba·chi Channel** \ˈbä-chē\. Strait bet. Batan Is. of the Philippines and S end of Taiwan; ab. 92 mi. (148 km.) wide; traversed at approx. 21°25′N by the boundary line as determined by Treaty of Paris 1898.

Bash·kor·to·stan \bȧsh-ˈkȯr-tə-ˌstän, -stan\ *or* **Bash·kir Republic** \bash-ˈkir\ *also* **Bash·kir·ia** \bash-ˈkir-ē-ə\ *or* **Bash·kir·i·ya** \bȧsh-ˈkē-rē-yə\. Republic, a subdivision of E Russia in Europe, bounded on N by Perm and Sverdlovsk oblasts, on E by Chelyabinsk Oblast, on S and SW by Orenburg Oblast, and on W by Tatarstan; 55,443 sq. mi. (143,597 sq. km.); pop. (1992e) 4,008,000; ✻ Ufa. A plateau and mountainous (Southern Urals) area, watered by the Belaya and its tributary the Ufa; has Ural River on its E border; has extensive forests and valuable mineral deposits in the mountains; rye, oats, corn, flax; oil production and refining; steel, chemicals. Bashkirs came under Russian control mid-16th cent., but have rebelled several times since; was an autonomous soviet socialist republic of the U.S.S.R. and became republic within Russia 1991 after Russian rejection of independence declaration; subsequently became member of Russian Federation.

Ba·si·gon \bä-'sē-g̲ōn\. River, cen. Camarines Norte prov., Luzon, Philippines; ab. 35 mi. (56 km.) long.

Ba·si·lan \bä-'sē-ˌlän\. **1.** Island group and province of Philippines, SW of Mindanao. See table at PHILIPPINES.
2. Largest island in Basilan group, separated from Zamboanga by Basilan Strait; 495 sq. mi. (1282 sq. km.). Mountainous, with highest point **Basilan Peak** 3320 ft. (1012 m.); has valuable timber, fishing; inhabitants mainly Moros.
3. *or* **Basilan City** *or* **Isa·be·la** \ˌē-sä-'b̲ā-lä, ˌi-zə-'be-lə\. Chartered city, ✱ of Basilan prov., NW Basilan I., Philippines.

Basilan Strait. Passage bet. Basilan I. and SW Mindanao, S Philippines; connects Moro Gulf with the Sulu Sea; ab. 10 mi. (16 km.) wide.

Bas·il·don \'ba-zil-dən\. Town, Essex, SE England, 25 mi. (40 km.) ENE of London; pop. (1991p) 157,500; developed as a new town.

Ba·si·li·ca·ta \bä-ˌzē-lē-'kä-tä\; *formerly* **Lu·ca·nia** \lü-'kän-yä\. Autonomous region, S Italy; 3857 sq. mi. (9990 sq. km.); pop. (1991p) 591,897; ✱ Potenza; wheat, rye. For provincial divisions, see table at ITALY.

Bas·i·lisk Harbour \'ba-sə-ˌlisk-, -zə-\. Large inlet in Utupua I., Santa Cruz Is., SW Pacific Ocean.

Ba·sin \'bās-^{ə}n\. Town, ⊗ of Big Horn co., N Wyoming; pop. (1990c) 1180.

Ba·sing·stoke \'bā-ziŋ-ˌstōk\. Town, Hampshire, S England, 46 mi. (74 km.) WSW of London; pop. (1981p) 67,447; an old town with many antiquities; grew rapidly in 1960s due to overspill from London; at **Ba·sing** \'bāz-iŋ\ parish to the E occurred Anglo-Saxon ruler Ethelred I's victory over the Danes 871; first charter granted 1227.

Ba·sir·hat \ˌbə-sər-'hät, ˌbä-\. Town, West Bengal, NE India, on Kalindi River 30 mi. (48 km.) E of Calcutta; pop. (1991p) 101,652.

Ba·sit, Cape \bə-'sēt\ *or Arab.* **Ras al–Basit** \ˌräs-ˌȧl-\. Cape, N coast of Latakia, Syria, 35°51′N.

Bas·ka·tong, Réservoir \'bas-kə-ˌtäŋ, -ˌtȯŋ\. Lake, SW Quebec, Canada; outlet S through Gatineau River.

Basle. See BASEL.

Ba·so·ko \bä-'sō-ˌkō\. Town, Haut-Zaïre administrative region, NE Democratic Rep. of the Congo, at junction of Aruwimi and Congo rivers.

Basque Country \'bäsk, 'bask\ *or Span.* **País Vasco** \'pīs-'b̲äs-kō\. Autonomous community and historical region, N Spain; bounded on N by Bay of Biscay, on E by Navarre, on SW by Castilla y León; ✱ Vitoria; comprises an autonomous community consisting of the modern provs. of Vizcaya, Álava, and Guipúzcoa; has Pyrenees on E and E end of Cantabrian Mts. on W; forests, orchards, vineyards; long a center of iron mining; fisheries. See table at SPAIN.
History: Inhabited by Basques, a people of obscure racial and linguistic origin who retained virtual autonomy until 19th cent.; little affected by Moorish conquest of Spain; Álava and Vizcaya successively dependent upon kingdoms of Asturias, Navarre, and Castile; took part in Carlist War 1834–76, but allowed by Alfonso XII to keep only limited administrative autonomy; given autonomy soon after outbreak of Spanish Civil War 1936 but occupied by Insurgents 1936–37; limited autonomy restored 1980.

Bas·ra \'bäs-rə, 'bəs-, 'bas-, 'bäz-, 'bəz-, 'baz-\ *or Arab.* **Al–Bas·rah** \ȧl-\ *also* **Bus·so·ra** *or* **Bus·so·rah** \'bə-sə-rə\; *formerly* **Bus·ra** *or* **Bus·rah** \'bäs-rə, 'bu̇s-, 'bəs-\. Port, at head of the Shatt al Arab, SE Iraq, ab. 75 mi. (121 km.) from the Persian Gulf; pop. (1985e) 616,700; a major center of oil refining and export before the 1980s war with Iran; connected by rail with Baghdad; administrative and commercial center; university (1967). Founded by Caliph 'Umar I 638 A.D.; famous under the Abbasids; known in *Arabian Nights* as **Bas·so·rah** \'ba-sə-rə\; taken by Turks 1668; during 17th–19th cents. had some business as trading center; in WWI taken by British; returned 1930; in WWII occupied by British 1941, became important for transshipment of supplies to Turkey and U.S.S.R.; heavily damaged during 1980s Iran-Iraq War and during 1991 Persian Gulf War.

Bas–Rhin \ˌbȧ-'ra^{n}\. Department of NE France. See table at FRANCE.

Bas·sac *or* **Ba·săk** \bä-'säk\. River, S cen. Cambodia; flows into the Mekong in Phnom Penh.

Bassae. See PHIGALIA.

Bassam. See GRAND BASSAM.

Bas·sa·no \bä-'sä-nō\ *or in full* **Bassano del Grap·pa** \del-'gräp-pä\. Commune, Vicenza prov., Veneto, NE Italy, on left bank of Brenta River 19 mi. (31 km.) NE of the commune of Vicenza; pop. (1991p) 38,659; has 12th cent. Romanesque church and 13th cent. castle. First mentioned 998; joined Venetian Republic 1402; 16th cent. painter Bassano made his home here; from 17th–19th cents. city well-known for Romondini printing house; scene of defeat of Austrians by French Emperor Napoléon Sept. 8, 1796; made duchy by Napoléon and conferred on diplomat Hugues-Bernard Maret 1809.

Bassas da India. See INDIA, BASSAS DA.

Bassée, La. See LA BASSÉE.

Bas·sein \bə-'sān\ *or* **Va·sai** \vä-'sī\. **1.** River, Irrawaddy div., Myanmar; ab. 160 mi. (257 km.) long; a navigable outlet of the Irrawaddy in W part of its delta.
2. City, ✱ of Irrawaddy div., Myanmar, in the Irrawaddy delta 90 mi. (145 km.) W of Yangon; pop. (1983c) 144,096; rice mills; badly damaged by Japanese 1942; reoccupied by British May 25, 1945.

Bassein, Donetski. See DONETS BASIN.

Basse–Nor·man·die \ˌbȧs-ˌnȯr-mä^{n}-'dē\. Region of NW France, on the English Channel. See table at FRANCE.

Bas·sen·thwaite \'bas-^{ə}n-ˌthwāt\. Lake in the Lake District in Cumberland co., NW England, E of Cockermouth; an expansion of Derwent River.

Basses–Alpes. See ALPES-DE-HAUTE PROVENCE.

Basse·terre \bȧs-'ter\. Seaport, ✱ of St. Kitts-Nevis, on St. Kitts I., Leeward Is., West Indies; pop. (1985e) 18,500; founded 1627.

Basse–Terre \ˌbȧs-'ter\. **1.** Island, the W part of the French dept. of Guadeloupe, West Indies, N of Dominica; 35 mi. (56 km.) long; pop. (1990c) 149,943.
2. Seaport on SW coast of Basse-Terre I., ✱ of the French dept. of Guadeloupe; pop. (1990c) 14,107; founded 1643.

Bas·sett \'ba-sət\. Village, ⊗ of Rock co., N Nebraska; pop. (1990c) 739.

Bassin d'Arcachon. See ARCACHON.

Bass Island \'bas\. Three islands in W Lake Erie, **North Bass I., Middle Bass I.,** and **South Bass I.,** N and E of Ottawa co., N Ohio; Put-in-Bay, scene of American officer Oliver Hazard Perry's naval victory 1813, is on South Bass I. and is the site of a national monument.

Bassorah. See BASRA.

Bass Rock. Large isolated greenstone rock, S of entrance to Firth of Forth, SE Scotland; lighthouse; site of ruins of 17th cent. castle, seized by Jacobites 1691 and held three years before surrendering to William of Orange.

Bass Strait. Strait separating Australia from Tasmania; 80 to 150 mi. (129 to 241 km.) wide, 185 mi. (298 km.) long; av. depth 230 ft. (70 m.); named 1798 for George Bass, British surgeon and navigator.

Bas·tar \'bəs-tər, 'bäs-\. Former Indian state, now part of Madhya Pradesh, E cen. India; 13,701 sq. mi. (35,486 sq. km.).

Bas·ti \'bəs-tē, 'bäs-\. Town, Uttar Pradesh, N India, 115 mi. (185 km.) NNE of Allahabad; pop. (1991p) 87,512; college.

Basti. See BAZA.

Ba·stia \bȧs-'tyȧ, 'bas-tē-ə, 'bäs-\. Seaport city, ✱ of Haute-Corse dept., France, on NE coast of island of Corsica 65 mi. (105 km.) NE of Ajaccio; pop. (1990c) 38,728; principal commercial and industrial city of Corsica; exports include wine and fish; citadel; cathedral. Became French 1768; ✱ of Corsica until 1791 (later superseded by Ajaccio).

Bas·togne \bȧ-'stȯn^{y}, -'stō-nyə\. Town, E Luxembourg prov., SE Belgium; pop. (1981c) 11,386; an upland town of the Ardennes 43 mi. (69 km.) S of Liége; important railroad and highway junction point. In WWII in the German offensive (Battle of the Bulge) of December 1944, an American division surrounded here; held after severe fighting until German forces driven back Jan. 1945.

Bas·trop \'bas-trəp\. **1.** County in S cen. Texas. See table at TEXAS.
2. City, ⊗ of Morehouse parish, N Louisiana, 24 mi. (39 km.) NNE of Monroe; pop. (1990c) 13,916.
3. City, ⊗ of Bastrop co., S cen. Texas, on Colorado River 28 mi. (45 km.) ESE of Austin; pop. (1990c) 4044; coal and oil deposits.

Basutoland. See LESOTHO.

Bas–Za·ïre \,bȧ-zä-'ēr\; *formerly* **Kon·go–Cen·tral** \kō^{n}-'gō-sä^{n}-'trȧl\. Administrative region of W Democratic Rep. of the Congo. See table at ZAIRE.

Ba·ta \'bä-tä\. Seaport, chief town of Mbini, Equatorial Guinea.

Ba·taan \bə-'tan, -'tän\. Province, W Luzon, Philippines, forming a peninsula 30 mi. (48 km.) long by 15 mi. (24 km.) wide on W side of Manila Bay; 530 sq. mi. (1373 sq. km.); pop. (1990p) 426,000; ✻ Balanga. Traversed by S end of Zambales Mts., highest point in province 4444 ft. (1355 m.); has many short streams and few indentations on its coast; Mariveles Bay at its S end is best harbor; its NW coast forms E shore of the large safe anchorage of Subic Bay; W half is covered with forests and jungle; E coastal plain is most populous. See table at PHILIPPINES.

Chief towns: Dinalupihan, Balanga, Orion, and Abucay.

History: Bet. 1600 and 1650 the scene of several conflicts with the Dutch; in early times a part of Pampanga; created separate province by Spanish governor-general 1754; civil government estab. March 1901 with Philippines coming under U.S. influence. In WWII scene of final struggle of American and Filipino forces under Gen. Douglas MacArthur against Japanese conquest of Philippines: N end occupied 1942, after fall of Manila, by American forces, who, after withdrawal southward toward Mariveles, surrendered Apr. 9, 1942; remnant of force retired to Corregidor (*q.v.*), which also gave up May 6; retaken by Americans early 1945.

Ba·ta·ba·nó, Gulf of \,bä-tä-bä-'nō\. Widemouthed gulf S of La Habana and Pinar del Río provs., W Cuba, and N of Isla de la Juventud.

Ba·tac \'bä-,täk\. Municipality, SW Ilocos Norte prov., Luzon, Philippines, 10 mi. (16 km.) S of Laoag; pop. (1980c) 37,579.

Bataille, Arques–la–. See ARQUES.

Bataisk. See BATAYSK.

Ba·tak·land \'bä-,täk-,land\ *or Du.* **Ba·tak·lan·den** \-,län-dən\. Region around Lake Toba, N Sumatra, Indonesia; original home of the Batak, an Indonesian people who once were practicing cannibals; country not controlled by Dutch until after middle of the 19th cent.

Ba·ta·la \bə-'tä-lə\. City, NW Punjab, NW India, ab. 25 mi. (40 km.) NE of Amritsar; pop. (1991p) 88,896.

Ba·ta·lha \bə-'tȧl-yə\. Commune, Leiria dist., W cen. Portugal, 6 mi. (10 km.) S of the commune of Leiria; pop. (1991p) 13,018; famous for its Dominican monastery, now a national monument containing tomb of John I of Portugal and other kings, built by John I of Portugal to commemorate his victory 1385 over John I of Castile at Aljubarrota nearby.

Batalpashinsk. See CHERKESSK.

Ba·tam \bä-'täm\. Island in Kepulauan Riau, Indonesia, opp. Singapore; 180 sq. mi. (466 sq. km.); its N shore borders on Singapore Strait.

Ba·tan \bä-'tän\. Island, E Albay prov., Luzon, Philippines, central of three islands N of Albay Gulf; forms part of S shore of Lagonoy Gulf; ab. 13 mi. (21 km.) long by 5 mi. (8 km.) wide; 35 sq. mi. (91 sq. km.); has valuable coal deposits.

Ba·ta·naea \,ba-tə-'nē-ə\. Roman name of S Bashan, ancient Palestine, forming the SW part of the region ruled over by Philip the Tetrarch (4 B.C.–34 A.D.).

Ba·ta·nes \bä-'tä-näs\. Province, comprising the **Ba·tan Islands** \bä-'tän\, N Philippines; N of Luzon; 81 sq. mi. (210 sq. km.); pop. (1990e) 14,435; ✻ Basco, on Batan I.; separated from Taiwan by Bashi Channel and from the Babuyan Is. to the S by Balintang Channel; comprises Itbayat, Batan, and Sabtang islands and 11 islets; mountainous, with an extinct volcano on Batan I. Long inhabited; first conquered by Spanish 1791; made a province 1909. See table at PHILIPPINES.

Ba·tang \'bä-,täŋ\. Town, Central Java prov., Indonesia, just E of Pekalongan.

Ba·tan·gas \bä-'täŋ-gäs\. **1.** Province, S Luzon, Philippines; 1222 sq. mi. (3165 sq. km.); pop. (1990p) 1,476,000; ✻ Batangas; numerous mountains, esp. in W and NE; many small streams; in cen. part is large Lake Taal with Taal volcano forming an island in its center; three large bays Balayan, Batangas, and Tayabas; sugar and other agricultural products. See table at PHILIPPINES.

Chief towns: Batangas, Lipa, Tanauan, Nasugbu, and Rosario.

History: Populous region in pre-Spanish times; explored by Spaniards 1570 and created a province 1581, much larger than at present; in 17th cent. suffered from Moro attacks and in 1911 from severe eruption of Taal volcano; active in revolution against Spanish; civil government estab. May 1901.
2. Municipality, its ✻, in S part of province on NE coast of Batangas Bay 58 mi. (93 km.) S of Manila; pop. (1990p) 184,000.

Batangas Bay. Inlet in S coast of Batangas prov., Luzon, Philippines; ab. 9 mi. (15 km.) across at mouth; island of Maricaban on SW; Batangas and Bauan at its head.

Batang Lu·par \'bä-,täŋ-'lü-,pär\. River, SW Sarawak, Malaysia; flows W into the South China Sea; 120 mi. (193 km.) long.

Batan Islands. See BATANES.

Ba·tan·ta \bä-'tän-tä\. Island off N coast of Salawati I., (*q.v.*) Irian Jaya, Indonesia; ab. 40 mi. (64 km.) long.

Ba·ta·via \bə-'tā-vē-ə\. **1.** City, Kane co., NE Illinois, 35 mi. (56 km.) W of Chicago; pop. (1990c) 17,076; nearby is the National Accelerator Laboratory.
2. City, ⊗ of Genesee co., W New York, 33 mi. (53 km.) WSW of Rochester; pop. (1990c) 16,310; service center; Genesee Community Coll. (1966); settled 1801; incorp. 1914.
3. Village, ⊗ of Clermont co., SW Ohio, 17 mi. (27 km.) E of Cincinnati; pop. (1990c) 1700.
4. \bä-'tä-vē-ä\. Former residency, Java, Netherlands Indies, now part of the Indonesian prov. of West Java; 3098 sq. mi. (8024 sq. km.); included lowlands along NW coast of Java on Java Sea and Jakarta Bay and the Thousand Is. group in SW Java Sea; region has many short streams; densely populated.
5. City, Indonesia. See JAKARTA.

Batavia Bay. See JAKARTA BAY.

Ba·ta·vi·an Republic \bə-'tā-vē-ən\. The name given to Holland by the French after its conquest in 1795; lasted until 1806 when kingdom of Holland was estab. with Louis Bonaparte, brother of French Emperor Napoléon, as its ruler. See *History* at NETHERLANDS.

Ba·taysk *or* **Ba·taisk** \bə-'tīsk\. City, SW Rostov Oblast, S Russia in Europe, 5 mi. (8 km.) S of Rostov-na-Donu; important railroad junction point with main line running SE to Caucasus. Key point in struggle for Rostov-na-Donu 1918 in Russian Civil War; seized by German armies July 1942 in WWII, recaptured Feb. 1943.

Bat·dam·bang. See BATTAMBANG.

Bates \'bāts\. County in W Missouri. See table at MISSOURI.

Bates·burg \'bāts-,bərg\. Town, W cen. South Carolina, 32 mi. (52 km.) W of Columbia; pop. (1990c) 4082.

Bates·ville \'bāts-,vil, -vəl\. **1.** City, ⊗ of Independence co., NE cen. Arkansas; pop. (1990c) 9187; marble and manganese in vicinity. Arkansas Coll. (1872); first settled 1812.
2. City, Franklin and Ripley cos., SE Indiana, 31 mi. (50 km.) ESE of Shelbyville; pop. (1990c) 4720.
3. City, a ⊗ of Panola co., NW Mississippi, 35 mi. (56 km.) ENE of Clarksdale; pop. (1990c) 6403.

Bath \'bath, 'bäth\. **1.** Name of counties in two states of the U.S. See tables at KENTUCKY and VIRGINIA.

\ə\ abut \ə\ matches \$^{ə}$\ kitten, Fr table \ər\ **further** \a\ ash \ā\ ace \ä\ cot, cart \ȧ\ Fr bac \au̇\ **out** \b\ Span Avila \ch\ **chin** \e\ bet \ē\ **easy** \g\ go \i\ hit \ī\ ice \j\ job \k\ Ger ich, Buch \$^{n}$\ Fr vin \ŋ\ sing \ō\ go \ö\ all \ȯ\ law \œ\ Fr bœuf \œ̄\ Fr **feu** \ȯi\ boy \th\ **thin** \t͟h\ **this** \ü\ loot \u̇\ foot \ue\ Ger füllen \ue̅\ Fr **rue** \y\ yet \$^{y}$\ Fr digne \'dēn^{y}\, nuit \'nw^{y}ē\ \yü\ **few** \yu̇\ **fury** \zh\ vision

2. City, ⊗ of Sagadahoc co., S Maine, on inlet of Atlantic Ocean 28 mi. (45 km.) NE of Portland; pop. (1990c) 9799; port of entry and trading center; shipbuilding; incorp. 1781.
3. Village, ⊗ of Steuben co., S New York, 19 mi. (31 km.) E of Hornell; pop. (1990c) 5801; settled 1793.
4. Borough, Northampton co., E Pennsylvania, 10 mi. (16 km.) NNE of Allentown; pop. (1990c) 2358.
5. Town, West Virginia. See BERKELEY SPRINGS.
6. *anc.* **Aquae Cal·i·dae** \ˈa-kwē-ˈka-lə-ˌdē, ˈä-kwī-ˈkä-li-ˌdī\ *or* **Aquae So·lis** \ˈsō-lis\. City and county borough, Avon, SW England, on the Avon River 12 mi. (19 km.) SE of Bristol; pop. (1991p) 79,900; health resort with thermal springs; Bath Univ. of Technology (1966); Roman remains (baths rediscovered 1775); received charter 1189.
History: Once popular as a Roman spa; Saxons arrived c. 6th cent. A.D., Normans c. 1100; in medieval times a center for cloth trade; experienced great social popularity 18th cent., which is reflected in literary works of Jane Austen, Tobias Smollett, Richard Brinsley Sheridan; extensive number of Georgian buildings remain; popular destination once again 20th cent.

Bath·gate \ˈbath-ˌgāt, -gət\. Burgh, Lothian region, SE Scotland; pop. (1981p) 14,388; coal deposits.

Bathinda. See BHATINDA.

Bath·urst \ˈba-thərst\. **1.** City, E New South Wales, SE Australia, on Macquarie River in Blue Mts., 100 mi. (161 km.) WNW of Sidney; pop. (1983c) 44,188; elev. 2206 ft. (672 m.); service center for agricultural area; food products, plastics; trout fishing; founded 1815.
2. City, ⊗ of Gloucester co., NE New Brunswick, Canada, on Nepisiguit Bay at mouth of Nepisiguit River; pop. (1991c) 14,409; summer resort; important salmon center and shipping port.
3. Seaport in Gambia. See BANJUL.
4. Village, S Eastern Cape prov., Rep. of South Africa, 90 mi. (145 km.) ENE of Port Elizabeth; first home and administrative center of British settlers of 1820.

Bathurst, Cape. Cape, NW mainland part of Northwest Territories, Canada, extending into Beaufort Sea, 70°35′N, 128°W.

Bathurst Inlet. Large inlet of Coronation Gulf, Nunavut, Canada.

Bathurst Island. **1.** Island, NW of Northern Terr., Australia, W of Melville I.; 30 mi. (48 km.) long; 786 sq. mi. (2036 sq. km.); separated from mainland by Clarence Strait.
2. Island, one of the Parry Is., Nunavut, N Canada; 7609 sq. mi. (19,707 sq. km.).

Ba·tis·can \ˌbä-ti-ˈskäⁿ\. River, S Quebec, Canada; rises in W Quebec co., flows S into St. Lawrence River near Batiscan in Champlain co.; ab. 50 mi. (81 km.) long.

Ba·tjan. See BACAN.

Bat·ley \ˈbat-lē\. Town, West Yorkshire, N England, 6 mi. (10 km.) SSW of Leeds; pop. (1981p) 42,572.

Bat·man \bät-ˈmän\. Province of Turkey in Asia. See table at TURKEY.

Bat·na \ˈbat-nə\. City, NE Algeria, on Toggourt-Annaba railroad line, 195 mi. (314 km.) SE of Algiers; pop. (1987p) 181,601.

Ba·to, Lake \bä-ˈtō\. Small lake on S boundary of Camarines Sur prov., Luzon, Philippines, partly in NW Albay prov.; total area 15 sq. mi. (39 sq. km.); receives many streams of Albay that rise near the foot of Mayon Volcano; outlet is the Bicol River.

Ba·to–Ba·to \bä-ˌtō-bä-ˈtō\. Municipality, ✻ of Tawi-tawi prov., SW Philippines.

Batoe. See BATU.

Bat·on Rouge \ˈbat-ᵊn-ˈrüzh\. **1.** For parishes in Louisiana, see *East Baton Rouge* and *West Baton Rouge* in table at LOUISIANA.
2. City, ✻ of Louisiana and ⊗ of East Baton Rouge parish, SE cen. Louisiana, on Mississippi River 78 mi. (126 km.) WNW of New Orleans; pop. (1990c) 219,531; 2d largest city in the state, located on bluffs on E side of the river; deepwater port facilities; petroleum refineries; distribution center for agricultural region. Louisiana State Univ. and Agricultural and Mechanical Coll. (1860), Southern Univ. and Agricultural and Mechanical Coll. (1880).
History: Transferred from France to Great Britain by Treaty of Paris 1763, and made a part of West Florida; conquered by Spain during American Revolution; ceded by Spain to France 1800; claimed again by Spain at time of Louisiana Purchase 1803; estab. independence by rebellion 1810, and declared itself county by the name of Feliciana; after admission of Louisiana to the Union 1812, incorp. as a town 1817; state ✻ 1849–61 and 1882 to date; held by Union forces for greater part of Civil War; consolidation of city and parish governments 1947.

Bat·tam·bang \ˈbät-täm-ˌbäŋ\ *also* **Bat·dam·bang** \-däm-\. Town, W Cambodia, W of Tonle Sap; pop. (1987e) 45,000; in a fertile plain in a large rice-growing area. Ceded to Siam by Cambodia 1809 and by Siam to French Indochina 1907; under Japanese pressure yielded by the French Vichy government to Siam 1941; returned to Cambodia 1946.

Bat·ten·berg \ˈbät-ᵊn-ˌberk\. Village, Hesse, Germany, 15 mi. (24 km.) NNW of Marburg; seat of family of counts whose title died out c. 1314 and was revived 1851 for a royal branch, English members of which renounced the title 1917 and assumed the surname Mountbatten.

Bat·ti·ca·loa \ˌbə-ti-kə-ˈlō-ə\. Seaport town, Sri Lanka on Bay of Bengal; pop. (1990e) 51,000; located on a lagoon once noted for its "singing fish," an unexplained natural phenomenon consisting of musical notes rising from the water. Captured by Portuguese, then by Dutch 17th cent.; taken by British 18th cent.; remains of forts.

Bat·ti·pa·glia \ˌbät-tē-ˈpäl-yä\. Commune, Salerno prov., S Campania, S Italy, 12 mi. (19 km.) ESE of the seaport of Salerno; pop. (1989c) 45,303.

Bat·tle \ˈbat-ᵊl\. **1.** River, cen. Alberta and Saskatchewan, Canada; flows E from cen. Alberta into North Saskatchewan at Battleford; ab. 340 mi. (547 km.) long.
2. Market town and parish, East Sussex, England, 6 mi. (10 km.) NW of Hastings; pop. (1981c) 5141; named from the battle of Hastings that took place 1066 on a hill SE of the town. The "Roll of Battle Abbey," a list of Norman surnames, probably compiled in 14th cent.

Battle Creek. City, Calhoun co., S Michigan, 22 mi. (35.4 km.) E of Kalamazoo; pop. (1990c) 53,540; known for manufacture of breakfast foods; Kellogg Community Coll. (1956); site of Battle Creek Sanitarium.

Bat·tle·ford \ˈbat-ᵊl-fərd, -ˌfōrd\. Town, W Saskatchewan, Canada, at junction of Battle and North Saskatchewan rivers opp. North Battleford; pop. (1991c) 4107. Founded 1875; ✻ of Northwest Territories 1876–82, and of Saskatchewan dist. 1882–1905; occupied briefly by Indians during 2d Riel Rebellion 1885.

Battle Ground \ˈbat-ᵊl-ˈgraund\. **1.** Town, Tippecanoe co., W cen. Indiana, ab. 7 mi. (11 km.) NNE of Lafayette; pop. (1990c) 806; on site of Prophetstown, founded 1808 by Shawnee Indian leader Tenskwatawa, brother of Tecumseh. Destroyed in battle of Tippecanoe 1811 but rebuilt.
2. City, Clark co., SW Washington; pop. (1990c) 3758.

Battle Harbour. Village on small island off SE Labrador coast, Canada, N of N end of Strait of Belle Isle, on sheltered roadstead; site of a Grenfell Mission Hospital, estab. 1893, which was destroyed by fire 1923.

Bat·tle·ment Mountain \ˈbat-ᵊl-mənt\. Peak, W Park co., NW Wyoming; 11,900 ft. (3627 m.).

Battle Mountain. **1.** Peak, Fall River co., SW corner of South Dakota; 4434 ft. (1351 m.).
2. Unincorporated settlement, ⊗ of Lander co., cen. Nevada; pop. (1990c) 3542.

Ba·tu *or Du.* **Ba·toe** \ˈbä-tü\. Island group, Indonesia, in the Indian Ocean off W cen. coast of Sumatra; 464 sq. mi. (1202 sq. km.); crossed by the Equator; contains about 48 islands with only three of any size, Tanahmasa, Tanahbala, and Pini.

Batu Anam \ˈbä-tü-ˈä-ˌnäm\. Village on railroad line, N Johor state, Malaysia, near Gemas; severe fighting bet. Australians and Japanese Jan. 1942 in WWII.

Ba·tu·da·ka \ˌbä-tü-ˈdä-kä\. See PENJU ISLANDS.

Batu Ga·jah \ˈbä-tü-ˈgä-jä\. Town, cen. Perak state, Malaysia, on railroad line just S of Ipoh; headquarters of Kinta Valley tin-bearing region.

Ba·tu·lao, Mount \bä-ˈtü-ˌlaů\. Mountain, NW Batangas prov., Luzon, Philippines, W of Lake Taal; 2894 ft. (882 m.).

Ba·tu·mi \bȧ-ˈtü-mē\; *formerly* **Ba·tum** \-ˈtüm\. City and seaport, ✻ of Adzhar Autonomous Rep., SW Republic of Georgia, on Black Sea near Turkish border; pop. (1991e) 137,500; has best port at E end of Black Sea; connected by rail and oil pipeline with Baku, Azerbaijan and Tbilisi; shipyard, oil refineries, engineering works; exports oil, manganese. Long a possession of Persia and Turkey; acquired by Russia 1878; occupied by British 1918; formerly one of the Black Sea bases of Soviet fleet.

Ba·tu Pa·hat \ˈbä-tü-ˈpä-hät\ *also* **Ban·dar Peng·ga·ram** \bän-ˈdär-peŋ-ˈgä-räm\. Seaport on the Strait of Malacca, W Johor state, Malaysia, SE of Muar; pop. (1980p) 277,995.

Bat Yam \ˈbät-ˈyäm\. Coastal city, W cen. Israel, a S suburb of Tel Aviv-Jaffa.

Ba·uan \ˈbä-ˌwän\. Municipality on N coast of Batangas Bay, Batangas prov., Luzon, Philippines, 4 mi. (6 km.) NW of the municipality of Batangas; pop. (1980c) 43,560.

Ba·uang \ˈbä-ˌwäŋ\. Municipality, S cen. La Union prov., Luzon, Philippines, at river mouth near the coast 6 mi. (10 km.) S of San Fernando; pop. (1980c) 41,859.

Bau·chi \ˈbaů-chē\. **1.** State of N cen. Nigeria. See table at NIGERIA.
2. Town, its ✻, 150 mi. (241 km.) SE of Kano; pop. (1991e) 76,070.

Bau·dette \bō-ˈdet\. Village, ⊗ of Lake of the Woods co., N Minnesota, on Rainy River; pop. (1990c) 1146.

Baudh \ˈbaůd\ *or* **Bod** \ˈbōd\. **1.** Former Indian state, now part of Orissa, E India; 1156 sq. mi. (2994 sq. km.).
2. *or* **Baudh Raj** \ˈräj\. Town, its ✻, on S bank of Mahanadi River 100 mi. (161 km.) WNW of Cuttack.

Baudissin. See BAUTZEN.

Bauld, Cape \ˈbȯld\. Cape at NE tip of Newfoundland, Canada, at N entrance to the Strait of Belle Isle.

Baule. See BAOULÉ.

Bau·res \ˈbaů-rās\. River in NE Bolivia; flows NW into Guaporé River on Brazilian border; with headstream Blanco ab. 360 mi. (579 km.) long.

Bau·ru \baů-ˈrü\. City, S cen. São Paulo state, SE Brazil, 175 mi. (282 km.) NW of the city of São Paulo; munic. pop. (1991p) 260,382.

Bau·ta \ˈbaů-tä\. Town and municipality, La Habana prov., W Cuba, 14 mi. (23 km.) SW of Havana; munic. pop. (1990e) 33,127.

Baut·zen \ˈbaůt-sən\ *or older* **Bu·dis·sin** \ˈbü-də-ˌsēn\ *or* **Bau·dis·sin** \ˈbaů-\. City, Saxony, E Germany; on Spree River 32 mi. (52 km.) ENE of Dresden; pop. (1992e) 47,131; became German c. 1030; scene of defeat of Prussian and Russian armies by French Emperor Napoléon May 20–21, 1813.

Baux-de-Provence, Les. See LES BAUX-DE-PROVENCE.

Bau·ya \ˈbaů-yä\. Town, W Sierra Leone; connected with Freetown by rail.

Bauzanum. See BOLZANO 2.

Ba·var·ia \bə-ˈvar-ē-ə\ *or Ger.* **Bay·ern** \ˈbī-ərn\. A state of S Germany; ✻ Munich; mountains include the Bavarian Alps, the Fichtelgebirge, and the Bohemian Forest (Böhmer Wald); grain; tourism; brewing. Largest cities: Munich, Nürnberg, Augsburg. See table at GERMANY.

History: Territory conquered by Romans first cent. B.C. (see NORICUM and RAETIA); invaded by Germanic peoples (Marcomanni) who became tributary to Franks in 6th cent. A.D.; conquered by Frankish King (later Holy Roman Emperor) Charlemagne and incorporated into his empire 788; assigned to East Frankish kingdom in divisions of Frankish empire 817, 843; one of great stem duchies of Holy Roman Empire; Bavarian East Mark became separate duchy of Austria (*q.v.*) 1156; taken from Saxony (*q.v.*) and given to house of Wittelsbach by Holy Roman Emperor Frederick Barbarossa 1180; divided into Upper and Lower Bavaria 13th cent.; under Louis IV of Upper Bavaria, who was crowned emperor 1328, added temporarily Brandenburg, Tirol, and Netherlandish counties; became electorate 1623; under Elector Maximilian I leader of Catholic League in Thirty Years' War; received Upper Palatinate 1648; allied with France 1701–04, during War of Spanish Succession; after War of Bavarian Succession 1778–79, united with Palatinate; its boundaries and make-up changed several times during Napoleonic era; granted constitution 1818; in 1833 merged its customs union with that of Prussia, laying basis of later Zollverein; joined Austria in war on Prussia 1866; joined North German Confederation 1870 and German Empire 1871; became a republic 1918; became a state of Weimar Republic 1919; Nazi leader Adolph Hitler's first power base during 1920s; constitution abolished by National Socialist (Nazi) regime 1933; part of U.S. occupation zone 1945; Palatinate removed and joined to Rhineland-Pfalz state; adopted new constitution 1946; became a state of Federal Republic of Germany (West Germany) 1949; remained a state in unified Germany 1990.

Ba·var·i·an Alps \bə-ˈvar-ē-ən\. Range of the Alps bet. S Bavaria, Germany, and Tirol, Austria, extending E and W from Lake Constance to Salzburg; highest point the Zugspitze 9720 ft. (2963 m.).

Bawd·win \ˈbȯ-ˌdwin\. Town, N Shan State, E cen. Myanmar, in mountains 30 mi. (48 km.) WNW of Lashio; has wolframite deposits that have been an important source of tungsten; ruby deposits.

Ba·we·an \ˈbä-wā-ˌän\. Island in the Java Sea, Indonesia, 100 mi. (161 km.) N of Surabaya; area 77 sq. mi. (199 sq. km.); invaded by Japanese in WWII 1942; just NE of the center of the naval battle of Java Sea Feb. 26–28, 1942 where Allies suffered severe defeat; surrendered to Allies Sept. 1945.

Baxar. See BUXAR.

Bax·ley \ˈbak-slē\. City, ⊗ of Appling co., SE Georgia, 38 mi. (61 km.) N of Waycross; pop. (1990c) 3841.

Bax·ter \ˈbak-stər\. County in N Arkansas. See table at ARKANSAS.

Baxter, Mount. Peak in the Sierra Nevada, on the boundary between Fresno and Inyo cos., SE cen. California; ab. 13,125 ft. (4000 m.).

Baxter Springs. City, Cherokee co., SE corner of Kansas; pop. (1990c) 4351; zinc and lead deposits nearby.

Bay \ˈbā\. Name of counties in two states of the U.S. See tables at FLORIDA and MICHIGAN.

Bay, La·gu·na de \lä-ˈgü-nä-thā-ˈbī\. Large crescent-shaped lake, cen. Luzon, Philippines, SE of Manila; ab. 32 mi. (52 km.) long; 344 sq. mi. (891 sq. km.); largest lake of the Philippines; its outlet is the Pasig at the NW.

Ba·yam·bang \ˌbī-äm-ˈbäŋ\. Municipality, S Pangasinan prov., Luzon, Philippines, 21 mi. (34 km.) SE of Lingayen on N bank of Agno River; pop. (1980c) 64,037.

Ba·ya·mo \bä-ˈyä-mō\. Town and municipality, ✻ of Granma prov., E Cuba; munic. pop. (1990e) 125,021; on **Bayamo River** (tributary of the Cauto) 27 mi. (43 km.) E of Manzanillo; founded 1513. A center of revolutionary movement against Spain 1868–98; here Cuban soldier Calixto García Íniguez received 1898 the "Message to Garcia."

Ba·ya·món \ˌbī-ä-ˈmōn\. **1.** River in E cen. Puerto Rico; flows N into Atlantic Ocean.
2. Town and municipality, NE cen. Puerto Rico; munic. pop. (1990c) 220,262, town pop. (1990c) 202,103; Bayamón Central Univ. (1970). According to tradition, the first municipality in Puerto Rico was founded near here; produces sugar.

Bay·ard \ˈbā-ərd\. City, Grant co., SW New Mexico, 75 mi. (121 km.) NW of Las Cruces; pop. (1990c) 2598.

Bay·bay \ˈbī-ˌbī\. Municipality, Leyte prov., on W coast of Leyte I., Philippines, on Camotes Sea 42 mi. (68 km.) SSW of Tacloban; historically important hemp port.

Bay·boro \ˈbā-ˌbər-ə\. Town, ⊗ of Pamlico co., E North Carolina, near Pamlico Sound; pop. (1990c) 733.

Bay Bulls \ˈbā-ˌbu̇lz\. Seaside resort, SE Newfoundland, Canada, on Atlantic Ocean 20 mi. (32 km.) S of St. John's.

Bay·burt \bī-ˈbu̇rt\. Province of Turkey in Asia. See table at TURKEY.

Bay City \ˈbā\. **1.** City, ⊗ of Bay co., E Michigan, at head of Saginaw Bay 13 mi. (21 km.) N of Saginaw; pop. (1990c) 38,936.

2. City, ⊗ of Matagorda co., SE Texas, 70 mi. (113 km.) WSW of Galveston; pop. (1990c) 18,170; sulfur and oil deposits.

Bayda, Al–. See BEIDA.

Bay de Verde \ˌbā-də-ˈvərd\. Seaport, SE Newfoundland, Canada, at mouth of Conception Bay; pop. (1991c) 679.

Bayern. See BAVARIA.

Ba·yeux \bá-ˈyœ\; *anc.* **Au·gus·to·du·rum** \ȯ-ˈgəs-tə-ˈdu̇r-əm, -ˈdyu̇r-\. Town, Calvados dept., Normandy, NW France, ab. 15 mi. (24 km.) WNW of Caen and ab. 5 mi. (8 km.) inland from the English Channel; pop. (1990c) 15,106. An old town, with bishopric after 4th cent.; taken by Norsemen 890; several times besieged and captured in wars bet. 12th and 16th cents. Has fine 13th cent. Gothic church and a museum containing the famous Bayeux tapestry (probably of 11th cent.), representing in 72 panels incidents in the life of William the Conqueror, duke of Normandy and king of England.

Bay·field \ˈbā-ˌfēld\. County in NW Wisconsin. See table at WISCONSIN.

Bay Harbor Islands. Town, Miami-Dade co., SE Florida, on coast ab. 3 mi. (4.8 km.) NE of Miami; pop. (1990c) 4703.

Bay Islands. See BAHÍA, ISLAS DE LA.

Baykal, Lake *also* **Baykal, Ozero.** See BAIKAL, LAKE.

Baykal Mountains *or* **Baykal'skiy Khrebet.** See BAIKAL MOUNTAINS.

Bay·ko·nur *or* **Bay·ko·nyr** *or* **Bai·ko·nur** \ˌbī-kə-ˈnu̇r\. Locality, Qaraghandy, cen. Kazakhstan, ab. 150 mi. (241 km.) NE of Aral Sea; site of principal Soviet missile- and rocket-testing facility, from which major Earth satellites and interplanetary probes were launched.

Bay·lor \ˈbā-lər\. County in N Texas. See table at TEXAS.

Bay Mi·nette \ˌbā-mi-ˈnet\. City, ⊗ of Baldwin co., SW Alabama, 22 mi. (35 km.) NE of Mobile; pop. (1990c) 7168.

Bay of Algiers. See ALGIERS 2.

Bay of Islands. 1. Inlet of Bering Sea, W coast of Adak I., Andreanof Is., Aleutian Is., Alaska.

2. Inlet of Gulf of St. Lawrence, W coast of Newfoundland, Canada; receives the Humber River.

3. Inlet of South Pacific Ocean, NE coast of North I., New Zealand.

Bay of Whales. See WHALES, BAY OF.

Ba·yom·bong \ˌbī-ōm-ˈbȯŋ\. Municipality, ✱ of Nueva Vizcaya prov., Luzon, Philippines, on Magat River; pop. (1980c) 32,066.

Bay·onne \bā-ˈōn\. City, Hudson co., NE New Jersey, on peninsula that separates Upper New York Bay from Newark Bay 5 mi. (8 km.) SW of Jersey City; pop. (1990c) 61,444; connected with Staten I. by Bayonne Bridge (steel arch, main span 1675 ft. or 511 m.; completed 1931) over Kill Van Kull; important petroleum-refining and exporting center; manufactures chemicals and radiators; extensive docks. Site visited by English navigator Henry Hudson 1609; original grant 1646; incorp. as city of Bayonne 1869.

Ba·yonne \bá-ˈyȯn\; *anc.* **La·pur·dum** \lə-ˈpər-dəm\. Port, Pyrénées-Atlantiques dept., SW France, at confluence of the Nive with the Adour near Bay of Biscay 55 mi. (89 km.) WNW of Pau; pop. (1990c) 41,846; fishing; oil and gas deposits nearby; cathedral (13th–16th cents.); citadel; arsenal.

History: Important port in Roman times; in Middle Ages held by English; held by French since 1451; meeting place of French Queen Catherine de Médicis and Spanish soldier Fernando Álvarez de Toledo, duke of Alva 1565 where Massacre of St. Bartholomew was once rumored to have been planned; famous in 16th and 17th cents. for manufacture of cutlery and armaments, the bayonet having been invented here (whence its name); meeting of French Emperor Napoléon, Charles IV of Spain, and prince of the Asturias 1808 which led to abdication of Spanish monarchs in favor of Napoléon's brother Joseph Bonaparte.

Bayou Barataria. See BARATARIA, BAYOU.

Bay·port \ˈbā-ˌpōrt\. City, Washington co., E Minnesota, on St. Croix River 15 mi. (24 km.) ENE of St. Paul; pop. (1990c) 3200; window manufacture; state prison.

Bay·reuth *also* **Bai·reuth** \bī-ˈrȯit, ˈbī-ˌ\. City, Bavaria, Germany, 41 mi. (66 km.) NE of Nürnberg; pop. (1992e) 72,777; 16th cent. and 18th cent. palaces; the Festspielhaus (designed by composer Richard Wagner), where the Wagner festivals have been held at irregular intervals since its opening 1876; burial place of Wagner and Hungarian composer Franz Liszt. Founded 1194 under Bishop Otto II of Bamberg; under burgrave of Nürnberg 1248–1398, margraves of Brandenburg-Kulmbach 1603–1769; to Prussia 1791, French Emperor Napoléon 1806, Bavaria 1810.

Bay Rob·erts \ˈrä-bərts\. Town on W shore of Conception Bay, Newfoundland, Canada, S of Harbour Grace and 27 mi. (43 km.) W of St. John's; pop. (1991c) 5474; port of entry.

Bayrūt. See BEIRUT.

Bay St. Lou·is \sānt-ˈlü-is, sənt\. City, ⊗ of Hancock co., S Mississippi, on Gulf of Mexico 15 mi. (24 km.) W of Gulfport; pop. (1990c) 8063; winter resort.

Baysān. See BET SHE'AN.

Bay Shore. Unincorporated settlement, Suffolk co., SE New York, on S shore of Long Island and Great South Bay ab. 40 mi. (64 km.) E of Brooklyn; pop. (1990c) 21,279.

Bay·side \ˈbā-ˌsīd\. Village, Milwaukee and Ozaukee cos., SE Wisconsin; pop. (1990c) 4789.

Bay Springs. Town, a ⊗ of Jasper co., SE cen. Mississippi; pop. (1990c) 1729.

Baytīn. See BETHEL 6.

Bayt Jālā. See BEIT JALA.

Bayt Laḥm. See BETHLEHEM 2.

Bay·town \ˈbā-ˌtau̇n\. City, Harris co., SE Texas, on Galveston Bay ab. 22 mi. (35 km.) ESE of Houston; pop. (1990c) 63,850; oil deposits; Lee Coll. (1934); area settled early 1800s; site of Confederate shipyard 1864; Baytown became part of Pelly 1945; Pelly and Goose Creek combined to be renamed Baytown 1948.

Bay Village. City, Cuyahoga co., N Ohio, on Lake Erie, W of Cleveland; pop. (1990c) 17,000.

Bay·ville \ˈbā-ˌvil\. Village on N shore of Long Island, Nassau co., SE New York; pop. (1990c) 7193.

Ba·za \ˈbä-thä, -sä\; *anc.* **Bas·ti** \ˈbas-ˌtī\. City, Granada prov., S Spain, 53 mi. (85 km.) NE of the city of Granada; pop. (1991p) 20,262. Important city in Moorish Grenada; besieged and finally taken by Queen Isabella of Castile 1489; scene of French victory over Spaniards 1810.

Ba·zan·court \ˌbá-zä^{n}-ˈkür\. Town, Marne dept., France, NE of Reims; scene of battle Oct. 7, 1918 when Germans were forced to evacuate it.

Ba·zar·dyu·ze \bə-ˈzär-dyu̇-ˈzē\. Peak in E Caucasus Mts., bet. Dagestan Rep., S Russia in Europe and Azerbaijan; 14,698 ft. (4480 m.).

Bazargic. See DOBRICH.

Baz·mān, Kūh–e– \ˌkü-hē-baz-ˈmän\. Peak of an extinct volcano, SE Iran; 11,447 ft. (3489 m.).

Beach \ˈbēch\. City, ⊗ of Golden Valley co., W North Dakota; pop. (1990c) 1205.

Beach Haven Inlet. Strait leading from Atlantic Ocean into S Barnegat Bay off SE tip of Ocean co., New Jersey.

Beach Park. Village, Lake co., NE corner of Illinois; pop. (1990c) 9513.

Beachwood \ˈbēch-ˌwu̇d\. **1.** Borough, Ocean co., E New Jersey, on Toms River 42 mi. (68 km.) NNE of Atlantic City; pop. (1990c) 9324.

2. City, Cuyahoga co., Ohio, E of Cleveland; pop. (1990c) 10,677.

Beachy Head \ˈbē-chē\. Headland on S coast of East Sussex, S England, projecting into English Channel; 575 ft. (175 m.) high; lighthouse. Scene 1690 of naval victory of French over British and Dutch.

Bea·con \ˈbē-kən\. City, Dutchess co., SE New York, on Hudson River opp. Newburgh; pop. (1990c) 13,243.

Beacon Falls. Town, New Haven co., S Connecticut; pop. (1990c) 5083; settled 1678; incorp. 1871.

Bea·cons·field \ˈbē-kənz-ˌfēld\. **1.** Municipality, N Tasmania, Australia, on Tamar River 25 mi. (40 km.) NW of Launceston; pop. (1991c) 17,076; important goldfields nearby 1877–1919.
2. City, Quebec, Canada, SW suburb of Montreal; pop. (1990c) 19,616.
3. \ *usu.* ˈbe-kənz-ˌfēld\. Town, Buckinghamshire, S cen. England, 22 mi. (35 km.) NW of London; pop. (1981p) 10,909; noted for its associations with statesman Edmund Burke, politician Benjamin Disraeli, and writer G. K. Chesterton.
4. Former town, E Northern Cape prov., Rep. of South Africa, SE suburb of Kimberley; united with Kimberley 1912.

Bea·dle \ˈbēd-ᵊl\. County in E cen. South Dakota. See table at SOUTH DAKOTA.

Bea·gle Channel \ˈbē-gəl\. Channel bet. S Tierra del Fuego I. and S group of Chilean islands off S tip of South America in Tierra del Fuego Archipelago.

Bear \ˈbar\. River, SE Idaho and N Utah; rises in Uinta Mts., N Utah, flows N crossing Wyoming border twice, turns NW into SE Idaho, bends S and empties into Great Salt Lake, N Utah; ab. 350 mi. (563 km.) long.

Bear Butte. Peak, Meade co., W South Dakota; 4422 ft. (1348 m.).

Beard·more Glacier \ˈbird-ˌmōr\. Glacier, Queen Maud Mts., Antarctica; 260 mi. (418 km.) long; one of world's largest glaciers.

Beards·town \ˈbirdz-ˌtau̇n\. City, Cass co., W cen. Illinois, on Illinois River 45 mi. (72 km.) WNW of Springfield; pop. (1990c) 5270.

Bearhaven. See CASTLETOWNBERE.

Bear Island \ˈbar\. **1.** Island, Ireland. See CASTLETOWNBERE.
2. *or* **Bjørn·øya** \ˈbyœr-ˌnȯi-yə\. Island in Barents Sea 240 mi. (386 km.) N of Norway; 69 sq. mi. (179 sq. km.); with Spitsbergen group forms Svalbard, Norway.

Bear Islands *or Russ.* **Med·ve·zhi Os·tro·va** \məd-ˈvʸā-zhē-ˌəs-trə-ˈvä\. Group of small islands, opp. mouth of Kolyma River, East Siberian Sea, off NE coast of Sakha Rep., Russia in Asia.

Bear Lake. **1.** Lake, E Idaho-Utah border; ab. 20 mi. (32 km.) long, 7 mi. (11 km.) wide; max. depth 36 ft. (11 m.); outlet is tributary of Bear River.
2. County in SE corner of Idaho. See table at IDAHO.

Bear Mountain. **1.** Peak, San Juan co., SW Colorado; 12,950 ft. (3947 m.).
2. Mountain in town of Salisbury, extreme NW Connecticut; 2316 ft. (706 m.).
3. Mountain on Hudson River in Bear Mountain Park (5066 acres or 2052 hectares, a section of Palisades Interstate Park), New York; 1305 ft. (398 m.); Bear Mountain Bridge, opened 1924, crosses Hudson here.
4. Mountain in NE Dauphin co., SE cen. Pennsylvania, on the edge of the Bear Valley coal basin; 2000 ft. (610 m.).
5. Peak, Pennington co., SW South Dakota; 7166 ft. (2184 m.).

Bé·arn \bā-ˈärn\ *or Lat.* **Ben·e·har·num** \ˌbe-ni-ˈhär-nəm\. Historical region of SW France; bounded anciently on W, on N, and on E by Gascony, and on S by Pyrenees; ✱ Pau. Part of Aquitania under Romans; devastated by Vandals, Visigoths, and later by Saracens; hereditary viscountship in 11th cent.; countship of Béarn held by Henry IV and retained when he became king of France 1589; united with French crown 1620; province of France 1620–1789.

Bear River. See BEAR.

Bear·wal·low Mountain \ˈbar-ˌwä-lō\. Peak, Yancey co., W North Carolina; 6487 ft. (1977 m.).

Be·as *or* **Bi·as** \ˈbē-ˌäs\; *anc.* **Hyph·a·sis** \ˈhi-fə-sis\. River, one of the "Five Rivers" of the Punjab, N India; rises in the Himalayas E of Dharmsala, Himachal Pradesh, flows W and SW to the Sutlej River in W Punjab state SW of city of Kapurthala; 290 mi. (467 km.) long.

Beas de Se·gu·ra \ˈbā-ˌäs-t͟hā-sā-ˈgü-rä\. Commune, Jaén prov., S Spain, 55 mi. (89 km.) NE of the commune of Jaén; pop. (1989c) 8261; in region producing wine.

Be·ata, Cape \bā-ˈä-tä\. Cape, SW Dominican Republic, extending into Caribbean Sea from S cen. coast of Hispaniola.

Beata Island. Small island, Dominican Republic, in the Caribbean Sea off S cen. coast of Hispaniola.

Be·aten·berg \bā-ˈät-ᵊn-ˌberk\ *or* **Sankt Beatenberg** \ˈzäŋkt\. Village, Bern canton, Switzerland, NW of Interlaken; pop. (1980c) 1176; resort.

Be·at·rice \bē-ˈa-trəs\. City, ⊗ of Gage co., SE Nebraska, 35 mi. (56 km.) S of Lincoln; pop. (1990c) 12,354.

Beat·tie Peak \ˈbē-tē, ˈbā-\. Mountain, San Juan and San Miguel cos., SW Colorado; 13,200 ft. (4023 m.).

Beat·ton \ˈbēt-ᵊn\. River, E British Columbia, Canada; flows E and S into Peace River; ab. 145 mi. (233 km.) long.

Beat·ty·ville \ˈbā-tē-ˌvil\. City, ⊗ of Lee co., E Kentucky; pop. (1990c) 1131; coal and oil deposits.

Beau Bas·sin \ˌbō-bə-ˈseⁿ\. Residential town, NW Mauritius, bet. Port Louis and Curepipe; closely linked with Rose Hill; pop. with Rose Hill (1991e) 95,711.

Beau·caire \bō-ˈkār\; *anc.* **Uger·num** \yü-ˈjər-nəm\; *later* **Bel·li Quad·rum** \ˈbe-ˌlī-ˈkwä-drəm\. Commune, Gard dept., S France, on right bank of Rhone River (opp. Tarascon) 15 mi. (24 km.) E of Nîmes; pop. (1990c) 13,600; 14th cent. churches. Formerly famous for great annual fair (founded 1217 by Raymond VI, count of Toulouse).

Beauce \ˈbōs\. Ancient district of N cen. France, now part of depts. of Loir-et-Cher and Eure-et-Loir; ✱ Chartres.

Beauce–Sar·ti·gan \ˌbōz-ˌsär-tē-ˈgäⁿ\. County, Quebec, Canada. See table at QUEBEC.

Beauce·ville \ˈbōs-ˌvil\. Town, ⊗ of Beauce-Sartigan co., S Quebec, Canada, on Chaudière River SSE of Quebec; pop. (1991c) 3869.

Beau·fort. **1.** \ˈbō-fərt\. County in E coastal North Carolina. See table at NORTH CAROLINA.
2. \ˈbyü-fərt\. County in S coastal South Carolina. See table at SOUTH CAROLINA.
3. \ˈbō-fərt\. Town and seaside resort, ⊗ of Carteret co., SE North Carolina, on inlet of Atlantic Ocean 35 mi. (56 km.) SE of New Bern; pop. (1990c) 3808; port of entry at terminus of an inland waterway; fishing; estab. 1722.
4. \ˈbyü-fərt\. City, ⊗ of Beaufort co., S South Carolina, on Port Royal 52 mi. (84 km.) SW of Charleston; pop. (1990c) 9576; tourist center; fishing; conquered by British in American Revolution; fell into hands of Union fleet 1861 in Civil War.
5. \ˈbō-fərt\. Town, SW Sabah, Malaysia, NE of Brunei Bay and on railroad line 45 mi. (72 km.) SSW of Kota Kinabalu; pop. (1980p) 37,126.

Beaufort Sea \ˈbō-fərt\. That part of the Arctic Ocean NE of Alaska, NW of Canada, and W of Banks I. in the Arctic Archipelago; max. depth ab. 15,000 ft. (4572 m.).

Beaufort West. Town, Western Cape prov., Rep. of South Africa, 260 mi. (418 km.) ENE of Cape Town; in Great Karoo region; founded 1818.

Beau·har·nois \ˌbō-ˌär-ˈnwä\. City, Quebec, Canada, on St. Lawrence River 20 mi. (32 km.) SW of Montreal; pop. (1991c) 6449.

Beau·har·nois–Sa·la·ber·ry \ˌbō-ˌär-ˈnwä-ˌsȧ-lȧ-be-ˈrē\. County, Quebec, Canada. See table at QUEBEC.

Beau·jo·lais \ˌbō-zhō-ˈlā\. Area in N Rhône dept. and NE Loire dept. of E cen. France; famous for its wines.

Beau·lieu \ˈbyü-lē\. Parish, New Forest rural dist., Southampton, S England; ruins of Beaulieu Abbey, wealthy Cistercian house founded by King John 1204.

Beau·ly \ˈbyü-lē\. Small river in N cen. Scotland, flowing NE into Moray Firth W of Inverness.

Beau·mar·is \bō-ˈmar-is\. Resort town, Gwynedd co., NW Wales, on **Beaumaris Bay;** pop. (1981p) 2088; 13th cent. castle.

Beau·mont \ˈbō-ˌmänt\. **1.** City, Riverside co., SE California, 21 mi. (34 km.) SE of San Bernardino; pop. (1990c) 9685.

\ə\ **abut** \ᵊ\ **kitten, F table** \ər\ **further** \a\ **ash** \ā\ **ace** \ä\ **cot, cart** \ȧ\ **F bac** \au̇\ **out** \b̲\ **Span Avila** \ch\ **chin** \e\ **bet** \ē\ **easy** \g\ **go** \i\ **hit** \ī\ **ice** \j\ **job** \k̲\ **Ger ich, Buch** \ⁿ\ **F vin** \ŋ\ **sing** \ō\ **go** \ȯ\ **law** \ȯi\ **boy** \œ\ **F bœuf** \œ̄\ **F feu** \th\ **thin** \t͟h\ **this** \ü\ **loot** \u̇\ **foot** \ue\ **Ger füllen** \ue̅\ **F rue** \y\ **yet** \ʸ\ **F digne** \ˈdēnʸ\, **nuit** \ˈnwʸē\ \yü\ **few** \yu̇\ **fury** \zh\ **vision**

2. \ *also* bō-ˈmänt\. City and port of entry, ⊗ of Jefferson co., SE Texas, on Neches River 73 mi. (118 km.) E of Houston; pop. (1990c) 114,323; connected with Gulf of Mexico by Sabine-Neches Canal; port of entry; shipyards, oil refineries; chemicals, paper; Lamar Univ. (1923); settled 1835; ⊗ 1838; incorp. 1881.

Beaumont–Ha·mel \ bō-ˌmōⁿ-ä-ˈmel\. Village, Somme dept., NE France, near the Ancre ab. 5 mi. (8 km.) N of Albert; fighting during WWI July–Nov. 1916 when taken by British, a phase of the first battle of the Somme.

Beaune \ ˈbōn\ *or Lat.* **Bel·na** \ ˈbel-nə\. City, Côte-d'Or dept., E France, 23 mi. (37 km.) SSW of Dijon; pop. (1990c) 22,171; 12th cent. church; large hospital (founded 1443); 15th cent. ramparts; school of viticulture; center for trading in Burgundy wines.

Beau·port \ bō-ˈpȯr\. City, Quebec co., S Quebec, Canada, NE suburb of Quebec City on St. Lawrence River; pop. (1991c) 69,158. Granted to Robert Gifford 1634, became first seigneury estab. in New France; served as French Gen. Louis-Joseph de Montcalm's headquarters 1759.

Beau·pré \ bō-ˈprā\. Town, S Quebec, Canada, on St. Lawrence River 27 mi. (43 km.) NE of Quebec City; pop. (1981c) 2740.

Beau·re·gard \ ˈbōr-ə-ˌgärd\. Parish in SW Louisiana. See table at LOUISIANA.

Beau·sé·jour \ ˌbō-ˌsā-ˈzhür\. Town, SE Manitoba, Canada, 30 mi. (48 km.) ENE of Winnipeg; pop. (1991c) 2633.

Beau·so·leil \ ˌbō-sȯ-ˈlā\. Commune, Alpes-Maritimes dept., SE France, near Ligurian Sea 8 mi. (13 km.) ENE of Nice; winter resort.

Beau·vais \ bō-ˈvā\; *anc.* **Bel·lov·a·cum** \ bə-ˈlä-və-kəm\ *also* **Cae·sar·om·a·gus** \ ˌsē-zə-ˈrä-mə-gəs\. Commune, ✻ of Oise dept., N France, 42 mi. (68 km.) NNW of Paris; pop. (1990c) 56,278; carpets, tractors; its tapestry factory famous for tapestries produced during 17th–18th cents. was destroyed in WWII; 13th cent. cathedral (unfinished); 10th and 12th cent. churches; 12th cent. palace; ancient Roman ramparts. Became commune 1096; made heroic resistance to large army of Burgundians under Duke Charles the Bold 1472; suffered damage during WWII; subsequently rebuilt.

Beaux, Les. See LES BAUX-DE-PROVENCE.

Bea·ver \ ˈbē-vər\. **1.** River, NW Oklahoma; flows E into Texas for 15 mi. (24 km.), then into Oklahoma again; joins Wolf Creek, forming North Canadian River; 280 mi. (451 km.) long.

2. River, W Pennsylvania; formed by confluence of Shenango and Mahoning rivers in Lawrence co., flows S into Ohio River at Rochester, cen. Beaver co.

3. Name of counties in three states of the U.S. See tables at OKLAHOMA, PENNSYLVANIA, UTAH.

4. Town, ⊗ of Beaver co., NW Oklahoma; pop. (1990c) 1584.

5. Residential borough, ⊗ of Beaver co., W Pennsylvania, on Ohio River 26 mi. (42 km.) NW of Pittsburgh; pop. (1990c) 5028.

6. City, ⊗ of Beaver co., SW Utah, 42 mi. (68 km.) SE of S end of Sevier Lake; pop. (1990c) 1998.

7. River, tributary of Churchill River in Saskatchewan and Alberta provs., Canada; 305 mi. (491 km.) long.

Beaver City. City, ⊗ of Furnas co., S Nebraska; pop. (1990c) 707.

Bea·ver·creek \ ˈbē-vər-ˌkrēk\. City, Greene co., SW Ohio; an E suburb of Dayton; pop. (1990c) 33,626.

Beaver Creek. River, NW Kansas and SW Nebraska; rises in Kit Carson co., E Colorado, flows NE across NW corner of Kansas into Nebraska and joins Sappa River 10 mi. (16 km.) before emptying into Republican River in Harlan co., S Nebraska; 200 mi. (322 km.) long.

Beaver Dam. **1.** City, Ohio co., W cen. Kentucky, 34 mi. (55 km.) NW of Bowling Green; pop. (1990c) 2904.

2. City, Dodge co., SE cen. Wisconsin, 29 mi. (47 km.) SSW of Fond du Lac; pop. (1990c) 14,196.

Beaver Dam Creek. See MECHANICSVILLE.

Beaver Dam Mountains. Range in extreme SW Utah.

Beaver Falls. City, Beaver co., W Pennsylvania, on Beaver River 18 mi. (29 km.) S of New Castle; pop. (1990c) 10,687; coal deposits, clay pits; Geneva Coll. (1848).

Bea·ver·head \ ˈbē-vər-ˌhed\. County in SW Montana. See table at MONTANA.

Beaverhead Mountains. Mountain range, part of Bitterroot Range, in Continental Divide, forming part of the boundary bet. SW Montana and E Idaho.

Bea·ver·hill Lake \ ˈbē-vər-ˌhil\. Lake in cen. Alberta, Canada, ab. 35 mi. (56 km.) E of Edmonton; 80 sq. mi. (207 sq. km.).

Beaver Island. **1.** Island in N Lake Michigan, a part of Charlevoix co., N Michigan, W of Emmet co., 56 sq. mi. (145 sq. km.).

2. One of the Falkland Is. (*q.v.*).

Beaver River. See BEAVER 1, 2, 7.

Bea·ver·ton \ ˈbē-vər-tən\. City, Washington co., Oregon, W of Portland; pop. (1990c) 53,310; diversified farming; high-tech industries.

Be·a·war \ bā-ˈä-wər\. Town, cen. Rajasthan, India, on affluent of Luni River 115 mi. (185 km.) SW of Jaipur; pop. (1991p) 105,357.

Beb·ing·ton \ ˈbe-biŋ-tən\. Town, Merseyside, NW England on the Mersey opp. Liverpool; pop. (1981p) 64,174.

Bec. Abbey. See LE BEC-HELLOUIN.

Bé·can·cour \ ˌbā-käⁿ-ˈkür\. **1.** County, Quebec, Canada. See table at QUEBEC.

2. Town, Nicolet-Yamaska co., S Quebec, Canada, on St. Lawrence River; pop. (1991c) 10,911.

Bec·cles \ ˈbe-kəlz\. Town, East Suffolk, E England, 100 mi. (161 km.) NE of London; pop. (1981p) 8903.

Be·čej \ ˈbe-ˌchā\. Town, Serbia, N Yugoslavia, ab. 60 mi. (97 km.) NNW of Belgrade.

Be·ce·lae·re \ ˌbā-sə-ˈlär-ə\. Small commune, West Flanders prov., NW Belgium; a stronghold in the German front line in WWI.

Bé·char \ bā-ˈshär\; *formerly* **Co·lomb** \ kȯ-ˈlōⁿ\ *or* **Colomb–Béchar.** Town, W Algeria, pop. (1987p) 107,311; coal deposits nearby; former French Foreign Legion post.

Bech·a·rof Lake \ ˈbe-chə-ˌrȯf\. Lake, N Alaska Penin., Alaska, SW of Katmai National Monument; ab. 30 mi. (48 km.) long; 458 sq. mi. (1186 sq. km.).

Bec–Hellouin, Le. See LE BEC-HELLOUIN.

Bech·u·a·na·land \ ˌbech-ˈwä-nä-ˌland\. **1.** Republic, S Africa. See BOTSWANA.

2. Former colony, Africa. See BRITISH BECHUANALAND.

Bechuanaland Protectorate. See BOTSWANA.

Beck·er \ ˈbe-kər\. County in NW cen. Minnesota. See table at MINNESOTA.

Beck·ham \ ˈbe-kəm\. County in W Oklahoma. See table at OKLAHOMA.

Beck·ley \ ˈbe-klē\. City, ⊗ of Raleigh co., S West Virginia, 35 mi. (56 km.) N of Bluefield; pop. (1990c) 18,296; coal deposits.

Beck·um \ ˈbe-kəm\. City, North Rhine-Westphalia, W Germany, 23 mi. (37 km.) SE of Münster; pop. (1980c) 37,899.

Bedd·gel·ert \ bāth-ˈgel-ərt, beth-\. Village, Caernarvon, NW Wales, S of Snowdon Mt.; resort, noted for its beautiful location; scene of legend of Prince Llewellyn and his hound.

Bed·ford \ ˈbed-fərd\. **1.** Name of counties in three states of the U.S. See tables at PENNSYLVANIA, TENNESSEE, VIRGINIA.

2. City, ⊗ of Lawrence co., S Indiana, 20 mi. (32 km.) S of Bloomington; pop. (1990c) 13,817; limestone deposits.

3. City, ⊗ of Taylor co., SW Iowa, 73 mi. (117 km.) SE of Council Bluffs; pop. (1990c) 1528.

4. City, ⊗ of Trimble co., N Kentucky; pop. (1990c) 761.

5. Town, Middlesex co., NE Massachusetts, 10 mi. (16 km.) S of Lowell; pop. (1990c) 12,996; Middlesex Community Coll. (1969).

6. Town, Hillsborough co., S New Hampshire, 3 mi. (5 km.) SW of Manchester; pop. (1990c) 12,563.

7. City, Cuyahoga co., N Ohio, 11 mi. (18 km.) SE of Cleveland; pop. (1990c) 14,822; a suburb of Cleveland.

8. Borough, ⊗ of Bedford co., S Pennsylvania, on branch of Juniata River 30 mi. (48 km.) S of Altoona; pop. (1990c)

3137; mineral springs nearby in **Bedford Springs,** a summer resort. Settled as **Rays·town** \ˈrāz-ˌtau̇n\ c. 1750; Fort Bedford, an important frontier station in last half of 18th cent., built 1750s; town laid out 1766.

9. City, Tarrant co., N Texas, 15 mi. (24 km.) ENE of Fort Worth; pop. (1990c) 43,762.

10. Independent city, ⊗ of Bedford co., SW cen. Virginia, 22 mi. (35 km.) WSW of Lynchburg; pop. (1990c) 6073.

11. County in England. See BEDFORDSHIRE.

12. Town, ⊗ of Bedfordshire, SE cen. England, on the Ouse 48 mi. (77 km.) NNW of London; pop. (1981p) 74,245; commercial center. Dates back to 6th cent.; scene of preacher and writer John Bunyan's imprisonment 1660–72 and 1675 (when he is supposed to have written *Pilgrim's Progress*).

Bedford Heights. Village, Cuyahoga co., Ohio, S of Cleveland; pop. (1990c) 12,131.

Bed·ford·shire \ˈbed-fərd-ˌshir, -shər\ *or* **Bedford** *or* **Beds** \ˈbedz\. **1.** Former county, SE cen. England; includes towns of Luton, Dunstable.

2. Administrative county, SE cen. England, approx. equivalent to the former county; watered by the Ouse River; estab. 1974. See table at ENGLAND.

Bed·ling·ton \ˈbed-liŋ-tən\. Parish, Northumberland, N England; known for its terriers; a part of **Bed·ling·ton·shire** \-ˌshir, -shər\, town on the Blyth near its mouth in North Sea 11 mi. (18 km.) N of Newcastle upon Tyne.

Bedloe's Island *or* **Bedloe Island.** See LIBERTY ISLAND.

Beds. See BEDFORDSHIRE.

Bed·well·ty \bed-ˈwel-tē\. Town, Gwent co., SE Wales, 31 mi. (50 km.) WNW of Bristol, England; pop. (1981p) 24,670; coal deposits.

Bed·worth \ˈbed-wərth\. Town, Warwickshire, cen. England; pop. (1981p) 41,991.

Będ·zin \ˈben-ˌjēn\ *or Russ.* **Ben·din** \ˈben-ˌdēn\ *or Ger.* **Bend·zin** \ˈbent-ˌsēn\. Commune, Katowice prov., S Poland, ab. 7 mi. (11 km.) NW of Katowice; pop. (1992e) 75,800; coal and iron deposits.

Bee \ˈbē\. County in S Texas. See table at TEXAS.

Bee·be \ˈbē-bē\. City, White co., NE cen. Arkansas, 27 mi. (43 km.) NE of Little Rock; pop. (1990c) 4455; Arkansas State Univ.–Beebe (1927).

Beech Grove \ˈbēch\. City, Marion co., cen. Indiana, 7 mi. (11 km.) SE of Indianapolis; pop. (1990c) 13,383.

Bee·croft Head \ˈbē-ˌkrȯft\. Peninsula and point of land, SE New South Wales, Australia, enclosing Jervis Bay on the N. See SAINT GEORGE, CAPE 2.

Bee·mer·ang, Mount \ˈbē-mə-ˌraŋ\. Mountain, Blue Mts., E New South Wales, Australia; 4100 ft. (1250 m.).

Bee·ren·berg \ˈber-ən-ˌbərg\. Extinct volcano on Jan Mayen I., Arctic Ocean; 7470 ft. (2277 m.); highest point on island.

Beeroth. See AL BĪRAH.

Be·er·she·ba \bir-ˈshē-bə, ber-, bər-\ *or Heb.* **Be·'er She·va'** \bə-ˈār-ˈshe-vä\ *or Arab.* **Bir es Sa·ba** \ˌbir-ˌes-ˈsȧ-bə\. Town, ✱ of Southern District, S Israel, ab. 45 mi. (72 km.) SW of Jerusalem; pop. (1992e) 128,400; glass; university (1965), Negev Institute for Arid Zone Research. Marked the extreme S limit of Palestine (*Judges* xx. 1): see DAN. Scene of victory of British over Turks 1917; part of British mandate to 1948; taken by Israelis 1948; important cultural and administrative center for Negev area of Israel.

Bees·ton and Sta·ple·ford \ˈbē-stən ... ˈstā-pəl-fərd\. Town, Nottinghamshire, N cen. England, 4 mi. (6 km.) SW of Nottingham; pop. (1981p) 64,599; pharmaceuticals.

Bee·ville \ˈbē-ˌvil\. City, ⊗ of Bee co., S Texas, 48 mi. (77 km.) NNW of Corpus Christi; pop. (1990c) 13,547; oil wells.

Bè·gles \ˈbeglᵊ\. Commune, Gironde dept., SW France, on Garonne River 4 mi. (6 km.) SSE of Bordeaux.

Beg·na \ˈbeŋ-nə\. River in S Norway; flows S into Tyrifjord Lake, whence it issues as the Dramselva.

Begovat. See BEKABAD.

Bé·hague, Pointe \ˌpwaⁿt-bē-ˈhȧg\. Cape extending into Atlantic Ocean from E coast of French Guiana.

Beharieh. See BAHARĪYA.

Beh·be·hān \ˌbā-bə-ˈhän\ *or* **Behbahan.** Town, Khūzestān prov., SW Iran, E of Bandar-e Shāhpūr; pop. (1986c) 78,694; oil fields nearby; near ruins of an ancient Persian city.

Be·hei·ra \be-ˈhā-rə\. Governorate, N Egypt. See table at EGYPT.

Behisni. See BESNI.

Behistun. See BĪSITŪN.

Behnesa. See OXYRHYNCHUS.

Behramköy. See ASSOS.

Bei *or W.-G.* **Pei** \ˈbā\. River, cen. Guangdong prov., SE China; rises in S Hunan and flows S to join the Xi delta W of Guangzhou; 217 mi. (349 km.) long.

Bei'an *or W.-G.* **Pei–an** *or* **Pei·an** \ˈbā-ˈän\ *also* **Pe·han·chen** \ˈbā-ˈhän-ˈchen\. Town, cen. Heilongjiang prov., NE China, ab. 170 mi. (275 km.) N of Harbin; pop. (1990c) 204,899; ✱ of former Pei-an prov.

Beibazar. See BEYPAZARI.

Bei·dai·he \ˈbā-ˈdī-ˈhə\ *or W.-G.* **Pei–tai–ho** *also* **Peh·tai·ho** \ˈbā-ˈdī-ˈhō\. Town, E Hebei prov., NE China, ab. 15 mi. (24 km.) SSW of Qinhuangdao; estab. 1894–95.

Bei·hai *or W.-G.* **Pei–hai** \ˈbā-ˈhī\ *also* **Pak·hoi** \ˈpäk-ˈhȯi\. Seaport, Guangxi Zhuangzu autonomous region, SE China, on Gulf of Tonkin ab. 350 mi. (565 km.) W of Hong Kong; pop. (1990c) 112,895; has good anchorage and is a natural port of entry for Yunnan and Guizhou provs. Open to foreign trade 1877.

Bei·jer·land \ˈbā-ər-ˌlänt\ *or* **Hoek·sche Waard** \ˈhu̇k-sə-ˌvärt\. Island attached to South Holland prov., Netherlands; 6 mi. (10 km.) S of Rotterdam.

Bei·jing \ˈbā-ˈjiŋ\ *or W.-G.* **Pe·king** \ˈpē-ˈkiŋ\; *from 1928 to 1949* **Pei·ping** \ˈpā-ˈpiŋ, ˈbā-\. City, ✱ of China, in an extensive plain of NE China; constitutes a special administrative unit (3386 sq. mi. or 8770 sq. km.); pop. (1990c) 10,819,407; administrative, cultural, and educational center of China; engineering; produces textiles, machinery, and petrochemicals; numerous educational institutions, incl. Peking Univ. (1898), People's Univ. of China (1950), and numerous specialized technical and party (political) schools. Inner part of city consists of Tatar City in N and Outer or Chinese City in S, having a combined area of ab. 25 sq. mi. (65 sq. km.) and formerly surrounded by 15th cent. walls (these were partially demolished during the "Great Cultural Revolution" 1966–67, several gates remaining intact). Tatar City contains old Imperial or "Forbidden City" with former imperial palace, former legations, parks, temples, hospitals, and various public buildings; abutting the Forbidden City is Tiananmen Square, world's largest public square; extensive development in modern times of residential suburbs to N and NW and industrial suburbs to E, esp. since 1949.

History: Had various names in ancient times; a frontier town for centuries, known as Ch'i (or Yen, from the district) under Chou dynasty (1122–255 B.C.) and later. Was ✱ of powerful monarchy, 10th to 12th cents. A.D., under the Khitan Mongols and the Kin Tatar dynasty; as Khanbalik became residence of Kublai Khan 1264–67 and ✱ of China 1267–1368 under Yuan dynasty; known to Europeans as Cambaluc, name given to it by Venetian traveler Marco Polo. Under Mings replaced as ✱ for a short time but in 1421 again chosen as ✱ with the name Beijing, and so continued under the Manchus (1644–1912). Occupied by European expeditionary forces and suffered considerable damage 1860 and during Boxer Rebellion 1900; in 1928 Nanjing made ✱ and name Beijing changed to Peiping. At the Marco Polo Bridge 9 mi. (14 km.) SW (see LUGOUQIAO) in 1937 fighting broke out bet. Japanese and Chinese troops, the incident that began the Sino-Japanese War (1937–45); surrendered to Communist forces in 1949 and again made ✱ and name restored to Beijing; municipal area radically expanded 1953 and 1958. In Tiananmen Square at the edge of the city, Chinese troops fired on students demonstrating for democratic reform June 4, 1989 killing over 200.

Bei Kem \ˈbā-ˈkem\. See YENISEY.

Beilan. See BELEN.

Beinn Dearg \ˈben-ˈjer-ək, -ˈdərg\ *or* **Ben Dearg** \ˈben\ *also* **Ben Derg** \ˈdərg\. Mountain, Highland region, N Scotland, SE of Loch Broom; 3547 ft. (1081 m.).

Bei·piao *or W.-G.* **Pei–piao** \ˈbā-ˈbyau̇\. Town, cen. Liaoning prov., NE China, 50 mi. (80 km.) NW of Jinzhou; in coal-bearing region.

Bei·ra \ˈbā-rə\. **1.** Former province, N cen. Portugal; ✻ Coimbra; soil rocky, except on coast; watered by Douro, Tagus, Mondego, and numerous other rivers; traversed by Serra da Estrela. Region produces grain, wine, lumber, fish, livestock, olives, wool, vegetables, dairy products, cork, fruit; coal, gold, silver, quartz, titanium, zinc, tin, uranium, feldspar, lead, arsenic, and wolfram; in 1835 was divided into the districts of Aveiro, Castelo Branco, Coimbra, Guarda, and Viseu.

2. Seaport, ✻ of Sofala prov., on SE coast of Mozambique, 120 mi. (193 km.) SW of mouth of the Zambezi; met. area pop. (1991e) 298,847; chief port for Zimbabwe, Malawi, and cen. Mozambique; exports ores.

Beira Al·ta \ˈäl-tə\. Former province of Portugal; lost most of its administrative functions 1959.

Beira Bai·xa \ˈbī-shə\. Former province of Portugal; lost most of its administrative functions 1959.

Beira Li·to·ral \ˌlē-tō-ˈräl\. Former province of Portugal; lost most of its administrative functions 1959.

Bei·rut *also* **Bay·rūt** \bā-ˈrüt\ *or Fr.* **Bey·routh** \bā-ˈrüt\; *anc.* **Be·ry·tus** \bə-ˈrī-təs\. City, ✻ of Lebanon, built on a promontory with Lebanon Mts. behind it; port facilities; connected by highway with Damascus and Baghdad; several universities and colleges incl. American Univ. of Beirut (1866, new charter 1920) and Lebanese Univ. (1951, reorganized 1953).

History: Ancient Phoenician settlement mentioned in Tell el-Amarna tablets; ruled by Romans until Arab capture of Syria (*q.v.*) 635 A.D.; captured for kingdom of Jerusalem (*q.v.*) by Baldwin I 1110; object of struggle bet. Crusaders and Saracens until latter finally captured it 1291; although came to be ruled by Druzes, technically belonged to Ottoman Empire; in 1840 bombarded and captured by British and French who intervened in Syria to quell revolt of Egyptian ruler Muḥammed ʻAlī Pasha against sultan (see EGYPT); captured by French in campaign against Turkey 1918; flourished esp. 1950s and 1960s as banking and cultural center for Middle East; a main target when civil war broke out in Lebanon 1975; has suffered heavy damage over many years; ✻ of Lebanon since 1920.

Beisān. See BET SHE'AN.

Bei·tang *or W.-G.* **Pei–t'ang** *also* **Peh·tang** \ˈbā-ˈtäŋ\. Town, Tianjin municipality, NE China, on Bo Hai, at mouth of Jiyun River 10 mi. (16 km.) N of Dagu. British and French forces landed in operations against Dagu forts 1860.

Beit Ja·la \bāt-ˈja-lə\ *or* **Bayt Jā·lā** \bāt-ˈjä-lə\; *bib.* **Gal·lim** \ˈga-lim\. Town, Jordan, ab. 1 mi. (1.6 km.) NW of Bethlehem; in area occupied by Israel 1967.

Beit Jibrin. See ELEUTHEROPOLIS.

Be·ja \ˈbā-zhə\. **1.** District of S Portugal. See table at PORTUGAL.

2. *anc.* **Pax Ju·lia** \ˈpaks-ˈjül-yə\. Commune, its ✻, 85 mi. (137 km.) SE of Lisbon; pop. (1981p) 39,616; copper and manganese deposits nearby. Roman ruins; cathedral c. 1300.

Bé·ja \bā-ˈzhä\ *or* **Bā·jah** \ˈbä-jə\; *anc.* **Vac·ca** \ˈva-kə\ *also* **Va·ga** \ˈvä-gə\. Town, N Tunisia, 65 mi. (105 km.) W of the city of Tunis; site of Roman colony; Byzantine ruins.

Be·jaïa \be-ˈjī-ə\ *or Fr.* **Bou·gie** \bü-ˈzhē\; *anc.* **Sal·dae** \ˈsal-ˌdē\. Seaport and commune, NE Algeria, on W shore of **Gulf of Bejaïa,** ab. 115 mi. (185 km.) E of Algiers; has good harbor; in 5th cent. a fortified city of Genseric the Vandal; in 11th cent. ✻ of powerful Berber dynasty; later under the Hafsids, Barbary pirates, and Spaniards; taken by French 1833.

Bejraburana. See PHETCHABUN.

Be·káa \be-ˈkä\. Former administrative division in E Lebanon.

Be·káa Valley \be-ˈkä\ *or* **Al Bi·qāʻ** \ˌal-be-ˈkä\ *also* **Be·qáa** \be-ˈkä\ *or Arab.* **Al Bi·gāʻ** *or* **Al–Bi·gaʻ** \ˌal-be-ˈkä\; *anc.* **Coe·le–Syr·ia** *or* **Coe·le·syr·ia** \ˌsē-lē-ˈsir-ē-ə\. Valley in Lebanon, bet. the Lebanon and Anti-Lebanon mountain ranges; 80 mi. (129 km.) long, 10 mi. (16 km.) wide; traversed by the upper Orontes (flowing N) and the Litani (flowing S) rivers. During the wars between the Seleucids and Egypt, Coele-Syria encompassed much of S Syria.

Bek·abad \ˈbā-kə-ˌbäd, ˈbe-kə-\; *before 1964* **Be·go·vat** \ˌbe-gə-ˈvät\. Town, Tashkent subdivision, Uzbekistan, ab. 80 mi. (129 km.) S of the city of Tashkent; pop. (1991e) 82,800.

Be·ka·si \bā-ˈkä-sē\. City, West Java prov., Indonesia, SE of Jakarta.

Bek–Budi. See KARSHI.

Bé·kés \ˈbā-ˌkāsh\. **1.** County of SE Hungary. See table at HUNGARY.

2. Commune, Békés co., SE Hungary; pop. (1991e) 22,500; trade center in agricultural region.

Bé·kés·csa·ba \ˈbā-ˌkāsh-ˌchȯ-ˌbȯ\. City, ⊗ of Békés co., SE Hungary, S of the commune of Békés; pop. (1992e) 67,913.

Bela Crk·va \ˈbe-lä-ˈtsər-kvä\ *or Hung.* **Fe·hér·tem·plom** \ˈfe-ˌhār-ˌtem-ˌplōm\ *or Ger.* **Weiss·kir·chen** \ˈvīs-ˌkir-kən\. Town, Serbia, Yugoslavia, 45 mi. (72 km.) E of Belgrade near border of Romania.

Bel Air \bel-ˈar\. Town, ⊗ of Harford co., NE Maryland, 23 mi. (37 km.) NE of Baltimore; pop. (1990c) 8860; Harford Community Coll. (1957).

Be·la·jan \bā-ˈlä-ˌyän\. River, E Borneo, Indonesia; ab. 150 mi. (241 km.) long; a N tributary of the Mahakam.

Be·lal·cá·zar \ˌbā-läl-ˈkä-thär\. Commune, Córdoba prov., S Spain, 51 mi. (82 km.) NNW of the city of Córdoba; pop. (1991c) 4143; argentiferous lead deposits.

Be·la·rus *or* **Bye·la·rus** \ˌbyā-lə-ˈrüs\. Republic, N cen. Europe, bounded on N by Russia and Latvia, on NW by Lithuania, on W by Poland, on S by Ukraine, and on E by Russia; 80,154 sq. mi. (207,599 sq. km.); pop. (1993e) 10,353,000; ✻ Minsk.

Chief rivers: The N part is crossed by the Western Dvina; upper course of Dnieper flows through E part from N to S; along the Pripyat in the S lies extensive marshy area (see POLESYE). In the W (former Poland) is upper course of Neman River and its tributaries and on the SW the Bug forms part of the boundary.

Chief products: potatoes, flax, timber; textiles, machine tools, food products.

Chief settlements: Minsk, Homyel', Mahilyow, Vitsyebsk.

History: In medieval times region was subject to Lithuanians and Poles; to Poland until late 18th cent.; E part to Russia in First Partition of Poland 1772 and remainder by Second 1793, and Third 1795; continual wars left country devastated and made worse by French Emperor Napoléon's campaign 1812 (see BEREZINA); again overrun in WWI and occupied by Poles 1919; comprised **Be·lo·rus·sian Soviet Socialist Republic** \ˌbe-lō-ˈrə-shən, ˌbye-\ 1919–91; in 1921 W part assigned to Poland; in 1922 became part of U.S.S.R.; in 1924 and 1926 E boundary adjusted by U.S.S.R. to include Vitsyebsk and Homyel'; in WWII overrun by German armies in summer of 1941; recovered by Soviet troops 1944; after WWII increased in area through Soviet annexation of part of NE Poland; as in past, sought to rebuild following war's devastation; became UN member 1945, despite being part of U.S.S.R.; large area suffered contamination as result of Chernobyl disaster 1986, forcing many to be evacuated in the following years; declared its independence from U.S.S.R. 1991; joined Commonwealth of Independent States 1991.

Belau. See PALAU.

Be·la·wan \bā-ˈlä-ˌwän\ *or* **Belawan–De·li** \ˈdā-lē\. Town and seaport, Sumatra, Indonesia; at mouth of Deli River; port of Medan.

Be·la·ya \ˈbye-lə-yə\. Navigable river, Bashkortostan, E Russia in Europe; rises in Southern Urals S of Zlatoust and flows S, W, and NW to the Kama River S of Sarapul; 882 mi. (1419 km.) long.

Belaya Tser·kov' \ˈtser-kəf\. Town, W Kiev subdivision, N Ukraine, on a tributary of the Dnieper 50 mi. (80 km.) S of the city of Kiev; commercial center on railroad line. Founded 11th cent.

Belbeis. See BILBEIS.

Bel·cha·tow \beu̇-ˈkä-tüf\. Commune, Piotrków prov., cen. Poland, W of Piotrków Trybunalski; pop. (1989e) 55,765.

Bel·cher Islands \ˈbel-chər\. Island group in SE Hudson Bay, off coast of Quebec, but administratively part of Nunavut, Canada; 1118 sq. mi. (2896 sq. km.).

Bel·cher·town \ˈbel-chər-ˌtau̇n\. Town, Hampshire co., W Massachusetts, 15 mi. (24 km.) NE of Springfield; pop. (1990c) 10,579.

Bel·chi·te \bel-ˈchē-tā\. Commune, Zaragoza prov., NE Spain, 22 mi. (35 km.) SSE of Saragossa; pop. (1991c) 1680; in Peninsular War scene of victory of French forces under Gen. Louis-Gabriel Suchet over Spanish forces, June 1809.

Bel·ding \ˈbel-diŋ\. City, Ionia co., S cen. Michigan, 25 mi. (40 km.) ENE of Grand Rapids; pop. (1990c) 5969.

Be·lém \be-ˈlem\ *or sometimes* **Pa·rá** \pȧ-ˈrä\. Seaport city, ✻ of Pará state, N Brazil, on Pará River 90 mi. (145 km.) from the sea; munic. pop. (1989e) 1,200,000; distribution center for Amazon Valley; exports include nuts; university (1957); founded 1616.

Be·len \be-ˈlen\; *formerly* **Bai·lan** \be-ˈlän\ *or* **Bei·lan** \bā-ˈlän\. Town, Hatay prov., S Turkey in Asia, just S of İskenderun.

Be·len \bə-ˈlen\. Village, Valencia co., W New Mexico, on the Rio Grande 30 mi. (48 km.) S of Albuquerque; pop. (1990c) 6547.

Bel·ep Islands \ˈbe-ləp\. Group of small islands, SW Pacific Ocean, bet. parallel coral reefs, 28 mi. (45 km.) NW of NW tip of New Caledonia.

Be·le·ri·um \bə-ˈlir-ē-əm\. Ancient name of Cornwall county, (*q.v.*) SW England.

Bel·fast \ˈbel-ˌfast\. **1.** Seaport city, ⊗ of Waldo co., S Maine, on Penobscot Bay 30 mi. (48 km.) SSW of Bangor; pop. (1990c) 6355; tourist center; settled c. 1770.
2. District, Northern Ireland centered on the city of Belfast; estab. 1974. See table at IRELAND, NORTHERN.
3. *also* bel-ˈ\. Seaport, ✻ of Northern Ireland and ⊗ of Belfast, Castlereagh, and Newtownabbey districts, E Northern Ireland; pop. (1991c) 279,237; shipbuilding,

food processing; linen, aircraft; Queen's Univ. of Belfast (1908).

History: Site of Norman castle in possession of earls of Ulster, granted to Sir Arthur Chichester 1604 who settled colonists (see ULSTER); town incorp. by James I of England (1603–25); settled by Scots from 17th cent.; had large immigration of French Huguenots after the rescinding of Edict of Nantes (1685) who contributed to furthering linen trade; became center of Irish Protestantism; site of sectarian conflict 19th and 20th cents., latest breaking out in 1960s and continuing more than 25 years later.

4. Town, Mpumalanga prov., Rep. of South Africa, 125 mi. (201 km.) E of Pretoria; alt. ab. 6465 ft. (1970 m.); summer resort.

Belfast Lough \ˈläk\. Inlet of the North Channel on E coast of Northern Ireland; the city of Belfast lies at its head.

Bel·fort \bel-ˈfȯr, bā-ˈ, ˈbel-ˌ, ˈbā-ˌ\. Fortified commune, ✻ of Territoire de Belfort, E France, 88 mi. (142 km.) ENE of Dijon; pop. (1990c) 51,913; commands pass (Belfort Gap, *q.v.*) bet. Vosges and Jura mountains; textiles. Ceded to France by Austria 1648; fortified by military engineer Sébastien de Vauban; unsuccessfully besieged by Allies 1814; besieged by Germans 1870–71; the only part of Alsace left to France after cession of 1871.

Belfort, Ter·ri·toire de \ˌter-ē-ˈtwär-də-\. Department of E France. See *Territoire de Belfort* in table at FRANCE.

Belfort Gap *or Fr.* **Trou·ée de Belfort** \trü-ˈā-də-\. Pass bet. Vosges and Jura mountains, E France, through which passes historic route from Saône Valley to the Rhine; highest point 1158 ft. (353 m.). Besieged many times over a long period because of its strategic location.

Belgard. See BIAŁOGARD.

Bel·gaum \bel-ˈgau̇m\. Town, Karnataka, SW India; pop. (1991p) 325,639; textiles.

Belgian Congo. See ZAIRE 1.

Belgian East Africa. See RUANDA-URUNDI.

Bel·gi·ca \ˈbel-ji-kə\. Ancient country, NE Gallia; one of the administrative areas into which Roman Emperors Augustus and Tiberius divided Gaul; corresponds in part with modern Belgium.

Bel·gium \ˈbel-jəm\ *or Fr.* **Bel·gique** \bel-ˈzhēk\ *or Flem.* **Bel·gië** \ˈbel-kē-ə\. Kingdom, NW Europe, bounded on NW by the North Sea (42 mi. or 68 km. of coastline), on N by Netherlands, on E by Germany, on SE by the Grand Duchy of Luxembourg, and on S and W by France; 11,781 sq. mi. (30,513 sq. km.); pop. (1991c) 9,978,681; ✻ Brussels.

Physical features: Schelde River and its tributaries (Leie, Dender, Senne, Rupel) in W cen. part and the Meuse in E and SE (also as boundary in NE along Limburg prov. of Netherlands); chief tributaries of the Meuse: Sambre, Ourthe, Amblève; extensive canal system connects many of the streams. Mostly plain with wooded hill region (Ardennes) in S; chief port on North Sea is Oostende, but Antwerp near mouth of Schelde has much greater trade.

Chief products: Wheat, barley, oats, rye, potatoes, sugar beets; livestock; coal; manufacturing: chemicals, textiles, iron and steel, paper; one of the world's most industrialized countries.

Chief cities: Antwerp, Ghent, Charleroi, Liège, Brussels.

Political divisions: Divided into the following three regions, which in turn are subdivided into a number of provinces (for pronunciation of their names, see their individual entries):

NAME	AREA (sq. mi.)	AREA (sq. km.)	POP. (1991c)	CAPITAL
Brussels	62	160	954,045	
Flanders	5,217	13,512	5,768,925	
Antwerp	1,104	2,859	1,605,167	Antwerp
Brabant (in part)	813	2,106	976,956[1]	
East Flanders	1,151	2,981	1,335,793	Ghent
Limburg	935	2,422	750,435	Hasselt
West Flanders	1,210	3,134	1,106,829	Brugge
Wallonia	6,504	16,845	3,255,711	
Brabant (in part)	421	1,090	325,621[1]	
Hainaut	1,463	3,789	1,278,791	Mons
Liège	1,497	3,877	999,646	Liège
Luxembourg	1,706	4,418	232,813	Arlon
Namur	1,413	3,660	423,317	Namur

[1] (1992e)

History: Inhabited in ancient times by Belgae, a people of Celtic stock, who were conquered by Roman Gen. Julius Caesar 57 B.C.; Belgica, a Roman province, erected by Emperor Augustus; invaded by Germanic peoples, incl. the Franks who incorp. territory in their kingdom; part of Carolingian kingdom of Lotharingia (see LORRAINE); except for duchy of Flanders which became dependency of France, attached to medieval empire as duchy of Lower Lorraine; broke up into semi-independent territories, such as Brabant, Limburg, Luxembourg (*qq.v.*); by 1484, territories of Netherlands, of which future Belgium was a part, gradually united into Burgundian state which passed to Hapsburgs 1477; the center of European commerce in 16th cent. (see ANTWERP); allotted to Spanish Hapsburgs 1555; basis of modern Belgium laid in S Catholic provinces, reclaimed from revolt against Spain and split from N Protestant provinces after Union of Utrecht 1579 (see NETHERLANDS); Artois, Lille, Maubeuge, and Cambrai lost to France in 17th cent.; Spanish Netherlands became Austrian 1713; overrun by French 1792 (see JEMAPPES) and incorp. in France 1801; reunited to Holland as independent kingdom of the Netherlands 1815; after revolt begun in 1830, recognized (by treaties of 1831 and 1839) as independent kingdom of Belgium, its neutrality guaranteed by the Great Powers; received half of duchies of Limburg and Luxembourg; under Leopold II, Congo Free State in personal union with Belgium 1885 and annexed in 1908 (see ZAIRE 1); invasion by Germany 1914 the occasion of British entrance into WWI; in peace treaty 1919, awarded Moresnet, Eupen-et-Malmédy, and mandate of Ruanda-Urundi (*qq.v.*); in WWII invaded May 1940 and occupied by Germans; cen. and E part overrun by Allied armies Sept. 1944; Battle of the Bulge in E Dec. 1944–Jan. 1945; formed customs union with Netherlands and Luxembourg 1947 which was later superseded by Benelux Union 1960; became a member of NATO 1949, EEC 1958; granted independence to Congo (now Democratic Rep. of the Congo) 1960; granted independence to Ruanda-Urundi (now countries of Rwanda and Burundi) 1962; adjusted provincial boundaries in accordance with distribution of the two national languages (Flemish in N, French in S) 1963; legislation enacted throughout 1970s and 1980s created three nearly autonomous regions: Flanders (Flemish-speaking), Wallonia (French-speaking), and Brussels (bilingual); became a federation comprised of three regions, Brussels, Flanders, and Wallonia 1993.

Bel·go·rod *also* **Byel·go·rod** \ˈbyel-gə-rət, ˈbel-gə-ˌräd\. City, ✻ of Belgorod Oblast, Russia, on upper Donets River and on railroad line 50 mi. (80 km.) N of Kharkiv, Ukraine; pop. (1992e) 314,000; food processing; iron ore deposits nearby. Of ecclesiastical importance in 17th cent. and later a fortified point in conflicts with the Tatars. Scene of bitter fighting bet. Germany and Soviets during WWII.

Belgorod–Dnes·trov·ski *or* **Belgorod–Dnes·trov·skiy** \-dne-ˈstrȯf-skē\; *formerly* **Ak·ker·man** \ˈä-kər-ˌmän\ *or Rom.* **Ce·ta·tea Al·bă** \chā-ˈtä-tyä-ˈäl-bə\; *anc.* **Ty·ras** \ˈtī-rəs\. City, Odessa subdivision, SW Ukraine, on right bank of Dniester estuary 28 mi. (45 km.) SE of Odessa; has shallow harbor but considerable trade; old fortifications.

History: On site of old Milesian colony of Tyras (founded 6th cent. B.C.); held by Macedonians and Romans; in medieval times under control of Tatars and Genoese, and in 1484 captured by Turks; seized several times by Russians who finally acquired it by treaty early 19th cent.; became a Romanian town 1918, a port of Bessarabia; ceded to U.S.S.R. June 1940 but seized by Germany 1941; retaken by U.S.S.R. 1944 and name subsequently changed from Akkerman.

Belgorod Oblast \ˈō-bləst, -ˌblast\. Subdivision, Russia in Europe; 10,463 sq. mi. (27,099 sq. km.); pop. (1992e)

1,408,000; ✻ Belgorod; winter and spring wheat; iron ore deposits; formed 1954.

Bel·grade \ˈbel-ˌgrād, -ˌgräd, -ˌgrad, bel-ˈ\ *or Serbo-Croat.* **Be·o·grad** \bā-ˈō-ˌgräd\. **1.** Former county, E Yugoslavia; 93 sq. mi. (241 sq. km.); ⊗ Belgrade; incorp. 1945 in Serbia, Yugoslavia.

2. *anc.* **Sin·gi·du·num** \ˌsin-jə-ˈdü-nəm, -ˈdyü-\. City, ✻ of Yugoslavia and of Serbia, on right bank of Danube River where the Sava joins it; pop. (1991p) 1,553,854; commercial and transportation center, one of most important for Balkans; textiles, electrical equipment, machine tools; food processing; mosque (16th cent.); citadel (1725–36); cathedral (1845); university (1863); seat of Serbian Academy of Sciences.

History: Roman fortification, Singidunum; destroyed by Avars 6th cent. A.D.; held by Avars to 9th cent., Bulgars in 10th, Byzantines from 11th to 13th, and by Serbs in 14th cent.; saved from siege by Turks when Hungarian national hero János Hunyadi defeated them nearby 1456 (see HUNGARY); captured by Ottoman Sultan Süleyman the Magnificent (see OTTOMAN EMPIRE) 1521; ceded to Austria 1718 by Treaty of Passarowitz and recovered by Turks in Peace of Belgrade 1739; in 19th cent. ✻ of independent principality of Serbia (*q.v.*); bombardment by Turks 1862 the cause of forced withdrawal of Turkish garrisons 1867; in WWI captured and lost by Austrians 1914, held by Central Powers 1915–18; scene of proclamation of Kingdom of Serbs, Croats, and Slovenes of which it became ✻ (see YUGOSLAVIA). In WWII devastated and captured by Germans 1941; retaken by Yugoslav and Soviet forces 1944. Following WWII, experienced large population growth as people moved in from countryside; remains ✻ of much-diminished Yugoslavia.

Bel·gra·no \bel-ˈgrä-nō\. Peak, NW Santa Cruz, S Argentina, NE of **Lake Belgrano;** 7526 ft. (2294 m.).

Bel·gra·via \bel-ˈgrā-vē-ə\. A fashionable residential district in the W end of London, SE England, centering at Belgrave Square.

Be·li·tung \bā-ˈlē-ˌtu̇ŋ\ *or* **Bil·li·ton** \bē-ˈlē-ˌtōn\ *or Du.* **Be·li·toeng** \bā-ˈlē-ˌtu̇ŋ\. Island, Indonesia, in the Java Sea off the SE coast of the island of Sumatra; 55 mi. (88 km.) long by 43 mi. (69 km.) wide; 1866 sq. mi. (4833 sq. km.); chief town Tanjungpandan; tin deposits.

Be·lize \bə-ˈlēz\ *or Span.* **Be·li·ce** \bā-ˈlē-sā\. **1.** *1840–1973* **British Honduras.** Independent country, Central America, bounded on N by Mexico, on E by the Caribbean Sea, and on S and W by Guatemala; 8867 sq. mi. (22,966 sq. km.); pop. (1990p) 184,340; ✱ Belmopan.

Physical features: Generally low and marshy along the coast, rising inland, hilly in S with highest point ab. 3681 ft. (1122 m.); separated from Quintana Roo, Mexico, on the N by the Hondo River and from Guatemala on the S by the Sarstoon; traversed in cen. part by the Belize River which rises in NE Guatemala and flows E to the Caribbean at Belize; off coast are many islets, reefs, and cays; in NE is Ambergris Cay, and opp. Belize are Turneffe Is.

Chief towns: Belize City and Orange Walk.

Chief products: Sugar, citrus fruits, bananas, corn, rice, honey; fish; timber; clothing; tourism.

Political divisions: Divided into the following six districts (for pronunciation of their names, see their individual entries):

NAME	AREA (sq. mi.)	AREA (sq. km.)	POP. (1990e)	CAPITAL
Belize	1,663	4,307	56,131	Belize City
Cayo	2,006	5,196	35,194	San Ignacio
Corozal	718	1,860	28,217	Corozal
Orange Walk	1,790	4,636	29,462	Orange Walk
Stann Creek	986	2,554	18,061	Dangriga
Toledo	1,704	4,413	17,275	Punta Gorda

History: Inhabited initially by Mayans, declining c. 900 A.D.; settled ab. 1638 by English logwood cutters from Jamaica; maintained existence despite Spanish opposition which was finally defeated 1798; made British superintendency of Belize 1786 to which Great Britain sought to add Bay Islands 1841; intended expansion by British (see also MOSQUITO COAST) part of background of Clayton-Bulwer Treaty bet. England and the U.S. 1850; attempted setting S boundary with Guatemala by treaty 1859, but not fully accepted by Guatemala; declared a colony subordinate to Jamaica 1862; independent of Jamaica since 1884; adopted new constitution 1960; achieved internal self-government 1964, independence 1981.

2. River, Belize; rises in NE Guatemala and flows E into the Gulf of Honduras at Belize City; 180 mi. (290 km.) long.

3. Administrative district, E Belize. See table at BELIZE 1.

Belize City *also* **Belize.** Seaport, ✱ of Belize district, Belize, at mouth of Belize River; pop. (1992e) 45,158; former ✱ of British Honduras; devastated by hurricanes 1961, 1978.

Beljak. See VILLACH.

Bel·knap \ˈbel-ˌnap\. County in cen. New Hampshire. See table at NEW HAMPSHIRE.

Belknap, Mount. Mountain, Piute co., SW cen. Utah; 12,139 ft. (3700 m.).

Bell \ˈbel\. **1.** Name of counties in two states of the U.S. See tables at KENTUCKY and TEXAS.

2. Residential city, Los Angeles co., SW California, 5 mi. (8 km.) S of the city of Los Angeles; pop. (1990c) 34,365; incorp. 1927.

Bell, Mount. Mountain, Antarctica, 84°04′S, 167°30′E; 14,117 ft. (4303 m.).

Bel·la Coo·la \ˌbe-lə-ˈkü-lə\. Short stream in SW British Columbia, Canada; flows W into Burke Channel.

Bellaire \be-ˈlar\. **1.** Village, ⊗ of Antrim co., NW Michigan; pop. (1990c) 1104.

2. City, Belmont co., E Ohio, on Ohio River 26 mi. (42 km.) S of Steubenville; pop. (1990c) 6028; coal, clay, limestone deposits.

3. City, Harris co., Texas, entirely within city of Houston; pop. (1990c) 13,842.

Bel·la·ry \bə-ˈlär-ē\ *or* **Bal·la·ri** \bə-ˈlär-ē\. Town, SW Karnataka, S cen. India, 270 mi. (434 km.) NW of Madras; pop. (1991p) 245,758; cotton and sugar trade.

Bel·la·vis·ta \ˌbā-yä-ˈvē-stä\. City, W Peru, W suburb of Lima; pop. (1981p) 69,113.

Belle·air \be-ˈlar\. Town, Pinellas co., W cen. Florida, 20 mi. (32 km.) W of Tampa; pop. (1990c) 3968.

Belle–Alliance, La. See LA BELLE-ALLIANCE.

Bel·leau \be-ˈlō\. Village, Aisne dept., N France, 9 mi. (14 km.) NW of Château-Thierry; WWI American military cemetery (dedicated 1923).

Belleau Wood *or Fr.* **Bois de Belleau** \bwä-də-be-ˈlō\ *also* **Bois de la Bri·gade Ma·rine** \lá-brē-ˌgäd-má-ˈrēn\. Wood, S of Belleau village, France; scene of WWI battle June 1918, in which five German divisions were defeated by 4th U.S. Marine Brigade, stopping German advance on Paris.

Belle·chasse \bel-ˈshás\. County, S Quebec, Canada. See table at QUEBEC.

Bel·leek \bə-ˈlēk\. Parish and village, Fermanagh dist., Northern Ireland, on the Erne River; famous for its china.

Belle·fon·taine \bel-ˈfaunt-ᵊn, -ˈfänt-\. City, ⊗ of Logan co., W Ohio, 30 mi. (48 km.) N of Springfield; pop. (1990c) 12,142; former site of Shawnee Indian village; settled by Europeans 1806.

Bellefontaine Neighbors. City, St. Louis co., Missouri, N of the city of St. Louis; pop. (1990c) 10,922.

Belle·fonte \ˈbel-ˌfänt\. Borough, ⊗ of Centre co., cen. Pennsylvania, 25 mi. (40 km.) NNW of Lewistown; pop. (1990c) 6358.

Belle Fourche \bel-ˈfüsh\. **1.** River, NE Wyoming and W South Dakota; rises in NE Wyoming, flows NE and E into Cheyenne River in E Meade co., South Dakota; ab. 350 mi. (563 km.) long; In S Butte co., South Dakota, a canal links river with **Belle Fourche Reservoir,** used for irrigation and formed by **Belle Fourche Dam** (completed 1911, height 112 ft. or 34 m. built across Owl Creek, a N tributary).

2. City, ⊗ of Butte co., W South Dakota, on Belle Fourche River 25 mi. (40 km.) N of Lead; pop. (1990c) 4355; bentonite deposits.

Belle Glade \ˈbel-ˌglād, bel-ˈglād\. City, Palm Beach co., SE Florida, on SE shore of Lake Okeechobee; pop. (1990c) 16,177; built 1925; laid waste by hurricane 1928; rebuilt.

Belle–Île–en–Mer \be-ˈlēl-äⁿ-ˈmer\. Island in N Bay of Biscay, off S coast of Morbihan dept. (to which it belongs), NW France; 35 sq. mi. (91 sq. km.).

Belle Isle \bel-ˈīl\. **1.** City, Orange co., cen. Florida; pop. (1990c) 5272.

2. Island, Newfoundland, Canada in Atlantic Ocean at entrance to Strait of Belle Isle; ab. 15 sq. mi. (39 sq. km.); lighthouse.

Belle Isle, Strait of. Channel bet. N tip of Newfoundland and SE Labrador, Canada, connecting Gulf of St. Lawrence with Atlantic Ocean; 10 to 20 mi. (16 to 32 km.) wide; ab. 90 mi. (145 km.) long.

Bellenz. See BELLINZONA.

Belle Plaine \ˈbel-ˌplān\. **1.** City, Benton co., E cen. Iowa, 34 mi. (55 km.) W of Cedar Rapids; pop. (1990c) 2834.

2. City, Scott co., SE Minnesota; pop. (1990c) 3149.

Belle·rive \ˈbel-ˌrēv\. Residential suburb of Hobart, Tasmania (*q.v.*), directly opp. on left bank of the Derwent.

Belle Ver·non \bel-ˈvər-nən\. Borough, Fayette co., SW Pennsylvania, on Monongahela River 24 mi. (39 km.) SSE of Pittsburgh; pop. (1990c) 1213; coal deposits; settled 1791.

Belle·ville \ˈbel-ˌvil\. **1.** City, ⊗ of St. Clair co., SW Illinois, 14 mi. (23 km.) SE of East St. Louis; pop. (1990c) 42,785; coal deposits nearby; Belleville Area Coll. (1946); Scott Air Force Base (*q.v.*) nearby.

2. City, ⊗ of Republic co., N Kansas, 17 mi. (27 km.) N of Concordia; pop. (1990c) 2517.

3. City, Wayne co., SE Michigan; pop. (1990c) 3270.

4. Township, Essex co., NE New Jersey, on Passaic River 4 mi. (6 km.) N of Newark; pop. (1990c) 34,213; an old Dutch settlement of 17th cent.; orig. known as Second River section of Newark; became separate community 1839.

5. City, ⊗ of Hastings co., SE Ontario, Canada, on Bay of Quinte 47 mi. (76 km.) W of Kingston; pop. (1991c) 37,243; fishing; site of Ontario School for the Deaf; founded 1790; became a city 1877.

Belle·vue \ˈbel-ˌvyü\. **1.** City, Campbell co., N Kentucky, on Ohio River just above Newport; pop. (1990c) 6997; a suburb of Covington, Kentucky, and Cincinnati, Ohio.

2. City, Sarpy co., E Nebraska, on Missouri River 8 mi. (13 km.) S of Omaha; pop. (1990c) 30,982; oldest town in Nebraska; on site of fur-trading post; missionary station 1833; Bellevue Coll. (1966).

3. City, Huron and Sandusky cos., N Ohio, 14 mi. (23 km.) SSW of the city of Sandusky; pop. (1990c) 8146; limestone deposits; settled 1815.

4. Borough, Allegheny co., SW Pennsylvania, on Ohio River; pop. (1990c) 9126; residential suburb of Pittsburgh.

5. City, King co., Washington, E of Seattle; pop. (1990c) 86,874; Bellevue Community Coll. (1966), City Univ. (1973).

6. Town, Brown co., E Wisconsin; pop. (1990c) 7541.

Bell·flow·er \ˈbel-ˌflau̇-ər\. City, Los Angeles co., California, N of Long Beach; pop. (1990c) 61,815.

Bell Gardens \ˈbel\. City, Los Angeles co., California, NW of Downey; pop. (1990c) 42,355.

Bel·li·court \ˌbe-lē-ˈkür\. Commune, Aisne dept., N France, 8 mi. (13 km.) N of St.-Quentin; in WWI part of Hindenburg Line, taken by Americans Sept. 1918; American military cemetery.

Bel·ling·ham \ˈbe-liŋ-ˌham\. **1.** Town, Norfolk co., E Massachusetts, 19 mi. (31 km.) SE of Worcester; pop. (1990c) 14,877; birthplace 1822 of William T. Adams ("Oliver Optic"), known popularly for his writing for children.

2. Commercial city, ⊗ of Whatcom co., NW Washington, on **Bellingham Bay** ab. 18 mi. (29 km.) S of Canadian border; pop. (1990c) 52,179; port of entry; Western Washington Univ. (1893); settled 1852 as **What·com** \ˈhwät-kəm, ˈwät-\ and became ⊗ 1854; eventually merged with nearby New Whatcom, Fairhaven, and Sehome to become Bellingham 1903.

Bel·lings·hau·sen Sea \ˈbe-liŋz-ˌhau̇-zᵊn\. Inlet of South Pacific Ocean on coast of Antarctica; extends along coast from Alexander I. to Thurston I., ab. long. 75° to 98°W and bet. lat. 70° and 72°S.

Bel·lin·zo·na \ˌbe-lən-ˈdzō-nə, -ˈtsō-\ *or Ger.* **Bel·lenz** \ˈbe-lents\. Commune, ✻ of Ticino canton, SE cen. Switzerland, near Ticino River 92 mi. (148 km.) SE of Bern; pop. (1989c) 17,142; tourism; railroad junction; castles dating to Milan's rule 14th–15th cent. Possibly fortified in Roman times; fought over by Como and Milan in Middle Ages; to Swiss Confederation 1503.

Belli Quadrum. See BEAUCAIRE.

Bell Island. **1.** Island in Atlantic Ocean, off NE coast of Newfoundland I., Newfoundland (prov.), Canada, 50°44′N, 55°35′W.

2. Island in Conception Bay, Newfoundland, Canada, W of city of St. John's, 47°36′N, 52°58′W.

Bell·mawr \bel-ˈmär\. Borough, Camden co., New Jersey, SW of the city of Camden; pop. (1990c) 12,603.

Bell·mead \ˈbel-ˌmēd\. City, McLennan co., Texas, NE suburb of Waco; pop. (1990c) 8336.

Bel·lo \ˈbā-yō\. Town, Antioquia dept., NW Colombia; munic. pop. (1985c) 208,439.

Bello Horizonte. See BELO HORIZONTE.

Bel·lo·na \be-ˈlō-nä\. Small island in SE Solomon Is., W Pacific Ocean, ab. 110 mi. (175 km.) S of Guadalcanal and ab. 20 mi. (32 km.) WNW of Rennell I.

Bellovacum. See BEAUVAIS.

Bel·lows Falls \ˈbe-ləz\. Village, in Rockingham town, Windham co., SE corner of Vermont, on Connecticut River 21 mi. (34 km.) N of Brattleboro; pop. (1990c) 3313; trucking terminal; communication and power supply cords; settled 1753.

Bell·port \ˈbel-ˌpōrt\. Village, Suffolk co., SE New York, on Great South Bay 13 mi. (21 km.) E of Islip; pop. (1990c) 2572.

Bell Rock \ˈbel\ *or* **Inch·cape Rock** \ˈinch-ˌkāp\. Rock in North Sea, Scotland, 12 mi. (19 km.) SE of Arbroath; covered by sea at high tide; has lighthouse built 1807–11 by the grandfather of writer Robert Louis Stevenson; subject of legends.

Bell Sound \ˈbel\. Large inlet on SW coast of Spitsbergen I., Svalbard.

Bel·lu·no \bel-ˈlü-nō\. **1.** Province of Veneto, NE Italy. See table at ITALY.

2. Commune, its ✻, on Piave River 50 mi. (80 km.) N of Venice; pop. (1981p) 36,513; tourism; 16th cent. cathedral. Became Roman 180 B.C.; in Middle Ages became Lombard duchy and later a Frankish countship; part of Venetian Republic 1405–1797; became part of Austria 1813; part of Italy 1866.

Bell·ville \ˈbel-ˌvil\. **1.** City, ⊗ of Austin co., SE cen. Texas; pop. (1990c) 3378.

2. Town, SW Western Cape prov., Rep. of South Africa, 12 mi. (19 km.) ENE of Cape Town; pop. (1985c) 68,915; Univ. of the Western Cape (1960).

Bell Ville \bel-ˈvēl, bezh-ˈvē-zhā\. Town, Córdoba prov., N cen. Argentina, 110 mi. (177 km.) WNW of Rosario; pop. (1980p) 26,559.

Bell·wood \ˈbel-ˌwu̇d\. Residential village, Cook co., NE Illinois, 13 mi. (21 km.) W of Chicago; pop. (1990c) 20,241.

Bel·ly \ˈbe-lē\. River, SW Alberta, Canada; rises in Glacier National Park, Montana, and flows NNE to Oldman River; 180 mi. (290 km.) long.

Bel·mar \ˈbel-ˌmär\. Borough, Monmouth co., E cen. New Jersey; pop. (1990c) 5877; seashore resort; fishing.

Bel·mond \ˈbel-ˌmänd\. City, Wright co., N cen. Iowa, 28 mi. (45 km.) SW of Mason City; pop. (1990c) 2500.

Bel·mont \ˈbel-ˌmänt\. **1.** County in E Ohio. See table at OHIO.

2. City, San Mateo co., W California, 10 mi. (16 km.) SSE of San Francisco; pop. (1990c) 24,127; Coll. of Notre Dame (1851).

3. Town, Middlesex co., NE Massachusetts, 7 mi. (11 km.) WNW of Boston; pop. (1990c) 24,720; residential suburb of Boston.

4. Village, Mississippi co., SE Missouri, 15 mi. (24 km.) S of Cairo, Illinois; scene of battle Nov. 7, 1861 in which Gen. Ulysses S. Grant's attacking force was driven back by Confederate forces under Gen. Leonidas Polk.
5. Town, Belknap co., New Hampshire; pop. (1990c) 5796.
6. Village, ⊗ of Allegany co., SW New York; pop. (1990c) 1006.
7. City, Gaston co., SW North Carolina, 7 mi. (11 km.) E of Gastonia; pop. (1990c) 8434; Belmont Abbey Coll. (1878).

Bel·mo·pan \ˌbel-mō-ˈpän\. Town, ✻ of Belize, 41 mi. (66 km.) SW of Belize City; pop. (1992e) 3687; became ✻ 1970 because former ✻ Belize City often subject to flooding.

Belna. See BEAUNE.

Bel–Nor \ˌbel-ˈnȯr\. Village, St. Louis co., Missouri; pop. (1990c) 2935.

Bel·oeil \be-ˈlœi\. Town, S Quebec, Canada, on Richelieu River NE of Montreal; pop. (1991c) 18,516.

Be·lo·gorsk \ˌbye-lə-ˈgȯrsk\. **1.** *1935–57* **Kui·by·shev·ka** \ˌküy-bi-ˈshef-kə\ *or* **Kuybyshevka–Vos·toch·na·ya** \-və-ˈstōch-nə-yə\; *earlier* **Alek·san·drov·ka** \ˌȧ-lik-sən-ˈdrəf-kə\. Town, Amur Oblast, S Russia in Asia, just NE of Blagoveshchensk; junction point on Trans-Siberian R.R. for Blagoveshchensk; pop. (1991e) 74,900.
2. *formerly* **Ka·ra·su·ba·zar** \ˌkär-ə-ˌsü-bə-ˈzär\. Town, S cen. Crimea, Ukraine, NE of Simferopol.

Be·lo Ho·ri·zon·te; *formerly* **Bel·lo Horizonte** \ˈbā-lō-rē-ˈzō^{n}n-tē\. City, ✻ of Minas Gerais state, E Brazil, 220 mi. (354 km.) N of Rio de Janeiro; munic. pop. (1989e) 2,300,000; alt. 2811 ft. (857 m.); steel, textiles, food products; federal university (1927), Catholic university (1959); region important for industry, cotton, and cattle; Brazil's first planned city.

Be·loit \bə-ˈlȯit\. **1.** City, ⊗ of Mitchell co., N cen. Kansas, on Solomon River 51 mi. (82 km.) NW of Salina; pop. (1990c) 4066; regional trading center.
2. City, Rock co., S Wisconsin, on Rock River on Illinois border; pop. (1990c) 35,573; Beloit Coll. (1846); Indian mounds nearby.

Be·lo·re·chensk \ˌbye-lə-ˈre-chinsk\. City, Krasnodar Kray, S Russia in Europe, ab. 50 mi. (81 km.) ESE of the city of Krasnodar; pop. (1991e) 56,900.

Be·lo·retsk \ˌbye-lə-ˈretsk\. City, E Bashkortostan, E Russia in Europe, on Belaya River in Southern Ural Mts.; pop. (1991e) 73,100.

Belorussian Soviet Socialist Republic *or* **Belorussia.** See BYELORUSSIAN SOVIET SOCIALIST REPUBLIC.

Belostok. See BIAŁYSTOK.

Belotsarsk. See KYZYL.

Belovar. See BJELOVAR.

Beloye More. See WHITE SEA.

Be·lo·ye Oze·ro \ˈbye-lə-yə-ˈȯ-zir-ə\ *or* **Byel·oze·ro** \bye-ˈlȯ-\. Lake (*ozero*) in W Vologda Oblast, NW cen. Russia in Europe; 433 sq. mi. (1122 sq. km.); outlet to Rybinsk Reservoir by Sheksna River; along its W and S shores is a part of the Volga-Baltic Waterway.

Bel·per \ˈbel-pər\. Town, Derbyshire, N cen. England, on the Derwent 8 mi. (13 km.) N of Derby; pop. (1981p) 16,453; cotton.

Bel·pre \ˈbel-ˌprā\. City, Washington co., SE Ohio, on Ohio River 10 mi. (16 km.) SSW of Marietta; pop. (1990c) 6796; Blennerhassett I. nearby.

Bel–Ridge \ˌbel-ˈrij\. Village, St. Louis co., Missouri; pop. (1990c) 3199.

Bel·sen \ˈbel-zən\ *or in full* **Ber·gen–Belsen** \ˈber-gən-\. Locality in Lower Saxony, N cen. Germany, ab. 12 mi. (19 km.) NNW of Celle; site of Nazi concentration camp taken by Allies Apr. 1945.

Belt, Great. See GREAT BELT.

Belt, Little. See LITTLE BELT.

Bel·ton \ˈbelt-^{ə}n\. **1.** City, Cass co., W Missouri, 12 mi. (19 km.) S of Kansas City; pop. (1990c) 18,150.
2. Village, Montana. See WEST GLACIER.
3. City, Anderson co., NW South Carolina, 9 mi. (15 km.) E of Anderson; pop. (1990c) 4646.
4. City, ⊗ of Bell co., cen. Texas, W of Temple; pop. (1990c) 12,476; Univ. of Mary Hardin–Baylor (1845).

Bel·trami \bel-ˈtra-mē\. County in N Minnesota. See table at MINNESOTA.

Belts·ville \ˈbelts-ˌvil\. Unincorporated settlement, Prince Georges co., Maryland, ab. 12 mi. (19 km.) NE of Washington, D.C.; pop. (1990c) 14,476; U.S. Dept. of Agriculture national research center.

Beltsy. See BĂIŢI.

Beluchistan. See BALUCHISTAN.

Be·lu·kha \bə-ˈlü-kə\ *also* **Bye·lu·kha** \byə-\. Highest peak in the Altay Shan on border bet. Kazakhastan and Gorno-Altay Rep., S Russia in Asia; 15,157 ft. (4620 m.).

Bel·vi·dere \ˈbel-və-ˌdir\. **1.** City, ⊗ of Boone co., N Illinois, 15 mi. (24 km.) E of Rockford; pop. (1990c) 15,958.
2. Town, ⊗ of Warren co., NW New Jersey, on Delaware River 11 mi. (18 km.) NNE of Phillipsburg; pop. (1990c) 2669.

Bel·yan·do \bel-ˈyan-dō\. River, E Queensland, NE Australia; flows N along E slope of Eastern Highlands; ab. 250 mi. (400 km.) long.

Bel·zo·ni \bel-ˈzō-nē\. City, ⊗ of Humphreys co., W Mississippi, 28 mi. (45 km.) SW of Greenwood; pop. (1990c) 2536.

Be·mid·ji \bə-ˈmi-jē\. City, ⊗ of Beltrami co., N Minnesota, 28 mi. (45 km.) S of Lower Red Lake; pop. (1990c) 11,245; resort; lumber; trade center for a large area; Bemidji State Univ. (1919).

Bemis Heights. See SARATOGA 3.

Ben–a–Bhuird \ˌben-ə-ˈbu̇rd\. Mountain, SW Grampian region, NE Scotland; 3924 ft. (1196 m.).

Benacus, Lacus. See GARDA, LAKE.

Ben·a·dir \ˌbe-nə-ˈdir\. Coastal region, S Somalia; its chief city is Mogadishu.

Ben Al·der \ben-ˈȯl-dər\. Mountain, S Highland region, N cen. Scotland, on W side of Loch Ericht; 3757 ft. (1145 m.).

Benares. See VARANASI.

Benas, Ras. See BANÂS, RAS.

Ben Avon \ben-ˈän\. Mountain in SW Grampian region, on boundary of Banff co., NE cen. Scotland; 3843 ft. (1171 m.).

Benbaun. See BENNEBEOLA, TWELVE BENS OF.

Ben·bec·u·la \ben-ˈbe-kyə-lə\. Island of the Outer Hebrides, Western Isles region, off NW coast of Scotland, bet. the islands of North Uist and South Uist; ab. 8 mi. (13 km.) long.

Ben·bon·yathe, Mount \ˌben-bən-ˈya-thē\. Peak in North Flinders Range, E South Australia, Australia; 3470 ft. (1058 m.).

Ben·brook \ˈben-ˌbru̇k\. City, Tarrant co., N Texas, 10 mi. (16 km.) SW of Fort Worth; pop. (1990c) 19,564.

Ben·bul·bin *or* **Ben·bul·ben** \ben-ˈbəl-bin\. Peak, N co. Sligo, Ireland; 1729 ft. (527 m.); poet William Butler Yeats is buried nearby.

Ben Cleuch. See OCHIL HILLS.

Ben Cru·a·chan \ben-ˈkrü-ə-kən, -kən\. Mountain, N Strathclyde region, W Scotland, SE of Loch Etive; 3689 ft. (1124 m.).

Bend \ˈbend\. City, ⊗ of Deschutes co., cen. Oregon, on Deschutes River 95 mi. (153 km.) E of Eugene; pop. (1990c) 20,469; Central Oregon Community Coll. (1949).

Ben Da·vis Point \ben-ˈdā-vis\. Point on SW coast of Cumberland co., SW New Jersey, in Delaware Bay.

Ben Dearg. See BEINN DEARG.

Bender *or* **Bendery.** See TIGHINA.

Ben·di·go \ˈben-di-ˌgō\; *formerly* **Sand·hurst** \ˈsand-ˌhərst\. City, cen. Victoria, SE Australia, 80 mi. (129 km.) NNW of Melbourne; pop. (1991p) 30,133; founded mid-19th cent.; one of earliest places where alluvial gold was discovered (1851).

Bendin. See BĘDZIN.

Ben Dou·ran \ben-ˈdu̇r-ən\ *or* **Ben Do·ran** \ˈdōr-ən\. Mountain in Grampian Mts., Strathclyde region, W Scotland; 3523 ft. (1074 m.).

Bendzin. See BĘDZIN.

Be·ne Be·raq \bə-ˈnā-bə-ˈräk\. City, W cen. Israel, NE suburb of Tel Aviv-Jaffa; pop. (1992e) 121,200.

Be·ne·dikt·beu·ern \ˌbā-nə-ˌdikt-ˈbȯi-ərn\. Village, Bavaria, S Germany, on railroad line 30 mi. (48 km.) S of Munich in N foothills of Alps; pop. (1980c) 2677; noted Benedictine monastery founded 733 where was discovered 13th cent. manuscript, the *Carmina Burana,* a collection of goliardic songs, now in Munich.

Beneharnum. See BÉARN.

Be·ne·lux Economic Union \ˈbe-nə-ˌləks\. Economic community, consisting of Belgium, Luxembourg, and Netherlands; headquarters Brussels, Belgium; purpose is to bring about economic union of members; treaty signed 1958, put into force 1960; border controls bet. members later abolished; while still in force, the three countries are also members of the EEC.

Be·ne·ven·to \ˌbā-nā-ˈven-tō\. **1.** Province of Campania, Italy. See table at ITALY.

2. *anc.* **Male·ven·tum** \ˌma-lə-ˈven-təm\ *also* **Bene·ven·tum** \ˌbe-nə-ˈven-təm\. Commune, its ✻, at confluence of Calore and Sabbato rivers 34 mi. (55 km.) NE of Naples; pop. (1991p) 62,683; in agricultural region; antiquities include a 9th cent. Lombard-Saracenic cathedral and the Porta Aurea (golden gate), a triumphal arch of Emperor Trajan, erected 114 A.D.

History: Ancient town of the Samnites; became Roman colony 268 B.C.; became seat of Lombard duchy of Benevento 571 A.D.; fell to Saracens and later to Normans; made a principality by French Emperor Napoléon 1806 and conferred upon statesman Charles-Maurice de Talleyrand Périgord; under papal control 1815 until its unification with the kingdom of Italy 1860.

Ben·e·wah \ˈben-ˌwä, -ˌwȯ\. County in NW Idaho. See table at IDAHO.

Ben·fleet \ˈben-ˌflēt\. Town, Essex, SE England, on inlet of Thames estuary 29 mi. (47 km.) E of London; pop. (1981p) 50,240.

Ben·gal \ben-ˈgȯl, beŋ-\; *earlier* **Bengal Presidency.** Former province, NE British India, now a region encompassing West Bengal, India and Bangladesh; 88,978 sq. mi. (230,453 sq. km.); ✻ Calcutta. Most of S part known as Sundarbans, occupied by delta of Ganges and Brahmaputra (see GANGES DELTA); S ranges of Himalayas in N and hills in Chittagong Hill Tracts and Tripura in SE.

History: Ancient Hindu region introduced to Buddhism by King Aśoka 3d cent. B.C.; NE part of older Bengal (see MAGADHA and BIHAR) nucleus of Maurya and Gupta empires; conquered by an Afghan ruler, Muʻizz-ud-Dīn Muḥammad (see GHOR), c. 1199; E Bengal made province under Tughlak dynasty 1324; Bengal under independent dynasty 1338–1539; in 1576 taken from Afghans by Moguls; first visited by factors of English East India Company 1633; Calcutta (*q.v.*) founded by English 1690 and Bengal made a presidency 1699; soon after British soldier and colonialist Robert Clive's victory at Plassey (*q.v.*) 1757 came to be under the Company's financial and military control; seat of authority of governor-general 1773–1834; Eastern Bengal and Assam separated from Bengal prov. 1905, but restored in 1912 when the whole was constituted as new presidency; made autonomous province 1937 (see INDIA 1); divided Aug. 15, 1947 into East Bengal, now Bangladesh, and West Bengal, part of India.

Bengal, Bay of. Part of Indian Ocean bet. E India and W coasts of Myanmar and the Malay Penin.

Beng·bu *or W.-G.* **Pang–pu** *or* **Peng–pu** \ˈbəŋ-ˈbü\. City, Anhui prov., E China, on Huai River 100 mi. (161 km.) NW of Nanjing; pop. (1990c) 449,245; Nationalist government base during civil war 1946 ff.; evacuated 1949.

Ben·gha·zi *also* **Ben·ga·si** \ben-ˈgä-zē, beŋ-, -ˈga-\. **1.** *or* **Ben·ga·zi** *same*\. Former province of N (Italian) Libya; 58,684 sq. mi. (151,992 sq. km.); ✻ Benghazi.

2. *also* **Ban·ghā·zī** \bän-ˈgä-zē, bäŋ-, baŋ-, -ˈga-\; *anc.* **Ber·e·ni·ce** \ˌber-ə-ˈnī-sē\. Coastal city, Libya, on NE shore of Gulf of Sidra; pop. (1988e) 446,250; university (1955); formerly a ✻ of Libya. Under Italian administration (1912–1942) developed as seaport and naval and air base. In WWII scene of severe fighting; changed hands several times before British finally took it late 1942.

Beng·ka·lis \beŋ-ˈkä-lis\. **1.** Island, E Sumatra, Indonesia, at S end of Strait of Malacca.

2. Town and fishing port on W side of island, ab. 120 mi. (195 km.) W of Singapore.

Beng·ku·lu \beŋ-ˈkü-lü\; *formerly* **Beng·koe·len** \beŋ-ˈkü-lən\ *or* **Ben·koe·len** *or* **Ben·ku·len** \beŋ-ˈkü-lən, ben-\. **1.** A province of Indonesia on the SW coast of Sumatra; ✻ Bengkulu; comprises the elevated region of the S Barisan Mts. and a narrow coastal strip. See table at INDONESIA. Was formerly a residency of the Netherland Indies.

2. Town, its ✻, a port at 3°48′S, 102°16′E, ab. 350 mi. (563 km.) NW of Jakarta; pop. (1990c) 170,327. Settlement estab. by British 1684 and fort built a few years later; in early years a center of pepper and spice trade; ceded to Dutch 1824 in exchange for Melaka. In 20th cent. during Indonesian fight for independence, nationalist leader Sukarno exiled here.

Ben·go \ˈbeŋ-gō\. Province of NW Angola. See table at ANGOLA.

Bengo, Bay of. Inlet of Atlantic Ocean on NW coast of Angola; Luanda is on it.

Ben·gore Head \ˌben-ˈgōr\. Cape, E of Giant's Causeway, Antrim dist., Northern Ireland.

Ben·guela *also* **Ben·guel·la** \beŋ-ˈgwe-lä\. **1.** Province of W Angola. See table at ANGOLA.

2. Seaport settlement, its ✻; railroad terminus. Fort built here 1587; town founded 1617.

Benguela Current. A cold ocean current, South Atlantic Ocean moving northward along the W coast of S Africa.

Ben·gué·rir \ˌben-gā-ˈrir\. Town, W cen. Morocco, ab. 45 mi. (72 km.) NNE of Marrakech on railroad line and highway to Casablanca.

Ben·guet \beŋ-ˈget\. Province, N Luzon, Philippines, in mountainous region of S Cordillera Central and Caraballo Mts.; ✻ La Trinidad; agriculture; gold deposits. Formed by Spanish as a military district (*comandancia*) 1846; made subprovince 1908, province 1968. Baguio, its most important town, administered separately. See table at PHILIPPINES.

Ben·ha \ˈben-hə\. City, ✻ of Qalyubīya governorate, N Egypt, on railroad line E of the Damietta branch of the Nile ab. 28 mi. (45 km.) N of Cairo.

Ben Hill \ˈben-ˈhil\. County in S cen. Georgia. See table at GEORGIA.

Be·ni \ˈbā-nē\. **1.** River, N and cen. Bolivia; rises in E cordillera of Andes in Cochabamba dept., flows N to unite with Mamoré River and form Madeira River; near its mouth receives large tributary from the W, the Madre de Dios; 994 mi. (1599 km.) long.

2. *also* **El Beni** \el-\. Department of N Bolivia. See table at BOLIVIA.

Be·ni Ab·bès \bā-ˈnē-ä-ˈbes\. Town, Algeria, near Moroccan border, ab. 100 mi. (160 km.) S of Béchar; pop. (1987p) 6469.

Be·ni·cia \bə-ˈnē-shə\. City, Solano co., cen. California, on N shore of Carquinez Strait 18 mi. (29 km.) NNE of Oakland; pop. (1990c) 24,437; fishing. Founded 1847; ✻ of California 1853–54; chartered as city 1861.

Beni Has·an \ˈbe-nē-ˈha-ˌsan\. Village on the Nile River, Egypt, 75 mi. (121 km.) N of Asyūt; site of rock tombs of XIIth dynasty, c. 1900 B.C., giving important information about ancient Egyptian society.

Be·nin \bə-ˈnēn, ˈbe-nin\. **1.** Formerly part of Upper Guinea, bet. the Volta River and Rio del Rey, incl. all of Slave Coast and the Niger delta region.

2. Name formerly given by French to their possessions on the Guinea coast incl. Dahomey.

3. Former native kingdom, one of the most highly organized of the states of W Africa before the coming of the Portuguese 1485; exerted great influence in 17th cent., then known to

Europeans as **Great Benin;** control taken over by British 1897–99; incorp. into British-ruled Nigeria.
4. River, S Nigeria, flowing into Bight of Benin; ab. 100 mi. (160 km.) long; connects with W part of Niger delta.
5. *or* **Benin City.** Town, ✱ of Edo state, S Nigeria, in W delta of the Niger ab. 150 mi. (240 km.) E of Lagos; pop. (1991e) 202,800; rubber-processing plants nearby.
6. *formerly* **Da·ho·mey** \də-'hō-mē\. Republic, W Africa, bounded on N by Niger, on E by Nigeria, on S by the Gulf of Guinea, on W by Togo, and on NW by Burkina Faso; 43,483 sq. mi. (112,621 sq. km.); pop. (1993e) 5,074,000; legal ✱ Porto-Novo, de facto ✱ Cotonou.

Physical features: Extending ab. 420 mi. (675 km.) inland from the Gulf of Guinea, the republic consists of a hilly region in the NW (max. elev. 2146 ft. or 654 m.), plains in the E and N, and a marshy coastal region in the S.

Chief exports: Palm products, cotton; other products: corn, cassava, yams; offshore oil.

Chief towns: Cotonou, Porto-Novo.

History: African kingdom which, in 17th cent., rose around Abomey; expanded N and to Slave Coast on S; French estab. trading presence in both Cotonou (1851) and Porto-Novo (1863); French finally captured Abomey and deposed ruler in 1892; made a French colony 1894 and part of French West Africa 1904; boundaries with Togo and Lagos determined in treaties with Germany and Great Britain late 19th cent.; made an overseas territory of France 1946; became an autonomous republic of the French Community; achieved independence 1960; name changed from Dahomey to Benin 1975.

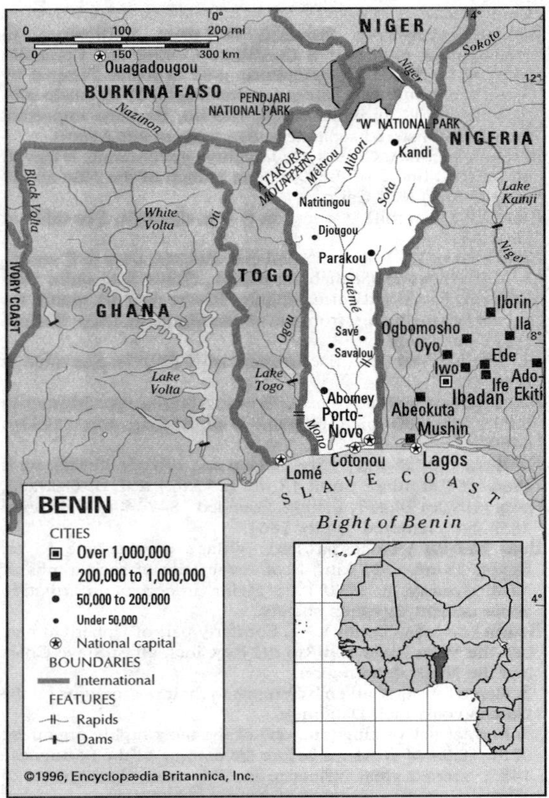

Benin, Bight of. Widemouthed bay in N section of the Gulf of Guinea, W Africa.
Be·ni Saf \'be-nē-'saf \. Seaport and commune, NW Algeria, ab. 50 mi. (80 km.) SW of Oran; pop. (1987p) 29,921; fishing.
Beni Su·ef *or* **Ba·nī Su·wayf** \'be-nē-sù-'āf\. **1.** Governorate of Upper Egypt. See table at EGYPT.
2. City, its ✱, on W bank of Nile 22 mi. (35 km.) SE of El Faiyūm; pop. (1991e) 174,000; trade center; cotton processing.
Ben·ja·min \'ben-jə-mən\. City, ⊗ of Knox co., N Texas; pop. (1990c) 225.
Ben·kel·man \'beŋ-kəl-mən\. City, ⊗ of Dundy co., S Nebraska; pop. (1990c) 1193.
Benkoelen *or* **Benkulen.** See BENGKULU.
Ben Laoigh. See BEN LUI.
Ben Law·ers \ben-'lȯ-ərz\. Mountain, Tayside region, cen. Scotland, NW of Loch Tay; 3984 ft. (1214 mi.).
Ben Ledi \ben-'le-dē\. Mountain in cen. Central region, cen. Scotland, NE of Loch Katrine; 2875 ft. (876 m.).
Ben Lo·mond \ben-'lō-mənd\. **1.** Mountain, N Utah, just N of Ogden; 9717 ft. (2962 m.).
2. Mountain, NE New South Wales, SE Australia; 4877 ft. (1487 m.); highest peak in New England Range.
3. Mountain, NE Tasmania, Australia, bet. the North Esk and South Esk rivers; 5160 ft. (1573 m.). in **Ben Lomond National Park.**
4. Mountain, Central region, S cen. Scotland, on E side of Loch Lomond; 3192 ft. (973 m.); dominating peak of the region.
Ben Lui \ben-'lü-ē\ *also* **Ben Laoigh** \'lə-ē\. Mountain, Central region, near Strathclyde region border, cen. Scotland, N of Ben Lomond; 3708 ft. (1130 m.).
Ben Mac·dhui \ˌben-mək-'dü-e\ *also* **Ben Muich·dhui** *same*\. Mountain, SW Grampian region, NE cen. Scotland; 4296 ft. (1309 m.); one of the Cairngorm group.
Ben More \ben-'mōr\. **1.** Mountain, cen. part of the island of Mull off W coast of Scotland; 3169 ft. (966 m.).
2. Mountain, N Central region, cen. Scotland; 3843 ft. (1171 m.).
3. *or* **Ben More As·synt** \'a-sint\. Mountain, N Highland region, N Scotland; 3273 ft. (998 m.).
Ben·more, Lake \ben-'mōr\. Lake, South I., New Zealand; 30.5 sq. mi. (79 sq. km.); max. depth 315 ft. (96 m.); largest artificial lake in New Zealand.
Ben·ne·be·o·la, Twelve Bens of \ˌbe-nə-'bē-ə-lə\ *also* **Twelve Pins of Bun·na·be·o·la** \ˌbə-\; *often shortened to* **The Twelve Bens** *or* **The Twelve Pins.** Mountain group in Connemara, W co. Galway, W Ireland; highest peak **Ben·baun** \ben-'bōn\ 2395 ft. (730 m.).
Ben·nett \'be-nit\. County in S South Dakota. See table at SOUTH DAKOTA.
Bennett, Lake. Lake, the W arm of Tagish Lake, on border bet. British Columbia and Yukon, Canada.
Bennett Island. Westernmost island of De Long group in Arctic Ocean, Sakha Rep., Russia, NE of New Siberian Is., 76°21′N, 148°56′E.
Ben·netts·ville \'be-nəts-ˌvil, -vəl\. City, ⊗ of Marlboro co., NE South Carolina, 30 mi. (48 km.) N of Florence; pop. (1990c) 9345.
Ben Nev·is \ben-'ne-vis\. Peak in Grampian Mts., Highland region, W cen. Scotland, E of N end of Loch Linnhe; 4406 ft. (1343 m.); highest peak in Great Britain.
Ben·ning·ton \'be-niŋ-tən\. **1.** County in SW corner of Vermont. See table at VERMONT.
2. Town, ⊗ of Bennington co., SW corner of Vermont, 31 mi. (50 km.) W of Brattleboro; pop. (1990c) 16,451; batteries, automobile parts, lubricating systems, publishing, plastics; Southern Vermont Coll. (1926), Bennington Coll. (1932).

History: Chartered by New Hampshire 1749, settled 1761; claimed by both New York and New Hampshire before Vermont became state; during the Revolution an important supply base for Continental Army; battle of Bennington fought nearby Aug. 16, 1777 in which Americans under Gen. John Stark defeated Col. Friedrich Baum, in command of a raiding force from Gen. John Burgoyne's army. See HOOSICK FALLS.
Be·no·ni \be-'nō-nē\. Town, NE Rep. of South Africa, in the Witwatersrand 20 mi. (32 km.) E of Johannesburg; pop.

(1985c) 94,926; alt. 5600 ft. (1707 m.); has some of the richest gold mines in the world; important industrial town.

Bénoué. See BENUE 1.

Bens·berg \ˈbens-ˌberk\. Commune, North Rhine-Westphalia, W Germany, 10 mi. (16 km.) ENE of Cologne; ruins of castle (1250).

Ben·sen·ville \ˈben-sən-ˌvil\. Village, Cook and Du Page cos., NE Illinois, 18 mi. (29 km.) WNW of Chicago; pop. (1990c) 17,767.

Bens·heim \ˈbens-ˌhīm\. City, Hesse, SW cen. Germany, 16 mi. (26 km.) S of Darmstadt; pop. (1980c) 32,964.

Ben·son \ˈben-sən\. **1.** County in N cen. North Dakota. See table at NORTH DAKOTA.

2. City, Cochise co., SE corner of Arizona, 42 mi. (68 km.) ESE of Tucson; pop. (1990c) 3824.

3. City, ⊗ of Swift co., W Minnesota; pop. (1990c) 3235.

4. Town, Johnston co., E North Carolina, 28 mi. (45 km.) S of Raleigh; pop. (1990c) 2810.

5. *also* **Ben·sing·ton** \ˈben-siŋ-tən\. Parish and village, SE Oxfordshire, cen. England, on the Thames; scene of battle late 8th cent. A.D. in which King Offa of Mercia defeated Cynewulf of Wessex, king of the West Saxons.

Ben·son·hurst \ˈbens-ᵊn-ˌhərst\. Neighborhood, S Brooklyn borough, New York City, New York.

Ben Sta·rav \ben-ˈstär-əv\. Mountain, N Strathclyde region, W Scotland, E of Loch Etive; 3541 ft. (1079 m.).

Bent \ˈbent\. County in SE Colorado. See table at COLORADO.

Ben·tinck Island \ˈben-tiŋk\. Island, cen. Mergui Archipelago (*q.v.*).

Bent·ley, Mount \ˈbent-lē\. Mountain, Antarctica, 78°07′S, 86°14′W; 13,934 ft. (4247 m.).

Bent·ley·ville \ˈbent-lē-ˌvil\. Borough, Washington co., SW Pennsylvania, 23 mi. (37 km.) S of Pittsburgh; pop. (1990c) 2673.

Ben·ton \ˈbent-ᵊn\. **1.** Name of counties in nine states of the U.S. See tables at ARKANSAS, INDIANA, IOWA, MINNESOTA, MISSISSIPPI, MISSOURI, OREGON, TENNESSEE, WASHINGTON.

2. City, ⊗ of Saline co., cen. Arkansas, 20 mi. (32 km.) SW of Little Rock; pop. (1990c) 18,177; founded 1836.

3. City, ⊗ of Franklin co., S Illinois, 25 mi. (40 km.) S of Mount Vernon; pop. (1990c) 7216; coal deposits.

4. City, ⊗ of Marshall co., W Kentucky, 22 mi. (35 km.) SE of Paducah; pop. (1990c) 3899.

5. City, ⊗ of Bossier parish, NW Louisiana; pop. (1990c) 2047.

6. Town, ⊗ of Scott co., SE Missouri; pop. (1990c) 575.

7. Town, ⊗ of Polk co., SE Tennessee; pop. (1990c) 992.

Benton Harbor. City, Berrien co., SW Michigan, on Lake Michigan 48 mi. (77 km.) WSW of Kalamazoo; pop. (1990c) 12,818; foundry products, household appliances; fruitpacking; Lake Michigan Coll. (1946). Seat of the religious colony the House of David (org. 1903).

Ben·ton·ville \ˈbent-ᵊn-ˌvil\. **1.** City, ⊗ of Benton co., NW corner of Arkansas, 22 mi. (35 km.) N of Fayetteville; pop. (1990c) 11,257; founded 1837.

2. Village, Johnston co., cen. North Carolina, 37 mi. (60 km.) SE of Raleigh; indecisive battle Mar. 19, 1865 bet. Confederates under Gen. Joseph E. Johnston and left wing of Gen. William T. Sherman's army.

Be·nue \ˈbā-nwā, ˈbe-\. **1.** *or in Cameroon* **Bénoué** \bā-ˈnwā\. River, W Africa, chief tributary of Niger River from E; rises in N Cameroon, flows W across E cen. Nigeria. ab. 870 mi. (1400 km.) long.

2. State of S cen. Nigeria. See table at NIGERIA.

Benue–Pla·teau \pla-ˈtō\. Former state of E cen. Nigeria; 39,206 sq. mi. (101,544 sq. km.); divided 1976 into Benue and Plateau.

Ben Ve·nue \ˌben-və-ˈnü, -ˈnyü\. Mountain, Central region, cen. Scotland, just S of Loch Katrine; 2393 ft. (729 m.).

Ben Vor·lich \ben-ˈvȯr-lik\. Mountain, SW Tayside region, cen. Scotland, S of Loch Earn; 3224 ft. (983 m.).

Ben Wyv·is \ben-ˈwi-vis\. Mountain, cen. Highland region, N Scotland; 3429 ft. (1045 m.).

Ben·xi *or W.-G.* **Pen–hsi** *or* **Pen–ch'i** \ˈben-ˈchē, -ˈchi\. Town, E cen. Liaoning prov., NE China, 30 mi. (48 km.) E of Liaoyang; pop. (1990c) 768,778; steel-producing center; cement; iron and coal mines; steel industry developed by Japanese c. 1915.

Ben–y–Gloe \ˌben-ē-ˈglō\. Mountain, N Tayside region, cen. Scotland; 3671 ft. (1119 m.).

Ben·zie \ˈben-zē\. County in NW Michigan. See table at MICHIGAN.

Beo \ˈbā-ō\. See TALAUD ISLANDS.

Beograd. See BELGRADE.

Bep·pu \ˈbe-pü\. City, on **Beppu Bay** (an arm of W end of Inland Sea), NE Kyūshū I., Japan, in Ōita prefecture; pop. (1990p) 130,323; hot springs.

Beqáa. See BEKÁA VALLEY.

Be·quia \ˈbe-ˌkwā\. An island of St. Vincent and the Grenadines; one of the N Grenadines.

Be·rar \bā-ˈrär, bə-\. Historical region, cen. India, in SW part N of Hyderabad; 17,809 sq. mi. (46,125 sq. km.); ✻ Amravati; crossed by Ajanta Range; bordered on E by Wardha River and on S by the Penganga. Founded 1484, one of the five Muslim kingdoms of the Deccan (*q.v.*); lasted until 1572 when it became part of Mogul Empire; overrun by Marathas near end of 17th cent.; with help of British commander Arthur Wellesley (later duke of Wellington), territory W of Wardha River acquired by ruler of Hyderabad; taken over by British government as Assigned Districts of Hyderabad 1853; transferred to administration of Central Provinces 1903. In Madhya Pradesh 1947–56; in Bombay state 1956–60; in Maharashtra since 1960.

Be·rat \bə-ˈrät\; *formerly* **Be·rati** \-ˈrä-tē\. **1.** District of S cen. Albania. See table at ALBANIA.

2. Town, its ✻; pop. (1990e) 43,800; thought to be the site of ancient **An·ti·pa·tria** \ˌan-ti-ˈpa-trē-ə, -ˈpā-\.

Berau. See DOBERAI.

Be·rau Bay \bə-ˈrau̇\; *formerly* **Mc·Cluer Gulf** \mə-ˈklu̇r\. Inlet on NW coast of New Guinea I., Irian Jaya, Indonesia; 125 mi. (201 km.) long by 15 to 30 mi. (24 to 48 km.) wide; almost cuts off Doberai Penin. from rest of New Guinea, being separated on E from Teluk Cenderawasih by isthmus only ab. 15 mi. (24 km.) wide.

Beraun. See BEROUNKA.

Ber·ber \ˈbər-bər\. Town, NE Sudan, on E bank of the Nile River ab. 30 mi. (48 km.) N of Ed Damer; in earlier days starting point for caravans going across the Nubian Desert to Suakin; occupied by Mahdists 1884–97.

Ber·be·ra \ˈbər-bə-rə\. Seaport, Somalia, on S shore of Gulf of Aden; pop. (1985e) 70,000.

Ber·bé·ra·ti \ˌber-bə-ˈrä-tē\. Town, SW Central African Rep.; pop. (1988e) 45,432.

Ber·bice \ˌbər-ˈbēs\. River, E Guyana; flows N into Atlantic Ocean near New Amsterdam; 370 mi. (595 km.) long; navigable for 125 mi. (201 km.).

Ber·chem \ber-ˈshem, ˈber-kəm\. Former commune, N Belgium; a S suburb that became part of Antwerp 1983.

Berch·tes·ga·den \ˈberk-təs-ˌgäd-ᵊn\. Town, SE Bavaria, Germany, in E Bavarian Alps ab. 10 mi. (16 km.) S of Salzburg; pop. (1992e) 7865; alt. 1889 ft. (576 m.); resort; site of villa built as retreat for dictator Adolf Hitler to which he often retired during WWII; scene of important conferences. Bombed by Allies Apr. 1945 and occupied May 7.

Berck \ˈberk\. Commune, Pas-de-Calais dept., N France, on English Channel ab. 50 mi. (81 km.) WNW of Arras; resort.

Ber·di·chev \bir-ˈdē-chif\. City, S Zhytomyr subdivision, W cen. Ukraine, 22 mi. (35 km.) S of the city of Zhytomyr; pop. (1991e) 93,000; railroad junction; engineering works, sugar refinery; tanning, food processing; settled 15th cent.; assigned to Lithuania 1546 by treaty, to Poland 1569; to Russia 1793.

\ə\ abut \ə\ matches \ᵊ\ kitten, Fr table \ər\ further \a\ ash \ā\ ace \ä\ cot, cart \a̍\ Fr bac \au̇\ out \b\ Span Avila \ch\ chin \e\ bet \ē\ easy \g\ go \i\ hit \ī\ ice \j\ job \k\ Ger ich, Buch \ⁿ\ Fr vin \ŋ\ sing \ō\ go \ȯ\ all \ȯ\ law \œ\ Fr bœuf \œ̄\ Fr feu \ȯi\ boy \th\ thin \t͟h\ this \ü\ loot \u̇\ foot \ue\ Ger füllen \ue̅\ Fr rue \y\ yet \ʸ\ Fr digne \ˈdēnʸ\, nuit \ˈnwʸē\ \yü\ few \yu̇\ fury \zh\ vision

Berdsk \ˈbyertsk\. Town, Novosibirsk Oblast, Russia in Asia, 20 mi. (32 km.) SSE of the city of Novosibirsk; pop. (1991e) 81,000.

Ber·dyansk \bir-ˈdyänsk\; *formerly* **Osi·pen·ko** \ˌä-si-ˈpyeŋ-kə\. Seaport town, SE Zaporozhye region, SE Ukraine, on N shore of Sea of Azov 45 mi. (72 km.) SW of Mariapol; pop. (1991e) 135,000; has good harbor; fishing; flour; oil refining; resort; large salt lagoons in vicinity.

Be·rea \bə-ˈrē-ə\. **1.** City, Madison co., E cen. Kentucky, 28 mi. (45 km.) E of Danville; pop. (1990c) 9126; Berea Coll. (1855).
2. City, Cuyahoga co., N Ohio, 12 mi. (19 km.) SW of Cleveland; pop. (1990c) 19,051; Baldwin-Wallace Coll. (1845).
3. Town, Greece. See VEROIA.

Be·re·go·vo \ˌber-ə-ˈgȯ-və\ *or Hung.* **Be·reg·szász** \ˈber-ˌek-ˌsäs\. Town, Zakarpatska subdivision, Ukraine; a Hungarian town included 1918 in Czechoslovakia; returned to Hungary 1939–45.

Bere·ha·ven. See CASTLETOWNBERE.

Ber·e·ni·ce \ˌber-ə-ˈnī-sē\. **1.** Ruined city, SE Egypt, on a bay of the Red Sea; ancient seaport sheltered on N by Cape Banas; founded by Ptolemy II 3d cent. B.C.
2. City, Libya. See BENGHAZI 2.

Be·re·stech·ko \ˌber-i-ˈstyech-kə\ *or Pol.* **Be·re·stecz·ko** \-ˈstech-kȯ\. Village, NW Ukraine, ab. 30 mi. (48 km.) S of Lutsk; scene of defeat 1651 of Cossack hetman Bohdan Khmelnytsky by Poles.

Be·ret·tyó \ˈber-ə-ˌtyō\ *or Rom.* **Be·re·tăul** \ˌber-ə-ˈtəl\. River, E Hungary and W Romania; rises in W Transylvania, flows W and SW to the Körös; ab. 150 mi. (240 km.) long.

Be·ret·tyó·új·fa·lu \ˈber-ə-ˌtyō-ˈüi-ˌfȯ-lü\. Commune, E Hungary, S of Debrecen; pop. (1980p) 16,406.

Be·re·zha·ny \bər-ə-ˈzhä-nē\ *or Pol.* **Brze·ża·ny** \bə-zhə-ˈzhä-nē\. Town, W Ukraine, 30 mi. (48 km.) WSW of Ternopol; formerly in Poland.

Be·re·zi·na \bə-ˈrāz-ᵊn-ə, -ˈrez-\. River, Belarus; flows SE into Dnieper River W of Homyel'. 365 mi. (587 km.) long; drainage basin 9471 sq. mi. (24,530 sq. km.). Battle fought at the crossing of the river near Barysaw 1812 by French Emperor Napoléon's army in the retreat from Moscow, when three Russian armies inflicted enormous losses on it. In WWII scene of fierce fighting 1941 during German advance on Smolensk.

Be·rez·ni·ki \bi-riz-ni-ˈkē\. City, cen. Perm Oblast, E Russia in Europe, at foot of W slope of Ural Mts. on left bank of Kama River; pop. (1992e) 197,000.

Be·re·zo·vo \bir-ˈyȯ-zə-və\; *formerly* **Be·re·zov** \-zəf\. Town, Tyumen Oblast, NW Russia in Asia, on left bank of lower Ob River where the Sosva joins it; estab. as Cossack trading post 1593.

Berg \ˈberk\. Former duchy on the Rhine E of Cologne, Germany, bounded on N by duchy of Kleve and on W by Jülich; ab. 1120 sq. mi. (2900 sq. km.); made countship 1108, became duchy 1380; associated with Jülich 1423, with Kleve 1511; became part of Prussia 1815. See DÜSSELDORF.

Ber·ga·ma \ˈber-gä-mä\. Town, İzmir prov., W Turkey in Asia, 50 mi. (81 km.) N of İzmir.
History: Important city, ancient Mysia, Asia Minor, ✻ of the kingdom of Pergamum (*q.v.*) and for a time of the Roman province of Asia, ab. 18 mi. (29 km.) inland from Aeolis coast opp. Lesbos. Flourished for ab. four centuries as a political and cultural center of the East, rivaling Ephesus and Smyrna in importance. An early seat of Christianity and one of the Seven Churches; remained a center of commercial activity under Byzantine and Ottoman empires; modern excavations begun 1878.

Ber·ga·mo \ˈber-gä-ˌmō\. **1.** Province of Lombardy, N Italy. See table at ITALY.
2. *anc.* **Ber·go·mum** \ˈbər-gə-ˌməm\. Commune, its ✻, in foothills of Alps 30 mi. (48 km.) NE of Milan; pop. (1991p) 115,655; textiles, cement; 12th cent. Romanesque cathedral; ancient walls. Settled by Gauls; became Roman municipium under Gen. Julius Caesar; destroyed by Attila, king of the Huns; became Lombard duchy; ruled by the Visconti of Lombardy 1329–1428, by Venetian Republic 1428–1797; conquered by French Emperor Napoléon 1796; under Austrian rule 1814–59, when it became part of Italian kingdom.

Bergara. See VERGARA.

Ber·ge·dorf \ˈber-gə-ˌdȯrf\. Section of Hamburg, Germany, on branch of Elbe River; observatory. Made a city 1275; belonged to Lübeck and Hamburg 1420–1868; became part of Hamburg 1938.

Ber·gen \ˈbər-gən\. County in NE corner of New Jersey. See table at NEW JERSEY.

Bergen. See MONS.

Bergen *or* **Bergen auf Rü·gen** \ˈber-gən-aủf-ˈrue-gən, -ˈrü-\. Chief town of island of Rügen, Mecklenburg-West Pomerania state, NE Germany; fisheries.

Bergen \ˈbar-gən\. Seaport city, ⊗ of Hordaland co., SW Norway; pop. (1990c) 211,826; 2d largest city in Norway; formerly constituted a county; after Oslo, Norway's most important port; processing center for North Sea oil; shipbuilding; tourism; exports include fish; university (1948); founded 1070; N outpost of Hanseatic League in 15th and 16th cents.; cathedral dating from 12th cent.; damaged by fire 1702, 1855, 1916. Occupied by Germans 1940 and held until end of WWII.

Bergen–Belsen. See BELSEN.

Ber·gen·field \ˈbər-gən-ˌfēld\. Borough, Bergen co., NE corner of New Jersey, 9 mi. (15 km.) E of Paterson; pop. (1990c) 24,458.

Bergen op Zoom \ˈber-kə-ȯp-ˈzōm\. Commune, North Brabant prov., S Netherlands, at mouth of small stream (Zoom) on Schelde estuary; pop. (1992e) 47,259; captured by Normans in 880; resisted Spanish 16th cent.; taken and held by French 1795–1814; formerly strongly fortified.

Ber·ge·rac \ˌber-zhə-ˈråk\. Commune, Dordogne dept., SW cen. France, on Dordogne River 25 mi. (40 km.) SSW of Périgueux; pop. (1990c) 27,886; wine; 19th cent. Gothic church; captured by English 1345 and fortified; taken by French 1450.

Ber·gisch Glad·bach \ˈber-gish-ˈglät-ˌbäk\. City, North Rhine-Westphalia, W Germany, 9 mi. (15 km.) NE of Cologne; pop. (1992e) 104,470; papermaking; made city 1856.

Berg·ka·men \berk-ˈkä-mən\. City, North Rhine-Westphalia, W Germany, 10 mi. (16 km.) NE of Dortmund; pop. (1980c) 47,977; coal deposits.

Bergomum. See BERGAMO 2.

Bergues \ˈberg\. Town, Nord dept., N France, ab. 5 mi. (8 km.) S of Dunkerque; built as a frontier fortress and often besieged in Flemish wars.

Ber·ha·la Strait \bər-ˈhä-lə\. Channel bet. the island of Singkep, Lingga Archipelago, and the E cen. coast of Sumatra, Indonesia.

Berhampore. See BAHARAMPUR.

Berhampur. See BRAHMAPUR.

Ber·ing Glacier \ˈbir-iŋ, ˈbar-\. Glacier, Chugach-St. Elias Mts., S Alaska; 126 mi. (203 km.) long; ab. 30 mi. (48 km.) wide near terminus; largest glacier in North America.

Be·rin·gia \bə-ˈrin-jē-ə\ *or* **Bering Land Bridge.** Hypothetical land bridge believed to have once connected Siberia and Alaska; the exposed Bering and Chukchi seas.

Bering Island *or* **Be·rin·ga Island** \ˈber-ən-gə\. See KOMANDORSKIYE OSTROVA.

Bering Sea. Part of North Pacific Ocean; 885,000 sq. mi. (2,292,150 sq. km.); max. depth 15,659 ft. (4773 m.); enclosed on E by mainland of Alaska, on SE and S by Aleutian Is., on SW by Kamchatka Penin., and on NW by E Siberia; connects by Bering Strait with Arctic Ocean; contains St. Lawrence I., Nunivak I., Pribilof Is. (all U.S.) and Komandorskiye Ostrova (Russia); latter two groups famous as fur-seal breeding grounds; receives Yukon River; crossed diagonally by International Date Line. Explorations of its waters and of Bering Strait 1728 and 1741 by Danish navigator Vitus Bering in employ of Russia formed chief basis for Russian claims to Alaska. Bering Sea Dispute bet. Great Britain and U.S. 1886–93 settled by court of arbitration at Paris 1893 in favor of Great Britain, denying U.S. the right to prohibit pelagic hunting of fur seals in Bering Sea. Subsequent arrangements for sealing restrictions made among interested parties, incl. U.S., Canada, and Japan, throughout 20th cent.

Bering Strait. Strait connecting Arctic Ocean and Bering Sea (*q.v.*), and separating Asia (Russia) from North America (Alaska); at narrowest point 53 mi. (85 km.) wide; Diomede Is. (*q.v.*) in middle. A drop in sea level during the Ice Age is believed to have exposed a land bridge (Beringia) connecting Asia and North America. Strait traversed by Danish navigator Vitus Bering 1728.

Be·ris·so \bā-ˈrēs-sō\. Town, Buenos Aires prov., Argentina, 5 mi. (8 km.) NE of La Plata.

Ber·ja \ˈber-ˌhä\. Commune, Almería prov., SE Spain, 20 mi. (32 km.) W of Almería; pop. (1991c) 12,054; viticulture; lead deposits.

Berke·ley \ˈbər-klē\. **1.** Name of counties in two states of the U.S. See tables at SOUTH CAROLINA and WEST VIRGINIA.

2. City, Alameda co., W California, on San Francisco Bay N of Oakland; pop. (1990c) 102,724; atomic research center nearby; Pacific School of Religion (1866), Univ. of California at Berkeley (1868), Armstrong Coll. (1918). Founded 1853; incorp. as city 1909; most of N section of city destroyed by fire 1923 and since rebuilt.

3. Village, Cook co., NE Illinois, 14 mi. (23 km.) W of Chicago; pop. (1990c) 5137.

4. City, St. Louis co., E Missouri, NW suburb of the city of St. Louis; pop. (1990c) 12,450; incorp. as a city 1937.

5. Plantation on left bank of the James River, Charles City co., E Virginia, at **Har·ri·son's Landing** \ˈhar-i-sənz\; birthplace (c. 1726) of Benjamin Harrison, signer of the Declaration of Independence, and (1773) of William Henry Harrison, 9th president of the U.S.; plundered by American traitor Benedict Arnold 1781; base for Union army after Malvern Hill battle July 1862.

Berkeley Springs *or legally* **Bath** \ˈbath, ˈbäth\. Town and health resort, ⊗ of Morgan co., NE West Virginia, near Potomac River 18 mi. (29 km.) NW of Martinsburg; pop. (1990c) 735.

Berk·ham·sted \ˈbər-kəm-sted, ˈbär-, -stid\; *formerly* **Great Berkhampstead.** Town, Hertfordshire, SE England, on Grand Union Canal 26 mi. (42 km.) NW of London; pop. (1981p) 15,461; remains of 11th cent. castle; birthplace of poet William Cowper 1731.

Berk·ley \ˈbər-klē\. **1.** Town, Bristol co., Massachusetts, at mouth of Taunton River, 4 mi. (6 km.) S of Taunton; pop. (1990c) 4237.

2. Residential city, Oakland co., SE Michigan, 12 mi. (19 km.) SSE of Pontiac; pop. (1990c) 16,960.

Berk·ner Island \ˈbərk-nər, ˈberk-\. Ice-covered island bet. Ronne Ice Shelf and Filchner Ice Shelf, Antarctica, S of Weddell Sea; ab. 230 mi. (370 km.) long and 90 mi. (140 km.) wide.

Berks \ˈbərks\. **1.** County in SE Pennsylvania. See table at PENNSYLVANIA.

2. \ˈbärks\. County in England. See BERKSHIRE 2, 3.

Berk·shire \ˈbərk-ˌshir, -shər\. **1.** County in W Massachusetts. See table at MASSACHUSETTS.

2. \ˈbärk-\ *or* **Berks** \ˈbärks\. Former county, S England; largely in the Thames River basin.

3. *or* **Berks.** Administrative county, S England, part of the former county; estab. 1974. See table at ENGLAND.

Berkshire Hills *or commonly* **Berk·shires** \ˈbərk-ˌshirz, -shərz\. Highlands in Berkshire co., W Massachusetts; highest peak Mt. Greylock 3491 ft. (1064 m.).

Bêrlad. See BÎRLAD.

Ber·len·ga \bər-ˈleŋ-gə\ *or* **Ber·len·gas Islands** \bər-ˈleŋ-gəsh\. Group of small islands off W coast of Portugal, 39°25′N; lighthouse.

Ber·lin \ˈbər-lən, -ˌlin\. **1.** Town, S Hartford co., cen. Connecticut, 11 mi. (18 km.) SSW of the city of Hartford; pop. (1990c) 16,787.

2. City, Coos co., N New Hampshire, in White Mts., at confluence of Dead and Androscoggin rivers 17 mi. (27 km.) S of Umbagog Lake; pop. (1990c) 11,824; fish hatchery nearby; winter sports.

3. Borough, Camden co., SW New Jersey, 15 mi. (24 km.) SE of the city of Camden; pop. (1990c) 5672.

4. City, Green Lake and Waushara cos., cen. Wisconsin, 20 mi. (32 km.) W of Oshkosh; pop. (1990c) 5371.

5. City, Canada. See KITCHENER.

6. Town, Eastern Cape prov., S Rep. of South Africa, 20 mi. (32 km.) WNW of East London; resort.

Berlin \ber-ˈlēn, bər-ˈlin\. City, comprising a state of Germany; served as national ✻ before 1945; partitioned into East Berlin and West Berlin 1945–90; official ✻ of reunified Germany since 1990 (see table at GERMANY); Charlottenburg Palace; Brandenburg Gate; German Academy of Science (1700); Humboldt Univ. (1810); several museums; Berlin Zoo.

History: Kölln and Berlin, both Wendish villages, founded in early 13th cent.; member of Hanseatic League 14th cent.; united under name of Berlin, it became residence of Hohenzollerns and ✻ of Brandenburg (*q.v.*); from 1701 ✻ of kingdom of Prussia (*q.v.*); grew to be industrial and commercial center, esp. under Frederick the Great (1740–86); entered by Austrians 1757 and by Russians 1760; occupied by French under Emperor Napoléon, who issued there the Berlin decree 1806; ✻ of German Empire 1871–1918, of Weimar Republic 1919–32, of Third Reich 1933–45; scene of Congress of Berlin 1878 and of Berlin Conference 1885; site of Summer Olympic Games 1936; much of city destroyed by Allied bombing 1941 and 1943–45; occupied by Soviet troops Apr.–May 1945; divided June 1945 into four occupation zones (American, British, French, and Soviet); Allied powers integrated their parts of city into one economic entity 1948; Soviets responded with blockade of W section of city, causing Allied powers to initiate airlift to supply area; blockade ended 1949; on setting up of independent governments in E and W Germany 1949, West Berlin became part of West Germany (made a state 1950 but not formally incorp.), and East Berlin was made ✻ of East Germany; continuing emigration through 1950s from Soviet East Berlin prompted erection of Berlin Wall 1961 dividing East Berlin from West Berlin; agreement among occupying powers early 1970s led to some regulation of border crossings; political unrest led to opening of wall Nov. 1989 and subsequent dismantling; reunified Berlin became official ✻ of reunified Germany 1990; provisions made to transfer government apparatus from Bonn to proceed over a number of years.

Berlin, East. Former city, ✻ of East Germany 1945–90 constituted a district of East Germany; see BERLIN.

Ber·lin, Mount \ˈbər-lin\. Peak, N Nye co., cen. Nevada; 9081 ft. (2768 m.).

Berlin, West. Former city, an exclave of West Germany lying wholly within East Germany; 185 sq. mi. (479 sq. km.); enjoyed close political, economic, and cultural ties with West Germany (but was not a constitutional part of West Germany); see BERLIN.

Berlin Wall. Former barrier, bet. East Germany and West Berlin, West Germany, N cen. Europe; constructed Aug. 1961 to stem the flow of emigrants out of East Germany; dismantled upon reunification of East Germany and West Germany 1990.

Ber·me·jo \ber-ˈmā-hō\ *also* **Ver·me·jo** *same*\. River, N Argentina; rises on the Bolivian frontier and flows SE into Paraguay River on the Paraguay-Argentina boundary; 650 mi. (1046 km.) long; its middle course known as the Teuco.

Ber·meo \ber-ˈmā-ō, -ˈmeu̇\. Commune, Vizcaya prov., N Spain, on Bay of Biscay 15 mi. (24 km.) NE of Bilbao; pop. (1991c) 17,923.

Ber·mu·da \bər-ˈmyü-də\ *also* **Bermuda Islands** *or* **Ber·mu·das** \-dəz\; *formerly* **Som·ers Islands** \ˈsə-mərz-\.

British colony comprising a group of about 300 islands (of which only some 20 are inhabited), in W North Atlantic Ocean ab. 640 mi. (1030 km.) ESE of Cape Hatteras; 20 sq. mi. (52 sq. km.); pop. (1994e) 61,700; principal island **Bermuda Island** *also called* **Great Bermuda** *or* **Long Island;** ✻ Hamilton, on Bermuda I.; tourism.

History: Visited by Spanish 1515 and named for Juan de Bermúdez who may have visited 1503; English called them Somers Is. after Sir George Somers who was forced to land there while on his way to Virginia 1609; first colonized by English (sent by members of Virginia Company) on St. George's I. 1612; settled and governed under the Somers Island Company 1615–84; taken over by British crown 1684; ✻ removed from St. George to Hamilton 1815; sites for military and naval bases leased to U.S. 1940; adopted new constitution 1968.

Bermuda Hundred. Village, Chesterfield co., SE cen. Virginia, on a peninsula bet. James and Appomattox rivers; orig. a settlement of Jamestown colony 1613; a Union base in Gen. Ulysses S. Grant's campaign against Richmond 1864.

Bermuda Triangle. Triangular area in North Atlantic Ocean bet. Bermuda, Florida, and Puerto Rico; site of numerous reported disappearances of planes and ships.

Bern *also* **Berne** \ˈbern, ˈbərn\. **1.** Canton, Switzerland. See table at SWITZERLAND.

2. City, ✻ of Switzerland and of Bern canton, on Aare River 59 mi. (95 km.) SW of Zürich; pop. (1989c) 135,825; pharmaceuticals, textiles, chocolate; university (1528, university status 1834); national library; 15th cent. Gothic cathedral; 15th cent. Gothic town hall; hall of Swiss Federal Council; headquarters of Universal Postal Union (founded 1874).

History: Founded as military post by Duke Berchtold V of Zäringen 1191; became free imperial city 1218; achieved final independence 1339; entered Swiss Confederation 1353 (see SWITZERLAND); accepted Reformation 1528; became powerful in 18th cent. when it ruled Vaud, Fribourg, Aargau, and the region of the Bernese Alps; after French occupation 1798, made member of Helvetic Republic; made ✻ of Switzerland 1848.

Ber·nal Hill \bər-ˈnäl\. Peak, SW San Miguel co., NE cen. New Mexico; 7020 ft. (2140 m.).

Ber·na·lil·lo \ˌbər-nə-ˈlē-yō\. **1.** County in cen. New Mexico. See table at NEW MEXICO.

2. Town, ⊗ of Sandoval co., NW cen. New Mexico, on the Rio Grande 12 mi. (19 km.) N of Albuquerque; pop. (1990c) 5960; inhabited by Pueblo Indians long before coming of the Spanish; approx. site of Spanish explorer Francisco Coronado's headquarters 1540–42; settled by Europeans 1698.

Ber·nam \ˈber-ˌnäm\. River on boundary bet. S Perak and N Selangor states, Malaysia; flows W into the Strait of Malacca; ab. 120 mi. (195 km.) long; navigable for over 100 mi. (161 km.).

Ber·nards·ville \ˈbər-nərdz-ˌvil\. Borough, Somerset co., N cen. New Jersey, 8 mi. (13 km.) SW of Morristown; pop. (1990c) 6597.

Ber·nay \ber-ˈnā\. Commune, Eure dept., France, 25 mi. (40 km.) WNW of Évreux; grew up around Benedictine abbey (founded 1013).

Bern·burg \ˈbern-ˌbu̇rk\. City, Saxony-Anhalt, cen. Germany, on Saale River 22 mi. (35 km.) W of Dessau; pop. (1992e) 39,006. Fortified town in 10th cent.; ✻ of duchy of Anhalt-Bernburg.

Berne \ˈbərn\. **1.** City, Adams co., E Indiana, 32 mi. (52 km.) S of Fort Wayne; pop. (1990c) 3559; founded 1852 by Mennonite immigrants from Bern, Switzerland; official publishing house for the Mennonite General Conference.

2. See BERN.

Ber·ne·ray \ˈbər-nə-ˌrā\. See BARRA.

Ber·nese Alps \bər-ˈnēz, -ˈnēs\ *or* **Bernese Ober·land** \ˈō-bər-ˌlänt\; *Ger.* **Ber·ner Al·pen** *or* **Berner Oberland** \ˌber-nər-ˈäl-pən\. See OBERLAND and table at ALPS.

Ber·ni·cia \bər-ˈni-shə, -shē-ə\. Kingdom, of Anglo-Saxon England, located bet. Tyne and Forth, with ✻ at Bamborough; by 7th cent. united with Deira (*q.v.*) to form kingdom of Northumbria (*q.v.*).

Ber·ni·er \ˈbər-nē-ər\. Island off W coast of Western Australia, Australia, at entrance to Shark Bay, 24°52′S, 113°08′E.

Ber·ni·na \ber-ˈnē-nə\. S extension of the Rhaetian Alps, on border bet. Italy and Switzerland; its highest peak and the highest in the Rhaetian Alps is **Piz Bernina** \ˈpēts\ *or* **Piz·zo Bernina** \ˈpēt-sō\ on the Italian border but in Switzerland. **Bernina Pass** is E of the peak. See table at ALPS.

Bern·kas·tel–Kues \ˈbern-ˌkäst-ᵊl-ˈküs\; *formerly* **Bernkastel.** Town, Rhineland-Palatinate, W Germany, on the Mosel 21 mi. (34 km.) NE of Trier; pop. (1992e) 7026; tourism; white wine (Bernkasteler); received charter 1291.

Beroea. 1. Town, Greece. See VEROIA.

2. Town, West Bank. See AL BĪRAH.

3. City, Syria. See ALEPPO 2.

Be·roun·ka \ˈber-au̇n-ˌkä\ *or Ger.* **Be·raun** \ˈbā-ˌrau̇n\. River, W Czech Republic; formed by union of several streams near Plzeň, flows E into Vltava River; ab. 140 mi. (225 km.) long.

Berre, Étang de \ā-ˌtäⁿ-də-ˈber\. Lagoon, S Bouches-du-Rhône dept., S France, E of the Rhone River; 13 mi. (21 km.) long, 3 to 8 mi. (5 to 13 km.) wide; has narrow outlet to Gulf of Lion.

Ber·ri·en \ˈber-ē-ən\. Name of counties in two states of the U.S. See tables at GEORGIA and MICHIGAN.

Berrien Springs. Village, Berrien co., SW Michigan, 47 mi. (76 km.) WSW of Kalamazoo; pop. (1990c) 1927; Andrews Univ. (1874).

Ber·ry *also* **Ber·ri** \be-ˈrē\. Historical region of cen. France, bounded anciently on N by Orléanais, on E by Nivernais, on SE by Bourbonnais, on SW by Marche, and on W by Touraine; ✻ Bourges. Orig. inhabited by the Bituriges Cubi who opposed Vercingetorix, Gallic chief of the Arverni; under Romans was part of Aquitania Prima; countship in Carolingian period; fell to crown in 11th cent.; made duchy 1360; returned to French crown 1601; province to 1789.

Ber·ry–au–Bac \be-ˌrē-ō-ˈbäk\. Village, Aisne dept., N France, 11 mi. (18 km.) NW of Reims; crossing of Aisne River here frequently of importance in WWI, esp. in Chemin des Dames battles 1917–18.

Berry Islands \ˈber-ē\. Group of small islands in Bahamas, N of Andros I.; 20 sq. mi. (52 sq. km.).

Ber·ry·ville \ˈber-ē-ˌvil, -vəl\. **1.** City, a ⊗ of Carroll co., NW Arkansas; pop. (1990c) 3212.

2. Town, ⊗ of Clarke co., N Virginia; pop. (1990c) 3097.

Ber·si·mis \ˌber-si-ˈmē\. River, tributary of the St. Lawrence River in Quebec, Canada; flows SSE; enters the St. Lawrence NE of Tadoussac; ab. 240 mi. (385 km.) long.

Ber·thier·ville \ˌber-tyā-ˈvēl\ *also* **Berthier.** Town, Quebec, Canada, on St. Lawrence River 37 mi. (60 km.) WSW of Trois-Riviéres; pop. (1990c) 3854.

Ber·thoud \ˈbər-thəd\. Town, Larimer co., N Colorado, 40 mi. (64 km.) N of Denver; pop. (1990c) 2990.

Ber·thoud Pass \ˌbər-thəd\. Mountain pass, Clear Creek and Grand cos., N Colorado, in Front Range of the Rocky Mts.; 11,315 ft. (3449 m.); ski runs; highway.

Ber·tie \bər-ˈtē, ˈbər-ˌ\. County in NE North Carolina. See table at NORTH CAROLINA.

Ber·tin·court \ˌber-ˌteⁿ-ˈkür\. Village, Pas-de-Calais dept., N France, ab. 6 mi. (10 km.) E of Bapaume. Fighting Mar. 1917 and Mar. 1918 in WWI.

Be·ru \ˈbā-rü\. Island (atoll) in S Gilbert Is., Kiribati, S of the Equator, W Pacific Ocean; 11 mi. (18 km.) long.

Ber·wick \ˈbər-wik\. **1.** Town, St. Mary parish, S Louisiana, 53 mi. (85 km.) S of Baton Rouge; pop. (1990c) 4375; fishing center.

2. Town, York co., SW Maine, on New Hampshire border 25 mi. (40 km.) SW of Biddeford; pop. (1990c) 5995.

3. Borough, Columbia co., E cen. Pennsylvania, on Susquehanna River 23 mi. (37 km.) WSW of Wilkes-Barre; pop. (1990c) 10,976; founded 1786.

4. City, S Victoria, Australia, a SE suburb of Melbourne; pop. (1991c) 69,144.

Ber·wick \ˈber-ik\ *or* **Ber·wick·shire** \-ˌshir, -shər\. Former county, SE Scotland. ⊗ Duns.

Berwick–upon–Tweed \ˈber-ik … ˈtwēd\. Town, Northumberland, N England, on North Sea at mouth of the Tweed near

Scottish border; pop. (1981p) 12,169; herring and salmon fishing; English from 1482.

Ber·wyn \ˈbər-ˌwin, -wən\. Residential city, Cook co., NE Illinois, just W of Cicero; pop. (1990c) 45,426.

Berwyn Heights. Town, Prince Georges co., S cen. Maryland, 8 mi. (13 km.) NE of Washington, D.C.; pop. (1990c) 2952.

Ber·wyn Mountains \ˈber-wən\. Range in N Wales, where Clwyd, Gwynedd, and Powys cos. come together; highest point Moel Sych 2713 ft. (827 m.).

Berytus. See BEIRUT.

Be·san·çon \bə-zäⁿ-ˈsōⁿ, bə-ˈzan-sən\; *anc.* **Ve·son·tio** \və-ˈzän-shē-ˌō\. City, ✻ of Doubs dept., E France, 47 mi. (76 km.) E of Dijon; pop. (1990c) 119,194; watch and clock industry; textiles, paper; university (1422); citadel by military engineer Sébastien de Vauban; school of artillery; Roman ruins, incl. triumphal arch of Emperor Marcus Aurelius, aqueduct, and amphitheater; captured by Gen. Julius Caesar 58 B.C.; became ✻ of Franche-Comté 1676.

Besi. See SANANA 1.

Be·şik·taş \be-ˈshēk-ˌtäsh\. District of İstanbul, Turkey in Europe, on the Bosporus NE of Beyoğlu.

Bes·kids, East *and* **West Beskids** \ˈbes-ˌkidz, be-ˈskēdz\. Mountain ranges, W Carpathians, on N boundary of Slovakia; highest peak Babia Góra, in West Beskids; 5659 ft. (1725 m.).

Bes·ni \bes-ˈnē\; *formerly* **Be·his·ni** \ˌbā-his-ˈnē\. Town, S Turkey in Asia, in mountains 53 mi. (85 km.) ENE of Maraş.

Besoeki. See BESUKI.

Bes·sa·ra·bia \ˌbe-sə-ˈrā-bē-ə\. **1.** Region of SE Europe, bet. Dniester and Prut rivers extending from Black Sea N to Poland. In Roman times a part of the colony of Dacia; later a borderland overrun by barbarian migrations; named after Basarab dynasty of Walachia, 14th cent. A.D.; became part of principality of Moldavia (*q.v.*) 15th cent.; fought over by Turks and Russians 1711–1812; ceded by Turkey to Russia 1812; part yielded 1856 to Moldavia after Crimean War but most of it recovered by Russia 1878 by Treaty of Berlin; formed a government under Russia 1812–1917 (17,147 sq. mi. or 44,411 sq. km.; ✻ Kishinev).

2. *or Rom.* **Ba·sa·ra·bia** \ˌbä-sə-ˈrä-byə\. Former province, E Romania; 17,151 sq. mi. (44,421 sq. km.); ✻ Chişinău (Kishinev). Proclaimed independence from Russia as Moldavian Republic (*q.v.*) 1917; joined Romania 1918 and recognized as Romanian by Treaty of Versailles 1919 but still claimed by U.S.S.R. Seized by U.S.S.R. June 1940; with Bukovina most of the area incorp. Aug. 1940 as Moldavian Federal Soviet Rep., renamed the Moldavian S.S.R. (*q.v.*), with a smaller part being incorp. in Ukrainian S.S.R. (*q.v.*), both parts of the U.S.S.R. Retaken by Germans and Romanians June 1941; recovered by U.S.S.R. 1944; returned to former S.S.R. status; for later information on the area see MOLDOVA and UKRAINE.

Bes·se·mer \ˈbe-sə-mər\. **1.** City, Jefferson co., Alabama, SW of Birmingham; pop. (1990c) 33,497.

2. City, ⊗ of Gogebic co., NW Upper Michigan Penin., 5 mi. (8 km.) E of Ironwood; pop. (1990c) 2272; area with iron deposits.

Bessemer City. City, Gaston co., SW North Carolina, 7 mi. (11 km.) W of Gastonia; pop. (1990c) 4698.

Be·su·ki *or Du.* **Be·soe·ki** \bā-ˈsü-kē\. Former residency, Java, Netherlands Indies; 3913 sq. mi. (10,135 sq. km.); ✻ Bondowoso; included E end of Java bet. Madura Strait on the N, Indian Ocean on the S; now part of the Indonesian prov. of East Java.

Besztercze. See BISTRIŢA 2.

Beszterczebánya. See BANSKÁ BYSTRICA.

Bet Guvrin. See ELEUTHEROPOLIS.

Beth·al \ˈbe-thəl\. Town, NE cen. Rep. of South Africa, ESE of Johannesburg.

Be·thal·to \bə-ˈthȯl-tō\. Village, Madison co., SW Illinois, 23 mi. (37 km.) NNE of East St. Louis; pop. (1990c) 9507.

Beth·a·ny \ˈbe-thə-nē\. **1.** Town, New Haven co., S Connecticut, 9 mi. (15 km.) NW of the city of New Haven; pop. (1990c) 4608.

2. City, ⊗ of Harrison co., N Missouri, 43 mi. (69 km.) NW of Chillicothe; pop. (1990c) 3005.

3. City, Oklahoma co., cen. Oklahoma, 7 mi. (11 km.) W of Oklahoma City; pop. (1990c) 20,075; Southern Nazarene Univ. (1899), Southwestern Coll. of Christian Ministries (1946).

4. Town, Brooke co., N West Virginia, ab. 12 mi. (19 km.) NE of Wheeling; pop. (1990c) 1139; Bethany Coll. (1840).

5. Village, Jordan. See AL-ʻAYZARĪYAH.

Beth·el \ˈbe-thəl\. **1.** Division in Alaska. See table at ALASKA.

2. City, W Alaska, near mouth of Kuskokwim River; pop. (1990c) 4674; began as a Moravian mission 1885.

3. Town, N cen. Fairfield co., SW Connecticut; pop. (1990c) 17,541.

4. Town, Oxford co., W Maine, 36 mi. (58 km.) WNW of Lewiston; pop. (1990c) 2329; alt. ab. 700 ft. (215 m.); in the Rangeley Lakes region; resort.

5. Town, Sullivan co., SE New York, W of Monticello; pop. (1990c) 3693; site of Woodstock music festival 1969.

6. Ancient city of Palestine now an archaeological site and village (*Arab.* **Bay·tīn** \bā-ˈtēn\), Jordan, in area occupied by Israel 1967, ab. 11 mi. (18 km.) N of Jerusalem; in early history of Israel considered a holy place (*Gen.* xii. 8; xxviii. 19).

Bethel Park. Borough, Allegheny co., Pennsylvania, S of Pittsburgh; pop. (1990c) 33,823.

Be·thes·da \bə-ˈthez-də\. Unincorporated settlement, Montgomery co., cen. Maryland, N of Washington, D.C.; pop. (1990c) 62,936; National Naval Medical Center, National Institutes of Health.

Beth–ho·ron, Lower *and* **Upper Beth–horon** \beth-ˈhōr-ən\. Twin towns, in mountain pass, ancient Palestine, ab. 11 mi. (18 km.) NW of Jerusalem; in Old Testament times a strategic place where there were often conflicts (*Josh.* x. 11; *1 Kings* ix. 17).

Bé·thin·court \ˌbā-ˌteⁿ-ˈkür\. Village, Meuse dept., NE France, 6 mi. (10 km.) NW of Verdun; held by Germans in siege of Verdun in WWI, 1916–17.

Beth·le·hem \ˈbeth-li-ˌhem, -lē-əm\. **1.** City, Lehigh and Northampton cos., E Pennsylvania, on Lehigh River 5 mi. (8 km.) E of Allentown; pop. (1990c) 71,428; formerly a major steel-producing center; Lehigh Univ. (1865), Moravian Coll. (1807), Northampton County Area Community Coll. (1966); founded by Moravians 1741; housed hospital for Continental soldiers during Revolution; incorp. as borough 1845; became city 1917. Music center (home of annual Bach festival); chief center of Moravian sect in U.S.

2. *or Arab.* **Bayt Laḥm** \bāt-ˈlä-k̲əm\. Town, Jordan, 5 mi. (8 km.) SSW of Jerusalem, Israel, in area occupied by Israel 1967; pop. (1987e) 34,180; ancient town of Judaea, the early home of King David. Regarded by Christendom as the site of the Nativity; under Israeli-Palestinian self-rule agreement turned over to Palestine Dec. 24, 1995.

3. Town, E cen. Rep. of South Africa, 150 mi. (241 km.) ENE of Bloemfontein; pop. (1985c) 12,871; railroad center; in fertile agricultural region; mountain scenery.

Beth·page \beth-ˈpāj\. Unincorporated settlement, Nassau co., New York, in cen. Long Island S of Hicksville; pop. (incl. Old Bethpage; 1990c) 15,761.

Beth·sa·i·da of Galilee \beth-ˈsā-ə-də … ˈga-lə-ˌlē, ˌga-lə-ˈ\ *or* **Bethsaida of Gau·lo·ni·tis** \ˌgȯ-lə-ˈnī-tis\ *also* **Bethsaida Ju·li·as** \ˈjü-lē-əs\. Ancient city, thought to have been in Galilee; its site disputed.

Bé·thune \bā-ˈtu̇en, -ˈtyün\. Commune, Pas-de-Calais dept., N France, 17 mi. (27 km.) NNW of Arras; pop. (1990c) 25,261; coal deposits. During WWI held by British and several times attacked, esp. Apr. 1918; heavily damaged in both WWI and WWII.

Be·tio \ˈbā-chē-ˌō\. Islet and village, S end of Tarawa (*q.v.*) Atoll, Kiribati, W Pacific Ocean.

Bet·pak–Da·la \ˌbyet-ˌpäk-də-ˈlä\ *also* **Go·lod·na·ya Steppe**

\gə-ˈlȯd-nə-yə\ *or* **Hun·ger·steppe** \ˈhəŋ-gər-ˌstep\. Desert region in SE Kazakhstan, W of Lake Balkhash; ab. 300 mi. (485 km.) wide; bordered on NW by Sarysu River.

Bet She'·an \ˌbāt-shə-ˈän\; *Arab.* **Bay·sān** *also* **Bei·sān** \bā-ˈsän\; *anc.* **Scy·thop·o·lis** \si-ˈthä-pə-lis\. Town, Northern District, Israel, W of the Jordan River ab. 18 mi. (29 km.) SE of Nazareth; pop. (1992e) 14,100. Site of settlement of Early Bronze Age (c. 3000–2000 B.C.) and rich in archaeological material of the pre-Israelite period; important in Hittite and early Egyptian history; important also in ancient Roman times; fell to Arabs 636 A.D. One of the 10 cities of Decapolis.

Bet She·mesh \ˌbāt-ˈshe-ˌmesh\. Urban settlement, Israel, ab. 15 mi. (24 km.) W of Jerusalem; next to an archaeological site having same name; ancient settlement built bet. 2400 and 2100 B.C., destroyed by Babylonian King Nebuchadrezzar II 6th cent. B.C.

Bet·si·bo·ka \ˌbet-sē-ˈbō-kä\. River, cen. Madagascar, flowing N into Bombetoka Bay.

Bet·ten·dorf \ˈbet-ᵊn-ˌdȯrf\. City, Scott co., E Iowa, on Mississippi 5 mi. (8 km.) E of Davenport; pop. (1990c) 28,132; Scott Community Coll. (1966).

Bet·ti·ah \ˈbe-tē-ə\. Town, NW Bihar, NE India, 100 mi. (161 km.) NNW of Patna; pop. (1991p) 92,583.

Be·tul \ˈbā-ˌtül\; *formerly* **Bad·nur** \ˈbäd-ˌnu̇r\. Town, Madhya Pradesh, cen. India, 103 mi. (166 km.) SSE of Bhopal; pop. (1991p) 63,489.

Bet·wa \ˈbā-ˌtwä\. River, cen. India; rises in W Madhya Pradesh, flows NE and E into Yamuna River near Hamirpur; 360 mi. (579 km.) long; feeds large irrigation system.

Bet·wys y Coed \ˌbe-təs-ē-ˈkȯid\. Resort village, Gwynedd co., NW Wales, on the Conway River ab. 16 mi. (26 km.) S of Llandudno; pop. (1981p) 658; in beautiful glen and river scenery; tourist and artist center.

Beu·el \ˈbȯi-əl\; *formerly* **Vi·lich** \ˈfē-lik\. Former city, North Rhine-Westphalia, W Germany, on Rhine River; since 1969 part of Bonn.

Beu·lah \ˈbyü-lə\. Village, ⊗ of Benzie co., NW Michigan; pop. (1990c) 421.

Beu·ron \ˈbȯi-ˌrōn\. Village and monastery, Baden-Württemberg, S Germany, on the N bank of the Danube ab. 8 mi. (13 km.) NE of Tuttlingen; pop. (1980c) 1198; monastery founded 1077 by Augustinians, secularized 1802, taken over by Benedictines 1863; library.

Beuthen. See BYTOM.

Be·ve·land \ˈbā-və-ˌlänt\. Peninsula, Zeeland prov., Netherlands; formerly comprised two islands, **North Beveland** (35 sq. mi. or 91 sq. km.) and **South Beveland** (144 sq. mi. or 373 sq. km.), in the estuary of the Schelde River, separated by narrow channel. In WWII South Beveland occupied by Allies Oct. 1944.

Be·ve·ren \ˈbā-və-rən\. Commune, East Flanders prov., NW cen. Belgium, 6 mi. (10 km.) N of Antwerp; pop. (1981c) 40,857.

Bev·er·ley \ˈbe-vər-lē\. Town, Humberside, N England, 7 mi. (11 km.) NNW of Hull; pop. (1991p) 109,500; received first charter 1129.

Bev·er·ly \ˈbe-vər-lē\. **1.** City, Essex co., NE corner of Massachusetts, 16 mi. (26 km.) NE of Boston; pop. (1990c) 39,195.

2. City, Burlington co., S cen. New Jersey, on Delaware River 13 mi. (21 km.) NE of Camden; pop. (1990c) 2973.

Beverly Hills. **1.** Residential city, Los Angeles co., SW California, W suburb of the city of Los Angeles; pop. (1990c) 31,971.

2. Village, Oakland co., SE Michigan, S of Pontiac; pop. (1990c) 10,610.

Be·ver·wijk \ˈbā-vər-ˌvīk\. Commune, North Holland prov., W Netherlands, NW of Amsterdam; pop. (1981e) 35,220.

Bew·cas·tle \ˈbyü-ˌka-səl\. Village, Cumbria, NW England, 10 mi. (16 km.) NE of Brampton; has remarkable cross of 7th or 8th cent., with runic inscriptions.

Bex \ˈbe\. Commune, Vaud canton, W Switzerland, near the Rhone SE of E end of Lake Geneva; pop. (1980c) 4843; salt deposits, brine baths.

Bexar \ˈbar\. County in S cen. Texas. See table at TEXAS.

Bex·hill \ˌbeks-ˈhil\. Town and resort, East Sussex, S England, on English Channel; pop. (1981p) 35,529.

Bex·ley \ˈbek-slē\. **1.** City, Franklin co., cen. Ohio, surrounded by Columbus; pop. (1990c) 13,088.

2. Borough of Greater London, SE England. See table at LONDON 4.

Bey Dağ·la·rı \ˈbā-ˌdä-glä-ˈrē\. Mountain range in SW Turkey in Asia, W of the Gulf of Antalya; highest point Akdağ 10,125 ft. (3086 m.).

Bey·koz \bā-ˈkȯz\. Town, NW Turkey in Asia, on E shore of the Bosporus N of Üsküdar.

Bey·o·ğlu \ˌbā-ō-ˈglü\; *formerly* **Pe·ra** \ˈper-ə\. District of İstanbul, Turkey in Europe; the section N of the Golden Horn.

Bey·pa·za·rı \ˌbā-ˌpä-zä-ˈrə\; *formerly* **Bei·ba·zar** \ˌbā-bä-ˈzär\ *also* **Bai·ba·zar** \ˌbā-i-bä-ˈzär\. Town, W cen. Turkey in Asia, 60 mi. (97 km.) W of Ankara; historically noted for its fruit; important under the Byzantine emperors.

Beyrouth. See BEIRUT.

Bey·şe·hir \ˌbā-she-ˈhir\. Town, SW cen. Turkey in Asia, on SE shore of Lake Beyşehir.

Beyşehir Lake *or Turk.* **Beyşehir Gö·lü** \gœ-ˈlue\. Lake, SW cen. Turkey in Asia, W of Konya; 35 mi. (56 km.) long; 250 sq. mi. (648 sq. km.).

Be·zen·gi \bə-ˈzeŋ-gē\. Glacier, Kabardino-Balkaria, Russia in Europe; 8 mi. (13 km.) long, .5 mi. (.8 km.) wide near its terminus.

Be·zhi·tsa \ˈbye-zhət-sə\; *during WWII until Jan. 1944* **Or·dzho·ni·kid·ze·grad** \ˌȯr-ˌjä-nə-ˈkid-zə-ˌgräd\. Former town, Bryansk Oblast, Russian S.F.S.R., U.S.S.R.; incorp. into the city of Bryansk 1956.

Bé·ziers \bā-ˈzyā\; *anc.* **Bae·ter·rae** \bē-ˈter-ē\. City, Herault dept., S France, 38 mi. (61 km.) SW of Montpellier; pop. (1990c) 72,362; regional trade center; surrounded by old walls; 12th cent. Gothic cathedral. Ancient Gallic fortress; captured by Romans 120 B.C.; massacre 1209 of 20,000 inhabitants for having harbored (1200) the Albigenses; episcopal see to 1790.

Be·zons \bə-ˈzōⁿ\. Commune, Val-d'Oise dept., N France, NW suburb of Paris.

Bezwada. See VIJAYAWADA.

Bha·dar \ˈbə-dər, ˈbä-\. River, Kathiawar Penin., W India; ab. 120 mi. (195 km.) long; flowing WSW into Arabian Sea.

Bhadgaon. See BHAKTAPUR.

Bhad·res·war \bə-ˈdres-wər\. Town, West Bengal, India, on Hugli River 20 mi. (32 km.) N of Calcutta; pop. (1991p) 72,414.

Bha·gal·pur \ˈbä-gəl-ˌpu̇r\. Town, Bihar, NE India, on right bank of Ganges River 205 mi. (330 km.) NNW of Calcutta; pop. (1991p) 254,993; rail center; silk; university (1960).

Bha·gi·ra·thi \bə-ˈgē-rə-tē\. **1.** Headstream of the Ganges River near Gangotri, N India.

2. Upper course of the Hugli (*q.v.*), West Bengal, NE India, one of the Ganges distributaries. See also GANGES DELTA.

Bha·kra Dam \ˈbə-krə, ˈbä-\. Dam in gorge of Sutlej River near village of Bhakra, Himachal Pradesh, N India, NW of Bilaspur; 740 ft. (226 m.) high. With **Nan·gal Dam** \ˌnəŋ-gəl-, ˌnäŋ-\ forms part of Bhakra-Nangal irrigation and hydroelectric project, completed 1954.

Bhak·ta·pur \ˈbək-tə-ˌpu̇r\; *formerly* **Bhad·ga·on** \ˈbəd-ˌgau̇n\. Town, cen. Nepal, 8 mi. (13 km.) E of Kathmandu; pop. (1981c) 48,472; palace (c. 1700).

Bha·mo \bə-ˈmō\. Town, N Myanmar, on E bank of upper Irrawaddy River 100 mi. (161 km.) S of Myitkyina and 65 mi. (105 km.) NW of Namhkam; pop. (1983c) 26,169; about 40 mi. (64 km.) from China border; head of navigation of the Irrawaddy, with connections with Yangon; was an important station on Stilwell Road (earlier Ledo Road) connecting Myitkyina with Burma Road; lost to Japanese Apr. 1942 and scene of much fighting before its recovery Oct.–Dec. 1944.

Bhan·da·ra \bən-ˈdär-ə\. Town, NE Maharashtra, cen. India, on branch of Wainganga River 33 mi. (53 km.) E of Nagpur; pop. (1991p) 71,762.

Bharat. See INDIA 2.

Bha·rat·pur \ˈbə-rət-ˌpu̇r\ *or* **Bhurt·pore** \ˈbərt-ˌpōr\. **1.** Former Indian state, now part of Rajasthan, NW India; 1978 sq. mi. (5123 sq. km.).

2. City, its ✻, 34 mi. (55 km.) W of Agra; pop. (1991p) 148,506; known for beauty and workmanship of its chowries, made from sandalwood, ivory, and silver. Strongly fortified; unsuccessfully besieged 1805 by British under Lord Gerard Lake; besieged by Sir Stapleton Cotton (Lord Combermere) 1825–26 and captured.

Bharuch. See BROACH.

Bha·tin·da *or* **Ba·thin·da** \bə-ˈtin-də\. Town, Punjab, N India, 100 mi. (161 km.) S of Amritsar; pop. (1991p) 159,114; rail center.

Bhat·pa·ra \bät-ˈpär-ə\. City, West Bengal, NE India, on Hugli River 22 mi. (35 km.) N of Calcutta; pop. (1991c) 315,976; jute processing.

Bhav·na·gar *or* **Bhau·na·gar** \bau̇-ˈnə-gər\. **1.** Former Indian state, E Kathiawar, on W shore of Gulf of Khombhat, now part of Gujarat, W India; 2961 sq. mi. (7669 sq. km.). Region first settled by Gohel Rajputs about 1260; came into close relations with Bombay government in 18th cent. and its lands consolidated by British in 1807.

2. Town and seaport, its ✻, on W coast of Gulf of Khombhat 200 mi. (322 km.) N of Bombay; pop. (1991c) 402,338; spinning mills, brick factories; several colleges; founded 1723; chief seaport of Kathiawar Penin.

Bhawalpur. See BAHAWALPUR.

Bhawanipatna. See KALAHANDI.

Bhe·ra \ˈbā-rə, ˈber-ə\. Town, N Punjab, Pakistan, on Jhelum River 105 mi. (169 km.) NW of Lahore; ancient Indian mounds nearby.

Bhi·lai \bi-ˈlī\. Town, Madhya Pradesh, cen. India, 160 mi. (257 km.) E of Nagpur.

Bhi·ma \ˈbē-mə\. River, S India; rises in Maharashtra state in Western Ghats E of Bombay, flows SE in S Maharashtra, N Karnataka, and cen. Andhra Pradesh to Krishna River near Raichur; ab. 400 mi. (645 km.) long.

Bhir *or* **Bir** \ˈbir\ *or* **Bid** \ˈbid\. Town, cen. Maharashtra, cen. India, 65 mi. (105 km.) SSE of Aurangabad; pop. (1991p) 112,351.

Bhi·wa·ni \bi-ˈwä-nē\. Town, W Haryana, N India, 70 mi. (113 km.) W of Delhi; pop. (1991p) 121,449.

Bho·pal \bō-ˈpäl\. **1.** Former state, S Central India States, India; 6921 sq. mi. (11,136 sq. km.); incorp. 1956 in Madhya Pradesh. Chief state of former Bhopal Agency and next to Hyderabad the most important Muslim state in India. Surface broken by Vindhya Mts.; Narmada River formed its S border. Founded 1723 by Dōst Moḥammad Khān, an Afghan chieftain who had served under Mogul Emperor Aurangzeb (ʻĀlamgīr I); made treaty arrangements with British government 1817; ruled by female line (begums of Bhopal) 1844–1926.

2. City, ✻ of Madhya Pradesh, India, ab. 182 mi. (295 km.) NW of Nagpur; pop. (1991c) 1,062,771; heavy electrical equipment; several colleges; ✻ of former Bhopal state; toxic gas accident Dec. 1984 resulted in ab. 2500 deaths.

Bhopal Agency. Subdivision, of former Central India Agency; 9073 sq. mi. (23,499 sq. km.); comprised a group of nine Indian states (including Bhopal); ✻ Bhopal.

Bhor \ˈbōr\. **1.** Former state, W India; 910 sq. mi. (2357 sq. km.). one of Deccan and Kolhapur States in Western Ghats, now part of Maharashtra,

2. Town, its ✻, in S cen. Maharashtra; 25 mi. (40 km.) S of Pune.

Bhot \ˈbōt\ *or* **Bho·ti·ya** \ˈbō-tē-ə\ *or* **Bho·ti·yal** \-ˌyäl\. Old names for Tibet.

Bhu·ba·nes·war *or* **Bhu·ba·nesh·war** \ˌbü-bə-ˈnesh-wər\ *also* **Bhu·va·nesh·war** \ˌbü-və-ˈnesh-\. Town, ✻ of Orissa, E India, 30 mi. (48 km.) N of Puri; pop. (1991c) 411,542; Utkal Univ. (1943), Orissa Univ. of Agriculture and Technology (1962); has ab. 500 (orig. several thousand) temples in Orissan style of architecture, erected bet. 7th and 16th cents. A.D.; the Great Temple one of the finest Hindu shrines in India.

Bhuj \ˈbüj\. Town, ✻ of former Kutch state, now in Gujarat, W India, 190 mi. (306 km.) W of Ahmadabad; pop. (1991p) 91,901; known for silverwork.

Bhuket. See PHUKET.

Bhurtpore. See BHARATPUR.

Bhu·sa·wal *or* **Bhu·sa·val** \bu̇-ˈsä-vəl\. Town, N Maharashtra, W India, on Tapti River; pop. (1991p) 144,804.

Bhu·tan \bü-ˈtän, -ˈtan\; *Bhutanese* **Druk–yul** \ˈdrük-ˈyül\. Kingdom in E Himalayas on NE border of India, bounded on N by Tibet, China, on E by Assam, India, on S by Assam and West Bengal, and on W by Sikkim and Tibet; ab. 16,000 sq. mi. (41,440 sq. km.); pop. (1993e) 1,546,000; ✻ Thimphu (Tashi Chho Dzong); crossed for most part by short high mountain ridges (peaks up to 24,000 ft. or 7315 m.) running N to S and separated by deep valleys (12,000 to 18,000 ft. or 3658 to 5486 m.). Inhabitants (Bhutanese) are mostly a branch of Tibetan Mongolians (chiefly Buddhists).

Chief products: Rice, corn, wheat, barley, timber, potatoes.

History: Though area long inhabited, became political entity perhaps 300 years ago; came under Chinese domination off and on from 1720; relations with British began about 1772; acts of violence against British subjects 1863 led to invasion 1865 when by treaty portions were annexed to India; since 1907 under rule of hereditary maharaja; responsibility for external relations assumed by Great Britain in treaty 1910; after 1949 accepted Indian guidance in foreign affairs; territorial claims to parts of the country advanced by China 1958; became a member of the UN 1971.

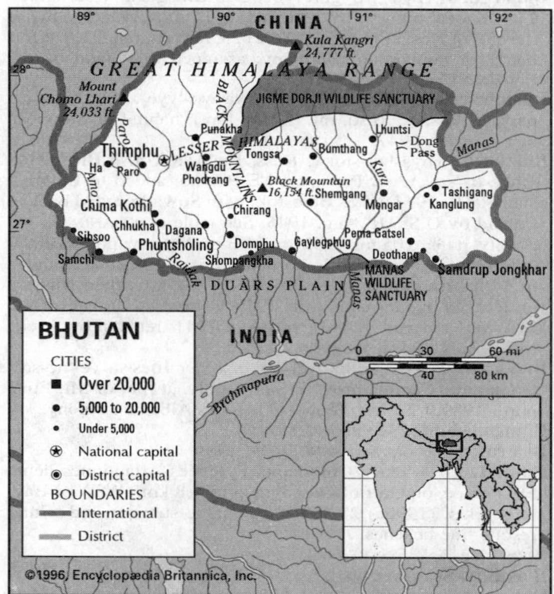

Bhuvaneshwar. See BHUBANESWAR.

Biache–Saint–Vaast \ˌbyȧsh-se^{n}-ˈvȧ\. Commune, Pas-de-Calais dept., N France, 7 mi. (11 km.) SW of Douai; severe fighting in July 1916 and Aug. 1918.

Biac·na·ba·to *or* **Biak–na–ba·to** \bē-ˌäk-nä-ˈbä-tō\. Village in mountains of NE Bulacan prov., Luzon, Philippines, 28 mi. (45 km.) NE of Malolos; noted for its caves. Scene Dec. 14, 1897 of signing of Pact of Biacnabato bet. Emilio Aguinaldo, head of provisional government, and Spanish governor-general in attempt to terminate the revolution.

Bia·fo Glacier \bē-'ä-fō\. Glacier, Karakoram Range, Pakistan (in region claimed by India); 36 mi. (58 km.) long; ab. 1.2 mi. (1.9 km.) wide near its terminus.

Bi·a·fra \bē-'a-frə, bē-'ä-, bī-'a-\ *or* **Republic of Biafra.** Former secessionist state, W Africa; inhabited chiefly by Ibo people. Its secession from Nigeria 1967 led to a costly civil war and resultant mass starvation; reincorporated into Nigeria 1970; region now divided into the Nigerian states Anambra, Imo, Cross River, and Rivers.

Biafra, Bight of *or* **Bight of Bon·ny** \'bä-nē\. Widemouthed bay in E section of the Gulf of Guinea, W Africa.

Bi·ak \bē-'äk\ *also* **Wi·ak** \wē-\. Island, largest of the Schouten Is., off N coast of Irian Jayra, Indonesia; 45 mi. (72 km.) long by 23 mi. (37 km.) wide; 948 sq. mi. (2455 sq. km.); NW part hilly; several populous towns on coast incl. Bosnik; three airfields. Seized by Japanese 1942; retaken after fierce fighting May–June 1944 by Allied forces.

Biak–na–bato. See BIACNABATO.

Bia·ła \'byä-wä\. **1.** River, E Kraków prov., Poland, a branch of the Dunajec River; 71 mi. (114 km.) long; battles May 1915 in German offensive under Field Marshal August von Mackensen.
2. River, W Kraków prov., Poland, tributary of the upper Vistula; 21 mi. (34 km.) long.

Biała, Bielsko. See BIELSKO BIAŁA.

Biała Pod·la·ska \pȯd-'läs-kä\. **1.** Province, E Poland. See table at POLAND.
2. Commune, its ✻, 60 mi. (97 km.) NNE of Lublin; pop. (1989e) 52,068.

Bia·ło·gard \byä-'wȯ-ˌgärt\ *or Ger.* **Bel·gard** \'bel-ˌgärt\. City, Koszalin prov., NW Poland, ab. 15 mi. (24 km.) SSW of the city of Koszalin; pop. (1989e) 23,968; church (1310); formerly in Pomerania, Germany; assigned to Poland by the Potsdam Conference 1945.

Bia·ło·wie·za National Park \ˌbyä-wȯ-'vye-zhä\. National park, E Poland; 20 sq. mi. (52 sq. km.); habitat of European bison; estab. 1947.

Bia·ły·stok \byä-'wi-stȯk\; *Russ.* **Be·lo·stok** *also* **Bie·lo·stok** \ˌbye-lə-'stȯk\. **1.** Province, NE Poland; added to Belorussian S.S.R. 1944–45 as Belostok; with Suwałki ceded back to Poland by U.S.S.R. Aug. 1945. See table at POLAND.
2. City, its ✻, 105 mi. (169 km.) NE of Warsaw; pop. (1989e) 268,085; textile center; important railroad junction. Founded in 14th cent.; annexed to Prussia 1795–1807, then Russian until taken by Germans Aug. 1915; restored to Poland 1919. In WWII overrun by Germans July 1941; retaken by Soviet troops July 1944.

Bian·ca·vil·la \bē-ˌäŋ-kä-'vēl-lä\ *or older* **Ines·sa** \ē-'ne-sə\. Commune, Catania prov., E Sicily, Italy, at foot of Mt. Etna; pop. (1989c) 22,767; founded 1480 as Albanian colony.

Bianco, Monte. See BLANC, MONT.

Bi·a·ro \bē-'är-ō\. See SANGIHE ISLANDS.

Biar·ritz \byä-'rēts\. Commune, Pyrénées-Atlantiques dept., SW France, on Gulf of Gascogne 5 mi. (8 km.) WSW of Bayonne; pop. (1990c) 28,887; fashionable summer and winter resort; fine beaches.

Bi·as \'bē-ˌäs\. See BEAS.

Bias Bay. See DAYA WAN.

Bi·bane Mountains \bē-'bän\. Range of the Little Atlas Mts., N Algeria.

Bibb \'bib\. Name of counties in two states of the U.S. See tables at ALABAMA and GEORGIA.

Bi·be·rach \'bē-bə-ˌräk\ *or in full* **Biberach an der Riss** \än-də-'ris\. City, Baden-Württemberg, S Germany, 56 mi. (90 km.) SE of Stuttgart; pop. (1980c) 28,284; founded 1170; scene of defeat of Austrians by French 1796 and 1800.

Bibi Eibat. See KHANLAR.

Bi·brac·te \bə-'brak-tē\. Ancient town, E Gaul, near modern Autun; ✻ of the Aedui; battlefield 58 B.C. where Roman Gen. Julius Caesar defeated the Helvetii.

Bi·brax \'bī-ˌbraks\. Ancient town of the Remi, Belgica, NE Gaul, near the Aisne on or near site of Laon.

Bices·ter \'bis-tər\. Town, Oxfordshire, England, 12 mi. (19 km.) NNE of Oxford; pop. (1981p) 14,436.

Biche, Lac la. See LA BICHE, LAC.

Bichitra. See PHICHIT.

Bick·nell \'bik-nəl\. City, Knox co., SW Indiana, 13 mi. (21 km.) ENE of Vincennes; pop. (1990c) 3357; coal deposits.

Bi·col. 1. *or* **Bi·kol** \'bē-ˌkōl\. River, W cen. Camarines Sur prov., Luzon, Philippines; flows NW from Lake Bato to San Miguel Bay; ab. 75 mi. (120 km.) long; fertile valley.
2. Region of the Philippines. See table at PHILIPPINES.

Bicol Peninsula. SE extension of Luzon, Philippines, inhabited principally by the Bikol; comprises Camarines Norte, Camarines Sur, Albay, and Sorsogon provs.

Bid. See BHIR.

Bida. See DOHA.

Bida \'bē-dä\. City, W cen. Nigeria, near left bank of the Niger; pop. (1991e) 110,800; noted for its brass and copper work. Settled since 16th cent.; conquering Emir Zaki made it his ✻ c. 1860; came under British 1901.

Bi·dar \'bē-dər\. Town, N Karnataka, India, 68 mi. (109 km.) NW of Hyderabad; pop. (1991p) 107,542; dynastic ✻ of Bidar kingdom in 16th cent.

Bi·das·soa \ˌbē-də-'sō-ə\. Stream, at N frontier of Spain; rises in Spain and flows W and N to Bay of Biscay at Fuenterrabía; for ab. 7 mi. (11 km.) its lower course forms boundary bet. France and Spain; 41 mi. (66 km.) long.

Bid·de·ford \'bi-də-fərd\. City, York co., SW Maine, across the Saco River from Saco; pop. (1990c) 20,710; Univ. of New England (1953); settled 1630.

Bid·dulph \'bi-ˌdəlf\. Town, Staffordshire, W cen. England, 8 mi. (13 km.) N of Stoke-on-Trent; pop. (1981p) 19,160.

Bid·e·ford \'bi-də-fərd\. Town, Devon, SW England, near mouth of Torridge River 45 mi. (72 km.) N of Plymouth; pop. (1981p) 12,211.

Bié \'byā\. Province of cen. Angola. See table at ANGOLA.

Bie·brza \'byeb-zhä\ *or Russ.* **Bobr** \'bȯ-bər\. River, N Poland; flows into Narew River; ab. 102 mi. (164 km.) long.

Biel \'bēl\ *or Fr.* **Bienne** \'byen\. Commune, N Bern canton, Switzerland, near Bielersee 17 mi. (27 km.) NNW of the city of Bern; pop. (1991e) 52,670; railroad junction; clocks. Founded c. 1200 by bishop of Basel; to France 1798; to Bern canton 1815.

Bie·la·wa \bye-'lä-vä\ *or Ger.* **Lang·en·bie·lau** \ˌläŋ-ən-'bē-ˌlau̇\. Town, Wałbrzych prov., SW Poland, 37 mi. (60 km.) SSW of Wrocław; pop. (1989e) 34,219.

Bie·le·feld \'bē-lə-ˌfelt\. City, North Rhine-Westphalia, Germany, 38 mi. (61 km.) E of Münster; pop. (1992e) 322,132; machine tools, chemicals, pharmaceuticals; founded c. 1214.

Bie·ler·see \'bē-lər-ˌzā\; *mostly formerly* **Lake of Bienne** \'byen\. Lake, Bern canton, W Switzerland, 3 mi. (4.8 km.) NE of Lake of Neuchâtel; 10 mi. (16 km.) long and bet. 1 and 3 mi. (1.6 and 4.8 km.) wide; 16 sq. mi. (26 sq. km.). Philosopher and writer J.J. Rousseau lived on an island in the lake.

Biel·la \bē-'el-lä\. Commune, Vercelli prov., Piedmont, NW Italy, 25 mi. (40 km.) NW of Vercelli; pop. (1991p) 48,277; railroad terminus; in rich agricultural area.

Bielostok. See BIAŁYSTOK.

Biel·sko–Bia·ła \'byel-skȯ-'byä-wä\ *or Ger.* **Bie·litz** \'bē-lits\. **1.** Province, S Poland. See table at POLAND.
2. Town, its ✻, at NW foot of Carpathian Mts. 26 mi. (42 km.) S of Katowice; pop. (1989e) 179,879; textiles.

Bielsk Pod·las·ki \'byelsk-pȯd-'lä-skē\. Commune, Białystok prov., NE Poland; pop. (1989e) 26,304.

Bien Hoa *also* **Bien·hoa** \'byen-'hwä\. Town, S Vietnam, 20 mi. (32 km.) NNE of Ho Chi Minh City; pop. (1986c) 273,879; wood products; formerly ✻ of Cambodia; site of large American air base during Vietnam War; Buddha statues.

Bienne. See BIEL.

Bienne, Lake of. See BIELERSEE.

Bi·en·ville \bē-'en-ˌvil, -vəl\. Parish in NW Louisiana. See table at LOUISIANA.

Bien·ville, Lac \ˌlák-byen-'vēl\ *or* **Lake Bienville.** Lake, N cen. Quebec, Canada; with outlet through Great Whale River into Hudson Bay; 392 sq. mi. (1015 sq. km.).

Bié Plateau \'byā\. Highland region, cen. Angola; alt. ab. 5000 ft. (1525 m.).

Bier·stadt, Mount \ˈbir-ˌstat\. Peak, Clear Creek co., N cen. Colorado; 14,060 ft. (4286 m.).

Bie·tig·heim \ˈbē-tig-ˌhīm\. City, Baden-Württemberg, S Germany, 13 mi. (21 km.) N of Stuttgart; received city charter 14th cent.

Big An·ne·mes·sex River \ˌa-nə-ˈme-siks\. Inlet of Tangier Sound, Somerset co., SE Maryland.

Big Bay Point. Point on N coast of Marquette co., N Michigan Penin., extending into Lake Superior.

Big Bear Lake. Reservoir in San Bernardino Mts., SW San Bernardino co., SW California, formed by damming small natural lake; center of resort area.

Big Ben \ˌbig-ˈben\. Active volcano, Heard I., S Indian Ocean; at 9006 ft. (2745 m.); highest point on Australian territory.

Big Bend National Park. See UNITED STATES, *National Parks.*

Big Beth·el \ˈbe-thəl\. Locality, Warwick co., Virginia, ab. 10 mi. (16 km.) NW of Fort Monroe; battle June 1861.

Big Black. 1. *also* **Great Black.** River, NW Maine; formed by junction of branches in NW Aroostook co., flows NE into St. John River; ab. 40 mi. (64 km.) long.
2. River, W cen. Mississippi; rises in Webster co., N cen. Mississippi, flows SW into the Mississippi River in NW Claiborne co., SW Mississippi; 330 mi. (531 km.) long.

Big Blue. River, Nebraska and Kansas; flowing from Hamilton co., SE cen. Nebraska, SE into Kansas River at Manhattan, Riley co., NE Kansas; 300 mi. (483 km.) long.

Big Bone Lick. Locality, Boone co., N Kentucky, just E of Ohio River; deposit of mammoth fossils discovered early 18th cent.; visited by pioneer Daniel Boone c. 1770.

Big Cypress Swamp. Swamp region, W part of the Everglades, S Florida; ab. 2400 sq. mi. (6215 sq. km.); a national preserve since 1974.

Big Delta. Unincorporated settlement, E Alaska, on Tanana River and on Alaska Highway at its junction with Richardson Highway, 65 mi. (105 km.) SE of Fairbanks; pop. (1990c) 400.

Big Diomede. See DIOMEDE ISLANDS.

Bi·gej \ˈbē-ˌgej\. Islet, SE Kwajalein Atoll, W Marshall Is., ab. 12 mi. (19 km.) NNE of Kwajalein I.; taken by Allies Feb. 1944.

Big Elk Peak. Mountain, E Bonneville co., SE Idaho; 9478 ft. (2889 m.).

Big·e·low Mountain \ˈbi-gə-lō\. Mountain, Somerset co., W Maine; 4150 ft. (1265 m.).

Big Equi·nox. \ˈē-kwi-ˌnäks, ˈe-\ *or* **Mount Equinox.** Peak in Taconic Range, in Bennington co., SW Vermont; 3816 ft. (1163 m.).

Big Flats. Town, Chemung co., S New York, ab. 9 mi. (15 km.) NW of Elmira near Chemung River; pop. (1990c) 7596.

Big Fork. River, N Minnesota; rises in NW Itasca co., flows N into Rainy River on U.S.-Canada boundary; ab. 120 mi. (195 km.) long.

Big·gles·wade \ˈbi-gəlz-ˌwād\. Town, Bedfordshire, SE cen. England, 42 mi. (68 km.) N of London; pop. (1981p) 10,928.

Big Hole National Battlefield. See UNITED STATES, *National Historical Parks.*

Big·horn \ˈbig-ˌhȯrn\. River, Wyoming and Montana; formed by confluence of Popo Agie and Wind rivers in Fremont co., W cen. Wyoming; flows N into Yellowstone River in SW Treasure co., SE cen. Montana; 336 mi. (541 km.) long.

Big Horn. Name of counties in two states of the U.S. See tables at MONTANA and WYOMING.

Bighorn Basin. Basin bet. Absaroka Range and Bighorn Mts. in N cen. Wyoming.

Bighorn Lake; *formerly* **Yel·low·tail Reservoir** \ˈye-lō-ˌtāl\. Reservoir in Bighorn River in Big Horn co., S Montana, formed by Yellowtail Dam (see UNITED STATES, *Dams and Reservoirs*).

Bighorn Mountain. Peak, Banner co., W Nebraska; 4713 ft. (1437 m.).

Bighorn Mountains. Range in N Wyoming extending N and S from Montana border to Natrona co.; highest point Cloud Peak 13,165 ft. (4013 m.).

Big Island, the. The island of Hawaii.

Big Kaweah. See KAWEAH PEAKS.

Big Lake. 1. Lake in cen. Washington co., E Maine.
2. City, ⊗ of Reagan co., W Texas; pop. (1990c) 3672.

Big Mountain; *formerly* **Pah·ute Peak** \ˈpä-yüt\. Mountain, W Humboldt co., NW Nevada; 8618 ft. (2627 m.); highest in Black Rock Range.

Big Muddy. River, SW Illinois; rises in S cen. Illinois, flows SW into Mississippi in W Jackson co., SW Illinois; ab. 100 mi. (160 km.) long.

Big Nemaha. See NEMAHA.

Bigorra. See TARBES.

Bi·gorre \bē-ˈgȯr\. Medieval county in W Pyrenees, SW France, in valley of the Adour; ✻ Tarbes.

Big Pine Key. One of the Florida Keys; site of a key deer refuge.

Big Rapids. City, ⊗ of Mecosta co., cen. Michigan, 35 mi. (56 km.) WNW of Mount Pleasant; pop. (1990c) 12,603; summer resort; natural gas and oil reserves; Ferris State Univ. (1884).

Big Sa·ble Point \ˈsā-bəl\. Point on W coast of Mason co., W Michigan, extending into Lake Michigan.

Big Sandy. 1. River, W Arizona; joins Santa Maria River on SE boundary of Mohave co. to form Williams River; ab. 80 mi. (130 km.) long.
2. Navigable river, E Kentucky; formed by confluence of Levisa Fork and Tug Fork (*qq.v.*) in E Lawrence co., E Kentucky, flows N forming N section of Kentucky-West Virginia boundary, and empties into Ohio River near Catlettsburg, NE Kentucky; 22 mi. (35 km.) long.

Big Sandy Creek. River, E Colorado; rises in N El Paso co., flows SE into Arkansas River; 200 mi. (322 km.) long.

Big Sioux \ˈsü\. River, South Dakota and Iowa; rises in W Grant co., NE South Dakota, flows S and SE to form South Dakota-Iowa boundary, and empties into Missouri River at extreme SE corner of South Dakota on W boundary of Sioux City; 420 mi. (676 km.) long.

Big Slide Mountain. Peak in the Adirondack Mts., Essex co., NE New York; 4255 ft. (1297 m.).

Big Southern Butte. Peak, S Butte co., SE cen. Idaho; ab. 7550 ft. (2301 m.).

Big Spring. City, ⊗ of Howard co., NW Texas, 78 mi. (126 km.) NW of San Angelo; pop. (1990c) 23,093; oil refineries; Howard Coll. (1945).

Big Stone. County in W Minnesota. See table at MINNESOTA.

Big Stone Gap. Town, Wise co., SW Virginia, in Cumberland Mts. 40 mi. (64 km.) WNW of Bristol; pop. (1990c) 4748.

Big Stone Lake. Narrow lake, bet. NE corner of South Dakota and W Minnesota; ab. 30 mi. (48 km.) long; created by **Big Stone Lake Dam** on Minnesota River.

Big Sur \ˈsər\. **1.** Village, Monterey co., California, near coast SE of Point Sur on **Big Sur River** (ab. 10 mi. or 16 km.) long).
2. Resort region, Monterey co., California, extending from vicinity of Point Sur ab. 80 mi. (130 km.) SE along coast W of Santa Lucia Range. Poet Robinson Jeffers' home in area.

Big Thicket. Wilderness area, E Texas, NE of Houston; 450 sq. mi. (1170 sq. km.).

Big Timber. City, ⊗ of Sweet Grass co., S cen. Montana, on Yellowstone River; pop. (1990c) 1557.

Big Tu·jun·ga \tə-ˈhəŋ-gə\. Dam across Big Tujunga Creek, Los Angeles co., California; height 250 ft. (76 m.); impounds water for flood control.

Big Tupper Lake. See TUPPER LAKES.

Big Wich·i·ta Dam \ˈwi-chə-ˌtȯ\ *or* **Wichita Falls Dam.** Dam across Wichita River, Baylor co., N Texas; height 100 ft. (31 m.); completed 1923; impounds water for irrigation, forming **Lake Kemp** \ˈkemp\.

Big Wood. River, S Idaho; rises on S slopes of Sawtooth Range, flows S, then W to Snake River; 95 mi. (153 km.) long.

\ə\ abut \ə̇\ matches \ᵊ\ kitten, Fr table \ər\ further \a\ ash \ā\ ace
\ä\ cot, cart \ȧ\ Fr bac \au̇\ out \b̲\ Span Avila \ch\ chin \e\ bet \ē\ easy
\g\ go \i\ hit \ī\ ice \j\ job \k̲\ Ger ich, Buch \ⁿ\ Fr vin
\ŋ\ sing \ō\ go \ö\ all \ȯ\ law \œ\ Fr bœuf \œ̄\ Fr feu \ȯi\ boy
\th\ thin \th̲\ this \ü\ loot \u̇\ foot \ue\ Ger füllen \ue̅\ Fr rue
\y\ yet \ʸ\ Fr digne \ˈdēnʸ\, nuit \ˈnwʸē\ \yü\ few \yu̇\ fury \zh\ vision

Bi·hać \ˈbē-ˌhäch\. Town, W Bosnia and Herzegovina, on Una River, near Croatian border; pop. (1991p) 70,896; under Turkish rule to 1878.

Bi·har \bi-ˈhär\. **1.** State, NE India; ✻ Patna; plateau region in S and Ganges Valley in N. See table at INDIA.

Chief products: Rice, corn, wheat; coal, iron ore.

Largest cities: Patna, Ranchi, Jamshedpur.

History: Its limits nearly the same as ancient kingdoms of Videha and Magadha with records dating back to c. 600 B.C. Under Magadha King Bimbisāra, Gautama Buddha began his preaching at Bodh Gayā (*q.v.*). Succeeded by Maurya empire, followed 320 A.D. by Gupta empire, with Pataliputra (Patna) as ✻. Native dynasty overcome c. 1200 by Muslims and about 1497 annexed to Delhi; taken over by British 1765 and made a part of Bengal; important in Indian mutiny against British mid-19th cent.; set up as part of prov. of Bihar and Orissa 1912 but made a separate province 1936; boundaries readjusted 1956.

2. *also* **Bihar Sha·rif** \shȧ-ˈrēf\. Town, cen. Bihar state, 40 mi. (64 km.) SE of Patna; pop. (1991p) 200,976; has many mosques and graves holy to Muslims and is a place of pilgrimage.

Bihar and Oris·sa \ȯ-ˈri-sə\. Former province of British India; 83,054 sq. mi. (215,110 sq. km.); ✻ Patna; geographically included Indian States, 28,648 sq. mi. (74,198 sq. km.); existed 1912–36.

Bi·hor \bē-ˈhȯr\. County of NW Romania. See table at ROMANIA.

Bihor Mountains *or Hung.* **Bi·har Mountains** \ˈbē-ˌhȯr\. Mountains, W cen. Transylvania, Romania, NW of the Transylvanian Alps; highest point ab. 6065 ft. (1850 m.).

Biisk. See BIYSK.

Bi·ja·gós, Ar·qui·pé·la·go dos \ˌär-ki-ˈpe-lə-ˌgü-ˌdüzh-ˌbē-zhə-ˈgȯsh\ *also* **Ilhas dos Bijagós** \ˈēl-yəzh\ *or Eng.* **Bis·sa·gos Islands** \bi-ˈsä-gəs\. Group of low islands, Guinea-Bissau, W Africa, off coast SW of Bissau; among them are Orango, Formosa, Caravéla, Bubaque; on easternmost island (Bolama) is town and port of Bolama.

Bijanagar. See VIJAYANAGAR.

Bi·ja·pur \bi-ˈjä-pu̇r\. Town, Karnataka, W India, 240 mi. (386 km.) SE of Bombay; pop. (1991p) 186,846. Became ✻ independent state estab. 1489 by Yusuf Adil Shah; one of the five Muslim kingdoms of the Deccan (*q.v.*). Has numerous pre-Muslim ruins and large mosques, palaces, and buildings in Islamic style, also an impressive citadel and fort. Kingdom conquered by Mogul Emperor Aurangzeb (ʻĀlamgīr I) 1686, ceded to Marathas 1760, and taken over by British 1818.

Bi·ja·war \bi-ˈjä-wər\. Former Indian state, now part of Madhya Pradesh, cen. India; 980 sq. mi. (2538 sq. km.).

Bi·je·lji·na \bē-ˈyel-yē-ˌnä\. Town, NE corner of Bosnia and Herzegovina.

Bij·nor \ˈbij-ˌnȯr\. Town, NW Uttar Pradesh, N India, 3 mi. (5 km.) from left bank of Ganges River 75 mi. (121 km.) NE of Delhi; pop. (1991p) 66,156.

Bi·ka·ner \ˌbi-kə-ˈnir, ˈbe-kə-ˌner\. **1.** Former Indian state, now part of Rajasthan, NW India; 23,181 sq. mi. (60,039 sq. km.); desolate tract, part of Thar Desert without a single stream; N part watered by irrigation canals. Founded ab. 1465 by Rajput chief; adhered loyally to Mogul Empire; waged wars with Jodhpur through 18th cent.; had British political influence during 19th cent.

2. City, its ✻, 240 mi. (386 km.) W of Delhi; pop. (1991c) 416,289; founded 1488 by Bika, a Rajput chief of Marwar; noted for its carpets and blankets; surrounded by stone wall and overlooked by citadel; its temples and palaces constructed of bright red sandstone.

Bi·ki·ni \bi-ˈkē-nē\. Atoll with ab. 20 islets, Marshall Is., Micronesia, 11°35′N, 165°23′E; lagoon 21.5 mi. (36 km.) long by 11 mi. (18 km.) wide. Largest islets Bikini, Enyu, and Namu; entrance to lagoon is through Enyu Channel on the SE, 9 mi. (15 km.) wide. Population of 167 removed to Rongerik before American tests of atomic bomb July 1 and 25, 1946; moved from Rongerik to Kili 1948; hydrogen bomb tested 1954, 1956; inhabitants returned 1969 but were evacuated again in 1978; because of high radiation, island remains uninhabited.

Bikol. See BICOL 1.

Bik·scho·te *or* **Bix·schoo·te** \ˈbik-ˌsk̲ō-tə\. Village, West Flanders prov., NW Belgium, 5 mi. (8 km.) N of Ieper (Ypres); scene of first effective German gas attack Apr. 1915, in WWI.

Bi·laa Point \bē-ˈlä\. Most northerly point of Mindanao, Philippines, at NE corner, Surigao del Norte prov.

Bilād–es–Sudan. See SUDAN.

Bilá Hora. See WHITE MOUNTAIN 3.

Bi·las·pur \bi-ˈläs-ˌpu̇r\. **1.** Former Indian state, now in Himachal Pradesh, N India; 450 sq. mi. (1167 sq. km.).

2. Town, its ✻, on Sutlej River.

3. Town, NE Madhya Pradesh, cen. India, on tributary of Mahanadi River 210 mi. (338 km.) ENE of Nagpur; pop. (1991p) 233,570.

Bi·lauk·taung Range \bi-ˈlau̇k-tau̇ŋ\. Mountain range along boundary bet. SE Myanmar and SW Thailand; elev. bet. 2000 and 5000 ft. (610 and 1524 m.).

Bil·bao \bil-ˈb̲ä-ˌō, -ˈbau̇\. City, ✻ of Vizcaya prov., N Spain, 7 mi. (11 km.) from the Bay of Biscay; pop. (1991c) 369,839; a major Spanish port; chemical and metallurgical industries; shipbuilding, fishing; university (1886); founded 1300; besieged by Carlists during 19th cent.

Bil·beis *or* **Bel·beis** *or* **Bil·bays** \bil-ˈbās\. Town, Sharqīya governorate, NE Egypt, ab. 30 mi. (48 km.) NE of Cairo.

Bilbilis. See CALATAYUD.

Bi·le·cik \ˌbē-le-ˈjēk\. **1.** Province of Turkey in Asia. See table at TURKEY.

2. Town, its ✻, 37 mi. (60 km.) NW of Eskişehir; pop. (1990p) 23,050.

Bíle Karpaty. See WHITE CARPATHIAN MOUNTAINS.

Bił·go·raj \bēu̇-ˈgȯ-rī\. Commune, Zamość prov. E Poland; pop. (1989e) 25,619.

Bí·li·na \ˈbē-lē-ˌnä\ *or Ger.* **Bi·lin** \bē-ˈlēn\. City, NW Czech Republic; pop. (1980p) 18,836; mineral springs.

Bi·li·ran \bē-ˈlē-ˌrän\. Island N of Leyte, cen. Philippines; 192 sq. mi. (497 sq. km.); comprises a subprovince of Leyte; chief town Caibiran. See table at PHILIPPINES.

Bilkas. See BILQĀS.

Bille·rica \bil-ˈrik-ə\. Town, Middlesex co., NE Massachusetts, 6 mi. (10 km.) S of Lowell; pop. (1990c) 37,609.

Bil·ling·ham \ˈbi-liŋ-əm\. Town, Cleveland, N England; pop. (1981c) 36,712; chemicals.

Bil·lings \ˈbi-liŋz\. **1.** County in W North Dakota. See table at NORTH DAKOTA.

2. City, ⊗ of Yellowstone co., S cen. Montana, on Yellowstone River; pop. (1990c) 81,151; alt. 3120 ft. (951 m.); trading and shipping point. Eastern Montana Coll. (1927), Rocky Mountain Coll. (1878).

Billiton. See BELITUNG.

Bill Wil·liams Mountain \ˈbil-ˈwil-yəmz\. Peak, SW Coconino co., N cen. Arizona; 9264 ft. (2824 m.).

Billy Chinook, Lake. See CHINOOK, LAKE.

Bil·ma \ˈbil-mə\. Town, E Niger; formerly an oasis on N to S route.

Bi·loxi \bi-ˈlək-sē, -ˈläk-\. City, a ⊗ of Harrison co., SE Mississippi, on Gulf of Mexico 13 mi. (21 km.) E of Gulfport; pop. (1990c) 46,319; casino gambling; resort; oyster and shrimp fishing; Keesler Air Force Base with U.S. Air Force technical school; first permanent white settlement in the Mississippi Valley nearby (1699).

Bil·qās *or* **Bil·kas** \bil-ˈkäs\ *or in full* **Bilqās Qism Aw·wal** \ˈkis-ᵊm-au̇-ˈwäl\. Town, Daqahlīya governorate, Egypt, in Nile Delta 30 mi. (48 km.) SW of Damietta; pop. (1986p) 73,162.

Bilt, de. See DE BILT.

Bi·ma \ˈbē-mä\. Seaport, NE Sumbawa I., Lesser Sunda Is., Indonesia; on Bima Bay adjacent to Raba.

Bima Bay. Inlet of Flores Sea on NE coast of Sumbawa I., Lesser Sunda Is., Indonesia; one of best harbors in Indonesia; town of Raba on it.

Bim·i·ni \ˈbi-mi-nē\ *or* **Bim·i·nis** \-nēz\. Two small islands and nearby cays of Bahamas, E of S Florida and separated from Florida by the Straits of Florida; 9 sq. mi. (15 km.); named for mythical island of Bimini, supposed site of "fountain of youth," the quest for which led to first European sighting of Florida 1513 by Spanish explorer Juan Ponce de León.

Bi·nal·ba·gan \ˌbē-näl-ˈbä-gän\. Municipality, W coast of Negros Occidental prov., Negros, Philippines, on Panay Gulf; pop. (1980c) 49,428.

Bi·na·lo·nan \ˌbē-nä-ˈlō-nän\. Municipality, E Pangasinan prov., Luzon, Philippines, 23 mi. (37 km.) E of Lingayen; pop. (1980c) 35,574.

Bi·ñan \bē-ˈnyän\. Municipality, W Laguna prov., Luzon, Philippines, near SW coast of Laguna de Bay; pop. (1980c) 83,684; important terminus for roads to Cavite.

Bi·nang·o·nan \ˌbē-näŋ-ˈō-nän\. Municipality, S Rizal prov., Luzon, Philippines, on W shore of peninsula on Laguna de Bay 10 mi. (16 km.) SE of Pasig; pop. (1980c) 80,980; large deposits of building stone nearby.

Binche \ˈbeⁿsh\. Town, Hainaut prov., SW Belgium, on Haine River 10 mi. (16 km.) E of Mons; pop. (1991c) 32,837.

Bindloe. See MARCHENA.

Bindraban. See VRINDAVAN.

Bing·en \ˈbiŋ-ən\. City, Rhineland-Palatinate, W Germany, at confluence of Rhine and Nahe rivers 17 mi. (27 km.) W of Mainz; pop. (1992e) 24,272; tourism; wine; 15th cent. Gothic church; Klopp Castle nearby; famous Drususbrücke (bridge; built by Roman Gen. Drusus Senior late first cent. B.C.) over the Nahe River; ancient Mäuseturm (Mouse Tower; according to legend, Archbishop Hatto I devoured by mice here 913); Rhenish Technical Coll.; inhabited by ancient Belgae; scene of defeat of Gauls by Romans 70 A.D.; Holy Roman Emperor Henry IV imprisoned in nearby castle 1105; under French rule 1797–1814; to Hesse 1815.

Bin·ger·ville \ˌbeⁿ-zhā-ˈvēl\. Seaport town, Ivory Coast; former territorial ✱.

Bing·ham \ˈbiŋ-əm\. County in SE Idaho. See table at IDAHO.

Bingham Canyon. Disincorporated town, Salt Lake co., N Utah, 20 mi. (32 km.) SSW of Salt Lake City; site of one of world's largest open-pit copper mines.

Bing·ham·ton \ˈbiŋ-əm-tən\. City, ⊗ of Broome co., S New York, at confluence of Chenango and Susquehanna rivers 65 mi. (105 km.) S of Syracuse; pop. (1990c) 53,008; Broome Community Coll. (1946), State Univ. of New York at Binghamton (1946). With Johnson City and Endicott one of so-called Triple Cities; first permanent settlement 1787; incorp. as village 1834, city 1867; site of first farm bureau in U.S. (1911).

Bingian, Slieve. See SLIEVE BINGIAN.

Bing·ley \ˈbiŋ-lē\. Town, West Yorkshire N England, on the Aire 7 mi. (11 km.) NNW of Bradford; pop. (1981p) 28,070.

Bin·göl \biŋ-ˈgœl\. **1.** Province of Turkey in Asia. See table at TURKEY.

2. Town, its ✱; pop. (1990p) 41,680.

Bingöl Da·ğı \dä-ˈgē\. Mountain range (*dağı*), Armenia, E Turkey in Asia, NW of Lake Van; highest point 11,975 ft. (3650 m.).

Bin·go Sea \ˈbiŋ-gō\ *or* **Sea of Bingo.** Expansion of the Inland Sea, Japan, in its central part, N of Shikoku I.

Binh Dinh. See AN NHON.

Bin·jai. \bin-ˈjī\. City, N Sumatra, Indonesia; pop. (1990c) 181,904.

Bin·ma·ley \ˌbēn-mä-ˈlā\. Municipality, cen. Pangasinan prov., Luzon, Philippines, in Agno delta 3 mi. (5 km.) E of Lingayen on S shore of Lingayen Gulf; pop. (1980c) 47,332.

Bin·tan \ˈbin-ˌtän\ *or* **Bin·tang** \-ˌtäŋ\ *also* **Rhio** \ˈrē-ō, rē-ˈō\ *or* **Ri·ou** *or* **Ri·ouw** \ˈrē-ˌaů, rē-ˈaů\. Island, largest of Kepulauan Riau, Indonesia, off S tip of the Malay Penin.; 415 sq. mi. (1075 sq. km.); bauxite deposits.

Bin·tu·lu \bēn-ˈtü-lü\. Coastal town, W Sarawak, East Malaysia, NW Borneo, Malaysia; pop. (1980p) 58,296.

Bío–Bío \ˌbē-ō-ˈbē-ō\. **1.** River, S cen. Chile; flows from the Andes into the Pacific Ocean at the city of Concepción; 238 mi. (383 km.) long.

2. Former province of S cen. Chile.

3. Region S cen. Chile, ✱ Concepción. See table at CHILE.

Bio·ko \bē-ˈō-kō\; *1973–79* **Ma·ci·as Ngue·ma Bi·yo·go** \mä-ˈthē-äs-əŋ-ˈgwā-mä-bē-ˈō-gō, mä-ˈsē-\; *earlier* **Fer·nan·do Póo** \fer-ˈnän-dō-ˈpō\. Island in Bight of Biafra, W Africa, ab. 60 mi. (96 km.) SW of Douala, Cameroon; 779 sq. mi. (2018 sq. km.); pop. (1983c) 57,740; belongs to Equatorial Guinea; chief town Malabo (✱ of Equatorial Guinea).

Bipontium. See ZWEIBRÜCKEN.

Biqā, Al–. See BEKÁA VALLEY.

Bir. See BHIR.

Bir, Cape \ˈbir\ *or Arab.* **Ras Bir** \räs\. Cape projecting from E coast of Djibouti into the Gulf of Aden at entrance to Bab el-Mandab.

Bīrah, Al. See AL BĪRAH.

Bir al–Go·bi \ˈbir-äl-ˈgō-bē\. Village and pass in the hills of Libya, 37 mi. (60 km.) S of Tobruk; fighting 1941–42.

Bi'r al–Hukayyim. See BIR HACHEIM.

Bi·rat·na·gar \bi-ˈrät-ˌnə-gər\. Town, SE Nepal, ab. 150 mi. (241 km.) SE of Kathmandu.

Bird Island. See AVES ISLAND.

Birds·boro \ˈbərdz-ˌbər-ō\. Borough, Berks co., SE Pennsylvania, on Schuylkill River 9 mi. (15 km.) SSE of Reading; pop. (1990c) 4222; founded 1740.

Bir·dum \ˈbər-dəm\. Settlement, N cen. Northern Terr., Australia, 270 mi. (434 km.) SE of Darwin; connected to Darwin by railroad 1929–76.

Bi·re·cik \ˌbir-ē-ˈjek\ *or* **Bi·ri·jik** \ˌbir-i-\. Town on left bank of the Euphrates River, SE Turkey in Asia, 45 mi. (72 km.) WSW of Urfa.

Bir es Saba. See BEERSHEBA.

Bir Ha·cheim \ˌbir-hä-ˈkām\ *or Arab.* **Bi'r al–Hu·kay·yim** \äl-hů-ˈkī-yim\. Village, Libya, 40 mi. (64 km.) SSW of Tobruk; in WWII scene of much fighting 1942, esp. when taken by Germans under Field Marshal Erwin Rommel June 1942.

Bir·han \bir-ˈhän\. Peak, cen. Ethiopia, NNW of Addis Ababa; 13,628 ft. (4154 m.).

Birijik. See BIRECIK.

Bīr·jand \bēr-ˈjänd\. Town, SE Khorāsān prov., NE Iran; on a plateau (alt. 4440 ft. or 1353 m.) and on the highway from Mashhad to Zāhedān; pop. (1986c) 81,798.

Bir·ke·nau \ˈbir-kə-ˌnaů\ *or Pol.* **Brze·zin·ka** \bzhe-ˈzēŋ-kä\. Village, S Poland, adjacent to Oświęcim (Auschwitz); site of a Nazi concentration camp in WWII.

Bir·ken·head \ˈbər-kən-ˌhed, ˌbər-kən-ˈ\. **1.** County borough, Merseyside, NW England, on the Mersey estuary opp. Liverpool; pop. (1981p) 123,907; shipbuilding and shipping center; has flourmills; technical college (1955). Connected with Liverpool by tunnel under the Mersey 2.1 mi. (3.4 km.) long. First iron vessel in England built here 1829; new docks opened 1847; Confederate privateer *Alabama* launched 1862; first European town to have streetcars.

2. Borough, North I., New Zealand; pop. (1981c) 21,324; suburb of Auckland on N shore of Waitemata Harbor.

Bir·ket Qā·rūn \ˈbir-ket-kä-ˈrün\; *Eng.* **Lake Qarun.** Shallow lake, along NW boundary of El Faiyûm governorate, Egypt; ab. 30 mi. (48 km.) long, 5 mi. (8 km.) wide; 85 sq. mi. (220 sq. km.); occupies part of basin of ancient Lake Moeris (*q.v.*).

Bir·kir·ka·ra \ˌbir-kir-ˈkär-ä\. Town, Malta, ab. 3 mi. (5 km.) W of Valletta; pop. (1988c) 20,711.

Bîr·lad *formerly* **Bâr·lad** *or* **Bêr·lad** \bər-ˈläd\. City, E Romania, 60 mi. (97 km.) NNW of Galaţi; pop. (1989c) 75,843; food processing; ball bearings.

Bir·ming·ham \ˈbər-miŋ-ˌham, *Brit. usu.* -miŋ-əm\. **1.** City, ⊗ of Jefferson co., N cen. Alabama; pop. (1990c) 265,968; area rich in coal, hematite, and many other minerals; steel, aircraft, chemicals; Samford Univ. (1841), Birmingham-Southern Coll. (1856), Miles Coll. (1907), Southeastern Bible Coll. (1935), Jefferson State Junior Coll. (1963), Lawson State Community Coll. (1965), Univ. of Alabama at Birmingham (1969); incorp. 1871.

2. Residential city, Oakland co., SE Michigan, 8 mi. (13 km.) SSE of Pontiac; pop. (1990c) 19,997.
3. City, ⊗ of West Midlands, W cen. England, 98 mi. (158 km.) NW of London; pop. (1991p) 934,900; a major manufacturing and transportation center; automobiles, electrical equipment, chocolate; Univ. of Birmingham (1900), Univ. of Aston in Birmingham (1966). Grammar school founded 1552 by King Edward VI. Before 13th cent. a market town; swept by plague 17th cent.; enfranchised by Reform Act 1832; suffered heavy bombing in WWII; subsequently rebuilt.

Bir·nie \ˈbər-nē\. Island in center of Phoenix Is. group, Kiribati, cen. Pacific Ocean, S of Kanton I.; 1 sq. mi. (1.6 sq. km.).

Bir·nin Keb·bi \ˈbēr-ˌnēn-ˈkeb-bē\. City, ✻ of Kebbi state, NW Nigeria; pop. (1991e) 53,330.

Bi·ro·bi·dzhan *or* **Bi·ro·bi·jan** \ˌbē-rō-bē-ˈjän, -ˈjan\. **1.** Administrative subdivision of Russia in Asia. See JEWISH AUTONOMOUS OBLAST.
2. City, ✻ of Jewish Autonomous Oblast, SE Russia in Asia on Trans-Siberian R.R. ab. 110 mi. (177 km.) W of Khabarovsk; pop. (1991e) 86,300.

Birr \ˈbər\; *formerly* **Par·sons·town** \ˈpärs-ᵊnz-ˌtau̇n\. Town, W co. Offaly, cen. Ireland; pop. (1991p) 3257; castle, historically noted as astronomical observatory.

Bir·žai \ˈbēr-ˌzhī\ *or Russ.* **Bir·zhai** \bir-ˈzhī\ *or Ger.* **Bir·sen** \ˈbir-zən\. Town, N Lithuania; alliance bet. Czar Peter the Great of Russia and Augustus II of Poland formed here 1701 against Sweden.

Bisanthe. See TEKİRDAĞ 2.

Bisayas. See VISAYAN ISLANDS.

Bis·bee \ˈbiz-bē\. City, ⊗ of Cochise co., SE corner of Arizona, 58 mi. (93 km.) E of Nogales; pop. (1990c) 6288; center of what was once one of richest copper-producing regions in America; gold, silver, lead deposits nearby also.

Biscari. See ACATE.

Biscay *or* **Biscaya.** See VIZCAYA.

Bis·cay, Bay of \ˈbis-kā, -kē\ *or* **Gulf of Gas·co·ny** \ˈgas-kə-nē\ *or Fr.* **Golfe de Gas·cogne** \ˌgȯlf-də-gà-ˈskȯnʸ\ *or Span.* **Gol·fo de Viz·ca·ya** \ˈgōl-fō-ˌt͟hā-b͟eth-ˈkä-yä\; *anc.* **Ma·re Can·tab·ri·cum** \ˈmā-rē-kan-ˈta-bri-kəm, ˈmär-ā-\ *or* **Aq·ui·tan·i·cus Si·nus** \ˌa-kwi-ˈta-ni-kəs-ˈsī-nəs\ *also* **Si·nus Can·tab·ri·cus** \ˈsī-nəs-kan-ˈta-bri-kəs\ *or* **Can·ta·ber Oce·a·nus** \ˈkan-tə-bər-ō-ˈsē-ə-nəs\. Large inlet of the Atlantic Ocean on W coast of France and N coast of Spain, from Île d'Ouessant on the N to Cape Ortegal, Spain, on the S; max. depth 15,525 ft. (4732 m.); receives the Loire, Garonne, and Adour rivers on the E.

Bis·cayne Bay \bis-ˈkān, ˈbis-ˌ\. Inlet of Atlantic Ocean on E coast of Miami-Dade co., SE Florida; the city of Miami is on its NW shore and the island of **Key Biscayne** is on the NE.

Biscayne National Park. See UNITED STATES, *National Parks.*

Biscayne Park. Village, Miami-Dade co., SE Florida; pop. (1990c) 3068.

Bi·sce·glie \bē-ˈshā-lyā\. Seaport, Bari prov., Puglia, SE Italy, on Adriatic Sea 21 mi. (34 km.) WNW of the seaport of Bari; pop. (1991p) 46,916. Architectural remains from Normans, Hohenstaufens, and Angevins.

Bisch·heim \bē-ˈshem, ˈbish-ˌhīm\. Commune, Bas-Rhin dept., NE France, NW suburb of Strasbourg.

Bish·en·pur \ˈbi-shən-ˌpu̇r\. Town, S cen. Manipur, NE India, ab. 20 mi. (32 km.) SSW of Imphal; severe fighting near here Apr. 1944 in which Japanese advance was stopped.

Bish·kek \bish-ˈkek\ *also* **Pish·pek** \pish-ˈpek\; *1926–91* **Frun·ze** \ˈfrün-zi\. City, ✻ of Kyrgyzstan, on Chu River, on Kazakhstan border 125 mi. (201 km.) WSW of Alma-Ata; pop. (1991e) 641,400; agricultural machinery; meatpacking; university (1951); site of Uzbek fort taken by Russians 1862; birthplace of Gen. Mikhail V. Frunze, for whom it was renamed 1926.

Bish·nu·pur \ˈbish-nu̇-ˌpu̇r\. Town, West Bengal, NE India, 75 mi. (121 km.) NW of Calcutta; pop. (1991p) 56,119; in ancient times an important city; ✻ of a Hindu kingdom founded in 8th cent.

Bi·sho \ˈbē-shō\. Town, Rep. of South Africa, ✻ of former Ciskei enclave.

Bish·op \ˈbi-shəp\. **1.** City, Inyo co., E California, in Owens River valley 35 mi. (56 km.) W of Nevada border; pop. (1990c) 3475; tungsten desposits.
2. City, Nueces co., S Texas, 30 mi. (48 km.) SW of Corpus Christi; pop. (1990c) 3337.

Bishop Auck·land \ˌbi-shəp-ˈȯ-klənd\. Town, Durham, N England, at confluence of Wear and Gaunless rivers 23 mi. (37 km.) S of Newcastle upon Tyne; pop. (1981p) 32,572; residence of bishops of Durham.

Bish·ops and Clerks \ˈbi-shəps … ˈklärks\. Group of small rocky islands in St. George's Channel, off Dyfed, SW coast of Wales; ab. 5 mi. (8 km.) W of St. David's Head.

Bish·op's Falls \ˈbi-shəps\. Waterfall in Exploits River, cen. Newfoundland, Canada, ab. 14 mi. (23 km.) from its mouth.

Bishop's Stort·ford \ˈstȯrt-fərd, ˈstȯ-\. Town, Hertfordshire, SE England, on the Stort 28 mi. (45 km.) NNE of London; pop. (1981p) 22,807; birthplace of colonial administrator Cecil Rhodes 1853.

Bishop's Wearmouth. See SUNDERLAND 2.

Bish·op·ville \ˈbi-shəp-ˌvil, -vəl\. Town, ⊗ of Lee co., NE cen. South Carolina, 22 mi. (35 km.) NNE of Sumter; pop. (1990c) 3560.

Bī·si·tūn *or* **Bi·su·tun** \ˌbē-si-ˈtün\ *or* **Be·his·tun** \ˌbā-his-\. Ruined town in W Iran, 22 mi. (35 km.) E of Bākhtarān; on limestone cliff above present village is monument of Persian King Darius the Great consisting of sculptures in relief and trilingual (cuneiform) inscriptions, the "Rosetta Stone of Asia"; decipherment by English army officer and Orientalist Sir Henry Rawlinson in 1840s furnished key to translation of Assyrian and Babylonian records.

Bis·kra \ˈbis-krə, -krä\. Town, NE Algeria, at an oasis ab. 120 mi. (193 km.) SSW of Constantine; pop. (1987p) 128,747; dates; winter resort; successively ruled by Romans, Arabs, Turks, and French.

Bis·ley \ˈbiz-lē\. Village, Surrey, S England, ab. 29 mi. (47 km.) SW of London and ab. 7 mi. (11 km.) NE of Aldershot; scene since 1890 of annual meet of National Rifle Association.

Bis·marck \ˈbiz-ˌmärk\. City, ✻ of North Dakota and ⊗ of Burleigh co., S cen. North Dakota, on Missouri River; pop. (1990c) 49,256; trading center in spring-wheat region; oil refinery; Bismarck State Coll. (1939), Univ. of Mary (1959); Kennedy Memorial Center (dedicated 1971). First settled 1873; became territorial ✻ 1883, state ✻ 1889.

Bismarck Archipelago. Island group in W Pacific Ocean N of E end of island of New Guinea; 19,173 sq. mi. (49,658 sq. km.); pop. (1989e) 371,400; includes islands of New Britain, New Ireland, New Hanover (Lavongai), Admiralty Is., and about 200 other islands and islets; part of Papua New Guinea. Islands are of volcanic origin with active volcanoes, esp. on New Britain; main part of archipelago is circular in form enclosing extensive Bismarck Sea and lies bet. 1° and 6°20′S lat. and 145° and 154°E long.; natives mainly Melanesians, with many different languages; produces copra.

History: First visited in early part of 17th cent.; coasts of New Britain explored by William Dampier 1700 and after 1767 other islands by Philip Carteret and others. Proclaimed German protectorate 1884. Occupied by Australians 1914 and included in mandate (Trust Terr. of New Guinea) to Australia 1920. Seized by Japanese Jan. 1942; Rabaul, Gasmata, Kavieng frequently bombed by Allied forces 1943–44; retaken by Allies 1944; to Australia as UN trust territory after WWII; became part of independent Papua New Guinea 1975.

Bismarckburg. See KASANGA.

Bismarck Range. Mountain range, E New Guinea I.; Papua New Guinea, highest peak Mt. Wilhelm 14,762 ft. (4500 m.).

Bismarck Sea. Part of the W Pacific Ocean enclosed by the islands of the Bismarck Archipelago; ab. 500 mi. (805 km.) across from E to W. In battle of Bismarck Sea Mar. 1943 Allied planes completely destroyed a large Japanese fleet, thus greatly hampering further Japanese control of area.

Bisnulok. See PHITSANULOK.

Bi·son \ˈbīs-ᵊn\. Town, ⊗ of Perkins co., NW South Dakota; pop. (1990c) 451.

Bissagos Islands. See BIJAGÓS, ARQUIPÉLAGO DOS.

Bis·sau \bis-ˈau̇\. Seaport, ✻ of Guinea-Bissau, on Gêba estuary; pop. (1988e) 125,000; founded by Portuguese 1687.

Bis·ti·neau, Lake \ˈbis-tə-ˌnō\. Lake on boundary bet. Bienville and Bossier parishes, NW Louisiana; ab. 30 mi. (48 km.) long and 2 mi. (3 km.) wide; navigable; connected by outlet stream S with Red River.

Bis·tri·ţa *or* **Bis·tri·tsa** \ˈbēs-trēt-ˌsä\. **1.** River, NE Romania; rises in SE Carpathian Mts., flows SE into Siret River near Bacău; 185 mi. (298 km.) long.
2. *or Hung.* **Besz·ter·cze** \ˈbes-tərt-ˌsā\. River, N Romania; ab. 60 mi. (97 km.) long; an upper tributary of the Someşul.
3. City, ⊗ of Bistriţa-Năsăud co., Romania, on Bristriţa River ab. 40 mi. (64 km.) N of Tîrgu-Mureş; pop. (1989c) 79,544; founded by German colonists in 12th cent.

Bistriţa–Nă·să·ud \ˌnə-sə-ˈüd\. County of N Romania. See table at ROMANIA.

Bisutun. See BĪSITŪN.

Bitche \ˈbēch\ *or Ger.* **Bitsch** \ˈbich\. Commune, Moselle dept., NE France, near Saar border 60 mi. (97 km.) NW of Strasbourg. Citadel on rocky hill dominating the town defended in several wars; in WWII a strong point of German defense, taken by U.S. troops Jan. 1945.

Bi·thyn·ia \bə-ˈthi-nē-ə\. Ancient country in NW Asia Minor, bordering on the Propontis and Euxine and adjoining Paphlagonia on the E and Galatia, Phrygia, and Mysia on the S. Mountainous and well-forested; on the W indented by two inlets and crossed by the Sangarius (*or mod.* Sakarya) River. Settled by a Thracian tribe. Its first king, Nicomedes I, founded Nicomedia (*or mod.* İzmit) as ✻ c. 264 B.C.; prosperous until extended warfare with Mithradates, king of Pontus; became Roman province 74 B.C. with varying boundaries; known as **Bithynia et Pon·tus** \et-ˈpän-təs\ 98–117 A.D.; under Byzantine Empire divided into two parts.

Bithynium. See CLAUDIOPOLIS.

Bit·lis \bit-ˈlēs\. **1.** Province of Turkey in Asia. See table at TURKEY.
2. Town, its ✻, ab. 16 mi. (26 km.) SW of Lake Van; pop. (1990p) 38,275; alt. 4700 ft. (1433 m.).

Bi·to·la \ˈbi-tȯ-lä\ *or Serbo-Croat.* **Bi·tolj** \ˈbē-tȯlʸ, -tōl-yə\ *or* **Mo·nas·tir** \ˌmä-nə-ˈstir\. City, Republic of Macedonia; pop. (1991p) 122,173; alt. 2019 ft. (615 m.); carpets; settled by Slavs c. 6th cent. A.D. near ancient **Her·a·clea Lyn·ces·tis** \ˌher-ə-ˈklē-ə-lin-ˈses-təs\; passed to Turks late 14th cent.; became important commercial city; taken from Turks in Second Balkan War and assigned to Serbia by Treaty of Bucharest 1913. In WWI taken 1915 by Bulgaria but retaken by Allies; again captured 1941 by Bulgarians in WWII.

Bi·ton·to \bē-ˈtȯn-tō\; *anc.* **Bu·tun·tum** \byü-ˈtən-təm\. Commune, Bari prov., Puglia, SE Italy, 11 mi. (18 km.) W of the seaport of Bari; pop. (1991p) 49,792; 12th cent. Romanesque cathedral.

Bitsch. See BITCHE.

Bit·ter·feld \ˈbi-tər-ˌfelt\. City, Saxony-Anhalt, E cen. Germany, 45 mi. (72 km.) SE of Magdeburg; pop. (1981c) 22,445; graphite, magnesium deposits. Founded 12th cent.; conquered by Landgrave Dietrich von Meissen 1476; under Saxon rule; passed to Prussia 1815.

Bit·ter Lakes \ˈbi-tər\. Two lakes, Isthmus of Suez, Egypt, just N of Suez; connected and traversed by the Suez Canal (23 mi. or 37 km. across). **Great Bitter Lake** (*or Arab.* **Al–Bu·hay·rah al–Mur·rah al–Ku·brā** \ˌal-bü-ˈhī-rə-al-ˈmu̇r-ə-al-ˈkü-brä\) and **Little Bitter Lake** (*or Arab.* **Al–Buhayrah al–Murrah as–Su·ghrā** \as-ˈsü-ˌgrä\). Orig. in ancient bed of Red Sea; in modern times marshy depressions until filled by the cutting of the canal.

Bit·ter·root *or* **Bitter Root** \ˈbi-tər-ˌrüt, -ˌru̇t\. River, W Montana; rises in S Ravalli co., flows N and joins Clark Fork near Missoula in cen. Missoula co.

Bitterroot Range *or* **Bitterroot Mountains** *also* **Bitter Root Range** *or* **Bitter Root Mountains.** A range of the Rocky Mts. extending along the Idaho-Montana boundary; 300 mi. (483 km.) long; highest point Scott Peak 11,393 ft. (3473 m.); pierced by **Bitterroot Tunnel,** a railroad tunnel nearly 2 mi. (3 km.) long.

Biv·ouac Peak \ˈbi-və-ˌwak\. Mountain in N Grand Teton National Park, NW Wyoming; 11,045 ft. (3367 m.).

Bi·wa \ˈbē-wä\ *also* **Omi** \ˈō-mē\. Lake in W cen. Honshū, Japan, NE of Kyōto; 40 mi. (64 km.) long and 12 mi. (19 km.) wide; 260 sq. mi. (673 sq. km.); largest lake in Japan; alt. 285 ft. (87 m.); noted for its scenic beauty and famous in Japanese legends; its outlet is the Yodo.

Bix·by \ˈbiks-bē\. City, Tulsa co., NE Oklahoma, 15 mi. (24 km.) SE of the city of Tulsa; pop. (1990c) 9502; oil wells.

Bixschoote. See BIKSCHOTE.

Bi·ya \ˈbē-ə\. River, Gorno-Altay Rep., S Russia in Asia; flows NW, joins the Katun to form the Ob; 190 mi. (306 km.) long.

Bi·ya·la \bi-ˈya-lə\. Town, Kafr ash Shaykh governorate, Egypt, ab. 14 mi. (23 km.) NW of El Mansûra.

Biysk *also* **Biisk** \ˈbēsk\. Town, E Altay Kray, S Russia in Asia, on the Biya River near its junction with the Katun; pop. (1992e) 235,000; food products.

Bi·zerte \bə-ˈzər-tē, bi-ˈzert\ *or* **Bi·zer·ta** \bə-ˈzər-tə\; *anc.* **Hip·po Za·ry·tus** \ˈhi-pō-zə-ˈrī-təs\. Fortified seaport, N Tunisia; fishing, oil refining; northernmost town in Africa; threefold harbor: outer harbor on Mediterranean with breakwater and two jetties, inner harbor (Bay of Sebra) connected with outer by canal, and Lake Bizerte (*q.v.*) with well-developed naval port and arsenal (Sidi Abdallah); military post, Menzel Bourguiba, on S shore of lake.
History: In early times a Roman colony; taken by Arabs 7th cent.; subject for many years to Tunis and Constantine and scene of frequent revolts. Harbor fell into neglect but after French seizure in 1881, remade and opened 1895. In WWII captured by Allies May 1943; French naval base evacuated 1963.

Bizerte, Lake *or* **Lake Bizerta.** Deepwater lagoon, 42 sq. mi. (109 sq. km.) forming a landlocked harbor for Bizerte (*q.v.*).

Bjarg·tan·gar, Cape \ˈbyärg-ˌtäŋ-ər\. Cape, W Iceland, N of Breidha Fjord.

Bje·lo·var \bye-ˈlȯ-ˌvär\ *also* **Bel·o·var** \ˈbe-lō-ˌvär\. Town, N Croatia, 43 mi. (69 km.) E of Zagreb; pop. (1991c) 42,066.

Bjeshkët e Nemuna. See NORTH ALBANIAN ALPS.

Björkö. See PRIMORSK.

Björneborg. See PORI.

Bjørnøya. See BEAR ISLAND.

Black \ˈblak\. **1.** River, E cen. Louisiana; formed by confluence of Ouachita and Tensas rivers; flows S into Red River forming section of boundary bet. Catahoula and Concordia parishes, E cen. Louisiana; 101 mi. (163 km.) long.
2. River, SE Missouri and NE Arkansas; navigable 100 mi. (161 km.); rises in Ozark Plateau in NE Reynolds co., SE Missouri, flows SE then SW into White River on boundary of Jackson and Independence cos., NE cen. Arkansas; 280 mi. (451 km.) long.
3. River, N cen. New York; rises in Herkimer co., flows W and NW into Lake Ontario near Watertown, Jefferson co.; 120 mi. (193 km.) long; navigable for 40 mi. (64 km.).
4. River, SE North Carolina; flows S from Sampson co. into Cape Fear River ab. 10 mi. (16 km.) above Wilmington; 150 mi. (241 km.) long.
5. River, E South Carolina; rises in Sumter co., flows SE into Winyah Bay in E Georgetown co.
6. River, N Vermont; rises in S Orleans co., flows N into Lake Memphremagog.
7. River, SE Vermont; flows S and SE in Windsor co. into Connecticut River; 40 mi. (64 km.) long.
8. River, W cen. Wisconsin; rises in Taylor co., flows SW into Mississippi River at La Crosse; 160 mi. (257 km.) long.
9. *or in China* **Amo** \ˈä-ˈmō\ *or in Vietnam* **Song Da** \ˈsȯŋ-ˈdä\. River, SE Asia; rises in cen. Yunnan, China, flowing SE and uniting with the Red River near Sontay, N Vietnam; ab. 500 mi. (805 km.) long.

Black Belt. A strip of rolling prairie land extending across cen. Alabama and Mississippi, with black clayey soil, formerly good for growing cotton.

Black Broth·ers \ˈbrə-thərz\. Mountain, Yancey co., W North Carolina; 6620 ft. (2018 m.).

Black·burn \ˈblak-bərn\. Town, Lancashire, NW England, 21 mi. (34 km.) NNW of Manchester; pop. (1991p) 132,800; engineering; textiles; technical college (1954); coalfields nearby.

Blackburn, Mount. Mountain, Wrangell Mts., SE Alaska, 120 mi. (193 km.) NE of mouth of Copper River; 16,390 ft. (4996 m.).

Black Canyon. **1.** Canyon of the Colorado River bet. Arizona and Nevada; ab. 15 mi. (24 km.) long; site of Hoover Dam; ab. 25 mi. (40 km.) SE of Las Vegas, Nevada. See *Hoover Dam* at UNITED STATES, *Dams and Reservoirs.*

2. Canyon of the Gunnison River in NE Montrose co., W Colorado, where the river cuts through granite, gneiss, and black schist; ab. 50 mi. (81 km.) long, averages 1300 ft. (396 m.) wide, walls 3000 ft. (914 m.) at highest point; most picturesque part is now the **Black Canyon of the Gunnison National Park.** See UNITED STATES, *National Parks.*

Black Country. The area around Birmingham, England—so called because of the once heavy grime from industrial pollutants.

Black Current. See JAPAN CURRENT.

Black Dome. Peak in the Catskill Mts., Greene co., SE New York; 3990 ft. (1216 m.).

Black Down. See MENDIP HILLS.

Black·foot \ˈblak-ˌfu̇t\. **1.** River, SE Idaho; flows out of **Blackfoot River Reservoir,** Caribou co., NW and W into Snake River in cen. Bingham co.; ab. 100 mi. (161 km.) long. **2.** City, ⊗ of Bingham co., SE Idaho, 23 mi. (37 km.) N of Pocatello; pop. (1990c) 9646.

Blackfoot Mountain. Peak in cen. Glacier National Park, NW Montana, SW of St. Mary Lakes; 9597 ft. (2925 m.); has glacier on N slope.

Black·ford \ˈblak-fərd\. County in E cen. Indiana. See table at INDIANA.

Black Forest *or Ger.* **Schwarz·wald** \ˈshfärts-ˌvält\. Mountainous region, Baden-Württemberg, SW Germany, along E bank of upper Rhine from the Neckar to the Swiss border; highest peak Feldberg 4905 ft. (1495 m.); higher parts thickly forested; has many lakes and mineral springs; contains sources of Neckar and Danube rivers; tourist resort.

Black Hawk \ˈblak-ˌho̊k\. County in NE cen. Iowa. See table at IOWA.

Black·head \ˈblak-ˌhed\. Peak, San Juan Mts., E Archuleta co., S Colorado; 12,500 ft. (3810 m.).

Black Head \ˈblak-ˌhed\. **1.** Cape on W coast of Ireland, on S side of entrance to Galway Bay.

2. Cape on NE coast of Northern Ireland, on N side of entrance to Belfast Lough; lighthouse.

Black Head Peak. Peak in the Catskill Mts., Greene co., SE New York; 3940 ft. (1201 m.).

Black·heath \ˈblak-ˌhēth\. Open common and residential district, SE London, England, mainly in Lewisham borough S of the Thames; area of common 267 acres (108 hectares); headquarters of Kentish rebels 1381 under Wat Tyler and again 1450 under Jack Cade; later notorious for its highwaymen. Here golf first introduced into England 1608.

Black Hills. Group of mountains in W South Dakota and NE Wyoming; total area ab. 6000 sq. mi. (15,540 sq. km.); contains gold, lead, and other mineral deposits; highest mountain 7242 ft. (2207 m.) Harney Peak, South Dakota; drained chiefly by the Belle Fourche and S fork of Cheyenne River.

Blackhope Scar. See MOORFOOT HILLS.

Black Jack. City, St. Louis co., E Missouri; pop. (1990c) 6128.

Black Kaweah. See KAWEAH PEAKS.

Black Lake. **1.** Lake, N Natchitoches parish, NW cen. Louisiana; ab. 13 mi. (21 km.) long; outlet is to Red River; part of a large fish and game preserve.

2. Lake, W St. Lawrence co., N New York; ab. 20 mi. (32 km.) long; outlet from N end into Oswegatchie River.

3. Town, S Quebec, Canada, 5 mi. (8 km.) SSW of Thetford Mines; pop. (1991c) 4449; asbestos deposits.

Black Me·sa \ˈmā-sə\. Elevation in Cimarron co., extreme NW Oklahoma; 4973 ft. (1516 m.); highest point in the state.

Black·more, Mount \ˈblak-ˌmōr\. Peak, cen. Gallatin co., S Montana; 10,196 ft. (3108 m.).

Black Mountain. **1.** Peak, Dawson and Gilmer cos., N Georgia; 3600 ft. (1097 m.).

2. Mountain, Harlan co., SE Kentucky; 4145 ft. (1263 m.); highest peak in the state.

3. Peak, N Grant co., SW New Mexico; 9020 ft. (2749 m.).

4. Town, Buncombe co., W North Carolina, 13 mi. (21 km.) E of Asheville; pop. (1990c) 5418; summer tourist center.

Black Mountains. **1.** Ridge in W Mohave co., NW cen. Arizona, along E bank of Colorado River.

2. Range of Blue Ridge, chiefly in Yancey and Buncombe cos., in W North Carolina; highest peak Mt. Mitchell 6684 ft. (2037 m.).

3. *or Welsh* **Y Myn·ydd Du** \ə-ˈmə-nith-ˈdē\. Range in Gwent and Powys cos., SE Wales, E of the Usk River; highest peak 2660 ft. (811 m.).

Black Pine Peak. Mountain, SE Cassia co., S Idaho; 9385 ft. (2861 m.).

Black·pool \ˈblak-ˌpül\. Town, Lancashire, NW England, on Irish Sea 28 mi. (45 km.) N of Liverpool; pop. (1991p) 144,500; seaside resort.

Black River. Name of several rivers. See BLACK.

Black River Falls. City, ⊗ of Jackson co., W cen. Wisconsin, on falls of Black River 25 mi. (40 km.) N of Sparta; pop. (1990c) 3490.

Black·rock \ˈblak-ˌräk\. Residential town, co. Dublin, E Ireland; a SE suburb of Dublin on the coast near Dun Laoghaire; seaside resort.

Black Rock Desert. Alkaline sink in NW Nevada; ab. 70 mi. (113 km.) long and 20 mi. (32 km.) wide; 1000 sq. mi. (2590 sq. km.); **Black Rock Range** (highest point Pahute Peak 8618 ft. or 2627 m.) extends along its W side, in Humboldt co.

Blacks·burg \ˈblaks-ˌbərg\. Town, Montgomery co., W Virginia, 28 mi. (45 km.) W of Roanoke; pop. (1990c) 34,590; Virginia Polytechnic Institute and State Univ. (1872).

Black Sea *also* **Eux·ine Sea** \ˈyük-sən, -sīn\ *or Russ.* **Cher·no·ye Mo·re** \ˈchȯr-nə-yə-ˈmȯr-yə\; *anc.* **Pon·tus** *or* **Pon·tus Eux·i·nus** \ˈpän-təs-yu̇k-ˈsī-nəs\. Sea bet. Europe and Asia; ab. 180,000 sq. mi. (466,200 sq. km.); max. depth 7250 ft. (2210 m.); connected with Aegean Sea through the Bosporus, Sea of Marmara, and Dardanelles, and with the Sea of Azov, its N arm, by Kerch Strait; receives many rivers, esp.: Danube, Dniester, Bug, Dnieper, Kuban' (of Europe); Kızıl Irmak and Sakarya (of Turkey in Asia); the Sea of Azov receives the Don. Most marine life exists in a shallow surface layer.

Black·shear \ˈblak-ˌshir\. City, ⊗ of Pierce co., SE Georgia, 10 mi. (16 km.) NE of Waycross; pop. (1990c) 3263.

Black·sod Bay \ˈblak-ˌsäd\. Inlet of Atlantic Ocean on W coast of Ireland, S of Erris Head, enclosed on the W by Mullet Penin.

Black·stock Knob \ˈblak-ˌstäk\. Peak, Buncombe co., W North Carolina; 6386 ft. (1947 m.).

Black·stone \ˈblak-ˌstōn\. **1.** River, S cen. Massachusetts and NE Rhode Island; rises in S cen. Worcester co., Massachusetts, flows SE across NE corner of Rhode Island, becomes the Sekonk at Pawtucket; 40 mi. (64 km.) long.

2. Town, Worcester co., cen. Massachusetts, 20 mi. (32 km.) SE of the city of Worcester; pop. (1990c) 8023.

3. Town, Nottoway co., S cen. Virginia, 36 mi. (58 km.) WSW of Petersburg; pop. (1990c) 3497.

Black·town \ˈblak-ˌtau̇n\. Town, E New South Wales, SE Australia, on railroad line 18 mi. (29 km.) NW of Sydney.

Black Volta. See VOLTA, BLACK.

Black War·ri·or \ˈwȯr-ē-ər, ˈwär-\. Navigable river, cen. Alabama; formed by confluence of Locust and Mulberry forks in Jefferson co., flows SW, through coalfields, into Tombigbee River near Demopolis; 178 mi. (286 km.) long; furnishes waterpower above Tuscaloosa.

Black·wa·ter \ˈblak-ˌwȯ-tər, -ˌwä-\. **1.** River, W cen. Missouri; rises in W Johnson co., flows E into Missouri River in N Cooper co.; ab. 85 mi. (137 km.) long.
2. River, SE Virginia; rises in Prince George co., joins Nottoway River on North Carolina boundary to form the Chowan.
3. River, S cen. British Columbia, Canada; flows E into Fraser River; ab. 130 mi. (209 km.) long.
4. River, S Ireland; rises 16 mi. (26 km.) NE of Killarney, flows E across co. Cork, then S to Youghal Bay; 100 mi. (161 km.) long.
5. River, co. Meath, E Ireland; flows SE from co. Cavan into the Boyne River at Navan; ab. 40 mi. (64 km.) long.
6. River, W Essex co., SE England; rises near Saffron Walden and flows SE into the North Sea; 40 mi. (64 km.) long.
7. River, SW cen. Northern Ireland; rises in Dungannon dist. and flows along boundary bet. Dungannon and Armagh dists. into SW Lough Neagh; 50 mi. (81 km.) long.

Blackwater Falls. Falls in Blackwater River (tributary of Cheat River), Tucker co., NE West Virginia; 63 ft. (19 m.) high; above **Blackwater Canyon** (gorge ab. 10 mi. (16 km.) long with rugged walls 1000 ft. or 305 m. high) in **Blackwater Falls State Park,** at N end of Monongahela National Forest.

Black·well \ˈblak-ˌwel\. City, Kay co., N Oklahoma; pop. (1990c) 7538. See WELFARE ISLAND.

Blackwells Island. See ROOSEVELT ISLAND 2.

Bla·den \ˈblā-dən\. County in S North Carolina. See table at NORTH CAROLINA.

Bla·dens·burg \ˌblā-dənz-ˌbərg\. Town, Prince Georges co., S cen. Maryland, 7 mi. (11 km.) ENE of Washington, D.C.; pop. (1990c) 8064; site of battle Aug. 1814 in which American defeat by British resulted in the subsequent burning of most of the public buildings of Washington.

Blaen·av·on *also* **Blaen·a·fon** \blīn-ˈa-vən\. Town, Gwent, SE Wales, 31 mi. (50 km.) NW of Bristol England; pop. (1981p) 6363.

Bla·go·ev·grad \blä-ˈgȯ-ev-ˌgrät\. Town, SW Bulgaria; pop. (1991e) 79,089; mineral springs.

Bla·go·vesh·chensk \ˌblə-gə-ˈvyāsh-chinsk\. City, ✱ of Amur Oblast, SE Russia in Asia, on Amur River, near junction with Zeya River; pop. (1992e) 214,000; on Trans-Siberian R.R.; founded 1856 by statesman and explorer Nikolai Muravyov; scene of Russo-Japanese naval incident 1937; base for Soviet advances in WWII into Manchuria Aug. 1945.

Blaine \ˈblān\. **1.** Name of counties in four states of the U.S. See tables at IDAHO, MONTANA, NEBRASKA, OKLAHOMA.
2. City, Anoka and Ramsey cos., Minnesota, NW of Minneapolis; pop. (1990c) 38,975.
3. City and port of entry, Whatcom co., NW Washington, near Canadian boundary 20 mi. (32 km.) NNW of Bellingham; pop. (1990c) 2489; tourist center.

Blair \ˈblar\. **1.** County in S cen. Pennsylvania. See table at PENNSYLVANIA.
2. City, ⊗ of Washington co., E Nebraska, on Missouri River 22 mi. (35 km.) N of Omaha; pop. (1990c) 6860; regional trade center; Dana Coll. (1884).

Blairs·ville \ˈblarz-ˌvil\. **1.** City, ⊗ of Union co., N Georgia; pop. (1990c) 564.
2. Borough, Indiana co., W cen. Pennsylvania, on Conemaugh River 21 mi. (34 km.) W of Johnstown; pop. (1990c) 3595.

Blakang Mati See SENTOSA.

Blake·ly \ˈblā-klē\. **1.** City, ⊗ of Early co., SW Georgia, 47 mi. (76 km.) WSW of Albany; pop. (1990c) 5595; founded 1821.
2. Borough, Lackawanna co., NE Pennsylvania, 7 mi. (11 km.) NE of Scranton; pop. (1990c) 7222; suburb of Scranton; coal.

Blake Point \ˈblāk\. Point at NE extremity of Isle Royale, Michigan, NW Lake Superior.

Blam·bang·an Peninsula \bläm-ˈbäŋ-ən\. Narrow strip of land forming southernmost point of Java, Indonesia, bet. S end of Bali Strait and Indian Ocean.

Blanc, Cape \ˈbläŋk, ˈblä^{n}\. **1.** *or* **Cape Blan·co** \ˈbläŋ-kō\. Cape on NW coast of Africa; a narrow peninsula extending S into Atlantic Ocean; bisected by the boundary bet. Western Sahara and Mauritania.
2. Cape on N tip of Tunisia, 37°20′N, 9°50′E.

Blanc, Mont \mȯ^{n}-ˈblä^{n}\ *or Ital.* **Mon·te Bian·co** \ˈmȯn-tā-bē-ˈäŋ-kō\. Massif, on border of France, Italy, and Switzerland. Its principal peak, Savoy Alps, Haute-Savoie dept., SE France, is highest mountain of the Alps; first climbed Aug. 1786 by Michel-Gabriel Paccard and Jacques Balmat. Beneath it is **Mont Blanc Tunnel** (8 mi. or 13 km.) connecting Chamonix-Mont-Blanc, France, with Courmayeur, Italy; one of longest vehicular tunnels in the world. See table at ALPS.

Blan·ca, La·gu·na \lä-ˈgü-nä-ˈbläŋ-kä\. Large freshwater lake in extreme S Chile, E of Skyring Water.

Blan·ca Peak \ˈblaŋ-kə\. Mountain, Castilla, Huerfano, and Alamosa cos., S Colorado; 14,345 ft. (4372 m.); highest peak in the Sangre de Cristo Mts.

Blanche Bay \ˈblanch\. Inlet of Pacific Ocean on NE coast of New Britain I., Bismarck Archipelago; its inner part is site of Rabaul.

Blanche Harbour. Protected body of water in Treasury Is., S of Bougainville I., Solomon Is., bet. Mono and Stirling islands; affords good anchorage.

Blan·ches·ter \ˈblan-ˌches-tər\. Village, Clinton co., SW Ohio, 29 mi. (47 km.) ENE of Cincinnati; pop. (1990c) 4206; settled 1832.

Blanc–Mesnil, Le. See LE BLANC-MESNIL.

Blanc–Nez \ˌblä^{n}-ˈnā\. White chalk cliff forming a cape on Strait of Dover, N France, 5 mi. (8 km.) SW of Calais; its companion cape is Gris-Nez (*q.v.*).

Blan·co \ˈblaŋ-kō\. County in cen. Texas. See table at TEXAS.

Blanco \ˈbläŋ-kō\. **1.** River, E Bolivia; 330 mi. (531 km.) long.
2. River, W Honduras; flows out of Lake Yojoa (*q.v.*) into the Ulúa River; ab. 45 mi. (72 km.) long.

Blanco, Cape \ˈblaŋ-kō\. Cape on NW coast of Curry co., SW corner of Oregon; westernmost point of Oregon, 42°50′N, 124°34′W.

Blanco, Cape \ˈbläŋ-kō\. **1.** Cape, Africa. See BLANC, CAPE 1.
2. Cape at S extremity of Nicoya Penin., on W coast of Costa Rica, at the entrance to the Gulf of Nicoya.
3. Cape at extreme NW tip of Peru.

Blanco, Pi·co \ˈpē-kō-ˈbläŋ-kō\. Mountain, SE Costa Rica, in the Cordillera de Talamanca; 11,693 ft. (3564 m.).

Blanc Sa·blon \ˌblä^{n}-sà-ˈblō^{n}\. Municipality, E Quebec, Canada, on **Blanc Sablon Bay,** inlet at S end of Strait of Belle Isle on boundary bet. Labrador and Quebec; pop. (1991c) 1211.

Bland \ˈbland\. **1.** County in W Virginia. See table at VIRGINIA.
2. Village, its ⊗.

Blan·ding \ˈblan-diŋ\. City, San Juan co., SE Utah; pop. (1990c) 3162; nearby are Hovenweep and Natural Bridges national monuments.

Blan·ken·ber·ge \ˈbläŋ-kən-ˌber-kə\. Commune, West Flanders prov., NW Belgium; pop. (1981c) 14,832; resort.

Blan·ken·burg *or* **Blankenburg am Harz** \ˈbläŋ-kən-ˌbu̇rk-äm-ˈhärts\. City, Saxony-Anhalt, cen. Germany, 35 mi. (56 km.) SW of Magdeburg; pop. (1992e) 18,231; founded c. 1200.

Blan·qui·lla \bläŋ-ˈkē-yä\. Island, Venezuela, in Caribbean Sea 74 mi. (119 km.) NNE of La Tortuga I.

Blan·tyre \blan-ˈtīr\. City, Shire Highlands, S Malawi; pop. (1987c) 333,120; distilling; cement, textiles; chief commercial center of Malawi; approx. alt. 3600 ft. (1097 m.); combined with Limbe forming single municipality 1956; founded 1876; named after explorer David Livingstone's birthplace in Scotland.

Blar·ney \ˈblär-nē\. Town, cen. co. Cork, SW Ireland, 4 mi. (6.4 km.) NW of Cork; pop. (1981c) 1980; in its 15th cent.

Blarney Castle is the "Blarney stone," which is said to make anyone who kisses it proficient in blarney (i.e., smooth, wheedling talk or flattery).

Blas·dell \ˈblāz-ˌdel\. Village, Erie co., W New York, on Lake Erie 7 mi. (11 km.) S of Buffalo; pop. (1990c) 2900.

Blas·ket Islands \ˈblas-kət\. Group of small islands in co. Kerry, off SW coast of Ireland, N of entrance to Dingle Bay; largest is Great Blasket.

Blå·vand, Cape \ˈblȯ-ˌvän\ *or Dan.* **Blå·vands Huk** \ˈblȯ-ˌväns-ˌhu̇k\. Cape on W cen. coast of Jutland Penin., Denmark.

Bla·vet \blä-ˈvā\. River, Brittany, NW France; rises in Côtes-du-Nord dept., flows SSW to the Bay of Biscay; its estuary forms the harbor of Lorient; 87 mi. (140 km.) long.

Blay·don \ˈblād-ᵊn\. Town, Tyne and Wear, N England, on the Tyne 5 mi. (8 km.) W of Newcastle upon Tyne; pop. (1981p) 30,563; coal.

Bleck·ley \ˈble-klē\. County in cen. Georgia. See table at GEORGIA.

Bled \ˈbled\. Village on glacial **Lake Bled** in NW Slovenia, ab. 30 mi. (48 km.) NW of Ljubljana.

Bled·soe \ˈbled-sō\. County in SE cen. Tennessee. See table at TENNESSEE.

Ble·kinge \ˈblā-kiŋ-ə\. Province of S Sweden. See table at SWEDEN.

Blencathara. See SADDLEBACK.

Blen·heim \ˈble-nim\. **1.** Urban area, NE South I., New Zealand; pop. (1992e) 23,800; harbor for smaller vessels.
2. *Eng. and Fr. form of Ger.* **Blind·heim** \ˈblint-ˌhīm\. Village W Bavaria, Germany, on Danube 23 mi. (37 km.) NNW of Augsburg; scene of victory Aug. 13, 1704 of English under John Churchill, first duke of Marlborough and Prince Eugene of Savoy over French and Bavarians under Marshals Tallard and Marsin in War of Spanish Succession; called also battle of Höchstädt (*q.v.*).

Blenheim Palace. Original seat of John Churchill, first duke of Marlborough, near Woodstock, Oxfordshire, cen. England; granted to duke by government in Queen Anne's reign.

Blen·ner·has·sett Island \ˌble-nər-ˈha-sət\. Island in Ohio River, West Virginia, 2 mi. (3.2 km.) below Parkersburg; famous as meeting place 1805 of political leader Aaron Burr and Harman Blennerhassett who had purchased part of island 1798.

Blesae. See BLOIS.

Bletch·ley \ˈblech-lē\. Town, Buckinghamshire, SE cen. England, 43 mi. (69 km.) NW of London; Open Univ. (1969).

Blibba. See BLITTA.

Bli·da \ˈblē-də\ *or* **El Bou·laï·da** \ˌel-bü-ˈlī-də\. City, N Algeria, ab. 10 mi. (16 km.) SW of the city of Algiers; situated on edge of a plain at base of Maritime Atlas Mts.; pop. (1987p) 170,182; active trade in oranges. Dates from 16th cent.; important under the Turks.

Blindheim. See BLENHEIM 2.

Blind River \ˈblīnd\. Town and port, Algoma dist., S Ontario, Canada, on North Channel at mouth of Mississagi River 70 mi. (113 km.) E of Sault Ste. Marie; pop. (1991c) 3355; railroad town in mineral district.

Bliss·field \ˈblis-ˌfēld\. Village, Lenawee co., S Michigan, 32 mi. (52 km.) S of Ann Arbor; pop. (1990c) 3172.

Bli·tar \ˈblē-ˌtär\. Town East Java prov., Indonesia, ab. 20 mi. (32 km.) SE of Kediri; pop. (1990c) 119,011.

Blit·ta \ˈblēt-tä\; *formerly* **Blib·ba** \ˈblib-bä\. Town, Togo, on railroad line ab. 143 mi. (230 km.) N of Lomé.

Block Island \ˈbläk\. **1.** Island, Rhode Island, in Atlantic Ocean at E entrance to Long Island Sound, ab. 9 mi. (15 km.) SW of Point Judith; 7 mi. (11 km.) long, 3.5 mi. (5.6 km.) wide; ab. 11 sq. mi. (29 sq. km.); part of Washington co., Rhode Island; coextensive with town of New Shoreham; summer resort and deep-sea fishing center; has two good harbors and two lighthouses. Called Manisses by original Indian inhabitants; first settlement by Europeans 1661; admitted to the colony of Rhode Island 1664.
2. Village in town of New Shoreham, Washington co., SE Rhode Island; resort.

Block Island Sound. Body of water bet. Washington co., S Rhode Island and Block I., connecting Atlantic Ocean on E with Long Island Sound on W.

Bloem·fon·tein \ˈblüm-ˌfän-ˌtān\. City, ✱ of Free State, Rep. of South Africa, 295 mi. (475 km.) W of Durban on a tributary of Modder River; pop. (1985c) 104,381; glassware, furniture, plastics; railway workshops; university (1855, present status 1950); founded 1846.

Bloem·hof \ˈblüm-ˌhȯf\. Town, NE Rep. of South Africa, on Vaal River 95 mi. (153 km.) NNE of Kimberley; diamond deposits.

Blois \ˈblwä\; *anc.* **Ble·sae** \ˈblē-sē\. City, ✱ of Loir-et-Cher dept., N cen. France, on right bank of Loire River 35 mi. (56 km.) SW of Orléans; pop. (1990c) 51,549; 17th cent. cathedral; ancient Roman aqueduct. Famous castle rich in historical associations: residence of counts of Blois; became a favorite residence of French kings.

Blom·i·don, Cape \ˈblä-mi-dən\. Cape and promontory on W coast of Nova Scotia, Canada, S of entrance to Minas Basin; 670 ft. (204 m.) high.

Bło·nie \ˈbwȯ-nye\. Village, Warszawa prov., Poland, ab. 17 mi. (27 km.) W of Warsaw; in WWI in Russian W defense line, taken by Germans July 20, 1915.

Bloods·worth Island \ˈblədz-wərth\. Island in Chesapeake Bay, S Dorchester co., Maryland.

Bloody Nose Ridge. Name given by U.S. marines to Umurbrogol Mt. on Peleliu I., S Palau, W Pacific Ocean; scene of severe fighting Sept. 1944 which resulted in isolation of Japanese.

Bloo·mer \ˈblü-mər\. City, Chippewa co., W Wisconsin, 13 mi. (21 km.) NNW of Chippewa Falls; pop. (1990c) 3085.

Bloom·field \ˈblüm-ˌfēld\. **1.** Town, cen. Hartford co., N Connecticut, NNW of the city of Hartford; pop. (1990c) 19,483; incorp. 1835.
2. Town, ⊗ of Greene co., SW Indiana, 24 mi. (39 km.) WSW of Bloomington; pop. (1990c) 2592.
3. City, ⊗ of Davis co., SE Iowa, 18 mi. (29 km.) S of Ottumwa; pop. (1990c) 2580; regional distribution point.
4. City, ⊗ of Stoddard co., SE Missouri; pop. (1990c) 1800.
5. Town, Essex co., NE New Jersey, 4 mi. (6 km.) NNW of Newark; pop. (1990c) 45,061; Bloomfield Coll. (1868); orig. part of Newark, made separate township following Revolutionary War; incorp. 1812.

Bloomfield Hills. City, Oakland co., SE Michigan, 20 mi. (32 km.) NW of Detroit; pop. (1990c) 4288; Oakland Community Coll. (1964).

Bloom·ing·dale \ˈblü-miŋ-ˌdāl\. **1.** Village, Du Page co., NE Illinois, 27 mi. (43 km.) W of Chicago; pop. (1990c) 16,614.
2. Borough, Passaic co., N New Jersey, 9 mi. (15 km.) WNW of Paterson; pop. (1990c) 7530.

Bloom·ing Grove \ˈblüm-iŋ-ˈgrōv\ *or formerly* **Cor·si·ca** \ˈkȯr-si-kə\. Village, Morrow co., cen. Ohio; birthplace of Warren G. Harding, 29th president of the U.S., 1865.

Bloom·ing·ton \ˈblü-miŋ-tən\. **1.** City, ⊗ of McLean co., cen. Illinois, 35 mi. (56 km.) ESE of Peoria; pop. (1990c) 51,972; in coal-bearing region; Illinois Wesleyan Univ. (1850).
2. City, ⊗ of Monroe co., S cen. Indiana, 45 mi. (72 km.) SW of Indianapolis; pop. (1990c) 60,633; limestone deposits; Indiana Univ. Bloomington (1820); settled c. 1815.
3. City, Hennepin co., SE cen. Minnesota, SW of Minneapolis; pop. (1990c) 86,335; Mall of America, largest enclosed shopping mall in U.S.; Normandale Community Coll. (1968).

Blooms·burg \ˈblümz-ˌbərg\. Town, ⊗ of Columbia co., E cen. Pennsylvania, 26 mi. (42 km.) NNW of Pottsville; pop. (1990c) 12,439; Bloomsburg Univ. of Pennsylvania (1839).

Blooms·bury \ˈblümz-bə-rē, *U.S. also* -ˌber-ē\. A central district of London, SE England; British Museum; Univ. of London; a fashionable area early 20th cent., noted esp. for its intellectuals with artistic and literary influence.

Blo·ra \ˈblō-rä\. Town, central Java prov., Indonesia, E of Semarang; in hilly region producing teak.

Blore Heath \ˈblōr\. Area in Staffordshire, W England, 3 mi. (5 km.) ENE of Market Drayton; site of Yorkist victory 1459 over Lancastrians in Wars of the Roses.

Bloss·burg \ˈblȯs-ˌbərg\. Borough, Tioga co., N Pennsylvania, on Tioga River 30 mi. (48 km.) N of Williamsport; pop. (1990c) 1571; coal deposits.

Blount \ˈblənt\. Name of counties in two states of the U.S. See tables at ALABAMA and TENNESSEE.

Blounts·town \ˈblənts-ˌtau̇n\. City, ⊗ of Calhoun co., NW Florida, on Apalachicola River 47 mi. (76 km.) W of Tallahassee; pop. (1990c) 2404.

Blu·cher Point \ˈblü-chər\. Point of land on NE coast of Huon Penin., Papua New Guinea.

Blu·denz \ˈblü-dents\. Town, Vorarlberg, SW Austria, on the Ill River 25 mi. (40 km.) S of Bregenz; pop. (1991c) 13,369; alt. ab. 1920 ft. (585 m.); tourist resort; 18th cent. castle; given municipal charter 1296.

Blue \ˈblü\. **1.** River, S Indiana; rises in Washington co., flows S into Ohio River; ab. 40 mi. (64 km.) long.
2. Upper course of E Fork of the White River, Indiana, to cen. Bartholomew co. See WHITE 3.

Blue Ash \ˈblü-ˌash\. City, Hamilton co., SW Ohio, NE of Cincinnati; pop. (1990c) 11,860.

Blue Earth. **1.** County in S Minnesota. See table at MINNESOTA.
2. City, ⊗ of Faribault co., S Minnesota, 18 mi. (29 km.) E of Fairmont; pop. (1990c) 3745.

Blue·field \ˈblü-ˌfēld\. **1.** Town, Tazewell co., SW Virginia, on border adjoining Bluefield, West Virginia, 32 mi. (52 km.) WNW of Pulaski; pop. (1990c) 5363; Bluefield Coll. (1922).
2. City, Mercer co., S West Virginia, in Blue Ridge contiguous with Bluefield, Virginia; pop. (1990c) 12,756; near coalfield, also iron, limestone, and silica deposits. Bluefield State Coll. (1895).

Blue·fields \ˈblü-ˌfēldz\. **1.** River in Nicaragua. See ESCONDIDO.
2. Town, ✻ of Zelaya dept., Nicaragua, on SE coast at mouth of the Escondido River; munic. pop. (1985e) 17,721; export center.

Blue·grass \ˈblü-ˌgras\. Region in central Kentucky where Kentucky bluegrass (*Poa pratensis*) abounds; noted for breeding of fine horses.

Blue Grot·to \ˈgrä-tō\. Cavern, N shore of island of Capri, in Bay of Naples, Italy; ab. 175 ft. (53 m.) long and 50 ft. (15 m.) high; renowned for the dazzling blue light inside.

Blue·hill Bay \ˈblü-ˌhil\. Inlet of Atlantic Ocean on S coast of Hancock co., Maine, W of Mt. Desert I.

Blue Island. City, Cook co., NE Illinois, just S of Chicago; pop. (1990c) 21,203; suburb of Chicago.

Blue Knob. Peak, Bedford co., S Pennsylvania, N of the borough of Bedford; 3130 ft. (954 m.).

Blue Licks \ˈliks\. Locality, incl. mineral springs (**Blue Licks Springs**), Nicholas co., NE Kentucky, on right bank of Licking River ab. 40 mi. (64 km.) NE of Lexington; scene of battle Aug. 1782 in which Kentucky pioneers were defeated by a force of Indians and Canadians; site now **Blue Licks Battlefield State Park.**

Blue Me·sa Dam *and* **Blue Mesa Reservoir** \ˈmā-sə\. See UNITED STATES, *Dams and Reservoirs.*

Blue, Mount. Peak, Franklin co., W Maine; 3187 ft. (971 m.).

Blue Mountain 1. *formerly* **Rich Mountain** \ˈrich\. Peak in Ouachita Mts., Polk and Scott cos., W Arkansas; 2623 ft. (800 m.); 2d highest point in state. See MAGAZINE MOUNTAIN.
2. Range in SE Pennsylvania, part of Kittatinny Mt. (*q.v.*).
3. Peak, N Clallam co., NW Washington; 6007 ft. (1831 m.).
4. Town, Tippah co., N Mississippi; pop. (1990c) 667; Blue Mountain Coll. (1873).

Blue Mountains. **1.** Mountain range, NE Oregon and SE Washington; highest peak Rock Creek Butte 9105 ft. (2775 m.).
2. *or* **Blue Plateau.** Part of Great Dividing Range, E New South Wales, SE Australia; 2000 to 3600 ft. (610 to 1097 m.).
3. City, New South Wales, SE Australia; pop. (1991c) 69,420; formed 1947.
4. Range in E Jamaica, West Indies; highest **Blue Mountain Peak** 7388 ft. (2252 m.)., on slopes of which Blue Mountain coffee grows.

Blue Mud Bay. Inlet on W Gulf of Carpentaria on Arnhem Land coast, N Northern Terr., Australia.

Blue Nile. **1.** River, Sudan. See NILE.
2. *or* **Al–Ja·zī·rah** \ˌal-jȧ-ˈzē-rə\ *also* **El Ge·zi·ra** \ˌel-jə-ˈzē-rə\. Former province of E Sudan; ✻ Wad Medani.

Blue Plateau. See BLUE MOUNTAINS 2.

Blue Point. Locality, Suffolk co., Long Island, New York, on Great South Bay, SW of Patchogue; noted for its oyster beds.

Blue Ridge. **1.** *or* **Blue Ridge Mountains.** The E and SE range of the Appalachian Mts., extending from near Harpers Ferry, West Virginia, SW across W Virginia and W North Carolina into N Georgia and NW South Carolina; by some considered to include the N extension into Maryland, Pennsylvania, and New York; its highest peaks are in the Black Mts. (*q.v.*) of North Carolina; av. elev. 2000 to 4000 ft. (610 to 1219 m.).
2. City, ⊗ of Fannin co., N Georgia; pop. (1990c) 1336.

Blue Ridge Dam. See table at TENNESSEE VALLEY AUTHORITY.

Blue Ridge Parkway. Scenic parkway, Virginia and North Carolina, extending 470 mi. (756 km.) along crest of Blue Ridge; administered by the U.S. National Park Service; parkway estab. 1936.

Blue River. Name of two rivers in Indiana. See BLUE.

Blue Springs. City, Jackson co., W Missouri, 10 mi. (16 km.) SE of Independence; pop. (1990c) 40,153.

Blue Sulphur Springs. Mineral springs Greenbrier co., SE West Virginia.

Bluff \ˈbləf\; *formerly* **Camp·bell·town** \ˈkam-bəl-ˌtau̇n\. Borough on peninsula (**The Bluff**), S South I., New Zealand, at entrance to **Bluff Harbour,** an inlet of Foveaux Strait; port of Invercargill; pop. (1981c) 2720.

Bluff, El. See EL BLUFF.

Bluff·ton \ˈbləf-tən\. **1.** City, ⊗ of Wells co., NE Indiana, 23 mi. (37 km.) S of Fort Wayne; pop. (1990c) 9020.
2. Village, Allen co., NW Ohio, 15 mi. (24 km.) NE of Lima; pop. (1990c) 3367; distribution point; crushed stone and limestone in vicinity; Bluffton Coll. (1899).

Blu·me·nau \ˌblü-mə-ˈnau̇\. Town on the Itajaí River, Santa Catarina state, S Brazil; munic. pop. (1991p) 211,677; founded c. 1850 by German immigrants.

Blüm·lis·alp \ˈblüm-lēs-ˌälp\. Range in the Bernese Alps. S cen. Switzerland; highest peak **Blüm·lis·alp·horn** \-ˌhȯrn\ 12,021 ft. (3664 m.).

Blunts Reef \ˈblənts-\. Reef just off Cape Mendocino, California.

Blyth \ˈblīth\. Port, Northumberland, N England, on North Sea at mouth of the **Blyth River** (20 mi. or 32 km. long) 12 mi. (19 km.) NNE of Newcastle upon Tyne; pop. (1981p) 36,466.

Blythe \ˈblīth\. City, Riverside co., SE California, near the Colorado River; pop. (1990c) 8428; Palo Verde Coll. (1947); settled 1910.

Blythe·ville \ˈblī-ˌvil, ˈblīth-, -vəl\. City, a ⊗ of Mississippi co., NE Arkansas, 5 mi. (8 km.) S of Missouri border; pop. (1990c) 22,906; a regional trade center.

Blyth River. See BLYTH.

Bo·ac \ˈbō-ˌäk\. Municipality, ✻ of Marinduque prov., Marinduque I., Philippines, on river 2 mi. (3 km.) from W coast; pop. (1980c) 37,005; an old Spanish-built town.

Bo·a·co \bō-ˈä-kō\. **1.** Department of SW cen. Nicaragua. See table at NICARAGUA.
2. Town, its ✻; munic. pop. (1985e) 15,645.

Boa Esperança, Cabo da. See GOOD HOPE, CAPE OF 2.

Bo·a·no \bō-ˈä-nō\. Small island off W end of Ceram I., Indonesia; 18 mi. (29 km.) long, 12 mi. (19 km.) wide.

Boars Head \ˈbōrz\. Peak, Schuylkill co., E cen. Pennsylvania; 2100 ft. (640 m.).

\ə\ **abut** \ə̇\ **matches** \ᵊ\ **kitten,** Fr **table** \ər\ **further** \a\ **ash** \ā\ **ace** \ä\ **cot, cart** \ȧ\ Fr **bac** \au̇\ **out** \b\ Span **Avila** \ch\ **chin** \e\ **bet** \ē\ **easy** \g\ **go** \i\ **hit** \ī\ **ice** \j\ **job** \k\ Ger **ich, Buch** \ⁿ\ Fr **vin** \ŋ\ **sing** \ō\ **go** \ȯ\ **all** \ȯ\ **law** \œ\ Fr **bœuf** \œ̄\ Fr **feu** \ȯi\ **boy** \th\ **thin** \th\ **this** \ü\ **loot** \u̇\ **foot** \ue\ Ger **füllen** \ue̅\ Fr **rue** \y\ **yet** \ʸ\ Fr **digne** \ˈdēnʸ\, **nuit** \ˈnwʸē\ \yü\ **few** \yu̇\ **fury** \zh\ **vision**

Boa Vis·ta \ˌbō-ə-ˈvēsh-tə\. **1.** Town, ✻ of Roraima state, W Brazil, on right bank of upper Rio Branco; pop. (1980c) 66,954.
2. Island, easternmost of Cape Verde Is.; 239 sq. mi. (619 sq. km.); pop. (1990p) 3457.

Bo·az \ˈbō-ˌaz\. City, Marshall and Etowah cos., NE Alabama, 17 mi. (27 km.) NW of Gadsden; pop. (1990c) 6928; Snead State Junior Coll. (1898).

Bob·bi·li \ˈbä-bi-lē\. Town, NE Andhra Pradesh, E India, 60 mi. (97 km.) N of Vishakhapatnam; when attacked by French and natives 1756, held out until every man was dead or mortally wounded.

Bober. See BÓBR.

Bo·bi·gny \ˌbò-bē-ˈnyē\. Commune, ✻ of Seine-St.-Denis dept., N France, NE suburb of Paris.

Böb·ling·en \ˈbœ-bliŋ-ən\. City, Baden-Württemberg, S Germany, 10 mi. (16 km.) SW of Stuttgart; pop. (1980c) 3090; founded c. 1250; heavily bombed in WWII, since rebuilt.

Bo·bo–Diou·las·so *or* **Bo·bo Diou·las·so** \ˈbò-bō-ˌdyü-lä-ˈsō, -ˈlä-sō\. City, W Burkina Faso; pop. (1990e) 300,000; terminus of railroad lines from Abidjan and Ouagadougou.

Bo·bo·tov Kuk \ˈbò-bò-ˌtòv-ˈku̇k\. Peak, Montenegro, SW Yugoslavia; 8274 ft. (2522 m.); highest in Durmitor and in Dinaric Alps (see table at ALPS).

Bóbr \ˈbü-bər\ *or Ger.* **Bo·ber** \ˈbō-bər\. River, chiefly in W Wrocław prov., SW Poland; flows N to the Odra (Oder) SE of Frankfurt, Germany; formerly in Silesia, Germany.

Bobr. River, Poland. See BIEBRZA.

Bobriki. See NOVOMOSKOVSK.

Bo·bruysk *or* **Ba·bruysk** *also* **Bo·bruisk** \bä-ˈbrü-isk\. City, SE cen. Belarus, 90 mi. (145 km.) SE of Minsk; pop. (1991e) 223,000; engineering; shoes; on Berezina River; fortified by Alexander I; withstood attack of French army 1812; nearly destroyed by great fire 1902; seized by Germans July 1941, recovered June 1944.

Boca, La. See LA BOCA.

Bo·ca Chi·ca \ˈbō-kə-ˈchē-kə\. Island in Florida Keys adjacent to Key West; U.S. Naval Air Station.

Boca Chica. See CORREGIDOR and NORTH CHANNEL.

Boca del Río \t͟hel-ˈrē-ō\. Municipality, Veracruz state, Mexico, 6 mi. (10 km.) S of the seaport of Veracruz; munic. pop. (1990p) 143,844; fishing.

Boca Grande. See CORREGIDOR and SOUTH CHANNEL.

Bo·cai·u·va *or* **Bo·cay·u·va** \ˌbü-kī-ˈü-və\. Town, Minas Gerais state, E Brazil, on railroad line ab. 190 mi. (306 km.) N of Belo Horizonte; visited by scientists to observe eclipse of the sun May 20, 1947.

Boca Ra·ton \ˌbō-kə-rə-ˈtōn\. City, Palm Beach co., SE Florida, on the coast 17 mi. (27 km.) N of Fort Lauderdale; pop. (1990c) 61,492; Coll. of Boca Raton (1963), Florida Atlantic Univ. (1964); incorp. 1925.

Bo·cas del To·ro \ˈbō-käs-del-ˈtō-rō\. **1.** Province of W Panama. See table at PANAMA.
2. Atlantic coast port, its ✻, on an island off NW coast of Panama; pop. (1990p) 5139.

Bocchetta. Pass, Apennines. See table at APENNINES.

Boch·nia \ˈbòk-nyä\. Commune, Tarnów prov., Poland, ab. 20 mi. (32 km.) ESE of Kraków; pop. (1989e) 28,845; salt and gypsum deposits. Taken 1702 by Swedish King Charles XII.

Bo·cholt \ˈbò-ˌkȯlt\. City, North Rhine-Westphalia, Germany, near Dutch border; pop. (1992e) 69,595.

Bo·chum \ˈbō-ku̇m\. City, North Rhine-Westphalia, W Germany, in Ruhr Valley 37 mi. (60 km.) SSW of Münster; pop. (1992e) 398,578; automobiles, chemicals; metallurgical industries; church (1599); university (1965); planetarium (1964); received municipal charter 1321; in WWII bombed by British; rebuilt after 1946.

Bock·um–Hö·vel \ˈbò-ku̇m-ˈhœ-fəl\. City, North Rhine-Westphalia, W Germany, 16 mi. (26 km.) NE of Dortmund; coal deposits. Founded in 12th cent.

Bod. See BAUDH 1.

Bo·day·bo *also* **Bo·dai·bo** \bə-ˌdī-ˈbò\. Town, NE Irkutsk Oblast, Russia in Asia, on right bank of Vitim River NE of Lake Baikal.

Bodegas. See BABAHOYO.

Bo·de·le \bō-ˈdā-lā\ *or Fr.* **Bo·dé·lé** \bò-dā-ˈlā\. Low area, N Chad, NE of Lake Chad and S of Tibesti Mts.; historically important for its forage grasses.

Bo·den \ˈbü-dən\. Town, Norrbotten prov., N Sweden, on Luleålv River 22 mi. (35 km.) NNW of Luleå; pop. (1980p) 28,848.

Bodensee. See CONSTANCE, LAKE.

Bo·derg, Lough \läk-ˈbō-ˌderg, -ˌdərg\. Lake in N cen. Ireland, S of Lough Allen; one of the chain of lakes traversed by the Shannon River.

Bodh Ga·yā \ˈbòd-ˈgī-ä\ *or* **Buddh Gaya** \ˈbu̇d-ˈgī-ə\ *or* **Bud·dha Ga·yā** \ˈbu̇-də-ˈgī-ä\. Village, cen. Bihar, NE India, 7 mi. (11 km.) S of Gaya; pop. (1991p) 21,686. One of the holiest sites of Buddhism; here Buddha (Siddhārtha Gautama) is said to have experienced his Enlightenment under the sacred Bo Tree. A temple and other structures built on the site 3d cent. B.C. have been destroyed and a rebuilt temple (orig. 2d cent. A.D.) now marks the place.

Bod·ie Island \ˈbä-dē\. Long narrow island, NE North Carolina, separating Albemarle and Roanoke sounds from the Atlantic Ocean; 37 sq. mi. (96 sq. km.); lighthouse at its S end.

Bo·di·na·yak·ka·nur \ˌbō-di-ˈnä-yə-kə-ˌnu̇r\. Town, Tamil Nadu, S India; 55 mi. (89 km.) W of Madurai; pop. (1991p) 66,028.

Bodincomagus. See CASALE MONFERRATO.

Bo·djo·ne·go·ro *or* **Bo·jo·ne·go·ro** \ˌbō-jō-nə-ˈgō-rō\. **1.** Former residency, Netherlands Indies, now part of the prov. of East Java, Indonesia; 2634 sq. mi. (6822 sq. km.); ✻ Bodjonegoro.
2. Town, its ✻, on Solo River 60 mi. (97 km.) W of Surabaya.

Bod·kin Point \ˈbäd-kin\. Point, Anne Arundel co., cen. Maryland, on S side of mouth of Patapsco River.

Bod·min \ˈbäd-min\. Town, ⊗ of former Cornwall co., SW England, 26 mi. (42 km.) WNW of Plymouth; pop. (1981p) 12,148.

Bodø \ˈbō-ˌdœ\. Seaport, ⊗ of Nordland co., N Norway, ab. 100 mi. (161 km.) SW of Narvik; pop. (1990c) 36,536; trade center; shipping point; tourist resort, with the midnight sun from June 1 to July 12.

Bodotria. See FORTH.

Bod·rog \ˈbòd-ˌròk\. Small river in NE Hungary; flows SW into Tisza River near Tokaj.

Bo·drum \bō-ˈdru̇m\ *also* **Bu·drum** \bu̇-ˈdrüm\; *anc.* **Hal·i·car·nas·sus** \ˌha-li-kär-ˈna-səs\. Seaport, SW Turkey in Asia, on S side of **Bodrum Peninsula** on Aegean Sea, opp. Kos Is. See HALICARNASSUS.

Bodza. See BUZĂU.

Boeleleng. See BULELENG.

Bo·èo, Cape \bō-ˈā-ō\ *or in full* **Cape Boèo o Li·li·beo** \ō-ˌlē-lē-ˈbā-ō\. Westernmost point of Sicily, Italy.

Boe·o·tia \bē-ˈō-shə, -shē-ə\. **1.** District and ancient republic in E cen. Greece, bounded on N by Locris Opuntia, on E by the Atalante Channel and the Evripos, on S by Attica, Megaris, and Gulf of Corinth, on W and NW by Phocis; chief cities Orchomenus (*q.v.*) and Thebes (*qq.v.*).

History: Inhabited by Boeotians, an Aeolian people from Thessaly; politically significant after formation of Boeotian League under headship of Thebes c. 600–550 B.C.; a Medized state during Greek war with Persia; hostile to Athens which succeeded in breaking up Boeotian League and forcing members, except Thebes, to join Delian League c. 457 B.C.; revolted against Athens and restored League c. 447 B.C.; in Peloponnesian War, defeated Athenians at Delium 424 B.C.; after battle of Leuctra (*q.v.*) 371 B.C., led by Thebes, dominated Greece; declined after King Philip II of Macedon's victory at Chaeronea 338 B.C. and the destruction of Thebes by his son, Alexander the Great, c. 335 B.C.

2. *or Gk.* **Voi·o·tia** \vyö-ˈtē-ə\. Department, Central Greece region, Greece. See table at GREECE.

Boer·ne \ˈbər-nē\. City, ⊗ of Kendall co., S cen. Texas; pop. (1990c) 4274; tourist and health resort.

Boeroe. See BURU.

Boetoeng. See BUTON.

Boeuf River \ˈbəf, ˈbu̇f\. River, NE Louisiana; rises just N of Arkansas border, flows SW into Ouachita River in N Catahoula parish; ab. 200 mi. (322 km.) long.

Bōfu. See HŌFU.

Bogadjim. See BOM.

Bo·ga·lu·sa \ˌbō-gə-ˈlü-sə\. City, Washington parish, E Louisiana, 60 mi. (97 km.) NNE of New Orleans; pop. (1990c) 14,280.

Bo·gaz·köy \bȯ-ˈä-kœi\ *or* **Bo·gaz·ka·le** \bȯ-ˈäz-kä-le\. Village in mountains of N cen. Turkey in Asia, 16 mi. (26 km.) NW of Yozgat and ab. 90 mi. (145 km.) E of Ankara; containing ancient Hittite ruins of **Hat·tu·shash** \ˈha-tə-ˌshash\ *or Gk.* **Pte·ria** \ˈtē-rē-ə\. Remarkable remains of probable ✻ of powerful Hattic dynasty (c. 16th–12th cents. B.C.); described by Greek historian Herodotus.

Bog·da Shan \ˈbōg-ˈdä-ˈshän\ *or W.-G.* **Po–ko–to Shan** \ˈbō-ˌkō-ˌtō-ˈshän\; *formerly* **Bog·do–ola** \ˈbōg-ˈdō-ō-ˈlä\. Mountain range, E Tian Shan, E of Ürümqi, cen. Xinjiang Uygur, W China; highest peak ab. 17,865 ft. (5445 m.); av. height 14,000 ft. (4267 m.).

Bo·gen·fels \ˈbō-gən-ˌfels\. Town, SW Namibia, on coast 50 mi. (81 km.) S of Lüderitz; has remarkable natural-rock archway.

Bog·nor Re·gis \ˈbäg-nər-ˈrē-jis\. Town, West Sussex, S England, on the coast ab. 17 mi. (27 km.) E of Portsmouth; pop. (1981p) 39,536; seaside resort.

Bo·go \bō-ˈgō\. Municipality on E coast of Cebu I., Phil., on inlet of Visayan Sea 54 mi. (87 km.) N of City of Cebu; pop. (1980c) 42,444; good harbor.

Bo·gong, Mount \ˈbō-ˌgäŋ\. Mountain, SE Victoria, SE Australia, in Darg Plateau at S end of Great Dividing Range; 6516 ft. (1986 m.); highest point in Victoria.

Bo·gor \ˈbō-ˌgȯr\ *or Du.* **Bui·ten·zorg** \ˈbœit-ᵊn-ˌzȯrk̲\. **1.** Residency of the prov. of West Java, Indonesia; 4484 sq. mi. (11,614 sq. km.); a residency of the former Netherlands Indies; in N of this area are mountains of cen. range of Java (see SALAK, GUNUNG and GEDE, MOUNT).

2. City, its ✻, 36 mi. (58 km.) S of Jakarta; pop. (1990c) 271,711; several universities and colleges, incl. Univ. of Bogor (1961); palace, formerly residence of the Dutch governor-general; at elev. of ab. 870 ft. (265 m.); notable botanical garden (founded 1817) with more than 10,000 kinds of plants. City founded 1745.

Bogorodsk. See NOGINSK.

Bo·go·slof \ˈbō-gə-ˌslȯf, -ˌsläf\. Small island, Alaska, in Bering Sea ab. 60 mi. (97 km.) W of N Unalaska I.; built up by submarine volcano; uninhabited; first reported by Russian navigators ab. 1796 when it appeared as a single peak. Violent eruptions in 19th and 20th cents. have changed its aspect; now has several peaks joined by a land strip.

Bo·go·ta \bə-ˈgō-tə\. Borough, Bergen co., NE corner of New Jersey, 8 mi. (13 km.) ESE of Paterson; pop. (1990c) 7824.

Bo·go·tá \ˌbō-gō-ˈtä, -ˈtȯ\. **1.** *formerly* **Fun·za** \ˈfün-sä\. River in W cen. Colombia; flows into Magdalena River near Bogotá. See TEQUENDAMA FALLS.

2. *orig.* **San·ta Fe** \ˈsän-tä-ˈfā\ *later* **Santa Fe de Bogotá.** City, ✻ of Colombia and ✻ of Cundinamarca dept., on plateau (alt. 8563 ft. or 2610 m.) of E Andes; pop. (1992e) 4,921,300; constitutes, with adjacent area, the Capital District (613 sq. mi. or 1588 sq. km.; pop. [1985c] 4,239,490); tobacco products; chemicals; commercial and financial center; several universities and colleges; cathedral (rebuilt 1814); observatory.

History: Orig. center of Chibcha culture; Spanish settlement founded 1538 by Gonzalo Jiménez de Quesada, conquistador; ✻ of viceroyalty of New Granada; audiencia estab. 1549; scene of revolt 1810–11 against Spanish rule; recovered by Spaniards 1816–19; freed by victory of South American revolutionary leader Símon Bolívar at Boyacá 1819; ✻ of Gran Colombia and later (1831) of New Granada (Colombia).

Bog·ra \ˈbō-grə\. Town, Bangladesh, 57 mi. (92 km.) NE of Rajshahi; pop. (1991p) 93,114.

Bogue Sound \ˈbōg\. Sound bet. S mainland of Carteret co., SE North Carolina, and barrier islands off the coast; connects at W end with Atlantic Ocean through the **Bogue Inlet.**

Bo·gu·szów \bȯ-ˈgü-shüf\ *or Ger.* **Got·tes·berg** \ˈgȯ-təs-ˌberk\. City, NW Wałbrzych prov., SW Poland, 47 mi. (76 km.) SW of Wrocław; pop. (1981p) 20,249; formerly in Germany; assigned to Poland by Potsdam Conference 1945.

Bo Hai *or W.-G.* **Po Hai** \ˈbō-ˈhī\ *or* **Gulf of Chih·li** \ˈjə-ˈlē\. The NW arm of the Yellow Sea enclosed by Liaoning, Hebei, and Shandong provs., and Tianjin municipality of China; its NE extension is the Gulf of Liaodong.

Bo·he·mia \bō-ˈhē-mē-ə\ *or Czech* **Če·chy** \ˈche-k̲ē\ *or Ger.* **Böh·men** \ˈbœ̄-mən\. Former kingdom, cen. Europe, since 1918 constitutes W part of Czech S.R. (now the Czech Republic); ✻ Prague. Encircled by mountains: Erzgebirge on NW, Sudety on NE, Bohemian-Moravian Highlands on SE, and the Bohemian Forest on SW; highest point 5256 ft. (1602 m.) in the Riesengebirge, a range of the Sudety.

Chief rivers: Elbe (here called the Labe) and its tributaries the Vltava (Moldau) and Ohře (Eger).

Chief products: Flax, hops; graphite, iron ore, coal.

Chief towns: Prague, Plzeň, České Budějovice, Pardubice.

History: Settled in ab. 5th cent. A.D. by W Slavic people, Czechs; tributary to Holy Roman Emperor Charlemagne's empire (see FRANCE); part of kingdom of Moravia (*q.v.*) founded 870; converted to Latin Christianity by German missionaries 9th cent.; after dissolution of Moravia c. 907, became duchy which in 10th cent. was forced to accept German suzerainty; under rule of Přemysl family, expanded to include Moravia, parts of Silesia, Slovakia, and Kraków (forced to yield Polish conquests by Holy Roman Emperor Henry III 1041); in 12th cent. raised to rank of electorate and hereditary kingdom within Holy Roman Empire; at height of power under Otakar II (1253–78) who conquered Styria from Hungary and Austrian territories but was defeated by Emperor Rudolf (of Hapsburg) 1278; last ruler of Přemysl line (d. 1306) also king of Poland; during reign of King Charles I 1347–78 (who was also Holy Roman Emperor Charles IV) of Luxembourg line (1308–1437) reached "golden age," controlling Upper and Lower Lusatia, Moravia, Silesia, and Brandenburg; alienated by anti-Hus Council of Constance (see KONSTANZ), plunged into Hussite Wars 1420–36; from election of Ferdinand I as king (see AUSTRIA) 1526, remained under Hapsburg rule to 1918; deposition of ruler (Defenestration of Prague) 1618 inaugurated Thirty Years' War (see GERMANY); Protestantism exterminated and independence lost at battle of White Mountain 1620; by 18th cent. completely incorp. in Austrian empire; battleground in wars of Prussian King Frederick the Great and in 1866 (see PRUSSIA); with Moravia and Slovakia, declared independence 1918 (see CZECHOSLOVAKIA); invaded by Germans and made part of German Protectorate of Bohemia and Moravia Mar. 1939; made a province of Czechoslovakia 1945; province dissolved 1949 and divided into several administrative units; became part of the Czech Socialist Republic 1968; subsequently, part of independent Czech Republic 1992.

Bohemia and Mo·ra·via \mȯ-ˈrā-vē-ə\. German protectorate comprising the two W divisions of Czechoslovakia; set up Mar. 1939, dissolved 1945.

Bo·he·mi·an Forest \bō-ˈhē-mē-ən\ *or Ger.* **Böh·mer Wald** \ˈbœ̄-mər-ˌvält\ *or Czech* **Čes·ký Les** \ˈches-kē-ˈles\. Mountain range along the boundary bet. Bavaria, Germany, and Bohemia, Czech Republic; highest peak Arber, in Bavaria, 4780 ft. (1457 m.).

Bohemian–Mo·ra·vi·an Highlands \mȯ-ˈrā-vē-ən\ *or Czech* **Čes·ko·mo·rav·ská Vrch·o·vi·na** \ˈches-kȯ-ˌmȯ-räf-skä-ˈvər-k̲ȯ-vē-nä\. Mountain range, Czech Republic; forms boundary bet. the former provinces of Bohemia and Moravia; highest point ab. 2700 ft. (823 m.); runs NE and SW.

\ə\ **abut** \ᵊ\ **matches** \ᵊ\ **kitten**, Fr **table** \ər\ **further** \a\ **ash** \ā\ **ace** \ä\ **cot, cart** \à\ Fr **bac** \au̇\ **out** \b̲\ Span **Avila** \ch\ **chin** \e\ **bet** \ē\ **easy** \g\ **go** \i\ **hit** \ī\ **ice** \j\ **job** \k̲\ Ger **ich, Buch** \ⁿ\ Fr **vin** \ŋ\ **sing** \ō\ **go** \ȯ\ **all** \ȯ\ **law** \œ\ Fr **bœuf** \œ̄\ Fr **feu** \ȯi\ **boy** \th\ **thin** \t͟h\ **this** \ü\ **loot** \u̇\ **foot** \ue\ Ger **füllen** \u̅e\ Fr **rue** \y\ **yet** \ʸ\ Fr **digne** \ˈdēnʸ\, **nuit** \ˈnwʸē\ \yü\ **few** \yu̇\ **fury** \zh\ **vision**

Böhmer Wald. See BOHEMIAN FOREST.

Böhmisch–Brod. See ČESKÝ-BROD.

Böhmisch–Leipa. See ČESKÁ LÍPA.

Bo·hol \bō-'hōl\. Island, one of the Visayan Is., S cen. Philippines, N of Mindanao; 1492 sq. mi. (3864 sq. km.); with smaller adjacent islands, forms a province (see table at PHILIPPINES). Has fairly regular coastline with many islands, largest Panglao on SW and Lapinin on W side of Canigao Channel; few good anchorages; highest peaks ab. 2600 ft. (793 m.); short rivers; produces rice, coconuts, hemp; chief settlements, mostly on the coast, Talibon, Tagbilaran, Ubay, Loon. Visited by Spanish explorer Miguel López de Legazpi 1565; under Spanish rule until late 19th cent.; civil government created Apr. 1901; came under Japanese control 1942; invaded and recovered Apr. 1945 by U.S. forces. See table at PHILIPPINES.

Bohol Strait. Passage bet. SE Cebu and W Bohol, Philippines; from 12 to 25 mi. (19 to 40 km.) wide; connects Camotes Sea on the N with Mindanao Sea on the S.

Bohotle Wein. See BUUHOODLE.

Boil·ing Springs \'bȯi-liŋ\. Town, Cleveland co., SW North Carolina, SW of Shelby; pop. (1990c) 2445; Gardner-Webb Coll. (1905).

Boinu. See KALADAN.

Boi·ro \'bȯi-rō\. Coastal commune, La Coruña prov., NW Spain, 54 mi. (87 km.) SSW of the seaport of La Coruña; pop. (1991c) 17,665; fishing.

Bois. See BOIS DE BOULOGNE.

Bois Blanc Island \'bä-ˌblō—*sic*\. **1.** Island in NW Lake Huron, a part of Mackinac co., Michigan; 35 sq. mi. (91 sq. km.).
2. Long, narrow island in Detroit River, SE Michigan opp. Amherstburg, Ontario, Canada.

Boisbriand \ˌbwä-brē-'äⁿ\. Town, S Quebec, Canada, ab. 15 mi. (24 km.) WNW of Montreal; pop. (1996c) 25,227.

Bois Brule. See BRULE.

Bois–Co·lombes \ˌbwä-kō-'lōⁿb\. Commune, Hauts-de-Seine dept., N France, NW suburb of Paris.

Bois d'Avocourt. See AVOCOURT.

Bois de Belleau. See BELLEAU WOOD.

Bois de Bou·logne \ˌbwä-də-bü-'lōnʸ\ *or familiarly* **Bois** \'bwä\. Park, formerly a forest, just W of Paris, France, in a loop of the Seine adjoining Neuilly on the N and Boulogne on the W; 2155 acres (873 hectares); acquired by the city of Paris 1852 and transformed into a recreational area; contains the racetracks of Longchamp and Auteuil (steeplechases).

Bois de la Brigade Marine. See BELLEAU WOOD.

Bois des Fi·li·on \ˌbwä-dā-fēl-'yōⁿ\. Village, S Quebec, Canada, 15 mi. (24 km.) NW of Montreal; pop. (1991c) 6337.

Bois de Sioux \ˌbȯi-də-'sü\. River, W Minnesota; flows N out of Lake Traverse, forms S section of North Dakota-Minnesota boundary, unites with Otter Tail River to form Red River of the North.

Bois–du–Roi \ˌbwä-dū-'rwä\. Highest peak in Morvan Mts., E cen. France; 2959 ft. (902 m.).

Boi·se \'bȯi-sē, -zē\. **1.** River, SW cen. Idaho; flows W through Boise (city) and Canyon co. into Snake River; ab. 60 mi. (97 km.) long; formed by forks uniting in NW Elmore co.
2. County in W cen. Idaho. See table at IDAHO.
3. City, ✱ of Idaho and ⊗ of Ada co., SW Idaho; pop. (1990c) 125,738; alt. 2704 ft. (824 m.); largest city in the state; packinghouses; food processing; Boise State Univ. (1932); founded 1863 on the site of an army camp; incorp. as city 1864; ✱ of Idaho Terr. 1864, and of the state from 1890.

Boi·se City \'bȯi-zā\. Town, ⊗ of Cimarron co., NW Oklahoma; pop. (1990c) 1509; oil deposits.

Bois–le–Duc. See 'S HERTOGENBOSCH.

Boj·a·dor, Cape \ˌbȯ-jə-'dȯr, ˌbō-hä-'dōr\. Cape extending into Atlantic Ocean on W cen. coast of Western Sahara, S of Canary Is., 26°08'N, 14°30'W.

Bojana. See BUENË.

Bo·je·a·dor, Cape \ˌbō-ˌhā-ä-'thȯr\. Point on NW coast of Ilocos Norte prov., Luzon, Philippines, fronting on South China Sea at 18°30'N, 120°34'E.

Boj·nūrd *also* **Buj·nurd** \bōj-'nu̇rd\. Town in mountains of N Khorāsān prov., NE Iran; pop. (1986c) 93,392.

Bo·jo·la·li \ˌbō-yō-'lä-lē\. Town, cen. Java, Indonesia, at foot of Gunung Merapi.

Bojonegoro. See BODJONEGORO.

Bo·ké \bō-'kā\. Town, W Guinea, on Nunez River, 110 mi. (177 km.) NW of Conakry.

Bokhara. See BUKHARA.

Bokn Fjord *also* **Bukn Fjord** \'bük-ᵊn\. Inlet of the North Sea on SW coast of Norway, N of Stavanger; ab. 35 mi. (56 km.) long; 10 to 15 mi. (16 to 24 km.) wide.

Bo·ko·ro \bō-'kō-rō\. Town, SW cen. Chad, 140 mi. (225 km.) E of Fort-Lamy.

Boks·burg \'bäks-ˌbərg\. Town, NE Rep. of South Africa, 15 mi. (24 km.) E of Johannesburg; pop. (1985c) 110,832; electrical equipment, freight cars, soap; fruit canning; important gold-mining center.

Bo·la·ma \bō-'lä-mä\ *or* **Bu·la·ma** \bu̇-\. **1.** Island of the Arquipélago dos Bijagós, Guinea-Bissau (see BIJAGÓS, ARQUIPÉLAGO DOS).
2. Town on Bolama I., former ✱ of Portuguese Guinea.

Bolangir. See PATNA 1.

Bo·lan Pass \'bō-län\. Mountain pass, Pakistan; bet. Sibi and Quetta in N Baluchistan; ab. 60 mi. (97 km.) long; elev. at crest 5900 ft. (1798 m.).

Bol·bē, Lake \'bȯl-bē\ *or Gk.* **Lím·ni Vól·vi** \'lēm-nē-'völ-vē\. Lake in N part of Chalcidice, Macedonia, Greece.

Bolbitine, Bolbitinic Mouth. See ROSETTA.

Bolbok. See SAN JUAN 13.

Bol·don \'bōl-dən\. Town, Tyne and Wear, NE England, 7 mi. (11 km.) SE of Newcastle upon Tyne; pop. (1981p) 24,171.

Bolerium. See LAND'S END.

Boleslav, Mladá. See MLADÁ BOLESLAV.

Bo·le·sła·wi·ce \ˌbȯ-le-swä-'vē-tse\ *or Ger.* **Bun·zel·witz** \'bu̇nt-səl-ˌvits\. Village, Wrocław prov., SW Poland, 7 mi. (11 km.) N of Świdnica; formerly in Silesia, Germany; battle 1761 bet. forces of Prussian King Frederick the Great and combined Austrian and Russian forces.

Bo·le·sła·wiec \ˌbȯ-le-'swä-vyets\ *or Ger.* **Bunz·lau** \'bu̇nts-ˌlau̇\. Town, N Jelenia Góra prov., SW Poland, on Bóbr River; pop. (1989e) 43,852; to Bohemian crown 1392, to Prussia 1742; assigned to Poland by Potsdam Conference 1945.

Bol·ga·tan·ga \ˌbōl-gä-'tän-gä\. Town, ✱ of Upper East Region, N Ghana; pop. (1984c) 32,495.

Bo·li·nao \ˌbō-lē-'nau̇\. **1.** Cape, NW point of the peninsula of W Pangasinan prov., Luzon, Philippines, 16°20'N, 119°52'E, on South China Sea coast W of Lingayen Gulf.
2. Municipality, NW Pangasinan, just E of the cape and opp. Santiago I.; pop. (1980c) 39,335.

Bo·ling·brook \'bōl-iŋ-ˌbru̇k\. Village, Will co., NE Illinois, ab. 14 mi. (22 km.) W of SW Chicago; pop. (1990c) 40,843.

Bo·li·var \'bä-li-vər\. **1.** County in NW Mississippi. See table at MISSISSIPPI.
2. City, ⊗ of Polk co., SW Missouri; pop. (1990c) 6845; Southwest Baptist Univ. (1878).
3. Town, ⊗ of Hardeman co., SW Tennessee; pop. (1990c) 5969.

Bo·lí·var \bō-'lē-ˌbär\. **1.** Town, Buenos Aires prov., E Argentina, ab. 170 mi. (274 km.) SW of the city of Buenos Aires; pop. (1980p) 16,382; trading center.
2. Department of N Colombia. See table at COLOMBIA.
3. Municipality, Cauca dept., SW Colombia, 47 mi. (76 km.) NNE of Pasto; alt. 6435 ft. (1961 m.).
4. Province of W Ecuador. See table at ECUADOR.
5. State of SE Venezuela. See table at VENEZUELA.

Bolívar, Cer·ro \'ser-rō\; *formerly* **La Pa·ri·da** \ˌlä-pä-'rē-thä\. Hill, Bolívar state, Venezuela, S of Ciudad Bolívar; ab. 6 mi. (9.6 km.) long; 2000 ft. (610 m.) high; iron deposits.

Bolívar, Pi·co \'pē-kō\. Mountain, Sierra Nevada National Park, Mérida state, W Venezuela; highest in the Cordillera Mérida and in Venezuela, 16,427 ft. (5007 m.).

Bolivar Peninsula \'bä-li-vər\. Peninsula at E entrance to Galveston Bay, Texas; ab. 23 mi. (37 km.) long; port at tip (**Bolivar Point**).

Bo·liv·ia \bə-ˈliv-ē-ə\. **1.** Town, ⊗ of Brunswick co., S North Carolina; pop. (1990c) 228.

2. Republic, W cen. South America, bounded on N and E by Brazil, on SE by Paraguay, on S by Argentina, and on W by Peru and Chile; 424,162 sq. mi. (1,098,579 sq. km.); pop. (1993e) 7,715,000; administrative ✱ La Paz, constitutional ✱ Sucre.

Physical features: In E part has low, hot, fertile land, watered by many rivers; in cen. part on E slope of mountains high plateau region; in W part the cen. ranges of the Andes, esp. the Cordillera Real E of Lake Titicaca, highest peaks Sorata (Ancohuma and Illampu) 20,958 ft. (6388 m.), Nevado Sajama 21,391 ft. (6520 m.), Illimani 21,201 ft. (6462 m.); many volcanic peaks; in SW in Oruro and Potosí depts. are elevated nitrate deserts, esp. Uyuni. Chief rivers are large headstreams of the Madeira: Guaporé (along Brazillian border) and its tributaries Baures and Itonamas; Mamoré, with many tributaries draining E slopes of the Andes; Beni and its tributary the Madre de Dios; Abuna (forming in N part of boundary with Brazil); upper Pilcomayo in the S. Includes part of Lake Titicaca (*q.v.*) which receives waters of Lake Poopó in SW cen. part through the Desaguadero River.

Chief products: Barley, coca, corn, wheat, rice, potatoes, sugarcane, coffee; tin, gold, lead, antimony, zinc, silver, oil, natural gas; textiles; food processing.

Chief cities: La Paz, Santa Cruz, El Alto, Cochabamba.

Political divisions: Divided into the following nine departments (for pronunciations, see their individual entries):

\ə\ **abut** \ᵊ\ **matches** \ᵊ\ **kitten, Fr table** \ər\ **further** \a\ **ash** \ā\ **ace**
\ä\ **cot, cart** \á\ **Fr bac** \au̇\ **out** \b\ **Span Avila** \ch\ **chin** \e\ **bet** \ē\ **easy**
\g\ **go** \i\ **hit** \ī\ **ice** \j\ **job** \k\ **Ger ich, Buch** \ⁿ\ **Fr vin**
\ŋ\ **sing** \ō\ **go** \ȯ\ **all** \ȯ\ **law** \œ\ **Fr bœuf** \œ̄\ **Fr feu** \ȯi\ **boy**
\th\ **thin** \th\ **this** \ü\ **loot** \u̇\ **foot** \ue\ **Ger füllen** \ue̅\ **Fr rue**
\y\ **yet** \ʸ\ **Fr digne** \ˈdēnʸ\, **nuit** \ˈnʷʸē\ \yü\ **few** \yu̇\ **fury** \zh\ **vision**

NAME	AREA (sq. mi.)	AREA (sq. km.)	POP. (1992p)	CAPITAL
Beni	82,457	213,564	251,390	Trinidad
Chuquisaca	19,893	51,523	451,722	Sucre
Cochabamba	21,479	55,631	1,093,625	Cochabamba
La Paz	51,732	133,986	1,883,122	La Paz
Oruro	20,690	53,587	338,893	Oruro
Pando	24,644	63,828	37,785	Cobija
Potosí	45,644	118,218	645,817	Potosí
Santa Cruz	143,097	370,621	1,351,191	Santa Cruz
Tarija	14,526	37,622	290,851	Tarija

History: Bolivian highlands location of advanced Tiahuanaco culture c. 7th cent.–c. 11th cent., and with its passing became home of the Aymaras, Indians with a high pre-Inca culture, who were conquered by Incas c. 15th cent.; conquered during 1530s by Hernando Pizarro, half brother of Francisco Pizarro, conqueror of Peru (*q.v.*); organized as dependency of Charcas or Upper Peru; joined to Viceroyalty of Buenos Aires 1776; although struggles against royalists continuous from 1809, achieved independence from Spain only in 1825 when Gen. Antonio José de Sucre invaded Charcas; long troubled by internal strife and series of unsuccessful wars; lost seacoast in War of the Pacific against Chile (*q.v.*) 1879–84; after dispute with Brazil, ceded Acre (*q.v.*) 1903; finally made peace 1904 with Chile which retained Arica (*q.v.*); renewed dispute 1920–29; lost most of Gran Chaco (*q.v.*) by treaty 1938 which settled war with Paraguay (1932–35); period 1952–64 marked by economic and political reforms (incl. land redistribution and nationalization of the largest tin mines); civilian government overthrown 1964; new constitution adopted 1967, but civil unrest has persisted; signed agreement with Peru 1993 to have access to Peruvian port Ilo, alleviating its over 100-year landlocked status.

Bol·la·te \bōl-'lä-tā\. Commune, Milano prov., Lombardy, N Italy, 6 mi. (9.6 km.) NNW of Milan; pop. (1989c) 43,392.

Bol·li·gen \'bȯ-li-gən\. Town, Bern canton, Switzerland, E suburb of the city of Bern; pop. (1980c) 32,312.

Bol·lin \'bä-lin\. River, Cheshire, NW England; 20 mi. (32 km.) long; tributary of the Mersey.

Bol·lin·ger \'bō-liŋ-gər, 'bu̇-, -ər; 'bä-lin-jər\. County in SE Missouri. See table at MISSOURI.

Bo·lo·gna \bō-'lō-nyä\. **1.** Province of Emilia-Romagna, N Italy. See table at ITALY.

2. *anc.* **Fel·si·na** \'fel-si-nə\; *later* **Bo·no·nia** \bə-'nō-nē-ə\. Commune, its ✻ and ✻ of Emilia-Romagna, at foot of Apennines 51 mi. (82 km.) NNE of Florence; pop. (1991p) 404,322; transportation center; food processing; university (11th cent.); 14th cent. Gothic church of San Petronio.

History: Site of Etruscan town Felsina; made Roman military colony c. 190 B.C.; belonged to Byzantine exarchate of Ravenna (*q.v.*); after short period of Lombard rule became free commune, receiving charter in 12th cent.; seat of oldest European university, founded c. 1088; joined Lombard League against Holy Roman Emperor Frederick Barbarossa 1167; helped break power of Frederick II; in course of 15th cent. ruled temporarily by Bentivoglio and Visconti families; incorp. in Papal States (*q.v.*) by Pope Julius II 1506; scene of crowning of Holy Roman Emperor Charles V 1530; after French occupation 1796, made ✻ of Cispadane Republic (*q.v.*); restored to Papal States 1815; occupied by Austria after revolts 1831, 1848; voted annexation to kingdom of Italy 1860. In WWII after surrender of Italy Sept. 1943, controlled by Germans until April 1945.

Bolos. See VOLOS.

Bol·se·na \bōl-'sā-nä\; *anc.* **Vol·sin·ii** \väl-'si-nē-ˌī\. Commune, Viterbo prov., N Lazio, Italy, on Lake Bolsena; pop. (1991p) 4834; 11th cent. church.

Bolsena, Lake. Lake, N Lazio, cen. Italy, 10 mi. (16 km.) NNW of Viterbo; 10 mi. (16 km.) long, 8 mi. (13 km.) wide; discharges through Marta River SW into N Tyrrhenian Sea.

Bolshaya. See MCKINLEY, MOUNT.

Bol'sha·ya Ki·nel' \bəlʸ-'shī-ə-kē-'nyelʸ\. River, E Russia in Europe; rises in N Orenburg Oblast and flows W to join the Samara River just E of the city of Samara; 220 mi. (354 km.) long.

Bol·'she·vik \ˌbȯl-she-'vik\. Island, SE Severnaya Zemlya, in Arctic Ocean off Taymyr Penin., N Russia in Asia.

Bolshoi Begichev. See BOL'SHOY BEGICHEV.

Bolshoi Berezovy Island. See PRIMORSK.

Bolshoi Irgiz. See BOL'SHOY IRGIZ.

Bolshoi Tyuters. See BOL'SHOY TYUTERS.

Bol'shoy Be·gich·ev *or* **Bol·shoi Begichev** \bȯlʸ-'shȯi-'byā-gi-chəf\. Island, NW Sakha Rep., N Russia in Asia, N of Nordvik Bay, at mouth of Khatanga River.

Bol'shoy Berezoviy Ostrov. See PRIMORSK.

Bol'shoy Ir·giz *also* **Bolshoi Irgiz** \ir-'gēz\ River, E Russia in Europe; rises in S Samara Oblast and flows W into Volga River opp. Vol'sk; ab. 300 mi. (485 km.) long; navigable except at low-water season.

Bol'shoy Lya·khov·skiy \lyə-'kȯf-skʸē\. Largest island of the Lyakhovskiye Ostrova. (*q.v.*).

Bol'shoy Tyu·ters *also* **Bolshoi Tyuters** \'tyü-tərs\; *formerly* **Ty·tär·saa·ri** \'tu̇e-tar-ˌsä-rē\. Island, W Russia in Europe, in Gulf of Finland, off coast of Estonia.

Bol'shoy Yenisei. See YENISEY.

Bolsón de Mapimí. See MAPIMÍ, BOLSÓN DE.

Bol·so·ver \'bäl-ˌsō-vər, 'bōl-ˌzō-\. Town, Derbyshire, N cen. England, 13 mi. (21 km.) SSE of Sheffield; pop. (1991p) 69,000.

Bolt Head \'bōlt\. Headland on S coast of Devon, SW England, W of Start Point.

Bol·ton \'bōlt-ᵊn\. **1.** Town, Tolland co., N Connecticut; pop. (1990c) 4575.

2. Town, Worcester co., Massachusetts; pop. (1990c) 3134.

3. *formerly* **Bolton–le–Moors** \lə-'mu̇rz\. Town, Greater Manchester, NW England, on the Croal 11 mi. (18 km.) NW of Manchester; pop. (1991p) 253,300; textile mills, papermills, chemical manufacturing; coal deposits nearby; one of the oldest centers of the woolen trade, where Richard Arkwright invented the spinning frame (1769) and Samuel Crompton the mule-jenny (1779).

Bol·ton Brown, Mount \'bōlt-ᵊn-'brau̇n\. Peak in the Sierra Nevada, E Fresno co., S cen. California; 13,527 ft. (4123 m.).

Bo·lu \bō-'lü\. **1.** Province of Turkey in Asia. See table at TURKEY.

2. Town, its ✻; pop. (1990p) 60,600.

Bo·lus Head \'bō-ləs\. Cape on SW coast of Ireland, on W side of entrance to Ballinskelligs Bay.

Bol·za·no \bōl-'tsä-nō, -'dzä-\. **1.** Province of Trentino-Alto Adige, Italy. See table at ITALY.

2. *or Ger.* **Bo·zen** \'bōt-sən\; *anc.* **Bau·za·num** \bȯ-'zā-nəm\. Commune, its ✻, in S Tirol at confluence of the Isarco River with the Adige 87 mi. (140 km.) NNW of Venice; pop. (1991p) 98,233; trade center for region producing wine and fruits; 14th cent. Gothic cathedral; Franciscan monastery. In medieval times, seat of Bavarian border countships; fell to episcopate of Trent 1027; because of location, continuously contested by Trent and the Tirol; to Tirolean counts 1531; united with Austria 1813; to Italy following WWI; area remains a mix of German and Italian speakers.

Bom \'bȯm\; *formerly* **Bo·ga·djim** \'bō-gä-jēm\. Village and port at head of Astrolabe Bay, Papua New Guinea, ab. 12 mi. (19 km.) S of Madang.

Bo·ma \'bō-mä\. Town, W Democratic Rep. of the Congo, ab. 60 mi. (96 km.) from the mouth of the Congo River on N bank; pop. (1991e) 246,207; rail terminus; exports timber, bananas, palm products; until 1926 ✻ of Belgian Congo. Founded as a slave market in 16th cent.

Bo·mar·sund \'bü-mär-ˌsənd\. **1.** Strait in the Åland Is. in the Gulf of Bothnia.

2. Russian-built fort on Åland, Finland; captured 1854 by British and French (Crimean War).

Bom·ba·la \bȯm-'bä-lə\. Town, SE New South Wales, SE Australia, 110 mi. (177 km.) S of Canberra and ab. 38 mi. (61 km.) W of Eden harbor; pop. (1991c) 3000; one of many sites considered 1903–04 for Commonwealth ✻.

Bom·bay \bäm-'bā\. **1.** Former state, W India; area (1956) 190,919 sq. mi. (494,480 sq. km.); ✻ Bombay. Extended along W coast from Pakistan boundary on the NW to Mysore on the S, with Western Ghats along most of its length (highest 4500 ft. or 1372 m.) and in N the lower courses of the Narmada and Tapti rivers flowing into Gulf of Cambay; sources of several large rivers (Godavari, Bhima, Krishna) of cen. India within its boundaries; chief industry cotton manufacturing.

Chief cities: Bombay, Pune, Ahmadabad, Nagpur, Sholapur, Vadodara.

History: Under various Hindu and Muslim dynasties during early Christian era down to c. 1500, but not an important center; Goa (*q.v.*) taken 1510 by Portuguese and Bombay town 1534; first English settlement at Surat 1613; territory much increased by districts from Gujarat 1805–18, from Kathiawar 1807–20, and from sections along E slope of Ghats 1819–27; received Aden 1839 and Sind 1843. Sind made separate province 1936 and Aden a crown colony 1937; constituted an autonomous province of British India 1937; became part of independent India Aug. 15, 1947; reorganized 1956 as state incorporating Kutch and Saurashtra and the Marathi-speaking parts of Hyderabad and Madhya Pradesh, small areas being transferred at that time to Mysore and Rajasthan states; divided May 1, 1960 into a Gujarati-speaking state (Gujarat, *q.v.* ✻ Ahmadabad) and a Marathi-speaking state (Maharashtra, *q.v.* ✻ Bombay).

2. *or* **Mum·bai** \ˈməm-ˌbī\. City, its ✻ and (since 1960) ✻ of Maharashtra state; (**Greater Bombay** pop. [1991c] 9,925,891); old part of city is on Bombay I.; good harbor, ocean gateway to W India; financial center; chemicals, textiles; filmmaking; Univ. of Bombay (1857), Indian Institute of Technology (1958); Sahar International Airport on Salsette I.

History: Town acquired by Portuguese 1534; ceded to English as part of dowry of Catherine of Braganza, wife of Charles II 1661; granted to East India Company 1668; developed by the Company's representative of city of Surat (*q.v.*) who made it headquarters 1672; in 1708 became center of British authority in India; first Indian railroad constructed 1853 bet. it and Thāne; after opening of Suez Canal 1869 and construction of other railroads, became largest distributing center in India; enlarged through municipal rezoning 1950.

Bombay Island. Island, India, 10 mi. (16 km.) off W cen. coast; 24 sq. mi. (62 sq. km.); coextensive with the old part of Bombay; encloses **Bombay Harbor** on the E; connected by bridges and causeways with Salsette I. to the N.

Bombay States. A former group of 151 mostly small states of India; later divided bet. Vadodara and the Gujarat States Agency, Kolhapur and Deccan States, and Western India States Agency.

Bom·be·to·ka Bay \ˌbȯm-be-ˈtō-kä\. Inlet of Mozambique Channel on NW coast of Madagascar.

Bombon, Lake. See TAAL, LAKE.

Bo·mi Hills \ˈbō-mē\. Group of low hills, N Liberia, N of Monrovia.

Bom Je·sus \ˈbōm-zhi-ˈzüs, ˌbōⁿ\. Small island in Guanabara Bay, N of the city of Rio de Janeiro, Brazil.

Bøm·lo \ˈbœm-lō\. Island, Hordaland co., SW Norway, S of Bergen; 21 mi. (34 km.) long; 70 sq. mi. (181 sq. km.).

Bommes \ˈbȯm\. Village, Gironde dept., SW France; produces wine (see SAUTERNES).

Bom·o·seen, Lake \ˈbä-mə-ˌzēn\. Lake, NW Rutland co., W Vermont; ab. 8 mi. (13 km.) long; ab. 4 sq. mi. (10 sq. km.); summer resort.

Bo·mu \ˈbō-mü\ *or in Central African Rep. often* **Mbo·mou** *also* **M'Bo·mu** \əm-ˈbō-mü\. River, cen. Africa; flows W forming boundary bet. N Democratic Rep. of the Congo and S Central African Rep. and unites with Uele River to form Ubangi River; ab. 500 mi. (800 km.).

Bomvanaland. See TEMBULAND.

Bon, Cape \ˈbōⁿ\ *or Arab.* **Ra's aṭ Ṭīb** \ˌrás-át-ˈtēb\. Peninsula, Tunisia, extending NE from extreme NE part of country; ab. 50 mi. (80 km.) long; occupied by German troops in retreat from Egypt and Libya May 1943; surrendered to Allied army that May.

Bona. See ANNABA.

Bo·na, Mount \ˈbō-nə\. Mountain in SE Alaska, at E end of Wrangell Mts. near Yukon border; 16,500 ft. (5029 m.).

Bonacca. See GUANAJA.

Bo·nai \ˈbō-ˌnī\. Former princely state, now part of Orissa, NE India; 1280 sq. mi. (3315 sq. km.); ✻ **Bo·nai·garh** \ˌbōn-i-ˈgär\.

Bon·aire \bə-ˈnar\ *or Span.* **Buen Ai·re** \bwān-ˈī-rā\. Island, Netherlands Antilles, off coast of Venezuela 30 mi. (48 km.) E of Curaçao; 111 sq. mi. (287 sq. km.); pop. (1990c) 11,058; beach resorts; chief town Kralendijk.

Bo·nan·za Peak \bə-ˈnan-zə\. Mountain, N Chelan co., cen. Washington; 9511 ft. (2899 m.).

Bo·nao \bō-ˈnaů\. Town, ✻ of Monseñor Nouel prov., Dominican Republic.

Bonaparte. See RÉUNION.

Bo·na·parte Archipelago \ˈbō-nə-ˌpärt\. Group of small islands off N coast of Western Australia, Australia.

Bon·a·ven·ture \ˌbä-nə-ˈven-chər\. **1.** River, Gaspé Peninsula, SE Quebec, Canada; flows S into Chaleur Bay; ab. 60 mi. (96 km.) long.

2. County, on Gaspé Penin., Quebec, Canada. See table at QUEBEC.

Bon·a·vis·ta \ˌbä-nə-ˈvis-tə\. Seaport, E Newfoundland, Canada, on E side of Bonavista Bay near Cape Bonavista; pop. (1991c) 4597; one of island's oldest fishing stations.

Bonavista Bay. Inlet of Atlantic Ocean in E Newfoundland, Canada, bet. Cape Freels on NW and **Cape Bonavista** on SE; ab. 40 mi. (64 km.) wide; contains numerous small islands.

Bond \ˈbänd\. County in SW cen. Illinois. See table at ILLINOIS.

Bon·di \ˈbän-ˌdī\. Part of Waverley municipality, city of Sydney, New South Wales, Australia; famous beach (**Bondi Beach**).

Bon·doc \bȯn-ˈdȯk\. Peninsula, SE end of Quezon prov., Luzon, Philippines; its S extremity is **Bondoc Point,** on N side of Sibuyan Sea; ab. 37 mi. (59 km.) long.

Bon·dou·kou \ˌbȯⁿ-dü-ˈkü\. Interior town, E Ivory Coast; pop. (1988c) 32,231.

Bon·do·wo·so \ˌbȯn-dō-ˈwō-sō\. Town, East Java prov., Indonesia, 90 mi. (145 km.) SE of Surabaya; in valley W of Idjen Mts.

Bon·dy \bōⁿ-ˈdē\. Commune, Seine-St.-Denis dept., N France, ENE suburb of Paris; near forest (**Forest of Bondy**) formerly notorious as haunt of brigands.

Bône. See ANNABA.

Bo·ne, Gulf of \ˈbō-nā\ *or* **Gulf of Bo·ni** \ˈbō-nē\. Large inlet of Flores Sea extending into S coast of Sulawesi, Indonesia.

Bo'ness. See BORROWSTOUNNESS.

Bo·ne·te \bō-ˈnā-tā\. Peak, N La Rioja prov., Argentina; 22,546 ft. (6872 m.).

Bong·a·bon \bȯŋ-ˈä-ˌbȯn, -ˈgä-\. Municipality, E cen. Nueva Ecija prov., Luzon, Philippines, 16 mi. (26 km.) NE of Cabanatuan; pop. (1980c) 32,451; an early ✻ of the province.

Bon·gor \bȯŋ-ˈgȯr\. Town, SW Chad, on Logone River opp. Cameroon; pop. (1988e) 19,914.

Bon·ham \ˈbä-nəm\. City, ⊗ of Fannin co., NE Texas, 23 mi. (37 km.) E of Sherman; pop. (1990c) 6686.

Bon Homme \ˈbä-nəm\. County in SE South Dakota. See table at SOUTH DAKOTA.

Boni, Gulf of. See BONE, GULF OF.

Bo·ni·fa·cio \ˌbō-nē-ˈfä-chō\. Commune, S point of Corsica, France, on Strait of Bonifacio; pop. (1990c) 2701; on narrow peninsula with steep cliffs on three sides; a historic town, said to have been settled 828; became Genoese late 12th cent., later practically an independent republic; remains Genoese in character.

Bonifacio, Strait of. Strait bet. islands of Corsica, France and Sardinia, Italy, in Mediterranean Sea; 7 mi. (11 km.) at narrowest part.

Bon·i·fay \ˈbä-nə-ˌfā\. Town, ⊗ of Holmes co., NW Florida, 96 mi. (154 km.) ENE of Pensacola; pop. (1990c) 2612.

Bo·nin Islands \ 'bō-nin\ *or* **Oga·sa·wa·ra Islands** \ ō-ˌgä-sä-'wär-ä\ *or Jp.* **Ogasawara–gun·tō** \ 'gün-tō\. Group of 27 volcanic islands in the W Pacific Ocean, 600 mi. (965 km.) S of Tokyo, Japan, bet. lat. 26°30′ and 27°44′N and long. 141° and 143°E; 40 sq. mi. (104 sq. km.); belongs to Tokyo prefecture. Largest island Chichi-Jima in center; other important islands Haha-Jima, Muko-Jima, and Yome-Jima. First known to Japanese c. 1600; first colonized 1830 by small group of Europeans and Hawaiians; formally annexed by Japanese 1876. In WWII attacked by U.S. task force Sept. 1944; frequently bombed by U.S. planes 1944–45. Administered by U.S. 1945–68; returned to Japan.

Bo·ni·rau \ ˌbō-nē-'raù\. Mountain, N Doberai Penin., NW Irian Jaya, Indonesia; 7546 ft. (2300 m.).

Bonn \ 'bòn, 'bän\. City, North Rhine-Westphalia, W Germany, on the left bank of Rhine River 16 mi. (26 km.) SSE of Cologne; pop. (1992e) 296,244; seat of German parliament and formerly ✻ of West Germany; chemicals, stoneware, light metal goods; 13th cent. Romanesque cathedral; 18th cent. town hall; university (1777, dissolved 1794, refounded 1818). Birthplace of composer Ludwig van Beethoven 1770; cultural center. Bombed by Allies 1944–45, captured Mar. 1945; meeting place of constituent assembly which drafted constitution, approved May 8, 1949, for West German republic (comprising American, British, and French occupation zones); chosen as ✻ of the new republic (sometimes called **Bonn Republic**) May 1949; with reunification of Germany 1990, ✻ moved to Berlin, but Bonn remained seat of German parliament until 1999.

Bonne Bay \ 'bòn\. Inlet of the Gulf of St. Lawrence, W Newfoundland, Canada.

Bon·ner \ 'bä-nər\. County in N Idaho. See table at IDAHO.

Bon·ners Ferry \ 'bä-nərz\. City, ⊗ of Boundary co., N Idaho, 75 mi. (121 km.) NNE of Coeur d'Alene; pop. (1990c) 2193.

Bonner Springs. City, Wyandotte co., NE Kansas, 15 mi. (24 km.) W of Kansas City; pop. (1990c) 6413; site of Agricultural Hall of Fame.

Bonne Terre \ bän-'ter\. City, St. Francois co., E Missouri, 52 mi. (84 km.) SSW of St. Louis; pop. (1990c) 3871; lead.

Bon·ne·ville \ 'bä-nə-ˌvil\. County in SE Idaho. See table at IDAHO.

Bonneville, Mount. Peak, E Sublette co., W Wyoming; 12,530 ft. (3819 m.).

Bonneville Dam. Dam across Columbia River on Washington-Oregon boundary, ENE of Portland, Oregon; height 170 ft. (52 m.); completed 1937.

Bonneville Salt Flats. A stretch of barren salt flat land, Tooele co., NW Utah; ab. 100 sq. mi. (260 sq. km.); part of bed of the Pleistocene **Lake Bonneville,** whose main remnant is the Great Salt Lake; several vehicular speed records estab. here since 1935.

Bon·ney Lake \ 'bä-nē\. City, Pierce co., W cen. Washington, 12 mi. (19 km.) E of Tacoma; pop. (1990c) 7494.

Bon·ny \ 'bä-nē\. Seaport village at mouth of **Bonny River** (one of the mouths of the Niger, *q.v.*), SE Nigeria; lost much of its trade to Port Harcourt, but still ships oil.

Bonny, Bight of. See BIAFRA, BIGHT OF.

Bononia. **1.** City, Bulgaria. See VIDIN 2.
2. Seaport city, France. See BOULOGNE.
3. Commune, Italy. See BOLOGNA 2.

Bon Se·cour Bay \ ˌbän-sə-'kùr\. Inlet of Gulf of Mexico on SW coast of Baldwin co., SW Alabama.

Bon·thain \ bòn-'tīn\. **1.** Port at S end of SW peninsula of Sulawesi, Indonesia.
2. Peak, Indonesia. See LOMPOBATANG.

Bon·the \ 'bän-tē\. Seaport town, Sierra Leone, on E coast of Sherbro I.; pop. (1985p) 7032; trading town.

Bon·toc \ bōn-'tōk\. Municipality, ✻ of Mountain Province, Luzon, Philippines, on upper Chico River, in W part of province; pop. (1980c) 17,091.

Bo·ny \ bō-'nē\. Village, Aisne dept., NE France, 10 mi. (16 km.) NNW of St.-Quentin; site of WWI battle Sept. 1918; American military cemetery.

Book·er T. Wash·ing·ton National Monument \ 'bù-kər-ˌtē-'wò-shiŋ-tən, -'wä-\. See UNITED STATES, *National Monuments.*

Boom \ 'bōm\. Commune, Antwerp prov., N Belgium, on the Rupel 8 mi. (13 km.) S of the city of Antwerp; pop. (1991c) 13,874.

Boom·plaats \ 'bōm-ˌpläts\. Locality, cen. Rep. of South Africa, near Jagersfontein, SW of Bloemfontein; scene Aug. 1848 of defeat of Boers led by Andries Pretorius.

Boone \ 'bün\. **1.** Name of counties in eight states of the U.S. See tables at ARKANSAS, ILLINOIS, INDIANA, IOWA, KENTUCKY, MISSOURI, NEBRASKA, WEST VIRGINIA.
2. City, ⊗ of Boone co., cen. Iowa, 35 mi. (56 km.) NNW of Des Moines; pop. (1990c) 12,392; American Indian antiquities discovered nearby.
3. Town, ⊗ of Watauga co., NW North Carolina; pop. (1990c) 12,915; Appalachian State Univ. (1903).

Boone Dam. See table at TENNESSEE VALLEY AUTHORITY.

Boones·boro; *earlier* **Boones·bor·ough** \ 'bünz-bər-ō\. Village, Madison co., E cen. Kentucky, on Kentucky River; site of a fort founded by pioneer Daniel Boone 1775.

Boone·ville \ 'bün-ˌvil\. **1.** City, a ⊗ of Logan co., W Arkansas, 34 mi. (55 km.) SE of Fort Smith; pop. (1990c) 3804.
2. City, ⊗ of Owsley co., E Kentucky; pop. (1990c) 232.
3. Town, ⊗ of Prentiss co., NE Mississippi; pop. (1990c) 7955; Northeast Mississippi Community Coll. (1948).

Boons·boro \ 'bünz-bər-ō\. Town, Washington co., N Maryland, ab. 10 mi. (16 km.) S of Hagerstown near a gap in South Mountain (*q.v.*); pop. (1990c) 2445; scene of Union victory Sept. 1862.

Boon·ton \ 'bünt-ᵊn\. Town, Morris co., N New Jersey, 8 mi. (13 km.) NNE of Morristown; pop. (1990c) 8343; settled 1762, incorp. 1867; important ironmaking center during middle of 19th cent.

Boon·ville \ 'bün-ˌvil\. **1.** City, ⊗ of Warrick co., SW Indiana, 17 mi. (27 km.) ENE of Evansville; pop. (1990c) 6724; coal deposits.
2. City, ⊗ of Cooper co., cen. Missouri, on Missouri River 25 mi. (40 km.) W of Columbia; pop. (1990c) 7095; Kemper Military School and Coll. (1844); scene nearby June 1861 of first land battle of Civil War in Missouri, in which Union troops under Gen. Nathaniel Lyon defeated Confederate force under Col. John S. Marmaduke.
3. Village, Oneida co., cen. New York, 20 mi. (32 km.) N of Rome; pop. (1990c) 4246.

Booth·bay Harbor \ 'büth-'bā\. Seaport town, Lincoln co., S Maine, on Atlantic Ocean 34 mi. (55 km.) ENE of Portland; pop. (1990c) 2347; fishing center and summer resort.

Boo·thia, Gulf of \ 'bü-thē-ə\. Gulf bet. Boothia Penin. and Melville Penin., S of NW Baffin I., Nunavut, Canada.

Boothia Peninsula; *formerly* **Boothia Fe·lix Peninsula** \ 'fē-liks\. Peninsula, almost an island, Nunavut, Canada; separated from Baffin I. on the E by Gulf of Boothia and from Prince of Wales I. on the NW by Franklin Strait. The North Magnetic Pole was formerly located on its W shore (see MAGNETIC POLE). Its N tip is northernmost point of mainland of North America, at 71°58′N.

Boo·tle \ 'büt-ᵊl\. Town, Merseyside, NW England, on the Mersey, suburb of Liverpool; pop. (1981p) 62,463; shipping center.

Bo·phu·tha·tswa·na \ ˌbō-pü-tä-'tswä-nä\. Former political entity consisting of a group of noncontiguous black enclaves within the Rep. of South Africa; pop. (1993e) 2,564,000; ✻ Mmabatho; platinum; granted independence 1977, but never recognized internationally; reintegrated with Rep. of South Africa 1994.

Bo·po·lu \ bō-'pō-lü\. Settlement, NW Liberia, ab. 70 mi. (113 km.) N of Monrovia.

Bo·que·rón \ ˌbō-kā-'rōn\. **1.** Department of NW Paraguay. See table at PARAGUAY.
2. Port, a barrio of Cabo Rojo municipality, SW Puerto Rico, on **Boquerón Bay.**

Bor \ 'bòr\. **1.** Town, Nizhegorod Oblast, cen. Russia in Europe, ab. 7 mi. (11 km.) NNE of Nizhniy Novgorod; pop. (1991e) 64,500.

2. Town, E Serbia, Yugoslavia, ab. 95 mi. (153 km.) SE of Belgrade; pop. (1991p) 60,008; copper deposits.

Bo·ra–Bo·ra *or* **Bo·ra·bo·ra** \ˌbōr-ä-ˈbōr-ä\. One of the Leeward Is. group of the Society Is., French Polynesia, 9 mi. (15 km.) WNW of Tahaa; ab. 14 sq. mi. (36 sq. km.); pop. (1988c) 4225.

Bo·rah Peak \ˈbōr-ə\. Mountain in Lost River Range, Custer co., cen. Idaho; 12,662 ft. (3859 m.); highest point in the state.

Bo·ran \ˈbōr-ən\. Region, S Ethiopia, bordering on Kenya.

Bo·rås \bü-ˈrōs\. Town, Älvsborg prov., SW Sweden, 35 mi. (56 km.) E of Göteborg; pop. (1993e) 102,840; textile mills; founded early 17th cent. by King Gustavus II Adolph.

Bo·rāz·jān \ˌbō-räz-ˈjän, -ˈjȯn\. Town, SW Iran, ab. 25 mi. (40 km.) NE of Būshehr; pop. (1986c) 67,061.

Borbetomagus. See WORMS 2.

Bor·bon \bȯr-ˈbȯn\. Municipality on NE coast of Cebu I., Philippines, 38 mi. (61 km.) N of City of Cebu; pop. (1980c) 20,137.

Borbonensis Ager. See BOURBONNAIS.

Bor·deaux \bȯr-ˈdō\; *anc.* **Bur·dig·a·la** \bər-ˈdi-gə-lə\. Commercial seaport, ✻ of Gironde dept., SW France, 13 mi. (21 km.) above confluence of Garonne and Dordogne rivers, 310 mi. (499 km.) SSW of Paris; pop. (1990c) 213,274; shipbuilding, oil refining; chemicals; food processing; archiepiscopal see; famous for its red and white wines; important structures include a 17-arch stone bridge (1821), Grand Théâtre; cathedral, 12th–15th cent.; bell towers; site of large square with statues of political philosopher Baron de Montesquieu and essayist Michel de Montaigne; university (1441).

History: Under Roman rule was ✻ of Aquitania Secunda; taken by Goths and Normans; passed to King Louis VII of France; held by England 1154–1453; suffered during Revolution as a Girondist center; joined with Bourbon forces 1814; seat of government of National Defense 1870; French government temporarily moved here at beginning of both World Wars; occupied by Germans during WWII; relieved 1944; university replaced 1970 by Universities of Bordeaux I, II, and III.

Bor·den \ˈbȯrd-ᵊn\. County in NW Texas. See table at TEXAS.

Borden Island. Island, N Parry Is., split bet. Northwest Territories and Nunavut, Canada.

Bor·den·town \ˈbȯrd-ᵊn-ˌtau̇n\. City, Burlington co., S cen. New Jersey, on Delaware River 6 mi. (10 km.) SSE of Trenton; pop. (1990c) 4341; settled 1682 by English Quakers.

Bor·ders \ˈbȯr-dərz\. Administrative region, SE Scotland; established 1975. See table at SCOTLAND.

Bor·di·ghe·ra \ˌbȯr-dē-ˈgā-rä\. Commune, Imperia prov., Liguria, NW Italy, ESE of Ventimiglia; pop. (1991p) 11,559; seaport; winter resort.

Bordj Bou Ar·re·ridj \ˌbȯrj-bü-á-rā-ˈrēj\. Commune, NE Algeria, ab. 110 mi. (177 km.) WSW of Constantine; pop. (1987p) 84,264.

Bordø \ˈbōr-t͟hœ̄\. One of the Faeroe Is. (*q.v.*).

Borgå. See PORVOO.

Bør·ge·fjell National Park \ˈbœr-gə-ˌfyel\. National park, cen. Norway; 386 sq. mi. (1000 sq. km.); alpine area; estab. 1963.

Bor·gen Bay \ˈbȯr-gən\. Inlet of Bismarck Sea on N coast of New Britain I., Bismarck Archipelago, at W end just E of Cape Gloucester; strategic elevation on the bay captured by U.S. marines 1944 after a ten-day battle.

Bor·ger \ˈbȯr-gər\. City, Hutchinson co., NW Texas, in the Panhandle; pop. (1990c) 15,675; gas and oil wells; Frank Phillips Coll. (1946).

Bor·ger·hout \ˈbȯr-k̲ər-ˌhau̇t\. Former commune, N Belgium; an E suburb that became part of Antwerp 1983.

Borg·holm \ˈbȯrʸ-ˌhȯlm, ˈbȯrg-ˌhōm\. Seaport, Kalmar prov., SE Sweden, on W coast of Öland I.; pop. (1980p) 11,030; chief town of island; seaside resort; ruins of c. 13th cent. castle.

Borgne, Lake \ˈbȯrn\. Inlet of Mississippi Sound in Orleans and St. Bernard parishes, SE Louisiana; connects Lake Pontchartrain with Gulf of Mexico.

Bor·go Mag·gio·re \ˈbōr-gō-mä-ˈjō-rā\. Town, cen. San Marino; pop. (1990e) 2172.

Borgo San Donnino. See FIDENZA.

Bor·go San Lo·ren·zo \ˈbōr-gō-ˌsän-lō-ˈrent-sō\. Commune, Firenze prov., Tuscany, cen. Italy, 14 mi. (23 km.) NNE of Florence; pop. (1981p) 14,690; sulfur springs; summer resort.

Borgo Val di Ta·ro \ˈväl-dē-ˈtä-rō\. Commune, Parma prov., Emilia-Romagna, N Italy, 36 mi. (58 km.) SW of the commune of Parma; pop. (1981p) 7337; lignite deposits nearby.

Bor·gu \ˈbȯr-gü\ *or Fr.* **Bor·gou** \bȯr-ˈgü\. Region, W Africa in N Benin and W Nigeria, bounded on NE and E by the Niger River; an area contested by France and Great Britain 1894–98; divided by convention of June 1898.

Bo·ri·nage \ˌbȯ-rē-ˈnäzh\. Coal-bearing district surrounding Mons, Hainaut prov., Belgium.

Borinquén, Point. Cape at NW end of Puerto Rico, at E side of entrance to Mona Passage.

Bo·ri·slav *or* **Bo·ry·slav** \ˌbə-rē-ˈsläf\ *or Pol.* **Bo·ry·sław** \bȯ-ˈri-släf\. City, W Ukraine, at N foot of Carpathian Mts. 44 mi. (71 km.) SW of L'viv; formerly in Poland; oil field; natural-gas deposits.

Bo·ri·so·glebsk \bə-ˌrē-sə-ˈglyepsk\. City, E Voronezh Oblast, Russia in Europe, at junction of Vorona and Khoper rivers; pop. (1991e) 72,100; estab. 1646 as a fort against the Crimean Tatars; center of grain-producing area.

Borisov. See BARYSAW.

Bo·ri·sov·ka \bə-ˈrē-səf-kə\. **1.** Town, S Kazakhstan, on railroad line 145 mi. (233 km.) NW of Tashkent.

2. Town, SW Belgorod Oblast, Russia in Europe, on left bank of Vorskla River near its source 52 mi. (84 km.) N of Kharkiv; held by Germans 1941–43.

Borkhaya. See BUORKHAYA.

Bor·kou *also* **Bor·ku** \ˈbȯr-ˌkü\. A region of the E Sahara in N Chad.

Bor·kum \ˈbȯr-kəm\. Island, Germany, in North Sea at mouth of Ems River 26 mi. (42 km.) NW of Emden, the westernmost of the East Frisian Is.; ab. 6 mi. (10 km.) long; 14 sq. mi. (36 sq. km.); a popular summer resort.

Bor·länge \ˈbȯr-ˌleŋ-ə\. Town, Kopparberg prov., cen. Sweden; pop. (1993e) 47,300.

Bor·mi·da \ˈbȯr-mē-dä\. River, mostly in Piedmont, NW Italy; rises at E end of Maritime Alps, flows NE to the Tanaro below Alessandria; ab. 100 mi. (160 km.) long.

Borm·la \ˈbȯrm-lä\ *or* **Co·spi·cua** \kȯ-ˈspē-kwä\. Settlement, SE Malta, across the harbor from Valletta; pop. (1991e) 7895; with adjacent **Sen·glea** \seŋ-ˈglā-ə\ and **Vit·to·rio·sa** \vi-ˌtȯr-ē-ˈō-sə\ often called the "Three Cities."

Bor·na \ˈbȯr-nä\. City, E Germany; pop. (1981c) 23,165; became city in 13th cent.

Bor·neo \ˈbȯr-nē-ˌō\. Island in the Malay Archipelago, E of Sumatra, N of Java, and W of Sulawesi; 290,320 sq. mi. (751,929 sq. km.); 3d largest island in the world; N part includes the Malaysian states of Sabah and Sarawak, and the sultanate of Brunei; S section (*Indonesian* **Ka·li·man·tan** \ˌkä-lē-ˈmän-ˌtän\) forms part of Indonesia, and is divided into the provs. of Central Kalimantan, East Kalimantan, South Kalimantan, and West Kalimantan (see table at INDONESIA).

Physical features: Touches South China Sea on W and NW, Sulu Sea on NE, Celebes Sea and Makassar Strait on E, and Java Sea on S. Crossed by the Equator in S cen. part; has indented coastline with numerous good harbors. Mountainous throughout N and cen. parts; chief ranges Muller, Schwaner, and Kapuas; highest point Mt. Kinabalu 13,455 ft. (4101 m.) in Sabah.

Chief rivers: Barito, Kapuas, Mahakam, and Rajang.

Chief products: Rice, tobacco, millet, copra, pepper; bauxite, coal, iron, and oil.

\ə\ **abut** \ˈə\ matches \ᵊ\ kitten, Fr table \ər\ **further** \a\ **ash** \ā\ **ace** \ä\ cot, cart \á\ Fr bac \au̇\ **out** \b̲\ Span Avila \ch\ **chin** \e\ **bet** \ē\ **easy** \g\ **go** \i\ **hit** \ī\ **ice** \j\ **job** \k̲\ **Ger ich, Buch** \ⁿ\ **Fr vin** \ŋ\ **sing** \ō\ **go** \ȯ\ **all** \ȯ\ **law** \œ\ **Fr bœuf** \œ̄\ **Fr feu** \ȯi\ **boy** \th\ **thin** \t͟h\ **this** \ü\ **loot** \u̇\ **foot** \ue\ **Ger füllen** \ue̅\ **Fr rue** \y\ **yet** \ʸ\ Fr digne \ˈdēnʸ\, nuit \ˈnwʸē\ \yü\ **few** \yu̇\ **fury** \zh\ **vision**

History: Invaded c. 5th cent. A.D. by people from S India; S part influenced by Sumatra and Java (*qq.v.*); sultanate of Brunei (*q.v.*) on N coast gave its name in altered form to entire island; visited by Portuguese, Dutch, and English traders 16th and 17th cents.; Sabah (North Borneo), Sarawak, and Brunei (sometimes called collectively **British Borneo**) declared British protectorates 1888 (see also LABUAN); rest (**Dutch Borneo**) claimed by Dutch who subdued coast, esp. in wars during mid-19th cent.; oil discovered in Brunei 1929. In WWII seized by Japanese late 1941; frequently bombed by U.S. planes 1944–45; invasion begun at Tarakan by Australian troops May 1945; finally retaken with surrender of Japanese late summer 1945. Dutch Borneo reorganized 1947 as a federation of autonomous provinces to be included in the projected United States of Indonesia; reorganized again as part of Republic of Indonesia 1950; Sabah and Sarawak made states of Malaysia 1963; hostilities bet. Indonesia and Malaysia 1963–66. Brunei became independent state 1983.

Borneo, South and East. Former residency of Dutch Borneo, Netherlands Indies, now divided into the Indonesian provinces of Central Kalimantan, East Kalimantan, and South Kalimantan (*qq.v.*).

Born·holm \ˌbȯrn-ˈhōlm\. Island, constituting a county of Denmark, in Baltic Sea 25 mi. (40 km.) S of Sweden; 227 sq. mi. (588 sq. km.); pop. (1989e) 45,991; ⊗ Rønne. Generally hilly; popular tourist resort. In early times the home of pirates; seized by the Hanseatic League 1510; down to 1660 held for varying periods by Denmark, Lübeck, Sweden; Danish since 1660.

Born·höved \bȯrn-ˈhœ-fət\. Village, SE Schleswig-Holstein, N Germany, 10 mi. (16 km.) E of Neumünster; pop. (1980c) 2590; battle here July 22, 1227, in which Danes under Waldemar II were defeated by Germans, decisively ending Danish dominion over Baltic region.

Bor·no \ˈbȯr-nō\. State of NE Nigeria. See table at NIGERIA.

Bor Nor. See BUIR NUR.

Bor·no·va \ˌbȯr-nȯ-ˈvä\. Town, W Turkey in Asia, 5 mi. (8 km.) NE of İzmir.

Bor·nu \ˈbȯr-nü\. A vast plain, NE Nigeria, sloping toward Lake Chad; inhabited chiefly by the Kanuri people; constituted a Muslim kingdom from ab. 11th cent.; together with Kanem formed an empire from ab. 13th cent., at height of its power c. 1571–1603; came in conflict with Fulani ab. 1808; after 1835 visited by Europeans and by 1900 French, Germans, and British had spheres of influence; in 1902 became part of Nigeria under British; cen. part of former kingdom became the state of Borno [sic] 1967.

Borny. See COLOMBEY.

Bo·ro·bu·dur *or Du.* **Bo·ro·boe·doer** \ˌbō-rō-bü-ˈdür\. Ruins of a great Buddhist temple, Central Java prov., Indonesia, 18 mi. (29 km.) NW of Yogyakarta; over 1000 years old, built of volcanic lava over a hill, with eight galleries of hundreds of exquisite bas-relief carvings and life-size images of Buddha; rediscovered 1835; restoration worked on during 20th cent.

Bo·ro·di·no \bə-rə-dē-ˈnȯ\. Village, W Moscow Oblast, W cen. Russia in Europe, 70 mi. (113 km.) WSW of the city of Moscow on the Moscow-Smolensk highway (now on railroad). Scene of great battle of Napoleonic Wars Sept. 7, 1812 in which French Emperor Napoléon defeated Gen. M.I. Kutuzov with heavy losses on both sides, allowing Napoléon to occupy Moscow.

Bo·ron·ga Islands \bō-ˈrȯŋ-gä\. Group of small islands, Myanmar, in Bay of Bengal off W coast of cen. part of the country, S of Sittwe.

Bo·rong·an \bō-ˈräŋ-än\. Municipality, ✻ of Eastern Samar prov., SE Samar, Philippines, on coast 36 mi. (58 km.) E of Catbalogan; pop. (1980c) 39,741.

Bo·ro·vi·chi \bə-rə-vē-ˈchē\. Town, SE Novgorod Oblast, W Russia in Europe, on Msta River 160 mi. (257 km.) SE of St. Petersburg; pop. (1991e) 62,800; coal deposits.

Bor·ro·me·an Islands \ˌbȯr-ə-ˈmē-ən\ *or Ital.* **Iso·le Bor·ro·meo** \ˈē-zō-lā-ˌbȯr-rō-ˈmā-ō\. Four small islands in Lake Maggiore, NW Italy; noted for their scenery.

Bor·row·dale \ˈbär-ō-ˌdāl, ˈbȯr-\. Valley in Cumbria, NW England, near Keswick, famed for its beauty; through it flows the Derwent.

Bor·row·stoun·ness \bō-ˈnes; ˌbär-ə-stō-ˈnes, ˌbȯr-\ *or officially* **Bo'·ness** \bō-ˈnes\. Seaport burgh, Central region, SE Scotland, on Firth of Forth; coal deposits.

Bor·sa \ˈbōr-sȧ\. Town, Maramureş co., N Romania; pop. (1989c) 30,609.

Bor·sip·pa \bȯr-ˈsi-pə\. Ancient Akkadian city near Babylon; its ruins are just S of Al Ḩillah.

Bor·sod–Abaúj–Zemp·lén \ˈbōr-shōd-ˈȯ-bȯ-üy-ˈzem-ˌplān\. County of N Hungary. See table at HUNGARY.

Bor·stal \ˈbōrst-ᵊl\. Village, Kent, SE England, near Rochester; site of Borstal Reformatory (founded 1902) which pioneered the segregation of young offenders from mature criminals, and other reforms.

Bo·rū·jerd *or* **Bu·ru·jird** \ˌbō-rü-ˈjerd\. City, W Iran, 200 mi. (322 km.) SW of Tehran; pop. (1986c) 183,879; alt. ab. 5500 ft. (1676 m.).

Borysław *or* **Boryslaw.** See BORISLAV.

Borysthenes. See DNIEPER.

Bor·zya \ˈbȯr-zhə\. Town, S Chita Oblast, S Russia in Asia, on Russian-Manchurian R.R. ab. 170 mi. (274 km.) SE of the city of Chita.

Bo·san·ska Gra·diš·ka \ˈbȯ-sän-skä-ˈgrä-dish-kä\. Town, N Bosnia and Herzegovina, on Sava River, near Croatian border.

Bos·ca·wen \ˈbäs-ˌkwīn\. Town, Merrimack co., S cen. New Hampshire, on Merrimack River 9 mi. (15 km.) N of Concord; pop. (1990c) 3586.

Boscawen. See TAFAHI.

Bos·co·bel \ˌbäs-kə-ˈbel\. **1.** City, Grant co., SW corner of Wisconsin, on Wisconsin River; pop. (1990c) 2706; trade center; founding place of the Gideons, society of commercial travelers (1899).

2. Locality, Shropshire, W England, E of Shrewsbury; site of Royal Oak in which Prince Charles (later Charles II) hid in his flight after battle of Worcester 1651.

Bos·co·re·a·le \ˌbȯs-kō-rā-ˈä-lā\. Commune, Napoli prov., Campania, Italy, at foot of S slope of Vesuvius near Pompeii; pop. (1989c) 29,815; important discoveries of antiquities have been made in vicinity.

Bos·ham \ˈbä-zəm\. Village, South Downs, West Sussex, England, on coast 4 mi. (6 km.) W of Chichester; resort and fishing village. A historical site said to have been associated with Canute (king of England early 11th cent.).

Bo·shan *or W.-G.* **Po–shan** \ˈbō-ˈshän\. Town in mountainous area, cen. Shandong prov., NE China, 55 mi. (88 km.) ESE of Jinan on branch of Jinan-Qingdao railroad.

Bos·hof \ˈbȯs-ˌhȯf\. Resort town, E cen. Rep. of South Africa, 30 mi. (48 km.) ENE of Kimberley.

Bo·si·le·grad *or* **Bo·silj·grad** \ˈbȯ-sēl-ˌgrät\. Town, SE Yugoslavia, near Bulgarian and Macedonian borders; with surrounding district, 320 sq. mi. (829 sq. km.), ceded to Yugoslavia by Bulgaria 1920.

Bos·koop \ˈbȯs-ˌkōp\. Commune, South Holland prov., Netherlands, 2 mi. (3.2 km.) NW of Gouda; pop. (1981e) 13,890; famous for its nurseries of roses and other flowering shrubs.

Bos·kop \ˈbȯs-ˌkȯp\. Locality, Rep. of South Africa, WSW of Johannesburg; site of discovery of fossilized skull 1913.

Bos·na \ˈbȯs-nä\. River, cen. Bosnia and Herzegovina; flows N into Sava River 24 mi. (39 km.) E of Slavonski Brod; 150 mi. (241 km.) long.

Bos·nia \ˈbäz-nē-ə\ *or Serbo-Croat.* **Bos·na** \ˈbȯs-nä\. Region, S Europe, separated from Croatia on N by the Sava River, from Serbia on E by the Drina River, borders Montenegro on S, Herzegovina on SW, and Croatia on W; Dinaric Alps along W border. For history, see BOSNIA AND HERZEGOVINA.

Bosnia and Her·ze·go·vi·na \ˈhert-se-ˌgȯ-vē-nä; ˌhərt-sə-ˈgō-vē-nə, -gō-ˈvē-nə\ *or* **Bosna i Her·ce·go·vi·na** \ē-ˈhert-se-ˌgȯ-vē-nä\ *or* **Bosnia and Hercegovina** *or* **Bosnia–Hercegovina.** Country, SE Europe; a constituent republic of Yugoslavia 1946–92; 19,904 sq. mi. (51,750 sq. km.); pop. (1993e) 4,422,000; ✻ Sarajevo.

History: Bosnia ruled by Croatian kings c. 958 A.D.; subject to Hungary during 12th cent.; organized c. 1200 under a ban (representative of Hungarian kings); Herzegovina (then known as Hum) independent, except for brief intervals, from 10th–14th cents., then conquered by Bosnia 14th cent.; independent kingdom with its ruler, Stephen Tvrtko, taking title "King of Bosnia and Serbia" c. 1376; took part in battle of Kosovo (*q.v.*) 1389; kingdom disintegrated from 1391, the S part becoming independent duchy Herzegovina; Bosnia conquered by Turks 1463; Herzegovina taken by Turks 1482; scene of insurrections against Turkish rule c. 1821–1850; by Treaty of Berlin 1878, placed under control of Austria-Hungary which made it new prov. of Bosnia-Herzegovina; formally annexed to Austria 1908; following WWI became part of Kingdom of Serbs, Croats, and Slovenes, later renamed Yugoslavia (*q.v.*); became a federated republic of Yugoslavia (✻ Sarajevo) in 1946 constitution; with collapse of Communist regimes in E Europe, Yugoslavia began to break up; Bosnia and Herzegovina declared its independence 1992; Serbian part of population objected, with conflict ensuing among Serbs, Croats, and Muslims; heavy fighting centered on Sarajevo and spread throughout country; peace accord signed 1995.

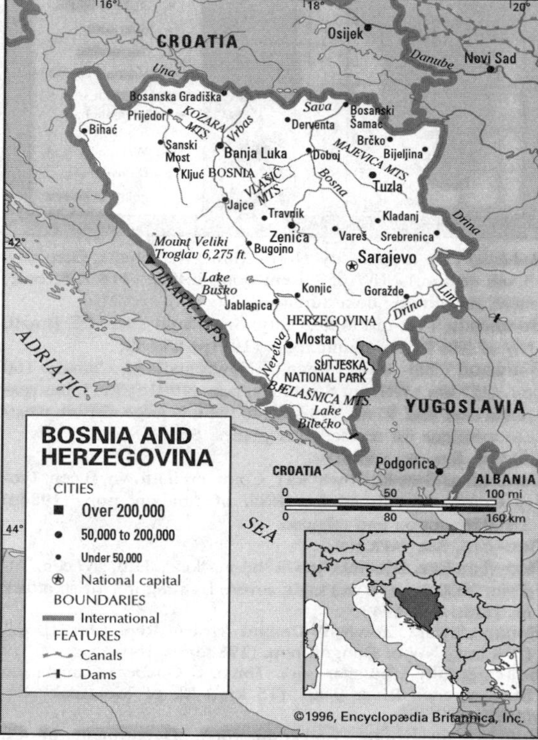

Bos·nik \ˈbȯz-nek, ˈbȯs-\. Village on SE coast of Biak I., Schouten Is., Irian Jaya, Indonesia; with Mokmer Airfield a few miles W taken by Allies May–June 1944.

Bosora. See BUSRA.

Bos·po·rus \ˈbäs-pə-rəs\ *or Turk.* **Ka·ra·de·niz Bo·ğa·zı** \ˌkä-rä-de-ˈnēz-ˌbō-ä-ˈzi\; *anc.* **Bosporus Thra·ci·us** \-ˈthrā-shəs, -shē-əs\ *or, incorrectly,* **Bos·pho·rus** \ˈbäs-fə-rəs\. Narrow strait bet. Turkey in Europe and Turkey in Asia connecting the Sea of Marmara with the Black Sea; 19 mi. (31 km.) long and from ab. .5 to 2.8 mi. (.8 to 4.4 km.) wide. Noted for its scenery on both banks and on European side lined with many residential suburban villages of İstanbul; spanned by two of the longest bridges in the world (completed 1973 and 1988). From ancient times, important as thoroughfare of commerce bet. Black Sea and Aegean and Mediterranean; of great importance in medieval trade of Constantinople; controlled by Turks from mid-15th cent., when they completed fortification of its shores. See also DARDANELLES and, for later history, STRAITS, THE 2.

Bosporus, Cimmerian *or* **Bosporus Cimmerius. 1.** Strait. See KERCH STRAIT.

2. Ancient kingdom. See CIMMERIAN BOSPORUS.

Bos·que \ˈbäs-kē\. County in cen. Texas. See table at TEXAS.

Bosra. See BUSRA.

Bos·san·goa \ˌbȯs-säŋ-ˈgwä\. Town, W cen. Central African Rep.; pop. (1988p) 120,330.

Bos·sier \ˈbō-zhər\. Parish in NW Louisiana. See table at LOUISIANA.

Bossier City. City, Bossier parish, NW Louisiana, E suburb of Shreveport; pop. (1990c) 52,721; oil refineries.

Bos·ton \ˈbȯs-tən\. **1.** Seaport city, ✻ of Massachusetts, and ⊗ of Suffolk co., E Massachusetts, on Massachusetts Bay and at mouths of Charles and Mystic rivers; pop. (1990c) 574,283; largest city in the state. Commercial, financial, medical, educational, and cultural center; insurance; business services; publishing; tourism. Home of the Unitarian movement in U.S.; birthplace of the Christian Science movement. Famous buildings include: Old North Church 1723 (Christ Church), from the steeple of which the signal was given to American patriot Paul Revere to inform him of the route taken by the British in their march on Concord, Old South Meetinghouse (1729), Faneuil Hall (1742, known as the "Cradle of Liberty"), the old State House (c. 1713), U.S. Custom House, Boston Public Library, Boston Museum of Fine Arts, Museum of Science; **Boston National Historical Park** estab. 1974 (see UNITED STATES, *National Historical Parks*). Massachusetts Coll. of Pharmacy and Allied Health Sciences (1823), Boston Conservatory (1867), New England Conservatory of Music (1867), Boston Univ. (1869), Massachusetts Coll. of Art (1873), Emerson Coll. (1880), Wheelock Coll. (1888), Boston Architectural Center (1889), Northeastern Univ. (1898), Simmons Coll. (1899), Fisher Coll. (1903), Wentworth Institute of Technology (1904), Suffolk Univ. (1906), Emmanuel Coll. (1919), Berklee Coll. of Music (1945), Univ. of Massachusetts–Boston (1964).

History: Settled by Gov. John Winthrop 1630 (see CHARLESTOWN 2); made ✻ of Massachusetts Bay Colony 1632; began first continuously published colonial newspaper 1704; leader in opposition to British trade restrictions and other policies leading to the outbreak of the American Revolution; scene of the Boston Massacre Mar. 5, 1770, and the so-called Boston Tea Party Dec. 16, 1773; trade shut off by Boston Port Bill 1774; battle of Bunker Hill June 17, 1775; British withdrew from city Mar. 17, 1776; opposed to President Thomas Jefferson's embargo policy and War of 1812; incorp. as a city 1822; center of antislavery movement 1830–65; important as manufacturing and textile center at end of 19th cent.; maintains its commercial and cultural importance for New England.

2. Village, ⊗ of Bowie co., NE Texas.

3. *formerly* **St. Bot·olph's Town** \sānt-ˈbä-təlfs, sənt\. Town, Lincolnshire, E England, on the Witham near its mouth 49 mi. (79 km.) E of Nottingham; pop. (1991p) 52,600; shipping, fisheries; trade center.

Boston Bay. W section of Massachusetts Bay, E Massachusetts; the city of Boston is situated at its W end on **Boston Harbor.**

Boston Corner. Town, Columbia co., New York; 1.5 sq. mi. (3.9 sq. km.); former SW corner of Massachusetts; ceded to New York mid-19th cent.

Boston Mountains. Ridge in Ozark Plateau in NW Arkansas; highest peak over 2800 ft. (853 m.).

Bostra. See BUSRA.

Bos·worth Field \ˈbäz-wərth\. Field in rural part of Leicestershire, cen. England; site of final battle 1485 in Wars of the Roses in which Richard III was defeated and killed by forces led by Henry Tudor, earl of Richmond (who became Henry VII).

Bo·ta·fo·go Bay \ˌbō-tä-ˈfō-gō\. Inlet of Guanabara Bay in S section of Rio de Janeiro, Brazil, enclosed on SE by Pão de Açúcar (Sugarloaf Mt.).

Bot·a·ny \ˈbät-^{ə}n-ē\. Municipality, E New South Wales, Australia, suburb of Sydney; pop. (1991c) 34,435.

Botany Bay. Inlet of South Pacific Ocean, on S border of city of Sydney, New South Wales, SE Australia, 9 mi. (15 km.) S of Port Jackson; ab. 6 mi. (10 km.) at greatest width. Scene of first landing on Australian soil by English explorer Capt. James Cook 1770; selected 1787 as site for penal settlement; landing made Jan. 1788; settlement transferred later to Port Jackson. Now location for many suburbs of Sydney.

Botany Point. Cape on W end of St. Thomas I., Virgin Is., West Indies.

Bot·e·tourt \ˈbä-tə-ˌtät\. County in W cen. Virginia. See table at VIRGINIA.

Bo·tev Peak \ˈbȯ-tef\. Mountain, Bulgaria, ab. 81 mi. (130 km.) E of Sofia; 7793 ft. (2375 m.); highest peak in Balkan Mts.

Both·ell \ˈbä-thəl\. City, King co., W cen. Washington, 12 mi. (19 km.) NE of Seattle; pop. (1990c) 12,345.

Both·nia \ˈbäth-nē-ə\. Former name of the region about the Gulf of Bothnia.

Bothnia, Gulf of. N arm of the Baltic Sea, extending bet. Sweden on the W and Finland on the E.

Both·well \ˈbäth-ˌwel, -wəl\. Parish and town, Strathclyde region, Scotland, ab. 7 mi. (11 km.) SE of Glasgow; ruins of 13th cent. Bothwell Castle; at **Bothwell Bridge** over the Clyde the Royalists under James Scott, duke of Monmouth and John Graham of Claverhouse defeated the Covenanters 1679.

Botocan. See PAGSANJAN.

Bo·to·şa·ni *or* **Bo·to·sha·ni** \ˌbō-tō-ˈshän^{y}\. **1.** County of NE Romania. See table at ROMANIA.
2. Commercial town, its ⊗; pop. (1989c) 119,563; textiles; trade center.

Bo·trange \bȯ-ˈträ^{n}zh\. Peak in Hohe Venn Mts., Liège prov., E Belgium; 2277 ft. (694 m.); highest peak in Belgium.

Bo·tswa·na \bȯt-ˈswä-nä, bät-\; *formerly* **Bech·u·a·na·land Protectorate** *or short form* **Bechuanaland** \ˌbech-ˈwä-nə-ˌland\. Republic, S Africa, bounded on W and N by Namibia, on NE by Zimbabwe, and on SE and S by the Rep. of South Africa; 219,916 sq. mi. (569,582 sq. km.); pop. (1993e) 1,406,000; linked with Zambia across Zambezi River; ✻ Gaborone.

Physical features: Essentially a tableland with mean elev. of ab. 3300 ft. (1006 m.); part of Kalahari Desert is in SW and W, Okavango Basin and salt lakes in N; av. yearly rainfall is 18 in. (46 cm.).

Chief products: Economy traditionally dependent on the export of cattle; crops include corn, sorghum, peanuts; became one of world's largest diamond producers in 1980s; copper, manganese, salt.

Chief towns: Gaborone and Francistown.

History: Region occupied by British at instigation of colonial administrator Cecil Rhodes 1884; organized as British protectorate 1885, divided into British Bechuanaland and Bechuanaland Protectorate (the latter lying N of Molopo River); included in grant to British South Africa Company 1889 but never administered by it; when British Bechuanaland (*q.v.*) was attached to Cape of Good Hope 1895, N part remained a protectorate until it became an independent republic 1966; member of the Commonwealth; diamond and copper discoveries late 1960s helped boost economy, making it one of Africa's strongest.

Bot·ti·neau \ˌbä-tə-ˈnō\. **1.** County in N North Dakota. See table at NORTH DAKOTA.
2. City, its ⊗, 59 mi. (95 km.) NE of Minot; pop. (1990c) 2598.

Bottom. See THE BOTTOM.

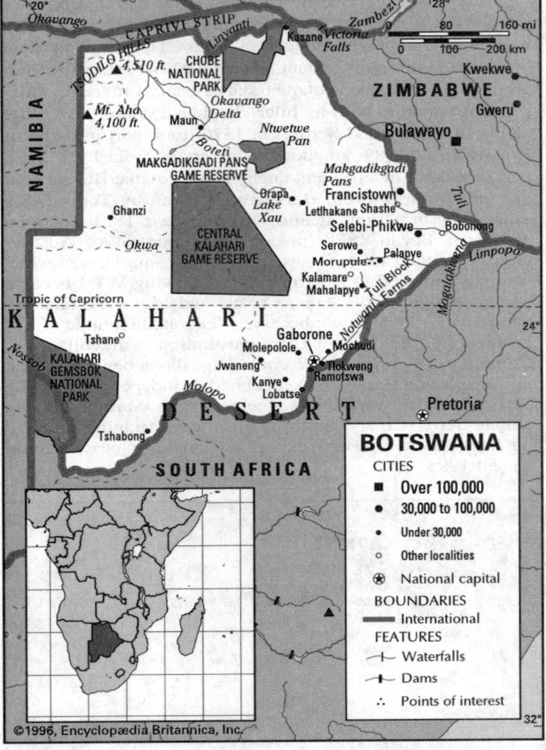

Bot·trop \ˈbȯ-ˌtrȯp\. City, North Rhine-Westphalia, Germany, 5 mi. (8 km.) NNW of Essen; pop. (1992e) 118,758; coal; steel, machinery; coke furnaces.

Bo·tu·ca·tu \ˈbü-tü-kä-ˈtü\. City, São Paulo state, SE Brazil, NW of São Paulo; munic. pop. (1991p) 85,689.

Bot·wood \ˈbät-ˌwu̇d\. Town, E Newfoundland, Canada, 160 mi. (257 km.) WNW of St. John's; pop. (1991c) 3663; has seaplane base and 30 mi. (48 km.) to the E is large airport, western terminus for transatlantic planes. See GANDER.

Bötzow. See ORANIENBURG.

Boua·ké *or* **Bwa·ke** \bwä-ˈkā\. Commercial town, S cen. Ivory Coast, on railroad line NNW of Abidjan; pop. (1984e) 220,000; cotton and tobacco.

Bou–Am. See TAFILALT.

Bou–Aou·kaz, Dje·bel \ˈjab-^{ə}l-ˈbü-au̇-ˈkaz\. Hill, NW cen. Tunisia; 2000 ft. (610 m.) high; severe fighting in British attack on Tunis Apr. 1943.

Bouar \ˈbwär\. Town, W Central African Rep., ab. 210 mi. (338 km.) NW of Bangui; pop. (1988e) 49,166.

Bou·cher·ville \ˈbü-shər-ˌvil\. Town, S Quebec, Canada, on St. Lawrence River 9 mi. (15 km.) NE of Montreal; pop. (1991c) 33,796.

Bouches–du–Rhône \ˌbüsh-dü̅-ˈrōn\. Department of SE France. See table at FRANCE.

Bou·fa·rik *or* **Bu·fa·rik** \ˌbü-fä-ˈrēk\. Commune, N Algeria, ab. 21 mi. (34 km.) SSW of Algiers; pop. (1987p) 41,305.

Bou·gain·ville \ˈbü-gən-ˌvil, ˈbō-; ˌbü-ge^{n}-ˈvēl\. Largest island of the Solomon Is., W Pacific Ocean; ab. 127 mi. (204 km.) long by ab. 49 mi. (79 km.) wide; 3880 sq. mi. (10,049 sq. km.); a part of Papua New Guinea. Traversed lengthwise by a mountain range called Emperor Range in N and Crown Prince Range in S, highest peak Mt. Balbi 8999 ft. (2743 m.) in N section; much of the interior was among the last places on earth to be explored. Has rich volcanic soil; coconut plantations; other products are coffee and cocoa. On N is Buka I. separated from it by narrow Buka Passage, and on the S are Shortland Is. Good harbors are at Kieta, Buka Passage, and

Buin at S end; on W coast is anchorage in Empress Augusta Bay.

History: Discovered by French navigator Louis de Bougainville 1768; came under control of a German trading company 1882 and was a German possession 1899–1914; taken by Australians in WWI and included 1920 in mandated New Guinea. Occupied 1942 by Japanese who developed harbors and made airfields; bombed by Allied air forces 1943 and landings made by U.S. marines on coast of Empress Augusta Bay, but most of island and Japanese forces bypassed 1944 until campaign by Australians in 1945; became part of UN Trust Terr. of New Guinea following WWII; became part of Papua New Guinea when it achieved independence 1975; during late 1980s and early 1990s secessionist movement grew.

Bougainville Strait. Channel bet. S Bougainville and NW Choiseul Is., W cen. Solomon Is.; ab. 30 mi. (48 km.) wide.

Bou·ga·roun, Cape \ˌbü-gȧ-ˈrün\. Cape on coast of NE Algeria.

Bougie. See BEJAÏA.

Bouil·lon \bü-ˈyōⁿ\. Town in the Ardennes, Luxembourg prov., Belgium, on the Semois ab. 7 mi. (11 km.) NNE of Sedan; pop. (1991c) 5468; made ✱ of small duchy of Crusader Godfrey of Bouillon, late 11th cent.; later attached successively to Liège, Sedan, France, Netherlands, Belgium.

Bou·ï·ra \bwē-ˈrä\. Commune, N Algeria, 58 mi. (93 km.) SE of Algiers; pop. (1987p) 36,550.

Boukhara. See BUKHARA.

Boulaïda, El. See BLIDA 2.

Boul·der \ˈbōl-dər\. **1.** County in N cen. Colorado. See table at COLORADO.
2. City, its ⊗, 25 mi. (40 km.) NW of Denver; pop. (1990c) 83,312; resort; in agriculturally rich region; mineral deposits; space-research industries; electronic equipment; a site of National Institute of Standards and Technology, National Center for Atmospheric Research, Univ. of Colorado at Boulder (1876); settled 1858; incorp. as town 1871.
3. Town, ⊗ of Jefferson co., SW cen. Montana; pop. (1990c) 1316; lead, zinc deposits.
4. Town, S Western Australia, Australia, in gold-bearing district 335 mi. (539 km.) ENE of Perth; pop. (1981c) 11,543.

Boulder Canyon. Former canyon of the Colorado River bet. Arizona and Nevada ab. 20 mi. (32 km.) above Black Canyon (site of Hoover Dam); now covered by Lake Mead.

Boulder City. City, Clark co., SE corner of Nevada; pop. (1990c) 12,567; built by U.S. government in 1932 as construction headquarters during work on Hoover Dam; an administrative headquarters for Bureau of Reclamation and for Lake Mead National Recreation Area; became self-governing c. 1960.

Boulder Dam. See *Hoover Dam* at UNITED STATES, *Dams and Reservoirs.*

Boulder Peak. Mountain, S Custer co., cen. Idaho; 10,966 ft. (3342 m.).

Bou·lin·da, Mount \bu̇-ˈlin-də\. Peak in cen. part of island of New Caledonia, SW Pacific Ocean; 4078 ft. (1243 m.).

Bou·logne \bü-ˈlōnʸ, -ˈlōn, -ˈlōn-yə, -ˈlȯin\ *or* **Bou·logne–sur–Mer** \sᵫr-ˈmer\; *anc.* **Ges·o·ri·a·cum** *or* **Ges·so·ri·a·cum** \ˌje-sə-ˈrī-ə-kəm\; *later* **Bo·no·nia** \bə-ˈnō-nē-ə\. Seaport city, Pas-de-Calais dept., N France, on English Channel 61 mi. (98 km.) NW of Arras; pop. (1990c) 44,244; important passenger port; fishing center; 13th cent. castle; Italian-Renaissance cathedral; Roman remains; large English population.

History: Inhabitants massacred by Normans 882 A.D.; taken by Henry VIII of England 1544; returned to France 1550; demolished by Holy Roman Emperor Charles V 1553; place where Emperor Napoléon gathered large army 1803–05 in preparation for attack on England. In WWII taken by Germans May 1940; stormed by Canadians Sept. 1944; suffered severe damage during WWII; largely rebuilt since.

Boulogne–Bil·lan·court \ˌbē-yäⁿ-ˈkür\; *formerly* **Bou·logne–sur–Seine** \sᵫr-ˈsen, -ˈsān\. Commune, Hauts-de-Seine dept., N France, SW suburb of Paris on the Seine River, near Bois de Boulogne; automobiles, airplanes, chemical products.

Bound·a·ry \ˈbau̇n-drē\. County in N Idaho. See table at IDAHO.

Boundary Bay. Inlet of Strait of Georgia in extreme SW British Columbia on U.S.-Canada border bet. Point Roberts and Blaine, Washington.

Boundary Peak. Mountain, W Esmeralda co., SW Nevada, on Nevada-California boundary; 13,140 ft. (4005 m.); highest point in Nevada.

Bound Brook \ˈbau̇nd-ˌbru̇k\. Borough, Somerset co., N cen. New Jersey, on Raritan River 7 mi. (11 km.) NW of New Brunswick; pop. (1990c) 9487; settled late 17th cent.; during American Revolution, scene of rout by British force under Gen. Charles Cornwallis 1777.

Boun·ti·ful \ˈbau̇n-ti-fəl\. City, Davis co., N Utah, 8 mi. (13 km.) N of Salt Lake City; pop. (1990c) 36,659; settled 1847.

Boun·ty Islands \ˈbau̇n-tē\. Group of 13 islets, 415 mi. (668 km.) ESE of Dunedin, New Zealand, 48°S, 178°30′E; .5 sq. mi. (1.3 sq. km.); uninhabited; under New Zealand administration; discovered 1788 by Capt. William Bligh in H.M.S. *Bounty.*

Bou·quet Canyon Dam \ˌbō-ˈkā, ˌbü-\. Dam across **Bouquet Creek,** California; height 225 ft. (69 m.); completed 1934; impounds water in **Bouquet Reservoir** for waterpower.

Bou·rail \bü-ˈrī\. Town, New Caledonia I., SW Pacific Ocean, 80 mi. (129 km.) NW of Nouméa; pop. (1980p) 3149.

Bour·bon \ˈbər-bən\. Name of counties in two states of the U.S. See tables at KANSAS and KENTUCKY.

Bourbon. See RÉUNION.

Bour·bon·nais \bər-ˈbō-nəs\. Village, Kankakee co., NE Illinois, 5 mi. (8 km.) N of Kankakee; pop. (1990c) 13,934.

Bourbonnais \bür-bȯ-ˈne\ *or Lat.* **Bor·bo·nen·sis Ager** \ˌbȯr-bə-ˈnen-sis-ˈā-jər\. Historical region of cen. France; bounded anciently on NE by Nivernais, on E by Burgundy, on SE by Lyonnais, on S by Auvergne, on SW by Marche, and on NW by Berry; ✱ (from late 15th cent.) Moulins.

History: Part of Celtic Gaul under Roman Gen. Julius Caesar, then of Aquitania under Emperor Augustus; gradually began separate existence in 10th cent. A.D. under Aimar, a lord of Bourbon; to Robert de France (1256–1318), comte de Clermont (6th son of Louis IX) responsible for most famous house of Bourbon; lordship raised to duchy (1327) under Robert's successor, Louis I; became part of royal domain 1527 and subsequently a province of France.

Bourbon–Vendée. See LA ROCHE-SUR-YON.

Bou·resches \bü-ˈresh\. Village, Aisne dept., NE France, 7 mi. (11 km.) WNW of Château-Thierry; taken by Americans June 1918 in battle of Belleau Wood.

Bourg \ˈbürk\ *also* **Bourg–en–Bresse** \äⁿ-ˈbres\. Commune, ✱ of Ain dept., E France, 45 mi. (72 km.) W of Geneva, Switzerland; pop. (1990c) 42,955; tourism; 16th cent. Gothic church; museum of antiquities. See BRESSE.

Bourges \ˈbürzh\; *anc.* **Avar·i·cum** \ə-ˈvar-i-kəm\. Commune, ✱ of Cher dept., cen. France., 126 mi. (203 km.) S of Paris; pop. (1990c) 78,773; in agriculturally rich region; 13th cent. Gothic cathedral; archiepiscopal palace; taken by Roman Gen. Julius Caesar 52 B.C.; under Emperor Augustus was a town of Roman prov. of Aquitania; important center in historical region of Berry; site of numerous medieval councils; university founded 1463 but abolished during Revolution.

Bour·get \bür-ˈzhe, -ˈzhā\. Lake in Savoie dept., E France; 11 mi. (18 km.) long.

Bourget, Le. See LE BOURGET.

Bourg–Ma·dame \ˌbür-mȧ-ˈdȧm\. Village, Pyrénées-Orientales dept., S France; international bridge over a tributary of the Segre to Puigcerdá marks the France-Spain frontier.

Bour·gogne \bür-'gȯn^{y}, -'gȯ-nyə\. **1.** Historical region, France. See BURGUNGY.
2. Region of E cen. France. See table at FRANCE.

Bourg–Saint–Mau·rice \ˌbür-se^{n}-mȯ-'rēs\. Commune, Savoie dept., E France; in a valley in Graian Alps at alt. 2668 ft. (813 m.); railroad terminal and French W terminus of Little St. Bernard Pass; tourism.

Bourke \'bərk\. Town, N New South Wales, SE Australia, on Darling River 410 mi. (660 km.) NW of Sydney; pop. (1991c) 4464; first settled as a fort 1835.

Bour·lon \bür-'lō^{n}\. Village and forested area (**Bourlon Wood**), Pas-de-Calais dept., N France, 5 mi. (8 km.) W of Cambrai; fighting Nov. 20–30, 1917.

Bourne \'bōrn\. Town, Barnstable co., SE Massachusetts, on Cape Cod Canal 14 mi. (23 km.) W of the town of Barnstable; pop. (1990c) 16,064; summer resort.

Bourne·mouth \'bōrn-məth, 'bu̇rn-\. Town, Dorset, S England, on English Channel; pop. (1991p) 154,400; resort.

Bouscat, Le. See LE BOUSCAT.

Bou·vet Island \bü-'vā\. Island, Norway, in S Atlantic Ocean 1600 mi. (2574 km.) SSW of Cape of Good Hope, Rep. of South Africa, 54°26′S, 3°24′E; claimed for Norway 1927.

Bou·vines \bü-'vēn\. Village, Nord dept., NE France, 10 mi. (16 km.) SE of Lille; battlefield July 27, 1214 where French under King Philip Augustus defeated Holy Roman Emperor Otto IV, King John of England, and their allies.

Bow \'bō\. **1.** Town, Merrimack co., New Hampshire; pop. (1990c) 5500; birthplace of Mary Morse Baker Eddy, founder of Christian Science Church, 1821.
2. River, SW Alberta, Canada; rises in Banff National Park on the E slopes of the Rocky Mts., flows SE through the park just E of Lake Louise then E past Calgary to unite with the Oldman and form the South Saskatchewan River; 315 mi. (507 km.) long.

Bow·bells \'bō-ˌbelz\. City, ⊗ of Burke co., NW North Dakota; pop. (1990c) 498.

Bow·doin Lake \'bōd-^{ə}n\. Lake, N cen. Phillips co., N Montana, 12 mi. (19 km.) ENE of Malta; ab. 5 mi. (8 km.) long; wildlife refuge nearby.

Bow·en \'bō-ən\. Seaport, E Queensland, NE Australia, 290 mi. (467 km.) NW of Rockhampton; pop. (1981c) 13,645.

Bow Fell \'bō-'fel\. Mountain, Cumbria, NW England, in the Lake District; 2960 ft. (902 m.).

Bow·ie \'bü-ē\. **1.** County in NE Texas. See table at TEXAS.
2. Town, Prince Georges co., Maryland, NE of Washington, D.C.; pop. (1990c) 37,589; racetrack; Bowie State Univ. (1865).
3. City, Montague co., N Texas, 42 mi. (68 km.) SE of Wichita Falls; pop. (1990c) 4990.

Bow Island. See HAO.

Bowling Green \ˌbō-liŋ-'grēn\. **1.** City, ⊗ of Warren co., S Kentucky, 64 mi. (103 km.) SE of Owensboro; pop. (1990c) 40,641; regional trade center; tobacco market; limestone deposits; Western Kentucky Univ. (1906).
2. City, ⊗ of Pike co., E Missouri; pop. (1990c) 2976.
3. City, ⊗ of Wood co., NW Ohio, 18 mi. (29 km.) S of Toledo; pop. (1990c) 28,176; Bowling Green State Univ. (1910).
4. Town, ⊗ of Caroline co., E Virginia; pop. (1990c) 727.

Bow·man \'bō-mən\. **1.** County in SW corner of North Dakota. See table at NORTH DAKOTA.
2. City, its ⊗; pop. (1990c) 1741.

Bow River. See BOW 2.

Box·bor·ough \'bäks-ˌbər-ō\. Town, Middlesex co., Massachusetts, 25 mi. (40 km.) NW of Boston; pop. (1990c) 3343.

Box Butte \'bäks-ˌbyüt\. County in NW Nebraska. See table at NEBRASKA.

Box El·der \'bäks-ˌel-dər\. **1.** County in NW corner of Utah. See table at UTAH.
2. City, Pennington co., W South Dakota; pop. (1990c) 2680.

Box·ford \'bäks-fərd\. Town, Essex co., NE Massachusetts, 20 mi. (32 km.) NNE of Boston; pop. (1990c) 6266.

Box Hill. Town, NE suburb of Melbourne, S Victoria, SE Australia; pop. (1991c) 45,139.

Bo Xian *or W.-G.* **Po·hsien** \'bō-'shyen\; *formerly* **Po·chow** \'pō-'chau̇\. Commercial city, NW Anhui prov., E China, ab. 160 mi. (255 km.) NW of Hefei.

Box·tel \'bȯks-təl\. Commune, North Brabant prov., S Netherlands, ab. 12 mi. (19 km.) E of Tilburg; pop. (1981e) 24,551.

Bo·ya·cá \ˌbō-yä-'kä\. **1.** Department of cen. Colombia. See table at COLOMBIA.
2. Town, Boyacá dept., cen. Colombia; battle in which Spanish were defeated by small army under South American revolutionary leader Simon Bolívar and Gen. Francisco de Paula Santander Aug. 7, 1819. See BOGOTÁ 2.

Boyana. See BUENË.

Boyd \'bȯid\. Name of counties in two states of the U.S. See tables at KENTUCKY and NEBRASKA.

Boyd·ton \'bȯid-tən\. Town, ⊗ of Mecklenburg co., S Virginia; pop. (1990c) 453.

Boy·er \'bȯi-ər\. River, W Iowa; rises in Buena Vista co., NW Iowa, flows SW into Missouri River in W Pottawattamie co., SW Iowa; 123 mi. (198 km.) long.

Bo·yer Ahmadī–ye Sardīr va Kohkīlūyeh. See KOHKĪLŪYEH VA BOYER AHMADĪ-YE SARDĪR.

Boy·er·town \'bȯi-ər-ˌtau̇n\. Borough, Berks co., SE Pennsylvania, 16 mi. (26 km.) E of Reading; pop. (1990c) 3759.

Boyle \'bȯil\. **1.** County in cen. Kentucky. See table at KENTUCKY.
2. Town, N co. Roscommon, N cen. Ireland; ruins of Cistercian abbey dating from c. 13th cent.

Boyls·ton \'bȯil-stən\. Town, Worcester co., cen. Massachusetts, NE of the city of Worcester; pop. (1990c) 3517.

Boyne \'bȯin\. River, E Ireland; rises in the Bog of Allen, co. Kildare, flows NNE into the Irish Sea just below Drogheda; 70 mi. (113 km.) long; important battle fought on its banks 3 mi. (5 km.) W of Drogheda July 1, 1690 in which the forces under King William III of England defeated the Jacobites under James II. See AUGHRIM.

Boyne City. City, Charlevoix co., NW Michigan, 40 mi. (64 km.) SW of Cheboygan; pop. (1990c) 3478; fishing; resort.

Boyn·ton Beach \'bȯint-^{ə}n\. City, Palm Beach co., SE Florida, S of West Palm Beach; pop. (1990c) 46,194.

Bo·yo·ma Falls \bō-'yō-mä\; *formerly* **Stan·ley Falls** \'stan-lē\. Seven cataracts of the upper Congo (Lualaba) River in N cen. Democratic Rep. of Congo, on the Equator, above Kisangani, extending ab. 60 mi. (97 km.).

Boz Bu·run \ˌbōz-bü-'rün\. Cape on NW coast of Turkey in Asia, projecting W into the Sea of Marmara, 40°24′N, 26°54′E.

Boz·caa·da \ˌbōz-jä-'dä\; *anc.* **Ten·e·dos** \'te-nə-ˌdäs\. Turkish island in NE Aegean Sea off W coast of Turkey in Asia, S of the island of Gökçeada and ab. 12 mi. (19 km.) S of the Dardanelles; in the Trojan legend the station of the Greek fleet; used as a base by Persian King Xerxes in the Persian War and later an ally of Athens. See GREECE.

Boz Dağ \bōz-'dä\; *anc.* **Tmo·lus** \tə-'mō-ləs\. Mountain range, W Turkey in Asia 20 mi. (32 km.) E of İzmir; ab. 6200 ft. (1890 m.) high; divides valleys of Gediz and Cayster.

Boze·man \'bōz-mən\. City, ⊗ of Gallatin co., S Montana; pop. (1990c) 22,660; Montana State Univ. (1893).

Bozeman Pass. Mountain pass near Bozeman, S Montana; alt. ab. 6000 ft. (1830 m.), on the **Bozeman Trail** which extended from Julesburg, Colorado, on the South Platte River to Virginia City, mining town in SW Montana; traced by American pioneer John M. Bozeman 1862 and later; its use by gold seekers opposed by Indians and abandoned after 1868; after 1877 became important cattle route.

Bozen. See BOLZANO 2.

Boz·rah \'bȯz-rə, 'bäz-\. **1.** Village, Syria. See BUSRA.
2. *or mod.* **Bu·ṣay·rā** \bü-'sī-rä\. Town, Jordan, SSE of Dead Sea and near Petra; perhaps same location of city mentioned in Old Testament (*Gen.* xxxvi. 33, among others) in ancient Edom.

Bra \'brä\. Commune, Cuneo prov., Piedmont, NW Italy, 25 mi. (40 km.) NE of the commune of Cuneo; pop. (1989c) 26,750.

Bra·bant \'brä-bänt; brə-'bant, -'bänt\. **1.** Old duchy of the Netherlands, covering territory of what is now S Netherlands and cen. and N Belgium.

History: Region settled by Franks in 5th cent. A.D.; in 9th cent. included. in kingdom of Lotharingia and after 959 in duchy of Lower Lorraine (see LORRAINE); in late 12th cent. became independent duchy; finally passed to house of Burgundy 1430; inherited by Hapsburgs 1477; from 15th cent. a center of culture and commerce (see ANTWERP and BRUSSELS); N section took part in revolt from Spain and by treaty of 1609 was awarded to United Provinces (see NETHERLANDS); S (and larger) section remained part of Spanish, later Austrian, Netherlands; united under French rule 1794–1814 and in kingdom of Netherlands 1815–30; provs. of Antwerp and S Brabant joined revolt of Belgium (*q.v.*) 1830.

2. Province, cen. Belgium; split bet. Flanders and Wallonia regions; one of Belgium's most densely populated provinces; rivers Senne, Dijle, Demer. Formerly, part of the old duchy of Brabant; overrun by the Germans in 1914 and 1940 and occupied by them through World Wars I and II. See table at BELGIUM.

Brabant Island. Island, Palmer Archipelago, Antarctica; 33 mi. (53 km.) long, 2d in size in the archipelago; discovered 1898 by Belgian explorer Adrian Gerlache de Gomery.

Brač *or* **Brach** \ˈbräch\ *or Ital.* **Braz·za** \ˈbrät-sä\. Island, Croatia, in the Adriatic Sea off the Dalmatian coast; 152 sq. mi. (394 sq. km.).

Bracara Augusta. See BRAGA 2.

Brac·cia·no, Lake \ˌbrä-chē-ˈä-nō\; *anc.* **Sab·a·ti·nus** \ˌsa-bə-ˈtī-nəs\. Lake, W cen. Italy, 17 mi. (27 km.) NW of Rome; 22 sq. mi. (57 sq. km.); drains SW into the Tyrrhenian Sea.

Brace·bridge \ˈbrās-ˌbrij\. Town, ⊗ of Muskoka dist., SE Ontario, Canada, 5 mi. (8 km.) E of S end of Lake Muskoka; pop. (1991c) 12,308; resort.

Brach. See BRAČ.

Brack·en \ˈbra-kən\. County in NE Kentucky. See table at KENTUCKY.

Brack·en·ridge \ˈbra-kən-rij\. Borough, Allegheny co., SW Pennsylvania, on Allegheny River 18 mi. (29 km.) NE of Pittsburgh; pop. (1990c) 3784.

Brack·ett·ville \ˈbra-kət-ˌvil\. City, ⊗ of Kinney co., SW Texas, 28 mi. (45 km.) E of Del Rio; pop. (1990c) 1740.

Brack·we·de \ˈbräk-ˌvā-də\. Town, North Rhine-Westphalia, Germany, 36 mi. (58 km.) E of Münster and just S of Bielefeld; first mentioned 1151.

Bra·da·no \ˈbrä-dä-nō\. River, S Italy; flows SE into the head of the Gulf of Taranto; 73 mi. (117 km.) long.

Brad·dock \ˈbra-dək\. Borough, Allegheny co., SW Pennsylvania, on Monongahela River 8 mi. (13 km.) E of Pittsburgh; pop. (1990c) 4682; scene of Gen. Edward Braddock's defeat July 9, 1755 by French and Indians during French and Indian War.

Bra·den·ton \ˈbrād-ᵊn-tən\. City, ⊗ of Manatee co., W Florida Penin., at S end of Tampa Bay 11 mi. (18 km.) N of Sarasota; pop. (1990c) 43,779; winter resort; travertine deposits; Manatee Community Coll. (1957).

Brad·ford \ˈbrad-fərd\. **1.** Name of counties in two states of the U.S. See tables at FLORIDA and PENNSYLVANIA.

2. City, McKean co., N Pennsylvania, 18 mi. (29 km.) W of Allegheny River as it crosses New York border; pop. (1990c) 9625; oil refineries; Univ. of Pittsburgh at Bradford (1963).

3. *locally* ˈbrat-fəd\. City, West Yorkshire, N England, near the Aire 10 mi. (16 km.) W of Leeds; pop. (1981p) 280,691; center of worsted industry; coal; wool exchange (1867); Univ. of Bradford (1966).

Bradford–on–Avon \ˈā-vən, ˈa-\. Town, Wiltshire, S England, 6 mi. (10 km.) ESE of Bath; pop. (1981p) 8752; ancient Saxon church.

Brad·ley \ˈbrad-lē\. **1.** Name of counties in two states of the U.S. See tables at ARKANSAS and TENNESSEE.

2. Village, Kankakee co., NE Illinois, 3 mi. (5 km.) N of the city of Kankakee; pop. (1990c) 10,792.

Bradley, Mount. Peak in the Sierra Nevada, NE Tulare co., S cen. California; 13,280 ft. (4048 m.).

Bradley Beach. Borough, Monmouth co., E cen. New Jersey, on Atlantic Ocean 2 mi. (3 km.) S of Asbury Park; pop. (1990c) 4475; seaside resort; fisheries.

Bra·dy \ˈbrā-dē\. City, ⊗ of McCulloch co., cen. Texas, 46 mi. (74 km.) SSW of Brownwood; pop. (1990c) 5946.

Brae·mar \brā-ˈmär\. Village, SW Grampian region, NE Scotland, 7 mi. (11 km.) W of Balmoral Castle; seat of the earls of Mar; standard of Jacobite revolt raised here 1715 by John Erskine, 6th earl.

Brae·ri·ach \brā-ˈrē-ək\. Peak, N cen. Scotland, on border bet. Grampian and Highland regions; 4248 ft. (1295 m.).

Bra·ga \ˈbrä-gə\. **1.** District of NW Portugal. See table at PORTUGAL.

2. *anc.* **Brac·a·ra Au·gus·ta** \ˈbra-kə-rə-ȯ-ˈgəs-tə\. Commune, its ✱, 30 mi. (48 km.) NNE of Porto; pop. (1990c) 63,033; ✱ of old prov. of Entre-Douro-e-Minho; said to have been founded by Carthaginians; Roman ruins; 12th cent. cathedral; pilgrimage church nearby; archiepiscopal see and primacy of Portugal; residence of Portuguese court 1093–1147.

Bra·ga·do \brȧ-ˈgä-dō\. Town, Buenos Aires prov., E Argentina; pop. (1980p) 27,101.

Bra·gan·ça \brȧ-ˈgäⁿ-sə\ *or Eng.* **Bra·gan·za** \brə-ˈgan-zə\. **1.** Town, NE Pará state, N Brazil, ab. 120 mi. (195 km.) E of Belém; pop. (1991p) 43,209.

2. District of NE Portugal. See table at PORTUGAL.

3. Commune, its ✱, near Spanish border 88 mi. (142 km.) ENE of Braga; pop. (1990c) 14,181; former ✱ of old prov. of Trás-os-Montes; episcopal see; castle of royal house of Braganza, long rulers of Portugal and Brazil.

Bragança Pau·lis·ta \pau̇-ˈlēs-tə\. City, São Paulo state, SE Brazil, 40 mi. (64 km.) N of the city of São Paulo; pop. (1991p) 85,799.

Braganza. See BRAGANÇA.

Brāh·man·bā·ria \ˌbrä-mən-ˈbär-ē-ə\. Town, SE Bangladesh, 50 mi. (80 km.) ENE of Dhaka.

Brah·ma·ni \ˈbräm-ə-nē\. River, Orissa, E India; rises in S Bihar and flows S to join the Mahanadi delta N of Cuttack; ab. 300 mi. (485 km.) long.

Brah·ma·pur \ˈbrä-mə-ˌpu̇r\ *or* **Ber·ham·pur** \ˈber-həm-ˌpu̇r\. Town, Orissa, E India, 103 mi. (166 km.) SW of Cuttack and 9 mi. (15 km.) from the Bay of Bengal; pop. (1981e) 162,407; college (1878).

Brah·ma·pu·tra \ˌbräm-ə-ˈpü-trə\; *anc.* **Dy·ar·da·nes** \ˌdī-ər-ˈdā-nēz\ *or* **Oe·da·nes** \ē-ˈdā-nēz\. River in Tibet, China (where its upper course is called Zangbo), NE India, and Bangladesh; rises in SW Tibet in the Gangdisê Range (Himalayas) near 82°E; as the Zangbo flows E 700 mi. (1126 km.) across S part of Tibet; on its S bank is Xigazê; at about 95°E turns abruptly S and breaks through E Himalayas in great gorges (known in this section as the **Di·hang** \ˈdē-ˈhäŋ\) and turns again SSW near Sadiya in NE Assam to flow W through Assam Valley and S in Bangladesh, where it becomes the Jamuna and merges with the Ganges in the Ganges-Brahmaputra Delta (*q.v.*); ab. 1800 mi. (2900 km.) long; area of 361,000 sq. mi. (934,990 sq. km.). Navigable for 800 mi. (1287 km.) to Dibrugarh, India; important for irrigation and transportation. Its upper course long unknown, esp. its identity with the Zangbo, first estab. by exploration 1884–86.

Braich–y–Pwll \ˌbrīk-i-ˈpül\. Cape, Lleyn Penin., NW coast of Wales.

Bră·i·la \brə-ˈē-lä\. **1.** County of SE Romania. See table at ROMANIA.

2. City, its ⊗, on Danube River, 12 mi. (19 km.) S of Galaţi; pop. (1989c) 242,595; important port; pulp and paper, food processing; important in wars of Turks, Walachians, and Russians.

Braine–l'Al·leud \ˌbren-lȧ-ˈlœ\. Commune, Brabant prov., cen. Belgium, 11 mi. (17.7 km.) S of Brussels; pop. (1991c) 32,458.

Brai·nerd \ˈbrā-nərd\. City, ⊗ of Crow Wing co., cen. Minnesota, on Mississippi River 53 mi. (85 km.) N of St. Cloud;

pop. (1990c) 12,353; paper; hospital; in resort area; Brainerd Community Coll. (1938).

Brain·tree \ˈbrān-ˌtrē\. **1.** Town, Norfolk co., E Massachusetts, 10 mi. (16 km.) S of Boston; pop. (1990c) 33,836; suburb of Boston; birthplace of John Adams 1735 and John Quincy Adams 1767 (2d and 6th U.S. presidents) in that part of town now Quincy.

2. Town, Essex, SE England, on the Blackwater 39 mi. (63 km.) NE of London; pop. (1981p) 30,110.

Brak·pan \ˈbrak-ˌpan, ˈbräk-ˌpän\. Town, NE Rep. of South Africa, in the Witwatersrand, 23 mi. (37 km.) E of Johannesburg; pop. (1985c) 88,696; became separate municipality 1919; rich gold fields.

Brambanan. See PRAMBANAN.

Bram·ham Moor \ˈbra-məm\. Locality, Yorkshire, N England, ENE of Leeds; battle Feb. 1408 in which Sir Henry Percy, earl of Northumberland, was defeated and killed.

Bramp·ton \ˈbramp-tən\. **1.** Town, ⊗ of Peel munic. region, SE Ontario, Canada, 20 mi. (32 km.) W of Toronto; pop. (1991c) 234,445; optical equipment.

2. Market town N Cumbria, England, 11 mi. (18 km.) NE of Carlisle.

Branch \ˈbranch\. County in S Michigan. See table at MICHIGAN.

Bran·co, Rio \ˌrē-ō-ˈbrȧŋ-kü\. River, N Brazil; formed by confluence of the Uraricoera and Tacutu; flows S into the Rio Negro; 350 mi. (563 km.) long.

Bran·den·burg \ˈbran-dən-ˌbərg\. City, ⊗ of Meade co., NW cen. Kentucky, on Ohio River, downstream from Louisville; pop. (1990c) 1857.

Brandenburg \ˈbrän-dən-ˌbu̇rk, ˈbran-dən-ˌbərg\. **1.** Historical region and province of Prussia; since 1945 the E section has been part of Poland, the W section part of East Germany and since 1990 reunited Germany.

History: Earliest Germanic inhabitants replaced by Slavic Wends who were unsubdued by Holy Roman Emperor Charlemagne; overcome in 12th cent. by Albert the Bear, margrave of Brandenburg, who established order, encouraged German colonists, and laid basis for expansion of territory secured by cooperation of his successors with Teutonic Order (see PRUSSIA); recognized as one of seven imperial electorates 1356; declined and lost territory latter part of 14th cent.; given by emperor to Frederick of Nürnberg who became elector 1417; helped Teutonic Order in war against Poland 15th cent.; extended boundaries and crushed nobility; accepted Reformation c. 1540; acquired Kleve and Ravensberg 1614 by marriage of Elector John Sigismund, who became duke of Prussia 1618; added East Friesland under Great Elector, Frederick William (1640–88), whose successful participation in wars against Sweden made Brandenburg-Prussia a leading power; its elector became king of Prussia 1701; its administration reorganized 1815; following WWII, E part to Poland; from 1952 W part constituted the East German districts of Potsdam, Frankfurt, and (in part) Cottbus; pre-1952 W area recreated German state 1990.

2. State of Germany. See table at GERMANY.

3. *or* **Brandenburg an der Ha·vel** \ˌän-dər-ˈhä-fəl\. City, Brandenburg (state), E Germany, on Havel River 38 mi. (61 km.) WSW of Berlin; pop. (1992e) 88,760; 12th cent. Romanesque cathedral; 14th cent. town hall; episcopal see intermittently 948–1598; seat of Prussian National Assembly 1848; former residence of reigning family of Prussia.

Bran·der, Pass of \ˈbran-dər\. Mountain pass, N Strathclyde region, W Scotland, through which the waters of Loch Awe pass to Loch Etive; ab. 7 mi. (11 km.) long.

Bran·don \ˈbran-dən\. **1.** City, ⊗ of Rankin co., S cen. Mississippi; pop. (1990c) 11,077.

2. Town, Rutland co., W Vermont, 14 mi. (23 km.) NNW of the city of Rutland; pop. (1990c) 4223; farming, electronic components, brushes; manufacture of woodworking; lumbering; resort.

3. City, SW Manitoba, Canada, on S bank of Assiniboine River; pop. (1991c) 38,567; railroad divisional point; grain elevators, oil refineries; Brandon Univ. (1899, university status 1967); government experimental farm. Founded 1879; named after Brandon House, a Hudson's Bay post 17 mi. (27 km.) E, estab. 1793.

4. Town, Durham, N England, on the Deerness 17 mi. (27 km.) S of Newcastle upon Tyne; pop. (1981p) 17,905.

5. Mountain in co. Kerry, SW Ireland; near the sea W of Brandon Bay; 3127 ft. (953 m.).

Brandon Bay. Inlet of Atlantic Ocean on SW coast of Ireland, W of Tralee Bay.

Bran·dy·wine \ˈbran-dē-ˌwīn\. A creek in Pennsylvania and Delaware uniting with Christina Creek (now Christina River) at Wilmington, Delaware; battlefield on the creek in Pennsylvania 10 mi. (16 km.) NW of Wilmington where on Sept. 11, 1777 the British under Gen. William Howe defeated the Americans under Gen. George Washington and entered Philadelphia later that month. See CHADDS FORD.

Bran·ford \ˈbran-fərd\. Town, New Haven co., S Connecticut, on Long Island Sound 6 mi. (10 km.) ESE of the city of New Haven; pop. (1990c) 27,603; resort; settled 17th cent.

Bra·nie·wo \brä-ˈnye-vō\ *or Ger.* **Brauns·berg** \ˈbrau̇ns-ˌberk\. City, NE Elbląg prov., N Poland, NE of the city of Elbląg; pop. (1981p) 15,007; founded 13th cent.; to Poland 1466, to Prussia 1772, to Poland 1945.

Brans·field Strait \ˈbranz-ˌfēld\. Channel bet. South Shetlands on N and Antarctic Penin. on S, Antarctica; ab. 175 mi. (280 km.) long, and 52 mi. (84 km.) wide.

Bran·son \ˈbrans-ᵊn\. City, Taney co., S Missouri; pop. (1990c) 3706; tourist center with music theaters, Silver Dollar City recreated Ozark pioneer settlement, and an outdoor amphitheater featuring summer performances of author Harold Bell Wright's *The Shepherd of the Hills.*

Brant \ˈbrant\. County, SE Ontario, Canada. See table at ONTARIO.

Bran·tas \ˈbrän-täs\. River, E cen. Java, Indonesia; flows W, N, and NE into Madura Strait, one branch (Kali Mas) at Surabaya and the other 25 mi. (40 km.) S at the town of Bangil; 195 mi. (314 km.) long.

Brant·ford \ˈbrant-fərd\. City, ⊗ of Brant co., SE Ontario, Canada, on Grand River 22 mi. (35 km.) WSW of Hamilton; pop. (1991c) 81,997; named orig. **Brant's Ford** for Mohawk Chief Joseph Brant; in gratitude for serving British cause during American Revolution given land here for the united Iroquois tribes of Six Nations 1784; first Europeans settled early 19th cent.; early home of inventor Alexander Graham Bell; founded 1830.

Brant·ley \ˈbrant-lē\. County in SE Georgia. See table at GEORGIA.

Bras d'Or \bra-ˈdȯr\. Salt lake, cen. Cape Breton I., Nova Scotia, Canada; ab. 50 mi. (80 km.) long; 360 sq. mi. (932 sq. km.). Its N extension is **Little Bras d'Or**.

Brasil. See BRAZIL.

Bra·sí·lia \brä-ˈzēl-yə\. City, ✻ of Brazil, on the Paraná (a headstream of the Tocantins); constitutes, with surrounding area, the Federal District (2245 sq. mi. or 5815 sq. km.; pop. [1989c] 1,803,478); presidential palace; cathedral; university (1961); construction begun 1956; ✻ moved from Rio de Janeiro 1960; nearby is **Brasília National Park.**

Bra·şov *or* **Bra·shov** \brä-ˈshōv\ *or Hung.* **Bras·só** \ˈbrȯsh-shō\. **1.** County of cen. Romania. See table at ROMANIA.

2. *or Ger.* **Kron·stadt** \ˈkrōn-ˌshtät\ *from 1950 to 1960* **Sta·lin** \ˈstä-lēn, ˈshtä-, -lin\. City, its ⊗, in the foothills of Transylvanian Alps; pop. (1989c) 352,640; textiles, tractors; town hall (1420, restored 1777); Gothic church (14th–15th cent.); university; founded by Teutonic Order 1211; a leader in Reformation in Transylvania in 16th cent.

Brass \ˈbras\. Town, Nigeria, at mouth of **Brass River** (100 mi. or 161 km. long, a channel of the Niger delta); formerly (19th cent.) a flourishing slave trading settlement, visited by Portuguese and British.

Bras·schaat *or* **Bras·schaet** \ˈbräs-ˌskät\. Commune, Antwerp prov., N Belgium; pop. (1991c) 35,231.

Brass·town Bald \ˈbras-ˌtau̇n\ *also* **Mount Eno·tah** \i-ˈnō-tə\. Mountain on boundary of Towns and Union cos., N Georgia; 4784 ft. (1458 m.); highest point in the state.

Bra·ti·sla·va \ˈbrä-tyē-ˌslä-vä; ˌbrä-ti-ˈslä-və, ˌbra-\ *or Ger.* **Press·burg** \ˈpres-ˌbu̇rk\ *or Hung.* **Po·zsony** \ˈpō-ˌzhōnʸ,

-ˌzhō-nyə\. City, ✻ of Slovakia and formerly of Slovak Socialist Rep. Czechoslovakia, on left bank of Danube ab. 30 mi. (48 km.) E of Vienna; pop. (1991p) 441,453; textiles; cultural center; Comenius Univ. (1919), technical university (1937); large Gothic cathedral (from 13th cent.) where kings of Hungary were formerly crowned.

History: As Pressburg an old town dating back to 9th cent.; ✻ of Hungary 1541–1784 and seat of Diet until 1848; scene of signing of Treaty of Pressburg Dec. 26, 1805 bet. France and Austria, by which Austria lost much territory and recognized French Emperor Napoléon as king of Italy. On formation of Czechoslovakia became ✻ of province of Slovakia 1918–39; ✻ of German protected state of Slovakia 1939–45; ✻ of Slovak Socialist Rep. 1969–92; ✻ of Slovakia since 1992.

Bratsk \ˈbrätsk\. City, Irkutsk Oblast, S cen. Russia in Asia, on Angara River; pop. (1992e) 259,000; important hydroelectric power installations.

Brat·tle·boro \ˈbrat-ᵊl-ˌbər-ō\. Town, Windham co., SE corner of Vermont, on Connecticut River 8 mi. (13 km.) N of Massachusetts border; pop. (1990c) 12,241; wood products, health and medical services, food distribution, publishing, paper; resort; School for International Training (1964); settled by garrison of Fort Dummer 1724; chartered 1753. Birthplace of architect Richard Morris Hunt (1827) and his brother, artist William Morris Hunt (1824); British author Rudyard Kipling had a home ("Naulahka") nearby where he lived in 1890s.

Braunsberg. See BRANIEWO.

Braunschweig. See BRUNSWICK.

Braun·ston \ˈbrȯn-stən, ˈbrän-\. Village, Northamptonshire, cen. England, 3 mi. (5 km.) NW of Daventry; terminus of the Grand Union Canal which here goes through a tunnel 1.5 mi. (2 km.) long.

Bra·va \ˈbrä-və\. Southernmost island of Cape Verde; 25 sq. mi. (65 sq. km.); pop. (1990p) 6980.

Brava Point. Cape on S coast of Uruguay near Montevideo extending into the Río de la Plata (56 mi. or 90 km. wide here) opp. Piedras Point in Argentina.

Bravo, Río *or* **Río Bravo del Norte.** See RIO GRANDE.

Braw·ley \ˈbrȯ-lē\. City, Imperial co., SE corner of California, in Imperial Valley S of Salton Sea; 115 ft. (35 m.) below sea level; pop. (1990c) 18,923.

Brax·ton \ˈbrak-stən\. County in cen. West Virginia. See table at WEST VIRGINIA.

Bray \ˈbrā\. **1.** Town and port, NE co. Wicklow, E Ireland; pop. (1991p) 25,101; resort, on wide bay, just N of Bray Head.

2. Civil parish, Berkshire, S England; residence of a vicar who is said in a popular song "The Vicar of Bray" to have been in turn both Roman Catholic and Protestant in order to keep his position in four successive English reigns bet. 1520 and 1560.

3. Small region in Somme dept., N France; chief town Neufchâtel.

4. *or* **Bray–sur–Somme** \ˈbrā-sᵫr-ˈsȯm\. Village, Somme dept., N France, on the Somme SE of Albert; battle in Allied retreat 1918.

Bray Head. 1. Cape at SW end of Valentia I., co. Kerry, SW coast of Ireland, S of entrance to Dingle Bay.

2. Point on E coast of Ireland, just S of Dublin.

Bra·zeau \brə-ˈzō\. River, SW Alberta, Canada; ab. 125 mi. (200 km.) long; a tributary of the upper North Saskatchewan.

Brazeau, Mount. Peak in Jasper National Park, SW Alberta, Canada, near source of Brazeau River; 11,386 ft. (3470 m.).

Bra·zil \brə-ˈzil\ *or Span.* **Bra·sil** \brä-ˈsēl\; *officially* **Federative Republic of Brazil** *or Port.* **Re·pú·bli·ca Fe·de·ra·ti·va do Bra·sil** \ri-ˈpü-bli-kə-ˌfā-di-rə-ˈtē-və-ˌdü-brə-ˈzil\; *from 1891 to 1967* **United States of Brazil. 1.** Federal republic, E cen. South America, bounded on NW by Colombia, on N by Venezuela, Guyana, Suriname, and French Guiana, on E by the Atlantic Ocean, on S by Uruguay, and on W by Argentina, Paraguay, Bolivia, and Peru; 3,284,426 sq. mi. (8,506,663 sq. km.); pop. (1989c) 150,051,784; ✻ Brasília.

Physical features: Mountain ranges (averaging less than 4000 ft. or 1219 m.) and plateau region are chiefly in E and S parts; highest point is the Pico da Bandeira, 9495 ft. (2894 m.) high, located in the E part on the border bet. the states of Minas Gerais and Espírito Santo; in N part on Guyana and Venezuela borders are Tumuc-Humac, Acaraí, Pacaraima, Parima, and other ranges (*serras*). Its entire N and cen. part is lowland region, occupied by the Amazon (*q.v.*) and its many great tributaries; other rivers: in plateau region in E the São Francisco, Parnaíba, and Jequitinhonha; in the SW the Paraguay, Alto Paraná, and Uruguay (each in part a boundary stream); in the Iguaçu, tributary of the Alto Paraná, are the famous Iguaçu Falls. Has few lakes of any size; largest is Lagoa dos Patos, in Rio Grande do Sul. Except for the large islands of Marajó and Caviana at the mouth of the Amazon and Maracá to the N there are no large islands along the 4603 mi. (7406 km.) of the Atlantic coastline; ab. 250 mi. (400 km.) NE of Cape São Roque, at 3°51′S, 32°25′W, is the important small island of Fernando de Noronha. Has good harbors at Belém, Salvador, Rio de Janeiro, Santos, and Pôrto Alegre. Its immense forests (*selvas*) of the Amazon region are source of many forest products (incl. balata, Brazil nuts); the savannas or grasslands (*campos*) are source of cattle and agricultural products; its plateau region in E and S is of great importance for its coffee, cocoa, tobacco, cotton, and yerba maté; also produces sugar, rice, corn, soybeans, oranges; fishing; large mineral deposits: bauxite, manganese, iron ore, beryllium, chrome, nickel; manufacturing: food processing; chemicals, pharmaceuticals, footwear, machinery, textiles, automobiles, cement, iron and steel.

Chief cities: São Paulo, Rio de Janeiro, Salvador, Belo Horizonte, Recife, Porto Alegre, Manaus, Goiânia, Curitiba, and Belem.

Political divisions: Divided into 26 states and the Federal District (for pronunciation of their names, see their individual entries):

NAME	AREA (sq. mi.)	AREA (sq. km.)	POP. (1991p)
Acre	59,343	153,698	417,437
Alagoas	11,238	29,184	2,512,515
Amapá	54,965	142,359	289,050
Amazonas	604,032	1,564,443	2,088,682
Bahia	216,612	561,025	11,801,810
Ceará	57,147	148,011	6,353,346
Espírito Santo	17,658	45,734	2,598,231
Goiás	131,339	340,168	4,024,547
Maranhão	127,242	329,557	4,922,339
Mato Grosso	352,400	912,716	2,020,581
Mato Grosso do Sul	140,219	363,167	1,778,494
Minas Gerais	226,707	587,171	15,746,200
Pará	481,869	1,248,041	5,084,726
Paraíba	20,833	53,957	3,200,620
Paraná	76,959	199,324	8,415,659
Pernambuco	39,005	101,023	7,109,626
Piauí	97,017	251,274	2,581,054
Rio de Janeiro	17,092	44,268	12,584,108
Rio Grande do Norte	20,528	53,168	2,413,618
Rio Grande do Sul	108,951	282,183	9,127,611
Rondônia	93,839	243,043	1,130,400
Roraima	88,843	230,181	215,790
Santa Catarina	37,060	95,985	4,536,433
São Paulo	95,852	248,257	31,192,818
Sergipe	8,441	21,862	1,492,400
Tocantins	116,573	301,294	920,133
Federal District	2,245	5,814	1,596,174

History: Inhabited orig. by indigenous peoples about whom little is known; N coast explored by Vicente Pinzón, a Spaniard, 1500; although theoretically allotted to Portugal by Treaty of Tordesillas 1494, not formally claimed by discovery until Portuguese navigator Pedro Álvars Cabral accidentally touched there 1500; title confirmed to John III of Portugal by Congress of Badajoz 1524; first settled at São Vicente under system of hereditary captaincies early 1530s;

80°
75°
70°
65°
60°
VENEZUELA
Mt. Roraima 9,219 ft.
Georgetown
Medellín
Bogotá
SERRA PACARAIMA
SERRA PARIMA
GUYANA
SURI
COLOMBIA
Orinoco
RORAIMA
Boa Vista
GUIANA HIGHLANDS
SERRA ACARAI
Magdalena
Branco
Trombetas
PICO DA NEBLINA NATIONAL PARK
Neblina Peak 9,886 ft.
Negro
Equator
Quito
ECUADOR
Putumayo
Balbina Reservoir
Lago de Erepecu
JAÚ NATIONAL PARK
TUPINAMBARAMA ISLAND
Urucará
Parintins
Guayaquil
Fonte Boa
Manaus
Itacoatiara
Maués
Amazon
São Paulo de Olivença
Tefé
Codajás
Nova Olinda do Norte
Coari
Borba
Juruá
AMAZONAS
Benjamin Constant
Carauari
Marañón
Jutaí
Manicoré
Tapajós
ANDES MOUNTAINS
Eirunepé
Juruá
Purus
Madeira
Humaitá
Lábrea
CACHIMBO
Teles Pires
Juruena
Cruzeiro do Sul
Jamari
Tarauacá
Bôca do Acre
Pôrto Velho
Samuel Reservoir
Roosevelt
PERU
ACRE
Ucayali
Rio Branco
RONDÔNIA
BRA
Brasiléia
Acre
Guajará-Mirim
Ji-Paraná
NORTE HILLS
SERRA DO TOMBADOR
Arinos
Cacoal
PACAÁS NOVOS NATIONAL PARK
Guaporé
SERRA DOS PARECIS
Lima
Paraguai
Várzea Grande
Cáceres
Lake Titicaca
BOLIVIA
Poconé
Cuiabá
São
La Paz
ALTIPLANO
ANDES MOUNTAINS
Lake Uberaba
PANT
Lake Poopó
Corumbá
PACIFIC OCEAN
CHACO
Paraguai
PARAGUAY
GRAN
ATCAMA DESERT
Antofagasta
Bermejo
Tropic of Capricorn
Asunción
CHILE
ARGENTINA
Paraná
Uruguaiana
Córdoba
Santiago
URUG
Buenos Aires

ATLANTIC OCEAN

FRENCH GUIANA
Paramaribo
Cayenne
CABO ORANGE NATIONAL PARK
Amapá
MARACÁ ISLAND
TUMUC-HUMAC MTS.
AMAPÁ
CAVIANA ISLAND
Macapá
Marajó Bay
MARAJÓ ISLAND
Belém
São Luís
LENÇÓIS MARANHENSES NATIONAL PARK
Santarém
Altamira
Tucuruí Reservoir
AMAZÔNIA NATIONAL PARK
PARÁ
CARAJÁS MTS.
Marabá
Imperatriz
MARANHÃO
Teresina
PIAUÍ
Fortaleza
CEARÁ
RIO GRANDE DO NORTE
Natal
PARAÍBA
João Pessoa
Recife
PERNAMBUCO
Maceió
ALAGOAS
Aracaju
SERGIPE
Salvador
BAHIA
Feira de Santana
Vitória da Conquista
TOCANTINS
Palmas
ARAGUAIA NATIONAL PARK
BANANAL ISLAND
MATO GROSSO
PLANALTO DO MATO GROSSO
Cuiabá
Brasília
FEDERAL DISTRICT
Goiânia
GOIÁS
MINAS GERAIS
Belo Horizonte
ESPÍRITO SANTO
Vitória
RIO DE JANEIRO
Rio de Janeiro
São Paulo
SÃO PAULO
MATO GROSSO DO SUL
Campo Grande
PARANÁ
Curitiba
SANTA CATARINA
Florianópolis
RIO GRANDE DO SUL
Pôrto Alegre
Lagoa Dos Patos
Montevideo
SAINT PETER AND SAINT PAUL ROCKS
ROCAS
PERNAMBUCO FERNANDO DE NORONHA ISLAND
Almas Peak 6,068 ft.
Mt. Igreja 5,930 ft.

BRAZIL

CITIES
- Over 5,000,000
- 500,000 to 5,000,000
- 100,000 to 500,000
- Under 100,000
- National capital
- Political subdivision capital

BOUNDARIES
- International
- Political subdivision

FEATURES
- Waterfalls
- Dams

0 150 300 mi
0 200 400 km

settled for short periods by French at Rio de Janeiro 1555–60 and at Maranhão (São Luís) 1612, by Dutch at Pernambuco 1630–54; neglected during period of Spanish rule of Portugal 1580–1640; fought war which resulted in expulsion of Dutch 1641–54; made viceroyalty with ✻ at Bahia 1640–1762 and at Rio de Janeiro from 1763; interior opened by Paulistas (people of São Paulo) and others who developed production of mineral wealth, gold and diamonds, and planting of sugar and coffee, esp. in 18th cent.; expanded Portuguese boundaries recognized in treaties of Madrid 1750 and San Ildefonso 1777; in 1808 became refuge and seat of government of John VI, prince regent, when French Emperor Napoléon invaded Portugal; opened to foreign commerce 1808; United Kingdom of Portugal, Brazil, and Algarve proclaimed and ruled from Brazil 1815–21; forced grant of constitution by John VI who returned to Portugal 1821; in 1822 proclaimed independence (see SÃO PAULO 2) under Pedro who became Emperor Pedro I (1822–31); fought war with Argentina over Banda Oriental 1825–28 (see URUGUAY); prosperous and internally peaceful during reign of Emperor Pedro II (succeeded 1831, ruled 1841–89); helped overthrow Argentinian dictatorship of Juan Manuel de Rosas 1852 (see ARGENTINA); allied with Argentina and Uruguay in war against Paraguay 1865–70; deposed Pedro II 1889 and adopted constitution for federal republic; settled peaceably numerous boundary disputes 1895–1909; declared war on Germany 1917; entered League of Nations 1920 but withdrew 1928; under President Getulio Vargas (first term 1930–45) set up constitutions 1934 and 1937, the second of which established dictatorial powers; joined Allies in WWII Aug. 1942; Vargas forced to resign 1945; democracy put in effect; elections led to second Vargas term 1951–54; Brasília made ✻ 1960; civilian government overthrown 1964; new constitution became effective 1969; civilian government returned 1985; economic scandal led President Fernando Collor de Mello to resign 1992.

2. City, ⊗ of Clay co., W Indiana, 15 mi. (24 km.) ENE of Terre Haute; pop. (1990c) 7640.

Brazil Current. A warm ocean current, South Atlantic Ocean, flowing S along the coast of Brazil.

Bra·zil·ian Highlands \brə-ˈzil-yən\ *also* **Plan·al·to Cen·tral** \plȧ-ˌnȧl-tü-sen-ˈträl\. Highland region in SE Brazil, chiefly in Minas Gerais, Goiás, Bahia, and São Paulo states.

Bra·zo·ria \brə-ˈzōr-ē-ə\. **1.** Coastal county in SE Texas. See table at TEXAS.

2. City, Brazoria co., Texas; pop. (1990c) 2717.

Braz·os \ˈbra-zəs\. **1.** River, cen. Texas; formed by confluence of Salt Fork and Double Mountain Fork in Stonewall co. N Texas, flows SE into Gulf of Mexico in S Brazoria co.; 840 mi. (1351 km.) long; navigable 40 mi. (64 km.) (300 mi. or 483 km. in high water); drainage area 42,800 sq. mi. (110,852 sq. km.).

2. County in E cen. Texas. See table at TEXAS.

Brazos Peak. Mountain, NE Rio Arriba co., N New Mexico; 11,274 ft. (3436 m.).

Brazza. See BRAČ.

Braz·za·ville \ˈbrä-zə-ˌvēl, ˈbra-zə-ˌvil\. River port, ✻ of Rep. of the Congo (see CONGO 3), on NW shore of Pool Malebo in the Congo River; pop. (1992e) 937,579; textiles; tanneries; university (1972); connected with Atlantic seaboard by railroad completed 1934; center for river trade for 1000 mi. (1609 km.) up the Congo; maintains boat link with Kinshasa. Founded 1883 by French explorer Pierre Brazza; used as a base for later claims of France to vast territory to NE; ✻ of former French Equatorial Africa.

Brč·ko \ˈbərch-kȯ\. Town, NE Bosnia and Herzegovina, ab. 70 mi. (115 km.) NNE of Sarajevo.

Brea \ˈbrā-ə\. City, Orange co., SW California, 22 mi. (35 km.) NE of Long Beach; pop. (1990c) 32,873.

Bread·al·bane \bre-ˈdȯl-bən, -ˈdal-\. Area and former district in Grampian Mountains, cen. Scotland.

Breath·itt \ˈbre-thit\. County in E Kentucky. See table at KENTUCKY.

Breaux Bridge \ˈbrō-ˈbrij\. Town, St. Martin parish, S Louisiana, 8 mi. (13 km.) ENE of Lafayette; pop. (1990c) 6515.

Bre·bes \ˈbrā-bes\. Town, cen. Java, Indonesia, W of Tegal; pop. (1980c) 54,829.

Brèche–de–Ro·land \ˌbresh-də-rȯ-ˈläⁿ\. Defile, Hautes-Pyrénées dept., SW France, in the Pyrenees on the France-Spain boundary 35 mi. (56 km.) S of Tarbes; alt. 9200 ft. (2804 m.); in medieval legend said to have been hewn by the knight Roland with one blow of his sword Durendal.

Bre·chin \ˈbrē-k̲in\. Burgh, Tayside region, E Scotland; pop. (1981p) 7674; papermills, distilleries; linen weaving.

Bre·chou \brə-ˈshü\. One of the Channel Islands, just W of Sark; 74 acres (30 hectares).

Breck·en·ridge \ˈbre-kən-rij\. **1.** Town, ⊗ of Summit co., cen. Colorado; pop. (1990c) 1285.

2. City, ⊗ of Wilkin co., W Minnesota; pop. (1990c) 3708.

3. City, ⊗ of Stephens co., N cen. Texas, 50 mi. (80 km.) ENE of Abilene; pop. (1990c) 5665.

Breckenridge Hills. Village, St. Louis co., Missouri, NW of the city of St. Louis; pop. (1990c) 5404.

Breck·in·ridge \ˈbre-kən-rij\. County in NW cen. Kentucky. See table at KENTUCKY.

Brecknock See BRECKNOCKSHIRE.

Brecknock Peninsula. Peninsula extending westward from SW Tierra del Fuego I., Chile.

Breck·nock·shire \ˈbrek-ˌnäk-ˌshir, -nək-, -shər\ *or* **Brec·on·shire** \ˈbrek-ən-ˌshir, -shər\ *or Welsh* **Bry·chein·iog** \brə-ˈk̲īn-yȯg, -ˈkān-\ *also* **Breck·nock** \ˈbrek-ˌnäk, -nək\ *or* **Brec·on** \ˈbre-kən\. Former county, SE Wales; mountainous region; rivers Usk and Wye. See POWYS 2.

Brecks·ville \ˈbreks-ˌvil\. Village, Cuyahoga co., N Ohio, 12 mi. (19 km.) S of Cleveland; pop. (1990c) 11,818.

Břec·lav \ˈbər-zhets-läf\ *or Ger.* **Lun·den·burg** \ˈlůn-dən-ˌbůrk\. Town, S Czech Republic, near Austrian and Slovakian borders.

Brecon. **1.** Former county of Wales. See BRECKNOCKSHIRE.

2. *or Welsh* **Ab·er·hond·du** \ˌa-bər-ˈhȯn-t̲h̲ē\. Market town, Powys co., SE Wales; pop. (1981c) 7467.

Brecon Beacons. Two sandstone peaks, Powys, Wales, highest point 2907 ft. (886 m.); highest massif in S Wales; included in **Brecon Beacons National Park.**

Breconshire See BRECKNOCKSHIRE.

Bre·da \brā-ˈdä, ˈbrā-də\. Commune, North Brabant prov., S Netherlands, on the Merk River 14 mi. (23 km.) W of Tilburg; pop. (1992e) 162,951; synthetic fabrics, food products, machinery, matches; Gothic church (15th cent.).

History: An old town (received municipal charter 1252), strongly fortified in early times; Compromise of Breda signed 1566 by the Dutch and Spanish; seized by duke of Parma 1581 but retaken 1590 by Maurice of Nassau, stadtholder of the Netherlands; after siege of a year surrendered 1625 to Spaniards; retaken by Dutch 1637; Declaration of Breda (amnesty proclamation) issued 1660 by exiled Charles II of England; Peace Treaties of Breda concluded 1667 bet. Britain, France, and Netherlands; important in wars of French Revolution 1793–95. In WWII occupied by Germans 1940–44.

Bree \ˈbrā\. River, SW Rep. of South Africa; flows SE into Indian Ocean. 165 mi. (266 km.) long.

Breed's Hill. See BUNKER HILL.

Breese \ˈbrēz\. City, Clinton co., SW cen. Illinois, 33 mi. (53 km.) E of East St. Louis; pop. (1990c) 3567.

Bre·genz \ˈbrā-ˌgens\; *anc.* **Bri·gan·ti·um** \bri-ˈgan-chē-əm\. City, ✻ of Vorarlberg, Austria, at E end of Lake Constance 78 mi. (126 km.) WNW of Innsbruck; pop. (1991c) 27,236; lake harbor and tourist resort; has a museum of Roman and Celtic antiquities. Ancient Celtic settlement; important station under Romans; became city c. 1200; in Middle Ages under counts of Bregenz, later under counts of Montfort; passed to Hapsburgs 1523.

Brei·dha Fjord \ˈbrā-t̲h̲ä\. Bay on W coast of Iceland.

Brei·sach am Rhein \ˈbrī-ˌzäk̲-äm-ˈrīn\; *sometimes shortened to* **Breisach;** *formerly* **Alt·brei·sach** \ˌält-ˈbrī-ˌzäk̲\; *anc.* **Mons Bri·si·a·cus** \ˈmänz-bri-ˈsī-ə-kəs\. Town, Baden-Württemberg, Germany, on right bank of Rhine across from

France; pop. (1992e) 10,891; an old fortified town of the Sequani on left bank of Rhine, captured by tribal chief Ariovistus c. 61 B.C.; one of chief fortresses of the German Empire during Middle Ages; resisted Protestants during Thirty Years' War but capitulated after siege by French 1638; ceded to France 1648 by Treaty of Westphalia; to Austria 1697; to Baden by Treaty of Pressburg 1805; badly damaged in WWII; subsequently rebuilt.

Breis·gau \ˈbrīs-ˌgau̇\. Historical region, now part of Baden-Württemberg, Germany, in area bet. the Rhine and the Black Forest; once part of Roman Empire; town of Freiburg im Breisgau founded 12th cent.; Breisgau to Hapsburgs 14th cent.; suffered great destruction during Thirty Years' War; divided bet. Württemberg and Baden 1805; all to Baden 1806.

Brei·ten·feld \ˈbrīt-ᵊn-ˌfelt\. Village, E Germany, 6 mi. (10 km.) N of Leipzig; scene of two battles of the Thirty Years' War: (1) Sept. 17, 1631 in which Swedes and Saxons under Swedish King Gustavus II Adolph completely defeated the Imperialist forces under Johann Tserclaes, count von Tilly; (2) Nov. 2, 1642 in which the Swedish army under Lennart Torstenson defeated the Imperialists under Archduke Leopold William and Prince Octavio Piccolomini.

Breit·horn \ˈbrīt-ˌhȯrn\. Peak on the Switzerland-Italy border S of Zermatt, Valais canton, Switzerland; 13,685 ft. (4171 m.).

Bre·men \ˈbrē-mən\. **1.** City, Carroll and Haralson cos., W Georgia, 40 mi. (64 km.) W of Atlanta; pop. (1990c) 4356.
2. Town, Marshall co., N Indiana; pop. (1990c) 4725.

Bremen \ˈbrā-mən, ˈbre-\. **1.** Former archbishopric and duchy, covering territory bet. lower Weser and lower Elbe rivers, Germany, NW of former duchy of Brunswick-Lüneburg; ab. 2000 sq. mi. (5180 sq. km.); made archbishopric in 13th cent.; created a duchy 1648 under supremacy of Sweden; became part of electorate of Hannover 1715.
2. Former German state, NW Germany; 99 sq.mi. (159 sq. km.); ✻ Bremen; comprised district around city of Bremen; lost sovereignty at accession of National Socialist (Nazi) regime 1933; in 1947 became part of new Bremen state, West Germany (see BREMEN 3).
3. A state of Germany and formerly of West Germany; includes cities of Bremen and Bremerhaven; ✻ Bremen; state estab. 1947. See table at GERMANY.
4. Commercial city, ✻ of Bremen state (not a part of earlier duchy), NW Germany, on Weser River 59 mi. (95 km.) SW of Hamburg; pop. (1992e) 552,746. A major port; historically important shipbuilding center; steel, electrical equipment; 11th cent. Romanesque cathedral; statue of legendary hero Roland (1404), university (1971); museum.
History: Became episcopal see 787, seat of an archbishopric 845; one of the important members of the Hanseatic League; became free city under elector of Brunswick; part of French First Empire 1810–13; joined North German Confederation 1866; joined German empire 1871; in WWII submarine and naval base; heavily damaged in WWII.

Bre·mer \ˈbrē-mər\. County in NE Iowa. See table at IOWA.

Brem·er·ha·ven \ˌbrā-mər-ˈhä-fən, ˈbre-mər-ˌhä-vən\. Seaport city, NW Germany, at the mouth of the Weser 35 mi. (56 km.) N of Bremen, forming an exclave of Bremen state; pop. (1992e) 130,938; historically important shipbuilding center; engineering works, fisheries; founded 1827; in 1939 united with **We·ser·mün·de** \ˌvā-zər-ˈmœn-də\ founded 1924, and known by that name until 1947 when it became, as Bremerhaven, part of the newly-created Bremen state. In WWII heavily damaged.

Bremersdorp. See MANZINI.

Brem·er·ton \ˈbre-mər-tən\. City, Kitsap co., W Washington, on Puget Sound 15 mi. (24 km.) W of Seattle; pop. (1990c) 38,142; Olympic Coll. (1946); site of Puget Sound Naval Shipyard (1891).

Bren·ham \ˈbre-nəm\. City, ⊗ of Washington co., SE cen. Texas, 35 mi. (56 km.) S of Bryan; pop. (1990c) 11,952; Blinn Coll. (1883).

Brenner \ˈbre-nər\ *or Ital.* **Bren·ne·ro** \ˈbren-nā-ˌrō\. **1.** Pass in Alps. See table at ALPS.
2. Village and customs station at Italian end of Brenner Pass.

Brent \ˈbrent\. A borough of Greater London, SE England, consisting of the former munic. boroughs of Wembley and Willesden. See table at LONDON 4.

Bren·ta \ˈbren-tä\; *anc.* **Me·do·a·cus Ma·jor** \mə-ˈdō-ə-kəs-ˈmā-jər\. River, Veneto, NE Italy; flows SE through Venezia into the lagoons of Venice. ab. 100 mi. (160 km.) long.

Brent·ford and Chis·wick \ˈbrent-fərd ... ˈchi-zik\. Urban area, SE England, part of the Greater London borough of Hounslow; Brentford was scene of defeat of the Danes 1016 by English King Edmund Ironside, and of the defeat of the Parliamentarians 1642 by Prince Rupert and the Royalist army.

Bren·ton Point \ˈbrent-ᵊn\ *also* **Bren·ton's Point** \ˈbrent-ᵊnz\. Southernmost point of the island of Rhode Island, Newport co., SE Rhode Island, SSW of Newport.

Brent·wood \ˈbrent-ˌwu̇d\. **1.** City, Contra Costa co., W California, 38 mi. (61 km.) E of San Francisco; pop. (1990c) 7563.
2. Town, Prince Georges co., S cen. Maryland, 5 mi. (8 km.) NE of Washington; pop. (1990c) 3005.
3. City, St. Louis co., E Missouri, 8 mi. (13 km.) W of the city of St. Louis; pop. (1990c) 8150; residential suburb of St. Louis.
4. Unincorporated settlement, in Islip town, Suffolk co., cen. Long Island, SE New York; pop. (1990c) 45,218.
5. Residential borough, Allegheny co., SW Pennsylvania, bordering on S of Pittsburgh; pop. (1990c) 10,823.
6. City, Williamson co., Tennessee, just S of Nashville; pop. (1990c) 16,392.
7. Town, Essex, SE England, 20 mi. (32 km.) ENE of London; pop. (1991p) 68,600; seat of a grammar school dating from the middle 16th cent.

Bre·scia \ˈbrā-shä, ˈbre-shə\. **1.** Province of Lombardy, N Italy. See table at ITALY.
2. *anc.* **Brix·ia** \ˈbrik-sē-ə\. Walled commune, its ✻, at foot of Alps 54 mi. (87 km.) ENE of Milan; pop. (1991p) 200,722; firearms, machinery, textiles; railroad junction; 11th cent. and 17th cent. cathedrals; the Broletto Palace (13th cent.) and the Palazzo della Loggia; many fine Roman remains.
History: Ancient Celtic town; became seat of Roman colony 27 B.C. and later a Roman municipium; devastated by Goths 412 A.D., plundered by Attila, king of the Huns, 452; fell to Lombardy; free city 936–1426; held variously from 15th cent. by Venice, France, and Austria until united with kingdom of Italy 1860.

Bres·kens \ˈbres-kəns\. Town, Zeeland prov., SW Netherlands, on S shore of Schelde estuary.

Breslau. See WROCŁAW 2.

Bres·sa·no·ne \ˌbrā-sä-ˈnō-nä\ *or Ger.* **Bri·xen** \ˈbrik-sən\. Commune, Bolzano prov., Trentino-Alto Adige, NE Italy, at S end of Brenner Pass in S Tirol on Isarco River, 20 mi. (32 km.) NE of Bolzano; pop. (1991p) 17,010; 18th cent. cathedral; many churches; tourist center; ceded to Italy 1919 by Austria.

Bresse \ˈbres\. Region, E France; ab. 60 mi. (97 km.) long, 20 mi. (32 km.) wide; fertile region specializing in poultry. Ancient countship comprised the plain around Bourg and the Revermont; under house of Savoy from 1272 with Bourg its ✻; ceded to French King Henry IV 1601.

Bres·so \ˈbres-sō\. Commune, Milano prov., Lombardy, N Italy, 5 mi. (8 km.) N of Milan; pop. (1989c) 30,872.

Bres·suire \ˌbre-ˈswēr\. Commune, Deux-Sèvres dept., W France, 38 mi. (61 km.) N of Niort; a historical town damaged and pillaged in wars 1214, 1598, 1794.

Brest \ˈbrest\. **1.** Subdivision of Belarus, in the SW; 12,471 sq. mi. (32,300 sq. km.); pop. (1991e) 1,483,700; ✻ Brest; hemp, flax; forestry; nearly coextensive with former Polesie dept. of Poland.

2. *formerly* **Brest Li·tovsk** \ˈbrest-li-ˈtȯfsk\ *or Pol.* **Brześć nad Bu·giem** \bə-ˈzhesch-näd-ˈbüg-ˌyem\. City, ✱ of Brest subdivision, SW Belarus, on right bank of Bug River; pop. (1991e) 277,000; important railroad junction; textiles; metal-working. From Poland to Russia 1795; taken by Germans 1915; scene of signing of treaty (Brest Litovsk) bet. Germany and Russia 1918; to Poland 1919–39; in WWII taken by Germans Sept. 28, 1939 but after division of Poland by Germany and U.S.S.R. remained in Soviet part 1939–41; taken by Germany 1941; retaken by U.S.S.R. 1944; remained ✱ of subdivision when Belarus became independent 1991.

3. Fortified seaport commune, Finistère dept., NW France on Atlantic Ocean 32 mi. (52 km.) NW of Quimper; pop. (1990c) 153,099; a major naval station of France, planned by Armand-Jean du Plessis, (Cardinal Richelieu) and fortified by military engineer Sébastien Vauban in 17th cent.; manufactures metal goods; exports produce; ship repairing; naval schools; botanical gardens.

History: Unsuccessfully attacked by English and Dutch 1694; blockaded by English, and French fleet defeated 1794 by forces led by Adm. Richard Howe; important debarkation point for American troops and supplies in WWI. In WWII occupied by Germans June 1940; used as submarine base and frequently bombed by Allies; retaken by Allies Sept. 1944; suffered severe damage.

Bre·tagne. \brə-ˈtänʸ, -ˈtän-yə\. **1.** Historical region, France. See BRITTANY.

2. Region of W France, lying within historical Brittany. See table at FRANCE.

Bre·ti·gny *or Fr.* **Bré·ti·gny** \brā-tē-ˈnyē\. Village of Normandy, Eure-et-Loir dept., N cen. France, just SE of Chartres; treaty May 8, 1360 bet. England and France, closing the first part of the Hundred Years' War.

Bret·on, Cape \ˈbret-ᵊn, ˈbrit-\. **1.** Cape, most easterly point of Cape Breton I., NE Nova Scotia, Canada.

2. County, Cape Breton I., E Nova Scotia, Canada. See table at NOVA SCOTIA.

Breton Sound \ˈbret-ᵊn\. Inlet of Gulf of Mexico off NE coast of Plaquemines parish, SE Louisiana.

Brett, Cape \ˈbret\. Cape on NE coast of N extension of North I., New Zealand, E of Bay of Islands.

Bret·ton Woods \ˈbret-ᵊn\. Fashionable resort, Coos co., N New Hampshire, ab. 18 mi. (29 km.) SSE of Littleton; site of UN Monetary and Financial Conference July 1–22, 1944 at which an International Monetary Fund was estab.

Bre·vard \brə-ˈvärd\. **1.** County in cen. E coast of Florida. See table at FLORIDA.

2. City and summer resort, ⊗ of Transylvania co., SW North Carolina, 26 mi. (42 km.) SSW of Asheville; pop. (1990c) 5388; Brevard Coll. (1853).

Bré·vent \brā-ˈväⁿ\. Peak in the Alps, Haute-Savoie dept., E France, near Mont Blanc; 8285 ft. (2525 m.).

Brew·er \ˈbrü-ər\. City, Penobscot co., E cen. Maine, on Penobscot River opp. Bangor; pop. (1990c) 9021.

Brewer, Mount. Peak on boundary bet. Fresno and Tulare cos., S cen. California, in the Sierra Nevada; ab. 13,570 ft. (4135 m.).

Brew·ster \ˈbrü-stər\. **1.** County in W Texas. See table at TEXAS.

2. Town, Barnstable co., SE Massachusetts, on Cape Cod Bay; pop. (1990c) 8440.

3. Village, ⊗ of Blaine co., cen. Nebraska; pop. (1990c) 22.

Brewster, Cape. Point on E coast of Greenland, 70°19′N, 22°05′W.

Brewster, Mount. Peak in Panama, E of the Panama Canal; 3018 ft. (920 m.).

Brew·ton \ˈbrüt-ᵊn\. City, ⊗ of Escambia co., S Alabama, 60 mi. (97 km.) ENE of Mobile Bay; pop. (1990c) 5885.

Brey·ten \ˈbrāt-ᵊn\. Town, NE cen. Rep. of South Africa, 120 mi. (193 km.) E of Johannesburg; railroad junction point.

Brezhnev. See NABEREZHNYE CHELNY.

Bri·an·çon \ˌbrē-äⁿ-ˈsōⁿ\; *anc.* **Bri·gan·tio** \bri-ˈgan-shē-ō\. Town, Hautes-Alpes dept., SE France, 48 mi. (77 km.) SE of Grenoble; pop. (1990c) 12,141; frontier town and tourist resort at N end of Cottian Alps; connects with Italy by the Col de Genèvre (alt. 6102 ft. or 1860 m.). In Roman times important station on road from N Italy to SE Gaul.

Briansk. See BRYANSK.

Briansk Oblast. See BRYANSK OBLAST.

Bri·an·za \brē-ˈänt-sä\. Hilly but fertile district S of Lake Como, Lombardy, N Italy.

Bri·ar·cliff Man·or \ˈbrī-ər-klif-ˈma-nər\. Residential village, Westchester co., SE New York, E of Hudson River 31 mi. (50 km.) N of New York City; pop. (1990c) 7070; The King's Coll. (1938).

Bri·dal·veil Fall *or* **Bridalveil Falls** \ˈbrīd-ᵊl-ˌvāl\. Waterfall in Yosemite National Park, E cen. California; 620 ft. (189 m.) high.

Bridge·burg \ˈbrij-ˌbərg\. Former town, SE Ontario, Canada; joined with Fort Erie village 1932 to form Fort Erie town.

Bridge City \ˈbrij\. City, Orange co., Texas, NNE of Port Arthur; pop. (1990c) 8034.

Bridg·end \brij-ˈend\. Town, Mid Glamorgan co., SE Wales; pop. (1981p) 15,699; regional trade center.

Bridge·port \ˈbrij-ˌpōrt\. **1.** City, Jackson co., NE corner of Alabama, on Tennessee River 3 mi. (5 km.) S of Tennessee border; pop. (1990c) 2936.

2. Village, ⊗ of Mono co., E California.

3. City, Fairfield co., SW corner of Connecticut, on Long Island Sound at mouth of Pequonnock River, 17 mi. (27 km.) SW of New Haven; pop. (1990c) 141,686; manufactures electrical goods, munitions, and metal goods. Univ. of Bridgeport (1927), Housatonic Community Coll. (1966). Settled 1639 as **Pe·quon·nock** \pi-ˈkwō-nək\, later called **New·field** \ˈnü-ˌfēld, ˈnyü-\, **Strat·field** \ˈstrat-ˌfēld\, and **Fair·field Village** \ˈfar-ˌfēld\; incorp. as town 1821, city 1836; industrial development accelerated after Civil War; site of P.T. Barnum Circus Museum; birthplace of Gen. Tom Thumb (Charles Sherwood Stratton) 1838.

4. Township, Lawrence co., SE Illinois, 17 mi. (27 km.) E of Olney; pop. (1990c) 2588.

5. City, ⊗ of Morrill co., W Nebraska, on North Platte River 32 mi. (52 km.) ESE of Scottsbluff; pop. (1990c) 1581.

6. Borough, Montgomery co., SE Pennsylvania, on Schuylkill River 14 mi. (23 km.) NW of Philadelphia; pop. (1990c) 4292.

7. City, Wise co., N Texas, 40 mi. (64 km.) NNW of Fort Worth; pop. (1990c) 3581; incorp. 1913.

8. City, Harrison co., N West Virginia, 5 mi. (8 km.) E of Clarksburg; pop. (1990c) 6739.

Bridgeport Dam. Dam across W fork of Trinity River, Wise co., N Texas; NE of Fort Worth; height 110 ft. (34 m.); completed 1931; impounds water, **Lake Bridgeport,** for flood control and water supply.

Bridg·er's Pass \ˈbri-jərz\. Mountain pass, S Wyoming, SSE of South Pass; discovered by frontiersman James Bridger and later used by pony express and Union Pacific R.R.

Bridges Creek. See WAKEFIELD 3.

Bridge·ton \ˈbrij-tən\. **1.** City, St. Louis co., Missouri, NW of the city of St. Louis; pop. (1990c) 17,779.

2. City, ⊗ of Cumberland co., SW New Jersey, 10 mi. (16 km.) N of mouth of Delaware River; pop. (1990c) 18,942; glass containers, textiles, food products; founded by Quakers c. 1686; first known as **Co·han·sey Bridge** \kō-ˈhan-zē\, later changed to **Bridge Town,** then **Bridgeton;** incorp. 1865.

Bridge·town \ˈbrij-ˌtau̇n\. Commercial port, ✱ of Barbados; pop. (1990p) 6070; exports sugar; tourism; founded 1628.

Bridge·view \ˈbrij-ˌvyü\. Village, Cook co., NE Illinois, W of Chicago; pop. (1990c) 14,402.

Bridge·ville \ˈbrij-ˌvil\. Borough, Allegheny co., SW Pennsylvania, 9 mi. (15 km.) SW of Pittsburgh; pop. (1990c) 5445.

Bridge·wa·ter \ˈbrij-ˌwȯ-tər, -ˌwä-\. **1.** Town, Plymouth co., SE Massachusetts, 7 mi. (11 km.) S of Brockton; pop. (1990c) 21,249; correctional facilities; Bridgewater State Coll. (1840).

2. Town, Rockingham co., N Virginia, SW of Harrisonburg; pop. (1990c) 3918; Bridgewater Coll. (1880).

3. Town, Lunenburg co., S Nova Scotia, Canada, on La Have River, 52 mi. (84 km.) WSW of Halifax; pop. (1991c) 7248;

founded ab. 1812; first school in Canada said to be estab. c. 1632 in this vicinity.

Bridg·north \ˈbrij-ˌnȯrth\. Market town, Shropshire, W England, on the Severn River 23 mi. (37 km.) W of Birmingham.

Bridg·ton \ˈbrij-tən\. Town, Cumberland co., SW Maine, 25 mi. (40 km.) W of Lewiston; pop. (1990c) 4307; in resort area.

Bridg·wa·ter \ˈbrij-ˌwȯ-tər, -ˌwä-\. Town, Somerset, SW England, on the Parret 10 mi. (16 km.) from Bristol Channel and 28 mi. (45 km.) SSW of Bristol; pop. (1981p) 26,132; seaport; Bath brick.

Brid·ling·ton \ˈbrid-liŋ-tən\. Town, Humberside, N England, on North Sea 25 mi. (40 km.) NNE of Hull; pop. (1981p) 29,329; excellent harbor; summer resort.

Brie \ˈbrē\. Agricultural district and historical region, NE France, E of Paris, now in depts. of Aisne, Marne, and Seine-et-Marne; chief town was Meaux; noted for its vineyards and pastures, and esp. for its cheese (Brie cheese).

Brieg. See BRZEG.

Bri·elle \brē-ˈel\. Borough, Monmouth co., E cen. New Jersey, 9 mi. (15 km.) SSW of Asbury Park; pop. (1990c) 4406.

Briel·le \ˈbrē-lə\ *also* **Briel** \ˈbrēl\ *or* **Bril** \ˈbril\ *or in English, esp. formerly,* **The Brill** \ˈbril\. Commune, South Holland prov., W Netherlands, on N coast of Voorne I. on the Nieuwe Maas, 14 mi. (23 km.) W of Rotterdam; pop. (1981e) 15,155; has good harbor; first mentioned 1280; first place seized by Dutch (led by William de la Marck in 1572) in reconquest of Netherlands from the Spanish, and held against attack by land and sea; occupied by British 1585–1616.

Bri·enne \brē-ˈen\. **1.** Small former county in the Champagne region, NE France, 23 mi. (37 km.) NNE of Troyes; held from 10th cent. to end of 18th cent. by Brienne family; its most famous member was the Crusader, John of Brienne (c.1148–1237), king of Jerusalem (1210–25).

2. *or* **Brienne–le–Châ·teau** \-lə-shȧ-ˈtō\. Town, Aube dept., France; site of military school at which the future Emperor Napoléon studied 1779–84; partly destroyed in battle early 1814 in which French gained a victory over Prussians.

Bri·enz \brē-ˈents\. Commune, Bern canton, Switzerland, at NE end of Brienzersee; pop. (1980c) 2759; noted for its scenery and traditionally for its wood-carving industry.

Bri·enz·er·see \brē-ˈent-sər-ˌzā\ *also* **Brienz, Lake of.** Lake, SE Bern canton, Switzerland; 11.5 sq. mi. (30 sq. km.); max. depth 856 ft. (261 m.); traversed by the Aare River.

Bri·er \ˈbrī-ər\. City, Snohomish co., NW cen. Washington; pop. (1990c) 5633.

Bri·er·field \ˈbrī-ər-ˌfēld\. Town, Lancashire, NW England, 23 mi. (37 km.) N of Manchester; pop. (1981p) 7755.

Bri·eulles–sur–Meuse \brē-ˌœl-sᵫr-ˈmœz\. Village, Meuse dept., NE France, 18 mi. (29 km.) NW of Verdun; monument marking crossing of Meuse 1918 by American forces in last phase of WWI.

Bri·ey \brē-ˈe, -ˈā\. Commune, Meurthe-et-Moselle dept., NE France, 12 mi. (19 km.) NW of Metz; center of **Briey Basin,** a district containing iron ore deposits.

Brig \ˈbrēk\ *or Fr.* **Brigue** \ˈbrēg\ *or Ital.* **Bri·ga** \ˈbrē-gä\. Commune, Valais canton, SW cen. Switzerland, on Rhone River 31 mi. (50 km.) ENE of Sion; tourist resort; station at Swiss end of Simplon Tunnel.

Brigade Marine, Bois de la. See BELLEAU WOOD.

Brig·an·tine \ˈbri-gən-ˌtēn\. City, Atlantic co., SE New Jersey, on Atlantic coast NE of Atlantic City; pop. (1990c) 11,354.

Brigantine Beach. Narrow sandy island off N Atlantic co., SE New Jersey.

Brigantinus Lacus. See CONSTANCE, LAKE.

Brigantio. See BRIANÇON.

Brigantium. See BREGENZ.

Bri·ga–Ten·da \ˌbrē-gä-ˈten-dä\. Region in Alpes-Maritimes dept., SE France, near the S end of the France-Italy border, ab. 32 mi. (52 km.) NE of Nice; formerly in NW Italy, comprises two small towns, **Briga Ma·rit·ti·ma** \mä-ˈrē-tē-mä\ and **Tenda,** on a small stream (Roja) in mountain area containing hydroelectric facilities. Demanded by France 1946 as reparation from Italy and ceded by treaty 1947.

Brig·ham City \ˈbri-gəm\. City, ⊗ of Box Elder co., NW Utah, 20 mi. (32 km.) N of Ogden; pop. (1990c) 15,644; settled by Mormons 1851.

Brig·house \ˈbrig-ˌhau̇s\. Town, West Yorkshire, N England, 20 mi. (32 km.) SW of Leeds; pop. (1981p) 35,241.

Brigh·ton \ˈbrīt-ᵊn\. **1.** City, ⊗ of Adams co., NE cen. Colorado, 18 mi. (29 km.) NE of Denver; pop. (1990c) 14,203; founded 1889.

2. City, Livingston co., SE Michigan; pop. (1990c) 5686.

3. Municipality, SE Tasmania, Australia, 12 mi. (19 km.) N of Hobart; pop. (1981c) 9441.

4. Municipality, S Victoria, SE Australia, on E side of Port Phillip Bay, suburb 8 mi. (13 km.) S of Melbourne; pop. (1991c) 32,230.

5. Village, Northumberland co., SE Ontario, Canada, near N shore of Lake Ontario 20 mi. (32 km.) WSW of Belleville; pop. (1991c) 4366; resort.

6. Town and seaside resort East Sussex, S England, on English Channel 50 mi. (81 km.) S of London; pop. (1991p) 133,400; has no harbor, but marina nearby; Univ. of Sussex (1961, located ab. 4 mi. or 6 km. NE of Brighton). Mentioned in Domesday Book; for several hundred years merely a fishing village; gained popularity as tourist destination following many visits by King George IV (first, as Prince of Wales) late 18th–early 19th cents.; Royal Pavillion (now a museum); racecourse; golf courses; theater.

Brighton Beach. Neighborhood, S Brooklyn borough, New York City, New York.

Bright·wa·ters \ˈbrīt-ˌwȯ-tərz, -ˌwä-\. Village, Suffolk co., SE New York, on Great South Bay on Long Island, 39 mi. (62 km.) E of New York City; pop. (1990c) 3265.

Brigue. See BRIG.

Brig·us \ˈbri-gəs\. Seaport, SE Newfoundland, Canada, on S shore of Conception Bay 25 mi. (40 km.) W of St. John's; pop. (1991c) 929; fishing.

Bri·hue·ga \brē-ˈwā-gä\. Commune, Guadalajara prov., cen. Spain, 17 mi. (27 km.) NE of the commune of Guadalajara; pop. (1991c) 3035; scene of English defeat by forces of Spanish King Philip V led by Louis-Joseph de Bourbon, duke of Vendôme, in War of Spanish Succession 1710.

Bri·ju·ni \brē-ˈyü-nē\ *or Ital.* **Bri·o·ni** \brē-ˈō-nē\. Island group belonging to Croatia, in the Adriatic Sea, off the W coast of Istria.

Bril *or* **The Brill.** See BRIELLE.

Bril·lion \ˈbril-yən\. City, Calumet co., E Wisconsin, 22 mi. (35 km.) WNW of Manitowoc; pop. (1990c) 2840.

Brindaban. See VRINDAVAN.

Brin·di·si \ˈbrēn-dē-zē\. **1.** Province of Puglia, SE Italy. See table at ITALY.

2. *anc.* **Brun·du·si·um** \ˌbrən-ˈdü-zē-əm, -ˈdyü-, -zhē-\ *or* **Brun·di·si·um** \-ˈdi-\. Seaport, its ✱, on Strait of Otranto in Adriatic, 66 mi. (106 km.) SE of Bari; pop. (1991p) 91,778; trades in wine; naval base during WWI; 11th cent. church; 11th cent. cathedral; 13th cent. castle built by Holy Roman Emperor Frederick II. Original settlement captured by Romans c. 267 B.C.; became Roman naval station; death place of poet Virgil 19 B.C.; taken by Saracens c. 836 and Normans 1071; important departure port for many Crusades; later lost much of its importance until opening of Suez Canal 1869; major port for tourist trade from Italy to Greece.

Brink·ley \ˈbriŋ-klē\. City, Monroe co., E Arkansas, 64 mi. (103 km.) E of Little Rock; pop. (1990c) 4234.

Brioni. See BRIJUNI.

Bri·on Island \brē-ˈōⁿ\. Small island in the Gulf of St. Lawrence, E Canada, N of Magdalen Is.

Bri·oude \brē-ˈüd\; *anc.* **Bri·vas** \ˈbrī-vəs\. Town, Haute-Loire dept., S cen. France, 36 mi. (58 km.) S of Clermont-Ferrand; trade center of a fertile plain; Romanesque church.

Briovera. See SAINT-LÔ.

\ə\ **abut** \ə\ matches \ᵊ\ kitten, Fr table \ər\ **further** \a\ **ash** \ā\ **ace** \ä\ cot, cart \ȧ\ Fr bac \au̇\ **out** \b̲\ Span Avila \ch\ **chin** \e\ **bet** \ē\ **easy** \g\ **go** \i\ **hit** \ī\ **ice** \j\ **job** \k̲\ Ger **ich**, Buch \ⁿ\ Fr **vin** \ŋ\ **sing** \ō\ **go** \ȯ\ **all** \ȯi\ **law** \œ\ Fr **bœuf** \œ̄\ Fr **feu** \ȯi\ **boy** \th\ **thin** \t̲h̲\ **this** \ü\ **loot** \u̇\ **foot** \ᵫ\ Ger **füllen** \ᵫ̄\ Fr **rue** \y\ **yet** \ʸ\ Fr digne \ˈdēnʸ\, nuit \ˈnwʸē\ \yü\ **few** \yu̇\ **fury** \zh\ **vision**

Bris·bane \ˈbriz-bən, -ˌbān\. **1.** City, San Mateo co., W California, on San Francisco Bay 5 mi. (8 km.) S of San Francisco; pop. (1990c) 2952.
2. River, SE Queensland, Australia; flows E to Moreton Bay; 215 mi. (346 km.) long.
3. Seaport city, ✻ of Queensland, Australia, on N bank of Brisbane River 13 mi. (21 km.) W of its mouth in Moreton Bay; pop. (1991c) 751,115; textiles; sugar and oil refineries; shipbuilding; Parliament House (1869); museum (1855); art gallery (1895); Univ. of Queensland (1909); founded 1824 as a penal colony; made ✻ of newly created colony of Queensland 1859.

Bris·coe \ˈbris-kō\. County in NW Texas. See table at TEXAS.

Bris·tol \ˈbrist-ᵊl\. **1.** Name of counties in two states of the U.S. See tables at MASSACHUSETTS and RHODE ISLAND.
2. City, SW Hartford co., N Connecticut, 15 mi. (24 km.) SW of the city of Hartford; pop. (1990c) 60,640; famous in its early history as clockmaking center; settled 1727; incorp. 1911; the town (incorp. 1785) is coextensive with the city.
3. City, ⊗ of Liberty co., NW Florida; pop. (1990c) 937.
4. Town, Grafton co., W New Hampshire, 14 mi. (23 km.) WNW of Laconia; pop. (1990c) 2537; summer resort.
5. Borough, Bucks co., SE Pennsylvania, on Delaware River 19 mi. (31 km.) ENE of Philadelphia in Bristol township; pop. (1990c) 10,405 (borough), 57,129 (township); carpets, paper, chemicals, metal products; early port of call for river traffic; settled 1697.
6. Town and port of entry, ⊗ of Bristol co., E Rhode Island, on Narragansett Bay 13 mi. (21 km.) ESE of Providence; pop. (1990c) 21,625; rubber goods; yachting; formerly important for whaling and shipbuilding; Roger Williams Univ. (1948); prior to coming of Europeans, area was headquarters for Philip, chief of Wampanoag Indians; first Europeans settled 1669; figured in King Philip's War (1675–76); incorp. by Plymouth Colony 1681; annexed to Rhode Island 1746; bombarded by British ships 1775; burned and pillaged by British 1778.
7. City, Sullivan co., NE Tennessee, 22 mi. (35 km.) NNE of Johnson City on Tennessee-Virginia line, pop. (1990c) 23,421; contiguous with Bristol, Virginia, the two cities having a common main thoroughfare through which the state line runs, but each city maintaining its own government structure; boundary finally settled 1903; King Coll. (1867), Bristol Univ. (1895).
8. Town, Addison co., W Vermont, 10 mi. (16 km.) NNE of Middlebury; pop. (1990c) 3762; settled 1786.
9. City, SW Virginia, contiguous with Bristol, Tennessee; in Washington co. but politically independent; pop. (1990c) 18,426; Virginia Intermont Coll. (1884).
10. Town, Kenosha co., SE Wisconsin; pop. (1990c) 3968.
11. City, ⊗ of Avon, SW cen. England, at confluence of Avon and Frome rivers 119 mi. (192 km.) by rail W of London; pop. (1991p) 370,300; seaport and important shipping center esp. for oil and food products; shipbuilding; aircraft; tobacco processing; Univ. of Bristol (1909); cathedral (1142); 14th cent. church; library (1613); art gallery; museum; theater; Clifton Suspension Bridge over the Avon.
History: From early times a place of commerce; received first charter 1155; active in medieval trade; point of departure 1497 of explorer John Cabot in search of a route to Asia; in English Civil War taken 1643 by Royalists under Prince Rupert and in 1645 captured by Parliamentarians; scene of Reform riots 1831; in WWII repeatedly bombed by German air force 1940 and 1941 with heavy destruction.

Bristol Bay. **1.** Arm of Bering Sea in its SE part, on W side of N end of Alaska Penin., SW Alaska; one of richest salmon-fishing areas in the world.
2. Division in Alaska. See table at ALASKA.

Bristol Channel. Arm of Atlantic Ocean extending bet. S Wales and SW England; ab. 85 mi. (135 km.) long and bet. 5 and 43 mi. (8 and 69 km.) wide.

Bris·tow \ˈbris-tō\. City, Creek co., E cen. Oklahoma, 20 mi. (32 km.) WSW of Sapulpa; pop. (1990c) 4062; supply and shipping center.

Brit·ain \ˈbrit-ᵊn\. **1.** Anglicized form of Latin **Bri·tan·nia** \brə-ˈta-nyə, -nē-ə\. Applied historically to the island of Great Britain (*q.v.*) esp. during its pre-Roman and Roman periods and in the early Anglo-Saxon period until the merging of the Heptarchy into the England of King Alfred. For additional history, see UNITED KINGDOM.
2. Kingdom of W Europe. See UNITED KINGDOM.

Britannia Inferior *and* **Britannia Superior.** See *History* at UNITED KINGDOM.

British America. **1.** *or specifically* **British North America.** Former designation for Canada.
2. Mostly former designation for all British possessions in, or adjacent to, North and South America.

British Antarctic Territory. British territory, Antarctica, consisting of possessions lying S of 60°S and bet. 80°W and 20°W; includes South Shetland Is. and South Orkney Is.; ab. 652,000 sq. mi. (1,688,680 sq. km.); administered formerly from Falkland Is., since 1989, from London; part of Falkland Is. Dependencies 1908, made separate colony 1962; although permanently uninhabited, the area has scientific research stations.

British Baluchistan. See BALUCHISTAN 2.

British Bechuanaland *or sometimes shortened to* **Bechuanaland.** Former British colony, S Africa, lying bet. Orange and Molopo rivers, bordering Griqualand West on SE; organized as part of British protectorate 1885 (see BOTSWANA); attached to Cape of Good Hope 1895 and with it became in 1910 part of the Union (now Rep.) of South Africa; chief towns: Mafikeng, Vryburg (*q.v.*), Taung, and Kuruman.

British Borneo. See BORNEO.

British Central Africa Protectorate. See MALAWI.

British Columbia. Province, Canada, on Pacific coast; ✻ Victoria.
Physical features: Most mountainous province of Canada; in N crossed by Rocky Mts. which on SE form boundary with Alberta; has several subsidiary ranges, nearly parallel, incl. Cariboo Mts., Selkirk Mts., Monashee Mts., and Purcell Mts.; farther W along the coast are the Coast Mts., a continuation of the Cascade Range of U.S. Its chief river is the Fraser which with tributaries waters most of cen. and S parts; in SE are Columbia and headstreams, and in NE the Liard and Peace rivers and tributaries, each a part of the Mackenzie River system; along the coast are many shorter streams (as Stikine, Skeena, Nass) and generally long narrow fjords. Lakes, mostly of the finger type, are numerous in all parts. Has 6 national parks and more than 250 provincial parks. Off its Pacific shores are many islands, notably Vancouver and the Queen Charlotte group; many good harbors; large ocean trade.
Chief products: Lumber; livestock, fishing; copper, zinc, lead, iron ore, oil, natural gas; tourism.
Chief cities: Vancouver, Surrey, Burnaby, Richmond. See table at CANADA.
History: Inhabited by indigenous peoples, among them Coast Salish, Nootka, Kwakiutl, and Haida when first visited by Europeans, probably Spanish, 1774; followed by English mariner Sir Francis Drake 1578–79 and by Capt. James Cook 1778; careful survey of coast made by Capt. George Vancouver 1792–94 and overland explorations made by several (Alexander Mackenzie, Meriwether Lewis and William Clark, David Thompson, and Simon Fraser) bet. 1793 and 1811; for a time (1849–58) known as **New Caledonia** and formed part of Hudson's Bay Company's concession; part claimed by U.S. (see OREGON); gold discovered in Fraser River basin 1857. Estab. as British crown colony 1858; united with Vancouver I. 1866, with N boundary extended to 60°N; became a province of Canada 1871.

British Commonwealth of Nations *or* **the British Commonwealth.** See COMMONWEALTH OF NATIONS.

British East Africa. **1.** Former name of Kenya (*q.v.*).
2. Name applied to the former British dependencies in E Africa: Kenya, Tanganyika, Uganda, and Zanzibar.

British Empire. See COMMONWEALTH OF NATIONS.

British Guiana. See GUYANA.

British Honduras. See BELIZE.

YUKON TERRITORY
NORTHWEST TERRITORIES
TATSHENSHINI-ALSEK NATIONAL WILDERNESS PARK
BRITISH COLUMBIA
CITIES
Provincial capital
City
BOUNDARIES
International
Provincial
FEATURES
Dams
ALASKA
UNITED STATES
PACIFIC OCEAN
ALBERTA
WASHINGTON
COAST MOUNTAINS
CASSIAR MOUNTAINS
ROCKY MOUNTAINS
SKEENA MTS
HAZELTON MTS
OMINECA MTS
CARIBOO MTS
COAST MOUNTAINS
QUEEN CHARLOTTE ISLANDS
Atlin
Atlin Lake
Lower Post
Liard R.
Cassiar
Juneau
Dease
Stikine R.
Continental Divide
Fort Nelson
Sikanni Chief R.
Ware
Finlay R.
Pink Mountain
Wonowon
Iskut R.
Nass R.
Skeena R.
Williston Lake
Hudson Hope
Fort St. John
Peace R.
Taylor
Rolla
Dawson Creek
Pouce-Coupé
Chetwynd
Tupper
Tumbler Ridge
Mackenzie
KUPREANOF I.
PRINCE OF WALES I.
REVILLAGIGEDO I.
Stewart
Portland Canal
Alice Arm
Kinkolith
Aiyansh
Kitwanga
Hazelton
New Hazelton
Takla Lake
Manson Creek
DALL I.
Portland Inlet
Dixon Entrance
DUNDAS I.
Port Simpson
Usk
Smithers
Telkwa
Babine Lake
Stuart Lake
Parsnip R.
Cape Knox
Masset
Prince Rupert
Port Edward
Skeena R.
Terrace
Quick
Houston
Fort St. James
PORCHER I.
Kitimat
Decker Lake
Burns Lake
Port Clements
GRAHAM I.
McCAULEY I.
François Lake
Nanika Dam
Fort Fraser
Fraser Lake
Vanderhoof
Willow River
Prince George
Giscome
Aleza Lake
Sinclair Mills
Queen Charlotte
Skidegate
PITT I.
Hecate Strait
Kemano
Kenney Dam
BANKS I.
GIL I.
Butedale
PRINCESS ROYAL I.
Tetachuck Lake
McBride
Wells
MORESBY I.
ARISTAZABAL I.
Klemtu
Quesnel
Dean R.
Alexandria
Likely
Quesnel Lake
KUNGHIT I.
Cape St. James
Ocean Falls
Hagensborg
Bella Coola
KING I.
Campbell Island
Queen Charlotte Sound
Chilcotin R.
Williams Lake
150 Mile House
HUNTER I.
Rivers Inlet
CALVERT I.
Alkali Lake
100 Mile House
Clearwater
Mount Waddington 13,104 ft.
Chilko Lake
Fraser R.
70 Mile House
Bridge Lake
Queen Charlotte Strait
Clinton
Thompson R.
Louis Creek
Cape Scott
Port Hardy
Simoom Sound
Gold Bridge
Bralorne
Lillooet
Cache Creek
Ashcroft
Savona
Kamloops
Sointula
Alert Bay
Lillooet R.
Quatsino Sound
Port Alice
VANCOUVER I.
Kelsey Bay
Cape Cook
Refuge Cove
Lytton
Merritt
Tahsis
Campbell River
Powell River
NOOTKA I.
Nootka Sound
Courtenay
Comox
Squamish
Harrison Lake
Princeton
Cumberland
Britannia Beach
FLORES I.
Tofino
Port Alberni
North Vancouver
Vancouver
Port Coquitlam
Hope
Chilliwack
Copper Mtn.
PACIFIC RIM NATIONAL PARK
Ucluelet
Nanaimo
Ladysmith
New Westminster
Delta
Mission City
White Rock
Barkley Sound
Bamfield
Youbou
Duncan
Esquimalt
Victoria
Cape Flattery
Strait of Juan de Fuca
UNITED STATES
0 40 80 mi
0 60 120 km
©1996 Encyclopædia Britannica, Inc.
140°
136°
132°
128°
124°
120°
60°
56°
52°
48°
ALBERTA
ROCKY MOUNTAINS
SELKIRK MTS
MONASHEE MTS
Mount Robson 12,972 ft.
Valemount
Blue River
52°
116°
Birch Island
Columbia Reach
Columbia R.
YOHO NATIONAL PARK
Golden
GLACIER NATIONAL PARK
Revelstoke
Chase
MT. REVELSTOKE NATIONAL PARK
KOOTENAY NATIONAL PARK
Edgewater
Salmon Arm
Enderby
Arrow
Invermere
Armstrong
Nakusp
Canal Flats
Vernon
Okanagan Lake
Kaslo
Kootenay Lake
Sparwood
Kelowna
Lakes
Kimberley
Fernie
Peachland
Summerland
Nelson
Cranbrook
Penticton
Castlegar
Warfield
Grasmere
Hedley
Oliver
Greenwood
Rossland
Fruitvale
Creston
Osoyoos
Grand Forks
Trail
UNITED STATES
Lake Koocanusa

British India. That part of India formerly under direct British administration. See INDIA 1.

British Indian Ocean Territory. British colony, Indian Ocean; formed 1965 from Chagos Archipelago (formerly part of Mauritius) and Aldabra, Farquhar, and Desroches Is. (returned to Seychelles June 1976); island residents resettled to Mauritius and Seychelles with the closing of copra plantations 1973.

British Isles. Island group in W Europe, comprising Great Britain, Ireland, and adjacent islands.

British Kaffraria. See KAFFRARIA.

British Malaya. Former British possessions in the Malay Penin. and the Malay Archipelago, SE Asia. See MALAYA, FEDERATION OF and STRAITS SETTLEMENTS.

British New Guinea. See PAPUA, TERRITORY OF.

British North America. See BRITISH AMERICA 1 and CANADA.

British North Borneo. See SABAH.

British Solomon Islands *or in full* **British Solomon Islands Protectorate.** Former British protectorate comprising the Solomon Is. (except Bougainville, Buka, and adjacent small islands) and the Santa Cruz Is.; ✻ Honiara. See SOLOMON ISLANDS 2.

British Somaliland *or* **Somaliland Protectorate.** Former British protectorate on S shore of the Gulf of Aden, E Africa; 67,936 sq. mi. (175,954 sq. km.); ✻ Hargeysa.

History: In Middle Ages a powerful Arab sultanate; broken up in 17th cent.; coast came under British influence in early 19th cent. but remained actually under Egyptian control until 1884; thereafter administered by British; in WWII occupied by Italian military forces 1940–41; retaken by British; united with former Italian Somaliland to form independent republic of Somalia (*q.v.*) 1960.

British Virgin Islands. See VIRGIN ISLANDS.

British West Indies. Name applied to the islands of the West Indies (*q.v.*) which were colonies of Great Britain, incl. Jamaica and its dependencies, Bahamas, Leeward Is., Windward Is., Barbados, Trinidad and Tobago. All of the British West Indies except the British Virgin Is. (in the Leeward Is.) and Bahamas united to form the West Indies (Federation) 1958–62; variation in political status among the islands: several now fully independent (e.g., Bahamas, Barbados, Trinidad and Tobago), others remain dependencies of Great Britain (e.g., Turks and Caicos, Anguilla, Montserrat).

Bri·to \ˈbrē-tō\. Small port on Pacific coast, SW Nicaragua; proposed as outlet with locks for W end of Nicaragua Canal (see NICARAGUA).

Brit·on Ferry \ˈbrit-ᵊn\. Seaport, part of the borough of Neath, West Glamorgan, S Wales, at mouth of the Neath River; port of Neath, center of export for region.

Brits \ˈbrits\. Town, NE Rep. of South Africa, ab. 28 mi. (45 km.) W of Pretoria.

Brit·ta·ny \ˈbrit-ᵊn-ē\ *or Fr.* **Bre·tagne** \brə-ˈtänʸ\. Historical peninsular region of NW France; bounded anciently on N by English Channel, on NE by Normandy, on E by Maine and Anjou, on SE by Poitou, on S and on W by Atlantic Ocean; exactly equivalent to modern depts. of Ille-et-Vilaine, Loire-Atlantique, Côtes-du-Nord, Morbihan, Finistère; ✻ Rennes; numerous short rivers; traditionally divided by Bretons into the *Armor* (coastal regions) and the *Argoat* (hinterland). The Breton language is still spoken esp. in rural W part of the region; present-day economic activity includes agriculture, fishing, and tourism.

History: For early history of region, see ARMORICA; region occupied by Bretons, Celtic people, whom the Anglo-Saxon invasion of Britain drove through SW England to NW corner of France 5th–6th cents. A.D.; subdued by Clovis, king of Franks, but never effectively part of Merovingian or Carolingian kingdoms; during 9th cent. ruled by Breton King Nominoë; at end of 10th cent., Geoffrey I, former count of Rennes, took title of duke of Brittany; acquired as fief of England 1169 through betrothal of its heiress to Geoffrey, son of Henry II; at death of Duke Arthur 1203, claimed as vassal state of France; territory expanded to include mouth of Loire; until 15th cent. practically a separate state; came to French crown through successive marriages of Duchess Anne of Brittany to Charles VIII 1491 and to Louis XII 1499 and of heiress, Claude de France, to Francis I 1514; incorp. into France 1532; up to French Revolution, a French province; involved in Wars of the Vendée (see POITOU).

Brit·ton \ˈbrit-ᵊn\. City, ⊗ of Marshall co., NE South Dakota, 45 mi. (72 km.) ENE of Aberdeen; pop. (1990c) 1394.

Briva Isarae. See PONTOISE.

Brivas. See BRIOUDE.

Brive–la–Gail·larde \ˌbrēv-lȧ-gȧ-ˈyȧrd\; *formerly* **Brive;** *anc.* **Bri·va Cur·re·tia** \ˈbrī-və-kü-ˈrē-shə, -shē-ə\. Commune, Corrèze dept., S cen. France, 12 mi. (19 km.) SW of Tulle; pop. (1990c) 52,677; ancient stone monuments; 12th cent. church; medieval houses.

Brixen. See BRESSANONE.

Brixia. See BRESCIA 2.

Br·no \ˈbər-nȯ\ *or Ger.* **Brünn** \ˈbrœn\. City, SE Czech Republic, 115 mi. (185 km.) SE of Prague; pop. (1991p) 387,986; textiles, metal goods; technical university (1899); university (1919). In area of habitation in prehistoric times; traces of Celts from before 500 A.D. remain; under Bohemian King Wenceslas I became imperial free city 1243; in various wars besieged or occupied by Swedes, Prussians, French from 15th–19th cents.; before WWI ✻ of Austrian crown land of Moravia.

Broa Bay \ˈbrō-ä\. Bay on SW coast of Matanzas prov. and SE coast of La Habana prov., W Cuba; enclosed on the S by Zapata Penin.

Broach \ˈbrōch\ *or* **Bha·ruch** \bə-ˈrōch\; *anc.* **Bar·y·ga·za** \ˌbar-i-ˈgā-zə\. City, Gujarat state, India, on N bank of Narmada River 30 mi. (48 km.) from Gulf of Cambay and 190 mi. (306 km.) N of Bombay; pop. (1991p) 132,312; for centuries one of most important travel and trade centers on India's W coast, noted for its fabrics and ivory objects. Annexed to Mogul Empire 1572; under rule of Marathas from 1685 until British capture late 18th cent.

Broad \ˈbrȯd\. **1.** River, W North Carolina and N South Carolina; rises in Blue Ridge, flows S into South Carolina and unites with Saluda River near Columbia to form Congaree River; ab. 220 mi. (355 km.) long.

2. River, S South Carolina; rises in Allendale co., flows SE into the Atlantic Ocean in Beaufort co.; ab. 70 mi. (115 km.) long.

Broad, Mount. Peak in the Himalayas, N India; 26,400 ft. (8047 m.).

Broad Channel Island. Island, New York City; largest in Jamaica Bay.

Broad Haven. Sea inlet on NW coast of co. Mayo, NW Ireland, E of Erris Head.

Broad·mead·ows \brȯd-ˈme-dōz\. City, Victoria, Australia, a NW suburb of Melbourne; pop. (1991c) 102,996.

Broads, The \ˈbrȯdz\. Low-lying district in Norfolk (**Norfolk Broads**) and Suffolk (**Suffolk Broads**), E England, characterized by lake-like expansions of the rivers, esp. along the lower courses of the **Yare** \ˈyar\, **Bure** \ˈbyu̇r\, and **Wave·ney** \ˈwāv-nē\, and by shallow lagoons connected with the rivers by channels; popular boating and fishing recreation area.

Broad Sound. Inlet of Pacific Ocean, on E coast of Queensland, Australia, S of Mackay.

Broad·stairs \ˈbrȯd-ˌstarz\. Resort town, Kent, SE England, on North Sea near Ramsgate.

Broad·top Mountain \ˈbrȯd-ˌtäp\. Coalfield in Bedford and Huntingdon cos., S Pennsylvania; 80 sq. mi. (207 sq. km.).

Broa·dus \ˈbrō-dəs\. Town, ⊗ of Powder River co., SE Montana; pop. (1990c) 572.

Broad·view \ˈbrȯd-ˌvyü\. Village, Cook co., Illinois, W of Chicago; pop. (1990c) 8713.

Broadview Heights. City, Cuyahoga co., NE Ohio, S of Cleveland; pop. (1990c) 12,219.

Broad·wa·ter \ˈbrȯd-ˌwȯ-tər, -ˌwä-\. County in SW cen. Montana. See table at MONTANA.

Brock·en \ˈbrä-kən\. Highest peak in the Harz Mts., cen. Germany, 32 mi. (52 km.) S of Brunswick; 3747 ft. (1142 m.); celebrated in legends, esp. in connection with the legend of Johann Faust.

Brock·port \ˈbräk-ˌpōrt\. Village, Monroe co., W New York, 18 mi. (29 km.) W of Rochester; pop. (1990c) 8749; State Univ. of New York Coll. at Brockport (1867).

Brock·ton \ˈbräk-tən\. City, Plymouth co., SE Massachusetts, 23 mi. (37 km.) S of Boston; pop. (1990c) 92,788; electronic equipment, machine tools, clothing, plastics; Massasoit Community Coll. (1966). Land deeded by Indians 1649; settled c. 1700; until 1821 a part of Bridgewater; name Brockton adopted 1874; incorp. 1881.

Brock·ville \ˈbräk-ˌvil\. Town, ⊗ of Leeds and Grenville co., SE Ontario, Canada, on the St. Lawrence 48 mi. (77 km.) ENE of Kingston; pop. (1991c) 21,582; summer resort area; pharmaceuticals.

Brod. See SLAVONSKI BROD.

Bro·deur Peninsula \brō-ˈdər\. NW section of Baffin I., Nunavut, Canada.

Brod·head \ˈbräd-ˌhed, ˈbrȯd-\. City, Green co., S Wisconsin, 13 mi. (21 km.) E of Monroe; pop. (1990c) 3165.

Brod·ni·ca \brȯd-ˈnēt-sä\. Commune, Toruń prov., N Poland; pop. (1989e) 25,988.

Bro·dy \ˈbrȯ-dē\. Commercial city, W Ukraine, 40 mi. (64 km.) NNW of Ternopol' (formerly in Poland); founded 1584; made city 1684; occupied by Russians in WWI, by Polish after the war; held by Germans 1941–44; to U.S.S.R. after WWII.

Bro·ken Ar·row \ˈbrō-kən-ˈar-ō\. City, Tulsa co., NE Oklahoma, 14 mi. (23 km.) SE of the city of Tulsa; pop. (1990c) 58,043; oil deposits.

Broken Bow \ˈbō\. **1.** City, ⊗ of Custer co., cen. Nebraska, 65 mi. (105 km.) ENE of North Platte; pop. (1990c) 3778.
2. City, McCurtain co., SE corner of Oklahoma, 47 mi. (76 km.) E of Hugo; pop. (1990c) 3961.

Broken Hill. 1. *or officially* **Broken Hill and Will·yama** \wil-ˈya-mə, -ˈyä-\. City, W New South Wales, SE Australia, in Main Barrier Range 260 mi. (418 km.) NE of Adelaide; pop. (1991c) 23,739; in subarid region at elev. of 1000 ft. (305 m.); center of district noted for production of lead, zinc, and silver; founded c. 1884.
2. Town, Zambia. See KABWE.

Bro·lo \ˈbrȯ-lō\. Village, Messina prov., NE Sicily, Italy, on N coast.

Bromberg. See BYDGOSZCZ.

Brome–Mis·sis·quoi \ˈbrōm-mi-ˈsis-kwȯi\. County, S Quebec, Canada. See table at QUEBEC.

Brom·ley \ˈbrəm-le, ˈbräm-\. A borough of Greater London, SE England. See table at LONDON 4.

Bro·mo \ˈbrō-mō\. Volcano, East Java prov., Indonesia, one of the Tengger Mts. (*q.v.*); famous for its frequent activity.

Bromp·ton \ˈbrämp-tən, ˈbrəmp-\. District of W cen. London, England, S of Hyde Park.

Broms·grove \ˈbrämz-ˌgrōv\. Town, Hereford and Worcester, W cen. England, 12 mi. (19 km.) SW of Birmingham; pop. (1991p) 89,800.

Bron \ˈbrōⁿ\. Commune, Rhône dept., E cen. France, ESE suburb of Lyon; airfield.

Brond·by \ˈbrȯn-ˌbü̅\. Commune, Sjælland I., Denmark; pop. (1989e) 34,359.

Brong–Aha·fo \ˈbrȯŋ-ä-ˈhä-fō\. Administrative region of cen. Ghana. See table at GHANA.

Bron·son \ˈbrän-sən\. Town, ⊗ of Levy co., NW Florida Penin.; pop. (1990c) 875.

Bron·te \ˈbrōn-tā\. Commune, Catania prov., E Sicily, Italy, at W foot of Mt. Etna; pop. (1991p) 18,659; British naval officer Horatio Nelson created duke of Bronte by Ferdinand IV of Naples 1799.

Bronx \ˈbräŋks\. **1.** River, New York City; rises in Westchester co., flows S into East River Strait, nearly bisecting Bronx borough.
2. County in SE New York. See table at NEW YORK.
3. *or* **The Bronx.** Borough, New York, forming N part of New York City; ⊗ of Bronx co. and coextensive with the county; 41 sq. mi. (106 sq. km.); pop. (1990c) 1,203,789; only borough of New York City on the mainland, comprising the section NE of Harlem River, with adjacent islands (City, Hart's, Riker's); traversed by Bronx River. Settled 1641; made separate county 1912; park system includes notably Pelham Bay (containing Orchard Beach), Van Cortlandt Park, and Bronx Park (containing Bronx Zoo and New York Botanical Gardens and museum); Yankee Stadium; Co-Op City housing development; educational institutions include Fordham Univ. (1841), Lehman Coll. of the City Univ. of New York (1931). Governed as part of New York City; has a borough president, with local and county functions conducted independently of central munic. government. See also NEW YORK 3.

Bronx·ville \ˈbräŋks-ˌvil\. Residential village, Westchester co., SE New York, 2 mi. (3.2 km.) N of Bronx borough; pop. (1990c) 6028; Concordia Coll. (1881), Sarah Lawrence Coll. (1926).

Brooke \ˈbru̇k\. County in Panhandle, N West Virginia. See table at WEST VIRGINIA.

Brooke's Point \ˈbru̇ks\. Coastal town, SE coast of Palawan, Philippines, on Sulu Sea; pop. (1980c) 46,320.

Brook Farm. See WEST ROXBURY.

Brook·field \ˈbru̇k-ˌfēld\. **1.** Town, Fairfield co., SW Connecticut, ab. 14 mi. (23 km.) WSW of Waterbury; pop. (1990c) 14,113.
2. Village, Cook co., NE Illinois, ab. 5 mi. (8 km.) W of Chicago; pop. (1990c) 18,876; site of Chicago Zoological Park (Brookfield Zoo).
3. Town, Worcester co., cen. Massachusetts, 15 mi. (24 km.) W of the city of Worcester; pop. (1990c) 2968.
4. City, Linn co., N Missouri, 27 mi. (43 km.) E of Chillicothe; pop. (1990c) 4888; coal deposits nearby.
5. City, Waukesha co., SE Wisconsin, a W suburb of Milwaukee; pop. (1990c) 35,184.

Brook·ha·ven \bru̇k-ˈhā-vən\. **1.** City, ⊗ of Lincoln co., SW Mississippi, 23 mi. (37 km.) N of McComb; pop. (1990c) 10,243.
2. Town, Suffolk co., Long Island, New York, E of Patchogue; pop. (1990c) 407,779; ab. 7 mi. (11 km.) to the NE is Upton, site of Brookhaven National (research) Laboratory.
3. Borough, Delaware co., SE Pennsylvania, SE of Philadelphia; pop. (1990c) 8567.

Brook·ings \ˈbru̇-kiŋz\. **1.** County in E South Dakota. See table at SOUTH DAKOTA.
2. City, Curry co., SW Oregon, 75 mi. (121 km.) SW of Medford; pop. (1990c) 4400; fishing.
3. City, ⊗ of Brookings co., E South Dakota, 53 mi. (85 km.) N of Sioux Falls; pop. (1990c) 16,270; South Dakota State Univ. (1881); became city 1883.

Brookland. See WEST COLUMBIA 1.

Brook·line \ˈbru̇k-ˌlīn\. Town, Norfolk co., E Massachusetts, just W of Boston; pop. (1990c) 54,718; Hebrew Coll. (1918), Hellenic Coll. and Holy Cross Greek Orthodox School of Theology (1937); birthplace of John F. Kennedy, 35th president of the U.S., 1917.

Brook·lyn \ˈbru̇-klin\. **1.** Residential town, cen. Windham co., NE corner of Connecticut; pop. (1990c) 6681.
2. Residential borough, New York forming part of New York City; ⊗ of Kings co. and coextensive with the county, in SW extremity of Long Island; 71 sq. mi. (184 sq. km.); pop. (1990c) 2,300,664 (largest in pop. of five boroughs of New York City); separated from Manhattan by East River; connected with Manhattan by Brooklyn Bridge (suspension; main span 1595 ft. or 486 m.; completed 1883) and with Staten I. by Verrazano-Narrows Bridge (suspension; main span 4260 ft. or 1298 m.; completed 1964); extensive facilities for oceangoing traffic; food products, machinery. Educational institutions include Brooklyn Coll. of the City Univ. of New York (1930), Polytechnic Univ. (1854), State Univ. of New York Health Science Center at Brooklyn (1858), Pratt Institute (1887), Long Island Univ.–Brooklyn Campus (1926), St.

Francis Coll. (1858, chartered 1884), St. Joseph's Coll. (1916), New York City Technical Coll. of the City Univ. of New York (1946), Kingsborough Community Coll. of the City Univ. of New York (1963), Medgar Evers Coll. of the City Univ. of New York (1969). Brooklyn Museum, Prospect Park, Marine Park, Botanic Garden; Coney Island; Greenwood Cemetery; Floyd Bennett Field (Brooklyn Coast Guard Air Station). Governed as part of New York City; has a borough president, with local and county functions conducted independently of central munic. government. See also NEW YORK 3.

History: Settlements made along Gowanus and Jamaica bays and at Wallabout Bay (later incorp. as Williamsburg) primarily by Dutch 1636 and 1637; settlement estab. 1645 near present site of borough hall and named *Breuckelen;* New Utrecht settled ab. 1650, Flatbush (at first called Midwout) ab. 1651; scene of battle of Long Island Aug. 27, 1776 in which British under Gen. William Howe defeated Americans under Gen. Israel Putnam; incorp. as city 1834; annexed Williamsburg and Bushwick 1855, included all of Kings co. by 1896; borough of New York City 1898.

3. City, Cuyahoga co., NE Ohio, SW of Cleveland; pop. (1990c) 11,706.

Brooklyn Center. City, Hennepin co., SE cen. Minnesota, a N suburb of Minneapolis; pop. (1990c) 28,887.

Brooklyn Park. City, Hennepin co., Minnesota, a suburb N and NW of Minneapolis; pop. (1990c) 56,381.

Brook Park \ˈbru̇k\. City, Cuyahoga co., NE Ohio, SW of Cleveland; pop. (1990c) 22,865; site of Cleveland's international airport.

Brooks \ˈbru̇ks\. **1.** Name of counties in two states of the U.S. See tables at GEORGIA and TEXAS.

2. Town, Alberta, Canada, 100 mi. (161 km.) SE of Calgary; pop. (1991c) 9433; gas wells.

Brooks Islands. See MIDWAY.

Brooks Range. Mountain range across N Alaska from Kotzebue Sound to Canadian border, forming NW end of Rocky Mts. and watershed bet. Yukon basin on S and Arctic coast on N; highest peak Mt. Isto ab. 9060 ft. (2760 m.); includes smaller groups or ridges of De Long, Baird, and Endicott Mts.

Brooks·ville \ˈbru̇ks-ˌvil\. **1.** City, ⊗ of Hernando co., W Florida Penin., 42 mi. (68 km.) N of Tampa; pop. (1990c) 7440.

2. City, ⊗ of Bracken co., NE Kentucky; pop. (1990c) 670.

Brook·ville \ˈbru̇k-ˌvil\. **1.** Town, ⊗ of Franklin co., E Indiana, 28 mi. (45 km.) SSW of Richmond; pop. (1990c) 2529.

2. Village, Nassau co., SE New York, 5 mi. (8 km.) SE of Glen Cove; pop. (1990c) 3716; Long Island Univ.–C.W. Post Campus (1954).

3. Village, Montgomery co., SW Ohio, 12 mi. (19 km.) WNW of Dayton; pop. (1990c) 4621.

4. Borough, ⊗ of Jefferson co., W cen. Pennsylvania, 18 mi. (29 km.) W of Du Bois; pop. (1990c) 4184.

Brook·wood \ˈbru̇k-wu̇d\. Village, Surrey, England, 4 mi. (6 km.) SW of Woking and 28 mi. (45 km.) SW of London; American military cemetery.

Broom, Loch \ˈbrüm, ˈbru̇m\. Sea inlet in Highland region, on NW coast of Scotland; **Little Loch Broom** is a parallel inlet just to the S.

Broome \ˈbrüm, ˈbru̇m\. **1.** County in S New York. See table at NEW YORK.

2. Seaport town, NW Western Australia, Australia, on Roebuck Bay; pop. (1991c) 8906; bombed by Japanese 1942.

Broom·field \ˈbrüm-ˌfēld\. City, Boulder and Jefferson cos., N cen. Colorado, 12 mi. (19 km.) NNW of Denver; pop. (1990c) 24,638.

Bros·sard \brȯ-ˈsär\. Town, S Quebec, Canada; pop. (1991c) 64,793; residential suburb of Montreal.

Broughton Bay. See TONGJOSŎN MAN.

Brough·ty Ferry \ˈbrȯ-tē\. District (formerly a suburb) of Dundee, Tayside region, E Scotland, on Firth of Tay ab. 3.5 mi. (6 km.) E of main part of the city; castle.

Brous·sard \brü-ˈsärd\. Town, Lafayette parish S Louisiana; pop. (1990c) 3213.

Brow·ard \ˈbrau̇-ərd\. County, on coast in SE Florida. See table at FLORIDA.

Brown \ˈbrau̇n\. Counties in nine states of the U.S. See tables at ILLINOIS, INDIANA, KANSAS, MINNESOTA, NEBRASKA, OHIO, SOUTH DAKOTA, TEXAS, WISCONSIN.

Brown, Mount. Peak in Glacier National Park, NW Montana; 8541 ft. (2603 m.).

Brown, Point. Point on SW coast of Grays Harbor co., W Washington, at N entrance to Grays Harbor.

Brown Clee Hill. See CLEE HILLS.

Brown Deer. Village, Milwaukee co., SE Wisconsin, N of the city of Milwaukee; pop. (1990c) 12,236.

Brown·field \ˈbrau̇n-ˌfēld\. City, ⊗ of Terry co., NW Texas, 38 mi. (61 km.) SSW of Lubbock; pop. (1990c) 9560; oil wells.

Brown·hills \ˈbrau̇n-ˌhilz\. Town, Staffordshire, England, NNE of Walsall.

Brown·ing \ˈbrau̇-niŋ\. Town, Glacier co., NW Montana; pop. (1990c) 1170; tourist resort; Museum of the Plains Indian (opened 1941); headquarters of the Blackfeet Indian Reservation.

Brown·lee Dam *and* **Brownlee Reservoir** \ˈbrau̇n-lē\. See UNITED STATES, *Dams and Reservoirs.*

Browns·burg \ˈbrau̇nz-ˌbərg\. Town, Hendricks co., cen. Indiana, ab. 3 mi. (4.8 km.) W of Indianapolis; pop. (1990c) 7628.

Browns·town \ˈbrau̇nz-ˌtau̇n\. Town, ⊗ of Jackson co., S Indiana, 32 mi. (52 km.) SE of Bloomington; pop. (1990c) 2872.

Browns·ville \ˈbrau̇nz-ˌvil, -vəl\. **1.** City, ⊗ of Edmonson co., cen. Kentucky; pop. (1990c) 897.

2. Neighborhood, E cen. Brooklyn borough, New York City, New York.

3. Borough, Fayette co., SW Pennsylvania, on Monongahela River 13 mi. (21 km.) NW of Uniontown; pop. (1990c) 3164.

4. City, ⊗ of Haywood co., W Tennessee, 27 mi. (43 km.) W of Jackson; pop. (1990c) 10,019.

5. City and port of entry, ⊗ of Cameron co., S Texas; on Rio Grande opp. Matamoros, Mexico, 25 mi. (40 km.) from Gulf of Mexico; pop. (1990c) 98,962; deepwater port (opened 1936); distribution point for nearby agricultural area; shrimp; tourism; Texas Southmost Coll. (1926). Began as trading post; Fort Brown, orig. Fort Taylor, estab. 1846 by Gen. Zachary Taylor (later, president of U.S.); involved in Mexican-American War; town founded 1848; served as one of principal ports of Confederacy during Civil War; site of Brownsville Affair (1906) in which racial tensions bet. black soldiers stationed at fort and white civilians resulted in President Theodore Roosevelt's having many black soldiers dishonorably discharged; although protested at the time, investigation and reversing of his order took place only in 1972.

Brown Wil·ly \brau̇n-ˈwi-lē\. Mountain, Cornwall, SW England, 4.5 mi. (7.2 km.) SE of Camelford; 1375 ft. (419 m.); highest point in Cornwall.

Brown·wood \ˈbrau̇n-ˌwu̇d\. City, ⊗ of Brown co., cen. Texas, 64 mi. (103 km.) SSE of Abilene; pop. (1990c) 18,387; oil wells; Howard Payne Univ. (1889).

Brox·bourne \ˈbräks-ˌbȯrn\. Borough, Hertfordshire, SE England, N of London; pop. (1991p) 79,500.

Bru·ay–en–Ar·tois \brūē-ˈā-äⁿ-när-ˈtwä\. Commune, Pas-de-Calais dept., N France, 17 mi. (27 km.) NW of Arras; coal deposits.

Bruce \ˈbrüs\. County, SE Ontario, Canada. See table at ONTARIO.

Bruce, Mount. Mountain in plateau region S of Fortescue River, Western Australia, Australia; 4024 ft. (1227 m.); highest point in state.

Bruce Peninsula *also* **Sau·geen Peninsula** \ˈsȯ-gēn\. Peninsula of SE Ontario, Canada; extends N bet. Lake Huron and Georgian Bay; contains **Bruce Peninsula National Park;** see CANADA, *National Parks.*

Bruch·sal \ˈbru̇k-ˌzäl\. City, Baden-Württemberg, Germany, on a tributary of the Rhine 11 mi. (18 km.) NE of Karlsruhe; pop. (1992e) 39,137; railroad junction; 18th cent. church. First mentioned 796 A.D.; to prince-bishops of Speyer 11th cent., their residence from 18th cent.; to Baden 1803; ab. 80 percent of city destroyed in WWII; subsequently rebuilt.

Bruck \ˈbru̇k\ *or* **Bruck an der Mur** \än-dər-ˈmür\. Commune, Styria, Austria, at confluence of Mürz and Mur rivers 25 mi. (40 km.) NNW of Graz; pop. (1991c) 14,155; chartered 13th cent.; old Gothic church.

Brug·ge \ˈbrœ-kə, ˈbru̇-gə\ *or* **Bruges** \ˈbrüzh\. Commune, ✻ of West Flanders prov., NW Belgium, ab. 55 mi. (89 km.) NW of Brussels; pop. (1992e) 116,700; an important commercial city on canals connecting with Zeebrugge and Oostende on the North Sea; shipbuilding, food processing; chemicals, electronic equipment, dies; tourism; has many old buildings; many museums.

History: First mentioned in 7th cent.; a member of Hanseatic League in 13th cent., Brugge developed into chief Hanseatic market; drove out French rulers 1302; as center of English wool trade and Flemish cloth industry, became commercial and financial hub of N Europe; residence of dukes of Burgundy who founded there Order of Golden Fleece 1430; art and cultural center in 15th cent. (painters such as Jan van Eyck and Hans Memling lived and worked there); sanding up of the Zwyn (small stream connecting it with North Sea), falling off of cloth industry, civil strife, and rise of rival Antwerp (*q.v.*) caused its decline from late 15th cent.; occupied by Germans in both World Wars.

Bru·ghe·rio \brü-ˈgā-rē-ˌō\. Commune, Milano prov., Lombardy, N Italy, 8 mi. (13 km.) NE of Milan; pop. (1989c) 29,636.

Brugh na Boinne \ˌbru̇-nə-ˈbȯin\. Locality, co. Meath, NE Ireland, on N bank of Boyne River, WSW of Drogheda; site of ancient royal cemetery with three great burial mounds, incl. Newgrange (*q.v.*).

Brühl \ˈbrǖl\. City, North Rhine-Westphalia, W Germany, 7 mi. (11 km.) S of Cologne; pop. (1992e) 42,194; foundries; became city 1285; its 18th cent. castle used for presidential receptions.

Bru·ja Point \ˈbrü-hä\. Cape, Panama on Gulf of Panama W of the Pacific terminus of the Panama Canal.

Bruk·ka·ros, Mount \ˈbru̇k-kä-ˌrōs\. Mountain, S cen. Namibia; ab. 5200 ft. (1585 m.); an extinct volcano.

Brule \ˈbrül, ˈbrü-lē\. County in S South Dakota. See table at SOUTH DAKOTA.

Brule \ˈbrül\ *or* **Bois Brule** \ˈbȯi\. **1.** River, Douglas co., NW corner of Wisconsin; flows N near E boundary of Douglas co., into Lake Superior; ab. 40 mi. (64 km.) long.
2. River, NE Wisconsin; rises in N Forest co., flows E and forms section of Wisconsin-Michigan boundary until it joins the Michigamme River to form the Menominee River on N boundary of Florence co.

Bru·nan·burh \ˈbrü-nən-ˌbərg\. Battlefield of uncertain location in S Scotland or N England; site of victory of Anglo-Saxon ruler Aethelstan over a league of Welsh, Scots, and Danes 937 A.D.

Brundusium *or* **Brundisium.** See BRINDISI 2.

Bru·nei \bru̇-ˈnī, ˈbrü-ˌnī\. **1.** River in Borneo. See LIMBANG.
2. *or officially* **State of Brunei Dar·us·sa·lam** \ˌdär-ə-sə-ˈläm\. Independent sultanate, SE Asia, in NE part of Borneo; 2226 sq. mi. (5765 sq. km.); pop. (1991p) 260,863; ✻ Bandar Seri Begawan; divided geographically into two parts, each entirely surrounded by Malaysian state of Sarawak and each having coastline on South China Sea and Brunei Bay; the two sections separated by Limbang River valley.

Chief products: Oil and natural gas.

History: In pre-Spanish times a powerful and populous state; visited by ships of Portuguese navigator Ferdinand Magellan 1521; declined in influence and became a resort for pirates; in return for British assistance dealing with unrest, its sultan in 1841 handed over Sarawak to British; English soldier James Brooke made raja; in 1847 sultanate entered into treaty with Great Britain, ceding Labuan; placed under British protection 1888; in 1906 definitely yielded all administration to a British Resident; oil discovered 1929; occupied by Japanese 1941, retaken by Australians 1945; rejected membership in federation with Malaysia 1963;

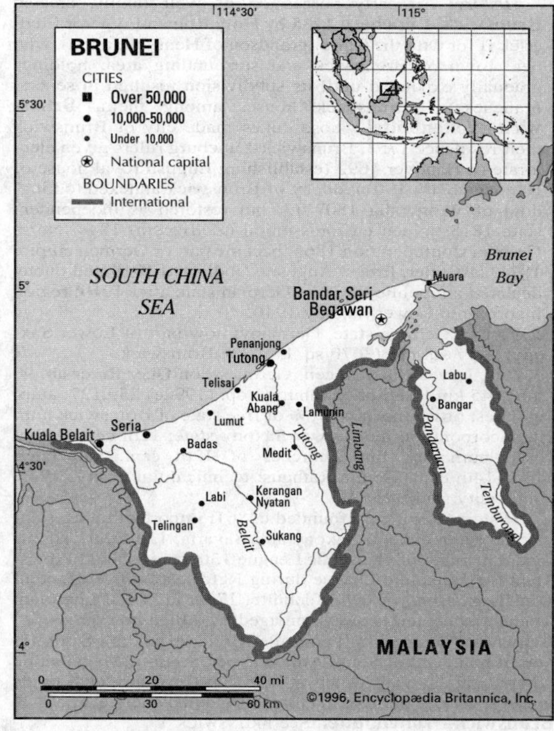

achieved independence and became a member of the Commonwealth Jan. 1, 1984.
3. *or* **Brunei Town.** Town, Brunei. See BANDAR SERI BEGAWAN.

Brunei Bay. Inlet of South China Sea on the NW coast of Borneo; its shores touched by East Malaysia and Brunei; in its N part is Labuan I.

Bruni. See BRUNY.

Brü·nig \ˈbrǖ-nik\. Mountain pass in Bernese Alps, Switzerland, E of Brienz; alt. 3396 ft. (1035 m.); connects valley of the Aare with Lake of Lucerne.

Brünn. See BRNO.

Bruns·büt·tel·koog \ˈbru̇ns-ˌbǖt-ᵊl-ˌkōk\. Town, Schleswig-Holstein, N Germany, on Elbe River at S entrance to Kiel Canal; oil pipeline terminal; founded 1762.

Bruns·sum \ˈbrœn-səm\. Commune, Limburg prov., SE Netherlands, 11 mi. (18 km.) NE of Maastricht; pop. (1981e) 29,715.

Bruns·wick \ˈbrənz-wik\. **1.** Name of counties in two states of the U.S. See tables at NORTH CAROLINA and VIRGINIA.
2. Seaport city, ⊗ of Glynn co., SE Georgia, on Atlantic Ocean; pop. (1990c) 16,433; seafood processing; Brunswick Coll. (1964).
3. Town, Cumberland co., SW Maine, 23 mi. (37 km.) NE of Portland; pop. (1990c) 20,906; trade center; medical facilities; Bowdoin Coll. (1794); Brunswick Naval Air Station.
4. Town, Frederick co., N Maryland, on Potomac River 15 mi. (24 km.) WSW of Frederick; pop. (1990c) 5117.
5. City, Medina co., Ohio, NW of Akron; pop. (1990c) 28,230.
6. City, S Victoria, SE Australia, N suburb of Melbourne; pop. (1991c) 39,886.

Brunswick *or Ger.* **Braun·schweig** \ˈbrau̇n-ˌshfīk\. **1.** Former duchy, cen. Germany, now part of Lower Saxony.

History: An early possession of Welf family, created **Brunswick–Lüneberg** 1235 by Holy Roman Emperor Frederick II for Otto the Child (grandson of Henry the Lion), who held town of Brunswick and surrounding area; holdings gradually expanded until its subdivision resulted in several branches of Brunswick house, among them, **Brunswick–Wolfenbüttel** whose dukes made city of Brunswick their residence 1753; Brunswick-Lüneburg rulers given electorate of Hanover 1692 (establishing English royal house of Hanover 1714–1901); duchy of Brunswick annexed to kingdom of Westphalia 1807–13, but restored as independent state 1815; joined customs union (*Zollverein*) 1844, North German Confederation 1866; became part of German empire 1871; last ruler, Ernest Augustus abdicated 1918 and duchy declared a republic; became German state after 1919; region incorp. into Lower Saxony 1946.

2. Former German state, Germany; now part of Lower Saxony; 1417 sq. mi. (3670 sq. km.); ✻ Brunswick.

3. City, Lower Saxony, cen. Germany, on Oker River ab. 90 mi. (145 km.) SSE of Hamburg; pop. (1992e) 259,127; automobiles, office machinery; ✻ of free state of Brunswick until its incorporation into Lower Saxony state; 12th cent. cathedral; numerous fine churches of 12th cent. and later; 13th–14th cent. Gothic Rathaus; technical university (1745, university status 1968).

History: Reputedly founded c. 861; important under Henry the Lion, duke of Saxony and Bavaria, 12th cent.; significant member of Hanseatic League 13th cent.; joined Protestant Schmalkaldic League during Reformation; residence of dukes of Brunswick-Wolfenbüttel 1753; in WWII important industrial center, heavily damaged by Allied bombing.

Brunswick Peninsula. Peninsula, Chile, extending S from S tip of mainland of South America, bet. Strait of Magellan on S and E and Otway Water on NW; Cape Froward, its S tip, is most southerly point of mainland of South America, 53°54′S.

Brunswick–Wolfenbüttel. See BRUNSWICK 1.

Bru·ny *or* **Bru·ni** \ˈbrü-nē\. Island off SE coast of Tasmania, Australia, SW of Storm Bay; its S point is Tasman Head; 149 sq. mi. (386 sq. km.); ab. 32 mi. (52 km.) long.

Brusa *or* **Brussa.** See BURSA.

Brush \ˈbrəsh\. City, Morgan co., NE Colorado, 10 mi. (16 km.) E of Fort Morgan; pop. (1990c) 4165.

Brus·sels \ˈbrə-səlz\ *or Fr.* **Bru·xelles** \brᵫ-ˈsel, brᵫk-\ *or Flemish* **Brus·sel** \ˈbrᵫ-səl\. **1.** Region of Belgium, comprising the city of Brussels and the surrounding area. See table at BELGIUM.

2. City, ✻ of Belgium, in Brussels region on Senne River; pop. (1991c) 136,424; commercial and political center; electrical equipment, machinery, rubber goods; city hall (15th cent.); palaces; cathedral (founded 1010); museums; churches; university (1834); site of World's Fair 1958; site of headquarters of European Union and of North Atlantic Treaty Organization (NATO).

History: Village grew up about chapel on island in Senne; among holdings of Louvain (Leuven) and later of dukes of Brabant (*q.v.*) who made it their residence; slower than Flemish towns to develop cloth industry, it had become, by 14th cent., chief town of Brabant; in 1530 made ✻ of Netherlands under Hapsburgs; took part in revolt against rulers 1576; won back for Hapsburgs by Alexander of Parma 1585; bombarded by French soldier François de Villeroi during wars of Louis XIV of France; under kingdom of the Netherlands 1815–30; center of Belgian revolution 1830 and ✻ of Belgium since 1830 when Belgium and Netherlands became independent states; occupied by Germans in both World Wars; officially a bilingual city (Flemish and French); became one of three regions in new federation of Belgium 1993.

Bruttium. See CALABRIA 2.

Brüx. See MOST.

Bruxelles. See BRUSSELS.

Bry·an \ˈbrī-ən\. **1.** Name of counties in two states of the U.S. See tables at GEORGIA and OKLAHOMA.

2. City, ⊗ of Williams co., NW corner of Ohio, 52 mi. (84 km.) W of Toledo; pop. (1990c) 8348.

3. City, ⊗ of Brazos co., E cen. Texas, 72 mi. (116 km.) SSE of Waco; pop. (1990c) 55,002; speedway nearby; Allen Academy (1886).

Bry·an·ka \brē-ˈän-kə\. Town, E Ukraine, 28 mi. (45 km.) WSW of Luhansk; pop. (1991e) 65,000; estab. 1962.

Bry·ansk *also* **Bri·ansk** \brē-ˈänsk\. City, ✻ of Bryansk Oblast, W Russia in Europe, on Desna River at head of navigation, W of Orel and 210 mi. (338 km.) SW of Moscow; pop. (1992e) 461,000; important railroad junction point; large ironworks, locomotive plant; first mentioned 12th cent.; independent principality; later subject to Lithuania but became Russian in 16th cent.

Bryansk Oblast *also* **Briansk Oblast** \ˈō-bləst, -ˌblast\; *Russ.* **Bry·an·ska·ya Oblast′** \brē-ˈän-skə-yə\ Subdivision, W Russia in Europe; 13,475 sq. mi. (34,900 sq. km.); pop. (1992e) 1,464,000; ✻ Bryansk; created 1946 from Orel Oblast.

Bryce, Mount \ˈbrīs\. Peak, E British Columbia, Canada, near Alberta border; 11,507 ft. (3507 m.).

Bryce Canyon National Park. See UNITED STATES, *National Parks.*

Brycheiniog. See BRECKNOCKSHIRE.

Bryn Ath·yn \brin-ˈa-thən\. Residential borough, Montgomery co., SE Pennsylvania, ab. 16 mi. (26 km.) NE of Philadelphia; pop. (1990c) 1081; seat of Bryn Athyn Cathedral, center of Swedenborgianism in the U.S.; Academy of the New Church Coll. (1876).

Bryn Mawr \brin-ˈmär\. Unincorporated settlement, Montgomery co., SE Pennsylvania, ab. 7 mi. (11 km.) S of Norristown; Bryn Mawr Coll. (1880), Harcum Junior Coll. (1915).

Bryson City \ˈbrī-sən\. Town, ⊗ of Swain co., W North Carolina, on edge of Great Smoky Mountains National Park 53 mi. (85 km.) W of Asheville; pop. (1990c) 1145; resort.

Brzeg \bə-ˈzhek\ *or Ger.* **Brieg** \ˈbrēk\; *anc.* **Civ·i·tas Al·tae Ri·pae** \ˈsi-vi-täs-ˈal-tē-ˈrī-pē\. City, Opole prov., SW Poland, on Odra (Oder) River 27 mi. (43 km.) SE of Wrocław; pop. (1989e) 38,440; formerly in Silesia, Germany; 14th cent. Gothic churches; town hall. Received city rights 1250; captured by Prussia in First Silesian War 1741; fortifications destroyed by French 1806; in WWII received heavy damage; taken by U.S.S.R. 1945; assigned to Poland by Potsdam Conference 1945.

Brześć nad Bugiem. See BREST 2.

Brzeżany. See BEREZHANY.

Brzezinka. See BIRKENAU.

Bua. See ČIOVO.

Buad \ˈbwäd\. Island off W coast of Samar, Philippines, across entrance to Maqueda and Villareal bays; 14 sq. mi. (36 sq. km.). Town of Zumarraga is on its W coast.

Bubaque. See BIJAGÓS, ARQUIPÉLAGO DOS.

Bu·bas·tis \byü-ˈbas-tis\. City of anc. Egypt, in Nile Delta; its ruins (excavated beginning late 19th cent.) near modern city of Zagazig, called **Tell Bas·ta** \tel-ˈbas-tə\; chief seat of worship of the goddess Bast, usually represented as lion-headed or cat-headed; chosen in 10th cent. B.C. by Sheshonk I as ✻ of XXIId (Bubastite) dynasty; declined after 4th cent. B.C.

Bū·bi·yān \ˌbü-bē-ˈyän\. Island at head of Persian Gulf off N coast of Kuwait and W of mouth of Shatt al Arab; administratively a part of Kuwait; historically claimed by Iraq.

Bu·ca \ˈbü-kə\. Town, W Turkey in Asia, just S of İzmir.

Bu·ca·ra·man·ga \ˌbü-kä-rä-ˈmäŋ-gä\. City, ✻ of Santander dept., N cen. Colombia; in the Cordillera Oriental of the Andes at alt. of 3340 ft. (1018 m.); pop. (1992e) 349,400; iron products; center of region producing coffee and tobacco; university (1947).

Bu·cas Gran·de \bü-ˈkäs-ˈgrän-dā\. Island off NE Mindanao, Philippines, a part of Surigao del Norte prov.; 50 sq. mi. (130 sq. km.); highest point 3012 ft. (918 m.).

Buc·ca·neer Archipelago \ˌbə-kə-ˈnir\. Group of islands off N coast of Western Australia, Australia, at entrance to King Sound.

Bu·chach \bu̇-ˈchäch\ *or Pol.* **Bu·czacz** \ˈbü-chäch\. Town, W Ukraine, on Strypa River 34 mi. (55 km.) SSW of Ternopol (formerly in Poland). Treaty bet. Poland and Turkey signed here 1672; in area long contested militarily; in WWI key point in Russian Gen. Aleksey Brusilov's effective offensive 1916; in WWII involved both in German eastern offensive 1941 and German western retreat 1944.

Buch·an \ˈbə-kən, -k̲ən\. Region NE Grampian region, Scotland, N of the Ythan River; includes Buchan Ness and the Bullers of Buchan (*qq.v.*).

Bu·chan·an \byü-ˈka-nən, bə-\. **1.** Name of counties in three states of the U.S. See tables at IOWA, MISSOURI, VIRGINIA. **2.** City, ⊗ of Haralson co., W Georgia; pop. (1990c) 1009. **3.** City, Berrien co., SW corner of Michigan, 53 mi. (85 km.) SW of Kalamazoo; pop. (1990c) 4992. **4.** *formerly* **Grand Bas·sa** \ˈba-sə\. Seaport, W Liberia, ab. 70 mi. (115 km.) SE of Monrovia; pop. (1988e) 25,000.

Buchanan Dam; *formerly* **Ham·il·ton Dam** \ˈha-mil-tən\. Dam across Colorado River, Burnet and Llano cos., cen. Texas; height 158 ft. (48 m.); completed 1937; impounds water for power, forming **Lake Buchanan,** *formerly* **Hamilton Lake.**

Buch·an Ness \ˈbə-k̲ən\. Headland on NE coast of Scotland, S of Peterhead; lighthouse; easternmost point of Scotland.

Bu·cha·rest \ˈbü-kə-ˌrest, ˈbyü-\ *or Rom.* **Bu·cu·reş·ti** \ˌbü-kü-ˈresht^y, -ˈresh-tē\. City, ✻ of Romania, on Dîmboviţa River; the municipality constitutes an administrative district (see table at ROMANIA); agricultural implements, railroad cars, motor vehicles, engineering products, engines, tires, radios and televisions, semiconductors and computers, precision instruments, plastics, chemicals, foodstuffs, furniture, metal goods, textiles, pharmaceuticals; university (1864); libraries; museums; parks; theaters; sports complex.

History: Evidence of longtime settlement in area; gained importance as residence of rulers of Walachia (*q.v.*) from 14th cent.; became ✻ of Romania (*q.v.*) 1862; scene of negotiation of several important treaties: (1) Peace of Bucharest 1812 bet. Russia and Turkey; (2) peace bet. Serbia and Bulgaria 1886 (see EASTERN RUMELIA); (3) Treaty of Bucharest 1913, stripping Bulgaria (*q.v.*) of its conquests. Occupied by Germans 1916–18; under Nazi control 1940–44; occupied by U.S.S.R. Aug. 1944; struck by powerful earthquake March 1977; scene of political demonstrations against government of Romanian leader Nicolae Ceauşescu 1989 culminating in his overthrow and execution.

Bu·chen·wald \ˈbü-k̲ən-ˌvält, ˈbü-kən-ˌwȯld\. Village, Thuringia, cen. Germany, near Weimar; site of concentration camp, taken Apr. 1945 by American forces. One of the worst of German camps for prisoners.

Buch·holz \ˈbük̲-ˌhȯlts\. Former town, Saxony, E Germany; now part of Annaberg-Buchholz.

Buchhorn. See FRIEDRICHSHAFEN.

Bück·e·burg \ˈbuē-kə-ˌbu̇rk\. Town, Lower Saxony, Germany; pop. (1980c) 20,574; was ✻ of Schaumburg-Lippe, former German state.

Buck·eye \ˈbək-ˌī\. Town, Maricopa co., SW cen. Arizona, 30 mi. (48 km.) W of Phoenix; pop. (1990c) 5038.

Buck·han·non \ˌbək-ˈha-nən\. **1.** River, NE cen. West Virginia; rises in SW Randolph co., flows N into Tygart River in Barbour co.; ab. 45 mi. (72 km.) long. **2.** City, ⊗ of Upshur co., NE cen. West Virginia, on Buckhannon River 14 mi. (23 km.) E of Weston; pop. (1990c) 5909; West Virginia Wesleyan Coll. (1890).

Buck·ha·ven and Meth·il \ˌbək-ˈhā-vən … ˈme-thil\. Burgh comprising two ports, Fife region, E Scotland, 7 to 8 mi. (11 to 13 km.) NE of Kirkcaldy.

Buck·ie \ˈbə-kē\. Seaport burgh, Grampian region, NE Scotland, ab. 13 mi. (21 km.) E of Elgin; pop. (1981p) 7763; fisheries.

Buck·ing·ham \ˈbə-kiŋ-əm, *U.S. also* -kiŋ-ˌham\. **1.** County in cen. Virginia. See table at VIRGINIA. **2.** Town, its ⊗, cen. Virginia. **3.** Town, Papineau co., SW Quebec, Canada, on Lièvre River 17 mi. (27 km.) NE of Ottawa; pop. (1991c) 10,548; phosphate, graphite, and mica deposits. **4.** County in England. See BUCKINGHAMSHIRE. **5.** Town, Buckinghamshire, SE cen. England, 20 mi. (32 km.) NE of Oxford; pop. (1981p) 6627; seat (Stowe, with famous gardens) of former dukes of Buckingham; location now of a public school.

Buck·ing·ham·shire \ˈbə-kiŋ-əm-ˌshir, -shər\ *or* **Buckingham** *or* **Bucks** \ˈbəks\. **1.** Former county, SE cen. England. **2.** Administrative county, SE cen. England, approx. equivalent to the former county; rivers Thames, Ouse, Thame; estab. 1974. See table at ENGLAND.

Buck Island Reef National Monument \ˈbək\. See UNITED STATES, *National Monuments.*

Buck·ley \ˈbə-klē\. **1.** City, Pierce and Thurston cos., W Washington, 20 mi. (32 km.) ESE of Tacoma; pop. (1990c) 3516. **2.** Town, Clwyd, NE Wales; pop. (1981p) 13,386.

Buckley, Mount. Peak, W North Carolina; 6599 ft. (2011 m.).

Buck Mountain \ˈbək\. **1.** Peak, Grayson co., SW Virginia; 4630 ft. (1411 m.). **2.** Peak, S cen. Grand Teton National Park, NW Wyoming; 11,923 ft. (3634 m.).

Buck·ner \ˈbək-nər\. City, Jackson co., W Missouri; pop. (1990c) 2873.

Buckner Bay. See NAKAGUSUKU BAY.

Bucks \ˈbəks\. **1.** County in SE Pennsylvania. See table at PENNSYLVANIA. **2.** County, England. See BUCKINGHAMSHIRE.

Buck·skin, Mount \ˈbək-ˌskin\. Peak, Lake and Park cos., cen. Colorado; 13,800 ft. (4206 m.).

Bucks·port \ˈbəks-ˌpōrt\. Town, Hancock co., SE Maine, on Penobscot River 17 mi. (27 km.) S of Bangor; pop. (1990c) 4825; across the river is Fort Knox (begun 1846).

Bucovina. See BUKOVINA.

Bucureşti. See BUCHAREST.

Bu·cy·rus \byü-ˈsī-rəs\. City, ⊗ of Crawford co., N cen. Ohio, on Sandusky River 17 mi. (27 km.) NNE of Marion; pop. (1990c) 13,496; settled c. 1820; became ⊗ 1830.

Buczacz. See BUCHACH.

Bu·da·fok \ˈbü-də-ˌfōk\. City, S suburb of Budapest, cen. Hungary, on Danube River; pop. (1980p) 40,623.

Bu·da·pest \ˈbü-də-ˌpest, ˈbyü-, *Hungarian* ˈbü-dö-ˌpesht\. City, ✻ of Hungary and ⊗ of Pest co.; 203 sq. mi. (526 sq. km.); pop. (1991e) 2,008,546; includes since 1873 former towns of **Bu·da** \ˈbü-də, -dö\ and **Óbu·da** \ˈō-bü-ˌdȯ\ on right bank of Danube and **Pest** \ˈpesht\ on left bank; precision instruments, textiles; several universities and colleges, incl. Loránd Eötvös Univ. (1635, moved to Buda 1745); opera house (1879–84); Academy of Sciences; libraries; theaters; museums.

History: Inhabited from Neolithic times; Buda site of Roman camp (*anc.* **Aquin·cum** \ə-ˈkwin-kəm\) set up in 2d cent. A.D.; Buda and Pest both towns inhabited by Germans in 13th cent.; Buda fortified by King Matthias Corvinus in 15th cent. and became ✻ of Hungary; captured and held by Turks 1541–1686; Buda (Pest almost destroyed earlier) retaken from Turks by Charles V, duke of Lorraine 1686; became free imperial city; in 1848–49 both towns disturbed by nationalistic revolt, Pest (which in 18th cent. had outstripped Buda) becoming ✻ of Lajos Kossuth's revolutionary government (see HUNGARY); a ✻ of Hungary under Dual Monarchy 1867 (see AUSTRIA-HUNGARY); united as Budapest 1873; center of revolt for independence of Hungary 1918; occupied by Romanians in war against government of Béla Kun 1919. In WWII an aircraft and supply center for German forces; bombed 1944–45 by U.S. Air Force and Buda badly damaged; taken by U.S.S.R. Feb. 1945 after long bitter fighting; center of anti-Communist uprising 1956 and again damaged by Soviet forces; in 1980s center of unrest with Hungarian Communist leadership; remained Hungarian ✻ when republic was declared 1989.

Bu·daun \bu̇-ˈdau̇n\. Town, NW cen. Uttar Pradesh, N India, 123 mi. (198 km.) ESE of Delhi; pop. (1991p) 116,706;

founded ab. 905 A.D.; has ruins of old fort and a splendid mosque converted in 13th cent. from an ancient Hindu temple by Iltutmish (Altamsh), king of Delhi.

Budd Coast \ˈbəd\. Mountainous section of Antarctica coast, 66°30′S, bet. 110°30′E and 114°E; part of Wilkes Land and part of Australian claim.

Buddh Gaya *or* **Buddha Gayā.** See BODH GAYĀ.

Bud·don Ness \ˌbəd-ᵊn-ˈnes\. Headland on E cen. coast of Scotland, at N entrance to Firth of Tay; lighthouse.

Bude \ˈbyüd\. Coast resort, N Cornwall, England, SW of Bideford on **Bude Bay.**

Budějovice, České. See ČESKÉ BUDĚJOVICE.

Budge Budge \ˈbəj-ˌbəj\. Town, West Bengal, NE India, on Hugli River; pop. (1991p) 73,361.

Budissin. See BAUTZEN.

Budrum. See BODRUM.

Budweis. See ČESKÉ BUDĚJOVICE.

Bu·ea \bü-ˈā-ə\. Town, W Cameroon, near the coast at foot of Cameroon Mt.; pop. (1987e) 39,064; connected by highway to the seaport town of Limbe; formerly ✻ of British Cameroons trust territory and before 1919 ✻ of German Cameroons (Kamerun).

Bued \ˈbwād\. River, NW Luzon, Philippines; ab. 35 mi. (56 km.) long.

Bue·na \ˈbyü-nə\. Borough, Atlantic co., SE New Jersey, 28 mi. (45 km.) NW of Atlantic City; pop. (1990c) 4441.

Buen Aire. See BONAIRE.

Buena Park \ˈbyü-nə\. City, Orange co., California, W of Anaheim; pop. (1990c) 68,784.

Bue·na·ven·tu·ra \ˌbwā-nä-ven-ˈtü-rä\. Important Pacific port, Valle dept., W Colombia, 210 mi. (338 km.) W of Bogotá on **Buenaventura Bay;** pop. (1985c) 174,397; is terminus of railroads in W Colombia; exports coffee, sugar, gold, and platinum; founded 1540.

Buena Vis·ta \ˌbyü-nə-ˈvis-tə\. **1.** County in NW Iowa. See table at IOWA.

2. City, ⊗ of Marion co., W Georgia; pop. (1990c) 1472.

3. Independent city, Rockbridge co., W cen. Virginia, 25 mi. (40 km.) NW of Lynchburg; pop. (1990c) 6406.

Buena Vista \ˌbwā-nä-ˈvē-stä\. **1.** Mountain, S Costa Rica; 10,820 ft. (3298 m.).

2. Battlefield, Coahuila state, NE Mexico, 8 mi. (13 km.) S of Saltillo; defeat of Gen. Antonio López de Santa Anna by U.S. forces under Zachary Taylor Feb. 1847 ended northern campaign in Mexican War.

Buena Vista Lake \ˌbyü-nə-ˈvis-tə\. Reservoir, in Kern co., S California, SW of Bakersfield, into which the lower course of the Kern River flows.

Buena Vista Peak. Mountain in the Sierra Nevada, cen. California, in S part of Yosemite National Park; 9709 ft. (2959 m.).

Bue·në \ˈbwā-nə\; *Serbo-Croat.* **Bo·ja·na** *or* **Bo·ya·na** \ˈbō-yä-ˌnä\. Small river in NW Albania, the N mouth of the Drin River; flows out of Lake Scutari SW into Adriatic Sea along boundary line bet. Albania and Yugoslavia.

Bue·nos Ai·res \ˌbwā-nəs-ˈar-ēz, ˈbwā-nōs-ˈī-rās\. **1.** Province of E cen. Argentina; ✻ La Plata. See table at ARGENTINA.

2. Viceroyalty, South America. See LA PLATA 3.

3. City, ✻ of Argentina and itself constituting the Federal District (77 sq. mi. or 199 sq. km.), E cen. Argentina, on estuary of the Río de la Plata, ab. 130 mi. (210 km.) from the sea; pop. (1991p) 2,960,976, met. area pop. 12,582,321; political, commercial, and industrial center; meat processing; flourmills, breweries, foundries, tanneries; extensive port facilities; several universities incl. Univ. of Buenos Aires (1821); numerous public buildings; museum; libraries; theaters; cathedral; opera house.

History: First colonized by Spanish soldier and explorer Pedro de Mendoza 1536 as **Santa María del Buen Aire;** not permanently settled until 1580; ✻ of subordinate division of viceroyalty of Peru, it became in 1776 the seat of viceroyalty of La Plata (*q.v.*) or Buenos Aires; blockaded by British in dispute over intervention in Uruguay 1845; drew up constitution separate from provinces in 1854 and began intermittent conflict with them over control of government of Argentina; erection into Federal District, as ✻ of Argentina but separate from province of Buenos Aires, settled war with provinces 1880; during 20th cent. continued to be most influential and largest city in country.

Buenos Aires, Lake *or in Chile* **La·go Ge·ne·ral Car·re·ra** \ˌlä-gō-ˌhā-nā-ˈräl-kär-ˈrā-rä\. Lake on the Chile-Argentina boundary, 46°35′S; ab. 75 mi. (120 km.) long; 865 sq. mi. (2240 sq. km.).

Buenos Aires, Point. Cape on NW point of Valdés Penin., enclosing Gulf of San José, NE coast of Chubut prov., S Argentina.

Buer \ˈbür\. Former city, Germany. See GELSENKIRCHEN.

Bu·et, Mont \mōⁿ-ˈbwā\. Peak in the Pennine Alps, E Haute-Savoie dept., E France; 10,200 ft. (3109 m.).

Buey \ˈbwā\. Cape on N coast of Tabasco state, SE Mexico, extending into the Bay of Campeche.

Bufarik. See BOUFARIK.

Buf·fa·lo \ˈbə-fə-ˌlō\. **1.** River, W Tennessee; rises in N Lawrence co., flows W, then N into Duck River in cen. Humphreys co.; ab. 100 mi. (160 km.) long.

2. Name of counties in three states of the U.S. See tables at NEBRASKA, SOUTH DAKOTA, WISCONSIN.

3. Village, ⊗ of Wright co., S cen. Minnesota, 31 mi. (50 km.) WNW of Minneapolis; pop. (1990c) 6856.

4. City, ⊗ of Dallas co., SW cen. Missouri; pop. (1990c) 2414.

5. City and port, ⊗ of Erie co., W New York, at NE point of Lake Erie and on Niagara River ab. 16 mi. (26 km.) SE of Niagara Falls; pop. (1990c) 328,123; W terminus of New York State Barge Canal; connected with Fort Erie, Canada, by Peace Bridge (opened 1927) across Niagara River; point of departure for Niagara Falls; a major center of U.S. trade with Canada; railroad and distribution center; grain and coal elevators; research laboratories. Albright-Knox Art Gallery; Grosvenor Library; State Univ. of New York at Buffalo (1846), State Univ. of New York Coll. at Buffalo (1867), Canisius Coll. (1870), D'Youville Coll. (1908), Medaille Coll. (1937), Erie Community Coll.-City Campus (1946), Trocaire Coll. (1958), Villa Maria Coll. of Buffalo (1960).

History: Settled by American Indians 1780; site platted by Joseph Ellicott 1799; sold in lots 1803; incorp. 1810; military post in War of 1812; burned by British and Indians 1813; rebuilt 1814–15; incorp. as village 1816; became W terminus of Erie Canal (opened 1825); became city 1832; important station on Underground Railroad. Scene of Pan-American Exposition 1901 where President William McKinley was assassinated; port on St. Lawrence Seaway since 1957.

6. Town, ⊗ of Harper co., NW Oklahoma; pop. (1990c) 1312.

7. Town, ⊗ of Harding co., South Dakota, on Grand River 36 mi. (58 km.) SE of NW corner of state; pop. (1990c) 488.

8. City, ⊗ of Johnson co., N Wyoming, 33 mi. (53 km.) S of Sheridan; pop. (1990c) 3302.

9. River, KwaZulu-Natal prov., Rep. of South Africa; rises in Drakensberg, flows SE, joining the Tugela River; ab. 200 mi. (320 km.) long.

Buffalo Bay. Inlet of Lake of the Woods in SE Manitoba, Canada; extends W from the American part of the lake.

Buffalo Bayou. Stream, flowing through Houston, Texas; 45 mi. (72 km.) long; lower course is Houston Ship Canal.

Buf·fa·lo Bill Dam \ˈbə-fə-ˌlō-ˈbil\ *or* **Sho·sho·ne Dam** \shə-ˈshō-nē\. Dam across Shoshone River in NW Wyoming, W of Cody; height 325 ft. (99 m.); completed 1910.

Buffalo Fork. River, N Arkansas; rises in SW Newton co., NW Arkansas, flows E and NE into White River on SE boundary of Marion co., N cen. Arkansas; 150 mi. (241 km.) long.

Buffalo Grove. Village, Cook and Lake cos., NE Illinois, ab. 12 mi. (19 km.) NW of Chicago; pop. (1990c) 36,427.

Buffalo National Park. See *Wood Buffalo National Park* at CANADA, *National Parks.*

Buffalo Peaks. Mountain in Chaffee and Park cos., cen. Colorado; 13,541 ft. (4127 m.).

Bu·ford \ˈbyü-fərd\. City, Gwinnett and Hall cos., N Georgia, ab. 28 mi. (45 km.) NE of Atlanta; pop. (1990c) 8771; trading center.

Bug \ˈbüg\. **1.** *or* **Western Bug.** River, E cen. Poland; rises in W Ukraine, flows N along Poland-Ukraine and Poland-Belarus borders to Brest, turns W and NW into Poland to the Vistula River 18 mi. (29 km.) NW of Warsaw; 481 mi. (774 km.) long; navigable below Brest. In WWI several battles fought along its course in 1915. About 200 mi. (322 km.) of its central course formed part of the Curzon Line, proposed by the Supreme Council after WWI Dec. 1919 as Poland's eastern frontier (ultimately, Poland's frontier stretched farther east); this same section included in the Russo-German boundary of 1939 and retained with a few changes after WWII in the boundary bet. U.S.S.R. and Poland.

2. *also* **Southern Bug;** *anc.* **Hyp·a·nis** \ˈhi-pə-nis\. River, SW Ukraine, rises in Khmel'nyts'kyy subdivision near former Polish border and flows SE to the Dnieper estuary; 532 mi. (856 km.) long; has many rapids and is not navigable above Voznesens'k; largest tributary is the Ingul, which joins it at Mykolayiv; its upper reaches utilized for hydroelectric power production.

Bu·ga \ˈbü-gä\. City, Vallee dept., W Colombia; munic. pop. (1985c) 86,513; trading center.

Bu·gan·da \bü-ˈgän-dä, byü-\. Former native kingdom of SE Uganda; ✻ Kampala; included islands in N part of Lake Victoria; part of British protectorate with considerable autonomy from 1900; monarchy abolished 1967 and kingdom made an integral part of Uganda.

Bu·gul'·ma *or* **Bu·gul·ma** \ˌbu̇-gəl-ˈmä\. Town, SE Tatarstan, E Russia in Europe, on railroad line 160 mi. (257 km.) SE of Kazan'; pop. (1991e) 91,100; oil.

Bu·gu·ru·slan \ˌbu̇-gə-ru̇-ˈslän\. Town, NW Orenburg Oblast, S Russia in Europe, on railroad line 95 mi. (153 km.) NE of Samara, on N bank of the Bol'shaya Kinel' River; pop. (1991e) 54,100; natural gas.

Bu·ḫay·rat \bu̇-ˈk̲ī-rət\. Arabic word meaning "lake." For names of lakes containing this word, see the 2d element.

Bu·hi \ˈbü-hē\. Municipality, SE Camarines Sur prov., Luzon, Philippines, on S shore of **Lake Buhi** (10 mi. or 16 km. long by 4 mi. or 6 km. wide); pop. (1980c) 48,625.

Buhl \ˈbyül\. City, Twin Falls co., S Idaho, 17 mi. (27 km.) W of Twin Falls; pop. (1990c) 3516.

Bui·es Creek \ˈbü-ēz\. Unincorporated settlement, Harnett co., cen. North Carolina, bet. Raleigh and Fayetteville; pop. (1990c) 2085; Campbell Univ. (1887).

Builth Wells \ˈbilth-ˈwelz\ *or Welsh* **Llan·fair–ym–Mu·allt** \ˈhlan-ˌvīr-ə-ˈmē-ält\. Town, Powys co., S cen. Wales, on the Wye; pop. (1981p) 1287; spa, market town; notable in Welsh history, dating back to 11th cent.; nearby, Welsh Prince Llewelyn ap Gruffudd defeated and killed 1282, leading to conquest of Wales by English.

Bu·in \bü-ˈēn\. Settlement at S end of Bougainville I., NW Solomon Is., W Pacific Ocean; held by Japanese as base, bypassed by Americans in conquest of the Solomon Is. 1942–43.

Bui·naksk *also* **Buy·naksk** \ˌbü-ē-ˈnäksk\; *formerly* **Temir–Khan–Shu·ra** \ti-ˈmir-ˌk̲än-shu̇-ˈrä\. Town, N cen. Dagestan, S Russia in Europe, on branch railroad 25 mi. (40 km.) WSW of Makhachkala.

Buir Nur \ˈbwir-ˈnȯr\ *or* **Buyr Nuur** \ˈbwir-ˈnu̇r\ *or W.-G.* **Pei–erh Hu** \ˈbā-ˈər-ˈhü\. Lake, E Asia, on border bet. Mongolia and Heilongjiang prov., NE China, S of Hulun Nur.

Buitengewesten. See OUTER PROVINCES.

Buitenzorg. See BOGOR.

Bu·ja·lan·ce \ˌbü-hä-ˈlän-thā\. Commune, Córdoba prov., S Spain, 23 mi. (37 km.) E of the city of Córdoba; pop. (1991c) 8487; ruins of 10th cent. Moorish castle.

Buj·nurd. See BOJNŪRD.

Bu·jum·bu·ra \ˌbü-jəm-ˈbu̇r-ə\; *formerly* **Usum·bu·ra** \ˌü-səm-ˈbu̇r-ə\. Town, ✻ of Burundi, on E side of N end of Lake Tanganyika; pop. (1990c) 236,334; Burundi's chief port; in agricultural region; textiles; university (1961); cultural center.

Bu·ka \ˈbü-kä\. One of the Solomon Is. just N of Bougainville I. (*q.v.*) and separated from it by **Buka Passage;** part of Papua New Guinea; 190 sq. mi. (492 sq. km.); contains excellent anchorage. Mostly level with mangrove swamps and some forest and grassland regions. Best anchorage is Queen Carola Harbour. Became part of Papua New Guinea 1975.

Bu·ka·ma \bü-ˈkä-mä\. Town, S cen. Katanga, SE Democratic Rep. of the Congo; trading town on navigable Lualaba River.

Bu·ka·vu \bü-ˈkäv-(ˌ)ü\; *formerly* **Cos·ter·mans·ville** \ˈkäs-tər-mənz-ˌvil\. Town, ✻ of Sud-Kivu administrative region, E Democratic Rep. of the Congo, at S end of Lake Kivu; pop. (1991e) 209,566; center of tourism for nearby national parks.

Bu·kha·ra *or* **Bo·kha·ra** *or* **Bou·kha·ra** \bȯ-ˈk̲ä-rä, bü-ˈkär-ə\. **1.** Former khanate occupying region around city of Bukhara, W Asia; later, a state in the region that became Soviet Central Asia. In early times region known as Sogdiana and Transoxiana (*qq.v.*). Ruled by Muslim Arabs from c. 710 A.D.; built into powerful Islamic kingdom by Samanids (9th–10th cent.); as ✻ of Samanid realm, which included territory from Baghdad to borders of India and from Bukhara to Persian Gulf, became an intellectual center of Islam and wealthy mart for trade of central Asia; destroyed by Mongol conqueror Genghis Khan c. 1220; under various dynasties, the prize of Mongols, Turks, Uzbeks (see TURKISTAN), and others; in 19th cent., its emir controlled khanates of Qŭqon and Khiva; conquered 1866–68 and made a Russian protectorate; proclaimed a Soviet republic 1920; became part of Uzbek S.S.R. (*q.v.*) 1924; part of independent Uzbekistan 1991.

2. Subdivision of S Uzbekistan; 55,290 sq. mi. (143,201 sq. km.); pop. (1991e) 1,708,000; ✻ Bukhara; formerly an oblast of Uzbek S.S.R.

3. City, ✻ of Bukhara subdivision, W Uzbekistan, E of the Amu Dar'ya and ab. 140 mi. (225 km.) W of Samarqand; pop. (1991e) 249,600; textiles; chief city of former khanate; has many mosques and minarets and was once noted as a holy place of Islam.

Bu·kid·non \bü-ˈkēd-ˌnȯn\. Province, N cen. Mindanao, Philippines; 3202 sq. mi. (8293 sq. km.); pop. (1980c) 631,634; ✻ Malaybalay. Mountainous and plateau region with no coastline; highest point is in Katanglad Mts., in W cen. part, ab. 9000 ft. (2745 m.); in N many short streams flowing N and NW to Gingoog and Macajalar bays; largest stream is the Pulangi in E and S forming the upper course of the Mindanao. Has fertile soil esp. suitable for grazing; important agriculturally, chief crops coffee, pineapples, and other fruit. Inhabitants include Bukidnons, with some Manobos and Moros. See table at PHILIPPINES.

Bu·kit Mer·ta·jam \ˈbü-kit-mer-ˈtä-jäm\. Town, Penang state, West Malaysia, on the island of Penang; pop. (1980p) 161,885.

Bu·kit·ting·gi \ˌbü-kit-ˈtiŋ-gē\; *formerly* **Fort de Kock** \ˌfōrt-də-ˈkȯk\. Inland town, W Sumatra, Indonesia, ab. 50 mi. (80 km.) N of Padang, in Padang Highlands; pop. (1990c) 83,811; important commercial center; original fortifications erected by Dutch 1825.

Bukn Fjord. See BOKN FJORD.

Bu·ko·ba \bü-ˈkō-bä\. Town, ✻ of Kagera region, Tanzania, on W shore of Lake Victoria.

Bu·ko·vi·na *or Rom.* **Bu·co·vi·na** \ˌbü-kō-ˈvē-nä\. Region, E cen. Europe; 3396 sq. mi. (8796 sq. km.). Occupies foothills of E Carpathian Mts., thickly wooded and source of Dniester, Prut, and Siret rivers flowing to Black Sea.

History: Inhabited by Ruthenians and Moldavians; part of principality of Moldavia (*q.v.*); occupied by Austria 1774 and formally ceded by Turkey 1777; ruled by Austria as part of Galicia until 1849 when Bukovina was made separate crown land; became independent for a brief time at collapse of Austria-Hungary 1918 and constituted a province of Romania 1918–40; seized by U.S.S.R. 1940 and incorp. with Bessarabia Aug. 1940 in Moldavian S.S.R.; held by German and Romanian forces 1941–45; N half became part of Ukrainian S.S.R. 1945 (chief town Chernivitsi), remaining in

Ukraine after independence 1991, and S half, incl. towns Rădăuţi and Siret, remained in Romania.

Būl, Kūh–e– \ˌkü-hē-ˈbül\. Mountain in SW cen. Iran, 175 mi. (282 km.) NE of Būshehr; 13,009 ft. (3965 m.).

Bu·la·can \ˌbü-lä-ˈkän\. **1.** Province, cen. Luzon, Philippines; 1032 sq. mi. (2673 sq. km.); pop. (1980c) 1,096,046; ✻ Malolos. W part is in cen. plain of Luzon; hills and mountains in the E, highest Mt. Oryod in SE 3838 ft. (1170 m.). Watered by the Angat, a large tributary of the Pampanga; delta of the latter covers a large area of swampy land in SW along shore of Manila Bay. See table at PHILIPPINES.

History: Had large towns before coming of the Spanish; one of earliest provinces created by them 1578; was center of opposition to British 1762–63; increased in population and trade during following century; scene of several notable events of revolution of 1897 (see BIACNABATO and MALOLOS); civil government estab. by Americans 1901. In WWII taken by Japanese 1942 but recovered 1945.

2. Municipality, SW Bulacan prov., Philippines, 7 mi. (11 km.) SE of Malolos; pop. (1980c) 34,920; former ✻ of the province.

Bulak. See BULAQ.

Bulama. See BOLAMA.

Bu·lan \ˈbü-ˌlän\. Municipality, SW Sorsogon prov., Luzon, Philippines; pop. (1980c) 60,911; port on Ticao Pass 22 mi. (35 km.) SSW of the municipality of Sorsogon.

Bu·land·shahr \ˌbü-ˈlənd-ˌshär\. Town, Uttar Pradesh, N India, on Kali Nadi River 45 mi. (72 km.) SE of Delhi; pop. (1991p) 126,737; taken over by British in 1805.

Bu·laq *also* **Bu·lak** \bü-ˈläk\. Port of Cairo, Egypt, located on the Nile; orig. site of museum (now in Cairo) founded c. 1860 by the Egyptian Ottoman ruler at the persuasion of the French archaeologist Auguste Mariette.

Bu·lat, Cape \bü-ˈlät\; *formerly* **Cape Ro·ma·nia** \rō-ˈmān-ē-ə, -ˈmān-yə\. Cape on SE extremity of the Malay Penin., Johor state, Malaysia, at E end of Singapore Strait.

Bu·la·wa·yo \ˌbü-lä-ˈwä-yō\ *also* **Bu·lu·wa·yo** \ˌbü-lü-\. Town, SW Zimbabwe, 240 mi. (386 km.) SW of Harare; textiles, radios, vehicle tires; chief town of Matabeleland; university; museum; important railroad center and trade headquarters for vast grazing area; gold and coal found in region; founded by British 1893.

Bul·dir \bu̇l-ˈdir\. Rocky islet in W Aleutian Is., Alaska, in channel bet. Kiska on E and Near Is. on W.

Buldur. See BURDUR.

Bu·le·leng *or Du.* **Boe·le·leng** \ˈbü-lə-ˌleŋ\. Seaport town, N coast of Bali I., Lesser Sunda Is., Indonesia; port of Singaraja.

Bul·gar Dağ·la·rı \bu̇l-ˈgär-ˌdä-lä-ˈrə\. Range in the Taurus Mts., S Turkey in Asia; highest peak Ardost 11,444 ft. (3488 m.). See CILICIAN GATES.

Bul·gar·ia \ˌbəl-ˈgar-ē-ə, bu̇l-\; *officially* **Republic of Bulgaria** *or Bulg.* **Re·pub·li·ka Bŭl·ga·ri·ya** \rā-ˈpu̇-bli-kä-bu̇l-ˈgär-ē-yä\. Republic, SE Europe, bounded on N by Romania, on E by Black Sea, on SE by Turkey, on S by Greece, and on W by Yugoslavia and Rep. of Macedonia; 42,823 sq. mi. (110,912 sq. km.); pop. (1993e) 8,466,000; ✻ Sofia.

Physical features: Crossed in cen. part by Balkan Mts. (locally, the Stara Planina) 3500 to 7793 ft. (1067 to 2375 m.); in SW and S by Rhodope Range; highest point Musala 9596 ft. (2925 m.); surface varied in plateau, plain, and river valley regions.

Chief rivers: Maritsa, flowing E into Turkey, and its tributary the Tundzha; Struma and Mesta in SW flowing S into Greece; Danube, forming most of N boundary with Romania.

Chief products: Wheat, corn, rye, tobacco, vegetables, fruits, oats, cotton; sheep, hogs; coal, copper, zinc, lead, iron,

manganese; manufacturing: metallurgical and chemical industries; cement, machinery, textiles.

Chief towns: Sofia, Plovdiv, Varna, Burgas, Ruse, Stara Zagora, Pleven.

Political divisions: Divided into the following nine regions (for pronunciation of their names, see their individual entries):

NAME	AREA (sq. mi.)	AREA (sq. km.)	POP. (1992e)	CAPITAL
Burgas	5,659	14,657	878,000	Burgas
Khaskovo	5,364	13,893	1,054,000	Khaskovo
Lovech	5,849	15,149	1,048,000	Lovech
Montana	4,095	10,606	653,000	Montana
Plovdiv	5,262	13,628	1,290,000	Plovdiv
Ruse	4,186	10,842	837,000	Ruse
Sofia (city commune)	506	1,310	1,220,000	
Sofia	7,328	18,980	1,004,000	Sofia
Varna	4,606	11,930	991,000	Varna

History: For earlier history of Bulgarian territory, see MOESIA and THRACE. Invaded by Bulgars, a Ural-Altaic people who in 6th cent. A.D. lived bet. Don River and Caucasus Mts. and in 7th cent. settled in Bessarabia, crossed Danube, became Slavicized, and founded first organized Slavic power in Balkans; soon after baptism of King Boris 865, joined Greek Church; powerful under Simeon the Great (893–927) who introduced Byzantine culture; invaded by Russians and Byzantines 10th cent.; W part erected by Bulgarian Czar Samuel (976–1014) into new state but lost independence 1014; part of Byzantine Empire 1018–1185; under Asen family, built 2d Bulgarian empire 1185 to mid-14th cent.; part of Ottoman Empire from Turkish conquest 14th to 20th cents.; revived nationalism in 19th cent.; premature rising in 1876 caused "massacres" by Turks which made Bulgarian problem a European concern; at close of Russo-Turkish War (1877–78), an autonomous Bulgarian principality (incl. most of Macedonia) erected by Treaty of San Stefano; divided by Congress of Berlin which returned Macedonia to Turkey and set up autonomous Eastern Rumelia 1878; annexed Eastern Rumelia 1885 thereby invoking war with Serbia; under Prince Ferdinand, reconciled with Russia 1896; declared complete independence from Turkey 1908; took a leading part in First Balkan War and, because of increased territory, caused Second Balkan War (see BALKAN STATES); forced to cede Dobruja to Romania and most of Macedonia to Serbia, Greece, and Turkey 1913; entered WWI on side of Central Powers 1915; King Ferdinand abdicated to son Boris III 1918; by Treaty of Neuilly (see NEUILLY-SUR-SEINE) lost position on Aegean seaboard 1919; recovered S Dobruja from Romania 1940; signed Axis pact 1941; invaded by U.S.S.R. Sept. 1944; abolished monarchy and became a people's republic 1946; member of Warsaw Pact and UN; resumed diplomatic relations with U.S. 1959 (broken since 1950); participated with the Soviet Union in the occupation of Czechoslovakia 1968; tensions bet. nationalists and ethnic Turk population led to emigration of large number of Turks 1980s; with other E European countries in late 1980s suffered political unrest resulting in resignation of ruling Communist leader, Todur Zhivkov 1989; new constitution proclaiming a republic 1991.

Bul·har \ˈbu̇l-ˌhär\. See BULLAXAAR.

Bulk·ley \ˈbəl-klē\. River, W cen. British Columbia, Canada, E of Bulkley Mts.; flows N into Skeena River; ab. 130 mi. (210 km.) long.

Bulkley Mountains. Range of the Coast Mts., W cen. British Columbia, Canada, W of Babine Mts.

Bul·lards Bar Dam *and* **Bullards Bar Reservoir.** See *New Bullards Bar Dam* at UNITED STATES, *Dams and Reservoirs.*

Bul·la·xaar \ˌbu̇l-lə-ˈk̲är\ *or* **Bul·har** \bu̇l-ˈhär\. Seaport town, N Somalia, on Gulf of Aden 40 mi. (64 km.) W of Berbera.

Bul·le·court \bül-ˈku̇(ə)r\. Village, Pas-de-Calais dept., N France, 9 mi. (14 km.) SE of Arras; severe fighting during WWI 1917–18.

Bul·ler \ˈbu̇-lər\. River, N South I., New Zealand; flows W to Tasman Sea; 110 mi. (177 km.) long.

Buller, Mount. Mountain at W end of Great Dividing Range, E Victoria, Australia; 5911 ft. (1802 m.).

Bul·lers of Buch·an \ˈbu̇-lərz ... ˈbə-k̲ən\. Basin in rocky coast of Buchan region, NE Grampian region, Scotland, 6 mi. (10 km.) S of Peterhead; ab. 200 ft. (61 m.) deep and 50 ft. (15 m.) wide.

Bull·frog \ˈbu̇l-ˌfrȯg, -ˌfräg\. Unpopulated county, S Nevada; 12 sq. mi. (31 sq. mi.); carved out of Nye co. 1987 to discourage placement of a federal nuclear waste dump there.

Bull·head City \ˈbu̇l-ˌhed\. City, Mohave co., NW Arizona, on Colorado River; pop. (1990c) 21,951.

Bull Hill \ˈbu̇l\. Peak, Lake co., cen. Colorado; 13,773 ft. (4198 m.).

Bull Island *or* **Bulls Island.** See BULLS BAY.

Bul·litt \ˈbu̇-lit\. County in cen. Kentucky. See table at KENTUCKY.

Bul·loch \ˈbu̇-lək\. County in E Georgia. See table at GEORGIA.

Bul·lock \ˈbu̇-lək\. County in SE Alabama. See table at ALABAMA.

Bull Point. Cape on extreme NW point of Devon, SW England, S of entrance to Bristol Channel; lighthouse.

Bull Run. Stream, NE Virginia; runs SE and forms boundary bet. Fairfax and Prince William cos., E of Manassas, and empties into Occoquan Creek; scene of Civil War battles: (1) July 21, 1861 in which Union leader Gen. Irvin McDowell was defeated by Confederate Gens. Joseph E. Johnston and Pierre Beauregard; and (2) Aug. 29–30, 1862 in which Gen. Robert E. Lee defeated Union forces under Gen. John Pope. Both battles called Manassas by Confederates.

Bulls Bay \ˈbu̇lz\. Inlet of Atlantic Ocean on NE coast of Charleston co., SE South Carolina; enclosed on SW by **Bull Island** *or* **Bulls Island.**

Bu·lo·lo \bü-ˈlō-lō\. **1.** River, an upper tributary of the Markham River, forming **Bulolo Valley,** part of the Morobe goldfields, SE New Guinea I., Papua New Guinea, in the mountains W of Huon Gulf. **2.** Mining town on the Bulolo River.

Bulsar. See VALSAD.

Bulshaia. See MCKINLEY, MOUNT.

Bu·lu·an \bü-ˈlü-ˌän\. Municipality, E cen. Sultan Kudarat prov., Mindanao, Philippines, near **Lake Buluan** (24 sq. mi. or 62 sq. km.); pop. (1980c) 38,313.

Bu·lu·san \bü-ˈlü-ˌsän\. Volcano, S cen. Sorsogon prov., Luzon, Philippines; 5118 ft. (1560 m.); 5 mi. (8 km.) inland; visible 60 mi. (97 km.) at sea and a landmark for ships in San Bernardino Strait; last eruption 1852.

Buluwayo. See BULAWAYO.

Bum·ba \ˈbüm-bä\. Town, Équateur prov., Zaire, on Congo River at its N point; airport.

Bum·bah \ˈbu̇m-bə\ *or* **Bun·bah** \ˈbu̇n-\. Town, NE Libya, on the **Gulf of Bumbah** *or* **Gulf of Bunbah.**

Bu·na \ˈbü-nä\. Village on Holnicote Bay, SE coast of New Guinea I., Papua New Guinea; formerly port for shipment of gold from inland goldfields; captured by Japanese July 1942; taken by Allies after severe fighting Jan. 1943.

Bun·bury \ˈbən-bər-ē\. Port, SW Western Australia, Australia, on Geographe Bay 90 mi. (145 km.) S of Perth; pop. (1981c) 21,749.

Bun·combe \ˈbəŋ-kəm\. County in W North Carolina. See table at NORTH CAROLINA.

Bun·da·berg \ˈbən-də-ˌbərg\. Seaport town, E Queensland, Australia, on Burnett River, 200 mi. (322 km.) N of Brisbane; pop. (1981c) 30,937.

Bün·de \ˈbu̵en-də\. City, North Rhine-Westphalia, Germany, 52 mi. (84 km.) WSW of Hannover; pop. (1980c) 40,056; settled early 18th cent.; headquarters of Allied Control Commission for Germany in 1945.

Bun·del·khand \ˈbu̇n-dəl-ˌkənd\. Formerly, one of the chief agency divisions, in E part of Central India Agency, now part of Madhya Pradesh, N cen. India; 10,081 sq. mi. (26,110 sq. km.); ✻ Nowgong (in Chhatarpur). Consisted of several states (most important Orchha) and estates. An uneven country of hills and plains; became subject c. 1500 to Delhi and to Marathas; rights transferred to the British by treaty 1817; became part of Madhya Pradesh 1956.

Bun·di \ˈbün-dē\. **1.** Former Indian state in Eastern Rajputana States; now part of Rajasthan, NW India; 2205 sq. mi. (5711 sq. km.); founded about mid-14th cent., it came under British protection by treaty in 1818. In 1948 became a part of Rajasthan.
2. Town, its ✻, 95 mi. (153 km.) SE of Ajmer; pop. (1991p) 65,016.

Bun·go Strait *also* **Bungo Channel** \ˈbüŋ-gō\; *formerly* **Ha·ya·sui Strait** \hä-ˈyä-sü-wē\. Channel, NE of Kyūshū, Japan, separating it from Shikoku; 20 to 25 mi. (32 to 40 km.) wide.

Bunguran Selatan Islands. See NATUNA ISLANDS.

Bun·ker Hill \ˈbəŋ-kər\. Height in Charlestown, Boston, Massachusetts; 107 ft. (33 m.) high; during early part of American Revolution, battle June 17, 1775 on adjacent **Breed's Hill** \ˈbrēdz\, where Bunker Hill Monument now stands.

Bunker Hill Village. City, Harris co., SE Texas, 11 mi. (18 km.) W of Houston; pop. (1990c) 3391.

Bun·kie \ˈbəŋ-kē\. Town, Avoyelles parish, cen. Louisiana, 28 mi. (45 km.) SSE of Alexandria; pop. (1990c) 5044; oil and natural gas.

Bunnabeola, Twelve Pins of. See BENNEBEOLA, TWELVE BENS OF.

Bun·nell \bə-ˈnel\. City, ⊗ of Flagler co., NE Florida; pop. (1990c) 1873.

Bunzelwitz. See BOLESŁAWICE.

Bunzlau. See BOLESŁAWIEC.

Bu·or·kha·ya \ˌbü-ȯr-ˈk̲ī-ə\ *or* **Bor·kha·ya** \bȯr-\. Cape, N Sakha Rep., Russia in Asia, extending into Laptev Sea at 133°20′E, just E of the Lena delta, and marking NE point of **Buorkhaya Gulf.**

Buq·buq \ˈbu̇k-bu̇k\. Coastal village, NW Egypt, E of Salūm and W of Sīdī Barrānī; fighting in WWII North African campaigns.

Buraida. See BURAYDAH.

Bu·ra·no \bü-ˈrä-nō\. Island and village in the Lagoon of Venice, NE Italy, ab. 5 mi. (8 km.) NE of Venice; part of Venice commune; noted for lacemaking.

Bu·ra·uen \bü-ˈrä-wān\. Municipality, cen. Leyte I., Philippines, W of Dulag and 21 mi. (34 km.) SW of Tacloban; pop. (1980c) 48,053; at foot of cen. mountain range and near sulfur deposits. Captured by Americans 1944 after severe fighting.

Bu·ray·dah *also* **Buraida** \bu̇-ˈrī-də, -ˈrā\. Town, N cen. Nejd, Saudi Arabia; commercial center; extensive palm groves.

Bur·bank \ˈbər-ˌbaŋk\. **1.** City, Los Angeles co., SW California, N of the city of Los Angeles; pop. (1990c) 93,643; television studios; Woodbury Univ. (1884).
2. City, Cook co., Illinois, just W of Chicago; pop. (1990c) 27,600.

Bur·de·kin \ˈbər-di-kən\. River, E Queensland, Australia; flows SE from Eastern Highlands and after junction with Belyando flows N and E to Pacific Ocean; 425 mi. (684 km.) long.

Burdigala. See BORDEAUX.

Bur·dur \bu̇r-ˈdu̇r\ *or* **Bul·dur** \bu̇l-ˈdu̇r\. **1.** Province of Turkey in Asia. See table at TURKEY.
2. Town, its ✻, 2 mi. (3 km.) SE of Lake Burdur, in hills (alt. 3150 ft. or 960 m.) and on railroad line to Antalya; pop. (1990p) 56,095.

Burdur, Lake *or Turk.* **Burdur Gö·lü** \gœ-ˈlue\. Lake in SW Turkey in Asia, SW of Eğridir Lake.

Burdwan. See BARDDHAMAN.

Bure. See BROADS, THE.

Bu·reau \ˈbyu̇r-ō\. County in N Illinois. See table at ILLINOIS.

Bu·re·ya \bü-ri-ˈyä\. River, a N tributary of the Amur in S Khabarovsk Kray, SE Russia in Asia; flows SW to the Amur below Blagoveshchensk; 445 mi. (716 km.) long.

Būr Fu'ād. See PORT FUAD.

Burg \ˈbu̇rk\. **1.** *also* **Burg bei Mag·de·burg** \bī-ˈmäk-də-ˌbu̇rk\. City, NE cen. Germany, on Elbe-Havel Canal near Elbe River 12 mi. (19 km.) NE of Magdeburg.
2. Chief town on Fehmarn I. See FEHMARN.

Bur·gas \bu̇r-ˈgäs\. **1.** Region of E Bulgaria. See table at BULGARIA.
2. Seaport, its ✻, on the Gulf of Burgas; pop. (1991e) 204,915; engineering works, fish canneries and other food-processing industries, oil refinery; one of Bulgaria's major ports.

Bur·gaski Za·liv \bür-ˈgä-skē-ˈzä-liv\ *or Eng.* **Burgaski Bay** *also* **Bur·gas, Gulf of** \bür-ˈgäs\. Inlet of the Black Sea on the cen. part of the coast of Bulgaria.

Bur Ga·vo \bür-ˈgä-vō\ *or* **Buur Gaa·bo** \bür-ˈgä-bō\; *formerly* **Port Durn·ford** \ˈdərn-fərd\. Seaport, S Somalia; in Jubaland, formerly part of Kenya.

Bur·gaw \ˈbər-ˌgä\. Town, ⊗ of Pender co., SE North Carolina; pop. (1990c) 1807.

Burg·dorf \ˈbu̇rk-ˌdȯrf\. Commune, Bern canton, Switzerland, on Emme River ab. 11 mi. (18 km.) NE of the city of Bern; pop. (1980c) 15,379; medieval castle; Swiss educational reformer Johann Pestalozzi principal of a school here 1799–1804.

Bur·gen·land \ˈbu̇r-gən-ˌlänt, ˈbər-gən-ˌland\. State, E Austria, on Hungarian border in foothills of the Alps and on edge of the Hungarian plain; ✻ Eisenstadt; corn, tobacco; sugar processing, textiles; includes N two thirds of Neusiedler Lake; before 1919 part of Hungary; by treaties of St.-Germain and Grand Trianon entire region was to be transferred to Austria but on Hungary's objection, a plebiscite was held Dec. 1921 and all but Sopron transferred Feb. 1922; as part of German Ostmark, absorbed by Styria. After WWII reconstituted as an Austrian state. See table at AUSTRIA.

Bur·gers·dorp \ˈbər-gərz-ˌdȯrp\. Town, Eastern Cape prov., S Rep. of South Africa, 70 mi. (113 km.) NNW of Queenstown; resort.

Bur·gess Hill \ˈbər-jəs\. Town, West Sussex, S England; pop. (1981p) 23,542.

Bürg·len \ˈbuer-glən\. Village, Uri canton, Switzerland, near SE tip of Lake of Lucerne SE of Altdorf; pop. (1980c) 3456; supposed birthplace of legendary hero William Tell.

Bur·gos \ˈbür-ˌgōs\. **1.** Province of N Spain. See table at SPAIN.
2. City, its ✻, 132 mi. (212 km.) N of Madrid; pop. (1991c) 160,278; tourism; noted for its old buildings, among them castle of counts of Castile and esp. the cathedral (1221), one of most noted examples of Gothic architecture in Europe; home and burial place of the military hero, El Cid (Rodrigo Díaz de Vivar). Founded 884; made ✻ of Old Castile; to 1560 a royal residence and ✻ of kingdom of León and Castile; seat of Falangist government 1936 led by Gen. Francisco Franco.

Bur·gun·dy \ˈbər-gən-dē\ *or Fr.* **Bour·gogne** \bür-ˈgȯnʸ, -ˈgȯ-nyə\. Region of varying limits in E Gaul and pre-Revolutionary France. Name was orig. applied to a kingdom in Rhone Valley and W Switzerland (see GENEVA 2) founded by a Germanic people, the Burgundians, who fled from Germany in early 5th cent. It was conquered by the Merovingians c. 534 and incorp. into the Frankish empire; in division of Carolingian empire by the Treaty of Verdun 843, included in Middle Kingdom (see LORRAINE) of Holy Roman Emperor Lothair I; region later divided into the kingdoms of Cisjurane (Lower) Burgundy or Provence, founded 879, and Transjurane (Upper) Burgundy, founded 888, which united 933 to form the kingdom of Burgundy or Arles (*q.v.*). After absorption of Arles by the Holy Roman Empire 1032, the name was retained in the Free County of Burgundy or Franche-Comté (*q.v.*) and esp. in the duchy of Burgundy which was formed in 9th cent. from lands in NW part of original kingdom S of 48th parallel chiefly bet. Saône and Loire rivers. On death of Duke Philippe I de Rouvre 1361, the duchy escheated to

French crown; given as appanage by King John II to his 4th son, Philip the Bold; passed in direct succession to John the Fearless, Philip the Good, and Charles the Bold, before whose death in 1477, the Burgundian house had controlled Nivernais, Franche-Comté, Lorraine (*qq.v.*), and Low Countries; seized from Charles's daughter, Duchess Mary of Burgundy, by King Louis XI and annexed to French crown; a province until the Revolution.

Bur·han·pur \bər-ˈhän-ˌpu̇r\. Town, Madhya Pradesh, cen. India, on the Tapti River S of Khandwa and 185 mi. (298 km.) W of Nagpur; pop. (1991p) 172,809; historically known for its brocades, gold and silver embroideries, flowered silks, and gold wire; a walled city of the Moguls, founded c. 1400, and for two centuries ✻ of independent Muslim princes; later the ✻ of the Deccan under the Moguls; captured 1803 by British but not retained; ceded to British 1861.

Bu·rias \ˈbür-ˌyäs\. Island just SE of Luzon, Philippines; 43 mi. (69 km.) long; 164 sq. mi. (425 sq. km.); forms part of Masbate prov. Long narrow mountainous island, N of Masbate and separated from Luzon on NE by Burias Pass; on NE border of Sibuyan Sea.

Burias Pass. Channel bet. E Burias I. and the mainland of SE Luzon, Philippines; ab. 12 mi. (19 km.) wide.

Buriat A.S.S.R. See BURYATIA.

Bu·ri·ca, Point \bü-ˈrē-kä\. Cape on S extremity of Costa Rica, on boundary with Panama, extending S into Pacific Ocean.

Bu·rin \ˈbyu̇r-in\. Town, S Newfoundland, Canada, on W shore of Placentia Bay at its mouth on E coast of **Burin Peninsula;** pop. (1991c) 2940; has landlocked harbor; fisheries.

Bu·ri·ram \ˌbü-rē-ˈräm\ *also* **Pu·ri·ram·ya** \ˌbü-rē-ˈräm —*sic*\. **1.** Province, SE Thailand; 4159 sq. mi. (10,772 sq. km.); pop. (1991e) 1,458,873.

2. Town, its ✻; pop. (1991e) 29,259.

Bur·ka·tów \bu̇r-ˈkä-tüf\ *or Ger.* **Bur·kers·dorf** \ˈbu̇r-kərz-ˌdȯrf\. Village, S Wrocław prov., SW Poland; formerly in Silesia, Germany; battle 1762 in which Prussian King Frederick the Great defeated the Austrians under Leopold von Daun during Seven Years' War.

Burk·bur·nett \ˌbərk-bər-ˈnet\. City, Wichita co., N Texas, near Red River 15 mi. (24 km.) N of Wichita Falls; pop. (1990c) 10,145.

Burke \ˈbərk\. **1.** Name of counties in three states of the U.S. See tables at GEORGIA, NORTH CAROLINA, NORTH DAKOTA.

2. City, ⊗ of Gregory co., S South Dakota; pop. (1990c) 756.

3. Town, Dane co., S Wisconsin; pop. (1990c) 3004.

Burke Channel. Inlet of Pacific Ocean, W British Columbia, Canada; ab. 52°N; ab. 45 mi. (72 km.) long.

Burke Mountain. Peak on boundary bet. Caledonia and Essex cos., NE Vermont; 3267 ft. (996 m.).

Burkersdorf. See BURKATÓW.

Burkes·ville \ˈbərks-ˌvil, -vəl\. City, ⊗ of Cumberland co., S Kentucky; pop. (1990c) 1815.

Bur·kett, Mount \ˈbər-kit\. Mountain, SE Alaska, near Alaska-British Columbia boundary, 30 mi. (48 km.) N of Wrangell; ab. 9730 ft. (2965 m.).

Bur·ki·na Fa·so \bu̇r-ˈkē-nə-ˈfä-sō, ˈfa-sō\; *formerly* **Upper Vol·ta** \ˈvōl-tə, ˈväl-\ *also* **Vol·ta·ic Republic** \vōl-ˈtā-ik, väl-\. Republic, W Africa, bounded on W and N by Mali, on E by Niger, on SE by Benin, and on S by Togo, Ghana, and Ivory Coast; 105,869 sq. mi. (274,201 sq. km.); pop. (1993e) 9,780,000; ✻ Ouagadougou.

Physical features: Plateau region; characterized by savanna, grassy in N, sparsley forested in S.

Chief products: Sorghum, corn, rice, cotton, peanuts, millet; livestock raising.

Chief settlements: Ouagadougou, Bobo-Dioulasso.

History: Inhabited and ruled for several centuries by Mossi, among others; French protectorate established over region 1895–97; S boundary demarcated through Anglo-French agreement 1898; part of Upper Senegal-Niger colony until 1919 (see *History* at MALI), when it became a separate colony; partitioned bet. other French possessions 1932; reconstituted an overseas territory within the French Union 1947; became an autonomous republic within the French

Community 1958; achieved total independence 1960; adopted new constitution 1970; border conflict with Mali 1985; experienced several coups throughout 1980s; military rule ended, new constitution adopted 1991.

Bur·leigh \ˈbər-lē\. County in S cen. North Dakota. See table at NORTH DAKOTA.

Bur·le·son \ˈbər-lə-sən\. **1.** County in E cen. Texas. See table at TEXAS.

2. City, Johnson and Tarrant cos., N Texas, 14 mi. (23 km.) S of Fort Worth; pop. (1990c) 16,113.

Bur·ley \ˈbər-lē\. City, ⊗ of Cassia co., S Idaho, on Snake River 38 mi. (61 km.) E of Twin Falls; pop. (1990c) 8702.

Bur·lin·game \ˈbər-liŋ-ˌgām\. Residential city, San Mateo co., W California, on W shore of San Francisco Bay; pop. (1990c) 26,801.

Bur·ling·ton \ˈbər-liŋ-tən\. **1.** County in S cen. New Jersey. See table at NEW JERSEY.

2. City, ⊗ of Kit Carson co., E Colorado; pop. (1990c) 2941.

3. Town, W Hartford co., N Connecticut; pop. (1990c) 7026; trout hatchery; settled 1780; incorp. 1806.

4. City, ⊗ of Des Moines co., SE Iowa, on Mississippi River; pop. (1990c) 27,208; settled c. 1832 on the site of an Indian village; incorp. as town 1836; temporary seat of government of Iowa Terr. 1838.

5. City, ⊗ of Coffey co., E Kansas, 28 mi. (45 km.) SE of Emporia; pop. (1990c) 2735; oil field nearby.

\ə\ abut \ə\ matches \ᵊ\ kitten, Fr table \ər\ further \a\ ash \ā\ ace
\ä\ cot, cart \å\ Fr bac \au̇\ out \b\ Span Avila \ch\ chin \e\ bet \ē\ easy
\g\ go \i\ hit \ī\ ice \j\ job \k\ Ger ich, Buch \ⁿ\ Fr vin
\ŋ\ sing \ō\ go \ȯ\ all \ȯ\ law \œ\ Fr bœuf \œ̄\ Fr feu \ȯi\ boy
\th\ thin \th\ this \ü\ loot \u̇\ foot \u̇\ Ger füllen \ue\ Fr rue
\y\ yet \ʸ\ Fr digne \ˈdēnʸ\, nuit \ˈnwʸē\ \yü\ few \yu̇\ fury \zh\ vision

6. Unincorporated settlement, ⊗ of Boone co., N Kentucky; pop. (1990c) 6070.
7. Town, Middlesex co., NE Massachusetts, 11 mi. (18 km.) SSE of Lowell; pop. (1990c) 23,302.
8. City, Burlington co., S cen. New Jersey, on Delaware River 11 mi. (18 km.) SSW of Trenton; pop. (1990c) 9835; shipping point. Settled by Quakers 1677; became ✱ of West Jersey 1681; alternated with Perth Amboy (*q.v.*) as provincial ✱ after union of East and West Jersey in 1702; invaded by Hessians 1776; bombarded by British 1778; many buildings from colonial period; birthplace of novelist James Fenimore Cooper 1789.
9. City, Alamance co., N cen. North Carolina, 20 mi. (32 km.) E of Greensboro; pop. (1990c) 39,498; textiles.
10. City and port of entry, ⊗ of Chittenden co., NW Vermont, on Lake Champlain 34 mi. (55 km.) WNW of Montpelier; pop. (1990c) 39,127; largest city in the state; center for education and medical services; shipping point; manufactures lumber and wooden products, electronic equipment, structural steel, business machines, processed foods; summer and winter resort; grave of Revolutionary soldier Ethan Allen. Univ. of Vermont (1791), Champlain Coll. (1878), Trinity Coll. (1925), Burlington Coll. (1972); chartered by province of New Hampshire 1763; settled 1773; organized 1797; figured as military center and base for naval activity on Lake Champlain in War of 1812; incorp. 1865.
11. City, Skagit co., NW Washington, 20 mi. (32 km.) S of Bellingham; pop. (1990c) 4349.
12. City, Racine co., SE Wisconsin, 24 mi. (39 km.) W of the city of Racine; pop. (1990c) 8855.
13. Town, Halton munic. region, SE Ontario, Canada, on Lake Ontario 7 mi. (4 km.) NE of Hamilton; pop. (1991c) 129,575; chemicals, lumber.

Burma. See MYANMAR.

Burma Road. Former highway, SE Asia, from Lashio (at railhead from Mandalay), E Burma (Myanmar), NE to Kunming in Yunnan, China; 681 mi. (1096 km.) long; crossed Burma-China border near Namhkam, Burma, and Wandingzhen (lowest point on road 3200 ft. or 975 m.), China; then proceeded generally E across Salween and Mekong river valleys through Baoshan and Tali to Kunming; alt. in Salween-Mekong region 6000 to 8500 ft. (1829 to 2591 m.). Extension (often considered a part of the Burma Road) E from Kunming to Guinyang in Guizhou, then N through Zunyi to Chongqing, ab. 700 mi. (1125 km.) by road. Total length, Chongqing to Yangon (in Burma by rail from Lashio through Hsipaw, Maymyo, and Mandalay), ab. 2100 mi. (3380 km.). In early part of WWII a vital transportation connecting link (opened 1938) for supplies to Chinese government; lower part in Burma and Yunnan seized by Japanese 1942. Reopened 1945 by completion of Stilwell Road (*q.v.*), earlier Ledo Road (see LEDO), connecting with India through Namhkam, Bhamo, and Myitkyina in Burma. Part in India and Burma abandoned after WWII; highway now in disrepair.

Bur·na·by \ˈbər-nə-bē\. Municipality, SW British Columbia, Canada; an E suburb of Vancouver; pop. (1991c) 158,858.

Bur·net \ˈbər-nət\. **1.** County in cen. Texas. See table at TEXAS.
2. City and resort, its ⊗, 43 mi. (69 km.) NNW of Austin; pop. (1990c) 3423.

Bur·nett \bər-ˈnet\. **1.** County in NW Wisconsin. See table at WISCONSIN.
2. River, SE Queensland, NE Australia; flows NE past Bundaberg and into Hervey Bay; 250 mi. (402 km.) long.

Burn·ham \ˈbər-nəm\. Village, Cook co., NE Illinois, on Indiana border, just S of Chicago; pop. (1990c) 3916.

Burnham–on–Sea. Resort town, Somerset, SW England, on Bristol Channel 24 mi. (39 km.) SW of Bristol; pop. (1981p) 14,920.

Bur·nie \ˈbər-nē\. Town on N coast of Tasmania, Australia, 75 mi. (121 km.) WNW of Launceston; pop. (1991c) 20,505.

Burn·ley \ˈbərn-lē\. Town, Lancashire, NW England, at confluence of Burn and Calder rivers 22 mi. (35 km.) N of Manchester; pop. (1991p) 89,000; engineering.

Burns \ˈbərnz\. City, ⊗ of Harney co., SE Oregon, 20 mi. (32 km.) N of Malheur Lake; pop. (1990c) 2913; center of old cattle empire.

Burns·ville \ˈbərnz-ˌvil\. **1.** City, SE Minnesota, S of Minneapolis; pop. (1990c) 51,288.
2. Town, ⊗ of Yancey co., W North Carolina; pop. (1990c) 1482.

Burnt·is·land \bərnt-ˈī-lənd\. Seaport burgh, Fife region, E Scotland, on the Firth of Forth opposite Edinburgh; pop. (1981p) 5875; fisheries.

Burnt Mountain \ˈbərnt\. Peak in the Sierra Nevada, E Fresno co., S cen. California; 10,602 ft. (3232 m.).

Bur·ra \ˈbər-ə\ *also* **Koo·rin·ga** \kü-ˈriŋ-gə\. Town, South Australia, Australia, ab. 80 mi. (130 km.) NE of Adelaide; pop. (1991c) 1191; nearby copper mines, of rich yield 1847–77, now closed.

Bur·rard Inlet \bə-ˈrärd\. Inlet of the Strait of Georgia, extending E into British Columbia, Canada; 9 mi. (15 km.) long; the city of Vancouver is on S side at its mouth and Port Moody at its head. One of the best natural harbors on the Pacific coast of North America.

Bur·rel \bu̇-ˈrel\. Town, ✱ of Mat dist., N cen. Albania.

Bur·ria·na \bür-ˈyä-nä\. Commune, Castellón de la Plana prov., E Spain, 8 mi. (13 km.) S of the city of Castellón de la Plana; pop. (1991c) 25,671.

Bur·rill·ville \ˈbər-əl-ˌvil\. Town, Providence co., N Rhode Island, 22 mi. (35 km.) NW of the city of Providence; pop. (1990c) 16,230; administrative center Harrisville; was part of Providence until 1731, part of Glocester 1731–1806; now includes several small villages.

Bur·row Head \ˈbər-ō\. Cape on S coast of Scotland, bet. Luce Bay and Wigtown Bay.

Burr·wood \ˈbər-ˌwu̇d\. U.S. Engineers' station at mouth of W course of Mississippi River in the delta, Louisiana; near southernmost point in state.

Bur·ry Inlet \ˈbər-ē\. E arm of Carmarthen Bay, SW Wales, bet. Dyfed and West Glamorgan.

Burry Port. Town, Dyfed co., S Wales; pop. (1981p) 5951.

Bur·sa \ˈbu̇r-sä\; *formerly* **Bru·sa** *or* **Brus·sa** \ˈbrü-sä\. **1.** Province of Turkey in Asia. See table at TURKEY.
2. *anc.* **Pru·sa** \ˈprü-sə\. City, its ✱, ab. 13 mi. (21 km.) from SE shore of Sea of Marmara; pop. (1990c) 834,576; connected by rail with its port Mudanya; noted for its carpets and silks; center of agricultural area; 15th cent. mosques; museums; university. As ancient Prusa founded at foot of (Mysian) Mt. Olympus as seat of Bithynian kings; flourished under Roman and Byzantine emperors and became ✱ of the Ottomans 14th cent.; plundered by Turkic ruler Timur 1402.

Bursa. See BYRSA.

Būr Saʻīd. See PORT SAID.

Burs·lem \ˈbərz-ləm\. Former municipal borough, Staffordshire, W cen. England; became part of Stoke-on-Trent 1910; known for manufacture of pottery since 17th cent.; home of Josiah Wedgwood; Wedgwood Institute. See POTTERIES, THE.

Burt \ˈbərt\. County in E Nebraska. See table at NEBRASKA.

Būr Tawfīq. See PORT TAUFIQ.

Burt Lake. Lake in W Cheboygan co., N Michigan; resort area in state park.

Bur·ton \ˈbərt-ᵊn\. **1.** City, SE cen. Michigan, SE of Flint; pop. (1990c) 27,617.
2. Parish, ⊗ of Sunbury co., S cen. New Brunswick, Canada, on right bank of St. John River 18 mi. (29 km.) E of Fredericton; pop. (1991c) 3833.

Burton, Lake. Reservoir in Tallulah River, Rabun co., NE Georgia; outlet into Chattooga River.

Burton upon Trent *or* **Burton on Trent** \ˈtrent\. Town, Staffordshire, W cen. England, 26 mi. (42 km.) NNE of Birmingham; pop. (1981p) 47,930; breweries.

Bu·ru *or Du.* **Boe·roe** \ˈbü-rü\. Island of the W Moluccas, Indonesia, Malay Archipelago, W of Ceram, 3°24′S, 126°40′E; area 3400 sq. mi. (8806 sq. km.); chief villages Namlea and Kajeli, on E coast; 90 mi. (145 km.) long by 50 mi. (81 km.) wide; generally elevated, esp. in the NW (highest point Mt. Tomahu 7969 ft. or 2429 m.); hardwood forests. Taken over by the Dutch mid-17th cent.; used by Indonesian officials for prison camp following 1965 revolt; most prisoners freed by 1980.

Burujird. See BORŪJERD.

Bu·rul·lus, Lake \bə-'rə-ləs\. Coastal lake in Nile Delta just E of Rosetta mouth, N Egypt; Baltīm is at its E end.

Bu·run·di \bu̇-'rün-dē\; *formerly* **Urun·di** \u̇-'rün-dē\. Republic, E cen. Africa, on NE side of Lake Tanganyika, bounded on N by Rwanda, on E and S by Tanzania, and on W by Democratic Rep. of the Congo; 10,759 sq. mi. (27,866 sq. km.); pop. (1993e) 5,665,000; ✻ Bujumbura.

Chief product: Coffee; other products include tea, cotton, corn, sorghum, beans, and bananas; livestock; ab. 95 percent of labor force is engaged in agriculture.

History: Inhabited for several centuries primarily by Hutu and Tutsi; Tutsi were politically dominant though fewer in number; at turn of 20th cent. to German-controlled East Africa; following WWI to Belgium, becoming known with Ruanda as mandate of Ruanda-Urundi (*q.v.*); following WWII became UN trust territory; achieved independence 1962; abolished monarchy and republic proclaimed 1966; from 1960s to 1990s suffered many coups and violent ethnic clashes bet. Hutu and Tutsi.

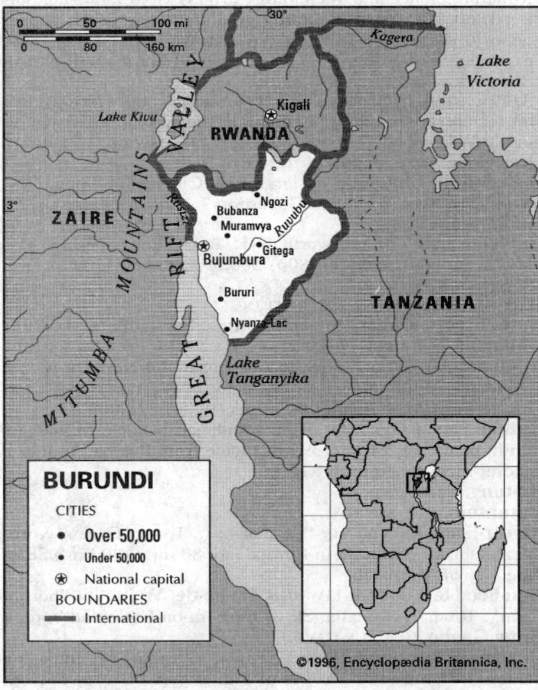

Bur·wash Landing \'bər-ˌwȯsh, -ˌwäsh\. Settlement on W shore of Kluane Lake, SW Yukon, Canada, on Alaska Highway; pop. (1991c) 77.

Bur·well \'bər-ˌwel, -wəl\. City, ⊗ of Garfield co., cen. Nebraska; pop. (1990c) 1278.

Burwell, Mount. Peak, S Park co., NW Wyoming; 11,738 ft. (3578 m.).

Bur·wood \'bər-ˌwu̇d\. Municipality, E New South Wales, SE Australia, W suburb of Sydney; pop. (1991c) 28,362.

Bury \'ber-ē\. Town, Greater Manchester, NW England, 10 mi. (16 km.) NNW of Manchester; pop. (1991p) 172,200; paper.

Bur·yat·ia \bu̇r-'yȧ-te-ə\ *or* **Bur·yat Republic** \bu̇r-'yät\; *formerly* **Buryat Autonomous Soviet Socialist Republic** *or* **Bur·iat Autonomous Soviet Socialist Republic** *or* **Bur·yat·ska·ya Autonomous Soviet Socialist Republic** \bu̇r-'yät-skȧ-yə\; *earlier* **Buryat–Mon·gol Autonomous Soviet Socialist Republic** \'mäŋ-gəl, -ˌgōl\. Autonomous republic, S Russia in Asia, E of Lake Baikal; 135,637 sq. mi. (351,300 sq. km.); pop. (1992e) 1,059,000; ✻ Ulan-Ude. Bounded on N and W by Irkutsk Oblast, on E and SE by Chita Oblast, on S by Mongolia; touches Tuva Rep. on SW. Includes practically all of Lake Baikal, Barguzin River, the lower courses of the Selenga and Khilok rivers, and the upper course of the Vitim. Main area consists of plateau and mountain ranges, the Yablonovyy Range along E border, the Barguzin and Baikal ranges near the lake. Products include wheat; fish, livestock; timber; molybdenum, wolfram; food products. Crossed in S by Trans-Siberian R.R. Buryats conquered by the Russians ab. 1700; for two centuries in W part of government known as Transbaikalia; with coming of railroad late 19th cent. began to gain some economic importance; organized as a region 1922, made an autonomous republic 1923; became republic within Russia 1991; subsequently became member of Russian Federation.

Bury Saint Ed·munds \'ber-ē-ˌsānt-'ed-məndz\. Town, Suffolk, E England, on the Lark 63 mi. (101 km.) NE of London; pop. (1981p) 28,914; burial place of King Edmund, known also as St. Edmund the Martyr (d. 870); ruins of a Benedictine abbey dating from c. 1020; received charter 1606; burial place of Mary of France (Mary Tudor) (d. 1533), sister of Henry VIII and wife of French King Louis XII.

Bur·zil Pass \bu̇r-'zēl\. Pass through the Himalayas, North-West Frontier prov., Pakistan, ab. 150 mi. (240 km.) NE of Islamabad; alt. 13,775 ft. (4199 m.).

Bu·sa, Cape \'bü-sä\ *or Gk.* **Ák·ra Voú·xa** \'ä-krä-'vük-sä\. Cape, NW point of Crete, Greece.

Busaco. See BUSSACO.

Bu·san·ga Swamp \bu̇-'säŋ-gä\. Large marsh area in W cen. Zambia.

Buṣayrā. See BOZRAH 2.

Bu·sen·to \bü-'sen-tō\. Small stream in Cosenza prov., S Italy, a tributary entering the Crati at Cosenza; Alaric, king of the Visigoths, traditionally believed to have been buried in its bed 410 A.D.

Bū·shehr \bü-'sher\. **1.** Province, SW Iran. See table at IRAN. **2.** *or* **Ban·dar–e–Bū·shehr** \'bän-där-e-bü-'sher\ *also* **Bushire** \bü-'shēr\. Seaport, Persian Gulf prov., SW Iran, on the Persian Gulf; pop. (1986c) 120,787; a port situated on a peninsula; has good anchorage and connections with many other ports; trade center for inland towns of Shīrāz, Eṣfahān, and Tehran; exports carpets, fruit, and cotton; founded c. 1736; important Gulf port esp. during 19th and early 20th cents.; suffered heavy damage during Iran-Iraq War 1980s.

Bush·ey \'bu̇-shē\. Town, Hertfordshire, SE England, 15 mi. (24 km.) WNW of London; pop. (1981p) 23,240.

Bush·man Land \'bu̇sh-mən\. Plateau region of W Northern Cape prov., W Rep. of South Africa, along the left bank of Orange River. **Great Bushman Land** lies chiefly to the W of 20°E long.; **Little Bushman Land** is lower on the course of the Orange; both are semidesert and rich in minerals.

Bush·nell \'bu̇sh-nəl\. **1.** City, ⊗ of Sumter co., cen. Florida Penin.; pop. (1990c) 1998. Museum and monument commemorate site of 1835 massacre by Seminoles, one of first battles beginning Second Seminole War.
2. City, McDonough co., W Illinois, 29 mi. (47 km.) S of Galesburg; pop. (1990c) 3288.

Bush·wick \'bu̇sh-wik\. Neighborhood of New York City, New York, in N Brooklyn borough, bordering on Queens. See *History* at BROOKLYN 3.

Bushy Run \'bu̇-shē\. Locality, Westmoreland co., SW Pennsylvania, near Greensburg; scene of battle 1763 in Pontiac's War in which Col. Henry Bouquet, on his way to the relief of Fort Pitt (Pittsburgh), defeated the Indians.

Bu·si·ra \bü-'sē-rä\. River, W cen. Democratic Rep. of the Congo; flows W and empties into Ruki River; 170 mi. (274 km.) long; chief headstream Tshuapa.

Bu·si·ris \byu̇-ˈsī-rəs\. City of ancient Egypt, in Nile Delta ab. 30 mi. (48 km.) SW of Tanis; seat of the worship of Osiris as god of nature.

Bus·ke·rud \ˈbu̇s-kə-ˌrü\. County of S Norway. See table at NORWAY.

Busk–Ivan·hoe Tunnel \ˈbəsk-ˈī-vən-ˌhō\. Automobile highway tunnel (orig. railroad tunnel) through Rocky Mts. in Colorado, near Leadville.

Bus·ra \bu̇s-rə, ˈbəs-\ *or* **Bos·ra** \ˈbȯs-rə, ˈbäs-\ *also* **Bos·o·ra** \ˈbȯ-sȯ-rə\ *also* **Boz·rah** \ˈbȯz-\. Ruins of town in the Hawrān, now a village in SW Syria on SW border of Jebel ed Druz; not the Bozrah of Edom (*Gen.* xxxvi. 33) or of Moab (*Jer.* xlviii. 24). In the time of the Maccabees (2d–1st cents. B.C.) a caravan junction point; known to Romans as **Bos·tra** \ˈbȯs-trə\ and became ✻ of Roman prov. of Arabia.

Busra *or* **Busrah.** See BASRA.

Bus·sa·co *or* **Bu·sa·co** \bü-ˈsä-kü\. Mountain on the boundary bet. Viseu and Coimbra districts, NE cen. Portugal; 1795 ft. (547 m.); site of a Peninsular War battle Sept. 27, 1810 in which British Gen. Arthur Wellesley, (later duke of Wellington) defeated French Emperor Napoléon's forces under Marshal André Masséna.

Bussahir. See BASHAHR.

Bus·sel·ton \ˈbə-səl-tən\. Town, SW Western Australia, Australia, on Geographe Bay; pop. (1993e) 15,628; resort.

Bus·se·to \büs-ˈsā-tō\. Town, Parma prov., Emilia-Romagna, N Italy; pop. (1981p) 7453; home of composer Giuseppe Verdi.

Bussora. See BASRA.

Bussorah. See BASRA.

Bus·sum \ˈbœ-səm\. Commune, North Holland prov., W Netherlands, SE of Amsterdam; pop. (1992e) 31,421; chocolate.

Bu·sto Ar·si·zio \ˈbü-stō-är-ˈsēt-sē-ˌō\. Commune, Varese prov., Lombardy, N Italy; pop. (1991p) 77,001; textiles; 16th cent. church designed by Donato Bramante.

Bu·suan·ga \bü-ˈswäŋ-gä\. Largest island of Calamian Group, Palawan prov., W Philippines; 344 sq. mi. (891 sq. km.); chief town Coron; on SW side of Mindoro Strait.

Busuitan. See MUSU-DAN.

Bu·ta \ˈbü-tä\. Town, W Haut-Zaïre administrative region, N Democratic Rep. of the Congo, 160 mi. (257 km.) N of Kisangani.

Bu·ta·re \bü-ˈtä-rā\. Town, S Rwanda; pop. (1991c) 28,645.

Bu·ta·ri·ta·ri. \bü-ˌtä-rē-ˈtä-rē\ *also* **Ma·kin** \ˈmä-kin, ˈmā-\. Island (atoll) at N end of Kiribati ab. 100 mi. (160 km.) N of Tarawa, W Pacific Ocean; 11 mi. (18 km.) at greatest width; lagoon and good anchorage; occupied by Japanese 1942; taken by U.S. troops 1943.

Bute \ˈbyüt\. **1.** Island in the Firth of Clyde off SW coast of Scotland; ab. 16 mi. (26 km.) long and bet. 2 and 5 mi. (3 and 8 km.) wide; 46 sq. mi. (119 sq. km.); chief town Rothesay.
2. *or* **Bute·shire** \-ˌshir, -shər\. Former county, SW Scotland, comprising Bute and Arran islands and the Cumbraes in the Firth of Clyde; ⊗ Rothesay on Bute.

Bute Inlet. Deep narrow fjord, SW British Columbia, Canada, 50°37′N, 124°53′W; ab. 40 mi. (64 km.) long; walls 4000 to 7000 ft. (1219 to 2134 m.) high.

Bu·thi·daung *or* **Bu·the·daung** \ˌbü-t͟hē-ˈdau̇ŋ\. Town, Rakhine state, Myanmar, on right bank of Mayu River near the coast 63 mi. (101 km.) NW of Sittwe; scene of fighting during WWII Japanese campaign against India.

Bu·thro·tum \byü-ˈthrō-təm\ *or Ital.* **Bu·trin·to** \bü-ˈtrēn-tō\. Ancient town of Epirus, NW Greece, on coast opp. N end of Corfu; has fair harbor. Modern town, **Bu·trint** \bü-ˈtrēnt\, is in Albania, on SW coast, and was overrun in Greek-Italian war of 1941 during WWII; has Greek and Roman ruins.

But·ler \ˈbət-lər\. **1.** Name of counties in eight states of the U.S. See tables at ALABAMA, IOWA, KANSAS, KENTUCKY, MISSOURI, NEBRASKA, OHIO, PENNSYLVANIA.
2. City, ⊗ of Choctaw co., W Alabama; pop. (1990c) 1872.
3. City, ⊗ of Taylor co., W cen. Georgia; pop. (1990c) 1673.
4. City, De Kalb co., NE Indiana, 28 mi. (45 km.) NE of Fort Wayne; pop. (1990c) 2601.
5. City, ⊗ of Bates co., W Missouri, 30 mi. (48 km.) N of Nevada; pop. (1990c) 4099.
6. Borough, Morris co., N New Jersey, 10 mi. (16 km.) WNW of Paterson; pop. (1990c) 7392.
7. City, ⊗ of Butler co., W Pennsylvania, 30 mi. (48 km.) N of Pittsburgh; pop. (1990c) 15,714; platted 1803.

Bu·to \ˈbyü-tō\. City of ancient Egypt, in the Nile Delta, S of Coastal Lake (now Lake Burullus); in early (predynastic) times ✻ of Lower Egypt.

Bu·ton \ˈbü-ˌtȯn\ *or* **Bu·tung** *or Du.* **Boe·toeng** \ˈbü-ˌtu̇ŋ\. Island off SE coast of Sulawesi, Indonesia; ab. 2000 sq. mi. (5180 sq. km.); ab. 100 mi. (160 km.) long; separated from Muna I. on the W by **Butung Strait** (ab. 65 mi. or 105 km. long); chief town Baubau.

Bütow. See BYTÓW.

Butrinto. See BUTHROTUM.

Butser Hill. See SOUTH DOWNS.

Butte \ˈbyüt\. **1.** Name of counties in three states of the U.S. See tables at CALIFORNIA, IDAHO, SOUTH DAKOTA.
2. City, ⊗ of Silver Bow co., SW Montana, in plateau of Rocky Mts.; pop. (1990c) 33,336; alt. 5765 ft. (1757 m.); 4th largest city in state; located over large mineral deposits (silver, zinc, manganese, and esp. copper). Montana Coll. of Mineral Science and Technology (1893). Settling began during 1860s, prospectors finding gold and later, silver; copper deposits discovered 1880; incorp. as town 1876, as city 1879; expanded its borders 1977 to include all but a small part of Silver Bow co.
3. Township, ⊗ of Boyd co., N Nebraska; pop. (1990c) 667.

But·ter·mere \ˈbə-tər-ˌmir\. Lake in the Lake District, Cumbria, NW England, 7 mi. (11 km.) SW of Keswick; 1.25 mi. (2 km.) long; max. depth 94 ft. (29 m.).

But·ter·milk Channel \ˈbə-tər-ˌmilk\. Channel in Upper New York Bay, New York, bet. Governors I. and Brooklyn; ab. 2.5 mi. (4 km.) long.

But·ter·worth \ˈbə-tər-ˌwərth\. **1.** Town, Penang state, Malaysia, on coast; pop. (1980p) 200,397.
2. See GCUWA.

Butt of Lewis. See LEWIS, BUTT OF.

Butts \ˈbəts\. County in cen. Georgia. See table at GEORGIA.

Buttsville. See GREENVILLE 2.

Bu·tu·an \bü-ˈtü-ˌän\. City, ✻ of Agusan del Norte prov., NE Mindanao, Philippines, on left bank of Agusan River ab. 5 mi. (8 km.) from its mouth; pop. (1990p) 228,000.

Butuan Bay. Large inlet of SE Mindanao Sea, NE Mindanao, Philippines; ab. 24 mi. (39 km.) wide from Diuata Point to E shore; receives Agusan River.

Bu·tung. See BUTON.

Butuntum. See BITONTO.

Bu·tur·li·nov·ka \bu̇-ˈtu̇r-ˈlyē-ˌnəf-kə\. Town, E cen. Voronezh Oblast, W Russia in Europe, ab. 80 mi. (130 km.) SE of the city of Voronezh.

Buu·hood·le \bü-ˈhōt-lā\ *also* **Bo·ho·tle Wein** \bō-ˈhōt-lā-ˈvīn\. Town, N Somalia, SE of Berbera on Ethiopian border.

Buur Gaabo. See BUR GAVO.

Bux·ar *or* **Bax·ar** \ˈbək-sər\. Town, W Bihar, NE India, on Ganges 77 mi. (124 km.) W of Patna; pop. (1991p) 55,660; victory 1764 of British under Maj. Hector Munro over forces of Shujā-ʻud-Dawlah and Mī Qāsim which established British control over Bengal.

Bux·te·hu·de \ˌbu̇k-stə-ˈhü-də\. City, Lower Saxony, N Germany, 14 mi. (23 km.) SW of Hamburg; pop. (1980c) 31,631; developed around Benedictine abbey founded 1197; made city 1237; member of Hanseatic League 1363.

Bux·ton \ˈbək-stən\. **1.** Town, York co., SW Maine, 15 mi. (24 km.) W of Portland; pop. (1990c) 6494.
2. Town, Derbyshire, N cen. England, 20 mi. (32 km.) SE of Manchester; pop. (1981p) 20,797; resort.
3. Coastal town, N Guyana, 11 mi. (18 km.) ESE of Georgetown.

Buynaksk. See BUINAKSK.

Buyr Nuur. See BUIR NUR.

Bü·yük·a·da \ˌbyœ-ˌyœk-ä-ˈdä\; *formerly* **Prin·ki·po** \ˌprēŋ-ki-ˈpō\. Island in E Sea of Marmara, W Turkey, SE of entrance to the Bosporus; largest of the Kızıl Is.

Bü·yük·de·re \ˌbyœ-ˌyœk-de-ˈrā\. Town, Turkey in Europe, on the Bosporus, 11 mi. (18 km.) NNE of İstanbul; residential suburb in valley from which İstanbul obtains part of its water supply.

Büyük Menderes. See MENDERES 1.

Bu·za·chi \bu̇-ˈzä-chē\. Large peninsula projecting into NE Caspian Sea, N of Mangyshlak Penin., Kazakhstan.

Bu·zău \bü-ˈzau̇\ *or Hung.* **Bod·za** \ˈbōd-ˌzȯ\. **1.** River, cen. Romania; rises in Braşov co. and flows SE through **Buzău Pass** in Transylvanian Alps and NE into Siret River near Galaţi; ab. 150 mi. (240 km.) long.
2. County of SE Romania. See table at ROMANIA.
3. City, its ⊗, on Buzău River 62 mi. (100 km.) NE of Bucharest; pop. (1989c) 145,423; textiles.

Bu·zu·luk \ˌbu̇-zu̇-ˈlük\. City, W Orenburg Oblast, E Russia in Europe, on left bank of Samara River and on railroad line 90 mi. (145 km.) ESE of Samara; pop. (1991e) 85,100; trading center at the edge of the steppe region.

Buz·zards Bay \ˈbə-zərdz\. **1.** Inlet of Atlantic Ocean, in SE Massachusetts; 30 mi. (48 km.) long and 5 to 10 mi. (8 to 16 km.) wide; the W end of Cape Cod Canal is at its NE extremity.
2. Unincorporated settlement, Barnstable co., SE Massachusetts, on Cape Cod Canal near entrance of inlet; pop. (1990c) 3250; Massachusetts Maritime Academy (1891).

Bwa·ga·oia \ˌbwä-gä-ˈȯi-ä\. See LOUISIADE ARCHIPELAGO.

Bwake. See BOUAKÉ.

Bwa·na M'kub·wa *or* **Bwa·na·mkub·wa** \ˈbwä-näm-ˈkü-bwä\. Town, cen. Zambia; copper deposits.

By·am Mar·tin \ˈbī-əm-ˈmärt-ᵊn\. Island in channel bet. Melville and Bathurst islands, Parry Is., Nunavut, Canada.

Byblos. See JUBAYL.

Byd·goszcz \ˈbid-ˌgȯshch\ *or Ger.* **Brom·berg** \ˈbrȯm-ˌberk\. **1.** Province of N cen. Poland. See table at POLAND.
2. City, its ✻, 67 mi. (108 km.) NE of Poznań; an inland port on **Bydgoszcz Canal** which connects basins of the Vistula and Oder rivers; pop. (1989e) 380,385; electronic equipment, textiles. Orig. a commercial city of the Teutonic Knights; enlarged and developed by Prussian King Frederick the Great in 18th cent.; under Prussian rule 1772–1919. In WWII held by Germans 1939–45.

Byel–. Literally "white" in Russian. For names beginning *Byel-*, see BEL-, as *Belgorod, Belogorsk, Belukha.*

Bye·lo·rus·sian Soviet Socialist Republic \ˌbye-lō-ˈrə-shən\ *or* **Be·lo·rus·sian Soviet Socialist Republic** \ˌbe-, ˌbye-\ *or* **Bye·lo·rus·sia** *or* **Be·lo·russia** \ˌbi-lə-ˈrü-sē-yə; ˌbye-lō-ˈrə-shə, be-\ *also* **White Russian Soviet Socialist Republic.** Constituent republic of U.S.S.R. 1919–91 when it gained independence as Belarus (*q.v.*).

Byelozero. See BELOYE OZERO.

By·lot Island \ˈbī-ˌlät\. Island, Nunavut, Canada, N of Baffin I. and W of Baffin Bay; 4200 sq. mi. (10,878 sq. km.).

Byrds·town \ˈbərdz-ˌtau̇n\. Town, ⊗ of Pickett co., N Tennessee; pop. (1990c) 998.

Byron. See NIKUNAU.

Byron, Cape \ˈbī-rən\. Cape, New South Wales, Australia, sheltering S part of **Byron Bay**; cape is extreme E point of continent, 28°39′S, 153°38′E.

Byr·sa *or* **Bur·sa** \ˈbər-sə\. The citadel of Carthage.

By·tom \ˈbi-ˌtȯm\ *or Ger.* **Beu·then** \ˈbȯit-ᵊn\. City, Katowice prov., SW Poland, ab. 8 mi. (13 km.) NW of the city of Katowice; pop. (1989e) 229,851; formerly in Silesia, Germany; iron, zinc, and lead works. Became part of Prussia mid-18th cent. Taken by U.S.S.R. Jan. 1945; in section assigned to Poland by Potsdam Conference 1945.

By·tów \ˈbi-tüf\ *or Ger.* **Bü·tow** \ˈbūē-tō\. Town, Słupsk prov., N Poland, ab. 55 mi. (89 km.) E of Koszalin; pop. (1981p) 13,419; railroad junction and market town; Polish town in 15th cent., came under Brandenburg 1657. Assigned to Poland by Potsdam Conference 1945.

Bytown. See OTTAWA 7.

By·za·ci·um \bə-ˈzā-shəm, -shē-əm\. The S part of the Roman prov. of Africa; corresponds to S half of Tunisia.

By·zan·tine Empire \ˈbiz-ᵊn-ˌtēn, bə-ˈzan-, ˈbīz-ᵊn-; ˌbiz-ᵊn-ˌtīn\. Empire of SE and S Europe and W Asia, 4th–15th cents., with boundaries varying greatly; in earliest period generally termed **Eastern Roman Empire,** 395–476, with ✻ at Constantinople (earlier Byzantium); first Byzantine emperor, so called, Zeno the Isaurian (474–491). Reached its greatest extent under Justinian (527–565), who reconquered large part of Western Empire, erected Church of St. Sophia, and issued basic codification of Roman law (*Corpus Juris Civilis*); divided into administrative districts (themes); withstood attacks of Persians, Arabs, and Bulgars 7th–10th cents.; ab. 1000 A.D. comprised S Balkans, Greece, Asia Minor, and parts of S Italy. Long controversy over iconoclasm within Eastern Church prepared for break with Roman Church; attained great wealth and cultural supremacy of Mediterranean world because of its control of commerce bet. East and West and its preservation of classical heritage; lost holdings in Italy and, as result of Manzikert (see MALAZGIRT), yielded Asia Minor to Seljuqs; declined under Comnenian dynasty and forced to give commercial control to Venice (*q.v.*) which profited most from Crusades; Constantinople sacked by Fourth Crusade 1204 and Empire split up into (1) Latin Empire (*q.v.*), Greek empires of (2) Trebizond and (3) Nicaea, and (4) miscellaneous Venetian, Latin, and Greek holdings (see ACHAEA, ATHENS 10, EPIRUS, and THESSALONÍKI); partly restored by capture of Constantinople by Michael VIII Palaeologus 1261; in 14th cent. gradually lost territory to Turks although Morea became cultural center for a while (see PELOPONNESE 1); capture of Constantinople in 1453 marked formal end of Byzantine Empire while smaller centers of resistance were shortly overcome (see OTTOMAN EMPIRE).

By·zan·ti·um \bə-ˈzan-shəm, -shē-əm, -tē-əm\. Ancient city, site of modern İstanbul (*q.v.*).

Bzu·ra \ˈbzü-rä\. River, Poland, flowing into Vistula River from the S; ab. 90 mi. (145 km.) long; its source is just N of Łódź.

C

Ca·a·cu·pé \ˌkä-ä-kü-ˈpā\. Town, ✻ of Cordillera dept., cen. Paraguay; munic. pop. (1992p) 12,368; agronomy institute; place of pilgrimage.

Ca·a·gua·zú \ˌkä-ä-g̅wä-ˈsü\. Department of E cen. Paraguay. See table at PARAGUAY.

Ca·a·ma·ño Sound \kä-ˈmä-nyō\. Inlet of Hecate Strait, off W coast of British Columbia, Canada, W of Princess Royal I. and N of Aristazabal I.

Ca·a·za·pá \ˌkä-ä-sä-ˈpä\. **1.** Department of S Paraguay. See table at PARAGUAY.
2. City, its ✻; munic. pop. (1985e) 3041.

Ca·bad·ba·ran \kä-ˌbäd-bä-ˈrän\. Municipality, Mindanao, Philippines, on E shore of Butuan Bay ab. 12 mi. (19 km.) N of Butuan; pop. (1980c) 42,695.

Ca·bai·guán \ˌkä-bī-ˈg̅wän\. Town and municipality, Las Villas prov., W cen. Cuba, 37 mi. (60 km.) SE of Santa Clara; munic. pop. (1990e) 43,326.

Ca·bal·lo \kä-ˈbä-yō\ *or* **Pu·lo Caballo** \ˈpü-lō\. Rocky islet in Corregidor group, Philippines, ab. 1 mi. (1.6 km.) SE of Corregidor I., in entrance to Manila Bay, Philippines; alt. 420 ft. (128 m.); lighthouse; site of Fort Hughes. Surrendered to Japanese May 1942; recaptured by U.S. Mar. 1945.

Ca·bal·lo Dam \kə-ˈbä-yō\. Secondary dam across Rio Grande River, Sierra co., New Mexico, below Elephant Butte Dam; height 96 ft. (29 m.); impounds water for irrigation.

Ca·ba·ñas \kä-ˈbä-nyäs\. **1.** Municipality on NE coast of Pinar del Río prov., W Cuba.
2. Department, N cen. El Salvador. See table at EL SALVADOR.

Ca·ba·na·tuan \ˌkä-bä-nä-ˈtwän\. Municipality, ✻ of Nueva Ecija prov., Luzon, Philippines, in S cen. part on left bank of Pampanga River; pop. (1990p) 173,000; a highway junction point and trade center. In WWII site of large Japanese prison camp (near Cabu village) for American and Filipino soldiers captured at Bataan and Corregidor.

Ca·ba·no \ˌka-bə-ˈnō\. Town, Témiscouata co., S Quebec, Canada, on Lake Témiscouata; pop. (1991c) 3145.

Ca·bar·ro·quis \ˌkä-bär-ˈrō-kēs\. Municipality, ✻ of Quirino prov., Luzon, Philippines.

Ca·bar·rus \kə-ˈbar-əs\. County in S cen. North Carolina. See table at NORTH CAROLINA.

Ca·bar·ru·yan Island \ˌkä-bä-ˈrü-yän\. Island on NW shore of Lingayen Gulf, Pangasinan prov., Luzon, Philippines; 30 sq. mi. (78 sq. km.); forested; chief town Anda.

Ca·ba·tu·an \ˌkä-bä-ˈtü-än\. Municipality, W cen. Iloilo prov., Panay, Philippines, NW of City of Iloilo; pop. (1980c) 34,468.

Ca·be·de·lo \ˌkä-bi-ˈde-lü\. Seaport, Paraíba state, E Brazil; munic. pop. (1980c) 19,007; port for João Pessoa.

Cab·ell \ˈka-bəl\. County in W West Virginia. See table at WEST VIRGINIA.

Cabellio. See CAVAILLON.

Ca·bes Point \ˈkä-bəs\. Cape on E coast of St. Thomas I., U.S. Virgin Is., West Indies, W of Pillsbury Sound.

Ca·be·za del Buey \kä-ˌbā-thä-t͟hel-ˈbwā\. Commune, Badajoz prov., SW Spain, 90 mi. (145 km.) E of the city of Badajoz; pop. (1991c) 6935.

Cabeza del Mo·ro \ˈmō-rō\. Highest peak in the Guadalupe Mts., Cáceres prov., W Spain; 5695 ft. (1736 m.).

Cabillonum. See CHALON-SUR-SAÔNE.

Ca·bi·mas \kä-ˈb̲ē-mäs\. Town, N Zulia state, NW Venezuela, on NE coast of Lake Maracaibo; pop. (1990c) 165,755.

Ca·bin·da *also* **Ka·bin·da** \kä-ˈbin-dä\. **1.** Province of Angola, N of the mouth of the Congo River; oil, timber, coffee, cocoa, palm oil; exclave attached to Angola, c. 1886, by agreement with Belgium. See table at ANGOLA.
2. Seaport, its ✻.

Cab·i·net Mountains \ˈkab-nit, ˈka-bə-\. A range of the Rocky Mts. in NW Montana and N Idaho; highest point ab. 9000 ft. (2743 m.).

Cabo Cruz. See CRUZ, CABO.

Cabo da Boa Esperança. See GOOD HOPE, CAPE OF 2.

Cabo de Hornos. See HORN, CAPE.

Cabo de la Aguja. See AGUJA, CAPE.

Ca·bo Del·ga·do \ˈkä-bü-del-ˈgä-dü\. **1.** Province of NE Mozambique. See table at MOZAMBIQUE.
2. Cape, Mozambique. See DELGADO, CAPE.

Cabo de São Vicente. See SAINT VINCENT, CAPE 2.

Ca·bo Gra·cias a Dios \ˈkä-bō-ˈgräs-yäs-ä-ˈdē-ōs\. Municipality, extreme NE Nicaragua; politically included in Zelaya dept.

Cabo Juby. See TARFAYA.

Ca·bo·ra Bas·sa \kȧ-ˈbȯr-ə-ˈbȧ-sə\ *or* **Ca·ho·ra Bassa** \kȧ-ˈhȯr-ə\. Dam on Zambezi River in cen. Tete prov., W Mozambique, impounding water to Zambia border; construction begun 1967, with work continuing during rest of 20th cent.; supplies power in Mozambique and also to South Africa, but transmission has been repeatedly interrupted by sabotage.

Ca·bor·ca \kä-ˈbȯr-kä\. City, Sonora state, Mexico, 150 mi. (241 km.) NW of Hermosillo; pop. (1990p) 58,516.

Ca·bo Ro·jo \ˈkä-bō-ˈrō-hō\. Municipality, SW Puerto Rico, S of Mayagüez; pop. (1990c) 38,521.

Cab·ot \ˈka-bət\. City, Lonoke co., cen. Arkansas, 18 mi. (29 km.) NE of Little Rock; pop. (1990c) 8319.

Cabot Head. Cape, SE Ontario, Canada; NE point of Bruce Penin. on Georgian Bay.

Cabot Strait. Channel in Canada, bet. SW Newfoundland and N Cape Breton I.; 68 mi. (109 km.) wide; connects St. Lawrence River with the Atlantic Ocean.

Ca·bourg \kȧ-ˈbür\. Village, Calvados dept., NW France; adjoins Dives-sur-Mer on the W; beach resort.

Cabo Verde, Ilhas do. See CAPE VERDE.

Cabo Yubi. See TARFAYA.

Ca·bra \ˈkä-brä\; *anc.* **Igab·rum** \i-ˈga-brəm\. Commune, Córdoba prov., S Spain, 37 mi. (60 km.) SE of the city of Córdoba; pop. (1991c) 20,306; captured from Moors by Ferdinand III c. 1240; recaptured 1311.

Cab·ras Island \ˈka-brəs\. Narrow island off W coast of Guam; ab. 2 mi. (3.2 km.) long and 0.25 mi. (0.4 km.) wide; forms part of N shelter of Apra Harbor.

Ca·bre·ra \kä-ˈbrā-rä\; *anc.* **Ca·prar·ia** \kə-ˈprar-ē-ə\. Small island of the Balearic Is., Baleares prov., Spain, 9 mi. (14 km.) S of Majorca; a part of Palma commune.

Ca·bri·el \ˌkä-b̲rē-ˈel\. River, E Spain; flows S through Cuenca prov. and into Júcar River; ab. 130 mi. (209 km.) long.

Ca·bril·lo National Monument \kə-ˈbri-lō\. See UNITED STATES, *National Monuments.*

Ca·bu \ˈkä-bü\. Village, cen. Nueva Ecija prov., Luzon, Philippines, ab. 7 mi. (11 km.) ENE of Cabanatuan. Site 1942–45 of Cabanatuan prison camp (see CABANATUAN).

Ca·bu·gao \kä-ˈbü-gau̇\. Municipality, N Ilocos Sur, Luzon, Philippines, on coast; pop. (1980c) 24,424.

Ca·ca·hua·mil·pa Caverns \ˌkä-kä-wä-ˈmēl-pä\. Large natural caverns in NE Guerrero state near Cuernavaca, cen. Mexico.

Ča·čak *or* **Cha·chak** \ˈchä-chäk\. Town, cen. Serbia, Yugoslavia, ab. 62 mi. (100 km.) S of Belgrade.

Ca·ca·pon \kə-ˈkā-pən\. River, NE West Virginia; rises in S Hardy co., flows N into Potomac River; ab. 130 mi. (209 km.) long.

Cac·cia, Cape \ˈkä-chä\. Cape on NW coast of the island of Sardinia, Italy.

Cá·ce·res \ˈkä-thā-ˌrās\. **1.** Province of W Spain. See table at SPAIN.
2. Commune, its ✻, on **Cáceres River;** pop. (1991c) 74,589; remains of Roman fortifications; held by Moors at various times during Middle Ages; captured by Alfonso IX of León 1229.

Ca·chan \kä-'shä^{n}\. Commune, Val-de-Marne dept., N France, S suburb of Paris on Bièvre River.

Cache \'kash\. **1.** River, NE Arkansas; rises in NE Arkansas and flows S into the White River in Monroe co., E cen. Arkansas; ab. 213 mi. (343 km.) long.
2. County in N Utah. See table at UTAH.

Cache la Pou·dre \ˌkash-lə-'pü-dər\. River, N Colorado; flows from a point near Milner Pass N and E to the South Platte near Greeley; ab. 125 mi. (200 km.) long.

Ca·chí, Ne·va·do de \nä-'bä-thō-thä-kä-'shē\. Peak in Salta prov., N Argentina; 22,047 ft. (6720 m.).

Ca·cho·ei·ra \kä-'shwā-rə\. City, Bahia state, E Brazil, near W coast of All Saints Bay ab. 45 mi. (72 km.) W of Salvador; munic. pop. (1980c) 27,977.

Cachoeira do Sul \dü-'sül\. City, Rio Grande do Sul state, S Brazil, on Jacuí River 110 mi. (177 km.) W of Pôrto Alegre; munic. pop. (1990c) 89,058.

Ca·cho·ei·ro de Ita·pe·mi·rim \kä-'shwā-rü-dē-ˌē-tä-pā-mē-'rē^{n}\. City, Espírito Santo state, E Brazil, 65 mi. (105 km.) SW of Vitória; munic. pop. (1991p) 143,763.

Ca·cou·na \kə-'kü-nə\. Summer resort, Quebec, Canada; on S shore of St. Lawrence NE of Rivière du Loup.

Cad·ca \'chät-sä\. Town, N Slovakia, near borders with Czech Republic and Poland; pop. (1989c) 24,727.

Cad·do \'ka-dō\. Name of a parish in NW corner of Louisiana and a county in W cen. Oklahoma. See tables at LOUISIANA and OKLAHOMA.

Caddo Lake. Lake on N Texas-Louisiana boundary; ab. 20 mi. (32 km.) long; connected with Red River; navigable.

Ca·de·rey·ta Ji·mé·nez \ˌkä-thä-'rā-tä-hē-'mā-nes\. Municipality, Nuevo León state, Mexico, 22 mi. (35 km.) ESE of Monterrey; pop. (1990p) 53,875.

Ca·der Fron·wen \'ka-dər-'frȯn-wen, 'kä-dər\. Peak in the Berwyn Mts., N Wales; 2568 ft. (783 m.).

Cader Id·ris \'i-dris\. Peak, Merionethshire, W Wales, S of Dolgellau; 2927 ft. (892 m.).

Cad·il·lac \'kad-ᵊl-ˌak\. City, ⊗ of Wexford co., NW Michigan, 36 mi. (58 km.) SSE of Traverse City; pop. (1990c) 10,104. Settled late 19th cent.; named for founder of Detroit, Antoine Laumet de La Mothe, Sieur de Cadillac.

Ca·diz. 1.\'kā-diz\. City, ⊗ of Trigg co., SW Kentucky; pop. (1990c) 2148.
2. \'ka-diz\. Village, ⊗ of Harrison co., E Ohio, 20 mi. (32 km.) WSW of Steubenville; pop. (1990c) 3439.
3. \'kä-thēs\. Chartered city, N Negros Occidental, Negros, Philippines, on Visayan Sea NE of City of Bacolod; pop. (1990e) 120,000.

Cá·diz \'kä-ˌthēth, -ˌthēs\ *or angl.* **Ca·diz** \kə-'diz; 'kā-diz, 'kä-, 'ka-\. **1.** Province of SW Spain. See table at SPAIN.
2. *anc.* **Ga·dir** \'gā-dər\; *later* **Ga·des** \'gād-(ˌ)ēz\. Seaport city, its ✻, on Bahía de Cádiz 58 mi. (93 km.) NW of Gibraltar and 62 mi. (100 km.) SSW of Seville; pop. (1991c) 154,347; naval and mercantile shipbuilding yards; exports sherry, olives, fish; 13th cent. and 18th cent. cathedrals (with paintings by Bartolomé Esteban Murillo), museums; Torre de Vigía signal tower; bullring.
History: Founded as Phoenician trading colony c. 1100 B.C.; outlet for mineral wealth, tin and amber from N; ruled by Carthaginians, Romans, Visigoths; held by Moors from 711 A.D. until captured 1262 by Alfonso of Castile; enjoyed great prosperity as one of two centers for Spanish trade with American colonies (see SEVILLE) 16th–18th cents.; scene of raid of Robert Devereux, earl of Essex, 1596; became seat of Casa de Contratación (clearinghouse for American trade) 1718; besieged by French 1810–12; seat of national assembly (Span. *Cortes*) which promulgated liberal constitution of 1812; witnessed beginning of revolution which deposed Queen Isabella II 1868; fell to Nationalists in Civil War during 1930s; late 20th cent. archaeological excavations established former Phoenician and Roman presence.

Cádiz, Ba·hía de \bä-'ē-ä-thä-\ *or Eng.* **Bay of Cádiz.** Inlet of Golfo de Cádiz on SW coast of Spain, affording excellent harbor for the city of Cádiz.

Cádiz, Gol·fo de \'gȯl-fō-thā\ *or Eng.* **Gulf of Cádiz.** Wide-mouthed inlet of Atlantic Ocean on SW coast of Spain.

Ca·do·re Alps \kä-'dō-rā\ *or* **Ca·dor·ic Alps** \kə-'dȯr-ik, -'där-\. A name of the Dolomites bet. Veneto and Friuli-Venezia Giulia, NE Italy.

Cadurcum. See CAHORS.

Cae·li·an \'sē-lē-ən\ *or Lat.* **Cae·li·us Mons** \'sē-lē-əs-'mänz\. One of the Seven Hills of Rome. See SEVEN HILLS.

Caen \'kä^{n}\. City, ✻ of Calvados dept., Normandy, NW France, on Orne River ab. 9 mi. (14 km.) from coast of English Channel and ab. 126 mi. (203 km.) WNW of Paris; pop. (1990c) 115,624; steel; electrical equipment; transportation center; notable structures include L'Abbaye-aux-Dames (founded 11th cent. by Matilda, wife of William the Conqueror), L'Abbaye-aux-Hommes (founded by William the Conqueror, duke of Normandy and king of England, 11th cent.), church of St.-Pierre; university (founded 1432 by Henry VI of England; having received much damage in WWII, it was later rebuilt on a new site); museum commemorating Normandy invasion of WWII. Under English rule 1346, 1417–50; suffered in Wars of Religion; captured by Protestants 1562. In WWII one of the main objects of Allied invasion; objective of British on D-day, June 6, 1944; Germans resisted forcefully; taken by Allies July 9; much of the city destroyed, but since rebuilt.

Caene *or* **Caenepolis.** See QENA 2.

Caerdydd. See CARDIFF 2.

Caere *or* **Agyl·la** \ə-'ji-lə\. Ancient city of Etruria at site of present-day commune of **Cer·ve·te·ri** \ˌcher-vā-'tā-rē\, Italy, near coast 18 mi. (29 km.) WNW of Rome; Etruscan tombs; according to legend, the refuge c. 390 B.C. of the vestal virgins when the Gauls took Rome.

Caerfyrddin. See CARMARTHEN.

Caer Gybi. See HOLYHEAD 2.

Caer·le·on \kär-'lē-ən, kīr-\; *anc.* **Is·ca Sil·u·rum** \'is-kə-'sil-yə-rəm\. Town, Gwent, SE Wales, on Usk River; pop. (1981p) 6711. Important Roman fortified outpost 1st–3d cents. A.D.; according to tradition may be "Carlion" (where King Arthur was crowned and held his court) of English writer Sir Thomas Malory's *Morte d'Arthur.*

Caer Luel. See CARLISLE 6.

Caer·nar·fon Bay *or* **Caer·nar·von Bay** *or* **Car·nar·von Bay** \kīr-'när-vən, kär-, kər-\. Bay, NW Wales; Menai Strait connects it with Beaumaris Bay.

Caer·nar·von *or* **Car·nar·von** \kīr-'när-vȯn, kär-, kər-\. **1.** Former county, Wales. See CAERNARVONSHIRE.
2. *or* **Caer·nar·fon** \-vən\. Town and seaport, ⊗ of Gwynedd co., NW Wales; pop. (1981p) 9506; famous 13th cent. castle, birthplace 1284 of Edward II (first heir to the English crown to be styled "Prince of Wales"); tourism.

Caer·nar·von·shire *or* **Car·nar·von·shire** \-ˌshir, -shər\ *or* **Caernarvon** *or* **Carnarvon.** Former county, NW Wales; ⊗ Caernarvon; rivers Conway, Ogwen, Glaslyn. See GWYNEDD.

Caer·phil·ly \kīr-'fi-lē, kär-, kər-\. Town, Mid Glamorgan co., SE Wales; pop. (1981p) 42,736; trade center in coal-bearing region; known esp. as place of origin of Caerphilly cheese; has 13th cent. castle.

Caesaraugusta. See SARAGOSSA.

Cae·sa·rea \ˌsē-zə-'rē-ə, ˌse-, -sə-\. **1.** Seaport, Algeria. See CHERCHELL.
2. Ancient seaport on coast of Samaria and Roman ✻ of Palestine, ab. 22 mi. (35 km.) S of Haifa, Israel, at site now called **Hor·bat Qe·sa·ri** \'kȯr-bät-'kā-sä-rē\; founded by Herod the Great, king of Judaea; made Roman ✻ after Emperor Vespasian's reign; site of an early Christian church and frequently mentioned in the New Testament; its fortifications strengthened 13th cent. by Crusader and French king, Louis IX; destroyed by Mamlūk Sultan Baybars I later in 13th cent.

Caesarea Mazaca. See KAYSERİ 2.

Caesarea Philippi. See BĀNIYĀS 2.

\ə\ abut \ᵊ\ kitten, Fr table \ər\ further \a\ ash \ā\ ace \ä\ cot, cart \ȧ\ Fr bac \au̇\ out \b̲\ Span Avila \ch\ chin \e\ bet \ē\ easy \g\ go \i\ hit \ī\ ice \j\ job \k̲\ Ger ich, Buch \$^{n}$\ Fr vin \ŋ\ sing \ō\ go \ȯ\ all \ȯ\ law \œ\ Fr bœuf \œ̄\ Fr feu \ȯi\ boy \th\ thin \th̲\ this \ü\ loot \u̇\ foot \ue\ Ger füllen \u̅e\ Fr rue \y\ yet \$^{y}$\ Fr digne \dēn^{y}\, nuit \nw^{y}ē\ \yü\ few \yu̇\ fury \zh\ vision

Cae·sar·i·en·sis \ˌsē-zə-rē-ˈen-sis\. Region, NW Africa; in Roman times, the E part of Mauretania.

Caesarodunum. See TOURS.

Caesaromagus. See BEAUVAIS.

Cae·sar's Head \ˈsē-zərz\. Range of the Blue Ridge, in N Greenville co., NW South Carolina; highest peak 3225 ft. (983 m.); the S face is a 1500-ft. (457-m.) precipice.

Caesena. See CESENA.

Ca·gar·ras Islands \kȧ-ˈgar-əs\. Islands in the Atlantic Ocean off Guanabara state, SE Brazil.

Ca·ga·yan \ˌkä-gä-ˈyän\. **1.** *or* **Rio Gran·de de Cagayan** \ˈrē-ō-ˈgrän-dā-ˌdā-\. River, NE Luzon, Philippines; flows N to Babuyan Channel; 220 mi. (354 km.) long; largest river in Luzon; chief tributary the Chico; valley 50 mi. (80 km.) wide bet. the Cordillera Central on the W and the Sierra Madre on the E; navigable for much of its course. Near its mouth is the port of Aparri.

2. River, Mindanao, Philippines; flows N from Bukidnon to Macajalar Bay; ab. 50 mi. (80 km.) long.

3. Province, NE Luzon, Philippines; ✻ Tuguegarao; occupies lower basin of Cagayan River, incl. part of its tributary the Chico, with Sierra Madre Range averaging ab. 3500 ft. (1070 m.) E of valley along Pacific Ocean; includes Babuyan Is. (*q.v.*) to the N; northernmost tip is Cape Engaño; valley region fertile, esp. suitable for tobacco. Chief towns: Tuguegarao, Aparri, Tuao, Baggao, Gattaran. See table at PHILIPPINES.

History: Visited and explored by Spaniards 1572–81; scene of several uprisings in 17th cent.; civil government estab. Sept. 1901. In WWII held by Japanese Dec. 1941–June 1945.

Cagayan de Oro \dā-ˈō-rō\. Chartered city, ✻ of Misamis Oriental prov., Mindanao, Philippines, in E part near S shore of Macajalar Bay ab. 3 mi. (5 km.) from mouth of Cagayan River; pop. (1990p) 340,000.

Cagayan Islands *or* **Ca·ga·ya·nes** \ˌkä-gä-ˈyä-nās\. Group of seven small islands in N part of Sulu Sea, Philippines, 70 mi. (113 km.) W of SW Negros, 9°40′N, 121°25′E; ab. 5 sq. mi. (13 sq. km.); only settlement **Ca·ga·yan·cil·lo** \ˌkä-gä-yän-ˈsēl-yō\; belong to Palawan prov.

Cagayan Su·lu \ˈsü-lü\. Small island in SW Sulu Sea, SW Philippines, ab. 70 mi. (113 km.) off the NE coast of Borneo; 26 sq. mi. (67 sq. km.); surrounded by 13 islets; noted for its scenery, fauna, and flora; suffered much in 19th cent. from Moro pirates. With Sibutu I. (*q.v.*) inadvertently omitted from Philippine lands sold by Spain to U.S. by treaty of 1898; acquired by U.S. by special agreement of 1900; part of Philippines at its independence 1935.

Cagayan Valley. Region of the Philippines. See table at PHILIPPINES.

Ca·gli \ˈkäl-yē\. Commune, Marche, cen. Italy, 29 mi. (47 km.) SSW of Pesaro; pop. (1981p) 9562.

Ca·glia·ri \ˈkäl-yä-rē\. **1.** Province of Sardinia, Italy. See table at ITALY.

2. *anc.* **Car·a·lis** \ˈkar-ə-lis\. Fortified seaport, its ✻, and ✻ of Sardinia, at head of Gulf of Cagliari on S coast of Sardinia 252 mi. (405 km.) SW of Rome; pop. (1989c) 219,095; exports include lead, zinc, salt; 14th cent. cathedral; ancient Roman remains; university (1606). Founded by Phoenicians; held successively by Romans, Saracens, Pisans, Spain, Austria, and (as kingdom of Sardinia) by Savoy. Bombed heavily in WWII; since rebuilt; now important port for Sardinia.

Cagliari, Gulf of. Inlet of Mediterranean Sea on S coast of the island of Sardinia.

Cagnes–sur–Mer \ˈkänʸ-sür-ˈmer\. Commune, Alpes-Maritimes dept., SE France; resort on the Riviera just W of Nice.

Ca·gra·ray \ˌkä-grä-ˈrī\. Island, E Albay prov., Luzon, Philippines, ab. 11 mi. (18 km.) NE of Legazpi; 28 sq. mi. (73 sq. km.); lies bet. Lagonoy Gulf and Albay Gulf.

Ca·gua \ˈkä-gwä\. Town, Aragua state, N Venezuela; pop. (1990c) 73,465.

Cagua, Mount. Mountain of volcanic origin, NE Cagayan prov., Luzon, Philippines, near N end of Sierra Madre Range; 3927 ft. (1197 m.).

Ca·guas \ˈkä-ˌgwäs\. Town and municipality, E cen. Puerto Rico; pop. (1990c) 92,429 (town), 133,447 (munic.); in fertile agricultural region.

Ca·ha·ba \kə-ˈhä-bə\. **1.** *also* **Ca·haw·ba** \-ˈhȯ-\. River, cen. Alabama; rises in St. Clair co., flows S through coalfields into Alabama River in Dallas co. ab. 10 mi. (16 km.) SW of Selma; ab. 200 mi. (320 km.) long.

2. Ruins, Dallas co., SW cen. Alabama; site of a town that served as the state's first ✻ and later as ⊗ of Dallas co.

Ca·ho·kia \kə-ˈhō-kē-ə\. Village, St. Clair co., SW Illinois, across the Mississippi from St. Louis, Missouri; pop. (1990c) 17,550; Parks Coll. of Saint Louis Univ. (1927); founded 1699 by the French, one of first permanent European settlements in Illinois. The **Cahokia Mounds,** a group of prehistoric Indian mounds incl. one which is among the largest prehistoric earthworks in the U.S., are located ab. 8 mi. (13 km.) away, NE of East St. Louis.

Cahora Bassa. See CABORA BASSA.

Ca·hors \kȧ-ˈȯr\; *anc.* **Ca·dur·cum** \kə-ˈdər-kəm\ *or* **Di·vo·na** \ˈdī-və-nə, ˈdi-\. City, ✻ of Lot dept., S cen. France, on Lot River 59 mi. (95 km.) N of Toulouse; pop. (1990c) 20,787; episcopal see (from 4th cent.); 12th cent. cathedral; 14th cent. fortified bridge; former episcopal palace. Important center of finance in Middle Ages; university (consolidated with Toulouse Univ. 1751) founded early 14th cent. by Pope John XXII, a native; under English rule 1360–1428.

Cahul. See KAGUL.

Cai·ba·rién \ˌkī-ˌbär-ˈyen\. Town, Las Villas prov., W cen. Cuba; pop. (1990e) 35,427; port on N coast 30 mi. (48 km.) E of Santa Clara.

Cai·cos Islands. See TURKS AND CAICOS ISLANDS.

Caicos Passage \ˈkā-kəs, -ˌkōs\. Channel in Bahamas, West Indies, NW of Caicos Is.; ab. 45 mi. (72 km.) wide.

Caieta. See GAETA.

Cail·lou Lake \ˈkā-lü, kā-ˈlü\. Lake in S Terrebonne parish, SE Louisiana; 5 mi. (8 km.) long.

Cai·ma·ne·ra \ˌkī-mä-ˈnā-rä\. Commune on W side of Guantánamo Bay, E Cuba; pop. (1981p) 7453.

Cainargeava–Mică. See KAYNARDZHA.

Caird Coast \ˈkard\. Ice-covered section of Antarctica, 76°S and 23° to 29°W, on SE coast of Weddell Sea NE of Luitpold Coast; part of Coats Land; included in British claim.

Cairn Eige. See CARN EIGE.

Cairn·gorm Mountains \ˈkarn-ˌgȯrm\. Range of the Grampians in NE cen. Scotland; highest peak Ben Macdhui, 4296 ft. (1309 m.) high; includes **Cairngorm,** 4084 ft. (1245 m.), on border of Highland and Grampian regions; chief source of a smoky-brown variety of quartz (cairngorm).

Cairn Hill \ˈkarn\. Peak in the Cheviot Hills along the border bet. England and Scotland; 2545 ft. (776 m.).

Cairns \ˈkarnz\. Seaport, NE Queensland, Australia, on Trinity Bay; pop. (1981c) 39,096; on narrow lowland strip E of Atherton Plateau; outlet and supply center for agricultural and mining region; sugar, tobacco, timber; black-marlin fishing; dairying; tin, fluorspar; tourism; founded 1870s.

Cairn·toul *also* **Carn·toul** \kärn-ˈtül, -ˈtau̇l\. Peak, SW Grampian region, N cen. Scotland, in the Cairngorm group; 4241 ft. (1293 m.).

Cai·ro \ˈker-ō, ˈkā-rō\. **1.** City, ⊗ of Grady co., SW Georgia, 50 mi. (80 km.) S of Albany; pop. (1990c) 9035.

2. City, ⊗ of Alexander co., SW Illinois, at confluence of Ohio and Mississippi rivers; pop. (1990c) 4846; port of entry; settled mid-19th cent.; depot for Union military supplies during Civil War. The "Eden" of English novelist Charles Dickens's *Martin Chuzzlewit.*

Cai·ro \ˈkī-rō\. **1.** Governorate of N Egypt. See CAIRO 2 and table at EGYPT.

2. *or Arab.* **Al–Qā·hi·rah** \ȧl-ˈkä-hē-rə\ *or* **El Qâ·hi·ra** \ˌel-ˈkä-hē-rə\. City, ✻ of Egypt, on right bank of Nile ab. 9 mi. (14 km.) above division into two main branches of the delta; pop. (1991e) 6,663,000; comprises most of the governorate of Cairo; chemicals, textiles; food and tobacco processing; largest city in Africa; several universities and colleges incl. Univ. of Cairo (1908); Museum of Islamic Art (1869), Egyptian Museum (1902); opera; zoo; has ab. 250 mosques (many in ruins), esp. Sultan Hasan Mosque (c. 1361), Muḥammad ʻAlī Mosque, and al-Azhar.

History: Near site of Roman city Babylon which was captured by Arabs 641 A.D.; Old Cairo (**Al–Fus·tāt** \ˌal-fu̇-ˈstät\) built by Arabs as military camp c. 642; new part (**Al–Qāhirah**) built by Fāṭimid dynasty (see EGYPT) c. 968 and made their ✻ 973, known as "City of Victory"; citadel erected in late 12th cent. by Saladin, ruler of Egypt and Syria at time of Third Crusade; while ✻ of Mamlūk sultans (from 13th cent.), reached greatest prosperity as trade and cultural center; taken by Ottoman Turks 1517 and began to decline in importance; with French Emperor Napoléon's invasion, held by French 1798–1801; ✻ of semi-independent pashalik (province) ruled by Muḥammad ʻAlī Pasha and of independent kingdom of Egypt (*q.v.*). British and U.S. base in North Africa campaign 1942. During WWII site of two conferences, the first Nov. 1943 bet. U.S. President Franklin D. Roosevelt, British Prime Minister Winston Churchill, and Nationalist Chinese Generalissimo Chiang Kai-shek, the second Dec. 1943 bet. Roosevelt, Churchill, and Turkish President İsmet İnönü; evacuated by British forces 1946; extensive population growth in later 20th cent. promoted expansion of both city and suburbs with related expansion of transportation systems.

Cairo, Mount \ˈkī-rō\. Mountain dominating Monte Cassino, Italy, on NNW; 5474 ft. (1668 m.).

Cai·ro·çu, Point \ˌkī-rō-ˈsü\. Cape on S coast of Guanabara state, SE Brazil, S of Ilha Grande Bay.

Caith·ness \ˈkāth-ˌnes, kāth-ˈ\. Former county, N Scotland; ⊗ Wick.

Cai·va·no \kī-ˈvä-nō\. Commune, Napoli prov., Campania, S Italy, 8 mi. (13 km.) NNE of Naples; pop. (1989c) 36,296; trade center.

Ca·ja·mar·ca; *formerly* **Ca·xa·mar·ca** \ˌkä-hä-ˈmär-kä\. Town, N Peru, on **Cajamarca River,** ab. 370 mi. (595 km.) NW of Lima; pop. (1990e) 92,600; alt. 8597 ft. (2620 m.); university (1962); hot sulfur springs (known as Baths of the Incas) nearby; 17th cent. church; 18th cent. cathedral; museums; important annual festival; Atahuallpa, last of the Inca sovereigns, executed here by Spanish conqueror Francisco Pizarro 1533.

Ca·jon Pass \kə-ˈhōn\. Pass bet. San Gabriel Mts. on W and San Bernardino Mts. on E, S California, N of the city of San Bernardino and ENE of Los Angeles; SE gateway for overland travel to the coast since 1831; now contains a major highway.

Cal·a·bar \ˈka-lə-ˌbär\. Town, ✻ of Cross River state, SE Nigeria, on left bank of **Calabar River** (flows into Cross estuary); pop. (1991e) 153,900; trades in palm oil, rubber, and timber; museum, university. Settled by the Efik; important trading center with Europeans, extending into 20th cent.

Ca·la·bo·zo \ˌkä-lä-ˈbō-sō\. Town, Guárico state, N cen. Venezuela, in the llanos, 110 mi. (177 km.) S of Caracas; pop. (1990c) 79,578.

Calabrese, Appennino. See table at APENNINES.

Ca·la·bria \kä-ˈlä-brē-ä, -ˈlā-\. **1.** Region of ancient Italy, a peninsula now forming the S part of Puglia.
2. *anc.* **Brut·ti·um** \ˈbrə-tē-əm\. Autonomous region, S Italy; ✻ Catanzaro; consists of marshy coastal flatlands, well-watered and fertile valleys, and a cen. ridge of granite mountains; heavily forested; subject to severe earthquakes (disastrous ones having occurred esp. 1783–87, 1905, 1908); citrus fruit; livestock.

History: Ancient Bruttium, founded as Greek colony, taken by Romans 3d cent. B.C.; retaken in 9th cent. A.D. by Byzantine Empire; conquered by Normans under Robert Guiscard who became duke of Apulia and Calabria 1059; united to Norman kingdom of Naples 11th cent. and with kingdom of Italy 1860; feudal land system extended into 20th cent.; major land reforms carried out after 1951; held elections for regional parliament 1970; despite the efforts following WWII to revitalize economy, area remains one of the poorer in the country. See table at ITALY.

Calabrian Apennines. See table at APENNINES.

Calae. See CHELLES.

Ca·la·fat \ˌkä-lä-ˈfät\. Town, Dolj co., S Romania, on the Danube opp. the Bulgarian city of Vidin; founded in 14th cent. by colonists from Genoa who developed the ship-repairing industry and whose workmen (*calfats*) gave the town its name; later became grain-trading center; battleground during Russo-Turkish conflicts in 19th cent.

Calagurris. See CALAHORRA.

Ca·lah See NIMRUD.

Ca·la·hor·ra \ˌkä-lä-ˈōr-rä\; *anc.* **Cal·a·gur·ris** \ˌka-lə-ˈgər-is\. Commune, Logroño prov., N Spain, on right bank of Ebro 26 mi. (42 km.) SE of the commune of Logroño. Roman ruins; place of pilgrimage. Ancient town, Calagurris, taken by Roman Gen. Pompey after a four–year siege 76–72 B.C. Birthplace of rhetorician Quintilian c. 35 A.D.

Cal·ais \ˈka-lis\. City, Washington co., E Maine, on St. Croix River; pop. (1990c) 3963; port of entry, connected with St. Stephen, New Brunswick, Canada, by International Bridge.

Ca·lais \ka̐-ˈle, ka-ˈlā\. Seaport, Pas-de-Calais dept., N France, on Strait of Dover 64 mi. (103 km.) NW of Arras; pop. (1990c) 75,836; important passenger port; nearby Sangatte, French terminus of Channel Tunnel, opened 1994; lacemaking; chemicals. Town of old county of Artois taken 1347 by Edward III of England; after 1450 only remaining English possession in France; recaptured 1558 by François de Lorraine, duke of Guise; held by Spanish 1596–98; objective, together with Dunkerque, of famous German "drive to the sea" in WWI. In WWII taken by Germans 1940; launching base for robot bombs against Britain 1944; heavily damaged during war; since rebuilt.

Calais, Pas de. See DOVER, STRAIT OF.

Ca·la·ma \kä-ˈlä-mä\. City, N Chile, on Loa River, on W slope of the Andes; pop. (1992p) 95,379; service center for mining area.

Ca·lam·ba \kä-ˈläm-bä\. Municipality on S shore of Laguna de Bay, W Laguna prov., Luzon, Philippines; pop. (1980c) 121,175; birthplace of patriot and writer José Rizal 1861.

Ca·la·mian Group \ˌkä-lə-mē-ˈän\ *also* **Ca·la·mia·nes** \ˌkä-lä-ˈmyä-nās\. Island group, SW Philippines, bet. Mindoro and Palawan islands; 600 sq. mi. (1554 sq. km.); comprises three large islands, Busuanga, Culion, and Coron, and ab. 95 small ones; part of Palawan prov. Mountainous and well-forested; chief town Coron.

Calamine, La. See MORESNET.

Ca·lam·i·ty, Mount \kə-ˈla-mi-tē\. Peak in the Adirondack Mts., Essex co., NE New York; 3641 ft. (1110 m.).

Cal·a·mus \ˈka-lə-məs\. River, N cen. Nebraska; rises in Brown co., flows SE into North Loup River in Garfield co., cen. Nebraska; ab. 70 mi. (113 km.) long.

Ca·lan·che \kä-ˈläŋ-kā\. Region on W cen. coast of Corsica, France; noted for its red-granite formations.

Ca·la·pan \ˌkä-lä-ˈpän\. Municipality, ✻ of Mindoro Oriental prov., Philippines, on NE coast of Mindoro I. at E end of Verde Island Passage; pop. (1980c) 67,370.

Ca·la·pe \kä-ˈlä-pē\. Municipality, W coast of Bohol, Philippines, on Bohol Strait N of Tagbilaran; pop. (1980c) 22,488.

Că·lă·ra·şi \kə-lə-ˈräshʸ\. **1.** County of SE Romania. See table at ROMANIA.
2. Town, its ⊗, on the Danube ab. 63 mi. (101 km.) ESE of Bucharest; pop. (1989c) 76,240; pulp.

Ca·lar·cá \ˌkä-lär-ˈkä\. Town, Quindío dept., W cen. Colombia; munic. pop. (1985c) 39,520.

Ca·la·si·ao \ˌkä-lä-sē-ˈau̇\. Municipality, cen. Pangasinan prov., Luzon, Philippines; on a branch of the Agno 7 mi. (11 km.) E of Lingayen; pop. (1980c) 48,101.

Ca·la·ta·fi·mi \kä-ˌlä-tä-ˈfē-mē\. Commune, Trapani prov., NW Sicily, Italy, 21 mi. (34 km.) ESE of the seaport of Trapani; pop. (1981p) 8159; site of military and nationalist leader Giuseppe Garibaldi's defeat May 1860 of Neapolitans, hastening ultimate unification of Italy.

\ə\ abut \ˈə\ matches \ᵊ\ kitten, Fr table \ər\ further \a\ ash \ā\ ace \ä\ cot, cart \a̐\ Fr bac \au̇\ out \b̲\ Span Avila \ch\ chin \e\ bet \ē\ easy \g\ go \i\ hit \ī\ ice \j\ job \k̲\ Ger ich, Buch \ⁿ\ Fr vin \ŋ\ sing \ō\ go \ȯ\ all \ȯ\ law \œ\ Fr bœuf \œ̄\ Fr feu \ȯi\ boy \th\ thin \th̲\ this \ü\ loot \u̇\ foot \ue\ Ger füllen \ue̅\ Fr rue \y\ yet \ʸ\ Fr digne \ˈdēnʸ\, nuit \ˈnwʸē\ \yü\ few \yu̇\ fury \zh\ vision

Ca·la·ta·gan \ˌkä-lä-tä-ˈgän\. Municipality on SW coast of Batangas prov., Luzon, Philippines; pop. (1980c) 27,578.

Ca·la·ta·yud \ˌkä-lä-tä-ˈyüth\. Commune, Zaragoza prov., NE Spain, 45 mi. (72 km.) SW of Saragossa; pop. (1991c) 17,432; trade center; sulfur baths; ruins of Moorish forts. Founded in 8th cent.; conquered 1120 by Alfonso I of Aragon. Birthplace c. 40 A.D. of the Latin poet Martial 2 mi. (3.2 km.) E at ancient **Bil·bi·lis** \ˈbil-bi-lis\.

Ca·la·tra·va \ˌkä-lä-ˈträ-vä\. **1.** Municipality, NE coast of Negros Occidental prov., Negros, Philippines, on Tanon Strait 36 mi. (58 km.) E of City of Bacolod; pop. (1980c) 58,163. **2.** Ancient fortress, cen. Spain, just ENE of Ciudad Real near Guadiana River; defended against Moors by two Cistercians who presented it to Sancho III of Castile 1158 and instituted Order of Calatrava; captured by Moors 1197, retaken 1212; taken over by Order of Alcántara 1218 when Order of Calatrava built new convent ab. 8 mi. (13 km.) S (New Calatrava); only a tower now on site.

Ca·lau·ag \ˌkä-lä-ˈwäg\. Municipality, Quezon prov., Luzon, Philippines; pop. (1980c) 57,907.

Cal·a·ver·as \ˌka-lə-ˈver-əs\. **1.** River, cen. California; flows SW into San Joaquin River; ab. 70 mi. (113 km.) long.
2. County in cen. California. See table at CALIFORNIA.

Ca·la·vi·te, Cape \ˌkä-lä-ˈvē-tä\. NW point of Mindoro I., Philippines, 13°26′N, 120°18′E; just to the E is **Mount Calavite,** 4990 ft. (1521 m.).

Ca·la·yan \ˌkä-lä-ˈyän\. Island in Babuyan group, N of Luzon, Philippines; 73 sq. mi. (189 sq. km.).

Cal·ba·yog \käl-ˈbä-ˌyȯg\. Chartered city, W Samar, Philippines, on Samar Sea 29 mi. (47 km.) NW of Catbalogan; pop. (1990p) 113,000.

Cal·be \ˈkäl-bə\ *or* **Calbe an der Saa·le** \än-dər-ˈzä-lə\. City, E cen. Germany, on Saale River 16 mi. (26 km.) S of Magdeburg; founded 12th cent.; to Brandenburg 1680.

Cal·ca·sieu \ˈkal-kə-ˌsü\. **1.** River, SW Louisiana; rises in N Vernon parish, flows in wide curve E, SE, and SW, through **Calcasieu Lake** (ab. 15 mi. or 24 km. long, in Cameron parish, surrounded by marshes which cover almost entire parish), and into Gulf of Mexico through **Calcasieu Pass** (ab. 5 mi. or 8 km. long); ab. 200 mi. (320 km.) long.
2. Parish in SW Louisiana. See table at LOUISIANA.

Calchi. See KHALKĒ.

Cal·cut·ta \kal-ˈkə-tə\. City, ✱ of West Bengal, NE India, on Hugli River ab. 90 mi. (145 km.) from its mouth; met. area pop. (1991c) 11,021,915; ✱ of former Bengal prov. and Presidency division and, until 1912, seat of government of India. Has one of world's most active ports; jute, iron, chemicals, textiles. Univ. of Calcutta (1857), Jadavpur Univ. (1955), Rabindra Bharati Univ. (1962). Has fine Maidan, (park, 2 sq. mi. or 5 sq. km.) which contains Fort William; Jain temple; botanical garden; government buildings; Indian museum; National Library.

History: English factory estab. by merchant Job Charnock on site 1690; Fort William erected 1696; seat of Bengal presidency 1707; captured by Sirāj-ud-Dawlah, nabob of Bengal, who imprisoned English (Black Hole of Calcutta) 1756; retaken by British soldier Robert Clive 1757; busy commercial center throughout 19th cent. and into 20th; ✱ of British India 1773–1912 (see DELHI); in 20th cent. began an economic decline esp. exacerbated after Bengal prov. was split 1947 bet. India and Pakistan; although poverty is notable, government in late 20th cent. tried to alleviate it through economic programs.

Cal·das \ˈkäl-däs\. Department of W cen. Colombia. See table at COLOMBIA.

Cal·das da Rai·nha \ˈkȧl-dȧzh-dȧ-rȧ-ˈē-nyə\. Town, Leiria dist., W Portugal; pop. (1991p) 21,923; spa; pottery.

Cal·dei·ra \käl-ˈdā-rä\. Mountain peak on Faial I. in the Azores; 3350 ft. (1021 m.).

Cal·der \ˈkȯl-dər\. **1.** River in Lancashire, NW England; flows into the Ribble River; 15 mi. (24 km.) long.
2. River in SW Yorkshire, N cen. England; flows NE into the Aire River at Castleford below Leeds.

Cal·de·ra \käl-ˈdā-rä\. Seaport and commune, Atacama region, N cen. Chile, ab. 40 mi. (64 km.) NW of Copiapó; chief port of region and the port of Copiapó (54 mi. or 87 km. by rail).

Cal·die·ro \käl-ˈdyā-rō\. Commune, Verona prov., SW Veneto, NE Italy; pop. (1981p) 4428; scene of battle of Napoleonic Wars (1805) in which the French defeated the Austrians.

Çal·dı·ran \ˌchäl-də-ˈrän\ *also* **Chal·di·ran** \ˌchäl-\. Town, E Turkey in Asia, S of Kars; battle 1514 in which Selim I, Ottoman sultan, defeated Persians and extended his empire.

Cald·well \ˈkȯl-ˌdwel, -dwəl, ˈkäl-\. **1.** Name of a parish in N cen. Louisiana and of counties in four states of the U.S. See tables at KENTUCKY, LOUISIANA, MISSOURI, NORTH CAROLINA, TEXAS.
2. City, ⊗ of Canyon co., SW Idaho, 25 mi. (40 km.) W of Boise; pop. (1990c) 18,400; Albertson Coll. (1891).
3. Borough, Essex co., NE New Jersey, 9 mi. (14 km.) NNW of Newark; pop. (1990c) 7549; Caldwell Coll. (1939); birthplace of Grover Cleveland, 22d and 24th president of the U.S., 1837.
4. Village, ⊗ of Noble co., SE Ohio, 21 mi. (34 km.) N of Marietta; pop. (1990c) 1786.
5. City, ⊗ of Burleson co., E cen. Texas, 20 mi. (32 km.) SW of Bryan; pop. (1990c) 3181.

Cal·dy Island *or* **Cal·dey Island** \ˈkäl-de\. Island, S Wales; at W entrance to Carmarthen Bay; lighthouse; site of monastery since c. 6th cent. A.D.; ancient stone inscribed in ogham and Latin.

Cal·e·don \ˈka-lə-dən\. **1.** River in SE Africa; rises in the Drakensberg near the NW boundary of KwaZulu-Natal, E Rep. of South Africa, flows WSW forming the boundary bet. Free State and Lesotho, and empties into Orange River; 240 mi. (386 km.) long.
2. Town, S Ontario, Canada, NW of Toronto; pop. (1991c) 34,965.
3. Town, SW Western Cape prov., S Rep. of South Africa, 70 mi. (113 km.) E of Cape Town; thermal springs.

Cal·e·do·nia \ˌka-lə-ˈdō-nyə, -nē-ə\. **1.** County in NE Vermont. See table at VERMONT.
2. Village, ⊗ of Houston co., SE corner of Minnesota, 30 mi. (48 km.) S of Winona; pop. (1990c) 2846; trade center.
3. Town, Racine co., SE Wisconsin; pop. (1990c) 20,999.
4. Ancient name for N Britain; roughly equivalent to present-day Scotland.

Cal·e·do·nian Canal \ˌkal-ə-ˈdō-nyən, -nē-ən\. Ship canal extending diagonally across N Scotland from Loch Linnhe on the SW to Moray Firth on the NE; built by uniting Lochs Ness, Oich, Lochy, and Eil with a navigable channel; begun 1803, opened 1822, completed 1847; 60.5 mi. (97 km.) long, incl. 22 mi. (35 km.) of channel construction and 38.5 mi. (62 km.) in the lochs; 110 ft. (34 m.) wide at water surface; locks have an av. lift of 8 ft. (2 m.); nowadays used by pleasure craft.

Ca·lex·i·co \kə-ˈlek-si-ˌkō, ka-\. City, Imperial co., S California, on Mexican border adjacent to Mexicali, Mexico; pop. (1990c) 18,633; incorp. 1908.

Calf of Man. See MAN, CALF OF.

Cal·ga·ry \ˈkal-gə-rē\. City, S Alberta, Canada, on Bow River; pop. (1991c) 710,677; trading and financial center of an extensive area of stock raising and gas and oil production; flour, building materials, lumber; oil refineries and meat-packing houses; railroad shops; botanical garden; zoo; museum. Univ. of Calgary (1945, reorganized 1966). Begun as a fort of the Northwest Mounted Police 1875; city charter 1893; city government reorganized 1952; site of Winter Olympic Games 1988 and annual Calgary Stampede (rodeo).

Cal·houn \kal-ˈhün\. **1.** Name of counties in 11 states of the U.S. See tables at ALABAMA, ARKANSAS, FLORIDA, GEORGIA, ILLINOIS, IOWA, MICHIGAN, MISSISSIPPI, SOUTH CAROLINA, TEXAS, WEST VIRGINIA.
2. City, ⊗ of Gordon co., NW Georgia, 22 mi. (35 km.) NNE of Rome; pop. (1990c) 7135; incorp. 1852; largely destroyed by Union Gen. William T. Sherman 1864 but rebuilt.
3. City, ⊗ of McLean co., W Kentucky; pop. (1990c) 854.

Ca·li \ˈkä-lē\. City, ✱ of Valle del Cauca dept., W Colombia; pop. (1992e) 1,624,400; alt. 3327 ft. (1014 m.); bisected by Cali River; connected by rail with port of Buenaventura 105 mi. (169 km.) to W; center of valley trade; manufactures paper and chemicals; livestock, coffee, sugarcane, cotton, and soybeans produced nearby; university (1945); founded 1536.

Ca·li·an Point *also* **Ka·li·an Point** \ˌkä-lē-ˈän\. Cape on SW coast of Davao del Sur prov., Mindanao, Philippines.

Cal·i·cut \ˈka-li-ˌkət\ *or* **Ko·zhi·kode** \ˈkō-zhi-ˌkōd\. City, cen. Kerala, S India, on the Malabar Coast 170 mi. (274 km.) SW of Bangalore; pop. (1991e) 456,618; wood processing; exports coconuts, coffee, tea, spices; gave its name to the cloth *calico;* several colleges.

History: Visited by Portuguese explorer Vasco da Gama 1498; unsuccessfully attacked by forces led by Portuguese soldier Alfonso de Albuquerque 1510; site of Portuguese fortified factory c. 1513–25 (abandoned); visited by British 1615; site of trading posts of British (estab. 1664), French (estab. 1698), Danish (estab. 1752); occupied by British troops 1790; transferred by treaty to British 1792.

Cal·i·for·nia \ˌka-li-ˈfȯr-nyə, -nē-ə\. **1.** A western state of U.S.A., bounded on N by Oregon, on E by Nevada and Arizona, on S by Mexican state of Baja California, and on W by the Pacific Ocean; 3d state in area, 158,706 sq. mi. (411,048 sq. km.) [land area 156,537 sq. mi. or 405,431 sq. km.]; first state in population, (1990c) 29,760,020; ✻ Sacramento; 31st state admitted to Union (1850). See table of states at UNITED STATES.

Nickname: Golden State.

State flower: Golden poppy.

Motto: Eureka (I Have Found It).

Rivers: Colorado, forming border in extreme SE with Arizona; Sacramento, flowing from near Mt. Shasta into San Francisco Bay; Pit, a tributary of the Sacramento; San Joaquin, flowing NW from the Sierra Nevada area to join the Sacramento.

Chief lakes: Tahoe in E on Nevada border, Owens in SE, and Salton Sea in Imperial Valley in extreme S.

Mountains and other features: Coast Ranges, in two parts, broken by San Francisco Bay and extending along most of the coast; a higher range, the Sierra Nevada, extends along E border and contains Mt. Whitney, highest peak in state, 14,494 ft. (4418 m.); in this range are Yosemite and Sequoia national parks, Lassen Peak, and Lassen Volcanic National Park; at its S end is Death Valley, a national monument and lowest spot in U.S., and Mojave and Colorado deserts.

Chief products: Tomatoes, lettuce, broccoli, strawberries, grapes, oranges, and other fruits and vegetables, cotton, rice, flowers; oil, natural gas, gypsum; manufacturing: transportation equipment, electrical machinery, electronics; movie and television industries; tourism; has important irrigation systems.

Chief cities: Los Angeles, San Diego, San Jose, San Francisco, Long Beach, Oakland, Sacramento, Fresno, Santa Ana, Anaheim.

Political divisions: Divided into the following 58 counties (for pronunciations of their names, see their individual entries):

NAME	AREA[1] (sq. mi.)	AREA[1] (sq. km.)	POP. (1990c)	CO. SEAT
Alameda	733	1,898	1,279,182	Oakland
Alpine	723	1,873	1,113	Markleeville
Amador	593	1,536	30,039	Jackson
Butte	1,668	4,320	182,120	Oroville
Calaveras	1,032	2,673	31,998	San Andreas
Colusa	1,152	2,984	16,275	Colusa
Contra Costa	733	1,898	803,732	Martinez
Del Norte[2]	1,007	2,608	23,460	Crescent City
El Dorado	1,726	4,470	125,995	Placerville
Fresno[3]	5,968	15,457	667,490	Fresno
Glenn	1,319	3,416	24,798	Willows
Humboldt[2]	3,586	9,288	119,118	Eureka
Imperial[4]	4,241	10,984	109,303	El Centro
Inyo[5]	10,130	26,237	18,281	Independence
Kern	8,152	21,114	543,477	Bakersfield
Kings	1,396	3,616	101,469	Hanford
Lake	1,261	3,266	50,631	Lakeport
Lassen[6]	4,561	11,813	27,598	Susanville
Los Angeles[7]	4,069	10,539	8,863,164	Los Angeles
Madera[8]	2,145	5,556	88,090	Madera
Marin	520	1,347	230,096	San Rafael
Mariposa[9]	1,453	3,763	14,302	Mariposa
Mendocino	3,511	9,093	80,345	Ukiah
Merced	1,981	5,131	178,403	Merced
Modoc	4,097	10,611	9,678	Alturas
Mono	3,027	7,840	9,956	Bridgeport
Monterey	3,324	8,609	355,660	Salinas
Napa	787	2,038	110,765	Napa
Nevada	975	2,525	78,510	Nevada City
Orange	782	2,025	2,410,556	Santa Ana
Placer	1,433	3,711	172,796	Auburn
Plumas	2,569	6,654	19,739	Quincy
Riverside	7,176	18,586	1,170,413	Riverside
Sacramento	975	2,525	1,041,219	Sacramento
San Benito	1,397	3,618	36,697	Hollister
San Bernardino[10]	20,119	52,108	1,418,380	San Bernardino
San Diego	4,262	11,039	2,498,016	San Diego
San Francisco[11]	45	117	723,959	San Francisco
San Joaquin	1,415	3,665	480,628	Stockton
San Luis Obispo	3,184	8,247	217,162	San Luis Obispo
San Mateo	447	1,158	649,623	Redwood City
Santa Barbara[12]	2,738	7,091	369,608	Santa Barbara
Santa Clara	1,300	3,367	1,497,577	San Jose
Santa Cruz	440	1,140	229,734	Santa Cruz
Shasta[13]	3,793	9,824	147,036	Redding
Sierra	958	2,481	3,318	Downieville
Siskiyou	6,264	16,224	43,531	Yreka
Solano	826	2,139	340,421	Fairfield
Sonoma	1,604	4,154	388,222	Santa Rosa
Stanislaus	1,511	3,913	370,522	Modesto
Sutter	603	1,562	64,415	Yuba City
Tehama	2,984	7,729	49,625	Red Bluff
Trinity	3,192	8,267	13,063	Weaverville
Tulare[14]	4,844	12,546	311,921	Visalia
Tuolumne[15]	2,279	5,903	48,456	Sonora
Ventura[16]	1,863	4,825	669,016	Ventura
Yolo	1,028	2,663	141,092	Woodland
Yuba	640	1,658	58,228	Marysville

[1] Area = land area.
[2] Contains part of Redwood National Park.
[3] SE part occupied by Kings Canyon National Park.
[4] Contains Imperial Valley and (in NW) most of Salton Sea, both below sea level.
[5] Death Valley in E and S.
[6] Part of Lassen Volcanic National Park in SW.
[7] Includes Santa Catalina and San Clemente Is., separated from mainland by San Pedro Channel.
[8] Part of Yosemite National Park in NE.
[9] E portion occupied by part of Yosemite National Park.
[10] Largest county in U.S.
[11] Coextensive with city of San Francisco.
[12] Includes northernmost group of Santa Barbara Is. (San Miguel, Santa Rosa, and Santa Cruz), separated from mainland by Santa Barbara Channel.
[13] SE corner contains part of Lassen Volcanic National Park, incl. Lassen Peak.
[14] NE portion contains Sequoia National Park.
[15] SE portion occupied by part of Yosemite National Park.
[16] Includes small islands of cen. part of chain of Santa Barbara Is.

History: Inhabited orig. by American Indians; first European coastal exploration by voyage of Spanish emissaries Juan Rodríguez Cabrillo and Bartolomé Ferrelo who established Spanish claim to region 1542–43; coast reached by English mariner Sir Francis Drake 1579; first Franciscan mission estab. by Junípero Serra at San Diego 1769; remained under Spanish control, and later under Mexican control until conquered by U.S. forces during Mexican War (1846–47); ceded to U.S. by Treaty of Guadalupe Hidalgo 1848; settlement by Americans begun in 1841, greatly accelerated after discovery of gold at Coloma (Sutter's Mill) in 1848 which brought influx of miners and adventurers (the "forty-niners"); admitted to Union Sept. 9, 1850 as a free state under Compromise Act; present constitution (many times amended) drawn up by constitutional convention 1878–79, ratified by people, and in force Jan. 1, 1880; with an already expanding population, state in 20th cent. grew even more with advent of the automobile; has more miles of freeway than any other state in U.S.; economy largest of all states in U.S.; subject to earthquakes, state suffered severe

CALIFORNIA
CITIES
State capital
County seat
City
BOUNDARIES
International
State
County
FEATURES
Canals
Dams
Points of interest
KEY TO NUMBERED COUNTIES
1 ALAMEDA
2 AMADOR
3 CALAVERAS
4 COLUSA
5 CONTRA COSTA
6 LAKE
7 MARIN
8 MERCED
9 NAPA
10 ORANGE
11 SACRAMENTO
12 SAN FRANCISCO
13 SAN JOAQUIN
14 SANTA CLARA
15 SANTA CRUZ
16 SOLANO
17 STANISLAUS
18 SUTTER
19 YOLO
20 YUBA
OREGON
NEVADA
ARIZONA
MEXICO
PACIFIC OCEAN
DEL NORTE
SISKIYOU
MODOC
HUMBOLDT
TRINITY
SHASTA
LASSEN
TEHAMA
PLUMAS
MENDOCINO
GLENN
BUTTE
SIERRA
NEVADA
PLACER
SONOMA
EL DORADO
ALPINE
TUOLUMNE
MONO
SAN MATEO
MARIPOSA
MADERA
SAN BENITO
FRESNO
INYO
MONTEREY
KINGS
TULARE
SAN LUIS OBISPO
KERN
SANTA BARBARA
VENTURA
LOS ANGELES
SAN BERNARDINO
RIVERSIDE
SAN DIEGO
IMPERIAL
Upper Klamath Lake
Clear Lake Reservoir
Goose Lake
LAVA BEDS NATIONAL MON.
FT. BIDWELL IND. RES.
REDWOOD NATIONAL PARK
HOOPA VALLEY IND. RES.
Mt. Shasta 14,163 ft.
Eagle Peak 9,934 ft.
LASSEN VOLCANIC NATIONAL PARK
Lassen Peak 10,456 ft.
Honey Lake
Eagle Lake
Pyramid Lake
ROUND VALLEY IND. RES.
Black Butte Reservoir
Clear Lake
Lake Tahoe
Carson City
POINT REYES NATIONAL SEASHORE
Mono Lake
YOSEMITE NATIONAL PARK
Boundary Peak 13,140 ft.
DEVILS POSTPILE NATIONAL MONUMENT
PAIUTE IND. RES.
KINGS CANYON NATIONAL PARK
SEQUOIA NATIONAL PARK
Mt. Whitney 14,495 ft.
DEATH VALLEY NATIONAL MONUMENT
Lowest point in North America 282 ft. below sea level
Owens Lake
PINNACLES NATIONAL MONUMENT
TULE RIVER IND. RES.
Searles Lake
Lake Mead
Lake Mohave
Soda Lake
MOJAVE DESERT
FORT MOHAVE IND. RES.
CHEMEHUEVI VALLEY IND. RES.
JOSHUA TREE NATIONAL MON.
COLORADO R. IND. RES.
Salton Sea
Imperial Reservoir
YUMA IND. RES.
CABRILLO NATIONAL MON.
Laguna Salada
Santa Barbara Channel
SAN MIGUEL I.
SANTA ROSA I.
SANTA CRUZ I.
CHANNEL ISLANDS NATIONAL PARK
SANTA BARBARA ISLANDS
SAN NICOLAS I.
SANTA CATALINA I.
SAN CLEMENTE I.
San Pedro Channel
Gulf of Santa Catalina
COAST RANGES
SIERRA NEVADA
SAN BERNARDINO MTS.
Los Angeles Aqueduct
California Aqueduct
Colorado R. Aqueduct
SEE INSET
Sacramento
Oakland
San Francisco
San Jose
Stockton
Modesto
Fresno
Bakersfield
Santa Barbara
Los Angeles
Long Beach
Anaheim
Santa Ana
Riverside
San Bernardino
Palm Springs
San Diego
Chula Vista
Escondido
Oceanside
MARIN
SONOMA
NAPA
SOLANO
CONTRA COSTA
ALAMEDA
SANTA CLARA
SANTA CRUZ
San Pablo Bay
JOHN MUIR NAT'L HIST. SITE
MUIR WOODS NAT'L MON.
GOLDEN GATE NAT'L REC. AREA
Fort Point N.H.S.
San Francisco Bay
Calaveras Reservoir
Mt. Hamilton 4,262 ft.
Leroy Anderson Reservoir
LOS ANGELES
SAN BERNARDINO
ORANGE
RIVERSIDE
Santa Monica Bay
San Pedro Bay
Lake Mathews
Lake Elsinore
0 20 40 60 80 100 mi
0 30 60 90 120 150 km
©2000, Encyclopædia Britannica, Inc.

ones in N around San Francisco esp. 1906 and 1989 and in S around Los Angeles 1994.
2. City, ⊗ of Moniteau co., cen. Missouri, 22 mi. (35 km.) W of Jefferson City; pop. (1990c) 3465.
3. Borough, Washington co., SW Pennsylvania, on Monongahela River 15 mi. (24 km.) NW of Uniontown; pop. (1990c) 5748; coal deposits; California Univ. of Pennsylvania (1852).

California, Gulf of *or in Mexico sometimes called* **Sea of Cor·tés** \kor-'tes, -'tez\; *formerly* **Ver·mil·ion Sea** \vər-'mil-yən\. Arm of the Pacific Ocean extending in NW direction bet. the Mexican states of Baja California and Baja California Sur on the W and Sonora and Sinaloa on the E; ab. 59,000 sq. mi. (152,810 sq. km.).

California, Lower. See BAJA CALIFORNIA.

California Aqueduct. Aqueduct, cen. California, carrying water from delta of the Sacramento River S through the San Joaquin Valley which it helps to irrigate.

California Current. An ocean current flowing S off W coast of North America.

Ca·li·ma \kä-'lē-mä\. River, W Colombia; flows into the San Juan N of Buenaventura; ab. 50 mi. (80 km.) long.

Cal·i·mere, Point \'ka-li-,mir\. Cape, E Tamil Nadu, SE coast of India, N of Palk Strait.

Calimno *or* **Calino.** See KALYMNOS.

Ca·li·nog \,kä-lē-'nȯg\. Municipality, N Iloilo prov., Panay, Philippines, N of City of Iloilo; pop. (1980c) 32,897.

Cal·i·pa·tria \,ka-li-'pā-trē-ə\. City, Imperial co., SE corner of California, 26 mi. (42 km.) N of El Centro; pop. (1990c) 2690.

Cal·i·sto·ga \,ka-li-'stō-gə\. City, Napa co., W cen. California, 12 mi. (19 km.) NE of Santa Rosa; pop. (1990c) 4468; hot springs and geysers; spa; in wine-producing area; settled 1859.

Calivo. See KALIBO.

Cal·la·han \'ka-lə-,han\. County in N cen. Texas. See table at TEXAS.

Cal·lan·der \'ka-lən-dər\. Village, Parry Sound dist., SE Ontario, Canada, on railroad line at E end of Lake Nipissing ab. 7 mi. (11 km.) SSE of North Bay.

Cal·lao \kä-'yä-ō\. City, chief seaport of Peru, on Callao Bay 8 mi. (13 km.) W of Lima; pop. (1990e) 588,600; metallurgical industries; breweries; exports include minerals, fish meal; well-equipped maritime terminal. Founded 1537; incorp. as a town 1671; destroyed by tidal wave and earthquake 1746; bombarded by Spanish 1866, and again c. 1880 by Chilean forces who took possession during War of the Pacific (1879–84); suffered heavy damage from earthquake 1940; major port expansion and modernization from mid-20th cent.

Cal·la·way \'ka-lə-,wā\. **1.** County in cen. Missouri. See table at MISSOURI.
2. City, Bay co., NW Florida; pop. (1990c) 12,253.

Calleva Atrebatum. See SILCHESTER.

Cal·lic·u·la \kə-'li-kyə-lə\. Mountain, Campania, Italy, N of Capua and ab. 4 mi. (6 km.) NE of Teanum Sidicinum (*or mod.* Teano); here Carthaginian Gen. Hannibal on his way back to Apulia 217 B.C. outwitted Roman commander Quintus Fabius Maximus Cunctator.

Cal·li·ni·cum \,ka-lə-'nī-kəm\. Ancient town on left bank of the Euphrates, N Syria, S of Edessa; on E frontier of Roman Empire in 6th and 7th cents. A.D.; Byzantine Gen. Belisarius defeated here 531 by Persian King Kavadh I.

Callipolis. See GELİBOLU.

Callithea. See KALLITHÉA.

Cal·lo·way \'ka-lə-,wā\. County in SW Kentucky. See table at KENTUCKY.

Calmar. See KALMAR.

Cal·no \'kal-,nō\ *or* **Cal·neh** \-nə\. Biblical city of N Syria (*Isa.* x. 9).

Ca·lo·o·can \,kä-lō-'ō-,kän\. Chartered city, NW Rizal prov., Luzon, Philippines, just N of Manila; pop. (1986e) 593,362.

Ca·loo·sa·hatch·ee \kə-,lü-sə-'ha-chē\. River, S Florida; rises in Glades co., S cen. Florida Penin., flows W past Fort Myers and into Gulf of Mexico; ab. 75 mi. (120 km.) long; connected by canal with Lake Hicpochee, constitutes W portion of the Okeechobee Waterway (*q.v.*).

Ca·lo·re \kä-'lō-rā\; *anc.* **Ca·lor** \'kā-,lȯr\. River, S Italy; E headstream of the Volturno.

Calpe. See GIBRALTAR, ROCK OF.

Cal·ta·gi·ro·ne \,käl-tä-jē-'rō-nē\. Commune, Catania prov., E Sicily, Italy, 37 mi. (60 km.) SW of the commune of Catania; pop. (1989c) 38,576.

Cal·ta·nis·set·ta \,käl-tä-nēs-'set-tä\. **1.** Province of cen. Sicily, Italy. See table at ITALY.
2. Commune, its ✻, 59 mi. (95 km.) SE of Palermo; pop. (1991p) 60,162; sulfur; mineral springs; cathedral; Norman monastery.

Ca·luire–et–Cuire \kȧl-'wēr-ā-'kwēr\. Commune, Rhône dept., E cen. France, N suburb of Lyon on left bank of Saône River.

Cal·u·met \'kal-yu̇-,met, -mət\. **1.** County in E Wisconsin. See table at WISCONSIN.
2. Area, NW Indiana and NE Illinois, SE of and adjacent to Chicago, Illinois; includes chiefly the cities of East Chicago, Gary, Hammond, and Whiting, Indiana, and Calumet City and Lansing, Illinois; historically known for its heavy industry.

Calumet City. City, Cook co., NE Illinois, 20 mi. (32 km.) S of Chicago on Indiana border; pop. (1990c) 37,840.

Calumet Harbor. Harbor district, SE Chicago, Illinois, on Lake Michigan at mouth of Calumet River (8 mi. or 13 km. long) draining **Lake Calumet** in S Chicago.

Calumet Park. Village, Cook co., NE Illinois, S suburb of Chicago; pop. (1990c) 8418.

Ca·lum·pit \,kä-lüm-'pēt\. Municipality, SW Bulacan prov., Luzon, Philippines, NW of Malolos.

Cal·va·dos \,kȧl-vȧ-'dōs; ,kal-və-'dōs, -'dōs, -'däs\. Department of NW France. See table at FRANCE.

Calvados Reef *or Fr.* **Ro·chers du Calvados** \rō-'shā-dᵫ-\. Long reef of rocks off village of Asnelles on Normandy coast, Calvados dept., France, W of the mouth of the Orne; was bet. the cen. and E beachheads on which Allies landed June 6, 1944 (D day).

Cal·va·ry \'kal-və-rē\ *or Heb.* **Gol·go·tha** \'gäl-gə-thə, gäl-'gä-thə\. The place, outside of the ancient city of Jerusalem, where Jesus, founder of Christianity, was crucified (*Luke* xxiii. 33); the traditional site is within the walls of modern Jerusalem and is occupied by the Church of the Holy Sepulcher; actual site is uncertain.

Cal·ven \'käl-vən\. Narrow gorge, NE Italy, near the border of Graubünden canton, Switzerland; scene of defeat 1499 of Holy Roman Emperor Maximilian I by the Swiss of the Grisons (Graubünden) who thereby gained their independence.

Cal·vert \'kal-vərt\. County in S Maryland. See table at MARYLAND.

Cal·vi \'käl-vē\. Seaport, NW Corsica, France; founded 13th cent.; under Genoese control during Middle Ages; repulsed forces of Henry II of France 1553; conquered by British naval officer Horatio Nelson 1794 after seven weeks' siege in which he lost an eye.

Calycadnus. See GÖKSU 1.

Cal·y·don \'ka-lə-,dän, -dən\. Ancient city, S Aetolia, cen. Greece, near coast of Gulf of Patras; scene in Greek legend of the Calydonian boar hunt.

Calydonius, Sinus. See PATRAS, GULF OF.

Calymna *or* **Calymnos.** See KALYMNOS.

Cam \'kam\. River, Cambridgeshire and Isle of Ely co., E cen. England; flows into the Ouse 3.5 mi. (6 km.) S of Ely; 40 mi. (64 km.) long; the city of Cambridge, on its banks, derives its name from the river.

Ca·ma·güey \,kä-mä-'gwā\; *formerly* **Puer·to Prín·ci·pe** \'pwer-tō-'prēn-sē-,pā\. **1.** Province of E cen. Cuba. See table at CUBA.

\ə\ abut \ˈə\ matches \ᵊ\ kitten, Fr table \ər\ further \a\ ash \ā\ ace \ä\ cot, cart \ȧ\ Fr bac \au̇\ out \b̵\ Span Avila \ch\ chin \e\ bet \ē\ easy \g\ go \i\ hit \ī\ ice \j\ job \k̟\ Ger ich, Buch \ⁿ\ Fr vin \ŋ\ sing \ō\ go \ȯ\ all \ȯ\ law \œ\ Fr bœuf \œ̄\ Fr feu \ȯi\ boy \th\ thin \t͟h\ this \ü\ loot \u̇\ foot \ue\ Ger füllen \ue̅\ Fr rue \y\ yet \ʸ\ Fr digne \'dēnʸ\, nuit \'nwʸē\ \yü\ few \yu̇\ fury \zh\ vision

2. Municipality and city, its ✻; munic. pop. (1990e) 283,008; distributing center. Founded on present site 1528; was early 19th cent. ✻ of Spanish West Indies. Its port is Nuevitas.

Camagüey, Ar·chi·pié·la·go de \ˌär-chē-ˈpye-lä-ˌgō-thā-\. Group of islands off N coast of Camagüey prov., E cen. Cuba; chief islands: Romano, Sabinal, Coco, and Guajaba.

Ca·ma·io·re \ˌkä-mä-ˈyō-rā\. Commune, Lucca prov., Tuscany, cen. Italy, 12 mi. (19 km.) NW of the commune of Lucca; pop. (1991p) 30,275.

Ca·ma·jua·ní \ˌkä-mä-wä-ˈnē\. Town, Las Villas prov., W cen. Cuba, E of Santa Clara.

Ca·ma·lig \kä-ˈmä-lēg\. Municipality, E Albay prov., Luzon, Philippines, at S base of Mayon Volcano and on railroad line ab. 6 mi. (10 km.) W of Legazpi.

Ca·ma·no Island \kə-ˈmā-nō\. Island in upper Puget Sound, off W coast of Snohomish co., NW Washington; ab. 14 mi. (23 km.) long; a part of Island co., Washington.

Ca·ma·rat, Cape \ˌkȧ-mȧ-ˈrȧ\. Cape, Var dept., SE France, NE of the Hyères Is.

Ca·ma·ret \ˌkȧ-mȧ-ˈrā\ *or in full* **Camaret–sur–Mer** \sūr-ˈmer\. Village, Finistère dept., NW France, at tip of a peninsula ab. 10 mi. (16 km.) S of Brest.

Camargo. See CIUDAD CAMARGO.

Ca·margue \kä-ˈmärg\ *or* **Île de la Camargue** \ˌēl-də-lȧ-\ *or* **The Camargue.** Marshy island in delta of the Rhone River, S France.

Cam·a·ril·lo \ˌka-mə-ˈri-lō\. City, Ventura co., SW California, 37 mi. (60 km.) ESE of Santa Barbara; pop. (1990c) 52,303.

Ca·ma·ri·nal, Cape \ˌkä-mä-rē-ˈnäl\. Cape on SW coast of Spain, S of Cape Trafalgar.

Ca·ma·ri·nes Nor·te \ˌkä-mä-ˈrē-nās-ˈnōr-tā\. Province, SE Luzon, Philippines, on Pacific coast; ✻ Daet. Mountains are volcanic and a continuation of ranges in Quezon and Camarines Sur; highest peak Labo 5066 ft. (1544 m.) on S border; soil very fertile; gold. Chief towns: Daet, Jose Pañganiban, Paracale. See table at PHILIPPINES.

Camarines Sur \ˈsür\. Province, comprising cen. part of long peninsula of SE Luzon, Philippines, with coasts on both the Pacific Ocean and inland waters of the archipelago; ✻ Naga. Mountain ranges extend along W coast and through Caramoan Penin.; volcanic peaks of Isarog and Iriga in cen. and S parts; the Bicol flows generally NW from Lake Bato to San Miguel Bay; on extreme E separated by narrow channel from Catanduanes I. (part of Albay). Chief towns: Naga, Iriga, Nabua, Libmanan, and Caramoan. United with Camarines Norte as one political unit until 1919 when made a separate province. See table at PHILIPPINES.

Camarões. See CAMEROONS.

Ca·ma·rón, Cape \ˌkä-mä-ˈrōn\. Cape on N coast of Honduras, projecting into the Caribbean Sea.

Cam·as \ˈka-məs\. **1.** County in S cen. Idaho. See table at IDAHO.

2. City, Clark co., SW Washington, on Columbia River 12 mi. (19 km.) E of Vancouver; pop. (1990c) 6442.

Camau. See QUAN LONG.

Ca Mau Peninsula. See MUI BAI BUNG.

Cam·ba·luc \ˈkam-bə-ˌlək\ *or* **Cam·ba·lu** \ˈkam-bə-ˌlü\. Venetian traveler Marco Polo's name for Khanbalik (*q.v.*), the Mongol ✻ of China.

Cam·bay \kam-ˈbā\. **1.** Former Indian state, now part of Gujarat, W India, at head of Gulf of Khambhat; 392 sq. mi. (1015 sq. km.).

2. Town, its ✻. See KHAMBHAT.

Cambay, Gulf of. See KHAMBHAT, GULF OF.

Camberiacum. See CHAMBÉRY.

Cam·ber·well \ˈkam-bər-ˌwel, -wəl\. Municipality, S Victoria, SE Australia, E suburb of Melbourne; pop. (1991c) 83,799.

Cam·bo·dia \kam-ˈbō-dē-ə\ *or* **Kam·pu·chea** \ˌkam-pù-ˈchē-ə, ˌkäm-\; *formerly* **Cam·bo·ja** \kam-ˈbō-jə\ *or* *1970–75* **Khmer Republic** \kə-ˈmer\; *1976–c. 1989* **Democratic Kampuchea** *or Fr.* **Cam·bodge** \käⁿ-ˈbȯj\. Constitutional monarchy, SE Asia, in S Indochina, bounded on N by Thailand and Laos, on E and SE by Vietnam, on SW by Gulf of Thailand, and on W and NW by Thailand; 69,898 sq. mi. (181,036 sq. km.); pop. (1993e) 9,287,000; ✻ Phnom Penh.

Physical features: Generally level with mountain range (Dangrek Mts.) along N border and peaks along the coast 2300 to 5700 ft. (700 to 1740 m.). Most of the republic lies in basin of lower Mekong River with the large lake, Tonle Sap, in its W part; has large jungle areas.

Chief products: Rice, corn, rubber, sugar, tobacco, timber; fishing; manufacturing: cement, paper, textiles.

Chief towns: Phnom Penh, Battambang, Kompong Cham.

History: In early times under Hindu and to lesser extent Buddhist influence; Khmer state gradually absorbed neighboring state early 7th cent. A.D.; at its height beginning with Jayavarman II and successors 9th–12th cents. when it ruled entire Mekong Valley and tributary Shan States and built Angkor Thom as ✻ (see ANGKOR); during 13th cent. more widespread adoption of Buddhism occurred, resulting in script change from Sanskrit to Pali; from 13th cent. attacked by Annamese and Siamese city-states; became province alternately of Annam or Siam; Batambang ceded to Siam 1809; became a French protectorate 1863; had border dispute with Siam, settled in favor of Cambodia 1907; during WWII occupied by Japanese along with much of Indochina; became fully independent 1954; member of UN 1955; border areas scene of fighting in Vietnam War from 1961; civilian government overthrown by military March 1970, forcing Prince Norodom Sihanouk into exile to China; NE and E areas subsequently occupied by North Vietnamese and penetrated by U.S. and South Vietnamese forces causing wider involvement in Vietnam War; Pol Pot came to power 1975 instituting regime of terror leading to mass slaughter of population; Vietnam involved in Cambodian civil wars through-

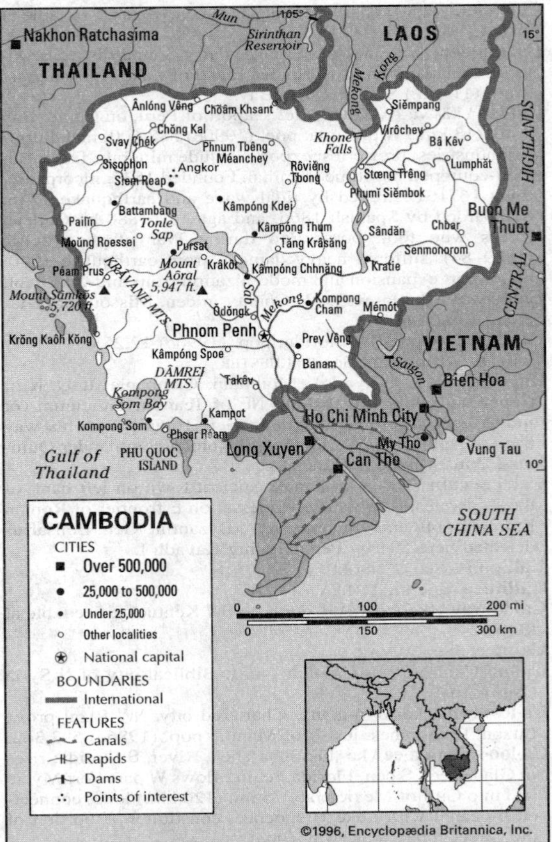

out 1980s; peace treaty among warring factions signed 1991; UN with temporary authority to administer country; elections held 1993; constitution adopted stipulating democratic government with limited monarchy; Sihanouk crowned king 1993; revolutionary movement members led by Pol Pot among others continued to fight.

Cambodia Point. See MUI BAI BUNG.

Cam·borne–Red·ruth \ˈkam-ˌbȯrn-ˈred-ˌrüth\. Area, Cornwall, SW England, 53 mi. (85 km.) WSW of Plymouth.

Cam·brai *or older* **Cam·bray** \kä^{n}-ˈbre, kam-ˈbrā\ *or Flem.* **Kam·bryk** \ˈkäm-brīk\; *anc.* **Cam·e·ra·cum** \ˌka-mə-ˈrā-kəm\. City, Nord dept., N France, on Schelde River 34 mi. (55 km.) SSE of Lille; pop. (1990c) 34,210; known for its linen goods (esp. cambric and cambresine—both named for the city); archiepiscopal see.

History: A Frankish ❋ 445 A.D.; league against Venice formed here 1508; Peace of Cambrai signed 1529; to France c. 1678. Occupied by Germans 1914–18; important battles of WWI fought in villages to SW: (1) a surprise British attack with first use of tanks on German lines and German counterattack 1917; in closing phase of war of attrition, a partial British success; (2) complete victory of British and Canadians 1918.

Cam·bria \ˈkām-brē-ə, ˈkam-\. **1.** County in SW cen. Pennsylvania. See table at PENNSYLVANIA.

2. Latin name of Wales, used by modern poets.

Cam·bri·an Mountains \ˌkam-brē-ən\. Range extending N to S through cen. Wales; highest peak Aran Mawddwy 2970 ft. (905 m.).

Cam·bridge \ˈkām-brij\. **1.** Village, ⊗ of Henry co., NW Illinois; pop. (1990c) 2601.

2. City and port, ⊗ of Dorchester co., SE Maryland, on E shore of Chesapeake Bay 38 mi. (61 km.) SE of Annapolis; pop. (1990c) 11,514; fishing. Settled 1684; colonial church.

3. City, a ⊗ of Middlesex co., NE Massachusetts, 3 mi. (5 km.) W of Boston; pop. (1990c) 95,802; educational center; also manufacturing and commercial center; electronics, computer programming, software, advanced computers, genetic engineering, consulting companies; museums; Harvard Univ. (1636), Radcliffe Coll. (1879, affiliated with Harvard Univ.), Massachusetts Institute of Technology (1861), Lesley Coll. (1909).

History: Founded 1630 as one of the Massachusetts Bay settlements and known as **New Towne** \ˈnü-ˌtau̇n, ˈnyü\ until 1638; Harvard Coll. (first institution of higher learning in U.S.) founded 1636 and first printing press in U.S. set up c. 1640 by Stephen Day; Gen. George Washington took command of American Army July 3, 1775 on Cambridge Common; Craigie House (built 1759) served as his headquarters 1775–76; poet Henry Wadsworth Longfellow lived at Craigie House, now known as Longfellow National Historic Site; in 19th cent. home of many American literary leaders; incorp. as city 1846; burial place of Longfellow, James Russell Lowell, Mary Baker Eddy, Oliver Wendell Holmes.

4. City, ⊗ of Isanti co., E Minnesota, 41 mi. (66 km.) N of Minneapolis; pop. (1990c) 5094.

5. City, Furnas co., S Nebraska, on Republican River; pop. (1990c) 1107; fossilized bones of saber-toothed tiger discovered 1947.

6. City, ⊗ of Guernsey co., E Ohio, 21 mi. (34 km.) ENE of Zanesville; pop. (1990c) 11,748; coal, pottery-clay, oil, and natural-gas deposits nearby; glass museum; settled c. 1806.

7. City, SE Ontario; Canada, pop. (1991c) 92,772; formed 1973 when Galt, Hespeler, and Preston were merged.

8. County in England. See CAMBRIDGESHIRE.

9. *or Lat.* **Can·ta·brig·ia** \ˌkan-tə-ˈbri-jə, -jē-ə\. City, ⊗ of Cambridgeshire co., E England, on Cam River 48 mi. (77 km.) NNE of London; pop. (1991c) 92,772; electronic equipment, cement; printing and publishing; many churches, esp. the Holy Sepulchre (round church, c. 1130) and St. Benedict; Fitzwilliam Museum. Dates from early times, its site probably occupied by Romans. Chiefly important because of Cambridge Univ. (dating from the 12th cent.). Royal Greenwich Observatory moved here 1990.

Cam·bridge·shire \ˈkām-brij-ˌshir, -shər\ *or* **Cambridge. 1.** Former county, E England; joined with Isle of Ely 1965–74 forming county of Cambridgeshire and Isle of Ely.

2. Administrative county, E England, incl. Isle of Ely and part of former Huntingdonshire; estab. 1974. See table at ENGLAND.

Cambridgeshire and Isle of Ely \ˈē-lē\. Former county in E England; chief rivers: Ouse, Cam, Lark, Nene; mainly agricultural.

Cam·bu·ni·an Mountains \kam-ˈbyü-nē-ən\. Mountain range on N border of Thessaly, NE Greece, and separating it from SW Macedonia; terminates in Mt. Olympus on the E.

Cam·den \ˈkam-dən\. **1.** Name of counties in four states of the U.S. See tables at GEORGIA, MISSOURI, NEW JERSEY, NORTH CAROLINA.

2. Town, ⊗ of Wilcox co., SW cen. Alabama; pop. (1990c) 2414.

3. City, ⊗ of Ouachita co., S Arkansas, on Ouachita River 29 mi. (47 km.) N of El Dorado; pop. (1990c) 14,380.

4. Town, Knox co., S Maine, on W shore of Penobscot Bay 37 mi. (60 km.) E of Augusta; pop. (1990c) 5060; resort.

5. City and port of entry, ⊗ of Camden co., SW New Jersey, on Delaware River across from Philadelphia, with which it is connected by bridge; pop. (1990c) 87,492; canned foods; settled c. 1681; incorp. as city 1828; railroad terminus 1834; made ⊗ of Camden co. 1844; grew rapidly in industrial expansion following Civil War; home of poet Walt Whitman 1873–92.

6. Village, Oneida co., cen. New York, 16 mi. (26 km.) WNW of Rome; pop. (1990c) 2552.

7. Village, ⊗ of Camden co., NE North Carolina, 4 mi. (6 km.) E of Elizabeth City.

8. City, ⊗ of Kershaw co., N cen. South Carolina, near Wateree River 31 mi. (50 km.) ENE of Columbia; pop. (1990c) 6696; noted steeplechase races; winter resort. First settled 1733–34; near scene during Revolution of American defeat (under Gen. Horatio Gates) and mortal wounding of Gen. Johann De Kalb in battle of Camden Aug. 16, 1780, and of British commander Francis Rawdon-Hastings' victory over Americans under Gen. Nathanael Greene at Hobkirk's Hill Apr. 25, 1781; in Civil War became Confederate storehouse, hospital, and haven of refuge until burned by Gen. William T. Sherman in 1865.

9. Town, ⊗ of Benton co., W Tennessee; pop. (1990c) 3643.

10. Municipality, E New South Wales, Australia, SW of Sydney; pop. (1991c) 22,473.

11. A borough of Greater London, SE England. See table at LONDON 4.

Cam·den·ton \ˈkam-dən-tən\. City, ⊗ of Camden co., S cen. Missouri; pop. (1990c) 2561.

Cam·el \ˈka-məl\. River in Cornwall, SW England; flows NW into Atlantic Ocean; ab. 30 mi. (48 km.) long.

Cam·el·ford \ˈka-məl-fərd\. Town, Cornwall, SW England, on the Camel River.

Cam·e·lot \ˈka-mə-ˌlät\. In the Arthurian legends, the place where King Arthur had his palace and court and where the Round Table was; has been variously located in Somersetshire, at Camelford, at or near Winchester, England, and in Wales.

Cam·els Hump \ˈka-məlz\. Peak of the Green Mts., Vermont, 20 mi. (32 km.) SE of Burlington; 4083 ft. (1244 m.).

Cam·em·bert \kȧ-mä^{n}-ˈber, ˈka-məm-ˌber\. Village, Orne dept., NW France, E of Falaise; Camembert cheese first made here attributed to Marie Harel; chief center for the cheese now in nearby Vimoutiers (*q.v.*).

Cameracum. See CAMBRAI.

Ca·me·ri·no \ˌkä-mā-ˈrē-nō\; *anc.* **Cam·e·ri·num** \ˌka-mə-ˈrī-nəm\. Commune, Macerata prov., Marche, cen. Italy, 23 mi. (37 km.) SW of the commune of Macerata; university (1727).

Cam·er·on \ˈka-mə-rən\. **1.** Name of a parish in SW corner of Louisiana and of counties in two states of the U.S. See tables at LOUISIANA, PENNSYLVANIA, TEXAS.
2. Town, ⊗ of Cameron parish, SW corner of Louisiana; pop. (1990c) 2041.
3. City, Clinton and De Kalb cos., NW Missouri, 47 mi. (76 km.) NNE of Kansas City; pop. (1990c) 4831.
4. City, ⊗ of Milam co., cen. Texas, 27 mi. (43 km.) SE of Temple; pop. (1990c) 5580.

Cameron, Mount. Peak, Park co., cen. Colorado; 14,238 ft. (4340 m.).

Cameron Pass. Mountain pass, Larimer and Jackson cos., N Colorado, in Medicine Bow Mts.; alt. 10,285 ft. (3135 m.).

Cam·er·oon \ˌka-mə-ˈrün\ *or Fr.* **Ca·me·roun** \kȧm-ˈrün\ *or officially* **Republic of Cameroon.** Republic, W Africa, bounded on N and NE by Chad, on E by Central African Rep., on S by Rep. of the Congo, Gabon, and Equatorial Guinea, on SW by the Bight of Biafra, and on W and NW by Nigeria; 183,591 sq. mi. (475,501 sq. km.); pop. (1993e) 13,103,000; ✱ Yaoundé.

Physical features: Plateau region inland, marshes along coast and lower courses of rivers; chief rivers Nyong and Sanaga.

Chief products: Cocoa, coffee, timber, bananas, peanuts, palm oil, cotton, rubber; petroleum, natural gas, bauxite; livestock.

Chief towns: Douala and Yaoundé.

History: For history prior to 1922, see CAMEROONS. French mandate 1922–46; became a UN trust territory under French administration 1946; achieved independence 1960; united with S part of former British trust territory of Southern Cameroons 1961; constitution implemented 1972; economic problems troubled the country through 1980s and 1990s.

Cameroon, Mount. Volcanic massif, W Cameroon, ab. 40 mi. (64 km.) NW of Douala; at 13,353 ft. (4070 m.), the highest mountain in sub-Saharan W Africa.

Cam·er·oons \ˌka-mə-ˈrünz\ *or Port.* **Ca·ma·rões** \ˌkȧ-mȧ-ˈrōi^{n}sh\ *or Ger.* **Ka·me·run** \ˌkä-mə-ˈrün\ *or Fr.* **Ca·me·roun** \kȧm-rün\. Former German protectorate, W Africa.

History: Long inhabited before European colonization, area was location of several kingdoms; Islam became important in N, esp. through the Fulani; Portuguese visited late 15th cent.; slave trading became important; missionaries arrived mid-19th cent., among them Englishman Alfred Saker; Germans arrived on coast and German protectorate proclaimed 1884; invaded by Anglo-French forces 1914; after WWI formally divided into British and French administrative zones 1919, which in 1922 became League of Nations mandates and in 1946 UN trust territories; French trust territory became independent republic 1960 (see CAMEROON); in 1961 S part of British trust territory voted for union with Cameroon, N part for union with Nigeria.

Ca·me·tá \ˌkä-mā-ˈtä\. Municipality, Pará state, N Brazil; pop. (1991p) 85,154.

Ca·mi·guin \ˌkä-mē-ˈgwēn\. **1.** Island in Babuyan group, N of Luzon, Philippines; 63 sq. mi. (163 sq. km.); mountainous.
2. Volcano, N part of Camiguin I., Babuyan Is., Philippines; 2602 ft. (793 m.).
3. Island, constituting a province of Philippines, in Mindanao Sea ab. 6 mi. (10 km.) off N coast of Mindanao; mountainous; highest peak 5620 ft. (1713 m.); produces rice; volcanic in formation; eruptions in 1871 and 1948; chief towns: Mambajao, Catarman, and Sagay. See table at PHILIPPINES.

Ca·mi·ling \ˌkä-mē-ˈlēŋ\. Municipality, NW Tarlac prov., Luzon, Philippines, on a tributary of the Agno 19 mi. (31 km.) NW of the municipality of Tarlac; important market town.

Ca·mil·la \kə-ˈmi-lə\. City, ⊗ of Mitchell co., SW Georgia, 25 mi. (40 km.) S of Albany; pop. (1990c) 5008.

Ca·mil·lus \kə-ˈmi-ləs\. Village, Onondaga co., cen. New York, 9 mi. (15 km.) W of Syracuse; pop. (1990c) 1150; claims title of "birthplace of the Republican party" (1852).

Ca·mi·ri \kä-ˈmē-rē\. Town, Santa Cruz dept., S Bolivia, 140 mi. (225 km.) SE of Sucre; oil refineries.

Ca·mi·rus \kə-ˈmī-rəs\. Ancient town on W coast of island of Rhodes; chief town of the island before Rhodes was founded.

Cam·lan \ˈkam-lən\. Locality, SW England, where King Arthur is said to have died in battle 537; site unidentified but possibly near Camelford in Cornwall.

Ca·mo·cim \ˌkȧ-mō-ˈsē^{n}\. City and port, Ceará state, NE Brazil; munic. pop. (1991p) 51,031.

Ca·mo·ghe \ˌkä-mō-ˈgā\. Peak, Ticino canton, SE cen. Switzerland; 7310 ft. (2228 m.).

Ca·mo·ni·ca \kä-ˈmȯ-nē-kä\. Valley in the Alps, in Brescia prov., Lombardy, N Italy; 50 mi. (81 km.) long.

Ca·mor·ta \kə-ˈmȯr-tə\. Island, cen. Nicobar Is., India, just N of Nancowry I.; 58 sq. mi. (150 sq. km.).

Ca·mo·tes Islands \kä-ˈmō-ˌtās\. Group of three islands (Poro, Pacijan, and Ponson), Cebu prov., Philippines, N of Camotes Sea near W coast of Leyte and ab. 20 mi. (32 km.) E of the N end of Cebu I., Visayan Is., E cen. Philippines; 86 sq. mi. (223 sq. km.); mountainous; largest town San Francisco on Pacijan I.; formerly part of Leyte prov.

Camotes Sea. Body of water in Visayan Is., E cen. Philippines, E of N end of Cebu I., N of Bohol, W of Leyte, and S of Camotes Is. Scene of several naval and air battles during WWII Leyte campaign 1944.

Camp \ˈkamp\. County in NE Texas. See table at TEXAS.

Cam·pa·gna \käm-ˈpä-nyä\. **1.** Region, Italy. See CAMPAGNA DI ROMA.
2. Commune, Salerno prov., Campania, S Italy, 18 mi. (29 km.) E of the seaport of Salerno; cathedral.

Campagna di Ro·ma \dē-ˈrō-mä\ *or Eng. often* **Roman Campagna.** Region surrounding Rome, Italy; ab. 800 sq. mi.

(2070 sq. km.); almost coextensive with Rome commune; in 20th cent. largely reclaimed and repopulated.

Cam·pal·di·no \ˌkäm-päl-ˈdē-nō\. Village, Tuscany, Italy, on upper Arno River ESE of Florence; scene of battle 1289 in which the Ghibelline supporters of Arezzo were severely defeated by the Guelphs of Florence, furthering Florentine power.

Cam·pa·na \käm-ˈpä-nä\. **1.** Town, Buenos Aires prov., E Argentina, on the Paraná River 45 mi. (72 km.) NW of the city of Buenos Aires; commercial center; oil refining and grain storage.

2. Island in Pacific Ocean off SW coast of Chile, NW of Wellington I.; ab. 55 mi. (89 km.) long, 10 mi. (16 km.) wide.

Cam·pa·na·rio \ˌkäm-pä-ˈnär-ē-ˌō\. Peak on Argentina-Chile boundary, bet. SW Mendoza prov., W Argentina, and E Maule region, cen. Chile; 13,284 ft. (4049 m.).

Cam·pa·nel·la, Point \ˌkäm-pä-ˈnel-lä\. Cape at S end of the Bay of Naples, Italy, opp. island of Capri.

Cam·pa·nia \käm-ˈpä-nyä\. **1.** Region, France. See CHAMPAGNE.

2. Autonomous region, S Italy; lies on Tyrrhenian Sea bet. Lazio and Basilicata; ✻ Naples; exceedingly fertile and generally mountainous region; produces principally wine, olives, citrus fruits, vegetables, and grain; fishing; chemical and metallurgical industries; tourism.

History: Noted in ancient times as a favorite resort of distinguished Romans; noted for its natural beauty and famous old towns (such as Cumae, Stabiae, Pompeii, Capua, Salernum, and Neapolis). Occupied successively by Greeks, Etruscans, Samnites, and from ab. 350 B.C. by Romans; later ruled by Goths, Byzantines, and Normans; region became part of kingdom of Italy 1860; held elections for regional parliament 1970. See table at ITALY.

Camp·bell \ˈkam-bəl, ˈka-məl\. **1.** Name of counties in five states of the U.S. See tables at KENTUCKY, SOUTH DAKOTA, TENNESSEE, VIRGINIA, WYOMING.

2. Former county in Georgia; part annexed to Fulton co. 1926, the rest 1932.

3. City, Santa Clara co., W California, SW of San Jose; pop. (1990c) 36,048.

4. City, Mahoning co., NE Ohio, on Mahoning River 4 mi. (6 km.) SE of Youngstown; pop. (1990c) 10,038.

Campbell, Cape. Cape on NE coast of South I., New Zealand, at W side of S Cook Strait.

Campbell, Mount. Peak, Antarctica, 84°55′S, 174°00′W; 12,434 ft. (3790 m.).

Camp·bell·ford \ˈkam-bəl-fərd, ˈka-məl-\. Town, Northumberland co., SE Ontario, Canada, on Trent River 28 mi. (45 km.) E of Peterborough; resort.

Campbell Hill. Elevation near Bellefontaine, Logan co., W Ohio; 1550 ft. (472 m.); highest point in the state.

Campbell Island. Island in S Pacific Ocean, 52°33′S, 169°9′E; 44 sq. mi. (114 sq. km.); discovered 1810; has good harbors; administered by New Zealand.

Campbell Mountain. Peak in Glacier National Park, NW Montana; 8207 ft. (2502 m.).

Camp·bell·pore \ˈkam-bəl-ˌpȯr\ *also* **Camp·bell·pur** \-ˌpu̇r\ *or* **At·tock** \ə-ˈtäk\. Town, N Punjab, Pakistan, ab. 50 mi. (81 km.) SE of Peshawar; has fortress built by Mogul Emperor Akbar 1581.

Campbell's Bay. Village, ⊗ of Pontiac co., SW Quebec, Canada, on Ottawa River opp. Calumet I. 50 mi. (81 km.) NW of Ottawa; pop. (1991c) 912.

Camp·bells·ville \ˈkam-bəlz-ˌvil, ˈka-məlz-\. City, ⊗ of Taylor co., cen. Kentucky, SW of Danville; pop. (1990c) 9577.

Camp·bell·ton \ˈkam-bəl-tən, ˈka-məl-\. City, Restigouche co., N New Brunswick, Canada, on Restigouche River 15 mi. (24 km.) from its mouth; pop. (1991c) 8699; at head of deepwater navigation; resort; founded late 18th cent.; almost completely destroyed by fire 1910, but rebuilt.

Camp·bell·town \ˈkam-bəl-ˌtau̇n, ˈka-məl-\. **1.** City, E New South Wales, Australia, on coast S of Sidney; pop. (1991c) 137,879.

2. *or* **Campbell Town.** Town and municipality, E Tasmania, Australia, 40 mi. (64 km.) SSE of Launceston.

3. Borough, New Zealand. See BLUFF.

Camp·bel·town \ˈkam-bəl-ˌtau̇n\. Seaport burgh, Strathclyde region, W Scotland, on the E side of S end of Kintyre Penin.; fishing.

Cam·pe·che \käm-ˈpā-chā\. **1.** State, SE Mexico. See table at MEXICO.

2. City, its ✻, on W coast of Yucatán Penin.; pop. (1990p) 172,208; service center for offshore oil facilities; exports cigars, cotton; museum; 16th cent. cathedral; Mayan remains in area; Spanish arrived 1517; founded 1540.

Campeche, Bank of *or Span.* **Ban·co Campeche** \ˈbäŋ-kō\. Shoal, N of Yucatán Penin., state of Yucatán, SE Mexico.

Campeche, Bay of *or Span.* **Ba·hía de Campeche** \bä-ˈē-ä-t͟hā-käm-ˈpā-chē\. SW section of the Gulf of Mexico, forming a wide shallow bay extending into SE Mexico; major oil well blowout June 3, 1979.

Cam·pe·chue·la \ˌkäm-pā-ˈchwā-lä\. Town, E Cuba, on coast of Golfo de Guacanayabo 15 mi. (24 km.) SW of Manzanillo.

Cam·per·down \ˈkäm-pər-ˌdau̇n\. Village, North Holland prov., W Netherlands, on North Sea coast 8 mi. (13 km.) NW of Alkmaar; nearby occurred naval battle 1797 in which British under Adm. Adam Duncan defeated Dutch under Adm. Jan Willem de Winter.

Camp Hill \ˈkamp\. Residential borough, Cumberland co., S Pennsylvania, 5 mi. (8 km.) WSW of Harrisburg; pop. (1990c) 7831; suburb of Harrisburg; correctional facility.

Cam·pi Bi·sen·zio \ˈkäm-pē-bē-ˈzent-sē-ˌō\. Commune, Firenze prov., Tuscany, cen. Italy, 7 mi. (11 km.) WNW of Florence; pop. (1989c) 34,558.

Cam·pi·da·no \ˌkäm-pē-ˈdä-nō\. Plain of SW Sardinia, Italy, extending ab. 70 mi. (113 km.) SE to NW across the island.

Campi Flegrei. See PHLEGRAEAN FIELDS.

Cam·pi·glia Ma·rit·ti·ma \käm-ˈpē-lyä-mä-ˈrēt-tē-mä\. Commune, Livorno prov., Tuscany, cen. Italy, 35 mi. (56 km.) SSE of the commune of Livorno.

Câmpina. See CÎMPINA.

Cam·pi·na Gran·de \kȧm-ˈpē-nə-ˈgrȧn-dē\. City, E Paraíba state, E Brazil, 100 mi. (161 km.) NW of Recife; munic. pop. (1991p) 326,153; leather, textiles.

Cam·pi·nas \kȧm-ˈpē-nəs\. City, E São Paulo state, SE Brazil, 68 mi. (109 km.) NNW of the city of São Paulo; munic. pop. (1991p) 846,084; distribution center for agricultural products; Catholic Univ., Univ. of Campinas (1962).

Cam·pli \ˈkäm-plē\. Commune, Teramo prov., Abruzzi, cen. Italy, 4 mi. (6 km.) N of the commune of Teramo.

Cam·po *or* **Kam·po** \ˈkäm-pō\. **1.** River, Africa. See NTEM.

2. Seaport town, Cameroon, at mouth of the Ntem River just N of the Equatorial Guinea boundary.

Cam·po·bas·so \ˌkäm-pō-ˈbäs-sō\. **1.** Province of Molise, cen. Italy. See table at ITALY.

2. Commune, its ✻, and ✻ of Molise, in Apennines ab. 95 mi. (153 km.) NE of Naples; pop. (1991p) 50,163; 15th cent. feudal castle; cathedral; archaeological museum.

Cam·po·bel·lo \ˌkam-pə-ˈbe-lō\. Island, Charlotte co., SW New Brunswick, Canada, just E of Eastport, Maine; ab. 10 mi. (16 km.) long, 2 to 3 mi. (3 to 5 km.) wide; separated from U.S. by Lubec Channel. Owned by Adm. William Owen and descendants 1767–1880; bought by New York syndicate and converted into summer resort; U.S. President Franklin D. Roosevelt summer home, now a memorial; Roosevelt Memorial Bridge to Lubec, Maine, completed 1962.

Cam·po de Crip·ta·na \ˈkäm-pō-t͟hā-krēp-ˈtä-nä\. Commune, Ciudad Real prov., S cen. Spain, 52 mi. (84 km.) NE of the commune of Ciudad Real; pop. (1991c) 13,727.

Cam·po·for·mi·do \ˌkäm-pō-ˈfȯr-mē-ˌdō\; *formerly* **Cam·po For·mio** \ˈfȯr-mē-ˌō\. Village, Udine prov., E Friuli-Venezia Giulia, NE Italy, SW of Udine; treaty Oct. 17, 1797 bet.

France and Austria ending first phase of Napoleonic Wars, recognizing most of French Emperor Napoléon's conquests.

Cam·po Gran·de \ˈkȧm-pü-ˈgrȧn-dē\. City, ✻ of Mato Grosso do Sul state, SW Brazil; munic. pop. (1991p) 525,612; on railroad line in center of S part of the state.

Cam·po Mai·or \ˈkȧm-pō-mī-ˈyȯr\. Municipality, Piauí state, NE Brazil, ab. 50 mi. (80 km.) NE of Teresina; pop. (1991p) 72,238.

Cam·pos \ˈkȧm-püs\. City, Rio de Janeiro state, SE Brazil, 35 mi. (56 km.) from mouth of the Paraíba River; in rich agricultural area.

Camp·ton \ˈkamp-tən\. **1.** City, ⊗ of Wolfe co., E Kentucky; pop. (1990c) 484.
2. Town, in Grafton co., cen. New Hampshire, 25 mi. (40 km.) NNW of Laconia; pop. (1990c) 2377; resort; settled 1765.

Câmpulung. See CÎMPULUNG.

Camp Upton. See UPTON 3.

Camp Verde \ˌkamp-ˈvər-dē\. Town, Yavapai co., cen. Arizona, 40 mi. (64 km.) SSW of Flagstaff; pop. (1990c) 6243.

Cam Ranh, Vinh \ˈvin-ˈkäm-ˈrän\ *or* **Cam Ranh Bay.** Inlet of South China Sea on SE coast of Vietnam, ab 12°N, bet. Phan Rang and Nha Trang. Former French naval base with large protected anchorage; during WWII used by Japanese 1940–45; major U.S. base (from 1965) during Vietnam War and later a major Soviet naval base.

Cam·rose \ˈkam-ˌrōz\. Town, S cen. Alberta, Canada, 44 mi. (71 km.) SSE of Edmonton; pop. (1991c) 13,420; grain elevators; Camrose Lutheran Coll. (1911).

Camulodunum. See COLCHESTER 4.

Ca·muy \kä-ˈmwē\. Town and municipality, NW Puerto Rico, W of Arecibo.

Ca·na \ˈkā-nə\ *or often* **Cana of Galilee.** Village, Israel, ab. 4 mi. (6 km.) NE of Nazareth; where Jesus performed his first miracle (*John* ii. 1).

Ca·naan \ˈkā-nən\. **1.** Town, Grafton co., W New Hampshire, on Indian River 11 mi. (18 km.) E of Lebanon; pop. (1990c) 3045; resort; Canaan Coll. (1955).
2. The ancient name of that part of Palestine (*q.v.*) bet. Jordan River and Mediterranean Sea, but sometimes vaguely used as the equivalent of all of Palestine; had civilization as far back as Neolithic time (c. 7000–c. 4000 B.C.); had settlements in Early Bronze Age (c. 3200–c. 2100 B.C.); later, invaded by Hebrews c. 1200 B.C., one group of which, the Israelites, eventually overcame its inhabitants (Canaanites) c. 10th cent. B.C.; the Promised Land of the Israelites (*Exod.* iii. 8).

Ca·naan Mountain \kə-ˈnān\. Peak, Preston co., N West Virginia; 3702 ft. (1128 m.).

Ca·ña·cao Bay \ˌkä-nyä-ˈkau̇\. Inlet of Manila Bay at end of Cavite Penin., Cavite prov., Luzon, Philippines; good anchorage; the N harbor of Cavite naval base.

Can·a·da \ˈka-nə-də\; *formerly, esp. before 1867, called* **British North America.** Independent country in N North America, bounded on N by Arctic Ocean, on E by Atlantic Ocean (incl. Davis Strait and Baffin Bay), on S by U.S., and on W by U.S. (Alaska) and Pacific Ocean; 3,851,809 sq. mi. (9,976,185 sq. km.); pop. (1991c) 27,296,859; ✻ Ottawa.

Physical features: Northernmost point (83°07′N) is Cape Columbia on Ellesmere I.; length of U.S.-Canada border 3987 mi. (6415 km.); includes many islands: Baffin, Ellesmere, Victoria, Newfoundland, Melville.

Rivers: St. Lawrence (draining Great Lakes and in part forming boundary with U.S.), Columbia (upper course, flows into Washington state, U.S.), Mackenzie (with great tributaries such as Liard, Slave, Peace, and Athabaska), Yukon (upper course, flows into Alaska), Nelson (with upper tributaries of North and South Saskatchewan), Red River of the North (lower course), Dubawnt, Fraser, Severn, Albany, Ottawa, and Saguenay.

Lakes: Parts of Lakes Ontario, Erie, Huron, Superior, and Lake of the Woods; Great Bear, Great Slave, Athabaska, Winnipeg, Winnipegosis, and many smaller ones such as Nipigon, Mistassini, and Louise (Banff National Park).

Mountains: Rocky Mts. in W with many high peaks extending from Alaska to U.S. border (incl. Selkirk, Cariboo, and other ranges), Coast Mts. along British Columbia coast, Laurentian Mts. in Quebec; highest point Mt. Logan 19,850 ft. (6050 m.) in Yukon Terr., 2d in height in North America.

Chief products: Wheat, oats, barley, fruits and vegetables, dairy products; livestock raising, fishing; petroleum, natural gas, copper, iron ore, nickel, zinc, uranium, platinum, silver, asbestos, potash; hydropower; manufacturing: iron and steel, pulp and paper, chemicals, motor vehicles; food processing.

Chief cities: Montreal, Calgary, Toronto, Winnipeg, Edmonton, North York, Scarborough, Vancouver, Mississauga, Hamilton.

Political divisions: Divided into 10 provinces and 3 territories—see table below (see also their individual entries):

NAME	AREA (sq. mi.)	AREA (sq. km.)	POP. (1991c)	CAPITAL
Provinces				
Alberta	246,422	638,232	2,545,553	Edmonton
British Columbia	344,663	892,677	3,282,061	Victoria
Manitoba	211,468	547,703	1,091,942	Winnipeg
New Brunswick	27,633	71,569	723,900	Fredericton
Newfoundland	143,488	371,634	568,474	St. John's
Nova Scotia	20,402	52,840	899,942	Halifax
Ontario	353,951	916,733	10,084,885	Toronto
Prince Edward I.	2,185	5,660	129,765	Charlottetown
Quebec	524,251	1,357,811	6,895,963	Quebec
Saskatchewan	220,121	570,113	988,928	Regina
Territories				
Northwest Territories	387,827	1,004,471	36,044	Yellowknife
Nunavut	865,605	2,241,917	21,605	Iqaluit
Yukon Territory	205,345	531,843	27,797	Whitehorse

History: Orig. inhabited by Indians and Inuit; early (c. 1000 A.D.) discovered by Norsemen; Atlantic coast frequented by European fishermen from 15th cent. (see NEWFOUNDLAND); mainland discovered by explorers in search of Northwest Passage to Asia (see HUDSON BAY and ARCTIC, THE); Gulf of St. Lawrence and river to sites of Quebec and Montreal discovered by French explorer Jacques Cartier 1534–42 under whom French attempted their first colony; Quebec (city) founded 1608 by Samuel de Champlain, who explored St. Lawrence River, discovered Lake Champlain, and penetrated interior to Georgian Bay 1603–15; Hudson Bay entered by English explorer Henry Hudson 1610; under influence of French missionaries after 1615; part of New France granted to Company of the Hundred Associates 1627; Montreal founded by French colonial administrator Paul de Maisonneuve 1642; expeditions of Jean Nicolet, Père Jacques Marquette and Louis Jolliet, and René-Robert Cavelier de La Salle; object of Anglo-French rivalry from 17th cent.; Acadia (see ACADIA 2), Newfoundland, and Hudson Bay region relinquished to England 1713; rest of country ceded by Treaty of Paris 1763; region of Ottawa and St. Lawrence rivers organized 1774 as Quebec prov. (*q.v.*). Boundaries with U.S. settled 1783 (see NORTHWEST TERRITORY), 1846 (see OREGON COUNTRY), and 1903 (see ALASKA). Dominion of Canada estab. 1867 by union of New Brunswick and Nova Scotia with Quebec, whose two parts (formerly known as Upper and Lower Canada or Canada West and Canada East) became present Ontario and Quebec provs.; purchased 1869 the W regions explored by Hudson's Bay Company (chartered 1670 by Charles II) and North West Company (consolidated with Hudson's Bay Company 1821); as a result of Riel's Rebellion 1869, Manitoba created province 1870; admitted as provinces British Columbia 1871, Prince Edward I. 1873, Alberta and Saskatchewan 1905, Newfoundland 1949; see NORTHWEST TERRITORIES, YUKON; entered WWI 1914; through Statute of Westminster recognized as equal partner of Great Britain 1931; entered WWII 1939; joined UN 1945, NATO 1949; reached agreement with U.S. on joint air defense of North America in years following WWII; constitution promulgated 1982; during 2d half of 20th cent., movement grew for Quebec separatism; referendums for more political autonomy for Quebec rejected 1992 and 1995, but issue remained unresolved; signed North American Free Trade Agreement (NAFTA) with U.S. and Mexico 1992.

CANADA—NATIONAL PARKS

NAME	ESTABLISHED	AREA (acres)	AREA (hectares)	LOCATION	FEATURES
Auyuittuq	1972[1]	5,305,600	2,148,768	Cumberland Penin., Baffin I., Northwest Territories	Mountainous landscape of fjords, glaciers, a large ice cap; many species of birds, abundant wildlife
Banff	1885	1,640,960	664,589	SW Alberta	Mountains, glaciers, game sanctuary; summer and winter sports center; resort area from Banff to Lake Louise
Bruce Peninsula	1987	66,560	26,957	Bruce Penin., SE Ontario	Marsh and forest lands
Cape Breton Highlands	1936	234,880	95,126	N Cape Breton I., Nova Scotia	Rugged highland and coastal scenery
Elk Island	1913	48,000	19,440	ab. 30 mi. (48 km.) E of Edmonton, Alberta	Fenced enclosure containing buffalo, moose, deer, wapiti; recreational and camping resort
Ellesmere Island	1986	9,760,640	3,953,059	NE Ellesmere I., Northwest Territories	Glaciers, tundra; Arctic wildlife
Forillon	1970	59,500	24,100	Gaspé Penin., Quebec	Scenic cliffs and highlands; cliff-nesting birds; hiking trails, campgrounds, snowshoeing, cross-country skiing
Fundy	1948	51,000	20,700	on Bay of Fundy, Nova Scotia	Interesting rock formations; recreational areas
Georgian Bay Islands	1929	3,200	1,296	30 islands in Georgian Bay, Ontario	Limestone formations; resort
Glacier	1886	333,440	135,043	SE British Columbia	Peaks, glaciers, valleys in heart of Selkirk Mts.
Grasslands	1981	224,000	90,720	SW Saskatchewan	Canadian short-grass prairie, badlands; rare species of birds and animals
Gros Morne	1973	458,000	185,490	Newfoundland I.	Mountains of Long Range, forests, beaches, shifting dunes, tidal inlet; saltwater and freshwater fishing, nature center, campgrounds, hiking trails
Jasper	1907	2,688,000	1,088,640	W Alberta	Mountains, lakes; big-game sanctuary; resorts
Kejimkujik	1968	94,080	38,102	SW cen. Nova Scotia	Varied fauna and flora; numerous lakes and streams
Kluane	1972	5,440,000	2,203,200	SW Yukon on Alaska border	Mt. Logan 19,850 ft. (6050 m.), highest peak in Canada; large glacier system; abundant wildlife
Kootenay	1920	347,520	140,746	SE British Columbia	Mountains, canyons, hot mineral springs
Kouchibouguac	1969	58,880	23,846	on Northumberland Strait, E New Brunswick	Dunes, salt marshes, tidewater lagoons, peat bogs; variety of wetland plant life
La Mauricie	1970	134,400	54,432	in Laurentian Mts., S Quebec	Numerous lakes, wilderness area; wildlife; campgrounds, beaches, canoeing
Mingan Archipelago	1984	37,100	15,026	bet. Anticosti I. and Quebec mainland	Island scenery and wildlife
Mount Revelstoke	1914	64,000	25,920	SE British Columbia	Plateau region on Mt. Revelstoke, slope of Selkirk Mts.
Nahanni	1972	1,177,700	476,968	SW Northwest Territories	Scenic area along the South Nahanni River incl. three large canyons and an extensive cataract; variety of birds, wildlife, wild flowers
Northern Yukon	1984	2,470,000	1,000,350	NW Yukon on Alaska border	Permafrost and fluvial features; diverse Arctic vegetation, abundant Arctic wildlife; Inuit archaeological sites
Pacific Rim	1970	123,500	50,018	in three sections, Vancouver I., British Columbia	Coastal scenery, 45 mi. (72 km.) long trail; sea mammals; campsites, shipwrecks
Point Pelee	1918	3,840	1,555	Ontario, on Lake Erie	Southernmost mainland point in Canada; resort
Prince Albert	1927	957,440	387,763	cen. Saskatchewan	Forested region with many lakes and waterways; resort
Prince Edward Island	1937	4,480	1,814	25 mi. (40 km.) long strip, N Prince Edward Island	Beaches and recreational area
Pukaskwa	1971	464,060	187,944	Ontario, on Lake Superior	Wilderness area accessible only by boat
Riding Mountain	1929	735,360	297,821	SW Manitoba	Forested highland area with many lakes; game preserve
St. Lawrence Islands	1904	988	400	mainland area and thirteen of the Thousand Is., SE Ontario	Recreational areas
South Moresby	1988	363,520	147,226	Queen Charlotte Is., W British Columbia	Mountains, spruce forest
Terra Nova	1957	97,920	39,658	on Bonavista Bay, 205 mi. (330 km.) N of St. John's, Newfoundland	Varied scenery; fishing; camping facilities
Waterton Lakes	1895	129,920	52,618	S Alberta; Canadian part of Waterton-Glacier International Peace Park (*q.v.*)	Mountain recreational area
Wood Buffalo[2]	1922	11,072,000	4,484,160	N Alberta and S Northwest Territories, W of Slave River and bet. Lake Athabaska and Great Slave Lake	Immense forested and plains region; large herd of buffalo and other game
Yoho	1886	324,480	131,414	SE British Columbia	Peaks, waterfalls, lakes, valleys, on W slopes of Rocky Mts.

[1] Estab. as Baffin Island National Park.
[2] Includes former Buffalo National Park, estab. 1908 and covering 126,400 acres (51,192 hectares) in Alberta.

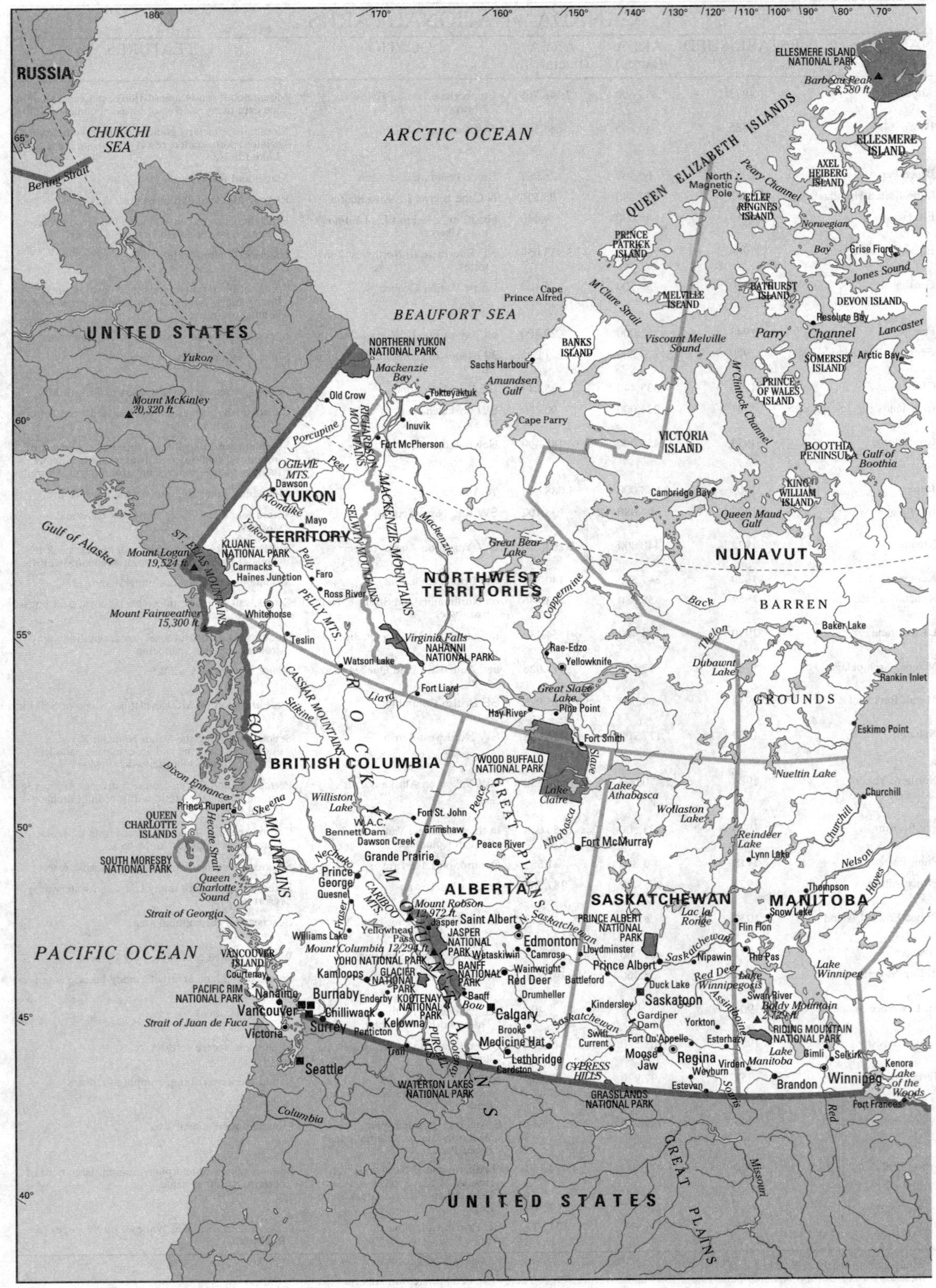

RUSSIA
CHUKCHI SEA
Bering Strait
ARCTIC OCEAN
UNITED STATES
Yukon
Mount McKinley 20,320 ft.
BEAUFORT SEA
NORTHERN YUKON NATIONAL PARK
Mackenzie Bay
Old Crow
Tuktoyaktuk
Inuvik
Fort McPherson
Porcupine
RICHARDSON MOUNTAINS
OGILVIE MTS.
Peel
Dawson
Klondike
YUKON TERRITORY
Mayo
MACKENZIE MOUNTAINS
SELWYN MOUNTAINS
Mackenzie
Gulf of Alaska
ST. ELIAS MOUNTAINS
Mount Logan 19,524 ft.
KLUANE NATIONAL PARK
Carmacks
Haines Junction
Pelly
Faro
Ross River
PELLY MTS.
Whitehorse
Mount Fairweather 15,300 ft.
Teslin
Virginia Falls
NAHANNI NATIONAL PARK
Watson Lake
CASSIAR MOUNTAINS
Stikine
Liard
Fort Liard
ROCKY MOUNTAINS
COAST MOUNTAINS
BRITISH COLUMBIA
Dixon Entrance
Prince Rupert
Skeena
QUEEN CHARLOTTE ISLANDS
Hecate Strait
SOUTH MORESBY NATIONAL PARK
Queen Charlotte Sound
Williston Lake
W.A.C. Bennett Dam
Fort St. John
Grimshaw
Dawson Creek
Peace River
Peace
Grande Prairie
Nechako
Prince George
Quesnel
CARIBOO MTS.
Fraser
Mount Robson 12,972 ft.
Jasper
Yellowhead Pass
Williams Lake
Mount Columbia 12,294 ft.
JASPER NATIONAL PARK
YOHO NATIONAL PARK
GLACIER NATIONAL PARK
BANFF NATIONAL PARK
KOOTENAY NATIONAL PARK
Strait of Georgia
PACIFIC OCEAN
VANCOUVER ISLAND
Courtenay
PACIFIC RIM NATIONAL PARK
Nanaimo
Kamloops
Burnaby
Enderby
Vancouver
Chilliwack
Kelowna
Strait of Juan de Fuca
Victoria
Surrey
Penticton
Trail
PURCELL MTS.
Kootenay
Seattle
WATERTON LAKES NATIONAL PARK
Columbia
Banff
Bow
Calgary
Red Deer
Wetaskiwin
Wainwright
Drumheller
Brooks
Medicine Hat
Lethbridge
Cardston
ALBERTA
Saint Albert
Edmonton
Camrose
Lloydminster
GREAT PLAINS
N. Saskatchewan
WOOD BUFFALO NATIONAL PARK
Lake Claire
Athabasca
Fort McMurray
Lake Athabasca
Slave
Fort Smith
Hay River
Pine Point
Great Slave Lake
Rae-Edzo
Yellowknife
NORTHWEST TERRITORIES
Great Bear Lake
Coppermine
Cape Parry
Amundsen Gulf
Sachs Harbour
BANKS ISLAND
Cape Prince Alfred
M'Clure Strait
PRINCE PATRICK ISLAND
MELVILLE ISLAND
Viscount Melville Sound
QUEEN ELIZABETH ISLANDS
North Magnetic Pole
Peary Channel
ELLEF RINGNES ISLAND
AXEL HEIBERG ISLAND
ELLESMERE ISLAND
ELLESMERE ISLAND NATIONAL PARK
Barbeau Peak 8,580 ft.
Norwegian Bay
Grise Fiord
Jones Sound
BATHURST ISLAND
DEVON ISLAND
Resolute Bay
Parry Channel
Lancaster
SOMERSET ISLAND
Arctic Bay
PRINCE OF WALES ISLAND
M'Clintock Channel
VICTORIA ISLAND
BOOTHIA PENINSULA
Gulf of Boothia
KING WILLIAM ISLAND
Cambridge Bay
Queen Maud Gulf
NUNAVUT
Back
BARREN GROUNDS
Thelon
Dubawnt Lake
Baker Lake
Rankin Inlet
Eskimo Point
Nueltin Lake
Churchill
Wollaston Lake
Reindeer Lake
Lynn Lake
Churchill
Nelson
Hayes
Thompson
Snow Lake
MANITOBA
SASKATCHEWAN
Lac la Ronge
PRINCE ALBERT NATIONAL PARK
Flin Flon
Saskatchewan
Nipawin
The Pas
Prince Albert
Battleford
Duck Lake
Red Deer Lake
Lake Winnipegosis
Lake Winnipeg
Saskatoon
Kindersley
Swan River
Baldy Mountain 2,729 ft.
Assiniboine
Gardiner Dam
Yorkton
RIDING MOUNTAIN NATIONAL PARK
Swift Current
Fort Qu'Appelle
Esterhazy
Moose Jaw
Regina
Virden
Lake Manitoba
Gimli
Selkirk
Weyburn
Brandon
Winnipeg
Estevan
Souris
CYPRESS HILLS
GRASSLANDS NATIONAL PARK
Kenora
Lake of the Woods
Fort Frances
Red
Missouri
UNITED STATES
GREAT PLAINS
180°
170°
160°
150°
140°
130°
120°
110°
100°
90°
80°
70°
65°
60°
55°
50°
45°
40°

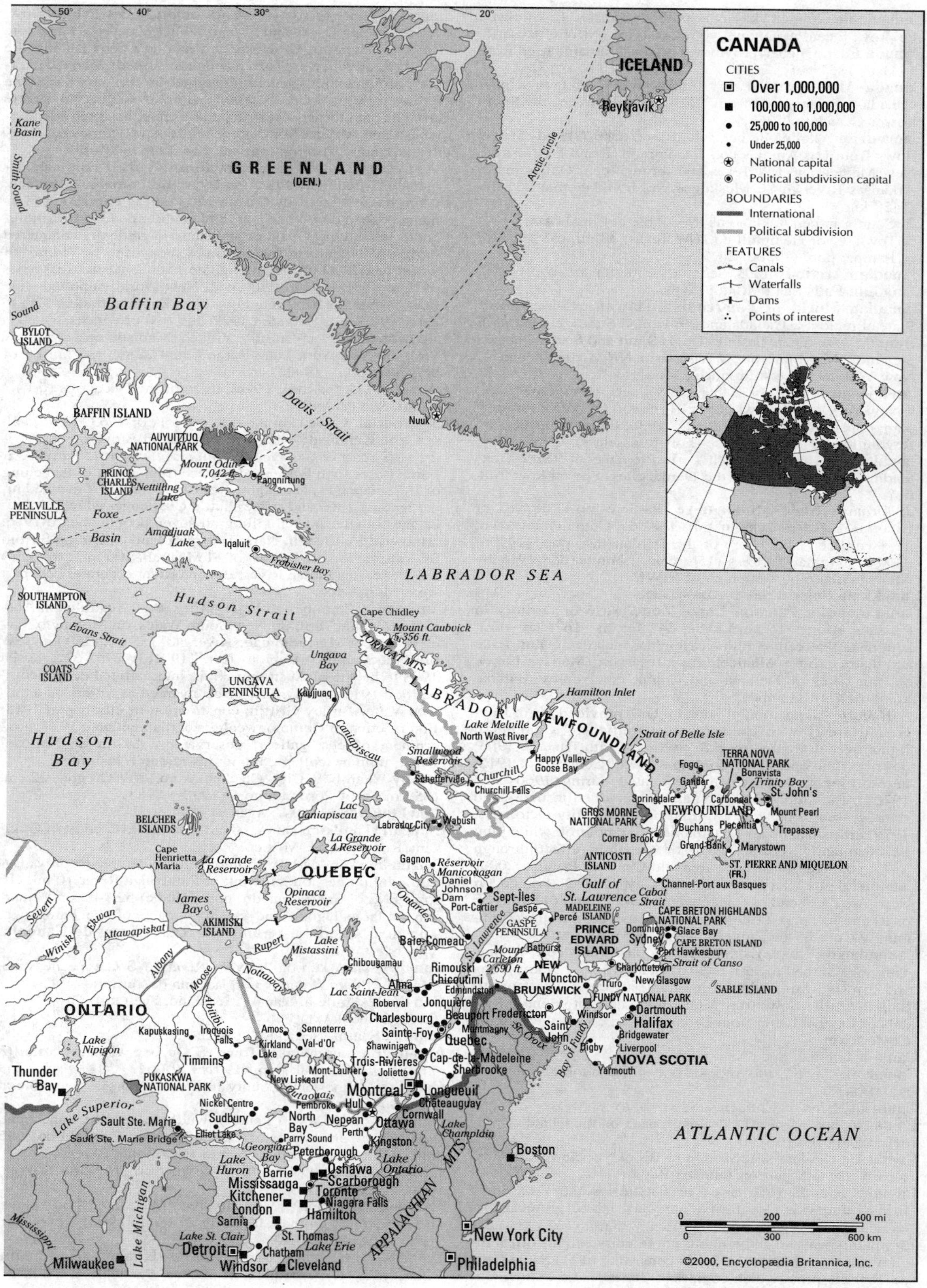
CANADA
CITIES
Over 1,000,000
100,000 to 1,000,000
25,000 to 100,000
Under 25,000
National capital
Political subdivision capital
BOUNDARIES
International
Political subdivision
FEATURES
Canals
Waterfalls
Dams
Points of interest
GREENLAND
(DEN.)
ICELAND
Reykjavík
Nuuk
Arctic Circle
Kane Basin
Smith Sound
Baffin Bay
Davis Strait
BYLOT ISLAND
BAFFIN ISLAND
AUYUITTUQ NATIONAL PARK
Mount Odin 7,042 ft.
Pangnirtung
PRINCE CHARLES ISLAND
Nettilling Lake
MELVILLE PENINSULA
Foxe Basin
Amadjuak Lake
Iqaluit
Frobisher Bay
LABRADOR SEA
SOUTHAMPTON ISLAND
Hudson Strait
Evans Strait
COATS ISLAND
Cape Chidley
Mount Caubvick 5,356 ft.
TORNGAT MTS.
Ungava Bay
UNGAVA PENINSULA
Kuujjuaq
LABRADOR
Hamilton Inlet
Lake Melville
North West River
NEWFOUNDLAND
Strait of Belle Isle
Hudson Bay
Caniapiscau
Smallwood Reservoir
Schefferville
Churchill
Churchill Falls
Happy Valley-Goose Bay
Fogo
TERRA NOVA NATIONAL PARK
Bonavista
Gander
Trinity Bay
St. John's
Springdale
Carbonear
Mount Pearl
NEWFOUNDLAND
GROS MORNE NATIONAL PARK
Buchans
Placentia
Trepassey
Corner Brook
Grand Bank
Marystown
BELCHER ISLANDS
Lac Caniapiscau
Labrador City
Wabush
La Grande 4 Reservoir
Cape Henrietta Maria
La Grande 2 Reservoir
QUEBEC
Gagnon
Réservoir Manicouagan
Daniel Johnson Dam
ANTICOSTI ISLAND
ST. PIERRE AND MIQUELON (FR.)
Channel-Port aux Basques
Opinaca Reservoir
James Bay
Outardes
Port-Cartier
Sept-Îles
Gulf of St. Lawrence
Cabot Strait
Gaspé
MADELEINE ISLAND
Percé
GASPÉ PENINSULA
CAPE BRETON HIGHLANDS NATIONAL PARK
Severn
Ekwan
Attawapiskat
Winisk
AKIMISKI ISLAND
Rupert
Lake Mistassini
Baie-Comeau
St. Lawrence
PRINCE EDWARD ISLAND
Dominion
Glace Bay
Sydney
CAPE BRETON ISLAND
Port Hawkesbury
Strait of Canso
Albany
Nottaway
Chibougamau
Rimouski
Bathurst
Mount Carleton 2,690 ft.
NEW BRUNSWICK
Charlottetown
Moose
Alma
Chicoutimi
Lac Saint-Jean
Roberval
Edmundston
Moncton
Truro
New Glasgow
SABLE ISLAND
ONTARIO
Jonquière
FUNDY NATIONAL PARK
Abitibi
Charlesbourg
Beauport
Fredericton
Windsor
Dartmouth
Halifax
Kapuskasing
Iroquois Falls
Amos
Senneterre
Sainte-Foy
Montmagny
St. Croix
Saint John
Bridgewater
Lake Nipigon
Kirkland Lake
Val-d'Or
Shawinigan
Quebec
Bay of Fundy
Digby
Liverpool
Timmins
Trois-Rivières
Cap-de-la-Madeleine
NOVA SCOTIA
Joliette
Sherbrooke
Yarmouth
Thunder Bay
PUKASKWA NATIONAL PARK
Mont-Laurier
New Liskeard
Outaouais
Montreal
Longueuil
Nickel Centre
Pembroke
Hull
Châteauguay
Lake Superior
Sault Ste. Marie
Sudbury
North Bay
Nepean
Ottawa
Cornwall
Sault Ste. Marie Bridge
Elliot Lake
Perth
Lake Champlain
ATLANTIC OCEAN
Georgian Bay
Parry Sound
Kingston
Boston
Peterborough
Lake Huron
Lake Ontario
Barrie
Oshawa
Scarborough
MTS.
Mississauga
Toronto
Kitchener
Niagara Falls
Lake Michigan
Mississippi
London
Hamilton
APPALACHIAN
Sarnia
Lake St. Clair
St. Thomas
New York City
Detroit
Chatham
Lake Erie
Milwaukee
Windsor
Cleveland
Philadelphia
0 200 400 mi
0 300 600 km
50°
40°
30°
20°
©2000, Encyclopædia Britannica, Inc.

Ca·ña·da de Gó·mez \kä-'nyä-t͟hä-t͟hā-'gō-mās\. Town, Santa Fe prov., E cen. Argentina, 40 mi. (64 km.) NNW of Rosario.

Canada East. Quebec province, Canada —a name used from 1841 to 1867.

Canada West. Region of Canada, equivalent to Upper Canada—a name used from 1841 when it was reunited with Lower Canada to 1867.

Ca·na·di·an \kə-'nā-dē-ən\. **1.** River, SW United States; flows from Las Animas co., S Colorado, S and E across NE New Mexico and NW Texas and through cen. Oklahoma to Arkansas River in SE Muskogee co., E Oklahoma; 906 mi. (1458 km.) long.
2. County in cen. Oklahoma. See table at OKLAHOMA.
3. Town, ⊗ of Hemphill co., NW Texas, 38 mi. (61 km.) NE of Pampa; pop. (1990c) 2417.

Canadian Arctic Islands. See ARCTIC ARCHIPELAGO.

Canadian Falls See NIAGARA FALLS.

Canadian Shield *or* **Lau·ren·tian Plateau** \lȯ-'ren-chən\. Plateau region, E Canada and NE United States, extending E from the Mackenzie basin to Davis Strait and S to S Quebec, S Ontario, NE Minnesota, N Wisconsin, NW Michigan, and NE New York incl. the Adirondack Mts.

Can·a·jo·har·ie \ˌka-nə-jō-'har-ē\. Village, Montgomery co., E New York, on Mohawk River 21 mi. (34 km.) W of Amsterdam; pop. (1990c) 3909; settled c. 1730; figured in American Revolution as meeting place (Fort Rensselaer).

Ça·nak·ka·le \ˌchä-näk-kä-'lā\. **1.** Province of Turkey, extending on both sides of the Dardanelles. See table at TURKEY.
2. *formerly* **Ka·le–i Sul·ta·ni·ye** \kä-ˌle-ē-ˌsu̇l-tä-nē-'ye\ *or* **Cha·nak Ka·les·si** \chä-'näk-kä-les-'sē\. Commercial town, its ✱, on the Asian shore of the Dardanelles; pop. (1990p) 53,887; Ottoman fortress (15th cent.); bombarded 1915 by Allies in Gallipoli campaign of WWI.

Çanakkale Boğazı. See DARDANELLES.

Canal Zone *or* **Panama Canal Zone.** Strip of territory in Panama; 10 mi. (16 km.) wide; 647 sq. mi. (1676 sq. km.); administrative center Balboa Heights; includes Gatun Lake and district above Alhajuela for a reservoir (Madden Lake), but not cities of Panama and Colón; chief cities: Balboa, Rainbow City, Gamboa.

History: Acquisition of zone by U.S. provided for in Hay-Herrán Treaty with Colombia (not ratified by Colombia); rights over it granted to U.S. by treaty with Panama 1903; governed and operated according to act of Congress of 1912; unrest over U.S. presence accelerated during 1960s and 1970s; negotiations bet. U.S. and Panama led to treaty and Zone ceased to exist as a formal political entity October 1, 1979; area since under Panamanian civil control, while joint Panamanian-U.S. supervision of Canal in effect through 1999; sole control of both area and Canal to Panama 2000.

Can·an·dai·gua \ˌka-nən-'dā-gwə\. City, ⊗ of Ontario co., W New York, at N end of Canandaigua Lake 26 mi. (42 km.) SE of Rochester; pop. (1990c) 10,725; carriage museum; Community Coll. of the Finger Lakes (1965); resort.

Canandaigua Lake. Lake in Ontario and Yates cos., W New York; one of the Finger Lakes (*q.v.*); ab. 15 mi. (24 km.) long and 2 mi. (3 km.) wide at its greatest extent. The **Canandaigua Outlet** flows from N end of the lake into Seneca River N of Cayuga Lake; from Lyons, Wayne co., also called the Clyde River.

Cana of Galilee. See CANA.

Ca·ñar \kä-'nyär\. Province of W cen. Ecuador. See table at ECUADOR.

Canarias, Islas *or* **Canaries.** See CANARY ISLANDS.

Ca·na·rio \kȧ-'nȧr-ē-ˌü\. Mountain peak on the island of Madeira; 5449 ft. (1661 m.).

Ca·nar·sie \kə-'när-sē\. Section of Brooklyn, New York City, New York, in S part on Jamaica Bay.

Ca·nary Islands \kə-'nar-ē\ *or* **Ca·nar·ies** \-ēz\ *or Span.* **Is·las Ca·na·rias** \'ēs-ˌläs-kä-'när-yäs\. Island group in Atlantic Ocean off NW coast of Africa, 823 mi. (1324 km.) SW of Spain; forms an autonomous community and historical region (*Span.* **Canarias**) of Spain consisting of (1) Santa Cruz de Tenerife prov. which comprises Tenerife, La Palma, Gomera, and Hierro (*qq.v.*) islands, and (2) Las Palmas prov. which comprises Grand Canary, Fuerteventura, Lanzarote (*qq.v.*), Alegranza, Graciosa, and Isla de Lobos islands, the last three of which are barren and uninhabited; volcanic in origin; mountainous, generally rugged in contour; has some fertile valleys; mild, pleasant climate; subject to severe droughts and tornadoes; irrigated farming; has both Mediterranean and African flora; produces bananas, tomatoes, ornamental plants; fishing; tourism. See table at SPAIN.

History: Known in ancient times as the "Fortunate Islands"; visited in Middle Ages by Arabs, Portuguese, French; taken possession of by Castile 1402 during expedition in its name of Jean de Béthencourt and Gadifer de La Salle; indigenous inhabitants Guanche and Canario gradually conquered during 15th cent.; in ancient times thought to be W limit of world (see HIERRO); beginning late 15th cent. on usual route of Spanish vessels in trade with New World; supplied wine in exchange for fish brought by New England traders 17th to early 19th cents.; divided 1927 into two provinces.

Can·a·sto·ta \ˌka-nə-'stō-tə\. Village, Madison co., cen. New York, on New York State Barge Canal 22 mi. (35 km.) E of Syracuse; pop. (1990c) 4673.

Ca·na·tha \kä-'nä-thä\. Greek town of the Decapolis (*q.v.*).

Canati. See FELANITX.

Ca·nav·er·al, Cape \kə-'na-vrəl, -və-rəl\ *or 1963–73 officially* **Cape Ken·ne·dy** \'ke-nə-dē\. Cape in Brevard co., Florida, on E coast of Canaveral Penin., E of Merrit I.; Patrick Air Force Base; John F. Kennedy Space Center, site of launching of U.S. manned space flights from 1961 incl. first manned lunar landing 1969 and space shuttle *Challenger* which exploded shortly after launch killing all seven people aboard 1986.

Canaveral Peninsula. Narrow strip of land extending S from SE Volusia co., off E coast of Florida; ab. 100 mi. (160 km.) long; encloses Indian River; Banana River separates cen. part from Merritt I.

Can·ber·ra \'kan-ˌber-ə, -bə-rə\. City, ✱ of Australia, in Australian Capital Terr., SE New South Wales, on Molonglo River, branch of Murrumbidgee River, ab. 155 mi. (250 km.) SW of Sydney; pop. (Capital Terr. [1991c]) 276,162; chosen 1908 to be site of Australian ✱; in international design competition 1912 for city, first place awarded to American architect Walter Burley Griffin; construction of city begun 1913; first meeting of Commonwealth's parliament held 1927; government offices; gallery; observatory; Australian National Univ., military college; numerous research institutes.

Can·by \'kan-bē\. City, Clackamas co., NW Oregon, 22 mi. (35 km.) S of Portland; pop. (1990c) 8983.

Canchungo. See TEIXEIRA PINTO.

Can·cún \kän-'kün, kan-\. Island resort, off NE coast of Quintana Roo state, SE Mexico.

Can·da·ba \kän-'dä-b͟ä\. Municipality, E Pampanga prov., Luzon, Philippines, on left bank of Pampanga River 10 mi. (16 km.) ENE of San Fernando; pop. (1980c) 52,945; on W margin of large lagoon and swamp area E of the Pampanga, known as **Candaba Swamp** (*or Span.* **Pi·nag de Candaba** \pē-'näg-t͟hā-)\).

Can·de·la·ria \ˌkän-dā-'lär-yä\. River in S Campeche state, Mexico; flows W and N into Laguna de Términos.

Can·dia \'kän-dē-ä, 'kan-\. **1.** Island. See CRETE 3.
2. City. See IRÁKLION.

Candia, Sea of. See CRETE, SEA OF.

Can·di·ac \'kan-dē-ˌak\. Town, S Quebec, Canada, 5 mi. (8 km.) S of Montreal; pop. (1991c) 11,064.

Can·dler \'kand-lər\. County in E cen. Georgia. See table at GEORGIA.

Can·dle·wood, Lake \'kand-ᵊl-ˌwu̇d\. Lake, W Connecticut, near New York border bet. Litchfield and Fairfield cos.; 15 mi. (24 km.) long; drains N into Housatonic River.

Can·do \'kan-ˌdü\. City, ⊗ of Towner co., N North Dakota; pop. (1990c) 1564.

Can·don \kän-'dȯn\. Municipality, NW Luzon, Philippines, near coast and on main highway 25 mi. (40 km.) S of Vigan; pop. (1980c) 36,802.

Ca·nea *also* **Ka·nea** \kə-'nē-ə\ *or Gk.* **Kha·niá** *also* **Cha·nia** \k͟än-'yä\. **1.** Department of Greece. See table at GREECE.

2. *anc.* **Cy·do·nia** \sī-'dō-nē-ə, -nyə\. Commercial seaport city, its ✻, on N coast of island at base of Akroteri Penin. on Kólpos Khaníon; pop. (1991c) 50,077; citrus fruits produced nearby; Orthodox and Catholic bishoprics. Prospered under Venetian rule; taken by Turks c. 1646; was ✻ of Crete 1841–1971; in WWII suffered heavily during German invasion 1941; commercial importance has since revived.

Canea Bay. See KHANÍON, KÓLPOS.

Ca·ne·lo·nes \ˌkä-nā-'lō-nās\. **1.** Department of S Uruguay. See table at URUGUAY.

2. *or* **Gua·da·lu·pe** \ˌgwä-thä-'lü-pā\. Town, its ✻, 27 mi. (43 km.) N of Montevideo; pop. (1985c) 17,325.

Ca·nen·di·yú \ˌkä-ˌnen-dē-'yü\. Department of E Paraguay. See table at PARAGUAY.

Ca·ñe·te \kä-'nyā-tā\. **1.** River, W cen. Peru; flows SW into Pacific Ocean 80 mi. (129 km.) S of Lima; 120 mi. (193 km.) long.

2. Town at mouth of the Cañete, Peru; pop. (1981p) 20,721.

Caney. See EL CANEY.

Ca·ney, Point \kä-'nā\. Cape on SE coast of Las Villas prov., W cen. Cuba.

Ca·ney Fork \'kā-nē\. River, cen. Tennessee; formed by confluence of branches in SE White co., flows W and NW into Cumberland River near Carthage, Smith co.; traverses Great Falls Lake (bet. White, Van Buren, and Warren cos.), formed by Great Falls Dam, one of the dams of the Tennessee Valley Authority (*q.v.*).

Can·field \'kan-ˌfēld\. Village, Mahoning co., NE Ohio, 10 mi. (16 km.) SW of Youngstown; pop. (1990c) 5409.

Can·gas \'käŋ-gäs\. Commune, Pontevedra prov., NW Spain, on Bay of Vigo 14 mi. (23 km.) SW of the commune of Pontevedra; pop. (1991c) 22,758.

Cangas de Nar·cea \thā-när-'sā-ä\ *also* **Cangas de Ti·neo** \thā-tē-'nā-ō\. Commune, Asturias prov., NW Spain, 37 mi. (60 km.) WSW of Oviedo; pop. (1991p) 19,152; coal.

Cangas de Onís \thā-ō-'nēs\. Commune, Asturias prov., NW Spain, 35 mi. (56 km.) E of Oviedo; pop. (1991c) 6404. Ancient seat of Asturian kings. See COVADONGA.

Can·go Caves \'käŋ-gō\. Stalactite caves in the Groote Swartberg, Western Cape prov., Rep. of South Africa, N of Oudtshoorn.

Can·i·a·pis·cau *or mostly formerly* **Kan·i·a·pis·kau** \ˌka-nē-ə-'pis-kō\. River, N Quebec, Canada; flows from **Lac Caniapiscau** *or mostly formerly* **Kaniapiskau Lake** (210 sq. mi. or 544 sq. km., 54°N, 69°W) in cen. Quebec; 575 mi. (925 km.) long; has significant potential for hydroelectric power generation.

Ca·ni·cat·tì \ˌkä-nē-kät-'tē\. Commune, Agrigento prov., SW Sicily, Italy, 16 mi. (26 km.) ENE of the commune of Agrigento; pop. (1989c) 34,582.

Ca·ni·gao Channel \ˌkä-nē-'gaủ\. Passage bet. SW Leyte and E Bohol, S cen. Philippines; connects NE Mindanao Sea with Camotes Sea; 18 to 28 mi. (29 to 45 km.) wide.

Ca·ni·gou \ˌkȧ-nē-'gü\. Peak, S Pyrénées-Orientales dept., S France, in the E Pyrenees ab. 20 mi. (32 km.) SW of Perpignan; 9135 ft. (2784 m.).

Ca·ni·no \kä-'nē-nō\. Village, Viterbo prov., W Lazio, cen. Italy, WNW of the commune of Viterbo; pop. (1981p) 5111; in 1814 made a principality for French Emperor Napoléon's brother, Lucien Bonaparte.

Can·is·teo \ˌka-nə-'stē-(ˌ)ō\. **1.** River, SW New York; rises in Allegany co., flows SE into Tioga River ab. 5 mi. (8 km.) SW of Corning in SE Steuben co.; ab. 60 mi. (97 km.) long.

2. Residential village, Steuben co., S New York, on Canisteo River 6 mi. (10 km.) SSE of Hornell; pop. (1990c) 3636. Former Indian village; permanent settlement begun 1788.

Can·ji·lon, Mount \ˌkan-hi-'lȯn\. Mountain, Rio Arriba co., N New Mexico; 10,700 ft. (3261 m.).

Çan·kırı \ˌchäŋ-kə-'rē\ *or* **Chan·ki·ri** \ˌchäŋ-\. **1.** Province of Turkey in Asia. See table at TURKEY.

2. *anc.* **Gan·gra** \'gaŋ-grə\; *later* **Ger·man·i·cop·o·lis** \gər-ˌma-nə-'kä-pə-ləs\. Town, its ✻, on tributary of Kızıl Irmak ab. 60 mi. (97 km.) NE of Ankara; pop. (1990p) 45,729; scene of Synod of Gangra c. 350 A.D.

Can·la·on \ˌkän-lä-'ȯn\. **1.** *formerly* **Ma·la·spi·na** \ˌmä-lä-'spē-nä\. Active volcano, N cen. Negros I., cen. Philippines; 8070 ft. (2460 m.); in eruption 1866 and 1893.

2. Chartered city, Negros I., Philippines, at the foot of Canlaon Volcano; pop. (1990p) 37,000.

Can·na \'ka-nə\. Island of the Inner Hebrides, Scotland, off W coast of Scottish mainland; part of Highland region; 4.5 mi. (7 km.) long.

Can·nae \'ka-nē\. Battlefield near modern Barletta, Bari prov., Puglia, SE Italy, where, in 216 B.C., during Second Punic War, Carthaginian Gen. Hannibal inflicted on Roman army one of the severest defeats ever sustained by Rome.

Can·na·nore \'ka-nə-ˌnōr\ *or* **Ka·na·nur** \ˌkə-nə-'nủr\. Town, N Kerala, SW India, on the Malabar Coast 50 mi. (80 km.) NNW of Calicut; pop. (1991p) 65,233; has some export trade. Visited by Portuguese explorer Vasco da Gama 1498; Portuguese fort built 1505; Dutch fort built 1656; captured by British 1783.

Cannanore Islands. See LACCADIVE ISLANDS.

Can·nel·ton \'ka-nəl-tən\. City, ⊗ of Perry co., S Indiana, on Ohio River 43 mi. (69 km.) E of Evansville; pop. (1990c) 1786.

Cannes \'kȧn\. Seaport and commune, Alpes-Maritimes dept., SE France, on Mediterranean 18 mi. (29 km.) SW of Nice; pop. (commune [1990c]) 69,363; international resort; site of annual international film festival. Subject to raids from sea, had fortifications built by monks in early Middle Ages; Emperor Napoléon landed nearby on his escape from Elba 1815; popular resort from mid-19th cent.

Cannet, Le. See LE CANNET.

Can·ning Stock Route \'ka-niŋ\. Track across N cen. Western Australia, Australia, extending through barren desert land ab. 1090 mi. (1750 km.) from Wiluna on the SW to Halls Creek on the NE; used for herding livestock in first half of 20th cent.

Can·nock \'ka-nək\. Town, Staffordshire, W cen. England, 16 mi. (26 km.) NNW of Birmingham; pop. (1981p) 59,235; engineering.

Can·non \'ka-nən\. **1.** River, SE Minnesota; rises in S Le Sueur co., flows NE to the Mississippi; ab. 95 mi. (153 km.) long.

2. County in cen. Tennessee. See table at TENNESSEE.

Can·non·ball \'ka-nən-ˌbȯl\. River, SW North Dakota; rises in Slope co., flows E into Missouri River on NW boundary of Sioux co.; ab. 140 mi. (225 km.) long.

Cannon Falls. City, Goodhue co., SE Minnesota, 24 mi. (39 km.) NE of Faribault; pop. (1990c) 3232.

Cannon Mountain. **1.** Peak in Glacier National Park, NW Montana; 8460 ft. (2579 m.).

2. *or* **Pro·file Mountain** \'prō-ˌfīl\. Peak, N Grafton co., W New Hampshire, in White Mts. on W side of Franconia Notch; 4077 ft. (1243 m.); on a SE shoulder is a natural formation (the Profile, or Old Man of the Mountain) which resembles a human face seen in profile; on NE is a formation resembling a cannon; aerial tramway; ski area.

Cannstatt. See BAD CANNSTATT.

Ca·no·as \kȧ-'nō-əs\. City, Rio Grande do Sul state, S Brazil, a N suburb of Pôrto Alegre; munic. pop. (1991p) 278,997.

Can·on City \'ka-nyən\. City, ⊗ of Fremont co., S cen. Colorado, on Arkansas River 35 mi. (56 km.) SW of Colorado Springs; pop. (1990c) 12,687; resort in mining district; state correctional facilities; museum; settled 1859.

Can·ons·burg \'ka-nənz-ˌbərg\. Borough, Washington co., SW Pennsylvania, 18 mi. (29 km.) SSW of Pittsburgh; pop. (1990c) 9200; platted 1787; active center of Whiskey Rebellion 1794.

Ca·no·pus \kə-'nō-pəs\. City of ancient Egypt, 15 mi. (24 km.) E of Alexandria at Abū Qīr; in early times of much importance because of its great temple of Serapis; the most

---

\ə\ **abut** \ˊə\ **matches** \ᵊ\ **kitten, Fr table** \ər\ **further** \a\ **ash** \ā\ **ace** \ä\ **cot, cart** \ȧ\ Fr **bac** \aủ\ **out** \b\ Span **Avila** \ch\ **chin** \e\ **bet** \ē\ **easy** \g\ **go** \i\ **hit** \ī\ **ice** \j\ **job** \k\ Ger **ich, Buch** \$^{n}$\ Fr **vin** \ŋ\ **sing** \ō\ **go** \ö\ **all** \ȯ\ **law** \œ\ Fr **bœuf** \œ̄\ Fr **feu** \ȯi\ **boy** \th\ **thin** \th\ **this** \ü\ **loot** \ủ\ **foot** \ue\ Ger **füllen** \ue̅\ Fr **rue** \y\ **yet** \$^{y}$\ Fr **digne** \'dēn^{y}\, **nuit** \'nw^{y}ē\ \yü\ **few** \yủ\ **fury** \zh\ **vision**

westerly branch of the Nile Delta then had its mouth here, **Ca·no·pic Mouth** \kə-ˈnō-pik\.

Ca·no·sa di Pu·glia \kä-ˈnō-sä-t͟hē- ˈpül-yä\; *anc.* **Ca·nu·si·um** \kə-ˈnü-zē-əm, -ˈnyü-, -zhē-\. Commune, Bari prov., Puglia, SE Italy, 43 mi. (69 km.) WNW of the seaport of Bari; pop. (1991p) 30,955; former see; Romanesque cathedral built 11th cent.; ruined castle; ancient Roman remains.

Canossa. See CIANO D'ENZA.

Ca·nou·an \ˌkä-nō-ˈwän\. Small island of the Grenadines, Windward Is., West Indies.

Canóvanas. See LOÍZA.

Can·so \ˈkan-sō\. Town, Guysborough co., E Nova Scotia, Canada, on Atlantic Ocean at mouth of Chedabucto Bay near Cape Canso; pop. (1991c) 1228; reputed to have been inhabited by European fishermen and fur traders shortly after explorer Christopher Columbus' discovery of America; raided during 18th cent. alternately by British and by French; frequently raided by Indians; settlement started to grow early 19th cent.; port of call for fishing fleet; American terminus of several Atlantic cables; causeway link to Cape Breton I. completed 1955.

Canso, Cape. Cape at NE end of Nova Scotia mainland, Canada, at S entrance to Chedabucto Bay.

Canso, Strait of *or* **Gut of Canso.** Deep, narrow channel bet. NE Nova Scotia mainland and S Cape Breton I., Canada; ab. 14.5 mi. (23 km.) long and 1 mi. (2 km.) wide.

Cantaber Oceanus. See BISCAY, BAY OF.

Can·ta·bria \kän-ˈtä-b͟rē-ä\. **1.** Historical region, of N Spain; early inhabited by Celts; because of isolation, little affected by Moorish invasions; came under Castilian influence during Middle Ages.

2. Autonomous community, N Spain. See table at SPAIN.

3. *formerly* **San·tan·der** \sän-ˈtän-der\. Province of N Spain, coextensive with Cantabria autonomous community. See table at SPAIN.

Can·ta·bri·an Mountains \kan-ˈtā-brē-ən\ *or Span.* **Cor·dil·le·ra Can·tá·bri·ca** \ˌkōr-t͟hēl-ˈyā-rä-kän-ˈtä-b͟rē-kä\. Range in N and NW Spain; highest peak Torre de Cerredo 8787 ft. (2678 m.).

Cantabrigia. See CAMBRIDGE 9.

Can·tal \kän-ˈtål\. Department of S cen. France. See table at FRANCE.

Can·ter·bury \ˈkan-tər-ˌber-ē\. **1.** Town, Windham co., NE Connecticut; pop. (1990c) 4467.

2. Municipality, E New South Wales, SE Australia, SW suburb of Sydney; pop. (1991c) 129,232.

3. *anc.* **Du·ro·ver·num** \ˌdu̇r-ə-ˈvər-nəm, ˌdyu̇r-\ *or ecclesiastical Lat.* **Can·tu·ar·ia** \ˌkan-chə-ˈwar-ē-ə\ *or O.E.* **Cant·wa·ra·burh** \ˈkant-ˌwar-ə-bu̇rk\. City, Kent, SE England, on Great Stour River 53 mi. (85 km.) ESE of London; tourism; Univ. of Kent at Canterbury; ecclesiastical metropolis of England since the founding 602 of a monastery by St. Augustine. Church, later the cathedral, destroyed by fire 1067, but rebuilt, destroyed again by fire 1174, rebuilt 1175–80; improved by changes and additions 1379–1503; scene of murder of Archbishop Thomas Becket 1170 and after his canonization 1172 made a place of pilgrimage (shrine, built after 1175, destroyed by Henry VIII 1538); background for English poet Geoffrey Chaucer's *Canterbury Tales*; town heavily damaged by German bombing 1942 but cathedral escaped for most part; birthplace of English dramatist Christopher Marlowe 1564.

Canterbury Bight. Wide inlet of Pacific Ocean, E cen. coast of South I., New Zealand, S of Banks Penin.

Can Tho \ˌkən-ˈtō\. Town, S Vietnam, on right bank of the Mekong River in its delta 90 mi. (145 km.) SW of Ho Chi Minh City; pop. (1989c) 208,078; produces coconut oil, milled rice.

Can·ti·gny \ˌkäⁿ-ˌtē-ˈnyē\. Village, Somme dept., N France, ab. 18 mi. (29 km.) S of Amiens; battle May 1918, first offensive by U.S. forces in WWI.

Can·ti·les Cay \kän-ˈtē-lās\. Island in N Caribbean Sea, E of Isla de la Juventud and S of W Cuba.

Can·ton \ˈkant-ᵊn\. **1.** Town, W Hartford co., N Connecticut; pop. (1990c) 8268; incorp. 1806; includes Collinsville (*q.v.*).

2. City, ⊗ of Cherokee co., NW Georgia, 33 mi. (53 km.) NNW of Atlanta; pop. (1990c) 4817.

3. City, Fulton co., W cen. Illinois, 25 mi. (40 km.) WSW of Peoria; pop. (1990c) 13,922; Spoon River Coll. (1959); settled 1825; incorp. 1849.

4. Town, Norfolk co., E Massachusetts, 14 mi. (23 km.) SSW of Boston; pop. (1990c) 18,530; site of American patriot Paul Revere's brass and bell foundry.

5. City, ⊗ of Madison co., cen. Mississippi, 25 mi. (40 km.) NNE of Jackson; pop. (1990c) 10,062.

6. City, Lewis co., NE Missouri, on Mississippi River 33 mi. (53 km.) N of Hannibal; pop. (1990c) 2623; Culver-Stockton Coll. (1853).

7. Village, ⊗ of St. Lawrence co., N New York, 18 mi. (29 km.) ESE of Ogdensburg; pop. (1990c) 6379; St. Lawrence Univ. (1856).

8. Town, Haywood co., W North Carolina, 15 mi. (24 km.) W of Asheville; pop. (1990c) 3790.

9. City, ⊗ of Stark co., NE Ohio, 20 mi. (32 km.) SSE of Akron; pop. (1990c) 84,161; Malone Coll. (1892), Walsh Coll. (1960), Kent State Univ., Stark campus (1967), Stark Technical Coll. (1970); site of Pro Football Hall of Fame, classic car museum; settled c. 1805; became ⊗ 1809; incorp. as city 1854. Home of President William McKinley, who is buried here with his family in National McKinley Memorial.

10. City, ⊗ of Lincoln co., SE South Dakota, on Big Sioux River 20 mi. (32 km.) S of Sioux Falls; pop. (1990c) 2787; shipping point.

11. City, ⊗ of Van Zandt co., NE Texas; pop. (1990c) 2949.

Canton. See GUANGZHOU.

Canton Island. See KANTON ISLAND.

Can·tù \kän-ˈtü\. Commune, Como prov., Lombardy, N Italy, 5 mi. (8 km.) SSE of the commune of Como; pop. (1991p) 35,930.

Cantuaria *or* **Cantwaraburh.** See CANTERBURY 3.

Cantyre. See KINTYRE.

Cantyre, Mull of. See KINTYRE, MULL OF.

Canusium. See CANOSA DI PUGLIA.

Can·vey Island \ˈkan-vē\. Island and town, Essex, SE England, ab. 30 mi. (48 km.) E of London; pop. (1981p) 35,293.

Can·yon \ˈka-nyən\. **1.** County in SW Idaho. See table at IDAHO.

2. City, ⊗ of Randall co., NW Texas, in the Panhandle 18 mi. (29 km.) S of Amarillo; pop. (1990c) 11,365; farming; West Texas State Univ. (1910); historical museum.

Canyon City. Town, ⊗ of Grant co., E cen. Oregon; pop. (1990c) 648.

Can·yon de Chel·ly National Monument \ˈka-nyən-də-ˈshā\. See UNITED STATES, *National Monuments.*

Canyon Di·ab·lo \dī-ˈa-blō\. Gorge, SE Coconino co., N Arizona, in **Canyon Diablo River;** ab. 225 ft. (69 m.) deep and 500 ft. (152 m.) wide; a tributary of the Little Colorado River.

Canyon Lake. See MORMON FLAT DAM.

Can·yon·lands National Park \ˈkan-yən-ˌlandz\. See UNITED STATES, *National Parks.*

Cao·bang \ˈkau̇-ˌbäŋ\. Town, N Vietnam, near Chinese border ab. 115 mi. (185 km.) NE of Hanoi.

Ca·or·le \kä-ˈōr-lē\. Commune, Venezia prov., Veneto, NE Italy, on Gulf of Venice at mouth of Livenza River; pop. (1981p) 11,452; fishing; resort; cathedral.

Cap, Le. See CAP HAITIEN.

Capac–Urcu. See ALTAR.

Ca·pan·no·ri \kä-ˈpän-nō-rē\. Commune, Lucca prov., Tuscany, cen. Italy, 4 mi. (6 km.) E of the commune of Lucca; pop. (1991p) 43,042; consists of a group of villages.

Ca·par·ra \kä-ˈpär-rä\. Former settlement on Puerto Rico near San Juan, founded 1508 by Spanish explorer Juan Ponce de León, later abandoned.

Ca·pas \ˈkä-päs\. Municipality, Luzon, Philippines; pop. (1980c) 46,523.

Cap–Chat \ˌkap-ˈshä\. Village, West Gaspé co., Gaspé Penin., SE Quebec, Canada, on St. Lawrence River 46 mi. (74 km.) ENE of Matane; pop. (1981c) 3464.

Cap–de–la–Ma·de·leine \ˌkȧp-də-ˌlȧ-ˌmȧd-ˈlen\. City, Champlain co., S Quebec, Canada, on N bank of St. Lawrence River 4 mi. (6 km.) ENE of Trois Rivières; pop. (1991c) 33,716; shrine.

Cape Bar·ren Island \-ˈbar-ən\. Second largest island in the Furneaux Group, NE of Tasmania, Australia.

Cape Bret·on \kāp-ˈbret-ᵊn, kə-ˈbret-, -ˈbrit-\. County, E Nova Scotia, Canada. See table at NOVA SCOTIA.

Cape Breton Highlands National Park. See CANADA, *National Parks.*

Cape Breton Island. Island, E part of Nova Scotia, E Canada; 3970 sq. mi. (10,282 sq. km.); pop. (1991c) 161,686; comprises four counties: Cape Breton, Inverness, Richmond, and Victoria; separated from mainland by narrow Strait of Canso; in central part are Bras d'Or salt lakes; its highest peak, North Barren 1747 ft. (532 m.), is highest peak in Nova Scotia; has many summer resorts and Cape Breton Highlands National Park; site of extensive Sydney coalfields. Claimed by French in 17th cent. and retained by Treaty of Utrecht 1713; ceded to England 1763; independent of Nova Scotia 1784–1820 (✱ Sydney); linked with mainland by causeway since 1955.

Cape Ca·nav·er·al \kə-ˈna-və-rəl\. **1.** Cape. See CANAVERAL, CAPE.

2. City, Brevard co., E Florida, 40 mi. (64 km.) ESE of Orlando; pop. (1990c) 8014.

Cape Charles \ˈchär-əlz\. Cape, Virginia. See CHARLES, CAPE.

Cape Coast; *formerly* **Cape Coast Castle.** Seaport town, ✱ of Central region, S Ghana, 75 mi. (121 km.) WSW of Accra; pop. (1984c) 57,224; university college. (1962); orig. an Ashanti center; first settlement by Portuguese c. 1600; site of castle (hence the early name) built by Swedes mid-17th cent.; seized by English c. 1664 and held against various attacks; ✱ of colony to 1877.

Cape Cod \ˈkäd\. **1.** Sandy peninsula, SE Massachusetts, nearly coextensive with Barnstable co.; 1 to 20 mi. (2 to 32 km.) wide, ab. 65 mi. (105 km.) long, extends E from the mainland and forms a wide curve toward the N enclosing Cape Cod Bay; has open ocean (Atlantic) on the E, Nantucket Sound on the S (separating it from Martha's Vineyard and Nantucket I.), Buzzards Bay on the SW; its base on the W is crossed by the Cape Cod Canal (8 mi. or 13 km. long); extending from its SE corner is Monomoy Point, a long narrow sand spit, and extending from its SW corner are the Elizabeth Is. Its N tip, N of Provincetown, discovered by English navigator Bartholomew Gosnold 1602; Pilgrims from *Mayflower* landed near Provincetown Nov. 1620.

2. The N tip of the peninsula.

Cape Cod Bay. S end of Massachusetts Bay off E coast of Massachusetts; formed within the northward sweep of Cape Cod. See CAPE COD CANAL.

Cape Cod Canal. Ship canal in Barnstable co., Massachusetts, crossing Cape Cod at its base; 17.5 mi. (28 km.) long (with dredged approaches), 500 ft. (152 m.) wide, 32 ft. (10 m.) deep; connects Buzzards Bay with Cape Cod Bay; completed 1914, owned by U.S. government.

Cape Colony. Former British colony, S Africa; estab. 1806; became Cape Prov. of Union of South Africa 1910.

Cape Coral. City, Lee co., SW coastal Florida on estuary of Caloosahatchee River; pop. (1990c) 74,991; grew rapidly in 1970s and 1980s.

Cape Eliz·a·beth \i-ˈli-zə-bəth\. Town, Cumberland co., SW Maine, on Atlantic Ocean 7 mi. (11 km.) S of Portland; pop. (1990c) 8854; summer resort.

Cape Fear \ˈfir\. River, cen. and SE North Carolina; formed by confluence of Deep and Haw rivers in Chatham co., flows SE into Atlantic Ocean in E Brunswick co.; 202 mi. (325 km.) long; navigable to Fayetteville.

Cape Gi·rar·deau \jə-ˈrär-dō\. **1.** County in SE Missouri. See table at MISSOURI.

2. City, Cape Girardeau co., SE Missouri, on Mississippi River 30 mi. (48 km.) NNW of its confluence with Ohio River; pop. (1990c) 34,438; Southeast Missouri State Univ. (1873).

Cape Hat·ter·as National Seashore Park \ˈha-tə-rəs\. See table, note 5, at NORTH CAROLINA.

Cape Horn Mountain \ˈhȯrn\. Peak in Salmon River Mts., W Custer co., cen. Idaho; 9500 ft. (2896 m.).

Cape Kru·sen·stern National Monument \ˈkrü-zən-ˌstərn\. See UNITED STATES, *National Monuments.*

Ca·pel·le aan de IJs·sel \kə-ˈpe-lə-ˌän-də-ˈā-səl, ˈī-səl\. Commune, South Holland prov., Netherlands, ab. 5 mi. (8 km.) E of Rotterdam; pop. (1992e) 58,541.

Cape May \ˈmā\. **1.** Cape, S New Jersey. See MAY, CAPE 1.

2. County in S New Jersey. See table at NEW JERSEY.

3. City, Cape May co., S New Jersey, ab. 40 mi. (64 km.) SW of Atlantic City on Atlantic Ocean; pop. (1990c) 4668; early settlement (from 17th cent.) known as Cape Island; one of oldest Atlantic coast resorts, prominent esp. in 19th and early 20th cents.; many restored Victorian structures.

Cape May Court House. Unincorporated settlement, ⊗ of Cape May co., S New Jersey, 28 mi. (45 km.) SW of Atlantic City; pop. (1990c) 4426.

Cape Melville National Park. See MELVILLE, CAPE 1.

Cape of Good Hope. **1.** Cape, Rep. of South Africa. See GOOD HOPE, CAPE OF 2.

2. Former province, Rep. of South Africa. See CAPE PROVINCE.

Cape Province *or officially* **Cape of Good Hope** *or Afrikaans* **Kaap·pro·vin·sie** \ˌkäp-ˌprō-ˈvin-sē\; *before 1910* **Cape Colony.** Former province, Rep. of South Africa; 278,380 sq. mi. (721,004 sq. km.); pop. (1991p) 5,514,420; ✱ Cape Town; part of its N boundary was formed by Orange River, its principal stream, which separated it from Free State on NE and from Namibia on NW; was bounded in extreme NE by Lesotho and KwaZulu-Natal; rivers included the Olifants and Great Berg in SW and streams flowing S or SE to South Atlantic and Indian oceans, as the Bree, Fish, Gourits, Great Kei, and Mzimvubu; had inner plateau bordered by an escarpment roughly parallel with the coast; many short ranges 6000 to 8500 ft. (1830 to 2590 m.) in height; S of the escarpment in cen. part was the Great Karoo, a dry tableland 2000 to 3000 ft. (610 to 915 m.) above sea level; its most southerly point—also most southerly point of continent of Africa—was Cape Agulhas 34°52′S (most southerly point of Cape of Good Hope, 92 mi. or 148 km. WNW of Cape Agulhas, is 34°21′S).

History: Original inhabitants of Cape of Good Hope included, among others, members of the Bantu, the San, and Khoikhoin; first European visit 1488 by Portuguese navigator Bartolomeu Dias while en route to India 1487–88; colony founded by Dutch who began settlement at Table Bay 1652; occupied by British 1795–1803 and 1806–14; ceded to British by Dutch 1814; Natal united with Cape Colony for administrative purposes c. 1843–56; annexed British Kaffraria mid-19th cent. and British Bechuanaland 1895; administered Lesotho (formerly Basutoland) 1871–84; received responsible government 1872; joined Union of South Africa 1910, subsequently Rep. of South Africa 1961; ceased to exist as an administrative entity 1994 and roughly split into Eastern Cape, Northern Cape, and Western Cape provs.

Ca·per·na·um \kə-ˈpər-nā-əm\. Ruined city of ancient Palestine, on the NW shore of the Sea of Galilee; home of Jesus during much of the period of his ministry.

Cape Sa·ble Island \ˈsā-bəl\. Small island off the SW tip of Nova Scotia, Canada.

Ca·pes·terre \ˌkȧ-pes-ˈter\. Commune, SE Marie-Galante I., Guadeloupe, West Indies.

Cape Town \ˈkāp-ˌtau̇n\ *or Afrikaans* **Kaap·stad** \ˈkäp-ˌstät\. Seaport city, legislative ✱ of Rep. of South Africa, in SW part on Table Bay; pop. (1985c) 776,617; formerly ✱ of Cape Prov.; exports oil and cereals; harbor sheltered by artificial breakwater; the republic's chief port; South African Museum (1825); botanical gardens; South African Public Library;

South African Cultural History Musuem; castle (17th cent.); Univ. of Cape Town (at Rondebosch, 1918).

History: First settlement at Table Bay founded 1652 by Dutch navigator Jan van Riebeeck for the Dutch East India Company; served as a stopover for ships plying the Europe-to-India route; under Dutch rule until 1795, when it was captured by a British force; returned to the Dutch by the Treaty of Amiens 1803, retaken by the British 1806.

Cape Verde *or* **Cape Verde Islands** \ˈvərd\ *or Port.* **Ilhas do Ca·bo Ver·de** \ˈēl-yəs-dü-ˌkȧ-bü-ˈver-də\. Republic consisting of a group of volcanic islands in the Atlantic Ocean, bet. 14°47′ and 17°13′N lat.; 1557 sq. mi (4033 sq. km.); pop. (1993e) 350,000; its ✻ is Praia, on São Tiago. Until 1975 constituted a Portuguese overseas province; chief islands: São Tiago, Santo Antão, São Vicente, São Nicolau, Sal, Boa Vista, Fogo, Maio, Brava, Santa Luzia. Generally mountainous, highest peak 9281 ft. (2829 m.) on Fogo; produces sugar, corn, beans, salt, fruits, coffee, peanuts, hides; fishing; chief towns are Praia, the ✻, and Mindelo on São Vicente. Discovered 1456 by Ca'da Mosto, Venetian navigator in service of Prince Henry of Portugal; visited 1460 by Portuguese navigator Diogo Gomes; first settled 1462; fought over by English and French during subsequent centuries, but remained under Portuguese control; on shipping route, enjoyed some prosperity late 19th cent.; status changed from colony to Portuguese overseas prov. 1951; became independent July 5, 1975; while once associated with Guinea-Bissau, broke with it legally 1981.

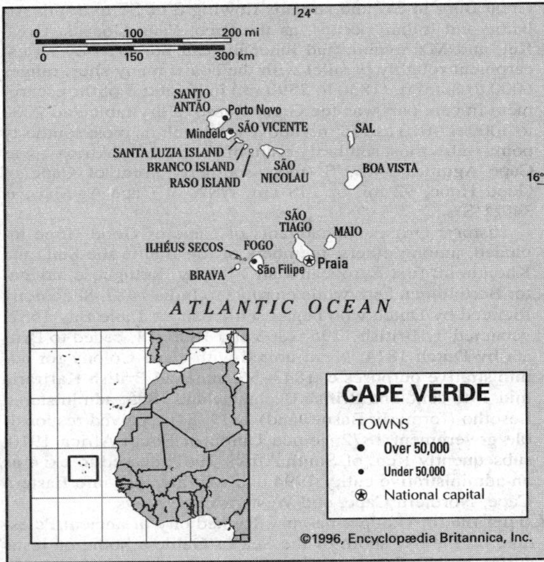

Cape York Peninsula \ˈyȯrk\. Peninsula forming NE part of Queensland, Australia; terminates in Cape York on Torres Strait; ab. 450 mi. (724 km.) long.

Cap Hai·tien \kāp-ˈhā-shən\ *or Fr.* **Cap–Ha·ï·tien** \kȧ-pī-ˈsyeⁿ\ *or locally* **Le Cap** \lə-ˈkȧp\. Seaport, N Haiti; pop. (1992e) 92,122; once ✻ of Haiti; destroyed during rebellion against French 1802; rebuilt by Haitian leader and self-proclaimed king Henri Christophe, whose most notable buildings nearby, now ruins, are Sans Souci palace and La Citadelle; suffered earthquake 1842.

Ca·pha·reus \kə-ˈfar-ˌyüs, -ˈfar-ē-əs\ *or Gk.* **Ka·fi·révs** \ˌkä-fē-ˈrefs\ *also* **Do·ro** \ˈdȯr-ō\. Cape, SE coast of Euboea I., Greece; extends into Aegean Sea as rocky and dangerous promontory.

Ca·pia·tá \ˌkä-pyä-ˈtä\. City, Central dept., S cen. Paraguay; munic. pop. (1992p) 83,189.

Ca·pi·ba·ri·be \ˌkȧ-pē-bȧ-ˈrē-bē\. River, Pernambuco state, NE Brazil; flows E into Atlantic Ocean at Recife; 140 mi. (225 km.) long.

Ca·pil·la del Mon·te \kä-ˈpē-zhä-thel-ˈmän-tā\. Mountain resort, W Córdoba prov., N cen. Argentina; alt. ab. 3000 ft. (914 m.).

Capital Federal. See FEDERAL DISTRICT 1.

Capitan, El. See EL CAPITAN.

Cap·i·tan Peak \ˌka-pi-ˈtan\. Mountain, Lincoln co., cen. New Mexico; 10,083 ft. (3073 m.).

Cap·i·to·la \ˌka-pi-ˈtō-lə\. City, Santa Cruz co., W California, 5 mi. (8 km.) E of the city of Santa Cruz; pop. (1990c) 10,171.

Cap·i·tol Heights \ˈka-pət-ᵊl\. Town, Prince Georges co., S cen. Maryland, 6 mi. (10 km.) E of Washington, D.C.; pop. (1990c) 3633.

Capitol Hill. 1. Hill, Washington, D.C., site of the U.S. Capitol.

2. Neighborhood, Washington, D.C., to the immediate E and SE of the U.S. Capitol.

Cap·i·to·line \ˈka-pət-ᵊl-ˌīn, *Brit. often* kə-ˈpit-ᵊl-\. One of the Seven Hills of Rome, Italy; once had two peaks, the Arx and the **Cap·i·to·li·um** \ˌka-pə-ˈtō-lē-əm\. See SEVEN HILLS.

Capitol Peak. Mountain, Pitkin co., W cen. Colorado; 14,130 ft. (4307 m.).

Capitol Reef National Park. See UNITED STATES, *National Parks.*

Ca·piz \ˈkä-pēs\. **1.** Province, N Panay, Philippines; borders Sibuyan Sea on the N with Jintotolo Channel on NE; ✻ Roxas; good harbors at Roxas and in Pilar Bay; mountainous in W and SW; fertile plain in the E in the Panay Valley. See table at PHILIPPINES.

2. Chartered city, its ✻. See ROXAS.

Capodistria. See KOPER.

Caporetto. See KOBARID.

Cap·pa·do·cia \ˌka-pə-ˈdō-shə\. Historical mountainous district of E Asia Minor (cen. modern Turkey) of varying boundaries; watered by the Halys River; a satrapy of the Persian Empire, it became a semi-independent kingdom under Ariarathes I, a contemporary of Macedonian King Alexander the Great; estab. as a separate dynasty c. 255 B.C.; aided Rome in its wars in Asia Minor; Roman province 17 A.D.; Caesarea Mazaca was its chief city.

Ca·pra·ia \kä-ˈprī-ä\. Island Genova prov., Italy; in Mediterranean Sea NNW of Elba and E of N tip of Corsica; ab. 7 sq. mi. (18 sq. km.); contains a penal colony.

Ca·pra·ra, Point \kä-ˈprä-rä\. N point of Asinara I. off NW coast of Sardinia, Italy.

Capraria. See CABRERA.

Ca·pra·ro·la \ˌkä-prä-ˈrō-lä\. Commune, Viterbo prov., N Lazio, cen. Italy, 9 mi. (14 km.) SE of the commune of Viterbo; pop. (1981p) 4777; castle built for Farnese family, finished (1559–72) by Italian architect Vignola (Giacomo Barozzi).

Capreae. See CAPRI.

Ca·pre·ra \kä-ˈprā-rä\. Island, Sassari prov., Sardinia, Italy; in Tyrrhenian Sea off NE coast of Sardinia; 6 sq. mi. (16 sq. km.); Italian nationalist leader Giuseppe Garibaldi's home 1856–82 and burial place.

Ca·pre·se \kä-ˈprā-sā\ *or* **Caprese Mi·chel·an·ge·lo** \ˌmē-ke-ˈlän-je-ˌlō\. Commune, Arezzo prov., E Tuscany, Italy; pop. (1981p) 1846; birthplace of Italian painter, sculptor, architect Michelangelo 1475.

Ca·pri \ˈkä-prē; kə-ˈprē, ka-\; *anc.* **Cap·re·ae** \ˈkap-rē-ˌē\. Island, Napoli prov., Italy, in the Bay of Naples; 4 sq. mi. (10 sq. km.); cliffs on E side rise 900 ft. (274 m.); highest point 1923 ft. (586 m.) is on W side; on N shore is the Blue Grotto (*q.v.*); chief town Capri; tourist resort. A favorite resort of ancient Romans; during Napoleonic Wars captured alternately by British and by French; returned to Ferdinand I of the Two Sicilies 1813.

Cap·ri·corn Channel \ˈka-prə-ˌkȯrn\. Passage in Pacific Ocean off E coast of Queensland, Australia; entrance to waters inside Great Barrier Reef at its S end.

Ca·pri·vi Strip \kä-ˈprē-vē\; *formerly* **Caprivi Concession** *or Ger.* **Ca·pri·vi·zip·fel** \kə-ˌprē-vē-ˈtsip-fəl\. Strip of land, S Africa, a NE extension of Namibia; runs E ab. 300 mi. (485 km.) bet. Angola and Zambia on N and Botswana on S, no more than 65 mi. (104 km.) at its widest; ab. 7000 sq. mi. (18,130 sq. km.); known also as "Caprivi's Finger"; obtained as part of German colony South-West Africa (now Namibia) 1890 by German Chancellor Count Georg Leo von Caprivi in negotiations with the British.

Capsa. See GAFSA.

Cap San·té \ˌkȧp-sä^{n}-ˈtā\. Undesignated municipality, ⊗ of Portneuf co., S Quebec, Canada, on N bank of St. Lawrence River 28 mi. (45 km.) WSW of the city of Quebec; pop. (1991c) 2563; an old parish dating back to 17th cent.

Cap·ua \ˈkä-pü-ä, ˈka-pyü-wə\. Commune, Caserta prov., Campania, S Italy, on Volturno River 19 mi. (31 km.) N of Naples; pop. (1991p) 17,967; 9th cent. cathedral (modernized).

History: Founded 856 A.D. on site of ancient **Cas·i·li·num** \ˌka-si-ˈlī-nəm\ 2.5 mi. (4 km.) NW of the original ancient city of Capua (devastated by Vandals led by Genseric 456 A.D., completely destroyed 840 by the Saracens); captured 1501 by Italian military leader Cesare Borgia; as fortified city, one of defenses of kingdom of Naples; fell to kingdom of Italy 1860; scene of heavy fighting 1943 in WWII.

Ca·pu·lin Volcano National Monument; *formerly* **Capulin Mountain National Monument** \ˈka-pyü-lin\. See UNITED STATES, *National Monuments.*

Ca·que·tá \ˌkä-kā-ˈtä\. **1.** Name for the upper course of the Japurá River in Colombia. See JAPURÁ.

2. Department of S Colombia. See table at COLOMBIA.

Car, Slieve. See SLIEVE CAR.

Ca·ra·bal·lo Mountains \ˌkä-rä-ˈbī-ō\ *also* **Ca·ra·bal·los** \-ōs\. Mountain group in cen. Luzon, Philippines, with general elev. of 2000 to 5000 ft. (600 to 1500 m.); joined from the N by the Cordillera Central and on the E by the Sierra Madre; the range extending to the S into Quezon prov. is sometimes called the **Caraballo Sur** \ˈsür\.

Ca·ra·bao \ˌkä-rä-ˈb̲aů\. Islet, Philippines, off Luzon I., on S side of entrance to Manila Bay. See CORREGIDOR.

Carabaya, Cordillera de. See CORDILLERA DE CARABAYA.

Ca·ra·bo·bo \ˌkä-rä-ˈb̲ō-b̲ō\. **1.** State of N Venezuela. See table at VENEZUELA.

2. Village in Carabobo state, Venezuela, ab. 20 mi. (32 km.) SW of Valencia; battle June 24, 1821 in which South American revolutionist Simón Bolívar defeated royalists thereby winning independence for Venezuela. Monument commemorating battle.

Ca·ra·cal \kä-ˈrä-käl\. City, Olt co., S Romania, 30 mi. (48 km.) ESE of Craiova; pop. (1989c) 39,522.

Ca·rac·as \kä-ˈrä-käs, kə-ˈra-kəs\. City, ✻ of Venezuela and of the Federal District, N Venezuela; met. area pop. (1990p) 1,824,892; alt. ab. 3000 ft. (900 m.); connected with its seaport La Guaira, 8 mi. (13 km.) directly N, by a railroad line ab. 23 mi. (37 km.) long; oil refining, storage, and export; rubber goods, textiles, glassware, chemicals; food processing; several universities and colleges incl. Central Univ. of Venezuela (1696, university status 1725) and Simón Bolívar Univ. (1970); cathedral (17th cent.); basilica; museums.

History: Founded 1567 by Diego de Losada; sacked by English commander Amyas Preston 1595; birthplace of revolutionists Francisco de Miranda 1750 and Simón Bolívar 1783; under Bolívar's leadership, first colony to revolt from Spain c. 1810; suffered earthquake which helped royalists to recover city 1812; reentered by Bolívar 1813 and occupied by him again June 1821 (after Carabobo); became ✻ of independent Venezuela.

Caralis. See CAGLIARI 2.

Caraman *or* **Caramania.** See KARAMAN.

Ca·ra·mo·an \ˌkä-rä-ˈmō-ˌän\. Municipality at E end of Caramoan Penin., SE Luzon, Philippines, near shore of Lagonoy Gulf; pop. (1980c) 32,659.

Caramoan Peninsula. Peninsula extending into Pacific Ocean, SE Luzon, Philippines; on W is San Miguel Bay and on SE Lagonoy Gulf; ab. 53 mi. (85 km.) long, 13 mi. (21 km.) wide.

Ca·ran·se·beş \ˌkä-rän-ˈse-besh\. Town, Caraş-Severin co., Romania; pop. (1989c) 34,594.

Carapacheta. See KARAPACHETA.

Car·a·quet \ˈkar-ə-ˌket\. Town, NE New Brunswick, Canada, on S shore of Chaleur Bay; pop. (1991c) 4556; in 19th cent. an important cod-fishing village, with 22 mi. (35 km.) of beach.

Ca·raş–Se·ve·rin \ˈkär-ˌäsh-ˌse-ve-ˈrēn\. County of SW Romania. See table at ROMANIA.

Ca·ra·tas·ca, La·gu·na de \lä-ˈgü-nä-ˌt̲h̲ā-ˌkä-rä-ˈtäs-kä\ *or* **Caratasca Lagoon.** Large lagoon on E coast of Honduras, an inlet of the Caribbean Sea.

Ca·ra·tin·ga \ˌkär-ə-ˈtēŋ-gə\. Municipality, Minas Gerais state, E Brazil, 120 mi. (193 km.) E of Belo Horizonte; pop. (1991p) 125,640.

Ca·ra·vag·gio \ˌkä-rä-ˈvä-jō\. Commune, Bergamo prov., Lombardy, N Italy, 13 mi. (21 km.) S of the commune of Bergamo; pop. (1981p) 13,877; formerly defended by walls, castle, and moat; birthplace of Italian painter Michelangelo Merisi, known as Caravaggio, 1573.

Car·a·van·ca Mons \ˌkar-ə-ˈvaŋ-kə-ˈmänz\ *or Ital.* **Ca·ra·van·che** \ˌkä-rä-ˈväŋ-kā\. See *Karawankan* in table at ALPS.

Ca·ra·vé·la \ˌkä-rä-ˈb̲ā-lä\. See BIJAGÓS, ARQUIPÉLAGO DOS.

Ca·ra·zo \kä-ˈrä-sō\. Department of SW Nicaragua. See table at NICARAGUA.

Car·bal·lo \kär-ˈbäl-yō, -ˈbī-ō\. Commune, La Coruña prov., NW Spain, 19 mi. (31 km.) SW of the commune of La Coruña; pop. (1991c) 26,033; thermal mineral springs and baths.

Car·ber·ry Hill \ˈkär-bə-rē\. Hill, Lothian, Scotland, E of Edinburgh; 500 ft. (152 m.); Mary, Queen of Scots, surrendered to barons here 1567.

Carbilo. See SAINT-NAZAIRE.

Car·bon \ˈkär-bən\. Name of counties in four states of U.S. See tables at MONTANA, PENNSYLVANIA, UTAH, WYOMING.

Car·bo·na·ra, Cape \ˌkär-bō-ˈnä-rä\. Cape on SE extremity of Sardinia, Italy, E of the Gulf of Cagliar.

Car·bon·ate Mountain \ˈkär-bə-ˌnāt, -nət\. Peak, Chaffee co., cen. Colorado; 13,900 ft. (4237 m.).

Car·bon·dale \ˈkär-bən-ˌdāl\. **1.** City, Jackson co., SW Illinois, ab. 80 mi. (130 km.) SE of St. Louis; pop. (1990c) 31,252; Southern Illinois Univ. at Carbondale (1874).

2. City, Lackawanna co., NE Pennsylvania, 14 mi. (23 km.) NE of Scranton; pop. (1990c) 10,664.

Car·bo·near \ˌkär-bə-ˈnir\. Seaport, SE Newfoundland, Canada, on W shore of Conception Bay 27 mi. (43 km.) WNW of St. John's; pop. (1991c) 5259; fishing.

Car·bo·nia \kär-ˈbō-nyə\. Town, Cagliari prov., SW Sardinia, Italy, near coast; pop. (1989c) 33,501.

Car·ca·gen·te \ˌkär-kä-ˈhān-tā\ *or* **Car·cai·xent** \ˌkär-kä-ˈshent, -kī-\. Commune, Valencia prov., E Spain, on Júcar River 29 mi. (47 km.) SSW of the commune of Valencia.

Car·car \ˈkär-ˌkär\. Municipality on E coast of Cebu I., Philippines, 22 mi. (35 km.) SW of City of Cebu; pop. (1980c) 57,822.

Car·ca·ra·ñá \ˌkär-kä-rä-ˈnyä\. River in cen. Argentina; formed by Saladillo and Tercero rivers, flows E into Paraná River above Rosario.

Car·cas·sonne \ˌkȧr-kȧ-ˈsȯn\; *anc.* **Car·ca·so** \ˈkär-kə-ˌsō\. City, ✻ of Aude dept., S France, on Aude River 57 mi. (92 km.) SE of Toulouse; pop. (1990c) 44,991; tourism; 12-arch bridge; partly surrounded by walls attributed in part to Visigoths; castle; 13th cent. Gothic cathedral. Taken by Muslims 728 A.D.; viscountship 11th–13th cents.; taken by English soldier Simon de Montfort c. 1209; joined to French crown 1247; pillaged and heavily damaged by Edward, Prince of Wales (the Black Prince) 1355; Huguenots massacred here

1566. Extensive reconstruction of medieval structures undertaken 19th–20th cents.

Car·che·mish \'kär-kə-ˌmish, kär-'kē-mish\. Ruined city on the W bank of the Euphrates River at Syria-Turkey border, 35 mi. (56 km.) SE of Gaziantep; ancient city of Mitanni kingdom in 2d millennium B.C.; later a chief city of the Hittites; captured by Egyptians under Thutmose III in 15th cent. B.C., came under Assyria after 717 B.C.; scene of great battle 605 B.C. in which Nebuchadrezzar II of Babylon defeated Necho II and destroyed Egyptian power in Asia (*Isa.* x. 9; *Jer.* xlvi. 2).

Car·chi \'kär-chē\. Province of N Ecuador. See table at ECUADOR.

Car·cross \'kär-ˌkrȯs\. Settlement, on N shore of Lake Bennett, S Yukon, Canada; pop. (1991c) 183; on railroad line; terminus of a short branch of the Alaska Highway.

Car·da·mom Hills \'kär-də-məm\. Range, S India, on E border of Kerala state; averages 2000 to 4000 ft. (610 to 1220 m.).

Cár·de·nas \'kär-t͟hā-ˌnäs\. Seaport city on **Cárdenas Bay,** W cen. Cuba, 23 mi. (37 km.) E of Matanzas; pop. (1990e) 75,651; sugar refining, rum distillation, rope manufacturing.

Car·diff \'kär-dif\. **1.** Town, Onondaga co., New York, S of Syracuse; the "Cardiff giant" reported found nearby 1869 was a rude figure of a man 10.5 ft. (3 m.) high, carved out of gypsum obtained at Fort Dodge, Iowa, exhibited for a time as a "petrified man."

2. *or Welsh* **Caer·dydd** \'kīr-ˌdit͟h\. Seaport city, ✻ of Wales and ⊗ of South Glamorgan and of Mid Glamorgan, SE Wales; pop. (1991p) 272,600; historically a center for steel manufacturing, shipbuilding, and coal export; now has papermills, chemical works, engineering works; Cardiff Castle (dating from c. 1090); Univ. of Wales, Univ. of Wales College of Cardiff; National Museum of Wales; officially recognized as ✻ of Wales 1955.

Car·di·gan \'kär-di-gən\. **1.** Former county, W Wales. See CARDIGANSHIRE and DYFED 2.

2. *or Welsh* **Ab·er·tei·fi** \ˌab-ər-'tī-vē, -'tā-\. Town, Dyfed co., W Wales; pop. (1981p) 4184; site of castle built by Normans and demolished by Oliver Cromwell's Parliamentarians.

Cardigan, Mount Mountain, S Grafton co., W New Hampshire; 3121 ft. (951 m.).

Cardigan Bay. Widemouthed inlet of St. George's Channel on W coast of Wales.

Car·di·gan·shire \'kär-di-gən-ˌshir, -shər\ *or* **Cardigan.** Former county, W Wales, on Cardigan Bay; ⊗ Cardigan; mountainous. See DYFED 2.

Car·di·nal Mountain \'kärd-ᵊn-əl\. Peak, E Fresno co., S cen. California, in the Sierra Nevada; 13,388 ft. (4081 m.).

Car·dross \'kär-ˌdrȯs, kär-'drȯs\. Parish and village, Dunbarton co., Scotland, on the Firth of Clyde ab. 4 mi. (6 km.) NW of Dumbarton; nearby is the castle where king of Scotland Robert I (the Bruce) died 1329.

Ca·rei \kä-'rā\ *also* **Ca·reŭ Ma·re** \kä-ˌrā-ů-'mär-ə\ *or Hung.* **Nagy·ká·roly** \nȯj-'kö-rȯi\. Commune, Satu Mare co., Romania, SW of the city of Satu Mare; pop. (1989c) 29,246; formerly belonged to Hungary; once seat of Hungarian politician Count Mihály Károlyi's family; monastery.

Ca·ren·cro \kə-'reŋ-krō\. Town, Lafayette parish, S Louisiana; pop. (1990c) 5429.

Ca·ren·tan \ˌkȧ-räⁿ-'täⁿ\. Town, Manche dept., NW France, at base of Cotentin Penin. 23 mi. (37 km.) W of Bayeux; has small port; strong fortress in Middle Ages; suffered much during 16th cent. Wars of Religion; during WWII captured by U.S. troops after severe battle June 1944.

Car·ew \'kar-ü, -ē\. Village, Dyfed, SW Wales, on Milford Haven 5 mi. (8 km.) E of Pembroke; 0.5 mi. (0.8 km.) N are ruins of a castle of ab. 13th cent.; 14-ft. (4-m.) Celtic cross near the castle entrance.

Car·ey \'kar-ē\. Village, Wyandot co., NW cen. Ohio, 14 mi. (23 km.) ESE of Findlay; pop. (1990c) 3684; limestone.

Carey, Lake. Dry salt lake, S cen. Western Australia, Australia.

Car·ga·dos Ca·ra·jos Shoals \kär-'gä-dōs-kä-'rä-zhōs\ *also* **Saint Bran·don Shoals** \ˌsānt-'bran-dən, sənt-\. Group of shoals in the Indian Ocean NE of Mauritius, to which they belong.

Car·ia \'kar-ē-ə\. Ancient division of SW Asia Minor bordering on the S and SW on the Aegean Sea, on the N on Lydia, and on the E on Phrygia and Lycia; coextensive with modern S Aydın and W Muğla, Turkey; coastline marked by several long peninsulas (esp. Bodrum) and gulfs and numerous Aegean Is. (now parts of the Dodecanese); covered with fairly high mountains; traversed in the N by the Menderes River. In early times settled by Doric and Ionic colonies; absorbed by Lydia but for a time under independent king, Mausolus (whose tomb is known as one of Seven Wonders of Ancient World), c. 377–353 B.C.; taken from Persia 334 B.C. by Macedonian King Alexander the Great; came under Syria and Pergamum and in 129 B.C. incorp. in the Roman prov. of Asia.

Chief cities: Halicarnassus (the ✻), Miletus, Cnidus, Magnesia, and Tralles.

Ca·ri·a·ci·ca \ˌkȧ-rē-ə-'sē-kə\. Municipality, Espírito Santo state, E Brazil, just W of Vitoria; pop. (1991p) 274,450.

Ca·ria·co, Gulf of \kär-'yä-kō\. Inlet of Caribbean Sea on NE coast of Venezuela, S of Araya Penin.

Ca·ri·ba·na, Point \ˌkä-rē-'b̲ä-nä\. Cape on NW coast of Colombia, at E side of Gulf of Urabá.

Ca·rib·be·an Community and Common Market \ˌkar-ə-'bē-ən, kə-'ri-bē-\ *or abbr.* **Car·i·com** \'kar-i-ˌkäm\. Economic community, consisting of Antigua and Barbuda, Bahamas, Barbados, Belize, Dominica, Grenada, Guyana, Jamaica, Montserrat, St. Kitts-Nevis, St. Lucia, St. Vincent and the Grenadines, Suriname, Trinidad and Tobago; purpose is to reduce customs barriers and promote free flow of labor within the region and coordinate foreign policies of the member states. Formed 1973 to replace **Caribbean Free Trade Association**.

Caribbean Sea. Arm of the Atlantic Ocean, bounded by the West Indies on the N and E, N South America on the S, and Central America on the W; connects with Gulf of Mexico on the NW through Yucatán Channel; ab. 1,049,500 sq. mi. (2,718,205 sq. km.); max. depth ab. 25,000 ft. (7620 m.) in Cayman Trench (*q.v.*).

Caribbees. See WEST INDIES.

Car·i·boo Mountains \'kar-ə-ˌbü\. Range of the Rocky Mts., E cen. British Columbia, Canada, in the great bend of the Fraser River; ab. 200 mi. (320 km.) long; highest point Mt. Sir Wilfrid Laurier 11,750 ft. (3581 m.); separated from main range of the Rocky Mts. by upper Fraser River; district in W foothills scene of famous gold rush of 1860s.

Cariboo Road *or* **Car·i·bou Road** \'kar-ə-ˌbü\. Highway, British Columbia, W Canada; follows Fraser River, turns NW at N end of Cariboo Mts. and ends at Hazelton (*q.v.*); modern highway is ab. 500 mi. (800 km.) long; original road (begun during gold rush 1862, opened 1865) was ab. 400 mi. (650 km.) long and opened the area for settlement.

Car·i·bou \'kar-ə-ˌbü\. **1.** County in SE Idaho. See table at IDAHO.

2. Town, Aroostook co., N Maine, on Aroostook River 13 mi. (21 km.) N of Presque Isle; pop. (1990c) 9413.

Caribou Mountain. Peak, SE Bonneville co., SE Idaho; 9816 ft. (2992 m.).

Caribou Mountains. Range, N Alberta, Canada, N of Peace River; av. height ab. 2000 ft. (610 m.); N part in Wood Buffalo National Park.

Caribou Road. See CARIBOO ROAD.

Ca·ri·ga·ra \ˌkä-rē-'g̅ä-rä\. Municipality on Carigara Bay, N Leyte I., Philippines, 22 mi. (35 km.) W of Tacloban; pop. (1980c) 34,377; taken by Americans Nov. 1944 during WWII Allied advance on the Philippines.

Carigara Bay. S part of Samar Sea at N end of Leyte I., Philippines; enclosed on NW by Biliran I.

Ca·rig·nan \ˌkä-rē-'nyäⁿ\. Town, S Quebec, Canada; pop. (1991c) 5386.

Ca·ri·huai·ra·zo \ˌkä-rē-wī-'rä-sō\. Peak, cen. Ecuador, NNE of Riobamba, in the Andes; 16,515 ft. (5034 m.).

Ca·ri·ni \kä-'rē-nē\. Commune, Palermo prov., NW cen. Sicily, Italy, 10 mi. (16 km.) W of the seaport of Palermo; pop. (1991c) 20,277; medieval castle.

Ca·rin·thia \kə-'rin-thē-ə\ *or Ger.* **Kärn·ten** \'kernt-ᵊn\. State of S Austria, bordering on Italy and Slovenia; bordered on S by Karawanken and Carnic Alps and separated from Salzburg state on NW by the Hohe Tauern; ✱ Klagenfurt; forms basin watered by the Drava with several lakes (such as Wörther See and Millstätter See); rye, oats, wheat; livestock; magnesite, iron ore, lead, zinc; center of a summer resort area.

History: Inhabited orig. by a Celtic people; part of Roman prov. of Noricum; invaded by Germans, then by Slovenes in period of migrations; in 8th cent. A.D. belonged to Carolingian empire (part of Bavaria); made a separate duchy 976 which, for a time, included Verona and Styria and finally came to Hapsburgs in 1335; parts of Carinthia belonged to Illyrian Provinces (*q.v.*) 1809–13; became Austrian crown land 1849; after 1918 parts went to Yugoslavia and Italy; in 1920, possession of S part by Yugoslavia confirmed by a plebiscite, but Klagenfurt region retained by Austria. See table at AUSTRIA.

Car·is·brooke \'kar-iz-ˌbru̇k, -is-\. Village and parish, Isle of Wight, S England; castle in which King Charles I was imprisoned 1647–48.

Carle·ton \'kärl-tən\. **1.** County, W New Brunswick, Canada. See table at NEW BRUNSWICK.

2. Former county, Ontario, Canada; now part of Ottawa-Carleton. See table at ONTARIO.

Carleton, Mount. Mountain, N New Brunswick, Canada; 2690 ft. (820 m.); highest peak in the province.

Carleton Place. Town, Lanark co., SE Ontario, Canada, on Mississippi River at foot of Mississippi Lake, 28 mi. (45 km.) SW of Ottawa; pop. (1991c) 7432; resort.

Car·ling·ford Lough \'kär-liŋ-fərd-'läk\. Inlet of Irish Sea on E coast of Ireland, on boundary bet. SE Northern Ireland and NE Ireland (republic).

Car·lin·ville \'kär-lin-ˌvil\. City, ⊗ of Macoupin co., SW cen. Illinois, 38 mi. (61 km.) SSW of Springfield; pop. (1990c) 5416; Blackburn Coll. (1837).

Car·lisle \kär-'līl, kər-, 'kär-ˌ\. **1.** County in SW Kentucky. See table at KENTUCKY.

2. City, ⊗ of Nicholas co., NE Kentucky; pop. (1990c) 1639.

3. Town, Middlesex co., NE Massachusetts, 18 mi. (29 km.) NW of Boston; pop. (1990c) 4333.

4. Village, Montgomery and Warren cos., SW Ohio, 15 mi. (24 km.) SW of Dayton; pop. (1990c) 4872.

5. Borough, ⊗ of Cumberland co., S Pennsylvania, 19 mi. (31 km.) W of Harrisburg; pop. (1990c) 18,419; settled 1720; scene of treaty bet. Ohio Indians and statesman Benjamin Franklin 1753; headquarters of President George Washington during Whiskey Rebellion 1794; station on Underground Railroad bringing slaves from the South to the North before Civil War; occupied by Confederates June 27–30, 1863. Site of Carlisle Indian School 1879–1918; Dickinson Coll. (1773), Dickinson School of Law (1834). Home and grave of American Revolutionary heroine Molly Pitcher (Mary McCauley).

6. *anc.* **Lu·gu·val·li·um** \ˌlü-gyu̇-'va-lē-əm\ *or* **Lu·gu·val·lum** \-'va-ləm\ *or later* **Caer Lu·el** \kär-'lü-əl\. City, ⊗ of Cumbria, NW England, on Eden River 8 mi. (13 km.) from Solway Firth and 108 mi. (174 km.) N of Liverpool; pop. (1991p) 99,800; textiles, coal deposits; railroad center; cathedral (begun in 12th cent.). Important Roman station; refounded by English King William II (William Rufus); as a border fortress often attacked by Scots; place of imprisonment of Mary, Queen of Scots, 1568.

Car·lo·for·te \ˌkär-lō-'fòr-tā\. See SAN PIETRO.

Carlota, La. See LA CARLOTA.

Car·low \'kär-lō\. **1.** County, Leinster prov., SE Ireland; ✱ Carlow; flour milling, malting. See table at IRELAND.

2. Town, its ⊗; pop. (1991p) 11,275; ruins of great Norman castle; St. Patrick's Coll. (c. 1795); burned by Irish rebel Rory Oge O'More late 16th cent.; taken by English Gen. Oliver Cromwell's forces 1650.

Carlowitz. See SREMSKI KARLOVCI.

Carls·bad \'kärlz-ˌbad\. **1.** City, San Diego co., SW California, NW of the city of San Diego; pop. (1990c) 62,126; popular beaches.

2. City, ⊗ of Eddy co., SE New Mexico, on Pecos River 70 mi. (113 km.) S of Roswell; pop. (1990c) 24,952; potash deposits; to the SW are Carlsbad Caverns (*q.v.*), and to the N is the Carlsbad Reclamation Project (developed by U.S. government at beginning of 20th cent.) consisting of **Ava·lon Dam** \'a-və-ˌlän\ and **Mc·Mil·lan Dam** \mək-'mi-lən\ across the Pecos River, with the lakes thus formed and miles of canals and ditches; founded 1887.

Carlsbad. See KARLOVY VARY.

Carlsbad Caverns. Series of limestone caves near Carlsbad, SE New Mexico; Big Room, one of world's largest natural underground chambers, over 0.5 mi. (0.8 km.) long, 650 ft. (198 m.) wide at its widest part, and 285 ft. (87 m.) high; now included in **Carlsbad Caverns National Park** (see UNITED STATES, *National Parks*).

Carls·berg Ridge \'kärlz-ˌbərg\. Ridge, NW Indian Ocean floor, extending approx. from SE of Socotra to W of Maldives in a general NW to SE direction; a center of oceanic crust formation according to the theory of plate tectonics.

Carlsruhe. See KARLSRUHE.

Carl·stadt \'kärl-ˌstat\. Borough, Bergen co., NE corner of New Jersey, 8 mi. (13 km.) SE of Paterson; pop. (1990c) 5510. Orig. bought cooperatively from American owners by German exiles and liberals seeking political freedom.

Carl·ton \'kärlt-ᵊn\. **1.** County in E Minnesota. See table at MINNESOTA.

2. Village, its ⊗; pop. (1990c) 923.

3. Town, Nottinghamshire, N cen. England, 4 mi. (6 km.) NE of Nottingham; pop. (1981p) 46,456.

Car·lyle \kär-'līl, 'kär-ˌ\. City, ⊗ of Clinton co., SW cen. Illinois, 40 mi. (64 km.) E of East St. Louis; pop. (1990c) 3474; trading center.

Car·ma·gno·la \ˌkär-mä-'nyō-lä\. Commune, Torino prov., Piedmont, NW Italy, on Po River 17 mi. (27 km.) S of Turin; pop. (1991c) 24,634; ruins of ancient castle; presumed to have given its name to the *carmagnole,* costume worn in S France by Piedmontese workmen and adopted, after 1792, by the French Revolutionaries, whose revolutionary song was *La Carmagnole.*

Car·man \'kär-mən\. Town, S Manitoba, Canada, 48 mi. (77 km.) SW of Winnipeg; pop. (1991c) 2567; railroad junction.

Carmana *or* **Carmania.** See KERMĀN.

Car·mar·then \kər-'mär-t͟hən, kär-\. **1.** Former county, Wales. See CARMARTHENSHIRE and DYFED 2.

2. Commercial seaport, ⊗ of Dyfed, S Wales; pop. (1991p) 54,800; ruins of Norman castle on site of ancient Roman station; received first town charter 1227; residence of British essayist and dramatist Sir Richard Steele at time of his death 1729.

Carmarthen Bay. Inlet of Bristol Channel on S coast of Wales; Caldy I. is at its W entrance.

Car·mar·then·shire \kər-'mär-t͟hən-ˌshir, kär-, -shər\ *or* **Carmarthen.** Former county, S Wales; ⊗ Carmarthen; hilly area; chief river the Towy. See DYFED 2.

Car·mel \'kär-məl\. **1.** Town, Hamilton co., cen. Indiana, 15 mi. (24 km.) N of Indianapolis; pop. (1990c) 25,380.

2. Town, ⊗ of Putnam co., SE New York, 20 mi. (32 km.) ESE of Newburgh; pop. (1990c) 28,816.

Car·mel \kär-'mel\ *or* **Carmel–by–the–Sea.** City, Monterey co., W California, on Pacific Ocean S of Monterey Bay; pop. (1990c) 4239; founded c. 1904 by several artists as rustic refuge; art and recreation center; tourism. Nearby is Mission San Carlos Borromeo del Rio Carmelo, burial place of its founder, Spanish missionary Junípero Serra.

Car·mel, Mount \ˈkär-məl\. Mountain, N Israel, near Mediterranean coast; extends southeasterly ab. 15 mi. (24 km.) along S bank of the Qishon River; Haifa is at its foot; 1789 ft. (545 m.); early became sacred; known to Egyptians in 2d millennium B.C.; mentioned several times in Bible, prominently as place where Hebrew prophet Elijah took on worshipers of Baal (*1 Kings* xviii. 19 ff.); after 6th cent. A.D. a favored site for monasteries, esp. that of the Order of Carmelites, founded in latter part of 12th cent.

Car·me·lo \kär-ˈmā-lō\. Town, Colonia dept., SW Uruguay, 140 mi. (225 km.) NW of Montevideo; at mouth of the Uruguay River.

Car·men \ˈkär-men\. **1.** Island enclosing Laguna de Términos, SE Bay of Campeche, Campeche state, SE Mexico.
2. Small island off SE coast of Baja California, NW Mexico, in the Gulf of California; salt deposits.
3. *or* **Ciu·dad del Carmen** \syü-ˈthäth-del-\. Town on W end of Carmen I., Campeche state, SE Mexico; has a good port.

Car·men de Pa·ta·go·nes \ˈkär-men-thā-ˌpä-tä-ˈgō-nās\. Town, E Argentina, SW of Buenos Aires; transfer of national ✻ to the towns of Carmen de Patagones and Viedma (across the Rio Negro) approved 1987.

Car·mi \ˈkär-ˌmī\. City, ⊗ of White co., SE Illinois, 45 mi. (72 km.) ESE of Mount Vernon; pop. (1990c) 5564.

Car·mi·chael \ˈkär-ˌmī-kəl\. Unincorporated settlement, Sacramento co., N cen. California, NE of the city of Sacramento; pop. (1990c) 48,702.

Car·mo·na \kär-ˈmō-nä\; *anc.* **Car·mo** \ˈkär-mō\. Commune, Sevilla prov., SW Spain, 18 mi. (29 km.) ENE of Seville; pop. (1991c) 23,617; ancient Roman necropolis; city gates; Moorish wall and alcazar; captured from Moors 1247 by Ferdinand III, king of Castile.

Car·nac \kȧr-ˈnȧk\. Commune, Morbihan dept., NW France, on Quiberon Bay ab. 17 mi. (27 km.) SE of Lorient; pop. (1990c) 4322; museum; region noted for many Neolithic stone monuments incl. dolmens and long rows of menhirs; mounds; remains of a Gallo-Roman town nearby.

Car·na·ro \kär-ˈnä-rō\ *also* **Fiu·me** \ˈfyü-mā\. Former province of Italy, incl. the islands of the Gulf of Quarnero (Cherso, Lussino, Unie)—name Canaro used by Italian writer and soldier Gabriele D'Annunzio when he occupied Fiume 1919. Now (by treaty of 1947) part of Croatia.

Car·nar·von \kär-ˈnär-vən, kər-\. Town, Wales. See CAERNARVON 2.

Carnarvon Bay. See CAERNARFON BAY.

Carnarvonshire. See CAERNARVONSHIRE.

Car·nat·ic \kär-ˈna-tik\ *or* **Kar·na·tik** \kər-ˈnä-tik\. A region and former administrative unit bet. Eastern Ghats and Coromandel Coast, S India, S of 16°N; now a part of Tamil Nadu and Andhra Pradesh, India; orig. the country of the Kanarese, an irregular area in S cen. India incl. Karnataka and parts of Andhra Pradesh. Historically of great importance; divided for centuries bet. Pāṇḍya and Chola kingdoms; from 14th–18th cents. under Muslims and the Delhi kings; for a time independent, with ✻ at Arcot; during 18th cent. the scene of Anglo-French rivalry, British gaining ascendancy after seizure of Arcot 1751 and defeat of Hyder Ali in Second Mysore War (1780–84); annexed by British 1801.

Car·nedd Da·fydd \ˈkär-ˌneth-ˈdä-vith\. Mountain, Gwynedd, NW Wales, NE of Snowdon; 3426 ft. (1044 m.).

Carnedd Llew·el·yn \hlə-ˈwe-lən, ˈhlwe-lin\. Mountain, Gwynedd, NW Wales; 3484 ft. (1062 m.).

Car·ne·gie \ˈkär-nə-gē, kär-ˈne-gē, *locally* kär-ˈnā-gē\. Borough, Allegheny co., SW Pennsylvania, 6 mi. (10 km.) WSW of Pittsburgh; pop. (1990c) 9278.

Car·ne·gie, Lake \kär-ˈne-gē\. Lake on W edge of Gibson Desert, cen. Western Australia, Australia; usually dry.

Carn Eige \ˌkärn-ˈāg\ *also* **Cairn Eige** \ˈkärn, ˈkarn\. Peak, Highland region, NW Scotland; 3877 ft. (1182 m.).

Car·ne·ro, Point \kär-ˈnā-rō\. Point on S coast of Spain extending into the Strait of Gibraltar at W entrance to the Bay of Gibraltar.

Carnes·ville \ˈkärnz-ˌvil\. City, ⊗ of Franklin co., NE Georgia; pop. (1990c) 514.

Carnic Alps. See table at ALPS.

Car Nic·o·bar *or* **Kar Nicobar** \ˈkär-ˈni-kə-ˌbär\. Most northerly island of Nicobar group, Andaman and Nicobar Is., India; 49 sq. mi. (127 sq. km.).

Car·nio·la \ˌkär-nē-ˈō-lə, kär-ˈnyō-\ *or Ger.* **Krain** \ˈkrīn\. **1.** Region of S Europe, NE of head of Adriatic Sea; mountainous, having E end of Carnic Alps in NW and traversed on W by the Julian Alps; chief town Ljubljana, Slovenia.
History: Belonged to Roman prov. of Pannonia; received influx of Slovenes c. 590 A.D.; with Carinthia, ruled by Carolingian mark of Bavaria; in 13th cent. a part of the Holy Roman Empire (**March of Carniola**) in SE bordering on kingdom of Hungary; came under the Hapsburgs 1335 who took title of duke of Carinthia; ceded to French Emperor Napoléon by Austria 1809–13 (see ILLYRIAN PROVINCES), remained duchy of Austria until 1849.
2. Austrian crown land 1849–1918, bounded on N by Carinthia, on NE by Styria, on E, SE, and S by Croatia, and on W by Italy (Istria and Gorizia); divided after WWI bet. Italy (782 sq. mi. or 2025 sq. km.) and Yugoslavia (3060 sq. mi. or 7925 sq. km.); by 1947 treaty entirely in Yugoslavia; with breakup of Yugoslavia late 20th cent. area included in Slovenia.

Carn Mairg. See MONADHLIATH MOUNTAINS.

Car·nous·tie \ˈkär-ˈnü-stē\. Seaport burgh, Tayside region, E Scotland, on North Sea ab. 11 mi. (18 km.) ENE of Dundee; pop. (1981p) 9217; resort with fine beach and golf course.

Carn·sore Point \ˈkärn-ˌsōr\. Cape on SE extremity of Ireland, projecting into St. George's Channel.

Carntoul. See CAIRNTOUL.

Car·nun·tum \kär-ˈnən-təm\. Ancient town, N Pannonia, Roman Empire, on S bank of the Danube; ruins near Hainburg, Austria; orig. Celtic, became important Roman post from the time of Emperor Augustus; used as base 171–173 A.D. by Emperor Marcus Aurelius in his campaign against the Marcomanni; destroyed by Germans 4th cent.

Caro \ˈkar-ō\. Village, ⊗ of Tuscola co., E Michigan, 28 mi. (45 km.) E of Saginaw; pop. (1990c) 4054.

Car·ol City \ˈkar-əl\. Unincorporated settlement, Miami-Dade co., SE Florida, NW of Miami Beach; pop. (1990c) 53,331.

Car·o·li·na \ˌkar-ə-ˈlī-nə\. Early American colony; as granted by British King Charles II to eight lords proprietors 1663 included land from ocean to ocean bet. 31st and 36th parallels; in 1665 boundaries extended to included area around Albemarle Sound where settlers from Virginia had located since ab. 1650. Fundamental constitutions by English philosopher John Locke adopted by proprietors in 1669 and later abandoned; first permanent settlement by English 1670 (in South Carolina); because of neglect of proprietors to defend colony in Tuscarora War (1711–12) and Yamassee War (1715–16) and other reasons, charter abrogated and separate royal governments ultimately estab. in North Carolina and South Carolina (*qq.v.*) 1729—hence, **the Carolinas.**

Ca·ro·li·na \ˌkä-rō-ˈlē-nä\. Municipality, NE Puerto Rico, 11 mi. (18 km.) ESE of San Juan; pop. (1990c) 177,806; sugar processing.

Carolina, La. See LA CAROLINA.

Car·o·li·na Beach \ˌkar-ə-ˈlī-nə\. Town, Brunswick co., SE North Carolina, on an island S of Wilmington; pop. (1990c) 3630.

Car·o·line \ˈkar-ə-ˌlīn\. Name of counties in two states of the U.S. See tables at MARYLAND and VIRGINIA.

Caroline Island. Small atoll, Kiribati, one of the Line Is. in cen. Pacific Ocean, ab. 400 mi. (645 km.) E of Penrhyn I., 9°58′S, 150°13′W; 6 mi. (10 km.) long by 1 mi. (2 km.) wide; shallow lagoon.

Caroline Islands *or* **Car·o·lines** \ˈkar-ə-ˌlīnz, -lənz\ *or Ger.* **Ka·ro·lin·en** \ˌkä-rō-ˈlē-nən\. Extensive archipelago in W Pacific Ocean, E of S Philippines; ab. 5° to 10°N and 130° to 166°E; 457 sq. mi. (1184 sq. km.), incl. lagoons 3740 sq. mi. (9687 sq. km.); formerly part of the U.S. Trust Terr. of the Pacific Islands; includes 550 to 680 islands (depending on definition of "island"); has many coral islets and reefs; most important islands: Yap, Pohnpei, Chuuk, Kosrae (the Federated States of Micronesia), and Palau. Some islands are fertile and populous; the larger are volcanic, the smaller are atolls, generally uninhabited; native inhabitants are Micronesians; on some islands are massive ruins, still unexplained, indicating presence of people centuries ago.

History: Explored by Spanish 17th cent.; rarely visited down to latter part of 19th cent.; German seizure of Yap 1885 aroused protest (dispute settled 1887 by decision of Pope Leo XIII); islands purchased by Germany 1899; seized by Japan 1914 and granted as mandate to Japan following WWI; after 1935 prohibited territory to all foreigners; fortified by Japan; Ulithi and S islands (Peleliu and Angaur) of the Palau group occupied by Americans 1944 during WWII; placed under U.S. trusteeship 1947; with exception of Palau (*q.v.*), islands became Federated States of Micronesia 1979.

Car·ol Stream \\'kar-əl\\. Village, Du Page co., NE Illinois, ab. 15 mi. (24 km.) W of Chicago; pop. (1990c) 31,716.

Ca·ro·ní \\ˌkä-rō-'nē\\. River, E Venezuela; rises in Pacaraima Mts. in SE Venezuela; flows N into Orinoco River near its mouth; 550 mi. (885 km.) long; contains Guri Dam (*q.v.*).

Ca·ro·ra \\kä-'rō-rä\\. Town, Lara state, NW Venezuela, ab. 53 mi. (85 km.) W of Barquisimeto.

Ca·rouge \\kä-'rüzh\\. Commune, Geneva canton, SW Switzerland; pop. (1980c) 13,100; suburb of Geneva.

Car·pa·thi·an Mountains \\kär-'pā-thē-ən\\ *or* **Car·pa·thi·ans** \\-ənz\\; *anc.* **Car·pa·tes** \\'kär-pə-ˌtēz\\. Mountain system of E Europe, along boundary bet. Slovakia and Poland and extending southward through Ukraine and E Romania; max. width 180 mi. (290 km.); highest peak Gerlachovka 8711 ft. (2655 m.); subdivided into East and West Beskids (see BESKIDS) and the Tatra Mts. (or High Tatra) in cen. part; extensions to SW are Little Carpathian Mts. and White Carpathian Mts. (*qq.v.*); Transylvanian Alps are sometimes called the South Carpathians. Source of Vistula, Dniester, and Tisza rivers; among best-known passes are Yablonitsa Pass and Lupków Pass.

Carpathian Ruthenia *or* **Carpatho–Ukraine.** See ZAKARPATS'KA.

Carpathus *or* **Carpathos.** See KARPATHOS.

Carpenisi. See KARPENISION.

Car·pen·tar·ia, Gulf of \\ˌkär-pən-'tar-ē-ə\\. Large gulf, NE Australia, inlet of Arafura Sea; bordered on W by Northern Terr., and on E by Cape York Penin. of Queensland; ab. 480 mi. (770 km.) N to S and 400 mi. (645 km.) E to W; for the most part shallow (av. 30 to 40 fathoms).

Carpenter Dam. See HAMILTON, LAKE 1.

Car·pen·ters·ville \\'kär-pən-tərz-ˌvil\\. Village, Kane co., NE Illinois, N of Elgin; pop. (1990c) 23,049.

Car·pen·tras \\ˌkȧr-pä^{n}-'trä\\; *anc.* **Car·pen·to·rac·te** \\kär-ˌpen-tə-'rak-tē\\. City, Vaucluse dept., SE France, 12 mi. (19 km.) NE of Avignon; Gothic cathedral; Roman remains, incl. triumphal arch, aqueduct. A former episcopal see; residence of Pope Clement V 1313; former ✱ of papal countship of Venaissin.

Car·pi \\'kär-pē\\. Commune, Modena prov., Emilia-Romagna, N Italy, 10 mi. (16 km.) NNW of the commune of Modena; pop. (1989c) 60,690; episcopal see; 16th cent. castle; 16th cent. church; citadel.

Car·pin·te·ria \\ˌkär-pən-tə-'rē-ə\\. City, Santa Barbara co., SW California, SE of the city of Santa Barbara; pop. (1990c) 13,747.

Car·qui·nez Strait \\kär-'kē-nās\\. Strait joining San Pablo and Suisun bays, California; 8 mi. (13 km.) long.

Carrae. See HARAN.

Car·ran·tuo·hill *also* **Car·ran·tu·al** \\ˌkar-ən-'tü-əl\\. Highest peak in Ireland, in Macgillicuddy's Reeks, co. Kerry; 3414 ft. (1041 m.).

Car·ra·ra \\kär-'rä-rä\\; *formerly* **Apua·nia** \\ä-'pwä-nyä\\. Commune, Massa-Carrara prov., Tuscany, cen. Italy; pop. (1989c) 68,528; Carrara marble used by notable sculptors, incl. Michelangelo; 13th cent. castle; 14th cent. cathedral; 16th cent. baroque palace.

Carr·bo·ro \\'kär-ˌbər-ō\\. Town, Orange co., N North Carolina, 10 mi. (16 km.) SW of Durham; pop. (1990c) 11,553.

Carreta, Point. See MANSO, POINT.

Carrhae. See HARAN.

Car·ri·a·cou \\ˌkar-ē-ə-'kü\\. Largest island of the Grenadines (*q.v.*); administered as part of Grenada; 13 sq. mi. (34 sq. km.); chief town Hillsborough.

Car·rick·fer·gus \\ˌkar-ik-'fər-gəs\\. **1.** District, E Northern Ireland; estab. 1974. See table at IRELAND, NORTHERN.

2. Town, its ⊗, Carrickfergus dist., NE Northern Ireland, on N shore of Belfast Lough 9.5 mi. (15 km.) NE of Belfast; pop. (1990e) 31,000; historically an important seaport; castle begun 12th cent., still much intact, used as refuge for Scots settlers during English Civl War.

Car·rick on Shan·non \\'kar-ik ... 'sha-nən\\. Town, ⊗ of co. Leitrim, N Ireland (republic), 28 mi. (45 km.) SE of Sligo; pop. (1981c) 360; recreational fishing.

Carrick on Suir \\'shu̇r\\. Town, SE co. Tipperary, S Ireland, 18 mi. (29 km.) WNW of Waterford; pop. (1991p) 5145; slate deposits; c. 14th cent. castle; at nearby Carrickbeg are ruins of a medieval abbey.

Car·ring·ton \\'kar-iŋ-ˌtən\\. City, ⊗ of Foster co., E cen. North Dakota, NNW of Jamestown; pop. (1990c) 2267.

Carr Inlet \\'kär\\. Inlet, S end of Puget Sound, W of Tacoma, Washington.

Car·ri·zal \\ˌkär-rē-'säl\\. Village, Chihuahua state, Mexico, ab. 85 mi. (135 km.) S of Ciudad Juárez; scene of skirmish 1916 during Mexican Revolution in which Mexican government troops defeated American Gen. John Pershing's forces who were in pursuit of revolutionary Francisco (Pancho) Villa in retaliation for his raid across Mexico-U.S. border.

Car·ri·zo Springs \\kə-'rē-zō\\. City, ⊗ of Dimmit co., S Texas, 47 mi. (76 km.) S of Uvalde; pop. (1990c) 5745; fruit packing, oil refining.

Car·ri·zo·zo \\ˌkär-ə-'zō-zō\\. Town, ⊗ of Lincoln co., cen. New Mexico, 75 mi. (121 km.) W of Roswell; pop. (1990c) 1075.

Car·roll \\'kar-əl\\. **1.** Name of counties in 13 states of the U.S. See tables at ARKANSAS, GEORGIA, ILLINOIS, INDIANA, IOWA, KENTUCKY, MARYLAND, MISSISSIPPI, MISSOURI, NEW HAMPSHIRE, OHIO, TENNESSEE, VIRGINIA. For parishes of Louisiana, see *East Carroll* and *West Carroll* in table at LOUISIANA.

2. City, ⊗ of Carroll co., W cen. Iowa, 47 mi. (76 km.) SW of Fort Dodge; pop. (1990c) 9579.

Car·roll·ton \\'kar-əl-tən\\. **1.** Town, ⊗ of Pickens co., W Alabama; pop. (1990c) 1170.

2. City, ⊗ of Carroll co., W Georgia, 40 mi. (64 km.) WSW of Atlanta; pop. (1990c) 16,029; wire cable, textiles; West Georgia Coll. (1933); incorp. 1856.

3. City, ⊗ of Greene co., W Illinois, 33 mi. (53 km.) NNW of Alton; pop. (1990c) 2507; settled 1818.

4. City, ⊗ of Carroll co., N Kentucky, on Ohio River 37 mi. (60 km.) N of Frankfort; pop. (1990c) 3715.

5. Town, a ⊗ of Carroll co., cen. Mississippi; pop. (1990c) 221.

6. City, ⊗ of Carroll co., NW cen. Missouri, 30 mi. (48 km.) S of Chillicothe; pop. (1990c) 4406.

7. Village, ⊗ of Carroll co., E Ohio, 21 mi. (34 km.) SE of Canton; pop. (1990c) 3042; coal deposits nearby.

8. City, Dallas and Denton cos., N Texas, 15 mi. (24 km.) NNW of Dallas; pop. (1990c) 82,169; population more than doubled bet. 1970 and 1980 and again bet. 1980 and 1990.

Car·ron \\'kar-ən\\. **1.** River, Central region, S cen. Scotland; flows E into the Firth of Forth; 20 mi. (32 km.) long.

2. Village, Central region, Scotland, on Carron River ab. 2 mi. (3 km.) NW of Falkirk; at one time noted for production of cannon called carronade.

Car·rot \\'kar-ət\\. River, cen. Saskatchewan, Canada; flows ENE across Manitoba border into Saskatchewan River; 250 mi. (402 km.) long.

Carso. See KRAS.

Car·son \'kärs-ᵊn\. **1.** River, W United States, rising in Alpine co., E California, and flowing N and E into Carson Sink, N Churchill co., W Nevada; ab. 170 mi. (275 km.) long.

2. County in NW Texas. See table at TEXAS.

3. City, Los Angeles co., California, SE of the city of Los Angeles; pop. (1990c) 83,995; California State Univ., Dominguez Hills (1960).

4. Village, ⊗ of Grant co., S North Dakota; 70 mi. (113 km.) SW of Bismarck; pop. (1990c) 383.

Carson City. City, ✱ of Nevada, near Lake Tahoe and Carson River 30 mi. (48 km.) S of Reno; pop. (1990c) 40,443; alt. 4697 ft. (1432 m.); gaming, recreation; tourism-related services; Western Nevada Community Coll. (1971); formerly important for processing of silver mined in area; site of branch of U.S. Mint 1870–93 (now a museum); settled 1858 and later renamed for American scout Christopher (Kit) Carson; became territorial ✱ 1861; became state ✱ 1864 when Nevada gained statehood; joined with former Ormsby co. to become independent city 1969.

Carson Lake. Lake, SW Churchill co., W Nevada, in S part of Carson Sink; ab. 12 mi. (19 km.) long; no outlet.

Carson Pass. Mountain pass, Alpine co., E California, in main range of the Sierra Nevada; elev. 8634 ft. (2632 m.); discovered during winter 1843–44 by explorer and soldier Capt. John Frémont and scout Christopher (Kit) Carson; used by the forty-niners on way to California goldfields.

Carson Peak. Mountain, Hinsdale co., SW Colorado; 13,600 ft. (4145 m.).

Carson Sink. Shallow marshy region in N Churchill co., W Nevada; contains a wildlife refuge and a restricted military area. See CARSON LAKE.

Carstensz, Mount. See JAYA, PUNCAK.

Car·ta·ge·na \,kär-tä-'hā-nä, -'kā-; ,kär-tə-'je-nə\. **1.** Seaport, ✱ of Bolívar dept., on NW coast of Colombia, 60 mi. (97 km.) SW of Barranquilla; pop. (1992e) 688,300; textiles, leather goods; has good harbor with narrow entrance; Colombia's principal oil port; 16th–17th cent. cathedral; several churches; 16th–17th cent. fort; university (1824); founded 1533, became one of the most important cities of Spanish America; in 17th cent. second only to Mexico City in Western Hemisphere; strongly fortified in Spanish times with evidence of structures remaining; often attacked by the French and esp. by English (naval officers Sir Francis Drake in 1585 and Edward Vernon in 1741); Spanish until 1815 when it was taken by South American revolutionary Simón Bolívar but soon lost, retaken by independence forces 1821; although declined in economic importance during 19th cent., regained prominence as oil-processing facility during 20th cent.

2. *anc.* **Car·tha·go No·va** \kär-'tä-gō-'nō-və\. Seaport city, Murcia prov., SE Spain, on Mediterranean 28 mi. (45 km.) ESE of the commune of Murcia; pop. (1991p) 166,736; naval arsenal; lead, iron, zinc, copper deposits; medieval Gothic cathedral; ancient castle; Roman ruins.

History: Founded by Carthaginians under Gen. Hasdrubal 227 B.C.; captured by Roman Gen. Scipio Africanus c. 209 B.C. and made a Roman colony; sacked by Goths 425 A.D.; taken by Byzantines 6th cent. and Visigoths 7th cent.; held by Moors from 711 until freed by James I of Aragon 1269; important Mediterranean naval base 16th–17th cents.; site of uprisings against central government 1873–74.

Car·ta·go \kär-'tä-gō\. **1.** Town, Valle del Cauca dept., W Colombia, 125 mi. (201 km.) W of Bogotá; pop. (1985c) 92,524.

2. Province of cen. Costa Rica. See table at COSTA RICA.

3. City, ✱ of Cartago prov., Costa Rica, at foot of Mt. Irazú 14 mi. (22 km.) SE of San José; alt. 4765 ft. (1452 m.); former ✱ of Costa Rica; founded 1563; suffered severe earthquakes 18th and 19th cents.

Car·ter \'kär-tər\. Name of counties in five states of the U.S. See tables at KENTUCKY, MISSOURI, MONTANA, OKLAHOMA, TENNESSEE.

Carter, Mount. Peak in Glacier National Park, NW Montana; 9834 ft. (2997 m.).

Car·ter·et \,kär-tə-'ret\. **1.** Coastal county in SE North Carolina. See table at NORTH CAROLINA.

2. Borough, Middlesex co., cen. New Jersey, 6 mi. (10 km.) NNE of Perth Amboy near Staten I.; pop. (1990c) 19,025.

Car·te·ret \,kär-tə-'rā\. Village, W coast of Manche dept., NW France, 20 mi. (32 km.) SW of Cherbourg; now part of Barneville-Carteret; small port. When reached by Allied forces June 18, 1944, N part of Cotentin Penin. (*q.v.*) was cut off; important point in battle of Normandy; Allied forces opened peninsula several days later.

Carter Lake. City, Pottawattamie co., SW Iowa; pop. (1990c) 3200.

Carter Notch. Notch in White Mts., N Carroll co., W New Hampshire; 1057 ft. (322 m.).

Cart·ers Dam *and* **Carters Reservoir** \'kär-tərz\. See UNITED STATES, *Dams and Reservoirs.*

Car·ters·ville \'kär-tərz-,vil\. City, ⊗ of Bartow co., NW Georgia, 35 mi. (56 km.) NW of Atlanta; pop. (1990c) 12,035; valuable mineral deposits nearby.

Car·ter·ville \'kär-tər-,vil\. City, Williamson co., S Illinois, 10 mi. (16 km.) W of Marion; pop. (1990c) 3630; John A. Logan Coll. (1967).

Car·thage \'kär-thij\. **1.** City, ⊗ of Hancock co., W Illinois, 38 mi. (61 km.) NNE of Quincy; pop. (1990c) 2657; place where Mormon founder Joseph Smith and his brother Hyrum were imprisoned for treason and killed by a mob 1844; jail preserved as a monument.

2. Town, ⊗ of Leake co., cen. Mississippi, 48 mi. (77 km.) NE of Jackson; pop. (1990c) 3819.

3. City, ⊗ of Jasper co., SW Missouri, 14 mi. (23 km.) NE of Joplin; pop. (1990c) 10,747; marble quarries; site of fierce fighting during Civil War, commemorated with monuments; outlaw Belle Starr born in the area 1848.

4. Village, Jefferson co., N New York, 16 mi. (26 km.) E of Watertown; pop. (1990c) 4344.

5. Town, ⊗ of Moore co., cen. North Carolina; pop. (1990c) 976; Sandhills Community Coll. (1863).

6. Town, ⊗ of Smith co., N cen. Tennessee, on Cumberland River 21 mi. (34 km.) E of Lebanon; pop. (1990c) 2386.

7. City, ⊗ of Panola co., E Texas, 28 mi. (45 km.) S of Marshall; pop. (1990c) 6496; Panola Coll. (1947).

8. *anc.* **Car·tha·go** \kär-'thä-gō, -'tä-\. Ancient city and state, N Africa, on coast NE of modern Tunis, Tunisia; built on tip of a peninsula, orig. around a citadel known as the Byrsa; comprised inner and outer harbor, extensive walls, old and new city (suburb of Megara). Ongoing archaeological investigation of many Roman ruins and some Phoenician.

History: Founded by colonists from Phoenician kingdom of Tyre traditionally late 9th cent. B.C. but probably occurred during 8th cent.; from 6th cent. B.C. began conquests in W Africa, Sicily, and Sardinia; after defeat at Himera (*q.v.*) 480 B.C., developed sea power and, under descendants of the general Hamilcar, came to dominate W Mediterranean; fought Sicily 4th cent. B.C.; engaged in series of bitter wars with Rome, known as Punic Wars: in First Punic War 264–241 B.C. lost Sicily to Rome; conquered Spain to Ebro 237–228 B.C.; in Second Punic War (led by Hannibal, Hamilcar's son) 218–201 B.C. fought battles of Cannae and Zama (*qq.v.*); at end of Third Punic War 149–146 B.C. city utterly destroyed by the younger Scipio; site of colony founded by Julius Caesar 44 B.C.; became important center of Roman African province; birthplace of ecclesiast Tertullian (c. 155 A.D.); center of controversy in early Christianity; embroiled in schism of ecclesiast Donatus 4th cent.; captured by Vandals 439 A.D.; won for Byzantine Empire by Gen. Belisarius 533–34; taken by Arabs at end of 7th cent. and with their emphasis on Tunis began to lose importance.

Carthago Nova. See CARTAGENA 2.

Car·ti·er Islet *or* **Cartier Island** \,kär-tē-'ā\. Small uninhabited island off N coast of Western Australia, Australia, SE of the Ashmore Is.

Cart·wright \'kärt-,rīt\. Coastal community and harbor, SE Labrador, Newfoundland, Canada; pop. (1991c) 611.

Ca·ru·a·ru \,kä-rü-ə-'rü\. City, E Pernambuco state, E Brazil; munic. pop. (1991p) 213,557; trade center for agricultural and livestock-raising area.

Ca·rú·pa·no \kä-'rü-pä-ˌnō\. Seaport, N Sucre state, N Venezuela, on Paria Penin. 100 mi. (161 km.) ENE of Barcelona; pop. (1990e) 78,593; coffee and cacao.

Ca·ruth·ers·ville \kə-'rə-thərz-ˌvil\. City, ⊗ of Pemiscot co., SE corner of Missouri, on Mississippi River 60 mi. (97 km.) SW of its conjunction with Ohio River; pop. (1990c) 7389.

Car·ver \'kär-vər\. **1.** County in SE cen. Minnesota. See table at MINNESOTA.

2. Town, Plymouth co., Massachusetts, SW of Plymouth; pop. (1990c) 10,590.

Car·vin \kär-'vеⁿ\. Commune, Pas-de-Calais dept., N France, 18 mi. (29 km.) NNE of Arras; coal nearby.

Car·vo·ei·ro, Cape \kȧr-'vwā-rü\. Cape on W coast of Portugal, 39°21′N, 9°24′W.

Cary \'kar-ē\. **1.** Village, McHenry co., N Illinois, 34 mi. (55 km.) W of Chicago; pop. (1990c) 10,043.

2. Town, Wake co., E cen. North Carolina, 7 mi. (11 km.) W of Raleigh; pop. (1990c) 43,858; pop. has more than quintupled since 1970.

Ca·rys·tus \kə-'ris-təs\ *or Gk.* **Ká·ris·tos** \'kä-rēs-ˌtös\. Town at S end of island of Euboea, Greece; inhabited since ancient times; has long been noted for marble.

Cas·a·blan·ca \ˌka-sə-'blaŋ-kə, ˌkä-sə-'bläŋ-, -zə-\; *Arab.* **Dar el Bei·da** *or* **Dar–al–Bai·da** \'där-el-'bī-dä\. Seaport city, W coast of Morocco, pop. (1989e) 3,102,000; largest city in Morocco; large harbor; textile manufacture; tourism; financial center.

History: Founded by Portuguese on site of ancient city of Anfa, destroyed in 1468; occupied 1757 by Moroccan sultan and in 1907 by French as result of murder of some French workers; while under French protectorate large-scale construction of new housing initiated 1920s; in WWII surrendered to Allies Nov. 1942; scene of conference bet. British Prime Minister Winston Churchill and U.S. President Franklin Roosevelt Jan. 1943, at which the "unconditional surrender" of Axis countries was determined upon.

Ca·sa Gran·de \'kä-sə-'grän-dā\. City, Pinal co., S Arizona, 43 mi. (69 km.) SSE of Phoenix; pop. (1990c) 19,082; historical museum.

Casa Grande Ruins National Monument. See UNITED STATES, *National Monuments.*

Ca·sa·lec·chio di Re·no Bo·lo·gna \ˌkä-sä-'lek-kyō-dē-'rā-nō-bō-'lō-nyä\. Commune, Bologna prov., Emilia-Romagna, N Italy, 4 mi. (6 km.) WSW of the commune of Bologna; pop. (1989c) 35,170; a suburb of Bologna.

Ca·sa·le Mon·fer·ra·to \kä-'sä-lā-ˌmȯn-fer-'rä-tō\. Commune, Alessandria prov., Piedmont, NW Italy, on Po River 18 mi. (29 km.) NNW of the commune of Alessandria; pop. (1989c) 39,568; 18th cent. palaces; 12th cent. cathedral; Gothic church; citadel (founded 1590 by Vicenzo Gonzag, duke of Mantua) one of strongest in Italy. Founded 8th cent. on site of ancient **Bo·din·com·a·gus** \ˌbō-diŋ-'kä-mə-gəs\; fell to marquises of Montferrat 13th cent., becoming ✻ of the duchy of Montferrat; fought over by Savoy, France 17th cent.; to Italy 1860.

Ca·sal·mag·gio·re \kä-ˌsäl-mä-'jō-rē\. Commune, Cremona prov., Lombardy, N Italy, on Po River; pop. (1981p) 13,159.

Ca·sa·mance \ˌkä-zä-'mäⁿs\ *also* **Ka·sa·man·sa** \ˌkä-zə-'män-sə\. River, Senegal, S of Gambia; 200 mi. (322 km.) long.

Ca·sa·na·re \ˌkä-sä-'nä-rā\. Department of cen. Colombia. See table at COLOMBIA.

Ca·sas, Ciu·dad de las. See SAN CRISTOBAL 6.

Ca·sas Gran·des \'kä-säs-'grän-dās\. Town, NW Chihuahua state, N Mexico, SSW of Nuevo Casas Grandes; munic. pop. (1990p) 10,678; nearby to the S are ruins of ancient city, perhaps settled first more than 1000 years ago by peoples from pueblo culture orig. estab. in SW United States; archaeological finds indicate later influence of Mexican Toltecs.

Cascadas, Las. See LAS CASCADAS.

Cas·cade \ka-'skād\. **1.** County in cen. Montana. See table at MONTANA.

2. City, ⊗ of Valley co., W cen. Idaho; pop. (1990c) 877.

Cascade Point. Cape on S cen. part of W coast of South I., New Zealand, 44°S, 168°22′E.

Cascade Range. Mountain range, W United States; N continuation of the Sierra Nevada, extending N from Lassen Peak, NE California, across Oregon and Washington; highest peak Mt. Rainier 14,410 ft. (4392 m.), in Washington; its continuation N in British Columbia, Canada, is known as the Coast Mts.

Cascade Tunnel. Railroad tunnel, Chelan and King cos., cen. Washington, ab. 55 mi. (88 km.) ENE of Seattle, through Cascade Range; 7.79 mi. (12.5 km.) long; completed 1929.

Ca·sci·na \'kä-shē-nä\. Commune, Pisa prov., Tuscany, cen. Italy, on Arno River 8 mi. (13 km.) ESE of the commune of Pisa; pop. (1991p) 36,006; Florentine victory over Pisans 1364.

Cas·co Bay \'kas-kō\. Inlet of Atlantic Ocean on SE coast of Cumberland co., SW Maine, containing many islands incl. Orrs I. and Chebeague I.; the city of Portland is situated on its W shore.

Case Inlet \'kās\. Inlet, bet. Mason and Pierce cos., Washington, at S end of Puget Sound.

Ca·se·ros \kä-'sā-rōs\. Town, W suburb of Buenos Aires, Argentina.

Ca·ser·ta \kä-'ser-tä, -'zer-\. **1.** Province of Campania, Italy. See table at ITALY.

2. Commune, ✻ of Caserta prov., Campania, S Italy, 16 mi. (26 km.) NNE of Naples; pop. (1991p) 68,811; palace (begun 1752; designed by architect Luigi Vanvitelli) built by Charles III of Spain. Headquarters of Garibaldian campaigns 1860. British Field Marshal Harold Alexander's headquarters during latter part of Italian campaign in WWII; here "Act of Surrender" of German Army Group in Italy and Yugoslavia signed Apr. 29, 1945.

Ca·sey. **1.** \'kā-sē\. County in cen. Kentucky. See table at KENTUCKY.

2. \'kā-zē, -sē\. City, Clark co., E Illinois, 67 mi. (108 km.) SE of Decatur; pop. (1990c) 2914.

Ca·seyr, Raas \'räs-kä-'sār\ *or* **Cape Gar·da·fui** \ˌgär-dä-'fwē, -'fü-ē\ *or* **Cape Guar·da·fui** \ˌgwär-\ *or* **Ras Asir** \ˌräs-ä-'sir\; *anc.* **Aro·ma·ta** \ə-'rō-mə-tə\. Cape extending into Indian Ocean from NE tip of Somalia, S of entrance to Gulf of Aden.

Ca·sey·ville \'kā-sē-ˌvil\. Village, St. Clair co., SW Illinois, 6 mi. (10 km.) E of East St. Louis; pop. (1990c) 4419.

Cash·el \'kash-əl\. Town, S cen. co. Tipperary, S Ireland; pop. (1991p) 2473; at the base of **Rock of Cashel** 306 ft. (93 m.) high, on which are the ruins of a 13th cent. cathedral, a 12th cent. chapel, and a round tower; 13th cent. abbey. Irish chieftains of Munster here submitted to Henry II of England 1171.

Ca·si·gu·ran \ˌkä-sē-'gü-ˌrän\. Port, SE Luzon, Philippines, on Sorsogon Bay.

Casiguran Sound. Long narrow inlet of Pacific Ocean on E coast of Luzon, Philippines, with Cape San Ildefonso marking its SE point of entrance.

Ca·sil·da \kä-'sēl-dä\. Town, Santa Fe prov., N cen. Argentina, 210 mi. (338 km.) NW of Buenos Aires and 34 mi. (55 km.) W of Rosario; pop. (1980p) 23,492.

Casilinum. See CAPUA.

Casinum. See CASSINO.

Ca·si·quia·re *or* **Cas·si·qui·are** \ˌkä-sē-'kyä-rā\. River, S Venezuela; connects the upper course (Guainía) of Rio Negro with the Orinoco River; 222 mi. (357 km.) long; a unique stream, not having a reversible current but flowing in a channel over marshy land of slight relief; strictly an arm of the Orinoco.

Cas·ket Mountain \'kas-kət\. Peak, Jeff Davis co., W Texas; 6180 ft. (1884 m.).

Čás·lav \'chäs-läf\ *or Ger.* **Tschas·lau** \'chäs-ˌlau̇\. City, cen. Czech Republic, 45 mi. (72 km.) ESE of Prague; pop. (1980p) 9950.

Caso. See KASOS.

\ə\ abut \ə\ matches \ə\ kitten, Fr table \ər\ **further** \a\ ash \ā\ ace \ä\ cot, cart \ȧ\ Fr bac \au̇\ out \b\ Span Avila \ch\ chin \e\ bet \ē\ easy \g\ go \i\ hit \ī\ ice \j\ job \k\ Ger ich, Buch \ⁿ\ Fr vin \ŋ\ sing \ō\ go \ȯ\ all \ȯ\ law \œ\ Fr bœuf \œ̄\ Fr feu \ȯi\ boy \th\ thin \th\ this \ü\ loot \u̇\ foot \ue\ Ger füllen \ue̅\ Fr rue \y\ yet \y\ Fr digne \'dēnʸ\, nuit \'nwʸē\ \yü\ few \yu̇\ fury \zh\ vision

Ca·so·ria \kä-ˈsōr-ē-ä\. Commune, Napoli prov., Campania, S Italy, 3 mi. (5 km.) N of Naples; pop. (1991p) 79,315.

Cas·per \ˈkas-pər\. City, ⊗ of Natrona co., cen. Wyoming, on North Platte River; pop. (1990c) 46,742; trade center; oil refineries; natural gas; tourism; Casper Coll. (1945). Fort from early settlement late 19th cent., reconstructed, now museum. Nearby Teapot Dome oil fields, source of 1920s federal scandal.

Cas·pi·an Gates \ˈkas-pē-ən\; *anc.* **Cas·pi·ae Py·lae** \ˈkas-pē-ˌē-ˈpī-ˌlē\. **1.** Pass, N Iran, N of Rhages (near modern Tehran) in Elburz Mts., known in ancient times; used by Macedonian King Alexander the Great in his pursuit of Persians c. 330 B.C.

2. *or anc.* **Al·ba·ni·ae Pylae** \al-ˈbā-nē-ˌē\. Narrow pass, S Russia in Europe, on N shore of Caspian Sea, near Derbent; used by Roman historian Tacitus in his *Annals* (vi, 33).

Caspian Sea; *anc.* **Cas·pi·um Ma·re** \ˈkas-pē-əm-ˈmā-rē, ˈmä-ˌrā\ *or* **Hyr·ca·num Mare** \hər-ˈkā-nəm\. Inland salt lake bet. Europe and Asia; basin is 746 mi. (1200 km.) long and 270 mi. (434 km.) wide; 143,550 sq. mi. (371,795 sq. km.); the largest inland body of water in the world; about 92 ft. (28 m.) below sea level. Receives the Volga, Ural, and Emba rivers at the N, and the Terek and Kura (with Araks) on the W. Has no outlet; loses more by evaporation than it receives from streams and siphoning for irrigation has resulted in a serious drop in level; enclosed by Azerbaijan, S Russia in Europe, Kazakhstan, Turkmenistan, and Iran. Chief ports Baku in Azerbaijan and Enzeli and Bandar-e Torkeman in Iran. Important as commercial route during Middle Ages when it formed a part of Mongol-Baltic trade route for goods from Asia; today is source of caviar and oil along its E shores.

Cass \ˈkas\. **1.** River, E Michigan; formed by union of headstreams in Tuscola co., flows W into the Saginaw River, Saginaw co., cen. Michigan; ab. 100 mi. (160 km.) long.

2. Name of counties in nine states of the U.S. See tables at ILLINOIS, INDIANA, IOWA, MICHIGAN, MINNESOTA, MISSOURI, NEBRASKA, NORTH DAKOTA, TEXAS.

Cassai. See KASAI.

Cassandreia. See POTIDAEA.

Cas·sa·no al·lo Io·nio \käs-ˈsä-nō-ˌäl-lō-ē-ˈō-nyō\. Commune, Cosenza prov., Calabria, S Italy, 33 mi. (53 km.) N of the commune of Cosenza; pop. (1981p) 19,217; episcopal see; castle.

Cassano d'Ad·da \ˈdäd-dä\. Commune, Milano prov., Lombardy, N Italy, on the Adda 16 mi. (26 km.) E of Milan; pop. (1981p) 15,319; scene of defeat of Ghibellines by Guelphs 1259; scene of victory of Louis-Joseph de Bourbon, duke of Vendôme over Austrian Gen. Eugene of Savoy 1705 in War of Spanish Succession; in Napoleonic Wars scene of victory of Russian Field Marshal Aleksandr Suvorov over French forces of Gen. Victor Moreau 1799.

Casscàta delle Marmore. See VELINO.

Cassel. See KASSEL.

Cas·sel·berry \ˈka-səl-ˌber-ē\. City, Seminole co., cen. Florida, 9 mi. (15 km.) NNE of Orlando; pop. (1990c) 18,911; pop. doubled bet. 1970 and 1990.

Cas·sia \ˈka-shə\. County in S Idaho. See table at IDAHO.

Cas·sian Way \ˈka-shən\ *or Lat.* **Via Cas·sia** \ˈvī-ə-ˈka-shə, -shē-ə\. Ancient Roman road from Rome to Florence, through Bolsena, Chiusi, and Arezzo; extension ran NW to the Aurelian Way near Luna.

Cas·si·no \kä-ˈsē-nō\; *before 1871* **San Ger·ma·no** \ˌsän-jer-ˈmä-nō\; *anc.* **Ca·si·num** \kə-ˈsī-nəm\. Commune, Frosinone prov., Lazio, cen. Italy, near Rapido River 28 mi. (45 km.) ESE of the commune of Frosinone; pop. (1991p) 32,803; ancient ruins; Benedictine monastery of Monte Cassino (*q.v.*) nearby; peace signed here by Holy Roman Emperor Frederick II and Pope Gregory IX 1230. In WWII a key position in the German Gustav Line, barring entrance to Allies into valley of Liri River and road to Rome; battle for it began early 1944, but through Feb. and Mar. infantry, artillery, and air assaults were unsuccessful; town finally captured in May; monastery and town completely destroyed, both rebuilt after WWII.

Cassiquiare. See CASIQUIARE.

Cas·si·ter·i·des \ˌka-sə-ˈter-ə-ˌdēz\. Ancient name of tin-producing (Gk. *kassiteros* tin) islands of W Europe; may have applied to Isles of Scilly off Great Britain, but location unknown.

Cass Lake \ˈkas\. **1.** Lake on NW boundary of Cass co., N cen. Minnesota, extending into Beltrami co.; ab. 10 mi. (16 km.) long.

2. City, Cass co., N cen. Minnesota, on Cass Lake 15 mi. (24 km.) ESE of Bemidji; pop. (1990c) 923.

Cas·sop·o·lis \kə-ˈsä-plis\. Village, ⊗ of Cass co., SW Michigan; pop. (1990c) 1822.

Cass·ville \ˈkas-ˌvil\. City, ⊗ of Barry co., SW Missouri; pop. (1990c) 2371.

Castalian Spring. See PARNASSUS 2.

Ca·stel·fi·dar·do \kä-ˌstel-fē-ˈdär-dō\. Commune, Ancona prov., Marche, cen. Italy, S of the seaport of Ancona; pop. (1981p) 14,285; musical instruments; scene of battle 1860 in which Italians (Piedmontese) decisively defeated papal forces.

Cas·tel·fran·co Ve·ne·to \käs-ˌtel-ˈfräŋ-kō-ˈve-nā-tō\. Commune, Treviso prov., Veneto, NE Italy, 15 mi. (24 km.) W of the commune of Treviso; pop. (1991p) 29,461; birthplace of painter Giorgione c. 1477.

Ca·stel Gan·dol·fo \käs-ˈtel-gän-ˈdȯl-fō\. Commune, Roma prov., Lazio, cen. Italy, on W shore of Lake Albano 13 mi. (21 km.) SE of Rome; pop. (1991p) 6784; includes a group of papal estates; papal palace begun by Urban VIII; summer residence of the popes. See VATICAN CITY.

Ca·stel·lam·ma·re, Gulf of \käs-ˌtel-läm-ˈmä-rā\. Inlet of Tyrrhenian Sea on NW coast of the island of Sicily, Italy.

Castellammare del Gol·fo \del-ˈgōl-fō\. Seaport, Trapani prov., NW Sicily, Italy, on Gulf of Castellammare E of the seaport of Trapani; pop. (1981p) 13,348.

Castellammare di Sta·bia \dē-ˈstä-byä\; *anc.* **Sta·bi·ae** \ˈstā-bē-ˌē\. Fortified seaport, Napoli prov., Campania, S Italy, on Bay of Naples 16 mi. (26 km.) SE of Naples; pop. (1991p) 68,720; episcopal see; ruins of 13th cent. castle; dockyards; summer resort. Built near ancient Stabiae, which was destroyed by the eruption of Vesuvius 79 A.D. in which Roman scholar Pliny the Elder perished.

Castellana, La. See LA CASTELLANA.

Ca·stel·la·ne·ta \käs-ˌtel-lä-ˈnā-tä\. Commune, Taranto prov., Puglia, SE Italy, 19 mi. (31 km.) NW of the seaport of Taranto; pop. (1981p) 15,512; medieval cathedral; birthplace of American actor Rudolph Valentino 1895.

Castell–nedd. See NEATH 2.

Cas·tel·lón \ˌkä-stel-ˈyōn\. Province of E Spain. See table at SPAIN.

Cas·te·llón de la Pla·na \ˌkäs-tel-ˈyōn-thā-lä-ˈplä-nä\. Mediterranean seaport, ✱ of Castellón, Spain, 40 mi. (64 km.) NNE of Valencia; pop. (1991p) 133,180; oranges; tourism; captured from Moors by James I of Aragon 1233.

Castellorizo. See KASTELLÓRIZON.

Cas·tel·nau·da·ry \kȧ-ˌstel-ˌnō-dȧ-ˈrē\. Commune, Aude dept., S France, ab. 22 mi. (35 km.) WNW of Carcassonne; important in ancient Languedoc and in the wars against the Albigenses in 13th cent.; battle 1632 in which Louis XIII defeated the rebellious Henri II, duke of Montmorency, and Gaston, duke of Orléans (the king's brother).

Castelnuovo. See HERCEGNOVI.

Cas·te·lo Bran·co \kȧ-ˈshte-lü-ˈbrȧŋ-kü\. **1.** District of E cen. Portugal. See table at PORTUGAL.

2. Commune, its ✱, 114 mi. (183 km.) NE of Lisbon; pop. (1991p) 54,439; cork, wool; cathedral; Roman ruins; medieval castle. A city of Knights Templars.

Castelrosso. See KASTELLÓRIZON.

Ca·stel San Gio·van·ni \käs-ˈtel-sän-jō-ˈvä-nē\. Commune, Piacenza prov., Emilia-Romagna, N Italy, 15 mi. (24 km.) W of the commune of Piacenza; pop. (1981p) 11,863.

Ca·stel·ve·tra·no \käs-ˌtel-vā-ˈträ-nō\. Commune, Trapani prov., NW Sicily, Italy, 29 mi. (47 km.) SSE of the seaport of Trapani; pop. (1991p) 30,193; ruins of ancient Selinus (*q.v.*) nearby.

Ca·sti·glio·ne del La·go \ˌkäs-tēl-ˈyō-nā-del-ˈlä-gō\. Commune, Perugia prov., Umbria, cen. Italy, on Lake Trasimeno

18 mi. (29 km.) WNW of the commune of Perugia; pop. (1981p) 12,999; castle.

Castiglione del·le Sti·vie·re \de-lə-stē-'vyā-rā\. Commune, Mantova prov., Lombardy, N Italy, 22 mi. (35 km.) NW of Mantua; pop. (1981p) 15,086; Austrians under Field Marshal Dagobert von Wurmser defeated by French under Napoléon Bonaparte (later Emperor Napoléon I) 1796.

Cas·tile \ka-'stēl\ *or Span.* **Cas·til·la** \kä-'stē-lyä\. Region and ancient kingdom, cen. and N cen. Spain; 53,463 sq. mi. (138,469 sq. km.); comprises the modern provs. of Ávila, Burgos, Guadalajara, Madrid, Palencia, Segovia, Soria, and Valladolid, and parts of Ciudad Real, Cuenca, and Toledo; divided into two historical regions: in the N, Old Castile (*q.v.*), and in the S, New Castile (*q.v.*); extensive plains, forming tablelands hemmed in on all sides by mountains; some fertile regions, esp. in the S, but in general arid; watered chiefly by the Duero, Guadiana, Tagus, and Júcar rivers.

History: Orig. an extension of kingdom of León (see LEÓN 5); in 10th cent. A.D. countship of Castile made hereditary and practically autonomous by Count González of Burgos; united with Navarre 1029 which began conquest of León; León united with Castile by Ferdinand I 1037; expanded by series of conquests of Moorish kingdoms: Toledo (New Castile) 1085, Córdoba 1236, Murcia 1243, and Seville 1248; took Canary Is. 1402 and Gibraltar 1462; union with Aragon (*q.v.*) 1479 (after marriage of Isabella of Castile to Ferdinand of Aragon 1469) completed with accession of their grandson, Charles I of Spain, 1516. See SPAIN.

Cas·til·la–La Man·cha \kä-'stē-lyä-lä-'män-chä\. Autonomous community and historical region of cen. Spain. See table at SPAIN.

Castilla la Nueva. See NEW CASTILE.

Castilla la Vieja. See OLD CASTILE.

Cas·til·la y Le·ón \kä-'stē-lyä-ē-lā-'ōn\. Autonomous community and historical region of N Spain. See table at SPAIN.

Cas·til·lo de San Mar·cos National Monument \kas-'tē-yō-dā-san-'mär-kōs\. See UNITED STATES, *National Monuments.*

Cas·til·lon \,kás-tē-'yōⁿ\ *or* **Castillon–la–Ba·taille** \-lá-bá-'tī\. Commune, Gironde dept., SW France, on the Dordogne River 26 mi. (42 km.) E of Bordeaux; scene of English defeat July 17, 1453 in last battle of Hundred Years' War.

Cas·tine \kas-'tēn\. Town, Hancock co., SE Maine, on E side of Penobscot Bay, 35 mi. (56 km.) S of Bangor; pop. (1990c) 1161; fishing and resort center; Maine Maritime Academy (1941); one of Maine's oldest towns with many historical markers. From early 17th cent. contended over by Indians, American colonists, British, and French; occupied by British in War of 1812.

Cas·tle·bar \,ka-səl-'bär\. Town, ⊗ of co. Mayo, NW Ireland; pop. (1991p) 6071; site of Norman castle, home of Anglo-Irish de Burghs; nearby is site of runaway victory ("Castlebar Races") of French auxiliaries and Irish insurrectionists over militia and yeomanry 1798.

Cas·tle Clin·ton National Monument \'ka-səl-'klint-ᵊn\. See UNITED STATES, *National Monuments.*

Castle Dale \'ka-səl-,dāl\. City, ⊗ of Emery co., E cen. Utah; pop. (1990c) 1704; castle-like sandstone formations nearby.

Cas·tle·ford \'ka-səl-fərd\. Town, West Yorkshire, N England, 11 mi. (18 km.) ESE of Leeds; pop. (1981p) 36,032.

Cas·tle·gar \,ka-səl-'gär\. Town, S British Columbia, Canada; pop. (1991c) 6579.

Castle Harbour. Gulf off NE Bermuda I., formed by St. George's I. and St. David I. on N and small islands on E.

Castle Hill. Elevation, Cassino, Italy; near the Benedictine monastery; after bitter fighting captured by Allied troops Mar. 1944.

Castle Hills. City, Bexar co., S cen. Texas, entirely within city limits of San Antonio; pop. (1990c) 4198.

Castle Island. One of the Bahamas, at SE entrance to Crooked Island Passage; lighthouse (estab. 1868).

Cas·tle·maine \,ka-səl-'mān\. Town, cen. Victoria, SE Australia, 65 mi. (105 km.) NW of Melbourne; pop. (1991p) 6812; one of Australia's first gold-mining towns.

Castle Mountain; *1946–79* **Mount Ei·sen·ho·wer** \'ī-zᵊn-,haù-ər\. Mountain, S Alberta, Canada, W of Calgary, in Banff National Park; 9029 ft. (2752 m.).

Castle Peak. **1.** Mountain in the Sierra Nevada, E Fresno co., S cen. California; 10,668 ft. (3252 m.).
2. Mountain, Gunnison and Pitkin cos., W cen. Colorado; 14,265 ft. (4348 m.).
3. Mountain, SW Custer co., cen. Idaho; 11,820 ft. (3603 m.).

Castle Point. Peak, W Klamath co., S Oregon, SW of Crater Lake; 6300 ft. (1920 m.).

Cas·tle·reagh \'ka-səl-,rā\. District, E Northern Ireland; estab. 1974. See table at IRELAND, NORTHERN.

Castle Rock. City, ⊗ of Douglas co., cen. Colorado; pop. (1990c) 8708.

Castle Shan·non \'sha-nən\. Borough, Allegheny co., SW Pennsylvania, 6 mi. (10 km.) S of Pittsburgh; pop. (1990c) 9135.

Cas·tle·ton \'ka-səl-tən\. Town and summer resort, Rutland co., W Vermont, ab. 10 mi. (16 km.) W of Rutland; pop. (1990c) 4278; Castleton State Coll. (1787); during American Revolution, mobilization center of Ethan Allen and Green Mountain Boys before attack on Fort Ticonderoga 1775.

Castleton on Hud·son *or* **Castleton–on–Hudson.** Village, Rensselaer co., E New York, on Hudson River 9 mi. (15 km.) S of Albany; pop. (1990c) 1491; high-level bridge, railroad cutoff, with channel span of 1008 ft. (307 m.).

Cas·tle·town \'ka-səl-,taùn\. Town, former ✽ of Isle of Man (*q.v.*), on S coast of the island; pop. (1991c) 3152.

Cas·tle·town·bere \'ka-səl-tən-,ber\ *also* **Cas·tle·town Bear·ha·ven** \'ka-səl-tən-'ber-,hā-vən\ *or* **Bearhaven** *or* **Bere·ha·ven** \'ber-,hā-vən\. Small town, co. Cork, SW Ireland, on N coast of Bantry Bay; has harbor partly enclosed by **Bere Island** *or* **Bear Island** \'bar\; formerly used as a British naval base.

Castor. See ZWILLINGE.

Cas·tor Peak \'kas-tər\. Mountain in Yellowstone National Park, NW Wyoming; 10,854 ft. (3308 m.).

Castra Regina. See REGENSBURG.

Cas·tres \'kástrᵊ\; *anc.* **Cas·tra Al·bi·en·si·um** \'kas-trə-,al-bē-'en-sē-əm\. City, Tarn dept., S France, on Agout River 24 mi. (39 km.) S of Albi; pop. (1990c) 46,292; architecturally notable town hall (former episcopal palace) with gardens on plan of Tuileries; 17th cent. church; museum. Founded on site of Roman camp around Benedictine monastery 647; to crown 1225; episcopal see 1317–late 18th cent.; made countship 1356; accepted Protestant Reformation 16th cent.; conquered by Louis XIII 1629. Birthplace of French politician Jean Jaurès 1859.

Cas·tries \ká-'strē, 'käs-,trēs\. Seaport, ✽ of St. Lucia, on NW coast of St. Lucia I., Windward Is., West Indies; pop. (1991c) 11,147.

Cas·tro. **1.** \'kas-trō\. County in NW Texas. See table at TEXAS.
2. \'kásh-trü\. Municipality, Paraná state, S Brazil, ab. 60 mi. (97 km.) NW of Curitiba; pop. (1991p) 63,935.
3. \'käs-trō\. Small port, Los Lagos region, S cen. Chile; on E shore of Chiloé I.

Castro Al·ves \'kásh-trü-'ál-vēs\. City, Bahia state, E Brazil, on railroad line ab. 68 mi. (109 km.) W of Salvador; munic. pop. (1980c) 50,661.

Castro del Río \'käs-trō-del-'rē-ō\. Commune, Córdoba prov., S Spain, 22 mi. (35 km.) SE of the city of Córdoba; pop. (1991c) 7963.

Castrogiovanni. See ENNA 2.

Ca·strop–Rau·xel *also* **Ka·strop–Rauxel** \'käs-,tróp-'raùk-səl\. City, North Rhine-Westphalia, W Germany, 32 mi. (52 km.) SSW of Münster; pop. (1992e) 79,065; coal deposits; chemicals; first known mention of Castrop 834.

Ca·stro·re·a·le \ˌkäs-trō-rā-ˈä-lā\. Commune, Messina prov., NE Sicily, Italy; pop. (1981p) 3199; castle ruins; churches; museum.

Ca·stro–Ur·dia·les \ˈkäs-trō-ür-ˈthyä-lās\. Seaport, Cantabria prov., N Spain, on Bay of Biscay 30 mi. (48 km.) ESE of Santander; pop. (1991c) 13,376; iron deposits.

Cas·tro Valley \ˈkas-trō\. Unincorporated settlement, Alameda co., W California, N of Hayward; pop. (1990c) 48,619.

Ca·stro·vil·la·ri \ˌkäs-trō-ˈvē-lä-rē\. Commune, Cosenza prov., Calabria, S Italy; pop. (1989c) 22,544.

Castrum. See AL-QASR.

Castua. See KASTAV.

Cas·tu·lo \ˈkas-tů-ˌlō\. Ancient Iberian town of Hispania Tarraconensis (in modern S Spain) on the Baetis (Guadalquivir) River; important Roman town near silver and lead mines. Roman Gen. Scipio Africanus defeated Carthaginians here 208 B.C. Site of modern **Caz·lo·na** \kath-ˈlō-nä\, Jaén prov., 2 mi. (3.2 km.) N of Linares.

Casus. See KASOS.

Cas·well \ˈkaz-ˌwel, -wəl\. County in N North Carolina. See table at NORTH CAROLINA.

Catabathmus Magna. See SALŪM.

Ca·ta·ca·os \ˌkä-tä-ˈkaůs\. Town, NW Peru, SW of Piura; pop. (1981p) 40,817.

Ca·ta·gua·ses \ˌkȧ-tȧ-ˈgwä-zēs\. Town, SE Minas Gerais state, E Brazil, 120 mi. (193 km.) NNE of Rio de Janeiro; munic. pop. (1991p) 58,162.

Cat·a·hou·la \ˌka-tə-ˈhü-lə\. Parish in cen. Louisiana. See table at LOUISIANA.

Catahoula Lake. Lake in S La Salle parish, Louisiana.

Ca·ta·in·gan \ˌkä-tä-ˈēŋ-ˌgän\. Municipality, SE coast of Masbate I., Philippines, on Samar Sea; pop. (1980c) 39,378.

Ça·tal·ca *or angl.* **Cha·tal·ja** \chä-ˈtäl-jä\. Town, İstanbul prov., Turkey in Europe, ab. 20 mi. (32 km.) W of the city of İstanbul; center of heavily fortified line across peninsula from Black Sea to Sea of Marmara, where Turks made stand 1912 in First Balkan War; part of W boundary of Turkey in Europe by Treaty of Sevrès 1920.

Ça·tal·hü·yük \chä-ˌtäl-hüē-ˈyüēk, -hü-ˈyük\. Locality, SW cen. Turkey in Asia, SE of Konya; archaeological site where remains of a large Neolithic settlement have been found.

Catalina. See SANTA CATALINA 1.

Cat·a·lo·nia \ˌkat-ᵊl-ˈō-nyə, -nē-ə\ *or Span.* **Ca·ta·lu·ña** \ˌkä-tä-ˈlü-nyä\ *or Catalan* **Ca·ta·lu·nya** \ˌkä-tä-ˈlü-nyä\. Autonomous community and historical region in NE corner of Spain, bounded on N by France and the Pyrenees, on E and S by the Mediterranean, on SW by Valencia, and on W by Aragon; comprises an autonomous community consisting of the modern provs. of Barcelona, Gerona, Lérida, and Tarragona; traversed by spur of Pyrenees; watered principally by the Ebro River; generally rugged land, but containing fertile valleys and coastlands; rich in minerals and agricultural products; its people retain own language (Catalan) and strong sense of regional unity. See table at SPAIN.

History: Orig. settled by numerous independent tribes, and subsequently by Phoenicians and Greeks; invaded by Carthaginians under Generals Hamilcar Barca and Hannibal 3d cent. B.C.; conquered by Romans under whom it became a wealthy province with its ✻ at Tarragona; invaded by Visigoths early 5th cent. A.D.; S portion taken by Arabs 712 but reconquered by Frankish King (later Holy Roman Emperor) Charlemagne who set up Spanish March 795 with its ✻ later (801) at Barcelona; became independent Frankish county of Barcelona (or Catalonia) 9th cent.; united with Aragon (*q.v.*) 1137; by 13th cent. had extensive territory N of Pyrenees (incl. Cerdaña, Roussillon, part of Provence); Barcelona became a European trade center and point of departure for Aragonese expansion in Mediterranean (see MAJORCA; SICILY); engaged in long struggle to maintain political and cultural autonomy against frequent attempts at centralization and unification by Castile; revolted 1640–59 as result of policy of Spanish politician Gaspar de Guzmán y Pimental, count Olivares; Cerdaña and Roussillon lost to France 1659; during War of the Spanish Succession (1701–14) sided with Archduke Charles of Austria; entered another movement for autonomy 1917–19; autonomous 1932–34; again autonomous after joining Loyalists in Spanish Civil War 1936; lost autonomy 1939 after fall of Barcelona (Loyalist ✻ from 1937) and forbidden use of Catalan by Gen. Francisco Franco's government; with Spain's return to monarchy under Juan Carlos I, became one of 18 autonomous communities; use of Catalan restored; first parliamentary elections held 1980.

Cat·a·mar·ca \ˌkä-tä-ˈmär-kä\. **1.** Province of NW Argentina. See table at ARGENTINA.

2. Town, its ✻, 115 mi. (185 km.) SSW of San Miguel de Tucumán; pop. (1991p) 110,489; at alt. of 1600 ft. (488 m.) in foothills of E Andes; agricultural and market center.

Catana. See CATANIA 2.

Ca·tan·dua·nes \ˌkä-tän-ˈdwä-nās\. Island off SE Luzon, E Philippines, constituting a province of Philippines; ✻ Virac; with Luzon coast forms Lagonoy Gulf; covered with hills and low mountain ranges, highest peak ab. 3000 ft. (915 m.); soil fertile producing rice, corn, and coconuts; formerly a subprovince of Albay prov., made separate province 1945. See table at PHILIPPINES.

Ca·tan·du·va \ˌkȧ-tän-ˈdü-və\. City, São Paulo state, SE Brazil, 230 mi. (370 km.) NW of the city of São Paulo; munic. pop. (1991p) 93,318.

Ca·ta·nia \kä-ˈtä-nyä\. **1.** Province of E Sicily, Italy. See table at ITALY.

2. *anc.* **Cat·a·na** \ˈka-tə-nə, ˈkä-\. Commune, its ✻, at foot of Mt. Etna on Gulf of Catania; pop. (1991p) 330,037; important port; chemicals, sulfur, processed foods, textiles; fishing; episcopal see; ancient Greek and Roman ruins; Norman cathedral (1091); university (1434); 13th cent. castle.

History: Founded by Greeks 729 B.C.; taken by Romans 263 B.C. (First Punic War); taken by Arabs 902 A.D. and by Normans c. 1090; devastated by earthquakes, esp. in 1169 and 1693, and by volcanic eruptions, esp. in 1669; off nearby coast scene of naval victory of French under commander Abraham Duquesne over the Spanish and Dutch fleet under Dutch Adm. Michiel de Ruyter 1676. In WWII a German defense point; under attack by British 1943 suffered heavy damage. Birthplace of Italian composer Vincenzo Bellini 1801.

Catania, Gulf of. Inlet of Mediterranean Sea on E coast of the island of Sicily, Italy; ab. 20 mi. (32 km.) long.

Ca·ta·ño \kä-ˈtä-nyō\. Municipality, San Juan dist., NE Puerto Rico, on S shore of San Juan harbor S of the city of San Juan; pop. (1990c) 34,587.

Ca·tan·za·ro \ˌkä-tänd-ˈzä-rō, -tänt-ˈsä-\. **1.** Province of Calabria, S Italy. See table at ITALY.

2. City, its ✻ and ✻ of Calabria, near Gulf of Squillace 183 mi. (295 km.) SE of Naples; pop. (1991p) 93,464; cathedral, museum; summer resort; founded 10th cent.; devastated by earthquake 1783 and early 20th cent.; heavily bombed in WWII.

Cat·a·o·nia \ˌka-tə-ˈō-nyə\. Ancient region of Asia Minor bet. Cappadocia and Cilicia, incl. NE part of Taurus Mts.

Ca·tar·man \ˌkä-tär-ˈmän\. Municipality, ✻ of Northern Samar prov., N coast of Samar I., Philippines, 55 mi. (89 km.) NNE of Catbalogan; pop. (1980c) 59,021.

Cat·a·sau·qua \ˌka-tə-ˈsȯ-kwə\. Borough, Lehigh co., E Pennsylvania, on Lehigh River 4 mi. (6 km.) N of Allentown; pop. (1990c) 6662.

Ca·tas·tro·phe, Cape \kə-ˈtas-trə-fē\. Cape at W entrance to Spencer Gulf, S South Australia, Australia.

Ca·ta·tum·bo \ˌkä-tä-ˈtüm-bō\. River in N South America; rises in N Colombia, flows NE across Venezuelan border and into Lake Maracaibo; ab. 210 mi. (340 km.) long.

Ca·taw·ba \kə-ˈtȯ-bə\. **1.** River, North Carolina and South Carolina; flowing from the Blue Ridge, W North Carolina, S into South Carolina, where it is known as the Wateree. See WATEREE.

2. County in W cen. North Carolina. See table at NORTH CAROLINA.

Cat·ba·lo·gan \ˌkät-bä-ˈlō-gän\. Municipality, ✻ of Western Samar prov., Philippines, on W coast of Samar I. in cen. part; pop. (1980c) 58,737; has harbor on Samar Sea.

Cateau, Le. See LE CATEAU.
Catelet, Le. See LE CATELET.
Ca·ter·ham and War·ling·ham \ˈkā-tər-əm ... ˈwȯr-liŋ-əm\. Town, Surrey, S England, 18 mi. (29 km.) S of London; pop. (1981p) 33,083.
Ca·thay \kə-ˈthā, ka-\. An old name for China, esp. N China, introduced to medieval Europe in the Latin form *Cathaia* by the Franciscan monk William of Rubrouck, who traveled to Mongolia in 1253–55. It comes through Arabic and Persian mediation from *Khitay*, the Turkic name for the Khitans, a non-Chinese steppe people who dominated much of N China from the 10th to early 12th cents. The Turkic word survives in the modern Russian name for China, *Kitai*.
Cat·head Point \ˈkat-ˌhed\. Point at N extremity of Leelanau co., NW Michigan, on Lake Michigan.
Ca·the·dral City \kə-ˈthē-drəl\. City, Riverside co., SE California; pop. (1990c) 30,085.
Cathedral Mountain. Peak, Brewster co., W Texas; 6860 ft. (2091 m.).
Cathedral Peak. Mountain in Yellowstone National Park, NW Wyoming; 10,760 ft. (3280 m.).
Cathedral Range. Mountain range, NE Mariposa co., California, in the Sierra Nevada in Yosemite National Park; highest point 11,516 ft. (3510 m.).
Cathedral Rocks. Mountain, Mariposa co., California; 7503 ft. (2287 m.).
Catherine, Mount. See KATHERINA, GEBEL.
Catherine Archipelago. See ALEUTIAN ISLANDS.
Cathkin Peak. See CHAMPAGNE CASTLE.
Cath·lam·et \kath-ˈla-mit\. Town, ⊗ of Wahkiakum co., SW Washington; pop. (1990c) 508.
Cat Island \ˈkat\. **1.** Island in Gulf of Mexico, off S coast of Harrison co., SE Mississippi.
2. One of the Bahamas, in Atlantic Ocean SE of Eleuthera I. and WNW of San Salvador; 150 sq. mi. (389 sq. km.); pop. (1980c) 2143; formerly identified with the San Salvador of Christopher Columbus (see SAN SALVADOR 1).
Cat·letts·burg \ˈkat-lits-ˌbərg\. City, ⊗ of Boyd co., NE Kentucky, 5 mi. (8 km.) S of Ashland; pop. (1990c) 2231.
Ca·to·che, Cape \kə-ˈtō-chē\. NE extremity of Yucatán Penin., SE Mexico, projecting into Yucatán Channel.
Ca·tons·ville \ˈkāt-ᵊnz-ˌvil, -vəl\. Unincorporated settlement, Baltimore co., Maryland; pop. (1990c) 35,233; Univ. of Maryland Baltimore County (1963).
Ca·too·sa \kə-ˈtü-sə\. **1.** County in NW Georgia. See table at GEORGIA.
2. City, Rogers co., Oklahoma, a suburb of Tulsa; pop. (1990c) 2954.
Ca·tron \kə-ˈträn\. County in W New Mexico. See table at NEW MEXICO.
Cats·kill \ˈkat-ˌskil\. Village, ⊗ of Greene co., SE New York, on W side of Hudson River 30 mi. (48 km.) S of Albany; pop. (1990c) 4690; summer resort, gateway to Catskill Mts.; settled by Dutch c. 1680; incorp. 1806.
Catskill Mountains. Group of the Appalachian system, SE New York, along W bank of Hudson chiefly in Greene, Ulster, and Delaware cos.; highest peak Slide Mt. 4204 ft. (1281 m.); heavily wooded; many resorts.
Cat·tail Peak \ˈkat-ˌtāl\. Mountain, Yancey co., W North Carolina, near Mt. Mitchell; 6600 ft. (2012 m.).
Cat·ta·rau·gus \ˌka-tə-ˈrȯ-gəs\. County in SW New York. See table at NEW YORK.
Cattaraugus Creek. River, W New York; forms boundary bet. Erie and Cattaraugus cos. and flows W into Lake Erie; ab. 70 mi. (115 km.) long.
Cattaro. See KOTOR.
Cattegat. See KATTEGAT.
Cau·a·bu·ri \ˌkau̇-á-bu̇-ˈrē\. River, NW Brazil; flows from S tip of Venezuela S into Rio Negro; ab. 100 mi. (160 km.) long.
Ca·ua·yan \kä-ˈwä-yän\. Municipality, Negros, Philippines, on Panay Gulf; pop. (1980c) 62,224.
Cau·ca \ˈkau̇-kä\. **1.** River, W Colombia; rises in Andes, flows N into Magdalena River; 838 mi. (1348 km.) long.
2. Department of SW Colombia. See table at COLOMBIA.
Cau·ca·sia \kȯ-ˈkā-zhə, -shə\ *or* **Cau·ca·sus** \ˈkȯ-kə-səs\ *or Russ.* **Kav·kaz** \kȧf-ˈkȧs\. Region bet. the Black and Caspian seas, comprising the Republic of Georgia, Azerbaijan, Armenia, and part of S Russia in Europe; ab. 154,250 sq. mi. (399,510 sq. km.); extends SE and NW ab. 750 mi. (1205 km.) from Apsheron Penin. to mouth of Kuban' River on Black Sea; contains the Caucasus Mts. (*q.v.*) which divide it into **Cis·cau·ca·sia** \ˌsis-\, N of the range, and **Trans·cau·ca·sia** \ˌtranz-\, on the S.
History: Inhabited from ancient times by indigenous peoples, among them Caucasians, to which successive invaders added numerous other elements; known to ancient Greeks (see COLCHIS); penetrated, during Middle Ages, by Christianity; E Caucasus later converted to Islam; under nominal Persian and Turkish suzerainty until gradually forced into connection with Russia which had expanded to the Caspian by the acquisition of Astrakhan (*q.v.*); conquered by Russia 18th–19th cents.; mountain people of Caucasus became Russian subjects after arrest of their leader Shāmil 1859; Circassians later surrendered; Kars, Ardahan, and Batum ceded by Turkey to Russia 1878. For later history of S part, see TRANSCAUCASIAN FEDERATION. In WWII its oil fields goal of German advance 1942; German armies driven out 1943. With breakup of U.S.S.R. 1991, much of the area was involved in interethnic conflict.
Caucasian Wall. See *History* at DERBENT.
Caucasus Indicus. See HINDU KUSH.
Cau·ca·sus Mountains \ˈkȯ-kə-səs\ *or Russ.* **Kav·kaz·skiy Khre·bet** \kəf-ˈkä-skē-kryi-ˈbyet\. Mountain range, bet. the Black and Caspian seas, in S Russia in Europe, the Republic of Georgia, Azerbaijan, and Armenia; ab. 700 mi. (1125 km.) long; often considered the SE limit of Europe; separates Ciscaucasia from Transcaucasia. Of volcanic origin; has many peaks above 15,000 ft. (4572 m.), highest Mt. Elbrus 18,481 ft. (5633 m.); crossed by high passes, the two best-known being Daryal and Mamison (*qq.v.*).
Cauda. See GAVDOS.
Cau·dé·ran \ˌkō-dā-ˈräⁿ\. Former commune, Gironde dept., SW France; now part of Bordeaux.
Caudine Forks \ˈkȯ-ˌdīn, -ˌdēn\. Mountain passes on the road bet. Capua and Benevento, Campania, S Italy, near Caudium; defeat of Romans by the Samnites 321 B.C.
Cau·di·um \ˈkȯ-dē-əm\. Ancient town, Samnium, S Italy, E of Benevento.
Caugh·ley \ˈkä-flē\. Village, E Shropshire, England; site of pottery factories where willow pattern was first made ab. 1780.
Ca·uit Point \ˈkä-wēt\. Point of land, NE Mindanao, Philippines, SE of entrance to Lanuza Bay.
Caul·field \ˈkȯl-ˌfēld\. Municipality, S Victoria, SE Australia, SE suburb of Melbourne; pop. (1991c) 67,776.
Cau·que·nes \kau̇-ˈkā-nās\. City, Maule region, S cen. Chile, ab. 198 mi. (320 km.) S of Santiago; formerly ✻ of Maule prov.; in area severely damaged by earthquake 1939.
Cau·ra \ˈkau̇-rä\. River, cen. Venezuela; rises in the Pacaraima Mts., flows N into the Orinoco; ab. 450 mi. (725 km.) long.
Cau·sap·scal \ˌkō-zäp-ˈskäl\. Town, Matane co., Gaspé Penin., SE Quebec, Canada, 37 mi. (60 km.) SSE of the town of Matane; pop. (1991c) 2160.
Causses \ˈkōs\. District, S cen. France, on S border of the Massif Central; a limestone region, noted for gorges and subterranean rivers.
Cau·te·rets \kō-ˈtrā\. Commune, SW Hautes-Pyrénées dept., SW France; hot sulfur springs.
Cau·tín \kau̇-ˈtēn\. Former province of S cen. Chile.
Cau·to \ˈkau̇-tō\. River, E Cuba; flows W into Golfo de Guacanayabo; 155 mi. (249 km.) long; navigable for ab. 70 mi. (115 km.); longest river in Cuba.

Cauvery. See KĀVERI.

Cauvery Falls. See KĀVERI.

Ca·va de' Tir·re·ni \ˈkä-vä-ˌdā-tē-ˈrā-nē\. Commune, Salerno prov., Campania, S Italy, 3 mi. (5 km.) WNW of Salerno; pop. (1991p) 52,610; cathedral; summer resort; famous Benedictine monastery (founded early 11th cent. by St. Alferius over a cave he occupied) nearby.

Ca·vail·lon \ˌkȧ-vȧ-ˈyōn\; *anc.* **Ca·bel·lio** \kə-ˈbe-lē-ˌō\. Commune, Vaucluse dept., SE France, on Durance River 13 mi. (21 km.) SE of Avignon; 12th cent. cathedral.

Cav·a·lier \ˌka-və-ˈlir\. **1.** County, in NE North Dakota. See table at NORTH DAKOTA.
2. City, ⊗ of Pembina co., NE corner of North Dakota; pop. (1990c) 1508.

Ca·val·ly \kə-ˈva-lē\ *or in Liberia* **Ca·val·la** \kə-ˈva-lə\. River, W Africa, forming part of boundary bet. Ivory Coast and Liberia; 320 mi. (515 km.) long.

Cav·an \ˈkav-ᵊn\. **1.** County, Ulster prov., N Ireland (republic); chiefly agricultural. See table at IRELAND.
2. Town, its ⊗; pop. (1991p) 3332; burned 1690 by Enniskillen partisans of William of Orange after their defeat of Jacobite forces.

Ca·va·ra·ya \ˌkä-vä-ˈrī-ä\. Peak, N Chile, W of Lake Poopó; 19,193 ft. (5850 m.).

Cave of the Winds. See NIAGARA FALLS.

Cave Spring. Unincorporated settlement, Roanoke co., W cen. Virginia, at a crossroads just S of the city of Roanoke; pop. (1990c) 24,053.

Ca·via·na \kȧ-ˈvyȧ-nə\. Island in N branch of the mouth of the Amazon River, NE Brazil; belongs to Pará state.

Ca·vi·te \kä-ˈvē-tē\. **1.** Province, SW Luzon, Philippines; ✻ Trece Martires; on S side of Manila Bay; W end of NW shore is on South Channel (see CORREGIDOR). A plain except for the low mountain range in S on Batangas border; its many streams flow N or NW to Manila Bay. Has volcanic soil. See table at PHILIPPINES.
History: Not populous in early Spanish times, but increased in importance with establishment of navy yard at Cavite; in 19th cent. the center of revolutionary activity led by Emilio Aguinaldo against Spanish and later, American governments; civil government estab. 1901.
2. *or officially* **City of Cavite.** Chartered city, in NE part of province, on narrow point of land (**Cavite Peninsula**) 8 mi. (13 km.) across Manila Bay, SW of Manila; pop. (1990e) 92,000; largest city in the province. A walled town with old forts and arsenals; its harbor part of Bacoor Bay (bet. the peninsula and the mainland); in early times made a naval base by the Spanish government.
History: Scene of defeat of Spanish fleet by American Adm. George Dewey May 1, 1898, known as the battle of Manila Bay (*q.v.*). Chief naval base of U.S. fleet in Pacific area 1898–1941. Created a chartered city 1940. Partly destroyed by Japanese air attacks Dec. 8–10, 1941; captured by Japanese Jan. 1942; retaken by Americans 1945.

Caw·dor \ˈkȯ-dər\. Parish, Highland region, N Scotland, 5 mi. (8 km.) SW of Nairn; famous castle where the murder of King Duncan in William Shakespeare's play *Macbeth* takes place.

Cawnpore. See KANPUR.

Ca·xi·as \kȧ-ˈshē-əs\. City, NE Maranhão state, NE Brazil, 182 mi. (293 km.) SE of São Luís; munic. pop. (1991p) 145,709.

Caxias do Sul \dü-sül\. City, Rio Grande do Sul state, S Brazil, 60 mi. (97 km.) N of Pôrto Alegre; munic. pop. (1991p) 290,968; metallurgy; viticulture.

Ca·xi·to \kä-ˈshē-tü\. Town, ✻ of Bengo prov., NW Angola, NE of Luanda.

Ca·yam·be \kä-ˈyäm-bā\. Dormant volcano in the Andes, N Ecuador; 18,996 ft. (3790 m.).

Cay·ce \ˈkā-sē\. City, Lexington co., W cen. South Carolina, SW of Columbia; pop. (1990c) 11,163.

Cay·enne \kī-ˈen, kā-\. City, ✻ of French Guiana, on NW coast of **Cayenne Island** (ab. 30 mi. or 48 km. in circumference); pop. (1990c) 37,097; island is formed by the **Cayenne River,** a small stream that divides into two channels before emptying into the Atlantic. City founded by French 1643; in 19th cent. penal colonies estab. there by French; penal colonies closed mid-20th cent.

Cayes *or* **Aux Cayes** \ō-ˈkā\. Seaport on S Tiburon Penin., SW Haiti; pop. (1982c) 105,383.

Ca·yey \kä-ˈyā\. Town and municipality, SE Puerto Rico, 9 mi. (14 km.) NNW of Guayama; pop. (1990c) 23,332 (town), 46,553 (munic.); Univ. of Puerto Rico, Cayey Univ. Coll. (1967); founded 1774.

Cay·man Islands \ˈkā-mən\. Island group in NW Caribbean Sea ab. 200 mi. (320 km.) NW of Jamaica; ab. 100 sq. mi. (260 sq. km.); pop. (1990c) 25,355; a British dependency. Group comprises three islands: **Grand Cayman,** the largest, 76 sq. mi. (197 sq. km.), pop. (1990c) 23,881, with George Town, ✻ of the group, on its W end; NE of Grand Cayman **Little Cayman,** 20 sq. mi. (52 sq. km.), pop. (1990c) 33; and **Cayman Brac** \ˈbrak\, 22 sq. mi. (57 sq. km.), pop. (1990c) 1441; tourism; finance. Discovered by Christopher Columbus 1503 but never occupied by Spaniards; to British 1670; subsequently colonized by English from Jamaica; administratively independent of Jamaica 1962; constitution providing for a governor enacted 1972.

Cayman Trench. Trench, NW Caribbean Sea, S of the Cayman Is., extending in a general E to W direction from ab. 75°W to ab. 85°W; contains deepest point in Caribbean Sea, 24,720 ft. (7535 m.), 19°12′N, 80°W.

Cayo. For names of islets beginning with Cayo, see the 2d element.

Ca·yo \ˈkä-yō\. **1.** Administrative district, W Belize. See table at BELIZE.
2. *or* **Cayo, El.** Town, Belize. See SAN IGNACIO 1.

Ca·yo Cos·ta \ˈkī-ō-ˈkäs-tə, -ˈkȯs-\ *or* **La·cos·ta Island** \lə-ˈkäs-tə, -ˈkȯs-\. Island, SW Florida, in Gulf of Mexico, off W coast of Lee co., at entrance to Charlotte Harbor.

Cay Sal Bank \ˈkē-ˈsal, ˈkā\. Bank in W Bahamas, bet. Straits of Florida and N cen. Cuba; separated from Great Bahama Bank on E by Santaren Channel; Cay Sal lighthouse (estab. 1839) in NW corner.

Ca·ÿs·ter \kā-ˈis-tər\ *or mod.* **Kü·çük Men·de·res** \kǖ-ˈchǖk-ˈmen-de-ˌres\. River, SW Asia Minor, (now W Turkey in Asia), N of the Menderes; flows W to Aegean Sea near Ephesus; ab. 85 mi. (135 km.) long; celebrated in works by Greek epic poet Homer.

Cay·u·ga \kä-ˈyü-gə, kē-\. County in cen. New York. See table at NEW YORK.

Cayuga Lake. Lake chiefly in Cayuga and Seneca cos., W cen. New York; one of the Finger Lakes (*q.v.*); 40 mi. (64 km.) long, av. width 2 mi. (3 km.); deepest point ab. 435 ft. (135 m.); connected at N end with Seneca Lake by the **Cayuga and Seneca Canal** \ˈse-ni-kə\, part of New York State Barge Canal system.

Ca·zal·la de la Sier·ra \kä-ˈthä-lyä-thä-lä-ˈsyer-rä\. Commune, Sevilla prov., SW Spain, on S slope of the Sierra Morena 40 mi. (64 km.) NNE of Seville; pop. (1991c) 5147.

Caz·e·no·via \ˌka-zə-ˈnō-vē-ə\. Village and resort, Madison co., cen. New York, 18 mi. (29 km.) ESE of Syracuse; pop. (1990c) 3007.

Cazlona. See CASTULO.

Ca·zor·la \kä-ˈthȯr-lä\. Commune, Jaén prov., S Spain, 42 mi. (68 km.) ENE of the commune of Jaén; pop. (1991c) 9046; reached peak of importance under Moors.

Ce·a·nan·nus Mór \ˌsē-ə-ˈna-nəs-ˈmȯr\; *formerly* **Kells** \ˈkelz\. Town, NW cen. co. Meath, E Ireland, 25 mi. (40 km.) W of Drogheda; pop. (1986c) 2413; site of monastery, founded c. 550 by St. Columba, dissolved 1551, where the Book of Kells, an elaborately illuminated manuscript of the Gospels in Latin, was kept for safekeeping before being sent to the library of Trinity Coll., Dublin.

Ce·a·rá \syä-ˈrä\. **1.** State of NE Brazil; ✻ Fortaleza; cotton, sugarcane. See table at BRAZIL.
2. City, its ✻. See FORTALEZA.

Ce·ba·co *or* **Cé·ba·co** \ˈsā-bä-ˌkō\. Island, Panama, at the entrance to the Gulf of Montijo.

Cebenna. See CÉVENNES.

Ce·bo·ru·co \ˌsā-bä-ˈrü-kō\. Active volcano, Nayarit state, W Mexico, SE of city of Tepic; 7098 ft. (2163 m.).

Ce·bu \sā-'bü\ *or Visayan* **Sug·bu** \süg-'bü\. **1.** Island, one of the Visayan Is., E cen. Philippines, constituting with adjacent islets a province (❋ City of Cebu); 1707 sq. mi. (4421 sq. km.); 139 mi. (224 km.) long by ab. 20 mi. (32 km.) wide, with mountain chain extending its entire length (highest 3324 ft. or 1013 m.), crossed by only six passes. Touches Visayan Sea on N and Camotes Sea on E, separated from Bohol on SE by Bohol Strait, and from Negros on W by Tanon Strait. Its more important adjacent islands are Bantayan W of N end and Camotes group and Mactan on the E. Produces corn, coconuts, tobacco, and coal. Its inhabitants are Visayans. See table at PHILIPPINES.

History: Before coming of Spaniards one of the more populous and prosperous islands; visited Apr. 7, 1521 by Portuguese explorer Ferdinand Magellan (see MACTAN); occupied by Spanish explorer Miguel de Legazpi 1565; evacuated by Spanish 1898; civil government created by U.S. 1901. Occupied by Japanese 1942; retaken by U.S. forces 1945.

2. *or officially* **City of Cebu.** Chartered city, ❋ of Cebu prov., in cen. part of E coast of Cebu I.; pop. (1990p) 610,000; exports include copra. Oldest Spanish town in the Philippines; has excellent harbor, sheltered on E by Mactan I.; contains Santo Niño church in front of which is the cross Portuguese explorer Ferdinand Magellan set up at the first Mass on the island; several universities; cathedral; old Spanish stone fort. Occupied by Spanish explorer Miguel de Legazpi 1565 and until 1571 ❋ of Spanish possessions in the Philippines. Seized by Japanese 1942; subsequently heavily damaged; recaptured by U.S. forces 1945.

Cec·ca·no \chā-'kä-nō\. Commune, Frosinone prov., Lazio, cen. Italy, on Sacco River 5 mi. (8 km.) S of the commune of Frosinone; pop. (1989c) 22,039.

Čechy. See BOHEMIA.

Ce·cil \'sē-səl\. County in NE corner of Maryland. See table at MARYLAND.

Ce·ci·na \'che-chē-,nä\. Coastal commune, Livorno prov., Tuscany, cen. Italy, near mouth of **Cecina River,** 20 mi. (32 km.) SE of the commune of Livorno; pop. (1989c) 24,836.

Ce·dar \'sē-dər\. **1.** River, Minnesota and Iowa; flows from SE Minnesota SE to Iowa River in Louisa co., SE Iowa; 329 mi. (529 km.) long.

2. River, E cen. Nebraska; rises in Garfield co., flows SE into Loup River in Nance co.; 120 mi. (193 km.) long.

3. Name of counties in three states of the U.S. See tables at IOWA, MISSOURI, NEBRASKA.

Cedar Bergen. See CEDAR MOUNTAINS.

Cedar Breaks National Monument. See UNITED STATES, *National Monuments.*

Ce·dar·burg \'sē-dər-,bərg\. City, Ozaukee co., E Wisconsin, 17 mi. (27 km.) N of Milwaukee; pop. (1990c) 9895.

Cedar City. Town, Iron co., SW Utah; pop. (1990c) 13,443; tourist center in area of Zion National Park to the S. Cedar Breaks National Monument to the E; coal deposits; Southern Utah Univ. (1897); settled 1851.

Cedar Creek. **1.** River, SW North Dakota; 200 mi. (322 km.) long; flows E into Cannonball River.

2. Small stream in Shenandoah co., N Virginia, flowing into the N fork of the Shenandoah River; battle Oct. 19, 1864 in which Union forces under Gen. Philip Henry Sheridan defeated the Confederates under Gen. Jubal Anderson Early.

Cedar Creek Dam. Dam and reservoir in Cedar Creek (branch of Salmon Falls Creek), SW Twin Falls co., SW Idaho. See SALMON DAM.

Cedar Creek Peak. Mountain, E Cassia co., S Idaho; 7586 ft. (2312 m.).

Cedar Falls. City, Black Hawk co., NE cen. Iowa, 6 mi. (10 km.) W of Waterloo; pop. (1990c) 34,298; Univ. of Northern Iowa (1876).

Cedar Grove. Township, Essex co., NE New Jersey, 6 mi. (10 km.) SSW of Paterson; pop. (1990c) 12,053.

Cedar Hill. City, Dallas co., NE Texas, 18 mi. (29 km.) SW of the city of Dallas; pop. (1990c) 19,976.

Ce·dar·hurst \'sē-dər-,hərst\. Residential village, Nassau co., SE New York, on Long Island 17 mi. (27 km.) ESE of New York City; pop. (1990c) 5716.

Cedar Keys. Small group of islands in Gulf of Mexico, off SW coast of Levy co., NW Florida Penin.

Cedar Lake. **1.** Town, Lake co., NW corner of Indiana, SW of Valparaiso; pop. (1990c) 8885.

2. Lake, W of N Lake Winnipeg, W Manitoba, Canada; 517 sq. mi. (1339 sq. km.); Saskatchewan River flows through it to Lake Winnipeg.

Cedar Mountain. Locality in Culpeper co., Virginia, 10 mi. (16 km.) S of the town of Culpeper; battle Aug. 9, 1862 in which Union forces under Gen. Nathaniel Prentiss Banks were defeated by Gen. Richard Stoddert Ewell's Confederate troops.

Cedar Mountains *or Afrikaans* **Ce·der Ber·gen** \'sā-dər-,ber-gə\ *or* **Cedar Bergen.** Range in Western Cape prov., Rep. of South Africa; highest peak ab. 6650 ft. (2025 m.).

Cedar Point. **1.** Point, SE Mobile co., Alabama, at W entrance to Mobile Bay; has ferry connection to Dauphin I.

2. Point, E St. Marys co., S Maryland, on S side of mouth of Patuxent River; located within Patuxent River Naval Air Warfare Center, estab. 1943–44.

3. Tip of long narrow peninsula on Lake Erie at entrance to Sandusky Bay, Erie co., Ohio.

Cedar Rapids. City, ⊗ of Linn co., E Iowa, 105 mi. (169 km.) ENE of Des Moines; pop. (1990c) 108,751; electronic equipment, farming machinery, cereals, meat products; Coe Coll. (1851), Mount Mercy Coll. (1928), Kirkwood Community Coll. (1966); settled 1838; incorp. 1856. Once home of American artist Grant Wood.

Cedar River. See CEDAR 1 and 2.

Ce·dar·town \'sē-dər-,taůn\. City, ⊗ of Polk co., NW Georgia, 17 mi. (27 km.) S of Rome; pop. (1990c) 7978.

Ce·dar·ville \'sē-dər-,vil\. Village, Greene co., SW cen. Ohio, NE of Xenia; pop. (1990c) 3210; Cedarville Coll. (1887).

Ceder Bergen. See CEDAR MOUNTAINS.

Ce·dros \'sā-drōs\. Island, Mexico, in the Pacific Ocean, off the coast of Baja California; ab. 30 mi. (48 km.) long.

Ce·fa·lù \,chā-fä-'lü\; *anc.* **Ceph·a·loe·di·um** \,se-fə-'lē-dē-əm\. Seaport, Palermo prov., NW cen. Sicily, Italy, on Tyrrhenian Sea 37 mi. (60 km.) ESE of the seaport of Palermo; pop. (1991p) 13,791; cathedral (begun 1131). Ancient city an ally of Carthage c. 396 B.C.; conquered by Siracusans Dionysius the Elder and later Agathocles; taken by Moors 9th cent. A.D.; taken by Normans led by Roger II 1130.

Ceg·léd *also* **Czeg·léd** \'tseg-,lād\. City, cen. Hungary, 42 mi. (68 km.) SE of Budapest; pop. (1991e) 38,700; trades in agricultural products.

Ce·glie Mes·sa·pi·co \'chel-yā-mās-'sä-pē-,kō\. Commune, Brindisi prov., Puglia, SE Italy, 22 mi. (35 km.) W of the seaport of Brindisi; pop. (1981p) 20,585; castle.

Cei·ba \'sā-bä\. Municipality, E Puerto Rico, SE of San Juan; pop. (1990c) 17,145.

Ceiba, La. See LA CEIBA.

Celaenae. See DINAR.

Ce·la·no \chā-'lä-nō\. **1.** Former lake, cen. Italy. See FUCINO.

2. Commune, Puglia prov., Abruzzi, cen. Italy, on N shore of the former Fucino 22 mi. (35 km.) SSE of L'Aquila; pop. (1981p) 10,605; castle.

Ce·la·ya \sä-'lī-ä\. City, Guanajuato state, cen. Mexico, 45 mi. (72 km.) SE of the city of Guanajuato; munic. pop. (1990p) 315,577; alt. 5750 ft. (1753 m.); cereal, beans, cattle, dairy products; railroad junction; 19th cent. cathedral. During Mexican Revolution site of defeat of bandit and revolutionary leader Francisco (Pancho) Villa by soldier and politician Álvaro Obregón 1915.

Celebes. See SULAWESI.

Celebes Sea. Part of the Pacific Ocean, enclosed on N by Sulu Archipelago and Mindanao of the Philippines, on E by Sangihe Is., on S by Sulawesi (Celebes), and on W by Borneo; connected with Java Sea by Makassar Strait on SW; ab. 420 mi.

(675 km.) from N to S and 520 mi. (835 km.) E to W at widest parts; ab. 165,000 sq. mi. (427,350 sq. km.).

Celestial Empire. See CHINA.

Ce·li·na \sə-'lī-nə\. **1.** City and summer resort, ⊗ of Mercer co., W Ohio, on W end of Lake St. Marys; pop. (1990c) 9650.

2. Town, ⊗ of Clay co., N Tennessee; pop. (1990c) 1493.

Ce·lje \'tsel-ye\ *or Ger.* **Cil·li** \'tsi-lē\. Town, E cen. Slovenia, 37 mi. (60 km.) NE of Ljubljana.

Cel·le \'tse-lə\. City, Lower Saxony, N cen. Germany, on Aller River 22 mi. (35 km.) NE of Hannover; pop. (1992e) 72,609; potash; textiles; 13th cent. ducal palace; 16th cent. town hall; founded 1292; residence of dukes of Brunswick and Lüneburg 14th cent. to 1705.

Celles \'sel\. Village, Namur prov., SE Belgium, ab. 8 mi. (13 km.) E of Dinant; pop. (1981c) 5511; farthest point W reached Dec. 1944 by German counteroffensive (Battle of the Bulge); soon thereafter retaken by Allies.

Ce·lo, Mount \'sē-lō\. Peak, Yancey co., W North Carolina; 6351 ft. (1936 m.).

Celt·i·be·ria \ˌsel-tə-'bir-ē-ə, ˌsel-tī-, ˌkel-\. Mountainous district of ancient Spain, in NE bet. the Ebro and Tagus rivers; came under Roman rule late 2d cent. B.C.

Cemenelum. See CIMIEZ.

Cemetery Ridge. Low ridge in Adams co., Pennsylvania, extending in N and S direction S of Gettysburg; at its N end just to the E and ab. 0.5 mi. (0.8 km.) S of the town are **Cemetery Hill** and **Culp's Hill** \'kəlps\ where much of the fighting of the first two days of the battle of Gettysburg July 1–2, 1863 took place, partly a Confederate success; meanwhile the ridge as far S as Round Top (*q.v.*) was occupied by the center of the Union defense and received on July 3 the Confederate assault led by Gen. George Edward Pickett, who was repulsed with loss of three fourths of his division.

Cen·chre·ae \seŋ-'krē-ē, 'seŋ-krē-ˌē\. Ancient town, NE coast of Peloponnese, S Greece, on Saronic Gulf SE of Corinth; visited by St. Paul on missionary journey (*Acts* xviii. 18).

Cen·de·ra·wa·sih, Te·luk \'te-lu̇k-ˌchen-də-rə-'wä-sē\ *also* **Teluk Cen·dra·wa·sih** \ˌchen-drə-\ *or* **Sa·re·ra Bay** \sä-'rer-ə\; *formerly* **Geel·vink Bay** \'gāl-viŋk\. Bay on N coast of Irian Jaya, Indonesia; ab. 250 mi. (400 km.) wide at mouth, Cape Perkam to Manokwari, extends ab. 150 mi. (240 km.) inland; contains Yapen and Numfoor islands.

Ce·nis, Mont \ˌmōⁿ-sə-'nē\ *or Ital.* **Mon·te Ce·ni·sio** \'mōn-tā-chā-'nē-zyō\. **1.** Massif in the Alps, SE France on Italian border; traversed by Mont Cenis Pass.

2. Alpine pass and tunnel. See table at ALPS.

Cen·ter \'sen-tər\. **1.** Village, ⊗ of Knox co., NE Nebraska; pop. (1990c) 112.

2. Village, ⊗ of Oliver co., North Dakota; pop. (1990c) 826.

3. City, ⊗ of Shelby co., E Texas, 45 mi. (72 km.) NE of Lufkin; pop. (1990c) 4950.

4. Town, Outagamie co., E Wisconsin; pop. (1990c) 2716.

Center. See also CENTRE.

Center City. Village, ⊗ of Chisago co., E Minnesota; pop. (1990c) 451.

Center Line *also* **Cen·ter·line** \'sen-tər-ˌlīn\. Residential city, Macomb co., SE Michigan, entirely surrounded by Warren; pop. (1990c) 9026.

Cen·ter·ville \'sen-tər-ˌvil\. **1.** Village, N New Castle co., Delaware, NW of Wilmington; elev. 442 ft. (135 m.); highest point in state.

2. City, Houston co., cen. Georgia; pop. (1990c) 3251.

3. City, ⊗ of Appanoose co., S Iowa, 30 mi. (48 km.) SW of Ottumwa; pop. (1990c) 5936.

4. Village, ⊗ of St. Joseph co., S Michigan; pop. (1990c) 1516.

5. Village, ⊗ of Reynolds co., SE Missouri; pop. (1990c) 89.

6. City, Montgomery co., SW Ohio, 10 mi. (16 km.) S of Dayton; pop. (1990c) 21,082.

7. Borough, Washington co., SW Pennsylvania, on Monongahela River 17 mi. (27 km.) WNW of Uniontown; pop. (1990c) 3842.

8. Town, ⊗ of Hickman co., Tennessee; pop. (1990c) 3616.

9. City, ⊗ of Leon co., E cen. Texas; pop. (1990c) 812.

10. City, Davis co., N Utah, ab. 7 mi. (11 km.) N of Salt Lake City; pop. (1990c) 11,500.

11. Unincorporated settlement, Fairfax co., Virginia. See CENTREVILLE 4.

Cen·to \'chen-tō\. Commune, Ferrara prov., Emilia-Romagna, N Italy; pop. (1989c) 29,026; notable church, museum; birthplace of painter Giovanni Barbieri 1591.

Centorbi. See CENTURIPE.

Cen·tral \sen-'träl\. **1.** Administrative region of S Ghana. See table at GHANA.

2. Department of S Paraguay. See table at PARAGUAY.

Central \'sen-trəl\. **1.** Town, Pickens co., NW South Carolina; pop. (1990c) 2438; Central Wesleyan Coll. (1906).

2. Administrative region, cen. Scotland; estab. 1975. See table at SCOTLAND.

Central African Republic *or Fr.* **Ré·pu·blique Cen·traf·ri·caine** \ˌrā-pü-'blēk-ˌsäⁿ-trȧ-frē-'ken\; *formerly* **Uban·gi-Sha·ri** \ü-ˌbäŋ-gē-'shär-ē, yü-\ *or Fr.* **Ou·ban·gui–Cha·ri** \ü-bäⁿ-'gē-shȧ-'rē\; *1976–79* **Central African Empire.** Republic, cen. Africa, bounded on N by Chad, on E by Sudan, on S by Democratic Rep. of the Congo and Rep. of the Congo, and on W by Cameroon; 240,376 sq. mi. (622,374 sq. km.); pop. (1993e) 2,998,000; ✱ and largest city Bangui.

Physical features: Landlocked republic, consisting of a plateau region having an av. alt. of ab. 2200 ft. (670 m.); N half is characterized by savanna and is drained by tributaries of Chari; S half is densely forested.

Chief products: Cotton, coffee, rice, rubber, peanuts, timber; livestock raising; diamonds.

History: Although seemingly inhabited for a long time, archaeological remains are scant; for several centuries before arrival of Europeans area subjected to slave traders; Bangui estab. by French 1889; united with Chad 1906 to form French colony of **Ubangi–Shari–Chad** \-'chad\ *or Fr.* **Oubangui–Chari–Tchad** \-'chȧd\; became part of French Equatorial Africa (now French Congo) 1910; separated from Chad 1920; status changed to that of overseas territory 1946; became an autonomous republic within French Community 1958; achieved independence 1960; civilian government overthrown in coup d'état 1966 led by Jean-Bedel Bokassa; Central African Empire decreed 1976 by Bokassa; government overthrown 1979; country reverted to republic; coup d'état 1981 with military in power; elections held 1993 led to civilian government.

Central America. The S portion of North America from S boundary of Mexico to NW Colombia, South America; 228,578 sq. mi. (592,017 sq. km.); pop. (1992e) 29,901,000; includes the countries of Guatemala, Belize, Honduras, El Salvador, Nicaragua, Costa Rica, and Panama (*qq.v.*); bordered on SW by Pacific Ocean and on NE by Caribbean Sea. By some geographers regarded as beginning at Isthmus of Tehuantepec and thus incl. also five states of Mexico: Quintana Roo, Yucatán, Campeche, Tabasco, and Chiapas. Its many mountains a connecting link bet. W North American system and the Andes; numerous volcanoes, many of them active; highest point Volcan Tajumulco, W Guatemala 13,845 ft. (4220 m.). See MIDDLE AMERICA.

History: Area long inhabited by indigenous peoples; among Indians with established civilizations were Maya who were influential through much of first millennium A.D.; Atlantic coast from Honduras to Gulf of Darien skirted by Christopher Columbus 1502; first European settlement 1510 on Gulf of Darien; explored by agents of Spanish soldier and administrator Pedro Arias Dávila (also known as Pedrarias) from Panama; coast of Nicaragua explored and Lake Nicaragua visited by Spanish historian Gil González Dávila 1522; Granada and León founded by Spanish conquistador Fernández de Córdoba 1523; Gulf of Honduras explored 1524 by Spaniards Olid and Las Casas sent by Hernán Cortés from Mexico; Guatemala and El Salvador conquered by Spanish soldier Pedro de Alvarado 1524; organized (except for Chiapas and Panama) into Spanish captaincy general of Guatemala; English arrived 17th cent. settling what would become British Honduras (now Belize); independent in 1821; joined Mexico under Mexican Emperor Augustín de Iturbide for

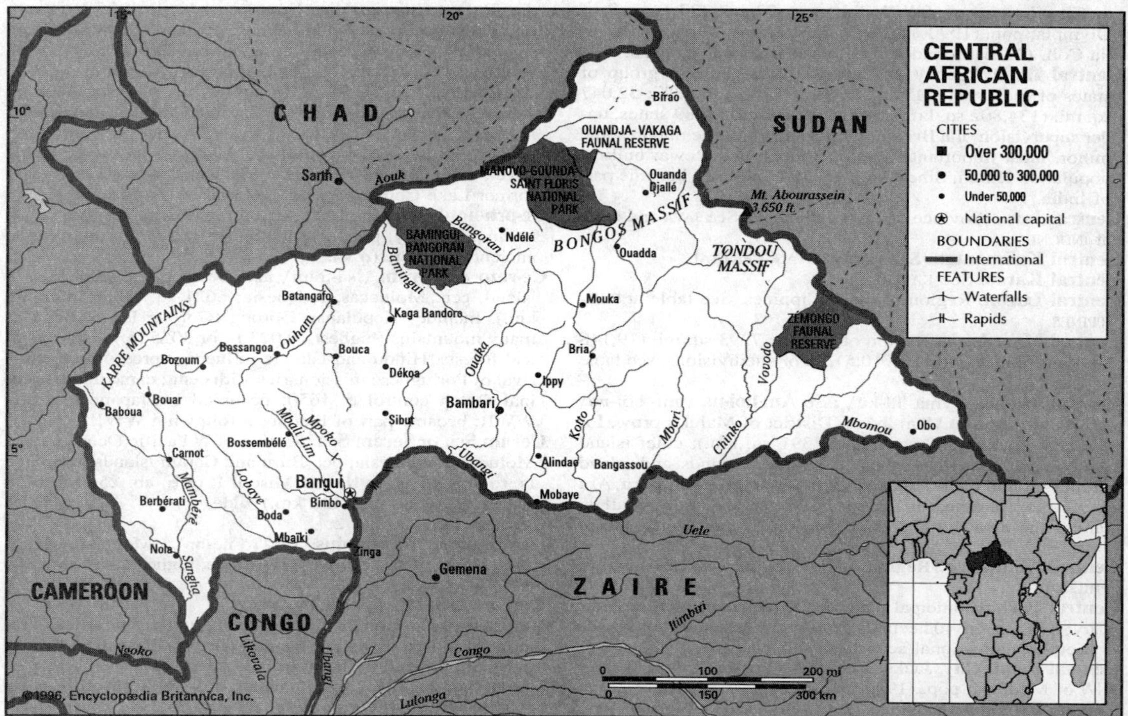

brief period during 1822–23; loosely united as **United Provinces of Central America** 1823–39; separated into independent republics 1838–39; from 1848 control of Isthmian transit an issue bet. U.S. and Great Britain (see NICARAGUA and PANAMA); organized as Greater Republic of Central America 1895–98; treaties of amity drawn up by Washington conference of Central American states 1923. See CENTRAL AMERICAN COMMON MARKET.

Central American Common Market. Economic community, consisting of Costa Rica, El Salvador, Guatemala, Honduras, Nicaragua; headquarters Guatemala City, Guatemala; purpose is creation of customs union and establishment of common external tariffs, but political unrest among member countries has made this difficult; formed 1960.

Central Asia, Soviet. Formerly used name referring to that part of the U.S.S.R. comprising the Uzbek, Turkmen, Tadzhik, and Kirgiz S.S.R.s and sometimes thought to include all or part of the Kazakh S.S.R. also.

History: Before 19th cent., part ruled by Muslim khanates of Bukhara, Khiva, and Qŭqon, and rest inhabited by uncontrolled nomad Turkmen tribes who were subdued by Russians under Alexander II c. 1865 when Russian prov. of Turkistan was constituted; khanates subsequently subdued later 19th cent., although small measure of independence allowed into 20th cent.; Turkmen tribes defeated by early 1880s; after Bolshevik Revolution, reorganized as constituent republics of the U.S.S.R.; on breakup of U.S.S.R. 1991 became independent republics.

Central Australia. A territory of Australia 1927–31, 20th to 26th parallels of S lat., in cen. part of continent; ✻ Stuart (now known as Alice Springs, *q.v.*); formerly S part of Northern Terr.

Central Black Earth Region *or Russ.* **Tsen·tral'·no–Cher·no·zem·nyy Ray·on** \tsen-ˈträl-nə-ˌchir-nə-ˌzyȯm-nē-rī-ˈȯn\. Region, W Russia in Europe and NE Ukraine; a rich agricultural area.

Central City. 1. Town, ⊗ of Gilpin co., N cen. Colorado; pop. (1990c) 335; center of important mining region after major discovery of gold c. 1858; 19th cent. opera house; tourism.

2. Village, Marion co., S cen. Illinois, suburb of Centralia; pop. (1990c) 1390.

3. City, Muhlenberg co., W Kentucky, 32 mi. (51 km.) S of Owensboro; pop. (1990c) 4979.

4. City, ⊗ of Merrick co., E cen. Nebraska, on Platte River 23 mi. (37 km.) ENE of Grand Island; pop. (1990c) 2868.

Central District. District of cen. Israel. See table at ISRAEL.

Central Europe. Indefinite and occasional term applied to the countries of the cen. part of Europe, approx. those bet. the Baltic Sea on N and Alps on S and bet. Russia, Belarus, Ukraine, and Moldova on E and North Sea and France on W. Sometimes in political sense the term (**Mit·tel·eu·ro·pa** \ˌmit-ᵊl-ȯi-ˈrō-pə\, that is, **Middle Europe**) is used; at times use extended to include also Poland and Romania.

Central Falls. City, Providence co., N Rhode Island, on Blackstone River just N of Pawtucket; pop. (1990c) 17,637; clock tower; site of clash 1934 bet. National Guard troops and striking textile workers.

Central Greece. Region of Greece; 6004 sq. mi. (15,550 sq. km.); pop. (1991c) 578,876. For subdivisions, see table at GREECE.

Cen·tra·lia \sen-ˈtrāl-yə\. **1.** City, Clinton and Marion cos., SW cen. Illinois, 58 mi. (93 km.) E of East St. Louis; pop. (1990c) 14,274; Kaskaskia Coll. (1940); coal mines, oil wells; founded 1853; incorp. 1859.

2. City, Boone co., cen. Missouri, 22 mi. (35 km.) NNE of Columbia; pop. (1990c) 3414.

3. Borough, Columbia co., E cen. Pennsylvania, 12 mi. (19 km.) NNW of Pottsville; pop. (1990c) 63; long-burning underground mine fire began 1962.

4. City, Lewis co., SW Washington, 23 mi. (37 km.) S of Olympia; pop. (1990c) 12,101; dairy farms; lumber; Centralia Coll. (1925); founded by a black freedman c. 1875.

Central India Agency *or* **Central India.** Former group of states of India, bet. 21° and 26°N and 74° and 83°E; 52,047 sq. mi. (134,802 sq. km.); ✻ Indore; comprised 89 states, under supervision of a British political agent, some major, some minor, most important: Indore, Bhopal, and Rewa; bulk of population Hindu. Since Aug. 15, 1947 all have become part of India.

Central Java. Province of Java, Indonesia. See JAVA and table at INDONESIA.

Central Kalimantan. See KALIMANTAN, CENTRAL.

Central Karoo. See KAROO.

Central Luzon. Region of the Philippines. See table at PHILIPPINES.

Central Macedonia. Region of Greece; 7393 sq. mi. (19,148 sq. km.); pop. (1991c) 1,710,513. For subdivisions, see table at GREECE.

Central Ma·lu·ku \mä-ˈlü-kü\ *also* **Am·boi·na** \am-ˈbȯi-nə\ *or Malay* **Am·bon** \ˈäm-ˌbȯn\. District of Maluku prov., Indonesia; area 11,348 sq. mi. (29,391 sq. km.); chief island Ambon; chief town Ambon. Comprises islands and island groups around the Banda Sea, esp. Ambon, Ceram, Buru, Aru Is., Kai Is., Tanimbar Is., Babar Is., Wetar, and many small islands, and also the S and SE portion of mainland of Irian Jaya.

Central Mindanao. Region of the Philippines. See table at PHILIPPINES.

Central Park. Municipal park, cen. Manhattan I., New York City; 840 acres (340 hectares); provides the setting for a wide variety of recreational activities.

Central Point. City, Jackson co., SW Oregon, 7 mi. (11 km.) NW of Medford; pop. (1990c) 7509.

Central Province. Province, cen. Kenya. See table at KENYA.

Central Provinces and Berar. See MADHYA PRADESH.

Central Range. See SREDINNYY KHREBET.

Central Sulawesi. Province of Sulawesi, Indonesia. See SULAWESI and table at INDONESIA.

Central Valley. Valley of Sacramento and San Joaquin rivers (*qq.v.*) in California, bet. the Sierra Nevada and Coast Ranges; over 400 mi. (644 km.) long, 20 to 50 mi. (32 to 80 km.) wide; contains productive irrigated farmland.

Central Vi·sa·yas \vē-ˈsī-äs\. Region of the Philippines. See table at PHILIPPINES.

Cen·tre \ˈsen-tər\. **1.** County in cen. Pennsylvania. See table at PENNSYLVANIA.

2. Town, ⊗ of Cherokee co., NE Alabama; pop. (1990c) 2893.

Centre \ˈsäntrᵊ\. Region of cen. France. See table at FRANCE.

Centre. See also CENTER.

Cen·tre·ville \ˈsen-tər-ˌvil\. **1.** City, ⊗ of Bibb co., cen. Alabama; pop. (1990c) 2508.

2. City, St. Clair co., SW Illinois, SE of St. Louis, Missouri; pop. (1990c) 7489.

3. Town, ⊗ of Queen Annes co., E Maryland; pop. (1990c) 2097.

4. *also* **Cen·ter·ville** \ˈsen-tər-ˌvil\. Unincorporated settlement, Fairfax co., Virginia, near field of first battle of Bull Run 1861; pop. (1990c) 26,585.

Centum Cellae. See CIVITAVECCHIA.

Cen·tu·ri·pe \chān-ˈtü-rē-pe\; *earlier* **Cen·tor·bi** \chān-ˈtȯr-bē\; *anc.* **Cen·tu·ri·pa** \sen-ˈtu̇r-i-pə, -ˈtyu̇r-\. Commune, Enna prov., cen. Sicily, Italy, SW of Mt. Etna; pop. (1991p) 6615; marble; many Greek and Roman ruins; destroyed by Holy Roman Emperor Frederick II c. 1232; rebuilt 1548.

Ceos. See KÉA.

Cephaloedium. See CEFALÙ.

Ceph·a·lo·nia \ˌse-fə-ˈlō-nyə, -nē-ə\ *or Gk.* **Ke·fal·li·nía** \ˌke-fä-lē-ˈnē-ä\; *anc.* **Ceph·al·le·nia** \ˌse-fə-ˈlē-nē-ə, -nyə\. One of Ionian Is., Greece; in Ionian Sea off W coast of mainland of Greece; 288 sq. mi. (746 sq. km.); with Ithaca forms Cephalonia dept. (see table at GREECE). Chief town Argostólion on inlet on SW coast. Mountainous, highest point 5341 ft. (1628 m.). Seized by Romans 189 B.C.; Norman soldier Robert Guiscard died here during battle 1085 A.D.; subsequently occupied by Venetians; British 1809–64, Greek since 1864. Suffered devastating earthquake 1953.

Ce·phi·sus \sə-ˈfī-səs\ *or* **Ce·phis·sus** \-ˈfi-səs\ *or Gk.* **Ki·fi·sós** \ˌkē-fē-ˈsȯs\. **1.** River, E cen. Greece, flowing from Mt. Pendelikon S into the Saronic Gulf, passing to W of Athens.

2. *or Gk.* **Ki·fis·sós Voio·ti·kós** \ˌkē-fē-ˈsȯs-ˌvyō-tē-ˈkȯs\. River, cen. Greece; rises near Mt. Oeta, flows E to site of former Lake Copais (*q.v.*); ab. 60 mi. (97 km.) long.

Ce·pra·no \chā-ˈprä-nō\. Commune, Frosinone prov., SE Lazio, cen. Italy; pop. (1981p) 8369; nearby are the ruins of ancient Fregellae (*q.v.*).

Ce·ram *or* **Se·ram** \ˈsā-ˌräm\ *also* **Se·rang** \ˈsā-ˌräŋ\. Large island, cen. Moluccas, Indonesia; 6621 sq. mi. (17,148 sq. km.). Includes Kepulauan Gorong (Gorong Is.) to SE. Has many mountains (highest 10,023 ft. or 3055 m.), dense tropical forests. Hindu and Islamic influences present before arrival of Portuguese missionaries 15th cent.; came under nominal Dutch control c. 1650; occupied by Japanese during WWII; became part of Indonesia following WWII.

Ceram Sea *or* **Seram Sea.** Section of W Pacific Ocean in cen. Moluccas, Indonesia; bet. Buru and Ceram islands to S, Sula Is. to W, Obi Is. to N, and Misool I. to E; ab. 250 mi. (400 km.) long by 80 mi. (130 km.) wide.

Cerasus. See GİRESUN 2.

Ce·rau·ni·an Mountains \sə-ˈrȯ-nē-ən\. Mountain range along coast of NW Epirus, NW Greece; highest peak ab. 6300 ft. (1920 m.).

Cercina. See KERKENNAH ISLANDS.

Cer·da·ña \ser-ˈdä-nyä\ *or Fr.* **Cer·dagne** \ser-ˈdänʸ\. Old region of Europe in the E Pyrenees, partly in France and partly in Spain; drained by the upper Segre River.

Ce·res \ˈsir-ēz\. **1.** City, Stanislaus co., cen. California, 6 mi. (10 km.) SE of Modesto; pop. (1990c) 26,314.

2. Town, Western Cape prov., Rep. of South Africa, 63 mi. (101 km.) ENE of Cape Town.

Ceresio, Lago *or* **Ceresius, Lacus.** See LUGANO, LAKE.

Ce·ri·gno·la \ˌchā-rē-ˈnyō-lä\. Commune, Foggia prov., Puglia, SE Italy, 22 mi. (35 km.) SE of the commune of Foggia; pop. (1991p) 54,971; defeat of French by Spanish 1503.

Cerigo. See KÍTHIRA.

Cernăuţi. See CHERNIVTSI.

Cer·na·vo·dă *or* **Cer·na–Vo·dă** \ˌcher-nä-ˈvō-də\. Commercial port, Constanţa co., SE Romania, on the Danube WNW of the city of Constanţa; terminus of canal (opened 1984) linking the Black Sea with the Danube.

Cer·ral·vo \ser-ˈräl-vō\. Small island off SE coast of Baja California, Mexico, at the mouth of the Gulf of California.

Cer·re·do, Tor·re de \ˈtȯr-rā-t͟hā-ser-ˈrā-t͟hō\ *or* **Pe·ña de Cerredo** \ˈpā-nyä\. Highest peak in the Cantabrian Mts., W Cantabria prov., N Spain; 8787 ft. (2678 m.).

Cer·ri·tos \sə-ˈrē-təs\. City, Los Angeles co., SW California, ab. 8 mi. (13 km.) SE of the city of Los Angeles; pop. (1990c) 53,240.

Cerro de Incahuási *or* **Cerro de Incaguassi.** See INCAHUÁSI, CERRO DE.

Cer·ro de las Me·sas \ˈser-rō-t͟hā-läs-ˈmā-säs\. Village, Veracruz state, E Mexico, SE of Veracruz; archaeological site, jades found here 1941.

Cerro del Toro. See TORO, CERRO DEL.

Cer·ro de Pas·co \ˈser-rō-t͟hā-ˈpäs-kō\. **1.** Mountain, cen. Peru; 15,100 ft. (4602 m.).

2. Town, cen. Peru, ab. 112 mi. (180 km.) NE of Lima; pop. (1990e) 170,500; alt. 14,436 ft. (4400 m.); university (1965); nearby deposits of copper, bismuth, zinc, lead, and historically important silver and gold.

Cer·ro de Pun·ta \ˈser-rō-t͟hā-ˈpün-tä\. Peak, in E Cordillera Central, cen. Puerto Rico; 4389 ft. (1338 m.); highest mountain in Puerto Rico.

Cer·ro Gor·do \ˈser-ō-ˈgȯr-dō\. County in N Iowa. See table at IOWA.

Cer·ro Gor·do \ˈser-rō-ˈgȯr-dō\. Mountain pass bet. Veracruz and Jalapa, E Mexico; battle Apr. 1847 in which Americans under Gen. Winfield Scott defeated Mexicans.

Cer·ro Lar·go \ˈser-rō-ˈlär-gō\. Department of E Uruguay. See table at URUGUAY.

Cer·ro Pal·pa·na \ˈser-rō-päl-ˈpä-nä\. Peak, N Chile, near Bolivian border; 19,833 ft. (6045 m.).

Cerro Santiago. See SANTIAGO, MOUNT.

Cer·tal·do \cher-ˈtäl-(ˌ)dō\. Commune, Firenze prov., Tuscany, cen. Italy, 18 mi. (29 km.) SW of Florence; pop. (1981p) 15,835; home of 14th cent. writer Giovanni Boccaccio.

Cerveteri. See CAERE.

Cer·via \ˈcher-vyä\. Commune, Ravenna prov., Emilia-Romagna, N Italy, on Adriatic Sea 14 mi. (23 km.) SSE of the commune of Ravenna; pop. (1981p) 24,613; salt deposits; bathing beaches.

Cervin, Mont *or* **Monte Cervino.** See MATTERHORN.

Ce·sa·no Ma·der·no \chā-ˈzä-nō-mä-ˈder-nō\. Commune, Milano prov., Lombardy, N Italy, 9 mi. (14 km.) N of Milan; pop. (1989c) 31,874.

César \ˈsā-sär\. Department of N Colombia. See table at COLOMBIA.

Ce·se·na \chā-ˈzā-nä\; *anc.* **Cae·se·na** \sə-ˈzē-nə\. Commune, Forlì prov., Emilia-Romagna, N Italy, 12 mi. (19 km.) SE of the commune of Forlì; pop. (1989c) 89,606; food processing; episcopal see (one of the oldest in Italy); citadel; library (founded 1452). Withstood attack by Spanish soldier and prelate Gil de Albornoz 1357; destroyed by Antipope Clement VII (Robert of Geneva) 1377; under the Malatestas through 1465; became part of the papal domain in the late 15th cent.; birthplace of Popes Pius VI (1717) and VII (1742).

Ce·se·na·ti·co \ˌchā-zā-ˈnä-tē-ˌkō\. Commune, Forlì prov., Emilia-Romagna, N Italy, on Adriatic Sea 18 mi. (29 km.) E of the commune of Forlì; fishing; bathing beaches.

Cēsis \ˈtsā-sə̇s\ *or* **Tse·sis** \ˈtsā-sə̇s\ *or Ger.* **Wen·den** \ˈven-dən\. Town, N Latvia, in the Gauja River Valley 45 mi. (72 km.) NE of Riga; pop. (1991e) 22,100.

History: Formerly seat of the Livonian Knights and member of Hanseatic League; variously under Swedish and Polish rule until it was taken over by Russia 1721; battlefield 1919 where Latvian army with Estonian aid defeated the Germans; held by Germans in WWII 1941–44.

Čes·ká Lí·pa \ˈches-kä-ˈlē-pä\ *or Ger.* **Böh·misch–Lei·pa** \ˈbœ̄-mish-ˈlī-pə\. Town, N Czech Republic, 40 mi. (64 km.) N of Prague; pop. (1989c) 40,177; castle (1583).

Česká Socialistická Republika. See CZECH SOCIALIST REPUBLIC.

Čes·ké Bu·dě·jo·vi·ce \ˈches-ke-ˈbu̇d-ye-ˌyȯ-vēt-ˌse\ *or Ger.* **Bud·weis** \ˈbu̇t-ˌvīs\. City, S Czech Republic, on Vltava River 75 mi. (121 km.) S of Prague; pop. (1991p) 97,283; founded c. 1265; Dominican abbey; arcaded town square; original home of Budweiser beer.

Českomoravská Vrchovina. See BOHEMIAN-MORAVIAN HIGHLANDS.

Československo *or* **Československá Socialistická Republika.** See CZECHOSLOVAKIA.

Čes·ký–Brod \ˈches-kē-ˈbrȯt\ *or Ger.* **Böh·misch–Brod** \ˈbœ̄-mish-ˈbrōt\. Commune, W cen. Czech Republic, 19 mi. (31 km.) E of Prague; Hussite leader Prokop Holý was killed in nearby battle of Lipany 1434.

Český Les. See BOHEMIAN FOREST.

Čes·ký Tě·šín \ˈches-kē-ˈtye-ˌshēn\; *formerly* **Tě·šín Čes·ký** \ˈtye-ˌshēn-ˈches-kē\. Town, E Czech Republic, ab. 15 mi. (24 km.) ESE of Ostrava on Polish border opp. Cieszyn (*q.v.*); pop. (1989c) 28,792.

Cess. See CESTOS.

Cess·nock \ˈses-ˌnäk\. Town, E New South Wales, SE Australia, 25 mi. (40 km.) W of Newcastle; pop. (1991c) 43,849; coal deposits.

Ces·tos \ˈses-təs\; *formerly* **Cess** \ˈses\. River, Liberia; flows into Atlantic Ocean ab. 100 mi. (160 km.) SE of Monrovia; ab. 200 mi. (320 km.) long.

Ce·ta·tea Al·bă \chā-ˌtä-tyä-ˈäl-bə\. **1.** Former department, S Bessarabia, Romania; 2932 sq. mi. (7594 sq. km.); now a part of Ukraine.

2. City, its ✻, now in Odessa region, Ukraine. See BELGOROD-DNESTROVSKI.

Ce·ti·nje \ˈtse-tē-nye\. Town, Montenegro, Yugoslavia, in mountainous region 19 mi. (31 km.) SE of Kotor; pop. (1991p) 20,258; the former ✻ of Montenegro; monastery; tombs of Montenegrin rulers; museum in former royal palace. Founded in latter part of 15th cent. by Ivan the Black Crnojevich; several times sacked and burned by Turkish invaders.

Cette. See SÈTE.

Ceu·ta \ˈthā-ü-tä, ˈsyü-tä\ *or Arabic* **Seb·ta** \ˈseb-tə\. Spanish enclave, N Morocco, at E end of Strait of Gibraltar opp. Gibraltar; pop. (1990p) 73,483; military station and seaport; with Melilla comprises an autonomous community of Spain. Long a flourishing trading town under the Arabs; taken by Portuguese 1415; first occupied by Spanish 1580. See PILLARS OF HERCULES.

Ceuta and Me·lil·la \mā-ˈlē-lyä, -ˈlē-yä\. Autonomous community of Spain. See table at SPAIN.

Cé·vennes \sā-ˈven\; *anc.* **Ce·ben·na** \sə-ˈbe-nə\. **1.** Mountain range in S France extending NE and SW, W of the Rhone, from N Ardèche dept. to SW Hérault dept.; highest peak Mt. Mézenc 5755 ft. (1754 m.).

2. Old district, France, NE part of Languedoc, comprising the region of the Cévennes Mts.; ✻ Mende. Inhabitants known as Cevenoles; scene of uprising of Camisards in early 18th cent. religious wars following the revocation of the Edict of Nantes (1685).

Cey·han \jā-ˈhän\. **1.** *formerly* **Ji·hun** \jī-ˈhün\; *anc.* **Pyr·a·mus** \ˈpir-ə-məs\. River, Turkey in Asia; flows from the Anti-Taurus Mts. S and SSW through Cilicia into Gulf of İskenderun; 316 mi. (508 km.) long.

2. Town, S Turkey in Asia, on Ceyhan River and on railroad line 25 mi. (40 km.) E of Adana.

Ceylon. See SRI LANKA.

Cha·blais \shȧ-ˈblā\. Ancient region of Savoy; now part of Haute-Savoie dept., E France, S of Lake Geneva; ✻ Thonon; gained by counts of Savoy; became Calvinist 16th cent.; won back 1594–98 to Catholicism by St. Francis of Sales under aegis of Charles Emmanuel, duke of Savoy; ultimately became part of France.

Cha·blis \shȧ-ˈblē; ˈsha-ˌblē, sha-ˈblē\. Commune, Yonne dept., NE cen. France, ab. 11 mi. (18 km.) E of Auxerre; white Burgundy wines produced in region.

Cha·ca·bu·co \ˌchä-kä-ˈbü-kō\. **1.** Town, Buenos Aires prov., E Argentina, ab. 120 mi. (193 km.) W of the city of Buenos Aires; pop. (1980p) 23,660; in important agricultural district.

2. Village just N of Santiago, cen. Chile; scene of battle Feb. 12, 1817 in which Argentinian soldier and statesman José de San Martín with Chilean patriot Bernardo O'Higgins defeated the Spanish royalists.

Cha·cao Channel \chä-ˈkau̇\. Strait bet. N Chiloé I. and the mainland of S cen. Chile, connecting the Gulf of Ancud with the Pacific Ocean.

Chachak. See ČAČAK.

Cha·cha·ni \chä-ˈchä-nē\. Peak, S Peru; 19,931 ft. (6075 m.); meteorological station.

Cha·cha·po·yas \ˌchä-chä-ˈpō-yäs\. Town, N Peru, ab. 160 mi. (257 km.) NE of Trujillo; pop. (1990e) 13,100; alt. 7638 ft. (2328 m.).

Cha·choeng·sao *or* **Cha·xerng·sao** \ˈchä-ˈchəŋ-ˈsau̇\. Town, S Thailand, on railroad line 40 mi. (64 km.) E of Bangkok; pop. (1991e) 42,233.

Cha·co \ˈchä-kō\. **1.** Region, S cen. South America. See GRAN CHACO.

2. Province of N Argentina; ✻ Resistencia. See table at ARGENTINA.

Chaco Austral. See GRAN CHACO.

Chaco Boreal. See GRAN CHACO.

Chaco Central. See GRAN CHACO.

Chaco Culture National Historical Park. See UNITED STATES, *National Historical Parks.*

Chad \ˈchad\ *or Fr.* **Tchad** \ˈchȧd\. Republic, N cen. Africa, bounded on N by Libya, on E by Sudan, on S by Central African Rep., on SW by Cameroon, and on W by Nigeria and Niger; 495,752 sq. mi. (1,283,998 sq. km.); pop. (1985e) 5,200,000; ✻ N'Djamena.

Physical features: Landlocked republic having the form of a shallow basin; N region mainly desert, S region is forested and supports agriculture; elevated areas are in N (Tibesti Mts., *q.v.*) and on E boundary.

Chief products: Cotton, peanuts, millet, rice, cassava; livestock, fish; salt.

Chief towns: N'Djamena, Sarh, Moundou, Abéché.

History: Formerly the kingdoms of Kanem-Bornu, Baguirmi, and Wadai; territory explored by French 1891; made part of French Equatorial Africa 1910; became a separate colony 1920; status changed to French overseas territory 1946; became a republic within French Community 1958; achieved independence 1960 followed by decades of civil war and frequent intervention by France and Libya.

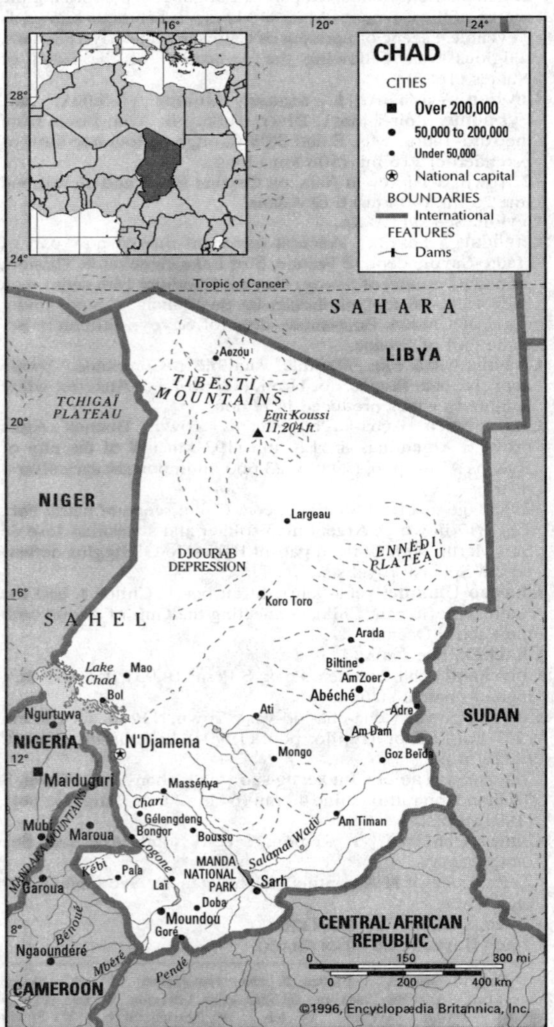

Chad, Lake. Lake, NW cen. Africa, at junction of boundaries of Nigeria, Niger, and Chad; its S part forms N extent of Cameroon; its area ranges from ab. 3800 to ab. 9900 sq. mi. (ab. 9842 to ab. 25,641 sq. km.); fed by Chari River from S and by numerous other streams, has no outlet but remains fresh; ab. 13 ft. (4 m.) deep in NW, 13 to 23 ft. (4 to 7 m.) in S where it is navigable. First explored by Europeans Dixon Denham, Dr. Walter Oudney, and Hugh Clapperton 1823. See FRENCH EQUATORIAL AFRICA.

Chad·der·ton \ˈcha-dər-tən\. Town, Lancashire, NW England, suburb of Oldham, on the Irk River 8 mi. (13 km.) NE of Manchester; pop. (1981p) 34,013.

Chadds Ford \ˈchadz\. Village, Delaware co., Pennsylvania, on Brandywine Creek; originally Chad's Ford, a crossing of the Brandywine, where in American Revolution the main action of the battle of Sept. 11, 1777 bet. forces of Gen. George Washington and Gen. William Howe was fought; Brandywine River Museum.

Cha·di·leo \chä-dē-ˈlā-ō\. Name given to lower course of Río Salado, La Pampa prov., S cen. Argentina. See SALADO, RÍO 1.

Chad·ron \ˈsha-drən\. City, ⊗ of Dawes co., NW Nebraska, 50 mi. (80 km.) N of Alliance; pop. (1990c) 5588; Chadron State Coll. (1911).

Chaer·o·nea \ˌker-ə-ˈnē-ə, ˌkir-\. Ancient city, now in ruins, of W Boeotia, E cen. Greece, SE of Mt. Parnassus and near Orchomenus; scene of victory of King Philip II of Macedon 338 B.C. over a confederation of Greek states and of the defeat of Mithradates VI, king of Pontus, by Roman Gen. Sulla 86 B.C.; birthplace of biographer Plutarch c. 46 A.D.

Cha·fa·ri·nas Islands \ˌchä-fä-ˈrē-näs\ *or* **Zaf·a·rin Islands** \ˈza-fə-rin\. Island group, Spain, in the Mediterranean Sea off N end of Morocco, near Melilla; lighthouse maintained on the only island that is inhabited.

Chaf·fee \ˈchā-fē, ˈcha-\. **1.** County in cen. Colorado. See table at COLORADO.
2. City, Scott co., SE Missouri, 12 mi. (19 km.) SW of Cape Girardeau; pop. (1990c) 3059.

Cha·gai \ˈchä-ˌgī\. Historical district, NW Baluchistan, Pakistan; 19,429 sq. mi. (50,321 sq. km.); pop. (1981p) 11,000; mountainous; desert region; annexed by Pakistan during the period of British colonial rule in the late 1800s.

Chagai Hills. Range, Pakistan, extending E and W along Afghan boundary of Chagai historical dist.; highest point 8061 ft. (2457 m.).

Cha·ghā Kūr \chä-ˈgä-ˈkür\ *also* **Chi·gha Khur** \chi-ˈgä\. Town, W Iran, in mountainous region.

Cha·gos Archipelago \ˈchä-gəs\. Group of islands in Indian Ocean S of Maldives; 23 sq. mi. (60 sq. km.); has no permanent population; acquired by Britain from France in 1814 and administered as a dependency of Mauritius; from 1965–76 part of and now the sole territory comprising the British Indian Ocean Terr.; chief island Diego Garcia.

Cha·gres \ˈchä-grəs, ˈcha-\. River in Panama; rises in cen. Panama E of Panama Canal, flows SW where it is dammed to form Gatun Lake, and drains NW out of Gatun Lake into the Caribbean Sea.

Cha·grin Falls \shə-ˈgrin, ˈsha-grin\. Residential village, Cuyahoga co., N Ohio, 15 mi. (24 km.) ESE of Cleveland; pop. (1990c) 4146.

Cha·gua·ra·mas \ˌchä-gwä-ˈrä-mäs\. Settlement, NW Trinidad, West Indies, on **Chaguaramas Bay,** inlet of the Gulf of Paria, WNW of Port of Spain; site of U.S. naval base during WWII.

Cha·har \ˈchä-ˈhär\. Former province, E Nei Monggol (Inner Mongolia), N China, bounded on NW and N by Mongolia, on E by Jehol and Manchuria, on S by Hebei and Shanxi provs. of China, and on SW and W by Suiyuan; ✻ Zhangjiakou. Taken over by Japanese 1937; returned to Chinese control after WWII. Partitioned 1952 among other provinces.

Cha·hār Ma·hāll va Bakh·tī·a·rī \chə-ˈhär-mə-ˈhäl-vä-bäk-ˈtē-ə-ˌrē\ *or* **Bakhtīarī va Chahār Mahāll.** Province of W cen. Iran; formerly a governorship. See table at IRAN.

Chāh Ba·hār \ˈchä-bə-ˈhär\ *also* **Chah·bar** *or* **Char·bar** \chä-ˈbär\. Seaport, on coast of Gulf of Oman, SE Iran, at S end of E Iranian highway from Mashhad.

Chai·ba·sa \chī-ˈbäs-ə\. Town, Bihar, India; pop. (1991p) 56,657.

Chai·nat *or* **Jai·nat** *also* **Jay·a·nath** \ˈchī-ˈnät\. Town, SW cen. Thailand; pop. (1991e) 14,001.
Chain Island. See ANAA ISLAND.
Ch'ai–ta–mu. See QAIDAM.
Chai·ya·phum *or* **Ja·ya·bum** \ˌchī-yä-ˈpüm\. Town, N Thailand; pop. (1991e) 25,607.
Cha·ke Cha·ke \ˈchä-kā-ˈchä-kā\. Settlement, ✻ of Pemba South region, cen. Pemba I., E Tanzania.
Cha·la·te·nan·go \ˌchä-lä-tā-ˈnäŋ-gō\. **1.** Department of NW El Salvador. See table at EL SALVADOR.
2. Town, its ✻; pop. (1992c) 27,600.
Chalcedon. See KADIKÖY.
Chal·chi·co·mu·la \ˌchäl-chē-kō-ˈmü-lä\. Village, Puebla state, SE cen. Mexico, at foot of Mt. Citlaltépetl.
Chal·chua·pa \ˌchäl-ˈchwä-pä\. City, Santa Ana dept., W El Salvador, near the city of Santa Ana; pop. (1986e) 63,700.
Chal·cid·i·ce \kal-ˈsi-di-sē\ *or Gk.* **Khal·ki·dhi·kí** \ˌkäl-kē-thē-ˈkē\. **1.** Peninsula of E Macedonia, NE Greece, projecting SE into N Aegean Sea bet. Strymonic Gulf on E and Gulf of Salonika on W; terminates in three long peninsulas: (from E to W) Acte, Sithonia, and Kassándra (*qq.v.*). In N part at its base are Lakes Bolbē and Korónia and the city of Thessaloníki. See ATHOS.
2. Department of Greece. See table at GREECE.
Chalcis. See KHALKÍS.
Chal·co \ˈchäl-kō\. Dry lake in cen. Mexico, ab. 25 mi. (40 km.) SE of Mexico City; alt. 7480 ft. (2280 m.).
Chal·dea *also* **Chal·daea** \kal-ˈdē-ə\. Ancient region on the Euphrates River and the Persian Gulf, Asia; orig. the S part of Babylonia. Frequently, and esp. in biblical use (*Gen.* xi. 28; *Dan.* ix. 1), equivalent to Babylonia (*q.v.*) after it was occupied by the Chaldeans, a Semitic people who had attacked it since 11th cent. B.C. and finally secured throne and established a Chaldean dynasty under Nabopolassar c. 625 B.C.; with help, brought about fall of Assyrian empire 612 B.C.; while ruled by Nebuchadrezzar II, subdued Judaea, and captured Jerusalem 597 and 586 B.C.; Chaldean (or Neo-Babylonian) empire fell when Persians captured Babylon 539 B.C.
Chaldiran. See ÇALDIRAN.
Cha·leur Bay \shə-ˈlœr, -ˈlu̇r\ *or Fr.* **Baie de Chaleur** \ˌbā-də-shə-ˈlœ̄r\. Inlet of W Gulf of St. Lawrence, SE Canada, extending bet. N New Brunswick and the Gaspé Penin. in SE Quebec; ab. 85 mi. (137 km.) long; its S extension is Nepisiguit Bay; receives the Restigouche River; famous as a fishing ground, esp. for salmon. Navigated and named by French explorer Jacques Cartier c. 1535.
Chal·font \ˈchal-ˌfänt\. Borough, Bucks co., Pennsylvania; pop. (1990c) 3069.
Chalkar–Tengis. See CHELKAR-TENGIZ.
Chalkis. See KHALKÍS.
Chalk River \ˈchȯk\. Village near Ottawa River, SE Ontario, Canada, 20 mi. (32 km.) NW of Pembroke; pop. (1991c) 874; atomic reactor and research center.
Chal·lis \ˈcha-lis\. City, ⊗ of Custer co., cen. Idaho; pop. (1990c) 1073.
Chal·mette \shal-ˈmet\. Unincorporated settlement, ⊗ of St. Bernard parish, SE Louisiana, on the Mississippi River downstream from New Orleans; pop. (1990c) 31,860.
Châ·lons–sur–Marne \shä-ˈlōⁿ-ˌsūr-ˈmärn\. Commune, ✻ of Marne dept., NE France, on Marne River 95 mi. (153 km.) E of Paris; pop. (1990c) 51,533; cathedral, restored under Louis XIV; 12th cent. Romanesque church. Chief town of the ancient Catalauni; fortified by Romans; on plains to the S (Catalaunian Plains) Attila, king of the Huns, defeated by a combined force of Romans and Visigoths 451; briefly occupied by the Germans 1914; occupied by the Germans and heavily bombed in WWII.
Cha·lon–sur–Saône \sha-ˈlōⁿ-ˌsūr-ˈsōn\; *anc.* **Cab·il·lo·num** \ka-bə-ˈlō-nəm\. City, Saône-et-Loire dept., E cen. France, on Saône River 35 mi. (56 km.) N of Mâcon; pop. (1990c) 56,259; 12th–15th cent. cathedral; 15th cent. episcopal palace; received communal charter 1256.
Chaltel. See FITZ ROY.
Chama, Rio. See RIO CHAMA.
Chamalhari. See CHOMO LHARI.
Cha·man \ˈchä-mən\. Town, W Baluchistan, Pakistan, 60 mi. (97 km.) NW of Quetta on Afghanistan border; pop. (1981p) 30,000; railroad terminus; on highway over **Chaman Pass.**
Cha·mar·tín de la Ro·sa \ˌchä-mär-ˈtēn-thā-lä-ˈrō-sä\. Former commune, cen. Spain, now part of Madrid.
Cham·ba \ˈchəm-bə\. **1.** Former state, N India; founded in 6th cent.; came under British influence 1846; made part of Himachal Pradesh 1948.
2. Town, Himachal Pradesh, N India, on gorge of upper Ravi River; pop. (1991p) 17,028.
Cham·bal \ˈchəm-bəl\. Unnavigable river, cen. India; rises in W Vindhya Mts. near Indore and flows NE, E, and SE into the Yamuna W of Kanpur.
Cham·ber·lain \ˈchām-bər-lin\. City, ⊗ of Brule co., S South Dakota, on Missouri River 10 mi. (16 km.) N of its confluence with White River; pop. (1990c) 2347; tourism.
Chamberlain Lake. Lake in N Piscataquis co., N cen. Maine; numerous campsites on its shores.
Cham·bers \ˈchām-bərz\. **1.** Island in middle of Green Bay, NE Wisconsin, in Door co.
2. Name of counties in two states of the U.S. See tables at ALABAMA and TEXAS.
Cham·bers·burg \ˈchām-bərz-ˌbərg\. Borough, ⊗ of Franklin co., S Pennsylvania, 50 mi. (80 km.) WSW of Harrisburg; pop. (1990c) 16,647; limestone, freestone, marble deposits. Wilson Coll. (1869); settled 1730; abolitionist John Brown's headquarters 1859; burned by Confederates 1864.
Cham·bé·ry \ˌshäⁿ-(ˌ)bā-ˈrē\ *or Lat.* **Cam·be·ri·a·cum** \ˌkam-bə-ˈrī-ə-kəm\. City, ✻ of Savoie dept., E France, 54 mi. (87 km.) E of Lyon; pop. (1990c) 55,603; ✻ of historical Savoy 1232–1562; cathedral; château of dukes of Savoy.
Cham·be·shi \chäm-ˈbā-shē, cham-ˈbē-\ *also* **Cham·be·zi** \chäm-ˈbā-zē, cham-ˈbē-\. A headstream of the Congo River, Africa; rises in N Zambia, flows SW, forms multiple channels in swamp S of Lake Bangweulu from which it emerges as the Luapula; ab. 300 mi. (480 km.) long.
Cham·bey·ron, Ai·guille de \ā-ˌgwē-də-ˌshäⁿ-bā-ˈrōⁿ\. Mountain in the Cottian Alps, Alpes-de-Haute Provence dept., SE France; 11,155 ft. (3400 m.).
Cham·bezi. See CHAMBESHI.
Cham·blee \ˈsham-blē\. City, De Kalb co., NW cen. Georgia, N of Atlanta; pop. (1990c) 7668.
Cham·bly \ˈsham-blē, shäⁿ-ˈblē\. City, S Quebec, Canada, on Richelieu River 14 mi. (23 km.) ESE of Montreal; pop. (1991c) 15,893; site of fort built 1665; defense post against Iroquois; captured by British in 1760 and Americans 1775; served as a main base of operations for British commanders Sir Guy Carleton and John Burgoyne following American withdrawal in 1776.
Chambly Canal. Canal, part of Richelieu River system, Quebec, Canada, from Chambly to St. Johns; 11.78 mi. (19 km.) long, with nine locks.
Cham·bolle–Mu·si·gny \shäⁿ-ˈbȯl-mū̄-zē-ˈnyē\. Commune, Côte-d'Or dept., E France, near Dijon; celebrated wines (red Burgundy) from vineyard of Musigny.
Chambon–Feugerolles, Le. See LE CHAMBON-FEUGEROLLES.
Cham·bord \shäⁿ-ˈbȯr\. Village, Loir-et-Cher dept., N cen. France, ab. 10 mi. (16 km.) NE of Blois; pop. (1990c) 214; château built by Francis I and his son Henry II.
Cha·me·le·cón \ˌchä-mā-lā-ˈkȯn\. River in NW Honduras; flows NE into the Gulf of Honduras; ab. 125 mi. (200 km.) long.
Cha·me Point \ˈchä-mā\. Cape on S coast of Panama, at W side of entrance to the Bay of Panama.
Cha·mi·zal \ˈsha-mə-ˌzal, ˌchä-mē-ˈsäl\. Tract of land N of the Rio Grande adjoining El Paso, Texas; 437 acres (177 hectares); originally in Mexico, later in U.S. because of change of

course of Rio Grande; after long controversy ceded to Mexico by U.S. in 1963.

Cham·lang \ˈchäm-ˈläŋ\. Mountain in the Himalayas, Nepal; 24,014 ft. (7319 m.).

Cha·mo, Lake \ˈchä-mō\ *or* **Ch'amo Hāyk'** \ˈchä-mō-ˈhīk\ *or* **Lake Sha·mo** \ˈshä-mō\. Lake, SW Ethiopia.

Cha·mo·nix *or* **Cha·mou·ni** \ˌsha-mō-ˈnē\. Noted valley in Haute-Savoie dept., E France, near NW entrance to Mont Blanc Tunnel; ab. 14 mi. (23 km.) long and bet. 1 and 2.5 mi. (0.6 to 4 km.) wide; winter sports; mountain climbing; site of Winter Olympic Games 1924; best starting point for ascent of Mont Blanc to the SE, at the town of **Chamonix–Mont–Blanc** \mōⁿ-ˈbläⁿ\.

Cha·mou·chou·ane \ˌshä-mü-shü-ˈän\ *also* **Ash·uap·mu·chuan** *or* **Ash·uap·mu·shuan** \ash-ˈwäp-mu̇-ˌshwän\. River, S Quebec, Canada; flows SE into Lac St.-Jean; 165 mi. (265 km.) long.

Cham·pa \ˈcham-pə\. Ancient coastal kingdom of Indochina, now part of cen. Vietnam; fl. 2d cent. A.D. to end of 14th cent. Its inhabitants were Chams, related to the Cambodians.

Cham·pagne \sham-ˈpān\ *or Lat.* **Cam·pa·nia** \kam-ˈpā-nyə, -nē-ə\. Historical region of NE France, bounded on N by Low Countries; ✻ Troyes; watered by Marne, Aube, Aisne, Meuse, Yonne rivers; famous for its wines. An important medieval French county, held by houses of Vermandois, Blois, and Navarre; by marriage 1284 of heiress Jeanne de Navarre to Prince Philip (later Philip IV) of France, came to French crown; province until c. 1790; scene of battles of WWI and WWII.

Champagne–Ar·denne \-ar-ˈden\. Region of NE France. See table at FRANCE.

Champagne Castle *formerly* **Cath·kin Peak** \ˈkath-kin\. Peak in Drakensberg, Rep. of South Africa; 11,073 ft. (3375 m.).

Cham·paign \sham-ˈpān\. **1.** Name of counties in two states of the U.S. See tables at ILLINOIS and OHIO.
2. City, Champaign co., E cen. Illinois; pop. (1990c) 63,502; adjoins Urbana; settled ab. 1855; incorp. 1860.

Champaign–Urbana. See URBANA 1.

Cham·pa·quí \ˌchäm-pä-ˈkē\. Peak, W Córdoba prov., N cen. Argentina; 9350 ft. (2850 m.); highest of the Sierras de Córdoba.

Champ·au·bert \ˌshäⁿ-pō-ˈber\. Village, Marne dept., NE France, ab. 17 mi. (27 km.) SSE of Épernay; scene of battle Feb. 1814 in which French Emperor Napoléon defeated the allies.

Cham·pe·ri·co \ˌchäm-pā-ˈrē-kō\. Seaport, Retalhuleu dept., SW Guatemala; pop. (1993e) 12,517; port for Retalhuleu and Quetzaltenango.

Cham·pi·gny–sur–Marne \ˌshäⁿ-pē-ˈnyē-ˌsu̇r-ˈmärn\. Residential commune, Val-de-Marne dept., N France, SSE suburb of Paris on Marne River; battles Nov. 30 and Dec. 2, 1870 in which the French attempted unsuccessful sorties from Paris during Franco-Prussian War.

Cham·pi·on's Hill \ˈcham-pē-ənz\. Hill, Hinds co., SW cen. Mississippi, 20 mi. (32 km.) E of Vicksburg; battle May 1863 in which Union forces under Gen. Ulysses S. Grant drove Confederates back toward Vicksburg.

Cham·plain \cham-plān\. County, S Quebec, Canada. See table at QUEBEC.

Champlain, Lake. Lake bet. Vermont and New York on N part of boundary, extending ab. 6 mi. (10 km.) into Canada; ab. 125 mi. (201 km.) long; 430 sq. mi. (1114 sq. km.); max. depth 399 ft. (122 m.). Visited 1609 by French explorer Samuel de Champlain; scene of first British and American naval battle Oct. 11, 1776 and American naval victory over British Sept. 11, 1814.

Champlain Canal. Canal, W New York, connecting Lake Champlain at Whitehall with the Erie Canal at Waterford; 60 mi. (97 km.) long, with 11 locks; part of the New York State Barge Canal system.

Cham·plin \ˈcham-plən\. City, Hennepin co., SE cen. Minnesota, on Mississippi River; pop. (1990c) 16,849.

Cham·po·eg \cham-ˈpō-eg\. Settlement in Willamette Valley, Oregon, S of Portland; "Champoeg meeting" held May 2, 1843 to organize the first provisional government in the Pacific Northwest; site commemorated by Champoeg Memorial State Park.

Cham·po·tón \ˌchäm-pō-ˈtōn\. Seaport, Campeche state, Mexico, on Campeche Bay 48 mi. (77 km.) SW of Campeche; munic. pop. (1990p) 70,264; fishing.

Chanak Kalessi. See ÇANAKKALE 2.

Chanar. See CHUNAR.

Cha·ña·ral \ˌchä-nyä-ˈräl\. Port, Atacama region, N cen. Chile; historically important exports of nitrates and copper.

Chança. See CHANZA.

Chan·ce·lade \shäⁿ-ˈslad\. Commune, Dordogne dept., SW cen. France; skeleton unearthed near here in 1888 considered to be of the Upper Paleolithic period.

Chan·cel·lor \ˈchan-sə-lər\; *formerly* **Chan·cel·lors·ville** \ˈchan-sə-lərz-ˌvil\. Locality in Spotsylvania co., Virginia, just W of Fredericksburg; scene of battle May 1863 which resulted in defeat of Union forces under Gen. Joseph Hooker by Confederates under Gens. Robert E. Lee and Thomas ("Stonewall") Jackson and death of Jackson May 10.

Chan Chan \ˈchän-ˈchän\. Ancient city, N Peru, near modern Trujillo; center of pre-Incan culture, the Chimú, flourished c. 13th cent. A.D.; submitted to Incans 15th cent.

Chan–chiang \ˈchän-ˈchyäŋ\. **1.** Name of Kwangchowan after its restoration to China by France 1945.
2. Town, Guangdong, China. See ZHANJIANG.

Chan–chiang Kang. See ZHANJIANG GANG.

Chan·da·lar \ˌshan-də-ˈlär\. River, NE Alaska; flows SE from Endicott Mts. to upper Yukon; 280 mi. (451 km.) long.

Chandannagar. See CHANDERNAGORE.

Chan·dau·si \ˌchən-ˈdau̇-sē\. Town, W Uttar Pradesh, N India, on affluent of Ganges River 95 mi. (153 km.) E of Delhi; pop. (1991p) 82,733; rail and trade center.

Chan·de·leur Islands \ˌshan-də-ˈlu̇r\. Chain of small islands in St. Bernard parish, off E coast of SE Louisiana, lying bet. **Chandeleur Sound** and the Gulf of Mexico.

Chan·der·na·gore \ˌchən-dər-nə-ˈgōr\ *or* **Chan·dan·na·gar** \ˌchən-də-ˈnə-gər\ *or* **Chan·der·na·gor** \ˌchən-dər-nə-ˈgōr\ *or* **Chan·dar·na·gar** \-ˈnə-gər\. Settlement and adjoining territory, SE India, on the Hugli River 21 mi. (34 km.) N of Calcutta; ab. 4 sq. mi. (10 sq. km.); pop. (1981e) 421,256.
History: Settled by French late 17th cent.; in 18th cent. a thriving center for trade; captured by English 1757 and again in 1794; restored to French 1816. Voted 1949 to join India; became part of Republic of India 1950.

Chan·di·garh \ˈchən-dē-gər\. **1.** Union territory of India. See table at INDIA.
2. City, joint ✻ of Punjab and Haryana states, and Chandigarh union terr., N India; pop. (1991c) 510,565; university (1947).

Chan·dler \ˈchand-lər\. **1.** City, Maricopa co., SW cen. Arizona, 17 mi. (27 km.) SE of Phoenix; pop. (1990c) 90,533; electronic components; winter resort.
2. City, ⊗ of Lincoln co., cen. Oklahoma, 26 mi. (42 km.) N of Shawnee; pop. (1990c) 2596.

Chan·dra·pur \ˌchən-drə-ˈpu̇r\; *formerly* **Chan·da** \ˈchən-də\. Town, E Maharashtra, cen. India; pop. (1991p) 225,841; ✻ of Gond dynasty 12th–18th cents.

Chang \ˈchäŋ\ *or W.-G.* **Yang·tze** \ˈyäŋ-ˈtsə; ˈyaŋ-ˈsē, ˈyäŋ-, -ˈtsē\. Principal river of China; rises in E Kunlun Shan in SW Qinghai, flows SE through deep gorges marking boundary bet. Tibet and Sichuan, then E across the plateau of Yunnan and finally ENE across the entire width of China Proper to the East China Sea near Shanghai; 3434 mi. (5525 km.) long. Known as the Jinsha (*q.v.*) in its upper course. Navigable for vessels of large draft 585 mi. (941 km.); above Yichang navigation difficult and dangerous because of rapids in the Chang Gorges (*q.v.*); on some sections above the gorges navigable for smaller vessels. Its chief tributaries on the N are the Yalong, Min, Jialing, and Han; on the S the Wu and the outlets of (lakes) Dongting Hu and Poyang Hu. In its upper course 8000 to 10,000 ft. (2450 to 3050 m.) above sea level, at Batang 8540 ft. (2603 m.), at Chongqing 650 ft. (198 m.), at Yichang (below the gorges) 131 ft. (40 m.) and for the last 200 mi. (322 km.) of its course practically at sea level.

Changan. See XI'AN.
Chan·ga·na·che·ri \ˌchəŋ-gə-ˈnä-chə-rē\. Town, cen. Kerala, S India, SE of Alleppey; pop. (1991p) 52,498.
Chang·bai Shan *or W.-G.* **Ch'ang–pai Shan** \ˈchäŋ-ˈbī-ˈshän\. Mountain range, Jilin prov., NE China, along N North Korean border; highest point 9003 ft. (2744 m.); source of Songhua, Yalu, and Tumen rivers. Many Manchu legends connected with it.
Chang·bha·kar \ˌchäŋ-bə-ˈkär\. Former princely state, NE Central Provinces, India; 899 sq. mi. (2328 sq. km.); now part of Madhya Pradesh.
Chang–chia–k'ou. See ZHANGJIAKOU.
Ch'ang–chih. See CHANGZHI.
Ch'ang–chou. **1.** See ZHANGZHOU.
2. See CHANGZHOU.
Changchuen. See SHANGCHUAN.
Chang·chun *or W.-G.* **Ch'ang–ch'un** \ˈchäŋ-ˈchu̇n\ *or Jp.* **Hsin·king** \ˈshin-ˈjiŋ\. City, ✻ of Jilin prov., NE China, on railroad line 165 mi. (266 km.) NNE of Shenyang; pop. (1990c) 1,679,270; on edge of fertile Songhua River plain; rail junction point; trucks and cars; processed foods; light engineering; university (1958), technical college (1958).
History: Small village until end of 18th cent. when small farmers came into district from Shandong and gained in importance after completion of Chinese Eastern Railway 1901; made ✻ of new Japanese state of Manchukuo 1932. In WWII captured by Russians Aug. 1945; scene of conflicts in Chinese Civil War 1946–48.
Chang·de *or W.-G.* **Ch'ang–te** \ˈchäŋ-ˈdə\. City, N Hunan prov., SE cen. China, on left bank of Yuan River near its mouth; pop. (1990c) 301,276; a former treaty port; center of China's "Rice Bowl." Has high mountains to the W. In WWII severely damaged in four unsuccessful attacks 1939–43 by Japanese in their campaigns against Changsha; finally fell 1944.
Chang Gorges *or* **Yangtze Gorges.** Series of gorges in the Chang (Yangtze) River, Hubei and Sichuan provs., cen. China bet. the cities of Chongqing (at 650 ft. or 198 m. above sea level) and Yichang (at 131 ft. or 40 m.), caused by the river forcing its passage through the Daba Shan. Most notable of the gorges are bet. Yichang and Fengjie.
Chang–kuang–tsai Ling. See ZHANGGUANGCAI LING.
Chang–ku Feng \ˈjäŋ-ˈgau̇-ˈfəŋ\ *or Russ.* **Go·ra Za·o·zer·na·ya** \ˈgər-ə-ˌzä-əz-ˈyȯr-nə-yə\. Hill on left bank of Tumen River near its mouth in disputed area on frontier of Russia, North Korea, and China; controls Russian Posyeta Bay to the NE; scene of fighting bet. Russians and Japanese July–Aug. 1938.
Ch'ang–pai Shan. See CHANGBAI SHAN.
Chang·sha *or W.-G.* **Ch'ang–sha** \ˈchäŋ-ˈshä\. City, ✻ of Hunan prov., SE cen. China, on right bank of the Xiang ab. 45 mi. (72 km.) S of Dongting Hu (lake); pop. (1990c) 1,113,212; machine tools, farm equipment, textiles, handicrafts; rice processing; university (1959). Formerly enclosed by wall built according to tradition ab. 202 B.C.; once famed as a literary and education center; made a treaty port 1904; successfully withstood a siege by Taiping rebels mid-19th cent. Site of statesman Mao Tse-tung's education and conversion to Communism; scene of major battles in Sino-Japanese War (1937–45); briefly occupied by Japanese (1941 and 1944–45). Han dynasty tomb and preserved corpse discovered 1972.
Chang·shu *or W.-G.* **Ch'ang–shu** \ˈchäŋ-ˈshü\. Town, Jiangsu prov., China, 119 mi. (192 km.) ESE of Nanjing; pop. (1990c) 181,805.
Ch'ang–te. See CHANGDE.
Chang·ting *or W.-G.* **Ch'ang–t'ing** \ˈchäŋ-ˈtiŋ\ *or* **Ting·zhou** *or W.-G.* **Ting·chow** *or* **Ting–chou** \ˈtiŋ-ˈjō\. City, SW Fujian prov., China, on upper Han Shui near Jiangxi border 165 mi. (266 km.) N of Shantou.
Chang–tzu \ˈchäŋ-ˈdzə\. North peak of Mt. Everest group, Himalayas, S Tibet, China, on Nepal border; 24,780 ft. (7553 m.).
Chan·gui·no·la \ˌchäŋ-gē-ˈnō-lä\. Town, NW Panama; pop. (1990p) 33,632.
Ch'ang–won \ˈchäŋ-ˈwän\. City, ✻ of South Kyŏngsang prov., South Korea; pop. (1985c) 173,508.
Chang·yang *or W.-G.* **Ch'ang–yang** \ˈchäŋ-ˈyäŋ\. Town, S Hubei prov., E cen. China, on tributary of the Chang 12 mi. (19 km.) S of Yichang.
Chang·zhi *or W.-G.* **Ch'ang–chih** \ˈchäŋ-ˈjē\; *formerly* **Lu–an** \ˈlü-ˈän\. Town, S Shanxi prov., E China, ab. 100 mi. (160 km.) NW of Kaifeng; pop. (1990c) 317,144; communications center and Chinese military base in Sino-Japanese War 1937–45.
Chang·zhou *or W.-G.* **Ch'ang–chou** \ˈchäŋ-ˈjō\; *formerly* **Wu·tsin** \ˈwü-ˈtsin\. City, S Jiangsu prov., E China, ab. 70 mi. (113 km.) ESE of Nanjing on the Grand Canal; pop. (1990c) 531,470; known in ancient times, received name of Changzhou under Sui dynasty.
Chan·has·sen \chan-ˈhas-ᵊn\. City, Carver and Hennepin cos., SE cen. Minnesota, 7 mi. (11 km.) W of Minneapolis; pop. (1990c) 11,732.
Chania. See CANEA.
Chankiri. See ÇANKIRI.
Channel, The. See ENGLISH CHANNEL.
Channel Country. Pastoral region, E cen. Australia, primarily in SW Queensland; crossed by many stream channels.
Channel Islands. **1.** Group of islands, United Kingdom, in the English Channel 10 to 30 mi. (16 to 48 km.) off W coast of Manche dept., France; 75 sq. mi. (194 sq. km.); pop. (1986c) 135,694; comprise Jersey, Guernsey, Alderney, Sark, and several islets. Domestically independent, not controlled by British government. Originated noted breeds of cattle, esp. Jersey and Guernsey breeds. Fertile islands, exporting fruit, vegetables, and flowers; tourism. Inhabitants are of part Norman descent, part English.
History: Structures such as cromlechs and menhirs indicate occupation by prehistoric people; became part of Normandy in 10th cent.; united to British crown at time of Norman Conquest 1066; remained under British control in 1204 when the French conquered Normandy; British claims recognized in Treaty of Bretigny 1360; occupied by Germans June 1940–May 1945.
2. *or* **Santa Barbara Islands** \ˌsan-tə-ˈbär-bə-rə\. Chain of islands, California, off S coast, separated from mainland by Santa Barbara and San Pedro channels, in Santa Barbara, Ventura, and Los Angeles cos.; includes islands of San Miguel, Santa Rosa, Santa Cruz, Anacapa, Santa Barbara, San Nicolas, Santa Catalina, and San Clemente.
Channel Islands National Park. See UNITED STATES, *National Parks.*
Channel–Port aux Basques \ˈcha-nəl-ˌpōr-tō-ˈbask\. Town, SW Newfoundland, Canada; pop. (1991c) 5644.
Channel Tunnel. Rail tunnel under English Channel from Folkstone, England to Sangatte (near Calais), France; opened 1994.
Chan·ning \ˈcha-niŋ\. City, ⊗ of Hartley co., NW Texas; pop. (1990c) 277.
Chantabun. See CHANTHABURI.
Chan·ta·da \chän-ˈtä-t͟hä\. Commune, Lugo prov., NW Spain, 32 mi. (52 km.) SSW of the commune of Lugo; pop. (1991c) 10,184.
Chan·tha·bu·ri \chän-ˌtä-bu̇-ˈrē\ *also* **Chan·ta·bun** \chän-tä-ˈbün\ *or* **Chan·ta·bu·ri** \chän-ˌtä-bu̇-ˈrē\. Commercial town, S Thailand, near NE coast of Gulf of Siam 140 mi. (225 km.) SE of Bangkok; pop. (1991e) 39,898; has good port.
Chan·til·ly \shan-ˈti-lē\. Unincorporated settlement, Fairfax co., Virginia, 20 mi. (32 km.) W of Washington, D.C.; pop. (1990c) 29,337; battle Sept. 1862 in which Gen. Thomas ("Stonewall") Jackson attempted unsuccessfully to prevent withdrawal of Gen. John Pope's Union troops after 2d battle of Bull Run; Dulles International Airport.

\ə\ abut \ᵊ\ kitten, Fr table \ər\ further \a\ ash \ā\ ace \ä\ cot, cart \à\ Fr bac \au̇\ out \b\ Span Avila \ch\ chin \e\ bet \ē\ easy \g\ go \i\ hit \ī\ ice \j\ job \k\ Ger ich, Buch \ⁿ\ Fr vin \ŋ\ sing \ō\ go \ȯ\ all \ȯ\ law \œ\ Fr bœuf \œ̄\ Fr feu \ȯi\ boy \th\ thin \t͟h\ this \ü\ loot \u̇\ foot \ue\ Ger füllen \ue̅\ Fr rue \y\ yet \ʸ\ Fr digne \ˈdēnʸ\, nuit \ˈnwʸē\ \yü\ few \yu̇\ fury \zh\ vision

Chantilly \ˌshä^{n}-tē-ˈyē\. Commune, Oise dept., N France; pop. (1990c) 11,525; château and park; gave its name to Chantilly lace, formerly made there.

Chan·trey Inlet \ˈchan-trē\. Inlet on N coast of mainland part of Nunavut, Canada.

Cha·nute \shə-ˈnüt\. City, Neosho co., SE Kansas, 44 mi. (71 km.) WSW of Fort Scott; pop. (1990c) 9488; Neosho County Community Coll. (1936); near oil, gas, and clay deposits.

Cha·ny, Lake \-ˈchän-ē\. Lake, SW Novosibirsk Oblast, SW Russia in Asia, E of Omsk; ab. 1000 sq. mi. (2590 sq. km.).

Chan·za \ˈchän-thä\ *or Port.* **Chan·ça** \ˈchan-sə\. River in SW Spain; flows SSW, forming a section of the Spain-Portugal boundary, and empties into Guadiana River ab. 20 mi. (32 km.) from its mouth.

Chao·'an \ˈchau̇-ˈän\ *or locally* **Chao·zhou** \ˈchau̇-ˈjō\ *or W.-G.* **Ch'ao–an** \ˈchau̇-ˈän\ *or* **Ch'–ao–chou** *or* **Chao·chow** \ˈchau̇-ˈjō\. City, E Guangdong prov., SE China, on Han River ab. 20 mi. (32 km.) above Shantou; made treaty port 1858 but river too shallow for large vessels; large river trade by junk. Scene of banishment of the great poet, philosopher, and opponent of Buddhism, Han Yü (768–824 A.D.), under the T'ang dynasty.

Chao–ch'ing. See ZHAOQING.

Chao Hu *or W.-G.* **Ch'ao–Hu** \ˈchau̇-ˈhü\; *Eng.* **Chao Lake.** Lake (*hu*), cen. Anhui, E China, S of Hefei; outlet on SE to the Chang River.

Cha·o·nia \kā-ˈō-nē-ə\. District of ancient Epirus, NW Greece, extending along the coast N of the Kalamas River.

Chao Phra·ya \chau̇-ˈprī-ə\; *often in English sources* **Me Nam** *or* **Me·nam** \mā-ˈnäm\. River, Thailand; flows S from highlands on N border to head of Gulf of Thailand near Bangkok; 227 mi. (365 km.) long; forms a highly productive agricultural valley; strictly, name applies only to lower course, 160 mi. (257 km.), from junction of Nan and Ping rivers at 15°42′N; lower course has many branches, the W branch being the Tha Chin (*q.v.*). See NAN and PING.

Chao–t'ung. See ZHAOTONG.

Cha·pa·la, Lake \chä-ˈpä-lä\. Lake, Jalisco state, Mexico; 50 mi. (81 km.) long; 651 sq. mi. (1686 sq. km.); largest lake in Mexico; traversed by the Río Santiago (see SANTIAGO, RÍO).

Cha·pa·ré \ˌchä-pä-ˈrā\. River, cen. Bolivia, flows N into the upper Mamoré River; ab. 180 mi. (290 km.) long.

Cha·pa·yevsk \chə-ˈpä-yefsk\. Town, S Samara Oblast, W Russia in Europe, on Samara-Syzran' railroad line 30 mi. (48 km.) W of the city of Samara; pop. (1991e) 96,000.

Chap·el Hill \ˈcha-pəl\. Town, Durham and Orange cos., N North Carolina, 11 mi. (18 km.) WSW of the city of Durham; pop. (1990c) 38,719; residential; Univ. of North Carolina at Chapel Hill (1789).

Chap·man, Mount \ˈchap-mən\. Peak in Great Smoky Mts., Sevier co., E Tennessee; 6425 ft. (1958 m.).

Chapman Peak. Mountain in Glacier National Park near N boundary, NW Montana; 9375 ft. (2858 m.).

Chap·pa·quid·dick Island \ˌcha-pə-ˈkwi-dik\. Island in Nantucket Sound, Massachusetts, off SE coast of Martha's Vineyard.

Chap·pell \ˈcha-pəl\. Village, ⊗ of Deuel co., W Nebraska; pop. (1990c) 979.

Cha·pra \ˈchə-prə\. Commercial town, W Bihar, NE India, on Ganges River just below junction with the Ghāghara; pop. (incl. adjoining communities, 1991p) 136,824.

Cha·pul·te·pec \chä-ˈpül-tā-ˌpek\. Fortified rocky hill, Mexico, 3 mi. (5 km.) SW of Mexico City, first developed by Aztec rulers; captured by American assault Sept. 1847 during the Mexican War; scene of meeting of Inter-American Conference 1945 that drafted Act of Chapultepec pledging use of combined force in preserving American boundaries. Site of 18th cent. castle, now museum, orig. built as summer home by Spanish viceroys and rebuilt by Emperor Maximillian; served as presidential residence until 1940; area now part of Mexico City's principal park.

Cha·ram·bi·rá Point \chä-ˌräm-bē-ˈrä\. Cape on Pacific coast of Colombia, 4°N.

Cha·ran–Ka·noa \ˈchär-än-kä-ˈnō-ä\. Village on SW coast of Saipan, Mariana Is.; beachheads 2 mi. (3.2 km.) S and 2 mi. (3.2 km.) N secured by U.S. marines June 15, 1944; base for advance N to Garapan and S to Aslito Airfield.

Charbar. See CHĀH BAHĀR.

Char·cas \ˈchär-käs\ *or* **Las Charcas** \läs-\. Early name for the Spanish audiencia of Upper Peru (*q.v.*).

Char·co Azul Bay \ˈchär-kō-ä-ˈzül\. Inlet of Gulf of Chiriquí on the N, in extreme SW Panama.

Char·cot Island \ˌshär-ˈkō\. Island in Palmer Archipelago, Antarctica, 69°45′S, 75°15′W.

Chard \ˈchärd\. Town, Somerset, SW England, N of Lyme Regis; pop. (1981p) 9384; market center; lace.

Char·don \ˈshärd-^{ə}n\. Village, ⊗ of Geauga co., NE Ohio, 24 mi. (39 km.) ENE of Cleveland; pop. (1990c) 4446.

Char·dzhou \chär-ˈjō\ **1.** Administrative subdivision of Turkmenistan; 36,178 sq. mi. (93,701 sq. km.); pop. (1991e) 774,700.

2. *or* **Chär·jew** \ˈchär-ˈjü\ *also* **Char·jui** \chär-ˈjü-ē\; *1926–27 called* **Len·insk** \ˈle-ˌninsk, ˈl^{y}ä-n^{y}insk\. Town, its ✱, on left bank of Amu Dar'ya ab. 60 mi. (97 km.) SW of Bukhara; pop. (1991e) 166,400; cotton processing; superphosphate; important port.

Cha·rente \shȧ-ˈrä^{n}t\. **1.** Navigable river, W France; rises in Haute-Vienne dept., flows W into the Bay of Biscay opp. Oléron I.; 224 mi. (360 km.) long.

2. Department of W France. See table at FRANCE.

Charente–Ma·ri·time \ˌmȧ-rē-ˈtēm\; *formerly* **Charente–In·fé·rieure** \e^{n}-fer-ˈyœr\. Department of W France. See table at FRANCE.

Cha·ren·ton–le–Pont \ˌshȧ-rä^{n}-ˈtō^{n}-lə-ˈpō^{n}\. Commune, Val-de-Marne dept., N France, SE suburb of Paris, at confluence of Marne and Seine rivers. Includes **Con·flans** \kō^{n}-ˈflä^{n}\ *or* **Con·flans–l'Ar·che·vêque** \-ˌlȧr-shā-ˈvek\ where treaty bet. Louis XI and the League of Public Weal was signed 1465.

Char·gog·ga·gogg·man·chaug·gaug·ga·gogg·chau·bu·na·gun·ga·maugg, Lake \chär-ˌgȯ-gə-ˌgȯg-man-ˌchȯ-ˌgȯ-gə-ˌgȯg-chȯ-ˌbə-nə-ˈgəŋ-gə-ˌmȯg\ *or* **Lake Chau·bu·na·gun·ga·maug** \chȯ-ˌbə-nə-ˈgəŋ-gə-ˌmȯg\ *or* **Lake Web·ster** \ˈweb-stər\ *or* **Lake Char·gog·ga·gogg·man·chaug·ga·gogg·chau·bu·na·gun·ga·maugg** \chär-ˌgȯ-gə-ˌgȯg-man-ˌchȯ-gə-ˌgȯg-chȯ-ˌbə-nə-ˈgəŋ-gə-ˌmȯg\. Lake, in S Worcester co., cen. Massachusetts, near Webster.

Cha·ri *or* **Sha·ri** \ˈshä-rē\. River, flowing from Central African Rep. NW into Lake Chad, Chad; ab. 590 mi. (949 km.) long; many tributaries in N Central African Rep. N'Djamena is at head of delta.

Chā·ri·kār \ˈchär-i-ˌkär\. Town, E Afghanistan; pop. (1988e) 26,500; alt. 5300 ft. (1615 m.).

Char·ing Cross \ˌchar-iŋ-ˈkrȯs\. District in London, England, S of Trafalgar Square; formerly site of an Eleanor Cross, destroyed 1647, now has a modern memorial cross, erected mid-19th cent.

Char·i·ton \ˈshar-ət-^{ə}n\. **1.** River, S Iowa and N cen. Missouri; rises in Clarke co., S Iowa, flows E then S across Missouri border and into the Missouri River; 280 mi. (451 km.) long.

2. County in N cen. Missouri. See table at MISSOURI.

3. City, ⊗ of Lucas co., S Iowa, 42 mi. (68 km.) SSE of Des Moines; pop. (1990c) 4616.

Chärjew *also* **Charjui.** See CHARDZHOU 2.

Char·kha·ri \chər-ˈkär-ē\. Former Indian state, NE Central India Agency, India, ab. 100 mi. (160 km.) W of Allahabad; 785 sq. mi. (2033 sq. km.); now part of Uttar Pradesh.

Charkhlik. See RUOQIANG.

Char·le·magne \ˈshär-lə-ˌmān\. Village, L'Assomption co., S Quebec, Canada, 9 mi. (15 km.) N of Montreal; pop. (1991c) 5598.

Charle·mont \ˈchärl-ˌmänt\. Village, Armagh dist., S Northern Ireland, on the Blackwater 6 mi. (10 km.) N of the town of Armagh; terminus of Ulster Canal.

Char·le·roi \ˌshär-lə-ˌrȯi\. Borough, Washington co., SW Pennsylvania, on Monongahela River 22 mi. (35 km.) S of Pittsburgh; pop. (1990c) 5014; coal deposits.

Char·le·roi \shär-lə-ˈrȯi, -ˈrwä\. Commune, Hainaut prov., SW Belgium; pop. (1992e) 206,800; industrial center in a coal- and iron-mining region; steel, glass; town hall (1936). Formerly a medieval village, fortress decreed 1666 and named for Charles II of Spain; strategically important in the 17th–19th cents. and held variously by France, Spain, Austria, and Holland; briefly French Emperor Napoléon's headquarters 1815; fortress dismantled late 19th cent.; captured by Germans after fierce fighting Aug. 1914.

Charles \ˈchärlz\. **1.** River, E Massachusetts; flows into Boston Bay; its estuary separates Boston from Cambridge; 47 mi. (76 km.) long; navigable for 7 mi. (11 km.).
2. County in S Maryland. See table at MARYLAND.

Charles, Cape. Cape at S tip of Northampton co., Virginia, N of entrance to Chesapeake Bay.

Charles·bourg \shärl-ˈbür\. City, Quebec co., S Quebec, Canada, a suburb, 3 mi. (5 km.) N of Quebec City; pop. (1991c) 70,788.

Charles City. **1.** County in E Virginia. See table at VIRGINIA.
2. City, ⊗ of Floyd co., N Iowa, 30 mi. (48 km.) ESE of Mason City; pop. (1990c) 7878.
3. Village, ⊗ of Charles City co., E Virginia; birthplaces nearby of William Henry Harrison (1773) and John Tyler (1790), 9th and 10th presidents of the U.S.

Charles Island. See SANTA MARÍA 3.

Charles Mix \ˈmiks\. County in S South Dakota. See table at SOUTH DAKOTA.

Charles Mound. Elevation, Jo Daviess co., NW Illinois; 1235 ft. (376 m.); highest point in the state.

Charles·ton \ˈchärl-stən\. **1.** Coastal county in SE South Carolina. See table at SOUTH CAROLINA.
2. City, a ⊗ of Franklin co., NW Arkansas; pop. (1990c) 2128.
3. City, ⊗ of Coles co., E cen. Illinois, 50 mi. (81 km.) ESE of Decatur; pop. (1990c) 20,398; Eastern Illinois Univ. (1895).
4. City, a ⊗ of Tallahatchie co., NW Mississippi, 31 mi. (50 km.) ESE of Clarksdale; pop. (1990c) 2328.
5. City, ⊗ of Mississippi co., SE Missouri, 28 mi. (45 km.) SSE of Cape Girardeau; pop. (1990c) 5085.
6. Seaport city, ⊗ of Charleston co., SE South Carolina; on Atlantic Ocean; pop. (1990c) 80,414; paper and pulp mills, oil refineries, tourism; ships coal, phosphates, petroleum products, cotton, cotton goods, tobacco, fertilizer; formerly protected by Forts Sumter and Moultrie; Coll. of Charleston (1770), Medical Univ. of South Carolina (1824), The Citadel (1842), Charleston Southern Univ. (1960), Trident Technical Coll. (1964).

History: Founded 1670 on Albemarle Point on W bank of Ashley River by an English colony under William Sayle and Joseph West; removed across Ashley River to present location 1680; became center of wealth and culture in the South; first American fire-insurance company estab. here early 18th cent.; successfully opposed attacks by British fleet 1776 and 1779, but was captured May 1780 by Sir Henry Clinton, and held by British until Dec. 1782; became center of movement for nullification 1832 and of other movements to resist federal authority; site of the convention which proclaimed secession of South Carolina from the Union Dec. 1860; scene of outbreak of hostilities in the Civil War 1861 (see FORT SUMTER); evacuated by Confederate forces Feb. 1865 after two years of siege; seriously damaged by earthquake Aug. 31, 1886 and hurricane Sept. 1989.
7. City, ✻ of West Virginia and ⊗ of Kanawha co., W cen. West Virginia, at confluence of Elk and Kanawha rivers; pop. (1990c) 57,287; distribution point for region producing coal, oil and gas, salt, hardwood timber; manufactures chemicals, glass, foundry products. Univ. of Charleston (1888). Settled around Fort Lee shortly after the Revolution; home, for a time, of pioneer Daniel Boone; state capitol designed by Cass Gilbert; incorp. 1794, as city 1870; ✻ of West Virginia 1870–75, and from 1885.

Charleston Peak. Mountain, W Clark co., SE Nevada; 11,919 ft. (3633 m.); highest in Spring Mts.

Charles·town \ˈchärlz-ˌtau̇n\. **1.** City, Clark co., S Indiana, NE of Jeffersonville; pop. (1990c) 5889.
2. Former city, Middlesex co., Massachusetts, since 1874 part of Boston; on Boston Harbor bet. mouths of Charles and Mystic rivers; former U.S. Navy Yard now part of Boston National Historical Park. Founded ab. 1628, oldest part of Boston; almost destroyed June 17, 1775 in battle of Bunker Hill (*q.v.*). Birthplace of telegraph inventor Samuel Morse 1791.
3. Town, Sullivan co., SW New Hampshire, on Connecticut River 10 mi. (16 km.) S of Claremont; pop. (1990c) 4630; military base for Colonial troops during last years of French and Indian War; rendezvous for Gen. John Stark and New Hampshire troops en route to battle of Bennington 1777 during Revolution.
4. Town and summer resort, Washington co., S Rhode Island, on inlet of Block Island Sound SW of Newport; pop. (1990c) 6478; taken from Westerly and incorp. 1738. Site of Indian burial ground and of Coronation Rock, where until 1770 Narraganset Indians crowned their chieftains.
5. Chief town on Nevis I., St. Kitts-Nevis, West Indies; pop. (1985e) 1700.

Charles Town. City, ⊗ of Jefferson co., NE West Virginia, 14 mi. (23 km.) S of Martinsburg; pop. (1990c) 3122; scene of trial and execution of abolitionist John Brown 1859.

Char·le·ville \ˈchär-lə-ˌvil, ˈchärl-ˌvil\. Town, S Queensland, Australia, on Warrego River 423 mi. (681 km.). WNW of Brisbane; pop. (1991c) 3513.

Charleville–Mé·zières \ˌshär-lə-ˈvēl-mā-ˈzher\. Commune, ✻ of Ardennes dept., NE France, on Meuse River; pop. (1990c) 59,439; Mézières fortified in Middle Ages; Charleville founded 1606; twin towns merged 1966. Birthplace of poet Arthur Rimbaud 1854. Severely damaged in WWI and WWII.

Char·le·voix \ˈshär-lə-ˌvȯi\. **1.** County in NW Michigan. See table at MICHIGAN.
2. City, its ⊗, on Lake Michigan 41 mi. (66 km.) NNE of Traverse City; pop. (1990c) 3116; resort; fishing.
3. County, S Quebec, Canada. See table at QUEBEC.

Charlevoix–Est \ˌshȧr-lə-ˈvwä-ˈest\ *or* **East Charlevoix** \ˈshär-lə-ˌvȯi\. County, S Quebec, Canada. See table at QUEBEC.

Char·lotte \ˈshär-lət\. **1.** Name of counties in two states of the U.S. See tables at FLORIDA and VIRGINIA.
2. City, ⊗ of Eaton co., S Michigan, SW of Lansing; pop. (1990c) 8083.
3. City, ⊗ of Mecklenburg co., S North Carolina, in Piedmont 15 mi. (24 km.) N of South Carolina border; pop. (1990c) 395,934; largest city in the state; important distribution point; textiles, machinery, food products, metal goods, chemicals. Johnson C. Smith Univ. (1867), Queens Coll. (1857), Univ. of North Carolina at Charlotte (1946), Central Piedmont Community Coll. (1963). Settled c. 1748, incorp. 1768, made ⊗ 1774; during Revolution occupied by British under Gen. Charles Cornwallis 1780; center of gold rush at end of 18th cent.; branch of U.S. Mint estab. c. 1836 (closed 1913); last meeting place of Confederate cabinet 1865. James Knox Polk, 11th president of the U.S., born nearby 1795.
4. Town, ⊗ of Dickson co., NW cen. Tennessee; pop. (1990c) 854.
5. Town, Chittenden co., Vermont, S of Burlington; pop. (1990c) 3148.
6. County, SW New Brunswick, Canada. See table at NEW BRUNSWICK.

Charlotte Ama·lie \ə-ˈmäl-yə, ˈa-mə-lē\; *formerly* **St. Thom·as** \ˈtä-məs\. Seaport, ✻ of St. Thomas I. and of the Virgin Is. of the U.S., West Indies; at head of St. Thomas Harbor on S shore of St. Thomas I.; pop. (1990c) 12,331; tourism.

Charlotte Courthouse. Town, ⊗ of Charlotte co., S Virginia; pop. (1990c) 531.

Charlotte Harbor. Inlet of Gulf of Mexico, in Charlotte and Lee cos., on W coast of SW Florida; receives Peace River in NE; Pine I. extends S of it.

Char·lot·ten·burg \shär-ˈlät-^{ə}n-ˌbu̇rk\. **1.** A former city of Germany, since 1920 a residential section of W Berlin; site of 17th cent. palace (damaged in WWII, now restored) of Queen Sophia Charlotte, wife of Frederick I of Prussia.
2. Coastal town, on Cottica River, NE Suriname.

Char·lottes·ville \ˈshär-ləts-ˌvil, -vəl\. City, ⊗ of Albemarle co., cen. Virginia, but politically independent, 70 mi. (113 km.) WNW of Richmond; 6 sq. mi. (16 sq. km.); pop. (1990c) 40,341; Univ. of Virginia (1819) founded and orig. designed by Thomas Jefferson, 3d president of the U.S., Piedmont Virginia Community Coll. (1972). Monticello (home of Jefferson; now national memorial) and Ash Lawn (home of James Monroe, 5th president of the U.S.) nearby; settled in 1730s; chartered as city 1888.

Char·lotte·town \ˈshär-lət-ˌtau̇n\. City, ✻ of Prince Edward I., and ⊗ of Queens co., Canada, in cen. part of island, on Hillsborough Bay; pop. (1991c) 15,396; commercial center of the province; produces potatoes, dairy products; fishing; tourism; Univ. of Prince Edward I. (1969); founded by French ab. 1720; became ✻ 1765.

Charlotte Town. See GOUYAVE.

Charl·ton \ˈchärl-tən\. **1.** County in SE Georgia. See table at GEORGIA.
2. Town, Worcester co., cen. Massachusetts, 12 mi. (19 km.) SW of the city of Worcester; pop. (1990c) 9576.

Charl·ton Kings \ˌchärl-tən-ˈkiŋz\. Town, Gloucestershire, SW cen. England; pop. (1981p) 10,785.

Char·ny \shär-ˈnē\. Town, S Quebec, Canada, on Chaudière River 8 mi. (13 km.) SSW of Quebec City; pop. (1991c) 10,239.

Charran. See HARAN.

Char·ters Tow·ers \ˈchär-tərz-ˈtau̇-ərz\. Town, E Queensland, Australia, near Burdekin River 75 mi. (121 km.) SW of Townsville; pop. (1991c) 9016; in gold-bearing region.

Char·tres \ˈshärt, ˈshärtr^{ə}\; *anc.* **Au·tri·cum** \ˈȯ-tri-kəm\ *also* **Civ·i·tas Car·nu·tum** \ˈsi-və-ˌtas-kär-ˈnü-təm, -ˈnyü-\. Commercial city, ✻ of Eure-et-Loir dept., N cen. France, on Eure River 48 mi. (77 km.) SW of Paris; pop. (1990c) 41,850; breweries, foundries; agricultural machinery, electronic equipment; 13th cent. Gothic cathedral, noted particularly for its two spires. Was ✻ and center of Druid worship for Celtic tribe, the Carnutes; burned by Normans 858; held by the counts of Blois and Champagne in Middle Ages; Second Crusade preached here by St. Bernard 1146; sold to France 1286; taken by English 1417; recovered 1432; Henry IV crowned in cathedral here 1594; occupied by Germans 1870; city damaged in WWII; since rebuilt.

Char·treuse, La Grande \lä-ˌgrä^{n}-shär-ˈtrœ̄z\. Chief house, until 1903, of Carthusian order, near the village of **Saint–Pierre–de–Char·treuse** \se^{n}-ˌpyer-də-shär-ˈtrœ̄z\, Isère dept., SE France, ab. 13 mi. (21 km.) N of Grenoble; religious settlement founded by St. Bruno of Cologne 1084; present buildings date from 17th cent.; monks expelled 1903 as result of Associations Law (1901) dissolving monastic associations, restored c. 1941; noted for liqueur.

Cha·ryb·dis \kə-ˈrib-dis\. Legendary site of ancient mythological whirlpool near Massina, Sicily, Italy; notable in Greek mythology. See SCILLA.

Chase \ˈchās\. Name of counties in two states of the U.S. See tables at KANSAS and NEBRASKA.

Chas·ka \ˈchas-kə\. City, ⊗ of Carver co., SE cen. Minnesota, on Minnesota River 20 mi. (32 km.) SW of Minneapolis; pop. (1990c) 11,339.

Chatalja. See ÇATALCA.

Cha·teau·bri·ant \ˌshä-tō-brē-ˈä^{n}\. Commune, Loire-Atlantique dept., NW France, 40 mi. (64 km.) NNE of Nantes; castle.

Châ·teau·dun \ˌsha-tō-ˈdœ̄^{n}\. Commune, Eure-et-Loir dept., N cen. France, 28 mi. (45 km.) SSW of Chartres; dates from Gallo-Roman period; castle.

Cha·teau·gay \ˈsha-tə-gē, -ˌgā\ *or in Canada* **Châ·teau·guay** \ˌsha-tə-ˈgā\. River, U.S. and Canada; rises in N New York in Chateaugay Lakes on border bet. Clinton and Franklin cos. and flows N through Châteauguay co. in S Quebec to the St. Lawrence ab. 14 mi. (23 km.) above Montreal; ab. 60 mi. (97 km.) long. On its banks in Canada about 15 mi. (24 km.) from its mouth a battle in War of 1812 was fought Oct. 26, 1813 in which the American forces under Gen. Wade Hampton were repulsed by the British.

Chateaugay Lakes. Two lakes in NE New York, **Upper Chateaugay** in W Clinton co. and **Lower Chateaugay** in E Franklin co.; outlet, Chateaugay River flowing out of N end of Lower Chateaugay; resort.

Châ·teau·guay \ˈsha-tə-gē, -ˌgā; ˌsha-tə-ˈgā\. **1.** River, New York and Canada. See CHATEAUGAY.
2. Town, S Quebec, Canada, on St. Lawrence River 14 mi. (23 km.) SW of Montreal; pop. (1991c) 39,833; near mouth of Châteauguay River and opp. the Ottawa.

Châ·teau·neuf–de–Ran·don \ˌshä-tō-ˈnœ̄f-də-ˌre^{n}-ˈdō^{n}\. Village, Lozère dept., S France, NE of Mende; besieged 1380 by soldier Bertrand du Guesclin who died here.

Châ·teau Ri·cher \shä-ˌtō-rē-ˈshā\. Town, S Quebec, Canada, on N bank of St. Lawrence River 25 mi. (40 km.) NE of Quebec City; pop. (1991c) 3690.

Châ·teau·roux \ˌshä-tō-ˈrü\; *during Revolution called* **In·dre·ville** \ˌe^{n}-drə-ˈvēl\. Commercial commune, ✻ of Indre dept., cen. France, on Indre River 80 mi. (129 km.) S of Orléans; pop. (1990c) 35,691; 10th cent. castle.

Château–Thier·ry \shä-ˌtō-tye-ˈrē\. Commune, Aisne dept., N France, on right bank of Marne River 37 mi. (60 km.) SSW of Laon; pop. (1990c) 15,830; trades in wine; ruins of castle said to have been built by Frankish ruler Charles Martel 8th cent.; birthplace of writer Jean de La Fontaine 1621. Battles 1814; last German offensive of WWI halted here by French and American forces 1918; American military monument. See MARNE.

Châtelard, Le. See LE CHÂTELARD.

Châ·te·let \ˌshä-tə-ˈlā\. Commune, Hainaut prov., SW Belgium, on Sambre River; pop. (1991c) 36,538.

Châ·tel·le·rault *or in Eng. usage* **Châ·tel·he·rault** \ˌshä-tel-ˈrō\. Commune, Vienne dept., W cen. France, on Vienne River 21 mi. (34 km.) NNE of Poitiers; pop. (1990c) 35,691. Built around 10th cent. castle; ✻ of a 16th cent. duchy.

Cha·te·nay–Ma·la·bry \ˌshät-ˈnā-ˌmä-lä-ˈbrē\. Commune, Hauts-de-Seine dept., N France, 7 mi. (11 km.) SSW of Paris.

Chat·ham \ˈchat-^{ə}m\. **1.** Name of counties in two states of the U.S. See tables at GEORGIA and NORTH CAROLINA.
2. Village, Sangamon co., cen. Illinois, 10 mi. (16 km.) SSW of Springfield; pop. (1990c) 6074.
3. Town, Barnstable co., SE Massachusetts, on Atlantic Ocean 18 mi. (29 km.) E of the town of Barnstable; pop. (1990c) 1916; resort.
4. Residential borough, Morris co., N New Jersey, on Passaic River 6 mi. (10 km.) SE of Morristown; pop. (1990c) 8007.
5. Town, ⊗ of Pittsylvania co., S Virginia; pop. (1990c) 1354.
6. Seaport town, Northumberland co., E New Brunswick, Canada, on estuary of Miramichi River; pop. (1991c) 6544; good harbor; center for fishing and hunting; founded c. 1800.
7. City, ⊗ of Kent co., SE Ontario, Canada, on Thames River 16 mi. (26 km.) E of Lake St. Clair; pop. (1991c) 43,557; settled in 1830s; a northern terminus of the Underground Railroad for slaves fleeing U.S. before Civil War.
8. Town, Kent, SE England, on the Medway 30 mi. (48 km.) ESE of London; pop. (1991c) 43,557; one of the chief naval and military stations of Great Britain; first used for naval purposes by Henry VIII; Royal Dockyard until early 1980s, now an historic trust.

Chatham Island. **1.** Island, Galapagos Is. See SAN CRISTÓBAL 4.
2. Island, New Zealand. See CHATHAM ISLANDS.

Chatham Islands. Island group belonging to New Zealand, in S Pacific Ocean 536 mi. (862 km.) E of South I.; 44°S, 176°W; 372 sq. mi. (964 sq. km.); pop. (1990e) 770; comprise two islands: Chatham (347 sq. mi. or 899 sq. km.) and Pitt (25 sq. mi. or 65 sq. km.); was inhabited by the Moriori when first visited by Europeans in 1791.

Chatham Strait. Narrow passage bet. Admiralty and Kuiu islands on E and Baranof and Chichagof islands on W, SE Alaska.

Châ·til·lon \ˌshä-tē-ˈyōⁿ\. Commune, Hauts-de-Seine dept., N France, S suburb of Paris; site 1949 of France's first nuclear reactor.

Châtillon–sur–Seine \-sūr-ˈsen, -ˈsān\. Commune, Côte-d'Or dept., E France, 43 mi. (69 km.) NW of Dijon; 10th cent. church; ruined medieval castle of dukes of Burgundy; unsuccessful conference Feb.–Mar. 1814 bet. French Emperor Napoléon and the allies. In WWII junction point Sept. 1944 of two American armies, one from N France, one from S France.

Chat·om \ˈchat-ᵊm\. Town, ⊗ of Washington co., SW Alabama; pop. (1990c) 1094.

Châ·tou \shä-ˈtü\. Commune, Yvelines dept., N France, NNW suburb of Paris on Seine River; summer resort; 13th cent. church.

Chats·worth \ˈchats-ˌwərth\. **1.** City, ⊗ of Murray co., N Georgia; pop. (1990c) 2865.
2. Seat of the dukes of Devonshire, Derbyshire, N cen. England, ab. 20 mi. (32 km.) N of Derby; one of the most splendid residences in England, open to visitors.

Chat·ta·hoo·chee \ˌcha-tə-ˈhü-chē\. **1.** Navigable river, rising in Towns co., NE Georgia, and flowing SW to Alabama border at West Point, W cen. Georgia, then S forming a section of Alabama-Georgia boundary and a section of Georgia-Florida boundary; 436 mi. (702 km.) long; dammed, forming Lake Seminole; section below Lake Seminole known as Apalachicola (*q.v.*).
2. County in W Georgia. See table at GEORGIA.
3. *before 1941* **River Junction.** Town, Gadsden co., NW Florida, NW of Tallahassee; pop. (1990c) 4382.

Chat·ta·noo·ga \ˌcha-tə-ˈnü-gə, ˌchat-ᵊn-ˈü-\. City, and port of entry, ⊗ of Hamilton co., SE Tennessee, on Tennessee River just N of Georgia border; pop. (1990c) 152,466; in scenic region, with Missionary Ridge to the E and Lookout Mt. to the SW; manufactures steel, farm implements, textiles, chemicals, nuclear reactors; railroad center; main headquarters of Tennessee Valley Authority (TVA) since 1930s; iron and coal deposits nearby; tourism; Univ. of Tennessee at Chattanooga (1886), Tennessee Temple Univ. (1946), Chattanooga State Technical Community Coll. (1963). Chickamauga and Chattanooga National Military Park nearby (see UNITED STATES, *National Historical Parks*).
History: First permanent nonnative settlement replaced Cherokee trading center c. 1835; became salt-trading center; chartered 1839, as city 1851; developed river trade (in commodities such as cotton); grew with arrival of railroads 1840s and 1850s; served as Union base during Civil War battle of Chickamauga Sept. 19–20, 1863 and battle of Chattanooga Nov. 23–25, 1863 (battle of Lookout Mt., called "Battle above the Clouds," and battle of Missionary Ridge).

Chat·too·ga \chə-ˈtü-gə\. **1.** River, Georgia; the upper course of the Tugaloo; setting of the film *Deliverance* (1972).
2. County in NW Georgia. See table at GEORGIA.

Cha·tu·ge Dam \chə-ˈtü-gə\. See table at TENNESSEE VALLEY AUTHORITY.

Chaubunagungamaug, Lake. See CHARGOGGAGOGGMANCHAUGGAUGGAGOGGCHAUBUNAGUNGAMAUGG, LAKE.

Chau·dière \shō-ˈdyer\. River, S Quebec, Canada; rises in Lake Megantic and flows N to the St. Lawrence just above Quebec City; ab. 120 mi. (193 km.) long.

Chaudière Falls. Falls in Ottawa River at Ottawa city, Ontario, Canada; river narrows to 200 ft. (61 m.), descends 50 ft. (15 m.); site of extensive waterpower development.

Chauk \ˈchau̇k\. Town, Magwe div., Myanmar, on Irrawaddy River ab. 60 mi. (97 km.) N of the town of Magwe.

Chau·kan Pass \ˈchau̇-ˌkän\. Pass over mountains, on NW boundary of Myanmar, NE of Patkai Range; alt. 7979 ft. (2432 m.).

Chaulnes \ˈshōn\. Commune, Somme dept., N France, 11 mi. (18 km.) SW of Péronne; scene of much fighting in WWI.

Chau·mont \shō-ˈmōⁿ\; *formerly* **Chaumont–en–Bas·si·gny** \-äⁿ-ˌbä-sē-ˈnyē\. Commune, ✻ of Haute-Marne dept., NE France, at confluence of Marne and Suize rivers 140 mi. (225 km.) ESE of Paris; pop. (1990c) 28,900; iron ore deposits nearby; 13th–16th cent. church. Treaty 1814 bet. Great Britain, Russia, Austria, and Prussia renewing and strengthening alliance against French Emperor Napoléon; headquarters of American Expeditionary Force under Gen. John Pershing in WWI. In WWII taken by Germans 1940; retaken by American armies 1944.

Cha·un Bay \ˌchə-ˈün\. Inlet of the Arctic Ocean, NW Chukchi Autonomous Okrug, NE Russia in Asia, 69°N, 170°E.

Chau·ny \shō-ˈnē\. Commune, Aisne dept., N France, on Oise River S of St.-Quentin; destroyed in WWI; subsequently rebuilt.

Chau·phu \ˈchau̇-ˈpu̇\. Town, S Vietnam, on Cambodian border 105 mi. (169 km.) W of Ho Chi Minh City.

Chau·tau·qua \shə-ˈtȯ-kwə\. **1.** Name of counties in two states of the U.S. See tables at KANSAS and NEW YORK.
2. Town, Chautauqua co., SW corner of New York, on Chautauqua Lake; pop. (1990c) 4554; Chautauqua system of popular education inaugurated 1874.

Chautauqua Lake. Lake, Chautauqua co., SW corner of New York; ab. 18 mi. (29 km.) long and from 1 to 2.5 mi. (1.6 to 4 km.) wide; outlet from SE end flows into Allegheny River.

Chaux–de–Fonds, La. See LA CHAUX-DE-FONDS.

Chav·es \ˈcha-vis, ˈsha-\. County in SE New Mexico. See table at NEW MEXICO.

Cha·ves \ˈshä-vēsh\; *anc.* **Aq·uae Fla·vi·ae** \ˈa-kwē-ˈflā-vē-ē, ˈä-\. Commune, Vila Real dist., N Portugal, near Spanish border 22 mi. (35 km.) NNE of the commune of Vila Real; pop. (1987e) 45,800; thermal salt baths and springs; medieval churches; remains of Roman bridge; castle of dukes of Bragança; manufactures linens and silks.

Cha·ville \shä-ˈvēl\. Commune, Hauts-de-Seine dept., N France, SW suburb of Paris.

Cha·vín de Huán·tar \chä-ˈvēn-thā-ˈwän-tär\. Site, W cen. Peru, of temple ruins of a pre-Columbian culture.

Chaxerngsao. See CHACHOENGSAO.

Cha·zy \shā-ˈzē\. Village, Clinton co., NE New York, near Lake Champlain ab. 13 mi. (21 km.) N of Plattsburg; pop. (1990c) 3890; nearby are limestone formations of geological interest.

Chazy Lake. Lake, Clinton co., NE corner of New York, source of Great Chazy River; ab. 4 mi. (6 km.) long.

Chea·dle and Gat·ley \ˈchēd-ᵊl … ˈgat-lē\. Town, Cheshire, NW England, S of Manchester; pop. (1981p) 58,683; bricks, pharmaceuticals.

Chea·ha \ˈchē-ˌhȯ\. Mountain, Cleburne co., E Alabama; 2407 ft. (734 m.); highest point in state.

Cheat \ˈchēt\. River, N West Virginia; formed by confluence of forks in S Tucker co., flows N across Pennsylvania border and into Monongahela River in SW Fayette co., SW Pa.; ab. 150 mi. (240 km.) long; E of Morgantown are lake, dam, and gorge; hydroelectric power development.

Cheat·ham \ˈchēt-ᵊm\. County in NW cen. Tennessee. See table at TENNESSEE.

Cheat Mountain \ˈchēt\. Mountain, Randolph co., NE cen. West Virginia; 3478 ft. (1060 m.).

Cheb \ˈkep, ˈhep\ *or Ger.* **Eger** \ˈā-gər\. City, W Czech Republic, in the valley of the Ohře ab. 50 mi. (80 km.) NW of Plzeň; pop. (1991p) 31,847; scene of assassination of Austrian Gen. Albrecht von Wallenstein 1634.

Che·beague \shə-ˈbēg\. Island, largest in Casco Bay, Cumberland co., off coast of SW Maine.

Che·bo·ksa·ry \ˌche-bäk-ˈsär-ē\. Town, ✻ of Chuvash Rep., E cen. Russia in Europe, on the Volga 80 mi. (129 km.) W of Kazan; pop. (1992e) 442,000; commercial and cultural center of the republic; textiles; hydroelectric power station; university (1967).

Che·boy·gan \shi-ˈbȯi-gən\. **1.** River, N Michigan; flows N into Lake Huron at Cheboygan; ab. 40 mi. (64 km.) long.
2. County in N Michigan. See table at MICHIGAN.

3. City, its ⊗, on Lake Huron at mouth of the Cheboygan River; pop. (1990c) 4999; summer resort; formerly a lumbering center.

Chech, Erg. See ERG, AL-.

Che·cheno–In·gush Autonomous Soviet Socialist Republic \chi-ˈche-nō-in-ˈgüsh\. Former autonomous republic, a subdivision of the Russian S.F.S.R., U.S.S.R., on N slopes of Caucasus Mts.; 7452 sq. mi. (19,301 sq. km.); ✱ Grozny; formed 1936 following the consolidation of the Chechen and Ingush autonomous areas; dissolved during WWII for collaboration with Germans; reconstituted 1957; split into separate Chechen and Ingush republics within Russia 1992.

Chech·nya *or* **Chech·e·nya** *or* **Chech·e·nia** \chech-ˈnyä, ˈchech-nyə\ *or* **Che·chen Republic** \chi-ˈchen\ *or less correctly transliterated* **Chech·e·ni·ya.** Subdivision of S Russia in Europe; formerly part of Checheno-Ingush A.S.S.R., U.S.S.R.; became republic within Russia 1992; subsequently became member of Russian Federation; demand of independence 1992 and subsequent resistance to Russian authority lead to invasion by Russian troops Jan. 1995.

Che·co·tah \chi-ˈkō-tə\. City, McIntosh co., E Oklahoma, 22 mi. (35 km.) SSW of Muskogee; pop. (1990c) 3290.

Ched·a·buc·to Bay \ˌshe-də-ˈbək-tō\. Inlet of Atlantic Ocean, NE tip of the mainland of Nova Scotia, Canada, SE of Strait of Canso.

Ched·dar \ˈche-dər\. Village, Somersetshire, SW England, 22 mi. (35 km.) SW of Bristol; cliffs and stalactite caverns; known also for its cheese (Cheddar cheese) orig. made here.

Che·du·ba \chə-ˈdü-bə\. Island, Rakhine, W Myanmar, in Bay of Bengal S of Ramree I.; 202 sq. mi. (523 sq. km.); held by Japanese 1942–45.

Cheek·to·wa·ga \ˌchēk-tə-ˈwä-gə\. Town, Erie co., W New York, E of Buffalo; pop. (1990c) 99,314.

Ch'e–erh–ch'en. See QARQAN 1.

Cheese·man Dam \ˈchēz-mən\. Dam across South Platte River, SW Douglas co., cen. Colorado; height 236 ft. (72 m.); completed 1904; forms **Cheeseman Lake.**

Che–fang. See ZHEFANG.

Chefoo. See YANTAI.

Che·gu·tu \chā-ˈgü-tü\; *formerly* **Hart·ley** \ˈhärt-lē\. Town NE Zimbabwe; pop. (1992p) 30,122; center of agricultural and gold-mining region.

Che·ha·lis \chi-ˈhā-ləs, shi-\. **1.** River, W Washington; rises in Lewis co., flows NW into Grays Harbor at Aberdeen; ab. 125 mi. (200 km.) long.

2. City, ⊗ of Lewis co., SW Washington, 5 mi. (8 km.) S of its sister city Centralia (*q.v.*); pop. (1990c) 6527.

Chehalis, Point. Point on SW coast of Grays Harbor co., W Washington, at S entrance to Grays Harbor.

Cheik–Sa·ïd \ˈshāk-sä-ˈēd\ *or Arab.* **Shaykh Sa'īd** \ˈshīk-sä-ˈēd\. Former French territory, SW tip of Arabian Penin. on Bab el-Mandeb opp. Perim I.; ab. 1 sq. mi. (2.6 sq. km.); first acquired 1868 by French commercial company; ceded to French government 1886.

Che·ju \ˈchā-ˈjü\. **1.** *or Jp.* **Sai·shu To** \ˈsī-ˈshü-ˈtō\; *formerly* **Quel·part** \ˈkwel-ˌpärt\. Island, a province of South Korea, N East China Sea; 706 sq. mi. (1829 sq. km.); pop. (1990p) 232,687; ✱ Cheju; oranges, cattle raising; fishing; tourism.

2. *or Jp.* **Saishu.** Town, its ✱; pop. (1985c) 202,911; largest settlement on the island.

Che·ka·lin \ˌchə-kə-ˈlyēn\ *or* **Likh·vin** \ˈlik-vin, ˈlyik-vyin\. Town, W Tula Oblast, W cen. Russia in Europe, 56 mi. (90 km.) W of the city of Tula; head of navigation of Oka River.

Chekiang. See ZHEJIANG.

Che·lan \shə-ˈlan\. **1.** County in cen. Washington. See table at WASHINGTON.

2. Town, Chelan co., cen. Washington, at S end of Lake Chelan; pop. (1990c) 2969; summer resort.

Chelan, Lake. Lake, Chelan co., cen. Washington; from 1 to 2 mi. (1.6 to 3 km.) wide; ab. 55 mi. (88 km.) long; outlet from S end flows into Columbia River.

Chelan Range. Range in Chelan co., cen. Washington, extending along the W shore of Lake Chelan.

Ché·lia, Dje·bel \ˈje-bəl-ˈshāl-ˌyä\ *or Arab.* **Je·bel She·lia** \ˈje-bəl-she-ˈlē-ə\. Peak in Aurès Mts., NE Algeria; 7648 ft. (2331 m.); highest peak in Algeria.

Cheliabinsk. See CHELYABINSK.

Che·lif *or* **Ché·liff** \shā-ˈlēf\ *also* **She·liff** \shə-ˈlēf\. River, Algeria; rises in Atlas Mts., flows N and W into Mediterranean Sea E of Oran; 422 mi. (679 km.) long; longest river in Algeria.

Cheliff, Ech–. See ECH-CHELIFF.

Chel·kar–Teng·iz \chel-ˈkär-tyen-ˈgēs\ *or* **Chal·kar–Ten·gis** \chäl-ˈkär-tyen-ˈgēs\. Lake, cen. Kazakhstan, ab. 110 mi. (177 km.) NE of the Aral Sea.

Chelles \ˈshel\; *anc.* **Ca·lae** \ˈkā-lē\. Commune, Seine-et-Marne dept., N France, near N bank of the Marne 7 mi. (11 km.) E of Paris; pop. (1990c) 45,495; prehistoric remains found nearby, whence the name "Chellean epoch"; site of famous convent, founded in the 7th cent. and destroyed in the French Revolution.

Chelly Canyon \ˈshā\. See *Canyon de Chelly National Monument* at UNITED STATES, *National Monuments.*

Chełm \ˈkeu̇m\. **1.** Province, E Poland. See table at POLAND.

2. *or Russ.* **Kholm** \ˈkȯlm\. Commune, its ✱, 42 mi. (68 km.) ESE of Lublin, just W of the Bug; pop. (1989e) 64,848; cathedral; trade center for fertile agricultural region. Founded 1233; to Poland 1377; to Austria 1795; to Russia 1815; battle 1915 resulting in German victory; occupied by Germans WWII; Polish People's Republic proclaimed here July 22, 1944.

Chełm·no \ˈkelm-nȯ\; *Ger.* **Culm** *or* **Kulm** \ˈkülm\. Commune, Toruń prov., N cen. Poland, on Vistula River 24 mi. (39 km.) NNW of the city of Toruń; pop. (1989e) 21,436. Founded c. 1230 by Teutonic Knights; belonged to Prussia 1773–1807, 1815–1919.

Chelms·ford \ˈchelmz-fərd, ˈchemz-\. **1.** Town, Middlesex co., NE Massachusetts, 4 mi. (6 km.) SSW of Lowell; pop. (1990c) 32,383.

2. Town, ⊗ of Essex, SE England, 30 mi. (48 km.) NE of London; pop. (1991p) 150,000; electrical equipment, roller bearings; 15th cent. cathedral; 16th cent. grammar school; first wireless telegraph broadcasting service 1920.

Chełm·ża \ˈkeu̇m-zhä, ˈkelm-\; *Ger.* **Culm·see** *or* **Kulm·see** \ˈku̇lm-ˌzā\. Town, Toruń prov., N cen. Poland, 12 mi. (19 km.) N of the city of Toruń; pop. (1981p) 14,872.

Chelny. See NABEREZHNYE CHELNY.

Chel·sea \ˈchel-sē\. **1.** City, Suffolk co., E Massachusetts, 3 mi. (5 km.) NNE of Boston; pop. (1990c) 28,710. Settled 1624, set off from Boston 1739; suffered great fire Apr. 12, 1908.

2. Village, Washtenaw co., SE Michigan, 15 mi. (24 km.) W of Ann Arbor; pop. (1990c) 3772.

3. Neighborhood, Manhattan borough, New York City, N of Greenwich Village.

4. Village in Chelsea town (township), ⊗ of Orange co., E Vermont, 14 mi. (23 km.) S of Barre; pop. (town, 1990c) 1166.

5. Former metropolitan borough of London, SE England; now part of Kensington and Chelsea.

6. City, S Victoria, Australia, a SE suburb of Melbourne; pop. (1991c) 25,822.

Chel·ten·ham \ˈchelt-ᵊn-ˌham, -ᵊn-əm\. **1.** Township, Montgomery co., SE Pennsylvania, NNE of Philadelphia; pop. (1990c) 34,923.

2. Municipal borough, Gloucestershire, SW cen. England, on the River Chelt 42 mi. (68 km.) S of Birmingham; pop. (1991p) 85,900; tourism; mineral springs; town first mentioned 1223.

Che·lya·binsk *also* **Che·lia·binsk** \chel-ˈyä-bənsk\. City, ✱ of Chelyabinsk Oblast, W Russia in Asia, 125 mi. (201 km.) S of Yekaterinburg; pop. (1992e) 1,143,000; industrial center; iron and steel, agricultural implements; on the Trans-Siberian R.R. Founded as a frontier outpost on the site of a Bashkir village 1736. Headquarters of Czechoslovak legion in fighting after Bolshevik Revolution of 1917.

Chelyabinsk Oblast \ˈō-bləst, -ˌblast\ *or* **Che·lya·bin·ska·ya**

Oblast' \chel-'yä-bin-skə-yə-'ȯ-bləst^y\. Subdivision of W Russia in Asia, E of S Urals; 33,938 sq. mi. (87,899 sq. km.); pop. (1992e) 3,638,000; ✻ Chelyabinsk. Has much fertile and forested land; wheat; coal, copper, zinc, chromite; heavy engineering; chemicals. Chief cities: Chelyabinsk, Magnitogorsk, Zlatoust, Kopeysk. Exploitation and subsequent depletion of great deposits of iron (see MAGNITOGORSK) began in 1929. Organized as an administrative subdivision 1934; in WWII greatly reduced by organization of Kurgan Oblast from its E part.

Che·lyus·kin, Cape \chel-'yüs-kən\ *or Russ.* **Mys Chelyuskin** \'məs\. Cape on Taymyr Penin., N Russia in Asia; northernmost point of Asia, 77°45'N, 104°20'E.

Che·min des Dames \shə-ˌme^n-dā-'dȧm\. Highway ab. 4 mi. (6 km.) N of and parallel with the Aisne River, N France, with its E end near Craonne; literally, "Ladies Road," so-called because it was traveled by the daughters of Louis XV. Scene of severe fighting throughout WWI. In WWII taken by Germans.

Chemmis. See AKHMĪM.

Chem·nitz \'kem-nits\. **1.** District of former East Germany. See KARL-MARX-STADT.

2. *1953–90* **Karl–Marx–Stadt** \ˌkärl-'märks-ˌshtät\. City, E Germany, on Chemnitz River at foot of Erzgebirge 43 mi. (69 km.) SE of Leipzig; pop. (1992e) 287,511; transportation center; textiles, machinery, chemicals, motor vehicles; made free imperial city 1125; given monopoly of bleaching 1357, making it an early center of textile industry; heavily damaged in WWII.

Chemulpo. See INCH'ŎN.

Che·mung \shi-'məŋ\. **1.** River, S New York; formed by confluence of Cohocton and Tioga rivers in Steuben co.; flows SE across Pennsylvania border and into Susquehanna River. See ELMIRA.

2. County in S New York. See table at NEW YORK.

Che·na \'chē-nə\. River, cen. Alaska, flowing to the Tanana River ab. 6 mi. (10 km.) WSW of Fairbanks; ab. 160 mi. (257 km.) long.

Che·nab \chə-'näb\; *anc.* **Aces·i·nes** \ə-'ses-ᵊn-ˌēz\. River, India and Pakistan; rises in Himachal Pradesh in the Himalayas, India, flows NW, then W and SW through Jammu and Kashmir and W cen. Punjab, Pakistan, to unite with the Sutlej to form the Panjnad; joined by the Jhelum in W Punjab; 599 mi. (964 km.) long; one of the "Five Rivers" of the Punjab; source of extensive canal and irrigation system.

Che·nan·go \shə-'naŋ-gō\. **1.** River, S cen. New York; rises near Madison-Oneida co. boundary, flows S into Susquehanna River at Binghamton; ab. 100 mi. (160 km.) long.

2. County in S cen. New York. See table at NEW YORK.

Chen–chiang. See ZHENJIANG.

Chê·née \she-'nā\. Commune, Liège prov., Belgium, SE suburb of the city of Liège.

Che·ney \'chē-nē\. City, Spokane co., E Washington, 14 mi. (23 km.) SSW of the city of Spokane; pop. (1990c) 7723; Eastern Washington Univ. (1890).

Cheney Cob·ble \'kä-bəl\. Peak in the Adirondack Mts., Essex co., NE New York; 3673 ft. (1120 m.).

Chen·gal·pat·tu \'cheŋ-gəl-ˌpə-tü\ *also* **Chin·gle·put** \'chiŋ-gəl-ˌpət\. Town, Tamil Nadu, S India, 14 mi. (23 km.) SW of Madras; pop. (1991p) 53,784; important as ✻ of Vijayanagar kings in 16th cent.; a strategic fort during wars bet. French and English in 18th cent.

Chengchiatun. See SHUANGLIAO.

Cheng–chou *or* **Chengchow.** See ZHENGZHOU.

Cheng·de *or W.-G.* **Ch'eng–te** \'chəŋ-'də\ *or* **Je·hol** \jə-'hōl, 'rō-'hō\. City, ✻ of former Jehol prov., now in Hebei prov., NE China, on Luan River ab. 110 mi. (177 km.) NE of Beijing; pop. (1990c) 246,799; textiles; copper and coal mines nearby; historically famous as the summer residence of the Manchu emperors of China. The imperial estates, begun 1703 by Emperor K'ang-hsi, are now a public park; here Emperor Ch'ien-lung received in 1793 the historic British trade mission under Lord George Macartney.

Cheng·du *or W.-G.* **Ch'eng–tu** \'chəŋ-'dü\. City, ✻ of Sichuan prov., S cen. China; pop. (1990c) 1,713,255; textiles, chemicals, aluminum, railway equipment; located on remarkable irrigation system of the Min and other streams devised more than 2000 years ago, the center of an exceptionally fertile region; university (1931), technical college (1954). One of the oldest cities of China; in early times for certain periods an imperial ✻; cottage of 8th cent. poet Tu Fu, tombs and other remains of early eras; WWII American air base for B-29 bombers 1944; experienced period of rapid industrial growth following Communist takeover in 1949.

Chenghsien. See ZHENGZHOU.

Chen–hai. See ZHENHAI.

Che·non·ceaux \shə-nȯ^n-'sō\. Village, Indre-et-Loire dept., W cen. France, on Cher River, ESE of Tours; notable 16th cent. chateau which bridges the river is now a tourist attraction.

Chenstokhov. See CZĘSTOCHOWA.

Chen–yüan. See ZHENYUAN.

Che·pach·et \chi-'pa-chit\. Village, Providence co., N Rhode Island, ab. 15 mi. (24 km.) NNW of Central Falls; governmental center of Glocester.

Che·po \'chā-pō\. River in E cen. Panama; flows W and SW into the Bay of Panama E of Panama City.

Chepping Wycombe. See HIGH WYCOMBE.

Cheq·uers \'che-kərz\. An historic Tudor mansion in Buckinghamshire, England 35 mi. (56 km.) NW of London; presented to the government by Lord and Lady Lee of Fareham 1917; the official country seat of the prime minister of Great Britain.

Cher \'sher\. **1.** River, cen. France; rises in Creuse dept., flows NW into Loire River; 217 mi. (349 km.) long.

2. Department of cen. France. See table at FRANCE.

Che·ra·sco \kā-'räs-kō\. Commune, Cuneo prov., Piedmont, Italy, on Tanaro River ab. 22 mi. (35 km.) NE of the commune of Cuneo; pop. (1981p) 6253; treaty 1631 bet. France and Spain; armistice Apr. 28, 1796 bet. France and Sardinia that ended Sardinian support of Austria.

Che·raw \chi-'rȯ, 'chē-rȯ\. Town, Chesterfield co., NE South Carolina, on Pee Dee River 14 mi. (23 km.) WNW of Bennettsville; pop. (1990c) 5505; settled mid-18th cent.; captured by Gen. William T. Sherman 1865.

Cher·bourg \sher-'bür, 'sher-ˌbu̇rg\. Seaport and naval arsenal, Manche dept., NW France, on N coast of Cotentin Penin. on English Channel; pop. (1990c) 28,773; strongly fortified; a major French naval station; consists of old or civil town and Port Militaire, the new or military town; transatlantic port of embarkation and debarkation; metallurgy. Believed to occupy site of ancient Roman station; fought over by the French and English in the Middle Ages; taken by English 1758; passed to France and extensively fortified by Louis XVI late 18th cent. In WWII held by Germans; attacked from S and taken by Allies June 1944; harbor practically destroyed by Germans; became an important supply port for the Allies.

Cher·chell *or* **Sher·shell** \sher-'shel\; *anc.* **Cae·sa·rea** \ˌsē-zə-'rē-ə, ˌse-, -zə-\. Seaport, N Algeria; WSW of Algiers.

Cherchen. See QIEMO.

Che·rem·kho·vo \chə-'rem-kə-ˌvō\. Town, S Irkutsk Oblast, S Russia in Asia, on Trans-Siberian R.R. 80 mi. (129 km.) NW of the city of Irkutsk; pop. (1991e) 73,600; large coalfields nearby.

Cheren. See KEREN.

Che·re·po·vets \ˌcher-ə-'pȯ-vyits, -pə-'vyets\. City, SW Vologda Oblast, W cen. Russia in Europe, 70 mi. (113 km.) W of the city of Vologda, near junction of Suda and Sheksna rivers just before they enter Rybinsk Reservoir (*q.v.*); pop. (1992e) 317,000; iron and steelworks; shipbuilding, timberwork; orig. a settlement (in Novgorod principality) which grew up near a monastery founded before 15th cent.; became a town c. 1780.

Cher·gui, Chott ech \ˈshät-ˌesh-ˈshər-gē\ *or Arab.* **Shatt al–Sher·gui** \ˈshȧt-ȧl-ˈsher-gē\. Marshy saline lake, NW Algeria.

Cheribon. See CIREBON.

Cher·kas·sy *or* **Cher·ka·sy** \chir-ˈkä-sē\. **1.** Administrative subdivision of cen. Ukraine; 8069 sq. mi. (20,899 sq. km.); pop. (1991e) 1,530,900; ✻ Cherkassy; important sugar-beet producing region; formed 1954.
2. City, its ✻, on the Dnieper 100 mi. (161 km.) SE of Kiev; pop. (1991e) 302,000. In 15th cent. an important Cossack town, esp. for trading; under Polish rule until Cossack leader Bohdan Khmelnytsky's revolt 1648; became Russian late 18th cent.; held by Germans 1941–43.

Cher·kess Autonomous Oblast \chir-ˈkyes ... ˈȯ-bləst, -ˌblast\. Former autonomous region, Russian S.F.S.R., U.S.S.R., in valley of upper Kuban' River; 1273 sq. mi. (3297 sq. km.); mountainous. See KARACHAYEV AUTONOMOUS OBLAST.

Cherkessia, Karachay–. See KARACHAY-CHERKESSIA.

Cher·kessk \chir-ˈkyesk\; *formerly* **Ba·tal·pa·shinsk** \ˌbə-təl-pə-ˈshinsk\; *later* **Su·li·mov** \sü-ˈlē-mȯf, sül-ˈyē-məf\. Town, ✻ of Karachay-Cherkessia, S Russia in Europe, on Kuban' River 160 mi. (257 km.) SE of Krasnodar; pop. (1992e) 119,000; railroad terminus. For a time before WWII known as **Ye·zho·vo–Cherkessk** \ˈyā-zhə-və-\ but name restored to Cherkessk in 1938.

Cherna. See CRNA.

Cher·na·ya \ˈchȯr-nə-yə\. Small river in the Crimean Penin., Ukraine, E of Sevastopol'; flows W into the Black Sea; scene of victory of allies over Russians 1855 during Crimean War.

Cherniakovsk. See CHERNYAKHOVSK.

Cher·ni·gov \chir-ˈnē-gəf\. Medieval principality, E cen. Europe, extending NE from Kiev to borders of Ryazan'; ✻ Chernigov; at height of power in 11th and 12th cents.

Chernihiv \cher-ˈnē-hē-ü\ *or Russ* **Chernigov** \chir-ˈnē-gəf\. **1.** Administrative subdivision of Ukraine; most of W boundary formed by the Dnieper River; 12,317 sq. mi. (31,901 sq. km.); pop. (1991e) 1,405,800; ✻ Chernihiv; corn, tobacco.
2. City, its ✻, on right bank of Desna River 77 mi. (124 km.) NNE of Kiev; pop. (1991e) 306,000; manufactures pianos.
History: A very old town, mentioned as early as 907; in 11th cent. became ✻ of Chernigov principality, at which time its cathedral (still preserved) was built; partly destroyed by Mongols c. 1240; annexed by Lithuania in 14th cent.; held by Russia 16th cent. and by Poland for part of 17th cent.; reoccupied by Russia late 17th cent.; captured by Germans Sept. 1941; retaken late in 1943.

Cher·niv·tsi \chir-ˈnift-sē\ *or* **Cher·nov·tsy** \chir-ˈnȯft-sē\. **1.** Administrative subdivision of Ukraine; 3217 sq. mi. (8332 sq. km.); pop. (1991e) 938,600; ✻ Chernivtsi; timber; formerly a part of Bukovina in N Romania; to U.S.S.R. 1940.
2. *or Rom.* **Cer·nă·u·ţi** \ˌcher-nə-ˈüts, -ˈüt-sē\ *or Ger.* **Czer·no·witz** \ˈcher-nə-ˌvits\. City, its ✻ and former ✻ of Bukovina, on right bank of Prut River; pop. (1991e) 259,000; textiles; university, opened by Germans 1875. First mentioned early 15th cent.; grew from small village after Austrian occupation in 1775; battlefield in WWI; became Romanian 1918; ceded to U.S.S.R. 1940.

Cher·no·byl \chər-ˈno-bəl, cher-\. Site, N Ukraine, of town abandoned after 1986 accident at nuclear power plant.

Cher·no·gorsk \ˌchir-nə-ˈgȯrsk\. Town, Krasnoyarsk Kray, cen. Russia in Asia, ab. 160 mi. (255 km.) SW of the city of Krasnoyarsk; pop. (1991e) 79,700.

Chernovtsy. See CHERNIVTSI.

Chernoye More. See BLACK SEA.

Cher·nya·khovsk *also* **Cher·nia·kovsk** \chir-ˈnyä-kəfsk\ *or Ger.* **In·ster·burg** \ˈin-stər-ˌbu̇rk\. City, Kaliningrad Oblast, W exclave of Russia in Europe, on Wegorapa River; railroad junction; formerly in East Prussia, Germany; 14th cent. castle. Founded c. 1336; taken by and became part of U.S.S.R. 1945 following WWII.

Cher·o·kee \ˈcher-ə-ˌkē, ˌcher-ə-ˈ\. **1.** Name of counties in eight states of the U.S. See tables at ALABAMA, GEORGIA, IOWA, KANSAS, NORTH CAROLINA, OKLAHOMA, SOUTH CAROLINA, TEXAS.
2. City, ⊗ of Cherokee co., NW Iowa; pop. (1990c) 6026.
3. City, ⊗ of Alfalfa co., N Oklahoma, 38 mi. (61 km.) NW of Enid; pop. (1990c) 1787.

Cherokee Dam. See table at TENNESSEE VALLEY AUTHORITY.

Cherokee Outlet. Strip of land along S border of Kansas; ab. 12,000 sq. mi. (31,100 sq. km.); guaranteed to Cherokee Indians by treaties in the 1820s and 30s; held by Cherokee Nation until c. 1891 when it was purchased by U.S. for ab. $8,596,000; opened to settlers Sept. 16, 1893; became part of Oklahoma Terr.; an adjoining region, **Cherokee Strip,** became part of Kansas.

Cherokees, Grand Lake O' the *or* **Cherokees, Lake O' The.** See PENSACOLA DAM.

Cher·ra·pun·ji; *earlier* **Cher·ra Poon·jee** \ˌcher-ə-ˈpu̇n-jē\. City and former British military station, S Meghalaya, NE India; pop. (1991p) 7833; alt. ab. 4590 ft. (1400 m.); noted for record rainfall (annual av. ab. 450 in. or 1140 cm.).

Cher·ry \ˈcher-ē\. County in N Nebraska. See table at NEBRASKA.

Cherry Hill; *formerly* **Del·a·ware** \ˈdel-ə-ˌwar\. Township, Camden co., W cen. New Jersey, E of the city of Camden; pop. (1990c) 69,348.

Cherry Hills Village. City, Arapahoe co., NE cen. Colorado, just S of Denver; pop. (1990c) 5245.

Cherry Island. See ANUDA ISLAND.

Cherry Valley. Village, Otsego co., New York, 50 mi. (80 km.) W of Albany; pop. (1990c) 1210; medicinal springs; raided by a combined force of Tories under Walter Butler and Iroquois under Chief Joseph Brant Nov. 11, 1778.

Cher·ry·ville \ˈcher-ē-ˌvil\. City, Gaston co., SW North Carolina, 10 mi. (16 km.) ENE of Shelby; pop. (1990c) 4756.

Cher·ski Range *or* **Cher·skiy Range** \ˈcher-skē\ *or Russ.* **Khrebet Cherskogo** \kri-ˈbyet-ˈcher-skə-və\. Mountain range, NE Sakha Rep. E Russia in Asia, N of the Sea of Okhotsk; runs NW and SE; highest point 10,217 ft. (3114 m.).

Cherso. See CRES.

Cher·so·nese, The \ˈkər-sə-ˌnēz, -ˌnēs\; *anc.* **Cher·so·ne·sus** \ˌkər-sə-ˈnē-səs\. Literally "peninsula"; in ancient geography applied to several peninsulas in Europe and Asia. See CRIMEA, GALLIPOLI PENINSULA, JUTLAND, KHERSON, and MALAY PENINSULA.

Chersonesus Aurea. See MALAY PENINSULA.

Chert·sey \ˈchərt-sē\. Town, Surrey, S England, on S bank of the Thames; pop. (1981p) 43,265.

Cher·well \ˈchär-wəl\. River, cen. England; rises in Northamptonshire, flows S through Oxfordshire into the Thames (Isis) at Oxford; 30 mi. (48 km.) long.

Ches·a·ning \ˈche-sə-ˌniŋ\. Village, Saginaw co., cen. Michigan, 20 mi. (32 km.) SW of the city of Saginaw; pop. (1990c) 2567.

Ches·a·peake \ˈche-sə-ˌpēk\. Independent city, SE Virginia, S of Norfolk; pop. (1990c) 151,976; cement, fertilizer, steel products; traversed by inland waterways; formed 1963 by merger of former city of South Norfolk and former county of Norfolk.

Chesapeake and Delaware Canal. Canal from Delaware City, Delaware, to Chesapeake City, Maryland, connecting Chesapeake and Delaware bays; ab. 14 mi. (23 km.) long, 90 ft. (27 m.) wide, and 12 ft. (4 m.) deep at medium low water.

Chesapeake and Ohio Canal National Historical Park. See UNITED STATES, *National Historical Parks.*

Chesapeake Bay. Inlet of Atlantic Ocean, its lower section in Virginia and its upper section in Maryland; 193 mi. (311 km.) long, from 3 to 25 mi. (5 to 40 km.) wide; ab. 3230 sq. mi. (8365 sq. km.); receives the Susquehanna River in the N, the Patuxent and Potomac on the W, the Chester, Choptank, and Nanticoke on the E, and the Rappahannock, York, and James rivers on the SW.

Chesapeake Bay Bridge Tunnel. Series of bridges and tunnels across and under Chesapeake Bay from Virginia Beach, Virginia to the southernmost tip of Delmarva Penin.

Chesapeake City. Town, Cecil co., NE Maryland; pop. (1990c) 735; terminus of Chesapeake and Delaware Canal.

Chesh·am \ˈche-shəm, -səm\. Town, Buckinghamshire, SE cen. England, 25 mi. (40 km.) WNW of London; pop. (1981p) 20,655.

Chesh·ire \ˈche-shər, -ˌshir\. **1.** County in SW corner of New Hampshire. See table at NEW HAMPSHIRE.
2. Town, N cen. New Haven co., S Connecticut, 5 mi. (8 km.) WNW of Wallingford; pop. (1990c) 25,684; incorp. 1780.
3. Town, Berkshire co., W Massachusetts, 9 mi. (15 km.) NNE of Pittsfield; pop. (1990c) 3479.

Cheshire *or* **Ches·ter** \ˈches-tər\. **1.** Former county, W England; rivers Dee, Weaver, and Mersey; towns included Birkenhead, Stockport, Wallasey, Crewe, Macclesfield.
2. Administrative county, W England, incl. most of the former county except parts now in Merseyside and Greater Manchester; estab. 1974. See table at ENGLAND.

Chesh·ska·ya Bay \ˈchesh-skə-yə\ *or Russ.* **Cheshskaya Gu·ba** \gü-ˈbä\. Inlet of the Arctic Ocean (Barents Sea), Arkhangel'sk Oblast, N coast of Russia in Europe, E Kanin Penin.

Ches·hunt \ˈche-sənt\. Town, Hertfordshire, SE England, 15 mi. (24 km.) N of London; pop. (1981p) 49,670; market gardens.

Chesnokovka. See NOVOALTAISK.

Ches·ter \ˈches-tər\. **1.** River, E Maryland; flows W along boundary of Kent and Queen Annes cos. into Chesapeake Bay; ab. 40 mi. (64 km.) long.
2. Name of counties in three states of the U.S. See tables at PENNSYLVANIA, SOUTH CAROLINA, TENNESSEE.
3. Town, S cen. Middlesex co., S Connecticut, on Connecticut River; pop. (1990c) 3417; tourism; light industry; settled as part of Deep River c. 1690; incorp. 1836.
4. City, ⊗ of Randolph co., SW Illinois, on Mississippi River; pop. (1990c) 8194; shipping center.
5. Town, ⊗ of Liberty co., N Montana; pop. (1990c) 942.
6. City and port of entry, Delaware co., SE Pennsylvania, on Delaware River 14 mi. (23 km.) WSW of Philadelphia; pop. (1990c) 41,856; shipbuilding yards, steelmills, chemicals, paper; site of Commodore John Barry Bridge (cantilever; main span 1644 ft. or 501 m., completed 1974) spanning Delaware River; Widener Univ. (1821; incorp. 1862). Settled by Swedes c. 1644 (one of the oldest settlements in Pennsylvania); under Dutch control 1655, English control 1664; William Penn arrived 1682; became borough 1701, ⊗ late 18th cent. to mid-19th cent., city c. 1866.
7. City, ⊗ of Cheshire co., N South Carolina, 18 mi. (29 km.) SSW of Rock Hill; pop. (1990c) 7158.
8. Town, Windsor co., S Vermont; pop. (1990c) 2832.
9. Residential city, Hancock co., N tip of West Virginia Panhandle, on Ohio River; pop. (1990c) 2905.
10. County in England. See CHESHIRE.
11. *anc.* **De·va** \ˈdē-və\ *or* **De·va·na Cas·tra** \di-ˈvā-nə-ˈkas-trə\. City and county borough, ⊗ of Cheshire, NW England, on the Dee River 15 mi. (24 km.) S of Liverpool; pop. (1991p) 115,000; active port and railroad center; tourism. Noted for its well-preserved walls, famous "Rows" of houses, and cathedral. For several centuries after 60 A.D. Roman "camp on the Dee," headquarters of the 20th Legion; after Romans left held by Anglo-Saxons and Danes; rebuilt 907 by Mercian ruler Aethelflaed; last place in England to surrender (1070) to William the Conqueror, duke of Normandy and successful claimant to the English throne; beginning c. 14th cent. scene of presentation of mystery plays of the Chester Cycle.

Ches·ter·field \ˈches-tər-ˌfēld\. **1.** Name of counties in two states of the U.S. See tables at SOUTH CAROLINA and VIRGINIA.
2. Town, Madison co., cen. Indiana, 12 mi. (19 km.) SW of Muncie; pop. (1990c) 2730.
3. City, St. Louis co., E Missouri, on the Missouri River, W of the city of St. Louis; pop. (1990c) 37,991; Logan Coll. of Chiropractic (1935).
4. Town, ⊗ of Chesterfield co., NE South Carolina; pop. (1990c) 1373; organized 1798.
5. Village, ⊗ of Chesterfield co., Virginia.
6. Town, Derbyshire, N cen. England, 11 mi. (18 km.) S of Sheffield; pop. (1991p) 99,700; coal; engineering; 14th cent. church with twisted spire. George Stephenson, inventor and founder of railways, lived and died here.

Chesterfield Inlet. 1. Inlet of Hudson Bay, E mainland portion of Nunavut, N Canada; 140 mi. (225 km.) long, 1 to 10 mi. (1.6 to 16 km.) wide; it extends in a northwesterly direction and expands into Baker Lake (*q.v.*).
2. Hamlet on NW coast of Hudson Bay, Canada, on S side of mouth of Chesterfield Inlet; pop. (1991c) 316.

Chesterfield Islands. Group of 11 coral islets in cen. Coral Sea, Australia, bet. N New Caledonia I. and E coast of Queensland; total area ab. 4 sq. mi. (10 sq. km.). Owned by France; uninhabited; guano deposits.

Ches·ter–le–Street \ˌches-tər-lə-ˈstrēt\. Town, Durham, N England, 10 mi. (16 km.) S of Newcastle upon Tyne; pop. (1991p) 51,000; coal nearby.

Ches·ter·ton \ˈches-tər-tən\. Town, Porter co., NW Indiana, 5 mi. (8 km.) S of Lake Michigan; pop. (1990c) 9124.

Ches·ter·town \ˈches-tər-ˌtau̇n\. Town, ⊗ of Kent co., NE Maryland, 32 mi. (52 km.) ESE of Baltimore; pop. (1990c) 4005; fisheries; seat of Washington Coll. (1782), named for George Washington, first U.S. president, who later contributed to the endowment and received an honorary degree.

Chest·nut, Mount \ˈches-ˌnət\. Peak, Rabun co., NE Georgia; 4600 ft. (1402 m.).

Chestnut Hill. 1. Unincorporated suburb of Boston, Massachusetts; Boston Coll. (1863), Pine Manor Coll. (1911).
2. Residential neighborhood, NW Philadelphia, Pennsylvania.

Chestnut Ridge. 1. Ridge extending from Preston co., West Virginia, NE to cen. Indiana co., W cen. Pennsylvania; ab. 130 mi. (210 km.) long; highest point 2293 ft. (699 m.).
2. Village, Rockland co., SE New York; pop. (1990c) 7517.

Che·sun·cook Lake \chə-ˈsən-ˌku̇k\. Lake, cen. Piscataquis co., N cen. Maine; ab. 20 mi. (32 km.) long; traversed by W branch of the Penobscot River.

Che·tu·mal \ˌchā-tu̇-ˈmäl\. Town, ✱ of Quintana Roo state, E Yucatán Penin., Mexico; pop. (1990c) 94,158.

Chetumal Bay. Inlet of NW Caribbean Sea, SE coast of Quintana Roo state, Mexico, and NE coast of Belize; ab. 70 mi. (115 km.) long.

Che·val Blanc, Pointe du \ˈpwe^{n}t-dᵫ-shə-ˌväl-ˈblä^{n}k\ *or* **Cap à Foux** \ˌkäp-ä-ˈfü\. Cape, Haiti, at NW tip of Hispaniola, on SE side of Windward Passage.

Chev·er·ly \ˈshe-vər-lē\. Town, Prince Georges co., S cen. Maryland, E of Washington, D.C.; pop. (1990c) 6023.

Chev·i·ot \ˈshi-vē-ət, ˈshe-\. City, Hamilton co., SW corner of Ohio, 8 mi. (13 km.) NW of Cincinnati; pop. (1990c) 9616.

Chev·i·ot Hills \ˈche-vē-ət, ˈshe-, ˈchi-\. Range of hills extending NE to SW along the England-Scotland border; highest peak **Cheviot** 2676 ft. (816 m.).

Chevy Chase \ˈche-vē-ˈchās\. Town, Montgomery co., cen. Maryland, N of Washington, D.C.; pop. (1990c) 2675.

Ch'ew Ba·hir *or* **Chew Bahir** \ˈchev-ˈbä-ˌhir\ *or* **Stef·a·nie** \ˈste-fə-nē\. Shallow saline lake, SW Ethiopia, E of N end of Lake Turkana; ab. 37 mi. (60 km.) long; elev. ab. 1900 ft. (580 m.).

Chey·enne \shī-ˈan, -ˈen\. **1.** River, Wyoming and South Dakota; rises in E Wyoming; enters South Dakota in Fall River co., and flows generally NE, joining Missouri River in cen. South Dakota; ab. 527 mi. (850 km.) long.
2. Name of counties in three states of the U.S. See tables at COLORADO, KANSAS, NEBRASKA.
3. Town, ⊗ of Roger Mills co., W Oklahoma; pop. (1990c) 948; Gen. George Custer attacked Cheyenne Indians in battle of Washita (Nov. 1868) nearby.
4. City, ✱ of Wyoming and ⊗ of Laramie co., SE Wyoming, 10 mi. (16 km.) N of Colorado border; pop. (1990c) 50,008; alt. 6100 ft. (1859 m.); Laramie County Community Coll. (1968); railroad center; ships cattle and sheep; oil refineries, plastics; tourism; Francis E. Warren Air Force Base adjoins the city; nation's first base for intercontinental ballistic missiles nearby; founded and incorp. 1867; made ✱ 1869.

\ə\ abut \ᵊ\ kitten, Fr table \ər\ further \a\ ash \ā\ ace \ä\ cot, cart \ȧ\ Fr bac \au̇\ out \b\ Span Avila \ch\ chin \e\ bet \ē\ easy \g\ go \i\ hit \ī\ ice \j\ job \k\ Ger ich, Buch \$^{n}$\ Fr vin \ŋ\ sing \ō\ go \ȯ\ all \ȯ\ law \œ\ Fr bœuf \œ̄\ Fr feu \ȯi\ boy \th\ thin \t͟h\ this \ü\ loot \u̇\ foot \ue\ Ger füllen \ᵫ\ Fr rue \y\ yet \$^{y}$\ Fr digne \ˈdēn^{y}\, nuit \ˈnw^{y}ē\ \yü\ few \yu̇\ fury \zh\ vision

Cheyenne Wells. Town, ⊗ of Cheyenne co., E Colorado; pop. (1990c) 1128.

Chey·ney \'chā-nē\. Village, Delaware co., SE Pennsylvania, W of Media; Cheyney Univ. of Pennsylvania (1837).

Chha·tar·pur \'chə-tər-,pu̇r\. Former Indian state, now part of Uttar Pradesh, N India; 1170 sq. mi. (3030 sq. km.); ✻ Chhatarpur.

Chhat·tis·garh \'chə-tis-,gär\. Former agency, forming a group of several Indian states, N, W, and S of Chhattisgarh div., geographically in E Central Provinces, India; 37,688 sq. mi. (97,612 sq. km.).

Chhin·dwa·ra \chin-'dwär-ə\. Town, S Madhya Pradesh, India, 64 mi. (103 km.) NNW of Nagpur.

Chhota Udepur. See CHOTA UDEPUR.

Chhung Kompong Som. See KOMPONG SOM.

Chi \'chē\ *also* **Si** \'sē\. River, E Thailand; ab. 300 mi. (480 km.) long; N, and chief tributary, of the Mun River, joining it at 50 mi. (81 km.) above its mouth.

Chiahsing. See JIAXING.

Chia–i \'chyä-'ē\. City, W cen. Taiwan; pop. (1993e) 258,664; trade center; wine, tires, cement; rice and timber produced nearby.

Chia–ling. See JIALING.

Chiambone, Ras. See DICKS HEAD.

Chiamis. See CIAMIS.

Chia–mu–ssu. See JIAMUSI.

Chi–an. See JI'AN.

Chiana. See CHIANI.

Chiang–ling. See JIANGLING.

Chiang Mai \'jyäŋ-'mī\ *also* **Chieng·mai** \'jyeŋ-'mī\ *or* **Kiang·mai** \'jyäŋ-'mī, kē-\. City, NW Thailand, on upper course of Ping River ab. 80 mi. (130 km.) E of Myanmar (Burma) border; pop. (1991e) 161,541; important trade center, esp. in teak; railroad terminus; university (1964); founded late 13th cent. as ✻ of independent Lan Na kingdom, later subject to Burma; came under the control of Bangkok in 18th cent., but remained semi-independent until late 19th cent.

Chiang–men. See JIANGMEN.

Chiang Rai \'chyäŋ-'rī\ *also* **Chieng·rai** \'chyeŋ-'rī\. **1.** Province, N Thailand; 7260 sq. mi. (18,803 sq. km.); pop. (1991e) 1,048,299; ✻ Chiang Rai.

2. Town, its ✻, on tributary of the Mekong River 90 mi. (145 km.) NE of Chiang Mai; pop. (1991e) 35,270; trading town on junction of highways N to Myanmar and NW Indochina and S to Lampang.

Ch'iang–t'ang. See QIANGTANG.

Chiang–yin. See JIANGYIN.

Chia·ni \kē-'ä-nē\ *or* **Chia·na** \-nä\. River, cen. Italy, flowing N from near Chiusi to the Arno River at Arezzo; ab. 25 mi. (40 km.) long; its valley **Val·le di Chiana** \'väl-lā-dē-\, formerly marshy and malarial, has been drained and canalized.

Chia–ning. See NANJING.

Chi·an·ti Mountains \kē-'än-tē\ *or Ital.* **Mon·ti Chianti** \'mōn-tē\. Mountain range the Apennines in Tuscany, cen. Italy. The region is noted for its wines, esp. a dry red variety.

Chiao–hsien. See JIAOXIAN.

Chiao Hsien. See JIAO XIAN.

Chiao–tso. See JIAOZUO.

Chi·a·pas \chē-'ä-päs\. State of SE Mexico. See table at MEXICO.

Chia·ri \kē-'är-ē\; *anc.* **Clar·i·um** \'klar-ē-əm\. Commune, Brescia prov., Lombardy, N Italy, 16 mi. (26 km.) W of the commune of Brescia; pop. (1981p) 16,191; scene of defeat of French and Spanish army by Austrians under Prince Eugene of Savoy 1701.

Chias·so \'kyäs-,sō\. Commune, Ticino canton, Switzerland, on Italian frontier W of SW end of Lake Como; pop. (1980c) 8583; on St. Gotthard railroad.

Chi·a·tu·ra \chē-'ä-tu̇r-ə\ *or* **Chi·a·tu·ri** \-rē\. Town, cen. Republic of Georgia, in S foothills of Caucasus Mts. ab. 85 mi. (135 km.) NW of Tbilisi; pop. (1991e) 68,900; rich manganese mines.

Chia·va·ri \kē-'ä-vä-rē\. Commune, Genova prov., Liguria, NW Italy, on Gulf of Rapallo 22 mi. (35 km.) ESE of the seaport of Genoa; pop. (1991p) 28,396.

Chia·ven·na \kyä-'ven-nä\. Town, Sondrio prov., N Lombardy, Italy, at N end of Lake Como; pop. (1981p) 7587; S terminal of Splügen Pass.

Chia–yü–kuan \'jyä-yü-'gwän\. See GREAT WALL.

Chiazza. See PIAZZA ARMERINA.

Chi·ba \'chē-bä\. **1.** Prefecture, Honshū, Japan; ✻ Chiba; rice; fisheries. See table at JAPAN.

2. City, its ✻, on E shore of Tokyo Bay; pop. (1990p) 829,467; steel; university (1949); ✻ of a powerful daimyo family 12th–16th cents.; now prosperous commercial city.

Chi·bou·ga·mau \shə-'bü-gə-,mō\. Town, Abitibi co., SW Quebec, Canada, 150 mi. (241 km.) NW of Roberval; pop. (1991c) 8855; gold deposits.

Chibyu. See UKHTA.

Chi·ca·go \shə-'kä-gō, -'kȯ-\. **1.** Small river in Chicago, Illinois, consisting of N branch and S branch; S branch connected with the Des Plaines River at Lockport by the **Chicago Sanitary and Ship Canal** (see ILLINOIS WATERWAY).

2. City, ⊗ of Cook co., NE Illinois, on Lake Michigan; pop. (1990c) 2,783,726; important port and 3d largest city in U.S.; a major industrial, commercial, and transportation center; steel, chemicals, electronic equipment; food processing, metalworking; printing and publishing; Chicago Board of Trade, Chicago Mercantile Exchange; Chicago Public Library, John Crerar Library; Shedd Aquarium, Planetarium, Field Museum of Natural History; Art Institute of Chicago; notable buildings include the Water Tower, the Wrigley Building, and the Sears Tower; its educational institutions include: St. Xavier Univ. (1847), School of the Art Institute of Chicago (1866), Chicago State Univ. (1869), Loyola Univ. of Chicago (1870), Illinois Coll. of Optometry (1872), American Conservatory of Music (1886), Moody Bible Institute (1886), Columbia Coll. (1890), North Park Coll. (1891), Univ. of Chicago (1891), Illinois Institute of Technology (1892), De Paul Univ. (1898), Vandercook Coll. of Music (1909), City Colleges of Chicago (1911), Spertus Coll. of Judaica (1925), DeVry Institute of Technology (1931), Roosevelt Univ. (1945), Northeastern Illinois Univ. (1961), Lutheran School of Theology (1962), Univ. of Illinois at Chicago (1965), Rush Univ. (1969), Keller Graduate School of Management (1973), American Schools of Professional Psychology (1976), East-West Univ. (1978).

History: In 17th cent. name associated with portage (bet. Des Plaines and Chicago rivers) which connected St. Lawrence-Great Lakes system with Mississippi; strategic position on route for travel to Mississippi important to French, British, and Americans; tract, 6 mi. (10 km.) square, at river mouth, acquired by U.S. from Indians 1795; Fort Dearborn built 1803, abandoned during War of 1812, rebuilt 1816; settled in the 1830s and received city charter 1837; expanded rapidly after completion of Illinois and Michigan Canal 1848, connecting Chicago and Mississippi rivers, and its connection with railroads from east c. 1852; rebuilt quickly after great fire of 1871; scene of Haymarket riot 1886; social reformer Jane Addams opened Hull House settlement 1889; site of World's Columbian Exposition 1893; scene of Pullman strike 1894; became a leading architectural center late 19th cent. and earned a literary reputation early 20th cent.; scene of race riots 1919; became notorious for organized crime in the prohibition era; site of Century of Progress Exposition 1933–34. Atomic-bomb scientists produced first nuclear chain reaction at Univ. of Chicago 1942; scene of antiwar protests and civil unrest during Democratic national convention 1968.

Chicago Heights. City, Cook co., NE Illinois, ab. 10 mi. (16 km.) S of Chicago; pop. (1990c) 33,072.

Chicago Ridge. Village, Cook co., NE Illinois, SW of Chicago; pop. (1990c) 13,643.

Chicago Sanitary and Ship Canal. See CHICAGO 1.

Chi·ca·pa \shē-'kä-pä\. River in the Congo basin, S Africa; rises in E cen. Angola, flows N into Kasai River; 310 mi. (499 km.) long.

Chich·a·gof \'chi-chə-,gȯf, -,gäf\. Island, NW Alexander Archipelago, SE Alaska, N of Baranof I.

Chichagof Harbor. Inlet on NE coast of Attu I. at W end of Aleutian Is., Alaska.

Chi·chén It·zá \chē-'chen-ēt-'sä\. Village in Yucatán state, Mexico, ab. 20 mi. (32 km.) W of Valladolid; once one of the principal centers of the Mayas; extensive ruins and well-preserved temples, pyramids, and towers, rich with sculptures; built around "cenotes" (natural wells); numerous artifacts, as well as evidence of human sacrifice, recovered in modern times.

Chich·es·ter \'chi-chə-stər\. Town, ⊗ of West Sussex, S England, 16 mi. (26 km.) ENE of Portsmouth; pop. (1981p) 24,189; early Norman cathedral (begun late 11th cent.); market cross 1501; remains of ancient city walls.

Ch'i–ch'i–ha–erh. See QIQIHAR.

Chi·chi–Ji·ma \'chē-chē-'jē-mä\ *also* **Chi·chi–shi·ma** \-'shē-mä\. **1.** Group of islands in the Bonin Is., Japan.
2. Largest island in the group and in the Bonin Is.

Chick·a·hom·i·ny \ˌchi-kə-'hä-mə-nē\. River, E Virginia; rises 16 mi. (26 km.) NW of Richmond, flows SE into James River; ab. 90 mi. (145 km.) long.

Chickamauga and Chattanooga National Military Park. See UNITED STATES, *National Historical Parks.*

Chick·a·mau·ga Creek \ˌchi-kə-'mȯ-gə\. Tributary of the Tennessee River, NW Georgia; site of battle fought Sept. 1863 in which Confederates under Gen. Braxton Bragg defeated Union troops under Gen. William Starke Rosecrans; part of the campaign for Chattanooga.

Chickamauga Dam. See table at TENNESSEE VALLEY AUTHORITY.

Chick·a·saw \'chi-kə-ˌsȯ\. **1.** Name of counties in two states of the U.S. See tables at IOWA and MISSISSIPPI.
2. City, Mobile co., SW Alabama, NW of Prichard; pop. (1990c) 6649.

Chickasaw Bayou. An arm of the Mississippi River, W Mississippi, just N of Vicksburg and near the lower Yazoo; attack Dec. 1862 by Union forces on heights (**Chickasaw Bluffs**) along its bank unsuccessful in attempt to capture Vicksburg.

Chick·a·sa·whay \ˌchi-kə-'sȯ-ˌwā\ *or* **Chick·a·sa·wha** \-wə\. River, SE Mississippi; rises in E cen. Mississippi, flows S to unite with Leaf River in N George co. and form Pascagoula River; 210 mi. (338 km.) long.

Chick·a·sha \'chi-kə-ˌshā\. City, ⊗ of Grady co., cen. Oklahoma, on Washita River 40 mi. (64 km.) SW of Oklahoma City; pop. (1990c) 14,988; oil and gas deposits; Univ. of Science and Arts of Oklahoma (1908).

Chi·cla·na de la Fron·te·ra \chē-'klä-nä-ˌthā-lä-'frōn-'tā-rä\. Commune, Cádiz prov., SW Spain, 12 mi. (19 km.) SE of the city of Cádiz; pop. (1991p) 44,620; thermal sulfur springs.

Chi·cla·yo \chē-'klī-ō\. Coastal city, NW Peru; pop. (1990e) 419,600; in rice and sugar district; university (1962), agricultural college (1963); its ports are Eten and Pimentel.

Chi·co \'chē-kō\. **1.** City, Butte co., N California, 80 mi. (129 km.) N of Sacramento; pop. (1990c) 40,079; founded 1860, incorp. 1872; California State Univ., Chico (1887).
2. Either of two rivers in S Argentina, one flowing NE out of Lake Musters in S Chubut prov. and emptying into Chubut River, the other in Santa Cruz prov. flowing SE into Atlantic Ocean at the port of Santa Cruz.
3. River, NE Luzon, Philippines, a W tributary of the Cagayan; 140 mi. (225 km.) long.
4. *or* **Pam·pan·ga Chico** \päm-'päŋ-gä\. River, cen. Luzon, Philippines, a W tributary of the Pampanga River; flows S; ab. 60 mi. (97 km.) long.

Chicomóztoc. See ZACATECAS 2.

Chi·con·te·pec \chē-'kōn-tā-ˌpek\. Municipality, Veracruz state, Mexico, 95 mi. (153 km.) SSW of Tampico; pop. (1990p) 60,137.

Chic·o·pee \'chi-kə-pē, -gə-, -bē\. **1.** River, SW cen. Massachusetts; formed by junction of Quaboag and Swift rivers in N Hampden co., flows W into Connecticut River.
2. City, Hampden co., SW Massachusetts, on Connecticut River just N of Springfield; pop. (1990c) 56,632; includes **Chicopee Falls, Chicopee Center, Wil·li·man·sett** \ˌwi-lə-'man-sət\, **Fair·view** \'far-ˌvyü\, and **Al·den·ville** \'ȯl-dən-ˌvil\; sporting goods, meat products; Coll. of Our Lady of the Elms (1928); Westover Air Reserve Base is mostly in Chicopee.

Chi·cot \'shē-kō\. County in SE corner of Arkansas. See table at ARKANSAS.

Chicot, Point. Point on E coast of St. Bernard parish, SE Louisiana, on Breton Sound.

Chi·cou·ti·mi \shi-'kü-ti-mē\. **1.** River, S Quebec, Canada, rises in Laurentides Provincial Park, flows N to Lake Kenogami and then E to the Saguenay River at Chicoutimi; ab. 100 mi. (160 km.) long; in its lower course drops nearly 500 ft. (152 m.); noted for its scenery.
2. City, Quebec, Canada, on Saguenay River at head of navigation at mouth of Chicoutimi River; pop. (1991c) 62,670; Univ. of Quebec (branch; 1969); center of great waterpower developments; founded 1676.

Chi·dam·ba·ram \chi-'dəm-bə-rəm\. Town, N cen. Tamil Nadu, S India, 125 mi. (201 km.) SSW of Madras; pop. (1991p) 58,927; has numerous pagodas and temples, the principal temple sacred to Siva, much visited by pilgrims.

Chid·ley, Cape \'chid-lē\. Cape at N tip of Labrador, Canada, on Killinek I. on S side of entrance to Hudson Strait.

Chief Mountain \'chēf\. Peak in Glacier National Park, NW Montana; 9066 ft. (2763 m.).

Chief's Head \'chēfs-ˌhed\. Peak, Boulder co., N cen. Colorado; 13,579 ft. (4139 m.).

Ch'ieh–mo. See QIEMO.

Chiem, Lake \'kēm\ *or Ger.* **Chiem·see** \'kēm-ˌzā\. Largest lake in Bavaria, S Germany, ab. 40 mi. (64 km.) ESE of Munich; 31 sq. mi. (80 sq. km.); 1699 ft. (518 m.) above sea level; has three islands; outlet is the Alz with course of 30 mi. (48 km.) to the Inn.

Chiengmai. See CHIANG MAI.

Chiengrai. See CHIANG RAI.

Chie·ri \kē-'är-ē\. Commune, Torino prov. Piedmont,, NW Italy, 8 mi. (13 km.) SE of Turin; pop. (1989c) 31,081; large Gothic church.

Chie·ti \kē-'ā-tē\. **1.** Province of Abruzzi, cen. Italy. See table at ITALY.
2. *anc.* **Te·a·te** \tē-'ā-tē\. Commune, its ✱, near right bank of Pescara River 93 mi. (150 km.) ENE of Rome; pop. (1991p) 55,709; archiepiscopal see; university (1961); 11th cent. cathedral; Roman remains. Formerly ruled by Romans, Lombards, and Normans; under Normans was ✱ of the Abruzzi; Theatine (Roman Catholic) order named for ancient city.

Chi·ga·sa·ki \ˌchē-gä-'sä-kē\. City, Kanagawa prefecture, Honshū, Japan, ab. 16 mi. (26 km.) SW of Yokohama; pop. (1990p) 201,672; manufactures chinaware.

Chigha Khur. See CHAGHĀ KŪR.

Chi·gha Sa·rāi \chi-'gä-sə-'rī\. Town, NE Afghanistan.

Chig·nec·to \shig-'nek-tō\. Isthmus joining Nova Scotia, Canada, to the mainland, comprising Cumberland co. and part of Colchester co.; in its narrowest part, at Amherst, ab. 12 mi. (19 km.) wide; on N borders on Northumberland Strait and on S on Chignecto Bay and Minas Basin.

Chignecto Bay. N extremity of Bay of Fundy, Canada, bet. SE New Brunswick and NW Nova Scotia mainland; 50 mi. (81 km.) long; extremely high tides.

Chig·nik \'chig-nik\. Bay, inlet on SE coast of Alaska Penin., S Alaska.

Chig·well \'chig-ˌwel, -wəl\. Town, Essex, SE England, a suburb of Greater London.

Chih–chiang, Chih·kiang. See ZHIJIANG.

Chih·li \'chē-'lē, 'chə-, 'jir-\. **1.** Former province in NE China; 115,830 sq. mi. (300,000 sq. km.); ✱ Peking; divided 1928 largely into Hebei, Jehol, and Chahar.
2. Province, China. See HEBEI.

Chihli, Gulf of. See BO HAI.

Chih–lieh–p'u. See JELEP–LA.

Chi–hsi. See JIXI.

\ə\ abut \ᵊ\ matches \ᵊ\ kitten, Fr table \ər\ further \a\ ash \ā\ ace \ä\ cot, cart \à\ Fr bac \aù\ out \b̲\ Span Avila \ch\ chin \e\ bet \ē\ easy \g\ go \i\ hit \ī\ ice \j\ job \k\ Ger ich, Buch \ⁿ\ Fr vin \ŋ\ sing \ō\ go \ȯ\ all \ȯ\ law \œ\ Fr bœuf \œ̄\ Fr feu \ȯi\ boy \th\ thin \th̲\ this \ü\ loot \u̇\ foot \ue\ Ger füllen \ue̅\ Fr rue \y\ yet \ʸ\ Fr digne \'dēnʸ\, nuit \'nwʸē\ \yü\ few \yu̇\ fury \zh\ vision

Chi·hua·hua \chē-ˈwä-wä, shə-, -wə\. **1.** State of N Mexico. See table at MEXICO.
2. City, its ✻; munic. pop. (1990p) 530,487; alt. 4600 ft. (1402 m.); founded 1709; university (1954); historically the center of a rich silver-mining district.

Chi·jol Canal \chē-ˈhōl\. Canal, E Veracruz state, Mexico, connecting Tampico (Pánuco River) with Tuxpan; 6 ft. (2 m.) deep, 25 ft. (8 m.) wide.

Chi·kas·kia \chi-ˈkas-kē-ə\. River, cen. U.S., flowing from S Kansas E and SE into Oklahoma where it joins a fork of Arkansas River.

Chik·ma·ga·lūr \ˈchik-mə-gə-ˌlu̇r\. Town, SW Karnataka, India; pop. (1991p) 60,814.

Chi·ku·ho \ˌchē-ku̇-ˈhō\. Municipal division, Fukuoka prefecture, N Kyūshū, Japan; pop. (1990p) 11,360; notable large coal mines.

Chilachap. See CILACAP.

Chi·la·pa \chē-ˈlä-pä\ *or in full* **Chilapa de Al·va·rez** \thä-ˈäl-bä-räs\. Town, Guerrero, S Mexico; munic. pop. (1990p) 85,621.

Chilatjap. See CILACAP.

Chi·law \chi-ˈlau̇\. Town, W coast of Sri Lanka; pop. (1989e) 25,000.

Chil·co·tin \chil-ˈkōt-ᵊn\. River, S cen. British Columbia, Canada; flows SE into Fraser River; 145 mi. (233 km.) long.

Chil·ders·burg \ˈchil-dərz-ˌbərg\. City, Talladega co., E cen. Alabama, 38 mi. (61 km.) SE of Birmingham; pop. (1990c) 4579.

Chil·dress \ˈchil-drəs\. **1.** County in NW Texas. See table at TEXAS.
2. City, its ⊗, 80 mi. (129 km.) E of Plainview; pop. (1990c) 5055; railroad division point.

Chile \ˈchē-lā, ˈchi-lē\. Republic, SW South America, bounded on N by Peru and Bolivia, on E by Argentina, on S by Drake Passage, and on W by the Pacific Ocean; 292,257 sq. mi. (756,946 sq. km.); pop. (1982c) 11,275,440; ✻ Santiago.

Physical features: Long, narrow country bet. Andes Mts. and the Pacific Ocean; approx. 2650 mi. (4265 km.) long (from ab. 17°30′S to Cape Horn at 55°59′S) and nowhere more than 221 mi. (356 km.) wide. Has low coastal ranges; N part is high plateau (Atacama Desert). In N includes several peaks above 19,000 ft. (5791 m.) (Copiapó, Palpana, Llullaillaco), but most of highest Andean peaks are on the boundaries with Bolivia and Argentina. Has no rivers of any size; largest Loa, Bío-Bío, Maipo, Itata, Maule, Copiapó; many lakes in S cen. part in resort region (Llanquihue, Ranco); S of 42° coast marked by many inlets, islands, and archipelagoes; owns W half of Tierra del Fuego and island on which is Cape Horn; also possesses small islets of Juan Fernández, Easter I., and others far out in the Pacific.

Chief export: Copper; other products: nitrates, iodine, coal, iron ore, molybdenum, precious metals, oil; wheat, fruit, potatoes, corn, sugar beets; fish, livestock; timber, wood products.

Chief cities: Santiago, Concepción, Viña del Mar, Valparaíso, Talcahuano, Antofagasta, Temuco.

Political divisions: Divided (1975) into the regions listed in the table below (for pronunciation of their names, see their individual entries). Prior to 1975 divided into the following 21 provinces (for pronunciation of their names, see their individual entries): Aconcagua, Antofagasta, Arauco, Atacama, Aysén, Bío-Bío, Cautín, Chiloé, Concepción, Curicó, Linares, Magallanes, Malleco, Maule, Ñuble, O'Higgins, Osorno, Santiago, Tarapacá, Valdivia, Valparaíso.

NAME	AREA (sq. mi.)	AREA (sq. km.)	POP. (1992c)	CAPITAL
Aisén del General Carlos Ibáñez del Campo	42,094	109,025	82,103	Coihaique
Antofagasta	48,820	126,444	407,409	Antofagasta
Atacama	29,179	75,573	230,786	Copiapó
Bío-Bío	14,258	36,929	1,731,837	Concepción
Coquimbo	15,697	40,656	503,734	La Serena
La Araucanía	12,300	31,858	774,959	Temuco
Libertador General Bernardo O'Higgins	6,318	16,365	692,408	Rancagua
Los Lagos	25,868	66,997	957,864	Puerto Montt
Magallanes y Antártica Chilena	50,978	132,034	143,486	Punta Arenas
Maule	11,700	30,302	834,178	Talca
Santiago	5,926	15,349	5,180,757	Santiago
Tarapacá	22,663	58,698	341,237	Iquique
Valparaíso	6,330	16,396	1,373,967	Valparaíso

History: Orig. inhabited by the Araucanians; in 15th cent. N part conquered by Incas; first invaded by Spanish under Diego de Almagro 1536–37; settlement begun at Santiago by Pedro de Valdivia 1541; governed under viceroyalty of Peru, becoming a separate captaincy general 1778; revolted against Spain 1810, but not finally independent until Feb. 12, 1818, after battle of Chacabuco (1817); independence assured by victory of soldier and statesman Jose de San Martín at Maipo Apr. 5, 1818; governed by Bernardo O'Higgins to 1823; under President Joaquin Prieto (1831–41) and chief minister Diego Portales (1830–37); received centralistic constitution 1833 and orderly conservative government; fought confederation of Peru and Bolivia (see YUNGAY) 1836–39; took part in war with Spain 1866; in War of the Pacific against Peru and Bolivia 1879–84, won the rich nitrate fields on coast of Bolivia (see ANTOFAGASTA and IQUIQUE) and occupied Tacna and Arica (*qq.v.*) which, until 1929, were subject of dispute with Peru; conflict bet. executive and legislative branches of government led to a brief civil war in 1891 followed by parliamentary rule and decreased presidential power; boundary dispute with Argentina settled 1902; neutral in WWI but affected financially because of trade; adopted new constitution 1925; in WWII severed relations with the Axis 1943 and declared war on Japan 1945; initiated reform program known as "Chileanization" in the 1960s; following national election, Marxist candidate Salvador Allende Gossens elected president 1970, ousted by military coup 1973 in which Allende died; new constitution 1981 provided for eventual return to civilian rule; 10-year state of emergency lifted 1983; elections held 1989 resulted in return to civilian government.

Chiledug. See TJILEDUG.

Chile Rise. Ridge, SE Pacific Ocean floor, extending approx. from S of Easter I. to W of S Chile in a general NW to SE direction; a center of oceanic crust formation according to theory of plate tectonics.

Chilia. See KILIYA.

Chilia–Nouă. See KILIYA 2.

Chi·li·an·wa·la *or* **Chil·li·an·wa·la** \ˌchi-lē-än-ˈwä-lə\. Village, Punjab, Pakistan, 5 mi. (8 km.) E of the Jhelum; indecisive but bloody battle 1849 in Sikh Wars bet. the English under Sir Hugh Gough and the Sikhs.

Ch'i–lien Shan. See QILIAN SHAN.

Chilika Lake. See CHILKA LAKE.

Chi–lin. See JILIN 2.

Ch'i–lin–ts'o. See SILING CO.

Chil·ka Lake \ˈchil-kə\ *or* **Chil·i·ka Lake** \ˈchi-li-\. Shallow inland gulf on the NE coast of India, in E Orissa state.

Chil·kat \ˈchil-ˌkat\. River, SE Alaska; flows SE to **Chilkat Inlet** at head of Lynn Canal (*q.v.*).

Chil·ko Lake \ˈchil-ˌkō\. Lake, S cen. British Columbia, Canada; outlet is the **Chilko River** flowing N into Chilcotin River; 75 sq. mi. (194 sq. km.).

Chil·koot Inlet \ˈchil-ˌküt\. E arm of Lynn Canal (*q.v.*), SE Alaska.

Chilkoot Pass. Pass in coast range, N Rocky Mts.; highest point 3502 ft. (1067 m.); extends 29 mi. (47 km.) from former village of Dyea at head of Taiya Inlet, Lynn Canal, SE Alaska, to Lake Bennett in Yukon Terr., Canada; formerly an American Indian route; used in the late 1890s by gold seekers until opening of White Pass Railway farther E; today used by recreational hikers.

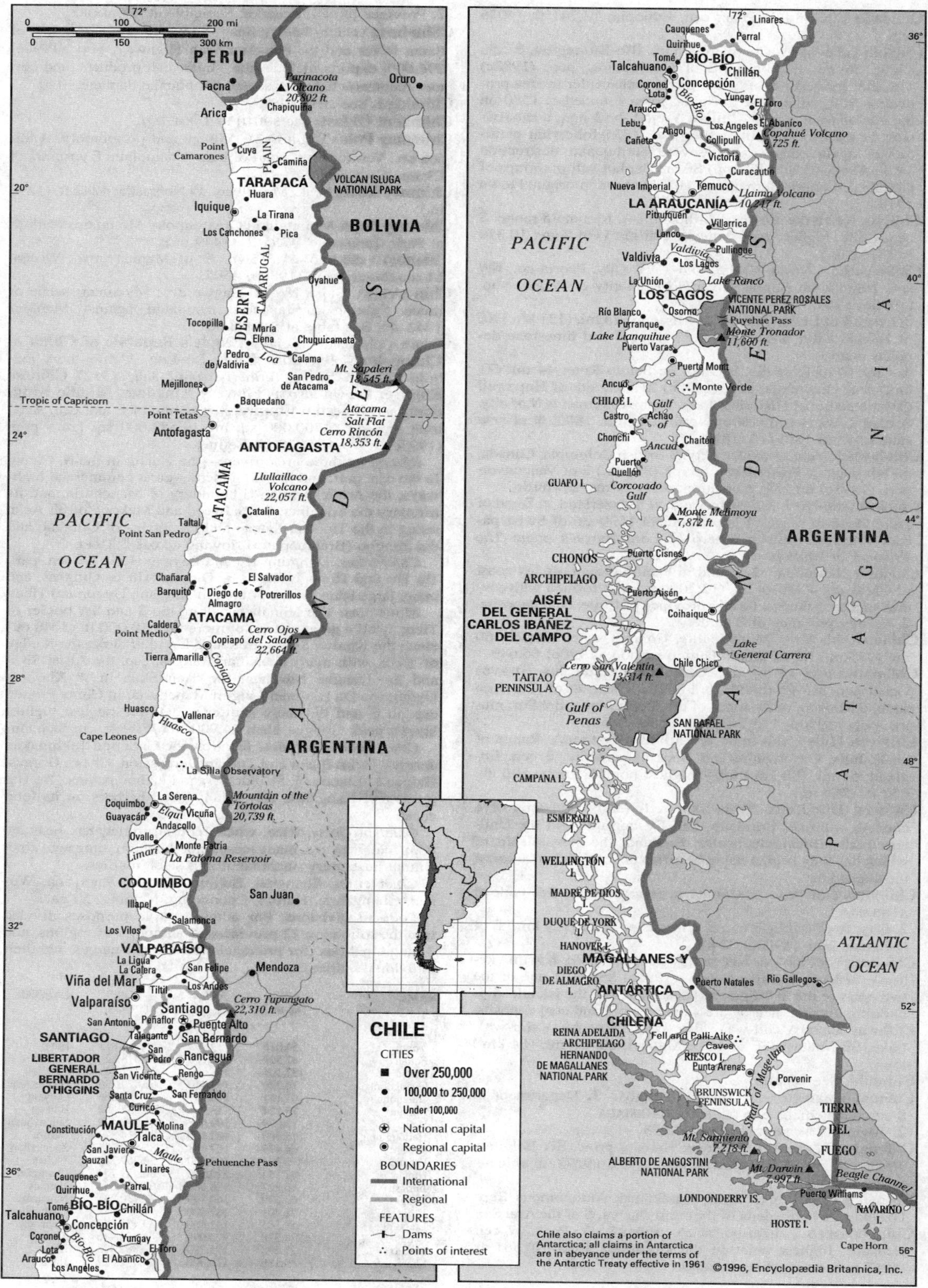
PERU
BOLIVIA
ARGENTINA
PACIFIC OCEAN
ATLANTIC OCEAN
ANDES
PATAGONIA
Tacna
Arica
Parinacota Volcano 20,802 ft.
Chapiquiña
Oruro
Point Camarones
Cuya
Camiña
VOLCAN ISLUGA NATIONAL PARK
TARAPACÁ
Huara
Iquique
La Tirana
Los Canchones
Pica
TAMARUGAL PLAIN
DESERT
Oyahue
Tocopilla
María Elena
Chuquicamata
Pedro de Valdivia
Loa
Calama
Mt. Sapaleri 18,545 ft.
San Pedro de Atacama
Mejillones
Baquedano
Tropic of Capricorn
Atacama Salt Flat
Point Tetas
Antofagasta
Cerro Rincón 18,353 ft.
ANTOFAGASTA
ATACAMA
Llullaillaco Volcano 22,057 ft.
Catalina
Taltal
Point San Pedro
Chañaral
El Salvador
Barquito
Diego de Almagro
Potrerillos
ATACAMA
Caldera
Point Medio
Copiapó
Cerro Ojos del Salado 22,664 ft.
Tierra Amarilla
Copiapó
Huasco
Vallenar
Huasco
Cape Leones
La Silla Observatory
La Serena
Mountain of the Tórtolas 20,739 ft.
Coquimbo
Guayacán
Elqui
Vicuña
Andacollo
Ovalle
Monte Patria
Limarí
La Paloma Reservoir
COQUIMBO
San Juan
Illapel
Salamanca
Los Vilos
VALPARAÍSO
La Ligua
La Calera
San Felipe
Mendoza
Viña del Mar
Tiltil
Los Andes
Valparaíso
Santiago
Cerro Tupungato 22,310 ft.
San Antonio
Peñaflor
Puente Alto
SANTIAGO
Talagante
San Bernardo
San Pedro
Rancagua
LIBERTADOR GENERAL BERNARDO O'HIGGINS
San Vicente
Rengo
Santa Cruz
San Fernando
Curicó
Constitución
MAULE
Molina
Talca
San Javier
Sauzal
Maule
Linares
Pehuenche Pass
Cauquenes
Quirihue
Parral
Tomé
BÍO-BÍO
Chillán
Talcahuano
Concepción
Coronel
Lota
Yungay
Arauco
Bío-Bío
El Abanico
El Toro
Los Angeles
72°
20°
24°
28°
32°
36°
0 100 200 mi
0 150 300 km
Linares
Cauquenes
Parral
Quirihue
Tomé
BÍO-BÍO
Chillán
Talcahuano
Concepción
Coronel
Lota
Yungay
El Toro
Arauco
El Abanico
Lebu
Los Angeles
Angol
Copahué Volcano 9,725 ft.
Cañete
Collipulli
Victoria
Curacautín
Nueva Imperial
Temuco
Llaima Volcano 10,247 ft.
LA ARAUCANÍA
Pitrufquén
Villarrica
Lanco
Pullingue
Valdivia
Los Lagos
La Unión
Lake Ranco
LOS LAGOS
VICENTE PEREZ ROSALES NATIONAL PARK
Puyehue Pass
Río Blanco
Osorno
Purranque
Monte Tronador 11,600 ft.
Lake Llanquihue
Puerto Varas
Puerto Montt
Ancud
Monte Verde
CHILOE I.
Gulf
Castro
Achao
of
Chonchi
Ancud
Chaitén
Puerto Quellón
GUAFO I.
Corcovado Gulf
Monte Melimoyu 7,872 ft.
CHONOS ARCHIPELAGO
Puerto Cisnes
Puerto Aisén
AISÉN DEL GENERAL CARLOS IBÁÑEZ DEL CAMPO
Coihaique
Lake General Carrera
Chile Chico
Cerro San Valentín 13,314 ft.
TAITAO PENINSULA
Gulf of Penas
SAN RAFAEL NATIONAL PARK
CAMPANA I.
ESMERALDA I.
WELLINGTON I.
MADRE DE DIOS I.
DUQUE DE YORK I.
HANOVER I.
DIEGO DE ALMAGRO I.
MAGALLANES Y ANTÁRTICA CHILENA
Puerto Natales
Rio Gallegos
REINA ADELAIDA ARCHIPELAGO
Fell and Palli-Aike Caves
HERNANDO DE MAGALLANES NATIONAL PARK
RIESCO I.
Punta Arenas
Strait of Magellan
Porvenir
BRUNSWICK PENINSULA
TIERRA DEL FUEGO
Mt. Sarmiento 7,218 ft.
ALBERTO DE ANGOSTINI NATIONAL PARK
Mt. Darwin 7,997 ft.
Beagle Channel
Puerto Williams
LONDONDERRY IS.
NAVARINO I.
HOSTE I.
Cape Horn
40°
44°
48°
52°
56°
CHILE
CITIES
Over 250,000
100,000 to 250,000
Under 100,000
National capital
Regional capital
BOUNDARIES
International
Regional
FEATURES
Dams
Points of interest
Chile also claims a portion of Antarctica; all claims in Antarctica are in abeyance under the terms of the Antarctic Treaty effective in 1961
©1996, Encyclopædia Britannica, Inc.

Chil·la·lo \chi-ˈlä-lō\. Peak, cen. Ethiopia; 13,241 ft. (4036 m.).

Chil·lán \chē-ˈyän\. Commercial city, Bío-Bío region, S cen. Chile, 56 mi. (90 km.) NE of Concepción; pop. (1982c) 118,163; formerly ✱ of Ñuble prov.; trade center in area producing fruit, wine, flour; original town founded c. 1580 on the site of what is now **Chillán Viejo** \-ˈvyā-hō\, a subdivision of the city; rebuilt farther N c. 1835 following earthquake; again rebuilt after severe earthquake destruction 1939. About 45 mi. (72 km.) SE are the hot sulfur springs of Chillán. Liberator Bernardo O'Higgins born in original town 1778.

Chillán, Ne·va·dos de \nā-ˈvä-t͟hōs-ˌt͟hā-\. Mountain range, S cen. Chile; highest peak **Vol·cán Chillán** \vōl-ˈkän\ 10,370 ft. (3161 m.).

Chil·li·cothe \ˌchi-lə-ˈkä-thē, -ˈkȯ-\. **1.** City, Peoria co., NW cen. Illinois, on Illinois River N of the city of Peoria; pop. (1990c) 5959.

2. City, ⊗ of Livingston co., N Missouri, 75 mi. (121 km.) NE of Kansas City; pop. (1990c) 8804; coal and limestone deposits nearby.

3. City, ⊗ of Ross co., S Ohio, on Scioto River 44 mi. (71 km.) S of Columbus; pop. (1990c) 21,923; site of Hopewell Culture National Historical Park. Camp Sherman is N of city. Settled 1796; became ✱ of Northwest Terr. 1800, ✱ of new state of Ohio 1803–10, 1812–16.

Chil·li·wack \ˈchi-lə-ˌwak\. City, S British Columbia, Canada, on left bank of Fraser River 55 mi. (88 km.) E of Vancouver; pop. (1991c) 60,251; recreation; dairy farms, sawmills.

Chil·lon \shē-ˈyōⁿ\. Castle in Vaud, W Switzerland, at E end of Lake Geneva; place of imprisonment 1530–36 of Swiss patriot François Bonivard, hero of Lord Byron's poem *The Prisoner of Chillon.*

Chi·loé \ˌchē-lō-ˈā\. **1.** Island in Pacific Ocean off SW coast of Chile; ab. 4700 sq. mi. (12,200 sq. km.); formed with several smaller islands a former province of Chile; coal deposits.

2. Former province of S Chile.

Chi·lón \chē-ˈlōn\. Municipality, Chiapas state, Mexico, 60 mi. (97 km.) NE of Tuxtla Gutierrez; pop. (1990p) 66,649.

Chil·pan·cin·go *or in full* **Chilpancingo de los Bra·vos** \ˌchēl-pän-ˈsēŋ-gō-t͟hā-lōs-ˈbrä-b͟ōs\. Town, ✱ of Guerrero state, S Mexico, on N slopes of the Sierra Madre del Sur; munic. pop. (1990p) 136,243; university (1869).

Chil·tern Hills \ˈchil-tərn\ *or* **Chil·terns** \-tərnz\. Range of chalk hills, Oxfordshire and Buckinghamshire, S cen. England; 55 mi. (88 km.) long; highest point Coombe Hill ab. 852 ft. (260 m.).

Chiltern Hundreds. Three *hundreds* (early divisions of a county) —Stoke, Burnham, and Desborough—in the Chiltern Hills, Buckinghamshire, England, the stewardship of which has long been a nominal office under the chancellor of the exchequer.

Chil·ton \ˈchilt-ᵊn\. **1.** County in cen. Alabama. See table at ALABAMA.

2. City, ⊗ of Calumet co., E Wisconsin, 18 mi. (29 km.) E of Oshkosh; pop. (1990c) 3240.

Chi–lung \ˈjē-ˈlu̇ŋ\ *or* **Kee·lung** \ˈkē-ˈlu̇ŋ\ *or Jp.* **Ki·run** \kē-ˈrün\. Seaport, N Taiwan; pop. (1992e) 356,501; one of the two ports of the ✱ Taipei; has best harbor in the island; shipbuilding, fishing; nearby are valuable gold and coal deposits.

Chil·wa, Lake \ˈchil-wä\ *also* **Lake Shir·wa** \ˈshir-wä\. Lake, SE Malawi, SE of Lake Malawi; ab. 40 mi. (64 km.) long.

Chimahi. See CIMAHI.

Chi·mal·te·nan·go \chē-ˌmäl-tā-ˈnäŋ-gō\. **1.** Department of S cen. Guatemala. See table at GUATEMALA.

2. Town, its ✱; pop. (1993e) 24,933.

Chi·may \shē-ˈmā\. Commune, Hainaut prov., SW Belgium, 30 mi. (48 km.) SW of Dinant; pop. (1981c) 9273; marble deposits; castle.

Chim·bai \chim-ˈbī\. Town, Karakalpak Autonomous Rep., Uzbekistan, in the delta of the Amu Dar'ya, S of the Aral Sea.

Chim·bo·ra·zo \ˌchēm-bō-ˈrä-zō, ˌshēm-\. **1.** Peak, W cen. Ecuador; highest point in the Cordillera Real, 20,561 ft. (6267 m.); an inactive volcano.

2. Province of cen. Ecuador. See table at ECUADOR.

Chim·bo·te \chēm-ˈbō-tā\. Seaport town, W Peru, at mouth of Santa River and on Pan-American Highway; pop. (1990e) 296,600; exports include rice, sugar, fish products, and cotton; reconstructed after severe earthquake damage 1970.

Chimkent. See SHYMKENT.

Chimkent Oblast. See SOUTH KAZAKHSTAN.

Chim·ney Point \ˈchim-nē\. Village and promontory, Addison co., Vermont, on S part of Lake Champlain; E terminal of Champlain Bridge.

Chimney Rock. Peak, Morrill co., W Nebraska; 4242 ft. (1293 m.).

Chimney Tops. Mountain in Great Smoky Mountains National Park, Tennessee; 4755 ft. (1449 m.).

Chi·moio \shē-ˈmȯi-ō\. Town, ✱ of Manica prov., W cen. Mozambique, pop. (1980p) 4507.

Chin \ˈchin\. State, NW of Magwe div., Myanmar; scene of much fighting in Japanese campaign against Manipur 1942–44. See table at MYANMAR.

Chi·na \ˈchī-nə\; *officially* **People's Republic of China** *or* **Chung–hua Jen–min Kung–ho–kuo** \ˈchu̇ŋ-ˈhwä-ˈjən-ˈmin-ˈku̇ŋ-ˈhō-ˈkwȯ\; *formerly (until Jan. 1912)* **Chinese Empire;** *known also as* **Flowery Kingdom, Middle Kingdom,** *and* **Celestial Empire.** A republic of E and cen. Asia; total area ab. 3,700,000 sq. mi. (9,583,000 sq. km.); pop. (1993e) 1,179,467,000; ✱ Beijing.

Rivers: Its three great rivers—the Huang in the N, Chang in the cen. part, and the Xi in the S—great commercial highways; the Amur forming N boundary of Manchuria, and its tributary the Songhua; the Salween and Mekong of SE Asia, rising in the Tibetan Plateau and mountains of Qinghai; and the Zangbo (Brahmaputra) flowing across S Tibet.

Chief lakes: Dongting Hu and Poyang Hu in SE cen. part, Tai Hu and Hongze Hu in E, Qinghai Hu in Qinghai, and many large lakes without outlet in Xinjiang Uygur and Tibet.

Mountains: The Himalayas along the S and SW border of Tibet, itself a great plateau of more than 10,000 ft. (3048 m.) elev.; the Kunlun Shan, stretching E and W along the N edge of Tibet, with many subsidiary ranges, esp. the Altun Shan and the Danghe Nanshan; the Tian Shan in W Xinjiang Uygur; the Da Hinggan Ling in Manchuria; in China Proper, esp. in S and W, many shorter and lower ranges; highest known peak Gongga Shan 24,900 ft. (7590 m.) in Sichuan.

Other notable physical features: the Gobi and Taklimakan deserts, Tarim Basin and Turpan Depression, Chang Gorges, Hainan I., Liaodong, Shandong, and Leizhou penins., Bo Hai (gulf) and Hangzhou Bay. Many good harbors on its long coast.

Chief products: Rice, wheat, cotton, millet, tea, peanuts, fish; coal, iron ore, manganese, molybdenum, tungsten, zinc; animal husbandry; manufacturing: steel, textiles.

Chief cities: Shanghai, Beijing, Tianjin, Shenyang, Wuhan, Guangzhou, Harbin, Chongqing, Nanjing, Xi'an.

Political divisions: For administrative purposes divided into the following 22 provinces, 5 autonomous regions, and 3 municipalities (for pronunciation of their names, see their individual entries):

NAME	AREA (sq. mi.)	AREA (sq. km.)	POP. (1990c)	CAPITAL
Provinces				
Anhui	54,015	139,899	56,180,813	Hefei
Fujian	47,529	123,100	30,048,224	Fuzhou
Gansu	137,104	355,099	22,371,141	Lanzhou
Guangdong	76,220	197,410	62,829,236	Guangzhou
Guizhou	67,181	173,999	32,391,066	Guiyang
Hainan	13,124	33,991	6,557,482	Haikou
Hebei	77,079	199,635	61,082,439	Shijiazhuang
Heilongjiang	178,996	463,600	35,214,873	Harbin
Henan	64,479	167,001	85,509,535	Zhengzhou
Hubei	73,394	190,090	53,969,210	Wuhan
Hunan	81,274	210,500	60,659,754	Changsha
Jiangsu	40,927	106,001	67,056,519	Nanjing
Jiangxi	63,629	164,799	37,710,281	Nanchang
Jilin	72,201	187,000	24,658,721	Changchun
Liaoning	58,301	151,000	39,459,697	Shenyang
Qinghai	278,378	720,999	4,456,946	Xining
Shaanxi	75,598	195,799	32,882,403	Xi'an
Shandong	59,189	153,300	84,392,827	Jinan

NAME	AREA (sq. mi.)	AREA (sq. km.)	POP. (1990c)	CAPITAL
Shanxi	60,656	157,099	28,759,014	Taiyuan
Sichuan	219,691	569,000	107,218,173	Chengdu
Yunnan	168,417	436,200	36,972,610	Kunming
Zhejiang	39,305	101,800	41,445,930	Hangzhou
Autonomous Regions				
Guangxi Zhuangzu	85,096	220,399	42,245,765	Nanning
Nei Monggol	454,633	1,177,499	21,456,798	Hohhot
Ningxia Huizu	30,039	77,801	4,655,451	Yinchuan
Tibet (Xizang)	471,660	1,221,599	2,196,010	Lhasa
Xinjiang Uygur	635,829	1,646,797	15,155,778	Ürümqi
Municipalities				
Beijing	3,386	8,770	10,819,407	
Shanghai	772	1,999	13,341,896	
Tianjin	4,400	11,396	8,785,402	

History: Early hominids were in China as far back as the Paleolithic period; Chinese civilization probably spread from Huang River valley where it existed c. 3000 B.C.; traditional Chinese history begins with the Hsia dynasty ab. 2000 B.C.; Shang dynasty (16th–17th cents. B.C.), the first vouched for by valid historical evidence, had writing system and calendar; succeeding Western Chou dynasty (11th–8th cents. B.C.) controlled a vast feudal society extending from mouth of Chang River to Great Wall; divided into warring states in Eastern Chou dynasty (8th–3d cents. B.C.), during which Taoism and Confucianism were founded; Ch'in dynasty (221–206 B.C.) expanded S of the Chang, unifying the area that came to be known as China Proper and establishing a centralized bureaucracy; members of Han dynasty (206 B.C.–220 A.D.) pursued a policy of military expansionism and gained first direct overland contact with West (Rome); Buddhism (see INDIA 1) introduced by first century A.D.; Han technical advances included paper and porcelain; split up bet. 220 and 265 into three kingdoms Shu (Han), Wu, and Wei, followed by a period of disunity characterized by minor regional dynasties and ongoing war with non-Chinese invaders; reunited by Sui dynasty (581–618); "Golden Age" of Chinese art and literature began under T'angs (618–907) whose authority extended beyond the boundaries of China Proper; declined into another period of fragmentation and warfare known as the Five Dynasties and Ten Kingdoms (907–960); ruled by Northern Sung dynasty (960–1127), and, after invasion of the Juchen in N, by Southern Sungs (1127–1279); Sung period remembered as a great age of cultural achievement; in 13th cent. conquered by Mongols whose empire eventually included all of China and stretched across Asia; Kublai Khan, first of Yüan (Mongol) dynasty (1279–1368), visited by Venetian traveler Marco Polo; S China drove out Mongols and founded Ming dynasty (1368–1644); reached in 16th cent. by Portuguese whose traders and missionaries were at first admitted to interior but were later strictly limited (see MACAO); under Manchus (Ch'ing dynasty 1644–1911/12) Chinese empire included Manchuria, Mongolia, Taiwan, Tibet, and Turkistan, and claimed various border states as tributaries; in first treaty with European power (see NERCHINSK) 1689, defined N boundary with Russia; from c. 1760 Canton (now Guangzhou) alone open to European trade until, at close of First Opium War 1842, China forced to cede Hong Kong and open five treaty ports; E Siberia, as far as Vladivostok (*q.v.*) ceded to Russia 1858–60; Ch'ing dynasty weakened by Taiping Rebellion 1851–64; lost Korea, Taiwan, and Penghu (Treaty of Shimonoseki) following the Chinese-Japanese War of 1894–95; lease of Kiaochow to Germany in 1898 began European scramble for concessions; N China scene of Boxer risings 1900; revolutionaries overthrew Ch'ing dynasty and estab. Chinese Republic 1912; forced to yield to Twenty-one Demands of Japan 1915; entered WWI 1917; Nine-Power Treaty, guaranteeing China's administrative and territorial integrity, signed after Washington Conference 1922; nationalist government formed at Nanjing by the Kuomintang party 1928 following more than a decade of warlordism and political strife; Manchuria (*q.v.*) invaded by Japan 1931, puppet state of Manchukuo created 1932; communist base estab. in the Shaanxi prov. following the Long March across China 1934–35; engaged in Sino-Japanese War 1937–45; one of the four Great Powers in WWII 1939–45; civil war 1945–49, during which Communist regime estab. control over mainland China; People's Republic of China proclaimed Oct. 1, 1949; suffered from the economic failure of the "Great Leap Forward" (massive communalization of agriculture and local industry 1958–60) and from famine 1959–c. 1961; suppressed Tibetan uprising 1959; U.S.S.R. withdrew its technicians and advisors 1960; fought border war with India 1962; exploded its first nuclear bomb 1964; deteriorating relations with U.S.S.R. culminated in a number of border clashes in the late 1960s; serious internal crises during "Great Cultural Revolution" (1966–76 radical agenda to revitalize leftist values); became a member of UN 1971; major earthquake 1976; moved toward economic reform and improved relations with the West following the Third Plenum of the Central Committee of the Eleventh National Party Congress 1978; estab. full diplomatic relations with the U.S. 1979; suppressed Tiananmen Square student demonstration with military force 1989, incurring international disapproval and temporary economic sanctions. See also HONG KONG, MACAO, MANCHUKUO, MANCHURIA, and TAIWAN.

China, Mainland. Name for the People's Republic of China (see CHINA) to distinguish it from Taiwan.

China Grove. Town, Rowan co., cen. North Carolina, 10 mi. (16 km.) SW of Salisbury; pop. (1990c) 2732.

Chinan. See JINAN.

Chi·nan·de·ga \ˌchē-nän-ˈdā-gä\. **1.** Department of NW Nicaragua. See table at NICARAGUA. **2.** Town, its ✻; pop. (1985e) 67,792; sugar.

China Proper. The parts of present-day People's Republic of China having provincial status with the exclusion of Hainan and the provs. comprising Manchuria (Liaoning, Jilin, and Heilongjiang).

China Sea. Part of Pacific Ocean reaching from Japan to S end of Malay Penin.; divided by Taiwan into **East China Sea** *or* **Eastern Sea** (482,300 sq. mi. or 1,249,157 sq. km., max. depth 9126 ft. or 2782 m., enclosed by E China, South Korea, Kyūshū I., Ryukyu Is., and Taiwan) and **South China Sea,** *often called simply* **China Sea** (895,400 sq. mi. or 2,319,086 sq. km.), max. depth ab. 15,000 ft. or 4600 m., enclosed by SE China, Indochina, Malay Penin., Borneo, Philippines, and Taiwan).

Chi·na·ti Peak \chə-ˈnä-tē\. Mountain, Presidio co., W Texas; 7730 ft. (2356 m.).

Chin·cha Al·ta \ˈchin-chə-ˈäl-tə\. Town, SW Peru; pop. (1981p) 38,718.

Chincha Islands. Group of small islands in Pacific Ocean off coast of W cen. Peru; guano.

Chinchaycocha. See JUNÍN 2.

Chin–chou *or* **Chin·chow** \ˈjin-ˈjō\. See JINZHOU.

Chin·co·teague \ˌshiŋ-kə-ˈtēg, ˌchiŋ-\. Town, NE Accomac co., E Virginia, on **Chincoteague Island,** bet. S end of Assateague I. and the mainland; pop. (1990c) 3572.

Chincoteague Bay. Long narrow bay bet. Assateague I. and the mainland (Maryland and Virginia).

Chin·de \ˈchēn-dā\. Seaport town on only navigable mouth of the Zambezi, SE cen. Mozambique; formerly chief port for Malawi and Zambia.

Chin·dwin \ˈchin-ˈdwin\. River, W Myanmar; rises in Kumon Range in N Myanmar, flows NW through Hukawng Valley, then S along India border and SE to the Irrawaddy at Myingyan; ab. 720 mi. (1158 km.) long; chief tributary of the Irrawaddy; generally navigable below its confluence with the Uyu, its chief tributary. Scene of much fighting in WWII.

Chi·nen Peninsula \chē-ˈnen\. Peninsula on E coast of Okinawa, Japan, at S end of island S of Nakagusuku Bay; Japanese on it cut off by U.S. troops June 1945.

\ə\ abut \ə̇\ matches \ᵊ\ kitten, Fr table \ər\ further \a\ ash \ā\ ace
\ä\ cot, cart \ȧ\ Fr bac \au̇\ out \b̲\ Span Avila \ch\ chin \e\ bet \ē\ easy
\g\ go \i\ hit \ī\ ice \j\ job \k̲\ Ger ich, Buch \ⁿ\ Fr vin
\ŋ\ sing \ō\ go \ȯ\ all \ȯ\ law \œ\ Fr bœuf \œ̄\ Fr feu \ȯi\ boy
\th\ thin \th̲\ this \ü\ loot \u̇\ foot \ue\ Ger füllen \üe\ Fr rue
\y\ yet \ʸ\ Fr digne \ˈdēnʸ\, nuit \ˈnwʸē\ \yü\ few \yu̇\ fury \zh\ vision

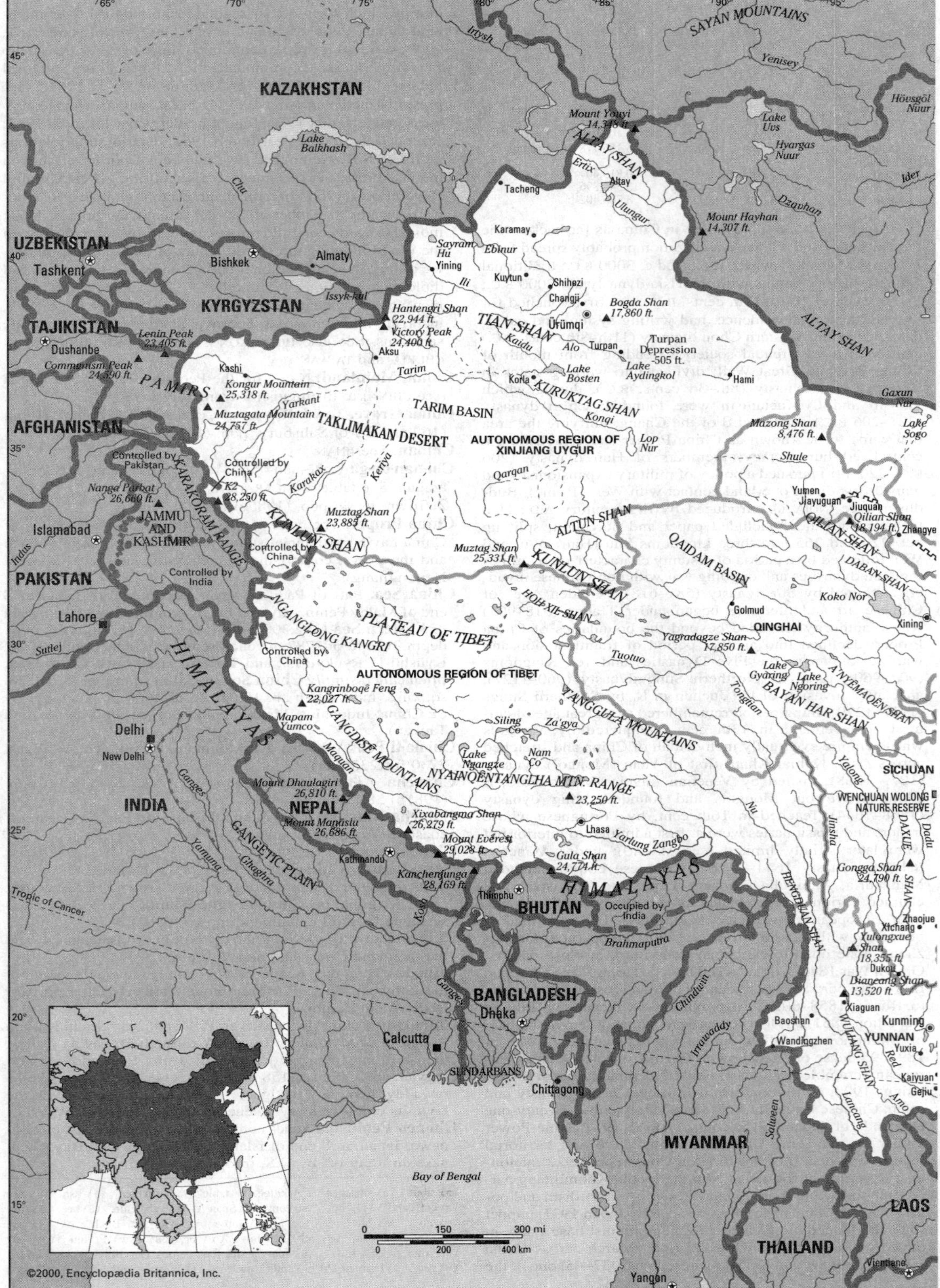
KAZAKHSTAN
UZBEKISTAN
KYRGYZSTAN
TAJIKISTAN
AFGHANISTAN
PAKISTAN
INDIA
NEPAL
BHUTAN
BANGLADESH
MYANMAR
THAILAND
LAOS
Tashkent
Bishkek
Almaty
Dushanbe
Islamabad
Lahore
Delhi
New Delhi
Kathmandu
Thimphu
Dhaka
Calcutta
Chittagong
Yangon
Vientiane
Lake Balkhash
Issyk-kul
PAMIRS
KARAKORAM RANGE
KUNLUN SHAN
HIMALAYAS
GANGETIC PLAIN
TIAN SHAN
ALTAY SHAN
TARIM BASIN
TAKLIMAKAN DESERT
AUTONOMOUS REGION OF XINJIANG UYGUR
PLATEAU OF TIBET
AUTONOMOUS REGION OF TIBET
QINGHAI
SICHUAN
YUNNAN
QAIDAM BASIN
ALTUN SHAN
QILIAN SHAN
DABAN SHAN
BAYAN HAR SHAN
A'NYEMAQEN SHAN
TANGGULA MOUNTAINS
GANGDISE MOUNTAINS
NYAINQENTANGLHA MTN. RANGE
HENGDUAN SHAN
WULIANG SHAN
DAXUE SHAN
WENCHUAN WOLONG NATURE RESERVE
SAYAN MOUNTAINS
Ürümqi
Lhasa
Kunming
Golmud
Xining
Kashi
Aksu
Hami
Turpan
Turpan Depression -505 ft.
Mount Everest 29,028 ft.
K2 28,250 ft.
Kanchenjunga 28,169 ft.
Nanga Parbat 26,660 ft.
Mount Dhaulagiri 26,810 ft.
Mount Manaslu 26,686 ft.
Xixabangma Shan 26,279 ft.
Muztag Shan 25,331 ft.
Kongur Mountain 25,318 ft.
Muztagata Mountain 24,757 ft.
Gula Shan 24,774 ft.
Gongga Shan 24,790 ft.
Victory Peak 24,400 ft.
Hantengri Shan 22,944 ft.
Lenin Peak 23,405 ft.
Communism Peak 24,590 ft.
Muztag Shan 23,885 ft.
Kangrinboqê Feng 22,027 ft.
Mount Youyi 14,348 ft.
Mount Hayhan 14,307 ft.
Bogda Shan 17,860 ft.
Qilian Shan 18,194 ft.
Mazong Shan 8,476 ft.
Yagradagze Shan 17,850 ft.
Yulongxue Shan 18,355 ft.
Diancang Shan 13,520 ft.
JAMMU AND KASHMIR
Controlled by Pakistan
Controlled by China
Controlled by India
Occupied by India
Bay of Bengal
SUNDARBANS
Tropic of Cancer
0 150 300 mi
0 200 400 km
©2000, Encyclopædia Britannica, Inc.

CHINA
CITIES
Over 3,000,000
1,000,000 to 3,000,000
Under 1,000,000
National capital
Provincial capital
BOUNDARIES
International
Disputed
Line of control
Provincial
FEATURES
Great Wall
Canals
100°
105°
110°
115°
120°
125°
130°
135°
140°
RUSSIA
MONGOLIA
NORTH KOREA
SOUTH KOREA
JAPAN
TAIWAN
VIETNAM
PHILIPPINES
Lake Baikal
Angara
Selenga
YABLONOVYY RANGE
Shilka
Onon
Orhon
Selenge
Egiyn
Ulaanbaatar
Kerulen
GOBI DESERT
Zeya
Bureya
Amur
Argun
HUZHONG NATURE RESERVE
Fengshui Shan 4,585 ft.
HANMA NATURE RESERVE
Nuomin
Nanweng
XIAO HINGGAN LING
SIKHOTE-ALIN MOUNTAINS
Wusuli
Manzhouli
Hailar
Xuguit
Hulun Nur
DA HINGGAN LING
Butha Qi
Nen
Yalu
Bei'an
Yichun
Hegang
Jiamusi
Shuangyashan
HEILONGJIANG
Qiqihar
Suihua
Songhua
Daqing
Anda
Qitaihe
Jixi
Zhaodong
Harbin
Daguokui Shan 5,543 ft.
Lake Khanka
Baicheng
Lake Qagan
Di'er Songhua
Mudanjiang
Mudan
MANCHURIAN PLAIN
JILIN
Horqin Youyi Qianqi
Tao'er
Jilin
Changchun
CHANGBAI NATURE RESERVE
Dunhua
Yanji
Tumen
Vladivostok
Huanggangliang Shan 6,655 ft.
Xiliao
Tongliao
Huaide
Siping
Liaoyuan
Songhua Reservoir
Erenhot
AUTONOMOUS REGION OF NEI MONGGOL
Laoha
Tiefa
Tieling
Hailong
Hunjiang
Mount Paektu 9,000 ft.
CHANGBAI MTS.
Chifeng
Fuxin
Fushun
Tonghua
Chaoyang
Beipiao
Shenyang
Liaoyang
Benxi
BEIJING MUNICIPALITY
Chengde
Anshan
Haicheng
Yingkou
SEA OF JAPAN
YIN SHAN
Lake Ulansuhai
Jining
Jinzhou
Jinxi
Liaoning
Dandong
Linhe
Baotou
Hohhot
Zhangjiakou
Yongding
Luan
Huang He
Datong
Beijing
Qinhuangdao
Bo Hai
P'yongyang
Wuhai
Dongsheng
Heng Shan 6,616 ft.
HEBEI
Zhuozhou
Tianjin
Tangshan
Fuxian
Korea Bay
HELAN SHAN
Jinchang
Shizuishan
MU US DESERT
Wutai Shan 10,030 ft.
Changzhou
TIANJIN MUNICIPALITY
Dalian
Seoul
Yinchuan
Baoding
Xinzhou
Hutuo
Ziya
Wuwei
Wuzhong
Taiyuan
Shijiazhuang
Longkou
Weihai
Yangquan
Hengshui
Dongying
Yantai
AUTONOMOUS REGION OF NINGXIA HUIZU
SHANXI
Yuci
Nangong
SHANDONG PENINSULA
GANSU
Xingtai
Dezhou
Binzhou
Zibo
Weifang
Qingdao
Huang He
Baiyin
Yan'an
TAIHANG SHAN
Jinan
Tai Shan 5,048 ft.
Tai'an
Laiwu
YELLOW SEA
Lanzhou
LOESS PLATEAU
LIUPAN SHAN
SHAANXI
LÜLIANG SHAN
Fen
Changzhi
Handan
Yidu
SHANDONG
Linxia
Pingliang
Hancheng
Hebi
Anyang
Qufu
Xintai
Linfen
Jincheng
Puyang
Houma
Xinxiang
Heze
Jining
Linyi
Rizhao
Yuncheng
Jiaozuo
Tianshui
Tongchuan
Weinan
Sanmenxia
Zhengzhou
Kaifeng
Zaozhuang
Lianyungang
Grand Canal
BAISHUI RIVER NATURE RESERVE
Baoji
Xianyang
Xi'an
Hua Shan 6,552 ft.
Luoyang
Song Shan 4,724 ft.
HENAN
Shangqiu
Huaibei
Huaiyin
Yancheng
Taibai Shan 12,356 ft.
QIN SHAN
Pingdingshan
Xuchang
Zhoukou
Xuzhou
Hongze Hu
JIANGSU
Taizhou
MIN SHAN
Hanzhong
Danjiangkou Reservoir
Nanyang
Zhumadian
Ying
Bengbu
Fuyang
Yangzhou
Guanghua
Huai
Huainan
ANHUI
Nanjing
Nantong
Min
Shiyan
Xiangfan
Xinyang
Hefei
Cangzhou
Yu Shan 12,956 ft.
Mianyang
DABIE SHAN
Chang Jiang
Wuhu
Wuxi
Suzhou
Shanghai
Tai Hu
SHANGHAI MUNICIPALITY
Deyang
Suizhou
Lu'an
Lake Chao
Chengdu
Daxian
HUBEI
Han
Tongling
Huzhou
Jiaxing
Suining
Wanxian
Nanchong
Guangming Shan 6,039 ft.
Hangzhou
SICHUAN BASIN
Lichuan
Yichang
Yingcheng
Wuhan
Ezhou
Anqing
HUANG SHAN
Shaoxing
Yuyao
Ningbo
EAST CHINA SEA
Huaying
Enshi
Shashi
Huangshi
Tunxi
Xin'anjiang Reservoir
Leshan
Emei Shan 10,167 ft.
Zigong
Fuling
Shishou
Jiujiang
Jingdezhen
Jinhua
Luzhou
Chongqing
Jinshi
Puqi
Poyang Hu
Lanxi
Haimen
Changde
Yueyang
Nanchang
Quzhou
Lishui
Yibin
Wu
Yuan
Dongting Hu
Shangrao
Jishou
Changsha
Fengcheng
ZHEJIANG
DALIANG SHAN
Xiangtan
Zhuzhou
Xinyu
Gan
Yingtan
Wenzhou
Yingchuan
Lengshuijiang
Loudi
Fuzhou
Zhaotong
Zunyi
Bozhou
Pingxiang
Shaowu
GUIZHOU
Huaihua
Heng Shan 4,232 ft.
JIANGXI
Guiyang
Hongjiang
Shaoyang
Ji'an
Nanping
Shuicheng
Lengshuitan
Hengyang
Min
Fuzhou
Kaili
HUNAN
Jinggangshan
Sanming
Anshun
Duyun
Yongzhou
Zixing
Yong'an
FUJIAN
Qujing
Beipan
Chenzhou
Ganzhou
Putian
Taipei
NAN SHAN
Quanzhou
Guilin
Longyan
Taiwan Strait
Hechi
Shaoguan
Zhangzhou
Xiamen
Liuzhou
Bei
Meizhou
Bose
Heshan
Chao'an
AUTONOMOUS REGION OF GUANGXI ZHUANGZU
Wuzhou
Xi
GUANGDONG
Shantou
Xun
Zhaoqing
Guangzhou
Huizhou
Yu
Nanning
Yulin
Jiangmen
Shenzhen
Pingxiang
Qinzhou
Zhuhai
HONG KONG (Special Administrative Region)
Maoming
MACAU (Special Administrative Region)
Beihai
Zhanjiang
Hanoi
Gulf of Tonkin
Haikou
SOUTH CHINA SEA
Danxian
Nandu
Qionghai
HAINAN
Wuzhi Shan 6,124 ft.
HAINAN ISLAND
Yaxian
Mekong

Chi·nese City \ˈchī-ˌnēz, -ˌnēs\ *or* **Outer City.** Section of Beijing, China, S of Tatar (Inner) City; designated mid-16th cent. during the Ming dynasty.

Chinese Tur·ke·stan \ˌtər-ki-ˈstan\ *or* **Kash·gar·ia** \kash-ˈgar-ē-ə\ *or* **East Turkistan.** The part of Turkistan (*q.v.*) under Chinese control; by some, thought to be coextensive with Xinjiang Uygur, but more properly the W and cen. parts of Xinjiang Uygur, W China; chief town was Kashgar, now Kashi. At various times occupied by among others the Chinese, Ephthalites, Uighurs, Muslims, and Mongols. Hotan was long the most important city. In 14th and 15th cents. visited by many Muslim scholars, but tolerance then established abolished by Chinese conquest in 18th cent.; under leadership of Uzbeks rebelled against China 1866; reconquered 1877–78.

Chinese Wall. See GREAT WALL.

Ching. See JING.

Ch'ing–chiang. See QINGJIANG.

Ch'ing–hai. 1. Lake, China. See QINGHAI.

2. Province, China. See QINGHAI.

Chingleput. See CHENGALPATTU.

Chin·go·la \chēŋ-ˈgō-lä\. Town, Zambia, 30 mi. (48 km.) NW of Kitwe; pop. (1990c) 281,183; service center in copper region.

Ch'ing–tao. See QINGDAO.

Ching–te–chen. See JINGDEZHEN.

Ch'ing–yüan. See BAODING.

Chin·hae \ˈchin-ˈhī\; *formerly* **Chin·kai** \-ˈkī\. Seaport town, South Kyŏngsang prov., South Korea, on inlet of Western Channel 22 mi. (35 km.) W of Pusan; pop. (1980p) 112,098; former Japanese naval base.

Chinhai. See ZHENHAI.

Chin Hills \ˈchin\. Range of hills along W border of Magwe div., Myanmar, part of Arakan Yoma system; from 7000 to 10,000 ft. (2134 to 3048 m.); inhabited by Chin peoples.

Chin·ho·yi \chēn-ˈhō-yē\. Town, N cen. Zimbabwe; pop. (1992p) 42,946.

Chinhsien. See JINZHOU.

Ch'in–huang–tao. See QINHUANGDAO.

Chin·i·ot \ˈchi-nē-ət\. Town, Pakistan, on E bank of Chenab River 80 mi. (129 km.) W of Lahore; pop. (1981p) 160,000.

Chin·ju \ˈjin-ˈjü\ *or* **Shin·shu** \ˈshin-ˈshü\. Town, South Kyŏngsang prov., South Korea, 55 mi. (88 km.) W of Pusan; pop. (1985c) 227,309.

Chinkai. See CHINHAE.

Chinkiang. See ZHENJIANG.

Ch'in Ling Shan. See QINLING SHANDI.

Chinnampo. See NAMP'O.

Chinnereth, Sea of. See GALILEE, SEA OF.

Chi·no \ˈchē-nō\. City, San Bernardino co., SE California, 30 mi. (48 km.) E of Los Angeles; pop. (1990c) 59,682; trade center; founded 1887.

Chi·non \shē-ˈnȯⁿ\. Commune, Indre-et-Loire dept., NW cen. France, on the Vienne River; pop. (1990c) 8961; wine; nuclear power plant; birthplace of writer François Rabelais 1483 is nearby.

Chi·nook \shə-ˈnu̇k, chə-\. Town, ⊗ of Blaine co., N Montana, 22 mi. (35 km.) E of Havre; pop. (1990c) 1512.

Chinook, Lake *or* **Lake Billy Chinook.** Reservoir in Deschutes River in Jefferson co., N cen. Oregon, formed by Round Butte Dam (see UNITED STATES, *Dams and Reservoirs*).

Chi·no Valley \ˈchē-nō\. Town, Yavapai co., cen. Arizona; pop. (1990c) 4837.

Chinsura. See HOOGHLY-CHINSURA.

Chinwangtao. See QINHUANGDAO.

Chiog·gia \kē-ˈȯj-jä\; *anc.* **Fos·sa Clau·dia** \ˈfä-sə-ˈklȯ-dē-ə\. Seaport, Venezia prov., Veneto, NE Italy, on island in Lagoon of Venice 15 mi. (24 km.) S of Venice; pop. (1991p) 52,582; major fishing port; built on piles and connected with mainland by bridge; 17th cent. cathedral; supremacy of Venice over Genoa decided here in naval campaign 1378–81.

Chi·os \ˈkī-ˌäs\ *or* **Khí·os** \ˈk̲ē-ȯs\ *or Turk.* **Sa·kız** \sä-ˈkə̇z\ *or Ital.* **Scio** \ˈshē-(ˌ)ō\. **1.** Island, Greece, in the Aegean Sea off W coast of Turkey in Asia; 30 mi. (48 km.) long by 8 to 15 mi. (13 to 24 km.) wide; 325 sq. mi. (842 sq. km.); by some included among the Southern Sporades (see SPORADES); with adjacent islets forms a department of Greece (see table at GREECE); hilly, fertile; produces figs, olives; marble.

History: Noted in antiquity for its claims as epic poet Homer's birthplace 9th cent. B.C. and for its school of epic poets, the Homeridae; also for its sculptors. Colonized by Ionians and became powerful state; became subject to Persia 546 B.C.; joined Delian League c. 478 B.C. but revolted several times against Athenian domination; prospered under Romans and Byzantines; later passed successively to Turks, Venetians, Genoese, and Ottomans; suffered massacre by Turks 1822; passed to Greece as a result of the Balkan Wars (1912–13). Birthplace of historian and rhetorician Theopompus c. 380 B.C. See AEGEAN ISLANDS.

2. City on E coast of Chios I., ✱ of Chios dept.; exports include wine and fruit.

Chi·pa·ta \chē-ˈpä-tä\; *formerly* **Fort James·son** \ˈjām-sən\. Town, Zambia, 290 mi. (467 km.) ENE of Lusaka, near Malawi border; pop. (1980p) 145,869.

Chip·ley \ˈchip-lē\. Town, ⊗ of Washington co., NW Florida, 105 mi. (169 km.) ENE of Pensacola; pop. (1990c) 3866.

Chi·po·la \chə-ˈpō-lə\. River, SE Alabama and W Florida; flows S from Henry co., SE Alabama, and empties into the Apalachicola River ab. 10 mi. (16 km.) from its mouth; ab. 130 mi. (209 km.) long; navigable for a short distance.

Chip·pen·ham \ˈchi-pə-nəm\. Town, Wiltshire, S England, on the Avon 20 mi. (32 km.) E of Bristol; pop. (1981p) 19,290; food processing, engineering; incorp. as town 1554.

Chip·pe·wa \ˈchi-pə-ˌwȯ, -ˌwä\. **1.** River, W cen. Minnesota; flows S into Minnesota River.

2. River, W cen. Wisconsin; rises in Sawyer co., flows S and SW into Mississippi River; 183 mi. (294 km.) long; navigable 50 mi. (80 km.) to Eau Claire, Wisconsin.

3. Name of counties in three states of the U.S. See tables at MICHIGAN, MINNESOTA, WISCONSIN.

4. Locality, SE Ontario, Canada, on Niagara River 2 mi. (3.2 km.) above Niagara Falls; American forces defeated the British here on July 5, 1814.

Chippewa Falls. City, ⊗ of Chippewa co., W Wisconsin, on Chippewa River 10 mi. (16 km.) NNE of Eau Claire; pop. (1990c) 12,727; recreation area; settled 1837.

Chippewa Lake. Lake in Sawyer co., NW Wisconsin; a source of Chippewa River.

Chipping Wycombe. See HIGH WYCOMBE.

Chip·ut·net·i·cook Lakes \ˌshi-pət-ˈne-ti-ˌku̇k, -kək\. Chain of lakes forming upper course of St. Croix River, on boundary bet. W New Brunswick, Canada, and E Maine; largest is Grand Lake (*q.v.*).

Chi·qui·mu·la \ˌchē-kē-ˈmü-lä\. **1.** Department of SE Guatemala. See table at GUATEMALA.

2. City, its ✱; munic. pop. (1993e) 31,243.

Chi·qui·mu·li·lla \ˌchē-kē-mü-ˈlē-yä\. Town, Santa Rosa dept., S Guatemala; pop. (1981c) 30,418.

Chi·quin·qui·rá \chē-ˌkēŋ-kē-ˈrä\. Town, Boyacá dept., cen. Colombia, 65 mi. (105 km.) N of Bogotá; alt. 8365 ft. (2550 m.); emerald deposits nearby; pilgrimages on the occasions when two religious feasts are celebrated.

Chi·ra \ˈchē-rä\. Island, Puntarenas prov., Costa Rica, in Gulf of Nicoya.

Chir·chik \chir-ˈchēk\. Town, Tashkent subdivision, Uzbekistan, ab. 20 mi. (32 km.) NE of the city of Tashkent.

Chire. See SHIRE.

Chir·i·ca·hua Mountains \ˌchir-i-ˈkä-wə\. Small range in E Cochise co., SE Arizona; includes Chiricahua National Monument.

Chiricahua National Monument. See UNITED STATES, *National Monuments.*

Chi·ri·quí \ˌchē-rē-ˈkē\. **1.** Volcanic peak. See BARÚ.

2. Province of W Panama. See table at PANAMA.

Chiriquí, Gulf of. Inlet of the Pacific Ocean in SW Panama.

Chiriquí Lagoon. Inlet of the Caribbean Sea on the NW coast of Panama, W of Mosquito Gulf.

Chir·ri·pó Gran·de \ˌchēr-rē-ˈpō-ˈgrän-dā\. Mountain in the Cordillera de Talamanca, SE cen. Costa Rica; 12,530 ft. (3819 m.); highest point in Costa Rica.

Chi·sa·go \shi-ˈsȯ-gō\. County in E Minnesota. See table at MINNESOTA.

Chishima Rettō. See KURIL ISLANDS.

Chis·holm \ˈchi-zəm\. City, St. Louis co., NE Minnesota, 4 mi. (6 km.) ENE of Hibbing; pop. (1990c) 5290.

Chisholm Trail. A cattle trail leading N from near San Antonio, Texas, to Abilene, Kansas; used esp. immediately after the Civil War when large herds of cattle were driven to markets in the north; fell into disuse with coming of railroads.

Chisimaio. See KISMAAYO.

Chi·şi·nău \ˌkē-shē-ˈnau̇\; *1940–91* **Ki·shi·nev** \ˈki-shi-ˌnef\. City, ✻ of Moldova, on a tributary of the Dniester 90 mi. (145 km.) NW of Odessa, Ukraine; pop. (1989p) 665,000; commercial town on railroad line from Iaşi to Odessa; exports leather, flour, tobacco, and wine; university (1945); cathedral. First mentioned 15th cent.; taken by Turks 16th cent.; acquired 1812 by Russia; scene of massacre of Jews 1903 instigated by Russian officials; as part of Bessarabia was under Romanians 1918–40; made ✻ of Moldavian S.S.R. 1940; held by Axis powers 1941–44; entered by U.S.S.R. Aug. 24, 1944.

Chi·sos Mountains \ˈchē-səs\. Range in Big Bend National Park, S Brewster co., W Texas; highest peak 7835 ft. (2388 m.).

Chi·sto·pol \ˌchis-ˈtȯ-pəl\. Town, cen. Tatarstan, E Russia in Europe, on left bank of Kama River 65 mi. (105 km.) SE of Kazan; pop. (1991e) 66,600; a trade center.

Chistyakovo. See TOREZ.

Chiswick. See BRENTFORD AND CHISWICK.

Chi·ta \chē-ˈtä\. City, ✻ of Chita Oblast, S Russia in Asia, on Chita River near its confluence with the Ingoda; pop. (1992e) 377,000; founded 1653.

Chi·ta \ˈchē-tä\. City, Aichi prefecture, S Honshū, Japan; pop. (1990p) 75,434.

Chi·ta, Ne·va·do de \nā-ˈvä-t͟hō-t͟hā-ˈchē-tä\. Peak in the Cordillera Oriental, N cen. Colombia, near Venezuelan border; 18,022 ft. (5493 m.).

Ch'i–t'ai. See QITAI.

Chitaldroog *or* **Chitaldrug.** See CHITRADURGA.

Chi·tam·bo \chē-ˈtäm-bō\. Village, NE Zambia, S of the marshes on S shore of Lake Bangweulu; Scottish missionary and explorer David Livingstone died 1873 at Old Chitambo, a small village NNW of Chitambo.

Chi·ta Oblast \chē-ˈtä-ˈȯ-bləst, -ˌblast\ *or* **Chi·tin·ska·ya Oblast'** \chē-ˈtin-skə-yə-ˈȯ-bləstʸ\. Administrative subdivision of S Russia in Asia; 166,602 sq. mi. (431,499 sq. km.); pop. (1992e) 1,391,000; ✻ Chita. Its chief streams are the Amur on its SE border, the Shilka and Argun (headstreams of the Amur), and the Olekma and Zeya. Region is a plateau area, with the Yablonovyy Mts. on the W and extensions of mountain ranges of Khabarovsk Kray in the E. Rich in mineral resources (gold, lead, zinc); timber; crossed by the Trans-Siberian R.R. in the S. Chief cities: Chita, Nerchinsk, Sretensk. Forms part of one of the earliest settled regions of E Siberia, then known as Transbaikalia; after the Bolshevik Revolution 1917 a part of the Far Eastern Region (*q.v.*); designated as a new administrative subdivision 1937.

Chi·to·se \chē-ˈtō-sā\. City, Hokkaidō, Japan, 8 mi. (13 km.) SW of Sapporo; pop. (1990p) 78,947.

Chit·ra·dur·ga \ˌchit-rə-ˈdər-gə\; *formerly* **Chit·al·droog** *or* **Chit·al·drug** \ˈchi-təl-ˌdrüg\. Town, N Karnataka, S India, 137 mi. (220 km.) N of Mysore; pop. (1991p) 87,053.

Chi·tral \chi-ˈträl\. **1.** *or* **Ku·nar** \ku̇-ˈnər, -ˈnär\ *or esp in Afghanistan* **Ko·nar** \ku̇-, kō-\. River, Pakistan and NE Afghanistan; flows S through Chitral and into Afghanistan and empties into Kabul River near Jalālābād; ab. 300 mi. (480 km.) long.
2. Town, its ✻, on Chitral River at over 5000 ft. (1524 m.). Small British force withstood siege 1895.

Chi·tré \chē-ˈtrā\. Town, ✻ of Herrera prov., S Panama; pop. (1990p) 21,585.

Chit·ta·gong \ˈchi-tə-ˌgäŋ, -ˌgȯŋ\. Town, principal port of Bangladesh, on Karnaphuli River 12 mi. (19 km.) from its mouth; pop. (1991p) 1,566,070; exports jute, tea; oil refinery, engineering works, jute mills; university (1966); in one of the regions of heaviest annual rainfall in the world. Known to early Portuguese mariners; conquered by nabob of Bengal 1666; ceded to British East India Company 1760; port facilities damaged in conflict bet. India and Pakistan 1971.

Chittagong Hill Tracts. Hilly region, Bangladesh; along border with Myanmar; 5093 sq. mi. (13,191 sq. km.); inhabited by descendants of Arakanese and aboriginal peoples. Established directly elected district councils 1989 following 14 years of conflict between guerrillas and government.

Chit·te·nan·go \ˌchit-ᵊn-ˈaŋ-gō\. Village, Madison co., cen. New York, 16 mi. (26 km.) E of Syracuse; pop. (1990c) 4734.

Chit·ten·den \ˈchit-ᵊn-dən\. County in NW Vermont. See table at VERMONT.

Chittenden, Mount. Peak in Yellowstone National Park, NW Wyoming; 10,189 ft. (3106 m.).

Chittenden Reservoir. Reservoir at upper end of East Creek tributary of Otter Creek, W cen. Vermont.

Chittim. See CITIUM.

Chit·toor \chi-ˈtu̇r\. Town, S Andhra Pradesh, SE India, ab. 90 mi. (145 km.) W of Madras; pop. (1991p) 133,233.

Chi·tun·gwi·za \ˌchē-tüŋ-ˈgwē-zä\. Town, NE cen. Zimbabwe, SSE of Harare; area pop. (1992p) 274,035.

Chiu–chiang. See JIUJIANG.

Chiu–ch'üan. See JIUQUAN.

Ch'iung–chou *or* **Ch'iung–shan.** See QIONGSHAN.

Chiu–san–shui. See HEKOU 1.

Chiu·si \ˈkyü-sē\; *anc.* **Clu·si·um** \ˈklü-zhē-əm, -zē-\. Commune, Siena prov., SE Tuscany, cen. Italy, ab. 40 mi. (64 km.) SE of the commune of Siena; pop. (1981p) 9206; one of the 12 cities of ancient Etruria, fl. 7th–5th cents. B.C.; became subject to Rome 3d cent. B.C.; declined in Middle Ages because of proximity to swamps of Chiani River.

Chi·u·ta, Lake \shē-ˈü-tä\. Lake in NW Mozambique, SE Africa; the Lugenda River issues from its N end.

Chi·vas·so \kē-ˈväs-sō\. Commune, Torino prov., Piedmont, NW Italy, on Po River NE of Turin; pop. (1989c) 25,257; sulfur baths.

Chi·vil·coy \ˌchē-vēl-ˈkȯi\. City, Buenos Aires prov., E Argentina, 90 mi. (145 km.) W of the city of Buenos Aires.

Chixoy. See USUMACINTA.

Ch'i–yang. See QIYANG.

Chi–yün. See JIYUN.

Chkalov. See ORENBURG.

Chkalovskaya Oblast'. See ORENBURG OBLAST.

Cho·a·pan \ˌchō-ä-ˈpän\. Municipality, Oaxaca state, Mexico, 55 mi. (88 km.) NE of the city of Oaxaca.

Choaspes. See KARKHEH.

Cho·be \ˈchō-bā\. Swamp and lower course of Kwando River in Caprivi Strip, Namibia.

Chobe National Park. Park, N Botswana; 4500 sq. mi. (11,655 sq. km.); noted for its wildlife; acquired national park status 1968.

Chocim. See KHOTIN.

Cho·có \chō-ˈkō\. Department of W Colombia. See table at COLOMBIA.

Cho·cor·ua, Mount \shə-ˈkȯr-ə-wə, -ˈkär-\. Peak, W cen. Carroll co., E New Hampshire, in Sandwich Range of the White Mts.; 3475 ft. (1059 m.).

Choc·taw \ˈchäk-ˌtȯ\. **1.** Name of counties in three states of the U.S. See tables at ALABAMA, MISSISSIPPI, OKLAHOMA.
2. Town, Oklahoma co., cen. Oklahoma, 17 mi. (27 km.) E of Oklahoma City; pop. (1990c) 8545.

Choc·taw·hatch·ee \ˌchäk-tə-ˈha-chē\. River, NW Florida; rises in S Alabama; flows S, forming boundary bet. Walton and

\ə\ abut \ᵊ\ kitten, Fr table \ər\ further \a\ ash \ā\ ace \ä\ cot, cart \ȧ\ Fr bac \au̇\ out \b\ Span Avila \ch\ chin \e\ bet \ē\ easy \g\ go \i\ hit \ī\ ice \j\ job \k\ Ger ich, Buch \ⁿ\ Fr vin \ŋ\ sing \ō\ go \ȯ\ all \ȯ\ law \œ\ Fr bœuf \ǣ\ Fr feu \ȯi\ boy \th\ thin \t͟h\ this \ü\ loot \u̇\ foot \ue\ Ger füllen \ue̅\ Fr rue \y\ yet \ʸ\ Fr digne \ˈdēnʸ\, nuit \ˈnwʸē\ \yü\ few \yu̇\ fury \zh\ vision

Washington cos., into **Choctawhatchee Bay,** inlet of Gulf of Mexico; 140 mi. (225 km.) long.

Chō·fu \ˈchō-ˌfü\. Town, Tokyo prefecture, Honshū, Japan; a suburb of the city of Tokyo; pop. (1990c) 197,680; electrical equipment, machinery; food products.

Choi·seul \shwä-ˈzœl\. One of the Solomon Is., W Pacific Ocean, ab. 32 mi. (51 km.) E of SE Bougainville I.; 85 mi. (137 km.) long and bet. 4 and 20 mi. (6 and 32 km.) wide; 1170 sq. mi. (3030 sq. km.); pop. (1986c) 12,549; was under German control 1886–99; became part of British Solomon Is. protectorate; chief settlement Bambatana on W coast; highest point 2470 ft. (753 m.); nearly surrounded by barrier reef.

Choi·sy–le–Roi \shwä-ˌzē-lə-ˈrwä\. Commune, Val-de-Marne dept., N France, SSE suburb of Paris on left bank of Seine River; Rouget de Lisle, composer of "La Marseillaise," buried here.

Choj·ni·ce \kȯi-ˈnēt-sə\ *or Ger.* **Ko·nitz** \ˈkō-nits\. Commune, Bydgoszcz prov., N cen. Poland, 45 mi. (72 km.) NW of the city of Bydgoszcz; pop. (1989e) 37,664; scene of last great victory of Teutonic Knights over Poles 1454; to Prussia 1772; to Poland after WWI.

Choj·nów \ˈkȯi-nüf\ *or Ger.* **Hay·nau** *also* **Hai·nau** \ˈhī-ˌnau̇\. City, W cen. Legnica prov., SW Poland, 11 mi. (18 km.) N of the city of Legnica; pop. (1981p) 12,076; formerly in Silesia, Germany; assigned to Poland 1945.

Chō·kai \ˈchō-ˌkī\. Volcano, N Yamagata prefecture, N Honshū, Japan, near coast; 7314 ft. (2229 m.).

Cho·la \ˈchō-lə\. Early kingdom encompassing much of SE India, Kerala, Mysore, Ceylon; known from antiquity, but esp. powerful under Chola dynasty of Tamil kings (c. 850–1279 A.D.); extended from Pudukkottai to Nellore, with capitals at Tiruchirapalli, Kumbakonam, and Thanjavur.

Cho·let \shō-ˈlā\. Commune, Maine-et-Loire dept., W France, on Maine River 32 mi. (51 km.) SSW of Angers; pop. (1990c) 56,540; 15th cent. bridge; completely destroyed in Wars of the Vendée 1793–96.

Cho·lu·la \chō-ˈlü-lä\ *or in full* **Cholula de Ri·va·da·bia** \t͟hä-ˌrē-vä-t͟hä-ˈbē-ä\. Town, Puebla state, SE cen. Mexico, 8 mi. (13 km.) W of the city of Puebla; site of the truncated Pyramid of Quetzalcoatl (base covers 42 acres or 17 hectares), used by the Aztecs; numerous other pyramids; area overrun by Spanish under Hernán Cortés 1519; Spanish subsequently built many churches (several remaining) on pyramid sites. See TEOTIHUACÁN.

Cho·lu·te·ca \ˌchō-lü-ˈtā-kä\. **1.** River, S Honduras; flows E, S, and SW to Gulf of Fonseca; ab. 150 mi. (240 km.) long.
2. Department of S Honduras. See table at HONDURAS.
3. Town, its ✻; pop. (1989e) 57,400.

Cho·mo Lha·ri \ˌchō-mō-ˈlär-ē\ *or* **Cha·ma·lha·ri** \ˌchä-mä-ˈlär-ē\ *or* **Chu·ma·lha·ri** \ˌchü-mä-ˈlär-ē\. Mountain peak in the Himalayas bet. Tibet, China, and NW Bhutan; 23,997 ft. (7314 m.).

Chomolungma. See EVEREST, MOUNT.

Cho·mu·tov \ˈk͟ō-mə-ˌtȯf\ *or Ger.* **Ko·mo·tau** \ˈkō-mə-ˌtau̇\. City, NW Czech Republic, 52 mi. (84 km.) NW of Prague; pop. (1991p) 53,191; coal deposits.

Ch'ŏn·an \ˈchən-ˈän\. Town, South Ch'ungch'ŏng prov., South Korea, ab. 39 mi. (63 km.) NNW of Taejŏn; pop. (1985c) 170,196.

Chon Bu·ri \ˈchən-bu̇-ˈrē\. Town, S Thailand, pop. (1991e) 45,763.

Cho·ne \ˈchō-nā\. **1.** River, W Ecuador; flows from Andes Mts. W into Pacific Ocean; ab. 60 mi. (97 km.) long.
2. City, Manabí prov., W Ecuador, 110 mi. (177 km.) WSW of Quito.

Ch'ŏng·jin \ˈchəŋ-ˈjin\. City and port, NE North Korea on Sea of Japan; pop. (1987e) 520,000.

Ch'ŏng·ju \ˈchəŋ-ˈjü\. Town, ✻ of North Ch'ungch'ŏng prov., South Korea; pop. (1985c) 350,256; processing and distribution center for rice, tobacco, and silk.

Chong·qing \ˈchu̇ŋ-ˈchiŋ\ *or traditionally* **Chung·king** \ˈchəŋ-ˈkiŋ, ˈchu̇ŋ-\ *or W.-G.* **Ch'ung–ch'ing** \ˈchu̇ŋ-ˈchiŋ\. City, S Sichuan prov., S China, on N bank of the Chang at its junction with the Jialing; pop. (1990c) 2,266,772; ✻ of China 1937–45; chemicals, cement, textiles, iron and steel, munitions, motor vehicles, paper; food products; trade center for much of W China. Declared open port c. 1891; made political ✻ of China during WWII by Kuomintang (Nationalist) party; bombed heavily by Japanese after 1938; taken by Chinese Communists 1949.

Chŏn·ju \ˈjən-ˌjü\; *formerly* **Zen·shu** \ˈzen-ˌshü\. Town, ✻ of North Chŏlla prov., South Korea, 120 mi. (193 km.) S of Seoul; pop. (1985c) 426,473; in rice-growing region.

Cho·nos Archipelago \ˈchō-nōs\ *or Span.* **Ar·chi·pié·la·go de los Chonos** \ˌär-chē-ˈpyā-lä-ˌgō-t͟hā-lōs-ˈchō-ˌnōs\. Group of islands in S Pacific Ocean off SW coast of Chile, N of Madre de Dios Archipelago.

Chon·ta·les \chōn-ˈtä-lās\. Department of S cen. Nicaragua. See table at NICARAGUA.

Cho Oyu \ˈchō-ō-ˈyü\. Mountain peak in the Himalayas bet. Tibet, China and Nepal, NW of Mt. Everest; 26,750 ft. (8153 m.); first scaled 1954.

Cho·pi·col·qui \ˌchō-pē-ˈkōl-kē\. Peak in the Cordillera Occidental, Peru; ab. 22,000 ft. (6700 m.).

Chop·tank \ˈchäp-ˌtaŋk\. River, cen. Delaware and E Maryland; rises in W cen. Delaware, flows SW across Maryland border to Chesapeake Bay in SE Talbot co.; ab. 65 mi. (105 km.) long.

Cho·ras·mia \kə-ˈraz-mē-ə\. Province of ancient Persia on the Oxus, W Asia, extending W to the Caspian Sea; in 12th cent. ab. equivalent to Shahdom of Khwārizm (*q.v.*) which became the khanate of Khiva (*q.v.*). The Chorasmians, who were Aryans, formed a contingent under 5th cent. B.C. King Xerxes the Great.

Chor·ley \ˈchȯr-lē\. Town, Lancashire, NW England, 19 mi. (31 km.) WNW of Manchester; pop. (1991p) 96,500; cotton weaving, engineering.

Chorlu. See ÇORLU.

Cho·rol·que \chō-ˈrōl-kā\. Peak, Potosí dept., SW Bolivia; 18,414 ft. (5616 m.).

Chorrera, La. See LA CHORRERA.

Chor·ril·los \chō-ˈrē-yōs\. Residential town, Peru, ab. 9 mi. (14 km.) S of Lima; pop. (1990e) 201,882; resort; scene of Chilean victory over Peruvians 1881 during War of the Pacific.

Chorum. See ÇORUM.

Cho·rzów \ˈk͟ō-ˌzhüf\. City, Katowice prov., SW Poland, 5 mi. (8 km.) NNW of the city of Katowice; pop. (1989e) 132,674; steelworks, foundries.

Chosen. See KOREA.

Chosen Strait. See WESTERN CHANNEL.

Chō·shi \ˈchō-ˌshē\. Seaport town, Chiba prefecture, on SE coast of Honshū, Japan, at mouth of Tone River 60 mi. (97 km.) E of Tokyo; pop. (1990p) 85,138; fishing.

Cho·shu \ˈchō-ˌshü\. The old province of Nagato, Japan, in SW extremity of Honshū, now part of Yamaguchi prefecture; the feudal territory of a Japanese clan, uniting in latter part of 19th cent. with several others in opposition to foreigners and in rebellion against the shogunate.

Cho·si·ca \chō-ˈsē-kä\. Town, Peru, 35 mi. (56 km.) NE of Lima; alt. 2800 ft. (853 m.); popular resort esp. for day trips from Lima.

Chosŏn. See KOREA.

Chosŏn Minjujuŭi In'min Konghwaguk. See KOREA, NORTH.

Choszcz·no \ˈk͟ōsht-ˌshnō\; *formerly* **Arns·wal·de** \ˈärns-väl-də\. Town, N Gorzów prov., NW Poland, 40 mi. (64 km.) SE of Szczecin; pop. (1981p) 13,599; before 1945 in Prussia, Germany; coal deposits.

Cho·ta Nag·pur States \ˈchō-tə-ˈnäg-ˌpu̇r\. A group of nine former states, NE India; earlier in Eastern States Agency.

Cho·ta Ude·pur *or* **Chho·ta Udepur** \ˈchō-tə-ü-ˈdā-ˌpu̇r\ *also* **Chota Udai·pur** \ü-ˈdī-ˌpu̇r\. **1.** Former Indian state, Gujarat States, W India; 894 sq. mi. (2315 sq. km.); ✻ Chota Udepur.
2. Town, its ✻, ab. 50 mi. (80 km.) E of Vadodara.

Cho·teau \ˈshō-ˌtō\. City, ⊗ of Teton co., NW cen. Montana; pop. (1990c) 1741.

Chotin. See KHOTIN.

Chott \ˈshȯt, ˈshät\. French form of Arabic *shatt* (saline lake). For names beginning **Chott** see the 2d element, as **Chott Djerid,** see DJERID, **Chott ech Chergui,** see CHERGUI.

Cho·tu·si·ce \ˈkȯ-tü-ˌsit-sə\ *or Ger.* **Cho·tu·sitz** \ˈkō-tə-ˌzits\. Village, cen. Czech Republic, near Čáslav; scene of victory of Prussian King Frederick the Great over Austrians 1742 as result of which Prussia acquired most of Silesia from Austrian Empress Maria Theresa.

Choukoutien *or* **Chou–k'ou–tien–chen.** See ZHOUKOUDIANZHEN.

Chou–shan. See ZHOUSHAN.

Chou·teau \ˈshō-ˌtō\. County in N cen. Montana. See table at MONTANA.

Cho·wan \chə-ˈwän\. **1.** River, NE North Carolina; formed by confluence of Blackwater and Nottoway rivers, flows SE into Albemarle Sound; ab. 50 mi. (80 km.) long.

2. County in NE North Carolina. See table at NORTH CAROLINA.

Chow·chil·la \chau̇-ˈchi-lə\. City, Madera co., cen. California, 35 mi. (56 km.) NW of Fresno; pop. (1990c) 5930.

Choy·bal·san \ˌchȯi-bäl-ˈsän\; *formerly* **Ker·u·len** \ˈker-ü-ˌlen\. Town, E Mongolia, on Kerulen River, ab. 360 mi. (580 km.) E of Ulaanbaatar.

Christ·church \ˈkrīst-ˌchərch\. **1.** Town, Dorset, S England, at confluence of Avon and Stour rivers 23 mi. (37 km.) WSW of Southampton; pop. (1991p) 40,500; seaside resort; received first charter c. 1150.

2. City, near E coast of South I., New Zealand, on small Avon River 8 mi. (13 km.) NW of its port, Lyttelton; pop. (1991c) 292,858; one of New Zealand's principal industrial centers; transportation equipment, carpets; meatpacking; woolens; founded 1850 by English Anglicans.

Chris·tian \ˈkris-chən\. Name of counties in three states of the U.S. See tables at ILLINOIS, KENTUCKY, MISSOURI.

Christiana. See CHRISTINA.

Chris·ti·a·na \ˌkris-tē-ˈä-nə\. Town, North-West prov., cen. Rep. of South Africa, on Vaal River 65 mi. (105 km.) NNE of Kimberley; diamonds.

Christiania. See OSLO 2.

Christiansand. See KRISTIANSAND.

Chris·tians·burg \ˈkris-chənz-ˌbərg\. Town, ⊗ of Montgomery co., Virginia, 27 mi. (43 km.) WSW of Roanoke; pop. (1990c) 15,004; founded 1792.

Christian Sound. Inlet of Pacific Ocean at S end of Chatham Strait, S of Baranof I., SE Alaska.

Chris·tian·sted \ˈkris-chən-ˌsted\. Town on NE coast of St. Croix I., Virgin Is. of the U.S., West Indies; pop. (1990c) 2555; ✻ of the former Danish West Indies.

Christiansund. See KRISTIANSUND.

Chris·ti·na \kris-ˈtē-nə\; *formerly* **Chris·ti·ana** \ˌkris-tē-ˈa-nə\. River in N Delaware uniting with Brandywine Creek and flowing into Delaware River at Wilmington.

Christ·mas Island \ˈkris-məs\. **1.** Island in Indian Ocean, an external territory of Australia, ab. 225 mi. (362 km.) S of W end of Java; 11 mi. (18 km.) long, 4.5 mi. (7 km.) wide; 52 sq. mi. (135 sq. km.); pop. (1993c) 1000; deposits of phosphate of lime. Known to navigators since ab. 1650; formally annexed by Great Britain 1888, placed under Straits Settlements 1889, and incorp. with Singapore settlement 1900; under Japanese occupation 1942–45; ceded to Australia 1958; rejected secession in an unofficial referendum 1994.

2. One of the Line Is. in cen. Pacific Ocean. See KIRITIMATI.

Chris·to·pher \ˈkris-tə-fər\. City, Franklin co., S Illinois, 28 mi. (45 km.) SSW of Mount Vernon; pop. (1990c) 2774.

Chrysopolis. See ÜSKÜDAR.

Chrysorrhoas. See BARADA.

Chrza·nów \ˈkshä-nüf\. Commune, W Kraków prov., S Poland, 27 mi. (43 km.) WNW of the city of Kraków; pop. (1989e) 42,205; lead and coal deposits.

Chu \ˈchü\. River, SE Kazakhstan; flows from the Tian Shan W to small lake in desert; 700 mi. (1126 km.) long.

Chu. See ZHU.

Ch'üan–chou *or* **Chuan–chow.** See QUANZHOU.

Chuapa. See TSHUAPA.

Chubb Crater. See NOUVEAU-QUÉBEC, CRATÈRE DU.

Chub·buck \ˈchə-bək\. City, Bannock co., SE Idaho; pop. (1990c) 7791.

Chū·bu \ˈchü-bü\. Administrative region of Japan, in cen. Honshū. For subdivisions, see table at JAPAN.

Chu·but \chü-ˈbüt\. **1.** River in S Argentina; rises in Andes, flows E across Chubut prov., and empties into Atlantic Ocean near Rawson.

2. Province of S cen. Argentina, ✻ Rawson. See table at ARGENTINA.

Chu–chou *or* **Chu·chow.** See ZHUZHOU.

Chuchow. See LISHUI.

Chuckchee Sea. See CHUKCHI SEA.

Chudskoye Ozero. See PEIPUS, LAKE.

Ch'ü–fu *or* **Ch'ü–fou.** See QUFU.

Chu·gach Mountains \ˈchü-ˌgach, -ˌgash\. Mountain range along coast of S Alaska, extending from head of Cook Inlet ab. 280 mi. (450 km.) eastward to W end of St. Elias Mts.

Chū·go·ku \ˌchü-ˈgō-kü\. Administrative region of Japan, in SW Honshū. For subdivisions, see table at JAPAN.

Chuguchak. See TACHENG.

Ch'ü–hsien. See QU XIAN.

Chuk·chi Autonomous Okrug \ˈchək-chē, ˈchu̇k-\ *or* **Chu·kot Autonomous Okrug** \chə-ˈkȯt ... ˈȯ-ˌkrük\ *or* **Chu·kot·ka** \chə-ˈkȯt-kə\. Administrative district, Magadan Oblast, NE Russia in Asia; 284,826 sq. mi. (737,699 sq. km.); pop. (1992e) 146,000; ✻ Anadyr; comprises Chukchi Penin. and territory occupied by Anadyr River system and Chukot Range E of Sakha Rep. and N of Koryak Autonomous Okrug; inhabited chiefly by Russians, as well as Chukchi, Evenk, Koryak, and Yakut; hunting and fishing; tin deposits; formed 1930 and formerly a part of Khabarovsk Kray.

Chukchi Peninsula *or Russ.* **Chu·kot·skiy Po·lu·os·trov** \chu̇-ˈkȯt-skyē-ˌpə-lə-ˈȯs-trəf\. Peninsula, E Chukchi Autonomous Okrug, NE Russia in Asia, bet. Bering Sea on the S and Chukchi Sea on the N; its E point is Dezhneva Mys (*q.v.*).

Chukchi Sea *also* **Chuck·chee Sea** \ˈchək-chē,ˈchu̇k-*or Russ.* **Chu·kot·sko·ye Mo·re** \chu̇-ˈkȯt-skə-yə-ˈmȯr-yə\. Sea, part of Arctic Ocean N of Bering Strait bet. Asia and North America.

Chukotskoye More. See CHUKCHI SEA.

Chu·kot·sko·ye Na·gor'·ye \chə-ˈkȯt-skə-yə-nə-ˈgȯr-yə\; *formerly* **Ana·dyr Range** *or* **Ana·dir Range** \ˌä-nä-ˈdir\ *or Russ.* **Ana·dyr·skiy Khre·bet** \ˌə-nə-ˈdir-skē-kri-ˈbyet\. Mountain range, NW Chukchi Autonomous Okrug, NE Russia in Asia; an extension of the Kolyma Mts.; runs NW and SE across Arctic Circle to Chukchi Penin.

Chu·la Vis·ta \ˌchü-lə-ˈvis-tə\. City, San Diego co., SW California, S of the city of San Diego; pop. (1990c) 135,163; Southwestern Coll. (1961).

Chu·lu·ca·nas \ˌchü-lü-ˈkä-näs\. Town, NW Peru, 32 mi. (51 km.) NE of Piura; pop. (1981p) 71,924.

Chu·lym *or* **Chu·lim** \chə-ˈlim\. Navigable river, W cen. Russia in Asia; rises in mountains of SW Krasnoyarsk Kray and flows N and W into Ob' River below Tomsk; 1177 mi. (1894 km.) long.

Chumalhari. See CHOMO LHARI.

Chumbi. See CH'U-MU-PI SHAN-KU.

Chum·phon *or* **Jum·porn** \ˈchu̇m-ˈpȯn\. Town, S Thailand; port on Malay Penin. on W shore of Gulf of Thailand 245 mi. (394 km.) S of Bangkok; pop. (1991e) 13,811.

Ch'u–mu–pi Shan–ku \ˈchü-ˈmü-ˈpē-ˈshän-ˈkü\ *also* **Chum·bi** \ˈchu̇m-bē\. Fertile valley in the Himalayas, in S Tibet, China, bet. Sikkim and Bhutan; alt. 9500 ft. (2896 m.).

Chu·na \chu̇-ˈnä\ *or* **Uda** \u̇-ˈdä\. River, Irkutsk Oblast and Krasnoyarsk Kray, S cen. Russia in Asia; flows N and W to Angara just above its junction with the Yenisey; 748 mi. (1204 km.) long.

Chu·nar *also* **Cha·nar** \chə-ˈnär\. Fortified and ancient town on S bank of Ganges, SE Uttar Pradesh, N India; 20 mi. (32 km.) SSW of Varanasi; important in 16th cent. struggles bet. Mogul Emperor Humāyūn and Afghan leader Shēr Shāh; recaptured by Mogul Emperor Akbar 1575; came under control of British c. 1763; treaty signed here 1781 bet. English colonial administrator Warren Hastings and nabob of Oudh.

Ch'un·ch'ŏn \ˈchün-ˈchən\. Town, ✻ of Kangwŏn prov., South Korea; pop. (1985c) 162,998.

Ch'ung–ch'ing. See CHONGQING.

Chungchow. See ZHONG XIAN.

Chung–hsien. See ZHONG XIAN.

Chung–hua Jen–min Kung–ho–kuo. See CHINA.

Chungking. See CHONGQING.

Chung–t'iao Shan. See ZHONGTIAO SHAN.

Chun–ko–erh. See JUNGGAR.

Chu·qui·ca·ma·ta \ˌchü-kē-kä-ˈmä-tä\. Subdivision of Calama commune, N Chile; pop. (1983p) 29,959; contains one of world's largest single copper-mining properties.

Chu·qui·sa·ca \ˌchü-kē-ˈsä-kä\. **1.** Department of S Bolivia. See table at BOLIVIA.

2. City, Bolivia. See SUCRE 1.

Chur \ˈku̇r\ *or Romansh* **Cue·ra** \ˈkwer-ä\ *or Ital.* **Co·i·ra** \ˈkȯi-rä\ *or Fr.* **Coire** \ˈkwär\; *anc.* **Cu·ria Rhae·to·rum** \ˈkyu̇r-ē-ə-rē-ˈtōr-əm\. Commune, ✻ of Graubünden canton, E Switzerland, 43 mi. (69 km.) E of Altdorf; pop. (1989c) 31,078; 11th–12th cent. cathedral; important tourist resort. Was an important center of the Roman prov. of Raetia; mentioned as episcopal see in 5th cent. A.D.; imperial city during the Holy Roman Empire; became ✻ of Graubünden canton early 19th cent. Birthplace of Swiss painter Angelica Kauffmann 1741.

Church \ˈchərch\. Town, Lancashire, NW England, on Leeds and Liverpool Canal 20 mi. (32 km.) N of Manchester; pop. (1981p) 4332.

Church Hill. Town, Hawkins co., NE Tennessee, 23 mi. (37 km.) NW of Johnson City; pop. (1990c) 4834.

Church·ill \ˈchər-ˌchil, -chəl\. **1.** County in W Nevada. See table at NEVADA.

2. Borough, Allegheny co., SW Pennsylvania, 9 mi. (15 km.) E of Pittsburgh; pop. (1990c) 3883.

3. River, cen. Canada; rises in Lake la Loche in NW Saskatchewan, flows E across Saskatchewan and N Manitoba and turns NE into Hudson Bay at Churchill; 1000 mi. (1609 km.) long; many rapids; passes through many large lakes, esp. **Churchill Lake** (213 sq. mi. or 552 sq. km.) and Snake in Saskatchewan and Granville and Southern Indian in Manitoba; chief tributaries the Reindeer and Beaver.

4. *formerly* **Hamilton** \ˈha-mil-tən, -məlt-ᵊn\. River, S cen. Labrador, Newfoundland, Canada; rises in Ashuanipi Lake, flows N to Dyke Lake, then SE through Dyke Lake and Lobstick Lake and finally NE into Lake Melville (*q.v.*); 208 mi. (335 km.) long; in its upper course called Ashuanipi; just below outlet from Lobstick Lake is Churchill Falls.

5. Seaport, NE Manitoba, Canada, on Hudson Bay at mouth of Churchill River; pop. (1991c) 1143; nature-oriented tourism; terminus of branch railroad line from the Pas; construction of port for direct shipment of wheat to Europe finished 1931. Settled as Fort Churchill 1688 by Hudson's Bay Company.

Churchill, Cape. Headland on W shore of Hudson Bay, NE Manitoba, Canada, E of Churchill.

Churchill, Mount. 1. Peak in the Wrangell Mts., SE Alaska; 15,638 ft. (4767 m.).

2. Mountain, SW British Columbia, Canada, ab. 60 mi. (100 km.) NW of Vancouver; 10,500 ft. (3200 m.).

Churchill Downs \ˈdau̇nz\. Racetrack, Louisville, Kentucky; scene of annual Kentucky Derby, foremost American horse-racing event, held since 1875.

Churchill Falls; *formerly* **Grand Falls.** Falls in Churchill River, W Labrador, Newfoundland, Canada; ab. 225 mi. (362 km.) from Lake Melville; ab. 300 ft. (90 m.) high, 200 ft. (60 m.) wide; hydroelectric power installations; first explored by John McLean of the Hudson's Bay Company 1839.

Churchill Lake. See CHURCHILL 3.

Churchill Peaks. Two principal peaks of Mt. McKinley, S cen. Alaska; N peak 19,470 ft. (5935 m.), S peak 20,320 ft. (6194 m.).

Church Mountain. Peak, W cen. Whatcom co., NW Washington; 6245 ft. (1904 m.).

Church Point. Town, Acadia parish, S Louisiana, 18 mi. (29 km.) NW of Lafayette; pop. (1990c) 4677.

Chu·ren Hi·mal \ˈchü-ˈren-hi-ˈmäl\. Mountain in the Himalayas, Nepal; 24,158 ft. (7363 m.).

Chu·ru \ˈchu̇r-ü\. Town, Rajasthan, NW India, 110 mi. (178 km.) NNW of Jaipur; pop. (1991p) 82,430.

Chu·ru·bus·co \ˌchü-rü-ˈbü-skō\. Locality near Mexico City, Mexico; battle Aug. 1847 in which American Gen. Winfield Scott defeated Mexican forces of Gen. Antonio López de Santa Anna.

Chusan *or* **Chu Shan.** See ZHOUSHAN.

Chu·so·va·ya \ˌchü-sə-ˈvī-ə\. River, Sverdlovsk and Perm' oblasts, W Russia; rises near Yekaterinburg and flows NW to Kama River; ab. 430 mi. (690 km.) long.

Chu·so·voy *also* **Chu·so·voi** \ˌchü-sə-ˈvȯi\. Town, Perm' Oblast, E Russia in Europe, ab. 60 mi. (97 km.) ENE of the city of Perm'; pop. (1991e) 58,000.

Chust. See KHUST.

Chuuk \ˈchu̇k\ *or* **Truk** \ˈtrək, ˈtru̇k\; *formerly* **Ho·go·lu** \ˈhō-gə-ˌlü\. Island group, cen. Caroline Is., W Pacific Ocean, ab. 925 mi. (1488 km.) E of Yap I., 1500 mi. (2414 km.) W of Tarawa in Kiribati, and 800 mi. (1287 km.) N of Rabaul; 45 sq. mi. (117 sq. km.); pop. (1989c) 38,341; group comprises ab. 11 major islands and many islets; chief islands Dublon, Weno, Tol, Udot, Fefan, and Uman; all within a lagoon ab. 38 mi. (61 km.) in diameter, encircled by a reef which is pierced by 20 passes (only 4 navigable) allowing access to several fine harbors and anchorages within. Chief anchorage is enclosed by Dublon I., Fefan I., and Uman I. and was developed by Japanese into major naval base; airfield on Dublon. Strongly fortified by Japanese after taken from Germany 1914 during WWI; in WWII raided and bombed by U.S. naval and air forces 1944.

Chu·vash Republic \chü-ˈväsh\ *also* **Chu·vash·ia** \chü-ˈvä-shē-ə\. Autonomous republic, E cen. Russia in Europe, S of the Volga; 7066 sq. mi. (18,301 sq. km.); pop. (1992e) 1,393,000; ✻ Cheboksary. In level country of Volga basin, crossed by lower Sura River, which also forms part of W boundary; spring wheat, corn, potatoes, peas, fruit, sugar beets, flax; livestock; lumbering and woodworking; textiles, leather; food products. Population predominantly Chuvashes, a Turkic people. Chief towns: Cheboksary and Alatyr. Suffered much during civil war 1918–20 and in the famine that followed; created an autonomous area 1920 and an autonomous republic (**Chuvash A.S.S.R.**) 1925; became republic within Russia 1991; subsequently became member of Russian Federation.

Chu·zen·ji, Lake \chü-ˈzen-jē\ *or* **Chuzenji Ko** \-ˈkō\. Lake in Tochigi prefecture, cen. Honshū, Japan, 7 mi. (11 km.) W of Nikkō; 15 mi. (24 km.) in circumference; alt. 4375 ft. (1334 m.); resort; noted for its mountain scenery; shrines.

Cia·les \sē-ˈä-lās\. Municipality, cen. Puerto Rico, 17 mi. (27 km.) SE of Arecibo; pop. (1990c) 18,084.

Ci·a·mis \chē-ˈä-mis\ *or* **Tji·a·mis** \chē-\ *also* **Chi·a·mis** \chē-\. Town, West Java prov., Indonesia, ab. 60 mi. (95 km.) SE of Bandung.

Ciam·pi·no \chäm-ˈpē-nō\. Village, cen. Italy, in Lazio 10 mi. (16 km.) SE of Rome; international airport.

Ci·an·jur \chē-ˈän-ju̇r\ *or* **Tji·an·djur** \chē-\ *or Du.* **Tji·an·djoer** \chē-\. Town, West Java prov., Indonesia, on railroad line 35 mi. (56 km.) SE of Bogor, in plateau region E of Mt. Gede.

Cia·no d'En·za \ˈchä-nō-ˈdent-sä\. Commune, Reggio nell'Emilia prov., Emilia-Romagna; N Italy, 12 mi. (19 km.) SW of the commune of Reggio nell'Emilia; pop. (1981p) 3304; includes village of **Ca·nos·sa** \kə-ˈnä-sə\ containing ruins of castle in which Holy Roman Emperor Henry IV submitted 1077 to Pope Gregory VII and did public penance, this humiliation of Henry giving rise to the phrase (reputedly first used by German Chancellor Otto von Bismarck 1872) "going to Canossa" meaning "humble submission."

Ci·a·nor·te \ˌsē-ə-ˈnȯr-tē\. Municipality, Paraná state, S Brazil.

Ci·bao \sē-ˈbau̇\. Fertile valley, cen. Dominican Republic, running E and W parallel with and N of the Cordillera Central; chief towns: Santiago de los Caballeros and La Vega.

Ci·bo·la \ˈsi-bə-lə\. County in W New Mexico, created 1981 from W part of Valencia co. See table at NEW MEXICO.

Cí·bo·la \ˈsē-bō-lä\. Vague historical region in present N New Mexico thought to include seven pueblos (the "Seven Cities of Cíbola") believed by earliest Spanish explorers of the region to contain vast treasures.

Ci·bo·lo \ˈsi-bə-ˌlō\. River, Texas; rises on Edwards Plateau, flows SE and enters San Antonio River in cen. Karnes co.; ab. 150 mi. (240 km.) long.

Cib·y·ra \ˈsi-bə-rə\. Important ancient city of Phrygia, on the border of Caria; became part of Roman Empire c. 83 B.C.

Cic·ero \ˈsi-sə-ˌrō\. Town, Cook co., NE Illinois, W suburb of Chicago; pop. (1990c) 67,436; horse racing; Morton Coll. (1924).

Ci·dra \ˈsē-drä\. Municipality, E cen. Puerto Rico; pop. (1990c) 35,601.

Cie·cha·nów \chə-ˈkä-nüf\. **1.** Province, NE cen. Poland. See table at POLAND.
2. Commune, its ✻, 49 mi. (79 km.) NNW of Warsaw; pop. (1989e) 43,208.

Cie·go de Avi·la \sē-ˈā-gō-thā-ˈä-bē-lä\. **1.** Province of E cen. Cuba. See table at CUBA.
2. City, its ✻; pop. (1990e) 88,102; railroad junction.

Cié·na·ga \ˈsyā-nä-gä\. Coastal town, N Magdalena dept., N Colombia, 40 mi. (64 km.) E of Barranquilla; munic. pop. (1985c) 57,250.

Cien·fue·gos \ˌsyen-ˈfwā-gōs\. **1.** Province of W cen. Cuba. See table at CUBA.
2. City, its ✻, on **Cienfuegos Bay;** pop. (1990e) 123,600; exports sugar. First visited by explorer Christopher Columbus; settled 1738; town founded by French colonists 1819; destroyed by storm 1825; subsequently rebuilt.

Cie·szyn \ˈche-shin\ *or Ger.* **Te·schen** \ˈte-shən\ *or Czech* **Tě·šín** \ˈtye-shēn\. City, Bielsko Biała prov., S Poland, 40 mi. (64 km.) SSW of Katowice; pop. (1989e) 36,629; divided 1920 bet. Poland (Cieszyn) and Czechoslovakia (Český Těšín); reunited under Polish rule 1938 but annexed by Germany during WWII; W town returned to Czechoslovakia 1945. Railroad junction; a Silesian stronghold from 12th cent.; seat of principality through 17th cent.; passed with Bohemia to Hapsburgs 1526; treaty ending War of the Bavarian Succession signed 1779; remained under Austrian control until end of WWI. See TESCHEN 3.

Cie·za \ˈthyā-thä, ˈsyā-sä\. Commune, Murcia prov., SE Spain, on Segura River 25 mi. (40 km.) NNW of the commune of Murcia; pop. (1991c) 30,875; remains of Roman fort.

Ci·fuen·tes \sē-ˈfwān-tās\. Municipality, Las Villas prov., W cen. Cuba; pop. (1981p) 35,288; railroad junction point 10 mi. (16 km.) S of Sagua la Grande.

Ci·ku·ray, Gu·nung \ˈgü-ˌnu̇ŋ-chē-ˈkü-rī\ *or* **Tji·ku·raj** \chē-\ *or Du.* **Tji·koe·raj** \chē-\. Mountain, West Java prov., Indonesia, SSW of Garut; 9255 ft. (2821 m.); highest extinct volcano in the mountain groups around Garut.

Ci·la·cap \chē-ˈlä-chäp\; *mostly formerly* **Chi·la·chap** \chē-\ *or* **Chi·la·tjap** \chē-\ *or* **Tji·la·tjap** \chē-\. Seaport on SW coast of Central Java prov., Indonesia; pop. (1980c) 1,333,211; only harbor on S coast of Java. In WWII used as port of Allied defense against Japanese invasion of Java Feb. 1942.

Ci·li·cia \sə-ˈli-shə, -shē-ə\. Ancient country and region in SE Asia Minor, extending along Mediterranean coast S of Taurus Mts. from the Nur Mts. to Pamphylia; under Assyrians until allied with Cyrus II and made satrapy of Persian Empire; subdued by Macedonian King Alexander the Great who entered it through Cilician Gates; conquered by Roman Gen. Pompey the Great and made a Roman province first cent. B.C.; administrative division of Byzantine Empire; invaded by Arabs 8th cent. A.D.; reconquered by Byzantium 10th cent.; an independent Armenian principality (also called Little Armenia) founded 1080, which later became kingdom; conquered by Mamlūks 1375; a scene of Armenian massacres at the hands of the Turks early 20th cent.; during WWI, occupied by French; to Turkey 1920s. As a modern region in Turkey, called also **Lesser Armenia,** it includes İçel prov. and part of Maraş prov.

Ci·li·cian Gates \sə-ˈli-shən\; *anc.* **Ci·li·ci·ae Py·lae** \sə-ˈli-shē-ˌē-ˈpī-ˌlē\; *Turk.* **Kü·lek Bo·ğa·zı** \kü̅-ˈlek-bō-ä-ˈzē\ *or* **Gü·lek Bo·gaz** \gü̅-ˈlek-bō-ˈäz\. Pass through Bulgar Dağları, a range in the Taurus Mts., S Turkey in Asia, 38 mi. (61 km.) NW of Adana; has been used for centuries by armies and traders.

Cilli. See CELJE.

Ci·ma·hi \chē-ˈmä-hē\ *or* **Tji·ma·hi** \chē-\ *also* **Chi·ma·hi** \chē-\. Town, West Java prov., Indonesia, on railroad line just NW of Bandung; pop. (1980c) 105,940.

Cim·ar·ron \ˈsi-mə-ˌrōn, -ˌrän, -rən\. **1.** River, cen. and SW United States; rises in Colfax co., NE New Mexico, and flows across SW Kansas and cen. Oklahoma into Arkansas River in SE Pawnee co., N Oklahoma; ab. 500 mi. (805 km.) long; upper reaches known as **Dry Cimarron,** 78 mi. (126 km.) long.
2. County in NW Oklahoma. See table at OKLAHOMA.
3. City, ⊗ of Gray co., SW Kansas; pop. (1990c) 1626.

Cim·bri·an Chersonese \ˈsim-brē-ən\ *or* **Cim·bric Chersonese** \ˈsim-brik\. Ancient name for Jutland.

Ci·miez \sē-ˈmyāz\; *anc.* **Cem·e·ne·lum** \ˌse-mə-ˈnē-ləm\. Fashionable residential section of Nice, France; Matisse museum, Chagall museum; has Gallo-Roman ruins.

Ci·mi·ni, Mon·ti \ˈmȯn-tē-ˈchē-mē-nē\ *or Eng.* **Ci·min·i·an Hills** \sə-ˈmi-nē-ən\. Small mountain range, Lazio, cen. Italy, just SE of Viterbo; highest point **Mon·te Ci·mi·no** \ˈmȯn-tā-ˈchē-mē-ˌnō\ 3454 ft. (1053 m.).

Ci·mi·te·ro \ˌchē-mē-ˈtā-rō\. Island in the Lagoon of Venice, NE Italy.

Cim·me·ri·an Bos·po·rus \sə-ˈmir-ē-ən-ˈbäs-pə-rəs\ *or* **Bosporus Cim·mer·i·us** \sə-ˈmir-ē-əs\. **1.** Strait, SE Europe. See KERCH STRAIT.
2. An ancient kingdom on and around the Cimmerian Bosporus (*or mod.* Kerch Strait); first settlement was by Milesians (6th cent. B.C.) at town of Panticapaeum, later ✻ of the kingdom; gradually included all of Crimea; maintained close ties with Athens 5th–3d cents. B.C.; came under Mithradates VI of Pontus c. 100 B.C.; under Roman Empire until 4th cent. A.D.

Ci·mo·lus \sə-ˈmō-ləs\ *or Gk.* **Kí·mo·los** \ˈkē-mō-ˌlōs\ *or Ital.* **Ar·gen·tie·ra** \ˌär-jen-ˈtyā-rä\. Island, SW Cyclades, S Aegean Sea, just NE of Melos, in Cyclades dept., Greece; 16 sq. mi. (41 sq. km.); has produced much cimolite, a mineral named for the island.

Ci·mo·ne, Mon·te \ˈmȯn-tā-chē-ˈmō-nē\. Highest peak in the Tuscan Apennines. See table at APENNINES.

Cîm·pi·na *or* **Câm·pi·na** \ˈkim-pē-nȧ\. Town, Prahova co., S cen. Romania; pop. (1989c) 44,240; oil, chemicals.

Cîm·pu·lung *or* **Câm·pu·lung;** *formerly* **Kim·po·lung** \ˌkim-pu̇-ˈlu̇ŋ\. Town, Argeş co., S cen. Romania; pop. (1989c) 42,678; motor vehicles; founded by German colonists in 12th cent.

Ci·na·ru·co \ˌsē-nä-ˈrü-kō\. River, NE Colombia and W Venezuela; flows E to the Orinoco; ab. 280 mi. (451 km.) long; joined on S by the **Ci·na·ru·qui·to** \ˌsē-nä-rü-ˈkē-tō\, ab. 250 mi. (402 km.) long, its main tributary.

Cin·ca \ˈsēŋ-kä\. River, NE Spain; rises in the Pyrenees on the French frontier, flows S into Segre River above its junction with the Ebro; 110 mi. (177 km.) long.

Cin·cin·nati \ˌsin-sə-ˈna-tē, -tə\. City, ⊗ of Hamilton co., SW corner of Ohio, on Ohio River; pop. (1990c) 364,040; railroad center and distribution port (esp. coal, iron, lumber, salt); electric motors, machine-shop products, soap products, jet engines; brewing, meatpacking; art, natural history, and historical museums; zoo; Univ. of Cincinnati (1819), Xavier Univ. (1831), Hebrew Union Coll.–Jewish Institute of Religion (1875), Coll. of Mount St. Joseph (1920), Cincinnati Bible Coll. and Seminary (1924), Union Institute (1964), Cincinnati Technical Coll. (1966).

History: Laid out 1788 as Losantiville (Fort Washington built 1789); became ⊗ 1790, renamed Cincinnati by Northwest Terr. Gov. Arthur St. Clair in honor of a Revolutionary War officers' society; incorp. as town 1802, as city 1819; developed esp. with opening of Miami and Erie Canal 1832; received influx of German and Irish immigrants mid-19th cent. Birthplace 1857 of William Howard Taft, 27th president of the U.S.

Ci·ni·sel·lo Bal·sa·mo \ˌchē-nē-ˈzel-lō-ˈbäl-sä-ˌmō\. Commune, Milano prov., Lombardy, N Italy, 4 mi. (6 km.) N of Milan; pop. (1989c) 78,046.

Cin·na·min·son \ˌsi-nə-ˈmin-sən\. Township, Burlington co., S cen. New Jersey, near Riverton; pop. (1990c) 14,583; site of first recorded sighting of Japanese beetle in U.S. 1916.

Cinque Ports \ˈsiŋk\. A number of seaport towns on the coast of Kent and Sussex in England important in medieval times, orig. five—Dover, Sandwich, Romney (now New Romney), Hastings, and Hythe—to which were later added Winchelsea, Rye, and other minor places; probably first enfranchised by Edward the Confessor (reigned 1042–66); granted many special privileges by the crown, most of which have since been annulled, in return for sea service in defense of the coast; gradually declined in importance after the 14th cent.

Cin·ta·la·pa \ˌsēn-tä-ˈlä-pä\. Town and municipality, Chiapas state, SE Mexico, 40 mi. (64 km.) W of San Andrés Tuxtla; munic. pop. (1990p) 59,037.

Cin·to, Monte \mȯnt-ˈchēn-tō\. Mountain, NW Corsica, France; 8888 ft. (2709 m.).

Cintra. See SINTRA.

Çiotat, La. See LA CIOTAT.

Či·o·vo \ˈchē-ō-ˌvō\ *or Ital.* **Bua** \ˈbü-ä\. Croatian island in the Adriatic Sea off the Dalmatian coast opp. Trogir.

Ci·pan·go \si-ˈpaŋ-gō\ *also* **Ci·pan·gu** \-gü\. In medieval legend an island, or islands, E of Asia; described by Venetian traveler Marco Polo by the name Zipangu. It was sought by Christopher Columbus and is generally identified with the modern Japan.

Circars, Northern. See NORTHERN CIRCARS.

Cir·cas·sia \sər-ˈka-shə, -shē-ə\. Region in S Russia in Europe, N of the W end of the Caucasus Mts. and on the NE coast of the Black Sea; has no political significance. Known from antiquity though early history is obscure. The Circassians were noted for their military prowess; Christianized in 6th cent., converted to Islam 17th cent. Taken over by Russia in the 19th cent.; after a long period of resistance to Russia in Russo-Turkish wars large numbers of Circassians emigrated to Turkey 1864. After 1917 Bolshevik Revolution autonomous areas estab. for some Circassians and other ethnic minorities (see ADYGEA, CHERKESS AUTONOMOUS OBLAST, KARACHAYEV AUTONOMOUS OBLAST, and KABARDINO-BALKARIA).

Cir·ceo, Mon·te \ˈmȯn-tā-chir-ˈchā-ō\; *anc.* **Cir·cae·um Prom·on·to·ri·um** \sər-ˈsē-əm-ˌprä-mən-ˈtōr-ē-əm\. Mountain and promontory on N side of the Gulf of Gaeta, W Italy, W of Terracina; 1775 ft. (541 m.); from very early times associated with the island of **Ae·aea** \ē-ˈē-ə\, legendary home of the sorceress Circe.

Cir·cle \ˈsər-kəl\. **1.** Unincorporated settlement, E Alaska, on upper Yukon River ab. 85 mi. (137 km.) above Ft. Yukon; pop. (1990c) 73; mining village settled 1890s, deserted during Klondike rush.

2. Town, ⊗ of McCone co., E Montana; pop. (1990c) 805.

Circle Pines. Village, Anoka co., E Minnesota, 10 mi. (16 km.) N of St. Paul; pop. (1990c) 4704.

Cir·cle·ville \ˈsər-kəl-ˌvil\. City, ⊗ of Pickaway co., S cen. Ohio, on Scioto River 25 mi. (40 km.) S of Columbus; pop. (1990c) 11,666; settled 1810 on site once occupied by Mound Builders; incorp. as city 1853.

Cir·cu·lar Head \ˈsər-kyə-lər\. **1.** A promontory at tip of a peninsula on N coast of Tasmania, Australia, ab. 40 mi. (64 km.) NW of Burnie; 478 ft. (146 m.) high; a steep mass of greenstone; at its foot on mainland side is the town of Stanley.

2. Town, Australia. See STANLEY 3.

Ci·re·bon \ˌchē-re-ˈbȯn\ *also* **Che·ri·bon** \ˌchē-\ *or* **Tji·re·bon** \ˌchē-\. **1.** Former residency of Netherlands Indies, on coast of Java Sea; 2097 sq. mi. (5431 sq. km.); now part of the Indonesian prov. of West Java; fertile coastal plain, with one high mountain, Tjiremaj, in the SE. A center of Islam in Java since 16th cent. but the sultanate became subject to the Dutch in 17th cent.

2. Seaport, W Java, Indonesia; pop. (1990c) 245,307.

Ci·re·may, Gu·nung \ˈgü-ˌnu̇ŋ-chē-ˈrā-mī\ *or* **Tji·re·maj** \chē-\. Volcano, West Java prov., Indonesia, SSW of Cirebon; 10,098 ft. (3078 m.).

Cirenaica. See CYRENAICA.

Ci·ren·ces·ter \ˈsīr-ən-ˌses-tər, ˈsi-sə-tər\; *anc.* **Co·rin·i·um** \kōr-ˈin-ē-əm, kȯr-\. Town, Gloucestershire, SW cen. England, 14 mi. (23 km.) SE of Gloucester; was 2d largest town in Roman Britain; Roman remains; Corinium Museum; remains of an abbey dating from 1117.

Cirene. See CYRENE.

Ci·rey *or in full* **Cirey–sur–Blaise** \sē-ˌrā-sūer-ˈblez\. Village, Haute-Marne dept., NE France, NW of Chaumont; on Blaise River, tributary of Marne; writer Voltaire resided here (1734–49) in the château of Mme. du Châtelet.

Ci·riè \chē-rē-ˈā\. Commune, Torino prov., Piedmont, NW Italy, 12 mi. (19 km.) NNW of Turin; pop. (1981p) 18,849.

Cirque de Gavarnie. See GAVARNIE.

Cirque Mountain \ˈsərk\. Highest point in Torngat Mts., Labrador, Newfoundland, Canada, at S end of the range; 5160 ft. (1573 m.).

Cirta. See CONSTANTINE.

Cisa *or* **La Cisa.** Pass in the Apennines. See table at APENNINES.

Cisalpine Gaul. See GAUL.

Cis·al·pine Republic \sis-ˈal-pīn\. Former republic in N Italy created by French Emperor Napoléon 1797 by combining the Cispadane and Transpadane republics; ✻ Milan; embraced lands around Milan N of Po River and around Ferrara and Bologna S of the Po; incorp. into kingdom of Italy 1805.

Cis·cau·ca·sia \ˌsis-kȯ-ˈkā-zhə, -shə\ *also* **Northern Caucasia** *or Russ.* **Pred·kav·kaz'·ye** \ˌprid-kəf-ˈkäsʸ-yə\. Region N of the Caucasus Mts. in S Russia in Europe; 82,600 sq. mi. or 213,934 sq. km. (see CAUCASIA); comprises Chechnya and Ingushetia, S half of Krasnodar Kray, and the Dagestan, Kabardino-Balkaria, and Alania republics.

Cis·co \ˈsis-kō\. City, Eastland co., N cen. Texas, 40 mi. (64 km.) E of Abilene; pop. (1990c) 3813.

Cis·kei \ˈsis-ˌkī\. Former black enclave, Rep. of South Africa, ✻ Bisho; granted independence 1981, but never internationally recognized; began reincorporation into South Africa Feb. 1991; now part of Eastern Cape prov.

Cis·lei·tha·nia \ˌsis-lī-ˈthā-nyə, -nē-ə\. Formerly, that part of Austria-Hungary W of Leitha River.

Cispadane Gaul. See GAUL.

Cis·pa·dane Republic \ˈsis-pə-ˌdān, sis-ˈpā-ˌdān\. Former republic in N Italy created by French Emperor Napoléon 1796 from lands S of Po River around Modena, Reggio nell'Emilia, Ferrara, and Bologna; ✻ Bologna; incorp. 1797 into Cisalpine Republic (*q.v.*).

Cistercium. See CÎTEAUX.

Cis·ter·na di La·ti·na \chēs-ˈter-nä-dē-lä-ˈtē-nä\. Commune, Latina prov., Lazio, W cen. Italy, 8 mi. (13 km.) NNW of the commune of Latina; pop. (1989c) 30,895.

Ci·ster·ni·no \ˌchēs-tər-ˈnē-nō\. Commune, Brindisi prov., Puglia, SE Italy, 28 mi. (45 km.) WNW of the seaport of Brindisi; pop. (1981p) 11,395.

Cit·a·del, Mount \ˈsit-ə-dəl, -ˌdel\. Peak in Glacier National Park, NW Montana; 9024 ft. (2751 m.).

Cî·teaux \sē-ˈtō\ *or Lat.* **Cis·ter·ci·um** \sis-ˈtər-shəm\. Village in the commune of **Saint–Ni·co·las–lès–Cîteaux** \ˌseⁿ-ˌnē-kə-ˈlä-lā-\, Côte-d'Or dept., E France, ab. 16 mi. (26 km.)

SSE of Dijon; abbey of Cistercian Order, founded 1098 by St. Robert de Molesmes.

Ci·thae·ron \sə-'thē-rən\ *or* **Ki·thai·rón** \,kē-the-'rön\ *also* **El·a·tea** \,e-lə-'tē-ə\. Mountain, Greece, on Attica-Boeotia boundary; 4623 ft. (1409 m.); sacred to Bacchus and the Muses.

Citharista. See LA CIOTAT.

Ci·ti·um \'si-shəm, -shē-əm\. Ancient city on SE coast of Cyprus, center of Phoenician influence in the island; part of its site is now port of Larnaca. Founded before Phoenician era; under control of Assyria in 7th cent. B.C. In the Bible known as **Kit·tim** \'ki-təm\, *also* **Chit·tim** \'ki-təm\. During period of Greek revolts was loyal to Persia. Birthplace of Greek Stoic philosopher Zeno c. 335 B.C.

Ci·tlal·té·petl. See ORIZABA 1.

Cit·ro·nelle \,si-trə-'nel\. Town, Mobile co., SW Alabama, 30 mi. (48 km.) NW of the city of Mobile; pop. (1990c) 3671; surrender of last Confederate army E of Mississippi River May 4, 1865.

Cit·rus \'si-trəs\. Coastal county in W peninsula of Florida. See table at FLORIDA.

Cit·ta·del·la \,chē-tä-'del-lä\. Commune, Padova prov., Veneto, NE Italy, 16 mi. (26 km.) NNW of Padua; pop. (1981p) 17,215; founded 1220; ancient city walls.

Cit·tà della Pie·ve \chē-'tä-del-lä-'pyā-vā\. Commune, Perugia prov., Umbria, cen. Italy; pop. (1981p) 6463; cathedral. Birthplace of painter Pietro Vannucci (Perugino) c. 1450.

Città del Vaticano. See VATICAN CITY.

Cit·tà di Cas·tel·lo \chē-'tä-dē-kä-'stel-lō\. Commune, Perugia prov., Umbria, cen. Italy, on Tiber River 27 mi. (43 km.) NNW of the commune of Perugia; pop. (1991p) 37,394; Renaissance cathedral; mineral springs.

Cittavecchia. See STARI GRAD.

Città Vecchia. See MDINA.

City Island. Island in Long Island Sound off E coast of the Bronx, New York City.

City of Davao. See DAVAO 2.

City of Refuge National Historical Park. See *Pu'uhonua o Honaunau* at UNITED STATES, *National Historical Parks.*

City of the Dalles. See DALLES, THE 1.

City Point. Former village, now part of Hopewell, Prince George co., Virginia, on James River; Union base of operations in Civil War.

Ciu·dad Acu·ña \syü-'t͟hät͟h-ä-'kü-nyä\; *formerly* **Vi·lla Acuña** \'vē-yä\. Town, NE Coahuila state, NE Mexico, on the Rio Grande opp. Del Rio, Texas.

Ciu·dad Bo·lí·var \syü-'thäth-bō-'lē-,vär\. River port, ✻ of Bolívar state, NE Venezuela, on the narrows (Span. *angosturas*) of the Orinoco River, whence its former popular name **An·gos·tu·ra** \,äŋ-gȯs-'tü-rä, ,aŋ-gəs-'tu̇r-ə\; pop. (1990p) 225,846; exports include cattle, hides, timber; gold; founded 1764.

Ciu·dad Ca·mar·go \syü-'t͟häth-kä-'mär-gō\. Town, SE Chihuahua state, N Mexico, 85 mi. (137 km.) SE of the city of Chihuahua; part of municipality of **Camargo**.

Ciudad del Carmen. See CARMEN 3.

Ciu·dad del Es·te \syü-'t͟hät͟h-t͟hel-'es-tā\; *formerly* **Puer·to Pre·si·den·te Stroess·ner** \'pwer-tō-,prā-sē-'den-tā-'stres-ner\. Town, ✻ of Alto Paraná dept., E Paraguay; pop. (1992p) 133,893.

Ciu·dad Del·ga·do \syü-'t͟hät͟h-t͟hel-'gä-t͟hō\. Town, San Salvador dept., SW cen. El Salvador; pop. (1986e) 96,815.

Ciudad de México, D.F. See MEXICO CITY.

Ciudad de Valles. See VALLES 2.

Ciu·da·de·la \,syü-t͟hä-'t͟hā-lä\ *or* **Ciu·ta·del·la** \,syü-tä-'t͟hel-yä\ *or in full* **Ciu·ta·del·la de Me·nor·ca** \,t͟hā-mā-'nōr-kä\. Seaport, Baleares prov., Spain, on W coast of Minorca I. 70 mi. (113 km.) NE of Palma.

Ciu·dad Gua·ya·na \,syü-'t͟hät͟h-gä-'yä-nä\ *or* **San To·mé de Guayana** \,sän-tō-'mā-t͟hā-\ *or* **San·to To·mé de Guayana** \,sän-tō-tō\. City, NE Bolívar state, E Venezuela, at confluence of Orinoco and Caroní rivers; pop. (1990e) 536,506; a planned city, founded 1961.

Ciu·dad Guz·mán \syü-'t͟hät͟h-güs-'män\. City, Jalisco state, W cen. Mexico; 35 mi. (56 km.) S of Lake Chapala; munic. pop. (1990p) 73,919.

Ciu·dad Hi·dal·go \syü-'t͟hät͟h-ē-'t͟häl-gō\. Town, Michoacán state, SW Mexico.

Ciu·dad Juá·rez \syü-'t͟hät͟h-'hwär-,es\ *or* **Juárez.** City, Chihuahua state, N Mexico, opp. El Paso, Texas; pop. (1990c) 789,522; alt. 3117 ft. (950 m.); connected with El Paso by bridges over the Rio Grande; founded in latter part of 17th cent.; important as early transportation center; headquarters of Mexican revolutionary and statesman Benito Juárez 1865; orig. called El Paso del Norte, name changed 1888 to honor Juárez.

Ciu·dad Ma·de·ro \syü-'t͟hät͟h-mä-'t͟hā-rō\ *also* **Vi·lla Ce·ci·lia** \'vē-yä-sā-'sēl-yä\. City, Tamaulipas state, E Mexico, N suburb of Tampico; munic. pop. (1990p) 159,644; museum.

Ciu·dad Man·te \syü-'t͟hät͟h-'män-tā\. Town, Tamaulipas state, E Mexico.

Ciu·dad Man·u·el Do·bla·do \syü-'t͟hät͟h-män-'wel-dō-'blä-t͟hō\. Municipality, Guanajuato state, Mexico, 50 mi. (81 km.) SW of the city of Guanajuato.

Ciu·dad Obre·gón \syü-'t͟hät͟h-,ō-brā-'gȯn\. Town, Sonora state, NW Mexico, 65 mi. (105 km.) SE of Guaymas; nearby irrigated farmland produces rice, cotton, and corn.

Ciu·dad Oje·da \syü-'t͟hät͟h-ō-'hā-t͟hä\. Municipality, Zulia state, NW Venezuela, 40 mi. (64 km.) SE of Maracaibo, on shore of Lake Maracaibo; pop. (1990e) 96,257.

Ciudad Porfirio Díaz. See PIEDRAS NEGRAS 2.

Ciu·dad Re·al \syü-'t͟hät͟h-rā-'äl\. **1.** Province of S cen. Spain. See table at SPAIN.

2. Commune, its ✻, near Guadiana River 99 mi. (159 km.) S of Madrid; pop. (1991p) 56,315; distribution center for agricultural products; Gothic cathedral; founded mid-13th cent. by Alfonso X (el Sabio); Spaniards defeated by French near-by 1809.

Ciu·dad Ro·dri·go \syü-'t͟hät͟h-rō-'t͟hrē-g͟ō\. Commune, Salamanca prov., W Spain, 53 mi. (85 km.) WSW of the commune of Salamanca; pop. (1991p) 14,857; cathedral (begun 12th cent.); taken by English 1706 but recovered 1707; in Peninsular War twice captured: by the French under Marshal Michel Ney 1810 and by the British under Gen. Arthur Wellesley (later duke of Wellington) 1812. The well-preserved portion of the city within medieval walls has been declared a historic monument.

Ciudad Trujillo. See SANTO DOMINGO 3.

Ciu·dad Val·les \syü-'t͟hät͟h-'bä-yās\. Municipality, San Luis Potosí state, Mexico, 80 mi. (129 km.) W of Tampico; pop. (1990p) 130,970.

Ciu·dad Vic·to·ria \syü-'t͟hät͟h-vēk-'tōr-yä\. Town, ✻ of Tamaulipas state, E cen. Mexico; in region producing henequen, lumber, and sugar, 150 mi. (241 km.) SE of Monterrey; university (1956); founded 1750.

Ciutadella *or* **Ciutadella de Menorca.** See CIUDADELA.

Ci·vi·ta Ca·stel·la·na \'chē-vē-,tä-,käs-tel-'lä-nä\; *anc.* **Fa·le·rii** \fə-'ler-ē-,ī\. Commune, Viterbo, N Lazio, cen. Italy, N of Rome; pop. (1991p) 15,357; cathedral (completed 13th cent.); ancient Falerii one of 12 cities of Etruria; built on a plateau surrounded except on W side by gorges 200 ft. (61 m.) deep; conquered by Romans 241 B.C.

Civita Lavinia. See LANUVIUM.

Ci·vi·ta·no·va Mar·che \,chē-vē-tä-'nȯ-vä-'mär-kā\. Commune, Macerata prov., Marche, E Italy, on coast, ab. 15 mi. (24 km.) E of the commune of Macerata; pop. (1991p) 37,070.

Civitas Altae Ripae. See BRZEG.

Civitas Carnutum. See CHARTRES.

Civitas Eburovicum. See ÉVREUX.

Civitas Nemetum. See SPEYER.

Ci·vi·ta·vec·chia \ˌchē-vē-tä-ˈvek-kyä\; *anc.* **Cen·tum Cel·lae** \ˈsen-təm-ˈse-lē\ *also* **Tra·ja·ni Por·tus** \trə-ˌjā-nī-ˈpōr-təs\. Fortified seaport, Roma prov., Lazio, cen. Italy, on Tyrrhenian Sea 39 mi. (63 km.) WNW of Rome; pop. (1991p) 50,856; maritime traffic; episcopal see; chief port of Rome; founded by Roman Emperor Trajan early 2d cent.; citadel (designed by Donato Bramante and completed by Michelangelo); arsenal; Etruscan and ancient Roman antiquities; heavily bombed in WWII.

Ciz·re \jēz-ˈre\; *formerly* **Je·zi·ret ibn Omar** \jə-ˈzir-et-ˌib-ᵊn-ˈō-mär\. Town, SE Turkey in Asia, on Tigris River on Syrian border.

Clack·a·mas \ˈkla-kə-məs\. **1.** River, NW Oregon; flows NW into Willamette River; ab. 80 mi. (130 km.) long.
2. County in NW Oregon. See table at OREGON.

Clack·man·nan \klak-ˈma-nən\. **1.** *or* **Clack·man·nan·shire** \-ˌshir, -shər\. Former county, cen. Scotland; ⊗ Alloa; associated with poet Robert Burns.
2. Parish and town, cen. Scotland, ab. 7 mi. (11 km.) E of Stirling; formerly served as ⊗ of Clackmannan.

Clac·ton–on–Sea \ˈklak-tən\. Town, Essex, SE England, on North Sea 59 mi. (95 km.) ENE of London; pop. (1981p) 43,571; seaside resort.

Clai·borne \ˈklā-bərn\. Name of a parish in N Louisiana and of counties in two states of the U.S. See tables at LOUISIANA, MISSISSIPPI, TENNESSEE.

Claire, Lake \ˈklar\. Lake, NE Alberta, Canada, W of Lake Athabaska; 545 sq. mi. (1412 sq. km.).

Claire·mont \ˈklar-ˌmänt\. Town, ⊗ of Kent co., NW Texas.

Clair Engle Lake. Reservoir in Trinity River in Trinity co., NW California, formed by Trinity Dam (see UNITED STATES, *Dams and Reservoirs*).

Clair·ton \ˈklart-ᵊn\. City, Allegheny co., SW Pennsylvania, on Monongahela River 12 mi. (19 km.) SSE of Pittsburgh; pop. (1990c) 9656; settled 18th cent.

Clair·vaux \kler-ˈvō\. Hamlet, Aube dept., NE France, 40 mi. (64 km.) ESE of Troyes; contains Cistercian abbey, founded 1115 by St. Bernard of Clairvaux, made into a prison 1808.

Clal·lam \ˈkla-ləm\. Coastal county of NW Washington. See table at WASHINGTON.

Cla·mart \klȧ-ˈmȧr\. Commune, Hauts-de-Seine dept., N France, a S suburb of Paris near Forest of Meudon.

Cla·me·cy \klȧm-ˈsē\. Commune, Nièvre dept., cen. France, 36 mi. (58 km.) NNE of Nevers on the Canal of Nivernais; former see.

Clan·ton \ˈklant-ᵊn\. City, ⊗ of Chilton co., cen. Alabama, 41 mi. (66 km.) NW of Montgomery; pop. (1990c) 7669.

Clara, Agua. See AGUA CLARA.

Clare \ˈklar\. **1.** County in cen. Michigan. See table at MICHIGAN.
2. City, Clare co., cen. Michigan, 15 mi. (24 km.) N of Mount Pleasant; pop. (1990c) 3021.
3. River, co. Galway, Ireland; flows S through center of county then W and into Lough Corrib near its S end.
4. County, Munster prov., W Ireland; ⊗ Ennis; oats, potatoes; livestock raising, fishing. See table at IRELAND.
5. Island off W coast of Ireland at entrance to Clew Bay and S of Achill I.; 6.3 sq. mi. (16 sq. km.); administratively in co. Mayo, Ireland (republic).

Clare·mont \ˈklar-ˌmänt\. **1.** City, Los Angeles co., SW California, 28 mi. (45 km.) E of the city of Los Angeles; pop. (1990c) 32,503; Pomona Coll. (1887), Claremont Graduate School (1925), Scripps Coll. (1926), Claremont McKenna Coll. (1946), Harvey Mudd Coll. (1955), Pitzer Coll. (1963).
2. City, Sullivan co., SW New Hampshire, 30 mi. (48 km.) N of Keene; pop. (1990c) 13,902; summer resort.
3. Town, W Western Australia, Australia W suburb of Perth on Melville Water, the estuary of Swan River; pop. (1981c) 8193.

Clare·more \ˈklar-ˌmōr\. City and health resort, ⊗ of Rogers co., NE Oklahoma, 25 mi. (40 km.) ENE of Tulsa; pop. (1990c) 13,280; mineral springs; gun museum; birthplace (1879) of actor and humorist Will Rogers nearby.

Clar·ence \ˈklar-əns\. **1.** River, NE New South Wales, SE Australia; flows SE to Pacific Ocean; 245 mi. (394 km.) long.
2. River, NE South I., New Zealand; flows NE, E, and SE to Pacific Ocean S of Waipapa Point; 130 mi. (209 km.) long.

Clarence Island. **1.** Small island in Scotia Sea, in NE part of South Shetlands, 54°05′W, 61°12′S; part of British Antarctic Terr.
2. Chilean island in Tierra del Fuego Archipelago (*q.v.*), SW of Brunswick Penin.

Clarence Strait. **1.** Narrow passage, SE Alaska, bet. Prince of Wales I. on W and Wrangell and Revillagigedo islands and mainland on E; ab. 135 mi. (217 km.) long.
2. Channel bet. Bathurst and Melville islands on N and mainland of Northern Terr., Australia, on S; connects Van Diemen Gulf with Timor Sea; ab. 90 mi. (145 km.) long.
3. *or* **Khū·rān Strait** \kü-ˈrän\. Strait in E Persian Gulf, extending bet. Qeshm I. and the mainland of Iran.

Clar·en·don \ˈklar-ən-dən\. **1.** County in E cen. South Carolina. See table at SOUTH CAROLINA.
2. City, ⊗ of Monroe co., E Arkansas; pop. (1990c) 2072.
3. City, ⊗ of Donley co., NW Texas, in the Panhandle; pop. (1990c) 2067; Clarendon Coll. (1927).
4. Parish, England. See CLARENDON PARK.

Clarendon Hills. Village, Du Page co., NE Illinois, SW of Chicago; pop. (1990c) 6994.

Clarendon Park *or* **Clarendon.** Parish, S Wiltshire, England, 2 mi. (3 km.) SE of Salisbury; scene 1164 of council of bishops and barons who issued the *Constitutions of Clarendon* defining and limiting the rights of the clergy, which actions ultimately led to the break bet. Henry II and his archbishop of Canterbury, Thomas Becket.

Cla·rens \klȧ-ˈräⁿ\. Village, one of the Montreux group, Vaud canton, Switzerland, at E end of Lake Geneva; winter resort; chief scene of author and philosopher Jean-Jacques Rousseau's *Nouvelle Héloïse.*

Clares·holm \ˈklarz-ˌhōm\. Town, Alberta, Canada, 75 mi. (121 km.) SSE of Calgary; pop. (1991c) 3297.

Cla·ri·den·stock \klä-ˈrēd-ᵊn-ˌshtȯk\. Peak in the Alps, Uri canton, cen. Switzerland; 10,730 ft. (3271 m.).

Cla·rin·da \klə-ˈrin-də\. City, ⊗ of Page co., SW Iowa; pop. (1990c) 5104.

Clar·ing·ton \ˈklar-iŋ-tən\; *formerly* **Newcastle.** Town, SE Ontario, Canada, on Lake Ontario; pop. (1991c) 49,479.

Clar·i·on \ˈklar-ē-ən\. **1.** River, NW cen. Pennsylvania; rises in McKean co., flows SW into Allegheny River.
2. County in W Pennsylvania. See table at PENNSYLVANIA.
3. City, ⊗ of Wright co., N cen. Iowa; pop. (1990c) 2703.
4. Borough, ⊗ of Clarion co., W Pennsylvania, on Clarion River; pop. (1990c) 6457; Clarion Univ. of Pennsylvania (1867).

Clarium. See CHIARI.

Clark \ˈklärk\. **1.** Name of counties in 12 states of the U.S. See tables at ARKANSAS, IDAHO, ILLINOIS, INDIANA, KANSAS, KENTUCKY, MISSOURI, NEVADA, OHIO, SOUTH DAKOTA, WASHINGTON, WISCONSIN.
2. Township, Union co., NE New Jersey, SW of Elizabeth; pop. (1990c) 14,692.
3. City, ⊗ of Clark co., NE South Dakota; pop. (1990c) 1292.

Clark, Mount. **1.** Peak in the Sierra Nevada, E Mariposa co., cen. California, in Yosemite National Park; 11,522 ft. (3512 m.).
2. Peak in Franklin Mts., W mainland part of Northwest Territories, Canada; 4798 ft. (1462 m.).
3. Peak, N South I., New Zealand; 7085 ft. (2160 m.).

Clarke \ˈklärk\. Name of counties in five states of the U.S. See tables at ALABAMA, GEORGIA, IOWA, MISSISSIPPI, VIRGINIA.

Clarkes·ville \ˈklärks-ˌvil\. City, ⊗ of Habersham co., NE Georgia; pop. (1990c) 1151.

Clark Fork. River, Montana and Idaho; rises near Butte, Silver Bow co., SW Montana, and flows NW across Idaho border to Pend Oreille Lake in N Idaho; ab. 300 mi. (480 km.) long.

Clarks·burg \ˈklärks-ˌbərg\. City, ⊗ of Harrison co., N West Virginia, on West Fork River; pop. (1990c) 18,059; coal, oil, and gas. Important supply depot for Union troops during Civil War; birthplace of Confederate Gen. T.J. ("Stonewall") Jackson 1824, when it was in state of Virginia.

Clarks·dale \ˈklärks-ˌdāl\. City, ⊗ of Coahoma co., NW Mississippi, 53 mi. (85 km.) NNW of Greenwood; pop. (1990c) 19,717; Coahoma Community Coll. (1926).

Clarks Fork \ˈklärks\. River, NW Wyoming and S Montana; rises in Absaroka Range in S Montana, flows E through NW Wyoming, then N into Yellowstone River in S cen. Montana; ab. 120 mi. (190 km.) long.

Clarks Hill Lake *or in S.C.* **Strom Thur·mond Lake** \ˈsträm-ˈthər-mənd\. Reservoir on Georgia-South Carolina boundary; ab. 35 mi. (56 km.) long; formed by damming of Savannah River.

Clarks Summit. Borough, Lackawanna co., NE Pennsylvania, 7 mi. (11 km.) N of Scranton; pop. (1990c) 5433; Baptist Bible Coll. and Theological Seminary (1932).

Clarks·ton \ˈklärk-stən\. **1.** City, De Kalb co., NW cen. Georgia; pop. (1990c) 5385; residential suburb of Atlanta.
2. City, Asotin co., SE Washington, on Snake River opp. Lewiston, Idaho; pop. (1990c) 6753.

Clarks·ville \ˈklärks-ˌvil, -vəl\. **1.** City, ⊗ of Johnson co., NW Arkansas, near Arkansas River 56 mi. (90 km.) E of Fort Smith; pop. (1990c) 5833. Univ. of the Ozarks (1834).
2. Town, Clark co., S Indiana, across Ohio River from Louisville, Kentucky; pop. (1990c) 19,833.
3. City, ⊗ of Montgomery co., N Tennessee, on peninsula at confluence of Cumberland and Red rivers 40 mi. (64 km.) WNW of Nashville; pop. (1990c) 75,494; formerly important tobacco-processing center; livestock; Austin Peay State Univ. (1927); settled 1784.
4. City, ⊗ of Red River co., NE Texas, 29 mi. (47 km.) E of Paris; pop. (1990c) 4311.

Clat·sop \ˈklat-səp\. Coastal county in NW Oregon. See table at OREGON.

Clauda. See GAVDOS.

Claude \ˈklȯd\. City, ⊗ of Armstrong co., NW Texas, in the Panhandle; pop. (1990c) 1199.

Clau·di·op·o·lis \ˌklȯ-dē-ˈä-pə-lis\; *earlier* **Bi·thyn·i·um** \bə-ˈthi-nē-əm\. Ancient city in Bithynia, Asia Minor, near modern Bolu, Turkey; thought to have been destroyed by earthquake.

Claus·thal–Zel·ler·feld *also* **Klaus·thal–Zel·ler·feld** \ˈklau̇s-täl-ˈtse-lər-ˌfelt\. City, Lower Saxony, Germany, in NW Harz Mts. 32 mi. (51 km.) SSW of Brunswick; pop. (1980c) 16,270; technical university (1775, university status 1912); formerly an important mining center: iron, lead, copper, silver, zinc; winter resort; city charter received by Clausthal 1554, by Zellerfeld 1532.

Claw·son \ˈklȯs-ᵊn\. City, Oakland co., SE Michigan, 11 mi. (18 km.) SE of Pontiac; pop. (1990c) 13,874.

Clax·ton \ˈklak-stən\. City, ⊗ of Evans co., SE cen. Georgia, 48 mi. (77 km.) W of Savannah; pop. (1990c) 2464.

Clay \ˈklā\. **1.** Name of counties in 18 states of the U.S. See tables at ALABAMA, ARKANSAS, FLORIDA, GEORGIA, ILLINOIS, INDIANA, IOWA, KANSAS, KENTUCKY, MINNESOTA, MISSISSIPPI, MISSOURI, NEBRASKA, NORTH CAROLINA, SOUTH DAKOTA, TENNESSEE, TEXAS, WEST VIRGINIA.
2. Town, ⊗ of Clay co., cen. West Virginia; pop. (1990c) 592.

Clay, Mount. Peak of the White Mts. in S Coos co., N New Hampshire, just N of Mt. Washington; ab. 5535 ft. (1687 m.).

Clay Center. **1.** City, ⊗ of Clay co., NE cen. Kansas, NW of Manhattan; pop. (1990c) 4613.
2. City, ⊗ of Clay co., S Nebraska; pop. (1990c) 825.

Clay·ton \ˈklāt-ᵊn\. **1.** Name of counties in two states of the U.S. See tables at GEORGIA and IOWA.
2. Town, a ⊗ of Barbour co., SE Alabama; pop. (1990c) 1564.
3. City, Contra Costa co., W California, SE of Concord; pop. (1990c) 7317.
4. City, ⊗ of Rabun co., NE corner of Georgia; pop. (1990c) 1613.
5. City, ⊗ of St. Louis co., E Missouri, 8 mi. (13 km.) W of the city of St. Louis; pop. (1990c) 13,874; residential suburb of St. Louis.
6. Borough, Gloucester co., SW New Jersey, 21 mi. (34 km.) S of Camden; pop. (1990c) 6155.
7. Town, ⊗ of Union co., NE corner of New Mexico; pop. (1990c) 2484; on high plateau.
8. Town, Jefferson co., N New York, on St. Lawrence River in Thousand Is. region; pop. (1990c) 4629; summer resort, fishing center; port of entry.
9. Town, Johnston co., E North Carolina, 13 mi. (21 km.) SE of Raleigh; pop. (1990c) 4756.

Clay·ton–le–Moors \-lə-ˈmu̇rz, -ˈmōrz\. Town, Lancashire, NW England, 21 mi. (34 km.) N of Manchester; pop. (1981p) 6309.

Cla·zom·e·nae \klə-ˈzä-mə-ˌnē\. Ancient city in Asia Minor, 20 mi. (32 km.) W of İzmir (Turkey), on the Gulf of İzmir; one of the 12 Ionian Cities, celebrated for its terra-cotta sarcophagi. Birthplace of Greek philosopher Anaxagoras 5th cent. B.C.

Clear, Cape \ˈklir\. Headland, S Clear I., off SW Ireland.

Clear Creek. **1.** River, cen. Colorado; rises in SW Clear Creek co., flows E into South Platte River; ab. 80 mi. (130 km.) long.
2. County in N cen. Colorado. See table at COLORADO.

Clear·field \ˈklir-ˌfēld\. **1.** County in W cen. Pennsylvania. See table at PENNSYLVANIA.
2. Borough, its ⊗, 20 mi. (32 km.) ESE of Du Bois; pop. (1990c) 6633; settled c. 1805.
3. City, Davis co., N Utah, S of Ogden; pop. (1990c) 21,435.

Clear Fork. River, N cen. Texas; flows E across Jones co., follows winding course through Shackelford, Throckmorton, and Stephens cos.; enters Brazos River in S Young co.; 220 mi. (354 km.) long.

Clear Island. Island off S coast of co. Cork, Ireland; 3 mi. (4.8 km.) long; its S point is Cape Clear; 4 mi. (6.4 km.) to the SW is Fastnet lighthouse.

Clear·lake \ˈklir-ˌlāk\. City, Lake co., W California, on Clear Lake; pop. (1990c) 11,804.

Clear Lake. **1.** Lake, Lake co., W California; 25 mi. (40 km.) long, 2 to 10 mi. (3.2 to 16 km.) wide.
2. Reservoir in California. See CLEAR LAKE RESERVOIR.
3. *or in full* **Clear Lake City.** City on Clear Lake, Cerro Gordo co., N Iowa, 14 mi. (22 km.) W of Mason City; pop. (1990c) 8183.
4. City, ⊗ of Deuel co., E South Dakota; pop. (1990c) 1247.

Clear Lake Reservoir *or* **Clear Lake.** Large reservoir in NW Modoc co., NE California, ab. 10 mi. (16 km.) S of Oregon border; its outlet, an upper tributary (Lost River) of the Klamath, flows NW into Oregon.

Clear·wa·ter \ˈklir-ˌwȯ-tər, -ˌwä-\. **1.** River, NW Idaho; formed by forks uniting in N Idaho co., flows N and W into Snake River at Lewiston, NW Nez Perce co.
2. Name of counties in two states of the U.S. See tables at IDAHO and MINNESOTA.
3. City, ⊗ of Pinellas co., W Florida Penin., on Gulf of Mexico; pop. (1990c) 98,784; tourism; sport fishing; connected by two-mile (three-kilometer) causeway with **Clearwater Beach Island,** a beach resort; incorp. 1891.
4. Lake, Quebec, Canada; 478 sq. mi. (1238 sq. km.); outlet on W connects it with Lac Guillaume-Delisle (*q.v.*).
5. River, SW Alberta, Canada; flows from N Banff National Park to North Saskatchewan River; 100 mi. (161 km.) long.
6. River, cen. Canada; rises in lakes in NW Saskatchewan and flows W to the Athabasca in NE Alberta; midway in its course is accessible from Lac La Loche (source of Churchill River) by La Loche Portage; ab. 130 mi. (210 km.) long.

Clearwater Mountains. Mountain group in Idaho co., N cen. Idaho; highest point ab. 8000 ft. (2400 m.).

Cle·burne \ˈklē-bərn\. **1.** Name of counties in two states of the U.S. See tables at ALABAMA and ARKANSAS.
2. City, ⊗ of Johnson co., N cen. Texas, 27 mi. (43 km.) S of Fort Worth; pop. (1990c) 22,205; tourism, agricultural area.

Clee Hills \ˈklē\. Range of hills, S Shropshire, W England; 14 mi. (22 km.) long; highest peaks **Brown Clee Hill** 1792 ft. (546 m.) and **Tit·ter·stone Clee Hill** \ˈti-tər-stən\ 1750 ft. (533 m.).

Cle El·um \klē-ˈe-ləm\. City, Kittitas co., cen. Washington, at junction of Cle Elum and Yakima rivers 35 mi. (56 km.) WSW of Wenatchee; pop. (1990c) 1778.

Cle Elum Lake. Lake, NW Kittitas co., cen. Washington; 8 mi. (13 km.) NE of city of Cle Elum; a widening of **Cle Elum River,** which flows into Yakima River at Cle Elum; **Cle Elum Dam** (135 ft. or 41 m.; completed 1933) at S end of lake aids in water conservation for irrigation.

Clee·thorpes \ˈklē-ˌthȯrps\. Town, Humberside, E England, at mouth of the Humber 18 mi. (29 km.) SE of Hull; pop. (1991p) 67,500; seaside resort.

Cleeve Cloud \ˈklēv-ˈklau̇d\. Highest point in the Cotswold Hills, in NE Gloucestershire, SW cen. England, 3.25 mi. (5.2 km.) NE of Cheltenham; 1031 ft. (314 m.).

Clem·en·ton \ˈkle-mən-tən\. Borough, Camden co., SW New Jersey, SSE of the city of Camden; pop. (1990c) 5601.

Clem·son \ˈklem-sən\; *formerly* **Clemson College.** City, Anderson and Pickens cos., NW South Carolina, WSW of Greenville; pop. (1990c) 11,096; peaches, apples, poultry; textiles; tourism; Clemson Univ. (1889).

Cleofás, María. See MARÍA CLEOFÁS.

Cler·mont \ˈkler-ˌmänt\. **1.** County in SW Ohio. See table at OHIO.

2. City, Lake co., cen. Florida Penin., 24 mi. (39 km.) W of Orlando; near Lake Apopka; pop. (1990c) 6910.

Clermont \kler-ˈmōⁿ\. Commune, Oise dept., N France, 41 mi. (66 km.) N of Paris; once seat of countship, united to crown by Louis IX who gave it 13th cent. to his son Robert de France, first of the house of Bourbon.

Cler·mont–Fer·rand \ˌkler-ˌmōⁿ-fe-ˈräⁿ\. City, ✻ of Puy-de-Dôme dept., S cen. France, 88 mi. (142 km.) E of Limoges; pop. (1990c) 140,167; tires and other rubber goods; university (1854, university status 1896); Gothic cathedral (begun 13th cent.); 12th cent. church. Birthplace of scientist and philosopher Blaise Pascal 1623.

History: **Clermont** (*anc.* **Au·gus·to·nem·e·tum** \ȯ-ˌgəs-tə-ˈne-mə-təm, ə-ˌgəs-\) founded by Romans; ✻ of the Arverni; made episcopal see c. 3d cent; scene of several councils, esp. the council 1095 giving rise to the Crusades; became ✻ of duchy of Auvergne 16th cent.; officially united 1731 with Montferrand, nearby town founded 11th cent.

Clermont–l'Hé·rault \-lā-ˈrō\. Commune, Hérault dept., S France; dates from Roman times; occupied by Saracens; scene of much conflict during 16th cent. religious wars in Languedoc.

Clermont–Tonnerre. See REAO.

Cleuch, Ben. See OCHIL HILLS.

Cleve. See KLEVE.

Cleve·don \ˈklēv-dən\. Town, Avon, SW England, on Bristol Channel 11 mi. (18 km.) W of Bristol; pop. (1981p) 17,915; seaside resort.

Cleve·land \ˈklēv-lənd\. **1.** Name of counties in three states of the U.S. See tables at ARKANSAS, NORTH CAROLINA, OKLAHOMA.

2. City, ⊗ of White co., NE Georgia; pop. (1990c) 1653.

3. City, a ⊗ of Bolivar co., NW Mississippi, 30 mi. (48 km.) NNE of Greenville; pop. (1990c) 15,384; Delta State Univ. (1924).

4. City and port of entry, ⊗ of Cuyahoga co., N Ohio, at mouth of Cuyahoga River on Lake Erie; pop. (1990c) 505,616; 2d largest city in the state; steel; industrial research; health care facilities; notable structures include Terminal Tower (708 ft. or 216 m.) and Jacob's Field baseball stadium. Case Western Reserve Univ. (1826), Dyke Coll. (1848), Cleveland Institute of Art (1882), John Carroll Univ. (1886), Cleveland Institute of Music (1920), Cleveland State Univ. (1923), Cuyahoga Community Coll. (1963). Surveyed by Moses Cleaveland for Connecticut Land Company 1796; incorp. as village 1814, as city 1836; expanded following opening of first section of Ohio and Erie Canal 1827 and arrival of railroads 1851; annexed rival Ohio City 1854; developed into a major industrial center and continued to thrive through the first half of the 20th cent.; emigration of population to suburbs began in the 1950s; city experienced financial difficulties in the 1970s, but has since undergone revitalization. Carl B. Stokes, the first African-American mayor of a major U.S. city, elected 1967.

5. City, Pawnee co., N Oklahoma, on Arkansas River 30 mi. (48 km.) WNW of Tulsa; pop. (1990c) 3156.

6. City, ⊗ of Bradley co., SE Tennessee, 26 mi. (42 km.) ENE of Chattanooga; pop. (1990c) 30,354; Lee College (1918), Cleveland State Community Coll. (1967); incorp. 1838 following eviction of Cherokee Indians.

7. City, Liberty co., E Texas, 42 mi. (68 km.) NNE of Houston; pop. (1990c) 7124.

8. Administrative county, N England, on North Sea N of North Yorkshire; includes Hartlepool, Middlesbrough, and Stockton-on-Tees; estab. 1974. See table at ENGLAND.

Cleveland, Mount. Peak, highest point in Glacier National Park, NW Montana; ab. 10,455 ft. (3185 m.).

Cleveland Heights. City, Cuyahoga co., N Ohio, 7 mi. (11 km.) E of Cleveland; pop. (1990c) 54,052; residential suburb.

Cleveland Hills. Highlands in North Yorkshire, N England; highest ab. 1400 ft. (425 m.); iron deposits; Cleveland bay horses first bred in this region.

Cleves *or* **Clèves.** See KLEVE.

Clew Bay \ˈklü\. Inlet of Atlantic Ocean in co. Mayo, NW Ireland; ab. 8 mi. (13 km.) wide, extends inland 15 mi. (24 km.).

Clew·is·ton \ˈklü-əs-tən\. City, Hendry co., S Florida, on Lake Okeechobee; pop. (1990c) 6085; formerly a sugar-processing center.

Cli·chy *or* **Cli·chy–la–Ga·renne** \klē-ˈshē-ˌlȧ-gȧ-ˈren\; *anc.* **Clip·pi·a·cum** \kli-ˈpī-ə-kəm\. Commune, Hauts-de-Seine dept., N France, NW suburb of Paris; pop. (1990c) 48,204; 17th cent. church; a residence of the Merovingian court in 7th cent.

Clif·den \ˈklif-dən\. Town and seaport, W co. Galway, W Ireland; pop. (1986c) 896; lobster fishing.

Cliffside Park \ˈklif-ˌsīd\. Borough, Bergen co., NE corner of New Jersey, on Hudson River 8 mi. (13 km.) NNE of Jersey City and opp. New York City; pop. (1990c) 20,393.

Clif·ton \ˈklif-tən\. **1.** Town, ⊗ of Greenlee co., SE Arizona, on San Francisco River 110 mi. (177 km.) NE of Tucson near New Mexico border; pop. (1990c) 2840; settled 1872.

2. City, Passaic co., N New Jersey, NNW of the city of Passaic; pop. (1990c) 71,742; formerly part of Passaic, made separate city 1917; manufactures steel, textiles, chemicals.

3. City, Bosque co., cen. Texas, NW of Waco; pop. (1990c) 3195.

4. City, Canada. See NIAGARA FALLS 3.

5. Residential suburb of Bristol, Gloucestershire, England, on the Avon where it forms a gorge 245 ft. (75 m.) deep which is crossed by a suspension bridge designed by British engineer I. K. Brunel; hot springs.

Clifton Forge \ˈklif-tən\. City in Alleghany co. but politically independent, W Virginia, 10 mi. (16 km.) E of Covington; 1 sq. mi. (2.6 sq. km.); pop. (1990c) 4679; Dabney S. Lancaster Community Coll. (1964).

Clifton Heights. Borough, Delaware co., SE Pennsylvania, 7 mi. (11 km.) W of Philadelphia; pop. (1990c) 7111.

Clifton Springs. Village, Ontario co., W New York, 29 mi. (47 km.) ESE of Rochester; pop. (1990c) 2175; sulfur springs.

Cli·max \ˈklī-ˌmaks\. Village, Lake co., cen. Colorado, NE of Leadville on Fremont Pass; Harvard Observatory; North America's largest molybdenum mine.

Clinch \ˈklinch\. **1.** River, Virginia and E Tennessee; rises in Tazewell co., SW Virginia, flows SW across Tennessee border and joins the Tennessee River in Roane co.; ab. 300 mi. (480 km.) long; passes through Norris Lake, formed by Norris Dam near junction of Powell and Clinch rivers, one of the dams of the Tennessee Valley Authority (*q.v.*).

2. County in S Georgia. See table at GEORGIA.

Clinch Mountain. Ridge, extending from SW Virginia SW across border into NE Tennessee, bet. Clinch and Holston rivers; 4724 ft. (1440 m.).

Cling·mans Dome \ˈkliŋ-mənz\. Mountain in the Great Smoky Mts., on Tennessee-North Carolina boundary; highest peak 6643 ft. (2025 m.), highest point in Tennessee.

Clin·ton \ˈklint-ᵊn\. **1.** Name of counties in nine states of the U.S. See tables at ILLINOIS, INDIANA, IOWA, KENTUCKY, MICHIGAN, MISSOURI, NEW YORK, OHIO, PENNSYLVANIA.
2. City, ⊗ of Van Buren co., N cen. Arkansas; pop. (1990c) 2213.
3. Town, SW Middlesex co., S Connecticut, on Long Island Sound and on Hammonasset River; pop. (1990c) 12,767; cosmetics; tourism.
4. City, ⊗ of De Witt co., cen. Illinois, 22 mi. (35 km.) N of Decatur; pop. (1990c) 7437.
5. City, Vermillion co., W Indiana, 12 mi. (19 km.) N of Terre Haute; pop. (1990c) 5040; coal deposits.
6. City, ⊗ of Clinton co., E Iowa, on Mississippi River 30 mi. (48 km.) NE of Davenport; pop. (1990c) 29,201; Mount St. Clare Coll. (1895), Clinton Community Coll. (1946); trade center.
7. City, ⊗ of Hickman co., SW Kentucky, 24 mi. (39 km.) WSW of Mayfield; pop. (1990c) 1547.
8. Town, ⊗ of East Feliciana parish, E Louisiana; pop. (1990c) 1904.
9. Town, Kennebec co., Maine; pop. (1990c) 3332.
10. Town, Worcester co., cen. Massachusetts, 12 mi. (19 km.) NNE of the city of Worcester; pop. (1990c) 13,222.
11. City, Hinds co., SW cen. Mississippi; pop. (1990c) 21,847; Mississippi Coll. (1826).
12. City, ⊗ of Henry co., W Missouri, 40 mi. (64 km.) SW of Sedalia; pop. (1990c) 8703; historically important coal mining.
13. Village, Oneida co., cen. New York, 9 mi. (14 km.) WSW of Utica; pop. (1990c) 2238; Hamilton Coll. (1793).
14. City, ⊗ of Sampson co., SE North Carolina; pop. (1990c) 8204.
15. City, Custer co., W Oklahoma, on Washita River 86 mi. (138 km.) W of Oklahoma City; pop. (1990c) 9298; shipping center; founded 1903.
16. City, Laurens co., NW South Carolina, 27 mi. (43 km.) NE of Greenwood; pop. (1990c) 7987; Presbyterian Coll. (1880).
17. Town, ⊗ of Anderson co., E Tennessee, 15 mi. (24 km.) NW of Knoxville; pop. (1990c) 8972.
18. City, Davis co., N Utah; pop. (1990c) 7945.

Clinton, Mount. Peak of the White Mts., in S Coos co., N New Hampshire, SW of Mt. Washington; 4275 ft. (1303 m.).

Clinton–Col·den Lake \ˈkōl-dən\. Lake, E mainland part of Northwest Territories, Canada, NE of Great Slave Lake; 253 sq. mi. (655 sq. km.)

Clin·ton·ville \ˈklint-ᵊn-ˌvil\. City, Waupaca co., E cen. Wisconsin, 30 mi. (48 km.) NNW of Appleton; pop. (1990c) 4351.

Clint·wood \ˈklint-ˌwu̇d\. Town, ⊗ of Dickenson co., SW Virginia; pop. (1990c) 1542.

Clio \ˈklī-ō\. City, Genesee co., SE cen. Michigan, 12 mi. (19 km.) N of Flint; pop. (1990c) 2629.

Clip·per·ton \ˈkli-pərt-ᵊn\. Uninhabited French island, E Pacific Ocean, 670 mi. (1078 km.) SW of Mexico, 10°17′N, 109°13′W; 2 sq. mi. (5.2 sq. km.); a low atoll bet. 2 and 3 mi. (3.2 and 4.8 km.) in diameter, enclosing a rock 82 ft. (25 m.) high. Discovered and used as a base by English pirate John Clipperton in early 18th cent.; claimed by France c. 1855; forcibly occupied by Mexico 1897; awarded to France 1930 by king of Italy as arbitrator; administered from French Polynesia but not part of that territory.

Clippiacum. See CLICHY.

Clith·er·oe \ˈkli-t͟hə-ˌrō\. Town, Lancashire, NW England, on the Ribble 28 mi. (45 km.) N of Manchester; pop. (1981p) 13,552; ruined Norman castle.

Cli·tun·no \klē-ˈtün-nō\; *formerly* **Cli·tum·nus** \klī-ˈtəm-nəs\. River, Umbria, cen. Italy; rises W of Spoleto and flows N into the Topino. There was once a spring in the area described by Roman author Pliny the Younger.

Cloates, Point \ˈklōts\. Cape on Indian Ocean, W Western Australia, Australia, S of North West Cape.

Clon·a·kil·ty \ˌklä-nə-ˈkil-tē\. Town, S coast of co. Cork, SW Ireland, at head of **Clonakilty Bay,** an inlet of Atlantic Ocean; pop. (1986c) 2567; fisheries. Birthplace of Irish nationalist leader Michael Collins 1890.

Clon·ard \ˈklä-nərd\. Village, co. Meath, E Ireland, on Boyne River 30 mi. (48 km.) WNW of Dublin; ruins of famous monastery, founded c. 520 by St. Finnian, at which Irish missionary St. Columba studied.

Clon·fert \ˈklän-fərt\. Village, SE co. Galway, W Ireland; has ruined cathedral on site of 6th cent. monastery founded by St. Brendan.

Clon·mac·noise \ˌklän-mək-ˈnȯiz\. Parish, NW co. Offaly, cen. Ireland, on Shannon River ab. 9 mi. (14 km.) S of Athlone; early center of Christianity, site of an abbey founded c. 545 by St. Ciaran; cathedral built c. 900 laid waste by English 1552; see merged with Meath 1568; ruins (known as "the Seven Churches") preserved as a national monument.

Clon·mel \klän-ˈmel\. Town, ⊗ of co. Tipperary, S Ireland, on Suir River; pop. (1986c) 11,759.

Clon·tarf \klän-ˈtärf\. Residential suburb of Dublin, Ireland, on N shore of Dublin Bay; scene 1014 of defeat of Danes by forces of Irish King Brian Boru, who was killed here.

Clo·quet \klō-ˈkā\. **1.** River, NE Minnesota; rises in Lake co., flows SW into St. Louis River in S St. Louis co.
2. City, Carlton co., E Minnesota, 17 mi. (27 km.) WSW of Duluth; pop. (1990c) 10,885.

Clos·ter \ˈkläs-ter\. Borough, Bergen co., NE corner of New Jersey, 11 mi. (18 km.) ENE of Paterson; pop. (1990c) 8094.

Cloud \ˈklau̇d\. County in N Kansas. See table at KANSAS.

Cloud·cap \ˈklau̇d-ˌkap\. Mountain, W Klamath co., SW Oregon, near E shore of Crater Lake; 8070 ft. (2460 m.).

Cloud Peak. Mountain on boundary bet. Big Horn and Johnson cos., N Wyoming; 13,165 ft. (4013 m.); highest point in Bighorn Mts.

Clouds Rest \ˈklau̇dz-ˈrest\. Mountain, Mariposa co., cen. California; 9930 ft. (3027 m.); rises 5964 ft. (1818 m.) above Yosemite Valley, in Yosemite National Park.

Cloud·veil Dome \ˈklau̇d-ˌvāl\. Peak in cen. Grand Teton National Park, NW Wyoming; 12,026 ft. (3666 m.).

Cloudy Bay \ˈklau̇-dē\. Inlet of Cook Strait on NE coast of South I., New Zealand; Blenheim is on its S shore.

Clo·vel·ly \klō-ˈve-lē\. Village, Devon, SW England, on SW shore of Barnstaple Bay ab. 11 mi. (18 km.) WSW of Bideford; on a cliff, its main street is like a staircase and is too steep for wheeled vehicles; resort.

Clo·ver \ˈklō-vər\. Town, York co., N South Carolina, 17 mi. (27 km.) NW of Rock Hill; pop. (1990c) 3422.

Clo·ver·dale \ˈklō-vər-ˌdāl\. City, Sonoma co., W California, 27 mi. (43 km.) NW of Santa Rosa; pop. (1990c) 4924.

Clo·vis \ˈklō-vis\. **1.** City, Fresno co., S cen. California, 10 mi. (16 km.) NE of the city of Fresno; pop. (1990c) 50,323.
2. City, ⊗ of Curry co., E New Mexico, near Texas boundary; pop. (1990c) 30,954; four-way railroad division point; regional trade center; settled 1907; railroad siding called Riley's Switch.

Cloyne \ˈklȯin\. Village, co. Cork, SW Ireland, 15 mi. (24 km.) ESE of the city of Cork; pop. (1986c) 506; ancient bishopric of which Irish philosopher and cleric George Berkeley was bishop 1734–53; 14th cent. cathedral.

Cluj \ˈklüzh\. County of NW cen. Romania. See table at ROMANIA.

Cluj–Na·po·ca \-ˈnä-pō-kä\ *or Ger.* **Klau·sen·burg** \ˈklau̇z-ᵊn-ˌbu̇rk\ *or Hung.* **Ko·lozs·vár** \ˈkō-lōzh-ˌvär\. City, ⊗ of Cluj co., Romania, in Transylvania in hills on right bank of the Someşul Mic; pop. (1989c) 317,914; textiles; university; begun 12th cent. as German settlement on site of older town; declared a free town 1405. Cluj was joined with neighboring Napoca in the mid-1970s.

Clunia. See FELDKIRCH.

Clu·ny \klü-'nē, 'klü-nē\. Commune, Saône-et-Loire dept., E cen. France; pop. (1990c) 4724; remains of Benedictine abbey of Cluny, founded 910 by William I, duke of Aquitaine; Cluny lace developed 19th cent., inspired by designs used formerly by monks of the abbey. The Romanesque basilica (or abbey church), of which only parts remain, was largest church in world until construction of St. Peter's in Rome.

Clusium. See CHIUSI.

Clute \'klüt\. City, Brazoria co., SE Texas, 53 mi. (85 km.) S of Houston; pop. (1990c) 8910.

Clu·tha \'klü-thə\. River in SE South I., New Zealand; flows SE into the Pacific Ocean; headstreams rise in Lakes Wanaka and Wakatipu; 200 mi. (322 km.) long.

Clw·yd \'klü-id\. **1.** River in N Wales; flows N into Irish Sea at Rhyl; 35 mi. (56 km.) long; vale of Clwyd noted for scenery.

2. County, NE Wales, formed 1974; includes former Flintshire and Denbighshire. See table at WALES.

Clyde \'klīd\. **1.** River, W New York, from Lyons in Wayne co. to Seneca River; part of Canandaigua Outlet.

2. Locality, SE Georgia; formerly a town and ⊗ of Bryan co.

3. City, Sandusky co., N Ohio, 17 mi. (27 km.) SW of the city of Sandusky; pop. (1990c) 5776; settled c. 1820.

4. Town, Callahan co., NW cen.Texas, 10 mi. (16 km.) E of Abilene; pop. (1990c) 3002.

5. River, S Scotland; 106 mi. (170 km.) long; catchment area ab. 1481 sq. mi. (3836 sq. km.); rises in SE Strathclyde region, flows N, near Lanark descends by four waterfalls a distance of 320 ft. (98 m.) in less than 4 mi. (6.4 km.); flows NW near Hamilton, past Glasgow (head of navigation for ocean-going vessels) and Renfrew; at Dumbarton expands into the **Firth of Clyde,** an estuary extending 64 mi. (103 km.) to the island of Ailsa Craig where it is ab. 37 mi. (60 km.) wide. **Clydes·dale** \'klīdz-,dāl\, the valley of the upper Clyde, ab. 50 mi. (80 km.) long, noted for agriculture and for a breed of heavy draft horses (*Clydesdale*).

Clyde·bank \'klīd-,baŋk\. Town, Strathclyde region, W cen. Scotland, on the Clyde; pop. (1991e) 46,920.

Clyde Hill. Town, King co., W cen. Washington; pop. (1990c) 2972.

Clyth Ness \'klīth-'nes\. Headland projecting into North Sea, E Highland region, on NE coast of Scotland, S of Wick; lighthouse.

Cni·dus \'nī-dəs\. Ancient Greek city, SW Asia Minor, at Cape Krio, end of long promontory of Caria; ruins. Noted for its wealth, temples, statues (incl. the famous statue of Aphrodite by Praxiteles), and educational institutions (esp. its medical school). Nearby was fought naval battle 394 B.C. in which Athenian leader Conon defeated Spartan forces.

Cnossus. See KNOSSOS.

Coa·chel·la \,kō-'che-lə\. City, Riverside co., SE California, 80 mi. (129 km.) NE of San Diego; pop. (1990c) 16,896.

Coachella Valley. Valley in SE California bet. Salton Sea and the San Bernardino Mts.

Coa·ho·ma \kō-'hō-mə\. County in NW Mississippi. See table at MISSISSIPPI.

Co·a·hui·la \,kō-ä-'wē-lä\. State, NE Mexico. See table at MEXICO.

Coal \'kōl\. County in S Oklahoma. See table at OKLAHOMA.

Coal City. Village, Grundy co., NE Illinois, 20 mi. (32 km.) SSW of Joliet; pop. (1990c) 3907; in coal-bearing region.

Coal·dale \'kōl-,dāl\. **1.** Borough, Schuylkill co., E cen. Pennsylvania, 20 mi. (32 km.) ENE of Pottsville; pop. (1990c) 2531.

2. Town, Alberta, Canada, 10 mi. (16 km.) E of Lethbridge; pop. (1991c) 5310.

Coal·gate \'kōl-,gāt\. City, ⊗ of Coal co., S Oklahoma, 33 mi. (53 km.) SE of Ada; pop. (1990c) 1895; oil and gas wells nearby.

Coa·lin·ga \kō-'liŋ-gə\. City, Fresno co., S cen. California, 50 mi. (80 km.) SW of the city of Fresno; pop. (1990c) 8212; West Hills Community Coll. (1932); oil fields.

Coal·ville \'kōl-,vil\. **1.** City, ⊗ of Summit co., NE Utah; pop. (1990c) 1065.

2. Town, Leicestershire, cen. England, 14 mi. (22 km.) WNW of Leicester; pop. (1981p) 30,832; coal deposits.

Co·a·mo \kō-'ä-mō\. Town and municipality, S cen. Puerto Rico, ENE of Ponce; pop. (1990c) 13,266 (town), 33,837 (munic.).

Coast \'kōst\. **1.** Province of SE Kenya. See table at KENYA.

2. Administrative region of Tanzania. See *Pwani* in table at TANZANIA.

Coastland. See KÜSTENLAND.

Coast Ranges. Mountains along the Pacific coast of North America from the S part of California, where they meet the Sierra Nevada (see SAN BERNARDINO MOUNTAINS), through Oregon and Washington, into British Columbia and Alaska (Vancouver I., Queen Charlotte Is., Alexander Archipelago, St. Elias and Chugach mountains, Kenai Penin., and Kodiak I.); in California peaks are from 3800 ft. (1158 m.) to 8831 ft. (2692 m.; Mt. Pinos); in Oregon from 2500 ft. (762 m.) to 7000 ft. (2134 m.); in Washington to 8150 ft. (2484 m.; highest point in the Olympic Mts.). The **Coast Mountains** of British Columbia, incl. Mt. Waddington 13,260 ft. (4042 m.), are not a continuation of the U.S. Coast Ranges but of the Cascade Range (*q.v.*).

Coat·bridge \'kōt-,brij\. Burgh, Strathclyde region, S cen. Scotland, 9 mi. (14 km.) E of Glasgow; pop. (1981p) 50,866; engineering.

Co·a·te·pec \kō-,ä-tā-'pek\. Town, Veracruz state, E Mexico, in the Sierra Madre Oriental, just S of Jalapa; munic. pop. (1990p) 61,647.

Co·a·te·pe·que \kō-,ä-tā-'pā-kā\. Town, Quetzaltenango dept., SW Guatemala; munic. pop. (1981c) 49,641; in coffee-growing region.

Coates·ville \'kōts-,vil\. City, Chester co., SE Pennsylvania, 28 mi. (45 km.) E of Lancaster; pop. (1990c) 11,038.

Co·at·i·cook \kō-'a-ti-,ku̇k\. **1.** County, S Quebec, Canada. See table at QUEBEC.

2. Town, S Quebec, Canada, 20 mi. (32 km.) S of Sherbrooke; pop. (1991c) 6637.

Coats Island \'kōts\. Island in N Hudson Bay, Nunavut, Canada; 2206 sq. mi. (5714 sq. km.).

Coats Land. Largely ice-covered section of Antarctica on SE coast of Weddell Sea from 18°W to 40°W; includes Caird Coast and Luitpold Coast.

Co·at·za·co·al·cos \kō-,ät-sä-kō-'äl-kōs\ *or* **Quet·zal·co·al·co** \ket-,säl-kō-'äl-kō\. **1.** River in the Isthmus of Tehuantepec, Mexico; rises in the Sierra Madre, flows NE into the Bay of Campeche; ab. 175 mi. (282 km.) long.

2. *formerly* **Puer·to Mé·xi·co** \'pwer-tō-'me-hē-,kō\. Town and port, Veracruz state, E Mexico; located on Coatzacoalcos River 1 mi. (1.6 km.) from its mouth; munic. pop. (1990p) 232,314; timber; oil.

Co·bá \kō-'bä\. Ancient Maya location covering a large area, NE Yucatán Penin., Mexico; ruins now in Quintana Roo state.

Co·balt \'kō-,bȯlt\. Town, Timiskaming dist., SE Ontario, Canada, just W of Lake Timiskaming; pop. (1991c) 1470. Extensive ore bodies containing silver and cobalt were discovered 1903, but have since been depleted. Mining museum; annual miners' festival.

Co·bán \kō-'bän\. City, ✻ of Alta Verapaz dept., cen. Guatemala; pop. (1993e) 25,715; in rich coffee-growing area; Mayan ruins nearby.

Co·bar \'kō-,bär\. Town, cen. New South Wales, SE Australia, 360 mi. (579 km.) WNW of Sydney; pop. (1991c) 5412; deposits of gold, copper, silver, lead, and zinc.

Cobb \'käb\. County in NW Georgia. See table at GEORGIA.

Cob·ble Mountain Dam \'kä-bəl\. Dam across Little River, W Hampden co., W Massachusetts; height 253 ft. (77 m.); constructed early 1930s; impounds water, **Cobble Mountain Reservoir,** for water supply and power.

Cob·e·quid Bay \'kä-bə-,kwid\. E arm of Minas Basin, cen. Nova Scotia, Canada; Truro is at its head.

Cobh \'kōv\; *formerly* **Queens·town** \'kwēnz-,tau̇n\. Town and seaport on Great I. in Cork Harbour, SE co. Cork, SW Ireland; pop. (1986c) 6369; port of call for ocean liners; cathedral. In 1838 the *Sirius* set out from here on one of the first transatlantic steamship crossings. Adjacent Haulbowline I.

was formerly an important British naval base, now Irish naval base.

Co·bi·ja \kō-'b̲ē-hä\. City, ✻ of Pando dept., NW Bolivia, on Acre River; pop. (1992p) 9973.

Coblenz. See KOBLENZ.

Co·bles·kill \'kō-bəlz-ˌkil\. Village, Schoharie co., E New York, SW of Amsterdam; pop. (1990c) 5268; State Univ. of New York Coll. of Agriculture and Technology at Cobleskill (1916).

Co·bourg \'kō-ˌbərg\. Town, ⊗ of Northumberland co., SE Ontario, Canada, on Lake Ontario 70 mi. (113 km.) ENE of Toronto; pop. (1991c) 15,079; good harbor; summer resort.

Cobourg Peninsula *also* **Co·burg Peninsula** \'kō-ˌbərg\. Peninsula, N Australia, on N side of Van Diemen Gulf; 50 mi. (80 km.) long, 20 mi. (32 km.) broad; part of a national park.

Co·bre \'kō-brā\ *or* **El Cobre** \el-\. Municipality, E Cuba, 8 mi. (13 km.) W of Santiago de Cuba; copper mines first worked 16th cent.

Co·burg \'kō-ˌbərg\. **1.** Municipality, S Victoria, SE Australia, N suburb of Melbourne; pop. (1991c) 50,625.

2. City, Bavaria, Germany, 36 mi. (58 km.) NW of Bayreuth; pop. (1992e) 44,693; machinery, toys; renovated castle with museum, refuge of religious reformer Martin Luther 1530; former ducal palace (the Ehrenberg) dating from 16th cent. First mentioned 1056; passed to the house of Wettin 1353, to Ernestine line of dukes of Saxony 1485; former ducal ✻ of Saxe-Coburg and (with Gotha) of Saxe-Coburg-Gotha; to Bavaria 1920. Albert, prince consort of British Queen Victoria, born nearby in 1819.

Coburg Island. Island, Northwest Territories, Canada, bet. Devon and Ellesmere islands, at entrance of Jones Sound; ab. 20 mi. (32 km.) long.

Coburg Peninsula. See COBOURG PENINSULA.

Cocanada. See KAKINADA.

Co·cha·bam·ba \ˌkō-chä-'b̲äm-bä\. **1.** Department of W cen. Bolivia. See table at BOLIVIA.

2. City, its ✻, ab. 80 mi. (129 km.) NE of Oruro; pop. (1992p) 404,102; 8392 ft. (2558 m.) above the sea; orig. known as **Oro·pe·za** \ˌōr-ō-'pā-sä\; cacao, coffee, sugar, fruit, potatoes, tobacco; cathedral, university (1832); chief distributing point for E Bolivia; founded 1574.

Co·chin \kō-'chin\. **1.** Region, SW India, on Malabar Coast; area 1493 sq. mi. (3867 sq. km.); ✻ Ernakulam. As with the town of Cochin (see COCHIN 2), possessed by the Portuguese, Dutch, and English in the centuries prior to India's independence 1947; subsequently merged with Travancore forming state of **Trav·an·core–Cochin** \'tra-vən-ˌkōr\ which became in 1956 part of new state of Kerala.

2. Town, N Kerala state, SW India; situated on a long strip of land of Malabar Coast 125 mi. (201 km.) W of Madurai; pop. (1991c) 582,588; maintains harbor facilities with difficulty, esp. during monsoon season from May to August; shipping and trade center.

History: First visited by Europeans c. 1500; trade estab. by Portuguese navigators Pedro Álvars Cabral and Vasco da Gama; fort built by Portuguese soldier Alfonso de Albuquerque 1503, first European fort in India; British settled 1635 but forced out by Dutch 1663, under whom town became important trade center; came under sovereignty of Indian ruler Hyder Ali but was surrendered by his son Tipu Sultan to the British 1792; occupied by British 1795–1947.

Co·chin China \'kō-ˌchin\ *or Fr.* **Co·chin·chine** \kȯ-she^{n}-'shē^{n}\. A former French possession, later that part of S Vietnam lying S of 10°50′N; 29,974 sq. mi. (77,633 sq. km.); ✻ Saigon; with exception of few hills (c. 3000 ft. or 900 m.) in N part, flat alluvial plain of Mekong Delta and several short streams; river channels and irrigation canals form one of the greatest rice-producing areas in Asia; fishing.

History: Vassal of Chinese empire; later part of Khmer kingdom of Cambodia (*q.v.*) and of empire of Annam; in French war with Annam, Saigon was occupied 1859; by Treaty of Saigon 1862, its three E provinces were ceded to French who occupied its W provinces in 1867 and made it a colony; united administratively with French protectorates of Annam, Tonkin, and Cambodia to form French Indochina 1887; made an autonomous republic within the French Union 1946; incorp. in Vietnam 1949; became part of South Vietnam 1954. See VIETNAM, SOUTH.

Cochinos, Bahía de. See PIGS, BAY OF.

Co·chi·nos Point \kō-'chē-nōs\. Point at S end of Bataan Penin., Luzon, Philippines, near Mariveles; actually formed by group of islets, Los Cochinos.

Co·chise \kō-'chēz, 'kō-ˌchēz\. County in SE corner of Arizona. See table at ARIZONA.

Coch·ran \'kä-krən\. **1.** County in NW Texas. See table at TEXAS.

2. City, ⊗ of Bleckley co., cen. Georgia; pop. (1990c) 4390.

Coch·rane \'kä-krən\. **1.** District, E Ontario, Canada. See table at ONTARIO.

2. Town, its ⊗, 48 mi. (77 km.) NNE of Timmins; pop. (1991c) 4585.

Cock·burn Channel \'kō-bərn\. Passage off S Chile extending S and W from Strait of Magellan to the Pacific bet. Clarence I. on W and SW Tierra del Fuego.

Cockburn Island. Island in N Lake Huron, off W tip of Manitoulin I., administratively a part of Manitoulin dist., S Ontario, Canada.

Cocke \'käk\. County in E Tennessee. See table at TENNESSEE.

Cock·er \'kä-kər\. River in Cumbria, NW England; flows out of Lake Buttermere N into the Derwent at Cockermouth; 15 mi. (24 km.) long.

Cock·er·mouth \'kä-kər-məth, -ˌmau̇th\. Town, Cumbria, NW England; pop. (1981p) 7149; birthplace of poet William Wordsworth 1770.

Cock·pit Country \'käk-ˌpit\. Region, W cen. Jamaica, containing karst topography.

Cock·rell Hill \'kä-krəl\. City, Dallas co., NE Texas, 8 mi. (13 km.) SW of the city of Dallas; pop. (1990c) 3746.

Co·clé \kō-'klā\. Province of cen. Panama. See table at PANAMA.

Co·co \'kō-kō\; *formerly* **Se·go·via** \sä-'g̲ō-b̲ē-ä\. River, N Nicaragua; flows NE into the Caribbean Sea; over 450 mi. (724 km.) long; greater part of its course forms boundary bet. Nicaragua and Honduras.

Coco, Isla de. See COCOS ISLAND.

Co·coa \'kō-kō\. City, Brevard co., E Florida, on Indian River 42 mi. (68 km.) SE of Orlando; pop. (1990c) 17,722; citrus-shipping center; fishing resort; Brevard Community Coll. (1960); incorp. 1895.

Cocoa Beach. City, Brevard co., E Florida, 45 mi. (72 km.) ESE of Orlando; pop. (1990c) 12,123; resort.

Co·co Cay \'kō-kō\ *or Span.* **Ca·yo Coco** \'kä-yō-'kō-kō\. Island, Cuba, off NW coast of Camagüey prov.

Coco Channel. Strait off N point of North Andaman I., Andaman Is., Bay of Bengal.

Co·co·ni·no \ˌkō-kə-'nē-nō\. County in N Arizona. See table at ARIZONA.

Coconino Plateau. Tableland in cen. Coconino co., N cen. Arizona, S of Grand Canyon National Park.

Co·co·nut Creek \'kō-kə-ˌnət\. City, Broward co., SE Florida; pop. (1990c) 27,485.

Co·co·nut Grove \'kō-kə-nət\. S suburban section of Miami, Florida, on Biscayne Bay.

Co·cos Island \'kō-kōs\ *or* **Is·la de Co·co** \'ēs-lä-t̲h̲ā-'kō-kō\. Uninhabited Costa Rican island, Pacific Ocean, at 5°32′N, 87°04′W; 18 sq. mi. (47 sq. km.).

Cocos Islands *or* **Kee·ling Islands** \'kē-liŋ\. External territory, consisting of a group of 27 small coral islands in the Indian Ocean belonging to Australia; ab. 580 mi. (930 km.) SW of Java, Indonesia; 12°5′S, 96°53′E; 5.5 sq. mi. (14 sq. km.); pop. (1993e) 600; coconuts and coconut products.

History: Discovered 1609; acquired by Great Britain 1857, placed under Ceylon governor 1878, under Straits Settlements 1886; incorp. with Singapore settlement 1903;

placed under Australian authority 1955; purchased 1978 by Australian government from John Clunies-Ross, whose family had received the islands in a 19th cent. grant; voted to integrate with Australia Apr. 6, 1984; in WWI scene of sinking of German cruiser *Emden* by Australian cruiser *Sydney* 1914.

Co·cu·la \kō-ˈkü-lä\. Town, Jalisco state, W cen. Mexico, 32 mi. (51 km.) SW of Guadalajara.

Cocuy, Sierra Nevada de. See SIERRA NEVADA DE COCUY.

Cod, Cape. See CAPE COD.

Co·de·ra, Cape \kō-ˈt͟hā-rä\. Cape extending into Caribbean Sea on N cen. coast of Venezuela, E of Caracas.

Cod·ing·ton \ˈkä-diŋ-tən\. County in NE South Dakota. See table at SOUTH DAKOTA.

Co·dó \kō-ˈdō\. Municipality, Maranhão state, NE Brazil, ab. 110 mi. (175 km.) SSE of São Luis; pop. (1991p) 111,537.

Co·do·gno \kō-ˈdō-nyō\. Commune, Milano prov., Lombardy, N Italy, 34 mi. (55 km.) SE of Milan; pop. (1981p) 15,142.

Cod·ring·ton \ˈkä-driŋ-tən\. Village, Antigua and Barbuda; chief settlement on Barbuda I.

Co·dy \ˈkō-dē\. City, ⊗ of Park co., NW Wyoming, on Shoshone River E of Buffalo Bill Reservoir; pop. (1990c) 7897; tourist resort at E entrance to Yellowstone Park.

Cody Peak. Mountain on E boundary of Yellowstone National Park, NW Wyoming; 10,267 ft. (3129 m.).

Coele–Syria *or* **Coelesyria.** See BEKÁA VALLEY.

Coe·neo \ˌkō-ā-ˈnā-ō\ *also* **Coeneo de la Li·ber·tad** \ˌt͟hā-lä-ˌlē-ber-ˈtät͟h\. Municipality, Michoacán state, Mexico, 45 mi. (72 km.) NE of Uruapan.

Coes·feld \ˈkōs-ˌfelt\ *also* **Koes·feld** \ˈkōs-\. City, North Rhine-Westphalia, Germany, 21 mi. (34 km.) W of Münster; pop. (1980c) 31,063. Became city 1197; member of Hanseatic League; to Prussia early 19th cent.

Coët·qui·dan \ˌkȯ-et-kē-ˈdä^{n}\. Military camp, Morbihan dept., NW France; site of French national military academy St.-Cyr after WWII.

Coeur d'Alene \ˌkȯrd-^{ə}l-ˈān\. **1.** River, N Idaho; flows W from Shoshone co. into Coeur d'Alene Lake; ab. 37 mi. (59 km.) long.

2. City, ⊗ of Kootenai co., N Idaho, 32 mi. (51 km.) E of Spokane, Washington; pop. (1990c) 24,563; discovery of silver and lead deposits c. 1882; North Idaho Coll. (1933); on site of military post estab. late 1870s.

Coeur d'Alene Lake. Lake in Kootenai co., N Idaho; ab. 30 mi. (48 km.) long; ab. 60 sq. mi. (155 sq. km.); center of large resort area.

Cof·fee \ˈkȯ-fē, ˈkä-\. Name of counties in three states of the U.S. See tables at ALABAMA, GEORGIA, TENNESSEE.

Cof·fee·ville \ˈkȯ-fē-ˌvil, ˈkä-\. Town, a ⊗ of Yalobusha co., N Mississippi; pop. (1990c) 825.

Cof·fey \ˈkȯ-fē, ˈkä-\. County in E Kansas. See table at KANSAS.

Cof·fey·ville \ˈkȯ-fē-ˌvil, ˈkä-\. City, Montgomery co., SE Kansas, 15 mi. (24 km.) S of Independence; pop. (1990c) 12,917; former frontier town and cattle-shipping point; near oil and gas fields; Coffeyville Community Coll. (1923). Most of the Dalton outlaw gang were killed here 1892 during an attempt to rob two banks at the same time.

Cof·fin Island \ˈkȯ-fən\. See MAGDALEN ISLANDS.

Coffs Harbour \ˈkȯfs, ˈkäfs\. Coastal city, NE New South Wales, Australia; pop. (1991c) 51,520; bananas.

Co·fre de Pe·ro·te \ˈkō-frā-t͟hā-pā-ˈrō-tā\ *or Indian name* **Nau·cham·pa·te·petl** \ˌnaů-ˌchäm-pä-ˈtā-ˌpet-^{ə}l\. Mountain, Veracruz state, Mexico; 15,816 ft. (4821 m.).

Co·ghi·nas \kō-ˈgē-näs\. River in N Sardinia, Italy; flows N into Gulf of Asinara; ab. 60 mi. (97 km.) long.

Coglians, Monte. See KELLERWAND.

Co·gnac \kȯ-ˈnyäk; ˈkōn-ˌyak, ˈkän-, ˈkȯn-\; *anc.* **Comp·ni·a·cum** \kämp-ˈnī-ə-kəm\. Commune, Charente dept., W France, on Charente River 24 mi. (39 km.) W of Angoulême; pop. (1990c) 19,932; famous for its distilleries producing cognac (named for it). Birthplace of King Francis I 1494; Protestant stronghold in latter part of 16th cent.

Cohansey Bridge. See BRIDGETON 2.

Co·has·set \kō-ˈha-sət\. Town, Norfolk co., E Massachusetts, on Atlantic Ocean 15 mi. (24 km.) SE of Boston; pop. (1990c) 7075; summer resort.

Cohasset Rocks. See MINOTS LEDGE.

Co·hoc·ton *or* **Con·hoc·ton** \kə-ˈhäk-tən\. River, S New York; flows SE and unites with Tioga River near Corning to form Chemung River; ab. 60 mi. (97 km.) long.

Co·hoes \kə-ˈhōz\. City, Albany co., E New York, at confluence of Mohawk and Hudson rivers near E terminus of New York State Barge Canal, 10 mi. (16 km.) N of Albany; pop. (1990c) 16,825; power from 70-foot (21-meter) falls of Mohawk River. First settled by Dutch 1665; incorp. 1869; headquarters of Gen. Horatio Gates in Revolutionary War.

Coi. See RED 4.

Coi·ba \ˈkȯi-bä\. Island in Pacific Ocean off SW coast of Panama; 20 mi. (32 km.) long.

Coig \ˈkȯig\; *formerly* **Coy·le** *or* **Coi·le** \ˈkȯi-lā\. River, Santa Cruz prov., S Argentina; rises near Chilean border, flows E and NE into Atlantic Ocean; ab. 180 mi. (290 km.) long.

Coi·hai·que \kȯi-ˈī-kā\. Town ✱ of Aisén del General Carlos Ibáñez del Campo region; S Chile, pop. (1982c) 29,163.

Coim·ba·tore \ˈkȯim-bə-ˌtōr\. City, W Tamil Nadu, S India, 280 mi. (451 km.) SW of Madras; on S slope of Nilgiri Hills; pop. (1991c) 816,321; teak; cottonmills; coffee; agricultural college; long important in commanding the approach to the Palghat Gap; nearby is temple of **Pe·rur** \pə-ˈrür\, of historical interest.

Co·im·bra \ˈkwēm-brə\. **1.** District of W cen. Portugal. See table at PORTUGAL.

2. *anc.* **Ae·min·i·um** \ē-ˈmi-nē-əm\. City, its ✱, on Mondego River 108 mi. (174 km.) NNE of Lisbon; munic. pop. (1991p) 145,724; pottery, fabrics, paper; tanning; former ✱ of Portugal (1139–c. 1260); several notable churches incl. 12th and 17th cent. cathedrals; museum in former episcopal palace; aqueduct; Univ. of Coimbra (Portugal's oldest, founded 1290 at Lisbon; permanently transferred to Coimbra 1537); Roman ruins of **Co·nim·bri·ge** \kə-ˈnim-bri-gə\ nearby. Along with its neighbor, ancient Conimbriga, important under Romans; variously held by Visigoths and Moors; finally recaptured 1064 by Ferdinand I (the Great) and Rodrigo Díaz de Vivar (El Cid); Spanish noblewoman Inés de Castro, mistress of the future Peter I and celebrated by novelists and poets, murdered here 1355.

Co·ín \kō-ˈēn\. Commune, Málaga prov., S Spain, 19 mi. (31 km.) W of the city of Málaga; pop. (1991p) 14,855; olive oil, wine; marble quarries nearby.

Coira *or* **Coire.** See CHUR.

Co·je·des \kō-ˈhā-thes\. State of NW cen. Venezuela. See table at VENEZUELA.

Co·ju·te·pe·que \kō-ˌhü-tā-ˈpā-kā\. City, ✱ of Cuscatlán dept., cen. El Salvador, 16 mi. (26 km.) E of San Salvador; pop. (1992c) 43,564.

Coke \ˈkōk\. County in W cen. Texas. See table at TEXAS.

Co·la·ti·na \ˌkō-lä-ˈtē-nə\. Municipality, Espírito Santo state, E Brazil, ab. 60 mi. (97 km.) NNW of Vitória; pop. (1991p) 106,712.

Col·bert \ˈkäl-bərt\. County in NW Alabama. See table at ALABAMA.

Col·by \ˈkōl-bē\. City, ⊗ of Thomas co., NW Kansas, 38 mi. (61 km.) E of Goodland; pop. (1990c) 5396; Colby Community Coll. (1964).

Colby Mountain. Peak in the Sierra Nevada, in SE Tuolumne co., cen. California; 9631 ft. (2935 m.).

Col·ches·ter \ˈkōl-ˌches-tər, -chəs-\. **1.** Town, NW New London co., SE Connecticut; pop. (1990c) 10,980; settled 1699; includes borough of Colchester (pop. 3212).

2. Town, Chittenden co., NW Vermont, 6 mi. (10 km.) NE of Burlington; pop. (1990c) 14,731; St. Michael's Coll. (1904).

3. County, cen. Nova Scotia, Canada. See table at NOVA SCOTIA.

4. *anc.* **Cam·u·lo·du·num** \ˌkam-yə-lō-ˈdü-nəm, -ˈdyü-\. Town, Essex, SE England, on the Colne River 53 mi. (85 km.) NE of London; pop. (1991p) 141,100; oyster fisheries; in agricultural region; Univ. of Essex (1961); Roman walls; castle (now houses museum of Romano-British antiquities);

remains of Augustinian priory. In ancient times ❋ of pre-Roman British ruler Cunobelinus; site of Roman settlement, the first Roman colony in Britain, founded by Emperor Claudius c. 43 A.D. and reestablished after it was burned by British Queen Boudicca's warriors c. 60 A.D.; received first charter 1189.

Col·chis \ˈkäl-kəs\. Ancient country on the Black Sea S of Caucasus Mts. corresponding to W part of the Republic of Georgia; watered by the Phasis (*or mod.* Rioni); ❋ Aea; settled by Milesians to whom native inhabitants gave support; Colchians claimed by Greek historian Herodotus to have been of black race; in Greek legend the home of Medea and magic, where in a sacred grove was the Golden Fleece sought by the Argonauts; in first cent. B.C. Colchians were overcome by Mithradates VI, king of Pontus; later came under Roman influence.

Col de Fréjus. See FRÉJUS, POINTE DE.

Col·den Mountain \ˈkōl-dən\. Peak in the Adirondack Mts., in Essex co., NE New York; 4713 ft. (1437 m.).

Col de Somport. See POTERLA, COLLADO DE LA.

Cold Harbor \ˈkōld\. Locality, Hanover co., E cen. Virginia, N of the Chickahominy River ab. 10 mi. (16 km.) ENE of Richmond; site of two battles of the Civil War: (1) in 1862, better known as Gaines' Mill (*q.v.*); (2) in 1864, in which Confederate Gen. Robert E. Lee forced Union troops to retire with heavy losses.

Cold·spring \ˈkōld-ˌspriŋ\. City, ⊗ of San Jacinto co., E Texas; pop. (1990c) 538.

Cold Spring. Village, Putnam co., SE New York, on Hudson River 20 mi. (32 km.) S of Poughkeepsie; pop. (1990c) 1998; made Parrott guns used in Civil War.

Cold·stream \ˈkōld-ˌstrēm\. Burgh, Borders region, SE Scotland, on English border; pop. (1981p) 1649; the Coldstream Guards orig. organized here by English Gen. George Monck for 1660 march into England, which resulted in the restoration of Charles II; once a popular resort for couples eloping.

Cold·water \ˈkōld-ˌwȯ-tər, -ˌwä-\. **1.** River, NW Mississippi; rises in NE Marshall co., flows SW and S into Tallahatchie River in Quitman co.; 220 mi. (354 km.) long.
2. City, ⊗ of Comanche co., S Kansas; pop. (1990c) 1223.
3. City, ⊗ of Branch co., S Michigan, 28 mi. (45 km.) S of Battle Creek; pop. (1990c) 9607.
4. Village, Mercer co., W Ohio, 33 mi. (53 km.) SW of Lima; pop. (1990c) 4335.

Cole \ˈkōl\. County in cen. Missouri. See table at MISSOURI.

Cole·brook \ˈkōl-ˌbru̇k\. Town, Coos co., N New Hampshire, on Connecticut River 33 mi. (53 km.) NNW of Berlin; pop. (1990c) 2444.

Cole·man \ˈkōl-mən\. **1.** County in cen. Texas. See table at TEXAS.
2. City, its ⊗, 28 mi. (45 km.) WNW of Brownwood; pop. (1990c) 5410.

Çö·le·me·rik \ˌjœ-le-me-ˈrēk\; *formerly* **Ha·kkâ·ri** *also* **Ha·kâ·ri** \hä-ˈkär-ē\. Town, ❋ of Hakkâri prov., SE Turkey in Asia; pop. (1980p) 18,514.

Co·len·so \kə-ˈlen-sō\. Village, W KwaZulu-Natal prov., Rep. of South Africa, on Tugela River, 65 mi. (105 km.) NW of Pietermaritzburg; scene of battle Dec. 1899 in Boer War which halted the British advance to relieve Ladysmith (*q.v.*) 14 mi. (23 km.) N; occupied by British Feb. 1900.

Cole·raine \kōl-ˈrān, ˈkōl-ˌrān\. **1.** District, N Northern Ireland; estab. 1973. See table at IRELAND, NORTHERN.
2. Town and shipping port, its ⊗, on Bann River; pop. (1990e) 48,600; fisheries, distilleries; food products; linen manufacture; New Univ. of Ulster (1965).

Cole·roon \kōl-ˈrün; ˈkōl-ˌrün, ˈkō-lə-\. The N and largest branch of the Kāveri River (*q.v.*), India, in its delta; empties into Bay of Bengal ab. 25 mi. (40 km.) S of Cuddalore.

Coles \ˈkōlz\. County in E cen. Illinois. See table at ILLINOIS.

Coles·berg \ˈkōlz-ˌbərg\. Town, Northern Cape prov., S cen. Rep. of South Africa, 130 mi. (209 km.) SW of Bloemfontein; during Boer War scene of repeated clashes 1899–1900.

Col·fax \ˈkōl-ˌfaks\. **1.** Name of counties in two states of the U.S. See tables at NEBRASKA and NEW MEXICO.
2. Town, ⊗ of Grant parish, cen. Louisiana; pop. (1990c) 1696.
3. City, ⊗ of Whitman co., SE Washington, 15 mi. (24 km.) NNW of Pullman; pop. (1990c) 2713.

Col·hué \kȯl-ˈwā\ *or* **Colhué Hua·pí** \wä-ˈpē\. Lake in S Chubut prov., S Argentina, E of Lake Musters.

Co·li·ma \kō-ˈlē-mä\. **1.** Volcano, Jalisco state, W cen. Mexico; 13,993 ft. (4265 m.).
2. State of SW Mexico. See table at MEXICO.
3. City, its ❋; pop. (1990c) 106,967; alt. 1600 ft. (488 m.); leather goods; in region producing cotton and rice; university; city founded 1522.

Coll \ˈkōl\. Island of the Inner Hebrides, W of N Mull I., off W coast of Scotland; ab. 12 mi. (19 km.) long; administratively a part of Strathclyde region.

Col·la·dor \ˌkō-yä-ˈthȯr\. Peak, N Peru; 12,835 ft. (3912 m.).

Col·la·tia \kə-ˈlā-shə, -shē-ə\. Ancient Sabine town, Latium, Italy, ab. 10 mi. (16 km.) NE of Rome; scene, in Roman legend, of the rape of Lucretia (Lucrece), wife of politician Tarquinius Collatinus; referred to as **Col·la·ti·um** \-shəm, -shē-əm\ in William Shakespeare's poem *The Rape of Lucrece.*

Col·le di Val d'El·sa \ˈkȯl-lā-dē-ˈväl-ˈdel-sä\. Commune, Siena prov., Tuscany, cen. Italy, 14 mi. (23 km.) NW of the commune of Siena; pop. (1981p) 15,937; cathedral.

Col·lege \ˈkä-lij\. Unincorporated settlement, W suburb of Fairbanks, Alaska; pop. (1990c) 11,249; seat of Univ. of Alaska (founded 1917, opened 1922); pop. more than doubled bet. 1980 and 1990.

Col·lege·dale \ˈkä-lij-ˌdāl\. Village, Hamilton co., SE Tennessee, E of Chattanooga; pop. (1990c) 5048; Southern Coll. of Seventh-Day Adventists (1892).

College Park. **1.** City, Clayton and Fulton cos., NW cen. Georgia, 8 mi. (13 km.) SSW of Atlanta; pop. (1990c) 20,457.
2. City, Prince Georges co., Maryland, 8 mi. (13 km.) NE of Washington, D.C.; pop. (1990c) 21,927; Univ. of Maryland at College Park (1856), Univ. of Maryland Univ. Coll. (1947).

College Place. City, Walla Walla co., SE Washington, 8 mi. (13 km.) SW of Walla Walla; pop. (1990c) 6308; Walla Walla Coll. (1892).

College Station. City, Brazos co., E cen. Texas, 4 mi. (6 km.) S of Bryan; pop. (1990c) 52,456; Texas A&M Univ., College Station (1876).

Col·lege·ville \ˈkä-lij-ˌvil\. **1.** Township, Stearns co., cen. Minnesota, 10 mi. (16 km.) W of St. Cloud; pop. (1990c) 1624; St. John's Univ. (1857).
2. Borough, Montgomery co., SE Pennsylvania, ab. 8 mi. (13 km.) NW of Norristown; pop. (1990c) 4227; Ursinus Coll. (1869).

Col·le·gno \kō-ˈlā-nyō\. Commune, Torino prov., Piedmont, NW Italy, NW of Turin; pop. (1989c) 48,483.

Col·le·ton \ˈkäl-ət-ᵊn\. Coastal county in S South Carolina. See table at SOUTH CAROLINA.

Col·ley·ville \ˈkä-lē-ˌvil\. Village, Tarrant co., N Texas; pop. (1990c) 12,724.

Col·lie \ˈkä-lē\. Town, SW Western Australia, Australia, 110 mi. (177 km.) S of Perth; pop. (1991c) 7684.

Col·lier \ˈkäl-yər\. County, SW coast of Florida. See table at FLORIDA.

Collier Bay. Large inlet of Indian Ocean, N coast of Western Australia, Australia.

Col·lier·ville \ˈkäl-yər-ˌvil\. Town, Shelby co., SW Tennessee, 22 mi. (35 km.) SE of Memphis; pop. (1990c) 14,427.

Colli Euganei. See EUGANEAN HILLS.

Col·lin \ˈkä-lən\. County in NE Texas. See table at TEXAS.

Col·ling·dale \ˈkä-liŋ-ˌdāl\. Borough, Delaware co., SE Pennsylvania, 7 mi. (11 km.) WSW of Philadelphia; pop. (1990c) 9175.

\ə\ abut \ə̇\ matches \ᵊ\ kitten, Fr table \ər\ further \a\ ash \ā\ ace \ä\ cot, cart \ȧ\ Fr bac \au̇\ out \b̶\ Span Avila \ch\ chin \e\ bet \ē\ easy \g\ go \i\ hit \ī\ ice \j\ job \k̲\ Ger ich, Buch \ⁿ\ Fr vin \ŋ\ sing \ō\ go \ȯ\ all \ȯ\ law \œ\ Fr bœuf \œ̄\ Fr feu \ȯi\ boy \th\ thin \t͟h\ this \ü\ loot \u̇\ foot \ue\ Ger füllen \ue̅\ Fr rue \y\ yet \ʸ\ Fr digne \ˈdēnʸ\, nuit \ˈnwʸē\ \yü\ few \yu̇\ fury \zh\ vision

Col·lings·wood \ˈkä-liŋz-ˌwu̇d\. Borough, Camden co., SW New Jersey, 3 mi. (5 km.) SE of the city of Camden; pop. (1990c) 15,289; settled by Quakers 1682; incorp. 1888; residential.

Col·lings·worth \ˈkä-liŋz-ˌwərth\. County in NW Texas. See table at TEXAS.

Col·ling·wood \ˈkä-liŋ-ˌwu̇d\. Town, Simcoe co., SE Ontario, Canada, on Nottawasaga Bay 29 mi. (47 km.) WNW of Barrie; pop. (1991c) 13,505; shipbuilding.

Collingwood Bay. Inlet of Solomon Sea on SE coast of island of New Guinea, Papua New Guinea.

Col·lins \ˈkä-lənz\. **1.** Short stream, cen. Tennessee; rises near W boundary of Sequatchie co., flows N into Caney Fork at Great Falls Lake; forms part of system of Tennessee Valley Authority (*q.v.*).
2. Town, ⊗ of Covington co., S Mississippi; pop. (1990c) 2541.

Collins, Mount. Peak in Great Smoky Mts., on boundary bet. Tennessee and North Carolina 2.5 mi. (4 km.) NE of Clingmans Dome; 6188 ft. (1886 m.).

Collins Landing. See THOUSAND ISLANDS 1.

Col·lins·ville \ˈkä-lənz-ˌvil\. **1.** Unincorporated subdivision of the town of Canton, Connecticut; pop. (1990c) 2591.
2. City, Madison and St. Clair cos., SW Illinois, 10 mi. (16 km.) E of East St. Louis; pop. (1990c) 22,446; in former coal-mining section.
3. City, Tulsa co., NE Oklahoma, 17 mi. (27 km.) NNE of the city of Tulsa; pop. (1990c) 3612; near oil and gas wells.

Col·lo \ˈkȯ-lō\. Coastal town, NE Algeria, 37 mi. (60 km.) NNE of the city of Constantine.

Col·mar \ˈkōl-ˌmär, kōl-ˈ\ *or Ger.* **Kol·mar** \ˈkōl-mär\. Commune, ✻ of Haut-Rhin dept., NE France, 105 mi. (169 km.) E of Chaumont; pop. (1990c) 64,889; textiles; tourism. Has well-preserved old section with many notable buildings and churches; museum. Became free imperial city 1226; briefly under Swedes during the Thirty Years' War; gradually annexed by France 17th cent.; to Germany 1871, France c. 1919; in WWII taken by Germans 1940, retaken by Allies 1945. Birthplace 1834 of Frédéric-Auguste Bartholdi, sculptor of the Statue of Liberty in New York.

Cöln. See COLOGNE.

Colne \ˈkōn, ˈkōln\. **1.** River, Essex, SE England; flows SE into North Sea; 35 mi. (56 km.) long.
2. River, Hertfordshire and Buckinghamshire, SE cen. England; flows into the Thames; 35 mi. (56 km.) long.
3. Town, Lancashire, NW England, 27 mi. (43 km.) N of Manchester; pop. (1981p) 18,203.

Col·nett \ˈkäl-nət\. Peak, NE coast of New Caledonia I., SW Pacific Ocean; 4954 ft. (1510 m.).

Co·lô·a·ne \ku̇-ˈlō-ȧ-nə\. See MACAO 1.

Co·logne \kə-ˈlōn\; *Ger.* **Köln** *or less often* **Cöln** \ˈkœln\; *anc.* **Op·pi·dum Ubi·o·rum** \ˈä-pi-dəm-ˌü-bē-ˈōr-əm, ˌyü-bē-\ *later, because birthplace of Agrippina the Younger, wife of Roman Emperor Claudius,* **Co·lo·nia Ag·rip·pi·na** \kə-ˈlō-nyə-ˌa-grə-ˈpī-nə\. City, North Rhine-Westphalia, W Germany, on W bank of Rhine River 20 mi. (32 km.) SSE of Düsseldorf; pop. (1992e) 956,690; chemicals, eau de cologne; engineering; important river port; banking center; has a number of Roman remains, incl. first cent. tower; numerous medieval churches; famous 13th cent. cathedral (completed 19th cent.); university (1388, dissolved 1798, refounded 1919); opera house (1957); botanical and zoological gardens.

History: Orig. settled by Romans together with a German tribe called the Ubii; Roman name, Colonia Agrippina, given to colony in 50 A.D.; became an episcopal see 4th cent.; captured by Franks 5th cent.; made an archiepiscopal see late 8th cent.; its archbishop increased holdings (acquired duchy of Lorraine 953 and of Westphalia 1180) until this became one of most powerful principalities of Germany; one of most important centers of Hanseatic League; after battle of Worringen 1288, citizenry established their independence of archbishop; a center of medieval German art and learning; archbishop confirmed as elector of the Holy Roman Empire 1356; city's prosperity declined, esp. after Thirty Years' War; occupied by French 1794; archbishopric secularized 1801; given to kingdom of Prussia by Congress of Vienna 1815; reorganized 1821; new period of prosperity, 19th cent.; after WWI occupied by Allied troops 1918–26. In WWII object of first great air raid of the war May 30, 1942; frequently bombed 1943–45 by British and American air forces; entered by American troops Mar. 1945; extensively damaged in WWII, but since rebuilt.

Co·lo·gno Mon·ze·se \kō-ˈlȯn-yō-mȯnt-ˈsā-zā\. Commune, Milano prov., Lombardy, N Italy, ab. 6 mi. (10 km.) NE of Milan; pop. (1989c) 52,838.

Co·lo·ma \kə-ˈlō-mə\. Village, El Dorado co., California, near Placerville 36 mi. (58 km.) NE of Sacramento; site of Sutter's Mill where gold was discovered Jan. 24, 1848.

Colomb *or* **Colomb–Béchar.** See BÉCHAR.

Co·lombes \kō-ˈlȯⁿb, kə-ˈlōm\. Commune, Hauts-de-Seine dept., N France, NW suburb of Paris; pop. (1990c) 79,058.

Co·lom·bey *or* **Colombey–Nouil·ly** \kō-lȯⁿ-ˈbā-nü-ˈyē\. Village, Moselle dept., NE France, ab. 4 mi. (6 km.) E of Metz; scene of battle 1870 during Franco-Prussian War.

Colombey–les–Deux–Églises \-lā-ˈdœz-ā-ˈglēz\. Commune, Haute-Marne dept., NE France; home and burial place of Charles de Gaulle, president of France 1958–69.

Co·lom·bia \kə-ˈləm-bē-ə, kō-ˈlōm-bē-ä\. Republic, NW South America, bounded on N by the Caribbean Sea, on E by Venezuela and Brazil, on S by Peru and Ecuador, on W by the Pacific Ocean and Panama; 439,735 sq. mi. (1,138,914 sq. km.); pop. (1985c) 26,525,670; ✻ Bogotá.

Physical features: Covered in W and cen. parts by N end of the Andes system, here separating into three parallel ranges: Cordillera Oriental (E), extending into NW Venezuela; Cordillera Central (cen.); and Cordillera Occidental (W); highest peak Cristóbal Colón 19,020 ft. (5797 m.); other peaks, above 16,000 ft. (4877 m.), are Tolima, Chita, Puracé; has many volcanoes.

Rivers: In cen. part the Magdalena and the Cauca (W tributary of the Magdalena), both flowing N bet. main ranges of the Andes; in W the Atrato flowing N to Gulf of Urabá and many short rapid streams on the coast flowing W to the Pacific; in E tributaries of the Orinoco (Meta, Vichada, Guaviare), the Vaupés (tributary of the Rio Negro), and in SE the Apaporis and Caquetá; in S the Putumayo forming most of boundary with Peru.

Chief products: Coffee, bananas, sugar, cotton, tobacco, rice, corn, potatoes, sorghum, cut flowers, livestock; oil, iron ore, platinum, gold, emeralds, silver; textiles; world's largest exporter of cocaine.

Chief cities: Bogotá, Cali, Medellín, Barranquilla, Cartagena, Cúcuta, Bucaramanga, Pereira, Ibagué, Manizales.

Political divisions: Divided into 32 departments and the Capital District (for pronunciation of their names, see their individual entries):

NAME	AREA (sq. mi.)	AREA (sq. km.)	POP. (1992e)	CAPITAL
Capital District	613	1,588	4,239,490[1]	Bogotá
Departments				
Amazonas	46,811	121,240	52,900	Leticia
Antioquia	24,274	62,870	4,467,900	Medellín
Arauca	9,069	23,489	97,000	Arauca
Atlántico	1,263	3,271	1,704,000	Barranquilla
Bolívar	10,190	26,392	1,451,700	Cartagena
Boyacá	8,919	23,100	1,274,400	Tunja
Caldas	2,812	7,283	909,800	Manizales
Caquetá	34,820	90,184	309,500	Florencia
Casanare	17,169	44,468	176,800	Yopal
Cauca	11,774	30,495	933,600	Popayán
César	9,186	23,792	799,900	Valledupar
Chocó	18,226	47,205	350,900	Quibdó
Córdoba	9,720	25,175	1,115,100	Montería
Cundinamarca	8,638	22,372	1,658,800	Bogotá
Guainía	30,141	78,065	13,100	San Felipe
Guaviare	16,280	42,165	63,900	Guaviare
Huila	7,718	19,990	777,900	Neiva
La Guajira	7,791	20,179	347,500	Riohacha
Magdalena	8,843	22,903	979,700	Santa Marta
Meta	33,116	85,770	564,300	Villavicencio
Nariño	11,986	31,044	1,163,400	Pasto
Norte de Santander	8,037	20,816	1,006,900	Cúcuta
Putumayo	9,873	25,571	221,900	Mocoa
Quindío	705	1,826	414,500	Armenia

COLOMBIA
CITIES
Over 200,000
50,000 to 200,000
Under 50,000
National capital
Political subdivision capital
BOUNDARIES
International
Political subdivision
FEATURES
Canals
Waterfalls
Rapids
Points of interest
CARIBBEAN SEA
PACIFIC OCEAN
VENEZUELA
ECUADOR
PERU
BRAZIL
PANAMA
SAN ANDRÉS Y PROVIDENCIA
ISLA DE PROVIDENCIA
SAN ANDRÉS ISLAND
ALBUQUERQUE KEYS
Bogotá
Medellín
Cali
Barranquilla
Cartagena
Maracaibo
Quito
Iquitos
Leticia
LLANOS
ANDES
0° Equator
©1996, Encyclopædia Britannica, Inc.

NAME	AREA (sq. mi.)	AREA (sq. km.)	POP. (1992e)	CAPITAL
Risaralda	1,530	3,963	735,700	Pereira
San Andrés y Providencia	17	44	41,600	San Andrés
Santander	11,950	30,950	1,642,600	Bucaramanga
Sucre	4,063	10,523	611,400	Sincelejo
Tolima	9,006	23,326	1,193,400	Ibagué
Valle del Cauca	8,203	21,246	3,335,800	Cali
Vaupés	25,103	65,017	34,400	Mitú
Vichada	38,212	98,969	19,400	Puerto Carreño

[1](1985c)

History: Coasts explored by Spaniards c. 1500; Santa Marta founded 1525; Cartagena founded 1533; Santa Fé de Bogotá founded 1538 after Spanish conquistador Gonzalo Jiménez de Quesada had defeated the Chibcha-speaking peoples of the Colombian plateau 1536–38; subject to viceroyalty of Peru until New Granada (*q.v.*) (which included modern Colombia, Panama, Ecuador, and Venezuela) was made a separate viceroyalty (temporarily in 1717, permanently in 1740); began struggle for independence from Spain 1810; achieved independence under leadership of Simón Bolívar 1819 (see BOYACÁ); together with Panama, Venezuela, and eventually Ecuador, formed Gran Colombia (*q.v.*); by 1830 had lost Venezuela and Ecuador through secession; remaining territory (called New Grenada from 1830) reorganized as: Grenadine Confederation 1858, United States of New Granada 1861, United States of Colombia 1863, and Republic of Colombia 1886; civil war 1899–1902; lost Panama (*q.v.*) through a U.S.-supported revolt after Colombia failed to ratify a treaty giving the U.S. development rights 1903; recognized Panama's independence 1914, received compensation from U.S. 1921; neutral in WWI; settled border disputes with Ecuador c. 1917, Venezuela 1922; following threat of war with Peru, settled dispute over town of Leticia (*q.v.*) through League of Nations 1934; in WWII broke off relations with Axis countries; entered decade-long period of political violence bet. Liberals and Conservatives known as "la violencia" beginning with 1948 assassination of Liberal leader Jorges Eliécer Gaitan; under military dictatorship 1953–57; Liberal and Conservative parties agreed to alternate power under the National Front 1958–74; from 1974 held regular two-party elections; joined Andean Group (*q.v.*) 1969; plagued by guerrilla activities and drug wars during late 20th cent.; new constitution adopted 1991.

Co·lom·bo \kə-'ləm-bō\. Seaport and commercial city, ✻ of Sri Lanka, near mouth of Kelani River on Indian Ocean; pop. (1990e) 615,000; largest city of Sri Lanka; has artificial harbor; financial services; food products; tobacco; many temples, mosques, and churches; university; national museum. Port probably known to voyagers in antiquity; settled by Arabs 8th cent. A.D.; occupied 1517 by Portuguese, captured by Dutch 1656, and taken over by English 1796 (see CEYLON); replaced Galle as Sri Lanka's leading port in the 1880s following completion of first breakwater; a British defense base in Indian Ocean 1942–45; site of conference 1950 leading to formation of Colombo Plan (economic assistance program for Asian countries).

Co·lón \kō-'lōn\. **1.** Town and municipality, Matanzas prov., W cen. Cuba, 27 mi. (43 km.) SE of Cárdenas; munic. pop. (1990e) 53,169.
2. Department of N Honduras. See table at HONDURAS.
3. Province of N cen. Panama. See table at PANAMA.
4. *formerly* **As·pin·wall** \'as-pən-ˌwȯl\. City, ✻ of Colón prov., N cen. Panama, on Limon Bay at N entrance to Panama Canal; pop. (1990p) 54,469; N terminus of Panama R.R. (completed 1855); city founded 1850 and named for William H. Aspinwall, one of builders of railroad; with its suburb Cristobal (*q.v.*) an important port.

Colón, Archipiélago de. See GALÁPAGOS ISLANDS.

Co·lo·nel Ovie·do \ˌkō-lō-'nel-ō-'vyā-t͟hō\. Settlement, S cen. Paraguay, E of Asunción; ✻ of Caaguazú dept.

Co·lo·nia \kō-'lōn-yä\. **1.** Department of SW Uruguay. See table at URUGUAY.
2. *or* **Colonia del Sa·cra·men·to** \t͟hel-ˌsä-krä-'men-tō\. Seaport and resort, its ✻, on La Plata River opp. Buenos Aires; pop. (1985c) 19,102; founded by Portuguese from Brazil 1680; fought over by Spanish and Portuguese; acquired by Spain in 1777; center of rich agricultural district.

Colonia Agrippina. See COLOGNE.

Colonia Julia Fanestris. See FANO.

Co·lo·ni·al Beach \kə-'lō-nyəl, -nē-əl\. Town and resort, Westmoreland co., E Virginia, on Potomac River 30 mi. (48 km.) E of Fredericksburg; pop. (1990c) 3132; fisheries.

Colonial Heights. Independent city, SE cen. Virginia, on Appomattox River opp. Petersburg; pop. (1990c) 16,064.

Colonial National Historical Park. See UNITED STATES, *National Historical Parks.*

Colonial Territories *or* **Colonias.** See PANDO 1.

Col·o·nie \ˌkä-lə-'nē\. Village, Albany co., New York, NW of the city of Albany; pop. (1990c) 8019.

Colonna, Cape. See SOUNION, CAPE.

Co·lon·ne, Cape \kō-'lȯn-nā\; *anc.* **La·cin·i·um Prom·on·to·ri·um** \lə-'si-nē-əm-ˌprä-mən-'tōr-ē-əm\. Cape on E coast of Calabria, S Italy, projecting into Ionian Sea S of Gulf of Taranto.

Col·on·say \'kä-lən-ˌzā, -ˌsā\. Island of the Inner Hebrides, W Scotland, N of Islay I. and W of Jura I.; ab. 16 sq. mi. (41 km.); part of Strathclyde region.

Co·lo·nus \kə-'lō-nəs\. Ancient village, Attica, Greece, ab. 1.5 mi. (2 km.) N of Athens; birthplace of Greek dramatist Sophocles c. 496 B.C.

Col·o·phon \'kä-lə-fən, -ˌfän\. Ancient city, one of the 12 Ionian Cities, in Lydia, Asia Minor; 15 mi. (24 km.) NW of Ephesus; famous for its troop of cavalry; conquered by Macedonian Gen. Lysimachus c. 302 B.C.; birthplace of philosopher Xenophanes c. 560 B.C.

Col·o·ra·do \ˌkä-lə-'ra-dō, -'rä-\. **1.** River, SW United States; rises in NE Grand co., N Colorado; flows SW across Colorado receiving the Gunnison from SE, across SE corner of Utah receiving Green River from N and the San Juan from E, across NW corner of Arizona receiving the Little Colorado from SE; turns S and becomes lower section of Arizona-Nevada boundary and entire California-Arizona boundary; joined in SW Arizona by Gila River from E; flows through Mexico ab. 90 mi. (145 km.), empties into Gulf of California; ab. 1450 mi. (2350 km.) long. Passes through two notable canyons, Grand Canyon and Black Canyon (*qq.v.*), and three national parks: Arches, Canyonlands, and Grand Canyon (see UNITED STATES, *National Parks*); dams include Glen Canyon (in Arizona, creating Lake Powell), Hoover (bet. Nevada and Arizona, creating Lake Mead), and Parker (bet. California and Arizona, creating Lake Havasu); water is diverted for irrigation and to supply the urban needs of esp. Los Angeles, San Diego, and Phoenix. See SALTON SEA.
2. River, cen. Texas; rises in Dawson co., flows SE into Matagorda Bay; ab. 600 mi. (950 km.) long; navigable to Austin.
3. A west central state of U.S.A., bounded on N by Wyoming and Nebraska, on E by Nebraska and Kansas, on S by Oklahoma and New Mexico, on W by Utah; 8th state in area, 104,247 sq. mi. (270,000 sq. km.); 26th state in population, (1990c) 3,294,394; ✻ Denver; 38th state admitted to Union (1876). See table of states at UNITED STATES.

Nickname: Centennial State.

State flower: Columbine.

Motto: Nil Sine Numine (Nothing Without Providence).

Rivers: Colorado (see COLORADO 1); Arkansas, from cen. region E into Kansas; South Platte, from cen. region NE into Nebraska; Rio Grande, rising in SW, flowing SE into New Mexico.

Highest point: Mt. Elbert 14,433 ft. (4399 m.), in Lake co.; has 55 peaks above 14,000 ft. (4267 m.) and 1090 above 10,000 ft. (3048 m.).

Chief products: Wheat, sugar beets, corn; livestock; oil, molybdenum, coal; manufacturing: food processing, printing; tourism; skiing and other outdoor recreation.

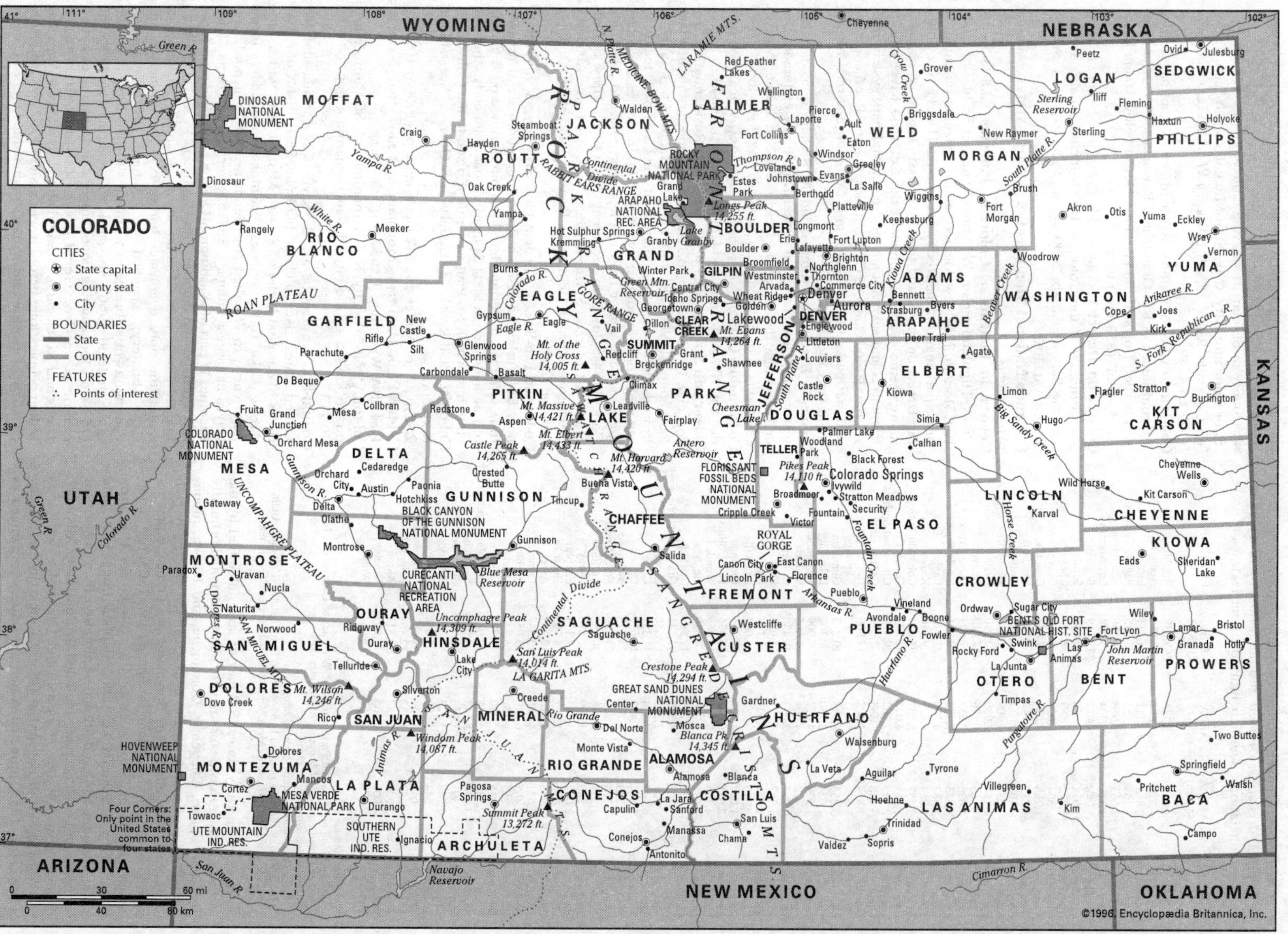

COLORADO
CITIES
State capital
County seat
City
BOUNDARIES
State
County
FEATURES
Points of interest
WYOMING
NEBRASKA
KANSAS
OKLAHOMA
NEW MEXICO
ARIZONA
UTAH
ROCKY MOUNTAINS
FRONT RANGE
SANGRE DE CRISTO MTS.
SAN JUAN MTS.
SAWATCH RANGE
PARK RANGE
MOFFAT
ROUTT
JACKSON
LARIMER
WELD
LOGAN
SEDGWICK
PHILLIPS
MORGAN
YUMA
WASHINGTON
ADAMS
BOULDER
GRAND
RIO BLANCO
GARFIELD
EAGLE
SUMMIT
CLEAR CREEK
GILPIN
JEFFERSON
DENVER
ARAPAHOE
ELBERT
DOUGLAS
KIT CARSON
CHEYENNE
LINCOLN
EL PASO
TELLER
PARK
LAKE
PITKIN
MESA
DELTA
GUNNISON
CHAFFEE
FREMONT
CUSTER
PUEBLO
CROWLEY
KIOWA
OTERO
BENT
PROWERS
MONTROSE
SAN MIGUEL
OURAY
HINSDALE
SAGUACHE
DOLORES
SAN JUAN
MINERAL
RIO GRANDE
ALAMOSA
HUERFANO
LAS ANIMAS
BACA
MONTEZUMA
LA PLATA
ARCHULETA
CONEJOS
COSTILLA
Denver
Colorado Springs
Pueblo
Grand Junction
Fort Collins
Boulder
Pikes Peak 14,110 ft.
Longs Peak 14,255 ft.
Mt. Elbert 14,433 ft.
Mt. Massive 14,421 ft.
Mt. Harvard 14,420 ft.
ROCKY MOUNTAIN NATIONAL PARK
MESA VERDE NATIONAL PARK
DINOSAUR NATIONAL MONUMENT
COLORADO NATIONAL MONUMENT
GREAT SAND DUNES NATIONAL MONUMENT
BLACK CANYON OF THE GUNNISON NATIONAL MONUMENT
FLORISSANT FOSSIL BEDS NATIONAL MONUMENT
HOVENWEEP NATIONAL MONUMENT
Four Corners: Only point in the United States common to four states
0 30 60 mi
0 40 80 km
©1996, Encyclopædia Britannica, Inc.

Chief cities: Denver, Colorado Springs, Aurora.

Political divisions: Divided into the following 63 counties (for pronunciations, see their individual entries):

NAME	AREA[1] (sq. mi.)	AREA[1] (sq. km.)	POP. (1990c)	CO. SEAT
Adams	1,245	3,225	265,038	Brighton
Alamosa	719	1,862	13,617	Alamosa
Arapahoe	815	2,111	391,511	Littleton
Archuleta	1,364	3,533	5,345	Pagosa Springs
Baca	2,563	6,638	4,556	Springfield
Bent	1,519	3,934	5,048	Las Animas
Boulder[2]	748	1,937	225,339	Boulder
Chaffee	1,038	2,688	12,684	Salida
Cheyenne	1,772	4,589	2,397	Cheyenne Wells
Clear Creek	394	1,020	7,619	Georgetown
Conejos	1,268	3,284	7,453	Conejos
Costilla	1,213	3,142	3,190	San Luis
Crowley	802	2,077	3,946	Ordway
Custer	737	1,909	1,926	Westcliffe
Delta	1,154	2,989	20,980	Delta
Denver[3]	68	176	467,610	Denver
Dolores	1,026	2,657	1,504	Dove Creek
Douglas	843	2,183	60,391	Castle Rock
Eagle	1,682	4,356	21,928	Eagle
Elbert	1,864	4,828	9,646	Kiowa
El Paso[4]	2,157	5,587	397,014	Colorado Springs
Fremont	1,561	4,043	32,273	Canon City
Garfield	2,997	7,762	29,974	Glenwood Springs
Gilpin	148	383	3,070	Central City
Grand[2]	1,854	4,802	7,966	Hot Sulphur Springs
Gunnison	3,236	8,381	10,273	Gunnison
Hinsdale	1,054	2,730	467	Lake City
Huerfano	1,574	4,077	6,009	Walsenburg
Jackson	1,622	4,201	1,605	Walden
Jefferson	785	2,033	438,430	Golden
Kiowa	1,767	4,577	1,688	Eads
Kit Carson	2,171	5,623	7,140	Burlington
Lake	379	982	6,007	Leadville
La Plata	1,684	4,362	32,284	Durango
Larimer[2]	2,611	6,762	186,136	Fort Collins
Las Animas	4,794	12,416	13,765	Trinidad
Lincoln	2,593	6,716	4,529	Hugo
Logan	1,822	4,719	17,567	Sterling
Mesa	3,303	8,555	93,145	Grand Junction
Mineral	921	2,385	558	Creede
Moffat	4,743	12,284	11,357	Craig
Montezuma[5]	2,094	5,423	18,672	Cortez
Montrose	2,238	5,796	24,423	Montrose
Morgan	1,278	3,310	21,939	Fort Morgan
Otero	1,254	3,248	20,185	La Junta
Ouray	540	1,399	2,295	Ouray
Park	2,002	5,185	7,174	Fairplay
Phillips	680	1,761	4,189	Holyoke
Pitkin	973	2,520	12,661	Aspen
Prowers	1,621	4,198	13,347	Lamar
Pueblo	2,405	6,229	123,051	Pueblo
Rio Blanco	3,263	8,451	5,972	Meeker
Rio Grande	915	2,370	10,770	Del Norte
Routt	2,330	6,035	14,088	Steamboat Springs
Saguache	3,144	8,143	4,619	Saguache
San Juan	391	1,013	745	Silverton
San Miguel	1,283	3,323	3,653	Telluride
Sedgwick	544	1,409	2,690	Julesburg
Summit	611	1,582	12,881	Breckenridge
Teller	553	1,432	12,468	Cripple Creek
Washington	2,526	6,542	4,812	Akron
Weld	4,002	10,365	131,821	Greeley
Yuma	2,379	6,162	8,954	Wray

[1] Area = land area.
[2] Rocky Mountain National Park occupies SW corner of Larimer co., NE corner of Grand co., and NW corner of Boulder co.
[3] Coextensive with city of Denver.
[4] Pikes Peak within county, near W boundary.
[5] Its SW point the only point in U.S. common to four states (Colorado, Utah, Arizona, and New Mexico). Mesa Verde National Park in SE cen. part.

History: In early times, SW part of state inhabited by the Anasazi; when Europeans arrived, plains inhabited primarily by the Arapaho, Cheyenne, Comanche, and Kiowa; mountains inhabited mainly by the Utes; explored chiefly by 18th cent. Spaniards; claimed by Spain and also France; E part acquired by U.S. in Louisiana Purchase (*q.v.*) 1803, rest in territory yielded by Mexico 1845–48; explored for U.S. government by Zebulon Pike 1806, Stephen Long 1820, and John Frémont 1842; additional exploration by a host of fur trappers and traders; parts included in Louisiana, Missouri, Utah, New Mexico, Kansas, and Nebraska territories 1805–61; gold, discovered at Cherry Creek (in present-day Denver) in 1858, attracted American settlers; organized as territory of Colorado 1861; admitted as state Aug. 1, 1876; constitution adopted 1876.

4. County in SE cen. Texas. See table at TEXAS.

5. *or* **Colorado City.** City, ⊗ of Mitchell co., NW cen. Texas, on Colorado River 25 mi. (40 km.) W of Sweetwater; pop. (1990c) 4749.

Co·lo·ra·do \ˌkō-lō-ˈrä-thō\. River in cen. Argentina; formed by confluence of Río Grande and Barrancas rivers near Chilean border, flows SE into Atlantic Ocean below Bahía Blanca; 530 mi. (853 km.) long.

Col·o·ra·do Desert \ˌkä-lə-ˈra-dō, -ˈrä-\. Arid region in SE California, W of the Colorado River; includes Palm Springs and the Salton Sea; ab. 2000 sq. mi. (5200 sq. km.). See IMPERIAL VALLEY.

Colorado National Monument. See UNITED STATES, *National Monuments.*

Col·o·ra·do Plateau *or* **Colorado Plateaus** \ˌkä-lə-ˈra-dō, -ˈrä-\. Highland region, W United States, in SE half of Utah, W Colorado, NW New Mexico, and N Arizona; bounded by principal ranges of the Rocky Mts. on the N and E, the Sonoran Desert on the S, and the Great Basin on the W; contains many scenic deep-cut gorges of the Colorado River and its tributaries and several units of the national park system incl. Arches, Bryce Canyon, Canyonlands, Capitol Reef, and Zion national parks (all in Utah), and Colorado National Monument (in Colorado).

Colorado River Aqueduct. Conduit, S California, carrying water from Lake Havasu at Parker Dam in the Colorado River W through the Colorado Desert and San Jacinto Mts. to reservoirs S of Riverside ab. 240 mi. (385 km.) long.

Co·lo·ra·dos, Cer·ro \ˈser-rō-ˌkō-lō-ˈrä-thōs\. Volcano on border bet. NW Argentina and Chile; 19,846 ft. (6049 m.).

Col·o·ra·do Springs \ˌkä-lə-ˈra-dō, -ˈrä-\. Residential and resort city, ⊗ of El Paso co., E cen. Colorado, at foot of Pikes Peak; pop. (1990c) 281,140; alt. 5980 ft. (1823 m.); tourism; Prorodeo Hall of Fame; Garden of the Gods park featuring red sandstone monoliths; founded 1871; incorp. as city 1886; grew as trade center for Cripple Creek goldfield. Colorado Coll. (1874), Colorado Technical Coll. (1965), Univ. of Colorado at Colorado Springs (1965); U.S. Air Force Academy (1954; transferred 1958 from Denver); site of an Olympic training facility.

Co·los·sae \kə-ˈlä-sē\. Ancient city, SW Phrygia, in what is now SW Turkey in Asia; a flourishing commercial town in time of Greek historian Herodotus but declined on founding of Laodicea (see DENIZLI 2) nearby; seat of an early Christian church to which St. Paul wrote the Epistle to the Colossians.

Col·quitt \ˈkäl-kwit\. **1.** County in S Georgia. See table at GEORGIA.

2. City, ⊗ of Miller co., SW Georgia; pop. (1990c) 1991.

Col·ter Peak \ˈkōl-tər\. Mountain in Yellowstone National Park, NW Wyoming; 10,683 ft. (3256 m.).

Col·ton \ˈkōlt-ᵊn\. City, San Bernardino co., SE California, 3 mi. (5 km.) S of the city of San Bernardino; pop. (1990c) 40,213.

Co·lum·bia \kə-ˈləm-bē-ə\. **1.** River, SW Canada and NW United States; rises in Columbia Lake, SE British Columbia, flows NW around N end of Selkirk Mts., turns S; widens into Arrow Lake (*q.v.*); crosses Washington boundary, forms large curve to W called Big Bend; near Oregon border receives its largest tributary, Snake River, from E; turns W and becomes W part of Washington-Oregon boundary; turns N below Portland and empties into Pacific; 1214 mi. (1953 km.) long; drainage area 258,000 sq. mi. (668,220 sq. km.); its mouth the only deepwater harbor bet. San Francisco and Cape Flattery; spanned by Astoria Bridge, longest continuous-truss bridge in world (main span 1232 ft. or 376 m., completed 1966), at Astoria, Oregon; navigable 95 mi. (153 km.) for seagoing boats; upper course source of hydroelectric power (see *Grand Coulee Dam* at UNITED STATES, *Dams and Reservoirs*). Area inhabited by various American Indian peoples long before it was visited 1792 by Capt. Robert Gray of Boston and named for his ship; a U.S.-Canada

treaty (1961, revised 1964) provides for cooperative development of the river.
2. Name of counties in eight states of the U.S. See tables at ARKANSAS, FLORIDA, GEORGIA, NEW YORK, OREGON, PENNSYLVANIA, WASHINGTON, WISCONSIN.
3. Town, Tolland co., N Connecticut, 20 mi. (32 km.) ESE of Hartford; pop. (1990c) 4510.
4. City, Monroe co., SW Illinois; pop. (1990c) 5524.
5. City, ⊗ of Adair co., S cen. Kentucky; pop. (1990c) 3845; Lindsey Wilson Coll. (1903).
6. City, ⊗ of Caldwell parish, Louisiana; pop. (1990c) 386.
7. Unincorporated settlement, Howard co., cen. Maryland; a planned city bet. Baltimore and Washington, D.C.; pop. (1990c) 75,883.
8. City, ⊗ of Marion co., S Mississippi, 32 mi. (51 km.) W of Hattiesburg; pop. (1990c) 6815.
9. City, ⊗ of Boone co., cen. Missouri, 27 mi. (43 km.) N of Jefferson City; pop. (1990c) 69,101; Stephens Coll. (1833), Univ. of Missouri–Columbia (1839), Columbia Coll. (1851).
10. Town, ⊗ of Tyrrell co., E North Carolina; pop. (1990c) 836.
11. Borough, Lancaster co., SE Pennsylvania, on Susquehanna River 11 mi. (18 km.) W of the city of Lancaster; pop. (1990c) 10,701; settled by Quakers 1726; proposed as site for national ✱ c. 1790.
12. City, ✱ of South Carolina and ⊗ of Richland co., in W cen. part of the state on Congaree River, 12 mi. (19 km.) E of Lake Murray; pop. (1990c) 98,052; electronic equipment, textiles; Univ. of South Carolina–Columbia (1801), Lutheran Theological Southern Seminary (1830), Columbia Coll. (1854), Benedict Coll. (1870), Columbia Bible Coll. (1923); founded to replace Charleston as ✱ of the state 1786; incorp. as village 1805, as city 1854; during Civil War, shelled, entered, and burned by Union troops under Gen. William T. Sherman 1865.
13. City, ⊗ of Maury co., W cen. Tennessee, on Duck River 43 mi. (69 km.) SSW of Nashville; pop. (1990c) 28,583; Columbia State Community Coll. (1966); settled 1807. Home at one time of James K. Polk, 11th president of the U.S.

Columbia, Cape. Northernmost point of Canada, on N coast of Ellesmere I., NE Arctic Archipelago, 83°07′N.

Columbia, District of. See DISTRICT OF COLUMBIA.

Columbia, Mount. Peak bet. SW Alberta and SE British Columbia, Canada, on S border of Jasper National Park; 12,294 ft. (3747 m.).

Columbia City. City, ⊗ of Whitley co., NE Indiana, 18 mi. (29 km.) WNW of Fort Wayne; pop. (1990c) 5706.

Columbia Falls. Town, Flathead co., NW Montana, 14 mi. (23 km.) NE of Kalispell; pop. (1990c) 2942; resort area.

Columbia Glacier. Glacier, Chugach Mts., S Alaska, W of Valdez; 41 mi. (66 km.) long; ab. 4 mi. (6 km.) wide near its terminus.

Columbia Heights. Residential city, Anoka co., E Minnesota, on Mississippi River just N of Minneapolis; pop. (1990c) 18,910.

Columbia Lake. Lake, SE British Columbia, W Canada; ab. 14 mi. (23 km.) long; elev. 2700 ft. (823 m.); source of Columbia River.

Co·lum·bi·ana \kə-ˌləm-bē-ˈa-nə\. **1.** County in E Ohio. See table at OHIO.
2. Town, ⊗ of Shelby co., cen. Alabama; pop. (1990c) 2968.
3. Village, Columbiana co., E Ohio, 15 mi. (24 km.) S of Youngstown; pop. (1990c) 4961.

Columbia Peak *or* **Mount Columbia.** Peak in Chaffee co., Colorado; 14,073 ft. (4289 m.).

Co·lum·bre·tes \ˌkō-lu̇m-ˈbrā-tās\. Group of small islands in Mediterranean Sea off E Spain.

Co·lum·bus \kə-ˈləm-bəs\. **1.** County in S North Carolina. See table at NORTH CAROLINA.
2. City, ⊗ of Muscogee co., W Georgia, on Chattahoochee River 80 mi. (129 km.) WSW of Macon; pop. (1990c) 179,278; textiles; Columbus Coll. (1958); estab. 1828 as frontier post on site of a Creek Indian village; Fort Benning (*q.v.*) ab. 8 mi. (13 km.) S.
3. City, ⊗ of Bartholomew co., cen. Indiana, 34 mi. (55 km.) E of Bloomington; pop. (1990c) 31,802; has several buildings designed by famous architects.
4. City, ⊗ of Cherokee co., SE corner of Kansas, 18 mi. (29 km.) SW of Pittsburg; pop. (1990c) 3268.
5. City, NW Hickman co., SW Kentucky, on Mississippi River just below confluence with the Ohio; pop. (1990c) 252; during Civil War, fortified 1861 by Confederates but evacuated 1862.
6. City, ⊗ of Lowndes co., E Mississippi, 7 mi. (11 km.) W of Alabama border; pop. (1990c) 23,799; Mississippi Univ. for Women (1884). Served as temporary ✱ of Mississippi 1863 when Jackson was occupied by Union troops.
7. Town, ⊗ of Stillwater co., S cen. Montana; pop. (1990c) 1573.
8. City, ⊗ of Platte co., E Nebraska, at confluence of Loup and Platte rivers; pop. (1990c) 18,480; hydropower-project headquarters; Central Community Coll.–Platte Campus (1968).
9. Village, Luna co., SW New Mexico; pop. (1990c) 641; raided by Mexican bandit and revolutionary Francisco (Pancho) Villa 1916.
10. Town, ⊗ of Polk co., SW North Carolina; pop. (1990c) 812.
11. City, ✱ of Ohio and ⊗ of Franklin co., cen. Ohio, on Scioto River ab. 107 mi. (170 km.) NE of Cincinnati; pop. (1990c) 632,910; automobile parts, electrical equipment, glass, food products, aircraft, coated fabrics, shoes; zoo, conservatory; Ohio State Capitol; Gallery of Fine Arts; Battelle Memorial Institute (1929); Ohio State Penitentiary; U.S. Defense Construction Supply Center; Capital Univ. (1850), Ohio State Univ.–Columbus (1870), Columbus Coll. of Art and Design (1879), Pontifical Coll. Josephinum (1888), Franklin Univ. (1902), Ohio Dominican Coll. (1911), DeVry Institute of Technology (1952), Columbus State Community Coll. (1963); first settlement at Franklinton (later absorbed by Columbus) 1797 on W bank of the Scioto; site opposite laid out 1812 as new ✱ and named Columbus; made ⊗ 1824; became city 1834; has annexed several surrounding communities.
12. Town, ⊗ of Colorado co., SE cen. Texas, on Colorado River 33 mi. (53 km.) S of Brenham; pop. (1990c) 3367.
13. City, Columbia co., S cen. Wisconsin, 25 mi. (40 km.) NE of Madison; pop. (1990c) 4093; settled 1839.

Co·lu·sa \ke-ˈlü-sə\. **1.** County in N cen. California. See table at CALIFORNIA.
2. City, its ⊗, on Sacramento River 53 mi. (85 km.) NW of the city of Sacramento; pop. (1990c) 4934.

Col·ville \ˈkōl-ˌvil, ˈkäl-\. **1.** River, N Alaska; flows E along N slope of Brooks Range, then N to Beaufort Sea; 375 mi. (603 km.) long.
2. City, ⊗ of Stevens co., NE Washington, ab. 68 mi. (109 km.) N of Spokane; pop. (1990c) 4360; silver deposits.

Colville, Cape. Cape on N coast of North I., New Zealand, on E side of Hauraki Gulf.

Col·vin, Mount \ˈkäl-vin\. Peak in the Adirondack Mts., Essex co., NE New York; 4074 ft. (1242 m.).

Col·vos Passage \ˈkäl-vəs\. Strait at S end of Puget Sound, Washington, W of Vashon I.

Col·wyn \ˈkäl-wən\. Borough, Delaware co., SE Pennsylvania, just W of Philadelphia; pop. (1990c) 2613.

Colwyn Bay. Town, Clwyd co., N Wales; pop. (1981p) 26,278; popular seaside resort.

Co·mac·chio \kō-ˈmä-kē-ˌō\; *anc.* **Co·mac·ti·um** \kə-ˈmak-shē-əm, -tē-əm\. Fortified commune, Ferrara prov., Emilia-Romagna, N Italy, 30 mi. (48 km.) ESE of the commune of Ferrara; pop. (1981p) 20,930; built on 13 islands connected by bridges; fisheries.

Comagene. See COMMAGENE.

Co·mal \ˈkō-ˌmȯl\. County in S cen. Texas. See table at TEXAS.

Co·mal·cal·co \ˌkō-mäl-ˈkäl-kō\. Municipality, Tabasco state, Mexico, 26 mi. (42 km.) NW of Villahermosa; pop. (1990p) 141,211; major late Mayan ruins incl. temples and tomb; museum.

Co·man, Mount \ˈkō-mən\. Mountain, Antarctica, 73°49′S, 64°18′W; 12,000 ft. (3658 m.).

Co·ma·na \kə-ˈmā-nə\. Ancient city of S Cappadocia, Asia Minor, in Taurus Mts. on upper Seyhan River; exact site uncertain; important religious center in pre-Roman and Roman times.

Co·man·che \kə-ˈman-chē\. **1.** Name of counties in three states of the U.S. See tables at KANSAS, OKLAHOMA, TEXAS.
2. City, ⊗ of Comanche co., cen. Texas, 24 mi. (39 km.) ENE of Brownwood; pop. (1990c) 4087.

Co·mar·ca de San Blas \kō-ˈmär-kä-thā-ˌsän-ˈbläs\. Administrative territory, NE Panama, consisting of a strip along the Caribbean coast. See table at PANAMA.

Co·ma·ya·gua \ˌkō-mä-ˈyä-gwä\. **1.** Department of S cen. Honduras. See table at HONDURAS.
2. Town, its ✻, 35 mi. (56 km.) W of Tegucigalpa; pop. (1989e) 39,500; former ✻ of Honduras.

Combaconum. See KUMBAKONAM.

Com·ba·hee \ˌkəm-ˈbē, ˈkəm-ˌbē\. River, S South Carolina; formed by confluence of Salkehatchie and Little Salkehatchie rivers; flows SE to Atlantic Ocean; ab. 140 mi. (225 km.) long.

Combarelles, Les. See EYZIES, LES.

Combe Ca·pelle \ˌkō^{n}b-kȧ-ˈpel\. Rock shelter, near Bergerac, Dordogne dept., SW cen. France; noted for discovery 1909 of a skeleton, the type specimen of the Combe-Capelle race of the Aurignacian period perhaps belonging to Cro-Magnon.

Com·ber·mere Bay \ˈkəm-bər-ˌmir\. Inlet of Bay of Bengal on W coast of Myanmar, SE of Sittwe.

Com·bles \ˈkō^{n}bl^ə\. Commune, Somme dept., NW France, 6 mi. (10 km.) NNW of Péronne; scene of much fighting during WWI; left in ruins.

COMECON. See COUNCIL FOR MUTUAL ECONOMIC ASSISTANCE.

Come·ragh Mountains \ˈküm-rə\. Mountain range in S Ireland, in co. Waterford; highest peak **Knock·a·naf·frin** \ˌnä-kə-ˈna-frən\ 2597 ft. (792 m.).

Co·me·río \ˌkō-mā-ˈrē-ō\. Municipality, E cen. Puerto Rico; pop. (1990c) 20,265.

Co·mil·la *or* **Ku·mil·la** \kü-ˈmi-lə\. Town, Bangladesh, on affluent of Meghna River 50 mi. (80 km.) SE of Dhaka; pop. (1991p) 164,509; basketry; jute milling; distribution point for hides and skins; thermal power.

Co·mi·no \kō-ˈmē-nō\. **1.** Cape on E coast of Sardinia, Italy, N of Gulf of Orosei.
2. Island of the Malta group in the Mediterranean Sea, bet. Malta and Gozo; 1 sq. mi. (2.6 sq. km.).

Co·mi·so \ˈkȯ-mē-ˌzō\. Commune, Ragusa prov., SE Sicily, Italy, 7 mi. (11 km.) W of the commune of Ragusa; pop. (1991p) 28,018; castle.

Co·mi·tán *or in full* **Comitán de Do·mín·guez** \ˌkō-mē-ˈtän-thā-dō-ˈmēŋ-gās\. Town, Chiapas state, SE Mexico; munic. pop. (1990p) 78,668.

Com·mack \ˈkä-ˌmak\. Unincorporated settlement, Suffolk co., New York, in cen. Long Island ESE of Huntington; pop. (1990c) 36,124.

Com·ma·ge·ne *or* **Com·a·ge·ne** \ˌkä-mə-ˈjē-nē\. District of ancient Syria, bet. Taurus Mts. and Euphrates River SE of Cappadocia; independent under a branch of the Seleucids; came under Romans in Emperor Vespasian's reign; ✻ Samosata.

Commander Islands. See KOMANDORSKIYE OSTROVA.

Commedagh, Slieve. See SLIEVE COMMEDAGH.

Com·merce \ˈkä-mərs\. **1.** City, Los Angeles co., SW California, NW of Downey; pop. (1990c) 12,135.
2. City, Jackson co., NE Georgia; pop. (1990c) 4108.
3. City, Hunt co., NE Texas, 15 mi. (24 km.) ENE of Greenville; pop. (1990c) 6825; East Texas State Univ. (1889).

Commerce City. City, Adams co., NE cen. Colorado, NE of Denver; pop. (1990c) 16,466.

Com·me·wij·ne *or* **Com·me·wy·ne** \ˌkȯ-mə-ˈvī-nə, -ˈvā-\. River, NE Suriname; flows NNW into the Suriname estuary near Paramaribo; ab. 100 mi. (160 km.) long.

Commonwealth, the *or* **Commonwealth of Nations;** *formerly* **British Commonwealth of Nations** *or* **the British Commonwealth.** An association of sovereign states, consisting of the United Kingdom and a number of its former dependencies; formerly constituted, with several other British-controlled territories, the **British Empire;** formally estab. by Statute of Westminster (1931) and consisting at the time of its formation of the United Kingdom, Australia, Canada, Irish Free State (withdrew 1949), Newfoundland (became a province of Canada 1949), New Zealand, and the Union (now Republic) of South Africa (withdrew 1961; readmitted 1994). After WWII the following countries (with year of independence) became members: India and Pakistan (1947; Pakistan withdrew 1972 and rejoined 1989), Ceylon (now Sri Lanka; 1948), Ghana (1957), Nigeria (1960; suspended 1995), Cyprus and Sierra Leone (1961), Jamaica, Trinidad and Tobago, Uganda, and Samoa (1962), Kenya and Malaysia (1963), Malawi, Malta, Tanzania, and Zambia (1964), Gambia and Singapore (1965), Barbados, Botswana, Guyana, Lesotho (1966), Mauritius, Nauru, and Swaziland (1968), Fiji (1970; withdrew 1987; readmitted 1997), Tonga (1970), Bangladesh (1972), Bahamas (1973), Grenada (1974), Papua New Guinea (1975), Seychelles (1976), Solomon Is., Tuvalu (special status), and Dominica (1978), St. Lucia, Kiribati, and St. Vincent and the Grenadines (1979), Zimbabwe and Vanuatu (1980), Belize and Antigua and Barbuda (1981), Maldives (1982), St. Kitts-Nevis (1983), Brunei (1984), Namibia (1990), Cameroon and Mozambique (1995).

History: (1) *Territorial development:* Territorial acquisition began in early 17th cent. with group of settlements in North America and the West Indian, East Indian, and African trading posts founded by private individuals and trading companies; captured Gibraltar 1704; by 18th cent., held 13 Atlantic seaboard colonies (see UNITED STATES) and began to add territory in India (see INDIA 1); as result of French defeat (completed by 1763) secured Canada, E Mississippi Valley, and supremacy in India; began to build power in Malaya 1786 (see PENANG); acquired Cape of Good Hope, Ceylon, and Malta as result of Napoleonic Wars; settled Australia 1788 and subsequently New Zealand; secured Aden 1839, Hong Kong 1842, and controlled Suez Canal (*q.v.*) 1875–1956; in 19th cent. European partition of Africa, acquired Nigeria, Egypt, and territories later comprising British East Africa and part of what became the Union (now Republic) of South Africa; after WWI, secured mandates to German East Africa, part of Cameroons, part of Togo, German South-West Africa, Mesopotamia, Palestine, and part of German Pacific islands. (2) *Political development:* Prior to 1783, crown and parliament claimed full authority over colonial legislatures; U.S. having achieved independence, crown and parliament gradually evolved system of self-government for some colonies ultimately set forth in Governor General of Canada Lord Durham's report 1839; gave dominion status to Canada 1867, then to Australia 1901, New Zealand 1907, Union of South Africa 1910, and Irish Free State 1921; by Statute of Westminster 1931 gave legal expression to the Commonwealth of Nations; since 1949 members have been allowed to continue membership upon attaining status as independent countries (for other territories with year of independence see above).

Commonwealth of Australia. See AUSTRALIA.

Commonwealth of Independent States. Association of the former constituent republics of the U.S.S.R. except for Lithuania, Latvia, and Estonia; formed 1991.

Commonwealth of the Bahamas. See BAHAMAS.

Communauté, La. See FRENCH COMMUNITY.

Com·mun·ism Peak \ˈkä-myə-ˌni-zəm\ *also* **Mount Communism** *or Russ.* **Pik Kom·mun·iz·ma** \ˈpēk-ˌkə-mü-ˈnēs-mə\; *formerly* **Sta·lin Peak** \ˈstä-lən, ˈsta-, -ˌlēn\ *or* **Gar·mo Peak** \ˈgär-mō\. Peak, NE cen. Tajikistan; 24,590 ft. (7495 m.); highest peak in Tajikistan and in the former U.S.S.R.

Co·mo \ˈkō-mō\. **1.** Province of Lombardy, N Italy. See table at ITALY.

2. *anc.* **Co·mum** \ˈkō-məm\. Commune, its ✻, at SW end of Lake Como 24 mi. (39 km.) N of Milan; pop. (1991p) 85,955; tourism; cathedral. Settled from ancient times; headquarters of Ghibelline party in Middle Ages; destroyed 1127 by Milanese and subsequently rebuilt by Holy Roman Emperor Frederick I; came under the Visconti family 1335; later under Spanish, French, and Austrian control; liberated by Italian nationalist Giuseppe Garibaldi 1859. Italian dictator Benito Mussolini arrested nearby Apr. 1945 and shot. Birthplace of Roman scholars Pliny the Elder (23 A.D.) and Pliny the Younger (c. 61 A.D.).

Como, Lake; *anc.* **La·cus Lar·i·us** \ˈlā-kəs-ˈlar-ē-əs\. Lake in Lombardy, N Italy, expansion of Adda River; 37 mi. (60 km.) by ab. 3 mi. (5 km.); 56 sq. mi. (145 sq. km.); surrounded by mountains 3000 to 7000 ft. (900 to 2100 m.) high; many resorts.

Co·mo·do·ro Ri·va·da·via \ˌkō-mō-ˈt͟hō-rō-ˌrē-vä-ˈt͟hä-vē-ä\. Seaport, Chubut prov., SE Argentina, on San Jorge Gulf; pop. (1980p) 96,865; oil.

Co·mon·dú \ˌkȯ-mȯn-ˈdü\. Municipality, Baja California Sur terr., Mexico; pop. (1990p) 74,165.

Co·mon·fort \ˌkō-mȯn-ˈfȯr, -ˈfȯrt\. Town, Guanajuato state, cen. Mexico, 38 mi. (61 km.) SE of the city of Guanajuato; munic. pop. (1990p) 56,573.

Com·o·rin, Cape \ˈkä-mə-rən\. Cape on S extremity of India, in Tamil Nadu.

Com·o·ros \ˈkä-mə-ˌrōz\ *also* **Com·o·ro Islands** \-ˌrō\ *or Fr.* **Îles Co·mores** \ˌēl-kȯ-ˈmȯr\. **1.** Group of volcanic islands in N Mozambique Channel, bet. NE Mozambique and NW Madagascar; 863 sq. mi. (2235 sq. km.); includes the islands of Grande Comore, Anjouan, Mayotte, and Mohéli. Long under Arab influence; indigenous population made up of Arabs, Asians, and peoples from African mainland; known to European navigators from 16th cent.; Mayotte occupied by French 1843, other islands secured as French protectorates late 19th cent.; became a colony attached administratively to Madagascar 1914; made a French overseas territory 1947; internal autonomy 1961 and independence 1975 except for Mayotte, which remained French.

2. *officially* **Federal Islamic Republic of the Comoros.** Republic, W Indian Ocean, off SE coast of Africa; includes all of the Comoros except Mayotte; 719 sq. mi. (1862 sq. km.); pop. (1990e) 519,527; ✻ Moroni; exports vanilla, copra, ylang-ylang and other esssential oils, cloves.

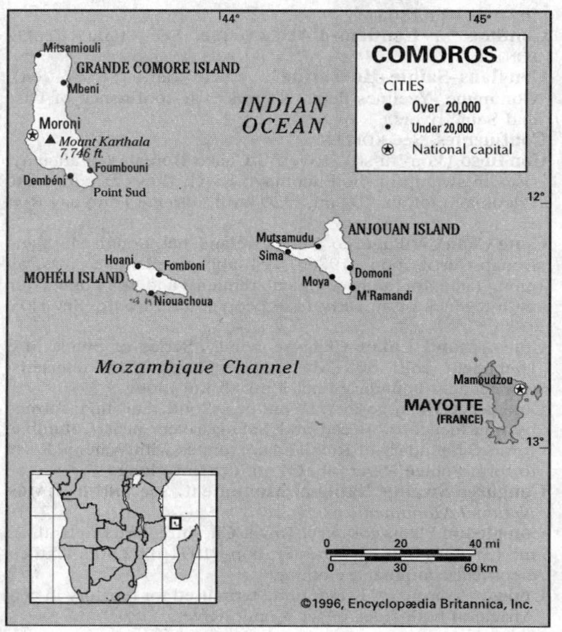

Co·mox \ˈkō-ˌmäks\. Village, British Columbia, Canada, on the Strait of Georgia 5 mi. (8 km.) E of Courtenay; pop. (1991c) 8253.

Com·piègne \kȯ^{n}p-ˈyen^y\. Commune, Oise dept., N France, on left bank of Oise River 34 mi. (55 km.) E of Beauvais; pop. (1990c) 44,703; Gothic town hall (restored); fine château.

History: Favorite residence and hunting grounds of royalty from the Middle Ages through the Second Empire of Napoléon III; scene of capture of French national heroine Joan of Arc by Burgundians and English 1430; during Franco-Prussian War, German headquarters 1870–71; armistice ending WWI signed in railway car in forest nearby Nov. 11, 1918; armistice bet. France and Germany signed here in same car June 22, 1940; retaken by Allies 1944.

Complutum. See ALCALÁ DE HENARES.

Compniacum. See COGNAC.

Com·po·ste·la \ˌkȯm-pȯ-ˈstā-lä\. Municipality, Nayarit state, Mexico, 25 mi. (40 km.) S of Tepic; pop. (1990p) 59,796; founded 16th cent.

Compostela, Santiago de. See SANTIAGO 14.

Comp·ton \ˈkämp-tən\. City, Los Angeles co., SW California, 2 mi. (3.2 km.) S of the city of Los Angeles; pop. (1990c) 90,454; steel castings; Compton Community Coll. (1927).

Com·stock Lode \ˈkäm-ˌstäk-ˈlōd\. See VIRGINIA CITY 2.

Com·tat Ve·nais·sin \kō^n-ˈtȧ-və-nā-ˈse^n\ *or* **Comtat** *or* **Venaissin.** Historical region of SE France, bounded on N by Dauphiné, on E and S by Provence, and on W by Languedoc; ✻ Carpentras; under papal rule 1274–1791.

Comum. See COMO 2.

Con·a·kry *also* **Kon·a·kri** \ˈkä-nə-krē, kȯ-nä-ˈkrē\. Seaport town, ✻ of Guinea, on Tombo I. (*q.v.*); pop. (1983c) 705,280; port facilities; exports include alumina and bananas; automobile assembly; technical college (1963).

Co·nan·i·cut Island \kə-ˈna-ni-kət\. Island in Narragansett Bay W of Rhode Island (island); a part of Newport co., Rhode Island; coextensive with Jamestown; Beaver Tail lighthouse at S tip.

Con·a·sau·ga \ˌkä-nə-ˈsȯ-gə\. River, NW Georgia; rises in SE Tennessee, flows S into Georgia, unites with Coosawattee River to form Oostanaula River.

Conca. See CUENCA 3.

Con·car·neau \ˌkō^n-kȧr-ˈnō\. Commune, Finistère dept., NW France, on Atlantic coast NW of Lorient; old part of town walled, on an island, new part on mainland a seaside resort; fishing.

Con·cep·cion *or Span.* **Con·cep·ción** \ˌkȯn-sep-ˈsyȯn\. Municipality, SE Tarlac prov., Luzon, Philippines, 13 mi. (21 km.) SSE of the municipality of Tarlac; pop. (1980c) 80,647.

Con·cep·ción. \ˌkȯn-sep-ˈsyȯn\. **1.** Former province of S cen. Chile.

2. Commercial city, ✻ of Bío-Bío region, S cen. Chile, on the Bío-Bío River 6 mi. (10 km.) from its mouth and 260 mi. (418 km.) SW of Santiago; pop. (1982c) 267,891; formerly ✻ of Concepción prov.; distribution center for S Chile; its ports are Tomé and Talcahuano; food products, textiles, glass, steel; coal mines nearby; university (1919).

History: Founded by Spanish soldier Pedro de Valdivia ab. 6 mi. (10 km.) from its present site 1550; laid waste by Araucanian Indians c. 1555; destroyed by earthquakes 1570, 1730, 1751; rebuilt on present location c. 1755; again hit by major earthquakes 1835, 1939, 1960.

3. Active volcano, Nicaragua; 5282 ft. (1610 m.); one of two peaks (see MADERA 4) on the island of Ometepe in Lake Nicaragua.

4. Department of E Paraguay. See table at PARAGUAY.

5. *or* **Vil·la Concepción** \ˈvē-yä\. Town and river port, ✻ of Concepción dept., E Paraguay, on E bank of Paraguay River 125 mi. (201 km.) N of Asunción; pop. (1992p) 35,485.

6. Island, West Indies. See GRENADA 3.
Concepción, La. See LA CONCEPCIÓN.
Concepción Bay. Inlet of Pacific Ocean in coast of S cen. Chile, near city of Concepción.
Concepción de la Vega. See LA VEGA 2.
Concepción del Uru·guay \t͟hel-ˌü-rü-ˈg̅wī\. River port, Entre Ríos prov., E Argentina, on the border of Uruguay; pop. (1980p) 46,065; national university (1778).
Concepción Strait *or* **Concepción Channel.** Strait, S of Duke of York I. (Madre de Dios Archipelago), off SW Chile, leading from Pacific Ocean NE into Trinidad Gulf.
Con·cep·tion, Point \kən-ˈsep-shən\. Point on SW extremity of Santa Barbara co., SW California.
Conception Bay. Inlet of Atlantic Ocean in SE Newfoundland, Canada, W of the city of St. John's; ab. 40 mi. (64 km.) long.
Con·cha·gua \kȯn-ˈchä-g̅wä\. Volcano, El Salvador, 95 mi. (153 km.) ESE of the city of San Salvador; 4101 ft. (1250 m.).
Conchas, Las. See TIGRE 1.
Con·chas Dam \ˈkän-chəs\. Dam across S Canadian River, E San Miguel co., New Mexico; height 188 ft. (57 m.); completed c. 1939; impounds water for flood control and irrigation, forming **Conchas Lake** *or* **Conchas Reservoir** (ab. 25 sq. mi. or 65 sq. km.).
Con·cho \ˈkän-chō\. **1.** River, Texas; rises in Tom Green co., flows E to join Colorado River; 53 mi. (85 km.) long; see MIDDLE CONCHO, NORTH CONCHO, and SOUTH CONCHO.
2. County in W cen. Texas. See table at TEXAS.
Con·chos \ˈkȯn-chōs\. River, Chihuahua state, N Mexico; flows N into the Rio Grande; ab. 300 mi. (485 km.) long.
Con·cord \ˈkäŋ-kərd, ˈkän-, -ˌkȯrd\. **1.** River, NE Massachusetts; formed by junction of Sudbury and Assabet rivers, flows N into the Merrimack River at Lowell.
2. City, Contra Costa co., W California, NNE of Berkeley; pop. (1990c) 111,348.
3. Residential town, Middlesex co., NE Massachusetts, 12 mi. (19 km.) S of Lowell; pop. (1990c) 17,076; tourism; historical museum; settled 1635; in 1775 had storehouse of munitions and military supplies which the British were marching to seize when they were checked by minutemen in battles at Lexington and Concord Apr. 19, 1775; statue of the *Minute Man of Concord* by Concord resident Daniel Chester French at the bridge over Concord River where battle was fought; residence of writers A. Bronson Alcott, Louisa May Alcott, Ralph Waldo Emerson, Nathaniel Hawthorne, Henry David Thoreau.
4. City, ✻ of New Hampshire and ⊗ of Merrimack co., S cen. New Hampshire, on Merrimack River 18 mi. (29 km.) N of Manchester; pop. (1990c) 36,006; electrical equipment, leather goods; granite quarries; St. Paul's School (preparatory school, 1856); New Hampshire Technical Institute (1961). Original grant 1659; settled 1727; incorp. by Massachusetts as Rumford 1733, by New Hampshire as town of Concord 1765, as city 1853; became ✻ 1808.
5. City, ⊗ of Cabarrus co., S cen. North Carolina, 18 mi. (29 km.) NE of Charlotte; pop. (1990c) 27,347; former gold-mining center (gold discovered 1799); manufactures cotton goods; Barber-Scotia Coll. (1867).
6. Municipality, E New South Wales, SE Australia, W suburb of Sydney on S bank of lower Parramatta River; pop. (1991c) 23,150.
Con·cor·dia. **1.** \kən-ˈkȯr-dē-ə\. Parish in E cen. Louisiana. See table at LOUISIANA.
2. \kän-ˈkȯr-dē-ə\. City, ⊗ of Cloud co., N Kansas, 50 mi. (80 km.) N of Salina; pop. (1990c) 6167.
Con·cor·dia \kən-ˈkȯr-dē-ə\. City, Entre Ríos prov., E Argentina, on right bank of Uruguay River opp. Salto in Uruguay; pop. (1991p) 138,905.
Con·da·mine \ˈkän-də-ˌmīn\. River, SE Queensland, Australia; flows W through Darling Downs; joins Maranoa to form Culgoa; 430 mi. (692 km.) long.
Con·da·te \kən-ˈdā-tē\. Name of Celtic origin, meaning "confluence (of two rivers)," given to numerous towns in ancient Gaul, esp. modern Cosne-sur-Loire, Montereau-faut-Yonne, Rennes, and St.-Claude (*qq.v.*), and retained in its modern French form **Con·dé** \kȯⁿ-ˈdā\ in many such names.
Con·dé–sur–l'Es·caut \kȯⁿ-ˌdā-sᵫr-les-ˈkō\. Commune, Nord dept., N France, 7 mi. (11 km.) NE of Valenciennes and 2 mi. (3 km.) from Belgian border; principality from which the Condé branch of house of Bourbon held their title.
Condé–sur–Noi·reau \kȯⁿ-ˌdā-sᵫr-nwä-ˈrō\. Commune, Calvados dept., NW France, 33 mi. (53 km.) SSW of Caen.
Condivincum. See NANTES.
Con·dom \kȯⁿ-ˈdȯⁿ\. Commune, Gers dept., SW France, 20 mi. (32 km.) SW of Agen; founded 8th cent.; episcopal see 1317–1790; sacked 1569 by Huguenots; trades in armagnac, the brandy made in this region.
Con·don \ˈkän-dən\. City, ⊗ of Gilliam co., N Oregon; pop. (1990c) 635.
Co·ne·cuh \kə-ˈnā-kə\. **1.** River, S Alabama; flows SW into the Escambia River; 145 mi. (233 km.) long.
2. County in S Alabama. See table at ALABAMA.
Co·ne·glia·no \ˌkō-nā-ˈlyä-nō\. Commune, Treviso prov., Veneto, NE Italy, 15 mi. (24 km.) N of the commune of Treviso; pop. (1991p) 35,301; wine. Birthplace of painter Giovanni Battista Cima c. 1459.
Co·ne·jos \kə-ˈnā-əs, -həs\. **1.** County in S Colorado. See table at COLORADO.
2. Village, its ⊗, on **Conejos River,** a tributary of the Rio Grande, in foothills of San Juan Mts.
Con·e·maugh \ˈkä-nə-ˌmȯ\. River, SW Pennsylvania; formed by confluence of **Little Conemaugh River** and Stony Creek at Johnstown, in Cambria co., flows W to unite with Loyalhanna Creek and form Kiskiminetas River; ab. 45 mi. (72 km.) long. See JOHNSTOWN 3.
Con·es·to·ga \ˌkä-nə-ˈstō-gə\. Township, Lancaster co., SE Pennsylvania, SSW of the city of Lancaster; pop. (1990c) 3470; Conestoga wagon developed in region ab. 1750.
Co·ney Island \ˈkō-nē\. Section of S Brooklyn, New York City, New York; formerly an island 5 mi. (8 km.) long, now part of Long Island (since silting up of Coney Island Creek); once considered a resort, now an amusement area; first pavilion and bathhouse erected 1844; boardwalk, aquarium.
Confederate States of America. Name of the 11 Southern states of the U.S. during their secession from the Union 1860–65: Alabama, Florida, Georgia, Louisiana, Mississippi, South Carolina, Texas, Arkansas, North Carolina, Tennessee, and Virginia; ✻ Montgomery, Alabama 1861, but soon moved to Richmond, Virginia; dissolved shortly after defeat in Civil War 1865.
Conflans *or* **Conflans–l'Archevêque.** See CHARENTON-LE-PONT.
Con·flans–Sainte–Ho·no·rine \kȯⁿ-ˌflän-seⁿ-tȯ-nȯ-ˈrēn\. Commune, Yvelines dept., N France, at confluence of Oise and Seine rivers.
Confluentes. See KOBLENZ.
Con·fu·so \kȯn-ˈfü-sō\. River, S Chaco Boreal, W Paraguay; rises in swamp of the Pilcomayo River, flows E, parallel to Pilcomayo for ab. 200 mi. (320 km.), into the Paraguay River.
Cong \ˈkäŋ\. Village, co. Mayo, Ireland, bet. Lough Mask and Lough Corrib; pop. (1986c) 194; abbey and stone cross; region noted for archaeological remains and for connection with legends of an early Irish people, the Firbolg. See MOYTURA.
Con·ga·mond Lakes \ˈkäŋ-gə-mənd\. Series of ponds in S Hampden co., SW Massachusetts, on Massachusetts-Connecticut boundary line; 3 mi. (5 km.) long.
Con·ga·ree \ˈkäŋ-gə-ˌrē\. River, cen. South Carolina; formed by confluence of Broad and Saluda rivers near Columbia; forms S boundary of Richland co.; unites with Wateree River to form Santee River; ab. 60 mi. (95 km.) long.
Congaree Swamp National Monument. See UNITED STATES, *National Monuments.*
Con·gle·ton \ˈkäŋ-gəl-tən\. Town, Cheshire, NW England, 22 mi. (35 km.) S of Manchester; pop. (1991p) 82,900; textiles, electrical equipment, clothing.
Con·go \ˈkäŋ-gō\. **1.** Indefinite term used for territory in cen. Africa on both sides of the Congo River.

2. Republic, Africa. See ZAIRE 1.
3. *officially* **Republic of the Congo;** *formerly* **Middle Congo.** Republic, equatorial Africa, bounded on N by Cameroon and Central African Rep., on E and S by Democratic Rep. of the Congo, on SW by Cabinda exclave of Angola and the Atlantic Ocean, and on W by Gabon; 132,047 sq. mi. (342,002 sq. km.); pop. (1993e) 2,775,000; ✻ Brazzaville.

Chief products: Peanuts, palm kernels, bananas, sugarcane, coffee, timber; lead, gold, petroleum (offshore).

Chief towns: Brazzaville, Pointe-Noire.

History: Prior to European colonization, area was home to several thriving kingdoms; slave trade began following Portuguese exploration of coast 15th cent. and continued through 19th cent.; area became a territory of French Equatorial Africa (*q.v.*) 1910; status changed to that of French overseas territory 1946; became an autonomous republic within the French Community 1958; achieved independence 1960; has suffered political instability with government changing hands several times late 20th cent.

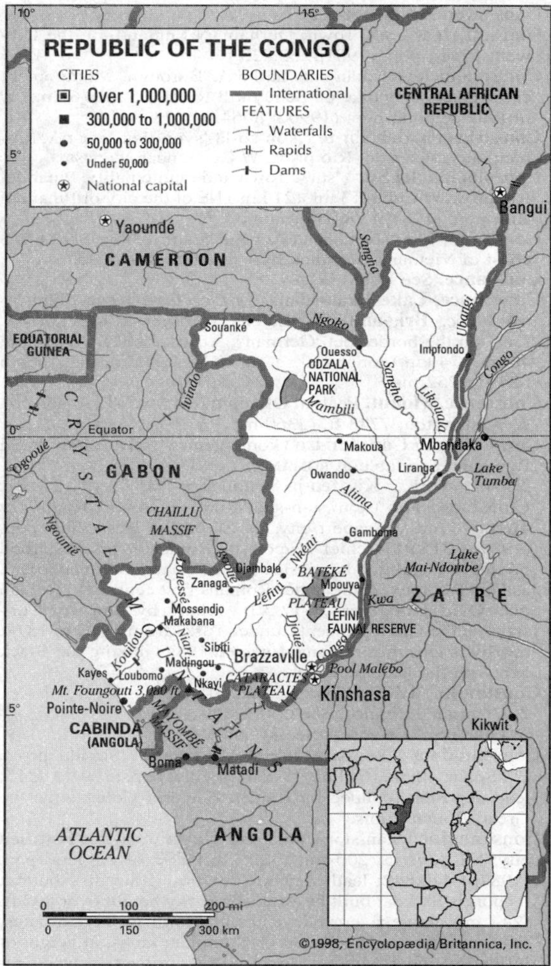

4. *also* **Kon·go** \ˈkòŋ-gō\; *in Angola called* **Za·i·re** \ zä-ˈir-ē\ *or in Democratic Rep. of the Congo* **Za·ïre** \zä-ˈir\. River, W cen. Africa; one of largest in the world; formed by confluence of Luapula and Lualaba rivers: the Luapula, flows N through Lake Mweru forming the boundary bet. Zambia and Democratic Rep. of the Congo; the Lualaba rises in SE Democratic Rep. of the Congo and flows N to join the Luapula at ab. 6°45′S, 26°50′E. From this junction to Boyoma Falls (*q.v.*), the Congo is sometimes known as the Lualaba; below Boyoma Falls, turns NW and W in a big curve, receiving the Lindi and Aruwimi rivers from the N and the Lomami from the S; begins to turn SW, receives Mongala from N, turns more sharply S and is joined by the Ubangi; from this point to ab. 200 mi. (320 km.) from mouth on Atlantic Ocean forms boundary bet. Rep. of the Congo and Democratic Rep. of the Congo; receives the Kasai from the E; more than 2700 mi. (4344 km.) long; drainage area 1,425,000 sq. mi. (3,690,750 sq. km.); at Pool Malebo (*q.v.*) ab. 330 mi. (530 km.) from its mouth are located Brazzaville and Kinshasa; navigable for 83 mi. (134 km.) from mouth to Matadi and for 1050 mi. (1689 km.) bet. Pool Malebo and Boyoma Falls, and for 585 mi. (941 km.) above the falls. Estuary ab. 7 mi. (11 km.) wide from Banana Point on N to Sharks Point on S; its mouth discovered 1482 by Portuguese navigator Diogo Cão; lower course ascended by British expedition 1816; headstreams traced by Scottish missionary and explorer David Livingstone during his last expedition 1867–73; entire river system explored by British journalist Henry M. Stanley 1874–84.
5. District, Angola. See ZAIRE 2.

Congo, Democratic Republic of the. See ZAIRE 1.
Congo Free State. See ZAIRE 1.
Congress Poland. See POLAND 1.
Conhocton. See COHOCTON.
Coni. See CUNEO 2.
Conimbriga See COIMBRA 2.
Con·is·brough \ˈkä-nəs-brə\. Town, South Yorkshire, N England, on the Don River near Doncaster; pop. (1981p) 16,114; has 12th cent. castle, home (Coningsburgh) of Athelstane in Scottish writer Sir Walter Scott's novel *Ivanhoe.*
Con·is·ton \ˈkä-nə-stən\. Village, N Lancashire, England, at N end of Coniston Water; burial place of English art critic and writer John Ruskin.
Coniston Fells. Mountain range in N Lancashire, NW England; highest peak **Coniston Old Man** *or* **Old Man of Coniston** 2633 ft. (803 m.); on W side of **Coniston Water** *or* **Coniston Lake,** ab. 5 mi. (8 km.) long, max. depth 184 ft. (56 m.).
Conjeeveram. See KANCHIPURAM.
Conn, Lough. \ˈkän\ Lake, co. Mayo, NW Ireland; 8 mi. (13 km.) long, 4 mi. (6 km.) wide.
Con·nacht \ˈkä-ˌnȯt\ *also* **Con·naught** \ˈkä-ˌnȯt, kə-ˈnȯt\. Province, NW Ireland; 6611 sq. mi. (17,122 sq. km.); pop. (1991c) 422,909; counties: Galway, Leitrim, Mayo, Roscommon, Sligo.

History: An ancient native kingdom in W Ireland; Christianized by St. Patrick 5th cent.; from 11th cent. dominated by the O'Connors of Roscommon whose feuds with other kingdoms led to Anglo-Norman invasion in 12th cent. (see IRELAND); passed to the de Burgh family 13th cent.; divided into counties late 16th cent.

Con·nah's Quay \ˈkä-nəz-ˈkē\. Town and port, Flintshire, NE Wales; pop. (1981p) 14,801.
Connaught. See CONNACHT.
Con·naught Tunnel \ˈkä-ˌnȯt\. Railroad tunnel through Selkirk Mts. at Rogers Pass, British Columbia, Canada; 5 mi. (8 km.) long; alt. 3790 ft. (1155 m.); completed 1916.
Con·ne·aut \ˈkä-nē-ˌät\. City, Ashtabula co., NE corner of Ohio, on Lake Erie; pop. (1990c) 13,241; ore and coal port.
Con·nect·i·cut \kə-ˈne-ti-kət\. **1.** River, NE United States; rises in Connecticut Lakes, N New Hampshire, near Canadian border, flows S, its W bank forming New Hampshire-Vermont boundary, crosses W cen. Massachusetts and cen. Connecticut, empties into Long Island Sound bet. the towns of Old Lyme and Old Saybrook; 407 mi. (655 km.) long; chief tributaries are White River in Vermont, Ashuelot in New Hampshire, Deerfield, Millers, Westfield, and Chicopee

rivers in Massachusetts, and Farmington in Connecticut; navigable to Windsor, Connecticut. See *History* at CONNECTICUT 2.

2. An eastern state of U.S.A., southernmost of the New England states, bounded on N by Massachusetts, on E by Rhode Island, on S by Long Island Sound, and on W by New York; 48th state in area, 5018 sq. mi. (12,997 sq. km.) [land area 4872 sq. mi. or 12,618 sq. km.]; 27th state in population, (1990c) 3,287,116; ✻ Hartford; original state of the Union, the 5th to ratify the U.S. Constitution (Jan. 9, 1788). See table of states at UNITED STATES.

Nicknames: Constitution State; Nutmeg State.

State flower: Mountain laurel.

Motto: Qui Transtulit Sustinet (He Who Transplanted Sustains).

Chief rivers: Connecticut (see CONNECTICUT 1), Housatonic in W, and Thames in E, flowing S into Long Island Sound.

Highest point: Mt. Frissell 2380 ft. (725 m.) in Litchfield co.

Chief products: Dairy products, shade-grown tobacco for cigar wrappers; manufacturing: jet engines, helicopters, submarines; guns and ammunition; insurance.

Chief cities: Bridgeport, Hartford, New Haven, Waterbury, Stamford.

Political divisions: Divided into the following eight counties (for pronunciation of their names, see their individual entries):

NAME	AREA[1] (sq. mi.)	AREA[1] (sq. km.)	POP. (1990c)	FORMER CO. SEAT(S)[2]
Fairfield	627	1,624	827,645	Bridgeport
Hartford	739	1,914	851,783	Hartford
Litchfield	930	2,409	174,092	Litchfield
Middlesex	372	963	143,196	Middletown
New Haven	605	1,567	804,219	New Haven and Waterbury
New London	667	1,728	254,957	New London and Norwich
Tolland	416	1,077	128,699	Tolland
Windham	516	1,336	102,525	Putnam and Willimantic

[1] Area = land area.
[2] County governments abolished 1960.

History: Orig. inhabited by the Algonquin Indians. Connecticut River expored 1614 by Dutch navigator Adriaen Block, and again 1632 by Edward Winslow of Plymouth; posts estab. 1633 by the Dutch at Hartford and by a Plymouth contingent at Windsor; a 3d post estab. at Wethersfield 1634 following 1633 exploration of the area by John Oldham of Massachusetts Bay Colony; permanent settlements estab. at the three river towns of Hartford, Windsor, and Wethersfield 1635–36, primarily by colonists from Massachusetts Bay; Saybrook Colony estab. 1635; Pequot tribe nearly extinguished in Pequot War 1636–37; New Haven Colony estab. 1638; three river towns formed Connecticut Colony and adopted Fundamental Orders, considered by some to be the first American constitution based on the consent of the governed, 1638–39; in New England Confederation 1643–84; Connecticut Colony absorbed Saybrook Colony 1644; received charter 1662 which united Connecticut and New Haven colonies and granted strip of land extending to Pacific; included in Dominion of New England, the government of Connecticut was briefly taken over by British colonial governor Sir Edmund Andros 1687–89; relinquished claims to W lands 1786 except for Western Reserve (situated in what is now Ohio) to which it abandoned jurisdiction 1800; participated in Hartford Convention 1814–15; adopted state constitution 1818, in force until 1965, when it was replaced by another.

Connecticut Farms. See UNION 5.

Connecticut Lakes. Four small lakes in N Coos co., N New Hampshire; the 4th lake, within half a mile of the Canadian border, and the 3d lake are the ultimate sources of the Connecticut River.

Connecticut Reserve. See WESTERN RESERVE.

Con·nells·ville \ˈkän-ᵊlz-ˌvil\. City, Fayette co., SW Pennsylvania, on Youghiogheny River 12 mi. (19 km.) NNE of Uniontown; pop. (1990c) 9229; settled c. 1770.

Con·ne·ma·ra \ˌkä-nə-ˈmär-ə, -ˈmar-\. Barren, mountainous coastal district in W co. Galway, W Ireland; bounded on N by Clew Bay, on E by Lough Mask and Lough Corrib, on S by Galway Bay, on W by Atlantic Ocean; Twelve Bens of Bennebeola in W (highest point 2395 ft. or 730 m.).

Con·ners·ville \ˈkä-nərz-ˌvil\. City, ⊗ of Fayette co., E Indiana, 18 mi. (29 km.) SW of Richmond; pop. (1990c) 15,550.

Con·ness, Mount \kə-ˈnes\. Peak in the Sierra Nevada, in E Tuolumne co., cen. California; ab. 12,590 ft. (3837 m.).

Con·o·ver \ˈkän-ˌō-vər\. Town, Catawba co., W cen. North Carolina, 40 mi. (64 km.) NW of Charlotte; pop. (1990c) 5465.

Con·rad \ˈkän-ˌrad\. City, ⊗ of Pondera co., NW Montana; pop. (1990c) 2891.

Con·roe \ˈkän-rō\. City, ⊗ of Montgomery co., E Texas, 38 mi. (61 km.) N of Houston; pop. (1990c) 27,610.

Con·se·lhei·ro La·fa·ie·te \ˌkȯn-si-ˈlyā-rü-ˌlȧ-fā-ˈyā-tē\. City, Minas Gerais state, E Brazil; munic. pop. (1991p) 88,827.

Consentia. See COSENZA 2.

Con·sett \ˈkän-sət\. Town, Durham, N England, on the Derwent River; pop. (1981p) 33,433.

Con·sho·hock·en \ˌkän-shə-ˈhä-kən\. Borough, Montgomery co., SE Pennsylvania, on Schuylkill River 3.5 mi. (6 km.) W of Philadelphia; pop. (1990c) 8064.

Con·so·la·ción del Nor·te \ˌkȯn-sō-lä-ˈsyōn-t͟hel-ˈnȯr-tā\. Municipality, Pinar del Río prov., W Cuba, near N coast.

Consolación del Sur \ˈsür\. Town and municipality, Pinar del Río prov., W Cuba, 13 mi. (21 km.) NE of the city of Pinar del Río; pop. (1981p) 78,054 (munic.).

Con Son \ˈkōn-ˈsōn\. Island in the South China Sea, off S coast of Vietnam; occupied by French c. 1861–1954.

Constance. See KONSTANZ.

Con·stance, Lake \ˈkän-stənts\ *or Ger.* **Bo·den·see** \ˈbōd-ᵊn-ˌzā\; *anc.* **Brig·an·ti·nus La·cus** \ˌbri-gən-ˈtī-nəs-ˈlā-kəs\. Lake on the border bet. Germany, Austria, and Switzerland; 46 mi. (74 km.) long; 210 sq. mi. (544 sq. km.); max. depth 827 ft. (252 m.).

Constance, Mount. Peak in Olympic Mts., in E Jefferson co., W Washington; 7743 ft. (2360 m.).

Con·stan·ţa *or* **Con·stan·tsa** \kōn-ˈstänt-sə\. **1.** County of SE Romania. See table at ROMANIA.

2. *or Turk.* **Küs·ten·ja** \ˌkūē-sten-ˈyä, ˌkyü-\; *anc.* **Con·stan·ti·a·na** \kən-ˌstan-shē-ˈā-nə\ *or* **To·mi** \ˈtō-ˌmī\ *or* **To·mis** \-məs\. Seaport city, its ⊗, on the Black Sea; pop. (1989c) 315,917; chief seaport of Romania; textiles, food products, metal goods; seaside resort. Founded 7th cent. B.C. as Greek colony; came under Romans first cent. A.D.; Roman poet Ovid exiled here 9–17 A.D.; rebuilt by Emperor Constantine the Great 4th cent.; under Turks from 1413 to 1878; nearby is terminus of canal (opened 1984) linking the Black Sea with the Danube River.

Constantia. 1. City, Cyprus. See SALAMIS 1.

2. Commune, France. See COUTANCES.

3. Lake port, Germany. See KONSTANZ.

Cons·tan·ti·na \ˌkȯn-stän-ˈtē-nä\. Commune, Sevilla prov., SW Spain, 40 mi. (64 km.) NNE of Seville; pop. (1991c) 7315; lead deposits; founded by Roman Emperor Constantine the Great; Roman ruins.

Cons·tan·tine \ˈkän-stən-ˌtēn\; *anc.* **Cir·ta** \ˈsər-tə\. Fortified city, NE Algeria, 200 mi. (322 km.) ESE of Algiers; pop. (1987p) 440,842; leather goods, textiles; grain distribution; its port is Skikda; built by Arabs on rocky height over 800 ft. (244 m.) above river valley; has medieval walls and gates; Roman ruins nearby. Was ✻ of Numidian kings, at height of influence under Micipsa 2d cent. B.C.; ruined in wars, restored by Roman Emperor Constantine the Great 313 A.D.; taken by French 1837 after long siege; occupied by U.S. troops Nov. 1942.

Constantine Harbor. Inlet at E end of Amchitka I. on N coast, Aleutian Is., Alaska; airport.

Constantinople. See İSTANBUL.

Constantiola. See OLTENIŢA.

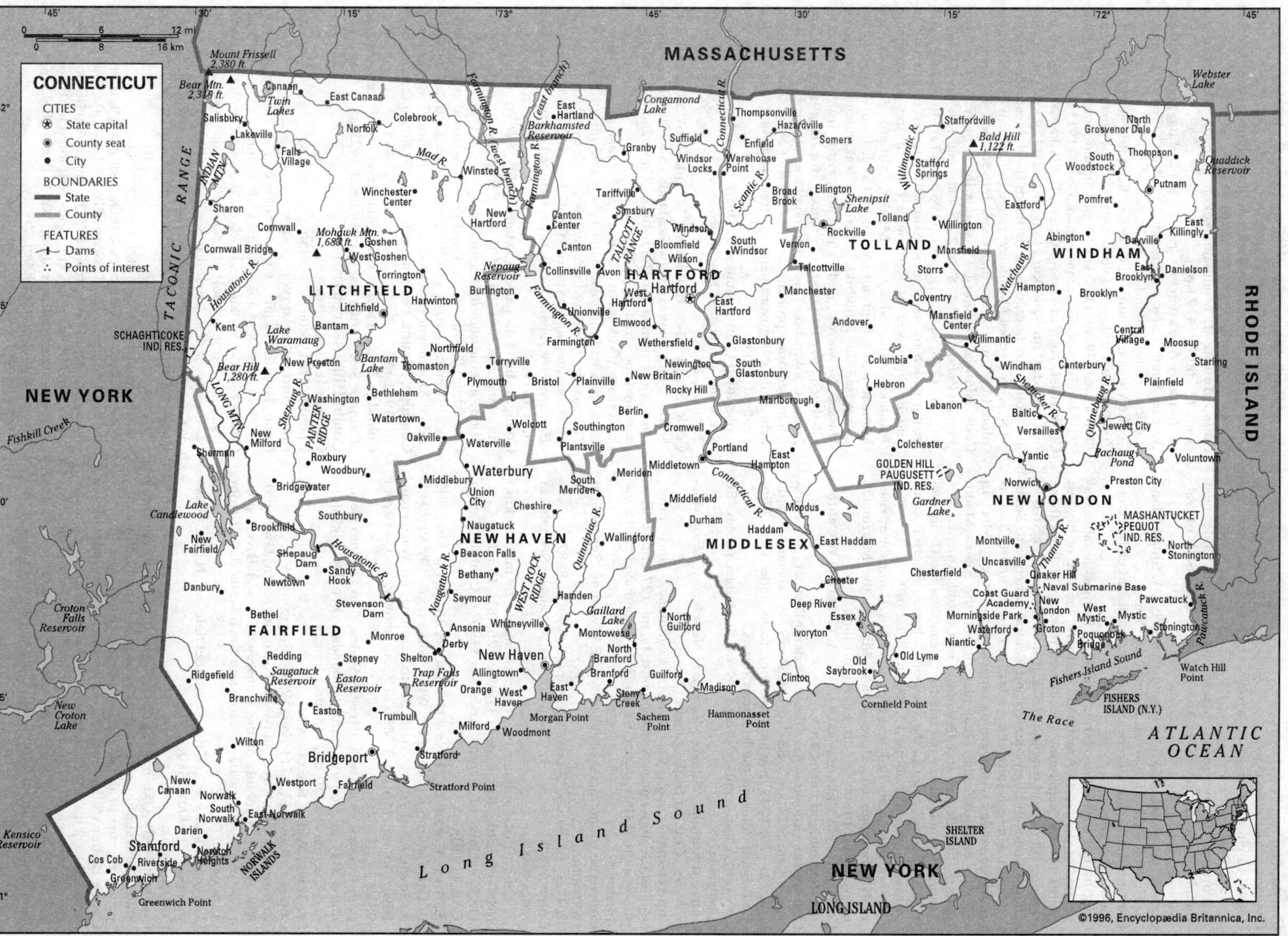
CONNECTICUT
CITIES
State capital
County seat
City
BOUNDARIES
State
County
FEATURES
Dams
Points of interest
0 6 12 mi
0 8 16 km
MASSACHUSETTS
RHODE ISLAND
NEW YORK
ATLANTIC OCEAN
Long Island Sound
LONG ISLAND
SHELTER ISLAND
FISHERS ISLAND (N.Y.)
Fishers Island Sound
The Race
LITCHFIELD
HARTFORD
TOLLAND
WINDHAM
NEW LONDON
MIDDLESEX
NEW HAVEN
FAIRFIELD
Hartford
New Haven
Bridgeport
Waterbury
Stamford
Connecticut R.
Housatonic R.
Thames R.
TACONIC RANGE
Mount Frissell 2,380 ft.
Bear Mtn. 2,316 ft.
Bald Hill 1,122 ft.
Mohawk Mtn. 1,683 ft.
Bear Hill 1,280 ft.
SCHAGHTICOKE IND. RES.
GOLDEN HILL PAUGUSETT IND. RES.
MASHANTUCKET PEQUOT IND. RES.
©1996, Encyclopædia Britannica, Inc.

Constantsa. See CONSTANŢA.
Constanz. See KONSTANZ.
Cons·ti·tu·ción \ˌkȯns-tē-tü-ˈsyōn\. **1.** Port, Argentina. See VILLA CONSTITUCIÓN.
2. Port and summer resort, Maule region, S cen. Chile, near mouth of the Maule River 163 mi. (262 km.) SSW of Valparaíso.
Con·sti·tu·tion Island \ˌkän-stə-ˈtü-shən, -ˈtyü-\. Small island in Hudson River opp. West Point, New York.
Continent, the. The European mainland as distinguished from the British Isles.
Continental Divide *also* **Great Divide.** The most notable watershed of the North American continent; the line of highest points of land separating the waters flowing W from those flowing N or E and extending SSE from NW Canada across W United States through Mexico and Central America to South America where it joins the Andes; in Canada and U.S. generally coincides with various ranges of the Rocky Mts.; in Mexico comprises the great plateau bet. the Sierra Madre ranges (Occidental and Oriental); in Central America lies generally much nearer the Pacific Ocean than the Caribbean Sea. Its central point is the state of Colorado where it comprises many peaks above 13,000 ft. (3962 m.).
Con·tooc·ook \kən-ˈtu̇-kək\. River, S New Hampshire; rises in Hillsborough co., flows N and NE into the Merrimack above Concord; ab. 80 mi. (129 km.) long.
Con·tra Cos·ta \ˈkän-trə-ˈkäs-tə, ˈkȯs-\. County in W California. See table at CALIFORNIA.
Con·tre·ras \kȯn-ˈtrā-räs\. Town, Federal District, cen. Mexico, 14 mi. (23 km.) SSW of Mexico City; scene of battle Aug. 19–20, 1847 in which the Americans under Gen. Winfield Scott defeated the Mexican forces.
Con·vent \ˈkän-ˌvent\. Village, ⊗ of St. James parish, SE Louisiana.
Convent Station. Village, Morris co., New Jersey, SE of Morristown; Coll. of St. Elizabeth (1899).
Con·ver·sa·no \ˌkȯn-ver-ˈsä-nō\. Commune, Bari prov., Puglia, SE Italy, near Adriatic coast 17 mi. (27 km.) ESE of the seaport of Bari; pop. (1981p) 20,507; medieval castle; cathedral.
Con·verse \ˈkän-vərs\. **1.** County in E Wyoming. See table at WYOMING.
2. City, Bexar co., S cen. Texas; pop. (1990c) 8887.
Con·way \ˈkän-wā\. **1.** County in cen. Arkansas. See table at ARKANSAS.
2. City, ⊗ of Faulkner co., cen. Arkansas, 25 mi. (40 km.) NNW of Little Rock; pop. (1990c) 26,481; Hendrix Coll. (1876), Univ. of Central Arkansas (1907), Central Baptist Coll. (1950).
3. Town, Carroll co., E New Hampshire, 36 mi. (58 km.) NNE of Laconia in S region of the White Mts.; pop. (1990c) 7940.
4. Town, ⊗ of Horry co., E South Carolina, on Waccamaw River 35 mi. (56 km.) NNE of Georgetown; pop. (1990c) 9819.
5. *or* **Con·wy** \ˈkän-wē\. River, N Wales; flows N, into Beaumaris Bay at Conwy; formed boundary bet. Denbighshire and Caernarvon; 30 mi. (48 km.) long.
6. Town, Wales. See CONWY 2.
Con·wy \ˈkän-wē\. **1.** River, Wales. See CONWAY 5.
2. *formerly* **Con·way** \ˈkän-wā\. Town and resort, Gwynedd, NW Wales, at mouth of the Conway (Conwy) River; pop. (1981p) 12,969; castle remains and town walls dating from 13th cent.
Con·yers \ˈkän-yərz\. City, ⊗ of Rockdale co., N cen. Georgia; pop. (1990c) 7380.
Coo. See KOS.
Coo·ber Pe·dy \ˈkü-bər-ˈpē-dē\. Town, cen. South Australia state, Australia, in barren, remote area of extreme high temperatures; one of the world's chief sources of opals.
Cooch Be·har \ˈküch-bə-ˈhär\. **1.** Former Indian state, NE India; 1321 sq. mi. (3421 sq. km.); ✱ Cooch Behar; once under the government of Bengal, later one of the states of the Eastern States Agency; since 1950 part of West Bengal state, India; in earlier times a powerful state in Assam; came under British control 1772.
2. *or* **Koch Bihar.** Town, its ✱, 265 mi. (426 km.) NNE of Calcutta; pop. (1991p) 71,028.
Cook \ˈku̇k\. Name of counties in three states of the U.S. See tables at GEORGIA, ILLINOIS, MINNESOTA.
Cook, Mount. **1.** Mountain, Yukon, Canada, SE of Mt. Logan; 13,760 ft. (4194 m.).
2. *formerly* **Ao·ran·gi** \au̇-ˈräŋ-ē\. Peak of the Southern Alps, W cen. South I., New Zealand; 12,349 ft. (3764 m.); highest peak in New Zealand.
Cooke \ˈku̇k\. County in N Texas. See table at TEXAS.
Cooke·ville \ˈku̇k-ˌvil, -vəl\. City, ⊗ of Putnam co., N cen. Tennessee, 79 mi. (127 km.) N of Chattanooga; pop. (1990c) 21,744; Tennessee Technological Univ. (1915).
Cook Inlet. Arm of Pacific Ocean, S Alaska, W of Kenai Penin.; ab. 150 mi. (240 km.) long; 80 mi. (129 km.) at its widest point; Anchorage is at its head; has largest tidal bore in U.S. with 45-foot (14-meter) range in one arm of it. First explored by English mariner Capt. James Cook 1778.
Cook Islands. Group of 15 islands in S Pacific Ocean, W of French Polynesia; lat. 8° to 23°S and long. 156° to 167°W; 92 sq. mi. (238 sq. km.); pop. (1986c) 17,614; includes a S group which by itself is occasionally referred to as Cook Is. and is comprised of Rarotonga (seat of the government), Aitutaki, Atiu, Mangaia, Mauke, Mitiaro, Takutea, and Manuae and a N group (Northern Cook Is. or Manihiki Is.) comprised of Manihiki, Penrhyn, Rakahanga, Pukapuka, Nassau, Suwarrow, and Palmerston; citrus fruit, copra; orig. inhabited by Polynesians; named for Englishman Capt. James Cook, who explored some of the islands in 1773; British protectorate proclaimed 1888; part of New Zealand 1901; achieved self-government in free association with New Zealand 1965.
Cooks·town \ˈku̇ks-ˌtau̇n\. **1.** District, cen. Northern Ireland. See table at IRELAND, NORTHERN.
2. Town, its ⊗.
Cook Strait *also* **Rau·ka·wa** \ˈrau̇-kə-wə\. Channel bet. North I. and South I., New Zealand; 16 to 90 mi. (26 to 145 km.) wide; named for Englishman Capt. James Cook, who explored the strait c. 1770.
Cook·town \ˈku̇k-ˌtau̇n\. Town, NE Queensland, Australia, on Coral Sea within Great Barrier Reef 295 mi. (475 km.) N of Townsville; trades with Papua New Guinea; place where English mariner and explorer Capt. James Cook beached the *Endeavor* for repairs 1770; town founded during Palmer gold rush 1873.
Cool·gar·die \kül-ˈgär-dē\. Municipality, SW Western Australia, Australia, 351 mi. (565 km.) E of Perth; pop. (1991c) 1063; in gold-mining region.
Coo·lidge \ˈkü-lij\. City, Pinal co., S Arizona; pop. (1990c) 6927; Central Arizona Coll. (1969); Casa Grande Ruins National Monument (see UNITED STATES, *National Monuments*).
Coolidge, Mount. Peak in Custer co., SW South Dakota; 6400 ft. (1951 m.).
Coolidge Dam. Dam across Gila River in SE cen. Arizona forming San Carlos Lake; completed 1928.
Coolin Hills. See CUILLIN HILLS.
Coomassie. See KUMASI.
Coombe Hill \ˈküm\. See CHILTERN HILLS.
Coon Butte. See METEOR CRATER.
Coon Rapids \ˈkün\. City, Anoka co., E Minnesota; pop. (1990c) 52,978; Anoka-Ramsey Community Coll. (1965).
Coo·per \ˈkü-pər, ˈku̇-\. **1.** River, S South Carolina; flows S into Charleston harbor; ab. 60 mi. (95 km.) long.
2. County in cen. Missouri. See table at MISSOURI.
3. City, ⊗ of Delta co., NE Texas; pop. (1990c) 2153.
Cooper City. City, Broward co., SE Florida; pop. (1990c) 20,791.
Cooper Mountain. See KENAI MOUNTAINS.
Cooper Creek *or* **Coo·pers Creek** \ˈkü-pərz, ˈku̇-\ *or esp. in its northeastern part* **Bar·coo River** \bär-ˈkü\. Intermittent river, Australia; flows from SW Queensland to NE South Australia; ab. 600 mi. (965 km.) long; explored by British 1845.
Coo·pers·burg \ˈkü-pərz-ˌbərg, ˈku̇-\. Borough, Lehigh co., E Pennsylvania; pop. (1990c) 2599.
Coo·pers·town \ˈkü-pərz-ˌtau̇n, ˈku̇-\. **1.** Residential village,

⊗ of Otsego co., cen. New York, at S end of Otsego Lake near Susquehanna River, 31 mi. (50 km.) SSE of Utica; pop. (1990c) 2180; founded late 1780s by William Cooper, father of novelist James Fenimore Cooper, who made it the setting of his *Leatherstocking Tales;* popularly believed to be site of origin of sport of baseball 1839; National Baseball Hall of Fame and Museum.

2. City, ⊗ of Griggs co., E North Dakota; pop. (1990c) 1247.

Coo·pers·ville \ˈkü-pərz-ˌvil, ˈku̇-, -vəl\. City, Ottawa co., Michigan, 14 mi. (22 km.) WNW of Grand Rapids; pop. (1990c) 3421.

Coorg *or* **Kurg** \ˈku̇rg\. Former kingdom in mountainous region of Western Ghats, S Asia. Ruled primarily by an independent Hindu dynasty from late 16th cent. until 1834 when overthrown by British; administered by chief commissioner of Mysore 1881–1947; area now in Karnataka state, India.

Coo·rong, The \kü-ˈräŋ\. Saltwater lagoon, the S arm of Lake Alexandrina, SE South Australia, Australia; 80 mi. (129 km.) long; extends SE parallel with the coast.

Coorong National Park. National park, SE South Australia, Australia, SSE of Adelaide; comprised of The Coorong and a long spit that separates it from the Indian Ocean; avian breeding grounds; kangaroos.

Co·os \kō-ˈäs, ˈkō-ˌäs\. County in N New Hampshire. See table at NEW HAMPSHIRE.

Coos \ˈküs\. Coastal county in SW Oregon. See table at OREGON.

Coo·sa \ˈkü-sə\. **1.** River, Alabama and Georgia; formed by confluence of Etowah and Oostanaula rivers, Floyd co., NW Georgia; flows W into Alabama and SW to join Tallapoosa River to form Alabama River; 286 mi. (460 km.) long.

2. County in E cen. Alabama. See table at ALABAMA.

Coosa Bald. Peak, Union co., N Georgia; 4287 ft. (1307 m.).

Coo·sa·wat·tee \ˌkü-sə-ˈwä-tē\. River, NW Georgia; rises in Gilmer co., flows SW to unite with the Conasauga River and form the Oostanaula River.

Coos Bay \ˈküs\. **1.** Inlet on coast of Coos co., SW Oregon, at mouth of the **Coos River.**

2. *until 1944* **Marsh·field** \ˈmärsh-ˌfēld\. City, Coos co., SW Oregon, on Coos Bay inlet of Pacific Ocean; pop. (1990c) 15,076; port of entry; Southwestern Oregon Community Coll. (1961).

Co·pa·ca·bana Beach \ˌkō-pə-kə-ˈba-nə\ *or Port.* **Praia de Co·pa·ca·bana** \ˈprī-ə-dē-ˌkō-pȧ-kȧ-ˈbȧ-nə\. Beach on Atlantic Ocean, SE part of city of Rio de Janeiro, Brazil, at W side of entrance to Guanabara Bay; resort.

Co·pa·hué \ˌkō-pä-ˈwā\. Volcanic peak, W Neuquén prov., W Argentina, on Chilean border; 9875 ft. (3010 m.).

Co·pa·is \kō-ˈpā-əs\; *Gk.* **Ko·pa·ïs** \ˌkō-pä-ˈēs\ *or* **To·po·lia** \tə-ˈpōl-yə\. Former lake in N Boeotia, Greece; received the Cephisus; formed extensive marshland, at several periods drained by underground channels to Euboean Sea; in 19th cent. properly drained and much ground reclaimed for agriculture.

Co·pán \kō-ˈpän\. **1.** Department of W Honduras. See table at HONDURAS.

2. Ruined city, W Honduras. See SANTA ROSA 6.

Cop·co No. 1 \ˈkäp-kō\. Dam across Klamath River, N Siskiyou co., N California; height 239 ft. (73 m.); completed 1922; impounds water for waterpower.

Co·pen·ha·gen \ˌkō-pən-ˈhā-gən, -ˈhä-, ˈkō-pən-ˌ\ *or Danish* **Kø·ben·havn** \ˌkœ-bən-ˈhau̇n\. **1.** County of Denmark, on Sjælland I. See table at DENMARK.

2. Commune, ✻ of Denmark, on E coast of Sjælland I., and N part of Amager I., Denmark; pop. (1989e) 467,850, with suburbs, **Greater Copenhagen,** (1990e) 1,337,114; Denmark's leading commercial center; shipping center; shipbuilding, brewing, machinery; Univ. of Copenhagen (1479), Technical Univ. of Denmark (1829); Amalienborg Palace (residence of the Danish monarch since 1794), Charlottenborg Palace (now Royal Academy of Art), Christiansborg Palace where parliament meets (rebuilt early 20th cent.); botanical gardens (1874); town hall (1894–1905); Tivoli amusement park; Trinity Church with noted round tower; National Museum, Thorvaldsen Museum; cathedral (rebuilt after 1807); statue of author Hans Christian Andersen's Little Mermaid; cultural center of northern literature and art.

History: A fishing village fortified by Bishop Absalon in 12th cent.; given municipal privileges 1254; frequently attacked and taken by Hanseatic League; made ✻ of kingdom of Denmark 1443; besieged unsuccessfully by Charles X Gustav of Sweden 1658–59; scene of treaty 1660 by which Denmark ceded to Sweden the S part of Scandinavian Penin.; fires 1728 and 1795; harbor scene of destruction of Danish fleet by British 1801; bombarded by British 1807; during WWII occupied by Germans 1940–45.

Cö·pe·nick *or* **Kö·pe·nick** \ˈkœ-pə-ˌnik\. Former commune, now part of E Berlin, Germany; scene of trial of Crown Prince Frederick of Prussia (later Frederick the Great) 1730 after his attempt to escape to England.

Co·per·ti·no \ˌkō-per-ˈtē-nō\. Commune, Lecce prov., Puglia, SE Italy; pop. (1989c) 23,711; Renaissance castle with Angevin traces.

Co·piague \ˈkō-ˌpāg, -ˌpeg\. Unincorporated settlement, Suffolk co., SE New York, on Long Island W of Lindenhurst; pop. (1990c) 20,769.

Co·pi·ah \kə-ˈpī-ə\. County in SW Mississippi. See table at MISSISSIPPI.

Co·pia·pó \ˌkō-pyä-ˈpō\ *also* **San Fran·cis·co de la Sel·va** \ˌsän-frän-ˈsēs-kō-ˌthā-lä-ˈsāl-bä\. **1.** River, Atacama prov., N cen. Chile; flows NW and W into the Pacific Ocean.

2. Town, ✻ of Atacama region, N cen. Chile, on the Copiapó River ab. 42 mi. (68 km.) N of Santiago; pop. (1992c) 79,268; silver and copper-processing center; formerly ✻ of Atacama prov.; settled 1540; frequently damaged by earthquakes.

Cop·lay \ˈkä-plē\. Borough, Lehigh co., E Pennsylvania, on Lehigh River; pop. (1990c) 3267.

Cop·pa·ro \kō-ˈpär-ō\. Commune, Ferrara prov., Emilia-Romagna, N Italy, ENE of the commune of Ferrara; pop. (1981p) 20,773; in Po Delta, formerly marshland.

Cop·pell \ˈkä-pəl\. City, Dallas co., Texas, N of Dallas-Fort Worth International Airport; pop. (1990c) 16,881.

Cop·pe·na·me \ˌkō-pə-ˈnä-mə\. River, N Suriname; flows N into Atlantic Ocean; 250 mi. (402 km.) long.

Cop·per \ˈkä-pər\. River, S Alaska; flows S around W end of Wrangell Mts. and through Chugach Mts. to Gulf of Alaska; ab. 300 mi. (480 km.) long.

Cop·per·as Cove \ˈkä-pə-rəs\. City, Coryell co., cen. Texas, 53 mi. (85 km.) SW of Waco; pop. (1990c) 24,079.

Cop·per·mine \ˈkä-pər-ˌmīn\. River, N mainland part of Canada; rises in Barren Grounds, along Northwest Territories - Nunavut border, flows NW and N to Coronation Gulf; 525 mi. (845 km.) long.

Coptos. See QIFT.

Co·pul·hué, Pa·so \ˈpä-sō-ˌkō-pül-ˈwā\. Mountain pass in Andes on boundary bet. Neuquén prov., W Argentina, and Bío-Bío prov., S cen. Chile; alt. 6891 ft. (2100 m.).

Co·quei·ros, Point \kō-ˈkā-rüs\ *or Braz.* **Pon·ta de Co·queiros** \ˈpōⁿ-tə-dē-\; *formerly* **Point Pe·dras** \ˈpā-drəs\. Cape extending into Atlantic Ocean on SE coast of Paraíba state, E Brazil; most easterly point of South America, 7°38′S, 34°47′W.

Co·quet \ˈkō-kət\. **1.** Island in the North Sea off NE coast of Northumberland, N England.

2. River, N Northumberland, N England; rises in the Cheviot Hills, flows E into the North Sea; ab. 40 mi. (65 km.) long.

Co·quil·hat·ville \ˌkō-kē-yät-ˈvēl, ˌkō-kē-ˈat-ˌvil, kō-ˈkē-ə-ˌvil\. **1.** Administrative region, Democractic Rep. of the Congo. See *Équateur* in table at ZAIRE.

2. Town, Democratic Rep. of the Congo. See MBANDAKA.

Co·quille \kō-ˈkēl\. **1.** River, SW Oregon; formed by confluence of branches in Coos co., flows N and W into Pacific Ocean; with longest branch ab. 70 mi. (113 km.) long; navigable to Coquille.

2. City, ⊗ of Coos co., SW Oregon, on Coquille River 13 mi. (21 km.) S of the city of Coos Bay; pop. (1990c) 4121.

Co·quim·bo \kō-'kēm-bō\. **1.** Region of cen. Chile. See table at CHILE.

2. Port, Coquimbo region, cen. Chile, 215 mi. (346 km.) N of Valparaíso; pop. (1982c) 62,186; the port for La Serena.

Cor·al Bay \'kȯr-əl, 'kär-\. Bay on E end of St. John I., Virgin Is. of the U.S., West Indies.

Coral Ga·bles \'gā-bəlz\. City, Miami-Dade co., SE Florida, on Biscayne Bay S and W of the S part of Miami; pop. (1990c) 40,091; resort; tropical botanical garden; Univ. of Miami (1925); a planned community with notable landscaping; incorp. 1925.

Coral Harbour. Hamlet, Nunavut, Canada, on inlet on S coast of Southampton I.; pop. (1991c) 578; airport.

Coral Sea. Part of the Pacific Ocean bet. Queensland, Australia, on the W, and Vanuatu and New Caledonia on the E; bordered on N by Papua New Guinea and Solomon Is.; N part known as the Solomon Sea (*q.v.*). Scene during WWII of U.S. victory over Japanese May 1942.

Coral Sea Islands Territory. External territory of Australia, consisting of several uninhabited islets bet. 10°S and 23°30′S and bet. 154°E and 158°E .

Coral Springs. City, Broward co., SE Florida, NW of Fort Lauderdale and on edge of the Everglades; pop. (1990c) 79,443.

Cor·al·ville \'kȯr-əl-ˌvil\. City, Johnson co., E Iowa, bordering Iowa City; pop. (1990c) 10,347.

Co·rang·a·mite, Lake \kə-'raŋ-gə-ˌmīt\. Lake, Victoria, Australia, 50 mi. (81 km.) W of Port Philip Bay; ab. 100 sq. mi. (259 sq. km.).

Corantijn. See COURANTYNE.

Co·ra·op·o·lis \ˌkȯr-ē-'ä-pə-lis\. Borough, Allegheny co., SW Pennsylvania, on Ohio River; pop. (1990c) 6747; Robert Morris Coll. (1921); settled c. 1760.

Co·rato \kō-'rä-tō\. Commune, Bari prov., Puglia, SE Italy, 25 mi. (40 km.) WNW of the seaport of Bari; pop. (1991p) 42,473.

Cor·beil–Es·sonnes \kȯr-ˌbā-e-'sȯn\. Commune, Essonne dept., N France, at confluence of Seine and Essonne rivers 16 mi. (26 km.) SSE of Paris; pop. (1990c) 40,768; long noted for flourmills. Under Carolingian kings **Corbeil** (*or anc.* **Cor·bi·li·um** \kȯr-'bē-lē-əm\) ✻ of a countship; annexed to France 1108; treaty bet. Louis IX of France and James I of Aragon signed here 1258.

Cor·bie \kȯr-'bē\. Commune, Somme dept., N France, 10 mi. (16 km.) NE of Amiens; ruins of Benedictine abbey, founded 7th cent. by Bathilde, queen of Clovis II; damaged in WWI.

Corbilium. See CORBEIL–ESSONNES.

Cor·bin \'kȯr-bən\. City, Knox and Whitley cos., SE Kentucky; pop. (1990c) 7419.

Cor·bridge \'kȯr-brij\. Market town, Northumberland, N England, on N bank of Tyne River; nearby is site of Corstopitum, Roman military post; ✻ of Northumbria in 8th cent.

Cor·by \'kȯr-bē\. Town, Northamptonshire, cen. England; pop. (1991p) 52,300.

Cor·co·ran \'kȯr-kə-rən\. City, Kings co., SW cen. California, 45 mi. (72 km.) SE of Fresno; pop. (1990c) 13,364.

Cor·co·va·do \ˌkȯr-kō-'vä-dü\. **1.** Peak on S side of city of Rio de Janeiro, SE Brazil; 2310 ft. (704 m.); has gigantic concrete figure of Christ the Redeemer on its top; funicular railway; part of a national park.

2. Volcanic peak in the Andes, S Chile, opp. Chiloé I.; 7550 ft. (2301 m.).

Corcovado Gulf. Inlet of Pacific Ocean lying bet. Chiloé I. and the mainland of SW Chile.

Corcyra. See CORFU.

Corcyra Nigra. See KORČULA 1.

Cor·dele \kȯr-'dēl, 'kȯr-ˌ\. City, ⊗ of Crisp co., SW cen. Georgia, 35 mi. (56 km.) NE of Albany; pop. (1990c) 10,321.

Cor·dil·le·ra \ˌkȯr-t͟hē-'yā-rä, -t͟hēl-\. **1.** Department of cen. Paraguay. See table at PARAGUAY.

2. Autonomous region of the Philippines. See table at PHILIPPINES.

Cordillera Cantábrica. See CANTABRIAN MOUNTAINS.

Cordillera Cen·tral \ˌsen-'träl\. **1.** Range of the Andes (*q.v.*) in Colombia.

2. Chief range of the Dominican Republic; includes Pico Duarte, 10,414 ft. (3174 m.) high.

3. Range of the Andes extending NW and SE in N cen. Peru, E of the Marañón.

4. The main mountain range of N Luzon, Philippines, extending from N edge of its cen. plain to N coast of the island; highest point Mt. Pulog 9606 ft. (2928 m.); unites with the Caraballo Mts. (*q.v.*) in cen. Luzon.

5. Mountain range in SW cen. Puerto Rico; highest peak Cerro de Punta 4389 ft. (1338 m.).

Cordillera de Agostini. See ANDES.

Cordillera de Amambay. See SERRA DE AMAMBAÍ.

Cordillera de Ca·ra·ba·ya \t͟hā-ˌkä-rä-'bä-yä\. A range of the Andes (*q.v.*), SE Peru, E of Cuzco; highest point Nevado Ausangate 20,945 ft. (6384 m.).

Cordillera de los Andes. See ANDES.

Cordillera de Mé·ri·da \t͟hā-'mā-rē-t͟hä\ *also* **Sier·ra Ne·va·da de Mérida** \'syār-rä-nā-'bä-t͟hä\. Range of mountains extending NE and SW in W Venezuela; highest point Pico Bolívar, 16,427 ft. (5007 m.); a NE extension of the Andes.

Cordillera de Ta·la·man·ca \t͟hā-ˌtä-lä-'mäŋ-kä\. Range in S Costa Rica, extending SE into W Panama; highest point Chirripó Grande 12,533 ft. (3820 m.).

Cordillera de Ve·ne·zue·la \t͟hā-ˌbā-nā-'thwā-lä\. Mountain range in N Venezuela; highest point ab. 8530 ft. (2600 m.).

Cordillera Domeyko. See ANDES.

Cordillera de Guanacaste. See GUANACASTE, CORDILLERA DE.

Cordillera Huayhuash. See ANDES.

Cordillera Ma·rí·ti·ma \mä-'rē-tē-mä\. Name of the Cordillera Occidental in Peru. See ANDES.

Cordillera Occidental. See ANDES.

Cordillera Orien·tal \ˌōr-yen-'täl\. **1.** E range of the Andes in cen. Bolivia.

2. E range of the Andes in Colombia. See ANDES.

3. E range of the Andes in N Peru.

4. E range of the Andes in SE Peru; highest point Salcantay 20,574 ft. (6271 m.).

Cordillera Re·al \rā-'äl\. **1.** Range of the Andes, W Bolivia. See ANDES.

2. Range of the Andes in Ecuador. See ANDES.

Cór·do·ba \'kȯr-t͟hō-bä\. **1.** Province of N cen. Argentina. See table at ARGENTINA.

2. City, its ✻, on the Primero River 387 mi. (623 km.) NW of Buenos Aires; munic. area pop. (1991p) 1,179,067; glass, leather, textiles; fruit and cereals grown nearby; transportation center; National Univ. of Córdoba (1613), Catholic Univ. (1956); cathedral; observatory; city founded 1573.

3. Department of N Colombia. See table at COLOMBIA.

4. Town, Veracruz state, E Mexico, 55 mi. (89 km.) WSW of the seaport of Veracruz; munic. pop. (1990p) 150,428; alt. 2700 ft. (823 m.); coffee and sugar processing. Treaty signed here 1821 granting Mexico independence from Spain.

5. *or Eng.* **Cor·do·va** \'kȯr-də-və\. Province of S Spain. See table at SPAIN.

6. *or Eng.* **Cor·do·va** \'kȯr-də-və\; *anc.* **Cor·du·ba** \'kȯr-dů-bə, -dyů-\. City, ✻ of Córdoba prov., S Spain, on Guadalquivir River 73 mi. (118 km.) ENE of Seville; pop. (1991p) 300,229; textiles; brewing and distilling; tourism. Roman and Moorish remains, incl. an 8th cent. mosque (now a cathedral) built by ‘Abd ar-Raḥmān I, an alcazar, and a Moorish bridge over the Guadalquivir.

History: Probably founded by Carthaginians; ruled by Romans, Visigoths, and 711–1236 by the Moors; in 756 A.D. became independent of Damascus caliphate and under Umayyad ruler ‘Abd ar-Raḥmān I and his successors, became seat of emirate, later the Western Caliphate of Córdoba; flourishing ✻ of the most powerful state in Spain (at height in 10th cent.); under Moorish rule became renowned throughout Europe as home of most brilliant intellectual achievements of its time; declined gradually after overthrow of caliphate 1031; captured by Ferdinand III of Castile 1236; pillaged by French 1808.

Cor·do·va \kȯr-ˈdō-və\. **1.** City, Walker co., NW cen. Alabama, 28 mi. (45 km.) NW of Birmingham; pop. (1990c) 2623.
2. Coast city, SE Alaska, on inlet at SE corner of Prince William Sound; pop. (1990c) 2110; founded and flourished as a railroad terminus for copper-mining operations prior to WWII.

Cór·do·va Island \ˈkȯr-thō-bä, ˈkȯr-də-və\. Tract of land on N bank of the Rio Grande forming an enclave of Mexico within the city of El Paso, Texas; 385 acres (156 hectares); N 193 acres (78 hectares) ceded to U.S. in return for Chamizal (*q.v.*) 1963.

Corduba. See CÓRDOBA 6.

Corduene. See GORDYENE.

Core Sound \ˈkōr\. Sound, SE North Carolina, in Atlantic Ocean, bet. mainland of Carteret co., and **Core Banks,** one of chain of islands or reefs, having Cape Lookout at S tip.

Cor·fin·i·um \kȯr-ˈfi-nē-əm\. Ancient town, Samnium, Italy, ab. 7 mi. (11 km.) N of Sulmo, on the Valerian Way; ✻ of short-lived republic of Italia, formed by allies during Social War (90–88 B.C.).

Cor·fu \kȯr-ˈfü; ˈkȯr-ˌfü, -ˌfyü\ *or Gk.* **Kér·ky·ra** \ˈker-kē-rä\; *anc.* **Cor·cy·ra** \kȯr-ˈsī-rə\. **1.** One of the Ionian Is. in the Ionian Sea off the coast of SW Albania and NW Greece; 40 mi. (64 km.) long by 7 to 17 mi. (11 to 27 km.) wide; 229 sq. mi. (593 sq. km.); with Paxos forms a department of Greece (see table at GREECE); fertile, produces olive oil, figs, oranges, lemons, and wine.

History: Settled by Corinthians c. 734 B.C.; probably the **Sche·ria** \ˈskir-ē-ə\ of epic poet Homer; off its coasts first naval battle of Greek history fought bet. Corfu and Corinth c. 664 B.C.; c. 435 B.C. sought help of Athens against Corinth, one of the causes of Peloponnesian War; became Roman possession 229 B.C.; Venetian from 1386 to 1797, when it took the name Corfu; under British administration 1815–64; since 1864 part of Greece. In WWI refuge of Serbs and scene of signing July 20, 1917 of pact which estab. new Serb, Croat, and Slovene state; in WWII occupied by Italians and Germans.

2. Seaport city, ✻ of Corfu dept., Ionian Is., W Greece, on E coast of the island; pop. (1991p) 36,875; palace, 16th cent. Venetian fortress.

Corfu Straits *or* **Corfu Channel.** Narrow channel bet. NE Corfu I. and SW coast of Albania.

Co·ria del Río \ˈkȯr-ē-ä-thel-ˈrē-ō\. Commune, Sevilla prov., SW Spain, on Guadalquivir River 9 mi. (15 km.) SSW of Seville; pop. (1991c) 21,928.

Co·ri·glia·no \ˌkō-rē-ˈlyä-nō\ *or in full* **Corigliano Ca·la·bro** \ˈkä-lä-ˌbrō\. Commune, Cosenza prov., Calabria, S Italy, near W shore of Gulf of Taranto 25 mi. (40 km.) NNE of the commune of Cosenza; pop. (1989c) 39,358; castle.

Corinium. See CIRENCESTER.

Cor·inth \ˈkȯr-ənth, ˈkär-\. **1.** City, ⊗ of Alcorn co., NE Mississippi; pop. (1990c) 11,820; textiles, dairy products; severe fighting Oct. 3–4, 1862, when Union forces under Gen. William Starke Rosecrans repulsed Confederates under Gen. Earl Van Dorn.
2. Village, Saratoga co., E New York, on Hudson River 28 mi. (45 km.) NE of Amsterdam; pop. (1990c) 2760.
3. *or Gk.* **Kó·rin·thos** \ˈkȯr-ēn-thōs\ *or Lat.* **Co·rin·thia** \kə-ˈrin-thē-ə\. Division of ancient Greece, occupying greater part of Isthmus of Corinth and part of NE Peloponnese; bounded on N and W by Gulf of Corinth, on NE by Megaris, on E by Saronic Gulf, on S by Argolis, and on W by Sicyonia.
4. Department of Peloponnese, Greece. See table at GREECE.
5. City, ✻ of Corinth dept., NE Peloponnese, Greece, on Gulf of Corinth; 3 mi. (5 km.) ENE of site of ancient city of Corinth; pop. (1991c) 28,903. See ACROCORINTHUS.

History: Although inhabited by c. 3000 B.C., ancient Corinth appears to have been founded c. 9th cent. B.C. by Dorian invaders of Greece; by position on Isthmus of Corinth became leading commercial city and founded Siracusa, Corcyra (see CORFU) c. 734 B.C., and numerous other colonies, incl. Potidaea c. 600 B.C.; member of Peloponnesian League in Peloponnesian War (see SPARTA 7); in Corinthian War 395–387 B.C., joined Athens, Thebes, and Árgos against Sparta; joined Achaean League 3d cent. B.C.; destroyed by Roman Gen. Mummius 146 B.C.; refounded by Roman colony sent out by Gen. Julius Caesar 44 B.C.; scene of early mission of St. Paul c. 51 A.D.; taken from Byzantine Empire by Latin Crusaders early 13th cent.; conquered by Ottoman Turks 1458; controlled by Venice 1687–1715, Turks 1715–1822, and Greece from 1822; old city destroyed by earthquake and new city founded 1858; excavation of ancient site begun 1896. In WWII occupied by Germans 1941–44.

Corinth, Gulf of *also* **Gulf of Le·pan·to** \ˈle-pän-ˌtō, li-ˈpan-tō\ *or Gk.* **Ko·rin·thi·a·kós Kól·pos** \kö-ˌrēn-thē-ä-ˈkös-ˈköl-ˌpös\; *anc.* **Si·nus Cor·in·thi·a·cus** \ˈsī-nəs-ˌkȯr-ən-ˈthī-ə-kəs\. Inlet of Mediterranean Sea, cen. Greece, NE of the Peloponnese, extending E from Lepanto Strait to Isthmus of Corinth (*q.v.*).

Corinth, Isthmus of *or Gk.* **Isth·mos Ko·rin·thou** \ēsth-ˈmös-kö-ˈrēn-thü\. Isthmus connecting Peloponnese with E cen. Greece; 4 to 8 mi. (6 to 13 km.) wide, 20 mi. (32 km.) long; crossed by a ship canal (4 mi. or 6 km. long; constructed 1881–93) connecting the Gulf of Corinth with the Saronic Gulf.

Corinthia. See CORINTH 3.

Co·rin·to \kə-ˈrēn-tō\. Seaport, Chinandega dept., NW Nicaragua; pop. (1985e) 24,250; most important port in Nicaragua; exports coffee and sugar.

Co·ri·o·li \kə-ˈrī-ə-ˌlī\. Ancient Volscian town, Latium, Italy; according to tradition, scene of siege 493 B.C. by Romans under the legendary hero Gnaeus Marcius Coriolanus.

Co·ris·co \kō-ˈris-kō\. Island, Equatorial Guinea, in Bight of Biafra, off SW coast of the country's mainland; 6 sq. mi. (16 sq. km.).

Corizza. See KORÇË.

Cork \ˈkȯrk\. **1.** County, Munster prov., SW Ireland; ⊗ Cork; dairy farming; livestock; tourism. See table at IRELAND.
2. City, its ⊗, at mouth of Lee River at head of Cork Harbour 15 mi. (24 km.) from the Atlantic Ocean; pop. (1991p) 127,024; seaport; leather goods; bacon curing; breweries, distilleries, oil storage depots; its deepwater port is Cobh (*q.v.*); seat of a constituent college of the National Univ. of Ireland (1908). Originated as monastery c. 7th cent.; frequently ravaged (esp. 9th cent.) and eventually settled by the Danes; passed to Henry II of England 1172; taken by Parliamentarian forces under Oliver Cromwell 1649 and John Churchill, earl (later duke) of Marlborough, 1690; heavily damaged 1920 during Irish uprising against English.

Cork Harbour. Harbor on S coast of Ireland; 1 mi. (2 km.) wide at the entrance, expands to width of 4 mi. (6 km.) inland.

Cor·le·o·ne \ˌkōr-lā-ˈō-nā\. Commune, Palermo prov., NW cen. Sicily, Italy; pop. (1991p) 11,261; possibly of Arabic origin.

Çor·lu *or* **Chor·lu** \chȯr-ˈlü\. Town, Tekirdağ prov., Turkey in Europe, NE of the seaport of Tekirdağ.

Cormantyne. See KORMANTINE.

Corn Belt \ˈkȯrn\. Region, E cen. U.S., of major corn production; usu. thought to include W Ohio, Indiana, Illinois, Iowa, S Minnesota, E South Dakota, E Nebraska, E Kansas, and N Missouri.

Cor·ne·lia \kȯr-ˈnēl-yə\. City, Habersham co., NE Georgia, 39 mi. (63 km.) NNW of Athens; pop. (1990c) 3219.

Cor·nell, Mount \kȯr-ˈnel\. Peak in the Catskill Mts., Ulster co., SE New York; 3906 ft. (1191 m.).

Cor·nel·lá de Llo·bre·gat \ˌkȯr-nā-ˈlyä-thā-ˌlyō-brā-ˈgät\; *sometimes shortened to* **Cornellá.** Commune, Barcelona prov., E Spain, ab. 5 mi. (8 km.) WSW of the city of Barcelona; pop. (1991c) 84,927; a suburb of Barcelona.

\ə\ abut \ˋə\ matches \ᵊ\ kitten, Fr table \ər\ further \a\ ash \ā\ ace \ä\ cot, cart \à\ Fr bac \au̇\ out \b\ Span Avila \ch\ chin \e\ bet \ē\ easy \g\ go \i\ hit \ī\ ice \j\ job \k\ Ger ich, Buch \ⁿ\ Fr vin \ŋ\ sing \ō\ go \ö\ all \ȯ\ law \œ\ Fr bœuf \œ̄\ Fr feu \ȯi\ boy \th\ thin \th\ this \ü\ loot \u̇\ foot \ue\ Ger füllen \ue̅\ Fr rue \y\ yet \ʸ\ Fr digne \ˈdēnʸ\, nuit \ˈnwʸē\ \yü\ few \yu̇\ fury \zh\ vision

Cor·ner Brook \'kȯ(ə)r-nər\. City, W Newfoundland, Canada, at head of estuary of Humber River; pop. (1991c) 22,410; fishing.

Corneto. See TARQUINIA.

Cor·niche \kȯr-'nēsh\. Road, actually three more or less parallel highways along the Riviera, France, from Nice to Menton; ab. 19 mi. (31 km.) long; cuts across the precipitous cliffs (Fr. *corniche,* "shelf, cornice") of the Maritime Alps: (1) Grande Corniche, the upper road, part of great military road built by French Emperor Napoléon 1806; for through and heavy traffic; (2) Petite Corniche, the lower road, along the coast; and (3) Moyenne Corniche, the middle road, affording better access to the towns.

Cor·ning \'kȯr-niŋ\. **1.** City, a ⊗ of Clay co., NE corner of Arkansas; pop. (1990c) 3323.
2. City, Tehama co., N California, 5 mi. (8 km.) W of Sacramento River and 21 mi. (34 km.) NW of Chico; pop. (1990c) 5870.
3. City, ⊗ of Adams co., SW Iowa; pop. (1990c) 1806.
4. City, Steuben co., S New York, on Chemung River 14 mi. (23 km.) W of Elmira; pop. (1990c) 11,938; manufactured the 200-inch (508-centimeter) lens for the telescope of Mt. Palomar observatory in California 1934; Corning Community Coll. (1956); settled c. 1789.

Corn Islands \'kȯrn\. Two small islands, **Is·la del Maíz Gran·de** \'ēs-lä-t͟hel-'mīs-'grän-dā\ (**Great Corn Island**) and **Isla del Maíz Pe·que·ña** \pā-'kā-nyä\ (**Little Corn Island**), in Caribbean Sea ab. 40 mi. (64 km.) off E coast of Nicaragua; 4 sq. mi. (10 sq. km.); leased by Nicaragua to U.S. 1916–71.

Cor·no, Mon·te \'mȯn-tā-'kȯr-nō\. Peak, in the Gran Sasso d'Italia, Abruzzi Apennines; highest peak in the Apennines. See table at APENNINES.

Cor·nouaille \kȯr-'nwī\. Ancient region and medieval county, W France, now part of Finistère, Côtes-du-Nord, and Morbihan depts.; ✻ Quimper. Settled by Celts from Cornwall 6th cent.; united with duchy of Brittany 1066.

Corn·wall \'kȯrn-,wȯl, -wəl\. **1.** Borough, Lebanon co., SE cen. Pennsylvania, 17 mi. (27 km.) N of Lancaster; pop. (1990c) 3231; iron ore deposits.
2. City, ⊗ of Stormont, Dundas, and Glengarry co., SE Ontario, Canada, on St. Lawrence River 53 mi. (85 km.) SE of Ottawa; pop. (1991c) 47,137; chemicals, paper.
3. Former county, extreme SW part of England; now part of Cornwall and Isles of Scilly co.; forms a peninsula ab. 75 mi. (120 km.) long (45 mi. or 72 km. wide at base), terminating in Land's End; has rocky coast, much indented. Highest point Brown Willy 1375 ft. (419 m.).
Rivers: Tamar, Camel.
Chief towns: St. Austell, Penzance, Falmouth, Truro.
Chief industries: Raising of dairy cattle, fishing; tourism; formerly a tin-mining region (thought by some to be source of tin for Phoenicians in ancient times).
History: Many remains (such as cromlechs and dolmens) of early inhabitants. Anciently called Belerium; given by William the Conqueror to his brother Robert as an earldom; created a duchy 1337 by Edward III for his son and still is appanage of the eldest living son of the sovereign.

Cornwall and Isles of Scil·ly \'si-lē\. County, SW England. See table at ENGLAND.

Corn·wal·lis Island \kȯrn-'wä-lis\. One of the Parry Is., cen. Arctic Archipelago, Nunavut, Canada, bet. Bathurst I. and Devon I., N of Barrow Strait; 2701 sq. mi. (6996 sq. km.); airfield, weather station; island discovered by English explorer Sir William Parry 1819.

Cornwall on Hudson; *formerly* **Cornwall.** Village, Orange co., SE New York, S of Newburgh; pop. (1990c) 3093; summer resort on Hudson River at foot of Storm King Mt.

Co·ro \'kō-rō\; *formerly* **San·ta Ana de Coro** \'sän-tä-'ä-nä-t͟hä-\. Town, ✻ of Falcón state, NW Venezuela, SE of Gulf of Coro at base of Paraguaná Penin.; pop. (1990p) 124,616; La Vela (La Vela de Coro), its port, ab. 7 mi. (11 km.) ENE; founded 1527; for a few years before 1578 ✻ of Venezuela; site of revolutionary Francisco de Miranda's unsuccessful attempt 1806 to free Venezuela from Spain.

Co·ro·a·tá \,kȯr-ü-ə-'tä\. Municipality, Maranhão state, NE Brazil, ab. 100 mi. (161 km.) WSW of São Luís; pop. (1991p) 70,348.

Coroch. See ÇORUH.

Cor·o·man·del Channel \,kȯr-ə-'man-dəl\. Strait bet. S end of Great Barrier I. and mainland of North I., New Zealand; ab. 10 mi. (16 km.) wide.

Coromandel Coast. Coast of SE India from Point Calimere N to mouths of Krishna River; this section of Bay of Bengal shoreline is low with no good harbors; beaten by heavy seas throughout the year, esp. during NE monsoon (Oct. to Apr.); chief ports: Nellore, Madras, Pondicherry, Cuddalore, Tranquebar, and Nagappattinam.

Co·ron \kō-'rōn\. **1.** Island, Calamian Group, W Philippines, off SE coast of Busuanga I.; 27 sq. mi. (70 sq. km.); high, rocky, and sparsely inhabited.
2. Municipality, N Palawan prov., Philippines, on SE coast; pop. (1980c) 25,129; chief town of Busuanga I.

Co·ro·na \kə-'rō-nə\. City, Riverside co., SE California, 12 mi. (19 km.) SW of San Bernardino; pop. (1990c) 76,095; shipping center for citrus fruits.

Cor·o·na·do \,kȯr-ə-'nä-dō\. Residential city, San Diego co., SW California, on bay opp. the city of San Diego; pop. (1990c) 26,540.

Co·ro·na·do Bay \,kō-rō-'nä-t͟hō\. Widemouthed inlet of Pacific Ocean on W coast of Costa Rica.

Cor·o·na·tion Gulf \,kȯr-ə-'nā-shən\. Gulf, Nunavut, Canada, bet. the mainland and S Victoria I., ab. 109° to 115°W.

Coronation Island. Largest island of the South Orkney group, South Atlantic Ocean, 60°37′S, 45°35′W; 193 sq. mi. (500 sq. km.).

Cor·o·nea \,kȯr-ə-'nē-ə\. Town in W part of ancient Boeotia, E cen. Greece, SW of Lake Copais; scene of battles: (1) 447 B.C. Boeotians defeated the Athenians, and (2) 394 B.C. Spartans under Agesilaus in the Corinthian War defeated the coalition led by Thebes.

Co·ro·nel \,kō-rō-'nel\. Seaport, Concepción prov., S cen. Chile, 17 mi. (27 km.) S of the city of Concepción; pop. (1992p) 74,090; important coal deposits; founded 1851, was granted city status 1875; scene of a naval battle Nov. 1, 1914 bet. British squadron under Rear Adm. Sir Christopher Cradock and German squadron under Adm. Maximilian von Spee in which British were defeated, Cradock himself going down with his flagship *Good Hope.* See *History* at FALKLAND ISLANDS.

Coronel Ovie·do \ō-'b͟yā-t͟hō\. City, ✻ of Caaguazú dept., E Paraguay; munic. pop. (1992p) 38,250.

Co·ro·pu·na, Ne·va·do \nā-'b͟ä-t͟hō-,kō-rō-'pü-nä\. Peak in Andes (Cordillera Occidental), S Peru, NW of Arequipa; 21,079 ft. (6425 m.).

Ço·ro·vo·dë \,chȯr-ō-'vō-də\. Town, ✻ of Skrapar dist., S cen. Albania.

Co·ro·zal \,kō-rō-'säl\. **1.** Administrative district, NE Belize. See table at BELIZE.
2. Seaport, its ✻; pop. (1990p) 7268; produces sugar, rum, corn.
3. Town, Panama, on the Panama Canal ab. 2 mi. (3 km.) NNW of Balboa.
4. Municipality, Sucre dept., N Colombia, ab. 80 mi. (129 km.) SSE of Cartagena.
5. Municipality, N cen. Puerto Rico, SW of San Juan; pop. (1990c) 33,095.

Cor·pus Chris·ti \'kȯr-pəs-'kris-tē\. City and port of entry, ⊗ of Nueces co., S Texas, on SW shore of Corpus Christi Bay at mouth of Nueces River, on Gulf Intracoastal Waterway; pop. (1990c) 257,453; chemicals; railroad and shipping center; seaside and fishing resort; oil and gas fields; oil refineries; fisheries; naval air station; Del Mar Coll. (1935), Corpus Christi State Univ. (1947); settled c. 1839; incorp. 1852; figured in Mexican and U.S. civil wars.

Corpus Christi Bay. Inlet of Gulf of Mexico in NE Nueces co., S Texas; sheltered from the gulf by Mustang I., its connection with the gulf being the strait **Corpus Christi Pass** (S of the island).

Cor·ral \kȯr-ˈräl\. Port and commune, Los Lagos region, S cen. Chile, near mouth of Valdivia River; scene of Chilean victory 1818 in War of Independence.

Cor·ra·lil·lo \ˌkȯr-rä-ˈlē-yō\. Municipality, Las Villas prov., W cen. Cuba, 40 mi. (64 km.) E of Cárdenas; pop. (1981p) 27,100.

Cor·reg·gio \kȯr-ˈre-jō\. Commune, Reggio nell'Emilia prov., Emilia-Romagna, N Italy, 8 mi. (13 km.) NE of the commune of Reggio; pop. (1981p) 20,011; birthplace of painter Correggio (Antonio Allegri) 1494.

Cor·reg·i·dor \kə-ˈre-gə-ˌdȯr\. Island in entrance to Manila Bay, Philippines, 3.5 mi. (6 km.) off S point of Bataan Penin. ab. 6 mi. (10 km.) SE of Mariveles and 28 mi. (45 km.) WSW of Manila; area ab. 2 sq. mi. (5 sq. km.); highest point 649 ft. (198 m.); belongs to Cavite prov.; rocky; divides entrance to Manila Bay into two channels: North Channel (also Boca Chica), 2 mi. (3.2 km.) wide, and South Channel (also Boca Grande), 6.5 mi. (10 km.) wide; site of Pacific War Memorial; nearby are two small islands La Monja and Caballo I.; before the war the small islands of El Fraile and Carabao I., site of Fort Frank, served as an American military defense unit. Four lighthouses, and American-built fortification, Fort Mills; extensive tunnels in the rock. First fortified by Spanish 18th cent.; made a U.S. military station after the Spanish-American War (1898) and later strengthened by other fortifications; after Japanese invasion of the Philippines Dec. 1941 chosen with Bataan (*q.v.*) by Gen. Douglas MacArthur as major defense position; after long resistance, surrendered May 6, 1942; retaken by Americans 1945.

Cor·rèze \kȯ-ˈrez\. Department of S cen. France. See table at FRANCE.

Cor·rib, Lough \ˈkȯr-əb, ˈkär-\. Lake in W co. Galway, W Ireland, S of Lough Mask; 27 mi. (43 km.) long; 65 sq. mi. (168 sq. km.); has outlet, **Corrib River,** on SE flowing into Galway Bay.

Corridor, Polish. See POLISH CORRIDOR.

Cor·rien·tes \kȯr-ˈyen-tās\. **1.** Province of NE Argentina. See table at ARGENTINA.

2. City, its ✻, on the Paraná River opp. Resistencia; pop. (1991p) 267,742; commercial center for agricultural area; museum (1854); university (1957); founded by Spanish 1588.

Corrientes, Cape. 1. Cape, SE Buenos Aires prov., extending into Atlantic Ocean from E Argentina.

2. Cape extending into Pacific Ocean from cen. part of W coast of Colombia.

3. Cape on SW coast of Pinar del Río prov., W Cuba.

4. W extremity of state of Jalisco, W cen. Mexico, projecting into the Pacific Ocean, 20°25′N.

Corrientes Bay. Bay in SW coast of Pinar del Río prov., W Cuba, W of Cape Corrientes.

Cor·ry \ˈkȯr-ē\. City, Erie co., NW corner of Pennsylvania, 28 mi. (45 km.) ESE of Erie; pop. (1990c) 7216.

Cor·ry·vreck·an *or* **Cor·rie·vrech·an** *or* **Cor·rie·vrek·in** \ˌkȯr-i-ˈvre-kən\. Whirlpool and strait off W coast of Scotland, N of Jura I.

Corse \ˈkȯrs\. **1.** Island belonging to France. See CORSICA 1.

2. Region, SE France, coextensive with the island of Corsica.

Corse, Cape; *anc.* **Sa·crum Pro·mon·to·ri·um** \ˈsa-krəm-ˌprä-mən-ˈtōr-ē-əm, ˈsā-\. N point of Corsica, France.

Corse–du–Sud \ˌkȯrs-dᵫ-ˈsᵫd\. Department of France, in S Corsica. See table at FRANCE.

Corse·wall Point \ˈkȯrs-ˌwȯl\. Cape on the N coast of The Rinns of Galloway, Dumfries and Galloway region, SW Scotland; lighthouse.

Cor·si·ca \ˈkȯr-si-kə\. **1.** *or Fr.* **Corse** \ˈkȯrs\. Island in the Mediterranean Sea belonging to France; W of N Italy and ab. 100 mi. (160 km.) SE of SE coast of France; 3360 sq. mi. (8702 sq. km.); pop. (1991e) 250,634; a department (Corse) of France 1815–1975 (✻ Ajaccio); since 1975 an administrative region (Corse) divided into two departments: Corse-du-Sud (✻ Ajaccio) and Haute-Corse (✻ Bastia); ab. 115 mi. (185 km.) long from Cape Corse in the N to the Strait of Bonifacio on the S separating it from Sardinia; mountainous with highest point Monte Cinto 8888 ft. (2709 m.); has numerous short streams; E coastline is unbroken by harbors or bays but W coast is quite irregular with Gulf of Ajaccio its largest inlet.

Chief products: cork, cheese, wine, olive oil, citrus fruits.

History: Settled in ancient times by Phocaeans, Etruscans, and Carthaginians; conquered and settled by Romans 3d and 2d cents. B.C.; conquered by Vandals 5th cent. A.D. and by Byzantines mid-6th cent.; in the following centuries, invaded, occupied, or claimed by Lombards, Franks, Arabs, and the Papacy; granted to Pisa by the pope 11th cent.; after a bitter struggle bet. Pisa and Genoa, and later Genoa and Aragon, ruled primarily by Genoa through the 18th cent.; revolted 1755 under Corsican patriot Pasquale Paoli; sold by Genoa to France 1768; occupied by British 1794–96. In WWII occupied by German and Italian forces 1942–43. Birthplace of French Emperor Napoléon I (known earlier as Napoléon Bonaparte) 1769.

2. Village, Ohio. See BLOOMING GROVE.

Cor·si·cana \ˌkȯr-sə-ˈka-nə\. City, ⊗ of Navarro co., NE cen. Texas, S of Dallas; pop. (1990c) 22,911; oil wells and refineries; Navarro Coll. (1946).

Cor·si·co \ˈkȯr-sē-ˌkō\. Commune, Milano prov., Lombardy, N Italy, 4 mi. (6 km.) SW of Milan; pop. (1989c) 39,590.

Cor·son \ˈkȯr-sən\. County in N South Dakota. See table at SOUTH DAKOTA.

Corson Inlet. Narrow strait leading from Atlantic Ocean through barrier islands off NE coast of Cape May co., S New Jersey.

Cor·stop·i·tum \kȯr-ˈstä-pi-təm\. See CORBRIDGE.

Cor·ta·zar \ˌkȯr-tä-ˈsär\. Municipality, Guanajuato state, cen. Mexico, just W of Querétaro; pop. (1990p) 74,325.

Cor·te \ˈkȯr-tā, kȯr-ˈtā\. Commune, cen. Corsica, France; partly built on steep, high rock; home 1755–69 of Corsican patriot Pasquale Paoli; marble deposits nearby; wine trade.

Cor·te Ma·dera \ˈkȯr-tə-mə-ˈder-ə\. Town, Marin co., W coastal California, N of San Francisco; pop. (1990c) 8272.

Cor·te·nuo·va \ˌkȯr-tā-ˈnwō-vä\. Commune, Bergamo prov., Lombardy, Italy, bet. the communes of Bergamo and Brescia; pop. (1981p) 1255; scene of victory 1237 of Holy Roman Emperor Frederick II over the Lombards.

Cor·tés \kȯr-ˈtās\. Department of NW Honduras. See table at HONDURAS.

Cortés, Sea of. See CALIFORNIA, GULF OF.

Cor·tez \kȯr-ˈtez\. City, ⊗ of Montezuma co., SW corner of Colorado; pop. (1990c) 7284.

Cor·ti·na \kȯr-ˈtē-nä\ *or in full* **Cortina d'Am·pez·zo** \däm-ˈpet-ˌsō\. Village in Belluno prov., N Italy, N of the commune of Belluno; noted ski resort, in the Dolomites; site of Winter Olympic Games 1956.

Cort·land \ˈkȯrt-lənd\. **1.** County in cen. New York. See table at NEW YORK.

2. City, its ⊗, 30 mi. (48 km.) S of Syracuse; pop. (1990c) 19,801; State Univ. of New York Coll. at Cortland (1868); settled 1791.

3. Village, Trumbull co., NE Ohio, 9 mi. (14 km.) E of Warren; pop. (1990c) 5666.

Cor·to·na \kȯr-ˈtō-nä\. Commune, Arezzo prov., Tuscany, cen. Italy, 14 mi. (23 km.) SSE of the commune of Arezzo; pop. (1991p) 22,352; cathedral; remains of Etruscan walls; Roman ruins; museum of Etruscan antiquities; tomb of St. Margaret. Ancient Etruscan city; confederated with Rome c. 310 B.C.; passed to Florence 15th cent. Birthplace of painter Luca Signorelli c. 1445.

Corubal. See GRANDE, RIO 1.

Ço·ruh \ˈchō-rüh\ *or* **Co·roch** \ˈchō-rȯk\. **1.** River in NE Turkey in Asia; flows ENE, then N across Russian border into Black Sea S of Batumi; 234 mi. (377 km.) long.

2. Province, Turkey in Asia. See RİZE.

3. Seaport, Turkey in Asia. See RİZE.

\ə\ **abut** \ᵊ\ **matches** \ᵊ\ **kitten, Fr table** \ər\ **further** \a\ **ash** \ā\ **ace** \ä\ **cot, cart** \à\ **Fr bac** \au̇\ **out** \b\ **Span Avila** \ch\ **chin** \e\ **bet** \ē\ **easy** \g\ **go** \i\ **hit** \ī\ **ice** \j\ **job** \k\ **Ger ich, Buch** \ⁿ\ **Fr vin** \ŋ\ **sing** \ō\ **go** \ȯ\ **all** \ȯ\ **law** \œ\ **Fr bœuf** \œ̄\ **Fr feu** \ȯi\ **boy** \th\ **thin** \t͟h\ **this** \ü\ **loot** \u̇\ **foot** \ue\ **Ger füllen** \ᵫ\ **Fr rue** \y\ **yet** \ʸ\ **Fr digne** \ˈdēnʸ\, **nuit** \ˈnwʸē\ \yü\ **few** \yu̇\ **fury** \zh\ **vision**

Ço·rum *or* **Cho·rum** \chō-ˈrům\. **1.** Province of Turkey in Asia. See table at TURKEY.
2. Town, its ✻, E of the Kızıl Irmak 116 mi. (187 km.) NE of Ankara; pop. (1980p) 76,020.

Co·rum·bá \ˌkòr-üm-ˈbä\. Commercial city on the Paraguay River, Mato Grosso state, SW Brazil, ab. 11 mi. (18 km.) from the border of SE Bolivia; munic. pop. (1991p) 88,279.

Coruña, La *or* **Corunna.** See LA CORUÑA.

Co·run·na \kə-ˈrü-nə\. City, ⊗ of Shiawassee co., S cen. Michigan, 23 mi. (37 km.) W of Flint; pop. (1990c) 3091.

Cor·u·pe·di·on \ˌkòr-ů-ˈpē-dē-ən, -yů-\ *or* **Cor·u·pe·di·um** \-əm\. Battlefield in ancient Lydia, Asia Minor, ENE of Magnesia, where Seleucus Nicator, founder of the Seleucid dynasty of Syria, defeated Macedonian Gen. Lysimachus 281 B.C.

Cor·val·lis \kòr-ˈva-lis\. City, ⊗ of Benton co., W Oregon, on Willamette River 30 mi. (48 km.) SSW of Salem; pop. (1990c) 44,757; lumber; Oregon State Univ. (1868); settled c. 1845.

Cor·vo \ˈkòr-vü\. Island, NW Azores, Portugal; 7 sq. mi. (18 sq. km.); smallest island of the group.

Corycian Cave. See PARNASSUS 2.

Cor·y·don \ˈkòr-ə-dən\. **1.** Town, ⊗ of Harrison co., S Indiana, 18 mi. (29 km.) WSW of New Albany; pop. (1990c) 2661; ✻ of Indiana Terr. 1813–16 and of the state of Indiana until 1825; captured and held for a short time 1863 by Confederate raiding party under Gen. John Hunt Morgan.
2. Town, ⊗ of Wayne co., S Iowa; pop. (1990c) 1675.

Cor·yell \kòr-ˈyel\. County in cen. Texas. See table at TEXAS.

Cos. See KOS.

Co·sa·ma·lo·a·pan \ˌkō-sä-mä-lō-ˈä-pän\. Municipality, Veracruz state, Mexico, 63 mi. (101 km.) S of the city of Veracruz; pop. (1990p) 76,640.

Cos Cob \ˈkäs-ˈkäb\. Subdivision of town of Greenwich, Connecticut.

Co·sen·za \kō-ˈzent-sä\. **1.** Province of Calabria, S Italy. See table at ITALY.
2. *anc.* **Con·sen·tia** \kən-ˈsen-chē-ə\. Commune, its ✻, at confluence of Busento and Crati rivers 150 mi. (241 km.) SE of Naples; pop. (1991p) 87,140; cathedral containing tombs of Louis III, duke of Anjou, and Isabella of Aragon; castle; college. Ancient ✻ of the Brutii; taken by Romans 204 B.C.; frequently devastated by earthquakes.

Co·shoc·ton \kə-ˈshäk-tən\. **1.** County in E cen. Ohio. See table at OHIO.
2. City, its ⊗, on Muskingum River; pop. (1990c) 12,193.

Co·si·güi·na Vol·cán \ˌkō-sē-ˈgwē-nä-vòl-ˈkän\. Volcano, Nicaragua, on the Gulf of Fonseca; 2818 ft. (859 m.); eruption 1835.

Cos·mo·le·do Islands \ˌkäz-mə-ˈlā-dō\. Group of small islands in the Aldabra Is. (*q.v.*), Seychelles.

Cosne–sur–Loire \ˈkōn-sūr-ˈlwär\; *anc.* **Con·da·te** \kän-ˈdā-tē\. Commune, Nièvre dept., cen. France, on the Loire River 37 mi. (60 km.) NNW of Nevers; military post in Middle Ages.

Cospicua. See BORMLA.

Cossimbazar. See BAHARAMPUR.

Cossyra. See PANTELLERIA.

Costa, Cayo. See CAYO COSTA.

Cos·ta Bra·va \ˈkōs-tä-ˈbrä-vä\. The coast of Catalonia, Spain, NE of Barcelona; resort area.

Cos·ta del Sol \ˈkòs-tä-thel-ˈsòl, -ˈsōl\. The S coast of Spain from Estepona to Motril.

Cos·ta Me·sa \ˈkōs-tə-ˈmā-sə\. City, Orange co., SW coastal California, SSW of Santa Ana; pop. (1990c) 96,357; Southern California Coll. (1920), Orange Coast Coll. (1947); automotive museum.

Cos·ta Ri·ca \ˈkòs-tä-ˈrē-kä\. Republic, S Central America, bounded on N by Nicaragua, on E by the Caribbean Sea and Panama, and on S and W by the Pacific Ocean; 19,652 sq. mi. (50,899 sq. km.); pop. (1993e) 3,199,000; ✻ San José.

Physical features: Traversed from NW to SE by the mountains of the Continental Divide, its SE section known as the Cordillera de Talamanca; highest point Chirripó Grande 12,533 ft. (3820 m.); chief volcanoes Irazú, Turrialba, and Barba. Only large river is the San Juan on NE boundary; its main tributaries are San Carlos and Sarapiquí. Its Caribbean coastline has only one good harbor, Puerto Limón; on Pacific coast has large penin. of Nicoya in NW and smaller penin. of Osa in S, the Gulf of Nicoya and Golfo Dulce, and the wide Coronado Bay.

Chief products: Coffee, bananas, rice, timber, sugar; livestock; textiles; food processing; fertilizer; tourism.

Chief towns: San José, Desamparados, Puerto Limón, Alajuela, Puntarenas.

Political divisions: Divided into seven provinces (for pronunciation of their names, see their individual entries):

NAME	AREA (sq. mi.)	AREA (sq. km.)	POP. (1991e)	CAPITAL
Alajuela	3,669	9,503	539,375	Alajuela
Cartago	1,004	2,600	340,298	Cartago
Guanacaste	4,015	10,399	242,681	Liberia
Heredia	1,120	2,901	243,679	Heredia
Limón	3,591	9,301	219,485	Puerto Limón
Puntarenas[1]	4,358	11,287	338,384	Puntarenas
San José	1,896	4,911	1,105,844	San José

[1]Includes islands of Chira and Coco.

History: Inhabited by several indigenous tribes when reached by explorer Christopher Columbus on last voyage 1502; became a Spanish province 1540 although the Spaniards failed to establish a permanent settlement until the 1560s; with other countries of Central America (*q.v.*), revolted against Spain 1821; in Augustín de Iturbide's Mexican empire 1822–23; nominally part of United Provinces of Central America 1823–38; declared itself independent republic mid-19th cent.; adopted constitution 1871; boundary with Panama arbitrated 1900 but not finally settled until 1941; revolution 1917 brought trouble with U.S.; entered WWI 1918; joined League of Nations 1920; in WWII declared war on Axis countries Dec. 1941; adopted new constitution 1949

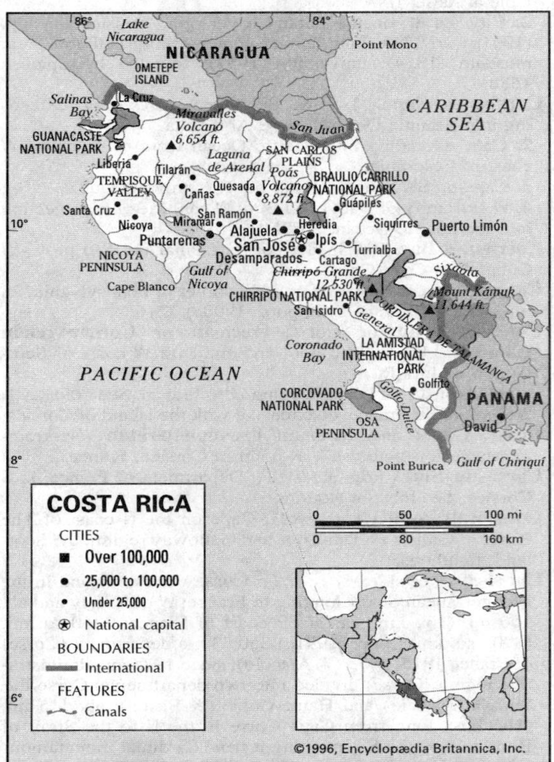

after 1948 rebellion; joined Central American Common Market 1962. In 1987 then president Oscar Arias Sánchez awarded Nobel Peace Prize for his efforts to negotiate peace among El Salvador, Nicaragua, and Guatemala.

Costermansville. **1.** Former province, Democractic Rep. of the Congo. See KIVU.

2. Town, Democratic Rep. of the Congo. See BUKAVU.

Cos·til·la \käs-'tē-yə\. County in S Colorado. See table at COLORADO.

Costilla Peak. Mountain, NW Colfax co., N New Mexico, in Sangre de Cristo Range; 12,634 ft. (3851 m.).

Co·sum·nes \kə-'səm-nəs\. River, N cen. California; rises in El Dorado co., flows SW into Mokelumne River.

Cos·wig *or* **Kos·wig** \'kȯs-,vik\. City, Saxony, E Germany, on the Elbe, NW of Dresden; pop. (1981c) 28,843.

Cosyra. See PANTELLERIA.

Co·ta·ba·to \,kō-tä-'bä-tō\. **1.** River, Mindanao, Philippines. See MINDANAO 2.

2. Region and former province, SW Mindanao, Philippines; ✻ Pagalungan; mountainous in S and on E and N borders; Mt. Apo (*q.v.*) on E boundary highest mountain 9690 ft. (2954 m.) in the Philippines; mountains densely wooded with fine, hard timber. Cen. and W part occupied with basin of the Mindanao River and lower course of its tributary, the Pulangi. Inhabitants chiefly the Magindanao. Muslim influence estab. before arrival of Spanish; now divided into Cotabato del Norte, Maguindanao, and Sultan Kudarat provs.

3. Province, SW Mindanao, Philippines; ✻ Kidapawan. See table at PHILIPPINES.

4. Chartered city, N Maguindanao prov. in the delta of the Mindanao, Mindanao I., Philippines; pop. (1990p) 127,000; has good harbor 7 mi. (11 km.) from town.

Cotabato, South. See SOUTH COTABATO.

Co·teau–Landing \kō-'tō\. Village, S Quebec, Canada, on St. Lawrence River; pop. (1991c) 1552.

Cote Blanche Bay \,kōt-'blä^{n}sh\. Inlet of Gulf of Mexico on SW coast of St. Mary parish, S Louisiana; divided into **East Cote Blanche Bay** and **West Cote Blanche Bay**.

Côte d'Azur \,kōt-,dȧ-'zu̇r\. The Mediterranean coast of France, esp. its E end; part of the Riviera (*q.v.*).

Côte des Allemands. See GERMAN COAST.

Côte d'Ivoire. See IVORY COAST.

Côte d'Or \kōt-'dȯr\. Range of hills, Côte-d'Or dept., E France, SW of Dijon; noted for rich vineyards.

Côte–d'Or. Department of E France. See table at FRANCE.

Co·ten·tin Peninsula \,kō-tä^{n}-'te^{n}\. Peninsula formed by N end of Manche dept., NW France, bet. Channel Is. and Bay of the Seine. In WWII scene of fighting from beginning of Allied invasion June 6, 1944 to capture of Cherbourg June 27.

Côte Saint Luc \,kōt-sānt-'lük, se^{n}-'lu̇k\. City, Montreal co., S Quebec, Canada; pop. (1991c) 28,700; residential suburb of Montreal.

Côtes–du–Nord \,kōt-dü-'nȯr\. Department of NW France. See table at FRANCE.

Cöthen. See KÖTHEN.

Co·tin·go \kō-'tēŋ-gü\. River, N Brazil; rises near border, flows S into the Tacutu; 180 mi. (290 km.) long.

Co·to \'kō-tō\. Small stream in SE Costa Rica, flowing into Golfo Dulce; 25 mi (40 km.) long; ownership of region has been disputed by Panama.

Co·to·nou *also* **Ko·to·nu** \,kō-tō-'nü\. Seaport, Benin; pop. (1985e) 402,290; commercial center; as former ✻ of Dahomey, retains a major role in governmental activities.

Co·to·paxi \,kō-tō-'päk-sē, -'pak-, -'pä-hē\. **1.** Active volcano, N cen. Ecuador; 19,347 ft. (5897 m.).

2. *formerly* **Le·ón** \lā-'ōn\. Province of cen. Ecuador. See table at ECUADOR.

Cotrone. See CROTONE.

Cots·wold Hills \'kät-,swōld, -swəld\ *or* **Cots·wolds** \-,swōldz, -swəldz\. Range of hills in Gloucestershire, SW cen. England; highest point Cleeve Cloud 1031 ft. (314 m.).

Cot·tage Grove \'kä-tij-'grōv\. **1.** Village, Washington co., E Minnesota, 11 mi. (18 km.) SE of St. Paul; pop. (1990c) 22,935; residential suburb of St. Paul.

2. City, Lane co., W Oregon, S of Eugene; pop. (1990c) 7402.

3. Town, Dane co., S Wisconsin; pop. (1990c) 3525.

Cott·bus *or* **Kott·bus** \'kät-bəs, -,bu̇s\. **1.** District of former East Germany.

2. City, Brandenburg, E Germany, on Spree River 64 mi. (103 km.) SE of Berlin; pop. (1992e) 123,321; formerly ✻ of Cottbus dist.; textiles, electrical machinery, leather, building materials; railroad center. First mentioned 1156; passed 1445 to elector of Brandenburg, 1807 to Saxony, 1813 to Prussia; in WWII captured by Soviet troops Apr. 1945.

Cottian Alps. See table at ALPS.

Cot·ti·ca \kȯ-'tē-kə\. Navigable river, N Suriname; flows W into the Commewijne near its mouth; ab. 80 mi. (130 km.) long.

Cot·tle \'kät-^{ə}l\. County in NW Texas. See table at TEXAS.

Cot·tle·ville \'kät-^{ə}l-,vil\. Town, St. Charles co., E Missouri; pop. (1990c) 2936.

Cot·ton \'kät-^{ə}n\. County in SW Oklahoma. See table at OKLAHOMA.

Cot·ton·wood \'kät-^{ə}n-,wu̇d\. **1.** River, S Minnesota; rises in Lyon co., flows E into Minnesota River below New Ulm in Brown co.; ab. 140 mi. (225 km.) long.

2. County in SW Minnesota. See table at MINNESOTA.

3. Town, Yavapai co., cen. Arizona, 15 mi. (24 km.) SW of Flagstaff; pop. (1990c) 5918.

Cottonwood Creek. Creek in S San Diego co., SW California; contains Barrett Dam and Morena Dam (*qq.v.*).

Cottonwood Falls. City, ⊗ of Chase co., E cen. Kansas; pop. (1990c) 889.

Cottonwood Heights. Unincorporated settlement, Salt Lake co., N Utah, 6 mi. (10 km.) S of Salt Lake City; pop. (1990c) 28,766.

Cottonwood Mountain. Peak, S Idaho co., N cen. Idaho; ab. 9320 ft. (2840 m.).

Co·tuí \kō-'twē\. Town, ✻ of Sánchez Ramírez prov., cen. Dominican Republic; pop. (1981p) 96,667.

Co·tu·it \kō-'tü-it\. Town, Barnstable co., SE Massachusetts, on Nantucket Sound.

Co·tul·la \kə-'tü-lə\. City, ⊗ of La Salle co., S Texas, 70 mi. (113 km.) N of Laredo; pop. (1990c) 3694.

Cotyora. See ORDU 2.

Cou·chi·ching, Lake \'kü-chə-chiŋ\. Lake, SE Ontario, Canada, joined on the S by larger Lake Simcoe.

Cou·cy–le–Châ·teau–Auf·frique \kü-,sēl-shȧ-'tō-ō-'frēk\; *often shortened to* **Coucy–Auffrique** *or* **Coucy–le–Chateau.** Commune, Aisne dept., N France, 18 mi. (29 km.) WSW of Laon; ruins of feudal castle, destroyed by Germans during WWI.

Cou·de·kerque–Branche \,kü-də-,kerk-'brä^{n}sh\. Commune, Nord dept., N France, SE suburb of Dunkerque.

Cou·ders·port \'kau̇-dərz-,pōrt\. Borough and mountain resort, ⊗ of Potter co., N Pennsylvania, on Allegheny River 36 mi. (58 km.) ESE of Bradford; pop. (1990c) 2854.

Cou·lee Dam \'kü-lē\. Town, Grant, Douglas, and Okanogan cos., NE cen. Washington, on Columbia River; includes former town of Mason City; pop. (1990c) 1087.

Coul·man Island \'kōl-mən\. Island in Ross Dependency off coast of Victoria Land, Antarctica, 73°28′S, 169°45′E.

Cou·lom·miers \,kü-lȯ-'myā\. Commune, N Seine-et-Marne dept., N France; 13th–16th cent. church.

Coun·cil \'kau̇n-səl\. Village, ⊗ of Adams co., W Idaho; pop. (1990c) 831.

Council Bluffs. City, ⊗ of Pottawattamie co., SW Iowa, on Missouri River opp. Omaha, Nebraska; pop. (1990c) 54,315; manufactures cast-iron pipes; Iowa Western Community Coll. (1923); site of Mormon settlement 1846–52; outfitting point for emigrants to California during gold rush 1849–50; selected as E terminus of Union Pacific R.R. 1863.

Council For Mutual Economic Assistance; *abbr.* **COMECON** \,kä-mē-'kän, -me-\. Former economic organi-

---

\ə\ abut \ᵊ\ kitten, Fr table \ər\ further \a\ ash \ā\ ace \ä\ cot, cart \ȧ\ Fr bac \au̇\ out \b\ Span Avila \ch\ chin \e\ bet \ē\ easy \g\ go \i\ hit \ī\ ice \j\ job \k\ Ger ich, Buch \$^{n}$\ Fr vin \ŋ\ sing \ō\ go \ȯ\ all \ȯ\ law \œ\ Fr bœuf \œ̄\ Fr feu \ȯi\ boy \th\ thin \t͟h\ this \ü\ loot \u̇\ foot \u̇e\ Ger füllen \ūe\ Fr rue \y\ yet \$^{y}$\ Fr digne \'dēn^{y}\, nuit \'nw^{y}ē\ \yü\ few \yu̇\ fury \zh\ vision

zation, consisting of Bulgaria, Cuba, Czechoslovakia, East Germany, Hungary, Mongolian People's Republic, Poland, Romania, U.S.S.R., Vietnam; headquarters Moscow, U.S.S.R. Formed 1949; purpose was to accelerate economic development and promote equality in levels of development of member countries; Albania became inactive 1961; Yugoslavia given limited membership 1964; formal disbandment June 28, 1991.

Council Grove. City, ⊗ of Morris co., E cen. Kansas, 25 mi. (40 km.) NW of Emporia; pop. (1990c) 2228. In 1825 site of meeting bet. Osage Indians and U.S. government officials leading to opening of Santa Fe Trail for settlers' use.

Council of Europe. Political organization, consisting of Albania, Andorra, Austria, Belgium, Bulgaria, Croatia, Cyprus, Czech Republic, Denmark, Estonia, Finland, France, Georgia, Germany, Greece, Hungary, Iceland, Ireland, Italy, Latvia, Liechtenstein, Lithuania, Luxembourg, Macedonia, Malta, Moldova, Netherlands, Norway, Poland, Portugal, Romania, Russia, San Marino, Slovakia, Slovenia, Spain, Sweden, Switzerland, Turkey, Ukraine, and the United Kingdom; headquarters Strasbourg, France; purpose is to promote cooperation among the members in safeguarding democratic political principles; estab. 1949; Greece withdrew 1969 and was readmitted 1974.

Coun·try Club Hills \ˈkən-trē-ˈkləb\. City, Cook co., NE Illinois, 7 mi. (11 km.) S of Chicago; pop. (1990c) 15,431.

Coun·try·side \ˈkən-trē-ˌsīd\. City, Cook co., NE Illinois, ab. 3 mi. (5 km.) W of Chicago; pop. (1990c) 5716.

Coupe·ville \ˈküp-ˌvil\. Town and resort, ⊗ of Island co., NW Washington, on Whidbey I.; pop. (1990c) 1377.

Cour·an·tyne *or Du.* **Co·ran·tijn** \ˈkōr-ən-ˌtīn\. River, N South America; rises in the Serra Acaraí, flows N to Atlantic Ocean forming boundary bet. Guyana and Suriname; 475 mi. (764 km.) long.

Cour·be·voie \ˌkür-bə-ˈvwä\. Commune, Hauts-de-Seine dept., N France, on the Seine, a NW suburb of Paris; pop. (1990c) 65,649.

Cour·ce·lette \ˌkür-sə-ˈlet\. Village, Somme dept., N France, 5 mi. (8 km.) NE of Albert; scene of heavy fighting in WWI.

Cour·celles \kür-ˈsel\. Commune, Hainaut prov., SW Belgium, just NNW of Charleroi; pop. (1981c) 29,757.

Cour·land \ˈkür-ˌlänt, ˈku̇r-lənd\ *also* **Kur·land** \ˈkür-ˌlänt\. Historical region, on E Baltic shore, in Latvia; included Kurzeme (*q.v.*). See BALTIC PROVINCES. In 13th cent. Lettish inhabitants conquered by Livonian Knights; upon dissolution of Livonian Order in 1561, transformed into duchy under Polish suzerainty; after 1737 its duke a client ruler of Russian throne; under Russian rule 1795; scene of severe fighting bet. Germans and Russians 1914–15; became part of Latvia (*q.v.*) 1918.

Courland Lagoon. See KURSKIY ZALIV.

Courland Spit. See KURSKAYA KOSA.

Cour·ma·yeur \ˌkür-mȧ-ˈyœr\. Village, Valle d'Aosta region, NW Italy, SE of Mont Blanc; pop. (1981p) 2741; resort.

Courneuve, La. See LA COURNEUVE.

Courte·nay \ˈku̇rt-nē\. City, E Vancouver I., British Columbia, Canada, on Strait of Georgia 90 mi. (145 km.) WNW of Vancouver; pop. (1991c) 11,652; resort.

Court·land \ˈkōrt-lənd\. Town, ⊗ of Southampton co., SE Virginia; pop. (1990c) 819; slave leader Nat Turner's insurrection took place nearby Aug. 1831 when town was known as Jerusalem.

Courtrai. See KORTRIJK.

Cou·shat·ta \ku̇-ˈsha-tə\. Town, ⊗ of Red River parish, NW Louisiana; pop. (1990c) 1845.

Cou·tances \kü-ˈtäⁿs\; *anc.* **Con·stan·tia** \kən-ˈstan-shə, -shē-ə\. Commune, Manche dept., NW France, 17 mi. (27 km.) WSW of St.-Lô; pop. (1990c) 11,827; 13th cent. cathedral; ancient Celtic town, in 3d cent. fortified by Roman Emperor Constantius Chlorus and named in his honor; often besieged in Middle Ages; in WWII captured by Allies July 1944.

Cou·tras \kü-ˈträ\. Commune, Gironde dept., SW France, 56 mi. (90 km.) NE of Bordeaux; scene Oct. 20, 1587 of battle in which Henry of Navarre (later Henry IV) defeated the Catholic army of Henry III.

Co·va·don·ga \ˌkō-bä-ˈt͟hȯŋ-gä\. Village, Asturias prov., NW Spain, 5 mi. (8 km.) from Cangas de Onís; scene of victory of Christian King Pelayo over the Moors c. 718.

Co·vas·na \kō-ˈväs-nä\. County of cen. Romania. See table at ROMANIA.

Cove Neck. See OYSTER BAY 2.

Cov·ent Garden \ˈkä-vənt\. Neighborhood, London, England, surrounding a square of the same name; site of Royal Opera House; the square was orig. the site of a convent's garden and was later an important produce market.

Cov·en·try \ˈkä-vən-trē, ˈkə-\. **1.** Town, S cen. Tolland co., N Connecticut; pop. (1990c) 10,063; incorp. c. 1712. Birthplace of American Revolutionary hero Nathan Hale 1755.
2. Town, Kent co., cen. Rhode Island, 15 mi. (24 km.) SW of Providence; pop. (1990c) 31,083; town's governmental seat is village of Washington; town taken from Warwick and incorp. 1741.
3. City, West Midlands, cen. England, near the Avon 18 mi. (29 km.) ESE of Birmingham; pop. (1991p) 292,500; motor vehicles, synthetic fibers, machinery, telecommunication equipment; Univ. of Warwick (1965). Home of Lady Godiva, who, with her husband, founded a Benedictine abbey here 1043; probably center of the presentation of the Coventry Mysteries (plays) 15th–16th cents. Heavily bombed by Germans Nov. 1940; spire of 15th cent. cathedral left standing and new cathedral built near it 1962.

Co·vi·lhã \ˌkü-vē-ˈlyäⁿ\. Commune, Castelo Branco dist., E cen. Portugal, N of the commune of Castelo Branco; munic. pop. (1991p) 22,028.

Coville, Lake. See NAKNEK LAKE.

Co·vi·na \kō-ˈvē-nə\. City, Los Angeles co., SW California, 15 mi. (24 km.) E of the city of Los Angeles; pop. (1990c) 43,207.

Cov·ing·ton \ˈkə-viŋ-tən\. **1.** Name of counties in two states of the U.S. See tables at ALABAMA and MISSISSIPPI.
2. City, ⊗ of Newton co., N cen. Georgia, 32 mi. (51 km.) ESE of Atlanta; pop. (1990c) 10,026; incorp. 1822.
3. City, ⊗ of Fountain co., W Indiana, on Wabash River 27 mi. (43 km.) WNW of Crawfordsville; pop. (1990c) 2747.
4. City, Kenton co., N Kentucky, at confluence of Ohio and Licking rivers opp. Cincinnati; pop. (1990c) 43,264; diversified manufacturing; founded 1815.
5. City, ⊗ of St. Tammany parish, SE Louisiana, 37 mi. (60 km.) N of New Orleans; pop. (1990c) 7691; fishing and hunting.
6. Village, Miami co., W Ohio; pop. (1990c) 2603.
7. Town, ⊗ of Tipton co., W Tennessee, 39 mi. (63 km.) NE of Memphis; pop. (1990c) 7487.
8. Independent city, ⊗ of Alleghany co., W Virginia; pop. (1990c) 6991.

Cow·an, Lake \ˈkau̇-ən\. Intermittent lake, S Western Australia, Australia, in E Swanland S of Kalgoorlie.

Cow·ans·ville \ˈkau̇-ənz-ˌvil\. Town, S Quebec, Canada, 48 mi. (77 km.) ESE of Montreal; pop. (1991c) 11,982.

Cow·den·beath \ˌkau̇d-ᵊn-ˈbēth\. Burgh, Fife region, E Scotland; pop. (1981p) 12,235.

Cow·en, Mount \ˈkau̇-ən\. Mountain, Park co., S Montana; 11,206 ft. (3416 m.).

Cowes \ˈkau̇z\. Town, N Isle of Wight, England, 9 mi. (14 km.) WSW of Portsmouth; pop. (1981p) 19,663; seaport and yachting resort.

Co·we·ta \kə-ˈwē-tə\. **1.** County in W Georgia. See table at GEORGIA.
2. City, Wagoner co., NE Oklahoma; pop. (1990c) 6159.

Cow·ley \ˈkau̇-lē\. County in S Kansas. See table at KANSAS.

Cow·litz \ˈkau̇-lits\. **1.** River, SW Washington; formed by confluence of forks in E Lewis co., flows W, then S into Columbia River in Cowlitz co.; 130 mi. (209 km.) long.
2. County in SW Washington. See table at WASHINGTON.

Cow·pas·ture \ˈkau̇-ˌpas-chər\. River, W Virginia; rises in Highland co., flows SW, unites with Jackson River to form the James; ab. 60 mi. (95 km.) long.

Cow·pens \ˈkau̇-ˌpenz\. Town, Spartanburg co., NW South Carolina, in the Piedmont 8 mi. (13 km.) ENE of Spartanburg; pop. (1990c) 2176; just N of town is scene of battle Jan. 17,

1781 in which Gen. Daniel Morgan defeated British under Col. Banastre Tarleton, commemorated by **Cowpens National Battlefield** (see UNITED STATES, *National Historical Parks*).

Cow·ra \ˈkau̇-rə\. Town, SE cen. New South Wales, SE Australia, 100 mi. (161 km.) N of Canberra; pop. (1992e) 12,440.

Cox·comb Mountain \ˈkäks-ˌkōm\. Peak, cen. Park co., NW Wyoming; 11,000 ft. (3353 m.).

Coxcomb Peak. Mountain, Hinsdale and Ouray cos., SW Colorado; 13,663 ft. (4164 m.).

Coxen Hole. See ROATÁN 2.

Cox·sack·ie \ku̇k-ˈsä-kē\. Village, Greene co., SE New York, on Hudson River 22 mi. (35 km.) S of Albany; pop. (1990c) 2789.

Coyle. See COIG.

Co·yo·a·cán \ˌkȯi-ō-ä-ˈkän\. City, Federal District, cen. Mexico, suburb of Mexico City; 16th cent. church and monastery; several museums; site from which Spanish conquistador Hernán Cortés set out to take Aztec ✻ of Tenochititlán; first seat of Spanish government; birthplace (1907) and lifelong home of painter Frida Kahlo.

Coy·o·te Peaks \kī-ˈōt-ē, ˈkī-ˌōt\. Mountain in the Sierra Nevada, E Tulare co., S cen. California; ab. 10,900 ft. (3320 m.).

Co·zad \kō-ˈzad\. City, Dawson co., S cen. Nebraska, on Platte River; pop. (1990c) 3823.

Cozie, Alpi. See *Cottian Alps* in table at ALPS.

Co·zu·mel \ˌkō-sü-ˈmel\. Resort island off NE coast of Quintana Roo state, SE Mexico; 24 mi. (39 km.) long, 7 mi. (11 km.) wide.

Crab Island. See VIEQUES 1.

Cracow. See KRAKÓW.

Cra·dle Mountain \ˈkrād-ᵊl\. Mountain, NW cen. Tasmania, Australia, on W edge of cen. highlands, in Cradle Mountain–Lake St. Clair National Park; 5069 ft. (1545 m.).

Cradle Mountain–Lake Saint Clair National Park. National park, NW cen. Tasmania, Australia; mountains and forest traversed by the Overland Track, a 50-mile (80-kilometer) hiking trail.

Crad·ock \ˈkra-dək\. Town, cen. Eastern Cape prov., S Rep. of South Africa, 125 mi. (201 km.) N of Port Elizabeth; at ab. 3000 ft. (915 m.) surrounded by mountains.

Craf·ton \ˈkraf-tən\. Borough, Allegheny co., SW Pennsylvania, 4 mi. (6 km.) W of Pittsburgh; pop. (1990c) 7188.

Craggy Dome, Craggy Gardens, Craggy Pinnacle. See GREAT CRAGGY MOUNTAINS.

Craig \ˈkrāg, ˈkreg\. **1.** Name of counties in two states of the U.S. See tables at OKLAHOMA and VIRGINIA.
2. Town on W coast of Prince of Wales I., SE Alaska; pop. (1990c) 1260.
3. City, ⊗ of Moffat co., NW corner of Colorado, on Yampa River; pop. (1990c) 8091.

Craig·a·vad \ˌkrā-gə-ˈvad\. Suburb of Belfast, Northern Ireland, on Belfast Lough 5.5 mi. (9 km.) NE of Belfast.

Craig·av·on \krā-ˈga-vən\. **1.** District, cen. Northern Ireland. See table at IRELAND, NORTHERN.
2. Town, its ⊗.

Crai·gen·put·tock \ˌkrā-gən-ˈpə-tək\. Farm near Dumfries, S Scotland; home of essayist and historian Thomas Carlyle 1828–34.

Craig·head \ˈkrāg-ˌhed\. County in NE Arkansas. See table at ARKANSAS.

Craig Head. Cape on N coast of Moray co., NE Scotland; lighthouse.

Crails·heim \ˈkrīls-ˌhīm\. City, Baden-Wurttemburg, cen. S Germany, roughly halfway bet. Stuttgart to the SW and Nürnburg to the NE; pop. (1992e) 28,588.

Cra·io·va \krä-ˈyō-vä\. City, ⊗ of Dolj co., S Romania, on the Jiu River 112 mi. (180 km.) W of Bucharest; pop. (1989c) 300,030; agricultural machinery, fertilizer, textiles, food processing, locomotives; restored church (orig. built 17th cent.), university (1966).

Cran·ber·ry Lake \ˈkran-ˌber-ē\. Lake, in S St. Lawrence co., N New York; 6 mi. (10 km.) long.

Cran·brook \ˈkran-ˌbru̇k\. City, SE British Columbia, Canada, in Kootenay Valley 70 mi. (113 km.) E of Nelson; pop. (1991c) 16,447; active trade center; lead and zinc deposits.

Cran·don \ˈkran-dən\. City, ⊗ of Forest co., NE Wisconsin, 25 mi. (40 km.) E of Rhinelander; pop. (1990c) 1958; built around and bet. four lakes.

Crane \ˈkrān\. **1.** County in W Texas. See table at TEXAS.
2. City, its ⊗, 128 mi. (206 km.) W of San Angelo; pop. (1990c) 3533.

Cran·ford \ˈkran-fərd\. Township, Union co., NE New Jersey, 5 mi. (8 km.) W of Elizabeth; pop. (1990c) 22,633; Union County Coll. (1933).

Cran·non \ˈkra-nän\ *or* **Cra·non** \ˈkrā-nän\. Ancient town in cen. Thessaly, NE Greece, ab. 13 mi. (21 km.) SW of Larisa; scene of battle 322 B.C. in which Macedonian Gen. Antipater defeated in the Lamian War the league of cities of cen. Greece.

Cran·ston \ˈkran-stən\. City, Providence co., N Rhode Island, on Pawtuxet River 5 mi. (8 km.) S of and adjoining Providence; pop. (1990c) 76,060; wire, rubber goods, machinery, textiles; breweries; settled c. 1636.

Craonne \ˈkrän\. Village, Aisne dept., N France, ab. 15 mi. (24 km.) SE of Laon; battle Mar. 7, 1814 in which French Emperor Napoléon repulsed the allies; in struggle for Chemin des Dames in WWI taken and retaken several times 1917–1918 and virtually destroyed.

Cratère du Nouveau–Québec. See NOUVEAU-QUÉBEC, CRATÈRE DU.

Cra·ter Lake \ˈkrā-tər\. Lake in Cascade Mts., W Klamath co., S Oregon; ab. 6 mi. (10 km.) long, 5 mi. (8 km.) wide, and 1932 ft. (589 m.) deep; occupies caldera of Mt. Mazama, an extinct volcano; remarkable esp. for the intensity of color of the water; region has been set aside as **Crater Lake National Park** (see UNITED STATES, *National Parks*).

Crater Peak. Mountain, W Klamath co., S Oregon, S of Crater Lake; 7265 ft. (2214 m.).

Craters of the Moon National Monument. See UNITED STATES, *National Monuments.*

Cra·ti \ˈkrä-tē\; *anc.* **Cra·this** \ˈkrā-thəs\. River, Calabria, S Italy; rises S of Cosenza, flows to Gulf of Taranto; ancient Sybaris may have been at its mouth; 58 mi. (93 km.) long.

Cra·to \ˈkra̐-tü\. City, S Ceará state, NE Brazil; munic. pop. (1991p) 90,360; a railroad terminus.

Cra·ven \ˈkrā-vən\. County in SE North Carolina. See table at NORTH CAROLINA.

Craw·ford \ˈkrȯ-fərd\. Name of counties in 11 states of the U.S. See tables at ARKANSAS, GEORGIA, ILLINOIS, INDIANA, IOWA, KANSAS, MICHIGAN, MISSOURI, OHIO, PENNSYLVANIA, WISCONSIN.

Crawford Notch. Defile in White Mts. (*q.v.*) in NW Carroll co., New Hampshire, traversed by Saco River.

Craw·fords·ville \ˈkrȯ-fərdz-ˌvil\. Commercial city, ⊗ of Montgomery co., W cen. Indiana, 43 mi. (69 km.) WNW of Indianapolis; pop. (1990c) 13,584; Wabash Coll. (1832).

Craw·ford·ville \ˈkrȯ-fərd-ˌvil\. **1.** Village, ⊗ of Wakulla co., NW Florida.
2. City, ⊗ of Taliaferro co., NE cen. Georgia; pop. (1990c) 577.

Craw·ley \ˈkrȯ-lē\. Town, West Sussex, S England; pop. (1991p) 87,100; Gatwick Airport serving London is nearby to the N.

Cra·zy Mountains \ˈkrā-zē\. Mountain group, Meagher, Park, and Sweet Grass cos., S Montana; highest point, **Crazy Peak** 11,214 ft. (3418 m.), is in N Sweet Grass co.

Crécy–en–Pon·thieu \krā-ˈsē-ˌäⁿ-pōⁿ-ˈtyœ\; *sometimes shortened to* **Crécy** *also Eng.* **Cres·sy** \ˈkre-sē\. Commune, Somme dept., N France, ab. 12 mi. (19 km.) N of Abbeville; scene Aug. 26, 1346 of first decisive battle of Hundred Years' War, a victory for Edward III of England over Philip VI of France; noted for weapons and tactics of the English, who used longbows and dismounted men-at-arms; established England as a military power.

Cred·i·ton \ˈkre-di-tən\. Town, cen. Devon, SW England, ab. 8 mi. (13 km.) NW of Exeter; pop. (1981p) 6169; episcopal see 909–c. 1049; formerly had important wool industries. Birthplace of St. Boniface c. 675.

Cree \ˈkrē\. Lake, N Saskatchewan, Canada; 446 sq. mi. (1155 sq. km.); discharges through **Cree River** (ab. 90 mi. or 145 km. long) to the Fond du Lac River.

Creede \ˈkrēd\. Town, ⊗ of Mineral co., S Colorado, in gorge of Rio Grande; pop. (1990c) 362; founded 1890 as mining camp (silver, gold, zinc) and within two to three years had a pop. of ab. 8000.

Creek \ˈkrēk\. County in E cen. Oklahoma. See table at OKLAHOMA.

Creil \ˈkrā\. Commune, Oise dept., N France, on Oise River 28 mi. (45 km.) N of Paris; pop. (1990c) 33,501.

Cre·ma \ˈkrā-mə, ˈkre-\. Commune, Cremona prov., Lombardy, N Italy, on Serio River 23 mi. (37 km.) NW of the commune of Cremona; pop. (1991p) 33,178; cathedral. Taken c. 1160 by Holy Roman Emperor Frederick Barbarossa; under Milan and then Venice; to Austria 1815, until becoming part of the kingdom of Italy.

Cre·mo·na \kre-ˈmō-nä\. **1.** Province of Lombardy, N Italy. See table at ITALY.
2. Fortified commune, its ✻, on Po River 49 mi. (79 km.) ESE of Milan; pop. (1991p) 73,404; 12th cent. cathedral; 13th cent. town hall; in 16th–18th cents. violins manufactured by the Amati and Guarnieri families and by Antonio Stradivari. Colonized by Romans 218 B.C. on site of Gallic village; destroyed c. 69 A.D. by Roman commander (later emperor) Titus Flavius Vespasianus; medieval town incorp. by Milan 1334.

Cren·shaw \ˈkren-ˌshȯ\. County in S Alabama. See table at ALABAMA.

Cré·py \krā-ˈpē\ *or in full* **Cré·py–en–Laon·nois** \-ˌäⁿ-läⁿ-ˈnwä\. Commune, Aisne dept., N France, ab. 6 mi. (10 km.) NW of Laon; Treaty of Crépy signed Sept. 1544 bet. Francis I of France and Holy Roman Emperor Charles V.

Crépy–en–Va·lois \-äⁿ-val-ˈwä\. Commune, Oise dept., N France, ab. 16 mi. (26 km.) S of Compiègne; ancient ✻ of Valois; remains of château; churches of St. Denis and St. Thomas.

Cres \ˈtsres\ *or Ital.* **Cher·so** \ˈker-sō\. Island, in the Kvarnerić Channel (Gulf of Quarnero), Croatia, at the head of the Adriatic Sea; 158 sq. mi. (409 sq. km.); belonged to Austria before WWI, then to Italy; since 1947 part of Croatia.

Cres·cent, Lake \ˈkres-ᵊnt\. Lake, Clallam co., NW Washington, N of Olympic Mts.

Crescent City. City, ⊗ of Del Norte co., NW corner of California, on coast; pop. (1990c) 4380; fishing.

Cres·co \ˈkres-kō\. City, ⊗ of Howard co., N Iowa, 18 mi. (29 km.) WNW of Decorah; pop. (1990c) 3669.

Cress·kill \ˈkres-ˌkil\. Borough, Bergen co., NE corner of New Jersey, 11 mi. (18 km.) E of Paterson; pop. (1990c) 7558.

Cressy. See CRÉCY–EN–PONTHIEU.

Crest \ˈkrest\. Commune, Drôme dept., SE France; keep of a 12th cent. castle.

Crest Hill. City, Will co., NE Illinois, W of Hammond, Indiana; pop. (1990c) 10,643.

Crest·line \ˈkrest-ˌlīn\. City, Crawford co., N cen. Ohio, 12 mi. (19 km.) W of Mansfield; pop. (1990c) 4934.

Cres·ton \ˈkres-tən\. **1.** City, ⊗ of Union co., S Iowa, 57 mi. (92 km.) SW of Des Moines; pop. (1990c) 7911; Southwestern Community Coll. (1926).
2. Town, British Columbia, Canada, 45 mi. (72 km.) SE of Nelson; pop. (1991c) 4205.

Cres·tone Needle \ˈkres-tōn\. Peak, Custer and Saguache cos., S cen. Colorado; 14,191 ft. (4325 m.).

Crestone Peak. Peak, Custer and Saguache cos., S cen. Colorado; 14,294 ft. (4357 m.).

Crest·view \ˈkrest-ˌvyü\. City, ⊗ of Okaloosa co., NW Florida, 47 mi. (76 km.) ENE of Pensacola; pop. (1990c) 9886.

Crest·wood \ˈkrest-ˌwu̇d\. **1.** Village, Cook co., NE Illinois, 4 mi. (6.4 km.) SW of Chicago; pop. (1990c) 10,823.
2. City, St. Louis co., E Missouri; pop. (1990c) 11,234.

Crete \ˈkrēt\. **1.** Village, Will co., NE Illinois, 14 mi. (22.5 km.) S of Chicago; pop. (1990c) 6773.
2. City, Saline co., SE Nebraska, 19 mi. (31 km.) SW of Lincoln; pop. (1990c) 4841; Doane Coll. (1872).
3. *or Gk.* **Krí·ti** \ˈkrē-tē\; *anc.* **Cre·ta** \ˈkrē-tə\ *also* **Can·dia** \ˈkan-dē-ə\. Greek island in E Mediterranean Sea, SSE of Greece; ab. 160 mi. (257 km.) long and from 6 to 35 mi. (10 to 56 km.) wide; 3189 sq. mi. (8260 sq. km.); pop. (1991p) 536,980; ✻ Iráklion; with several smaller islands forms an administrative division of Greece, comprising the departments of Canea, Iráklion, Lasithion, and Rethýmnē. Has high central range of mountains, highest Mt. Ida 8058 ft. (2456 m.); many short streams, watering districts that produce citrus fruits and olives; tourism; has several prominent capes (as Busa, Krio, Sidero) and is indented by many bays, esp. Suda, Canea, Messara. Chief towns Iráklion, Canea, Rethymnon.
History: Inhabited from Neolithic times; in the Bronze Age, developed an advanced civilization (the Minoan civilization c. 3000–c. 1100 B.C.); palaces built at Knossos, Phaestus, and Mallia c. 2000 B.C.; at peak of power c. 16th cent. B.C., with influence extending to surrounding islands and to the mainland (see MYCENAE); declined from 15th cent. B.C., perhaps as result of invasion from the Greek mainland; annexed to Rome 67 B.C.; part of Byzantine Empire from 395 A.D.; taken by Saracens 9th cent.; reconquered for Byzantines by Emperor Nicephorus Phocas 961; passed to Venice as a result of Fourth Crusade 1204; conquered 1669 by Ottoman Turks; in the late 19th cent., sought to expel Turks and unite with Greece; after a series of insurrections, achieved limited self-rule 1898; officially united with Greece 1913; in WWII captured by German airborne forces May 1941.

Crete, Sea of; *formerly* **Sea of Can·dia** \ˈkan-dē-ə\ *or Gk.* **Krē·ti·kòn Pé·la·gos** \ˌkrē-tē-ˈkön-ˈpā-lä-ḡōs\. Part of the E Mediterranean Sea N of Crete and S of the Cyclades.

Crêt de la Neige. See NEIGE, MOUNT.

Cré·teil \krā-ˈtā\. Commune, ✻ of Val-de-Marne dept., N France, SE suburb of Paris on Marne River.

Creus, Cape \ˈkrā-əs\. Cape on extreme NE coast of Spain; W limit of Gulf of Lion.

Creuse \ˈkrœ̄z, ˈkrüz\. **1.** River, France; rises in Creuse dept., flows NW into Vienne River; 160 mi. (257 km.) long.
2. Department of cen. France. See table at FRANCE.

Creusot, Le. See LE CREUSOT.

Cre·val·co·re \ˌkrā-väl-ˈkȯ-rā\. Commune, Bologna prov., Emilia-Romagna, N Italy; pop. (1981p) 11,742.

Creve Coeur. **1.** \ˈkrēv-ˈku̇r\. Village, Tazewell co., cen. Illinois; pop. (1990c) 5938.
2. \ˈkrēv-ˌkȯr, -ˌkär\. City, St. Louis co., E Missouri, W of the city of St. Louis; pop. (1990c) 12,304.

Crewe \ˈkrü\. Town, Cheshire, NW England, 30 mi. (48 km.) SE of Liverpool; pop. (1981p) 47,759; important railroad center; incorp. 1877.

Crick·lade \ˈkrik-ˌlād\. Market town, Wiltshire, England, on the Thames 9 mi. (14 km.) NW of Swindon; Romans estab. fort first cent. A.D.; received city charter under Henry II 12th cent.

Crieff \ˈkrēf\. Burgh, Tayside region, cen. Scotland; pop. (1981p) 5442; resort.

Cril·lon, Mount \ˈkri-lən\. Peak, S Alaska, on Fairweather Penin. S of Mt. Fairweather; 12,726 ft. (3879 m.); summit reached for first time 1934.

Cri·mea \krī-ˈmē-ə\ *or Russ.* **Krym** \ˈkrim\ *or since 1992 officially* **Cri·me·an Republic** \krī-ˈmē-ən\; *1954–91* **Crimean Oblast.** Administrative subdivision of Ukraine; 10,425 sq. mi. (27,001 sq. km.); pop. (1991e) 2,549,800; ✻ Simferopol; coextensive with **Crimean Peninsula,** extending into the Black Sea and having the Sea of Azov to the NE; joined to mainland by Isthmus of Perekop which has Karkinit Bay on W and Sivash or Putrid Sea on E; its E extension is the Kerch Penin., separated from Russian mainland (Krasnodar Kray) by Kerch Strait, the entrance to the Sea of Azov; from W end of Kerch Penin. a long narrow spit of land, the Arabat, extends NW bet. Sea of Azov and Sivash Sea; N two thirds is steppe country, with good soil for agriculture; along SE shore extends the Yaila Range reaching a height of 5000 ft. (1524 m.); its rivers are short unnavigable streams.

Chief products: Wheat, corn, tobacco, flowers for essential oils; fishing; vineyards; iron ore; tourism.

Chief towns: Sevastopol', Simferopol', Kerch, Yevpatoriya.

History: Inhabitants in very early times were Cimmerians, who were expelled by Scythians 7th cent.; settled by Greeks 6th cent. B.C. (see KERCH and FEODOSIYA); from 5th cent. B.C., under kingdom of the Cimmerian Bosporus, eventually becoming subject to Rome; in the first millennium A.D., invaded by Goths, Huns, and by Khazars; partially in Byzantine Empire; invaded by Tatars 13th cent., who became subject to Ottoman Turks late 15th cent.; annexed by Russia 1783. Scene of Crimean War (Turkey, England, France, Sardinia against Russia) 1854–56; became an autonomous republic of the Russian S.F.S.R. 1921; in WWII overrun by Nazi armies 1941 (see SEVASTOPOL'); retaken 1944; republic liquidated and ab. 200,000 Tatars exiled to Soviet Central Asia and Siberia 1945 for alleged collaboration with Nazis; status changed to oblast; reconstituted as a Ukrainian oblast 1954; exiled Tatars began to return in the late 1980s. Following the dissolution of the Soviet Union in 1991, Crimea obtained some degree of autonomy, although its exact status remained a subject of debate bet. Russia and Ukraine.

Cri·mi·sus \krə-ˈmī-səs\ *or* **Cri·mis·sus** \-ˈmi-səs\. River, W Sicily, Italy; scene of battle in which Greek statesman and general Timoleon defeated the Carthaginians 341 B.C.

Crim·mit·schau *or* **Krim·mit·schau** \ˈkri-mət-ˌshau̇\. City, Saxony, Germany, 36 mi. (58 km.) S of Leipzig; pop. (1992e) 22,245.

Crip·ple Creek \ˈkri-pəl\. City, ⊗ of Teller co., cen. Colorado, SW of Colorado Springs; pop. (1990c) 584; tourism; developed as a gold-mining boomtown.

Cri·sa \ˈkrī-sə\. Ancient city of Phocis, cen. Greece, near Delphi and bet. it and its port on the Gulf of Corinth; destroyed by Amphictyonic League in First Sacred War c. 590 B.C. See DELPHI 2.

Cris·field \ˈkris-ˌfēld\. City, Somerset co., SE Maryland, on Chesapeake Bay 32 mi. (52 km.) SW of Salisbury; pop. (1990c) 2880; oysters, crabs.

Crisp \ˈkrisp\. County in SW cen. Georgia. See table at GEORGIA.

Cris·to·bal *or Span.* **Cris·tó·bal** \krēs-ˈtō-b̲äl\. **1.** Former district in NW Canal Zone, Panama.
2. Town, N cen. Panama; a suburb of Colón and Rainbow City, at Atlantic entrance to Panama Canal.

Cristóbal Co·lón, Pi·co \ˈpē-kō-krēs-ˈtō-b̲äl-kō-ˈlōn\. Peak in the Sierra Nevada de Santa Marta, N Colombia; ab. 19,020 ft. (5795 m.); highest peak in Colombia.

Crit·ten·den \ˈkrit-ᵊn-dən\. Name of counties in two states of the U.S. See tables at ARKANSAS and KENTUCKY.

Cr·na \ˈtsər-nä\ *or* **Cher·na** \ˈcher-nä\. River, Rep. of Macedonia; flows SE and N into Vardar River; 125 mi. (201 km.) long.

Crna Gora. See MONTENEGRO 1.

Croagh Pat·rick \krō-ˈpa-trik\. Mountain in S co. Mayo, W Ireland; 2510 ft. (765 m.); according to tradition, place where St. Patrick began his missionary work in Ireland.

Cro·atan Sound \ˌkrō-ə-ˈtan\. Strait bet. Roanoke I. and the mainland of Dare co., E North Carolina.

Cro·a·tia \krō-ˈā-shə\ *or Croat.* **Hr·vat·ska** \hər-ˈvät-skä\. Independent country, SE Europe, a constituent republic of Yugoslavia 1946–91; 21,829 sq. mi. (56,537 sq. km.); pop. (1993e) 4,821,000; ✻ Zagreb; bauxite, coal, oil. Boundaries have varied greatly at different periods. Chief towns: Zagreb, Split, Rijeka, Osijek.

History: For earlier history of region, see PANNONIA. From 7th cent. A.D., inhabited by Croats, a S Slavic people, whom Holy Roman Emperor Charlemagne made tributary to Franks early 9th cent.; converted to Roman Catholicism; formed into kingdom under Tomislav c. 925; joined with Hungary in dynastic union (1102); retained varying degrees of autonomy in union with Hungary over the next eight centuries; most of Croatia taken by Turks 1526, remaining part accepted Hapsburg rule 1527, Turkish part restored by Treaty of Karlowitz 1699; parts of Croatia included in French Emperor Napoléon's Illyrian Provinces (*q.v.*) 1809–13; helped Austria put down Hungarian revolution 1848–49 and as a result formed with Slavonia separate Austrian crown land which was reunited to Hungary as part of *Ausgleich* (compromise) 1867 (see AUSTRIA-HUNGARY) and set up as a Hungarian crown land **Croatia–Sla·vo·nia** \-slə-ˈvō-nē-ə, -nyə\; united with other Yugoslav areas to proclaim kingdom of Serbs, Croats, and Slovenes 1918 (see YUGOSLAVIA); resisted the centralizing policies of Serb-dominated Yugoslavia and in 1939 was united with Dalmatia and parts of Bosnia and Herzegovina to form an autonomous region within Yugoslavia; nominally independent state 1941–45; became a constituent republic of Yugoslavia in 1946 constitution; declared independence June 25, 1991, precipitating war with Serbia; recognized by the international community 1992.

Crock·ett \ˈkrä-kət\. **1.** Name of counties in two states of the U.S. See tables at TENNESSEE and TEXAS.
2. City, ⊗ of Houston co., E Texas, 32 mi. (52 km.) S of Palestine; pop. (1990c) 7024.

Croc·o·dile \ˈkrä-kə-ˌdīl\. **1.** River, Africa. See LIMPOPO.
2. A headstream of the Komati River, Mpumalanga prov., Rep. of South Africa.

Crocodilopolis. See ARSINOË 2.

Croia. See KRUJË.

Croix \ˈkrwä\. Commune, Nord dept., N France, NE suburb of Lille; pop. (1990c) 20,308.

Cro·ker Island \ˈkrō-kər\. Island off N coast of Cobourg Penin., Northern Terr., Australia; 30 mi. (48 km.) long.

Cro–Magnon. See EYZIES, LES.

Crom·ar·ty Firth \ˈkrä-mər-tē\. Inlet of Moray Firth, Highland region, N Scotland.

Cro·mer \ˈkrō-mər\. Resort town, Norfolk, England, on North Sea coast 24 mi. (39 km.) N of Norwich; pop. (1981p) 6192; coast guard and lifeboat station.

Comp·ton \ˈkrəmp-tən\. Town, Greater Manchester, NW England, NE of Manchester; pop. (1981p) 19,938.

Crom·well \ˈkräm-ˌwel, -wəl\. **1.** Town, NW Middlesex co., S Connecticut, on Connecticut River; pop. (1990c) 12,286; Holy Apostles Coll. (1956); town incorp. 1851.
2. Borough, S South I., New Zealand, on upper Clutha River in lake region; pop. (1991c) 4294.

Crook \ˈkru̇k\. **1.** Name of counties in two states of the U.S. See tables at OREGON and WYOMING.
2. Town, Durham, N England, 20 mi. (32 km.) SSW of Newcastle upon Tyne.

Crook·ed \ˈkru̇-kəd\. River, cen. Oregon; flows W and NW into Deschutes River; 105 mi. (169 km.) long.

Crooked Creek. River, SW Illinois; flows into Kaskaskia River; ab. 50 mi. (80 km.) long.

Crooked Island. One of the Bahamas, in cen. part of group S of San Salvador (Watling); 76 sq. mi. (197 sq. km.).

Crooked Island Passage. Deepwater channel in Bahamas, S and SE of Long I. and NW of Crooked I. and Acklins I.; ab. 40 mi. (64 km.) wide.

Crooks·ton \ˈkru̇k-stən\. City, ⊗ of Polk co., NW Minnesota, 32 mi. (52 km.) SW of Thief River Falls; pop. (1990c) 8119.

Crooks·ville \ˈkru̇ks-ˌvil\. Village, Perry co., SE cen. Ohio, 13 mi. (21 km.) S of Zanesville; pop. (1990c) 2601.

Crop·redy \ˈkräp-ˌre-dē\. Village, N Oxfordshire, cen. England, ab. 4 mi. (6 km.) N of Banbury; scene of battle (Cropredy Bridge) 1644 in which the Royalists defeated the Parliamentarians under Sir William Waller.

Cros·by \ˈkrȯz-bē\. **1.** County in NW Texas. See table at TEXAS.
2. City, ⊗ of Divide co., NW North Dakota; pop. (1990c) 1312.
3. *or* **Great Crosby.** Town, Merseyside, NW England, on Irish Sea at mouth of the Mersey 6 mi. (10 km.) NNW of Liverpool; pop. (1981p) 53,660.

Crosby, Mount. Peak, S Park co., NW Wyoming; 12,435 ft. (3790 m.).

Cros·by·ton \ˈkrȯz-bēt-ᵊn\. City, ⊗ of Crosby co., NW Texas, E of Lubbock; pop. (1990c) 2026.

Cross \ˈkrȯs\. **1.** County in E Arkansas. See table at ARKANSAS.
2. River, W Africa; flows from Cameroon W and S through Nigeria to Bight of Biafra; ab. 300 mi. (485 km.) long.

Cross, Cape. Cape on NW coast of Namibia; point farthest S (22°S) reached by Portuguese navigator Diogo Cão during 2d voyage (1485–86); cross erected here by him.

Cross Bay. Bay on NW coast of Spitsbergen I., Norway.

Cross City. Town, ⊗ of Dixie co., NW Florida Penin., 50 mi. (81 km.) W of Gainesville; pop. (1990c) 2041.

Cros·sett \ˈkrȯ-sət\. City, Ashley co., SE Arkansas, 42 mi. (68 km.) E of El Dorado; pop. (1990c) 6282.

Cross Fell. See PENNINE CHAIN.

Cross–Florida Waterway. See OKEECHOBEE WATERWAY.

Cross Keys. Former post village, S Rockingham co., Virginia, 20 mi. (32 km.) NE of Staunton; battle June 8, 1862 in which Confederates under Gen. Richard Stoddert Ewell defeated Union troops under Gen. John Charles Frémont.

Cross Mountain. Peak in the Sierra Nevada, in N Tulare co., S cen. California; 12,140 ft. (3700 m.).

Cross River. **1.** See CROSS 2.
2. *formerly* **South–Eastern.** State of SE Nigeria. See table at NIGERIA.

Cross Sound. Inlet of Pacific Ocean bet. SE Alaska and N Chichagof I.; joins S end of Glacier Bay.

Cross·ville \ˈkrȯs-ˌvil\. City, ⊗ of Cumberland co., E cen. Tennessee, 28 mi. (45 km.) W of Harriman; pop. (1990c) 6930.

Cro·ton \ˈkrōt-ᵊn\. River, SE New York; flows from Dutchess co. S and SW through Putnam and Westchester cos. into Hudson River; ab. 60 mi. (95 km.) long; important source of water supply for New York City since 1842, when **Croton Aqueduct** (tunnel 31 mi. or 50 km. long when completed) first brought in water from original reservoir near its mouth; contains a system of dams and reservoirs incl. Croton Falls and New Croton.

Cro·to·ne \krō-ˈtō-nā\ *or sometimes* **Co·tro·ne** \kō-ˈtrō-nā\; *anc.* **Cro·to·na** \krə-ˈtō-nə\ *or* **Cro·ton** \ˈkrō-ˌtän, ˈkrōt-ᵊn\. Commune, Catanzaro prov., Calabria, S Italy, on Gulf of Taranto; pop. (1991p) 55,633; cathedral; old castle. Ancient Greek republic, founded by Achaeans c. 710 B.C.; 6th cent. home of renowned Olympic athlete Milo and, from c. 530 B.C., of philosopher and mathematician Pythagoras; destroyed rival town of Sybaris 510 B.C.; declined as a result of wars, most notably the war with Pyrrhus, king of Epirus, 3d cent. B.C.

Cro·ton Falls Dam \ˈkrōt-ᵊn\. Dam across W branch of Croton River, Putnam co., SE New York, height 167 ft. (51 m.); forms **Croton Falls Reservoir,** part of Croton system of water supply for New York City.

Croton–on–Hudson. Village, Westchester co., SE New York, on Hudson River 34 mi. (55 km.) N of New York City; pop. (1990c) 7018.

Crow \ˈkrō\. River, S Minnesota; flows NE into Mississippi River above Anoka; formed by junction of N and S forks on boundary bet. Hennepin and Wright cos.; ab. 50 mi. (80 km.) long.

Crow·bor·ough \ˈkrō-ˌbər-ō\. Town, East Sussex, SE England, SSE of London; pop. (1981c) 15,082.

Crow·ell \ˈkrō-əl\. City, ⊗ of Foard co., N Texas, 30 mi. (48 km.) SW of Vernon; pop. (1990c) 1230.

Crow·ley \ˈkrau̇-lē\. **1.** County in E Colorado. See table at COLORADO.
2. City, ⊗ of Acadia parish, S Louisiana, 24 mi. (39 km.) W of Lafayette; pop. (1990c) 13,983.
3. City, Tarrant co., N Texas, 10 mi. (16 km.) S of Fort Worth; pop. (1990c) 6974.

Crown Heights \ˈkrau̇n\. Neighborhood, N cen. Brooklyn borough, New York City.

Crown Mountain. **1.** Peak, Hinsdale and San Juan cos., SW Colorado; 13,600 ft. (4145 m.).
2. Peak, S Brewster co., W Texas; 7186 ft. (2190 m.).
3. *or* **Crown Hill.** Peak, W cen. St. Thomas I., in the Virgin Is. of the U.S., West Indies; 1556 ft. (474 m.); highest point in the Virgin Is.

Crown Point. **1.** City, ⊗ of Lake co., NW Indiana, 13 mi. (21 km.) S of Lake Michigan; pop. (1990c) 17,728.
2. Town, Essex co., NE New York, on Lake Champlain ab. 7 mi. (11 km.) S of Ticonderoga; pop. (1990c) 1963; the French built **Fort St. Fré·dér·ic** \ˌseⁿ-frā-dā-ˈrēk, ˌsānt-ˈfre-də-rik, -drik\ here 1731 as proposed ✱ of territory; in French and Indian War, resisted English attacks 1755–56; taken 1759 by Gen. Jeffrey Amherst who began Fort Amherst (renamed Fort Crown Point); captured by Seth Warner and Green Mountain Boys at beginning of American Revolution 1775; again briefly held by British 1777; ruins of forts, now part of an historic site.

Crown Prince Range. Mountain range in S part of Bougainville I., NW Solomon Is., Papua New Guinea; highest peak 7383 ft. (2250 m.).

Crown Prince Rudolf Island \ˈrü-ˌdȯlf\. Northernmost island of Franz Josef Land, Arctic Ocean.

Crown Princess Martha Land. See PRINCESS MARTHA COAST.

Crow Peak \ˈkrō\. Mountain, Lawrence co., W South Dakota; 5787 ft. (1764 m.).

Crow's Nest \ˈkrōz-ˌnest\. **1.** Mountain, Orange co., New York, on W bank of the Hudson above West Point; 1396 ft. (426 m.).
2. Mountain, Pennington co., SW South Dakota; 7048 ft. (2148 m.).

Crows·nest Pass \ˈkrōz-ˌnest\. Pass through Rocky Mts., in SE British Columbia, Canada, on Alberta border; lat. 49°35′N; alt. 5500 ft. (1676 m.).

Crow Wing \ˈkrō-ˌwiŋ\. **1.** River, Minnesota; formed by branches in N Wadena co., cen. Minnesota; flows SE and E into the Mississippi on SW boundary of Crow Wing co.

2. County in cen. Minnesota. See table at MINNESOTA.

Croy·don \'krȯid-^{ə}n\. **1.** City, Victoria, Australia, an E suburb of Melbourne; pop. (1991c) 45,807.

2. A borough of Greater London, SE England. See table at LONDON 4.

Cro·zet Islands \krō-'zā\. Five small French islands in S Indian Ocean, 46°S, 52°E; 195 sq. mi. (505 sq. km.); discovered 1772 by French navigator Marion-Dufresne.

Cruachan, Ben. See BEN CRUACHAN.

Cru·ces \'krü-ses\. Town and municipality, Las Villas prov., W cen. Cuba; munic. pop. (1990e) 22,175.

Crum El·bow \ˌkrəm-'el-bō\. Double bend in Hudson River ab. 4 mi. (6 km.) above Poughkeepsie, New York.

Crum·mock Water \'krə-mək\. Lake in Cumberland co., NW England; 3 mi. (5 km.) long, max. depth 144 ft. (44 m.).

Cruz, Cabo *or* **Cruz, Cape** \'krüs\. Cape at SW point of SE Cuba, projecting into Caribbean Sea.

Cruz, Point \'krüz\. Small coral promontory just W of mouth of Mataniko River, NW coast of Guadalcanal I., SE Solomon Is.; in WWII scene of considerable fighting.

Cruz Al·ta \krü-'zäl-tə\. City, Rio Grande do Sul state, S Brazil; munic. pop. (1991p) 68,794.

Cruz Bay \'krüz\. Town at W end of St. John I., Virgin Is. of the U.S., West Indies.

Cruz del Eje \'krüs-t͟hel-'ā-hā\. Town, Córdoba prov., N cen. Argentina.

Cru·zei·ro \krü-'zā-rü\. **1.** City, Santa Catarina, Brazil. See JOAÇABA.

2. City, São Paulo state, S Brazil, WNW of Rio de Janeiro; pop. (1991p) 65,862.

Cruz Gran·de \'krüs-'grän-dā\. Seaport, cen. Chile, 32 mi. (52 km.) N of Coquimbo.

Crys·tal \'krist-^{ə}l\. City, Hennepin co., SE cen. Minnesota, 15 mi. (24 km.) W of Minneapolis; pop. (1990c) 23,788.

Crystal Beach. Village, Niagara munic. region, Ontario, Canada, on shore of Lake Erie.

Crystal City. **1.** City, Jefferson co., E Missouri, on Mississippi River 30 mi. (48 km.) S of St. Louis; pop. (1990c) 4088.

2. City, ⊗ of Zavala co., S Texas, 35 mi. (56 km.) S of Uvalde; pop. (1990c) 8263; shipping center for agriculturally productive region called "Winter Garden," growing esp. spinach.

Crystal Falls. City, ⊗ of Iron co., NW Michigan, 23 mi. (37 km.) NNW of Iron Mountain (city); pop. (1990c) 1922; iron deposits in nearby Menominee Range area.

Crystal Lake. City, McHenry co., N Illinois, 28 mi. (45 km.) WSW of Waukegan; pop. (1990c) 24,512; McHenry County Coll. (1967).

Crystal River. City, Citrus co., W Florida Penin.; pop. (1990c) 4044.

Crystal Springs. City, Copiah co., SW Mississippi, 23 mi. (37 km.) SSW of Jackson; pop. (1990c) 5643.

Csallóköz. See GREAT SCHÜTT.

Cse·pel \'che-ˌpel\. **1.** Island in Danube River S of Budapest, cen. Hungary; 30 mi. (48 km.) long.

2. Commune on N tip of Csepel I.

Cson·grád \'chōŋ-ˌgräd\. County of S Hungary. See table at HUNGARY.

Ctes·i·phon \'te-sə-ˌfän, 'tē-\. Ancient ruined city in cen. Iraq, on E bank of the Tigris opp. Seleucia and 20 mi. (32 km.) SSE of Baghdad; ✻ of the ancient kingdom of Parthia (*q.v.*) and of later Sassanid empire (see IRAN); part of the great vaulted hall of this later period still standing. Captured by Arabs 637 A.D.; declined after building of Arab ✻ at Baghdad (*q.v.*); scene of WWI battle won by Turks over the British Nov. 1915.

Cua·ji·mal·pa \ˌkwä-hē-'mäl-pä\. Municipality, Federal District, Mexico, 11 mi. (18 km.) SW of Mexico City.

Cuando. See KWANDO.

Cuan·do–Cu·ban·go \'kwän-dō-kü-'bäŋ-gō\. Province of SE Angola. See table at ANGOLA.

Cuango. See KWANGO.

Cuan·za *or* **Kwan·za** \'kwän-zä\. River, cen. Angola; rises in S cen. part of the country, flows NW into Atlantic Ocean near Luanda; 600 mi. (965 km.) long.

Cuanza Nor·te \'nȯr-tē\. Province of NW Angola. See table at ANGOLA.

Cuanza Sul \'sül\. Province of W Angola. See table at ANGOLA.

Cuauh·té·moc \kwau̇-'tā-mäk\. Municipality, Chihuahua state, Mexico, 55 mi. (89 km.) W of the city of Chihuahua; pop. (1990p) 112,631.

Cuau·tla \'kwau̇t-lä\. Town, Morelos state, S cen. Mexico, ab. 18 mi. (29 km.) SE of Cuernavaca; munic. pop. (1990p) 120,301; alt. 4350 ft. (1326 m.); sulfur springs; resort.

Cu·ba \'kyü-bə, *Span.* 'kü-b͟ä\. **1.** Island in the Greater Antilles, West Indies, S of Florida and N of W Caribbean Sea; ab. 41,620 sq. mi. (107,800 sq. km.); with adjacent islands forms Republic of Cuba.

2. *officially* **Republic of Cuba.** Independent country, comprising the island of Cuba and surrounding small islands; 42,804 sq. mi. or 110,862 sq. km.; pop. (1993e) 10,892,000; ✻ Havana.

Physical features: Island 746 mi. (1200 km.) long from Cape Maisí on E to Cape San Antonio on W; varies in width from 25 to 125 mi. (40 to 201 km.); has coastline of ab. 2000 mi. (3200 km.) with many cays and islands (largest Isla de la Juventud off SW); largely flat or rolling country; highest point in Santiago de Cuba prov. (Pico Turquino 6560 ft. or 2000 m.); rivers mostly short and rapid.

Chief export: Sugar; other products: fruit, coffee, rice, tobacco, nickel, manganese; livestock raising, fishing; manufacturing: food processing (esp. sugar refining), tobacco products esp. cigars (considered among the world's best), textiles, cement.

Chief cities: Havana, Santiago de Cuba, Camagüey, Holguín, Guantánamo, Santa Clara.

Political divisions: Divided into the following 14 provinces and the special municipality of Isla de la Juventud (for pronunciation of their names, see their individual entries):

NAME	AREA (sq. mi.)	AREA (sq. km.)	POP. (1990e)	CAPITAL
Provinces				
Camagüey	5,654	14,644	740,314	Camagüey
Ciego de Avila	2,594	6,718	364,000	Ciego de Avila
Cienfuegos	1,660	4,299	364,069	Cienfuegos
Granma	3,381	8,757	789,336	Bayamo
Guantánamo	2,546	6,594	496,548	Guantánamo
Holguín	3,642	9,433	992,661	Holguín
La Habana	2,268	5,874	643,422	Güira de Melena
La Habana, Ciudad de	296	767	2,096,054	
Las Tunas	2,549	6,602	491,967	Victoria de las Tunas
Matanzas	4,668	12,090	608,832	Matanzas
Pinar del Río	4,344	11,251	690,625	Pinar del Río
Sancti Spíritus	2,695	6,980	428,262	Sancti Spíritus
Santiago de Cuba	2,537	6,571	990,621	Santiago de Cuba
Villa Clara	3,228	8,360	807,705	Santa Clara
Special Municipality				
Isla de la Juventud	1,182	3,061	72,505	

History: Inhabited by the Ciboney and Taino, among others, when explorer Christopher Columbus arrived during his first voyage 1492; conquest by Spaniards began 1511 with the founding of Baracoa by Diego Velázquez; following depletion of indigenous population, importation of African slaves began; captured by British 1762, but restored to Spain 1763; revolted unsuccessfully 1868–78 (the Ten Years' War); abolished slavery 1886; rose again in 1895, as result of which U.S. entered Spanish-American War 1898; Spain relinquished its claim to Cuba under Treaty of Paris Dec. 10, 1898; Cuba took over its own government May 20, 1902 following a three-year American military occupation, although the U.S. retained intervention rights under the Platt Amendment of the 1901 constitution; signed treaty leasing Guantánamo Bay to U.S., which used it as naval base; occupied

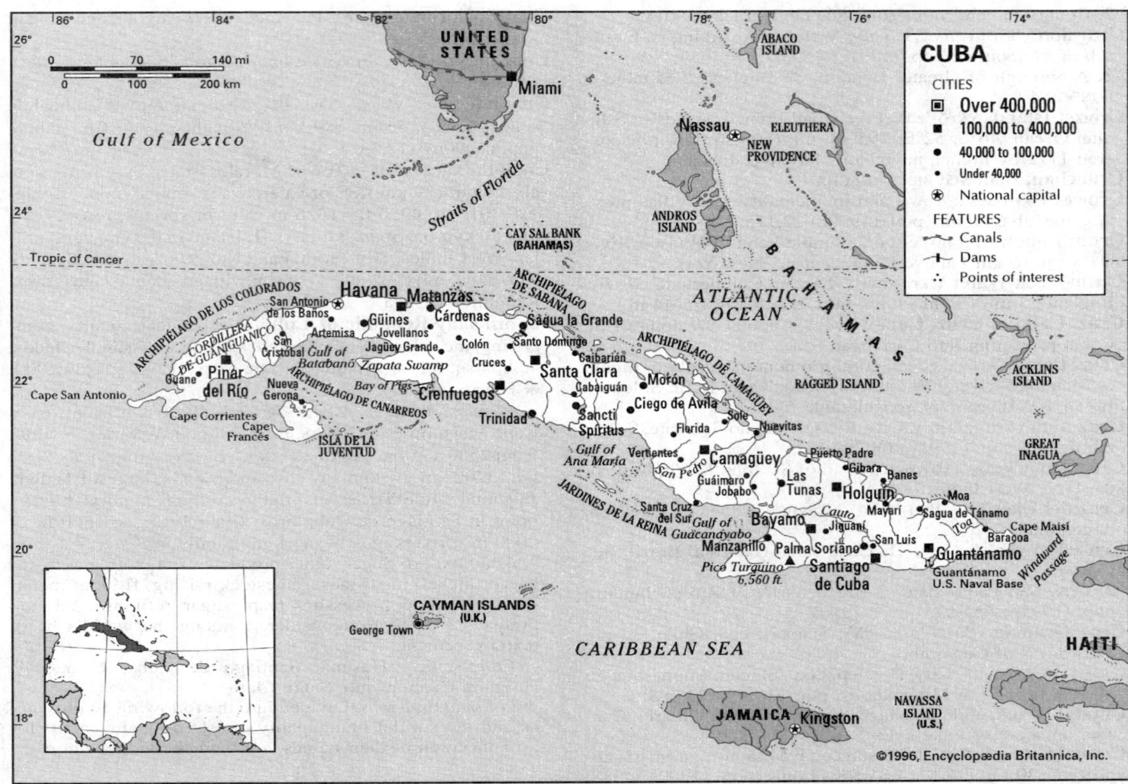

1906–09 by U.S. troops, who also intervened on other occasions; entered WWI 1917; given full claim to Isla de la Juventud 1925; Cuban sovereignty unrestricted after U.S. abrogation of Platt Amendment 1934; declared war on Axis powers Dec. 1941. Regime of dictator Fulgencio Batista y Zaldívar fell Jan. 1959 to forces of Fidel Castro, who began implementing Communist rule; following sharp U.S. reaction U.S.S.R. forced to remove its missiles from Cuban soil 1962, but U.S.S.R remained an economic backer; massive emigration followed easing of restrictions 1980; in late 1980s as Communism collapsed in U.S.S.R., lost significant financial backing and economy suffered greatly.

3. City, Crawford co., Missouri; pop. (1990c) 2537.

Cubango. See OKAVANGO.

Cu·ba·tão \ˌkü-bə-ˈtau̇^{n}\. City, São Paulo state, S Brazil, SE of the city of São Paulo; pop. (1991p) 90,572.

Çu·buk \chü-ˈbük\. **1.** River, tributary of the Ankara, N Turkey in Asia; 52 mi. (84 km.) long; dam and reservoir (completed 1935) furnish water for irrigation around Ankara.

2. Town, N Turkey in Asia, on river 8 mi. (13 km.) N of Ankara.

Cuck·field \ˈkək-ˌfēld\. Town, West Sussex co., S England; pop. (1981p) 28,254.

Cú·cu·ta \ˈkü-kü-tä\ *also* **San Jo·sé de Cúcuta** \ˌsän-hō-ˈsā-t̲h̲ā-\. City, ✻ of Norte de Santander dept., N Colombia, near the Venezuelan border, on Colombia-Venezuela highway; pop. (1992e) 450,300; in coffee- and oil-producing region; destroyed by earthquake 1875, rebuilt.

Cud·a·hy \ˈkə-də-ˌhē\. **1.** City, Los Angeles co., SW California, 4 mi. (6.4 km.) E of S part of the city of Los Angeles; pop. (1990c) 22,817.

2. City, Milwaukee co., SE Wisconsin, on Lake Michigan 7 mi. (11 km.) S of the city of Milwaukee; pop. (1990c) 18,659.

Cud·da·lore \ˈkəd-^{ə}l-ˌōr\. Town, E Tamil Nadu, S India, on Coromandel Coast 18 mi. (29 km.) S of Pondicherry; pop. (1991p) 143,774; seaport with mostly coastal trade; fishing, shipbuilding. Just to the N are ruins of Fort St. David (*q.v.*).

Cud·da·pah \ˈkə-də-pə\. Town, SW Andhra Pradesh, S India, near Penner River 140 mi. (225 km.) NW of Madras; pop. (1991p) 121,422.

Cu·dil·le·ro \ˌkü-t̲h̲ēl-ˈyā-rō, -t̲h̲ē-\. Commune, Asturias prov., NW Spain, on Bay of Biscay 22 mi. (35 km.) NW of Oviedo; pop. (1991c) 6657; manganese deposits nearby.

Cud·worth \ˈkəd-ˌwərth\. Town, South Yorkshire, N England; pop. (1981p) 9361.

Cuen·ca \ˈkweŋ-kä\. **1.** City, ✻ of Azuay prov., S Ecuador, ab. 68 mi. (109 km.) SE of Guayaquil; pop. (1990c) 194,981; alt. 8468 ft. (2581 m.); Panama hats, leather, textiles; university, cathedral. Founded by Spanish 1557 on site of native town called Tumibamba; made episcopal see 1786.

2. Province of cen. Spain. See table at SPAIN.

3. *anc.* **Con·ca** \ˈkōŋ-kə\. Commune, ✻ of Cuenca prov., E cen. Spain, on Júcar River 89 mi. (143 km.) ESE of Madrid; pop. (1991p) 42,615; 13th cent. Gothic cathedral; famous "hanging houses" built on steep hillsides; museum of abstract art; captured from Moors by Alfonso VIII of Castile 1177; under attack by French 1808 and 1810, and by Carlists 1874.

Cuenca, Serranía de. See SERRANÍA DE CUENCA.

Cuera. See CHUR.

Cuer·na·va·ca \ˌkwer-nä-ˈb̲ä-kä; ˌkwer-nə-ˈvä-kə, -ˈva-\. Town, ✻ of Morelos state, S cen. Mexico; pop. (1990p) 281,752; alt. 5058 ft. (1542 m.); flour; textiles, cement; university; 16th cent. cathedral; palace once lived in by Spanish conquistador Hernán Cortés; resort. Orig. inhabited by Aztecs; overrun by Spanish under Cortés 1521; a favorite retreat of Emperor Maximilian.

Cuer·nos of Ne·gros \ˈkwer-nōs … ˈnā-grōs\. Highest peak in Negros Oriental prov., Negros I., Philippines, in SE part W of city of Dumaguete; 6101 ft. (1860 m.).

Cue·ro \ˈkwer-ō\. City, ⊗ of De Witt co., S Texas, on

Guadalupe River 27 mi. (43 km.) NNW of Victoria; pop. (1990c) 6700.

Cue·vas del Al·man·zo·ra \ˈkwā-bä-t͟hel-ˌäl-män-ˈsō-rä\; *formerly* **Cuevas de Ve·ra** \t͟hā-ˈber-ä\. Commune, Almería prov., SE Spain, 42 mi. (68 km.) NE of the seaport of Almería; pop. (1991c) 9167.

Cu·gir \ˈkü-jēr\. Town, Alba co., Romania; pop. (1989c) 34,832.

Cu·ia·bá; *formerly* **Cu·ya·bá** \ˌkü-yə-ˈbä\. **1.** River, Mato Grosso state, SW Brazil; rises near Diamantino, flows S into São Lourenço River; ab. 300 mi. (485 km.) long.

2. City, ✻ of Mato Grosso state, SW Brazil, on Cuiabá River; munic. pop. (1991p) 401,112; in cattle raising and agricultural area; active river trade; on highway at W edge of plateau; founded in 18th cent.

Cuicuilco. See SAN CUICUILCO.

Cui·la·pa \kwē-ˈlä-pä\. Town, ✻ of Santa Rosa dept., S Guatemala, SE of Guatemala City; munic. pop. (1993e) 9861.

Cuil·lin Hills *or* **Coo·lin Hills** \ˈkü-lən\. Hills on Skye I., NW Scotland; highest peak 3309 ft. (1009 m.).

Cuillin Sound. Body of water off NW coast of Scotland, bet. Skye and Rum islands, Inner Hebrides.

Cuí·to \ˈkwē-tō\. River, SW Africa; rises in cen. Angola, flows through marshland, S and SE into Okavango River on Angola border; ab. 400 mi. (645 km.) long.

Cuit·zeo, Lake \kwit-ˈsā-ō\. Lake, Michoacán state, SW Mexico; 31 mi. (50 km.) long.

Cularo. See GRENOBLE.

Cul·ber·son \ˈkəl-bər-sən\. County in W Texas. See table at TEXAS.

Cu·le·bra \kü-ˈlā-brä; kü-ˈle-brə, kyü-\. Island off E coast of Puerto Rico; 10 sq. mi. (26 sq. km.); pop. (1990c) 1542; belongs to Puerto Rico; formerly site of a U.S. naval base.

Culebra Cut. See CULEBRA MOUNTAIN.

Culebra Gulf. See MURCIÉLAGOS, GULF OF.

Culebra Mountain. Hill, Panama, in SE part of former Canal Zone, through which **Culebra Cut** (see GAILLARD CUT) was made.

Culebra Peak. Mountain, Costilla and Las Animas cos., S Colorado; 14,069 ft. (4288 m.); in cen. part, called the **Culebra Range,** of the Sangre de Cristo Range.

Cul·goa \ˈkəl-ˌgō-ə\. River, SE Queensland and NE New South Wales, Australia; formed by junction of Maranoa and Condamine rivers, flows SW; with these streams the longest tributary of the Darling; ab. 200 mi. (320 km.) long.

Cu·lia·cán \ˌkül-yä-ˈkän\ *or officially* **Culiacán–Ro·sa·les** \-rō-ˈsä-les, -ˈzä-ləs\. Commercial city, ✻ of Sinaloa state, W Mexico, on **Culiacán River** (ab. 175 mi. or 280 km. long) 40 mi. (64 km.) from its mouth; munic. pop. (1990p) 602,114; winter vegetables; university; city founded on site of earlier Indian settlement by Spanish early 16th cent.

Cu·lion \kül-ˈyōn\. **1.** Island, S part of Calamian Group, N Palawan prov., Philippines; 150 sq. mi. (389 sq. km.).

2. Town on NE coast of island.

Cul·le·ra \kü-ˈlyer-ä, -ˈyer-\. Commune, Valencia prov., E Spain, on Júcar River near its mouth on the Mediterranean 24 mi. (39 km.) SSE of the commune of Valencia; captured 13th cent. from Moors by James I of Aragon.

Cul·li·nan \ˈkəl-ə-nən, -ˌnan\. Town, Gauteng prov., NE Rep. of South Africa, 20 mi. (32 km.) E of Pretoria; site of the Premier diamond mine in which was discovered 1905 the Cullinan diamond, at the time the largest found.

Cull·man \ˈkəl-mən\. **1.** County in N Alabama. See table at ALABAMA.

2. City, its ⊗, 45 mi. (72 km.) N of Birmingham; pop. (1990c) 13,367.

Cul·lod·en Moor \kə-ˈläd-ᵊn, -ˈlōd-\ *also* **Drum·mos·sie Moor** \ˌdrəm-ˈmō-sē\. Moor, Highland region, NW Scotland; battle Apr. 16, 1746 in which British force under William Augustus, duke of Cumberland, defeated Highland Jacobite force under Prince Charles Edward Stuart, thus ending last armed outbreak of the Stuart cause; notorious for slaughter of Highland wounded after battle.

Cul·lo·whee \ˈkə-lə-ˌwē\. Unincorporated settlement, Jackson co., SW North Carolina, ab. 16 mi. (26 km.) SW of Waynesville; pop. (1990c) 4029; Western Carolina Univ. (1889).

Culm. See CHEŁMNO.

Culmsee. See CHEŁMŻA.

Cul·pep·er \ˈkəl-ˌpep-ər\. **1.** County in N Virginia. See table at VIRGINIA.

2. Town, its ⊗, W of Fredericksburg; pop. (1990c) 8581; muster place in 1775 for Culpeper minutemen.

Culp's Hill. See CEMETERY RIDGE.

Cul·ver City \ˈkəl-vər\. City, Los Angeles co., SW California, SW of the city of Los Angeles; pop. (1990c) 38,793; aircraft production; motion-picture studios.

Cu·mae \ˈkyü-mē\. Ancient town, Campania, Italy, on coast W of Neapolis (Naples); one of oldest Greek colonies in Italy, founded c. 750 B.C.; allied with Hiero I of Syracusae (Siracusa) in his defeat of Etruscans in naval battle 474 B.C.; conquered by Samnites late 5th cent. B.C.; came under supremacy of Rome 338 B.C.; destroyed by Neapolitans 1205 A.D. On the site near the shore is the acropolis containing caves said to have been seat of the oracle of the Cumaean Sibyl; many Greek and Roman remains.

Cu·ma·ná \ˌkü-mä-ˈnä\. Seaport city, ✻ of Sucre state, N Venezuela, 185 mi. (298 km.) E of Caracas; pop. (1990p) 212,492; exports tobacco, cacao, fish, cotton textiles, coffee; university (1958).

History: Settled c. 1520 by Spanish missionary and historian Bartolomé de Las Casas who established a model Indian colony; destroyed by natives 1522; resettled shortly thereafter; thought by many to be oldest existing European settlement in South America; has often suffered from earthquakes and political upheaval.

Cum·bal, Ne·va·do de \nā-ˈbä-t͟hō-ˌt͟hā-küm-ˈbäl\. Volcano in the Andes, Nariño dept., SW Colombia, on border of Ecuador; 16,039 ft. (4889 m.).

Cum·ber·land \ˈkəm-bər-lənd\. **1.** Navigable river, S Kentucky and N Tennessee; formed by confluence of forks in Harlan co., SE Kentucky, flows W through S Kentucky, turns S in Monroe co. and makes great loop in N Tennessee, reenters Kentucky running N into Ohio River in W Livingston co., W Kentucky; 687 mi. (1105 km.) long. The **Cumberland Falls** *or* **Great Falls** (92 ft. or 28 m. high, over 100 ft. or 30 m. wide) are in cen. Whitley co., Kentucky. See *Great Falls Dam* in table at TENNESSEE VALLEY AUTHORITY.

2. Name of counties in eight states of the U.S. See tables at ILLINOIS, KENTUCKY, MAINE, NEW JERSEY, NORTH CAROLINA, PENNSYLVANIA, TENNESSEE, VIRGINIA.

3. Town, Hancock and Marion cos., Indiana, on E edge of Indianapolis; pop. (1990c) 2933.

4. City, Harlan co., SE Kentucky, 21 mi. (34 km.) SSE of Hazard; pop. (1990c) 3112.

5. Town, Cumberland co., SW Maine, 14 mi. (23 km.) NNW of Portland; pop. (1990c) 5836.

6. City, ⊗ of Allegany co., NW Maryland, on Potomac River; pop. (1990c) 23,706; railroad center; coal deposits nearby; textiles, rubber, glass, paper products; Allegany Community Coll. (1961). Col. George Washington's and British Gen. Edward Braddock's headquarters during French and Indian War.

7. Town, Providence co., N Rhode Island, 4 mi. (6 km.) SE of Woonsocket; pop. (1990c) 29,038; governmental center Valley Falls. Orig. part of Massachusetts; annexed to Rhode Island 1746; incorp. 1747.

8. Village, ⊗ of Cumberland co., cen. Virginia, ab. 50 mi. (80 km.) W of Richmond.

9. County in N Nova Scotia, Canada. See table at NOVA SCOTIA.

\ə\ **abut** \ˈə\ **matches** \ᵊ\ **kitten, Fr table** \ər\ **further** \a\ **ash** \ā\ **ace** \ä\ **cot, cart** \å\ **Fr bac** \aů\ **out** \b̶\ **Span Avila** \ch\ **chin** \e\ **bet** \ē\ **easy** \g\ **go** \i\ **hit** \ī\ **ice** \j\ **job** \k̟\ **Ger ich, Buch** \ⁿ\ **Fr vin** \ŋ\ **sing** \ō\ **go** \ȯ\ **all** \ȯ\ **law** \œ\ **Fr bœuf** \œ̄\ **Fr feu** \ȯi\ **boy** \th\ **thin** \t͟h\ **this** \ü\ **loot** \u̇\ **foot** \ue\ **Ger füllen** \üe\ **Fr rue** \y\ **yet** \ʸ\ **Fr digne** \ˈdēnʸ\, **nuit** \ˈnwʸē\ \yü\ **few** \yu̇\ **fury** \zh\ **vision**

10. Former county, NW England; lakes included Derwent Water, Ullswater, Thirlmere; rivers included Derwent, Ehen, Esk; towns included Whitehaven, Workington, Penrith.

Cumberland Caverns. Caves, Warren co., cen. Tennessee 10 mi. (16 km.) SE of McMinnville; contains one of largest cave rooms in E United States.

Cumberland Falls. See CUMBERLAND 1.

Cumberland Gap. Pass through Cumberland Plateau in Claiborne co., NE Tennessee; alt. 1640 ft. (500 m.); first discovered by nonnatives 1750, became an early emigrant route; used by Daniel Boone in his pioneer trips into Kentucky 1767–71 and when he led settlers to site of Boonesboro 1775 blazing and clearing the Wilderness Road; strategic point in Civil War; estab. as **Cumberland Gap National Historical Park** (see UNITED STATES, *National Historical Parks*).

Cumberland Island. Island in Atlantic Ocean, off mainland of Camden co., SE Georgia; 34 sq. mi. (88 sq. km.).

Cumberland Islands. Group of small islands off E coast of Queensland, Australia, SE of Townsville.

Cumberland Lake. Lake, E Saskatchewan, Canada; 166 sq. mi. (430 sq. km.); drains S into Saskatchewan River.

Cumberland Peninsula. Peninsula, E Baffin I., E Nunavut, Canada; its easternmost point, Cape Dyer, on Davis Strait.

Cumberland Plateau *also* **Cumberland Mountains.** Tableland extending NE to SW from S West Virginia to NE Alabama N of Birmingham; extends along border bet. Kentucky and Virginia and in E Tennessee W of the Tennessee River; av. height ab. 2000 ft. (600 m.), av. width ab. 50 mi. (80 km.); structurally the W section of the Appalachian Mts. and a part of the Allegheny Plateau. Rich deposits of bituminous coal in the Tennessee area.

Cumberland Road *or* **National Road.** First federal road in the U.S.; construction started at Cumberland, Maryland in 1811, opened to Wheeling (then part of Virginia) 1818, and eventually extended to St. Louis, Missouri .

Cumberland Sound. **1.** Inlet of Atlantic Ocean, on Georgia-Florida boundary; receives the St. Marys River.

2. Inlet of Davis Strait, SE Baffin I., Nunavut, N Canada, SW of Cumberland Penin.

Cum·ber·nauld \ˌkəm-bər-ˈnȯld\. Town, Strathclyde region, S cen. Scotland; pop. (1991e) 50,700; estab. as a new town 1955.

Cum·braes, The \ˌkəm-ˈbrāz, ˈkəm-ˌ\. Two islands in the Firth of Clyde, Strathclyde region, SW Scotland: **Great Cumbrae Island,** WSW of Largs; 5 sq. mi. (13 sq. km.); summer resort; **Little Cumbrae Island,** S of Great Cumbrae; 1 sq. mi. (3 sq. km.); lighthouse.

Cumbre, La. See USPALLATA PASS.

Cum·bre Ne·gra \ˌküm-brā-ˈnā-grä\. Peak, W Chubut prov., S Argentina, on Chilean border; 6273 ft. (1912 m.).

Cum·bria \ˈkəm-brē-ə\. **1.** Ancient Celtic kingdom, NW Britain; S part (Cumberland, Westmorland, and Lancashire [in part]) under Anglo-Saxon control c. 944, N part (Ayr, Dumfries, Lanark, Kirkcudbright, Renfrew, and Wigton) to Scotland 1018.

2. Administrative county, NW England; includes former counties of Cumberland and Westmorland, and Furness district formerly in Lancashire; estab. 1974. See table at ENGLAND.

Cum·bri·an Mountains \ˈkəm-brē-ən\. Range of hills in Cumberland, Westmorland, and Lancashire, NW England; highest peak Scafell Pike 3210 ft. (978 m.), highest mountain in England.

Cu·mières *or in full* **Cumières–le–Mort–Homme** \kü-ˌmyer-lə-ˌmȯr-ˈtȯm\. Former village, Meuse dept., NE France, ab. 6 mi. (10 km.) NW of Verdun just E of Le Mort Homme, on the Meuse River; destroyed in fighting around Verdun during WWI.

Cu·mi·na·pa·ne·ma \ˈkü-mə-ˌnä-ˌpä-nə-ˈmä\. River, N Brazil; flows S and unites with Curuapanema River to form Curuá River emptying into the Amazon; ab. 150 mi. (240 km.) long.

Cum·ing \ˈkə-miŋ\. County in NE Nebraska. See table at NEBRASKA.

Cum·ming \ˈkə-miŋ\. Town, ⊗ of Forsyth co., N Georgia; pop. (1990c) 2828.

Cu·naxa \kyü-ˈnak-sə\. Town, ancient Babylonia, E of the Euphrates River ab. 87 mi. (140 km.) NW of Babylon; scene of battle 401 B.C. bet. Artaxerxes II of Persia and his brother Cyrus the Younger in which the latter was killed; as a result of the demoralization of Cyrus' army, the Greek mercenary force, orig. led by Clearchus, made (401–399 B.C.) their famous Retreat of the Ten Thousand under historian Xenophon (described in his *Anabasis*) to Cotyora on the Black Sea.

Cun·di·na·mar·ca \ˌkün-di-nə-ˈmär-kə\. Department of cen. Colombia. See table at COLOMBIA.

Cu·ne·ne *or* **Ku·ne·ne** \kü-ˈnā-nə\. **1.** River, SW Angola; flows S and W to Atlantic Ocean; 700 mi. (1126 km.) long; in its lower course forms a section of the boundary bet. Angola and Namibia; in its westward descent to coast are several cataracts, esp. the **Ru·a·ca·na Falls** \ˌrü-ə-ˌkän-ə\ (17°22′S, 14°12′E), which fall 406 ft. (124 m.).

2. Province of S Angola. See table at ANGOLA.

Cu·neo \ˈkü-nē-ˌō\. **1.** Province of Piedmont, NW Italy. See table at ITALY.

2. *or Fr.* **Co·ni** \kȯ-ˈnē\. Commune, its ✻, 69 mi. (111 km.) W of Genoa; pop. (1989c) 55,746; Gothic cathedral; 13th cent. church.

Cu·par \ˈkü-pər, -pär\. Burgh, Fife region, E Scotland; pop. (1981p) 6642; was site of a 12th cent. castle of the MacDuffs, earls of Fife.

Cu·per·ti·no \ˌkü-pər-ˈtē-nō, ˌkyü-\. City, Santa Clara co., W California, 8 mi. (13 km.) W of San Jose; pop. (1990c) 40,263; Cogswell Polytechnical Coll. (1887).

Ću·pri·ja *or* **Chu·pri·ya** \ˈchü-prē-yə\. Town, Serbia, E cen. Yugoslavia, ab. 70 mi. (115 km.) SE of Belgrade.

Cura. See VILLA DE CURA.

Cu·ra·çao \ˌku̇r-ə-ˈsō, ˌkyu̇r-, -ˈsau̇\. **1.** Territory, West Indies. See NETHERLANDS ANTILLES.

2. Largest island of the Netherlands Antilles (*q.v.*), in the Caribbean Sea, 60 mi. (97 km.) N of NW Venezuela; 36 mi. (58 km.) long by 8 mi. (13 km.) wide; 182 sq. mi. (471 sq. km.); pop. (1992e) 143,816; chief town Willemstad (✻ of the Netherlands Antilles); surface generally flat, highest point 1220 ft. (372 m.); chief industry refining of oil from Venezuela; tourism.

History: Inhabited orig. by native Indian peoples who were displaced by Europeans, Spanish first arriving 1499; first settled by Spanish 1527; captured by Dutch West India Company 1634; held by British 1807–15; with Aruba awarded to Netherlands by Treaty of Paris 1815; internal self-government granted 1954.

Cu·ra·ray \ˌku̇r-ə-ˈrī\. River, NW South America, rising in E cen. Ecuador and flowing E into Napo River in NE Peru; ab. 500 mi. (800 km.) long.

Cu·re·pipe \ku̇r-ˈpēp\. Town and health resort, cen. Mauritius; pop. (1991e) 66,790; cultural center.

Cu·res \ˈkyu̇r-ēz\. Ancient town, Latium, Italy, NE of Rome; famous in legend as original home of Sabines who settled the Quirinal; associated with Numa Pompilius, king 715–673 B.C. of Rome.

Curia Rhaetorum. See CHUR.

Cu·ri·có \ˌkü-rē-ˈkō\. **1.** Former province of cen. Chile.

2. City, Maule region, Chile, 110 mi. (177 km.) S of Santiago; pop. (1992c) 103,919; founded 1743; formerly ✻ of Curicó prov.

Cu·ri·ti·ba; *formerly* **Cu·ry·ti·ba** \ˌku̇r-ə-ˈtē-bə\. City, ✻ of Paraná state, S Brazil, ab. 70 mi. (115 km.) from the coast; met. area pop. (1990e) 1,966,426; tobacco; paper, matches, textiles, motor vehicles, cement; Federal Univ. (1912), Catholic Univ. (1959); founded 1654.

Cur·ragh, The \ˈkər-ə\. Plain, co. Kildare, E Ireland, on W bank of the Liffey; site of a racecourse and many racing stables.

Cur·ral das Frei·ras \ku̇-ˌräl-dəs-ˈfrer-əs\. Vast natural amphitheater in cen. Madeira I., Portugal.

Cur·rent \ˈkər-ənt\. River, Missouri and Arkansas; flows from Texas co., S Missouri, E and SE into Black River in Randolph co., NE Arkansas; ab. 250 mi. (400 km.) long.

Cur·ri·tuck \ˈkər-ə-ˌtək\. **1.** County in NE North Carolina. See table at NORTH CAROLINA.

2. Village, its ⊗.

Currituck Sound. Sound, W of barrier island in E Currituck co., NE North Carolina, extends N ab. 35 mi. (56 km.) from mouth of Albemarle Sound.

Cur·ry \ˈkər-ē\. Name of counties in two states of the U.S. See tables at NEW MEXICO and OREGON.

Cur·tea de Ar·geş \ˌku̇r-tyä-dā-ˈär-jesh\. Commune, S cen. Romania, on Argeş River, SW of Cîmpulung; pop. (1992p) 35,823; 13th cent. Byzantine church; 14th cent. palace ruins; 15th cent. church. 13th cent. ✻ of Walachia.

Cu·ruá \ku̇r-ˈwä\. River, N Brazil; flows S into the Amazon; 65 mi. (105 km.) long.

Cu·ru·a·pa·ne·ma \ku̇r-ˌwä-ˌpä-nə-ˈmä\. River, N Brazil; flows S and unites with Cuminapanema River to form Curuá River emptying into the Amazon; ab. 170 mi. (275 km.) long.

Curupira, Serra. See SERRA CURUPIRA.

Cu·ru·zú Cua·tiá \ˌkü-rü-ˈsü-kwä-ˈtyä\. Town, Corrientes prov., NE Argentina, 160 mi. (257 km.) SSE of the city of Corrientes.

Cur·wens·ville \ˈkər-wənz-ˌvil\. Borough, Clearfield co., W cen. Pennsylvania, on W branch of Susquehanna River 16 mi. (26 km.) ESE of Du Bois; pop. (1990c) 2924; settled 1812.

Curytiba. See CURITIBA.

Curzola. See KORČULA.

Cur·zon Line \ˈkərz-ᵊn\. A line suggested by English politician Lord George Nathaniel Curzon to the Supreme Council in Dec. 1919 as a practical line of demarcation bet. Soviet Russia and the then new state of Poland; began at the S tip of Lithuania just N of Hrodna, extended S to the right bank of the Bug River near Brest, then followed the Bug for ab. 200 mi. (320 km.), turned W near Sokal and SSW across E Galicia to the N boundary of Czechoslovakia at a point ab. 50 mi. (80 km.) S of Przemyśl; primarily an ethnic boundary with areas to W inhabited chiefly by Poles and those to E by Russians. Again used 1920 as basis for armistice bet. Russians and Poles, but final E boundary of Poland, fixed by Treaty of Riga 1920, was approx. parallel but 120 to 160 mi. (193 to 257 km.) farther E. Used in part by Germany and U.S.S.R. for partition of Poland Sept. 1939 but with W extensions at N and S ends; by Yalta Conference 1945 and later action claimed by U.S.S.R. as basis for new boundary bet. U.S.S.R. and Poland.

Cus·ca·tlán \ˌküs-kə-ˈtlän\. Department, cen. El Salvador. See table at EL SALVADOR.

Cusco. See CUZCO.

Cush *or* **Kush** \ˈkəsh, ˈku̇sh\. Ancient country in Nubia region of Nile Valley; in 2d millennium B.C. subject to Egypt; in 8th cent. B.C. its King Piankhi invaded and conquered Egypt; ruled by Piankhi's brother Shabaka from 716 B.C. who also invaded Egypt and set up XXVth dynasty and made Memphis his ✻; other important cities included Meroë.

Cush·ing \ˈku̇-shiŋ\. City, Payne co., N cen. Oklahoma, 40 mi. (64 km.) W of Sapulpa; pop. (1990c) 7218; founded 1892.

Cushing, Mount. Mountain, N British Columbia, Canada; 8676 ft. (2644 m.); highest peak in Stikine Mts.

Cush·man, Lake \ˈku̇sh-mən\. Reservoir across N fork of Skokomish River, Mason co., W Washington; created by dams (275 and 240 ft. or 84 and 73 m. high) completed 1926; supplies waterpower.

Cus·se·ta \kə-ˈsē-tə\. Town, ⊗ of Chattahoochee co., W Georgia; pop. (1990c) 1107.

Cus·ter \ˈkəs-tər\. **1.** Name of counties in six states of the U.S. See tables at COLORADO, IDAHO, MONTANA, NEBRASKA, OKLAHOMA, SOUTH DAKOTA.

2. City and summer resort, ⊗ of Custer co., SW South Dakota, 30 mi. (48 km.) SW of Rapid City; pop. (1990c) 1741; tourist center (near Wind Cave National Park and other scenic spots); mica.

Custer, Mount. Peak, NW Montana, in Glacier National Park on Continental Divide; ab. 8885 ft. (2710 m.).

Custer Battlefield National Monument. Former name (1879–1991) of *Little Bighorn Battlefield National Monument.* See UNITED STATES, *National Monuments.*

Custer Peak. Mountain, Lawrence co., W South Dakota; ab. 6800 ft. (2070 m.).

Cu·sto·za \ku̇-ˈstōt-sə\ *also* **Cu·stoz·za** \-ˈstȯt-\. Village, Verona prov., Veneto, NE Italy, 11 mi. (18 km.) SW of the commune of Verona; scene of two Italian defeats in wars for unity and independence: (1) July 24, 1848 by Austrians under Count Joseph Radetzky, and (2) June 24, 1866 by Austrian forces of Archduke Albert.

Cüstrin. See KOSTRZYN.

Cut Bank \ˈkət-ˌbaŋk\. Town, ⊗ of Glacier co., NW Montana, 95 mi. (153 km.) NNW of Great Falls; pop. (1990c) 3329.

Cutch, Gulf of. See KACHCHH, GULF OF.

Cutch, Rann of. See KACHCHH, RANN OF.

Cu·thah \ˈkyü-thə\. Ancient city, Babylonia; devoted to worship of Nergal, ruler of Aralu, the abode of the dead; one of cities from which people were taken by the king of Assyria to colonize Samaria (2 *Kings* xvii. 24).

Cuth·bert \ˈkəth-bərt\. City, Randolph co., SW Georgia, 38 mi. (61 km.) WNW of Albany; pop. (1990c) 3730; Andrew Coll. (1854); city incorp. 1834.

Cut·off Peak \ˈkət-ˌȯf\. Mountain, S Montana, in Yellowstone National Park; ab. 10,300 ft. (3140 m.).

Cut·tack \ˈkə-tək\. City, Orissa, E India, on Mahanadi River 220 mi. (354 km.) SW of Calcutta; pop. (1991c) 440,295; historically noted for its excellent silver filigree work; jute processing, milling, handicrafts are important today; several colleges. Successively ✻ of Orissa for Hindu kings, the Moguls, and Maratha governors; captured by British in Second Maratha War 1803.

Cutts Peak \ˈkəts\. Mountain, Washington co., N cen. Vermont; 4080 ft. (1244 m.).

Cut·ty·hunk Island \ˈkə-tē-ˌhəŋk\. Island, SW Elizabeth Is., Buzzards Bay, SE Massachusetts.

Cux·ha·ven \ku̇ks-ˈhäf-ᵊn\. Seaport, Lower Saxony, Germany, on North Sea at mouth of Elbe River; pop. (1992e) 56,328; fisheries; resort; shipbuilding; 14th cent. castle; frequently bombed by Allied air forces in WWII.

Cuyabá. See CUIABÁ.

Cuy·a·ho·ga \ˌkī-ə-ˈhō-gə, kī-ˈhō-, kə-ˈhō-, -ˈhȯ-, -ˈhä-\. **1.** River, NE Ohio; rises in Geauga co., flows SW through Portage co. into Summit co., turns abruptly N and flows into Lake Erie at Cleveland; near Akron receives the **Little Cuyahoga River**; ab. 80 mi. (130 km.) long.

2. County in N Ohio. See table at OHIO.

Cuyahoga Falls. City, Summit co., NE Ohio, on Cuyahoga River 5 mi. (8 km.) N of Akron; pop. (1990c) 48,950; chemicals, rubber goods, machinery, tools and dies.

Cu·ya·po \ˌkü-yä-ˈpō\. Municipality, NW Nueva Ecija prov., Luzon, Philippines; pop. (1980c) 39,654.

Cu·yo \ˈkü-yō\. **1.** Island group, cen. Philippines, N of Sulu Sea and ab. 65 mi. (105 km.) E of N end of Palawan I.; ab. 50 sq. mi. (130 sq. km.); comprises Cuyo and Agutaya islands, and ab. 45 islets; forms part of Palawan prov.

2. Largest island in group; 22 sq. mi. (57 sq. km.); volcanic in origin; highest point ab. 600 ft. (185 m.).

3. Municipality, coextensive with Cuyo I. and nearby islets; pop. (1980c) 14,692.

Cuy·u·na Range \kī-ˈyü-nə\. Iron-ore belt, in Crow Wing and Aitkin cos., cen. Minnesota, NW of Mille Lacs.

Cu·yu·ni \kü-ˈyü-nē\. River, N South America; rises in E Venezuela, flows N, then E forming section of Venezuela-Guyana boundary, continues E across N Guyana to Essequibo River near its mouth; just before entering the Essequibo, is joined by Mazaruni River; 350 mi. (563 km.) long.

Cuz·co *also* **Cus·co** \ˈkü-skō\. **1.** Peak, Potosí dept., SW Bolivia; 17,830 ft. (5435 m.).

2. City, SE Peru, ab. 350 mi. (565 km.) SE of Lima; pop. (1990e) 316,804; alt. 11,024 ft. (3360 m.); university (1672); Renaissance cathedral. Was once ✻ of vast Inca empire and known as the "City of the Sun"; traditionally thought to have been founded c. 11th cent. by Manco Capac; taken by the

Spanish under conquistador Francisco Pizarro 1533; nearby are remains of ancient fortress of early Inca construction and of the city of Machu Picchu (*q.v.*) and of the Temple of the Sun; suffered major earthquake damage 1950; many sites since restored.

Cwm·bran \ku̇m-ˈbrän\. Town, ⊗ of Gwent co., SE Wales, 15 mi. (24 km.) NNE of Cardiff; estab. as a new town 1949.

Cyc·la·des \ˈsi-klə-ˌdēz\ *or Gk.* **Ki·klá·dhes** \kē-ˈklä-t͟hes\. Group of ab. 220 islands and islets in S Aegean Sea, bet. the Peloponnese and the Dodecanese; 993 sq. mi. (2572 sq. km.); pop. (1991p) 95,083; administratively a department of Greece; ✱ Ermoupolis; chief islands: Ándros, Tínos, Naxos, Amorgos, Melos, Páros, Syros, Kéa, Kíthnos, Sérifos, Ios, and Thira. So called according to ancient tradition because they formed a ring or circle (*Gk. kyklos*) around the sacred island of Delos.

History: Thought to have been orig. inhabited by Carians; under Mycenaean culture 2d millennium B.C.; held successively by Persians, Athenians (after Mycale [*q.v.*] 479 B.C.), Ptolemaic Egypt, and Macedonia; ruled by Venetians as duchy of Naxos after early 13th cent.; for rest of history, see as part of AEGEAN ISLANDS.

Cy·clone Mountain \ˈsī-ˌklōn\. Peak, Chaffee co., cen. Colorado; 13,800 ft. (4206 m.).

Cyd·nus \ˈsid-nəs\ *or* **Tar·sus** \ˈtär-səs\. Historic river in Cilicia, in modern İçel prov., Turkey in Asia; flows SE from Taurus Mts. past town of Tarsus to the Mediterranean.

Cy·do·nia \sī-ˈdō-nē-ə, -nyə\. Ancient city on NW coast of Crete, on whose site is modern Canea (*q.v.*).

Cydweli. See KIDWELLY.

Cyl·le·ne \sə-ˈlē-nē\ *or mod.* **Kil·lí·ni** \kē-\ *or* **Zir·ia** \ˈzir-ē-ə\. Mountain, NE Peloponnese, S Greece; 7789 ft. (2374 m.); in ancient times was on border bet. Achaea and Arcadia; in Greek legend sacred to the god Hermes as his birthplace.

Cy·me \ˈsī-mē\. City of ancient Aeolis, in Asia Minor, on the W coast N of the mouth of the Gediz. Birthplace of Greek historian Ephorus c. 405 B.C.

Cymru. See WALES 1.

Cyn·os·ceph·a·lae \ˌsi-nə-ˈse-fə-(ˌ)lē, ˌsī-\. Two hills, SE Thessaly, NE Greece; in a low range ab. 18 mi. (29 km.) SSE of Larissa. Scene of battles: (1) 364 B.C. in which the Thebans under Pelopidas defeated Alexander, despot of Pherae; and (2) 197 B.C., the decisive battle of the Second Macedonian War, in which the Roman Gen. T. Quinctius Flamininus defeated King Philip V of Macedon.

Cy·nos·se·ma \ˌsi-nə-ˈsē-mə, ˌsī-\. Promontory on E side of Chersonesus Thracica (Gallipoli Penin.), Turkey in Europe; naval battle in which Athenians under generals Alcibiades and Thrasybulus defeated Spartans occurred off promontory 411 B.C.

Cyn·o·su·ra \ˌsi-nə-ˈsu̇r-ə, ˌsī-\ *or* **Kyn·o·su·ra** \ˌki-nə-ˈsu̇r-ə, ˌkī-\. Promontory, E Salamis I., Greece, just SE of Salamis town and opp. Mt. Aegaleos on coast of Attica; battle of Salamis, in which Persian fleet of Xerxes the Great beaten by Greek fleet led by Gen. Themistocles, occurred off promontory 480 B.C.

Cyn·thi·ana \ˌsin-thē-ˈa-nə\. City, ⊗ of Harrison co., N Kentucky, 27 mi. (43 km.) NNE of Lexington; pop. (1990c) 6497.

Cyn·thus \ˈsin-thəs\. Mountain, Delos I., Cyclades Is., Aegean Sea; legendary birthplace of the god Apollo and the goddess Artemis.

Cy·press \ˈsī-prəs\. City, Orange co., SW California, just E of NE Long Beach; pop. (1990c) 42,655.

Cypress Hills. Hilly region, SE Alberta and SW Saskatchewan, Canada; extends ab. 100 mi. (160 km.) E to W; contains two provincial parks; has highest peak in Saskatchewan, 4546 ft. (1386 m.).

Cy·prus \ˈsī-prəs\ *or Gk.* **Ky·pros** \ˈkē-prȯs\ *or Turk.* **Ki·bris** \ˈkē-bris\. Island, a republic, E Mediterranean Sea, 60 mi. (97 km.) W of coast of Syria and 40 mi. (64 km.) S of coast of Turkey; area 3572 sq. mi. (9251 sq. km.); pop. (1993e) 764,000; ✱ Nicosia (Lefkosia); of irregular shape with a number of wide bays and prominent capes, esp. Cape Andreas which terminates a long narrow peninsula on the NE; in cen. part has a plain, enclosed on N by mountain range which reaches 3357 ft. (1023 m.) and on S by range culminating in Mt. Olympus 6403 ft. (1952 m.); no rivers or lakes of any size.

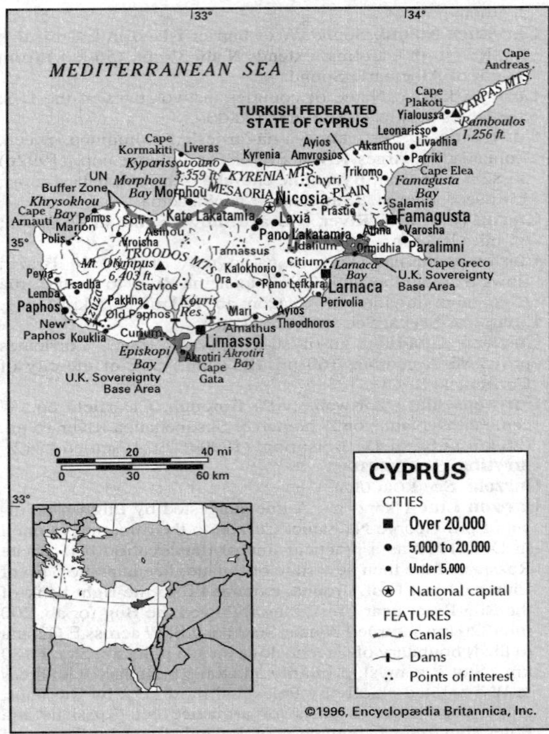

Chief products: Cereals, grapes, potatoes, citrus fruits, tobacco; chrome, asbestos; tourism; in early times famous for its copper (the English word ultimately from Greek name of island, *Kypros*, through Latin *cuprum*).

Chief towns: Nicosia (Lefkosia), Limassol, Larnaca; has ruins of several famous towns of ancient times, esp. Citium and Paphos.

History: Evidence of inhabitation dates from c. 6000 B.C.; remains from Bronze Age 2d millennium B.C.; influenced by Minoan and Mycenaean cultures; colonized by ancient Greeks and Phoenicians; ruled by Assyrian, Persian (after 525 B.C.), Ptolemaic, and Roman empires (see PAPHOS); as part of Byzantine Empire, frequently raided or captured by Arabs 7th–10th cents. A.D.; captured by Richard I (Lion-Hearted) of England during Third Crusade 1191; sold to Lusignan dynasty which ruled 1192–1474; Famagusta, leading port, held by Genoese 1376–1464; 1489 acquired by Venetians whom Turks expelled 1571; according to convention with Turkey, administered by Great Britain 1878–1914; annexed by British at outbreak of war with Turkey 1914; made a crown colony 1925; became an independent republic 1960; unrest prompted by Turkish inhabitants' fears that Greek inhabitants seek ultimate union of island with Greece; establishment of UN peacekeeping mission 1964 following period of armed strife bet. Greek and Turkish sectors of population; Turkish soldiers invaded 1974, ultimately taking N part of island; a separate Turkish Federated State of Cyprus was proclaimed 1975 with fighting continuing; Turkish Republic of Northern Cyprus proclaimed 1985, but only Turkey gave it international recognition; settlement talks headed by UN continued 1980s into 1990s.

Cy·re·na·ica *also* **Ci·re·na·ica** \ˌsir-ə-ˈnā-ə-kə, ˌsī-rə-\. Easternmost part of Libya.

History: Ancient Cyrenaica settled by Greeks who founded Cyrene (Cirene) c. 630 B.C.; under Greek dynasty estab. by Battus of Thera, kingdom of Cyrene or Cyrenaica took form, and other cities were founded; known at one time as Pentapolis because it included five cities (Cyrene, Arsinoë, Berenice, Barka, Apollonia); after death of Macedonian King Alexander the Great, ruled by Ptolemies; bequeathed to Romans 96 B.C. and in 67 B.C. made Roman province which included Crete; overrun by Arabs in 7th cent. A.D.; nominally under Ottoman Empire after conquest of Egypt (*q.v.*); part of Tripoli (*q.v.*) which was annexed to Italy 1911 (see LIBYA). Scene of many battles in WWII 1940–42: see BARDĪYAH, DERNA, TOBRUK, BENGHAZI, and BIR HACHEIM; a province of Libya 1951–63 (330,258 sq. mi. or 855,368 sq. km.; ❋ Benghazi).

Cy·re·ne \sī-'rē-nē\ *or Ital.* **Ci·re·ne** \chē-'rā-nē\. Ancient city in N Africa, at present-day settlement of Shaḩḩāt, Libya; founded by Greeks c. 630 B.C.; original ❋ of Cyrenaica and a city of the Pentapolis; taken by Macedonian King Alexander the Great 331 B.C. and soon after came under the Ptolemies; belonged to Romans after 96 B.C.; has interesting ruins.

Cyrus. See KURA.

Cythera. See KÍTHIRA.

Cyz·i·cus \'si-zi-kəs\. **1.** Peninsula, Turkey in Asia. See KAPIDAĞI.

2. Ancient city, Mysia, Asia Minor, on isthmus leading to Kapıdağı Penin. on Sea of Marmara; possibly founded by Greeks from Miletus 756 B.C.; in naval battle off its shore 410 B.C. Athenian forces led by Gen. Alcibiades destroyed Spartan fleet.

Czecho·slo·va·kia \ˌchek-ə-slō-'väk-ē-ə, -'vak-\ *or Czech* **Čes·ko·slo·ven·sko** \ˌches-kə-'slȯ-vən-ˌskȯ\; *officially* **Czecho·slo·vak Socialist Republic** \ˌchek-ə-'slō-ˌväk, -ˌvak\ *or Czech* **Čes·ko·slo·ven·ská So·ci·a·lis·tická Re·pu·bli·ka** \ˌches-kə-'slȯ-vən-skä-ˌsō-tsē-ə-'lēs-ti-kä-rä-'pu̇b-li-kə\. Former republic, cen. Europe; comprising two constituent republics: the Czech Socialist Republic and the Slovak Socialist Republic; 49,371 sq. mi. (127,871 sq. km.); pop. (1991p) 15,567,666; ❋ Prague.

History: See BOHEMIA, MORAVIA, SLOVAKIA, SILESIA, and ZAKARPATS'KA; republic formed in 1918 by Czechs and Slovaks from territories formerly part of the Austro-Hungarian Empire; Tomáš G. Masaryk first president 1918–35; received Teschen after dispute with Poland 1919–20; ratified constitution and began its operation 1920; political life disturbed by minority demands for autonomy, incl. those of Sudeten Germans who were supported by Nazi leader Adolf Hitler's Germany; after Munich agreement which settled German-Czech crisis of 1938, Sudetenland annexed to Germany, Teschen (now Český Těšín) to Poland, and a strip of Slovakia and of Ruthenia to Hungary; Slovakia and Ruthenia, given autonomy 1938, declared independence 1939; remainder of Czech state became German protectorate of Bohemia and Moravia 1939–45; after WWII lost Carpathian Ruthenia (Zakarpatska) to the U.S.S.R.; formed close political and economic union with U.S.S.R., and by Communist coup Feb. 1948 came under Soviet domination; member of Warsaw Pact 1955; its political liberalization (1967–68) suppressed by Soviet invasion Aug. 1968; federal constitution adopted 1968 with country comprised of constituent Czech Socialist Republic and Slovak Socialist Republic; breakup of U.S.S.R. late 1980s resulted in move toward more political freedom; new government formed 1989 but Czechs and Slovaks remained at odds over maintaining the union; decision to form two countries arrived at 1992; divided Jan. 1, 1993 into separate countries of Czech Republic and Slovakia.

Czechoslovak Socialist Republic. See CZECHOSLOVAKIA.

Czech·o·wi·ce–Dzie·dzi·ce \ˌchek-ə-'vēt-sə-je-'jēt-sə\. Town, Katowice prov., S Poland, ab. 25 mi. (40 km.) S of the city of Katowice; pop. (1981p) 32,482.

Czech Republic \'chek\. Country, cen. Europe, bounded on NE by Poland, on SE by Slovakia, on S by Austria, and on W

and NW by Germany; 30,450 sq. mi. (78,866 sq. km.); pop. (1993e) 10,332,000; ✻ Prague.

Physical features: Mountainous country, Bohemia shut in on SW by the Bohemian Forest (Böhmer Wald), on the NW by Erzgebirge, and on NE by the Sudety which also extend into N Moravia; Moravia crossed by several ranges NE to SW, esp. the Bohemian-Moravian Highlands on the W.

Rivers: Labe (upper Elbe) in Bohemia and its important branches, the Ohře, Berounka, and Vltava; in Moravia the upper courses of the Oder (*Czech* Odra) and March (*Czech* Morava).

Chief products: cereal grains, sugar beets, potatoes; coal; motor vehicles, steel, machinery, chemicals.

Chief cities: Prague, Brno, Ostrava.

History: Largely shares history of Bohemia (*q.v.*) and Moravia (*q.v.*) up to 1918; became part of Czechoslovakia (*q.v.*) 1918–92; proclaimed Czech Republic 1992, effective 1993.

Czech Socialist Republic *or Czech* **Čes·ká So·ci·a·lis·tická Re·pu·bli·ka** \ˈches-kä-ˌsō-tsē-ə-ˈlēs-ti-kä-rä-ˈpu̇b-li-kə\. Constituent republic of former Czechoslovakia; became independent Czech Republic Jan. 1, 1993.

Czegléd. See CEGLÉD.

Cze·ladź \ˈchel-ˌäj\ *or Ger.* **Tsche·li·ads** \ˈchā-lē-ˌäts\. Commune, Katowice prov., S Poland, 5 mi. (8 km.) N of the city of Katowice; pop. (1981p) 36,690; coal deposits.

Czenstochau. See CZĘSTOCHOWA.

Czernowitz. See CHERNIVTSI.

Czę·sto·cho·wa \ˌchen(t)-stə-ˈkō-və\ *or Russ.* **Chen·sto·khov** \ˌchen(t)-stə-ˈkȯf, -ˈkȯv\; *Ger.* **Czen·sto·chau** *or* **Tschen·sto·chau** \ˈchen(t)-stə-ˌkau̇\. **1.** Province, S Poland. See table at POLAND.
2. City, its ✻, on Warta River ab. 40 mi. (64 km.) N of Katowice; pop. (1992e) 258,700; railroad junction, manufactures include textiles, paper, steel, iron; food products; famous shrine of Virgin, Our Lady of Częstochowa ("The Black Madonna"), in ancient monastery; several museums. A historic town, very wealthy in 15th cent.; resisted siege by Swedes 1655 and 1705; occupied by Germans WWI and WWII.

D

Da·an·ban·ta·yan \dä-ˈän-bän-tä-ˈyän\. Municipality on coast at N tip of Cebu I., Philippines, 69 mi. (111 km.) N of City of Cebu; pop. (1980c) 45,926.

Dabʻa, El *or* **Dabah, Ad.** See AD DABAH.

Daban. See BAIRIN YOUQI.

Da·ba Shan \ˈdä-ˈbä-ˈshän\ *or W.-G.* **Ta–pa Shan** \ˈdä-ˈbä\. Mountain range, cen. China, on border bet. SE Shaanxi, W Hubei, and NE Sichuan; highest peak 8884 ft. (2708 m.); its E end forms W edge of Hubei basin and on S it is cut by the Chang Gorges (*q.v.*).

Dabbah, Ad. See ED DEBBA.

Da·bhoi \də-ˈbȯi\. Town, SE Gujarat state, W India, 20 mi. (32 km.) SE of Vadodara; pop. (1991p) 50,619; has fine architectural remains of Hindu structures such as temples and gates.

Da·bob Bay \ˈdā-ˌbäb\. Inlet of Hood Canal, Jefferson co., W Washington.

Dą·bro·mierz \dȯ^{n}-ˈbrȯ-myesh\ *or Ger.* **Ho·hen·frie·de·berg** \ˌhō-ən-ˈfrē-də-ˌberk\. Village, SW Poland, near Strzegom; formerly in Silesia, Prussia, Germany; in Second Silesian War scene of victory of Prussians under Frederick the Great over Austrians and Saxons under Charles, prince of Lorraine, June 1745.

Dą·bro·wa Gór·ni·cza \dȯ^{n}-ˈbrȯ-vä-gu̇r-ˈnē-chä\ *or Ger.* **Dom·brau** \ˈdȯm-ˌbrau̇\. Commune, Katowice prov., S Poland, 8 mi. (13 km.) ENE of the city of Katowice; pop. (1992e) 139,200; coal-mining center since 1796.

Dacca. See DHAKA.

Da·chau \ˈdä-ˌk̲au̇\. Town, Bavaria, Germany, 10 mi. (16 km.) NNW of Munich on the Amper River; pop. (1992e) 35,892; electrical equipment; site, prior to and during WWII, of large concentration camp, the first in Germany, captured by Allies Apr. 1945.

Dach·stein, Mount \ˈdäk̲-ˌshtīn\. Highest peak in the **Dachstein Mountains** in W cen. Austria, ab. 35 mi. (56 km.) SE of Salzburg; 9829 ft. (2996 m.).

Da·cia \ˈdā-shə, -shē-ə\. Ancient country, cen. Europe; bounded on N by Carpathians, on NE by the Tyras (Dniester), on E and S by Danubius (Danube), and on W by the Tissus (Tisza); roughly equivalent to modern Romania; ✻ Sarmizegetusa.

History: Inhabited before Roman conquest by Getae and Dacians, peoples of Thracian stock, who invaded Roman Empire in Emperor Domitian's reign; conquered by Emperor Trajan, and following death of Dacian King Decebalus, made Roman province 107 A.D.; fortified and colonized by Rome as its trans-Danube frontier; abandoned to Goths when Emperor Aurelian withdrew Roman colonists to Moesia (*q.v.*) 270; region of Dacia invaded by Goths, Huns, Avars, Bulgars, Magyars, Pechenegs, and Cumans before founding of principalities, Walachia and Moldavia (*qq.v.*).

Dade \ˈdād\. **1.** Name of counties in two states of the U.S. See tables at GEORGIA and MISSOURI.

2. Former county in SE Florida; renamed Miami-Dade in 1997.

Dade City. City, ⊗ of Pasco co., W Florida Penin., 35 mi. (56 km.) NE of Tampa; pop. (1990c) 5633; kaolin deposits nearby.

Dade·ville \ˈdād-ˌvil\. City, ⊗ of Tallapoosa co., E Alabama; pop. (1990c) 3276.

Da·dra and Na·gar Ha·ve·li \də-ˈdrä … ˌnə-gər-ə-ˈve-lē\. Union territory of India, bordering on Gujarat and Maharashtra; ✻ Silvassa. See table at INDIA.

Da·et \ˈdä-ˌāt\. Municipality, ✻ of Camarines Norte, near coast, Luzon, Philippines; pop. (1980c) 54,789; chief commercial town of province.

Dafana, Tall al–. See DAPHNAE.

Da·ga·mi \dä-ˈgä-mē\. Municipality, Leyte prov., N cen. Leyte I., Philippines, 16 mi. (26 km.) SSW of Tacloban; on E slope of mountains; pop. (1980c) 22,021.

Da·ge·stan *or* **Da·ghe·stan** \ˌda-gə-ˈstan, ˌdä-gə-ˈstän\. Republic, a subdivision of S Russia in Europe; bounded on NW and N by Chechnya, on E by Caspian Sea, on S by Azerbaijan, and on W by Republic of Georgia; 19,421 sq. mi. (50,300 sq. km.); pop. (1992e) 1,890,000; ✻ Makhachkala. Along its S and SW border stretch the Caucasus Mts.; the S two thirds a mountainous region, the N part and along the Caspian mostly sandy plain and salt marsh; the rivers are comparatively short mountain streams; forests small, little good agricultural land; main occupation raising cattle and sheep; wine; large but undeveloped mineral resources, esp. iron, oil, natural gas; glassworks, hydroelectric power plants.

Chief towns: Makhachkala, Derbent.

History: From early times inhabited by peoples in conflict with one another; ceded by Persia to Russia 1813; not subjugated until 1859 (see GUNIB); rose again during Russo-Turkish War 1877; formed separate republic 1917; became autonomous soviet socialist republic 1921 in North Caucasus region of U.S.S.R.; N part to Checheno-Ingush A.S.S.R. 1943–57; became republic within Russia 1991; subsequently became member of Russian Federation.

Dag·gett \ˈda-gət\. County in NE Utah. See table at UTAH.

Dagö. See HIIUAMAA.

Da·go Peak \ˈdā-ˌgō\. Mountain, in Shoshone co., NE Idaho; 4999 ft. (1524 m.).

Da·gu *or W.-G.* **Ta–ku** *or* **Ta·ku** \ˈdä-ˈgü\. Town, E Tianjin municipality, NE China, on right bank of mouth of Hai River 37 mi. (60 km.) ESE of Tianjin (city); formerly site of forts guarding approach to Tianjin which were several times attacked by foreign forces, esp. in 1860 and in 1900 in the Boxer Rebellion; forts finally demolished by terms of Boxer Protocol of 1901.

Da·gu·pan \dä-ˈgü-ˌpän\. Municipality, N Pangasinan prov., Luzon, Philippines, on S shore of Lingayen Gulf 6 mi. (9.6 km.) E of Lingayen; pop. (1990p) 122,000; seaport.

Da·ha·na \ˈdȧ-hȧ-nə\. See AD DAHNĀʼ.

Da Hing·gan Ling \ˈdä-ˈhiŋ-ˈgän-ˈliŋ\ *or W.-G.* **Ta-hsing-an Ling** \ˈdä-ˈshiŋ-ˈän\ *or Eng.* **Great Khin·gan Mountains** \ˌkiŋ-ˈgän\. Mountain range running N and S in Nei Monggol (Inner Mongolia), China, averaging 3000 to 5000 ft. (914 to 1524 m.); forms a barrier bet. Mongolia and Manchuria; together with Xiao Hinggan Ling sometimes referred to as the Khingan.

Dah·lak Archipelago \dä-ˈläk\ *or Ital.* **Iso·le Da·ha·lach** \ˈē-zō-lā-ˌdä-hä-ˈläk\. Island group, Eritrea, in S Red Sea, off Mitsʼiwa Channel; **Dahlak Ke·bir** \ke-ˈbēr\, chief island, 290 sq. mi. (751 sq. km.).

Dah·lon·e·ga \də-ˈlä-nə-gə\. City, ⊗ of Lumpkin co., N Georgia; pop. (1990c) 3086; North Georgia Coll. (1873); former gold-mining town; site of a branch of U.S. Mint 1838–61; settled c. 1830.

Dah·na \ˈdȧ-nə\. See AD DAHNĀʼ.

Dahomey. See BENIN.

Dah·shûr *or* **Da·shur** \dä-ˈshu̇r\. Site near Memphis, Egypt, of many pyramids, incl. first true pyramid built by King Snefru (27th–26th cents. B.C.).

Daido. See TAEDONG.

Daihoku. See TAIPEI.

Dai·miel \dīm-ˈyel\. Commune, Ciudad Real prov., S cen. Spain, 19 mi. (30 km.) ENE of the commune of Ciudad Real;

\ə\ abut \ə\ matches \ᵊ\ kitten, Fr table \ər\ further \a\ ash \ā\ ace \ä\ cot, cart \ȧ\ Fr bac \au̇\ out \b\ Span Avila \ch\ chin \e\ bet \ē\ easy \g\ go \i\ hit \ī\ ice \j\ job \k̲\ Ger ich, Buch \$^{n}$\ Fr vin \ŋ\ sing \ō\ go \ȯ\ all \ȯ\ law \œ\ Fr bœuf \œ̄\ Fr feu \ȯi\ boy \th\ thin \th̲\ this \ü\ loot \u̇\ foot \ue\ Ger füllen \ue̅\ Fr rue \y\ yet \$^{y}$\ Fr digne \ˈdēn^{y}\, nuit \ˈnw^{y}ē\ \yü\ few \yu̇\ fury \zh\ vision

pop. (1991c) 16,688; manufactures include linens and liquors; Gothic and Doric parish churches.

Dainan. See T'AI-NAN.

Dain·ger·field \ˈdān-jər-ˌfēld\. Town, ⊗ of Morris co., NE Texas; pop. (1990c) 2572.

Dai·qui·rí \ˌdī-kē-ˈrē\. Commune, El Caney municipality, E Cuba, on coast 14 mi. (22 km.) E of Santiago Bay; American troops landed here during Spanish-American War 1898.

Dairen. See DALIAN.

Dai–sen \ˈdī-ˈsān\ *also* **Oya·ma** \ō-ˈyä-mä\. Peak in Tottori prefecture, W Honshū, Japan, SE of Matsue; 5620 ft. (1713 m.); a beautiful cone-shaped peak, the highest of the volcanic peaks of SW Honshū.

Dai·se·tsu·zan National Park \dī-ˈsā-tsü-ˌzän\. National park, cen. Hokkaido, Japan; 892 sq. mi. (2309 sq. km.); contains volcanoes and scenic lakes.

Dai·tō \ˌdī-ˈtō\. City, Ōsaka prefecture, Honshū, Japan, 8 mi. (13 km.) E of the city of Ōsaka; pop. (1992e) 127,130; electrical appliances, metal goods.

Da·ja·bón \ˌdä-kä-ˈbōn\. **1.** Province of N Dominican Republic. See table at DOMINICAN REPUBLIC.

2. Commune, its ✻; pop. (1981p) 21,331.

Dakahliya. See DAQAHLIYA.

Da·kar \dä-ˈkär, ˈda-ˌkär\. Seaport, ✻ of Senegal and of former French West Africa, on S side of Cap Vert Penin.; capital region pop. (1992e) 1,729,823; with Île de Gorée, Rufisque, and adjacent area formed from 1924 to 1946 an autonomous circumscription, **Dakar and Dependencies** (60 sq. mi. or 155 sq. km.); flour milling, fish canning; oil refining; textiles; peanut oil; zoological garden (1903); university (1957); has one of best harbors on Atlantic coast of Africa; of strategic importance as dominating W tip of Africa.

History: Founded 1857 opp. settlement of Île de Gorée (*q.v.*) which had been French since 17th cent.; railroad built from Dakar to St.-Louis 1882–85; became naval base and, in 1902, ✻ of French West Africa (*q.v.*); after defeat of France at beginning of WWII attacked unsuccessfully by forces of Free French and British Sept. 23–25, 1940; by decree 1946 reunited with Senegal; became ✻ of Senegal c. 1960.

Da·khin Shāh·bāz·pur \də-ˈkin-shə-ˈbaz-pu̇r, -ˈbäz-\; *formerly* **Dak·shin** \ˈdək-shin\. Island in Meghna River, Bangladesh; 615 sq. mi. (1593 sq. km.).

Dakh·la \ˈdä-klə\. **1.** Oasis, Egypt, 25°30′N, 29°E; chief town Al-Qasr.

2. *formerly* **Vi·lla Cis·ne·ros** \ˈvēl-yə-sis-ˈner-ōs, ˈvē-yə-\. Seaport on Río de Oro Bay, Western Sahara; airport.

Da·ko·ta \də-ˈkō-tə\. **1.** *or often called* **James** \ˈjāmz\. River in North Dakota and South Dakota; rises in Wells co., cen. North Dakota, flows S across E cen. South Dakota and empties into Missouri River at Yankton, Yankton co., SE South Dakota; 710 mi. (1142 km.) long.

2. Name of counties in two states of the U.S. See tables at MINNESOTA and NEBRASKA.

Dakota City. **1.** Town, ⊗ of Humboldt co., NW cen. Iowa; pop. (1990c) 1024.

2. Village, ⊗ of Dakota co., NE Nebraska; pop. (1990c) 1470.

Dakota Territory. Former territory, U.S.A., named from group of Siouan tribes; comprised the region on both sides of the middle course of Missouri River and W of the Red River of the North. First visited by La Vérendrye brothers 1742–43; greater part included in Louisiana Purchase 1803; N limit of NE section determined by treaty with Great Britain 1818; parts included in several U.S. territories 1805–1861; Dakota Territory (✻ Yankton 1861–1883, Bismark 1883–89) organized Mar. 2, 1861 incl. North and South Dakota and much of Wyoming and Montana; reduced to area of present two states 1868; settlement hastened by discovery of gold c. 1874 in the Black Hills; admitted to the Union Nov. 2, 1889, by division into North Dakota and South Dakota (*qq.v.*).

Đa·ko·vi·ca *or* **Dja·ko·vi·ca** \dyä-ˈkȯ-vit-sə\. Town, SW Serbia, S Yugoslavia.

Đa·ko·vo *or* **Dja·ko·vo** \ˈjä-kȯ-ˌvȯ\. Town, E Croatia, 22 mi. (35 km.) SW of Osijek; pop. (1991c) 29,493; episcopal see, one of whose bishops was Joseph G. Strossmayer, leader of Croatian National Party.

Dakshin. See DAKHIN SHAHBAZPUR.

Dal \ˈdəl\. Lake near Srinagar (*q.v.*), Jammu and Kashmir, N India.

Dal \ˈdȧl\ *also* **Dal·elf** \ˈdȧl-ˌelf\ *or* **Dal·älv** \-ˌelv\. River, S cen. Sweden; formed by two forks, the **Ös·ter Dal** \ˈœs-tər\ and **Väs·ter Dal** \ˈves-tər\; flows SE into Gulf of Bothnia; 250 mi. (402 km.) long.

Da·la·gue·te \ˌdä-lä-ˈgā-tā\. Municipality on E coast of Cebu I., Philippines, near S end on Bohol Strait 46 mi. (74 km.) SSW of City of Cebu.

Dalai Nor. See HULUN NUR.

Dalälv. See DAL.

Da·la·man \ˌdä-lä-ˈmän\. River, SW Turkey in Asia; flows S to the Mediterranean; 116 mi. (187 km.) long.

Da·lar·na *also* **Da·lar·ne** \ˈdȧ-lȧr-nä\; *mostly formerly* **Dal·e·car·lia** \ˌdä-lə-ˈkär-lē-ə\. Region in W cen. Sweden, approx. coextensive with Kopparberg prov. (see table at SWEDEN); region of many historical associations; its people noted for their dialect, colorful costumes, and patriotism, esp. in 15th and 16th cents. (revolted against Erik of Pomerania 1434–36, were strong supporters of Gustavus Vasa 1519–23). Rich in forests; iron and copper deposits.

Da Lat *or* **Da·lat** \ˈdä-ˈlät\. Town, S Vietnam, 48 mi. (77 km.) NE of Ho Chi Minh City; pop. (1989c) 102,583; developed by the French as a resort.

Dalbo. See VÄNERN.

Dal·by \ˈdȯl-bē\. Town, SE Queensland, Australia, in Darling Downs region on Condamine River 115 mi. (185 km.) WNW of Brisbane; pop. (1981c) 8784.

Dale \ˈdāl\. County in SE Alabama. See table at ALABAMA.

Dale·garth Force \ˈdāl-ˌgärth-ˈfōrs\. Waterfall in W Cumberland, NW England, in the Lake District.

Dalelf. See DAL.

Dale·ville \ˈdāl-ˌvil\. City, Dale co., SE Alabama, 22 mi. (35 km.) WNW of Dothan; pop. (1990c) 5117.

Dal·hart \ˈdal-ˌhärt\. City, Dallam and Hartley cos., ⊗ of Dallam co., NW corner of Texas, in the Panhandle; 70 mi. (113 km.) NNW of Amarillo; pop. (1990c) 6246.

Dal·hou·sie \dal-ˈhau̇-zē\. **1.** Seaport town, ⊗ of Restigouche co., N New Brunswick, Canada, on Chaleur Bay at mouth of Restigouche River; pop. (1991c) 4775; formerly extensive lumber trade; chemicals; salmon fishing; resort; settled c. 1810.

2. \ *or locally* dəl-ˈhau̇-zē\. City and hill station, Himachal Pradesh, N India, in Himalayas just E of upper Ravi River; elev. 7700 ft. (2347 m.); pop. (1991p) 6855.

Dali. See IDALIUM.

Da·li *or W.-G.* **Ta–li** \ˈdä-ˈlē\. **1.** *formerly* **Tung·chow** \ˈtu̇ŋ-ˈchau̇\. Town, E Shaanxi prov., E cen. China, 60 mi. (97 km.) ENE of Xi'an.

2. City, W cen. Yunnan prov., S China, on W shore of Er Hai 180 mi. (290 km.) W of Kunming; located at 6900 ft. (2103 m.) above sea level bet. lake and high mountains; ancient city noted for its marble; known to Chinese from first cent. B.C.; long a center of Yunnan; conquered by Mongols 13th cent.

Da·lian *or W.-G.* **Ta–lien** \ˈdä-ˈlyen\ *or administrative* **Lü·da** *or W.-G.* **Lü–ta** \ˈlue-ˈdä\; *conventional* **Dai·ren** \ˈdī-ˈren\; *Russ.* **Dal·ny** \ˈdȧl-nē\. City on S coast of Liaodong Penin., Liaodong prov., China, 20 mi. (32 km.) E of Lüshun (Port Arthur); pop. (1990c) 1,723,302; has one of finest harbors on East Asia coast and is NE China's leading port; sheltered on N, W, and S by hills; connects by rail with Shenyang and railroad system of E China; fishing; oil refining, shipbuilding; machine tools, textiles, chemicals, fertilizer, locomotives and rolling stock; medical college (1949), technical college (1950).

History: Leased to Russia 1898 (see GUANGDONG); made a free port and terminus of Siberian railroad by edict of Russian czar 1899; in Russo-Japanese War occupied by Japanese 1904; lease transferred to Japan by Treaty of Portsmouth Sept. 1905; again a free port 1906; taken by Soviet troops Aug. 1945; by Chinese-Soviet treaty of Aug. 1945 remained under Chinese sovereignty but a port with preferential rights for U.S.S.R.; Soviet troops withdrawn from area 1955.

Da·lí·as \dä-'lē-äs\. Commune, Almería prov., SE Spain, 18 mi. (29 km.) WSW of the seaport of Almería; pop. (1991c) 3511; lead deposits; mineral baths nearby.

Dal·keith \dal-'kēth\. Burgh, Lothian region, SE Scotland; pop. (1981p) 11,077; engineering; Dalkeith Palace, residence of several British monarchs, has a noted picture gallery.

Dall \'dȯl\. Narrow island, S Alexander Archipelago, SE Alaska, SW of Prince of Wales I.; 43 mi. (69 km.) long.

Dal·lam \'da-ləm\. County in NW corner of Texas. See table at TEXAS.

Dal·las \'da-ləs\. **1.** Name of counties in five states of the U.S. See tables at ALABAMA, ARKANSAS, IOWA, MISSOURI, TEXAS.

2. City, ⊗ of Paulding co., NW Georgia, 30 mi. (48 km.) WNW of Atlanta; pop. (1990c) 2810; scene of indecisive Civil War battle bet. the armies of Gen. Ulysses S. Grant and Gen. Robert E. Lee May 1864.

3. Town, Gaston co., SW North Carolina, 5 mi. (8 km.) N of Gastonia; pop. (1990c) 3012; Gaston Coll. (1963); was ⊗ 1846–1911.

4. City, ⊗ of Polk co., NW Oregon, 15 mi. (24 km.) W of Salem; pop. (1990c) 9422; settled c. 1845.

5. Residential borough, Luzerne co., E Pennsylvania, 9 mi. (14 km.) NNW of Wilkes-Barre; pop. (1990c) 2567; College Misericordia (1924).

6. City, ⊗ of Dallas co., NE Texas, on Trinity River ab. 33 mi. (53 km.) E of Fort Worth; pop. (1990c) 1,006,877; commercial, financial, and transportation center; manufactures cotton gins and other machinery, aircraft parts, electronic equipment, transportation equipment, apparel; printing and publishing; insurance; Cotton Bowl football stadium; Southern Methodist Univ. (1911), Univ. of Texas Southwestern Medical Center at Dallas (1943), Dallas Baptist Univ. (1965), El Centro Coll. (1966), Richland Coll. (1972). Site first settled 1841; became ⊗ 1846; incorp. as town 1856, as city 1871. President John F. Kennedy assassinated in city Nov. 22, 1963; important airline hub; Dallas-Fort Worth Airport opened 1973.

Dallas Peak. Mountain in Ouray and San Miguel cos., SW Colorado; 13,800 ft. (4206 m.).

Dal·las·town \'da-ləs-ˌtaùn\. Borough, York co., S Pennsylvania, 6 mi. (9.6 km.) SE of York; pop. (1990c) 3974.

Dalles, The \'dalz\. **1.** *also* **City of the Dalles.** City, ⊗ of Wasco co., N Oregon, on Columbia River 13 mi. (21 km.) W of its confluence with Deschutes River ab. 72 mi. (116 km.) E of Portland; pop. (1990c) 11,060; E terminus of 200-mile (322-kilometer) waterway from the sea; flour and lumber mills; ships fruit, grain, meat, wool. Indian village found here by explorers Meriwether Lewis and William Clark 1805; first settled by people of European ancestry 1838; incorp. 1857.

2. River, Wisconsin and Minnesota. See SAINT CROIX 2.

Dal·ma·tia \dal-'mā-shə, -shē-ə\ *or Serbo-Croat.* **Dal·ma·ci·ja** \ˌdäl-'mät-sē-yä\. A region, S Europe, on the Adriatic coast, in Yugoslavia, Bosnia and Herzegovina, and Croatia; ab. 4916 sq. mi. (12,732 sq. km.); pop. (1991p) 943,308; former Austrian crown land; extends from Montenegro near Albanian border on the S to Zadar, Croatia on the N and includes many islands; name sometimes applied to most of the coast of the former Yugoslavia; mountainous (Dinaric Alps), many good harbors.

History: Orig. inhabited by Illyrian peoples; conquered for Rome by Emperor Augustus c. 34 B.C.; province of prefecture of Illyricum (*q.v.*) under Emperor Diocletian (d. 313 A.D.); in Western part of Roman Empire after division of 395; part of Gothic kingdom of King Odoacer; reconquered by Eastern Roman Empire under Emperor Justinian; settled by Slavonic peoples in 7th cent.; possession of coastal towns the goal of successive rulers of Croatia, Hungary, and Serbia, with Venetians endeavoring to gain foothold from 10th cent.; coast came under rule of Venice, 1420–1699; province, incl. interior, finally ceded to Venice by Turkey 1718; with suppression of Venetian Republic, held by Austria 1797–1805, 1815–1918 (ceded to French Emperor Napoléon 1805; part of Illyrian Provinces 1809–15; returned to Austria by Congress of Vienna 1815); partly occupied by Italy 1918–19; joined Kingdom of Serbs, Croats, and Slovenes 1918 (see YUGOSLAVIA); Zara (Zadar) and several islands held by Italy which was forced to give up its other Dalmatian claims in Treaty of Rapallo 1920; held by Italy during WWII but returned to Yugoslavia after the war; included in federated republic of Croatia (*q.v.*) 1946 and, later (1991) in independent Croatia.

Dal·meny \dal-'me-nē\. Village, West Lothian co., Scotland, on Firth of Forth; pop. (1991c) 1436; cathedral; Forth Bridge (cantilever; main span 1710 ft. or 521 m.; completed 1890) spanning Firth of Forth.

Dal'·ner·e·chensk \däl^{y}-ˌner-ə-'chensk\; *before 1972* **Iman** \ē-'män\. City, W Primorskiy Kray, E Russia in Asia, on Ussuri River 212 mi. (341 km.) NNE of Vladivostok; on Trans-Siberian R.R.

Dalnevostochny Rayon. See FAR EASTERN REGION.

Dalny. See DALIAN.

Da·loa \dä-'lō-ä\. Town, SW cen. Ivory Coast; pop. (1988c) 122,530.

Dal·ri·a·da \ˌdal-rē-'ā-də\. Ancient kingdom, NE Ireland in the traditional county of Antrim and from late 5th cent. extending across the North Channel into Kintyre Penin. and the island of Islay in W Scotland; by the 9th cent. the Irish part had lost its identity, but the Scottish part continued to flourish.

Dal·ten·ganj *also* **Dal·ton·ganj** \'dȯlt-^{ə}n-ˌgənj, 'dält-\. Town, W Bihar state, NE India; pop. (1991p) 56,408; in coal-bearing region.

Dal·ton \'dȯlt-^{ə}n\. **1.** City, ⊗ of Whitfield co., NW Georgia, 38 mi. (61 km.) N of Rome; pop. (1990c) 21,761; incorp. 1847; ⊗ 1851; headquarters of Gen. Joseph E. Johnston during Civil War; cotton and lumber mills; center of carpet and candlewick-bedspread industries.

2. Town, Berkshire co., W Massachusetts, 5 mi. (8 km.) ENE of Pittsfield; pop. (1990c) 7155.

Dal·ton·ganj See DALTENGANJ.

Dalton–in–Fur·ness \'fər-nəs\. Town, Lancashire, NW England, near Irish Sea 52 mi. (84 km.) N of Liverpool; pop. (1981p) 10,931.

Da·lu·pi·ri \ˌdä-lü-'pē-rē\. **1.** Island in Babuyan group, Philippines, N of Luzon; 24 sq. mi. (62 sq. km.).

2. Island off NW coast of Samar, Philippines, on S side of San Bernardino Strait bet. Capul I. and Samar coast; 11 sq. mi. (28 sq. km.).

Da·ly \'dā-lē\. River, N Northern Terr., Australia; formed by the confluence of three smaller rivers in the hills W of Arnhem Land; flows W to Anson Bay; 225 mi. (362 km.) long; navigable for 70 mi. (113 km.).

Daly City. Residential city, San Mateo co., W California, S suburb of San Francisco; pop. (1990c) 92,311; absorbed town of Colma 1936.

Daly Waters. Village and station along N to S transportation route and on upper Roper River, N cen. Northern Terr., Australia.

Da·man \də-'män\ *or Port.* **Da·mão** \də-'maù^{n}\. **1.** A constituent part of the union terr. of **Daman and Diu** \'dē-ü\ on the W coast of India (see table at INDIA); 22 sq. mi. (57 sq. km.); captured by Portuguese 16th cent.; annexed by India 1961; a constituent part of the union terr. of Goa, Daman, and Diu until 1987.

2. Its chief town, a seaport, on Gulf of Khambat, W India, at mouth of Damanganga River 100 mi. (161 km.) N of Bombay; pop. (1991p) 26,895; once an active harbor, but now of decreasing importance; fishing.

Da·man·hūr \ˌdä-män-'hür, ˌda-man-\; *anc.* **Her·mop·o·lis Par·va** \hər-'mä-pə-ləs-'pär-və\. City, ✻ of Beheira governorate, Egypt, on railroad line E of Alexandria and W of Rosetta branch of the Nile; pop. (1991e) 216,000; cotton.

Da·man·sky Island \də-'män-skē\. Island in Ussuri River on China-Russia border; claims by China and U.S.S.R. led to border clashes 1969.

Damão. See DAMAN.

Damar. See DHAMAR.

Da·mar \dä-'mär\. Group of small islands in S Banda Sea, S Moluccas, Indonesia, NW of Babar Is.; part of the Serawatti Is. Chief island Damar, ab. 11 mi. (18 km.) in diameter, has active volcano.

Da·ma·ra·land \də-'mär-ə-ˌland, 'da-mə-rə-\ *also* **Her·re·ro·land** \hə-'rer-ō-ˌland\. Region, cen. Namibia; a plateau region inhabited chiefly by the Damara people. Chief occupation cattle raising.

Dam·a·ri·scot·ta \ˌdam-ri-'skä-tə, ˌda-mə-\. Narrow inlet of the Atlantic Ocean, on the coast of Lincoln co., S Maine; 22 mi. (35 km.) long.

Da·mas·cus \də-'mas-kəs\ *or French* **Da·mas** \dȧ-'mäs\; *Arab.* **Ash Shām** \esh-'shäm\ *or* **Di·mashq** \di-'mäshk\. City, ❋ of Syria, on the Barada River, with Anti-Lebanon Mts. to the W and desert to the E; munic. pop. (1992e) 1,451,000; cement, glass, textiles, furniture; sugar refineries; university (1923), technical college (1963); believed to be the oldest city in the world having continuous existence; for centuries a great trade mart; situated on edge of an oasis near beautiful gardens and groves; has Great Mosque (partly ruined), many small mosques.

History: Ancient city ruled by Egyptians and Hittites before it became an independent Aramaean kingdom c. 1000 B.C.; prominent in Hebrew history; conquered by Assyrians, Babylonians, Persians, Macedonian King Alexander the Great, Seleucids, Romans, and others; fell to Arabs 635 A.D.; 661 became residence of caliph until overthrow of Umayyad line 750; frequently attacked during Crusades; taken by Ottoman Turks 1516 and remained in Ottoman Empire 400 years; occupied 1918 by British and Arabs as part of campaign in Syria; center of Syrian independence movement until seized by French 1920 under League of Nations mandate; after long resistance forced by bombardment to submit to French after its occupation 1925 by Druze; captured by Free French and British June 1941; ❋ of independent Syria c. 1943.

Da·ma·tu·ru \ˌdä-mä-'tü-rü\. City, NE Nigeria; ❋ of Yobe state.

Da·mā·vand *or* **Dem·a·vend** \ˌdä-mä-'vänd\. Peak, N Iran, NE of Tehran; 18,934 ft. (5771 m.); highest point in the Elburz Mts.

Damer, Ed. See ED DAMER.

Dames, Chemin des. See CHEMIN DES DAMES.

Dām·ghān \däm-'gän\. Town, NW Khorāsān prov., NE Iran; pop. (1986c) 34,057; on main highway and railroad line from Tehran to Khorāsān; was of greater importance in the Middle Ages; destroyed in Afghan invasion 1723; has mosque dating from 9th cent.; has interesting ruins dating from the 11th cent. See HECATOMPYLOS.

Dam·i·et·ta \ˌda-mē-'e-tə\ *or Arab.* **Dum·yāṭ** \du̇m-'yät\. **1.** *anc.* **Phat·nit·ic** \fat-'ni-tik\. E mouth of the Nile, W of Port Said, Egypt; partly silted up and not navigable to large vessels.

2. Governorate of N Egypt. See table at EGYPT.

3. Commercial city, ❋ of governorate, N Egypt, port at mouth of the Damietta branch of the Nile, on E bank in the Nile Delta 8 mi. (13 km.) from the sea; pop. (1986p) 89,498; market center; cotton, silk, glassware; rice, fish; conquered and held by Crusaders 1219–21 and 1249–50.

Damir, Ad. See ED DAMER.

Dam·loup \dä^n-'lü\. Village, Meuse dept., NE France, 5 mi. (8 km.) NE of Verdun; severe fighting 1916 during WWI.

Dammam. See AD DAMMĀM.

Dam·ma·rie, Cape \ˌdȧ-mȧ-'rē\. Cape at NW point of Tiburon Penin., SW Haiti, on S side of entrance to Golfe de la Gonâve.

Dammarie–les–Lys \-lā-'lēs\. Commune, Seine-et-Marne dept., N France, near Melun; ruins of 13th cent. abbey founded by Blanche of Castile, mother of Louis IX.

Da·mo·dar \'dä-mō-ˌdär\. Navigable river, cen. Bihar and West Bengal states, NE India; flows ESE into Hugli River just below Navadwip; 368 mi. (592 km.) long; several dams provide power esp. for extensive mining and irrigation.

Da·moh \də-'mō\. Town, N Madhya Pradesh, India, 190 mi. (306 km.) N of Nagpur; pop. (1991p) 95,553; marketplace for cattle and farm produce of district.

Dam·pier Archipelago \'dam-pyər\. Group of ab. 20 small rocky islands off NW coast of Western Australia, Australia, 20°40′S.

Dampier Land. Peninsula, N Western Australia, Australia, bet. Indian Ocean and King Sound; Cape Leveque at tip.

Dampier Strait. **1.** Passage off W end of New Britain I., Bismarck Archipelago, W Pacific Ocean; separates New Britain from Umboi I.; ab. 15 mi. (24 km.) wide.

2. Channel bet. Waigeo I. and W end of the island of New Guinea, Malay Archipelago, W Pacific Ocean; ab. 100 mi. (161 km.) long and 35 mi. (56 km.) wide.

Dan \'dan\. **1.** River, S Virginia; rises in Patrick co., flows S into North Carolina, then E crossing state border several times before joining Roanoke River in S Virginia; 180 mi. (290 km.) long.

2. Ancient village at N extremity of Palestine on Lebanese border N of the Waters of Merom; mentioned in Bible (*Judges* xx.1); now a mound 2 mi. (3.2 km.) W of Bāniyās, Syria. See BEERSHEBA.

Da·na, Mount \'dā-nə\. Peak in the Sierra Nevada, in E Tuolumne co., cen. California; 13,053 ft. (3978 m.).

Dan·a·kil \'da-nə-ˌkil\ *or* **Den·a·kil** \'de-\ *or Ital.* **Dan·ca·lia** \dän-'käl-yä\. Desert region, E Africa, in NE Ethiopia, SE Eritrea, and N Djibouti; mostly in Great Rift Valley; inhabited by the Danakil, or Afar, people.

Da Nang \'dä-'näŋ\; *formerly* **Tou·rane** \tü-'rän\. Seaport city, cen. Vietnam; pop. (1989c) 369,734; excellent deepwater harbor; manufactures textiles and machinery; site of U.S. military base during Vietnam War.

Da·nao \də-'nau̇\. Chartered city on E coast of Cebu I., Philippines, 17 mi. (27 km.) NNE of City of Cebu; pop. (1990p) 73,000; port; coal deposits nearby.

Dana Point. City, Orange co., California, on coast SE of Los Angeles; pop. (1990c) 31,896.

Dan·a·pur \'də-nə-ˌpu̇r\ *or* **Din·a·pore** \'di-\ *also* **Din·a·pur.** Town, NW Bihar, NE India, on Ganges River 12 mi. (19 km.) W of Patna; pop. (1991p) 84,104; includes military cantonment; Sepoy troops stationed here joined mutiny in 1857.

Danastris. See DNIESTER.

Dan·bury \'dan-ˌber-ē, -bə-rē\. **1.** City, Fairfield co., SW Connecticut, 20 mi. (32 km.) NW of Bridgeport; pop. (1990c) 65,585; formerly notable hat industry; plastics, machinery; Western Connecticut State Univ. (1903). Settled c. 1685; served as military depot for American armies and was attacked and burned by British 1777 during Revolutionary War; incorp. as city 1889; point of origin of Danbury Hatters Case 1902 (Supreme Court decision 1908 against boycott by labor organizations); federal prison.

2. Town, ⊗ of Stokes co., N North Carolina; pop. (1990c) 119.

Dancalia. See DANAKIL.

Dandarah. See DENDERA.

Dan·de·nong \'dan-də-ˌnȯŋ\. City, Victoria, Australia, a SE suburb of Melbourne; pop. (1991c) 57,275.

Dan·dong \'dän-'du̇ŋ\ *or W.-G.* **Tan–tung** \'dän-'du̇ŋ\ *also* **An·tung** \'än-'du̇ŋ\. City, Liaoning prov., NE China, on Yalu River; pop. (1990c) 523,699; chemicals, paper; opened as a treaty port 1907; occupied by Japanese 1931–45; industrialization continued following WWII.

Dan·dridge \'dan-drij\. Town, ⊗ of Jefferson co., E Tennessee; pop. (1990c) 1540.

Dane \'dān\. County in S Wisconsin. See table at WISCONSIN.

Dane·law *also* **Dane·lagh** \'dān-ˌlȯ\. The NE part of England where Danish law was in force c. 9th–c. 11th cents.; covered East Anglia, Essex, a large part of Mercia, and most of Northumbria. See WEDMORE.

Dan·ger, Point \'dān-jər\. Cape on E coast of Australia, most northerly point of New South Wales, at 28°09′S, 153°34′E.

Danger Islands. Island group, Cook Is., cen. Pacific Ocean, in W part of N group; chief island Pukapuka.

Dangerous Archipelago. See TUAMOTU ARCHIPELAGO.

Dang·he Nan·shan \ˈdäŋ-ˈhə-ˈnän-ˈshän\ *or W.-G.* **Tang–ho–nan Shan** \ˈdäŋ-ˈhə-ˈnän-ˈshän\. Mountain range, NW cen. China, on border bet. Gansu and Qinghai provs.

Dangla. Mountain range, Tibet. See TANGGULA 1.

Dang Raek, Phanom. See DANGREK MOUNTAINS.

Dangra Yum Tso. See T'ANG-KU-LA-YU-MU-TS'O.

Dang·rek Mountains \ˈdäŋ-ˌrek, ˈdȯŋ-\ *or* **Pha·nom Dang Raek** \ˈfä-ˌnȯm-ˈdäŋ-ˌrek, -ˈdȯŋ-\ *or* **Thiu Khao Phanom Dong·rak** \ˈtyü-ˈkau̇-ˈfä-ˌnȯm-ˈdȯŋ-ˌrak\. Mountain range, extending E and W along SE boundary of Thailand, separating it from N Cambodia; ab. 200 mi. (320 km.) long; averages 1200 to 2500 ft. (366 to 762 m.). Its W end continues into S Thailand; highest point 4167 ft. (1270 m.).

Dan·gri·ga \dän-ˈgrē-gä\; *formerly* **Stann Creek** \ˈstan\. Coastal town, E cen. coast of Belize; ✱ of Stann Creek dist.; pop. (1990p) 6838.

Dangs, The \ˈdaŋz\. Former group of 14 small Indian states, subordinate to Gujarat States Agency, W India; 689 sq. mi. (1784 sq. km.); since 1960 part of Gujarat.

Da·nia \ˈdā-nē-ə\. City, Broward co., SE Florida, on Atlantic Ocean 20 mi. (32 km.) N of Miami; pop. (1990c) 13,024; resort; orig. settled by Danes c. 1896.

Dan·iels \ˈdan-yəlz\. County in NE Montana. See table at MONTANA.

Dan·iel·son \ˈdan-yəl-sən\. Borough in town of Killingly, Connecticut; pop. (1990c) 4441; incorp. 1854.

Dan·iels·ville \ˈdan-yəlz-ˌvil\. City, ⊗ of Madison co., NE Georgia; pop. (1990c) 318.

Danish West Indies. See VIRGIN ISLANDS.

Dan·lí \dän-ˈlē\. Town, El Paraíso dept., S Honduras, 45 mi. (72 km.) E of Tegucigalpa; pop. (1989e) 31,000.

Danmark. See DENMARK 1.

Dan·ne·mo·ra \ˌda-ni-ˈmōr-ə\. **1.** Village, Clinton co., NE corner of New York, 13 mi. (21 km.) W of Plattsburg; pop. (1990c) 4005; iron deposits; correctional facility (1845).
2. Commune, Uppsala prov., SE Sweden, 22 mi. (35 km.) N of the city of Uppsala; iron deposits.

Dan·ne·virke \ˈda-nə-ˌvərk\. Borough, SE North I., New Zealand, 110 mi. (177 km.) NE of Wellington; pop. (1981c) 5663; founded by Scandinavians.

Dan·no–ura *or* **Dan·no·u·ra** \ˌdän-ˌnō-ü-ˈrä\. Locality, E end of Shimonoseki (*q.v.*), Japan; naval battle 1185 in which the Taira clan was totally defeated by the Minamoto.

Dan River. See DAN 1.

Dansalan. See MARAWĪ.

Dans·ville \ˈdanz-ˌvil\. Village, Livingston co., W New York, NW of Hornell; pop. (1990c) 5002; health resort; birthplace of American Red Cross (founded by Clara Barton 1881).

Dan·ta \ˈdän-tə\. Former Indian state, Rajputana, NW India, NW of Jaipur; 347 sq. mi. (899 sq. km.).

Dantzig. See GDAŃSK.

Dan·ube \ˈdan-ˌyüb\ *or Bulg.* **Du·nav** \ˈdü-näv\ *or Ger.* **Do·nau** \ˈdō-ˌnau̇\ *or Hung.* **Du·na** \ˈdu̇-nȯ\ *or Rom.* **Du·nă·rea** \ˈdü-nər-ˌyä\ *or Russ.* **Du·nay** \dü-ˈnī\; *anc.* **Da·nu·bi·us** \da-ˈnü-bē-əs, -ˈnyü-\ *or in lower course* **Is·ter** \ˈis-tər\. River in cen. Europe; formed by confluence of Breg and Brigach rivers in the Black Forest, Baden-Württemberg, Germany, 37 mi. (60 km.) WNW of Lake Constance; flows E across S Germany, across N Austria and Hungary; ab. 20 mi. (32 km.) N of Budapest turns S and traverses cen. Hungary before forming part of border bet. Croatia and Yugoslavia and entering Yugoslavia where it turns SE; flows E as it forms section of the Romania-Bulgaria boundary; finally turns N across SE Romania and E into the Black Sea through several mouths (delta ab. 1000 sq. mi. or 2590 sq. km. in area), the northernmost channel, the Kiliya mouth, now forming boundary bet. Romania and Ukraine; 1771 mi. (2850 km.) long; drainage area 315,444 sq. mi. (817,000 sq. km.); 2d longest river in Europe (Volga is longest). Has many tributaries (approx. 300) draining the various ranges of the Alps and the Carpathians; chief tributaries on the left (N): Altmühl, Naab (Germany), Morava (Austria and Czech Republic) Váh, Nitra, Hron (Slovakia), Tisza (Yugoslavia and Hungary), Olt, Argeş, Siretul (Romania), and Prut (Romania and Moldova); on the right (S): Iller, Lech, Isar, Inn (Germany), Enns, Leitha (Austria), Rába (Hungary), Drava (Hungary, Croatia, Slovenia, and Austria), Sava, (Slovenia, Croatia, Croatia-Bosnia and Herzegovina border, Yugoslavia), Morava (Yugoslavia), and Iskŭr (Bulgaria). Navigable as far as Ulm by boats of limited draft; in Austria bet. Linz and Vienna passes through defiles with picturesque scenery; just W of Turnu-Severin in Romania passes through the famous defile of the Iron Gate (*q.v.*).

History: Long an important highway for trade bet. cen. and E Europe, its significance increased with development of steam navigation in 19th cent.; free navigation of Danube estab. in 1856 (Treaty of Paris) and placed under supervision of a European Commission; internationalized 1919 by Treaty of Versailles; regulated by postwar commission operating under Danube Convention of 1921; following WWII, new regulatory body consisting only of riparian nations was estab. 1948 with its headquarters in Budapest, Hungary; hydroelectric and navigation complex built at Iron Gate in 1970s.

Da·nu·bia \da-ˈnyü-bē-ə\. Occasional name for countries and regions of the Danube basin.

Da·nu·bi·an Principalities \da-ˈnyü-bē-ən\. Former name for Moldavia and Walachia (*qq.v.* for earlier history); ruled by Turkish governors although by Treaty of Kuchuk Kainarji 1774, Russian intervention permitted; following Russo-Turkish War, guaranteed withdrawal of Turkish troops and greater autonomy 1829; occupied by Russia 1829–34; popular revolt 1848 put down by joint Russo-Turkish forces; occupied by Russia 1849–51; occupied during Crimean War by Russia 1853–54 then by Austria 1854–56; as United Principalities of Moldavia and Walachia, had separate but identical administrations 1858–61; Alexandru Cuza elected prince in both principalities 1859; completely united and named Romania 1861; union recognized by sultan 1862; for later history, see ROMANIA.

Danubius. See DANUBE.

Danum. See DONCASTER.

Dan·vers \ˈdan-vərz\. Town, Essex co., NE corner of Massachusetts, 16 mi. (26 km.) NNE of Boston; pop. (1990c) 24,174; birthplace of Revolutionary commander Israel Putnam 1718; settled 1630s.

Dan·ville \ˈdan-ˌvil\. **1.** City, a ⊗ of Yell co., W cen. Arkansas; pop. (1990c) 1585.
2. City, Contra Costa co., W California, 10 mi. (16 km.) E of Oakland; pop. (1990c) 31,306.
3. City, ⊗ of Vermilion co., E Illinois, 33 mi. (53 km.) E of Champaign; pop. (1990c) 33,828; commercial center of farming and dairy region; Danville Area Community Coll. (1946); made ⊗ 1827; incorp. 1869.
4. Town, ⊗ of Hendricks co., cen. Indiana, 20 mi. (32 km.) W of Indianapolis; pop. (1990c) 4345.
5. City, ⊗ of Boyle co., cen. Kentucky, 32 mi. (51 km.) SSW of Lexington; pop. (1990c) 12,420; market center for tobacco and livestock, esp. horses. Centre Coll. (1819); settled 1775; seat of government for the area 1785–92.
6. Town, Rockingham co., New Hampshire; pop. (1990c) 2534.
7. Borough, ⊗ of Montour co., E cen. Pennsylvania, 30 mi. (48 km.) SE of Williamsport; pop. (1990c) 5165; iron ore, coal, limestone deposits; settled 1792.
8. City, Pittsylvania co., S Virginia, on Dan River 3 mi. (4.8 km.) N of North Carolina border; 14 sq. mi. (36 sq. km.); pop. (1990c) 53,056; politically independent; tobacco market; shipping and trading center; manufactures textiles; Averett Coll. (1859), Danville Community Coll. (1936); Danville Museum of Fine Arts and History housed in Confederate Memorial Mansion. Founded 1793; site of Confederate prison

during Civil War; seat of government briefly during last days of Southern Confederacy 1865.

Dan·zhu *or W.-G.* **Tan·chu** \ˈdän-ˈjü\. Town, SE Guangxi Zhuangzu, SE China, ab. 60 mi. (95 km.) W of Wuzhou; in WWII site of U.S. air base which was abandoned to Japanese Nov. 1944 and retaken by Chinese July 1945.

Danzig. See GDAŃSK.

Danzig, Gulf of. See GDAŃSK, GULF OF.

Dao \ˈdau̇, ˈdä-ō\. **1.** Municipality, S Antique prov., Panay, Philippines, on coastal highway 16 mi. (26 km.) S of San Jose de Buenavista.

2. Municipality, E cen. Capiz prov., Panay, Philippines, on the Panay River and on railroad line 15 mi. (24 km.) SSW of Roxas; pop. (1980c) 23,921; trades in forest products.

Da·peng Wan \ˈdä-ˈpəŋ-ˈwän\ *or W.-G.* **Tai Peng Wan** \ˈdī-ˈpəŋ-ˈwän\; *Eng.* **Mirs Bay** \ˈmərz\. Bay on the coast of Guangdong prov., SE China, E of New Territories, Hong Kong (*q.v.*); its waters leased by China to Great Britain 1898–1997.

Daph·nae \ˈdaf-nē\; *bib.* **Tah·pan·hes** \ˈtä-pən-ˌhēz, tə-ˈpan-\ *or mod.* **Tall al–Da·fa·na** \ˈtȧl-ȧl-ˈdȧ-fȧ-nə\. Ancient fortress, NE Egypt, W of Suez Canal near Al Qanṭarah; archaeological site.

Daph·ne \ˈdaf-nē\. City, Baldwin co., SW Alabama, across Mobile Bay from the city of Mobile; pop. (1990c) 11,290.

Daph·nē \ˈdaf-nē\. Town on coast near tip of Acte Penin., Chalcidice, Greece; has famous monastery.

Da·piak, Mount \ˈdäp-ˌyäk\. Mountain, Zamboanga del Sur prov., Mindanao, Philippines, 25 mi. (40 km.) SSE of Dipolog; 8416 ft. (2565 m.).

Da·pi·tan \də-ˈpē-ˌtän\. Chartered city, N Zamboanga del Norte prov., Mindanao, Philippines, on **Dapitan Bay** (inlet of S side of passage bet. Sulu Sea and Mindanao Sea); pop. (1990p) 59,000; trade center with good harbor; one of the oldest towns in the Philippines; controversial political writer José Rizal spent four years of exile here 1893–96.

Dapsang. See K2.

Da·qah·lī·ya *also* **Da·kah·lī·ya** \ˌdä-kä-ˈlē-yə\. Governorate of N Egypt. See table at EGYPT.

Da·ra \ˈdar-ə\. Ancient fortress in N Mesopotamia; captured by Persians 573 A.D. during war of Khosrow I against Justin II, ruler of Byzantine Empire.

Dā·rāb \də-ˈräb\. Town, Fārs prov., SW Iran, 130 mi. (209 km.) SE of Shīrāz; pop. (1986c) 33,718; noted for its groves of oranges and lemons and for the large sculptured Sassanid bas-relief nearby.

Dar–al–Baida. See CASABLANCA.

Da·ram \də-ˈräm\. Largest of coastal islands of Samar, Philippines, off W coast in Samar Sea, W of Buad I.; 39 sq. mi. (101 sq. km.).

Dar·bhan·ga \dər-ˈbəŋ-gə\. City, N Bihar, NE India, 70 mi. (113 km.) NE of Patna; pop. (1991p) 218,274; chief distribution and trade point for district's agricultural products; university (1961).

Dar·by \ˈdär-bē\. Borough, Delaware co., SE Pennsylvania, 5 mi. (8 km.) W of Philadelphia; pop. (1990c) 11,140.

Darchan. See DARHAN.

Dar·da·nelle \ˌdärd-ᵊn-ˈel\. City, a ⊗ of Yell co., W cen. Arkansas, on Arkansas River; pop. (1990c) 3722.

Dar·da·nelles \ˌdärd-ᵊn-ˈelz\ *or Turk.* **Ça·nak·ka·le Bo·ğa·zı** \ˌchä-näk-kä-ˈlā-ˌbō-gä-ˈzē, -ˌbō-ä-\; *anc.* **Hel·les·pon·tus** \ˌhe-lə-ˈspän-təs\ *or angl.* **Hel·les·pont** \ˈhe-lə-ˌspänt\. Narrow strait, bet. Europe (Gallipoli Penin.) and Turkey in Asia; 38 mi. (61 km.) long, .75 to 4 mi. (1 to 6 km.) wide; connects Sea of Marmara with Aegean Sea.

History: Ancient Hellespont the scene of Persian King Xerxes' crossing to Europe in invasion of Greece 480 B.C. (see IRAN); crossed by Macedonian King Alexander the Great 334 B.C.; part of Eastern Roman (Byzantine) Empire until 14th cent.; held and fortified by Ottoman Turks 15th cent.; with expansion of Russia to Black Sea, increased in strategic importance as only outlet for Russian fleet to Mediterranean; for history of control as an issue of European politics, see STRAITS, THE; scene of Allied campaign during WWI 1915 (for land attack see GALLIPOLI PENINSULA).

Dar·di·stan \ˌdär-di-ˈstän\. Region, NW Jammu and Kashmir, N India, and N North-West Frontier prov., Pakistan; inhabited by the Dards, a group of Indo-Aryan peoples of the upper Indus Valley.

Dardo. See KANGDING.

Dare \ˈdar\. Coastal county in E North Carolina. See table at NORTH CAROLINA.

Dar el Beida. See CASABLANCA.

Dar·ent \ˈdar-ənt\. River, W Kent, SE England; flows NE to the Thames; navigable to Dartford; 20 mi. (32 km.) long.

Dar es Sa·laam \ˌdär-ˌes-sä-ˈläm\. **1.** Region of E Tanzania; formerly part of Pwani region. See table at TANZANIA.

2. *or* **Dar·es·sa·lam.** Seaport city on Indian Ocean; ✻ of Tanzania, also ✻ of Pwani and Dar es Salaam regions; pop. (1988p) 1,360,850; cement, textiles, footwear; food processing; university (1961); founded 1862 by sultan of Zanzibar; taken by German East Africa Company, 1887; made ✻ of German East Africa 1891; captured by British 1916; ✻ of Tanganyika 1961–64; became ✻ of Tanzania 1964.

Dar·field \ˈdär-ˌfēld\. Town, South Yorkshire, N England; pop. (1981p) 8051.

Dar·fur \där-ˈfür, ˈdär-ˌfür\. **1.** Former province of W Sudan; ✻ El Fasher.

2. Region of W Sudan, coextensive with the former province; ✻ El Fasher; pastoralism; an independent kingdom until conquered by Egypt 1874; made part of Sudan (formerly Anglo-Egyptian Sudan) 1898.

Dar·ga·ville \ˈdär-gə-ˌvil\. Borough, North I., New Zealand, on Wairoa River near W coast 80 mi. (129 km.) NNW of Auckland; pop. (1981c) 4747.

Darg Plateau \ˈdärg\. Highland region, S end of Great Dividing Range, E Victoria, SE Australia; highest Mt. Bogong 6508 ft. (1984 m.).

Dar Ha·mid \ˈdär-ha-ˈmēd\. Desert region, cen. Sudan, SW of Khartoum.

Dar·han *also* **Dar·chan** \ˈdär-ˌkän\. Town, N Mongolia, ab. 117 mi. (188 km.) NNW of Ulaanbaator; pop. (1989p) 85,800.

Darial Pass *or* **Dariel Pass.** See DARYAL PASS.

Dar·i·en \ˌdar-ē-ˈen\. **1.** Residential town, SW Fairfield co., SW Connecticut, on Long Island Sound; pop. (1990c) 18,196; raided by British during Revolutionary War; incorp. 1820.

2. City, ⊗ of McIntosh co., SE Georgia; pop. (1990c) 1783.

3. City, Du Page co., NE Illinois, W of Chicago, pop. (1990c) 18,341.

Da·rién \där-ˈyen\. **1.** *orig.* **San·ta Ma·ría la An·ti·gua del Darién** \ˈsän-tä-mä-ˈrē-ä-lä-än-ˈtē-gwä-ˌdel-där-ˈyen\. Settlement and colony estab. by Spaniards on W shore of Gulf of Urabá on N coast of Isthmus of Darien (later Isthmus of Panama, first visited by Europeans early in 16th cent.); colony founded 1510; from here Spanish explorer Vasco Núñez de Balboa crossed the isthmus 1513 and was first European to view the South Sea (Pacific) from the New World; center of early Spanish exploration until replaced by Panama (Panamá); part of prov. of New Granada; in 1698 site of settlement founded by Darien company, a Scottish undertaking under William Paterson which sought to cut off Spanish colonies but was not maintained. For later history, see PANAMA.

2. Province of E Panama. See table at PANAMA.

3. Village, Panama, on SE shore of Gatun Lake.

Darien, Gulf of. Inlet of the Caribbean Sea extending bet. E Panama and NW Colombia; receives the Atrato River; its inner section is the Gulf of Urabá.

Darien, Isthmus of. See PANAMA, ISTHMUS OF.

Da·rién, Ser·ra·nía del \ˌser-rä-ˈnē-ä-ˌdel-där-ˈyen\. Range in E Panama, extending in part along the Panama-Colombia boundary; av. height ab. 3000 ft. (914 m.).

Dar·jee·ling *or* **Dar·ji·ling** \där-ˈjē-liŋ\. Town, NE India, in West Bengal; pop. (1991p) 73,008, incl. cantonments of Jalapahar and Lebong; on Sikkim border at av. elev. of 7500 ft. (2286 m.); commands one of finest views in the world incl. Mt. Kanchenjunga, 40 mi. (64 km.) directly N, and Mt. Everest (visible on clear days from nearby **Ti·ger Hill** \ˌtī-gər-\ 8515 ft. or 2595 m.) 110 mi. (177 km.) to the NW. Inhabitants chiefly Nepalese and Bhutanese. Summer headquarters of Bengal government. See SHILIGURI.

Darke \ˈdärk\. County in W Ohio. See table at OHIO.

Dar·kot Pass \ˈdär-kət, ˈdər-kōt\. Mountain pass in a range of the E Hindu Kush, from Gilgit, in Jammu and Kashmir, to Chitral, in North-West Frontier prov., Pakistan; elev. 15,380 ft. (4688 m.).

Dar·ling \ˈdär-liŋ\. River, S Queensland and N and W New South Wales, SE Australia; flows SW into Murray River near South Australian border; 1702 mi. (2739 km.) long; navigable in part and at certain seasons; volume is very irregular; has headstreams in Great Dividing Range and Darling Downs.

Darling Downs \ˈdaùnz\. Agriculturally productive tableland, SE Queensland, Australia, W of Brisbane; ab. 25,000 sq. mi. (64,750 sq. km.); drained by upper tributaries of Darling River.

Darling Range. Mountain range, SW Western Australia, Australia, parallel with the coast; ab. 250 mi. (402 km.) long; highest point 1910 ft. (582 m.).

Dar·ling·ton \ˈdär-liŋ-tən\. **1.** County in NE South Carolina. See table at SOUTH CAROLINA.
2. City, its ⊗, 10 mi. (16 km.) NW of Florence; pop. (1990c) 7311; trade center for agricultural region; manufactures veneers; stock-car raceway; settled 1798.
3. City, ⊗ of Lafayette co., S Wisconsin, 18 mi. (29 km.) E of Platteville; pop. (1990c) 2235.
4. Town, Durham, N England, on the Skerne 50 mi. (81 km.) N of Leeds; pop. (1991p) 96,700; railroad center; engineering; woolen mills.

Darm·stadt \ˈdärm-ˌshtät\. City, S Hesse state, Germany, 17 mi. (27 km.) S of Frankfurt-am-Main; pop. (1992e) 140,040; chemicals, machinery; museum; 16th cent. town hall; technical university (1836, university status 1895). Made city 1330; to Hesse 1479; became ✻ of Hesse-Darmstadt 1567; ✻ of Hesse 1919–45; in WWII taken by Americans 1945.

Dar·nah \ˈdär-nə\ *or* **Der·na** \ˈder-nə\. Coastal city, Libya, ab. 165 mi. (265 km.) ENE of Benghazi. Captured by U.S. marines 1805 in war with Barbary pirates; damaged severely in WWII, occupied by British 1942.

Dar·rell Island \ˈdar-əl\ *also* **Dar·rell's Island** \-rəlz\. Small island in Great Sound, Bermuda, SW of Hamilton; transatlantic air base.

Dart \ˈdärt\. River, S Devon, SW England; flows SE to English Channel at Dartmouth; 46 mi. (74 km.) long (incl. estuary).

Dart, Cape. Cape at foot of Mt. Siple promontory, Marie Byrd Land, Antarctica, 123°W.

Dart·ford \ˈdärt-fərd\. Town, Kent, SE England, on the Darent 15 mi. (24 km.) ESE of London; pop. (1991p) 78,400; scene of outbreak of Peasants' Revolt (Wat Tyler's Rebellion) June 1381; site of the first papermill in England.

Dart·moor \ˈdärt-ˌmùr, -ˌmōr\. Tableland, S Devon, SW England; 365 sq. mi. (945 sq. km.); mean elev. 1700 ft. (518 m.); has wild open places, many tors (highest High Willhays 2039 ft. or 622 m.), and morasses; source of all principal Devonshire rivers; its forests, in cen. part, are only small tracts of dwarf oaks; estab. as a national park 1951; prison at Princetown built early 1800s for French captives from Napoleonic Wars, convict prison since 1850.

Dart·mouth \ˈdärt-məth\. **1.** Town, Bristol co., SE Massachusetts, 6 mi. (10 km.) SW of New Bedford; pop. (1990c) 27,244; formerly a shipbuilding center; fishing.
2. Coastal town, Halifax co., S Nova Scotia, Canada, on Halifax harbor across from the city of Halifax; pop. (1991c) 67,798; beer; aircraft parts; shipbuilding, oil refineries; former whaling port; settled c. 1750.
3. Town, Devon, SW England, on English Channel at mouth of the Dart 25 mi. (40 km.) E of Plymouth; pop. (1981p) 6298; boatbuilding yards; Royal Naval Coll.

Dar·ton \ˈdärt-ᵊn\. Town, South Yorkshire, N England; pop. (1981p) 17,491.

Da·ru \ˈdä-rü\. Town and port of entry on a small island, Papua New Guinea, 9°04′S, 143°12′E, on N side of Torres Strait; pop. (1980c) 7127.

Da·ru·var \ˈdä-rü-ˌvär\. Commune, Croatia, 64 mi. (103 km.) ESE of Zagreb; thermal springs.

Dar·vel Bay \ˈdär-vəl\. Inlet of Celebes Sea, on SE coast of Sabah, East Malaysia, opp. W end of Sulu Archipelago of the Philippines.

Dar·wen \ˈdär-win, *by residents also* ˈdar-ən\. Town, Lancashire, NW England, 17 mi. (27 km.) NNW of Manchester; pop. (1981p) 30,048; cotton goods, chemicals, paint.

Dar·win \ˈdär-win\; *orig.* **Palm·er·ston** \ˈpäl-mər-stən, ˈpä-\; *later* **Port Darwin.** Seaport, ✻ of Northern Terr., Australia, on **Port Darwin** (an inlet of Clarence Strait); pop. (1991c) 70,071; one of the best harbors in Australia; supply and shipping point for N Australia; terminus of overland telegraph and highway from Adelaide; center of sparsely populated and largely undeveloped region. Settled c. 1869; small boom followed discovery of gold in 1880s; Allied base in WWII; bombed by Japanese 1942, then rebuilt; devastated by cyclone Dec. 25, 1974, rebuilt a second time.

Darwin, Mount. Peak in the Sierra Nevada, on boundary bet. Fresno and Inyo cos., SE cen. California; 13,830 ft. (4215 m.).

Daryācheh–ye Namak. See NAMAK, DARYĀCHEH-YE.

Daryācheh–ye Orūmīyeh *and* **Daryācheh–ye Rezā'īyeh.** See ORŪMĪYEH, DARYĀCHEH-YE.

Daryācheh–ye Sīstān. See HELMAND 1.

Dar·yal Pass *or* **Dar·i·al Pass** \dər-ˈyäl, där-\ *or* **Dar·i·el Pass** \där-ˈyel\. Gorge in the Caucasus Mts., S Russia in Europe, E of Mt. Kazbek; traversed by Terek River; has vertical rock walls 5900 ft. (1798 m.) high. Probably the only early passage across the Caucasus Mts.; through it was constructed the Georgian Military Road from Tbilisi to Vladikavkaz.

Dar''yoi Amu. See AMU DAR'YA.

Dash·howuz \ˌdəsh-hə-ˈwüs\ *or* **Ta·sha·uz** \ˌtə-shə-ˈüs\. Town, N Turkmenistan, on Uzbekistan border; pop. (1991e) 117,000.

Dashiqiao. See YINGKOU 2.

Dasht \ˈdȧsht\. River, SW Baluchistan, Pakistan; flows SW into Arabian Sea; 265 mi. (426 km.) long.

Dasht–e–Ka·vīr \-ˌē-kə-ˈvēr\ *or* **Great Salt Desert.** Salt desert, a plateau, in N cen. Iran; alt. 2500 ft. (762 m.).

Dasht–e–Lūt \-ē-ˈlüt\. Tableland, cen. and E cen. Iran; alt. 1000 ft. (305 m.); largely desert.

Dashur. See DAHSHŪR.

Da·sol Bay \dä-ˈsōl\. Inlet of South China Sea on SW coast of Pangasinan prov., Luzon, Philippines.

Das·pal·la \dəs-ˈpə-lə\. Former Indian state, SE Eastern States, NE India, W of Cuttack; region now in Orissa state; 556 sq. mi. (1440 sq. km.).

Da·ta \ˈdä-tä\. Mountain in S part of Cordillera Central, N Luzon, Philippines; 7577 ft. (2310 m.).

Date Line. See INTERNATIONAL DATE LINE.

Da·tia *also* **Dut·tia** \ˈdə-tē-ə\. **1.** Former Indian state, now part of Madhya Pradesh, N cen. India; 846 sq. mi. (2191 sq. km.); ✻ Datia; came under British government by treaty early 1800s.
2. Town, its ✻, 45 mi. (72 km.) SSE of Gwalior; pop. (1991p) 65,565; has 17th cent. Hindu palace.

Dat·il Mountains \ˈda-til\. Range in W cen. New Mexico, extending across N part of boundary bet. Catron and Socorro cos.

Datoek, Tandjoeng. See DATU, CAPE.

Da·tong \ˈdä-ˈtùŋ\ *or W.-G.* **Ta–t'ung** \ˈdä-ˈtùŋ\; *formerly* **Ta·tung–fu** \ˈdä-ˌtùŋ-ˈfü\. City, N Shanxi prov., NE China, 180 mi. (290 km.) W of Beijing; pop. (1990c) 798,319; has rail connections with Taiyuan to the SSW and trades in livestock, coal, and furs; ancient buildings remain dating back to Lino period (c. 11th cent.). Nearby, ab. 10 mi. (16 km.) distant, are the notable Buddhist cave temples of Yungang. City dates back to Han dynasty (c. 200 B.C.–c. 220 A.D.); 4th cent. became ✻ of Northern Wei dynasty; scene of fighting in Chinese Civil War bet. Nationalists and Communists (1945 ff.).

Dat·teln \ˈdät-əln\. Commune, North Rhine-Westphalia, Germany, in the valley of the Lippe 24 mi. (39 km.) SSW of Münster; pop. (1980c) 37,192; coal deposits.

Da·tu, Cape \ˈdä-tü\ *or Du.* **Tan·djoeng Da·toek** \ˈtän-ˌjuŋ-ˈdä-tu̇k\. Cape, W Borneo, projecting into South China Sea at ab. 109°30′E, marking the boundary bet. W Sarawak, East Malaysia and the NW part of the Indonesian prov. of West Kalimantan.

Datu Bay. Inlet of South China Sea in SW Sarawak, Malaysia bet. delta of Rajang River and mouth of Sarawak River, N of Kuching; receives the Batang Lupar.

Daugava. See DVINA, WESTERN.

Dau·gav·grī·va \ˈdau̇-gəf-ˌgrē-və\ *or Russ.* **Dau·ga·va** \ˈdau̇-gə-və\ *or Ger.* **Dü·na·mün·de** \ˌdu̅e̅-nə-ˈmu̅en-də\; *formerly* **Ust Dvinsk** \ˈüst-ˈdvinsk\. Harbor and fortress at mouth of the Western Dvina on the Gulf of Riga, cen. Latvia, 8 mi. (13 km.) N of Riga; serves as Riga's port in winter; held by Germans 1917–18 in WWI and 1941–44 in WWII.

Dau·gav·pils \ˈdau̇-gəf-ˌpils\ *or Russ.* **Dvinsk** \ˈdvinsk\ *or Ger.* **Dü·na·burg** \ˈdu̅e̅-nə-ˌbu̇rk\. City, E Latvia, on Western Dvina River; pop. (1991e) 129,000; railroad junction 136 mi. (219 km.) SE of Riga; trade center for lumber and food products; textiles. Founded in 1270s by Teutonic Knights; under Polish rule 1559–1772, Russian rule 1772–1915; resisted repeated attacks by Germans 1915–18; under independent Latvian rule 1918–1940; under U.S.S.R. rule 1940–1991; held 1941–44 by Germans in WWII.

Dau·lat·a·bad \ˌdau̇-lə-tə-ˈbäd\. Town, NW cen. Maharashtra state, S cen. India, ab. 10 mi. (16 km.) NW of Aurangabad; has remarkable fortress on rock ab. 600 ft. (183 m.) high within which are ruins of tower, palace, temple, and other structures. As **De·o·gi·ri** \ˌdā-ō-ˈjir-ē\ founded late 12th cent.; captured late 13th cent. by Sultan ʻAlāʼ-ud-Dīn Muḥammad Khaljī of the Khaljī dynasty; made ✻ of India mid-14th cent. by Muḥammad ibn Tughluq who gave it its present name; later, held by various Muslim rulers; after 1707 came into possession of nizam of Hyderabad.

Dau·le \ˈdau̇-lā\. **1.** River, NW Ecuador; flows S into Guayas River; 55 mi. (89 km.) long.

2. Town, Guayas prov., W Ecuador, on E bank of Daule River 22 mi. (35 km.) N of Guayaquil.

Dau·lis \ˈdȯ-lis\. Ancient city of Phocis, cen. Greece, 12 mi. (19 km.) E of Delphi; scene of legend of Philomela.

Daung Island \ˈdau̇ŋ\; *formerly* **Ross Island** \ˈrȯs\. Island, N Mergui Archipelago (*q.v.*), Myanmar.

Dau·phin \ˈdȯ-fin\. **1.** County in SE cen. Pennsylvania. See table at PENNSYLVANIA.

2. River, S cen. Manitoba, Canada, connecting Lake Manitoba with Lake Winnipeg; ab. 70 mi. (113 km.) long; passes through Lake St. Martin.

3. Town, SW cen. Manitoba, Canada, 10 mi. (16 km.) W of S end of Lake Dauphin; pop. (1991c) 8453; fishing.

Dauphin, Lake. Lake, SW Manitoba, Canada, W of N Lake Manitoba; 200 sq. mi. (518 sq. km.).

Dau·phi·né \ˌdō-fē-ˈnā\. Historical region and former province of SE France; bounded anciently on N by Burgundy, on E by Savoy (kingdom of Sardinia), on S by Provence, on SW by Comtat Venaissin, on W by Languedoc, and on NW by Lyonnais; equivalent to modern depts. of Drôme, Hautes-Alpes, Isère; ✻ Grenoble; watered by Drôme, Isère, and Durance rivers; mountainous in E.

History: Region occupied by Burgundians, later by Franks; formed part of Holy Roman Emperor Lothair I's kingdom (see LORRAINE) and of kingdom of Arles (*q.v.*); from 10th to 13th cents. consolidated and expanded by counts of Vienne who were vassals of Holy Roman Empire; sold 1349 to Philip VI of France who transferred it to his grandson, the future Charles V of France; became appanage of eldest son of French king who assumed title (*dauphin*) attached to the land; quasi-independent status until annexed 1457 by Charles VII of France.

Dauphiné Alps. See table at ALPS.

Dauphin Island \ˈdȯ-fin\. Island at entrance to Mobile Bay, off SW coast of Alabama; included in Mobile co.; discovered by French soldier and colonist Pierre Le Moyne, sieur d'Iberville 1699; seized by U.S. from French 1813.

D'Au·tray \dō-ˈtrā\. County, Quebec, Canada. See table at QUEBEC.

Da·van·ge·re \ˈdä-veŋ-ger-ˌā\. Town, E Karnataka state, S India, 155 mi. (249 km.) NW of Bangalore; pop. (1991p) 265,971; textiles; distribution point for cereals and cotton.

Da·vao \ˈdä-ˌvau̇\. **1.** Former province, SE Mindanao, Philippines, now consisting of the provs. of Davao, Davao del Sur, and Davao Oriental; region very mountainous with high peaks in E and Mt. Apo 9690 ft. (2954 m.), highest in the Philippines, on W border. Agusan River rises in SE and flows N, other short streams flow E to Pacific or S or E to Davao Gulf; at N end of Davao Gulf is large Samal I. and off Tinaca Point in SW are Sarangani Is.

History: Visited by Spaniards in 16th cent. but region under jurisdiction of sultanate of Mindanao until middle of 19th cent.; organized as a Spanish province 1849 and changed to a military district 1860; under Americans granted civil government 1914; from ab. 1902 large Japanese population; held by Japanese1941–45; partitioned into the provs. Davao del Norte, Davao del Sur, and Davao Oriental 1969.

2. Province, Mindanao, Philippines; ✻ Tagum. See table at PHILIPPINES.

3. *or officially* **City of Davao.** Chartered city, ✻ of former Davao prov., Mindanao, Philippines, on NW shore of Davao Gulf opp. Samal I.; pop. (1990p) 850,000; shipping point for agricultural products; university (1965). Founded 1849; in 20th cent. developed as part of Japanese colony; seized by Japanese 1941 and made a naval base; retaken by Allied forces May 1945.

Davao del Sur \del-ˈsu̇r\. Province, Mindanao, Philippines; ✻ Digos. See DAVAO 1 and table at PHILIPPINES.

Davao Gulf. Large inlet of Pacific Ocean, Mindanao, Philippines; ab. 80 mi. (129 km.) long by 45 mi. (72 km.) wide; marked on SE side of entrance by Cape San Agustin and on SW by Calian Point; Samal I. is at its N end.

Davao Ori·en·tal \ˌō-rē-en-ˈtäl\. Province, Mindanao, Philippines; ✻ Mati. See DAVAO 1 and table at PHILIPPINES.

Dav·en·port \ˈda-vən-ˌpōrt\. **1.** City, ⊗ of Scott co., E Iowa, on Mississippi River across from Rock Island, Illinois; pop. (1990c) 95,333; railroad and commercial center; manufactures food products; clothing; St. Ambrose Univ. (1882), Palmer Coll. of Chiropractic (1895), Teikyo Marycrest Univ. (1939). Founded c. 1836; site of the first railroad bridge across the Mississippi River, completed 1856; suffered significant damage in floods 1993.

2. Town, ⊗ of Lincoln co., E Washington; pop. (1990c) 1502.

Dav·en·try \ˈda-vən-trē\. Town, Northamptonshire, cen. England; pop. (1991p) 61,600.

Da·vid \dä-ˈvēth\. Town, ✻ of Chiriquí prov., W Panama; pop. (1990p) 65,635; its port, Pedregal, is 5 mi. (8 km.) to the S.

David City \ˈdā-vid\. City, ⊗ of Butler co., E Nebraska, 39 mi. (63 km.) NNW of Lincoln; pop. (1990c) 2522; trade center.

David–Go·ro·dok \dä-ˈvēd-ˌgȯr-ȯ-ˈdȯk\ *or Pol.* **Da·wid-gró·dek** \ˌdä-vid-ˈgrü-ˌdek\. Town, S Belarus, on Goryn River 49 mi. (79 km.) E of Pinsk; formerly in Poland.

David Point \ˈdā-vid\. Cape on S side of W St. Thomas I., Virgin Is., West Indies, W of Fortuna Bay.

Da·vids Island \ˈdā-vidz\. Island in Long Island Sound, New York, near New Rochelle.

Da·vid·son \ˈdā-vid-sən\. **1.** Name of counties in two states of the U.S. See tables at NORTH CAROLINA and TENNESSEE.

2. Town, Mecklenburg co., S North Carolina, 18 mi. (29 km.) N of Charlotte; pop. (1990c) 4046; Davidson Coll. (1837).

Davidson, Mount. Peak, site of Virginia City, Storey co., W Nevada; 7870 ft. (2399 m.).

Da·vie \ˈdā-vē\. **1.** County in cen. North Carolina. See table at NORTH CAROLINA.

2. Town, Broward co., SE Florida; pop. (1990c) 47,217.

Da·viess \ˈdā-vis\. Name of counties in three states of the U.S. See tables at INDIANA, KENTUCKY, MISSOURI.

Da·vis \ˈdā-vis\. **1.** Name of counties in two states of the U.S. See tables at IOWA and UTAH.

2. City, Yolo co., N cen. California, 15 mi. (24 km.) W of Sacramento; pop. (1990c) 46,209; Univ. of California, Davis (1906); agricultural research farm.
3. City, Murray co., S Oklahoma, on Washita River 23 mi. (37 km.) N of Ardmore; pop. (1990c) 2543; oil wells.

Davis, Mount *also* **Davis Mountain;** *formerly* **Ne·gro Mountain** \ˈnē-grō\. Elevation, Somerset co., S Pennsylvania; 3213 ft. (979 m.); highest point in the state.

Davis Bridge Dam. See HARRIMAN DAM.

Davis Island. Man-made island, Tampa, Florida, at mouth of Hillsborough River; munic. hospital and several recreational centers.

Davis Mountain. See DAVIS, MOUNT.

Davis Mountains. Small range in Jeff Davis co., W Texas; includes Mt. Livermore 8382 ft. (2555 m.).

Da·vi·son \ˈdā-vi-sən\. **1.** County in SE South Dakota. See table at SOUTH DAKOTA.
2. City, Genesee co., SE cen. Michigan, 10 mi. (16 km.) E of Flint; pop. (1990c) 5693.

Davis Peak. Mountain, N Cascade Range, NW Washington; 7150 ft. (2179 m.).

Davis Strait. Strait bet. SW Greenland and E Baffin I., connecting Baffin Bay with the Atlantic Ocean; width at its narrowest point 200 mi. (322 km.). Discovered by English navigator John Davis during voyage in search of Northwest Passage (*q.v.*) c. 1585; Greenland side of strait explored by Davis in 1587 when he sailed through it into Baffin Bay.

Da·vos \dä-ˈvōs\. Commune, Graubünden canton, E Switzerland, in Alpine **Davos Valley** 13 mi. (21 km.) ESE of Chur; pop. (1990c) 11,610; consists of villages of **Davos–Platz** \-ˈpläts\ and **Davos–Dorf** \-ˈdȯrf\; famous as a center for winter sports and as a health resort.

Da·wa \ˈdä-wä\. River, S Ethiopia; flows SE to join the Genale and Wabē Gestro rivers and form the Jubba; also forms part of the boundary bet. Ethiopia and Kenya.

Da·wa·sīr, Wa·di ad \ˈwä-dē-ȧd-dȧ-ˈwä-sir\. Watercourse in SW cen. Saudi Arabia; flows NE, then NW; dry at some seasons.

Dawes \ˈdȯz\. County in NW Nebraska. See table at NEBRASKA.

Dawhah, Ad–. See DOHA.

Dawidgródek. See DAVID-GORODOK.

Daw·lish \ˈdȯ-lish\. Coast town, Devon, SW England, on the English Channel 12 mi. (19 km.) S of Exeter; pop. (1981p) 10,755; seaside resort.

Daw·na Range \ˈdȯ-nə\. Mountain range extending NW and SE along boundary bet. E cen. Myanmar and W Thailand, W of Thaungyin River; highest point 6819 ft. (2078 m.).

Daw·ros Head \ˈdȯ-ˌräs\. Cape on W coast of co. Donegal, N Ireland (republic), N of Donegal Bay.

Daw·son \ˈdȯs-ᵊn\. **1.** Name of counties in four states of the U.S. See tables at GEORGIA, MONTANA, NEBRASKA, TEXAS.
2. City, ⊗ of Terrell co., SW Georgia, 22 mi. (35 km.) NW of Albany; pop. (1990c) 5295.
3. River, E Queensland, Australia, S tributary of Fitzroy River; flows N; 312 mi. (502 km.) long.
4. *formerly* **Dawson City.** City, Yukon Terr., N Canada, on right bank of the Yukon near where it is joined by the Klondike, ab. 50 mi. (81 km.) E of Alaska boundary; pop. (1991c) 972; elev. 1400 ft. (427 m.); tourism; temperature frequently averages –40°F for several days. Had its beginnings in 1896 in the Klondike gold rush; at its height 1898 it was much larger than now; ✽ of Yukon Terr. 1898–1953; last gold-dredging operation closed 1966.
5. Island, Chile, in Tierra del Fuego Archipelago (*q.v.*) off W coast of Tierra del Fuego I.; separated from Brunswick Penin. on W by Strait of Magellan.

Dawson, Mount. Mountain, SE British Columbia, Canada; in Selkirk Mts., in Glacier National Park; 11,122 ft. (3090 m.).

Dawson Creek. City, NE British Columbia, Canada, 315 mi. (507 km.) NW of Edmonton near Alberta border; pop. (1991c) 10,981; grains, livestock; timber; starting point of the Alaska Highway (*q.v.*).

Dawson Springs. City, Hopkins co., W Kentucky, 53 mi. (85 km.) E of Paducah; pop. (1990c) 3129; mineral springs.

Daw·son·ville \ˈdȯs-ᵊn-ˌvil\. Town, ⊗ of Dawson co., N Georgia; pop. (1990c) 467.

Dax \ˈdaks\ *or* **Ax** \ˈaks\; *anc.* **Aq·uae Tar·bel·li·cae** \ˈa-kwē-tär-ˈbe-lə-ˌsē, ˈā-\; *later* **Aquae Au·gus·tae** \ȯ-ˈgəs-tē\. Commune, Landes dept., SW France, on Adour River 30 mi. (48 km.) SW of Mont-de-Marsan; pop. (1990c) 20,119; hot saline springs; mineral baths; 14th cent. castle; 18th cent. cathedral. Ancient Gallic town; made episcopal see early in Christian era; ✽ of viscountship in Béarn during Middle Ages.

Day \ˈdā\. County in NE South Dakota. See table at SOUTH DAKOTA.

Da·ya Wan *or W.-G.* **Ta–ya Wan** \ˈdä-ˈyä-ˈwän\; *Eng.* **Bi·as Bay** \ˈbī-əs\. Inlet of South China Sea, on coast of Guangdong prov., SE China, E of Kowloon.

Da·ye *or W.-G.* **Ta–yeh** \ˈdä-ˈyā\. Town, Hubei prov., E cen. China, SW of Huangshi.

Da·ying *or W.-G.* **Ta–ying** \ˈdä-ˈyiŋ\; *Burmese* **Ta·ping** \ˈtä-ˈpiŋ\. River, China and Myanmar; flows SW out of Yunnan prov., China, crosses Myanmar border and empties into the Irrawaddy River at Bhamo; ab. 170 mi. (275 km.) long.

Dayr az Zawr *or* **Deir ez Zor** \ˈdār-ez-ˈzȯr\. Town, E Syria, on right bank of Euphrates River; most important town of a large area; lies at junction of river route from Aleppo to Baghdad and from Damascus NE to Mosul.

Day·ton \ˈdāt-ᵊn\. **1.** City, Campbell co., N Kentucky, on Ohio River 3 mi. (5 km.) above Newport; pop. (1990c) 6576.
2. Village, Lyon co., W Nevada, ab. 11 mi. (18 km.) NE of Carson City; gold discovered here 1849.
3. City, ⊗ of Montgomery co., SW Ohio, on Miami River 47 mi. (76 km.) N of Cincinnati; pop. (1990c) 182,044; aviation and aeronautical research center, site of Wright-Patterson Air Force Base; distribution center for fertile region; manufactures include air-conditioning equipment, paper, tools, rubber products, computers, household appliances; printing and publishing. United Theological Seminary (1871), Sinclair Community Coll. (1887), Univ. of Dayton (1850), Wright State Univ. (1964). Settled 1796; became ⊗ 1803; incorp. as town 1805, as city 1841; suffered from disastrous flood 1913; first large city to adopt commission-manager form of government (1913). Home of aviation pioneers Wilbur and Orville Wright and the writer Paul Lawrence Dunbar.
4. City, ⊗ of Rhea co., E cen. Tennessee; pop. (1990c) 5671; coal deposits. Bryan Coll. (1930); scene of Scopes test case evolution trial July 1925.
5. City, Liberty co., E Texas, 43 mi. (69 km.) NE of Houston; pop. (1990c) 5151.
6. City, ⊗ of Columbia co., SE Washington, 27 mi. (43 km.) NE of Walla Walla; pop. (1990c) 2468.

Day·to·na Beach \dā-ˈtō-nə\. Resort city, Volusia co., E Florida, on Atlantic Ocean 92 mi. (148 km.) SSE of Jacksonville; pop. (1990c) 61,921; noted esp. for its hard, white beach; Daytona International Speedway (site of Daytona 500); Bethune-Cookman Coll. (1904), Embry-Riddle Aeronautical Univ. (1926), Daytona Beach Community Coll. (1958); settled c. 1870; formed 1926 by consolidation of municipalities of Seabreeze, Daytona Beach, and Daytona.

Dayton Aviation Heritage National Historical Park. See UNITED STATES, *National Historical Parks.*

Da Yunhe. See GRAND CANAL.

De Aar \də-ˈär\. Town, S Rep. of South Africa, 240 mi. (386 km.) NNW of Port Elizabeth; important railroad junction of main lines from Cape Town and Port Elizabeth.

Dead Indian Peak. Mountain, W Park co., NW Wyoming, in the Absaroka Range, 28 mi. (45 km.) WNW of Cody; 12,263 ft. (3738 m.).

Dead·man Mountain \ˈded-ˌman\. Peak, N Lincoln co., W Wyoming; 10,365 ft. (3159 m.).

Dead·mans Bay \ˈded-ˌmanz\. Inlet of Gulf of Mexico on coast of upper Dixie and lower Taylor cos., NW Florida Penin.

Dead Man's Hill. See LE MORT HOMME.

Dead Sea; *anc.* **La·cus As·phal·ti·tes** \ˈlā-kəs-ˌas-ˌfȯl-ˈtī-tēz\ *or Arab.* **Bah·ret Lut** \ˈbä-ret-ˈlüt\. Salt lake on the boundary bet. Israel and Jordan; 51 mi. (82 km.) long, 11 mi. (18 km.) wide at its greatest breadth; 394 sq. mi. (1020 sq. km.); surface 1312 ft. (400 m.) below the level of the Mediterranean Sea; lowest point on Earth's surface; receives the Jordan River at N end; has had many names and has figured in many events of biblical history.

Dead·wood \ˈded-ˌwu̇d\. **1.** River in Valley and Boise cos., W cen. Idaho; tributary of S fork of Payette River; **Deadwood Dam** (height 165 ft. or 50 m.; completed 1931) and **Deadwood Reservoir** in S Valley co. impound its waters for irrigation.

2. City, ⊗ of Lawrence co., W South Dakota, in **Deadwood Gulch** in N Black Hills, 4 mi. (6 km.) N of Lead; pop. (1990c) 1830; trade center for surrounding mining camps and cattle ranches; mining, ore smelting and refining, lumbering, livestock raising; tourist center; settled c. 1876 following discovery of gold in Deadwood Gulch; grave sites of Wild Bill Hickok (killed here in 1876) and Calamity Jane (Martha Jane Burk).

Deaf Smith \ˈdef-ˈsmith\. County in NW Texas. See table at TEXAS.

Deal \ˈdēl\. **1.** Borough and summer resort, Monmouth co., E cen. New Jersey, on Atlantic Ocean ab. 4 mi. (6 km.) S of Long Branch; pop. (1990c) 1179.

2. Town, Kent, SE England, on Strait of Dover 8 mi. (13 km.) NNE of Dover; pop. (1981p) 25,989; large safe anchorage; boatbuilding; tourism; fishing; two castles built by Henry VIII; reputed landing place of Roman Gen. Julius Caesar 55 B.C.

Deal Island. Small island, partly marshland, in Tangier Sound, Chesapeake Bay, NW Somerset co., Maryland.

Dean, Forest of \ˈdēn\. Ancient royal forest, since 1938 a National Forest Park, W Gloucestershire, SW cen. England, bet. Severn and Wye rivers; ab. 20 mi. (32 km.) long, 10 mi. (16 km.) wide; contains coal deposits.

Dean Channel. Inlet of Pacific Ocean (Queen Charlotte Sound), W British Columbia, Canada; ab. 75 mi. (120 km.) long; receives **Dean River** (ab. 150 mi. or 240 km. long) from the E; connects with Burke Channel on S.

De·án Fu·nes \dā-ˈän-ˈfü-nes\. Town, Córdoba prov., N cen. Argentina, on railroad line 75 mi. (121 km.) NNW of the city of Córdoba; pop. (1980p) 16,306.

Dear·born \ˈdir-ˌbȯrn\. **1.** County in SE Indiana. See table at INDIANA.

2. City, Wayne co., SE Michigan, 10 mi. (16 km.) W of Detroit; pop. (1990c) 89,286; Henry Ford Community Coll. (1938), Univ. of Michigan–Dearborn (1959), Detroit Coll. of Business (1962); site of the Ford Motor Company headquarters; incorp. as city 1925; home of Henry Ford (1863–1947).

Dearborn Heights. City, Wayne co., SE Michigan, 8 mi. (13 km.) E of Detroit; pop. (1990c) 60,838.

Dearg, Beinn *or* **Dearg, Ben.** See BEINN DEARG.

Dearne \ˈdərn\. River, West Yorkshire, N England; tributary of the Don; 25 mi. (40 km.) long.

Dease \ˈdēz\. River, British Columbia, Canada; flows N from small Dease Lake to the Liard River at Lower Post on the Alaska Highway; ab. 120 mi. (195 km.) long.

Dease Strait. Channel, Canada, bet. S Victoria I. and N Canada mainland, E of Coronation Gulf.

Death Valley \ˈdeth\. Valley in Inyo co., E California, bet. Panamint Mts. on W and Amargosa Range on E; ab. 140 mi. (225 km.) long; Amargosa River flows into it from S; contains small pool, Badwater, lowest point in U.S., 282 ft. (86 m.) below sea level, less than 80 mi. (129 km.) from Mt. Whitney (14,494 ft. or 4418 m., highest point in U.S. outside of Alaska); estab. 1933 as **Death Valley National Park** (see UNITED STATES, *National Parks*).

Deau·ville \dō-ˈvēl\. Commune, Calvados dept., NW France, on the Bay of the Seine ab. 20 mi. (32 km.) NE of Caen; pop. (1990c) 4380; resort, racecourse.

De Ba·ca \dē-ˈbä-kə\. County in E cen. New Mexico. See table at NEW MEXICO.

De·ba Ha·be \ˈdā-bä-ˈhä-bā\. Town, Bauchi state, NE cen. Nigeria; pop. (1993e) 128,400.

De·bar \ˈde-bär\. Fortified town, W Rep. of Macedonia, near Drin River and Albanian border; commercial center; nearby sulfurous springs.

Debba, Ed. See ED DEBBA.

Deb·dou \deb-ˈdü\. Town, NE Morocco, ab. 80 mi. (129 km.) SW of Oujda.

Dę·bi·ca \de-ˈbēt-sə\. Town, E Tarnów prov., SE Poland; pop. (1989e) 45,292.

De Bilt \də-ˈbilt\. Commune, Utrecht prov., cen. Netherlands, a suburb of the city of Utrecht; pop. (1981e) 31,970.

Dę·blin \ˈde^{n}-blēn\; *Russ.* **Ivan·go·rod** \ē-ˈvän-gə-ˌrət\. Town, Lublin prov., E Poland, at junction of Wieprz and Vistula rivers; pop. (1981p) 16,052.

De·bo, Lake \ˈdā-bō\. Lake, cen. Mali, ab. 150 mi. (240 km.) SW of Tombouctou; traversed from SW to N by Niger River.

De·bre·cen \ˈde-bret-ˌsen\. City, ⊗ of Hajdú-Bihar co., E Hungary, 120 mi. (193 km.) E of Budapest; 172 sq. mi. (446 sq. km.); pop. (1991e) 222,300; commercial center in agricultural and livestock-raising region; furniture, pharmaceuticals, pottery, ball bearings; university (1912); founded in 14th cent.; scene of patriot and statesman Lajos Kossuth's proclamation 1849 of Hungary's independence from the Hapsburgs; in WWII taken by Soviet troops 1944; seat of provisional Hungarian government 1944–45.

De·bre Mar·kos \ˈde-bre-ˈmär-kōs\. Town, W Ethiopia, 110 mi. (177 km.) NW of Addis Ababa; pop. (1989e) 50,152.

De·bre Zey·it *or* **Debre Zeit** \ˈde-brə-ˈzāt\. Town, Ethiopia, 25 mi. (40 km.) SE of Addis Ababa; pop. (1989e) 67,852.

De·cap·o·lis \di-ˈka-pə-lis\. Region in N of ancient Palestine, beginning W of Jordan River at E end of Plain of Esdraelon and stretching to the E and NE of the Sea of Galilee; settled by many Greeks following Macedonian King Alexander the Great's conquests, but got its name *(Gk.*, literally, "ten cities") from the league of 10 (original) Greek cities formed after Roman Gen. Pompey the Great's campaign 64–63 B.C.; generally under Roman control. Damascus was only important city; Scythopolis (Bet She'an) the only one W of the Jordan; others were Gadara, Pella, Jarash, Philadelphia, Hippos, Raphana, Dion, and Canatha.

De·ca·tur \di-ˈkā-tər\. **1.** Name of counties in five states of the U.S. See tables at GEORGIA, INDIANA, IOWA, KANSAS, TENNESSEE.

2. City, ⊗ of Morgan co., N Alabama, on Tennessee River 75 mi. (121 km.) N of Birmingham; pop. (1990c) 48,761; shipyard; John C. Calhoun State Community Coll. (1965); chartered as city 1826; nearly destroyed in Civil War; consolidated 1927 with city of Albany; Stone Mt. nearby.

3. City, ⊗ of De Kalb co., NW cen. Georgia, 5 mi. (8 km.) E of Atlanta; pop. (1990c) 17,336; residential suburb of Atlanta; Agnes Scott Coll. (1889), DeVry Institute of Technology (1969); incorp. 1823.

4. City, ⊗ of Macon co., cen. Illinois, on Sangamon River 35 mi. (56 km.) E of Springfield; pop. (1990c) 83,885; in corn-growing region; manufactures corn and soybean products, tires, tractors; coal deposits; railroad center; Millikin Univ. (1901), Richland Community Coll. (1971); in May 1860 Abraham Lincoln here received his first endorsement by a party convention for the presidential nomination.

5. City, ⊗ of Adams co., E Indiana, 20 mi. (32 km.) SSE of Fort Wayne; pop. (1990c) 8644.

6. Town, ⊗ of Newton co., E cen. Mississippi; pop. (1990c) 1248; East Central Community Coll. (1928).

7. Town, ⊗ of Meigs co., SE Tennessee; pop. (1990c) 1361.

8. City, ⊗ of Wise co., N Texas, 25 mi. (40 km.) W of Denton; pop. (1990c) 4252; trade center for region.

Decatur, Lake. Lake, Macon co., cen. Illinois; 13 mi. (21 km.) long, .5 mi. (.8 km.) wide; made by damming Sangamon River E of Decatur.

De·ca·tur·ville \di-ˈkā-tər-ˌvil\. Town, ⊗ of Decatur co., W Tennessee; pop. (1990c) 879.

De·caze·ville \də-kȧz-ˈvēl\. Commune, Aveyron dept., S France, on Lot River 20 mi. (32 km.) NW of Rodez; coal deposits.

Dec·can *also* **Dek·kan** \ˈde-kən, -ˌkan, -ˌkän\. The peninsula of India S of Narmada River; in a more restricted sense the tableland bet. the Narmada and Krishna rivers, comprising Maharashtra and parts of Madhya Pradesh, Andhra Pradesh, Karnataka, and Orissa. See SOUTHERN DECCAN and UNITED DECCAN STATE.

History: Region of predominantly Dravidian population not reached by Aryan invasion (see INDIA 1); states of Deccan vassals of Maurya rulers c. 3d cent. B.C.; gradually passed under rule of kings of Andhra, a state which expanded from original location on E coast of Deccan to become paramount in cen. and N India 1st cent. B.C.–3d cent. A.D.; invaded by Muslims in 13th cent. and conquered in 14th cent.; ruled by independent Muslim Bahmanī sultanate which later split up into five Muslim sultanates of Deccan (Ahmadnagar, Berar, Bidar, Bijapur, and Golconda); largely conquered by Mogul dynasty in 17th cent.; scene in 18th cent. of rivalry of British and French and subsequently of British struggle against Marathas; under British control until 1947.

Deccan and Kol·ha·pur States \ˈkō-lə-ˌpu̇r\. Former agency division, W India, comprising 18 Indian states, now part of Maharashtra; chief state Kolhapur, with former agency headquarters at city of Kolhapur; several of the states formed 1947 a new state, the United Deccan State.

Deccan Proper. See SOUTHERN DECCAN.

De·cep·tion Island \di-ˈsep-shən\. See SOUTH SHETLAND ISLANDS.

Dě·čín \ˈdye-chēn\ *or Ger.* **Tet·schen** \ˈte-chən\. City, N Czech Republic, on the Labe (Elbe) opp. Podmokly, near border of Germany; pop. (1991p) 55,112; manufactures chemicals, paper, textiles, metal goods; 17th cent. castle.

De·cize \də-ˈsēz\. Commune, S Nièvre dept., cen. France; S terminus of the Canal du Nivernais.

De·co·rah \di-ˈkōr-ə\. City, ⊗ of Winneshiek co., NE Iowa, 62 mi. (100 km.) NE of Waterloo; pop. (1990c) 8063; Luther Coll. (1861).

Dede Agach. See ALEXANDROÚPOLIS.

Ded·ham \ˈde-dəm\. Town, ⊗ of Norfolk co., E Massachusetts, on Charles River 9 mi. (14 km.) SW of Boston; pop. (1990c) 23,782; primarily residential; one of oldest towns in state, settled 1635; Fairbanks house (1636) is believed to be oldest existing frame dwelling in U.S.; first free school in America supported by general tax, built 1649; scene of Sacco-Vanzetti trial 1921.

Dee \ˈdē\. **1.** River, NE Scotland; rises on the slopes of the Cairngorm Mts., flows E into North Sea at Aberdeen; noted for its scenery and its salmon fishing; 87 mi. (140 km.) long.
2. River, S Scotland; flows S in Dumfries and Galloway region into Solway Firth; 50 mi. (80 km.) long.
3. *or Welsh* **Dyfr·dwy** \ˈdə-vər-ˈdü-ē\. River, N Wales and W England; rises in Bala Lake, N Wales; flows E, NE, and N, forming a section of the England-Wales boundary; crosses into W England, passes through Chester, and empties into Irish Sea through **Dee Estuary;** 70 mi. (113 km.) long.

Deel \ˈdēl\. River, co. Limerick, SW Ireland; flows into Shannon River; 26 mi. (42 km.) long.

Deep \ˈdēp\. River, N cen. North Carolina; rises in Guilford co., flows SE and E to unite with Haw River in Chatham co. and form Cape Fear River; ab. 125 mi. (200 km.) long.

Deep Bay. **1.** Bay, NW of Kowloon Penin., Hong Kong.
2. Inlet on SE cen. coast of Malaita I., SE Solomon Is.

Deep Bot·tom \ˈbä-təm\. Hamlet, Henrico co., E cen. Virginia; scene of fighting during Civil War 1864.

Deep Creek Lake. Artificial lake, Garrett co., NW corner of Maryland; 4000 acres (1620 hectares); formed by a hydroelectric-power dam in **Deep Creek** near its confluence with the Youghiogheny River.

Deep·ha·ven \ˈdēp-ˌhā-vən\. Village, Hennepin co., SE cen. Minnesota, W of Minneapolis; pop. (1990c) 3653.

Deep Hole Harbor. Inlet of Nantucket Sound on S coast of W Barnstable co., SE Massachusetts.

Deep River. **1.** River, North Carolina. See DEEP.
2. *formerly* **Say·brook** \ˈsā-ˌbru̇k\. Town, S cen. Middlesex co., S Connecticut, on Connecticut River; pop. (1990c) 4332; settled 1635; united with Connecticut 1644.
3. Town, Renfrew co., SE Ontario, Canada, on Ottawa River 25 mi. (40 km.) NW of Pembroke; pop. (1991c) 4571.

Deep South. Region of SE U.S. variably considered to include Alabama, Georgia, Louisiana, Mississippi, the Carolinas, and all or part of the adjacent states of Florida, Virginia, Tennessee, Arkansas, and Texas.

Deer, Old \ōld-ˈdir\. Parish, Aberdeen co., NE Scotland, 9 mi. (14 km.) W of Peterhead; site of ancient abbey the founding of which is related in the *Book of Deer,* a manuscript copy of portions of the Gospels in Latin containing c. 12th cent. marginal notes in Scottish Gaelic; the oldest Scottish document containing Gaelic, it was discovered c. 1860 at Cambridge Univ. Library; no part of the original abbey remains.

Deer Creek. River, cen. Ohio; rises in Madison co., flows SE through Pickaway co., enters Scioto River in N Ross co.; 80 mi. (129 km.) long.

Deer Creek Dam. Dam across Provo River, N cen. Utah; height 235 ft. (72 m.); completed 1941; impounds water, **Deer Creek Reservoir,** for irrigation.

Deer·field \ˈdir-ˌfēld\. **1.** River, NW Massachusetts; rises in Windham co., SE Vermont, flows S across Massachusetts border and E into Connecticut River in cen. Franklin co., NW Massachusetts; ab. 100 mi. (161 km.) long.
2. Village, Cook and Lake cos., NE corner of Illinois, 18 mi. (29 km.) S of Waukegan; pop. (1990c) 17,327; Trinity Coll. (1897).
3. Town, Franklin co., NW Massachusetts, 4 mi. (6 km.) S of Greenfield; pop. (1990c) 5018; one of oldest towns in Connecticut Valley, settled c. 1669; suffered from two serious Indian attacks, the Bloody Brook Massacre 1675, and the raid of 1704 when a band of Indians and French burned the town, killed 49 and carried ab. 100 captive to Canada. Seat of Deerfield Academy (estab. 1797), now a coed preparatory school.

Deerfield Beach. Town, Broward co., SE Florida, on Atlantic Ocean 38 mi. (61 km.) N of Miami; pop. (1990c) 46,325; incorp. 1925; pop. is five times what it was in 1960.

Deer Flat Dam. Earth-embankment dam in Canyon co., SW Idaho; forms **Lake Low·ell** \ˈlō-əl\ *also* **Deer Flat Reservoir;** reservoir filled by water diverted through canal from Boise River.

Deer Island. **1.** Island bet. Boston Bay and Boston Harbor, Massachusetts.
2. Island, Charlotte co., SW New Brunswick, Canada, in S part of Passamaquoddy Bay near coast of Maine.

Deer Isle. **1.** *also* **Deer Island.** Island on E side of entrance to Penobscot Bay, S Maine; part of Hancock co.; chief town Deer Isle.
2. Town, Hancock co., SE Maine, on Deer I. in Penobscot Bay; pop. (1990c) 1829; fishing and summer resort.

Deer Lodge. **1.** County in SW Montana. See table at MONTANA.
2. City, ⊗ of Powell co., W Montana, 37 mi. (60 km.) WSW of Helena; pop. (1990c) 3378.

Deer Mountain. **1.** Peak, W North Carolina; 6233 ft. (1900 m.).
2. Peak, Pennington co., SW South Dakota; 5500 ft. (1676 m.).

Deer Park. **1.** Unincorporated settlement, Suffolk co., New York, in cen. Long Island N of Babylon; pop. (1990c) 28,840.
2. City, Hamilton co., SW corner of Ohio, 9 mi. (14 km.) NNE of Cincinnati; pop. (1990c) 6181.
3. City, Harris co., SE Texas, 15 mi. (24 km.) E of Houston; pop. (1990c) 27,652; chemicals, plastics.

De·fi·ance \di-ˈfī-əns\. **1.** County in NW Ohio. See table at OHIO.
2. City, its ⊗, at confluence of Auglaize and Maumee rivers 40 mi. (64 km.) NNW of Lima; pop. (1990c) 16,768; on site of Fort Defiance built by Gen. Anthony Wayne 1794; iron castings; Defiance Coll. (1850); incorp. 1836.

De Fu·ni·ak Springs \də-ˈfyü-nē-ˌak\. Town, ⊗ of Walton co., NW Florida, 70 mi. (113 km.) ENE of Pensacola; pop. (1990c) 5120; large freshwater spring; site of Florida Chautauqua educational institution (2d in U.S.).

Degh \ˈdāg\. River, India and Pakistan; flows SW out of S Jammu and Kashmir, India, through Punjab, Pakistan, to Ravi River SW of Lahore; ab. 200 mi. (320 km.) long.

De·go \ˈdā-gō\. Commune, Savona prov., W cen. Liguria, NW Italy; scene 1796 of defeat of Austrians by French Emperor Napoléon's forces.

De Grey \də-ˈgrā\. River, NW Western Australia, Australia; flows N and NW to Indian Ocean near Point Larrey; ab. 190 mi. (305 km.) long.

De·hi·bat \de-hē-ˈbät\. Town, SE Tunisia, on boundary with Libya 95 mi. (153 km.) S of Médenine.

De·hi·wa·la–Mount La·vin·ia \ˈdā-hē-ˈwə-lə … lə-ˈvi-nē-ə\. Town, W Sri Lanka, on Indian Ocean 8 mi. (13 km.) S of Colombo; historically a health and pleasure resort located on rock ledge.

Dehli. See DELHI.

DeHonte. See WESTERSCHELDE.

Deh·ra Dun \ˈder-ə-ˈdün\. Town, NW Uttar Pradesh, N India, 140 mi. (225 km.) NNE of Delhi; pop. (1991p) 270,028; tea processing; headquarters of Government Forest Department and Survey of India; also seat of Indian Forest Coll. and its associated Research Institute and India Military Coll. (1934); has large military cantonment; fine temple in Muslim style erected 1699 by a Sikh guru.

De·hua *or W.-G.* **Te–hua** \ˈdā-ˈhwä\. Town, S cen. Fujian prov., SE China, 75 mi. (121 km.) SW of Fuzhou; noted for its white porcelain (*blanc de chine*).

De·i·ra \ˈdā-rə\. Former Anglian kingdom, extending from Tees River to Humber Estuary, in E part of modern Yorkshire, England; emerged in 2d half of 6th cent. A.D.; after a long conflict united with its N neighbor, Bernicia, in 7th cent. to form kingdom of Northumbria (*q.v.*).

Deir el–Bah·ri \ˈdār-el-ˈbä-rē\. Temple site, Egypt, on W bank of Nile near Thebes and opp. Karnak; important archaeological site; tombs opened by French Egyptologist Gaston-Camille-Charles Maspero 1881; temple built by Queen Hatshepsut (1503–1482 B.C.); situated at base of a cliff 400 ft. (122 m.) high; contains pictorial representations on its walls of expedition to land of Punt.

Deir ez Zor. See DAYR AZ ZAWR.

Dej \ˈdezh\ *or Hung.* **Dés** \ˈdāsh\. City, Cluj co., NW Romania, on Someşul River; pop. (1989c) 41,415; railroad junction.

Dejima. See DESHIMA.

De Kaap \də-ˈkäp\. Mountain, N Drakensberg, NE Rep. of South Africa; goldfields in **De Kaap Valley** where town of Barberton was founded during the gold rush in the 1880s.

De Kalb \di-ˈkalb\. **1.** Name of counties in six states of the U.S. See tables at ALABAMA, GEORGIA, ILLINOIS, INDIANA, MISSOURI, TENNESSEE.
2. City, De Kalb co., N Illinois, 28 mi. (45 km.) SSE of Rockford; pop. (1990c) 34,925; manufactures electrical equipment; Northern Illinois Univ. (1895).
3. Town, ⊗ of Kemper co., E Mississippi; pop. (1990c) 1073.

Dekkan. See DECCAN.

De la Beche \ˌde-lə-ˈbesh\. Mountain, Southern Alps, South I., New Zealand, 9 mi. (14 km.) NE of Mt. Cook; 9817 ft. (2992 m.).

Del·a·goa Bay \ˌdel-ə-ˈgō-ə\. Inlet of the Indian Ocean on extreme SE coast of Mozambique; 55 mi. (88 km.) long; the city of Maputo (*q.v.*), ✻ of Mozambique, lies at its head. Discovered by Portuguese 1502; neighboring territory explored 1544 by Lourenço Marques; claimed by Portuguese and British until attempt of Transvaal to occupy it 1868 brought dispute to a head; awarded to Portugal by arbitration 1875.

De Land \di-ˈland\. City, ⊗ of Volusia co., E Florida, 22 mi. (35 km.) WSW of Daytona Beach; pop. (1990c) 16,491; center of citrus-growing region; winter resort; Stetson Univ. (1883); founded 1876.

De·la·no \də-ˈlā-nō\. City, Kern co., S California, 30 mi. (48 km.) NNW of Bakersfield; pop. (1990c) 22,762; ships grain and fruit.

Del·a·no, Mount \ˈde-lə-ˌnō\. Peak of Rocky Mts., in Beaverhead co., SW Montana; 10,200 ft. (3109 m.).

Del·a·no Peak \ˈde-lə-ˌnō\. Mountain on boundary bet. Piute and Beaver cos., SW cen. Utah; 12,173 ft. (3710 m.).

Delatyn. See DELYATIN.

Delatyn Pass. See JABLONICA PASS.

Del·a·van \ˈde-lə-van\. City and summer resort, Walworth co., S Wisconsin, 19 mi. (31 km.) E of Janesville; pop. (1990c) 6073.

Del·a·ware \ˈde-lə-ˌwar\. **1.** River, Pennsylvania and Delaware; formed by junction of E and W branches in Delaware co., S New York, flows SE to form Pennsylvania-New York, Pennsylvania-New Jersey, and Delaware-New Jersey boundaries, and empties into Delaware Bay; 280 mi. (451 km.) long; navigable to Trenton, New Jersey. Spanned by Commodore John Barry Bridge (cantilever; main span 1644 ft. or 501 m.; completed 1974) at Chester, Pennsylvania. See WASHINGTON CROSSING.
2. Middle Atlantic state of the U.S.A., bounded on N and NW by Pennsylvania, on E by Delaware River and Delaware Bay and Atlantic Ocean, and on S and W by Maryland; 49th state in area, 2057 sq. mi. (5328 sq. km.) [land area 1983 sq. mi. or 5136 sq. km.]; 46th state in population, (1990c) 666,168; ✻ Dover; an original state of the Union, the first state to ratify the U.S. Constitution (Dec. 7, 1787). See table of states at UNITED STATES.

Nicknames: First State; Diamond State.
State flower: Peach blossom.
Motto: Liberty and Independence.
River: Delaware (see DELAWARE 1).
Highest point: Centerville (442 ft. or 135 m.), in New Castle co.
Chief industries: Chemicals; food processing; poultry raising, fishing; soybeans, corn.
Chief cities: Wilmington, Dover, Newark.
Political divisions: Divided into the following three counties (for pronunciations, see their individual entries):

NAME	AREA[1] (sq. mi.)	AREA[1] (sq. km.)	POP. (1990c)	CO. SEAT
Kent	594	1,538	110,993	Dover
New Castle	439	1,137	441,946	Wilmington
Sussex	950	2,461	113,229	Georgetown

[1] Area = land area.

History: Region orig. inhabited by several Algonquian tribes; earliest European settlements made by Dutch 1631 at present site of Lewes; first permanent settlements made by Swedes 1638 (see NEW SWEDEN and WILMINGTON 1); New Sweden captured by Dutch 1655 and, as part of New Netherland, by English 1664; part of New York until it became part of a grant made to William Penn (see PENNSYLVANIA) 1682; in 1704 received right to separate legislative assembly, but remained under governor of Pennsylvania until 1776; active in American Revolution; formulated first state constitution 1776, adopted present constitution 1897; remained in Union during Civil War.
3. Name of counties in six states of the U.S. See tables at INDIANA, IOWA, NEW YORK, OHIO, OKLAHOMA, PENNSYLVANIA.
4. Township, New Jersey. See CHERRY HILL.
5. City, ⊗ of Delaware co., cen. Ohio, 23 mi. (37 km.) N of Columbus; pop. (1990c) 20,030; mineral springs; Ohio Wesleyan Univ. (1842); birthplace 1822 of Rutherford B. Hayes, 19th president of the U.S.; founded 1808.

Delaware Bay. Arm of Atlantic Ocean, bet. SW coast of New Jersey and E coast of Delaware.

Delaware City. Town, New Castle co., N Delaware; pop. (1990c) 1682; terminus of Chesapeake and Delaware Canal.

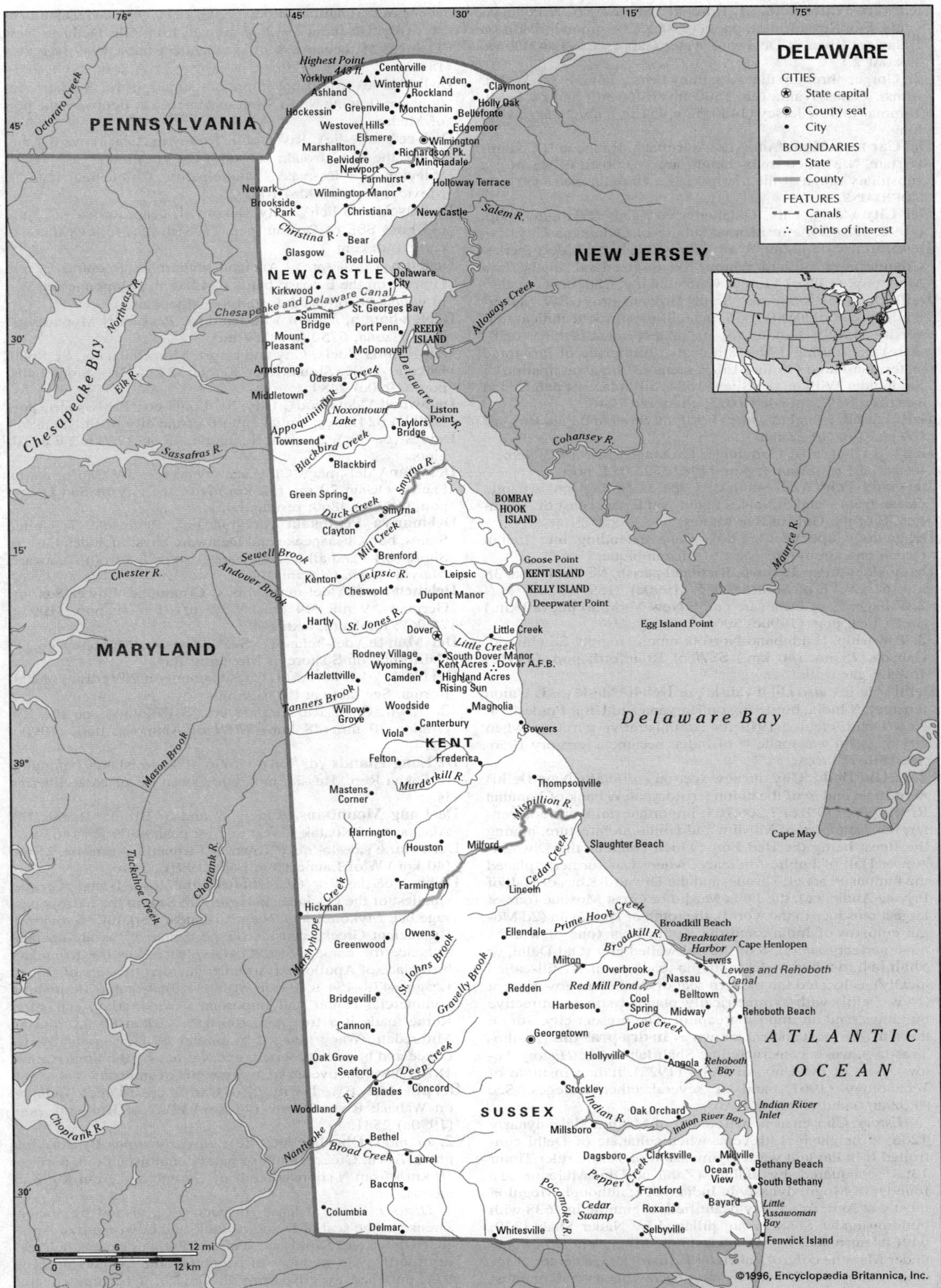
DELAWARE
CITIES
State capital
County seat
City
BOUNDARIES
State
County
FEATURES
Canals
Points of interest
PENNSYLVANIA
NEW JERSEY
MARYLAND
NEW CASTLE
KENT
SUSSEX
Delaware Bay
ATLANTIC OCEAN
Chesapeake Bay
76°
45′
30′
15′
75°
39°
Highest Point 443 ft.
Centerville
Yorklyn
Winterthur
Arden
Claymont
Ashland
Rockland
Holly Oak
Hockessin
Greenville
Montchanin
Bellefonte
Westover Hills
Edgemoor
Elsmere
Wilmington
Marshallton
Richardson Pk.
Belvidere
Minquadale
Newport
Farnhurst
Holloway Terrace
Newark
Wilmington Manor
Brookside Park
Christiana
New Castle
Salem R.
Christina R.
Bear
Glasgow
Red Lion
Delaware City
Kirkwood
Chesapeake and Delaware Canal
St. Georges Bay
Summit Bridge
Port Penn
REEDY ISLAND
Mount Pleasant
McDonough
Alloways Creek
Octoraro Creek
Northeast R.
Elk R.
Armstrong
Odessa
Middletown
Appoquinimink Creek
Delaware R.
Noxontown Lake
Liston Point
Taylors Bridge
Townsend
Blackbird Creek
Sassafras R.
Cohansey R.
Blackbird
Smyrna R.
Green Spring
Duck Creek
Smyrna
BOMBAY HOOK ISLAND
Clayton
Mill Creek
Maurice R.
Sewell Brook
Brenford
Chester R.
Andover Brook
Leipsic
Kenton
Leipsic R.
Goose Point
KENT ISLAND
KELLY ISLAND
Cheswold
Dupont Manor
Deepwater Point
Hartly
St. Jones R.
Egg Island Point
Dover
Little Creek
Little Creek
Rodney Village
South Dover Manor
Wyoming
Kent Acres
Dover A.F.B.
Hazlettville
Camden
Highland Acres
Rising Sun
Tanners Brook
Willow Grove
Woodside
Magnolia
Canterbury
Bowers
Viola
Mason Brook
Felton
Frederica
Murderkill R.
Thompsonville
Mastens Corner
Mispillion R.
Cape May
Harrington
Houston
Milford
Slaughter Beach
Cedar Creek
Tuckahoe Creek
Choptank R.
Farmington
Lincoln
Hickman
Marshyhope Creek
Prime Hook Creek
Broadkill Beach
Owens
Ellendale
Broadkill R.
Breakwater Harbor
Cape Henlopen
Greenwood
Lewes
St. Johns Brook
Milton
Overbrook
Lewes and Rehoboth Canal
Redden
Red Mill Pond
Nassau
Gravelly Brook
Belltown
Bridgeville
Harbeson
Cool Spring
Midway
Rehoboth Beach
Love Creek
Cannon
Georgetown
Oak Grove
Deep Creek
Hollyville
Angola
Rehoboth Bay
Seaford
Blades
Concord
Stockley
Woodland
Indian R.
Indian River Inlet
Oak Orchard
Choptank R.
Nanticoke R.
Indian River Bay
Bethel
Millsboro
Broad Creek
Laurel
Dagsboro
Clarksville
Millville
Bethany Beach
Pepper Creek
Ocean View
South Bethany
Bacons
Pocomoke R.
Frankford
Cedar Swamp
Roxana
Bayard
Little Assawoman Bay
Columbia
Delmar
Whitesville
Selbyville
Fenwick Island
0 6 12 mi
0 6 12 km
©1996, Encyclopædia Britannica, Inc.

Delaware Water Gap. **1.** Borough, Monroe co., E Pennsylvania, E of Stroudsburg; pop. (1990c) 733; summer resort on Delaware River at Delaware Water Gap. (see DELAWARE WATER GAP 2.)

2. Gorge, through the Kittatinny Mts., having on W Mt. Minsi, Pennsylvania (ab. 1500 ft. or 460 m.) and on E Mt. Tammany, New Jersey (1480 ft. or 451 m.); ab. 2 mi. (3 km.) long.

Del Car·men Mountains \del-ˈkär-mən\. Range in N Coahuila state, N Mexico; max. height ab. 10,000 ft. (3048 m.); a subsidiary range of the Sierra Madre Oriental. See SANTIAGO MOUNTAINS.

Del City \ˈdel\. City, Oklahoma co., cen. Oklahoma; pop. (1990c) 23,928; a residential suburb of Oklahoma City.

De·lé·mont \də-lā-ˈmōⁿ\ *or Ger.* **Dels·berg** \ˈdels-ˌberk\. Commune, ✻ of Jura canton, NW Switzerland, in the Jura Mts.; pop. (1989c) 11,467; watchmaking; 18th cent. castle.

Delft \ˈdelft\. Commune, South Holland prov., SW Netherlands; pop. (1990c) 90,066; penicillin, spirits; technical university (1905); famous for its pottery manufacture (delftware) esp. during 17th–18th cents.; birthplace of jurist and statesman Hugo Grotius 1583; scene of the assassination of Stadholder William the Silent 1584; birthplace of painter Jan Vermeer 1632; founded 1075; chartered 1246.

Delft Island. Island in waters bet. Palk Strait and Palk Bay, off NW coast of Sri Lanka.

Delf·zijl \delf-ˈzīl\. Commune, Groningen prov., NE Netherlands, on Ems estuary; pop. (1981e) 25,052; port.

Del·ga·da Point \del-ˈgä-t͟hä\. Cape extending into Atlantic Ocean from S end of Valdés Penin., off E cen. coast of Argentina, S of the Gulf of San Matías.

Del·ga·do, Cape \del-ˈgä-dō\. Cape extending into Indian Ocean on extreme NE coast of Mozambique.

Del·hi \ˈdel-ˌhī\. **1.** Town, Richland parish, NE Louisiana, 38 mi. (61 km.) E of Monroe; pop. (1990c) 3169.

2. Village, ⊗ of Delaware co., S New York, 50 mi. (80 km.) S of Utica; pop. (1990c) 3064.

3. Township, Haldimand-Norfolk munic. region, SE Ontario, Canada, 25 mi. (40 km.) SSW of Brantford; pop. (1991c) 15,852; gas wells.

Delhi \ˈde-lē\ *also* **Dil·li** \ˈdi-lē\ *or* **Deh·li** \ˈde-lē\. **1.** Union territory, N India, bordering on Haryana and Uttar Pradesh; ✻ New Delhi; created 1912 for administrative purposes when city of Delhi was made ✻ of India; became a territory 1956. See table at INDIA.

2. *or* **Old Delhi.** City, its new section (*officially* **New Delhi**) ✻ of India and ✻ of the union territory, on W bank of Yamuna River; pop. (1991c) 7,206,704; important rail and trade center; has examples of Muslim and Hindu architecture, among the finest being the Red Fort (which contains the Diwan-i-Am or Hall of Public Audience, where was formerly placed the famous Peacock Throne, and the Diwan-i-Khas or Hall of Private Audience), the Jama Masjid or Great Mosque (one of largest mosques in the world), the tomb of Humāyūn (2d Mogul emperor of India), and the Kutb Minar (one of world's most perfect towers). S of the old walled city (Old Delhi, or **Shah·ja·han·a·bad** \ˌshä-jə-ˈhä-nə-ˌbäd\, as it is still called locally), is located the modern seat of the Indian government (New Delhi) with symmetrically planned streets, attractive buildings, and an imposing capitol. The present city, 7th on this site (the most ancient known as **In·dra·pras·tha** \ˌin-drə-ˈprəs-tə\), was reconstructed by Shāh Jahān (see *History*, below). Seat of the Univ. of Delhi (1922), Indian Institute of Technology (1961), and of several other colleges. See FIROZABAD and TUGHLAKABAD.

History: Chosen as ✻ by founder of Muslim Slave dynasty 1206; at height in 13th cent. when sultanate of Delhi controlled N India; laid waste by invasion of Turkic ruler Timur 1398; conquered by Bābur (Ẓahīr-ud-Dīn Muḥammad), founder of Mogul dynasty in India, 1526; although Mogul ✻ mostly at Agra (*q.v.*), city beautified, beginning in 1638 with building under Shāh Jahān; pillaged by Nāder Shāh 1739; with its surrender to Marathas 1771, Mogul emperor came under Maratha control; taken by British 1803; a center of Indian mutiny 1857, held by mutineers for several months; scene of coronation durbars 1903, 1911; replaced Calcutta as ✻ of British India 1912, ✻ moved from Old Delhi to New Delhi 1931, became ✻ of independent India 1947 (see NEW DELHI).

De·li \ˈdā-lē\. Short but important stream of NE Sumatra, Indonesia; flowing NE to Strait of Malacca at Belawan, the port of Medan.

De·li·ce \de-lē-ˈje\. River, cen. Turkey in Asia; flows NW and N into the Kızıl Irmak; 265 mi. (426 km.) long.

De·li·cias \dā-ˈlēs-ˌyäs\. Municipality, Chihuahua state, N Mexico; pop. (1990p) 104,026.

De·litzsch \ˈdā-lich\. City, Saxony, E cen. Germany, 22 mi. (35 km.) SSE of Dessau; pop. (1981c) 25,746; city dates to early 14th cent.

De·li·um \ˈdē-lē-əm\. Ancient seaport in Boeotia, E cen. Greece, on the E coast; battle 424 B.C. in Peloponnesian War in which Boeotians defeated the Athenians.

Del·len·baugh, Mount \ˈde-lən-ˌbȯ\. Peak in N Mohave co., NW Arizona; 6750 ft. (2057 m.).

Dell Rapids \ˈdel\. City and resort, Minnehaha co., SE South Dakota, on Big Sioux River 20 mi. (32 km.) N of Sioux Falls; pop. (1990c) 2484.

Dell·wood \ˈdel-ˌwu̇d\. City, St. Louis co., E Missouri; pop. (1990c) 5245; residential suburb of the city of St. Louis.

Del·lys \de-ˈlēs\. Seaport, N Algeria, 45 mi. (72 km.) E of Algiers.

Del Mar \ˈdel-ˌmär\. City, San Diego co., SW California, on Pacific Ocean 20 mi. (32 km.) N of the city of San Diego; pop. (1990c) 4860; residential.

Del·mar·va Peninsula \del-ˈmär-və\. Peninsula, E United States, bet. Chesapeake and Delaware bays; includes Eastern Shore (*q.v.*) and all of Delaware— so called from *Del*aware, *Mar*yland, *Va.* (Virginia).

Del·men·horst \ˈdel-mən-ˌhȯrst\. Commune, Lower Saxony, Germany, 9 mi. (14 km.) WSW of Bremen; pop. (1992e) 75,967; linoleum, textiles.

Del Mon·te \del-ˈmän-tē\. Seaside resort, Monterey co., W California, on S shore of Monterey Bay.

Del Norte \del-ˈnōrt\. **1.** Coastal county in NW corner of California. See table at CALIFORNIA.

2. Town, ⊗ of Rio Grande co., S Colorado, on the Rio Grande 30 mi. (48 km.) WNW of Alamosa; pop. (1990c) 1674.

De Long Islands \di-ˈlȯŋ\. Group of small islands belonging to Sakha Rep., Russia, in Arctic Ocean NE of New Siberian Is.

De Long Mountains. Range, W end of Brooks Range, NW Alaska, N of Noatak River; highest peak 4800 ft. (1463 m.).

Del·o·raine \ˌde-lə-ˈrān\. Town, N Tasmania, Australia, 25 mi. (40 km.) W of Launceston; pop. (1991c) 5540.

De·los \ˈdē-ˌläs\ *or Gk.* **Dhí·los** \ˈt͟hē-ˌlōs\. Island, Greece, smallest of the Cyclades in S Aegean Sea, in the narrow passage bet. Mykonos and Rhenea islands; 2 sq. mi. (5 sq. km.). By ancient Greeks considered the center of the archipelago (whence the name: see CYCLADES), sacred as the legendary birthplace of Apollo and Artemis; guarded treasure of Delian League 478–454 B.C. (see ATHENS 10); became flourishing commercial center and important slave market, esp. after Rome made it a free port 166 B.C.; sacked 88 B.C. during Mithradatic Wars; ravaged by pirates 69 B.C.; gradually declined and became deserted; excavations by the French since 1870s have uncovered many remains of interest.

Del·phi \ˈdel-ˌfī\. **1.** City, ⊗ of Carroll co., NW cen. Indiana, on Wabash River 30 mi. (48 km.) WNW of Kokomo; pop. (1990c) 2531.

2. *or mod.* **Dhel·foí** \t͟hel-ˈfē\; *in early times* **Py·tho** \ˈpī-ˌthō\. Town, Greece, situated nearly equidistant (ab. 6 mi. or 10 km.) from N shore of Gulf of Corinth and from Mt. Parnassus.

History: From at least 7th cent. B.C., visited by ancient Greeks as the seat of Delphic oracle and of worship of Apollo, Pythius, and Dionysus; scene of Pythian games, held every fourth year; member of Amphictyonic League 6th cent. B.C.; enriched by gifts from all Greece, it became coveted booty, as when Phocians used its wealth to finance Third Sacred War (355–346 B.C.); plundered repeatedly in Roman times.

Del·phos \ˈdel-fəs\. City, Allen and Van Wert cos., NW Ohio, 13 mi. (21 km.) WNW of Lima; pop. (1990c) 7093.

Del·ray Beach \ˈdel-ˌrā\. City, Palm Beach co., SE Florida, on Atlantic Ocean 18 mi. (29 km.) S of West Palm Beach; pop. (1990c) 47,181; tourist resort.

Del Rio \del-ˈrē-ō\. City and port of entry, ⊗ of Val Verde co., SW Texas, on Rio Grande 37 mi. (60 km.) SE of its confluence with Pecos River; pop. (1990c) 30,705; market and distributing center for livestock and agricultural area; international flood-control dam dedicated 1969.

Delsberg. See DELÉMONT.

Del·son \ˈdel-sən\. Town, S Quebec, Canada, 5 mi. (8 km.) S of Montreal; pop. (1991c) 6063.

Del·ta \ˈdel-tə\. **1.** Name of counties in three states of the U.S. See tables at COLORADO, MICHIGAN, TEXAS.
2. City, ⊗ of Delta co., W Colorado, on Gunnison River 35 mi. (56 km.) SE of Grand Junction; pop. (1990c) 3789.
3. Village, Fulton co., NW Ohio, 24 mi. (39 km.) W of Toledo; pop. (1990c) 2849.
4. State of Nigeria. See table at NIGERIA.
5. District municipality, S British Columbia, Canada, S and SE of Vancouver; pop. (1991c) 88,978.

Delta Ama·cu·ro \ˈdel-tä-ˌä-mä-ˈkü-rō\. Territory of NE Venezuela. See table at VENEZUELA.

Del·ville Wood \del-ˈvēl, ˈdel-ˌvil\. Forested area near Longueval, Somme dept., N France; taken by Allies in battle of the Somme 1916.

De·lya·tin \dyi-ˈlyä-tyin\ *or* **De·la·tyn** \de-ˈlä-tin\. Town, SW Ukraine, at E end of Yablonitsa Pass on Prut River, 28 mi. (45 km.) SSW of Ivano-Frankivs'k; salt deposits, mineral baths; formerly in Poland.

De·mar·ca·tion Point \ˌdē-ˌmär-ˈkā-shən\. Cape, NE Alaska, extending N into Beaufort Sea, marking boundary bet. Alaska and Yukon Terr., Canada, 69°40′N, 141°15′W.

Dem·a·rest \ˈde-mə-ˌrest\. Borough, Bergen co., NE New Jersey, 13 mi. (21 km.) ENE of Paterson; pop. (1990c) 4800.

Demavend. See DAMĀVAND.

De·mer \ˈdā-mər\. River, E cen. Belgium; flows W in Limburg and Brabant provs., empties into Dijle River 6 mi. (10 km.) N of Louvain; 47 mi. (76 km.) long.

Dem·e·rara \ˌde-mə-ˈrar-ə, -ˈrär-\. River, Guyana; flows N parallel with and E of Essequibo River, empties into Atlantic Ocean at Georgetown; ab. 200 mi. (320 km.) long; navigable for ab. 65 mi. (105 km.).

De·me·tri·as \di-ˈmē-trē-əs\. Ruined city, SE Thessaly, NE Greece, near modern Volos; founded c. 290 B.C. by Macedonian King Demetrius I Poliorcetes and a favorite residence of Macedonian kings until c. 168 B.C.

Dem·ing \ˈde-miŋ\. Village, ⊗ of Luna co., SW New Mexico, W of Las Cruces; pop. (1990c) 10,970; in farming and ranching area; copper deposits nearby.

Demir Hissár *or* **Demir Hisar.** See SIDEROKASTRON.

Dem·min \de-ˈmēn\. City, Mecklenburg-West Pomerania, NE Germany, on Peene River ab. 40 mi. (64 km.) ESE of Rostock; pop. (1981c) 16,967. One of the oldest Slavic settlements in Pomerania; unsuccessfully besieged by Germans 1148; conquered by Henry the Lion, duke of Saxony, c. 1164; became member of Hanseatic League 1283; to Sweden 1648, to Prussia 1720, to Mecklenburg 1946–52.

Dem·o·crat, Mount \ˈde-mə-ˌkrat\. Peak, Park and Lake cos., cen. Colorado; 14,148 ft. (4312 m.).

Democratic and Popular Republic of Algeria. See ALGERIA.

Democratic Kampuchea. See CAMBODIA.

Democratic People's Republic of Korea. See KOREA, NORTH.

Democratic Republic of Vietnam. See VIETNAM, NORTH.

Demonesi Insulae. See KIZIL ISLANDS.

De·mop·o·lis \di-ˈmä-pə-lis\. City, Marengo co., W Alabama, on Tombigbee River 48 mi. (77 km.) W of Selma; pop. (1990c) 7512.

Dem·o·rest \ˈde-mə-ˌrest\. Town, Habersham co., NE Georgia; pop. (1990c) 1088; Piedmont Coll. (1897).

Dem·po, Gu·nung \ˈgü-ˌnu̇ŋ-ˈdem-ˌpō\. Volcanic peak, S Sumatra, Indonesia, in the Barisan Mts. E of Bengkulu; 10,361 ft. (3158 m.).

De·nain \də-ˈneⁿ\. Commune, Nord dept., N France, 26 mi. (42 km.) SE of Lille; coal deposits. Fortified at early date; scene of battle 1712 (during War of Spanish Succession) in which French under Marshal Claude-Louis-Hector de Villars defeated Austrians under Prince Eugene of Savoy.

Denakil. See DANAKIL.

Denali. See MCKINLEY, MOUNT.

Denali National Park; *formerly* **Mount McKinley National Park.** See UNITED STATES, *National Parks.*

Den·bigh \ˈden-bē\. **1.** Former village, ⊗ of former Warwick co., SE Virginia; now part of city of Newport News.
2. Former county in Wales. See DENBIGHSHIRE.
3. *or Welsh* **Din·bych** \ˈdin-bik\. Town, Clwyd co., N Wales; pop. (1981p) 9040; ruined 13th cent. castle besieged by Oliver Cromwell's Parliamentarians before it capitulated 1646; birthplace of explorer Sir Henry Morton Stanley 1841.

Den·bigh·shire \ˈden-bē-ˌshir, -shər\ *or* **Denbigh.** Former county, N Wales; ⊗ Ruthin; hilly area; rivers: Dee, Conway, Clwyd; chief towns: Wrexham, Colwyn Bay. See CLWYD.

Den·by Dale \ˈden-bē-ˈdāl\. Town, West Yorkshire, N England; pop. (1981p) 13,476.

Den·der \ˈden-dər\ **1.** *or Fr.* **Dendre** \ˈdänd-rᵊ\. Navigable river, W cen. Belgium; flows N out of Hainaut prov. into Schelde River at Dendermonde; 42 mi. (68 km.) long.
2. River, E Africa. See DINDER.

Den·de·ra \ˈden-də-ˌrä\ *or* **Dan·da·rah** \ˈdan-\; *anc.* **Ten·ty·ra** \ˈten-tə-rə\. Village, Upper Egypt, on left side of the Nile opp. Qena; ancient city dedicated to worship of goddess Hathor; temple was begun first cent. B.C. and added to by the Romans; among temple decorations was a celebrated zodiac now in the Louvre in Paris.

Den·der·mon·de \ˈden-dər-ˌmȯn-də\ *or Fr.* **Ter·monde** \ter-ˈmōⁿd\. Commune, East Flanders prov., NW cen. Belgium, at the confluence of the Schelde and Dender rivers; taken by English military commander John Churchill, duke of Marlborough, 1706; pillaged by Germans 1914.

Dendre. See DENDER 1.

Den·ham Springs \ˈde-nəm\. Town, Livingston parish, SE Louisiana, E of Baton Rouge; pop. (1990c) 8381.

Den Hel·der \dən-ˈhel-dər\. Commune, North Holland prov., W Netherlands; pop. (1993e) 61,149; fortified port on the Mars Diep, an outlet from Waddenzee into North Sea; Dutch naval station.

De·nia \ˈdā-(ˌ)nyä\; *anc.* **Di·a·ni·um** \dī-ˈā-nē-əm, -ˈan-ē-\. Seaport commune, Alicante prov., SE Spain, on Mediterranean Sea 45 mi. (72 km.) NE of the city of Alicante; pop. (1991c) 24,764.

Den·i·son \ˈde-nə-sən\. **1.** City, ⊗ of Crawford co., W Iowa, 58 mi. (93 km.) NNE of Council Bluffs; pop. (1990c) 6604.
2. City, Grayson co., NE Texas, in valley of Red River 10 mi. (16 km.) N of Sherman; pop. (1990c) 21,505; railroad center; shipping point for agricultural region; manufactures include clothing and plastic products; Grayson County Coll. (1963); birthplace 1890 of Dwight D. Eisenhower, 34th president of the U.S.

Denison Dam. Dam across Red River on Oklahoma-Texas boundary, NNW of Denison, Texas; completed 1944.

De·nis–Ri·ve·rin \dā-ˈnē-rēv-ˈreⁿ\. County, Quebec, Canada. See table at QUEBEC.

De·niz·li \ˌde-niz-ˈlē\. **1.** Province of Turkey in Asia. See table at TURKEY.
2. City, its ✻, on a tributary of the Menderes ab. 112 mi. (180 km.) SE of İzmir, with which it has rail connections; pop. (1990c) 204,118; in agricultural region; during wars bet. Seljuq Turks and Byzantines in 12th cent. replaced ancient

La·od·i·cea \(,)lā-,äd-ə-'sē-ə\ *or* **Laodicea ad Ly·cum** \-,ad-'lī-kəm\, now in ruins nearby; founded by Syrian King Antiochus II and several times destroyed by earthquake or conquest, but recovered; one of the Seven Churches of Asia Minor (*Rev.* i–iii); captured by Ottoman Empire 1389.

Den·mark \'den-,märk\. **1.** *or Dan.* **Dan·mark** \'dån-,märk\. Kingdom, NW Europe, bounded on the N by the Skagerrak, on the E by the Kattegat, Øresund, and Baltic Sea, on the S by Germany, and on the W by the North Sea; 16,629 sq. mi. (43,069 sq. km.); pop. (1989e) 5,129,778; ✻ Copenhagen; comprises most of Jutland (*Dan.* Jylland) Penin. and a group of islands in Baltic Sea, the most prominent of which are Sjælland, Fyn, Falster, Lolland, Langeland, and Bornholm (90 mi. or 145 km. E of Sjælland); self-governing entities included in the Danish realm are Greenland (839,999 sq. mi. or 2,175,597 sq. km.) and the Faeroe Is. (540 sq. mi. or 1399 sq. km.).

Physical features: Low, flat land with highest point (on E coast of Jutland) not above 550 ft. (168 m.); has no large rivers and few lakes, but its shoreline, esp. in N and W of Jutland, is indented by many lagoons and fjords; most important is Limfjorden extending across N Jutland from North Sea to Kattegat. Great Belt is passage bet. Sjælland and Fyn, and Little Belt a narrower channel bet. Fyn and mainland.

Chief products: Wheat, rye, barley, dairy products, fish; livestock; oil and gas; manufacturing: chemicals, textiles, machinery, electrical equipment, transportation equipment; food processing.

Chief cities: Copenhagen, Århus, Odense, Ålborg, Frederiksberg.

Political divisions: Divided into the following 14 counties and 2 communes (for pronunciation of their names, see their individual entries):

NAME	AREA (sq. mi.)	AREA (sq. km.)	POP. (1989c)	CAPITAL
Counties				
Århus	1,761	4,561	594,184	Århus
Bornholm[1]	227	588	46,105	Rønne
Copenhagen	203	526	602,046	Copenhagen
Frederiksborg	520	1,347	340,513	Hillerød
Fyn	1,346	3,486	458,111	Odense
Nordjylland	2,383	6,173	483,754	Ålborg
Ribe	1,209	3,131	218,460	Ribe
Ringkøbing	1,874	4,853	266,834	Ringkøbing
Roskilde	344	891	215,993	Roskilde
Sønderjylland	1,520	3,938	250,158	Åbenrå
Storstrøm	1,312	3,398	257,007	Nykøbing Falster
Vejle	1,157	2,997	329,847	Vejle
Vestsjælland	1,152	2,984	283,271	Sorø
Viborg	1,592	4,122	230,318	Viborg
Communes				
Copenhagen	34	88	467,850	
Frederiksberg	3	9	85,327	

[1]Coextensive with Bornholm I.

History: Settled by Danes, a Scandinavian branch of Teutons, c. 6th cent. A.D.; participated in Viking raids on England, France, and Low Countries 8th–10th cents.; Christianized 10th–11th cents.; 11th cent. united Danish kingdom included Schleswig (*q.v.*), S Sweden, England, and intermittently Norway; expansion begun along S shore of Baltic by dynasty founded by Valdemar the Great (1157–82); Erik V forced by nobles to grant first written constitution 1282, establishing annual parliaments; following Treaty of Stralsund 1370, was dominated by Hanseatic League; Scandinavia united under Margaret of Denmark 1388 (Union of Kalmar 1397); Danish monarchy of the Oldenburg line 1448–1863; Sweden (*q.v.*) became independent 1523 and began to threaten Danish supremacy; accepted Protestant Reformation with sanctioning of Danish Lutheran Church 1536; lost power and territory in wars with Sweden in 17th cent.; in Leagues of

Armed Neutrality 1780 and 1800; after bombardment of Copenhagen 1807, joined French Emperor Napoléon; forced to cede Norway and Helgoland 1814; duchies of Schleswig and Holstein (*qq.v.*) lost in war with Austria and Prussia 1864; neutral in WWI; sold Danish West Indies (see VIRGIN ISLANDS) to U.S. 1917; recognized Iceland (*q.v.*) as sovereign state in personal union with Denmark 1918 (union terminated 1944); received Northern Schleswig (*Dan.* Nord Slesvig) by plebiscite 1920; member of League of Nations 1920; in 1933 was awarded E Greenland (occupied by Norway 1931); occupied by Germany Apr. 1940–May 1945; member of UN 1945; member of NATO 1949; adopted new constitution 1953; signed treaty of accession to European Economic Community 1972.

2. Town, Bamburg co., SW South Carolina, 21 mi. (34 km.) SW of Orangeburg; pop. (1990c) 3762; Voorhees Coll. (1897).

Denmark Strait. Channel bet. SE Greenland and Iceland; 130 mi. (209 km.) wide; connects Arctic Ocean with the North Atlantic; here in WWII on May 24, 1941 the German battleship *Bismarck* sank the British *Hood.*

Den·ne·witz \ˈde-nə-ˌvits\. Village, Brandenburg, E Germany, 42 mi. (68 km.) SSW of Berlin; scene of victory Sept. 6, 1813 of Prussians under Gen. Friedrich Wilhelm von Bülow over the French forces of Marshal Michel Ney.

Den·nis \ˈde-nis\. Town, Barnstable co., SE Massachusetts, on Cape Cod 7 mi. (11 km.) ENE of the town of Barnstable; pop. (1990c) 13,864; summer and fishing resort; site of the Cape Playhouse.

Dennis Ness \ˈnes\. Headland on N coast of North Ronaldsay I., Orkney Is., off N Scotland; lighthouse.

Den·ni·son \ˈde-ni-sən\. Village, Tuscarawas co., E Ohio, 27 mi. (43 km.) S of Canton; pop. (1990c) 3282. See UHRICHSVILLE.

De·nou·sa \t͟hē-ˈnü-sä\. Small island, E Cyclades, S Aegean Sea, Greece, 12 mi. (19 km.) E of Naxos; in Cyclades dept.

Den·pa·sar *also* **Den Pa·sar** \den-ˈpä-ˌsär\. Town, ✻ of Bali prov., S Bali, Lesser Sunda Is., Indonesia; administrative and commercial center; seaport and airport.

Dent \ˈdent\. County in SE cen. Missouri. See table at MISSOURI.

Dent Blanche \ˈdä^{n}-ˈblä^{n}sh\. Peak in the Pennine Alps, S Switzerland; 14,293 ft. (4357 m.).

Dent d' Hérens. See HÉRENS, DENT D'.

Dent du Mi·di \ˈdä^{n}-dūe-mē-ˈdē\. Mountain, SW Switzerland, near French border SSW of Bex; 10,686 ft. (3257 m.).

Den·ton \ˈdent-ᵊn\. **1.** County in N Texas. See table at TEXAS.

2. Town, ⊗ of Caroline co., E Maryland, 40 mi. (64 km.) E of Annapolis; pop. (1990c) 2977.

3. City, ⊗ of Denton co., N Texas, 35 mi. (56 km.) NNW of Dallas; pop. (1990c) 66,270; trade and research center; Univ. of North Texas (1890), Texas Woman's Univ. (1901).

4. Town, Lancashire, NW England, 6 mi. (10 km.) ESE of Manchester; pop. (1981p) 37,729; plastics.

D'En·tre·cas·teaux Channel \ˌdȯn-trə-ˈkas-(ˌ)tō\. Strait separating S end of Bruny I. from Tasmania mainland, Australia.

D'Entrecasteaux Islands. Island group, Papua New Guinea, in the W Pacific Ocean, off SE coast of New Guinea I.; 1200 sq. mi. (3108 sq. km.); chief settlement Dobu; include Goodenough, Fergusson, and Normanby islands and many islets, small coral atolls, and reefs; separated from the mainland by Ward Hunt and Goschen straits; copra; mountainous, with many extinct volcanoes; first recorded visit by a Westerner 1793.

D'Entrecasteaux Point. Cape, SW point of Australia, in Western Australia.

Den·ver \ˈden-vər\. **1.** County in NE cen. Colorado. See table at COLORADO.

2. City, its ⊗ and ✻ of Colorado, in NE cen. part of the state on South Platte River; pop. (1990c) 467,610; alt. 5280 ft. (1609 m.); largest city in the state; commercial and transportation center; aerospace industry; stockyard; tourism; U.S. Mint; Botanical Gardens; Colorado State Historical Museum, Denver Art Museum; Univ. of Denver (1864), Iliff School of Theology (1892), Regis Univ. (1877), Univ. of Colorado at Denver (1912), Metropolitan State Coll. of Denver (1963), Community Coll. of Denver (1970). Settlement called Auraria (*q.v.*) made 1858 by gold prospectors and miners and united with two other villages to form Denver 1860; incorp. as city 1861; made territorial ✻ 1867.

3. Borough, Lancaster co., Pennsylvania, NE of Ephrata; pop. (1990c) 2861.

Denver City. Town, Yoakum co., NW Texas, 72 mi. (116 km.) SW of Lubbock; pop. (1990c) 5145; oil wells.

De·o·band \ˈdā-ə-ˌbənd\. Town, NE Uttar Pradesh, N India, 75 mi. (121 km.) NNE of Delhi; pop. (1991p) 62,461; an ancient town with numerous temples.

De·o·ghar *or* **De·o·garh** \ˈdā-ō-gər\. Town, E Bihar, NE India, 170 mi. (274 km.) NW of Calcutta; pop. (1991p) 85,846; has temples dedicated to Hindu god Siva; visited by many pilgrims.

Deogiri. See DAULATABAD.

De Pere \di-ˈpir\. City, Brown co., E Wisconsin, on Fox River 5 mi. (8 km.) S of Green Bay (city); pop. (1990c) 16,569; manufactures paper, medicines; site of St. Francis Xavier Mission (estab. 1671); St. Norbert Coll. (1898).

De·pew \di-ˈpyü\. Village, Erie co., W New York, 9 mi. (14 km.) E of Buffalo; pop. (1990c) 17,673; suburb of Buffalo.

De·pos·it \di-ˈpä-zit\. Village and summer resort, Broome and Delaware cos., S New York; pop. (1990c) 1936.

De Queen \də-ˈkwēn\. City, ⊗ of Sevier co., SW Arkansas; pop. (1990c) 4633; incorp. 1897; made ⊗ 1905.

De Quin·cy \də-ˈkwin-sē\. Town, Calcasieu parish, SW Louisiana, 20 mi. (32 km.) NW of Lake Charles (city); pop. (1990c) 3474; natural-gas deposits nearby.

De·ra Gha·zi Khan \ˈdā-rə-ˌgä-zē-ˈk̲än\. Town, Punjab, Pakistan, on Indus River 45 mi. (72 km.) W of Multan; pop. (1981p) 103,000; cement; founded at close of 15th cent. by Ghāzi Khān, son of a Baluchi chieftain.

Dera Is·mail Khan \i-ˈsmīl-ˈk̲än\. Town, North-West Frontier prov., Pakistan, on right bank of Indus River 155 mi. (249 km.) S of Peshawar; pop. (1981p) 116,000; founded at close of the 15th cent.; active bazaar; conducts trade with Afghanistan through the Gumal Pass (*q.v.*).

Deraiyeh. See AD DIRʻĪYAH.

Der·be \ˈdər-bē\. Ancient town, S Lycaonia, Asia Minor, on border of Cilicia; visited by St. Paul on first and second journeys.

Der·bent *or* **Der·bend** \dyir-ˈbyent\; *anc.* **Al·ba·na** \al-ˈbā-nə\. Town, SE Dagestan Rep., S Russia in Europe, on Caspian Sea 70 mi. (113 km.) SE of Makhachkala; pop. (1991e) 81,500; in narrow strip of land with high hills immediately behind, and Caspian Gates (pass) nearby; hills covered with orchards and vineyards; chief industries wine making and wool spinning.

History: At S end of pass are remains of Caucasian Wall, a Persian defense against inroads of nomadic tribes of the N, believed to have been built (6th cent.) by Khosrow I; seized by Arabs 728 and made into a cultural center; captured by Mongols 1220; held briefly by Russian Czar Peter the Great 1722; besieged by Russians 1796 and finally annexed from Persia 1813; damaged in civil war of 1917–21.

Der·by \ *U.S.* ˈdər-bē, *Brit. usu.* ˈdär-bē\. **1.** City, New Haven co., S Connecticut, at confluence of Naugatuck and Housatonic rivers opp. Shelton, 8 mi. (13 km.) W of New Haven; pop. (1990c) 12,199; manufactures copper goods and pins; the town (incorp.) is coextensive with the city; settled 1642; incorp. 1893.

2. City, Sedgwick co., S cen. Kansas, ab. 13 mi. (21 km.) SE of Wichita; pop. (1990c) 14,699.

3. Town in Vermont. See DERBY LINE.

4. Former county, N cen. England. See DERBYSHIRE 1.

5. Administrative county in England. See DERBYSHIRE 2.

\ə\ **abut** \ᵊ\ **kitten**, Fr **table** \ər\ **further** \a\ **ash** \ā\ **ace**
\ä\ **cot, cart** \ȧ\ Fr **bac** \au̇\ **out** \b\ Span **Avila** \ch\ **chin** \e\ **bet** \ē\ **easy**
\g\ **go** \i\ **hit** \ī\ **ice** \j\ **job** \k̲\ Ger **ich, Buch** \$^{n}$\ Fr **vin**
\ŋ\ **sing** \ō\ **go** \ȯ\ **all** \ȯ\ **law** \œ\ Fr **bœuf** \œ̄\ Fr **feu** \ȯi\ **boy**
\th\ **thin** \t͟h\ **this** \ü\ **loot** \u̇\ **foot** \ue\ Ger **füllen** \ūe\ Fr **rue**
\y\ **yet** \$^{y}$\ Fr **digne** \ˈdēn^{y}\, **nuit** \ˈnw^{y}ē\ \yü\ **few** \yu̇\ **fury** \zh\ **vision**

6. Town, N Western Australia, Australia, on King Sound; pop. (1986c) 3258; service center for nearby oil fields.

7. City, ⊗ of former Derbyshire co., N cen. England, on Derwent River 37 mi. (60 km.) NNE of Birmingham; pop. (1991p) 214,000; railroad center; manufactures aircraft engines, chemicals, textiles, plastics; historically notable for pottery (Royal Crown Derby); birthplace of philosopher Herbert Spencer 1820.

Derby Line \ˈdər-bē-ˈlīn\. Village in Derby town (pop. [1990c] 4479), Orleans co., N Vermont, on Canadian border ab. 7 mi. (11 km.) NE of Newport; pop. (1990c) 855; is closely associated with nearby Stanstead and Rock Island in Quebec, Canada.

Der·by·shire \ˈdär-bē-ˌshir, -shər\ *or* **Derby. 1.** Former county, N cen. England; ⊗ Derby; rivers included the Derwent and the Trent.

2. Administrative county, N cen. England, approx. equivalent to the former county; major settlements: Derby, Chesterfield, Ilkeston, Glossop; estab. 1974. See table at ENGLAND.

Derg, Ben. See BEINN DEARG.

Derg, Lough \ˈdərg\. **1.** Lake in SE co. Donegal, Ireland; according to legend, the entrance to St. Patrick's Purgatory was on a small island in this lake.

2. Lake in cos. Galway, Clare, and Tipperary, SW cen. Ireland; traversed N to S by Shannon River; ab. 24 mi. (39 km.) long, bet. 2 and 6 mi. (3 and 10 km.) wide; site of large hydropower station.

De Rid·der \də-ˈri-dər\. City, ⊗ of Beauregard parish, SW Louisiana, 42 mi. (68 km.) N of Lake Charles (city); pop. (1990c) 9868.

Der·mott \ˈdər-mət\. City, Chicot co., SE corner of Arkansas, 12 mi. (19 km.) W of Mississippi River; pop. (1990c) 4715.

Derna. See DARNAH.

Dern·berg, Cape \ˈdərn-ˌbərg, ˈdern-ˌberg\. Cape extending into Atlantic Ocean on SW coast of Namibia.

Der·ry \ˈder-ē\. **1.** Town, Rockingham co., SE New Hampshire, 10 mi. (16 km.) SE of Manchester; pop. (1990c) 29,603.

2. Borough, Westmoreland co., SW Pennsylvania, 21 mi. (34 km.) W of Johnstown; pop. (1990c) 2950.

3. *or* **Lon·don·der·ry** \ˈlən-dən-ˌder-ē\. District, NW Northern Ireland; estab. 1974. See table at IRELAND, NORTHERN.

4. *or* **Lon·don·der·ry** \ˈlən-dən-ˌder-ē\. Seaport, its ⊗, on Foyle River near head of Lough Foyle 95 mi. (153 km.) NW of Belfast; good harbor; tanneries; flour; textiles (esp. linens). Has two cathedrals (Anglican and Roman Catholic); Magee University Coll. (1865).

History: Began with an abbey founded by St. Columba mid-6th cent.; subject to Norse invasions several times before 13th cent.; resisted attack 1566 of Hugh O'Neill, earl of Tyrone in rebellion against the English; granted to Corporation of London 1613 and renamed Londonderry; held out 105 days in unsuccessful siege 1689 by army of James II; naval base in World Wars I and II; official name changed back to Derry 1984.

Derryfield. See MANCHESTER 7.

Dertona. See TORTONA.

Dertosa. See TORTOSA 1.

Der·went \ˈdər-wənt\. **1.** River, S cen. Tasmania, Australia; rises in Lake St. Clair and flows SE to Storm Bay; 107 mi. (172 km.) long; has many affluents on its left bank, outlets of the lakes of the cen. highlands, esp. the Dee, Ouse, Clyde, and Jordan; navigable to Hobart on its right bank on the estuary (4 mi. or 6 km. wide).

2. River, Cumberland, NW England; flows N through lakes Derwent Water and Bassenthwaite, turns WSW to Solway Firth at Workington; 33 mi. (53 km.) long.

3. River, N Derbyshire, N cen. England; flows SE into the Trent on border of Leicestershire; 60 mi. (97 km.) long.

4. River, Durham and Northumberland, N England; flows NE to the Tyne 3 mi. (5 km.) W of Gateshead; 30 mi. (48 km.) long.

5. River, Yorkshire, N England; flows N into the Ouse; 57 mi. (92 km.) long.

Derwent Water. Lake in the Lake District, Cumberland, NW England; 3 mi. (5 km.) long; max. depth 72 ft. (22 m.); has several islands on one of which, Lord I., was the residence of the earls of Derwentwater; traversed from S to N by the Derwent River; in S receives also the brook which contains Lodore waterfall.

Dés. See DEJ.

Des·a·gua·de·ro \ˌdā-ˌsä-gwä-ˈt͟hā-rō\. **1.** Name given to upper course of Río Salado (see SALADO, RÍO 1) in W Argentina.

2. River, W Bolivia; flows from Lake Titicaca on the Peruvian border to Lake Poopó; 200 mi. (322 km.) long.

Des·a·güe, Ca·nal del \kä-ˈnäl-ˌdel-dā-ˈsä-gwā\. Canal, cen. Mexico; ab. 30 mi. (50 km.) long; built bet. 1879 and 1900 to drain the Valley of Mexico; removed danger of floods from Mexico City.

Des Al·le·mands, Lake \dez-ˈäl-mənz\. Lake in S St. John the Baptist parish, SE Louisiana.

De·sam·pa·ra·dos \dā-ˌsäm-pä-ˈrä-t͟hōs\. Town, cen. Costa Rica, a suburb S of San Jose; pop. (1992e) 54,668.

Des Arc \ˈdez-ˌärk\. Town, a ⊗ of Prairie co., E cen. Arkansas, on White River; pop. (1990c) 2001; river port.

Des·ca·be·za·do \ˌdes-ˌkä-bə-ˈsä-dō\. Two mountains in E cen. Chile, near Argentine border: **Descabezado Gran·de** \ˈgrän-dā\ 12,565 ft. (3830 m.) and **Descabezado Chi·co** \ˈchē-kō\ 10,660 ft. (3249 m.).

Des·chutes \di-ˈshüts\. **1.** River, cen. and N Oregon; rises in SW Deschutes co., flows N into Columbia River forming part of boundary bet. Wasco and Sherman cos.; 250 mi. (402 km.) long.

2. County in cen. Oregon. See table at OREGON.

De·se \ˈdā-sā\ *or* **Des·se** \ˈdes-sā\. Town, N cen. Ethiopia; pop. (1989e) 87,246.

De·se·a·do \ˌdā-sā-ˈä-t͟hō\. River, S Argentina; flows E from the Andes in NW Santa Cruz terr. on the Chilean border and empties into Atlantic Ocean at Puerto Deseado; 380 mi. (611 km.) long.

De·se·cheo Island \ˌdā-sā-ˈchā-ō\. Small island off NW Puerto Rico.

De·sen·ga·ño, Cape \ˌdā-sen-ˈgä-nyō\. Cape on E coast of Santa Cruz prov., S Argentina, extending into Atlantic Ocean.

De·sen·za·no del Gar·da \ˌdā-send-ˈzä-nō-del-ˈgär-dä\. Commune, Brescia prov., Lombardy, N Italy, on S shore of Lake Garda 16 mi. (26 km.) ESE of the commune of Brescia; pop. (1989c) 20,746; important harbor.

Des·er·et \ˌde-zə-ˈret\. The provisional state comprising the greater part of the SW United States S of the 42d parallel and W of the Rocky Mts.; organized 1849 by a convention of Mormons; ✱ Salt Lake City; refused recognition by the U.S. Congress and Utah Terr. created in its stead 1850.

De·ser·tas \də-ˈzer-təsh\. Small group of rocky islets, Portugal, in the Madeira Is. (*q.v.*), 30 mi. (48 km.) SE of Madeira; 32°31′N, 16°30′W.

Des·ert Hot Springs \ˈde-zərt\. City, Riverside co., SE California, 8 mi. (13 km.) N of Palm Springs; pop. (1990c) 11,668; health resort.

De·sha \də-ˈshā\. County in SE Arkansas. See table at ARKANSAS.

De·shi·ma \dā-ˈshē-mä, ˈdā-shē-ˌmä\ *also* **De·ji·ma** \dā-ˈjē-mä, ˈdā-jē-mä\. Former island, at the head of Nagasaki harbor, Kyūshū, Japan; now a reclaimed part of mainland; the residence of representatives of the Dutch East India Company 1641–1858; during these two centuries, when Japan was closed to all foreigners, the only point of contact bet. the Japanese and the outside world; Dutch agents were allowed to carry on a restricted trade.

Desiderii Fanum. See SAINT-DIZIER.

De·sio \ˈdā-zyō\. Commune, Milano prov., Lombardy, N Italy, 11 mi. (18 km.) NNW of Milan; pop. (1991p) 33,782.

Dé·si·rade \ˌdā-zē-ˈräd\. Island in West Indies, a dependency of Guadeloupe (*q.v.*); 11 sq. mi. (28 sq. km.).

Des·jar·dins \ˌdā-zhär-ˈdeⁿ\. County, Quebec, Canada. See table at QUEBEC.

De Smet \də-ˈsmet\. City, ⊗ of Kingsbury co., E South Dakota; pop. (1990c) 1172.

Des Moines \di-ˈmȯin\. **1.** River, formed by junction of E and W forks in Humboldt co., NW cen. Iowa; flows SE diagonally across Iowa to empty into the Mississippi at Keokuk, SE extremity of Iowa; 327 mi. (526 km.) long; incl. W fork, which rises in Murray co., SW Minnesota, it is 535 mi. (861 km.) long; forms extreme E section of Iowa-Missouri boundary.
2. County in SE Iowa. See table at IOWA.
3. City, ✻ of Iowa, and ⊗ of Polk co., S cen. Iowa, at confluence of Des Moines and Raccoon rivers; pop. (1990c) 193,187; largest city in the state; in the Iowa corn belt; farm equipment, tires; insurance; publishing; Drake Univ. (1881), Grand View Coll. (1896), Univ. of Osteopathic Medicine and Health Sciences (1898), American Institute of Business (1921); Fort Des Moines built on this site 1843; settlement incorp. as Fort Des Moines 1851; made ✻ of Iowa and chartered as city of Des Moines 1857. Army post, Fort Des Moines, estab. c. 1900, S of the city, was location in WWII of first WAC training center.
4. City, King co., W cen. Washington, on Puget Sound 15 mi. (24 km.) S of Seattle; pop. (1990c) 17,283.

Des·mond \ˈdez-mənd\. Ancient kingdom, S Munster, S Ireland; comprised present cos. Cork and Kerry.

Des·na \dyis-ˈnä\. River, W Russia in Europe and Ukraine; rises E of Smolensk and flows generally S to join the Dnieper near Kiev; ab. 550 mi. (885 km.) long; navigable to Bryansk and is an important channel for the lumber trade; chief tributary the Seim.

De·so·la·ción \ˌdā-sō-lä-ˈsyōn\ *also Eng.* **Des·o·la·tion** \ˌde-sə-ˈlā-shən\. Uninhabited Chilean island, northernmost of the Tierra del Fuego Archipelago; 70 mi. (113 km.) long.

Désolation, Îles de *or* **Desolation Islands.** See KERGUELEN ISLANDS.

Des·o·la·tion Point \ˌde-sə-ˈlā-shən\. Point at N end of Dinagat I., Surigao del Norte prov., Mindanao, Philippines, on E side of Surigao Strait.

De So·to \di-ˈsō-tō\. **1.** Name of a parish in NW Louisiana and of counties in two states of the U.S. See tables at FLORIDA, LOUISIANA, MISSISSIPPI.
2. City, Jefferson co., E Missouri, 38 mi. (61 km.) SSW of St. Louis; pop. (1990c) 5993; determined by U.S. Census Bureau as 1980 center location of U.S. population; lead and zinc deposits nearby.
3. City, Dallas co., NE Texas, 14 mi. (23 km.) S of the city of Dallas; pop. (1990c) 30,544.

De·spair, Mount \di-ˈspar\. Peak in Glacier National Park, NW Montana; ab. 8582 ft. (2616 m.).

Des·patch \di-ˈspach\. Town, S Rep. of South Africa, ab. 18 mi. (29 km.) NW of Port Elizabeth.

Des Peres \də-ˈper\. City, St. Louis co., E Missouri, 8 mi. (13 km.) W of the city of St. Louis; pop. (1990c) 8395.

Des Plaines \des-ˈplānz\. **1.** River, NE Illinois; rises in SE Wisconsin, flows S to unite with Kankakee River and form Illinois River; 150 mi. (241 km.) long. See ILLINOIS WATERWAY.
2. City, Cook co., NE Illinois, NW of Chicago; pop. (1990c) 53,223.

Despoto Planina. See RHODOPE.

Des·roches \dā-ˈrȯsh\. Island belonging to Seychelles in Indian Ocean NNE of Madagascar; until 1976 part of British Indian Ocean Terr.

Des·sau \ˈde-ˌsau̇\. City, Saxony-Anhalt, E cen. Germany, on Mulde River 71 mi. (114 km.) SW of Berlin; pop. (1992e) 95,097; 16th cent. palace; munic. theater; old and new town halls; 16th cent. church. First mentioned 1213; ✻ of Anhalt-Dessau 1603; scene of victory of Austrian Gen. Albrecht von Wallenstein over German Count Peter von Mansfeld 1626 (Thirty Years' War); ✻ of Anhalt 1863–1945; site of Bauhaus art school 1925–32, headed by architect Walter Gropius until 1928; suffered severe damage in WWII; in Halle dist. of East Germany 1945–1990.

Desse. See DESE.

Destêrro. See FLORIANÓPOLIS.

De·struc·tion Island \di-ˈstrək-shən\. Island in Pacific Ocean, Jefferson co., W Washington.

Det·mold \ˈdet-ˌmȯlt\. City, North Rhine-Westphalia, Germany, 54 mi. (87 km.) E of Münster; pop. (1992e) 70,970; 16th cent. castle; 18th cent. castle; summer resort; formerly ✻ of Lippe; large statue to Arminius, conqueror of Varus (9 A.D.), nearby; Frankish King (later Holy Roman Emperor) Charlemagne defeated Saxons nearby (at ancient Theotmalli) 783 A.D.

De·tour \ˈdē-ˌtu̇r, di-ˈtu̇r\. Village, SE tip of Chippewa co., E and NE Upper Penin. of Michigan; pop. (1990c) 806; at mouth of St. Marys River which enters Lake Huron through **Detour Passage,** a strait bet. the mainland and Drummond I.

Detour, Point. Point at SE extremity of Delta co., S Upper Penin. of Michigan, extending into Lake Michigan.

De·troit \di-ˈtrȯit, *locally also* ˈdē-ˌtrȯit\. **1.** River, SE Michigan; connects Lake St. Clair with Lake Erie and forms part of U.S.-Canada boundary; ab. 31 mi. (50 km.) long; crossed by railroad tunnel (2668 ft. or 813 m. long) and vehicular tunnel (2200 ft. or 671 m. long), connecting Detroit, Michigan with Windsor, Ontario.
2. City, ⊗ of Wayne co., SE Michigan, on Detroit River just W of Lake St. Clair; pop. (1990c) 1,027,974; largest city in the state; health care; automobile manufacturing (although the automotive industry is no longer as highly concentrated in Detroit as it once was, the city is still closely associated with it); foundry products, paints, pharmaceuticals, chemicals; Univ. of Detroit Mercy (1877), Marygrove Coll. (1906), Wayne State Univ. (1868), Center for Creative Studies–Coll. of Art and Design (1926), Shaw Coll. at Detroit (1962).
History: Fort Pontchartrain du Détroit (Ft. Pontchartrain of the Straits) founded by French 1701; from foundation, it was trading and political center for Great Lakes region; surrendered to English during Seven Years' War 1760; besieged by the Ottawa under Chief Pontiac 1763–64; turned over to U.S. 1796; almost destroyed by fire 1805; surrendered by army officer William Hull to British 1812 but reoccupied by Americans under Gen. William Henry Harrison 1813; ✻ of Michigan Terr. 1805–37 and of state 1837–47; auto manufacturing begun in the city 1899; scene of major race riots 1943 and 1967.

Detroit Dam *and* **Detroit Reservoir.** See UNITED STATES, *Dams and Reservoirs.*

Detroit Lakes. City, ⊗ of Becker co., NW cen. Minnesota, 42 mi. (68 km.) E of Fargo, North Dakota; pop. (1990c) 6635; trade center and summer resort in a lake region.

Detskoye Selo. See PUSHKIN.

Det·ti·foss \ˈde-tē-ˌfȯs\. Waterfall in Jökulsá á Fjöllum River, NE Iceland; 144 ft. (44 m.) high.

Det·ting·en \ˈde-tiŋ-ən\. Village, Bavaria, Germany; scene in War of the Austrian Succession of victory of George II of England, commanding an army of English, Hannoverian, and Hessian troops, over the French 1743.

Deu·el \ˈdü-əl, ˈdyü-\. Name of counties in two states of the U.S. See tables at NEBRASKA and SOUTH DAKOTA.

Deur·ne \ˈdœr-nə\. **1.** Former commune, N Belgium; an E suburb that became part of Antwerp 1983.
2. Commune, North Brabant prov., S Netherlands, just E of Eindhoven; pop. (1981e) 28,351.

Deutsch–Brod. See HAVLÍČKŮV BROD.

Deutsches Reich. See GERMANY.

Deutsch–Eylau. See IŁAWA.

Deutschland. See GERMANY.

Deutz \ˈdȯits\. Part of Cologne, Germany, on right bank of Rhine; separate town until 1888; castle, made Benedictine monastery 11th cent.

Deux–Mon·tagnes \ˌdœ-mōⁿ-ˈtänʸ\ *or* **Two Mountains. 1.** County, Quebec, Canada. See table at QUEBEC.
2. City, Deux-Montagnes, Quebec, Canada; pop. (1991c) 13,035.

Deux–Montagnes, Lac des \ˌlàk-dā-ˌdœ̄-mȯⁿ-ˈtänʸ\ *or* **Lake of Two Mountains.** Expansion of the Ottawa River at its junction with the St. Lawrence, W of Montreal I., Quebec, Canada; bordered on SE by Île Perrot and has two outlets to the NE, the Rivière des Mille Îles and Rivièredes Prairies.

Deuxponts. See ZWEIBRÜCKEN.

Deux–Sè·vres \ˌdœ̄-ˈsevrᵊ\. Department of W France. See table at FRANCE.

Deva. See CHESTER 10.

De·va \ˈdā-vä\ *or Ger.* **Diem·rich** \ˈdēm-rik\. City, ⊗ of Hunedoara co., W cen. Romania, on the Mureşul River 78 mi. (126 km.) ESE of Arad; pop. (1989c) 77,336; in fruit-growing region; food processing.

De Valls Bluff \dē-ˈvalz\. Town, a ⊗ of Prairie co., E cen. Arkansas, on White River; pop. (1990c) 702.

Devana. See ABERDEEN 2.

Devana Castra. See CHESTER 10.

Dé·va·vá·nya \ˈdā-vö-ˌvä-nyö\. Commune, Békés co., SE Hungary, 47 mi. (76 km.) SW of Debrecen; pop. (1980p) 11,208.

De·ven·ter \ˈdā-vən-tər\. Commercial commune, Overijssel prov., E Netherlands, on IJssel River; pop. (1992e) 68,004; founded 8th cent.; belonged to Hanseatic League.

Dev·er·on \ˈde-və-rən\. River in NE Scotland; flows into North Sea at Banff; 61 mi. (98 km.) long.

De·vies Mountain \də-ˈvēs\. Peak, Fayette co., SW Pennsylvania; 2760 ft. (841 m.).

Dé·ville–lès–Rou·en \dā-ˈvēl-lā-ˈrwäⁿ, rü-ˈaⁿ\. Commune, Seine-Maritime dept., N France, ab. 2 mi. (3 km.) W of Rouen of which it is a suburb.

Devil Mountain. See AUYÁN-TEPUÍ.

Dev·ils \ˈde-vilz\. River, SW Texas; rises in NW Sutton co., flows S; 100 mi. (161 km.) long.

Dev·il's Bit Mountains \ˈde-vilz-ˈbit\. Range in N co. Tipperary, S Ireland; highest peak 1583 ft. (482 m.).

Devil's Bridge *or Welsh* **Pont·ar·fy·nach** \ˌpȯn-tär-ˈvə-näk\. Locality, Dyfed, W Wales, on Rheidol River; noted for scenery, stone bridges, chasm 114 ft. (35 m.) deep.

Devil's Ear Mountain. Peak in the Adirondack Mts., NE New York; 3903 ft. (1190 m.).

Devil's Island *or Fr.* **Île du Dia·ble** \ˌēl-dūē-ˈdyáblᵊ\. One of the Safety Is. (*q.v.*) off the N coast of French Guiana; became a penal colony of the French government in 2d half of 19th cent.; here Capt. Alfred Dreyfus, convicted of treason, was a prisoner 1895–99; penal colonies abolished 1938.

Devils Lake. 1. Saline lake bet. Ramsey and Benson cos., NE cen. North Dakota.
2. City, ⊗ of Ramsey co., NE North Dakota, on former N shore of Devils Lake; pop. (1990c) 7782; railroad and trading center; Univ. of North Dakota, Lake Region (1941).

Dev·ils Post·pile National Monument \ˈde-vilz-ˈpōst-ˌpīl\. See UNITED STATES, *National Monuments.*

Devils River. See DEVILS.

Devils Tower National Monument. See UNITED STATES, *National Monuments.*

De·vine \də-ˈvīn\. City, Medina co., S cen. Texas, 33 mi. (53 km.) SW of San Antonio; pop. (1990c) 3928.

De·vi·zes \di-ˈvī-zəz\. Town, Wiltshire, S England, on the Kennet 28 mi. (45 km.) ESE of Bristol; pop. (1981p) 10,629; market center.

Dev·on \ˈde-vən\. **1.** Former county in England. See DEVONSHIRE.
2. Administrative county, SW England, comprising the former county; ⊗ Exeter; estab. 1974. See table at ENGLAND.
3. River, E Scotland; rises in Ochil Hills, Perth co., flows into Forth River in Clackmannan co. ab. 3 mi. (5 km.) NW of Alloa; ab. 34 mi. (55 km.) long.

Devon Island *also* **North Devon Island.** Island, E cen. Arctic Archipelago, Nunavut, Canada, N of Baffin I. and at the head of Baffin Bay; 20,861 sq. mi. (54,030 sq. km.).

Dev·on·port \ˈde-vən-ˌpōrt\. **1.** Town, on N coast of Tasmania, Australia, at mouth of Mersey River 50 mi. (80 km.) WNW of Launceston; munic. pop. (1991c) 22,660; active port; recreational resort.
2. Seaport, Devon, SW England; on E side of Tamar estuary NW of Plymouth, of which it is a part; dockyard, military and naval station.
3. Borough, North I., New Zealand, suburb of Auckland on N side of Waitemata Harbor; pop. (1981c) 10,410; important naval station.

Dev·on·shire \ˈde-vən-ˌshir, -shər\ *or* **Devon.** Former county, SW England; ⊗ Exeter; rivers Exe and Dart.

De·vrez \de-ˈvrez\. River, N cen. Turkey in Asia; flows E into the Kızıl Irmak; 115 mi. (185 km.) long.

De·was \dā-ˈwäs\. **1.** Two former Indian states, now part of Madhya Pradesh, cen. India: **Dewas Senior,** 449 sq. mi. (1163 sq. km.); **Dewas Junior,** 419 sq. mi. (1085 sq. km.). Founded in first half of 18th cent. by two brothers, Maratha chieftains; merged with Madhya Pradesh 1956.
2. Town, their joint ❋, 23 mi. (37 km.) NE of Indore; pop. (1991p) 163,699.

Dew·ey \ˈdü-ē, ˈdyü-\. **1.** Name of counties in two states of the U.S. See tables at OKLAHOMA and SOUTH DAKOTA.
2. City, Washington co., NE Oklahoma, 6 mi. (10 km.) NE of Bartlesville; pop. (1990c) 3326.

De Witt \di-ˈwit\. **1.** Name of counties in two states of the U.S. See tables at ILLINOIS and TEXAS.
2. City, a ⊗ of Arkansas co., E Arkansas, 40 mi. (64 km.) E of Pine Bluff; pop. (1990c) 3553; shipping point.
3. City, Clinton co., E Iowa, 18 mi. (29 km.) W of the city of Clinton; pop. (1990c) 4514.
4. City, Clinton co., Michigan, N of Lansing; pop. (1990c) 3964.

Dews·bury \ˈdüz-ˌber-ē, ˈdyüz-, -bə-rē\. Town, West Yorkshire, N England, on Calder River 9 mi. (14 km.) S of Leeds; pop. (1981p) 48,339; wool, leather, carpets.

Dex·ter \ˈdek-stər\. **1.** Town, Penobscot co., E cen. Maine, 30 mi. (48 km.) WNW of Bangor; pop. (1990c) 4419.
2. City, Stoddard co., SE Missouri, 26 mi. (42 km.) E of Poplar Bluff; pop. (1990c) 7559; trade center.

Dez \ˈdez\ *also* **Ab–i–Diz** \ˌäb-i-ˈdēz\. River, W Iran; 250 mi. (402 km.) long; tributary of Kārūn River. See DEZFŪL.

Dez·fūl \dez-ˈfül\ *or* **Diz·ful** \diz-ˈfül\. Town, Khūzestān prov., SW Iran, ab. 130 mi. (209 km.) N of Khorramshahr; pop. (1986c) 151,420; on Dez River, a dam 20 mi. (32 km.) upstream providing power and water for irrigation. The ruins of ancient Susa are ab. 15 mi. (24 km.) S; scene of riots 1978 prior to Iranian Revolution; attacked by Iraqi aircraft in Iran-Iraq War of 1980s.

Dezh·ne·va, Mys \ˈməs-dezh-ˈnyȯ-və\ *or* **Cape Dezh·nev** \ˈdezh-nyif\ *also* **East Cape.** Cape at E end of Chukchi Penin., Chukchi Autonomous Okrug, NE Russia in Asia, projecting into Bering Strait; most easterly point in Asia, 169°40′W.

De·zhou *or W.-G.* **Te–chou** \ˈdə-ˈjō\; *formerly* **Teh·sien** \ˈdə-ˈshyen\. Town, NW Shandong prov., NE China, on Grand Canal near Hebei border 65 mi. (105 km.) NW of Jinan.

Dhah·ran \ˌthä-ˈhrän, dä-ˈrän\ *or Arab.* **Aẓ Ẓah·rān** \ˌáth-thä-ˈhrän\. Town, E Saudi Arabia, near W coast of Persian Gulf near Bahrain; adjacent to Ad Dammām in extensive oil regions; university (1963); pipeline connection with Abqaiq oil field 40 mi. (64 km.) to the SW; air base; target of Iraqi Scud missile attacks in Gulf War 1991.

Dha·ka *also* **Dac·ca** \ˈda-kə, ˈdä-\. City, ❋ of Bangladesh, just W of Meghna River in cen. part of the country; pop. (1991p) 3,637,892; river port; textiles, rope and string, baskets, embroidery work; boatbuilding; ships jute, rice, sugar; Univ. of Dhaka (1921), Univ. of Engineering and Technology (1961). Site of French, Dutch, and English trading posts at various times; ❋ of Mogul prov. of Bengal 1608–1704 and of former British prov. of Eastern Bengal and Assam 1905–12; scene of surrender of Pakistani forces to Indian troops 1971.

Dha·mār *or* **Da·mar** \thá-ˈmär, da-\. Town, S cen. Yemen, SSE of San'a, in a valley bet. two volcanic peaks; market in grain-producing area; noted horse-breeding center; ancient Islamic theological school.

Dha·nush·ko·di \ˌdə-nüsh-ˈkō-dē\. Seaport at E tip of Rameswaram I., Tamil Nadu, SE India, bet. Palk Strait and Gulf of Mannar.

Dhar \'där\. **1.** Former Indian state, now part of Madhya Pradesh, cen. India; 1798 sq. mi. (4657 sq. km.); founded by Rajputs 9th cent. A.D.; conquered by Muslims 13th cent.; made a fief of the Marathas mid-18th cent.; came under British control 1819; merged with Madhya Bharat 1948.
2. Town, its ✱, 33 mi. (53 km.) SW of Indore; pop. (1991p) 59,089; of great antiquity; famous in medieval India as ✱ of Rajput dynasty of Malwa; long a center of culture and learning; has fine Pillar Mosque and other structures of interest.

Dha·ram·pur \'dər-əm-,pu̇r\. **1.** Former Indian state, now part of Gujarat state, W India; 719 sq. mi. (1862 sq. km.).
2. Town, its ✱, 115 mi. (185 km.) N of Bombay.

Dharm·sa·la \dərm-'sä-lə\ *or* **Dhar·am·sala** \,dər-əm-\. Town, Himachal Pradesh, N India; pop. (1991p) 17,320; residence of the Dalai Lama since his exile from Tibet 1959.

Dharwar. See HUBLI-DHARWAR.

Dhau·la·gi·ri, Mount \,dau̇-lə-'gir-ē\. Peak in the Himalayas, W cen. Nepal; 26,810 ft. (8172 m.); first scaled 1960.

Dhaulpur. See DHOLPUR.

Dhe·ké·lia \t͟he-'kāl-yä\ *also* **Ta·toi** *or* **Ta·tóï** \tä-'tȯi\. Town, Greece, ab. 16 mi. (26 km.) N of Athens; royal palace.

Dhelfoí. See DELPHI 2.

Dhen·ka·nal \den-'kä-näl\. Town, Orissa, E India, 25 mi. (40 km.) NW of Cuttack; pop. (1991p) 46,250.

Dhī·bān \'thē-,bän, 'zē-\. Settlement, Jordan, SSW of Amman; site of ruins of ancient Dibon (*q.v.*).

Dhík·ti \'t͟hēk-tē\ *or Eng.* **Dic·te** \'dik-tē\. Mountain peak in Dhíkti Mts., E Crete, Greece; 7045 ft. (2147 m.); in Greek mythology one possible place where Zeus was reared.

Dhíkti Mountains. Mountains, E Crete, Greece; highest point Dhíkti (*q.v.*) 7045 ft. (2147 m.).

Dhílos. See DELOS.

Dhodhekánisos. See DODECANESE.

Dho·far \dō-'fär\ *or Arab.* **Zu·fār** \t͟hō-'fär\. Province, S Oman; ✱ Salalah; scene of unsuccessful revolt (1960s–1970s) against rule of sultans of Oman.

Dhol·pur \'dōl-,pu̇r\. **1.** Former Indian state, now part of Rajasthan state, NW India; 1173 sq. mi. (3038 sq. km.); settled 11th cent.; under Mogul emperors 16th to early 18th cents.
2. *or* **Dhaul·pur** \'dau̇l-\. Town, its ✱, 34 mi. (55 km.) S of Agra; pop. (1991p) 68,524.

Dhonburi. See THON BURI.

Dho·ra·ji \dō-'rä-jē\. Town, Gujarat, W India, 250 mi. (402 km.) NW of Bombay; pop. (1991p) 77,683.

Dhran·ga·dhra \'dräŋ-gə-,drä\. **1.** Former Indian state, now part of Gujarat state, W India; 1167 sq. mi. (3023 sq. km.).
2. Town, its ✱, 75 mi. (121 km.) W of Ahmadabad; pop. (1991p) 54,281.

Dhrol \'drōl\. Former Indian state, now part of Gujarat state, W India; 283 sq. mi. (733 sq. km.).

Dhu·bu·ri *or* **Dhu·bri** \'du̇-brē\. Town, NW Assam, NE India, on right bank of Brahmaputra River ab. 260 mi. (420 km.) NNE of Calcutta; pop. (1991p) 65,861.

Dhu·lia \'dü-lē-ə\. Town, N Maharashtra, W India, on Panjhra River 200 mi. (322 km.) NE of Bombay; pop. (1991p) 277,957; cotton goods, cigarettes.

Día \'t͟hē-ä, 'dē-\. Small island off N coast of Crete, Greece, E Mediterranean Sea, ab. 10 mi. (16 km.) NNE of Iráklion.

Diablatins, Morne. See DIABLOTIN, MORNE.

Diable, Île du. See DEVIL'S ISLAND.

Dia·ble·rets \,dyä-blə-'rä\. Peak in the Bernese Alps, Valais canton, SW cen. Switzerland; 10,531 ft. (3210 m.).

Diablo, Canyon. See CANYON DIABLO.

Di·ab·lo, Mount \dē-'ä-blō, dī-'a-\. Isolated peak, Contra Costa co., W California, 32 mi. (51 km.) E of Oakland; 3849 ft. (1173 m.).

Dia·blo·tin, Morne \'mȯrn-,dyä-blȯ-'teⁿ\ *or* **Morne Dia·bla·tins** \-'teⁿ\. Peak on the island of Dominica; 4747 ft. (1447 m.).

Diala. See DIYALA.

Di·a·lao Point \,dē-ä-'lau̇\. Point on N coast of Ilocos Norte prov., Luzon, Philippines; marks NE point of Bangui Bay.

Di·al Mountain \'dīl\. Peak in the Adirondack Mts., Essex co., NE New York; 4023 ft. (1226 m.).

Diamant. See JAMBUAIR.

Dia·man·te \,dē-ä-'män-tā\. River in Mendoza prov., W Argentina; rises in Andes near Chile-Argentina border, flows E to the Río Salado.

Di·a·man·ti·na \,dī-ə-,man-'tē-nə\. Intermittent river, SW Queensland, Australia; 560 mi. (901 km.) long; upper tributary of the Warburton River.

Di·a·man·ti·na \,dē-ə-,mȧn-'tē-nə\. City, cen. Minas Gerais state, E Brazil; munic. pop. (1991p) 26,075; diamonds.

Di·a·man·ti·no \,dē-ə-,mȧn-'tē-nü\. Town, Mato Grosso state, SW Brazil, near source of Paraguay River 80 mi. (129 km.) NNW of Cuiabá.

Diamond. See JAMBUAIR.

Di·a·mond, Cape \'dī-mənd, 'dī-ə-\. Promontory, E end of city of Quebec, Canada; alt. 333 ft. (101 m.); site of citadel.

Diamond Bar. City, Los Angeles co., California, bordering SW Pomona; pop. (1990c) 53,672.

Diamond Harbour. Port, West Bengal, NE India, at the head of the estuary of the Hugli, 30 mi. (48 km.) SSW of Calcutta with which it is connected by rail; pop. (1991p) 30,260.

Diamond Head. Cape and landmark, SE Oahu I., Hawaii, SE of Honolulu; 761 ft. (232 m.) high.

Diamond Mountains. 1. Range in E cen. Nevada, extending from SW Elko co. S along boundary bet. Eureka and White Pine cos.
2. Mountain peaks, North Korea. See KŬMGANG MOUNTAINS.

Diamond Peak. 1. Mountain in the Sierra Nevada, in E Fresno co., S cen. California; 13,105 ft. (3994 m.).
2. Mountain, SE tip of Lane co., W Oregon; 8744 ft. (2665 m.).

Dian Chi *or W.-G.* **Tien Ch'ih** *or* **Tien Chih** \'dyen-'chē, -'chi\. Lake, cen. Yunnan prov., S China, just S of Kunming.

Dianium. See DENIA.

Diarbekr. See DİYARBAKIR.

Di·bang \dē-'bäŋ\ *or* **Di·bong** \-'bȯŋ\. Tributary of the Brahmaputra River, in NE India and SW Tibet, China; flows into the Brahmaputra at the great bend in NE Assam.

Di·bër \'dē-bər\ *or* **Di·brë** \-brə\ *or Ital.* **Di·bra** \'dē-brä\. District of NE Albania. See table at ALBANIA.

Dibio. See DIJON.

Di·boll \'dī-bəl\. City, Angelina co., E Texas, 15 mi. (24 km.) SSW of Lufkin; pop. (1990c) 4341.

Di·bon \'dī-,bän\. Ancient city of Palestine, at present-day Dhībān; place where the Moabite stone was found 1868, a block of basalt bearing an inscription of 34 lines, dating from the 9th cent. B.C. and written in the Moabite alphabet, an important representative of Phoenician script. See MOAB.

Dibong. See DIBANG.

Dibra *or* **Dibrë.** See DIBËR.

Di·bru·garh \'di-bru̇-gər\. Town, NE Assam, NE India, head of navigation on left bank of Brahmaputra River; pop. (1991p) 118,374; university (1965); center of tea-raising region; in WWII an Allied air base.

Dibse. See THAPSACUS.

Dicaearchia. See POZZUOLI.

Dick·ens \'di-kənz\. **1.** County in NW Texas. See table at TEXAS.
2. City, its ⊗; pop. (1990c) 322.

Dick·en·son \'di-kən-sən\. County in SW Virginia. See table at VIRGINIA.

Dick·er·son, Mount \'di-kər-sən\. Mountain, Antarctica, 84°20′S, 167°09′E; 13,517 ft. (4120 m.).

Dick·ey \'di-kē\. County in S North Dakota. See table at NORTH DAKOTA.

Dick·in·son \'di-kən-sən\. **1.** Name of counties in three states of the U.S. See tables at IOWA, KANSAS, MICHIGAN.
2. City, ⊗ of Stark co., SW North Dakota; pop. (1990c) 16,097; lignite coal deposits, clay deposits; Dickinson State Univ. (1918); founded c. 1880; became ⊗ 1884.
3. City, Brazoria co., SE Texas; pop. (1990c) 9497.

\ə\ abut \ə\ matches \ᵊ\ kitten, Fr table \ər\ further \a\ ash \ā\ ace \ä\ cot, cart \ȧ\ Fr bac \au̇\ out \b\ Span Avila \ch\ chin \e\ bet \ē\ easy \g\ go \i\ hit \ī\ ice \j\ job \k\ Ger ich, Buch \ⁿ\ Fr vin \ŋ\ sing \ō\ go \ȯ\ all \ȯ\ law \œ\ Fr bœuf \œ̄\ Fr feu \ȯi\ boy \th\ thin \t͟h\ this \ü\ loot \u̇\ foot \ue\ Ger füllen \u̅e\ Fr rue \y\ yet \ʸ\ Fr digne \'dēnʸ\, nuit \'nwʸē\ \yü\ few \yu̇\ fury \zh\ vision

Dicks Head \ˈdiks\ *or Arab.* **Ras Chiam·bo·ne** *also* **Ras Kiam·bo·ne** \ˌräs-kyäm-ˈbō-nē\. Promontory extending into Indian Ocean at boundary bet. SE Somalia and NE Kenya.

Dick·son \ˈdik-sən\. **1.** County in NW cen. Tennessee. See table at TENNESSEE.

2. Town, Dickson co., NW cen. Tennessee, 35 mi. (56 km.) WSW of Nashville; pop. (1990c) 8791.

Dickson City. Borough, Lackawanna co., NE Pennsylvania, 5 mi. (8 km.) NE of Scranton; pop. (1990c) 6276; coal deposits.

Dickson Island *or Russ.* **Os·trov Dik·son** \ˈȯs-trəf-ˈdēk-sən\. Small island off NW coast of Siberia, NW Russia in Asia, at mouth of Yenisey River, ab. 73°30′N, 80°20′E; has settlement and harbor.

Dic·le Ne·hri \dij-ˈlā-ne-ˈhrē\. Turkish name of upper Tigris River.

Dicte. See DHÍKTI.

Did·y·ma \ˈdi-də-mə\. Ruins of town on W coast of Asia Minor, S of Miletus; in ancient times was in Caria; oracle of Apollo; famous temple.

Didyme. See SALINA.

Diedenhofen. See THIONVILLE.

Die·go Gar·cia \dē-ˈā-gō-gär-ˈsē-ä\. Chief island of the Chagos Archipelago (*q.v.*), British Indian Ocean Terr., 7°20′S, 72°25′E; site of Anglo-American naval support and communication facilities.

Diego Ra·mí·rez \rä-ˈmē-res\. Island group, Chile, southernmost of the Tierra del Fuego Archipelago (*q.v.*), 60 mi. (97 km.) SW of Cape Horn.

Diégo–Suarez. See ANTSIRANANA.

Die·kirch \ˈdē-ˌkirk\. Town, Grand Duchy of Luxembourg; pop. (1981e) 5600.

Diemrich. See DEVA.

Dien Bien Phu \ˈdyen-ˈbyen-ˈfü\. Village, NW Vietnam near Laos border; French military post in Indochina War, fell to Vietminh after 56-day siege 1954.

Dien Khanh \ˈdyen-ˈkän\ *or* **Khanh-hoa** \ˈkän-ˈhwä\. Coastal town, S Vietnam, 45 mi. (72 km.) N of Phan Rang.

Di·eppe \ˈdyep, dē-ˈep\. **1.** Town, New Brunswick, Canada; pop. (1991c) 10,463.

2. \ˈdyep\. Seaport, Seine-Maritime dept., N France, on English Channel 34 mi. (55 km.) N of Rouen; shipbuilding; known for manufacture of ivory and bone goods, which dates from 15th cent. Important naval base in 17th cent.; suffered from plague 1668, 1670; bombarded by English and Dutch 1694; occupied by Prussians 1870–71 in Franco-Prussian War; occupied by Germans 1940–44 in WWII; site of Allied commando raid to test German defenses 1942.

Diest \ˈdēst\. Commune, Brabant prov., cen. Belgium; pop. (1991c) 21,461.

Die·ti·kon \ˈdē-ti-ˌkōn\. Commune, Zürich canton, Switzerland, NE of the city of Zürich; pop. (1989c) 21,426.

Die Vier Waldstatter. See FOREST CANTONS, THE FOUR.

Dif·fer·dange \ˌdē-fer-ˈdä^{n}zh\ *or Ger.* **Dif·fer·ding·en** \ˈdi-fər-ˌdiŋ-ən\. Town, SW Grand Duchy of Luxembourg, 12 mi. (19 km.) SW of the city of Luxembourg; pop. (1990e) 16,050.

Dig \ˈdēg\. Town, NE Rajasthan, NW India; scene of battle c. 1803 in which British defeated Marathas.

Dig·by \ˈdig-bē\. **1.** County, W Nova Scotia, Canada. See table at NOVA SCOTIA.

2. Resort town, its ⊗, on Annapolis Basin 57 mi. (92 km.) NNE of Yarmouth; pop. (1991c) 2311; founded 1783 by Loyalists from New England; a variety of herring became known as "Digby chickens" because of their export from here.

Digby Gut. Passage in W Nova Scotia, Canada; 2 mi. (3 km.) long and 0.5 mi. (0.8 km.) wide; forms outlet of Annapolis Basin into Bay of Fundy; actually a gap or cleft in elevated ridge along SW coast of Nova Scotia, its steep sides 400 to 600 ft. (122 to 183 m.) high; strong tides and winds.

Digh·ton \ˈdīt-^{ə}n\. **1.** City, ⊗ of Lane co., W Kansas; pop. (1990c) 1565.

2. Town, Bristol co., SE Massachusetts, 7 mi. (11 km.) N of Fall River; pop. (1990c) 5631. On E bank of Taunton River opp. the town is **Dighton Rock,** a boulder with curious markings believed to be of American Indian origin.

Dignano d'Istria. See VODNJAN.

Digne \ˈdēn^{y}\. Commune, ✻ of Alpes-de-Haute Provence dept., SE France, 71 mi. (114 km.) NE of Marseille; pop. (1990c) 17,425; 13th cent. cathedral; mineral springs nearby.

Di·gos \ˈdē-gōs\. Municipality, ✻ of Davao del Sur prov., Mindanao, Philippines; pop. (1980c) 70,065.

Di·gul *or Du.* **Di·goel** \dē-ˈgül\. Navigable river, SE Irian Jaya, Indonesia; rises in E end of Maoke Mts. and flows S and W to Arafura Sea, N of Dolak I.; ab. 400 mi. (640 km.) long; its basin largely swampy jungle.

Di·hang \dē-ˈhäŋ\ *or* **Di·hong** \-ˈhȯŋ\ *or Chin.* **Yar·lung** \ˈyär-ˈlu̇ŋ\. Name applied to the Brahmaputra River (*q.v.*) in its middle course, where it turns and breaks through the Himalayas in Tibet, China, and Assam, India.

Dij·le \ˈdī-lə\ *or* **Dy·le** \ˈdī-lə, ˈdēl\. River, Belgium; flows N and W in Brabant and Antwerp provs. and unites with the Nethe River 4 mi. (6 km.) NW of Mechelen to form the Rupel River; ab. 50 mi. (80 km.) long.

Di·jon \dē-ˈzhō^{n}\; *anc.* **Dib·io** \ˈdi-bē-ˌō\. City, ✻ of Côte-d'Or dept., E France, on Ouche River 168 mi. (270 km.) SE of Paris; pop. (1990c) 151,636; food products (noted esp. for mustard); surrounded by eight forts; 13th cent. church; 14th cent. town hall (former palace of dukes of Burgundy); university (1722); birthplace of prelate Jacques-Bénigne Bossuet (1627) and composer Jean-Philippe Rameau (1683). Site occupied from pre-Roman times; ✻ of Burgundy from 11th cent.; great prosperity under Valois dynasty 1364–1477; annexed by Louis XI late 15th cent.

Dikh Tau. See DYKH TAU.

Diks·mui·de *or* **Dix·mui·de** \dik-ˈsmī-də\ *or Fr.* **Dix·mude** \dēk-ˈsmu̅e̅d\. Commune, W Flanders prov., Belgium, 13 mi. (21 km.) N of Ieper; pop. (1991c) 15,273; destroyed in WWI when intentionally flooded 1914 to halt German advance.

Dikson, Ostrov. See DICKSON ISLAND.

Dik·wa \di-ˈkwä\. **1.** District, Borno State, NE Nigeria; 5149 sq. mi. (13,336 sq. km.); part of Bornu kingdom from 19th cent.; came under British control 1914; joined Nigeria by plebiscite 1961.

2. Town, its ✻, near SW shore of Lake Chad.

Di·la Point \ˈdē-lä\. Most westerly point of Ilocos Sur prov., Luzon, Philippines, ab. 4 mi. (6 km.) W of Vigan.

Dil·ā·rām \ˌdi-lä-ˈräm\. Town, SW cen. Afghanistan, on main highway 140 mi. (225 km.) WNW of Kandahār.

Di·li *or* **Dil·li** \ˈdi-lē\. Town, ✻ of East Timor prov., Timor I., Indonesia; on N coast; good harbor for small craft; held by Japanese during WWII; until 1975 ✻ of Portuguese Timor.

Dil·len·burg \ˈdi-lən-ˌbu̇rk\. Town, Hesse, Germany, ab. 25 mi. (40 km.) WSW of Marburg; pop. (1980c) 23,485; birthplace of Dutch Stadholder William the Silent 1533.

Dil·ley \ˈdi-lē\. City, Frio co., S Texas, 70 mi. (113 km.) SW of San Antonio; pop. (1990c) 2632.

Dil·li \ˈdi-lē\. **1.** Territory and city, India. See DELHI.

2. Town, Timor. See DILI.

Dil·ling·en \ˈdi-liŋ-ən\. **1.** *or in full* **Dillingen an der Do·nau** \ˌän-dər-ˈdō-ˌnau̇\. Town, Bavaria, Germany, on the N bank of the Danube 19 mi. (31 km.) NE of Ulm; pop. (1980c) 15,882; became town in 13th cent.

2. *or in full* **Dillingen an der Saar** \ˌän-dər-ˈzär\. Town, Saarland, Germany, on the Saar River 28 mi. (45 km.) S of Trier; pop. (1980c) 20,742.

Dil·ling·ham \ˈdi-liŋ-ˌham\. Division in Alaska. See table at ALASKA.

Dil·lon \ˈdi-lən\. **1.** County in NE South Carolina. See table at SOUTH CAROLINA.

2. City, ⊗ of Beaverhead co., SW Montana, 53 mi. (85 km.) S of Butte; pop. (1990c) 3991; Western Montana Coll. (1893).

3. Town, ⊗ of Dillon co., NE South Carolina, 29 mi. (47 km.) ENE of Florence; pop. (1990c) 6829.

Dillon Bay. Bay with good anchorage on W coast of Erromango I., Vanuatu, SW Pacific; site of Martyrs' Memorial Church, in memory of several missionaries killed on the island by natives in mid-19th cent.

Di·lo·lo \dē-ˈlō-lō\. Lake in E Angola, near border of Democratic Rep. of the Congo, 11°31′S, 22°20′E.

Di·ma·pur \ˈdē-mə-ˌpu̇r\. Town, Nagaland, NE India, at foot of W slope of Naga Hills and key point on Bengal-Assam railroad line; pop. (1991p) 56,918.

Dimash. See DAMASCUS.

Dîm·bo·vi·ţa \'dim-bō-,vēt-sä\. **1.** River, S cen. Romania; flows out of the Transylvanian Alps SSE past Bucharest into the Argeş River; 155 mi. (249 km.) long.

2. County of S cen. Romania. See table at ROMANIA.

Di·mi·trov·grad \di-'mē-trəf-,grät\. **1.** Town, Khaskovo region, S Bulgaria; pop. (1991e) 56,882; coal mines nearby; chemicals, cement; founded 1947.

2. *formerly* **Me·le·kess** \,mi-li-'kyes\. Town, Ul'yanovsk Oblast, E cen. Russia in Europe; pop. (1992e) 129,000.

Dim·mit \'di-mit\. County in S Texas. See table at TEXAS.

Dim·mitt \'di-mit\. Town, ⊗ of Castro co., NW Texas; pop. (1990c) 4408.

Di·na·gat \dē-'nä-gät\. **1.** Island, N of extreme NE point of Mindanao, SE Philippines, a part of Surigao del Norte prov.; 309 sq. mi. (800 sq. km.); separated from Mindanao by channel ab. 5 mi. (8 km.) wide, from Siargao I. on E by **Dinagat Sound,** and from S Leyte and Panaon islands on W by Surigao Strait (*q.v.*); has chain of mountains from N to S with several peaks above 1700 ft. (518 m.) and highest 3300 ft. (1006 m.); chief towns Dinagat and Loreto.

2. Municipality and chief town of Dinagat I., on SW coast; pop. (1980c) 36,726.

Di·naj·pur \di-'näj-,pu̇r\. **1.** Historical district, Bangladesh; 2609 sq. mi. (6757 sq. km.); ✻ Dinajpur; formerly a province of British India; partitioned bet. India and Pakistan 1947 (Indian sector constitutes the district **West Dinajpur** 1418 sq. mi. or 3673 sq. km.); wheat, jute, rice, sugarcane.

2. Town, its ✻; pop. (1991p) 136,657.

Di·na·lu·pi·han \,dē-nä-lü-'pē-,hän\. Municipality, N Bataan prov., Luzon, Philippines, near Pampanga border and ab. 14 mi. (23 km.) NNW of Balanga; pop. (1980c) 41,415.

Di·nan \dē-'nä^n\. City, Côtes-du-Nord dept., NW France, on Rance River 35 mi. (56 km.) E of St.-Brieuc; pop. (1990c) 12,873; remains of medieval ramparts; 12th cent. churches; 14th cent. castle; tourism.

Di·nant \dē-'nä^n\. Commune, Namur prov., S Belgium, on the Meuse; pop. (1991c) 12,183; in the Ardennes Forest region; sacked by Charles the Bold, duke of Burgundy, 1466 and by the Germans 1914.

Dinapore *or* **Dinapur.** See DANAPUR.

Di·nar \di-'när\; *anc.* **Ce·lae·nae** \sə-'lē-,nē\. Town, W cen. Turkey in Asia, on railroad line 50 mi. (80 km.) SSW of Afyon; ancient Celaenae a great city of Phrygia at the source of the Maeander (Menderes); setting of legend of Apollo and Marsyas.

Di·na·ra Pla·ni·na \'dē-nä-,rä-'plä-,nē-,nä\. See table at ALPS.

Di·nard \dē-'när\. Commune, Ille-et-Vilaine dept., NW France, on the Gulf of St.-Malo at the mouth of the Rance, opp. St.-Malo; resort.

Di·nar·ic Alps \də-'nar-ik\. See table at ALPS.

Dinbych. See DENBIGH 3.

Dinbych–y–pysgod. See TENBY.

Din·der \'din-,der\ *also* **Den·der** \'den-\ River, E Africa; rises in Ethiopia; flows NW across border of Sudan where it is also known as **Din·dar** \-,der\ and into Blue Nile N of Sennar; 300 mi. (483 km.) long.

Din·di·gul \'din-di-,gəl\. Town, S Tamil Nadu, S India, 35 mi. (56 km.) NNW of Madurai; pop. (1991p) 182,293; trade center; cigars, jewelry and other handicrafts, cotton goods; includes overlooking fort formerly of great strategic importance during the wars of the 17th and 18th cents.

Din·dy·mus, Mount \'din-də-məs\. See PESSINUS.

Din·ga·lan Bay \dēŋ-'gä-län\. Inlet of Pacific Ocean on E coast of Luzon, Quezon prov., Philippines, S of Baler Bay.

Ding·hai *or W.-G.* **Ting–hai** \'diŋ-'hī\. Commercial seaport, ✻ of Zhoushan Archipelago, on S shore of Zhoushan I., Zhejiang prov., E China.

Din·gle \'diŋ-gəl\. Seaport, W co. Kerry, SW Ireland; on a small harbor on NW shore of **Dingle Bay** (an inlet of Atlantic Ocean extending ab. 30 mi. or 48 km. inland); pop. (1986c) 1253.

Din·gras \dēŋ-'gräs\. Municipality, S cen. Ilocos Norte prov., Luzon, Philippines, on a tributary of the Laoag River 8 mi. (13 km.) ESE of Laoag; pop. (1980c) 26,511.

Ding·wall \'diŋ-,wȯl, -wəl\. Burgh, Highland region, N Scotland, at head of Cromarty Firth; pop. (1981p) 4815.

Din·kels·bühl \'diŋ-kəls-,bu̅e̅l\. Town, W Bavaria, Germany, ab. 45 mi. (72 km.) SW of Nürnberg; pop. (1992e) 11,271; first mentioned in 10th cent.; made free imperial city 1273; medieval walls, towers, and churches, esp. the Gothic church of St. George.

Di·no·saur National Monument \'dī-nə-,sȯr\. See UNITED STATES, *National Monuments.*

Dins·la·ken \'dins-,lä-kən\. City, North Rhine-Westphalia, Germany, near Rhine River 10 mi. (16 km.) N of Duisburg; pop. (1992e) 66,087; coal mining; manufactures wire, nails, lumber; received city charter 1273; heavily damaged in WWII.

Di·nu·ba \dī-'nü-bə\. City, Tulare co., S cen. California, 25 mi. (40 km.) SE of Fresno; pop. (1990c) 12,743; in irrigated region.

Din·wid·die \'din-,wi-dē, ,din-'wi-\. **1.** County in SE Virginia. See table at VIRGINIA.

2. Village, its ⊗, 15 mi. (24 km.) SW of Petersburg; scene of Union Gen. Philip Sheridan's defeat of Confederate Gen. George Pickett near Dinwiddie Courthouse before fall of Petersburg 1865, a part of the battle of Five Forks.

Di·oc·lea \dī-'ä-klē-ə\. See SALONAE.

Di·o·mede Islands \'dī-ə-,mēd\. Two islands **Big Diomede** (also known as **Rat·ma·nov** \rət-'mä-nəf\; belongs to Russia) and **Little Diomede** (belongs to U.S.) in middle of Bering Strait, ab. 2 mi. (3 km.) apart; separated by International Date Line. First European visitor Vitus Bering, Danish explorer in the employ of Russia, on Aug. 16, 1728 (St. Diomedes' Day); Big Diomede has important Russian weather station.

Di·on \'dī-,än\. Greek town, ancient Palestine; in the Decapolis (*q.v.*).

Dio·ny·si·a·des \,dī-ə-nə-'sī-ə-,dēz\. Group of small islands in Mediterranean Sea just W of Cape Sidero, NE point of Crete; belong to Greece.

Dioscurias. See SUKHUMI.

Diospolis *or* **Diospolis Magna.** See THEBES 1.

Diour·bel \dyür-'bel\. Town, Senegal, E of Dakar; pop. (1988c) 77,550.

Di·po·log \dē-'pō-,lōg\. Municipality, ✻ of Zamboanga del Norte prov., Mindanao, Philippines, on S coast of passage bet. Sulu Sea and Mindanao Sea; pop. (1990p) 80,000.

Di·rec·tion, Cape \də-'rek-shən\. Cape, cen. E coast of Cape York Penin., Queensland, NE Australia.

Di·re Da·wa *or* **Di·re·da·wa** \,dē-rā-'dau̇-ä\. City, E Ethiopia, on the Addis Ababa-Djibouti railroad line; pop. (1989e) 121,887; meat and coffee processing; hides and textiles, cement; railroad workshops; taken by British Mar. 30, 1941.

Di·ri·am·ba \,dē-rē-'äm-bä\. Town, Carazo dept., SW Nicaragua, 20 mi. (32 km.) S of Managua; munic. pop. (1985e) 19,728.

Diriyah *or* **Dir'īyah, ad.** See AD DIR'ĪYAH.

Dirk Har·tog Island \'dərk-'här-,tȯg, -,täg\. Island off W coast of Western Australia, Australia, 25°48′S, 113°E; 239 sq. mi. (619 sq. km.).

Dirschau. See TCZEW.

Dis·ap·point·ment, Cape \,di-sə-'pȯint-mənt\. Cape on SW extremity of Pacific co., SW Washington, on N side of entrance to Columbia River.

Disappointment, Lake. Dry salt lake, N cen. Western Australia, Australia, crossed by Tropic of Capricorn.

Disappointment Islands. Small island group, N Tuamotu Archipelago, French Polynesia, S Pacific Ocean.

Dis·cov·ery Bay \dis-'kə-və-rē\. Inlet of Indian Ocean, S coast of Australia, at boundary bet. Victoria and South Australia.

\ə\ abut \ə\ matches \ᵊ\ kitten, Fr table \ər\ further \a\ ash \ā\ ace \ä\ cot, cart \á\ Fr bac \au̇\ out \b\ Span Avila \ch\ chin \e\ bet \ē\ easy \g\ go \i\ hit \ī\ ice \j\ job \k\ Ger ich, Buch \$^n$\ Fr vin \ŋ\ sing \ō\ go \ȯ\ all \ȯ\ law \œ\ Fr bœuf \œ̄\ Fr feu \ȯi\ boy \th\ thin \th\ this \ü\ loot \u̇\ foot \ue\ Ger füllen \u̅e̅\ Fr rue \y\ yet \$^y$\ Fr digne \'dēn^y\, nuit \'nw^{y}ē\ \yü\ few \yu̇\ fury \zh\ vision

Dis·gra·zia, Mon·te \'mōn-tā-dēs-'grät-syä\. Peak in the Bernina Alps, N Italy, NNW of Sondrio; 12,067 ft. (3678 m.).

Dis·ko. See QEQERTARSUAQ.

Disko Bay. See QEQERTARSUUP TUNUA BAY.

Dis·mal Swamp *or* **Great Dismal Swamp** \'diz-məl\. Swamp area, SE Virginia and NE North Carolina; ab. 30 mi. (48 km.) long, 10 mi. (16 km.) wide; traversed by **Dismal Swamp Canal** (22 mi. or 35 km. long) connecting Chesapeake Bay with Albemarle Sound.

Dis·na \dyis-'nä, 'dyēs-nə\ *or Pol.* **Dzis·na** \'jēs-nä\. **1.** River, Belarus, flows E into Western Dvina River at Disna.
2. Town, N Belarus, 128 mi. (206 km.) NE of Vilnius, Lithuania; formerly in Poland; on Russian border following First Partition of Poland 1772; passed to Russia with Second Partition 1793.

Dis·pur \dis-'pu̇r\. City, ✻ of Assam, India, near Meghalaya border.

Dis·raë·li \diz-'rā-lē\. Village, S Quebec, Canada, 43 mi. (69 km.) NNE of Sherbrooke; pop. (1991c) 2749.

Dis·te·ghil \ˌdēs-tə-'gēl\. Peak in the Himalayas, in region controlled by Pakistan, 36°22′N, 75°12′E; 25,871 ft. (7885 m.).

District Heights. Town, Prince Georges co., S cen. Maryland, SE of Washington, D.C.; pop. (1990c) 6704.

District of Co·lum·bia \kə-'ləm-bē-ə\. Federal district of U.S.A., coextensive with the city of Washington (see WASHINGTON 5), bounded on N, E, and S by Maryland, and on W by Virginia; 69 sq. mi. (179 sq. km.) [land area 61 sq. mi. or 158 sq. km.]; pop. (1990c) 609,909; estimated pop. during WWII 1,250,000.
Official flower: American Beauty rose.
Motto: E Pluribus Unum (One Out of Many).
History: Territory for seat of federal government orig. 100 sq. mi. (259 sq. km.); authorized by congressional act 1790 and granted by Maryland and Virginia; site of Washington chosen by President George Washington, occupied by government 1800; part (see ALEXANDRIA 6) retroceded to Virginia 1847; slave trade forbidden in District 1850 and slavery abolished 1862; territorial government abolished 1874 in favor of government by a commission appointed by the President (formalized by Act of Congress 1878); by annexing Georgetown (*q.v.*), city of Washington became coterminous with federal district; granted suffrage in national elections 1961 by 23d Amendment to U.S. Constitution; mayor-council government estab. 1967; orig. appointees of the President, mayor and councillors became elected officials 1973, and received local legislative powers 1974.

Distrito Federal Spanish and Portuguese form of *Federal District.* See FEDERAL DISTRICT.

Di·sūq \di-'sük\. Town, Kafr ash Shaykh governorate, Lower Egypt, on Rosetta branch of the Nile E of Damanhūr; pop. (1986p) 78,119.

Dith·mar·schen \'dit-ˌmär-shən\ *or Eng.* **Dit·marsh** \-ˌmärsh\. Region, SW Schleswig-Holstein, Germany, bet. the Elbe and Eider rivers; partly marsh, partly sandy; in Holy Roman Emperor Charlemagne's time known as **Nord·al·bin·gia** \ˌnȯr-dal-'bin-jē-ə, -jə\; peasant independent self-government formed in Middle Ages, finally overcome in 1559 and divided; annexed with Schleswig-Holstein to Prussia 1866.

Diu \'dē-ü\. A constituent part of the union terr. of Daman and Diu, W India, 170 mi. (274 km.) NW of Bombay; 14 sq. mi. (36 sq. km.); comprises island, seaport town, and two small towns on the mainland; formerly part of the union terr. of Goa, Daman, and Diu. Came into Portuguese possession in 1535; invaded and annexed by India 1961.

Di·ua·ta Mountains \dē-'wä-tä\. Mountain range, NE Mindanao, Philippines, running N and S along boundary of Agusan del Norte prov.; highest peak Mt. Hilonghilong 6599 ft. (2011 m.).

Diuata Point. Point on NE coast of Mindanao, Philippines, marking boundary bet. Agusan del Norte and Misamis Oriental provs. and also W side of entrance to Butuan Bay.

Dives \'dēv\ *or in full* **Dives–sur–Mer** \-sᵫr-'mer\. Town, Calvados dept., NW France; on the Bay of the Seine; site from which William the Conqueror, duke of Normandy, set sail on his first attempt to reach England 1066 (see SAINT-VALÉRY-SUR-SOMME).

Di·vide \də-'vīd\. County in NW corner of North Dakota. See table at NORTH DAKOTA.

Divide Mountain. Peak, E border of Glacier National Park, NW Montana; ab. 8655 ft. (2638 m.).

Di·vid·ing Ridge \də-'vīd-iŋ\. Ridge extending along W section of boundary bet. Virginia and West Virginia.

Di·vion \dē-'vyōⁿ\. Commune, Pas-de-Calais dept., N France, 17 mi. (27 km.) NW of Arras; pop. (1968c) 10,407; coal deposits.

Di·vi·sion Peak \də-'vi-zhən\. Mountain, W Humboldt co., NW Nevada; 8585 ft. (2617 m.).

Divisões, Serra das. See SERRA DAS DIVISÕES.

Divodurum *or* **Divodurum Mediomatricum.** See METZ.

Divona. See CAHORS.

Di·wa·ni·yah, Ad. See AD DĪWĀNĪYAH.

Dix \'diks\. River, cen. Kentucky; flows N into Kentucky River. See DIX RIVER DAM.

Dix·ie \'dik-sē\. **1.** The states of the SE United States and esp. those which comprised the Confederacy.
2. Coastal county in NW peninsula of Florida. See table at FLORIDA.

Dix·moor \'diks-ˌmȯr\. Village, Cook co., NE Illinois, S of Chicago; pop. (1990c) 3647.

Dix Mountain. Peak in the Adirondack Mts., Essex co., NE New York; 4857 ft. (1480 m.).

Dixmuide *or* **Dixmude.** See DIKSMUIDE.

Dix·on \'dik-sən\. **1.** County in NE Nebraska. See table at NEBRASKA.
2. City, Solano co., cen. California, 20 mi. (32 km.) SW of Sacramento; pop. (1990c) 10,401.
3. City, ⊗ of Lee co., N Illinois, 40 mi. (64 km.) SSW of Rockford; pop. (1990c) 15,144; cement, electronic equipment; Sauk Valley Coll. (1965); founded 1830. Here, on the site of Fort Dixon, stands a statue of Abraham Lincoln as captain in Black Hawk War (1832).
4. City, ⊗ of Webster co., W Kentucky; pop. (1990c) 552; coal deposits.

Dixon Entrance. Strait bet. N Queen Charlotte Is., Canada, and S Prince of Wales I., SE Alaska, and W British Columbia; ab. 40 mi. (64 km.) wide; connects Hecate Strait with the Pacific Ocean.

Dix River Dam. Dam across Dix River in Kentucky; height 275 ft. (84 m.); completed 1925; waterpower.

Di·ya·la *or* **Di·a·la** \dē-'ä-lä\. River, cen. Iraq; rises in mountains of N Iraq, flows SW into the Tigris River at Baghdad; ab. 275 mi. (440 km.) long; navigable for 50 mi. (80 km.); traverses a fertile region.

Di·yar·ba·kır \di-ˌyär-bä-'kər\ *or* **Di·ar·bekr** \-'be-kər\. **1.** Province of Turkey in Asia. See table at TURKEY.
2. *anc.* **Am·i·da** \'a-mi-də\. Commercial city, its ✻, on right bank of the Tigris; pop. (1990c) 381,144; trades in wool, copper, grains, melons, cotton, and petroleum; esp. flourishing in 19th cent. As Amida became Roman colony 230 A.D.; captured 4th cent. by Shapur II of Persia; held at various times by Romans, Persians, and Arabs before finally being taken by Ottoman Turks 1515.

Diz, Ab–i–. See DEZ.

Dizful. See DEZFŪL.

Djailolo. See HALMAHERA.

Djai·lo·lo Passage \jī-'lō-lō\. Strait bet. SE Halmahera I. on the W and the small islands off W Waigeo I. on the E, in the Moluccas, E Malay Archipelago, E Indonesia; connects Ceram Sea with the Pacific Ocean; extreme width is ab. 100 mi. (160 km.).

Djaja Peak. See JAYA, PUNCAK.

Djajapura. See JAYAPURA.

Djajawidjaja Range. See JAYAWIJAYA RANGE.

Djakarta. See JAKARTA.

Djakarta Bay. See JAKARTA BAY.

Djakovica. See ĐAKOVICA.

Djakovo. See ĐAKOVO.

Djam·bi \'jäm-bē\. **1.** River, Sumatra, Indonesia. See HARI.

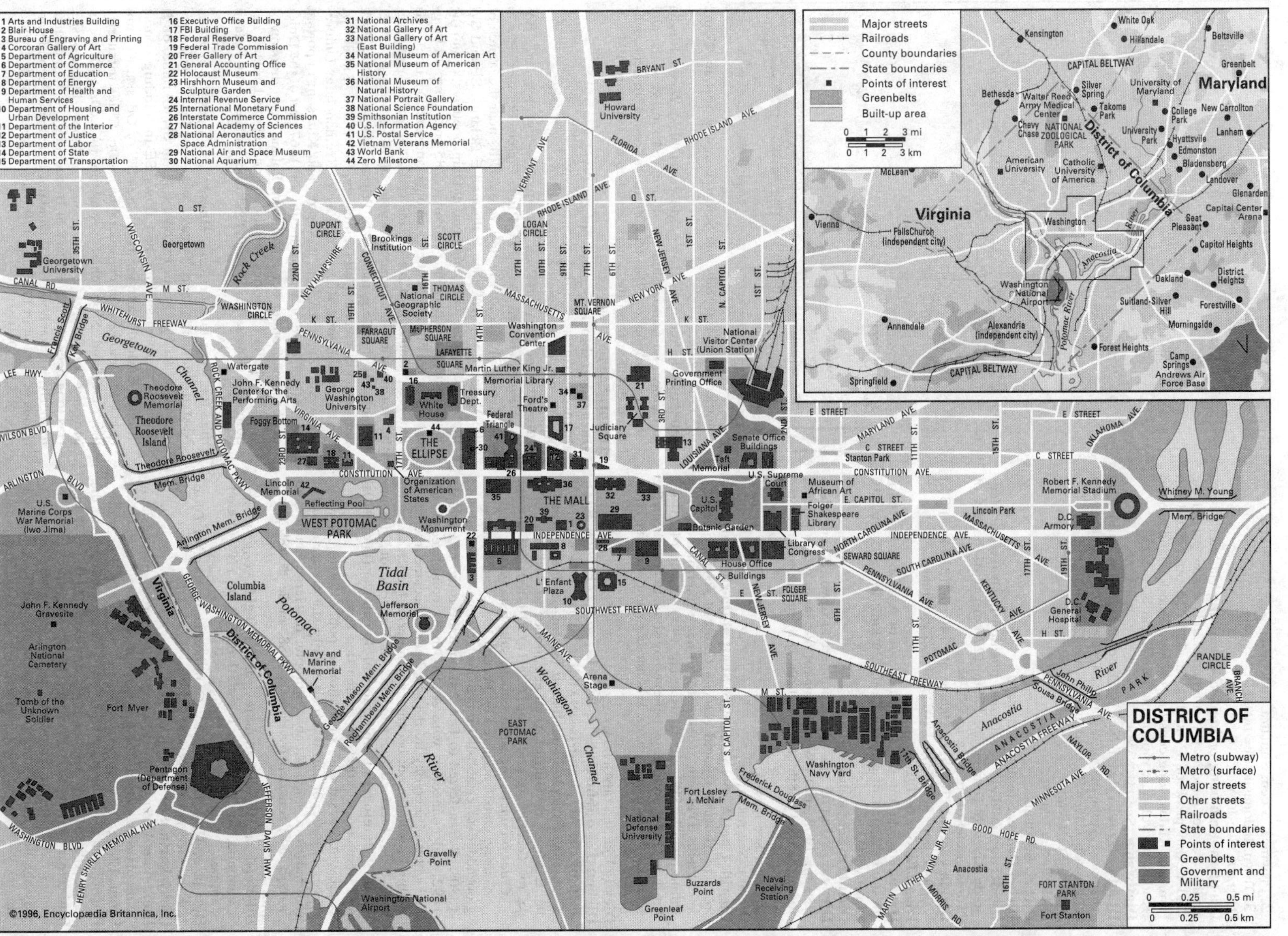
DISTRICT OF COLUMBIA
Metro (subway)
Metro (surface)
Major streets
Other streets
Railroads
State boundaries
Points of interest
Greenbelts
Government and Military
0 0.25 0.5 mi
0 0.25 0.5 km
1 Arts and Industries Building
2 Blair House
3 Bureau of Engraving and Printing
4 Corcoran Gallery of Art
5 Department of Agriculture
6 Department of Commerce
7 Department of Education
8 Department of Energy
9 Department of Health and Human Services
10 Department of Housing and Urban Development
11 Department of the Interior
12 Department of Justice
13 Department of Labor
14 Department of State
15 Department of Transportation
16 Executive Office Building
17 FBI Building
18 Federal Reserve Board
19 Federal Trade Commission
20 Freer Gallery of Art
21 General Accounting Office
22 Holocaust Museum
23 Hirshhorn Museum and Sculpture Garden
24 Internal Revenue Service
25 International Monetary Fund
26 Interstate Commerce Commission
27 National Academy of Sciences
28 National Aeronautics and Space Administration
29 National Air and Space Museum
30 National Aquarium
31 National Archives
32 National Gallery of Art
33 National Gallery of Art (East Building)
34 National Museum of American Art
35 National Museum of American History
36 National Museum of Natural History
37 National Portrait Gallery
38 National Science Foundation
39 Smithsonian Institution
40 U.S. Information Agency
41 U.S. Postal Service
42 Vietnam Veterans Memorial
43 World Bank
44 Zero Milestone
Major streets
Railroads
County boundaries
State boundaries
Points of interest
Greenbelts
Built-up area
0 1 2 3 mi
0 1 2 3 km
Maryland
Virginia
District of Columbia
Kensington
White Oak
Hillandale
Beltsville
Greenbelt
CAPITAL BELTWAY
Bethesda
Walter Reed Army Medical Center
Silver Spring
Takoma Park
University of Maryland
College Park
New Carrollton
Lanham
Chevy Chase
NATIONAL ZOOLOGICAL PARK
University Park
Hyattsville
Edmonston
Bladensberg
Landover
Glenarden
American University
Catholic University of America
McLean
Vienna
FallsChurch (independent city)
Washington
Anacostia
Seat Pleasant
Capital Center Arena
Capitol Heights
Oakland
District Heights
Washington National Airport
Suitland-Silver Hill
Forestville
Annandale
Alexandria (independent city)
Potomac River
Morningside
Forest Heights
Camp Springs
Andrews Air Force Base
Springfield
Georgetown University
Georgetown
Rock Creek
WISCONSIN AVE.
CANAL RD.
M ST.
WHITEHURST FREEWAY
Francis Scott Key Bridge
Georgetown Channel
Theodore Roosevelt Memorial
Theodore Roosevelt Island
LEE HWY.
WILSON BLVD.
ARLINGTON BLVD.
U.S. Marine Corps War Memorial (Iwo Jima)
John F. Kennedy Gravesite
Arlington National Cemetery
Tomb of the Unknown Soldier
Fort Myer
Pentagon (Department of Defense)
WASHINGTON BLVD.
HENRY SHIRLEY MEMORIAL HWY.
JEFFERSON DAVIS HWY.
GEORGE WASHINGTON MEMORIAL PKWY
Columbia Island
Potomac
Navy and Marine Memorial
George Mason Mem. Bridge
Rochambeau Mem. Bridge
Gravelly Point
Washington National Airport
River
EAST POTOMAC PARK
Washington Channel
Tidal Basin
Jefferson Memorial
Arlington Mem. Bridge
Theodore Roosevelt Mem. Bridge
ROCK CREEK AND POTOMAC PKWY
Watergate
John F. Kennedy Center for the Performing Arts
Foggy Bottom
George Washington University
WASHINGTON CIRCLE
DUPONT CIRCLE
Brookings Institution
SCOTT CIRCLE
THOMAS CIRCLE
National Geographic Society
LOGAN CIRCLE
FARRAGUT SQUARE
McPHERSON SQUARE
LAFAYETTE SQUARE
Martin Luther King Jr. Memorial Library
Washington Convention Center
MT. VERNON SQUARE
White House
Treasury Dept.
THE ELLIPSE
Federal Triangle
Ford's Theatre
Judiciary Square
Lincoln Memorial
Reflecting Pool
WEST POTOMAC PARK
Organization of American States
Washington Monument
THE MALL
L'Enfant Plaza
SOUTHWEST FREEWAY
MAINE AVE.
Arena Stage
Howard University
BRYANT ST.
RHODE ISLAND AVE.
FLORIDA AVE.
NEW YORK AVE.
NEW JERSEY AVE.
MASSACHUSETTS AVE.
PENNSYLVANIA AVE.
CONNECTICUT AVE.
NEW HAMPSHIRE AVE.
VERMONT AVE.
VIRGINIA AVE.
CONSTITUTION AVE.
INDEPENDENCE AVE.
Government Printing Office
National Visitor Center (Union Station)
Senate Office Buildings
Taft Memorial
U.S. Capitol
Botanic Garden
U.S. Supreme Court
Library of Congress
Folger Shakespeare Library
Museum of African Art
House Office Buildings
FOLGER SQUARE
CANAL ST.
Stanton Park
SEWARD SQUARE
MARYLAND AVE.
NORTH CAROLINA AVE.
SOUTH CAROLINA AVE.
E. CAPITOL ST.
Lincoln Park
KENTUCKY AVE.
POTOMAC AVE.
SOUTHEAST FREEWAY
Robert F. Kennedy Memorial Stadium
Whitney M. Young Mem. Bridge
D.C. Armory
D.C. General Hospital
OKLAHOMA AVE.
RANDLE CIRCLE
BRANCH AVE.
John Philip Sousa Bridge
PARK
Anacostia
ANACOSTIA FREEWAY
Anacostia Bridge
11th St. Bridge
Washington Navy Yard
Frederick Douglass Mem. Bridge
Fort Lesley J. McNair
National Defense University
Buzzards Point
Greenleaf Point
Naval Receiving Station
S. CAPITOL ST.
M ST.
MARTIN LUTHER KING JR. AVE.
MORRIS RD.
GOOD HOPE RD.
MINNESOTA AVE.
NAYLOR RD.
FORT STANTON PARK
Fort Stanton
©1996, Encyclopædia Britannica, Inc.

2. Province, S cen. Sumatra, Indonesia. See JAMBI 1.
3. Town, Indonesia. See JAMBI 2.

Djapara. See JEPARA.

Dja·pa·ra–Rem·bang *or* **Ja·pa·ra–Rembang** \jä-'pä-rä-'rem-ˌbäŋ\. Former residency, Netherlands Indies, now part of the Indonesian prov. of Central Java; 2339 sq. mi. (6058 sq. km.); ✻ Kudus; long coastline on Java Sea; lowland around Kudus but volcanic mountains in NW and S.

Djatiwangi. See JATIWANGI.

Djaul *or* **Dyaul** \'dyau̇l, 'jau̇l\. Island, Papua New Guinea, in Bismarck Archipelago, W Pacific Ocean; 30 mi. (48 km.) off NW coast of New Ireland; ab. 14 mi. (23 km.) long.

Djawa. See JAVA.

Djebeïl. See JUBAYL.

Djebel. See JEBEL.

Djebel Druze. See JEBEL ED DRUZ.

Dje·dei·da \je-'dā-də\. Railroad junction town on the Medjerda River, N Tunisia, ab. 17 mi. (27 km.) W of the city of Tunis; scene of fighting in WWII.

Djel·fa \'jel-fə\. Town, N Algeria, ab. 140 mi. (225 km.) S of Algiers; pop. (1987p) 84,207; railroad terminal.

Djem, El. See EL DJEM.

Dje·ma·dja \je-'mä-jä\. Largest island of Anambas Is., Indonesia, in W part of group; 15 mi. (26 km.) long, 10 mi. (16 km.) wide.

Djember. See JEMBER.

Djen·né *or* **Jen·né** \je-'nā\. Commercial town, S cen. Mali, 250 mi. (402 km.) NW of Bamako; has large mud mosque; town founded c. 8th cent.; fl. 12th–16th cents.; taken by the French 1893.

Djepara. See JEPARA.

Djerba. See JERBA.

Dje·rid, Chott \ˌshȯt-je-'rēd\ *or* **Shaṭṭ al–Ja·rīd** \ˌshat-al-jä-'rēd\ *or* **Shott el Dje·rid** \el-\ *or* **Chott el Je·rid** \je-'rēd\; *anc.* **Pa·lus Tri·to·nis** \'pā-ləs-trī-'tō-nəs\. Intermittently wet saline plain in SW cen. Tunisia; ab. 1900 sq. mi. (4920 sq. km.); in Greek mythology believed by some to have been the scene of the birth of Athena, whence her name *Athena Tritogeneia.*

Djevdjelija See GEVGELIJA.

Dji·bou·ti *also* **Ji·bu·ti** \ji-'bü-tē\. **1.** *1967–77* **French Territory of the Afars and Is·sas** \ä-'fär, -'färz … ē-'sä, -'säz\; *1885–1967* **French So·ma·li·land** \sō-'mä-lē-ˌland\. Republic, E Africa, on Gulf of Aden at entrance to Red Sea; 8880 sq. mi. (22,999 sq. km.); pop. (1991e) 510,000; ✻ Djibouti.

Chief products: hides, livestock, salt; fishing.

History: Obock acquired by French 1862; surrounding region added to establish French protectorate of Somaliland 1880s; ✻ transferred to Djibouti on trade route to Ethiopia 1892; rail connection with Addis Ababa completed 1917; had status of a colony until 1946 when it became a territory within French Union; became a member of French Community 1958; received independence as Republic of Djibouti, June 1977; refugees from Ethiopian-Somali war (late 1970s) and from civil conflicts in Eritrea fled here.

2. City, its ✻, on Gulf of Tadjoura; pop. (1991e) 300,000; serves as entrepôt and transport supply station; terminus of railroad from Addis Ababa, Ethiopia; has large landlocked harbor; salt; founded by French 1888; made ✻ 1892, free port 1949.

Dji·djel·li *or* **Ji·jel·li** \ˌjē-je-'lē\; *anc.* **Igil·gi·li** \ē-ˌjil-je-'lē\. Commune, NE Algeria, on coast 50 mi. (80 km.) NW of Constantine.

Djoc·ja *or* **Djok·ja** \'jȯ-kyə\. Common short form of *Djokjakarta.* See YOGYAKARTA.

Djokjakarta. See YOGYAKARTA.

Djom·bang \'jȯm-ˌbäŋ\. Town, East Java prov., Indonesia, in wide plain ab. 40 mi. (64 km.) SW of Surabaya.

Djouf, El. See EL DJOUF.

Djur·dju·ra *also* **Jur·jura** \ju̇r-'ju̇r-ə\. Mountain range of the Little Atlas Mts., N Algeria; highest point 7572 ft. (2308 m.).

Dmi·tri·ya Lap·te·va, Pro·liv \'prȯ-lyif-də-'mē-trē-ə-'läp-tyi-və\ *or* **Dmi·tri Lap·tev Strait** \də-'mē-trē-'läp-tyif\. Passage bet. mainland of N Sakha Rep., and Bol'shoy Lyakhovskiy Ostrov of the Lyakhovskiye Ostrova, N Russia in Asia; connects East Siberian Sea and Laptev Sea; ab. 27 mi. (43 km.) wide.

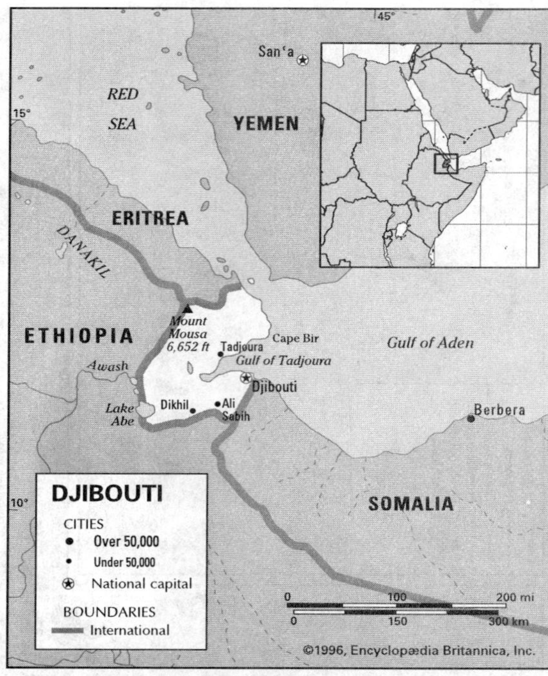

Dmi·trov \də-'mē-trəf\. Town, Moscow Oblast, W cen. Russia in Europe, on railroad line ab. 40 mi. (64 km.) N of the city of Moscow; pop. (1991e) 65,600; dates from 12th cent.; suffered damage from the Tatars; reached by Germans 1941.

Dnepr. See DNIEPER.

Dneprodzerzhinsk. See DNIPRODZERZHYNS'K.

Dnepropetrovsk. See DNIPROPETROVS'K.

Dnestr. See DNIESTER.

Dnie·per \'nē-pər\ *or Russ.* **Dne·pr** \də-'nyeprᵊ\; *anc.* **Bo·rys·the·nes** \bȯ-'ris-thə-ˌnēz\. River, E cent. Europe; rises in Smolensk Oblast, Russia in S Valdai Hills near the source of the Volga, flows SW, then S through E Belarus, SE and SW through Ukraine, with a big bend at Dnipropetrovs'k, into the Black Sea near Kherson; 1420 mi. (2285 km.) long; 3d longest river of Europe (after the Volga and the Danube), has drainage basin of 194,208 sq. mi. (502,999 sq. km.); navigable for most of its course to a point above Smolensk. Chief tributaries: the Berezina, Sozh, Pripyat', Desna, Sula, Psel, and Vorskla rivers. Chief cities on its course: Smolensk, Orsha, Mahilyow, Kiev, Cherkassy, Kremenchug, Dnipropetrovs'k, Zaporizhzhya, Nikopol', and Kherson; important for hydroelectric power production. In 1667 part of the Dnieper became frontier bet. Russia and Poland upon division of Ukraine; large territories on upper and middle Dnieper acquired by Russia in First and Second partitions of Poland 1772 and 1793.

Dnies·ter \'nēs-tər\ *or Russ.* **Dnes·tr** \də-'nyestrᵊ\ *or Rom.* **Ni·stru** \'nē-ˌstrü\; *anc.* **Ty·ras** \'tī-rəs\ *or* **Da·nas·tris** \də-'nas-trəs\. River, S cen. Europe; rises in SW Ukraine, on N slope of Carpathian Mts. and flows SE in winding course through E Moldova to the Black Sea SW of Odessa; 877 mi. (1411 km.) long; has considerable traffic. Chief tributaries the Seret and Stry; chief towns on its course: Khotin, Mogilev-Podol'skiy, Tighina, and Belgorod-Dnestrovski. Has long been the E boundary of Bessarabia; much of course formerly in or on border of Poland until First and Second partitions of Poland in 1772 and 1793; its entire course fell within U.S.S.R. 1940–91.

Dni·pro·dzer·zhyns'k *or* **Dne·pro·dzer·zhinsk** \də-ˌnye-prə-dzir-ˈzhēnsk\; *formerly* **Ka·men·sko·ye** \ˈkä-min-skə-yə\. City, cen. Dnipropetrovs'k Region, E cen. Ukraine, on right bank of the Dnieper ab. 20 mi. (32 km.) W of the city of Dnipropetrovs'k; pop. (1991e) 284,000; cement, chemicals; founded c. 1750; renamed 1936; dam on Dnieper completed 1964.

Dni·pro·pe·trovs'k *or* **Dne·pro·pe·trovsk** \də-ˌnye-prə-pē-ˈtrȯfsk\. **1.** Administrative subdivision of Ukraine, crossed by the Dnieper River; 12,317 sq. mi. (31,901 sq. km.); pop. (1991e) 3,908,700; ✻ Dnipropetrovs'k; manganese, iron ore; winter wheat, corn; formed 1932.

2. *formerly* **Eka·te·ri·no·slav** \i-ˌkä-ti-ˈrē-nə-ˌsläf, -ˌsläv\. City, its ✻, on right bank of the Dnieper at its big bend, 120 mi. (193 km.) SW of Kharkiv; pop. (1991e) 1,189,000; railroad junction, a center of the wheat trade of cen. Ukraine, also handles coal, iron; chemicals, footwear, steel, heavy machinery, food products; has railroad bridge across the Dnieper; cathedral; museum; library; university (1919). Founded by Russian statesman Grigory Potemkin 1787 and named Ekaterinoslav after Empress Catherine the Great; renamed 1926; held by Germans 1941–43.

Do·ab \dō-ˈäb\. Tract of land, N India, in Uttar Pradesh bet. the Ganges and the Yamuna rivers from the Siwalik Hills to their junction.

Doane, Mount \ˈdōn\. Peak in Yellowstone National Park, NW Wyoming; 10,656 ft. (3248 m.).

Doane Mountain. Peak, Pennington co., SW South Dakota; 5500 ft. (1676 m.).

Dobbs Ferry \ˈdäbz\. Village, Westchester co., SE New York, on Hudson River 20 mi. (32 km.) N of New York City; pop. (1990c) 9940; residential suburb of New York City; place 1781 where Gen. George Washington and Gen. Jean-Baptiste-Donatien de Vimeur, comte de Rochambeau, planned the Yorktown campaign.

Dö·beln \ˈdœ-bəln\. City, Saxony, E Germany, on the Mulde River 36 mi. (58 km.) ESE of Leipzig; pop. (1981c) 26,866; railroad junction; 15th cent. church.

Do·be·rai \ˈdō-bə-ˌrī\; *formerly* **Vo·gel·kop** \ˈvō-gəl-ˌkäp\ *or* **Be·rau** \bä-ˈrau̇\. Peninsula, NW extension of Irian Jaya, Indonesia, N of Berau Bay; Arfak Mts. extend along N coast; highest point Kwoka 8042 ft. (2451 m.); chief towns Sorong and Manokwari.

Doberan. See BAD DOBERAN.

Do·bo \ˈdō-bō\. Village and only port of Aru Is., Indonesia, on small island off W coast of Wokam I.

Do·brich \ˈdȯ-brēch\ *or Rom.* **Ba·zar·gic** \bä-ˈzär-jēk\ *or 1949–91* **Tol·bu·khin** \tōl-ˈbü-k̲ēn\. City, NE Bulgaria, ab. 25 mi. (40 km.) N of Varna; pop. (1991e) 115,789; in Romania 1913–40.

Do·bru·ja *or* **Do·bru·dja** \ˈdȯ-brü-ˌjä\ *or Rom.* **Do·bro·gea** \ˈdȯ-brü-ˌjä\. Region, SE Romania and NE Bulgaria, comprising Black Sea coastal strip S of Danube River; area 8979 sq. mi. (23,256 sq. km.). Colonized by Greeks and later inhabited by Romans; an autonomous state 14th cent.; in Ottoman Empire 15th cent.; N half given to Romania by Congress of Berlin 1878; S half ceded to Romania by Bulgaria 1913, returned to Bulgaria 1940.

Dob·son \ˈdäb-sən\. Town, ⊗ of Surry co., N North Carolina; pop. (1990c) 1195; Surry Community Coll. (1965).

Do·bu \ˈdō-bü\. Chief settlement of D'Entrecasteaux Is. (*q.v.*), Papua New Guinea, on small island bet. Fergusson and Normanby islands.

Do·ce \ˈdō-sə\. River, E Brazil; rises in S cen. Minas Gerais state, flows E across border of Espírito Santo state and into Atlantic Ocean N of Vitória; ab. 360 mi. (580 km.) long; in a region of many rich iron ore deposits.

Doch·art, Loch \ˈdä-k̲ərt\. Lake, Perth co., cen. Scotland; 3 mi. (5 km.) long.

Doc·tor Pe·dro P. Pe·ña \ˈdȯk-tȯr-ˈpā-t͟hrō-ˈpā-ˈpā-nyä\. Town, W Paraguay, across Pilcomayo River from Argentina.

Doda Betta, Mount. See NILGIRI HILLS.

Dod·dridge \ˈdä-drij\. County in N West Virginia. See table at WEST VIRGINIA.

Do·dec·a·nese \dō-ˈde-kə-ˌnēz, -ˌnēs\ *or* **Do·dec·a·ne·sus** \dō-ˌde-kə-ˈnē-səs\ *or Gk.* **Dho·dhe·ká·ni·sos** \ˌt͟hō-t͟he-ˈkä-nē-ˌsȯs\ *or* **Southern Spor·a·des** \ˈspȯr-ə-ˌdēz, ˈspär-\. Group of islands in SE Aegean Sea, forming a department of Greece (see table at GREECE); included in the Sporades; formerly part of Italian Aegean Is. (Isole Italiane dell 'Egeo); includes 12 main islands (Greek and Italian names): Astipálaia (Stampalia), Kalymnos (Calino), Karpathos (Scarpanto), Kasos (Caso), Khalkē (Calchi), Kos (Coo), Leros (Lero), Lipsos (Lisso or Lipso), Nīsiros (Nisiro), Patmos (Patmo), Sími (Simi), Tílos, and numerous small islands; administrative center Rhodes. Held as part of Ottoman Empire from 16th cent. until 1912; seized (with Rhodes) by Italy in war with Turkey over Tripoli 1912; promised by Italians to Greece 1913 but not surrendered; turned over to Greece after Turkey had ceded them to Italy by Treaty of Sèvres 1920; Rhodes, Dodecanese, and Kastellorizon (*q.v.*) given to Italy in Treaty of Lausanne 1923, restored to Greece by treaty 1947. See AEGEAN ISLANDS, and RHODES.

Dodge \ˈdäj\. Name of counties in four states of the U.S. See tables at GEORGIA, MINNESOTA, NEBRASKA, WISCONSIN.

Dodge City. City, ⊗ of Ford co., S Kansas, on Arkansas River 120 mi. (193 km.) E of Colorado border; pop. (1990c) 21,129; alt. 2480 ft. (756 m.); agricultural implements; wheat, livestock; Dodge City Community Coll. (1935), St. Mary of the Plains Coll. (1952); formerly frontier town and cattle-shipping point on the old Santa Fe Trail; lawmen Wyatt Earp and Bat Masterson worked here; incorp. 1875.

Dodge·ville \ˈdäj-vil\. City, ⊗ of Iowa co., SW Wisconsin, 24 mi. (39 km.) NE of Platteville; pop. (1990c) 3882; lead and zinc deposits nearby.

Dod·man Point \ˈdäd-mən\. Cape on SE coast of Cornwall, SW England.

Do·do·ma \dō-ˈdō-ˌmä\. **1.** Administrative region of NE cen. Tanzania. See table at TANZANIA.

2. Town, its ✻ and since 1974 designated future ✻ of Tanzania.

Do·do·na \də-ˈdō-nə\. Ancient town, on Mt. Tomarus, Epirus, NW Greece, in E part of Thesprotia; a center of Pelasgic worship; site of legendary oracle dedicated to Zeus and consulted from very early times.

Doe·tin·chem \ˈdü-ti-k̲əm\. Commune, Gelderland prov., E Netherlands, E of Arnhem; pop. (1981e) 38,586.

Dog·ger Bank \ˈdȯ-gər, ˈdä-\. Submerged sandbank in cen. North Sea, ab. 60 mi. (97 km.) E of England; fishing; naval battle bet. cruiser squadrons nearby 1915 in which the Germans escaped with one cruiser, the *Blücher,* lost.

Dog Island \ˈdȯg\. Island off S Franklin co., NW Florida; ab. 7 mi. (11 km.) long; separated from mainland by St. George Sound.

Dō·go \ˈdō-gō\. See OKI ARCHIPELAGO.

Do·ha \ˈdō-hə\ *also* **Bi·da** \ˈbē-də\ *or Arab.* **Ad–Daw·hah** \ȧd-ˈdau̇-hə\. Town, ✻ of Qatar, Arabian Penin., on the Persian Gulf; pop. (1986c) 217,294; residence of the sultan; university; 19th cent. Turkish fort; deepwater port since 1970s.

Do·had \ˈdō-ˌhəd\. Town, E Gujarat, W India, 105 mi. (169 km.) ESE of Ahmadabad; pop. (1991p) 66,444.

Doi In·tha·non \ˈdȯi-ˈin-tä-ˌnȯn\. Mountain, NW Thailand, near the upper course of the Ping River 35 mi. (56 km.) WSW of Chiang Mai; 8512 ft. (2594 m.); highest mountain in Thailand.

Doj·ran, Lake *or* **Lake Doi·ran** \ˈdȯi-ˌrän\. Small lake on boundary line bet. N Macedonia, Greece, and the Rep. of Macedonia, E of the Vardar; 18 sq. mi. (47 sq. km.); divided bet. the two countries; scene 1916–18 of conflict bet. Allies (British and French armies) and Central Powers (Germans and Bulgarians). On W shore is the commune of **Dojran**.

Dok·kum \ˈdȯ-kəm\. Town, Friesland prov., N Netherlands, ab. 12 mi. (19 km.) NE of Leeuwarden; pop. (1981e) 12,289; textiles, wire; scene of death of St. Boniface c. 754.

Dol \ˈdȯl\ *or in full* **Dol–de–Bre·tagne** \-də-brə-ˈtän^{y}, -ˈtän-yə\. Commune, Ille-et-Vilaine dept., NW France, SE of St.-Malo; 13th cent. cathedral. On frontier bet. Normandy and Brittany, formerly an important fortress.

Do·lak Island \ˈdō-läk\; *formerly* **Fre·de·rik Hen·drik** \ˈfrā-də-rik-ˈhen-drik\ *also* **Fred·e·rick Hen·ry** \ˈfre-də-rik-ˈhen-rē\. Island in Arafura Sea, off S coast of island of New Guinea; ab. 110 mi. (175 km.) by 55 mi. (90 km.); 3000 sq. mi. (7770 sq. km.); administratively a part of Irian Jaya, Indonesia; low, covered with swamps and jungles.

Dol·beau \dȯl-ˈbō\. Town, S Quebec, Canada, on Mistassini River 8 mi. (13 km.) N of Lac St.-Jean; pop. (1991c) 8181.

Dole \ˈdōl\. Commune, Jura dept., E France, on Doubs River 30 mi. (48 km.) N of Lons-le-Saunier; pop. (1990c) 27,860; 16th cent. church; hospital in Renaissance style; Roman ruins. Important as ✱ of Franche-Comté until taken from Spanish Hapsburgs by Louis XIV 1674 and ✱ moved to Besançon; birthplace of chemist and microbiologist Louis Pasteur 1822.

Dole \ˈdōl\ *or* **La Dôle** \lȧ-\. Peak, Vaud canton, W Switzerland, on French border ab. 16 mi. (26 km.) N of Geneva; 5502 ft. (1677 m.).

Dol·gel·lau \dōl-ˈge-hlī, -hlä, -hle; däl-ˈgeth-li, -lī\. Market town, S Gwynedd, W Wales; formerly ⊗ of Merionethshire co.

Dol·go·prud·nyy *also* **Dol·go·prud·ny** \ˌdȯl-gə-ˈprüd-nē\. Town, Moscow Oblast, W cen. Russia in Europe, 14 mi. (23 km.) NNW of the city of Moscow; pop. (1991e) 71,100.

Do·linsk \dō-ˈlyēnsk\ *or Jp.* **Ochi·ai** \ˌō-chē-ˈī\. Town, Sakhalin I., SE Russia in Asia, on coast 50 mi. (80 km.) N of Korsakov, with which it is connected by rail; formerly Japanese.

Dolisie. See LOUBOMO.

Dolj \ˈdälzh\. County of S Romania. See table at ROMANIA.

Dol·lard des Or·meaux \dō-ˈlȧr-dā-zȯr-ˈmō\. Town, Montreal co., S Quebec, Canada; pop. (1991c) 46,922; residential suburb of the city of Montreal.

Dol·lar Law \ˈdäl-ər-ˌlȯ\. Mountain, Borders region, S Scotland; 2680 ft. (817 m.).

Dol·lart \ˈdȯl-ˌärt\. Basin of upper (S) end of estuary of Ems River, NW Germany and NE Netherlands; 10 mi. (16 km.) long by 7 mi. (11 km.) wide; Emden is on its N shore.

Dolnja Tuzla. See TUZLA.

Do·lo·mites \ˈdō-lə-ˌmīts, ˈdä-\ *or Ital.* **Do·lo·mi·ti** \ˌdō-lō-ˈmē-tē\. See table at ALPS.

Dolonnur *or* **Dolon–nor.** See DUOLON.

Do·lo·res \də-ˈlōr-əs\. **1.** River, SW Colorado and E Utah; rises in NW end of San Juan Mts., Colorado, flows SW, then N and NW across Utah boundary into Colorado River in E cen. Grand co., E Utah; 230 mi. (370 km.) long.
2. County in SW Colorado. See table at COLORADO.
3. \dō-ˈlō-res\. Port, Soriano dept., SW Uruguay, on San Salvador River ab. 18 mi. (29 km.) above its confluence with the Uruguay, ab. 145 mi. (235 km.) NW of Montevideo; shipping point for grain.

Dolores Hi·dal·go \dō-ˈlō-res-ē-ˈt͟häl-gō\. Municipality, Guanajuato state, cen. Mexico, on railroad line 30 mi. (48 km.) NE of the city of Guanajuato; pop. (1990p) 102,200.

Dolores Peak \də-ˈlōr-əs\. Mountain, Dolores and San Miguel cos., SW Colorado; 13,502 ft. (21,725 m.).

Dol·phin, Cape \ˈdäl-fin, ˈdȯl-\. Cape, East Falkland I., extending into South Atlantic Ocean from NW coast.

Dolphin and Un·ion Strait \ˈyü-nyən\. Channel bet. SW Victoria I. and N Canada mainland; connects Coronation Gulf with Amundsen Gulf.

Dolphin Head. **1.** Promontory extending into Atlantic Ocean on SW cen. coast of Namibia.
2. Peak, W Jamaica, West Indies; 1788 ft. (545 m.).

Dol·ton \ˈdōlt-^{ə}n\. Village, Cook co., NE Illinois, just S of Chicago; pop. (1990c) 23,930.

Dom \ˈdōm\. Highest peak in Mischabelhörner, Valais canton, SW cen. Switzerland; 14,913 ft. (4545 m.).

Domb·ås \ˈdȯm-ˌbȯs, ˈdȯ-ˌmȯs\. Village, Oppland co., S cen. Norway, on S edge of Dovrefjell; scene of fighting bet. Allies and Germans Apr. 30–May 2, 1940.

Dombes \ˈdō^{n}b\. Region, S Ain dept., E France, bet. the Ain, Rhone, and Saône rivers; has many low hills and stagnant ponds. Once part of kingdom of Arles, later principality with ✱ at Trévoux; united to crown 1762.

Dombrau. See DĄBROWA GÓRNICZA.

Dôme, Puy de \ˌpwē-də-ˈdōm\. Peak, Puy-de-Dôme dept., S cen. France, W of Clermont-Ferrand; 4806 ft. (1465 m.).

Domel Island. See LETSÔK-AW ISLAND.

Dome Peak \ˈdōm\. **1.** Mountain, N Washington, on boundary bet. Chelan and Skagit cos.; 8920 ft. (2719 m.).
2. Mountain, Yakima co., S Washington; 6586 ft. (2007 m.).

Dome Rock. Height in Scotts Bluff co., W Nebraska; 4560 ft. (1390 m.).

Domeyko, Cordillera. See ANDES.

Dom·front \dȯ^{n}-ˈfrō^{n}\. Commune, W Orne dept., NW France, 30 mi. (48 km.) E of Avranches; Norman stronghold of Middle Ages; scene of fighting in WWII.

Dom·i·ni·ca \ˌdä-mə-ˈnē-kə\. Island republic, West Indies, formerly a self-governing state in association with Great Britain; in center of Lesser Antilles bet. Guadeloupe (S Leeward Is.) and Martinique (N Windward Is.); 289 sq. mi. (749 sq. km.); ab. 29 mi. (47 km.) from N to S, 16 mi. (26 km.) wide; pop. (1993e) 74,000; ✱ Roseau; mountainous and volcanic; highest peak Morne Diablotin 4747 ft. (1447 m.), highest point in the Lesser Antilles; bananas, cocoa, coconuts, limes; soap.

History: Inhabited by Caribs when first sighted by explorer Christopher Columbus 1493; Caribs left in possession until 18th cent.; settled by French from whom English took it 1759 (formally ceded to Britain by Treaty of Paris 1763); captured by French 1778 but restored to Great Britain 1783; incorp. with Leeward Is. 1833; administration transferred to Windward Is. 1940; member of West Indies (Federation) 1958–62; achieved internal self-government 1967; became

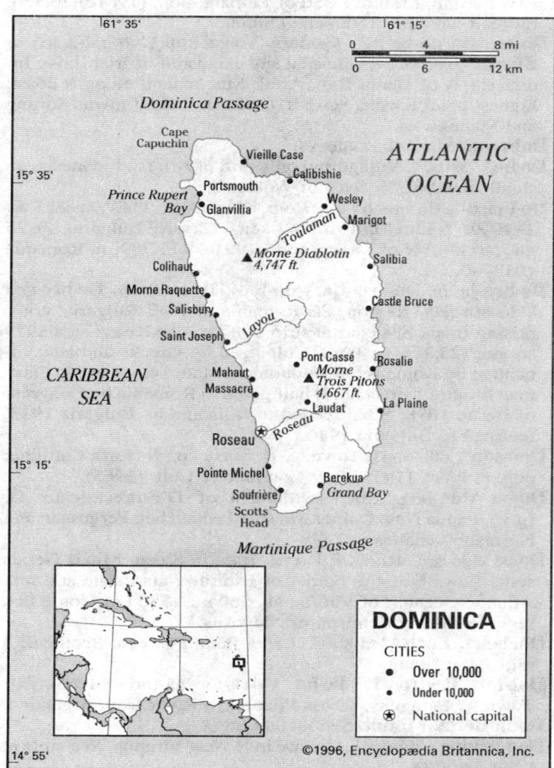

independent 1978; economy ravaged by hurricane damage 1979 and 1980.

Do·min·i·can Republic \də-ˈmi-ni-kən\ *or Sp.* **Re·pú·bli·ca Do·mi·ni·ca·na** \rā-ˈpü-blē-kä-dō-ˌmē-nē-ˈkä-nä\. Republic occupying E two thirds of Hispaniola I., West Indies; 18,657 sq. mi. (48,322 sq. km.); pop. (1993e) 7,634,000; ✱ Santo Domingo.

Physical features: On E terminates in Cape Engaño on Mona Passage (separates Hispaniola from Puerto Rico); Capes Isabela and Francés Viejo are prominent points on N coast and Cape Beata on SW; coastline generally regular except for long peninsula enclosing Bay of Samaná; N part covered by rich Vega Real Valley formed by two streams flowing in opposite directions; cen. part traversed by the Cordillera Central; highest point Pico Duarte, 10,414 ft. (3174 m.), several peaks above 5000 ft. (1500 m.); mountainous SW part contains Lake Enriquillo.

Chief products: Sugar, bananas, cocoa, coffee, rice, cigars and tobacco; nickel; cement.

Chief towns: Santo Domingo and Santiago de los Caballeros.

Political divisions: Divided into the National District and 29 provinces (for pronunciation of their names, see their individual entries):

NAME	AREA (sq. mi.)	AREA (sq. km.)	POP. (1990e)	CAPITAL
National District[1]	570	1,477	2,411,895	
Provinces				
Azua	938	2,430	195,420	Azua
Bahoruco	531	1,376	87,376	Neiba
Barahona	976	2,528	152,405	Barahona
Dajabón	344	890	64,123	Dajabón
Duarte	499	1,292	261,725	San Francisco de Macorís
El Seibo	641	1,659	97,590	El Seibo
Espaillat	386	1,000	182,248	Moca
Hato Mayor	514	1,330	77,823	Hato Mayor
Independencia	719	1,861	43,077	Jimaní
La Altagracia	1,191	3,084	111,241	Higüey
La Estrelleta	690	1,788	72,651	Elías Piña
La Romana	209	541	169,223	La Romana
La Vega	916	2,373	303,047	La Vega
María Trinidad Sánchez	506	1,310	125,148	Nagua
Monseñor Nouel	388	1,004	124,794	Bonao
Monte Cristi	768	1,989	92,678	Monte Cristi
Monte Plata	841	2,179	174,799	Monte Plata
Pedernales	373	967	18,896	Pedernales
Peravia	626	1,622	186,810	Baní
Puerto Plata	726	1,881	229,738	Puerto Plata
Salcedo	206	533	110,216	Salcedo
Samaná	382	989	73,002	Samaná
Sánchez Ramírez	453	1,174	140,635	Cotuí
San Cristóbal	604	1,564	320,921	San Cristóbal
San Juan	1,375	3,561	266,628	San Juan de la Maguana
San Pedro de Macorís	450	1,166	197,862	San Pedro de Macorís
Santiago	1,205	3,122	704,835	Santiago
Santiago Rodríguez	394	1,020	61,570	Sabaneta
Valverde	220	570	111,470	Mao

[1]Comprises the capital city of Santo Domingo and surrounding area.

History: For earlier history, see HISPANIOLA. Created 1844 after revolt against Haitian politician Jean-Pierre Boyer's rule of entire island of Hispaniola; except for brief period (1861–65) of annexation to Spain, has since then been independent, although its customs were controlled by U.S. 1905–41, and it was under U.S. military occupation 1916–24; termination of dictatorship of Rafael Trujillo 1961; civil war 1965, leading to U.S. military intervention; adoption of new constitution 1966; severe hurricane 1979; riots 1984 to protest food price increases.

Do·min·ion \də-ˈmin-yən\. Town, Cape Breton co., E Nova Scotia, Canada, on Atlantic Ocean 7 mi. (11 km.) ENE of Sydney; pop. (1991c) 2517; coal deposits.

Dom·joch \ˈdōm-ˌyȯk\. Mountain pass over the Mischabelhörner, S of the Dom, Valais canton, SW cen. Switzerland; elev. 14,060 ft. (4285 m.).

Dom·mel \ˈdȯ-məl\. River, S Netherlands; rises in Belgium, flows N across the border through cen. North Brabant prov., S Netherlands, into the Meuse; ab. 62 mi. (100 km.) long.

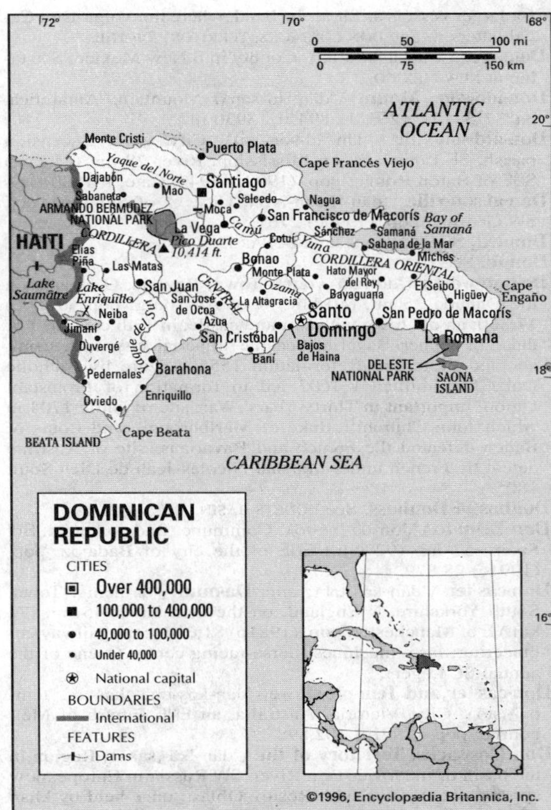

Do·mo \ˈdō-mō\. Small village, E Ethiopia, near the border of Somalia.

Do·mo·dos·so·la \ˌdō-mō-ˈdȯs-sō-lä\; *anc.* **Do·mus Dei** \ˈdō-məs-ˈdē-ˌī, ˈdā-ˌē\. Commune, Novara prov., Piedmont, NW Italy, in river valley 47 mi. (76 km.) N of Novara near Italian end of Simplon Tunnel; pop. (1981p) 20,069.

Dom·ré·my–la–Pu·celle \ˌdōⁿ-rā-ˈmē-lä-pue-ˈsel\. Village, Vosges dept., NE France, on the Meuse; birthplace of French national heroine Joan of Arc c. 1412.

Domus Dei. See DOMODOSSOLA.

Do·mu·yo \dō-ˈmü-yō\. Volcanic peak in the Andes, N Neuquén prov., Argentina, near Chilean boundary; 15,446 ft. (4708 m.).

Don \ˈdän\. **1.** River, Yorkshire, N cen. England; flows NE into the Ouse at Goole; 70 mi. (113 km.) long.

2. River, Grampian region, NE Scotland; flows E into North Sea 1.5 mi. (2.4 km.) N of Aberdeen; 82 mi. (132 km.) long.

3. \ˈdȯn\ *or Tatar* **Du·na** \ˈdü-nə\; *anc.* **Tan·a·is** \ˈta-nē-is\. River, SW Russia in Europe; rises just SE of Tula, flows SE in a big bend to within 48 mi. (77 km.) of the Volga, then turns SW to the Sea of Azov (Gulf of Taganrog) at Rostov-na-Donu; 1224 mi. (1969 km.) long; its drainage basin of 170,849 sq. mi. (442,499 sq. km.) covers E part of rich black-earth region; has abundant fish (salmon and herring) and along its banks are many fishing villages; the only cities of size along its course are Rostov-na-Donu and Voronezh; chief tributaries: Manych, Donets, Chir, Medveditsa, Khoper, Voronezh, and Sosna rivers. Although shallow it is navigable for larger vessels as far as the bend, where the Volga-Don Canal enters it. See DON COSSACKS, TERRITORY OF THE.

Do·na Ana \ˈdō-nyə-ˈa-nə\. County in S New Mexico. See table at NEW MEXICO.

Don·ald·son, Mount \ˈdän-ᵊld-sən\. Mountain, Antarctica, 84°37′S, 172°12′E; 12,894 ft. (3930 m.).

Don·ald·son·ville \ˈdän-ᵊld-sən-ˌvil\. City, ⊗ of Ascension parish, SE Louisiana, on Mississippi River 28 mi. (45 km.) SSE of Baton Rouge; pop. (1990c) 7949; state ✻ 1830–31.

Don·al·son·ville \ˈdän-ᵊl-sən-ˌvil\. City, ⊗ of Seminole co., SW Georgia; pop. (1990c) 2761.

Donard, Slieve. See SLIEVE DONARD.

Donau. See DANUBE.

Do·nau·wörth \ˈdō-naů-ˌvœrt\. Town, Bavaria, Germany, on the Danube 25 mi. (40 km.) N of Augsburg; pop. (1980c) 17,860; an old town with fort and castle; in 13th cent. seat of duke of Upper Bavaria; became imperial city 14th cent.; adopted Protestant Reformation 1555; seizure by Catholic Duke Maximillian I 1607 led to formation of Protestant Union; important in Thirty Years' War; site of battle 1704 in which John Churchill, duke of Marlborough, and Louis of Baden defeated the French and Bavarians; site of Austrian defeat by French under Marshal Nicolas-Jean de Dieu Soult 1805.

Donbas *or* **Donbass.** See DONETS BASIN.

Don Be·ni·to \ˈdōn-bā-ˈnē-tō\. Commune, Badajoz prov., SW Spain, 57 mi. (92 km.) ENE of the city of Badajoz; pop. (1991c) 28,879.

Don·cas·ter \ˈdäŋ-kəs-tər\; *anc.* **Da·num** \ˈdā-nəm\. Town, South Yorkshire, N England, on the Don River 45 mi. (72 km.) E of Manchester; pop. (1981p) 81,610; coal; railway engineering; farm machines; horse-racing center (scene of the annual St. Leger).

Don·cas·ter and Tem·ple·stowe \ˈdäŋ-kəs-tər, -ˌkas- ... ˈtem-pəl-ˌstō\. City, Victoria, Australia, an ENE suburb of Melbourne; pop. (1991c) 102,898.

Don Cos·sacks, Territory of the \ˈdän-ˈkä-ˌsaks\. Region in the basin of the lower Don River, SW Russia in Europe, now approx. coextensive with Rostov Oblast; once held by khan of the Crimea (see CRIMEA); settled by Cossacks by 16th cent.; lower Don basin, although controlled by Russia in early 17th cent., not formally acquired until Turkey ceded to Russia its claim to Azov 1739; Cossack communities had special political status in return for military service; in 1918, erected Republic of the Don, soon defeated by Bolsheviks; part of North Caucasus Region 1923–36.

Don·do \ˈdōn-ˌdō\. **1.** Town, NW Angola, on Cuanza River at head of navigation; pop. (1991e) 54,163.
2. Town, SE cen. Mozambique, ab. 30 mi. (48 km.) NNW of Beira; railroad junction.

Don·dra Head \ˈdōn-drə\. Cape on S extremity of Sri Lanka, 6°N, projecting into Indian Ocean.

Don·e·gal \ˌdä-ni-ˈgȯl, ˌdə-\. **1.** County, Ulster prov., N Ireland (republic); ⊗ Lifford; rivers: Foyle, Derg, Finn; oats, potatoes; livestock grazing, fishing; fishing nets, carpets, synthetic fibers, tweeds, woolen goods; tourism. See table at IRELAND.
2. Town, S co. Donegal, N Ireland (republic), at head (25 mi. or 40 km. inland) of **Donegal Bay;** pop. (1986c) 2242; ancient seat of the O'Donnell clan; ruins of a Franciscan monastery (founded 1474) and of a 17th cent. castle.

Do·nets \də-ˈnyets, -ˈnets\ *also* **Northern Donets.** River, E Ukraine and SW Russia in Europe; rises in E Kursk Oblast N of Belgorod and flows SE into Don River ENE of Rostov-na-Donu; 631 mi. (1015 km.) long; drainage area 38,439 sq. mi. (99,557 sq. km.); chief tributary the Oskol; navigable for ab. three quarters of its course and flows through the Donets Basin, affording means of transportation of heavy products. See DONETS BASIN.

Donets Basin *or Russ.* **Do·net·skiy Bas·seyn** \də-ˈnyet-skē-bə-ˈsyān\; *Russ. short form* **Don·bass** *or angl.* **Don·bas** \dən-ˈbäs, ˈdän-ˌbas\. Region in plain of Donets River and lower Dnieper, E Ukraine and SW Russia in Europe, producing a large amount of coal; adjoins the rich iron field of Krivoi Rog; contains many cities historically noted for industry as Artemovsk, Donets'k, Luhans'k, Makeyevka, Gorlovka, Yenakiyeve; in WWII occupied by Germans 1941 to 1943.

Do·nets'k *or* **Do·netsk** \də-ˈnyetsk\. **1.** *formerly* **Sta·li·no Oblast** \ˈstȧ-lyi-nō-ˈȯ-bləst, -ˌblast\. Administrative subdivision of Ukraine, cen. part of Donets Basin, touches on N shore of Sea of Azov; 10,232 sq. mi. (26,501 sq. km.); pop. (1991e) 5,346,700; ✻ Donets'k; important industrial area; iron and steel, chemicals; coal mining, heavy engineering; winter wheat, corn; formed 1938.
2. *formerly* **Stalino** *or* **Sta·lin** \ˈstȧ-lyin; ˈstä-lin, ˈsta-, -ˌlēn\ *also* **Yu·zov·ka** \ˈyü-zəf-kə\. City, its ✻, on Kalmius River 100 mi. (161 km.) NW of Rostov-na-Donu; pop. (1991e) 1,121,000; has foundries, chemical works, coking plants, steel mills, coal mines; several technical colleges, also university (1965). Founded c. 1870 by a British subject named Hughes (hence **Hughes·ov·ka** \ˈhyü-zəf-kə\, or in Russia Yuzovka); developed rapidly up to WWI and then again after 1924. In WWII held by Germans 1941–43.

Donetskiy Basseyn. See DONETS BASIN.

Don Fernando de Taos. See TAOS 2.

Dong *or W.-G.* **Tung** \ˈdůŋ\. River, Guangdong prov., SE China; rises in Jiangxi and flows SW and W into upper Zhu River ab. 25 mi. (40 km.) below Guangzhou; ab. 280 mi. (450 km.) long.

Dong·ga·la \dōŋ-ˈgä-lä, däŋ-\. Town and port, Sulawesi, Indonesia, on W coast on Makassar Strait 310 mi. (499 km.) N of Ujung Pandang.

Dong–nai \ˈdȯŋ-ˈnī\ *or* **Don·nai** \ˈdȯŋ-\. River, S Vietnam; flows W and S to unite with other streams (on one of which is Ho Chi Minh City) and form an extensive delta just N of the Mekong Delta; ab. 300 mi. (480 km.) long.

Don·go·la \ˈdȯŋ-gō-lä, dȯŋ-ˈgō-\ *also* **Dun·qu·lah** \ˈdȯn-kȯ-lə\. Town, cen. N Sudan, on the Nile ab. 47 mi. (76 km.) above the 3d of several cataracts; an old town, ✻ of the Nubian kingdom (see NUBIA) 6th to 14th cents.

Dongrak, Thiu Khao Phanom. See DANGREK MOUNTAINS.

Dong Thap Muoi. See REEDS, PLAIN OF.

Dong·ting Hu *or W.-G.* **Tung·ting Hu** *or* **Tung–t'ing Hu** \ˈdůŋ-ˈtiŋ-ˈhü\. Shallow lake (*hu*), NE Hunan, SE cen. China; 1430 sq. mi. (3704 sq. km.), 3500 to 4000 sq. mi. (9065 to 10,360 sq. km.) at high water in summer; ab. 75 mi. (120 km.) long; receives the Xiang, Yuan, Zi, and Li rivers; main outlet on NE at Yueyang; also connects with the Chang on NW by the Songzi Hu.

Don·i·phan \ˈdä-ni-fən\. **1.** County in NE corner of Kansas. See table at KANSAS.
2. City, ⊗ of Ripley co., S Missouri, 28 mi. (45 km.) WSW of Poplar Bluff; pop. (1990c) 1713.

Don·jek \ˈdän-ˌjek\. River, SW Yukon Terr., NW Canada; flows into White River; crossed by Alaska Highway NW of Burwash Landing.

Don·ley \ˈdän-lē\. County in NW Texas. See table at TEXAS.

Don·na \ˈdä-nə\. City, Hidalgo co., S Texas, 12 mi. (19 km.) E of McAllen; pop. (1990c) 12,652.

Døn·na \ˈdœn-nə\ *also* **Døn·naesø** \-ne-ˌsœ\. Island in Nordland co., in Norwegian Sea off W coast of Norway.

Don·na·co·na \ˌdä-nə-ˈkō-nə\. Town, Portneuf co., S Quebec, Canada, on St. Lawrence River 27 mi. (43 km.) W of Quebec City; pop. (1991c) 5659.

Donnai. See DONG-NAI.

Don·nells Dam \ˈdän-ᵊlz\ *and* **Donnells Reservoir.** See UNITED STATES, *Dams and Reservoirs.*

Don·ner Lake \ˈdä-nər\. Small lake, Nevada co., E California, in the Sierra Nevada ab. 13 mi. (21 km.) NW of Lake Tahoe; W of the lake are **Donner Peak** 8315 ft. (2534 m.) and **Donner Pass** ab. 7090 ft. (2160 m.), traversed by highway and site of U.S. Weather Bureau observatory.

Don·ners·berg \ˈdȯ-nərs-ˌberk\. Mountain, N Rhineland-Palatinate, Germany, at N end of Vosges Mts.; 2254 ft. (687 m.).

Don·ny·brook \ˈdä-nē-ˌbrůk\. Suburb of city of Dublin, E Ireland; scene of an annual fair, founded 1204 by King John of England and suppressed 1855, notorious for debauchery and fighting.

Do·no·ra \də-ˈnōr-ə\. Borough, Washington co., SW Pennsylvania, on Monongahela River 20 mi. (32 km.) SSE of Pittsburgh; pop. (1990c) 5928.

Do·nos·tia–San Se·bas·tián \ˌthō-nō-ˈstē-ä-ˌsän-ˌsā-bäs-ˈtyän\. Commercial seaport and resort, ✱ of Guipúzcoa prov., N. Spain, on Bay of Biscay 48 mi. (77 km.) E of Bilbao; pop. (1991p) 189,933; episcopal see; produces chemicals, cement, beer, chocolate, metal goods; commercial fisheries; 16th and 18th cent. churches; first mentioned 1014; received charter c. 1174, burned during occupation by Anglo-Portuguese army under Arthur Wellesley, duke of Wellington 1813; former summer residence of Spanish court.

Don Pe·dro Chris·to·pher·sen, Mount \dōn-ˈpā-drō-kri-ˈstä-fər-sən\. Peak, Antarctica, 85°31′S, 165°43′W; 12,355 ft. (3766 m.).

Don Pe·dro Dam *and* **Don Pedro Reservoir** \dän-ˈpā-drō\. See UNITED STATES, *Dams and Reservoirs*

Don·sol \dōn-ˈsōl\. Municipality, NW Sorsogon prov., Luzon, Philippines, on W coast at N end of Ticao Pass 28 mi. (45 km.) W of the municipality of Sorsogon; pop. (1980c) 33,785.

Doobaunt. See DUBAWNT.

Doo·ly \ˈdü-lē\. County in SW cen. Georgia. See table at GEORGIA.

Doon \ˈdün\. River, Strathclyde region, SW Scotland; flows through Loch Doon and empties into Firth of Clyde 3 mi. (5 km.) S of Ayr; ab. 25 mi. (40 km.) long; immortalized by poet Robert Burns.

Doon, Loch. Lake, Strathclyde region, SW Scotland, 22 mi. (35 km.) SSE of Ayr; ab. 5 mi. (8 km.) long.

Doone Valley \ˈdün\. Valley, N Devon, SW England, just N of Exmoor, Somerset; scene of legend of the Doones, a band of outlaws of 17th cent. who figured in Richard Doddridge Blackmore's novel *Lorna Doone.*

Door \ˈdōr\. County in NE Wisconsin. See table at WISCONSIN.

Doorman *or* **Doorman Top.** See SIMANGGELA.

Doorn \ˈdōrn\. Commune, Utrecht prov., cen. Netherlands, ab. 10 mi. (16 km.) SE of the city of Utrecht; pop. (1981e) 10,627; residence of Emperor William II of Germany (after his abdication) 1920–41.

Doornik. See TOURNAI.

Doorn·kop \ˈdȯrn-ˌkȯp\. Village, NE Rep. of South Africa, 15 mi. (24 km.) SW of Johannesburg; scene 1896 of Sir Leander Starr Jameson's surrender to Boer leader Piet Arnoldus Cronjé after the raid on Johannesburg.

Door Peninsula. Peninsula, E Wisconsin, bet. Green Bay and Lake Michigan; includes Door co. and parts of Kewaunee and Brown cos; 80 mi. (129 km.) long, 25 mi. (40 km.) wide at its base; cherries; tourism.

Dor \ˈdȯr\ *or Arab.* **Tan·tu·ra** \tän-ˈtu̇r-ə\; *anc.* **Do·ra** \ˈdōr-ə\. Settlement on Mediterranean coast, Israel, 15 mi. (24 km.) S of Haifa; pop. (1989e) 206; marked S limit of Phoenician rule at height of its power. A kingdom in the time of the judges of Israel c. 1200–1000 B.C. (*Josh.* xi. 2; *Judges* i. 27), but excavations show that it was a very old settlement; fortified during the Crusades.

Do·ra Bal·tea \ˈdōr-ə-ˈbȯl-tē-ə\. River, NW Italy; rises at foot of Little St. Bernard Pass and flows E and SE into Po River ab. 20 mi. (32 km.) below Turin; ab. 110 mi. (175 km.) long.

Dorada, La. See LA DORADA.

Do·ra·do \dō-ˈrä-thō\. Town and municipality, N Puerto Rico; town near coast 10 mi. (16 km.) W of San Juan; munic. pop. (1990c) 30,759.

Do·rah Pass \ˈdōr-ə\ *or* **Du·rah Pass** \ˈdu̇r-ə\. Mountain pass in Hindu Kush, from Afghanistan to Chitral in Pakistan; alt. 14,711 ft. (4484 m.).

Doran, Ben. See BEN DOURAN.

Dora Ri·pa·ria \ˈdō-rä-rē-ˈpä-rē-ä\. River, Piedmont, NW Italy; rises in Cottian Alps, flows E into Po River near Turin; ab. 60 mi. (97 km.) long.

Do·ra·ville \ˈdōr-ə-ˌvil\. City, De Kalb co., NW cen. Georgia; pop. (1990c) 7626.

Dor·cheat \ˈdȯr-ˌchēt\. Bayou, S United States; rises in S Nevada co., SW Arkansas, flows S into N end of Bistineau Lake, Webster parish, NW Louisiana; ab. 100 mi. (160 km.) long.

Dor·ches·ter \ˈdȯr-chəs-tər, -ˌches-\. **1.** Name of counties in two states of the U.S. See tables at MARYLAND and SOUTH CAROLINA.

2. Former town, now a ward of the city of Boston, E Massachusetts; extended nearly to Rhode Island boundary; included **Dorchester Heights** (a hill SE of Boston), the fortification of which resulted in the evacuation of Boston by the British Mar. 17, 1776.

3. Unincorporated settlement, ⊗ of Westmoreland co., SE New Brunswick, Canada, near mouth of Petitcodiac estuary 6 mi. (10 km.) W of Sackville; pop. (1991c) 4830.

4. *anc.* **Dur·no·var·ia** \ˌdər-nə-ˈvar-ē-ə\. Town, ⊗ of Dorset, S England, on Frome River; pop. (1981p) 14,049; remains of prehistoric settlement are nearby; site of Roman village; the Casterbridge of Thomas Hardy's Wessex novels.

Dor·dogne \dȯr-ˈdōnʸ\. **1.** *anc.* **Du·ra·ni·us** \du̇-ˈrā-nē-əs, dyu̇-\. River, SW France; formed by confluence of Dor and Dogne rivers in Puy-de-Dôme dept., S cen. France, flows SW and W to unite with Garonne River 13 mi. (21 km.) N of Bordeaux and form the Gironde Estuary; 293 mi. (471 km.) long; navigable for ab. 190 mi. (305 km.).

2. Department of SW cen. France. See table at FRANCE.

Dor·drecht \ˈdȯr-ˌdrekt\. **1.** *also* **Dordt** *or* **Dort** \ˈdȯrt\. Commune, South Holland prov., SW Netherlands, on Meuse River ab. 12 mi. (19 km.) ESE of Rotterdam; pop. (1993e) 112,687; commercial and shipping center; chemical and metallurgical works; 14th cent. church. Founded 1008, received town charter c. 1200; scene of meeting of first congress of Protestant provinces of the Netherlands 1572; scene of religious congress known as Synod of Dort 1618–19; birthplace of painters Albert Cuyp (1620) and Nicolaes Maes (1634).

2. Town, NE cen. Eastern Cape prov., S Rep. of South Africa, 120 mi. (193 km.) NNW of East London; met. area pop. (1993e) 212,164; alt. 5389 ft. (1643 m.); health and pleasure resort.

Dore, Monts \mōⁿ-ˈdȯr\. Mountain group in Auvergne Mts., Puy-de-Dôme dept., S cen. France; highest peak Puy de Sancy 6186 ft. (1885 m.).

Dör·gön Nuur \ˈdœr-ˌgœn-ˈnür\ *also* **Dur·ge Nur** \ˈdu̇r-gə-ˈnu̇r\. Salt lake, W Mongolia, 47°40′N, 93°30′E.

Do·ri·on \ˈdōr-ē-ˌōⁿ\. Town, Vaudreuil-Soulanges co., S Quebec, Canada, 25 mi. (40 km.) SW of Montreal; pop. (1991c) 5920.

Do·ris \ˈdōr-əs, ˈdär-\. **1.** Small country in cen. part of ancient Greece, bet. Oeta and Parnassus mountains and containing sources of Cephisus River; important in Greek history only as alleged home of the Hellenic people that entered and conquered Greece 12th cent. B.C.; Corinth and Sparta were Dorian cities.

2. District or region on coast of Caria, Asia Minor, and adjacent islands, made up of Dorian settlements.

Dor·king \ˈdȯr-kiŋ\. Town, Surrey, S England, 22 mi. (35 km.) SSW of London; pop. (1981p) 21,654; home of novelist and poet George Meredith (at Box Hill, just N).

Dor·ma·gen \ˈdōr-ˌmä-gən\. City, North Rhine-Westphalia, Germany, 10 mi. (16 km.) S of Düsseldorf; pop. (1992e) 58,843.

Dor·mont \ˈdȯr-ˌmänt\. Residential borough, Allegheny co., SW Pennsylvania, 4 mi. (6 km.) S of Pittsburgh; pop. (1990c) 9772.

Dorn·birn \ˈdȯrn-ˌbirn\. Commune, Vorarlberg, Austria, 6 mi. (10 km.) S of Bregenz; pop. (1991c) 40,735; textiles, machinery, electrical equipment; brewing.

Dor·noch \ˈdȯr-ˌnäk, -nək\. Burgh on Dornoch Firth, Highland region, N Scotland; pop. (1981p) 1006; health resort; scene 1722 of last execution in Scotland for witchcraft.

Dornoch Firth. Inlet of North Sea, Highland region, on NE coast of Scotland.

Doro. See CAPHAREUS.

Do·ro·hoi \ˌdȯr-ō-ˈhȯi\. Commercial city, Botoşani co., NE Romania, 75 mi. (121 km.) NW of Iaşi; pop. (1989c) 32,313.

Dorpat. See TARTU.

Dorris Bridge. See ALTURAS.

Dor·set \ˈdȯr-sit\. Administrative county, S England, approx. equivalent to the former Dorsetshire county; rivers Stour and Frome; barley, wheat, oats, beans; dairy farming, sheep, pigs, poultry; building-stone quarries; tourism; chief towns: Poole, Weymouth, Dorchester, Sherborne, Swanage; estab. 1974. See table at ENGLAND.

Dorset, Cape. Cape, SW Baffin I., Nunavut, Canada, at S tip of Foxe Penin.

Dor·set·shire \ˈdȯr-sət-ˌshir, -shər\ *or* **Dorset.** Former county, S England (see DORSET).

Dor·sten \ˈdōr-stən\. City, North Rhine-Westphalia, Germany, 14 mi. (23 km.) N of Essen; pop. (1992e) 78,814; coal mines; textiles. Founded 11th cent., made city 1251; heavily bombed in WWII.

Dort. See DORDRECHT 1.

Dort·mund \ˈdȯrt-ˌmu̇nt, -mənd\. City, North Rhine-Westphalia, Germany, in the Ruhr Valley 31 mi. (50 km.) S of Münster; pop. (1992e) 601,007; connected with North Sea by Dortmund-Ems Canal; well-developed harbor; important railroad center; manufactures machinery, steel; breweries, coal deposits; university (1966).

History: Ancient walled city; first mentioned c. 885 A.D. as **Throt·man·nia** \thrät-ˈma-nē-ə\; in 12th cent. called **Tre·mo·nia** \trē-ˈmō-nē-ə\; member of Hanseatic League; to Prussia 1815; occupied by French troops 1923–24; phenomenal growth after WWI; bombed and largely destroyed in WWII.

Dor·val \dȯr-ˈvȧl\. Residential town, Montreal I., S Quebec, Canada, 10 mi. (16 km.) WSW of the city of Montreal; pop. (1991c) 17,249.

Dorylaeum. See ESKİŞEHİR 2.

Dos Ba·hí·as, Cape \ˌdōs-bä-ˈhē-äs\. Cape extending into Atlantic Ocean on E coast of Chubut prov., S Argentina, at N side of entrance to San Jorge Gulf.

Dos Her·ma·nas \ˌdōs-er-ˈmä-näs\. Commune, Sevilla prov., SW Spain, 10 mi. (16 km.) SSE of Seville; pop. (1991p) 76,923.

Dospad Dagh. See RHODOPE.

Dos Pal·os \dȯs-ˈpa-ləs\. City, Merced co., California; pop. (1990c) 4196.

Do·than \ˈdō-thən\. **1.** City, ⊗ of Houston co., SE Alabama, 15 mi. (24 km.) N of Florida border and 15 mi. (24 km.) W of Chattahoochee River; pop. (1990c) 53,589; trading center for large agricultural region; George C. Wallace State Community Coll. at Dothan (1949); settled c. 1858; incorp. 1885; became ⊗ 1903.

2. Ancient town of Samaria, Palestine, on the highway N of Samaria at a pass leading to the Plain of Esdraelon; here Joseph, son of Hebrew patriarch Jacob, was sold into slavery by his brothers (*Gen.* xxxvii. 17).

Dou·ai \du̇-ˈā\; *formerly* **Dou·ay** \du̇-ˈā\; *anc.* **Du·a·cum** \du̇-ˈā-kəm, dyu̇-\. City, Nord dept., N France, on Scarpe River 19 mi. (31 km.) S of Lille; pop. (1990c) 44,195; automobiles, chemicals; printing; site of university from mid-16th cent. until 1887; gives its name to the Douay Version, an English version of the Bible from the Latin Vulgate for Roman Catholics (New Testament published at Rheims 1582, Old Testament at Douai 1609–10). Taken by Louis XIV 1667; suffered much damage in World Wars I and II.

Dou·a·la *also* **Du·a·la** \dü-ˈä-lä\. Seaport, Cameroon, on Bight of Biafra; pop. (1987c) 810,000; textiles; most important port of country; terminus of railroad inland; former ✻ of Kamerun (German) and later of Cameroun (French); taken from Germans Sept. 1914 in WWI.

Dou·ar·ne·nez \ˌdwȧr-nə-ˈnā\. Commune, Finistère dept., NW France, 12 mi. (19 km.) NW of Quimper; pop. (1990c) 16,701; fishing.

Dou·au·mont \dwō-ˈmō^{n}\. Fort in Meuse dept., NE France, just N of Verdun; scene of fighting bet. French and Germans 1916.

Douay. See DOUAI.

Double Mountain Fork. River, SW U.S. rising in E New Mexico, uniting with Salt Fork in Stonewall co., NW Texas to form Brazos River; ab. 200 mi. (320 km.) long.

Double Springs. Town, ⊗ of Winston co., NW Alabama; pop. (1990c) 1138.

Dou·ble·top Peak \ˈdə-bəl-ˌtäp\. Mountain, N Sublette co., W Wyoming; 11,713 ft. (3570 m.).

Doubs \ˈdü\. **1.** *anc.* **Du·bis** \ˈdü-bis, ˈdyü-\. River, E France; rises in Jura Mts., flows NE; becomes France-Switzerland border; flows into Switzerland, turns W then, in France, N and finally SW to enter the Saône; ab. 270 mi. (435 km.) long.

2. Department of E France. See table at FRANCE.

Doubt, River of. See ROOSEVELT, RIO.

Dougga. See THUGGA.

Dou·gher·ty \ˈdȯ-ər-tē\. County in SW Georgia. See table at GEORGIA.

Doug·las \ˈdə-gləs\. **1.** Island on Gastineau Channel, SE Alaska, opp. Juneau.

2. Name of counties in 12 states of the U.S. See tables at COLORADO, GEORGIA, ILLINOIS, KANSAS, MINNESOTA, MISSOURI, NEBRASKA, NEVADA, OREGON, SOUTH DAKOTA, WASHINGTON, WISCONSIN.

3. Former town on Douglas I., SE Alaska; merged with Juneau 1970.

4. City, Cochise co., SE corner of Arizona, on border with Mexico; pop. (1990c) 12,822; stock raising; Cochise Coll. (1962).

5. City, ⊗ of Coffee co., S Georgia, 35 mi. (56 km.) WNW of Waycross; pop. (1990c) 10,464; agricultural trading center; South Georgia Coll. (1906).

6. Town, Worcester co., cen. Massachusetts, 14 mi. (23 km.) S of the city of Worcester; pop. (1990c) 5438.

7. Town, ⊗ of Converse co., E Wyoming, on North Platte River 50 mi. (80 km.) E of Casper; pop. (1990c) 5076; livestock trade.

8. Town, ✻ of Isle of Man, England, in SE part of island; pop. (1991c) 22,214; seaside resort.

Douglas, Mount. Peak, S Sweet Grass co., S cen. Montana; 11,300 ft. (3444 m.).

Douglas Channel. Inlet of Pacific Ocean, W British Columbia, Canada, joining Gardner Canal at its mouth, N of Princess Royal I.; ab. 60 mi. (97 km.) long.

Douglas Dam. See table at TENNESSEE VALLEY AUTHORITY.

Doug·lass Hills \ˈdə-gləs\. City, Jefferson co., Kentucky; pop. (1990c) 5549.

Doug·las·ville \ˈdə-gləs-ˌvil\. City, ⊗ of Douglas co., W Georgia, 20 mi. (32 km.) W of Atlanta; pop. (1990c) 11,635.

Douglas Water. River in S cen. Scotland, flowing NE in Strathclyde region to empty into Clyde River.

Dou·ka·to, Cape *or* **Cape Du·ca·to** \dü-ˈkä-tō\ *or Gk.* **Ák·ra Dou·ká·ton** \ˈä-krä-thü-ˈkä-tōn\; *anc.* **Leu·ca·tes** \lü-ˈkā-tēz\. Promontory and S point of island of Levkás, Ionian Is., Greece; traditional scene of lyric poet Sappho's leap into the sea.

Doul·lens \dü-ˈlä^{n}\. Commune, Somme dept., N France, N of Amiens; medieval stronghold.

Dou·ra·dos \dō-ˈrä-düs\. Municipality, Mato Grosso state, cen. Brazil, 120 mi. (193 km.) SW of Campo Grande; pop. (1991p) 116,754.

Douran, Ben. See BEN DOURAN.

Dou·ro \ˈdō-ˌrü\ *or Span.* **Due·ro** \ˈdwā-rō\; *anc.* **Du·ri·us** \ˈdu̇r-ē-əs, ˈdyu̇r-\. River in Spain and Portugal; rises in Soria prov., N cen. Spain; flows W to NE Portugal, then turns S, forming section of Portugal-Spain boundary, then W into Atlantic Ocean 2 mi. (3 km.) S of Pôrto; 556 mi. (895 km.) long; in Portugal goes through deep gorges; Portuguese section developed for hydroelectric power production.

Douve \ˈdüv\. River in Manche dept., Normandy, NW France; flows S and E into Bay of the Seine NE of Carentan, which is near it on a tributary; ab. 40 mi. (64 km.) long.

Dou·vres \ˈdüvr^{ə}\. **1.** Commune, Calvados dept., NW France, N of Caen; held by Germans against Allied advance June 7–11, 1944.

2. Port, England. See DOVER 7.

Dove \ˈdəv, ˈdōv\. River, Derbyshire and Staffordshire, cen. England; flows S from near Buxton and empties into the Trent below Burton; ab. 39 mi. (63 km.) long; favorite stream of writer and fishing enthusiast Izaak Walton.

Dove Creek \ˈdəv\. Town, ⊗ of Dolores co., SW Colorado; pop. (1990c) 643.

Do·ver \ˈdō-vər\. **1.** Commercial city, ✱ of Delaware and ⊗ of Kent co., cen. Delaware, 40 mi. (64 km.) S of Wilmington; pop. (1990c) 27,630; shipping point for fruits; Wesley Coll. (1873), Delaware State Coll. (1891), Delaware Technical and Community Coll. (1967); laid out 1717; made state ✱ 1777; incorp. as town 1829, as city 1929.

2. City, ⊗ of Stafford co., SE New Hampshire, 11 mi. (18 km.) NNW of Portsmouth; pop. (1990c) 25,042; insurance; automobile parts, printing presses; settled c. 1622; attacked by Indians June 28, 1689; incorp. as city 1855.

3. Town, Morris co., N New Jersey, 8 mi. (13 km.) NNW of Morristown; pop. (1990c) 15,115; center of iron-ore area; government munition depot nearby; settled 1722.

4. City, Ohio. See WESTLAKE 2.

5. City, Tuscarawas co., E Ohio; pop. (1990c) 11,329; coal.

6. Town, ⊗ of Stewart co., NW Tennessee; pop. (1990c) 1341; burned by Union forces 1862.

7. *or Fr.* **Dou·vres** \ˈdüvrᵊ\; *anc.* **Du·bris Por·tus** \ˈdü-bris-ˈpōr-təs, ˈdyü-\. Port, Kent, SE England, on the Strait of Dover 67 mi. (108 km.) ESE of London; pop. (1981p) 32,843; chief of the Cinque Ports; naval base, resort, and the leading passenger port in Great Britain.

History: In Roman times an important landing place; Dover Castle, a stronghold of medieval England, besieged by Dauphin Louis (later Louis VIII of France) and rebellious barons 1216; held by Parliamentarians during Civil War; scene of secret treaty bet. English King Charles II and French King Louis XIV 1670; naval base during WWI; bombed and shelled by Germans in WWII.

Dover, Strait of *also* **Straits of Dover** *or Fr.* **Pas de Ca·lais** \ˌpäd-kȧ-ˈlā\; *anc.* **Fre·tum Gal·li·cum** \ˈfrē-təm-ˈga-li-kəm\. Channel bet. SE England and N France; 20 mi. (32 km.) wide at narrowest point; the easternmost and narrowest section of the English Channel.

Dover–Fox·croft \ˈdōv-ər-ˈfäks-ˌkrȯft\. Town, ⊗ of Piscataquis co., N cen. Maine, 34 mi. (55 km.) NW of Bangor; pop. (1990c) 4657.

Dovey. See DYFI.

Dov·re·fjell \ˈdȯ-vrə-ˌfyel\. Plateau in cen. Norway; highest point ab. 7565 ft. (2306 m.).

Do·wa·giac \dō-ˈwȯ-ˌjak\. City, Cass co., SW Michigan; pop. (1990c) 6409; Southwestern Michigan Coll. (1964).

Down \ˈdau̇n\. **1.** Former county, SE Northern Ireland; chief towns: Bangor, Newtownards, Newry, Downpatrick.

2. District, Northern Ireland; carved from traditional county 1974. See table at IRELAND, NORTHERN.

Dow·ners Grove \ˈdau̇-nərz\. Village, Du Page co., NE Illinois, ab. 10 mi. (16 km.) W of Chicago; pop. (1990c) 46,858.

Dow·ney \ˈdau̇-nē\. City, Los Angeles co., SW California, SE of the city of Los Angeles; pop. (1990c) 91,444; aircraft, chemicals.

Dow·nie·ville \ˈdau̇-nē-ˌvil\. Village, ⊗ of Sierra co., NE California, 78 mi. (126 km.) NNE of Sacramento.

Dow·ning·town \ˈdau̇-niŋ-ˌtau̇n\. Borough, Chester co., SE Pennsylvania, on E branch of Brandywine Creek 32 mi. (51 km.) W of Philadelphia; pop. (1990c) 7749.

Down·pat·rick \dau̇n-ˈpa-trik\. County town, ⊗ of Down dist., SE Northern Ireland, at SW end of Strangford Lough; pop. (1981c) 8245; cathedral; textiles; reputed burial place of St. Patrick, St. Columba, and St. Brigid.

Downs, The \ˈdau̇nz\. **1.** Range of hills in S England. See NORTH DOWNS, SOUTH DOWNS.

2. Roadstead in English Channel, along E coast of Kent bet. North and South Foreland; ab. 9 mi. (14 km.) long and 6 mi. (10 km.) wide; affords excellent anchorage, protected by a natural breakwater, the Goodwin Sands; scene of English naval victory over Dutch 1652 and of drawn battle bet. English and Dutch 1666.

Down Under. Australia or New Zealand.

Doyles·town \ˈdȯilz-ˌtau̇n\. Borough, ⊗ of Bucks co., SE Pennsylvania, 25 mi. (40 km.) N of Philadelphia; pop. (1990c) 8575; Delaware Valley Coll. (1896); settled 1735.

Drâa *or* **Dra** \ˈdrä\. River (often dry), SW Morocco; empties into Atlantic Ocean at **Cape Dra.**

Drabescus. See DRAMA 2.

Dra·chen·fels \ˈdrä-k̲ən-ˌfels\. Peak in the Siebengebirge, W Germany, on E bank of Rhine S of Bonn; 1053 ft. (321 m.) high; resort; in German legend said to be scene of the slaying of the dragon by the hero Siegfried.

Dra·cut \ˈdrā-kət\. Town, Middlesex co., NE Massachusetts, 2 mi. (3 km.) N of Lowell; pop. (1990c) 25,594.

Dra·go·ne·ra \ˌdrä-gō-ˈnā-rä, ˌdrag-ə-ˈner-ə\. Spanish island in Mediterranean Sea off W coast of Majorca; 1.67 sq. mi. (4.3 sq. km.).

Drag·on's Mouths *or* **Dragon's Mouth** \ˈdra-gənz\. Strait, North Atlantic Ocean, bet. Paria Penin., NE Venezuela, and NW coast of Trinidad, Trinidad and Tobago; ab. 10 mi. (16 km.) wide; so called because of the many small rocky islands in its several channels.

Dra·gui·gnan \ˌdrä-gē-ˈnyäⁿ\. Commune, Var dept., SE France, 40 mi. (64 km.) NE of Toulon; textiles; resort.

Dra·kens·berg \ˈdrä-kənz-ˌbərk\ *or Zulu* **Kwath·lam·ba** \kwät-ˈläm-bä\; *also* **Kah·lam·ba** \kä-ˈläm-bä\. Mountain range extending from SW to NE in Lesotho and SE Rep. of South Africa; highest peak Thabana Ntlenyana 11,425 ft. (3482 m.).

Drake Passage \ˈdrāk\. Strait bet. Cape Horn on N and South Shetland Is., connecting South Atlantic Ocean (Scotia Sea) and South Pacific Ocean.

Drake's Bay \ˈdrāks\. Inlet of Pacific Ocean E of Point Reyes, Marin co., W California; visited by Sir Francis Drake 1579.

Drakhmani. See ELATEIA.

Dra·ma \ˈdrä-mə\ *or Gk.* **Drá·ma** \ˈt̲h̲rä-mä\. **1.** Department of Greece. See table at GREECE.

2. *anc.* **Dra·bes·cus** \drə-ˈbes-kəs\. City, its ✱, in fertile valley bet. Strymon and Mesta rivers; pop. (1991p) 39,914; in tobacco-growing area.

Dram·men \ˈdräm-mən\. Seaport, ⊗ of Buskerud co., S Norway, at mouth of the **Drams·el·va** \ˈdräms-ˌel-və\ on a branch of the Oslo Fjord; pop. (1990c) 51,978; sawmills, papermills, cellulose factories; plastics, textiles, leather goods, beer.

Dran·cy \dräⁿ-ˈsē\. Commune, Seine-St.-Denis dept., N France, a NE suburb of Paris; pop. (1990c) 60,928; site in WWII of German concentration camp.

Dran·gi·a·na \ˌdran-jē-ˈā-nə, -ˈa-\. Ancient region of Asia, a part of Ariana and a province of ancient Persian Empire and of the Grecian empire of Macedonian King Alexander the Great; now included in W Afghanistan and E Iran. See SEISTAN.

Dra·no·va Island \ˈdrä-nȯ-vȧ\. Island, E Romania, in S part of Danube Delta.

Dra·per \ˈdrā-pər\. City, Salt Lake co., Utah; pop. (1990c) 7257.

Dra·va *or* **Dra·ve** \ˈdrä-və\ *or Ger.* **Drau** \ˈdrau̇\; *anc.* **Dra·vus** \ˈdrā-vəs\. River in S cen. Europe; rises in the Carnic Alps, S Austria, flows E into and across NE Slovenia, then SE into northernmost Croatia, and forming section of Croatia-Hungary boundary, empties into Danube River 14 mi. (23 km.) E of Osijek, Croatia; 447 mi. (719 km.) long; navigable for small boats for ab. 350 mi. (563 km.).

Drav·ska \ˈdräv-skə\. Former county (1929–45), NW Yugoslavia; 6151 sq. mi. (15,931 sq. km.); ⊗ Ljubljana; since 1945 approx. coextensive with Slovenia.

Dravus. See DRAVA.

Dray·ton Valley \ˈdrāt-ᵊn\. Town, Alberta, Canada, 63 mi. (101 km.) SW of Edmonton; pop. (1991c) 5983.

Dreketi. See NDREKETI.

Dren·the \ˈdren-tə\. Province, NE Netherlands; ✻ Assen; potatoes, rye; livestock raising; oil. See table at NETHERLANDS. Region inhabited from prehistoric times; under bishops of Utrecht (*q.v.*); passed to Charles V, the Hapsburg king of Spain, 1536; in United Provinces of the Netherlands 1581, gained provincial status 1796; under French rule 1795–1813; occupied by Germany in WWII.

Drepanum. See TRAPANI 2.

Dres·den \ˈdrez-dən\. **1.** Town, ⊗ of Weakley co., NW Tennessee; pop. (1990c) 2488.

2. Town, Kent co., SE Ontario, Canada, 13 mi. (21 km.) N of Chatham; pop. (1991c) 2646; gas wells.

3. \ˈdrās-dən\. District of former East Germany.

4. \ˈdrās-dən\. City, ✻ of Saxony state, E Germany, and formerly of Dresden dist., East Germany, on Elbe River 63 mi. (101 km.) ESE of Leipzig; pop. (1992e) 485,132; electrical equipment, precision tools, optical instruments, adding machines; Dresden china manufactured at Meissen (*q.v.*); technical university (1828, university status 1961); conservatory of music; academy of fine arts; opera house (completed 1878); world-famous art galleries and museums containing collections which include porcelain, medieval artifacts, and zoological specimens.

History: Orig. a Slavonic settlement; residence of margraves of Meissen at beginning of 13th cent.; residence of Albertine dukes of Saxony 1485–1918; bombarded by Prussian King Frederick the Great 1760; scene of famous battle Aug. 26–27, 1813, in which allies unsuccessfully attempted to wrest it from Napoleonic troops in occupation; occupied by Prussians 1866; very severely damaged in WWII; captured by U.S.S.R. forces 1945.

Dreux \ˈdrœ\; *anc.* **Du·ro·cas·ses** \ˌdu̇r-ə-ˈka-sēz, ˌdyu̇r-\; *later* **Dro·cae** \ˈdrō-ˌsē\. Commune, Eure-et-Loir dept., N cen. France, 20 mi. (32 km.) NNW of Chartres; pop. (1990c) 35,866; chemicals.

Drew \ˈdrü\. County in SE Arkansas. See table at ARKANSAS.

Drew·ry's Bluff; *formerly* **Dru·ry's Bluff** \ˈdru̇r-ēz\. Height on right bank of James River 5 mi. (8 km.) S of Richmond, Virginia, near Bermuda Hundred; Union gunboats repulsed May 1862; in campaign for Richmond May 1864 Union advance under Gen. Benjamin Franklin Butler halted by Confederate forces under Gen. Pierre Beauregard.

Driggs \ˈdrigz\. Village, ⊗ of Teton co., E Idaho; pop. (1990c) 846.

Drin \ˈdrēn, ˈdrin\ *or* **Dri·ni** \ˈdrē-nē\; *anc.* **Dri·lo** \ˈdrī-ˌlō\. River, Albania; flows N out of Lake Ohrid into E Albania, turns W in N Albania and empties into Adriatic Sea; 175 mi. (282 km.) long; its N mouth is the Buenë River.

Dri·na \ˈdrē-nə\; *anc.* **Dri·nus** \ˈdrī-nəs\. River, S Europe; flows N into Sava River ab. 60 mi. (97 km.) W of Belgrade; 285 mi. (459 km.) long; constitutes a large section of the boundary bet. Bosnia and Herzegovina and the Yugoslavian republic of Serbia.

Drin·ska \ˈdrēns-kə, ˈdrins-\. Former county (1929–45), cen. Yugoslavia; 11,417 sq. mi. (29,570 sq. km.); ⊗ Sarajevo; since 1945 divided bet. Serbia and Bosnia and Herzegovina.

Dris·kill Mountain \ˈdris-kəl\. Elevation, Bienville parish, Louisiana; 535 ft. (163 m.); highest peak in the state.

Drø·bak \ˈdrœ-ˌbäk\. Seaport town, Akershus co., SE Norway; used as a winter port for Oslo; summer resort.

Dro·be·ta–Tur·nu Se·ve·rin \drō-ˈbā-tä-ˈtür-nü-ˌsā-ve-ˈrēn\. City, ⊗ of Mehedinţi co., SW Romania, on Danube River near Iron Gate; pop. (1992p) 115,526; commercial center; shipbuilding, food processing. Ancient Roman town of Drobeta had commemorative tower (Turris Severi) named for Emperor Lucius Septimus Severus (146–211); site of Roman Emperor Trajan's bridge over the Danube (2d cent. A.D.).

Drocae. See DREUX.

Dro·court \drō-ˈkür\. Commune, Pas-de-Calais dept., N France, 9 mi. (14 km.) NE of Arras; important point of strong German defense line 1917, extending N from Quéant in the Hindenburg Line; taken by Allies 1918.

Dro·ghe·da \ˈdrȯ-ə-də, ˈdrȯi-də\. Town and port, S co. Louth, NE Ireland, on Boyne River; pop. (1991p) 23,845; salmon fisheries, cottonmills; beer, linen, cement. Site of noted synod 1152; besieged 1649 by English Parliamentarian commander Oliver Cromwell who stormed it and put most of the Royalist garrison to the sword; surrendered to William of Orange immediately after the nearby battle of the Boyne 1690.

Dro·go·bych \ˌdrə-gə-ˈbich\ *or* **Dro·ho·bych** \ˌdrȯ-kȯ-ˈbich\ *or Pol.* **Dro·ho·bycz** \drȯ-ˈhȯ-bich\. City, SW Ukraine, 39 mi. (63 km.) SW of L'viv (formerly in Poland); pop. (1991e) 79,000; oil refining; oil and natural gas deposits nearby. Passed to Austria in First Partition of Poland 1772; returned to Poland 1919; in WWII taken by U.S.S.R. Sept. 1939 and by Germany June 1941; ceded to U.S.S.R. 1945.

Droit·wich \ˈdrȯit-(ˌ)wich\. Town, Hereford and Worcester, W cen. England; pop. (1981p) 18,073; brine springs; health resort.

Drôme \ˈdrōm\. **1.** River, SE France; rises in Hautes-Alpes dept., flows NW and W into Rhone River 12 mi. (19 km.) SSW of Valence; ab. 60 mi. (97 km.) long.

2. Department of SE France. See table at FRANCE.

Dro·more \drə-ˈmōr\. Town, co. Banbridge, SE Northern Ireland, on Lagan River 17 mi. (27 km.) SW of Belfast; pop. (1981c) 3089; linen weaving.

Dron·field \ˈdrän-ˌfēld\. Town, Derbyshire, N cen. England; pop. (1981p) 23,304.

Drott·ning·holm \ˈdru̇t-niŋ-ˌhȯlm\. Village, E Sweden, on an island in Mälaren; site of palace, formerly the royal summer residence.

Droyls·den \ˈdrȯilz-dən\. Town, Lancashire, NW England, E suburb of Manchester; pop. (1981p) 22,513; chemicals, textiles; engineering.

Drug. See DURG.

Druk–yul. See BHUTAN.

Drum·clog \ˌdrəm-ˈkläg\. Moorland in Strathclyde region, S cen. Scotland, 16 mi. (26 km.) SE of Glasgow; scene of defeat of Royalists under John Graham of Claverhouse by the Covenanters June 1679.

Drum·hel·ler \ˈdrəm-ˌhe-lər\. City, S Alberta, Canada, on Red Deer River 62 mi. (100 km.) ENE of Calgary; pop. (1991c) 6277; formerly a center of lignite mining.

Drum·mond \ˈdrə-mənd\. County, S Quebec, Canada. See table at QUEBEC.

Drummond, Lake. Lake in Dismal Swamp, SE Virginia, near North Carolina border; ab. 7 mi. (11 km.) long by 5 mi. (8 km.) wide; ab. 20 ft. (6 m.) above sea level.

Drummond Island. Island in N Lake Huron, a part of Chippewa co., NE Michigan, off SE extremity of mainland; site of fort built by the British 1815 and held by them until 1822.

Drum·mond·ville \ˈdrə-mənd-ˌvil\. City, ⊗ of Drummond co., S Quebec, Canada, on St. Francis River 32 mi. (51 km.) S of Trois-Riviéres; pop. (1991c) 35,462; Coll. Marie-de-la-Présentation (1955).

Drummossie Moor. See CULLODEN MOOR.

Drum·moyne \drə-ˈmȯin\. Municipality, E New South Wales, SE Australia, W suburb of Sydney on S bank of Parramatta River; pop. (1991c) 30,192.

Drum·right \ˈdrəm-ˌrīt\. City, Creek and Payne cos., E cen. Oklahoma, 30 mi. (48 km.) W of Sapulpa; pop. (1990c) 2799.

Drury's Bluff. See DREWRY'S BLUFF.

Druze, Jeb·el \ˈje-bəl-ˈdrüz\ *or* **Ja·bal ad Du·rūz** \ˈjà-bȧl-ˌȧd-du̇-ˈrüz\ *or* **Jebel ed Druz** \ˌed-ˈdrüz\. **1.** Mountain, SW Syria; 5907 ft. (1800 m.).

2. Region, Syria. See JEBEL ED DRUZ 1.

Druzh·kov·ka \drüsh-ˈkȯf-kə, -ˈkəf-\. Town, Donetsk subdivision, Ukraine, 43 mi. (69 km.) NNW of the city of Donetsk; pop. (1991e) 74,000.

Drwę·ca \dər-ˈvenⁿ-sä\. River, N Poland; flows SW into the Vistula at Toruń; ab. 75 mi. (121 km.) long.

Dry·burgh Abbey \ˈdrī-bə-rə\. Ruin on the Tweed, Borders region, SE Scotland; tombs of writer Sir Walter Scott and British Field Marshal Lord Douglas Haig.

Dry Cimarron. See CIMARRON 1.

Dry·den \ˈdrīd-ᵊn\. Town, Kenora dist., W Ontario, Canada, 76 mi. (122 km.) E of the town of Kenora; pop. (1991c) 6505; provincial experimental farm.

Dry·gal·ski Island \drē-ˈgäl-skē, dri-ˈgal-\. Island off Queen Mary Coast, Antarctica, 66°45′S, 92°30′E; named after German explorer Erich von Drygalski.

Dry Tor·tu·gas \tȯr-ˈtü-gəz\. Small group of islands at entrance to Gulf of Mexico, a part of Monroe co., SW Florida, W of Marquesas Keys; site of **Dry Tortugas National Park** (see UNITED STATES, *National Parks*).

Duacum. See DOUAI.

Duala. See DOUALA.

Duar·te \ˈdwärt-ē, dü-ˈärt-\. City, Los Angeles co., SW California, E of Pasadena; pop. (1990c) 20,688.

Duar·te \ˈdwär-tē\. Province, N cen. Dominican Republic. See table at DOMINICAN REPUBLIC.

Duarte, Pi·co \ˈpē-kō-dü-ˈär-tā\; *formerly* **Monte Tru·jil·lo** \ˈmōn-tā-trü-ˈhē-yō\. Mountain in Cordillera Central, Dominican Republic; 10,414 ft. (3174 m.).

Du·bai \dü-ˈbī\. **1.** Emirate. See *Dubayy* in table at UNITED ARAB EMIRATES.

2. Coastal town, Dubayy emirate. See DUBAYY 2.

Du·bawnt *also* **Doo·baunt** \dü-ˈbȯnt\. River, N cen. Canada; rises in lakes in SE corner of Northwest Territories, flows N into Nunavut through **Dubawnt Lake** (1600 sq. mi. or 4144 sq. km.) and E through Aberdeen Lake into Baker Lake; 580 mi. (933 km.) long.

Du·bayy *or* **Du·bai** \dü-ˈbī\. **1.** Emirate. See table at UNITED ARAB EMIRATES.

2. Coastal town, its ✻; pop. (1981p) 265,702; deepwater port.

Dub·bo \ˈdə-bō\. Town, E cen. New South Wales, SE Australia, on Macquarie River 165 mi. (265 km.) NW of Sydney; pop. (1991c) 28,064; center of coal- and copper-bearing region; zoo.

Dü·ben·dorf \ˈdūē-bən-ˌdȯrf\. Commune, Zürich canton, NE cen. Switzerland, NE of the city of Zürich; pop. (1989c) 20,803; chemicals.

Dubis. See DOUBS 1.

Dub·lin \ˈdə-blin\. **1.** City, Alameda co., W California, 12 mi. (19 km.) SE of Oakland; pop. (1990c) 23,229.

2. City, ⊗ of Laurens co., cen. Georgia, 47 mi. (76 km.) ESE of Macon; pop. (1990c) 16,312; lumber industry; incorp. 1812.

3. Town, Cheshire co., SW corner of New Hampshire, ab. 12 mi. (19 km.) SSE of Keene; pop. (1990c) 1474; summer resort.

4. Village, in Delaware and Franklin cos., cen. Ohio, NW of Columbus; pop. (1990c) 16,366.

5. City, Erath co., N cen. Texas, 43 mi. (69 km.) NE of Brownwood; pop. (1990c) 3190.

6. County in Leinster prov., E Ireland. See table at IRELAND.

7. *or Gaelic* **Bai·le Atha Cli·ath** \blä-ˈklē-ə\; *anc.* **Eb·la·na** \ˈe-blə-nə\. City and seaport, ✻ of Ireland and ⊗ of co. Dublin, E Ireland, at mouth of Liffey River on **Dublin Bay;** pop. (1991p) 477,675; iron founding, shipbuilding, glass manufacture, stout brewing; noted castle, founded c. 1200; Christ Church Cathedral (Anglican), started 1053, the only one of Danish foundation in British Isles; St. Patrick's Cathedral (Anglican), which had writer Jonathan Swift as dean 1713–45; seat of Trinity Coll. (called also Univ. of Dublin), founded 1591, and of University Coll. of the National Univ. of Ireland (1909); birthplace of writers James Joyce (1882), Sean O'Casey (1880), and William Butler Yeats (1865).

History: Stronghold of Norse power in Ireland from 9th cent.; in battle of Clontarf (suburb of Dublin) occurred the Danish defeat at hands of Irish led by High King Brian Boru 1014; given charter and made center of English Pale by Henry II in expedition of 1171–72; besieged 1646 and surrendered to Parliamentarians 1647; scene of Phoenix Park murders 1882 and of Easter Rebellion 1916 (see IRELAND).

Dublon. See TONOAS.

Dub·na \ˈdüb-nə\. City, Moscow Oblast, W cen. Russia in Europe, on the Volga; pop. (1991e) 67,200; founded 1956 as a planned city for scientific research.

Dub·no \ˈdüb-nə\. Town, Rivne subdivision, Ukraine, 30 mi. (48 km.) SE of Luts'k; formerly in Poland. Passed to Russia in Third Partition of Poland 1795; changed hands several times in WWI; taken by Germany in WWII.

Du·bois \dü-ˈbȯis\. **1.** County in SW Indiana. See table at INDIANA.

2. Village, ⊗ of Clark co., E Idaho; pop. (1990c) 420.

Du Bois \dü-ˈbȯis\. City, Clearfield co., W cen. Pennsylvania, 46 mi. (74 km.) NNW of Altoona; pop. (1990c) 8286; in coal-mining and agricultural region.

Du·bov·ka \dü-ˈbȯf-kə\. Town, cen. Volgograd Oblast, S Russia in Europe, on the Volga 33 mi. (53 km.) N of the city of Volgograd; formerly an important Cossack center.

Dubris Portus. See DOVER 7.

Du·brov·nik \ˈdü-ˌbrȯv-nik\ *also Ital.* **Ra·gu·sa** \rä-ˈgü-sä\. Seaport, Croatia, on the coast ab. 90 mi. (145 km.) SSW of Sarajevo, Bosnia and Herzegovina; pop. (1991c) 55,638; tourism; alcoholic beverages, cheese; silk; 15th cent. palace. Founded 7th cent. by Romans; independent republic until conquered by French Emperor Napoléon 1808 and included in Illyrian Provinces; center of art and literature in Middle Ages; passed to Austria 1815; incorp. into Yugoslavia 1918.

Du·buque \də-ˈbyük\. **1.** County in E Iowa. See table at IOWA.

2. City, its ⊗, on Mississippi River; pop. (1990c) 57,546; river port in agricultural area; packinghouses; heavy equipment; health care; Univ. of Dubuque (1852), Clarke Coll. (1843), Loras Coll. (1839); first settled permanently 1833 (one of the oldest cities in Iowa); incorp. as city 1841.

Ducato, Cape. See DOUKATO, CAPE.

Ducatus Romae. See ROME, DUCHY OF.

Duch·cov \ˈdu̇k-ˌtsȯf\ *or Ger.* **Dux** \ˈdu̇ks\. City, NW Czech Republic, in foothills of Erzgebirge 48 mi. (77 km.) NW of Prague; pop. (1980p) 10,554.

Du·chesne \dü-ˈshān\. **1.** River, NE Utah; rises in Uinta Mts., flows S and E into Green River; ab. 120 mi. (193 km.) long.

2. County in NE cen. Utah. See table at UTAH.

3. City, ⊗ of Duchesne co., NE cen. Utah; pop. (1990c) 1308.

Du·cie Island \ˈdü-sē, ˈdyü-\. Uninhabited coral island 325 mi. (523 km.) E of Pitcairn I., in S Pacific Ocean, 24°40′S, 124°48′W; 2.5 sq. mi. (6 sq. km.); annexed by Great Britain 1902 and attached to Pitcairn I. colony.

Duck \ˈdək\. River, W cen. Tennessee; rises in Coffee co., flows W and NW into Tennessee River; 250 mi. (402 km.) long.

Duckwater Peak. See WHITE PINE MOUNTAINS.

Dud·don \ˈdəd-ᵊn\. River bet. Lancashire (Furness) and Cumberland, NW England; flows into the Irish Sea by an estuary 7 mi. (11 km.) long; ab. 20 mi. (32 km.) long.

Du·de·lange \dūēd-ˈläⁿzh\ *or Ger.* **Dü·de·ling·en** \ˈdūē-də-ˌliŋ-ən\. Commune, S Luxembourg, on French border 10 mi. (16 km.) S of the city of Luxembourg; pop. (1990e) 14,230.

Du·din·ka \dü-ˈdyiŋ-kə\. Town, ✻ of Taymyr Autonomous Okrug, N Russia in Asia, on Yenisey River near its mouth; pop. (1991e) 36,400; port; coal deposits nearby.

Dud·ley \ˈdəd-lē\. **1.** Town, Worcester co., cen. Massachusetts, 16 mi. (26 km.) SSW of the city of Worcester; pop. (1990c) 9540; Nichols Coll. (1815).

2. Town, West Midlands, W cen. England, 10 mi. (16 km.) WNW of Birmingham; pop. (1991p) 300,400; bricks, leather goods.

Dud·na \ˈdüd-nə\. River, E Maharashtra, S cen. India; flows SE into Godavari River W of Nander.

Dud·wei·ler \ˈdüt-ˌvī-lər\. Town, Saarland, Germany, just N of Saarbrücken.

Dueim, Ed. See ED DUEIM.

Due·ñas \dü-ˈā-nyäs\. Municipality, N cen. Iloilo prov., Panay, Philippines, near Jalaud River 25 mi. (40 km.) N of City of Iloilo; pop. (1980c) 23,962.

Duero. See DOURO.

Due West. Town in Due West township, Abbeville co., W South Carolina, ab. 17 mi. (27 km.) NW of Greenwood; pop. (1990c) 1220; Erskine Coll. (1839).

\ə\ **abut** \ᵊ\ **matches** \ᵊ\ kitten, Fr table \ər\ **further** \a\ **ash** \ā\ **ace** \ä\ cot, cart \á\ Fr bac \au̇\ **out** \b\ Span Avila \ch\ **chin** \e\ **bet** \ē\ **easy** \g\ **go** \i\ **hit** \ī\ **ice** \j\ **job** \k\ Ger **ich, Buch** \ⁿ\ Fr vin \ŋ\ **sing** \ō\ **go** \ȯ\ **all** \ò\ **law** \œ\ Fr bœuf \œ̄\ Fr feu \ȯi\ **boy** \th\ **thin** \t͟h\ **this** \ü\ **loot** \u̇\ **foot** \ue\ Ger füllen \ūē\ Fr **rue** \y\ **yet** \ʸ\ Fr digne \ˈdēnʸ\, nuit \ˈnwʸē\ \yü\ **few** \yu̇\ **fury** \zh\ **vision**

Duf·fel \ˈdü-fəl, ˈdə-\. Commune, Antwerp prov., N Belgium, 10 mi. (16 km.) SSE of the city of Antwerp; pop. (1991c) 15,194; a coarse woolen cloth (*duffel*) orig. made here.

Duf·fer·in \ˈdə-fə-rin\. County in SE Ontario, Canada. See table at ONTARIO.

Duff Islands \ˈdəf\. Small island group in N part of Santa Cruz Is., SW Pacific Ocean; 9°50′S, 167°10′E.

Du·four·spit·ze \dü-ˈfu̇r-ˌshpit-sə\. Highest peak of Monte Rosa and of Pennine Alps, on the Switzerland-Italy border; 15,203 ft. (4634 m.).

Du·gi Otok \ˈdü-gē-ˈō-ˌtȯk\ *or Ital.* **Iso·la Lun·ga** \ˈē-zȯ-lä-ˈlüŋ-gä\. Island belonging to Croatia, in the Adriatic Sea off the Dalmatian coast; 27 mi. (43 km.) long; 46 sq. mi. (119 sq. km.).

Dui·da \ˈdwē-dä\. Mountain, cen. Amazonas terr., S Venezuela; 7952 ft. (2424 m.).

Duis·burg \ˈdu̅e̅s-ˌberk, ˈdüz-bərg, ˈdyüz-\; *from 1929 to 1934* **Duisburg–Ham·born** \ˈhäm-ˌbȯrn\. City and river port, North Rhine-Westphalia, Germany, on the Rhine River at confluence of the Ruhr 12 mi. (19 km.) NNW of Düsseldorf; pop. (1992e) 537,441; Europe's largest inland river port (above tidewater); on W border of Ruhr industrial district; manufactures steel, machinery, chemicals, textiles; shipbuilding; coal; birthplace of sculptor Wilhelm Lehmbruck 1881. Ancient Roman town; passed to duchy of Kleve 1290, then to Brandenburg 1614; became member of Hanseatic League; site of a university 1655–1818; formed by consolidation of former city of Duisburg (residence from 1552 and burial site of cartographer Gerhardus Mercator) with surrounding communities in 1905, 1929 (incl. Hamborn), and 1975; occupied by Belgian and French troops 1921–25; severely bombed in WWII.

Dui·ve·land \ˈdœi-və-ˌlänt\. East part of Schouwen I., Zeeland prov., SW Netherlands; pop. (1981e) 5324.

Duke of Clarence. See NUKUNONO.

Duke of Glouces·ter Islands \ˈglȯs-tər, ˈgläs-\. Group of three small uninhabited islands, French Polynesia, in S Pacific Ocean, 470 mi. (756 km.) SE of Tahiti and 360 mi. (579 km.) NE of Raevavae in the Austral Is.; generally considered a part of the Tuamotu Archipelago.

Duke of York Island \ˈyȯrk\. **1.** Island, in Madre de Dios Archipelago, SW Chile, in S Pacific Ocean at entrance to Concepción Strait.

2. Island belonging to New Zealand, in Tokelau, cen. Pacific Ocean. See ATAFU.

Duke of York Islands. Group of 13 small islands, Papua New Guinea, in Bismarck Archipelago, W Pacific Ocean, at N end of St. George's Channel bet. NE New Britain I. and SW New Ireland I.; total area 23 sq. mi. (60 sq. km.).

Dukes \ˈdüks, ˈdyüks\. County in SE Massachusetts. See table at MASSACHUSETTS.

Duk·in·field \ˈdə-kin-ˌfēld\. Town, Greater Manchester, NW England, 6 mi. (10 km.) E of Manchester; pop. (1981p) 18,063; textiles.

Du·kla \ˈdü-klä\. Town, Krosno prov., SE Poland, 43 mi. (69 km.) SE of Tarnów; pop. (1981p) 1539; just N of **Dukla Pass** in Carpathian Mts., through which Russian army entered Hungary 1849 and which was used again by Russians in both World Wars.

Du·lag \ˈdü-ˌläg\. Municipality on E coast of Leyte I. on Leyte Gulf, Philippines, 19 mi. (31 km.) S of Tacloban; pop. (1980c) 28,219.

Dul·ce \ˈdül-ˌsā\. **1.** River, N cen. Argentina; rises in Tucumán prov., flows SE through several channels into the marsh region N of Mar Chiquita in N Córdoba prov.; 400 mi. (644 km.) long; in upper course called the **Sa·la·dil·lo** \ˌsäl-ə-ˈdē-(ˌ)(y)ō\.

2. River in SE Guatemala; flows from Lake Izabal (or Dulce Gulf) into Honduras Bay; link in commercial waterway from Panzós on the Polochic River to the Caribbean Sea.

Dulce, Gol·fo \ˈgȯl-fō\. Inlet of Pacific Ocean in S Costa Rica, E of Osa Penin.

Dulce Gulf. See IZABAL, LAKE.

Dulcigno. See ULCINJ.

Dül·men \ˈdu̇el-mən\. City, North Rhine-Westphalia, Germany, 16 mi. (26 km.) SW of Münster; pop. (1980c) 38,712.

Du·luth \də-ˈlüth\. **1.** City, Gwinnett co., Georgia; pop. (1990c) 9029.

2. City, ⊗ of St. Louis co., NE Minnesota, at W end of Lake Superior; pop. (1990c) 85,493; commercial center; excellent harbor; ships iron ore, grain, crude oil; medical facilities; tourism. Univ. of Minnesota, Duluth (1947); Coll. of St. Scholastica (1912). Region orig. inhabited by Sioux and Ojibwa; probably explored by Pierre Radisson and Médard Chouort des Groseilliers 1654–60; site of city visited by Daniel Greysolon, Sieur Duluth, in 1679; first permanent settlement c. 1852; incorp. 1870.

Dul·wich \ˈdə-lij, -lich\. District of Southwark borough, S London, England; residential; Dulwich Coll., founded and endowed 1619 by English actor Edward Alleyn, contains notable picture gallery of works esp. of Dutch and Flemish masters.

Du·ma·gue·te \ˌdü-mä-ˈgā-tā\. Chartered city, ✻ of Negros Oriental, Negros, Philippines, in SE part on coast at S end of Tanon Strait; pop. (1990p) 80,000; university (1901).

Du·ma·lag \dü-ˈmä-läg\. Municipality, S Capiz prov., Panay, Philippines, on upper Panay River 21 mi. (34 km.) SSW of Roxas; pop. (1980c) 22,198.

Du·man·gas \dü-ˈmäŋ-gäs\. Municipality, SE Iloilo prov., Panay, Philippines, near coast E of Jalaud River 13 mi. (21 km.) ENE of City of Iloilo; pop. (1980c) 41,241.

Du·man·jug \ˌdü-män-ˈhüg\. Municipality, Cebu prov., W coast of Cebu I., Philippines, on Tanon Strait 37 mi. (60 km.) SW of City of Cebu; pop. (1980c) 25,258.

Du·ma·ran \ˌdü-mä-ˈrän\. Island in Sulu Sea off NE coast of Palawan I., Palawan prov., W Philippines; 120 sq. mi. (311 sq. km.); chief town Araceli on E coast; thickly wooded.

Du·mas \ˈdü-məs\. **1.** City, Desha co., SE Arkansas, 39 mi. (63 km.) SE of Pine Bluff; pop. (1990c) 5520.

2. City, ⊗ of Moore co., NW Texas, 30 mi. (48 km.) WNW of Borger; pop. (1990c) 12,871.

Dum·bar·ton \ˌdəm-ˈbärt-ᵊn\. **1.** *or* **Dum·bar·ton·shire** \-ˌshir, -shər\. Former county, W cen. Scotland. See DUNBARTON.

2. Burgh, Strathclyde region, Scotland, on Leven River near its junction with the Clyde; pop. (1991e) 79,750; distilling; engineering works; in S part rising abruptly from the bank of the Clyde is Dumbarton Rock, a twin-peaked hill, site of Pictish and Norse fortresses and of a Scottish castle, which was prison of patriot Sir William Wallace before his removal to London for trial and execution (1305) and residence from which infant Mary, Queen of Scots, was spirited away to France 1548; ✻ of medieval Celtic kingdom of Strathclyde.

Dumbarton Oaks \ˈōks\. Mansion, Georgetown, Washington, D.C., where representatives of China, U.S.S.R., United Kingdom, and U.S. met Aug. 21 to Oct. 7, 1944 and formulated proposals for a world organization which were the basis of the organization of the United Nations as created at San Francisco in 1945.

Dum·béa \düm-ˈbā-ä\ *or* **La Dum·béa** \ˌlä-\. Village, SE New Caledonia I., NNW of Nouméa; pop. (1989c) 10,052.

Dum Dum *or* **Dum–Dum** \ˈdəm-ˌdəm\. Town, West Bengal, NE India, near Calcutta; pop. (four municipalities [1991p]) 427,666; headquarters of Bengal artillery 1783–1853; dumdum bullets were first made here.

Du·mei·ra \dü-ˈmā-rä\. Small island off coast of NE Africa, in Bab el Mandeb Strait.

Dum·fries \ˌdəm-ˈfrēs\. **1.** Town, Prince William co., Virginia; pop. (1990c) 4282.

2. *or* **Dum·fries·shire** \-ˌshir, -shər\. Former county, S Scotland, ⊗ Dumfries; contained the rivers Nith, Annan, Esk.

3. Burgh, ⊗ of Dumfries and Galloway region, S Scotland; pop. (1981p) 32,084; trade center; manufactures esp. hosiery and tweeds; residence (1791–96) and burial place of poet Robert Burns.

Dumfries and Galloway. Administrative region, S Scotland; estab. 1975. See table at SCOTLAND.

Du·mont \'dü-ˌmänt\. Borough, Bergen co., NE corner of New Jersey, 9 mi. (14 km.) E of Paterson; pop. (1990c) 17,187.
Dümrek. See SIMOÏS.
Dumyāṭ. See DAMIETTA.
Du·na \'dü-nö, -nə\. **1.** River, Hungary. See DANUBE.
2. River, Russia. See DON 3.
Düna. See DVINA, WESTERN.
Dünaburg. See DAUGAVPILS.
Du·na·gi·ri \ˌdü-nə-'gir-ē\. Mountain in the Himalayas, Uttar Pradesh, N India; 23,184 ft. (7066 m.).
Du·na·jec \dü-'nä-yets\. River, S Poland; flows N from Carpathian Mts. into Vistula River; 156 mi. (251 km.) long; scene of heavy fighting in WWI in the Austro-German offensive under Gen. August von Mackensen against Russia 1915.
Du·na·ke·szi \'dü-nö-ˌke-sē\. Town, Pest co., cen. Hungary; pop. (1991e) 27,800.
Dünamünde. See DAUGAVGRĪVA.
Dunărea. See DANUBE.
Du·na·új·vá·ros \'dü-nö-ˌüy-ˌvä-rōsh\. Town, W cen. Hungary, ab. 35 mi. (56 km.) SSW of Budapest, on the Danube; pop. (1991e) 60,000; iron and steel, textiles.
Dunav. See DANUBE.
Du·nav·ska \'dü-nəv-skə, -nəf-\. Former county (1929–45), NE Yugoslavia; 11,461 sq. mi. (29,684 sq. km.); ⊗ Novi Sad; since 1945 divided bet. Serbia and Vojvodina.
Dunay. See DANUBE.
Dun·bar \'dən-ˌbär\. City, Kanawha co., W cen. West Virginia, on Kanawha River W of Charleston; pop. (1990c) 8697.
Dun·bar \ˌdən-'bär\. Burgh, Lothian region, SE Scotland, at mouth of the Firth of Forth E of Edinburgh; pop. (1981p) 6015; fishing port and summer resort; scene of Parliamentarian commander Oliver Cromwell's victory Sept. 3, 1650 over Lord Alexander Leslie's Covenanters.
Dun·bar·ton \dən-'bärt-ᵊn\ *or* **Dun·bar·ton·shire** \-ˌshir, -shər\ *or* **Dum·bar·ton** \dəm-\ *or* **Dum·bar·ton·shire.** Former county, W cen. Scotland; ⊗ Dumbarton; its only important river the Clyde.
Dun·can \'dəŋ-kən\. **1.** City, ⊗ of Stephens co., S Oklahoma, 27 mi. (43 km.) E of Lawton; pop. (1990c) 21,732; oil wells; manufactures gasoline, oil-well machinery; founded c. 1892.
2. City, SE Vancouver I., British Columbia, Canada, 28 mi. (45 km.) NNW of Victoria; pop. (1991c) 4301; lake resort.
Duncan Passage. Channel separating Rutland and Great Andaman islands on the N from Little Andaman I. on the S, E Bay of Bengal; ab. 32 mi. (51 km.) wide.
Dun·cans·by Head \'dəŋ-kənz-bē\. Extreme NE point of the mainland in Highland region, Scotland; alt. 210 ft. (64 m.).
Dun·can·ville \'dəŋ-kən-ˌvil\. Town, Dallas co., NE Texas, 12 mi. (19 km.) SW of the city of Dallas; pop. (1990c) 35,748.
Dun·dalk \'dən-ˌdȯk\. Unincorporated settlement, Baltimore co., N Maryland; pop. (1990c) 65,800; Dundalk Community Coll. (1970).
Dun·dalk \dən-'dȯk, -'dȯlk\. Town and seaport, ⊗ of co. Louth, NE Ireland, on Dundalk Bay near mouth of Castletown River; pop. (1986c) 26,669; fisheries; trades in livestock and farm products. Captured c. 1315 by Scottish nobleman Edward Bruce who proclaimed himself king of Ireland here; nearby was scene of Bruce's defeat and death in battle against forces of English King Edward II 1318; damaged by fire during 1922–23 civil war.
Dundalk Bay. Inlet of Irish Sea on extreme NE coast of Ireland.
Dun·das \ˌdən-'das, 'dən-dəs\. **1.** Former county of Ontario, Canada; now part of Stormont, Dundas and Glengarry co.
2. Town, Hamilton-Wentworth munic. region, SE Ontario, Canada, a W suburb of the city of Hamilton; pop. (1991c) 21,868.
Dundas Strait \'dən-dəs\. Passage from Van Diemen Gulf to Arafura Sea, separating Cobourg Penin. from Melville I., Australia; ab. 18 mi. (29 km.) wide.
Dun·dee \ˌdən-'dē\. **1.** Village, Monroe co., SE corner of Michigan, 23 mi. (37 km.) S of Ann Arbor; pop. (1990c) 5376.
2. Seaport and burgh, ⊗ of Tayside region, E Scotland, on N bank of Firth of Tay; pop. (1991e) 172,860; electronics, textiles; service center for North Sea oil drilling; Univ. of Dundee (1967); ravaged many times in Scottish-English wars.
3. Town, E Rep. of South Africa, 120 mi. (193 km.) NNW of Durban; center of rich iron and coal district; occupied by British forces prior to the battle of Talana Hill, early in the Boer War, fought nearby Oct. 20, 1899.
Dun·drum Bay \ˌdən-'drəm\. Inlet of Irish Sea in co. Down, on SE coast of Northern Ireland, S of Strangford Lough.
Dun·dy \'dən-dē\. County in S Nebraska. See table at NEBRASKA.
Dun·e·din \ˌdə-'nē-din\. **1.** City, Pinellas co., W Florida Penin., on Gulf of Mexico 20 mi. (32 km.) NW of St. Petersburg; pop. (1990c) 34,012; distribution center for citrus fruit; winter resort; settled 1850s.
2. City, SE South I., New Zealand, at head of Otago Harbor 190 mi. (306 km.) SW of Christchurch; pop. (1991c) 116,577; port; manufactures furniture; exports include frozen meat and wool; Univ. of Otago (1869); founded by Scottish Presbyterians 1848; gold discovered nearby 1861.
Dun·el·len \də-'ne-lən\. Borough, Middlesex co., cen. New Jersey, 7 mi. (11 km.) N of New Brunswick; pop. (1990c) 6528.
Dun·ferm·line \dən-'fərm-lin, dəm-\. Burgh, Fife region, E Scotland; pop. (1991e) 129,910; manufactures linen and metal products; coal mining; Dunfermline Abbey, burial place of Malcolm III, Robert I (the Bruce), and other Scottish kings (11th–17th cents.); birthplace of Charles I of England (1600) and of industrialist Andrew Carnegie (1835).
Dun·gan·non \dən-'ga-nən\. **1.** District, Northern Ireland; estab. 1974. See table at IRELAND, NORTHERN.
2. Town, its ⊗, 8 mi. (13 km.) W of Lough Neagh; pop. (1990e) 43,800; linen.
Dun·gar·pur \'du̇ŋ-gər-ˌpu̇r\. **1.** Former state, NW India; 1460 sq. mi. (3781 sq. km.); under British protection 1818; became part of Rajasthan 1948.
2. Town, its ✻, 90 mi. (145 km.) NE of Ahmadabad; pop. (1991p) 35,608.
Dun·gar·van \dən-'gär-vən\. Town and seaport, S co. Waterford, S Ireland, on **Dungarvan Harbour** at mouth of Colligan River; pop. (1986c) 6849; remnants of a castle built by King John of England and of a medieval priory.
Dunge·ness *also* **Dunge Ness** \'dən-jə-'nes, dənj-'nes\. Headland on SE coast of England, projecting into Strait of Dover.
Dungeness Point. Cape in S Argentina, at N side of entrance to Strait of Magellan.
Dun·geon Gill Force \'dən-jən-gil-'fōrs\. Waterfall, Westmorland, NW England, E of Bow Fell in Lake District; 90 ft. (27 m.) high.
Dunheved. See LAUNCESTON.
Dunholme. See DURHAM 9.
Dun·huang *or W.-G.* **Tun–huang** \'du̇n-'hwäŋ\. Town, W Gansu prov., N cen. China. An important trading center on the Silk Road from first millennium B.C.; its location as crossroads promoted cultural exchange with W Asia; became important Buddhist center with nearby founding 4th cent. A.D. of caves dedicated to Buddha; a place of pilgrimage into 2d millennium A.D., caves later became disregarded; in early 20th cent. rediscovered, yielding thousands of cultural objects, among them manuscripts dealing with Buddhism and other religions.
Dun·keld \dən-'keld\. Town, Tayside region, cen. Scotland, on Tay River NW of Perth; early site of Celtic Christianity; ruins of 12th cent. cathedral.
Dun·kerque \dœⁿ-'kerk\ *or Eng.* **Dun·kirk** \'dən-ˌkərk, dən-'\ *or earlier French* **Dun·querque** \dœⁿ-'kerk\. Fortified seaport and city, Nord dept., N France, on Strait of Dover 44 mi. (71 km.) NW of Lille; pop. (1990c) 71,071; shipbuilding

yard; oil refining; foodstuffs; exports include cement; daily ferry to Dover, England; 16th cent. church; 15th cent. chapel.

History: Founded before 9th cent. A.D.; as part of Flanders, ruled by Burgundy and Spain; taken by English Lord Protector Oliver Cromwell following siege by English and French who defeated Spanish in "Battle of the Dunes" June 4, 1658; formally awarded to England by Pyrenees Treaty 1659 and sold to France by Charles II 1662; served as a base in 17th cent. for privateer Jean Bart (born here 1650); in Treaties of Utrecht 1713, Aix-la-Chapelle 1748 and Paris 1763, France agreed to demolish and to not rebuild its fortifications; in WWI object of German drives and target of German shelling; in WWII scene of evacuation of over 300,000 Allied soldiers from Flanders after fall of France May–June 1940; at end of war surrendered by Germans May 1945; largely rebuilt after the war.

Dun·kirk \ˈdən-ˌkərk\. **1.** City, Blackford and Jay cos., E Indiana, 11 mi. (18 km.) NE of Muncie; pop. (1990c) 2739.
2. City and port of entry, Chautauqua co., SW corner of New York, on Lake Erie 35 mi. (56 km.) SW of Buffalo; pop. (1990c) 13,989; in grape-growing region.
3. City, France. See DUNKERQUE.

Dunk Island \ˈdəŋk\. Island, 2.5 mi. (4 km.) off E coast of Queensland, NE Australia, ab. 60 mi. (97 km.) S of Cairns; Capt. James Cook first spotted the island 1770; home for 25 years of the Australian naturalist and journalist Edmund James Banfield, author of *The Confessions of a Beachcomber.*

Dunk·lin \ˈdən-klin\. County in SE Missouri. See table at MISSOURI.

Dun Laoghai·re \ˌdün-ˈler-ə, ˌdən-, -ˈlir-\ *or* **Dun·lea·ry** \dən-ˈlir-ē\; *formerly* **Kings·town** \ˈkiŋz-ˌtaün\. Borough, SE co. Dublin, E Ireland, on S shore of Dublin Bay; pop. (1986c) 54,715; seaport; fisheries; noted yachting center.

Dun·lap \ˈdən-ˌlap\. City, ⊗ of Sequatchie co., SE Tennessee; pop. (1990c) 3731.

Dun·man·us Bay \dən-ˈma-nəs\. Inlet of Atlantic Ocean on SW coast of Ireland, S of Bantry Bay.

Dun·more \ˈdən-ˌmōr\. Borough, Lackawanna co., NE Pennsylvania, 3 mi. (5 km.) E of Scranton; pop. (1990c) 15,403; center of once heavily mined anthracite region.

Dunmore Head. Promontory, co. Kerry, Munster prov., SW Ireland, N of Dingle Bay; most W point of mainland of Ireland, 10°30′W.

Dun·mow \ˈdən-ˌmō\ *or* **Little Dunmow.** Village, Essex, SE England, ab. 35 mi. (56 km.) NE of London; known for the custom (originated c. 13th cent.) of awarding a flitch of bacon to any couple who will swear that they have not quarreled or repented of their marriage within a year and a day of its celebration.

Dunn \ˈdən\. **1.** Name of counties in two states of the U.S. See tables at NORTH DAKOTA and WISCONSIN.
2. Town, Harnett co., cen. North Carolina, 24 mi. (39 km.) NE of Fayetteville; pop. (1990c) 8336.

Dun·net Head \ˈdə-nət\. Cape on NE coast of Scotland; the northernmost point of the Scottish mainland, 58°39′N; lighthouse.

Dunn·ville \ˈdən-ˌvil\. Town, Haldimand-Norfolk munic. region, SE Ontario, Canada, on Grand River 29 mi. (47 km.) SSE of Hamilton; pop. (1991c) 12,131; summer resort.

Dun·oon \də-ˈnün\. Coastal burgh, Strathclyde region, W Scotland; pop. (1981p) 9372; resort; ruins of ancient castle; statue of "Highland Mary" (Mary Campbell, the subject of several songs by Robert Burns), who was born nearby.

Dunquerque. See DUNKERQUE.

Dun·qu·lah. See DONGOLA.

Dun·ra·ven, Mount \dən-ˈrā-vən\. Mountain, Larimer co., N cen. Colorado, in Rocky Mountain National Park; 12,548 ft. (3825 m.).

Duns \ˈdənz\. Burgh, NE Borders region, SE Scotland; formerly ⊗ of Brewick co.

Dun·score \dən-ˈskōr\. Village, Dumfries co., S Scotland; site of Craigenputtock, farm home of essayist and historian Thomas Carlyle.

Dun·si·nane \dən-ˈsi-nən; *in "Macbeth"*, ˌdən-si-ˈnān\. Hill in Sidlaw Hills, Tayside region, cen. Scotland; 1012 ft. (308 m.); topped by ruins of a fort, purported scene of defeat of King Macbeth by Danish warrior Siward 1054.

Duns·muir \ˈdənz-ˌmyu̇r\. City, Siskiyou co., N California, near Mt. Shasta ab. 100 mi. (161 km.) ENE of Eureka; pop. (1990c) 2129; summer resort (hunting and fishing).

Dun·sta·ble \ˈdən-stə-bəl\. Town, Bedfordshire, SE cen. England, 32 mi. (51 km.) NNW of London; pop. (1981p) 30,912; motor vehicles, paper; engineering; Stone Age and Bronze Age ruins nearby; church built on remains of 12th cent. priory; venue of court at which Archbishop of Canterbury Thomas Cranmer ruled Catherine of Aragon's marriage to Henry VIII invalid (1533).

Dun·veg·an, Loch \ˈläk-dən-ˈve-gən\. Sea inlet on W coast of Skye I. in the Inner Hebrides, off NW coast of Scotland; enclosed on W by peninsula ending in **Dunvegan Head,** 100 ft. (30 m.) high.

Duo·lun \ˈdwō-ˈlu̇n\ *or W.-G.* **To–lun** \ˈdō-ˈlün\ *or* **Do·lon·nur** \ˈdō-ˌlōn-ˈnu̇r\ *mostly formerly* **Do·lon–nor** \-ˈnu̇r\. Town, Nei Monggol (Inner Mongolia), N China, ab. 120 mi. (195 km.) NW of Chengde.

Du Page \dü-ˈpāj\. County in NE Illinois. See table at ILLINOIS.

Du·plin \ˈdə-plin\. County in SE North Carolina. See table at NORTH CAROLINA.

Du·po \ˈdü-ˌpō\. Village, St. Clair co., SW Illinois, 10 mi. (16 km.) S of East St. Louis; pop. (1990c) 3164; limestone.

Du·pont \dü-ˈpänt\. Borough, Luzerne co., E Pennsylvania, 9 mi. (14 km.) NE of Wilkes-Barre; pop. (1990c) 2984; coal.

Düppel. See DYBBØL.

Du·pree \dü-ˈprē\. Town, ⊗ of Ziebach co., NW cen. South Dakota; pop. (1990c) 484.

Du·que de Bra·gan·ça Falls \ˈdü-kē-dē-brá-ˈgäⁿn-sə\. Falls in the Lucala River, NW Angola, 188 mi. (302 km.) E of Luanda; 344 ft. (105 m.) high.

Du·que de Ca·xi·as \ˈdü-kē-dē-ká-ˈshē-əs\. City, Rio de Janeiro state, SE Brazil; munic. pop. (1991p) 664,643.

Du·quesne \du̇-ˈkān\. City, Allegheny co., SW Pennsylvania, on Monongahela River 10 mi. (16 km.) ESE of Pittsburgh; pop. (1990c) 8525; former steelmaking center.

Du Quoin \dü-ˈkȯin\. City, Perry co., SW Illinois, ab. 20 mi. (32 km.) N of Carbondale; pop. (1990c) 6697.

Du·ra–Eu·ro·pos \ˈdu̇r-ə-yu̇-ˈrō-pəs, ˈdyu̇r-\. Ancient town of Mesopotamia on right bank of the Euphrates; inhabited esp. as a fortress by Seleucids (c. 300 B.C.), Romans (c. 165 A.D.), and others; destroyed by Sassanids c. 256; now village of **Sa·la·hi·yeh** \ˌsä-lə-ˈhē-yə\ in SE Syria near Iraqi border; important archaeological site.

Durah Pass. See DORAH PASS.

Durán. See ALFARO.

Du·rance \dæ̅-ˈräⁿs\. River, SE France; rises in Hautes-Alpes dept., flows SW into Rhone River 3 mi. (5 km.) SW of Avignon; ab. 180 mi. (290 km.) long.

Du·rand \du̇-ˈrand, dyu̇-\. **1.** City, Shiawassee co., S cen. Michigan, 17 mi. (27 km.) WSW of Flint; pop. (1990c) 4283.
2. City, ⊗ of Pepin co., W Wisconsin, 16 mi. (26 km.) S of Menomonie; pop. (1990c) 2003.

Du·ran·go \du̇-ˈraŋ-gō, dyu̇-\. **1.** City, ⊗ of La Plata co., SW Colorado, 18 mi. (29 km.) N of New Mexico border and 70 mi. (113 km.) ENE of SW corner of Colorado; pop. (1990c) 12,430; alt. ab. 6505 ft. (1985 m.); oil and natural-gas wells; tourism; Fort Lewis Coll. (1911); settled 1880.
2. State of NW cen. Mexico. See table at MEXICO.
3. *or officially* **Vic·to·ria de Durango** \vik-ˈtō-rē-ä-ˌthā-dü-ˈräŋ-gō\. City, its ✻, NW cen. Mexico; munic. pop. (1990p) 414,015; alt. 6314 ft. (1925 m.); center of mining and farming district; university (1856, university status 1957). Settled 1556; important political and religious center in early history of N Mexico.

Duranius. See DORDOGNE 1.

Du·rant \du̇-ˈrant, dyu̇-\. **1.** Town, Holmes co., W cen. Mississippi, 36 mi. (58 km.) SE of Greenwood; pop. (1990c) 2838.

2. City, ⊗ of Bryan co., S Oklahoma, 46 mi. (74 km.) ESE of Ardmore; pop. (1990c) 12,823; cotton, peanuts; oil; Southeastern Oklahoma State Univ. (1909).

Du·raz·no \dü-ˈräs-nō\. **1.** Department of cen. Uruguay. See table at URUGUAY.

2. *or* **San Pe·dro del Durazno** \sän-ˈpā-thrō-del-\. Town, its ✱, near Yi River 105 mi. (169 km.) N of Montevideo; pop. (1985c) 27,835.

Durazzo. See DURRËS.

Dur·ban \ˈdər-bən\. Seaport, E Rep. of South Africa, on landlocked lagoon, inlet of Indian Ocean; pop. (1985c) 634,301; the republic's leading port; shipbuilding, oil refining; chemicals, fertilizers, food products, footwear, textiles; resort; Univ. of Natal (1949); Univ. of Durban-Westville (1960); large Indian and Malayan population. Settled 1824; township laid out 1835 and named after Sir Benjamin D'Urban, then governor of Cape Colony; British garrison, besieged by Boers 1842. See NATAL 2.

Dü·ren \ˈdūē-rən\; *anc.* **Mar·co·du·rum** \ˌmär-kō-ˈdu̇r-əm, -ˈdyu̇r-\. City, North Rhine-Westphalia, Germany, on Rur River 18 mi. (29 km.) E of Aachen; pop. (1992e) 86,888; paper, sugar; botanical garden; astronomical observatory. First mentioned as Frankish settlement 8th cent.; scene of diets held by Holy Roman Emperor Charlemagne; passed to count of Jülich mid-13th cent.; burned by Holy Roman Emperor Charles V 1543; to France 1801, Prussia 1814; severely damaged in WWII; expanded 1970s by annexing adjacent communities.

Durg \ˈdu̇rg\; *formerly* **Drug** \ˈdrüg\. Town, SE Madhya Pradesh, E cen. India, 150 mi. (241 km.) E of Nagpur; pop. (1991p) 150,513.

Dur·ga·pur \ˈdu̇r-gə-ˌpu̇r\. Town, West Bengal, NE India; pop. (1991c) 425,836; steelmaking center.

Durge Nur. See DÖRGÖN NUUR.

Dur·ham \ˈdər-əm, ˈdu̇r-\. **1.** County in NE cen. North Carolina. See table at NORTH CAROLINA.

2. Town, Middlesex co., S Connecticut, 6 mi. (10 km.) S of Middletown; pop. (1990c) 5732; eggs and dairy products; settled c. 1699.

3. Town, Strafford co., SE New Hampshire, 5 mi. (8 km.) SSW of Dover; pop. (1990c) 11,818; Univ. of New Hampshire (founded at Hanover as part of Dartmouth Coll. 1866, removed to Durham 1893); settled 1635; scene of Indian attacks, notably 1675, 1694, 1704.

4. City, ⊗ of Durham co., NE cen. North Carolina, 20 mi. (32 km.) NW of Raleigh; pop. (1990c) 136,611; research center with historically notable cigarette and textile industries; Duke Univ. (1838), North Carolina Central Univ. (1909), Durham Technical Community Coll. (1961); region settled c. 1750; town founded c. 1853; incorp. 1869; made ⊗ 1881.

5. Municipal region in SE Ontario, Canada. See table at ONTARIO.

6. Town, Grey co., SE Ontario, Canada, 28 mi. (45 km.) S of Owen Sound; pop. (1991c) 2558.

7. Former county, N England.

8. County, N England, incl. most of former county; rivers include Tees and Wear; estab. 1974. See table at ENGLAND.

9. *or Saxon* **Dun·holme** \ˈdə-nəm\. City, ⊗ of Durham co., N England, on the Wear 15 mi. (24 km.) S of Newcastle upon Tyne; pop. (1991p) 85,000; important fortress and religious center following Norman Conquest; 11th cent. cathedral and castle, Univ. of Durham (1832).

Durius. See DOURO.

Dürkheim. See BAD DÜRKHEIM.

Durle·ston Head \ˈdərl-stən\. Headland on S coast of Dorset, S of Bournemouth, S England; lighthouse.

Dur·mi·tor \ˈdür-mē-ˌto̊r\. Mountain mass, cen. Montenegro, Yugoslavia, ESE of Mostar; highest peak Bobotov Kuk 8274 ft. (2522 m.); highest point of Dinaric Alps.

Durnovaria. See DORCHESTER 5.

Durobrivae. See ROCHESTER 8.

Durocasses. See DREUX.

Durocortorum. See REIMS.

Durostorum. See SILISTRA.

Durovernum. See CANTERBURY 3.

Dur·rës \ˈdu̇r-əs\ *or Ital.* **Du·raz·zo** \dü-ˈrät-sō\. **1.** District of W Albania. See table at ALBANIA.

2. *anc.* **Ep·i·dam·nus** \ˌe-pi-ˈdam-nəs\; *later* **Dyr·ra·chi·um** *or* **Dyr·rha·chi·um** \də-ˈrā-kē-əm\. Seaport, its ✱, on Adriatic Sea; pop. (1990e) 85,500; Albania's major port; outlet for Tiranë and shipping point for products incl. olive oil, tobacco, rubber products, and leather goods; has large Muslim population; Grand Mosque.

History: Ancient Epidamnus a colony founded by Corcyra and Corinth c. 625 B.C.; dispute over it a cause of Peloponnesian War; under Romans (after 229 B.C.) an important port at start of overland route across Greece; administrative subdivision of Dyrrachium a division of Byzantine Empire; taken by Norman military leader Robert Guiscard 1081–82 and by Normans 1185; after its capture by Angevins 1272, changed hands frequently bet. Albanians, Serbians, and Angevins; ruled by Venice 1392–1501, and by Turks 1501–1913; after occupation by Serbs 1912–13, made part of principality of Albania (*q.v.*); occupied by Italians and Austrians in WWI; heavily damaged in WWII; martial law imposed March 1991 to halt mass emigrations in commandeered ships.

Dur Shar·ru·kin \ˈdu̇r-shä-ˈrü-kin\. See KHORSABAD.

Durūz, Jabal ad. See DRUZE, JEBEL.

d'Urville, Cape. See PERKAM, CAPE.

D'Ur·ville Island \ˈdər-ˌvil\. Island, lying bet. Tasman Bay and Cook Strait off N coast of South I., New Zealand.

Dur·yea \ˈdu̇r-ˌyā, ˌdu̇r-ˈyā\. Borough, Luzerne co., E Pennsylvania, 7 mi. (11 km.) SW of Scranton; pop. (1990c) 4869; coal deposits.

Du·shan·be \ˈdyü-ˌshäm-bə, ˌdyü-shäm-ˈbā\; *until 1929* **Du·sham·be** *or* **Dyu·sham·be** *same*\; *from 1929 to 1961* **Sta·lin·a·bad** \ˌstä-lyi-nə-ˈbäd, ˌsta-li-nə-ˈbad\. City, ✱ of Tajikistan; pop. (1989p) 595,000; textiles; railroad terminus, connecting via Termez with Bukhara; Academy of Sciences (1951); earthquake Jan. 1989 (epicenter ab. 30 mi. or 48 km. SW) caused mudslide that killed hundreds in nearby village.

Düs·sel \ˈdūē-səl\. River, North Rhine-Westphalia, Germany; flows SW into the Rhine at Düsseldorf; ab. 20 mi. (32 km.) long.

Düs·sel·dorf \ˈdūē-səl-ˌdo̊rf, ˈdü-, ˈdyü-\. City and river port, ✱ of North Rhine-Westphalia, Germany, on Rhine River 21 mi. (34 km.) NNW of Cologne; pop. (1992e) 577,561; iron and steel, automobiles, paper, clothing, chemicals, machinery; 14th cent. Gothic church; Academy of Art (1767); university (1965). Birthplace of poet Heinrich Heine 1797. Founded before 11th cent.; became city 1288; residence of dukes of Berg, electors of the Palatinate; 1805 became ✱ of grand duchy of Berg created by French Emperor Napoléon; transferred to Prussia 1815; occupied by Allies 1921–25; heavily damaged in WWII.

Dutch Borneo. See BORNEO.

Dutch East Indies. See INDONESIA 2.

Dutch·ess \ˈdə-chəs\. County in SE New York. See table at NEW YORK.

Dutch Guiana. See SURINAME 2.

Dutch Harbor \ˈdəch\. Port and village, SW Alaska, on E Amaknak I. in Unalaska Bay, on N side of E end of Unalaska I., E Aleutian Is.; has harbor 1.75 mi. (3 km.) long by .75 mi. (1 km.) wide; the port, ab. 1.5 mi. (2 km.) N of Unalaska village, is used as port of call; crab fishing; in early days the center of the fur-sealing industry; U.S. naval base estab. 1940; attacked by Japanese aircraft June 1942; annexed by Unalaska 1965.

Dutch New Guinea. See IRIAN JAYA.

Du·tse \ˈdü-tsā\. City, ✱ of Jigawa State, N cen. Nigeria.

Duttia. See DATIA.

Dut·ton, Mount \ˈdət-ᵊn\. Peak, NW Garfield co., S Utah; 10,800 ft. (3292 m.).

Du·val \dü-ˈvȯl, də-, -ˈval\. Name of counties in two states of the U.S. See tables at FLORIDA and TEXAS.
Du·vall \dü-ˈvȯl, də-, -ˈval\. City, King co., Washington, 15 mi. (24 km.) ENE of Seattle; pop. (1990c) 2770.
Dúvida, Rio da. See ROOSEVELT, RIO.
Du·wa·mish \də-ˈwä-mish\ *or* **Dwa·mish** \ˈdwä-\. Navigable river, W cen. Washington; formed by confluence of Green and White rivers in SW King co., flows N into Puget Sound at Seattle.
Duwaym, Ad. See ED DUEIM.
Duweir, Tell ed–. See LACHISH.
Dux. See DUCHCOV.
Dux·bury \ˈdəks-ˌber-ē, -bər-\. Residential town, Plymouth co., SE Massachusetts, on Plymouth Bay 17 mi. (27 km.) ESE of Brockton; pop. (1990c) 13,895; summer resort.
Duzdab. See ZĀHEDĀN.
Dvi·na, Northern \dvē-ˈnä\ *or Russ.* **Se·ver·na·ya Dvina** \ˈse-vər-nə-yə\. River, N Russia in Europe; 466 mi. (750 km.) long; drainage basin 140,000 sq. mi. (362,600 sq. km.); navigable length 342 mi. (550 km.); chief river of White Sea basin; major tributaries: Pinegskaya Yentala, Vaga, Vychegda.
Dvina, Western *or Russ.* **Za·pad·na·ya Dvina** \ˈzä-pəd-nə-yə\ *or Lettish* **Dau·ga·va** \ˈdau̇-gə-və\ *or Ger.* **Dü·na** \ˈdūē-nə, ˈdü-, ˈdyü-\. River, N cen. Europe; rises in Russia's Valdai Hills, near sources of the Volga and the Dnieper, flows SW and W across N Belarus and SE and S Latvia to Gulf of Riga near Riga; 634 mi. (1020 km.) long; drainage basin 32,900 sq. mi. (85,211 sq. km.); generally navigable to Vitsyebsk; has many short tributaries; connected by canal systems with the Neva, Volga, and Dnieper rivers.
Dvina Gulf *or* **Dvina Bay** *or Russ.* **Dvin·ska·ya Gu·ba** \ˈdvin-skə-yə-gə-ˈbä\; *formerly* **Gulf of Arch·an·gel** \ˈär-ˌkān-jəl\. Southeast arm of White Sea, Arkhangel'sk Oblast, N Russia in Europe; receives Northern Dvina River; port of Arkhangel'sk at its head.
Dvinsk. See DAUGAVPILS.
Dvůr Krá·lo·vé nad La·bem \ˈdvür-ˈkrä-lȯ-ˌvā-ˌnäd-ˈlä-ˌbem\ *or Ger.* **Kö·ni·gin·hof** \ˈkœ-ni-gin-ˌhōf\. Town, N Czech Republic, 65 mi. (105 km.) ENE of Prague on Elbe River; pop. (1991p) 16,972.
Dwamish. See DUWAMISH.
Dwar·ka \ˈdwär-kə\. Seaport, Gujarat, W India, at W end of Kathiawar Penin.; pop. (1991p) 27,823; temple of Krishna; one of the seven sacred cities of India.
Dwight \ˈdwīt\. Village, Livingston co., NE cen. Illinois, 35 mi. (56 km.) SW of Joliet; pop. (1990c) 4230.
Dwor·shak Dam *and* **Dworshak Reservoir** \ˈdwȯr-ˌshäk\. See UNITED STATES, *Dams and Reservoirs.*
Dwy·ka \ˈdwī-kä\. River in Great Karoo region of Rep. of South Africa; flows into the Gamka NW of Oudtshoorn; ab. 90 mi. (145 km.) long; has given its name to a geological division of South Africa.
Dyardanes. See BRAHMAPUTRA.
Dyaul. See DJAUL.
Dyb·bøl \ˈdu̇eb-bœl\ *or Ger.* **Düp·pel** \ˈdue-pəl\. Town, Sønderjylland co., Denmark, on coast 6 mi. (10 km.) SW of Sønderborg; historically in duchy of Schleswig; scene of several struggles bet. Danes and Germans 1848 and 1849; held by Denmark 1850 until recaptured by Prussians 1864; held by Germany until returned to Denmark under plebiscite 1920.
Dy·ea \ˈdī-ˌā\. Former village, SE Alaska, at head of Taiya Inlet, N end of Lynn Canal; after discovery of gold (1896–97) in Klondike region, became supply center and starting point for trail over Chilkoot Pass to Dawson and northern mining fields; just NW of Skagway, which superseded it on opening of White Pass.
Dy·er \ˈdī-ər\. **1.** County in NW Tennessee. See table at TENNESSEE.
2. Town, Lake co., NW Indiana; pop. (1990c) 10,923.
Dyer, Cape. Easternmost point of Cumberland Penin., Baffin I., Canada, on Davis Strait, 61°18′W.
Dy·ers·burg \ˈdī-ərz-ˌbərg\. City, ⊗ of Dyer co., NW Tennessee, 45 mi. (72 km.) NW of Jackson; pop. (1990c) 16,317; cotton, cottonseed oil.
Dy·ers·ville \ˈdī-ərz-ˌvil\. City, Delaware and Dubuque cos., E Iowa, 25 mi. (40 km.) W of the city of Dubuque; pop. (1990c) 3703.
D'Yeu, Île. See YEU, ÎLE D'.
Dy·fed \ˈdə-ved, -vid\. **1.** Ancient region in SW Wales, now part of Dyfed co.
2. County, SW Wales, estab. 1974; includes former counties of Cardigan, Carmarthen, and Pembroke. See table at WALES.
Dy·fi *or* **Dov·ey** \ˈdə-vē\. River, W Wales; flows S and SW into Cardigan Bay; 30 mi. (48 km.) long.
Dyfrdwy. See DEE 3.
Dyke Ack·land Bay *or* **Dyke Ac·land Bay** \ˈdīk-ˈa-klənd\. Inlet of Solomon Sea on SE coast of island of New Guinea, SE of Holnicote Bay. See ORO BAY.
Dyke Lake \ˈdīk\. Large lake in W Labrador, Canada; forms part of course of Churchill River.
Dykh Tau *or* **Dykh·tau** *or* **Dikh Tau** \ˈdik-ˌtau̇\. Mountain in a N spur of the Caucasus Mts., S Kabardino-Balkaria, S Russia in Europe, 43°03′N, 43°08′E; 17,070 ft. (5203 m.).
Dyle. See DIJLE.
Dyrrachium *or* **Dyrrhachium.** See DURRËS 2.
Dy·sart \ˈdī-zərt\. Former burgh and seaport, SE cen. Scotland, on the Firth of Forth; since 1930 part of Kirkcaldy; ruins of chapel of St. Serf; in 15th and 16th cents. manufactured salt.
Dyushambe. See DUSHANBE.
Dza–chu. See MEKONG.
Dzaudzhikau. See VLADIKAVKAZ.
Dzer·zhinsk \dzir-ˈzhēnsk\. City, W Nizhegorod Oblast, cen. Russia in Europe, just W of Nizhniy Novgorod, on Oka River; pop. (1992e) 287,000; chemicals; engineering.
Dzer·zhins'k \dzir-ˈzhēnsʸk\. Town, Donets'k subdivision, Ukraine, ab. 25 mi. (40 km.) N of the city of Donets'k; pop. (1991e) 51,000.
Dzhalal Abad. See JALAL-ABAD.
Dzhambul *and* **Dzhambul Oblast.** See ZHAMBYL.
Dzhan·koy *also* **Dzhan·koi** \jəŋ-ˈkȯi\. Town, N Crimea, 55 mi. (88 km.) N of Simferopol'; pop. (1991e) 55,500; railroad junction; in WWII held by Germans 1941–44.
Dzhez·kaz·gan \ˌjes-kəz-ˈgän\. Town, Qaraghandy region, Kazakhstan, ab. 280 mi. (451 km.) SW of the city of Qaraghandy; pop. (1991e) 111,100; copper deposits.
Dzhirgalantu. See HOVD.
Dzhul'·fa; *formerly* **Jul·fa** \jül-ˈfä\. Town, Naxcıvan Rep., Azerbaijan, on Araks River 25 mi. (40 km.) SE of the town of Naxcıvan; junction point of Russian railroad lines for Tabrīz in Iran.
Dzier·żo·niów \jer-ˈzhȯ-ˌnyüf\ *or Ger.* **Rei·chen·bach** \ˈrī-kən-ˌbäk\. Town, Wałbrzych prov., SW Poland, ab. 30 mi. (48 km.) SW of Wrocław; pop. (1989e) 37,840; machinery, textiles. Founded in 12th cent.; scene of battle of Reichenbach 1762 in which Prussian King Frederick the Great defeated the Austrians; scene of Austro-Prussian diplomatic congress 1790 and of conference of coalition against French Emperor Napoléon 1813; assigned to Poland by Potsdam Conference 1945.
Dzisna. See DISNA.
Dzungaria. See JUNGGAR.
Dzun·gar·ian Ala Tau \zu̇ŋ-ˈgar-ē-ən-ˈä-lä-ˈtau̇, dzu̇ŋ-, zəŋ-\ *or Chin.* **Ala·taw Shan** *or W.-G.* **A–la–t'ao Shan** \ˈä-lä-ˈtau̇-ˈshän\. Mountain range bet. E Kazakhstan and NW Xinjiang Uygur, W China; highest peak 16,550 ft. (5044 m.).
Dzungarian Basin. See JUNGGAR.
Dzungarian Gate *or Chin.* **Ala·taw Shan·kou** \ˈä-lä-ˈtau̇-ˈshän-ˈkau̇\ *or W.-G.* **A–la Shan–k'ou** \ˈä-lä-ˈshän-ˈkau̇\. Pass in Dzungarian Ala Tau on border bet. Kazakhstan and Xinjiang Uygur, China; used for centuries as a migration and invasion route.

E

Eads \ˈēdz\. Town, ⊗ of Kiowa co., E Colorado; pop. (1990c) 780; natural gas.

Ea·gan \ˈē-gən\. City, Dakota co., SE Minnesota; pop. (1990c) 47,409.

Ea·gle \ˈē-gəl\. **1.** County in NW cen. Colorado. See table at COLORADO.
2. Town, its ⊗; pop. (1990c) 1580.

Eagle Grove. City, Wright co., N cen. Iowa, 20 mi. (32 km.) NE of Fort Dodge; pop. (1990c) 3671.

Eagle Lake. **1.** Lake in cen. Lassen co., NE California.
2. Lake in N Aroostook co., N Maine; drains into a tributary of Aroostook River.
3. Lake in N Piscataquis co., N cen. Maine.
4. City, Colorado co., SE cen. Texas, 40 mi. (64 km.) S of Brenham; pop. (1990c) 3551.
5. Lake, Kenora dist., SW Ontario, Canada; 140 sq. mi. (363 sq. km.); chief outlet through Rainy Lake.

Eagle Mountain. **1.** Peak, Cook co., NE Minnesota; 2301 ft. (701 m.); highest peak in the state.
2. Peak, Hudspeth co., W Texas; 7516 ft. (2291 m.).

Eagle Pass. City and port of entry, ⊗ of Maverick co., SW Texas, on the Rio Grande 52 mi. (84 km.) SSE of Del Rio; pop. (1990c) 20,651; site of U.S. Army encampment (Camp Eagle Pass) during war with Mexico; on one of favorite routes to California during gold rush of 1849; resort.

Eagle Peak. Mountain in SE Yellowstone National Park, NW Wyoming; 11,358 ft. (3462 m.).

Eagle River. **1.** Village, ⊗ of Keweenaw co., N Upper Penin. of Michigan, on Lake Superior.
2. City, ⊗ of Vilas co., N Wisconsin; pop. (1990c) 1374; summer resort.

Eagles Rest \ˈē-gəlz\. Peak in N Grand Teton National Park, NW Wyoming; ab. 11,257 ft. (3431 m.).

Ea·ling \ˈē-liŋ\. A borough of Greater London, SE England; pop. (1991p) 263,600; birthplace of biologist Thomas Huxley 1825. See table at LONDON 4.

Earle \ˈərl\. City, Crittenden co., E Arkansas, 27 mi. (43 km.) WNW of Memphis, Tennessee; pop. (1990c) 3393.

Ear·ling·ton \ˈər-liŋ-tən\. City, Hopkins co., W Kentucky, 28 mi. (45 km.) N of Hopkinsville; pop. (1990c) 1833; coal deposits.

Earl's Seat. See LENNOX HILLS.

Earls·ton \ˈərl-stən\; *orig.* **Er·cel·doune** *also* **Er·cil·doune** \ˈər-səl-ˌdün\. Parish and market town, E cen. Borders region, SE Scotland, near Melrose; pop. (1981p) 1599; ruin of ancient tower, the "Rhymer's Castle," residence of Thomas of Erceldoune or Thomas Learmont, seer and poet.

Ear·ly \ˈər-lē\. County in SW Georgia. See table at GEORGIA.

Earn \ˈərn\. River, Tayside region, cen. Scotland; flows out of Loch Earn and into the Tay River; 46 mi. (74 km.) long.

Earn, Loch. Lake, Central and Tayside regions, cen. Scotland; 7 mi. (11 km.) long.

Earns·law, Mount \ˈərnz-ˌlȯ\. Peak in Southern Alps, SW cen. South I., New Zealand; 9261 ft. (2823 m.).

Ear of Di·o·ny·si·us \ˌdī-ə-ˈni-shē-əs, -shəs; -ˈnī-sē-əs\. A narrow cavern in one of the ancient quarries of Siracusa, Sicily, Italy, tapering to an orifice above, where the tyrant Dionysius the Elder is said to have listened, as one still may, to conversation below.

Earth \ˈərth\. The planet on which we live; believed to be ab. 4,600,000,000 years old; equatorial circumference 24,902 mi. (40,067 km.); divided into continental masses and oceanic depressions with oceans covering 71 percent; total land area ab. 57,000,000 sq. mi. (147,630,000 sq. km.).

Earthquake Lake. See QUAKE LAKE.

Eas·ley \ˈēz-lē\. City, Pickens co., NW South Carolina, 13 mi. (21 km.) W of Greenville; pop. (1990c) 15,195; textiles.

East, The. **1.** The countries of Asia and of the Asian archipelagoes; the countries E of Europe; the Orient. See FAR EAST, MIDDLE EAST, and NEAR EAST.
2. In U.S. history and geography, formerly the part of the U.S. located E of the Allegheny Mts., esp. the New England states; now, often, the region E of the Mississippi River.

East Africa. A term often used of the area now comprising the countries of Tanzania, Kenya, Uganda, Rwanda, Burundi, and Somalia; sometimes used to include also other neighboring countries of E Africa.

East African Community. Former economic organization, consisting of Kenya, Tanzania, Uganda; formed 1967 to strengthen economic cooperation; disbanded 1977.

East Africa Protectorate. See KENYA.

East Al·ton \ˈȯlt-ᵊn\. Village, Madison co., SW Illinois, on Mississippi River 5 mi. (8 km.) E of Alton; pop. (1990c) 7063.

East An·glia \ˈaŋ-glē-ə\. **1.** Ancient division, incl. modern Norfolk and Suffolk, England; probably settled by Angles (see ANGELN), it emerged as one of kingdoms in Anglo-Saxon Heptarchy (*q.v.*); Christianized and subjugated by Mercia 7th cent.; practically absorbed in Mercia by 8th cent.; Danish territory according to the Peace of Wedmore 878; conquered by Wessex 10th cent.; Danish earldom under King Canute.
2. Geographical region of England comprising the counties of Norfolk and Suffolk.

East Antarctica. See ANTARCTICA.

East Aurora. Village, Erie co., W New York, 15 mi. (24 km.) ESE of Buffalo; pop. (1990c) 6647; seat of former Roycroft colony (handicrafts) and Roycroft Press, estab. by American writer, editor, and printer Elbert Hubbard 1895; settled 1804.

East Australian Current. Warm ocean current, South Pacific Ocean, flowing S off E coast of Australia.

East Avon. See AVON 7.

East Azerbaijan. Province of NW Iran. See AZERBAIJAN 1.

East Bat·on Rouge \ˌbat-ᵊn-ˈrüzh\. Parish in SE cen. Louisiana. See table at LOUISIANA.

East Bengal. Region, approx. coextensive with Bangladesh; formerly part of Bengal prov., British India; to Pakistan 1947; subsequently became East Pakistan prov.; part of Bangladesh 1971.

East Berlin. See BERLIN, EAST.

East Beskids. See BESKIDS, EAST.

East Beth·el \ˈbe-thəl\. City, Anoka co., E Minnesota, 27 mi. (43 km.) N of Minneapolis; pop. (1990c) 8050.

East Boston. Section of Boston, Massachusetts, on E side of Charles River estuary; site of Boston's Logan International Airport.

East·bourne \ˈēst-ˌbȯrn\. Town, East Sussex, S England, on English Channel 57 mi. (92 km.) S of London; pop. (1991p) 83,200; resort.

East Bridgewater. Town, Plymouth co., SE Massachusetts, 5 mi. (8 km.) SSE of Brockton; pop. (1990c) 11,104.

East Caicos See TURKS AND CAICOS ISLANDS.

East Cape. **1.** Most easterly point of the island of New Guinea, 151°E; marks NE corner of Milne Bay.
2. Cape on E coast of North I., New Zealand, easternmost point of North I., 178°33′E.
3. Cape, Russia. See DEZHNEVA MYS.

East Car·roll \ˈkar-əl\. Parish in NE corner of Louisiana. See table at LOUISIANA.

East–Central. Former state of S Nigeria; 11,548 sq. mi. (29,909 sq. km.); divided 1976 into Anambra and Imo.

East Charlevoix. See CHARLEVOIX-EST.

East Chicago. City, Lake co., NW corner of Indiana, on Lake Michigan 18 mi. (29 km.) SE of Chicago; pop. (1990c) 33,892; formerly notable center of manufacturing (esp. steel, chemicals, railroad equipment); refines oil.

East Chicago Heights. See FORD HEIGHTS.

East China Sea. See CHINA SEA.

East Chosen Bay. See TONGJOSŎN MAN.

East Cleveland. City, Cuyahoga co., N Ohio, 5 mi. (8 km.) ENE of Cleveland; pop. (1990c) 33,096; residential suburb; electrical research laboratories.

East Coast Bays. Borough, North I., New Zealand; NNW of Auckland; pop. (1981c) 28,866.

East Cote Blanche Bay. See COTE BLANCHE BAY.

East Dere·ham \ˈdir-əm\. Town, Norfolk, E England, 14 mi. (23 km.) W of Norwich; pop. (1981p) 11,845; home of poet William Cowper 1796–1800.

East Detroit. See EASTPOINTE.

East Dun·dee \dən-ˈdē\. Village, Kane co., NE Illinois, 35 mi. (56 km.) WNW of Chicago; pop. (1990c) 2721.

East Ems. See EMS.

Eas·ter Island \ˈē-stər\ *or Span.* **Is·la de Pas·cua** \ˈēs-lä-thā-ˈpäs-kwä\ *or native* **Ra·pa Nui** \ˈrä-pä-ˈnü-ē\. Island in S Pacific Ocean, 27°08′S, 109°23′W, ab. 2000 mi. (3218 km.) W of the Chilean coast; 46 sq. mi. (119 sq. km.); pop. (1985e) 1928; highest point 1765 ft. (538 m.); has hundreds of monolithic statues of human form averaging ab. 15 ft. (4.6 m.) in height. First European discovery made on Easter Sunday 1722 by Dutch Adm. Jacob Roggeveen; previously settled by Polynesians; annexed by Chile 1888.

East·ern \ˈē-stərn\. Region of NE Sudan; ✱ Kassala.

Eastern Bay. Inlet of Chesapeake Bay on SW coast of Queen Annes co., E Maryland.

Eastern Bengal. Former province of India. See *History* at ASSAM and BENGAL.

Eastern Cape. Province of S Rep. of South Africa. See table at SOUTH AFRICA, REPUBLIC OF.

Eastern Desert. See ARABIAN DESERT.

Eastern Empire. See BYZANTINE EMPIRE.

Eastern Euphrates. See MURAT NEHRI.

Eastern Fle·vo·land \ˈflā-vō-ˌlänt\. See ZUIDER ZEE.

Eastern Ghats. See GHATS.

Eastern Group. See LAU GROUP.

Eastern Hemi·sphere \ˈhe-mi-ˌsfir\. The part of Earth E of the Atlantic Ocean incl. Europe, Asia, Australia, and Africa; longitudes 20°W and 160°E often considered as its boundaries.

Eastern Highlands. See GREAT DIVIDING RANGE.

Eastern Island. See MIDWAY.

Eastern Ka·thi·a·war \ˈkä-tē-ə-ˌwär, -ˌvär\. Former agency, subdivision of Western India States Agency, W India, now part of Gujarat state.

Eastern Locris. See LOCRIS.

Eastern Macedonia and Thrace. Region of Greece; 5466 sq. mi. (14,157 sq. km.); pop. (1991c) 570,261. For subdivisions, see table at GREECE.

Eastern Manych. See MANYCH 3.

Eastern Province. Province, E Kenya. See table at KENYA.

Eastern Rajputana States. E part of former Rajputana Agency, NW India, comprising states of Bharatpur, Bundi, Dholpur, Jhalawar, Karauli, and Kotah (*qq.v.*). See RAJPUTANA AGENCY.

Eastern Range. Mountain range, Kamchatka (*q.v.*), E Russia in Asia; has several high volcanic peaks, incl. Klyuchevskaya Sopka 15,580 ft. (4749 m.), highest peak in Siberia.

Eastern Region 1. English name for El Oriente (*q.v.*). **2.** Administrative region of SE Ghana. See table at GHANA.

Eastern Roman Empire. See BYZANTINE EMPIRE.

Eastern Ru·me·lia \rü-ˈmē-lē-ə, -lyə\. Balkan region, now S part of Bulgaria, incl. Rhodope Mts. and valley of the Maritsa River; 12,585 sq. mi. (32,595 sq. km.); chief town Plovdiv (Philippopolis); estab. as autonomous province of Turkey 1878; annexed to Bulgaria 1885; Bulgarian annexation caused Serbian war against Bulgaria 1885–86 and a crisis in European diplomacy (1885–88) in which Russia failed to achieve separation of region from Bulgaria.

Eastern Sa·mar \ˈsä-ˌmär\. Province, E Samar, Philippines; ✱ Borongan. See table at PHILIPPINES.

Eastern Samoa. See AMERICAN SAMOA.

Eastern Schelde. See OOSTERSCHELDE.

Eastern Sea. See CHINA SEA.

Eastern Sea·board \ˈsē-ˌbōrd\. Region, E United States; usu. considered as incl. that part of the U.S. bordering on the Atlantic coast.

Eastern Shore. Region of Maryland and Virginia comprising that part of Maryland E of Chesapeake Bay and the counties of Accomac and Northampton in Virginia; by some thought to include all of Delaware and thus equivalent to the Delmarva Penin.

Eastern Siberian Region. Former subdivision of the U.S.S.R., consisting of the cen. and E parts of Siberia; 1,591,813 sq. mi. (4,122,769 sq. km.); chief town Irkutsk.

Eastern Sierra Madre. See SIERRA MADRE ORIENTAL.

Eastern Silesia. Former duchy in N Austria-Hungary, bet. Prussian Silesia and Moravia; chief town Opava; in 20th cent. its W two thirds became Czech prov. of Slezsko (Silesia); its E section was nearly equivalent to Teschen (*q.v.*).

Eastern States. 1. The New England states: Maine, New Hampshire, Vermont, Massachusetts, Rhode Island, and Connecticut— unofficially so called; in certain groupings, as in the former Federal Land Bank system, New York and New Jersey are included.
2. The states of the U.S. along the Atlantic seaboard E of the Allegheny Mts.— a term occasionally used in the Mississippi Valley and in states W of it. See EAST, THE 2.
3. Former group of Indian states, NE India; area 66,989 sq. mi. (173,502 sq. km.); comprised 42 states, two of which, Cooch Behar and Tripura (*qq.v.*), were on E border of Bengal prov.; others in region bet. Bihar on NE and Central India on SW, at one time part in Central Provinces and part (Orissa Feudatory States; 18,151 sq. mi. or 47,011 sq. km.) in Orissa. Under the British government had direct relations with the crown representative through resident at Calcutta; July 15, 1947, 39 of the 42 states formed an administrative union within India for more coordinated action on matters of common interest.

Eastern Thrace. See THRACE.

Eastern Townships. Towns of S Quebec, Canada, E of Montreal and S of the St. Lawrence—popularly so called; chief center Sherbrooke.

Eastern Trans·vaal \trans-ˈväl, tranz-\. See *Mpumalanga* in table at SOUTH AFRICA, REPUBLIC OF.

Eastern Vi·sa·yas \vē-ˈsī-yäs\. Region of the Philippines. See table at PHILIPPINES.

East Falkland. See FALKLAND ISLANDS.

East Fe·li·ci·ana \fə-ˌli-shē-ˈa-nə\. Parish in E Louisiana. See table at LOUISIANA.

East Flanders. Province, NW cen. Belgium; ✱ Ghent; formerly part of the region of Flanders (*q.v.*); rivers Schelde, Leie, Dender; potatoes, flax, hops, sugar beets; livestock; manufactures textiles, leather, food products. See table at BELGIUM.

East Florida. See *History* at FLORIDA.

East Fremantle. See FREMANTLE.

East Friesland. See OSTFRIESLAND.

East Frisian Islands. See FRISIAN ISLANDS.

East Gary. See LAKE STATION.

East Germany. See GERMANY, EAST.

East Gran·by \ˈgran-bē\. Town, Hartford co., N Connecticut, 12 mi. (19 km.) N of the city of Hartford; pop. (1990c) 4302; incorp. 1858; nearby is Newgate Prison, used in Revolutionary days and one of early state prisons, now a tourist site.

East Grand Forks. City, Polk co., NW Minnesota, on Red River opp. Grand Forks, North Dakota; pop. (1990c) 8658.

East Grand Lake. See GRAND LAKE 8.

East Grand Rapids. City, Kent co., W Michigan, suburb of Grand Rapids; pop. (1990c) 10,807; incorp. as a village 1891, as a city 1926.

East Green·wich \ˈgre-nich\. Town and summer resort, ⊗ of

Kent co., cen. Rhode Island, 12 mi. (19 km.) WSW of Providence; pop. (1990c) 11,865.

East Grin·stead \ˈgrin-stəd\. Town, West Sussex, S England; pop. (1981c) 22,394.

East Had·dam \ˈha-dəm\. Town, E Middlesex co., S Connecticut, on Connecticut River; pop. (1990c) 6676; recreation, tourism; Goodspeed Opera House, off-Broadway theater; incorp. 1734.

East·ham \ˈēst-ˌham, ˈēs-təm\. Town, Barnstable co., SE Massachusetts, ab. 25 mi. (40 km.) from Provincetown; pop. (1990c) 4462.

East·hamp·ton \ˌēst-ˈhamp-tən\. Town, Hampshire co., W Massachusetts, 12 mi. (19 km.) NNW of Springfield; pop. (1990c) 15,537; Williston Northampton School (coed preparatory school, 1971).

East Hamp·ton \ˈhamp-tən\. **1.** Town, NE Middlesex co., S Connecticut; pop. (1990c) 10,428; manufactures bells, netting, machine parts and tools; incorp. as Chatham 1767.
2. Village and summer resort, Suffolk co., SE New York, on Long Island, on Atlantic Ocean 20 mi. (32 km.) W of Montauk Point; pop. (1990c) 16,132; Clinton Academy (estab. 1784) was first academy of higher education in New York; home of John Howard Payne, composer of *Home, Sweet Home;* settled 1648; considered part of Connecticut until 1664.

East Hartford. Town, E cen. Hartford co., N Connecticut, on E side of Connecticut River opp. Hartford; pop. (1990c) 50,452; airplane engines; settled c. 1640.

East Haven. Suburban residential town, S New Haven co., Connecticut, on Long Island Sound; pop. (1990c) 26,144; summer resort; includes Lake Saltonstall, site of first iron mill in Connecticut; incorp. 1785.

East Hills. Village, Nassau co., New York, in SW cen. Long Island; pop. (1990c) 6746.

East In·dies \ˈin-ˌdēz\. **1.** *also* **East In·dia** \ˈin-dē-ə\. Collective name applied, loosely and vaguely, to India, Indochina, and the Malay Archipelago.
2. In better usage, politically, name applied to the Republic of Indonesia, formerly the Netherlands East Indies. See INDIES. By some writers used to include all the islands of the Malay Archipelago.

East Indonesia. State of the former United States of Indonesia (see INDONESIA 2), now part of the Republic of Indonesia; included Celebes (Sulawesi), the Moluccas, Bali, Lombok, Flores, Timor (Dutch sector), and other smaller islands of cen. Malay Archipelago; ✱ Ujung Pandang. Estab. Dec. 25, 1946, first state to be set up with the approval of the Netherlands in movement to form the United States of Indonesia.

East Islip \ˈī-slip\. Village, Suffolk co., SE New York, on S shore of Long Island; pop. (1990c) 14,325.

East Jaffrey. See JAFFREY.

East Java. Province, Java I., Indonesia. See JAVA and table at INDONESIA.

East Jer·sey \ˈjər-zē\. E and N part of New Jersey constituting a proprietary colony from 1676 to 1702 when it was united with West Jersey to form the royal province of New Jersey (*q.v.*); ✱ (from 1686) Perth Amboy; held by English colonialist William Penn and associates from 1682.

East Kalimantan. See KALIMANTAN, EAST.

East Ka·zakh·stan \ˌkä-zäk-ˈstän, ˌka-zak-ˈstan\. Subdivision of Kazakhstan; bounded on N by Altay Kray, Russia, on NE by Gorno-Altay Rep., Russia, on E and S by Xinjiang Uygur, China, and on W by Semey subdivision; 37,568 sq. mi. (97,301 sq. km.); ✱ Öskemen; silver, lead, and zinc deposits.

East Kil·bride \kil-ˈbrīd\. Burgh, Strathclyde region, Scotland, ab. 9 mi. (15 km.) SE of Glasgow; pop. (1991e) 70,500; engineering; electronics; clothing.

East·lake \ˈēst-ˌlāk\. City, Lake co., NE Ohio, on Lake Erie 20 mi. (32 km.) NE of Cleveland; pop. (1990c) 21,161; residential suburb of Cleveland.

East·land \ˈēst-lənd\. **1.** County in N cen. Texas. See table at TEXAS.
2. City, its ⊗, 50 mi. (81 km.) E of Abilene; pop. (1990c) 3690; trade center.

East Lans·downe \ˈlanz-ˌdau̇n\. Borough, Delaware co., SE Pennsylvania, near Philadelphia; pop. (1990c) 2691.

East Lansing. City, Ingham co., S Michigan, 5 mi. (8 km.) E of Lansing; pop. (1990c) 50,677; Michigan State Univ. (1855).

East Las Vegas. See LAS VEGAS 2.

East·leigh \ˈēst-ˌlē\. Town, Hampshire, S England, 6 mi. (10 km.) NNE of city of Southampton; pop. (1991p) 103,200; engineering.

East Liverpool. City, Columbiana co., E Ohio, on Ohio River 18 mi. (29 km.) N of Steubenville; pop. (1990c) 13,654; center of ceramic industry; settled 1798; incorp. 1834.

East London *or Afrikaans* **Oos–Lon·den** \ˌōs-ˈlən-dən\; *orig.* **Port Rex** \ˈreks\. City, S Rep. of South Africa, at mouth of Buffalo River 150 mi. (241 km.) ENE of Port Elizabeth; pop. (1985c) 85,699; wool; furniture, glass, textiles; fishing, fruit canning; resort; founded 1847, a military post in British Kaffraria.

East Long·mead·ow \ˈlȯŋ-ˌme-dō\. Town, Hampden co., SW Massachusetts, 5 mi. (8 km.) SE of Springfield; pop. (1990c) 13,367.

East Los Angeles. Unincorporated settlement, Los Angeles co., SW California; pop. (1990c) 126,379.

East Lo·thi·an \ˈlō-t͟hē-ən\ *or* **Had·ding·ton** \ˈha-diŋ-tən\ *or* **Had·ding·ton·shire** \-ˌshir, -shər\. Former county, SE Scotland; ⊗ Haddington; now part of Lothian region.

East Lyme \ˈlīm\. Residential town, SW New London co., SE Connecticut, on Long Island Sound; pop. (1990c) 15,340; incorp. 1839; tourism.

East Mc·Kees·port \mə-ˈkēz-ˌpōrt\. Residential borough, Allegheny co., SW Pennsylvania, 12 mi. (19 km.) E of Pittsburgh; pop. (1990c) 2678.

East·main \ˈēst-ˌmān\. River, W Quebec, Canada; flows W into James Bay; 510 mi. (821 km.) long; dammed for hydroelectric power generation.

East Malaysia. See MALAYSIA 1.

East·man \ˈēst-mən\. City, ⊗ of Dodge co., S cen. Georgia, 52 mi. (84 km.) SE of Macon; pop. (1990c) 5153.

East Mas·sa·pe·qua \ˌma-sə-ˈpē-kwə\. Unincorporated settlement, Nassau co., New York, on Long Island, SE of Mineola; pop. (1990c) 19,550.

East Mauch Chunk. See JIM THORPE.

East Meadow. Unincorporated settlement, Nassau co., New York, on Long Island E of Hempstead; pop. (1990c) 36,909.

East Moline. City, Rock Island co., NW Illinois, a suburb of Moline on Mississippi River; pop. (1990c) 20,147; state hospital.

East Naples. Unincorporated settlement, ⊗ of Collier co., SW Florida; pop. (1990c) 22,951.

East New Britain. See NEW BRITAIN 2.

East Nishnabotna. See NISHNABOTNA.

East North·port \ˈnȯrth-ˌpōrt\. Unincorporated settlement, Suffolk co., New York, on Long Island E of Huntington; pop. (1990c) 20,411.

East Nu·sa Teng·ga·ra \ˈnü-sə-teŋ-ˈgär-ə\. Province of Indonesia, in Lesser Sunda Is. See table at INDONESIA.

East Okoboji. See OKOBOJI.

Eas·ton \ˈē-stən\. **1.** Town, Fairfield co., SW Connecticut, 6 mi. (10 km.) E of Bridgeport; pop. (1990c) 6303.
2. Town, ⊗ of Talbot co., E Maryland, on E shore of Chesapeake Bay 28 mi. (45 km.) ESE of Annapolis; pop. (1990c) 9372.
3. Town, Bristol co., SE Massachusetts, 7 mi. (11 km.) SW of Brockton; pop. (1990c) 19,807.
4. City, ⊗ of Northampton co., E Pennsylvania, at junction of Lehigh and Delaware rivers 15 mi. (24 km.) ENE of Allentown; pop. (1990c) 26,276; paper, textiles, machinery, steel, cement; Lafayette Coll. (1826); became ⊗ 1752; incorp. as borough 1789, as city 1887.

East Orange. City, Essex co., NE New Jersey, residential suburb WNW of Newark; pop. (1990c) 73,552; electric motors, paint; largest of "The Oranges" (Orange, East Orange, West Orange, South Orange); incorp. as separate township 1863, as city 1899.

East Pacific Rise. Ridge, SE Pacific Ocean floor, extending from S of Mexico to approx. 120°W, 50°S in a general N to S direction; a center of oceanic crust formation according to theory of plate tectonics.

East Pakistan. See BANGLADESH.

East Palestine. City, Columbiana co., E Ohio, 18 mi. (29 km.) S of Youngstown; pop. (1990c) 5168; clay; estab. 1828.

East Palo Al·to \ˌpa-lō-ˈal-tō\. City, San Mateo co., W California; pop. (1990c) 23,451.

East Paterson. See ELMWOOD PARK 2.

East Peoria. City, Tazewell co., cen. Illinois, across Illinois River from Peoria; pop. (1990c) 21,378; Illinois Central Coll. (1966).

East Petersburg. Borough, Lancaster co., SE Pennsylvania, 3 mi. (5 km.) NW of the city of Lancaster; pop. (1990c) 4197.

East·pha·lia \ēst-ˈfā-lyə, -lē-ə\. E section of the ancient duchy of Saxony, Germany; bordered on the E by the Elbe River and on the S by the Harz Mts.

East Point. **1.** City, Fulton co., NW cen. Georgia, 7 mi. (11 km.) SSW of Atlanta; pop. (1990c) 34,402; textiles; Atlanta Christian Coll. (1937); incorp. 1887.
2. Point at E tip of Prince Edward I., Canada, extending into the Gulf of St. Lawrence.
3. Cape at E end of Anegada I. in the British Virgin Is., West Indies.
4. Cape at E end of St. Croix in the Virgin Is. of the U.S.
5. Cape at E end of Vieques I., Puerto Rico, E of the main island of Puerto Rico.

East·pointe \ˈēst-ˌpȯint\; *formerly* **East Detroit.** City, Macomb co., SE Michigan, 10 mi. (16 km.) NE of Detroit; pop. (1990c) 35,283.

East·port \ˈēst-ˌpōrt\. City, Washington co., SE corner of Maine, on island in Passamaquoddy Bay 24 mi. (39 km.) SE of Calais; pop. (1990c) 1965; fisheries.

East Prairie. City, Mississippi co., SE Missouri, 38 mi. (61 km.) S of Cape Girardeau; pop. (1990c) 3416.

East Providence. City, Providence co., N Rhode Island; pop. (1990c) 50,380; chemicals, jewelry, machinery; oil refining; suburb of Providence; orig. part of Seekonk, Massachusetts; set apart and incorp. 1862.

East Prussia *or Ger.* **Ost·preus·sen** \ˈȯst-ˌprȯis-ᵊn\. Historical region and former province of Prussia, E of Pomerania on SE Baltic shore; inhabited by Old Prussians, conquered by Teutonic Knights 13th cent. (see PRUSSIA); after (Second) Treaty of Torún 1466, retained by Teutonic Knights as vassal of Poland; included in duchy of Prussia secularized by Albert of Brandenburg 1525; province of kingdom of Prussia; scene of Gen. Paul von Hindenburg's successful resistance against Russians (see STĘBARK and MASURIA) in WWI; 1919 separated from rest of Germany by Polish Corridor (*q.v.*) and S part returned to Germany by plebiscite; reunited with territory of the Reich by German conquest of Poland 1939; invaded by Soviet armies in fall of 1944 and overrun Jan.–May 1945; by decision of Potsdam Conference 1945, divided bet. U.S.S.R. and Poland, with Kaliningrad (Königsberg), Chernyakhovsk (Insterburg), and all N of a line drawn E to W just S of the Pregolya (Pregel) River assigned to U.S.S.R. and S two thirds to Poland.

East Punjab. E part of former Punjab prov., India; after 1947 a province (later **Punjab** state, ✱ Chandigarh) of N India; 47,456 sq. mi. (122,911 sq. km.). In 1966 divided into states of Punjab and Haryana (*qq.v.*).

East Ret·ford \ˈret-fərd\. Town, Nottinghamshire, N cen. England, 23 mi. (37 km.) E of Sheffield; pop. (1981p) 19,348.

East Ridge. City, Hamilton co., SE Tennessee, on Georgia border 5 mi. (8 km.) ESE of Chattanooga; pop. (1990c) 21,101.

East Riding. See YORKSHIRE.

East River. Strait connecting Long Island Sound and Upper New York Bay, New York; separates Manhattan and the Bronx from Brooklyn and Queens on Long Island; numerous port facilities.

East River Mountain. Mountain, Bland co., SW Virginia; 3388 ft. (1033 m.); tunnel.

East Rochester. Village, Monroe co., W New York, 7 mi. (11 km.) E of Rochester; pop. (1990c) 6932.

East Rock·a·way \ˈräk-ə-ˌwā\. Residential village and resort, Nassau co., SE New York, on cen. Long Island 20 mi. (32 km.) ESE of New York City; pop. (1990c) 10,152.

East Rutherford. Borough, Bergen co., NE corner of New Jersey, 8 mi. (13 km.) NNE of Newark; pop. (1990c) 7902.

East Saint Louis. City, St. Clair co., SW Illinois, on Mississippi River opp. St. Louis, Missouri; pop. (1990c) 40,944; railroad center; once major industrial center, still produces steel, glass, chemicals.

East Schel·de. See OOSTERSCHELDE.

East Siberian Sea. Part of Arctic Ocean, N of Sakha Rep. and Chukchi Autonomous Okrug, NE Russia in Asia; extends from New Siberian Is. to Wrangel I.

East Side. The E part of Manhattan borough, New York City, New York esp. below 14th Street (Lower East Side); site of headquarters of UN (42d Street to 48th Street).

East Stoke. See STOKE, EAST.

East Stroudsburg. Borough, Monroe co., E Pennsylvania, 32 mi. (52 km.) NNE of Allentown; pop. (1990c) 8781; East Stroudsburg Univ. (1893).

East Suffolk. See SUFFOLK 3.

East Sussex. **1.** See SUSSEX 6.
2. County, SE England, approx. equivalent to the former county of the same name; estab. 1974. See table at ENGLAND.

East Syracuse. Village, Onondaga co., cen. New York, 5 mi. (8 km.) E of Syracuse; pop. (1990c) 3343.

East Ta·was \ˈtȯ-wəs, ˈtä-\. City, Iosco co., NE Michigan, at N side of mouth of Saginaw Bay; pop. (1990c) 2887.

East Ti·mor \-ˈtē-ˌmȯ(ə)r, -tē-ˈ\ *or* **Ti·mor Ti·mur** \ˌtē-mōr-ˈtē-mu̇r\. Province of Indonesia, Lesser Sunda Is.; comprises the E half of Timor and the former exclave Oé-Cusse on the N coast of W Timor; ✱ Dili; coffee, sandalwood, copra, rubber; formerly a Portuguese overseas province (**Portuguese Timor**).
History: Inhabited by indigenous peoples when Portuguese arrived in 16th cent.; scene of conflict 17th cent. after W end of island seized by Dutch; negotiations over Portuguese-Dutch boundary line begun 1859, but not concluded until 1914; occupied by Japanese Feb. 1942; given up by Portugal 1975 and immediately invaded by Indonesian troops; annexed by Indonesia 1976 without recognition of UN; insurgent movement active through 1980s and 1990s; independence approved in referendum Aug. 1999. See table at INDONESIA.

East Ti·rol \tə-ˈrōl, tī-; ˈtī-ˌrōl; ˈtir-əl\ *or Ger.* **Ost·ti·rol** \ˌȯst-ti-ˈrōl\. The E part of Tirol state, Austria; 763 sq. mi. (1976 sq. km.).

East Turkistan. See CHINESE TURKESTAN.

Eastview. See VANIER 1.

East·ville \ˈēst-ˌvil\. Town, ⊗ of Northampton co., E Virginia, S part of Delmarva Penin.; pop. (1990c) 185.

East Williston. Village, Nassau co., SE New York, 7 mi. (11 km.) S of Glen Cove; pop. (1990c) 2515.

East Windsor. Town, N cen. Hartford co., N Connecticut, on Connecticut River; pop. (1990c) 10,081; trolley museum; split off from Windsor 1768.

East·wood \ˈēst-wu̇d\. Town, Nottinghamshire, N cen. England, 8 mi. (13 km.) NW of Nottingham; pop. (1991e) 61,010; birthplace of novelist D.H. Lawrence 1885.

East York. Borough, SE Ontario, Canada, near Toronto; pop. (1991c) 102,696.

Ea·ton \ˈēt-ᵊn\. **1.** County in S Michigan. See table at MICHIGAN.
2. City, ⊗ of Preble co., SW Ohio, 22 mi. (35 km.) W of Dayton; pop. (1990c) 7396; founded 1806.

Eaton Rapids. City, Eaton co., S Michigan, 15 mi. (24 km.) SSW of Lansing; pop. (1990c) 4695.

Ea·ton·ton \'ēt-ᵊn-tən\. City, ⊗ of Putnam co., cen. Georgia, 38 mi. (61 km.) NNE of Macon; pop. (1990c) 4737.

Ea·ton·town \'ēt-ᵊn-ˌtau̇n\. Borough, Monmouth co., E cen. New Jersey, 6 mi. (10 km.) NNW of Asbury Park; pop. (1990c) 13,800.

Ea·ton·ville \-ˌvil\. Town, cen. Florida Penin., N of Orlando; pop. (1990c) 2170; became 1887 first town in U.S. incorp. by blacks.

Eau·bonne \ō-'bȯn\. Commune, Val-d'Oise dept., N France.

Eau Claire \ō-'klar\. **1.** River, W cen. Wisconsin; rises in Clark co., flows W into Chippewa River at Eau Claire; ab. 70 mi. (113 km.) long.
2. County in W Wisconsin. See table at WISCONSIN.
3. City, its ⊗, on Chippewa River; pop. (1990c) 56,856; tires, food products; Chippewa Valley Technical Coll. (1912), Univ. of Wisconsin—Eau Claire (1916); settled in 1840s; developed as outlet for Chippewa lumber district.

Eaux–Bonnes \ō-'bȯn\. Town, Pyrénées-Atlantiques dept., SW France, ab. 23 mi. (37 km.) S of Pau; thermal mineral waters famous since 14th cent.; ab. 5 mi. (8 km.) to the SW is the watering place of **Eaux–Chaudes** \ō-'shōd\, with warm sulfur springs.

Eaux Vives \ō-'vēv\. Former commune, Geneva canton, Switzerland; now in E part of city of Geneva.

Eauze \ā-'ōz\. Commune, W Gers dept., SW France, 15 mi. (24 km.) NW of Auch; ancient ✻ of Aquitania Tertia.

Ebal, Mount \'ē-bəl\ *or Arab.* **Ja·bal 'Ay·bāl** \'ja-bȧl-ˌī-'bäl\. Mountain, Jordan, N of Nābulus, in area occupied by Israel 1967; 3084 ft. (940 m.).

Eb·bw \'e-bü\. River, SE Wales; flows S from S Powys through W Gwent into the Usk S of Newport; 24 mi. (39 km.) long.

Ebbw Vale. Town, Gwent co., SE Wales, on the Ebbw 35 mi. (56 km.) NW of Bristol; pop. (1981p) 24,422; once notable for coal mining; now manufactures tinplate.

Eben Emael, Fort. See FORT EBEN EMAEL.

Eb·ens·burg \'eb-ᵊnz-ˌbərg\. Borough, ⊗ of Cambria co., SW cen. Pennsylvania, 15 mi. (24 km.) NE of Johnstown; pop. (1990c) 3872.

Eben·see \'āb-ᵊn-ˌzā\. Town, cen. Austria, at place where Traun River flows into Lake Traun; pop. (1991c) 8734; resort.

Ebers·wal·de–Fi·now \ˌā-bərs-'väl-də-'fē-nō\. City, Brandenburg, Germany, 28 mi. (45 km.) NE of Berlin and near border with Poland; foundries; forestry school; 14th cent. Gothic church; prehistoric (c. 11th–9th cents. B.C.) gold artifacts found here 1913; received charter mid-13th cent.

Ebe·tsu \ā-'bā-tsü\. City, Hokkaidō prefecture, Hokkaidō, Japan; E of Sapporo; pop. (1990p) 97,201.

Ebi·na \ā-'bē-nä\. City, Kanagawa prefecture, Honshū, Japan; pop. (1990p) 105,816.

Ebing·en \'ā-biŋ-ən\. City, Baden-Württemberg, Germany, 41 mi. (66 km.) S of Stuttgart.

Ebi·nur \e-'bē-'nür\ *or W.-G.* **Ai–pi** \'ī-'bē\. Salt Lake, W Junggar, NW Xinjiang Uygur, W China, bet. Alataw and N ranges of Tian Shan; alt. 2300 ft. (701 m.).

Eb·la \'e-blə\. Ancient city, Syria, S of modern Aleppo; flourished mid-3d millennium B.C.; 20th cent. excavations have recovered thousands of stone tablets with cuneiform writing providing information on area's way of life.

Eblana. See DUBLIN 7.

Eb·o·la \'e-bō-lä\. Headstream of the Mongala River (*q.v.*), N Democratic Rep. of the Congo; flows W.

Ebo·li \'ā-bȯ-lē\. Commune, Salerno prov., Campania, S Italy, 16 mi. (26 km.) ESE of Salerno; pop. (1991p) 32,154; castle.

Eb·on \'e-bən\. Atoll at S end of Ralik Chain, Marshall Is., W Pacific Ocean; 4°38'N, 168°43'E; 22 islets (largest Ebon).

Ebora. See ÉVORA 2.

Eboracum. See YORK 13.

Ebro \'ā-ˌbrō\; *anc.* **Ibe·rus** \ī-'bir-əs\. River, NE Spain; rises in the Cantabrian Mts. in Cantabria prov., flows ESE into Mediterranean Sea ab. 80 mi. (129 km.) SW of Barcelona; 565 mi. (909 km.) long; 2d longest river in Spain; has drainage basin of 33,600 sq. mi. (87,024 sq. km.); chief tributaries the Aragon, Segre, and Jalón rivers; has long been used for irrigation; navigable to seafaring vessels as far as Tortosa (ab. 22 mi. or 35 km. from its mouth) and to small boats as far as Tudela (in Navarra prov.).

Ebudae. See HEBRIDES.

Eburacum. See YORK 13.

Eburodunum. See EMBRUN and YVERDON.

Ebusus. See IBIZA.

EC. See EUROPEAN COMMUNITY.

Eca·te·pec de Mo·re·los \ā-ˌkä-tā-'pek-t͟hā-mō-'rā-lōs\. City, México state, Mexico, 11 mi. (18 km.) NE of Mexico City; commercial center for agricultural region.

Ecbatana. See HAMADĀN 2.

Ec·cle·fech·an \ˌe-kəl-'fe-kən, -k̲ən\. Village, Dumfries and Galloway region, S Scotland, near Dumfries; birthplace of essayist and historian Thomas Carlyle 1795.

Ec·cles \'e-kəlz\. Town, Greater Manchester, W England, on the Irwell 4 mi. (6 km.) W of Manchester; pop. (1981p) 37,166; textiles; 12th cent. church (restored).

Ec·cle·shall \'e-kəl-shəl, -ˌshȯl\. Market town, Staffordshire, England, 7 mi. (11 km.) NW of Stafford; walls and moat of castle which was episcopal residence 13th cent. to 1867.

Echa·gue \ā-'chä-gwā\. Municipality, S Isabela prov., Luzon, Philippines, on W bank of Cagayan River 34 mi. (55 km.) S of Ilagan; pop. (1980c) 41,390; taken by Americans June 1945.

Ech–Che·liff \ˌesh-shə-'lēf\; *formerly* **Al–As·nam** \ȧl-'ȧs-nȧm\. Town, N Algeria; pop. (1987p) 129,976; devastated by earthquake Oct. 10, 1980.

Ech·mi·a·dzin \ˌech-mē-ə-'dzēn\ *or* **Ej·mi·a·dzin** \ˌej-\ *or* **Yej·mi·a·dzin** \ˌyej-\; *formerly* **Va·gar·sha·pat** \ˌvä-gär-shä-'pät\. Town, Armenia, 12 mi. (19 km.) W of Yerevan, in valley of the Araks; pop. (1987e) 53,040. An old town dating from c. 6th cent. B.C.; ✻ of ancient kingdom of Armenia 184 to 344 A.D.; seat of the Armenian patriarch, founded by St. Gregory the Illuminator c. 302 A.D.; 6th cent. monastery; historically notable collection of Armenian literature some of which has been relocated to Yerevan.

Echo, Lake \'e-kō\. Lake, cen. Tasmania, Australia, ab. 60 mi. (97 km.) NW of Hobart; ab. 7 mi. (11 km.) long; source of Dee River, a tributary of the Derwent.

Echo Canyon. Ravine in Summit co., NE Utah, with walls 800 to 1200 ft. (244 to 366 m.) high; railroad passes through it; important in prestatehood and early history of the state.

Echo Dam. Dam across Weber River, Summit co., N Utah, NE of Salt Lake City; height 158 ft. (48 m); completed 1931; impounds water for irrigation, forming **Echo Reservoir.**

Ech·ols \'e-kəlz\. County in S Georgia. See table at GEORGIA.

Ech·ter·nach \'ek̲-tər-ˌnäk̲\. Town, NE Luxembourg, on the Sûre River 18 mi. (29 km.) NE of the city of Luxembourg; pop. (1991c) 4211; tourism; an old town famous for its festival on Whit-Tuesday; burial place of St. Willibrord (d. 739). Figured in fighting in Battle of the Bulge 1944–45.

Eci·ja \'ā-thē-ˌhä\; *anc.* **As·ti·gi** \'as-tə-ˌjī\. City, Sevilla prov., SW Spain, 48 mi. (77 km.) ENE of Seville; pop. (1991p) 35,566; cereals, olives, cotton grown nearby; episcopal see; ancient Roman colony; Roman ruins.

Eck·ern·för·de \ˌe-kərn-'fœr-də\. Seaport, Schleswig-Holstein, Germany, on Kiel Bay, just NW of Kiel; pop. (1980c) 23,081; fisheries; became town late 13th cent.

Eckmühl. See EGGMÜHL.

Écluse. See SLUIS.

Econ·o·my \i-'kä-nə-mē\. Borough, Beaver co., W Pennsylvania, NW of Pittsburgh; pop. (1990c) 9519. See AMBRIDGE.

Eco·po·ran·ga \ˌe-kȯ-pȯ-'räⁿn-gə\. Municipality, Espírito Santo state, E Brazil.

Ecorse \'ē-ˌkȯrs\. City, Wayne co., SE Michigan, on Detroit River S of Detroit; pop. (1990c) 12,180; steel manufacturing.

Écrins, Barre des. See BARRE DES ÉCRINS.

Ec·tor \'ek-tər\. County in W Texas. See table at TEXAS.

Ec·ua·dor \'e-kwə-ˌdȯr, *Span.* ˌe-kwä-'thōr\. Republic, NW South America; bounded on N by Colombia, on E and S by Peru, and on W by the Pacific Ocean; 109,483 sq. mi. (283,561 sq. km.); pop. (1993e) 10,985,000; ✽ Quito.

Physical features: Mountains include cen. range of the Andes with highest volcanic peaks Chimborazo 20,561 ft. (6267 m.), Cotopaxi 19,347 ft. (5897 m.), Cayambe 18,996 ft. (5790 m.), Sangay 17,159 ft. (5230 m.); country subject often to volcanic disturbances and earthquakes. Short streams flowing W to Pacific, incl. the Esmeraldas, and the Guayas flowing to wide Gulf of Guayaquil in SW; streams on E slope of Andes in El Oriente, tributaries of the Amazon and of its headstream the Marañón, most important being the Napo and its tributary the Curaray, the Tigre, Pastaza, Morona (Macuma in Ecuador), and Santiago (Zamora in Ecuador).

Island possessions: The Galápagos Is. (*q.v.*) ab. 600 mi. (965 km.) off the coast, constituting Archipiélago de Colón terr.

Chief products: Corn, coffee, rice, bananas, cotton, cocoa, sugar; livestock, fish; oil; manufacturing: food processing, textiles.

Chief cities: Guayaquil, Quito, Cuenca, Machala, Portoviejo, Manta, Ambato, Santo Domingo de los Colorados.

Political divisions: Divided into the following 21 provinces (for pronunciation of their names, see their individual entries):

NAME	AREA (sq. mi.)	AREA (sq. km.)	POP. (1990c)	CAPITAL
Azuay	2,973	7,701	506,090	Cuenca
Bolívar	1,256	3,254	155,088	Guaranda
Cañar	1,509	3,908	189,347	Azogues
Carchi	1,428	3,699	141,482	Tulcán
Chimborazo	2,176	5,637	364,682	Riobamba
Cotopaxi	2,041	5,287	276,324	Latacunga
El Oro	2,312	5,988	412,572	Machala
Esmeraldas	5,875	15,216	306,628	Esmeraldas
Galápagos	3,093	8,010	9,785	Barquerizo Moreno
Guayas	8,070	20,902	2,515,146	Guayaquil
Imbabura	1,925	4,986	265,499	Ibarra
Loja	4,167	10,793	384,698	Loja
Los Ríos	2,415	6,254	527,559	Babahoyo
Manabí	7,104	18,400	1,031,927	Portoviejo
Morona-Santiago	11,164	28,915	84,216	Macas
Napo	12,899	33,409	103,387	Tena
Pastaza	11,398	29,520	41,811	Puyo
Pichincha	6,409	16,599	1,756,228	Quito
Sucumbíos	7,186	18,612	76,952	Nueva Loja
Tungurahua	1,118	2,896	361,980	Ambato
Zamora-Chinchipe	7,985	20,681	66,167	Zamora

History: Quito, ancient name of Ecuador, conquered by the Incas before arrival of Spanish; conquered by Spanish 1534; a presidency under viceroyalty of Peru, later of New Granada; after earlier unsuccessful insurrections, won final independence from Spain at battle of Mt. Pichincha May 24, 1822; part of Gran Colombia until 1830 when it seceded to become republic of Ecuador; its political history a turbulent one; its boundaries, esp. with Peru, a long-standing cause of friction with its neighbors; boundary with Colombia settled 1916 but that with Peru, in spite of attempts of several treaties during 2d half of 19th cent., not settled until 1942 when the larger part of the region bet. the Marañón and the Putumayo was assigned to Peru; member of UN 1945; new constitution adopted 1979; struck by severe earthquakes March 1987.

Edam \'ā-ˌdäm, 'ē-dəm, -ˌdam\. Commune and seaport, North Holland prov., W Netherlands, on the IJsselmeer; pop. (1981e) 23,853; market for the cheese to which it gives its name (Edam cheese); textiles, ceramics; tourism.

Ed·couch \ˌed-'kau̇ch\. City, Hidalgo co., S Texas, 20 mi. (32 km.) ENE of McAllen; pop. (1990c) 2878.

Ed Da·mer \ed-'dȧ-mər\ *or* **Ad Dā·mir** \ȧd-\. Town, N Sudan, on the Nile.

Ed Deb·ba \ed-'de-bə\ *or* **Ad Dab·bah** \ȧd-'dȧ-bə\. Town, N cen. Sudan, on the Nile WSW of Marawī.

Ed·dra·chil·lis Bay \ˌe-drə-'ki-lis, -'ki-\. Bay, Highland region, on NW coast of Scotland.

Ed Du·eim \ed-dü-'ām\ *or* **Ad Du·waym** \ȧd-dü-'wām, -'wīm\. Town, Central region, E Sudan, on the White Nile; ✽ of former White Nile prov.

Ed·dy \'e-dē\. Name of counties in two states of the U.S. See tables at NEW MEXICO and NORTH DAKOTA.

Eddy, Mount. Peak, S cen. Siskiyou co., N California; 9038 ft. (2755 m.).

Ed·dy·stone \'e-dē-ˌstōn\. Borough, Delaware co., SE Pennsylvania, on Delaware River 12 mi. (19 km.) WSW of Philadelphia; pop. (1990c) 2446; munitions center during WWI.

Eddystone Rocks. Rocky islet, England, in the English Channel, 14 mi. (23 km.) SW of Plymouth; lighthouse.

Ed·dy·ville \'e-dē-ˌvil\. City, ⊗ of Lyon co., W Kentucky, on Cumberland River 30 mi. (48 km.) E of Paducah; pop. (1990c) 1889.

Ede \'ā-də\. Commune, Gelderland prov., E Netherlands, 13 mi. (21 km.) NW of Arnhem; pop. (1992e) 96,044; rayon-yarn factory, metallurgical works; pianos, food products.

Ede \'ā-ˌdā\. City, Oyo state, Nigeria, 45 mi. (72 km.) NNE of Ibadan; pop. (1991e) 271,000; cocoa; a Yoruba city.

Edéa \ā-'dā-ə\. Town, E Cameroon, on railroad line ab. 40 mi. (64 km.) SE of Douala; pop. (1987e) 40,792.

Eden \'ēd-ᵊn\. **1.** Town, Rockingham co., N North Carolina, 28 mi. (45 km.) N of Greensboro; pop. (1990c) 15,238.

2. Seaport town with large harbor on Twofold Bay, SE New South Wales, SE Australia; pop. (1991c) 3277.

3. River, Cumbria, NW England; flows N into head of Solway Firth; 65 mi. (105 km.) long.

4. River, Fife region, E Scotland; flows NE into St. Andrews Bay; 29.5 mi. (47.5 km.) long.

Eden Prairie. City, Hennepin co., SE cen. Minnesota; pop. (1990c) 39,311; residential suburb of Minneapolis.

Eden Valley Reservoir. Reservoir in a tributary of Green River, NW Sweetwater co., SW Wyoming.

Eden·ton \'ēd-ᵊn-tən\. Town, ⊗ of Chowan co., NE North Carolina, on Albemarle Sound near mouth of Chowan River; pop. (1990c) 5268; formerly horse-racing center. Settled c. 1658; ✽ of colony for part of 18th cent.; scene of "Edenton Tea Party" Oct. 25, 1774, a meeting of 51 ladies who signed a pact resolving not to drink tea or wear clothing made in England until the tax on tea should be repealed.

Eden·vale \'ēd-ᵊn-ˌvāl\. Town, NE Rep. of South Africa, suburb of Johannesburg.

Eder \'ā-dər\. River, chiefly in Hesse, Germany; flows E to join the Fulda just S of Kassel; 110 mi. (177 km.) long; in its course is **Eder Reservoir Dam,** which was bombed by British May 1943.

Edes·sa \i-'de-sə\. **1.** *or Gk.* **Édhes·sa** \'ā-the-sä\ *also* **Vo·de·na** \ˌvö-the-'nä\. City, ✽ of Pella dept., W Macedonia, Greece, 48 mi. (77 km.) WNW of Thessaloníki; pop. (1991p) 17,624; textiles; once widely considered site of ancient ✽ of Macedonian kings, but ✽ now thought to have been at Vergina.

2. Ancient city, Asia Minor. See URFA 2.

Edfu. See IDFU.

Ed·gar \'ed-gər\. County in E Illinois. See table at ILLINOIS.

Ed·gard \'ed-ˌgärd\. Unincorporated settlement, ⊗ of St. John the Baptist parish, SE Louisiana; pop. (1990c) 3115.

Ed·gar·town \'ed-gər-ˌtau̇n\. Town, ⊗ of Dukes co., SE Massachusetts, E Martha's Vineyard on **Edgartown Harbor,** on inlet of Nantucket Sound; pop. (1990c) 3062; settled 1642.

Edge·combe \'ej-kəm\. County in NE North Carolina. See table at NORTH CAROLINA.

Edge·cumbe, Mount \'ej-kəm\. Extinct volcano at S end of Kruzof I. opp. Sitka, SE Alaska; 2638 ft. (804 m.); nearby is **Cape Edgecumbe.**

Edge·field \'ej-ˌfēld\. **1.** County in W South Carolina. See table at SOUTH CAROLINA.

2. Town, its ⊗, 21 mi. (34 km.) NW of Aiken; pop. (1990c) 2563.

Edge·hill \'ej-ˌhil\ *or* **Edge Hill.** Ridge in S Warwickshire, cen. England, 7 mi. (11 km.) NW of Banbury; scene of an indecisive battle Oct. 1642 bet. Royalists under Charles I and Parliamentarian forces under Robert Devereux, 3d earl of Essex.

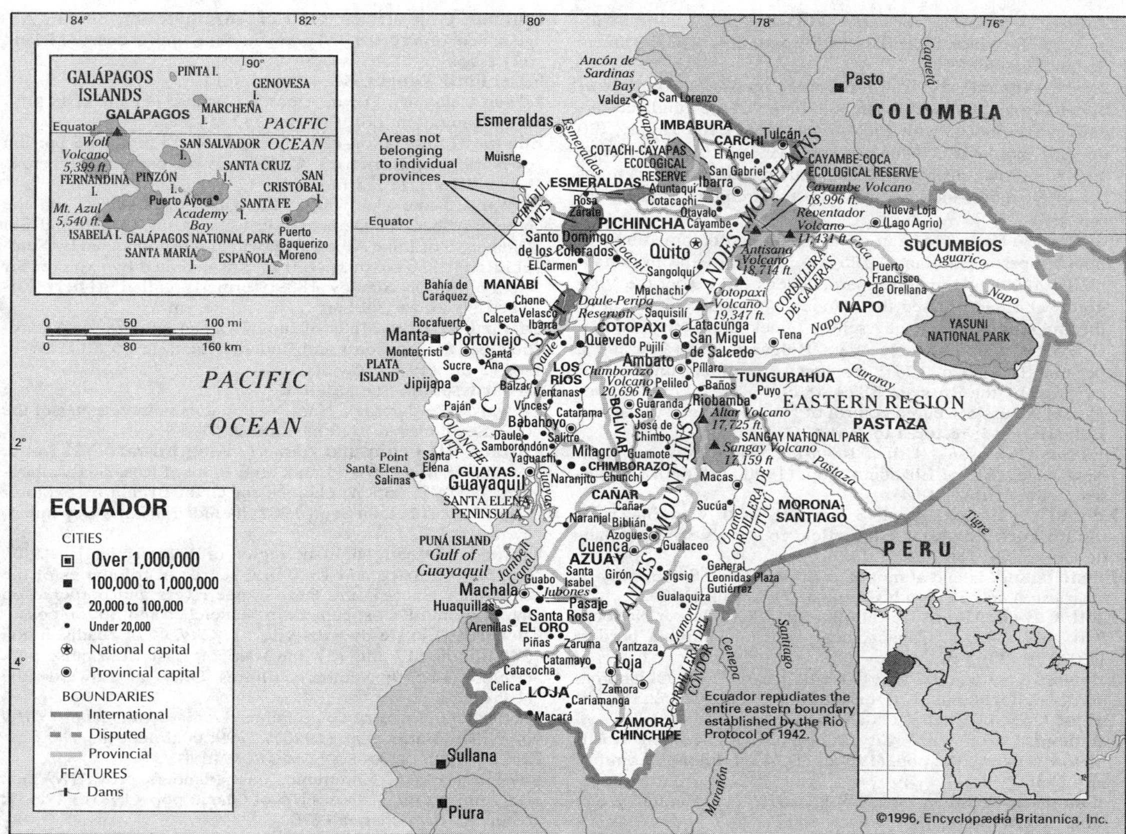

Edge Island. Island, SE Spitsbergen Archipelago, Norway, Arctic Ocean; 1970 sq. mi. (5102 sq. km.).

Edge·mont \ˈej-ˌmänt\. City, Fall River co., SW corner of South Dakota, near Black Hills 22 mi. (35 km.) WSW of Hot Springs; pop. (1990c) 906.

Edg·er·ton \ˈe-jər-tən\. City, Rock co., S Wisconsin, 11 mi. (18 km.) N of Janesville; pop. (1990c) 4254.

Edge·wa·ter \ˈej-ˌwȯ-tər, -ˌwä-\. **1.** Town, Jefferson co., cen. Colorado, 5 mi. (8 km.) W of Denver; pop. (1990c) 4613.
2. Town, Volusia co., E Florida; pop. (1990c) 15,337.
3. Borough, Bergen co., NE corner of New Jersey, on Hudson River 7 mi. (11 km.) NNE of Jersey City; pop. (1990c) 5001.

Edge·wood \ˈej-ˌwu̇d\. **1.** City, Kenton co., N Kentucky; pop. (1990c) 8143.
2. Unincorporated settlement, S Harford co., NE Maryland, 18 mi. (29 km.) NE of Baltimore; pop. (1990c) 23,903; site of **Edgewood Arsenal.**
3. Borough, Allegheny co., SW Pennsylvania, 7 mi. (11 km.) E of Pittsburgh; pop. (1990c) 3581.

Edge·worth \ˈej-wərth\. Borough, Allegheny co., SW Pennsylvania, on Ohio River 13 mi. (21 km.) WNW of Pittsburgh; pop. (1990c) 1670; birthplace of composer Ethelbert Nevin 1862.

Édhessa. See EDESSA 1.

Edi·na \i-ˈdī-nə\. **1.** City, Hennepin co., SE cen. Minnesota, 8 mi. (13 km.) SW of Minneapolis; pop. (1990c) 46,070.
2. City, ⊗ of Knox co., NE Missouri, 22 mi. (35 km.) E of Kirksville; pop. (1990c) 1283.

Ed·in·boro \ˈe-din-ˌbər-ə\. Borough, Erie co., NW corner of Pennsylvania, on a lake ab. 18 mi. (29 km.) S of Erie; pop. (1990c) 7736; Edinboro Univ. of Pennsylvania (1857).

Ed·in·burg \ˈe-din-ˌbərg\. City, ⊗ of Hidalgo co., S Texas, 10 mi. (16 km.) NNE of McAllen; pop. (1990c) 29,885; citrus-fruit canning; Univ. of Texas–Pan American (1927).

Ed·in·burgh. **1.** \ˈe-din-ˌbərg\. Town, Bartholomew and Johnson cos., cen. Indiana, 30 mi. (48 km.) SSE of Indianapolis; pop. (1990c) 4536.
2. *or* **Edinburghshire.** See MIDLOTHIAN 2.
3. \ˈed-ᵊn-ˌbər-ə\. City and burgh, ✱ of Scotland and ⊗ of Lothian region, SE Scotland, on S shore of Firth of Forth; pop. (1991e) 434,520; printing and publishing; tourism; built on several hills; the Old Town is on a rock, very steep on W end where castle stands and sloping toward the E where Holyrood Palace is located; New Town is W of the castle rock, separated from it by a valley, now site of public gardens; Univ. of Edinburgh (1583), Heriot-Watt Univ. (1966).
History: Possibly originated with castle erected by King Edwin of Northumbria who defeated the Picts early in 7th cent. A.D.; royal residence of Malcolm III MacDuncan (Canmore) in 11th cent.; Canongate, later annexed to Edinburgh, rose about the abbey of Holyrood; granted charter and rights over town of Leith by King Robert the Bruce; ✱ of Scottish kingdom and meeting place of parliament after 1437; lost political importance after accession of James VI to English throne as James I 1603 and union of Scotland (*q.v.*) with England 1707; proclaimed Charles II king 1649 and captured by Parliamentarian commander Oliver Cromwell 1650; New Town built in 18th cent.; became a literary and educational center.

Ed·ing·ton \ˈe-diŋ-tən\. Village and parish, Wiltshire, S England; 14th cent. priory church; scene of King Alfred the Great's victory over the Danes 878.

Edir·ne \ā-ˈdir-nə\; *formerly* **Adri·an·o·ple** \ˌā-drē-ə-ˈnō-pəl\. **1.** Province of Turkey in Europe, a part of E Thrace. See table at TURKEY.

2. *anc.* **Adri·an·op·o·lis** \ˌā-drē-ə-ˈnä-pə-lis\ *or* **Ha·dri·an·op·o·lis** \ˌhā-\. City, its ✻, on both banks of the Tundzha River at its confluence with the Maritsa (Meriç), NW Turkey, 130 mi. (209 km.) NW of İstanbul; pop. (1990c) 102,345; cereals and fruit grown nearby; cheese, leather, soap, cotton; a number of mosques, incl. one built by the architect Sinan (16th cent.).

History: Early Thracian town rebuilt and renamed by Roman Emperor Hadrian c. 125 A.D.; scene of the important battle in which Roman Emperor Valens fell before the Visigoths who had crossed the Danube 378; scene of defeat of the Bulgarian dynasty of Asen by Greek Emperor Theodore II 1255; conquered by the Avars, Bulgarians, and Crusaders, became Turkish c. 1361; residence of sultans until 1453; captured by the Russians 1829, 1879; by Treaty of Adrianople 1829 Russia secured control of Danube mouths; taken by Bulgaria 1913; restored to Turks 1922.

Ed·i·son \ˈe-di-sən\. Urban township, Middlesex co., cen. New Jersey, SW of Elizabeth; pop. (1990c) 88,680; Middlesex County Coll. (1964).

Ed·is·to \ˈe-di-ˌstō\. River, S and SW South Carolina; rises (**South Fork Edisto**) in E Edgefield co., flows SE into Atlantic Ocean; ab. 150 mi. (240 km.) long.

Edisto Island. Island at mouth of Edisto River, S extremity of Charleston co., SE South Carolina; 54 sq. mi. (140 sq. km.).

Edith Cav·ell, Mount \ˈē-dith-ˈka-vil\. Peak, Jasper National Park, SW Alberta, Canada, near British Columbia border; 11,033 ft. (3363 m.).

Ed·mond \ˈed-mənd\. City, Oklahoma co., cen. Oklahoma, bordering Oklahoma City on the N; pop. (1990c) 52,315; oil wells; Univ. of Central Oklahoma (1890).

Ed·monds \ˈed-məndz\. City, Snohomish co., NW cen. Washington, N of Seattle; pop. (1990c) 30,744; Edmonds Community Coll. (1967).

Ed·mon·son \ˈed-mən-sən\. County in SW cen. Kentucky. See table at KENTUCKY.

Ed·mon·ton \ˈed-mən-tən\. **1.** City, ⊗ of Metcalfe co., S Kentucky; pop. (1990c) 1477.

2. City, ✻ of Alberta, Canada, in S cen. part of province on both banks of North Saskatchewan River; pop. (1991c) 616,741; petrochemicals; oil refineries, meatpacking plants; retailing center of rich agricultural area; Univ. of Alberta (1906), Concordia Coll. (1921), St. Joseph's Coll. (1927), Christian Training Institute (1939); portion on S bank is former town of **Strath·co·na** \strath-ˈkō-nə\, annexed 1912; a leading railroad and air center of W Canada; orig. estab. 1795 as a fort and trading post of the Hudson's Bay Company; major oil reserves discovered nearby 1947.

3. Former municipal borough, now part of the Greater London borough of Enfield, England; residence of essayist Charles Lamb and poets William Cowper and John Keats.

Ed·munds \ˈed-məndz\. County in N South Dakota. See table at SOUTH DAKOTA.

Ed·munds·ton \ˈed-mən-stən\. City, ⊗ of Madawaska co., NW New Brunswick, Canada, on upper St. John River across from NE Maine; pop. (1991c) 10,835; fishing; École de Musique (1950).

Ed·na \ˈed-nə\. City, ⊗ of Jackson co., SE Texas, 25 mi. (40 km.) ENE of Victoria; pop. (1990c) 5343.

Edo. **1.** \ˈā-dō\. City, Japan. See TOKYO 2.

2. \ˈe-dō\. State of S Nigeria. See table at NIGERIA.

Edom \ˈē-dəm\ *also* **Se·ir** \ˈsē-ər\. Ancient country S of Dead Sea, along both sides of the Wadi al-ʻArabah, with indefinite boundaries; mountainous and largely barren; included summits of Hor and Seir; according to Bible (*Gen.* xxxvi) the land given to Esau (or Edom); chief town and ✻ Sela (Petra); with some shifting of boundaries to include S Judaea, became known in Maccabean and Roman times as Idumaea (*q.v.*).

Edre·mit \ˌe-drə-ˈmēt\; *anc.* **Ad·ra·myt·ti·um** \ˌa-drə-ˈmi-tē-əm\. Town, NW Turkey in Asia, near Aegean Sea at head of Gulf of Edremit.

Edremit, Gulf of; *anc.* **Gulf of Adramyttium.** Inlet of Aegean Sea, on W coast of Turkey in Asia, opp. N coast of island of Lesbos.

Edsel Ford Ranges. See FORD RANGES.

Ed·son \ˈed-sən\. Town, Alberta, Canada, 117 mi. (188 km.) W of Edmonton; pop. (1991c) 7323.

Edu·ni, Mount \i-ˈdü-nē, -ˈdyü-\. Peak, W mainland portion of Northwest Territories, Canada, in NE part of Mackenzie Mts.; 7716 ft. (2352 m.).

Ed·ward, Lake \ˈe-dwərd\. Lake in E cen. Africa, on the boundary bet. NE Democractic Rep. of the Congo and SW Uganda, S of Lake Albert with which it is connected by Semliki River; 830 sq. mi. (2150 sq. km.); visited by explorer Sir Henry Morton Stanley 1889; formerly called **Al·bert Ed·ward Ny·an·za** \ˈal-bərt ... nē-ˈan-zə, -nī-\.

Edward VIII Bay. Inlet of Indian Ocean on coast of Antarctica, bet. Kemp Coast and Enderby Land, at 66°50′S, 57°E; ab. 12 mi. (19 km.) wide.

Edwardesabad. See BANNU 2.

Ed·wards \ˈe-dwərdz\. Name of counties in three states of the U.S. See tables at ILLINOIS, KANSAS, TEXAS.

Edward VII Peninsula; *formerly* **King Edward VII Land.** Peninsula, Marie Byrd Land, on E shore of Ross Sea, Antarctica, 77°44′S, 155°W; claimed for Great Britain by explorer Capt. Robert Falcon Scott 1902; included in Ross Dependency (*q.v.*).

Edwards Plateau. Highland region of W Texas; alt. bet. 2000 and 5000 ft. (610 and 1520 m.); source of tributaries of the Colorado, Nueces, and Rio Grande rivers and bordered on the W by the Pecos; centers in Schleicher and Sutton cos.

Ed·wards·ville \ˈe-dwərdz-ˌvil\. **1.** City, ⊗ of Madison co., SW Illinois, 17 mi. (27 km.) NE of East St. Louis; pop. (1990c) 14,579; Southern Illinois Univ. at Edwardsville (1957).

2. Borough, Luzerne co., E Pennsylvania, 3 mi. (5 km.) WNW of Wilkes-Barre; pop. (1990c) 5399; coal deposits.

EEC. See EUROPEAN ECONOMIC COMMUNITY.

Eek·loo \ˈā-klō\. Commune, East Flanders prov., NW cen. Belgium, 11 mi. (18 km.) NW of Ghent; pop. (1981c) 19,637; received town charter 1270.

Eel \ˈēl\. River, NW California, rises in N Mendocino co., flows NW into Pacific Ocean.

Eesti. See ESTONIA.

Efa·te \ā-ˈfä-tā\ *or Fr.* **Va·té** \vä-ˈtā\; *formerly* **Sand·wich Island** \ˈsan-ˌdwich\. Island, cen. Vanuatu, SW Pacific Ocean; 26 mi. (42 km.) long by 14 mi. (23 km.) wide; 353 sq. mi. (914 sq. km.); pop. (1991e) 30,422; chief town Port-Vila, which is the administrative center of Vanuatu; good harbors at Port-Vila and Havannah.

Ef·fi·gy Mounds National Monument \ˈe-fi-jē\. See UNITED STATES, *National Monuments.*

Ef·fing·ham \ˈe-fiŋ-ˌham\. **1.** Name of counties in two states of the U.S. See tables at GEORGIA and ILLINOIS.

2. City, ⊗ of Effingham co., SE cen. Illinois; pop. (1990c) 11,851; electrical appliances.

Ef·fon–Alai·ye \ˈe-fȯn-ä-ˈlī-ä\. Town, SW Nigeria; pop. (1991e) 135,000.

Efo·gi \e-ˈfō-gē\. Village in Owen Stanley Range, Papua New Guinea, New Guinea I., 20 mi. (32 km.) NE of Port Moresby; severe fighting bet. Japanese and Allied forces 1942.

Ega·di, Iso·le \ˈē-zȯ-lā-ˈā-gä-dē\ *or* **Egadi Islands** *also* **Ae·ga·di·an Islands** \ē-ˈgā-dē-ən\; *anc.* **Ae·ga·tes** \ē-ˈgā-tēz\. Group of islands in Mediterranean Sea off W coast of Sicily, Italy; 15 sq. mi. (39 sq. km.); pop. (1991p) 4335; politically constitute Favignana commune in Trapani prov., NW Sicily; chief islands Marettimo and Favignana. Scene of naval battle in which Romans destroyed the Carthaginian fleet thus terminating the First Punic War 241 B.C.

Egedesminde. See AASIAAT.

Egeo, Isole Italiane dell'. See AEGEAN ISLANDS 2.

Eger \ˈā-gər\. **1.** River, Germany and Czech Republic. See OHŘE.

2. City, Czech Republic. See CHEB.

Eger \ˈe-ger\ *or Ger.* **Er·lau** \ˈer-ˌlau̇\. City, ⊗ of Heves co., N cen. Hungary, 25 mi. (40 km.) SW of Miskolc; pop. (1991e)

66,300; machinery; exports wine; processes tobacco; mineral springs nearby; invaded by Tatars 13th cent.; occupied by Turks 1596–1687; has many historic buildings.

Egerdir. See EĞRIDIR.

Eger·sund \ˈā-gər-ˌsůn\. Seaport town, Rogaland co., SW Norway, 35 mi. (56 km.) S of Stavanger; pop. (1980c) 11,863; fisheries.

Egg Harbor \ˈeg\. Early name of Somers Point (*q.v.*), New Jersey.

Egg Harbor City. City, Atlantic co., SE New Jersey, 17 mi. (27 km.) NW of Atlantic City; pop. (1990c) 4583; founded by German immigrants 1850.

Egg Island Point. Point on S coast of Cumberland co., SW New Jersey, extending into Delaware Bay.

Egg·mühl *or* **Eck·mühl** \ˈek-ˌmuēl\. Village, Bavaria, Germany, S of Regensburg; scene of battle Apr. 1809 in which French, Bavarians, and Württembergers under French Emperor Napoléon defeated Austrians under Archduke Charles.

Eg·ham \ˈe-gəm\. Town, Surrey, S England, on the Thames 20 mi. (32 km.) WSW of London; pop. (1981p) 27,817; the field of Runnymede (*q.v.*) lies along the riverside.

Eg·ma Plateau \ˈeg-mə\. Highland region, cen. Sinai Penin., (*q.v.*) NE Egypt; highest point Ras al-Geneina 5334 ft. (1626 m.).

Egmont, Cape. Cape on SW cen. coast of North I., New Zealand, at end of W bulge of North I.

Egmont Cape. 1. Cape, NE Cape Breton I., Nova Scotia, SE Canada.
2. Cape at S end of **Egmont Bay** (inlet of Northumberland Strait), W Prince Edward I., SE Canada.

Eg·mont, Mount \ˈeg-ˌmänt\ *or Maori* **Ta·ra·na·ki** \ˌtä-rä-ˈnä-kē\. Volcanic peak, in **Egmont National Park,** W cen. North I., New Zealand; 8260 ft. (2518 m.); noted for its symmetry and beauty.

Egorevsk. See YEGORYEVSK.

Eğ·ri·dir \ˌā-ri-ˈdir, -ḡri-\ *or* **Eger·dir** \ˌā-er-ˈdir, -ḡer-\ *also* **Ig·ri·dir** \ˌi-rə-ˈdir, -ḡrə-\. Town, İsparta prov., Turkey in Asia, at S end of Eğridir Lake.

Eğridir Lake *or Turk.* **Eğridir Gö·lü** \gœ-ˈlue\. Lake (*gölü*) in W Turkey in Asia, NE of İsparta; 30 mi. (48 km.) long by 3 to 10 mi. (5 to 16 km.) wide; no known outlet.

Egripos. See EVRIPOS.

Egypt \ˈē-jipt\; *officially* **Arab Republic of Egypt;** *formerly* **United Arab Republic;** *Arab.* **Mişr** \ˈmisr\; *anc.* **Ae·gyp·tus** \ē-ˈjip-təs\. Republic, NE Africa (with small part [Sinai Penin.] in Asia), bounded on N by the Mediterranean Sea, on E by Israel and the Red Sea, on S by Sudan, and on W by Libya; 386,900 sq. mi. (1,002,071 sq. km.), total habitable area ab.

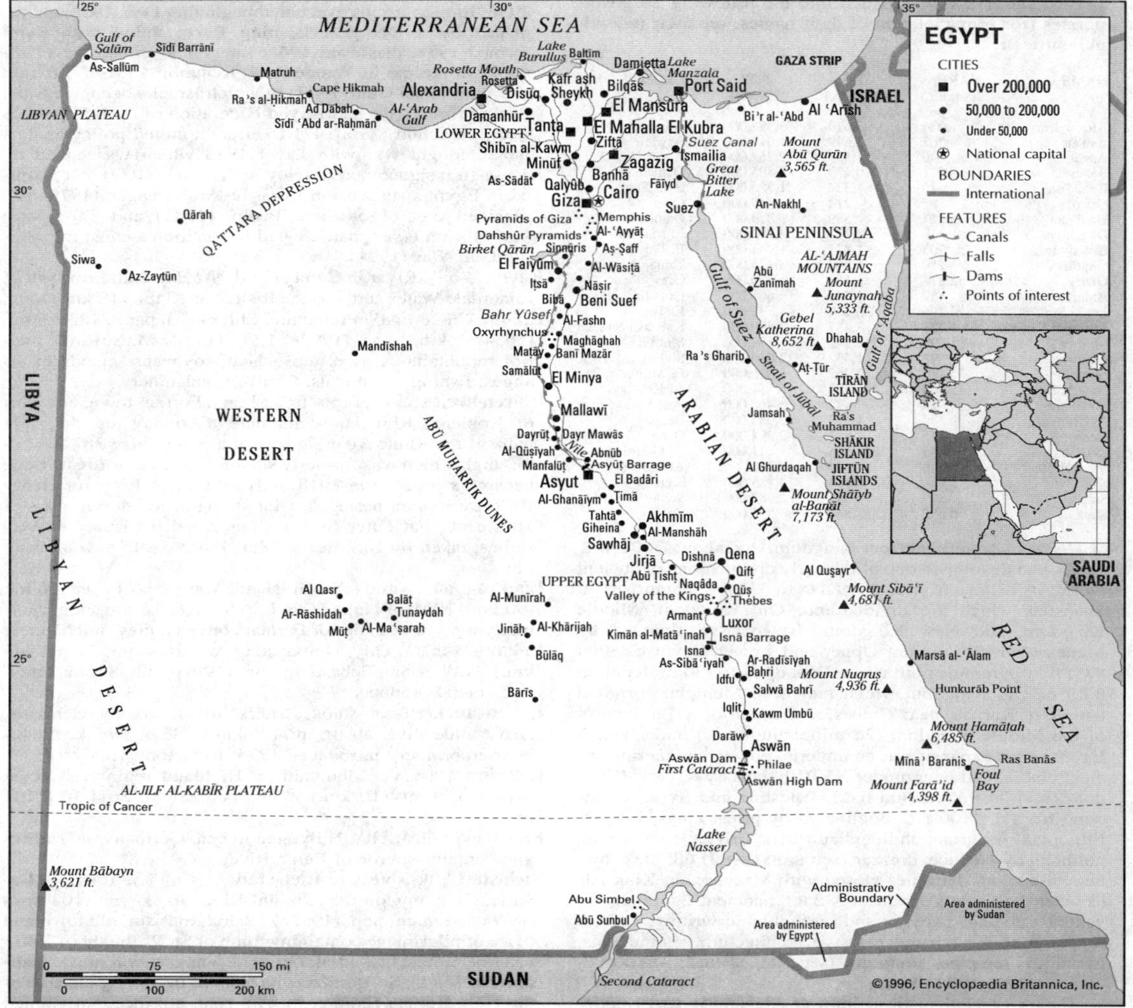

13,835 sq. mi. (35,833 sq. km.); pop. (1986c) 48,205,049; ✻ Cairo.

Physical features: Only mountains are those in Sinai Penin. in NE (bet. Gulf of Suez on W and Gulf of Aqaba on E) where Egma Plateau culminates in Ras al-Geneina 5328 ft. (1624 m.) and Gebel Musa group (highest point Gebel Katherina, 8652 ft. or 2637 m.) and in the range (3000 to 7150 ft. or 914 to 2179 m.) extending along Red Sea coast from Suez to border of Sudan.

Deserts: Has three large deserts: (1) Arabian, in E bet. the Nile and the mountains along the Red Sea and Gulf of Suez; (2) Western, in W cen. part; (3) E part of Libyan Desert along SW border; best known oases the Khārga (S cen. part), Dakhla (cen.), Farafra (W cen.), and Siwa (NW); bet. Western Desert and Mediterranean coast is Qattara Depression.

Nile River: Of critical importance to the life of the country is the Nile; its delta traditionally referred to as **Lower Egypt** and its valley S of 30°N is known as **Upper Egypt;** in S Aswān High Dam forms Lake Nasser.

Chief products: Cotton, wheat, sugarcane, corn, fruit, rice, onions; food processing; oil, manganese, phosphates, iron ore, salt; manufactured products include: textiles, iron and steel, chemicals, cement.

Chief cities: Cairo, Alexandria, Giza, Shubrā al-Khaymah, Port Said.

Political divisions: Divided into the following 26 governorates (for pronunciation of their names, see their individual entries):

NAME	AREA (sq. mi.)	AREA (sq. km.)	POP. (1994e)	CAPITAL
Alexandria	1,034	2,679	3,382,000	Alexandria
Aswān	262	679	1,017,000	Aswān
Asyūṭ	600	1,553	2,762,000	Asyūṭ
Beheira	3,911	10,130	3,895,000	Damanhūr
Beni Suef	510	1,322	1,785,000	Beni Suef
Cairo	83	214	6,849,000	Cairo
Damietta	227	589	879,000	Damietta
Daqahlīya	1,340	3,471	4,144,000	El Mansûra
El Faiyûm	705	1,827	1,943,000	El Faiyûm
Gharbīya	750	1,942	3,373,000	Tanta
Giza	32,878	85,153	4,400,000	Giza
Ismailia	557	1,442	665,000	Ismailia
Janūb Sīnā'	12,796	33,140	34,000	El Tûr
Kafr ash Shaykh	1,327	3,437	2,209,000	Kafr ash Shaykh
Matruh	81,897	212,112	179,000	Matruh
Minūfīya	592	1,532	2,619,000	Shibīn al-Kawm
Minya	873	2,262	3,288,000	El Minya
New Valley	145,369	376,505	134,000	Al Khārijah
Port Said	28	72	460,000	Port Said
Qalyubīya	387	1,001	2,983,000	Benha
Qena	715	1,851	2,694,000	Qena
Red Sea	78,643	203,685	111,000	Al Ghurdaqah
Shamāl Sīnā'	10,646	27,574	213,000	Al 'Arīsh
Sharqīya	1,614	4,180	4,125,000	Zagazig
Sohâg	597	1,547	2,982,000	Sohâg
Suez	6,888	17,840	393,000	Suez

History: A very ancient kingdom, by about 3000 B.C. Egypt had developed one of the early civilizations of ancient world; its history from c. 3000 B.C. to 332 B.C. comprises 30 dynasties which are divided into Old Kingdom, Middle Kingdom, and New Kingdom; Ist dynasty, founded by Menes (Narmer), united Upper and Lower Egypt c. 3000 B.C.; first pyramids built under IVth dynasty (3d millennium B.C.) of Old Kingdom which had ✻ at Memphis; original temple of Karnak, near Thebes, monument of XIIth dynasty of the Middle Kingdom (2d millennium B.C.) under which Egypt began expansion as an imperial power, conquering ancient Nubia, and later, under XVIIIth dynasty of New Kingdom (mid-2d millennium B.C.), Palestine and Syria; in decline from c. 1100 B.C. dominated by priest-kings, Libyan, Ethiopian, Assyrian, and Persian rulers; driven from Asiatic holdings by Nebuchadrezzar (see BABYLON 2) 605 B.C.; history of ancient dynasties closed with Macedonian King Alexander the Great's conquest 332 B.C.; ancient Egyptians invented calendar, papyrus and hieroglyphic writing, earliest seagoing ships; created massive architectural monuments, pyramids, temples, sculpture (see ABU SIMBEL, ABYDOS 2, GIZA, KARNAK, and LUXOR).

Center of Hellenistic culture at Alexandria (*q.v.*) under Ptolemies 332–30 B.C.; part of Roman Empire from 30 B.C. until Arab conquest 640 A.D.; Cairo (*q.v.*) seat of Fatimid caliphate which ruled Egypt 969–1171; ruled by Mamlūks 1250–1517; nominally part of Ottoman Empire 1517–1914; invaded by French Gen. (later Emperor) Napoléon Bonaparte, during which campaign he successfully waged Battle of the Pyramids, July 21, 1798, but French forced to withdraw (see ABŪ QĪR); became virtually independent with accession of Muḥammad 'Alī Pasha 1805; by revolts against sultan 1832 and 1839, obtained status of autonomous hereditary principality; under Khedive Ismā'īl Pasha, Suez Canal (*q.v.*) completed 1869; occupied 1882 by British, who shared dual control with France 1879–82; (for problem of Sudan, see *History* at SUDAN 2); administered by Evelyn Baring (Lord Cromer) 1883–1907; declared British protectorate 1914. Achieved independence 1922, but issues of British military occupation and Sudan only settled by treaty of 1936; 1923 constitution reintroduced 1935. Neutral in WWII; invaded Sept. 1940 by Italians, who were driven out by British Dec. 1940; invaded by Germans Nov. 1941 and again June–July 1942 when they reached El Alamein, but they were driven out after battle of Oct. 1942. For 1948–49 clash with Israelis, see *History* at ISRAEL 2; estab. a republic 1953, a year after overthrow of King Farouk by a military coup; intervention by British, French, and Israeli forces (Oct.–Nov.) following nationalization of Suez Canal Company July 1956; foreign troops evacuated beginning Dec. 1956 and replaced by a UN peacekeeping force; union with Syria formed 1958, dissolved 1961; intervened in support of republican regime in Yemen Arab Republic 1962–67; fought war with Israel (June 1967) in which Israelis occupied Sinai Penin.; formed the short-lived Federation of Arab Republics with Libya and Syria 1971 to effect a united policy against Israel; fought war with Israel 1973 which was ended by cease-fire; signed peace treaty with Israel (1979) that resulted in Egypt's suspension from the Arab League (1979–89); regained control of Sinai Penin. (1982) and Taba Strip (1989) from Israel; participated in coalition against Iraq during Gulf War (1991).

Ehen \ˈē-ən\. River in Cumberland, NW England; flows out of Ennerdale Water and S to the Irish Sea; 12 mi. (19 km.) long.

Ehi·me \ˈā-hē-ˌmā\. Prefecture, Shikoku, Japan; 2183 sq. mi. (5654 sq. km.); pop. (1992e) 1,511,000; ✻ Matsuyama; interior mountainous; rice, tea, wheat, soybeans, mandarin oranges; fishing; chemicals, fertilizer, machinery.

Eh·ren·breit·stein \ˌā-rən-ˈbrīt-ˌshtīn\. Former town, now part of Koblenz, Rhineland-Palatinate, Germany, on the right bank of the Rhine River, at foot of a rocky ridge 387 ft. (118 m.) high which was formerly site of an ancient fortress; ridge became a possession 1018 of Holy Roman Emperor Henry II; fortress often besieged, later strengthened during wars of 18th cent., but outer fortifications razed by Treaty of Versailles; taken by U.S. troops Mar. 1945; castle now a museum.

Eïao \ā-ˈyau̇, -ˈyä-ˌō\. Small island, Marquesas Is., ab. 56 mi. (90 km.) NNW of Nuku Hiva I.; 6.5 mi. (10.5 km.) long; formerly a place of exile for French convicts; now uninhabited.

Ei·bar \ˈā-ˌbär\. City, Guipúzcoa prov., N Spain, 27 mi. (43 km.) WSW of San Sebastián; pop. (1991p) 32,189; manufactures metal products.

Ei·ben·stock \ˈī-bən-shtȯk, -ˌstäk\. Town, Saxony, Germany, near Mulde River ab. 16 mi. (26 km.) SSE of Zwickau; tambour embroidery introduced 1775; to Saxony 1534.

Ei·bhinn \ˈā-vin\. Mountain, S Highland region, NW cen. Scotland, 6 mi. (10 km.) W of Loch Ericht; 3611 ft. (1101 m.).

Eichs·feld \ˈīks-ˌfelt\. Hilly area in cen. Germany, in Thuringia; contains source of Leine River.

Eich·stätt \ˈīk-ˌshtet\ *or* **Eich·stadt** \-ˌs(h)tät\. Town, W Bavaria, Germany, on the Altmühl River ab. 67 mi. (108 km.) NNW of Munich; pop. (1992e) 12,362; tourism; old town and place of pilgrimage containing tomb of St. Willibald (d. 786); has fine Gothic cathedral. Orig. a Roman station; made bishopric c. 745 by St. Boniface, its bishops becoming electors of the Holy Roman Empire; in 19th cent. a princedom granted to Eugène de Beauharnais, stepson of French Emperor Napoléon, subject to Bavaria.

Eick·el \ˈī-kəl\. Former town; since 1927 part of Wanne-Eickel (*q.v.*), Germany.

Ei·der \ˈī-dər\. River, N Germany, forming boundary bet. Schleswig and Holstein; rises E of Rendsburg and flows W into North Sea S of the Eiderstedt Penin.; 117 mi. (188 km.) long; importance decreased since completion of the Kiel Canal (Nord-Ost see Kanal). In 19th cent. gave its name to a Danish party (the *Eider Danes*) which advocated the incorporation of Schleswig into Denmark.

Ei·der·stedt \ˈī-dər-ˌshtet\. Peninsula extending into Heligoland Bight on W coast of Schleswig-Holstein, N Germany.

Eids·voll *also* **Eids·vold** \ˈāts-ˌvȯl\. Commune, Akershus co., SE Norway, 30 mi. (48 km.) NE of Oslo; pop. (1992e) 16,695; new constitution drawn up here May 17, 1814 providing for a unicameral national assembly and denying the king an absolute veto; constitution, with some modifications, still in effect.

Ei·el·son Air Force Base \ˈī-əl-sən\. U.S. airfield, E Alaska, on Tanana River on Alaska Highway, 26 mi. (42 km.) SE of Fairbanks; formerly known as **Mile 26.**

Ei·er·land *also* **Ei·jer·land** \ˈī-ər-ˌlänt\. North section of Texel I., Netherlands.

Ei·fel \ˈī-fəl\. Hilly region in W Germany, W of the Rhine River, NW of the Moselle River and NE of Luxembourg; ab. 40 mi. (64 km.) long, 20 mi. (32 km.) wide; highest point 3280 ft. (1000 m.) in E part; a barren region, chiefly of geologic interest; shows evidence of volcanic action; limestone moors, many lakes (called crater lakes).

Ei·ger \ˈī-gər\. Peak in the Bernese Alps, W cen. Switzerland, NW of the Finsteraarhorn; 13,025 ft. (3970 m.).

Eigg \ˈeg\. Small island of the Inner Hebrides, off W coast of Scotland; administratively a part of Highland region.

Eighty Mile Beach \ˈā-tē\. Stretch of Indian Ocean coast in NW Western Australia, Australia, bet. Port Hedland and Broome and bordering on a desolate part of Great Sandy Desert.

Eijerland. See EIERLAND.

Eil \ˈāl\. Coastal town, NE Somalia; terminus of road from Mogadishu.

Eil, Loch \ˈēl\. Sea inlet, Highland region, W Scotland, extending 8.5 mi. (14 km.) W from N end of Loch Linnhe; connects on E with Caledonian Canal system.

Eilat. See ELAT.

Eil·don Hills \ˈēl-dən\. Three conical peaks, Borders region, SE Scotland, S of Melrose; highest 1385 ft. (422 m.); prehistoric and Roman remains.

Ei·len·burg \ˈī-lən-ˌbu̇rk\. City, Saxony, Germany, on the Mulde River 13 mi. (21 km.) NE of Leipzig; pop. (1981c) 21,678; railroad junction; castle dating at least from the 10th cent.; town hall 1544–45; town dates from early 13th cent.; passed to Prussia 1815.

Ei·len·dorf \ˈī-lən-ˌdȯrf\. Commune, North Rhine-Westphalia, Germany, 4 mi. (6 km.) E of Aachen.

Eil Malk \ˈāl-ˈmälk\. Island, S cen. Palau, W Pacific Ocean, S of Urukthapel; bet. it and Peleliu I. 10 mi. (16 km.) to the SW are many islets and reefs.

Ei·meo \ī-ˈmā-ō\. One of the Windward Is., Society Is., French Polynesia. See MOORÉA.

Ein·beck \ˈīn-ˌbek\. Town, S Lower Saxony, Germany, ab. 40 mi. (64 km.) S of Hannover; pop. (1980c) 28,867; important esp. 15th–17th cents. Grew up around monastery founded 1080; seat of princes of Grubenhagen (branch of the ducal house of Brunswick) 14th cent. to 1596; member of Hanseatic League.

Eind·ho·ven \ˈīnt-ˌhō-vən, ˈānt-\. Commune, North Brabant prov., S Netherlands, 55 mi. (88 km.) SE of Rotterdam; pop. (1992e) 193,966; produces electrical and radio apparatus, motor vehicles, tobacco products, textiles; technical university (1956); received charter 1232; rapid pop. increase followed establishment of an electrical-apparatus factory in late 19th cent.; in WWII marked S point of region invaded by Allied airborne troops Sept. 1944.

Ein·sie·deln \ˈīn-ˌzēd-ᵊln\. Commune, Schwyz canton, E cen. Switzerland, 9 mi. (14 km.) NNE of the commune of Schwyz; pop. (1990c) 10,620; furniture; 18th cent. Benedictine abbey (founded 10th cent.) containing a famous image of the Virgin which is the object of annual pilgrimages; religious reformer Huldrych Zwingli was parish priest here 1516–18; birthplace 1493 of alchemist and physician Paracelsus.

Eipel. See IPEL'.

Eire. See IRELAND.

Ei·se·nach \ˈīz-ᵊn-ˌäk, -ˌäk\. City, Thuringia, cen. Germany, 31 mi. (50 km.) W of Erfurt; pop. (1992e) 44,266; machinery, electrical equipment, metal goods, wood products, chemicals; tourism; 16th cent. town hall. Birthplace 1685 of composer Johann Sebastian Bach; place where religious reformer Martin Luther attended school 1498–1501. Originated in 12th cent.; ✻ of Thuringian landgraves; residence 1572 ff. of Ernestine line of princes; ✻ of duchy of Eisenach 1672–1741; united with Weimar 1741; part of Thuringia 1815.

Ei·sen·berg \ˈīz-ᵊn-ˌberk, -ˌbərg\. City, Thuringia, W cen. Germany, 38 mi. (61 km.) E of Erfurt; 16th cent. town hall; palace (1677–92); first mentioned 12th cent.

Eisenburg. See VASVÁR.

Ei·sen·erz \ˈīz-ᵊn-ˌerts\. Commune, N Styria, Austria, 16 mi. (26 km.) NW of Leoben; pop. (1991c) 7759; mining school; nearby is the Erzberg (*q.v.*); became city 1948.

Ei·sen·how·er, Mount \ˈīz-ᵊn-ˌhau̇-ər\. **1.** *formerly* **Mount Pleas·ant** \ˈplez-ᵊnt\. Peak, S Coos co., N New Hampshire, in Presidential Range of the White Mts., SW of Mt. Washington; 4775 ft. (1455 m.).

2. Mountain, Alberta, Canada. See CASTLE MOUNTAIN.

Ei·sen·hut \ˈīz-ᵊn-ˌhüt\. Mountain, SW Styria, Austria, NW of Klagenfurt; 8006 ft. (2440 m.); highest peak in Noric Alps.

Ei·sen·hüt·ten·stadt \ˈīz-ᵊn-ˌhu̇e̅t-ᵊn-ˌshtät\. City, Brandenburg, E Germany, on the Oder River and border with Poland; pop. (1992e) 49,063; metallurgical works; pig iron; formed 1961 by the union of three towns.

Ei·sen·stadt \ˈīz-ᵊn-ˌshtät\. Town, ✻ of Burgenland, Austria, just W of Neusiedler Lake; pop. (1991c) 10,349; textiles; in wine-producing region; home of composer Joseph Haydn latter part of 18th cent.; until 1920 in Hungary.

Ei·ser·feld \ˈi-zər-ˌfelt\. City, North Rhine-Westphalia, Germany, 56 mi. (90 km.) NW of Frankfurt am Main; founded 1966.

Eisernes Tor. See IRON GATE.

Eis·le·ben \ˈīs-ˌlā-bən\. City, Saxony-Anhalt, E cen. Germany, in the E spurs of Harz Mts. 22 mi. (35 km.) NW of Merseburg; pop. (1992e) 25,228; apparel, furniture; 16th cent. town hall; houses in which religious reformer Martin Luther was born (a museum since 1917) and died; first mentioned 994.

Eitape. See AITAPE.

Eivissa. See IBIZA.

Ejmiadzin. See ECHMIADZIN.

Eka·laka \ˌē-kə-ˈla-kə\. Town, ⊗ of Carter co., SE corner of Montana; pop. (1990c) 439.

Ekaterinburg. See YEKATERINBURG.

Ekaterinenstadt. See MARKS.

Ekaterinodar. See KRASNODAR.

Ekaterinoslav. See DNEPROPETROVS'K.

Eke Crater \ˈā-ˌkā\. See MAUI 1.

Ekhmīm. See AKHMĪM.

Eki·bas·tuz \ˌe-kē-ˈbäs-tüs\. Town, Pavlodar subdivision, Kazakhstan, ab. 80 mi. (129 km.) SW of Pavlodar; pop. (1991e) 93,460.

Ek·ron \ˈe-ˌkrän\. City of ancient Palestine; its site now in Israel; one of the five chief city-kingdoms of Philistia.

El Aaiún. See AAIÚN, EL.

Elabuga. See YELABUGA.

El Agheila. See AL 'UQAYLAH.
Elah, Vale of \ˈē-lə\. Valley of middle course of N branch of Nahr Suqreir, Israel, ab. 15 mi. (24 km.) W of Bethlehem; probable site of the combat bet. David and Goliath (*1 Sam.* xvii. 2, 19).
El Ala·mein \ˌel-ˌa-lə-ˈmān\ *also* **Ala·mein.** Village on coastal road, N Egypt, ab. 65 mi. (104 km.) W of Alexandria and N of NE corner of Qattara Depression; farthest German advance July 1, 1942 in campaign to seize Alexandria, Cairo, and the Suez Canal; scene of battle Oct.–Nov. 1942 in which Allies defeated Germans. See AL-AQQAQIR.
El Al·to \ˌel-ˈäl-tō\. City, W Bolivia, a SW suburb of La Paz; pop (1989e) 307,400.
Elam \ˈē-ləm\ *also* **Su·si·a·na** \ˌsü-zē-ˈa-nə, -ˈä-, -ˈā-\. Ancient kingdom at head of Persian Gulf E of Babylonia; from c. 3000 B.C. there was a conflict bet. Elamites, non-Semitic inhabitants of Elam, and the Sumerians and Akkadians; with its ✱ at Susa, kingdom of Elam flourished c. 13th–12th cents. B.C.; absorbed 7th cent. B.C. by Assyria, which destroyed Susa; Susa later became one of capitals of Persian Empire of Cyrus the Great (see IRAN).
Elands·laag·te \ˈē-ˌlänts-ˌläk-tə\. Settlement, E Rep. of South Africa; scene of battle Oct. 1899 in which Boers under Petrus Joubert were temporarily repulsed by British.
El Aqqaqir. See AL-AQQAQIR.
el Arab, Bahr. See BAHR EL ARAB.
El 'Arīsh. See AL-'ARĪSH.
El Ashmūnein. See AL-ASHMŪNEIN.
Elat \ˈē-ˌlat\ *also* **Elath** \ˈē-ˌlath\ *or* **Ei·lat** \ā-ˈlät\. Seaport, S Israel, W of Aqaba at head of Gulf of Aqaba; pop. (1992e) 29,900; Israel's leading oil port; fishing; built since 1949.
Elatea. 1. Mountain. See CITHAERON.
2. Town. See ELATEIA.
Ela·teia *or* **Elá·tia** \e-ˈlä-tē-ä\ *or* **Drakh·ma·ni** \thräk-ˈmä-nē\; *anc.* **El·a·tea** \ˌe-lə-ˈtē-ə\. Town, E cen. Greece, NE of Mt. Parnassus.
Elath \ˈē-ˌlath\. **1.** Town, Jordan. See AQABA.
2. Seaport, S Israel. See ELAT.
Elaver. See ALLIER.
Elâ·zığ \ˌe-lä-ˈzə\; *formerly* **Elâ·ziz** \-ˈzēz\. **1.** Province of Turkey in Asia. See table at TURKEY.
2. Town, its ✱; pop. (1990e) 204,603.
El·ba \ˈel-bə\. **1.** City, a ⊗ of Coffee co., SE Alabama; pop. (1990c) 4011.
2. \ˈel-bä\; *anc.* **Il·va** \ˈil-və\ *also* **Ae·tha·lia** \i-ˈthā-lē-ə\. Island, Italy, in Mediterranean Sea bet. NE coast of Corsica and mainland of Italy; 86 sq. mi. (223 sq. km.); pop. (1984e) 28,907; politically a part of Italian prov. of Livorno, Tuscany; chief town Portoferraio; has iron-ore deposits which have been worked since ancient times. Residence of French Emperor Napoléon after his first abdication May 1814 to Feb. 1815 when he left secretly to begin his career of the "Hundred Days"; in WWII taken from Germans by French June 1944.
Elba, Cape. See HADARBA, RAS.
El Ba·dâ·ri \ˌel-bə-ˈdä-rē\. Village, Egypt, ab. 19 mi. (30 km.) SE of Asyūṭ; in region where excavations by English Egyptologist Sir Flinders Petrie revealed evidences of a predynastic Neolithic culture, dated c. 4000 B.C.
El Ban·co \el-ˈbäŋ-kō\. Town, Magdalena dept., N Colombia, ab. 148 mi. (238 km.) SE of Cartagena; munic. pop. (1985c) 23,807.
El·ba·san \ˌel-bä-ˈsän\; *formerly* **El·ba·sa·ni** \-ˈsä-nē\. **1.** District of cen. Albania. See table at ALBANIA.
2. Town, its ✱, on Shkumbin River 20 mi. (32 km.) SE of Tiranë; pop. (1990e) 83,300; market center in agricultural region producing esp. tobacco, fruit, and olive oil; cement, timber; E terminus of railroad line from Durrës; Italian base in early part of WWII.
El·be \ˈel-bə, ˈelb\ *or Czech* **La·be** \ˈlä-be\; *anc.* **Al·bis** \ˈal-bis\. River in Czech Republic and Germany; rises on S slopes of the Riesengebirge, Czech Republic, flows S, W, and NW in Czech Republic, then N across Germany, turning NW to flow into North Sea at Cuxhaven; 724 mi. (1165 km.) long; navigable to beyond Czech border; just N of Litoměřice cuts through the Erzgebirge in a narrow gorge. Chief tributaries Vltava and Ohře in Czech Republic, and Mulde, Saale, Schwarze Elster, Havel, and Elde in Germany; connected by canals with Oder River and Baltic Sea. Meeting point April 1945 of British and American armies with Soviet armies (see TORGAU); part of lower course estab. 1945 as line of demarcation bet. British and Soviet zones of administration in Germany.
Elbe–Havel Canal. Canal, NE cen. Germany, connecting the Elbe and Havel rivers.
El Be·ni \el-ˈbā-nē\ *or* **Beni.** Department of N Bolivia. See table at BOLIVIA.
El·bert \ˈel-bərt\. Name of counties in two states of the U.S. See tables at COLORADO and GEORGIA.
Elbert, Mount. Peak, Lake co., cen. Colorado; 14,433 ft. (4399 m.); highest peak in the state and in the Rocky Mts.
El·ber·ton \ˈel-bərt-ᵊn\. City, ⊗ of Elbert co., NE Georgia, E of Athens; pop. (1990c) 5682; granite deposits.
El·beuf \el-ˈbœf\. Commune, Seine-Maritime dept., N France, on Seine River 14 mi. (23 km.) SSW of Rouen; pop. (1990c) 16,750; textiles, automobiles, chemicals; Renaissance churches.
El·bląg \ˈel-ˌblȯŋk\ *or Ger.* **El·bing** \ˈel-biŋ\. **1.** Province, N Poland. See table at POLAND.
2. Seaport and City, its ✱, 30 mi. (48 km.) ESE of Gdańsk; pop. (1989e) 125,154; important shipbuilding and repair yards; metallurgical industries; machinery. Founded 1237; became member of Hanseatic League; taken by Poland 1454; annexed to Prussia 1772; captured by Soviet troops Jan.–Feb. 1945 after severe fighting; in section of East Prussia assigned to Poland by Potsdam Conference 1945.
El Bluff \el-ˈblüf\. Port, SE Nicaragua, at tip of a peninsula E of Bluefields.
El Boulaïda. See BLIDA 2.
El·bow Lake \ˈel-bō\. Village, ⊗ of Grant co., W Minnesota, 29 mi. (47 km.) W of Alexandria; pop. (1990c) 1186.
El·brus, Mount *or* **El'·brus, Gora** *also*, **Mount El·bruz** \el-ˈbrüs, ˈel-ˌbrüs\. Peak in the Caucasus Mts., S Russia in Europe, on Republic of Georgia border; 18,510 ft. or 5642 m. (W peak; E peak slightly lower); highest peak in Europe; actually in a N subsidiary spur of the main range of the Caucasus.
El·burz Mountains \el-ˈbu̇rz\. Range in N Iran, extending W to E parallel with S shore of Caspian Sea, from which it is separated by a lowland strip not at any point more than 25 mi. (40 km.) wide; highest peak Damāvand 18,934 ft. (5771 m.); has many peaks above 10,000 ft. (3048 m.).
El Ca·jon \ˌel-kə-ˈhōn\. City, San Diego co., SW coastal California, E of the city of San Diego; pop. (1990c) 88,693; aircraft components, electronic equipment; Grossmont Coll. (1961), Christian Heritage Coll. (1970).
El Cam·po \el-ˈkam-pō\. City, Wharton co., SE Texas, 25 mi. (40 km.) NW of Bay City; pop. (1990c) 10,511; oil, sulfur.
El Ca·ney \ˌel-kä-ˈnā\ *or* **Caney.** Municipality, E Cuba; scene of battle in the Spanish-American War in which Gen. Henry Lawton's division defeated the Spaniards July 1898; this and victory at San Juan Hill (*q.v.*) on same day led to American control of Santiago de Cuba and destruction of Adm. Pascual Cervera y Topete's fleet July 3.
El Cap·i·tan \ˌel-ˌka-pi-ˈtan\. **1.** Peak in the Sierra Nevada, Yosemite Valley, Yosemite National Park, cen. California; 7569 ft. (2307 m.); rises 3604 ft. (1098 m.) above the valley floor.
2. Peak, Ravalli co., W Montana; 9983 ft. (3043 m.).
3. Peak, Guadalupe Mts., NW Culberson co., W Texas; 8078 ft. (2462 m.).
El Capitan Dam. Dam across San Diego River, California; height 270 ft. (82 m.); completed 1934; impounds water for water supply.
El Cayo. See SAN IGNACIO 1.
El Cen·tro \el-ˈsen-trō\. City, ⊗ of Imperial co., SE corner of California, in Imperial Valley 86 mi. (138 km.) E of San Diego, near Mexican border; pop. (1990c) 31,384; 52 ft. (16 m.) below sea level; shipping point for fruits and vegetables; settled early 20th cent.

El Cer·ri·to \ˌel-sə-ˈrē-tō\. Residential city, Contra Costa co., W California, on San Francisco Bay 6 mi. (10 km.) N of Oakland; pop. (1990c) 22,869.

El Chaco. See GRAN CHACO.

El·chaig \el-ˈkāg, -ˈkäg\. Stream, Highland Region, Scotland; 6.5 mi. (10 km.) long. See GLOMACH, FALLS OF.

El·che \ˈel-chā\; *anc.* **Il·i·ci** \ˈi-li-ˌsī\. City, Alicante prov., SE Spain, 13 mi. (21 km.) SW of the seaport city of Alicante; pop. (1991c) 188,062; dates, palm fronds; manufactures olive oil, soap, shoes; episcopal palace; scene of annual mystery play; ancient Roman colony; held by Moors 8th–13th cents.

El Cobre. See COBRE.

El·da \ˈel-dä\. Commune, Alicante prov., SE Spain, 18 mi. (29 km.) NW of the seaport city of Alicante; pop. (1991c) 54,350; agricultural produce; manufactures paper and esparto articles; remains of old Moorish castle.

El Dabʽa See AD DABAH.

El·de \ˈel-də\. River, E cen. Germany; flows SW through several lakes into Elbe River ab. 65 mi. (105 km.) NW of Magdeburg; ab. 135 mi. (215 km.) long.

El·den Mountain \ˈel-dən\. Peak, cen. Coconino co., N cen. Arizona; 9280 ft. (2829 m.).

El Djem *or* **El Jem** \el-ˈjem\. Town, NE Tunisia, 40 mi. (64 km.) S of Sousse.

El Djouf *also* **Al–Juf** \el-ˈjüf, ȧl-\. Desert region in E Mauritania and W Mali; at W end of the Sahara.

El·don \ˈel-dən\. **1.** City, Wapello co., SE Iowa, 12 mi. (19 km.) SE of Ottumwa on Des Moines River; pop. (1990c) 1070.
2. City, Miller co., cen. Missouri, 23 mi. (37 km.) SW of Jefferson City; pop. (1990c) 4419.

El·do·ra \el-ˈdōr-ə\. City, ⊗ of Hardin co., N cen. Iowa, 24 mi. (39 km.) NNW of Marshalltown; pop. (1990c) 3038.

El·do·ra·do \ˌel-də-ˈrā-ˌdō\. **1.** Commercial city, Saline co., SE Illinois, 25 mi. (40 km.) W of confluence of Ohio and Wabash rivers; pop. (1990c) 4536; coal deposits.
2. Town, ⊗ of Schleicher co., W cen. Texas, 45 mi. (72 km.) S of San Angelo; pop. (1990c) 2019; oil and gas deposits.

El Do·ra·do \ˌel-də-ˈrä-dō\. County in E California. See table at CALIFORNIA.

El Do·ra·do \ˌel-də-ˈrā-dō\. **1.** City, ⊗ of Union co., S Arkansas, 80 mi. (129 km.) ESE of Texarkana; pop. (1990c) 23,146; settled 1843; made ⊗ 1844; after discovery of oil in 1921, became chief city of Arkansas oil industry.
2. City, ⊗ of Butler co., S Kansas, 28 mi. (45 km.) ENE of Wichita; pop. (1990c) 11,504; Butler County Community Junior Coll. (1927).

El·do·ra·do Range \ˌel-də-ˈrä-dō\. Range in extreme S tip of Nevada, running N to S along Colorado River.

El Do·ra·do Springs \ˌel-də-ˈrā-dō\. City, Cedar co., W Missouri, 18 mi. (29 km.) E of Nevada; pop. (1990c) 3830; mineral springs.

El·do·ret \ˌel-dō-ˈret\. Town, W cen. Kenya, on railroad line ab. 50 mi. (80 km.) NE of Kisumu; pop. (1983e) 55,300.

El·dridge \ˈel-drij\. City, Scott co., Iowa; pop. (1990c) 3378.

Elea. See VELIA.

Electoral Hesse. See *History* (3) at HESSE 3.

Elec·tra \i-ˈlek-trə\. City, Wichita co., N Texas, 25 mi. (40 km.) WNW of Wichita Falls; pop. (1990c) 3113; oil.

Elec·tric Peak \i-ˈlek-trik\. Mountain, S Montana, near Wyoming border, in Yellowstone National Park; 10,992 ft. (3350 m.); highest point in Gallatin Range.

Elek·tro·stal \el-ˌyek-trə-ˈstäl\; *formerly* **Za·tish·ye** \zä-ˈtē-shyə\. Town, Moscow Oblast, W cen. Russia in Europe, ab. 30 mi. (48 km.) E of the city of Moscow; pop. (1992e) 153,000.

Elektrovoz. See STUPINO.

El·e·phant \ˈe-lə-fənt\. **1.** Island in Scotia Sea, in NE part of South Shetland Is., British Antarctic Terr., ab. 61°10′S, 55°14′W.
2. *or* **Oli·fants** \ˈä-lə-fənts\. River, SE cen. Namibia; ab. 250 mi. (400 km.) long.

El·e·phan·ta \ˌe-lə-ˈfan-tə\ *or Hind.* **Gha·ra·pu·ri** \ˌgär-ə-ˈpu̇r-ē\. Small island in Bombay Harbor, W India, ab. 6 mi. (10 km.) E of the city of Bombay; famous for its Temple Caves, excavations cut out of solid rock probably 1000 to 1200 years ago; contains colossal carved figures of the Trimurti, Siva, Parvati, and other Hindu deities.

Elephant Butte Dam. Dam across the Rio Grande in SW New Mexico, NE of Truth or Consequences; completed 1916.

El·e·phan·ti·ne \ˌe-lə-ˌfan-ˈtī-nē, -ˈtē-\. Island in Nile River, in Upper Egypt, opp. Aswān just below the first of several cataracts; ruins of many structures—Egyptian, Roman, Saracen, and Arabic; at its upper end had ancient Nilometer; site of discovery 1903 of the *Elephantine papyri,* dating from end of 5th cent. B.C. and containing varied information about the Jewish people.

Elephant Mound. Prehistoric earthwork 4 mi. (6 km.) S of Wyalusing, NW Grant co., SW Wisconsin, on Mississippi River; once thought to resemble an elephant; first noticed 1872.

Elephant Mountain. Peak, W Brewster co., W Texas; 6200 ft. (1890 m.).

El Es·co·ri·al \ˌel-ˌes-kōr-ˈyäl\. Commune, Madrid prov., cen. Spain, 25 mi. (40 km.) NW of the city of Madrid in SW Sierra de Guadarrama; pop. (1991c) 6916; site of the Escorial, a vast structure erected 1563–84 at the direction of Philip II, comprising a royal palace, a royal mausoleum, a church, a college, and a monastery; containing many works of art.

Elets. See YELETS.

Eleu·sis \i-ˈlü-səs\ *or Gk.* **Elev·sís** \ˌe-lef-ˈsēs\. Village with ruins of an ancient city, E Greece, ab. 14 mi. (23 km.) NW of Athens, on N shore of Bay of Eleusis opp. Salamis I.; a place of great antiquity; in early times independent of Athens; seat of the Eleusinian Mysteries, the most famous of the Greek religious mysteries, in honor of Demeter; sacred buildings destroyed 395 A.D. by Alaric I, king of the Visigoths.

Eleusis, Bay of *or Gk.* **Kól·pos Elev·sí·nos** \ˈköl-pös-ˌe-lef-ˈsē-ˌnös\. Inlet of Saronic Gulf, Attica and Boeotia dept., Greece, almost completely shut in by Salamis I.

Eleu·thera \i-ˈlü-thə-rə\. One of the Bahamas, in the Atlantic Ocean E of New Providence I.; ab. 80 mi. (130 km.) long; 164 sq. mi. (425 sq. km.); one of the earliest islands in the Bahamas to be colonized, in mid-17th cent.

Eleu·ther·op·o·lis \i-ˌlü-thə-ˈrä-pə-lis\; *mod.* **Bet Gu·vrin** \ˈbāt-gə-ˈvrēn\ *or* **Beit Ji·brin** \ˈbāt-jə-ˈbrēn\. Ancient city in Palestine, ab. 40 mi. (64 km.) WNW of Hebron; site of Roman ruins; sacked or destroyed several times; rebuilt and renamed by Emperor Septimius Severus 200 A.D.; important in time of Crusades.

Eleven Thousand Virgins, Cape of the. See VÍRGENES.

Elevsínos, Kólpos. See ELEUSIS, BAY OF.

Elevsís. See ELEUSIS.

El Faiyûm \ˌel-fī-ˈyüm\ *or* **Al Fay·ūm** \ˌal-\. **1.** Governorate of N Upper Egypt. See table at EGYPT.
2. Town, its ✱, N Upper Egypt, ab. 70 mi. (115 km.) SW of Cairo; pop. (1986p) 212,523; cotton ginning, tanning; important modern town on the Bahr Yûsef bet. the Nile and Birket Qārūn; lies in bed of ancient Lake Moeris near site of Arsinoë, in region rich in archaeological objects and papyri.

El Fa·sher \el-ˈfa-shir\ *also* **Al–Fa·shir** \ȧl-\. Town, ✱ Darfur region, W Sudan.

Elfeld. See ELTVILLE.

El Fe·rrol \ˌel-fer-ˈrōl\ *also shortened to* **Ferrol;** *formerly* **El Ferrol del Cau·dil·lo** \ˌdel-kau̇-ˈdēl-yō, -ˈdē-\. City, La Coruña prov., NW Spain, 11 mi. (18 km.) NE of the seaport commune of La Coruña on a fine natural harbor; pop. (1991c) 83,045; important naval station; shipbuilding; chosen as site of naval arsenal by Philip V 1726; shipbuilding estab. in mid-18th cent.; surrendered to English 1805; occupied by French Jan.–June 1809.

El Frai·le \el-ˈfrī-lā\. Rocky islet, part of entrance to Manila Bay, Philippines, on S side of South Channel, ab. 2 mi. (3 km.) from Cavite shore; had American fortification, Fort Drum (see CORREGIDOR).

Elfsborg. See ÄLVSBORG.

El Fung. See AL-FUNG.

El Gazala. See AL-GAZALA.

El Geneina. See AL JUNAYNAH.

El Gezira. **1.** Region, E cen. Sudan. See GEZIRA.

2. Former province, E cen. Sudan. See BLUE NILE 2.

El·gin \ˈel-jin\. City, Cook and Kane cos., NE Illinois, 38 mi. (61 km.) WNW of Chicago; pop. (1990c) 77,010; dairy farming nearby; formerly a major center of watch manufacture; Elgin Community Coll. (1949), Judson Coll. (1963).

Elgin \ˈel-gin\. **1.** City, Bastrop co., S cen. Texas, 23 mi. (37 km.) E of Austin; pop. (1990c) 4846; oil wells.

2. County in SE Ontario, Canada. See table at ONTARIO.

3. *or* **Elginshire** \-ˌshir, -shər\. Former county in Scotland. See MORAY.

4. Burgh, NW Grampian region, NE Scotland; pop. (1981p) 18,905; distilleries; ruins of noted cathedral.

El Gîza. See GIZA.

El·gon, Mount \ˈel-ˌgän\. Volcanic peak on the Uganda-Kenya boundary, NE of Lake Victoria; 14,178 ft. (4321 m.).

El Ḩammâm. See AL-HAMMĀM.

El Ḩasa. See AL-HASA.

Elí·as Pi·ña \ā-ˈlē-äs-ˈpē-nyä\. **1.** Province, W Dominican Republic. See *La Estrelleta* in table at DOMINICAN REPUBLIC.

2. Commune, ✻ of La Estrelleta prov., Dominican Republic; pop. (1981p) 65,384.

Elichpur. See ACHALPUR.

Elikón. See HELICON.

Elimberrum. See AUCH.

Eliocroca. See LORCA.

El·i·ot \ˈe-lē-ət\. Town, York co., SW Maine, 28 mi. (45 km.) SSW of Biddeford; pop. (1990c) 5329.

Elis \ˈē-lis\. **1.** Ancient country in NW Peloponnese, Greece; bounded on N by Achaea, on E by Arcadia, on S by Messenia, and on W by Ionian Sea; extent varied in accordance with changes in its political influence; dist. of Triphylia in S for a time held by Arcadia. Watered by Peneus and Alpheus rivers; mountain range on E border included Mt. Erymanthus (at NE corner); chief town Elis; in S was plain of Olympia (*q.v.*). After First Peloponnesian War involved in most of the wars of Greece, usu. but not always as ally of Sparta; control of Olympian games for several centuries gave Eleans considerable prestige.

2. Department of Greece. See table at GREECE.

3. City, ✻ of ancient Elis, in W cen. part on Peneus River; now only ruins.

Elis·a·beth·ville \i-ˈli-zə-bəth-ˌvil\. **1.** Administrative region, Democratic Rep. of the Congo. See SHABA.

2. City, Democratic Rep. of the Congo. See LUBUMBASHI.

Elisavetgrad. See KIROVOHRAD 2.

Elisavetpol. See GÄNCÄ.

Elis·ta \e-ˈlyē-stə, ē-ˈlis-tə\; *formerly* **Step·noi** \styip-ˈnȯi\. Town, ✻ of Kalmykia Rep., S Russia in Europe, 220 mi. (354 km.) ESE of Rostov-na-Donu; pop. (1991e) 95,200; in WWII occupied by German forces Aug. 1942 but retaken by U.S.S.R. before the end of the war.

Eliz·a·beth \i-ˈli-zə-bəth\. **1.** Navigable river, Norfolk co., SE Virginia, emptying into Hampton Roads; the cities of Norfolk and Portsmouth are on its banks.

2. City, ⊗ of Union co., NE New Jersey; residential suburb of New York City on Newark Bay 5 mi. (8 km.) S of Newark; pop. (1990c) 110,002; connected with Staten I. by Goethals Bridge; manufactures machinery, chemicals, foundry products, sewing machines, textiles, automobiles.

History: Purchased by English from Indians 1664 and settled as Elizabethtown; until 1686 ✻ of New Jersey; meeting place of colonial assembly 1668–82; important point in Gen. George Washington's maneuvers during Revolution; chartered as borough of Elizabeth 1740 and 1789, as city 1855; original seat of Princeton Univ.; home of statesman Alexander Hamilton and political leader Aaron Burr.

3. Borough, Allegheny co., SW Pennsylvania, on Monongahela River 14 mi. (23 km.) SSE of Pittsburgh; pop. (1990c) 1610; formerly important boatbuilding center.

4. Town, ⊗ of Wirt co., W West Virginia; pop. (1990c) 900.

Elizabeth, Cape. **1.** Cape, Cumberland co., on coast of SW Maine, 8 mi. (13 km.) S of Portland.

2. *or Russ.* **Mys Ye·li·za·ve·ty** \ˈməs-yi-ˌli-zə-ˈvye-tē\. Point, Sakhalin I., Russia in Asia, See YELIZAVETY, MYS.

Elizabeth, Mount. Mountain, Antarctica, 83°54′S, 168°23′E; 14,698 ft. (4480 m.).

Elizabeth City. **1.** Former county in Virginia; since 1958, comprises independent city of Hampton.

2. Town, ⊗ of Pasquotank co., NE North Carolina, on N arm of Albemarle Sound; pop. (1990c) 14,292; excellent harbor; shipping point for area farm products; manufactures textiles, veneer. U.S. Coast Guard support center; Elizabeth City State Univ. (1891), Coll. of the Albemarle (1960); became ⊗ 1799; naval victory won near here by Union 1862.

Elizabeth Islands. Group of small islands in Dukes co., SE Massachusetts; extending SW from SW point of Cape Cod; separated from Martha's Vineyard by Vineyard Sound and from mainland of Massachusetts by Buzzards Bay.

Elizabeth Point. Cape on SW coast of Namibia, S of Lüderitz.

Eliz·a·beth·ton \i-ˌli-zə-ˈbeth-tən\. City, ⊗ of Carter co., NE Tennessee, on Watauga River 9 mi. (14 km.) E of Johnson City; pop. (1990c) 11,931; manufactures rayon and rayon yarn; nearby lakes provide recreational use.

Eliz·a·beth·town \i-ˈli-zə-bəth-ˌtau̇n\. **1.** Village, ⊗ of Hardin co., SE Illinois; pop. (1990c) 427.

2. City, ⊗ of Hardin co., cen. Kentucky, 40 mi. (64 km.) S of Louisville; pop. (1990c) 18,167; plastics, metal products; limestone deposits.

3. Village, ⊗ of Essex co., NE New York, in Adirondack Mts. 32 mi. (51 km.) S of Plattsburg; pop. (1990c) 1314.

4. Town, ⊗ of Bladen co., S North Carolina, on Cape Fear River 35 mi. (56 km.) SSE of Fayetteville; pop. (1990c) 3704.

5. Borough, Lancaster co., SE Pennsylvania, 18 mi. (29 km.) WNW of the city of Lancaster; pop. (1990c) 9952; Elizabethtown Coll. (1899); founded 1732.

El Ja·di·da \el-ˈjä-dē-də\ *also* **Al–Ja·di·da** \äl-\; *formerly* **Ma·za·gan** \ˌmä-zä-ˈgän\. Seaport, W Morocco, ab. 60 mi. (96 km.) SW of Casablanca; founded 1502 by Portuguese and held by them until 1769.

El Jem. See EL DJEM.

El Jerid, Chott. See DJERID, CHOTT.

Elk \ˈelk\. **1.** River, Pennsylvania and Maryland; flows S from Chester co., SE Pennsylvania, into N Chesapeake Bay in NE corner of Maryland; ab. 40 m. (64 km.) long; has wide estuary ab. 13 mi. (21 km.) long.

2. River, Tennessee and Alabama; flows SW from Grundy co., S Tennessee, into Tennessee River near upper end of Muscle Shoals, N Alabama; ab. 200 mi. (320 km.) long.

3. River, cen. West Virginia; rises in Pocahontas co., flows N, NW, and W into Kanawha River at Charleston in Kanawha co.; 172 mi. (277 km.) long.

4. Name of counties in two states of the U.S. See table at KANSAS and PENNSYLVANIA.

Ełk \ˈelk\ *or Ger.* **Lyck** \ˈlɪk\. City, Suwałki prov., NE Poland, ab. 60 mi. (97 km.) NW of Białystok; pop. (1989e) 50,236; railroad junction; formerly in East Prussia, Germany; assigned to Poland by Potsdam Conference 1945.

El·ka·der \el-ˈkā-dər\. Town, ⊗ of Clayton co., NE Iowa, 46 mi. (74 km.) NW of Dubuque; pop. (1990c) 1510.

El Kala \el-ˈkä-lä\; *formerly* **La Calle** \lä-ˈkäl\. Seaport, NE Algeria, 10 mi. (16 km.) from Tunisian border; lost by French and burned 1827; rebuilt 1836.

El Kan·ta·ra \el-ˈkan-tə-rə\. Oasis, N of Biskra, Algeria, at S end of gorge through Atlas Mts. on edge of the Sahara.

El–Katif. See AL QAṬĪF.

Elk City \ˈelk\. City, Beckham co., W Oklahoma, 27 mi. (43 km.) WSW of Clinton; pop. (1990c) 10,428; service center for livestock-raising area.

Elk Grove Village. Village, Cook and Du Page cos., NE Illinois, NW suburb of Chicago; pop. (1990c) 33,429.

El Khârga. See AL KHĀRIJAH.

Elk·hart \ˈel-ˌkärt, ˈelk-ˌhärt\. **1.** County in N Indiana. See table at INDIANA.
2. City, Elkhart co., N Indiana, 15 mi. (24 km.) E of South Bend; pop. (1990c) 43,627; band instruments, proprietary medicines, mobile homes.
3. City, ⊗ of Morton co., Kansas; pop. (1990c) 2318.

Elk Hills. Group of hills in Kern co., S California, W of Bakersfield; site of a U.S. naval oil reservation leased by Secretary of the Interior Albert B. Fall at time of Teapot Dome oil scandals (1920s) but lease canceled when scheme became public knowledge.

Elk·horn \ˈelk-ˌhȯrn\. **1.** River, NE Nebraska; rises in Rock co., flows SE into Platte River; 333 mi. (536 km.) long.
2. City, ⊗ of Walworth co., S Wisconsin, 24 mi. (39 km.) E of Janesville; pop. (1990c) 5337.

Elk·horn Peak \ˈelk-ˌhȯrn\. Mountain in Blue Mts., NE Oregon; 8922 ft. (2719 m.).

El Khroub *also* **El Kroub** \el-ˈkrüb\. Commune, NE Algeria, just SE of Constantine.

El·kin \ˈel-kin\. Town, Surry and Wilkes cos., N North Carolina, on Yadkin River; pop. (1990c) 3790.

El·kins \ˈel-kinz\. City, ⊗ of Randolph co., NE cen. West Virginia, 37 mi. (60 km.) SE of Clarksburg; pop. (1990c) 7420. Davis and Elkins Coll. (1904).

Elk Island National Park. See CANADA, *National Parks.*

Elk Mountain. 1. Peak, San Miguel co., NE cen. New Mexico; 11,661 ft. (3554 m.).
2. Peak, S cen. Wyoming; 11,162 ft. (3402 m.); one of the highest peaks in Medicine Bow Mts.

El·ko \ˈel-kō\. **1.** County, NE corner of Nevada. See table at NEVADA.
2. City, its ⊗, on Humboldt River 32 mi. (51 km.) NNW of Franklin Lake; pop. (1990c) 14,736; gold-mining; tourism; stock farms; Northern Nevada Community Coll. (1967); estab. 1868 as a construction camp for Central Pacific R.R.

Elk Point. City, ⊗ of Union co., SE corner of South Dakota; pop. (1990c) 1423.

Elk River. 1. Name of three rivers in the U.S. See ELK.
2. City, ⊗ of Sherburne co., cen. Minnesota, on Mississippi River NW of Minneapolis; pop. (1990c) 11,143.

El Kroub. See EL KHROUB.

Elk·ton \ˈelk-tən\. **1.** City, ⊗ of Todd co., SW Kentucky; pop. (1990c) 1789.
2. Town, ⊗ of Cecil co., NE Maryland, on Elk River; pop. (1990c) 9073. American "Gretna Green" (see GRETNA 2) until passage (1938) of a law requiring a 48-hour waiting period before marriage.

El Kuneitrah. See AL QUNAYTIRAH.

El La·go \el-ˈlä-gō\. City, Harris co., SE Texas, SE of Houston; pop. (1990c) 3269.

El·land \ˈe-lənd\. Town, West Yorkshire, N England; pop. (1981p) 18,011.

Ellás. See GREECE.

Ellasar. See LARSA.

El·la·ville \ˈe-lə-ˌvil\. City, ⊗ of Schley co., SW cen. Georgia; pop. (1990c) 1724.

El·lef Ring·nes Island \ˈe-lef-ˈriŋ-ˌnās\. One of the Sverdrup Is. (*q.v.*), Arctic Archipelago, Nunavut, Canada; 5139 sq. mi. (13,310 sq. km.).

El·len, Mount \ˈe-lən\. **1.** Peak, NE Garfield co., S Utah; 11,506 ft. (3507 m.).
2. Peak, Washington co., N cen. Vermont; ab. 4083 ft. (1245 m.).

El·len·dale \ˈe-lən-ˌdāl\. City, ⊗ of Dickey co., S North Dakota, 64 mi. (103 km.) S of Jamestown; pop. (1990c) 1798.

El·lens·burg \ˈe-lənz-ˌbərg\. City, ⊗ of Kittitas co., cen. Washington, on Yakima River 27 mi. (43 km.) N of Yakima; pop. (1990c) 12,361; meatpacking; Central Washington Univ. (1891).

El·len's Isle \ˈe-lənz\. Small island in Loch Katrine, Central region, Scotland; Ellen's haunt in Sir Walter Scott's poem *Lady of the Lake.*

El·len·ville \ˈe-lən-ˌvil\. Residential village, Ulster co., SE New York, in Shawangunk Mts. 26 mi. (42 km.) W of Poughkeepsie; pop. (1990c) 4243.

Elles·mere, Lake \ˈelz-ˌmir\. Coastal lake in E South I., New Zealand, on S side of Banks Penin.; 70 sq. mi. (181 sq. km.); 14 mi. (23 km.) long; tidal.

Ellesmere Island. Island, NE Nunavut, Canada, W of NW Greenland; 82,119 sq. mi. (212,688 sq. km.); its N point, Cape Columbia, is the northernmost point of Canada (83°08′N); in the NE is **Ellesmere Island National Park Reserve** (see CANADA, *National Parks*).

Ellesmere Port. Town, Cheshire, NW England, on the Mersey River 10 mi. (16 km.) SSE of Liverpool; pop. (1991p) 78,800; paper; oil refineries.

Ellice Islands See TUVALU.

Ellichpur. See ACHALPUR.

El·li·cott City \ˈe-li-kət\. Unincorporated settlement, ⊗ of Howard co., cen. Maryland; pop. (1990c) 41,396.

El·li·jay \ˈe-li-ˌjā\. City, ⊗ of Gilmer co., N Georgia; pop. (1990c) 1178.

El·ling·ton \ˈe-liŋ-tən\. Town, NW Tolland co., N Connecticut; pop. (1990c) 11,197; incorp. 1786.

El·li·ot \ˈe-lē-ət\. County in NE Kentucky. See table at KENTUCKY.

Elliott Bay. Inlet of Puget Sound, waterfront of the city of Seattle, Washington.

El·li·ott Lake \ˈe-lē-ət\. City, S Ontario, Canada, in an area dotted with lakes; pop. (1991c) 14,089.

El·lis \ˈe-lis\. Name of counties in three states of the U.S. See tables at KANSAS, OKLAHOMA, TEXAS.

Ellis Island. Island, Upper New York Bay, SE New York, ab. 1 mi. (1.6 km.) SW of Manhattan I.; sold by New York state to national government 1808; served as immigrant station 1892–1954 and for many years received great majority of immigrants and nonimmigrant aliens entering the U.S.; constitutes part of Statue of Liberty National Monument. See UNITED STATES, *National Monuments.*

El·lis·land \ˈe-lis-ˌland\. Farm, Dumfries and Galloway region, S Scotland, on the Nith River 6 mi. (10 km.) NW of Dumfries; home of poet Robert Burns 1788–91; property of British nation since 1928.

El·lis·ville \ˈe-lis-ˌvil\. **1.** City, a ⊗ of Jones co., SE Mississippi, 8 mi. (13 km.) SW of Laurel; pop. (1990c) 3634; Jones County Junior Coll. (1911).
2. City, St. Louis co., E Missouri; pop. (1990c) 7545.

El·lo·ra \e-ˈlōr-ə\ *also* **Elu·ra** \-ˈlu̇r-ə\. Village, cen. Maharashtra state, S cen. India, 15 mi. (24 km.) NW of Aurangabad; famous for its rock temples, a series of caves carved out of the rocky hillside 1.25 mi. (2 km.) long; in three sections: Buddhist, Brahmanical, and Jain; finest is Kailas of the Brahmanical group.

Ellore. See ELURU.

Ells·worth \ˈelz-wərth\. **1.** County in cen. Kansas. See table at KANSAS.
2. City, ⊗ of Ellsworth co., cen. Kansas, 36 mi. (58 km.) W of Salina; pop. (1990c) 2294.
3. City, ⊗ of Hancock co., SE Maine, 27 mi. (43 km.) SE of Bangor; pop. (1990c) 5975; trade center for tourist area.
4. Village, ⊗ of Pierce co., W Wisconsin; pop. (1990c) 2706.

Ellsworth, Mount. Peak in Glacier National Park, NW Montana; 8595 ft. (2620 m.).

Ellsworth Land; *formerly* **Ellsworth Highland** *or* **James W. Ellsworth Land.** High plateau, Antarctica, extending E from Marie Byrd Land to W coast of Weddell Sea S of Antarctic Penin., bet. 60° and 100°E.

Ellsworth Mountains. Mountain range, consisting of Sentinel Range and Heritage Range, Antarctica, S of Ellsworth Land; highest peak Vinson Massif 16,860 ft. (5139 m.).

Ell·wang·en \ˈel-väŋ-ən\. Town, E Baden-Württemberg, Germany, 46 mi. (74 km.) ENE of Stuttgart; pop. (1980c) 21,242; textiles; church 1182–1233; became town c. 1229; in WWII captured by Allies Apr. 1945.

Ell·wood City \ˈel-ˌwu̇d\. Borough, Beaver and Lawrence cos., W Pennsylvania, 11 mi. (18 km.) S of New Castle; pop. (1990c) 8894.

El Ma·hal·la El Ku·bra \ˌel-ma-ˈhal-lə-ˌel-ˈkü-brə\. City, Gharbīya governorate, Egypt, in Nile Delta W of Damietta branch 16 mi. (26 km.) NE of Ṭanṭa; pop. (1991e) 400,000; cotton gins, rice and flour mills.

El·ma·lı \ˌel-mä-ˈlə\. Town, SW Turkey in Asia, on highway in mountains 45 mi. (72 km.) W of Antalya; important archaeological discoveries of ancient remains in the area.

El Mal·pa·is National Monument \ˌel-ˌmäl-pä-ˈēs\. See UNITED STATES, *National Monuments.*

El Man·sû·ra \ˌel-mȧn-ˈsü-rə\ *or* **Al Man·ṣū·rah** \ˌȧl-\. Commercial City, ✻ of Daqahlīya governorate, Lower Egypt, on right bank of Damietta branch of the Nile SW of Lake Manzala; pop. (1986p) 316,870; scene of battle Feb. 8, 1250 in which Crusaders (Seventh Crusade) under King Louis IX of France were severely defeated and Louis was captured.

El Mar del Sur. See SOUTH SEA.

El Matarīya. See AL-MATARĪYA.

El·men·dorf Air Force Base \ˈel-mən-ˌdȯrf\. U.S. airfield, S cen. Alaska; just E of Anchorage, at head of Cook Inlet.

Elm Grove \ˈelm\. Village, Waukesha co., Wisconsin, 10 mi. (16 km.) W of Milwaukee; pop. (1990c) 6261.

Elm·hurst \ˈelm-ˌhərst\. Residential city, Du Page co., NE Illinois, W of Chicago; pop. (1990c) 42,029; museum of lapidary art; Elmhurst Coll. (1871).

el Milk, Wadi. See MILK, WADI EL.

El·mi·na \el-ˈmē-nə\. Seaport town, S Ghana; founded by Portuguese traders 15th cent.

El Min·ya \el-ˈmin-yə\ *or* **Al Min·ya** \ˌȧl-\. City, ✻ of Minya governorate, Upper Egypt, on left bank of the Nile 90 mi. (145 km.) S of El Faiyûm; pop. (1986p) 179,136.

El·mi·ra \el-ˈmī-rə\. City, ⊗ of Chemung co., S New York, on Chemung River 48 mi. (77 km.) W of Binghamton; pop. (1990c) 33,724; manufactures business machines, firefighting apparatus, electronic equipment, automobile parts, steel; Elmira Coll. (1855), one of first in U.S. to grant degrees to women; Elmira state reformatory for men (1876), pioneer in modern penological methods. Nearby at Newtown (name also of the city 1815–28) was fought Aug. 29, 1779 the battle in which forces of expedition under Gen. John Sullivan and Gen. James Clinton defeated Indians and Tories who had been harassing New York and Pennsylvania frontiers, also sometimes known as battle of Chemung River; settled c. 1788; became ⊗ 1836; chartered as city 1864; home and burial place of writer Samuel Clemens (Mark Twain).

El Mi·rage \ˌel-mə-ˈräzh\. Town, Maricopa co., SW cen. Arizona, 5 mi. (8 km.) NW of Phoenix; pop. (1990c) 5001.

Elmira Heights. Village, Chemung co., S New York, N suburb of Elmira; pop. (1990c) 4359.

El Misti. See MISTI, VOLCÁN.

El·mont \ˈel-ˌmänt\. Unincorporated settlement, Nassau co., SE New York, on Long Island SW of Garden City; pop. (1990c) 28,612.

El Mon·te \el-män-tē\. City, Los Angeles co., SW California, 12 mi. (19 km.) E of the city of Los Angeles; pop. (1990c) 106,209; electronic equipment, airplane accessories.

El·more \ˈel-ˌmōr\. Name of counties in two states of the U.S. See tables at ALABAMA and IDAHO.

El Mor·ro National Monument \el-ˈmōr-ō\. See UNITED STATES, *National Monuments.*

Elms·ford \ˈelmz-fərd\. Village, Westchester co., SE New York, 26 mi. (42 km.) N of New York City; pop. (1990c) 3938.

Elms·horn \ˈelms-ˌhȯrn, ˈelmz-\. City, Schleswig-Holstein, Germany, 20 mi. (32 km.) NW of Hamburg; pop. (1980c) 41,439; food processing; radio communication center; destroyed by Swedish forces mid-17th cent.

Elm·wood \ˈelm-ˌwu̇d\. **1.** Subdivision of town of West Hartford, Connecticut.

2. City, Peoria co., NW cen. Illinois, 20 mi. (32 km.) WNW of the city of Peoria; pop. (1990c) 1841; birthplace of sculptor Lorado Taft 1860.

Elmwood Park. **1.** Residential village, Cook co., NE Illinois, suburb of Chicago; pop. (1990c) 23,206.

2. *formerly* **East Paterson.** Borough, Bergen co., NE New Jersey, 2 mi. (3 km.) SE of Paterson; pop. (1990c) 17,623.

Elmwood Place. Village, Hamilton co., SW corner of Ohio, 7 mi. (11 km.) N of Cincinnati; pop. (1990c) 2937.

Elne \ˈeln\; *anc.* **Il·lib·e·ris** \i-ˈli-bə-ris\. Commune, Pyrénées-Orientales dept., S France, 10 m. (16 km.) SSE of Perpignan; 11th–12th cent. cathedral; scene of murder of Roman Emperor Constans 350 A.D.

El Obeid \ˌel-ō-ˈbīd, -ˈbād\ *also* **Al U·bay·yid** \ˌȧl-ō-ˈbī-id\. Town, ✻ of Kordofan region, cen. Sudan; battle fought nearby Nov. 1883 in which British Gen. William Hicks and Egyptian army were defeated by Sudanese leader Muḥammad Aḥmad (al-Mahdī).

Elo·bey, Is·las \ˈēs-läs-ˌe-lō-ˈbā\. Two islands in Gulf of Guinea, W Africa; combined area ab. 1 sq. mi. (2.6 sq. km.); part of Equatorial Guinea.

Elon College \ˈē-ˌlän\. Town, Alamance co., N cen. North Carolina, ab. 3 mi. (5 km.) NNW of Burlington; pop. (1990c) 4394; Elon Coll. (1889).

El Ori·en·te \ˌel-ˌō-rē-ˈen-tā\ *or* **Oriente** *or Eng.* **Eastern Region.** The part of Ecuador beyond (E of) the Andes; boundaries of region have been in dispute bet. Ecuador, Colombia, and Peru since 1860; by settlement of 1942 at Rio de Janeiro Conference now comprises the provs. of Morona-Santiago, Napo, Pastaza, and Zamora-Chinchipe, but Ecuador has disputed those borders since 1960.

El Oro \el-ˈōr-ō\. Province of SW Ecuador. See table at ECUADOR.

El Oued \ˌel-ˈwed\ *also* **Al–Oued** \ˌal-\. Town and oasis, NE Algeria, on highway 50 mi. (80 km.) NE of Touggourt; town pop. (1987p) 70,073.

Eloy \ˈē-ˌlȯi\. Town, Pinal co., S Arizona, 48 mi. (77 km.) NW of Tucson; pop. (1990c) 7211; nearby state park commemorates a Civil War battle fought here.

El Pa·ra·í·so \el-ˌpä-rä-ˈē-sō\. Department of S Honduras. See table at HONDURAS.

El Paso \el-ˈpa-sō\. **1.** Name of counties in two states of the U.S. See tables at COLORADO and TEXAS.

2. City and port of entry, ⊗ of El Paso co., W tip of Texas, on Rio Grande opp. Ciudad Juárez, Mexico; pop. (1990c) 515,342; alt. 3695 ft. (1126 m.); commercial and manufacturing center in region growing vegetables and cotton (irrigation furnished by Elephant Butte Dam); railroad center and gateway to Mexico; ore smelters, copper and oil refineries; meatpacking, food products, clothing; tourism; Univ. of Texas at El Paso (1913), El Paso Community Coll. (1969); Fort Bliss (*q.v.*) and Biggs Army Airfield nearby. First settled 1827; alternately occupied by Union and Confederate troops during Civil War; incorp. 1873. See CHAMIZAL.

El Paso del Nor·te \del-ˈnȯr-tā\. Gorge of the Rio Grande, Texas; near El Paso.

El Paso de Robles. See PASO ROBLES.

Elphinstone Island. See THAYAWTHADANGYI ISLAND.

El Por·ve·nir \ˌel-ˌpȯr-vā-ˈnēr\. Town, ✻ of Comarca de San Blas special terr., N Panama, on Point San Blas.

El Pro·gre·so \ˌel-prō-ˈgrā-sō\. **1.** Department of SE cen. Guatemala. See table at GUATEMALA.

2. Town, ✻ of El Progreso dept., Guatemala, on a tributary of the Usumacinta River; pop. (1981c) 11,693.

3. Town, Yoro prov., NW Honduras, on Ulúa River 48 mi. (77 km.) WNW of the town of Yoro; pop. (1989e) 63,400.

El Puerto de Santa María. See PUERTO DE SANTA MARÍA.

El Qantara. See AL QANṬARAH.

El Qasr. See AL-QASR.

El Qatrana. See AL-QATRĀNAH.

El Qunaytirah *or* **El Quneitra.** See AL QUNAYTIRAH.

El Quseir. See QUSEIR.

El Re·no \el-ˈrē-nō\. City, ⊗ of Canadian co., cen. Oklahoma, bordering Oklahoma City on the W; pop. (1990c) 15,414; distribution center for agricultural products grown nearby;

railroad shops; metal goods; Fort Reno and U.S. correctional institution nearby.

El·sa \'el-sə\. City, Hidalgo co., S Texas, 40 mi. (64 km.) NW of Brownsville; pop. (1990c) 5242.

El·sah \'el-sə\. Village, Jersey co., W Illinois, on Mississippi River; pop. (1990c) 851; Principia Coll. (1910).

El Sal·va·dor \ˌel-ˌsäl-vä-'t͟hōr, el-'sal-və-ˌdȯr\. Republic, Central America, bounded on NW by Guatemala, on N, NE, and E by Honduras, and on S and SW by the Pacific Ocean; 8260 sq. mi. (21,393 sq. km.); pop. (1993e) 5,517,000; ✻ San Salvador.

Physical features: Smallest and most densely populated of the Central American republics and the only one without an Atlantic seaboard. Crossed from NW to SE by two mountain ranges with many volcanic peaks, highest Santa Ana 7724 ft. (2354 m.), San Miguel 6957 ft. (2120 m.), and San Vicente ab. 7155 ft. (2180 m.); narrow coastal region is low plain, but most of country is plateau averaging 2000 ft. (610 m.). Only river the Lempa; several lakes in plateau region, largest Lake Ilopango.

Chief products: Coffee, sugar, cotton, corn; livestock; petroleum products, food products; textiles; clothing; chemicals; fishing.

Chief towns: San Salvador, Santa Ana, San Miguel, Mejicanos, Nueva San Salvador.

Political divisions: Divided into the following 14 departments (for pronunciation of their names, see their individual entries):

NAME	AREA (sq. mi.)	AREA (sq. km.)	POP. (1987e)	CAPITAL
Ahuachapán	686	1,777	286,140	Ahuachapán
Cabañas	420	1,088	207,573	Sensuntepeque
Chalatenango	622	1,611	267,201	Chalatenango
Cuscatlán	299	774	228,965	Cojutepeque
La Libertad	646	1,673	464,724	Nueva San Salvador
La Paz	478	1,238	292,009	Zacatecoluca
La Unión	841	2,178	361,737	La Unión
Morazán	519	1,344	244,550	San Francisco
San Miguel	773	2,002	502,113	San Miguel
San Salvador	341	883	1,150,531	San Salvador
Santa Ana	702	1,818	226,524	Santa Ana
San Vicente	477	1,235	510,565	San Vicente
Sonsonate	465	1,204	384,078	Sonsonate
Usulután	829	2,147	453,586	Usulután

History: Populated by native Indians when first Europeans arrived 1524 led by Spaniard Pedro de Alvarado; subsequently controlled by Guatemala; with rest of Central America (*q.v.*), became independent of Spain 1821, of Mexico upon collapse of Mexican empire 1823; member of United Provinces of Central America 1823–c. 1840; remained neutral in WWI but declared war on Axis powers 1941 in WWII; under military rule 1931–1979; became a founding member of the Central American Common Market 1960; adopted new constitution 1962; fought brief border war with Honduras 1969; scene of civil war 1980s after a period of increasing unrest during the 1970s; elected legislative asssembly 1982; adopted new constitution 1983; peace agreement among warring factions reached 1992.

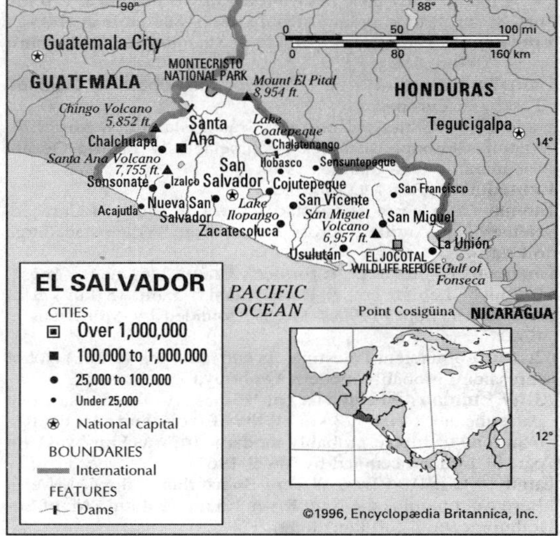

Elsass. See ALSACE.

Elsass–Lothringen. See ALSACE-LORRAINE.

El Se·gun·do \ˌel-sə-'gu̇n-ˌdō\. City, Los Angeles co., SW California, 14 mi. (23 km.) SW of the city of Los Angeles; pop. (1990c) 15,233; oil refining; founded by Standard Oil Company; incorp. 1917.

El Sei·bo *or* **El Sey·bo** \el-'sā-bō\. **1.** Province, E Dominican Republic. See table at DOMINICAN REPUBLIC.

2. *formerly* **San·ta Cruz del Seibo** *or* **Santa Cruz del Seybo** \ˌsän-tä-'krüs-del-\. Municipality, its ✻; pop. (1981p) 68,149; produces cacao, coffee, beeswax, sugar.

El·si·nore \'el-sə-ˌnōr\. **1.** City, SE California. See LAKE ELSINORE.

2. Seaport, Denmark. See HELSINGØR.

Elsinore Lake. Lake, SE California, near Lake Elsinore (city). See LAKE ELSINORE.

Els·mere \'elz-ˌmir\. **1.** Residential town, New Castle co., N Delaware, suburb of Wilmington; pop. (1990c) 5935.

2. City, Kenton co., N Kentucky, 8 mi. (13 km.) SW of Covington; pop. (1990c) 6847.

El·ster \'el-stər\. Name of two rivers in Germany: (1) **Schwar·ze Elster** \ˌshvärt-sə\, literally "Black Elster," in E part, 117 mi. (188 km.) long; flows N and NW into Elbe River 8 mi. (13 km.) E of Wittenberg; (2) **Weis·se Elster** \'vī-sə\, literally "White Elster," 153 mi. (246 km.) long; rises in NW Czech Republic and flows N past Leipzig to the Saale near Halle.

El·stow \'el-ˌstō\. Village, Bedfordshire, S England, ab. 1 mi. (2 km.) S of Bedford; birthplace of preacher and author John Bunyan 1628.

Els·tree \'el-strē\. Village, S Hertfordshire, England, NW of London; motion-picture industry in area.

El·te·keh \'el-tə-ˌkā\. Ancient village; its site now in Israel, W of Jerusalem and near Ekron; scene of battle 701 (or 700) B.C. in which Assyrian King Sennacherib defeated Egyptians.

El Tell el Kebîr. See TEL EL KEBIR.

El Te·ni·en·te \ˌel-ˌtā-nē-'en-tā\. Town, cen. Chile, 45 mi. (72 km.) S of Santiago; has extensive copper deposits. See SEWELL.

El Ti·gre \el-'tē-grā\. Town, Anzoátegui state, Venezuela, ab. 200 mi. (320 km.) SE of Caracas; pop. (1990c) 93,229.

El Tih. See AL-TIH.

El To·cu·yo \ˌel-tō-'kü-ˌyō\. Town, Lara state, NW Venezuela, in the Cordillera Mérida 40 mi. (64 km.) SW of Barquisimeto; pop. (1990c) 31,785.

El·ton, Lake \'elt-ᵊn\ *or Russ.* **Oze·ro El'·ton** \'ó-zer-ə-elʸ-'tȯn\ *or Kalmuck* **Al·tan–Nor** \ˌäl-tän-'nȯr\. Salt lake, Volgograd Oblast, S Russia in Europe, in steppe E of Volga River; very shallow, much of it dry in the summer; yields large quantities of salt.

El Tronador. See TRONADOR, MONTE.

El Tûr \el-'tür\. Town, ✻ of Janūb Sīnā' governorate, Egypt, on Gulf of Suez.

Elt·ville \'elt-ˌvil\; *formerly* **El·feld** \'el-ˌfelt\. Town, Hesse, Germany, on the Rhine 5 mi. (8 km.) SW of Wiesbaden; pop. (1980c) 15,764; received town rights 1332; Johannes Gutenberg estab. his printing press here c. 1465.

Elura. See ELLORA.

Elu·ru \e-'lůr-,ü\; *formerly* **El·lore** \e-'lōr\. City, NE Andhra Pradesh, E India, 225 mi. (362 km.) NNE of Madras at junction of Godavari and Krishna canal systems; pop. (1991p) 212,918; large rice trade, important carpet manufactures; leather, textiles; nearby ruins of Pedda Vegi.

El Va·do Dam \el-'vä-dō\. Dam across Rio Chama, NW cen. Rio Arriba co., NW New Mexico; height 175 ft. (53 m.); completed 1955; impounds water, **El Vado Reservoir,** for irrigation.

El·vas \'el-vəsh\ *or Lat.* **Al·pe·sa** \al-'pē-sə\ *or Arab.* **Ba·lesh** \'bá-lesh\. Fortified city, Portalegre dist., E cen. Portugal, near Spanish frontier 30 mi. (48 km.) SSE of the commune of Portalegre; pop. (1990c) 12,880; manufactures jewelry; 16th cent. cathedral; Moorish aqueduct (1498–1622; largest in Portugal). Fortified by Moors; taken by Portugal c. 1226; conquered by French 1808; ceded to Portugal by Convention of Sintra 1808.

Elvend, Mount. See ALWAND, MOUNT.

El·ve·rum \'el-və-,rům\. Town, Hedmark co., E Norway, SE of Lillehammer; pop. (1980c) 16,611; temporary meeting place of Norwegian government Apr. 1940 following successful German invasion of Oslo; government subsequently relocated temporarily to London.

El Vie·jo \,el-vē-'ā-hō\. Town, a NW suburb of Chinandega, NW Nicaragua.

El·wood \'el-,wůd\. **1.** City, Madison co., cen. Indiana, 25 mi. (40 km.) WNW of Muncie; pop. (1990c) 9494; tomatoes grown nearby; canneries.

2. Village, ⊗ of Gosper co., S Nebraska; pop. (1990c) 679.

Ely \'ē-lē\. **1.** City, St. Louis co., NE Minnesota, 40 mi. (64 km.) NE of Virginia; pop. (1990c) 3968; Vermilion Community Coll. (1922); tourism.

2. City, ⊗ of White Pine co., E Nevada, 63 mi. (101 km.) SSE of Ruby Lake; pop. (1990c) 4756; Great Basin National Park nearby.

3. Town, Cambridgeshire co., E England, on the Ouse River 18 mi. (29 km.) NNE of Cambridge; pop. (1981p) 10,268; engineering; its cathedral, begun c. 1083, one of the most notable in architecture in England; stronghold of rebel and outlaw Hereward the Wake 1070–71.

Ely, Isle of. Area of high ground amid fenlands, East Anglia, England.

Ely, Mount. Peak, N cen. Lincoln co., E Nevada; 7310 ft. (2228 m.).

El·y·ma·ïs \,e-li-'mā-is\. Greek form of Elam (*q.v.*), sometimes used to designate a district of ancient Elam, in its S part at head of Persian Gulf, inhabited by the Elymeans.

Elyr·ia \i-'lir-ē-ə\. City, ⊗ of Lorain co., N Ohio, 23 mi. (37 km.) WSW of Cleveland; pop. (1990c) 56,746; electrical machinery, plastics, automobile parts, tools, motors, metal goods; Lorain County Community Coll. (1963); settled 1817.

El Yun·que \el-'yůŋ-kā\. **1.** *also* **Ro·ca El Yunque** \'rō-kä\. Anvil-shaped peak, on Más a Tierra in Juan Fernández group, Chile, in the Pacific Ocean, ab. 420 mi. (676 km.) W of Valparaíso; 3002 ft. (915 m.) high.

2. Peak in the Luquillo Mts., E Puerto Rico; 3496 ft. (1066 m.).

Ema \'e-mə\. River, Estonia, outlet of Vorts-Jarv flowing E to Lake Peipus; 130 mi. (209 km.) long.

Emamrud. See SHAHRUD.

Eman·u·el \i-'man-yə-wəl\. County in E cen. Georgia. See table at GEORGIA.

Emaus. See EMMAUS 1.

Em·ba \'em-bə\. River, W Kazakhstan; flows SW into NE corner of Caspian Sea; ab. 350 mi. (565 km.) long; extensive oil fields on its lower course.

Em·bar·ca·de·ros, Point \em-,bär-kä-'dā-rōs\. Cape on NE coast of Puerto Rico, W of Cape San Juan.

Em·bar·ras *or* **Em·bar·rass** \'am-,brō—*sic*\. River, E Illinois; rises in Champaign co., flows S and SE into Wabash River; 185 mi. (298 km.) long.

Em·brun \äⁿ-'brœⁿ, -breⁿ\; *anc.* **Eb·u·ro·du·num** \,e-byů-rō-'dü-nəm, -'dyü-\. Commune, Hautes-Alpes dept., SE France, on the Durance ab. 100 mi. (160 km.) NE of Marseille; archiepiscopal see c. 800–1791; 12th cent. church, former cathedral.

Em·bu \'em-,bü\. Town, ✱ of Eastern Province, Kenya, ab. 25 mi. (40 km.) S of Mt. Kenya.

Em·den \'em-dən\. Seaport and city, Lower Saxony, Germany, at mouth of Ems River on N coast of the Dollart, 46 mi. (74 km.) WNW of Oldenburg; pop. (1992e) 51,103; shipbuilding, fishing; connected with interior by means of Dortmund-Ems and other canals; protected by dikes; 12th cent. church; 16th cent. town hall.

History: Founded 9th cent.; annexed to Hamburg 1453; made free city 1595, free port 1751; passed to Holland 1806 and to Hannover 1815; to Prussia 1866; heavily bombed in WWII, since rebuilt.

Emei Shan \'ə-'mā-'shän\ *or W.-G.* **O–mei Shan** \'ō-'mā, 'ə-\. Mountain, cen. Sichuan, S cen. China, SW of Chengdu; 10,167 ft. (3099 m.); sacred to Buddhists and visited by many pilgrims. Consists of three peaks, on one of which is a great precipice several thousand feet high; top and pathway to it has many pagodas and temples.

'Emeq Yizre'el. See ESDRAELON, PLAIN OF.

Emerald Isle. See IRELAND.

Emerita Augusta. See MÉRIDA.

Em·er·son \'e-mər-sən\. **1.** Borough, Bergen co., NE New Jersey, NE of Paterson; pop. (1990c) 6930.

2. Town, SE Manitoba, Canada, on Red River of the North, at Minnesota border 63 mi. (101 km.) S of Winnipeg; pop. (1991c) 721; Canadian port of entry.

Em·ery \'e-mə-rē\. County in E cen. Utah. See table at UTAH.

Em·er·y·ville \'e-mə-rē-,vil\. Town, Alameda co., W California, on San Francisco Bay; pop. (1990c) 5740; suburb of Oakland.

Emesa. See HOMS (Syria).

Em·i·grant Peak \'e-mi-grənt\. **1.** Mountain, S Park co., S Montana; 10,921 ft. (3329 m.).

2. Mountain, Esmeralda co., SW Nevada; 6790 ft. (2070 m.).

Emi Kous·si \ā-'mē-'kü-sē\. Extinct volcano, N Chad, 11,204 ft. (3415 m.); highest point of Tibesti massif.

Emi·lia–Ro·ma·gna \ā-'mēl-yä-rō-'män-yä\; *formerly* **Emilia;** *anc.* **Æmil·ia** \ē-'mi-lē-ə\. Autonomous region, N Italy, on Adriatic Sea bet. Tuscany and Lombardy; ✱ Bologna; mountainous in S, fertile plain (**Emil·ian Plain** \ē-'mil-yən\) in N; important agriculturally, producing wheat, corn, sugar beet, wine, vegetables, dairy products, food products; farm machinery, chemicals, pharmaceuticals, motor vehicles; oil and natural gas; formerly formed duchies of Parma and Modena and the papal Romagna; named for ancient Æmilian Way (built c. 187 B.C., ran from Rimini to Piacenza, 176 mi. or 283 km.); to kingdom of Italy 1860. See table at ITALY.

Em·i·nence \'e-mi-nəns\. City, ⊗ of Shannon co., S Missouri; pop. (1990c) 582.

Emin·ö·nü \,e-mi-nœ-'nɛ\. District and suburb of İstanbul, Turkey in Europe.

Emi·ra \,ā-mē-'rä\ *or* **Emi·rau** \-'raů\. Island in S part of St. Matthias Group, Bismarck Archipelago, W Pacific Ocean; occupied by U.S. marines 1944.

Emmahaven. See TELUKBAJUR.

Em·ma·stad \'e-mə-,stät, -,stad\. Town on island of Curaçao, Netherlands Antilles, across harbor from Willemstad; large oil refinery.

Em·ma·us \e-'mā-əs\. **1.** *formerly* **Emaus** \'ē-,maůs, -,mȯs\. Borough, Lehigh co., E Pennsylvania, 5 mi. (8 km.) S of Allentown; pop. (1990c) 11,157; founded by Moravians c. 1740.

2. Town of ancient Palestine, its site ab. 4 mi. (6 km.) NW of Jerusalem; probably modern **Qa·lun·ya** \kə-'lün-yə\.

3. *or* **Emmaus Ni·cop·o·lis** \ni-'kä-pə-lis\. Town of ancient Palestine, ab. 14 mi. (23 km.) WNW of Jerusalem near the Roman road to Joppa; probably modern **'Im·was** \im-'was\ (in part of Jordan occupied by Israel 1967).

Em·me \'e-mə\. River, W cen. Switzerland; flows NNW in Bern canton, joins the Aare River 1.5 mi. (2.4 km.) NE of Solothurn; 50 mi. (80 km.) long.

Em·men \ˈe-mən\. **1.** Commune, Drenthe prov., NE Netherlands, near German border ab. 28 mi. (45 km.) SE of Groningen; pop. (1992e) 93,107; textiles, pharmaceuticals; natural gas nearby.
2. Commune, Lucerne canton, Switzerland; pop. (1989c) 24,405.

Em·me·rich \ˈe-mə-rik\. City, North Rhine-Westphalia, Germany, near the Dutch border on Rhine River 61 mi. (98 km.) WSW of Münster; pop. (1980c) 29,336; river port; 15th cent. town hall. To counts of Gelder 1233; member of Hanseatic League 14th cent.; passed to Kleve 1402; with Kleve, passed to Brandenburg 1614; in WWII frequently bombed; in 1945 one of the crossings of the Rhine made here by Allies.

Em·met \ˈe-mət\. Name of counties in two states of the U.S. See tables at IOWA and MICHIGAN.

Em·mets·burg \ˈe-məts-ˌbərg\. City, ⊗ of Palo Alto co., N Iowa, 48 mi. (77 km.) NW of Fort Dodge; pop. (1990c) 3940.

Em·mett \ˈe-mət\. City, ⊗ of Gem co., SW Idaho, 23 mi. (37 km.) NW of Boise; pop. (1990c) 4601; settlement began 1864.

Em·mits·burg \ˈe-mits-ˌbərg\. Town, Frederick co., N Maryland, 20 mi. (32 km.) N of the city of Frederick; pop. (1990c) 1688; Mount St. Mary's Coll. (1808).

Em·mons \ˈe-mənz\. County in S North Dakota. See table at NORTH DAKOTA.

Emmons, Mount *also* **Emmons Peak.** Mountain, N Duchesne co., NE cen. Utah; 13,428 ft. (4093 m.).

Emona. See LJUBLJANA.

Em·o·ry \ˈe-mə-rē\. **1.** Village, ⊗ of Rains co., NE Texas; pop. (1990c) 963.
2. Unincorporated settlement, Washington co., SW Virginia; Emory and Henry Coll. (1838).

Emory Peak. Mountain, S Brewster co., W Texas; 7835 ft. (2388 m.); highest peak in Chisos Mts.

Em·pal·me \em-ˈpäl-mā\. Municipality, Sonora state, Mexico, 5 mi. (8 km.) NE of Guaymas.

Em·pan·ge·ni \ˌem-päŋ-ˈgā-nē\. Town, E Rep. of South Africa, ab. 92 mi. (148 km.) NE of Durban; pop. (1985c) 11,403.

Em·pe·dra·do \ˌem-pā-ˈthrä-thō\. Town, Corrientes prov., NE Argentina, on left bank of the Paraná ab. 30 mi. (48 km.) S of the city of Corrientes; pop. (1980p) 4732.

Em·per·or Range \ˈem-pər-ər\. Mountains forming N part of range that traverses Bougainville I., Papua New Guinea; includes Mt. Balbi 8999 ft. (2743 m.), highest point in entire range; S extension is Crown Prince Range.

Em·po·li \ˈem-pō-lē\. Commune, Firenze prov., Tuscany, cen. Italy, on Arno River 18 mi. (29 km.) WSW of Florence; pop. (1989c) 43,588; textiles, glass, pasta products; 11th cent. church.

Em·po·ria \em-ˈpōr-ē-ə\. **1.** City, ⊗ of Lyon co., E Kansas, 52 mi. (84 km.) SW of Topeka; pop. (1990c) 25,512; railroad division point; distribution point for farm products; Emporia State Univ. (1863); home of William Allen White, editor and proprietor of Emporia *Gazette* from 1895 to his death 1944; founded 1857.
2. Town, ⊗ of Greensville co. but politically independent, S Virginia, 38 mi. (61 km.) S of Petersburg; pop. (1990c) 5306; composed of **North Emporia** and **South Emporia.**

Em·po·ri·um \em-ˈpōr-ē-əm\. Borough, ⊗ of Cameron co., N cen. Pennsylvania, 38 mi. (61 km.) SSE of Bradford; pop. (1990c) 2513.

Em·press Au·gus·ta Bay \ˈem-prəs-ȯ-ˈgəs-tə\. Widemouthed inlet of Solomon Sea on W coast of Bougainville I., Papua New Guinea, W Pacific Ocean; scene Nov. 1943 of first landing by U.S. marines in invasion of Bougainville (*q.v.*).

Ems \ˈems, ˈemz\. **1.** *anc.* **Ami·sia** \ə-ˈmi-zhə, -zhē-ə\. River, NW Germany; rises in NE North Rhine-Westphalia, flows NW and N to the North Sea; 231 mi. (372 km.) long; its mouth is a wide estuary bordering on NE Netherlands, the upper part forming the Dollart (*q.v.*) and the lower comprising the navigable main channel which divides, passing to the W (**West Ems**) and E (**East Ems**) of Borkum I. in the East Frisian Is.; connected with the Ruhr region by the Dortmund-Ems canal system.
2. Town, Germany. See BAD EMS.

Ems·det·ten \ˈems-ˌdet-ᵊn, ˈemz-\. Commune, North Rhine-Westphalia, Germany, on Ems River 16 mi. (26 km.) NNW of Münster; pop. (1980c) 31,026; became town 1938.

Ems·worth \ˈemz-wərth\. Residential borough, Allegheny co., SW Pennsylvania, on Ohio River 8 mi. (13 km.) WNW of Pittsburgh; pop. (1990c) 2892.

Enard Bay \ˈe-ˌnärd\. Bay on NW coast of Scotland, S of Point of Stoer and N of Loch Broom.

Enare. See INARI.

Enare, Lake. See INARI, LAKE.

En·can·to, Cape \en-ˈkän-tō\ *or* **Encanto Point.** Cape on E coast of Luzon, Philippines, at SE point of Baler Bay.

En·car·na·ción \ˌen-kär-ˌnä-ˈsyōn\. Town, ✻ of Itapúa dept., SE Paraguay, on Paraná River opp. Posadas, Argentina, with which it is connected by bridge, 180 mi. (290 km.) SE of Asunción; munic. pop. (1992p) 55,359; in agricultural and grazing district; founded 1614.

En·ci·ni·tas \ˌen-si-ˈnē-təs\. City, San Diego co., S California, on coast N of the city of San Diego; pop. (1990c) 55,386.

En·con·tra·dos \ˌen-kōn-ˈträ-thōs\. Town, Zulia state, NW Venezuela, on Catatumbo River 125 mi. (201 km.) SW of Maracaibo.

En·coun·ter Bay \in-ˈkau̇n-tər\. Inlet of Indian Ocean, SE South Australia, Australia, at outlet of Murray River.

En·cru·ci·ja·da \en-ˌkrü-sē-ˈhä-dä\. Town and municipality, Las Villas prov., W cen. Cuba, 15 mi. (24 km.) N of Santa Clara; munic. pop. (1981p) 33,719.

En·dau \ˈen-ˌdau̇\. River, NE Johor and SE Pahang states, S Malay Penin.; Malaysia; flows NE into South China Sea near SE boundary of Pahang state.

En·de \en-ˈde\. Town and port on S coast of Flores I., Lesser Sunda Is., Indonesia.

En·der·bury \ˈen-dər-ˌber-ē\. One of the more important of the Phoenix Is., Kiribati, cen. Pacific Ocean, 3°08′S, 171°05′W; an atoll 3 mi. (5 km.) long by 0.75 mi. (1.2 km.) wide; 4 sq. mi. (10 sq. km.); formerly worked for guano. As an important airplane base visited and claimed 1937–39 by both Great Britain and U.S.; with Kanton I. placed 1939 under joint control; has no good anchorage and no seaplane facilities, its lagoon being merely a shallow pool.

En·der·by Land \ˈen-dər-bē\. Semicircular projection of Antarctica, extending from Prince Olav Coast (ab. 45°E) to Edward VIII Bay at ab. 57°20′E and extending N from ab. 67°30′S; first sighted by Europeans 1831; claimed by Australia.

En·di·cott \ˈen-di-kət, -ˌkät\. Village, Broome co., S New York, on Susquehanna River 8 mi. (13 km.) W of Binghamton; pop. (1990c) 13,531; with Binghamton and Johnson City, one of so-called Triple Cities; manufactures shoes, business machines.

Endicott Mountains. Subsidiary mountain range, cen. part of Brooks Range, N Alaska; highest peak ab. 9000 ft. (2740 m.).

En·dor \ˈen-ˌdȯr\ *or* **ʻEn Dor** \-ˈdȯr\. Town of ancient Palestine, its site now in Israel near Mt. Tabor 6 mi. (10 km.) SE of Nazareth (*1 Sam.* xxviii. 7).

En·dröd \ˈen-drœd\. Former commune, SE Hungary. See GYOMAENDRÖD.

Ene·we·tak *or* **Eni·we·tok** \ˌe-ni-ˈwē-ˌtäk, e-ˈnē-wə-\. Atoll at extreme NW end of Ralik Chain, NW Marshall Is., W Pacific Ocean, 11°30′N, 162°15′E; circular in shape with 40 islets around lagoon 23 mi. (37 km.) in diameter; good anchorage; main isles Enewetak in S and Engebi in N; taken by Americans from Japanese Feb. 1944 and made into a naval base; in 1947 designated by U.S. Atomic Energy Commission as permanent mid-Pacific proving ground for atomic weapons.

Enez \e-ˈnez\; *anc.* **Ae·nos** \ˈē-nəs\. Town and port, SW Turkey in Europe, on Meriç (Maritsa) River in its delta.

\ə\ abut \ˈə\ matches \ᵊ\ kitten, Fr table \ər\ further \a\ ash \ā\ ace \ä\ cot, cart \å\ Fr bac \au̇\ out \b\ Span Avila \ch\ chin \e\ bet \ē\ easy \g\ go \i\ hit \ī\ ice \j\ job \k\ Ger ich, Buch \ⁿ\ Fr vin \ŋ\ sing \ō\ go \ȯ\ all \ȯi\ law \œ\ Fr bœuf \œ̄\ Fr feu \ȯi\ boy \th\ thin \th\ this \ü\ loot \u̇\ foot \ue\ Ger füllen \ue̅\ Fr rue \y\ yet \ʸ\ Fr digne \ˈdēnʸ\, nuit \ˈnwʸē\ \yü\ few \yu̇\ fury \zh\ vision

En·fi·da \en-ˈfē-də\ *or* **En·fi·da·ville** \äⁿ-fē-də-ˈvēl\. Town, NE Tunisia, near the coast ab. 30 mi. (48 km.) SW of Hammamet; in WWII center of fighting Apr. 1943.

En·field \ˈen-ˌfēld\. **1.** Town, NE Hartford co., N Connecticut, on E bank of Connecticut River on Massachusetts border; pop. (1990c) 45,532; formerly extensive shade-grown tobacco production; Asnuntuck Community Coll. (1972); settled c. 1680 as part of Massachusetts; annexed to Connecticut 1749; includes Thompsonville (*q.v.*).

2. Town, Grafton co., W New Hampshire, 6 mi. (10 km.) E of Lebanon; pop. (1990c) 3979; formerly site of Shaker settlements.

3. Town, Halifax co., NE North Carolina, 18 mi. (29 km.) NNE of Rocky Mount; pop. (1990c) 3082; ⊗ of Edgecombe co. 1745–58.

4. A borough of Greater London, SE England. See table at LONDON 4.

En·ga·dine \ˌeŋ-gə-ˈdēn\ *or Ger.* **En·ga·din** \ˌeŋ-gä-ˈdēn\ *or Ital.* **En·ga·di·na** \ˌeŋ-gä-ˈdē-nä\. Swiss portion of valley of the Inn River, in E Graubünden canton, E Switzerland; ab. 60 mi. (97 km.) long; SW part is called the **Upper Engadine** and NE part the **Lower Engadine;** St.-Moritz is near SW end.

Engannim. See JENIN.

Engano. See ENGGANO.

En·ga·ño, Cape \en-ˈgä-nyō\. **1.** Cape Dominican Republic, at E end of island of Hispaniola, on NW side of Mona Passage.

2. NE point of Cagayan prov., Luzon, Philippines, formed by N tip of Palaui I., 18°35′N; lighthouse; important naval battle off this cape Oct. 1944 in which American fleet defeated Japanese force.

En·ge·bi \en-ˈgā-bē\. Islet of Enewetak Atoll (*q.v.*), Marshall Is.; captured by Americans Feb. 1944.

En–ge·di \en-ˈgē-ˌdī, -ˈge-dē\ *or* **ʻEn Ge·di** \ˈen-ˈge-dē\. Village and spring on W shore of Dead Sea, Israel, 18 mi. (29 km.) E of Hebron (*1 Sam.* xxiv. 1).

Eng·el·berg \ˈeŋ-əl-ˌberk\. Valley in the Alps, in Unterwalden canton, cen. Switzerland.

En·gel·mann Peak \ˈeŋ-gəl-mən\. Mountain in Clear Creek co., N cen. Colorado; 13,500 ft. (4115 m.).

Eng·el's *or* **Eng·els** \ˈeŋ-gilz\; *formerly* **Po·krovsk** \pə-ˈkrôfsk\. Town, Saratov Oblast, SE cen. Russia in Europe, on the Volga opp. the city of Saratov; pop. (1992e) 183,000; chemicals; food processing; ✱ of former Volga German A.S.S.R.; founded 1747; renamed 1931 in honor of socialist Friedrich Engels.

Eng·ga·no *or* **En·ga·no** \eŋ-ˈgä-nō\. Island in the Indian Ocean off SW coast of Sumatra, Indonesia; 18 mi. (29 km.) long by 11 mi. (18 km.) wide; area (with nearby islets) 171 sq. mi. (443 sq. km.); produces copra.

Enghien. See MONTMORENCY 3.

En·ghien–les–Bains \äⁿ-ˈgeⁿ-lā-ˈbeⁿ\. Commune, Val-d'Oise dept., N France, N suburb of Paris; pop. (1991c) 10,258; mineral springs.

En·gland \ˈiŋ-glənd, -lənd\. **1.** *or Lat.* **An·glia** \ˈaŋ-glē-ə\. South part of the island of Great Britain, excluding Wales; largest unit of the United Kingdom of Great Britain and Northern Ireland; 50,333 sq. mi. (130,362 sq. km.); pop. (1991p) 46,161,000; ✱ London.

Physical features: In N the Pennine Chain, Cumbrian Mts. (incl. Scafell Pike 3210 ft. or 978 m., highest in country), and Cheviot Hills (along Scottish border); in SW the Cotswold Hills and plateau regions of Exmoor and Dartmoor; in SE the Downs, and in S Salisbury Plain.

Chief rivers: Thames in S, Ouse in cen. and E, Humber (with Ouse and Trent) in NE, Mersey in W, and Severn in SW.

Chief lakes: Bassenthwaite, Derwent Water, Ullswater, Windermere.

Chief products: Barley, wheat, sugar beets, vegetables; livestock raising, fishing; coal, offshore petroleum; manufacturing: iron and steel, chemicals, textiles, transportation equipment, pharmaceuticals; engineering, publishing; tourism.

Chief cities: London, Birmingham, Leeds, Sheffield, Liverpool, Manchester. For history, see UNITED KINGDOM.

Political Divisions: Divided into the following 46 counties (for pronunciation of their names, see their individual entries):

NAME[1]	AREA (sq. mi.)	AREA (sq. km.)	POP. (1991p)	CO. SEAT
Avon	535	1,386	919,800	Bristol
Bedfordshire	494	1,279	514,200	Bedford
Berkshire	502	1,300	716,500	Reading
Buckinghamshire	753	1,950	252,900	Aylesbury
Cambridgeshire	1,364	3,533	640,700	Cambridge
Cheshire	929	2,406	937,300	Chester
Cleveland	233	603	541,100	Middlesbrough
Cornwall and Isles of Scilly	1,418	3,673	469,300	Truro
Cumbria	2,724	7,055	486,900	Carlisle
Derbyshire	1,052	2,725	914,600	Matlock
Devon	2,686	6,957	998,200	Exeter
Dorset	1,062	2,750	645,200	Dorchester
Durham	974	2,523	589,800	Durham
East Sussex	718	1,860	670,600	Lewes
Essex	1,470	3,807	1,495,600	Chelmsford
Gloucestershire	1,055	2,732	520,600	Gloucester
Greater London[2]	632	1,637	6,377,900	London
Greater Manchester[2]	514	1,331	2,454,800	Manchester
Hampshire	1,509	3,908	1,511,900	Winchester
Hereford and Worcester	1,571	4,069	667,800	Worcester
Hertfordshire	654	1,694	951,500	Hertford
Humberside	1,405	3,639	835,200	Hull
Isle of Wight	152	394	126,600	Newport
Kent	1,493	3,867	1,485,100	Maidstone
Lancashire	1,217	3,152	1,365,100	Preston
Leicestershire	1,021	2,644	860,500	Leicester
Lincolnshire	2,354	6,097	573,900	Lincoln
Merseyside[2]	261	676	1,376,800	Liverpool
Norfolk	2,152	5,574	736,400	Norwich
Northamptonshire	947	2,453	572,900	Northampton
Northumberland	2,013	5,214	300,600	
North Yorkshire	3,327	8,617	698,700	Northallerton
Nottinghamshire	866	2,243	980,600	Nottingham
Oxfordshire	1,044	2,704	553,800	Oxford
Shropshire	1,396	3,616	401,600	Shrewsbury
Somerset	1,383	3,582	459,100	Taunton
South Yorkshire[2]	624	1,616	1,248,500	Barnsley
Staffordshire	1,086	2,813	1,020,300	Stafford
Suffolk	1,520	3,937	629,900	Ipswich
Surrey	662	1,714	998,000	
Tyne and Wear[2]	216	559	1,087,000	Newcastle
Warwickshire	792	2,051	477,000	Warwick
West Midlands[2]	360	932	2,499,300	Birmingham
West Sussex	806	2,088	692,800	Chichester
West Yorkshire[2]	816	2,113	1,984,700	Wakefield
Wiltshire	1,392	3,605	553,300	Trowbridge

[1] For county names ending in *-shire*, the *-shire* is often omitted in common usage when there is no ambiguity. In legal use, the styling *county of Hertford*, not *Hertfordshire*, is preferred. The redundant *county of Hertfordshire* is incorrect.
[2] The former metropolitan counties lost their administrative functions in 1986 and now exist in name only.

Prior to 1974 divided into the following counties (for pronunciation of their names, see their individual entries): Bedfordshire, Berkshire, Buckinghamshire, Cambridgeshire and Isle of Ely, Cheshire, Cornwall, Cumberland, Derbyshire, Devonshire, Dorsetshire, Durham, Essex, Gloucestershire, Greater London, Hampshire, Herefordshire, Hertfordshire, Huntingdon and Peterborough, Kent, Lancashire, Leicestershire, Lincolnshire (The Parts of Holland, The Parts of Kesteven, The Parts of Lindsey), Norfolk, Northamptonshire, Northumberland, Nottinghamshire, Oxfordshire, Rutland, Shropshire, Somersetshire, Staffordshire, Suffolk (East Suffolk, West Suffolk), Surrey, Sussex (East Sussex, West Sussex), Warwickshire, Westmorland, Wight (Isle of), Wiltshire, Worcestershire, Yorkshire (East Riding, North Riding, West Riding).

2. City, Lonoke co., cen. Arkansas, 22 mi. (35 km.) SE of Little Rock; pop. (1990c) 3351.

En·gle·wood \ˈeŋ-gəl-ˌwu̇d\. **1.** City, Arapahoe co., NE cen. Colorado, a S suburb of Denver; pop. (1990c) 29,387.

2. City, Bergen co., NE corner of New Jersey, W of Hudson River 10 mi. (16 km.) E of Paterson; pop. (1990c) 24,850; incorp. as city 1895; Palisades Interstate Park nearby.

3. Village, Montgomery co., SW Ohio, 10 mi. (16 km.) NW of Dayton; pop. (1990c) 11,432.

Englewood Cliffs. Borough, Bergen co., NE New Jersey, 12 mi. (19 km.) SSE of Paterson; pop. (1990c) 5634; residential.

En·glish \ˈiŋ-glish\. **1.** Town, ⊗ of Crawford co., S Indiana, 33 mi. (53 km.) W of New Albany; pop. (1990c) 614.

2. River, largest tributary of the Winnipeg, in SW Ontario, Canada; flows W through chain of lakes; ab. 100 mi. (160 km.) long.

English Channel *or often* **The Channel** *or Fr.* **La Manche** \lȧ-ˈmä^{n}sh\. Strait bet. S England and N France; connects with Atlantic Ocean on the W and with North Sea (through the Strait of Dover) on the NE.

En·gui·ne·gatte \ä^{n}-gēn-ˈgät\; *formerly* **Gui·ne·gate** *or* **Gui·ne·gaste** \gēn-ˈgät\. Commune, Pas-de-Calais dept., N France, S of St.-Omer; scene of two battles: (1) bet. French King Louis XI and Holy Roman Emperor Maximilian I 1479, and (2) bet. English King Henry VIII and France 1513 in which the French were defeated, known as "Battle of the Spurs" from hasty flight of the French.

Engyum. See GANGI.

Enid \ˈē-nid\. City, ⊗ of Garfield co., N Oklahoma, 68 mi. (109 km.) NNW of Oklahoma City; pop. (1990c) 45,309; meatpacking; dairy farming; oil refineries; wheat; poultry; Phillips Univ. (1906); founded 1893.

Eni·peus \i-ˈnī-ˌpyüs\ *or* **Eni·pévs** \ˌe-nē-ˈpefs\. River in Thessaly, Greece, tributary of the Pinios.

Enisei. See YENISEY.

Eniwetok. See ENEWETAK.

Enk·hui·zen \ˈeŋk-hœiz-ᵊn, -ˈhīz-\. Commune and seaport, North Holland prov., W Netherlands, on W shore of IJsselmeer 28 mi. (45 km.) NE of Amsterdam; pop. (1993e) 16,081.

En·na \ˈe-nə\. **1.** Province of cen. Sicily, Italy. See table at ITALY.
2. *before 1927* **Ca·stro·gio·van·ni** \ˌkäs-trō-jō-ˈvä-nē\; *anc.* **En·na** \ˈe-nə\ *or* **Hen·na** \ˈhe-nə\. Commune, its ✱, 64 mi. (103 km.) SE of Palermo; pop. (1991p) 28,296; summer resort; trades in sulfur and rock salt; cathedral (founded 1307); old citadel; tower built by Frederick II of Aragon. Ancient site of principal temple of Ceres (Demeter); headquarters of slaves in First Servile War c. 134–32 B.C.; nearby Lake of Pergusa site of fabled rape of Proserpine by Dis (Pluto), god of the underworld; captured by Saracens 9th cent. and by Normans 11th cent.

En Na·hud \ˌen-nȧ-ˈhüd\ *or* **An Nu·hūd** \ˌȧn-nȯ-\. Commercial town, cen. Sudan, 120 mi. (193 km.) WSW of El Obeid.

En Na·qu·ra \ˌen-nä-ˈkü-rə\ *or* **An Nā·qū·rah** \ˌȧn-\. Village and cape on SW coast of Lebanon.

En Nasira. See NAZARETH 2.

En·ne·di \ˌe-ne-ˈdē\. Plateau, NE Chad; highest point 4298 ft. (1310 m.).

En·ne·pe·tal \ˈe-nə-pə-ˌtäl\. City, North Rhine-Westphalia, Germany; pop. (1980c) 35,729; formed 1949.

En·ner·dale Water \ˈe-nər-ˌdāl\. Lake in the Lake District, Cumberland, NW England; 2.5 mi. (4 km.) long; max. depth 148 ft. (45 m.).

En·nis \ˈe-nis\. **1.** City, Ellis co., NE cen. Texas, 20 mi. (32 km.) N of Corsicana; pop. (1990c) 13,883; cotton processing.
2. Town, ⊗ of co. Clare, W Ireland; pop. (1991p) 13,746; limestone; brewing, whiskey distilling; ruins of two abbeys nearby: Franciscan abbey (c. 1242; now a national monument), Clare Abbey (c. 1195).

En·nis·cor·thy \ˌe-ni-ˈskȯr-thē\. Town, cen. co. Wexford, SE Ireland, on River Slaney; pop. (1991p) 4127; remains of 13th cent. castle.

En·nis·kil·len \ˌe-ni-ˈski-lən\ *or* **In·nis·kil·ling** \ˌi-ni-ˈski-liŋ\. Town, ✱ of Fermanagh dist., SW Northern Ireland, on an island in the Erne River just S of Lough Erne; pop. (1981c) 10,429; trading center for agricultural region; manufactures hosiery. Scene of battle 1689 in which forces of William III defeated those of James II; famous regiment of Enniskillen Dragoons formed at the time.

En Nofilia. See NOFILIA.

Enns \ˈens\. **1.** River, cen. Austria; flows E and N from Styria into Danube River 11 mi. (18 km.) SE of Linz; forms section of boundary bet. Upper Austria and Lower Austria; 158 mi. (254 km.) long.
2. Town, Austria, on Enns River near its confluence with the Danube; pop. (1991c) 10,192; one of the oldest towns in Austria, receiving charter 1212; on old trade route across the Danube; in medieval times a prosperous market town; nearby is famous Augustinian monastery of St. Florian, with fine manuscript library.

Enon \ˈē-nən\. Village, Clark co., W cen. Ohio, 15 mi. (24 km.) NE of Dayton; pop. (1990c) 2605.

En·o·ree \ˈe-nə-ˌrē\. River, NW South Carolina; rises in the Blue Ridge in Greenville co., flows SE into Broad River; ab. 80 mi. (130 km.) long.

Enotah, Mount. See BRASSTOWN BALD.

En·ri·qui·llo, Lake \ˌen-rē-ˈkēl-yō, -ˈkē-\. Salt lake, SW Dominican Republic, E Hispaniola I., West Indies; 150 ft. (46 m.) below sea level.

En·sche·de \ˈen-skə-ˌdā\. Commune, Overijssel prov., E Netherlands, near German frontier; pop. (1992e) 147,199; textiles, rubber goods; natural history museum; technical university (1961); first mentioned 1118.

En·se·na·da \ˌen-sā-ˈnä-thä\. **1.** Town on Río de la Plata, Buenos Aires prov., E Argentina, ab. 35 mi. (56 km.) SE of the city of Buenos Aires; forms part of the port of La Plata.
2. Seaport, N Baja California, NW Mexico, on Pacific Ocean; munic. pop. (1990p) 260,905; shipping point for cotton and fish; tourism.

Ensham. See EYNSHAM.

En·shū Bight \ˈen-ˌshü\; *formerly* **To·to·mi Sea** \tō-ˈtō-mē\. Inlet of W Pacific Ocean, S coast of Honshū, Japan.

En·teb·be \en-ˈte-bə\. Town, formerly administrative ✱ of Uganda, 19 mi. (31 km.) SW of Kampala, on N shore of Lake Victoria; pop. (1991p) 41,638; alt. 3760 ft. (1146 m.); on the Equator; botanical gardens; in region producing bananas, coffee, cotton; connected by rail via Nairobi with Mombasa; founded 1893; was ✱ of Uganda 1894–1962.

En·ter·prise \ˈen-tər-ˌprīz\. **1.** City, Coffee co., SE Alabama, 27 mi. (43 km.) W of Dothan; pop. (1990c) 20,123; diversified industries; Enterprise State Junior Coll. (1965).
2. City, ⊗ of Wallowa co., NE corner of Oregon, 54 mi. (87 km.) NE of Baker City; pop. (1990c) 1905.

En·tre–Dou·ro–e–Mi·nho \ˌen-trē-ˈdō-rü-ē-ˈmē-nyü\. Former province, NW Portugal; 2749 sq. mi. (7120 sq. km.); ✱ Braga.

En·tre Rí·os \ˈen-trā-ˈrē-ōs\. Province of E Argentina; ✱ Paraná. See table at ARGENTINA.

Enu·gu \ā-ˈnü-gü\. **1.** State of S Nigeria. See table at NIGERIA.
2. City, its ✱; pop. (1993e) 293,200; educational center; coal.

Enum·claw \ˈē-nəm-ˌklȯ\. Town, King co., W cen. Washington, 23 mi. (37 km.) E of Tacoma; pop. (1990c) 7227; gateway to recreation areas of Mt. Rainier.

En·yu, Enyu Channel \ˈen-yü\. See BIKINI.

Enzeli. See BANDAR-E ANZALI.

Eolie, Isole. See LIPARI ISLANDS.

Eo·lus, Mount \ē-ˈō-ləs\. Peak, La Plata co., SW Colorado; 14,083 ft. (4292 m.).

Éparges, Les. See LES ÉPARGES.

Ep·au·let Mountain \ˈep-ə-ˌlet, -lət\. Peak, Clear Creek co., N cen. Colorado; 13,500 ft. (4115 m.).

Epe \ˈā-pə\. Commune, Gelderland prov., E Netherlands, 9 mi. (14 km.) N of Apeldoorn; pop. (1991e) 89,020.

Epe·cuén, Lake \ˌā-pā-ˈkwen\. Lake, S Buenos Aires prov., E Argentina; 15 sq. mi. (39 sq. km.); resort.

Epe·hy \e-ˈpē\. Village, Somme dept., N France, S of Cambrai; destroyed in WWI; taken by the British Sept. 1918.

Epeiros. See EPIRUS.

Éper·nay \ˌā-per-ˈnā\; *anc.* **Spar·na·cum** \ˈspär-nə-kəm\. Commune, Marne dept., NE France, on Marne River 21 mi. (34 km.) WNW of Châlons-sur-Marne; pop. (1990c) 27,738; in region famous for production of champagne wines; manufactures earthenware; railway workshops. Fortified city in Middle Ages; besieged by Henry IV 1592; scene of violent fighting and air raids 1914–18.

\ə\ **abut** \ə̇\ **matches** \ᵊ\ **kitten, Fr table** \ər\ **further** \a\ **ash** \ā\ **ace** \ä\ **cot, cart** \ȧ\ **Fr bac** \au̇\ **out** \b\ **Span Avila** \ch\ **chin** \e\ **bet** \ē\ **easy** \g\ **go** \i\ **hit** \ī\ **ice** \j\ **job** \k\ **Ger ich, Buch** \$^{n}$\ **Fr vin** \ŋ\ **sing** \ō\ **go** \ȯ\ **all** \ȯ\ **law** \œ\ **Fr bœuf** \œ̄\ **Fr feu** \ȯi\ **boy** \th\ **thin** \t͟h\ **this** \ü\ **loot** \u̇\ **foot** \ue\ **Ger füllen** \ue̅\ **Fr rue** \y\ **yet** \$^{y}$\ **Fr digne** \ˈdēn^{y}\, **nuit** \ˈnw^{y}ē\ \yü\ **few** \yu̇\ **fury** \zh\ **vision**

Eph·e·sus \ˈe-fə-səs\. Ruins of ancient Ionian city, W Asia Minor, near coast of Aegean Sea 35 mi. (56 km.) SSE of İzmir, in fertile plain near the mouth of the Caÿster River. Traditionally founded by Carians; one of the 12 Ionian Cities; conquered by Lydians and later by Persians; invaded by Macedonian King Alexander the Great 334 B.C.; had famous temple, a center of cult of Diana; finally came to Romans from king of Pergamum (*q.v.*); ✱ of Roman prov. of Asia; early seat of Christianity (visited by St. Paul on 2d and 3d missionary journeys, church to which was written the *Epistle to the Ephesians*); sacked by Goths 262 A.D.; seat of church council which condemned heresy of Nestorius 431.

Ephra·im \ˈē-frē-im\. **1.** City, Sanpete co., cen. Utah, 43 mi. (69 km.) WSW of Price; pop. (1990c) 3363; Snow Junior Coll. (1888); settled 1854.
2. Sometimes, the Northern Kingdom, or Kingdom of Israel (see ISRAEL 1).
3. Mountainous region or range (**Mount Ephraim**) of Jordan, orig. the country allotted to the tribe of Ephraim; extended S from near Shechem to neighborhood of Bethel.

Eph·ra·ta \ˈe-frə-tə\. Borough, Lancaster co., SE Pennsylvania, 13 mi. (21 km.) NE of the city of Lancaster; pop. (1990c) 12,133. Founded c. 1732 as German Seventh-Day Baptist monastic community (Society of the Solitary) by Johann Conrad Beissel; Ephrata Cloisters built; printing press estab. 1745.

Ephra·ta \ē-ˈfrā-tə\. City, ⊗ of Grant co., cen. Washington, at S end of the Grand Coulee Valley; pop. (1990c) 5349.

Epi *or* **Api** \ˈā-pē\. Island, SW Pacific Ocean, in E part of Vanuatu, 25 mi. (40 km.) SE of Malekula; 27 mi. (43 km.) long by 11 mi. (18 km.) wide; pop. (1991e) 3626; has mountain peak 2770 ft. (844 m.); fertile soil.

Epidamnus. See DURRËS 2.

Ep·i·dau·rus \ˌe-pi-ˈdȯr-əs\. Ancient seaport town in Greece, on E coast of Argolis on Saronic Gulf, 25 mi. (40 km.) E of Árgos; site of famous temple dedicated to Aesculapius, Greek god of medicine and healing; also site of theater and a Greek round structure (*tholos,* rotunda); much visited for centuries; until Roman times town and vicinity were semi-independent.

Épi·nal \ˌā-pē-ˈnäl\. Commune, ✱ of Vosges dept., NE France, on Moselle River 65 mi. (105 km.) E of Chaumont; pop. (1990c) 39,480; textiles; printing; metallurgical works; freestone and marble deposits nearby; founded 10th cent.; in WWII captured by U.S. forces Sept. 1944.

Épi·nay–sur–Seine \ˌā-pē-ˈne-sür-ˈsen\. Commune, Seine-St.-Denis dept., N France, N suburb of Paris on the Seine; pop. (1990c) 48,851.

Epiphania. See HAMĀH.

Epi·rus \i-ˈpī-rəs\ *or Gk.* **Epei·ros** \ˈē-pē-ˌrös\. **1.** An ancient country in NW Greece, bounded on N by Illyria, on E by Macedonia and Thessaly, on S by Aetolia and Acarnania, and on W by Ionian Sea, extending along coast of latter from Acroceraunia promontory on N to the Amvrakitós Kólpos on S; mountainous, traversed by main range of Pindus Mts. and parallel ranges; mountains cut by Inachus, Achelous, and Thíamis rivers; more important of its districts were Athamania, Thesprotia (*q.v.*), Molossis, and Chaonia; chief towns Phoenice, Dodona, Buthrotum.
History: United by King Pyrrhus (d. 272 B.C.); made a republic c. 200 B.C.; after Roman defeat of Macedonians 197 B.C. retained independence; punished by Rome for supporting Perseus, last king of Macedonia, 168 B.C.; set up as Roman province 146 B.C.; under Byzantine Empire until establishment of an independent state 1204; conquered by Turks 1430–40; Greece received E part 1881, captured Ioánnina 1913, and was awarded 1919 the W part as far N as a point on the coast off N Corfu; N part is now in S Albania; formed battleground for Greeks and Italians 1940–41.
2. Region of modern Greece; 3553 sq. mi. (9202 sq. km.); pop. (1991c) 339,210. For subdivisions, see table at GREECE.

Epo·meo, Mon·te \ˈmȯn-tē-ˌā-pō-ˈmā-ō\. Highest point on island of Ischia (*q.v.*), Italy; 2585 ft. (788 m.).

Eporedia. See IVREA.

Ep·per·ly, Mount \ˈe-pər-lē\. Mountain, Antarctica, 78°26′S, 85°53′W; 15,100 ft. (4600 m.).

Ep·ping \ˈe-piŋ\. **1.** Town, Rockingham co., SE New Hampshire, 15 mi. (24 km.) W of Portsmouth; pop. (1990c) 5162.
2. Town, Essex, SE England, 17 mi. (27 km.) NE of London; pop. (1981p) 11,413; on N edge of **Epping Forest,** a former royal forest of large extent, now a public park.

Ep·som \ˈep-səm\. **1.** Town, Merrimack co., S cen. New Hampshire, 11 mi. (18 km.) E of Concord; pop. (1990c) 3591.
2. Town, Surrey, S England, on the edge of Banstead Downs; nearby is **Epsom Downs** racecourse; magnesia springs in the vicinity from which Epsom salts formerly were made.

Ep·worth \ˈep-ˌwərth\. Parish in the Parts of Lindsey, Lincolnshire, E England; birthplace of religious leader John Wesley 1703.

Équa·teur \ˌā-kwä-ˈtœr\; *formerly* **Co·quil·hat·ville** \ˌkō-kē-lä-ˈvēl\. Administrative region of NW Democratic Rep. of the Congo. See table at ZAIRE.

Equa·tor \i-ˈkwā-tər, ˈē-ˌkwā-\. The great circle of Earth that is everywhere equally distant from the poles and divides the surface into Northern and Southern hemispheres.

Equa·to·ria \ˌē-kwə-ˈtōr-ē-ə, ˌe-\. **1.** Occasional name used somewhat indefinitely for the equatorial regions of Africa.
2. Former province of S Sudan; ✱ Juba; scene of sporadic antigovernment activity 1955–72.

Equa·to·ri·al Africa \ˌē-kwə-ˈtōr-ē-əl, ˌe-\. See FRENCH EQUATORIAL AFRICA.

Equatorial Countercurrent. The surface current moving E in a few places in the oceans near the Equator.

Equatorial Current. The surface current moving W in the oceans near the Equator.

Equatorial Guin·ea \ˈgi-nē\; *formerly* **Spanish Guinea.** Republic, W Africa, consisting of: (1) Mbini, the chiefly mainland portion bounded on N by Cameroon, on E and S by Gabon, and on W by the Atlantic Ocean; includes Corisco I. and Islas Elobey. (2) The islands of Bioko and Pagulu (1°25′S, 5°36′E). Total area 10,825 sq. mi. (28,037 sq. km.); total pop. (1993e) 376,000; ✱ Malabo, on the island of Bioko.
Physical features: (1) Mbini has a coastal plain varying in width from 10 to 15 mi. (16 to 24 km.); cen. and E regions

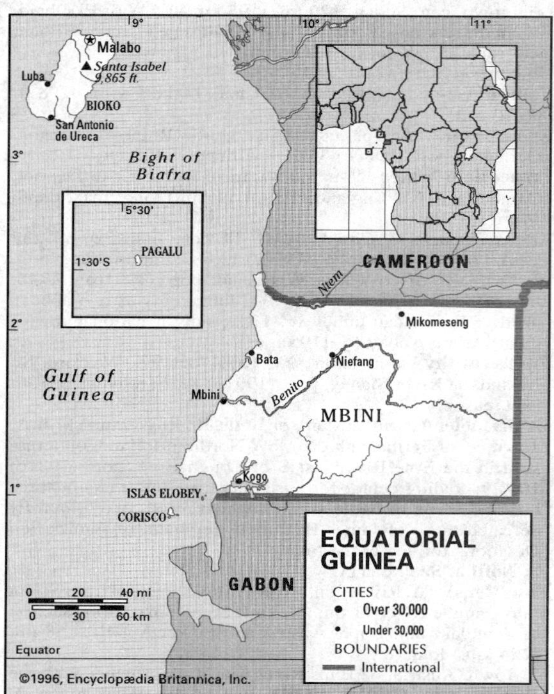

consist of a series of plateaus, reaching a max. height of ab. 4000 ft. (1220 m.); soils less fertile than those of Bioko. (2) Bioko has volcanic formations; soils highly fertile; av. annual rainfall ab. 100 in. (250 cm.); highest peak, Santa Isabel, 9865 ft. (3007 m.).

Chief products: Cocoa, coffee, palm oil, timber; fishing.

History: Island of Bioko (formerly Fernando Póo) orig. inhabited by the Bubi people; discovered by Portuguese c. 1472; ceded to Spain along with commercial rights on mainland 1778; Bioko under British administration 1827, returned to Spain 1843; period 1857–77 marked by Spanish exploration of mainland territory; Franco-Spanish agreement regarding borders of mainland territory 1900; was granted limited self-government 1963; achieved independence 1968; first president Francisco Macías Nguemo elected 1971, assumed dictatorial power 1973; government overthrown by military coup 1979; new constitution adopted 1982.

Equinox, Mount. See BIG EQUINOX.

Erath \'ē-ˌrath\. County in N cen. Texas. See table at TEXAS.

Erbil. See ARBĪL.

Erceldoune *or* **Ercildoune.** See EARLSTON.

Er·ci·yas \'er-jē-yäs\ *or* **Er·ci·yes** \-yes\; *anc.* **Ar·gae·us** \är-'jē-əs\. Peak, cen. Turkey in Asia, S of Kayseri; 12,848 ft. (3916 m.).

Er·co·la·no \ˌer-kō-'lä-nō\; *formerly* **Re·si·na** \rā-'zē-nä\. Commune, Napoli prov., Campania, S Italy; pop. (1989c) 63,571.

Erd \'erd\. Town, cen. Hungary; pop. (1991e) 47,800.

Erdély. See TRANSYLVANIA 2.

Er·e·bus, Mount \'er-ə-bəs\. Active volcano on Ross I. in Ross Sea, Antarctica, 77°32′S, 167°09′E; 12,448 ft. (3794 m.); site of airliner crash killing all 257 aboard 1979.

Erech \'ē-ˌrek\ *or Akkadian* **Uruk** \'ü-ˌrůk\. Ancient Sumerian city (c. 2300 B.C.) in S Babylonia, on Euphrates River NW of Ur of the Chaldees; in S cen. part of modern Iraq; in the Bible a city of Nimrod's kingdom in land of Shinar (*Gen.* x. 10); excavations on the site have been considerable, uncovering walls, a temple, base of a ziggurat, and a valuable library.

Ereğ·li \ˌe-re-'ḡlē, -'lē\. **1.** Town, SW cen. Turkey in Asia, 85 mi. (137 km.) ESE of Konya; pop. (1990p) 74,332; textile manufacturing.

2. *anc.* **Her·a·clea Pon·ti·ca** \ˌher-ə-'klē-ə-'pän-ti-kə\. Seaport, NW Turkey in Asia, on Black Sea 40 mi. (64 km.) ENE of mouth of Sakarya River; pop. (1990p) 63,776.

Ere·pe·cu, La·go do \'lä-gü-ˌdü-ˌer-i-pi-'kü\. Lake, NW Pará state, N Brazil, N of the Amazon; traversed by Trombetas River, a tributary of the Amazon.

Erepecurú. See PARU DE OESTE.

Ere·tria \e-'rē-trē-ə\. City of ancient Greece, on S coast of Euboea I. ab. 15 mi. (24 km.) ESE of Khalkis, its rival in the early period. Founded as an Ionian colony; destroyed by Persians 490 B.C. (before battle of Marathon) for earlier assistance to revolting Ionian Greeks; rebuilt but less significant.

Erft \'erft\. River, W Germany; rises in Eifel region and flows N to the Rhine near Neuss; 71 mi. (114 km.) long.

Er·furt \'er-ˌfůrt\. **1.** District of former East Germany; 2837 sq. mi. (7348 sq. km.); ✱ Erfurt.

2. City, ✱ of Thuringia state, cen. Germany and formerly of Erfurt dist., East Germany, 64 mi. (103 km.) WSW of Leipzig; pop. (1992e) 204,912; food processing; metal goods, electrical equipment, shoes, clothing; commercial flower growing, large trade in plants and seed; 12th cent. cathedral.

History: Episcopal see founded by St. Boniface 742; famous university opened 1392 (closed 1812); signed protective treaty with Saxony 1483; residence of religious reformer Martin Luther as Augustinian monk 1505–08; passed to elector of Mainz 17th cent.; scene of Congress of Erfurt (French Emperor Napoléon, Czar Alexander of Russia, numerous German sovereigns) 1808; taken by Prussia 1813; Prussian rule confirmed by Congress of Vienna 1814; captured by American forces Apr. 1945; scene of first meeting of heads of government of East and West Germany 1970.

Erg, Al– \ȧl-'erg\. Any of certain regions of sand dunes in the Sahara, N Africa, incl.: **Erg Igui·di** *also* **Erg Igi·di** \ˌē-gē-'dē\ in W Algeria and N Mauritania; **Erg Chech** \'shesh\ in SW Algeria and N Mali; **Great Western Erg** *or* **Grand Erg Oc·ci·den·tal** \grä^{n}-'derg-ˌȯk-sē-ˌdä^{n}-'tȧl\ in N cen. Algeria; **Great Eastern Erg** *or* **Grand Erg Orien·tal** \ˌōr-yä^{n}-'tȧl\ in E Algeria.

Er·ge·ne \ˌer-ge-'ne\. River, NW Turkey in Europe; rises near Black Sea coast, flows W into Maritsa (Meriç) River on Greek border; 175 mi. (282 km.) long.

Ergun. See ARGUN.

Er Hai *or W.-G.* **Erh Hai** \'er-'hī\. Lake in W Yunnan prov., S China; 30 mi. (48 km.) long by 10 to 15 mi. (16 to 24 km.) wide; alt. ab. 6600 ft. (2010 m.); has the city of Dali on W shore; resorts, many white marble pagodas built 1000 years ago by Sung dynasty; outlet to Yangbi River, a tributary of the Mekong.

Er·icht, Loch \'er-ikt\. Lake, Highland and Tayside regions, N cen. Scotland; 14 mi. (23 km.) long.

Er·ics·son, Mount \'er-ik-sən\. Peak in the Sierra Nevada, in N Tulare co., S cen. California; 13,625 ft. (4153 m.).

Eridanus. See PO.

Eri·du \'er-i-ˌdü, 'ā-rē-\. Ancient city, the chief seaport of Sumer and Babylonia, close to shore of Persian Gulf; its site now in Iraq, 120 mi. (193 km.) from the gulf near the lower Euphrates, S of An Nāsirīyah and near Ur of the Chaldees; the first royal city of Sumerian tradition; perhaps dates back to the 5th millennium B.C.; seat of worship of the god Ea.

Erie \'ir-ē\. **1.** Name of counties in three states of the U.S. See tables at NEW YORK, OHIO, PENNSYLVANIA.

2. City, ⊗ of Neosho co., SE Kansas; pop. (1990c) 1615.

3. City and port of entry, ⊗ of Erie co., NW corner of Pennsylvania, on Lake Erie; pop. (1990c) 108,718; large harbor, ships lumber, coal, iron ore, petroleum, grain; manufactures machinery, electric locomotives, ships, rubber products, plastics, clothing, paper products; Gannon Univ. (1925), Mercyhurst Coll. (1926), Pennsylvania State Univ. at Erie, The Behrend Coll. (1948). Laid out 1795 near site of old French Fort Presque Isle (1753); incorp. as borough and became ⊗ 1803; headquarters of Commodore Oliver Hazard Perry (most of whose vessels were built here) in War of 1812; incorp. as city 1851.

Erie, Lake. Lake in U.S. and Canada, bounded on W and N by Ontario prov., Canada, on E by New York, on S by Pennsylvania and Ohio, and on SW by Michigan, the U.S.-Canada boundary passing through the lake; ab. 240 mi. (385 km.) long; 9910 sq. mi. (3021 sq. km.); 4th in size of the five Great Lakes (*q.v.*); greatest depth 210 ft. (64 m.); elev. 570 ft. (174 m.); area of drainage basin 40,000 sq. mi. (103,600 sq. km.); at W end connected through Detroit River, Lake St. Clair, and St. Clair River with Lake Huron, and at E end through Niagara River and Welland Canal with Lake Ontario. Battle of Lake Erie, in which Commodore Oliver Hazard Perry defeated British naval force, fought in Put-in-Bay Sept. 10, 1813. See ERIE CANAL and NEW YORK STATE BARGE CANAL.

Erie Canal. Canal, from Buffalo, New York, on Lake Erie to Albany, New York, on Hudson River; 363 mi. (584 km.) long; 40 ft. (12 m.) wide at surface and 4 ft. (1 m.) deep; built 1817–25; enlarged several times and finally (work begun 1909) made a barge canal and became main waterway (340 mi. or 547 km. long, 150 ft. or 46 m. wide, and 12 ft. or 4 m. deep) of the New York State Barge Canal (*q.v.*).

Erímanthos. See ERYMANTHUS.

Eri·mo, Cape \ā-'rē-mō\. Cape on SE coast of Hokkaidō I., Japan.

Erin \'ir-in\. Town, ⊗ of Houston co., NW Tennessee; pop. (1990c) 1586.

Er·in \'er-in\. Ireland —now a poetic name.

Er·i·trea \ˌer-ə-'trē-ə, -'trā-\. Independent state, NE Africa, bounded on W by Sudan, on N and E by Red Sea, on SE by Djibouti, and on S by Ethiopia of which it was formerly part;

45,405 sq. mi. (117,599 sq. km.); pop. (1992e) 3,317,611; ✱ Asmara.

Physical features: Includes the many islands of the Dahlak Archipelago; has low coastal plain and interior mountain range with peaks 5300 ft. to 9882 ft. (1615 to 3012 m.); has two streams in the N, the Anseba and Baraka; headstreams of the Baraka flow N to Red Sea in Sudan, and cross its W part the Gash, tributary of Atbara.

Chief products: Cotton, salt, food products.

History: Part of ancient Ethiopia (*q.v.*); Aseb (*q.v.*) taken over by Italian government 1882; became a colony of Italy 1890; used as base for Italian invasion of Ethiopia 1935; made part of Italian East Africa 1936; conquered by British forces 1941; became federated with Ethiopia 1952; was made a province of Ethiopia 1962; after 1962, sporadic guerrilla warfare carried out by Eritrean secessionist groups; provisional government of Eritrea estab. 1991 upon overthrow of Ethiopian government; gained independence 1993.

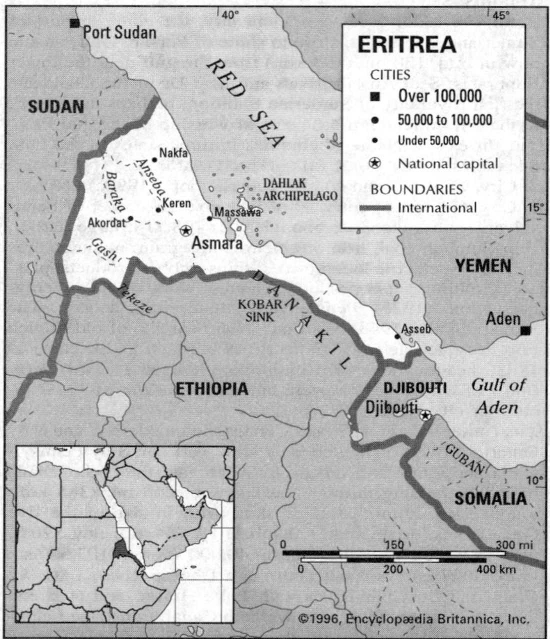

Erivan. See YEREVAN.

Er·lang·en \ˈer-ˌläŋ-ən\. City, Bavaria, Germany, on Regnitz River 12 mi. (19 km.) NNW of Nürnberg; pop. (1992c) 102,433; electronic equipment, textiles, medical machinery, gloves, hats, curtain fabric; brewing; 18th cent. baroque town hall; 18th cent. castle; university (1743). Chartered 1398; passed to burgraves of Nürnberg 1402, margraves of Bayreuth 1541, Prussia 1791, Bavaria 1810.

Er·lang·er \ˈər-laŋ-gər\. Residential city, Kenton co., N Kentucky, 7 mi. (11 km.) SW of Covington and 4 mi. (6 km.) SE of Greater Cincinnati airport; pop. (1990c) 15,979.

Erlau. See EGER.

Er·me·land \ˈer-mə-ˌlänt\ *or* **Erm·land** \ˈerm-ˌlänt\ *or Pol.* **War·mia** \ˈvär-myä\. Region, Elbląg and Olsztyn provs., N Poland; ab. 1650 sq. mi. (4274 sq. km.); formerly in East Prussia, Germany; extends SE from Vislinski Zaliv; became bishopric under Teutonic Knights 1250; attached to Poland by Treaty of Toruń (Thorn) 1466; became part of Prussia 1772; to Poland 1945.

Er·me·lo \ˈer-mə-ˌlō\. **1.** Commune, Gelderland prov., E Netherlands, 14 mi. (23 km.) NE of Amersfoort; pop. (1993e) 26,603; plastics.
2. Town, NE Rep. of South Africa, 120 mi. (193 km.) E of Johannesburg near source of Vaal River.

Er·mine Street \ˈər-min\. Ancient Roman road from London to York, Britain, passing through Lincoln and Doncaster; from York had an extension past Hadrian's Wall to Scotland; one of four great Roman roads of Britain (see FOSSE WAY, ICKNIELD WAY, and WATLING STREET).

Er·mont \er-ˈmōⁿ\. Commune, Val-d'Oise dept., N France.

Er·moú·po·lis *or* **Her·moú·po·lis** \er-ˈmü-pō-ˌlēs\ *or* **Sí·ros** \ˈsē-ˌrōs\. Commercial seaport city, ✱ of Cyclades dept., Cyclades Is., Greece, on E coast of Syros I.; pop. (1981c) 13,877.

Er·na·ku·lam \er-ˈnä-ku̇-ləm\. Town, cen. Kerala state, S India, on Malabar Coast 120 mi. (193 km.) W of Madurai; fishing; several colleges.

Erne \ˈərn\. River, N Ireland (island); rises in co. Cavan, N Ireland (republic), flows N across border of Northern Ireland, turns NW and widens into **Upper Lough Erne** \ˌläk\, 13 mi. (21 km.) long; continues as a winding river past Enniskillen and expands into **Lower Lough Erne** (18 mi. or 29 km. long; 53 sq. mi. or 137 sq. km.), then flows W into Donegal Bay; 72 mi. (116 km.) long; fine waterfall bet. Lough Erne and the bay.

Erode \i-ˈrōd\. Town, cen. Tamil Nadu, S India, on right bank of Kāveri River 75 mi. (121 km.) WNW of Tiruchchirappalli; pop. (1991p) 357,427; trade center.

Er Ramle. See RAMLA.

Er Riad. See RIYADH.

Er·ri·boll, Loch \ˈer-i-ˌbȯl\. Inlet of Atlantic Ocean on extreme N coast of Scotland; ab. 10 mi. (16 km.) long.

Er Rif \er-ˈrif\ *or* **Rif** *also* **Er Riff** *or* **Riff.** Hilly coastal region in N Morocco, constituting cen. and E parts of former Spanish Morocco, extending from a point E of Melilla to Ceuta; inhabited by Berber tribes (Riffs), who rose in revolt 1921; at first they defeated Spanish forces and, under leadership of Abd el-Krim from 1923, they held out until overcome by combined Spanish and French forces 1926.

Er·ri·gal Mountain \ˈer-ə-ˌgȯl\. Peak, co. Donegal, N Ireland (republic); 2466 ft. (752 m.).

Er·ris Head \ˈer-is\. Cape on NW coast of co. Mayo, NW Ireland, projecting into Atlantic Ocean.

Er·ro·man·go \ˌer-ō-ˈmäŋ-gō\ *or* **Er·ro·man·ga** *also* **Er·o·man·ga** \-ˈmäŋ-gä\. Island in S group of Vanuatu, SW Pacific Ocean, 62 mi. (100 km.) SSE of Efate; 35 mi. (56 km.) long, 25 mi. (40 km.) wide; has several mountain ranges, highest point 2600 ft. (792 m.), and several bays with good anchorages, esp. Dillon Bay on W coast.

Er·se·kë \er-ˈsā-kə\. **1.** Former province of Albania; now comprises Kolonjë district. See *Kolonjë* in table at ALBANIA.
2. *or* **Ko·lon·jë** \kȯ-ˈlȯnyə\. Town, ✱ of Kolonjë dist., SE Albania.

Érsekújvár. See NOVÉ ZÁMKY.

Ertis. See IRTYSH.

Er·win \ˈər-win\. **1.** Town, Harnett co., cen. North Carolina, ab. 4 mi. (6 km.) NW of Dunn; pop. (1990c) 4061.
2. Town, ⊗ of Unicoi co., NE Tennessee, 12 mi. (19 km.) S of Johnson City; pop. (1990c) 5015.

Er·y·man·thus \ˌer-ə-ˈman-thəs\; *Gk.* **Erí·man·thos** \e-ˈrē-män-ˌthȯs\ *or* **Olo·nos** \ˌō-lō-ˈnōs\. Peak in Achaea dept., NW Peloponnese, S Greece; 7296 ft. (2224 m.); in ancient times was where Arcadia, Achaea, and Elis met; in Greek mythology, scene of killing of the Erymanthian boar by Hercules.

Ery·ri \e-ˈrə-rē\. Region of NW Wales. See SNOWDON.

Er·y·thrae \ˈer-ə-ˌthrē\. Ancient city of Lydia, on coast of the peninsula opp. island of Chios; one of the 12 Ionian Cities; dwelling place of a sibyl, Herophile, regarded by some as identical with the Cumaean sibyl.

Er·y·thrae·an Sea \er-ə-ˈthrē-ən\ *or Lat.* **Ma·re Ery·thrae·um** \ˈmā-rē-ˌer-ə-ˈthrē-əm, ˈmär-ē\. In ancient geography, the part of the Indian Ocean now known as the Arabian Sea and the Persian Gulf; also called the Red Sea, the **Mare Ru·brum** \ˈrü-brəm\.

Er·y·thrai·on, Cape \ˌer-ə-ˈthrī-ˌän\. The SE point of Crete, Greece, extending into the Mediterranean Sea.

Erz·berg \ˈerts-ˌberk\. Mountain at Eisenerz, Styria, Austria; 5032 ft. (1534 m.); rich in iron ore; the mines have been worked for over 1000 years.

Erzerum. See ERZURUM.

Erz·ge·bir·ge \ˈerts-gə-ˌbir-gə\ *or Eng.* **Ore Mountains** \ˈōr\ *or Czech* **Kruš·né·ho·ry** \ˈkru̇sh-nyə-ˈhȯr-ē\. Mountain range bet. Germany and NW Czech Republic; highest peak Klínovec 4080 ft. (1244 m.).

Er·zin·can *or* **Er·zin·jan** \ˌer-zin-ˈjän\. **1.** Province of Turkey in Asia. See table at TURKEY.
2. Town, its ✻, on N bank of the Karasu 96 mi. (154 km.) W of Erzurum, in Turkish Armenia; pop. (1990p) 90,799; in fertile river plain in midst of orchards and gardens; chief agricultural products wheat, fruit, and cotton; cotton and silk industries; a military station with barracks and hospital; nearby in 4th cent. A.D. was home of St. Gregory the Illuminator. Came under control of Seljuqs 1071 but they were defeated here by Mongols 1243; added to Ottoman Empire by Sultan Mehmed II 1473; suffers frequent earthquakes, one of the most destructive of which occurred in 1939.

Er·zu·rum *or* **Er·ze·rum** \ˌer-zu̇-ˈrüm\. **1.** Province of Turkey in Asia. See table at TURKEY.
2. City, its ✻, on Turkish-Russian railroad; in mountains of W Turkish Armenia, a military station of strategic importance; pop. (1990c) 242,391; leather; trade center for sugar beets, cereals, and vegetables grown nearby; university (1957). Of great antiquity, important in Armenian and Arabic history; seized by Seljuqs 1071; came under Ottoman Turks 1515; three times captured by Russians—1828, 1878, 1916; site of meeting of First Turkish Nationalist Congress July 1919.

Esan, Cape \ˈā-sän\ *or* **Cape Ezan** \ˈā-ˌzän\. Cape on S coast of Hokkaidō, Japan, at S of entrance to Uchiura Bay.

Es·bjerg \ˈes-byer\. Seaport, Ribe co., SW Jutland Penin., Denmark, on North Sea; pop. (1992e) 81,843; Denmark's largest fishing port; exports meats and dairy products; base for North Sea oil exploration; only good harbor on W coast of Jutland; received munic. charter 1899.

Esbo. See ESPOO.

Es·ca·lan·te \ˌes-kə-ˈlan-tē\. River, S Utah; flows SE into Lake Powell; ab. 80 mi. (129 km.) long.

Escalante \ˌes-kä-ˈlän-tā\. Municipality, NE Negros Occidental, Negros, Philippines, on coast at N end of Tanon Strait; pop. (1980c) 71,293; important local trade center, founded ab. 1860.

Es·cam·bia \e-ˈskam-bē-ə\. **1.** Navigable river, SE United States; flows S from SW Alabama into Florida, where it forms boundary bet. Escambia and Santa Rosa cos.; empties into Pensacola Bay; ab. 75 mi. (121 km.) long.
2. Name of counties in two states of the U.S. See tables at ALABAMA and FLORIDA.

Es·ca·na·ba \ˌes-kə-ˈnä-bə\. **1.** River, Upper Penin., Michigan; rises in Marquette co., flows SE into Little Bay de Noc; ab. 100 mi. (161 km.) long.
2. City, ⊗ of Delta co., S Upper Penin., Michigan, on Little Bay de Noc; pop. (1990c) 13,659; port of entry; ships coal and oil products; Bay de Noc Community Coll. (1963).

Es·car·pa·do, Point \ˌes-kär-ˈpä-dō\. Cape on SW coast of Panama, at S side of entrance to Gulf of San Miguel.

Escaut. See SCHELDE.

Esch \ˈesh\ *or in full* **Esch–sur–Al·zette** \-ˌsu̅e̅r-äl-ˈzet\. Commune, S Luxembourg, on French border 10 mi. (16 km.) SW of the city of Luxembourg; pop. (1991c) 24,012; 2d largest city of Luxembourg; steel; in coal-bearing region.

Esch·we·ge \ˈesh-ˌvā-gə\. City, NE Hesse, Germany, on Werra River 25 mi. (40 km.) ESE of Kassel; pop. (1980c) 23,882; 16th cent. castle; varied manufactures, incl. soap, esp. a mottled type known as Eschwege, or Eschweger, soap; first mentioned 974; received city charter 13th cent.

Esch·wei·ler \ˈesh-ˌvī-lər\. City, North Rhine-Westphalia, Germany, 11 mi. (18 km.) NE of Aachen; pop. (1992e) 55,129; manufactures include iron and steel, textiles, plastics; limestone; coal deposits nearby. In WWII town and vicinity scene of severe fighting 1944.

Es·co·bal \ˌes-kō-ˈbäl\. Town, Colón prov., Panama, on W shore of Gatun Lake on border of former Canal Zone.

Es·co·ce·sa Bay \ˌes-kō-ˈsā-sä\. Bay on NE coast of Dominican Republic, NW of Cape Samaná, Hispaniola I., West Indies.

Es·con·di·do \ˌes-kən-ˈdē-dō\. City, San Diego co., SW corner of California, 28 mi. (45 km.) N of the city of San Diego; pop. (1990c) 108,635; vineyards; citrus fruit; founded 1885; incorp. 1888.

Escondido *or* **Blue·fields** \ˈblü-ˌfēldz\. Navigable river, S cen. Nicaragua; formed by the Siquia and other headstreams, flows E into the Caribbean Sea at Bluefields; 60 mi. (97 km.) long.

Escorial, El. See EL ESCORIAL.

Es·cu·dil·la Mountain \ˌes-kə-ˈdē-ə\. Peak in E Arizona, SE extremity of Apache co.; 10,955 ft. (3339 m.).

Es·cui·na·pa \ˌes-kwē-ˈnä-pä\ *or in full* **Escuinapa de Hi·dal·go** \t͟hā-ē-ˈt͟häl-gō\. Municipality, Sinaloa state, W Mexico, on railroad line ab. 40 mi. (64 km.) SE of Mazatlán.

Es·cuin·tla \es-ˈkwint-lä\. **1.** Department of S Guatemala. See table at GUATEMALA.
2. City, its ✻, 30 mi. (48 km.) SSW of Guatemala; munic. pop. (1993e) 66,424; medicinal baths; fruit growing.

Es·cu·mi·nac, Point \e-ˈskyü-mə-ˌnak\. Cape, E Northumberland co., E New Brunswick prov., SE Canada, on S side of entrance to Miramichi Bay.

Es·dra·e·lon, Plain of \ˌez-drə-ˈē-lən\ *also* **Valley of Jez·re·el** \ˈjez-rē-ˌel, -ˌrēl\ *or Heb.* **ʽEm·eq Yiz·re·ʽel** \ˈe-mek-ˌyēz-rā-ˈel\. Plain, N Israel, separating Galilee in the N from Samaria in the S; important agricultural region; formerly swampy, drained in 1920s and 1930s. See MEGIDDO.

Eş·fa·hān \ˌes-fä-ˈhän\; *formerly* **Is·pa·han** \ˌis-pä-\. **1.** Province of W cen. Iran. See table at IRAN.
2. *or* **Is·fa·han** \ˌis-fä-ˈhän\; *anc.* **As·pa·da·na** \ˌas-pə-ˈdā-nə\. City, its ✻; pop. (1986c) 986,753; on main highways S to Shīrāz, N to Tehran, and E to Yazd; in center is Maidan-i-Shāh, a great rectangular garden enclosing royal mosque, Masjid-i-Shāh, built by Shāh ʽAbbās I at end of 16th cent.; has large bazaar; particularly noted for silver filigree and metalwork; brocades and other textiles, carpets, steel; oil refining; university.
History: As Aspadana, ancient Median town; captured by Arabs during their conquest of Persia 641–650 A.D.; Seljuk ✻ in late 11th cent.; captured by Turkic ruler Timur 1388; ✻ of Persia 1598–1722; reached height of prosperity during 17th cent. when it was residence of Shāh ʽAbbās I; declined after capture by Afghans 1722.

Esher \ˈē-shər\; *formerly* **Esher and The Dit·tons** \ˈdit-ᵊnz\. Town, Surrey, S England, 15 mi. (24 km.) SW of London; pop. (1981p) 61,446; residential; site of the mansion, Esher Place, occupied 1529 by Thomas Cardinal Wolsey.

Eshnunna. See TELL ASMAR.

Esh·o·we \ˈe-shō-ˌwā\. Village, chief town of Zululand, E Rep. of South Africa, 70 mi. (113 km.) NNE of Durban; resort.

Esh Shām. See SYRIA 1.

Esk \ˈesk\. **1.** River in NE England, flowing E into North Sea at Whitby; 24 mi. (39 km.) long.
2. River, S Scotland; rises in Dumfries and Galloway region and flows S into the head of Solway Firth; its lower course for a few miles lies in Cumberland, England; 28 mi. (45 km.) long; Gretna Green is on N bank of Sark.
3. River, Lothian region, SE Scotland; formed by confluence of **North Esk** and **South Esk** in Dalkeith, flows N to Firth of Forth at Musselburgh; 3.5 mi. (6 km.) long (see NORTH ESK 3 and SOUTH ESK 3).

Esk Hause \ˈesk-ˌhȯs\. Mountain pass, W Cumberland, NW England, in the Lake District; 2490 ft. (759 m.).

Es·ki·fjör·dhur \ˈes-kē-ˌfyœr-t͟hər\. Fjord on E coast of Iceland.

Eski Foça. See FOÇA 2.

Eskije. See XÁNTHI 2.

Eskil·stu·na \ˈes-kil-ˌstüē-nə\. City, Södermanland prov., SE Sweden, S of Lake Mälaren 45 mi. (72 km.) W of Stockholm; pop. (1993e) 89,584; steelworks; manufactures cutlery and swords, precision instruments, machinery.

Es·ki·şe·hir \ˌes-ki-she-ˈhir\ *or* **Es·ki·shehr** \-ˈsher\. **1.** Province of Turkey in Asia. See table at TURKEY.

2. City, its ✱, on tributary of Sakarya River, 128 mi. (206 km.) W of Ankara; pop. (1990c) 413,082; agricultural equipment, cement and bricks, textiles, chemicals; sugar refining; famous for its deposits of meerschaum; nearby are ruins of what is believed to be ancient Phrygian city of **Dor·y·lae·um** \ˌdȯr-ə-ˈlē-əm\, a city that acquired importance in Byzantine times; scene of defeat of Seljuq Sultan Kilij Arslan, 1097 by Godfrey of Bouillon, duke of Lower Lorraine; taken by Ottoman Turks ab. 1176.

Es·la \ˈäz-lə, ˈez-\. River, NW Spain; rises in N León prov., flows SSW into Duero River ab. 15 mi. (24 km.) below Zamora; 171 mi. (275 km.) long.

Es·me·ral·da \ˌez-mə-ˈral-də\. County in SW Nevada. See table at NEVADA.

Es·me·ral·das \ˌes-mä-ˈräl-thäs\. **1.** River, NW Ecuador; flows W from Andes into Pacific Ocean; ab. 150 mi. (241 km.) long.

2. Province of NW Ecuador. See table at ECUADOR.

3. Town, its ✱, 2 mi. (3 km.) from mouth of Esmeraldas River 118 mi. (190 km.) NW of Quito; pop. (1990c) 98,558; gold deposits in vicinity.

Esna. See ISNA.

Eso·pus Creek \i-ˈsō-pəs\. Creek in Ulster co., SE New York; rises in Catskill Mts., flows SE then N into Hudson River ab. 10 mi. (16 km.) above Kingston. See ASHOKAN DAM.

Es·pail·lat \ˌes-pī-ˈyä\. Province, N cen. Dominican Republic. See table at DOMINICAN REPUBLIC.

España. See SPAIN.

Es·pa·no·la \ˌes-pən-ˈyō-lə\. **1.** Village, Rio Arriba and Santa Fe cos., N cen. New Mexico, 23 mi. (37 km.) NNW of the city of Santa Fe; pop. (1990c) 8389.

2. \ˌes-pə-ˈnō-lə\. Town, Sudbury dist., SE Ontario, Canada, 45 mi. (72 km.) WSW of the city of Sudbury; pop. (1991c) 5527.

Es·pa·ño·la \ˌes-pä-ˈnyō-lä\. **1.** *also* **Hood Island** \ˈhu̇d\. One of the Galápagos Is. (*q.v.*).

2. Island, West Indies. See HISPANIOLA.

Es·pe·rance, Cape \ˈes-pə-rəns\. Cape on NW coast of Guadalcanal I., SE Solomon Is., W Pacific Ocean; landing place for Japanese forces 1942–43; naval battle off coast near here Oct. 1942. See SAVO.

Es·pe·ran·za \ˌes-pā-ˈrän-sä\. Town, Santa Fe prov., E cen. Argentina, 20 mi. (32 km.) NW of the city of Santa Fe; pop. (1980p) 22,838.

Esperanza, La. See LA ESPERANZA.

Es·pi·chel, Cape \ˌish-pē-ˈshel\. Promontory on SW coast of Portugal, 21 mi. (34 km.) S of Lisbon.

Es·pi·nal \ˌes-pē-ˈnäl\. Municipality, Tolima dept., W cen. Colombia, on the upper Magdalena 30 mi. (48 km.) SE of Ibagué.

Es·pí·ri·to San·to \i-ˈshpē-rē-tü-ˈsäⁿn-tü\. **1.** Island, E Brazil, in Atlantic Ocean a few hundred yards off mainland of Espírito Santo state; site of the city of Vitória.

2. State, E Brazil; ✱ Vitória; in E part has swampy coastal plain; coffee, sugarcane, timber, food products. See table at BRAZIL.

Es·pí·ri·tu Santo \e-ˈspē-rē-ˌtü-ˈsän-tō\. **1.** *also* **Santo;** *formerly* **Ma·ri·na** \mä-ˈrē-nä\. Island, NW Vanuatu, SW Pacific Ocean; 76 mi. (122 km.) long by 45 mi. (72 km.) wide, 1420 sq. mi. (3678 sq. km.); largest island in group; has mountain range along W coast, highest point Mt. Tabwemasana 6167 ft. (1880 m.); coastline marked on the N by two peninsulas, largest on NW, with St. Philip and St. James Bay bet. them; agriculturally well developed; principal settlement Santo on SE coast. During WWII site of military and naval bases estab. by Americans.

2. Island, Mexico, off SE coast of Baja California, near mouth of Gulf of California; 13 mi. (21 km.) long.

Es·pi·ri·tu San·to, Cape \e-ˈspē-rē-ˌtü-ˈsän-tō\. NE point of Samar I., E Philippines 12°35′N, 125°11′E.

Espíritu Santo, Cape. Cape, Chile and Argentina, on N coast of Tierra del Fuego I. (*q.v.*), S of entrance to Strait of Magellan.

Espíritu Santo Bay. Inlet of Caribbean Sea on E coast of Yucatán Penin., Quintana Roo state, Mexico, S of Ascensión Bay.

Es·poo \ˈes-pō\ *or Swed.* **Es·bo** \ˈes-bü\. Town, Uusimaa prov., S Finland, ab. 11 mi. (18 km.) W of Helsinki; pop. (1992e) 175,806; granite; estab. 1963.

Es·qui·line \ˈes-kwə-ˌlīn, -lin\. One of the Seven Hills of Rome, Italy See SEVEN HILLS.

Es·qui·malt \ə-ˈskwī-ˌmȯlt\. Municipality, seaport, and naval station, SE Vancouver Is., British Columbia, Canada, on Strait of Juan de Fuca 4 mi. (6 km.) W of Victoria of which it is a suburb; pop. (1991c) 16,192; spacious harbor; British navy station until 1905 after which Canadian government took it over; its dry dock (built 1888) transferred to Canada 1910; shipyard, salmon cannery.

Es·qui·pu·las \ˌes-kē-ˈpü-läs\. Town, Chiquimula dept., SE Guatemala, 73 mi. (117 km.) E of Guatemala; pop. (1993c) 10,095; church contains a famous black image of Christ (the "Black Christ").

Es·rum \ˈes-rəm\. Lake in NE Sjælland I., Denmark.

Es Salt \es-ˈsȯlt\. Town, NW Jordan, W of Amman.

Es·sa·oui·ra \ˌe-sä-ˈwē-rä\; *formerly* **Mog·a·dor** \ˈmō-gä-ˌdōr\. City and seaport, SW cen. coast of Morocco; fish processing, tanning; landing place of U.S. forces Nov. 1942.

Es·sen \ˈes-ᵊn\ *also* **Essen an der Ruhr** \ˌän-dər-ˈrür\. City, North Rhine-Westphalia, Germany, 18 mi. (29 km.) NNE of Düsseldorf, near right bank of the Ruhr River ab. 13 mi. (21 km.) from where it enters the Rhine; pop. (1992e) 626,989; contains the most extensive ironworks and steelworks in Europe; coal mining; glass, chemicals, precision instruments, textiles; railroad center; cathedral; opera house; technical colleges. Founded 9th cent.; made a city 10th cent.; passed to Prussia 1802; bombed in WWI; heavily bombed by Allies 1943–45, esp. the Krupp steelworks; taken with other cities in fall of the Ruhr Apr.–May 1945.

Es·sen·don \ˈes-ᵊn-dən\. Municipality, S Victoria, SE Australia, NW suburb of Melbourne; pop. (1991c) 52,721.

Essentuki. See YESSENTUKI.

Es·se·qui·bo \ˌe-se-ˈkwē-bō\. River, Guyana; rises in Serra Uaçari on Brazilian border, flows N into Atlantic Ocean; 630 mi. (1014 km.) long; the republic's longest river; has wide estuary; navigable for some distance; main tributaries all from W: the Cuyuni and Mazaruni near its mouth, Potaro in cen. part, and Rupununi in S cen. part.

Es·sex \ˈe-siks\. **1.** Name of counties in five states of the U.S. See tables at MASSACHUSETTS, NEW JERSEY, NEW YORK, VERMONT, VIRGINIA.

2. Town, SE Middlesex co., S Connecticut, on W bank of Connecticut River near its mouth; pop. (1990c) 5904; settled 1690, incorp. 1852; as maritime trade center, attacked by British in War of 1812.

3. Unincorporated settlement, Baltimore co., Maryland, E of Baltimore; pop. (1990c) 40,872; Essex Community Coll. (1957).

4. Town, Essex co., NE Massachusetts, 23 mi. (37 km.) NE of Boston; pop. (1990c) 3260.

5. Town in Vermont. See ESSEX JUNCTION.

6. County, in SE Ontario, Canada. See table at ONTARIO.

7. Town, Essex co., SE Ontario, Canada, 16 mi. (26 km.) ESE of Windsor; pop. (1991c) 6759.

8. Former county, SE England.

History: Region a Roman center before invasion by East Saxons; Anglo-Saxon kingdom of The Heptarchy (*q.v.*) with its center at London; received Christianity and submitted to Mercia (*q.v.*) 7th cent. A.D.; its subkings later disappeared; included in territory under the Danelaw 9th cent.; reconquered by Wessex, it became a shire and later a powerful English earldom.

9. County, SE England, comprising the former county; rivers Thames, Stour, Colne, Blackwater, Lea, Crouch; chief towns

Southend-on-Sea, Colchester, Chelmsford, Harwich; estab. 1974. See table at ENGLAND.

Essex Junction. Village in Essex town, Chittenden co., NW Vermont, on Winooski River 5 mi. (8 km.) E of Burlington; pop. (1990c) 8396 (village), 16,498 (town).

Es·sex·ville \ˈe-siks-ˌvil\. City, Bay co., E Michigan, on Saginaw Bay 4 mi. (6 km.) E of Bay City; pop. (1990c) 4088.

Ess·ling \ˈes-liŋ\. Village, Austria, near Vienna. See ASPERN.

Ess·ling·en \ˈes-liŋ-ən\. City, Baden-Württemberg, Germany, on the Neckar River 6 mi. (10 km.) ESE of Stuttgart; pop. (1992e) 91,829; metalworking; machinery, electrical equipment, textiles, leather goods; distribution center for the area's fruits and wines; founded in 8th cent.; free imperial city; became part of Swabian League of cities.

Es·sonne \e-ˈsȯn\. **1.** River, N France; rises in Loiret dept., flows N to the Seine at Corbeil-Essonnes; ab. 56 mi. (90 km.) long.

2. Department of N France. See table at FRANCE.

Es Suweida *or* **Es Suweidiya.** See AS SUWAYDĀ.

Estado Libre Asociado Puerto Rico. See PUERTO RICO.

Es·ta·dos, Is·la de los \ˈēs-lä-t͟hā-ˌlōs-es-ˈtä-thōs\ *also* **Stat·en Island** \ˈsta-tən\. Island, Argentina, S Atlantic Ocean off E tip of Tierra del Fuego; ab. 45 mi. (72 km.) long; chief town San Juan de Salvamento, at E end. See TIERRA DEL FUEGO 2.

Estados Unidos de Venezuela. See VENEZUELA.

Estados Unidos Mexicanos. See MEXICO.

Es·tan·cia \e-ˈstan-chə\. Town, ⊗ of Torrance co., cen. New Mexico; pop. (1990c) 792.

Es·tân·cia \ē-ˈshtäⁿn-syə\. Town on coast, S Sergipe state, E Brazil; munic. pop. (1991p) 53,849.

Est·court \ˈest-ˌkōrt\. Town, E Rep. of South Africa, 85 mi. (137 km.) NW of Durban.

Este \ˈes-tā\; *anc.* **Ates·te** \ə-ˈtes-tē\. Commune, Padova prov., Veneto, NE Italy, 17 mi. (27 km.) SW of Padua; pop. (1991p) 17,714; medieval fortress; cathedral; campanile. Ancient Roman military colony; seat of Este family until their expulsion by Paduans in 12th cent.; with Padua fell to Venetians 1405.

Es·te·ban Eche·ver·ría \e-ˈstā-b̲än-ˌā-chā-vā-ˈrē-ä\. Town, S suburb of Buenos Aires, Argentina; pop. (1991p) 276,017.

Es·te·lí \ˌes-tā-ˈlē\. **1.** Department of W Nicaragua. See table at NICARAGUA.

2. Town, its ✻, 65 mi. (105 km.) N of Managua; munic. pop. (1985e) 30,635.

Es·te·po·na \ˌes-tā-ˈpō-nä\. Seaport commune, Málaga prov., S Spain, on Mediterranean Sea 46 mi. (74 km.) SW of the city of Málaga; pop. (1991c) 34,965.

Es·te·rel \ˌes-te-ˈrel\. Mountainous forested region, S France, on coast of depts. of Var and Alpes-Maritimes, bet. Fréjus and Cannes; highest point Mont Vinaigre 2020 ft. (616 m.).

Es·ter·ha·zy \ˈes-tər-ˌhā-zē\. Town, Saskatchewan, Canada, 120 mi. (193 km.) E of Regina; pop. (1991c) 2896.

Es·té·rias, Cape \e-ˈstā-rē-äs\. Cape extending into Gulf of Guinea on coast of Gabon, W equatorial part of Africa, bet. Corisco Bay on the N and Gabon River on the S; Libreville is on its S coast.

Es·tes Park \ˈes-tēz\. **1.** A high-level valley of the Front Range, Rocky Mts., N Colorado just E of east entrance of Rocky Mountain National Park.

2. Village in Larimer co., N Colorado, 28 mi. (45 km.) SW of Fort Collins; pop. (1990c) 3184; alt. 7500 ft. (2286 m.); entrance to Rocky Mountain National Park.

Es·te·van \ˈes-tə-ˌvan\. Town, SE Saskatchewan, Canada, on Souris River 54 mi. (87 km.) SE of Weyburn; pop. (1991c) 10,240; brickworks, oil wells, clay, coal deposits.

Es·ther, Mount \ˈes-tər\. Peak in the Adirondack Mts., Essex co., NE New York; 4270 ft. (1301 m.).

Es·ther·ville \ˈes-tər-ˌvil\. City, ⊗ of Emmet co., N Iowa, 58 mi. (93 km.) NE of Cherokee; pop. (1990c) 6720; Iowa Lakes Community Coll. (1967).

Esthonia. See ESTONIA.

Es·till \ˈest-ᵊl\. County in E Kentucky. See table at KENTUCKY.

Es·to·nia \e-ˈstō-nē-ə, -nyə\ *also less correctly* **Es·tho·nia** \e-ˈstō-, es-ˈthō-\; *Estonian* **Ees·ti** \ˈā-stē\. Republic, N Europe, bounded on N by Gulf of Finland, on E by Russia, on S by Latvia, and on W by the Baltic Sea; 17,413 sq. mi. (45,100 sq.

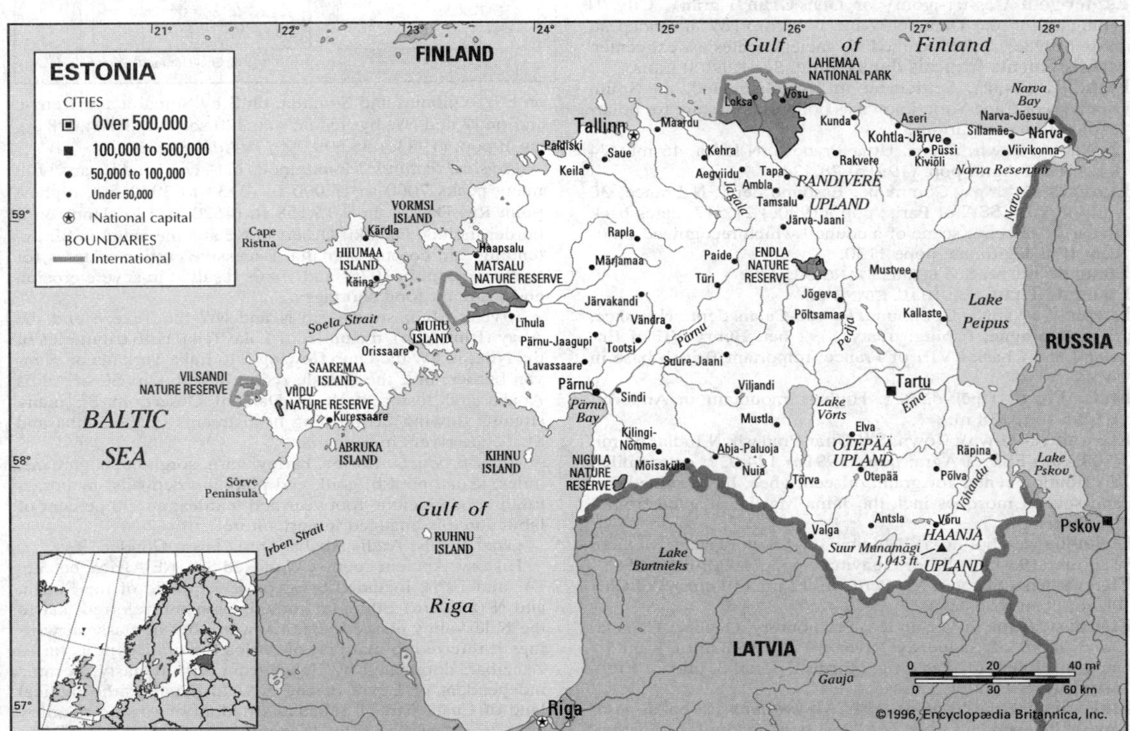

km.); pop. (1993e) 1,536,000; ✻ Tallinn; comprised **Estonian Soviet Socialist Republic** 1940–91.

Physical features: Coast is low and there are no heights of land; its SW coast is N shore of Gulf of Riga; includes four islands in Baltic Sea off W coast: Saaremaa, Hiiumaa, Muhu, and Vormsi; on E shares ab. one half of Lakes Peipus (*q.v.*) and Pskov with Russia; has many other lakes, largest of which is Vorts-Jarv, in S cen. part.

Chief rivers: Pärnu, Kasari, and Narva.

Chief products: Dairy produce, potatoes, rye; shale oil; cement, textiles; shipbuilding.

Chief towns: Tallinn and Tartu.

History: Estonians conquered by Danes who founded Reval (see TALLINN) 1219; after ferocious revolt of peasantry 1343–45, taken over by Teutonic Knights 1346; under rule of Swedish in N from 1558 and entirely from 1629; ceded to Russia (see BALTIC PROVINCES) 1721; became independent republic Feb. 1918; recognized by U.S.S.R. 1920 (peace signed at Tartu); joined League of Nations 1921; ruled as dictatorship 1934–37; joined nonaggression pact with Germany (see *History* at LATVIA) 1939; occupied by Soviet army and annexed to U.S.S.R. as Estonian S.S.R. 1940; overrun by German army 1941 and retaken by U.S.S.R. 1944; declared independence from U.S.S.R. Aug. 1991.

Es·to·ril \ˌēsh-tü-ˈril\. Resort town, Portugal, on coast W of Lisbon; pop. (1991p) 2524.

Estrada, A. See A ESTRADA.

Estrela, Serra da. See SERRA DA ESTRELA.

Es·tre·ma·du·ra \ˌish-tri-mə-ˈdu̇r-ə\. **1.** Former province, W Portugal; ✻ Lisbon; comprised S Leiría, part of Lisboa, and N Setúbal districts.

2. Region, W cen. Spain. See EXTREMADURA.

Es·tre·moz \ēsh-tri-ˈmȯsh\. Town, Évora dist., Portugal, ab. 25 mi. (40 km.) NE of the commune of Évora; pop. (1991p) 15,593; ruins of ancient castle; marble deposits; pottery; Portuguese victories over Spanish nearby 1663, 1665.

Estrondo, Serra do. See SERRA DO ESTRONDO.

Esutoru. See UGLEGORSK.

Esz·ter·gom \ˈes-tər-ˌgōm\ *or Ger.* **Gran** \ˈgrän\. City, N Hungary, on the Danube 27 mi. (43 km.) NW of Budapest; pop. (1992e) 29,705; cathedral, ancient ecclesiastical center.

Établissements français dans l'Inde. See FRENCH INDIA.

Etah. 1. \ˈē-ˌtä\. Settlement in NW Greenland, on Smith Sound N of Cape York; known as point of departure for polar exploration expeditions.

2. \ˈā-tə\. Town, W cen. Uttar Pradesh, N India, 46 mi. (74 km.) NE of Agra; pop. (1991p) 78,424.

Étampes \ā-ˈtäⁿp\. Commune, Essonne dept., N France, 30 mi. (48 km.) SSW of Paris; pop. (1990c) 21,547; dates back to early 7th cent.; scene of a council which recognized Innocent II as legitimate pope 1130.

Étang de Berre. See BERRE, ÉTANG DE.

Étang de Thau. See THAU, ÉTANG DE.

Éta·ples \ā-ˈtȧplᵊ\. Commune, Pas-de-Calais dept., N France, S of Boulogne; fishing; treaty 1492 bet. Henry VII of England and Charles VIII of France; important British base in WWI.

Etats, Pic d' \ˌpēk-dā-ˈtä\. Highest mountain in Andorra; 10,295 ft. (3138 m.).

Eta·wah \ā-ˈtä-wə\. Town, SW Uttar Pradesh, N India, 67 mi. (108 km.) ESE of Agra; pop. (1991p) 124,032; cottonmills; distribution center for grain, oilseed, ghee; has a ruined fort and several mosques incl. the Jama Masjid, adapted from a Hindu temple.

Etcho·joa \ˌe-chō-ˈhō-ä\. Municipality, Sonora state, Mexico, 120 mi. (193 km.) SE of Guaymas; pop. (1990p) 73,959.

Eten \ā-ˈten\. Seaport, NW Peru, ab. 12 mi. (19 km.) S of Chiclayo; open roadstead.

Eter·ni·ty, Cape \i-ˈtər-nə-tē\. Promontory, Quebec, Canada, on S shore of Saguenay River 39 mi. (63 km.) from its mouth; 1400 ft. (427 m.) high; forms E portal of inlet of **Eternity Bay**. See TRINITY, CAPE.

Ethi·o·pia \ˌē-thē-ˈō-pē-ə\ *also* **Ab·ys·sin·ia** \ˌa-bə-ˈsi-nē-ə, -nyə\. Independent state, E Africa, bounded on N by Eritrea,

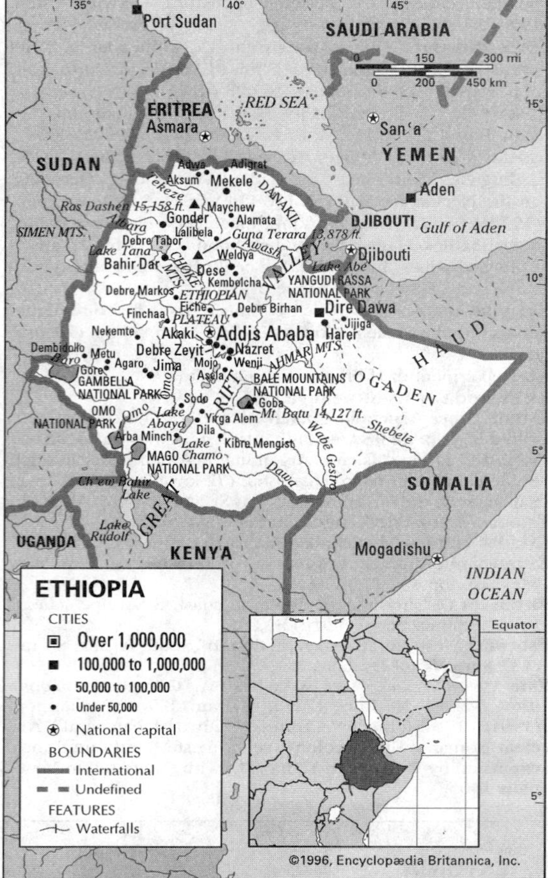

on E by Djibouti and Somalia, on S by Somalia and Kenya, and on W and NW by Sudan; 426,370 sq. mi. (1,104,298 sq. km.); pop. (1993e) 55,699,000; ✻ Addis Ababa.

Physical features: Mountainous in N, cen., and S parts with many peaks 7000 to 13,000 ft. (2134 to 3962 m.), highest point Ras Dashen in N 15,158 ft. (4620 m.); lowlands on E border include Danakil Desert in NE and the Haud in SE extending into coastal Somalia. Excessive cutting of trees for fuelwood esp. in 1970s and 1980s resulted in severe erosion and resultant food shortages.

Rivers: Main streams in N and NW the Tekeze and the Abay (Blue Nile), the outlet of Lake Tana, both tributaries of the Nile; in SW the Omo flowing S to Lake Turkana on Kenyan border; in E the Awash, rising in cen. part SE of Addis Ababa and losing itself in Danakil Desert; in SE many streams flowing SE forming headstreams of the Jubba and Shabeelle rivers in Somalia.

Chief products: Coffee, barley, corn, sorghum, sugarcane, hides, skins; potash, gold, and platinum deposits; manufactured goods include footwear and textiles; ab. 90 percent of labor force is engaged in agriculture.

Chief towns: Addis Ababa, Dire Dawa, Gonder.

History: Ancient country W of Red Sea, NE Africa, bet. ab. 24° and 10°N; included S Egypt, E Republic of the Sudan, and N (modern) Ethiopia; sometimes name referred just to the Nile Valley above Syene (Aswān), but in classical writings it referred to that part of Africa S from Egypt as far as Zanzibar; dominated by Egypt from XIth dynasty; became independent of Egypt during XXIIId dynasty; the biblical land of Cush; part of Sabaean kingdom of Aksum ruled by dynasty descended from Menelik, traditionally son of Hebrew King Solomon and Queen of Sheba; under Jewish influence until Christianized by Bishop Frumentius 4th cent. A.D.; from 675 cut off from rest of Christian world by Muslim conquest of Egypt and Nubia; after 1490 resumed contact when visited by Portuguese explorer Pero da Covilhã who was believed to have found kingdom of Prester John; Portuguese arrived 1541 to assist in expelling Muslim sultan of the Somali; center of missionary activity of Roman Catholics until their expulsion 1633; explored 1768–73 by Scotsman James Bruce who reported decayed empire restricted to region N of Blue Nile. Modern Ethiopia began with reign of Tewodros II, estab. by conquest of other chiefs 1855 and terminated by British army officer Robert Napier's expedition 1868; cut off from Red Sea by Egypt 1875–79; Aseb (*q.v.*) made Italian 1882; claimed as an Italian protectorate (through Treaty of Ucciali 1889); coastal region made separate Italian colony 1890 (see ERITREA); under Emperor Menelik II, defeated Italians at Adwa 1896; territorial integrity recognized by Great Britain, France, and Italy 1906; admitted to League of Nations 1923; promulgated first constitution 1931; after failure of League to settle an Italo-Ethiopian clash at Welwel 1934, invaded by Italy 1935; formally annexed to Italy and organized with Eritrea and Italian Somaliland as Italian East Africa (1936–41); regained independence after being liberated by British 1941; became federated with Eritrea 1952; adopted revised constitution 1955; Eritrea made a province 1962; founding member of Organization of African Unity 1963; border conflict with Somalia 1964; Emperor Haile Selassie deposed and provisional military government set up Sept. 1974; crown abolished Mar. 21, 1975; prov. of Eritrea overrun by rebels and Ogaden region invaded by Somalis 1977; Eritrean rebels and Somalis driven back 1978; experienced severe droughts and famine during the 1970s and 1980s; new constitution adopted 1987; peace accord signed with Somalia 1988; Eritrea and Tigray (*qq.v.*) taken over by rebels 1989; government overthrown and transitional government formed 1991; Eritrea officially declared an independent nation 1993.

Et·ive, Loch \'e-tiv\. Inlet of Atlantic Ocean on W coast of Scotland, extending from Firth of Lorn inland E (8.5 mi. or 14 km.) and NE (10.5 mi. or 17 km.) in Strathclyde region.

Et·na \'et-nə\. Borough, Allegheny co., SW Pennsylvania, on Allegheny River 5 mi. (8 km.) N of Pittsburgh; pop. (1990c) 4200.

Etna \'et-nə\ *also Sicilian* **Mon·gi·bel·lo** \ˌmän-jē-'be-lō\. Active volcano in NE Sicily, Italy, near the coast; 10,902 ft. (3323 m.); notably destructive eruptions 1169, 1669, and 1852.

Etna, Mount. Peak, Chaffee co., cen. Colorado; 13,800 ft. (4206 m.).

Eto·bi·coke \i-'tō-bə-ˌkōk\. City, SE Ontario, Canada, just W of Toronto; pop. (1991c) 309,993.

Eto·lin Strait \'e-tə-lin\. Passage in Bering Sea separating Nunivak I. from mainland of SW Alaska.

Eton \'ēt-^{ə}n\. Town, Buckinghamshire, SE cen. England, on the Thames opp. Windsor; Eton Coll. founded by Henry VI 1440.

Etorofu. See ITURUP.

Eto·sha Pan \ē-'tō-shə-'pan\. Large salt basin in N Namibia.

Et·o·wah \'e-tə-ˌwȯ, 'ā-, -ˌwä\. **1.** River, NW Georgia; rises in SE extremity of Tennessee, flows S across Georgia border, then W to unite with the Oostanaula near Rome in Floyd co. and form Coosa River; ab. 150 mi. (241 km.) long. **2.** County in NE Alabama. See table at ALABAMA. **3.** Town, McMinn co., SE Tennessee, 25 mi. (40 km.) NE of Cleveland; pop. (1990c) 3215.

Etowah Mound. Prehistoric earthwork, Bartow co., NW Georgia, 3 mi. (5 km.) SE of Cartersville, on Etowah River; a quadrilateral, truncated pyramid, base covers ab. 3 acres (1 hectare), top ab. 170 by 176 ft. (52 by 54 m.); 61 ft. (19 m.) high; copper plates with repoussé figures have been found in it.

Étre·tat \ˌā-trə-'tä\. Town, Seine-Maritime dept., N France, on coast N of Le Havre; resort.

Etru·ria \i-'trůr-ē-ə\. Ancient country in cen. Italy, covering region now comprising Tuscany and part of Umbria; home of Etruscans, a people of uncertain origin who established a civilization by ab. 7th cent. B.C.; their chief confederation, traditionally of 12 cities, included Veii, Florentia, and Volsinii, among others; traded extensively and built up civilization, noted for its art, at height c. 500 B.C.; at its peak Etruscan power extended into N and S Italy; gradually declined after defeat of its sea power off Cumae (*q.v.*) and absorption of its cities, one by one, by Rome (by 3d cent. B.C.); kingdom of Etruria erected by French Emperor Napoléon in 1801 incorp. in French First Empire 1808.

Etsch. See ADIGE.

Et·ten en Leur \'e-tən-ən-'lœr\. Commune, North Brabant prov., Netherlands, just W of Breda; pop. (1981e) 30,174.

Et·ter·beek \'e-tər-ˌbāk\. Commune, Brabant prov., cen. Belgium, a suburb of Brussels; pop. (1991c) 38,894.

Ett·ling·en \'et-liŋ-ən\. City, Baden-Württemberg, Germany, 6 mi. (10 km.) S of Karlsruhe; pop. (1992e) 38,082; paper, textiles. Roman foundation; city 1192; to Baden 1219.

Et·trick \'e-trik\. River, SE Scotland, flows NE through Borders region into the Tweed; 32 mi. (51 km.) long.

Ettrick Forest. Former forest and hunting ground in Borders region, SE Scotland; now converted into a pastoral region; James Hogg (1770–1835), Scottish poet, a native of the region, was known as "The Ettrick Shepherd."

Etymander. See HELMAND.

Etzina. See KHARA KHOTO.

Eu \'œ\. Commune, Seine-Maritime dept., N France, 17 mi. (27 km.) NE of Dieppe; ancient countship, supposedly descended from dukes of Normandy, which passed successively to houses of Brienne, Artois, Kleve, Lorraine-Guise, and Orléans; château begun in 16th cent., largely destroyed by fire 1902; extensive forest nearby.

EU. See EUROPEAN UNION.

'Eua \ā-'ü-ä\. Island of the Tongatapu group in S Tonga, SW Pacific Ocean, 9 mi. (14 km.) SE of Tongatapu I.; 34 sq. mi. (88 sq. km.); pop. (1986c) 4393.

Eu·boea \yů-'bē-ə\ *or* **Év·voia** \'e-vē-ä\ *also* **Ne·gro·pon·te** \ˌnā-grō-'pȯn-tā\. One of the largest islands of Greece, in the Aegean Sea; 90 mi. (145 km.) long by 4 to 30 mi. (6 to 48 km.) wide; 1411 sq. mi. (3654 sq. km.); with Northern Sporades forms a department of the Central Greece region (see table at GREECE). Separated on N from Magnesia and Achaea Phthiotis by narrow strait, on NW from Locris by the Atalante Channel, and in cen. part of W coast separated from Boeotia by narrow Evripos Strait, on which Khalkís and ruins of Aulis are situated; its mountains (highest 5718 ft. or 1743 m.) are part of the chain in Thessaly and the Cyclades; on NE coast is promontory of Artemisium and on SE Cape Caphareus. Connected with Boeotia by a bridge built by Chalcidians; dominated by Athens in 5th cent. B.C.; from 146 B.C. in Roman prov. of Macedon; to Venice 1204 but not subdued until 1366; conquered by Turks 1470; to Greece 1830. See CHALCIS and ERETRIA.

Eu·boe·an Sea \yů-'bē-ən\; *anc.* **Ma·re Eu·bo·i·cum** \'mā-rē-yů-'bō-i-kəm, 'mä-rā-\. See ATALANTE.

Eu·clid \'yü-klid\. City, Cuyahoga co., N Ohio, on Lake Erie, a NE suburb of Cleveland; pop. (1990c) 54,875; formerly notable grape culture; manufactures machinery, airplane parts, metal goods, electrical equipment; settled 1798.

Eu·do·ra \yü-'dōr-ə\. **1.** City, Chicot co., SE corner of Arkansas, 85 mi. (137 km.) E of El Dorado; pop. (1990c) 3155. **2.** City, Douglas co., Kansas; pop. (1990c) 3006.

Eu·fau·la \yů-'fȯ-lə\. **1.** City, Barbour co., SE Alabama, on Chattahoochee River 75 mi. (121 km.) SE of Montgomery; pop. (1990c) 13,220; shipping center; before 1843 known as Irwinton.

2. City, ⊗ of McIntosh co., E Oklahoma, on Canadian River 27 mi. (43 km.) NNE of McAlester; pop. (1990c) 2652.

Eu·ga·ne·an Hills \yü-ˈgā-nē-ən, ˌyü-gə-ˈnē-\ *or Ital.* **Col·li Eu·ga·nei** \ˈkȯl-lē-eu̇-ˈgä-nā-ˌē\. Range of hills, W Padova prov., Veneto, NE Italy; ab. 2000 ft. (610 m.) high.

Eu·gene \yü-ˈjēn\. City, ⊗ of Lane co., W Oregon, on Willamette River 62 mi. (100 km.) S of Salem; pop. (1990c) 112,669; lumber, food products; tourism; Univ. of Oregon (1872), Northwest Christian Coll. (1895), Lane Community Coll. (1965); settled 1851; became ⊗ 1853; incorp. as city 1862.

Eu·ge·nia, Point \yu̇-ˈjē-nyə\ *or* **Point San·ta Eugenia** \ˈsän-tä-eu̇-ˈkā-nyä\. Cape on W coast of Baja California Sur terr., Mexico, S of Sebastián Vizcaíno Bay.

Eugubium. See GUBBIO.

Eu·len·ge·bir·ge \ˈȯi-lən-gə-ˌbir-gə\. See SUDETY.

Eu·less \ˈyü-ləs\. Village, Tarrant co., N Texas, 16 mi. (26 km.) NE of Fort Worth; pop. (1990c) 38,149.

Eumolpias. See PLOVDIV 2.

Eu·nice \ˈyü-nis\. **1.** Town, St. Landry and Acadia parishes, S cen. Louisiana, 32 mi. (51 km.) NW of Lafayette; pop. (1990c) 11,162; oil nearby.

2. City, Lea co., SE corner of New Mexico, ab. 18 mi. (29 km.) S of Hobbs; pop. (1990c) 2676; oil (discovered in nearby Jal 1927); ranching; gas; founded 1909, made city 1937.

Euonymus. See PANAREA.

Eupatoria. See YEVPATORIYA.

Eu·pen \œ-ˈpen, ˈȯi-pən\. Commune, E Liège prov., E Belgium, 21 mi. (34 km.) E of the city of Liège; pop. (1991c) 17,161; cables, soap; brewing; formerly in Germany; transferred with Malmédy and Moresnet to Belgium by Treaty of Versailles 1919; in WWII taken in Allied advance Sept. 1944; with Malmédy (*q.v.*) forms **Eupen–et–Mal·mé·dy** \œ-ˈpen-ā-ˌmȧl-mā-ˈdē\ dist., 382 sq. mi. (989 sq. km.).

Eu·phra·tes \yu̇-ˈfrā-tēz\ *or Turk.* **Fı·rat Neh·ri** \fə-ˈrät-ne-ˈrē\ *or Arab.* **Al–Fu·rāt** \ˌal-fu̇-ˈrät\. River, SW Asia; formed by confluence of the Murat Nehri (Eastern Euphrates) and the Karasu (Western Euphrates, the main stream) in E Turkey; flows S and SE across NE Syria, through W and cen. Iraq to unite with the Tigris and continues, as Shatt al Arab, to Persian Gulf; 2235 mi. (3596 km.) long; has few important tributaries but in Syria on the N receives the Balīkh and the Khābūr; in middle course crosses Syrian Desert; in lower course in Iraq is used for irrigation, expands into swamps and side streams; navigable for small vessels below Hit; flow diverted by Turkey Jan.–Feb. 1990 to fill the newly created reservoir behind Ataturk Dam. Has on its banks several modern cities of importance: Erzincan (on the Karasu), Ar Raqqah, Dayr az Zawr, An Najaf, An Nāsirīyah, and ruins of many ancient cities. Its valley was extensively irrigated in ancient times and gave growth to civilizations of Babylonia, Assyria, Chaldea (see MESOPOTAMIA).

Eur·a·sia \yu̇-ˈrā-zhə, -shə\. Name given to Europe and Asia as one continent.

Euratom. See EUROPEAN ATOMIC ENERGY COMMUNITY.

Eure \ˈœr\. **1.** River, NW France; rises in Orne dept., flows N into the Seine above Rouen; 140 mi. (225 km.) long; navigable for ab. 50 mi. (80 km.).

2. Department of N France. See table at FRANCE.

Eure–et–Loir \ˌœr-ā-ˈlwär\. Department of N cen. France. See table at FRANCE.

Eu·re·ka \yu̇-ˈrē-kə\. **1.** County in cen. Nevada. See table at NEVADA.

2. City, ⊗ of Humboldt co., NW California, on Humboldt Bay 83 mi. (134 km.) S of Oregon border; pop. (1990c) 27,025; port of entry; dairy products; tourism; fisheries; redwood mills, chief redwood outlet for Pacific coast; Coll. of the Redwoods (1964); settled 1850; incorp. as city and made ⊗ 1856.

3. City, ⊗ of Woodford co., N cen. Illinois, 17 mi. (27 km.) E of Peoria; pop. (1990c) 4435; Eureka Coll. (1855).

4. City, ⊗ of Greenwood co., SE Kansas, 40 mi. (64 km.) S of Emporia; pop. (1990c) 2974.

5. Village, ⊗ of Eureka co., cen. Nevada, 42 mi. (68 km.) SSW of Ruby Lake; lead deposits; was a mining boomtown in 1870s.

6. City, McPherson co., N South Dakota, 62 mi. (100 km.) WNW of Aberdeen; pop. (1990c) 1197.

7. City, Juab co., W Utah, 30 mi. (48 km.) SW of Provo; pop. (1990c) 562; gold, silver, copper, lead, zinc deposits.

Eureka Springs. City, a ⊗ of Carroll co., NW Arkansas, 35 mi. (56 km.) NE of Fayetteville; pop. (1990c) 1900; notable for numerous medicinal springs.

Euripos. See EVRIPOS.

Euripus. See KHALKÍS.

Eu·ro·pa \yu̇-ˈrō-pə\. **1.** Small French island, S cen. Mozambique Channel, 22°20′S, 40°22′E; administratively part of Réunion.

2. Latin, German, Italian, and Spanish form of Europe (*q.v.*).

Europa Point. Southernmost tip of Gibraltar, on Strait of Gibraltar.

Eu·rope \ˈyu̇r-əp\. Continent, smallest except Australia; 3,997,929 sq. mi. (10,354,636 sq. km.); pop. (1990e) 498,000,000.

Boundaries: On N, Arctic Ocean (chief subdivisions Kara Sea, Barents Sea, White Sea); most northerly point North Cape, Norway, 71°10′20″N; chief islands: Vaygach, Novaya Zemlya, Kolguyev (Russia), Svalbard (Norway). On E, Asia, with which it is sometimes considered as one continent, Eurasia, the conventional boundary being Ural Mts. and Ural River; on SE Caspian Sea. On S, Caucasus Mts., Black Sea, and Mediterranean (chief subdivisions Aegean Sea, Ionian Sea, Adriatic Sea, Tyrrhenian Sea, Ligurian Sea); marked by Crimean, Balkan, Italian, and Iberian penins.; most southerly point Cape Tarifa, Spain, 36°01′N; chief islands: Aegean Is., Crete, Ionian Is. (Greece), Sicily, Sardinia (Italy), Corsica (France), and Balearic Is. (Spain). On W, Atlantic Ocean (chief subdivisions Bay of Biscay, North Sea, Norwegian Sea); indented on NW by Baltic Sea (subdivisions Gulf of Bothnia, Gulf of Finland) which is connected with North Sea by the Kattegat and the Skagerrak; marked by peninsulas of Jutland (Denmark) and Scandinavia; most westerly point of mainland Cape Roca, Portugal, 9°30′W, of British Isles, Dunmore Head, Ireland, 10°30′W; chief islands British Isles, with smaller groups: Shetland, Orkney, and Outer Hebrides; Faeroes (Denmark), Lofoten Is. (Norway). Chief islands of Baltic Sea: Åland Is. (Finland), Saaremaa, Hiiumaa (Estonia), Gotland, Öland (Sweden), Bornholm, Sjælland, Fyn, Falster, Lolland (Denmark), and Rügen (Germany). European mainland separated from British Isles by English Channel and Strait of Dover; from NE Africa by Strait of Gibraltar; from Turkey in Asia by Dardanelles, Sea of Marmara, and Bosporus.

Mountains: Numerous high mountain regions; Pyrenees (bet. Spain and France), Alps (Switzerland, France, Italy, Austria), Apennines (Italy), Bohemian Forest, Erzgebirge (Germany and Czech Republic), Sudetic Mts. (Poland and Czech Republic), Carpathian Mts. (Slovakia, Poland, and Romania), Kjølen Mts. (Norway and Sweden), Transylvanian Alps (Romania), Rhodope Mts., Balkan Mts. (Bulgaria), Caucasus (incl. highest point of continent, Mt. Elbrus, 18,510 ft. or 5642 m.) and Ural Mts. (Russia).

Other physical features: High plateau of Spain with several mountain ranges (Cantabrian, Sierra de Guadarrama, Sierra Nevada) and extensive level plain of much of Russia and Ukraine; lowest point is Caspian Sea (ab. 92 ft. or 28 m. below sea level).

Rivers: Volga, Don, Northern Dvina (Russia), Dnieper (Russia, Belarus, and Ukraine), Dniester (Ukraine and Moldova), Vistula (Poland), Oder, Elbe (Germany and Czech Republic), Rhine (chiefly Germany), Thames (England), Seine, Loire, Rhone (France), Ebro, Guadalquivir (Spain), Douro, Tagus (Spain and Portugal), Po, Tiber (Italy), Danube (Germany, Austria, Hungary, Yugoslavia, Romania, Bulgaria, Ukraine).

Lakes: Many small lakes in Switzerland (esp. Geneva, Neuchâtel, Zürich); Constance (Switzerland and Germany), Balaton (Hungary), Como, Garda, Maggiore (Italy), Scutari

(Yugoslavia and Albania), Vänern, Vättern, Mälaren (Sweden), numerous lakes in Finland, and the large lakes of Ladoga, Onega, and Peipus (Estonia and Russia).

Political divisions: Albania, Andorra, Austria, Belarus, Belgium, Bosnia and Herzegovina, Bulgaria, Croatia, Czech Republic, Denmark, Estonia, Finland, France, Germany, Gibraltar, Greece, Hungary, Iceland, Ireland, Italy, Latvia, Liechtenstein, Lithuania, Luxembourg, Macedonia, Malta, Moldova, Monaco, Netherlands, Norway, Poland, Portugal, Romania, Russia (part), San Marino, Slovakia, Slovenia, Spain, Sweden, Switzerland, Turkey (part), Ukraine, United Kingdom, Vatican City, and Yugoslavia. See EUROPEAN ECONOMIC COMMUNITY, EUROPEAN FREE TRADE ASSOCIATION, and WARSAW TREATY ORGANIZATION.

European Atomic Energy Community *or frequently* **Eur·at·om** \yu̇-ˈra-təm\. Scientific-economic organization; purpose is to promote and regulate nonmilitary European nuclear research; formed 1958.

European Coal and Steel Community. Economic organization; purpose is to promote cooperation in the area of heavy industry; formed by treaty ratified 1952.

European Community *or* **European Communities;** *abbr.* **EC.** See EUROPEAN UNION.

European Economic Community *or frequently* **Common Market;** *abbr.* **EEC.** Economic organization; purpose is to promote economic cooperation among the members; formed 1957; has created free movement of labor among members and, 1968, customs union with common external tariff.

European Free Trade Association; *abbr.* **EFTA.** Economic community, consisting of Austria, Finland, Iceland, Liechtenstein, Norway, Sweden, Switzerland; headquarters Geneva, Switzerland; formed 1960; eliminated industrial import duties 1966; founding members Denmark, United Kingdom, and Portugal withdrew upon entry into the European Community.

European Union; *formerly* **European Communities** *or* **European Community;** *abbr.* **EU.** Political and economic organization comprising the European Atomic Energy Community, the European Coal and Steel Community, and the European Economic Community; consists of France, Germany, Italy, Belgium, Netherlands, Luxembourg, which joined together (in the European Coal and Steel Community) 1951, Denmark, Ireland, the United Kingdom, which were admitted in 1973, Greece, which was admitted in 1981, Portugal and Spain, which were admitted in 1986, and Austria, Finland, and Sweden which were admitted in 1995; headquarters Brussels, Belgium; Norwegian voters rejected membership 1972; Greenland voters rejected membership (as part of Denmark) 1982 leading to Greenland's withdrawal 1985; name changed to European Union 1993; Norwegian voters again rejected membership 1994.

Europos, Dura–. See DURA-EUROPOS.

Europus. See RHAGAE.

Euros. See EVROS.

Eu·ro·tas \yu̇-ˈrō-təs\ *or Gk.* **Ev·ró·tas** \e-ˈvrō-täs\; *formerly* **Iri** \ˈēr-ē\. River, S Peloponnese, Greece, flowing S into Gulf of Laconia; ab. 60 mi. (97 km.) long; ancient Sparta was on it.

Eu·rym·e·don \yu̇-ˈri-mə-ˌdän\. Ancient name of a small river in S Asia Minor; scene of battle 466 B.C. in which the Greek leader Cimon defeated the Persians.

Eu·ry·ta·nia \ˌyu̇r-ə-ˈtā-nē-ə\. Department of Greece. See table at GREECE.

Eus·kir·chen \ˈȯis-ˌkir-kən\. City, North Rhine-Westphalia, Germany, 20 mi. (32 km.) SSW of Cologne; pop. (1992e) 50,084; received city rights 1302.

Eus·tis \ˈyü-stis\. City, Lake co., cen. Florida, on **Lake Eustis** 30 mi. (48 km.) NW of Orlando; pop. (1990c) 12,967.

Eu·taw \ˈyü-ˌtȯ\. City, ⊗ of Greene co., W Alabama; pop. (1990c) 2281.

Eutaw Springs. Locality on **Eutaw Creek**, a tributary of the Santee River, in Berkeley co., South Carolina, ab. 45 mi. (72 km.) N of Charleston; scene of battle in Revolutionary War Sept. 8, 1781, last important conflict in South Carolina, its results more favorable to Americans.

Eu·tin \ȯi-ˈtēn\. Commune, Schleswig-Holstein, Germany, ab. 20 mi. (32 km.) N of Lübeck; pop. (1992e) 16,845; agricultural college; founded c. 1143.

Eut·suk Lake \ˈüt-sək\. Lake in W cen. British Columbia, Canada; 96 sq. mi. (249 sq. km.); drains E through Nechako River; largest lake in Tweedsmuir (Provincial) Park.

Euxine Sea. See BLACK SEA.

Evan·ge·line \i-ˈvan-jə-ˌlēn\. Parish in S cen. Louisiana. See table at LOUISIANA.

Ev·ans \ˈe-vənz\. **1.** County in SE cen. Georgia. See table at GEORGIA.

2. Town, Weld co., N Colorado, 4 mi. (6 km.) S of Greeley; pop. (1990c) 5877.

Evans, Mount. 1. Peak, Clear Creek co., N cen. Colorado; 14,264 ft. (4348 m.); on its crest is a scientific laboratory of Univ. of Denver, built 1936; jointly sponsored 1948 with four other universities as the Inter-University High-Altitude Laboratory; road to summit.

2. Peak, Park and Lake cos., cen. Colorado; 13,580 ft. (4139 m.).

Ev·ans·dale \ˈe-vənz-ˌdāl\. Town, Black Hawk co., NE cen. Iowa, SE of Waterloo; pop. (1990c) 4638.

Ev·ans·ton \ˈe-vən-stən\. **1.** City, Cook co., NE Illinois, on Lake Michigan, N of Chicago; pop. (1990c) 73,233; Northwestern Univ. (1851), Garrett-Evangelical Theological Seminary (1853), National-Louis Univ. (1886), Seabury-Western Theological Seminary (1933), Kendall Coll. (1934); lighthouse.

2. Town, ⊗ of Uinta co., SW corner of Wyoming, on Bear River 5 mi. (8 km.) E of Utah border; pop. (1990c) 10,903; coal, iron, and petroleum deposits.

Ev·ans·ville \ˈe-vənz-ˌvil\. **1.** City, ⊗ of Vanderburgh co., SW Indiana, on Ohio River 29 mi. (47 km.) ENE of confluence with Wabash River; pop. (1990c) 126,272; 3d largest city in the state; aluminum, air-conditioning equipment, pharmaceuticals, refrigerators, plastics; Univ. of Evansville (1854), Univ. of Southern Indiana (1965).

2. City, Rock co., S Wisconsin, 15 mi. (24 km.) WNW of Janesville; pop. (1990c) 3174; settled 1839.

Ev·e·leth \ˈe-və-ləth\. City, St. Louis co., NE Minnesota, 5 mi. (8 km.) S of Virginia; pop. (1990c) 4064; iron ore nearby; site of U.S. Hockey Hall of Fame.

Even·ki Autonomous Okrug \e-ˈveŋ-kē ... ˈȯ-ˌkrük\ *also* **Even·kiy·skiy Autonomous Okrug** \e-ˈveŋ-kē-skʸē\. Administrative district in E part of Krasnoyarsk Kray, cen. Russia in Asia; 296,370 sq. mi. (767,598 sq. km.); pop. (1992e) 25,000; ✱ Tura; in N cen. Siberia, crossed by the Lower (Nizhnyaya) Tunguska River; graphite, coal; timber; formed 1930; inhabited by Evenkis, a people of Mongol origin.

Ev·er·ard, Lake \ˈe-və-ˌrärd\. Lake, S South Australia, Australia, W of Lake Gairdner.

Eve·re \ˈā-və-rə\. Commune, Brabant prov., cen. Belgium, NE of Brussels; pop. (1991c) 13,443.

Ev·er·est, Mount \ˈe-vrəst, -və-rəst\ *or Tibetan* **Cho·mo·lung·ma** \ˌchō-mō-ˈlu̇ŋ-mə\. Highest mountain in the world, in the Himalayas bet. Nepal and Tibet, China, at 27°59′N, 86°56′E; 29,028 ft. (8848 m.); scene of numerous climbing attempts 1921–52; summit first photographed from airplane 1933 and first reached May 29, 1953 by New Zealander Edmund Hillary, Nepalese Tenzing Norgay, and other members of a British-led expedition; summit first reached via east face, 1983.

Ev·er·ett \ˈe-vrət, -və-rət\. **1.** City, Middlesex co., NE Massachusetts, N of Boston; pop. (1990c) 35,701; petroleum storage; manufactures metal goods, paper products, chemicals, truck bodies, foundry products.

2. Borough, Bedford co., S Pennsylvania, 28 mi. (45 km.) S of Altoona; pop. (1990c) 1777; coal deposits.

EUROPE
CITIES
National capital
Country capital
BOUNDARIES
International
FEATURES
Canals
Dams
Glaciers
ARCTIC
ICELAND
Reykjavík
Fontur Point
Vatna Glacier
Hvannadalshnúkur 6,952 ft.
Arctic Circle
NORWEGIAN SEA
LOFOTEN ISLANDS
KOLEN MOUNTAINS
Lake Hornavan
FAROE ISLANDS (DEN.)
NORWAY
SWEDEN
Galdhopiggen 8,100 ft.
JOTUNHEIM MTS.
SHETLAND ISLANDS (U.K.)
ORKNEY ISLANDS
HEBRIDES
HARDANGER PLATEAU
Oslo
Lake Vänern
Stockholm
UNITED KINGDOM
Ben Nevis 4,406 ft.
Buchan Ness
SCOTLAND
Lindesnes Cape
Skagerrak
Kattegat
Lake Vättern
SMÅLAND HIGHLANDS
Donegal Bay
NORTHERN IRELAND
Edinburgh
SOUTHERN UPLANDS
NORTH SEA
Belfast
JUTLAND
DENMARK
Copenhagen
BALTIC
Shannon
Dublin
IRISH SEA
ISLE OF MAN
PENNINE CHAIN
IRELAND
Dursey Head
NORTH FRISIAN ISLANDS
EAST FRISIAN ISLANDS
BORNHOLM (DEN.)
CELTIC SEA
St. George's Channel
WALES
ENGLAND
Cardiff
NETHERLANDS
ATLANTIC OCEAN
London
Amsterdam
Thames
Land's End
Strait of Dover
PLAIN
Elbe
Berlin
Warta
HARZ MTS.
Oder
English Channel
Brussels
CHANNEL ISLANDS (U.K.)
BELGIUM
GERMANY
EUROPEAN
ARDENNES
Rhine
Seine
BRITTANY
LUXEMBOURG
Luxembourg
Saar
Ohře
Elbe
Prague
Paris
CZECH REPUBLIC
Loire
Meuse
BOHEMIAN FOREST
VOSGES MTS.
BLACK FOREST
Danube
FRANCE
Bay of Biscay
Lake Constance
Inn
Bratislava
JURA MTS.
Bern
LIECHTENSTEIN
Vienna
LITTLE ALFOLD
Cape Finisterre
MASSIF CENTRAL
Lake Geneva
SWITZERLAND
Vaduz
ALPS
AUSTRIA
HUNG
Mont Blanc 15,771 ft.
Matterhorn 14,691 ft.
Drava
Lake Balaton
CANTABRIAN MTS.
AQUITAINE BASIN
Ljubljana
Lake Garda
Adige
JULIAN ALPS
Zagreb
SLOVENIA
CROATIA
Douro
IBERIAN CORDILLERA
PYRENEES
Pico Aneto 11,168 ft.
CÉVENNES
Rhône
Po
Gulf of Venice
MESETA CENTRAL
Duero
IBERIAN
ANDORRA
Andorra la Vella
Monaco
MONACO
Gulf of Genoa
BOSNIA AND HERZEGOVINA
Sarajevo
DINARIC ALPS
PORTUGAL
San Marino
SAN MARINO
Ebro
Gulf of Lion
APENNINES
Madrid
LIGURIAN SEA
Arno
Lisbon
Tagus
SPAIN
CORSICA (FR.)
ITALY
Tiber
ADRIATIC SEA
Guadiana
PENINSULA
Monte Corno 9,560 ft
Mont L'Incudine 7,008 ft.
VATICAN CITY
Rome
SIERRA MORENA
Gulf of Valencia
BALEARIC ISLANDS
Cape Saint Vincent
Guadalquivir
Vesuvius 4,189 ft.
SARDINIA (IT.)
TYRRHENIAN SEA
SALENTINA PENINSULA
Gulf of Cadiz
Mount Marmara 6,016 ft.
Gulf of Taranto
SIERRA NEVADA
Mulhacén Peak 11,407 ft.
Strait of Gibraltar
GIBRALTAR (U.K.)
MEDITERRANEAN SEA
IONIAN
Etna 10,902 ft.
SICILY
MALTA
Valletta

OCEAN
BARENTS SEA
KOLGUYEV ISLAND
KANIN PENINSULA
TIMAN RIDGE
URAL MOUNTAINS
Mount Narodnaya 6,214 ft.
FINNMARK PLATEAU
Lake Inari
KOLA PENINSULA
Kebnekaise Peak 6,965 ft.
LAPLAND
WHITE SEA
POHJANMAA LOWLAND
Gulf of Bothnia
Northern Dvina
FINLAND
Lake Saimaa
Lake Onega
Sukhona
Vyatka
Kama Reservoir
Lake Päijänne
Lake Ladoga
ÅLAND ISLANDS
Helsinki
Gulf of Finland
Rybinsk Reservoir
Kama
Ural
Tallinn
ESTONIA
Lake Peipus
VALDAI HILLS
Gorky Reservoir
Volga
Kuybyshev Reservoir
SAAREMAA
GOTLAND
Gulf of Riga
LATVIA
Riga
Moscow
RUSSIA
Oka
VOLGA HILLS
SEA
EUROPEAN PLAIN
Western Dvina
CENTRAL RUSSIAN UPLAND
LITHUANIA
Dnieper
RUSSIA
Vilnius
Minsk
BELORUSSIAN RIDGE
Neman
BELARUS
Vistula
Bug
Polesye Marshlands
Warsaw
LAND
Don
Volgograd Reservoir
DONETS BASIN
Kiev
Tsimlyansk Reservoir
Gerlachovsky Peak 8,711 ft.
UKRAINE
Kremenchuk Reservoir
CARPATHIAN MOUNTAINS
Southern Bug
AZOV UPLAND
OVAKIA
Kakhovka Reservoir
KUMA-MANYCH DEPRESSION
Dniester
MOLDOVA
Chişinău
Budapest
SEA OF AZOV
STAVRAPOL UPLAND
ARY
GREAT ALFOLD
Prut
Siretul
CASPIAN SEA
ROMANIA
CRIMEAN PENINSULA
Tisza
TRANSYLVANIAN ALPS
CAUCASUS
Danube
Bucharest
Belgrade
Olt
BLACK SEA
YUGOSLAVIA
BALKAN MOUNTAINS
Sofia
BULGARIA
Scopje
RHODOPE MTS.
MACEDONIA
TURKEY
Bosporus
Tirane
ALBANIA
PINDUS MTS.
CORFU
SEA
GREECE
AEGEAN SEA
Athens
0 150 300 mi
0 200 400 km
PELOPONNESE
RHODES
CYPRUS
Nicosia
CRETE
©1996, Encyclopædia Britannica, Inc.

3. City and seaport, ⊗ of Snohomish co., NW cen. Washington, on Puget Sound at mouth of Snohomish River 28 mi. (45 km.) N of Seattle; pop. (1990c) 69,961; aircraft; lumbering center; fisheries; Everett Community Coll. (1941).

Everett, Mount. Peak, Berkshire co., SW corner of Massachusetts; 2624 ft. (800 m.).

Ev·er·glades, The \ˈe-vər-ˌglādz\. A vast tract of marshland in Palm Beach, Broward, Miami-Dade, Monroe, and Collier cos., S Florida, lying S of Lake Okeechobee; ab. 40 mi. (64 km.) wide; large area has been reclaimed by drainage canals with locks and levees; the S part has been set aside as **Everglades National Park** (see UNITED STATES, *National Parks*).

Ev·er·green \ˈe-vər-ˌgrēn\. City, ⊗ of Conecuh co., S Alabama, 80 mi. (129 km.) NE of Mobile Bay; pop. (1990c) 3911.

Evergreen Park. Village, Cook co., NE Illinois, surrounded on three sides by SW Chicago; pop. (1990c) 20,874.

Ev·er·man \ˈe-vər-mən\. Village, Tarrant co., N Texas, bordering on S Fort Worth; pop. (1990c) 5672.

Ev·ers·ley \ˈe-vərz-lē\. Village, NE Hampshire, S England, NW of Aldershot; residence of clergyman and novelist Charles Kingsley.

Eve·sham \ˈēv-shəm\. Town, Hereford and Worcester, W cen. England, on the Avon 27 mi. (43 km.) S of Birmingham; pop. (1981p) 15,271; trade center in section raising fruit and vegetables; scene of battle Aug. 4, 1265 in which English soldier and statesman Simon de Montfort was defeated and killed by royalist forces.

Évian–les–Bains \ā-ˈvyäⁿ-le-ˈbeⁿ\; *sometimes shortened to* **Évian** \ā-ˈvyäⁿ\. Commune, Haute-Savoie dept., E France, on S shore of Lake Geneva; pop. (1990c) 7027; fashionable health resort.

Évo·ra \ˈe-vu̇-rə\. **1.** District of SE cen. Portugal. See table at PORTUGAL.

2. *anc.* **Eb·o·ra** \ˈe-bō-rə\ *or* **Lib·er·al·i·tas Ju·li·a** \ˌli-bə-ˈra-lə-ˌtas-ˈjül-yə\. Commune, its ✻, 68 mi. (109 km.) E by S of Lisbon; munic. pop. (1990c) 34,851; manufactures cotton, cloth; iron founding; 12th–13th cent. cathedral; Roman temple of Diana; archiepiscopal see. Captured by Roman Gen. Quintus Sertorius 80 B.C., by Moors c. 712 A.D., by Portuguese 1166; residence of Portuguese court 15th and 16th cents.

Evpatoria. See YEVPATORIYA.

Évreux \ā-ˈvrœ\; *anc.* **Civ·i·tas Ebu·ro·vi·cum** \ˈsi-vi-ˌtas-i-ˌbyu̇r-ō-ˈvī-kəm\. Commune, ✻ of Eure dept., N France, 55 mi. (88 km.) WNW of Paris; pop. (1990c) 51,452; metal and rubber products; one of oldest towns in France; ancient Norman church; 11th–18th cent. cathedral; Roman ruins nearby. Pillaged by Normans 892; taken and burned by Henry I of England 1119; captured by Philip Augustus of France 1194, 1199; alternated bet. English and French control in 15th cent.

Ev·ri·pos \ˈe-vrē-ˌpös\ *also* **Eu·ri·pos** \yu̇-ˈrī-pəs\ *or* **Egripos** \ˈe-gri-pəs\. Narrow strait bet. cen. part of W Euboea I. and the mainland of Greece, S of Atalante Channel; the tidal current flows through it violently.

Év·ros \ˈe-ˌvrȯs\. **1.** River, SE Europe. See MARITSA.

2. *or* **Eu·ros** \ˈyu̇r-ˌȯs\ *or mod. Gk.* **He·bras** *or* **He·vros** \ˈe-ˌvrös\. Department of Greece. See table at GREECE.

Evrótas. See EUROTAS.

Évry \ā-ˈvrē\. Town, ✻ of Essonne dept., N France, ab. 15 mi. (24 km.) S of Paris; pop. (1990c) 45,854.

Ev·ry·khou \ˌe-vrē-ˈkü\. Village, W cen. Cyprus; former terminus of railroad line from Famagusta.

Evstrátios, Áyios *or* **Evstrátios, Hagios.** See HAGIOS EVSTRÁTIOS.

Evstrátios, Hagios. See HAGIOS EVSTRÁTIOS.

Évvoia. See EUBOEA.

Ewa Beach \ˈā-vä, -wä\. Unincorporated settlement, Honolulu co., Hawaii, 10 mi. (16 km.) W of the city of Honolulu; pop. (1990c) 14,315.

Ewab Islands. See KAI ISLANDS.

Ewaso Ng'iro *or* **Ewaso Nyiro.** See NG'IRO, EWASO.

Ewau·na, Lake \i-ˈwȯ-nə\. Small lake, SW Klamath co., S Oregon, just S of Upper Klamath Lake; source of Klamath River.

Ewe, Loch \ˈyü\. Inlet of the Atlantic Ocean on coast of Highland region, N Scotland; 10 mi. (16 km.) long; connected with Loch Maree by Ewe River, 3 mi. (5 km.) long.

Ewe·land \ˈā-wā-ˌland\. Region extending ab. 80 mi. (129 km.) along coast of W Africa, bet. mouth of Volta River and Grand Popo at mouth of the Mono; ab. 10,000 sq. mi. (25,900 sq. km.); inhabited by the Ewe people; part of former Slave Coast.

Ew·ing \ˈyü-iŋ\. Township, Mercer co., W cen. New Jersey, NNW of Trenton; pop. (1990c) 34,185.

Ex·cel·si·or Mountain \ik-ˈsel-sē-ər\. Peak in the Sierra Nevada, in Mono co., E California; 12,446 ft. (3794 m.).

Excelsior Mountains. Mountain range in Mineral co., SW Nevada; highest Pilot Peak ab. 9187 ft. (2800 m.).

Excelsior Springs. City, Clay co., NW Missouri, 25 mi. (40 km.) NE of Kansas City; pop. (1990c) 10,354; plastics; mineral springs; resort.

Exe \ˈeks\. River, SW England; rises in NW Somerset, flows S past Tiverton and Exeter into English Channel at Exmouth; 55 mi. (88 km.) long.

Ex·e·ter \ˈek-sə-tər\. **1.** City, Tulare co., S cen. California, 45 mi. (72 km.) SE of Fresno; pop. (1990c) 7276.

2. Town, ⊗ of Rockingham co., SE New Hampshire, 12 mi. (19 km.) WSW of Portsmouth; pop. (1990c) 12,481; settled and incorp. 1638; ✻ of New Hampshire in Revolutionary days 1775 ff.; Phillips Exeter Academy (estab. 1781, opened 1783).

3. Borough, Luzerne co., E Pennsylvania, on Susquehanna River 9 mi. (14 km.) W of Scranton; pop. (1990c) 5691; coal deposits.

4. Town, Washington co., S Rhode Island, 13 mi. (21 km.) WNW of Newport; pop. (1990c) 5461; formerly part of North Kingstown.

5. Village, Huron co., SE Ontario, Canada, 27 mi. (43 km.) W of Stratford; pop. (1991c) 4338.

6. *anc.* **Is·ca Dum·no·ni·o·rum** \ˈis-kə-dəm-ˌnō-nē-ˈōr-əm\. City and county borough, ⊗ of Devon, SW England, on the Exe River 37 mi. (60 km.) NE of Plymouth; pop. (1991p) 101,100; has cathedral housing the Exeter Book, the largest collection of Old English poetry; railroad center; agricultural center; shipping (city connected with tidal estuary of the Exe by a ship canal); Univ. of Exeter (1955). Probably a trading center and fort existed here even before Roman times; a center of resistance of Britons to Anglo-Saxon invasion; withstood Danish attack 1001, but captured by Danish King Sweyn I 1003; capitulated to William the Conqueror, first Norman king of England, 1068; Royalist stronghold in Civil War 1642–46; in WWII site of largest U.S. Navy supply depot in England.

Ex·moor \ˈeks-ˌmu̇r, -ˌsmōr\. Tract of moorland in Somerset and Devon, SW England; 32 sq. mi. (83 sq. km.); highest point 1707 ft. (520 m.); contains **Exmoor National Park** estab. 1954; 265 sq. mi. (686 sq. km.).

Ex·mouth \ˈeks-ˌmau̇th\. Resort town, Devon, SW England, on English Channel at mouth of the Exe, 10 mi. (16 km.) SSE of Exeter; pop. (1981p) 28,787; fishing and yachting.

Exmouth Gulf. Inlet of Indian Ocean, W Western Australia, bet. 21° and 23°S; North West Cape is its NW point.

Exmouth Peninsula. Peninsula extending S from SW coast of Chile, E of Wellington I.

Ex·ploits \ˈek-ˌsplȯits\. River, Newfoundland, Canada; flows NE through Red Indian Lake into Notre Dame Bay; 153 mi. (246 km.) long.

Ex·plor·ing Isles \ik-ˈsplōr-iŋ\. Island group, N end of Lau group, E Fiji, SW Pacific Ocean, 17°15′S, 178°52′W; ab. 10 islands, largest Vanua Mbalavu.

Ex·port \ˈek-spōrt\. Borough, Westmoreland co., SW Pennsylvania, 20 mi. (32 km.) E of Pittsburgh; pop. (1990c) 981; coal deposits.

Ex·tre·ma·du·ra \ˌes-trā-mä-ˈt͟hü-rä\ *also* **Es·tre·ma·du·ra** \ˌes-\. Region, W cen. Spain; bounded on N by León, E by New Castile, S by Andalusia, W by Portugal; comprises an autonomous community (✱ Mérida) consisting of the modern provs. of Cáceres and Badajoz; tableland; watered by Tagus and Guadiana rivers; raises sheep and swine, large forests in N portion, agricultural land in S; deposits of silver, coal, copper. See table at SPAIN.

Ex·u·ma \ik-ˈsü-mə, ig-ˈzü-\. Island group of Bahamas, in Atlantic Ocean SE of New Providence I.; 130 sq. mi. (337 sq. km.); pop. (1980c) 3672; consists of **Great Exuma, Little Exuma,** and adjacent cays.

Exuma Sound. Body of water in Bahamas, SE of New Providence and Eleuthera islands and W of Cat I.

Eya·si, Lake \ā-ˈyä-sē\. Lake, N Tanzania; 45 mi. (72 km.) long and 10 mi. (16 km.) wide; fossils of Africanthropus hominids found nearby 1935.

Eye \ˈī\. Peninsula extending into North Minch on NE coast of island of Lewis with Harris, Outer Hebrides, off NW coast of Scotland.

Ey·ja Fjord \ˈä-yä\. Inlet of Arctic Ocean on N coast of Iceland, E of Skaga Fjord.

Eylau, Deutsch–. See IŁAWA.

Eylau, Preussisch *or* **Eylau.** See BAGRATIONOVSK.

Eyn·sham \ˈen-shəm, ˈān-\ *or* **En·sham** \ˈen-\. Parish and village, Oxfordshire, cen. England, 7.5 mi. (12 km.) NW of Oxford; few remains of ancient Benedictine abbey of which Ælfric Grammaticus was first abbot (1005).

Ey·rar·bak·ki \ˈā-ˌrär-ˌbäk-kē\. Village, SW coast of Iceland, ab. 32 mi. (51 km.) SE of Reykjavík.

Eyre, Lake \ˈar\. Salt lake, NE South Australia, Australia; comprised of two sections, **Lake Eyre North** and the smaller **Lake Eyre South;** total area 3600 sq. mi. (9324 sq. km.); max. depth 4 ft. (1 m.); largest salt lake in Australia; contains lowest point in Australia; 52 ft. (16 m.) below sea level.

Eyre Peninsula. Large peninsula, S South Australia, Australia, W of Spencer Gulf; ab. 200 mi. (322 km.) long.

Ey·zies, Les \ˌlā-zā-ˈzē\ *or in full* **Les Eyzies–de–Ta·yac** \-də-tī-ˈäk\. Commune, Dordogne dept., SW cen. France, ab. 22 mi. (35 km.) SE of Périgueux on the Vézère; region containing many caves, notably **Cro–Ma·gnon** \ˌkrō-mä-ˈnyōⁿ\, where type specimens of the Cro-Magnon race dating from the Aurignacian period were found 1868, and **Les Com·ba·relles** \ˌkōⁿ-bə-ˈrel\ and **Font–de–Gaume** \ˌfōⁿ-də-ˈgōm\ discovered 1901, decorated with Paleolithic paintings and engravings. See also LE MOUSTIER and LA MADELEINE 1.

Ezan, Cape. See ESAN, CAPE.

Ezi·on–ge·ber \ˌē-zē-ən-ˈgē-bər\. Ancient town, now an archaeological site, near Aqaba at head of Gulf of Aqaba, SW corner of Jordan; place where Solomon, king of Israel, built a navy (*1 Kings* ix. 26); came under control of Edomites in middle of 8th cent. B.C.

Ezo. See HOKKAIDŌ.

Ez·ra Church \ˈez-rə\. Site in SW Atlanta, Georgia, of battle July 28, 1864 in which Confederates tried unsuccessfully to check Gen. William T. Sherman's advance.

Ez Zuetina. See QARYAT AZ ZUWAYTĪNAH.

F

Fa·bri·a·no \ˌfä-brē-ˈä-nō\. Commune, Ancona prov., Marche, cen. Italy, 38 mi. (61 km.) SW of the seaport of Ancona; pop. (1989c) 28,588; paper manufacture and electrical appliances; sulfur springs.

Fa·ca·ta·ti·vá \ˌfä-kä-ˌtä-tē-ˈvä\. City, Cundinamarca dept., cen. Colombia, 25 mi. (40 km.) NW of Bogotá; alt. 8270 ft. (2521 m.).

Fachan. See FOSHAN.

Fad·de·yev·ski \fə-ˈdā-əf-skē\. One of New Siberian Is. (*q.v.*).

Fæmund. See FEMUND.

Fa·en·za \fä-ˈen-zä, -ˈent-sä\; *anc.* **Fa·ven·tia** \fə-ˈven-chə, -chē-ə\. Commune, Ravenna prov., Emilia-Romagna, N Italy, 19 mi. (31 km.) SW of the commune of Ravenna; pop. (1989c) 54,118; medieval palace; early Renaissance cathedral; iron and salt springs; pottery center; International Museum of Ceramics. Scene of victory of the Ostrogoths over the Byzantines c. 542 A.D.; became famous in 15th and 16th cents. for its manufacture of Faenza ware and faïence (both named for the town); in Papal States 16th–19th cents.; suffered damage during WWII.

Faer·oe Islands *or* **Far·oe Islands** \ˈfar-ō\ *or Dan.* **Fær·ø·er·ne** \fa-ˈroe-ər-nə\. Island group in Atlantic Ocean N of British Isles, ab. 200 mi. (322 km.) NW of Shetland Is.; 540 sq. mi. (1399 sq. km.); pop. (1989e) 47,653; comprised of 17 inhabited islands and a few that are uninhabited, largest Strømø; constitute a self-governing unit within the Danish realm; ✻ Tórshavn; islands generally hilly and precipitous; highest point 2894 ft. (882 m.); fishing and sheep raising. Settled by Irish monks c. 7th cent.; colonized by Norsemen c. 8th cent.; ruled by Norway from 11th cent.; passed to Denmark 1380; inhabitants, of Norse descent, are represented in Danish parliament; unsuccessfully sought independence 1946; received self-government 1948.

Faesulae. See FIESOLE.

Fa·e·te, Mon·te \ˈmȯn-tā-fä-ˈā-tā\. Mountain, Italy, S of Rome; 3136 ft. (956 m.); taken by American forces just before capture of Rome June 1944.

Fă·gă·raş \fə-gə-ˈräsh\. Town, Braşov co., N cen. Romania, on Olt River NW of the city of Braşov; pop. (1989c) 45,426; fertilizers, plastic goods.

Fa·ga·to·go \ˌfäŋ-gä-ˈtōŋ-gō\. Village on Pago Pago Harbor, Tutuila Is., American Samoa.

Fa·ger·sta \ˈfä-gər-ˌstä\. Town, Västmanland prov., E cen. Sweden, 37 mi. (60 km.) N of Västerås; pop. (1980p) 15,121; manufactures pig iron.

Fa·gui·bine, Lake \ˌfä-gē-ˈbēn\ *or* **Lake Fa·gi·bi·ni** \ˌfä-gē-ˈbē-nē\. Lake, Mali, W of Tombouctou and N of Niger River; ab. 70 mi. (113 km.) long.

Fahlun. See FALUN.

Fa·ial *also* **Fa·yal** \fä-ˈyäl\. Westernmost island of cen. group of the Azores, W of Pico I.; 38°34′N, 28°42′W; 66 sq. mi. (171 sq. km.); pop. (1991p) 15,155; chief town, Horta; settled by Flemish late 15th cent.

Fa·ïd Pass \ˌfa-ˈēd\. Mountain pass, N Tunisia, E of Sbeïtla and on highway to Sfax; scene of Allied defeat by Germans under Field Marshall Erwin Rommel Feb. 14, 1943; retaken in April.

Faifo. See HOI AN.

Fails·worth \ˈfālz-ˌwərth\. Town, Greater Manchester, NW England, 5 mi. (8 km.) NE of Manchester; pop. (1981p) 21,751.

Fair·banks \ˈfar-ˌbaŋks\. Town, cen. Alaska, at junction of Tanana and Chena rivers; pop. (1990c) 30,843; alt. 448 ft. (137 m.); chief town of cen. Alaska; port of entry; terminus of railroad to Seward and of Alaska Highway; Univ. of Alaska, Fairbanks (1917) at suburban village of College (ab. 2 mi. or 3 km. W); gold deposits, lumber; the trans–Alaska oil pipeline is nearby. Founded 1902 as result of a gold rush.

Fairbanks North Star. Division in Alaska. See table at ALASKA.

Fair·born \ˈfar-ˌbȯrn\. City, Greene co., SW Ohio, NE of Dayton; pop. (1990c) 31,300; formed 1950 by consolidation of former villages of Fairfield and Osborn.

Fair·burn \ˈfar-bərn\. City, Fulton co., NW cen. Georgia, 18 mi. (29 km.) SW of Atlanta; pop. (1990c) 4013.

Fair·bury \ˈfar-ˌber-ē\. **1.** City, Livingston co., NE cen. Illinois, 33 mi. (53 km.) NE of Bloomington; pop. (1990c) 3643.
2. City, ⊗ of Jefferson co., SE Nebraska; pop. (1990c) 4335.

Fair·fax \ˈfar-ˌfaks\. **1.** County in NE Virginia. See table at VIRGINIA.
2. Town, Marin co., W California, 15 mi. (24 km.) NW of San Francisco; pop. (1990c) 6931.
3. Town, Osage co., N Oklahoma, 25 mi. (40 km.) ESE of Ponca City; pop. (1990c) 1749; oil.
4. City, ⊗ of Fairfax co., but politically independent, NE Virginia; 6 sq. mi. (16 sq. km.); pop. (1990c) 19,622; George Mason Univ. (1957).

Fair·field \ˈfar-ˌfēld\. **1.** Name of counties in three states of the U.S. See tables at CONNECTICUT, OHIO, SOUTH CAROLINA.
2. City, Jefferson co., cen. Alabama, 5 mi. (8 km.) W of Birmingham; pop. (1990c) 12,200; Miles Coll. (1905); founded 1910; planned city, laid out by U.S. Steel Corp. (see also GARY); once known as Corey.
3. City, ⊗ of Solano co., cen. California, 40 mi. (64 km.) SW of Sacramento; pop. (1990c) 77,211; textiles; wine, livestock, fruit; Travis Air Force Base.
4. Town, SE Fairfield co., SW Connecticut, on Long Island Sound; pop. (1990c) 53,418; Bridgeport Engineering Institute (1924), Fairfield Univ. (1942), Sacred Heart Univ. (1963); port of entry; settled 1639; burned by British during Revolutionary War.
5. City, ⊗ of Camas co., S cen. Idaho; pop. (1990c) 371.
6. City, ⊗ of Wayne co., SE Illinois, 30 mi. (48 km.) E of Mount Vernon; pop. (1990c) 5439.
7. City, ⊗ of Jefferson co., SE Iowa, 24 mi. (39 km.) E of Ottumwa; pop. (1990c) 9768.
8. Town, Somerset co., W Maine, on Kennebec River 4 mi. (6 km.) N of Waterville; pop. (1990c) 6718.
9. Township, Essex co., NE New Jersey, 6 mi. (10 km.) SSW of Paterson; pop. (1990c) 7615.
10. City, Butler co., SW Ohio, 18 mi. (29 km.) N of Cincinnati; pop. (1990c) 39,729.
11. Town, ⊗ of Freestone co., E cen. Texas; pop. (1990c) 3234.
12. Town, Franklin co., NW Vermont, 8 mi. (13 km.) E of St. Albans; pop. (1990c) 1680; birthplace of Chester A. Arthur, 21st president of the U.S., 1829.
13. Municipality, E New South Wales, SE Australia, W suburb of Sydney; pop. (1991c) 175,099.

Fairfield Village. See BRIDGEPORT 3.

Fair·ha·ven \ˈfar-ˌhā-vən, far-ˈ\. **1.** Town, Bristol co., SE Massachusetts, on Buzzards Bay across harbor from New Bedford; pop. (1990c) 16,132; former whaling center; boatyards.
2. Town, Washington. See BELLINGHAM 2.

Fair Ha·ven \ˈfar-ˌhā-vən\. **1.** Borough and resort, Monmouth co., E cen. New Jersey, 16 mi. (26 km.) SE of Perth Amboy; pop. (1990c) 5270.
2. Town, Rutland co., W Vermont, on Poultney River 15 mi. (24 km.) W of the city of Rutland; pop. (1990c) 2887; slate; chartered 1779.

Fair Ha·vens \ˈhā-vənz\. Sheltered harbor on S coast of Crete, Greece, E of Bay of Messara; port where St. Paul's ship touched on his journey to Rome (*Acts* xxvii 8).

Fair Head. Basaltic headland projecting into North Channel on extreme NE coast of Ireland; 636 ft. (194 m.) high.

Fair·hope \ˈfar-ˌhōp\. City, Baldwin co., SW Alabama, on Mobile Bay SE of Mobile; pop. (1990c) 8485; resort; settled 1893–94 on basis of single-tax doctrine promulgated by economist Henry George.

Fair·lawn \ˈfar-ˌlȯn\. Village, Summit co., NE Ohio; pop. (1990c) 5779; residential suburb of Akron.

Fair Lawn. Borough, Bergen co., NE corner of New Jersey, 3 mi. (5 km.) ENE of Paterson; pop. (1990c) 30,548.

Fair·mont \ˈfar-ˌmänt\. City, ⊗ of Martin co., S Minnesota, 41 mi. (66 km.) SSW of Mankato; pop. (1990c) 11,265; lake resort.

2. City, ⊗ of Marion co., N West Virginia, on Monongahela River 18 mi. (29 km.) NNE of Clarksburg; pop. (1990c) 20,210; aluminum, glass, coal-mining machinery; center of coal-mining region; Fairmont State Coll. (1865); site settled 1793; city formed by merger of previous communities of Middletown and Palatine 1843; a Union supply depot in Civil War, raided by Confederate cavalry 1863.

Fair·mount \ˈfar-ˌmau̇nt\. Town, Grant co., N cen. Indiana, 9 mi. (14 km.) S of Marion; pop. (1990c) 3130.

Fair Oaks. Locality just E of Richmond, Virginia; battlefield (called also Seven Pines), scene of engagement May 31–June 1, 1862 in which Union troops under Gen. George McClellan repulsed Confederates under Gen. Joseph E. Johnston (Johnston was wounded, and on June 1 Gen. Robert E. Lee took command of Confederate forces).

Fair·play \ˈfar-ˌplā\. Town, ⊗ of Park co., cen. Colorado; pop. (1990c) 387; alt. 9964 ft. (3037 m.).

Fair·port \ˈfar-ˌpōrt\. Village, Monroe co., W New York, 10 mi. (16 km.) E of Rochester; pop. (1990c) 5943.

Fairport Harbor. Village, Lake co., NE Ohio, on Lake Erie 28 mi. (45 km.) NE of Cleveland; pop. (1990c) 2978; fishing.

Fair·view \ˈfar-ˌvyü\. **1.** City, Nelson co., cen. Kentucky; pop. (1990c) 119; birthplace of Confederate President Jefferson Davis 1808.

2. Community, Massachusetts. See CHICOPEE 2.

3. Borough, Bergen co., NE corner of New Jersey, 7 mi. (11 km.) N of Jersey City; pop. (1990c) 10,733.

4. Unincorporated settlement, Dutchess co., SE New York, NE of New York City; pop. (1990c) 4811.

5. City, ⊗ of Major co., NW Oklahoma, 37 mi. (60 km.) WSW of Enid; pop. (1990c) 2936.

Fairview Heights. City, St. Clair co., SW Illinois, 10 mi. (16 km.) E of East St. Louis; pop. (1990c) 14,351.

Fairview Park. City, Cuyahoga co., N Ohio, SW suburb of Cleveland; pop. (1990c) 18,028.

Fair·way \ˈfar-ˌwā\. City, Johnson co., E Kansas, S of Kansas City; pop. (1990c) 4173.

Fair·weath·er, Cape \ˈfar-ˌwe-t͟hər\. Cape on SE coast of Alaska, 58°55′N, 138°W, ab. 35 mi. (55 km.) S of Mt. Fairweather.

Fairweather, Mount *or* **Fairweather Mountain.** Peak on boundary bet. Alaska and NW British Columbia, Canada, on NW border of Glacier Bay National Monument; 15,300 ft. (4663 m.).

Fai·sa·la·bad \ˈfī-sə-lə-bad\; *before 1980* **Lyall·pur** \ˈlīl-ˌpu̇r\. Town, Punjab, Pakistan, 75 mi. (121 km.) W of Lahore; pop. (1981c) 1,184,209; market for cloth and grain; center of textile, hosiery, and flour-milling industries; also produces vegetable oils, sugar; fertilizer, pharmaceuticals; university (1961); founded c. 1890.

Fa·i·si \fä-ˈē-sē, -zē\. Town, E coast of Shortland I., NW Solomon Is., W Pacific Ocean; government station, chief town of Shortland Is.; became Japanese base in WWII.

Faiyûm, El. See EL FAIYÛM.

Fai·yûm Depression \fī-ˈyüm\. Low area, N cen. Egypt, in the vicinity of El Faiyûm.

Faiz·ā·bād *also* **Fyz·a·bad** \ˈfī-zä-ˌbäd, ˈfī-zə-ˌbad\. **1.** Town, NE Afghanistan. See FEYZĀBĀD.

2. *formerly* **Faizābād–cum–Ajodh·ya** \-ˌkəm-ə-ˈyō-dyə\. City, E cen. Uttar Pradesh, N India, on Ghagara River 75 mi. (121 km.) E of Lucknow; pop. (1991p) 125,012; rail center; refines sugar. Founded c. 1730 as ✻ of Oudh; later became residence of the nabobs of Oudh; ✻ moved to Lucknow 1775; station for troops. Includes nearby Ajodhya (*q.v.*).

Fa·jar·do \fə-ˈhär-dō\. Town, NE Puerto Rico; pop. (1990c) 36,882.

Fa·ka·o·fo \ˌfä-kä-ˈō-fō\. Atoll of Tokelau group, cen. Pacific Ocean, N of Samoa; lagoon 7 mi. (11 km.) by 4 mi. (6 km.); has chief settlement (**Fakaofo**) of the group.

Fa·ka·ra·va \ˌfä-kä-ˈrä-vä\. Atoll in Tuamotu Archipelago, French Polynesia, South Pacific Ocean, 16°S, 145°31′W; 32 mi. (51 km.) long by 10 mi. (16 km.) wide; pop. (1988c) 651; chief settlement Rotoava.

Fak·fak \ˈfäk-ˌfäk\. Coastal settlement at W end of Irian Jaya, Indonesia, just S of entrance to Berau Bay.

Fa·laise \fȧ-ˈlez\. Commune, S Calvados dept., NW France, 19 mi. (31 km.) SE of Caen; pop. (1990c) 8387; ruined castle. Seat of dukes of Normandy, probably birthplace of William the Conqueror c. 1028; conquered by English under Henry V 1417; recovered by France c. 1450; suffered heavy damage in WWII, captured by Allies Aug. 1944 and formed N point of Falaise pocket (see ARGENTAN).

Fa·la·lop \fə-ˈlä-ləp\. See ULITHI.

Fa·lam \fə-ˈläm\. Town, W Myanmar, on Manipur River 175 mi. (282 km.) NW of Mandalay.

Fal·cón \fäl-ˈkōn\. State of Venezuela. See table at VENEZUELA.

Fal·co·na·ra Ma·rit·ti·ma \ˌfäl-kō-ˈnä-rä-ˌmä-rēt-ˈtē-mä\. Commune, Ancona prov., Marche, E Italy, ab. 10 mi. (16 km.) W of the seaport of Ancona; pop. (1989c) 30,060.

Fal·con·er \ˈfal-kə-nər, ˈfȯl-\. Village, Chautauqua co., SW New York; pop. (1990c) 2653.

Fal·con Heights \ˈfal-kən\. City, Ramsey co., E Minnesota, N suburb of St. Paul; pop. (1990c) 5380.

Fa·lé·mé \ˌfä-lā-ˈmā\. River, Senegal; ab. 250 mi. (402 km.) long; tributary of Senegal River.

Falerii. See CIVITA CASTELLANA.

Fal·fur·ri·as \fal-ˈfyu̇r-ē-əs\. City, ⊗ of Brooks co., S Texas, 58 mi. (93 km.) SW of Corpus Christi; pop. (1990c) 5788; gypsum, oil.

Falkenau. See SOKOLOV.

Fal·ken·see \ˈfäl-kən-ˌzā\. City, E Germany, just W of Berlin.

Fal·ken·stein \ˈfäl-kən-ˌshtīn\ *also* **Falkenstein in Sachsen** \in-ˈzäk-sən\. City, Saxony, Germany, 36 mi. (58 km.) SW of Chemnitz.

Fal·kirk \ˈfȯl-ˌkərk\. Burgh, Central region, Scotland, 20 mi. (32 km.) ENE of Glasgow; pop. (1981p) 36,875. Scene of two battles: (1) 1298, in which Edward I of England defeated Scots under Sir William Wallace; (2) 1746, in which Prince Charles Edward Stuart and his Highlander Jacobites defeated the English.

Falk·land Current \ˈfȯ-klənd, ˈfȯl-\. A cold ocean current flowing N along the coast of Argentina.

Falkland Islands *or Span.* **Is·las Mal·vi·nas** \ˈēs-ˌläs-mäl-ˈbē-näs\. British colony in South Atlantic Ocean, 300 mi. (483 km.) E of Strait of Magellan; 4700 sq. mi. (12,173 sq. km.); pop. (1993e) 2100; ✻ Stanley; comprises two principal islands, **East Falkland** (2550 sq. mi. or 6605 sq. km.; with adjacent small islands 2610 sq. mi. or 6760 sq. km.) and **West Falkland** (1750 sq. mi. or 4533 sq. km.; with adjacent small islands 2090 sq. mi. or 5413 sq. km.); the smaller islands include Weddell I., Pebble I., and Jason Is.; main islands of quite irregular shape with wide channel (**Falkland Sound**) bet. them; many fjords and bays; highest point Mt. Usborne 2312 ft. (705 m.) on East Falkland; sheep raising; claimed by Argentina.

History: Discovered 1592; settled by French 1764, also settled by English 1765; French settlement purchased by Spain 1770 and English expelled; settlement restored to English 1771 but soon withdrawn by England for economic reasons; claimed by Argentina after winning independence from Spain (and still claimed), but occupied by British since 1833; in nearby waters during WWI a British fleet destroyed

German Pacific fleet Dec. 8, 1914; brief war followed Argentine invasion Apr. 1982 before the British regained possession in June; exclusive fishing zone implemented by United Kingdom Feb. 1, 1987.

Falkland Islands Dependencies. Collective name for South Georgia I., South Sandwich Is., (*qq.v.*), and several other islets; total area ab. 1570 sq. mi. (4065 sq. km.); administered from the Falkland Is. (*q.v.*).

Falknov. See SOKOLOV.

Fal·kö·ping \ˈfäl-ˌshœ-piŋ\. Town, Skaraborg prov., S Sweden, W of Lake Vättern; pop. (1989c) 31,722; scene of battle 1389 in which Albert, duke of Mecklenburg and king of Sweden, was defeated and taken prisoner by forces of Margaret of Denmark.

Fal·la, Mount \ˈfa-lə\. Mountain, Antarctica, 84°22′S, 164°55′E; 12,549 ft. (3825 m.).

Fall·en Tim·bers \ˈfȯ-lən-ˈtim-bərz\. Locality, NW Ohio, on Maumee River SW of Toledo; scene of victory Aug. 20, 1794 of U.S. Gen. Anthony Wayne over the Indians of the Northwest Terr. which led to British evacuation of border forts in accordance with Jay's Treaty (Nov. 1794).

Fal·lon \ˈfa-lən\. **1.** County in E Montana. See table at MONTANA.
2. City, ⊗ of Churchill co., W Nevada, near Carson Lake and Carson Sink 53 mi. (85 km.) E of Reno; pop. (1990c) 6438.

Fall River \ˈfȯl\. **1.** County in SW corner of South Dakota. See table at SOUTH DAKOTA.
2. Seaport, a ⊗ of Bristol co., SE Massachusetts, on Mt. Hope Bay at mouth of Taunton River 12 mi. (19 km.) NW of New Bedford; pop. (1990c) 92,703; Bristol Community Coll. (1966); in 19th cent. one of largest centers in U.S. for cotton mills and textile-machinery works. Orig. part of Plymouth Colony; settled 1656; birthplace and scene (1892) of murder trial of Lizzie Borden.

Falls \ˈfȯlz\. County in cen. Texas. See table at TEXAS.

Falls Church. Independent city, NE Virginia, 10 mi. (16 km.) NW of Alexandria; 2 sq. mi. (5 sq. km.); pop. (1990c) 9578; incorp. as town 1875; became an independent city 1948. The church (1767–69) for which it was named served as recruiting center during Revolution and as a hospital during Civil War.

Falls City. City, ⊗ of Richardson co., SE corner of Nebraska, 65 mi. (105 km.) ESE of Beatrice; pop. (1990c) 4769.

Falluja, Al–. See AL FALLŪJAH.

Fal·mouth \ˈfal-məth\. **1.** City, ⊗ of Pendleton co., N Kentucky, 30 mi. (48 km.) SSE of Covington; pop. (1990c) 2378.
2. Town, Cumberland co., SW Maine, 6 mi. (10 km.) N of Portland; pop. (1990c) 7610.
3. Residential and resort town, Barnstable co., SE Massachusetts, 16 mi. (26 km.) ESE of New Bedford near E shore of Buzzards Bay; pop. (1990c) 27,960; formerly whaling and boatbuilding center; Otis Air National Guard Base; includes **Woods Hole,** seat of Woods Hole Oceanographic Institution (founded 1930); attacked from sea by British in Revolutionary War and War of 1812; birthplace of Katherine Lee Bates, author of "America the Beautiful," 1858.
4. Seaport town on S coast of island of Antigua, Antigua and Barbuda, West Indies.
5. Port, Cornwall, SW England, on English Channel at mouth of the Fal River 44 mi. (71 km.) WSW of Plymouth; pop. (1981p) 18,525; fishing center, seaside resort; taken from Royalists 1646 by Baron Thomas Fairfax following five-month siege in English Civil War.
6. Coastal town, Jamaica, West Indies; pop. (1991p) 7245.

False Bay \ˈfȯls\. Bay on SW coast of Rep. of South Africa, E of Cape of Good Hope.

False Cape. See VALS, TANJUNG.

False Cape Horn. Cape at SE tip of Hoste I., Chile, S of Tierra del Fuego I. and NW of Cape Horn.

False Di·vi, Point \ˈdi-vē\. Cape, E coast of India, E of Krishna delta and S of Machilipatnam.

False Pass. Village on E coast of Unimak I., Aleutian Is., opp. tip of Alaska Penin.

False Point. Cape, in Orissa on NE coast of India, projecting into Bay of Bengal just N of mouth of Mahanadi River.

Fal·so, Cape \ˈfäl-sō\. SW extremity of Baja California, Mexico, extending into Pacific Ocean.

Fal·ster \ˈfäl-stər\. Island forming a part of Denmark, lying in Baltic Sea S of the island of Sjælland (with which it is connected by a bridge over 10,000 ft. or 3000 m. long), SW of Møn, and E of Lolland; 198 sq. mi. (513 sq. km.); pop. (1989e) 42,841.

Fa·lun *or* **Fah·lun** \ˈfä-ˌlün\. City, ⊗ of Kopparberg prov., cen. Sweden, 130 mi. (209 km.) NW of Stockholm; pop. (1989c) 53,110; iron; former copper-mining center.

Fa·ma·gu·sta \ˌfä-mə-ˈgüs-tə, ˌfa-\ *or Turk.* **Ma·go·sa** \ˌmä-gȯ-ˈsä\. Seaport, E Cyprus, on Famagusta Bay, in Turkish Republic of Northern Cyprus (see *History* at CYPRUS), 3 mi. (5 km.) S of ruins of Salamis (*q.v.*); has medieval fortifications, castle, and large cathedral (now a mosque); connected by rail with Nicosia. Important during Crusades, receiving many refugees after fall of Acre 1291; taken by Genoese c. 1372 and by Turks 1571; nearby was British internment camp for Jews attempting to enter Palestine illegally 1946–48.

Famagusta Bay. Broad inlet of Mediterranean Sea on E coast of Cyprus.

Famatina, Sierra de. See SIERRA DE FAMATINA.

Fa·na \ˈfä-nə\. Coastal commune, Hordaland co., SW Norway, SSE of Bergen.

Fan·ad Head \ˈfa-nəd\. Cape on N coast of Ireland, at W of entrance to Lough Swilly; lighthouse.

Fan·nin \ˈfa-nin\. Name of counties in two states of the U.S. See tables at GEORGIA and TEXAS.

Fanning. See TABUAERAN.

Fa·no \fä-ˈnō\; *anc.* **Pha·nos** \ˈfā-ˌnäs\ *or Gk.* **Otho·noí** \ˌō-thō-ˈnē\. Island of the Ionian Is., Greece, 14 mi. (23 km.) NW of Corfu.

Fano \ˈfä-nō\; *anc.* **Fa·num For·tu·nae** \ˈfā-nəm-fȯr-ˈtü-nē, -ˈtyü-\; *later* **Co·lo·nia Ju·lia Fa·nes·tris** \kə-ˈlō-nē-ə-ˈjül-yə-fə-ˈnes-tris\. Commune, Pesaro e Urbino prov., Marche, cen. Italy, on Adriatic Sea near mouth of Metauro River, 6 mi. (10 km.) SE of Pesaro; pop. (1991p) 53,281; manufactures silk; vegetables, sugar beets; fisheries; cathedral; remains of triumphal arch and city walls. Under Papal States 1463–1860; first printing press with movable Arabic type set up here c. 1514. See PENTAPOLIS.

Fanø \ˈfä-ˌnœ\. Island, North Frisian Is., Denmark, in North Sea off SW coast of Jutland Penin.; 22 sq. mi. (57 sq. km.); pop. (1981c) 2687.

Fan–si–pan \ˈfa^{n}-sē-ˈpa^{n}\. Mountain, N Vietnam, 155 mi. (249 km.) NW of Hanoi; 10,306 ft. (3141 m.); highest mountain in Vietnam.

Fan·wood \ˈfan-ˌwu̇d\. Borough, Union co., NE New Jersey, 9 mi. (14 km.) W of Elizabeth; pop. (1990c) 7115.

Fao. See AL FĀW.

Fara. See SHURUPPAK.

Faradofay. See TÔLAÑARO.

Fa·ra·fan·ga·na \ˌfär-ä-fän-ˈgä-nə\. Town, SE coast of Madagascar, S of Manakara.

Fa·raf·ra \fä-ˈrä-frə\ *or* **Fa·ra·fi·rah** \fä-ˈrä-fi-rə\. Oasis, Matrūh governorate, Egypt, in Libyan Desert, 27°N, 28°E.

Fa·rāh \fə-ˈrä\. **1.** River, W cen. Afghanistan, rising in mountains and flowing SW into Lake Helmand; ab. 200 mi. (320 km.) long; drainage area 12,500 sq. mi. (32,375 sq. km.).
2. Town, SW Afghanistan; pop. (1988e) 22,200.

Fa·ral·lo·nes de Ca·li National Park \ˌfär-ə-ˈyō-nās-də-ˈkäl-ē\. National park, Cauca dept., Colombia; 463 sq. mi. (1199 sq. km.); estab. 1962.

Far·al·lon Islands \ˈfar-ə-ˌlän\. Small group of islands in Pacific Ocean, a part of San Francisco co., W cen. California, ab. 30 mi. (48 km.) W of Golden Gate.

Fa·ra·sān, Ja·zā·'ir \jä-ˈzä-ˌer-ˌfä-rä-ˈsän\ *or Eng.* **Fa·ra·san Islands** \ˌfär-ə-ˈsan\. Group of islands in SE Red Sea, off SW coast of Asir, Saudi Arabia.

Far East. **1.** The countries of E and SE Asia: Myanmar, Cambodia, China, Indonesia, Japan, Korea (North and South), Laos, Malaysia, Philippines, Taiwan, and Vietnam; term

sometimes expanded to include E Siberia (Russia) and Mongolia.
2. The E strip of Siberia along the coast, in 19th cent. a viceroyalty of Russian empire, later known as Maritime Province. See FAR EASTERN REGION and SIBERIA.

Far Eastern Region *or* **Far Eastern Territory** *or Russ.* **Dal·ne·vos·toch·ny Ra·yon** \ˈdäl-nyə-və-ˈstȯch-nyi-rä-ˈyȯn\. Economic region, Russia in Asia; 2,399,958 sq. mi. (6,215,891 sq. km.); coextensive with Khabarovsk Kray and Primorskiy Kray and Amur, Kamchatka, Magadan, and Sakhalin oblasts; greater part of region first known as **Far Eastern Republic,** a state formed 1920 from Russian territory of E Siberia with ✻ at Chita; republic dissolved and region incorp. into Soviet Russia 1922; reorganized 1926 as Far Eastern Terr.; reorganized again 1938 when it was divided.

Fa·regh \fä-ˈreg\. Short river in NE Libya; drains W into marshes S of Al ʻUqaylah.

Fare·ham \ˈfar-əm\. Town, Hampshire, S England, on NW Portsmouth harbor 6 mi. (10 km.) NNW of Portsmouth; pop. (1991p) 97,300; boatbuilding; engineering.

Fare·well, Cape \ˈfar-ˌwel\ **1.** *or Dan.* **Kap Far·vel** \ˌkap-fär-ˈvel\. S point of Greenland, 59°45′N, 44°W.
2. Northernmost point of South I., New Zealand, 40°30′S.

Farghona. See FERGANA 2.

Far·go \ˈfär-gō\. City, ⊗ of Cass co., E North Dakota, on Red River at head of navigation; pop. (1990c) 74,111; largest city in the state; agricultural implements; meatpacking plants (in suburb of **West Fargo,** pop. [1990c] 12,287); North Dakota State Univ. (1890); founded 1871; incorp. 1875.

Fargues \ˈfärg\. Village, Gironde dept., SW France; produces wine (see SAUTERNES).

Far·i·bault \ˈfar-ə-ˌbō\. **1.** County in S Minnesota. See table at MINNESOTA.
2. City, ⊗ of Rice co., S Minnesota, 47 mi. (76 km.) S of Minneapolis; pop. (1990c) 17,085; flower nurseries; on site of trading post estab. 1826 by Alexander Faribault.

Fa·ri·da·bad \fä-ˈrē-dä-ˌbäd\. Town, Haryana, N India; pop. (1991c) 617,717.

Fa·rid·kot \fə-ˈrēd-ˌkōt\. **1.** Former Indian state, now part of Punjab, N India, S of the Sutlej; 637 sq. mi. (1650 sq. km.); under British influence 1809–1947.
2. Town, its ✻; pop. (1991p) 56,038.

Fa·rid·pur \fə-ˈrēd-ˌpu̇r\. District, Bangladesh, on S bank of an old channel of the Ganges.

Fa·ri·lhões \ˌfȧ-rēl-ˈyȯiⁿsh\. Group of Portuguese islets off W cen. coast of Portugal, just N of the Berlengas Is.

Farm·ers Branch \ˈfär-mərz\. City, Dallas co., NE Texas, NNE suburb of the city of Dallas; pop. (1990c) 24,250.

Farm·ers·ville \ˈfär-mərz-ˌvil\. **1.** City, Tulare co., S cen. California, 45 mi. (72 km.) SE of Fresno; pop. (1990c) 6235.
2. City, Collin co., NE Texas, W of Greenville; pop. (1990c) 2640.

Farm·er·ville \ˈfär-mər-ˌvil\. Town, ⊗ of Union parish, N Louisiana; pop. (1990c) 3334.

Farm·ing·dale \ˈfär-miŋ-ˌdāl\. Village, Nassau co., SE New York, on Long Island 30 mi. (48 km.) E of New York City; pop. (1990c) 8022; State Univ. of New York Coll. of Technology at Farmingdale (1912).

Farm·ing·ton \ˈfär-miŋ-tən\. **1.** River, N Connecticut; formed by confluence in NE Litchfield co. of E and W branches both of which rise in Massachusetts; flows into Connecticut River at Windsor.
2. Town, W cen. Hartford co., N Connecticut; pop. (1990c) 20,608; watered by Farmington River; Tunxis Community Coll. (1970), Charter Oak Coll. (1973); settled 1640; incorp. 1645. Includes two communities: (1) former industrial center, now residential suburb; and (2) Unionville (*q.v.*).
3. City, Fulton co., W cen. Illinois; pop. (1990c) 2535.
4. Town, ⊗ of Franklin co., W Maine; pop. (1990c) 7436; Univ. of Maine at Farmington (1863).
5. City, Oakland co., SE Michigan, 14 mi. (23 km.) SSW of Pontiac; pop. (1990c) 10,132.
6. Village, Dakota co., SE Minnesota, 22 mi. (35 km.) S of St. Paul; pop. (1990c) 5940.
7. City, ⊗ of St. Francois co., E Missouri, 59 mi. (95 km.) S of St. Louis; pop. (1990c) 11,598; lead deposits.
8. Town, Strafford co., SE New Hampshire, 6 mi. (10 km.) NW of Rochester; pop. (1990c) 5739; summer resort.
9. City, San Juan co., NW corner of New Mexico, on San Juan River near NE corner of large Navajo Indian reservation; pop. (1990c) 33,997; regional trade center; near oil, gas, and coal fields; has oil refineries.
10. City, ⊗ of Davis co., N Utah, on Great Salt Lake 15 mi. (24 km.) N of Salt Lake City; pop. (1990c) 9028; settled by Mormons 1848.

Farmington Hills. City, Oakland co., SE Michigan; NW suburb of Detroit; pop. (1990c) 74,652.

Farm·ville \ˈfärm-ˌvil, -vəl\. **1.** Town, Pitt co., E North Carolina, 21 mi. (34 km.) SSE of Wilson; pop. (1990c) 4392.
2. Town, ⊗ of Prince Edward co., S cen. Virginia, 45 mi. (72 km.) E of Lynchburg; pop. (1990c) 6046; Longwood Coll. (1884).

Farn·bor·ough \ˈfärn-bə-rə\. Town, Hampshire, S England, 31 mi. (50 km.) WSW of London; pop. (1981p) 45,453; site of Royal Aircraft Establishment.

Farne Islands \ˈfärn\ *also* **The Sta·ples** \ˈstā-pəlz\. Group of 17 small islands off NE coast of Northumberland, N England; scene of wreck of the *Forfarshire* 1838 and the rescue, from Longstone lighthouse, by Victorian heroine Grace Darling and her father.

Farn·ham \ˈfär-nəm\. **1.** City, S Quebec, Canada, on Yamaska River 35 mi. (56 km.) ESE of Montreal; pop. (1991c) 6146; important railroad junction.
2. Town, Surrey, S England, on Wey River 38 mi. (61 km.) SW of London; pop. (1981p) 35,289; castle.

Farnham, Mount. See PURCELL MOUNTAINS.

Farn·worth \ˈfärn-ˌwərth\. Town, Greater Manchester, NW England, 7 mi. (11 km.) NW of Manchester; pop. (1981p) 24,589; collieries; textiles; engineering.

Fa·ro \ˈfȧ-rü\. **1.** District of S Portugal. See table at PORTUGAL.
2. Seaport commune, its ✻, on Atlantic Ocean 137 mi. (220 km.) SSE of Lisbon; munic. pop. (1991p) 31,966; trades in fish, wine, cork, figs and other dried and fresh fruits, basketry; antimony deposits; cathedral; taken from Moors 1249; sacked by English 1596; earthquakes 1722, 1755.

Faro, Cape \ˈfä-rō\ *or Ital.* **Pun·ta del Faro** \ˈpün-tä-del-\; *anc.* **Pe·lo·rus** \pə-ˈlōr-əs\. Cape on NE extremity of Sicily, Italy.

Faroe Islands. See FAEROE ISLANDS.

Fårön \ˈfȯr-ˌœn\. Island in Baltic Sea off NE coast of Gotland I.; a part of Gotland prov., Sweden; 56 sq. mi. (145 sq. km.).

Far·quhar, Cape \ˈfär-kər, -kwər\. Point on W coast of Western Australia, Australia, near Tropic of Capricorn.

Farquhar Islands. Group of small islands belonging to Seychelles in Indian Ocean NE of Madagascar; 3 sq. mi. (8 sq. km.); formerly (1965–76) part of British Indian Ocean Terr.

Far·ra·gut \ˈfar-ə-gət\. Town, Knox co., E Tennessee, 10 mi. (16 km.) SW of Knoxville; pop. (1990c) 12,793.

Far·rell \ˈfar-əl\. City, Mercer co., W Pennsylvania, on Shenango River 17 mi. (27 km.) NNW of New Castle; pop. (1990c) 6841.

Far Rock·a·way \ˈfär-ˈrä-kə-ˌwā\. Neighborhood, Queens borough, New York City, on S shore of Long Island SE of Jamaica Bay; formerly a seashore resort.

Far·rukh·a·bad \fə-ˈrü-kä-ˌbad\. City, Uttar Pradesh, N India, on right bank of Ganges River 90 mi. (145 km.) WNW of Lucknow; with Fategarh (*q.v.*) forms joint municipality; sugar, tobacco, potatoes; saltpeter; cotton cloth, perfume. Farrukhabad founded 1714; scene of defeat of Marathas by Gen. Gerard Lake 1804; in Indian mutiny 1857–58 scene of a massacre of English and of several engagements.

Fārs \ˈfärz\; *anc.* **Per·sis** \ˈpər-sis\. Province, SW Iran; 51,465 sq. mi. (133,294 sq. km.); ✻ Shīrāz; cotton, rice, tobacco; ancient Persis the original home of Persians and nucleus of later Persian Empire, in extent corresponded closely with modern Fārs; chief cities were Persepolis and Pasargadae. See table and *History* at IRAN.

Fársala. See PHARSALUS.

Far·shut \fär-ˈshüt\. Town, Upper Egypt, near left bank of the Nile ab. 35 mi. (56 km.) W of Qena.

Far·tak, Cape \fär-ˈtak\ *or Arab.* **Ras Fartak** \ˌräs\. Cape on coast of Ḥaḑramawt, Yemen, SW of Qamr Bay projecting into Arabian Sea.

Farther Pomerania. See POMERANIA.

Farvel, Kap. See FAREWELL, CAPE 1.

Far·well \ˈfär-ˌwel, -wəl\. City, ⊗ of Parmer co., NW Texas; pop. (1990c) 1373.

Far West. The part of the United States W of the Mississippi River, or, now more generally, the part W of the Great Plains.

Fās. See FÈS.

Fa·sa·no \fä-ˈzä-nō\. Commune, Brindisi prov., Puglia, SE Italy, near Adriatic Sea 33 mi. (53 km.) NW of the seaport of Brindisi; pop. (1989c) 38,564.

Fasher, El *or* **Fashir, Al–.** See EL FASHER.

Fashoda. See KODOK.

Fa·stiv \ˈfá-stəf\ *or* **Fa·stov** \-stəf\. Town, W Kiev subdivision, N cen. Ukraine 35 mi. (56 km.) SW of the city of Kiev.

Fast·net \ˈfast-nət\. Rocky islet, S Ireland, in Atlantic Ocean 4 mi. (6 km.) SW of Cape Clear, 51°24′N, 9°35′W; lighthouse.

Fastov. See FASTIV.

Fa·te·garh \fə-ˈtā-gər\. City, Uttar Pradesh, N India; pop. (1991p) with Farrukhabad (*q.v.*) 193,624.

Fa·teh·pur \ˈfə-tə-ˌpu̇r\. **1.** Town, Uttar Pradesh, N India, 50 mi. (80 km.) SE of Kanpur; pop. (1991p) 117,203.
2. Town, E Rajasthan, NW India, formerly in NW Jaipur state, Rajputana; pop. (1991p) 66,398.

Fatehpur Si·kri \ˈsē-krē\. Town, SW Uttar Pradesh, N India, 23 mi. (37 km.) W of Agra; pop. (1991p) 25,459; ancient city founded 1569 by Mogul Emperor Akbar, who made it his ✻ of the Mogul Empire; abandoned after his death 1605; remains include magnificent structures, partly in ruins: palaces, audience halls, tombs, great gate of victory (Buland Darwaza).

Father, The *or* **Ula·wun** \ü-ˈlä-ˌwün\. Active volcano, Whiteman Range, on the island of New Britain, near N coast at E end, W Pacific Ocean; 7546 ft. (2300 m.); highest point on the island.

Fá·ti·ma \ˈfa-ti-mə, ˈfä-tē-mə\. Village, cen. Portugal, SE of Leiria; shrine of the Virgin, destination of pilgrimage; visited by Pope Paul VI 1967.

Fatshan. See FOSHAN.

Fa·tu Hi·va \ˈfä-tü-ˈhē-və\; *formerly* **Mag·da·le·na** \ˌmag-də-ˈlē-nə\. Island, Marquesas Is., South Pacific Ocean, ab. 36 mi. (58 km.) S of E end of Hiva Oa I., French Polynesia; 31 sq. mi. (80 sq. km.); pop. (1988c) 497.

Faulk \ˈfȯk\. County in N cen. South Dakota. See table at SOUTH DAKOTA.

Faulk·ner \ˈfȯk-nər\. County in cen. Arkansas. See table at ARKANSAS.

Faulk·ton \ˈfȯk-tən\. City, ⊗ of Faulk co., N cen. South Dakota; pop. (1990c) 809.

Fau·quier \ˈfȯ-ˌkir\. County in N Virginia. See table at VIRGINIA.

Faure·smith \ˈfau̇r-ˌsmith\. Town, cen. Rep. of South Africa, just W of Jagersfontein and 70 mi. (113 km.) SW of Bloemfontein; founded 1848, year of nearby battle of Boomplaats (*q.v.*).

Fau·ro \ˈfau̇-rō\. Island, one of Shortland Is. group S of Bougainville I., Solomon Is., W Pacific Ocean; ab. 10 mi. (16 km.) long.

Fa·va·ra \fä-ˈvä-rä\. Commune, Agrigento prov., SW Sicily, Italy, 5 mi. (8 km.) E of the commune of Agrigento; pop. (1989c) 33,213; castle; sulfur, marble.

Faventia. See FAENZA.

Fav·er·sham \ˈfa-vər-shəm\. Town, Kent, SE England, on Faversham Creek 45 mi. (72 km.) ESE of London; pop. (1981p) 16,098; brewing, engineering; member of Cinque Ports; tomb of King Stephen.

Fa·vi·gna·na \ˌfä-vē-ˈnyä-nä\. An island and commune of Isole Egadi (*q.v.*).

Fāw, Al. See AL FĀW.

Faxa Bay \ˈfäk-sä\ *or Icel.* **Fax·a·flói** \ˈfäk-sä-ˌflō-ē, -ˌflȯi\. Bay on SW coast of Iceland; Reykjavík is situated on its SE shore.

Fayal. See FAIAL.

Fay·ette \fā-ˈet, ˈfā-ət\. **1.** Name of counties in 11 states of the U.S. See tables at ALABAMA, GEORGIA, ILLINOIS, INDIANA, IOWA, KENTUCKY, OHIO, PENNSYLVANIA, TENNESSEE, TEXAS, WEST VIRGINIA.
2. City, ⊗ of Fayette co., NW Alabama, 35 mi. (56 km.) NNW of Tuscaloosa; pop. (1990c) 4909.
3. City, Fayette co., NE Iowa, 32 mi. (51 km.) S of Decorah; pop. (1990c) 1317; Upper Iowa Univ. (1857).
4. City, ⊗ of Jefferson co., SW Mississippi; pop. (1990c) 1853.
5. City, ⊗ of Howard co., N cen. Missouri, 25 mi. (40 km.) NW of Columbia; pop. (1990c) 2888; Central Methodist Coll. (1854).
6. Town, Seneca co., W cen. New York; pop. (1990c) 3636; scene of organization by Joseph Smith 1830 of Church of Jesus Christ of Latter-day Saints.

Fay·ette·ville \ˈfā-ət-ˌvil, -vəl\. **1.** City, ⊗ of Washington co., NW Arkansas, 50 mi. (80 km.) N of Fort Smith; pop. (1990c) 42,099; trade center; summer mountain resort; Univ. of Arkansas, Fayetteville (1871), Agricultural Experiment Station. Settled 1828; incorp. as city 1906; several battles of Civil War fought nearby, incl. battle of Pea Ridge (Mar. 7–8, 1862).
2. City, ⊗ of Fayette co., W Georgia; pop. (1990c) 5827.
3. Village, Onondaga co., cen. New York, 10 mi. (16 km.) E of Syracuse; pop. (1990c) 4248.
4. City, ⊗ of Cumberland co., S cen. North Carolina, on Cape Fear River at head of navigation, 50 mi. (80 km.) S of Raleigh; pop. (1990c) 75,695; wood products, textiles; formerly important turpentine and lumber center; Fayetteville State Univ. (1867), Methodist Coll. (1956), Fayetteville Technical Community Coll. (1961); Fort Bragg and Pope Air Force Base are nearby. Founded by Scottish colonists 1739; occupied by British Gen. George Cornwallis 1781; state ✻ 1789–93; occupied by Union Gen. William T. Sherman 1865.
5. City, ⊗ of Lincoln co., S Tennessee, 44 mi. (71 km.) SE of Columbia; pop. (1990c) 6921.
6. Town, ⊗ of Fayette co., S cen. West Virginia; pop. (1990c) 2182; New River Gorge Bridge, world's longest steel-arch bridge (main span 1700 ft. or 518 m.; completed 1977), spanning New River nearby.

Fayyūm, Al. See EL FAIYÛM.

Fa·zogl \fä-ˈzȯg-lə\ *or* **Faz·og·li** \fä-ˈzȯg-lē\ *or* **Fa·zokl** \fä-ˈzȯk-lə\. District, E Sudan, on Ethiopian border S of Sennar; traversed by the Blue Nile.

Fazzān. See FEZZAN.

Fear, Cape \ˈfir\. Cape on Smith I., SE coast of Brunswick co., North Carolina, at mouth of Cape Fear River.

Feath·er \ˈfe-t͟hər\. River, N cen. California; rises in Plumas co. and flows SW into Sacramento River above city of Sacramento; ab. 100 mi. (160 km.) long; incl. its forks 250 mi. (400 km.) long.

Feather Falls. Falls in middle fork of Feather River, N cen. California; 640 ft. (195 m.) high.

Feath·er·stone \ˈfe-t͟hər-stən, -ˌstōn\. Town, West Yorkshire, N England, E of Wakefield; pop. (1981p) 14,043; coal.

Feath·er·top, Mount \ˈfe-t͟hər-ˌtäp\. Peak, E cen. Victoria, SE Australia; 6307 ft. (1922 m.).

Fé·camp \fā-ˈkäⁿ\; *anc.* **Fis·cam·num** \fis-ˈkam-nəm\. Seaport, Seine-Maritime dept., N France, on English Channel 40 mi. (64 km.) NW of Rouen; pop. (1990c) 21,143; fisheries; Benedictine liqueurs, still made (now by secular corporation) in same place where formula was discovered in early 16th cent. by monks of Benedictine monastery.

Fedala. See MOHAMMEDIA.

Fe·dchen·ko Glacier \fed-'cheŋ-kō\. Glacier in the Pamirs, Tajikistan; 44 mi. (71 km.) long; ab. 1.5 mi. (2 km.) wide at its terminus.

Federal Capital Territory. 1. Administrative subdivision, Australia. See AUSTRALIAN CAPITAL TERRITORY.

2. Administrative subdivision, Nigeria. See table at NIGERIA.

Federal District *or Span.* **Dis·tri·to Fe·de·ral** \dē-'strē-tō-,fā-th̲ā-'räl\ *or Port.* **Dis·tri·to Fe·de·ral** \dish-'trē-tü-,fā-di-'räl\. **1.** *also* **Federal Capital** *or Span.* **Ca·pi·tal Federal** \,kä-pē-'täl-,fā-th̲ā-'räl\. The city of Buenos Aires, ✱ of Argentina, not included in prov. of Buenos Aires. See table at ARGENTINA.

2. Former seat of national government, SE Brazil; 451 sq. mi. (1168 sq. km.); coextensive with city of Rio de Janeiro.

3. Large area on plateau of SE Goiás state, cen. Brazil; site of Brasília, ✱ (since Apr. 21, 1960) of Brazil. See table at BRAZIL.

4. Area, Mexico, containing Mexico City, the nation's ✱. See table at MEXICO.

5. Area, Venezuela, containing Caracas, the nation's ✱. See table at VENEZUELA.

Federal Heights. City, Adams co., Colorado, 5 mi. (8 km.) N of Denver; pop. (1990c) 9342.

Federal Islamic Republic of the Comoros. See COMOROS.

Federal Republic of Germany. See GERMANY.

Federal Republic of Yugoslavia. See YUGOSLAVIA.

Federated Ma·lay States \mə-'lā, 'mā-,lā\. Former federation of the states of Pahang, Perak, Selangor, and Negeri Sembilan at S extremity of Malay Penin.; ✱ Kuala Lumpur. Entered treaties providing for their protection by British government (Perak 1874, the other states later); federated 1896; occupied by Japanese in WWII; joined Federation of Malaya 1948, Malaysia 1963. See MALAYA, FEDERATION OF and MALAYSIA.

Federated Shan States. See SHAN.

Federated States of Micronesia. See MICRONESIA, FEDERATED STATES OF.

Federation of Arab Republics. See ARAB REPUBLICS, FEDERATION OF.

Federation of Malaya. See MALAYA, FEDERATION OF.

Federation of South Arabia. See SOUTH ARABIA, FEDERATION OF.

Federative Republic of Brazil. See BRAZIL.

Fe·djadj, Chott al– \,shät-'al-fe-'jäj\. Marshy saline lake, S cen. Tunisia; an E extension of Chott Djerid; ab. 60 mi. (95 km.) long.

Fe·fan \'fā-,fän\. Island, Federated States of Micronesia, W Pacific Ocean; in E part of Chuuk (*q.v.*); highest point 1026 ft. (313 m.).

Fehértemplom. See BELA CRKVA.

Feh·marn \'fā-,märn\. Island, Schleswig-Holstein, Germany; separated by **Fehmarn Sound** from the mainland; in W Baltic Sea, on NW side of entrance to Mecklenburg Bay; 71 sq. mi. (184 sq. km.).

Fehr·bel·lin \,fār-be-'lēn\. Town, NE cen. Germany, NW of Berlin; scene 1675 of victory of Great Elector Frederick William of Brandenburg over the Swedes under Karl Gustav Wrangel.

Feil·ding \'fēl-diŋ\. Borough, SW North I., New Zealand, 85 mi. (137 km.) NNE of Wellington; pop. (1992e) 13,500.

Fei·ra de San·ta·na \'fā-rə-dē-sä^n-'tä^n-nə\; *formerly* **Feira.** City, Bahia state, E Brazil, 60 mi. (97 km.) NNW of Salvador; munic. pop. (1991p) 405,691; produces dried beef, tobacco, beans, corn; bicycles, furniture.

Fe·jér \'fe-,yār\. County of W cen. Hungary. See table at HUNGARY.

Fe·la·nitx \,fā-lä-'nēch\ *or* **Fe·la·ni·che** \,fā-lä-'nē-chā\; *anc.* **Ca·na·ti** \kə-'nä-,tī\. Commune, Baleares prov., Spain, SE Majorca I., 27 mi. (43 km.) ESE of Palma; pop. (1991c) 14,176.

Feld·berg \'felt-,berk\. Highest peak in Black Forest, Baden-Württemberg, Germany, SE of Freiburg; 4905 ft. (1495 m.).

Feld·kirch \'felt-,kirk\; *anc.* **Clu·nia** \'klü-nē-ə\. City, Vorarlberg, W Austria, on Liechtenstein frontier on Ill River 20 mi. (32 km.) SSW of Bregenz; pop. (1991c) 26,743; castle; railroad junction, on the route over the Arlberg Pass to the E.

Félegyháza. See KISKUNFÉLEGYHÁZA.

Felicitas Julia. See LISBON 6.

Fe·li·pe Car·ril·lo Puer·to \fā-'lē-pā-kä-'rē-yō-'pwer-tō\; *formerly* **San·ta Cruz de Bra·vo** \'sän-tä-'krüs-th̲ā-'brä-vō\. Town, E cen. Quintana Roo state, Yucatán Penin., Mexico.

Fe·lix·stowe \'fē-lik-,stō\. Port, Suffolk, E England; pop. (1981p) 20,858; seaside resort.

Fell·bach \'fel-,bäk\. City, Baden-Württemberg, Germany, E of Stuttgart; pop. (1980c) 41,383.

Fel·le·tin \fel-'te^n\. Commune, S Creuse dept., cen. France, S of Aubusson; noted for tapestry-weaving.

Fellin. See VILJANDI.

Fel·ling \'fe-liŋ\. Town, Tyne and Wear, N England, 4 mi. (6 km.) S of Newcastle upon Tyne; pop. (1981p) 36,431.

Felsina. See BOLOGNA 2.

Fel·sted *or* **Fel·stead** \'fel-sted\. Village, Essex, SE England; school here founded mid-16th cent.

Fel·tre \'fel-trā\; *anc.* **Fel·tria** \-trē-ə\. Commune, Belluno prov., Veneto, NE Italy, 17 mi. (27 km.) SW of the commune of Belluno; pop. (1989c) 20,003; cathedral; trades in agricultural products, textiles; besieged by Austrians 1917–18.

Fe·mund *or* **Fæ·mund** \'fā-,mu̇n\. Lake, Hedmark co., E Norway, 85 mi. (137 km.) SE of Trondheim; 78 sq. mi. (202 sq. km.).

Fen \'fen, 'fən\. River, cen. Shanxi prov., NE China; ab. 300 mi. (480 km.) long; an E tributary of the Huang, flows SSE.

Fen Country. See FENS, THE.

Feng·cheng *or W.-G.* **Feng–ch'eng** \'fəŋ-'chəŋ\ *or Jp.* **Feng·hwang·cheng** \'fəŋ-'hwäŋ-'chəŋ\. Town, S Liaoning prov., NE China; former treaty port; held by Japanese in Russo-Japanese War 1904–05.

Feng·du *or W.-G.* **Feng–tu** \'fəŋ-'dü\. City, SE Sichuan prov., S cen. China, on N bank of the Chang River 85 mi. (137 km.) ENE of Chongqing.

Feng·hua \'fəŋ-'hwä\. Town, NE Zhejiang prov., E China, ab. 10 mi. (16 km.) SSW of Ningbo; birthplace of Nationalist leader Generalissimo Chiang Kai-shek 1887.

Feng·jie \'feŋ-'jye\ *or W.-G.* **Feng–chieh** \-'jye\ *or* **Feng·kieh** \-'jye\; *formerly* **Kwei·chow** \'gwā-'jō\. City, E Sichuan, S cen. China, on N bank of Chang River at head of Chang Gorges (*q.v.*), 120 mi. (193 km.) WNW of Yichang; has long been of great strategic importance.

Feng·tai *or W.-G.* **Feng–t'ai** \'fəŋ-'tī\. Railroad junction town, NE China, part of Beijing municipality.

Feng·tien \'fəŋ-'tyen\. **1.** Province of China. See LIAONING.

2. City, China. See SHENYANG.

3. Former province (1932–45), S Manchukuo; 29,263 sq. mi. (75,791 sq. km.); ✱ Shenyang.

Feng–tu. See FENGDU.

Fe·ni Islands \'fā-nē\. Group of small islands, Papua New Guinea, in Bismarck Archipelago, W Pacific Ocean, ab. 40 mi. (64 km.) off SE coast of New Ireland.

Fen·no·scan·dia *also* **Fen·no–Scan·dia** \,fe-nō-'skan-dē-ə\. The part of N Europe consisting of Norway, Sweden, Finland, and the adjacent part of Russia —specifically used in geology.

Fens, The \'fenz\ *also* **Fen Country** \'fen\. Low-lying districts in E England, esp. in Lincolnshire near shores of the Wash; max. length ab. 73 mi. (117 km.); once marshland but long since drained and cultivated.

Fen·ton \'fent-ᵊn\. **1.** Village, Genesee co., SE cen. Michigan, 15 mi. (24 km.) S of Flint; pop. (1990c) 8444; summer resort.

2. City, St. Louis co., Missouri; pop. (1990c) 3346.

3. District, England. See POTTERIES, THE.

Fen·tress \'fen-trəs\. County in N Tennessee. See table at TENNESSEE.

Fen·yang *or W.-G.* **Fen–yang** \'fən-'yäŋ\. City, cen. Shanxi prov., NE China, 60 mi. (97 km.) SW of Taiyuan.

Fe·o·do·si·ya \ˌfē-ə-ˈdō-sē-ə\ *or Ital.* **Kaf·fa** \ˈkä-fä\ *or Tatar* **Ke·fe** \ke-ˈfā\; *anc.* **The·o·do·sia** \ˌthē-ə-ˈdō-shə, -shē-ə\. Seaport town, SE Crimea, Ukraine, 55 mi. (88 km.) WSW of Kerch; pop. (1991e) 86,000; fine harbor, rail connections with Kerch and Dzhankoy; exports grain; important esp. for its oyster fishing and preparation of caviar; health resort. Site of Greek colony founded by Milesians by 6th cent. B.C.; formed part of kingdom of Cimmerian Bosporus (*q.v.*); as Kaffa was a flourishing Genoese trading colony 13th cent.; captured by Turks 1475; to Russia 1783; held by Germans during WWII.

Fer, Cape \ˈfer\ *or Fr.* **Cap de Fer** \ˌkap-də-ˈfer\. Cape on NE coast of Algeria, 35 mi. (56 km.) NW of Annaba.

Fère, La. See LA FÈRE.

Fère–en–Tar·de·nois \ˈfer-ä^{n}-ˌtär-də-ˈnwä\. Town, Aisne dept., N France; type station for Tardenoisian culture; just E, at village of **Se·ringes–et–Nesles** \sə-ra^{n}zh-ā-nel\, is an American military cemetery; scene of fighting in WWI.

Fe·ren·ti·no \ˌfer-ren-ˈtē-nō\; *anc.* **Fer·en·ti·num** \ˌfer-ən-ˈtī-nəm\. Commune, Frosinone prov., Lazio, cen. Italy, 6 mi. (10 km.) NW of the commune of Frosinone; pop. (1991p) 19,137; cathedral; ancient city walls; mineral baths.

Fer·ga·na *also* **Fer·gha·na** \fir-ˌgə-ˈnä\. **1.** Administrative subdivision of Uzbekistan, formerly an oblast of Uzbek S.S.R.; 2741 sq. mi. (7099 sq. km.); pop. (1991e) 2,226,400; ✻ Fergana; cotton, fruit; sericulture; oil fields.

2. *or* **Far·gho·na** \fər-ˈgō-nə\ *formerly* **Sko·be·lev** \ˈskō-bi-lif\. City, ✻ of Fergana administrative division, E Uzbekistan, in fertile valley of region of the Alai Mts. 40 mi. (64 km.) E of Qŭqon; pop. (1991e) 226,500; light industries; deposits of ferganite (a uranium mineral) in vicinity; founded c. 1876; built by Russians 10 mi. (16 km.) SE of old town of Margelan and earlier known as **No·vyy Mar·ge·lan** \ˈnō-vē-mər-gyi-ˈlän\ (*or Eng.* **New Mar·ge·lan** \ˈmär-gi-ˌlän\).

Fergana Valley *or* **Fergana Basin.** Region, W cen. Asia, W of the Tian Shan; overrun by Arabs in 8th cent.; conquered by Mongol leader Genghis Khan 13th cent. and Turkic ruler Timur 14th cent.; in 16th cent. conquered by the Uzbeks and became part of Qŭqon; taken by Russians 1875–76 and made a division of Russian Turkestan (see TURKISTAN); divided under Soviet government, now has parts in Uzbekistan, Tajikistan, and Kyrgyzstan.

Fer·gus \ˈfər-gəs\. **1.** County in cen. Montana. See table at MONTANA.

2. Town, Wellington co., SE Ontario, Canada, 13 mi. (21 km.) NW of Guelph; pop. (1991c) 7940.

Fergus Falls. City, ⊗ of Otter Tail co., W cen. Minnesota, 50 mi. (80 km.) SE of Moorhead; pop. (1990c) 12,362; flour; summer resort; hydroelectric power plant; Fergus Falls Community Coll. (1960).

Fer·gu·son \ˈfər-gə-sən\. City, St. Louis co., E Missouri, 10 mi. (16 km.) NNW of the city of St. Louis; pop. (1990c) 22,286.

Fer·gus·son \ˈfər-gə-sən\ *or* **Ka·lu·wa·wa** \ˌkä-lä-ˈwä-wä\. One of the D'Entrecasteaux Is., Papua New Guinea, in W Pacific Ocean 4 mi. (6 km.) E of Goodenough I.; ab. 38 mi. (61 km.) long and 16 mi. (26 km.) wide; 518 sq. mi. (1342 sq. km.); several good harbors; fumaroles and geysers.

Fer·i·ana \ˌfer-yä-ˈnä\. Town, W Tunisia, SSW of Kasserine Pass; briefly held by Germans 1943.

Fer·man·agh \fər-ˈma-nə\. **1.** Former county, SW Northern Ireland; chief river the Erne.

2. District, SW Northern Ireland; estab. 1974. See table at IRELAND, NORTHERN.

Fer·mo \ˈfer-mō\; *anc.* **Fir·mum Pi·ce·num** \ˈfər-məm-pī-ˈsē-nəm\. Commune, Ascoli Piceno prov., Marche, cen. Italy, near Adriatic Sea 23 mi. (37 km.) NNE of the commune of Ascoli Piceno; pop. (1991p) 34,434; Gothic cathedral; bronze foundry. Founded by Sabines; taken by Romans 3d cent. B.C.; part of papal domain mid-16th cent. to 1860.

Fer·moy \fər-ˈmȯi\. Town, NE co. Cork, SW Ireland, on Blackwater River; pop. (1991p) 2297; agricultural trading center; sport fishing.

Fer·nan·di·na \ˌfer-nän-ˈdē-nä, ˌfər-\. **1.** An early name of Cuba (*q.v.*).

2. *also* **Nar·bor·ough Island** \ˈnär-bə-rə\. One of the Galápagos Is. (*q.v.*), Ecuador.

Fer·nan·di·na Beach \ˌfər-nən-ˈdē-nə\. City, ⊗ of Nassau co., on Amelia I., NE corner of Florida, 25 mi. (40 km.) NE of Jacksonville; pop. (1990c) 8765.

Fer·nan·do de la Mo·ra \fer-ˈnän-dō-ˌthā-lä-ˈmō-rä\. City, S Paraguay, a suburb of Asunción; pop. (1992p) 95,287.

Fer·nan·do de No·ro·nha \fer-ˈnän-dü-dē-nō-ˈrō-nyə\. Island, Brazil, in Atlantic Ocean ab. 250 mi. (400 km.) NE of Cape São Roque; 10 sq. mi. (26 sq. km.); pop. (1980c) 1342; constitutes a territory; used as a penal colony from 18th cent.; discovered c. 1501; **Fernando de Noronha Marine National Park** (estab. 1988) comprises part of the island and surrounding waters.

Fernando Póo. See BIOKO.

Fer·não Ve·lo·so Bay \fər-ˈnau̇^{n}-və-ˈlō-zü\. Inlet of Mozambique Channel on NE coast of Mozambique, S of Cape Loguno.

Fern·dale \ˈfərn-ˌdāl\. Residential city, Oakland co., SE Michigan, just N of Detroit; pop. (1990c) 25,084; automobile and aircraft parts, machinery, tools.

Fer·ney \fer-ˈnā\ *or in full* **Ferney–Vol·taire** \vōl-ˈtar\. Town, Ain dept., E France, on shore of Lake Geneva ab. 4 mi. (6 km.) from Geneva; grew up around the colony of watchmakers estab. by the writer Voltaire, who lived here 1758–78.

Fer·nie \ˈfər-nē\. City, SE British Columbia, Canada, E of Kootenay River, on W slope of Rocky Mts.; pop. (1991c) 5012; coal deposits.

Ferns \ˈfərnz\. Village, co. Wexford, E Ireland, ab. 8 mi. (13 km.) N of Enniscorthy; once ✻ of kingdom of Leinster; cathedral.

Fe·rolle, Point \fə-ˈrōl\. Cape, NW Newfoundland, Canada, on SE of entrance to Strait of Belle Isle.

Fe·roze·pur *or* **Fe·roze·pore.** See FIROZPUR.

Ferozeshah. See FĪROZ SHĀH.

Fer·ra·ra \fer-ˈrä-rä\. **1.** Province of Emilia-Romagna, N Italy. See table at ITALY.

2. *anc.* **Fo·rum Ali·e·ni** \ˈfōr-əm-ˌa-lē-ˈē-ˌnī\. Commune, its ✻, near the Po 57 mi. (92 km.) SW of Venice; pop. (1991p) 137,336; chemicals, plastics, sugar; seven-mile city wall; cathedral; castle; fortified citadel; art gallery, university (1391); birthplace of religious reformer Girolamo Savonarola 1452. In 1240 came to be ruled by Este family; to Papal States 1598; incorp. into kingdom of Italy 1859; suffered severe damage in WWII; taken by Allies Apr. 1945.

Fer·ri·day \ˈfer-i-ˌdā\. Town, Concordia parish, E cen. Louisiana, 10 mi. (16 km.) NW of Natchez, Mississippi; pop. (1990c) 4111.

Ferro. See HIERRO.

Ferrol, El *or* **Ferrol.** See EL FERROL.

Fer·ry \ˈfer-ē\. County in NE Washington. See table at WASHINGTON.

Fer·ry·land \ˈfer-ē-ˌland\. Town, SE Newfoundland, Canada, on Atlantic Ocean 38 mi. (61 km.) S of St. John's; pop. (1991c) 717; harbor; site of colony estab. early 1620s by Sir George Calvert, lord Baltimore, abandoned 1629.

Ferryville. See MENZEL BOURGUIBA.

Ferté–Bernard, La. See LA FERTÉ-BERNARD.

Ferté–Milon, La. See LA FERTÉ-MILON.

Fertile Crescent. A semicircle of fertile land, stretching from SE coast of the Mediterranean around Syrian Desert N of Arabian Penin. to Persian Gulf; term sometimes expanded to include Nile Valley; scene of struggles and migrations of some of the earliest known peoples (Sumerians, Assyrians, Semitic tribes)—a term used by some historians of the prehistory of SW Asia.

Fertő tó. See NEUSIEDLER, LAKE.

Fès \ˈfes\ *or* **Fez** \ˈfez\ *or Arab.* **Fās** \ˈfas\. Commercial city, N cen. Morocco, ab. 150 mi. (241 km.) NE of Casablanca; pop. (1982c) 448,823; leather goods; one of the sacred cities of Islam, founded late 8th cent.; many mosques, incl. Qarawiyin, center of university; the tomb of Idrīs II, the city's founder, is a national shrine; for many years a traditional ✻ of Morocco.

Fes·sen·den \ˈfes-ᵊn-dən\. City, ⊗ of Wells co., cen. North Dakota; pop. (1990c) 655.

Festiniog. See FFESTINIOG.

Fes·tu·bert \ˌfes-tᵫ-ˈber\. Village, Pas-de-Calais dept., N France, near Béthune; scene of several battles during WWI.

Fes·tus \ˈfes-təs\. Commercial and residential city, Jefferson co., E Missouri, on Mississippi River 29 mi. (47 km.) S of St. Louis; pop. (1990c) 8105.

Fe·teşti \fə-ˈtesht\. Town, Ialomiţa co., SE Romania; pop. (1989c) 34,139; ships fruit and other agricultural products.

Fet·lar \ˈfet-ˌlär\. One of Shetland Is., NE of Scotland.

Fet·za·ra \fet-ˈsä-rə\ *also* **Fez·za·ra** \fə-\. Lake, Algeria, SW of Annaba; ab. 30 mi. (48 km.) long.

Fey·zā·bād \ˈfā-zä-ˌbäd\ *or* **Fai·zā·bād** \ˈfī-zä-ˌbäd\ *also* **Fyz·a·bad** \ˈfī-zə-ˌbad\. Town, in Badakhshān region, NE Afghanistan; alt. 4000 ft. (1220 m.); flourmills.

Fez. See FÉS.

Fé·zen·sac \ˌfā-ˌzäⁿ-ˈsak\. See ARMAGNAC.

Fez·zan \fe-ˈzan\ *or Arab.* **Faz·zān** \fá-ˈzän\; *anc.* **Pha·za·nia** \fə-ˈzā-nē-ə\. Region of desert and oases in SW Libya; area ab. 212,805 sq. mi. (551,170 sq. km.); date palms; region conquered by Romans first cent. B.C.; taken by Arabs 7th cent. A.D.; to Ottoman Empire 1842; made part of Tripoli by Italians 1912; prov. of Libya 1951–63.

Ffes·tin·i·og *or* **Fes·tin·i·og** \fes-ˈtin-yȯg\. Village, Gwynedd co., W Wales; pop. (1981p) 5437; slate deposits.

Fia·na·ran·tsoa \fyä-nä-räⁿ-ˈtsō-ə\. Commune, SE Madagascar; pop. (1990e) 124,489; in rich agricultural region.

Fich·tel·berg \ˈfik-təl-ˌberk\. Mountain, Erzgebirge, Germany; 3982 ft. (1214 m.); highest peak in former East Germany.

Fich·tel·ge·bir·ge \ˈfik-təl-gə-bir-gə\ *or Czech* **Smr·či·ny** \ˈsmər-chə-nē\. Mountain range in NE Bavaria, Germany; highest peak Schneeberg 3453 ft. (1052 m.).

Ficks·burg \ˈfiks-ˌbərg\. Town, E cen. Rep. of South Africa, on Caledon River 105 mi. (169 km.) ENE of Bloemfontein.

Fi·den·za \fē-ˈdent-sä\; *before 1927* **Bor·go San Don·ni·no** \ˈbȯr-gō-ˌsän-dȯn-ˈnē-nō\; *anc.* **Fi·den·tia** \fī-ˈden-chə, -chē-ə, fi-\; *later* **Fi·den·ti·o·la** \-ˌden-chē-ˈō-lə\. Commune, Parma prov., Emilia-Romagna, N Italy, 14 mi. (23 km.) WNW of the commune of Parma; pop. (1991p) 23,008; St. Domninus said to have been beheaded here 304 A.D.—whence its former name; part of duchy of Parma and Piacenza 1545–1859.

Fi·er \fē-ˈer\. **1.** District of SW Albania. See table at ALBANIA.
2. Town, its ✱.

Fier \ˈfyer\. River, Haute-Savoie dept., E France; flows W through Annecy to the Rhone; 41 mi. (66 km.) long; connected with Lake Annecy by Thiou Canal which runs through Annecy; noted for scenery of its gorges.

Fie·scher Glacier \ˈfē-shər\. Glacier, S cen. Switzerland, S side of Bernese Alps; 10 mi. (16 km.) long.

Fie·so·le \ˈfyā-zō-lā\; *anc.* **Fae·su·lae** \ˈfē-zu̇-lē\. Commune, Firenze prov., Tuscany, cen. Italy, 4 mi. (6 km.) NE of Florence; pop. (1991p) 15,056; health resort; 11th cent. Romanesque cathedral; episcopal palace; ruins of Etruscan city walls, Roman baths and theater; home of painter Fra Angelico. Ancient Etruscan town; conquered by Romans 3d cent. B.C.; declined with rise of Florence (*q.v.*).

Fife \ˈfīf\. **1.** *or* **Fife·shire** \-ˌshir, -shər\. Former county, E Scotland, bet. Firths of Tay and Forth; ⊗ Cupar.
2. Administrative region, E Scotland, approx. equivalent to the former county; rivers Eden and Leven; chief towns: Dunfermline, Kirkcaldy, and Buckhaven and Methil; estab. 1975. See table at SCOTLAND.

Fife Ness \ˈnes\. Headland on E coast of Fife region, E Scotland.

Fi·gue·res \fē-ˈgā-res\ *also* **Fi·gue·ras** \-res\. City, Gerona prov., NE Spain, in E Pyrenees Mts. 24 mi. (39 km.) N of the commune of Gerona; pop. (1991c) 34,573; citadel built by Ferdinand VI; occupied repeatedly by French late 18th and early 19th cents.

Fi·ji \ˈfē-jē\ *also* **Fiji Islands.** Independent republic, consisting of an island group in the SW Pacific Ocean, E of Vanuatu and SW of Samoa, bet. 16° and 19°20′S lat. and 178°W and 177°E long.; includes Rotuma (*q.v.*); 7055 sq. mi. (18,272 sq. km.); pop. (1986c) 715,735; ✱ Suva (on Viti Levu I.); crossed by 180th meridian but lies W of International Date Line; group contains over 800 islands and islets, of which ab. 100 are inhabited. Volcanic in origin, with fertile soil; highest point Mt. Tomaniivi, on Viti Levu, 4341 ft. (1323 m.).

Chief islands: Viti Levu, Vanua Levu, Taveuni, Kandavu, Koro, Gau, and Ovalau; important groups Lau Group (incl. Lakeba Is.), Yasawa Group.

Chief products: sugar, copra, fruit; gold; tourism; chief occupations fishing and agriculture.

History: According to archaeological evidence, inhabited from ancient times; first European sighting by Dutch navigator Abel Tasman 1643; visited by English explorer Capt. James Cook 1774; used by escaped convicts from Australia as early as 1804; offered to Great Britain 1858 by native ruler; annexed by Great Britain 1874; achieved independence as a member of the Commonwealth 1970; declared a republic Oct. 1987 following a military coup; membership in Commonwealth ended.

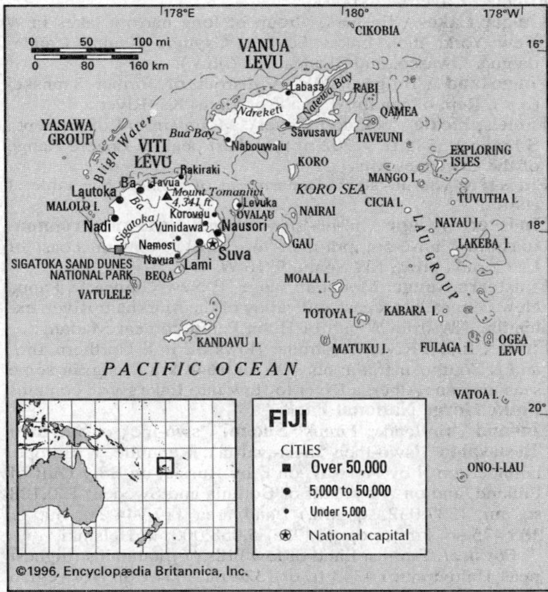

Fi·la·del·fia \ˌfē-lä-t͟hel-ˈfē-ä\. Town, ✱ of Boquerón dept., NW cen. Paraguay.

Filch·ner, Cape \ˈfilk-nər\. Point on coast of Antarctica extending into Indian Ocean at 91°53′E and ab. 66°27′S; forms dividing point bet. Queen Mary Coast and Wilhelm II Coast.

Filchner Ice Shelf. Large area of shelf ice at head of Weddell Sea, Antarctica, bet. Coats Land and Berkner I., ab. 79°S, 40°W; extends inland ab. 250 mi. (400 km.); discovered 1912.

Filipinas, Islas *or* **Filipinas, República de.** See PHILIPPINES.

Fílippoi. See PHILIPPI.

Filitrá. See PHILIATRA.

Fill·more \ˈfil-mōr\. **1.** Name of counties in two states of the U.S. See tables at MINNESOTA and NEBRASKA.
2. City, Ventura co., SW California, 43 mi. (69 km.) WNW of Los Angeles; pop. (1990c) 11,992.
3. City, ⊗ of Millard co., W Utah, 20 mi. (32 km.) NW of Richfield; pop. (1990c) 1956; founded 1851; ✱ of Utah territorial government 1851–56.

Fi·mi \ˈfē-mē\. River, W Democratic Rep. of the Congo; the section of Lukenie River bet. Lake Leopold II outlet and Kasai River.

Fi·na·le Emi·lia \fē-ˈnä-lā-ā-ˈmē-lyä\. Commune, Modena prov., Emilia-Romagna, N Italy, on Panaro River 22 mi. (35 km.) NE of the commune of Modena; pop. (1981p) 15,276.

Finale Li·gu·re \lē-ˈgü-rā\. Commune, Savona prov., Liguria, NW Italy, on Ligurian Sea 11 mi. (18 km.) SW of the seaport of Savona; pop. (1981p) 13,824; fish processing; health resort.

Fin·cas·tle \ˈfin-ˌka-səl\. Town, ⊗ of Botetourt co., W cen. Virginia; pop. (1990c) 236.

Find·horn \ˈfind-ˌhȯrn\. River, NE Scotland; flows NE in Highland and Grampian regions to empty into Moray Firth; 62 mi. (100 km.) long.

Find·lay \ˈfind-lē\. City, ⊗ of Hancock co., NW Ohio, 40 mi. (64 km.) S of Toledo; pop. (1990c) 35,703; in heart of once productive petroleum and gas region; manufactures petroleum products, tires, and machinery; Univ. of Findlay (1882); incorp. 1887.

Fingal's Cave. See STAFFA.

Fin·ger Lakes \ˈfiŋ-gər\. Group of long narrow lakes in W New York, incl. Lakes Seneca, Cayuga, Keuka, Canandaigua, Owasco, and Skaneateles (*qq.v.*).

Fin·go·land \ˈfiŋ-gō-ˌland\. A district of former Transkei (*q.v.*), Rep. of South Africa, E of Great Kei River.

Fi·niels, Pic de \ˌpēk-də-fē-ˈnyel\. Mountain in Lozère dept., S France; 5585 ft. (1702 m.); highest peak in Lozère Range of the Cévennes Mts.

Fin·is·tère \ˌfē-nē-ˈster\. Department of France. See table at FRANCE.

Fin·is·terre, Cape \ˌfē-nē-ˈster-e\; *anc.* **Ne·ri·um Pro·mon·to·ri·um** \ˈnir-ē-əm-ˌprä-mən-ˈtōr-ē-əm\. Point on coast of La Coruña prov., NW Spain, 9°16′W.

Finisterre Range. Mountain range, E New Guinea I., Papua New Guinea, bet. coast and valley of the Markham River, extending NW from W part of Huon Penin. to near Madang.

Finke \ˈfiŋk\. River, Australia; flows SE in S Northern Terr. and N South Australia; ab. 400 mi. (644 km.) long; in some seasons joins Alberga River to flow into Lake Eyre; contains **Finke Gorge National Park.**

Fin·land \ˈfin-lənd\; *Finnish* **Suo·mi** \ˈswȯ-mē\ *or* **Suo·men Ta·sa·val·ta** \ˈswȯ-men-ˈtä-sä-ˌväl-tä\. Republic, N Europe, bounded on N by Norway, on E by Russia, on S by Gulf of Finland, and on W by Gulf of Bothnia and Sweden; 130,128 sq. mi. (337,032 sq. km.) [land area 117,944 sq. mi. or 305,475 sq. km.]; pop. (1993e) 5,058,000; ✱ Helsinki.

Physical features: Land of few hills or mountains (highest peak Haltiatunturi 4343 ft. or 1324 m., in NW on Norwegian border) but of many lakes (nearly one tenth of total area) and streams (esp. Oulu and Kemi in the N).

Chief lakes: Oulujärvi, Saimaa, Näsijärvi, Keitele, Pielinen (all in S or cen. part), and Inari (in the N). Has long coastline with several excellent ports.

Chief islands: The Åland group (formerly Swedish), and Kimito, Vallgrund, and Karlö, in Gulf of Bothnia.

Chief products: Timber, oats, barley, potatoes, rye; copper, iron ore, zinc; fishing, livestock raising; manufacturing: paper, paperboard, wood pulp, clothing, textiles, chemicals; food processing, shipbuilding, machinery.

Chief cities: Helsinki, Espoo, Tampere, Turku, Vantaa.

Political divisions: Divided into the following 12 provinces (for pronunciation of their names, see their individual entries):

NAME	AREA (sq. mi.)	AREA (sq. km.)	POP. (1993e)	CAPITAL
Åland[1]	581	1,505	25,008	Mariehamn
Häme	7,499	19,422	688,355	Hämeenlinna
Keski-Suomi	7,080	18,337	255,879	Jyväskylä
Kuopio	7,727	20,013	258,712	Kuopio
Kymi	4,960	12,846	335,093	Kouvola
Lappi	38,326	99,264	202,434	Rovaniemi
Mikkeli	8,363	21,660	207,875	Mikkeli
Oulu	23,583	61,080	445,632	Oulu
Pohjois-Karjala	8,278	21,440	177,803	Joensuu
Turku ja Pori	8,886	23,015	731,792	Turku
Uusimaa	4,000	10,360	1,277,800	Helsinki
Vaasa	10,845	28,088	448,363	Vaasa

[1] An autonomous province.

History: Region widely settled by Finnish people by the beginning of the 8th cent. A.D.; conquered and Christianized by Swedes in 12th and 13th cents.; E part (see KARELIA) ceded to Russia 1721; ceded to Russia by Sweden following defeat in war of 1808–09, organized as autonomous grand duchy of the czar; 1899–1917 suffered from policy of Russification which took away constitution and other rights; proclaimed independence 1917; after civil war in which Germans helped drive out Russian forces 1918–19, independence recognized by U.S.S.R. 1920; awarded Åland Archipelago 1921 after dispute with Sweden; invaded by Soviet forces 1939 and forced to cede Karelian Isthmus and other border districts to U.S.S.R. as result of defeat 1940; joined Germany against U.S.S.R. 1941; regained lost territory temporarily 1941–44 but again forced to yield to U.S.S.R. the same territory, with slight changes (retention of Hangö by Finland in exchange for Porkkala Penin. near Helsinki and loss of Pechenga terr.); Porkkala Penin. returned to Finland 1956; member of UN and Nordic Council 1955; associate member of the European Free Trade Association 1961, full member 1986; admitted to European Community 1995.

Finland, Gulf of. Arm of Baltic Sea, S of Finland and N of Estonia; 260 mi. (418 km.) long, from 45 to 85 mi. (72 to 137 km.) wide; chief islands: Gogland, Lavansaari, and Kotlin; chief cities on it: Helsinki and Kotka (Finland), Vyborg and St. Petersburg (Russia), Narva and Tallinn (Estonia).

Fin·lay \ˈfin-lē\. River, N British Columbia, Canada; from N cen. British Columbia flows S and E to unite with Parsnip River at 56°N and form Peace River; 250 mi. (402 km.) long; regarded as ultimate headstream of Mackenzie River.

Fin·ley \ˈfin-lē\. City, ⊗ of Steele co., E North Dakota; pop. (1990c) 543.

Finmarken. See FINNMARK.

Finn \ˈfin\. **1.** River, co. Donegal, N Ireland (republic); flows E out of **Lough Finn** across co. Donegal to unite with Mourne River on Northern Ireland border and form Foyle River; 25 mi. (40 km.) long.
2. River, N Ireland; flows from SE Fermanagh district, Northern Ireland, into cos. Monaghan and Cavan in Ireland (republic) and into Upper Lough Erne, Northern Ireland.

Fin·ney \ˈfi-nē\. County in W Kansas. See table at KANSAS.

Finn·mark \ˈfin-ˌmärk\ *also* **Fin·mark·en** \-ˌmär-kən\. County of N Norway. See table at NORWAY.

Finsch·ha·fen \ˈfinch-ˌhä-fən\. Settlement on SE coast of New Guinea I., Papua New Guinea, at extremity of Huon Penin. 65 mi. (105 km.) ENE of Lae; early headquarters of German trading company; occupied by Japanese 1942 and used as an air base; retaken by Australians 1943.

Fin·ster·aar·horn \ˌfin-stə-ˈrär-ˌhȯrn\. Peak, S Switzerland; 14,019 ft. (4273 m.); highest of the Bernese Alps.

Fin·ster·wal·de \ˌfin-stər-ˈväl-də\. City, E Germany, 61 mi. (98 km.) SSE of Berlin; pop. (1981c) 23,723; 16th cent. Gothic church; to electorate of Saxony 1635; to Prussia 1815.

Fiord·land National Park \fē-ˈȯrd-ˌland, ˈfyȯrd-\. National park, SW corner of South I., New Zealand; 4725 sq. mi. (12,238 sq. km.); extends 200 mi. (322 km.) along coast indented with many sounds that resemble fjords.

Fırat Nehri. See EUPHRATES.

Fir·crest \ˈfər-ˌkrest\. Town, Pierce co., W cen. Washington, just W of Tacoma; pop. (1990c) 5258.

Fire·baugh \ˈfīr-ˌbȯ\. City, Fresno co., S cen. California, 35 mi. (56 km.) WNW of the city of Fresno; pop. (1990c) 4429.

Fire Island \ˈfīr\ *also* **Fire Island Beach.** Long narrow sandy spit of land off S cen. Long Island, New York, bet. Great South Bay and Atlantic Ocean; ab. 30 mi. (48 km.) long, 0.25 to 0.5 mi. (0.4 to 0.8 km.) wide; lighthouse on W tip; summer resort.

Fi·ren·ze \fē-ˈrent-sā\. **1.** Province of Tuscany, Italy. See table at ITALY.

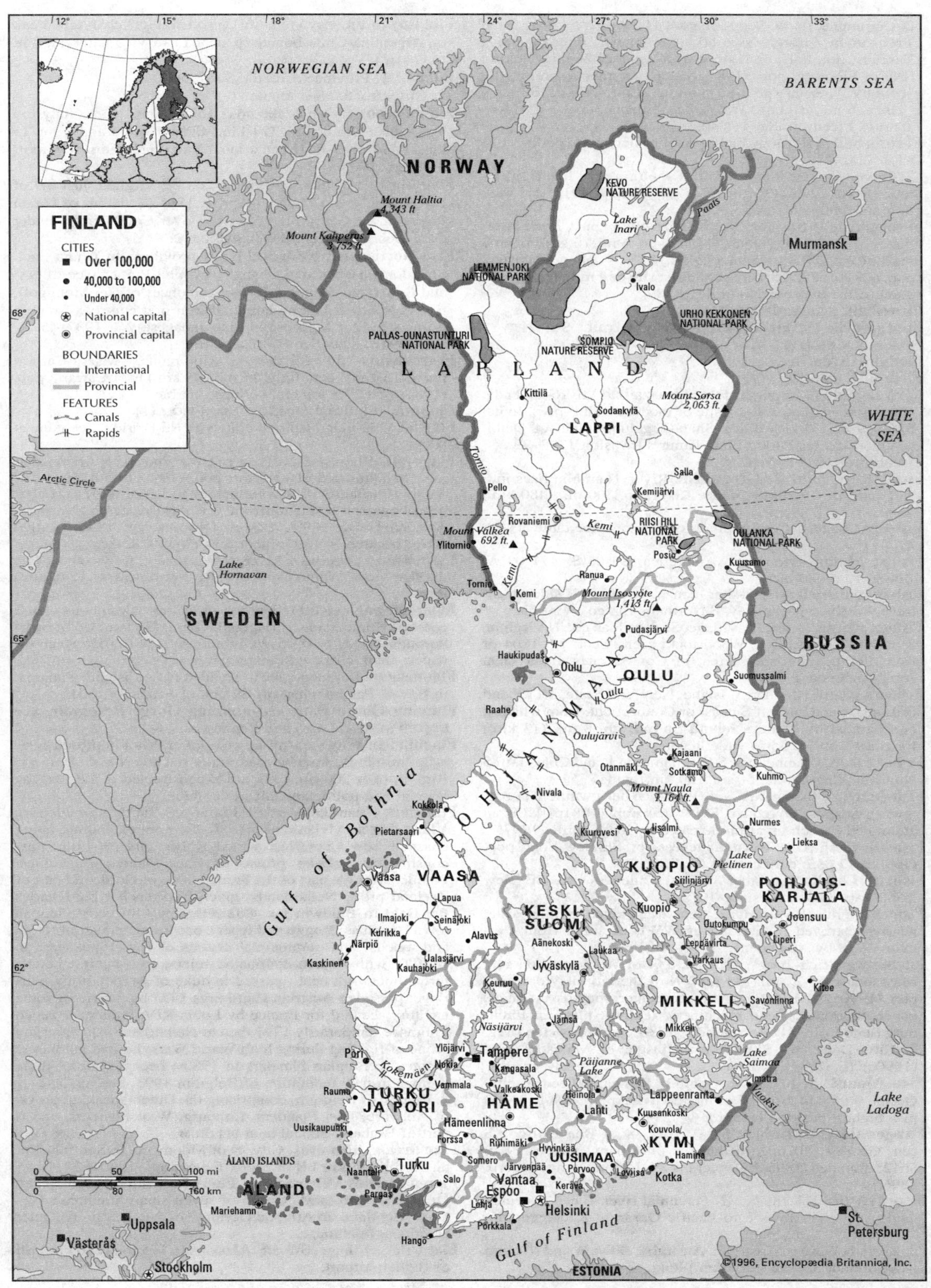

FINLAND
CITIES
Over 100,000
40,000 to 100,000
Under 40,000
National capital
Provincial capital
BOUNDARIES
International
Provincial
FEATURES
Canals
Rapids
NORWEGIAN SEA
BARENTS SEA
WHITE SEA
NORWAY
SWEDEN
RUSSIA
ESTONIA
Gulf of Bothnia
Gulf of Finland
Lake Ladoga
Arctic Circle
Mount Haltia 4,343 ft
Mount Kahperas 3,752 ft
KEVO NATURE RESERVE
Lake Inari
Paatsjoki
Murmansk
LEMMENJOKI NATIONAL PARK
Ivalo
URHO KEKKONEN NATIONAL PARK
PALLAS-OUNASTUNTURI NATIONAL PARK
SOMPIO NATURE RESERVE
LAPLAND
Kittilä
Mount Sorsa 2,063 ft
Sodankylä
LAPPI
Tornio
Salla
Pello
Kemijärvi
Rovaniemi
Kemi
RIISI HILL NATIONAL PARK
OULANKA NATIONAL PARK
Mount Valkea 692 ft.
Ylitornio
Posio
Kuusamo
Lake Hornavan
Ranua
Mount Isosyöte 1,413 ft
Pudasjärvi
Haukipudas
Oulu
OULU
POHJANMAA
Suomussalmi
Raahe
Oulujärvi
Kajaani
Otanmäki
Sotkamo
Kuhmo
Nivala
Mount Naula 1,164 ft
Kokkola
Pietarsaari
Kiuruvesi
Iisalmi
Nurmes
Lieksa
Lake Pielinen
Vaasa
VAASA
KUOPIO
Siilinjärvi
POHJOIS-KARJALA
Lapua
Kuopio
Ilmajoki
Seinäjoki
KESKI-SUOMI
Outokumpu
Joensuu
Kurikka
Alavus
Liperi
Närpiö
Äänekoski
Laukaa
Leppävirta
Jalasjärvi
Kaskinen
Kauhajoki
Jyväskylä
Varkaus
Keuruu
Kitee
MIKKELI
Savonlinna
Näsijärvi
Jämsä
Mikkeli
Ylöjärvi
Pori
Tampere
Kokemäen
Nokia
Kangasala
Päijänne Lake
Lake Saimaa
Vammala
Imatra
Vuoksi
Rauma
TURKU JA PORI
Valkeakoski
HÄME
Heinola
Lappeenranta
Lahti
Kuusankoski
Uusikaupunki
Hämeenlinna
Kouvola
Forssa
Riihimäki
Hyvinkää
KYMI
ÅLAND ISLANDS
UUSIMAA
Hamina
Somero
Järvenpää
Porvoo
Loviisa
Kotka
Naantali
Turku
Salo
Vantaa
Kerava
ÅLAND
Pargas
Espoo
Lohja
Helsinki
Mariehamn
Porkkala
Uppsala
Västerås
Hangö
St. Petersburg
Stockholm
0 50 100 mi
0 80 160 km
©1996, Encyclopædia Britannica, Inc.
12° 15° 18° 21° 24° 27° 30° 33°
68° 65° 62°

2. Commune, its ✻. See FLORENCE 11.

Fi·ren·zuo·la \fē-rent-'swō-lä\. Commune, Firenze prov., Tuscany, cen. Italy, on N slope of Apennines 24 mi. (39 km.) NNE of Florence; pop. (1981p) 5260; summer resort.

Fir·mi·ny \ˌfēr-mē-'nē\. Commune, Loire dept., SE cen. France, 6 mi. (10 km.) WSW of St.-Étienne; coal.

Firmum Picenum. See FERMO.

Fi·roz·a·bad \fi-'rō-zə-ˌbad\. **1.** Former city, India. See FĪRŪZĀBĀD.

2. Town, W Uttar Pradesh, N India, on railroad line N of Yamuna River 22 mi. (35 km.) E of Agra; pop. (1991p) 215,089; in grain-producing area.

Fi·roz·pur \fi-'rōz-ˌpu̇r\ *also* **Fe·roze·pur** \-ˌpu̇r\ *or* **Fe·roze·pore** \-ˌpōr\. City, Punjab, N India, ab. 4 mi. (6 km.) from S bank of Sutlej River 45 mi. (72 km.) SSE of Lahore, Pakistan; pop. (1991p) 77,505; three colleges; site of a military cantonment; came under British rule 1835.

Firozshah. See FEROZESHAH.

First Kurile Strait *or* **First Kuril Strait.** See PERVYY KURIL'SKIY PROLIV.

Firth of Clyde. See CLYDE 4.

Firth of Forth. See FORTH.

Fī·rū·zā·bād \fē-'rü-zä-ˌbäd\ *or* **Fi·ro·za·bad** \fi-'rō-zə-ˌbad\. One of the earlier cities on site of modern Delhi (*q.v.*), India; founded c. 1354 by Fīrūz Shāh Tughluq, sultan of Delhi; abandoned after Turkic ruler Timur's invasion 1398–99.

Fiscamnum. See FÉCAMP.

Fish \'fish\; *formerly* **Great Fish.** River, Namibia; rises in S cen. part, flows S into Orange River; ab. 300 mi. (480 km.) long.

Fish·er \'fi-shər\. County in NW cen. Texas. See table at TEXAS.

Fisher, Mount. Mountain, Antarctica, 85°06′S, 171°03′W; 13,386 ft. (4080 m.).

Fish·er·mans Island \'fi-shər-mənz\. Island at N side of entrance to Chesapeake Bay, S Northampton co., Virginia.

Fish·er's Hill \'fi-shərz\. Village, Shenandoah co., N Virginia, 8 mi. (13 km.) NNE of Woodstock; scene Sept. 22, 1864 of Gen. Philip Sheridan's defeat of Confederates under Gen. Jubal Anderson Early.

Fish·ers Island \'fi-shərz\. Island, New York state, off NE end of Long Island and off S coast of Connecticut, from which it is separated by **Fishers Island Sound;** ab. 8 mi. (13 km.) long, ab. 1 mi. (2 km.) wide; resort.

Fisher Strait. Channel bet. S Southampton I. and Coats I. in S Nunavut, Canada; ab. 50 mi. (80 km.) wide.

Fish·guard \'fish-ˌgärd\ *or Welsh* **Aber·gwaun** \ˌa-bər-'gwīn\. Seaport, Dyfed co., SW Wales; pop. (1981p) 4908; an attempted French invasion defeated by local militia 1797.

Fish·kill \'fish-ˌkil\. Town, Dutchess co., SE New York; pop. (1990c) 17,655; correctional facility.

Fishkill Landing. Former village, Dutchess co., SE New York; part of Beacon since 1913.

Fismes \'fēm\. Town, Marne dept., NE France, on the Vesle; nearly destroyed in fighting of WWI; captured from Germans 1918 by Americans.

Fitch·burg \'fich-ˌbərg\. **1.** City, a ⊗ of Worcester co., cen. Massachusetts, 22 mi. (35 km.) N of the city of Worcester; pop. (1990c) 41,194; transportation center; foundry products, paper, fabricated steel, machinery, textiles, plastics; Fitchburg State Coll. (1894); settled c. 1730; incorp. as city 1872.

2. City, Dane co., S Wisconsin, just S of Madison; pop. (1990c) 15,648.

Fi·to, Mount \'fē-tō\. Peak, Upolu I., Samoa, SW cen. Pacific Ocean, 9 mi. (14 km.) SE of the town of Apia; 3608 ft. (1100 m.); highest peak on Upolu I.

Fitz·ger·ald \fits-'jer-əld, 'fits-ˌ\. City, ⊗ of Ben Hill co., S cen. Georgia, 50 mi. (80 km.) E of Albany; pop. (1990c) 8612; founded 1895 by veterans of Union Army; incorp. 1896.

Fitz·roy \'fits-ˌrȯi, fits-'\. **1.** Perennial river, E cen. Queensland, Australia; flows E to Pacific Ocean at Rockhampton; 180 mi. (290 km.) long.

2. River, N Western Australia, Australia; flows W and NW into King Sound; 350 mi. (563 km.) long.

Fitz Roy *or* **Fitz·roy** \fēts-'rȯi\ *also* **Chal·tel** \chäl-'tel\. Peak on Argentina-Chile boundary, near Lake Viedma; 11,070 ft. (3374 m.).

Fiume. 1. Province, Croatia. See CARNARO.

2. City, Croatia. See RIJEKA.

Fiu·mi·ci·no \ˌfyü-mē-'chē-nō\. Town, Lazio, cen. Italy, on Tyrrhenian Sea 15 mi. (24 km.) SW of Rome and 3 mi. (5 km.) WNW of Ostia; Leonardo da Vinci International Airport (opened 1961).

Five Forks. Locality, Dinwiddie co., SE Virginia, just SW of Petersburg; scene Mar. 31–Apr. 1, 1865 of victory of Union forces under Gen. Philip Sheridan over Confederates under Gen. George Pickett. See DINWIDDIE 2.

Five Northern Provinces. Five N provinces of China, incl. Shandong, Hebei, and Shanxi of China Proper (see CHINA) and Cahar and Suiyuan (former provinces of Nei Monggol); rich deposits of coking coal and iron ore; control of region primary aim of Japanese in Sino-Japanese War 1937–45.

Five Towns, The. See POTTERIES, THE.

Fi·viz·za·no \ˌfē-vēd-'zä-nō\. Commune, Massa-Carrara prov., Tuscany, cen. Italy, 15 mi. (24 km.) N of Carrara; pop. (1981p) 10,271; mineral springs; marble.

Fjöllum, Jökulsá á. See JÖKULSÁ Á FJÖLLUM.

Flag·ler \'fla-glər\. Coastal county in NE Florida. See table at FLORIDA.

Flag·staff \'flag-ˌstaf\. City, ⊗ of Coconino co., N Arizona, 63 mi. (101 km.) NE of Prescott; pop. (1990c) 45,857; in Coconino Plateau S of San Francisco Peaks at 6907 ft. (2105 m.) above sea level; tourism; scientific research; Northern Arizona Univ. (1899), Lowell Observatory (1894); settled 1876; became ⊗ 1891; incorp. as city 1928.

Flam·beau \'flam-bō\. River, N Wisconsin; flows out of Lac du Flambeau SW into Chippewa River; ab. 150 mi. (240 km.) long.

Flam·bor·ough Head \'flam-ˌbər-ə, -bə-rə\. Promontory on E coast of Humberside, N England, 18 mi. (29 km.) SE of Scarborough; 54°07′N, 0°05′W; lighthouse, 214 ft. (65 m.) above water; chalk cliffs with many caverns.

Fla·men·co \flə-'meŋ-(ˌ)kō\. Small fortified island, Panama, in Bay of Panama, just off SE end of Panama Canal.

Flaming Gorge Dam *and* **Flaming Gorge Reservoir.** See UNITED STATES, *Dams and Reservoirs.*

Fla·min·i·an Way \flə-'mi-nē-ən\ *or Lat.* **Via Fla·min·ia** \ˌvē-ə-flə-'mi-nē-ə\. Ancient road, Italy; ran due N from Rome to Rimini, over 200 mi. (322 km.); constructed c. 220 B.C. by general and politician Gaius Flaminius.

Flan·ders \'flan-dərz\ *or Fr.* **Flan·dre** \'flä^{n}dr^{ə}\ *or Flemish* **Vlaan·de·ren** \'vlän-də-rən\. **1.** Region extending along coast of Low Countries; a medieval county (✻ Lille) now constituting Belgian provs. of East Flanders and West Flanders (*qq.v.*), part of the French dept. of Nord, and part of Zeeland prov., Netherlands; given by French King Charles the Bald to Baldwin I c. 862 A.D.; by 14th cent. Flemish towns (such as Brugge and Ieper), becoming industrial (cloth and metals) and commercial centers of N Europe, were in conflict with French-dominated rulers; rose against counts throughout 14th cent.; passed to duke of Burgundy by marriage; passed to Austrian Hapsburgs 1477 by marriage; some territory secured for France by Louis XIV; remainder ceded to France temporarily 1797 then to Netherlands (*q.v.*); region scene of fighting during both World Wars; limited autonomy granted to Belgian Flanders in 1980s; became one of three regions in new federation of Belgium 1993. See ARTOIS.

2. Region of Belgium; comprising the Dutch-speaking provs. of Antwerp, East Flanders, Limburg, West Flanders, and N part of Brabant. See table at BELGIUM.

Flan·dreau \'flan-drü\. City, ⊗ of Moody co., E South Dakota, 35 mi. (56 km.) N of Sioux Falls; pop. (1990c) 2311.

Flan·nan Isles \'fla-nən\ *or* **Flan·nan Islands** *also* **Seven Hunt·ers** \'hən-tərz\. Group of seven small uninhabited islands, Scotland, in Atlantic Ocean W of Lewis I. in the Outer Hebrides; lighthouse.

Flat \'flat\. Village, SW cen. Alaska, ab. 175 mi. (280 km.) NE of Bethel; airport.

Flat·bush \ˈflat-ˌbu̇sh\. Neighborhood of cen. Brooklyn, New York. See *History* at BROOKLYN 2.

Flat·head \ˈflat-ˌhed\. **1.** River, S Canada and W Montana; rises in SE British Columbia, flows S across U.S.-Canada boundary to **Flathead Lake** (ab. 30 mi. or 48 km. long, 12 to 14 mi. or 19 to 23 km. wide; 197 sq. mi. or 510 sq. km.), thence S and W into Clark Fork; 245 mi. (394 km.) long.
2. County in NW Montana. See table at MONTANA.

Flat River. City, St. Francois co., E Missouri, 55 mi. (88 km.) SSW of St. Louis; pop. (1990c) 4823; lead deposits; Mineral Area Community Coll. (1922).

Flat Rock. City, Wayne co., SE Michigan, 22 mi. (35 km.) SSW of Detroit; pop. (1990c) 7290.

Flat·tery, Cape \ˈfla-tə-rē\. Cape, NW Clallam co., NW Washington, on S side of entrance to Strait of Juan de Fuca.

Flat Top. See OTTER, PEAKS OF.

Flat·woods \ˈflat-wu̇dz\. City, Greenup co., NE Kentucky; pop. (1990c) 7799.

Flèche, La. See LA FLÈCHE.

Fleet \ˈflēt\. Town, Hampshire, S England; pop. (1981p) 26,004.

Fleet·wood \ˈflēt-ˌwu̇d\. **1.** Borough, Berks co., SE Pennsylvania, 10 mi. (16 km.) NE of Reading; pop. (1990c) 3478.
2. Port, Lancashire, NW England, on Morecambe Bay at mouth of the Wyre 20 mi. (32 km.) N of Blackpool; pop. (1981p) 28,467; trading port; seaside resort.

Flegrei, Campi. See PHLEGRAEAN FIELDS.

Fleisch·manns \ˈflīsh-mənz\. Village and summer resort, Delaware co., S New York, in Catskill Mts. ab. 32 mi. (51 km.) NW of Kingston; pop. (1990c) 351.

Flé·malle \flā-ˈmäl\. Commune, Liège prov., Belgium, SW of the city of Liège; pop. (1991c) 26,500; nearby is Flémalle fort, one of circle of forts around Liège.

Flem·ing \ˈfle-miŋ\. County in NE Kentucky. See table at KENTUCKY.

Flem·ings·burg \ˈfle-miŋz-ˌbərg\. City, ⊗ of Fleming co., NE Kentucky; pop. (1990c) 3071.

Flem·ing·ton \ˈfle-miŋ-tən\. Borough, ⊗ of Hunterdon co., NW cen. New Jersey, 21 mi. (34 km.) N of Trenton; pop. (1990c) 4047; scene of trial of Bruno R. Hauptmann 1935 for kidnapping and murder of Charles Lindbergh Jr.; settled mid-18th cent.

Flens·burg \ˈflents-ˌbu̇rk, ˈflenz-ˌbərg\. Seaport city, Schleswig-Holstein, Germany, at head of a 30-mile-long (48-kilometer-long) inlet (**Flens·burg·er För·de** \-ˌbu̇r-gər-ˈfœr-də\) of Baltic Sea near Danish border; pop. (1992e) 87,241; shipbuilding; foundries, rolling mills; paper; fish; rum; 13th cent. church. Chartered 1284; passed from Denmark to Prussia 1864; by plebiscite Mar. 1920 voted to remain in Germany; in WWII a naval base, frequently bombed.

Flers \ˈfler\. Commune, Orne dept., NW France, 38 mi. (61 km.) NW of Alençon.

Fletch·er \ˈfle-chər\. Town, Henderson co., W North Carolina, 10 mi. (16 km.) S of Asheville; pop. (1990c) 2787.

Fletsch·horn \ˈflech-ˌho̊rn\. Peak in Pennine Alps, S Switzerland, S of Simplon Pass; 13,107 ft. (3995 m.).

Fleu·rus \flœ-ˈrᵫs\. Commune, Hainaut prov., SW Belgium; pop. (1991c) 22,507; scene of battles, 1690 in which French under Francois-Henri de Montmorency-Bouteville, duc de Luxembourg, defeated Dutch and Germans, and 1794 in which French under Marshal Jean-Baptiste Jourdan defeated Austrians.

Fleu·ry \flœ-ˈrē\ *or in full* **Fleury–de·vant–Dou·au·mont** \-də-ˌvä^{n}-dwō-ˈmō^{n}\. Commune, Meuse dept., NE France; 2 mi. (3 km.) NE of Verdun; severe fighting 1916, changed hands several times.

Flevo Lacus. See ZUIDER ZEE.

Flevo·land \ˈflā-vō-ˌlänt\. Province, cen. Netherlands. See table at NETHERLANDS.

Flin·ders \ˈflin-dərz\. **1.** Largest island of the Furneaux Group off NE Tasmania, Australia; 769 sq. mi. (1992 sq. km.); 20 mi. (32 km.) wide by 40 mi. (64 km.) long; place where aboriginal Tasmanians were forced to take refuge 1831.
2. River, N Queensland, Australia; flows NW to Gulf of Carpentaria; 520 mi. (837 km.) long.

Flinders Ranges. Mountain region, E South Australia, Australia.

Flinders Reefs. Group of reefs outside Great Barrier Reef, Queensland, Australia, 17°37′S.

Flin Flon \ˈflin-ˌflän\. Town, on Manitoba-Saskatchewan border, Canada, ab. 148 mi. (238 km.) NE of Prince Albert; pop. (1991c) 7449; copper and zinc deposits.

Flinsch Peak \ˈflinch\. Mountain on Continental Divide in Glacier National Park, NW Montana; 9225 ft. (2812 m.).

Flint \ˈflint\. **1.** River, W Georgia; formed by junction of Mud and Camp creeks in Fayette co., flows into Lake Seminole; 265 mi. (426 km.) long.
2. River, SE Michigan; flows NW to unite with Shiawassee River to form Saginaw River.
3. City, ⊗ of Genesee co., SE cen. Michigan, 58 mi. (93 km.) NNW of Detroit; pop. (1990c) 140,761; historically notable automobile manufacturing center; first estab. 1904; Baker Coll. (1911), GMI Engineering and Management Institute (1919), Charles Mott Community Coll. (1923), Univ. of Michigan–Flint (1956); settled 1819; incorp. as city 1855.
4. Small island at S end of Line Is. in cen. Pacific Ocean S of Hawaii, ab. 450 mi. (725 km.) NNW of Tahiti; now part of Kiribati; U.S. claim dropped with ratification (1983) of treaty signed in 1979.
5. Former county of Wales. See FLINTSHIRE.
6. Seaport, Clwyd co., NE Wales; pop. (1981p) 16,454; coal and lead deposits; manufactures rayon, paper; received first charter 1284; scene 1399 of Richard II's submission to Henry Bolingbroke, duke of Hereford, and soon after, king of England as Henry IV.

Flint·shire \ˈflint-ˌshir, -shər\ *or* **Flint.** Former county, NE Wales; ⊗ Mold; rivers Dee, Clwyd; chief towns Rhyl, Flint. See CLWYD 2.

Flod·den \ˈfläd-^{ə}n\. Hill in N Northumberland, N England, 12 mi. (19 km.) E of Kelso near Scottish border; site (also known as **Flodden Field**) of battle 1513 in which English under Thomas Howard, 2d duke of Norfolk, defeated with great slaughter Scots under James IV, who was killed.

Flo·ra \ˈflōr-ə\. City, Clay co., SE cen. Illinois, 33 mi. (53 km.) NE of Mt. Vernon; pop. (1990c) 5054.

Flo·ral Park \ˈflōr-əl\. Residential village, Nassau co., SE New York, on Long Island 15 mi. (24 km.) E of New York City; pop. (1990c) 15,947; flower culture.

Flor·ence \ˈflo̊r-əns\. **1.** Name of counties in two states of the U.S. See tables at SOUTH CAROLINA and WISCONSIN.
2. Subdivision of town of Northampton, Massachusetts.
3. City, ⊗ of Lauderdale co., NW corner of Alabama, on Tennessee River by Wilson Dam; pop. (1990c) 36,426; Univ. of North Alabama (1872); founded 1818; incorp. as city 1889.
4. Town, ⊗ of Pinal co., S Arizona, on Gila River 50 mi. (80 km.) SE of Phoenix; pop. (1990c) 7510; copper deposits; founded 1866.
5. City, Fremont co., S cen. Colorado, on Arkansas River 35 mi. (56 km.) SSW of Colorado Springs; pop. (1990c) 2990; in oil-bearing region; founded as coal-mining center c. 1860; incorp. as city 1887.
6. City, Boone co., N Kentucky, SW of Cincinnati, Ohio; pop. (1990c) 18,624.
7. Unicorporated settlement, Burlington co., S cen. New Jersey, on Delaware River 7 mi. (11 km.) SSW of Trenton; pop. (with Roebling, 1990c) 10,266.
8. Coastal city, Lane co., Oregon, WSW of Eugene; pop. (1990c) 5162.
9. City, ⊗ of Florence co., E South Carolina, 40 mi. (64 km.) ENE of Sumter; pop. (1990c) 29,813; transportation and trade

center; tobacco, cotton; Francis Marion Univ. (1970); in Civil War shipping center and point of embarkation for troops, hospital, and prison; national Civil War cemetery is nearby.
10. Town, ⊗ of Florence co., NE Wisconsin; pop. (1990c) 2097.
11. *or Ital.* **Fi·ren·ze** \fē-ˈrent-sā\; *anc.* **Flo·ren·tia** \flə-ˈren-chə, -chē-ə\. Commune, ✻ of Firenze prov. and of Tuscany, cen. Italy, at head of navigation on Arno River at foot of Apennines, 146 mi. (235 km.) NNW of Rome; pop. (1991p) 402,316; ornamental glass and pottery, furniture, art reproductions, shoes, clothing; tourism; archiepiscopal see; university (1321); seat of Accademia della Crusca; contains ab. 40 museums. Notable structures include 13th cent. Duomo or Cathedral of Santa Maria del Fiore with 15th cent. dome, the Baptistery of St. John, churches of Santa Croce (13th cent.), Santa Maria del Carmine, Santa Maria Novella (13th cent.), San Lorenzo (with Medici chapel), San Marco, and Orsanmichele, the 14th cent. Ponte Vecchio, the Campanile, the Bargello or Palazza del Podestà (national museum), the Strozzi Palace, the Rucellai Palace, the Pitti Palace, the Boboli Gardens, the Loggia dei Lanzi, the Accademia Gallery, the Uffizi Gallery, the Laurentian Library, the Medici-Riccardi Palace, and the Palazzo Vecchio.

History: Founded at foot of hill on top of which stood Etruscan town of Faesulae (see FIESOLE); in Roman times located on Cassian Way; controlled in turn by Goths, Byzantines, and Lombards; in medieval margravate of Tuscany (*q.v.*); by end of 12th cent. a flourishing trade and industrial center; came to be governed chiefly by members of wealthy guilds; torn by bitter civil strife which reflected Guelph-Ghibelline (papal-imperial) struggle in Italy; republic gradually secured control of extensive surrounding territory, incl. Pistoia, Arezzo, Volterra, Pisa, and Livorno; after 1434 ruled by the Medici (Cosimo 1434–64, Lorenzo the Magnificent 1469–92), members of powerful banking family, who fostered development of Italian Renaissance in which Florence was a leader; republic under religious reformer Girolamo Savonarola 1494–98; final expulsion of Medici occurred 1527 but they were restored as dukes of Florence 1531 and as grand dukes of Tuscany 1569; probably greatest cultural and artistic center of W Europe (14th–16th cents.); its language diffused throughout Italy, subsequently becoming standard language of the country; ✻ of Italy 1865–71. In WWII abandoned 1944 by Germans, who destroyed all but one (Ponte Vecchio) of the Arno bridges; suffered severe flood damage to buildings and works of art 1966, now largely restored; Uffizi Gallery damaged by car bomb 1993.

Florence Lake *and* **Florence Lake Dam.** See SAN JOAQUIN 1.

Flo·ren·cia \flō-ˈren-sē-ä\. Town, ✻ of Caquetá dept., S Colombia, 120 mi. (193 km.) ENE of Pasto; munic. pop. (1992e) 108,300.

Flo·ren·cio Va·re·la \flō-ˈren-sē-ˌō-bä-ˈrā-lä\. Town, Buenos Aires prov., E Argentina, ab. 15 mi. (24 km.) SE of the city of Buenos Aires; pop. (1991p) 253,554.

Florentia. See FLORENCE 11.

Flo·res \ˈflōr-əs\. **1.** Island, NW Azores (*q.v.*); 58 sq. mi. (150 sq. km.); pop. (1991p) 4435.
2. Municipality, Pernambuco state, E Brazil, on a tributary of the São Francisco 200 mi. (322 km.) W of Recife; pop. (1980c) 22,431.
3. Town, ✻ of Petén dept., N Guatemala, on an island in a lake; pop. (1993e) 3493; stronghold of Itza Indians who were not conquered by Spaniards until 1697.
4. Island of the Lesser Sunda Is., Indonesia; ab. 224 mi. (360 km.) long; 37 mi. (60 km.) wide near W end; 6622 sq. mi. (17,151 sq. km.); largest island in the chain extending from Java to Timor, lies E of Sumbawa and bet. Flores Sea and Savu Sea; chief towns Ende and Ruteng. Volcanic in origin; several isolated peaks above 5000 ft., (1524 m.), highest 7872 ft. (2399 m.) in W cen. part; coastline has few inlets; no large rivers; exports chiefly copra, grows maize. In early times subject to the princes of Celebes (now Sulawesi); came partly under Dutch influence 17th cent., although the E end was claimed and held by Portugal until mid-19th cent.; entire island came under Dutch control 1907; under Japanese control during WWII; to Indonesia 1949.
5. Department of SW Uruguay. See table at URUGUAY.

Flores, Lago de. See PETÉN ITZÁ, LAGO.

Flores, Las. See LAS FLORES.

Flores Sea. Body of water bet. E end of Java Sea and W end of Banda Sea, bet. S Sulawesi and Lesser Sunda Is. in Indonesia; ab. 150 mi. (240 km.) wide; in SW merges with Bali Sea.

Flo·res·ville \ˈflōr-əs-ˌvil\. City, ⊗ of Wilson co., S cen. Texas, 30 mi. (48 km.) SSE of San Antonio; pop. (1990c) 5247.

Flor·ham Park \ˈflȯr-əm, ˈflär-\. Borough, Morris co., N New Jersey, 4 mi. (6 km.) E of Morristown; pop. (1990c) 8521.

Flo·ri·a·na \ˌflōr-ē-ˈä-nə, -ˈa-\. Suburb of Valletta, on island of Malta.

Flo·ri·a·nó·po·lis \ˌflō-rē-ə-ˈnȯ-pü-lis\; *formerly* **Des·têr·ro** \dēsh-ˈter-ü\. City, ✻ of Santa Catarina state, S Brazil, on Santa Catarina I.; munic. pop. (1991p) 254,944; university 1955; excellent harbor; considerable coastwise trade.

Flor·i·da \ˈflōr-ə-də, ˈflär-\. **1.** Southeast state of U.S.A., bounded on N by Alabama and Georgia, on E by Atlantic Ocean, on S by Straits of Florida and the Gulf of Mexico, on W by Gulf of Mexico and Alabama; 22d state in area, 58,664 sq. mi. (151,940 sq. km.) [land area 54,136 sq. mi. or 140,212 sq. km.]; 4th state in population, (1990c) 12,937,926; ✻ Tallahassee; 27th state admitted to Union (1845). See table of states at UNITED STATES.

Nickname: Sunshine State.

State flower: Orange blossom.

Motto: In God We Trust.

Rivers: St. Johns, rising in E cen. part and flowing N into Atlantic Ocean; Caloosahatchee, outlet of Lake Okeechobee in the S flowing W; Indian River (actually a tidal inlet) in the E extending 165 mi. (265 km.) along the coast; Kissimmee, chief headstream of the lake of same name; Withlacoochee, in the W; Suwannee and Apalachicola in the N, and the boundary rivers Perdido in the NW and St. Marys in the NE.

Highest point: 345 ft. (105 m.), located in Walton co.

Chief products: Citrus fruits, vegetables, dairy products, cattle; phosphates; electronic equipment. Tourism is a major industry.

Chief cities: Jacksonville, Miami, Tampa, St. Petersburg, Hialeah, Orlando, Fort Lauderdale.

Political divisions: Divided into the following 67 counties (for pronunciation of their names, see their individual entries):

NAME	AREA[1] (sq. mi.)	AREA[1] (sq. km.)	POP. (1990c)	CO. SEAT
Alachua	916	2,372	181,596	Gainesville
Baker	585	1,515	18,486	Macclenny
Bay	747	1,935	126,994	Panama City
Bradford	294	761	22,515	Starke
Brevard[2]	1,011	2,618	398,978	Titusville
Broward[3]	1,219	3,157	1,255,488	Fort Lauderdale
Calhoun[4]	561	1,453	11,011	Blountstown
Charlotte	703	1,821	110,975	Punta Gorda
Citrus	560	1,450	93,515	Inverness
Clay	593	1,536	105,986	Green Cove Springs
Collier[3]	2,006	5,196	152,099	East Naples
Columbia	784	2,031	42,613	Lake City
De Soto	648	1,678	23,865	Arcadia
Dixie	692	1,792	10,585	Cross City
Duval	766	1,984	672,971	Jacksonville
Escambia	665	1,722	262,798	Pensacola
Flagler	487	1,261	28,701	Bunnell
Franklin[6]	536	1,388	8,967	Apalachicola
Gadsden[6]	512	1,326	41,105	Quincy
Gilchrist	346	896	9,667	Trenton
Glades	753	1,950	7,591	Moore Haven
Gulf[4]	565	1,463	11,504	Wewahitchka
Hamilton	514	1,331	10,930	Jasper
Hardee	629	1,629	19,499	Wauchula
Hendry	1,187	3,074	25,773	La Belle
Hernando	484	1,254	101,115	Brooksville
Highlands	1,043	2,701	68,432	Sebring
Hillsborough	1,038	2,688	834,054	Tampa
Holmes	482	1,248	15,778	Bonifay
Indian River[2]	507	1,313	90,208	Vero Beach
Jackson[4]	935	2,422	41,375	Marianna
Jefferson	605	1,567	11,296	Monticello
Lafayette	549	1,422	5,578	Mayo

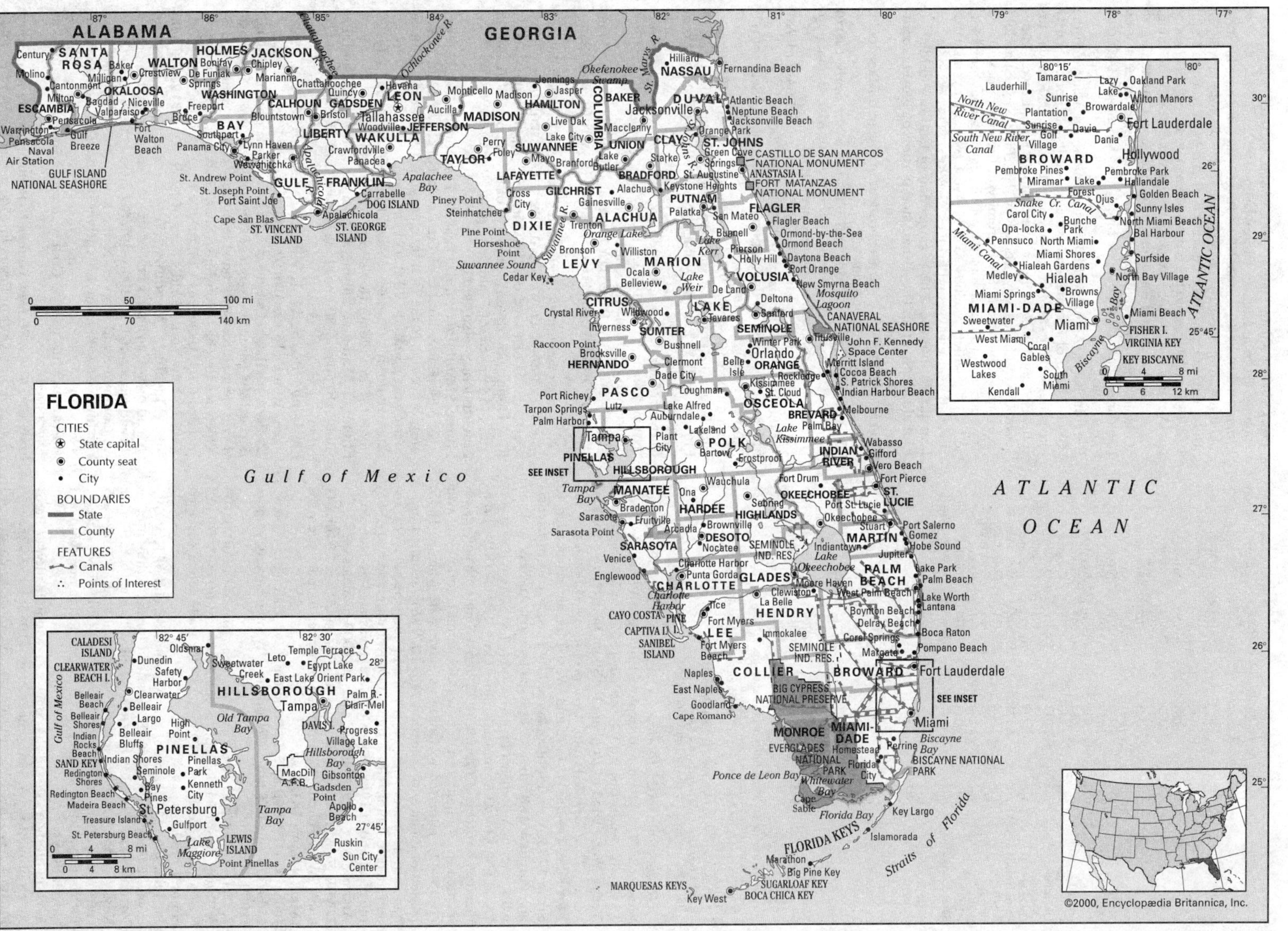

FLORIDA
CITIES
State capital
County seat
City
BOUNDARIES
State
County
FEATURES
Canals
Points of Interest
0 50 100 mi
0 70 140 km
ALABAMA
GEORGIA
ATLANTIC OCEAN
Gulf of Mexico
Straits of Florida
FLORIDA KEYS
SEE INSET
Tallahassee
Jacksonville
Orlando
Tampa
Miami
Fort Lauderdale
Pensacola
Gainesville
St. Augustine
Daytona Beach
Key West
Apalachee Bay
Tampa Bay
Lake Okeechobee
Ponce de Leon Bay
Florida Bay
Biscayne Bay
BIG CYPRESS NATIONAL PRESERVE
EVERGLADES NATIONAL PARK
BISCAYNE NATIONAL PARK
CANAVERAL NATIONAL SEASHORE
GULF ISLAND NATIONAL SEASHORE
CASTILLO DE SAN MARCOS NATIONAL MONUMENT
FORT MATANZAS NATIONAL MONUMENT
John F. Kennedy Space Center
ESCAMBIA
SANTA ROSA
OKALOOSA
WALTON
HOLMES
WASHINGTON
JACKSON
BAY
CALHOUN
GULF
LIBERTY
GADSDEN
FRANKLIN
LEON
WAKULLA
JEFFERSON
MADISON
TAYLOR
HAMILTON
SUWANNEE
LAFAYETTE
DIXIE
COLUMBIA
GILCHRIST
LEVY
BAKER
UNION
BRADFORD
ALACHUA
NASSAU
DUVAL
CLAY
ST. JOHNS
PUTNAM
FLAGLER
MARION
CITRUS
VOLUSIA
LAKE
SUMTER
HERNANDO
PASCO
SEMINOLE
ORANGE
BREVARD
OSCEOLA
POLK
HILLSBOROUGH
PINELLAS
MANATEE
HARDEE
HIGHLANDS
INDIAN RIVER
OKEECHOBEE
ST. LUCIE
MARTIN
SARASOTA
DESOTO
GLADES
CHARLOTTE
LEE
HENDRY
PALM BEACH
BROWARD
COLLIER
MONROE
MIAMI-DADE
BROWARD
MIAMI-DADE
Hialeah
Hollywood
Miami Beach
KEY BISCAYNE
ATLANTIC OCEAN
0 4 8 mi
0 6 12 km
PINELLAS
HILLSBOROUGH
St. Petersburg
Clearwater
Old Tampa Bay
Hillsborough Bay
Gulf of Mexico
0 4 8 mi
0 4 8 km
©2000, Encyclopædia Britannica, Inc.

NAME	AREA[1] (sq. mi.)	AREA[1] (sq. km.)	POP. (1990c)	CO. SEAT
Lake	961	2,489	152,104	Tavares
Lee	785	2,033	335,113	Fort Myers
Leon	670	1,735	192,493	Tallahassee
Levy	1,183	3,064	25,923	Bronson
Liberty[6]	839	2,173	5,569	Bristol
Madison	703	1,821	16,569	Madison
Manatee	739	1,914	211,707	Bradenton
Marion	1,599	4,141	194,833	Ocala
Martin	556	1,440	100,900	Stuart
Miami-Dade[3,5]	2,042	5,289	1,937,094	Miami
Monroe[3,5]	1,034	2,678	78,024	Key West
Nassau[7]	650	1,684	43,941	Fernandina Beach
Okaloosa	944	2,445	143,776	Crestview
Okeechobee	777	2,012	29,627	Okeechobee
Orange	910	2,357	677,491	Orlando
Osceola	1,310	3,393	107,728	Kissimmee
Palm Beach[3]	1,978	5,123	863,518	West Palm Beach
Pasco	742	1,922	281,131	Dade City
Pinellas	265	686	851,659	Clearwater
Polk	1,861	4,820	405,382	Bartow
Putnam	779	2,018	65,070	Palatka
Saint Johns	605	1,567	83,829	St. Augustine
Saint Lucie[2]	584	1,513	150,171	Fort Pierce
Santa Rosa	1,032	2,673	81,608	Milton
Sarasota	587	1,520	277,776	Sarasota
Seminole	305	790	287,529	Sanford
Sumter	555	1,437	31,577	Bushnell
Suwannee	686	1,777	26,780	Live Oak
Taylor	1,051	2,722	17,111	Perry
Union	241	624	10,252	Lake Butler
Volusia	1,062	2,751	370,712	De Land
Wakulla	601	1,557	14,202	Crawfordville
Walton	1,053	2,727	27,760	De Funiak
Washington	585	1,515	16,919	Chipley

1 Area = land area.
2 Indian River (inlet) along full extent of shoreline.
3 These counties include Everglades region.
4 On E bounded by Apalachicola River, former boundary of old colonies of East and West Florida.
5 Includes part of Florida Keys (island chain).
6 On W bounded by Apalachicola River.
7 Includes Amelia I., S end of Sea Islands chain.

History: Spanish Florida, which included SE part of present U.S., sighted and explored by Juan Ponce de León 1513; St. Augustine (*q.v.*) settled 1565; following Seven Years' War, ceded to England by Spain in exchange for Havana 1763; divided into two provinces (known as the **Flor·i·das** \-ə-dəz\), East and West Florida; retroceded to Spain 1783; West Florida claimed by U.S. as part of Louisiana Purchase 1803; border crossed by Gen. Andrew Jackson who captured Pensacola 1814 and 1818; purchased for $5,000,000 by U.S. under Adams-Onís Treaty 1819; organized as territory of Florida 1822; most Seminole natives relocated to Indian Terr. (now Oklahoma) following war (1835–42); admitted to Union as slave state Mar. 3, 1845; passed ordinance of secession Jan. 10, 1861; annulled ordinance of secession Oct. 28, 1865 and abolished slavery; readmitted to Union 1868; present constitution adopted 1885, much amended 1968; S part of state devastated by Hurricane Andrew Aug. 1992 leaving over 200,000 homeless.

2. Village, Monroe co., NE Missouri, on Salt River 28 mi. (45 km.) SW of Hannibal; birthplace of writer Samuel Clemens (Mark Twain) 1835.

Flo·ri·da \flō-ˈrē-t͟hä\. **1.** Municipality, Camagüey prov., Cuba, 23 mi. (37 km.) NW of the city of Camagüey; pop. (1990e) 50,793.

2. Department of S cen. Uruguay. See table at URUGUAY.

3. Town, ✱ of Florida dept., S cen. Uruguay, 60 mi. (97 km.) N of Montevideo; pop. (1985c) 28,445; trade center for agricultural products.

Flor·i·da, Cape \ˈflōr-ə-də, ˈflär-\. Point, SE end of Key Biscayne, Biscayne Bay, off SE coast of Florida; lighthouse.

Florida, Straits of *also* **Florida Strait.** Channel bet. Florida Keys (S end of Florida) and N coast of Cuba; ab. 90 mi. (145 km.) wide; connects Atlantic Ocean and Gulf of Mexico.

Florida Bay. Body of water bet. S tip of Florida mainland and Florida Keys.

Flo·ri·da·blan·ca \flō-ˌrē-t͟hä-ˈbläŋ-kä\. Municipality, W Pampanga prov., Luzon, Philippines; pop. (1985c) 137,975.

Florida City. City, Miami-Dade co., SE Florida, 25 mi. (40 km.) SSW of Miami; pop. (1990c) 5806; suffered widespread damage from hurricane Andrew Aug. 1992.

Florida Island \ˈflōr-ə-də, ˈflär-; flō-ˈrē-t͟hä\ *or* **Ngge·la Su·le Ai·lan** \əŋ-ˈge-lä-ˈsü-le-ˈī-län\. Island in SE Solomon Is. in SW Pacific Ocean, N of Guadalcanal and W of Malaita I.; 22 mi. (35 km.) long and ab. 6 mi. (10 km.) wide; off its W shore is Olevuga I. and close to its S shore are the islands of Tulagi (*q.v.*), Gavutu, and Tanambogo; off SE coast stretching to Guadalcanal are shoals and reefs, interrupted in center by Sealark Channel. Occupied briefly by Japanese 1942 (see also SAVO).

Florida Keys. A chain of islands extending in a curve to the SW off S tip of Florida, on N side of Straits of Florida; partly in Miami-Dade co. but chiefly in Monroe co., Florida; includes Key Largo, Upper Matecumbe Key, Lower Matecumbe Key, Long Key, Vaca Key, Big Pine Key, Sugarloaf Key, and Key West at SW extremity of the group; devastated by hurricane 1935; traversed by Overseas Highway, completed 1938, which extends to Key West over many miles of landfill, causeways, and bridges. See KEY WEST.

Florida Panhandle. The W projection of land in Florida.

Florida Peninsula. The E mainland portion of Florida, comprising the greater part of the state's area.

Flo·ri·na \ˈflō-rē-nä\. **1.** Department of Western Macedonia, Greece. See table at GREECE.

2. *also* **Fló·ri·na** *or* **Phló·ri·na** \ˈflō-rē-nä\ *or Serb.* **Le·rin** \le-ˈrēn\. City, its ✱, near border of Rep. of Macedonia; pop. (1991p) 12,768; seized by Germans 1941.

Flor·is·sant \ˈflōr-ə-sənt\. City, St. Louis co., E Missouri, NW of the city of St. Louis; pop. (1990c) 51,206.

Florissant Fossil Beds National Monument. See UNITED STATES, *National Monuments.*

Floss·moor \ˈfläs-ˌmu̇r, ˈflȯs-\. Village, Cook co., NE Illinois, ab. 8 mi. (13 km.) S of Chicago; pop. (1990c) 8651.

Flow·er Hill \ˈflau̇-ər\. Village, Nassau co., SE New York; pop. (1990c) 4490.

Flower Mound. Town, Denton co., N Texas, 15 mi. (24 km.) NW of Dallas; pop. (1990c) 15,527.

Flowery Kingdom. See CHINA.

Floyd \ˈflȯid\. **1.** River, NW Iowa; ab. 80 mi. (130 km.) long; rises in O'Brien co., flows SW into Missouri River at Sioux City.

2. Name of counties in six states of the U.S. See tables at GEORGIA, INDIANA, IOWA, KENTUCKY, TEXAS, VIRGINIA.

3. Town, ⊗ of Floyd co., SW Virginia; pop. (1990c) 396.

Floyd·a·da \flȯi-ˈdā-də\. Town, ⊗ of Floyd co., NW Texas, 28 mi. (45 km.) SE of Plainview; pop. (1990c) 3896.

Fluchthorn. See SILVRETTA.

Flume Mountain \ˈflüm\. Peak in Franconia Mts., Grafton co., New Hampshire, E of Franconia Notch; 4327 ft. (1319 m.); on W side is the **Flume,** a canyon, 12 ft. (4 m.) wide at narrowest point, ab. 70 ft. (21 m.) deep.

Flu·men·do·sa \ˌflü-men-ˈdō-sä\. River, SE Sardinia, Italy; 79 mi. (127 km.) long; flows into Tyrrhenian Sea.

Flu·mi·ni Man·nu \ˈflü-mē-nē-ˈmän-nü\. River, S Sardinia, Italy; ab. 50 mi. (80 km.) long; enters Gulf of Cagliari at Cagliari.

Flush·ing \ˈflə-shiŋ\. **1.** Village, Genesee co., SE cen. Michigan, 10 mi. (16 km.) WNW of Flint; pop. (1990c) 8542.

2. Former village, Queens co., SE New York, on Long Island; since 1898 part of borough of Queens, New York City; mostly residential; formerly notable nursery center; scene of U.S. Open tennis championships; Shea Stadium; Coll. of Aeronautics (1932), Queens Coll. of the City Univ. of New York (1937); New York World's Fairs of 1939–40 and 1964–5 held in **Flushing Meadows,** now site of **Flushing Mead·ows–Co·ro·na Park** \ˈme-dōz-kə-ˈrō-nə\; temporary headquarters of UN (1946–49). See also QUEENS 2.

3. Commune and seaport, Netherlands. See VLISSINGEN.

Flushing Bay. Inlet of East River, N shore of Long Island, New York.

Flu·van·na \flü-ˈva-nə\. County in cen. Virginia. See table at VIRGINIA.

Fly \ˈflī\. River, SE New Guinea I., Papua New Guinea; flows S and SE into Gulf of Papua in wide estuary; part of its middle course forms boundary with Irian Jaya, Indonesia; ab. 650 mi. (1045 km.) long; one of the largest rivers in New Guinea, navigable for more than 500 mi. (805 km.).

Foa \ˈfō-ä\. Island in Haapai group, Tonga, SW cen. Pacific Ocean.

Foard \ˈfōrd\. County in N Texas. See table at TEXAS.

Fo·ça *or* **Fo·cha** \fō-ˈchä\. Two seaports İzmir prov., W Turkey in Asia, on Gulf of İzmir: (1) **Ye·ni·fo·ça** \ye-ˌnē-fō-ˈchä\ (New Foça), founded 1421 by Genoese. (2) **Foça;** *formerly* **Es·ki Foça** \es-ˌkē\ (Old Foça); *anc.* **Pho·caea** \fō-ˈsē-ə\, ab. 5 mi. (8 km.) S of Yenifoça; most northerly of the 12 Ionian Cities on W coast of Asia Minor; a flourishing maritime state c. 800–600 B.C.; estab. several colonies, incl. Massilia (Marseille) 600 B.C.; abandoned to conquering Persians 540 B.C.

Foc·şa·ni \fōk-ˈshänʸ, -ˈshä-nyə\. City, ⊗ of Vrancea co., E cen. Romania; pop. (1989c) 101,799; wine; scene of battles: (1) 1789 in which a combined Austrian-Russian army defeated the Turks; (2) 1917 when it was taken by Austrian and German forces; German-Romanian armistice signed here Dec. 6, 1917.

Fog·gia \ˈfò-jä\. **1.** Province of Puglia, SE Italy. See table at ITALY.
2. Commune, its ✻, 162 mi. (261 km.) ESE of Rome; pop. (1991p) 155,042; cellulose; wool market; cheese; in region producing olives, grapes, tobacco, wheat; center of great Puglia plain or "tavoliere"; ruins of 13th cent. castle of Frederick II; airfields captured by British 1943.

Fog·gy Bot·tom \ˈfò-gē-ˈbät-ᵊm, ˈfä-\. Area of bottomland along Potomac River in Washington, D.C.; site of U.S. Department of State headquarters.

Fo·go \ˈfō-gü\. One of Cape Verde Is., in S part of group; ab. 190 sq. mi. (490 sq. km.); pop. (1990p) 33,860; contains active volcano ab. 9281 ft. (2829 m.), highest point in islands.

Fogo \ˈfō-gō\. Seaport town, E Newfoundland, Canada, on N shore of **Fogo Island,** E of entrance to Notre Dame Bay; pop. (1991c) 1030.

Föhr \ˈfœr\. Island off W coast of Schleswig-Holstein, N Germany, one of North Frisian Is.; 32 sq. mi. (83 sq. km.); chief town Wyk.

Foix \ˈfwä\. Commune, ✻ of Ariège dept., S France, at foot of the Pyrenees 47 mi. (76 km.) S of Toulouse; pop. (1990c) 10,446; tourism.

Foix, Countship of. Historical region of S cen. France; bordered anciently on N and E by Languedoc, on SE by Roussillon, on S by the Pyrenees, and on W by Gascony; capitals Foix and Pamiers; watered by Ariège River; made countship 11th cent.; became connected with Navarre 15th cent. by marriage; joined to French crown at ascension of Henry IV to throne of France 1589.

Fol·croft \ˈfäl-ˌkrȯft\. Borough, Delaware co., SE Pennsylvania, 1.3 mi. (2 km.) W of S Philadelphia; pop. (1990c) 7506.

Fo·ley \ˈfō-lē\. **1.** Town, Baldwin co., SW Alabama, 30 mi. (48 km.) SE of Mobile; pop. (1990c) 4937.
2. Village, ⊗ of Benton co., cen. Minnesota, 15 mi. (24 km.) ENE of St. Cloud; pop. (1990c) 1854.

Fo·li·gno \fō-ˈlēn-yō\; *anc.* **Ful·gin·i·um** \ˌfu̇l-ˈji-nē-əm, ˌfəl-\. Commune, Perugia prov., Umbria, cen. Italy, 18 mi. (29 km.) SE of Perugia; pop. (1991p) 50,947; paper, sugar; 12th cent. cathedral; two Renaissance palaces. Ancient Umbrian settlement; ruled by the Guelph (papal-supporting) Trinci family 1305–1439; part of Papal States 1439–1860, of Italy from 1860.

Folke·stone \ˈfōk-stən\. Seaport and summer resort, Kent, SE England, on Strait of Dover 6 mi. (10 km.) WSW of Dover; pop. (1981p) 43,742; fisheries; terminus of Channel Tunnel; restored medieval church; dates back to Roman and Saxon times.

Folk·ston \ˈfōk-stən\. City, ⊗ of Charlton co., SE Georgia; pop. (1990c) 2285.

Fol·lans·bee \ˈfä-lənz-bē\. City, Brooke co., N West Virginia, on Ohio River 19 mi. (31 km.) N of Wheeling; pop. (1990c) 3339.

Fol·som \ˈfōl-səm\. **1.** City, Sacramento co., California, NE of the city of Sacramento; pop. (1990c) 29,802; state prison.
2. Village, Union co., NE New Mexico, E of Raton; pop. (1990c) 71; nearby is site where in 1926 were first found artifacts, esp. chipped stone projectile points (*Folsom points*), considered as representative of culture of a Stone Age people of North America from approx. 9000 B.C. (late Pleistocene).

Fom·bo·ni \fȯm-ˈbō-nē\. See MWALI.

Fo·men·to \fō-ˈmen-tō\. Town and municipality, Las Villas prov., W cen. Cuba; munic. pop. (1981p) 32,356.

Fon·da \ˈfän-də\. Village, ⊗ of Montgomery co., E New York, on Mohawk River 12 mi. (19 km.) W of Amsterdam; pop. (1990c) 1007; settled by Dutch 18th cent.; burned by Loyalist troops 1780; became ⊗ 1836.

Fond du Lac \ˈfänd-ᵊl-ˌak, ˈfän-jə-ˌlak\. **1.** County in E Wisconsin. See table at WISCONSIN.
2. City and resort, its ⊗, at S end of Lake Winnebago; pop. (1990c) 37,757; machine tools, outboard motors, leather, automobile parts; dairy products; Marian Coll. of Fond du Lac (1936); cathedral. French trading post 18th cent.; settled 1836; lumbering town until railroad brought industrialization.
3. River, N Saskatchewan, Canada; flows W to Lake Athabaska; ab. 100 mi. (160 km.) long.

Fon·di \ˈfōn-dē\; *anc.* **Fun·di** \ˈfən-ˌdī\. Commune, Latina prov., Lazio, cen. Italy, 29 mi. (47 km.) ESE of the commune of Latina; pop. (1991p) 31,122; on ancient Appian Way; 15th cent. castle; Gothic cathedral.

Fon·ga·fa·le \ˌfȯŋ-gä-ˈfä-lā\. Administrative center, Funafuti Atoll, Tuvalu.

Fon·sa·gra·da \ˌfän-sä-ˈgrä-t͟hä\. Commune, Lugo prov., NW Spain, 27 mi. (43 km.) ENE of the commune of Lugo; pop. (1991c) 6986.

Fon·se·ca, Gulf of \fȯn-ˈsā-kä\ *also* **Fonseca Bay.** Large inlet of Pacific Ocean with El Salvador on N, Honduras on E, and Nicaragua on S.

Fon·taine \fōⁿ-ˈten\. Commune, Isère dept., France; in Franche-Comté historical region.

Fon·taine·bleau \ˌfōⁿ-ten-ˈblō\. Commune, Seine-et-Marne dept., N France, near left bank of the Seine 35 mi. (56 km.) SSE of Paris; pop. (1990c) 18,037; in forest of Fontainebleau; barracks, military college, communal college, school of designing and engineering; famous for its château (SE of town), former residence of French kings, now summer residence of presidents of France; place where revocation of Edict of Nantes was signed 1685, where Pope Pius VII was held prisoner by Emperor Napoléon 1812–14, and where Napoléon signed his first abdication 1814.

Fon·tana \fän-ˈta-nə\. City, San Bernardino co., S California, W of the city of San Bernardino; pop. (1990c) 87,535.

Fontana Dam. See table at TENNESSEE VALLEY AUTHORITY.

Fontanet. See FONTENOY 2.

Fontarabia. See FUENTERRABÍA.

Font–de–Gaume. See EYZIES, LES.

Fon·te·nay–aux–Roses \fōⁿt-ˌnā-ō-ˈrōz\. Commune, Hauts-de-Seine dept., N France; a S suburb of Paris.

Fontenay–le–Comte \-lə-ˈkōⁿt\. Town, SE Vendée dept., W France; 25 mi. (40 km.) NE of La Rochelle; scene of much fighting during 16th cent. Wars of Religion; ✻ of dept. of Vendée 1790–1806.

Fontenay–sous–Bois \-sü-ˈbwä\. Commune, Val-de-Marne dept., N France; a SE suburb of Paris.

Fon·te·noy \fōⁿt-ˈnwä\. **1.** Commune, Hainaut prov., SW Belgium, 5 mi. (8 km.) ESE of Tournai; scene of battle May 11, 1745 during War of Austrian Succession in which French under Maurice of Saxony (Marshal Saxe) with help of Irish Brigade defeated a combined force of British, Hannoverians, Austrians, and Dutch under William Augustus, duke of Cumberland.

\ə\ **abut** \ᵊ\ matches \ᵊ\ kitten, Fr table \ər\ **further** \a\ **ash** \ā\ **ace** \ä\ **cot, cart** \å\ Fr bac \au̇\ **out** \b\ Span Avila \ch\ **chin** \e\ **bet** \ē\ **easy** \g\ **go** \i\ **hit** \ī\ **ice** \j\ **job** \k\ Ger **ich, Buch** \ⁿ\ Fr vin \ŋ\ **sing** \ō\ **go** \ȯ\ **all** \ȯi\ **law** \œ\ Fr **bœuf** \œ̄\ Fr **feu** \ȯi\ **boy** \th\ **thin** \t͟h\ **this** \ü\ **loot** \u̇\ **foot** \ue\ Ger **füllen** \ue̅\ Fr **rue** \y\ **yet** \ʸ\ Fr digne \ˈdēnʸ\, nuit \ˈnwʸē\ \yü\ **few** \yu̇\ **fury** \zh\ **vision**

2. *formerly* **Fon·ta·net** \ˌfȯⁿ-tə-ˈnā\. Town, Yonne dept., NE cen. France, S of Sens; scene of defeat of Emperor Lothair I by his brothers Charles the Bald and Louis the German 841.

Fon·te·vrault \ˌfȯⁿ-tə-ˈvrō\ *or in full* **Fontevrault–l'Ab·baye** \-lȧ-ˈbā\. Town, Maine-et-Loire dept., W France, ESE of Saumur; pop. (1990c) 1818; abbey, founded 1099, where early Plantagenet kings were buried, made a prison under Emperor Napoléon.

Font·vieille \ˌfȯⁿ-ˈvyā\. Commune, Monaco, SW of Monaco-Ville.

Foochow. See FUZHOU.

Foots·cray \ˈfu̇ts-ˌkrā\. Municipality, S Victoria, SE Australia, W suburb of Melbourne; pop. (1991c) 46,844; bluestone deposits.

For·a·ker, Mount \ˈfȯr-i-kər, ˈfär-\. Mountain in Alaska Range in Denali National Park, S cen. Alaska, SW of Mt. McKinley; 17,400 ft. (5304 m.).

For·bach \fȯr-ˈbȧk\. Commune, Moselle dept., NE France, 32 mi. (51 km.) E of Metz; pop. (1990c) 27,357; paper; coal deposits nearby; scene of battle Aug. 6, 1870 in which French under Gen. Charles-Auguste Frossard were defeated by the Prussians.

Forbes \ˈfȯrbz\. Town, E cen. New South Wales, SE Australia, 185 mi. (298 km.) WNW of Sydney; pop. (1991c) 10,343; flour mills, sawmills.

Forbes, Mount. Peak in Banff National Park, SW Alberta, Canada; 11,852 ft. (3612 m.).

Forbidden City. **1.** City, Tibet, China. See LHASA.

2. The walled enclosure, Beijing, China (ab. 0.33 sq. mi. or 0.85 sq. km.), containing the Imperial Palace, with its pleasure grounds, reception halls, pavilions, and offices of state — so called because it was formerly closed to the public.

For·ca·dos \fȯr-ˈkä-dōs\. **1.** The main navigable channel of Niger River, S Nigeria.

2. Town, S Nigeria, on coast 160 mi. (257 km.) SE of Lagos; main port of entry at mouth of Niger River.

Forch·heim \ˈfōrk-ˌhīm\. City, Bavaria, Germany, 20 mi. (32 km.) N of Nürnberg; pop. (1980c) 29,021; 14th cent. bishop's palace and remains of 16th–17th cent. fortifications; first mentioned c. 8th cent.; to Bavaria early 19th cent.

Ford \ˈfōrd\. Name of counties in two states of the U.S. See tables at ILLINOIS and KANSAS.

Ford City. Borough, Armstrong co., W Pennsylvania, on Allegheny River 34 mi. (55 km.) NE of Pittsburgh; pop. (1990c) 3413.

Ford·ham \ˈfōr-dəm\. Former village now included in Bronx borough, New York City, New York; Fordham Univ. (1841).

Ford Heights; *formerly* **East Chicago Heights.** Village, Cook co., NE Illinois, 9 mi. (14 km.) S of Chicago; pop. (1990c) 4259.

Ford Island. Island in Pearl Harbor, S Oahu, Hawaiian Is., N Pacific Ocean.

Ford·lan·dia \ˌfōrd-ˈlan-dē-ə\. Abondoned town, Pará state, NE Brazil, on Tapajós River ab. 110 mi. (177 km.) S of Santarém; formerly one of the Ford rubber plantations.

Ford Ranges; *formerly* **Ed·sel Ford Ranges** \ˈed-səl\. Mountain groups and ranges, NW Marie Byrd Land, Antarctica; extend S from shelf ice at 140° to 145°W and 76° to 78°S; highest peak ab. 14,000 ft. (4270 m.).

For·dyce \ˈfōr-ˌdīs\. City, ⊗ of Dallas co., S cen. Arkansas, 30 mi. (48 km.) NE of Camden; pop. (1990c) 4729.

Fo·rel, Mount \fō-ˈrel\. Mountain, E Greenland, near coast N of Angmagssalik; 11,024 ft. (3360 m.).

Fore·land, North \ˈfōr-lənd\ *and* **South Foreland.** Two headlands in Kent, SE England: North Foreland, 2.5 mi. (4 km.) SE of Margate; South Foreland, 3 mi. (5 km.) NE of Dover; both have lighthouses; nearby naval battle 1666 in which British defeated a Dutch fleet under Adm. Michiel de Ruyter.

Foreland Sound. See PRINCE CHARLES FORELAND.

Fore River \ˈfōr\ *or in full* **Wey·mouth Fore River** \ˈwā-məth\. Inlet of Boston Bay on coast of Norfolk co., E Massachusetts; formerly site of large shipyards at Quincy.

For·est \ˈfȯr-əst, ˈfär-\. **1.** Name of counties in two states of the U.S. See tables at PENNSYLVANIA and WISCONSIN.

2. City, ⊗ of Scott co., cen. Mississippi, 41 mi. (66 km.) E of Jackson; pop. (1990c) 5060.

3. *or* **Vorst** \ˈvȯrst\. Commune, Brabant prov., cen. Belgium, a suburb of Brussels; pop. (1991c) 46,437.

Forest Acres. Town, Richland co., W cen. South Carolina, 6 mi. (10 km.) W of Columbia; pop. (1990c) 7197.

Forest Cantons, The Four *or Ger.* **Die Vier Wald·stät·ter** \dē-ˈfir-ˈvält-ˌshte-tər\. Uri, Schwyz, Unterwalden, and Lucerne cantons, Switzerland, surrounding Lake of Lucerne (Lake of the Four Forest Cantons); Uri, Schwyz and Unterwalden, first to unite against Hapsburgs 1291, were nucleus of Swiss Confederation. See SWITZERLAND.

Forest City. **1.** City, ⊗ of Winnebago co., N Iowa, 25 mi. (40 km.) WNW of Mason City; pop. (1990c) 4430; Waldorf Coll. (1903).

2. Town, Rutherford co., SW North Carolina, 20 mi. (32 km.) W of Shelby; pop. (1990c) 7475.

Forest Grove. City, Washington co., NW Oregon, 22 mi. (35 km.) W of Portland; pop. (1990c) 13,559; Pacific Univ. (1849).

Forest Heights. Town, Prince Georges co., S cen. Maryland, bordering on SE Washington, D.C.; pop. (1990c) 2859.

Forest Hill. Village, Tarrant co., Texas, 6 mi. (10 km.) SE of Fort Worth; pop. (1990c) 11,482.

Forest Hills. **1.** Residential community in Queens borough, New York City, New York; on Long Island; formerly scene of national tennis tournaments.

2. Borough, Allegheny co., SW Pennsylvania, ab. 2 mi. (3.2 km.) E of Pittsburgh; pop. (1990c) 7335.

Forest Lake. Village, Washington co., E Minnesota, 25 mi. (40 km.) N of St. Paul; pop. (1990c) 5833; resort.

Forest of Ardennes. See ARDENNES 1.

Forest Park. **1.** Town, Clayton co., NW cen. Georgia, SSE suburb of Atlanta; pop. (1990c) 16,925; large farmers market.

2. Residential village, Cook co., NE Illinois, W suburb of Chicago; pop. (1990c) 14,918.

3. Residential suburb, Hamilton co., SW Ohio, 12 mi. (19 km.) N of Cincinnati; pop. (1990c) 18,609.

For·est·ville \ˈfȯr-əst-ˌvil, ˈfär-\. Subdivision of town of Bristol, Connecticut. See BRISTOL 2.

Fo·rez \fō-ˈrez\. Ancient region, cen. France, a plain bet. the upper Loire and the Allier rivers, W of Lyon; bordered on W by **Forez Mountains;** medieval countship dependent on Burgundy; united with France 1527.

For·far \ˈfȯr-fər\. **1.** *or* **For·far·shire** \-ˌshir, -shər\. Former county of Scotland. See ANGUS.

2. Burgh, E Tayside region, E Scotland; pop. (1981p) 12,742; jute, linen goods; site of castle, residence of early Scottish kings, destroyed early 14th cent. by Robert I the Bruce.

Fo·ril·lon National Park \ˌfō-rē-ˈyōⁿ\. See CANADA, *National Parks.*

Fork·ed Deer \ˈfȯr-kəd-ˈdir\. River, W Tennessee; formed by confluence of long N and S forks in S Dyer co.; flows W into Mississippi River; ab. 15 mi. (24 km.) long. See OBION 1.

Forks \ˈfȯrks\. Town, Clallam co., Washington, WSW of Port Angeles; pop. (1990c) 2862.

For·lì \fȯr-ˈlē\. **1.** Province of Emilia-Romagna, N Italy. See table at ITALY.

2. *anc.* **Fo·rum Liv·ii** \ˌfōr-əm-ˈli-vē-ˌī\. Commune, its ✱, 168 mi. (270 km.) SE of Milan; pop. (1991p) 109,228; household appliances, furniture; episcopal see; 14th–15th cent. citadel; cathedral; allied with Ravenna 12th cent.; became part of Papal States 1504; to Italy 1861.

For·man \ˈfōr-mən\. City, ⊗ of Sargent co., SE North Dakota; pop. (1990c) 586.

Form·by \ˈfȯrm-bē\. Town, Merseyside; NW England, on Irish Sea 10 mi. (16 km.) N of Liverpool; pop. (1981p) 25,798.

For·men·te·ra \ˌfȯr-men-ˈtā-rä\; *anc.* **Oph·i·u·sa** \ˌä-fē-ˈyü-sə, ˌō-\. Fourth largest island of the Balearic group, Baleares prov., Spain, in W Mediterranean Sea S of Ibiza I. and 82 mi. (132 km.) SW of Majorca; 40 sq. mi. (104 sq. km.); pop. (1991c) 4333; fishing. See BALEARIC ISLANDS.

For·men·tor, Cape \ˌfōr-men-ˈtōr\. Cape on N extremity of island of Majorca, W Mediterranean Sea.

For·mia \ˈfōr-mē-ä\; *formerly* **Mo·la di Ga·e·ta** \ˈmō-lä-dē-gä-ˈā-tä\; *anc.* **For·mi·ae** \ˈfȯr-mē-ˌē\. Commune, Latina prov., Lazio, cen. Italy, on Gulf of Gaeta 41 mi. (66 km.) ESE of the commune of Latina; pop. (1991p) 33,982; summer resort; active seaport. Ancient town of the Volsci; later taken by Romans; on Appian Way; site of a villa of Roman statesman Cicero, who was murdered nearby 43 B.C. (see ASTURA); in WWII suffered much damage, since rebuilt.

For·mi·ga \fu̇r-ˈmē-gə\. City, Minas Gerais state, E Brazil, 100 mi. (161 km.) WSW of Belo Horizonte; munic. pop. (1991p) 61,727.

For·mi·gny \ˌfȯr-mē-ˈnyē\. Village, Calvados dept., NW France, ab. 27 mi. (43 km.) WNW of Caen; scene of battle 1450 in which French defeated English near the end of Hundred Years' War (see CASTILLON).

For·mo·sa \fȯr-ˈmō-sä\. **1.** Province of N Argentina. See table at ARGENTINA.
2. Town, its ✻, on a tributary of the Paraguay River; pop. (1991p) 62,974.

Formosa. See TAIWAN.

Formosa Bay. See UNGAMA BAY.

Formosa Strait. See TAIWAN STRAIT.

For·mo·so, Cape \fȯr-ˈmō-sō\. Cape on coast of Nigeria, near Nun mouth of Niger River.

For·res \ˈfȯr-is, ˈfär-\. Burgh, Grampian region, NE Scotland, 11 mi. (18 km.) SW of Elgin; pop. (1981p) 8346; site of castle at which Macbeth is said to have killed Duncan; nearby is the heath where, in the Shakespeare play, Macbeth met the three witches.

For·rest \ˈfȯr-əst, ˈfär-\. County in SE Mississippi. See table at MISSISSIPPI.

Forrest City. Commercial city, ⊗ of St. Francis co., E Arkansas; pop. (1990c) 13,364; corn, sweet potatoes, cotton.

Forst \ˈfȯrst\ *or in full* **Forst in der Lau·sitz** \in-der-ˈlau̇-zits\. City, Brandenburg, E Germany, on Polish border 14 mi. (23 km.) E of Cottbus; textiles.

For·syth \ˈfōr-ˌsīth, fōr-ˈsīth\. **1.** Name of counties in two states of the U.S. See tables at GEORGIA and NORTH CAROLINA.
2. City, ⊗ of Monroe co., cen. Georgia, 22 mi. (35 km.) NW of Macon; pop. (1990c) 4268.
3. City, ⊗ of Taney co., S Missouri; pop. (1990c) 1175.
4. City, ⊗ of Rosebud co., SE Montana; pop. (1990c) 2178.

Fort Al·ba·ny \ˈȯl-bə-nē\. Trading post, Cochrane dist., E Ontario, Canada, on James Bay at mouth of Albany River; estab. late 17th cent. by Hudson's Bay Company.

Fort Aleksandrovsk. See FORT SHEVCHENKO.

For·ta·le·za \ˌfōr-tə-ˈlā-zə\ *also* **Ce·a·rá** \ˌsā-ə-ˈrä\. City and port, ✻ of Ceará state, NE Brazil, ab. 270 mi. (435 km.) NW of Natal; munic. pop. (1989e) 1,700,000; port works at Point Mucuripe 5 mi. (8 km.) E; manufactures textiles; exports sugar, coffee, cotton, hides, carnauba wax; university (1954); founded early in 17th cent.; made ✻ 1810.

Fort Am·herst National Historic Park \ˈa-mərst\. Reservation, cen. Prince Edward I., Canada, across the harbor from Charlottetown.

Fort An·cient \ˈān-shənt, -chənt\. Prehistoric American Indian fortification, Warren co., SW Ohio; overlooks Little Miami River; earth wall over 3.5 mi. (6 km.) long, 6 to 10 ft. (2 to 3 m.) high, encloses ab. 100 acres (41 hectares) in two divisions, the Old Fort and the New Fort.

Fort Anne National Park \ˈan\. Reservation, Annapolis Royal, W Nova Scotia, Canada.

Fort–Archambault. See SARH.

Fort At·kin·son \ˈat-kin-sən\. City, Jefferson co., SE Wisconsin; pop. (1990c) 10,227.

Fort Bat·tle·ford National Historic Park \ˈbat-ᵊl-ˌfōrd, -fərd\. Reservation, W cen. Saskatchewan, Canada.

Fort Beau·fort \ˈbō-fərt\. Town, S Rep. of South Africa, 105 mi. (169 km.) NE of Port Elizabeth.

Fort Beau·sé·jour National Historic Park \ˌbō-ˌsā-ˈzhür\. Reservation, E New Brunswick, Canada; French defeated here 1755 by British.

Fort Bel·voir \ˈbel-ˌvȯr\; *formerly* **Fort Hum·phreys** \ˈhəm-frēz\. Military post, SE Fairfax co., NE Virginia, on the Potomac; Defense Mapping School.

Fort Bend \ˈbend\. County in SE Texas. See table at TEXAS.

Fort Ben·ning \ˈbe-niŋ\. Military post, Muscogee co., W Georgia, 8 mi. (13 km.) S of Columbus; 97,000 acres (39,285 hectares); largest infantry post in the U.S.; estab. during WWI, infantry school from 1919.

Fort Ben·ton \ˈbent-ᵊn\. City, ⊗ of Chouteau co., N cen. Montana, on Missouri River; pop. (1990c) 1660; founded 1846 as Fort Lewis; renamed 1850.

Fort Bliss \ˈblis\. Military post, El Paso co., W Texas, within the city of El Paso; 50 sq. mi. (130 sq. km.); Air Defense Artillery Center.

Fort Bragg \ˈbrag\. **1.** City, Mendocino co., W California, on Pacific coast 96 mi. (154 km.) S of Eureka; pop. (1990c) 6078; redwood trees; army post founded 1857.
2. Military reservation, Cumberland co., S cen. North Carolina, ab. 10 mi. (16 km.) NW of Fayetteville; estab. 1918; includes Pope Air Force Base; scene of battle of Monroes Crossroads 1865.

Fort Bridg·er \ˈbri-jər\. Village, Uinta co., SW Wyoming; nearby is the site of trading post opened 1843 by frontiersman James Bridger, an important station on Oregon Trail and a U.S. Army post 1858–90, site now a state park.

Fort Brown \ˈbrau̇n\. Historical military reservation, Cameron co., Texas, just E of Brownsville; 288 acres (117 hectares); fort estab. 1846; military post 1865–1944.

Fort Car·il·lon \ˈkar-ə-ˌlän\. See TICONDEROGA.

Fort Car·o·line National Memorial \ˈkar-ə-ˌlīn, -lən\. Fortified settlement, NE Florida, on S side of mouth of St. Johns River; estab. by French Huguenots 1564, destroyed the next year by the Spanish under Menéndez de Avilés.

Fort Cham·bly National Historic Park \ˈsham-blē, shäⁿ-ˈblē\. Reservation, S Quebec, Canada, E of Montreal.

Fort Christiansborg. See ACCRA.

Fort Chris·ti·na \kris-ˈtē-nə\. Swedish settlement on site of Wilmington, Delaware; estab. by Dutch colonial official Peter Minuit 1638. See WILMINGTON 1.

Fort Clark. See PEORIA 3.

Fort Clay·ton \ˈklāt-ᵊn\. Military reservation, Panama, on E shore of Miraflores Lake, Panama, ab. 5 mi. (8 km.) from Pacific terminus of Panama Canal; an American installation up to 1999.

Fort Col·lins \ˈkä-linz\. City, ⊗ of Larimer co., N Colorado, 40 mi. (64 km.) NNE of Boulder; pop. (1990c) 87,758; sugar, lambs; tourism; Colorado State Univ. (1870); settled 1864 around a military post.

Fort Con·ger \ˈkäŋ-gər\. Arctic post on Hall Basin, Grant Land, Ellesmere I., N Canada, ab. 81°45′N; station estab. by American explorer A.W. Greely 1881; a monthly average (Feb.) of –40°F (–40°C) has been recorded. See VERKHOYANSK and OIMYAKON.

Fort Crève·cœur \ˌkrēv-ˈkür\. **1.** See ILLINOIS 3.
2. Seaport, Ghana. See ACCRA.

Fort Dauphin. See TÔLAÑARO.

Fort Da·vis \ˈdā-vis\. Village, ⊗ of Jeff Davis co., W Texas.

Fort Dearborn. See CHICAGO 2.

Fort de Char·tres \də-ˈchär-tərz\. Old fort, SW Illinois, near Kaskaskia, on the Mississippi; estab. 1720; in state park.

Fort–de–France \ˌfȯr-də-ˈfräⁿs\. City, ✻ of the French overseas dept. of Martinique, West Indies, on large **Fort–de–France Bay** on SW coast of island; partially destroyed by earthquake 1839 and by fire 1890.

Fort de Kock. See BUKITTINGGI.

Fort De·pos·it \di-ˈpä-zət\. Town, Lowndes co., S cen. Alabama, 30 mi. (48 km.) SW of Montgomery; pop. (1990c) 1240; estab. as military post c. 1813.

Fort Des Moines. See DES MOINES 3.

Fort Dodge \ˈdäj\. City, ⊗ of Webster co., N cen. Iowa, 68 mi. (109 km.) NW of Des Moines; pop. (1990c) 25,894; chemical fertilizers, farm equipment; meatpacking; Iowa Central Community Coll. (1921); near gypsum deposits from which the Cardiff giant was carved (see CARDIFF 1).

Fort Don·el·son National Battlefield; *formerly* **Fort Donelson National Military Park** \ˈdä-nəl-sən\. See UNITED STATES, *National Historical Parks.*

Fort Drum \ˈdrəm\. See CORREGIDOR.

Fort Duf·fer·in \ˈdə-fə-rin\. See MANDALAY 3.

Fort Du·quesne \dü-ˈkān\. French fort, completed 1754 on site of modern Pittsburgh, Pennsylvania; captured by British 1758 and renamed Fort Pitt.

Fort Eben Emael \ˈā-bən-ˈā-ˌmäl\. Former fort, N of Liège, Belgium, on Albert Canal; captured by Germans 1940.

Fort Ed·ward \ˈed-wərd\. Village, Washington co., E New York, on Hudson River 38 mi. (61 km.) N of Troy; pop. (1990c) 3561; on site of colonial Fort Edward.

Fort Erie \ˈir-ē\. Town, Niagara munic. region, SE Ontario, Canada, on Lake Erie as it empties into Niagara River; pop. (1991c) 8891; connected with Buffalo, New York, by International Bridge (railroad), by Peace Bridge (dedicated 1927), and by ferries; manufactures automobile accessories, paint. Formed 1932 by amalgamation of Bridgeburg town and Fort Erie village; on site of old Fort Erie, which was captured by American forces during War of 1812 and destroyed by American troops 1814 following British siege.

For·tes·cue \ˈfȯr-tə-ˌskyü\. River, W Western Australia, Australia; in flood seasons flows NW to Indian Ocean near Dampier Archipelago; 340 mi. (547 km.) long.

Fort Es·te·ros \es-ˈtā-rōs\. Former Bolivian post in the Gran Chaco, on Pilcomayo River; now in Paraguay.

Fort Fair·field \ˈfar-ˌfēld\. Town and village, Aroostook co., N Maine, on Aroostook River 10 mi. (16 km.) NE of Presque Isle; pop. (1990c) 3998; port of entry.

Fort Fish·er \ˈfi-shər\. Air Force station and former fort, S New Hanover co., SE North Carolina, near Cape Fear; designed to protect port of Wilmington; captured by Union forces Jan. 15, 1865.

Fort Fran·ces \ˈfran-səs, -səz\. Town, ⊗ of Rainy River dist., SW Ontario, Canada, on Rainy River across from International Falls, Minnesota; pop. (1991c) 8891; lumber and paper mills, large power plant; site of 18th cent. French fort and trading post.

Fort Frank \ˈfraŋk\. See CORREGIDOR.

Fort Fred·er·i·ca National Monument \ˌfre-də-ˈrē-kə\. See UNITED STATES, *National Monuments.*

Fort Fron·te·nac \frōⁿt-ˈnák\. French fort from 17th cent. on site of modern Kingston (*q.v.*), Ontario, Canada; captured and destroyed by British 1758.

Fort Gaines \ˈgānz\. City, ⊗ of Clay co., SW Georgia; pop. (1990c) 1248.

Fort Gar·ry \ˈgar-ē\. Fort and post of Hudson's Bay Company in Canada, estab. 1821 at junction of Assiniboine and Red rivers; now Winnipeg (*q.v.*).

Fort George \ˈjȯrj\. River, cen. and W Quebec, Canada; flows W into lower James Bay; 480 mi. (772 km.) long.

Fort George G. Meade \ˈjȯrj-ˌjē-ˈmēd\. Military reservation, NW Anne Arundel co., Maryland; 7500 acres (3038 hectares); estab. 1917; during WWII site of a WAC training school.

Fort Good Hope *or* **Good Hope.** Trading station on lower Mackenzie River, W mainland portion of Northwest Territories, Canada, ab. 130 mi. (210 km.) NW of Norman Wells; pop. (1991c) 602.

Forth \ˈfōrth\. River, S cen. Scotland; 116 mi. (187 km.) long; rises on NE slope of Ben Lomond, flows E into **Firth of Forth;** (*anc.* **Bo·do·tria** \bə-ˈdō-trē-ə\), an estuary extending inland from North Sea 48 mi. (77 km.) and varying in width from 1.5 to 17.5 mi. (2.4 to 28 km.). The firth is spanned by Forth Bridge (cantilever; main span 1710 ft. or 521 m.; completed 1890) at Dalmeny near Edinburgh.

Fort Hall \ˈhȯl\. **1.** Former fort at a junction point on the Oregon Trail, on Snake River N of Pocatello, SE Idaho; original fort built 1834. Present village of Fort Hall and Fort Hall Indian Reservation are nearby.

2. Town in Kenya. See MURANG'A.

Fort Hen·ry \ˈhen-rē\. Locality, Stewart co., NW Tennessee, on Tennessee River S of Fort Donelson National Battlefield; site of Fort Henry, captured by Gen. Ulysses S. Grant Feb. 6, 1862.

Fort Hertz. See PUTAO.

Fort Hughes \ˈhyüz\. See CORREGIDOR.

Fort Humphreys. See FORT BELVOIR.

For·tín Bo·que·rón \fōr-ˈtēn-ˌbō-kā-ˈrōn\. Fort in S Boquerón dept., W Paraguay, in the Chaco Boreal.

Fort Jameson. See CHIPATA.

Fort Jef·fer·son National Monument \ˈje-fər-sən\. Former national monument; redesignated Dry Tortugas National Park 1992. See UNITED STATES, *National Parks.*

Fort Johnston. See MANGOCHI.

Fort Kent \ˈkent\. Town, Aroostook co., N Maine, on St. John River across from New Brunswick, Canada; pop. (1990c) 4268; port of entry; Univ. of Maine at Fort Kent (1878).

Fort Knox \ˈnäks\. **1.** Military reservation, N Hardin co., N cen. Kentucky; 33,000 acres (13,365 hectares); estab. 1917 as training camp, permanent military post since 1932; Godman Army Airfield; location since 1936 of U.S. Gold Bullion Depository.

2. Former military post, SE Maine, across the Penobscot from Bucksport; now a tourist site.

Fort–Lamy. See N'DJAMENA.

Fort Lang·ley National Historic Park \ˈlaŋ-lē\. Reservation, S British Columbia, Canada, on Fraser River, E of Vancouver.

Fort Lau·der·dale \ˈlȯ-dər-ˌdāl\. City, ⊗ of Broward co., SE Florida, on Atlantic Ocean 25 mi. (40 km.) N of Miami; pop. (1990c) 149,377; Fort Lauderdale Coll. (1940), Broward Community Coll. (1960), Nova Univ. (1964); yachting and fishing resort; deepwater harbor of Port Everglades is just S; estab. as a military post 1838; incorp. 1911.

Fort Leav·en·worth \ˈle-vən-ˌwərth\. Military reservation, Leavenworth co., E Kansas, adjoining Leavenworth; 8000 acres (3240 hectares); one of oldest military posts W of the Mississippi, estab. 1827; federal penitentiary; U.S. Army Command and General Staff Coll.

Fort Le·Boeuf \lə-ˈbœf\. Fort erected by the French 1753 on site of Waterford, Pennsylvania, just S of Erie; visited 1753 by George Washington with message from Gov. Robert Dinwiddie of Virginia.

Fort Lee \ˈlē\. Borough, Bergen co., NE corner of New Jersey, on Hudson River 10 mi. (16 km.) NNE of Jersey City; pop. (1990c) 31,997; film processing; formerly notable center of motion-picture production; site of fort built, with Fort Washington, to prevent British use of Hudson River in Revolutionary War, and abandoned after fall of Fort Washington 1776; connected to New York City by George Washington Bridge.

Fort Len·nox National Historic Park \ˈle-nəks\. Reservation, Quebec, Canada.

Fort Lew·is \ˈlü-is\. **1.** Former name of Fort Benton (*q.v.*), Montana.

2. Military post, Pierce co., W cen. Washington, SW of Tacoma; 62,000 acres (25,110 hectares); McChord Air Force Base; estab. 1917.

Fort Li·ard \ˈlē-ˌärd\ *or* **Liard.** Trading post, SW mainland portion of Northwest Territories, Canada, on the Liard River ab. 130 mi. (210 km.) SSW of Fort Simpson; pop. (1991c) 485.

Fort Lou·doun Dam \ˈlau̇d-ᵊn\. See table at TENNESSEE VALLEY AUTHORITY.

Fort Lup·ton \ˈləp-tən\. Town, Weld co., N Colorado, on South Platte River 25 mi. (40 km.) N of Denver; pop. (1990c) 5159.

Fort Mc·Clel·lan \mə-ˈkle-lən\. Military installation, Calhoun co., NE Alabama; 20,000 acres (8100 hectares).

Fort Mc·Hen·ry National Monument and Historic Shrine \mək-ˈhen-rē\. See UNITED STATES, *National Monuments.*

Fort Mac·leod \mə-ˈklau̇d\ *also* **Macleod.** Town, Alberta, Canada, on Oldman River 28 mi. (45 km.) W of Lethbridge; pop. (1991c) 3112.

Fort Mc·Mur·ray \mək-ˈmər-ē\. Town, NE Alberta, W Canada, on Athabaska River; pop. (1991c) 34,706; oil sands nearby.

Fort Mc·Pher·son \mək-ˈfər-sən\ *or* **McPherson.** Hamlet, NW mainland part of Northwest Territories, Canada, on Peel River S of Aklavik; pop. (1991c) 759; trade center.

Fort Mad·i·son \ˈma-di-sən\. City, a ⊗ of Lee co., SE corner of Iowa, on the Mississippi; pop. (1990c) 11,618; site of penitentiary.

Fort Mal·den National Historical Park \ˈmȯl-dən\. Reservation, Amherstburg, Ontario, Canada; contains restored **Fort Malden,** built late 18th cent. and used as a frontier post in War of 1812.

Fort Mar·i·on National Monument \ˈmar-ē-ən\. See SAINT AUGUSTINE.

Fort Ma·tan·zas National Monument \mə-ˈtan-zəs\. See UNITED STATES, *National Monuments.*

Fort Max·im Gor·ki \ˈmak-səm-ˈgȯr-kē\. Former Soviet defense fort of Sevastopol', Crimea, Ukraine; taken from U.S.S.R. by Germans June 1942.

Fort Meade \ˈmēd\. City, Polk co., cen. Florida Penin., 25 mi. (40 km.) S of Lakeland; pop. (1990c) 4976; site of military post during Seminole War.

Fort Meigs \ˈmegz\. Former fort at rapids in Maumee River, NW Ohio; besieged unsuccessfully May 1–9, 1813 by force of British and Indians.

Fort Mill \ˈmil\. Town, York co., N South Carolina, 7 mi. (11 km.) NNE of Rock Hill; pop. (1990c) 4930.

Fort Mills \ˈmilz\. Former fort on Corregidor I. at entrance to Manila Bay, Philippines.

Fort Mims \ˈmimz\. Temporary stockade erected near junction of Alabama and Tombigbee rivers, Alabama; scene of a massacre of settlers by Creek Indians under their chief Red Eagle, (William Weatherford), Aug. 30, 1813.

Fort Mitch·ell \ˈmi-chəl\. City, Kenton co., N Kentucky, 3 mi. (5 km.) S of Cincinnati, Ohio; pop. (1990c) 7438.

Fort Mon·mouth \ˈmän-məth\. Military installation, E Monmouth co., E cen. New Jersey, SE of Red Bank.

Fort Mon·roe \mən-ˈrō\. Military installation, Hampton, SE Virginia, at Old Point Comfort at entrance to Hampton Roads; 19th cent. fortress surrounded by a moat; before 1946 site of coast artillery school; Confederate President Jefferson Davis held prisoner here 1865–67 after Civil War.

Fort Mor·gan \ˈmȯr-gən\. City, ⊗ of Morgan co., NE Colorado, on South Platte River 70 mi. (113 km.) ENE of Denver; pop. (1990c) 9068.

Fort Moul·trie \ˈmül-trē, ˈmōl-\. Fort in Charleston harbor, SE South Carolina, on N side of entrance, on Sullivans I.; Seminole leader Osceola imprisoned here 1837 and died here 1838 during Seminole War; evacuated by Union garrison Dec. 26, 1860 to strengthen Fort Sumter; seized by state authorities Dec. 27, 1860 and held by Confederates throughout Civil War.

Fort My·er \ˈmī-ər\. Military installation, N Virginia, bordering on Arlington National Cemetery.

Fort My·ers \ˈmī-ərz\. City, ⊗ of Lee co., SW Florida, on estuary of Caloosahatchee River just S of Charlotte Harbor; pop. (1990c) 45,206; ships citrus fruit, flowers, and vegetables; tourism; home and laboratory of inventor Thomas Edison, now a museum; Edison Community Coll. (1962); fort built c. 1841 to protect area settlers from Seminole raids.

Fort Nas·sau \ˈna-ˌsȯ\. **1.** Fort built 1623 by the Dutch on left bank of Delaware River (in what is now New Jersey) opp. site of Philadelphia, Pennsylvania; used as trading post; abandoned mid-17th cent.

2. Fort built 1614 by the Dutch on Hudson River just S of present city of Albany, New York; destroyed 1617 by flood; replaced by Fort Orange 1624 (see ALBANY 6).

Fort–National. See L'ARBAA NAÏT IRATHEN.

Fort Ne·ces·si·ty \ni-ˈse-sə-tē\. Small fortification, Great Meadows, Pennsylvania; erected 1754 by English colonial expeditionary force under Maj. George Washington; attacked by French and Indians July 3, 1754 and forced to surrender; site has been set aside as **Fort Necessity National Battlefield** (see UNITED STATES, *National Historical Parks*).

Fort Nel·son \ˈnel-sən\. **1.** River, N British Columbia, Canada; has several headstreams rising on E slopes of Rocky Mts. in N British Columbia; flows NW into Liard River; 260 mi. (418 km.) long.

2. Town, NE British Columbia, Canada, 225 mi. (362 km.) N of Dawson Creek on Fort Nelson River, 58°49′N, 122°39′W; pop. (1991c) 3804; formerly a Hudson's Bay Company post, now an important station on Alaska Highway; gas fields.

Fort Ni·ag·a·ra \nī-ˈa-grə, -gə-rə\. Fort at mouth of Niagara River, New York; built by French 1726 on site of earlier fortification; captured by British 1759; passed to U.S. 1796; again captured by British 1813 and returned to U.S. 1815.

Fort Norman. See TULITA.

Fort Ogle·thorpe \ˈōg-əl-ˌthȯrp\. City, Catoosa and Walker cos., NW Georgia, 20 mi. (32 km.) NW of Dalton; pop. (1990c) 5880.

Fort Olimpo. See FUERTE OLIMPO.

Fort Or·ange \ˈȯr-inj, ˈär-, -ənj\. Former Dutch fort on site of modern Albany (*q.v.*), New York.

Fort Pat·rick Hen·ry Dam \ˈpat-rik-ˈhen-rē\. See table at TENNESSEE VALLEY AUTHORITY.

Fort Payne \ˈpān\. City, ⊗ of De Kalb co., NE Alabama, 35 mi. (56 km.) NE of Gadsden; pop. (1990c) 11,838.

Fort Peck Dam \ˈpek\ *and* **Fort Peck Lake.** See UNITED STATES, *Dams and Reservoirs.*

Fort Pick·ens \ˈpi-kənz\. Fort on Santa Rosa I. at entrance to Pensacola harbor, Florida; held by Union troops during Civil War (1861–65).

Fort Pierce \ˈpirs\. City, ⊗ of St. Lucie co., E Florida, on Indian River 30 mi. (48 km.) NE of Lake Okeechobee; pop. (1990c) 36,830; citrus fruit; fish; recreation; Indian River Community Coll. (1960); fort built 1838 during Seminole War.

Fort Pierre \ˈpir\. City, ⊗ of Stanley co., cen. South Dakota; pop. (1990c) 1854; settled around fort built 1817 (see SOUTH DAKOTA).

Fort Pil·low \ˈpi-lō\. Fort, Tennessee, on Mississippi River 40 mi. (64 km.) N of Memphis; scene of Union defeat Apr. 12, 1864.

Fort Pitt \ˈpit\. Name given to Fort Duquesne after capture by British 1758. See PITTSBURGH.

Fort Plain \ˈplān\. Village, Montgomery co., E New York, on Mohawk River 23 mi. (37 km.) W of Amsterdam; pop. (1990c) 2416; settled by German Palatines 1722; site of Fort Plain (1776) nearby.

Fort Pont·char·train du Dé·troit \ˌpän-chər-ˈtrān-dü-dē-ˈtrȯit\. See DETROIT 2.

Fort Por·tal \ˈpōrt-ᵊl\. Town, Uganda, 160 mi. (257 km.) W of Entebbe; pop. (1991p) 32,627.

Fort Presque Isle \presk-ˈīl, ˈēl\. French fort on site of Erie, Pennsylvania; built 1753, burned by Indians 1763.

Fort Prince of Wales National Historic Park \ˈwālz\. Reservation, NE Manitoba, Canada, on Hudson Bay; contains ruins of fort built by English 1733–71 to control Hudson Bay.

Fort Prov·i·dence \ˈprä-vi-dəns\ *also* **Providence.** Hamlet, S mainland part of Northwest Territories, Canada, on Mackenzie River at its outlet from Great Slave Lake; pop. (1991c) 645.

Fort Pu·las·ki National Monument \pə-ˈlas-kē, pyü-\. See UNITED STATES, *National Monuments.*

Fort Ran·dall Dam \ˈrand-ᵊl\. See UNITED STATES, *Dams and Reservoirs.*

Fort Ran·dolph \ˈran-ˌdälf\. Former U.S. fort at Caribbean terminus of Panama Canal, Panama, on E side of entrance to Limon Bay.

Fort Re·cov·ery \ri-ˈkə-və-rē\. Village, Mercer co., W Ohio, 41 mi. (66 km.) SW of Lima; pop. (1990c) 1313; on site of Gen. Arthur St. Clair's defeat by Indians 1791 and of Gen. Anthony Wayne's "recovery" of the area 1793–94.

\ə\ **abut** \ə̇\ **matches** \ᵊ\ **kitten, Fr table** \ər\ **further** \a\ **ash** \ā\ **ace**
\ä\ **cot, cart** \ȧ\ Fr **bac** \au̇\ **out** \b̲\ Span **Avila** \ch\ **chin** \e\ **bet** \ē\ **easy**
\g\ **go** \i\ **hit** \ī\ **ice** \j\ **job** \k̲\ Ger **ich, Buch** \ⁿ\ Fr **vin**
\ŋ\ **sing** \ō\ **go** \ö\ **all** \ȯ\ **law** \œ\ Fr **bœuf** \œ̄\ Fr **feu** \ȯi\ **boy**
\th\ **thin** \t̲h̲\ **this** \ü\ **loot** \u̇\ **foot** \ue\ Ger **füllen** \ue̅\ Fr **rue**
\y\ **yet** \ʸ\ Fr **digne** \ˈdēnʸ\, **nuit** \ˈnwʸē\ \yü\ **few** \yu̇\ **fury** \zh\ **vision**

Fort Res·o·lu·tion \re-zə-ˈlü-shən\ *also* **Resolution.** Settlement, S mainland part of Northwest Territories, Canada, at mouth of Slave River on S shore of Great Slave Lake; pop. (1991c) 515; formerly a fort of Hudson's Bay Company.

Fort·ress Mountain \ˈfȯr-trəs\. Peak, cen. Park co., NW Wyoming; ab. 12,075 ft. (3680 m.).

Fort Ri·ley \ˈrī-lē\. Military installation, Riley and Geary cos., E Kansas; 24,000 acres (9720 hectares); cavalry museum.

Fort Rosebery. See MANSA.

Fort Saint Da·vid \sānt-ˈdā-vəd, sənt\. Ruins of British fort on Coromandel Coast, Tamil Nadu, SE India, just N of town of Cuddalore; sold by Marathas to the English 1690; became British headquarters for S India 1746; Robert Clive appointed its governor 1756; captured by French 1758, 1782; finally passed to British 1785.

Fort Sainte Anne \sānt-ˈan, sənt\. Fort on Isle La Motte, Lake Champlain, NW Vermont; built by French 1666; first settlement in Vermont (only temporary).

Fort Saint Fré·dér·ic See CROWN POINT 2.

Fort Saint George. See MADRAS 2.

Fort Saint John \sānt-ˈjän, sənt\. Town, NE British Columbia, Canada, ab. 40 mi. (64 km.) NW of Dawson Creek on Peace River; pop. (1991c) 14,156.

Fort San Lo·ren·zo \ˌsan-lə-ˈren-zō\. Former U.S. fort, Panama, at mouth of Chagres River, W of Limon Bay.

Fort Sas·katch·e·wan \sə-ˈska-chə-wən, sa-, -ˌwän\. Town, Alberta, Canada, 18 mi. (29 km.) NE of Edmonton; pop. (1991c) 12,078.

Fort Schuy·ler \ˈskī-lər\. **1.** Former military post at Throgs Neck, New York; one of N defenses of New York harbor.
2. Fort, Rome, New York. See FORT STANWIX.

Fort Scott \ˈskät\. City, ⊗ of Bourbon co., SE Kansas, 85 mi. (137 km.) S of Kansas City; pop. (1990c) 8362; Fort Scott Community Coll. (1919).

Fort Shaw·nee \shȯ-ˈnē, shä-\. Village, Allen co., NW Ohio, 65 mi. (104 km.) NW of Columbus; pop. (1990c) 4128.

Fort Sher·man \ˈshər-mən\. Military reservation, Panama, at Caribbean terminus of Panama Canal, on W side of entrance to Limon Bay; an American installation up to 1999.

Fort Shev·chen·ko \shif-ˈcheŋ-kə\; *earlier* **Fort Ale·ksan·drovsk** \ˌá-lik-ˈsán-ˌdrəvsk\. Former Soviet military station, SW Kazakh S.S.R., U.S.S.R., at tip of Mangyshlak Penin. on NE shore of Caspian Sea.

Fort Sill \ˈsil\. Military installation, Comanche co., SW Oklahoma, ab. 5 mi. (8 km.) N of Lawton; estab. 1869; field artillery school; scene of surrender of the Comanche and Kiowa Indians c. 1875.

Fort Simp·son \ˈsimp-sən\ *also* **Simpson.** Village, SW mainland part of Northwest Territories, Canada, on Mackenzie River where it is joined by the Liard; pop. (1991c) 1142; site of administration headquarters for Nahanni National Park.

Fort Smith \ˈsmith\. **1.** Region, W cen. Canada, an administrative subdivision of Northwest Territories, consisting of the S part of former dist. of Mackenzie; area 235,697 sq. mi. (610,456 sq. km.); pop. (1991c) 27,553.
2. City, a ⊗ of Sebastian co., W Arkansas, at confluence of Arkansas and Poteau rivers on Oklahoma border; pop. (1990c) 72,798; auto bodies, metal goods, refrigerators, glass; Westark Community Coll. (1928); U.S. Army post 1817–71; important supply and departure point after discovery of gold in California in 1848; incorp. as city 1851.
3. Town, S mainland part of Northwest Territories, Canada, on Slave River at Alberta boundary; pop. (1991c) 2480; former headquarters of Northwest Territories.

Fort Snel·ling \ˈsne-liŋ\. Former military post in Minnesota, bet. Minnesota and Mississippi rivers S of Minneapolis; site acquired from Sioux by explorer Zebulon Pike 1805; fort, called Fort St. Anthony until 1825, built 1820.

Fort Stan·wix \ˈstan-wiks\. Fort on site of Rome, New York, built 1758 by English on site of earlier French post; called **Fort Schuy·ler** \ˈskī-lər\ from 1776; treaties with Iroquois signed here 1768, 1784; **Fort Stanwix National Monument** estab. 1935 (see UNITED STATES, *National Monuments*).

Fort Stock·ton \ˈstäk-tən\. City, ⊗ of Pecos co., W Texas, 73 mi. (118 km.) SSW of Odessa; pop. (1990c) 8524.

Fort Sum·ner \ˈsəm-nər\. Village, ⊗ of De Baca co., E cen. New Mexico, 58 mi. (93 km.) W of Clovis; pop. (1990c) 1269; nearby are ruins of fort, built 1862, and grave of outlaw William Bonney (Billy the Kid).

Fort Sum·ter \ˈsəm-tər\. Fort on S side of entrance to Charleston harbor, South Carolina; subjected to Confederate bombardment Apr. 12–13, 1861 which began the Civil War, surrendered to Confederates Apr. 14, 1861; evacuated upon Union advance on Charleston 1865; **Fort Sumter National Monument** estab. 1948 (see UNITED STATES, *National Monuments*).

Fort Thom·as \ˈtä-məs\. Residential city, Campbell co., N Kentucky, 5 mi. (8 km.) SE of Covington; pop. (1990c) 16,032.

Fort Ticonderoga. See TICONDEROGA.

For·tu·na \fȯr-ˈtü-nə\. City, Humboldt co., NW California, 14 mi. (23 km.) S of Eureka; pop. (1990c) 8788.

Fortuna Bay. Bay S of W end of St. Thomas I., U.S. Virgin Is., West Indies.

For·tu·nate Islands \ˈfȯr-chə-nət\ *or* **Fortunate Isles;** *anc.* **For·tu·na·tae In·su·lae** \ˌfȯr-chə-ˈnā-tē-ˈin-sə-ˌlē\. In early times, a name applied to Canary Is.

For·tune \ˈfȯr-chən\. Seaport, S Newfoundland, Canada, on S shore at mouth of Fortune Bay; pop. (1991c) 2177.

Fortune Bay. Inlet of Atlantic Ocean in S Newfoundland, Canada; ab. 80 mi. (130 km.) long; extensive fishing grounds; scene 1878 of conflict over fishing rights.

Fortune Island. See LONG CAY.

Fort Un·ion \ˈyü-nyən\. Former trading post, NE Montana, on Missouri River near mouth of the Yellowstone; built 1828 by Kenneth McKenzie of the American Fur Company and orig. called Fort Floyd; dismantled 1868.

Fort Union National Monument. Ruined fort, S Mora co., NE New Mexico, N of Watrous; estab. 1851, became one of most important military posts in SW United States; a Confederate objective (not reached) in Civil War; evacuated 1891. See UNITED STATES, *National Monuments.*

Fort Valley. City, ⊗ of Peach co., cen. Georgia; pop. (1990c) 8198; chemicals; Fort Valley State Coll. (1895).

Fort Van·cou·ver \van-ˈkü-vər\. W terminus of Oregon Trail, now the city of Vancouver, Washington, on Columbia River.

Fort Victoria. See MASVINGO.

Fort Wads·worth \ˈwädz-ˌwərth\. Former military post on Staten I., New York, at entrance to New York Bay.

Fort Wag·ner \ˈwag-nər\. Fort on Morris I. in Charleston harbor, South Carolina; attacked by Union forces July 1863; captured Sept. 7, 1863.

Fort Wal·ton Beach \ˈwȯlt-ᵊn\. City, Okaloosa co., NW Florida, E of Pensacola; pop. (1990c) 27,471; resort; Eglin Air Force Base is nearby.

Fort Wash·ing·ton \ˈwȯ-shiŋ-tən, ˈwä-\. Military post during American Revolution, on upper Manhattan I., New York, on Hudson; captured by British Nov. 1776.

Fort Wayne \ˈwān\. City, ⊗ of Allen co., NE Indiana, 105 mi. (169 km.) NE of Indianapolis; pop. (1990c) 173,072; railroad center; manufactures electrical equipment, car parts; St. Francis Coll. (1890), Indiana Univ.–Purdue Univ. at Fort Wayne (1917), Indiana Institute of Technology (1930). Site orig. occupied by Miami Indians; French fur-trading post and fort built in 17th cent.; seized by British 1760; lost briefly to followers of Ottawa Chief Pontiac; new fort built 1794 by Gen. Anthony Wayne; incorp. as city 1840.

Fort Wel·ling·ton \ˈwe-liŋ-tən\. Town, NE Guyana, 51 mi. (82 km.) by rail SE of Georgetown.

Fort Wellington National Historic Park. Reservation, Prescott, Ontario, Canada, on the St. Lawrence; contains defense post built 1812–13.

Fort Whoop–up. See LETHBRIDGE.

Fort Wil·liam \ˈwil-yəm\. **1.** City, Ontario, Canada. See THUNDER BAY 5.
2. Burgh, Highland region, NW Scotland, on Loch Linnhe; pop. (1981p) 11,079; tourist center.

Fort Wood \ˈwu̇d\. Former military post on Liberty I., New York harbor, New York; site of **Statue of Liberty National Monument** (See UNITED STATES, *National Monuments*).

Fort Worth \ˈwərth\. City, ⊗ of Tarrant co., N Texas, on Trinity River ab. 33 mi. (53 km.) W of Dallas; pop. (1990c) 447,619; commercial and transportation center of stock-raising and oil-producing region; manufactures aircraft, aerospace equipment, electronic equipment, food products; Texas Christian Univ. (1873), Texas Wesleyan Univ. (1891), Southwestern Baptist Theological Seminary (1908), Tarrant County Junior Coll. (1965); planetarium; settled around military post (but never a fort) founded 1849.

Fort Wright \ˈrīt\. City, Kenton co., N Kentucky; pop. (1990c) 6570.

For·ty Fort \ˈfȯr-tē\. Residential borough, Luzerne co., E Pennsylvania, 3 mi. (5 km.) N of Wilkes-Barre; pop. (1990c) 5049. See WYOMING VALLEY.

Fort Yu·kon \ˈyü-ˌkän\. Village, E Alaska, at junction of Porcupine River with the Yukon; a Hudson's Bay Company trading post from 1847 until the U.S. purchased Alaska.

Fort Zea·lan·dia \zē-ˈlan-dē-ə\. Fort built by the Dutch near T'ai-nan on SW coast of Taiwan; captured by Chinese pirate leader Koxinga (Cheng Ch'eng-kung) 1661–62.

Forum Alieni. See FERRARA 2.

Forum Julii. **1.** Commune, SE France. See FRÉJUS.
2. Former duchy, NE Italy. See FRIULI.

Forum Livii. See FORLÌ 2.

Fo·shan \ˈfō-ˈshän\; *formerly* **Nam·hoi** \ˈnäm-ˈhȯi\ *or* **Fat·shan** \ˈfät-ˈshän\ *also* **Fa·chan** \ˈfä-ˈchän\. City, cen. Guangdong prov., SE China, ab. 12 mi. (19 km.) above Guangzhou in Xi delta; pop. (1990c) 303,160.

Fossa Claudia. See CHIOGGIA.

Fos·sa·no \fȯs-ˈsä-nō\. Commune, Cuneo prov., Piedmont, NW Italy, 13 mi. (21 km.) NE of the commune of Cuneo; pop. (1991p) 23,358; episcopal see; mineral baths.

Fosse Way *or* **Foss Way** \ˈfäs\. Ancient Roman road in Britain; extended from Lincoln to Exeter, passing through Leicester and Bath and intersecting Watling Street in S cen. Britain; one of the four great Roman roads of Britain (see ERMINE STREET, ICKNIELD STREET, and WATLING STREET).

Fos·sil \ˈfä-səl\. City, ⊗ of Wheeler co., N cen. Oregon, ab. 17 mi. (27 km.) S of Condon; pop. (1990c) 399.

Fossil Butte National Monument. See UNITED STATES, *National Monuments.*

Fossil Mountain. Peak in Teton Range, W Teton co., NW Wyoming; 10,912 ft. (3326 m.).

Fos·som·bro·ne \ˌfōs-sōm-ˈbrō-nā\. Commune, Pesaro e Urbino prov., Marche, cen. Italy, near Metauro River 18 mi. (29 km.) SSE of the seaport of Pesaro; pop. (1981p) 10,032; episcopal see.

Foss Way. See FOSSE WAY.

Fos·ter \ˈfȯs-tər, ˈfäs-\. **1.** County in E cen. North Dakota. See table at NORTH DAKOTA.
2. Town, Providence co., N Rhode Island; pop. (1990c) 4316.

Foster City. City, San Mateo co., W California; pop. (1990c) 28,176.

Fos·to·ria \fȯ-ˈstōr-ē-ə\. City, Hancock, Seneca, and Wood cos., NW Ohio, 15 mi. (24 km.) NE of Findlay; pop. (1990c) 14,983.

Foth·er·in·ghay \ˈfä-t͟hə-riŋ-ˌgā\. Village, Northamptonshire, England; remains of castle where Richard III was born 1452 and where Mary, Queen of Scots was imprisoned, tried, and executed Feb. 8, 1587.

Fou·gères \fü-ˈzher\. City, Ille-et-Vilaine dept., NW France, 29 mi. (47 km.) NE of Rennes; pop. (1990c) 23,138.

Fou·la \ˈfü-lə\. One of the Shetland Is., NE of N Scotland; Old Norse language survived here until the early 19th cent.

Foul Bay \ˈfau̇l\. Inlet of Red Sea on E coast of Egypt, at Tropic of Cancer.

Fou–ling. See FULING.

Foul·ness Point \ˈfau̇l-ˌnes\. Cape on **Foulness Island,** Essex, SE coast of England, N of entrance to the Thames estuary.

Foul·wind, Cape \ˈfau̇l-ˌwind\. Cape on NW coast of South I., New Zealand, forming S side of Karamea Bight.

Foun·tain \ˈfau̇nt-ᵊn\. **1.** County in W Indiana. See table at INDIANA.
2. City, El Paso co., E cen. Colorado, 11 mi. (18 km.) SSE of Colorado Springs; pop. (1990c) 9984.

Fountain Hill. Borough, Lehigh co., E Pennsylvania, on Lehigh River 4 mi. (6 km.) E of Allentown; pop. (1990c) 4637.

Fountain Hills. Town, Maricopa co., SW cen. Arizona, just E of Scottsdale; pop. (1990c) 10,030.

Fountain Inn. Town, Greenville and Laurens cos., NW South Carolina, 16 mi. (26 km.) SE of Greenville; pop. (1990c) 4388; manufactures chemicals, airplane parts, tennis balls, air conditioners, garden hoses, screwdrivers, copiers, printers, plastics, paint, capacitors, machine parts.

Fountain Valley. City, Orange co., SW California, 28 mi. (45 km.) SE of Los Angeles; pop. (1990c) 53,691; Coastline Community Coll. (1976).

Four Corners. Locality in SW United States, the point of intersection of 37°N with 109°W, the only place in the U.S. where boundaries of four states—Colorado, New Mexico, Arizona, and Utah—come together.

Four Forest Cantons, Lake of the. See LUCERNE, LAKE OF.

Four Forest Cantons, The. See FOREST CANTONS, THE FOUR.

Four Lakes. Chain of four connected lakes in Dane co., S Wisconsin, named Mendota (or Fourth Lake), Monona (or Third Lake), Waubesa (or Second Lake), and Kegonsa (or First Lake).

Four League Bay. Inlet of Gulf of Mexico on W coast of Terrebonne parish, SE Louisiana.

Four Mountains, Islands of the. See ISLANDS OF THE FOUR MOUNTAINS.

Foúrnoi. See PHOURNOI.

Four Peaks. Mountain, E Maricopa co., S cen. Arizona; 7645 ft. (2330 m.).

Fou·ta Djal·lon *also* **Fu·ta Jal·lon** \ˈfü-tä-jä-ˈlōn\. Mountainous district, W Guinea; highest point 4970 ft. (1515 m.); ab. 30,000 sq. mi. (77,700 sq. km.); source of many streams, esp. the Niger and Senegal; inhabitants chiefly Fulani; chief town Labé.

Foux, Cap à. See CHEVAL BLANC, POINTE DU.

Fo·veaux Strait \ˈfō-vō\. Channel bet. South I. and Stewart I., New Zealand; 18 to 20 mi. (29 to 32 km.) wide.

Fowl·er \ˈfau̇-lər\. **1.** City, Fresno co., S cen. California, 10 mi. (16 km.) SE of the city of Fresno; pop. (1990c) 3208.
2. Town, ⊗ of Benton co., W Indiana, 25 mi. (40 km.) NW of Lafayette; pop. (1990c) 2333.

Fowliang. See JINGDEZHEN.

Fox \ˈfäks\. **1.** River, SE Wisconsin and NE Illinois; flows S to the Illinois River at Ottawa in La Salle co., N Illinois; ab. 220 mi. (354 km.) long.
2. River, SE cen. Wisconsin; rises in N Columbia co., flows SW to a point ab. 1.5 mi. (2 km.) from Wisconsin River with which it is connected by canal (see PORTAGE 5), then N and NE into Lake Winnebago and out of N end of lake into Green Bay at city of Green Bay; 175 mi. (282 km.) long.

Fox Basin. See FOXE BASIN.

Foxborough *or* **Foxboro** \ˈfäks-ˌbər-ō\. Town, Norfolk co., E Massachusetts, 11 mi. (18 km.) W of Brockton; pop. (1990c) 14,637.

Fox Channel. See FOXE BASIN.

Fox Chapel. Borough, Allegheny co., SW Pennsylvania, 9 mi. (15 km.) NE of Pittsburgh; pop. (1990c) 5319.

Foxcroft. See DOVER-FOXCROFT.

Foxe Basin \ˈfäks\; *formerly* **Fox Basin.** Large body of water bet. Melville Penin. and W Baffin I., E Nunavut, Canada; connects with N end of Hudson Bay by **Foxe Channel** (*formerly* **Fox Channel;** ab. 110 mi. or 177 km. wide), bet. Southampton I. and **Foxe Peninsula** (*formerly* **Fox Peninsula),** SW part of Baffin I.

\ə\ **abut** \ə̇\ matches \ᵊ\ kitten, Fr table \ər\ **further** \a\ **ash** \ā\ **ace** \ä\ **cot, cart** \ȧ\ Fr bac \au̇\ **out** \b̲\ Span Avila \ch\ **chin** \e\ **bet** \ē\ **easy** \g\ **go** \i\ **hit** \ī\ **ice** \j\ **job** \k̲\ Ger **ich**, Bu**ch** \ⁿ\ Fr vi**n** \ŋ\ si**ng** \ō\ g**o** \ȯ\ **all** \ȯ\ **law** \œ\ Fr b**œu**f \œ̄\ Fr f**eu** \ȯi\ **boy** \th\ **thin** \t͟h\ **this** \ü\ **loot** \u̇\ **foot** \ue\ Ger f**ü**llen \üe\ Fr **rue** \y\ **yet** \ʸ\ Fr digne \ˈdēnʸ\, nuit \ˈnwʸē\ \yü\ **few** \yu̇\ **fury** \zh\ vi**s**ion

Fox Islands. **1.** Island group off SW tip of Alaska Penin., E Aleutian Is., Alaska; includes Unimak, Akutan, Unalaska, and Umnak islands; chief settlements Unalaska and Dutch Harbor (*q.v.*).

2. Two islands, **North Fox Island** and **South Fox Island,** in N Lake Michigan, part of Leelanau co., NW Michigan.

Fox Lake. Village, Lake co., NE Illinois, 16 mi. (26 km.) W of Waukegan; pop. (1990c) 7478.

Fox Peninsula. See FOXE BASIN.

Fox Point. Village, Milwaukee co., Wisconsin, on Lake Michigan E and N of the city of Milwaukee; pop. (1990c) 7238.

Fox River Grove. Village, McHenry co., Illinois, 30 mi. (48 km.) NW of Chicago; pop. (1990c) 3551.

Foyle \ˈfȯil\. River, N Ireland (republic); 16 mi. (26 km.) long; formed by confluence of Finn and Mourne rivers on border bet. Limavady and Derry dists., Northern Ireland; flows N past Derry and expands into the estuary **Lough Foyle** \ˈläk, ˈläk\, 18 mi. (29 km.) long, on boundary bet. Derry, Northern Ireland, and co. Donegal, Ireland (republic).

Foynes \ˈfȯinz\. Village, NW coast of co. Limerick, SW Ireland, on S shore of Shannon estuary 22 mi. (35 km.) W of Limerick; pop. (1986c) 707; former transatlantic seaplane terminal, now superseded by nearby Shannon Airport.

Frack·ville \ˈfrak-ˌvil\. Borough, Schuylkill co., E cen. Pennsylvania, 7 mi. (11 km.) N of Pottsville; pop. (1990c) 4700.

Fra·go·so Cay \frä-ˈgō-sō-ˈkē, ˈkā\. Island off NE coast of Las Villas prov., W cen. Cuba.

Fraile, El. See EL FRAILE.

Frakes, Mount \ˈfrāks\. Mountain, Antarctica, 76°48′S, 117°42′W; 12,064 ft. (3677 m.).

Fra·me·ries \fràm-ˈrē\. Commune, Hainaut prov., SW Belgium, ab. 5 mi. (8 km.) SSW of Mons; pop. (1991c) 21,270.

Fra·ming·ham \ˈfrā-miŋ-ˌham\. Town, Middlesex co., NE Massachusetts, 20 mi. (32 km.) WSW of Boston; pop. (1990c) 64,989; computer components; printing and publishing; Framingham State Coll. (1839); settled 1650.

Fran·ca \ˈfrȧŋ-kə\. City, NE São Paulo state, SE Brazil, 160 mi. (257 km.) N of Campinas; munic. pop. (1991p) 232,656.

Fran·ca·vil·la Fon·ta·na \ˌfräŋ-kä-ˈvēl-lä-fōn-ˈtä-nä\. Commune, Brindisi prov., Puglia, SE Italy, 20 mi. (32 km.) WSW of the seaport of Brindisi; pop. (1989c) 35,172; cathedral; imperial palace.

France \ˈfrans, ˈfrāⁿs\ *or officially* **Ré·pu·blique fran·çaise** \rā-pǖ-ˈblēk-frāⁿ-ˈsez\; *earlier* **Gaul** \ˈgȯl\ *or Fr.* **Gaule** \ˈgōl\ *or Lat.* **Gal·lia** \ˈga-lē-ə, ˈgä-\. Republic of W Europe, bounded on N by English Channel, on NE by Belgium and Luxembourg, on E by Germany, Switzerland, and Italy, on S by the Mediterranean Sea, Spain, and Andorra, and on W by Bay of Biscay; principality of Monaco forms an enclave on Mediterranean coast; 212,918 sq. mi. (551,458 sq. km.); pop. (1982c) 54,257,300; ✻ Paris.

Chief mountains: Alps (*q.v.*) on SE (Italian border), Pyrenees on S (Spanish border), Jura Mts. on E (Swiss border), Vosges in NE, Massif Central and Auvergne Mts. in SE cen. part; highest point Mont Blanc 15,781 ft. (4810 m.), in the Alps.

Chief rivers: Seine, with its tributaries the Yonne, Marne, and Oise, flowing into English Channel; Loire, Garonne, and Adour, flowing into Bay of Biscay; Rhone, with its chief tributary the Saône, flowing S into Mediterranean Sea.

Islands: Île d'Ouessant (Ushant) off tip of Brittany; Belle-Île, Noirmoutier, Yeu, Ré, and Oléron in Bay of Biscay; Hyères Is. in Mediterranean Sea.

Chief products: Wheat, barley, potatoes, sugar beets, wine; fish; timber; bauxite, coal, iron ore; manufacturing: iron and steel, chemicals, textiles, transportation equipment; engineering; food processing, power production; tourism.

Chief cities: Paris, Marseille, Lyon, Toulouse, Nice, Strasbourg, Nantes, Bordeaux, Montpellier, Rennes.

Political divisions: Divided into the following 22 regions which in turn are subdivided into a number of departments (for pronunciation of their names, see their individual entries):

NAME	AREA (sq. mi.)	AREA (sq. km.)	POP. (1991e)	CAPITAL
Alsace				
Bas-Rhin	1,848	4,786	959,903	Strasbourg
Haut-Rhin	1,360	3,522	675,190	Colmar
Aquitaine				
Dordogne	3,546	9,184	388,053	Périgueux
Gironde	3,861	10,000	1,226,133	Bordeaux
Landes	3,566	9,236	313,187	Mont-de-Marsan
Lot-et-Garonne	2,069	5,359	306,480	Agen
Pyrénées-Atlantiques	2,946	7,630	583,472	Pau
Auvergne				
Allier	2,829	7,327	355,933	Moulins
Cantal	2,217	5,742	158,195	Aurillac
Haute-Loire	1,917	4,965	206,207	Le Puy
Puy-de-Dôme	3,071	7,954	597,504	Clermont-Ferrand
Basse-Normandie				
Calvados	2,137	5,535	618,678	Caen
Manche	2,296	5,947	480,702	Saint-Lô
Orne	2,355	6,099	296,658	Alençon
Bourgogne				
Côte-d'Or	3,384	8,764	497,917	Dijon
Nièvre	2,640	6,838	231,787	Nevers
Saône-et-Loire	3,307	8,565	556,480	Mâcon
Yonne	2,867	7,426	325,242	Auxerre
Bretagne				
Côtes-du-Nord	2,655	6,876	538,594	Saint-Brieuc
Finistère	2,620	6,786	839,092	Quimper
Ille-et-Vilaine	2,609	6,757	808,516	Rennes
Morbihan	2,611	6,762	624,206	Vannes
Centre				
Cher	2,791	7,229	322,842	Bourges
Eure-et-Loir	2,269	5,877	400,818	Chartres
Indre	2,617	6,778	237,566	Châteauroux
Indre-et-Loire	2,364	6,123	534,506	Tours
Loiret	2,603	6,742	588,644	Orléans
Loir-et-Cher	2,438	6,314	308,469	Blois
Champagne-Ardenne				
Ardennes	2,014	5,216	295,146	Charleville-Mézières
Aube	2,317	6,001	290,434	Troyes
Haute-Marne	2,400	6,216	203,410	Chaumont
Marne	3,152	8,164	557,400	Châlons-sur-Marne
Corse				
Corse-du-Sud	1,650	4,274	118,779	Ajaccio
Haute-Corse	1,700	4,403	131,855	Bastia
Franche-Comté				
Territoire de Belfort	235	609	135,391	Belfort
Doubs	2,019	5,229	487,996	Besançon
Haute-Saône	2,063	5,343	227,828	Vesoul
Jura	1,934	5,009	252,023	Lons-le-Saunier
Haute-Normandie				
Eure	2,318	6,004	521,300	Évreux
Seine-Maritime	2,415	6,255	1,226,531	Rouen
Île-de-France				
Essonne	699	1,810	1,104,712	Évry
Hauts-de-Seine	63	163	1,398,795	Nanterre
Seine-et-Marne	2,284	5,916	1,109,963	Melun
Seine-St.-Denis	91	236	1,395,027	Bobigny
Val-de-Marne	94	243	1,224,759	Créteil
Val-d'Oise	482	1,248	1,070,811	Pontoise
Ville-de-Paris	41	106	2,156,766	Ville-de-Paris
Yvelines	877	2,271	1,327,485	Versailles
Languedoc-Roussillon				
Aude	2,406	6,232	301,794	Carcassonne
Gard	2,258	5,848	594,974	Nîmes
Hérault	2,360	6,112	811,384	Montpellier
Lozère	1,995	5,167	72,360	Mende
Pyrénées-Orientales	1,589	4,116	369,425	Perpignan
Limousin				
Corrèze	2,263	5,861	236,575	Tulle
Creuse	2,146	5,558	129,453	Guéret
Haute-Vienne	2,128	5,512	353,578	Limoges
Lorraine				
Meurthe-et-Moselle	2,021	5,234	710,119	Nancy
Meuse	2,402	6,221	195,402	Bar-le-Duc
Moselle	2,399	6,213	1,010,129	Thionville
Vosges	2,267	5,872	384,269	Épinal
Midi-Pyrénées				
Ariège	1,888	4,890	136,837	Foix
Aveyron	3,372	8,733	268,501	Rodez
Gers	2,415	6,255	175,309	Auch
Haute-Garonne	2,433	6,301	945,155	Toulouse
Hautes-Pyrénées	1,740	4,507	224,673	Tarbes
Lot	2,019	5,229	157,394	Cahors
Tarn	2,221	5,752	341,576	Albi
Tarn-et-Garonne	1,435	3,717	203,270	Montauban
Nord-Pas-de-Calais				
Nord	2,216	5,739	2,532,387	Lille
Pas-de-Calais	2,563	6,638	1,435,749	Arras
Pays de la Loire				
Loire-Atlantique	2,631	6,814	1,061,487	Nantes

NAME	AREA (sq. mi.)	AREA (sq. km.)	POP. (1991e)	CAPITAL
Maine-et-Loire	2,753	7,130	710,162	Angers
Mayenne	1,997	5,172	278,965	Laval
Sarthe	2,397	6,208	515,105	Le Mans
Vendée	2,594	6,718	513,467	La Roche-sur-Yon
Picardie				
Aisne	2,849	7,379	535,097	Laon
Oise	2,261	5,856	738,781	Beauvais
Somme	2,384	6,174	548,629	Amiens
Poitou-Charentes				
Charente	2,298	5,952	341,533	Angoulême
Charente-Maritime	2,644	6,848	530,709	La Rochelle
Deux-Sèvres	2,318	6,004	345,640	Niort
Vienne	2,697	6,985	382,508	Poitiers
Provence-Alpes-Côte d'Azur				
Alpes-de-Haute-Provence	2,681	6,944	132,976	Digne
Alpes-Maritimes	1,658	4,294	990,944	Nice
Bouches-du-Rhône	1,974	5,113	1,775,076	Marseilles
Hautes-Alpes	2,131	5,519	115,029	Gap
Var	2,316	5,998	838,098	Toulon
Vaucluse	1,377	3,566	475,909	Avignon
Rhône-Alpes				
Ain	2,222	5,755	481,422	Bourg
Ardèche	2,132	5,522	278,333	Privas
Drôme	2,519	6,524	418,624	Valence
Haute-Savoie	1,696	4,393	584,962	Annecy
Isère	2,886	7,475	1,026,838	Grenoble
Loire	1,843	4,773	747,262	Saint-Étienne
Rhône	1,241	3,214	1,522,075	Lyons
Savoie	2,330	6,035	357,863	Chambéry

French overseas departments include: French Guiana, Guadeloupe, Martinique, and Réunion (*qq.v.*).

History: Region inhabited by Celtic Gauls from at least 7th cent. B.C.; S part (Gallia Narbonensis) Roman province from 121 B.C.; N and cen. part conquered and subdued by Gen. Julius Caesar 58–51 B.C. See GAUL 2. Subjected to repeated invasions of Germanic peoples (as Franks, Burgundians, and Visigoths) throughout Roman period; most came under kingdom of Salian Franks during reign of Clovis I (Merovingian dynasty) 481–511 A.D., who defeated last Roman governor of Gaul; kingdom divided among Clovis' four sons, and over next 500 years repeatedly united only to be redivided in similar fashion; Frankish kingdom expanded under Merovingians to include Burgundy and Provence; effective rule passed to Carolingians 7th cent. under fainéant Merovingian kings; Pépin III (the Short) was first Carolingian king, crowned 751; expanded under Charlemagne (reigned 768–814) to include parts of modern Spain, Italy, Germany, and the Low Countries; new conquests lost when realm divided by Treaty of Verdun 843. During medieval feudal period, in which central authority was merely nominal, divided into several domains (incl. Normandy, Aquitaine, Burgundy, and Flanders); after Norman conquest of England 1066 duchy of Normandy in personal union with England; also lost to England during 12th cent.: Anjou, Maine, and Touraine (by inheritance) and Aquitaine (by marriage); all lands except Aquitaine recovered by France early 13th cent. under the sword of King Philip Augustus; in course of Hundred Years' War (1337–1453) regained all lands from English except Calais (regained 1558); civil wars of religion (1562–98) resulted in Edict of Nantes (1598) granting religious toleration to Protestants (Huguenots), revoked by Louis XIV 1685; territorial gains under Louis XIV (reigned 1643–1715) included Alsace, Franche-Comté, and Lorraine; power, prestige, and overseas possessions decreased by Treaty of Paris 1763 ending Seven Years' War. Royal government overthrown by French Revolution 1789, country becoming a republic (First Republic 1792–99), followed by the Consulate (1799–1804) under Napoléon Bonaparte who proclaimed himself emperor (First Empire 1804–15); during period of Napoleonic Wars (1796–1815), acquired by conquest most of W and cen. Europe, but lost all after final defeat of Napoléon at Waterloo 1815. Monarchy reestablished under Bourbons, but overthrown by revolution of 1848 and succeeded by Second Republic (1848–52) under Louis-Napoléon, proclaimed Emperor Napoléon III 1852; Second Empire (1852–70) overthrown in bloodless revolution, a result of French defeat in Franco-Prussian War (1870–71); Third Republic estab. 1870. N part of country ravaged by fighting in WWI (1914–18); in WWII occupied 1940–44 by Germans, the S nominally under a French government with ✻ at Vichy, repudiated by the Free French under Charles de Gaulle, which actively continued resistance to Axis forces and assumed authority over liberated French territories; country invaded by Allies at Normandy June 6, 1944, completely liberated by Sept. 1944; under provisional government until establishment of Fourth Republic 1946; member of UN 1945, Council of Europe 1949, NATO 1949, EEC 1958 (merged into EC 1967); several overseas possessions lost to independence movements 1940s and 1950s, incl. French Indochina, Morocco, and Tunisia; crisis over Algerian independence (1954–61) brought an end to Fourth Republic; Fifth Republic estab. under Charles de Gaulle 1958 (see FRENCH COMMUNITY); independence granted to Algeria 1962; withdrew from integrated NATO command system 1966; resignation of President de Gaulle April 1969 followed defeat of referendum on constitutional reforms; Socialist party brought to power 1981 with election of François Mitterrand as president.

Fran·cés, Cape \frän-ˈses\. Cape on SW coast of Pinar del Río prov., W Cuba, S of Cortés Bay.

Francés, Point. Cape on SW coast of Isla de la Juventud, Caribbean Sea; encloses Siguanea Bay.

Francés Vie·jo, Cape \frän-ˈses-vē-ˈā-hō\. Cape, N coast of Hispaniola I., in Dominican Republic.

France·ville \frä^{n}s-ˈvēl, ˈfrans-ˌvil\. Town, SE Gabon, on a tributary of the Ogooué River.

Franche–Com·té \ˌfrä^{n}sh-kō^{n}-ˈtā\. Region, E cen. France, comprised of the depts. of Doubs, Haute-Saône, Jura, and Territoire de Belfort; bounded anciently on N by Lorraine, on E by Swiss Confederation, on W by duchy of Burgundy, and on S by Savoy; ✻ Besançon; included in original kingdom of Burgundy founded 5th cent. A.D.; later became county of Burgundy as distinct from duchy of Burgundy; part of kingdom of Arles; belonged to Holy Roman Empire from 11th cent.; brought under control of duchy of Burgundy by Philip the Bold 1384; passed to Holy Roman Emperor Maximilian I late 15th cent., and from him to Spanish Hapsburgs; occupied 1667 and 1674 by Louis XIV of France to whom Spain finally ceded it 1678; a province of France until the Revolution, when it was broken into several departments. See table at FRANCE.

Franche·ville \frä^{n}sh-ˈvēl\. County, Quebec, Canada. See table at QUEBEC.

Franchise. See ARRAS.

Fran·cia \ˈfran-chē-ə\. **1.** The kingdom of the Franks (Austrasia, Neustria, and Aquitaine), from c. 481 to 768.
2. Duchy of N cen. France, c. 1000; chief towns Paris, Orléans, and Tours.

Franciade. See SAINT-DENIS 1.

Fran·cis, Cape \ˈfran-sis\ *also* **Cape Saint Francis.** Cape, SE Newfoundland, Canada, E of entrance to Conception Bay N of St. John's.

Fran·cis Case, Lake \ˈfran-sis-ˈkās\. See *Fort Randall Dam* at UNITED STATES, *Dams and Reservoirs.*

Fran·cis·co I. Ma·de·ro \frän-ˈsēs-kō-ē-mä-ˈthā-rō\. Municipality, Coahuila state, Mexico, 24 mi. (39 km.) NE of Torreón; pop. (1990p) 51,470.

Fran·cis·co Mo·ra·zán \frän-ˈsēs-kō-ˌmō-rä-ˈsän\; *formerly* **Te·gu·ci·gal·pa** \tā-ˌgü-sē-ˈgäl-pä\. Department of S cen. Honduras. See table at HONDURAS.

Fran·cis·town \ˈfran-sis-ˌtau̇n\. Chief town of N Botswana, near Zimbabwe border; pop. (1991c) 65,244; trade center for farming area.

\ə\ **abut** \ə\ matches \ᵊ\ kitten, Fr table \ər\ **further** \a\ **ash** \ā\ **ace**
\ä\ **cot, cart** \å\ Fr bac \au̇\ **out** \b\ Span Avila \ch\ **chin** \e\ **bet** \ē\ **easy**
\g\ **go** \i\ **hit** \ī\ **ice** \j\ **job** \k\ Ger **ich, Buch** \$^{n}$\ Fr vin
\ŋ\ **sing** \ō\ **go** \ȯ\ **all** \ȯi\ **law** \œ\ Fr bœuf \œ̄\ Fr **feu** \ȯi\ **boy**
\th\ **thin** \th\ **this** \ü\ **loot** \u̇\ **foot** \ue\ Ger füllen \üē\ Fr **rue**
\y\ **yet** \$^{y}$\ Fr digne \ˈdēn^{y}\, nuit \ˈnw^{y}ē\ \yü\ **few** \yu̇\ **fury** \zh\ **vision**

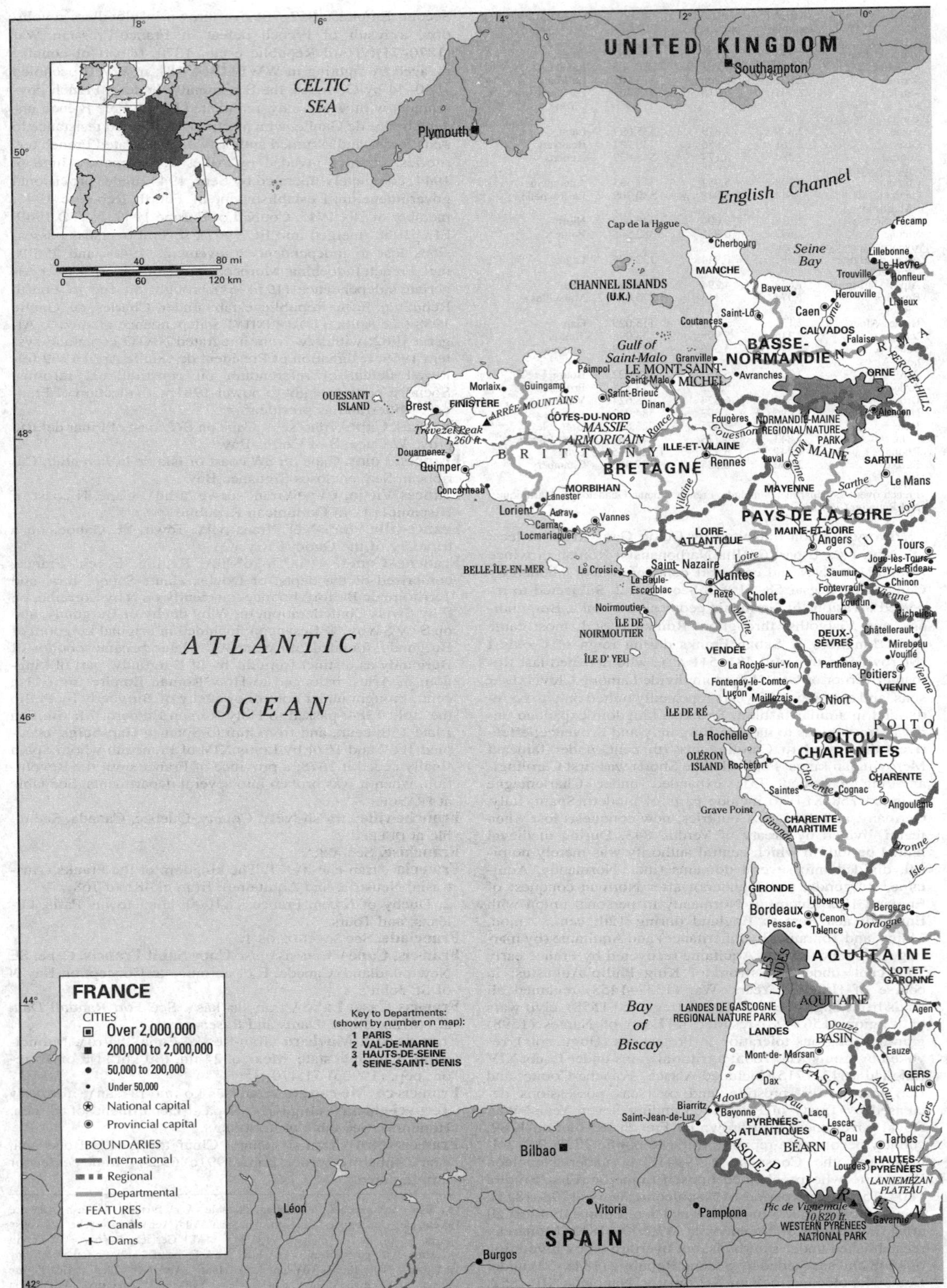
UNITED KINGDOM
Southampton
CELTIC SEA
Plymouth
English Channel
ATLANTIC OCEAN
Cap de la Hague
Cherbourg
Seine Bay
Fécamp
Lillebonne
Le Havre
Honfleur
Trouville
Lisieux
MANCHE
CHANNEL ISLANDS (U.K.)
Bayeux
Herouville
Caen
Saint-Lô
Coutances
CALVADOS
Falaise
Gulf of Saint-Malo
BASSE-NORMANDIE
NORMA
PERCHE HILLS
Granville
Paimpol
LE MONT-SAINT-MICHEL
Saint-Malo
Avranches
ORNE
OUESSANT ISLAND
Morlaix
Guingamp
Saint-Brieuc
Dinan
Brest
FINISTÈRE
ARRÉE MOUNTAINS
CÔTES-DU-NORD
MASSIF ARMORICAIN
Fougères
NORMANDIE-MAINE REGIONAL NATURE PARK
Alençon
Trévezel Peak 1,260 ft.
Rance
Couesnon
MAINE
Douarnenez
Quimper
BRITTANY
ILLE-ET-VILAINE
BRETAGNE
Rennes
Laval
Mayenne
SARTHE
Concarneau
MORBIHAN
MAYENNE
Sarthe
Le Mans
Lorient
Lanester
Auray
Vannes
Carnac
Locmariaquer
Vilaine
PAYS DE LA LOIRE
Loir
LOIRE-ATLANTIQUE
MAINE-ET-LOIRE
Angers
ANJOU
Tours
BELLE-ÎLE-EN-MER
Le Croisic
Saint-Nazaire
Loire
Joué-lès-Tours
Azay-le-Rideau
La Baule-Escoublac
Nantes
Saumur
Chinon
Rezé
Cholet
Fontevrault
Loudun
Vienne
Noirmoutier
ÎLE DE NOIRMOUTIER
Maine
Thouars
Richelieu
Châtellerault
DEUX-SÈVRES
Mirebeau
Vouillé
ÎLE D' YEU
VENDÉE
La Roche-sur-Yon
Parthenay
Poitiers
VIENNE
Fontenay-le-Comte
Luçon
Maillezais
Niort
ÎLE DE RÉ
POITO
La Rochelle
POITOU-CHARENTES
OLÉRON ISLAND
Rochefort
CHARENTE
Charente
Saintes
Cognac
Angoulême
Grave Point
Gironde
CHARENTE-MARITIME
Dronne
Isle
GIRONDE
Libourne
Bergerac
Bordeaux
Cenon
Pessac
Talence
Dordogne
LES LANDES
AQUITAINE
LOT-ET-GARONNE
Bay of Biscay
LANDES DE GASCOGNE REGIONAL NATURE PARK
Agen
LANDES
Douze
BASIN
Mont-de-Marsan
Eauze
GASCONY
Adour
GERS
Auch
Dax
Gers
Biarritz
Bayonne
Pau
Lacq
Saint-Jean-de-Luz
PYRÉNÉES-ATLANTIQUES
Lescar
Pau
Tarbes
BÉARN
BASQUE
PYRENEES
Bilbao
Lourdes
HAUTES-PYRÉNÉES
LANNEMEZAN PLATEAU
Léon
Vitoria
Pamplona
Pic de Vignemale 10,820 ft.
Gavarnie
WESTERN PYRENEES NATIONAL PARK
SPAIN
Burgos
8°
6°
4°
2°
0°
50°
48°
46°
44°
42°
0 40 80 mi
0 60 120 km
FRANCE
CITIES
Over 2,000,000
200,000 to 2,000,000
50,000 to 200,000
Under 50,000
National capital
Provincial capital
BOUNDARIES
International
Regional
Departmental
FEATURES
Canals
Dams
Key to Departments: (shown by number on map):
1 PARIS
2 VAL-DE-MARNE
3 HAUTS-DE-SEINE
4 SEINE-SAINT- DENIS

Channel Tunnel
Strait of Dover
Dunkerque
Saint-Pol-sur-Mer
Gravelines
Calais
Ghent
Brussels
NETHERLANDS
Bonn
BELGIUM
Boulogne-sur-Mer
PAS-DE-CALAIS
Saint-Omer
Aire-sur-la-Lys
Armentières
Tourcoing
Wattrelos
Roubaix
Lille
Lillers
Croix
Béthune
Lens
Saint-Amand-les-Eaux
Liévin
Douai
Valenciennes
ARTOIS
Canche
Hesdin
NORD-PAS-DE-CALAIS
Arras
NORD
Maubeuge
Cambrai
Sambre
Meuse
Escaut
ARDENNES
Rhine
Frankfurt am Main
Abbeville
Somme
PICARDY
Péronne
Saint-Quentin
Oise
Rocroi
LUXEMBOURG
GERMANY
Mosel
Dieppe
Bresle
Amiens
SOMME
Charleville-Mézières
Sedan
Luxembourg
SEINE-MARITIME
HAUTE-NORMANDIE
AISNE
Laon
PICARDIE
BRAY
Montdidier
Noyon
ARDENNES
Longwy
OISE
Coucy-le-Château-Auffrique
WOËVRE PLATEAU
Saar
Beauvais
Compiègne
Aisne
Thionville
Forbach
Seine
Rouen
Le Petit-Quevilly
Soissons
ARGONNE
LORRAINE
MOSELLE HILLS
Elbeuf
Gisors
PARIS BASIN
Creil
Oise
Reims
Verdun
Metz
Sarreguemines
Wissembourg
Stuttgart
Chantilly
Senlis
Montigny-lès-Metz
Vernon
Epte
VAL-D'OISE
Pontoise
Paris
Château-Thierry
Marne
MOSELLE
BAS-RHIN
Évreux
Saint-Denis
Meaux
Bobigny
Épernay
Châlons-sur-Marne
MEUSE
Saint-Mihiel
MEURTHE-ET-MOSELLE
Haguenau
EURE
Nanterre
ÎLE-DE-FRANCE
Ornain
Bar-le-Duc
Nancy
Strasbourg
Boulogne-Billancourt
Saint-Maur-des-Fossés
MARNE
CHAMPAGNE
Vandœuvre
Avre
Versailles
Créteil
BRIE
Saint-Dizier
Toul
Lunéville
Rosheim
Obernai
Dreux
YVELINES
Évry
SEINE-ET-MARNE
Provins
LORRAINE
ALSACE
Rambouillet
Corbeil-Essonnes
CHAMPAGNE-ARDENNE
Sélestat
Eure
ESSONNE
Melun
Saint-Dié
VOSGES MOUNTAINS
Fontainebleau
Moselle
Ribeauvillé
Chartres
Étampes
Troyes
HAUTE-MARNE
VOSGES
Épinal
Kaysersberg
BEAUCE
Nemours
AUBE
Seine
Aube
Clairvaux
Munster
Colmar
EURE-ET-LOIR
Sens
Yonne
BARS PLATEAU
Chaumont
FAUCILLES MTS.
Remiremont
Mount de Guebwiller 4,670 ft.
ANJOU
LOIRET
Langres
Mulhouse
Orléans
Saint-Benoît-sur-Loire
HAUT-RHIN
Rhine
Vendôme
Loire
Auxerre
TERR. DE BELFORT
Belfort
Zürich
AUSTRIA
Beaugency
YONNE
LANGRES PLATEAU
Vesoul
Saône
HAUTE SAÔNE
Montbéliard
SUNDGAU
Ill
LIECHTENSTEIN
Vaduz
Blois
Chambord
Cure
CÔTE-D'OR
Doubs
INDRE-ET-LOIRE
LOIR-ET-CHER
Vézelay
Dijon
Amboise
BOURGOGNE
DOUBS
Besançon
TOURAINE
Chenonceaux
Cher
Sancerre
MORVAN REGIONAL NATURE PARK
MORVAN
FRANCHE-COMTÉ
Bern
Vierzon
CHER
NIÈVRE
Beaune
Dole
Loches
CENTRE
Bourges
BERRY
Nevers
BURGUNDY
JURA MOUNTAINS
Mount Preneley 2,955 ft.
Autun
JURA
SWITZERLAND
INDRE
Châteauroux
Le Creusot
Chalon-sur-Saône
Ain
Indre
Saint-Amand-Montrond
Blanzy
Montceau
Lons-le-Saunier
Lake Geneva
Creuse
Allier
BOURBONNAIS
SAÔNE-ET-LOIRE
BRESSE
Évian-les-Bains
Cher
Moulins
Cluny
Thonon-les-Bains
Gartempe
ALLIER
Montluçon
Mount Saint-Rigaud 3,309 ft.
Mâcon
Oyonnax
Annemasse
Geneva
Mount Neige 5,652 ft.
Bonneville
Chamonix-Mont-Blanc
Guéret
Bourg-en-Bresse
AIN
Rhône
HAUTE-SAVOIE
Midi Tunnel
HAUTE-VIENNE
CREUSE
AUVERGNE
Vichy
Roanne
BEAUJOLAIS MTS.
RHÔNE
Annecy
Lake Annecy
Mont Blanc 15,771 ft.
Oradour-sur-Glane
Aubusson
Riom
LYONNAIS
Villefranche-sur-Saône
SAVOY
Limoges
Clermont-Ferrand
Lyon
Vaulx-en-Velin
Villeurbanne
Lake Bourget
Aix-les-Bains
Isère
LIMOUSIN
MONTS DORE
LOIRE
Vénissieux
Saint-Priest
Bourgoin
Chambéry
VANOISE NATIONAL PARK
SAVOIE
Tignes
Col du Mont Cenis
Puy de Sancy 6,186 ft.
PUY-DE-DÔME
Saint-Chamond
Vienne
RHÔNE-ALPES
MAURIENNE
CORRÈZE
MASSIF CENTRAL
Firminy
Saint-Étienne
DAUPHINÉ
Isère
VALLEY
Vézère
Tulle
Dordogne
AUVERGNE
AUVERGNE VOLCANO REGIONAL NATURE PARK
ISÈRE
Fontaine
Grenoble
Échirolles
Fréjus Tunnel
Montgenèvre Pass
ITALY
Périgueux
CANTAL
HAUTE-LOIRE
Romans-sur-Isère
Mont Pelvoux 12,920 ft.
PÉRIGORD
Brive-la-Gaillarde
Le Puy
Valence
Briançon
Drac
Cère
Allier
DAUPHINÉ ALPS
Drôme
DORDOGNE
Aurillac
Sarrans Dam
Privas
Rhône
ÉCRINS NATIONAL PARK
Durance
ARDÈCHE
DRÔME
Gap
MERCANTOUR NATIONAL PARK
LOT
LOZÈRE
Mende
Montélimar
HAUTES-ALPES
Serre-Ponçon Reservoir
Decazeville
Lot
CÉVENNES
AVEYRON
Rodez
CÉVENNES NATIONAL PARK
VAUCLUSE
ALPES-DE-HAUTE-PROVENCE
Gelas Peak 10,315 ft.
MARITIME ALPS
Cahors
Digne
Villeneuve-sur-Lot
Orange
ALPES-MARITIMES
QUERCY
Alès
Carpentras
PROVENCE-ALPES-CÔTE D'AZUR
Tinée
TARN-ET-GARONNE
Millau
GARD
VAUCLUSE
Menton
Montauban
Avignon
Durance
Villefranche
MONACO
Monaco
Nîmes
Beaucaire
Tarascon
Verdon
Nice
Tarn
Albi
Saint-Affrique
LANGUEDOC-ROUSSILLON
Les Baux-de-Provence
Arles
Salon-de-Provence
PROVENCE ALPS
Grasse
Le Cannet
Antibes
Cannes
MIDI-PYRÉNÉES
TARN
Montpellier
BOUCHES-DU-RHÔNE
CAMARGUE
Aix-en-Provence
Draguignan
ESTÉREL MASSIF
Saint-Raphaël
Arrats
Colomiers
Toulouse
Castres
HÉRAULT
Aigues-Mortes
Saintes-Maries-de-la-Mer
Istres
Martigues
Marignane
VAR
Fréjus
Saint-Tropez
HAUTE-GARONNE
NOIRE MOUNTAINS
Béziers
LANGUEDOC
Sète
Agde
Marseille
Aubagne
La Ciotat
MONTS DES MAURES
Hyères
CÔTE D'AZUR
La Seyne-sur-Mer
Toulon
Garonne
Carcassonne
AUDE
Narbonne
Gulf of Lion
Foix
Aude
ARIÈGE
Têt
Perpignan
MEDITERRANEAN SEA
PYRÉNÉES-ORIENTALES
ROUSSILLON
Andorra la Vella
ANDORRA
Cape Corse
Gulf of Saint-Florent
Bastia
Calvi
HAUTE-CORSE
Monte Cinto 8,876 ft.
Golo
Corte
CORSE
Gulf of Sagone
CORSE-DU-SUD
Aleria
Ajaccio
Taravo
Mont l'Incudine 6,980 ft.
CORSICA
Sartène
Porto-Vecchio
Bonifacio
Strait of Bonifacio
©2000, Encyclopædia Britannica, Inc.

Fran·co·nia \fraŋ-ˈkō-nē-ə, -nyə\. **1.** Resort village, Grafton co., W New Hampshire, in Franconia Mts. ab. 5 mi. (8 km.) S of Littleton; pop. (1990c) 811.

2. *or Ger.* **Fran·ken** \ˈfräŋ-kən\. Former duchy of S cen. Germany, now included chiefly in the German states of Bavaria, Baden-Württemberg, and Hesse.

History: A medieval Frankish duchy, part of Austrasia (*q.v.*) and, after 843 A.D. (see FRANCE), of German part of former Carolingian empire; its duke, Conrad, was raised to German throne 911; divided into Rhenish (west) and East Franconia, the latter alone retaining name of Franconia after 12th cent.; Franconian circle of empire formed 1512; name abolished 1806 but revived 1837 by kingdom of Bavaria in its subdivisions (government districts) of Upper, Middle, and Lower Franconia.

Franconia Mountains. W range of White Mts., in Grafton co., W New Hampshire; highest peak Mt. Lafayette 5249 ft. (1600 m.), on E side of **Franconia Notch** through which Pemigewasset River flows and which is flanked on W by Cannon Mt. (*q.v.*).

Fra·ne·ker \ˈfrä-nə-kər\. Commune, Friesland prov., N Netherlands; pop. (1981e) 12,804; site of university 1585–1811.

Franken. See FRANCONIA 2.

Fran·ken·berg \ˈfräŋ-kən-ˌbu̇rk, ˈfraŋ-kən-ˌbərg\. City, Saxony, E Germany, 10 mi. (16 km.) NE of Chemnitz; 13th–14th cent. church.

Frank·en·muth \ˈfraŋ-kən-ˌmüth\. City, Saginaw co., cen. Michigan, 15 mi. (24 km.) SE of the city of Saginaw; pop. (1990c) 4408.

Frankenstein *or* **Frankenstein in Schlesien.** See ZĄBKOWICE.

Fran·ken·thal \ˈfräŋ-kən-ˌtäl\. City, Rhineland-Palatinate, Germany, 28 mi. (45 km.) SSW of Darmstadt; pop. (1992e) 47,087; metalworking; railroad junction. First mentioned 772; site of monastery 12th–16th cents.; destroyed by French 1689 and later rebuilt; devastated in WWII, since rebuilt.

Frank·ford \ˈfraŋk-fərd\. District, E Philadelphia, Pennsylvania.

Frank·fort \ˈfraŋk-fərt\. **1.** City, ⊗ of Clinton co., cen. Indiana, 20 mi. (32 km.) WSW of Kokomo; pop. (1990c) 14,754.

2. City, ✻ of Kentucky and ⊗ of Franklin co., N cen. Kentucky, on Kentucky River 52 mi. (84 km.) E of Louisville; pop. (1990c) 25,968; electronic equipment, furniture, textiles, bourbon whiskey; tobacco and Thoroughbred horses produced in area; gravesite of pioneer Daniel Boone; founded 1786; became ✻ 1792 after state admitted to Union earlier that year; briefly held by Confederates 1862; Kentucky State Univ. (1886).

3. City, Benzie co., NW Michigan, on Lake Michigan at mouth of Betsie River 28 mi. (45 km.) N of Manistee; pop. (1990c) 1546; fishing center.

4. Village, Herkimer co., NE cen. New York, 10 mi. (16 km.) ESE of Utica; pop. (1990c) 2693; forms single community with Mohawk, Ilion, and Herkimer; settled 1723.

5. Anglicized form of *Frankfurt* as in **Frankfort on the Main** and **Frankfort on the Oder.** See FRANKFURT 2 and 3.

Frank·furt \ˈfräŋk-ˌfu̇rt, ˈfraŋk-fərt\. **1.** District of former East Germany.

2. *or in full* **Frankfurt an der Oder** \ˌän-dər-ˈō-dər\ *or Eng.* **Frankfort on the Oder** \ˈō-dər\. City, E Brandenburg, Germany, on the Oder River 50 mi. (80 km.) ESE of Berlin; pop. (1992e) 85,357; formerly ✻ of Frankfurt dist.; machinery, textiles; birthplace of dramatist Heinrich von Kleist 1777. Chartered 1253; joined Hanseatic League 1368; site of university 1506–1811, when moved to Wrocław; captured by Swedes 1631 in Thirty Years' War; shelled and taken 1945 by Soviet forces in WWII. See SŁUBICE.

3. *or in full* **Frankfurt am Main** \äm-ˈmīn\ *or Eng.* **Frankfort on the Main** \ˈmīn, ˈmān\. City, Hesse, Germany, on Main River 17 mi. (27 km.) N of Darmstadt; pop. (1992e) 654,679; chemicals and pharmaceuticals, leather goods; financial center with stock exchange; annual book fair; notable buildings include Römer (old town hall), Saalhof and Taxis imperial palaces, cathedral, Senckenberg museum, academy of art; university (1914).

History: Region inhabited by Celtic and Germanic peoples c. first cent. B.C.; site of Roman military settlement first cent. A.D.; important center under Carolingian empire; often site of election and/or coronation of emperors from Middle Ages through 18th cent.; free imperial city 1372–1806; lost free city status under French Emperor Napoléon, restored to autonomy 1815; a partisan of Austria, it was occupied by and annexed to Prussia 1866; scene of signing of final peace of Franco-Prussian War 1871; occupied briefly by French troops 1920; in WWII frequently bombed by Allies and greatly damaged; occupied by Allies 1945. Birthplace of writer Johann Wolfgang von Goethe (1749), of financier Meyer Amschel Rothschild (1744), and of Nobel chemist Otto Hahn (1879).

Fränkische Saale. See SAALE, FRÄNKISCHE.

Frank·lin \ˈfraŋ-klin\. **1.** Name of a parish in Louisiana and of counties in 24 states of the U.S. See tables at ALABAMA, ARKANSAS, FLORIDA, GEORGIA, IDAHO, ILLINOIS, INDIANA, IOWA, KANSAS, KENTUCKY, LOUISIANA, MAINE, MASSACHUSETTS, MISSISSIPPI, MISSOURI, NEBRASKA, NEW YORK, NORTH CAROLINA, OHIO, PENNSYLVANIA, TENNESSEE, TEXAS, VERMONT, VIRGINIA, WASHINGTON.

2. City, ⊗ of Heard co., W Georgia; pop. (1990c) 876.

3. City, ⊗ of Johnson co., cen. Indiana, ab. 10 mi. (16 km.) S of Indianapolis; pop. (1990c) 12,907; Franklin Coll. of Indiana (1834).

4. City, ⊗ of Simpson co., S Kentucky, 21 mi. (34 km.) S of Bowling Green; pop. (1990c) 7607.

5. City, ⊗ of St. Mary parish, S Louisiana; pop. (1990c) 9004.

6. Town, Norfolk co., E Massachusetts, 19 mi. (31 km.) W of Brockton; pop. (1990c) 22,095; Dean Junior Coll. (1865).

7. Village, Oakland co., SE Michigan, 20 mi. (32 km.) NW of Detroit; pop. (1990c) 2626.

8. City, ⊗ of Franklin co., S Nebraska; pop. (1990c) 1112.

9. City, Merrimack co., S cen. New Hampshire, on Merrimack River (*q.v.*) 10 mi. (16 km.) SW of Laconia; pop. (1990c) 8304; settled as part of Salisbury 1764 on site of former Abenaki Indian village; incorp. 1895.

10. Borough, Sussex co., N corner of New Jersey, 10 mi. (16 km.) ENE of Newton; pop. (1990c) 4977; as source of zinc ores franklinite and willemite, formerly an important center of zinc-mining industry.

11. Town, ⊗ of Macon co., SW North Carolina, on Little Tennessee River 55 mi. (89 km.) WSW of Asheville; pop. (1990c) 2873.

12. City, Warren co., SW Ohio, on Miami River 15 mi. (24 km.) S of Dayton; pop. (1990c) 11,026.

13. City, ⊗ of Venango co., NW Pennsylvania, 8 mi. (13 km.) WSW of Oil City; pop. (1990c) 7329; site of early Indian village; site of several 18th cent. forts; founded c. 1795.

14. City, ⊗ of Williamson co., cen. Tennessee, 19 mi. (31 km.) S of Nashville; pop. (1990c) 20,098; scene of Civil War battle 1864 in which Union forces under Gen. John M. Schofield defeated Confederates under Gen. John Bell Hood.

15. Town, ⊗ of Robertson co., E cen. Texas; pop. (1990c) 1336.

16. Politically independent town, Southampton co., SE Virginia, on Blackwater River 21 mi. (34 km.) W of Suffolk; 4 sq. mi. (10 sq. km.); pop. (1990c) 7864; paper.

17. Town, ⊗ of Pendleton co., E West Virginia; pop. (1990c) 914.

18. City, Milwaukee co., SE Wisconsin, SSW suburb of the city of Milwaukee; pop. (1990c) 21,855.

19. Former administrative district, N Northwest Territories, Canada; area incl. water 549,253 sq. mi. (1,422,565 sq. km.); includes Baffin I., all other Arctic islands and Boothia and Melville penins.; sparsely populated; administered from Ottawa. Formed 1895, boundaries defined 1918, ceased to exist 1979.

Franklin, Mount. **1.** Peak of White Mts., in S Coos co., N New Hampshire, SSW of Mt. Washington; 5028 ft. (1532 m.).

2. Peak, New South Wales, Australia, 24 mi. (39 km.) SW of Canberra; 5392 ft. (1644 m.).

Franklin, State of. A temporary state organized 1784 in W lands of North Carolina (now part of E Tennessee) which it had ceded to the U.S. (act of cession later repealed); ✱ estab. at Greenville 1785; last legislative session 1787; ceased to exist 1788.

Franklin Bay. Inlet of Amundsen Gulf, coast of Northwest Territories, Canada.

Franklin D. Roo·se·velt Island \ˈfraŋ-klin-ˌdē-ˈrō-zə-ˌvelt, ˈrü-, -vəlt-\. See ROOSEVELT ISLAND 2.

Franklin D. Roosevelt Lake *or* **Roosevelt Lake** *also infrequently* **Grand Cou·lee Reservoir** \ˈkü-lē\. Lake, N cen. Washington; formed in Columbia River by Grand Coulee Dam, N end near Canadian border; 151 mi. (243 km.) long.

Franklin Falls Dam. Dam across Pemigewasset River near Franklin, S cen. New Hampshire; height 146 ft. (45 m.); completed 1943; impounds water for flood control.

Franklin Lake. Dry salt lake in S Elko co., NE Nevada.

Franklin Lakes. Borough, Bergen co., NE New Jersey, 5 mi. (8 km.) NW of Paterson; pop. (1990c) 9873.

Franklin Mountains. Range, in W cen. mainland part of Northwest Territories, Canada, W of Great Bear Lake; highest peak Mt. Clark 4798 ft. (1462 m.).

Franklin Park. **1.** Village, Cook co., NE Illinois, suburb of Chicago; pop. (1990c) 18,485.
2. Borough, Allegheny co., SW Pennsylvania, 12 mi. (19 km.) NW of Pittsburgh; pop. (1990c) 10,109.

Franklin Square. Unincorporated settlement, Nassau co., New York, in SE Long Island W of Hempstead; pop. (1990c) 28,205.

Franklin Strait. Channel bet. SE Prince of Wales I. and Boothia Penin., Nunavut, Canada.

Frank·lin·ton \ˈfraŋ-klin-tən\. **1.** Town, ⊗ of Washington parish, E Louisiana, N of New Orleans; pop. (1990c) 4007.
2. City, Ohio. See COLUMBUS 11.

Franks Peak \ˈfraŋks\. Highest peak in the Absaroka Range, at S end in S Park co., NW Wyoming; 13,140 ft. (4005 m.).

Franks·ton \ˈfraŋks-tən\. City, S Victoria, Australia; pop. (1991c) 84,986.

Fran·tiš·ko·vy Láz·ně \ˈfrän-tyēsh-ˌkȯ-vē-ˈläz-nye\ *or Ger.* **Fran·zens·bad** \ˈfrän-səns-ˌbät\. Village, W Czech Republic, ab. 24 mi. (39 km.) WSW of Karlovy Vary; mineral baths and springs.

Franz Jo·sef Fjord \ˈfrän(t)s-ˈjō-zəf, -səf\ *also* **Kej·ser Franz Jo·sephs Fjord** \ˈkī-sər-ˈfräns-ˈyō-sefs\. Inlet of Greenland Sea, NE coast of Greenland, ab. 73°15′N; 125 mi. (201 km.) long.

Franz Josef Land *or Russ.* **Zem·lya Fran·tsa Io·si·fa** \zim-ˈlyä-ˈfrant-sə-ˈyȯ-sə-fə\ *also* **Fridt·jof Nan·sen Land** \ˈfrid-ˌyȯf-ˈnän-sən\. Archipelago in Arctic Ocean, part of Arkhangel'sk Oblast, N Russia in Europe; 80° to 82°N, 43° to 65°E, N of Novaya Zemlya; ab. 8000 sq. mi. (20,720 sq. km.); consists of ab. 187 islands, largest: Aleksandra Land, George Land, Wilczek Land, and Graham Bell I.; most northerly land of Eastern Hemisphere; covered with ice. Discovered 1873 by Austro-Hungarian expedition of Julius von Payer and Carl Weyprecht; claimed by U.S.S.R. 1926. See ARCTIC, THE.

Franz Josef–Spitze. See GERLACHOVKA.

Fra·sca·ti \frä-ˈskä-tē\. Commune, Roma prov., Lazio, cen. Italy, on NW side of Alban Hills 11 mi. (18 km.) SE of Rome; pop. (1991p) 20,043; cathedral; summer resort; ancient Roman ruins, incl. villa of orator and statesman Cicero; near ruins of ancient Tusculum.

Fra·ser \ˈfrā-zer, -zhər\. **1.** Town, Grand co., N Colorado, NNW of Berthoud Pass; pop. (1990c) 575; alt. 8568 ft. (2612 m.); sometimes called "Icebox of the Nation" because of its low year-round mean temperature.
2. City, Macomb co., SE Michigan, NE suburb of Detroit; pop. (1990c) 13,899.
3. River, S cen. British Columbia, Canada; rises in Rocky Mts. near Yellowhead Pass, flows NW bet. Rocky and Cariboo ranges, then in sharp turn S around N of Cariboo Mts. nearly to U.S. border and finally W, breaking through Coast Mts. in long canyon, to empty into Strait of Georgia just S of Vancouver; 850 mi. (1368 km.) long; drainage area ab. 84,100 sq. mi. (217,819 sq. km.); navigable for ab. 90 mi. (145 km.); chief tributaries: the Nechako, Chilcotin, Thompson, Blackwater, and Lillooet; spanned by Alex Fraser Bridge (cable-stayed; main span 1526 ft. or 465 m.; completed 1986) near Vancouver, British Columbia. Discovered by Alexander Mackenzie 1793, explored to its mouth by Simon Fraser 1808.

Fra·ser·burgh \ˈfrā-zər-ˌbər-ə, -zhər-\. Seaport burgh, Grampian region, NE Scotland, near Kinnairds Head on NE coast 57°40′N, 2°W; pop. (1981p) 12,478; herring fisheries.

Fraser Island *or* **Great Sandy Island.** Island off SE coast of Queensland, Australia; 70 mi. (113 km.) long; 66 sq. mi. (171 sq. km.); timber.

Frat·ta·mag·gio·re \ˌfrät-tä-mä-ˈjō-rā\. Commune, Napoli prov., Campania, S Italy, 7 mi. (11 km.) N by E of Naples; pop. (1989c) 37,430; resort.

Frauenburg. See FROMBORK.

Frau·en·feld \ˈfrau̇-ən-ˌfelt\. Commune, ✱ of Thurgau canton, NE Switzerland, 21 mi. (34 km.) NE of Zürich; pop. (1989c) 19,538; textiles; medieval castle; armory; became city in mid-13th cent.

Fray Ben·tos \frī-ˈb̲ān-tȯs\. Town and river port, ✱ of Río Negro dept., W Uruguay, on E bank of Uruguay River ab. 175 mi. (282 km.) NW of Montevideo; pop. (1985c) 20,135; meatpacking; estab. 1859; Uruguay's first industrialized meatpacking plant estab. here 1861.

Fray Jor·ge National Park \ˌfrī-ˈhȯr-hā\. National park, N cen. Chile, SW of La Serena; a pocket of subtropical forest; park estab. 1941.

Fray·ser's Farm \ˈfrā-zərz, -zhərz\ *or* **Glen·dale** \ˈglen-ˌdāl\. Battlefield near Richmond, Virginia, where Gens. James Longstreet and A. P. Hill lost over 3000 men in an encounter with Union forces June 30, 1862.

Fre·chen \ˈfrek̲-ᵊn\. Town, North Rhine-Westphalia, Germany, SW suburb of Cologne; pop. (1980c) 43,483.

Fred·er·i·cia \ˌfrā-t̲h̲ə-ˈrād-syä\. Seaport, Vejle co., SE Jutland Penin., Denmark; pop. (1989e) 45,992; textiles; oil refinery; estab. as fortress 1650; scene of battle July 6, 1849 in which Danes defeated Prussians.

Fred·er·ick \ˈfre-drik, -də-rik\. **1.** Name of counties in two states of the U.S. See tables at MARYLAND and VIRGINIA.
2. City, ⊗ of Frederick co., N Maryland, 24 mi. (39 km.) SE of Hagerstown; pop. (1990c) 40,148; in agricultural region; residence of poet Francis Scott Key and Civil War heroine Barbara Frietchie; Hood Coll. (1893), Frederick Community Coll. (1957). See MONOCACY 2.
3. City, ⊗ of Tillman co., SW Oklahoma, 25 mi. (40 km.) SE of Altus; pop. (1990c) 5221.

Frederick Henry. See DOLAK ISLAND.

Fred·er·icks·burg \ˈfre-driks-ˌbərg, -də-riks-\. **1.** City, ⊗ of Gillespie co., cen. Texas; pop. (1990c) 6934; noted for Sunday houses in which farm families from outlying areas stayed in town on weekends from the late 1800s; settled 1846.
2. City, NE Virginia, in Spotsylvania co. but politically independent, on Rappahannock River 41 mi. (66 km.) SW of Alexandria; 6 sq. mi. (16 sq. km.); pop. (1990c) 19,027; Mary Washington Coll. (1908); settled 1671; incorp. as city 1879; scene of battle Dec. 1862, when Union army under Gen. Ambrose Burnside was defeated by Confederates under Gen. Robert E. Lee.

Fredericksburg and Spot·syl·va·nia County Battlefields Memorial National Military Park \ˌspät-səl-ˈvān-yə\. See UNITED STATES, *National Historical Parks.*

Fred·er·ick·town \ˈfre-drik-ˌtau̇n, -də-rik-\. City, ⊗ of Madison co., SE Missouri, 45 mi. (72 km.) WNW of Cape Girardeau; pop. (1990c) 3950; lead deposits nearby.

Frederick Wil·liam IV Falls \ˈfre-drik-ˈwil-yəm\. Falls on Courantyne River, on boundary bet. Guyana and Suriname.

\ə\ **abut** \ᵊ\ **kitten**, Fr table \ər\ **further** \a\ **ash** \ā\ **ace** \ä\ **cot, cart** \à\ Fr bac \au̇\ **out** \b̲\ Span Avila \ch\ **chin** \e\ **bet** \ē\ **easy** \g\ **go** \i\ **hit** \ī\ **ice** \j\ **job** \k̲\ Ger **ich**, **Buch** \ⁿ\ Fr vin \ŋ\ **sing** \ō\ **go** \ȯ\ **all** \ȯ\ **law** \œ\ Fr bœuf \œ̄\ Fr feu \ȯi\ **boy** \th\ **thin** \t̲h̲\ **this** \ü\ **loot** \u̇\ **foot** \ue\ Ger füllen \ue̅\ Fr **rue** \y\ **yet** \ʸ\ Fr digne \ˈdēnʸ\, nuit \ˈnwʸē\ \yü\ **few** \yu̇\ **fury** \zh\ **vision**

Fred·er·ic·ton \ˈfre-drik-tən, -də-rik-\. City, ✱ of New Brunswick and ⊗ of York co., New Brunswick, Canada, in SW part of province at head of navigation of St. John River 55 mi. (89 km.) NNW of St. John; pop. (1991c) 46,466; government and education center; railroad center; 19th cent. cathedral; Univ. of New Brunswick (1859). Laid out as provincial ✱ 1785 across river from village of **Sainte Anne's Point** \sānt-ˈanz\, which was settled by French c. 1740, earliest settlement in region, and received many Acadian refugees.

Frederik Hendrik. See DOLAK ISLAND.

Fred·er·iks·berg \ˌfret͟h-regz-ˈber\. Commune, Sjælland I., Denmark; 3 sq. mi. (8 sq. km.); pop. (1989e) 85,327; a suburb of Copenhagen; Royal Copenhagen Porcelain factory; founded 1651.

Fre·de·riks·borg \ˌfret͟h-regz-ˈbȯr\. County of Denmark. See table at DENMARK.

Fre·de·riks·håb \ˌfret͟h-regz-ˈhȯp\. Settlement on S coast of Greenland, NNW of Ivigtut; pop. (1991e) 2162.

Fre·de·riks·havn \ˌfret͟h-regz-ˈhau̇n\. Seaport, Nordjylland co., NE Jutland Penin., Denmark, on the Kattegat 37 mi. (60 km.) NE of Ålborg; pop. (1991e) 35,448.

Frederiksnagar. See SERAMPORE.

Fred·er·ik·sted \ˈfre-drik-ˌsted, -də-rik-\. City on W coast of St. Croix I., Virgin Is. of the U.S., West Indies; pop. (1990c) 1064.

Fre·do·nia \fri-ˈdō-nē-ə, -nyə\. **1.** City, ⊗ of Wilson co., SE Kansas, N of Independence; pop. (1990c) 2599; oil, gas.
2. Village, Chautauqua co., SW corner of New York, near Lake Erie 23 mi. (37 km.) N of Jamestown; pop. (1990c) 10,436; grape juice, wine; State Univ. of New York Coll. at Fredonia (1826); site of first local Grange unit 1868.

Fredrikshald. See HALDEN.

Fredrikshamn. See HAMINA.

Fred·rik·stad \ˈfre-drik-ˌstä\. Seaport, Østfold co., SE Norway, on E shore of Oslo Fjord at mouth of Glåma River; pop. (1992e) 26,473; shipping point for wood products and chemicals; founded 1567 as a fortress by Frederick II.

Free·born \ˈfrē-ˌbȯrn\. County in S Minnesota. See table at MINNESOTA.

Free·burg \ˈfrē-ˌbərg\. Village, St. Clair co., SW Illinois, 18 mi. (29 km.) SE of East St. Louis; pop. (1990c) 3115.

Free City of Danzig. See *History* at GDAŃSK 2.

Free·dom \ˈfrē-dəm\. Borough, Beaver co., W Pennsylvania; pop. (1990c) 1897; founded 1832.

Free·hold \ˈfrē-ˌhōld\. Borough, ⊗ of Monmouth co., E cen. New Jersey, 18 mi. (19 km.) S of Perth Amboy; pop. (1990c) 10,742; first white settlement 1650; village estab. by Scots 1715, called Monmouth Court House, later changed to Freehold 1801; incorp. as town 1869, as borough 1919. See MONMOUTH COURT HOUSE.

Free·land \ˈfrē-lənd\. Borough, Luzerne co., E Pennsylvania, S of Wilkes-Barre; pop. (1990c) 3909; coal deposits.

Freels, Cape \ˈfrēlz\. Cape on E coast of Newfoundland, Canada, marking NW point of Bonavista Bay, 49°15′N.

Freels Peak. Mountain, E El Dorado co., E California; 10,880 ft. (3316 m.).

Free·man Lake \ˈfrē-mən\. Lake, NW cen. Indiana, formed in Tippecanoe River by Oakdale Dam. See SHAFER LAKE.

Free·man's Farm \ˈfrē-mənz\. Locality, near Bemis Heights on W bank of Hudson River bet. villages of Saratoga and Stillwater, Saratoga co., New York; center of fighting in two battles of Saratoga (*q.v.*) 1777.

Free·port \ˈfrē-ˌpōrt\. **1.** City, ⊗ of Stephenson co., N Illinois, 28 mi. (45 km.) W of Rockford; pop. (1990c) 25,840; Highland Community Coll. (1962); settled 1835; chartered 1855; scene of Lincoln-Douglas debate (1858) in which politician Stephen Douglas expounded his "Freeport Doctrine" that local legislation could be effective against slavery despite the Supreme Court's Dred Scott decision.
2. Town, Cumberland co., SW Maine, 16 mi. (26 km.) NNE of Portland; pop. (1990c) 6905; factory outlets; incorp. 1789; final papers for separation of Maine from Massachusetts signed here 1820, establishing Maine as an independent state.
3. Residential village, Nassau co., SE New York, on S shore of Long Island 25 mi. (40 km.) ESE of New York City; pop. (1990c) 39,894; oysters.
4. City and port of entry, Brazoria co., SE Texas, at mouth of Brazos River on Gulf of Mexico 40 mi. (64 km.) WSW of Galveston; pop. (1990c) 11,389; chemicals; plant for extracting magnesium from seawater.
5. Town on SW coast of Grand Bahama I., Bahamas; pop. (1990c) 26,574; tourism.

Freer \ˈfrir\. City, Duval co., S Texas, 60 mi. (97 km.) ENE of Laredo; pop. (1990c) 3271.

Free State *or Afrikaans* **Vry·staat** \ˈfrā-ˌstät, ˈfrī-\; *formerly* **Or·ange Free State** \ˈȯr-inj, ˈär-, -ənj\. Province, E cen. Rep. of South Africa, bounded on SE by Lesotho, and by all of the South African provinces except for Western Cape and Northern; forms part of inner plateau of South Africa; 4000 to 5000 ft. (1219 to 1524 m.) above sea level, with higher W slopes of Drakensberg along E border. Traversed along S border by Orange River, along N by the Vaal and separated for most part from Lesotho by Caledon River; crossed by tributaries of the Vaal River (Modder, Riet, Vet), flowing generally W. Wide plains afford excellent grazing; chief industry stock raising; chief agricultural products grains and fruits; gold, coal. See table at SOUTH AFRICA, REPUBLIC OF.

History: Region inhabited by Bantu-speaking peoples when first visited by Europeans toward end of 18th cent.; a few settlements made early 19th cent. but occupancy really began c. 1835 with Great Trek of Boers out of Cape Colony; annexed by British 1848 as **Orange River Sovereignty;** became independent Orange Free State 1854; engaged in conflicts with Basothos 2d half of 1860s; joined Boers of South African Republic (Transvaal) against British in Boer War (1899–1902); again annexed to British dominions as **Orange River Colony** 1900; granted responsible government 1907; joined Union (now Republic) of South Africa 1910, name changed back to Orange Free State. See HEILBRON.

Free·stone \ˈfrē-ˌstōn\. County in E cen. Texas. See table at TEXAS.

Free Territory of Trieste. See TRIESTE 3.

Free·town \ˈfrē-ˌtau̇n\. **1.** Town, Bristol co., SE Massachusetts, 10 mi. (16 km.) N of New Bedford; pop. (1990c) 8522.
2. Seaport town, ✱ of Sierra Leone, on N shore of Sierra Leone Penin.; pop. (1985p) 469,776; best harbor in W Africa, at mouth of Sierra Leone River; fish processing, oil refining; footwear, diamonds; cathedral (1852); university (1967); settled 1787 chiefly by freed slaves who were granted land by a native chieftain.

Fre·gel·lae \fri-ˈje-lē\. Ancient Volscian town, Latium, Italy; a few ruins near modern Ceprano; near Liris (*mod.* Liri) River; colony estab. by Romans 328 B.C.; revolted against Rome 125 B.C. and was destroyed.

Fre·ge·nal de la Sier·ra \ˌfre-k͟ā-ˈnäl-ˌt͟hā-lä-ˈsyer-rä\. Commune, Badajoz prov., SW Spain, 47 mi. (76 km.) SSE of the city of Badajoz; pop. (1991c) 5585.

Fré·hel, Cape \frā-ˈel\. Cape on coast of Côtes-du-Nord dept., NW France, 15 mi. (24 km.) W by N of St.-Malo.

Frei·berg \ˈfrī-berk\. City, Lower Saxony, E Germany, 21 mi. (34 km.) SW of Dresden near W bank of Mulde River; pop. (1992e) 47,582; precision instruments, leather, porcelain; lead and zinc mines nearby; mining academy (founded 1765); 13th cent. relic called the Golden Portal; 15th cent. Gothic cathedral. Founded 12th cent. as silver-mining camp; scene of Prussian victory 1762 during Seven Years' War.

Frei·burg \ˈfrī-ˌbu̇rk, -ˌbərg\. **1.** Canton and commune, Switzerland. See FRIBOURG.
2. *also* **Freiburg im Breis·gau** \im-ˈbrīs-ˌgau̇\. City, Baden-Württemberg, Germany, at W foot of Black Forest 80 mi. (129 km.) SW of Stuttgart; pop. (1992e) 193,775; chemicals; Gothic cathedral; university (1457); ducal palace. Founded 1120; Austrian 1368–1806; scene during Thirty Years' War of several battles Aug. 1644 in which French under Louis II, duc d'Enghien and Henri de La Tour d'Auvergne (Marshal Turenne) forced the retreat of Bavarians under Field Marshal Franz von Mercy; passed to Baden 1806.

Freienwalde. See BAD FREIENWALDE.

Frei·sing \ˈfrī-ziŋ\. City, Bavaria, Germany, 20 mi. (32 km.) NNE of Munich; pop. (1992e) 38,433; 12th cent. cathedral. Founded by Romans; episcopal see 8th–19th cents.

Frei·tal \ˈfrī-ˌtäl\. City, Lower Saxony, E Germany, 6 mi. (10 km.) SW of Dresden; founded 1921.

Fré·jus \frā-ˈzhūēs\. **1.** *anc.* **Fo·rum Ju·lii** \ˈfōr-əm-ˈjü-lē-ˌī\. Commune, Var dept., SE France; pop. (1990c) 42,613; Roman ruins include amphitheater and aqueduct; cathedral has 5th cent. baptistery. Founded first cent. B.C. by Roman Gen. Julius Caesar; severe flood 1959 following failure of nearby dam.

2. Alpine pass and tunnel. See table at ALPS.

Fre·man·tle \frē-ˈmant-^{ə}l\. City, SW Western Australia, Australia, on Indian Ocean at mouth of Swan River, part of the Perth met. area; pop. (1991c) 23,834; founded 1829; seaport for Perth; shipbuilding; exports chiefly wool, wheat; site of 1987 America's Cup yacht races; suburbs are **East Fremantle** and **North Fremantle.**

Fre·mont \ˈfrē-ˌmänt\. **1.** Name of counties in four states of the U.S. See tables at COLORADO, IDAHO, IOWA, WYOMING.

2. City, Alameda co., W California, SSE of Oakland; pop. (1990c) 173,339; automobiles; Ohlone Coll. (1966).

3. City, Newaygo co., W Michigan, 22 mi. (35 km.) NE of Muskegon; pop. (1990c) 3875; baby food.

4. City, ⊗ of Dodge co., E Nebraska, on Platte River 33 mi. (53 km.) WNW of Omaha; pop. (1990c) 23,680; flour mills; Midland Lutheran Coll. (1883).

5. Town, Rockingham co., New Hampshire; pop. (1990c) 2576.

6. City, ⊗ of Sandusky co., N Ohio, 21 mi. (34 km.) WSW of the city of Sandusky; pop. (1990c) 17,648; sugar-beet and cannery center; site of two Wyandot Indian villages; later site of Fort Stevenson (built 1812), successfully defended against British attack 1813; home and burial place of President Rutherford B. Hayes in state park here.

Fremont Peak. **1.** Mountain peak, N Arizona. See SAN FRANCISCO PEAKS.

2. Mountain in Wind River Range, W cen. Wyoming; ab. 13,745 ft. (4189 m.).

French \ˈfrench\. River, SE Ontario, Canada, bet. Sudbury and Parry Sound dists.; outlet of Lake Nipissing to Georgian Bay; 60 mi. (97 km.) long.

French Antilles. See FRENCH WEST INDIES.

French Broad \ˈbrȯd\. River, E United States; formed by junction of N and W forks in Transylvania co., SW North Carolina, flows NW through Great Smoky Mts. across Tennessee border, turns W to unite with Holston River near Knoxville and form Tennessee River; 210 mi. (338 km.) long; near its junction with Holston River is Douglas Dam, one of dams of Tennessee Valley Authority (*q.v.*).

French·burg \ˈfrench-ˌbərg\. City, ⊗ of Menifee co., E Kentucky; pop. (1990c) 625.

French Community *or Fr.* **Com·mu·nau·té fran·çaise** \kō-mūē-nō-ˈtā-frä^{n}-ˈsez\ *or* **La Communauté.** The former federation comprising metropolitan France, its overseas departments and territories, and those of its former African territories (Central African Rep., Chad, Congo, Dahomey, Gabon, Malagasy Rep., and Senegal) which, on becoming republics, chose to maintain their ties with France; formed under the Constitution of the Fifth Republic promulgated Oct. 5, 1958, superseding the French Union; formal operation was short-lived.

French Congo. Name used before 1910 for the French possessions comprising French Equatorial Africa and restricted to Middle Congo between 1910 and its independence in 1960.

French Creek. River, New York and Pennsylvania; flows from SW New York SW and SE into Allegheny River at Franklin, cen. Venango co., NW Pennsylvania; ab. 140 mi. (225 km.) long.

French Equatorial Africa; *occas. shortened to* **Equatorial Africa** *or earlier* **French Congo.** Former federation of French possessions, W cen. Africa, consisting of Chad, Gabon, Middle Congo, and Ubangi-Shari; 969,112 sq. mi. (2,510,000 sq. km.); ✻ Brazzaville.

History: Coast explored by Portuguese 15th cent.; French settlement of region began on Gabon River c. 1841 and continued throughout 19th cent.; borders of French possessions determined by series of international agreements; region divided 1910 into three federated colonies, Gabon, Middle Congo, and Ubangi-Shari-Chad, and name changed from French Congo (Chad made a separate fourth colony of the federation 1920); ab. 100,000 sq. mi. (259,000 sq. km.) of territory ceded to Germany 1911 in return for recognition of French rights to Morocco, territory recovered 1919 by Treaty of Versailles; declared its independence of Vichy government 1940; Brazzaville became center of operations of Free French in Africa; by the new French constitution of 1946 status of the four colonies changed to that of overseas territories of France within the French Union; territories became autonomous republics within French Community 1958, and each achieved total independence 1960.

French Frigate Shoals. Group of islets, Hawaiian Is., 100 mi. (161 km.) W of Necker I., 23°45′N, 166°10′W.

French Gui·a·na \gē-ˈa-nə, -ˈä-; gī-ˈa-nə\ *or Fr.* **Guy·ane fran·çaise** \gwē-ˈyȧn-frä^{n}-ˈsez\. French overseas department on NE coast of South America, having Suriname on the W and Brazil on E and S; 35,126 sq. mi. (90,976 sq. km.); pop. (1993e) 128,000; ✻ Cayenne; chief mountains the Tumuc-Humac Mts. on the S border separating it from Brazil; hinterland largely plateau.

Chief rivers: The Maroni, forming boundary with Suriname on W, the Oyapock, forming boundary with Brazil on E, and the Mana and Sinnamary rivers.

Chief products: Timber, shrimp, rice.

History: For early history of region see GUIANA. First French settlement at Cayenne early 17th cent.; largely neglected until 18th cent. when French made unsuccessful attempts to settle; occupied by British and Portuguese 1809 but restored to France after 1817; early development hindered by presence of penal colonies, the first estab. 1852; boundary with Brazil settled by arbitration 1900; reconstituted as overseas department of France 1946; penal colonies closed by 1947.

French Guinea. See GUINEA 2.

French India *or officially* **Éta·blisse·ments fran·çais dans l'Inde** \ā-tȧ-blē-ˈsmä^{n}-frä^{n}-ˈse-dä^{n}-le^{n}d\. Five settlements in India that formerly constituted a territory of France: Chandernagore, Pondicherry (Pondichéry), Karikal, Yanam, all on E coast, and Mahé on W coast; 197 sq. mi. (510 sq. km.); ✻ Pondicherry.

History: French stations in India founded by French East India Company (chartered 1664); under leadership of Governor-General Joseph-François Dupleix, Deccan and Carnatic (*qq.v.*) came under French control by 1750, but that control quickly waned until Robert Clive's victory at Plassey 1757 gave British ascendancy in India (see INDIA 1); Pondicherry and other ports captured and restored several times, until by Paris treaties of 1814 and 1815 French possessions in India were returned (reoccupied by French by 1817); ceded to India 1949–56.

French In·do·chi·na \ˌin-dō-ˈchī-nə\. Former name for the E part of the peninsula of Indochina (*q.v.*), SE Asia, bordering on China on the N, Myanmar on the NW, Thailand on the W; 291,793 sq. mi. (755,744 sq. km.); ✻ Hanoi.

History: Corresponds approx. to empire of Annam as it existed at beginning of 19th cent., then owing suzerainty to China. French-controlled Cochin China, Cambodia, Annam, and Tonkin (*qq.v.*) were united for administration 1887, Laos and Kwangchowan added 1893 and 1898; occupied by Japanese 1940; clashed with Siamese forces; forced to cede territory in Cambodia and Laos to Siam 1941; after WWII occupied for a time by British and Chinese troops until French control reestablished 1946; scene of warfare 1946–54 as extreme nationalist group sought independence from France; by 1955 Vietnam had become divided at 17th parallel into two states and Cambodia and Laos were independent. See CAMBODIA; LAOS; VIETNAM, NORTH and VIETNAM, SOUTH.

French Lick \'french-'lik\. Resort town, Orange co., S Indiana, SSW of Bedford; pop. (1990c) 4902; sulfur springs; birthplace of basketball player Larry Bird 1956.

French·man Bay \'french-mən\. Inlet of Atlantic Ocean on SE coast of Maine, E of Mt. Desert I.

French Morocco. See MOROCCO 1.

French Pol·y·ne·sia \ˌpä-lə-'nē-zhə, -shə\ *or Fr.* **Po·ly·né·sie fran·çaise** \pȯ-lē-nā-'zē-frä^{n}-'sez\; *formerly* **French Ocean·ia** \ˌō-shē-'a-nē-ə, -'ā-\ *or Fr.* **Éta·blisse·ments (fran·çais) de l'Océ·a·nie** \ˌā-tȧ-blē-'smä^{n}-(frä^{n}-'se)-də-lō-sā-ȧ-'nē\. French overseas territory in South Pacific Ocean, comprising Marquesas, Society, Gambier, and Austral island groups and Tuamotu Archipelago (*qq.v.*); 1261 sq. mi. (3266 sq. km.); pop. (1993e) 212,000; ✻ Papeete on Tahiti, Society Is.; covers wide area, approx. from 7°S to 29°S and 132°W to 156°W; exports include copra, coconut oil, and vanilla.

History: Islands discovered and explored by Europeans throughout 16th–18th cents.; visited by French missionaries in late 18th cent.; French protectorates estab. 1840s; colony of French Oceania estab. 1880s; administration reorganized 1903; became overseas territory of France 1946; French nuclear tests conducted in region since 1966, but moved underground 1975.

French River. See FRENCH.

French Shore. Former neutralized territory on W and N coasts of Newfoundland, Canada, from Cape Ray in SW to Cape St. John (50°N); estab. 1713 when Newfoundland was ceded to Great Britain with certain rights granted to French fishermen, esp. that of drying fish on land; above limits defined 1783; source of much friction 19th cent. bet. England and France; France relinquished its claims 1904; surrounding waters also source of dispute over fishing rights with American fishermen (settled by arbitration 1910).

French Somaliland. See DJIBOUTI 1.

French Southern and Antarctic Territories *or Fr.* **Terres Au·strales et Ant·arc·tiques fran·çaises** \ˌter-ō-'strȧl-zā-ȧnt-ärk-'tēk-frä^{n}-'sez\. French overseas territory, consisting of Adélie Coast and the following S Indian Ocean islands: Amsterdam I., Crozet Is., Kerguelen Is., and St. Paul I. (*qq.v*); estab. 1955.

French Sudan. See MALI.

French Territory of the Afars and the Issas. See DJIBOUTI 1.

French Union. The French federation formed by the Constitution of the Fourth Republic of Sept. 29, 1946 (confirmed by referendum of Oct. 13, 1946), comprising France with its overseas departments and territories and the associated states; superseded 1958 by the French Community (*q.v.*).

French·ville \'french-ˌvil\. Town, Aroostook co., N Maine, on St. John River E of Fort Kent; pop. (1990c) 1338.

French West Africa. Former federation of French dependencies, W Africa, consisting of what are now the independent republics of Benin, Burkina Faso, Guinea, Ivory Coast, Mali, Mauritania, Niger, and Senegal; 1,739,034 sq. mi. (4,504,098 sq. km.); ✻ Dakar; estab. 1895, reorganized several times; federation dissolved 1958–59.

French West Indies; *also* **French An·til·les** \an-'ti-lēz\ *or Fr.* **An·tilles fran·çaises** \ä^{n}-'tēl-frä^{n}-'sez\. Islands of the Lesser Antilles, West Indies; comprise Martinique, Guadeloupe (*qq.v.*), and the five dependencies of Guadeloupe.

Fresh·wa·ter \'fresh-ˌwȯ-tər, -ˌwä-\. Village, W Isle of Wight, England; resort; site of Farringford estate, home of poet Alfred, Lord Tennyson from 1853.

Fresnes \'fren\. Commune, Val-de-Marne dept., N France.

Fres·nil·lo \fres-'nē-yō\ *or in full* **Fresnillo de Gon·zá·lez Eche·ver·ría** \thā-gōn-'sä-lās-ā-chā-ver-'rē-ä\. Municipality, Zacatecas state, cen. Mexico; pop. (1990p) 160,208; school of mines; silver mines nearby; founded 1554.

Fres·no \'frez-nō\. **1.** County in S cen. California. See table at CALIFORNIA.

2. City, its ⊗, 155 mi. (249 km.) SE of San Francisco, in San Joaquin valley; pop. (1990c) 354,202; marketing and shipping center; fruitpacking (esp. raisins); cotton, sugar beets, dairy products; Fresno City Coll. (1910), California State Univ., Fresno (1911), Fresno Pacific Coll. (1944); founded 1872; made ⊗ 1874; incorp. as city 1885.

Fresno Dam. Dam across Milk River, N Montana; height 111 ft. (34 m.); completed 1939; impounds water for irrigation.

Fretum Gallicum. See DOVER, STRAIT OF.

Fretum Herculeum. See GIBRALTAR, STRAIT OF.

Frey·ci·net Peninsula \ˌfrās-^{ə}n-ˌā\. Peninsula on E coast of Tasmania, Australia, 42°13′S; ab. 20 mi. (32 km.) long; its tip preserved as **Freycinet National Park.**

Fria, Cape \'frē-ə\. Cape extending into Atlantic Ocean on NW coast of Namibia, S of Angola boundary.

Fri·ant Dam \'frī-ənt\. See SAN JOAQUIN 1.

Friaul. See FRIULI.

Fri·bourg \frē-'bür\ *or Ger.* **Frei·burg** \'frī-ˌbu̇rk, -ˌbərg\. **1.** Canton of Switzerland; ✻ Fribourg; cheese; tourism. Remained Catholic during Reformation; under French rule 1798–1814; joined Sonderbund 1845 (see *History* at SWITZERLAND), surrendered to Swiss army 1847. See table at SWITZERLAND.

2. Commune, its ✻, on peninsula in Saane River 17 mi. (27 km.) SW of Bern; pop. (1991e) 33,913; chocolate and other food products; 13th cent. cathedral; university (1889); founded as military post 1157; held by Hapsburgs 13th–15th cents.; became member of Swiss Confederation 1481.

Fri·court \frē-'kür\. Village, Somme dept., N France, near Albert; taken by Allies 1916 in WWI, shelled by Germans.

Fri·day Harbor \'frī-dā\. Town, ⊗ of San Juan co., NW Washington, NE of Victoria, British Columbia; on San Juan I.; pop. (1990c) 1492.

Frid·ley \'frid-lē\. City, Anoka co., E Minnesota, SE of the city of Anoka; pop. (1990c) 28,335.

Fridt·jof Nan·sen, Mount \'frēd-yȯf-'nän-sən\. Mountain, Antarctica, 85°21′S, 167°33′W; 13,087 ft. (3989 m.).

Fridtjof Nansen Land. See FRANZ JOSEF LAND.

Fried·berg \'frēt-berk, 'frēd-ˌbərg\. City, Hesse, Germany, near Usa River 15 mi. (24 km.) N of Frankfurt am Main; pop. (1980c) 24,233.

Friedek–Mistek. See FRÝDEK-MÍSTEK.

Friedland. See PRAVDINSK.

Fried·ling·en \'frēt-liŋ-ən\. Battlefield in SW corner of Baden, Germany, on the Rhine N of Basel and SE of Mulhouse; scene 1702 of victory of French under duc de Villars over Margrave Louis William I of Baden during War of Spanish Succession.

Frie·drichs·ha·fen \'frē-driks-'häf-^{ə}n\; *before 1811* **Buchhorn** \'bük-ˌhȯrn\. City, SE Baden-Württemberg, Germany, on Lake Constance 14 mi. (23 km.) E of Konstanz; pop. (1992e) 54,764; automobiles; tourism; important harbor; passed to Württemberg 1810. Chief center of manufacture of Zeppelins during and for some years after WWI; suffered heavy damage during WWII.

Frie·drichs·ruh \ˌfrē-driks-'rü\. Village, Schleswig-Holstein, Germany, 15 mi. (24 km.) SE of Hamburg; home of statesman and chancellor Otto von Bismarck on his retirement 1890.

Frie·drichs·thal \'frē-driks-ˌtäl\. Town, Saarland, Germany, ab. 8 mi. (13 km.) N of Saarbrücken; pop. (1980c) 12,560; coal.

Friedrich–Wilhelmshafen. See MADANG 2.

Friendly Islands. See TONGA.

Friend·ship \'frend-ship\. Village, ⊗ of Adams co., cen. Wisconsin; pop. (1990c) 728.

Friends·wood \'frendz-ˌwu̇d\. City, Galveston co., SE Texas, 20 mi. (32 km.) SE of Houston; pop. (1990c) 22,814.

Friesche Eilanden. See FRISIAN ISLANDS.

Fries·land \'frēs-lənd, 'frēz-, -ˌland\ *also* **Vries·land** \'vrēs-, 'vrēz-\. Province, N Netherlands; ✻ Leeuwarden; dairy farming, livestock raising. See table at NETHERLANDS.

Frin·ton–on–Sea \'frint-^{ə}n\. Town, Essex, SE England; resort on North Sea coast.

Frio \ˈfrē-ō\. **1.** River, S Texas; flows into Nueces River; 220 mi. (354 km.) long.
2. County in S Texas. See table at TEXAS.

Frio, Cape. Cape extending into Atlantic Ocean from coast of Rio de Janeiro state, SE Brazil.

Fri·o·na \frē-ˈō-nə\. City, Parmer co., NW Texas, 65 mi. (105 km.) SW of Amarillo; pop. (1990c) 3688.

Frische Nehrung *or* **Frisches Haff.** See VISLINSKI ZALIV.

Fris·co \ˈfris-kō\. City, Collin co., NE Texas, just N of Plano; pop. (1990c) 6141.

Fri·sia \ˈfri-zhē-ə, ˈfrē-, -zhə\. Former country, W Europe, situated along SE coast of North Sea at time of Frankish empire; corresponded approx. to modern Netherlands.

Fri·sian Islands \ˈfri-zhən-, ˈfrē-\ *or Du.* **Frie·sche Ei·lan·den** \ˈfrē-sə-ˈā-ˌlän-dən\. Chain of islands in North Sea, bet. 3 and 20 mi. (5 and 32 km.) from European mainland, incl.: (1) **North Frisian Islands** off NW coast of Schleswig-Holstein, Germany, and the SW coast of Denmark; chief islands: (German) Sylt, Föhr, Nordstrand, Pellworm, and Amrum; (Danish) Rømø, Fanø, and Mandø. (2) **East Frisian Islands** off Lower Saxony state, Germany; chief islands: Borkum, Juist, Norderney, Langeoog, Spiekeroog, and Wangerooge. (3) **West Frisian Islands** off Waddenzee and N Netherlands coast; chief islands: Texel, Vlieland, Terschelling, Ameland, and Schiermonnikoog. Helgoland (*q.v.*) belongs to German group of North Frisian Is.

Fris·sell, Mount \frə-ˈzel\. Mountain, Litchfield co., NW Connecticut; 2380 ft. (725 m.); highest point in the state.

Fritz·lar \ˈfrits-ˌlär\. Town, N Hesse, Germany, on Eder River; pop. (1980c) 15,158; church of St. Peter and monastery, both founded 8th cent. by St. Boniface.

Fri·u·li \ˈfrē-ü-ˌlē, frē-ˈü-lē\ *or Ger.* **Fri·aul** \frē-ˈau̇l\; *anc.* **Fo·rum Ju·lii** \ˈfōr-əm-ˈjü-lē-ˌī\. Former duchy in NE Italy; became Lombard duchy 6th cent.; made Frankish King Charlemagne's territory 8th cent.; at close of 11th cent., part of patriarchate of Aquileia (*q.v.*); W part occupied by Venice in 15th cent.; E part (under Gorizia) acquired 1500 by Austria which received rest 1797; in French Emperor Napoléon's Illyrian Provinces (*q.v.*); Venetian part returned to Italy 1866 and rest after WWI; now part of Friuli-Venezia Giulia.

Friuli–Ve·ne·zia Giu·lia \-vā-ˈnet-sē-ä-ˈjül-yä\. Autonomous region, NE Italy; ✻ Trieste; dairy products, textiles; was granted limited autonomy 1963. See table at ITALY.

Fro·bish·er Bay \ˈfrō-bi-shər\. **1.** Inlet extending NW in SE Baffin I., E Nunavut, N Canada; first entered by English mariner Martin Frobisher 1576; airfield at its head.
2. Town, Nunavut, Canada. See IQALUIT.

From·bork \ˈfrȯm-ˌbȯrk\ *or Ger.* **Frau·en·burg** \ˈfrau̇-ən-ˌbu̇rk\. Town, Olsztyn prov., N Poland, on the Vislinski Zaliv, ab. 40 mi. (64 km.) E of Gdańsk; pop. (1981p) 1957; cathedral (1329–88); monument to Polish astronomer Nicolaus Copernicus who was canon of cathedral; formerly in East Prussia.

Frome \ˈfrüm\. **1.** River, Herefordshire, W England; flows into the Lugg; 20 mi. (32 km.) long.
2. Town, Somerset, SW England, on the **Frome River** (tributary of the Avon) 20 mi. (32 km.) SSE of Bristol; pop. (1981p) 14,527.

Frome, Lake \ˈfrōm\. Shallow lake, E South Australia, Australia, E of Lake Torrens; ab. 60 mi. (97 km.) long.

Fron·te·nac \ˈfrän-tə-ˌnak\. **1.** City, Crawford co., SE Kansas, 4 mi. (6 km.) N of Pittsburg; pop. (1990c) 2588.
2. City, St. Louis co., E Missouri, 9 mi. (15 km.) W of the city of St. Louis; pop. (1990c) 3374.
3. County in SE Ontario, Canada. See table at ONTARIO.

Frontenac, Lac. See ONTARIO, LAKE.

Fron·te·ra \frȯn-ˈtā-rä\; *formerly* **Ál·va·ro Obre·gón** \ˈäl-bä-rō-ō-brā-ˈg̅ōn\. Town, Tabasco state, SE Mexico, on Grijalva River near its mouth; pop. (1990p) 61,466.

Fron·tier \frən-ˈtir\. County in S Nebraska. See table at NEBRASKA.

Fron·ti·gnan \ˌfrōⁿ-tē-ˈnyäⁿ\. Commune, Hérault dept., S France, on a narrow lagoon just E of Étang de Thau; muscatel.

Front Range \ˈfrənt\. A range of Rocky Mts. in N cen. Colorado; highest peak Grays Peak 14,270 ft. (4350 m.).

Front Royal \ˈrȯi-əl\. Town, ⊗ of Warren co., N Virginia, 20 mi. (32 km.) S of Winchester; pop. (1990c) 11,880; scene of capture of Union troops by Confederates 1862.

Fro·si·no·ne \ˌfrō-zē-ˈnō-nā\. **1.** Province of Lazio, cen. Italy. See table at ITALY.
2. *anc.* **Fru·si·no** \ˈfrüz-ᵊn-ˌō, ˈfrüs-\. Commune, its ✻, 48 mi. (77 km.) ESE of Rome; pop. (1991p) 45,525; wine; remains of ancient Volscian town.

Frost·burg \ˈfrȯst-ˌbərg\. City, Allegany co., NW Maryland, 9 mi. (15 km.) W of Cumberland; pop. (1990c) 8075; Frostburg State Univ. (1898).

Frost·proof \ˈfrȯst-ˌprüf\. City, Polk co., cen. Florida Penin., 35 mi. (56 km.) SE of Lakeland; pop. (1990c) 2808.

Fro·ward, Cape \ˈfrō-wərd\. South tip of Brunswick Penin., Chile, on N side of Strait of Magellan; most S point of mainland of South America, 53°54′S, 71°18′W.

Frøya \ˈfrœ-yä\. Island in Norwegian Sea off W coast of Norway, W of Trondheim Fjord and N of Hitra I.

Frunze. See BISHKEK.

Frusino. See FROSINONE 2.

Frý·dek–Mís·tek \ˈfrē-dek-ˈmēs-tek\ *or Ger.* **Frie·dek–Mis·tek** \ˈfrē-dek-ˈmis-tek\. Town, E Czech Republic, just S of Ostrava; pop. (1991p) 65,067.

Frye·burg \ˈfrī-ˌbərg\. Town, Oxford co., W Maine, on New Hampshire border 38 mi. (61 km.) W of Lewiston; pop. (1990c) 2968; Fryeburg Academy (1791).

Fu'ād, Būr. See PORT FUAD.

Fu·cec·chio \fü-ˈchek-kyō\. Commune, Firenze prov., Tuscany, cen. Italy, on Arno River 23 mi. (37 km.) W by S of Florence; pop. (1989c) 20,499.

Fuchau. See FUZHOU.

Fu·chun *or W.-G.* **Fu–ch'un** \ˈfü-ˈchu̇n\ *or* **Tsien Tang** \ˈchyen-ˈtäŋ\. Navigable river, Zhejiang prov., E China; flows NE into Hangzhou Bay; ab. 140 mi. (225 km.) long; remarkable for its tidal bore.

Fu·ci·no \ˈfü-chē-ˌnō\; *anc.* **Fu·ci·nus** \ˈfyü-si-nəs\ *or mod.* **Ce·la·no** \chā-ˈlä-nō\. Former lake in L'Aquila prov., cen. Italy; 60 sq. mi. (155 sq. km.); drained 1854–75, providing 42,000 acres (17,010 hectares) for cultivation.

Fue·go \ˈfwē-g̅ō\. Volcano, Guatemala, SW of Guatemala City; 12,346 ft. (3763 m.); eruptions 1880, 1974.

Fuen·te de Can·tos \ˈfwān-tā-t͟hā-ˈkän-tōs\. Commune, Badajoz prov., SW Spain, 53 mi. (85 km.) SE of the city of Badajoz; pop. (1991c) 5075.

Fuente Obe·ju·na; *formerly* **Fuen·te·o·ve·ju·na** \ˈfwān-tā-ˌō-b̲ā-ˈhü-nā\. City, Córdoba prov., S Spain, 46 mi. (74 km.) NW of the city of Córdoba; pop. (1991c) 6322; formerly seat of Knights of Calatrava.

Fuen·ter·ra·bía \ˌfwān-tār-rä-ˈb̲ē-ä\ *or Eng.* **Fon·ta·ra·bia** \ˌfȯn-tə-ˈrā-bē-ə\. Town, Guipúzcoa prov., N Spain, at mouth of Bidassoa just N of Irún; medieval fortress town with ruins; often a scene of conflict since the Middle Ages.

Fuer·te \ˈfwer-tā\. River, SW Chihuahua and N Sinaloa states, Mexico; flows into Gulf of California; ab. 180 mi. (290 km.) long.

Fuerte Olim·po \ˈfwer-tā-ō-ˈlēm-pō\ *or Eng.* **Fort Olimpo.** Town, ✻ of Alto Paraguay dept., N Paraguay, on Paraguay River.

Fuer·te·ven·tu·ra \ˌfwer-tā-b̲en-ˈtü-rä\. One of the Canary Is. (*q.v.*), Las Palmas prov., Spain, 75 mi. (121 km.) ENE of Grand Canary I.; 668 sq. mi. (1730 sq. km.); of volcanic origin.

Fu·ga \ˈfü-g̅ä\. Island in Babuyan group, N of Luzon, Philippines; 36 sq. mi. (93 sq. km.); good anchorage.

Fuhkien. See FUJIAN.

Fu–hsin. See FUXIN.

Fujairah *or* **Fujayrah, Al.** See AL FUJAYRAH.

Fu·ji \'fü-jē\. **1.** *or* **Fu·ji·ya·ma** \,fü-jē-'yä-mä\ *or more correctly* **Fu·ji–no–Ya·ma** \'fü-jē-,nō-'yä-mä\ *or* **Fu·ji·san** \,fü-jē-'sän\. Sacred mountain in S cen. Honshū, Japan, ab. 70 mi. (113 km.) WSW of Tokyo; 12,388 ft. (3776 m.); an isolated peak, highest in Japan; almost a perfect cone; its crater has diameter of nearly 2000 ft. (610 m.); a quiescent volcano, last eruption 1707.

2. City, Shizuoka prefecture, Honshū, Japan; pop. (1992e) 226,587.

Fu·jian \'fü-'jyen\ *or W.-G.* **Fu·kien** *also* **Fuh·kien** \'fü-'kyen\. Maritime province, SE China, bounded on N by Zhejiang, on E and SE by East China Sea and Taiwan Strait, on SW by Guangdong, and on W by Jiangxi; ✻ Fuzhou; chief river the Min flowing SE to East China Sea near Fuzhou; subtropical climate; important agriculturally, tea and rice the chief crops; extensive forests which produce fir, pine, and camphor; fruit processing; chief cities: Fuzhou, Zhangzhou, Xiamen. In early times home of barbaric tribes; boundaries estab. during reign of Sung dynasty 10th–13th cents.; according to Venetian traveler Marco Polo, under Kublai Khan (13th cent.) it had an immense trade through the port of Zaytūn; taken by the Communist regime 1949. See table at CHINA.

Fu·ji·eda \,fü-jē-'ā-dä\. City, Shizuoka prefecture, Honshū, Japan, 12 mi. (19 km.) SW of Shizuoka; pop. (1992e) 122,322.

Fu·ji·no·mi·ya \,fü-jē-nō-'mē-yä\. City, Shizuoka prefecture, Honshū, Japan, 22 mi. (35 km.) NE of the city of Shizuoka; pop. (1992e) 118,735.

Fuji–no–Yama *or* **Fujisan** *or* **Fujiyama.** See FUJI 1.

Fu·ji·sa·wa \,fü-jē-'sä-wä\. City, Kanagawa prefecture, Honshū, Japan; pop. (1992e) 358,757; iron goods.

Fukae. See FUKUE.

Fu·ka·ya \fü-'kä-yä\. City, Saitama prefecture, Honshū, Japan, 46 mi. (74 km.) NW of Tokyo; pop. (1990c) 94,023.

Fukien. See FUJIAN.

Fu·ku·chi·ya·ma \fü-,kü-chē-'yä-mä\. City, Kyōto prefecture, Honshū, Japan, 35 mi. (56 km.) NW of the city of Kyōto; pop. (1980c) 63,788.

Fu·kue \fü-'kü-ā\ *or* **Fu·kae** \fü-'kä-ā\. **1.** Largest island of Gotō Archipelago, off W coast of Kyūshū, Japan; 1342 sq. mi. (3476 sq. km.).

2. Town, on E coast of Fukue I., Japan; largest town of Gotō Archipelago.

Fu·kui \fü-'kü-ē, 'fü-,\. **1.** Prefecture, Honshū, Japan; ✻ Fukui. See table at JAPAN.

2. City, its ✻, near the coast ab. 70 mi. (113 km.) NNW of Nagoya; pop. (1992e) 254,008; in feudal period seat of a daimyo; after Meiji Restoration 1868 became large industrial center; produces textiles, esp. habutai (a thin, soft Japanese silk); university (1949); devastated by earthquake 1948.

Fu·ku·o·ka \,fü-kü-'ō-kä\. **1.** Prefecture, N Kyūshū, Japan; ✻ Fukuoka; coal. See table at JAPAN.

2. Seaport city, its ✻, on Hakata Bay; pop. (1992e) 1,261,658; fishing; Kyūshū Univ. (1910). Ancient trade port; at time (1274–81) of attempted invasions of Mongol ruler Kublai Khan, the scene of much fighting; heavily bombed 1945.

Fu·ku·shi·ma \,fü-kü-'shē-mä\. **1.** Prefecture, N cen. Honshū, Japan; ✻ Fukushima; mountainous region; rice, tobacco; fishing. See table at JAPAN.

2. City, its ✻, pop. (1992e) 280,958; railroad junction; trade center. In feudal times the castle town of a daimyo.

Fu·ku·ya·ma \,fü-kü-'yä-mä\. **1.** City, Hiroshima prefecture, SW Honshū, Japan, on Inland Sea 33 mi. (53 km.) W of Okayama; pop. (1990c) 365,615.

2. Town, Hokkaidō, Japan. See MATSUMAE.

Fu·la·ni Empire \fü-'lä-nē\. See SOKOTO.

Ful·da \'fu̇l-də\. **1.** River, cen. Germany; flows N from E Hesse state to unite with Werra River at Münden and form the Weser River; 135 mi. (217 km.) long.

2. City, E Hesse, cen. Germany, on Fulda River 54 mi. (87 km.) NE of Frankfurt am Main; pop. (1992e) 57,180; textiles; 8th cent. abbey, around which town grew; 18th cent. cathedral contains tomb of St. Boniface; formerly seat of university (1734–1803); made episcopal see 1752; passed to Prussia 1866; in WWII taken by U.S. troops 1945.

Fulginium. See FOLIGNO.

Fu·ling *or W.-G.* **Fu–ling** *or* **Fou–ling** \'fü-'liŋ\. Town, SE Sichuan, S cen. China, on S bank of the Chang, ab. 50 mi. (80 km.) E of Chongqing.

Ful·ler·ton \'fu̇l-ər-tən\. **1.** City, Orange co., SW California, 17 mi. (27 km.) NE of Long Beach; pop. (1990c) 114,144; transportation equipment, aircraft parts, paper products; oil wells; Southern California Coll. of Optometry (1904), Fullerton Coll. (1913), Pacific Christian Coll. (1928), California State Univ., Fullerton (1957).

2. City, ⊗ of Nance co., E cen. Nebraska; pop. (1990c) 1452.

Ful·ton \'fu̇lt-ᵊn\. **1.** Name of counties in eight states of the U.S. See tables at ARKANSAS, GEORGIA, ILLINOIS, INDIANA, KENTUCKY, NEW YORK, OHIO, PENNSYLVANIA.

2. City, Whiteside co., NW Illinois, on Mississippi River 35 mi. (56 km.) N of Rock Island; pop. (1990c) 3698.

3. City, Fulton co., SW corner of Kentucky, on Tennessee border 23 mi. (37 km.) SW of Mayfield; pop. (1990c) 3078.

4. City, ⊗ of Itawamba co., NE Mississippi; pop. (1990c) 3387; Itawamba Community Coll. (1948).

5. City, ⊗ of Callaway co., cen. Missouri, 25 mi. (40 km.) NNE of Jefferson City; pop. (1990c) 10,033; mineral springs; Westminster Coll. (1851), William Woods Coll. (1870).

6. City, Oswego co., cen. New York, 24 mi. (39 km.) NNW of Syracuse; pop. (1990c) 12,929.

Fulton Chain Lakes. Chain of small lakes in NE cen. New York, chiefly in Herkimer co.

Ful·ton·dale \'fu̇lt-ᵊn-,dāl\. City, Jefferson co., cen. Alabama, 5 mi. (8 km.) N of Birmingham; pop. (1990c) 6400.

Ful·wood \'fu̇l-wu̇d\. Town, Lancashire, NW England, NE suburb of Preston; pop. (1981p) 23,769.

Fu·na·ba·shi \,fü-nä-'bä-shē\. City, Chiba prefecture, Honshū, Japan; pop. (1992e) 537,614; suburb of Tokyo; fish market.

Fu·na·fu·ti \,fü-nä-'fü-tē\. Atoll, cen. Tuvalu, W Pacific Ocean, 8°31′S, 179°13′E; 30 islets; lagoon area 84 sq. mi. (218 sq. km.), land area 17 sq. mi. (44 sq. km.); contains chief village and government headquarters of the group. Occupied by U.S. marines 1943 and U.S. base estab.; U.S. claim dropped 1983.

Fun·chal \fün-'shäl, fən-\. **1.** Former district of Portugal, coextensive with Madeira Is.

2. Seaport commune, ✻ of Madeira Is., Portugal, at head of large bay on SE coast of Madeira I.; munic. pop. (1991p) 126,021; winter resort; 15th–16th cent. cathedral; tomb of Portuguese navigator João Goncalves Zarco, discoverer of island and founder of the town 1421.

Fun·dão \füⁿ-'dau̇ⁿ\. Commune, Castelo Branco dist., E cen. Portugal, 24 mi. (39 km.) N of the commune of Castelo Branco; pop. (1981p) 31,906.

Fundi. See FONDI.

Fun·dy, Bay of \'fən-dē\. Inlet of Atlantic Ocean in SE Canada, extending bet. S New Brunswick and Nova Scotia; at upper end branches into Chignecto Bay and Minas Basin; 94 mi. (151 km.) long, 32 mi. (52 km.) wide at its mouth; remarkable for swift tidal currents; tides reaching 70 ft. (21 m.) recorded at head of bay; St. John (New Brunswick) on it.

Fundy National Park. See CANADA, *National Parks.*

Fünen. See FYN.

Fünfkirchen. See PÉCS.

Fung, Al– *or* **Fung, El.** See AL-FUNG.

Fu·niu Shan *or W.-G.* **Fu Niu Shan** \'fü-'nyü-'shän\. Mountain range in E cen. China, chiefly in N Henan prov., an E extension of Qinling Shandi; includes peaks ab. 9000 ft. (2745 m.) high.

Funza. See BOGOTÁ 1.

Fu·quay–Va·ri·na \'fü-kwā-və-'rī-nə\. Town, Wake co., E cen. North Carolina, 18 mi. (29 km.) SW of Raleigh; pop. (1990c) 4562.

Furāt, Al–. See EUPHRATES.

Füred. See BALATONFÜRED.

Fur·ka Pass \'fu̇r-kä\. Mountain pass bet. Uri and Valais cantons, S cen. Switzerland; 7994 ft. (2437 m.).

Fur·nas \ˈfər-nəs\. County in S Nebraska. See table at NEBRASKA.

Fur·neaux Group \ˈfər-nō\. Island group off NE Tasmania, Australia, at E end of Bass Strait; separated from Tasmania by Banks Strait; ab. 900 sq. mi. (2330 sq. km.); pop. (1986c) 1010; largest Flinders I. and Cape Barren I. Discovered 1773 by Capt. Tobias Furneaux in command of the *Adventure,* one of English explorer Capt. James Cook's ships.

Furnes. See VEURNE.

Fur·ness \ˈfər-nəs\. District, NW Cumbria, NW England, N of Morecambe Bay; S portion a peninsula with Barrow-in-Furness the chief town, N portion in Lake District; iron ore in SW; ruins of famous abbey, founded 1127 by a Benedictine order which later joined Cistercian order and became largest Cistercian abbey in England.

Fur Seal Islands. See PRIBILOF ISLANDS.

Fürst·en·feld·bruck \ˌfuerst-ᵊn-ˈfelt-ˌbrůk\. City, Bavaria, Germany, 15 mi. (24 km.) W of Munich; pop. (1980c) 31,887; notable 18th cent. church.

Fürstentum Liechtenstein. See LIECHTENSTEIN.

Für·sten·wal·de \ˌfuerst-ᵊn-ˈväl-də\. City, Brandenburg, E Germany, on Spree River 24 mi. (39 km.) ESE of Berlin; pop. (1992e) 34,163. Chartered 1285; episcopal see 1385–1571; bombed during WWII.

Fürth \ˈfuert\. City, Bavaria, Germany, at confluence of Regnitz and Pegnitz rivers 5 mi. (8 km.) NW of Nürnberg; pop. (1992e) 105,297; electronic equipment, toys; 14th cent. church; city hall (1840–50); Germany's first railway line opened 1835 bet. Fürth and Nürnberg; city bombed by Allies 1944–45.

Further India. See INDOCHINA.

Fu·ry and Hec·la Strait \ˈfyůr-ē ... ˈhe-klə\. Passage, Canada, from Gulf of Boothia to Foxe Basin, bet. Melville Penin. and NW Baffin I., ab. 100 mi. (161 km.) long.

Fusan. See PUSAN.

Fu·sa·ro \fü-ˈsä-rō, -ˈzä-\; *anc.* **Pa·lus Ach·e·ru·sia** \ˈpā-ləs-ˌa-kə-ˈrü-zhə, -zhē-ə\. Small lake, Campania, Italy, on peninsula bet. Gulf of Gaeta and Bay of Pozzuoli.

Fushih. See YAN'AN.

Fu·shi·mi \ˈfü-shē-mē\. Suburb of Kyōto, Kyōto prefecture, Honshū, Japan; historically important as residence (1594–98) of the shogun Toyotomi Hideyoshi.

Fu·shun *or W.-G.* **Fu–shun** \ˈfü-ˈshün\. City, Liaoning prov., NE China, 30 mi. (48 km.) E of Shenyang; pop. (1990c) 1,202,388; on rich bituminous coalfield. Mines known to Chinese since c. 13th cent. A.D.; modern development begun by Russians 1902.

Füs·sen \ˈfues-ᵊn\. Commune, SW Bavaria, Germany, near Tirol border; pop. (1992e) 14,050; castle; treaty signed here 1745 bet. Elector Maximilian III Joseph of Bavaria and Empress Maria Theresa of Austria which led to Bavaria's withdrawal from War of the Austrian Succession.

Fustāt, Al–. City, Egypt. See CAIRO 2.

Futa Jallon. See FOUTA DJALLON.

Futa *or* **La Futa.** Apennine pass. See table at APENNINES.

Fu·tu·na Islands \fü-ˈtü-nä\ *or* **Hoorn Islands** \ˈhōrn\. Island group in SW Pacific Ocean, NE of Fiji; 35 sq. mi. (91 sq. km.); pop. (1990c) 4732; a part of Wallis and Futuna Is. group, a French overseas territory; before 1959 a protectorate under the authority of the French overseas territory of New Caledonia; comprises **Futuna** (8 mi. by 5 mi. or 13 km. by 8 km.) and Alofi (6 mi. by 3 mi. or 10 km. by 5 km.) islands; discovered by Dutch 1616; annexed by France 1887.

Fu·xin *or W.-G.* **Fu–hsin** \ˈfü-ˈshin\. City, Liaoning prov., NE China, WNW of Shenyang.

Fu·yu *or W.-G.* **Fu–yü** \ˈfü-ˈyue\; *formerly* **Pe·tu·na** \pi-ˈtü-nə\. Town, Jilin prov., NE China, 100 mi. (161 km.) SW of Harbin.

Fu·zhou \ˈfü-ˈjō\ *or W.-G.* **Foo·chow** *or* **Fu·chau** \ˈfü-ˈchaů\; *formerly* **Min·how** \ˈmin-ˈhaů\. Seaport, ✱ of Fujian prov., SE China, on Min River 34 mi. (55 km.) from its mouth, ab. halfway bet. Hong Kong (455 mi. or 732 km. by sea) and Shanghai; pop. (1990c) 874,809; chief part is walled city ab. 2 mi. (3.2 km.) from N bank of river. For years, famous as chief port for export of black tea; fishing, food processing (esp. sugarcane, tea, and rice). In the city and on nearby hills are beautiful examples of Chinese architecture incl. pagodas and temples. Site of a city from at least 2d cent. B.C.; named Fuzhou during T'ang dynasty c. 8th cent. A.D.; one of first five treaty ports opened to trade by Treaty of Nanking 1842; changed hands several times bet. Japanese and Chinese in WWII.

Fyn \ˈfuen\ *also* **Fu·nen** \ˈfue-nən\. One of the islands of Denmark, bet. Sjælland on E and lower Jutland Penin. on W; with small adjacent islands constitutes a county; wheat, dairy products. See table at DENMARK.

Fyne, Loch \ˈfīn\. Inlet of Firth of Clyde, W Scotland, in Strathclyde region; 41 mi. (66 km.) long; herrings.

Fyzabad. 1. Town, Afghanistan. See FAIZĀBĀD 1. **2.** City, India. See FAIZĀBĀD 2.

G

Gab·a·rus Bay \ˈga-bə-ˌrüs\. Inlet of Atlantic Ocean, E coast of Cape Breton I., Nova Scotia, Canada, SW of Louisbourg.

Gabelhorn. See OBER-GABELHORN.

Gabe Rock \ˈgāb\. Height, SW Banner co., W Nebraska; 5006 ft. (1526 m.).

Gaberones. See GABORONE.

Ga·bès \ˈgä-ˌbes, gä-ˈbes\ *or* **Qā·bis** *also* **Qa·bes** \ˈkä-ˌbes\; *anc.* **Tac·a·pe** \ˈta-kə-ˌpē\. Seaport town and oasis, SE Tunisia, on the **Gulf of Gabès** (*or Fr.* **Golfe de Gabès;** *anc.* **Syr·tis Minor** \ˈsər-təs\); pop. (1989e) 83,610; peaches; fishing.

Ga·bii \ˈgā-bē-ˌī\. Ancient city, Latium, Italy, 12 mi. (19 km.) E of Rome; important city in ancient times until conquered by probably Tarquinius Superbus, last Roman king, late 6th cent. B.C.

Ga·ble, Great \ˈgā-bəl\. Mountain, W Cumberland, NW England, in the Lake District; 2949 ft. (899 m.).

Gable Mountain. Peak in Glacier National Park, NW Montana; ab. 9260 ft. (2822 m.).

Gablonz. See JABLONEC NAD NISOU.

Ga·bon \gȧ-ˈbō^{n}\ *or* **Ga·bun** \gə-ˈbün\ *or Eng.* **Ga·boon** \gə-ˈbün\. **1.** *or officially* **Gab·o·nese Republic** \ˌga-bə-ˈnēz\ *or Fr.* **Ré·pu·blique Ga·bo·naise** \rā-pue-ˈblēk-gȧ-bȯ-ˈnez\. Republic, W equatorial part of Africa, bounded on NW by Equatorial Guinea, on N by Cameroon, on E and S by Rep. of the Congo, and on W by the Atlantic Ocean; 102,317 sq. mi. (265,001 sq. km.); pop. (1993e) 1,280,000; ✱ Libreville.

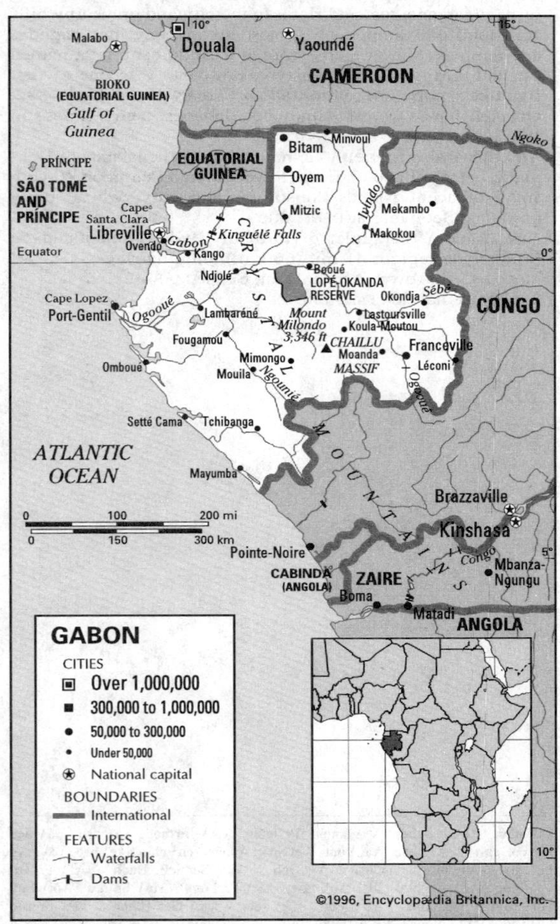

Physical features: Narrow coastal plain; hilly in S and on N border; highest point Mt. Iboundji 5167 ft. (1575 m.) in N. Chief river the Ogooué, whose basin covers most of the republic.

Chief products: Cocoa, coffee, cassava, palm oil, timber; manganese, iron ore, uranium, oil.

Chief towns: Libreville, Port-Gentil.

History: Neolithic artifacts in area; indigenous population Bantu tribes; Fang entered area in 18th cent.; French traders settled (1839–41); Libreville founded 1849; became a colony 1903 and part of French Equatorial Africa 1910; changed to a territory 1946; became a republic within the French Community 1958; achieved independence 1960; government overthrown by army, restored with aid of French troops 1964; Gabonese Democratic Party established as sole political party by President Omar Bongo; adopted new constitution 1966; initiated major economic development program 1971; growing discontent with single party system in 1980s led to riots in Libreville and Port-Gentil 1989 and legalization of opposition parties; first multiparty elections 1990.

2. Estuary, Gabon (republic); 7 mi. (11 km.) wide, extending ab. 40 mi. (64 km.) inland; Libreville is at its mouth; visited by Portuguese at end of 15th cent.

Ga·bo·ro·ne \ˌgä-bō-ˈrō-nā\; *formerly* **Ga·be·ro·nes** \ˌgä-bə-ˈrō-nəs\. Town, ✱ of Botswana, in SE part near border with Rep. of South Africa; pop. (1991c) 133,468; government is chief economic activity; university.

Ga·bro·vo \ˈgä-brō-ˌvō\. Town, cen. Bulgaria, on upper Yantra River; pop. (1991e) 80,694; textiles; first Bulgarian national school opened here 1835.

Gabun. See GABON.

Ga·dag \ˈgə-dəg\. Town, Karnataka, SW India, 310 mi. (499 km.) SE of Bombay; important rail junction; in area of archaeologically notable Hindu temples.

Gad·a·ra \ˈga-də-rə\. Greek town of the Decapolis (*q.v.*), NE Palestine, ab. 6 mi. (10 km.) SE of Sea of Galilee; gave its name to the Gadarenes (*Mark* v. 1; *Luke* viii. 26).

Gade \ˈgād\. Short river, Hertfordshire, SE England, just NW of Greater London.

Gades. See CÁDIZ 2.

Gads·den \ˈgadz-dən\. **1.** County in N Florida. See table at FLORIDA.

2. City, ⊗ of Etowah co., NE Alabama, on Coosa River 60 mi. (97 km.) ENE of Birmingham; pop. (1990c) 42,523; textiles, automobile tires; in area rich in manganese, iron ore, coal, limestone, sandstone, timber; Gadsden State Community Coll. (1965); settled c. 1840.

Gadsden Purchase. A tract of land, now in S New Mexico and S Arizona; 29,640 sq. mi. (76,768 sq. km.); purchased 1853 by U.S. from Mexico for $10,000,000 after negotiations conducted by James Gadsden, U.S. minister to Mexico.

Gads·hill \ˈgadz-ˌhil\. Low hill in Kent, SE England, 3 mi. (5 km.) WNW of Rochester; home of novelist Charles Dickens.

Gael·tacht \ˈgāl-ˌtəkt\. The Irish-speaking parts of Ireland, primarily on or near the W coast.

Ga·e·ta \gä-ˈā-tä\; *anc.* **Ca·ie·ta** \kā-ˈē-tə, kī-ˈē-\. Fortified seaport, Latina prov., Lazio, cen. Italy, on Gulf of Gaeta 41 mi. (66 km.) ESE of Littoria; pop. (1991p) 22,393; glass manufacture; fisheries; ancient ruins, incl. a Roman theater, a Roman amphitheater, and a campanile. Center of commercial prosperity after dissolution of Roman and Eastern empires; withstood numerous invasions, esp. by Lombards and Saracens; fell to Norman Sicily mid-12th cent.; papal refuge

1848–50 from Roman revolutions; last stronghold of Neapolitan Bourbons in Italy; fell to Gen. Enrico Cialdini after long siege 1861.

Gaeta, Gulf of. Inlet of Tyrrhenian Sea on W coast of Italy, N of Bay of Naples and E of Ponza Is.

Gae·tu·lia \ji-ˈtü-lē-ə, -ˈtyü-\. Ancient district, N Africa, N part of Libya and of Sahara region; inhabited by nomadic tribes of the Gaetuli who were part of the Berber peoples of Numidia.

Gaff·ney \ˈgaf-nē\. City, ⊗ of Cherokee co., N South Carolina, 19 mi. (31 km.) ENE of Spartanburg; pop. (1990c) 13,145; textile mills; Limestone Coll. (1845).

Gäfle. See GÄVLE.

Gäfleborg. See GÄVLEBORG.

Gaf·sa \ˈgaf-sə\ *or* **Qaf·sah** \ˈkäf-sə\; *anc.* **Cap·sa** \ˈkap-sə\. Town and oasis, W cen. Tunisia, ab. 115 mi. (185 km.) W of Sfax; pop. (1989e) 58,773; olives, dates; phosphates; thermal springs; discoveries of prehistoric artifacts nearby have given name *Capsian* to a Mesolithic culture of N Africa. In WWII scene of some of first fighting by American troops in African campaign (see AL-QAṢRAYN).

Ga·ga·rin \gȧ-ˈgȧ-rin\; *formerly* **Gzhatsk** \ˈgzhätsk\. Town, NE Smolensk Oblast, W Russia in Europe, 90 mi. (145 km.) W of Moscow; birthplace 1934 of Yuri Alekseyevich Gagarin, first person to travel in space; name changed after Gagarin's death in 1968.

Gage \ˈgāj\. County in SE Nebraska. See table at NEBRASKA.

Gage·town \ˈgāj-ˌtau̇n\. Village, ⊗ of Queens co., S New Brunswick, Canada, on St. John River 36 mi. (58 km.) N of St. John; pop. (1991c) 607.

Ga·gnoa \gä-ˈnyō-ä\. Town, S cen. Ivory Coast; pop. (1988c) 84,911.

Ga·gny \gȧ-ˈnyē\. Commune, Seine-St.-Denis dept., N France, 6 mi. (10 km.) ENE of Paris.

Ga·han·na \gə-ˈha-nə\. City, Franklin co., cen. Ohio, a NE suburb of Columbus; pop. (1990c) 27,791; pop. more than doubled bet. 1970 and 1990.

Gaidaro. See ANGATHONÍSI.

Gail \ˈgāl\. Town, ⊗ of Borden co., NW Texas.

Gail·lac \gȧ-ˈyȧk\ *or* **Gaillac–sur–Tarn** \-sụr-ˈtȧrn\. Commune, Tarn dept., S France, on Tarn River ab. 12 mi. (19 km.) W of Albi; Benedictine abbey founded 960; a wine-producing area since ancient times.

Gail·lard Cut \gil-ˈyärd, ˈgāl-ˌyärd, ˈgā-ˌlärd\; *formerly* **Cu·le·bra Cut** \kü-ˈlā-brə, kyü-, -ˈle-\. SE section of Panama Canal, ab. 8 mi. (13 km.) through Continental Divide at Culebra Mt., from Gamboa to locks at Pedro Miguel; 45 ft. (14 m.) deep, width at bottom 300 ft. (91 m.); name changed by President Woodrow Wilson in honor of David Du Bose Gaillard (d. 1913) who had charge of excavation of this most difficult part in construction of the canal.

Gain·er Memorial Dam \ˈgā-nər\; *formerly* **Scit·u·ate Dam** \ˈsi-chə-ˌwət\. Dam across Pawtuxet River, N cen. Rhode Island; height 180 ft. (55 m.); completed 1928; impounds water, **Scituate Reservoir,** for water supply of Providence.

Gaines \ˈgānz\. County in NW Texas. See table at TEXAS.

Gaines·boro \ˈgānz-ˌbər-ō\. Town, ⊗ of Jackson co., N Tennessee; pop. (1990c) 1002.

Gaines' Mill \ˈgānz\. Battlefield just ENE of Richmond, Virginia; scene June 27, 1862 of defeat of Union forces under Gen. Fitz-John Porter by Gen. Robert E. Lee's Confederates; sometimes known as Cold Harbor (*q.v.*).

Gaines·ville \ˈgānz-ˌvil, -vəl\. **1.** City, ⊗ of Alachua co., N Florida Penin., 65 mi. (105 km.) SW of Jacksonville; pop. (1990c) 84,770; Univ. of Florida (established 1853 and site of state museum), Santa Fe Community Coll. (1966).
2. City, ⊗ of Hall co., N Georgia, 35 mi. (56 km.) NW of Athens; pop. (1990c) 17,885; poultry; Brenau Coll. (1878), Gainesville Coll. (1965); incorp. 1821.
3. City, ⊗ of Ozark co., S Missouri; pop. (1990c) 659.
4. City, ⊗ of Cooke co., N Texas, 30 mi. (48 km.) W of Sherman; pop. (1990c) 14,256; settled c. 1851 on route of the 1849 gold seekers.
5. Village, Prince William co., NE Virginia; battle Aug. 28, 1862, a part of 2d battle of Bull Run.

Gains·bor·ough \ˈgānz-ˌbər-ō\. Town, Parts of Lindsey, Lincolnshire, E England, on the Trent 30 mi. (48 km.) SW of Hull; pop. (1981p) 18,691; the St. Ogg's of novelist George Eliot's *Mill on the Floss;* the Dane Sweyn Forkbeard began conquest of England here in 1013.

Gaïon. See PAXOS.

Gaird·ner, Lake \ˈgard-nər\. Lake, S South Australia, Australia, N of Eyre Penin.; ab. 90 mi. (145 km.) long; 1840 sq. mi. (4766 sq. km.).

Gair Loch \ˈgar\. Inlet of Atlantic Ocean in Strathclyde region, NW coast of Scotland; the village of **Gair·loch** \ˈgar-ˌläk\ is at its head.

Gai·thers·burg \ˈgā-thərz-ˌbərg\. Town, Montgomery co., W Maryland, 20 mi. (32 km.) NW of Washington, D.C.; pop. (1990c) 39,542.

Ga·la \ˈgä-lə\ *or* **Gala Water.** River, SE Scotland; rises in Moorfoot Hills, S of Edinburgh; flows SSW into the Tweed 3 mi. (5 km.) W of Melrose; 21 mi. (34 km.) long.

Ga·la·na \gä-ˈlä-nä\. River, E Africa; rises in S Kenya, flows SE across S Kenya into Indian Ocean S of Ungama Bay; 340 mi. (547 km.) long.

Ga·lá·pa·gos Islands \gə-ˈlä-pə-gəs-, -ˈla-\ *or Span.* **Archi·pié·la·go de Co·lón** \ˌär-chē-ˈpyā-lä-gō-t͟hā-kō-ˈlōn\ *also* **Tor·toise Islands** \ˈtȯr-təs\. Island group constituting a province of Ecuador, in Pacific Ocean on the Equator ab. 600 mi. (965 km.) W of mainland; administrative center in Baquerizo Moreno on San Cristóbal; tourism; biological research; fishing; comprises many small islands and ab. 15 large ones; noted for its flora and fauna, a large portion of which is endemic, and esp. for its giant tortoise (*Span.* galápago), Darwin's finches, marine iguanas, and flightless cormorants. Discovered 1535 by Spanish; Inca pottery shards indicate earlier human presence; claimed by Ecuador 1832; visited by English naturalist Charles Darwin in 1835 resulting in studies of the endemic wildlife that figure importantly in his theory of natural selection; part designated a wildlife sanctuary in 1935 and 1959 by Ecuador; important U.S. airbase during WWII; sanctuary became Galapagos National Park in 1968; administered by Charles Darwin Biological Research Station opened 1964. See table at ECUADOR.

Gal·a·shiels \ˌga-lə-ˈshēlz\. Burgh, Borders region, SE Scotland; pop. (1981p) 12,294; manufactures tweeds; Scottish Coll. of Textiles.

Gal·a·ta \gä-ˈlä-tä, ˈgä-lə-tə\. Chief business section of İstanbul, Turkey, on the Golden Horn S of Beyoğlu; foreign and esp. Genoese traders' settlement 10th–15th cents.; taken over by the Turks 1453.

Ga·la·ţi \gä-ˈläts, -ˈlät-sē\; *formerly* **Ga·latz** \ˈgä-ˌläts\. **1.** County of E Romania. See table at ROMANIA.
2. City, its ⊗, on lower Danube ab. 115 mi. (185 km.) NE of Bucharest; pop. (1989c) 307,376; port, food processing; shipyards, iron and steel plant; chemicals, textiles; university; seat of European Danube Commission 1856–1945.

Ga·la·tia \gə-ˈlā-shə, -shē-ə\. Ancient country of cen. Asia Minor, orig. incl. parts of Phrygia and Cappadocia; settled by Gauls in 3d cent. B.C.; expanded by them until checked by Attalus I of Pergamum c. 230 B.C.; became dependent upon Romans in 2d cent. B.C. and Roman province 25 B.C.; visited by St. Paul (*Epistle to the Galatians*). See ANKARA 2.

Ga·la·ti·na \ˌgä-lä-ˈtē-nä\. Commune, Lecce prov., Puglia, SE Italy, 10 mi. (16 km.) S of the commune of Lecce; pop. (1989c) 29,280.

Galatz. See GALAŢI.

Gala Water. See GALA.

Ga·lax \ˈgā-ˌlaks\. City, SW Virginia, in Carroll and Grayson cos. but politically independent; 3 sq. mi. (8 sq. km.); pop. (1990c) 6670.

Gald·hø·pig·gen \ˈgäl-ˌhœ̄-ˌpē-gən\. Peak in the Jotunheimen, S cen. Norway, S of Glittertind; 8100 ft. (2469 m.).

G H

Ga·le·na \gə-ˈlē-nə\. **1.** City, ⊗ of Jo Daviess co., NW corner of Illinois, on Galena River; pop. (1990c) 3647; tourism; important lead- and zinc-mining center first half of 19th cent.; home of Ulysses S. Grant, 18th U.S. president.
2. City, Cherokee co., SE corner of Kansas, 22 mi. (35 km.) S of Pittsburg; pop. (1990c) 3308.
3. City, ⊗ of Stone co., SW Missouri; pop. (1990c) 401.

Galena Park. City, Harris co., SE Texas; pop. (1990c) 10,033.

Ga·len·stock \ˈgä-lən-ˌshtȯk, ˈga-lən-ˌstäk\. Peak in Valais and Uri cantons, S cen. Switzerland; 11,755 ft. (3583 m.).

Ga·le·ra Point \gə-ˈlir-ə\. Cape at NE tip of island of Trinidad.

Ga·le·ras \gä-ˈlā-räs\ *also* **Pas·to** \ˈpäs-tō\. Volcano at S end of Cordillera Occidental in SW Colombia, near Ecuador border; erupted Jan. 14, 1993.

Gales·burg \ˈgālz-ˌbərg\. City, ⊗ of Knox co., W Illinois, 45 mi. (72 km.) WNW of Peoria; pop. (1990c) 33,530; Knox Coll. (1837), Carl Sandburg Coll. (1967); settled 1836 by pioneers from Whitesboro, New York; incorp. as city 1857; birthplace of author Carl Sandburg 1878.

Gales Ferry \ˈgālz\. Subdivision of town of Ledyard, Connecticut. See LEDYARD.

Ga·li·cia \gə-ˈli-shə, -shē-ə\. **1.** *or Pol.* **Ha·licz** \ˈhäl-ich\ *or* **Ga·li·cja** \gä-ˈlēt-syä\ *or Russ.* **Ga·li·tsi·ya** \gə-ˈlēt-sē-yə\. Historic area and former Austrian crown land in E cen. Europe; 30,645 sq. mi. (79,371 sq. km.); includes N slopes of Carpathian Mts. and the valleys of upper Vistula and of upper Dniester, Bug, and Seret rivers; has rich oil fields.

History: Orig. small medieval principality; united with Lodomeria early 13th cent.; series of Mongol invasions through 13th cent.; annexed to Poland mid-14th cent. by Casimir III; annexed to Austria and named Galicia in partitions of Poland of 1772, 1795, and 1815; Polish uprising in W led to annexation of independent republic of Kraków to Galicia by Austria in 1846; mid-19th cent. revolts against Austria led to limited autonomy; Polish and Ukrainian languages recognized in addition to German; site of much WWI fighting; Poland regained region after war; during WWII E Galicia organized by U.S.S.R. into Ukrainian S.S.R.; after war, E remained with Ukrainian S.S.R. (Ukraine since 1990) and W remained with Poland by Polish-Soviet treaty.

2. *anc.* **Gal·lae·cia** \gə-ˈlē-shə, -shē-ə\. Region and ancient kingdom, NW Spain, bounded on N and W by Atlantic Ocean, on S by Portugal, on SE by León, on NE by Asturias; comprises an autonomous community consisting of the modern provs. of La Coruña, Lugo, Orense, Pontevedra; deeply indented coastline with good harbors; mountainous; chief river the Miño. Independent kingdom under the Suevi 5th–6th cents.; overthrown first by Visigoths, later by Moors; became part of kingdom of Asturias 8th–9th cents. See table at SPAIN.

Gal·i·lee \ˈga-lə-ˌlē, ˌga-lə-ˈ\. Hilly region of ancient Palestine, coextensive with N part of modern Israel, bounded on E by Jordan River and Sea of Galilee, and extending S to Plain of Esdraelon; in early times corresponded to land of tribe of Naphtali; in first cent. B.C. a Roman province, divided into Upper Galilee and Lower Galilee, and forming a tetrarchy under rule of Herod family; childhood home of Jesus, site of Jesus' ministry; major cities included Cana, Tiberias, and Nazareth.

Galilee, Sea of; *usu. name in Gospels for mod.* **Lake Ti·be·ri·as** \tī-ˈbir-ē-əs\ *or Arab.* **Bu·ḩay·rat Ţa·ba·rī·yā** \bü-ˈkī-rət-ˌtä-bä-ˈrē-yə\; *in Bible also called* [*Deut.* iii. 17] **Sea of Chin·ne·reth** \ˈki-nə-ˌreth\ *or* [*Luke* v. 1] **Lake of Gen·nes·a·ret** \gə-ˈne-sə-ˌret, -rət\ *or* [*John* vi. 1] **Sea of Tiberias.** Freshwater lake, N Israel; 13 mi. (21 km.) long, 7 mi. (11 km.) wide; ab. 700 ft. (212 m.) below sea level; derives most of its inflow from the Jordan River; economically significant (irrigation, fishing); rich in biblical associations; numerous archaeological sites in region.

Ga·li·na Point \gə-ˈlē-nə\. Cape on NE coast of island of Jamaica, West Indies.

Gal·ion \ˈgal-yən\. City, Crawford co., N cen. Ohio, 15 mi. (24 km.) W of Mansfield; pop. (1990c) 11,859; settled c. 1830.

Galitsiya. See GALICIA 1.

Gallabat. See QALLĀBĀT.

Gallaecia. See GALICIA 2.

Gal·lan Head \ˈga-lən\. Cape on W coast of island of Lewis with Harris, in the Outer Hebrides, off NW coast of Scotland.

Gal·la·ra·te \ˌgäl-lä-ˈrä-tā\. Commune, Varese prov., Lombardy, N Italy, 10 mi. (16 km.) S of the commune of Varese; pop. (1991p) 44,869; produces textiles.

Gal·la·tin \ˈga-lət-ᵊn\. **1.** River, Wyoming and S Montana; rises in NW corner of Wyoming, flows N into Montana to unite with Jefferson and Madison rivers and form the Missouri River; 125 mi. (201 km.) long; has formed a deep narrow canyon ab. 70 mi. (113 km.) long, at entrance to which is a small village **Gallatin Gateway,** cen. Gallatin co., the canyon being one of the entrances to Yellowstone National Park.
2. Name of counties in three states of the U.S. See tables at ILLINOIS, KENTUCKY, MONTANA.
3. City, ⊗ of Daviess co., NW Missouri, 25 mi. (40 km.) WNW of Chillicothe; pop. (1990c) 1864.
4. City, ⊗ of Sumner co., N Tennessee, 26 mi. (42 km.) NE of Nashville; pop. (1990c) 18,794; tobacco; clothing, locks.

Gallatin Peak. Peak, S Montana; 11,015 ft. (3357 m.).

Gallatin Range. Mountains, Gallatin and Park cos., S Montana and NW Wyoming, bet. the Gallatin and Yellowstone rivers; highest point Electric Peak 10,992 ft. (3350 m.), in NW corner of Yellowstone National Park.

Galle \ˈgäl, ˈgal\; *formerly* **Point de Galle** \ˌpȯint-də-\. Town, Sri Lanka, on Indian Ocean ab. 55 mi. (89 km.) SSE of Colombo; pop. (1990e) 84,000; seaport on rocky promontory. Occupied by Portuguese late 16th cent.; taken mid-17th cent. by Dutch, who erected fort; many old Buddhist monasteries.

Gal·le·gos \gä-ˈyā-gōs, gäl-\. River, S Argentina; flows E across S Santa Cruz prov. into **Gallegos Bay** opp. Falkland Is.; 180 mi. (290 km.) long.

Gal·ley Head \ˈga-lē-ˌhed\. Cape on SW coast of Ireland, E of Cape Clear; castle ruins; lighthouse.

Gal·lia \ˈga-lē-ə\. County in S Ohio. See table at OHIO.

Gal·lia \ˈga-lē-ə, ˈgä-\. Latin for "Gaul"; for compound names beginning with Gallia, see GAUL.

Gallicum, Fretum. See DOVER, STRAIT OF.

Gallim. See BEIT JALA.

Gal·li·nas, Point \gä-ˈyē-näs, gäl-\. Northernmost point of South America, La Guajira Penin., N Colombia; 12°25′N.

Gal·lip·o·li \gə-ˈli-pə-lē\. **1.** \gäl-ˈlē-pō-lē\. Fortified seaport and commune, Lecce prov., Puglia, SE Italy, on E shore of Gulf of Taranto 21 mi. (34 km.) SSW of the commune of Lecce; pop. (1989p) 20,921.
2. Seaport, Turkey. See GELİBOLU.

Gallipoli Peninsula *or Turk.* **Ge·li·bo·lu Ya·rı·ma·da·sı** \ˌge-lē-bȯ-ˈlü-ˌyä-rə-ˌmä-dä-ˈsē\. Narrow tongue of land extending SW from S coast of Turkey in Europe, bet. the Dardanelles on the SE and Saros Gulf and Aegean Sea on the NW and W; 63 mi. (101 km.) long. Scene of battles 1915–16 in Allied campaign in WWI, in conjunction with naval bombardment of Dardanelles forts; troops, mainly Anzacs, landed Apr. 1915; severe fighting in several peninsula locations; unsuccessful issue led to withdrawal (last troops left Jan. 1916). Location of **Gallipoli National Park;** many war memorials and Turkish and Allied cemeteries.

Gal·li·po·lis \ˌga-lə-pə-ˈlēs\. City, ⊗ of Gallia co., S Ohio, on Ohio River 30 mi. (48 km.) NE of Ironton; pop. (1990c) 4831; settled by French immigrants 1790.

Gal·li·tzin \gə-ˈlit-sən\. Borough, Cambria co., SW cen. Pennsylvania, 10 mi. (16 km.) W of Altoona; pop. (1990c) 2003; railroad tunnel at crest of Alleghenies above Altoona.

Gäl·li·va·re *also* **Gel·li·vare** \ˈye-lē-ˌvär-ə\. Rural commune, Norrbotten prov., N Sweden, in the Arctic Circle; pop. (1989c) 22,562; iron deposits.

Gal·lo, Cape \ˈgä-lō\. **1.** *or Gk.* **Ák·ra Akrí·tas** \ˈä-krä-ä-ˈkrē-täs\. Cape on SW coast of Peloponnese, S Greece, on W side of Gulf of Messenia.
2. Point on NW coast of Sicily, Italy, NW of Palermo.

Gal·loo Island \ˈga-lü\. Island in NE Lake Ontario, off W cen. coast of Jefferson co., N New York.

Gal·lops Island \ˈga-ləps\. One of the smaller and outer islands in Boston Harbor, Massachusetts.

Gal·lo·way \ˈga-lə-ˌwā\. Area in SW Scotland, comprising the former Wigtown and Kirkcudbright cos.; dairy farming.

Galloway, Mull of \ˈməl\. Cape on SW extremity of Scotland, projecting into Irish Sea W of entrance to Luce Bay; lighthouse.

Gal·lup \ˈga-ləp\. City, ⊗ of McKinley co., NW New Mexico, on Puerco River, bet. Southern Navajo and Zuñi Indian reservations; pop. (1990c) 19,154; railroad division point; coal mines; wool combing and packing, cattle raising; tourism; regional headquarters of U.S. Bureau of Indian Affairs; incorp. 1891; made ⊗ 1901.

Gal Oya National Park \ˈgäl-ˈō-yə\. National park, Sri Lanka; 98 sq. mi. (254 sq. km.); habitat of wide variety of wildlife, incl. bear, elephant, leopard; estab. 1954.

Galt \ˈgȯlt\. **1.** City, Sacramento co., N cen. California, 22 mi. (35 km.) SSW of the city of Sacramento; pop. (1990c) 8889.

2. Former city, SE Ontario, Canada, on Grand River 11 mi. (18 km.) SE of Kitchener; in rich farming area. Founded as **Shade's Mills** \ˈshādz-ˈmilz\ c. 1817; many early settlers were Scottish; renamed 1827 after Scottish novelist John Galt; merged 1973 with Preston to form Cambridge (*q.v.*).

Gal·ty Mountains *or* **Gal·tee Mountains** \ˈgȯl-tē\. Range, extending E to W in cos. Tipperary and Limerick, Ireland; ab. 15 mi. (24 km.) long; highest peak **Gal·ty·more** \ˌgȯl-tē-ˈmōr\, 3018 ft. (920 m.), in SW co. Tipperary.

Ga·lung·gung \gä-ˈlu̇ŋ-ˌgu̇ŋ\. Mountain, W Java, Indonesia, ab. 10 mi. (16 km.) E of Garut; 7113 ft. (2168 m.).

Gal·va \ˈgal-və\. City, Henry co., NW Illinois, 35 mi. (56 km.) SE of Rock Island; pop. (1990c) 2742.

Gal·ves·ton \ˈgal-və-stən\. **1.** County in SE Texas. See table at TEXAS.

2. City and port of entry, its ⊗, on E end of **Galveston Island** (30 mi. or 48 km. long) at S side of entrance to **Galveston Bay** (inlet of Gulf of Mexico) 48 mi. (77 km.) SSE of Houston; pop. (1990c) 59,070; connected with mainland by causeway and bridge; extensive port facilities, exports esp. cotton, sulfur, grain; food products; oil refineries; fisheries; resort; Univ. of Texas Medical Branch at Galveston (1891), Galveston Coll. (1967).

History: Probably where Spanish explorer Cabeza de Vaca was shipwrecked 1528; used as rendezvous by the pirate Jean Laffite 1817–21; made naval base during Texas revolt against Mexico 1835; temporary ✱ of the republic before and after battle of San Jacinto 1836; incorp. as city 1839; scene of Civil War battle 1863; first city to adopt (1901) commission plan of municipal government, sometimes called Galveston plan; suffered severe hurricanes esp. 1900, 1961, and 1980s.

Gal·way \ˈgȯl-ˌwā\. **1.** County, Connacht prov., W Ireland; ⊗ Galway; mountainous; chief river the Shannon; agriculture, fishing. See table at IRELAND.

2. Municipal borough and seaport, its ⊗, at head of **Galway Bay** (extends inland ab. 20 mi. or 32 km. on border bet. cos. Galway and Clare); pop. (1991p) 50,842; black-marble quarrying; fishing; tourism; textiles, electronics. Ruins of a 13th cent. Franciscan friary; 14th cent. church; seat of University Coll. (1845).

Ga·ma·gō·ri \gä-ˈmä-ˌgō-rē, ˌgä-mä-ˈgō-rē\. City, Aichi prefecture, Honshū, Japan, 32 mi. (52 km.) SE of Nagoya; pop. (1990p) 84,819.

Gam·bē·la *also* **Gam·bei·la** \gäm-ˈbā-lä\. Town, W Ethiopia; pop. (1989e) 5202.

Gam·bia \ˈgam-bē-ə, ˈgäm-\ **1.** *or* **The Gambia** *or in full* **Republic of the Gambia.** Republic, W Africa; 4003 sq. mi. (10,368 sq. km.); pop. (1983c) 687,817; ✱ Banjul (formerly Bathurst); consists of a strip of land extending ab. 6 mi. (10 km.) on both sides of the Gambia River and ab. 200 mi. (322 km.) inland from river mouth; constitutes an enclave in Senegal.

Chief products: Peanuts, palm kernels, rice, millet; livestock; forestry; fish.

Chief towns: Serekunda; Banjul.

History: Inhabited by Malinke, Fulani, and Wolof since 13th cent.; first Europeans to visit were Portuguese in mid-15th cent.; British acquired trade rights from Portuguese 1588; Fort James, collection site during slave trade, built mid-17th cent. on small island ab. 20 mi. (32 km.) from mouth of Gambia River; captured by French 1779; British claims to region recognized by Treaty of Versailles 1783; Gambia settlement placed under government of Sierra Leone 1807–43; became a British colony 1843; reverted to former status under Sierra Leone 1866; again made a separate colony 1888; boundaries settled 1889; territory upstream made a British protectorate 1894; became self-governing 1963; achieved full independence 1965; became a republic 1970; entered limited confederation with Senegal called Senegambia 1982, which was dissolved 1989.

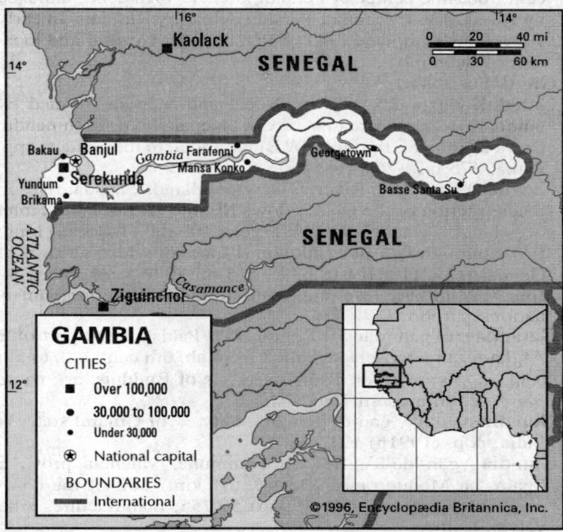

2. River, W Africa; rises in Fouta Djallon, Guinea; flows NW through Senegal and W through Gambia (republic) and into Atlantic Ocean at Banjul; ab. 700 mi. (1126 km.) long; lower 200 mi. (322 km.), which are navigable at all seasons, are in Republic of the Gambia.

Gam·bier \ˈgam-ˌbir\. Village, Knox co., cen. Ohio, E of Mount Vernon; pop. (1990c) 2073; Kenyon Coll. (1824).

Gambier, Mount. See MOUNT GAMBIER.

Gambier Islands. Island group, French Polynesia, S Pacific Ocean; 23°09′S, 134°58′W; 12 sq. mi. (31 sq. km.); pop. (1988c) 620; chief island Mangareva; nearly enclosed by barrier reef 40 mi. (64 km.) in circumference; generally considered a SE extension of the Tuamotu Archipelago.

Gam·boa \gäm-ˈbō-ə, gam-\. Town, Panama, on Panama Canal at SE corner of Gatun Lake; to the W is **Gamboa Reach,** channel (8 mi. or 13 km.) of canal in arm of Gatun Lake.

Game·well \ˈgām-ˌwel, -wəl\. Town, Caldwell co., North Carolina, 60 mi. (96 km.) NE of Asheville; pop. (1990c) 3357.

Gam·ka \ˈgam-kə\. River, Great Karoo region of S Rep. of South Africa; 160 mi. (257 km.) long; unites with the Olifants River to form the Gourits.

Gam·toos \gam-ˈtüs\. River in S Rep. of South Africa; flows SE to Indian Ocean; incl. Groot River, its main headstream, ab. 300 mi. (483 km.) long.

Ga·mu \gä-ˈmü\. Municipality, W cen. Isabela prov., Luzon, Philippines, 7 mi. (11 km.) S of Ilagan; pop. (1980c) 16,922.

Gan *or W.-G.* **Kan** \ˈgän\. River in Jiangxi prov., SE China; flows N through Poyang Hu (lake) into the Chang; 537 mi. (864 km.) long.

Gana. See GHANA 1.

Ganale Dorya. See GENALE.

Gan·a·noq·ue \ˌga-nə-ˈnä-kwē, -kwə\. Town, SE Ontario, Canada, on St. Lawrence River 20 mi. (32 km.) E of Kingston; pop. (1991c) 5209; adjacent to the Thousand Is.

Gän·cä \gän-ˈjä\ *or* **Gyan·dzha** \gyän-ˈjä\ *also* **Gan·dzha** \gän-\; *c. 1935–90* **Ki·ro·va·bad** \ˌkē-rə-və-ˈbät\; *c. 1813–1920* **Eli·sa·vet·pol** *or* **Ye·li·za·vet·pol** \ji-li-zə-ˈvyet-ˌpȯl\. City, W Azerbaijan, S of Kura River, on railroad line 110 mi. (177 km.) SE of Tbilisi; pop. (1991e) 282,200; on N spur of plateau region of Armenia at alt. of ab. 1440 ft. (439 m.); textiles. An old Armenian town founded as early as 5th cent.; destroyed by earthquake 12th cent. and by Mongols 13th cent.; became center of Persian khanate 17th cent.; annexed by Russia 1804; scene of Persian defeat by Russians in early 19th cent. Birthplace 1141 of Persian poet Neẓāmī and location of his tomb.

Gand. See GHENT.

Gan·dak \ˈgən-ˌdək\. River, Nepal and N India; formed by union of several streams in cen. Nepal W of Kathmandu, flows SW and SE through NW Bihar, India, to the Ganges opp. Patna; 475 mi. (764 km.) long.

Gan·der \ˈgan-dər\. River, E Newfoundland, Canada; rises in S cen. section of the island, flows NE into **Gander Bay,** inlet of Atlantic Ocean W of Cape Freels; 102 mi. (164 km.) long; flows through **Gander Lake** on N shore of which at town of Gander (pop. [1991c] 10,339), 215 mi. (346 km.) NW of St. John's, is air base (esp. important during WWII); large international airport.

Gan·dha·ra \gən-ˈdär-ə\. Region, NW Pakistan and part of E Afghanistan—loosely so called from ab. 6th cent. B.C. to 5th cent. A.D.; known for distinctive style of Buddhist art; name preserved in modern *Kandahār.*

Gan·dhi·na·gar \ˌgən-di-ˈnə-gər\. City, ✻ of Gujarat state, W India; pop. (1991p) 121,746.

Gan·día \gän-ˈdē-ä\. Seaport commune, Valencia prov., E Spain, on Mediterranean 38 mi. (61 km.) SSE of the commune of Valencia; pop. (1991p) 50,755; manufactures silk, velvet, leather.

Gan·do \ˈgän-dō\. **1.** *or* **Gwan·du** \ˈgwän-dü\. Traditional emirate, NW Nigeria; orig. settled by a little-known people; became emirate of Fulani Empire early 19th cent.; came under control of Nigeria (then a British protectorate) 1903; chief town Gwandu.

2. Town of NW Nigeria. See GWANDU.

Gandzha. See GÄNCÄ.

Gan·ga·na·gar \ˈgəŋ-gə-ˌnə-gər\. Town, Rajasthan, NW India; pop. (1981e) 121,516.

Gang·di·sê *or W.-G.* **Kang–ti–ssu** \ˈgäŋ-ˈdē-ˈsə\; *Eng.* **Kai·las** \kī-ˈläs\. Mountain range, SW Tibet, China; highest peak Kangrinboqê Feng; contains sources of the Indus and Sutlej rivers and headstreams of the Brahmaputra.

Gan·ges \ˈgan-ˌjēz\ *or Sanskrit and Hind.* **Gan·ga** \ˈgəŋ-gə\. Sacred river of N and NE Indian subcontinent; rises in the Himalayas near Gangotri, NE border of Tehri dist., Uttar Pradesh; flows S through the district as the Bhagirathi, then out into the plain of India at Hardwar in NW Uttar Pradesh, thence SE through Uttar Pradesh, Bihar, West Bengal, and Bangladesh to merge with the Brahmaputra River and flow into the Bay of Bengal through the vast Ganges Delta (*q.v.*); ab. 1557 mi. (2505 km.) long. Unites with the Yamuna at Allahabad; receives from the S the Son and from the N the tributaries Somati, Ghaghara, and Gandak; in upper course is source of extensive irrigation canals. On its banks are the sacred cities of Allahabad and Varanasi.

Ganges Canals. Irrigation canals, W Uttar Pradesh, India.

Ganges Delta *or* **Ganges–Brah·ma·pu·tra Delta** \-ˌbrä-mə-ˈpü-trə\. Region in West Bengal, India and in Bangladesh; ab. 220 mi. (354 km.) wide along Bay of Bengal; covered by the streams forming the mouths of the Ganges and Brahmaputra rivers. On entering Bangladesh the Brahmaputra is joined by the Tista from the NW and from there to its junction with the Ganges is known as the Jamuna. The main streams, Ganges and Jamuna, unite to form the **Pad·ma** \ˈpəd-mə\, which below Dhaka is joined by the Meghna; from this point to the Bay of Bengal the E mouth of the delta is known as the Meghna; the W outlet of the Meghna, W of Dakhin Shahbazpur I., is the **Te·tu·lia** \ti-ˈtül-yə\. Above Rajbari the **Mad·hu·ma·ti** \ˌmə-də-ˈmə-tē\ leaves the Ganges entering the Bay of Bengal at the **Ba·les·war** \bə-ˈles-wər\ mouth. The stream farthest W is the Hugli which leaves the Ganges near Murshidabad, passing Calcutta (90 mi. or 145 km. from the sea) and entering the Bay of Bengal by the largest mouth of the delta; its upper course above Santipur is an old channel of the Ganges, generally known as the **Bha·gi·ra·thi** \bä-ˈgir-ə-tē\. Many smaller streams of the delta bet. the Tetulia and Hugli mouths form a swamp region (ab. 6526 sq. mi. or 16,902 sq. km.) known as the **Sun·dar·bans** \ˈsu̇n-dər-ˌbənz\ *also* **Sun·der·bunds** \-ˌbəndz\. Delta struck Nov. 1970 by one of history's most devastating cyclones.

Gan·ge·tic Plain \gan-ˈje-tic\ *also* **Ganges Plain** *or* **In·do–Gangetic Plain** \ˈin-dō-\. A fertile region in N India and in Bangladesh, traversed by the Ganges River and its tributaries; one of the world's most densely populated areas.

Gan·gi \ˈgän-jē\; *anc.* **En·gy·um** \ˈen-jē-əm\. Commune, Palermo prov., NW cen. Sicily, Italy, 52 mi. (84 km.) ESE of the seaport of Palermo; pop. (1981p) 8451.

Gan·go·tri \ˈgəŋ-gə-ˌtrē\. Mountain temple, NW Uttar Pradesh, N India, near source of Bhagirathi River; elev. 10,319 ft. (3145 m.).

Gangra. See ÇANKIRI 2.

Gan·gri \ˈgäŋ-grē, ˈgəŋ-\. Mountain in the Himalayas, Bhutan; 24,742 ft. (7541 m.).

Gang·tok \ˈgəŋ-ˌtȯk\. Town, ✻ of Sikkim, NE Indian subcontinent; 28 mi. (45 km.) NE of Darjeeling; pop. (1991p) 24,971.

Gan·nett Peak \ˈga-nət\. Mountain, Fremont co., cen. Wyoming, in Wind River Range; 13,804 ft. (4208 m.); highest point in the state.

Gann·val·ley \ˈgan-ˌva-lē\. Village, ⊗ of Buffalo co., S cen. South Dakota.

Ga·nong·ga \gä-ˈnȯŋ-gä\. Small island of the New Georgia Is., cen. Solomon Is., W Pacific Ocean; S of Vella Lavella I.

Gans·ho·ren \ˈgäns-ˌhȯr-ən\. Commune, suburb of Brussels, Brabant prov., Belgium; pop. (1991c) 20,422.

Gan·su *or W.-G.* **Kan·su** \ˈgän-ˈsü\. Province of N cen. China, forming a long narrow wedge bet. Ningxia Huizu on N and Qinghai on S, touching Shaanxi on E, Sichuan on SE, and Xinjiang Uygur on W; ✻ Lanzhou. Crossed by the upper Huang River from SW to NE, whose tributaries and the Ruo (in N cen. part) afford valleys for highways. Mountainous, includes N ranges of Danghe Nanshan in W (20,000 ft. or 6096 m.) and E extension (Min Shan) of Kunlun Shan in S (17,000 ft. or 5182 m.); at lower levels characterized by sandy plains and (esp. in the E) by rich loess terraces. Great part of it traversed by W end of Great Wall, with its branches. Produces wheat, cotton, tobacco, oil. Served as corridor for great highway to the W, the old Silk Road (*q.v.*)—to Turkistan, India, Persia; for several centuries a part of the kingdom of Wei; came under Kublai Khan in 13th cent.; under the Mings a part of Shensi; scene of Muslim rebellions 1862–73; made a separate province 1911; suffered from great earthquake 1920. See table at CHINA.

Gan·zhou *or W.-G.* **Kan–chou** \ˈgän-ˈjō\; *formerly* **Kan-hsien** \ˈgän-ˈshyen\. Town, S Jiangxi prov., SE China, on upper Gan River ab. 200 mi. (322 km.) NNE of Guangzhou; in WWII fought over by Japanese and Chinese 1945.

Gao \ˈgau̇\. Town and port, E Mali, on Niger River; pop. (1987p) 54,874.

Gao·mi *or W.-G.* **Kao–mi** \ˈgau̇-ˈmē\. Town, E cen. Shandong prov., NE China, on railroad line 40 mi. (64 km.) NW of Qingdao.

Gap \ˈgäp\; *anc.* **Va·pin·cum** \və-ˈpiŋ-kəm\. Commune, ✻ of Hautes-Alpes dept., SE France, 96 mi. (155 km.) NNE of Marseille; pop. (1990c) 35,647; wood products; tourism.

Ga·pan \gä-ˈpän\. Municipality, S Nueva Ecija prov., Luzon, Philippines, S of Cabanatuan; pop. (1980c) 60,014.

Gar \ˈgär\ *or W.-G.* **Ka–erh** \ˈgä-ˈər\; *formerly* **Gar·tok** \ˈgär-ˈtȯk\. Town, SW Tibet, China, on upper Indus at W end of Gangdisê Range; alt. 15,200 ft. (4633 m.); trading center opened by British 1904.

Ga·ra Gor·fu \ˈgär-ə-gȯr-ˈfü\. Peak, cen. Ethiopia, N of Addis Ababa; 11,482 ft. (3500 m.).

Ga·ra·ka·yo \ˌgä-rä-ˈkä-yō\. Island, S Palau Is., SW Pacific Ocean, near Peleliu, 1 mi. (1.6 km.) in diameter; occupied by U.S. forces Oct. 1944.

Garam. See HRON.

Ga·ra·nhuns \ˌgȧ-rȧ-ˈnyü^{n}s\. City, Pernambuco state, E Brazil, 120 mi. (193 km.) SW of Recife; munic. pop. (1991p) 103,293.

Gar·a·pan \ˌgä-rä-ˈpän, ˌgar-ə-ˈpan\. Town on W coast of Saipan, Mariana Is., W Pacific Ocean; heavy fighting between Japanese and American forces 1944.

Gar·ba·gna·te Mi·la·ne·se \ˌgär-bä-ˈnyä-tā-ˌmē-lä-ˈnā-zā\. Commune, Milano prov., Lombardy, N Italy; pop. (1989c) 25,201.

Garbieh. See GHARBĪYA.

Garb·sen \ˈgärp-sən\. Municipality, Lower Saxony, Germany, 8 mi. (13 km.) W of Hannover; pop. (1992e) 61,182; formed 1967.

Garches \ˈgȧrsh\. Commune, Hauts-de-Seine dept., N France, ab. 8 mi. (13 km.) W of Paris; Lafayette Escadrille monument in memory of American aviators killed in WWI.

Gar·cía Caves \gär-ˈsē-ə\. Large natural caves, Nuevo León state, NE Mexico, near Monterrey; stalactites and an underground lake.

Gard \ˈgȧr\. Department of S France. See table at FRANCE.

Gar·da, Lake \ˈgär-dä\; *anc.* **La·cus Be·na·cus** \ˈlā-kəs-bə-ˈnā-kəs\. Lake in E Lombardy, N Italy, its E shore on Veneto boundary; 32 mi. (52 km.) long and 2 to 11 mi. (3 to 18 km.) wide; 143 sq. mi. (370 sq. km.); drains S through Mincio River into the Po; tourism; noted for scenic beauty.

Gardafui, Cape. See CASEYR, RAAS.

Gardaia. See GHARDAÏA.

Gar·den \ˈgard-^{ə}n\. County in W Nebraska. See table at NEBRASKA.

Gar·de·na \gär-ˈdē-nə\. City, Los Angeles co., SW California, S suburb of the city of Los Angeles; pop. (1990c) 49,847.

Gardena, Val di \ˈväl-dē-gär-ˈdā-nä\ *or Ger.* **Gröd·ner·tal** \ˈgrœt-nər-ˌtäl\. Valley, Trentino-Alto Adige, NE Italy; 18 mi. (29 km.) long.

Garden City. **1.** City, Chatham co., SE Georgia, 2 mi. (3.2 km.) N of Savannah; pop. (1990c) 7410.

2. City, ⊗ of Finney co., W Kansas, on Arkansas River; pop. (1990c) 24,097; Garden City Community Coll. (1919).

3. City, Ada co., SW Idaho, on Boise River and surrounded on three sides by Boise (city); pop. (1990c) 6369.

4. City, Wayne co., SE Michigan, 15 mi. (24 km.) W of Detroit; pop. (1990c) 31,846.

5. Residential village, Nassau co., SE New York, on Long Island 18 mi. (29 km.) E of New York City; pop. (1990c) 21,686; founded 1867; Protestant Episcopal Cathedral of the Incarnation; Adelphi Univ. (founded 1896 in Brooklyn), Nassau Community Coll. (1959); Roosevelt Field, airport where Charles A. Lindbergh began his historic transatlantic flight, 1927; printing and publishing center.

6. Village, ⊗ of Glasscock co., W Texas.

Gar·den·dale \ˈgärd-^{ə}n-ˌdāl\. City, Jefferson co., cen. Alabama, 10 mi. (16 km.) N of Birmingham; pop. (1990c) 9251.

Garden Grove. City, Orange co., SW California, S of Anaheim; pop. (1990c) 143,050; citrus groves nearby.

Garden Island. Island in N Lake Michigan N of Beaver I.; part of Charlevoix co., NW Michigan.

Garden of the Gods. A region near Colorado Springs, Colorado; ab. 500 acres (203 hectares); noted for numerous unusual and colorful rock formations of sandstone.

Garden Reach \ˈrēch\. SW suburb of Calcutta, West Bengal, NE India, on E bank of Hugli River.

Garden Wall. Mountain in Glacier National Park, NW Montana; 8600 ft. (2621 m.); a narrow ridge with glaciers on either side.

Gar·dēz *or* **Gar·deyz** \gər-ˈdāz\. Town, E Afghanistan; pop. (1988e) 11,300; elev. 7500 ft. (2286 m.); lumbering.

Gardinas. See HRODNA 2.

Gar·di·ner \ˈgärd-nər, -^{ə}n-ər\. **1.** City, Kennebec co., SW Maine, on Kennebec River 8 mi. (13 km.) S of Augusta; pop. (1990c) 6746.

2. Town, S Park co., S Montana; N entrance to Yellowstone National Park; alt. ab. 5267 ft. (1605 m.); nearby are **Gardiner River** and **Gardiner Canyon.**

Gar·di·ners Bay \ˈgärd-nərz, -^{ə}n-ərz\. Inlet of Long Island Sound on E end of Long Island, New York.

Gardiners Island. Island in Gardiners Bay, E Long Island, New York, W of Montauk Point; settled 1639; first English settlement in New York; privately owned game preserve; reputed burial place of pirate loot by Captain William Kidd.

Gard·ner \ˈgärd-nər\. **1.** City, Worcester co., cen. Massachusetts, 9 mi. (15 km.) W of Fitchburg; pop. (1990c) 20,125; furniture; woodworking; high-technology industries; Mount Wachusett Community Coll. (1963).

2. One of the Phoenix Is. See NIKUMARORO.

Gardner, Mount. Mountain, Antarctica, 78°23′S, 86°02′W; 15,375 ft. (4686 m.).

Gardner Canal *or* **Gardner Channel.** Inlet of Pacific Ocean, W British Columbia, Canada, joining Douglas Channel at its mouth; ab. 80 mi. (129 km.) long.

Gardner Lake. Lake in W cen. New London co., SE Connecticut.

Gardner Pinnacles. Group of islets, Hawaiian Is., in cen. Pacific Ocean 25°N, 167°55′W; consists of lava rock columns 170 ft. (52 m.) high; in Hawaiian Is. Bird Reservation.

Gare Loch \ˈgar\. Branch of the Firth of Clyde, SW Scotland; 7 mi. (11 km.) long.

Garenne–Colombes, La. See LA GARENNE-COLOMBES.

Gar·field \ˈgär-ˌfēld\. **1.** Name of counties in six states of the U.S. See tables at COLORADO, MONTANA, NEBRASKA, OKLAHOMA, UTAH, WASHINGTON.

2. City, Bergen co., NE corner of New Jersey, on Passaic River 5 mi. (8 km.) SE of Paterson; pop. (1990c) 26,727; machinery, paper products, rubber goods.

Garfield, Mount. **1.** Peak, San Juan co., SW Colorado; 13,072 ft. (3984 m.).

2. Peak, Franconia Mts., N cen. New Hampshire, in N Grafton co.; 4488 ft. (1368 m.).

Garfield Heights. City, Cuyahoga co., N Ohio, 6 mi. (10 km.) SSE of Cleveland; pop. (1990c) 31,739; steel; oil refineries.

Garfield Mountain. **1.** Peak, Chaffee and Pitkin cos., W cen. Colorado; 13,800 ft. (4206 m.).

2. Peak in Bitterroot Range on Idaho-Montana state boundary; 10,961 ft. (3341 m.).

Gar·forth \ˈgär-ˌfōrth\. Town, West Yorkshire, N England; pop. (1981p) 28,405.

Gar·ga·no Promontory \gär-ˈgä-nō\; *or* **Pro·mon·to·rio del Gar·ga·no** \ˌprō-mȯn-ˈtōr-ē-ō-ˌdel-gär-ˈgä-nō\; *anc.* **Gar·ga·num** \gär-ˈgā-nəm\. Promontory extending into Adriatic Sea from E coast of Foggia prov., Puglia, SE Italy; ab. 30 mi. (48 km.) long; highest point 3465 ft. (1056 m.); easternmost point is **Te·sta del Gargano** \ˈtes-tä-ˌdel-\.

Gar·i·bal·di Provincial Park \ˌgar-ə-ˈbȯl-dē\. Provincial park in SW British Columbia, Canada, N of Vancouver; contains **Mount Garibaldi** 8786 ft. (2678 m.), glaciers, snowfields.

Ga·ri·glia·no \ˌgä-rē-ˈlyä-nō\. River, SE Lazio, cen. Italy; flows SE, then SW on Campania border to Gulf of Gaeta; ab. 100 mi. (160 km.) long; its main headstream the Liri; in WWII formed German defense line 1943–44; crossed by Allies May 1944 after long and severe fighting.

Ga·ris·sa \gä-ˈrē-sä\. Town, ✻ of North-Eastern prov., NE Kenya.

Gar·land \ˈgär-lənd\. **1.** County in W cen. Arkansas. See table at ARKANSAS.

2. City, Dallas co., NE Texas, bordering Dallas on the NE; pop. (1990c) 180,650; oil-field equipment, electronic equipment, chemicals; Amber Univ. (1971).

\ə\ abut \$^{ə}$\ kitten, Fr table \ər\ further \a\ ash \ā\ ace \ä\ cot, cart \ȧ\ Fr bac \au̇\ out \b̶\ Span Avila \ch\ chin \e\ bet \ē\ easy \g\ go \i\ hit \ī\ ice \j\ job \k\ Ger ich, Buch \$^{n}$\ Fr vin \ŋ\ sing \ō\ go \ȯ\ all \ȯ\ law \œ\ Fr bœuf \œ̄\ Fr feu \ȯi\ boy \th\ thin \t͟h\ this \ü\ loot \u̇\ foot \u̵\ Ger füllen \ue̅\ Fr rue \y\ yet \$^{y}$\ Fr digne \ˈdēn^{y}\, nuit \ˈnw^{y}ē\ \yü\ few \yu̇\ fury \zh\ vision

Gar·misch–Par·ten·kir·chen \ˈgär-mish-ˌpärt-ᵊn-ˈkirk-ᵊn\. Commune, Bavaria, S Germany, in foothills of Bavarian Alps near Oberammergau; pop. (1992e) 27,094; noted as resort and center for winter sports; scene of Winter Olympic Games 1936.

Garmo Peak. See COMMUNISM PEAK.

Gar·ner \ˈgär-nər\. **1.** City, ⊗ of Hancock co., N Iowa, 21 mi. (34 km.) W of Mason City; pop. (1990c) 2916.

2. Town, Wake co., E cen. North Carolina, 5 mi. (8 km.) SSE of Raleigh; pop. (1990c) 14,967.

Gar·nett \ˈgär-nit\. City, ⊗ of Anderson co., E Kansas, 42 mi. (68 km.) NW of Fort Scott; pop. (1990c) 3210.

Garoet. See GARUT.

Ga·ro Hills \ˈgär-ō\. Hilly region, Meghalaya, NE India, in bend of Brahmaputra; highest point ab. 5000 ft. (1525 m.).

Ga·ronne \gȧ-ˈrȯn\; *anc.* **Ga·rum·na** \gə-ˈrəm-nə\. River, SW France; rises on slopes of the Pyrenees, in Spain; flows NW past Toulouse and Bordeaux to unite with Dordogne River 13 mi. (21 km.) N of Bordeaux and form Gironde estuary; 357 mi. (574 km.) long.

Garonne, Haute– \ˈōt\. Department of S France. See *Haute-Garonne* in table at FRANCE.

Ga·roua *or* **Ga·rua** \gä-ˈrü-ä\. Town, N Cameroon, on the Benue River at head of navigation in the summertime; pop. (1987c) 142,000; commercial center, airport; junior college.

Garove. See WITU.

Gar·rard \ˈgar-əd, -ərd\. County in E cen. Kentucky. See table at KENTUCKY.

Gar·rett \ˈgar-it\. **1.** County in NW corner of Maryland. See table at MARYLAND.

2. City, De Kalb co., NE Indiana, 20 mi. (32 km.) N of Fort Wayne; pop. (1990c) 5349.

Garrison Dam. See UNITED STATES, *Dams and Reservoirs.*

Garrison Reservoir. See SAKAKAWEA, LAKE.

Gar·ron Point \ˈgar-ən\. Headland in Antrim dist., NE Northern Ireland, on the Irish Sea.

Gar·ry Lake \ˈgar-ē\. Lake, mainland part of Nunavut, Canada; 980 sq. mi. (2538 sq. km.); traversed by Black River.

Gar·stedt \ˈgär-ˌshtet\. City, Schleswig-Holstein, N Germany, 9 mi. (15 km.) N of Hamburg.

Gartok. See GAR.

Garua. See GAROUA.

Garumna. See GARONNE.

Ga·rut *or Du.* **Ga·roet** \gä-ˈrüt\. Town, West Java prov., Indonesia, ab. 32 mi. (52 km.) SE of Bandung; on plateau (alt. 2300 ft. or 701 m.) surrounded by mountains; resort.

Gar·vel·loch's \gär-ˈve-ləks\ *or* **Isles of the Sea.** Island group Firth of Lorn, W Scotland.

Gar·vin \ˈgär-vin\. County in S cen. Oklahoma. See table at OKLAHOMA.

Gar·wood \ˈgär-ˌwu̇d\. Borough, Union co., NE New Jersey, 6 mi. (10 km.) W of Elizabeth; pop. (1990c) 4227.

Gary \ˈgar-ē\. City, Lake co., NW corner of Indiana, on Lake Michigan; pop. (1990c) 116,646; formerly a major steel-producing center; Indiana Univ. Northwest (1922); site purchased and laid out by U.S. Steel Corp. 1905 (see also FAIRFIELD 2); incorp. 1906; scene of origin and development of the platoon school (*Gary plan*); decline in steel industry 1980s led to plant closings and high unemployment; revitalization efforts 1990s; airport; civic center.

Gar·za \ˈgär-zə\. County in NW Texas. See table at TEXAS.

Garza Dam *or* **Lake Dal·las Dam** \ˈda-ləs\. Dam across Elm Fork of Trinity River, Denton co., N Texas; height 80 ft. (24 m.); completed 1927; impounds water for water supply of Dallas.

Garza Gar·cía \ˈgär-sä-gär-ˈsē-ä\. City, Nuevo León state, Mexico, 8 mi. (13 km.) SW of Monterrey; munic. pop. (1990p) 112,394.

Ga·san \gä-ˈsän\. Municipality, SW coast of Marinduque I., Philippines, 11 mi. (18 km.) S of Boac; pop. (1980c) 23,185.

Gas City \ˈgas\. City, Grant co., N cen. Indiana, 5 mi. (8 km.) SSE of Marion; pop. (1990c) 6296.

Gascogne. See GASCONY.

Gascogne, Golfe de. See BISCAY, BAY OF.

Gas·con·ade \ˌgas-kə-ˈnād\. **1.** River, S cen. Missouri; rises in Ozark Plateau, flows N into Missouri River in N Gasconade co.; ab. 265 mi. (426 km.) long.

2. County in E cen. Missouri. See table at MISSOURI.

Gas·co·ny \ˈgas-kə-nē\ *or Fr.* **Gas·cogne** \gȧ-ˈskōnʸ\ *or Lat.* **Vas·co·nia** \vas-ˈkō-nē-ə, -nyə\. Historical region of SW France; bounded anciently on N by Guienne, on E by Languedoc, on SE by Countship of Foix, on S by Béarn and Pyrenees, and on W by Atlantic Ocean; ✻ Auch. Part of Roman Aquitania Tertia, later called Novempopulana; Basque population conquered by Visigoths 5th cent. A.D.; Franks conquered area 6th cent. A.D.; Basques regained area early 7th cent. and set up duchy of Gascony recognized by Franks; became attached to Aquitaine (*q.v.*) in 11th cent.; passed into English control mid-12th cent.; remained a stronghold of English allegiance until France gained control mid-15th cent.; up to 1789, formed, with Guienne (*q.v.*), part of French *gouvernement* of Guienne and Gascony.

Gascony, Gulf of. See BISCAY, BAY OF.

Gas·coyne \ˈgas-ˌkȯin\. River, W Western Australia, Australia; upper course in desert, flows W to Geographe Channel; 475 mi. (764 km.) long; nearly dry except in flood time.

Gash. See MAREB.

Ga·sher·brum \ˈgə-shər-ˌbrüm, -ˌbru̇m\ *also* **Gu·shar·brum** \ˈgu̇-\. Peak in the Himalayas, Jammu and Kashmir, in region controlled by Pakistan, just SE of K2; 26,470 ft. (8068 m.); first climbed 1958.

Gashiun Nor. See GAXUN NUR.

Gas·ma·ta \gäs-ˈmä-tä, gaz-\. Coastal town and government station, S New Britain I., Bismarck Archipelago, Papua New Guinea, ab. 200 mi. (322 km.) SW of Rabaul; Japanese air base in WWII.

Gas·pa·ril·la Island \ˌgas-pə-ˈri-lə\. Island in Gulf of Mexico, at N of entrance to Charlotte Harbor, off W coast of Charlotte co., SW Florida.

Gaspar Strait. See KELASA STRAIT.

Gas·pé \gȧ-ˈspā\. Town, SE Quebec, Canada, on Gaspé Penin., 115 mi. (185 km.) NE of Dalhousie, New Brunswick; pop. (1991c) 16,402.

Gaspé, Cape. E tip of Gaspé Penin., at NE of entrance to Gaspé Bay, SE Quebec, Canada.

Gaspé Bay. Inlet of Gulf of St. Lawrence at E end of Gaspé Penin., SE Quebec, Canada; ab. 18 mi. (29 km.) long.

Gaspé Peninsula. Peninsula in SE Quebec, Canada, N of New Brunswick and Chaleur Bay and S of mouth of St. Lawrence River; ab. 11,390 sq. mi. (29,500 sq. km.), 170 mi. (274 km.) long; a tableland (highest peak 4159 ft. or 1268 m.), thickly forested with many lakes and rivers; excellent hunting and fishing; famous for its scenery. Visited by French explorer Jacques Cartier 1534.

Gas·pé·sie Provincial Park \ˌga-spā-ˈzē\ *or* **Gas·pe·sian Provincial Park** \ga-ˈspē-zhən\. Provincial park, West Gaspé co., N cen. Gaspé Penin., SE Quebec, Canada; 514 sq. mi. (1331 sq. km.); Mt. Jacques Cartier, fishing lakes and streams.

Gastein. See BADGASTEIN.

Ga·stein·er Ache \gä-ˈstī-nər-ˈä-kə\. Stream, Salzburg, Austria; flows N from Hohe Tauern to Salzach River; ab. 25 mi. (40 km.) long; flows through beautiful valley (alt. 3000 to 3500 ft. or 915 to 1065 m.) noted for its mineral springs; contains two notable waterfalls: **Upper Ga·stein** \gä-ˈstīn\ 207 ft. (63 m.) and **Lower Gastein** 279 ft. (85 m.).

Gasteiz. See VITORIA.

Gas·ti·neau Channel \ˈgas-tə-ˌnō\. Short channel, SE Alaska, bet. mainland and Douglas I. Both Juneau and Douglas are situated on it.

Gas·ton \ˈgast-ᵊn\. County in SW North Carolina. See table at NORTH CAROLINA.

Gas·to·nia \ga-ˈstō-nē-ə, -nyə\. City, ⊗ of Gaston co., SW North Carolina, 20 mi. (32 km.) W of Charlotte; pop. (1990c) 54,732; textiles.

Ga·ta, Cape \ˈgä-tä\. **1.** S point of Cyprus, tip of peninsula W of Akrotiri Bay.

2. *or Span.* **Ca·bo de Gata** \ˈkä-bō-thā-\. Cape on SE coast of Spain, forming E side of Gulf of Almería.

Gata, Sierra de. See SIERRA DE GATA.

Gat·chi·na \ˈga-chi-nə\; *formerly* **Kras·no·gvar·deisk** \ˌkräs-nəg-vər-ˈdāsk\ *also (1923–29)* **Trot·sko·ye** \ˈtrȯt-skə-yə\. Town, St. Petersburg Oblast, W Russia in Europe, 25 mi. (40 km.) SSW of the city of St. Petersburg; pop. (1991e) 81,300. Town grew around palace, begun 1766 for Count Grigory Orlov, later became summer residence of czars. Site of fighting during Russian Revolution and WWII; much damage to palace, now under restoration and functioning as a museum.

Gate City \ˈgāt\. Town, ⊗ of Scott co., SW Virginia, 24 mi. (39 km.) W of Bristol; pop. (1990c) 2214.

Gates \ˈgāts\. County in NE North Carolina. See table at NORTH CAROLINA.

Gates·head \ˈgāts-ˌhed\. Town, Tyne and Wear, N England, on the Tyne opp. Newcastle; pop. (1991p) 196,500; glass, chemicals, plastics, paints; electrical engineering; technical college.

Gates of the Arctic National Park. See UNITED STATES, *National Parks.*

Gates·ville \ˈgāts-ˌvil, -vəl\. **1.** Town, ⊗ of Gates co., NE North Carolina; pop. (1990c) 308.
2. City, ⊗ of Coryell co., cen. Texas, 35 mi. (56 km.) W of Waco; pop. (1990c) 11,492.

Gath \ˈgath\. City of ancient Philistia, Palestine, ab. 12 mi. (19 km.) E of Ashdod; one of five Philistine city-kingdoms; biblical birthplace of Philistine champion Goliath.

Ga·ti·co \gä-ˈtē-kō\. Port, Antofagasta prov., N Chile; formerly belonged to Bolivia; ceded to Chile as a result of War of the Pacific (1879–1883).

Gat·i·neau \ˌgat-^{ə}n-ˈō\. **1.** River, SW Quebec, Canada; rises in chain of lakes S of the height of land, flows S through Réservoir Baskatong into the Ottawa River at Hull opp. Ottawa; 240 mi. (386 km.) long; source of waterpower.
2. Town, SW Quebec, Canada, just NE of Hull near mouth of Gatineau River; pop. (1991c) 92,284.

Gat·lin·burg \ˈgat-lən-ˌbərg\. City, Sevier co., E Tennessee, near Great Smoky Mountains National Park; pop. (1990c) 3417.

Gatooma See KADOMA.

Gat·ta·ran \ˌgät-tä-ˈrän\. Municipality, W cen. Cagayan prov., Luzon, Philippines, on Cagayan River 20 mi. (32 km.) S of Aparri; pop. (1980c) 35,477.

Gatukai. See NGGATOKAE.

Ga·tun·cil·lo \gä-ˌtün-ˈsē-yō\. River in Panama E of the Panama Canal; flows S joining Chagres River.

Ga·tun Lake \gä-ˈtün\ *or Span.* **La·go Ga·tún** \ˈlä-gō-gä-ˈtün\. Lake, Panama, in Isthmus of Panama; 166 sq. mi. (430 sq. km.); constitutes part of Panama Canal system and was formed by **Gatun Dam** (across Chagres River; completed 1912; max. height 115 ft. or 35 m.; length of crest 8324 ft. or 2537 m.); nearby are **Gatun Locks** and the town of **Gatun,** 7 mi. (11 km.) S of Colón.

Gat·wick \ˈgat-ˌwik\. Locality, West Sussex, S England, S of London; site of an international airport serving London.

Gau \ˈgau̇\ *or* **Ngau** \əŋ-ˈgau̇\. Island, Fiji, SW Pacific Ocean, E of Viti Levu.

Gaua. Island, Vanuatu. See SANTA MARÍA 5.

Gauḍa. See GAUR.

Gaud–i–Zirreh. See GAWD-I-ZIRREH.

Gau·ga·me·la \ˌgȯ-gə-ˈmē-lə\. Ancient village in Assyria, ab. 32 mi. (51 km.) W of Arbela (see ARBĪL); scene of battle 331 B.C. in which Macedonian King Alexander the Great defeated Persians under Darius III.

Gau·ha·ti \gau̇-ˈhä-tē\ *or* **Gu·wa·ha·ti** \ˌgü-wə-ˈhä-tē\. Town, NW Assam, NE India, on Brahmaputra River 335 mi. (539 km.) NE of Calcutta; pop. (1991c) 584,342; commercial center; university (1948); nearby temples of Kamakhya and Umananda are places of Hindu pilgrimage. Ceded to British 1826; British seat of administration for Assam 1826–74.

Gau·ja *or Russ.* **Gau·ya** \ˈgau̇-yä\ *or Ger.* **Aa** \ˈä\. River, Latvia, rises SE of Cēsin, flows in wide bend to Gulf of Riga NE of Riga; 260 mi. (418 km.) long; longest river in Latvia.

Gaul \ˈgȯl\ *or Fr.* **Gaule** \ˈgōl\ *or Lat.* **Gal·lia** \ˈga-lē-ə\. Ancient country of Europe, commonly the part S and W of the Rhine, W of Alps, and N of Pyrenees, inhabited from ab. 600 B.C. by Celtic tribes (Lat. *Galli*); in earliest times also N Italy.

Early divisions: **Cis·al·pine Gaul** \sis-ˈal-ˌpīn\; *Lat.* **Gallia Cis·al·pi·na** \ˌsis-ˌal-ˈpī-nə\ *also* **Gallia Ci·te·ri·or** \sə-ˈtir-ē-ər, sī-\. N Italy in valley of Po N of Apennines; settled by Celts c. 4th–3d cents. B.C.; conquered by Rome c. 222 B.C.; made Roman province c. 80 B.C., its SE boundary being the Rubicon (*q.v.*). Divided c. first cent. B.C. into: (a) **Cis·pa·dane Gaul** \ˈsis-pə-ˌdān, sis-ˈpā-ˌdān\ *or Lat.* **Gallia Cis·pa·da·na** \ˌsis-pə-ˈdā-nə\. Region S of lower Po, ab. coextensive with modern Emilia-Romagna autonomous region. (b) **Trans·pa·dane Gaul** \ˈtrans-pə-ˌdān, trans-ˈpā-ˌdān\ *or Lat.* **Gallia Trans·pa·da·na** \ˌtrans-pə-ˈdā-nə\. Region N of upper Po, ab. coextensive with modern W Lombardy and N Piedmont. See CISALPINE REPUBLIC, CISPADANE REPUBLIC, and TRANSPADANE REPUBLIC. **Trans·al·pine Gaul** \trans-ˈal-ˌpīn, tranz-\; *Lat.* **Gallia Trans·al·pi·na** \ˌtrans-ˌal-ˈpī-nə, ˌtranz-\ *also* **Gallia Ul·te·ri·or** \ˌəl-ˈtir-ē-ər\; *later* **Gallia Cel·ti·ca** \ˈsel-ti-kə, ˈkel-\; *also known as* **Gallia Proper** *or Fr.* **Gaule.** Practically all of modern France (incl. Gallia Narbonensis [see below]) and Belgium and parts of Switzerland, Germany, and Netherlands. Conquered by Roman Gen. Julius Caesar 58–51 B.C. and divided into three parts according to native inhabitants—Aquitania (in SW), Gallia (in W and center), Belgica (in NE) collectively known as **Gallia Co·ma·ta** \kō-ˈmā-tə\ *or* **Tres Gal·li·ae** \ˈtrās-ˈga-lē-ī\; entire area reorganized by Emperors Augustus and Tiberius as administrative areas of Narbonensis, Aquitania, Lugdunensis, Belgica, and the military districts of Germania Inferior and Germania Superior. **Gallia Nar·bo·nen·sis** \ˌnär-bə-ˈnen-səs\ *or* **Narbonensis**. SE part of Gallia Proper, formed as Roman province c. 121 B.C.; ❋ Narbo Martius (see NARBONNE); named **Pro·vin·cia Ro·ma·na** \prə-ˈvin-shə-rō-ˈmä-nə, -shē-ə\, which became Provence (*q.v.*); renamed Gallia Narbonensis under Emperor Augustus.

Gaule. See GAUL.

Gau·ley \ˈgȯ-lē\. River, cen. West Virginia; rises in Pocahontas co., flows W and S, joins New River in N Fayette co. to form Kanawha River; 104 mi. (167 km.) long.

Gaulus. See GOZO.

Gaur \ˈgau̇r\ *or* **Gau·ḍa** \ˈgau̇-də\ *or* **Lakh·nau·ti** \lək-ˈnau̇-tē\. Ancient city, former ❋ (c. 1200–1340, 1455–1563) of Bengal, in West Bengal, NE India, 8 mi. (13 km.) S of English Bazar and ab. 163 mi. (262 km.) N of Calcutta. Famed for its size and splendor as Muslim seat of government. Ruins of mosques and fortifications remain.

Gau·ri San·kar *or* **Gau·ri·san·kar** \ˌgau̇r-ē-ˈsəŋ-kər\. Peak in the Himalayas, on the Nepal-China border; ab. 35 mi. (56 km.) W of Mt. Everest; 23,440 ft. (7144 m.).

Gauss·berg \ˈgau̇s-ˌbərg\ Extinct volcano on Wilhelm II coast, Antarctica, 66°48′S, 89°12′E; 1120 ft. (341 m.); discovered during expedition 1901–1903 under German explorer Dr. Erich von Drygalski and named for its ship, the *Gauss.*

Gau·sta \ˈgau̇-stä\. Peak, Telemark co., S Norway; 6178 ft. (1883 m.).

Gau·teng \ˈgau̇-ˌteŋ\; *formerly* **Pre·to·ria–Wit·wa·ters·rand–Ver·een·ig·ing** \pri-ˈtōr-ē-ə-ˈvit-ˌvä-tərz-ˌränd-fə-ˈrā-ni-ˌgiŋ\. Province, cen. NE Rep. of South Africa; ❋ Johannesburg; estab. 1993. See table at SOUTH AFRICA, REPUBLIC OF.

Gau·tier \ˈgō-ˌshā\. City, Jackson co., SE Mississippi, on the Pascagoula River where it flows into Mississippi Sound; pop. (1990c) 10,088.

Gauya. See GAUJA.

Ga·var·nie \ˌgȧ-vȧr-ˈnē\. Village, Hautes-Pyrénées dept., SW France, near the Spanish border at head of the Gave de Pau whose valley here forms the **Cirque de Gavarnie** \ˌsērk-də\, most famous of the characteristic cirques of the Pyrenees, a vast amphitheater 2 mi. (3 km.) wide with steep wall, in places reaching 5600 ft. (1707 m.), over which the *gave* (mountain torrent) comes in a spectacular waterfall 1384 ft. (422 m.) high.

\ə\ **abut** \ə̇\ matches \$^{ə}$\ kitten, Fr table \ər\ **further** \a\ **ash** \ā\ **ace**
\ä\ cot, cart \ȧ\ Fr bac \au̇\ **out** \b̲\ Span Avila \ch\ **chin** \e\ **bet** \ē\ **easy**
\g\ **go** \i\ **hit** \ī\ **ice** \j\ **job** \k̲\ Ger **ich**, Buch \$^{n}$\ Fr vin
\ŋ\ sing \ō\ **go** \ȯ\ **all** \ȯ\ **law** \œ\ Fr **bœuf** \œ̅\ Fr **feu** \ȯi\ **boy**
\th\ **thin** \th̲\ **this** \ü\ **loot** \u̇\ **foot** \ue\ Ger **füllen** \ue̅\ Fr **rue**
\y\ **yet** \$^{y}$\ Fr digne \ˈdēn^{y}\, nuit \ˈnw^{y}ē\ \yü\ **few** \yu̇\ **fury** \zh\ **vision**

Gav·dos \ˈgäv-dəs\ *or* **Gāv·dhos** \ˈgäv-ˌthös\; *anc.* **Cau·da** \ˈkȯ-də\ *or* **Clau·da** \ˈklȯ-də\. Small island, Greece, in E Mediterranean Sea 22 mi. (35 km.) S of W end of Crete; refuge of St. Paul's ship during tempest (*Acts* xxvii. 16).

Gave de Pau. See PAU, GAVE DE.

Gäv·le *also* **Gäf·le** *or* **Gef·le** \ˈyev-lə\. Seaport city, ⊗ of Gävleborg prov., E Sweden, NNW of Stockholm; pop. (1993e) 89,194; exports iron ore and wood pulp; paper; received city charter 1446; 16th cent. castle; 18th cent. courthouse.

Gäv·le·borg *also* **Gäf·le·borg** *or* **Gef·le·borg** \ˈyev-lə-ˌbȯrʸ, -ˌbȯr-ē\. Province of E Sweden. See table at SWEDEN.

Ga·vu·tu \gä-ˈvü-tü\. Small island in SE Solomon Is., in W Pacific Ocean, off S coast of Florida I. just E of Tulagi I.

Gawd–i–Zir·reh *or* **Gaud–i–Zirreh** \ˈgȯd-ē-ˈzir-ə, ˈgau̇d-\. Lake and swamp, SW Afghanistan, near Pakistan and Iran borders; in wet season connected with Lake Helmand to NW.

Gaw·ler \ˈgȯ-lər\. Town, SE South Australia, Australia, 20 mi. (32 km.) NNE of Adelaide; pop. (1991c) 13,835; wheat grown nearby.

Ga·xun Nur \ˈgä-ˈshuen-ˈnür\ *or W.-G.* **Ka–shun–no–erh** \ˈgä-ˈshün-ˈnō-ˈər\; *mostly formerly* **Ga·shiun Nor** \ˈgä-ˈshyün-ˈnōr\. Large salt lake, W Gobi Desert, N China.

Ga·ya \gə-ˈyä\. City, cen. Bihar, NE India, 57 mi. (92 km.) S of Patna; pop. (1991p) 291,220; large trade with Calcutta; important Hindu pilgrimage center with numerous Hindu temples; ab. 7 mi. (11 km.) S is Bodh Gayā (*q.v.*), one of the holiest sites of Buddhism.

Gay Head \ˈgā\. Promontory, W end of Martha's Vineyard, Massachusetts; proposal to change name to the Wampanoag name *Aquinnah* rejected 1991.

Gay·lord \ˈgā-lərd, -ˌlȯrd\. **1.** City, ⊗ of Otsego co., N Michigan, 43 mi. (69 km.) S of Cheboygan; pop. (1990c) 3256.
2. City, ⊗ of Sibley co., S cen. Minnesota, 30 mi. (48 km.) NNW of Mankato; pop. (1990c) 1935.

Ga·za \ˈgä-zə, ˈga-, ˈgā-\; *Arab.* **Ghaz·ze** *or* **Ghaz·zah** \ˈgȧ-zə, ˈgə-\. Seaport, Gaza Strip, near coast, with small harbor 3 mi. (5 km.) distant; pop. (1988e) 57,000.

History: Town was prosperous trade center for much of its history; earliest reference as Egyptian garrison 15th cent. B.C.; mentioned in records from Tell el-ʻAmârna; important Philistine city; biblical site of Philistine temple of Dagon, destroyed by Samson (*Judges* xvi. 23–31); besieged throughout its history by Israelites, Assyrians, Egyptians, Babylonians, Persians; taken by Macedonian King Alexander the Great 332 B.C.; besieged during Maccabean Wars and Crusades after which it declined; controlled by Ottoman Turks 16th cent.; site of three major WWI battles bet. Turks and British 1917, taken by British Gen. Edmund Allenby. After war, town and area of strip became part of British mandate 1917–1948; under Egyptian control 1948–67 (except for Israeli occupation Nov. 1956–Mar. 1957; occupied by Israel 1967 with town as administrative center; town site of major uprisings known as the Intifada 1987 and 1988 with continued unrest and violence throughout strip; accord bet. Palestine Liberation Organization and Israel signed May 1994 gave self-rule to Gaza Strip and Jericho, followed by withdrawal of most Israeli troops.

Gaza. Province, of S Mozambique. See table at MOZAMBIQUE.

Gaz·a·ca \ˈga-zə-kə\. Ancient city, ✻ of Media Atropatene, Media, in mountains SE of Lake Matianus (*mod.* Daryācheh-ye Orūmīyeh) and W of Zanjān—exact location not known.

Gazala, Al– *or* **Gazala, El.** See AL-GAZALA.

Gaza Strip. Strip of land on SE Mediterranean Sea; ab. 26 mi. (42 km.) long, 4 to 5 mi. (6.4 to 8 km.) wide, 140 sq. mi. (225 sq. km.). For history, see GAZA.

Ga·zelle Peninsula \gə-ˈzel\. Peninsula at NE end of New Britain I., Bismarck Archipelago, W Pacific Ocean; has ports at Rabaul and Kokopo on Blanche Bay; volcanically active.

Ga·zi·an·tep *also* **Gazi Antep** \ˌgä-zē-än-ˈtep\. **1.** Province of Turkey. See table at TURKEY.
2. *formerly* **Ain·tab** \īn-ˈtȧb\. Town, its ✻, ab. 60 mi. (97 km.) N of Aleppo, Syria; pop. (1990c) 603,434; strategic importance in time of Crusades; center of Turkish resistance against French 1920–21; occupied by French; returned to Turkey 1922; renamed (*gazi*, Turkish "Defender of the Faith") in recognition of strong resistance. Has 6th cent. citadel.

Gcu·wa \ˈkü-wə\; *formerly* **But·ter·worth** \ˈbə-tər-ˌwərth\. Town, SE Rep. of South Africa, in former Transkei enclave.

Gdańsk \gə-ˈdänsk, -ˈdansk\ *or Ger.* **Dan·zig** \ˈdänt-sik\ *or Fr.* **Dant·zig** \dȧⁿt-ˈsēk\. **1.** Province of N Poland. See table at POLAND.
2. City and commercial seaport, its ✻, on Gulf of Gdańsk just W of mouth of the Vistula, situated on delta arm of the Vistula; pop. (1989e) 464,649; formerly an important shipbuilding center; chemicals, lumber; food processing, metalworking; important cultural center.

History: First mentioned late 10th cent. A.D. as Polish town of Gdańsk; ✻ of dukes of Pomerania 13th cent.; taken by Teutonic Knights 1308; joined Hanseatic League 13th cent. and became a leading trade center; in 1466, after revolt of part of W Prussia, became free city under Polish protection; captured by Russia 1734; ceded to Prussia in Second Partition of Poland 1793; became free city again by French-Prussian agreement 1807; recovered by Prussia 1815; by Treaty of Versailles (1919), the city, with adjoining territory (731 sq. mi. or 1893 sq. km.), estab. as free state (**Free City of Danzig**) under League of Nations; within Polish customs territory, it served as Polish outlet to sea; after 1933, threatened by competition of Gdynia (*q.v.*) and by rise of Nazis in Germany; under Nazi control 1935; German demands for cession of city to Germany the immediate issue of conflict bet. Poland and Germany which precipitated WWII; incorp. in Germany 1939; renamed by Germany **Hanseatic City of Danzig** 1940; recovered 1945 by Allies, and made part of Poland; in 1980, strikes precipitated by worsening economic conditions led to formation of the independent labor union Solidarity, which in turn led to national political turmoil during the next several years.

Gdańsk, Gulf of. Wide inlet of S Baltic Sea; N Poland.

Gdy·nia \gə-ˈdi-nē-ə\ *or Ger.* **Gding·en** \gə-ˈdiŋ-ən\. Seaport city, N Gdańsk prov., Poland, on Gulf of Gdańsk 10 mi. (16 km.) NNW of the city of Gdańsk; pop. (1989e) 250,936; prior to WWI a small German fishing village; returned to Poland by Treaty of Versailles 1920; became major port and naval base because of loss of Gdańsk as port; occupied by Germany 1939; port damaged in WWII; restored to Poland 1945; port rebuilt and now one of Europe's most modern ports.

Gé·ant, Ai·guille du \ā-ˈgwē-dᵫ-zhā-ˈäⁿ\. Peak in the Savoy Alps, Haute-Savoie dept., E France, NE of Mont Blanc; 13,166 ft. (4013 m.); nearby is the **Col du Géant** \ˌkȯl\, mountain pass, alt. 11,145 ft. (3397 m.), through the Alps from Chamonix-Mont-Blanc SE to Italy.

Gea·ry \ˈgir-ē\. County in NE cen. Kansas. See table at KANSAS.

Ge·au·ga \jē-ˈȯ-gə\. County in NE Ohio. See table at OHIO.

Gê·ba \ˈgā-bä\. River, W Africa; rises in Guinea; flows into Atlantic Ocean in Guinea-Bissau; ab. 190 mi. (306 km.) long.

Gebal. See JUBAYL.

Gebel. See JEBEL.

Gebweiler. See GUEBWILLER.

Geb·ze \geb-ˈze\. Town, NW Turkey in Asia, on NE coast of Sea of Marmara ab. 30 mi. (48 km.) SE of İstanbul.

Ge·da·ref \gə-ˈdär-əf\ *or* **Al–Qa·ḍā·rif** \ˌal-kə-ˈdär-if\. Town, S Eastern region, E Sudan; on Port Sudan-Sennar railroad line.

Ged·ding·ton \ˈge-diŋ-tən\. Village, N Northamptonshire, cen. England; site of one of several Eleanor Crosses marking a stage of the funeral procession to Westminster Abbey of Eleanor of Castile (d. 1290), queen of Edward I.

Ge·de, Gunung *or* **Gunung Ge·deh** \ˈgü-nu̇ŋ-ˈgā-də\. Active volcano, W Java, Indonesia, 45 mi. (72 km.) SE of Jakarta; 9705 ft. (2958 m.); many eruptions since 1832, the most severe in 1840; twin peak of Gunung Pangrango (*q.v.*).

Gedi. See MALINDI.

Ge·diz \ge-ˈdēz\ *also* **Sa·ra·bat** \ˌsä-rä-ˈbät\; *anc.* **Her·mus** \ˈhər-məs\. River, W Turkey in Asia; rises in mountains S of Kütahya, flows W into Gulf of İzmir; 217 mi. (349 km.) long.

Ge·dro·sia \jə-ˈdrō-zhə, -zhē-ə\. Ancient country of SW Asia, a subdivision of Ariana and a province of the Persian and Alexandrian empires, bounded on N by Drangiana and Arachosia, on E by India, on S by Arabian Sea, and on W by Carmania; largely desert; known in history chiefly for the hardships experienced by Macedonian King Alexander the Great's army crossing it on his return from India 325–324 B.C.; region now in Baluchistan prov., Pakistan and bordering part of SE Iran.

Geel *or* **Gheel** \ˈk̲āl\. Commune, Antwerp prov., N Belgium; pop. (1991c) 32,487; noted for its system of care of mentally ill persons; scene 7th cent. of murder of the Irish princess St. Dympna, patron saint of the mentally ill.

Gee·long \jə-ˈlȯŋ\. Seaport, S Victoria, SE Australia, at W end of Port Phillip Bay 50 mi. (80 km.) SW of Melbourne; pop. (1991c) 13,036; education center; automobiles, fertilizers; ships esp. wool; tourism.

Geelvink Bay. See CENDERAWASIH, TELUK.

Geel·vink Channel \ˈgāl-ˌviŋk\. Channel, Australia, in Indian Ocean, bet. Houtman Abrolhos and W Western Australia.

Gee·raards·ber·gen \ˈk̲ār-ərts-ˌber-k̲ə\ *or* **Gram·mont** \grä-ˈmō^{n}\. Commune, East Flanders prov., NW cen. Belgium, 22 mi. (35 km.) W of Brussels; pop. (1991c) 30,280.

Gefle. See GÄVLE.

Gefleborg. See GÄVLEBORG.

Gehenna. See HINNOM.

Ge Hu \ˈgə-ˈhü\ *or W.-G.* **Ko Hu** \ˈkō-ˈhü\ *or* **Ho Hu** \ˈhō-ˈhü\. Lake, S Jiangsu prov., E China, just SW of Changzhou.

Geis·ling·en an der Stei·ge \ˈgī-sliŋ-ən-ˌän-dər-ˈshtī-gə\. City, Baden-Württemberg, Germany, 34 mi. (55 km.) ESE of Stuttgart; pop. (1980c) 27,344; metal goods; 15th cent. church; to Württemberg 1810.

Geis·town \ˈgīs-ˌtau̇n\. Borough, Cambria co., SW cen. Pennsylvania, 4 mi. (6 km.) SE of Johnstown; pop. (1990c) 2749.

Ge·la \ˈjā-lä\; *formerly* **Ter·ra·no·va di Si·ci·lia** \ˌter-rä-ˈnȯ-vä-ˌdē-sē-ˈchēl-yä\; *anc.* **Gela** \ˈjē-lə\. Commune, Caltanissetta prov., Sicily, Italy, on S coast 30 mi. (48 km.) SSE of the commune of Caltanissetta; pop. (1991p) 72,079; petrochemicals; fisheries; remains of ancient city nearby. Founded c. 689 B.C. by Greek colonists from Rhodes and Crete; flourished under the tyrant Hippocrates; home of the poet Aeschylus; destroyed by Carthaginians; rebuilt by Greek Gen. Timoleon c. 340 B.C. and again destroyed c. 282 B.C.; refounded 1230s by Holy Roman Emperor Frederick II; known as Terranova di Sicilia until 1928; site of WWII American landings July 1943. Site of 5th cent. Greek temple and fortification; known for ancient Greek vases.

Gel·der·land *also* **Guel·der·land** \ˈk̲el-dər-ˌlänt, ˈgel-dər-ˌland\. Province, E Netherlands; ✱ Arnhem; mixed agriculture; bricks, textiles. See table at NETHERLANDS.

History: The larger part of the county incl. Zutphen, Nijmegen, Arnhem, and Roermond which had grown up around the county of Gelder (or Gelre) of the Holy Roman Empire and which became duchy 1339, was held by Charles the Bold, duke of Burgundy 1473–77, and ceded to Charles V of Spain 1543; joined Union of Utrecht of Netherlands (*q.v.*) against Spain 1579; SE part incl. Geldern fell to Prussia 1713; remainder became part of kingdom of Netherlands 1815.

Gel·dern \ˈgel-dərn\. Town, North Rhine-Westphalia, Germany, 28 mi. (45 km.) NW of Düsseldorf; pop. (1980c) 26,230; seat of counts and dukes of Gelder (see GELDERLAND) 11th to 14th cents.; to Prussia 1713.

Gel·drop \ˈk̲el-ˌdrȯp\. Commune, North Brabant prov., SE Netherlands, 4 mi. (6 km.) SE of Eindhoven; pop. (1981e) 26,600; woolen manufacturing.

Ge·leen \k̲ə-ˈlān\. Commune, Limburg prov., SE Netherlands, NE of Maastricht; pop. (1992e) 183,256; textiles.

Ge·li·bo·lu \ge-ˈlē-bȯ-ˌlü\ *or angl.* **Gal·lip·o·li** \gə-ˈli-pə-lē\; *anc.* **Cal·lip·o·lis** \kə-ˈli-pə-lis\. Seaport, Turkey in Europe, at entrance to Sea of Marmara on narrow neck of Gallipoli Penin. Ancient Callipolis colonized by Greeks; medieval trading center; first European conquest of Turks c. 1354.

Gelibolu Yarımadası. See GALLIPOLI PENINSULA.

Gel·i·do·nya, Cape \ˌge-lə-ˈdō-nyə\ *or Turk.* **Ge·li·do·nya Bu·run** \ˌge-lē-dȯ-ˈnyä-bu̇-ˈrün\. Cape on S coast of Turkey in Asia, on W side of entrance to Gulf of Antalya.

Gel·li·gaer \ˌge-lə-ˈgīr\. Town, Mid Glamorgan co., SE Wales; pop. (1981p) 34,118; coal deposits.

Gellivare. See GÄLLIVARE.

Gel·sen·kir·chen \ˌgel-zən-ˈkir-k̲ən\. City, North Rhine-Westphalia, Germany, 15 mi. (24 km.) W of Dortmund; pop. (1992e) 293,839; in Ruhr coal-bearing region; chemicals, glass; steelworks, foundries; includes since 1928 the city of Buer and the town of Horst; Castle Horst and Castle Berge, 16th through 18th cents.; chartered 1875; heavy bombing WWII.

Gem \ˈjem\. County in SW Idaho. See table at IDAHO.

Ge·mas \je-ˈmäs\. Town, SE Negeri Sembilan state, Malaysia, near border of Johor 35 mi. (56 km.) NE of Melaka; railroad junction.

Gem·bloux \zhä^{n}-ˈblü\. Commune, Namur prov., S Belgium, 10 mi. (16 km.) NW of the commune of Namur; pop. (1991c) 19,163; manufactures cutlery; state institute of agriculture; site of 1578 defeat of Dutch by Don John of Austria.

Gem·i·ni Peaks \ˈje-mə-ˌnī\. Mountain, Lake and Park cos., cen. Colorado; 13,900 ft. (4237 m.).

Gem·lik Gulf \gem-ˈlēk\. Inlet of SE Sea of Marmara, Turkey in Europe; Mudanya is on it.

Gem·mi Pass \ˈge-mē\. Mountain pass in the Bernese Alps, SW cen. Switzerland, 25 mi. (40 km.) S of Thun; 7598 ft. (2316 m.).

Gems·bok National Park \ˈgemz-ˌbȯk\. National park, SW Botswana, bordering on Rep. of South Africa's Kalahari Gemsbok National Park; wildlife.

Ge·na·den·dal \kə-ˈnäd-ᵊn-ˌdäl\. Town, SW Rep. of South Africa, 68 mi. (109 km.) E of Capetown.

Ge·na·le \je-ˈnä-lā\ *also* **Ga·na·le Dor·ya** \ˈdȯr-yä\. River, S Ethiopia, flows SE, then S to join the Wabē Gestro and Dawa and form the Jubba; ab. 225 mi. (362 km.) long.

Ge·nappe \zhə-ˈnäp\ *or* **Ge·ne·pi·ën** \k̲ə-ˈnā-pē-ən\. Town, Brabant prov., Belgium, SSE of Brussels; pop. (1991c) 12,822; ab. 2.5 mi. (4 km.) S is Quatre Bras (*q.v.*).

Genck. See GENK.

Gen·dring·en \ˈk̲en-driŋ-ə\. Commune, Gelderland prov., E Netherlands, 20 mi. (32 km.) ESE of Arnhem on German border; pop. (1981e) 20,103.

Geneina *or* **Geneina, El.** See AL JUNAYNAH.

Genepiën. See GENAPPE.

General Alvarado See MIRAMAR.

General Carrera, Lago. See BUENOS AIRES, LAKE.

Gen·er·al Grant National Park \ˌjen-rəl-ˈgrant\. Former national park, SE cen. California; 4 sq. mi. (10 sq. km.); included two groves of giant sequoias; estab. 1890; since 1940 a part of Kings Canyon National Park (see UNITED STATES, *National Parks*) and now known as **Grant Grove.**

General J. F. Uriburu. See ZÁRATE.

General Manuel Belgrano. See SIERRA DE FAMATINA.

Ge·ne·ral Pi·co \ˌkā-nā-ˈräl-ˈpē-kō\. Town, La Pampa prov., S cen. Argentina, 290 mi. (467 km.) WSW of Buenos Aires; pop. (1980p) 30,180.

Ge·ne·ral Ro·ca \ˌkā-nā-ˈräl-ˈrō-kä\. Town, Río Negro prov., Argentina; pop. (1980p) 38,296.

Ge·ne·ral San Mar·tín \ˌk̲ā-nā-ˈräl-ˌsän-mär-ˈtēn\ *also* **San Martín.** City, Buenos Aires prov., E Argentina, a suburb of Buenos Aires; pop. (1991p) 407,506.

Ge·ne·ral San·tos \ˌk̲ā-nā-ˈräl-ˈsän-tōs\. Chartered city, South Cotabato prov., Mindanao, Philippines; pop. (1990p) 250,000.

Ge·ne·ral Sar·mien·to \ˌk̲ā-nā-ˈräl-ˌsär-ˈmyen-tō\ *also* **Sarmiento.** Town, Buenos Aires prov., E Argentina, a W suburb of Buenos Aires; pop. (1991p) 646,891.

\ə\ abut \ᵊ\ matches \ᵊ\ kitten, Fr table \ər\ further \a\ ash \ā\ ace \ä\ cot, cart \à\ Fr bac \au̇\ out \b\ Span Avila \ch\ chin \e\ bet \ē\ easy \g\ go \i\ hit \ī\ ice \j\ job \k̲\ Ger ich, Buch \$^{n}$\ Fr vin \ŋ\ sing \ō\ go \ȯ\ all \ȯ\ law \œ\ Fr bœuf \œ̄\ Fr feu \ȯi\ boy \th\ thin \th̲\ this \ü\ loot \u̇\ foot \ue\ Ger füllen \ue̅\ Fr rue \y\ yet \$^{y}$\ Fr digne \ˈdēn^{y}\, nuit \ˈnw^{y}ē\ \yü\ few \yu̇\ fury \zh\ vision

Ge·ne·ral Tri·as \ˌkā-nā-ˈräl-ˈtrē-äs\. Municipality, Cavite prov., Luzon, Philippines, 7 mi. (11 km.) S of City of Cavite; pop. (1980c) 39,745.

Gen·e·see \ˌje-nə-ˈsē, ˈje-nə-ˌ\. **1.** River, Pennsylvania and New York; rises in Potter co., N Pennsylvania, flows N into Lake Ontario near Rochester, W New York; 144 mi. (232 km.) long.

2. Name of counties in two states of the U.S. See tables at MICHIGAN and NEW YORK.

Gen·e·seo \ˌje-nə-ˈsē-ō\. **1.** City, Henry co., NW Illinois, 24 mi. (39 km.) E of Rock Island; pop. (1990c) 5990.

2. Village, ⊗ of Livingston co., W New York, on Genesee River 26 mi. (42 km.) SSW of Rochester; pop. (1990c) 7187; State Univ. of New York Coll. at Geneseo (1867).

Ge·ne·va \jə-ˈnē-və\. **1.** County in SE Alabama. See table at ALABAMA.

2. City, ⊗ of Geneva co., SE Alabama, 2 mi. (3 km.) N of Florida border; pop. (1990c) 4681.

3. City, ⊗ of Kane co., NE Illinois, 36 mi. (58 km.) W of Chicago; pop. (1990c) 12,617; founded ab. 1833; incorp. as city 1887.

4. City, ⊗ of Fillmore co., SE Nebraska, 44 mi. (71 km.) E of Hastings; pop. (1990c) 1486.

5. City, Ontario co., W New York, at N end of Seneca Lake; pop. (1990c) 14,143; Hobart and William Smith Colleges (1822); settled c. 1785 on site of American Indian village.

6. City, Ashtabula co., NE corner of Ohio, 8 mi. (13 km.) WSW of the city of Ashtabula; pop. (1990c) 6597.

Geneva *or Fr.* **Ge·nève** \zhə-ˈnev, -ˈnāv\ *or Ger.* **Genf** \ˈgenf\ *or Ital.* **Gi·ne·vra** \jē-ˈnā-vrä\. **1.** Canton, Switzerland. See table at SWITZERLAND.

2. City, ✱ of Geneva canton, SW Switzerland, at S tip of Lake Geneva on Rhone River; pop. (1989c) 167,934; manufactures watches, jewelry, precision instruments, chemicals; banking; tourism; cultural center. Birthplace 1712 of Jean-Jacques Rousseau, author and philosopher; Reformation monument 1917; buildings include the Palais des Nations (orig. headquarters of the League of Nations, now offices of the United Nations), 10th–12th cent. Gothic cathedral, university (see below).

History: By 6th cent. B.C. a center of Allobroges, a Celtic-speaking people later conquered by Romans; seat of Burgundian kingdom 5th cent. A.D.; conquered by Franks 6th cent.; returned to Burgundy 9th–11th cents.; struggle bet. bishop and Savoyards who constantly threatened the city's independence 12th–15th cents.; in 16th cent., alliance with Protestant cantons of Bern and Fribourg protected it from Savoy; home of French theologian John Calvin, who established a theocratic state (1541) and made 16th cent. Geneva the intellectual center of Protestant Europe; Calvin's Academy, founded 1559, became university 1873; united with France 1798; in 1814, with expanded territory, joined Swiss Confederation as canton of Geneva; scene of conference which drew up Geneva (Red Cross) Convention 1864; League of Nations estab. here 1919, its buildings later taken over by UN; site of many international conferences dealing with diplomatic and political initiatives.

Geneva, Lake *or* **Lake Le·man** \ˈlē-mən, lā-ˈmän\; *anc.* **Le·man·nus** \li-ˈma-nəs\ *or* **Le·ma·nus** \li-ˈmā-nəs\. Lake in SW Switzerland and E France, extending in an arc along the boundary, only its S shore in France; 45 mi. (72 km.) long, 1.5 to 9 mi. (2.4 to 14 km.) wide; 224 sq. mi. (580 sq. km.); traversed E to W by Rhone River.

Ge·nè·vre, Col de \ˌkȯl-də-zhə-ˈnevrᵊ\. Mountain pass, N part of Cottian Alps, bet. France and Italy, E of Briançon; 6102 ft. (1860 m.).

Genf. German form of Geneva, Switzerland. See GENEVA.

Ge·nil *or* **Je·nil** \hā-ˈnēl\. River, S Spain; flows into Guadalquivir River 33 mi. (53 km.) SW of Córdoba; 209 mi. (336 km.) long.

Genk; *formerly* **Genck** \ˈkeŋk\. Commune, Limburg prov., NE Belgium, 11 mi. (18 km.) N of Liège; pop. (1992e) 61,600; automobiles; in coal-bearing region.

Gen·nar·gen·tu \ˌjen-när-ˈjen-tü\. Mountain group, E cen. Sardinia, Italy; highest point 6017 ft. (1834 m.).

Gennesaret, Lake of. See GALILEE, SEA OF.

Gen·ne·vil·liers \ˌzhen-vēl-ˈyā\. Commune, Hauts-de-Seine dept., N France, NNW suburb of Paris; has port facilities on the Seine.

Ge·noa \jə-ˈnō-ə\. **1.** City, De Kalb co., N Illinois, 22 mi. (35 km.) SE of Rockford; pop. (1990c) 3083.

2. Town, Douglas co., W Nevada, 12 mi. (19 km.) SSW of Carson City; oldest permanent settlement in Nevada.

Ge·noa \ˈje-nō-ə\ *or Ital.* **Ge·no·va** \ˈje-nō-vä\; *anc.* **Gen·ua** \ˈje-nyü-ə\. Seaport, ✱ of Genova prov. and ✱ of Liguria, NW Italy, at head of Gulf of Genoa at foot of Apennines 71 mi. (114 km.) SSW of Milan; pop. (1991p) 675,639; archiepiscopal see; one of most important Italian seaports; exports chiefly wine, olive oil, silk, paper; manufactures include iron and steel, textiles, fertilizers; oil refining, shipbuilding; cathedral of San Lorenzo; 16th cent. church of Sant'Ambrogio; 16th cent. Palazzo Doria; Palace of the Doges; university (1471); several museums incl. Galleria di Palazzo Rosso and Galleria di Palazzo Bianco. Birthplace of explorer Christopher Columbus 1451.

History: Ancient settlement on Ligurian coast; became Roman municipium; trading center of Liguria even in Roman times; invaded c. 600 A.D. by Lombards; became independent city 10th cent. and soon became chief commercial city of Mediterranean and Levant; gained special privileges at Constantinople in return for its assistance against Venice 1261 (see GALATA); defeated its trade rival, Pisa, after wars over control of Corsica and Sardinia 1284; early European banking center (Bank of St. George); established commercial colonies at Chios, Lesbos, Sámos, Kaffa (see FEODOSIYA), and Azov 13th–14th cents.; in War of Chioggia c. 1378–81, lost century-long struggle with Venice for control of Levant; declined commercially 14th–15th cents. and began to lose control of colonies; became object of French rivalry with Milan (*q.v.*) 14th–15th cents.; under Andrea Doria threw off French rule 1528 and initiated an economic recovery that included alliance with Spain; ceded Corsica (*q.v.*) to France 1768; with surrounding coastal strip set up as Ligurian Republic by French Emperor Napoléon 1797 and incorp. with France 1805; given to kingdom of Sardinia 1815; became important trade center again 19th cent.; scene of international economic conference 1922; in WWII badly damaged by Allied bombings 1942–44; subsequently rebuilt, achieving much economic importance for Italy.

Genoa, Gulf of. Inlet on Ligurian coast, NW Italy; N part of Ligurian Sea.

Ge·no·va \ˈje-nō-vä\. **1.** Province of Liguria, Italy. See table at ITALY.

2. Seaport, Italy. See GENOA.

Ge·no·ve·sa \ˌkā-nō-ˈbā-sä\ *also* **Tow·er Island** \ˈtau̇-ər\. One of the Galápagos Is. (*q.v.*), Ecuador.

Gent. See GHENT.

Gente Hermosa. See SWAINS.

Gen·tof·te \ˈgen-ˌtȯf-tə\. City, Copenhagen co., island of Sjælland, Denmark; part of Greater Copenhagen; pop. (1989e) 65,032.

Gen·try \ˈjen-trē\. County in NW Missouri. See table at MISSOURI.

Genua. See GENOA.

Genzan. See WŎNSAN.

Ge·og·ra·phe Bay \jē-ˈä-grə-fē\. Inlet of Indian Ocean, SW Western Australia, Australia, just E of Cape Naturaliste.

Geographe Channel. Passage bet. Bernier I. and mainland, W Western Australia, Australia; connects with Shark Bay on S.

Geok–Te·pe *or* **Gök–Té·pé** \ˌgœk-tā-ˈpā\. Town, S Turkmenistan, ab. 40 mi. (64 km.) NW of Ashkhabad; scene of victory of Russians over Tekke people of Turkmen 1881.

George \ˈjȯrj\. **1.** County in SE Mississippi. See table at MISSISSIPPI.

2. River, NE Quebec, Canada; flows N to Ungava Bay; 365 mi. (587 km.) long.

3. Town, S Rep. of South Africa, 235 mi. (378 km.) E of Cape Town; pop. (1985c) 41,920; founded 1811; residential.

George, Cape. Cape on N Nova Scotia, Canada, at W entrance to St. Georges Bay.

George, Lake. **1.** Lake in SE Putnam co., NE Florida Penin.; an expansion of St. Johns River.

2. Lake bet. Warren and Washington cos., E New York; ab. 33 mi. (53 km.) long, 0.75 to 3 mi. (1.2 to 5 km.) wide; outlet to N into Lake Champlain; center of a tourist and recreation area; scene of a number of engagements in French and Indian War 1754–63 and in American Revolution; Fort Ticonderoga at N end. Called **Lake Hor·i·con** \ˈhȯr-i-kən, ˈhär-\ by novelist James Fenimore Cooper.

3. Small lake, SW Uganda, NE of Lake Edward.

George V Coast *also* **King George V Land.** Section of coast of Antarctica E of Wilkes Land; 142° to 153°E and bet. 67° and 71°S; part of Australian claim.

George Land. See FRANZ JOSEF LAND.

George Rog·ers Clark National Historical Park \ˈjȯrj-ˈräjərz-ˈklärk\. See UNITED STATES, *National Historical Parks.*

Georg·es \ˈjȯr-jəz\. River, SE New South Wales, SE Australia; flows into Botany Bay S of Sydney.

Georges Bank. Submerged sandbank, Atlantic Ocean E of Massachusetts; fishing ground made dangerous by crosscurrents and fog; closed to commercial fishing late 1994 to replenish depleted stock.

Georges Island. Island in outer Boston Harbor, Massachusetts, NNW of Hull; Fort Warren where Confederate soldiers were held during Civil War is on it.

Georges Islands. Group of small islands, in Knox co., S Maine, at mouth of Muscongus Bay.

George·town \ˈjȯrj-ˌtau̇n\. **1.** Coastal county in E South Carolina. See table at SOUTH CAROLINA.

2. Town, ⊗ of Clear Creek co., N cen. Colorado; pop. (1990c) 891; nearby is Georgetown Loop, restored narrow gauge railroad.

3. Town, ⊗ of Sussex co., S Delaware, 33 mi. (53 km.) S of Dover; pop. (1990c) 3732.

4. Former town in District of Columbia (*q.v.*), now part of city of Washington. Georgetown Univ. (1789). Settled c. 1665; town laid out 1751; incorp. 1789; merged into District of Columbia 1871.

5. Town, ⊗ of Quitman co., SW Georgia; pop. (1990c) 913.

6. City, Vermilion co., E Illinois, 10 mi. (16 km.) S of Danville; pop. (1990c) 3678.

7. City, ⊗ of Scott co., N cen. Kentucky, 12 mi. (19 km.) N of Lexington; pop. (1990c) 11,414; automobile-manufacturing plant; Georgetown Coll. (1829).

8. Town, Essex co., NE Massachusetts, NE of Lowell; pop. (1990c) 6384.

9. Village, ⊗ of Brown co., SW Ohio, 35 mi. (56 km.) ESE of Cincinnati; pop. (1990c) 3627; boyhood home of President Ulysses S. Grant.

10. City and port of entry, ⊗ of Georgetown co., E South Carolina, at head of Winyah Bay 57 mi. (92 km.) NE of Charleston; pop. (1990c) 9517; settled c. 1729.

11. City, ⊗ of Williamson co., cen. Texas, 27 mi. (43 km.) N of Austin; pop. (1990c) 14,842; mineral springs; Southwestern Univ. (1840).

12. Settlement, Ascension I., on W coast.

13. Coast town, ⊗ of Kings co., E Prince Edward I., Canada; pop. (1991c) 716.

14. City, ✱ of Guyana, at mouth of Demerara River; pop. (1986e) 150,368; chief port of Guyana; exports include sugar, bauxite, rice, diamonds; cathedral; university (1963); botanical gardens. Founded by English 1781; called **Sta·broek** \ˈstä-ˌbru̇k\ during Dutch occupation when it was made seat of government 1784; renamed Georgetown 1812 on return to English.

15. Town on island of St. Vincent, Windward Is., West Indies.

George Town \ˈjȯrj-ˌtau̇n\. **1.** Municipality, N Tasmania, Australia, near mouth of Tamar River 35 mi. (56 km.) NNW of Launceston; pop. (1991c) 6921; resort; harbor.

2. Town on Exuma I., Bahamas, West Indies.

3. Town, ✱ of Cayman Is., on Grand Cayman I., West Indies.

4. *or* **Georgetown** *or* **Pe·nang** \pə-ˈnaŋ, pē-, -ˈnäŋ\. Seaport city, ✱ of Penang state, Malaysia. The first British settlement in Malaysia, founded by the East India Company 1786.

George Wash·ing·ton Birthplace National Monument \ˈjȯrj-ˈwȯsh-iŋ-tən\. See UNITED STATES, *National Monuments* and WAKEFIELD 3.

George Washington Car·ver National Monument \ˈkär-vər\. See UNITED STATES, *National Monuments.*

George West \jȯrj-ˈwest\. City, ⊗ of Live Oak co., S Texas; pop. (1990c) 2586.

Geor·gia \ˈjȯr-jə\. A southern state of U.S.A., bounded on N by Tennessee and North Carolina, on E by South Carolina and the Atlantic Ocean, on S by Florida, and on W by Alabama; 21st state in area, 58,910 sq. mi. (152,577 sq. km.) [land area 58,197 sq. mi. or 150,730 sq. km.]; 11th state in population, (1990c) 6,478,216; ✱ Atlanta; an original state of the Union, the 4th to ratify the U.S. Constitution, Jan. 2, 1788. See table of states at UNITED STATES.

Nicknames: Empire State of the South; Peach State.

State flower: Cherokee rose.

Motto: Wisdom, Justice, Moderation.

Rivers: Chattahoochee and Flint, uniting in SW to form the Apalachicola; Ocmulgee and Oconee, uniting in SE to form the Altamaha; Savannah, forming E boundary bet. Georgia and South Carolina.

Highest point: Brasstown Bald 4784 ft. (1458 m.) on boundary of Towns and Union cos.

Other important natural feature: Okefenokee Swamp 660 sq. mi. (1709 sq. km.) in SE.

Chief products: Processed foods, peanuts, pecans, peaches, tobacco; poultry, livestock; clays; manufacturing: textiles, pulp, carpets and rugs, automobile assembly.

Chief cities: Atlanta, Columbus, Macon, Savannah, Albany, Augusta.

Political divisions: Divided into the following 159 counties (for pronunciation of their names, see their individual entries):

NAME	AREA[1] (sq. mi.)	AREA[1] (sq. km.)	POP. (1990c)	CO. SEAT
Appling	513	1,329	15,744	Baxley
Atkinson	318	824	6,213	Pearson
Bacon	293	759	9,566	Alma
Baker	355	919	3,615	Newton
Baldwin	255	660	39,530	Milledgeville
Banks	231	598	10,308	Homer
Barrow	171	443	29,721	Winder
Bartow	461	1,194	55,911	Cartersville
Ben Hill	255	660	16,245	Fitzgerald
Berrien	468	1,212	14,153	Nashville
Bibb	254	658	149,967	Macon
Bleckley	219	567	10,430	Cochran
Brantley	447	1,158	11,077	Nahunta
Brooks	490	1,269	15,398	Quitman
Bryan	443	1,147	15,438	Pembroke
Bulloch	685	1,774	43,125	Statesboro
Burke	831	2,152	20,579	Waynesboro
Butts	185	479	15,326	Jackson
Calhoun	289	749	5,013	Morgan
Camden[2]	653	1,691	30,167	Woodbine
Candler	250	648	7,744	Metter
Carroll	495	1,282	71,422	Carrollton
Catoosa	167	433	42,464	Ringgold
Charlton	796	2,062	8,496	Folkston
Chatham[2]	445	1,153	216,935	Savannah
Chattahoochee	253	655	16,934	Cusseta
Chattooga	317	821	22,242	Summerville
Cherokee	415	1,075	90,204	Canton
Clarke	122	316	87,594	Athens
Clay	224	580	3,364	Fort Gaines
Clayton	149	386	182,052	Jonesboro
Clinch	797	2,064	6,160	Homerville
Cobb	343	888	447,745	Marietta
Coffee	612	1,585	29,592	Douglas
Colquitt	563	1,458	36,645	Moultrie
Columbia	290	751	66,031	Appling
Cook	233	603	13,456	Adel
Coweta	442	1,145	53,853	Newnan
Crawford	315	816	8,991	Knoxville

\ə\ **abut** \ə̇\ matches \ᵊ\ kitten, Fr table \ər\ **further** \a\ **ash** \ā\ **ace** \ä\ cot, cart \ȧ\ Fr bac \au̇\ **out** \b̲\ Span Avila \ch\ **chin** \e\ bet \ē\ **easy** \g\ **go** \i\ **hit** \ī\ **ice** \j\ **job** \k̲\ Ger **ich**, **Buch** \ⁿ\ Fr vin \ŋ\ **sing** \ō\ **go** \ȯ\ **all** \ȯi\ **law** \œ\ Fr bœuf \œ̄\ Fr **feu** \ȯi\ **boy** \th\ **thin** \th̲\ **this** \ü\ **loot** \u̇\ **foot** \ue\ Ger füllen \ue̅\ Fr **rue** \y\ yet \ʸ\ Fr digne \ˈdēnʸ\, nuit \ˈnwʸē\ \yü\ **few** \yu̇\ **fury** \zh\ **vision**

GEORGIA
CITIES
State capital
County seat
City
BOUNDARIES
State
County
FEATURES
Dams
Points of Interest
NORTH CAROLINA
TENNESSEE
SOUTH CAROLINA
ALABAMA
FLORIDA
ATLANTIC OCEAN
Gulf of Mexico
Fontana Lake
Chickamauga Lake
Tennessee R.
Thorpe Lake
Chatuge Lake
Lake Jocassee
Lake Keowee
Chattooga R.
Hartwell Reservoir
Hartwell Dam
Savannah R.
Clark Hill Lake
Salkehatchie R.
CHICKAMAUGA & CHATTANOOGA NATIONAL MIL. PARK
DADE
Chickamauga
Trenton
Ringgold
CATOOSA
MURRAY
WHITFIELD
Chatsworth
Dalton
WALKER
La Fayette
FANNIN
McCaysville
Blue Ridge
Blairsville
UNION
Choestoe
TOWNS
Hiawassee
RABUN
Clayton
Brasstown Bald 4,784 ft.
GILMER
Ellijay
Springer Mountain 3,782 ft.
HABERSHAM
Clarkesville
WHITE
Cleveland
Toccoa
STEPHENS
LUMPKIN
Dahlonega
Trion
CHATTOOGA
Summerville
GORDON
Calhoun
Oostanaula R.
Jasper
PICKENS
Dawsonville
DAWSON
HALL
Cornelia
BANKS
FRANKLIN
Hartwell
HART
Adairsville
FLOYD
Shannon
Alto Park
Rome
Lindale
BARTOW
Cartersville
CHEROKEE
Canton
FORSYTH
Cumming
Lake S. Lanier
Homer
Gainesville
Carnesville
Royston
Commerce
JACKSON
Jefferson
Danielsville
Elberton
ELBERT
MADISON
Weiss Reservoir
Etowah R.
Allatoona Lake
Cedartown
POLK
Acworth
COBB
Rockmart
Dallas
Marietta
Sugar Hill
Buford
GWINNETT
BARROW
Winder
Lawrenceville
CLARKE
Athens
OGLETHORPE
Watkinsville
OCONEE
Lexington
Tignall
WILKES
LINCOLN
Lincolnton
PAULDING
Smyrna
Decatur
Buchanan
HARALSON
Bremen
Douglasville
DOUGLAS
Atlanta
Forest Park
DE KALB
Monroe
WALTON
Washington
CARROLL
Carrollton
FULTON
Conyers
ROCKDALE
Social Circle
GREENE
Madison
Greensboro
TALIAFERRO
COLUMBIA
Appling
CLAYTON
Porterdale
Covington
NEWTON
MORGAN
Crawfordville
Bowdon
Jonesboro
Fayetteville
McDonough
Thomson
Grovetown
Augusta
Warrenton
McDUFFIE
Fort Gordon
Gracewood
Tallapoosa R.
Newnan
FAYETTE
HENRY
PUTNAM
Lake Oconee
WARREN
RICHMOND
HEARD
COWETA
SPALDING
Jackson
Monticello
Eatonton
Sparta
GLASCOCK
Franklin
Experiment
Griffin
BUTTS
Lake Sinclair
HANCOCK
Gibson
Wrens
Grantville
JASPER
Hogansville
Zebulon
LAMAR
BALDWIN
JEFFERSON
Waynesboro
La Grange
MERIWETHER
Greenville
PIKE
Barnesville
Forsyth
Ocmulgee R.
Milledgeville
Hardwick
Gray
WASHINGTON
Sandersville
Louisville
BURKE
Sardis
West Point Reservoir
TROUP
Woodbury
UPSON
Thomaston
MONROE
JONES
Gordon
Oconee R.
Tennille
Wadley
West Point Dam
West Point
Manchester
Macon
OCMULGEE NAT'L MON.
Irwinton
JENKINS
Millen
Sylvania
Hamilton
Lincoln Park
BIBB
WILKINSON
Wrightsville
SCREVEN
Lake Harding
Bartletts Ferry Dam
HARRIS
TALBOT
Knoxville
CRAWFORD
TWIGGS
Jeffersonville
JOHNSON
Goat Rock Dam
Talbotton
Warner Robins
Robins A.F.B.
Swainsboro
Twin City
Newington
Ogeechee R.
MUSCOGEE
Bibb City
Butler
Reynolds
Fort Valley
Dublin
East Dublin
EMANUEL
Columbus
Fort Benning
TAYLOR
PEACH
Perry
LAURENS
CANDLER
Statesboro
EFFINGHAM
HOUSTON
BLECKLEY
TREUTLEN
Soperton
Metter
Springfield
CHATTAHOOCHEE
MARION
Buena Vista
MACON
Montezuma
Cochran
BULLOCH
Rincon
Cusseta
SCHLEY
Ellaville
Oglethorpe
Unadilla
Hawkinsville
MONTGOMERY
Vidalia
Lyons
EVANS
FORT PULASKI NATIONAL MONUMENT
STEWART
Richland
PULASKI
Eastman
Mt. Vernon
Alamo
Claxton
Pembroke
Savannah
Preston
Americus
DOOLY
DODGE
WHEELER
TOOMBS
BRYAN
CHATHAM
Lumpkin
WEBSTER
SUMTER
Vienna
WILCOX
McRae
Reidsville
TATTNALL
Fort Stewart
Cordele
Abbeville
TELFAIR
Glennville
LIBERTY
Richmond Hill
Georgetown
CRISP
Rochelle
Lumber City
Hinesville
SIDWAY I.
QUITMAN
TERRELL
Cuthbert
Dawson
LEE
BEN HILL
JEFF DAVIS
Hazlehurst
Altamaha R.
Baxley
LONG
OSSABAW I.
Lake Eufaula
RANDOLPH
Shellman
Leesburg
TURNER
Fitzgerald
APPLING
Ludowici
Ashburn
ST. CATHERINES I.
Walter F. George Dam
Fort Gaines
Edison
Albany
Ocilla
Broxton
BACON
Jesup
WAYNE
Morgan
DOUGHERTY
Sylvester
IRWIN
COFFEE
Alma
McINTOSH
Sapelo Sound
SAPELO I.
CLAY
CALHOUN
Putney
WORTH
TIFT
Douglas
Patterson
Darien
Arlington
Blakely
Phillipsburg
Tifton
Alapaha R.
Satilla R.
Willacoochee
PIERCE
Doboy Sound
Altamaha Sd.
EARLY
BAKER
Newton
Doerun
BERRIEN
Pearson
Blackshear
GLYNN
ST. SIMONS I.
Chattahoochee R.
Choctawhatchee R.
Colquitt
Camilla
COLQUITT
Nashville
ATKINSON
Deenwood
Nahunta
FORT FREDERICA NATIONAL MON.
Flint R.
MILLER
MITCHELL
Moultrie
Sparks
Adel
Waycross
BRANTLEY
Arco
Brunswick
Donalsonville
COOK
LANIER
WARE
JEKYLL I.
Meigs
Hahira
Lakeland
Homerville
Woodbine
St. Andrew Sound
CUMBERLAND I.
SEMINOLE
GRADY
Pavo
Moody A.F.B.
CLINCH
CHARLTON
CAMDEN
CUMBERLAND ISLAND NATIONAL SEASHORE
Lake Seminole
Bainbridge
Cairo
THOMAS
BROOKS
LOWNDES
Valdosta
Folkston
Kingsland
DECATUR
Thomasville
St. Marys R.
St. Marys
Jim Woodruff Dam
Calvary
Boston
Quitman
Statenville
Okefenokee Swamp
ECHOLS
AMELIA I.
Nassau Sound
TALBOT I.
Apalachicola R.
Tallahassee
Lake Talquin
Suwannee R.
Ochlockonee R.
St. Johns R.
Apalachee Bay
Bald Point Lighthouse Point
0 20 40 mi
0 30 60 km
30'
85°
84°
83°
82°
81°
35°
34°
33°
32°
31°
30°
©1996, Encyclopædia Britannica, Inc.

NAME	AREA[1] (sq. mi.)	AREA[1] (sq. km.)	POP. (1990c)	CO. SEAT
Crisp	292	756	20,011	Cordele
Dade	168	435	13,147	Trenton
Dawson	211	546	9,429	Dawsonville
Decatur	575	1,489	25,511	Bainbridge
De Kalb	269	697	545,837	Decatur
Dodge	498	1,290	17,607	Eastman
Dooly	394	1,020	9,901	Vienna
Dougherty	324	839	96,311	Albany
Douglas	202	523	71,120	Douglasville
Early	525	1,360	11,854	Blakely
Echols	425	1,101	2,334	Statenville
Effingham	480	1,243	25,687	Springfield
Elbert	358	927	18,949	Elberton
Emanuel	686	1,777	20,546	Swainsboro
Evans	186	482	8,724	Claxton
Fannin	394	1,020	15,992	Blue Ridge
Fayette	199	515	62,415	Fayetteville
Floyd	514	1,331	81,251	Rome
Forsyth	218	565	44,083	Cumming
Franklin	269	697	16,650	Carnesville
Fulton	530	1,373	648,951	Atlanta
Gilmer	439	1,137	13,368	Ellijay
Glascock	143	370	2,357	Gibson
Glynn[2]	412	1,067	62,496	Brunswick
Gordon	358	927	35,072	Calhoun
Grady	466	1,207	20,279	Cairo
Greene	403	1,044	11,793	Greensboro
Gwinnett	437	1,132	352,910	Lawrenceville
Habersham	282	730	27,621	Clarkesville
Hall	378	979	95,428	Gainesville
Hancock	478	1,238	8,908	Sparta
Haralson	285	738	21,966	Buchanan
Harris	465	1,204	17,788	Hamilton
Hart	256	663	19,712	Hartwell
Heard	302	782	8,628	Franklin
Henry	331	857	58,741	McDonough
Houston	380	984	89,208	Perry
Irwin	372	963	8,649	Ocilla
Jackson	337	873	30,005	Jefferson
Jasper	373	966	8,453	Monticello
Jeff Davis	331	857	12,032	Hazlehurst
Jefferson	530	1,373	17,408	Louisville
Jenkins	351	909	8,247	Millen
Johnson	313	811	8,329	Wrightsville
Jones	402	1,041	20,739	Gray
Lamar	181	469	13,038	Barnesville
Lanier	177	458	5,531	Lakeland
Laurens	810	2,098	39,988	Dublin
Lee	355	919	16,250	Leesburg
Liberty[2]	514	1,331	52,745	Hinesville
Lincoln	193	500	7,442	Lincolnton
Long	402	1,041	6,202	Ludowici
Lowndes	507	1,313	75,981	Valdosta
Lumpkin	292	756	14,573	Dahlonega
McDuffie	253	655	20,119	Thomson
McIntosh[2]	426	1,103	8,634	Darien
Macon	403	1,044	13,114	Oglethorpe
Madison	281	728	21,050	Danielsville
Marion	365	945	5,590	Buena Vista
Meriwether	499	1,292	22,411	Greenville
Miller	287	743	6,280	Colquitt
Mitchell	509	1,318	20,275	Camilla
Monroe	398	1,031	17,113	Forsyth
Montgomery	237	614	7,163	Mount Vernon
Morgan	356	922	12,883	Madison
Murray	342	886	26,147	Chatsworth
Muscogee	220	570	179,278	Columbus
Newton	271	702	41,808	Covington
Oconee	186	482	17,618	Watkinsville
Oglethorpe	435	1,123	9,763	Lexington
Paulding	318	824	41,611	Dallas
Peach	151	391	21,189	Fort Valley
Pickens	225	583	14,432	Jasper
Pierce	342	886	13,328	Blackshear
Pike	230	596	10,224	Zebulon
Polk	312	808	33,815	Cedartown
Pulaski	253	655	8,108	Hawkinsville
Putnam	340	881	14,137	Eatonton
Quitman	171	443	2,209	Georgetown
Rabun	368	953	11,648	Clayton
Randolph	436	1,129	8,023	Cuthbert
Richmond	323	837	189,719	Augusta
Rockdale	128	332	54,091	Conyers
Schley	162	420	3,588	Ellaville
Screven	651	1,686	13,842	Sylvania
Seminole	246	637	9,010	Donalsonville
Spalding	201	521	54,457	Griffin
Stephens	180	466	23,257	Toccoa
Stewart	463	1,199	5,654	Lumpkin
Sumter	489	1,267	30,228	Americus
Talbot	390	1,010	6,524	Talbotton
Taliaferro	195	505	1,915	Crawfordville
Tattnall	490	1,269	17,722	Reidsville
Taylor	403	1,044	7,642	Butler
Telfair	440	1,140	11,000	McRae
Terrell	329	852	10,653	Dawson
Thomas	541	1,401	38,986	Thomasville
Tift	266	689	34,998	Tifton
Toombs	368	953	24,072	Lyons
Towns	166	430	6,754	Hiawassee
Treutlen	194	502	5,994	Soperton
Troup	446	1,155	55,536	La Grange
Turner	293	759	8,703	Ashburn
Twiggs	364	943	9,806	Jeffersonville
Union	309	800	11,993	Blairsville
Upson	334	865	26,300	Thomaston
Walker	445	1,153	58,340	La Fayette
Walton	330	855	38,586	Monroe
Ware	912	2,362	35,471	Waycross
Warren	284	477	6,078	Warrenton
Washington	674	1,746	19,112	Sandersville
Wayne	645	1,671	22,356	Jesup
Webster	195	505	2,263	Preston
Wheeler	306	793	4,903	Alamo
White	243	629	13,006	Cleveland
Whitfield	281	728	72,462	Dalton
Wilcox	383	992	7,008	Abbeville
Wilkes	468	1,212	10,597	Washington
Wilkinson	458	1,186	10,228	Irwinton
Worth	579	1,500	19,745	Sylvester

[1]Area = land area.
[2]Includes islands of Sea Islands chain.

History: Inhabited by Creek and Cherokee peoples when explored by Spanish and penetrated by Spanish missions 16th cent.; English colony, last of original 13 colonies to be founded, chartered 1732 and settled 1733 at Savannah by English philanthropist James E. Oglethorpe as refuge for debtors and as buffer state bet. Spanish Florida and the Carolinas; surrendered charter to crown 1752; became royal colony 1754; Savannah held by British 1778–82; chartered Univ. of Georgia 1785, the oldest state university; first southern state to ratify U.S. Constitution Jan. 2, 1788; ceded claims to western lands (now Alabama and Mississippi) 1802; Creek and Cherokee tribes forcibly removed to Indian Terr. 1830s; seceded from Union Jan. 19, 1861; scene of battle of Chickamauga 1863, campaign bet. Chattanooga and Atlanta, and Gen. William T. Sherman's "March to the Sea" 1864; ordinance of secession repealed Oct. 30, 1865 and slavery abolished; last state to be readmitted to Union July 15, 1870; adopted present constitution 1945.

Georgia, Republic of *or Georgian* **Sa·kart·ve·lo** \sä-ˈkärt-ve-ˌlō\ *or Russ.* **Gru·zi·ya** \ˈgrü-zē-ə\; *anc.* **Ibe·ria** \ī-ˈbir-ē-ə\. Republic, SW Asia, bounded on SE by Azerbaijan, on S by Armenia and Turkey, and on W by the Black Sea; comprised Georgian Soviet Socialist Rep. 1936–91; 26,911 sq. mi. (69,699 sq. km.); pop. (1993e) 5,493,000; ✱ Tbilisi; includes Abkhaz Rep., Adjarian Autonomous Rep., and South Ossetian Autonomous Region. Separated from Russia on N and NE by main range of Caucasus Mts.; comprises mainly the S slopes of W and cen. Caucasus, and valleys of the Rioni and upper Kura rivers.

Chief products: Wheat, sugar beets, barley, tea, citrus fruit, wine grapes; livestock; manganese; manufacturing: textiles, chemicals, steel products; hydroelectric power plants.

Chief towns: Tbilisi, Kutaisi, Rustavi.

History: Region contained ancient kingdoms of Colchis and Iberia; dependent upon Rome after first cent. B.C.; Christianized in 4th cent. A.D.; under Armenian control 6th and 7th cents.; conquered by Arabs 8th cent.; controlled by Armenians 9th–12th cents.; period of great expansion and cultural growth under Queen Tamara (1184–1212); suffered disintegration under impact of Mongol and Turkish invasions 13th–14th cents.; under Armenian, Turkish, and Persian control until it sought Russian protection in 18th cent.; annexation to Russia 1801 caused Russian war with Persia 1804–13 (see GULISTAN); became vassal of Russia 1783;

\ə\ **abut** \ə̇\ matches \ᵊ\ kitten, Fr **table** \ər\ **further** \a\ **ash** \ā\ **ace**
\ä\ **cot, cart** \ȧ\ Fr **bac** \au̇\ **out** \b̲\ Span A**v**ila \ch\ **chin** \e\ **bet** \ē\ **easy**
\g\ **go** \i\ **hit** \ī\ **ice** \j\ **job** \k̲\ Ger **ich**, **Buch** \ⁿ\ Fr **vin**
\ŋ\ **sing** \ō\ **go** \ȯ\ **all** \ȯ\ **law** \œ\ Fr **bœuf** \œ̄\ Fr **feu** \ȯi\ **boy**
\th\ **thin** \t̲h̲\ **this** \ü\ **loot** \u̇\ **foot** \ue\ Ger **füllen** \ue̅\ Fr **rue**
\y\ **yet** \ʸ\ Fr **digne** \ˈdēnʸ\, **nuit** \ˈnwʸē\ \yü\ **few** \yu̇\ **fury** \zh\ **vision**

when Russia collapsed 1917, entered short-lived federation; declared independent republic 1918; estab. Soviet government 1921; in 1922 joined Transcaucasian S.F.S.R. and entered U.S.S.R.; became constituent republic 1936; declared independence April 9, 1991; internal conflicts esp. with Abkhaz Rep. began 1992.

Georgia, Strait of. Channel in SW Canada and NW United States; has Vancouver I. on the W and mainland of SW British Columbia and Whatcom co., Washington on the E; connects by Johnstone Strait with Queen Charlotte Strait and extends S to Haro Strait (*q.v.*); 150 mi. (241 km.) long, 30 mi. (48 km.) wide at its widest part; forms part of inland ship passage from the Lower 48 to Alaska.

Geor·gi·an Bay \ˈjȯr-jən\. Inlet of Lake Huron, SE Ontario, Canada; has entrance ab. 20 mi. (32 km.) wide bet. E Manitoulin I. and Cape Hurd; ab. 125 mi. (200 km.) long, 50 mi. (80 km.) wide; 860 sq. mi. (2227 sq. km.). Thirty islands in SE included in **Georgian Bay Islands National Park** (see CANADA, *National Parks*).

Georgian Soviet Socialist Republic. See GEORGIA, REPUBLIC OF.

Geor·gi·na \jȯr-ˈjē-nə\. Intermittent river, Simpson Desert, E Northern Terr. and W Queensland, Australia; in some seasons flows to the Warburton; ab. 700 mi. (1125 km.) long.

Georgiu–Dezh. See LISKI.

Ge·or·giy·evsk *or* **Ge·or·gi·evsk** \gē-ˈȯr-gē-ˌyifsk\. Town, S Stavropol' Kray, S Russia in Europe, 18 mi. (29 km.) E of Pyatigorsk; pop. (1991e) 72,000; trade center for farm products. Founded 1777; scene of signing of treaty making Georgia a vassal of Russia 1783.

Ge·ra \ˈgā-rä\. **1.** District of former East Germany.
2. City, Thuringia, E Germany, on the Weisse Elster, 47 mi. (76 km.) ESE of Erfurt; pop. (1992e) 126,521; formerly ✻ of Gera district; textiles, metal goods; chartered early 13th cent.; Trinity Church 1611; Osterstein Palace 1686–1735; 16th cent. town hall; destroyed by fire 1639, 1686, and 1780; formerly ✻ of a principality.

Geral, Serra. See SERRA GERAL.

Ger·ald·ton \ˈjer-əld-tən\. Town, W Western Australia, Australia, 210 mi. (338 km.) NNW of Perth; pop. (1991c) 20,587; good harbor.

Gé·rard·mer \ˌzhā-ˌrär-ˈmā\. Commune, Vosges dept., NE France, on a lake in the Vosges Mts. 20 mi. (32 km.) SE of Épinal; resort.

Gerasa. See JARASH.

Ger·go·vie \ˌzhār-gō-ˈvē\. Plateau, Puy-de-Dôme dept., S cen. France, S of Clermont-Ferrand; above village of Gergovie; site of **Ger·go·via** \jər-ˈgō-vē-ə\, ancient settlement of the Arverni people where their chief Vercingetorix repulsed Roman Gen. Julius Caesar's forces 52 B.C.

Ge·ring \ˈgir-iŋ\. City, ⊗ of Scotts Bluff co., W Nebraska, on N Platte River opp. Scottsbluff; pop. (1990c) 7946.

Ger·i·zim, Mount \ˈger-ə-ˌzim, gə-ˈrī-zəm\ *or Arab.* **Je·bel at Tur** \ˈje-bəl-ȧt-ˈtür\. Mountain just S of Nābulus, Palestine, in region occupied by Israel 1967; sacred place for Samaritans.

Ger·la·chov·sky \ˈger-lə-ˌkȯf-skē\ *or* **Ger·la·chov·ka** \ˈger-lə-ˌk̲ȯf-kə\ *or Ger.* **Gerls·dor·fer Spit·ze** \ˈgerls-ˌdȯr-fər-ˈshpit-sə\; *formerly* **Franz Jo·sef–Spitze** \ˈfränts-ˈyō-zəf-ˈshpit-sə\ *or* **Sta·lin Peak** \ˈstä-lin, ˈsta-, -lēn\. Peak in Tatra Mts., Carpathians, N Slovakia; 8711 ft. (2655 m.).

Ger·man Coast \ˈjər-mən\ *or Fr.* **Côte des Al·le·mands** \ˈkōt-dā-zȧ-lə-ˈmäⁿ\. District in Louisiana, extending ab. 40 mi. (64 km.) along banks of Mississippi River from a point ab. 30 mi. (48 km.) above New Orleans; settled c. 1720 by Alsatians who had come to America under inducements of Scottish financier John Law's Mississippi Scheme, which collapsed 1720.

German Confederation. See *History* at GERMANY.

German Democratic Republic. See GERMANY, EAST.

German East Africa. See TANZANIA.

German Empire. See *History* at GERMANY.

Ger·ma·nia \jər-ˈmā-nē-ə, -nyə\. Historical name for ancient region of cen. Europe, comprising territory E of the Rhine and N of the Danube which never became part of Roman Empire.

Germania Inferior. Roman province of E Gallia (modern NE France and part of Belgium and Netherlands). See TRANSALPINE GAUL at GAUL.

Germania Superior. Roman province of NE Gallia (nearly equivalent to Alsace-Lorraine). See TRANSALPINE GAUL at GAUL.

Germanicopolis. See ÇANKIRI 2.

Germanicum, Mare. See NORTH SEA.

German New Guinea. See NEW GUINEA, TRUST TERRITORY OF.

German Ocean. See NORTH SEA.

German Southwest Africa. See NAMIBIA.

Ger·man·town \ˈjər-mən-ˌtau̇n\. **1.** Unincorporated settlement, Montgomery co., SW cen. Maryland, NW of Gaithersburg; pop. (1990c) 41,145; U.S. Dept. of Energy headquarters.
2. City, Montgomery co., SW Ohio; pop. (1990c) 4916.
3. Residential section of Philadelphia, Pennsylvania, on Wissahickon Creek; orig. settled by German colonists c. 1683; battle of Germantown Oct. 4, 1777 in which Gen. George Washington tried unsuccessfully to dislodge British troops

stationed there under Sir William Howe; consolidated with Philadelphia 1854; early printing and publishing center.
4. City, Shelby co., SW Tennessee, 14 mi. (23 km.) ESE of Memphis; pop. (1990c) 32,893.
5. Village, Washington co., SE Wisconsin, 17 mi. (27 km.) NW of Milwaukee; pop. (1990c) 13,658.

German Volga Republic. See VOLGA GERMAN AUTONOMOUS SOVIET SOCIALIST REPUBLIC.

Ger·ma·ny \'jər-mə-nē\; *or Ger.* **Deutsch·land** \'dȯich-ˌlänt\. Country, cen. Europe; bounded on N by North Sea, Denmark, and Baltic Sea, on E by Poland and Czech Republic, on SE by Austria, on S by Austria and Switzerland, on SW by France, and on W by Luxembourg, Belgium, and the Netherlands; 137,735 sq. mi. (356,734 sq. km.); pop. (1993e) 80,974,900; ✱ Berlin.

Physical features: Generally flat in N, hilly in NE and cen. region, and mountainous in S (highest peak Zugspitze 9720 ft. or 2963 m. in Bavarian Alps).

Chief rivers: Elbe, Rhine, Danube, Oder (forms section of boundary with Poland), Weser, Saale, Spree, Ems, and Havel.

Chief products: Corn, wheat, barley, sugar beets, potatoes, wine; coal, iron; motor vehicles.

Chief cities: Berlin, Hamburg, Munich, Cologne, Frankfurt, Essen, Dortmund, Stuttgart, Düsseldorf, Bremen, Duisburg, Hannover.

Political divisions: Divided into the following 16 states (for pronunciation of their names, see their individual entries):

NAME	AREA (sq. mi.)	AREA (sq. km.)	POP. (1991e)	CAPITAL
Baden-Württemberg	13,803	35,750	9,822,000	Stuttgart
Bavaria	27,239	70,549	11,448,800	Munich
Berlin	343	888	3,433,700	
Brandenburg	11,219	29,057	2,578,300	Potsdam
Bremen	156	404	681,700	Bremen
Hamburg	289	748	1,652,400	Hamburg
Hesse	8151	21,111	5,763,300	Wiesbaden
Lower Saxony	18,305	47,410	7,387,200	Hannover
Mecklenburg-West Pomerania	9,096	23,559	1,924,000	Schwerin
North Rhine-Westphalia	13,142	34,038	17,349,700	Düsseldorf
Rhineland-Palatinate	7,659	19,837	3,763,500	Mainz
Saarland	991	2,567	1,073,000	Saarbrücken
Saxony	7,081	18,340	4,764,300	Dresden
Saxony-Anhalt	7,956	20,606	2,874,000	Magdeburg
Schleswig-Holstein	6,046	15,659	2,626,100	Kiel
Thuringia (Thüringen)	6,275	16,252	2,611,300	Erfurt

History: Region E of Rhine and N of Danube (ancient Germania), inhabited from early times by Teutonic peoples, never included in Roman Empire; began as political entity with the division of Carolingian empire (see FRANCE) allotted to Louis the German 843 A.D. by Treaty of Verdun; one hundred years of Saxon rule began 918 with Henry I; Germany, with N Italy, included in Holy Roman Empire (*q.v.*); even at height of emperor's influence divided into numerous secular and ecclesiastical feudal units which increased their power during papal-imperial struggle; accession of first ruler of Hapsburg line, Rudolf I, 1273; expanded eastward, Prussia being conquered 13th cent. by Teutonic Knights; weakness and political dissolution of Empire accelerated by Reformation which began with Lutheran revolt 1517; Germany split into Catholic and Protestant states which suffered greatly from disastrous Thirty Years' War 1618–48 (see BOHEMIA); Empire yielded territory to France, Sweden, Brandenburg, and recognized practical sovereignty of feudal princes of its separate states 1648; in 18th cent. Prussia under the Hohenzollerns prospered and soon became strong military state and weakened Austria in Silesian Wars; Holy Roman Empire forcibly dissolved during Napoleonic Wars 1806, German states becoming dependents of France. Congress of Vienna redefined borders 1814–15 and formed **German Confederation** under Austrian hegemony opposed to unification; Zollverein or Customs Union estab. by Prussia 1834 to promote economic unity among the states; failed to achieve unity in Frankfurt National Assembly 1848–49; after victory in Seven Weeks' War against Austria 1866, Prussia under Prime Minister Otto von Bismarck became leader of German unification; **German Empire** (**Deutsch·es Reich** \'dȯi-chəs-'rīk, -'rīk\), a federal state dominated by Prussia proclaimed at close of Franco-Prussian War 1871 with Bismarck first chancellor (1871–90), united all German states except Austria; acquired Alsace-Lorraine (*q.v.*); allied with Austria-Hungary (*q.v.*) 1879 and with Italy 1882, thus forming Triple Alliance; adopted policy of colonial expansion 1884; supported Austria in the situation with Serbia (*q.v.*) that precipitated WWI 1914; forced Kaiser William II's abdication and proclaimed republic 1918; by Treaty of Versailles 1919 lost: Alsace-Lorraine, Moresnet, Eupen, Malmédy, most of Posen and West Prussia (incl. Danzig), Memel, N Schleswig and parts of Upper Silesia by plebiscites (see SILESIA), and all its colonies; also according with the Treaty of Versailles the Saar was placed temporarily under administration of the League of Nations; adopted Weimar Constitution 1919 and became known as Weimar Republic; Ruhr (*q.v.*) region occupied by French 1923; signed Locarno (*q.v.*) treaties 1925; member of League of Nations 1926–33. Ceased to be federal republic 1933 and became, under Chancellor Adolf Hitler, a centralized, unitary, totalitarian state known as the Third Reich, dominated by National Socialist (Nazi) party; recovered the Saar by plebiscite 1935; Nürnberg Laws passed denying Jews full citizenship 1935; reoccupied Rhineland and formed Rome-Berlin Axis and alliance with Japan 1936; annexed Austria and German Sudetenland 1938, rest of Czechoslovakia (*q.v.*) and Memel 1939; entered German-Soviet Nonaggression Pact 1939. Initiated WWII with invasion of Poland resulting in declarations of war by Great Britain and France Sept. 1939; overran Denmark, Norway, Netherlands, Belgium, Luxembourg, and France 1940; attacked U.S.S.R. June 1941; declared war on U.S. 1941; defeated at Stalingrad (now Volgograd) Jan. 1943, gradually forced out of U.S.S.R. 1943–44; defeated in North Africa May 1943; driven out of France and finally forced to surrender to Allies May 8, 1945; by Potsdam Conference July 17–Aug. 2, 1945, lost territory in E to Poland and the U.S.S.R. (see EAST PRUSSIA); divided 1945 into U.S., British, French, and Soviet zones of occupation; in 1949 U.S., British, and French zones were reconstituted forming West Germany (*q.v.*), Soviet zone forming East Germany (*q.v.*). Reunified Oct. 3, 1990.

Germany, East; *officially* **German Democratic Republic.** Former republic, N cen. Europe, bounded on N by the Baltic Sea, on E by Poland, on S by Czechoslovakia and West Germany, and on W by West Germany; 41,766 sq. mi. (108,174 sq. km.); pop. (1989e) 16,674,632; ✱ East Berlin.

Chief cities: East Berlin, Leipzig, Dresden, Karl-Marx-Stadt, Magdeburg, Halle, Erfurt, Rostock.

Political divisions: Divided into the following 15 districts (*Bezirke*)—for pronunciation of their names, see their individual entries: Cottbus, Dresden, East Berlin, Erfurt, Frankfurt, Gera, Halle, Karl-Marx-Stadt, Leipzig, Magdeburg, Neubrandenburg, Potsdam, Rostock, Schwerin, Suhl.

History: For history prior to 1945, see GERMANY. Following the partition of Germany (1945), region administered as occupation zone by U.S.S.R.; initial postwar period marked by the establishment of Soviet-type institutions and the confiscation of private property. Republic estab. as Communist state 1949; recognized frontier (Oder-Neisse Line) with Poland as final German boundary in cen. Europe 1950; initiated collectivization of agriculture 1952; anticommunist demonstrations suppressed with aid of Soviet forces 1953; was declared a sovereign state in treaty with U.S.S.R. and became

GERMANY
CITIES
Over 1,000,000
500,000 to 1,000,000
100,000 to 500,000
Under 100,000
National capital
State capital
BOUNDARIES
International
State
FEATURES
Canals
Dams
5°
7°
9°
11°
13°
15°
55°
53°
51°
49°
DENMARK
NORTH SEA
BALTIC SEA
NETHERLANDS
BELGIUM
LUXEMBOURG
FRANCE
SWITZERLAND
AUSTRIA
CZECH REPUBLIC
POLAND
NORTH FRISIAN ISLANDS
SYLT
SCHLESWIG-HOLSTEIN NATIONAL PARK
HELGOLAND
NIEDERSACHSISCHES WATTENMEER NATIONAL PARK
EAST FRISIAN ISLANDS
Waddenzee
Dollart Basin
Jade Bay
SCHLESWIG-HOLSTEIN
Flensburg
Maasholm
Schleswig
Petersdorf
FEHMARN
Oldenburg
Eider
Rendsburg
Kiel
Nord-Ostsee Kanal
Eutin
Neumünster
Lübeck
Cuxhaven
Glückstadt
Elmshorn
Norderstedt
Oste
Elbe
Alster
Stade
Wedel
Mölln
Hamburg
HAMBURG
Elbe Bridge
Seevetal
Lüneburg
Mecklenburg Bay
Warnemünde
Rostock
Stralsund
RÜGEN
Peenemünde
Greifswald
Peene
Wismar
Warnow
Recknitz
MECKLENBURG-WEST POMERANIA
Güstrow
Lake Kummerow
Torgelow
Grevesmühlen
Schwerin
Lake Schwerin
Neubrandenburg
Helpter Hill 587 ft
Waren
Lake Müritz
Hagenow
Parchim
Lake Plau
MECKLENBURG
Neustrelitz
Prenzlau
UCKERMARK
Oder
Elde
Schwedt
Hohensaaten-Friedrichsthal Canal
Zehdenick
Eberswalde-Finow
Neuruppin
PRIGNITZ
Wittenberge
Havelburg
Norden
Wilhelmshaven
Aurich
Nordenham
Bremerhaven
Emden
Weser
Osterholz-Scharmbeck
Oldenburg
BREMEN
Bremen
Delmenhorst
Papenburg
Ganderkesee
Achim
Verden
Weyhe
LÜNEBURG
HEATH
Uelzen
Aller
Walsrode
Cloppenburg
Vechta
LOWER SAXONY
EMSLAND
Ems
Lingen
Lake Dümmer
Leine
Celle
Nordhorn
Mittelland Canal
Lake Steinhude
Garbsen
Hannover
Wolfsburg
Osnabrück
Minden
Peine
Lehrte
Braunschweig
Rheine
TEUTOBURG FOREST
Herford
Bad Salzuflen
Hildesheim
Wolfenbüttel
Salzgitter
Hameln
Bielefeld
Detmold
Gandersheim
Lutter
Goslar
Wernigerode
Münster
MÜNSTERLAND
Bocholt
Gütersloh
NORTH RHINE-WESTPHALIA
Höxter
Kleve
Wesel
Dorsten
Marl
Recklinghausen
Hamm
Lippe
Lippstadt
Paderborn
Oberhausen
Gelsenkirchen
Herne
Dortmund
Duisburg
Essen
Bochum
Menden
Ruhr
Brilon
Krefeld
Mülheim
Hagen
Arnsberg
Düsseldorf
Wuppertal
Remscheid
Mönchen-gladbach
Solingen
SAUERLAND
Leverkusen
Bergisch Gladbach
ROTHAAR HILLS
Jülich
Hürth
Cologne
Eschweiler
Kerpen
Brühl
Sankt Augustin
Aachen
Stolberg
Bonn
Königswinter
Siegen
Lahn
SEVEN HILLS
WESTERWALD
Dill
Marburg
Remagen
Andernach
Giessen
Wetzlar
VOGELSBERG
Koblenz
Limburg
HESSE
Bad Ems
TAUNUS MTS.
Bad Homburg
Frankfurt am Main
RHINELAND-PALATINATE
Cochem
EIFEL
Moselle
Rhine
Zell
Wiesbaden
Hanau
Offenbach
Bingen
Mainz
Bernkastel-Kues
Trier
HUNSRÜCK
Bad Kreuznach
Aschaffenburg
Darmstadt
SPESSART
Nahe
Idar-Oberstein
Worms
Lorsch
Luxembourg
Saar
Frankenthal
ODENWALD
SAARLAND
Kaiserslautern
Mannheim
Amorbach
Neunkirchen
Ludwigshafen
Heidelberg
Homburg
Zweibrücken
Saarlouis
Saarbrücken
Sankt Ingbert
Pirmasens
Speyer
Neckar
HAARDT
Bruchsal
Karlsruhe
Heilbronn
Ettlingen
Pforzheim
Baden-Baden
Stuttgart
Esslingen
Calw
Sindelfingen
Strasbourg
Offenburg
BADEN-WÜRTTEMBERG
Tübingen
Reutlingen
Freudenstadt
ORTENAU
Hechingen
BLACK FOREST
KAISERSTUHL MASSIF
Triberg
Rottweil
Breisach
Furtwangen
Villingen-Schwenningen
Freiburg
Tuttlingen
Feldberg 4,905 ft
Singen
Lörrach
Wehr
REICHENAU
Konstanz
Ravensburg
Friedrichshafen
Lindau
Lake Constance
SWABIAN JURA
Danube
Ulm
Neu-Ulm
Iller
Memmingen
Kaufbeuren
Kempten
Füssen
Garmisch-Partenkirchen
Zugspitze 9,720 ft
BAVARIAN ALPS
Mittenwald
ALPS
Schwäbisch Hall
Crailsheim
Dinkelsbühl
Ellwangen
Schwäbisch Gmünd
Aalen
Göppingen
Nördlingen
Heidenheim
Wörnitz
Donauwörth
Lech
Augsburg
Friedberg
Dachau
Fürstenfeldbruck
Munich
Ottobrunn
Germering
Ammer Lake
Starnberger See
Rosenheim
Inn
Lake Chiem
Tegernsee
Bad Reichenhall
Berchtesgaden
Königssee
BERCHTESGADEN NATIONAL PARK
Erding
Freising
Landshut
Isar
BAVARIA
Ingolstadt
Eichstätt
Kelheim
Regensburg
Straubing
Deggendorf
Passau
BAVARIAN FOREST
BAVARIAN FOREST NATIONAL PARK
Regen
BOHEMIAN FOREST
Naab
Weiden
Amberg
Neumarkt
FRANCONIAN JURA
Rednitz
Nürnberg
Fürth
Erlangen
Forchheim
Main-Danube Canal
Ansbach
Rothenburg
Bad Mergentheim
Würzburg
Main
Bamberg
Bayreuth
Schneeberg 3,447 ft
FICHTEL GEBIRGE
Kulmbach
Coburg
Schweinfurt
Bad Kissingen
Hof
FRANCONIAN FOREST
Sonneberg
RHÖN MTS.
WASSERKUPPE
Fulda
Meiningen
Suhl
Mount Grosser Beer 3,221 ft
THURINGIA
Bad Hersfeld
Eisenach
Gotha
Arnstadt
Erfurt
Weimar
Apolda
Jena
Rudolstadt
Saalfeld
Eschwege
Mühlhausen
Sömmerda
Sondershausen
KYFFHÄUSER MTS.
THURINGIA
Korbach
Kassel
Münden
Werra
Leinefelde
Nordhausen
Göttingen
Northeim
HARZ MTS.
Brocken Peak 3,747 ft
Fulda
Lutter
Quedlinburg
Halberstadt
Aschersleben
Mansfeld
Harzgerode
Eisleben
Halle-Neustadt
Halle
Merseburg
Leuna
Weissenfels
Naumburg
Eisenberg
Gera
Crimmitschau
Greiz
Reichenbach
Plauen
VOGTLAND
Oelsnitz
Zwickau
Aue
Glauchau
Meerane
Altenburg
Chemnitz
Freiberg
ERZGEBIRGE
Fichtelberg 3,982 ft
Borna
Leipzig
Delitzsch
Eilenberg
Torgau
Döbeln
Riesa
Meissen
Grossenhain
Coswig
Dresden
Freital
Pirna
Bautzen
Löbau
Zittau
Görlitz
OBERLAUSITZ
Hoyerswerda
LUSATIA
Weisswasser
Senftenberg
Lauchhammer
Spremberg
Cottbus
Forst
Guben
Neisse
Schwarze Elster
Mulde
Saale
Elster
Wittenberg
Dessau
Zerbst
Köthen
Wolfen
Bitterfeld
Stassfurt
Schönebeck
Magdeburg
Burg
Genthin
Elbe-Havel Canal
FLÄMING HILLS
BRANDENBURG
SAXONY-ANHALT
Stendal
ALTMARK
Salzwedel
Havel
Rathenow
Falkensee
Berlin
BERLIN
Oranienburg
Strausberg
Potsdam
Brandenburg
Fürstenwalde
Frankfurt
Schönefeld
Oder-Spree Canal
Eisenhüttenstadt
Luckenwalde
Spree
Prague
0 40 80 mi
0 60 120 km
©1996, Encyclopædia Britannica, Inc.

a founding member of the Warsaw Pact 1955; constructed wall along East Berlin-West Berlin border in order to stem flight of its citizens to West; signed 20-year friendship treaty with U.S.S.R. 1964; participated with other Warsaw Pact members in invasion of Czechoslovakia 1968; diplomatic recognition not granted by most noncommunist governments until the early 1970s; signed treaty of cooperation with West Germany 1972; joined UN 1973; civil unrest and decreasing Soviet influence led to mass emigration, demonstrations, and ultimately the dismantling of the Communist government, 1989–90; first free elections held Mar. 1990; reunited with West Germany Oct. 3, 1990.

Germany, West; *officially* **Federal Republic of Germany.** Former republic, W cen. Europe, bounded on N by North Sea and Denmark, on E by East Germany and Czechoslovakia, on SE by Austria, on S by Austria and Switzerland, on SW by France, and on W by Luxembourg, Belgium, and the Netherlands; 95,936 sq. mi. (248,474 sq. km.); pop. (1989e) 62,259,700; ✱ Bonn.

Political divisions: Divided into the following 10 states (*Länder*)—for pronunciation of their names, see their individual entries: Baden-Württemburg, Bavaria, Bremen, Hamburg, Hesse, Lower Saxony, North Rhine-Westphalia, Rhineland-Palatinate, Saarland, Schleswig-Holstein.

History: For history prior to 1945, see GERMANY. Establishment of federal republic 1949; gained sovereignty and became member of NATO 1955; Saarland united with West Germany as 10th state 1957; member of the European Economic Community and of the European Atomic Energy Community 1958; signed friendship treaty with France 1963; signed nonaggression treaties with U.S.S.R. and Poland (1970) and Czechoslovakia (1973) that recognized inviolability of existing European frontiers; signed treaty of cooperation with Democratic Republic 1972; joined UN 1973; during 1980s played important role in European Community (EC), presented reunification plan to Democratic Republic 1989; reunited with former Democratic Republic Oct. 3, 1990.

Ger·mis·ton \ˈjər-mə-stən\. City, Gauteng prov., NE Rep. of South Africa, 9 mi. (14 km.) E of Johannesburg; pop. (1985c) 116,718; goldfields; world's largest gold refinery; engineering; textiles, chemicals.

Ge·rol·stein \ˈger-əl-ˈshtīn\. Village, Rhineland-Palatinate, Germany, 28 mi. (45 km.) N of Trier; pop. (1980c) 6680; health resort.

Ge·ro·na \hā-ˈrō-nä\. **1.** Municipality, NE cen. Tarlac prov., Luzon, Philippines, 10 mi. (16 km.) N of the municipality of Tarlac; pop. (1980c) 50,433.

2. Province of NE Spain. See table at SPAIN.

3. *or* **Gi·ro·na** \hē-ˈrō-nä\; *anc.* **Ge·run·da** \jə-ˈrən-də\. Fortified commune, ✱ of Gerona prov., NE Spain, 52 mi. (84 km.) NE of Barcelona; pop. (1991c) 68,656; textiles, chemicals; 13th cent. Gothic cathedral; under Moorish rule during 8th cent.; became principality under kingdom of Aragon; often besieged by both Spain and France in 17th–18th cent. wars.

Ger·ra *or* **Ger·rha** \ˈjer-ə\. Ancient port on SW coast of Sinus Persicus (Persian Gulf); mentioned by Greek geographer Strabo and Roman scholar Pliny the Elder; site probably at modern Oqair, Saudi Arabia.

Gers \ˈzher\. **1.** River, SW France; flows N into Garonne River near Agen; 111 mi. (179 km.) long.

2. Department of SW France. See table at FRANCE.

Ger·sau \ˈger-ˌzau̇\. Village, Schwyz canton, E cen. Switzerland, on Lake of Lucerne; pop. (1980c) 1702; resort.

Gersoppa, Falls of. See JOG FALLS.

Gerunda. See GERONA 3.

Geserich, Lake. See JEZIORAK.

Ge·shur \ˈgē-shər\. Region in ancient Palestine from NE shore of Sea of Galilee E to Bashan; in the time of King David an Aramaean kingdom (*2 Sam.* xiii. 37).

Gesoriacum *or* **Gessoriacum.** See BOULOGNE.

Ge·ta·fe \hā-ˈtä-fā\. Commune, Madrid prov., cen. Spain, ab. 20 mi. (32 km.) S of the city of Madrid; pop. (1991p) 138,704; nearby is the geographical center of Spain.

Geth·sem·a·ne \geth-ˈse-mə-nē\. The enclosure or garden on the Mount of Olives outside of Jerusalem (*q.v.*) which was the scene of the agony and arrest of Jesus (*Matt.* xxvi. 36–47).

Get·tys·burg \ˈge-tēz-ˌbərg\. **1.** Borough, ⊗ of Adams co., S Pennsylvania, 30 mi. (48 km.) WSW of York; pop. (1990c) 7025; tourism; Lutheran Theological Seminary (1826), Gettysburg Coll. (1832). Laid out in 1780s; became ⊗ 1800; incorp. 1806; scene of battle July 1–3, 1863, in which Union forces under Gen. George G. Meade defeated Confederates under Gen. Robert E. Lee, stopping Lee's invasion of the North (see CEMETERY RIDGE); scene of President Abraham Lincoln's Gettysburg Address, Nov. 19, 1863; site now comprising **Gettysburg National Military Park** (see UNITED STATES, *National Historical Parks*).

2. City, ⊗ of Potter co., N cen. South Dakota; pop. (1990c) 1510.

Ge·vels·berg \ˈgā-fəls-ˌberk\. City, North Rhine-Westphalia, Germany, 32 mi. (51 km.) NE of Cologne; pop. (1992e) 33,591.

Gev·ge·li·ja \gev-ˈge-lē-yä\ *also* **Djev·dje·li·ja** \dyev-ˈdye-lē-yä\. Town, SE Republic of Macedonia, on Vardar River at Greek border.

Gex \ˈzheks\. Town, Ain dept., E France, 10 mi. (16 km.) NNW of Geneva, Switzerland; in the **Pa·ys de Gex** \pā-ˌē-də-\, region bet. Alps and Jura Mts., at different times under control of counts of Geneva, dukes of Savoy, and Switzerland, ceded to France 1601.

Ge·yik Da·ğı \ge-ˈyēk-dä-ˈē\. Peak, SW Turkey in Asia, E of Gulf of Antalya; 10,270 ft. (3130 m.).

Gey·sir \ˈgā-sir\ *or Eng.* **Great Gey·ser** \ˈgī-zər, *Brit. sometimes* ˈgā- *or* ˈgē-\. Inactive geyser in SW cen. Iceland; active for short while following earthquake 1896.

Ge·zer \ˈgē-zər\. Ancient Canaanite city; Israel, ab. 6 mi. (10 km.) S of Lod, at Tel Gezer; excavations have revealed evidence of occupation from Paleolithic period until c. 10th cent. B.C.

Ge·zi·ra \jə-ˈzē-rə\ *or* **El Gezira** \ˌel-\ *or* **Al-Ja·zī·rah** \ˌal-jə-ˈzē-rə\. Region, E cen. Sudan, bet. Blue Nile and White Nile rivers; an irrigated plain producing cotton, peanuts, and other crops.

Gezira, El. See BLUE NILE 2.

Ghadāmis \gə-ˈdä-mes\ *or* **Gha·da·mes** *or* **Ghu·da·mis** \gə-ˈdä-mis\. Oasis and town, NW Libya, on Libya-Algeria boundary; pop. (1981e) 30,000.

Ghaem Shahr \ˈgīm-ˈshär\; *formerly* **Shā·hī** \shä-ˈhē\. Town, Māzandarān prov., N Iran, ab. 94 mi. (151 km.) NE of Tehran; pop. (1986c) 109,288.

Ghā·gha·ra \ˈgä-gə-rə\; *formerly* **Gog·ra** \ˈgō-grə\. River, N India, Nepal, and China; rises in SW Tibet, China, flows S through the Himalayas in Nepal, then SE in Uttar Pradesh, India into the Ganges near Chapra on NW Bihar border; ab. 570 mi. (915 km.) long. In Nepal called the **Kar·na·li** \kär-ˈnä-lē\ *also* **Kau·ri·ala** \ˌkau̇-rē-ˈä-lə\.

Gha·na \ˈgä-nə, ˈga-\. **1.** *or* **Ga·na** \ˈgä-nə\. Ancient and medieval kingdom in W Sahara, Africa.

2. *formerly* **Gold Coast.** Republic, W Africa, bounded on NW and N by Burkina Faso, on E by Togo, on S by the Gulf of Guinea, and on W by Ivory Coast; 92,100 sq. mi. (238,539 sq. km.); pop. (1993e) 15,636,000; ✱ Accra.

Physical features: Generally flat; highest peak Mt. Afadjato 2905 ft. (885 m.), in SE; traversed by Volta River; major lake: Lake Volta; N area characterized by grassland plains, S part heavily forested.

Chief products: Cocoa, palm oil, cassava, corn; fish; bauxite, diamonds, gold, manganese.

Chief towns: Accra, Kumasi, Tamale, Tema.

Political divisions: Divided into the following 10 regions (for pronunciation of their names, see their individual entries):

NAME	AREA (sq. mi.)	AREA (sq. km.)	POP. (1984c)	CAPITAL
Ashanti	9,417	24,390	2,090,100	Kumasi
Brong-Ahafo	15,273	39,557	1,206,608	Sunyani
Central	3,815	9,881	1,142,335	Cape Coast
Eastern	7,698	19,938	1,680,890	Koforidua
Greater Accra	995	2,577	1,431,099	Accra
Northern	27,175	70,383	1,164,583	Tamale
Upper East	3,414	8,842	772,744	Bolgatanga
Upper West	7,134	18,477	438,008	Wa
Volta	7,943	20,572	1,211,907	Ho
Western	9,236	23,921	1,157,807	Sekondi-Takoradi

History: Akan states founded 13th cent.; Ashanti empire estab. in S by 18th cent.; visited by Portuguese traders who founded Elmina 1482; a center for slave trade which was carried on by rival Dutch, English, French, and Danish companies; became British crown colony 1874; frontier with Togoland determined by treaties with Germany late 19th cent.; British protectorates estab. in Ashanti (*q.v.*) and Northern Territories 1901 and annexed to Gold Coast colony 1902; British trust territory of Togo united with Gold Coast 1956; achieved independence as Ghana 1957; estab. republic 1960; civilian government overthrown in coup d'état 1966, restored 1969, again overthrown 1972; military regime overthrown 1978; control seized by Jerry Rawlings 1979 who was elected president in the free election of 1992.

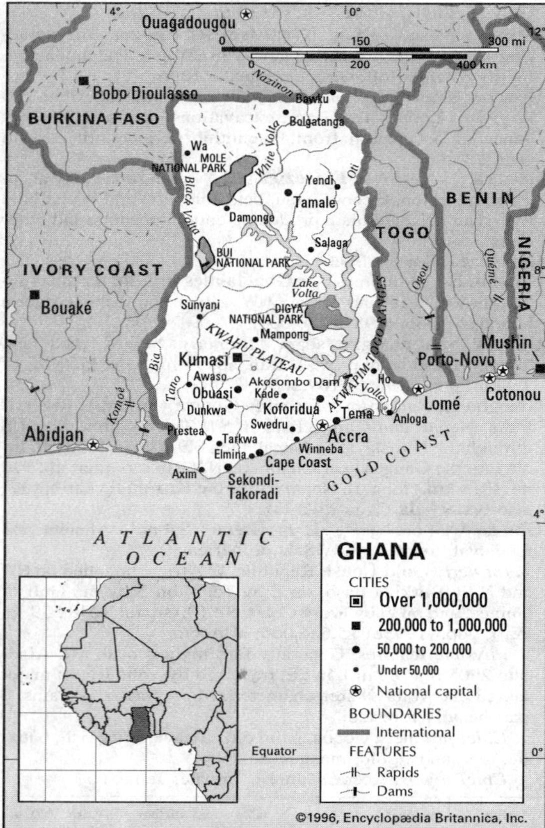

Ghan·si \ˈgän-sē\ *or* **Ghan·zi** \ˈgän-zē\ *or* **Ghan·si·land** \-ˌland\ *also* **Khan·zi** \ˈkän-zē\. Plateau region, NW Kalahari Desert, Botswana; on NE is Lake Ngami, on W Namibia.

Ghār al–Milḥ \ˈgär-ȧl-ˈmilk̲\; *formerly* **Por·to Fa·ri·na** \ˈpōr-tō-fȧ-ˈrē-nä\. Town, Tunisia, ab. 20 mi. (32 km.) E of Bizerte on a lagoon; pirate ships bombarded by English Adm. Robert Blake 1655; ruins of ancient Utica (*q.v.*) 10 mi. (16 km.) to the SE.

Gharapuri. See ELEPHANTA.

Gharaq as–Sultani, Al–. See AL-GHARAQ AS-SULTANI.

Ghar·bī·ya *or* **Gar·bi·eh** \gär-ˈbē-ə, gər-\. Governorate of N Lower Egypt. See table at EGYPT.

Ghar·da·ïa \gär-ˈdä-yə\ *also* **Gar·daia** \gär-ˈdī-ə\. Commune, Algeria, 300 mi. (483 km.) S of Algiers; pop. (1987p) 89,415.

Ghā·rib, Ge·bel \ˈje-bəl-ˈgär-ib\. Mountain, E Egypt, near S end of Gulf of Suez SW of **Ras Ghārib** \ˈräs\, point on the gulf; 5745 ft. (1751 m.).

Ghāt *or* **Ghat** \ˈgät\. Town and oasis, SW Libya; near Algerian border.

Ghats, Eastern *and* **Western Ghats** \ˈgȯts\. Two mountain ranges in S India: **Eastern Ghats** (av. height 1500 to 2000 ft. or 460 to 610 m.) extending for ab. 500 mi. (800 km.) along SE and E coast as far N as mouth of Mahanadi River; **Western Ghats** (av. height 3000 to 5000 ft. or 910 to 1520 m.) extending 800 mi. (1290 km.) along SW and W coast as far N as mouth of Tapti River; bet. them is the Deccan (*q.v.*).

Ghaudex *or* **Ghawdex.** See GOZO.

Gha·zi·a·bad \ˈgä-zē-ə-ˌbäd\. Town, N India, ab. 7 mi. (11 km.) NE of New Delhi; pop. (1991c) 454,156.

Gha·zi·pur \ˈgä-zi-ˌpu̇r\. Town, SE Uttar Pradesh, N India, on Ganges River 40 mi. (64 km.) ENE of Varanasi; pop. (1991p) 77,069; former licensed center for collecting and processing opium; has perfume distilleries. Important during British rule; burial place of Indian governor-general, Lord Charles Cornwallis (d. 1805).

Ghaz·nī *or* **Ghaz·ni** \ˈgäz-nē\. City, E Afghanistan, 92 mi. (148 km.) SW of Kabul; pop. (1988e) 35,900; trades in corn, fruit, and wool.

History: Estab. by the 7th cent.; ruled by the Muslim Ghaznavid dynasty 10th to mid-12th cents.; its most famous ruler was Maḥmūd of Ghazna who conquered neighboring regions and made the city ✳ of a kingdom extending from the Tigris to the Ganges early 11th cent.; under Ghūrids (inhabitants of Ghūr, now NW Afghanistan) by mid-12th cent.; taken by Ögödei, son of Genghis Khan, early 13th cent. Declined politically under the Moguls of India until 1747 when it became part of new Afghan kingdom; in Afghan Wars of 19th cent. captured by British; strategic target during Afghanistan War 1979–92.

Ghazzah *or* **Ghazze.** See GAZA.

Gheel. See GEEL.

Ghent \ˈgent\ *or Flemish* **Gent** \ˈkent\ *or Fr.* **Gand** \ˈgäⁿ\. Commercial city, ✳ of East Flanders prov., NW cen. Belgium, at confluence of Schelde and Leie rivers and at junction of several canals; pop. (1991c) 230,246; metallurgical industries, textiles, chemicals; fortifications; occupies a number of islands connected by bridges; important port; a center of flower-seed and bulb market; cathedral of St. Bavo has many notable works of art incl. the van Eyck brothers' *Adoration of the Lamb* altarpiece; university (1817). Scene of signing of Pacification of Ghent Nov. 8, 1576, which united the provinces of the Low Countries against Spain, and of Treaty of Ghent Dec. 24, 1814, marking end of War of 1812 bet. Great Britain and U.S.; occupied by Germans in both World Wars.

Gheor·ghe Gheor·ghiu–Dej \ˈgyȯr-gyə-gyȯr-ˈgyü-ˈdezh\. Town, Bacău co., E cen. Romania, ab. 25 mi. (40 km.) SSW of the city of Bacău; pop. (1989c) 57,057; chemicals.

Ghe·ri·ah \ˈgar-ē-ə\. Locality, Maharashtra state, India, S of Bombay; site of pirate stronghold reduced by British Baron Robert Clive 1756.

Ghilan. See GĪLĀN.

Ghor \ˈgȯr\ *or* **Ghūr** \ˈgu̇r\. Ancient kingdom, SW Asia, in what is now NW Afghanistan. Closely connected with Ghaznavid dynasty by 11th cent. A.D.; taken by its greatest ruler Mu'izz-ud-Din Muḥammed of Ghūr, who conquered all N India (1186–1206).

Ghor, The. The valley of the Dead Sea and lower Jordan River, Israel and Jordan; 4 to 12 mi. (6 to 19 km.) wide, ab. 65 mi. (105 km.) long.

Ghubbat al Qamar. See QAMAR, GHUBBAT AL.

Ghudamis. See GHADĀMIS.

Ghurdaqah, Al. See AL GHURDAQAH.

Gia Dinh \ˈzhä-ˈdin\. Town, S Vietnam, just N of Ho Chi Minh City.

Gian·nu·tri \jän-ˈnü-trē\. Small island in Tyrrhenian Sea off SW coast of Tuscany, cen. Italy.

Gi·ant Mountain \ˈjī-ənt\. Peak in the Adirondack Mts., Essex co., NE New York; 4622 ft. (1409 m.).

Giant Mountains. See RIESENGEBIRGE.

Gi·ant's Castle \ˈjī-ənts\. Peak in Drakensberg, E Rep. of South Africa, on border bet. Lesotho and KwaZulu-Natal; 10,902 ft. (3323 m.).

Giant's Causeway. Formation of prismatic basaltic columns on N coast of Moyle dist., Northern Ireland, making a rough platform extending for 300 yds. (274 m.) along coast and at one point ab. 500 ft. (150 m.) into the sea.

Giar·re \ˈjär-rā\. Commune, Catania prov., E Sicily, Italy, at E foot of Mt. Etna; pop. (1989c) 27,349.

Gia·ve·no \jä-ˈvā-nō\. Commune, Torino prov., Piedmont, NW Italy, 17 mi. (27 km.) SW of Turin; pop. (1981p) 11,265.

Gi·ba·ra \hē-ˈbä-rä\. Municipality, N coast of Holguín prov., E Cuba; pop. (1981p) 66,629; port for town of Holguín; exports esp. bananas. See HOLGUÍN.

Gib·bon Falls \ˈgi-bən\. Waterfall on **Gibbon River,** Yellowstone National Park, NW Wyoming; ab. 80 ft. (24 m.) high.

Gib·e·ah \ˈgi-bē-ə\. Town, ancient Palestine, site now N of Jerusalem in West Bank; residence of Saul, first king of Israel (*1 Sam.* xxii. 6).

Gib·e·on \ˈgi-bē-ən\. **1.** City of Canaan, 6 mi. (10 km.) NW of Jerusalem; the modern village of Al-Jib in West Bank; its inhabitants (Gibeonites) made an alliance with Israelite military leader Joshua but were made slaves (*Josh.* ix. 3–27).
2. Town, S cen. Namibia, on Fish River 180 mi. (290 km.) SSE of Windhoek.

Gi·bral·tar \jə-ˈbrȯl-tər\. **1.** City, Wayne co., SE Michigan, ab. 12 mi. (19 km.) S of Detroit; pop. (1990c) 4297.
2. British colony, a peninsula in S part of Spain; 2.5 mi. (4 km.) long, 2.25 sq. mi. (6 sq. km.); pop. (1981c) 26,479; administrative center Gibraltar (town); British naval and air base.
History: Captured 711 A.D. and fortified by Ṭāriq ibn Ziyād, Moorish invader of Spain; taken by Spanish 1462; captured by British 1704 during War of Spanish Succession and retained by treaty 1713; unsuccessfully besieged by French and Spanish 1779–83; made a British crown colony 1830; strategically important during WWI and WWII; adopted new constitution 1969, maintaining ties with Britain and continuing to allow for extensive self-rule; Spanish claims to colony rejected by Great Britain; Spain closed its border 1969–85; all residents granted British citizenship 1981; sovereignty dispute bet. Spain and United Kingdom continues.

Gibraltar, Bay of *also* **Bay of Al·ge·ci·ras** \ˌäl-hä-ˈthē-räs, ˌal-jə-ˈsir-əs\. Bay in S extremity of Spain, bet. Algeciras and Gibraltar.

Gibraltar, Rock of; *anc.* **Cal·pe** \ˈkal-pē\. Mountain on E end of Strait of Gibraltar, constituting with S part of isthmus linking it with Spain the British colony of Gibraltar; highest point 1398 ft. (426 m.).

Gibraltar, Strait of *also* **Straits of Gibraltar;** *Lat.* **Fre·tum Her·cu·le·um** \ˈfrē-təm-hər-ˈkyü-lē-əm\; *Arab.* **Bab al–Za·kak** \ˈbȧb-äz-zȧ-ˈkȧk, ȧl-zȧ-\. Passage connecting Mediterranean Sea and Atlantic Ocean, bet. Spain and Africa, with Gibraltar and Ceuta on either side at E end, Capes Trafalgar and Spartel at W end; 36 mi. (58 km.) long; ab. 8 mi. (13 km.) wide in narrowest part, ab. 23 mi. (37 km.) in widest. See PILLARS OF HERCULES.

Gibraltar Point. Cape on N side of entrance to the Wash, E cen. England, S of Skegness.

Gib·son \ˈgib-sən\. **1.** Name of counties in two states of the U.S. See tables at INDIANA and TENNESSEE.
2. *or* **Gibson City.** City, ⊗ of Glascock co., E cen. Georgia; pop. (1990c) 679.
3. City, NE cen. Illinois. See GIBSON CITY 2.

Gib·son·burg \ˈgib-sən-ˌbərg\. Village, Sandusky co., N Ohio, 20 mi. (32 km.) SSE of Toledo; pop. (1990c) 2579.

Gibson City. **1.** City, E cen. Georgia. See GIBSON 2.
2. *or* **Gibson.** Residential city, Ford co., NE cen. Illinois, 32 mi. (51 km.) E of Bloomington; pop. (1990c) 3396.

Gibson Dam. Dam across N fork of Sun River in NW cen. Montana; forms **Gibson Reservoir**.

Gibson Desert. Desert, cen. and E Western Australia, Australia, S of Great Sandy Desert; N to S extent ab. 250 mi. (400 km.), E to W extent ab. 520 mi. (840 km.); salt lakes.

Gibson Peak. Mountain in Custer and Saguache cos., S cen. Colorado; 13,729 ft. (4185 m.).

Gib·son·ville \ˈgib-sən-ˌvil\. Town, Alamance and Guilford cos., N cen. North Carolina; pop. (1990c) 3441.

Gid·dings \ˈgi-diŋz\. City, ⊗ of Lee co., cen. Texas, 30 mi. (48 km.) W of Brenham; pop. (1990c) 4093.

Gien \ˈzhyeⁿ\. Commune, Loiret dept., N cen. France, on the Loire 38 mi. (61 km.) ESE of Orléans; 15th cent. castle.

Giens \ˈzhyeⁿ\. Peninsula on SE coast of Var dept., S France, S of Hyères; forms E side of the **Gulf of Giens.**

Giess·bach \ˈgēs-ˌbäk\. Waterfall, SE Bern canton, Switzerland, E of Brienzersee; total drop 1312 ft. (400 m.).

Gies·sen \ˈgēs-ᵊn\. City, cen. Hesse, Germany, on Lahn River 35 mi. (56 km.) N of Frankfurt am Main; pop. (1992e) 73,763; castle ruins (14th cent.); university (1607). Chartered as city 1248; passed to Hesse later in 13th cent.; passed to Hesse-Darmstadt 1604; home and site of laboratory of chemist Justus von Liebig 1824–52.

Gif·horn \ˈgif-ˌhȯrn\. City, Lower Saxony, Germany, 16 mi. (26 km.) N of Brunswick; pop. (1980c) 33,154.

Gi·fu \ˈgē-fü\. **1.** Prefecture, cen. Honshū, Japan; ✻ Gifu; automobiles, chemicals, machinery, textiles. See table at JAPAN.
2. City, its ✻, 20 mi. (32 km.) NNW of Nagoya on Nagara River; pop. (1990p) 410,318; manufactures paperwares (esp. lanterns). Headquarters of Gen. Oda Nobunaga 16th cent.; rebuilt after earthquake 1831; noted for cormorant fishing on the Nagara.

Gi·gan·te \hē-ˈgän-tā\. Mountain, Guanajuato state, cen. Mexico; 10,653 ft. (3247 m.).

Gi·gha \ˈgē-ə\. Small island of the Inner Hebrides, SW Scotland, ab. 3.5 mi. (6 km.) W of Kintyre Penin.

Gi·glio \ˈjē-lyō\; *anc.* **Igil·i·um** \ī-ˈji-lē-əm\. Italian island in Mediterranean Sea off SW coast of Tuscany, cen. Italy; ab. 15 sq. mi. (39 sq. km.), highest point 1634 ft. (498 m.); has two towns: **Giglio Ca·stel·lo** \kä-ˈstel-lō\, on the height, and the port of **Giglio Por·to** \ˈpōr-tō\; granite quarrying began in Roman times.

Gi·hei·na \jē-ˈhā-nə\ *or* **Ju·hay·nah** \jü-\. Town, Sohâg governorate, Upper Egypt, near Nile.

Gihulngan. See GUIHULNGAN.

Gi·jón \kē-ˈkōn\. Seaport, Asturias autonomous community, NW Spain, on Bay of Biscay 16 mi. (26 km.) NE of Oviedo; pop. (1991c) 259,067; good harbor; manufactures glass; exports include iron ore and coal. Founded before Roman times; captured by Moors early 8th cent.; taken from Moors and made ✻ of kingdom of Asturias until 791; port of refuge of Spanish Armada after its defeat by British 1588.

Gi·la \ˈhē-lə\. **1.** River, New Mexico and Arizona; flows from SW New Mexico W across S Arizona to Colorado River near Yuma in SW corner of Arizona; 500 mi. (805 km.) long; its valley is chief habitat of the Gila monster, a large poisonous lizard.
2. County in E cen. Arizona. See table at ARIZONA.

Gila Bend. Town, Maricopa co., SW Arizona, SW of Phoenix at point where Gila River makes a sharp bend westward; pop. (1990c) 1747.

Gila Cliff Dwellings National Monument. See UNITED STATES, *National Monuments.*

Gī·lān *or* **Ghi·lan** *also* **Gui·lan** \ gē-'län\. Province of NW Iran, SW of Caspian Sea. See table at IRAN.

Gil·bert \'gil-bərt\. **1.** Town, Maricopa co., Arizona; pop. (1990c) 29,188; pop. more than quintupled bet. 1980 and 1990.

2. City, St. Louis co., NE Minnesota, 3 mi. (5 km.) ESE of Virginia; pop. (1990c) 1934; former iron-mining center.

3. Seasonally intermittent river, N Queensland, Australia; flows NW into Gulf of Carpentaria; 320 mi. (515 km.) long.

Gilbert and El·lice Islands Colony \'e-lis\. Former British colony in W Pacific Ocean, consisting of the Gilbert Is., Tuvalu, Ocean I., three islands (Tabuaeran, Washington, and Christmas) of the Line Is., and the Phoenix Is.; 283 sq. mi. (733 sq. km.); ✻ Tarawa. The two main groups proclaimed a British protectorate 1892 and made a colony 1915; Fanning I. (now Tabuaeran), Washington I., Christmas I., and Ocean I. (now Banaba) added 1916–19, and the Phoenix group 1937; divided 1976 bet. Gilbert Islands and Ellice Islands territories, now parts of Kiribati and Tuvalu (*qq.v.*).

Gilbert Grosvenor Range. See GROSVENOR MOUNTAINS.

Gilbert Islands. Island group containing 16 atolls, Kiribati, W Pacific Ocean on the Equator, SSE of Marshall Is. and NE of Solomon Is.; 102 sq. mi. (264 sq. km.); pop. (1985c) 63,848; ✻ Tarawa; until 1976 part of British Gilbert and Ellice Islands Colony; most important islands: Tarawa (largest), Butaritari, Abaiang, Abemama, Tabiteuea, Nonouti, and Beru. Islands have long been densely populated.

History: Possibly sighted by Spanish explorers in the 16th cent.; various islands visited by British navigators bet. 1765 and 1824; scene of missionary labors of Hiram Bingham 1857–64, 1873–75. Proclaimed a British protectorate 1892, made part of Gilbert and Ellice Islands Colony 1915; occupied by Japanese 1941–43 (see TARAWA). Made a separate territory 1976; became part of independent Kiribati July 1979. See TUVALU and KIRIBATI.

Gilbert Peak. Mountain in Uinta Mts., NE Utah, bet. Summit and Duchesne cos.; 13,422 ft. (4091 m.).

Gil·boa, Mount \ gil-'bō-ə\. Mountain, Israel, W of the Jordan and S of the Plain of Esdraelon near source of the Qishon; 1631 ft. (497 m.); place where King Saul was defeated by the Philistines and slew himself (*1 Sam.* xxxi. 1, 4).

Gil·christ \'gil-krist\. County in NW peninsula of Florida. See table at FLORIDA.

Gil·e·ad \'gi-lē-əd\. **1.** Mountainous region E of Jordan River in ancient Palestine, extending approx. from the Yarmūk to the Wadi al-Mawjib; now in NW Jordan.

2. Ancient city of the Gilead, S of the Zarqa.

Gilead, Mount. Peak, Jordan, NNE of the Dead Sea; 3597 ft. (1096 m.); in ancient Palestine in cen. Gilead.

Giles \'jīlz\. Name of counties in two states of the U.S. See tables at TENNESSEE and VIRGINIA.

Gil·ford \'gil-fərd\. Town, Belknap co., New Hampshire; pop. (1990c) 5867.

Gil·gal \'gil-,gal\. Name of several places in ancient Palestine, some yet unidentified; esp. village near Jericho, the first encampment of the Israelites W of Jordan River (*Josh.* iv. 19–24).

Gil·git \'gil-gət\. **1.** Region in NW Himalayas; 3118 sq. mi. (8076 sq. km.); under Pakistani control; prior to the partition of India was a district.

2. Town in the region, on **Gilgit River** (tributary of the Indus, ab. 150 mi. or 240 km. long) at elev. of 4890 ft. (1490 m.); once a Buddhist center, now an important strategic station on the highway to Chitral on W and to Hindu Kush passes on N.

Gil·les·pie \ gi-'les-pē\. **1.** County in cen. Texas. See table at TEXAS.

2. City, Macoupin co., SW cen. Illinois, 27 mi. (43 km.) NE of Alton; pop. (1990c) 3645.

Gil·lette \ji-'let\. City, ⊗ of Campbell co., NE Wyoming, 80 mi. (129 km.) ESE of Sheridan; pop. (1990c) 17,635; coal.

Gil·li·am \'gil-yəm\. County in N Oregon. See table at OREGON.

Gil·ling·ham \'ji-liŋ-əm\. Town, Kent, SE England, on the Medway 30 mi. (48 km.) ESE of London; pop. (1991p) 93,300; light industries.

Gillis Island. See KVITØYA.

Gil·ly \ zhē-'lē\. Commune, Hainaut prov., SW Belgium, on the Sambre just E of Charleroi.

Gil·mer \'gil-mər\. **1.** Name of counties in two states of the U.S. See tables at GEORGIA and WEST VIRGINIA.

2. City, ⊗ of Upshur co., NE Texas, 34 mi. (55 km.) NE of Tyler; pop. (1990c) 4822.

Gilolo. See HALMAHERA.

Gī·lo Wenz \'gē-lō-'wents\. River, SW Ethiopia; flows NW into the Pibor River on Sudan border.

Gil·pin \'gil-pin\. County in N cen. Colorado. See table at COLORADO.

Gilpin Peak. Mountain, Ouray and San Miguel cos., SW Colorado; 13,682 ft. (4170 m.).

Gil·roy \'gil-,ròi\. City, Santa Clara co., W California, 30 mi. (48 km.) SE of San Jose; pop. (1990c) 31,487; Gavilan Coll. (1919).

Gi·mie, Mount \ zhē-'mē\. Peak in S cen. St. Lucia I., West Indies; 3117 ft. (950 m.).

Gimma. See JIMA.

Gin·chy \ zhe^n-'shē\. Village, Somme dept., N France, 25 mi. (40 km.) NE of Amiens; captured by British in battle of the Somme Sept. 9, 1916.

Ginevra. Italian form of Geneva, Switzerland. See GENEVA.

Gin·go·og \ hēŋ-'gō-,òg\. Chartered city, E Misamis Oriental prov., N Mindanao, Philippines; pop. (1990p) 82,000; on S shore of **Gingoog Bay,** inlet of Mindanao Sea ab. 22 mi. (35 km.) wide at mouth.

Gi·no·wan \ gē-'nō-wän\. City, Okinawa prefecture, on Okinawa I., Japan; pop. (1990p) 75,899.

Gin·seng Mountain \'jin-,seŋ\. Peak in the Catskill Mts., SE New York; 3790 ft. (1155 m.).

Gin·za \'gēn-zä\. Street and surrounding district, Tokyo, Japan; a popular shopping and entertainment area.

Giofra. See AL JUFRAH.

Gio·ia del Col·le \'jò-yä-del-'kòl-lā\. Commune, Bari prov., Puglia, SE Italy, 20 mi. (32 km.) SE of the seaport of Bari; pop. (1989c) 27,621; 12th cent. castle.

Gio·io·sa Io·ni·ca \ jō-'yō-sä-'yò-nē-kä\. Commune, Reggio di Calabria prov., S Calabria, S Italy, on Ionian Sea; pop. (1981p) 6750; beaches.

Gio·vi·naz·zo \ ,jō-vē-'nät-sō\. Seaport, Bari prov., Puglia, SE Italy, on Adriatic Sea 10 mi. (16 km.) WNW of the seaport of Bari; pop. (1981p) 19,001; episcopal see (from 951).

Gio·vi·net·to, Mount \ ,jō-vē-'net-tō\. Mountain, Antarctica, 78°16′S, 86°10′W; 13,412 ft. (4088 m.).

Giovi. Pass, Apennines. See table at APENNINES.

Gipps·land \'gips-,land\. Region, SE coast of Victoria, SE Australia; ab. 14,000 sq. mi. (36,260 sq. km.); chief town Sale; fertile, rich in minerals; includes **Gippsland Lakes.**

Gi–ran. See I-LAN 2.

Gi·rard \ jə-'rärd\. **1.** City, ⊗ of Crawford co., SE Kansas, 10 mi. (16 km.) NW of Pittsburg; pop. (1990c) 2794.

2. City, Trumbull co., NE Ohio, NW of Youngstown; pop. (1990c) 11,304.

3. Borough, Erie co., NW corner of Pennsylvania, on Lake Erie 16 mi. (26 km.) WSW of the city of Erie; pop. (1990c) 2879.

Gi·rar·dot \ ,kē-,rär-'thòt\. City, Cundinamarca dept., cen. Colombia, ab. 50 mi. (80 km.) SE of Bogotá; pop. (1985c) 70,991; coffee.

Gi·rard·ville \ jə-'rärd-,vil\. Borough, Schuylkill co., E cen. Pennsylvania, 9 mi. (14 km.) NNW of Pottsville; pop. (1990c) 1889.

Gir·dle Ness \'gərd-ᵊl-'nes\. Headland on E cen. coast of Scotland, 2 mi. (3.2 km.) S of Aberdeen; lighthouse.

Gi·re·sun \ ,gē-re-'sün\ *or* **Ke·ra·sun** \ ,ke-rä-\. **1.** Province of Turkey in Asia. See table at TURKEY.

2. *to Romans* **Cer·a·sus** \'ser-ə-səs\; *to anc. Greeks* **Phar·na·cia** \ fär-'nā-shə, -shē-ə\. Seaport, its ✻, on the

Black Sea 70 mi. (113 km.) W of Trabzon; pop. (1990p) 67,536; exports hides, nuts, timber; site of Byzantine fortress.

Gir·ga \ˈgir-gə\ *or* **Jir·jā** \ˈjir-jä\ *also* **Gir·geh** \ˈgir-gə\. City, Egypt, on the Nile SE of Sohâg; noted for pottery; site of ancient Coptic monastery and one of the oldest Roman Catholic monasteries in Egypt.

Girgenti. See AGRIGENTO.

Gi·ri·dih \ˈgir-i-dē\. Town, E Bihar, NE India, 170 mi. (274 km.) NW of Calcutta; pop. (1991p) 77,912.

Gi·rishk \gi-ˈrishk\. Town, S cen. Afghanistan, on Helmand River 75 mi. (121 km.) WNW of Kandahār; center of rich agricultural district.

Gir·nar Hills \gir-ˈnär\. Mountains, India. See JUNAGADH.

Girne. See KYRENIA.

Girona. See GERONA 3.

Gi·ronde \zhē-ˈrōⁿd, ji-ˈränd\. **1.** Estuary on W coast of France, formed by confluence of Garonne and Dordogne rivers near Bordeaux; extends 45 mi. (72 km.) inland.

2. Department of SW France. See table at FRANCE.

Gir·van \ˈgər-vən\. Seaport burgh, Strathclyde region, SW Scotland, 17 mi. (27 km.) SSW of Ayr at mouth of Firth of Clyde; pop. (1981p) 7878; tourism; fishing port.

Gis·borne \ˈgiz-bərn\. Seaport city, E North I., New Zealand, on Poverty Bay; pop. (1992e) 31,400; first landing site in New Zealand of English explorer Capt. James Cook 1769.

Gi·sors \zhē-ˈzȯr\. Commune, Eure dept., N France, 20 mi. (32 km.) NW of Paris; pop. (1990c) 9673; as medieval ✻ of the Vexin dist. on frontier of Normandy was subject of many disputes bet. English and French 12th. cent.; ruins of 11th–12th cent. castle; 13th–16th cent. church.

Gi·te·ga \gē-ˈtā-gä\. Town, cen. Burundi, E of Bujumbura; pop. (1990c) 101,827.

Gitschin. See JIČÍN.

Giuba. See JUBBA .

Giuba, Oltre. See JUBALAND.

Giu·dec·ca \jü-ˈdek-kä\ *or* **La Giudecca** \lä-\. Long, narrow island, forming S part of city of Venice, Italy; separated from main island by channel, **Ca·na·le del·la Giudecca** \kä-ˈnä-lā-ˌdel-lä-\; 16th cent. church designed by Andrea Palladio.

Giu·glia·no in Cam·pa·nia \jü-ˈlyä-nō-in-käm-ˈpä-nyä\. Commune, Napoli prov., Campania, S Italy, 6 mi. (10 km.) NNW of Naples; pop. (1989c) 57,041.

Giu·lia·no·va \ˌjü-lyä-ˈnȯ-vä\. Commune, Teramo prov., Abruzzi, cen. Italy, on Adriatic Sea 16 mi. (26 km.) ENE of the commune of Teramo; pop. (1989c) 22,548.

Giu·lie, Al·pi \ˈäl-pē-ˈjül-yā\. See *Julian Alps* in table at ALPS.

Giur·giu \ˈjür-jü\ *or Bulg.* **Giur·ge·vo** \ˈju̇r-jā-ˌvȯ\. **1.** County of S Romania. See table at ROMANIA.

2. City, its ✻, on the Danube; munic. pop. (1989c) 72,275; shipyards; food processing; construction materials, chemicals, textiles; ruins of medieval fortress.

Gi·vet \zhē-ˈvā\. Commune, Ardennes dept., NE France, near Belgian frontier; divided by the Meuse River into **Grand–Givet** \ˈgräⁿ-\ and **Pe·tit–Givet** \pə-ˈtē-\.

Gi·za \ˈgē-zə\ *or* **El Gîza** \el-ˈgē-zə\ *or* **Al Jīzah** \ȧl-ˈjē-zə\. **1.** Governorate of Upper Egypt. See table at EGYPT.

2. City, its ✻, on W bank of the Nile near Cairo; pop. (1991e) 2,096,000; cotton textiles, footwear; brewing; motion-picture industry; 5 mi. (8 km.) W lie the Great Sphinx and the three pyramids built during Egypt's IVth dynasty, c. 26th cent. B.C.: The Great Pyramid, built by Khufu (or Cheops), 2nd king of the dynasty; the smaller pyramid of Khafra (or Chephren), 4th king; and the smallest and most perfect of the three, built by Menkure (or Mycerinus).

Gi·zo \ˈgē-zō\. Small island of the New Georgia Is., cen. Solomon Is., W Pacific Ocean, bet. Ganongga I. and Kolombangara I.

Gi·życ·ko \gi-ˈzhit-skȯ\ *or Ger.* **Löt·zen** \ˈlœt-sən\. City, W Suwałki prov., N Poland, at S end of Lake Mamry; pop. (1989e) 28,868.

Gjels·vik Peak \ˈgēls-vik\. Peak, Antarctica, 85°19′S, 167°54′W; 12,008 ft. (3660 m.).

Gji–i–Vlorës. See VLORË, BAY OF.

Gji·ro·kas·tër \ˌgyi-rō-ˈkäs-tər\ *or* **Gji·no·kas·tër** \ˌgyē-nō-\ *or Gk.* **Ar·gy·ro·ka·stron** \ˌär-yē-ˈrō-kä-ˌstrōn\ *or Ital.* **Ar·gi·ro·ca·stro** \ˌär-jē-ˈrȯ-kä-ˌstrō\. **1.** District of S Albania. See table at ALBANIA.

2. Town, its ✻; pop. (1990e) 24,900; under Turkish rule 15th cent. until taken by Greece 1913; occupied successively by Italy, Greece, and Germany during WWII; birthplace of Albanian Communist party leader Enver Hoxha 1908.

Gjø·vik \ˈyœ-vik\. Town, Oppland co., S cen. Norway, on Lake Mjøsa; pop. (1990c) 26,083.

Gju·hë·zës, Cape \ju̇-ˈhə-ˌzəs\; *formerly* **Cape Lin·guet·ta** \liŋ-ˈgwe-tä\ *or* **Cape Glos·sa** \ˈglȯ-sä\. Cape and promontory, SW Albania, 40°25′N, 19°18′E.

Glace Bay \ˈglās\. Town, Cape Breton co., E Nova Scotia, Canada, on Atlantic Ocean 12 mi. (19 km.) E of Sydney; pop. (1991c) 19,501; fishing; formerly mined coal.

Gla·cier \ˈglā-shər\. County in NW Montana. See table at MONTANA.

Glacier Bay. Narrow inlet of Pacific Ocean in N part of SE Alaska, NE extension of Cross Sound; ab. 60 mi. (97 km.) long; in center of **Glacier Bay National Park** (see UNITED STATES, *National Parks*).

Glacier National Park. **1.** National park, NW Montana. See UNITED STATES, *National Parks*.

2. National park, SE British Columbia, Canada. See CANADA, *National Parks*.

Glacier Peak. Mountain, E Snohomish co., NW cen. Washington; 10,541 ft. (3213 m.).

Gla·ciers, Ai·guille des \ā-ˈgwē-ˌdā-glȧ-ˈsyä\. Mountain in the Alps, France, just SW of Mont Blanc; 12,517 ft. (3815 m.).

Glad·beck \ˈglät-ˌbek\. City, North Rhine-Westphalia, Germany, 22 mi. (35 km.) WNW of Dortmund; pop. (1992e) 80,127.

Glades \ˈglādz\. County in S cen. peninsula of Florida. See table at FLORIDA.

Glade·wa·ter \ˈglād-ˌwȯ-tər, -ˌwä-\. City, Gregg and Upshur cos., NE Texas, 25 mi. (40 km.) ENE of Tyler; pop. (1990c) 6027.

Glad·sak·se \ˈgläth-ˌsäk-sə\. Commune, Sjælland I., Denmark; pop. (1989e) 61,198.

Glad·stone \ˈglad-ˌstōn\. **1.** City, Delta co., S Upper Penin., Michigan, on W side of Little Bay de Noc 8 mi. (13 km.) N of Escanaba; pop. (1990c) 4565.

2. City, Clay co., NW Missouri, N of Kansas City; pop. (1990c) 26,243.

3. City, Clackamas co., NW Oregon, on Clackamas River ab. 4 mi. (6 km.) S of Portland; pop. (1990c) 10,152.

Glad·stone \ˈglad-ˌstōn, -stən\. Town, E Queensland, Australia, on Pacific Ocean 270 mi. (434 km.) NNW of Brisbane; pop. (1981c) 22,712; aluminum; named for British statesman and prime minister William Ewart Gladstone, mid-19th cent.

Gladstone Peak. Mountain, Dolores and San Miguel cos., SW Colorado; 13,900 ft. (4237 m.).

Glad·win \ˈglad-win\. **1.** County in cen. Michigan. See table at MICHIGAN.

2. City, its ⊗, 30 mi. (48 km.) NNE of Mount Pleasant; pop. (1990c) 2682; lake resort.

Glå·ma \ˈglȯ-mə\. River, E Norway; rises in Dovrefjell Plateau; flows S into Skagerrak at Fredrikstad; 380 mi. (611 km.) long; longest river in Norway.

Gla·mis \ˈglämz; ˈglä-məs, ˈgla-\. Village, E Tayside region, E Scotland, N of Dundee; 17th cent. castle on site of an 11th cent. settlement.

Gla·mor·gan·shire \glə-ˈmȯr-gən-ˌshir, -shər\ *or* **Gla·mor·gan.** Former county, S Wales; ⊗ Cardiff; rivers Taff, Neath, Tawe; divided (1974) into new counties of **Mid Glamorgan, South Glamorgan,** and **West Glamorgan.**

Gla·mu·jö·kull \ˈglau̇-mü-ˌyœ-ˌku̇l\. Glacier in NW Iceland.

Gla·rus \ˈglä-ru̇s\. **1.** Canton, Switzerland. See table at SWITZERLAND.

2. Commune, its ✻, E cen. Switzerland, 36 mi. (58 km.) E of Lucerne; pop. (1989c) 5623; reformer Huldrych Zwingli parish priest here 1506–16.

Glas·cock \ˈglas-ˌkäk\. County in E cen. Georgia. See table at GEORGIA.

Glas·gow \ˈglas-gō\. **1.** City, ⊗ of Barren co., S Kentucky, 30 mi. (48 km.) E of Bowling Green; pop. (1990c) 12,351.

2. City, ⊗ of Valley co., NE Montana, 15 mi. (24 km.) NNW of Fort Peck Dam on Missouri River; pop. (1990c) 3572.

Glas·gow \ˈgläz-gō, ˈglaz-, ˈgläs-, ˈglas-\. City, ⊗ of Strathclyde region, W cen. Scotland, WSW of Edinburgh, on both banks of the Clyde; pop. (1993e) 681,470; the largest city in Scotland; seaport, extensive docks; textiles; engineering; 13th cent. cathedral; Univ. of Glasgow (1451), Univ. of Strathclyde (1964); museums; libraries; art galleries; botanical gardens.

History: According to tradition, settled 6th cent. by St. Kentigern (St. Mungo); chartered 12th cent.; became royal burgh 1450; prosperous commercial center from 18th cent., developed shipbuilding and iron industries 19th cent.

Glass·boro \ˈglas-ˌbər-ō\. Borough, Gloucester co., SW New Jersey, 17 mi. (27 km.) S of Camden; pop. (1990c) 15,614; settled by German glassmakers 1775; Glassboro State Coll. (1923), Rowan Coll. of New Jersey (1923); scene of meeting between U.S. President Lyndon Johnson and Soviet Premier Aleksey Kosygin 1967.

Glass·cock \ˈglas-ˌkäk\. County in W Texas. See table at TEXAS.

Glass Mountains \ˈglas\. Range, N Brewster co., W Texas; highest peak 6487 ft. (1977 m.).

Glass·port \ˈglas-ˌpōrt\. Borough, Allegheny co., SW Pennsylvania, on Monongahela River 10 mi. (16 km.) SSE of Pittsburgh; pop. (1990c) 5582.

Glas·ten·bury Mountain \ˈglas-tən-ˌber-ē\. Mountain, Bennington co., SW Vermont; 3748 ft. (1142 m.).

Glas·ton·bury. **1.** \ˈglas-tən-ˌber-ē\. Town, SE Hartford co., N Connecticut, 5.5 mi. (9 km.) SE of Hartford; pop. (1990c) 27,901; settled 1650; incorp. 1690.

2. \ˈglas-tən-ˌber-ē, -bə-rē\. Town, Somerset, SW England; pop. (1981p) 6773. Iron Age artifacts excavated from nearby mounds; site of early Christian abbey, rebuilt 12th–14th cents.; important pilgrimage site 16th cent.

Glatz. See KŁODZKO.

Glatzer Neisse. See NYSA 1.

Glau·chau \ˈglau̇-ˌkau̇\. City, Saxony, E Germany, on Mulde River 16 mi. (26 km.) W of Chemnitz; pop. (1981c) 29,762.

Gla·zov \ˈglȧ-zəf\. Town, N Udmurtia, E Russia in Europe, ab. 120 mi. (195 km.) E of Vyatka; pop. (1992e) 107,000.

Gleiwitz. See GLIWICE.

Glen·ar·den \glen-ˈär-dən\. Town, Prince Georges co., S cen. Maryland; pop. (1990c) 5025.

Glen·brook \ˈglen-ˌbru̇k\. Subdivision of town of Stamford, Connecticut; residential.

Glen Canyon \ˈglen\. Gorge along the Colorado River, S Utah and N Arizona, above Marble Canyon; site of **Glen Canyon Dam** in Colorado River (see UNITED STATES, *Dams and Reservoirs*).

Glen·coe \ˈglen-ˌkō\. **1.** Town, Etowah co., NE Alabama, 6 mi. (10 km.) E of Gadsden; pop. (1990c) 4670.

2. Residential village, Cook co., NE Illinois, ab. 9 mi. (14 km.) N of Chicago; pop. (1990c) 8499; Chicago Botanical Garden.

3. City, ⊗ of McLeod co., S cen. Minnesota, 45 mi. (72 km.) WSW of Minneapolis; pop. (1990c) 4648.

4. Town, KwaZulu-Natal prov., Rep. of South Africa, NW of Durban.

Glen·coe \glen-ˈkō\ *or* **Glen Coe.** Narrow valley in S Highland region, W Scotland; site of notorious massacre of Macdonald clan of Glencoe by soldiers under Archibald Campbell 1692.

Glen Cove \ˈglen-ˈkōv\. Residential city, Nassau co., SE New York, on N shore of Long Island 22 mi. (35 km.) ENE of New York City; pop. (1990c) 24,149; Webb Institute of Naval Architecture (1889).

Glen·dale \ˈglen-ˌdāl\. **1.** City, Maricopa co., SW cen. Arizona, 8 mi. (13 km.) NW of Phoenix; pop. (1990c) 148,134; trading center for cotton-growing area; Glendale Community Coll. (1965).

2. City, Los Angeles co., SW California, just N of the city of Los Angeles; pop. (1990c) 180,038; occupies part of first Spanish land grant in California (Rancho San Rafael 1784); manufactures airplanes and medical supplies; Glendale Community Coll. (1927); founded 1886.

3. City, St. Louis co., E Missouri, 11 mi. (18 km.) SW of the city of St. Louis; pop. (1990c) 5945.

4. Battlefield, Virginia. See FRAYSER'S FARM.

5. City, Milwaukee co., SE Wisconsin; pop. (1990c) 14,088.

Glendale Heights. Village, Du Page co., NE Illinois, ab. 13 mi. (21 km.) W of Chicago; pop. (1990c) 27,973.

Glen·da·lough, Vale of \ˈglen-də-ˌläk\. Valley in co. Wicklow, E Ireland, containing two small lakes; ruins of several 11th and 12th cent. ecclesiastical structures and the monastery founded by St. Kevin 6th cent.

Glen·dive \ˈglen-ˌdīv\. City, ⊗ of Dawson co., E Montana, on Yellowstone River 72 mi. (116 km.) NE of Miles City; pop. (1990c) 4802; Dawson Community Coll. (1940).

Glen·do·ra \glen-ˈdōr-ə\. City, Los Angeles co., SW California, ab. 17 mi. (27 km.) ENE of the city of Los Angeles; pop. (1990c) 47,828.

Glen·elg \gle-ˈnelg\. **1.** River, W Victoria, SE Australia; flows into Discovery Bay just over the border in South Australia; lower course flows through Lower Glenelg National Park (*q.v.*); 290 mi. (467 km.) long.

2. Suburb of Adelaide, SE South Australia, Australia, on Gulf St. Vincent; pop. (1991c) 4060.

3. Town, Highland region, NW Scotland, on Sound of Sleat.

Glen El·lyn \gle-ˈne-lən\. Village, Du Page co., NE Illinois, ab. 15 mi. (24 km.) W of Chicago; pop. (1990c) 24,944; Coll. of DuPage (1966).

Glen·gar·riff \glen-ˈgar-əf\. Town, SW co. Cork, SW Ireland, on N inlet of Bantry Bay; resort.

Glen·gar·ry \glen-ˈgar-ē\. Former county, of Ontario, Canada; now part of Stormont, Dundas and Glengarry co.

Glen In·nes \ˈi-nis\. Municipality, NE New South Wales, SE Australia, in New England Range; pop. (1991c) 6140.

Glen Ly·on \glen-ˈlī-ən\. Narrow valley, Tayside region, cen. Scotland, N of Loch Tay; ab. 30 mi. (48 km.) long.

Glen More \glen-ˈmōr\ *or in full* **Glen More nan Al·bin** \nän-ˈäl-bin\ **(Great Glen of Scotland).** Valley, Highland region, Scotland, extending from Loch Linnhe on the SW to Moray Firth on the NE; Caledonian Canal lies within it.

Glenn \ˈglen\. County in N California. See table at CALIFORNIA.

Glenn Highway. Highway, S Alaska; running ENE from Anchorage to Copper Center on Richardson Highway; ab. 170 mi. (274 km.) long.

Glenn·ville \ˈglen-ˌvil\. City, Tattnall co., SE cen. Georgia, 50 mi. (80 km.) W of Savannah; pop. (1990c) 3676.

Glen·ol·den \gle-ˈnōl-dən\. Borough, Delaware co., SE Pennsylvania, 8 mi. (13 km.) WSW of Philadelphia; pop. (1990c) 7260.

Glen·or·chy \gle-ˈnȯr-kē\. City, SE Tasmania, Australia, N suburb of Hobart; pop. (1991c) 42,172.

Glen·pool \ˈglen-ˌpül\. City, Tulsa co., NE Oklahoma, S of Tulsa; pop. (1990c) 6688.

Glen Ridge \ˈglen-ˈrij\. Residential borough, Essex co., NE New Jersey, 5 mi. (8 km.) NNW of Newark; pop. (1990c) 7076.

Glen·rock \ˈglen-ˌräk\. Town, Converse co., E Wyoming, on North Platte River; pop. (1990c) 2153.

Glen Rock. Borough, Bergen co., NE corner of New Jersey, 4 mi. (6 km.) NNE of Paterson; pop. (1990c) 10,833.

Glen Rose \ˈglen-ˌrōz\. City, ⊗ of Somervell co., N cen. Texas, 40 mi. (64 km.) SSW of Fort Worth; pop. (1990c) 1949.

Glen·roth·es \glen-ˈrä-this\. Town, ⊗ of Fife region, E Scotland; pop. (1991e) 38,000; electronic products, paper; estab. as a new town 1948.

Glen Roy \glen-ˈrȯi\. Narrow valley in Highland region, NW Scotland, NE of Fort William; noted for its *parallel roads,* horizontal ledges of glacial origin.

Glens Falls \ˈglenz\. City, Warren co., E New York, at falls (60 ft. or 18 m.) in Hudson River 38 mi. (61 km.) NE of Amsterdam; pop. (1990c) 15,023; Adirondack Community Coll. (1961); Hyde Collection of art; settled 1760s; destroyed by British 1780 during the Revolutionary War; incorp. as city 1908. Cooper's Cave (at foot of falls), named for novelist James Fenimore Cooper, setting for an episode of his *The Last of the Mohicans.*

Glen·side \ˈglen-ˌsīd\. Unincorporated settlement, Montgomery co., SE Pennsylvania, N and W of Philadelphia; pop. (1990c) 8704; Beaver Coll. (1853).

Glens of An·trim \ˈglenz ... ˈan-trim\ *also* **Glynns of Antrim** \ˈglinz\. Series of valleys on NE coast of Antrim, Northern Ireland.

Glen·view \ˈglen-ˌvyü\. Village, Cook co., NE Illinois, ab. 4 mi. (6.4 km.) NNW of Chicago; pop. (1990c) 37,093.

Glen·ville \ˈglen-ˌvil\. Town, ⊗ of Gilmer co., cen. West Virginia; pop. (1990c) 1923; Glenville State Coll. (1872).

Glen·wood \ˈglen-ˌwu̇d\. **1.** Village, Cook co., NE Illinois, ab. 7 mi. (11 km.) S of Chicago; pop. (1990c) 9289.

2. City, ⊗ of Mills co., SW Iowa, 18 mi. (29 km.) SSE of Council Bluffs; pop. (1990c) 4571.

3. City, ⊗ of Pope co., W cen. Minnesota, at N end of Lake Minnewaska; pop. (1990c) 2573; summer resort.

Glenwood Springs. City, ⊗ of Garfield co., W Colorado, on Colorado River; pop. (1990c) 6561; Colorado Mountain Coll.–Spring Valley Campus (1967); thermal mineral springs.

Glevum. See GLOUCESTER 7.

Glit·ter·tind \ˈgli-tər-ˌtin\. Peak in the Jotunheimen, S cen. Norway; 8110 ft. (2472 m.); highest peak in Norway.

Gli·wi·ce \gli-ˈvēt-se\ *or Ger.* **Glei·witz** \ˈglī-ˌvits\. City, Katowice prov., SW Poland, 14 mi. (23 km.) W of the city of Katowice; pop. (1989e) 222,084; blast furnaces, coal mines; chemicals; technical university (1945); chartered as city 1276; passed to Prussia 1742; returned to Poland after WWII.

Globe \ˈglōb\. City, ⊗ of Gila co., E cen. Arizona, 70 mi. (113 km.) E of Phoenix; pop. (1990c) 6062; important copper mines; historically important silver, gold, asbestos, manganese, vanadium, and tungsten mining in vicinity; incorp. 1907.

Gloces·ter \ˈgläs-tər, ˈglȯs-\. Town, Providence co., N Rhode Island, near Connecticut border; pop. (1990c) 9227; governmental center Chepachet.

Gloe, Ben–y–. See BEN-Y-GLOE.

Gło·gów \ˈgwȯ-ˌgüf\ *or Ger.* **Glo·gau** \ˈglō-ˌgau̇\. City, N Legnica prov., SW Poland, on Odra (Oder) River; pop. (1989e) 72,064; chartered as city mid-13th cent.; to Prussia 1742; returned to Poland after WWII.

Glo·mach, Falls of \ˈglä-mək\. Waterfall in headstream of the Elchaig, Highland region, Scotland; 370 ft. (113 m.) high.

Glo·rieuses, Îles \ˌēl-glȯr-ˈyœ̄z\ *or Eng.* **Glo·ri·o·so Islands** \ˌglōr-ē-ˈō-sō, -zō\. Group of small French islands in Indian Ocean, WNW of N Madagascar.

Glossa, Cape. See GJUHËZËS, CAPE.

Glos·sop \ˈglä-səp\. Town, Derbyshire, N cen. England, 16 mi. (26 km.) ESE of Manchester; pop. (1981p) 25,339.

Glouces·ter \ˈgläs-tər, ˈglȯs-\. **1.** Name of counties in two states of the U.S. See tables at NEW JERSEY and VIRGINIA.

2. City, Essex co., NE Massachusetts, on coast of Cape Ann 27 mi. (43 km.) NE of Boston; pop. (1990c) 28,716; port of entry; summer resort; important fishing port. Visited by French explorer Samuel de Champlain 1605; settled 1623; incorp. as city 1873; has bronze statue, "Fisherman at the Wheel," by Leonard Craske.

3. Village, ⊗ of Gloucester co., E Virginia.

4. County in NE New Brunswick, Canada. See table at NEW BRUNSWICK.

5. City, SE Ontario, Canada, SSE of Ottawa; pop. (1991c) 101,677.

6. County in England. See GLOUCESTERSHIRE.

7. *anc.* **Gle·vum** \ˈglē-vəm\. County town, ⊗ of Gloucestershire, SW cen. England, on the Severn 94 mi. (151 km.) WNW of London; pop. (1991p) 91,800; distribution point for timber and cereals; late-Gothic cathedral on site of an abbey founded 681. Founded by Roman Emperor Nerva 96–98 A.D.; began early to trade in iron and cloth; incorp. as town 1483; scene of first Sunday school, founded by Robert Raikes 1780.

Gloucester, Cape. Cape at NW corner of New Britain I., Bismarck Archipelago, on Dampier Strait.

Gloucester City. City, Camden co., SW New Jersey, on Delaware River 3 mi. (5 km.) S of the city of Camden; pop. (1990c) 12,649; settled by Irish Quakers 1682; scene of skirmishes during Revolutionary War; incorp. 1868.

Glouces·ter·shire \ˈgläs-tər-ˌshir, ˈglȯs-, -shər\ *or* **Gloucester.** **1.** Former county, SW cen. England.

2. Administrative county, SW cen. England, comprising the former county; rivers Severn, Avon, Wye; chief towns include Bristol, Tewkesbury, Cheltenham, Stroud; estab. 1974. See table at ENGLAND.

Glov·ers·ville \ˈglə-vərz-ˌvil\. City, Fulton co., E New York, 12 mi. (19 km.) NW of Amsterdam; pop. (1990c) 16,656; concentration of glove manufacturing gave it its name.

Głub·czy·ce \gwüp-ˈchit-se\ *or Ger.* **Le·ob·schütz** \ˈlā-ȯp-ˌshœts\. City, Opole prov., SW Poland; pop. (1981p) 12,934; formerly in Germany.

Glu·gor \glü-ˈgȯr\. Town, Penang state, Malaysia; university (1969).

Glu·khov \ˈglü-kəf\ *or* **Hlu·khiv** \ˈklü-kif\. Town, NE Ukraine, ab. 65 mi. (105 km.) NW of Sumy.

Gly·der Fach \ˈgli-dər-ˌväk\ *or* **Gly·der–fach.** Mountain, Gwynedd, NW Wales; 3262 ft. (994 m.).

Glyder Fawr \ˈgli-dər-ˌvau̇r\ *or* **Glyder–fawr.** Mountain, Gwynedd, NW Wales; 3279 ft. (999 m.).

Glynn \ˈglin\. Coastal county in SE Georgia. See table at GEORGIA.

Glynns of Antrim. See GLENS OF ANTRIM.

Gmünd. See SCHWÄBISCH GMÜND.

Gmun·den \ˈgmu̇n-dən\. Commune, Upper Austria, Austria; on Lake Traun at outlet into Traun River; pop. (1991c) 13,133; summer resort.

Gmundner See. See TRAUN, LAKE.

Gna·den·hut·ten \jə-ˈnā-dən-ˌhə-tən\. Village, Tuscarawas co., E Ohio, on Tuscarawas River; pop. (1990c) 1226; founded 1772 under leadership of Moravians by Christian Indians who were forced to move to Sandusky 1781; scene Mar. 7, 1782 of massacre by white men of a group of the Indians who had returned now marked by a nine-acre (four-hectare) memorial park.

Gniez·no \ˈgnyez-nȯ\ *or Ger.* **Gne·sen** \ˈgnāz-ᵊn\. Commune, Poznań prov., Poland, 28 mi. (45 km.) ENE of the city of Poznań; pop. (1989e) 69,969; manufactures sugar, leather, beer; ancient cathedral containing relics of St. Adalbert (*Pol.* Wojciech), patron saint of Poland. According to legend, site of Poland's first ✻; first king of Poland, Bolesław the Brave, crowned here 1000 and 1025; coronation place of kings of Poland to 1320; to Prussia 1793, to Poland 1919.

Gnossus. See KNOSSOS.

Goa *or Port.* **Gôa** \ˈgō-ə\. **1.** State, India, on W coast; formerly a constituent part of the centrally administered territory of Goa, Daman, and Diu; ✻ Panaji; 62 mi. (100 km.) of coastline; traversed by a spur of the Western Ghats ab. 4000 ft. (1219 m.) high, from which several short but navigable streams flow to the marshy coast, the two largest the Mandavi and the Juari; rice, fruit, iron ore, manganese. Former Portuguese possession; annexed by India 1961; became a state 1987. See table at INDIA.

2. *or* **Old Goa.** Seaport, India; a former ✻ of Goa, Daman, and Diu; founded 1440 by Bahmanī dynasty (see DECCAN);

under king of Bijapur 1482–1510; taken by Portuguese under Alfonso de Albuquerque 1510 and made ✻ of Portuguese India; scene of beginning of St. Francis Xavier's missionary labors 1542; greatest prosperity late 16th cent.; blockaded by Dutch fleets 1603, 1639; site abandoned for New Goa (see PANAJI) by most Portuguese inhabitants early 18th cent. as result of cholera epidemics; now mostly in ruins but has 16th–17th cent. cathedral and several churches and convents still standing.

3. Municipality, E Camarines Sur prov., Luzon, Philippines, at foot of Mt. Isarog; pop. (1980c) 36,254.

Goa, Da·man, and Diu \də-ˈmän ... ˈdē-ü\. A former union territory of India, consisting of the earlier Portuguese possessions of Goa, Daman, and Diu; 1441 sq. mi. (439 sq. km.); ✻ Panaji; formally annexed by India 1961; split into Goa state and Daman and Diu union territory 1987. See GOA 1, DAMAN 1, and DIU.

Goat Haunt Mountain \ˈgōt-ˌhȯnt, ˌhänt\. Peak in Glacier National Park, NW Montana; 8613 ft. (2625 m.).

Goat Island. **1.** Island in Niagara River, W New York, just above Niagara Falls; 0.75 mi. (1.2 km.) long; divides Niagara Falls (*q.v.*) into American Falls and Horseshoe Falls.

2. Island, California. See YERBA BUENA ISLAND.

3. Island, Chile. See JUAN FERNÁNDEZ.

Goat Mountain. **1.** Peak in Glacier National Park, NW Montana; 8790 ft. (2679 m.).

2. Peak, Culberson co., W Texas; 8600 ft. (2621 m.).

Go·ba \ˈgō-bə\. Town, S cen. Ethiopia; pop. (1989e) 28,112.

Go·ba·bis \gō-ˈbä-bis\. Town, E Namibia, 130 mi. (209 km.) E of Windhoek; pop. (1988c) 6500; alt. 4740 ft. (1445 m.); in pastoral region.

Gobannium. See ABERGAVENNY.

Gö·bels·berg \ˈgœ-bəls-ˌberk\. Highest peak in the Hausruck Mts., Upper Austria, Austria; 2625 ft. (800 m.).

Go·bi \ˈgō-bē\; *formerly also* **Sha·mo** \ˈshä-ˈmō\. Desert, cen. Asia, mostly in Mongolia (republic) and Nei Monggol (Inner Mongolia), China; ab. 500,000 sq. mi. (1,295,000 sq. km.); a broad depression (av. alt. 3000 to 5000 ft. or 900 to 1525 m.) in plateau region, bounded on S by ranges of N Tibetan Plateau (Qilian Shan in Qinghai and the Helan Shan in Ningxia Huizu), on W and NW by Altay Shan, on E by mountains of Nei Monggol and Mongolia (republic); SW part entirely sand but on other borders is steppe land; by some, taken to include Tarim basin also.

Goch \ˈgōk\. City, NW North Rhine-Westphalia, Germany, on Dutch border 66 mi. (106 km.) WSW of Münster; pop. (1980c) 28,778.

God·al·ming \ˈgäd-ᵊl-miŋ\. Town, Surrey, S England, on the Wey 30 mi. (48 km.) SW of London; pop. (1981p) 18,209; light engineering; since 1872 seat of Charterhouse School (notable charitable institution and school), founded in London in 17th cent.; birthplace of writer Aldous Huxley 1894.

Go·da·va·ri \gō-ˈdä-və-rē\. River, cen. India; rises in NW Maharashtra state, flows SE across the Deccan, crossing N Andhra Pradesh, and thence SE into Bay of Bengal through several mouths; its chief tributaries Dudna, Pranhita, Indravati, and Sabari on the N and Manjra on the S; ab. 900 mi. (1448 km.) long; navigable in lower course; source of reservoirs, canals, and irrigation systems; a sacred river of the Hindus.

God·dard, Mount \ˈgä-dərd\. Peak in the Sierra Nevada, in E Fresno co., S cen. California; 13,555 ft. (4132 m.).

Gode·rich \ˈgäd-ˌrich\. Resort town, ⊗ of Huron co., SE Ontario, Canada, on SE shore of Lake Huron 65 mi. (105 km.) NNE of Sarnia-Clearwater; pop. (1991c) 7452; harbor; salt mined nearby; founded c. 1828; built around a hexagonal town square.

Godesberg. See BAD GODESBERG.

God·havn. See QEQERTARSUAQ 2.

Godh·ra \ˈgo-drə\. Town, Gujarat, W India, 68 mi. (109 km.) ESE of Ahmadabad; pop. (1991p) 96,514; trades in timber.

Göding. See HODONÍN.

Gö·döl·lö \ˈgœ-dœl-ˌlœ\. Commune, 12 mi. (19 km.) NE of Budapest, cen. Hungary; pop. (1991e) 29,700; former royal palace (now part of university).

Go·doy Cruz \gō-ˈthȯi-ˈkrüs\. Town, Mendoza prov., W Argentina; S suburb of the city of Mendoza; wine making.

Gods Lake \ˈgädz\. Lake, E Manitoba, Canada; 319 sq. mi. (826 sq. km.); its outlet is **Gods River,** a tributary of Hayes River.

Godthåb *or* **Godthaab.** See NUUK.

Godwin Austen. See K2.

Godwin Island \ˈgä-dwin, ˈgȯ-\. Island in Atlantic Ocean, SE coast of Northampton co., Virginia.

Goenoeng Agoeng. See AGUNG, MOUNT.

Goenoeng Api. See GUNUNGAPI.

Goenoeng Awoe. See AWU, GUNUNG.

Goenoengsitoli. See GUNUNGSITOLI.

Goentoer. See GUNTUR 2.

Goe·ree \kü-ˈrā\. Island, South Holland prov., Netherlands, in estuary of the Maas (Meuse) River; 83 sq. mi. (215 sq. km.); W section is called Goeree and E section **Over·flak·kee** \ˈō-vər-flä-ˌkā\.

Goes \ˈkṳ̈s\. Commune, Zeeland prov., SW Netherlands, on South Beveland I.; pop. (1981e) 30,841.

Goffs·town \ˈgäfs-ˌtau̇n\. Town, Hillsborough co., S New Hampshire, 5 mi. (8 km.) WNW of Manchester; pop. (1990c) 14,621.

Go·ge·bic \gō-ˈgē-bik\. County in NW Michigan, in Upper Penin. See table at MICHIGAN.

Gogebic, Lake. Lake, Ontonagon and Gogebic cos., NW Michigan, in Upper Penin.; ab. 12 mi. (19 km.) long.

Gogebic Range. Iron-bearing region, N Wisconsin and NW Michigan (in Upper Penin.), extending E to W in Gogebic co., Michigan, and Bayfield, Ashland, and Iron cos., Wisconsin; highest point 1823 ft. (556 m.), in Gogebic co.

Gog·land \ˈgȯg-ˌländ\; *mostly formerly* **Hog·land** \ˈhüg-ˌländ\; *Finn.* **Sur Sa·ri** \ˈsür-ˌsä-rē\. Island, Russia in Europe, in Gulf of Finland, S of seaport of Kotka, Finland and ab. 110 mi. (175 km.) W of St. Petersburg.

Gogra. See GHĀGHARA.

Goi·â·nia; *formerly* **Goy·a·nia** \gȯi-ˈyȧ-nyə\. City, ✻ of Goiás state, SE cen. Brazil; munic. pop. (1991p) 920,838; trade center in livestock-raising region; Catholic university (1959), federal university (1964); a planned city, inaugurated as ✻ 1942.

Goi·ás; *formerly* **Goi·az** *or* **Goy·az** \gȯi-ˈyȧs\. **1.** State, cen. Brazil; ✻ Goiânia; produces coffee and rice; explored by Portuguese in 17th cent. See table at BRAZIL.

2. Town, Goiás state, cen. Brazil, 75 mi. (121 km.) NW of Goiânia; munic. pop. (1980c) 43,027; formerly ✻ of Goiás state.

Goil, Loch \ˈgȯil\. Inlet of Firth of Clyde in Strathclyde region, W cen. coast of Scotland, an arm of Loch Long.

Going–to–the–Sun Mountain. Peak in Glacier National Park, NW Montana, N of **Going–to–the–Sun Highway** which crosses the park; 9604 ft. (2927 m.).

Gök \ˈgərk\. River in N Turkey in Asia; flows E into Kızıl Irmak.

Gök·çe·a·da \ˌgœk-chā-ä-ˈdä\ *or Eng.* **Gök·çe Island** \ˈgœk-chā\; *before 1973* **İm·roz** \ə̇m-ˈrȯz\ *or Gk.* **Im·bros** \ˈēm-brös\. Turkish island in NE Aegean Sea, W of Gallipoli Penin. and NW of entrance to Dardanelles; 110 sq. mi. (285 sq. km.); pop. (1990p) 7947; Turkish island before being occupied by Greece 1912–14 and then by British during Gallipoli campaign (see GALLIPOLI PENINSULA); given back to Turkey 1923.

Gökcha. See SEVAN.

Gök·su \ˌgœk-ˈsü\. **1.** *anc.* **Sa·leph** \ˈsä-lif\; *earlier* **Cal·y·cad·nus** \ˌka-lə-ˈkad-nəs\. River, S Turkey in Asia (Cilicia); flows into Mediterranean at ruins of ancient Seleucia (Tracheotis) SW of İçel; 155 mi. (249 km.) long; the river, then called Saleph, in which Holy Roman Emperor Frederick Barbarossa drowned 1190 during Third Crusade.

2. River, E cen. Turkey in Asia; rises in Anti-Taurus Mts.; flows SW into Seyhan River; 125 mi. (201 km.) long.

Gök–Tépé. See GEOK-TEPE.

Go·lan Heights \ˈgō-ˌlän, -lən\ *or Arabic* **Al–Jaw·lān** \ȧl-ˌjau̇-ˈlän\. Hilly region, SW Syria; highest point 7297 ft.

(2224 m.); since 1967 under Israeli control; annexed by Israel 1981; tension bet. Syria and Israel over annexed land remained high during 1980s, with UN peacekeeping forces deployed; a series of peace talks took place early 1990s but situation remained unresolved.

Go·la·sec·ca \ˌgō-lä-ˈsek-kä\. Village, W Lombardy, N Italy, near S end of Lake Maggiore; pop. (1981p) 2565; site of 7th–6th cent. B.C. cremation cemeteries.

Gol·borne \ˈgōl-bərn\. Town, Lancashire, NW England, 15 mi. (24 km.) W of Manchester; pop. (1981p) 27,609.

Gol·con·da \gäl-ˈkän-də\. **1.** City, ⊗ of Pope co., SE corner of Illinois; pop. (1990c) 823; fluorite deposits.
2. Ruined town and fortress, W Andhra Pradesh, S cen. India, 5 mi. (8 km.) W of Hyderabad city. In 1512 became ✻ of one of the five ancient Muslim sultanates of the Deccan (*q.v.*) which was later conquered by Aurangzeb (ʽĀlamgīr) 1687 and annexed to Mogul Empire; famous for its diamonds.

Gold Beach \ˈgōld\. City, ⊗ of Curry co., SW corner of Oregon, on Pacific Ocean; pop. (1990c) 1546.

Gold Coast. **1.** Country, W Africa. See GHANA 2.
2. Coastal city, Queensland, Australia; pop. (1991c) 225,773; tourism.
3. Coast of the Gulf of Guinea, along shore of Ghana, W of the Slave Coast—so called from large quantities of gold formerly taken from sands and mines along the coast.

Gold Coast Colony. Former British colony on the Gold Coast; now part of Ghana; area now divided into the Greater Accra, Eastern, Central, and Western regions and part of the Volta region to the mouth of the Volta River; on N bordered on Ashanti and on W on Ivory Coast; ✻ Accra.

Gold Dust Peak. Mountain, Eagle co., NW cen. Colorado; 13,500 ft. (4115 m.).

Gold·en \ˈgōl-dən\. **1.** City, ⊗ of Jefferson co., cen. Colorado, 10 mi. (16 km.) W of Denver; pop. (1990c) 13,116; brewing; Colorado School of Mines (1874), Red Rocks Community Coll. (1967); National Earthquake Information Center; geology museum; founded 1859 as mining camp; ✻ of territory of Colorado 1862–67.
2. Town, SE British Columbia, Canada, on Canadian Pacific R.R. and on Columbia River; pop. (1991c) 3721; alt. 2585 ft. (788 m.).

Golden Bay. W arm of upper Tasman Bay on N coast of South I., New Zealand.

Golden Chersonese. See MALAY PENINSULA.

Gold·en·dale \ˈgōl-dən-ˌdāl\. City, ⊗ of Klickitat co., S Washington, 57 mi. (92 km.) SSW of Yakima; pop. (1990c) 3319.

Golden Fall. See GULLFOSS.

Golden Gate. Strait leading from Pacific Ocean into San Francisco Bay; San Francisco on its S shore; ab. 2 mi. (3 km.) wide; named 1849 during the gold rush; spanned by Golden Gate Bridge (suspension; main span 4200 ft. or 1280 m.; completed 1937).

Golden Gate Highlands National Park. National park, Free State, Rep. of South Africa, near border with Lesotho; ab. 16 sq. mi. (41 sq. km.); colorful sandstone formations, wildlife; estab. 1963.

Golden Hinde \ˈhīnd\. Mountain, cen. Vancouver I., British Columbia, Canada; 7219 ft. (2200 m.); highest mountain on Vancouver I.

Golden Horn. **1.** Peak, San Juan and San Miguel cos., SW Colorado; 13,600 ft. (4145 m.).
2. *or Turk.* **Ha·liç** \hä-ˈlēch\. Inlet of the Bosporus, Turkey in Europe, forming harbor of İstanbul; ab. 5 mi. (8 km.) long; separates Beyoğlu and Galata from older part of city.
3. *or Russ.* **Zo·lo·toy Rog** \ˌzə-lə-ˈtȯi-ˈrȯk\. Harbor of Vladivostok, Primorskiy Kray, SE Russia in Asia; an inlet of Amur Bay.

Golden Meadow. Town, Lafourche parish, SE Louisiana, on Bayou Lafourche; pop. (1990c) 2049.

Golden Throne. Peak in Karakoram Range of the Himalayas, N Jammu and Kashmir, in region controlled by Pakistan, SE of K2; 23,600 ft. (7193 m.).

Golden Triangle. Mountainous region, SE Asia where the borders of Thailand, Myanmar, and Laos meet; source of opium production.

Golden Valley. **1.** Name of counties in two states of the U.S. See tables at MONTANA and NORTH DAKOTA.
2. Village, Hennepin co., SE cen. Minnesota, 5 mi. (8 km.) W of Minneapolis; pop. (1990c) 20,971.

Gold·field \ˈgōld-ˌfēld\. Village, ⊗ of Esmeralda co., SW Nevada, 26 mi. (42 km.) S of Tonopah; grew after 1902 gold find; declined after peak production in 1910.

Golds·boro \ˈgōldz-ˌbər-ō\. City, ⊗ of Wayne co., E North Carolina, on Neuse River 46 mi. (74 km.) SE of Raleigh; pop. (1990c) 40,709; processes tobacco; Wayne Community Coll. (1957); Seymour Johnson Air Force Base.

Gold·stone Mountain \ˈgōld-ˌstōn\. Peak on NE boundary of Lemhi co., E cen. Idaho; 9892 ft. (3015 m.).

Gold·thwait, Mount \ˈgōld-ˌthwāt\. Mountain, Antarctica, 77°59′S, 86°03′W; 12,510 ft. (3813 m.).

Gold·thwaite \ˈgōld-ˌthwāt\. City, ⊗ of Mills co., cen. Texas; pop. (1990c) 1658.

Go·le·niów \gȯ-ˈle-ˌnyüf\ *or Ger.* **Goll·now** \ˈgȯl-ˌnō\. City, W Szczecin prov., NW Poland, 16 mi. (26 km.) NE of the seaport of Szczecin; pop. (1989e) 21,868.

Goletta. See HALQ AL-WADI.

Golfe de Gabès. See GABÈS.

Golfe de Gascogne. See BISCAY, BAY OF.

Golfe de la Gonâve. See GONAÏVES.

Gol·fi·to \gȯl-ˈfē-tō\. City, Puntarenas prov., S Costa Rica; pop. (1982e) 29,171; an important port handling esp. bananas.

Golf Manor \ˈgälf, ˈgȯlf, ˈgäf, ˈgȯf\. Village, Hamilton co., SW Ohio, 7 mi. (11 km.) NE of Cincinnati; pop. (1990c) 4154; residential suburb.

Golfo de Vizcaya. See BISCAY, BAY OF.

Golfo Dulce. See DULCE, GOLFO.

Golgotha. See CALVARY.

Go·li·ad \ˈgō-lē-ˌad\. **1.** County in S Texas. See table at TEXAS.
2. City, its ⊗, 22 mi. (35 km.) W of Victoria; pop. (1990c) 1946; historic resort, built up around mission and presidio estab. by Spaniards in 1749; figured in the Mexican revolt against Spain 1812–13, and in the Texas Revolution 1835–36.

Gol·ling·er \ˈgȯ-liŋ-ər\. Waterfall in Salzach River, Salzburg, Austria, ab. 10 mi. (16 km.) S of Salzburg near village of **Gol·ling** \ˈgȯ-liŋ\; 200 ft. (61 m.) high.

Gollnow. See GOLENIÓW.

Golodnaya Steppe. See BETPAK-DALA.

Gol·pāy·e·gān *or* **Gul·pai·gan** \ˌgōl-pī-ˈgän\. Town, W cen. Iran, 90 mi. (145 km.) NW of Eşfahān; pop. (1986c) 35,253.

Go·ma \ˈgō-mä\. Town, ✻ of Nord-Kivu administrative region, E Democratic Rep. of the Congo.

Gomal. See GUMAL.

Gomal Pass. See GUMAL PASS.

Go·ma·ti \ˈgȯ-mə-tē\; *formerly* **Gum·ti** \ˈgüm-tē\. River, N India; rises in NE Uttar Pradesh, flows SE past Lucknow to the Ganges below Varanasi; ab. 500 mi. (805 km.) long; navigable for small vessels.

Gom·be National Park \ˈgȯm-bā\. National park, westernmost Tanzania, on Lake Tanganyika; 20 sq. mi. (52 sq. km.); a chimpanzee reserve.

Gombroon. See BANDAR ʽABBĀS.

Gomel. See HOMYEL'.

Go·me·ra \gō-ˈmā-rä\. One of Canary Is. (*q.v.*), in Santa Cruz de Tenerife prov., Spain; 22 mi. (35 km.) W of Tenerife I.; 146 sq. mi. (378 sq. km.); chief town and port San Sebastián.

Gó·mez Pa·la·cio \ˈgō-ˌmes-pä-ˈlä-syō\. Municipality, Durango state, NW cen. Mexico, 195 mi. (314 km.) W of Monterrey; pop. (1990p) 232,550.

Go·mor·rah \gə-ˈmȯr-ə, -ˈmär-\. See SODOM.

Go·na \'gō-nə\. Settlement and mission station on SE coast of New Guinea I., Papua New Guinea, on Holnicote Bay just NNW of Buna; scene of fighting WWII 1942–43; see BUNA.

Go·na·ïves \ˌgō-nä-'ēv\ *or* **Les Gonaïves** \lā-\. Commercial town, W Haiti, on **Golfe de la Go·nâve** \'gȯlf-də-lȧ-gō-'näv\ 68 mi. (109 km.) NNW of Port-au-Prince; pop. (1992e) 63,291; harbor; exports cotton, coffee, cabinet woods. Independence of Haiti proclaimed here Jan. 1, 1804.

Go·nâve, Île de la \'ēl-də-lȧ-gō-'näv\. Island of the West Indies, in Golfe de la Gonâve, Haiti; 287 sq. mi. (743 sq. km.).

Gon·bad–e Kā·vūs \gōn-'bäd-ē-kō-'vüs\. Town, Māzandarān prov., N Iran; pop. (1986c) 87,100.

Gon·da \'gōn-də\. Town, E Uttar Pradesh, N India, 65 mi. (105 km.) ENE of Lucknow; pop. (1991p) 106,078.

Gon·dal \'gōnd-ᵊl\. **1.** Former Indian state, cen. Kathiawar, now part of Gujarat, W India; 1024 sq. mi. (2652 sq. km.).
2. Town, its ✱, Gujarat state, on tributary of the Bhadar ab. 250 mi. (402 km.) NNW of Bombay; pop. (1991p) 80,506.

Gon·der \'gȯn-dər\ *or* **Gon·dar** \-dər, -ˌdär\. City, NW Ethiopia, 21 mi. (34 km.) N of Lake Tana; pop. (1989e) 98,352; founded as Abyssinian ✱ by Emperor Fasilides 1632; remained ✱ through mid-19th cent.; noted for its ruins.

Gon·dia \'gȯn-dē-ə, -dyə\. Town, Maharashtra, cen. India; pop. (1991p) 109,271.

Gon·do·ko·ro \gən-'dȯ-kə-ˌrō\. Locale, S Sudan; on right bank of the Nile (White Nile).

Gond·wa·na \gȯn-'dwä-nə\. **1.** *also* **Gond·wa·na·land** \-ˌland\. Supercontinent, believed to have been of early Paleozoic origin, that comprised the current major landmasses of the Southern Hemisphere plus the Indian Subcontinent; believed to have merged with Laurussia (*q.v.*) and other major landmasses in late Paleozoic era to form Pangaea (*q.v.*); believed to have separated from Pangaea in early Mesozoic era, and throughout Mesozoic era and into Cenozoic era fragmented and separated into present landmasses.
2. Region of India, now divided bet. Andhra Pradesh, Madhya Pradesh, and Maharashtra; inhabited chiefly by the Gonds, a Dravidian people; has given its name to the supercontinent of Gondwana (see GONDWANA 1).

Go·nesse \gȯ-'nes\. Commune, Val-d'Oise dept., N France.

Gong·ga Shan \'gu̇ŋ-gä-'shän\; *traditionally* **Min·ya Kon·ka** \min-'yä-kȯn-'kä\. Mountain, Sichuan prov., S China, 30 mi. (48 km.) S of Kangding; 24,790 ft. (7556 m.).

Gon·zal·es \gən-'za-lis, -'zä-\. **1.** County in S cen. Texas. See table at TEXAS.
2. City, Monterey co., California; pop. (1990c) 4660.
3. Town, Ascension parish, SE Louisiana, 22 mi. (35 km.) SE of Baton Rouge; pop. (1990c) 7003.
4. City, ⊗ of Gonzales co., S cen. Texas, 60 mi. (97 km.) E of San Antonio; pop. (1990c) 6527; clay pits; scene of first battle in Texas Revolution 1835.

Gooch·land \'güch-lənd\. **1.** County in E cen. Virginia. See table at VIRGINIA.
2. Village, its ⊗.

Good·e·nough \'gu̇d-ᵊn-ˌəf\; *formerly* **Mo·ra·ta** \mö-'rä-tä\. Island, W D'Entrecasteaux Is., Papua New Guinea, in W Pacific Ocean off E extremity of New Guinea I., ab. 20 mi. (32 km.) long and 10 to 12 mi. (16 to 19 km.) wide; has cen. peak, **Mount Goodenough,** 8419 ft. (2566 m.).

Goodenough Bay. Inlet at NW end of Ward Hunt Strait (Solomon Sea), on N coast of E extremity of New Guinea I.

Good Harbor Bay. Inlet of Lake Michigan on N shore of Leelanau co., NW Michigan.

Good Hope. See FORT GOOD HOPE.

Good Hope, Cape of. **1.** Cape, Indonesia. See JAMURSBA, CAPE.
2. *or Port.* **Ca·bo da Boa Es·pe·ran·ça** \'kȧ-bü-dȧ-'bō-ə-ˌēs-pā-'rāⁿ-sə\. Cape on SW coast of Western Cape prov., S Rep. of South Africa, W of False Bay and 30 mi. (48 km.) S of Cape Town; alt. 840 ft. (256 m.). First sighted 1488 by Portuguese navigator Bartolomeu Dias who, according to legend, named it **Cabo Tor·men·to·so** \ˌtu̇r-mən-'tō-zü\ ("Cape of Storms"); passed by Vasco da Gama, another Portuguese navigator, 1497 on voyage to India; first Dutch settlement at Table Bay nearby 1652.
3. Former province, Rep. of South Africa. See CAPE PROVINCE.

Good·hue \'gu̇d-ˌhyü\. County in SE Minnesota. See table at MINNESOTA.

Good·ing \'gu̇-diŋ\. **1.** County, in S Idaho. See table at IDAHO.
2. City, its ⊗, ab. 12 mi. (19 km.) E of junction of Big Wood River with the Snake; pop. (1990c) 2820.

Good·land \'gu̇d-lənd\. City, ⊗ of Sherman co., NW Kansas, 20 mi. (32 km.) E of Colorado border; pop. (1990c) 4983.

Good·news Bay \'gu̇d-ˌnüz, -ˌnyüz\. City, SW Alaska, on inlet of Bering Sea just S of Kuskokwim Bay; pop. (1990c) 241; platinum deposits.

Good·well \'gu̇d-ˌwel\. Town, Texas co., NW Oklahoma, in Panhandle ab. 12 mi. (19 km.) SW of Guymon; pop. (1990c) 1065; Oklahoma Panhandle State Univ. (1909).

Good·win Sands \'gu̇d-win\. Dangerous shoals in N Strait of Dover, ab. 7 mi. (11 km.) E of Deal, England; 10 mi. (16 km.) long; encloses the Downs, famous roadstead where Dutch fleet under Adm. Maarten Harpertszoon Tromp was defeated by English 1652; scene of numerous shipwrecks.

Good·year \'gu̇d-ˌyir\. City, Maricopa co., SW cen. Arizona, 8 mi. (13 km.) W of Phoenix; pop. (1990c) 6258.

Goole \'gül\. Town, Humberside, N England, at confluence of Ouse and Don rivers 25 mi. (40 km.) W of Hull; pop. (1981p) 17,127; shipping center.

Goose \'güs\. River, E North Dakota; formed by confluence of forks in Steele co., flows E into Red River in E Traill co.; ab. 85 mi. (137 km.) long.

Goose Creek. Town, Berkeley co., SE South Carolina, 15 mi. (24 km.) NNW of Charleston; pop. (1990c) 24,692.

Goose Lake. Lake in E part of Oregon-California boundary.

Göp·ping·en \'gœ-piŋ-ən\. City, Baden-Württemberg, Germany, 24 mi. (39 km.) ESE of Stuttgart; pop. (1992e) 55,642; 15th cent. church; 16th cent. castle; founded mid-12th cent. by Hohenstaufen family; burned 1425 and 1782.

Go·rakh·pur \'gōr-ək-ˌpu̇r\. City, SE Uttar Pradesh, N India, on Rapti River 100 mi. (161 km.) N of Varanasi; pop. (1991c) 505,566; textiles, dyes; railroad divisional point, railroad workshops; univ. (1956); founded c. 1400.

Gora Shkhara. See SHKHARA, MOUNT.

Gora Zaozernaya. See CHANG-KU FENG.

Gor·da, Pun·ta \'pün-tä-'gȯr-t͟hä\. Cape on W tip of Zapata Penin., SW Matanzas prov., W cen. Cuba, at S of entrance to Broa Bay.

Gor·di·um \'gȯr-dē-əm\. Ancient city, ✱ of Phrygia; according to tradition founded by the peasant Gordius, said to have been king of Phrygia; scene of episode of the cutting of the Gordian knot by Macedonian King Alexander the Great; now ruins on right bank of the Sakarya 50 mi. (80 km.) WSW of Ankara, Turkey in Asia.

Gor·don \'gȯrd-ᵊn\. **1.** County in NW Georgia. See table at GEORGIA.
2. River, SW Tasmania, Australia; rises in central highlands, flows S, then W, to Macquarie Harbour; ab. 85 mi. (137 km.) long.

Gordon, Lake. Reservoir, S cen. Tasmania, Australia, WNW of Hobart.

Gor·dons Bay \'gȯrd-ᵊnz\. Inlet of South Pacific Ocean, New South Wales, SE Australia, on SE edge of Sydney.

Gor·dy·e·ne \ˌgȯrd-ē-'ē-nē\ *also* **Cor·du·e·ne** \ˌkȯr-jü-'ē-nē\. Mountainous region of ancient Armenia, in S part S of Thospitis Lacus (Lake Van).

Gore, The \'gōr\. NE tip of Vermont, E of Halls Stream; 1 sq. mi. (3 sq. km.); projects E into New Hampshire ab. 2 mi. (3 km.).

Gore Bay. Town, ⊗ of Manitoulin dist., S Ontario, Canada, on N shore of Manitoulin I.; pop. (1991c) 916.

Go·rée, Île de \'ēl-də-gȯ-'rā\. Island, Senegal, formerly in the circumscription of Dakar and Dependencies, which was united with Senegal 1946; in the harbor formed by peninsula of Cap Vert; inhabited by Lebu people when occupied by Portuguese mid-15th cent.; occupied by Dutch early 17th cent.; captured by French in 1677; major slave-trading center through 18th cent.; held by British during Napoleonic Wars;

restored to France 1817; lost importance with growth of Dakar and St.-Louis (*qq.v.*).

Gore Mountain. Peak in the Adirondack Mts., Warren co., E New York; 3595 ft. (1096 m.).

Gor·gān \gōr-ˈgòn\ *also* **Gur·gan** \gůr-\. River, N Iran; flows W into SE Caspian Sea N of Bander-e Shāh; 150 mi. (241 km.) long.

Gorgān *also* **Gurgan;** *formerly* **As·ter·a·bad** *or* **As·tar·a·bad** \ˌäs-tə-rə-ˈbäd, ˈas-tə-rə-ˌbad\ *or* **As·tra·bad** \ˌäs-trə-ˈbäd, ˈas-trə-ˌbad\. **1.** Former province of N Iran, now part of Māzandarān prov.; its ancient name **Hyr·ca·nia** \hər-ˈkā-nē-ə\.

2. City, Māzandarān prov., N Iran, ab. 23 mi. (37 km.) inland from Caspian Sea; pop. (1986c) 139,430.

Gor·go·na \gòr-ˈgō-nä\. Island in Ligurian Sea belonging to Italy, situated bet. Livorno and N tip of Corsica; ab. 2 sq. mi. (5 sq. km.).

Gor·gon·zo·la \ˌgòr-gòn-ˈzō-lä\. Town, Milano prov., SW cen. Lombardy, N Italy, 12 mi. (19 km.) ENE of Milan; pop. (1991p) 16,260; produces Gorgonzola cheese.

Gor·ham \ˈgòr-əm\. **1.** Town, Cumberland co., SW Maine, 10 mi. (16 km.) W of Portland; pop. (1990c) 11,856.

2. Town, Coos co., N New Hampshire, at confluence of Androscoggin and Peabody rivers 5 mi. (8 km.) S of Berlin; pop. (1990c) 3173; tourist center in White Mts.

Gori \ˈgòr-ē\. Town, E cen. Republic of Georgia, on Kura River ab. 40 mi. (64 km.) NW of Tbilisi; pop. (1991e) 70,100; alt. 2010 ft. (613 m.); center of a district producing corn and lumber; birthplace of Soviet dictator Josef Stalin 1879. Founded 7th cent. as Tontio; site of 12th cent. fortress.

Go·rin·chem \ˈk̲òr-kəm—*sic*\ *or* **Gor·kum** *same*\. Commune, South Holland prov., SW Netherlands, at confluence of the Waal and Maas (Meuse) rivers; pop. (1981e) 28,021; metalworking; nearby is castle where Dutch politician and humanist Hugo Grotius was imprisoned 1619–21.

Go·ri·zia \gō-ˈrēt-syä\. **1.** Province of NW Friuli-Venezia Giulia, NE Italy. See table at ITALY.

2. *or Ger.* **Görz** \ˈgœrts\. Commune, its ✻, on Isonzo River on Slovenian border, 74 mi. (119 km.) ENE of Venice; pop. (1991p) 37,999; machinery, textiles; 14th cent. Gothic cathedral; tourist resort; ✻ of former Austrian crown land of Görz and Gradisca; strategic point in Isonzo campaign in WWI; captured by Italians 1916; recaptured by German-Austrian offensive 1917; ceded to Italy by Treaty of St.-Germain 1919; treaty 1947 ceded part of town to Yugoslavia which became Nova Gorica.

Gorj \ˈgòrzh\. County of SW Romania. See table at ROMANIA.

Gorkha. See GURKHA.

Gorki, Gor'kii, Gor'kiy, Gorky. 1. *or* **Gor'·kov·ska·ya** \gər-ˈkòf-skə-yə\. Oblast, Russia in Europe. See NIZHEGOROD.

2. City, Russia in Europe. See NIZHNIY NOVGOROD.

Gorkum. See GORINCHEM.

Gor·li·ce \gòr-ˈlēt-se\. Commune, E Nowy Sącz prov., SE Poland, 58 mi. (93 km.) ESE of Kraków; pop. (1989c) 29,036.

Gör·litz \ˈgœr-ˌlits\. City, Saxony, E Germany, on the Polish border chiefly on W bank of the Neisse River; pop. (1992e) 70,448; railway cars; since 1945 the small part on E bank of the river belongs to Poland (Wrocław prov.) and is called **Zgor·ze·lec** \zgò-ˈzhe-lets\; first mentioned 11th cent.

Gor·lov·ka \ˈgòr-ləf-kə\ *or* **Hor·liv·ka** \ˈhòr-ləf-kə\. City, E Donets'k subdivision, E Ukraine, just N of the city of Donets'k; pop. (1991e) 337,000; chemicals; coal-mining center.

Gor·ner Grat \ˈgòr-nər-ˈgrät\. Ridge, Valais canton, SW cen. Switzerland, 3 mi. (5 km.) SE of Zermatt; 10,289 ft. (3136 m.); affords one of the finest views in the Alps.

Gor·no–Al·tay \ˈgòr-nə-ȧl-ˈtī\ *or* **Altay** *also* **Gor·no–Al·tai** *same*\ *or* **Altai.** Republic, S Russia in Asia, bordering on Mongolia; 35,753 sq. mi. (92,600 sq. km.); pop. (1993e) 197,000; ✻ Gorno-Altaysk; comprised **Gorno–Altay Autonomous Oblast** 1948–91 and earlier **Oy·rot Autonomous Oblast** \ˈòi-rət ... ˈò-bləst, -ˌblast\; a mountainous region, comprising the ranges of the NW Altay Shan; on the S on Kazakh border is Mt. Belukha, 15,157 ft. (4620 m.), highest of the Altays; its two main streams are the Katun' and Biya which join to form the Ob' River in SE Altay Kray; gold, mercury; created an autonomous oblast 1922; became republic within Russia 1991; subsequently became member of Russian Federation.

Gor·no–Al·taysk *or* **Gor·no–Al·taisk** \ˈgòr-nə-ȧl-ˈtīsk\; *formerly* **Oi·rot Tu·ra** \ˈòi-rət-tů-ˈrä\ *or* **Ula·la** \ü-ˈlä-lə\. Town, ✻ of Gorno-Altay Rep., S Russia in Asia, on Katun' River; pop. (1991c) 47,500; furniture, meat processing.

Gor·no–Ba·dakh·shan \ˈgòr-nə-ˌbə-dək̲-ˈshän\ *or* **Badakhshan.** Autonomous subdivision of Tajikistan, bordering on Afghanistan and Xinjiang Uygur, China; 24,595 sq. mi. (63,701 sq. km.); pop. (1991c) 167,100; ✻ Khorog; wheat; livestock; formed as autonomous oblast of U.S.S.R. 1925.

Go·ro·dok \gə-ˌrə-ˈdòk\ *or* **Gorodok Ya·gel·lon·ski** \yə-ˈge-lən-skē\ *or Pol.* **Gró·dek Ja·giel·loń·ski** \ˈgrò-ˌdek-ˌyä-gye-ˈlòn-skē\. Town, L'viv subdivision, W Ukraine, 16 mi. (26 km.) WSW of the city of L'viv (formerly in Poland).

Gorodok, David–. See DAVID-GORODOK.

Go·ro·ka \ˌgō-rō-ˈkä\. Town, E cen. Papua New Guinea, in E highlands; pop. (1990c) 17,855.

Go·rong, Ke·pu·lau·an \ˌke-pů-ˈlaů-ən-gò-ˈròŋ\ *or* **Gorong Islands.** See CERAM.

Go·ron·go·sa National Park \ˌgōr-òn-ˈgō-sä\. National park, Mozambique; 2135 sq. mi. (5530 sq. km.); abundant wildlife incl. buffalo, eland, elephant, hippopotamus, kudu, zebra.

Go·ron·ta·lo \ˌgō-ròn-ˈtä-lō\. Town on S coast of N peninsula of Sulawesi, Indonesia; pop. (1990c) 119,780; harbor; important trade center.

Gorontalo, Gulf of. See TOMINI, GULF OF.

Gor·tyn \ˈgòr-ˌtīn\ *also* **Gor·ty·na** \gòr-ˈtī-nə\. Ruins of ancient town, S cen. Crete, Greece, SW of Iráklion and ancient Knossos near S coast; many temples; long a rival of Knossos; civic law inscription discovered here 19th cent.

Go·ryn \gə-ˈrēn\ *or Pol.* **Ho·ryń** \hò-ˈrin\. River, W Ukraine and Belarus; flows N into Pripyat' River in the Polesye; 404 mi. (650 km.) long.

Góry, Tarnowskie. See TARNOWSKIE GÓRY.

Görz. See GORIZIA 2.

Gor·zów \ˈgò-ˌzhüf\. Province, W Poland. See table at POLAND.

Gor·zów Wiel·ko·pol·ski \ˈgò-zhüf-ˌvyel-kò-ˈpòl-skē\; *Ger.* **Lands·berg** \ˈlänts-ˌberk\ *also* **Landsberg an der War·the** \ˌän-dər-ˈvär-tə\. City, ✻ of Gorzów prov., W Poland, on Warta River; pop. (1989e) 123,350; chemical and timber industries; 13th and 18th cent. churches; founded as German city c. 1257; destroyed in Thirty Years' War, but rebuilt; assigned to Poland after WWII.

Gosainthan *or* **Gosaithan.** See XIXABANGMA FENG.

Gösch·e·nen \ˈgœ-shə-nən\. Village, Uri canton, cen. Switzerland, at N entrance to St. Gotthard Tunnel; pop. (1980c) 708.

Go·schen Strait \ˈgō-shən\. Channel bet. East Cape, SE New Guinea I. and Normanby I. of the D'Entrecasteaux Is., Papua New Guinea; ab. 10 mi. (16 km.) wide.

Gos·ford \ˈgäs-fərd\. Town, New South Wales, Australia, 35 mi. (56 km.) N of Sydney; pop. (1991c) 128,956.

Gos·forth \ˈgäz-ˌfōrth, -fərth\. Town, Northumberland, N England, N suburb of Newcastle upon Tyne; pop. (1981p) 23,835; residential.

Go·shen \ˈgō-shən\. **1.** County in SE Wyoming. See table at WYOMING.

2. City, ⊗ of Elkhart co., N Indiana, 22 mi. (35 km.) ESE of South Bend; pop. (1990c) 23,797; recreational vehicles and components, prefabricated houses, kitchen cabinets; Goshen Coll. (1894).

3. Village, ⊗ of Orange co., SE New York, 18 mi. (29 km.) WSW of Newburgh; pop. (1990c) 5255; one of the oldest racetracks for harness horses. While teaching school here in

1782 lexicographer Noah Webster worked on his *Blue-Backed Speller* (published 1783).
4. District of ancient Egypt E of the Nile delta; granted to Hebrew patriarch Jacob and his family by the king of Egypt; place where Jacob's descendants lived until the Exodus (*Gen.* xlvi–xlvii).
5. Boer republic, S Africa, now part of Rep. of South Africa; estab. in W Transvaal 1882 as part of westward expansion of Boers; became part of British Bechuanaland 1885. See STELLALAND.

Gos·lar \ˈgȯs-ˌlär\. City, SE Lower Saxony, Germany, 23 mi. (37 km.) S of Brunswick in N Harz Mts.; pop. (1992e) 46,497; chemicals; 11th cent. palace of Holy Roman Emperor Henry III; 12th cent. town hall; 16th cent. fortress towers. Founded 922; member Hanseatic League; imperial free city 1290 until passed to Prussia 1802; passed to Westphalia 1807; passed to Hannover 1815; with Hannoverian kingdom became part of Prussia 1866.

Gos·per \ˈgäs-pər\. County in S Nebraska. See table at NEBRASKA.

Gos·port \ˈgäs-ˌpōrt\. Town, Hampshire, S England, on Portsmouth harbor opp. Portsmouth; pop. (1991p) 72,800; naval base; engineering.

Gos·sau \ˈgȯ-saù\. Commune, St. Gall canton, Switzerland, 6 mi. (10 km.) W of the commune of St. Gall; pop. (1980c) 14,584.

Gö·ta \ˈyœ-tä\. Navigable river, S Sweden; drains Lake Vänern and flows SSW into the Kattegat; 58 mi. (93 km.) long; locks at the falls of Trollhättan (*q.v.*); part of **Göta Canal** connecting Göteborg on the W with Stockholm on the E; 58 locks, highest point 300 ft. (91 m.), uses many lakes (total distance ab. 360 mi. or 579 km., constructed part ab. 54 mi. or 87 km.).

Gö·ta·land \ˈyœ-tä-ˌländ\ *or* **Gö·ta·ri·ke** \-ˌrē-kə\. The S part of Sweden; 35,762 sq. mi. (92,624 sq. km.); pop. (1992e) 4,146,898; comprises the 12 provinces of Älvsborg, Blekinge, Göteborg and Bohus, Gotland, Halland, Jönköping, Kalmar, Kristianstad, Kronoberg, Malmöhus, Östergötland, and Skaraborg.

Gö·te·borg \ˈyœ-tä-ˌbȯrʸ, -ˌbȯr-ē\ *or* **Goth·en·burg** \ˈgäth-ᵊn-ˌbərg, ˈgät-\. Seaport, ⊗ of Göteborg and Bohus prov., SW Sweden, at mouth of Göta River on the Kattegat; pop. (1993e) 433,811; 2d largest city in Sweden; Sweden's chief seaport; fishing; exports automobiles and wood products; cathedral (1633, restored 1956–57); university (1891), technical university (1829); founded 1603; destroyed in Kalmar War 1611–13; refounded 1619 by King Gustavus II Adolph; originated 1865 what is known as the Göteborg licensing system for the regulation of liquor sales; became a free port 1921.

Göteborg and Bo·hus \ˈbü-hüs\. Province of SW Sweden. See table at SWEDEN.

Go·tem·ba \gō-ˈtām-bä\. City, Shizuoka prefecture, Honshū, Japan, 40 mi. (64 km.) NE of the city of Shizuoka; pop. (1990p) 79,560.

Go·tha \ˈgō-tə\. City, Thuringia, cen. Germany, 15 mi. (24 km.) W of Erfurt; pop. (1992e) 53,372; chemicals, machinery, textiles; 11th cent. town hall; 12th cent. church; 17th cent. castle; publishing (incl. the geographical publishing house of Hermann Haack founded by Johann Perthes 1785); city first mentioned 8th cent.; received charter 1189; residence of dukes of Saxe–Gotha 1640–1825, and of dukes of Saxe-Coburg-Gotha 1826–1918; site of congress 1875 where the Socialist Labor Party of Germany formed.

Go·tham \ˈgä-thəm, ˈgō-; *Brit.* ˈgō-təm, ˈgä-\. **1.** Village, Nottinghamshire, England, 7 mi. (11 km.) SW of Nottingham; inhabitants were given the name "the wise men of Gotham" for their reputed simplicity, since according to tradition when King John visited the village to select a site for a palace, the people, not wishing to support such a royal residence, feigned stupidity.
2. Name sometimes used for New York City; first popularly so called in *Salmagundi* (1807–08), a humorous work by Washington Irving, William Irving, and James Kirke Paulding, in reference to the proverbial folly of the inhabitants of Gotham, England.

Goth·en·burg \ˈgä-thən-ˌbərg\. **1.** City, Dawson co., S cen. Nebraska, on Platte River 36 mi. (58 km.) ESE of North Platte; pop. (1990c) 3232.
2. Seaport, Sweden. See GÖTEBORG.

Goth·ic Line \ˈgä-thik\. German defense line in WWII, in N cen. Italy, extending from Pisa to Rimini along heights above the Arno River, 150 mi. (241 km.) N of Rome; attacked by Allies Sept. 1944; penetrated after severe fighting by Dec. 1944.

Got·land *formerly also* **Gott·land** \ˈgȯt-ˌlänt; ˈgät-ˌland, -lənd\ *or* **Goth·land** \ˈgäth-ˌland, -lənd\. Island in Baltic Sea off SE coast of Sweden; with several islands (incl. Farön and Karlsö), constitutes the Swedish prov. of Gotland; ⊗ Visby; tourism; barley, rye; sugar beets; fisheries, cement works. See table at SWEDEN.
History: Center of trade as early as Bronze Age; part of Sweden since 9th cent.; estab. trading house at Novgorod 12th cent.; attracted German merchants to Visby (*q.v.*) which joined Hanseatic League; at height of importance 14th cent.; attacked by Danish 1361; became base for pirates; to Denmark by Peace of Stettin 1570; to Sweden by Treaty of Brömsebro 1645; fortified late 19th cent.

Go·tō Islands \ˈgō-ˌtō\ *or Jp.* **Go·tō–Ret·tō** \ˈgō-ˌtō-ˈret-ˌtō\. Chain of islands extending for ab. 100 mi. (161 km.) SW from NW Kyūshū, Japan; five main islands Fukue, Uku, Nakadōri, Naru, Hisaka; part of Nagasaki prefecture; ✻ Fukue; fishing.

Gottesberg. See BOGUSZÓW.

Göt·ting·en \ˈgœ-tiŋ-ən\. City, S Lower Saxony, Germany, on the Leine River 55 mi. (88 km.) SSW of Brunswick; pop. (1992e) 124,331; optical and scientific instruments; univ. (1737); headquarters of Max Planck Society, named for German physicist; first mentioned 953.

Gottland. See GOTLAND.

Gottschee. See KOČEVJE.

Gottwaldov. See ZLÍN.

Gou·da \ˈk̲aù-də\. Commune, South Holland prov., SW Netherlands, NE of Rotterdam; pop. (1992e) 67,146; manufactures pottery; cheese market (Gouda cheese); 16th cent. Groote Kerk, known esp. for its stained-glass windows; received charter 1272.

Gough Island \ˈgäf\ *or* **Gough's Island** \ˈgäfs\. Small island in South Atlantic Ocean, one of the Tristan da Cunha group, 40°20′S, 10°W; a British claim, became a dependency of St. Helena 1938.

Gouin, Réservoir \ˌrā-zer-ˌvwär-ˈgweⁿ\. Lake in SW Quebec, Canada, NW of city of Quebec; its outlet St.-Maurice River.

Goul·burn \ˈgōl-bərn\. **1.** River, E cen. Victoria, SE Australia; flows NW to Murray River; 280 mi. (451 km.) long; along its banks is **Goulburn River National Park**.
2. City, SE New South Wales, SE Australia, 50 mi. (80 km.) NE of Canberra; pop. (1991c) 21,451; made a city 1864.

Gould, Mount \ˈgüld\. Peak in Glacier National Park, NW Montana; 9551 ft. (2911 m.).

Goulette, La. See HALQ AL-WADI.

Goulimine \ˌgü-lē-ˈmēn\ *or* **Goulimime.** See GUELMIM.

Gou·rin \gü-ˈreⁿ\. Commune, Morbihan dept., NW France, 25 mi. (40 km.) NE of Quimper; 15th–16th cent. Gothic church; 16th cent. chapel.

Gou·rits \ˈgaù-rits\. River, SW Rep. of South Africa; formed by confluence of Groot and Olifants rivers, flows S into Indian Ocean near Mosselbaai in Western Cape prov.; 80 mi. (129 km.) long.

Gour·nia \ˈgùr-nē-ə\. Ancient town, NE Crete, Greece, at head of Mirabella Bay; on a low hill; fully excavated ruins of ancient Minoan town.

Gour·ock \ˈgùr-ək\. Burgh, Strathclyde region, SW Scotland, on S shore of Firth of Clyde; pop. (1981p) 11,158; seaport; summer resort, yachting center.

Gouv·er·neur \ˌgə-vər-ˈnùr, ˌgù-, -ˈnər\. Village, St. Lawrence co., N New York, 24 mi. (39 km.) S of Ogdensburg; pop. (1990c) 4604.

Gou·yave \gü-ˈyäv\ *or* **Char·lotte Town** \ˈshär-lət\. Town, W coast of Grenada I., Windward Is., West Indies.

Gove \ˈgōv\. **1.** County in W Kansas. See table at KANSAS.
2. *or* **Gove City.** City, its ⊗; pop. (1990c) 103.

Gove Peninsula. Peninsula, Arnhem Land, Northern Terr., Australia; inhabited by aboriginal people; bauxite deposits.

Go·ver·na·dor Island \ˌgü-vər-nə-ˌdōr\. Island in Guanabara Bay, Brazil, N of Rio de Janeiro; 12 sq. mi. (31 sq. km.); airport.

Governador Va·la·dar·es \ˌvà-lə-ˈdàr-is\. Municipality, Minas Gerais state, E Brazil, 150 mi. (241 km.) NE of Belo Horizonte; pop. (1991p) 230,487.

Gov·ern·ment Mountain \ˈgə-vər-mənt\. Peak, cen. Coconino co., N cen. Arizona; 8347 ft. (2544 m.).

Gov·er·nor's Harbour \ˈgə-vər-nərz\. Town on Eleuthera I. in Bahamas.

Governors Island. 1. Island in inner part of Boston Harbor, Massachusetts; site of Fort Winthrop.
2. Fortified island in New York Bay, New York, off end of East River; 173 acres (70 hectares); Fort Jay 1806, Castle William 1807–11.

Go·wan·da \gə-ˈwän-də\. Village, Cattaraugus and Erie cos., SW New York, 28 mi. (45 km.) S of Buffalo; pop. (1990c) 2901. Settled 1810, called Lodi until 1848.

Go·wa·nus Bay \gə-ˈwä-nəs\. Inlet of Upper New York Bay extending into S Brooklyn, W Long Island, New York.

Gow·er \ˈgau̇-ər\. Peninsula extending S into Bristol Channel from S cen. coast of Wales.

Go·ya \ˈgō-yä\. Town, Corrientes prov., NE Argentina, on E bank of Paraná River 112 mi. (180 km.) S of Corrientes; pop. (1980p) 47,357.

Goyania. See GOIÂNIA.

Goyaz. See GOIÁS.

Go·zo \ˈgȯd-zō, ˈgȯt-sō\ *or* **Maltese Ghau·dex** *or* **Ghaw·dex** \ˈgau̇-desh\; *anc.* **Gau·lus** \ˈgȯ-ləs\. Island of Malta, in Mediterranean Sea 58 mi. (93 km.) S of Sicily; 26 sq. mi. (67 sq. km.); pop. (1983e) 21,773; lacemaking; chief town Victoria. See MALTA.

Graaff Rei·net \ˈgräf-ˈrī-nət\. Town, S Rep. of South Africa, on Sundays River 135 mi. (217 km.) NNW of Port Elizabeth, in center of the Great Karoo; pop. (1985c) 18,106; distribution center in sheep-raising area; founded by the Dutch in 1786.

Grace·ville \ˈgrās-ˌvil\. City, Jackson co., NW Florida, 16 mi. (26 km.) NW of Marianna; pop. (1990c) 2675; Florida Baptist Theological Coll. (1943).

Gra·cias \ˈgrä-syäs\. **1.** See LEMPIRA.
2. Town, ✻ of Lempira dept., W Honduras, 100 mi. (161 km.) WNW of Tegucigalpa; pop. (1988p) 3678.

Gra·cias a Di·os \ˈgrä-syäs-ä-ˈthē-ōs\. Department of E Honduras. See table at HONDURAS.

Gracias a Dios, Cape. NE extremity of Nicaragua, extending into Caribbean Sea near Honduras border.

Gra·cio·sa \grà-ˈsyò-zə\. Island in cen. Azores, NW of Terceira; 24 sq. mi. (62 sq. km.); pop. (1991p) 5100; chief town Santa Cruz da Graciosa.

Graciosa Bay \ˌgräs-ē-ˌō-sə-\. Inlet on NW coast of Nendo I., Santa Cruz Is., SW Pacific Ocean; good harbor.

Gra·di·sca d'Ison·zo \grä-ˈdēs-kä-dē-ˈzōnt-sō\. Commune, Gorizia prov., Friuli-Venezia Giulia, NE Italy, SW of the commune of Gorizia on opp. side of the Isonzo; pop. (1981p) 6355; formerly part of Austrian crown land of Görz and Gradisca (see GORIZIA).

Gra·do \ˈgrä-dō\. Commune, Friuli-Venezia Giulia, NE Italy, on a small island in NW part of Gulf of Trieste, N Adriatic Sea; pop. (1981p) 9744; resort; has 6th cent. cathedral with a mosaic pavement.

Grado \ˈgrä-thō\. Commune, Asturias prov., NW Spain, 12 mi. (19 km.) WNW of Oviedo; pop. (1991c) 12,045.

Gra·dy \ˈgrā-dē\. Name of counties in two states of the U.S. See tables at GEORGIA and OKLAHOMA.

Graecia, Magna. See MAGNA GRAECIA.

Gra·fen·wöhr \ˈgräf-ᵊn-ˌvœr\. Village, Bavaria, Germany, ab. 21 mi. (34 km.) SE of Bayreuth; pop. (1980c) 5813.

Graf·ton \ˈgraf-tən\. **1.** County in W New Hampshire. See table at NEW HAMPSHIRE.
2. Town, Worcester co., cen. Massachusetts, 6 mi. (10 km.) ESE of the city of Worcester; pop. (1990c) 13,035; residential. Site of an Indian village estab. by Puritan clergyman John Eliot ("Apostle to the Indians") 1654.
3. City, ⊗ of Walsh co., NE North Dakota, 38 mi. (61 km.) NNW of Grand Forks; pop. (1990c) 4840; settled late 19th cent.
4. Village, Lorain co., N Ohio; pop. (1990c) 3344.
5. City, ⊗ of Taylor co., N West Virginia, on Tygart River 12 mi. (19 km.) SSE of Fairmont; pop. (1990c) 5524.
6. Village, Ozaukee co., E Wisconsin, 22 mi. (35 km.) N of Milwaukee; pop. (1990c) 9340.
7. Town, NE New South Wales, SE Australia, on Clarence River 45 mi. (72 km.) from its mouth and 150 mi. (241 km.) S of Brisbane; pop. (1991c) 17,124; port.

Gra·gna·no \grä-ˈnyä-nō\. Commune, Napoli prov., Campania, S Italy, 18 mi. (29 km.) SE of Naples; pop. (1989c) 29,781.

Gra·ham \ˈgrā-əm, ˈgra-əm, ˈgram\. **1.** Name of counties in three states of the U.S. See tables at ARIZONA, KANSAS, NORTH CAROLINA.
2. City, ⊗ of Alamance co., N cen. North Carolina, 21 mi. (34 km.) E of Greensboro; pop. (1990c) 10,426.
3. City, ⊗ of Young co., N Texas, 57 mi. (92 km.) S of Wichita Falls; pop. (1990c) 8986.

Graham, Mount. 1. Peak, in Pinaleno Mts., Graham co., Arizona; ab. 10,713 ft. (3265 m.).
2. Peak in Catskill Mts., Ulster co., SE New York; 3868 ft. (1179 m.).

Graham Bell Island \ˈbel\. See FRANZ JOSEF LAND.

Graham Coast. See GRAHAM LAND.

Graham Island. Northernmost and largest island of the Queen Charlotte Is., off W British Columbia, Canada; 2491 sq. mi. (6452 sq. km.).

Graham Land *formerly* **Graham Coast.** Part of the Antarctic Penin., British Antarctic Terr., extending from ab. 65°S to 66°15′S; once thought to be two islands, but on later exploration found to be part of the mainland; claimed by Britain 1832; also claimed by Argentina and Chile.

Gra·hams·town \ˈgrā-əmz-ˌtau̇n, ˈgra-əmz-, ˈgramz-\ *or Afrikaans* **Gra·hams·tad** \-ˌstät\. Town, S Eastern Cape prov., S Rep. of South Africa, 75 mi. (121 km.) ENE of Port Elizabeth; pop. (1985c) 19,188; summer resort; important legal and educational center; cathedral; Rhodes Univ. (1904, before 1951 part of Univ. of South Africa). Founded 1812 as a British military outpost in a region which for many years was scene of almost constant struggle bet. Europeans and Africans in the Cape Frontier Wars; settled by British 1820.

Graian Alps. See table at ALPS.

Grain Coast \ˈgrān\. Section of coast of Upper Guinea, W Africa, now Liberia, from Cape Palmas to Sierra Leone border —so called from the old trade in grains of paradise (*Aframomum melegueta*), a member of the ginger family.

Grain·ger \ˈgrān-jər\. County in NE Tennessee. See table at TENNESSEE.

Gra·jaú \ˌgrà-zhà-ˈü\. River, Maranhão state, NE Brazil; flows NNE to Mearim River; ab. 300 mi. (483 km.) long.

Grajaú, Lake. Lake in N cen. Maranhão state, NE Brazil, bet. the Pindaré and Grajaú rivers.

Gram·bling \ˈgram-bliŋ\. Village, Lincoln parish, N Louisiana, 34 mi. (55 km.) W of Monroe; pop. (1990c) 5484; Grambling State Univ. (1901).

Gram·mi·che·le \ˌgräm-mē-ˈke-lā\. Commune, Catania prov., E Sicily, Italy, 32 mi. (51 km.) SW of the commune of Catania; pop. (1981p) 13,607.

Grammont. See GEERAARDSBERGEN.

Gram·pi·an \ˈgram-pē-ən\. **1.** *or* **Grampian Hills.** Mountain system of Scotland, extending NE to SW across cen. Scotland, forming a natural boundary bet. the Scottish Highlands and the Scottish Lowlands; highest peak Ben Nevis 4409 ft. (1344 m.), highest mountain in Great Britain. See GRAUPIUS, MOUNT.

2. Administrative region, NE Scotland; estab. 1975. See table at SCOTLAND.

Gram·pi·ans, the \ˈgram-pē-ənz\. Mountain range, W Victoria, SE Australia; highest Mt. William 3829 ft. (1167 m.); contains **Grampians National Park.**

Gramsh \ˈgrämsh\. **1.** District of cen. Albania. See table at ALBANIA.

2. Town, its ✱.

Gran. 1. River, Slovakia. See HRON.

2. City, Hungary. See ESZTERGOM.

Gra·na·da \grä-ˈnä-t͟hä\. **1.** Department of SW Nicaragua. See table at NICARAGUA.

2. City, ✱ of Granada dept., SW Nicaragua, on NW shore of Lake Nicaragua; pop. (1985e) 88,636; rum, furniture, clothing, soap; founded by Spanish explorer Francisco Fernández de Córdoba 1523.

3. Ancient kingdom, Upper Andalusia, S Spain; 11,100 sq. mi. (28,749 sq. km.); divided 1833 into modern provs. of Granada, Almería, and Málaga. For its history, see GRANADA 5 and ANDALUSIA 2.

4. Province of S Spain. See table at SPAIN.

5. City, ✱ of Granada prov., S Spain, in the Sierra Nevada 80 mi. (129 km.) SE of Córdoba; pop. (1991p) 254,034; divided into three sections: Antequeruela (founded 1410), Albaicín, and Granada; manufactures textiles, paper, soap, woolens, liqueurs; archiepiscopal see (from 1493); university (1531); the Alhambra palace complex, begun c. 1230, one of finest examples of Moorish architecture in Spain; 16th cent. cathedral containing tombs of Ferdinand of Aragon and Isabella of Castile; the Cartuja, a 16th cent. Carthusian monastery; palace of Holy Roman Emperor Charles V (who was also king of Spain as Charles I).

History: Taken by Moors 711; seat of independent Moorish kingdom of Granada ruled by Nasrid dynasty 1238–1492; the last Moorish stronghold in Spain until captured 1492 by Ferdinand of Aragon and Isabella of Castile, ending Moorish power in Spain.

Gran·bury \ˈgrän-ˌber-ē\. City, ⊗ of Hood co., N cen. Texas; pop. (1990c) 4045.

Gran·by \ˈgran-bē\. **1.** Town, NW Hartford co., N Connecticut; pop. (1990c) 9369; settled 1664; incorp. 1786.

2. Town, Hampshire co., W Massachusetts, 20 mi. (32 km.) NNE of Springfield; pop. (1990c) 5565; St. Hyacinth Coll. (1927).

3. City, S Quebec, Canada, 45 mi. (72 km.) E of Montreal; pop. (1991c) 42,804; rubber and plastic products, textiles.

Gran Canaria. See GRAND CANARY.

Gran Cha·co \grän-ˈchä-kō\; *Span.* **Chaco** *or* **El Chaco** \el-\. Region, S cen. South America; ab. 300,000 sq. mi. (777,000 sq. km.); thinly populated, swampy, drained by Paraguay River and its chief W tributaries the Pilcomayo and Bermejo; principal divisions: (1) **Chaco Bo·re·al** \ˌbō-rā-ˈäl\, main part of region, in fork of the Paraguay and Pilcomayo; its ownership was cause of the Chaco War bet. Bolivia and Paraguay 1932–35; by peace treaty (signed at Buenos Aires 1938) larger cen. and E part (95,313 sq. mi. or 246,861 sq. km.) to Paraguay, smaller W part (ab. 46,561 sq. mi. or 120,593 sq. km.) to Bolivia. Paraguayan region divided administratively into three departments; Bolivian region attached to Tarija dept. (2) **Chaco Cen·tral** \sen-ˈträl\, part of the Gran Chaco in N Argentina bet. the Pilcomayo and Bermejo rivers; ab. 40,000 sq. mi. (103,600 sq. km.); comprises Formosa prov. (27,825 sq. mi. or 72,067 sq. km.) and N part of Salta prov. (ab. 12,000 sq. mi. or 31,080 sq. km.). (3) **Chaco Aus·tral** \aůs-ˈträl\, S part of Gran Chaco in N Argentina S of Bermejo River; ab. 66,000 sq. mi. (170,940 sq. km.); coextensive with NE part of Santiago del Estero prov., cen. part of Salta prov., and prov. of Chaco.

Gran Co·lom·bia \ˈgrän-kō-ˈlōm-bē-ä\ *or* **Great Colombia** \kə-ˈləm-bē-ə, -ˈlōm-\. Country of NW South America, 1819–30; formed as result of wars of Latin American states against Spain for independence, chiefly by activities of Gen. Simón Bolívar. Created by proclamation of Congress of Angostura Aug. 1819; comprised what is now Colombia, Panama, Venezuela, and Ecuador (not completely independent of Spain until May 1822); ✱ Bogotá; terminated by secession of Venezuela and Ecuador 1830. See COLOMBIA.

Grand \ˈgrand\. **1.** Former name of Colorado River from its source to its junction with Green River in SE Utah.

2. River in Iberville parish, S Louisiana; empties into Atchafalaya River.

3. River, SW Michigan; flows from Jackson co. N and W into Lake Michigan at Grand Haven; 260 mi. (418 km.) long; furnishes waterpower; navigable 40 mi. (64 km.) from mouth.

4. River, NW Missouri; rises in Adair co., SW cen. Iowa, flows SE across NW Missouri into Missouri River; 300 mi. (483 km.) long.

5. River, N South Dakota; formed by confluence of N and S forks in N Perkins co., flows E into Missouri River; ab. 200 mi. (322 km.) long.

6. The lower course of the Neosho River (*q.v.*) in Oklahoma. See PENSACOLA DAM.

7. Name of counties in two states of the U.S. See tables at COLORADO and UTAH.

8. River, SE Ontario, Canada; rises in Grey co. and flows S and SE to Lake Erie; 140 mi. (225 km.) long.

Grand Andely, Le. See LES ANDELYS.

Grand Atlas. See ATLAS MOUNTAINS.

Grand Ba·ha·ma \bə-ˈhä-mə\. One of the Bahamas; 530 sq. mi. (1373 sq. km.); pop. (1990c) 40,898; tourism.

Grand Bank. Seaport, S Newfoundland, Canada, on S shore and near mouth of Fortune Bay; pop. (1991c) 3528; is a supply depot for fishing fleets.

Grand Banks. Shallow section of North American continental shelf in Atlantic Ocean E and S of Newfoundland, Canada; extends ab. 350 mi. (563 km.) from W to E, ab. 200 mi. (322 km.) wide; av. depth 50 fathoms (92 m.); crossed by the Labrador Current from the N mingling with the Gulf Stream along its E edge; major cod-fishing region; for centuries frequented by fishing fleets of Canada, Great Britain, France, and U.S., since 1977 mostly within Canada's offshore territorial claim; made dangerous by fog, icebergs, and the fact that it is in the path of the transatlantic liners.

Grand Bassa. See BUCHANAN 4.

Grand Bas·sam \bä-ˈsäm\ *also* **Bassam.** City, Ivory Coast, adjoining Bingerville and just E of Abidjan; pop. (1988c) 41,825; served as first ✱ of Ivory Coast colony; important seaport until ab. 1950.

Grand Blanc \ˌgrand-ˈblaŋk\. City, Genesee co., SE cen. Michigan, 7 mi. (11 km.) SSE of Flint; pop. (1990c) 7760.

Grand–Bourg *or* **Grand–Bourg** \grän-ˈbür\. Commune, ✱ of Marie-Galante I., Guadeloupe overseas dept. of France, in West Indies; on SW coast of the island.

Grand Caicos. See TURKS AND CAICOS ISLANDS.

Grand Canal. 1. *or* **Da Yun·he** \ˈdä-ˈyʊn-ˈhə\ *or W.-G.* **Yün Ho** \ˈyʊn-ˈhō\. Inland waterway, NE China; ab. 1000 mi. (1609 km.) long, from Tianjin to Hangzhou (airline distance ab. 650 mi. or 1046 km.). Cen. part from the Chang (at Zhenjiang) to Huang River finished as early as the 4th cent. B.C.; extended S to Hangzhou early 7th cent. A.D.; N section finished by Kublai Khan late 13th cent.; later extended to Tongxian and Beijing. Called by the Chinese "Imperial River" or "Transport River." Now silted up in part and superseded somewhat by coast transport and the Tianjin-Pukou railroad.

2. *or Ital.* **Il Ca·na·le Gran·de** \ˌēl-kä-ˈnä-lā-ˈgrän-dā\. Main water thoroughfare of Venice, in winding course, 80 to 175 ft. (24 to 53 m.) wide; crossed by Rialto, Scalzi, and Accademia bridges; lined with palaces and fine buildings.

Grand Ca·nary \kə-ˈnar-ē\ *or Span.* **Gran Ca·na·ria** \ˌgräŋ-kä-ˈnär-yä\. One of the Canary Is. (*q.v.*), Las Palmas prov., Spain, 40 mi. (64 km.) ESE of Tenerife I.; 592 sq. mi. (1533 sq. km.); pop. (1991c) 666,150; chief city Las Palmas; bananas, tomatoes, tobacco.

Grand Canyon. **1.** Gorge in the Colorado River where it flows across NW corner of Arizona; usually taken as extending from mouth of Little Colorado River to Grand Wash Cliffs near Arizona-Nevada boundary but sometimes taken as also incl. Marble Canyon, above, and when measured thus, ab. 280 mi. (451 km.) long; 4 to 18 mi. (6 to 29 km.) wide, in places more than a mile (1.6 km.) deep; many peaks and smaller canyons within the main canyon; surrounding plateau 5000 to 9000 ft. (1500 to 2750 m.) above sea level; estab. as a national park 1919; a separate area mostly N of the canyon in NE Mohave co. set aside 1932 as **Grand Canyon National Monument** which was abolished 1975 and absorbed by **Grand Canyon National Park** (see UNITED STATES, *National Parks*).
2. Unincorporated settlement, Coconino co., N Arizona, in Grand Canyon National Park; pop. (1990c) 1499; park administration headquarters.

Grand Canyon of the Snake. See HELLS CANYON.

Grand Canyon of the Tuolumne. See TUOLUMNE 1.

Grand Canyon of the Yellowstone. See YELLOWSTONE 1.

Grand Cayman \ˈkā-mən, -ˌman\. See CAYMAN ISLANDS.

Grand Cess \ˈses\. Coastal town, SE Liberia, 40 mi. (64 km.) WNW of Cape Palmas.

Grand Com·bin \ˌgräⁿ-kōⁿ-ˈbeⁿ\. Peak in Pennine Alps, S Switzerland; 14,154 ft. (4314 m.).

Grand Comoros. See GRANDE COMORE.

Grand Cor·nier \ˌgräⁿ-kȯr-ˈnyā\. Peak in Pennine Alps, S Switzerland; 13,008 ft. (3965 m.).

Grand Cou·lee \ˌgrand-ˈkü-lē\. **1.** Valley bet. ranges of cliffs in cen. Washington, extending N to S in Douglas co.
2. City, Grant co., cen. Washington, at site of Grand Coulee Dam on Columbia River 78 mi. (126 km.) WNW of Spokane; pop. (1990c) 984; comprises former towns of Coulee Heights, Coulee Center, and Grand Coulee.

Grand Coulee Dam. See UNITED STATES, *Dams and Reservoirs.*

Grand Coulee Reservoir. See FRANKLIN D. ROOSEVELT LAKE.

Grand Cou·ron·né \ˌgräⁿ-ˌkü-rȯ-ˈnā\. Wooded heights E and NE of Nancy, France.

Grand–Duché de Luxembourg *or* **Grand Duchy of Luxembourg.** See LUXEMBOURG 2.

Gran·de, Ba·hía \bä-ˈē-ä-ˈgrän-dā\. Widemouthed bay on SE coast of Santa Cruz prov., S Argentina.

Gran·de, Ilha \ˌēl-yə-ˈgrȧn-də\. Island in Atlantic Ocean off S coast of Rio de Janeiro state, SE Brazil; 15 mi. (24 km.) long, 8 mi. (13 km.) wide.

Grande, Rio \ˌrē-ō-ˈgrand, ˈgran-dē\. River in S United States. See RIO GRANDE 1.

Gran·de, Rio \ˌrē-ō-ˈgrän-dā\. **1.** River, W Africa; rises in Fouta Djallon, W Guinea, flows by winding course W into Gêba estuary, Guinea-Bissau; ab. 250 mi. (402 km.) long; lower course (in Guinea-Bissau) sometimes called **Co·ru·bal** \ˌkō-rü-ˈbäl\, upper course (in Guinea), the **Kom·ba** \ˈkȯm-bä\.
2. River, W Bahia state, E Brazil; flows NE into São Francisco River; ab. 300 mi. (483 km.) long.
3. River, SW Minas Gerais state, E Brazil; flows W to unite with Paranaíba River and form Paraná River; forms section of boundary bet. Minas Gerais and São Paulo states; ab. 680 mi. (1094 km.) long.

Gran·de, Río \ˌrē-ō-ˈgrän-dā\. **1.** River, Mendoza prov., W cen. Argentina; rises near Chilean border, flows SE to unite with Barrancas River and form Colorado River; ab. 80 mi. (129 km.) long.
2. A name of the Mamoré (*q.v.*) in its upper course, Bolivia.
3. *or* **Río Grande de Santiago.** River, Mexico. See SANTIAGO, RIO.
4. River, Nicaragua; flows E to Caribbean Sea; ab. 200 mi. (322 km.) long.

Gran·de Añas·co \ˈgrän-dā-ä-ˈnyäs-kō\. River in W Puerto Rico; flows W into Añasco Bay.

Grande Casse, Pointe de la \ˌpweⁿt-də-lä-ˈgräⁿd-ˈkäs\. Peak, W Graian Alps, Savoie dept., E France; 12,638 ft. (3852 m.).

Grande Chartreuse, La. See CHARTREUSE, LA GRANDE.

Grande Co·more \ˌgräⁿd-kō-ˈmȯr\ *or* **Nja·zi·dja** \nyä-ˈzē-jä\ *also* **Grand Com·o·ros** \ˌgrand-ˈkä-mə-ˌrōz\. Island, largest of the Comoros, in N Mozambique Channel; 443 sq. mi. (1147 sq. km.); pop. (1990e) 243,122; N part a plateau, alt. ab. 2000 ft. (610 m.); in S is volcanic Mt. Karthala; chief town Moroni.

Gran·de de Are·ci·bo \ˈgrän-dā-t͟hā-ˌä-rā-ˈsē-b͟ō\. River in N Puerto Rico; flows N through Arecibo municipality into Atlantic Ocean; 40 mi. (64 km.) long.

Gran·de de Lo·í·za \ˈgrän-dā-t͟hā-lō-ˈē-sä\. River in NE Puerto Rico; flows N and NE into Atlantic Ocean.

Gran·de Island \ˈgrän-dā\. Island, Luzon, Philippines, in center of entrance to Subic Bay (*q.v.*); 0.5 sq. mi. (1 sq. km.).

Grande Prai·rie \ˈgrand-ˈprar-ē\. City, W Alberta, Canada, 235 mi. (378 km.) WNW of Edmonton; pop. (1991c) 28,271; forest products.

Grand Erg Occidental *and* **Grand Erg Oriental.** See ERG, AL-.

Grande Ronde \ˈgrand-ˈränd\. River, NE Oregon; rises in SW Union co., flows NE across Washington border and into Snake River; 175 mi. (282 km.) long.

Grandes Jo·rasses \ˌgräⁿ-jȯ-ˈrȧs\. Mountain having two peaks (higher one 13,799 ft. or 4206 m.) in Pennine Alps, on France-Italy boundary, NE of Mont Blanc.

Grande Soufrière. See SOUFRIÈRE 1.

Grande–Terre \gräⁿd-ˈter\. Island forming E part of Guadeloupe, West Indies.

Grand Falls. **1.** Waterfall, Canada. See CHURCHILL FALLS.
2. Town, Victoria co., W New Brunswick, Canada, on St. John River 35 mi. (56 km.) SE of Edmundston; pop. (1991c) 6083.

Grand Forks. **1.** County in E North Dakota. See table at NORTH DAKOTA.
2. City, its ⊗, on Red River 73 mi. (117 km.) N of Fargo; pop. (1990c) 49,425; trade center in hard-wheat belt; processing and distribution of cereals, potatoes, and sugar beets; Univ. of North Dakota (1883); Grand Forks Air Force Base is nearby. Estab. as fur-trading post 1801; settled 1871; incorp. as city 1881.
3. City, British Columbia, Canada, 60 mi. (97 km.) SW of Nelson; pop. (1991c) 3610.

Grand–Fort–Phi·lippe \ˌgräⁿ-fȯr-fē-ˈlēp\. Coastal commune, Nord dept., N France, ab. 11 mi. (18 km.) ENE of Calais.

Grand Haven. City, ⊗ of Ottawa co., W Michigan, on Lake Michigan at mouth of Grand River 12 mi. (19 km.) S of Muskegon; pop. (1990c) 11,951; summer resort; port of entry.

Grand Island. **1.** Island in upper Niagara River; part of Erie co., W New York; 8 mi. (13 km.) long.
2. City, ⊗ of Hall co., SE cen. Nebraska, near Platte River 90 mi. (145 km.) W of Lincoln; pop. (1990c) 39,386; flour mills, packinghouses. Central Community Coll.–Grand Island Campus (1976).

Grand Isle \ˈgrand-ˈīl\. **1.** Island in Jefferson parish, off coast of SE Louisiana, at SW entrance to Barataria Bay.
2. Island in Lake Champlain, Grand Isle co., NW corner of Vermont; ab. 10 mi. (16 km.) long.
3. County in NW corner of Vermont. See table at VERMONT.

Grand Junction. City, ⊗ of Mesa co., W Colorado, at junction of Gunnison and Colorado rivers; pop. (1990c) 29,034; alt. ab. 4590 ft. (1399 m.); trade center and distribution point for irrigated valley; peach orchards; tourist services; Mesa State Coll. (1925); incorp. as a town 1881.

Grand Lac. See TONLE SAP.

Grand La·hou \ˌgräⁿ-lä-ˈü\ *also* **Grand La·hu** \lä-ˈü\. Seaport, Ivory Coast, 70 mi. (113 km.) W of Abidjan.

Grand Lake. 1. Lake, NE Grand co., N Colorado, on SW border of Rocky Mountain National Park; the town of Grand Lake (pop. [1990c] 259) is on it.
2. Lake in NE Cameron parish, SW Louisiana; outlet SW into Gulf of Mexico.
3. Lake, chiefly in Iberia and St. Mary parishes, S Louisiana; ab. 30 mi. (48 km.) long, 9 mi. (14 km.) wide; drains through Atchafalaya River into Atchafalaya Bay.
4. Lake, Maine. See WEST GRAND LAKE.
5. *or* **Grand Reservoir.** Lake, Ohio. See SAINT MARYS, LAKE.
6. Lake, Queens co., S New Brunswick, Canada; 65 sq. mi. (168 sq. km.); outlet St. John River.
7. *formerly* **East Grand Lake.** Largest of the Chiputneticook Lakes, on SW border of York co., SW New Brunswick, Canada; borders on Maine.
8. Lake, W Newfoundland, Canada; ab. 56 mi. (90 km.) long; 205 sq. mi. (531 sq. km.); outlet through Humber River.
Grand Lake Métascouac. See MÉTASCOUAC.
Grand Lake O' the Cherokees. See PENSACOLA DAM.
Grand Ledge \'lej\. City, Eaton co., S Michigan, W of Lansing; pop. (1990c) 7579.
Grand Liban. See LEBANON 1.
Grand Ma·nan Island \mə-'nan\. Island at entrance to Bay of Fundy and S of Passamaquoddy Bay, off SW coast of New Brunswick, SE Canada; ab. 20 mi. (32 km.) long; separated from coast of Maine by **Grand Manan Channel** (ab. 8 mi. or 13 km. wide), which has strong currents; fine cliff scenery; summer resort; chief village North Head; fishing.
Grand Manitoulin. See MANITOULIN ISLAND.
Grand Ma·rais \mə-'rā\. City, ⊗ of Cook co., NE corner of Minnesota, on Lake Superior 23 mi. (37 km.) S of Canadian border; pop. (1990c) 1171.
Grand'Mère \grä^{n}-'mer\. City, Champlain co., S Quebec, Canada, on St.-Maurice River 20 mi. (32 km.) NNW of Trois-Rivières; pop. (1991c) 14,287; paper and pulp, shirts.
Grand Monadnock. See MONADNOCK, MOUNT.
Grand–Montrouge, Le. See MONTROUGE.
Grand Paradis. See GRAN PARADISO.
Grand Pass. See BARATARIA PASS.
Grand Po·po \,grä^{n}-pò-'pō, 'grand-'pō-pō\. Seaport, SW Benin, at mouth of the Mono River; on coastal railroad line bet. Porto-Novo and Lomé.
Grand Port·age National Monument \'pōr-tij\. See UNITED STATES, *National Monuments.*
Grand Prairie. City, Dallas and Tarrant cos., NE Texas, 13 mi. (21 km.) W of Dallas; pop. (1990c) 99,616; incorp. 1909.
Grand Pré \'gran-'prā\. Site, Kings co., W Nova Scotia, Canada, on S shore of Minas Basin near Wolfville; contains **Grand Pré National Historic Park;** founded c. 1675; early home of the Acadians; scene of poet Henry Wadsworth Longfellow's *Evangeline.* See ACADIA 2.
Grand Rapids. 1. City, ⊗ of Kent co., W Michigan, on Grand River 61 mi. (98 km.) WNW of Lansing; pop. (1990c) 189,126; manufactures furniture (esp. office furniture), auto parts; aluminum; Davenport Coll. of Business (1866), Calvin College (1876), Calvin Theological Seminary (1876), Grand Rapids Community Coll. (1914), Aquinas Coll. (1922), Kendall Coll. of Art and Design (1928), Reformed Bible Coll. (1940), Grand Rapids Baptist Coll. and Seminary (1941), Grace Bible Coll. (1946); Gerald R. Ford Museum. Orig. site of an Ottawa Indian settlement; trading post 1826; became lumbering center; incorp. as city 1850.
2. Village, ⊗ of Itasca co., N Minnesota, 32 mi. (51 km.) WSW of Hibbing; pop. (1990c) 7976; Itasca Community Coll. (1922).
Grand Reservoir. See SAINT MARYS, LAKE.
Grand River. See GRAND.
Grand River Dam. See PENSACOLA DAM.
Grand–Saint–Ber·nard \,grä^{n}-,se^{n}-ber-'när\. Alpine pass in Pennine Alps bet. Switzerland and Italy. See table at ALPS.
Grand Sa·line \sə-'lēn\. City, Van Zandt co., NE Texas, 30 mi. (48 km.) NW of Tyler; pop. (1990c) 2630.
Grand Sen·ti·nel \'sent-^{ə}n-əl\. Peak in the Sierra Nevada, E Fresno co., S cen. California; 8514 ft. (2595 m.).
Grand·son *or* **Gran·son** \grä^{n}-'sō^{n}\. Commune, Vaud canton, W Switzerland, SW of Neuchâtel; pop. (1980c) 1938; castle; 12th cent. church; scene of defeat of Charles the Bold, duke of Burgundy, by Swiss Confederation 1476.
Grand Ter·race \grand-'ter-əs\. City, San Bernardino co., SE California, N of Riverside; pop. (1990c) 10,946.
Grand Terre Island \,gran-'ter\. Island in Jefferson parish at entrance to Barataria Bay off coast of SE Louisiana; Barataria lighthouse.
Grand Te·ton \'tē-,tän\. Peak in cen. Grand Teton National Park, Teton co., NW Wyoming; 13,770 ft. (4197 m.); highest point in Teton Range.
Grand Teton National Park. See UNITED STATES, *National Parks.*
Grand Trav·erse \'tra-vərs\. County in NW Michigan. See table at MICHIGAN.
Grand Traverse Bay. Inlet of Lake Michigan, bet. Leelanau and Antrim cos., NW Michigan.
Grand Trianon. See VERSAILLES.
Grand Turk \'tərk\. Island ✱ of Turks and Caicos Is., West Indies; 7 mi. (11 km.) long; (pop. [1990c] 3761); believed by some to have been site of Christopher Columbus' first landfall in the New World.
Grand·view \'grand-,vyü\. **1.** City, Jackson co., W Missouri, 5 mi. (8 km.) S of Kansas City; pop. (1990c) 24,967.
2. City, Yakima co., S Washington, 39 mi. (63 km.) SE of the city of Yakima; pop. (1990c) 7169.
Grandview Heights. City, Franklin co., cen. Ohio, 6 mi. (10 km.) NNW of Columbus; pop. (1990c) 7010.
Grand·ville \'grand-,vil\. City, Kent co., W Michigan, 5 mi. (8 km.) SW of Grand Rapids; pop. (1990c) 15,624.
Grand Wash Cliffs. Chain of cliffs in NW Mohave co., NW Arizona, near Lake Mead.
Grange·mouth \'grānj-məth, -,mau̇th\. Seaport burgh, Central region, Scotland, on Forth estuary at terminus of the Forth and Clyde Canal 3 mi. (5 km.) NE of Falkirk; pop. (1981p) 21,666; shipbuilding yards, oil refinery; chemicals.
Granges. See GRENCHEN.
Grange·ville \'grānj-,vil\. City, ⊗ of Idaho co., N cen. Idaho; pop. (1990c) 3226.
Gra·ni·cus \grə-'nī-kəs\ *or mod.* **Ko·ca·baş** \kò-'jä-,bäsh\. River in Turkey in Asia; flowing N into the Propontis (Sea of Marmara); 56 mi. (90 km.) long; near its mouth Macedonian King Alexander the Great defeated the Persians 334 B.C.
Gran·ite \'gra-nit\. County in W Montana. See table at MONTANA.
Granite City. City, Madison co., SW Illinois, 7 mi. (11 km.) N of East St. Louis; pop. (1990c) 32,862; steel products; U.S. Army support center.
Granite Dome. Peak in the Sierra Nevada, in NE Tuolumne co., cen. California; 10,321 ft. (3146 m.).
Granite Falls. 1. Waterfall in Mount Rainier National Park, W cen. Washington; 350 ft. (107 m.) high.
2. City, ⊗ of Yellow Medicine co., Chippewa and Yellow Medicine cos., SW Minnesota, on Minnesota River 13 mi. (21 km.) SE of Montevideo; pop. (1990c) 3083; hydroelectric power plant.
3. Town, Caldwell co., W North Carolina, 10 mi. (16 km.) SSE of Lenoir; pop. (1990c) 3253.
Granite Peak. 1. Mountain, SE Park co., S Montana; 12,799 ft. (3901 m.); highest point in state.
2. Mountain, cen. Washoe co., NW Nevada; ab. 9055 ft. (2760 m.).
Granja, La. See SAN ILDEFONSO 2.
Gran·ma \grän-'mä\. Province of E Cuba. See table at CUBA.
Gran Malindang. See MALINDANG, MOUNT.
Gra·nol·lers \,grä-nō-'lyers\. Commune, Barcelona prov., NE Spain, 16 mi. (26 km.) NNE of the city of Barcelona; pop. (1991c) 51,873.
Gran Pa·ra·di·so \'grän-,pä-rä-'dē-zō\ *or Fr.* **Grand Pa·ra·dis** \,grä^{n}-pà-rà-'dē\. Peak, highest of the Graian Alps, in Gran Paradiso National Park, NW Piedmont, NW Italy. See table at ALPS.

Gran Paradiso National Park. National park, Piedmont, NW Italy; 240 sq. mi. (622 sq. km.); alpine vegetation, glaciers; estab. 1922.

Gran Piedra, La. See LA GRAN PIEDRA.

Gran Qui·vi·ra \ˌgran-kə-ˈvir-ə\. Site, cen. New Mexico containing ruins of pueblo now preserved in Salinas Pueblo Missions National Monument.

Gran Quivira National Monument. See *Salinas Pueblo Missions* at UNITED STATES, *National Monuments.*

Gran Sas·so d'Ita·lia \ˌgrän-ˈsä-sō-dē-ˈtäl-yä\. Mountain group, N Abruzzi, cen. Italy; includes Monte Corno 9560 ft. (2914 m.), highest peak in the Apennines.

Granson. See GRANDSON.

Grant \ˈgrant\. **1.** Name of a parish in cen. Louisiana and of counties in 14 states of the U.S. See tables at ARKANSAS, INDIANA, KANSAS, KENTUCKY, LOUISIANA, MINNESOTA, NEBRASKA, NEW MEXICO, NORTH DAKOTA, OKLAHOMA, OREGON, SOUTH DAKOTA, WASHINGTON, WEST VIRGINIA, WISCONSIN.
2. City, ⊗ of Perkins co., SW Nebraska; pop. (1990c) 1239.

Grant, Mount. **1.** Peak, Flathead co., NW Montana; 8620 ft. (2627 m.).
2. Peak, E Churchill co., W Nevada; ab. 8850 ft. (2700 m.).
3. Peak, W Mineral co., SW Nevada; 11,245 ft. (3427 m.); highest in Wassuk Range.

Grant City. Town, ⊗ of Worth co., NW Missouri; pop. (1990c) 988.

Grant Grove. See GENERAL GRANT NATIONAL PARK.

Gran·tham \ˈgran-thəm\. Town, Parts of Kesteven, Lincolnshire, E England, on the Witham 23 mi. (37 km.) E of Nottingham; pop. (1981p) 30,084; engineering; battlefield where Parliamentarian Gen. Oliver Cromwell had one of his first skirmishes with Royalists 1643.

Grant Land. N section of Ellesmere I., N Nunavut, Canada—a former designation.

Grant Peak. Mountain, E Yellowstone National Park, NW Wyoming; 11,015 ft. (3357 m.).

Grants \ˈgrants\. City, ⊗ of Cibola co., W New Mexico, ab. 70 mi. (115 km.) NW of Belen; pop. (1990c) 8626; uranium deposits; tourism.

Grants·burg \ˈgrants-ˌbərg\. Village, ⊗ of Burnett co., NW Wisconsin; pop. (1990c) 1144.

Grants Pass. City, ⊗ of Josephine co., SW Oregon, on Rogue River 25 mi. (40 km.) WNW of Medford; pop. (1990c) 17,488; trade center for fruit-growing, dairying, lumbering, and mining area.

Grants·ville \ˈgrants-ˌvil\. **1.** City, Tooele co., NW Utah, 45 mi. (72 km.) SW of Salt Lake City; pop. (1990c) 4500; settled 1850.
2. Town, ⊗ of Calhoun co., cen. West Virginia; pop. (1990c) 671.

Gran Valira. See VALIRA.

Gran·ville \ˈgran-ˌvil, -vəl\. **1.** County in N North Carolina. See table at NORTH CAROLINA.
2. Village, Washington co., E New York, on Vermont border 50 mi. (80 km.) NNE of Troy; pop. (1990c) 2646.
3. Village, Licking co., cen. Ohio, 6 mi. (10 km.) W of Newark; pop. (1990c) 4353; Denison Univ. (1831).

Granville \grä^{n}-ˈvēl\. Fortified seaport and commune, Manche dept., NW France, on Gulf of St.-Malo 30 mi. (48 km.) SW of St.-Lô; pop. (1990c) 13,340; resort; 15th cent. church.

Granville Lake \ˈgran-vil\. Lake, NW Manitoba, Canada; 392 sq. mi. (1015 sq. km.); an expansion of Churchill River.

Grape·vine \ˈgrāp-ˌvīn\. City, Tarrant co., N Texas, 20 mi. (32 km.) NE of Fort Worth; pop. (1990c) 29,202.

Grap·pa, Mount \ˈgräp-pä\ *or Ital.* **Mon·te Grappa** \ˈmȯn-tā\. Peak, Veneto, NE Italy, 10 mi. (16 km.) N of Bassano; 5823 ft. (1775 m.).

Gras, Lac de \ˌlak-də-ˈgrä\. Lake, mainland Northwest Territories, Canada, near Nunavut border; 345 sq. mi. (894 sq. km.); a source of the Coppermine River.

Graslitz. See KRASLICE.

Gras·mere \ˈgras-ˌmir\. Lake in the Lake District, Westmorland, NW England; 1 mi. (2 km.) long; poet William Wordsworth's home for many years was nearby.

Gras·moor \ˈgras-ˌmu̇r\ *or* **Grass·moor** *also* **Grasmoor Hill.** Mountain, Cumberland, NW England, in Lake District; 2791 ft. (851 m.).

Gräsö \ˈgre-ˌsœ\. Island off SE coast of Sweden, in Gulf of Bothnia N of Väddö I.; 34 sq. mi. (88 sq. km.).

Grasse \ˈgrȧs, ˈgräs\. Commune, Alpes-Maritimes dept., SE France, 17 mi. (27 km.) W of Nice; pop. (1990c) 42,077; winter resort; manufactures perfumes and essences; cathedral, museums. Independent republic in 12th cent.; became part of countship of Provence 1227; birthplace of painter Jean-Honoré Fragonard 1732.

Grass·lands National Park \ˈgras-ləndz, -ˌlandz\. See CANADA, *National Parks.*

Grassmoor. See GRASMOOR.

Grass Valley \ˈgras\. City, Nevada co., E California, 45 mi. (72 km.) W of Lake Tahoe; pop. (1990c) 9048.

Grassy Bay \ˈgra-sē\. Bay off NW coast of Bermuda I.

Grassy Knob. Peak, Union co., N Georgia; 4768 ft. (1453 m.).

Grå·sten \ˈgrȯ-ˌstān\ *or Ger.* **Grav·en·stein** \ˈgräv-^{ə}n-ˌshtīn\. Village, Sønderjylland co., SE Jutland, Denmark, SSE of Åbenrå; pop. (1981c) 6783; summer residence of Danish monarch; formerly in Germany.

Gratianopolis. See GRENOBLE.

Gra·tiot \ˈgra-shət\. County in cen. Michigan. See table at MICHIGAN.

Gratz. See GRAZ.

Grau·bün·den \grau̇-ˈbu̇e-dən\ *or Fr.* **Gri·sons** \grē-ˈzō^{n}\. Canton, E Switzerland; ✻ Chur; in Alps (Rhaetian Alps in E); includes Engadine Valley and sources of Rhine and Inn rivers; numerous mountain passes (such as Bernina and Oberalp); corn, wine; tourism. Formed part of ancient Roman prov. of Raetia (*q.v.*); conquered by Franks 6th cent.; became part of Germany; part of population accepted Reformation 1524–26; joined Swiss Confederation 1803. See table at SWITZERLAND.

Graudenz. See GRUDZIĄDZ.

Grau·pi·us, Mount \ˈgrȯ-pē-əs\ *or Lat.* **Mons Graupius** \ˈmänz\. Mountain in ancient Caledonia, of uncertain location; scene of battle in which Caledonians commanded by Galgacus were defeated 84 A.D. by Romans under Agricola, mentioned by historian Tacitus in his *Agricola;* has also been called Mt. Grampius, the name which became applied to the Grampians of Scotland.

Grave Creek Mound. See MOUNDSVILLE.

Gra·ve·lines \ˌgrȧv-ˈlēn\. Seaport commune, Nord dept., N France, 15 mi. (24 km.) SW of Dunkerque; pop. (1990c) 12,650; fish.

Grav·el Mountain \ˈgra-vəl\. Peak, Hinsdale co., SW Colorado; 13,600 ft. (4145 m.).

Gra·ve·lotte \ˌgrȧv-ˈlȯt\. Village, Moselle dept., NE France, near Metz; with St.-Privat-la-Montagne scene of one of most important battles of Franco-Prussian War Aug. 1870 in which the French under Marshal Achille-François Bazaine were forced by the Prussians to retreat into Metz (*q.v.*).

Gravenhage, 's. See HAGUE, THE.

Gra·ven·hurst \ˈgrā-vən-ˌhərst\. Town, Muskoka dist., SE Ontario, Canada, at foot of Lake Muskoka 10 mi. (16 km.) SSW of Bracebridge; pop. (1991c) 9988; center for campers and sportsmen.

Gravenstein. See GRÅSTEN.

Graves \ˈgrāvz\. County in SW Kentucky. See table at KENTUCKY.

Graves \ˈgrȧv\. District, Gironde dept., SW France; extends ab. 25 mi. (40 km.) along the Garonne W and S of Bordeaux; gravelly soil, hence the name; wine; adjoining on the SE is Sauternes (*q.v.*).

Graves·end \ˈgrāvz-ˈend\. Town, Kent, SE England, on Thames estuary 22 mi. (35 km.) E of London; paper manufacture, printing, engineering; here (1617) American Indian princess Pocahontas died and was buried.

Gravesend Bay. Inlet of Lower New York Bay, SW Long Island, New York.

Gra·vi·na in Pu·glia \grä-ˈvē-nä-ēn-ˈpül-yä\. Commune, Bari prov., Puglia, SE Italy, 30 mi. (48 km.) SW of the seaport of Bari; pop. (1989c) 39,047; cathedral; castle; limestone quarries nearby.

Gray \ˈgrā\. **1.** Name of counties in two states of the U.S. See tables at KANSAS and TEXAS.
2. City, ⊗ of Jones co., cen. Georgia; pop. (1990c) 2189.
3. Town, Cumberland co., SW Maine, 11 mi. (18 km.) N of Portland; pop. (1990c) 5904.
4. Commune, Haute-Saône dept., E France, river port on Saône 30 mi. (48 km.) SW of Vesoul; gave its name to distinguished English family of Grey, or de Grey; church of 13th–15th cents.; 17th cent. château.

Gray Kaweah. See KAWEAH PEAKS.

Gray·ling \ˈgrā-liŋ\. City, ⊗ of Crawford co., N Michigan, 45 mi. (72 km.) E of Traverse City; pop. (1990c) 1944; outdoor recreation.

Gray Peak. **1.** Mountain in Adirondack Mts., Essex co., NE New York; 4840 ft. (1475 m.).
2. Mountain in Yellowstone National Park, NW Wyoming; 10,300 ft. (3139 m.).

Grays Harbor \ˈgrāz\. **1.** Inlet of Pacific Ocean on SW coast of Grays Harbor co., W Washington.
2. Coastal county in W Washington. See table at WASHINGTON.

Grays·lake \ˈgrāz-ˈlāk\. Village, Lake co., NE Illinois, 11 mi. (18 km.) W of Waukegan; pop. (1990c) 7388; Coll. of Lake County (1967).

Grays Lake. Lake bet. Bonneville and Caribou cos., SE Idaho.

Gray·son \ˈgrā-sən\. **1.** Name of counties in three states of the U.S. See tables at KENTUCKY, TEXAS, VIRGINIA.
2. City, ⊗ of Carter co., NE Kentucky; pop. (1990c) 3510; Kentucky Christian Coll. (1919).

Grays Peak. Mountain, Clear Creek co., cen. Colorado; 14,270 ft. (4349 m.).

Graz; *earlier* **Gratz** \ˈgräts\. City, ✱ of Styria, Austria, on left bank of Mur River 87 mi. (140 km.) SSW of Vienna; pop. (1991c) 232,155; railroad shops; steel, machinery, paper, leather, textiles; 11th cent. castle; 15th cent. Gothic cathedral; 15th–16th cent. fortifications converted into parks 19th cent.; 16th cent. clock tower; 17th cent. arsenal; university (1585), technical university (1811); residence of early rulers of Styria; the astronomer Johannes Kepler taught here 1594–1600.

Great Abaco. See ABACO.

Great American Desert. Orig., a vaguely defined region, W United States, W of the Missouri River and sometimes incl. region W of the Rocky Mts.—so named from reports of early explorers to whom the territory appeared uninhabitable; later, the semiarid region bet. the Sierra Nevada and the Rockies, incl. the Great Basin; now, the region of deserts in SW Arizona and SE California.

Great Ar·te·sian Basin \är-ˈtē-zhən\. Basin, E cen. Australia, primarily in Queensland; one of the world's largest artesian basins.

Great Australian Bight. Bay on S coast of Australia; part of Indian Ocean; ab. 600 mi. (965 km.) wide.

Great Bahama Bank. See BAHAMA BANKS.

Great Banda. See BANDA BESAR.

Great Banjak. See BANJAK ISLANDS.

Great Barrier Island *or* **Otea** \ō-ˈtā-ä\. Island off E coast of N extension of North I., New Zealand, at E entrance to Hauraki Gulf.

Great Barrier Reef *also* **Barrier Reef.** Long stretch of coral reefs off NE coast of Queensland, Australia; ab. 1250 mi. (2000 km.) long; the largest deposit of coral in the world; N end close to coast, S end ab. 150 mi. (240 km.) out to sea; shallow waters inside reef strewn with coral islets or atolls, outside in Coral Sea waters of great depth; high tides and tremendous surf on outer edge; most of area designated a marine park 1983.

Great Bar·ring·ton \ˈbar-iŋ-tən\. Town, Berkshire co., W Massachusetts, on Housatonic River 18 mi. (29 km.) S of Pittsfield; pop. (1990c) 7225; ski slopes nearby; resort; Simon's Rock Coll. of Bard (1964); American poet and editor William Cullen Bryant town clerk here 1815–25; birthplace of American educator and writer W.E.B. Du Bois 1868.

Great Basin. Elevated region bet. the Wasatch Range and the Sierra Nevada, incl. Nevada and parts of Utah, California, Idaho, Wyoming, and Oregon; ab. 189,000 sq. mi. (489,500 sq. km.); chief rivers the Humboldt, N Nevada, and the Sevier, SW cen. Utah; has no drainage to the ocean, chief drainage center Great Salt Lake; includes Great Salt Lake Desert, Carson Sink, Mojave Desert (*qq.v.*), and Death Valley (see UNITED STATES, *National Monuments*).

Great Basin National Park. See UNITED STATES, *National Parks.*

Great Bay. Inlet at extreme S tip of Ocean co., New Jersey; connecting with Atlantic Ocean through Little Egg Inlet.

Great Bear Lake \ˈbar\. Lake, mainland part of Northwest Territories, Canada; 12,275 sq. mi. (31,792 sq. km.); largest lake entirely within Canada; of very irregular shape, with several long arms, its greatest length 192 mi. (309 km.); max. depth 1356 ft. (413 m.); its outlet is **Great Bear River** (70 mi. or 113 km. long), flowing W to the Mackenzie; frozen ab. eight months in the year; abounds in fish. Explored by European fur traders c. 1800, later followed by English explorer Sir John Franklin 1825; radium ores discovered on its E shore 1929.

Great Belt. See STORE STRAIT.

Great Bend. City, ⊗ of Barton co., cen. Kansas, on Arkansas River 53 mi. (85 km.) WNW of Hutchinson; pop. (1990c) 15,427; oil; wheat; Barton County Community Coll. (1965); on old Santa Fe Trail; Spanish explorer Francisco Coronado's Quivira (*q.v.*) generally located nearby.

Great Benin. See BENIN 3.

Great Berg \ˈbərg\. River, W Western Cape prov., S Rep. of South Africa; rises E of Cape Town, flows N and W into St. Helena Bay; 140 mi. (225 km.) long.

Great Berkhampstead. See BERKHAMSTED.

Great Bermuda. See BERMUDA.

Great Bitter Lake. See BITTER LAKES.

Great Black. See BIG BLACK 1.

Great Blasket. See BLASKET ISLANDS.

Great Brit·ain *or* **Britain** \ˈbrit-ᵊn\. Kingdom, W Europe, comprising England, Scotland, and Wales; ab. 88,150 sq. mi. (228,300 sq. km.); pop. (1991p) 53,917,000; together with Northern Ireland constitutes the United Kingdom of Great Britain and Northern Ireland; largest island in Europe. For additional information, see ENGLAND; IRELAND, NORTHERN; SCOTLAND; UNITED KINGDOM; WALES.

Great Bushman Land. See BUSHMAN LAND.

Great Cha·zy \shā-ˈzē\. River, Clinton co., NE corner of New York; flows out of Chazy Lake NE into Lake Champlain.

Great Co·co \ˈkō-kō\. Small island of the Andaman Is., Bay of Bengal; separated from North Andaman I. by Coco Channel.

Great Colombia. See GRAN COLOMBIA.

Great Corn Island. See CORN ISLANDS.

Great Crag·gy Mountains \ˈkra-gē\. Range, W North Carolina; includes **Craggy Dome** 6105 ft. (1861 m.), Buncombe co., and nearby **Craggy Pinnacle** 5944 ft. (1812 m.). Extending 10 mi. (16 km.) along crest of the range are the **Craggy Gardens,** a dense stand of purple rhododendron.

Great Crosby. See CROSBY 3.

Great Cumbrae Island. See CUMBRAES, THE.

Great Dayak. See KAHAYAN.

Great Dismal Swamp. See DISMAL SWAMP.

Great Divide. Watershed, North America. See CONTINENTAL DIVIDE.

Great Divide Basin. Elevated basin in Rocky Mts., S cen. Wyoming; forms a split in the Continental Divide.

Great Dividing Range *also* **Great Divide** *or* **Eastern Highlands.** Entire extent of mountain ranges in Queensland, New

South Wales, and Victoria, along E border of Australia; from 100 to 200 mi. (161 to 322 km.) wide; includes Australian Alps (*q.v.*) in SE part, with highest summit in Australia (Mt. Kosciusko 7310 ft. or 2228 m.); at N end is Atherton Plateau (*q.v.*).

Great Eastern Erg. See ERG, AL-.

Great Egg Harbor Inlet \ˈeg, ˈāg\. Narrow strait bet. Cape May and Atlantic cos., S New Jersey, leading from Atlantic Ocean into **Great Egg Harbor;** receives the **Great Egg River** *or* **Great Egg Harbor River** (ab. 40 mi. or 64 km. long, flows SE, lower part in Atlantic co.).

Great End. Mountain, Cumbria, NW England, in Lake District; 2984 ft. (910 m.).

Greater Ac·cra \ˈä-krä\. Region of Ghana. See table at GHANA.

Greater Antilles. See WEST INDIES.

Greater Armenia. **1.** *or* **Armenia Ma·jor** \ˈmā-jər\. In Roman times a province in the Byzantine Empire.
2. Name sometimes given, esp. in medieval times, to region of Armenia.

Greater Bombay. See BOMBAY 2.

Greater Copenhagen. See COPENHAGEN 2.

Greater London. See LONDON 4.

Greater Manchester. Metropolitan county, NW England; includes city of Manchester and towns of Bolton, Oldham, Rochdale, Salford, and Stockport; estab. 1974. See table at ENGLAND.

Greater Sunda Islands. See SUNDA ISLES.

Greater Tunb. See TUNB.

Greater Walachia. See MUNTENIA.

Great Exuma. See EXUMA.

Great Falls. **1.** Falls, Kentucky. See CUMBERLAND 1.
2. Cataract in the Potomac River on boundary bet. Maryland and Virginia; in a series of rapids ab. 15 mi. (24 km.) above Washington, D.C. where the river descends ab. 90 ft. (27 m.); 35 ft. (11 m.) high.
3. Dam in Caney Fork River, forming **Great Falls Lake** bet. White and Warren cos., cen. Tennessee. See table at TENNESSEE VALLEY AUTHORITY.
4. City, ⊗ of Cascade co., cen. Montana, on Missouri River 12 mi. (19 km.) WSW of the **Great Falls of the Missouri,** now in modified form; pop. (1990c) 55,097; copper refining and smelting, oil refining, flour milling, aluminum rolling; Coll. of Great Falls (1932).

Great Falls of the Passaic. See PASSAIC 1.

Great Fish \ˈfish\. **1.** River in Canada. See BACK RIVER.
2. River, SE Eastern Cape prov., Rep. of South Africa; flows SSE into Indian Ocean NE of Port Alfred; 400 mi. (644 km.) long.
3. River in Namibia. See FISH.

Great Gable. See GABLE, GREAT.

Great Geyser. See GEYSIR.

Great Glen of Scotland. Valley, Scotland. See GLEN MORE.

Great Grimsby. See GRIMSBY 2.

Great Gua·na Cay \ˈgwä-nä\. One of the Bahamas, in Atlantic Ocean bet. SE Andros I. and Cat I.

Great Gull Island \ˈgəl\. Island at E end of Long Island Sound, New York, just NE of Plum I.

Great Har·wood \ˈhär-wu̇d\. Town, Lancashire, NW England, 22 mi. (35 km.) N of Manchester; pop. (1981p) 10,921.

Great Himalayas. See HIMALAYAS, THE.

Great Inagua. See INAGUA.

Great Indian Desert. See THAR DESERT.

Great Island. Island in Cork Harbour, S coast of Ireland; site of town of Cobh (Queenstown).

Great Kai Island. See KAI ISLANDS.

Great Kanawha. See KANAWHA.

Great Kapela. See KAPELA, GREAT.

Great Karimata. See KARIMATA ISLANDS.

Great Karoo. See KAROO.

Great Kei \ˈkā, ˈkī\. River, Eastern Cape prov., S Rep. of South Africa; flows SE to Indian Ocean; ab. 150 mi. (240 km.) long; served as SW boundary of Transkei.

Great Khingan Mountains. See DA HINGGAN LING.

Great Lake. Largest lake in Tasmania, Australia, in cen. part S of the Great Western Tiers; 44 sq. mi. (114 sq. km.); ab. 15 mi. (24 km.) long; 2880 ft. (878 m.) above sea level; largest natural freshwater lake in Australia; drained by Ouse River.

Great Lakes. **1.** Chain of five lakes, Superior, Michigan, Huron, Erie, and Ontario (*qq.v.*), cen. North America; through the chain (except for Lake Michigan, which is wholly within the U.S.) runs the U.S.-Canada boundary; drained by St. Lawrence River. Visited by French early 17th cent., Samuel de Champlain and Étienne Brûlé reached Lake Huron and Lake Ontario 1615; Lake Michigan explored by Jean Nicolet 1634; founding of Detroit (*q.v.*) 1701 assured French control of region until Canada was ceded to British 1763; Lakes Ontario and Erie scenes of naval warfare bet. U.S. and British during War of 1812; disarmament effected under terms of Rush-Bagot Agreement 1817; came to be of great importance as commercial link bet. E and NW U.S., esp. after building of steamships and of Erie Canal 1825; St. Lawrence Seaway (*q.v.*) opened 1959.
2. Group of large lakes chiefly in Great Rift Valley, E cen. Africa, incl. esp. Lakes Turkana, Albert, Victoria, Tanganyika, and Malawi.

Great Lakes Naval Training Center. See WAUKEGAN.

Great Mal·vern \ˈmȯl-vərn\. Town, Hereford and Worcester, W cen. England, in Malvern Hills, SW of Worcester; resort with mineral springs; developed as spa early 19th cent.

Great Meadows. Level area on the Youghiogheny River, SW Pennsylvania, ab. 10 mi. (16 km.) ESE of present Uniontown; nearby is site of Fort Necessity, built 1754 under George Washington's supervision in campaign against French at Fort Duquesne.

Great Miami. See MIAMI 1.

Great Miquelon. See MIQUELON ISLAND.

Great Namaqualand. See NAMAQUALAND.

Great Natoena. See NATUNA ISLANDS.

Great Neck \ˈgrāt-ˌnek\. Residential village, Nassau co., SE New York, on N shore of Long Island; pop. (1990c) 8745; setting for F. Scott Fitzgerald's novel *The Great Gatsby.*

Great Neck Estates. Residential village, Nassau co., SE New York, on N shore of Long Island; pop. (1990c) 2790.

Great Neck Plaza. Residential village, Nassau co., SE New York, on N shore of Long Island, near Great Neck; pop. (1990c) 5897.

Great Nemaha. See NEMAHA.

Great Nethe. See NETHE.

Great Nic·o·bar \ˈni-kə-ˌbär\. One of the Nicobar Is. (*q.v.*).

Great Novgorod. See NOVGOROD 2.

Great Ormes Head \ˈȯrmz\. Cape extending into Irish Sea on N coast of Wales, E of Anglesey I.; lighthouse.

Great Ouse. See OUSE 1.

Great Pat·er·nos·ter Point \ˌpa-tər-ˌnäs-tər, ˌpä-\. Cape on W coast of Western Cape prov., Rep. of South Africa, S of St. Helena Bay.

Great Peconic Bay. See PECONIC BAY.

Great Pee Dee \ˈpē-ˌdē\. Name often used for stretch of Pee Dee River in South Carolina.

Great Plains. The continental slope of cen. North America (U.S. and Canada) extending E from the Rocky Mts. to the margin of the Canadian Shield in Canada; N to S extent is from delta of Mackenzie River to S Texas; characterized by smooth, treeless plains traversed by broad, shallow valleys of rivers rising in Rocky Mts., but in some sections with sand hills (esp. in NW Nebraska), buttes, and badlands.

Great Point. NE point of Nantucket I., Massachusetts.

Great Rann of Kachchh. See KACHCHH, RANN OF.

Great Re·dang \ˈrā-ˌdäŋ\ *or* **Redang.** Island, Malaysia, in South China Sea, off E coast of Malay Penin. in Terengganu state; thinly populated.

Great Rift Valley \ˈrift\ *also* **Rift Valley.** A great depression extending from valley of the Jordan in SW Asia S to Mozambique, SE Africa—a geological rather than a geographical term; marks a series of geological faults which are the result of great volcanic action; includes Dead Sea, Gulf of Aqaba, Red Sea, the chain of lakes in S Ethiopia, Lake Turkana and the chain of small lakes S of it in Kenya and Tanzania which are in E rift valley, and Lakes Albert, Edward, Kivu, Tanganyika, and Malawi in W rift valley. Below sea level at Dead Sea but in Africa in some places at over 6000 ft. or 1829 m. (as at Lake Naivasha in the E rift which has elev. of 6135 ft. or 1870 m.); esp. marked in cen. Kenya in the E rift valley bet. 1°N and 1°S where it has high perpendicular cliffs.

Great River Road. Scenic road system, U.S. and Canada, extending from S Manitoba and W Ontario to the Gulf of Mexico, mostly along the Mississippi River.

Great Ru·a·ha \rü-ˈä-hä\. River in cen. Tanzania; flows E into Rufiji River; ab. 300 mi. (475 km.) long.

Great Sac·an·da·ga Lake \ˌsa-kən-ˈdȯ-gə\; *formerly* **Sacandaga Reservoir.** Reservoir in Sacandaga River, E Fulton and W Saratoga cos., E New York; 42 sq. mi. (109 sq. km.) and 27 mi. (43 km.) long; formed by Conklingville Dam; completed 1930; regulates flow of upper Hudson. Now a summer resort.

Great Saint Ber·nard \ˌsānt-bər-ˈnärd\. Pass in the Alps. See table at ALPS.

Great Salt Desert. See DASHT-E-KAVĪR.

Great Salt Lake. Lake in Great Basin of U.S., in Box Elder, Tooele, Salt Lake, Davis, and Weber cos., N Utah; ab. 80 mi. (130 km.) long, 35 mi. (55 km.) wide; roughly 2000 sq. mi. (5180 sq. km.), but area fluctuates considerably; max. depth ab. 35 ft. (11 m.); waters strongly saline; mean elev. 4200 ft. (1280 m.); receives Bear, Jordan, and Weber rivers from E; no outlet; has a number of islands, incl. Antelope I. (36 sq. mi. or 93 sq. km.). First nonnative to visit and report on it was fur trader James Bridger 1824.

Great Salt Lake Desert. Broad, flat, low area SW of Great Salt Lake, N Utah; ab. 110 mi. (175 km.) long; barren and uncultivated; contains off-limits military test ranges.

Great Salt Plains Dam. Dam across Salt Fork of Arkansas River in Grant co., N Oklahoma, forming reservoir 10 mi. (16 km.) long for flood control and conservation.

Great Sand Dunes National Monument. See UNITED STATES, *National Monuments.*

Great Sandy Desert. **1.** Desert, Arabian Penin. See RUBʻ AL-KHALI.
2. Large tract of arid country, N cen. Western Australia, Australia; traversed by Canning Stock Route.

Great Sandy Island. See FRASER ISLAND.

Great Sangir. See SANGIHE ISLANDS.

Great Sark. See SARK 1.

Great Scheidegg. See SCHEIDEGG.

Great Schütt \ˈshüt\ *or Slovak* **Os·trov** \ˈȯs-ˌtrȯf\; *formerly* **Vel'·ký Žit·ný** \ˈvel-kē-ˈzhit-nē\ *or Hung.* **Csal·ló·köz** \ˈchȯ-lō-ˌkœz\. Island, SW Slovakia; 728 sq. mi. (1886 sq. km.); 53 mi. (85 km.) long, bet. 9 and 18 mi. (14 to 29 km.) wide; formed by arms of Danube River to the N of the main stream extending from Bratislava to Komárom.

Great Sea, The. The Mediterranean—esp. in biblical usage (as in *Num.* xxxiv. 6).

Great Sit·kin \ˈsit-kin\. Small island NE of Adak I. in Andreanof Is., Aleutian Is., Alaska.

Great Skellig. See SKELLIGS.

Great Slave Lake \ˈslāv\. Lake in S mainland part of Northwest Territories, Canada; outlet the Mackenzie, flowing from its W end; on S receives Slave River, the outlet of Lake Athabaska, and on SW the Hay River; 10,980 sq. mi. (28,438 sq. km.); 298 mi. (479 km.) long; max. depth 2015 ft. (614 m.); of irregular shape, with several long arms. Visited by English explorer Samuel Hearne 1771.

Great Slave River. See SLAVE.

Great Smoky Mountains \ˈsmō-kē\; *often shortened to* **Great Smok·ies** \-kēz\ *or* **Smokey Mountains** *or* **Smokies.** Range of the Appalachian Mts. extending along North Carolina-Tennessee boundary; highest peak Clingmans Dome 6643 ft. (2025 m.); remarkable for its flora, incl. large virgin forest of red spruce. Has been set aside as **Great Smoky Mountains National Park** (see UNITED STATES, *National Parks*).

Great Sound. Body of water enclosed by curve at W end of Bermuda I.

Great South Bay. Long narrow inlet of Atlantic Ocean bet. Fire I. and S shore of Long Island, New York.

Great Stour *or* **Stour** \ˈstu̇r\. River, Kent, SE England; flows NE past Canterbury and empties into North Sea through two arms which cut off the Isle of Thanet; 40 mi. (64 km.) long; navigable as far as Canterbury.

Great Vic·to·ria Desert \vik-ˈtōr-ē-ə\. Desert region in SE Western Australia and W South Australia, Australia; ab. 450 mi. (725 km.) E to W; av. height 500 to 1000 ft. (150 to 300 m.), sloping to Nullarbor Plain on S.

Great Wall *also* **Great Wall of China** *or* **Chinese Wall.** Defensive wall with towers at intervals, N China, extending for ab. 1500 mi. (2400 km.) from Gansu prov. to Bo Hai; 20 to 50 ft. (6 to 15 m.) high, 15 to 25 ft. (5 to 8 m.) thick; built in 3d cent. B.C. by Emperor Shih Huang Ti (Cheng); actual length, incl. branches and windings, more than 2000 mi. (3218 km.); important gates at Shanhaiguan (at E end), and Jiayuguan (at extreme W in Gansu).

Great Wass \ˈwäs\. Island in Atlantic Ocean off coast of Washington co., SE Maine.

Great Western Erg. See ERG, AL-.

Great Western Tiers \ˈtirz\. Mountain range in N cen. Tasmania, Australia, extending NW and SE along N border of the lake region; highest peak ab. 4200 ft. (1280 m.).

Great Whale \ˈhwāl, ˈwāl\. River, cen. and W Quebec, Canada; flows W into SE Hudson Bay; 230 mi. (370 km.) long; outlet of Lac Bienville.

Great Yar·mouth; *sometimes shortened to* **Yarmouth** \ˈyär-məth\. Town, Norfolk, E England, on North Sea at mouth of the Yare 110 mi. (177 km.) NE of London; pop. (1981p) 48,273; seaside resort; support center for North Sea oil and gas operations; old town noted for its "rows" (narrow lanes). A chartered and walled town from 13th cent.; church of St. Nicholas, founded 12th cent., destroyed by bombs during WWII and subsequently restored.

Great Zab. See ZAB, GREAT.

Great Zimbabwe. See ZIMBABWE.

Gre·co, Cape \ˈgre-kō, ˈgrā-\. SE point of Cyprus, at S end of Famagusta Bay.

Gredos, Sierra de. See SIERRA DE GREDOS.

Greece \ˈgrēs\ *or Gk.* **El·lás** \e-ˈläs\; *anc.* **Hel·las** \ˈhe-ləs\. Republic, S Europe, SW part of Balkan Penin., bounded on N by Albania, Republic of Macedonia, and Bulgaria, on NE by Turkey in Europe, on E by Aegean Sea, on S by Mediterranean, and on W by Ionian Sea; 50,944 sq. mi. (131,945 sq. km.); pop. (1993e) 10,310,000; ✻ Athens; includes Aegean Is., Ionian Is., and Crete.

Physical features: Forms a peninsula of irregular shape, with many deep indentations in coastline and two large peninsulas projecting from it: in NE Chalcidice with its three long projections, in S the Peloponnese (in medieval times Morea), joined to N part by Isthmus of Corinth and ending in three long peninsulas, the central one ending in Cape Taínaron, the southernmost point of the mainland.

Islands: Near coast the Ionian Is. on W and S and Euboea on E; in Aegean Sea the large groups of Cyclades, North and South Sporades, and Dodecanese (*q.v.*); Thásos, Samothrace, and Lemnos in N Aegean; Lesbos, Chios, and Sámos in E Aegean off W coast of Turkey in Asia; Crete to the SE in the Mediterranean.

Mountains: Pindus Mts. in Epirus; peaks of Olympus and Ossa on E coast; Othrys Range, Oeta and Parnassus in cen. part; and Cyllene and Erymanthus, with many ranges, in the Peloponnese.

Chief rivers: Peneus, Achelous, Arakhthos, Cephisus, and Alpheus; most rivers short.

Chief products: Wheat, tobacco, olives, corn, processed foods; viticulture; ab. 25 percent of total land area is cultiva-

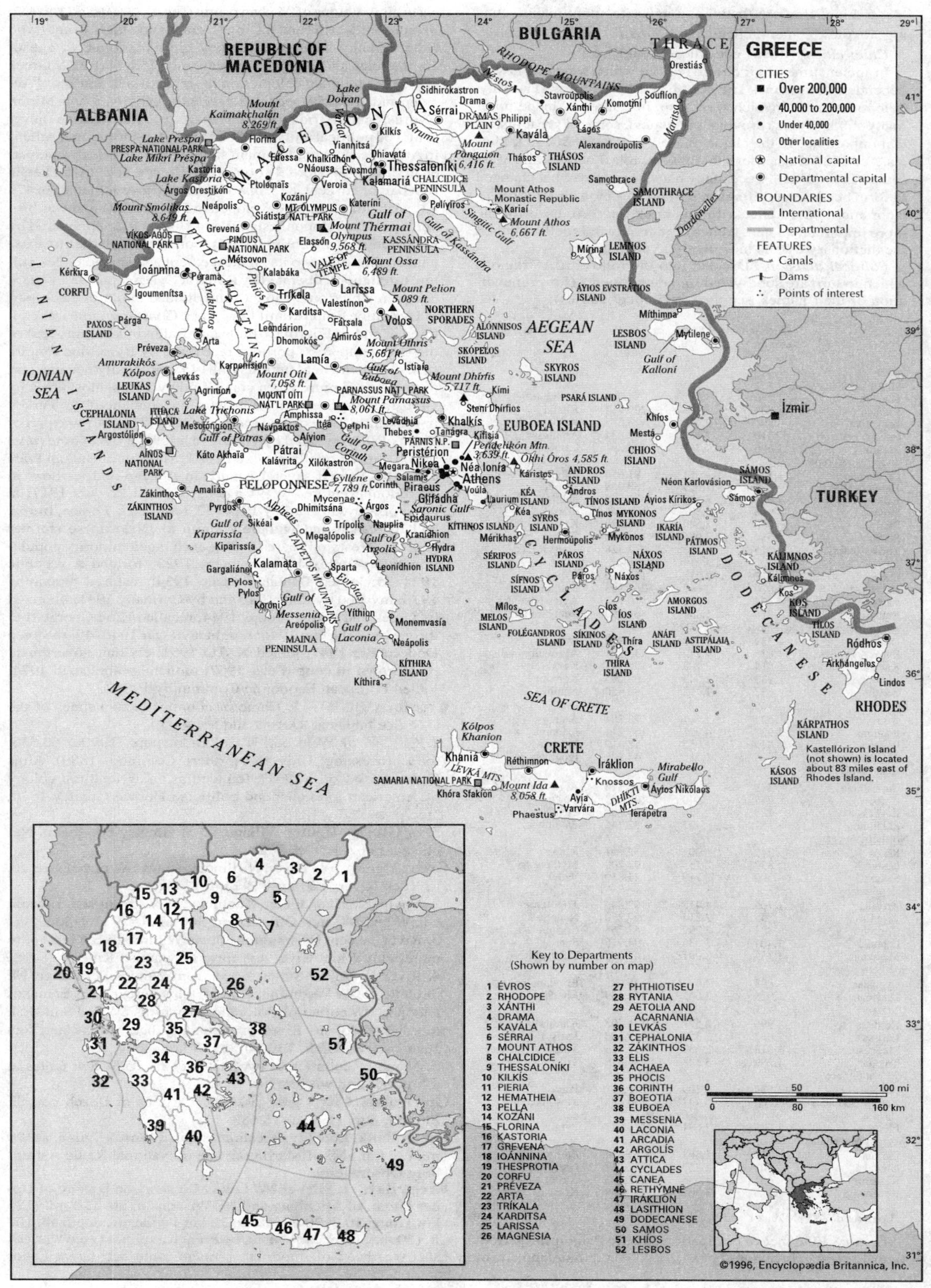

GREECE
CITIES
Over 200,000
40,000 to 200,000
Under 40,000
Other localities
National capital
Departmental capital
BOUNDARIES
International
Departmental
FEATURES
Canals
Dams
Points of interest
BULGARIA
REPUBLIC OF MACEDONIA
ALBANIA
TURKEY
THRACE
MACEDONIA
RHODOPE MOUNTAINS
AEGEAN SEA
IONIAN SEA
IONIAN ISLANDS
MEDITERRANEAN SEA
SEA OF CRETE
CYCLADES
DODECANESE
PELOPONNESE
PINDUS MOUNTAINS
EUBOEA ISLAND
CRETE
RHODES
Athens
Thessaloníki
Piraeus
Pátrai
Lárissa
Iráklion
Vólos
Kavála
Ioánnina
Khaniá
Kalamáta
Sérrai
Dráma
Xánthi
Komotiní
Alexandroúpolis
Orestiás
Kérkira
CORFU
Igoumenítsa
Árta
Préveza
Agrinion
Mesolóngion
Lamía
Trípolis
Sparta
Kórinthos
Khalkís
Mytilene
Khíos
Sámos
Ródhos
İzmir
Mount Olympus 9,568 ft.
Mount Ossa 6,489 ft.
Mount Pelion 5,089 ft.
Mount Athos 6,667 ft.
Mount Parnassus 8,061 ft.
Mount Ida 8,058 ft.
Mount Smólikas 8,649 ft.
Mount Kaimakchalán 8,269 ft.
Mount Óiti 7,058 ft.
Mount Pangaion 6,416 ft.
Mount Dhírfis 5,717 ft.
Mount Othris 5,661 ft.
Cyllene 7,789 ft.
Ókhi Óros 4,585 ft.
Pendelikón Mtn. 3,639 ft.
Gulf of Thérmai
Gulf of Corinth
Gulf of Patras
Saronic Gulf
Gulf of Argolis
Gulf of Laconia
Gulf of Messenia
Gulf of Kiparissía
Gulf of Kalloní
Kastellórizon Island (not shown) is located about 83 miles east of Rhodes Island.
0 50 100 mi
0 80 160 km
Key to Departments (Shown by number on map)
1 ÉVROS
2 RHODOPE
3 XÁNTHI
4 DRAMA
5 KAVÁLA
6 SÉRRAI
7 MOUNT ATHOS
8 CHALCIDICE
9 THESSALONÍKI
10 KILKÍS
11 PIERIA
12 HEMATHEIA
13 PELLA
14 KOZÁNI
15 FLORINA
16 KASTORIA
17 GREVENÁ
18 IOÁNNINA
19 THESPROTIA
20 CORFU
21 PRÉVEZA
22 ARTA
23 TRÍKALA
24 KARDITSA
25 LARISSA
26 MAGNESIA
27 PHTHIOTISEU
28 RYTANIA
29 AETOLIA AND ACARNANIA
30 LEVKÁS
31 CEPHALONIA
32 ZÁKINTHOS
33 ELIS
34 ACHAEA
35 PHOCIS
36 CORINTH
37 BOEOTIA
38 EUBOEA
39 MESSENIA
40 LACONIA
41 ARCADIA
42 ARGOLÍS
43 ATTICA
44 CYCLADES
45 CANEA
46 RETHYMNE
47 IRÁKLION
48 LASITHION
49 DODECANESE
50 SAMOS
51 KHÍOS
52 LESBOS
©1996, Encyclopædia Britannica, Inc.

ble; fishing; iron ore, bauxite, magnesite, zinc; manufacturing: textiles, cement, chemicals; tourism.

Chief cities: Athens and Thessaloníki.

In ancient times divided into regions which were at times independent kingdoms: Thrace, Macedonia, Epirus, Thessaly, Peloponnese, and which were, esp. in S Greece, made up of many subdivisions (provinces or states), some of great historical importance in the classic period, as Attica, Boeotia, Phocis, Aetolia, Achaea, Corinth, Elis, Arcadia, Laconia, and Messenia. (In modern Greece many names are somewhat changed in form because of difference in transliteration systems of ancient and modern Greek. In this book the form used for the more important ancient names is generally the spelling which the dictionary user is most likely to encounter.)

Political divisions: Divided into the following 13 regions which in turn are subdivided into departments (for pronunciation of their names, see their individual entries):

NAME	AREA (sq. mi.)	AREA (sq. km.)	POP. (1991c)	CAPITAL
Attica				
Central Greece				
Boeotia	1,240	3,212	134,034	Levádhia
Euboea	1,509	3,908	209,132	Khalkí
Eurytania	790	2,046	23,535	Karpenision
Phocis	819	2,121	43,884	Amphissa
Phthiotis	1,686	4,368	168,291	Lamía
Central Macedonia				
Chalcidice	1,178	3,051	91,654	Polygyros
Hematheia	656	1,699	138,068	Veroia
Kilkís	1,003	2,598	81,845	Kilkís
Pella	968	2,507	138,261	Edessa
Pieria	598	1,549	116,820	Kateríni
Sérrai	1,539	3,986	191,890	Sérrai
Thessaloníki	1,375	3,561	977,528	Thessaloníki
Crete				
Canea	917	2,375	133,060	Canea
Iráklion	1,020	2,642	263,868	Iráklion
Lasithion	702	1,818	70,762	Áyios Nikólaos
Rethýmnē	578	1,497	69,290	Rethymnon
Eastern Macedonia and Thrace				
Drama	1,339	3,468	96,978	Drama
Évros	1,638	4,242	143,791	Alexandroúpolis
Kavála	814	2,108	135,747	Kavála
Rhodope	982	2,543	103,295	Komotinē
Xánthi	692	1,792	90,450	Xánthi
Epirus				
Arta	622	1,611	78,884	Arta
Ioánnina	1,927	4,991	157,214	Ioánnina
Préveza	419	1,085	58,910	Préveza
Thesprotia	585	1,515	44,202	Igoumenítsa
Ionian Islands				
Cephalonia[1]	339	878	32,314	Argostólion
Corfu	247	640	105,043	Corfu
Levkás	125	324	20,900	Levkás
Zákinthos	157	407	32,746	Zákinthos
Northern Aegean				
Khíos	349	904	52,691	Khíos
Lesbos	832	2,155	103,700	Mytilene
Samos	300	777	41,850	Vathy
Pelopónnisos				
Arcadia	1,706	4,418	103,840	Tripolis
Argolis	855	2,214	97,250	Nauplia
Corinth	884	2,290	142,365	Corinth
Laconia	1,404	3,636	94,916	Sparta
Messenia	1,155	2,991	167,292	Kalamata
Southern Aegean				
Cyclades	993	2,572	95,083	Ermoúpolis
Dodecanese	1,028	2,662	162,439	Rhodes
Thessaly				
Karditsa	995	2,577	126,498	Karditsa
Larissa	2,067	5,354	269,300	Larissa
Magnesia	1,018	2,637	197,613	Volos
Tríkala	1,289	3,338	137,819	Tríkala
Western Greece				
Achaea	1,239	3,209	297,318	Patras
Aetolia and Acarnania	2,103	5,447	230,688	Mesolóngion
Elis	1,035	2,681	174,021	Pyrgos
Western Macedonia				
Florina	719	1,862	52,854	Florina
Grevená	903	2,339	37,017	Grevená
Kastoria	651	1,686	52,721	Kastoria
Kozáni	1,375	3,561	150,159	Kozáni

[1]Comprised of Cephalonia I. and Ithaca I.

History: Evidence of occupation dates to Paleolithic period; Indo-European invasions began c. 2000 B.C.; mainland site of early civilizations of Aegean origin (see MYCENAE and TIRYNS); invaded mid-11th cent. B.C. by Dorians and others from N who formed many small independent city-kingdoms; in age of commercial and industrial advance c. 750–500 B.C., Greek city-states founded colonies on shores of Black Sea and N Aegean, and in S Italy (see MAGNA GRAECIA), Sicily, S Asia Minor, Cyprus, and Africa (see CYRENE); ancient Greece never achieved political unity, but Sparta in Peloponnese, and Athens in Attica became predominant states while all states participated in shifting and loosely organized leagues; at war with Persia first half of 5th cent. B.C., major Greek victory at Plataea in 479 B.C.; Athenian empire developed in 5th cent. B.C. and was broken by Great Peloponnesian War 431–404 B.C.; conquered by Macedonian King Philip II whose son Alexander the Great expanded the empire to its greatest extent and spread Greek culture throughout; liberated by Rome at Cynoscephalae 197 B.C.; conquered by Rome 146 B.C. and divided into provinces; part of Byzantine Empire until 1204 when Constantinople was captured at end of Fourth Crusade and Baldwin I became first of the Latin emperors; portions recovered by Byzantine Empire (*q.v.*) 1261 and held until its fall 1453; gradually became part of Ottoman Empire when conquered by Turks, most areas by 1456; modern Greek kingdom won independence from Turkey in war 1821–29; received Ionian Is. 1864, Thessaly and part of Epirus 1881; defeated by Turkey in brief war over Crete (*q.v.*) which Greece finally annexed 1913; as result of Balkan Wars 1912–13, gained several islands in Aegean and territory in Macedonia; entered WWI against Central Powers 1917; at close of war with Turkey 1920–22, returned E Thrace, İmroz, and Bozcaada and withdrew claim to Dodecanese (former gains by Treaty of Sèvres 1920); exchanged minority population with Turkey by agreement 1923; formed a republic 1924–35; joined Balkan Entente 1934; restored monarchy 1935; invaded by Italy 1940 and by Germany 1941; liberated by Greek and British troops 1944; recalled King George II to throne by plebiscite 1946; fought civil war 1946–49; received Dodecanese 1947; joined NATO 1951; civilian government overthrown in coup d'état 1967; monarchy abolished 1974; joined European Economic Community 1981.

Gree·ley \ˈgrē-lē\. **1.** Name of counties in two states of the U.S. See tables at KANSAS and NEBRASKA.

2. City, ⊗ of Weld co., N Colorado; pop. (1990c) 60,536; food processing; Univ. of Northern Colorado (1889), Aims Community Coll. (1967); founded as an agricultural colony by American journalist and politician Horace Greeley 1870; incorp. as a city 1885.

3. *or* **Greeley Center.** Village, ⊗ of Greeley co., E cen. Nebraska; pop. (1990c) 562.

Green \ˈgrēn\. **1.** River, N Illinois; flows SW out of Lee co. to Rock River; 120 mi. (193 km.) long.

2. Navigable river, E cen. Kentucky; flows from cen. Lincoln co., W and NW into Ohio River; 360 mi. (579 km.) long.

3. River, W cen. Washington; flows W through S King co. to unite with White River and form Duwamish River.

4. River, W United States; flows from Wind River Range, NE Sublette co., W Wyoming, S into Utah where it turns E, makes a loop in NW corner of Colorado, then turns SW and S in Utah to enter Colorado River on boundary bet. Wayne and San Juan cos., SE Utah; 730 mi. (1175 km.) long.

5. Name of counties in two states of the U.S. See tables at KENTUCKY and WISCONSIN.

Green·acres City \ˈgrēn-ˌā-kərz\. City, Palm Beach co., SE Florida; pop. (1990c) 18,683.

Green Bank. Locality, Pocahontas co., E West Virginia, ab. 20 mi. (32 km.) NE of Marlinton; site of National Radio Astronomy Observatory.

Green Bay. **1.** Inlet of NW Lake Michigan, on S shore of Upper Penin. of Michigan and NE Wisconsin; ab. 120 mi. (195 km.) long; 10 to 20 mi. (16 to 32 km.) wide; av. depth ab. 100 ft. (30 m.); from early visits by French explorers (see WISCONSIN) was head of important portage route bet. Great Lakes

and Mississippi River by way of Fox and Wisconsin rivers (*qq.v.*).
2. City, ⊗ of Brown co., E Wisconsin, on S end of Green Bay at mouth of Fox River; pop. (1990c) 96,466; port of entry; fishing; manufactures paper; dairy products; National Railroad Museum; Northeast Wisconsin Technical Coll. (1913), Univ. of Wisconsin–Green Bay (1968). Visited by French explorer Jean Nicolet 1634; settled by fur traders, first half of 18th cent.; in region controlled by British 1763; ceded to U.S. 1783; important fur-trading community through early 19th cent.; occupied by British in War of 1812; Fort Howard, U.S. military post, built 1816; platting begun 1829; incorp. as city 1854.

Green·belt \ˈgrēn-ˌbelt\. City, Prince Georges co., S cen. Maryland, NE of Washington, D.C.; pop. (1990c) 21,096; Goddard Space Flight Center, National Agricultural Research Center nearby; city built late 1930s as a federal project in low-cost housing; population grew rapidly in 1940s and again in 1960s.

Green·bri·er \ˈgrēn-ˌbrī-ər\. **1.** River, SE West Virginia; rises in N Pocahontas co., flows SW into New River near Hinton; ab. 175 mi. (280 km.) long.
2. County in SE West Virginia. See table at WEST VIRGINIA.

Green·cas·tle \ˈgrēn-ˌka-səl\. **1.** City, ⊗ of Putnam co., W cen. Indiana, 32 mi. (51 km.) ENE of Terre Haute; pop. (1990c) 8984; lumbering; DePauw Univ. (1837).
2. Borough, Franklin co., S Pennsylvania, 12 mi. (19 km.) S of Chambersburg; pop. (1990c) 3600.

Green Cove Springs \ˈgrēn-ˌkōv\. City, ⊗ of Clay co., NE Florida, on St. Johns River 25 mi. (40 km.) S of Jacksonville; pop. (1990c) 4497.

Green·dale \ˈgrēn-ˌdāl\. **1.** Town, Dearborn co., SE Indiana, suburb of Lawrenceburg on Ohio River; pop. (1990c) 3881.
2. Residential village, Milwaukee co., SE Wisconsin; pop. (1990c) 15,128; built late 1930s as a federal-government project in low-cost housing.

Greene \ˈgrēn\. Name of counties in 14 states of the U.S. See tables at ALABAMA, ARKANSAS, GEORGIA, ILLINOIS, INDIANA, IOWA, MISSISSIPPI, MISSOURI, NEW YORK, NORTH CAROLINA, OHIO, PENNSYLVANIA, TENNESSEE, VIRGINIA.

Greene·ville \ˈgrēn-ˌvil, -vəl\. Town, ⊗ of Greene co., NE Tennessee, 30 mi. (48 km.) WSW of Johnson City; pop. (1990c) 13,532; burley tobacco market; electronic equipment; Tusculum Coll. (1794). Served as ✻ of State of Franklin 1785–87 which had seceded from North Carolina; home of Andrew Johnson, 17th president of the U.S., his homestead, tailor shop, and burial place set aside as a national historic site.

Green·field \ˈgrēn-ˌfēld\. **1.** City, Monterey co., W California, 32 mi. (51 km.) SE of Salinas; pop. (1990c) 7464.
2. City, ⊗ of Hancock co., cen. Indiana, 20 mi. (32 km.) E of Indianapolis; pop. (1990c) 11,657; tomatoes; birthplace of poet James Whitcomb Riley 1849.
3. City, ⊗ of Adair co., SW cen. Iowa, 50 mi. (80 km.) WSW of Des Moines; pop. (1990c) 2074.
4. Town, ⊗ of Franklin co., NW Massachusetts, on Connecticut River 34 mi. (55 km.) N of Springfield; pop. (1990c) 18,666; manufactures taps and dies and other hardware, silverware; Greenfield Community Coll. (1962); founded 1686, orig. part of Deerfield; incorp. 1753; birthplace of architect Asher Benjamin 1773.
5. City, ⊗ of Dade co., SW Missouri; pop. (1990c) 1416.
6. Village, Highland co., S Ohio, 21 mi. (34 km.) W of Chillicothe; pop. (1990c) 5172.
7. City, Milwaukee co., SE Wisconsin; a suburb of Milwaukee; pop. (1990c) 33,403; residential.

Greenfield Park. Town, S Quebec, Canada, 4 mi. (6 km.) E of Montreal on opp. side of the St. Lawrence; pop. (1991c) 17,652.

Green·hills \ˈgrēn-ˌhilz\. Village, Hamilton co., SW corner of Ohio, near Cincinnati; pop. (1990c) 4393; built late 1930s as a federal-government project in low-cost housing.

Green Island. Village, Albany co., E New York, on an island in Hudson River 8 mi. (13 km.) N of the city of Albany; pop. (1990c) 2490.

Green Islands. Group of small islands in extreme N Solomon Is., W Pacific Ocean, 45 mi. (72 km.) NNW of Buka I.; largest Nissan I., ab. 30 sq. mi. (78 sq. km.); administratively part of Papua New Guinea.

Green Lake. **1.** Lake, Green Lake co., cen. Wisconsin, 25 mi. (40 km.) W of Fond du Lac; ab. 7 mi. (11 km.) long.
2. County in cen. Wisconsin. See table at WISCONSIN.
3. Village, ⊗ of Green Lake co., cen. Wisconsin, at NE end of Green Lake; pop. (1990c) 1335.

Green·land \ˈgrēn-lənd, -ˌland\ *or Dan.* **Grøn·land** \ˈgrœn-ˌlän\ *or native* **Ka·laal·lit Nu·naat** \kä-ˈlät-lēt-nu̇-ˈnät, -ˈlä-\. Island, NE North America; 839,999 sq. mi. or 2,175,597 sq. km. (of which ab. 135,000 sq. mi. or 349,650 sq. km. are ice-free); pop. (1989e) 55,171; ✻ Godthåb; an integral part of the Danish realm.

Physical features: Largest island in the world (exclusive of Australia); greater part lies within Arctic Circle; max. length ab. 1650 mi. (2655 km.), max. breadth ab. 800 mi. (1285 km.); max. ice thickness ab. 11,000 ft. (3355 m.); numerous islands (largest is Qeqertarsuag) along coastline, which is deeply indented with fjords; highest peak is Mt. Gunnbjørn 12,139 ft. (3700 m.).

Chief products: Cryolite (largest deposits in the world), coal, lead, zinc; fishing, hunting.

Chief communities: Godthåb, Holsteinsborg, Julianehåb, Jakobshavn.

History: Inuit migration to Greenland began c. 2000 B.C.; visited by Norse leader Erik the Red, c. 982 who established colonies; his son, Leif Eriksson, introduced Christianity to Greenland and possibly landed in North America on his way to Greenland; came under Norwegian control 1261; original Norse settlements disappeared; came under Danish rule with Norway late 14th cent.; visited by numerous explorers 16th–19th cents. looking for Northwest Passage and North Pole; recolonization began 1721 with mission and trading company founded by Norwegian Hans Egede on SW coast; remained part of Denmark after Norway united with Sweden 1814; Denmark claimed full sovereignty 1921; Norway annexed part of E coast 1931, awarded to Denmark 1933; after occupation of Denmark by Germany in 1940, agreement made Apr. 9, 1941 permitting U.S. to establish air bases, radio, and weather stations to protect the island and preserve Danish sovereignty there during WWII; U.S.-Danish agreement signed 1951 providing joint defense of Greenland; made integral part of Denmark 1953; home rule began 1979.

Greenland Sea. Section of Arctic Ocean off NE Greenland; now generally considered as part of Norwegian Sea.

Green·lawn \ˈgrēn-ˌlȯn, -ˌlän\. Unincorporated settlement, Suffolk co., New York, on Long Island E of Huntington; pop. (1990c) 13,208.

Green·lee \ˈgrēn-lē\. County in SE Arizona. See table at ARIZONA.

Green Lowther. See LOWTHER HILLS.

Green·ly \ˈgrēn-lē\. Small island in Quebec, Canada, at W end of Strait of Belle Isle opp. the Labrador border.

Green Mountain. **1.** Peak, Lawrence co., W South Dakota; 5101 ft. (1555 m.).
2. Crater, Ascension. See ASCENSION 2.

Green Mountain Reservoir. Reservoir, N cen. Colorado in Summit co.

Green Mountains. A range of the Appalachian system, extending from Canada through Vermont into W Massachusetts; highest peak Mt. Mansfield 4393 ft. (1339 m.) in N Vermont.

Green·ock \ˈgrē-nək, ˈgri-, ˈgre-\. Seaport and burgh, Strathclyde region, SW Scotland, on S shore of the Firth of Clyde; pop. (1981p) 57,324; shipbuilding; electronics; sugar refineries; historically notable textile mills; birthplace of engineer and inventor James Watt 1736.

Green Pe·ter Dam *and* **Green Peter Reservoir** \ˈpē-tər\. See UNITED STATES, *Dams and Reservoirs.*

Green·point \ˈgrēn-ˌpȯint\. Neighborhood, N Brooklyn borough, New York City, bounded on W by the East River; Civil War shipbuilding center where the ironclad battleship *Monitor* was built.

Green Point. Town, W suburb of Cape Town, Western Cape prov., Rep. of South Africa. See SEA POINT.

Green·port \ˈgrēn-ˌpōrt\. Village, Suffolk co., SE New York, on N extension of Long Island bet. Long Island Sound and Gardiners Bay; pop. (1990c) 2070; summer resort.

Green River. 1. For rivers see GREEN.
2. Town, ⊗ of Sweetwater co., SW Wyoming, on Green River 15 mi. (24 km.) W of Rock Springs; pop. (1990c) 12,711; soda ash produced from trona mines nearby.

Green River Mountain. Peak, N Sublette co., W Wyoming; 10,175 ft. (3101 m.).

Green Rock. City, Henry co., NW Illinois; pop. (1990c) 2615.

Greens·boro \ˈgrēnz-ˌbər-ō\. **1.** Town, ⊗ of Hale co., W Alabama, 35 mi. (56 km.) S of Tuscaloosa; pop. (1990c) 3047; settled c. 1816; incorp. 1823; former site (1856–1918) of Southern Univ. (now Birmingham-Southern Coll. at Birmingham); antebellum mansions.
2. City, ⊗ of Greene co., NE cen. Georgia, 29 mi. (47 km.) SSE of Athens; pop. (1990c) 2860.
3. City, ⊗ of Guilford co., N cen. North Carolina, 26 mi. (42 km.) E of Winston-Salem; pop. (1990c) 183,521; chemicals; textile mills; insurance; Guilford Coll. (1834), Greensboro Coll. (1838), Bennett Coll. (1873), Univ. of North Carolina at Greensboro (1891), North Carolina Agricultural and Technical State Univ. (1891); made ⊗ 1808; Guilford Courthouse National Military Park (see UNITED STATES, *National Historical Parks*) nearby; birthplace of writers O. Henry (William Sydney Porter) 1862 and Wilbur Daniel Steele 1886.

Greens·burg \ˈgrēnz-ˌbərg\. **1.** City, ⊗ of Decatur co., SE cen. Indiana, 18 mi. (29 km.) SE of Shelbyville; pop. (1990c) 9286.
2. City, ⊗ of Kiowa co., S Kansas; pop. (1990c) 1792.
3. City, ⊗ of Green co., cen. Kentucky; pop. (1990c) 1990.
4. Town, ⊗ of St. Helena parish, E Louisiana; pop. (1990c) 583.
5. City, ⊗ of Westmoreland co., SW Pennsylvania, 27 mi. (43 km.) ESE of Pittsburgh; pop. (1990c) 16,318; historically notable coal mines; Seton Hill Coll. (1883), Univ. of Pittsburgh at Greensburg (1963); founded mid-1780s.

Greens Peak \ˈgrēnz\. Mountain, S Apache co., E Arizona; 10,115 ft. (3083 m.).

Greens·ville \ˈgrēnz-ˌvil, -vəl\. County in S Virginia. See table at VIRGINIA.

Green Tree \ˈgrēn-ˌtrē\. Borough, Allegheny co., SW Pennsylvania, just SW of Pittsburgh; pop. (1990c) 4905.

Green·up \ˈgrē-nəp\. **1.** County in NE Kentucky. See table at KENTUCKY.
2. City, its ⊗; pop. (1990c) 1158.

Green·ville \ˈgrēn-ˌvil, -vəl\. **1.** County in NW South Carolina. See table at SOUTH CAROLINA.
2. Commercial city, ⊗ of Butler co., S Alabama, 42 mi. (68 km.) SW of Montgomery; pop. (1990c) 7492; settled 1819; incorp. 1820 as Buttsville; name changed to Greenville shortly after.
3. City, ⊗ of Meriwether co., W Georgia; pop. (1990c) 1167.
4. City, ⊗ of Bond co., SW cen. Illinois, 47 mi. (76 km.) ENE of East St. Louis; pop. (1990c) 4806; Greenville Coll. (1892).
5. City, ⊗ of Muhlenberg co., W Kentucky, 30 mi. (48 km.) NNE of Hopkinsville; pop. (1990c) 4689.
6. City, Montcalm co., cen. Michigan, 25 mi. (40 km.) ENE of Grand Rapids; pop. (1990c) 8101.
7. City, ⊗ of Washington co., W Mississippi, on Mississippi River; pop. (1990c) 45,226; tools, concrete products, lumber; incorp. 1886; nearby is Winterville Mounds State Park, a preserved Indian ceremonial site.
8. City, ⊗ of Wayne co., SE Missouri; pop. (1990c) 437.
9. City, ⊗ of Pitt co., E North Carolina, 33 mi. (53 km.) SE of Rocky Mount; pop. (1990c) 44,972; market for tobacco, cotton, corn; East Carolina Univ. (1907); art museum; Voice of America broadcasting headquarters.
10. City, ⊗ of Darke co., W Ohio, 32 mi. (51 km.) NW of Dayton; pop. (1990c) 12,863. On site of Fort Greenville (built 1793) where Gen. Anthony Wayne's treaty with Indians was signed 1795, and of Shawnee Indian village, home of Chief Tecumseh; became ⊗ 1809.
11. Borough, Mercer co., W Pennsylvania, 27 mi. (43 km.) N of New Castle; pop. (1990c) 6734; Thiel Coll. (1866); settled 1796.
12. City, ⊗ of Greenville co., NW South Carolina, 100 mi. (161 km.) NW of Columbia; pop. (1990c) 58,282; electronics, chemicals, plastics, pharmaceuticals; metal fabrication; tourist resort in Piedmont Region of Blue Ridge; Furman Univ. (1826), Greenville Technical Coll. (1962).
13. City, ⊗ of Hunt co., NE Texas, 43 mi. (69 km.) NE of Dallas; pop. (1990c) 23,071; incorp. 1874.

Green·wich. 1. \ˈgre-nich, ˈgrēn-ˌwich, ˈgrin-ˌwich\. Residential town, SW Fairfield co., SW Connecticut, on Long Island Sound on New York border; pop. (1990c) 58,441; settled c. 1640; orig. in New Amsterdam, ceded to Connecticut 1650; site of headquarters of Montessori Society of America; Audubon Center.
2. \ˈgri-nij, ˈgre-, -nich\. A borough of Greater London, SE England. See table at LONDON 4. Site of Royal Greenwich Observatory bet. 1675 and 1950s; the meridian that passes through Greenwich serves as the basis for standard time throughout much of the world and for reckonings of longitude.
3. \ˈgre-nich, ˈgri-, -nij\. Island in South Shetland Is. (*q.v.*), South Atlantic Ocean.

Greenwich Village \ˈgre-nich, ˈgri-, -nij\. Former village on Manhattan I., now a part of Manhattan borough, New York City, New York, bounded approx. by W 14th Street, Spring Street, Broadway, and the Hudson River; New York Univ.; Washington Square; historically frequented by authors, artists, and students.

Green·wood \ˈgrēn-ˌwu̇d\. **1.** Name of counties in two states of the U.S. See tables at KANSAS and SOUTH CAROLINA.
2. Town, a ⊗ of Sebastian co., W Arkansas; pop. (1990c) 3984.
3. City, Johnson co., cen. Indiana, 10 mi. (16 km.) S of Indianapolis; pop. (1990c) 26,265.
4. City, ⊗ of Leflore co., W Mississippi, 50 mi. (80 km.) E of Greenville; pop. (1990c) 18,906; long-staple cotton.
5. City, ⊗ of Greenwood co., W South Carolina, 36 mi. (58 km.) SE of Anderson; pop. (1990c) 20,807; cotton, textiles, vegetable and flower seeds; Lander Coll. (1872), Piedmont Technical Coll. (1966).

Greenwood Lake. 1. Lake in N Passaic co., N New Jersey, and Orange co. SE New York; ab. 9 mi. (14 km.) long; summer resort.
2. Village, Orange co., SE New York, near tip of Greenwood Lake; pop. (1990c) 3208.

Greenwood Village. Town, Arapahoe co., NE cen. Colorado, bordering SE Denver; pop. (1990c) 7589.

Greer \ˈgrir\. **1.** Former county, Oklahoma, coextensive with present Beckham (S part), Greer, Harmon, and Jackson cos.; subject of long dispute bet. Texas and U.S., which was settled by the Supreme Court 1896.
2. County in SW Oklahoma. See table at OKLAHOMA.
3. Town, Greenville and Spartanburg cos., NW South Carolina, 12 mi. (19 km.) ENE of Greenville; pop. (1990c) 10,322.

Gregg \ˈgreg\. County in NE Texas. See table at TEXAS.

Greg·o·ry \ˈgre-gə-rē\. County in S South Dakota. See table at SOUTH DAKOTA.

Gregory, Lake. Shallow salt lake, NE South Australia, Australia, ESE of Lake Eyre.

Greifenberg. See GRYFICE.

Greifs·wald \ˈgrīfs-ˌvält\. City, Mecklenburg-West Pomerania, NE Germany, 19 mi. (31 km.) SE of Stralsund; pop. (1992e) 65,529; trades in coal and lumber; town hall (1350); university (1456); several 13th and 14th cent. churches; chartered 1250; to Sweden 1648, to Prussia 1815.

Greiz \ˈgrīts\. City, Thuringia, Germany, 14 mi. (23 km.) WSW of Zwickau; pop. (1981c) 36,770; medieval castle; until 1918 ✻ of a principality.

Gre·na·da \grə-ˈnā-də\. **1.** County in N cen. Mississippi. See table at MISSISSIPPI.

2. City, its ⊗, 28 mi. (45 km.) NE of Greenwood; pop. (1990c) 10,864.

3. Island, southernmost of the Windward Is., West Indies, 90 mi. (145 km.) N of Trinidad; 120 sq. mi. (311 sq. km.); ✻ St. George's on SW coast; of volcanic origin; has many short streams; mountainous, highest point Mt. St. Catherine 2757 ft. (840 m.).

4. Self-governing state in Windward Is., West Indies; comprises Grenada I. (see GRENADA 3) and the S Grenadines (incl. Carriacou); 133 sq. mi. (344 sq. km.); pop. (1989e) 98,000; ✻ St. George's on Grenada I.; chief products: cocoa, nutmegs, mace, bananas, and other fruits; tourism.

History: Island of Grenada sighted 1498 by explorer Christopher Columbus, who named it **Con·cep·ci·ón** \kòn-ˌsep-sē-ˈōn, -ˈsep-shən\; settlement founded by French governor of Martinique 1650; passed to French crown 1672; captured by British 1762 and ceded to them 1763; held by French 1779–83; returned to British 1783; scene of native uprising suppressed by British 1795–96; member of West Indies Federation 1958–62; was (with dependent islands) an associate state of Great Britain 1967–74; became an independent nation within the Commonwealth Feb. 7, 1974; government overthrown 1979; assassination of prime minister Oct. 19, 1983 led to invasion by Caribbean and U.S. troops Oct. 24–28, 1983.

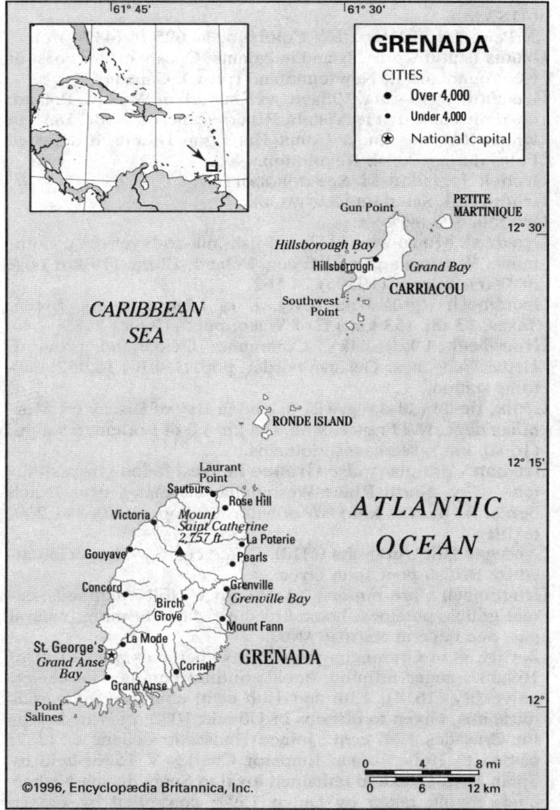

Gren·a·dier Island \ˌgre-nə-ˈdir\. Island in NE Lake Ontario, Jefferson co., N New York, NW of Sackets Harbor.

Grenadine Confederation. See *History* at COLOMBIA.

Gren·a·dines, The \ˌgre-nə-ˈdēnz\. Group of 600 small islands, Windward Is., at E end of Caribbean Sea, bet. Grenada and St. Vincent; 30 sq. mi. (78 sq. km.); largest Carriacou; S part (13 sq. mi. or 34 sq. km.; pop. [1991p] 5315) belongs to Grenada, N part (17 sq. mi. or 44 sq. km.; pop. [1991p] 8756, incl. Bequia and Union islands) to St. Vincent.

Gren·chen \ˈgren-k̲ən\ *or Fr.* **Granges** \ˈgräⁿzh\. Commune, Solothurn canton, NW Switzerland, 7 mi. (11 km.) W of the commune of Solothurn; pop. (1980c) 16,800.

Gre·no·ble \grə-ˈnōblᵊ, -ˈnō-bəl\; *anc.* **Cu·la·ro** \ˈkü-lä-ˌrō, ˈkyü-\; *later* **Gra·ti·an·op·o·lis** \ˌgrā-shē-ə-ˈnä-pə-lis\. City, ✻ of Isère dept., SE France, on Isère River 133 mi. (214 km.) NNE of Marseille; pop. (1990c) 153,973; electrical machinery, gloves, cement; tourism; 12th–13th cent. cathedral; 14th–15th cent. Palais de Justice (law courts); university (1339); nuclear research center; site of Winter Olympic Games 1968. La Grande Chartreuse (*q.v.*) ab. 12.5 mi. (20 km.) N of here; was ✻ of the Dauphiné (*q.v.*); birthplace of novelist Marie-Henri Beyle (Stendhal) 1783; important in French resistance movement during WWII.

Grenz·mark Po·sen–West·preus·sen \ˈgrents-ˌmärk-ˈpōz-ᵊn-ˈvest-ˌprȯis-ᵊn\. Former Prussian province, E Germany, on border of Poland; formed 1919 out of parts of former Posen and West Prussia provs.; since 1945 divided among several provinces of W Poland.

Gresh·am \ˈgre-shəm\. City, Multnomah co., NW Oregon, 14 mi. (23 km.) E of Portland; pop. (1990c) 68,235; Mt. Hood Community Coll. (1965).

Gre·sik \gre-ˈsēk\; *formerly* **Gris·see** *or* **Gri·see** \gri-ˈsē\. Seaport, East Java prov., Indonesia, ab. 8 mi. (13 km.) NW of Surabaya, on Surabaja Strait opp. Madura I.

Gret·na \ˈgret-nə\. City, ⊗ of Jefferson parish, SE Louisiana, on Mississippi River opp. New Orleans; pop. (1990c) 17,208.

Gretna Green \ˈgrēn\. Village Dumfries and Galloway region, S Scotland; long famous as marrying place of eloping couples from England.

Gre·ve \ˈgre-vā, ˈgrā-\. Commune, Firenze prov., Tuscany, cen. Italy, 15 mi. (24 km.) SE of Florence; pop. (1981p) 10,294.

Gre·ve \ˈgrā-və\. Town, Roskilde co., Denmark; pop. (1989e) 45,287.

Gre·ve·ling·en \ˈk̲rā-və-ˌliŋ-ən\. Inlet on SW coast of the Netherlands bet. Schouwen and Goeree islands.

Gre·ven \ˈgrā-vən\. City, North Rhine-Westphalia, Germany, 10 mi. (16 km.) N of Münster; pop. (1980c) 28,743.

Gre·ve·ná \ˌgre-ve-ˈnä\. **1.** Department of Western Macedonia, Greece. See table at GREECE.

2. Town, its ✻; pop. (1981p) 7726.

Gre·ven·broich \ˌgrā-vən-ˈbrōk̲\. Town, North Rhine-Westphalia, Germany; pop. (1992e) 62,030; railroad junction; aluminum products.

Grey \ˈgrā\. **1.** County in SE Ontario, Canada. See table at ONTARIO.

2. River, NW South I., New Zealand; flows SW into Tasman Sea at Greymouth; 75 mi. (121 km.) long.

Grey·beard \ˈgrā-ˌbird\. Mountain, Buncombe co., W North Carolina; 5448 ft. (1661 m.).

Grey·bull \ˈgrā-bəl\. **1.** River, NW Wyoming; rises in S Park co., flows NE into Bighorn River; ab. 100 mi. (160 km.) long.

2. Town, Big Horn co., N Wyoming, on Bighorn River 33 mi. (53 km.) N of Worland; pop. (1990c) 1789; oil refineries.

Greyerz. See GRUYÈRES.

Grey·lock, Mount \ˈgrā-ˌläk\. Peak in Berkshire Hills, Berkshire co., NW Massachusetts; 3491 ft. (1064 m.); highest point in state; war memorial tower on summit.

Greylock Mountain. **1.** Peak, La Plata co., SW Colorado; 13,578 ft. (4139 m.).

2. Peak, N Elmore co., SW cen. Idaho; 9317 ft. (2840 m.).

\ə\ abut \ᵊ\ kitten, F table \ər\ further \a\ ash \ā\ ace \ä\ cot, cart \á\ Fr bac \aù\ out \b\ Span Avila \ch\ chin \e\ bet \ē\ easy \g\ go \i\ hit \ī\ ice \j\ job \k̲\ Ger ich, Buch \ⁿ\ Fr vin \ŋ\ sing \ō\ go \ȯ\ all \ȯ\ law \œ\ Fr bœuf \œ̄\ Fr feu \ȯi\ boy \th\ thin \th\ this \ü\ loot \u̇\ foot \ue\ Ger füllen \ue̅\ Fr rue \y\ yet \ʸ\ Fr digne \ˈdēnʸ\, nuit \ˈnwʸē\ \yü\ few \yu̇\ fury \zh\ vision

3. Peak, SW Klamath co., S Oregon; 7850 ft. (2393 m.).

Grey·mouth \ˈgrā-ˌmau̇th, -məth\. Seaport urban area, W South I., New Zealand, at mouth of Grey River; pop. (1992e) 10,500; exports coal and timber.

Greys \ˈgrāz\. River, W Wyoming; flows N in N Lincoln co. into Snake River; ab. 65 mi. (105 km.) long.

Grey·town \ˈgrā-ˌtau̇n\. **1.** Seaport, Nicaragua. See SAN JUAN DEL NORTE.

2. Town, cen. KwaZulu-Natal prov., E Rep. of South Africa, 58 mi. (93 km.) NNW of Durban.

Grid·ley \ˈgrid-lē\. City, Butte co., N California, 55 mi. (88 km.) N of Sacramento; pop. (1990c) 4631.

Gridley Mountain. Mountain in Salisbury, extreme NW Connecticut; 2200 ft. (671 m.).

Gries Pass \ˈgrēs\. Mountain pass in Alps bet. Piedmont, NW Italy, and Valais canton, Switzerland; 8089 ft. (2466 m.).

Grif·fin \ˈgri-fən\. City, ⊗ of Spalding co., W cen. Georgia, 42 mi. (68 km.) SSE of Atlanta; pop. (1990c) 21,347; textile mills.

Grif·fith \ˈgri-fəth\. Town, Lake co., NW corner of Indiana, 8 mi. (13 km.) S of Gary; pop. (1990c) 17,916; metal products.

Grigan. See AGRIHAN.

Griggs \ˈgrigz\. County in E North Dakota. See table at NORTH DAKOTA.

Gri·jal·va \grē-ˈhäl-b̲ä\ *also* **Ta·bas·co** \tä-ˈb̲äs-kō, tə-ˈbas-kō\. River, Chiapas and Tabasco states, SE Mexico; flows N into Bay of Campeche; ab. 300 mi. (480 km.) long.

Grim, Cape \ˈgrim\. NW point of Tasmania, Australia.

Gri·mal·di \grē-ˈmäl-dē\. Caves in commune of Ventimiglia, Imperia prov., W Liguria, NW Italy, just across the border from Menton, France; evidence of prehistoric occupation includes human skeletal remains.

Grimes \ˈgrīmz\. **1.** County in E cen. Texas. See table at TEXAS.

2. City, Polk co., S cen. Iowa, 5 mi. (8 km.) WNW of Des Moines; pop. (1990c) 2653.

Grim·ma \ˈgri-mə\. City, Saxony, Germany, on left bank of the Mulde River 16 mi. (26 km.) SE of Leipzig; pop. (1981c) 17,474; 13th cent. church; 13th cent. castle; 16th cent. town hall; founded c. 1170.

Grims·by \ˈgrimz-bē\. **1.** Town, Niagara regional municipality, SE Ontario, Canada, on SW shore of Lake Ontario 18 mi. (29 km.) E of Hamilton; pop. (1991c) 18,520.

2. *or* **Great Grimsby.** Port, Humberside, E England, near mouth of the Humber 18 mi. (29 km.) SSE of Hull; fisheries; fertilizers; steel.

Grim·sel Pass \ˈgrim-zəl\. Mountain pass in Bernese Alps, SW cen. Switzerland; elev. 7159 ft. (2182 m.).

Gríms·ey \ˈgrēm-sā\. Island NE of Eyja Fjord, N Iceland, in Arctic Ocean.

Grin·del·wald \ˈgrind-ᵊl-ˌvält, -ˌwȯld\. Valley and town in Bernese Alps, cen. Switzerland, E of Interlaken; pop. (1988e) 3600; cattle raising; tourist resort; elev. of valley 3400 to 3500 ft. (1036 to 1067 m.), town at 3412 ft. (1040 m.).

Grin·nell \grə-ˈnel\. City, Poweshiek co., SE cen. Iowa, 23 mi. (37 km.) SSE of Marshalltown; pop. (1990c) 8902; farm equipment; livestock; Grinnell Coll. (1846); settled 1854; incorp. as town 1865, as city 1882.

Grinnell, Mount. Peak in Glacier National Park, NW Montana; 8848 ft. (2697 m.).

Grinnell Land. Cen. section of Ellesmere I., northernmost Nunavut, Canada.

Grinnell Peninsula. NW portion of Devon I., Nunavut, Canada, SW of Ellesmere I.

Gri·qua·land East \ˈgri-kwə-ˌland, ˈgrē-\. Historical division, KwaZulu-Natal prov., S Rep. of South Africa; 7722 sq. mi. (20,000 sq. km.); chief town Kokstad; agricultural country; settled 1862 by Griquas, a people of mixed European and African descent, under their leader, Adam Kok III; annexed to Cape Colony 1879.

Griqualand West. Historical division, Northern Cape prov., S Rep. of South Africa, N of Orange River and W of Free State; 15,444 sq. mi. (40,000 sq. km.); chief town Kimberley; dry, desert country, noted for its diamond fields. Settled by Griquas, a people of mixed European and African descent, late 18th cent.; diamonds discovered 1867; became subject of dispute bet. Orange Free State and British, who annexed it 1871; joined to Cape Colony 1880.

Gri·qua·town \ˈgri-kwə-ˌtau̇n, ˈgrē-\. Town, Northern Cape prov., Rep. of South Africa, 90 mi. (145 km.) W of Kimberley; in district yielding diamonds, asbestos, wool, mohair, and cereals; occupied several times by Boers during Boer War; remains of old fort.

Grisee. See GRESIK.

Grise Fiord \ˈgrīs\. Hamlet, S Ellesmere I., Nunavut, Canada; Canada's northernmost civilian settlement; pop. (1991c) 130.

Gris–Nez, Cape \grē-ˈnā\. Headland, Pas-de-Calais dept., N France, extending into Strait of Dover 15 mi. (24 km.) SW of Calais; point nearest to Great Britain; lighthouse. See BLANC-NEZ.

Grisons. See GRAUBÜNDEN.

Grissee. See GRESIK.

Gris·wold \ˈgriz-wəld, -ˌwȯld\. Town, NE New London co., E Connecticut, on E bank of Quinebaug River; pop. (1990c) 10,384; includes borough of Jewett City (*q.v.*).

Grive·gnée \ˌgrēv-ˈnyā\. Commune, Liège prov., E Belgium, a suburb of the city of Liège.

Griz·zly Mountain \ˈgriz-lē\. **1.** Peak, Chaffee co., cen. Colorado; 13,800 ft. (4206 m.).

2. Peak, Pitkin and Chaffee cos., W cen. Colorado; 13,988 ft. (4264 m.).

3. Peak in Glacier National Park, NW Montana; 9070 ft. (2765 m.).

Grizzly Peak. **1.** Mountain in the Sierra Nevada, on boundary bet. Tuolumne and Mono cos., E cen. California; 10,369 ft. (3160 m.).

2. Peak, Dolores and San Juan cos., SW Colorado; 13,738 ft. (4187 m.).

3. Peak, La Plata co., SW Colorado; 13,695 ft. (4174 m.).

Groais Island \ˈgrā\. Island in Atlantic Ocean, off NE coast of Newfoundland I., Newfoundland (prov.), Canada.

Gro·chów \ˈgrō-küf\. Village, an E suburb of Warsaw, Poland, on right bank of the Vistula River; scene of battle 1831 in which Russians under Count Hans von Diebitsch defeated Poles during Polish Revolution.

Gródek Jagielloński. See GORODOK.

Grödnertal. See GARDENA, VAL DI.

Grodno. See HRODNA.

Gro·dzisk Ma·zo·wiec·ki \ˈgrȯd-jisk-ˌmä-zȯ-ˈvyet-skē\. Commune, Warszawa prov., NE cen. Poland, 12 mi. (19 km.) SW of Warsaw; pop. (1989e) 24,562.

Groes·beck \ˈgrōs-ˌbek\. City, ⊗ of Limestone co., E cen. Texas, 33 mi. (53 km.) E of Waco; pop. (1990c) 3185.

Groes·beek \ˈk̲rüs-bāk\. Commune, Gelderland prov., E Netherlands, near German border; pop. (1981e) 18,452; customs station.

Groix, Île de \ˌēl-də-ˈgrwä\. Island in Bay of Biscay off Morbihan dept., NW France, 9 mi. (14 km.) S of Lorient; 6 sq. mi. (16 sq. km.); sea caves, dolmens.

Gro·nau \ˈgrō-ˌnau̇\ *also* **Gronau in West·fa·len** \in-vest-ˈfä-lən\. City, North Rhine-Westphalia, Germany, near Dutch border 32 mi. (51 km.) NW of Münster; pop. (1980c) 41,209; textiles.

Gron·gar Hill \ˈgräŋ-gər\. Hill, Dyfed co., S Wales; celebrated by British poet John Dyer.

Gro·ning·en \ˈk̲rō-niŋ-ən\. **1.** Province, NE Netherlands; cereal grains, potatoes; horse breeding, dairy farming; natural gas. See table at NETHERLANDS.

2. City, ✻ of Groningen prov., NE Netherlands; pop. (1992e) 169,387; sugar refining, book printing; commercial center; university (1614); 13th and 15th cent. churches; numerous museums. Given to bishops of Utrecht 1040; provided ships for Crusades 12th cent.; joined Hanseatic League c. 1282; passed to Holy Roman Emperor Charles V 1536; held by Spain from 1580 and remained loyal to Spain during Netherlands revolt; taken by Dutch 1594; controlled by France 1795–1814; occupied by Germany and suffered heavy damage during WWII.

Grønland. See GREENLAND.

Grøn·sund \ˈgrœn-ˌsu̇n\. Channel bet. Falster and Møn islands, SE Denmark.

Groot \ˈgrüt\. **1.** River, Western Cape prov., Rep. of South Africa; joins Gourits River.

2. River, Eastern Cape prov., Rep. of South Africa, main headstream of the Gamtoos (*q.v.*).

Groo·te Ey·landt \grüt-ˈī-lənd\. Island, W Gulf of Carpentaria, Northern Terr., Australia; 950 sq. mi. (2461 sq. km.); now part of an aboriginal reserve; tropical fruit, manganese.

Groot·fon·tein \ˈgrüt-ˌfȯn-ˌtān\. Town, N Namibia, 220 mi. (354 km.) NNE of Windhoek; pop. (1988e) 9000; copper- and lead-mining center; world's largest known meteorite is on nearby farm.

Groot–Swartberge. See SWARTBERGE, GROOT-.

Gros Is·let Bay \ˈgrōs-ˈī-lət\. Inlet of Caribbean Sea, NW coast of St. Lucia I., West Indies, ab. 5 mi. (8 km.) N of Castries.

Gros Morne \grō-ˈmȯrn\. Peak, W Newfoundland I., Canada; 2644 ft. (806 m.); included in **Gros Morne National Park** (see CANADA, *National Parks*).

Gross·bee·ren \grōs-ˈbā-rən, -ˈber-ən\. Village, Brandenburg, E Germany; scene of battle 1813 in which French were defeated by Prussians.

Grosse Mythe. See MYTHEN.

Grosse Pointe \ˈgrōs-ˈpȯint\. Residential city, Wayne co., SE Michigan, on Lake St. Clair just E of Detroit; pop. (1990c) 5681.

Grosse Pointe Farms. Residential city, Wayne co., SE Michigan, on Lake St. Clair just E of Detroit; pop. (1990c) 10,092.

Grosse Pointe Park. Residential city, Wayne co., SE Michigan, on Lake St. Clair just E of Detroit; pop. (1990c) 12,857.

Grosse Pointe Shores. Village, Macomb and Wayne cos., SE Michigan, 4 mi. (6.4 km.) E of Detroit; pop. (1990c) 2955.

Grosse Pointe Woods. Village, Wayne co., SE Michigan; pop. (1990c) 17,715; residential suburb of Detroit.

Gros·ser Aletsch \ˈgrō-sər-ˈä-lech\. Glacier in Bernese Alps, Switzerland; ab. 14 mi. (23 km.) long, ab. 1 mi. (1.6 km.) wide near its terminus.

Grosser Belchen. See GUEBWILLER, BALLON DE.

Gros·ser Feld·berg \ˈgrō-sər-ˈfelt-ˌberk\. Highest peak in Taunus Range, SW cen. Germany; 2886 ft. (880 m.).

Grosser Plöner See. Lake, Schleswig-Holstein, N Germany, near base of Jutland Penin., SE of Kiel.

Grosse Scheidegg. See SCHEIDEGG.

Gros·se·to \grō-ˈsā-tō\. **1.** Province of Tuscany, cen. Italy. See table at ITALY.

2. Commune, its ✻, 94 mi. (151 km.) NW of Rome; pop. (1991p) 70,096; 13th cent. Gothic cathedral; fortified citadel; museum of Etruscan antiquities; ruins of **Ru·sel·lae** \rü-ˈse-lē\, an ancient Etruscan city; sulfur baths.

Gross·glock·ner \ˈgrōs-ˌglȯk-nər\. Peak in the Hohe Tauern Range of the Alps, S Austria, bet. E Tirol and Carinthia; 12,470 ft. (3801 m.); highest point in Austria.

Gross·gör·schen \grōs-ˈgœr-shən\. Village, Saxony-Anhalt, E cen. Germany, SE of Lützen; formerly in Saxony prov., Prussia; battle, often called battle of Lützen (*q.v.*), May 2, 1813.

Grossherzogtum Luxemburg. See LUXEMBOURG 2.

Gross–Jä·gers·dorf \ˈgrōs-ˈyā-garz-ˌdōrf\ *or* **Gross–Jä·gern·dorf** \-ˈyā-gərn-\. Village, formerly in Prussia, Germany, now in Kaliningrad Oblast exclave of Russia in Europe, W of Chernyakhovsk; in Seven Years' War scene of battle 1757 in which Russians under Count Fyodor Apraksin defeated Prussians.

Gross Schreckhorn. See SCHRECKHORN, GROSS.

Gross Strehlitz. See STRZELCE OPOLSKIE.

Gross·ve·ne·di·ger \ˌgrōs-və-ˈnā-di-gər\. Peak in Hohe Tauern Range of the Alps, bet. E Tirol and Carinthia, Austria, and near Italian border; 12,054 ft. (3674 m.).

Grosswardein. See ORADEA.

Gros·ve·nor Dale \ˈgrō-və-nər\. Subdivision of Thompson, Connecticut. See THOMPSON 1.

Grosvenor Mountains *also* **Grosvenor Range;** *formerly* **Gil·bert Grosvenor Range** \ˈgil-bərt\. Mountain range, Antarctica, S of Ross Ice Shelf, bet. it and the South Pole; 86°S lat., just E of the 180th meridian; on the W touches Queen Alexandra Range and on E the Queen Maud Mts.

Gros Ventre \ˈgrō-ˌvänt\. River, W Wyoming; rises in Wind River Range, N Sublette co., flows W into Snake River in cen. Teton co.; ab. 100 mi. (160 km.) long.

Grot·on \ˈgrät-ᵊn\. **1.** Town, S New London co., SE corner of Connecticut, on Long Island Sound at mouth of Thames River opp. New London; pop. (1990c) 45,144; settled 1649; incorp. 1705; deep-sea fishing; builds submarines; Nautilus Museum at U.S. submarine base; town burned when Fort Griswold was attacked and taken by British under American traitor Benedict Arnold 1781. Includes borough of Groton.

2. Town, Middlesex co., NE Massachusetts, 11 mi. (18 km.) E of Fitchburg; pop. (1990c) 7511; Groton Preparatory School (1884), Lawrence Acad. (1793).

Grot·ta·glie \grō-ˈtä-lyā\. Commune, Taranto prov., Puglia, SE Italy, 11 mi. (18 km.) ENE of the seaport of Taranto; pop. (1991p) 30,752; pottery.

Grouse Hill \ˈgrau̇s\. Peak, W Klamath co., S Oregon, N of Crater Lake; 7401 ft. (2256 m.).

Grouse Mountain. Peak, SW Catron co., W New Mexico; ab. 10,135 ft. (3090 m.).

Grove City \ˈgrōv\. **1.** Village, Franklin co., cen. Ohio, 8 mi. (13 km.) SSW of Columbus; pop. (1990c) 19,661; diversified agriculture.

2. Borough, Mercer co., W Pennsylvania, 18 mi. (29 km.) ENE of New Castle; pop. (1990c) 8240; Grove City Coll. (1876); settled 1798.

Grove Hill. Town, ⊗ of Clarke co., SW Alabama; pop. (1990c) 1551.

Grove·land \ˈgrōv-lənd\. Town, Essex co., NE corner of Massachusetts, 16 mi. (26 km.) ENE of Lowell; pop. (1990c) 5214.

Grove·port \ˈgrōv-ˌpōrt\. Village, Franklin co., cen. Ohio, 10 mi. (16 km.) SE of Columbus; pop. (1990c) 2848.

Gro·ver City \ˈgrō-vər\. City, San Luis Obispo co., SW California, S of the city of San Luis Obispo; pop. (1990c) 11,656.

Groves \ˈgrōvz\. City, Jefferson co., SE coastal Texas, E of Port Arthur; pop. (1990c) 16,513.

Grove·ton \ˈgrōv-tən\. **1.** City, ⊗ of Trinity co., E Texas; pop. (1990c) 1071.

2. Stream, Virginia. See BULL RUN.

Grove·town \ˈgrōv-ˌtau̇n\. City, Columbia co., E Georgia, 20 mi. (32 km.) W of Augusta; pop. (1990c) 3596.

Groz·ny *or* **Groz·nyy** \ˈgrȯz-nē, ˈgräz-\. City, ✻ of Chechnya, S Russia in Europe, on a tributary of the Terek River 50 mi. (80 km.) ENE of Vladikavkas; pop. (1992e) 388,000; a major oil center, connected by pipelines with Makhachkala, Dagestan, on the Caspian Sea and with Tuapse, Krasnodar Kray, on the Black Sea and Rostov-na-Donu, Rostov Oblast, to the NW; petrochemicals; food processing. Founded as fortress 1818; oil discovered 1823; was ✻ of Checheno-Ingush A.S.S.R., U.S.S.R.; goal, but never reached, of German drive during WWII; scene of severe fighting and much damaged during civil war 1994–95.

Grubeshov. See HRUBIESZÓW.

Gru·dziądz \ˈgrü-ˌjȯnts\ *or Ger.* **Grau·denz** \ˈgrau̇-dents\. City, Toruń prov., N cen. Poland, on Vistula River 30 mi. (48 km.) N of the city of Toruń; pop. (1989e) 100,861; manufactures iron goods, agricultural machinery, shoes. Given municipal rights by Teutonic Knights 1291; to Poland 1466; passed to Prussia 1772; returned to Poland 1919; held by Germany in WWII.

Gru·gli·as·co \ˌgrü-glē-ˈäs-kō\. Commune, Torino prov., Piedmont, NW Italy, 5 mi. (8 km.) W of Turin; pop. (1989e) 40,464.

Gruin·ard Bay \ˈgrin-yərd\. Bay on NW coast of Highland region, N Scotland.

Gru·mo Ap·pu·la \ˈgrü-mō-ˈä-pu̇-lə\. Commune, Bari prov., Puglia, SE Italy; pop. (1981p) 11,531.

Grünberg *or* **Grünberg in Schlesien.** See ZIELONA GÓRA 2.

Grun·dy \ˈgrən-dē\. **1.** Name of counties in four states of the U.S. See tables at ILLINOIS, IOWA, MISSOURI, TENNESSEE. **2.** Town, ⊗ of Buchanan co., SW Virginia; pop. (1990c) 1305.

Grundy Center. City, ⊗ of Grundy co., NE cen. Iowa, 25 mi. (40 km.) WSW of Waterloo; pop. (1990c) 2491.

Grushevski, Aleksandrovsk–. See SHAKHTY.

Grütli. See RÜTLI.

Gru·yère \grē-ˈyer, grü-, grē-\. District, SE Fribourg canton, W cen. Switzerland; 192 sq. mi. (497 sq. km.); noted esp. for its cheese (Gruyère cheese) orig. made here.

Gru·yères \grē-ˈyer, grü-, grē-\ *or Ger.* **Grey·erz** \ˈgrī-ərts\. Commune, Fribourg canton, Switzerland, 16 mi. (26 km.) SW of the commune of Fribourg; pop. (1985e) 1250; medieval castle, seat of counts of Gruyère.

Gruziya. See GEORGIA, REPUBLIC OF.

Gry·fi·ce \gri-ˈfēt-sə\; *Ger.* **Grei·fen·berg** \ˈgrī-fən-ˌberk, -ˌbərg\ *or* **Greifenberg in Pom·mern** \in-ˈpȯ-mərn\. Town, N Szczecin prov., NW Poland, NE of the seaport of Szczecin; pop. (1981p) 15,351; founded 1262.

Gryt·vi·ken Harbour \ˈgrit-ˌvē-kən, ˈgrüt-\. See SOUTH GEORGIA.

Gstaad \ˈkshtät\. Resort village, Bern canton, W cen. Switzerland, in Bernese Alps; area pop. (1990c) 6090.

Gua·ca·na·ya·bo, Gulf of *or Sp.* **Gol·fo de Guacanayabo** \ˈgȯl-fō-ˌthā-ˌgwä-kä-nä-ˈyä-bō\. Gulf, E Cuba; the city of Manzanillo is on it.

Gua·chi·ría \ˌgwä-chē-ˈrē-ä\. River, NE cen. Colombia; flows E into Meta River; ab. 110 mi. (177 km.) long.

Gua·da·la·ja·ra \ˌgwä-thä-lä-ˈhä-rä, ˌgwä-də-\. **1.** Province of cen. Spain. See table at SPAIN. **2.** *anc.* **Ar·ri·a·ca** \ˌar-ē-ˈā-kə\. Commune, ✻ of Guadalajara prov., cen. Spain, 34 mi. (55 km.) NE of Madrid; pop. (1991p) 62,943; agriculture; manufactures woolens, leather, soap; Roman bridge; 13th and 17th cent. churches; 15th cent. palace of Mendoza family (patrons of the arts). Held by Rome in ancient times; held by Moors 8th–11th cents.; seat of Mendoza family 15th–17th cents. **3.** City, ✻ of Jalisco state, W cen. Mexico, 280 mi. (451 km.) WNW of Mexico City; munic. pop. (1990p) 1,628,617; alt. 5141 ft. (1567 m.); center of rich agricultural and industrial area; produces chemicals, footwear, textiles; noted for its handicrafts; cathedral (built c. 1560–1618); Univ. of Guadalajara (1792), Autonomous Univ. of Guadalajara (1935).

Guadalaviar. See TURIA.

Gua·dal·ca·nal \ˌgwäd-ᵊl-kə-ˈnal\. Island, Solomon Is., W Pacific Ocean, ab. 100 mi. (160 km.) SE of New Georgia and 35 mi. (56 km.) SW of Malaita; 2180 sq. mi. (5646 sq. km.); 92 mi. (148 km.) long and 33 mi. (53 km.) wide at its widest part; pop. (1986c) 80,244; has no good harbors and only a few at all usable; traversed lengthwise by Kavo Mts.; highest peak 8028 ft. (2447 m.); many short streams are along coast, the best known the Mataniko, Lunga, and Tenaru rivers in N. Has many coconut plantations; in some of the low coast regions mangrove swamps.

History: Visited by Spanish explorer Álvaro de Mendaña de Neira 1568; explored by English 1788; settled by English traders; annexed by Great Britain 1893; scene of WWII battle in which U.S. troops defeated occupying Japanese forces 1942–43.

Gua·da·le·te \ˌgwä-thä-ˈlā-tā\. River, SW Spain; flows SW into Gulf of Cádiz through two mouths; 86 mi. (138 km.) long.

Gua·da·li·mar \ˌgwä-thä-lē-ˈmär\. River, S Spain; flows into the Guadalquivir, 14 mi. (23 km.) N of Jaén; 104 mi. (167 km.) long.

Gua·dal·quiv·ir \ˌgwä-thäl-kē-ˈvēr\ *or Arab.* **Wadi al–Ke·bir** \ˈwä-dē-ˌal-kə-ˈbir\; *anc.* **Bae·tis** \ˈbē-təs\. River in S Spain; flows W and SW into Gulf of Cádiz at Sanlúcar de Barrameda; 408 mi. (656 km.) long.

Gua·da·lu·pe \ˌgwä-thä-ˈlü-pā, *in U.S.* ˈgwä-də-ˌlüp\. **1.** \ˌgwä-də-ˈlü-pē; ˈgwä-də-ˌlüp, ˈgä-\. River, SE Texas; ab. 250 mi. (400 km.) long; rises in Kerr co., flows SE into San Antonio River ab. 9 mi. (14 km.) from its mouth. **2.** Name of counties in two states of the U.S. See tables at NEW MEXICO and TEXAS. **3.** \ˌgwä-də-ˈlü-pā, -pē\. Town, Maricopa co., S cen. Arizona, surrounded by Tempe on three sides; pop. (1990c) 5458. **4.** City, Santa Barbara co., SW California, 50 mi. (80 km.) NW of the city of Santa Barbara; pop. (1990c) 5479. **5.** City, Costa Rica, suburb of San José. **6.** Island, Mexico, in Pacific Ocean 180 mi. (290 km.) off coast of W cen. Baja California; 80 sq. mi. (207 sq. km.); an extinct volcano, height ab. 4500 ft. (1375 m.); set aside ab. 1923 by Mexican government as a game reserve, esp. for protection of elephant seals. **7.** City, Nuevo León state, Mexico, 10 mi. (16 km.) E of Monterrey; pop. (1990p) 534,782. **8.** Municipality, Zacatecas state, Mexico, 4 mi. (6 km.) SE of the city of Zacatecas; pop. (1990c) 46,433. **9.** Town, Uruguay. See CANELONES 2.

Guadalupe Hi·dal·go \ē-ˈthäl-gō, -ˈdäl-gō\. Mostly former name for the city of Villa Gustavo A. Madero (*q.v.*), Mexico; gave its name to Treaty of Guadalupe Hidalgo signed here Feb. 2, 1848 terminating Mexican War.

Guadalupe Mountains \ˌgwä-də-ˈlü-pā\. **1.** Mountain range, S New Mexico and SW Texas; highest Guadalupe Peak 8749 ft. (2667 m.); contains **Guadalupe Mountains National Park** (see UNITED STATES, *National Parks*). **2.** *or Span.* **Sie·rra de Guadalupe** \sē-ˈer-ä-thā-ˌgwä-thä-ˈlü-pā\. Range, mostly in S Cáceres prov., SW cen. Spain; highest peak Cabeza del Moro 5695 ft. (1736 m.).

Guadalupe Peak. Mountain, Culberson co., W Texas, in Guadalupe Mts.; 8749 ft. (2667 m.); highest point in Texas.

Guadalupe y Cal·vo \ē-ˈkäl-bō\. Municipality, Chihuahua state, Mexico, 40 mi. (64 km.) SE of Ciudad Juárez.

Guadarrama, Sierra de. See SIERRA DE GUADARRAMA.

Gua·dar·ra·ma Pass \ˌgwä-thär-ˈrä-mä\. Mountain pass in the Sierra de Guadarrama, cen. Spain, S of Segovia; elev. ab. 4151 ft. (1265 m.).

Gua·de·loupe \ˈgwä-də-ˌlüp, ˌgwä-də-ˈ\. French overseas department, E West Indies; comprises two islands, Basse-Terre (or Guadeloupe proper) and Grande-Terre, separated by narrow channel and the dependencies Marie-Galante, Désirade, Îles des Saintes, St. Barthélemy, and part of St. Martin; 582 sq. mi. (1507 sq. km.); pop. (1993e) 418,000; ✻ Basse-Terre; highest peak Soufrière 4813 ft. (1467 m.); exports sugar, rum, bananas.

History: Sighted by Christopher Columbus 1493; indigenous Caribs resisted Spanish settlement 16th cent.; colony estab. by French 1635; held by British for short periods during 18th and 19th cents.; status changed from colony to overseas department 1946.

Gua·dia·na \gwä-ˈthyä-nä\; *anc.* **Anas** \ˈā-nəs\. River, Spain and Portugal; rises in S cen. Spain; flows W to Portuguese border; turns S, forming two sections of the boundary bet. Spain and Portugal, and empties into Gulf of Cádiz; 515 mi. (829 km.) long.

Guadiana Bay. Bay in N coast of W tip of Pinar del Río prov., W Cuba, E of Cape San Antonio.

Guadiana Me·nor \mā-ˈnȯr\. River, S Spain; unites with the Guadalquivir 4 mi. (6 km.) ESE of Úbeda; 58 mi. (93 km.) long.

Gua·dia·ro \gwä-ˈthyä-rō\. River, S Spain; flows S into Mediterranean Sea 11 mi. (18 km.) NE of Gibraltar; 49 mi. (79 km.) long.

Gua·dia·to \gwä-ˈthyä-tō\. River, S Spain; flows into the Guadalquivir 17 mi. (27 km.) WSW of Córdoba; ab. 70 mi. (113 km.) long.

Gua·dix \gwä-ˈdēks, -ˈdēsh\. City, Granada prov., S Spain, 26 mi. (42 km.) ENE of the city of Granada; pop. (1991p) 19,105; in wheat- and olive-producing region; Roman remains, Moorish fortress, 18th cent. cathedral.

Gua·fo \ˈgwä-fō\. Island off SW coast of Chile, SW of Chiloé I. and W of **Gulf of Guafo.**

Gua·gua \ˈgwä-gwä\. Municipality, Luzon, Philippines, on N edge of Pampanga Delta 7 mi. (11 km.) SW of San Fernando; pop. (1980c) 72,609.

Guahan. See GUAM.

Guái·ma·ro \ˈgwī-mä-ˌrō\. Municipality, E Camagüey prov., E cen. Cuba, 44 mi. (71 km.) SE of the city of Camagüey; pop. (1981p) 51,549.

Guai·nía \gwī-ˈnē-ä\. **1.** River, South America. See NEGRO, RIO 3.

2. Department of E Colombia. See table at COLOMBIA.

Guai·rá \gwī-ˈrä\. Department of S cen. Paraguay. See table at PARAGUAY.

Guaíra. See SETE QUEDAS.

Guaira, La. See LA GUAIRA.

Guai·te·cas Islands *or* **Guay·te·cas Islands** \gwī-ˈtā-käs\. Group of islands in Pacific Ocean off SW coast of Chile, comprising N part of Chonos Archipelago.

Gua·ja·ba Cay \gwä-ˈhä-bä\. Island, Camagüey Archipelago, off N coast of Camagüey prov., E cen. Cuba.

Guajira, La. See LA GUAJIRA.

Gua·ji·ra Peninsula *or* **Pe·nín·su·la de Gua·ji·ra** \pā-ˈnēn-sü-lä-t͟hā-gwä-ˈhē-rä\. Peninsula projecting NE on NW coast of South America, bet. the Caribbean Sea and the Gulf of Venezuela; split bet. Colombia and Venezuela.

Gua·lán \gwä-ˈlän\. Town, Zacapa dept., E Guatemala, on Motagua River ab. 15 mi. (24 km.) NE of the town of Zacapa; munic. pop. (1981c) 25,916.

Gual·do Ta·di·no \ˈgwäl-dō-tä-ˈdē-nō\. Commune, Perugia prov., Umbria, cen. Italy, 20 mi. (32 km.) ENE of the commune of Perugia; pop. (1981p) 13,467.

Gua·le·guay \ˌgwä-lā-ˈgwī\. **1.** River, Entre Ríos prov., E Argentina; flows S into the Paraná; ab. 220 mi. (354 km.) long.
2. Town, Entre Ríos prov., E Argentina, 80 mi. (129 km.) ESE of Rosario; pop. (1980p) 24,883.

Gua·le·guay·chú \ˌgwä-lā-gwī-ˈchü\. Town, Entre Ríos prov., E Argentina, near Uruguay River 125 mi. (201 km.) E of Rosario; pop. (1980p) 51,057.

Gual·la·ti·ri \ˌgwä-yä-ˈtē-rē\. Volcano, N Chile; 19,882 ft. (6060 m.); erupted 1960.

Guam \ˈgwäm\ *also* **Gua·han** \gwä-ˈhän\. Unincorporated U.S. territory, largest and southernmost of Mariana Is., W Pacific Ocean; 32 mi. (51 km.) long, bet. 4 and 10 mi. (6 and 16 km.) wide; 209 sq. mi. (541 sq. km.); pop. (1993e) 143,000; ✻ Agana; in S half are hills (highest 1329 ft. or 405 m.) with several streams and fertile areas, N half mainly plateau ab. 500 ft. (150 m.); has reef along much of the coast; on W coast is best anchorage, Apra Harbor, bet. Orote Penin. and Cabras I.; struck occasionally by earthquakes and typhoons; extensive U.S. military facilities; chief crops bananas, sweet potatoes, corn, sugarcane; tourism; Univ. of Guam (1952).

History: Possibly visited by Portuguese navigator Ferdinand Magellan 1521; occupied by Spain 1565; ceded to U.S. by Spain Dec. 1898 after Spanish-American War; administered by U.S. Navy until 1950; developed by U.S. as naval station and civil aviation stop 1930s; occupied by Japanese 1941; recovered by U.S. forces 1944; administration transferred to U.S. Department of the Interior 1950; strategic air base in Vietnam War.

Guam·blin \ˈgwäm-ˌblēn\ *also* **So·cor·ro** \sō-ˈkȯr-ō\. Island off SW coast of Chile, NW of Chonos Archipelago.

Gua·na·ba·coa \ˌgwä-nä-bä-ˈkō-ä\. Town and municipality, W Cuba, just E of Havana; munic. pop. (1990e) 100,452.

Gua·na·ba·ra \ˌgwä-nȧ-ˈbȧ-rə\. Former state, SE Brazil; created from former federal district 1960; combined with Rio de Janeiro state 1975.

Guanabara Bay *also* **Rio de Ja·nei·ro Bay** \ˈrē-ō-ˌdē-zhȧ-ˈnā-rü, -dā-zhä-ˈner-ō\. Inlet of Atlantic Ocean in SE Brazil; the city of Rio de Janeiro is on its SW shore; 16.5 mi. (27 km.) long, 11 mi. (18 km.) wide; spanned near its neck by longest plate-and-box-girder bridge in world (main span 984 ft. or 300 m., total length 8.6 mi. or 13.9 km.; completed 1974), bet. Rio de Janeiro and Niterói.

Gua·na·cas·te \ˌgwä-nä-ˈkäs-tā\. Province of NW Costa Rica. See table at COSTA RICA.

Guanacaste, Cor·dil·le·ra de \ˌkōr-t͟hē-ˈyä-rä-ˌt͟hā-, -t͟hēl-\. Range, NW Costa Rica; highest peak 6627 ft. (2020 m.).

Guanahani. See SAN SALVADOR 1.

Gua·na·ja \gwä-ˈnä-hä\ *also* **Bo·nac·ca** \bō-ˈnä-kä\. One of the Islas de la Bahía, N of N cen. Honduras in the Caribbean Sea.

Gua·na·jay \ˌgwä-nä-ˈhī\. Town and municipality, Pinar del Río prov., W Cuba, 25 mi. (40 km.) SW of Havana; munic. pop. (1981p) 25,801.

Gua·na·jua·to \ˌgwä-nä-ˈhwä-tō\. **1.** State of cen. Mexico. See table at MEXICO.
2. City, its ✻, 170 mi. (274 km.) NW of Mexico City; munic. pop. (1990p) 113,580; alt. 6726 ft. (2050 m.); in mountainous region noted for centuries for its gold and silver mines, still being worked; university (1732, university status 1945); numerous churches and museums.

Gua·nal, Point \gwä-ˈnäl\. Cape on S coast of Isla de la Juventud, Cuba.

Gua·na·re \gwä-ˈnä-rā\. **1.** River, W Venezuela; flows ESE to join the Portuguesa River.
2. Town, ✻ of Portuguesa state, W cen. Venezuela, ab. 75 mi. (121 km.) SSW of Barquisimeto; pop. (1990p) 83,380; in coffee-producing region.

Gua·ne \ˈgwä-nā\. Municipality, Pinar del Río prov., W Cuba, 28 mi. (45 km.) SW of the city of Pinar del Río; pop. (1981p) 32,595.

Guang·de *or W.-G.* **Kuang–te** \ˈgwäŋ-ˈdə\ *also* **Kwang·teh** \ˈkwäŋ-ˈte\. Town, SE Anhui prov., E China, ab. 65 mi. (105 km.) NW of Hangzhou; scene of considerable fighting in WWII, esp. in 1943.

Guang·dong *or W.-G.* **Kwang·tung** \ˈgwäŋ-ˈdu̇ŋ\. Province, SE China, bounded on N by Hunan and Jiangxi provs., on NE by Fujian, on E and S by South China Sea, and on W by Guangxi Zhuangzu; ✻ Guangzhou. Lies largely in the tropics and has both mountain and plains regions, with four large rivers, Xi, Bei, Dong, and Han; chiefly agricultural; textiles; industrial development limited by lack of fuel and mineral resources. Coastline almost 800 mi. (1290 km.) long, provides several excellent harbors; has many islands, esp. those in the Xi Delta. Chief cities Guangzhou, Shantou, Shaoguan. See table at CHINA.

History: Inhabited by independent tribes; conquered by Chinese 222 B.C.; colonized for military and agricultural purposes into 12th cent. A.D.; Canton (Guangzhou) developed into important foreign trade center; rapid population growth led to increasing emigration by 17th cent.; site of illicit opium importation by Great Britain which led to First Opium War 1841–42; war ended by Treaty of Nanking by which Hong Kong was ceded to Great Britain and five ports were opened to British trade; ceded Kowloon to British 1860 and Macao to Portugal 1887; Bay of Kwangchowan (now Zhanjiang Gang) (*q.v.*) leased to France 1898–1945; marked by much unrest at time of revolution 1911; site of formation of the Kuomintang (Nationalist Party) under Sun Yat-sen 1912; occupied by Japanese 1938 through end of WWII 1945.

Guang·hua \ˈgwäŋ-ˈhwä\ *or W.-G.* **Kuang–hua** \ˈgwäŋ-ˈhwä\ *or locally* **Lao·he·kou** \ˈlau̇-ˈhə-ˈkō\ *or* **Lao–ho–k'ou** \ˈlau̇-ˈhō-ˈkō\. City, N Hubei prov., E cen. China, ab. 200 mi. (320 km.) NW of Wuhan; pop. (1985e) 71,200.

Guang·xi Zhuang·zu \ˈgwäŋ-ˈshē-ˈjwäŋ-ˈdzü\ *or* **Guangxi Zhuang** \ˈjwäŋ\; *often shortened to* **Guangxi;** *W.-G.* **Kwang·si Chuang** \ˈgwäŋ-ˈshē-ˈjwäŋ\; *often shortened to* **Kwangsi.** Autonomous region, SE China, bounded on N by Guizhou and Hunan provs., on E and S by Guangdong, on SW by Vietnam, and on W by Yunnan; ✻ Nanning; hilly; traversed by the Xiang, Hongshui, and Gui rivers, all tributaries of the Xi; produces much rice in the river valleys and has valuable forest products. See table at CHINA.

Guang·zhou *or W.-G.* **Kuang–chou** \ˈgwäŋ-ˈjō\; *Eng.* **Can·ton** \ˈkan-ˌtän, kan-ˈ\. Commercial city and port, ✱ of Guangdong prov., SE China, on Zhu River in Xi Delta ab. 80 mi. (130 km.) from the sea; pop. (1990c) 2,914,281; chief port and city of S China; city proper (Old City) enclosed by walls with 12 gates; has very large population living on riverboats; medical college (1953), university (1958).

History: In early history of China an outpost of minor importance; incorp. in empire 3d cent. B.C.; became important city under Ming dynasty (1368–1644); first seaport of China opened to foreigners; regularly visited for centuries by Arab and Hindu traders, in 16th cent. by Portuguese; in late 17th cent. granted right to British East India Company to establish factory (trading and residence facility); later opened to French and Dutch and (except for Macao) remained the only Chinese trading port open to foreigners down to 1842; its resistance to English opium trade led to war with Great Britain 1839–42; became one of the first treaty ports by Treaty of Nanking 1842; scene of incident 1856 that led to 2d war with Great Britain; occupied by British and French 1856–61; granted 1859 new concession area (Shamien) to foreigners; its commercial prosperity affected by growth of Hong Kong; in 19th cent. seat of nationalist ideas and Guomindong (Kuomintang) (see GUANGDONG); scene of modernization programs 1920s; occupied by Japanese 1938–45; taken by Communists 1949; industrial growth continued; with Communist China's renewed ties to West, designated as one of several economic investment areas 1984.

Gua·nía \gwä-ˈnē-ä\. Department of Colombia. See table at COLOMBIA.

Guá·ni·ca \ˈgwä-nē-kä\. Municipality, SW Puerto Rico, on Guánica Harbor W of Ponce; pop. (1990c) 18,984.

Guánica Harbor. Bay on S coast of Mayagüez municipality, W Puerto Rico.

Gua·ni·quil·la Point \ˌgwä-nä-ˈkē-yä\. Cape on SW coast of Puerto Rico, N of Boquerón Bay.

Guan·tá·na·mo \gwän-ˈtä-nä-ˌmō\. **1.** Province of E Cuba. See table at CUBA.
2. Town and municipality, its ✱; town ab. 10 mi. (16 km.) N of Guantánamo Bay; municipality includes seaport barrio Caimanera on W side of Guantánamo Bay; munic. pop. (1990e) 200,381; sugar center.

Guantánamo Bay. Bay, E Cuba; 30 sq. mi. (78 sq. km.); site of U.S. naval station estab. 1903; landing place of U.S. naval units in Spanish-American War 1898.

Guapay. See MAMORÉ.

Gua·po·ré \ˌgwä-pō-ˈrā\. **1.** *or in Brazil* **Ité·nez** \ē-ˈtā-nes\. River, W cen. South America; rises in W Mato Grosso state, SW Brazil, flows NW, forming section of Brazil-Bolivia boundary, to join the Mamoré River; 1087 mi. (1749 km.) long.
2. State, Brazil. See RONDÔNIA.

Gua·qui \ˈgwä-kē\. Lake port, La Paz dept., W Bolivia, at S end of Lake Titicaca near mouth of Desaguadero River; railroad terminus 61 mi. (98 km.) from La Paz.

Gua·ran·da \gwä-ˈrän-dä\. City, ✱ of Bolívar prov., W Ecuador, 72 mi. (116 km.) NE of Guayaquil; pop. (1990c) 15,730.

Gua·ra·pua·va \ˌgwä-rä-ˈpwä-və\. Town, S cen. Paraná state, S Brazil, 140 mi. (225 km.) W of Curitiba; munic. pop. (1991p) 159,573.

Gua·ra·tin·gue·tá \ˌgwär-ə-ˌtēŋ-gə-ˈtä\. City, São Paulo state, SE Brazil, 125 mi. (201 km.) W of Rio de Janeiro; munic. pop. (1991p) 98,251; commercial center of agricultural district producing esp. coffee.

Guar·da \ˈgwär-də\. **1.** District of NE Portugal. See table at PORTUGAL.
2. Commune, its ✱, 65 mi. (105 km.) ENE of Coimbra; munic. pop. (1991p) 39,145; cathedral; 12th cent. castle.

Guarda, Ángel de la. See ÁNGEL DE LA GUARDA.

Guardafui, Cape. See CASEYR, RAAS.

Guard·house, The \ˈgärd-ˌhau̇s\. Mountain in Glacier National Park, NW Montana; 9300 ft. (2835 m.).

Guar·dia·gre·le \ˌgwär-dyä-ˈgrā-lā\. Commune, Chieti prov., Abruzzi, cen. Italy, 12 mi. (19 km.) S of the commune of Chieti; pop. (1981p) 10,223.

Guard·i·an, The \ˈgär-dē-ən\. Peak, San Juan co., SW Colorado; 13,624 ft. (4153 m.).

Guá·ri·co \ˈgwä-rē-ˌkō\. **1.** River, W Venezuela; flows SW and S into Apure River; ab. 300 mi. (480 km.) long.
2. State of N cen. Venezuela. See table at VENEZUELA.

Gua·ri·ti·co \ˌgwä-rē-ˈtē-kō\. River, W Venezuela; flows ENE into Apure River; ab. 160 mi. (260 km.) long.

Gua·ru·já \ˌgwȧ-ru̇-ˈzhä\. See SANTOS.

Gua·rul·hos \gwȧ-ˈrül-yüs\. Municipality, São Paulo state, SE Brazil, 9 mi. (14 km.) NE of the city of São Paulo; pop. (1991p) 781,499.

Gua·sa·ve \gwä-ˈsä-vā\. Municipality, Sinaloa state, Mexico, 95 mi. (153 km.) NE of Culiacán; pop. (1990p) 257,821.

Guásimas, Las. See LAS GUÁSIMAS.

Gua·stal·la \gwä-ˈstä-lä\; *anc.* **War·da·stal·la** \ˌwȯr-də-ˈsta-lə\. Commune, Reggio nell'Emilia prov., Emilia-Romagna, N Italy, on Po River 14 mi. (23 km.) NE of Reggio; pop. (1991p) 13,356; cathedral; palace of Gonzaga princely family.

History: Probably founded by Lombards in 7th cent.; passed to Gonzaga family 1539; made center of duchy 1621; passed to duchy of Parma 1748; passed to Napoleonic family 1806; became part of duchy of Modena 1847; became part of kingdom of Italy 1859.

Gua·te·ma·la \ˌgwä-tā-ˈmä-lä, ˌgwä-tə-ˈmä-lə\. **1.** Republic, Central America, bounded on W and N by Mexico, on E by Belize and the Gulf of Honduras, on SE by Honduras and El Salvador, and on S by the Pacific Ocean; 42,042 sq. mi. (108,889 sq. km.); pop. (1993e) 9,713,000; ✱ Guatemala.

Physical features: Mountainous; main range the SE extension of the Sierra Madre of Mexico, roughly parallel with Pacific coast ab. 40 mi. (64 km.) distant; highest peaks include Volcan Tajumulco 13,845 ft. (4220 m.), Tacaná 13,428 ft. (4093 m.), Acatenango 13,044 ft. (3976 m.), Santa María 12,375 ft. (3772 m.), Atitlán 11,604 ft. (3537 m.); interior is extensive tableland 2000 to 5000 ft. (610 to 1520 m.); regions on both Pacific and Atlantic coasts are hot lowlands. Chief rivers: the Usumacinta in NW on Mexican border, the Sarstoon flowing E into Amatique Bay, the Polochic (through Lake Izabal) and Motagua flowing to Gulf of Honduras. Chief lakes: Lake Izabal in E, Petén Itza in N, and Atitlán in SW cen. part.

Chief products: Coffee, cotton, bananas, corn, rice, sugar, timber, cattle; lead, zinc, oil; garments, textiles, prepared foods.

Chief city: Guatemala.

Political divisions: Divided into the following 22 departments (for pronunciation of their names, see their individual entries):

NAME	AREA (sq. mi.)	AREA (sq. km.)	POP. (1985e)	CAPITAL
Alta Verapaz	3,354	8,687	539,400	Cobán
Baja Verapaz	1,206	3,124	170,300	Salamá
Chimaltenango	764	1,979	315,500	Chimaltenango
Chiquimula	917	2,375	237,100	Chiquimula
El Progreso	742	1,922	102,000	El Progreso
Escuintla	1,693	4,385	495,800	Escuintla
Guatemala	821	2,126	1,853,700	Guatemala
Huehuetenango	2,857	7,400	650,100	Huehuetenango
Izabal	3,490	9,039	296,700	Puerto Barrios
Jalapa	797	2,064	177,000	Jalapa
Jutiapa	1,243	3,219	332,200	Jutiapa
Petén	13,843	35,853	215,300	Flores
Quetzaltenango	753	1,950	513,100	Quetzaltenango
Quiché	3,235	8,379	523,100	Santa Cruz del Quiché
Retalhuleu	717	1,857	218,600	Retalhuleu
Sacatepéquez	180	466	164,900	Antigua Guatemala
San Marcos	1,464	3,792	644,600	San Marcos
Santa Rosa	1,141	2,955	251,700	Cuilapa
Sololá	410	1,062	220,500	Sololá
Suchitepéquez	969	2,510	333,600	Mazatenango
Totonicapán	410	1,062	273,000	Totonicapán
Zacapa	1,039	2,691	152,900	Zacapa

History: Settlement dates to c. 2500 B.C.; Mayan civilization developed in region and in Yucatan Penin., declined 10th cent. A.D.; conquered by Spanish forces under Pedro de

Alvarado 1524; captaincy general of Guatemala estab. (included most of Central America) 1524; revolted against Spain 1821 and joined Mexican empire under Gen. Augustín de Iturbide 1822–23; withdrew from United Provinces (see CENTRAL AMERICA) and became independent republic under dictator Rafael Carrera 1839; under President Justo Rufino Barrios 1873–85, tried by force to form a union of Central American states; ruled by Manuel Estrada Cabrera 1898–1920; declared war on Germany during WWI; in 1933 settled century-old boundary dispute with Honduras; in WWII declared war on Axis powers 1941; government overthrown 1944 and 1954; civil war erupted 1960; promulgated new constitution 1965; government coup 1983; peace talks late 1980s into 1990s.

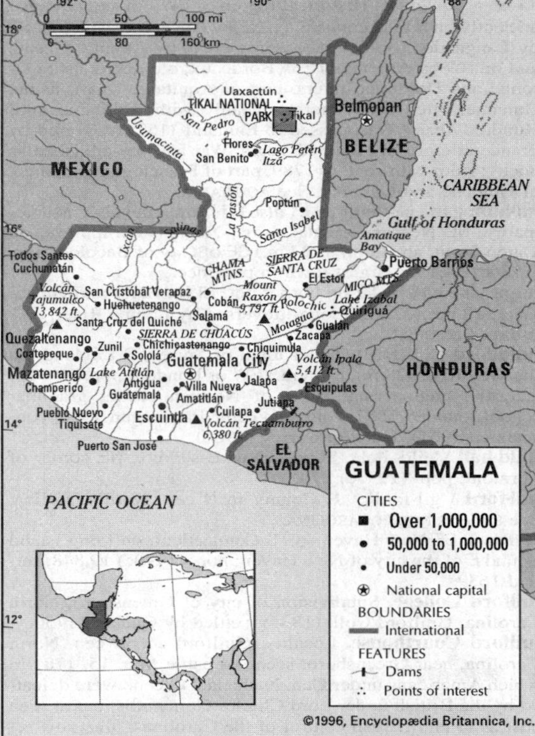

2. Department of S cen. Guatemala. See table at GUATEMALA 1.

3. *or* **Guatemala City.** City, ✱ of Guatemala and of Guatemala dept.; met. area pop. (1993e) 1,132,730; alt. ab. 5000 ft. (1525 m.); largest city in Central America; in volcanic area; center of fertile agricultural region; several colleges incl. San Carlos Univ. of Guatemala (1676). Founded 1776 to replace earthquake-damaged Antigua Guatemala (*q.v.*) and became ✱ of captaincy general of Guatemala; ✱ of the prov. of Central America in Mexican empire 1822–23; ✱ of the United Provinces of Central America 1823–33; severely damaged in earthquakes 1917–18 and 1976.

Guatemala, Antigua. City, Guatemala. See ANTIGUA GUATEMALA.

Guaura. See HUAURA.

Gua·via·re \gwäv-ˈyä-rā\. **1.** River, Colombia; flows E from its source in Andes Mts. in SW cen. Colombia; empties into Orinoco River on Colombia-Venezuela boundary; ab. 650 mi. (1050 km.) long.

2. Department of cen. Colombia. See table at COLOMBIA.

3. Town, its ✱, on the Guaviare.

Gua·ya·ma \gwä-ˈyä-mä\. Town and municipality, SE Puerto Rico, near coast 32 mi. (51 km.) E of Ponce; pop. (1990c) 21,692 (town), 41,588 (munic.); its port is Arroyo.

Guayana. See GUIANA.

Gua·ya·ne·co Islands \ˌgwī-ä-ˈnā-kō\. Group of small islands in Pacific Ocean off SW coast of Chile, S of Gulf of Penas.

Gua·ya·nil·la \ˌgwī-ä-ˈnē-yä\. Municipality, SW Puerto Rico; pop. (1990c) 21,581; on coast W of Ponce on **Guayanilla Harbor.**

Gua·ya·quil \ˌgwī-ä-ˈkēl, -ˈkil\ *or officially* **San·tia·go de Guayaquil** \ˌsän-tē-ˈä-gō-t͟hā-\. Seaport, ✱ of Guayas prov., SW Ecuador, its old part on Guayas River ab. 40 mi. (64 km.) from the coast; munic. pop. (1990c) 1,508,444; chief port of Ecuador; sugar refineries, iron foundries, tanneries; Univ. of Guayaquil (1867), technical college (1958); 16th cent. church; cathedral. Orig. founded 1530s; moved to present site 1537; named in honor of St. James on whose day it was founded and of Indian chief Guaya and his wife Quila; frequently attacked by buccaneers 17th cent.; severely damaged in repeated fires 18th–19th cents.; scene of historic meeting bet. statesmen Simón Bolívar and José de San Martín 1822; damaged by earthquake 1942.

Guayaquil, Gulf of. Inlet of Pacific Ocean in SW coast of Ecuador, and bounded on S by tip of NW Peru; receives Guayas River from the N; contains many islands in inner part, the largest Puná I.

Gua·yas \ˈgwī-äs\. **1.** River, Guayas prov., W Ecuador; an arm of Gulf of Guayaquil and the estuary of Babahoyo River; ab. 180 mi. (290 km.) long; with Babahoyo River navigable for ab. 200 mi. (325 km.).

2. Province of W Ecuador. See table at ECUADOR.

Guay·mas \ˈgwī-mäs\. Town, Sonora state, NW Mexico; pop. (1990p) 128,960; port on Gulf of California; railroad terminus; fishing; the port for Hermosillo.

Guay·na·bo \gwī-ˈnä-b̠ō\. Town and municipality, NE Puerto Rico; town 8 mi. (13 km.) S of San Juan; pop. (1990c) 73,385 (town), 92,886 (munic.).

Guayra. See SETE QUEDAS.

Guaytecas Islands. See GUAITECAS ISLANDS.

Gu·ba·kha \gü-ˈbä-k̠ə\. Town, Perm' Oblast, E Russia in Europe, ab. 35 mi. (56 km.) NE of the city of Perm'.

Gu·ban \ˈgü-ˌbän\. Plateau region, NW Somalia; parallels Gulf of Aden.

Gu·bat \ˈgü-ˌbät\. Municipality and port, NE Sorsogon prov., Luzon, Philippines, ab. 10 mi. (16 km.) ESE of Sorsogon; pop. (1980c) 43,866.

Gub·bio \ˈgü-bē-ˌō\; *anc.* **Eu·gu·bi·um** \yu̇-ˈgü-bē-əm, -ˈgyü-\ *also* **Igu·vi·um** \i-ˈgü-vē-əm, ī-, -ˈgyü-\. Commune, Perugia prov., Umbria, cen. Italy, 23 mi. (37 km.) NE of the commune of Perugia; pop. (1989c) 31,748; ceramics; 13th cent. cathedral; 13th cent. church of St. Francis; 14th cent. Palazzo dei Consoli; 15th cent. ducal palace; ancient Roman theater. See UMBRIA.

Gu·ben \ˈgü-bən\. **1.** Former city, of Germany, now comprising the separate cities of Guben, Germany and **Gubin,** Poland.

History: In origin a Wendish town; successively a possession of Brandenburg early 14th cent., Bohemia c. 1367, Saxony 1635, and Prussia 1815; following Potsdam Conference (1945) E section assigned to Poland and W section assigned to then East Germany as Wilhelm-Pieck-Stadt Guben (now Guben).

2. *or* **Wil·helm–Pieck–Stadt Gu·ben** \ˈvil-ˌhelm-ˈpēk-ˌshtät-ˈgüb-ᵊn\. City, Brandenburg, E Germany, across Polish border from Gubin; pop. (1981c) 36,806.

Gub·kin \ˈgüp-kin\. Town, Belgorod Oblast, Russia in Europe, ab. 65 mi. (105 km.) NE of the city of Belgorod; pop. (1991e) 76,400; iron ore deposits nearby.

\ə\ abut \ə̇\ matches \ᵊ\ kitten, Fr table \ər\ further \a\ ash \ā\ ace \ä\ cot, cart \ȧ\ Fr bac \au̇\ out \b̠\ Span Avila \ch\ chin \e\ bet \ē\ easy \g\ go \i\ hit \ī\ ice \j\ job \k̠\ Ger ich, Buch \ⁿ\ Fr vin \ŋ\ sing \ō\ go \ȯ\ all \ȯ\ law \œ\ Fr bœuf \œ̄\ Fr feu \ȯi\ boy \th\ thin \t͟h\ this \ü\ loot \u̇\ foot \ue\ Ger füllen \ue̅\ Fr rue \y\ yet \ʸ\ Fr digne \ˈdēnʸ\, nuit \ˈnwʸē\ \yü\ few \yu̇\ fury \zh\ vision

Gud·brands·da·len \ˈgu̇d-ˌbräns-ˌdä-lən\ *also* **Gud·brands·dal** \-ˌdäl\. Valley in Oppland co., S cen. Norway; extends NW and SE above Lake Mjøsa and Lillehammer, N part bet. the Jotunheimen and Dovrefjell; ab. 140 mi. (225 km.) long; scene of severe WWII fighting Apr. 1940; setting for dramatist Henrik Ibsen's play *Peer Gynt.*

Gu·de·nå \ˈgü-t͟hə-nȯ\. Longest river in Denmark; rises in N cen. Jutland, empties into Randers Fjord, 98 mi. (158 km.) long; an inlet of the Kattegat on E coast.

Gu·di·ya·ttam \ˌgu̇-dē-ˈyä-təm\. Town, N Tamil Nadu, S India, near Palar River 100 mi. (161 km.) W of Madras.

Gueb·wil·ler \ˌgeb-vē-ˈler\ *or Ger.* **Geb·wei·ler** \ˈgāp-ˌvī-lər\. Commune, Haut-Rhin dept., NE France, 15 mi. (24 km.) SSW of Colmar; 13th cent. church; 16th cent. town hall.

Guebwiller, Mount de *or Ger.* **Gros·ser Bel·chen** \ˈgrō-sər-ˈbel-k͟ən\ *or* **Sul·zer Belchen** \ˈzu̇lt-sər\. Mountain in Haut-Rhin dept., NE France, W of Guebwiller; 4670 ft. (1423 m.); highest in Vosges Mts.

Gue·cho \ˈgwā-chō\. Commune, Vizcaya prov., N Spain, on Bay of Biscay 8 mi. (13 km.) NW of Bilbao.

Guéc·ké·dou \ge-ˈkā-dü\. Town, S Guinea, near Liberian border; pop. (1983p) 31,641.

Guelderland. See GELDERLAND.

Guel·ma \gel-ˈmä\. Commune, NE Algeria, ab. 40 mi. (64 km.) E of Constantine.

Guel·mim \gül-ˈmēm\ *or* **Gou·li·mime** \ˌgü-lē-ˈmēm\ *or* **Gou·li·mine** \-ˈmēn\. Town, SW Morocco, in Anti-Atlas Range of Atlas Mts. (*q.v.*); pop. (1982c) 38,140.

Guelph \ˈgwelf\. City, ⊗ of Wellington co., SE Ontario, Canada, 15 mi. (24 km.) ENE of Kitchener; pop. (1991c) 87,976; rubber goods, electrical apparatus, iron and steel products; high-tech industry; Univ. of Guelph (1964); founded 1827.

Gué·rande \gā-ˈräⁿd\. Commune, Loire-Atlantique dept., NW France, ab. 10 mi. (16 km.) W of St.-Nazaire; 14th–15th cent. fortifications; 12th–16th cent. church.

Gué·ret \gā-ˈrā\. Commune, ✱ of Creuse dept., cen. France, 124 mi. (200 km.) S of Orléans.

Guer·ni·ca \ger-ˈnē-kä\ *or* **Guernica y Lu·no** \ē-ˈlü-nō\. Town, E Vizcaya prov., N Spain, ENE of Bilbao; once seat of a Basque parliament, now symbolized by a sacred oak tree; bombed 1937 by German planes in Spanish Civil War; its destruction the subject of a noted painting by Spanish painter and sculptor Pablo Picasso.

Guern·sey \ˈgərn-zē\. **1.** County in E Ohio. See table at OHIO.
2. One of the Channel Is., in the English Channel; 24 sq. mi. (62 sq. km.); pop. (1986c) 55,421; constitutes, with Alderney, Sark, and adjacent islands, a bailiwick with area 30 sq. mi. (78 sq. km.), pop. (1993e) 63,500, and ✱ St. Peter Port; market gardening, cattle breeding (the *Guernsey* breed of cattle originated here).

Guernsey Dam. Dam across North Platte River, NE Platte co., SE Wyoming; height 135 ft. (41 m.); forms **Guernsey Reservoir** completed 1928.

Guer·re·ro \gär-ˈrā-rō\. **1.** State of S Mexico. See table at MEXICO.
2. Municipality, Chihuahua state, Mexico, 95 mi. (153 km.) W of the city of Chihuahua.

Gü·fer·horn \ˈgue̅-fər-ˌhȯrn\. Peak in the Adula group, on Switzerland-Italy border; 11,103 ft. (3384 m.).

Gu·gu \ˈgü-gü\. Mountain range, cen. Ethiopia, E of Addis Ababa; highest peak Gugu 11,886 ft. (3623 m.).

Gu·guan \gü-ˈgwän\. Island, cen. Mariana Is., W Pacific Ocean; ab. 2.5 mi. by 1 mi. (4 km. by 1.6 km.).

Gui \ˈgwē\ *or W.-G.* **Kuei** *also* **Kwei** \ˈgwā\. River, E Guangxi Zhuangzu, S China; flows S to join the Xi at Wuzhou; ab. 200 mi. (320 km.) long.

Gui·a·na \gē-ˈä-nə, gī-, -ˈa-\ *also* **Gua·ya·na** \gwä-ˈyä-nä\. **1.** Region bet. the Orinoco, Negro, and Amazon rivers and the Atlantic Ocean, N South America, incl. Suriname, Guyana, French Guiana, S and E Venezuela, and N Brazil; ab. 690,000 sq. mi. (1,787,100 sq. km.). Earliest known inhabitants were Surinen Indians; coast sighted by Christopher Columbus c. 1498; explored by Spanish early 16th cent.; orig. was thought to include El Dorado; settlements founded by Dutch c. 1580 and by French and English first half of 17th cent. For later history see FRENCH GUIANA, GUYANA, and SURINAME 2.
2. Coastal strip of French Guiana. See FRENCH GUIANA.

Guiana Highlands. Highland area in N South America, extending from E Venezuela E across N Brazil, Guyana, Suriname, and French Guiana; sparsely populated; produces cabinet woods, medicinal plants; contains gold, diamonds.

Gui·a·nas, the \gē-ˈä-nəz, gī-, -ˈa-\. Section of N South America comprising British Guiana (now Guyana), Dutch Guiana (now Suriname), and French Guiana.

Gui·do·nia Mon·te·ce·lio \gwē-ˈdȯn-yä-ˌmȯn-tā-ˈchāl-yō\. Commune, Roma prov., Lazio, W cen. Italy; pop. (1989c) 56,052.

Gui·enne *or* **Guy·enne** \gē-ˈen\ *or Lat.* **Aq·ui·ta·nia** \ˌa-kwə-ˈtā-nē-ə, ˌä-, -nyə\. Historical region of SW France; bounded anciently on N by Limousin, on NE by Auvergne, on E and SE by Languedoc, on S by Gascony, on W by Atlantic Ocean, and on NW by Angoumois; ✱ Bordeaux; old duchy near Garonne and Dordogne rivers, part of Aquitaine (*q.v.*); name, Guienne, often used interchangeably with Aquitaine until Hundred Years' War; passed to England 1152; recovered by France at close of Hundred Years' War and reestablished as duchy; from 17th cent. to 1789, part of French *gouvernement* of Guienne and Gascony. See AQUITANIA.

Gui·huln·gan \gē-ˈhu̇lŋ-ˌgän\ *also* **Gi·hulng·an** \hē-\. Municipality, NE Negros Oriental prov., Negros, Philippines, on Tanon Strait, ab. 45 mi. (72 km.) SE of City of Bacolod; pop. (1980c) 84,156; largest town in province.

Gui·ja \ˈgē-hä\. Lake on border bet. El Salvador and Guatemala; 20 mi. (32 km.) long; traversed by Lempa River.

Guilan. See GĪLĀN.

Guild·ford \ˈgil-fərd\. Chief town of Surrey, S England, on the Wey River 28 mi. (45 km.) SW of London; pop. (1991p) 121,500; engineering; ruins of Norman castle; grammar school founded 1557; Anglican cathedral (begun 1936, consecrated 1961); Univ. of Surrey (1966).

Guild·hall \ˈgild-ˌhȯl\. Town, ⊗ of Essex co., NE corner of Vermont; pop. (1990c) 270.

Guil·ford \ˈgil-fərd\. **1.** County in N cen. North Carolina. See table at NORTH CAROLINA.
2. Town, SE New Haven co., S Connecticut; on Long Island Sound E of the city of New Haven; pop. (1990c) 19,848; settled 1639.

Guilford College. Subdivision of city of Greensboro, North Carolina; Guilford Coll. (1834); settled by Quakers 1750.

Guilford Courthouse. Locality, Guilford co., N cen. North Carolina, near Greensboro; scene of battle Mar. 15, 1781 in which Americans under Gen. Nathanael Greene were defeated by the British under Lord Charles Cornwallis, but at such cost as to end British control of the Carolinas; area now set aside as **Guilford Courthouse National Military Park** (see UNITED STATES, *National Historical Parks*).

Gui·lin \ˈgwē-ˈlin\ *or W.-G.* **Kuei–lin** *also* **Kwei·lin** \ˈgwā-ˈlin\. City, NE Guangxi Zhuangzu, SE China, 235 mi. (378 km.) NW of Guangzhou, Guangdong; pop. (1990c) 364,130; former ✱ of Guangxi Zhuangzu; agriculture; machinery, textiles; noted for its beautiful setting. Settlement possibly dates to Ch'in dynasty (221–206 B.C.); gained importance with construction of Ling Canal c. 215 B.C.; made ⊗ under Han dynasty (206 B.C.–220 A.D.) known as Shih-an; provincial ✱ 1644–1911 and 1936–49; strongly resisted Japanese in Sino-Japanese War 1939–45; site of U.S. air base which was abandoned 1944; Chinese retook city 1945.

Guil·laume–De·lisle, Lac \lák-gē-ˌyōm-də-ˈlēl\ *or* **Rich·mond Gulf** \ˈrich-mənd\. Lake, near SE coast of Hudson Bay, Quebec, Canada, opposite Belcher Is., bet. Clearwater Lake and the bay.

Guil·le·mont \ˌgē-yə-ˈmȯⁿ\. Village, Somme dept., N France; scene of severe fighting in WWI.

Güí·mar \ˈgwē-ˌmär\. Village, E coast of Tenerife, Canary Is.; resort.

Gui·ma·rães \ˌgē-mȧ-ˈrīⁿsh\. Commune, Braga dist., NW Portugal, 12 mi. (19 km.) SE of the commune of Braga; pop.

(1987e) 158,400; 10th cent. castle; 14th cent. church; birthplace (c. 1109) of Afonso I, first king of Portugal; besieged and taken 1127 by Alfonso VII of León.

Gui·ma·ras \ˌgē-mä-ˈräs\. Island off S coast of Panay I., cen. Philippines, separated from it by narrow Iloilo Strait; 223 sq. mi. (578 sq. km.); comprises a subprovince of Iloilo; chief town Jordan. See table at PHILIPPINES.

Guimaras Strait. Channel, extending NE and SW bet. SE Panay I. and NW Negros I., cen. Philippines; connects Visayan Sea with Sulu Sea; width varies from 7 to 20 mi. (11 to 32 km.).

Guim·ba \gēm-ˈbä\. Municipality, W Nueva Ecija prov., Luzon, Philippines, 17 mi. (27 km.) NW of Cabanatuan; pop. (1980c) 58,847; on main highway bet. Pangasinan and Nueva Ecija provs.

Gui·na·yan·gan \ˌgē-nä-ˈyäŋ-gän\. Municipality, SE Quezon prov., SE Luzon, Philippines, on coast at head of Ragay Gulf; pop. (1980c) 29,174.

Guin·ea \ˈgi-nē\ *or Fr.* **Gui·née** \gē-ˈnā\ *or Span.* **Gui·nea** \gē-ˈnā-ä\ *or Port.* **Gui·né** \gē-ˈnā\. **1.** Term applied to coastal region of W Africa bet. 15°N and 15°S; bet. Gambia and Cameroon (**Upper Guinea**) and bet. Cameroon and S Angola (**Lower Guinea**); name, from an ancient kingdom, not in general European use until after 1500. See EQUATORIAL GUINEA and GUINEA-BISSAU. Various sections of coast of Upper Guinea given different names by early traders: Slave Coast, Gold Coast, Ivory Coast, Grain Coast (*qq.v.*).

2. *formerly* **French Guinea.** Republic, W Africa, bounded on N by Senegal and Mali, on E by Mali and Ivory Coast, on S by Liberia and Sierra Leone, on W by the Atlantic Ocean, and on NW by Guinea-Bissau; 94,925 sq. mi. (245,856 sq. km.); pop. (1991e) 7,300,000; ✻ Conakry, on Tombo I.

Physical features: Includes Los Is. group opp. Conakry. Has marshy seacoast, ab. 170 mi. (274 km.) long, the coastal plain rising to hilly and plateau regions in the interior which form a tableland that is source of upper tributaries of Niger and Senegal rivers, also of many streams flowing SW to Atlantic. In N is Fouta Djallon tableland and on S borders are ranges that reach 3500 ft. (1067 m.) near coast and 6000 ft. (1829 m.) on Liberian border.

Chief products: Rice, bananas, coffee, pineapples, cassava, corn, palm products, peanuts; livestock; bauxite, iron ore, diamonds.

Chief towns: Conakry, Kankan, Labé, Kindia, Nzerekore.

History: Original settlers forced out c. 900 A.D.; numerous kingdoms estab.; visited by Portuguese mid-15th cent. and slave trade estab.; Fouta Djallon area part of Fulani Empire 16th–19th cents.; British, French, Portuguese active in trade 17th cent.; coastal region proclaimed French protectorate 1849; boundary agreements with Great Britain and Portugal late 19th cent.; administered with Senegal under name of **Ri·vières du Sud** \ˌrē-vē-ˌe(ə)r-dəs-ˈ(y)üd\ until its establishment as a separate colony 1893; became part of French West Africa 1904; status changed to that of overseas territory of France 1946; achieved independence 1958; government overthrown by military coup 1984; new constitution calling for democratization adopted 1991; first multiparty elections 1993.

Guinea, Gulf of. Great inlet of Atlantic Ocean on W cen. coast of Africa, bet. Upper Guinea and Lower Guinea and incl. Bights of Benin and Biafra.

Guin·ea–Bis·sau \ˈgi-nē-bi-ˈsau̇, gē-ˌnā-bē-ˈsau̇\; *formerly* **Portuguese Guinea.** Independent state, W Africa, bounded on N by Senegal, on E and SE by Guinea, and on SW and W by the Atlantic Ocean; 13,948 sq. mi. (36,125 sq. km.); pop. (1993e) 1,036,000; ✻ and chief town Bissau.

Physical features: Includes Arquipélago dos Bijagós; most of country consists of low, marshy terrain with a max. elev. of ab. 800 ft. (244 m.) in SE; traversed in cen. part by Gêba River.

Chief products: Peanuts, rice, fish, timber, coconuts, palm oil.

History: Part of Mali empire by 13th cent. A.D.; visited by Portuguese mid-15th cent.; active in supplying slave trade into 18th cent.; became Portuguese colony 1879 although not completely subjugated until 1936; boundaries estab. by convention with France 1886; made overseas territory of Portugal 1951; movement for independence began early 1960s; independence declared 1973; government overthrown by military coup 1980; new constitution adopted 1984; first multiparty elections 1994.

\ə\ **abut** \ᵊ\ kitten, Fr table \ər\ **further** \a\ ash \ā\ ace \ä\ cot, cart \a̐\ Fr bac \au̇\ **out** \b\ Span Avila \ch\ **chin** \e\ bet \ē\ easy \g\ go \i\ hit \ī\ ice \j\ job \k\ Ger **ich, Buch** \ⁿ\ Fr vin \ŋ\ sing \ō\ go \ȯ\ all \ȯ\ **law** \œ\ Fr bœuf \œ̄\ Fr feu \ȯi\ boy \th\ thin \t͟h\ **this** \ü\ loot \u̇\ **foot** \ue\ Ger füllen \ūe\ Fr rue \y\ yet \ʸ\ Fr digne \ˈdēnʸ\, nuit \ˈnwʸē\ \yü\ few \yu̇\ fury \zh\ vision

Guinea Current. Warm ocean current in the Atlantic, flowing E along the Guinea coast, W Africa.

Guinée. See GUINEA 1.

Guinegaste *or* **Guinegate.** See ENGUINEGATTE.

Güi·nes \ˈgwē-nās\. Municipality, W Cuba; pop. (1990e) 57,053; in tobacco-producing region; railroad junction 30 mi. (48 km.) SE of Havana.

Guînes \ˈgēn\. Commune, Pas-de-Calais dept., N France, 7 mi. (11 km.) SE of Calais; held by English 1352–1558; residence of English King Henry VIII in 1520 during meeting of "Field of the Cloth of Gold" bet. him and French King Francis I. See ARDRES.

Guin·gamp \geⁿ-ˈgäⁿ\. Commune, Côtes-du-Nord dept., NW France, 17 mi. (27 km.) WNW of St.-Brieuc; tourist center; former ✻ of countship, later the duchy, of Penthièvre; noted for church (14th–16th cents.) where annual pardons are granted to pilgrims.

Gui·no·ba·tan \ˌgē-nō-bä-ˈtän\. Municipality, E cen. Albay prov., Luzon, Philippines, ab. 9 mi. (14 km.) WNW of Legazpi; pop. (1990c) 58,926.

Gui·o·nes, Pun·ta \ˈpün-tä-gē-ˈō-nās\. Cape on W coast of Nicoya Penin., W Costa Rica.

Gui·ping \ˈgwē-ˈpiŋ\ *or W.-G.* **Kuei–p'ing** *also* **Kwei·ping** \ˈgwā-ˈpiŋ\. Town, E cen. Guangxi Zhuangzu, SE China, 23°24′N, 110°05′E, at a river junction.

Gui·púz·coa \gē-ˈpüth-kō-ä, -ˈpüs-\. Province of N Spain. See table at SPAIN.

Guir, Cape. See RHIR, CAPE.

Güi·ra de Me·le·na \ˈgwē-rä-thā-mā-ˈlā-nä\. Town and municipality, ✻ of La Habana prov., W Cuba, 25 mi. (40 km.) SSW of Havana; munic. pop. (1990e) 27,226.

Guis·bor·ough \ˈgiz-bə-rō\. Town, Cleveland, N England, 10 mi. (16 km.) ESE of Middlesbrough; pop. (1981p) 19,903; remains of a 12th cent. priory.

Guise \ˈgēz, ˈgwēz\. Commune, Aisne dept., N France, on the Oise 23 mi. (37 km.) N of Laon; ruins of 16th cent. chateau of dukes of Guise; formerly noted for its cooperative ironworks estab. 1859 by French industrialist and reformer Jean-Baptiste-André Godin.

Gui·uan \ˈgē-ˌwän\. Municipality, SE tip of Samar, Philippines, on NE coast of Leyte Gulf 76 mi. (122 km.) SE of Catbalogan.

Gui·yang \ˈgwē-ˈyäŋ\ *or W.-G.* **Kuei–yang** *also* **Kwei·yang** \ˈgwā-ˈyäŋ\; *formerly* **Kwei·chu** \ˈgwā-ˈchü\. City, ✻ of Guizhou prov., S China, 220 mi. (354 km.) S of Chongqing, Sichuan ab. halfway on highway bet. Chongqing and Kunming, Yunnan; pop. (1990c) 1,018,619; on plateau at 3400 ft. (1036 m.) elev.; administrative and transportation center of the province.

Gui·zhou \ˈgwē-ˈjō\ *or W.-G.* **Kuei–chou** \ˈgwā-ˈjō\ *or* **Kwei·chow** \ˈgwā-ˈchau̇\. Province, S China, bounded on N by Sichuan prov., on E by Hunan, on S by Guangxi Zhuangzu, and on W by Yunnan; ✻ Guiyang; a plateau region bet. the tributaries of the Chang and Xi rivers; contains many aboriginal peoples, chiefly the Miao; wheat, corn, potatoes; has rich mercury deposits. Chief towns: Guiyang, Zunyi, Anshun, Duyun; made a province in 17th cent.; scene of many revolts by the Miao; remained in Chinese hands during WWII. See table at CHINA.

Gu·ja·rat *or* **Gu·je·rat** \ˌgü-jə-ˈrät, ˌgu̇-\. **1.** *or* **Gujarat Plains.** Extensive area of plains, cen. Gujarat state, W India. **2.** Historical region, W India, in Gujarat Plains; in widest use includes Gujarati-speaking regions of Kathiawar, Kutch, Vadodara, Palanpur, and other areas geographically located in or near the N part of former Bombay state (now adjacent areas of Gujarat and Maharashtra states).

History: Annexed to Sultanate of Delhi late 13th cent.; became independent kingdom c. 1401; territory extended by Aḥmad Shāh of Gujarat early 15th cent. who built Ahmadabad; annexed 1572–73 by Mogul Emperor Akbar; in 18th cent., overrun by Marathas who later ceded to British much of old kingdom of Gujarat; British later reorganized part of area into **Gujarat States Agency** 1933, incl. Baroda among large number of states and estates; became part of Republic of India 1947, and part of Bombay state (*q.v.*) which was divided 1960 into Gujarat (see below) and Maharashtra (*q.v.*) states.
3. State, W India; 72,236 sq. mi. (187,091 sq. km.); pop. (1991c) 41,309,582; ✻ Gandhinagar; comprises the Gujarati-speaking NW portion of the former Bombay state (*q.v.*); rice, cotton, wheat, salt; chemicals, pharmaceuticals, textiles. Formed 1960; borders extended after settlement of dispute with Pakistan 1968; religious strife bet. Hindus and Muslims became protracted 1980s and continued into 1990s. See MAHARASHTRA 2 and table at INDIA.

Guj·ran·wa·la \ˌgu̇j-rən-ˈwä-lə, ˌgu̇j-\. Town, Punjab, Pakistan, 42 mi. (68 km.) N of Lahore; pop. (1981c) 785,000; grain trade; brass and copper utensils; tanneries; birthplace of Sikh ruler Ranjit Singh 1780; ✻ of Sikh power until 1799; included in territory annexed by British after Second Sikh War (1848–49).

Guj·rat \ˈgu̇j-ˌrät\. Town, Punjab, Pakistan, near Chenab River 68 mi. (109 km.) N of Lahore; pop. (1981p) 214,000; known for work in gold and silver inlay; ceramics, electric fans. Founded c. 1580; scene of battle 1849 during Second Sikh War in which Sikh power was broken.

Gu·ko·vo \ˈgü-kə-və\. Town, Rostov Oblast, S Russia in Europe, ab. 60 mi. (97 km.) NNE of Rostov-na-Donu; pop. (1991e) 67,700; coal mining.

Gul·bar·ga \ˈgu̇l-bər-ˌgä\. Town, N cen. Karnataka, S cen. India, 120 mi. (193 km.) W of Hyderabad; pop. (1991p) 303,139; cotton, flour, paint, and oil. Seat of Bahmanī kings of the Deccan 1347–1422; remains of this era include a mosque said to be patterned after that of Córdoba in Spain.

Gülek Bogaz. See CILICIAN GATES.

Gulf \ˈgəlf\. County on NW coast of Florida. See table at FLORIDA.

Gulf Breeze \ˌbrēz\. City, Santa Rosa co., NW Florida, 5 mi. (8 km.) SE of Pensacola; pop. (1990c) 5530; residential suburb of Pensacola.

Gulf Cooperation Council. Economic and political organization, consisting of Bahrain, Kuwait, Oman, Qatar, Saudi Arabia, and the United Arab Emirates; headquarters Riyadh, Saudi Arabia; estab. 1981.

Gulf Intracoastal Waterway. System of inland waterways incl. rivers, bays, and canals from Apalachee Bay, Florida, to Brownsville, Texas; includes Mobile Bay and Mississippi Sound, goes through New Orleans, takes in the Sabine-Neches Waterway (*q.v.*) and the ship canal at Houston, Texas; ab. 1100 mi. (1770 km.) long.

Gulf Islands. Group of islands in Strait of Georgia off SE coast of Vancouver I., British Columbia, Canada.

Gulf·port \ˈgəlf-ˌpōrt\. **1.** City, Pinellas co., W Florida Penin.; suburb of St. Petersburg; pop. (1990c) 11,727.
2. City, a ⊗ of Harrison co., SE Mississippi, on Gulf of Mexico; pop. (1990c) 40,775; resort; ships textiles, lumber; seafood canneries.

Gulf Shores. City, Baldwin co., SW Alabama, 45 mi. (62 km.) SE of Mobile; pop. (1990c) 3261.

Gulf States. The U.S. states bordering on the Gulf of Mexico: Florida, Alabama, Mississippi, Louisiana, and Texas.

Gulf Stream. Warm ocean current in North Atlantic Ocean; flows out of Gulf of Mexico through Straits of Florida, where it is a current 50 mi. (80 km.) wide and more than 2000 ft. (610 m.) deep, continues NE along coast of U.S. to Nantucket I. and thence eastward; in N mid-Atlantic (40°N, 45°W) merges with North Atlantic Drift Current, a warm current flowing NE to the Barents Sea and influencing climate of W Europe as far as Norway; at ab. 30°W sends off Southeast Drift Current touching coasts of Iberian Penin. and NW Africa; rate of flow, more than 4 mi. (6 km.) an hour in the S and between 10 and 15 mi. (16 and 24 km.) a day farther N. Strictly, the term *Gulf Stream* does not apply beyond 60°W.

Gu·lis·tan \ˌgü-lə-ˈstan, -ˈstän\. Village, cen. Azerbaijan; treaty bet. Russia and Persia signed here 1813 by which Persia gave up Georgia, most of Azerbaijan, and neighboring districts to Russia.

Gu·li·ston \ˈgü-li-stən\ *or* **Gu·li·stan** \ˌgü-li-ˈstän\. City, ✻ of Syr Dar'ya subdivision of Uzbekistan; pop. (1991e) 56,900.

Gulja. See YINING.

Gul·kana \gəl-ˈka-nə\. Village on Copper River, SE Alaska, on Richardson and Glenn highways; pop. (1990c) 103; junction for cutoff to Tanacross on Alaska Highway.

Gull·foss \ˈgœd-ᵊl-ˌfōs\ *or Eng.* **Golden Fall.** Waterfall in Hvítá River, SW Iceland, near Geysir; 101 ft. (31 m.) high.

Gull Lake \ˈgəl\. Lake, Cass and Crow Wing cos., N cen. Minnesota; outdoor recreation.

Gulpaigan. See GOLPĀYEGĀN.

Gu·lu \ˈgü-lü\. Town, N cen. Uganda; pop. (1991p) 42,841.

Gu·mal \gə-ˈməl\ *or* **Go·mal** \gō-\. River, S North-West Frontier prov., Pakistan; flows from E Afghanistan E and SE to the Indus near Dera Ismail Khan; provides water for irrigation; chief tributary the Zhob.

Gumal Pass *or* **Gomal Pass.** Mountain pass at N end of Sulaiman Range, in S North-West Frontier prov., Pakistan, WNW of Dera Ismail Khan; elev. 7500 ft. (2286 m.).

Gumbinnen. See GUSEV.

Gu·mel \gü-ˈmel\. Town, N Nigeria, not far from Niger border; pop. (1991e) 49,780.

Gum·ma \ˈgu̇m-mä\. Prefecture, Honshū, Japan; ✻ Maebashi; sericulture; manganese. See table at JAPAN.

Gum·mers·bach \ˈgu̇-mərz-ˌbäḵ\. City, North Rhine-Westphalia, Germany, 28 mi. (45 km.) E of Cologne; pop. (1992e) 51,304.

Gumti. See GOMATI.

Gümüljina. See KOMOTINÍ.

Gü·mü·şha·ne *or* **Gü–mü·şa·ne** \gᵫ-ˈmᵫ-shä-ne\ *or* **Gü·müsh Kha·neh** \gᵫ-ˈmᵫsh-kä-ˈne\. **1.** Province of Turkey in Asia. See table at TURKEY.
2. Town, its ✻, 40 mi. (64 km.) SSW of Trabzon; pop. (1990p) 25,877.

Gu·na Te·ra·ra \ˈgü-nə-ˈter-ə-rə\. Mountain, N cen. Ethiopia, E of Lake Tana; 13,878 ft. (4230 m.).

Gun Cay \ˈgən\. Island in Bahamas, S of the Biminis; lighthouse on S end (estab. 1836).

Gun·flint \ˈgən-ˌflint\. Village, Cook co., NE Minnesota, at W end of **Gunflint Lake** on the U.S.-Canada boundary; iron ore in the region to the S, first to be discovered in the state but never mined because of its high titanium content.

Gu·nib \gü-ˈnib\. Village, W Dagestan Rep., S Russia in Europe, in E Caucasus Mts.; scene of capture 1859 of the Caucasian leader, Shāmil, which ended resistance of mountain peoples to Russian domination.

Gunn·bjørn Fjeld \ˈgœn-ˌbyœrn-ˈfyeld\; *angl.* **Mount Gunn·bjørn** \ˈgu̇n-ˌbyȯrn\. Mountain, near coast of E cen. Greenland, one of its highest; 12,139 ft. (3700 m.).

Gun·ni·son \ˈgə-nə-sən\. **1.** River, W cen. Colorado; rises in SE Gunnison co., flows W and NW into Colorado River in cen. Mesa co.; 150 mi. (241 km.) long; Black Canyon of the Gunnison is a national monument (see UNITED STATES, *National Monuments*). See also BLACK CANYON 2.
2. County in W cen. Colorado. See table at COLORADO.
3. Town, ⊗ of Gunnison co., W cen. Colorado, on Gunnison River 50 mi. (80 km.) W of Salida; pop. (1990c) 4636; incorp. 1880 as mining center; resort; Western State Coll. of Colorado (1911).

Gunong. See GUNUNG.

Gun·pow·der \ˈgən-ˌpau̇-dər\. River, N Maryland; rises in NE Carroll co., flows SE into upper Chesapeake Bay; ab. 60 mi. (97 km.) long.

Gun·sight Mountain \ˈgən-ˌsīt\. Peak in Glacier National Park, NW Montana; 9250 ft. (2819 m.).

Gun·ters·ville \ˈgən-tərz-ˌvil\. Town, ⊗ of Marshall co., NE Alabama, on Tennessee River, 30 mi. (48 km.) NW of Gadsden; pop. (1990c) 7038; river port.

Guntersville Dam. See table at TENNESSEE VALLEY AUTHORITY.

Gun·tur \gu̇n-ˈtu̇r\. **1.** City, cen. Andhra Pradesh, E India, NW of mouths of Krishna River; pop. (1991c) 471,051; important cotton and tobacco trade. Apparently founded in 18th cent. by French; ceded to British 1788.
2. \ˈgu̇n-ˌtu̇r\ *or Du.* **Goen·toer** \gu̇n-ˈtu̇r\. Volcano, W cen. Java, Indonesia; 7377 ft. (2249 m.).

Gu·nung \ˈgü-ˌnu̇ŋ\ *or* **Gu·nong** \-ˌnȯŋ\. Indonesian and Malaysian terms respectively, meaning "mountain," as in **Gunung Awu, Gunong Ta·han.** See 2d element of the name.

Gu·nung·api *or Du.* **Goe·noeng Api** \ˈgü-ˌnu̇ŋ-ˈä-pē\. Volcanic island, one of the Banda Is., Malay Archipelago, Indonesia; with Banda Besar (*q.v.*) and Bandanaira I. forms harbor of Bandanaira; an active volcano, 1858 ft. (566 m.) high; notable eruptions dating back to 18th cent.

Gu·nung·si·to·li *or Du.* **Goe·noeng·si·to·li** \ˌgü-ˌnu̇ŋ-sē-ˈtō-lē\. Chief village of Nias I. off W coast of Sumatra, Indonesia.

Gur, Lough \läḵ-ˈgu̇r\. Small lake, co. Limerick, S Ireland, S of Limerick; prehistoric settlement on shores with numerous stone monuments; 16th cent. castle nearby.

Gu·ra·bo \gü-ˈrä-bō\. Municipality, E Puerto Rico, SE of San Juan; pop. (1990e) 28,737.

Gur·das·pur \gu̇r-ˈdäs-ˌpu̇r\. Town, Punjab, N India, bet. Beas and Ravi rivers; pop. (1991p) 54,575.

Gurev. See ATYRAŪ.

Gurgan. See GORGĀN.

Gur·gaon \ˈgu̇r-ˌgau̇n\. City, SE Haryana state, India, SW of New Delhi; pop. (1991c) 121,486.

Gu·ri Dam \ˈgü-rē\. Dam in Caroní River, E cen. Venezuela; forms reservoir with large capacity.

Gurk \ˈgu̇rk\. River, Carinthia, S Austria; flows E and S into Drau (Drava) River 10 mi. (16 km.) E of Klagenfurt; 99 mi. (159 km.) long.

Gur·kha \ˈgu̇r-kə\ *or* **Gor·kha** \ˈgȯr-kə\. Village, E cen. Nepal, 50 mi. (80 km.) WNW of Kathmandu; ancestral home of Nepal's ruling house.

Gurla Mandhata. See KUA-LA-MAN-TA-T'A.

Gurn Peak. See ABU, MOUNT 1.

Gur·nards Head \ˈgər-nərdz\. Promontory on SE coast of Cornwall, SW England, N of Land's End.

Gur·nee \ˈgər-nē, gər-ˈnē\. Village, Lake co., NE Illinois, just W of Waukegan; pop. (1990c) 13,701.

Gur·net Point \ˈgər-nət\. Cape on N side of Plymouth Bay, Massachusetts.

Gu·ru·pi \ˌgü-rü-ˈpē\. River, NE Brazil; flows N from W Maranhão state, forming boundary bet. Pará and Maranhão; empties into Atlantic Ocean; ab. 300 mi. (483 km.) long.

Guryev. See ATYRAŪ.

Gu·sau \gü-ˈzau̇\. Town, Sokoto state, NW Nigeria, 130 mi. (209 km.) W of Kano; pop. (1991e) 139,400.

Gu·sev \ˈgü-sif\ *or Ger.* **Gum·bin·nen** \gu̇m-ˈbi-nən\. City, Kaliningrad Oblast, exclave of Russia in Europe, 68 mi. (109 km.) E of the city of Kaliningrad. Formerly part of East Prussia; scene of WWI Russian victory over Germans 1914; assigned to U.S.S.R. by Potsdam Conference 1945.

Gusharbrum. See GASHERBRUM.

Gus'–Khru·stal'·nyy *or* **Gus–Khru·stal·ny** \ˈgu̇sʸ-krü-ˈstälʸ-nē\. Town, Vladimir Oblast, cen. Russia in Europe, ab. 40 mi. (64 km.) SSE of the city of Vladimir; pop. (1991e) 77,000.

Gus·tav Line \ˈgu̇s-täf\. In WWII the main German defense line across Italy S of Rome, following the Garigliano River, running through Cassino to the Adriatic just N of the Sangro River; reached by Allies early 1944, taken May 1944.

Gus·ta·vo A. Ma·de·ro, Vil·la \ˈvē-yä-gü-ˈstä-bō-ä-mä-ˈt͟hā-rō\ *also* **Gua·da·lu·pe Hi·dal·go** \ˌgwä-t͟hä-ˈlü-pā-ē-ˈt͟häl-gō, ˌgwä-də-ˈlü-pā-hē-ˈdäl-gō\. City, Federal District, cen. Mexico; important Christian pilgrimage site due to visions of Virgin Mary reported 1531; Treaty of Guadalupe Hidalgo signed here Feb. 2, 1848 terminating Mexican War.

Gus·ta·vus \gəs-ˈtā-vəs\. Unincorporated settlement, SE Alaska, on Cross Sound N of Chichagof I. and W of Juneau; pop. (1990c) 258; entrance to Glacier Bay National Park; airport.

Gus·tine \gəs-ˈtēn\. City, Merced co., cen. California, 27 mi. (43 km.) W of the city of Merced; pop. (1990c) 3931.

Gü·strow \ˈgᵫs-trō\. City, Mecklenburg-West Pomerania, N Germany, 50 mi. (80 km.) SW of Stralsund; pop. (1992e) 36,951; engineering, food processing; 13th cent. cathedral; 16th cent. ducal castle; received city rights 1228.

\ə\ abut \ᵊ\ matches \ᵊ\ kitten, Fr table \ər\ further \a\ ash \ā\ ace \ä\ cot, cart \à\ Fr bac \au̇\ out \b\ Span Avila \ch\ chin \e\ bet \ē\ easy \g\ go \i\ hit \ī\ ice \j\ job \ḵ\ Ger ich, Buch \ⁿ\ Fr vin \ŋ\ sing \ō\ go \ȯ\ all \ȯ\ law \œ\ Fr bœuf \ᵫ\ Fr feu \ȯi\ boy \th\ thin \t͟h\ this \ü\ loot \u̇\ foot \ᵫ\ Ger füllen \ᵫ\ Fr rue \y\ yet \ʸ\ Fr digne \dēnʸ\, nuit \nwʸē\ \yü\ few \yu̇\ fury \zh\ vision

Gü·ters·loh \ˈgüē-tərz-ˌlō\. City, NE North Rhine-Westphalia, Germany, 31 mi. (50 km.) E of Münster; pop. (1992e) 88,537; manufactures foodstuffs, textiles, furniture; botanical gardens; city chartered 1825.

Guth·rie \ˈgə-thrē\. **1.** County in SW cen. Iowa. See table at IOWA.

2. City, ⊗ of Logan co., cen. Oklahoma, 28 mi. (45 km.) N of Oklahoma City; pop. (1990c) 10,518; oil wells; founded 1889; ✱ of Oklahoma Terr. and state of Oklahoma 1890–1910.

3. Village, ⊗ of King co., NW Texas.

Guthrie Center. City, ⊗ of Guthrie co., SW cen. Iowa, 50 mi. (80 km.) W of Des Moines; pop. (1990c) 1614.

Gut·ten·berg \ˈgət-ᵊn-ˌbərg\. **1.** City, Clayton co., NE Iowa, on Mississippi River 30 mi. (48 km.) NW of Dubuque; pop. (1990c) 2257; settled 1834; colonized by German immigrants 1845.

2. Town, Hudson co., NE New Jersey, on Hudson River just N of West New York; pop. (1990c) 8268.

Guwahati. See GAUHATI.

Guy·ana \gī-ˈä-nə\; *formerly* **British Gui·a·na** \gē-ˈä-nə, gī-, -ˈa-\. Republic, N South America, bounded on N and NE by the Atlantic Ocean, on E and SE by Suriname, on S and SW by Brazil, and on W by Brazil and Venezuela; 83,000 sq. mi. (214,970 sq. km.); pop. (1993e) 755,000; ✱ and chief town Georgetown.

Physical features: Has low-lying, marshy coastal region (coastline ab. 270 mi. or 434 km.) with inland plains sloping up to mountain ranges on W and S; highest range Pakaraima Mts., the NE extension of the Pacaraima Mts. along the Venezuela-Brazil boundary, culminating in Mt. Roraima 9219 ft. (2810 m.) near the junction of the Venezuela-Brazil-Guyana boundaries; in S is Serra Acaraí, highest peak ab. 2000 ft. (610 m.), densely wooded, and the W extension of the Tumuc-Humac Mts. along the Brazilian border. Has many rivers, all flowing to the Atlantic; among them the Essequibo, in cen. part with main tributaries: Cuyuni, Mazaruni, and Potaro (containing the Kaieteur Falls); the Courantyne on Suriname boundary in E; and the commercially important, but shorter streams, Demerara and Berbice, in the NE.

Chief products: Bauxite, diamonds, gold; sugar, rice, shrimp; timber.

History: For early history of region, see GUIANA. Dutch trading settlements founded c. 1580; Dutch colonies founded early 17th cent.; captured by British 1796; returned to Dutch but ceded to Great Britain 1814; became crown colony of British Guiana 1831; its boundary with Venezuela, long subject of controversy, became serious issue, involving U.S. (Olney Doctrine) in 1895; in arbitration award 1899, most of British claims upheld, although Venezuela continues to make claims; achieved independence 1966; became republic 1970; mass suicide of cult members following American Jim Jones in Jonestown 1978; adopted new constitution 1980.

Guy·an·dotte \ˈgī-ən-ˌdät\. River, SW West Virginia; rises in Wyoming co., flows NW into Ohio River near Huntington; ab. 150 mi. (241 km.) long.

Guyane française. See FRENCH GUIANA.

Guyenne. See GUIENNE.

Guy·mon \ˈgī-mən\. City, ⊗ of Texas co., NW Oklahoma; pop. (1990c) 7803.

Guy·ot, Mount \ˈgē-ō\. **1.** Mountain on E boundary of Tulare co., California, SW of Mt. Whitney; 12,300 ft. (3749 m.).

2. Peak, Grafton co., N cen. New Hampshire; 4589 ft. (1399 m.).

3. Peak in Great Smoky Mts., on boundary bet. Tennessee and North Carolina; 6621 ft. (2018 m.).

Guys·bor·ough \ˈgīz-ˌbər-ō\. **1.** County, E Nova Scotia, Canada. See table at NOVA SCOTIA.

2. Municipal district, its ⊗, at head of Chedabucto Bay; pop. (1991c) 6518.

Gwa·dar *or* **Gwa·dur** \ˈgwä-dər\. Port on Makran coast, SW Baluchistan, Pakistan; pop. (1981p) 17,000; belonged to sultanate of Muscat and Oman from 1797 until ceded to Pakistan 1958.

Gwa·li·or \ˈgwä-lē-ˌȯr\. **1.** Former state, India, now part of Madhya Pradesh state; 26,367 sq. mi. (68,291 sq. km.); ✱ Lashkar; one of the five chief Indian states, formerly the dominion of the Sindhia family of Marathas; larger part bet. Rajputana on W and United Provinces and Central India on E, with Chambal River forming its N and NW boundary; other smaller sections in SW Central India.

2. Town, N Madhya Pradesh, N cen. India, 65 mi. (105 km.) SSE of Agra; pop. (1991c) 690,765; footwear, textiles; university (1964); old part of city, which has many fine Mogul architectural remains, overlooked by famous fort of Gwalior, on a sandstone cliff 300 ft. (91 m.) high, first attested 525 A.D., featuring numerous 15th cent. rock-cut Jain and Hindu sculptures and several palaces, temples, and reservoirs. Fort was controlled by Hindus until 1232; control alternated bet. Muslims and Hindus until taken by Marathas 1751; captured by British 1780, 1843, 1858; returned by British 1886. To the S is the new city, Lashkar, founded c. 1810.

Gwan·du \ˈgwän-dü\. **1.** Historical emirate of Nigeria. See GANDO.

2. *formerly* **Gan·do** \ˈgän-dō\. Town, NW Nigeria, ab. 60 mi. (96 km.) SW of Sokoto; chief town of Gando emirate.

Gwa·tar Bay \ˈgwə-tər, ˈgwä-\. Inlet of Arabian Sea on Iran-Pakistan border; ab. 20 mi. (32 km.) long.

Gwee·bar·ra Bay \gwē-ˈbar-ə\. Inlet of Atlantic Ocean in W co. Donegal, N Ireland (republic), N of Donegal Bay.

Gwelo. See GWERU.

Gwent \ˈgwent\. **1.** Old region, SE Wales, incl. Glamorganshire, Monmouthshire, and adjoining areas.

2. County, SW Wales, formed 1974; comprises most of former Monmouthshire and a small part of former Glamorganshire. See table at WALES.

Gwe·ru \ˈgwā-rü\; *formerly* **Gwe·lo** \ˈgwā-lō\. Town, SW Zimbabwe, 90 mi. (145 km.) ENE of Bulawayo; pop. (1982p) 24,715; gold, chrome ore, asbestos fiber produced nearby.

Gwin·nett \gwi-ˈnet\. County in N Georgia. See table at GEORGIA.

Gwy. See WYE 1.

Gwy·dir \ˈgwī-dər\. River, NE New South Wales, SE Australia; flows W into Barwon River; 415 mi. (668 km.) long.

Gwyn·edd *or* **Gwyn·eth** \ˈgwi-ˌneth\. **1.** Ancient region in NW Wales comprising most of N Wales.

2. County, NW Wales, formed 1974; includes former Anglesey county, Caernarvonshire, and parts of Denbighshire and Merionethshire. See table at WALES.

Gyandzha. See GÄNCÄ.

Gya·ring *or W.-G.* **Kya·ring** \ˈgyä-ˈriŋ\. Lake, E cen. Tibet, China, 31°10′N, 88°15′E; ab. 40 mi. (64 km.) long.

Gy·a·ros \ˈyē-ə-ˌrȯs\ *or Gk.* **Yi·oú·ra** \yē-ˈü-rä\. Mountainous island, NW Cyclades, Greece, S Aegean Sea, NW of Syros; 7 sq. mi. (18 sq. km.); in Cyclades dept.

Gym·pie \ˈgim-pē\. Town, E Queensland, Australia, 90 mi. (145 km.) N of Brisbane; pop. (1981c) 10,768; in mining region.

Gyō·da \ˈgyō-dä\. City, Saitama prefecture, Honshu, Japan, 35 mi. (56 km.) NW of Tokyo; pop. (1990p) 83,181.

Gyo·ma \ˈjō-mö\. Former commune, SE Hungary. See GYOMAENDRÖD.

Gyo·ma·en·dröd \ˈjō-mö-ˌen-drœd\. Commune, SE Hungary, SW of Debrecen; formed 1981 by a consolidation of Gyoma and Endröd.

Gyön·gyös \ˈjœn-ˌjœsh\. City, N cen. Hungary, 45 mi. (72 km.) NE of Budapest; pop. (1991e) 37,200.

Győr \ˈjœr\ *or Ger.* **Raab** \ˈräp\. City, ⊗ of Győr-Moson-Sopron co., NW Hungary, 67 mi. (108 km.) WNW of Budapest; pop. (1991e) 134,200; textiles; flour milling, distilling; 12th–17th cent. cathedral, 13th cent. bishop's palace; became free royal town 1743.

Győr–Mo·son–So·pron \ˈjœr-ˈmō-ˌsōn-ˈshō-ˌprōn\. County of NW Hungary. See table at HUNGARY.

Gy–Paraná. See JIPARANÁ.

Gythium. See YÍTHION.

Gyu·la \ˈjü-lö\. City, SE Hungary, NE of Szeged near Romanian border; pop. (1991e) 35,100.

Gyulafehérvár. See ALBA IULIA.

Gyum·ri \ˈgyu̇m-rē\ *or* **Ku·may·ri** \ˈkü-mī-rē\; *1924-90* **Le·nin·a·kan** \li-ˌnēn-ȧ-ˈkän\; *before 1924* **Alek·san·dro·pol** *or* **Alex·an·dro·pol** \ˌȧ-lik-sän-ˈdrȯ-pəl\. City, NW Armenia, on a tributary of the Araks 55 mi. (88 km.) NW of Yerevan; pop. (1989c) 120,000; textiles, machinery; suffered devastation by earthquake Dec. 1988.

Gy·zyl·ar·bat \gi-ˌzil-är-ˈbät\ *or* **Ki·zyl–Ar·vat** \ki-ˌzil-är-ˈvät\. Town, SW Turkmenistan, on railroad line.

Gzhatsk. See GAGARIN.

\ə\ abut \ə\ matches \ᵊ\ kitten, Fr table \ər\ further \a\ ash \ā\ ace \ä\ cot, cart \ȧ\ Fr bac \au̇\ out \b\ Span Avila \ch\ chin \e\ bet \ē\ easy \g\ go \i\ hit \ī\ ice \j\ job \k\ Ger ich, Buch \ⁿ\ Fr vin \ŋ\ sing \ō\ go \ȯ\ all \ȯ\ law \œ\ Fr bœuf \œ̄\ Fr feu \ȯi\ boy \th\ thin \th\ this \ü\ loot \u̇\ foot \ue\ Ger füllen \ue̅\ Fr rue \y\ yet \ʸ\ Fr digne \ˈdēnʸ\, nuit \ˈnwʸē\ \yü\ few \yu̇\ fury \zh\ vision

H

Haabai. See HAAPAI.

Haa·kon \ˈha-kən\. County in W cen. South Dakota. See table at SOUTH DAKOTA.

Haan \ˈhän\. City, North Rhine-Westphalia, Germany, NW suburb of Solingen; pop. (1980c) 28,571.

Ha·a·no \ˈhä-ä-nō\. Island in NE Ha'apai group, Tonga, SW cen. Pacific Ocean.

Ha·'a·pai \hä-ä-ˈpī\ *or* **Ha·a·bai** \-ˈbī\. Island group in cen. Tonga (*q.v.*), SW cen. Pacific Ocean, ab. 60 mi. (97 km.) S of Vava'u group; pop. (1986c) 8919; ab. 50 islands, incl. Haano, Foa, Lifuka, Uiha, and Tofua; chief village Pangai on Lifuka I.

Haar·lem; *formerly* **Har·lem** \ˈhär-ləm\. City, ❋ of North Holland prov., W Netherlands, 12 mi. (19 km.) W of Amsterdam; pop. (1992e) 149,788; printing; textiles, machinery; center of tulip-growing and exporting region; 15th cent. cathedral of St. Bavo; Frans Hals and Teyler art museums. Chartered 1245; forced to yield to Spaniards after siege of seven months 1572–73; recaptured 1577 by Stadholder William I of Orange.

Haarlem Meer *and* **Haarlemmermeer.** See HOOFDDORP.

Hab \ˈhəb\. River, Pakistan; flows S into Arabian Sea, in its lower course forming boundary bet. Baluchistan and Sind; ab. 250 mi. (400 km.) long.

Habana, La. See LA HABANA 2 and HAVANA 2.

Habbaniyah, Lake. See HAWR AL HABBĀNĪYAH.

Hab·er·sham \ˈha-bər-ˌsham, -shəm\. County in NE Georgia. See table at GEORGIA.

Ha·bi·ki·no \ˌhä-bē-ˈkē-nō\. City, Ōsaka prefecture, Honshū, Japan, 11 mi. (18 km.) SSE of the city of Ōsaka; pop. (1990p) 115,035.

Ha·bor \ˈhā-ˌbȯr\. Biblical name (*2 Kings* xvii. 6) for the Khābūr River (*q.v.*).

Habs·burg \ˈhaps-ˌbərg, ˈhäps-ˌbu̇rk\. Hamlet in Aargau canton, N cen. Switzerland, NE of the commune of Aarau; pop. (1980c) 243; original seat of the Hapsburgs (*Ger.* Habsburgs).

Ha·chi·jō \ˈhä-chē-ˌjō\. **1.** Group of islands off SE Honshū, Japan, ab. 180 mi. (290 km.) S of Tokyo; ab. 32 sq. mi. (83 sq. km.); pop. (1980c) 10,436; forms an administrative unit of Tokyo prefecture; consists of Hachijō I. and three islets. **2.** Chief island of the group; 27 sq. mi. (70 sq. km.); pop. (1980c) 10,244.

Ha·chi·no·he \ˌhä-chē-ˈnō-hā\. Coastal town, Aomori prefecture, N Honshū, Japan; pop. (1990p) 241,065; chemicals; fisheries.

Ha·chi·ō·ji \ˌhä-chē-ˈō-jē\. City, Tokyo prefecture, SE cen. Honshū, Japan, 27 mi. (43 km.) W of the city of Tokyo; pop. (1990p) 466,373; noted for its weaving industry, esp. of silk fabrics; synthetic textiles, chemicals.

Hack·en·sack \ˈha-kən-ˌsak\. **1.** River, New York and New Jersey; flows from Rockland co., SE New York, S across New Jersey border and into Newark Bay; ab. 40 mi. (64 km.) long. **2.** City, ⊗ of Bergen co., NE corner of New Jersey, on Hackensack River 7 mi. (11 km.) ESE of Paterson; pop. (1990c) 37,049; foundry products, furniture, chemicals. Settled by Dutch 1647 as New Barbados; taken by English 1668; served as Revolutionary camping ground in turn for Americans and British; incorp. as town 1868; chartered as city and name changed to Hackensack 1921.

Hack·etts·town \ˈha-kəts-ˌtau̇n\. Town, Warren co., NW New Jersey, 19 mi. (31 km.) W of Morristown; pop. (1990c) 8120; Centenary Coll. (1867).

Hack·ney \ˈhak-nē\. A borough of Greater London, SE England. See table at LONDON 4.

Ha·da·no \hä-ˈdä-nō\. City, Kanagawa prefecture, Honshū, Japan, 37 mi. (60 km.) SW of Tokyo; pop. (1990p) 155,619.

Ha·dar·ba, Ras \ˌräs-hə-ˈdär-bə\; *formerly* **Cape El·ba** \-ˈel-bə\. Cape extending into Red Sea, NE Sudan.

Ḥadd, Ra's al \ˌrȧs-ȧl-ˈhȧd\; *angl.* **Cape Hadd** \ˈhad\. Easternmost extremity of Oman, and of Arabian Penin.; projects into the Arabian Sea.

Had·dam \ˈha-dəm\. Town, cen. Middlesex co., S Connecticut, on Connecticut River; pop. (1990c) 6769; incorp. 1668.

Had·ding·ton \ˈha-diŋ-tən\ *or* **Had·ding·ton·shire** \-ˌshir, -shər\. **1.** Former county, SE Scotland. See EAST LOTHIAN. **2.** Burgh, Lothian region, SE Scotland; pop. (1981p) 8117; includes Giffordgate, birthplace of religious reformer John Knox c. 1514.

Had·don \ˈhad-ᵊn\. Township, Camden co., SW New Jersey, SSE of the city of Camden; pop. (1990c) 14,837.

Had·don·field \ˈhad-ᵊn-ˌfēld\. Residential borough, Camden co., SW New Jersey, 6 mi. (10 km.) SE of the city of Camden; pop. (1990c) 11,628; founded c. 1701 by Elizabeth Haddon, an English Quaker; meeting place of New Jersey's first legislature 1777.

Haddon Heights. Borough, Camden co., SW New Jersey, 5 mi. (8 km.) SSE of the city of Camden; pop. (1990c) 7860.

Ha·de·jia \hä-ˈdā-jē-ä\. **1.** River, N Nigeria; rises W of Kano and flows ENE to the Yobe on Niger border; 375 mi. (603 km.) long. **2.** Town, Kano state, NE Nigeria, on Hadejia River 110 mi. (177 km.) E of the city of Kano; pop. (1991e) 47,400.

Ḥa·de·ra \hə-ˈdär-ə\. Town, W Israel, near coast 26 mi. (42 km.) S of Haifa; pop. (1992e) 48,400; paper.

Ha·ders·lev \ˈhȧ-t͟hərz-ˌleu̇\ *or Ger.* **Ha·ders·le·ben** \ˈhä-dərz-ˌlā-bən\. Seaport, Sønderjylland co., Denmark, SE Jutland; pop. (1989e) 30,220; railroad center; breweries, tanneries; 13th–15th cent. church; first mentioned 1228; under Prussian rule 1864–1920.

Hadhramaut. See ḤAḌRAMAWT.

Hadibu. See TAMRIDAH.

Hadī·thah, Al *or* **Haditha.** See AL HADĪTHAH.

Had·ley \ˈhad-lē\. Town, Hampshire co., W Massachusetts, on Connecticut River 16 mi. (26 km.) N of Springfield; pop. (1990c) 4231; birthplace of Gen. Joseph Hooker 1814; settled 1659, incorp. 1661.

Hadley Falls Dam. See HOLYOKE DAM.

Ḥaḍr, Al. See AL ḤAḌR.

Ḥaḍ·ra·mawt *or* **Hadh·ra·maut** \ˌhä-drä-ˈmau̇t\. Region, S Arabian Penin.; near coast in E Yemen; ab. 58,000 sq. mi. (150,220 sq. km.); parallel to coast is mountain range with av. alt. of 3500 ft. (1067 m.) (highest peak ab. 8000 ft. or 2440 m.); cen. part contains fertile valley along **Wa·di Ḥaḍramawt** \ˈwä-dē\ (ab. 400 mi. or 645 km. long); produces dates, honey, tobacco; chief town port of Al Mukallā.

Hadranum. See ADRANO.

Hadria. See ADRIA.

Hadrianopolis. See EDİRNE.

Hadria Picena. See ATRI.

Hadrumetum. See SOUSSE.

Hae·ju \ˈhī-jü\ *or Jp.* **Kai·shu** \ˈkī-shü\. Coastal town, SW North Korea; pop. (1987e) 195,000.

Haemus. See BALKAN MOUNTAINS.

Ha–erh–pin. See HARBIN.

Haf·nar·fjör·dhur \ˈhäp-när-ˌfyœr-t͟hu̇r\. Town, SW Iceland, ab. 10 mi. (16 km.) S of Reykjavík; pop. (1992e) 16,107; fishing port.

Hafren. See SEVERN 4.

Ha·fun, Ras \ˌrȧs-hä-ˈfün\; *angl.* **Cape Ha·fun** \ha-ˈfün\ *or* **Raas Xaa·fuun** \ˈräs-kä-ˈfün\. Cape on coast of NE Somalia; the E extremity of Africa, 10°27′N and 51°26′E.

Hafun Bay North. Inlet of Indian Ocean on NE coast of Somalia, N of Ras Hafun; S of cape is **Hafun Bay South.**

Ha·gen \ˈhä-gən\. City, North Rhine-Westphalia, Germany, 30 mi. (48 km.) ENE of Düsseldorf; pop. (1992e) 214,085; iron and steel, machinery, chemicals, paper; received munic. rights 1746.

Ha·ger·man Fossil Beds National Monument \ˈhā-gər-mən\. See UNITED STATES, *National Monuments.*

Ha·gers·town \ˈhā-gərz-ˌtau̇n\. City, ⊗ of Washington co., N Maryland, 68 mi. (109 km.) WNW of Baltimore; pop. (1990c) 35,445; manufactures organs, furniture, aircraft; Hagerstown Junior Coll. (1946).

Ha·gia Tri·a·da *or* **Agía Tri·á·da** \ä-ˈyē-ä-trē-ˈä-thä\. Ruins of ancient town, near Tympákion and shore of Bay of Messara, S Crete, Greece; important archaeological site.

Hagion *or* **Hagios.** See SAINT.

Hagion Oros. See ATHOS, MOUNT.

Ha·gi·os Eli·as, Mount \ˈä-yē-ös-ē-ˈlē-äs\ *or* **Mount Áyi·os-ilí·as** \ˌä-yē-ös-ē-ˈlē-äs\ *also* **Mount Saint Eli·as** \i-ˈlī-əs\. Name of several mountains in Greece; incl.: (1) a peak 7904 ft. (2409 m.) in the Taíyetos Mts., W Laconia, S Peloponnese; (2) a peak 5663 ft. (1726 m.) in Othrys Mts., S Thessaly.

Ha·gi·os Ev·strá·ti·os *also* **Áyi·os Ev·strá·ti·os** \ˈä-yē-ös-ef-ˈsträ-tē-ös\. Island, part of Lesbos dept., Greece, in N cen. Aegean Sea, ab. 25 mi. (40 km.) S of Lemnos; chief town Hagios Evstrátios, near NW tip of island.

Hagios Nikólaos. See ÁYIOS NIKÓLAOS.

Ha·go·noy \ˌhä-gō-ˈnȯi, ˌä-\. Municipality, SW Bulacan prov., Luzon, Philippines, in Pampanga Delta 7 mi. (11 km.) W of Malolos; pop. (1980c) 73,176.

Hague, Cap de la \ˌkȧp-də-lȧ-ˈȧg\. Headland on coast of Manche dept., NW France, W of Cherbourg, projecting into the English Channel.

Hague, The \thə-ˈhāg\ *or Du.* **'s Gra·ven·ha·ge** \ˌskräv-ᵊn-ˈhä-kə\. City, de facto seat of the Dutch government and ✻ of South Holland prov., SW Netherlands, 33 mi. (53 km.) SW of Amsterdam and 4 mi. (6 km.) inland from North Sea; pop. (1992e) 445,287; food processing, printing; site of headquarters of many international companies; meeting place of the International Peace Conference 1899 and the Second International Peace Conference 1907; site of the international courts of arbitration and justice, housed in the Peace Palace (gift of American philanthropist Andrew Carnegie); Royal Palace, 15th–16th cent. cathedral, The Haags Commune Museum, Mauritshuis Royal Art Gallery. Orig. a hunting seat of the counts of Holland; in WWII occupied by Germans and suffered much damage.

Ha·gue·nau \ȧg-ˈnō\. Commune, Bas-Rhin dept., NE France, 11 mi. (18 km.) N of Strasbourg; pop. (1990c) 30,384; textiles, glass; breweries; 12th and 13th cent. churches; built around hunting lodge of dukes of Swabia 12th cent.; became imperial city 1257; annexed to France 1648; fortresses razed by Louis XIV.

Ha·ha·ji·ma \ˌhä-hä-ˈjē-mä\. Island group of the Bonin Is., Japan.

Ha·ha–Ji·ma. Largest island of the Hahajima island group, Japan.

Hahn·ville \ˈhän-ˌvil\. Village, ⊗ of St. Charles parish, SE Louisiana; pop. (1990c) 2599.

Hai \ˈhī\. The lower course of the Bai (*q.v.*), China.

Haidarabad. See HYDERABAD.

Hai·ding·er \ˈhī-diŋ-ər\. Mountain, Southern Alps, South I., New Zealand; N of Mt. Cook; 10,059 ft. (3066 m.).

Haï·dra \ˈhī-drə\; *anc.* **Am·moe·da·ra** \a-ˈmē-də-rə\. Town, W Tunisia, on Algerian boundary; phosphates.

Hai·fa \ˈhī-fə\ *also* **Kaif·fa** *or* **Khai·fa** \ˈkī-fə\. **1.** District of NW Israel. See table at ISRAEL.

2. *anc.* **Syc·a·mi·num** \ˌsi-kə-ˈmī-nəm\. Seaport, its ✻, at S end of Bay of Haifa at foot of Mt. Carmel; pop. (1992e) 251,000; Israel's chief port; steel mill, chemical plants, oil refinery; textiles, glass, cement; technical institute (1924), university (1963).

Haifong. See HAIPHONG.

Hai·kou *or W.-G.* **Hai–k'ou** \ˈhī-ˈkō\ *or* **Hoi·how** \ˈhȯi-ˈkō\ *or Fr.* **Hoï–Hao** \ȯi-ˈau̇\. Port, ✻ of Hainan I., on its NE coast, SE China; pop. (1990c) 280,153; made an open port 1876.

Ḥā'il \ˈhī(ə)l\ *or* **Hail** \ˈhīl\. Town and oasis, N Nejd, Saudi Arabia, 250 mi. (402 km.) NE of Medina; a traditional stopping place for pilgrims traveling the road bet. Baghdad and Mecca.

Hai·lar \ˈhī-ˈlär\ *or W.-G.* **Hai–la–erh** \-ˈlä-ˈe(ə)r\. **1.** River, Heilongjiang prov., China; ab. 240 mi. (386 km.) long; upper course of the Argun (*q.v.*).

2. *formerly* **Hu·lun** \ˈhü-ˈlün\. Town, Heilongjiang prov., China, on Hailar River; ✻ of former North Hsingan prov., Manchukuo.

Hai·ley \ˈhā-lē\. City, ⊗ of Blaine co., S cen. Idaho; pop. (1990c) 3687.

Hai·ley·bury \ˈhā-lē-ˌber-ē\. Residential town, ⊗ of Timiskaming dist., SE Ontario, Canada, on W shore of Lake Timiskaming 80 mi. (129 km.) N of North Bay; pop. (1991c) 4962; founded c. 1883.

Hai·lun *or W.-G.* **Hai–lun** \ˈhī-ˈlün\. Town, SE cen. Heilongjiang prov., NE China, ab. 110 mi. (177 km.) N of Harbin.

Hai·nan *or W.-G.* **Hai–nan** \ˈhī-ˈnän\. Island constituting a province of China, in South China Sea off S coast of Guangdong prov., SE China, and E of Gulf of Tonkin; a part of Guangdong prov. until 1988; ✻ Haikou; separated from Leizhou Penin. by **Hainan Strait** (15 mi. or 24 km. wide). Mountainous (cen. range, 2500 to 5100 ft. or 762 to 1555 m.), much of area thickly forested; products include rubber, coffee, pepper. Under Chinese rule since late 2d cent. B.C.; not closely controlled until T'ang dynasty (617–907 A.D.); Qiongshan (*q.v.*) opened to foreign trade 1858, Haikou (*q.v.*) soon followed; occupied by Japanese 1939–45; came under Chinese Communist control 1950; became province of China 1988. See table at CHINA.

Hainau. See CHOJNÓW.

Hai·naut \ā-ˈnō\ *or Flem.* **He·ne·gou·wen** \ˈhā-nə-ˌkau̇-ə\. **1.** Medieval county in the Low Countries, now included in Belgium (Hainaut prov.) and N France (Nord dept.); estab. by late 9th cent. A.D.; united with county of Flanders several times 11th–13th cents. and with Holland late 13th cent.; in 14th cent. came to be held by Wittelsbach house of Bavaria; taken by Philip III, duke of Burgundy 1433; became in turn part of Spanish and Austrian Netherlands; gradually annexed to France 17th–18th cents.; part remained with France (now the Nord dept.), remainder passed to the Kingdom of the Netherlands 1814 and to Belgium 1831.

2. Province, SW Belgium; ✻ Mons; wheat, sugar beets; livestock raising, coal mining; steel, textiles, chemicals, glass, machine tools. See table at BELGIUM.

Hain·burg \ˈhīn-ˌbu̇rk\ *or in full* **Hainburg an der Do·nau** \än-dər-ˈdō-nau̇\. Town, Lower Austria, Austria; on the Danube near its confluence with the Morava W of Bratislava; has many Roman remains; captured by Turks 1529, 1683.

Haine \ˈan, ˈen\. River, S Hainaut prov., Belgium; flows W into Schelde River in France; 40 mi. (64 km.) long.

Haines \ˈhānz\. **1.** Division in Alaska. See table at ALASKA.
2. City, SE Alaska, on W side of Lynn Canal ab. 20 mi. (32 km.) S of Skagway; pop. (1990c) 1238; site of Presbyterian mission 1881; former U.S. Army base.

Haines City. City, Polk co., cen. Florida Penin., 20 mi. (32 km.) E of Lakeland; pop. (1990c) 11,683.

Hai·phong *also* **Hai Phong** *or* **Hai·fong** \ˈhī-ˈfȯŋ\. Seaport, N Vietnam, in the delta of the Red River ab. 20 mi. (32 km.) from the Gulf of Tonkin and ab. 60 mi. (97 km.) E of Hanoi; pop. (1989c) 449,747; harbor suffers from silting in its channels; rice; plastics, textiles, phosphates; naval station; connected by railway with Kunming in Yunnan, China. Estab. 1874; heavily bombed and harbor mined by U.S. during Vietnam War late 1960s into 1970s.

Hai·ti \ˈhā-tē\ **1.** *or Fr.* **Ha·ï·ti** \ˌȧ-ē-ˈtē\. Republic occupying W third of Hispaniola I., West Indies; 10,714 sq. mi. (27,749

\ə\ **abut** \ᵊ\ matches \ᵊ\ kitten, Fr table \ər\ **further** \a\ **ash** \ā\ **ace** \ä\ **cot, cart** \ȧ\ Fr bac \au̇\ **out** \b\ Span Avila \ch\ **chin** \e\ **bet** \ē\ **easy** \g\ **go** \i\ **hit** \ī\ **ice** \j\ **job** \k\ Ger **ich, Buch** \ⁿ\ Fr vin \ŋ\ **sing** \ō\ **go** \ȯ\ **all** \ȯ\ **law** \œ\ Fr **bœuf** \œ̄\ Fr **feu** \ȯi\ **boy** \th\ **thin** \th\ **this** \ü\ **loot** \u̇\ **foot** \ue\ Ger **füllen** \ue̅\ Fr **rue** \y\ **yet** \ʸ\ Fr digne \ˈdēnʸ\, nuit \ˈnwʸē\ \yü\ **few** \yu̇\ **fury** \zh\ **vision**

sq. km.); pop. (1993e) 6,902,000; ✱ and largest city Port-au-Prince. Official language French.

Physical features: NW separated from E tip of Cuba by Windward Passage; coastline irregular with large indentation (Golfe de la Gonâve) on W coast enclosed by two peninsulas (the one on the S being the long, mountainous Tiburon Penin.) and containing Île de la Gonâve I; off N coast is Tortuga I. Highest point in SE, in La Selle Mts., 8793 ft. (2680 m.); only large river the Artibonite.

Chief products: Coffee, cocoa, sisal, sugarcane; clothing, flour, cement.

History: For earlier history, see HISPANIOLA. Independent republic of Haiti, encompassing entire island of Hispaniola, estab. 1804 following slave revolt; E part of island restored to Spanish control 1809, island reunited under Haitian President Jean-Pierre Boyer 1822–43; E part of island revolted 1843 and formed Dominican Republic 1844; occupied by U.S. forces 1915–34; military coup 1950; François Duvalier elected president 1957 and became president for life 1963; Jean-Claude Duvalier succeeded his father as president for life 1971 but was forced into exile 1986; Jean-Bertrand Aristide, a Roman Catholic priest, elected president 1990 and deposed by military coup 1991; thousands of Haitians sought asylum in U.S.; international trade embargoes and other sanctions imposed; Aristide returned from exile 1994 and resumed presidency.

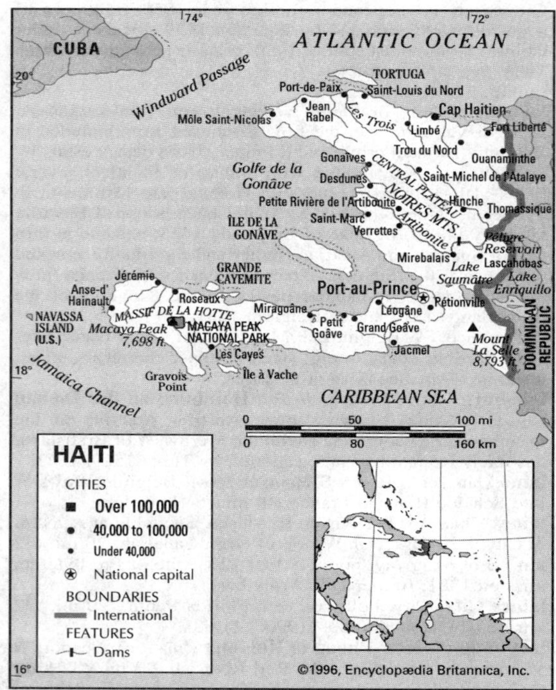

2. Original name for Hispaniola island. See HISPANIOLA.

Haitien, Cap *or* **Haïtien, Cap–.** See CAP HAITIEN.

Hai·yang *or W.-G.* **Hai–yang** \ˈhī-ˈyäŋ\. Island in Korea Bay, China, SE of Liaodong Penin. and 90 mi. (145 km.) ENE of Dalian.

Ḥajārah, al. See ḤIJĀRAH, AL.

Haj·dú–Bi·har \ˈhȯi-dü-ˌbē-hör\. County of E Hungary. See table at HUNGARY.

Haj·dú·bö·ször·mény \ˈhȯi-dü-ˌbœ-sœr-ˌmān\. City, E Hungary, 10 mi. (16 km.) NW of Debrecen; pop. (1991e) 37,200.

Haj·du·szo·bosz·ló \ˈhȯi-dü-ˌsō-bō-ˌslō\. City, E Hungary, 13 mi. (21 km.) SW of Debrecen; pop. (1991e) 24,800; health resort.

Ha·ji·pur \ˈhä-jē-ˌpu̇r\. Town, Bihar state, NE India, NE of Patna; pop. (1991p) 87,669.

Haj·now·ka \kī-ˈnüf-kä\. Commune, Białystok prov., NE Poland; pop. (1989e) 23,545.

Ha·ka *also* **Ha·kha** \ˈhä-kə\. Town, ✱ of Chin state; W Myanmar; pop. (1983c) 12,670.

Hakapehi. See TAIOHAE.

Ha·ka·ta Bay \hä-ˈkä-tä\. Inlet of Sea of Japan, NW coast of Kyūshū, Japan; forms outer harbor of Fukuoka.

Hakha. See HAKA.

Hak·kâ·ri; *formerly* **Ha·kâ·ri** \hä-ˈkä-rē\. **1.** Province of Turkey in Asia; ✱ Cölemerik. See table at TURKEY.
2. Town, SE Turkey in Asia. See CÖLEMERİK.

Ha·ko·da·te \ˌhä-kō-ˈdä-tā\. Seaport city, SW Hokkaidō, Japan, on Tsugaru Strait; pop. (1990p) 307,251; for many years chief city of the island and once ✱ of Hokkaidō prefecture; built on rocky peninsula; excellent harbor; site of Goryokaku Park orig. built as fort 19th cent.; N terminus of Seikan Tunnel; opened to foreign trade mid-19th cent.

Ha·ko·ne \hä-ˈkō-nā\. Village and mountain resort in SE Honshū, Japan, in Kanagawa prefecture 23 mi. (37 km.) ESE of Fuji and ab. 35 mi. (56 km.) SW of Yokohama; on **Lake Hakone;** numerous hot springs; good views of Fuji.

Ha·ku·pu \hä-ˈkü-pü\. Village, SE Niue I.; pop. (1989c) 240.

Ha·ku·san \ˌhä-kü-ˈsän\. Mountain, Ishikawa prefecture, W Honshū, Japan, on Gifu border, in **Hakusan National Park** (183 sq. mi. or 474 sq. km.); 8862 ft. (2701 m.); an extinct volcano; comprises five peaks.

Hal. See HALLE 1.

Ha·la \ˈhə-lə\. Town, Sind prov., Pakistan, 30 mi. (48 km.) N of Hyderabad; pop. (1981p) 57,000.

Halab. See ALEPPO.

Halas. See KISKUNHALAS.

Ha·la·wa \hä-ˈlä-vä, -wä\. Cape at NE end of Molokai I., Hawaii.

Halawa Bay. Bay on NE coast of Molokai I., Hawaii, W of Halawa.

Hal·ber·stadt \ˈhäl-bər-ˌshtät\. City, Saxony-Anhalt, cen. Germany, 33 mi. (53 km.) SE of Brunswick; pop. (1981c) 47,713; machinery; metalworking, food processing; made bishopric c. 814; center for manufacture of bombers in WWII.

Hal·con, Mount \häl-ˈkȯn\. Highest peak in Mindoro I., Philippines, in N part ab. 15 mi. (24 km.) SW of Calapan; 8469 ft. (2581 m.).

Hal·cott, Mount \ˈhȯl-kət\. Peak in Catskill Mts., Greene co., SE New York; 3537 ft. (1078 m.).

Hal·den \ˈhäl-dən\; *formerly* **Fred·riks·hald** \ˈfre-driks-ˌhäl\. Seaport, Østfold co., SE Norway, on the Skagerrak near Swedish border; pop. (1990c) 25,816; wood products; quarrying; textile mills.

Hal·di·mand \ˈhȯl-də-mənd\. Town, S Ontario, Canada, S of Hamilton; pop. (1991c) 20,573.

Haldimand–Nor·folk \-ˈnȯr-fək\. Municipal region, Ontario, Canada. See table at ONTARIO.

Hale \ˈhāl\. **1.** Name of counties in two states of the U.S. See tables at ALABAMA and TEXAS.
2. Village, Cheshire, NW England, 10 mi. (16 km.) S of Manchester; pop. (1981p) 16,247.

Ha·le·a·ka·la Crater \ˌhä-lā-ä-kä-ˈlä\. Crater in E Maui I., Hawaii; area ab. 19 sq. mi. (49 sq. km.), depth more than 2500 ft. (762 m.); chiefly a result of stream erosion. Area formerly part of Hawaii National Park; designated **Haleakala National Park** 1960; astrophysical research facilities. See UNITED STATES, *National Parks.*

Haleb. See ALEPPO.

Hale·don \ˈhāl-dən\. Borough, Passaic co., N New Jersey, just N of Paterson; pop. (1990c) 6951.

Ha·le·i·wa \ˌhä-lā-ˈē-vä\. Unincorporated settlement, Honolulu co., Hawaii, on Waialua Bay on N coast of Oahu; pop. (1990c) 2442; home to many artists.

Ha·le·pa \hä-ˈle-pə\ *or Gk.* **Kha·lé·pa** \kä-ˈle-pä\. E suburb of Canea, on island of Crete, Greece; Pact of Halepa granting broader rights to Greeks living on Crete signed here Oct. 1878.

Hales Corners \ˈhālz\. Village, Milwaukee co., SE Wisconsin, SW of the city of Milwaukee; pop. (1990c) 7623.

Hales·ow·en \ˈhāl-ˌzō-ən\. Town, West Midlands, W cen. England, on the Stour River 8 mi. (13 km.) SW of Birmingham; pop. (1981p) 57,453; iron foundries; machinery.

Ha·ley·ville \ˈhā-lē-ˌvil\. City, Winston co., NW Alabama, 46 mi. (74 km.) SW of Decatur; pop. (1990c) 4452; lumber.

Halfa. See WADI HALFA.

Hal·fa·ya Pass \hal-ˈfī-ə\ *or Arab.* **Nagb Al–Halfāyah** \ˌnäk-bal-\. Pass through the coast range of hills just S of Salūm, extreme NW Egypt; scene of heavy WWII fighting 1941.

Half Dome. Peak in the Sierra Nevada, in E Mariposa co., cen. California; 8842 ft. (2695 m.).

Half Moon Bay. City, San Mateo co., W California, on Half Moon Bay (inlet); pop. (1990c) 8886.

Haliacmon. See ALIÁKMON.

Hal·i·ar·tus \ˌha-lē-ˈär-təs\. Ancient town, Boeotia, Greece, 15 mi. (24 km.) NW of Thebes; place where Spartan commander Lysander was killed 395 B.C.

Hal·i·bur·ton \ˈha-lə-ˌbərt-ᵊn\. County, in SE Ontario, Canada. See table at ONTARIO.

Haliç. See GOLDEN HORN 2.

Hal·i·car·nas·sus \ˌha-lə-kär-ˈna-səs\ *or mod.* **Bo·drum** \bō-ˈdrüm\. Ancient city in SW Caria, Asia Minor (now in Turkey in Asia), on S coast of a peninsula; original site of Mausoleum of Halicarnassus, tomb of Persian Satrap Mausolus, erected c. 350 B.C. and ranked as one of the Seven Wonders of the Ancient World (its remains in the British Museum); birthplace of Greek historian Herodotus c. 484 B.C.

Ha·licz \ˈhä-lich\. Historic area of E cen. Europe. See GALICIA 1.

Hal·i·don Hill \ˈha-ləd-ᵊn\. Hill near Berwick-upon-Tweed, N England; battle July 19, 1333 in which Edward III, assisting Edward de Baliol, claimant to the throne of Scots King David II, defeated the Scots.

Hal·i·fax \ˈha-lə-ˌfaks\. **1.** Name of counties in two states of the U.S. See tables at NORTH CAROLINA and VIRGINIA.
2. Town, Plymouth co., Massachusetts, 10 mi. (16 km.) WNW of the town of Plymouth; pop. (1990c) 6526.
3. Town, ⊗ of Halifax co., NE North Carolina, 29 mi. (47 km.) NNE of Rocky Mount; pop. (1990c) 327; settled c. 1723; scene of North Carolina's first constitutional convention.
4. Town, ⊗ of Halifax co., S Virginia; pop. (1990c) 688.
5. County, in S Nova Scotia, Canada. See table at NOVA SCOTIA.
6. Commercial city, ✻ of Nova Scotia, Canada, and ⊗ of Halifax co.,on Atlantic Ocean in cen. part of S coast of province; pop. (1991c) 114,455, met. area pop. (1991c) 320,501; natural harbor; dry docks, dockyards; in winter Canada's most active port; used by fishing fleets; iron foundries; clothing, furniture; food processing; oil refining; railroad terminus; 19th cent. citadel; Dalhousie Univ. (1818), St. Mary's Univ. (1841), Technical Univ. of Nova Scotia (1907), Mount St. Vincent Univ. (1914).
History: Founded 1749 as British stronghold to rival French Louisbourg and made ✻ of Nova Scotia in place of Annapolis Royal; incorp. as city 1841; garrisoned by British troops until its defense was taken over by dominion forces 1906; greatly damaged by an explosion caused by a harbor collision 1917; important naval base esp. in WWI and WWII.
7. Town, West Yorkshire, N England, on the Hebble 22 mi. (35 km.) NE of Manchester; pop. (1981p) 87,488; has manufactures of cotton, wool, and worsted goods, iron and steel.

Halifax Bay. Inlet of Pacific Ocean on E coast of Queensland, Australia, 18°50′S, 146°30′E; Townsville is on it.

Halifax Citadel National Historic Park. Reservation, Halifax, Nova Scotia, Canada.

Ha·li·sa·har \ˈhä-lə-sə-ˌhər\. Town, West Bengal, NE India, just N of Calcutta; pop. (1991p) 113,670.

Hall \ˈhȯl\. **1.** Small island, cen. Bering Sea, Alaska, off NW tip of St. Matthew I.
2. Name of counties in three states of the U.S. See tables at GEORGIA, NEBRASKA, TEXAS.

Hall. See SCHWÄBISCH-HALL.

Hal·land \ˈhä-lənd\. Province of SW Sweden. See table at SWEDEN.

Hal·lan·dale \ˈha-lən-ˌdāl\. City, Broward co., SE Florida, on Atlantic Ocean 15 mi. (24 km.) N of Miami; pop. (1990c) 30,996; horseracing track; incorp. 1927.

Hal·la·ni·ya \ˌhȧ-lə-ˈnē-ə\. Island, Oman, largest of the Khurīyā Murīyā Jazā'ir (*q.v.*).

Hal·la San \ˈhä-ˌlä-ˈsän\ *or Jp.* **Kan·ra** \ˈkän-ˌrä\. Extinct volcano on Cheju I., in East China Sea off S coast of South Korea; 6398 ft. (1950 m.).

Hall Basin. Expansion of passage bet. Ellesmere I. and NW Greenland; connects Kennedy Channel with Robeson Channel.

Hal·le \ˈhä-lə\. **1.** *or Fr.* **Hal** \ˈȧl\. Commune, Brabant prov., Belgium; pop. (1991c) 32,768; paper.
2. District of former East Germany.
3. *or in full* **Halle an der Saa·le** \ˌän-dər-ˈzä-lə\. City, E cen. Germany, on the Saale 31 mi. (50 km.) WNW of Leipzig; pop. (1981c) 232,396; formerly ✻ of Halle dist.; coal mining, food processing; important railroad junction; medieval town hall; 15th cent. tower; former archiepiscopal residence; university (formed 1817 through merger of two older universities). Site of prehistoric settlements; first mentioned early 9th cent.; member of Hanseatic League 1281–1478; accepted Reformation 1522; annexed by Brandenburg 1648; birthplace of composer George Frideric Handel 1685.

Hal·le Neu·stadt \ˈhä-lə-ˈnȯi-ˌshtät\. City, Saxony-Anhalt, E cen. Germany, just NE of Halle from which it broke off 1964; pop. (1990e) 90,956.

Hal·letts·ville \ˈha-ləts-ˌvil\. City, ⊗ of Lavaca co., SE cen. Texas, 45 mi. (72 km.) N of Victoria; pop. (1990c) 2718.

Hal·li·gen \ˈhä-li-gən\. Island group off W coast of Schleswig-Holstein, N Germany; consists of the S islands of the North Frisian group; largest islands Nordstrand and Pellworm.

Hal·lock \ˈha-lək\. Village, ⊗ of Kittson co., NW corner of Minnesota, 55 mi. (89 km.) NW of Thief River Falls; pop. (1990c) 1304.

Hal·lo·well \ˈhä-lə-ˌwel, -wəl\. City, Kennebec co., SW Maine, on Kennebec River 3 mi. (5 km.) S of Augusta; pop. (1990c) 2534.

Hall Peninsula. Peninsula, N of Frobisher Bay, SE Baffin I., E Nunavut, Canada.

Halls Creek \ˈhȯlz\. Town, NE Western Australia, Australia; the N terminus of Canning Stock Route; pop. (1991c) 1305.

Halls Stream. Tributary of the Connecticut River; running bet. Quebec, Canada, and New Hampshire, U.S.; 20 mi. (32 km.) long.

Hall·statt \ˈhäl-ˌshtät, ˈhȯl-ˌstat\. Village, Austria, on shore of **Hall·stät·ter Lake** \ˈhäl-ˌshte-tər, ˈhal-ˌste-\ (ab. 3 sq. mi. or 8 sq. km., max. depth 410 ft. or 125 m.); Bronze and Iron Age archaeological site for which the Hallstatt culture of cen. and W Europe is named, known from discovery and excavation 1846–99 of more than 2000 graves which yielded artifacts dating back to as early as c. 1100 B.C.

Hal·luin \ȧl-ˈweⁿ\. Commune, Nord dept., N France, on Belgian border 13 mi. (21 km.) N of Lille.

Hall·wil, Lake \ˈhäl-ˌvil, -vəl\ *or Ger.* **Hall·wi·ler See** \ˈhäl-ˌvē-lər-ˈzā\. Lake, Aargau canton, N cen. Switzerland; ab. 4 sq. mi. (10 sq. km.), max. depth 154 ft. (47 m.); formed by expansion of the Aa River.

Hal·ma·he·ra \ˌhal-mə-ˈhər-ə, ˌhäl-\; *Du.* **Djai·lo·lo** \jī-ˈlō-lō\ *also* **Gi·lo·lo** \ji-ˈlō-lō\. Largest island of the Moluccas, in Indonesia, lying on the Equator; 6928 sq. mi. (17,944 sq. km.); no sizable towns; in NE is the port Galela. On E has four peninsulas enclosing three large bays; on W coast are the small islands of Ternate and Tidore (*qq.v.*); all peninsulas have mountains, 3000 to 5000 ft. (914 to 1524 m.), those in W being volcanic; some trade in coconuts. Known early to Spanish and Portuguese; under sultan of Ternate who yielded it to

Dutch 1683; in WWII taken by Japanese whose bases were frequently bombed by Allies 1944.

Halm·stad \ˈhälm-ˌstäd\. Seaport, ⊗ of Halland prov., SW Sweden, on the Kattegat; pop. (1993e) 81,084; paper, textiles; breweries; 14th cent. church.

Halq al–Wa·di \ˈhȧlk-ȧl-ˈwä-dē\ *or* **Halq el Oued** \el-ˈwed\ *or* **La Gou·lette** \ˌlä-gü-ˈlet\ *also* **Go·let·ta** \gō-ˈle-tə\. Seaport town, NE Tunisia; pop. (1989e) 67,685; the port of Tunis.

Häl·sing·borg *or* **Hel·sing·borg** \ˈhel-siŋ-ˌbȯrʸ, -ˌbȯr-ē\. Seaport, Malmöhus prov., SW Sweden, on Øresund opp. Helsingør, Denmark; pop. (1989c) 108,359; ships timber, paper, and chemicals; food processing; copper smelters; textiles. First mentioned 1085; ceded to Sweden 1710.

Häl·sing·land \ˈhel-siŋ-ˌländ\. Historic region, E cen. Sweden, largely in Gävleborg prov.

Hal·stead \ˈhȯl-ˌsted\. Town, Essex, SE England, on the Colne River 46 mi. (74 km.) NE of London; pop. (1981p) 9276.

Hal·tem·price \ˈhȯl-təm-ˌprīs\. Town, Humberside, NE England; pop. (1981p) 53,633.

Haltia, Mount \ˈhäl-tē-ä\ *or* **Hal·tia·tun·tu·ri** \-ˌtün-tü-rē\. Peak, NW Finland, on Norwegian border; 4343 ft. (1324 m.); highest point in Finland.

Hal·tom City \ˈhȯl-təm\. City, Tarrant co., N Texas, NE of Fort Worth; pop. (1990c) 32,856.

Hal·ton \ˈhȯlt-ᵊn\. Municipal region, Ontario, Canada. See table at ONTARIO.

Halton Hills. Town, S Ontario, Canada, SW of Brampton; pop. (1991c) 36,816.

Halys. See KIZIL IRMAK.

Ham \ˈȧm\. Village, Somme dept., N France, on the Somme 35 mi. (56 km.) SE of Amiens; ruins of medieval castle where Emperor Napoléon III was imprisoned 1840–46; suffered greatly during WWI.

Hama. See HAMĀH.

Hamad, Al–. See SYRIAN DESERT.

Ha·ma·dān \ˌha-mə-ˈdan, ˌhä-mä-ˈdän\. **1.** Province (formerly a governorship) of W Iran. See table at IRAN.

2. *anc.* **Ec·bat·a·na** \ek-ˈbat-ᵊn-ə\ *or* **Ag·bat·a·na** \ag-\. City, its ✻, in plain at foot of Mt. Alwand ab. 180 mi. (290 km.) WSW of Tehran; pop. (1986c) 272,499; important commercial city noted esp. for its leather goods and rugs; mentioned in the Bible (*Ezra* vi. 2); held to be site of tomb of Jewish heroine Esther and her relative Mordecai; residence and burial place of Arab philosopher Avicenna.

History: Ancient Ecbatana ✻ of Media and summer residence of Achaemenian kings; taken by Cyrus II, king of Persia, from Astyages, last king of Media, 550 B.C.; captured by Macedonian King Alexander the Great 330 B.C., by Arabs 7th cent.; taken by Seljuq Turks 12th cent.; destroyed 1220 by Mongols; sacked by Turkic ruler Timur 1386; passed bet. Iranian rulers and Ottomans; damaged in war with Iraq 1980s.

Ha·māh *or* **Hama** \ˈhȧ-mə\; *bib.* **Ha·math** \ˈhā-ˌmath\; *classical* **Ep·i·pha·nia** \ˌe-pə-fə-ˈnī-ə\. Commercial city, W Syria, 75 mi. (121 km.) SSW of Aleppo; pop. (1989e) 229,000; on railroad line; in rich agricultural region; noted for its waterwheels dating from Middle Ages; frequently mentioned in the Bible as on the N boundary of Israel. Site of prehistoric settlement; under Aramaeans 11th cent. B.C.; taken by Assyrians 9th cent. B.C.; later passed to Persians and Macedonians; taken by Seleucids and renamed Epiphania 2d cent. B.C.; came under Roman and Byzantine control; captured by Arabs 7th cent. A.D.; held by Crusaders 1108–15; occupied by Muslim hero Saladin 1188; passed to Egyptian Mamlūk dynasty c. 1300; home of Arab historian Abū al-Fidā, who was its prince 1310–31; to Ottomans 16th cent.; became part of modern Syria 1941; badly damaged in suppression of Muslim revolt 1982.

Ha·ma·ki·ta \ˌhä-mä-ˈkē-tä\. City, Shizuoka prefecture, Honshū, Japan, 12 mi. (19 km.) NE of Hamamatsu; pop. (1990p) 81,159.

Ha·ma·ma·tsu \ˌhä-mä-ˈmät-sü\. Industrial city, Shizuoka prefecture, S Honshū, Japan, near coast 56 mi. (90 km.) SE of Nagoya; pop. (1990p) 534,624; motorcycles; musical instruments.

Ha·mar \ˈhä-ˌmär\. City, ⊗ of Hedmark co., E Norway, on W shore of Lake Mjøsa N of Oslo; pop. (1990c) 16,129; in agricultural area; seat of bishopric. Original town founded 1152 by Nicholas Breakspear who later became Pope Adrian IV; destroyed by Swedes 1567; rebuilt and chartered mid-19th cent.

Hamath. See HAMĀH.

Ham·bach \ˈhäm-ˌbäk\. Commune, Rhineland-Palatinate, Germany, 15 mi. (24 km.) W of Speyer; to SW lie ruins of Hambach Castle, scene of the Hambacher Fest May 1832, a gathering of ab. 25,000 persons demanding a republic and national unity of Germany.

Ham·blen \ˈham-blən\. County in NE Tennessee. See table at TENNESSEE.

Ham·born \häm-ˈbȯrn\. Formerly separate community, Prussia, Germany; became part of Duisburg-Hamborn 1929. See DUISBURG.

Ham·burg \ˈham-ˌbərg\. **1.** City, ⊗ of Ashley co., SE Arkansas; pop. (1990c) 3098.

2. Village, Erie co., W New York, 10 mi. (16 km.) S of Buffalo; pop. (1990c) 10,442; Hilbert Coll. (1928).

3. Borough, Berks co., SE Pennsylvania, on Schuylkill River 15 mi. (24 km.) N of Reading; pop. (1990c) 3987; founded 1779.

4. \ *also* ˈhäm-ˌbu̇rk\. Maritime commercial city, constituting a state of Germany (see table at GERMANY), on Elbe River ab. 68 mi. (109 km.) from its mouth at Cuxhaven; pop. (1992e) 1,668,800; one of Europe's major ports; shipbuilding, oil refining, chemicals, machinery, electronic equipment; exports include industrial equipment, chemicals, food products; has extensive harbor and dock installations and outport at Cuxhaven; noteworthy buildings include the stock exchange, 19th cent. Rathaus in Neo-Renaissance style, 19th cent. Gothic-style church, and an 18th cent. baroque-style church; university (1919); numerous museums; birthplace of composers Felix Mendelssohn (1809) and Johannes Brahms (1833).

History: City grew around castle of Hammaburg, built c. 825; made episcopal see 831, archiepiscopal see 834; served as missionary center for N Europe; treaties with Lübeck 1241 and 1249 led to formation of Hanseatic League; became independent 1292; declared imperial city 1510; accepted Reformation 1529; joined Schmalkaldic League 1536; incorp. into French First Empire 1810–14; became member of German Federation as free city 1815; devastated by fire 1842; by decree of Jan. 26, 1937 reorganized incorporating the cities of Altona, Harburg, and Wandsbek; severely damaged by Allied bombings in WWII; taken by British forces May 1945.

Ham·den \ˈham-dən\. Suburban residential town, cen. New Haven co., S Connecticut; pop. (1990c) 52,434; Quinnipiac Coll. (1929), Paier Coll. of Art (1946), South Central Community Coll. (1967).

Hä·me \ˈha-mə\ *or Swed.* **Ta·vas·te·hus** \tä-ˈväs-tə-ˌhüs\. Province of S Finland. See table at FINLAND.

Hä·meen·lin·na \ˈha-ˌmān-ˌli-nə\ *or Swed.* **Ta·vas·te·hus** \tä-ˈväs-tə-ˌhüs\. City, ✻ of Häme prov., SW Finland; pop. (1989c) 43,098; textiles; birthplace of composer Jean Sibelius 1865. Orig. developed N of a castle built mid-13th cent.; chartered 1639; moved to present location c. 1779.

Ha·meln \ˈhä-məln\; *formerly* **Ham·e·lin** \ˈha-mə-lən\. City, Lower Saxony, Germany, on Weser River 25 mi. (40 km.) SW of Hannover; pop. (1992e) 58,906; machinery, chemicals, carpets; famous as scene of legend of Pied Piper of Hamelin.

Ham·ers·ley Range \ˈha-mərz-lē\. Mountain range, NW Western Australia, Australia; its highest peak (also highest peak in the state) is Mt. Bruce (*q.v.*); iron deposits; contains **Hamersley Range National Park** (2385 sq. mi. or 6177 sq. km.) featuring gorges and colorful exposed sandstone.

Ham·hŭng \ˈhäm-ˌhu̇ŋ\ *or Jp.* **Kan·ko** \ˈkän-ˌkō\. City, ✻ of South Hamgyŏng prov., North Korea; pop. (1987e) 701,000; textiles.

Ha·mi *or W.-G.* **Ha–mi** \ˈhä-ˈmē\; *formerly* **Qo·mul** \chō-ˈmül\. Town and oasis, E Xinjiang Uygur, W China; ancient frontier trading center; over the centuries under the rule of various Chinese dynasties, incl. Mongols and Uighurs.

Ha·mid \ˈhä-ˈmēt\. District of the Ottoman Empire, S Asia Minor, W of Karaman; roughly equivalent to modern İsparta prov. and W Konya, Turkey.

Ham·il·ton \ˈha-məl-tən\. **1.** Name of counties in ten states of the U.S. See tables at FLORIDA, ILLINOIS, INDIANA, IOWA, KANSAS, NEBRASKA, NEW YORK, OHIO, TENNESSEE, TEXAS.

2. City, ⊗ of Marion co., NW Alabama; pop. (1990c) 5787.

3. City, ⊗ of Harris co., W Georgia; pop. (1990c) 454.

4. City, Hancock co., W Illinois, on Mississippi River 33 mi. (53 km.) N of Quincy; pop. (1990c) 3281.

5. Town, Essex co., NE corner of Massachusetts, 21 mi. (34 km.) NE of Boston; pop. (1990c) 7280.

6. City, ⊗ of Ravalli co., W Montana, 45 mi. (72 km.) S of Missoula; pop. (1990c) 2737.

7. *or* **Hamilton Square.** Township, Mercer co., W cen. New Jersey, E of Trenton; pop. (1990c) 86,553.

8. Village, Madison co., cen. New York, 26 mi. (42 km.) SW of Utica; pop. (1990c) 3790; incorp. 1816; Colgate Univ. (1819).

9. *also* **Hamilton!.** City, ⊗ of Butler co., SW Ohio, 18 mi. (29 km.) N of Cincinnati; pop. (1990c) 61,368; chemicals, machinery, paper products; Miami Univ.–Hamilton campus (1968); on site of Fort Hamilton, built by Gen. Arthur St. Clair 1791, used as garrison post in Gen. Anthony Wayne's campaign of 1793–94; settled c. 1803, and became ⊗; incorp. 1810.

10. City, ⊗ of Hamilton co., cen. Texas, 47 mi. (76 km.) E of Brownwood; pop. (1990c) 2937.

11. Seaport town, ✻ of Bermuda, on Bermuda I.; pop. (1991c) 1100; tourism; founded 1790; made ✻ 1815; made free port 1956.

12. River, Canada. See CHURCHILL 4.

13. City, ⊗ of Hamilton-Wentworth munic. region, SE Ontario, Canada, at W end of Lake Ontario ab. 40 mi. (64 km.) SW of Toronto; pop. (1991c) 318,499; important transportation center: harbor, railroad terminus, airport; manufactures steel, iron, electrical equipment, textiles; McMaster Univ. (1887) in nearby Westdale; Royal Botanical Gardens (estab. 1941); town laid out c. 1815.

14. City, cen. North I., New Zealand; on Waikato River 70 mi. (113 km.) SSE of Auckland; pop. (1993e) 103,600; livestock; lumbering; dairy farms; Univ. of Waikato (1964).

15. Burgh, Strathclyde region, S cen. Scotland; pop. (1993e) 107,500; museums; mid-18th cent. church; nearby Strathclyde Country Park.

Hamilton, Lake. **1.** Lake in S Garland and NW Hot Spring cos., SW cen. Arkansas, formed by **Car·pen·ter Dam** \ˈkär-pən-tər\ across Ouachita River.

2. Lake in cen. Texas. See BUCHANAN DAM.

Hamilton, Mount. **1.** Peak, Santa Clara co., W California, 13 mi. (21 km.) E of San Jose; site of Lick Observatory.

2. Peak, White Pine co., E Nevada; ab. 10,740 ft. (3275 m.).

Hamilton Dam. See BUCHANAN DAM.

Hamilton Inlet. Inlet of Atlantic Ocean, SE Labrador, Newfoundland, Canada, estuary of Churchill River; with Lake Melville ab. 150 mi. (241 km.) long; one of the largest fjords on the Labrador coast, 14 to 25 mi. (23 to 40 km.) wide. Visited by early explorers (English navigator John Davis, 1586); site of French and English trading posts in 18th cent.; at its head Rigolet trading post was estab. 1837 by Hudson's Bay Company.

Hamilton Square. See HAMILTON 7.

Hamilton–Went·worth \-ˈwent-ˌwərth\. Municipal region, Ontario, Canada. See table at ONTARIO.

Ha·mi·na \ˈhä-mē-nä\ *or Swed.* **Fre·driks·hamn** \ˈfrā-driks-ˌhäm\. Town, Kymi prov., SE Finland, on Gulf of Finland; scene of signing of peace treaty 1809 by which Sweden ceded Finland to Russia.

Ha·mir·pur \hə-ˈmir-ˌpu̇r\. Town, SW Uttar Pradesh, N India, on the Yamuna 38 mi. (61 km.) SSW of Kanpur; pop. (1991p) 27,161; 11th cent. ruins.

Ham·let \ˈham-lət\. City, Richmond co., S North Carolina, 48 mi. (77 km.) WSW of Fayetteville; pop. (1990c) 6196.

Ham·lin \ˈham-lən\. **1.** County in E South Dakota. See table at SOUTH DAKOTA.

2. City, Fisher and Jones cos., NW cen. Texas, 40 mi. (64 km.) NNW of Abilene; pop. (1990c) 2791.

3. Town, ⊗ of Lincoln co., W West Virginia; pop. (1990c) 1030.

Hamm \ˈhäm\ *also* **Hamm in West·fa·len** \in-vest-ˈfä-lən\. City, North Rhine-Westphalia, Germany, on Lippe River 21 mi. (34 km.) SSE of Münster; pop. (1992e) 180,323; iron and wire mills; textiles. Founded 1227; member of Hanseatic League; heavily bombed in WWII with much damage.

Ḥammām, al– *or* **Ḥammâm, El.** See AL-ḤAMMĀM.

Ham·ma·met \ˌha-mə-ˈmet\ *also* **al–Ham·mā·māt** \al-ˌha-ma-ˈmat\. Coastal town, NE Tunisia, on **Gulf of Hammamet,** (inlet of the Mediterranean, at S base of peninsula ending in Cape Bon); pop. (1989e) 32,762.

Ham·mam Lif \ha-ˈmäm-ˈlēf\. Town, Tunisia, on Gulf of Tunis; pop. (1989e) 58,180.

Ḥam·mār, Hawr al \ˈhau̇r-ȧl-ˌhȧm-ˈmär\. Marshy lake, SE Iraq, S of the Euphrates before it joins the Tigris at Al Qurnah; ab. 70 mi. (113 km.) long; has connection with the Euphrates and with the Shatt al Arab above Basra.

Ham·me \ˈhä-mə\. Commune, East Flanders prov., NW cen. Belgium, 14 mi. (23 km.) SW of Antwerp; pop. (1991c) 22,799.

Ham·me·ren, Cape \ˈhȧ-mə-rən\. Cape on N tip of Bornholm I., Denmark; lighthouse.

Ham·mer·fest \ˈhä-mər-ˌfest\. City, Finnmark co., N Norway; located on Kvaløy I., 70°40′N, 23°42′E; pop. (1990e) 6934; northernmost city in Europe; manufactures cod-liver oil; has uninterrupted daylight May 17 to July 29; sun not visible Nov. 21 to Jan. 21; received charter 1789; destroyed by British bombardment 1809, by fire 1891, and by retreating Germans 1944.

Ham·mer·smith and Ful·ham \ˈha-mər-ˌsmith … ˈfu̇-ləm\. A borough of Greater London. See table at LONDON 4.

Hamm in Westfalen. See HAMM.

Ham·mo·nas·set \ˌha-mə-ˈna-sət\. River, S Connecticut; forms S part of boundary bet. New Haven and Middlesex cos. and empties into Long Island Sound just E of **Hammonasset Point**; ab. 18 mi. (29 km.) long.

Ham·mond \ˈha-mənd\. **1.** City, Lake co., NW corner of Indiana, on Illinois border adjacent to Calumet City; pop. (1990c) 84,236; incorp. as city 1884.

2. City, Tangipahoa parish, SE Louisiana, 45 mi. (72 km.) E of Baton Rouge; pop. (1990c) 15,871; Southeastern Louisiana Univ. (1925).

Ham·monds·port \ˈha-məndz-ˌpōrt\. Village, Steuben co., S New York, at S end of Keuka Lake; pop. (1990c) 929; vineyards; birthplace of aviator and inventor Glenn Hammond Curtiss 1878.

Ham·mon·ton \ˈha-mən-tən\. Town, Atlantic co., SE New Jersey, 27 mi. (43 km.) SE of Camden; pop. (1990c) 12,208.

Hamp·den \ˈham-dən\. **1.** County in W Massachusetts. See table at MASSACHUSETTS.

2. Town, Penobscot co., E cen. Maine, on Penobscot River 7 mi. (11 km.) S of Bangor; pop. (1990c) 5974.

Hampden–Syd·ney \-ˈsid-ne, ˈsid-nē\. Unincorporated settlement, Prince Edward co., S cen. Virginia; pop. (1990c) 1240; Hampden-Sydney Coll. (1776).

Ham·pi \ˈhəm-pē\. Town, Karnataka state, SW India, on S bank of the Tungabhadra, ab 30 mi. (48 km.) WNW of Bellary; ruins of Vijayanagar (*q.v.*).

Ham·pole \ˈham-ˌpōl\. Village, South Yorkshire, N England, 6 mi. (10 km.) NW of Doncaster; home of hermit, mystic, and writer Richard Rolle de Hampole (d. 1349).

Hamp·shire \ˈhamp-ˌshir, -shər\. Name of counties in two states of the U.S. See tables at MASSACHUSETTS and WEST VIRGINIA.

Hampshire; *abbr.* **Hants** \ˈhants\. **1.** Formerly a county in S England, comprising the later administrative counties of Hampshire (see HAMPSHIRE 2) and the Isle of Wight (*q.v.*).
2. Former administrative county, S England, mainland part of earlier county of Hampshire (see HAMPSHIRE 1).
3. Administrative county, S England, approx. equivalent to the former administrative county; estab. 1974. See table at ENGLAND.

Hamp·stead \ˈhamp-stəd, -ˌsted\. **1.** Town, Carroll co., N Maryland; pop. (1990c) 2608.
2. Town, Rockingham co., New Hampshire, NNE of Salem; pop. (1990c) 6732.
3. Residential town, Montreal I., S Quebec, Canada, W of the city of Montreal; pop. (1991c) 8645.
4. Former metropolitan borough of London, SE England, now part of the borough of Camden.

Hamp·ton \ˈhamp-tən\. **1.** County in SW South Carolina. See table at SOUTH CAROLINA.
2. City, ⊗ of Calhoun co., S Arkansas; pop. (1990c) 1562.
3. City, ⊗ of Franklin co., N cen. Iowa, 27 mi. (43 km.) S of Mason City; pop. (1990c) 4133.
4. Town, Rockingham co., SE New Hampshire, on Atlantic Ocean 10 mi. (16 km.) S of Portsmouth; pop. (1990c) 12,278; incorp. 1639; outpost of Massachusetts Bay Colony. **Hampton Beach** (resort on Atlantic) nearby.
5. Town, ⊗ of Hampton co., SW South Carolina; pop. (1990c) 2997.
6. Independent city, SE Virginia, on Hampton Roads 7 mi. (11 km.) NE of Newport News; 57 sq. mi. (148 sq. km.); pop. (1990c) 133,793; fisheries, packing plants (oysters, crabs). Hampton Univ. (1868), Langley Air Force Base, Old Point Comfort, and Fort Monroe in environs. Settled c. 1610 (oldest continuous community of English origin in America); burned by British in War of 1812 and by its own inhabitants to prevent occupation by Union troops 1861; incorp. as city 1908; consolidated with Elizabeth City co. 1952.
7. Unincorporated settlement, ⊗ of Kings co., S New Brunswick, Canada, 22 mi. (35 km.) NNE of St. John; pop. (1991c) 3590.
8. Locality, SE England, SW of London on the Thames, now part of the Greater London borough of Richmond upon Thames; nearby is Hampton Court Palace, one of largest of the royal residences, begun 1514 by Thomas Cardinal Wolsey and which passed to Henry VIII.

Hampton Bay. Inlet of Atlantic Ocean on S side of E Long Island, New York.

Hampton Roads. Channel through which the James, Elizabeth, and Nansemond rivers flow into Chesapeake Bay; 40 ft. (12 m.) deep, 4 mi. (6 km.) wide; site of Civil War naval battle bet. ironclad ships *Merrimac* and *Monitor* Mar. 9, 1862. The **Port of Hampton Roads,** comprising harbors of Newport News, Norfolk, and Portsmouth, is under local jurisdiction of State Port Authority of Virginia, created 1926.

Hamrā', Hammāda al–. See HAMMĀDA AL-HAMRĀ'.

Ham·run \ḣam-ˈrün\. Town, E cen. Malta I., Malta, just W of Valletta; pop. (1988c) 13,651.

Ham·tramck \ham-ˈtra-mik\. City, Wayne co., SE Michigan, entirely within city of Detroit; pop. (1990c) 18,372; automobile manufacturing.

Ha·mun–i–Lo·ra \hä-ˈmün-ē-lō-ˈrä\. Large lake (*hamun*) with no outlet, SW Asia, lying mostly in Pakistan, but extending into Afghanistan; receives the Pishin Lora.

Hamun–i–Mash·kel \-ṁash-ˈkel\; *anc.* **Ar·ia Pa·lus** \ˈar-ē-ə-ˈpā-ləs\. Lake (*hamun*), morass, and desert region, Chagai, NW Baluchistan, Pakistan, on Iranian border; receives Mashkel River from the SE.

Han \ˈhän\. **1.** River, Shaanxi and Hubei provs., E cen. China, flowing SE into the Chang River at Hankou; ab. 750 mi. (1205 km.) long; navigable for large vessels for ab. 370 mi. (595 km.).
2. Lower course of river system, E Guangdong prov., SE China; flows S past Chao'an to South China Sea at Shantou; ab. 100 mi. (161 km.) long.
3. *formerly* **Kan** \ˈkän\. River, South Korea, flowing WNW into Yellow Sea N of Inch'ōn; 292 mi. (470 km.) long.

Han·a·han \ˈha-nə-ˌhan, -hən\. City, Berkeley co., SE South Carolina, N of Charleston; pop. (1990c) 13,176.

Ha·na·lei Bay \ˌhä-nä-ˈlā-ē\. Bay on N coast of Kauai I., Hawaii.

Ha·na·ma·ni·oa, Cape \ˌhä-nä-ˌmä-nē-ˈō-ä\. Cape on S coast of Maui I., Hawaii, on Alalakeiki Channel opp. Kahoolawe I.

Ha·na·ma·u·lu \ˌhä-nä-ˈmä-ü-ˌlü\. Village, E coast of Kauai I., Hawaii, N of Nawiliwili Bay; pop. (1990c) 3611.

Ha·na·pe·pe \ˌhä-nä-ˈpā-pā\. Town, S coast of Kauai I., Hawaii; pop. (1990c) 1395; on **Hanapepe Bay** (W of Wahiawa Bay) adjoining Port Allen.

Ha·nau \ˈhä-ˌnau̇\. City, Hesse, Germany, on Main River 11 mi. (18 km.) E of Frankfurt am Main; pop. (1992e) 87,724; diamond polishing; manufactures jewelry, rubber goods, chemicals; 14th cent. St. Mary's church; 17th cent. Dutch-Walloon church; early 18th cent. castle; birthplace of folklorists Brothers Grimm 18th cent.; chartered 1303; scene of Napoleonic victory over Austro-Bavarians under Bavarian Gen. Karl Philipp Wrede nearby 1813; badly damaged in WWII.

Han–chung. See HANZHONG.

Han·cock \ˈhan-ˌkäk\. **1.** Name of counties in ten states of the U.S. See tables at GEORGIA, ILLINOIS, INDIANA, IOWA, KENTUCKY, MAINE, MISSISSIPPI, OHIO, TENNESSEE, WEST VIRGINIA.
2. Town, Berkshire co., W Massachusetts, 7 mi. (11 km.) NW of Pittsfield; pop. (1990c) 628; site of Shaker village.
3. City, Houghton co., NW part of Michigan's Upper Penin., 70 mi. (113 km.) NW of Marquette; pop. (1990c) 4547; copper mines; manufactures machinery, iron and brass products; Suomi Coll. (1896).

Hancock, Mount. Peak, near S boundary of Yellowstone National Park, NW Wyoming; 10,214 ft. (3113 m.).

Hand \ˈhand\. County in E cen. South Dakota. See table at SOUTH DAKOTA.

Han·da \ˈhän-dä\. City, Aichi prefecture, Honshū, Japan, 20 mi. (32 km.) S of Nagoya; pop. (1990p) 99,550.

Han·dan *or W.-G.* **Han–tan** \ˈhän-ˈdän\. Town, Hebei prov., NE China, ab. 100 mi. (160 km.) S of Shijiazhuang; pop. (1990c) 837,552; settlement goes back to ancient times; ruins of ancient cities nearby.

Han·dies Peak \ˈhan-dēz\. Peak, Hinsdale co., SW Colorado; 14,048 ft. (4282 m.).

Hand·lo·vá \ˈhänd-lȯ-ˌvä\ *or Hung.* **Nyi·tra·bán·ya** \ˈnyē-trö-ˌbän-ˌyö\. Town, W cen. Slovakia, in mountains 90 mi. (145 km.) NE of Bratislava; pop. (1980p) 17,777.

Hand·öl \ˈhän-ˌdœl\. Waterfall on **Handöl Creek,** W Jämtland, W Sweden; total drop 345 ft. (105 m.); highest waterfall in Sweden.

HaNegev. See NEGEV.

Han·ford \ˈhan-fərd\. **1.** City, ⊗ of Kings co., SW cen. California, 30 mi. (48 km.) S of Fresno; pop. (1990c) 30,897.
2. Site, Benton co., S Washington, on Columbia River NNW of Richland; made site 1942 of industrial plant (Hanford Engineer Works) of the Manhattan Project which produced the first atomic bombs. See RICHLAND 5.

Hang–chou *or* **Hangchow.** See HANGZHOU.

Hang–chou Bay *or* **Hangchow Bay.** See HANGZHOU BAY.

Hang·klip, Cape \ˈhäŋ-ˌklip\. Cape on SW coast of Western Cape prov., Rep. of South Africa, on SE side of entrance to False Bay.

Hangö \ˈhäŋ-ˌœ\ *or Finnish* **Han·ko** \ˈhäŋ-kȯ\. Seaport and peninsula, Uusimaa prov., S Finland, on Baltic Sea; resort; founded 1874; leased to U.S.S.R. as a military base 1940; relinquished by U.S.S.R. in exchange for lease of Porkkala 1944.

Hang·zhou *or W.-G.* **Hang–chou** \ˈhäŋ-ˈjō\ *or* **Hang·chow** \ˈhaŋ-ˈchau̇\. City, ✻ of Zhejiang prov., E China, at mouth of Fuchun River at head of Hangzhou Bay ab. 110 mi. (175 km.) SW of Shanghai; pop. (1990c) 1,099,660; iron and steel, machinery; important coastal trade; center of rice and silk production; S terminus of Grand Canal (Da Yun-he); university (1958). Was ✻ of Southern Sung dynasty c. 1126–1279. Visited 13th cent. by Venetian traveler Marco Polo who knew it as **Kin·sai** \ˈkin-ˈsā\; devastated in Taiping Rebellion 1861; opened to foreign trade 1896; under Japanese control 1937–45; fell to Chinese Communist forces 1949.

Hangzhou Bay *or W.-G.* **Hang–chou Bay** *or* **Hangchow Bay.** Funnel-shaped bay at mouth of Fuchun River, Zhejiang prov., E China; 60 mi. (97 km.) wide at entrance, extends inland 70 mi. (113 km.); famous for its bore; Zhoushan Archipelago lies across S entrance.

Han·hai *or W.-G.* **Han–hai** \ˈhän-ˈhī\. Chinese literary name for the vast Gobi and Xinjiang Uygur desert area in cen. Asia.

Hanko. See HANGÖ.

Han·kou *or W.-G.* **Han–k'ou** \ˈhän-ˈkō\ *or* **Han·kow** \ˈhaŋ-ˈkau̇\. Port of the tri-city conurbation of Wuhan, SE Hubei prov., E cen. China, on N bank of the Chang E of the Han and opp. Wuchang, 585 mi. (941 km.) by river from Shanghai. Existed for centuries as a fishing village; opened to trade 1861; grew rapidly after 1900; involved in industrial strike of Feb. 7, 1923; fell to Nationalist government 1926; occupied by Japanese 1938–45; came under Communist rule 1949.

Han·ley \ˈhan-lē\. Former county borough, Staffordshire, W cen. England, since 1910 part of Stoke-on-Trent; manufactures pottery; birthplace of writer Arnold Bennett 1867. See POTTERIES, THE.

Hann, Mount \ˈhan\. Mountain in Kimberley Plateau, NE Western Australia, Australia; 2800 ft. (853 m.).

Han·na \ˈha-nə\. Town, SE Alberta, Canada, 100 mi. (161 km.) ENE of Calgary; pop. (1991c) 2996.

Han·nas·town \ˈha-nəz-ˌtau̇n\. Locality, Westmoreland co., SW Pennsylvania, ab. 5 mi. (8 km.) NNE of Greensburg; coal mining; pre-Revolutionary ✻ of W Pennsylvania.

Han·ni·bal \ˈha-nə-bəl\. City, Marion and Ralls cos., NE Missouri, on Mississippi River; pop. (1990c) 18,004; river port; tourism; manufactures stoves; boyhood home of writer Samuel Clemens (Mark Twain).

Han·no·ver \ˈha-ˌnō-vər, -nə-, *Ger.* hä-ˈnō-vər, -ˈnō-fər\ *or Eng.* **Han·o·ver** \ˈha-ˌnō-vər, -nə-\. **1.** Former state of NW Germany; roughly equivalent to present-day Lower Saxony.

History: An electorate of the Holy Roman Empire officially known as Brunswick-Lüneburg 1692–1806; Elector George Louis became King George I of England 1714 (first of the house of Hanover); acquired Bremen and Verden from Sweden 1715; in Seven Years' War (1756–63) supported by England as ally of Prussia; occupied by French 1803; divided bet. Emperor Napoléon's kingdom of Westphalia and the French First Empire 1807–13; designated a kingdom 1814–66; with accession of Victoria to English throne 1837, became separate from England with which it had had a personal union since 1714; received constitution 1833 which was suspended by King Ernest Augustus (1837–51); kingdom extinguished and became province of Prussia as a result of Austro–Prussian War 1866; became state of West Germany and later incorp. into Lower Saxony state 1946.

2. City, ✻ of Lower Saxony and of the former Hannover state, Germany, on the Leine River 35 mi. (56 km.) WNW of Brunswick; pop. (1992e) 517,476; machinery, rubberworks; motor vehicles, electronic apparatus, textiles, chemicals; railway junction; zoological gardens; palace (orig. built 17th cent.); technical university (1831, university status 1880), medical school (1963). First mentioned 1100; chartered 1241; joined Hanseatic League 1386; became seat of dukes of Brunswick-Lüneburg 1636 (see HANNOVER 1); was ✻ of kingdom of Hannover 1815–66; passed with kingdom of Hannover to Prussia 1866; heavily bombed in WWII; became ✻ of Lower Saxony 1946.

Hannoversch–Münden. See MÜNDEN.

Hanö Bay \ˈhä-ˌnœ\. Inlet of Baltic Sea on SE coast of Sweden.

Ha·noi \ha-ˈnȯi, hə-\ *or Fr.* **Ha·noï** \á-nȯ-ˈē\. City, ✻ of Vietnam, on Red River ab. 75 mi. (120 km.) from the sea; its port is Haiphong; met. area pop. (1989c) 1,089,760; metalworking; textiles, chemicals, leather goods; university (1956). Dates back to era before Chinese invasions; made ✻ under Ly dynasty 1010; occupied by French 1883; was ✻ of French Indochina 1902–45; occupied by Japanese 1940–45 in WWII; scene of heavy fighting bet. French and Vietminh 1946–54; became ✻ of North Vietnam 1954; bombed by U.S. in Vietnam War; became ✻ of Vietnam 1976.

Han·o·ver \ˈha-ˌnō-vər\. **1.** County in E cen. Virginia. See table at VIRGINIA.

2. Town, Jefferson co., SE Indiana, on Ohio River; pop. (1990c) 3610; Hanover Coll. (1827).

3. Town, Plymouth co., SE Massachusetts, 10 mi. (16 km.) E of Brockton; pop. (1990c) 11,912.

4. Town, Grafton co., W New Hampshire, on Connecticut River 5 mi. (8 km.) NNW of Lebanon; pop. (1990c) 9212; chartered 1761; settled 1765; Dartmouth Coll. (chartered 1769, opened 1770).

5. Borough, York co., S Pennsylvania, 18 mi. (29 km.) SW of York; pop. (1990c) 14,399; manufactures shoes, textiles, furniture; horses; scene of battle bet. Union and Confederate cavalry 1863.

6. Village, ⊗ of Hanover co., E cen. Virginia; birthplace of American Revolutionary leader Patrick Henry (1736); birthplaces of politician Henry Clay (1777) and novelist and diplomat Thomas Nelson Page (1853) nearby.

7. Town, Grey co., SE Ontario, Canada, 30 mi. (48 km.) S of Owen Sound; pop. (1991c) 6711.

8. English form of Hannover (*q.v.*).

Hanover Island. Island off SW coast of Chile, S of Concepción Strait.

Hanover Park. Village, Cook and Du Page cos., NE Illinois, 17 mi. (27 km.) WNW of Chicago; pop. (1990c) 32,895.

Han·pan, Cape \ˈhan-ˌpan\. Northernmost point of Buka I., NW Solomon Is., Papua New Guinea, in W Pacific Ocean; 5°01′S, 154°37′E.

Han·sa Bay \ˈhän-sə\. Inlet on NE coast of New Guinea I., Papua New Guinea, halfway bet. Madang and Wewak.

Han·ság \ˈhön-ˌshäg\. Marshy region, E Austria and W Hungary, SE of Neusiedler Lake; 147 sq. mi. (381 sq. km.).

Hanseatic City of Danzig. See GDAŃSK 2.

Han·se·at·ic League \ˌhan-sē-ˈa-tik\ *or* **Hanse Towns** \ˈhans\. A defensive commercial confederacy of Europe, founded by N German towns in 13th cent.; grew out of treaties bet. Lübeck and Hamburg for mutual defense in trading; Lübeck made administrative center of Hanseatic League 1358; membership fluctuated constantly and included: Bremen, Cologne, Danzig (Gdańsk), Hamburg, Lübeck, Lüneburg, Magdeburg, Reval (Tallinn), Riga, Rostock; foreign trade centers included: Brugge, Bergen, London, and Novgorod; contributed to defeat of King Valdemar IV of Denmark whose attack on Gotland 1361 instigated warfare that ended in Treaty of Stralsund (1370) upholding Hanse trade hegemony in Baltic area; reached height of power mid-14th cent.; began to decline mid-15th cent.; last general assembly held 1669; Bremen and Hamburg still known as Hanseatic cities.

Han·sen Dam \ˈhan-sən\. Flood-control dam, Los Angeles co., S California.

Hans·ford \ˈhans-fərd, ˈhanz-\. County in NW Texas. See table at TEXAS.

Han·si \ˈhän-sē\. City, Haryana state, NW India, NW of Delhi; pop. (1991p) 59,638.

Hans Lol·lik Island \ˈhänz-ˈlä-lik\. One of the Virgin Is. of the U.S., West Indies, N of St. Thomas and separated from it by Leeward Passage.

Han·son \ˈhan-sən\. **1.** County in SE South Dakota. See table at SOUTH DAKOTA.

2. Town, Plymouth co., SE Massachusetts, 8 mi. (13 km.) ESE of Brockton; pop. (1990c) 9028.

Han–tan. See HANDAN.

Hants \ˈhans\. **1.** County in cen. Nova Scotia, Canada. See table at NOVA SCOTIA.

2. County, England. See HAMPSHIRE.

Ha·nu·man·garh \ˌhə-nu̇-ˈmän-gər\. City, Rajasthan state, NW India; pop. (1991p) 78,504.

Han·yang *or W.-G.* **Han–yang** \ˈhän-ˈyäŋ\. Part of the tri-city conurbation of Wuhan, SE Hubei prov., E cen. China, on N bank of the Chang W of Han River mouth and opp. Hankou and Wuchang; has grown rapidly since 1900 as part of industrial development of Hankou; iron and steel works.

Han·zhong *or W.-G.* **Han–chung** \ˈhän-ˈjüŋ\; *formerly* **Nan·cheng** \ˈnan-ˈcheŋ\. City, S Shaanxi prov., NE cen. China, on N bank of the Han 135 mi. (217 km.) SW of Xi'an; pop. (1990c) 169,930; important commercial center.

Hao \ˈhau̇\ *also* **Bow Island** \ˈbō\. Atoll in cen. Tuamotu Archipelago, French Polynesia, S Pacific Ocean, 18°15′S, 140°54′W; 30 mi. (48 km.) long, 5 to 9 mi. (8 to 14 km.) wide; pop. (1988c) 1333.

Haora. See HOWRAH.

Hapar. See HAPUR.

Ha·pa·ran·da \ˌhä-pä-ˈrän-dä\. Seaport, Norrbotten prov., NE Sweden, at mouth of Torneälven River on Gulf of Bothnia opp. Finnish town of Tornio; pop. (1989c) 10,343.

Hape·ville \ˈhāp-ˌvil, -vəl\. Residential city, Fulton co., NW cen. Georgia, 8 mi. (13 km.) S of Atlanta; pop. (1990c) 5483; Atlanta's international airport is located just S; incorp. 1891.

Hap·py Valley–Goose Bay \ˈha-pē\. Town, Newfoundland, E Canada; pop. (1991c) 8610. The separate towns of Happy Valley and Goose Bay united 1973.

Ha·pur \ˈhä-pər\; *formerly* **Ha·par** \ˈhä-pər\. Town, W Uttar Pradesh, N India, 35 mi (56 km.) E of Delhi; pop. (1991p) 146,591.

Har·a·han \ˈhar-ə-ˌhan\. City, Jefferson parish, SE Louisiana, W of New Orleans; pop. (1990c) 9927.

Har·al·son \ˈhar-əl-sən\. County in W Georgia. See table at GEORGIA.

Ha·ra·mosh \ˌhär-ə-ˈmōsh\. Mountain in the Karakoram Range, in Pakistani-controlled sector of Jammu and Kashmir; 24,270 ft. (7397 m.).

Ha·ra·mukh *or* **Ha·ra·muk** \ˈhär-ə-ˌmu̇k, -ˌmu̇k\. Peak in the Himalayas, N India, 25 mi. (40 km.) N of Srinagar; 16,015 ft. (4881 m.).

Ha·ran *or* **Har·ran** \hə-ˈrän, ˈhā-ran\; *anc.* **Car·rhae** *also* **Car·rae** \ˈkar-ē\. Town, Urfa prov., SE Turkey in Asia, ab. 22 mi. (35 km.) SSE of the city of Urfa. In ancient times a strategically important city (**Char·ran** \ˈkar-ˌan\ in *Acts* vii. 2) of N Mesopotamia, on the main trade route from Nineveh to Carchemish; residence of Terah and his son, the Hebrew patriarch Abraham (*Gen.* xi. 31–32). Scene of defeat of Roman Governor Crassus 53 B.C. by the Parthians and the defeat of Roman Emperor Galerius 296 A.D. by the Persians.

Ha·rap·pa \hə-ˈra-pə\. Locality, Punjab, Pakistan, in the Indus Valley; a site of the Indus Valley civilization c. 2500–1600 B.C. with excavated remains incl. a citadel and granary buildings. See MOHENJO DARO.

Harar. See HĀRER.

Ha·ra·re \hä-ˈrä-rā\; *formerly* **Salis·bury** \ˈsȯlz-bə-rē, ˈsalz-\. City, ✻ of Zimbabwe, 240 mi. (386 km.) NE of Bulawayo; pop. (1992p) 1,184,169; a commercial, industrial, and transportation center; gold mines nearby; distribution center for tobacco and other agricultural products; two cathedrals; library; museum; Univ. of Zimbabwe (1955); founded 1890; chartered as a city 1935.

Har·bel \ˈhär-bel\. Town, Liberia, E of Monrovia.

Har·bin \ˈhär-bən, här-ˈbin\ *or W.-G.* **Ha–erh–pin** \ˈhä-ˈər-ˈbin\ *also* **Khar·bin** \k̲är-ˈbin\; *formerly* **Pin·kiang** \ˈbin-ˈjyäŋ\ *or* **Ping·kiang** \ˈbiŋ-\. City, ✻ of Heilongjiang prov., NE China, on Songhua River 145 mi. (233 km.) NNE of Changchun; pop. (1990c) 2,443,398; machinery; food processing; almost in exact center of Manchuria. A small fishing village before 1896; entered treaty with Russia for building of railways through Harbin to Vladivostok and Dalian and grew rapidly; Russian military headquarters in Russo-Japanese War 1904–05; received many White Russian refugees 1917; occupied by Japanese 1932; taken by U.S.S.R. 1945; taken by Chinese Communist forces 1946.

Har·bor Beach \ˈhär-bər\. City, Huron co., E Michigan, on Lake Huron 20 mi. (32 km.) S of mouth of Saginaw Bay; pop. (1990c) 2089.

Har·bour Grace \ˈhär-bər-ˈgrās\. Seaport, SE Newfoundland, Canada, on W shore of Conception Bay 27 mi. (43 km.) W of St. John's; pop. (1991c) 3419; important departure point for pioneering transatlantic flights.

Harbour Island. One of the Bahamas, just off N Eleuthera I.; 2 sq. mi. (5 sq. km.).

Har·burg \ˈhär-ˌbu̇rk\. Former city, Prussia, Germany; since 1937 part of Hamburg. See HAMBURG 4.

Har·dang·er Fjord \här-ˈdäŋ-ər\. Inlet of North Sea, Hordaland co., on SW coast of Norway; extends inland NE and E 114 mi. (183 km.).

Har·dang·er·vid·da \här-ˈdäŋ-ər-ˌvi-də\. Large plateau in S Norway, E of Hardanger Fjord.

Har·dee \ˈhär-dē\. County in cen. Florida. See table at FLORIDA.

Har·de·man \ˈhär-də-mən\. Name of counties in two states of the U.S. See tables at TENNESSEE and TEXAS.

Har·den·berg \ˈhär-den-ˌberk̲\. Commune, Overijssel prov., E Netherlands; pop. (1981e) 31,676.

Har·der·wijk \ˈhär-dər-ˌvīk, -ˌvāk\. Commune and seaport, Gelderland prov., E Netherlands, on the IJsselmeer (*q.v.*); pop. (1992e) 36,282; metalworking; rubber goods; formerly a member of Hanseatic League; important port prior to 20th cent. Zuiderzee damming and reclamation projects.

Har·din \ˈhärd-ᵊn\. **1.** Name of counties in six states of the U.S. See tables at ILLINOIS, IOWA, KENTUCKY, OHIO, TENNESSEE, TEXAS.
2. Village, ⊗ of Calhoun co., W Illinois; pop. (1990c) 1071.
3. City, ⊗ of Big Horn co., S Montana, 45 mi. (72 km.) E of Billings; pop. (1990c) 2940.

Har·ding \ˈhär-diŋ\. Name of counties in two states of the U.S. See tables at NEW MEXICO and SOUTH DAKOTA.

Har·dins·burg \ˈhärd-ᵊnz-ˌbərg\. City, ⊗ of Breckenridge co., NW cen. Kentucky; pop. (1990c) 1906.

Har·doi \ˈhär-ˌdȯi\. Town, cen. Uttar Pradesh, N India, 60 mi. (97 km.) NW of Lucknow; pop. (1991p) 88,632.

Hardwar. See HARIDWAR.

Hard·wick \ˈhärd-ˌwik\. Town, Caledonia co., NE Vermont, 20 mi. (32 km.) NNE of Montpelier; pop. (1990c) 2964; settled 1797.

Hard·wicke Bay \ˈhärd-ˌwik\. Inlet in Yorke Penin., SE Spencer Gulf, South Australia, Australia.

Har·dy \ˈhär-dē\. **1.** County in NE West Virginia. See table at WEST VIRGINIA.

Hardy Dam. Dam across Muskegon River, W Michigan; height 130 ft. (40 m.); constructed early 1930s; impounds water for waterpower, forming **Hardy Dam Pond** in Newaygo and Mecosta cos.

Hare Bay \ˈhar\. Inlet of Atlantic Ocean near N tip of Newfoundland, Canada.

Hare Island. Island in St. Lawrence River opp. Rivière du Loup, S Quebec, Canada.

Ha·rel·be·ke \ˈhär-əl-ˌbā-kə\ *or* **Har·le·beke** \ärl-ˈbek, -ˈbāk\. Commune, West Flanders prov., NW Belgium, on Leie River 22 mi. (35 km.) SW of Ghent; pop. (1991c) 25,836.

Ha·rer *or* **Hā·rer** *also* **Ha·rar** *or* **Har·rar** \ˈhär-ər\. City, E Ethiopia; pop. (1989e) 76,890; trades in coffee; agricultural college.

Har·fleur \är-ˈflœr\. Seaport, Seine-Maritime dept., N France, 4 mi. (6 km.) E of Le Havre; 15th–16th cent. church; before rise of Le Havre, a chief port of France; captured by English King Henry V 1415; control shifted bet. France and England several times mid-15th cent.; pillaged by Huguenots 1562; damaged in WWII.

Har·ford \ˈhär-fərd\. County in NE Maryland. See table at MARYLAND.

Har·gey·sa *or* **Har·gei·sa** \här-ˈgā-sə\. Town, N Somalia, 50 mi. (80 km.) SW of Berbera; pop. (1985e) 85,000; was ✻ of former British Somaliland; heavy damage led to widespread abandonment during civil war late 1980s.

Har·ghi·ta \ˌhər-ˈgē-tə\. County of N cen. Romania. See table at ROMANIA.

Har HaZofim. See SCOPUS, MOUNT.

Har Horin. See KARAKORUM.

Ha·ri \ˈhär-ē\; *formerly* **Djam·bi** \ˈjäm-bē\. River, S cen. Sumatra, Indonesia; rises in Barisan Mts., flows E to Berhala Strait; ab. 450 mi. (724 km.) long.

Ha·rī \ˈhar-ē\ *or* **Ha·rī·rūd** *or* **Ha·ri Rud** \ˌhar-ē-ˈrüd\ *also* **He·ri Rud** \ˈher-ē\; *anc.* **Ar·i·us** \ˈar-ē-əs, ə-ˈrī-əs\. River, SW Asia; rises in mountains (Koh-i-Baba) W of Kabul, Afghanistan, flows W through fertile valley at Herāt, turns N forming part of boundary bet. Afghanistan and Turkmenistan on E and Iran on W, and then is lost in sands of Kara-Kum Desert of S Turkmenistan; 700 mi. (1126 km.) long. Its lower course called by the Turkmenian name, Tedzhen.

Hariana. See HARYANA.

Har·i·dwar \ˈhär-i-ˌdwär, ˈhər-\ *or* **Har·dwar** \ˈhär-ˌdwär, ˈhər-\. Town, NW Uttar Pradesh, N India, on the Ganges 110 mi. (177 km.) NNE of Delhi; pop. (1991p) 148,882; railroad center; known by many names in course of its long history; location of Ganges canal system headworks; Dakshewar temple and bathing ghat believed to be imprinted with Hindu god Vishnu's footprint are major pilgrimage sites; every 12 years scene of a large bathing pilgrimage, the Kumbh Mela.

Ha·ri·ma Sea \ˈhä-rē-mä\. Body of water at E end of Inland Sea bet. S Honshū and N Shikoku, Japan; bounded on E by Awaji I. and on W by Shōdo I.

Harimukotan. See KHARIMKOTAN.

Har·in·gey \ˈhar-iŋ-ˌgā\. A borough of Greater London, SE England. See table at LONDON 4.

Har·ing·vliet \ˈhar-iŋ-ˌvlēt\. Inlet of North Sea on SW coast of Netherlands; ab. 2.5 mi. (4 km.) wide; the W extension of Hollandsch Diep to the sea.

Har·kány \ˈhȯr-kän-yə\. Town, S Hungary, S of Pécs and SW of Mohács; in area of important Hungarian-Turk battles (see MOHÁCS).

Har·ker Heights \ˈhär-kər\. City, Bell co., cen. Texas, 20 mi. (32 km.) W of Temple; pop. (1990c) 12,841.

Har·lan \ˈhär-lən\. **1.** Name of counties in two states of the U.S. See tables at KENTUCKY and NEBRASKA.
2. City, ⊗ of Shelby co., W Iowa, 40 mi. (64 km.) NE of Council Bluffs; pop. (1990c) 5148.
3. City, ⊗ of Harlan co., SE Kentucky, 28 mi. (45 km.) NE of Middlesborough; pop. (1990c) 2686; coal mining; bet. 1900 and 1938 and in 1974 the scene of violent labor disputes bet. miners and mine operators.

Harlebeke. See HARELBEKE.

Har·lech \ˈhär-lek\. Village, W Wales, on coast 8 mi. (13 km.) N of Barmouth; ancient ✻ of Merionethshire. Harlech Castle built c. 1283 by English King Edward I; captured by Welsh rebellion leader Owen Glendower 1404; surrendered to Yorkists in Wars of the Roses 1468; last Welsh fortress to be held for King Charles I until its fall 1647.

Har·lem \ˈhär-ləm\. **1.** River channel, NE of Manhattan I., New York; with Spuyten Duyvil Creek connects the Hudson and East rivers.
2. District of Manhattan borough, New York City, New York, N of Central Park bet. Eighth Avenue and the East and Harlem rivers; a former village created 1658 and named New Haarlem; site of battle of Harlem Heights in American Revolution 1776; farm area in 18th cent.; became fashionable residential district 19th cent.; Italian community formed 1880s; bet. c. 1900 and WWI became a predominantly black residential area; site of Harlem Renaissance 1920s which included writers Countee Cullen, Langston Hughes, and Zora Neal Hurston; Latino community grew following WWI. For many years scene of high unemployment, overcrowding, and physical decline.
3. City, Netherlands. See HAARLEM.

Har·lin·gen \ˈhär-lən-jən\. City, Cameron co., S Texas, 21 mi. (34 km.) NNW of Brownsville; pop. (1990c) 48,735; ships citrus fruit, vegetables, cotton.

Har·ling·en \ˈhär-liŋ-ən\. Commune and seaport, Friesland prov., N Netherlands, on Waddenzee 16 mi. (26 km.) W of Leeuwarden; pop. (1981e) 15,733.

Har·low \ˈhär-lō\. Town, Essex, S England; pop. (1991p) 73,500; scientific apparatus, glass; printing; founded 1947.

Har·low·ton \ˈhär-lō-ˌtau̇n, -tən\. City, ⊗ of Wheatland co., cen. Montana, 48 mi. (77 km.) SSW of Lewistown; pop. (1990c) 1049.

Har·mon \ˈhär-mən\. County in SW Oklahoma. See table at OKLAHOMA.

Harmozia. See HORMUZ.

Har·nett \ˈhär-nət\. County in cen. North Carolina. See table at NORTH CAROLINA.

Har·ney \ˈhär-nē\. County in SE Oregon. See table at OREGON.

Harney Basin. Former lake bottom, Harney co., SE Oregon; 2500 sq. mi. (6475 sq. km.).

Harney Lake. Marshy lake, Harney Basin, cen. Harney co., SE Oregon; ab. 10 mi. (16 km.) long; connected with Malheur Lake.

Harney Peak. Mountain in Black Hills, Pennington co., SW South Dakota; 7242 ft. (2207 m.); highest point in state and highest point in United States E of Rocky Mts., although by some the Black Hills are considered a part of the Rocky Mountain system.

Härn·ö·sand *or* **Hern·ö·sand** \ˌher-nœ-ˈsand\. Seaport, ⊗ of Västernorrland prov., E Sweden, at mouth of Ångerman River; pop. (1989c) 27,204; ships forest products; chartered 1585; plundered and burned by Russians 1721.

Har Nuur \ˈhär-ˈnu̇r\ *or* **Kha·ra Nur** \ˈkär-ə\. Salt lake (*nuur, nur*), W Mongolia, just E of the larger lake Har Us Nuur.

Haro Strait \ˈhar-ō\. Strait SE of Vancouver I., in W part of Washington Sound, connecting Juan de Fuca Strait with Strait of Georgia, the three straits being traversed by the U.S.-Canada boundary.

Har·pen·den \ˈhär-pən-dən\. Town, Hertfordshire, SE England, 25 mi. (40 km.) NNW of London; pop. (1981p) 27,896; Rothamsted Experimental Station (founded 1843), noted for biological and agricultural research located nearby.

Har·per \ˈhär-pər\. **1.** Name of counties in two states of the U.S. See tables at KANSAS and OKLAHOMA.
2. Commercial seaport, extreme SE Liberia, at Cape Palmas.

Har·pers Ferry \ˈhär-pərz\. Residential town and tourist resort, Jefferson co., NE West Virginia, in Blue Ridge at confluence of Potomac and Shenandoah rivers ab. 55 mi. (88 km.) NW of Washington, D.C.; pop. (1990c) 308; settled c. 1734; site of U.S. arsenal estab. 1796 and seized in abolitionist John Brown's raid 1859; strategic base in Civil War. See *Harpers Ferry National Historical Park* at UNITED STATES, *National Historical Parks.*

Harper Woods. City, Wayne co., SE Michigan, NE of Detroit; pop. (1990c) 14,903.

Har·peth \ˈhär-pəth\. River, W cen. Tennessee; rises in SW Rutherford co., flows NW into Cumberland River; ab. 90 mi. (145 km.) long.

Harps·well \ˈhärps-ˌwel, -wəl\. Town, Cumberland co., SW Maine, 22 mi. (35 km.) NE of Portland; pop. (1990c) 5012; seaside resort.

Har·put \här-ˈpüt\; *formerly* **Khar·put** \kär-\. Town, Elâzığ prov., E cen. Turkey in Asia, near banks of upper Euphrates; Jacobite convent; ancient church; scene of Armenian massacre 1895.

Har·rah \ˈhar-ə\. Town, Oklahoma co., cen. Oklahoma, E of Oklahoma City; pop. (1990c) 4206.

Harran. See HARAN.

Harrar. See HARER.

Har·ri·can·aw \ˌhar-i-ˈka-nȯ\. River, SW Quebec, Canada; flows NNW to S end of James Bay in Ontario; ab. 250 mi. (400 km.) long.

Har·ri·man \ˈhar-ə-mən\. City, Roane co., E Tennessee, 38 mi. (61 km.) W of Knoxville; pop. (1990c) 7119.

Harriman, Mount. Peak, SW Klamath co., S Oregon; 7950 ft. (2423 m.).

Harriman Dam *also* **Davis Bridge Dam** \ˈdā-vəs\. Dam across Deerfield River in S Vermont; height 220 ft. (67 m.); completed 1924; impounds water for power.

Har·ring·ton Park \ˈhar-iŋ-tən\. Borough, Bergen co., NE New Jersey, 12 mi. (19 km.) NE of Paterson; pop. (1990c) 4623.

Harrington Sound. Body of water in NE cen. Bermuda I.

Har·ris \ˈhar-əs\. **1.** Name of counties in two states of the U.S. See tables at GEORGIA and TEXAS.

2. S section of island of Lewis with Harris, a part of Western Isles region, in Outer Hebrides, off NW coast of Scotland; 195 sq. mi. (505 sq. km.); place where Harris tweed was orig. made.

Harris, Sound of. Channel bet. Lewis with Harris I. and North Uist I. in the Outer Hebrides, NW Scotland.

Har·ris·burg \ˈhar-əs-ˌbərg\. **1.** City, ⊗ of Poinsett co., NE Arkansas; pop. (1990c) 1943.

2. City, ⊗ of Saline co., SE Illinois, 22 mi. (35 km.) E of Marion; pop. (1990c) 9289; coal mining; Southeastern Illinois Coll. (1961).

3. Village, ⊗ of Banner co., W Nebraska.

4. City, ✻ of Pennsylvania and ⊗ of Dauphin co., SE cen. Pennsylvania, on Susquehanna River 98 mi. (158 km.) WNW of Philadelphia; pop. (1990c) 52,376; manufactures steel products, machinery; state museum; Harrisburg Area Community Coll. (1964). Settled c. 1718; known as **Harris' Ferry** \ˈhar-i-səz, ˈhar-is\ until renamed Harrisburg when laid out in 1785; scene of noted conventions, esp. Harrisburg Convention of 1788; became borough 1791, state ✻ 1812, city 1860; site of Camp Curtin, first camp for Union forces during Civil War.

Har·ri·smith \ˈhar-ə-ˌsmith\. Town, Free State, E cen. Rep. of South Africa, 153 mi. (246 km.) NW of Durban.

Har·ri·son \ˈhar-ə-sən\. **1.** Name of counties in eight states of the U.S. See tables at INDIANA, IOWA, KENTUCKY, MISSISSIPPI, MISSOURI, OHIO, TEXAS, WEST VIRGINIA.

2. City, ⊗ of Boone co., N Arkansas, ab. 64 mi. (103 km.) ENE of Fayetteville; pop. (1990c) 9922; ships lumber; marble deposits. Caves with stalactite and stalagmite formations nearby.

3. City, ⊗ of Clare co., cen. Michigan; pop. (1990c) 1835; Mid Michigan Community Coll. (1965).

4. Village, ⊗ of Sioux co., NW Nebraska; pop. (1990c) 291.

5. Town, Hudson co., NE New Jersey, on Passaic River opp. Newark; pop. (1990c) 13,425.

6. Village, Westchester co., SE New York, ENE of Yonkers; pop. (1990c) 23,308.

7. City, Hamilton co., SW corner of Ohio, on Indiana border 18 mi. (29 km.) WNW of Cincinnati; pop. (1990c) 7518.

8. Township, Allegheny co., SW Pennsylvania, NE suburb of Pittsburgh; pop. (1990c) 11,763.

Harrison Bay. Inlet of Arctic Ocean N coast of Alaska, E of Point Barrow, 70°30′N, 151°30′W.

Har·ri·son·burg \ˈhar-ə-sən-ˌbərg\. **1.** Village, ⊗ of Catahoula parish, cen. Louisiana; pop. (1990c) 453.

2. City, ⊗ of Rockingham co. but politically independent, N Virginia, 23 mi. (37 km.) NNE of Staunton; 3 sq. mi. (8 sq. km.); pop. (1990c) 30,707; James Madison Univ. (1908), Eastern Mennonite Coll. (1917); city estab. 1780.

Harrison Lake. See LILLOOET.

Harrison's Landing. See BERKELEY 5.

Harrison Stickle. See LANGDALE PIKES.

Har·ri·son·ville \ˈhar-ə-sən-ˌvil\. City, ⊗ of Cass co., W Missouri, 30 mi. (48 km.) S of Independence; pop. (1990c) 7683.

Har·ris·ville \ˈhar-əs-ˌvil\. **1.** City, ⊗ of Alcona co., NE Michigan; pop. (1990c) 470.

2. Unincorporated settlement, Providence co., N Rhode Island, ab. 17 mi. (27 km.) NW of the city of Providence; pop. (1990c) 1654; administrative center of town of Burrillville.

3. City, Weber co., N Utah, just NW of Ogden; pop. (1990c) 3004.

4. Town, ⊗ of Ritchie co., NW West Virginia; pop. (1990c) 1839.

Har·rods·burg \ˈhar-ədz-ˌbərg\. City, ⊗ of Mercer co., cen. Kentucky, 9 mi. (14 km.) NNW of Danville; pop. (1990c) 7335; founded 1774; settled 1775; oldest city in the state; site of cabin in which Nancy Hanks and Thomas Lincoln, parents of U.S. President Abraham Lincoln, were married. See SPRINGFIELD 5.

Har·ro·gate \ˈhar-ə-ˌgāt\. Village, Claiborne co., NE Tennessee, on Kentucky border ab. 48 mi. (77 km.) NE of Knoxville; formerly a summer resort; Lincoln Memorial Univ. (1897).

Har·ro·gate \ˈhar-ə-gət, -ˌgāt\. Town, North Yorkshire, N England, 13 mi. (21 km.) N of Leeds; pop. (1981p) 66,475; fashionable resort; many mineral springs.

Har·row \ˈhar-ō\. A borough of Greater London, SE England. See table at LONDON 4.

Har·språng·et \ˈhär-ˌsprȯŋ-ət\ *or Lapp* **Njom·mel·sas·ka** \ˈnyȯ-məl-ˌsäs-kə\. Waterfall in Luleälv River, Norrbotten prov., N Sweden; 110 ft. (34 m.) high.

Hart \ˈhärt\. **1.** Name of counties in two states of the U.S. See tables at GEORGIA and KENTUCKY.

2. City, ⊗ of Oceana co., W Michigan, 18 mi. (29 km.) S of Ludington; pop. (1990c) 1942.

Har Tavor. See TABOR, MOUNT.

Hart·ford \ˈhärt-fərd\. **1.** County in N Connecticut. See table at CONNECTICUT.

2. City, ✻ of Connecticut, at head of navigation on Connecticut River 36 mi. (58 km.) NNE of New Haven; pop. (1990c) 139,739; port of entry; a major insurance center; electrical equipment; numerous parks with recreational facilities; State Capitol, Old State House (designed by Charles Bulfinch), State Armory, Wadsworth Atheneum (art museum), Mark Twain House, Harriet Beecher Stowe House; Soldiers and Sailors Civil War Memorial Arch; Phoenix Building (first two-sided building in U.S.); Trinity Coll. (1823), Morse School of Business (1860), Hartford Coll. for Women (1933), Hartford State Technical Coll. (1946), Greater Hartford Community Coll. (1967).

History: Estab. as trading post and fort by Dutch 1633; settled by band of colonists from Massachusetts Bay 1635–36; given present name 1637; first constitution of Connecticut Colony drawn up 1639; according to tradition royal charter protected from Governor Edmund Andros in famous Charter Oak incident 1687; ✻ of Connecticut (*q.v.*) with New Haven as co-capital 1701–1875; during Revolution important military supply depot; home of poets known as the "Hartford Wits" in 18th cent.; site of Hartford Convention Dec. 1814–Jan. 1815. Separate town and city incorp. 1784 and consolidated 1896; circus fire July 1944 claimed dozens of lives.

3. Village, Madison co., SW Illinois, on Mississippi River 15 mi. (24 km.) N of East St. Louis; pop. (1990c) 1676.

4. City, ⊗ of Ohio co., W cen. Kentucky; pop. (1990c) 2532.

5. Town, Windsor co., E Vermont; pop. (1990c) 9404.

6. City, Washington co., SE Wisconsin, 30 mi. (48 km.) NW of Milwaukee; pop. (1990c) 8188.

Hartford City. City, ⊗ of Blackford co., E Indiana, 17 mi. (27 km.) ESE of Marion; pop. (1990c) 6960.

Har·ting·ton \ˈhär-tiŋ-tən\. City, ⊗ of Cedar co., NE Nebraska, 42 mi. (68 km.) N of Norfolk; pop. (1990c) 1583.

Hart Island \ˈhärt\ *also* **Hart's Island** \ˈhärts\. Island in Long Island Sound, SE New York; off E coast of the Bronx, New York City; attached to Bronx borough; New York City's potter's field cemetery.

Hart·land \ˈhärt-lənd\. Village, Waukesha co., SE Wisconsin; pop. (1990c) 6906.

Hartland Point. Cape on W coast of Devon, SW England, on S side of entrance to Bristol Channel; lighthouse.

Har·tle·pool \ˈhärt-lē-ˌpül, ˈhärt-ᵊl-\. Seaport, Cleveland, N England, on North Sea 26 mi. (42 km.) SSE of Newcastle upon Tyne; pop. (1991p) 88,200; extensive docks; manufactures iron and steel; received charter 1201.

Hart·ley \ˈhärt-lē\. **1.** County in NW Texas. See table at TEXAS.

2. See CHEGUTU.

Hart·manns·wei·ler·kopf \ˌhärt-mänz-ˌvī-lər-ˈkȯf, ˈärt-mäns-ˌvē-ler-ˌkȯpf\. Commanding height in the Vosges Mts., Haut-Rhin dept., NE France, 8 mi. (13 km.) NW of Mulhouse; 3700 ft. (1128 m.).

Hart·selle \ˈhärt-səl\. City, Morgan co., N Alabama, 11 mi. (18 km.) S of Decatur; pop. (1990c) 10,795; founded 1870.

Hart's Island. See HART ISLAND.

Harts·ville \ˈhärts-ˌvil, -vəl\. **1.** City, Darlington co., NE South Carolina, 21 mi. (34 km.) NW of Florence; pop. (1990c) 8372; manufactures packaging products, fertilizer, textiles; Coker Coll. (1894).
2. Town, ⊗ of Trousdale co., N Tennessee; pop. (1990c) 2188.

Hart·ville \ˈhärt-ˌvil\. City, ⊗ of Wright co., S Missouri; pop. (1990c) 495.

Hart·well \ˈhärt-ˌwel, -wəl\. City, ⊗ of Hart co., NE Georgia, 37 mi. (60 km.) NE of Athens; pop. (1990c) 4555; incorp. 1856.

Hārūn, Jabal. See HOR, MOUNT.

Har Us Nuur \ˈhär-ˌüs-ˈnu̇r\ *or* **Kha·ra Usu Nur** *also* **Ka·ra Usu Nur** \ˈkär-ə-ˌü-su̇-ˈnu̇r\. Salt lake (*nuur, nur*), W Mongolia, E of Hovd; 40 mi. (64 km.) long.

Har·vard \ˈhär-vərd\. **1.** City, McHenry co., N Illinois, 28 mi. (45 km.) ENE of Rockford; pop. (1990c) 5975; in lake region.
2. Town, Worcester co., cen. Massachusetts, 11 mi. (18 km.) ESE of Fitchburg; pop. (1990c) 12,329; location of transcendentalist and teacher Bronson Alcott's Utopian community 1843–44.

Harvard, Mount. Peak in Sawatch Range, in Chaffee co., cen. Colorado; 14,420 ft. (4395 m.).

Har·vey \ˈhär-vē\. **1.** County in SE cen. Kansas. See table at KANSAS.
2. City, Cook co., NE Illinois, 4 mi. (6.4 km.) S of Chicago; pop. (1990c) 29,771.

Har·well \ˈhär-ˌwel, -wəl\. Village, Berkshire, S England, ab. 12 mi. (19 km.) S of Oxford; site of first nuclear reactor in England, estab. 1947.

Har·wich \ˈhär-wich\. Town, Barnstable co., SE Massachusetts, 12 mi. (19 km.) E of the town of Barnstable; pop. (1990c) 10,275; summer resort.

Har·wich \ˈhar-ij, -ich, *U.S. also* ˈhär-wich\. Seaport, Essex, SE England, on North Sea 68 mi. (109 km.) ENE of London; pop. (1981p) 15,076; fishing.

Har·wich Port \ˈhär-wich-ˌpōrt\. Unincorporated settlement, Barnstable co., SE Massachusetts, on Atlantic Ocean; part of town of Harwich; pop. (1990c) 1742; summer resort.

Har·win·ton \ˈhär-wən-tən\. Town, Litchfield co., NW Connecticut, 15 mi. (24 km.) W of Hartford; pop. (1990c) 5228.

Har·wood Heights \ˈhär-ˌwu̇d\. Village, Cook co., NE Illinois, NW suburb of Chicago; pop. (1990c) 7680.

Ha·ry·a·na *also* **Ha·ri·a·na** \ˌhär-ē-ˈä-nə\. State, N India; pop. is mostly Hindi-speaking; ✱ Chandigarh; largely part of Indo-Gangetic plain; drained by Yamuna River which forms its boundary with Uttar Pradesh; corn, rice, millet; cattle; sugar refining; formed 1966 when the former Punjab state was split. See table at INDIA.

Harz \ˈhärts\. Mountain group, cen. Germany, bet. Elbe and Weser rivers S of Brunswick; before reunification, crossed border bet. West Germany and East Germany; highest peak Brocken 3747 ft. (1142 m.); has many summer resorts; well forested; profitable mines of varied kinds; region, long a stronghold of paganism, has been source of many legends.

Harzburg. See BAD HARZBURG.

Hasa *or* **Hasa, Al–** *or* **Hasa, El.** See AL-HASA.

Ḥasakah, Al. See AL ḤASAKAH.

Ha·san Dağ \hä-ˈsän-ˈdä\. Peak, cen. Turkey in Asia, SE of Tuz Lake; 10,670 ft. (3252 m.).

Ha·san·lu \ˈhä-sən-ˌlü\. Archaeological site, Azerbaijan, NW Iran, ab. halfway bet. Daryācheh-ye Orūmīyeh and Iraq border; excavations have revealed evidence of an advanced culture dating from 2d to first millennia B.C.

Ḥāṣ·bay·ya \häs-ˈbā-yə\. Town, Lebanon, just W of Mt. Hermon.

Has·brouck Heights \ˈhaz-bru̇k\. Residential borough, Bergen co., NE corner of New Jersey, 7 mi. (11 km.) SE of Paterson; pop. (1990c) 11,488; founded 1685.

Hashemite Kingdom of Jordan. See JORDAN 1.

Has·kell \ˈhas-kəl\. **1.** Name of counties in three states of the U.S. See tables at KANSAS, OKLAHOMA, TEXAS.
2. Town, Muskogee co., E Oklahoma, on Arkansas River 19 mi. (31 km.) W of Muskogee; pop. (1990c) 2143.
3. City, ⊗ of Haskell co., N Texas, 50 mi. (80 km.) N of Abilene; pop. (1990c) 3362.

Haskovo. See KHASKOVO.

Ha·sle·mere \ˈhā-zəl-ˌmir\. Town, Surrey, S England, 11 mi. (18 km.) S of Aldershot; pop. (1981p) 13,900; in high valley bet. two ridges: Hindhead, on N side of which is "Devil's Punch Bowl," a curious depression, and Blackdown, on E slope of which is Aldworth, a house built by poet Alfred, Lord Tennyson 1868–69 and in which he died 1892.

Has·li \ˈhäs-lē\. Valley, SE Bern canton, W cen. Switzerland, E of the Grindelwald, through which passes upper course of the Aare (*q.v.*).

Has·ling·den \ˈhaz-liŋ-dən\. Town, Lancashire, NW England, 17 mi. (27 km.) N of Manchester; pop. (1981p) 15,900; textiles.

Has·san \ˈhəs-ᵊn\. Town, S Karnataka, S India, 63 mi. (101 km.) NW of Mysore; pop. (1991p) 90,719.

Has·sa·yam·pa River \ˌha-səm-ˈyam-pə\. Intermittent stream, W cen. Arizona; rises S of Prescott and flows S into Gila River.

Has·selt \ˈhä-səlt\. Commune, ✱ of Limburg prov., NE Belgium, 42 mi. (68 km.) E of Brussels; pop. (1991c) 66,611; distilleries; received charter 1232; important pilgrimage site of septennial fete on Assumption Day, Aug. 15; site of battle 1831 in which Dutch defeated Belgian nationalists.

Has·si R'Mel \ˈhä-sēr-ˈmel\. Town, N cen. Algeria, NW of Ghardaïa; located in major oil fields and on pipeline to coastal port of Arzew.

Has·su·na \ha-ˈsü-nə\. Archaeological site, N Iraq, on W bank of the Tigris 25 mi. (40 km.) S of Mosul; excavations of 1943–44 revealed evidence of occupation dating back to c. 5750 B.C.

Hasta Colonia. See ASTI 2.

Hasta Pompeia. See ASTI 2.

Ha·sten·beck \ˈhäs-tən-ˌbek\. Village, Lower Saxony, Germany, 3 mi. (5 km.) SE of Hameln; scene of French victory over the English in Seven Years' War 1757 which led to Convention of Kloster-Zeven (see ZEVEN).

Has·tings \ˈhā-stiŋz\. **1.** City, ⊗ of Barry co., SW Michigan, 29 mi. (47 km.) NE of Kalamazoo; pop. (1990c) 6549.
2. City, ⊗ of Dakota co., SE Minnesota, on Mississippi River 20 mi. (32 km.) SE of St. Paul; pop. (1990c) 15,445.
3. City, ⊗ of Adams co., S Nebraska, 23 mi. (37 km.) S of Grand I.; pop. (1990c) 22,837; manufactures farm implements; grain and dairy processing; Hastings Coll. (1882); Central Community Coll.–Hastings Campus (1966).
4. River, New South Wales, Australia; 108 mi. (174 km.) long.
5. Municipality, E New South Wales, Australia; pop. (1991c) 50,058.
6. County in SE Ontario, Canada. See table at ONTARIO.
7. Resort town, East Sussex, S England, on English Channel at entrance to Strait of Dover; pop. (1991p) 78,100; one of the Cinque Ports; scene of the battle of Hastings Oct. 14, 1066 in which William the Conqueror, duke of Normandy, defeated English King Harold II.
8. City, E North I., New Zealand, near Napier 160 mi. (257 km.) NE of Wellington; pop. (1981c) 36,083; beer; rebuilt after earthquake of 1931.

Has·tings–on–Hud·son \-ˈhəd-sən\. Residential village, Westchester co., SE New York, on Hudson River 18 mi. (29 km.) N of New York City, opp. the Palisades; pop. (1990c) 8000.

\ə\ abut \ᵊ\ kitten, Fr table \ər\ further \a\ ash \ā\ ace \ä\ cot, cart \á\ Fr bac \au̇\ out \b̲\ Span Avila \ch\ chin \e\ bet \ē\ easy \g\ go \i\ hit \ī\ ice \j\ job \k̲\ Ger ich, Buch \ⁿ\ Fr vin \ŋ\ sing \ō\ go \ȯ\ all \ȯ\ law \œ\ Fr bœuf \œ̄\ Fr feu \ȯi\ boy \th\ thin \th̲\ this \ü\ loot \u̇\ foot \ue\ Ger füllen \ue̅\ Fr rue \y\ yet \ʸ\ Fr digne \ˈdēnʸ\, nuit \ˈnwʸē\ \yü\ few \yu̇\ fury \zh\ vision

Ha·tay \hä-ˈtī\. Province of S Turkey in Asia, on Mediterranean coast; ✱ Antakya; coextensive with former sanjak (district) of Alexandretta (*q.v.*); ceded to Turkey 1939 by agreement bet. France and Turkey. See table at TURKEY.

Hat·boro \ˈhat-ˌbər-ō\. Borough, Montgomery co., SE Pennsylvania, 15 mi. (24 km.) NNE of Philadelphia; pop. (1990c) 7382.

Hatch·ie \ˈha-chē\. River, flowing from N Mississippi NW into Mississippi River on NW boundary of Tipton co., Tennessee; ab. 180 mi. (290 km.) long.

Hat·field \ˈhat-ˌfēld\. **1.** Town, Hampshire co., W Massachusetts, on Connecticut River 18 mi. (29 km.) N of Springfield; pop. (1990c) 3184; birthplace (1688) of Rev. Jonathan Dickinson, first president of the Coll. of New Jersey (now Princeton Univ.), and (1796) of Sophia Smith, founder of Smith Coll., Northampton, Massachusetts.

2. Borough, Montgomery co., SE Pennsylvania; NNW of Philadelphia; pop. (1990c) 2650.

3. Town, Hertfordshire, SE England, N of London; pop. (1981c) 25,150; Hatfield House, an early 17th cent. Jacobean mansion of the Cecil family, is open to the public.

Ha·thras \ˈhä-trəs\. Town, W Uttar Pradesh, N India, 85 mi. (137 km.) SSE of Delhi; pop. (1991p) 113,653; railroad center; has ruined Jat fort.

Ha·tia *or* **Ha·tya** \ˈhä-tē-ə\. Island group, formerly one island, Bangladesh, in main E mouth of the Ganges River; 171 sq. mi. (443 sq. km.); suffered severe cyclone damage 1970.

Ha·ti·llo \ä-ˈtē-ō\. Municipality, NW Puerto Rico, W of Arecibo; pop. (1990c) 32,703.

Ha·to Ma·yor \ˈä-tō-mä-ˈyȯr\. **1.** Province, Dominican Republic. See table at DOMINICAN REPUBLIC.

2. *or in full* **Hato Mayor del Rey** \t͟hel-ˈrā\. Commune, its ✱.

Hatra. See AL ḤAḌR.

Hatria. See ADRIA.

Hatria Picena. See ATRI.

Hat·ten·heim \ˈhät-ᵊn-ˌhīm\. Village, W Hesse, Germany, in the Rheingau; noted wine-producing region.

Hat·ter·as, Cape \ˈha-tə-rəs, ˈha-trəs\. Cape, SE **Hatteras Island,** Dare co., North Carolina; a long, narrow sand bar, one of the chain of islands off E coast of North Carolina; extends into Atlantic Ocean at a dangerous navigation point; tallest lighthouse in U.S., 208 ft. (63 m.); much of area included in **Cape Hatteras National Seashore** (authorized 1937); to the SW, near S tip of the island, is village of **Hatteras.**

Hatteras Inlet. Narrow strait leading from Atlantic Ocean into Pamlico Sound bet. S tip of Hatteras I. and Ocracoke I., North Carolina; during Civil War guarded by two forts built by Confederates but captured by Union forces Aug. 1861.

Hat·ties·burg \ˈha-tēz-ˌbərg\. City, ⊗ of Forrest co., SE Mississippi, 28 mi. (45 km.) SSW of Laurel; pop. (1990c) 41,882; chemicals, textiles; William Carey Coll. (1906), Univ. of Southern Mississippi (1910).

Hat·ting·en \ˈhä-tiŋ-ən\ *also* **Hattingen an der Ruhr** \ˌän-der-ˈrür\. City, cen. North Rhine-Westphalia, Germany, SE suburb of Essen on Ruhr River; pop. (1992e) 58,029; machinery; steel; ruins of 13th cent. castle; first mentioned 1019.

Hattushash. See BOGAZKÖY.

Ha·tu·tu \hä-ˈtü-tü\. Island, Marquesas Is., French Polynesia, S Pacific Ocean, 10 mi. (16 km.) NE of Eïao I.; 4 sq. mi. (10 sq. km.).

Hat·van \ˈhȯt-ˌvȯn\. Commune, cen. Hungary, 30 mi. (48 km.) E of Budapest; pop. (1991e) 24,800; railroad center.

Hatya. See HATIA.

Hat Yai \ˈhät-ˈyī\. Town, S Thailand, on Malay Penin.; pop. (1992e) 124,295.

Hau·bour·din \ˌō-bu̇r-ˈde^{n}\. Commune, Nord dept., N France, 6 mi. (10 km.) SW of Lille.

Haud *or* **Hawd** \ˈhau̇d\. Region, SE Ethiopia and SW Somalia; semidesert plateau, also has grassy plains.

Hau·ge·sund \ˈhœi-gə-ˌsu̇n\. Seaport, Rogaland co., SW Norway, on a fjord opp. Stavanger; pop. (1990c) 27,600; exports fish; shipbuilding yards, woolen mills, aluminum plant; site nearby held to be burial place of Harold I (died c. 940), first king of Norway.

Hau·ki·ve·si, Lake \ˈhau̇-kē-ˌve-sē\. Large lake, SE Finland.

Haul·bow·line \hȯl-ˈbō-lən\. Small island, Cork Harbour, SE co. Cork, SW Ireland; Irish naval base.

Hau·ra·ki Gulf \hau̇-ˈrä-kē\. Large bay, inlet of Pacific Ocean, on N coast of North I., New Zealand; in SW has inlet, Waitemata Harbor, on which Auckland is situated.

Hauran. See HAWRĀN.

Hauran, Wadi. See ḤAWRĀN, WĀDĪ.

Hau·sa states \ˈhau̇-sə, -zə\ *or* **Hau·sa·land** \-ˌland\. Region in Africa N of the Niger and Benue rivers, now corresponding to N Nigeria; chief town Kano; inhabited by the Hausa people. Conquered early 19th cent. by Fulani; became part of Protectorate of Nigeria early 20th cent.

Haus·ruck Mountains \ˈhau̇s-ˌru̇k\. Range, Austria, S of the Danube; highest peak Göbelsberg 2625 ft. (800 m.).

Haute–Corse \ˌōt-ˈkȯrs\. Department of France, on Corsica. See table at FRANCE.

Haute–Ga·ronne \ˌōt-gȧ-ˈrȯn\. Department of S France. See table at FRANCE.

Haute–Loire \ˌōt-ˈlwär\. Department of S cen. France. See table at FRANCE.

Haute–Marne \ˌōt-ˈmärn\. Department of NE France. See table at FRANCE.

Haute–Nor·man·die \ˌōt-ˌnȯr-mä^{n}-ˈdē\. Region of N France, on the English Channel. See table at FRANCE.

Hautes–Alpes \ˌōt-ˈzalp\. Department of SE France. See table at FRANCE.

Haute–Saône \ˌōt-ˈsōn\. Department of E France. See table at FRANCE.

Haute–Sa·voie \ˌōt-sȧ-ˈvwȧ\. Department of E France. See table at FRANCE.

Hautes Fagnes. See HOHE VENN MOUNTAINS.

Hautes–Py·ré·nées \ˌōt-ˌpē-rā-ˈnā\. Department of SW France. See table at FRANCE.

Haute–Vienne \ˌōt-ˈvyen\. Department of W cen. France. See table at FRANCE.

Haut–Rhin \ō-ˈre^{n}\. Department of NE France. See table at FRANCE.

Hauts–de–Seine \ˌō-də-ˈsān, -ˈsen\. Department of N France. See table at FRANCE.

Haut–Za·ïre \ˈō-zä-ˈir\; *formerly* **Ori·en·tale** \ˌȯr-ē-ä^{n}-ˈtäl\. Administrative region of NE Democratic Rep. of the Congo. See table at ZAIRE.

Ha·vana \hə-ˈva-nə\. **1.** City, ⊗ of Mason co., cen. Illinois, on Illinois River 38 mi. (61 km.) SW of Peoria; pop. (1990c) 3610.

2. *or Span.* **La Ha·ba·na** \ˌlä-ä-ˈbä-nä\. Seaport, ✱ of Cuba, on NW coast of Cuba, 90 mi. (145 km.) SSW of Key West, Florida; pop. (1990e) 2,096,054; constitutes a province of Cuba; largest city of the West Indies; harbor (ab. 3 mi. by 1.5 mi. or 5 km. by 2 km.), one of best in Western Hemisphere, its entrance through narrow channel having Morro Castle (begun 1589) and lighthouse on E and La Punta Fortress in old city on W; old city or commercial section on peninsula bet. harbor and ocean, new city, largely residential, on hills to W and S; railroad center; exports sugar, tobacco, cigars, coffee; textile mills; prior to 1961 tourism a major source of revenue; La Fuerza fortification (mid-16th cent.); cathedral (1704); Palace of the Captains General (late 18th cent.); Univ. of Havana (1728); fine squares and drives, esp. the Prado boulevard and the Malecón along N shore.

History: Founded by Spanish conquistador Diego Velásquez 1515; moved to present location 1519; became ✱ of Cuba 1592; chief naval station of Spain in New World and suffered esp. in 16th cent. in wars bet. Spain and England; captured by English 1762, restored 1763; since 1700 its history the same generally as that of Cuba (*q.v.*); its outer harbor scene of blowing up of U.S. battleship *Maine* Feb. 15, 1898, immediate cause of Spanish-American War.

Ha·van·nah \hə-ˈvä-nə\. Village on N coast of Efate I., Vanuatu, SW Pacific Ocean; good harbor.

Hav·ant \ˈha-vənt\. Town, Hampshire, S England, NE of Portsmouth; pop. (1991p) 117,400.

Hav·a·su, Lake \ˈha-və-ˌsü, hə-ˈvä-sü\. Lake on Arizona-California boundary created by a dam across the Colorado River.

Ha·vel \ˈhäf-ᵊl\. River, NE Germany; flows S out of Mecklenburg to Spandau, where it is joined by the Spree, and on into Elbe River; 212 mi. (341 km.) long.

Have·lock \ˈhav-ˌläk, -lək\. **1.** Former city, Lancaster co., SE Nebraska, now part of Lincoln.
2. Town, Craven co., SE North Carolina, 16 mi. (26 km.) SSE of New Bern; pop. (1990c) 20,268.

Havelock Island. See RITCHIE'S ARCHIPELAGO.

Hav·er·ford \ˈhav-ər-fərd\. **1.** Township, Delaware co., SE Pennsylvania; pop. (1990c) 49,848; residential.
2. Residential community in Lower Merion township, Montgomery co., SE Pennsylvania, NW of Philadelphia; settled 1680s; Haverford Coll. (1833).

Hav·er·ford·west \ˌha-vər-fərd-ˈwest\. Seaport, Dyfed co., SW Wales; pop. (1981p) 9936; ruins of 12th cent. castle and of 13th cent. Augustinian priory.

Ha·ver·hill \ˈhā-və-rəl\. **1.** City, Essex co., NE corner of Massachusetts, on Merrimack River 15 mi. (24 km.) NE of Lowell; pop. (1990c) 51,418; shoes, electrical products; Northern Essex Community Coll. (1961); birthplace of poet John Greenleaf Whittier 1807.
2. Town, Grafton co., W New Hampshire, on Connecticut River 22 mi. (35 km.) SSW of Littleton; pop. (1990c) 4164; chartered 1763.
3. Town, Suffolk, E England; pop. (1981p) 17,146.

Ha·ver·ing \ˈhā-və-riŋ\. A borough of Greater London, SE England. See table at LONDON 4.

Hav·er·straw \ˈha-vər-ˌstrȯ\. Village, Rockland co., SE New York, on W shore of Hudson River 32 mi. (51 km.) N of New York City; pop. (1990c) 9438.

Ha·ví·řov \ˈhä-vēr-ˌzhȯf\. Town, E Czech Republic, E of Ostrava; pop. (1991p) 86,267.

Hav·líč·kův Brod \ˈhäv-lēch-ˌküv-ˈbrȯt\; *formerly* **Ně·mec·ký Brod** \ˈnye-met-skē\ *or Ger.* **Deutsch–Brod** \ˈdȯich-ˈbrōt\. City, cen. Czech Republic, 60 mi. (97 km.) SE of Prague; pop. (1989c) 25,294.

Hav·re \ˈha-vər\. City, ⊗ of Hill co., N Montana, 108 mi. (174 km.) NE of Great Falls; pop. (1990c) 10,201; ships livestock, wheat; Northern Montana Coll. (1913).

Havre, Le *or* **Havre.** See LE HAVRE.

Ha·vre–Au·bert \ˌȧ-vrō-ˈber\. Chief village of Magdalen Is., Quebec, Canada, on Amherst I.; pop. (1991c) 3502.

Hav·re de Grace \ˌha-vər-də-ˈgras, -ˈgrās\. City, Harford co., NE Maryland, at mouth of Susquehanna River; pop. (1990c) 8952.

Haw \ˈhȯ\. River, N cen. North Carolina; formed by forks uniting in Alamance co., flows SE and unites with Deep River to form Cape Fear River; ab. 130 mi. (210 km.) long.

Ha·waii \hə-ˈwä-yē, -ˈwä-ˌē, -ˈvä-, -ˈwȯ-\. **1.** Largest of the Hawaiian Is. (see HAWAII 2), southernmost large island of the group, constituting a county of the state of Hawaii; 4021 sq. mi. (10,414 sq. km.); pop. (1990c) 120,317; ⊗ Hilo; top of a gigantic submarine mountain; contains four volcanic mountains: Mauna Kea, Hualalai, Mauna Loa, and Kilauea (the last two in Hawaii Volcanoes National Park).
2. *also* **Ha·wai·ian Islands** \-yən\; *formerly* **Sand·wich Islands** \ˈsand-wich\. A state of U.S.A.; chain of volcanic and coral islands in N cen. Pacific Ocean, comprising eight major and 114 minor islands; 2090 mi. (3363 km.) WSW of San Francisco; 47th state in area, 6471 sq. mi. (16,760 sq. km.); 41st state in population, (1990c) 1,108,229; ✻ Honolulu (on Oahu I.) is by far the state's largest settlement; admitted to Union 1959 as 50th state, incl. entire chain except Midway Is. See table of states at UNITED STATES.
Nickname: Aloha State.
State flower: Red hibiscus.
Motto: Ua Mau Ke Ea O Ka Aina I Ka Pono (The Life of the Land is Perpetuated in Righteousness).
Highest point: Mauna Kea 13,796 ft. (4205 m.) on Hawaii I.
Chief economic activities: Sugarcane production, food processing, tourism, military bases.
Political divisions: Divided into the following four counties (for pronunciation of their names, see their individual entries):

NAME	AREA[1] (sq. mi.)	AREA[1] (sq. km.)	POP. (1990c)	CO. SEAT
Hawaii	4,021	10,414	120,317	Hilo
Honolulu[2]	598	1,549	836,231	Honolulu
Kalawao	14	36	130	
Kauai	623	1,614	51,177	Lihue
Maui	1,173	3,038	100,374	Wailuku

[1] Area = land area.
[2] Includes the uninhabited islands of the archipelago (such as Kaula, Kure, Necker, French Frigate Shoal, and Gardner Pinnacles).

History: Original settlers came from the Marquesas Is. c. 400 A.D.; groups from Tahiti arrived c. 900–1000 A.D.; first European encounter 1778 with English Capt. James Cook who named it the Sandwich Is. and was killed here 1779; most of island group united under rule (1795–1819) of King Kamehameha I; frequented by American whalers from early 19th cent.; first visited by Christian missionaries from New England 1820; recognized as independent by U.S., Great Britain, and France 1840s; secured reciprocity treaty with U.S. 1875; Queen Liliuokalani overthrown and provisional government estab. with U.S. assistance 1893; declared republic 1894; annexed to U.S. by joint resolution 1898; estab. as U.S. territory 1900; scene of Japanese attack on Pearl Harbor Dec. 7, 1941; admitted as a state Aug. 21, 1959.
3. County in Hawaii. See HAWAII 1 and table at HAWAII 2.

Hawaiian Gardens. City, Los Angeles co., SW California, 12 mi. (19 km.) SE of the city of Los Angeles; pop. (1990c) 13,639.

Hawaii Volcanoes National Park. See UNITED STATES, *National Parks.*

Ha·wal·li \hə-ˈwä-lē\. Town, Kuwait, ab. 5 mi. (8 km.) SE of the seaport of Kuwait; pop. (1985c) 145,215.

Ha·wa·ra \hə-ˈwär-ə\. Archaeological site, SE of Birket Qārūn, Lower Egypt; tomb of Amenemhet III of XIIth dynasty, and of ruins of the labyrinth, which was reported by Greek historian Herodotus.

Ha·war·den \ˈhā-ˌwȯrd-ᵊn\. City, Sioux co., NW Iowa, on Big Sioux River 35 mi. (56 km.) N of Sioux City; pop. (1990c) 2439.

Haw·ar·den \ˈhärd-ᵊn, ˈhȯ-ər-dən\. Parish, Clwyd co., N Wales, near Chester, England; site of Hawarden Castle, built 1752, residence of Prime Minister William E. Gladstone; St. Deniol's Library, founded by Gladstone; ruins of 14th cent. castle.

Hawash. See AWASH.

Hawd. See HAUD.

Ha·wea, Lake \ˈhä-wē-ə\. Lake, S cen. South I., New Zealand; 46 sq. mi. (119 sq. km.); 19 mi. (31 km.) long; max. depth 1285 ft. (392 m.).

Ha·we·ra \ˈhä-wə-rə\. Seaport, W North I., New Zealand, on South Taranaki Bight 120 mi. (193 km.) N of Wellington; pop. (1981c) 8400.

Hawes·ville \ˈhȯz-ˌvil\. City, ⊗ of Hancock co., NW cen. Kentucky; pop. (1990c) 998.

Hawes Water \ˈhȯz\. Lake in Lake District, NW England, in Westmorland 5 mi. (8 km.) N of Kendal; 2.5 mi. (4 km.) long; max. depth 103 ft. (31 m.); provides part of Manchester water supply.

Ha·wi \ˈhä-wē\. Unincorporated settlement, Hawaii co., Hawaii, near Upolu Point on N coast of Hawaii I.; pop. (1990c) 924.

Ha·wick \ˈhȯ-ik\. Burgh, Borders region, SE Scotland, on the Teviot River 40 mi. (64 km.) NE of Dumfries; pop. (1981p) 16,333; manufactures wool textiles.

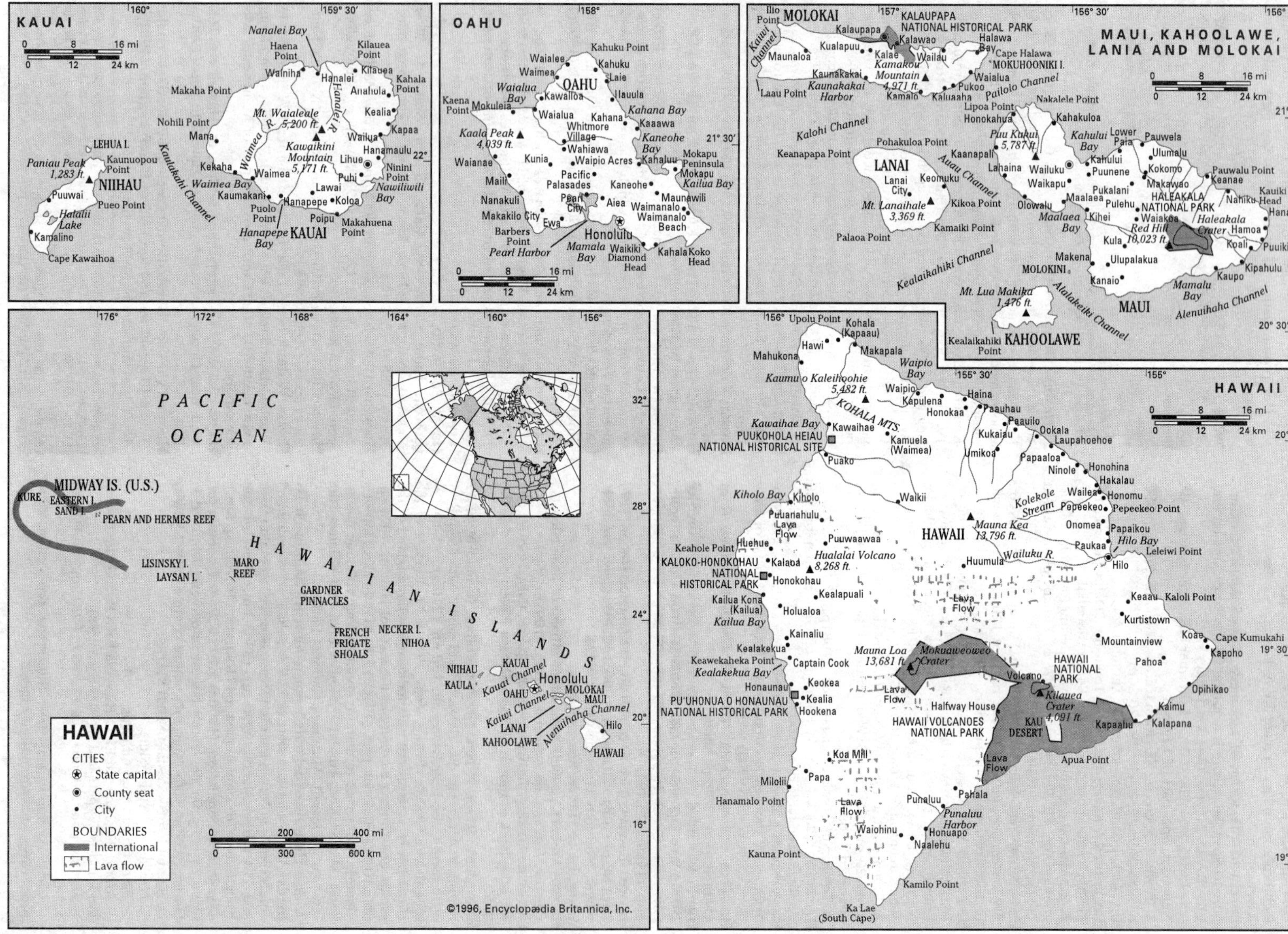
KAUAI
NIIHAU
OAHU
Honolulu
MAUI, KAHOOLAWE, LANIA AND MOLOKAI
MOLOKAI
LANAI
MAUI
KAHOOLAWE
PACIFIC OCEAN
MIDWAY IS. (U.S.)
HAWAIIAN ISLANDS
HAWAII
HAWAII VOLCANOES NATIONAL PARK
HAWAII
CITIES
State capital
County seat
City
BOUNDARIES
International
Lava flow
©1996, Encyclopædia Britannica, Inc.

Hawk Channel \ˈhȯk\. Channel, Atlantic Ocean, bet. Florida Keys (S end of Florida) and offshore coral reefs to the E and S.

Hawke Bay \ˈhȯk\. Large inlet of South Pacific Ocean on E cen. coast of North I., New Zealand; has city of Napier on SW shore.

Hawkes·bury \ˈhȯks-ˌber-ē, -bə-rē\. **1.** River, E New South Wales, SE Australia; flows NE and E to Pacific Ocean N of Sydney; 293 mi. (471 km.) long; navigable for small boats for ab. 70 mi. (115 km.).
2. Town, Prescott and Russell co., SE Ontario, Canada, on Ottawa River 54 mi. (87 km.) ENE of Ottawa; pop. (1991c) 9706.
3. City, E New South Wales, Australia; pop. (1991c) 51,319.

Haw·kins \ˈhȯ-kinz\. **1.** County in NE Tennessee. See table at TENNESSEE.
2. City, Wood co., NE Texas, ESE of Quitman; pop. (1990c) 1309; Jarvis Christian Coll. (1912).

Haw·kins·ville \ˈhȯ-kinz-ˌvil\. City, ⊗ of Pulaski co., S cen. Georgia, 38 mi. (61 km.) SSE of Macon; pop. (1990c) 3527.

Hawks·bill Mountain \ˈhȯks-ˌbil\. Peak in the Blue Ridge, Page co., N Virginia; ab. 4050 ft. (1235 m.); highest point in Shenandoah National Park.

Ha·worth \ˈhȯ-ərth, ˈhȯ-ˌwərth, ˈhau̇-ərth\. **1.** Borough, Bergen co., NE New Jersey, 9 mi. (14 km.) NE of Paterson; pop. (1990c) 3384.
2. Village in West Yorkshire, N England, WNW of Bradford; home of writers Charlotte, Emily, and Anne Brontë 19th cent., now a museum.

Hawr al Hab·bā·nī·yah \ˈhau̇r-ˌal-ˌha-ˌbä-ˈnē-yə\ *or Eng.* **Lake Habbaniyah** \ˌha-bə-ˈnē-yə\. Lake along S bank of the Euphrates, cen. Iraq, 50 mi. (80 km.) W of Baghdad; 54 sq. mi. (140 sq. km.); former British airfield estab. near its N shore.

Hawr al Ḥammār. See ḤAMMĀR, HAWR AL.

Haw·rān *also* **Hau·ran** \hau̇-ˈrän\. Plateau region in S Syria, S of Damascus and E of Jordan River; fertile. In Greco-Roman period a part of it known as Auranitis (*q.v.*).

Ḥaw·rān, Wā·dī *also* **Wa·di Hau·ran** \ˈwä-dē-hau̇-ˈrän\. River (*wadi*) in Syrian Desert, W Iraq; flows ENE to the Euphrates near Khan Baghdadi; ab. 240 mi. (385 km.) long.

Hawtah, al–. See LAḤIJ.

Ḥawṭah, Al. See AL ḤAWṬAH.

Haw·thorn \ˈhȯ-ˌthȯrn\. Municipality, S Victoria, SE Australia, E suburb of Melbourne; pop. (1991c) 30,006.

Haw·thorn·den \ˈhȯ-ˌthȯrn-dən\. Estate, 8 mi. (13 km.) SE of Edinburgh, Lothian region, Scotland; home of poet William Drummond (1585–1649).

Haw·thorne \ˈhȯ-ˌthȯrn\. **1.** Residential city, Los Angeles co., SW California, 5 mi. (8 km.) S of the city of Los Angeles; pop. (1990c) 71,349.
2. Village, ⊗ of Mineral co., SW Nevada, on S end of Walker Lake; pop. (1990c) 4162.
3. Borough, Passaic co., N New Jersey, 2 mi. (3 km.) NNE of Paterson; pop. (1990c) 17,084.

Hay \ˈhā\. **1.** Town, S New South Wales, SE Australia, on Murrumbidgee River 230 mi. (370 km.) WNW of Canberra; pop. (1991c) 3808; railroad terminus in sheep-raising region.
2. River, NW Canada; rises in NE British Columbia, flows E and N through NW Alberta to SW Great Slave Lake; 530 mi. (853 km.) long; its valley contains highway from point where it turns N in Alberta to the lake.

Hay·ange \ā-ˈyäⁿzh\. Commune, Moselle dept., NE France, 16 mi. (26 km.) N of Metz; an historically notable ironworking city.

Hayasdan. See ARMENIA 2.

Hayasui Strait. See BUNGO STRAIT.

Hay Canyon Butte. Isolated peak, Fall River co., SW corner of South Dakota; 3440 ft. (1049 m.).

Hay·den \ˈhād-ᵊn\. City, Kootenai co., Idaho, in Panhandle, N of Coeur d'Alene; pop. (1990c) 3744.

Hayden's Ferry. See TEMPE.

Hay·dock \ˈhā-ˌdäk\. Town, Merseyside, NW England, 15 mi. (24 km.) ENE of Liverpool; pop. (1981p) 16,584.

Haye–du–Puits, La. See LA HAYE-DU-PUITS.

Hayes \ˈhāz\. **1.** County in S Nebraska. See table at NEBRASKA.
2. River, E Manitoba, Canada; rises in chain of lakes and flows NE to Hudson Bay at York Factory; 300 mi. (483 km.) long.

Hayes, Mount. Mountain, E Alaska, at E end of Alaska Range, 63°37′N, 146°43′W; 13,832 ft. (4216 m.).

Hayes Center. Village, ⊗ of Hayes co., S Nebraska; pop. (1990c) 259.

Hayes Peninsula. Large projection of land, NW Greenland, bet. Baffin Bay on S and Kane Basin on N; Cape York its SW point, Qaanaag its chief settlement; largely covered with glaciers.

Hayes·ville \ˈhāz-ˌvil\. Town, ⊗ of Clay co., SW North Carolina; pop. (1990c) 279.

Haynau. See CHOJNÓW.

Haynes·ville \ˈhānz-ˌvil, -vəl\. Town, Claiborne parish, N Louisiana, 48 mi. (77 km.) NE of Shreveport; pop. (1990c) 2854.

Hayne·ville \ˈhān-vil, -vəl\. Town, ⊗ of Lowndes co., S cen. Alabama; pop. (1990c) 969.

Hay River. **1.** River, Canada. See HAY 2.
2. Town, S Northwest Territories, Canada, on S shore of Great Slave Lake; pop. (1991c) 3206.

Hays \ˈhāz\. **1.** County in S cen. Texas. See table at TEXAS.
2. City, ⊗ of Ellis co., cen. Kansas, 48 mi. (77 km.) NW of Great Bend; pop. (1990c) 17,767; oil fields; Fort Hays State Univ. (1902).

Hay·stack, Mount \hā-ˌstak\. Peak in Adirondack Mts., Essex co., NE New York; 4960 ft. (1512 m.).

Haystack Butte. Peak in Glacier National Park, NW Montana; 7405 ft. (2257 m.).

Haystack Mountain. Peak, S Windham co., SE Vermont; 3420 ft. (1042 m.).

Haystack Peak. Mountain in the Sierra Nevada, in Yosemite National Park, cen. California; ab. 10,000 ft. (3050 m.).

Hays·ville \ˈhāz-ˌvil\. City, Sedgwick co., S cen. Kansas, S of Wichita; pop. (1990c) 8364.

Hay·ti \ˈhā-ˌtī\. **1.** City, Pemiscot co., SE corner of Missouri, 5 mi. (8 km.) NW of Caruthersville; pop. (1990c) 3280.
2. Town, ⊗ of Hamlin co., E South Dakota; pop. (1990c) 372.

Hay·ward \ˈhā-wərd\. **1.** City, Alameda co., W California, 5 mi. (8 km.) E of San Francisco Bay; pop. (1990c) 111,498; California State Univ., Hayward (1957), Chabot Coll. (1961); city founded 1854.
2. City, ⊗ of Sawyer co., NW Wisconsin, 38 mi. (61 km.) N of Rice Lake (city); pop. (1990c) 1897.

Hay·wood \ˈhā-ˌwu̇d\. Name of counties in two states of the U.S. See tables at NORTH CAROLINA and TENNESSEE.

Hā·zār·ān, Kūh–e– \ˌkü-hē-hä-ˈzär-än\. Peak, Kermān prov., SE Iran; 14,500 ft. (4420 m.).

Haz·ard \ˈha-zərd\. City, ⊗ of Perry co., SE Kentucky, 53 mi. (85 km.) NE of Middlesborough; pop. (1990c) 5416; natural gas, coal.

Haz·ard·ville \ˈha-zərd-ˌvil\. Subdivision of town of Enfield, Connecticut. See ENFIELD 1.

Ha·za·ri·bag *or* **Ha·za·ri·bagh** \hə-ˈzär-i-ˌbäg\. Town, cen. Bihar, NE India, 210 mi. (338 km.) WNW of Calcutta; pop. (1991p) 97,712.

Hazaribagh National Park. National park, Bihar, NE India; 150 sq. mi. (389 sq. km.); wildlife refuge (bear, leopard, tiger); estab. 1955.

Ha·ze·brouck \äz-ˈbrük\. Commune, Nord dept., N France, 24 mi. (39 km.) WNW of Lille.

Ha·zel Crest \ˈhā-zəl\. Village, Cook co., NE Illinois, NNW of Chicago Heights; pop. (1990c) 13,334.

Hazel Park. City, Oakland co., SE Michigan, N of Detroit; pop. (1990c) 20,051

Ha·zel·ton \ˈhā-zəl-tən\. Village, N cen. British Columbia, W Canada, on Bulkley River at its junction with Skeena River; pop. (1991c) 339.

Hazelton Peak. Mountain, W Johnson co., N Wyoming; 10,552 ft. (3216 m.).

Ha·zel·wood \ˈhā-zəl-ˌwu̇d\. Village, St. Louis co., E Missouri, NW of the city of St. Louis; pop. (1990c) 15,324.

Ha·zle·hurst \ˈhā-zəl-ˌhərst\. **1.** City, ⊗ of Jeff Davis co., SE cen. Georgia, 48 mi. (77 km.) NNW of Waycross; pop. (1990c) 4202.
2. City, ⊗ of Copiah co., SW Mississippi, 32 mi. (51 km.) SSW of Jackson; pop. (1990c) 4221.

Ha·zle·ton \ˈhā-zəl-tən\. City, Luzerne co., E Pennsylvania, 20 mi. (32 km.) S of Wilkes-Barre; pop. (1990c) 24,730; textiles, shoes, steel products; Pennsylvania State Univ.–Hazleton campus (1934).

HaZofim, Har. See SCOPUS, MOUNT.

Head·land \ˈhed-lənd\. City, Henry co., SE Alabama, 10 mi. (16 km.) N of Dothan; pop. (1990c) 3266; founded 1817.

Healds·burg \ˈhēldz-ˌbərg\. City, Sonoma co., W California, 14 mi. (23 km.) NNW of Santa Rosa; pop. (1990c) 9469; founded 1852.

Heald·ton \ˈhēld-tən\. Town, Carter co., S Oklahoma, 22 mi. (35 km.) W of Ardmore; pop. (1990c) 2872.

Hea·nor \ˈhē-nər, ˈhā-\. Town, Derbyshire, N cen. England, 10 mi. (16 km.) WNW of Nottingham; pop. (1981p) 24,655.

Heard \ˈhərd\. County in W Georgia. See table at GEORGIA.

Heard Island. Island in S Indian Ocean, ab. 310 mi. (500 km.) SE of Kerguelen I., 53°10′S, 74°35′E; contains highest point in Australian territory (ab. 9000 ft. or 2750 m.); discovered by British 1833; came under Australian control 1947; together with the McDonald Is. (53°02′S, 72°36′E) constitutes the Australian external territory **Heard and McDonald Is.** \mək-ˈdän-ᵊld\ (total area 113 sq. mi. or 293 sq. km.).

Hearne \ˈhərn\. City, Robertson co., E cen. Texas, 18 mi. (29 km.) NNW of Bryan; pop. (1990c) 5132.

Hearst \ˈhərst\. Town, Cochrane dist., SE Ontario, Canada; pop. (1991c) 6079.

Hearst Island. Island in Weddell Sea, Antarctica, off E coast of Antarctic Penin.; at ab. 69°25′S, 62°10′W; ab. 42 mi. (68 km.) long, ab. 12 mi. (19 km.) wide; highest point 1200 ft. (366 m.).

Heart \ˈhärt\. River, SW North Dakota; rises in S Billings co., flows E into Missouri River opp. Bismarck; ab. 200 mi. (320 km.) long.

Heart Lake. Lake in Yellowstone National Park, NW Wyoming; S of Yellowstone Lake.

Heart's Con·tent \ˈhärts-kən-ˈtent\. Town, SE Newfoundland, Canada, on E shore of Trinity Bay 35 mi. (56 km.) WNW of St. John's; pop. (1991c) 567; terminus of several transatlantic cables.

Heath \ˈhēth\. **1.** City, Licking co., cen. Ohio, 30 mi. (48 km.) E of Columbus; pop. (1990c) 7231.
2. River forming part of boundary bet. Peru and Bolivia; flows N to Madre de Dios River.

Heath Point. E tip of Anticosti I., at mouth of St. Lawrence River, E Canada.

Heaths·ville \ˈhēths-ˌvil\. Village, ⊗ of Northumberland co., E Virginia.

Heave·ner \ˈhēv-nər\. City, Le Flore co., E Oklahoma, 13 mi. (21 km.) S of Poteau; pop. (1990c) 2601.

Heav·ens Peak \ˈhe-vənz\. Mountain in Glacier National Park, NW Montana; 9008 ft. (2746 m.).

Heb·bron·ville \ˈhe-brən-ˌvil\. Town, ⊗ of Jim Hogg co., S Texas, 50 mi. (80 km.) ESE of Laredo; pop. (1990c) 4465.

Heb·burn \ˈhe-bərn\. Town, Tyne and Wear, N England, on Tyne River 7 mi. (11 km.) E of Newcastle upon Tyne; pop. (1981p) 22,103; chemicals; shipbuilding; engineering works.

He·bei \ˈhə-ˈbā\ *or W.-G.* **Ho·peh** *also* **Ho·pei** \ˈhō-ˈbā\; *formerly* **Chih·li** \ˈjə̇-ˈlē, ˈjər-\. Province, NE China, bounded on NE by Liaoning, on SE by Bo Hai and by Shandong prov., on S by Henan, on W by Shanxi, and on NW by Nei Monggol (Inner Mongolia), with Beijing munic. forming an enclave in the center, and Tianjin munic. forming an enclave on Bo Hai; ✻ Shijiazhuang; mostly a level plain; contains part of the Great Wall and part of the Grand Canal (Da Yun-he). Produces coal, iron ore, and cotton. For centuries chief defense area against Mongols and Manchus to the N. Chief cities: Shijiazhuang, Tangshan, Handan. See table at CHINA.

He·ber City \ˈhē-bər\. City, ⊗ of Wasatch co., N cen. Utah, 30 mi. (48 km.) SE of Salt Lake City; pop. (1990c) 4782.

Heber Springs. City, ⊗ of Cleburne co., N cen. Arkansas, 50 mi. (80 km.) NNE of Little Rock; pop. (1990c) 5628.

Heb·gen Dam \ˈheb-gən\. Dam across Madison River, S Gallatin co., S Montana; forming **Hebgen Lake** 21 mi. (34 km.) long.

Heb·ri·des \ˈhe-brə-ˌdēz\ *or* **Western Isles** *also* **Western Islands;** *anc.* **Ebu·dae** \i-ˈbyü-dē\ *or* **He·bu·dae** \hi-\. Islands in the Atlantic Ocean W of Scotland; 2900 sq. mi. (7511 sq. km.); pop. (1991c) 30,660; divided by the Little Minch Strait into two groups: **Outer Hebrides** *or* **Long Island,** principal islands Lewis with Harris, North Uist, South Uist, and Barra; **Inner Hebrides,** principal islands Skye, Mull, and Islay. Scene of frequent incursions of Norse settlers from 8th cent. A.D.; ceded by Norway to Scotland in 1266.

Hebrides, Sea of the *also* **Gulf of the Hebrides.** Body of water off NW coast of Scotland, bet. S part of Outer Hebrides and the N part of Inner Hebrides.

He·bron \ˈhē-brən\. **1.** Town, Tolland co., N Connecticut, 17 mi. (27 km.) SE of Hartford; pop. (1990c) 7079.
2. Town, Porter co., NW Indiana; pop. (1990c) 3183.
3. City, ⊗ of Thayer co., S Nebraska, 47 mi. (76 km.) W of Beatrice; pop. (1990c) 1765.
4. *or Arab.* **Al–Kha·līl** \ˌȧl-kȧ-ˈlēl\; *anc.* **Kir·jath–Ar·ba** \ˈkər-jath-ˈär-bə, ˌkir-\. Town, Jordan, in region occupied by Israel 1967; 20 mi. (32 km.) SSW of Jerusalem; pop. (1987e) 79,087; leather tanning.
History: Sacred city of Judaism and Islam as home of patriarch Abraham and site of his burial place with wife Sarah at **Cave of Mach·pe·lah** \mak-ˈpē-lə\; home and ✻ of King David for seven and a half years; captured by Jewish patriot Judas Maccabaeus. Under Roman rule as part of Judea; taken by Arabs c. 635; held by Crusaders c. 1100–1260; part of mandated Palestine 1923–48; site of Arab riots 1929; in area annexed by Jordan 1950; part of West Bank (*q.v.*) from 1967; scene of terrorist attack on Palestinians 1994; under Palestinian authority since 1997.

Heb·ros \ˈe-ˌvrös\. See *Évros* in table at GREECE.

Hebrus. See MARITSA.

Hebudae. See HEBRIDES.

Hec·ate Strait \ˈhe-kət\. Channel bet. the Queen Charlotte Is. and mainland of W British Columbia, Canada, connecting Dixon Entrance with Queen Charlotte Sound; 35 to 80 mi. (56 to 129 km.) wide.

Hec·a·tom·py·los \ˌhe-kə-ˈtäm-pə-ˌläs\. Ancient city, for a time ✻ of kingdom of Parthia, at foot of S slope of E Elburz Mts.; center of ancient highways, hence, its name (literally, *Gk.* "hundred-gated"); probably located near modern Dāmghān, NW Khorāsān prov., NE Iran.

Hech·ing·en \ˈhe-kiŋ-ən\. Commune, cen. Baden-Württemberg, Germany, 25 mi. (40 km.) SSW of Stuttgart; pop. (1992e) 17,573; textiles, wood products; Hohenzollern castle (rebuilt 1850–56), church (1779–83).

Heck·mond·wike \ˈheck-mənd-ˌwīk\. Town, West Yorkshire, N England, SW of Leeds; pop. (1981p) 9738; carpets.

Hecla. See HEKLA.

Hec·la and Gri·per Bay \ˈhe-klə … ˈgrī-pər\. Bay, Melville I., Arctic Archipelago, Canada; 75°40′N, 111°W.

Hecla Island. Island in S Lake Winnipeg, SE Manitoba, S Canada.

Hedemarken. See HEDMARK.

Hedge·hope Hill \ˈhe-jəp\. Peak in Cheviot Hills along border bet. England and Scotland; 2348 ft. (716 m.).

Hedjaz. See HEJAZ.

Hed·mark \ˈhed-ˌmärk, ˈhād-\; *formerly* **He·de·mar·ken** \ˈhā-də-ˌmär-kən\. County of SE Norway. See table at NORWAY.

Hed·on \ˈhed-ᵊn\. Town, Humberside, N England, ab. 5 mi. (8 km.) E of Hull; pop. (1981p) 4525; in 13th cent. an important port; notable church of St. Augustine.

Hed·wig Village \'hed-wig\. City, Harris co., SE Texas, surrounded by Houston; pop. (1990c) 2616.

Heems·kerk \'hāms-ˌkerk\. Commune, North Holland prov., Netherlands; pop. (1981e) 31,753.

Heem·ste·de \'hām-ˌstā-də\. Commune, North Holland prov., W Netherlands, S suburb of Haarlem; pop. (1992e) 26,598.

Hee·ren·veen \'her-ən-ˌvān\. Commune, Friesland prov., N Netherlands, 17 mi. (27 km.) SSE of Leeuwarden; pop. (1992e) 38,649; bicycles.

Heer·len \'her-lə\. Commune, Limburg prov., SE Netherlands, just NE of Maastricht 5 mi. (8 km.) from German border; pop. (1992e) 95,001; chemicals.

He·fei \'hə-'fā\ *or W.-G.* **Ho–fei** \'hō-'fā\; *formerly* **Lu·chow** \'lü-'chaü\. City, ✻ of Anhui prov., E China; pop. (1990c) 733,278; chemicals, steel, textiles.

Hef·lin \'he-flin\. Town, ⊗ of Cleburne co., NE Alabama; pop. (1990c) 2906; settled 1883.

He·gang \'hə-'gäŋ\ *or W.-G.* **Ho–kang** \'hō-'gäŋ\. Town, Heilongjiang prov., NE China, ab. 40 mi. (64 km.) N of Jiamusi.

Hegoumenitsa. See IGOUMENÍTSA.

Heian–kyo. See KYŌTO.

Hei·de \'hī-də\ *also* **Heide in Hol·stein** \-in-'hōl-ˌstīn, -ˌstēn\. City, Schleswig-Holstein, Germany, 28 mi. (45 km.) SW of the city of Schleswig; pop. (1980c) 21,104.

Hei·del·berg \'hīd-ᵊl-ˌbərg, *Ger.* -ˌberk\. **1.** Borough, Allegheny co., SW Pennsylvania, 3 mi. (4.8 km.) WSW of Pittsburgh; pop. (1990c) 1238.
2. Town, Gauteng prov., NE Rep. of South Africa, 30 mi. (48 km.) ESE of Johannesburg.
3. City, Baden-Württemberg, Germany, on Neckar River 11 mi. (18 km.) ESE of Mannheim; pop. (1992e) 139,392; electrical equipment, metal goods; tourism; university (1386); ruins of Heidelberg Castle (13th–17th cents.); first mentioned 1196; ✻ of the Palatinate until 1720; center of German Calvinism in 16th cent. (*Heidelberg Catechism* 1563); passed to Baden 1803; site of U.S. military headquarters in Europe since 1948.
4. City, Victoria, Australia, a NE suburb of Melbourne; pop. (1991c) 60,468.

Hei·de·nau \'hīd-ᵊn-ˌaü\. City, Saxony, E Germany, SE suburb of Dresden on Elbe River; pop. (1981c) 20,067; founded 1920.

Hei·den·heim \'hīd-ᵊn-ˌhīm\. City, Baden-Württemberg, Germany, 41 mi. (66 km.) NW of Augsburg; pop. (1992e) 51,012; partly ruined 16th cent. castle (Hellenstein); manufactures machinery, textiles; place where St. Walburga died 779.

Heihe. See AIHUI.

Hei·ho \'hā-'hə\. **1.** Former province (1932–45), N Manchukuo; 42,388 sq. mi. (109,785 sq. km.).
2. Town, N Manchuria. See AIHUI.

Heijo. See P'YŎNGYANG.

Heil·bron \'hīl-ˌbrän\. Town, N Free State, E cen. Rep. of South Africa, 73 mi. (117 km.) S of Johannesburg.

Heil·bronn \'hīl-ˌbrän, hīl-'brȯn\. City, Baden-Württemberg, Germany, on Neckar River 27 mi. (43 km.) N of Stuttgart; pop. (1992e) 117,427; chemicals, paper, wine; residence of Carolingian princes 8th cent.; became free imperial city 1281; passed to Württemberg 1802; severely damaged during WWII.

Hei·lig·en·haus \'hī-li-gən-ˌhaůs\. City, North Rhine-Westphalia, Germany, 9 mi. (14 km.) NE of Düsseldorf; pop. (1980c) 29,661.

Heilong. See AMUR.

Hei·long·jiang \'hā-'lȯŋ-'jyäŋ\ *or W.-G.* **Hei·lung·kiang** \'hā-'lůŋ-'jyäŋ\. Province, NE China, in N part bordering on Amur (Heilong) River; ✻ Harbin; grain, sugar beets, timber; coal, gold; under Japanese control 1932–45; border with Russia has long been scene of periodic military incidents. See table at CHINA.

Heilsberg. See LIDZBARK WARMIŃSKI.

Hei–lung. See AMUR.

Heilungkiang. See HEILONGJIANG.

Hei·maey \'hā-ˌmī\. Volcanic island off S coast of Iceland; largest of Vestmannaeyjar group.

He·jaz *also* **He·djaz** \he-'jaz, hi-\ *or Arab.* **Al–Hi·jaz** \ˌal-hē-'jȧz\. W region of Saudi Arabia, extending along Red Sea coast, bounded on the N by Jordan, on E by Nejd, on S by Asir, and on W by Red Sea; 134,600 sq. mi. (348,614 sq. km.); NW coast extends along Gulf of Aqaba. Its coastal plain generally desolate; on its E edge is mountain range (highest point in N 7000 ft. or 2134 m.) with inland basins that have little drainage; most fertile part in S around Mecca and Medina. Chief products dates, millet, wheat. Ports include Jidda, Yanbu‘ al Baḩr, and Al Wajh.
History: Seat of Mecca and Medina (*qq.v.*), original centers of Islam; as province of Arabia, fell under Egyptian domination 1258; became Ottoman dependency after conquest of Egypt 1517; restored to order 1811–20 under Muḥammad ‘Ali Pasha, viceroy of Egypt, after Wahhabi revolt; resisted extension of railroad by Turks before WWI; revolted and proclaimed independence under King Ḥusayn ibn ‘Alī 1916; Ibn Sa‘ūd proclaimed king 1926; united with Nejd 1926 as dual kingdom which became Saudi Arabia (*q.v.*) 1932.

Hek·la *or* **Hec·la** \'he-klä\. Volcano in SW Iceland; 4747 ft. (1447 m.); largest crater ab. 1.25 mi. (2 km.) in circumference and 200 to 300 ft. (60 to 90 m.) deep; several eruptions recorded since 12th cent. incl. one Aug. 17, 1980.

He·kou *or W.-G.* **Ho–k'ou** \'hə-'kō\. **1.** *or* **Jiu·san·shui** *or W.-G.* **Chiu–san–shui** \'jyü-'sän-'shwē\; *formerly* **Sam·shui** \'säm-'shwē\. Walled town and port, cen. Guangdong prov., SE China, on N bank of Xi River at its junction with the Bei ab. 27 mi. (43 km.) W of Guangzhou; opened as treaty port 1897.
2. *mostly earlier* **Ho·kow** \'hə-'kō\. Frontier town, SE Yunnan prov., S China, on Yuan River opp. Lao Cai, Vietnam.

He·lan Shan *or W.-G.* **Ho–lan Shan** \'hə-'län-'shän\ *also* **A–la Shan** \'ä-'lä\. Mountain range, E Ningxia Huizu, N China, W of Huang River; highest peak ab. 12,000 ft. (3660 m.).

Helder, Den. See DEN HELDER.

Hel·der·berg Mountains \'hel-dər-ˌbərg\. Range of hills in Albany and Schoharie cos., E New York; ab. 1000 ft. (300 m.) high.

Hel·e·na \'he-lə-nə\. **1.** City, ⊗ of Phillips co., E Arkansas, on Mississippi River 88 mi. (142 km.) ENE of Pine Bluff; pop. (1990c) 7491; river port and railroad terminus; Phillips County Community Coll. (1965); scene of Civil War battle July 4, 1863 won by Union forces; incorp. 1833.
2. City, ✻ of Montana and ⊗ of Lewis and Clark co., W cen. Montana, 48 mi. (77 km.) NNE of Butte; pop. (1990c) 24,569; alt. 4155 ft. (1266 m.); paints; Carroll Coll. (1909); city founded 1864 after gold was discovered at Last Chance Gulch; incorp. as city 1881; became ✻ of territory of Montana 1875, and undisputed ✻ of the state 1894.

Hel·ens·burgh \'he-lənz-ˌbər-ə\. Coastal burgh, Strathclyde region, W cen. Scotland, on N shore of Firth of Clyde; pop. (1981p) 16,478; resort.

Hel·ford \'hel-fərd\. Small river in S Cornwall, England; flows S and E to English Channel; 10 mi. (16 km.) long; marks N limit of the Lizard.

Hel·go·land \'hel-gō-ˌland\ *or Eng.* **Hel·i·go·land** \'he-li-gō-\. Island in North Sea off W coast of Schleswig-Holstein, N Germany, 28 mi. (45 km.) from nearest mainland; 0.25 sq. mi. (0.6 sq. km.); pop. (1980c) 2166; resort; attached to North Frisian Is. and a part of Schleswig-Holstein state. Held by dukes of Schleswig–Holstein from 1402; passed to Danes 1714; seized by British 1807; formally ceded to British 1814; ceded to Germany 1890; became naval base; fortifications destroyed after WWI, but rebuilt and used in WWII; under British control 1945–52; fortifications again destroyed 1947; returned to West Germany 1952.

Hel·go·länd·er Bucht \ˈhel-gō-ˌlen-dər-ˈbu̇kt\ *or Eng.* **Hel·i·go·land Bight** \ˈhe-li-gō-ˌland\. Arm of the North Sea extending S and E of the island of Helgoland.

Hel·i·ce \ˈhe-lə-sē\. Ancient city, one of chief cities of Achaea, N Peloponnese, S Greece, on shore of Gulf of Corinth, near Aigion; noted for its sanctuary of Poseidon; destroyed 4th cent. B.C. by earthquake.

Hel·i·con \ˈhe-lə-ˌkän, -kən\ *or Gk.* **Eli·kón** \ˌe-lē-ˈkön\. Mountain, E cen. Greece, near Gulf of Corinth; 5738 ft. (1749 m.); was in SW part of ancient Boeotia on border of Phocis; supposed by ancient Greeks to be the home of the Muses; on it were the fountains of Aganippe and Hippocrene, supposed sources of poetic inspiration.

Heligoland. See HELGOLAND.

Heligoland Bight. See HELGOLÄNDER BUCHT.

He·li·op·o·lis \ˌhē-lē-ˈä-pə-lis\. **1.** *bib.* **On** \ˈän\. Ancient holy city in Lower Egypt; its ruins lie 6 mi. (10 km.) NE of Cairo; site of temple of the sun god, Ra, which later became repository for historical records; one obelisk remains at the site, two others from the site are known as Cleopatra's Needles and are now located at the Thames Embankment, London, and Central Park, New York City.

2. Village, Lebanon. See BAALBEK.

Hellas. See GREECE.

Hel·lemmes–Lille \e-ˌlem-ˈlēl\. Commune, Nord dept., N France, E suburb of Lille.

Hel·len·doorn \ˈhe-lən-ˌdȯrn\. Commune, Overijssel prov., E Netherlands, 17 mi. (27 km.) SE of Zwolle; pop. (1981e) 33,363; textile manufactures.

Hel·ler·town \ˈhe-lər-ˌtau̇n\. Borough, Northampton co., E Pennsylvania, 8 mi. (13 km.) ESE of Allentown; pop. (1990c) 5662.

Hellespont *or* **Hellespontus.** See DARDANELLES.

Hell·fire Pass \ˈhel-ˌfīr\. See HALFAYA PASS.

Hell Gate \ˈhel\. A narrow part of the East River, New York City, New York, bet. Long Island and Manhattan I., and also bet. Ward's I. and Long Island and bet. Ward's I. and Manhattan I.; made safe for navigation by removal, begun mid-19th cent., of rock reefs and by dredging; channel 200 ft. (61 m.) wide at narrowest part, 26 ft. (8 m.) deep; spanned by the Hell Gate Bridge (railroad, completed 1917) and the Triborough Bridge (highway, completed 1936).

Hel·lín \ā-ˈyēn\. Commune, Albacete prov., SE Spain, 35 mi. (56 km.) SSE of the commune of Albacete; pop. (1991c) 24,246.

Hells Canyon \ˈhelz\ *also* **Grand Canyon of the Snake** \ˈsnāk\. Canyon of the Snake River on Idaho-Oregon border; 40 mi. (64 km.) long; at max. depth 8032 ft. (2448 m.), the deepest canyon in U.S.

Hel·mand *or* **Hel·mund** \ˈhel-mənd\; *anc.* **Et·y·man·der** \ˌe-tə-ˈman-dər\. River, SW Afghanistan; 870 mi. (1400 km.) long; flows SW and W into **Lake Helmand** (*Pers.* **Dar·yā·cheh–ye Sī·stān** \ˌdär-yä-ˈchā-yə-si-ˈstän\), swampy region on border bet. Iran and Afghanistan. See GAWD-I-ZIRREH.

Helmantica. See SALAMANCA 3.

Hel·mond \ˈhel-ˌmȯnt\. Commune, North Brabant prov., S Netherlands, 9 mi. (14 km.) ENE of Eindhoven; pop. (1992e) 70,574; food processing; castle, built 1402.

Helm·stedt \ˈhelm-ˌshtet\. City, Lower Saxony, Germany, 21 mi. (34 km.) E of Brunswick; pop. (1992e) 27,072; brickworks; 13th cent. church; city rights confirmed 1228; seat of university 1576–1810.

Helmund. See HELMAND.

Hel Peninsula \ˈhel\. Spit of land, Gdańsk prov., N Poland, on W side of Gulf of Danzig; ab. 22 mi. (35 km.) long.

Hel·per \ˈhel-pər\. City, Carbon co., E cen. Utah, on Price River 7 mi. (11 km.) N of Price; pop. (1990c) 2148; named for locomotives used to pull trains over a summit there.

Helsingborg. See HÄLSINGBORG.

Hel·sing·ør \ˌhel-siŋ-ˈœr\ *or Eng.* **El·si·nore** \ˈel-sə-ˌnōr\. Seaport, Frederiksborg co., N Sjælland I., Denmark; pop. (1989e) 56,754; shipbuilding; brewing; site of Kronborg Castle (1574–85), famous as scene of English dramatist William Shakespeare's *Hamlet.*

Hel·sin·ki \ˈhel-ˌsiŋ-kē, hel-ˈ\ *or Swed.* **Hel·sing·fors** \ˈhel-siŋ-ˌfȯrs\. Seaport, ✻ of Finland and ✻ of Uusimaa prov., S Finland, on Gulf of Finland on a peninsula surrounded by islands and protected by fortifications at Suomenlinna (*q.v.*); pop. (1989c) 490,629; chemicals, clothing, metal goods, foodstuffs; Univ. of Helsinki (transferred from Turku 1828), technical university (1849, university status 1908); Lutheran cathedral (completed 1852), Russian Orthodox cathedral.

History: Founded N of present site by King Gustavus I Vasa of Sweden 1550; removed to present site 1640; fortified 1748; with Finland (*q.v.*) passed to Russia 1809; made Finnish ✻ instead of Turku 1812; damaged in bombings by U.S.S.R. 1939–40; site of Summer Olympic Games 1952; scene of Conference on Security and Cooperation in Europe 1975, resulting in Helsinki Accords.

Hel·ston \ˈhel-stən\. Town, Cornwall, SW England, 11 mi. (18 km.) WSW of Falmouth; pop. (1981p) 10,741; formerly a tin-mining center.

Hel·vel·lyn \hel-ˈve-lən\. Mountain in SE Cumberland, NW England, in Lake District 9 mi. (14 km.) SE of Keswick; 3118 ft. (950 m.).

Helvetia *or* **Helvetica.** See SWITZERLAND 1.

Hel·vick Head \ˈhel-vik\. Cape on S coast of Ireland, S of entrance to Dungarvan Harbour.

He·ma·theia \ˌē-mä-ˈthē-ä\. Department of Central Macedonia, Greece. See table at GREECE.

Hem·el Hemp·stead \ˈhe-məl-ˈhemp-stəd\. Town, Hertfordshire, SE England, near Gade River 23 mi. (37 km.) NW of London; pop. (1981p) 77,695; engineering.

He·mer \ˈhā-mər\. City, North Rhine-Westphalia, Germany, 35 mi. (56 km.) E of Essen; pop. (1980c) 32,745. First mentioned 1072.

Hem·et \ˈhe-mət\. City, Riverside co., SE California, 31 mi. (50 km.) SE of San Bernardino; pop. (1990c) 36,094; incorp. 1910.

Hem·lock Lake \ˈhem-ˌläk\. Lake, W New York, bet. Ontario and Livingston cos.; ab. 7 mi. (11 km.) long, 1 mi. (2 km.) wide; outlet from N end joins outlet from Honeoye Lake and flows into Genesee River.

Hemp·field \ˈhemp-ˌfēld\. Township, Westmoreland co., SW Pennsylvania, SE of Pittsburgh; pop. (1990c) 42,609.

Hemp·hill \ˈhemp-ˌhil\. **1.** County in NW Texas. See table at TEXAS.

2. City, ⊗ of Sabine co., E Texas; pop. (1990c) 1182.

Hemp·stead \ˈhemp-ˌsted, -stəd\. **1.** County in SW Arkansas. See table at ARKANSAS.

2. Residential village, Nassau co., SE New York, on Long Island 20 mi. (32 km.) E of New York City; pop. (1990c) 49,453; Hofstra Univ. (1935); village settled c. 1643.

3. Town, ⊗ of Waller co., SE Texas, 20 mi. (32 km.) E of Brenham; pop. (1990c) 3551.

Hems·worth \ˈhemz-ˌwərth\. Town, West Yorkshire, N England, SE of Wakefield; pop. (1981p) 14,138.

He·nan *or W.-G.* **Ho·nan** \ˈhə-ˈnän\. Province, E cen. China, bounded on N by Shanxi, Hebei, and Shandong provs., on E by Jiangsu and Anhui, on S by Hubei, and on W by Shaanxi; ✻ Zhengzhou; one of China's most densely populated provinces. Rivers include the Huang, forming NW boundary and flowing SE, the Luo in NW, and the upper course of the Huai. In the SW are the most easterly spurs of the Kunlun Shan with highest point at 7800 ft. (2375 m.). Has rich agricultural regions; wheat, cotton, tobacco. Chief cities include Zhengzhou, Anyang, Xinxiang, and Jiaozuo. Region of earliest settlements in China from which its culture spread; capitals of ancient dynasties at Luoyang and Kaifeng (*qq.v.*). See table at CHINA.

He·na·res \ā-ˈnär-äs\. River, cen. Spain; flows SW into Jarama River 10 mi. (16 km.) ESE of Madrid; ab. 75 mi. (120 km.) long.

Hen·daye \äⁿ-ˈdī\. Commune, Pyrénées-Atlantiques dept., SW corner of France near Spanish border, on Bidassoa River 13 mi. (21 km.) SW of Biarritz.

Hen·der·son \ˈhen-dər-sən\. **1.** Name of counties in five states of the U.S. See tables at ILLINOIS, KENTUCKY, NORTH CAROLINA, TENNESSEE, and TEXAS.

2. Commercial city, ⊗ of Henderson co., NW Kentucky, on Ohio River 10 mi. (16 km.) S of Evansville, Indiana; pop. (1990c) 25,945; oil, coal. Founded 1797; incorp. as city 1867.
3. City, Clark co., SE corner of Nevada, SE of Las Vegas; pop. (1990c) 64,942; titanium plant; incorp. 1953.
4. City, ⊗ of Vance co., N North Carolina, 40 mi. (64 km.) NNE of Raleigh; pop. (1990c) 15,655; tobacco market; manufactures textiles; incorp. 1841.
5. City, ⊗ of Chester co., W Tennessee, 17 mi. (27 km.) SW of Jackson; pop. (1990c) 4760; Freed-Hardeman Univ. (1869).
6. City, ⊗ of Rusk co., E Texas, 31 mi. (56 km.) ESE of Tyler; pop. (1990c) 11,139.

Henderson Island. Uninhabited British coral island in S Pacific Ocean, SE of Tuamotu Archipelago, 24°22′S, 128°16′W; ab. 120 mi. (190 km.) NE of Pitcairn I.; 12 sq. mi. (31 sq. km.); attached to Pitcairn I. colony.

Henderson Lake. Lake, W Essex co., NE New York; ab. 2.5 mi. (4 km.) long; a source of Hudson River.

Hen·der·son·ville \ˈhen-dər-sən-ˌvil\. **1.** City, ⊗ of Henderson co., SW North Carolina, in Blue Ridge 21 mi. (34 km.) SSE of Asheville; pop. (1990c) 7284; summer and health resort.
2. City, Sumner co., Tennessee, 10 mi. (16 km.) NE of Nashville; pop. (1990c) 32,188; pop. exploded in 1970s.

Hen·dricks \ˈhen-driks\. County in cen. Indiana. See table at INDIANA.

Hen·dry \ˈhen-drē\. County in S Florida. See table at FLORIDA.

Hen Egg Mountain \ˈhen-ˈeg,-ˈāg\. Peak, W Brewster co., W Texas; 5002 ft. (1525 m.).

Henegouwen. See HAINAUT.

Hengchow. See HENGYANG.

Heng·e·lo \ˈheŋ-ə-ˌlō\. Commune, Overijssel prov., E Netherlands, near German border; pop. (1992e) 76,726; salt, textiles, electronic apparatus; brewing.

Heng·feng *or W.-G.* **Heng–feng** \ˈhəŋ-ˈfəŋ\. Town, NE Jiangxi prov., SE China, on railroad line E of Nanchang.

Heng Shan \ˈhəŋ-ˈshän\. Mountain, E cen. Hunan prov., China, N of Hengyang; 4232 ft. (1290 m.); site of several Buddhist temples.

Heng·yang *or W.-G.* **Heng–yang** \ˈhəŋ-ˈyäŋ\; *formerly* **Heng·chow** \-ˈjō\. Town, S cen. Hunan prov., SE cen. China, ab. 150 mi. (240 km.) S of Changsha; pop. (1990c) 487,148; important rail and river junction point; scene of severe fighting in WWII 1944.

Hé·nin–Beau·mont \ā-ˈneⁿ-bō-ˈmōⁿ\; *formerly* **Hénin–Lié·tard** \-lyā-ˈtär\. Commune, Pas-de-Calais dept., N France, 4 mi. (6 km.) N of Arras.

Hen·kel Mountain \ˈheŋ-kəl\. Peak in Glacier National Park, NW Montana; 8700 ft. (2650 m.).

Hen·ley \ˈhen-lē\ *or* **Henley–on–Thames.** Town, Oxfordshire, cen. England, 35 mi. (56 km.) W of London; scene of annual Henley Royal Regatta, estab. 1839.

Hen·lo·pen, Cape \hen-ˈlō-pən\. Cape on E coast of Sussex co., Delaware, at S of entrance to Delaware Bay.

Henna. See ENNA 2.

Hen·ne·bont \ˌen-ˈbōⁿ\. Commune, Morbihan dept., NW France, on Blavet River 6 mi. (10 km.) NE of Lorient; Gothic church (built 1513–30); famous in War of Breton Succession for its defense by French nobleman John of Montfort when besieged by Charles of Blois, duke of Brittany, 1342; much damaged in WWII 1944–45.

Hen·ne·pin \ˈhe-nə-pən\. **1.** County in SE cen. Minnesota. See table at MINNESOTA.
2. Village, ⊗ of Putnam co., N cen. Illinois; pop. (1990c) 1111.

Hen·ni·ker \ˈhe-ni-kər\. Town, Merrimack co., S cen. New Hampshire, W of Concord; pop. (1990c) 4151; New England Coll. (1946).

Hen·ri·co \hen-ˈrī-kō\. County in E cen. Virginia. See table at VIRGINIA.

Hen·ri·et·ta \ˌhen-rē-ˈe-tə\. Town, ⊗ of Clay co., N Texas, 19 mi. (31 km.) ESE of Wichita Falls; pop. (1990c) 2896.

Henrietta Ma·ria, Cape \mə-ˈrē-ə\. Cape, N coast of Ontario, Canada, at W of entrance to James Bay.

Hen·ri Pit·tier National Park \än-ˈrē-pē-ˈtyer\. National park, N Venezuela, along the Caribbean coast just W of Caracas; 413 sq. mi. (1070 sq. km.); estab. 1937; a biologically diverse area of coastal mountains.

Hen·ry \ˈhen-rē\. **1.** Name of counties in 10 states of the U.S. See tables at ALABAMA, GEORGIA, ILLINOIS, INDIANA, IOWA, KENTUCKY, MISSOURI, OHIO, TENNESSEE, VIRGINIA.
2. City, Marshall co., N cen. Illinois, on Illinois River 30 mi. (48 km.) N of Peoria; pop. (1990c) 2591.

Henry, Cape. Cape on E coast of Virginia in city of Virginia Beach, S of entrance to Chesapeake Bay, opp. Cape Charles; connected with Cape Charles by Chesapeake Bay Bridge Tunnel; Fort Story; lighthouse; landing place of first permanent English settlers 1607.

Henry, Mount. **1.** Peak in the Sierra Nevada, E Fresno co., S cen. California; 12,196 ft. (3717 m.).
2. Peak in Glacier National Park, NW Montana; 8870 ft. (2704 m.).

Hen·ry·et·ta \ˌhen-rē-ˈe-tə\. City, Okmulgee co., E cen. Oklahoma, 13 mi. (21 km.) S of Okmulgee; pop. (1990c) 5872.

Henry Mountains. Mountains, Garfield co., S Utah; highest peak Mt. Ellen 11,506 ft. (3507 m.).

Hens·low, Cape \ˈhenz-lō\. Cape, SE extremity of Guadalcanal, Solomon Is., W Pacific Ocean.

Hen·tiyn Nu·ruu \hen-ˈtēn-ˈnu̇r-ü\ *or* **Ken·tei Mountains** \ˈgen-ˈtā\. Mountain range, N Mongolia, NE of Ulaanbaatar, in part parallel with Russian border; highest peak 8494 ft. (2589 m.).

Hen·za·da \ˌhen-zə-ˈdä\. Town, Myanmar, on Irrawaddy River 75 mi. (121 km.) NNW of Yangon; pop. (1983c) 82,005; at head of Irrawaddy Delta; connected by rail with Bassein; center of rice and tobacco cultivation.

Hep·pen·heim \ˈhe-pən-ˌhīm\. Commune, SE Hesse, Germany, 18 mi. (29 km.) S of Darmstadt; pop. (1980c) 23,786; first mentioned 755.

Hepp·ner \ˈhep-nər\. City, ⊗ of Morrow co., N Oregon, 45 mi. (72 km.) WSW of Pendleton; pop. (1990c) 1412.

Heptanesus. See IONIAN ISLANDS.

Hep·tarchy, The \ˈhep-ˌtär-kē\. The seven kingdoms of Anglo-Saxon England in historical convention: Kent, Sussex, Wessex, Essex, Northumbria, East Anglia, Mercia (*qq.v*).

Her·a·clea \ˌher-ə-ˈklē-ə\. **1.** Ancient city, Lucania, Italy, near Gulf of Taranto; founded by Greeks from Tarentum (*mod.* Taranto); battle 280 B.C. in which Pyrrhus, king of Epirus, defeated the Romans but with heavy losses, hence, a "Pyrrhic victory."
2. Town, Turkey in Asia. See AYVALIK.

Heraclea Lyncestis. See BITOLA.

Heraclea Pontica. See EREĞLİ 2.

Her·a·cle·op·o·lis \ˌher-ə-klē-ˈä-pə-lis\. Ancient city in Egypt; ✱ under IXth and Xth (Heracleopolitan) dynasties (c. 2130–c. 1970 B.C.).

Heracleum. See IRÁKLION.

He·radhs·vötn \ˈher-äths-ˌvœt-ᵊn\. River, N Iceland, flowing N into Skaga Fjord.

Hē·rá·klei·on \ē-ˈrä-klē-ˌön, hi-ˈra-klē-ən\. See IRÁKLION 2.

Heraklion. See IRÁKLION.

Her·ald Island \ˈher-əld\. Small island belonging to Russia, in Chukchi Sea, Arctic Ocean, 40 mi. (64 km.) E of Wrangel I.

He·rāt \he-ˈrät, hə-\; *anc.* **Ar·ia** \ˈar-ē-ə, ə-ˈrī-ə\. City, NW Afghanistan, on the Harī River; pop. (1988e) 177,300; commercial center; carpets; ancient citadel; 15th cent. mosque; noted for style of miniature painting (15th cent.) and for handwoven carpets (16th–17th cents.).

History: An old city, for centuries on trade route from India to Persia, Mesopotamia, and Europe; controlled by Arabs from 660 A.D.; invaded by Mongols 13th cent.; taken by Turkic ruler Timur 1383; ✻ and cultural center of Persia 15th cent.; control alternated several times bet. Persia and Afghanistan; passed to Afghanistan 1863; occupied by Soviet troops 1980.

Hé·rault \ā-ˈrō\. **1.** River, S France; rises in Cévennes Mts., flows SSW into Gulf of Lion near Agde; 100 mi. (161 km.) long.

2. Department of S France. See table at FRANCE.

Her·bert Hoo·ver Lake \ˈhər-bərt-ˈhü-vər\. Small lake, New Guinea I., on border bet. Irian Jaya, Indonesia, and Papua New Guinea, W of Fly River.

Herbertshöhe. See KOKOPO.

Her·ceg·no·vi \ˈhert-seg-ˈnò-vē\ *or Ital.* **Ca·stel·nuo·vo** \käs-ˌtel-ˈnwō-vō\. Seaport, Montenegro, SW Yugoslavia, on N shore of Gulf of Kotor.

Hercegovina. See HERZEGOVINA.

Her·cu·la·ne·um \ˌhər-kyu̇-ˈlā-nē-əm\. Ancient city (now an archaeological site), Campania, Italy, on coast SE of Neapolis, at NW foot of Vesuvius; with Pompeii, just S of the mountain, destroyed by eruption of 79 A.D.

Her·cu·les \ˈhər-kyə-ˌlēz\. City, Contra Costa co., California, 15 mi. (23 km.) NE of Oakland; pop. (1990c) 16,829.

Hercules, Pillars of. See PILLARS OF HERCULES.

Herculeum, Fretum. See GIBRALTAR, STRAIT OF.

He·re·dia \ā-ˈrā-thyä\. **1.** Province of cen. Costa Rica. See table at COSTA RICA.

2. Town, its ✻, just NW of San José; pop. (1991e) 27,390.

Her·e·ford \ˈhər-fərd\. City, ⊗ of Deaf Smith co., NW Texas, 40 mi. (64 km.) SW of Amarillo; pop. (1990c) 14,745; cattle.

Her·e·ford \ˈher-i-fərd, *US also* ˈhər-fərd\. **1.** Former county, W England. See HEREFORDSHIRE.

2. Town, Hereford and Worcester, W England, on the Wye 47 mi. (76 km.) SW of Birmingham; pop. (1991p) 49,800; center of agricultural area; glass, furniture, nickel alloys; founded by West Saxons in 7th cent.; ⊗ of former Herefordshire; cathedral begun 11th cent.

Hereford and Worcester. Administrative county, W England, comprising most of former Herefordshire and Worcestershire. See table at ENGLAND.

Her·e·ford·shire \ˈher-i-fərd-ˌshir, -shər\ *or* **Hereford.** Former county, W England, on border of Wales; rivers Wye, Teme, Frome. See HEREFORD AND WORCESTER.

Hé·rens, Dent d' \ˈdäⁿ-dā-ˈräⁿ\. Peak in Pennine Alps, on Switzerland-Italy boundary; 13,715 ft. (4180 m.).

He·rent·hals *or* **He·rent·als** \ˈher-ənt-ˌhäls\. Commune, Antwerp prov., N Belgium, 18 mi. (29 km.) E of the city of Antwerp; pop. (1991c) 24,500.

Her·ford \ˈher-ˌfȯrt\. City, North Rhine-Westphalia, Germany, 43 mi. (69 km.) ENE of Münster; pop. (1992e) 64,732; carpets, furniture, chocolate.

Hé·ri·court \ˌer-ē-ˈkür\. Commune, Haute-Saône dept., E France, near Belfort; scene of battle 1871, in Franco-Prussian War, in which French Gen. Charles-Denis-Sauter Bourbaki failed to raise the siege of Belfort.

Her·ing·ton \ˈher-iŋ-tən\. City, Dickinson co., E cen. Kansas, 40 mi. (64 km.) ESE of Salina; pop. (1990c) 2685.

Heri Rud. See HARĪ.

He·ri·sau \ˈher-i-ˌzau̇\ *or Fr.* **Hé·ri·sau** \ā-rē-ˈzō\. Commune, ✻ of Appenzell Outer Rhodes demicanton, NE Switzerland, 5 mi. (8 km.) SW of St. Gall; pop. (1989c) 15,560; railroad junction; textiles (esp. cotton goods).

Héristal. See HERSTAL.

Her·it·age Range \ˈher-ə-tij\. Mountain range, Antarctica. See ELLSWORTH MOUNTAINS.

Her·ki·mer \ˈhər-kə-mər\. **1.** County in NE cen. New York. See table at NEW YORK.

2. Village, its ⊗, on Mohawk River 14 mi. (23 km.) ESE of Utica; pop. (1990c) 7945; forms single community with Mohawk, Ilion, and Frankfort across river; dairy products; Herkimer County Community Coll. (1966). Settled by Palatines c. 1725; raided in French and Indian War; site of Fort Dayton (1776), from which Gen. Nicholas Herkimer marched to battle of Oriskany 1777; attacked by Indians under Mohawk Chief Joseph Brant 1778.

Herlen. See KERULEN 1.

Herm \ˈhərm\. One of the Channel Is., United Kingdom, 3 mi. (5 km.) E of Guernsey; in Guernsey bailiwick; 0.5 sq. mi. (1.3 sq. km.); pop. (1991c) 113.

Her·mann \ˈhər-mən\. City, ⊗ of Gasconade co., E cen. Missouri, on Missouri River 44 mi. (71 km.) E of Jefferson City; pop. (1990c) 2754; settled 1837 by colonists sent out by German Settlement Society of Philadelphia, Pennsylvania.

Hermanos, Los. See LOS HERMANOS.

Her·man·town \ˈhər-mən-ˌtau̇n\. City, St. Louis co., NE Minnesota, just W of Duluth; pop. (1990c) 6761.

Her·man·us \hər-ˈma-nəs\. Town, Western Cape prov., SW Rep. of South Africa, 60 mi. (97 km.) ESE of Cape Town; sport fishing.

Her·mis·ton \ˈhər-mə-stən\. City, Umatilla co., NE Oregon, ab. 6 mi. (10 km.) S of the Columbia; pop. (1990c) 10,040.

Her·mit·age \ˈhər-mə-tij\. **1.** City, ⊗ of Hickory co., SW cen. Missouri; pop. (1990c) 512.

2. City, Mercer co., W Pennsylvania, NE of Youngstown, Ohio; pop. (1990c) 15,300.

Hermitage Bay. Inlet of Atlantic Ocean, S coast of Newfoundland, Canada; ab. 25 mi. (40 km.) long; has several long arms.

Her·mit Islands \ˈhər-mət\. See NORTHWESTERN ISLANDS.

Her·mon, Mount \ˈhər-mən\ *or Arab.* **Ja·bal ash–Shaykh** \ˈjá-bál-ásh-ˈshīk, -ˈshāk\. Mountain, on boundary bet. Lebanon and SW Syria 28 mi. (45 km.) WSW of Damascus, Syria; 9232 ft. (2814 m.); highest point in Anti-Lebanon Range; has snow-covered crest; the N limit of Israelite conquests; since 1967 Israeli-administered territory has extended to its S and W slopes; mentioned in the Bible (*Ps.* lxxxix. 12; cxxxiii. 3).

Her·mon·this \hər-ˈmän-thəs\. Ancient city in Upper Egypt, on W bank of the Nile near Thebes. Part has been archaeologically explored during 20th cent.

Hermopolis Magna. See AL-ASHMŪNEIN.

Hermopolis Parva. See DAMANHŪR.

Her·mo·sa \er-ˈmō-sä\. Municipality, NE Bataan prov., Luzon, Philippines, ab. 2 mi. (3 km.) from NW coast of Manila Bay; pop. (1980c) 25,672.

Her·mo·sa Beach \hər-ˈmō-sə\. Resort city, Los Angeles co., SW California, on Pacific Ocean 15 mi. (24 km.) SSW of the city of Los Angeles; pop. (1990c) 18,219.

Her·mo·sil·lo \ˌer-mō-ˈsē-yō\. Town, ✻ of Sonora state, NW Mexico, on Sonora River ab. 65 mi. (105 km.) from Gulf of California; munic. pop. (1990p) 449,472; in fruit-growing region; university (1938).

Hermoupolis. See ERMOÚPOLIS.

Hermus. See GEDİZ.

Her·nád \ˈher-ˌnäd\ *or in Slovakia* **Hor·nád** \ˈhȯr-\. River, cen. Europe, in Slovakia and Hungary; rises in E cen. Slovakia, flows E and S into the Sajó (tributary of the Tisza) in NE Hungary; 165 mi. (266 km.) long.

Her·nan·da·rias \ˌer-nän-ˈdär-yäs\; *formerly* **Ta·cu·ru·pu·cú** \ˌtäk-ə-ˌrü-pə-ˈkü\. Town, E Paraguay, on the Paraná River; pop. (1992p) 28,464; former ✻ of Alto Paraná dept.

Her·nan·do \hər-ˈnan-dō\. **1.** County on W coast of Florida Penin., Florida. See table at FLORIDA.

2. City, ⊗ of De Soto co., NW corner of Mississippi; pop. (1990c) 3125.

Hern·don \ˈhərn-dən\. Town, Fairfax co., NE Virginia, 20 mi. (32 km.) NW of Washington, D.C.; pop. (1990c) 16,139.

Her·ne \ˈher-nə\. City, North Rhine-Westphalia, Germany, in Ruhr Valley 33 mi. (53 km.) SSW of Münster; pop. (1992e) 179,137; coal mines; chemicals, iron and steel; chartered 1897.

Herne Bay \ˈhərn\. Town, Kent, SE England, on North Sea 53 mi. (85 km.) E of London; pop. (1981c) 26,827; resort.

Her·ning \ˈher-neŋ\. Commercial city, Ringkøbing co., W cen. Jutland, Denmark, E of the town of Ringkøbing; pop. (1989e) 56,376; machinery, textiles.

Hernösand. See HÄRNÖSAND.

He·ro·op·o·lis \ˌhē-rō-ˈä-pə-lis\. Ancient town on E edge of Nile Delta, N Egypt; probably identical with ancient Pithom; terminus of canal from Bubastis on the Nile and port at head of **Gulf of Heroopolis** (now Bitter Lakes and Gulf of Suez).

Her·re·ra \är-ˈrā-rä\. Province on the Azuero Penin., S Panama. See table at PANAMA.

Her·re·ro \är-ˈrā-rō\. Cape on E cen. coast of Yucatán Penin., SE Mexico, at S of entrance to Espíritu Santo Bay.

Herreroland. See DAMARALAND.

Her·rin \ˈher-in\. City, Williamson co., S Illinois, 5 mi. (8 km.) NE of Marion; pop. (1990c) 10,857; trading center in former coal-mining area; scene of a coal-miners' strike 1922 in which several people were killed.

Herrn·hut \ˈhern-ˌhüt\. Town, Saxony, E Germany, 18 mi. (29 km.) SE of Bautzen; seat of a persecuted colony of Moravians who settled here 1722 on estate of religious leader Graf Nikolaus Ludwig von Zinzendorf.

Her·schel \ˈhər-shəl\. Small island in NW Mackenzie Bay, off coast of N Yukon Terr., Canada.

Hersfeld. See BAD HERSFELD.

Her·shey \ˈhər-shē\. Unincorporated settlement, Dauphin co., SE cen. Pennsylvania, ab. 13 mi. (21 km.) E of Harrisburg; pop. (1990c) 11,860; privately developed as workers' community by Hershey Chocolate Corporation 1903.

Her·stal \ˈher-ˌstäl\ *or Fr.* **Hé·ris·tal** \ā-rē-ˈstȯl\. Commune, Liège prov., E Belgium; pop. (1992e) 36,500; electrical equipment, firearms; birthplace of Pépin II (Pépin of Herstal), a ruler of the Franks.

Herst·mon·ceux \ˌhərst-mən-ˈsyü, -ˈsü\ *or* **Hurst·mon·ceux** \ˌhərst-\. Village, S England, in East Sussex 9 mi. (14 km.) NE of Eastbourne; Royal Greenwich Observatory (now in Cambridge) operated here in 15th cent. castle bet. 1950s and 1990.

Her·ten \ˈhert-ᵊn\ *also* **Herten in West·fa·len** \ˌin-vest-ˈfä-lən\. Commune, North Rhine-Westphalia, Germany, 10 mi. (16 km.) N of Essen; pop. (1992e) 69,374; coal mining, manufacturing of machinery.

Hert·ford \ˈhərt-fərd\. **1.** County in NE North Carolina. See table at NORTH CAROLINA.
2. Town, and port of entry, ⊗ of Perquimans co., NE North Carolina, on arm of Albemarle Sound 17 mi. (27 km.) WSW of Elizabeth City; pop. (1990c) 2105.

Hert·ford \ˈhär-fərd *also* ˈhärt-\. **1.** County, SE England. See HERTFORDSHIRE.
2. Town, ⊗ of Hertfordshire, SE England, on the Lea 22 mi. (35 km.) N of London; pop. (1981p) 21,412; site of first English synod held 673 by Theodore of Tarsus, archbishop of Canterbury.

Hert·ford·shire \ˈhär-fərd-ˌshir, ˈhärt-, -shər\ *or* **Hertford** *or* **Herts** \ˈhärts, ˈhərts\. **1.** Former county, SE England.
2. Administrative county, SE England, approx. equivalent to the former county; rivers Lea, Colne; towns include Hertford, Watford, St. Albans, Hemel Hempstead. See table at ENGLAND.

Hertogenbosch, 's. See 'S HERTOGENBOSCH.

Hertseliya. See HERZLIYYA.

Her·vey Bay \ˈhər-vē\. **1.** Inlet of Pacific Ocean in SE Queensland, Australia, N of Brisbane, bet. Fraser I. and mainland.
2. City, SE Queensland, E Australia, on Hervey Bay (inlet); pop. (1993e) 32,941.

Her·ze·go·vi·na \ˌhert-sə-ˈgō-vē-nə, -gō-ˈvē-nə, ˌhərt-\ *or Serb.* **Her·ce·go·vi·na** \ˈhert-sä-ˈgō-vē-nä\. Region, a constituent part of the republic of Bosnia and Herzegovina. See BOSNIA AND HERZEGOVINA.

Her·zliy·ya *also* **Her·tsel·i·ya** \ˌhert-sə-ˈlē-ə\. Town, W Israel, on Mediterranean Sea, 35 mi. (56 km.) NW of Jerusalem; pop. (1992e) 80,200; residential; estab. 1924; named after Theodor Herzl, founder of political Zionism.

Hes·din \ā-ˈdeⁿ\. Town, Pas-de-Calais dept., N France, NE of Abbeville; founded 1554 by Charles V; birthplace of writer Abbé Prévost 1697.

Heshbon. See ḤISBĀN.

Hes·pe·ler \ˈhes-pə-lər\. Formerly separate community, Waterloo co., SE Ontario, Canada; now part of Cambridge (*q.v.*).

Hes·per·ia \he-ˈspir-ē-ə\. City, SW San Bernardino co., SE California, N of the city of San Bernardino; pop. (1990c) 50,418.

Hes·pe·rus Peak \ˈhes-pə-rəs\. Mountain, NE Montezuma co., SW Colorado; ab. 13,230 ft. (4030 m.); highest in La Plata Mts.

Hesse \ˈhes, ˈhe-sē\ *or Ger.* **Hes·sen** \ˈhes-ᵊn\. **1.** Region in SW Germany, comprising the state of Hesse and the former Prussian prov. of Hesse-Nassau.
2. Former state of Germany; 2969 sq. mi. (7690 sq. km.); ✻ Darmstadt; now part of German states of Hesse and Rhineland-Palatinate.
3. A state of Germany; ✻ Wiesbaden; electrical equipment, motor vehicles, chemicals, textiles.
History: (1) Medieval landgraviate expanded from original holdings W to the Rhine and S to the Main; 1567, according to will of Landgrave Philip I, divided among four sons, two of whom founded houses of Hesse-Darmstadt *or* Hesse and Hesse-Cassel. (2) **Hesse–Darm·stadt** \-ˈdärm-ˌshtät\ (*Ger.* **Hessen–Darmstadt**) inherited by George I in 1567, extended its territory and became grand duchy of Hesse in French Emperor Napoléon's Confederation of the Rhine 1806; joined Prussian customs union (*Zollverein*) 1828; in 1866, after supporting Austria in Austro-Prussian (Seven Weeks') War forced to cede N areas to Prussia; joined North German Confederation 1867; proclaimed republic 1918; following WWII partitioned bet. newly formed states of Hesse and Rhineland-Palatinate. (3) **Hesse–Cas·sel** \-ˈkäs-ᵊl\ (*Ger.* **Hessen–Kas·sel** \-ˈkä-səl\), came from line of William IV, eldest son of Landgrave Philip I; also called **Electoral Hesse** because it was the only state to remain an electorate after breakup of Holy Roman Empire 1806; part of kingdom of Westphalia 1807; restored as independent state 1815; joined Prussian customs union 1831; united with Prussia in 1866 as result of siding with Austria in Seven Weeks' War and became part of new prov. of Hesse-Nassau. (4) **Hesse–Nas·sau** \-ˈnä-ˌsau̇\ (*Ger.* **Hessen–Nassau**) formerly a Prussian province formed from territories annexed in 1866 incl. Hessen-Kassel, duchy of Nassau, free city of Frankfurt am Main, and after 1929, former republic of Waldeck; divided into two provinces 1944; reconstituted 1945 and united with E parts of Hesse-Darmstadt as West German state of Hesse. See table at GERMANY.

Hess·ton \ˈhes-tən\. City, Harvey co., SE cen. Kansas, NW of Newton; pop. (1990c) 3012.

Hest·mona \ˈhest-ˌmȯ-nə\. Small island in Norwegian Sea, off W coast of Norway.

Hetch Hetchy Reservoir \ˈhech-ˌhe-chē\. See *O'Shaughnessy Dam* at UNITED STATES, *Dams and Reservoirs* and TUOLUMNE 1.

Het·ting·er \ˈhe-tən-jər\. **1.** County in SW North Dakota. See table at NORTH DAKOTA.
2. City, ⊗ of Adams co., SW North Dakota; pop. (1990c) 1574.

Het·ton–le–Hole \ˈhet-ᵊn-lə-ˈhōl\. Town, Tyne and Wear, N England, 13 mi. (21 km.) SSE of Newcastle upon Tyne; pop. (1981p) 15,903.

Hett·stedt \ˈhet-ˌshtet\. City, Saxony-Anhalt, cen. Germany, 23 mi. (37 km.) NW of Halle; pop. (1981c) 20,845; was a major center of the East German copper industry.

Heumar. See PORZ AM RHEIN.

Heu·ne·burg \ˈhȯi-nə-ˌbu̇rk\. Archaeological site, E of Sigmaringen, Germany; Celtic fortified settlement dating from c. 600 B.C.; evidence of trade with Greeks of Massilia (now Marseille).

Heuvelton. See OGDENSBURG.

He·ves \ˈhe-vesh\. County of N Hungary. See table at HUNGARY.

Hev·ros \ˈe-ˌvrȯs\. See *Évros* in table at GREECE.

Hex·ham \ˈhek-səm\. Town, Northumberland, N England, on the Tyne 20 mi. (32 km.) W of Newcastle upon Tyne; pop. (1981p) 9630; present abbey church of St. Andrew dates from 12th cent.

Hex·ham·shire \-ˌshir, -shər\. District around Hexham, S Northumberland, N England.

Hey·burn \ˈhā-bərn\. City, Minidoka co., S Idaho, on Snake River; pop. (1990c) 2714.

Hey·wood \ˈhā-ˌwu̇d\. Town, Greater Manchester, NW England, 9 mi. (15 km.) NNW of Manchester; pop. (1981p) 30,672; textiles; engineering.

Hi·a·le·ah \ˌhī-ə-ˈlē-ə\. City, Miami-Dade co., SE Florida, 5 mi. (8 km.) N and W of Miami; pop. (1990c) 188,004; incorp. 1925; Hialeah Park race track.

Hialeah Gardens. City, Miami-Dade co., SE Florida, W of Hialeah; pop. (1990c) 7713.

Hi·a·was·see \ˌhī-ə-ˈwä-sē\. **1.** River, SE United States. See HIWASSEE.
2. Town, ⊗ of Towns co., N Georgia; pop. (1990c) 547.

Hi·a·wa·tha \ˌhī-ə-ˈwȯ-thə, -ˈwä-\. **1.** City, Linn co., E Iowa, just N of Cedar Rapids; pop. (1990c) 4986.
2. City, ⊗ of Brown co., NE Kansas, 28 mi. (45 km.) NW of Atchison; pop. (1990c) 3603.

Hib·bing \ˈhi-biŋ\. City, St. Louis co., NE Minnesota, 58 mi. (93 km.) NW of Duluth, in the Mesabi Range; pop. (1990c) 18,046; taconite deposits; Hibbing Community Coll. (1916); just N is one of world's largest open-pit mines.

Hibernia. See IRELAND.

Hibernicus, Oceanus. See IRISH SEA.

Hick·man \ˈhik-mən\. **1.** Name of counties in two states of the U.S. See tables at KENTUCKY and TENNESSEE.
2. City, ⊗ of Fulton co., SW corner of Kentucky, on Mississippi River; pop. (1990c) 2689.

Hick·o·ry \ˈhi-kə-rē\. **1.** County in SW cen. Missouri. See table at MISSOURI.
2. City, Catawba co., W cen. North Carolina, 25 mi. (40 km.) W of Statesville; pop. (1990c) 28,301; manufactures cordage, textiles, furniture, and formerly wagons; Lenoir-Rhyne Coll. (1891).

Hickory Hills. City, Cook co., NE Illinois, 7 mi. (11 km.) W of Chicago; pop. (1990c) 13,021.

Hicks·ville \ˈhiks-ˌvil\. **1.** Unincorporated settlement, Nassau co., SE New York, on Long Island NE of Mineola; pop. (1990c) 40,174.
2. Village, Defiance co., NW Ohio, 50 mi. (81 km.) NW of Lima; pop. (1990c) 3664.

Hi·da·ka–Sam·mya·ku \hē-ˈdä-kä-ˈsä-myä-ˌkü\ *or* **Hi·da·ka Mountains.** Range in S Hokkaidō, Japan; highest peak Horoshiri 6730 ft. (2051 m.).

Hi·dal·go \hi-ˈdal-gō\. **1.** Name of counties in two states of the U.S. See tables at NEW MEXICO and TEXAS.
2. City, Hidalgo co., S Texas, on the Rio Grande across from Mexico; pop. (1990c) 3292.
3. \ *or Span.* ē-ˈt͟häl-gō\. State of cen. Mexico. See table at MEXICO.

Hidalgo del Parral. See PARRAL.

Hiddekel. See TIGRIS.

Hi·ei–zan \hē-ˈā-ˌzän\. Mountain, Kyōto prefecture, W cen. Honshū, Japan, just N of the city of Kyōto and near SW shore of Lake Biwa; 2800 ft. (853 m.); site of monastery built by religious leader Saichō, early 9th cent.

Hiera. See VULCANO.

Hi·e·ra·kon·po·lis \ˌhī-ə-rə-ˈkän-pə-lis\. Ancient city of Upper Egypt, on left bank of Nile, S of Thebes; important archaeological site where palette (ceremonial carved slate) of Narmer (leader of Egypt c. 3100 B.C.) was found.

Hierápetra. See IERÁPETRA.

Hi·er·ap·o·lis \ˌhī-ə-ˈra-pə-lis\. Ancient city of Phrygia, Asia Minor, near Maeander (Menderes) River; center for worship of goddess Leto in ancient times.

Hierosolyma. See JERUSALEM 3.

Hier·ro \ˈyār-rō\ *also* **Fer·ro** \ˈfer-rō\. Westernmost of the Canary Is. (*q.v.*), in Santa Cruz de Tenerife prov., Spain; 78 mi. (126 km.) WSW of Tenerife I.; 107 sq. mi. (277 sq. km.); chief town Valverde; volcanic in origin; rocky, unfertile soil; warm springs; produces wines. Thought by ancient geographers to mark W limit of world and hence they reckoned longitude from it.

Hi·ga·shi·hi·ro·shi·ma \hē-ˈgä-shē-hē-ˈrō-shē-mä\. City, Hiroshima prefecture, SW Honshū, Japan; pop. (1990p) 94,206.

Hi·ga·shi·ku·ru·me \hē-ˈgä-shē-kü-ˈrü-mā\. City, Tokyo prefecture, SE cen. Honshū, Japan; pop. (1990p) 113,800.

Hi·ga·shi·ma·tsu·ya·ma \hē-ˈgä-shē-ˌmät-sü-ˈyä-mä\. City, Saitama prefecture, Honshū, Japan; pop. (1990p) 84,395.

Hi·ga·shi·mu·ra·ya·ma \hē-ˈgä-shē-ˌmü-rä-ˈyä-mä\. City, Tokyo prefecture, Honshū, Japan, 18 mi. (29 km.) NW of the city of Tokyo; pop. (1990p) 134,002.

Hi·ga·shi·ōsa·ka \hē-ˈgä-shē-ˈō-sä-kä\. City, Ōsaka prefecture, Honshū, Japan; pop. (1990p) 518,251.

Hi·ga·shi·ya·ma·to \hē-ˈgä-shē-yä-ˈmä-tō\. City, Tokyo prefecture, SE cen. Honshū, Japan; pop. (1990p) 75,124.

Hig·ga·num \ˈhi-gə-nəm\. Subdivision of town of Haddam, Connecticut. See HADDAM.

Hig·gins Lake \ˈhi-gənz\. Lake, N Roscommon co., N cen. Michigan; ab. 7 mi. (11 km.) long; has outlet into Houghton Lake to the S.

Hig·gins·ville \ˈhi-gənz-ˌvil\. City, Lafayette co., W Missouri, 39 mi. (61 km.) NW of Sedalia; pop. (1990c) 4693.

High Atlas. See ATLAS MOUNTAINS.

High Bridge. Borough, Hunterdon co., NW cen. New Jersey, 15 mi. (24 km.) E of Phillipsburg; pop. (1990c) 3886.

High·gate \ˈhī-ˌgāt\. Town, Franklin co., NW Vermont, near Canadian boundary; pop. (1990c) 3020; settled 1787.

High·gate \ˈhī-gət\. Part of Haringey, London, England, NE of Hampstead Heath in Hornsey. A number of well-known persons, among them the novelist George Eliot (Mary Ann Evans) and German political philosopher Karl Marx are buried in Highgate Cemetery.

High Island. Island in N Lake Michigan, NW of Beaver I.; part of Charlevoix co., NW Michigan.

High Knob. Peak, Wise co., SW Virginia; 4162 ft. (1269 m.).

High·land \ˈhī-lənd\. **1.** Name of counties in two states of the U.S. See tables at OHIO and VIRGINIA.
2. City, San Bernardino co., SE California; pop. (1990c) 34,439.
3. City, Madison co., SW Illinois, 27 mi. (43 km.) ESE of East St. Louis; pop. (1990c) 7525.
4. Town, Lake co., NW corner of Indiana, 7 mi. (11 km.) S of Lake Michigan; pop. (1990c) 23,696.
5. City, Utah co., N cen. Utah; pop. (1990c) 5002.
6. Administrative region, NW Scotland. See table at SCOTLAND.

Highland Beach. Coastal town, Palm Beach co., SE Florida, N of Boca Raton; pop. (1990c) 3209.

Highland Falls. Village, Orange co., SE New York, on Hudson River 5 mi. (8 km.) SSW of Newburgh; pop. (1990c) 3937; adjoins West Point.

Highland Heights. **1.** City, Campbell co., N Kentucky; pop. (1990c) 4223; Northern Kentucky Univ. (1968).
2. City, Cuyahoga co., N Ohio, 14 mi. (22 km.) NE of Cleveland; pop. (1990c) 6249.

Highland Lake. Lake in NE Litchfield co., NW Connecticut, W of Winsted.

Highland Park. **1.** City, Lake co., NE Illinois, on Lake Michigan 12 mi. (19 km.) N of Chicago; pop. (1990c) 30,575.
2. City, Wayne co., SE Michigan, entirely within city of Detroit; pop. (1990c) 20,121; tractors, automobiles.
3. Borough, Middlesex co., cen. New Jersey, on Raritan River 2 mi. (3 km.) E of New Brunswick; pop. (1990c) 13,279.
4. Town, Dallas co., NE Texas, entirely within the city of Dallas; pop. (1990c) 8739.

Highland Peak. Mountain, N cen. Lincoln co., E Nevada; 9395 ft. (2864 m.).

High·lands \ˈhī-ləndz\. **1.** County in cen. Florida Penin., Florida. See table at FLORIDA.
2. Borough, Monmouth co., E cen. New Jersey, on Sandy Hook Bay 17 mi. (27 km.) ESE of Perth Amboy; pop. (1990c) 4849; fishing village, summer resort; first U.S. Navy wireless station erected on nearby Monmouth Hills 1903.
3. Town, Orange co., SE New York; pop. (1990c) 13,667.

4. That portion of Scotland lying NW of a line drawn from Dumbarton to Stonehaven; term sometimes includes the islands of Arran, Bute, the Cumbraes, and the Hebrides, but excludes the Orkney Is., Shetland Is., Caithness, the flat coastal areas of Nairn, Elgin, Banff, and E Grampian. The area below the Dumbarton-Stonehaven line is known as **The Low·lands** \ˈlō-landz\.

Highlands of the Hudson. Hilly region on both sides of Hudson River in Rockland, Orange, Putnam, and Dutchess cos., SE New York.

Highland Village. City, Denton co., NE Texas, NNW of Dallas; pop. (1990c) 7027; pop. more than doubled in 1980s.

High·more \ˈhī-ˌmōr\. City, ⊗ of Hyde co., cen. South Dakota; pop. (1990c) 835.

High Peak. **1.** Mountain in the Catskill Mts., Greene co., SE New York; 3654 ft. (1114 m.).
2. Highest peak of Zambales Mts., in N cen. Zambales prov., Luzon, Philippines, ab. 17 mi. (27 km.) NE of Iba; 6683 ft. (2037 m.).

High Plains. The Great Plains esp. from Nebraska southward.

High Point. **1.** Elevation in N Sussex co., N New Jersey; 1803 ft. (550 m.); highest point in New Jersey, in High Point (State) Park; New Jersey War Memorial, stone tower 225 ft. (69 m.) high.
2. City, Guilford co., N cen. North Carolina, 14 mi. (23 km.) WSW of Greensboro; pop. (1990c) 69,496; in Piedmont upland belt; furniture-manufacturing center; hosiery; High Point Univ. (1924); city incorp. 1859.

High Rock Lake. Reservoir for waterpower in Yadkin River (*q.v.*) bet. Rowan and Davidson cos., cen. North Carolina; formed by **High Rock Dam.**

High Sierra. The Sierra Nevada in California. See SIERRA NEVADA.

High·spire \ˈhī-ˌspīr\. Borough, Dauphin co., SE cen. Pennsylvania, on Susquehanna River 7 mi. (11 km.) SE of Harrisburg; pop. (1990c) 2668.

High Springs. City, Alachua co., N Florida Penin., 22 mi. (35 km.) NW of Gainesville; pop. (1990c) 3144; founded 1885.

High Tatra Mountains. See TATRA MOUNTAINS.

High·tow·er Bald \ˈhī-ˌtau̇-ər-ˈbȯld\. Peak, Towns co., N Georgia; 4517 ft. (1377 m.).

Hights·town \ˈhīts-ˌtau̇n\. Borough, Mercer co., W cen. New Jersey, 13 mi. (21 km.) ENE of Trenton; pop. (1990c) 5126; The Peddie School (1864); borough founded 1721.

High Will·hays \ˈwi-lēz\. Highest point in Dartmoor, Devon, SW England; 2039 ft. (622 m.).

High·wood \ˈhī-ˌwu̇d\. City, Lake co., NE corner of Illinois, on Lake Michigan 12 mi. (19 km.) S of Waukegan; pop. (1990c) 5331.

High Wyc·ombe \hī-ˈwi-kəm\; *formerly* **Chep·ping Wyc·ombe** *or* **Chip·ping Wycombe** \ˈchi-piŋ\. Town, Buckinghamshire, SE cen. England, on the Wye 29 mi. (47 km.) WNW of London; pop. (1981p) 60,516; furniture, paper; printing works.

Higuera, La. Commune, cen. Chile. See CRUZ GRANDE.

Hi·güe·ro, Point \ē-ˈgwā-rō\ *also* **Point Ji·güe·ro** \hē-\. Cape at NW end of Puerto Rico, SW of Point Borinquén and on E side of Mona Passage.

Hi·güey \ē-ˈgwā\. Town, ✻ of La Altagracia prov., E Dominican Republic; pop. (1981p) 83,755.

Hii·u·maa \ˈhē-ə-mä\ *or Russ.* **Khi·u·ma** \ˈkē-ə-mə\ *or Swed.* **Dagö** \ˈdä-gœ̄\. Island in Baltic Sea off W coast of Estonia; 373 sq. mi. (966 sq. km.).

Ḥi·jā·rah, al *or* **al Ḥa·jā·rah** \ˌȧl-hə-ˈjä-rə\. Extensive desert region, S Iraq, S of the Euphrates. Sometimes considered as extending across border into Saudi Arabia.

Hijaz, Al–. See HEJAZ.

Hi·ko·ne \hē-ˈkō-nē\. Town in Shiga prefecture, W cen. Honshū, Japan, on E shore of Lake Biwa; pop. (1990p) 99,518; noted for its scenery and early 17th cent. castle; birthplace 1815 of statesman Ii Naosuke who signed Japan's first trade agreement with U.S. 1858.

Hi·ko Range *or* **Hy·ko Range** \ˈhī-kō\. Small range in cen. Lincoln co., E Nevada.

Hi·kue·ru \hē-ˈkwā-rü\. Island, cen. Tuamotu Archipelago, French Polynesia, S Pacific Ocean, 17°36′S, 142°37′W.

Hild·burg·hau·sen \ˈhilt-ˌbu̇rk-ˌhau̇z-ᵊn\. Town, Thuringia, cen. Germany, on Werra River SE of Meiningen; ✻ of a principality which was united to Saxe-Meiningen 1826; late 17th cent. ducal palace.

Hil·den \ˈhil-dən\. City, North Rhine-Westphalia, Germany, near Rhine River 7 mi. (11 km.) SE of Düsseldorf; pop. (1992e) 55,189; textiles.

Hil·des·heim \ˈhil-dəs-ˌhīm\. City, Lower Saxony, Germany, 18 mi. (29 km.) SSE of Hannover; pop. (1992e) 105,674; dairy and agricultural machinery; St. Michael's church and Hildesheim Cathedral, both orig. 11th cent.; city received charter 1300.

Hill \ˈhil\. Name of counties in two states of the U.S. See tables at MONTANA and TEXAS.

Hilla. See ḤILLAH, AL.

Hil·la·by, Mount \ˈhi-lə-bē\. Peak, N cen. Barbados; 1104 ft. (337 m.); highest peak in the country.

Ḥil·lah, Al \äl-ˈhi-lə\ *also* **Hil·la** \ˈhi-lə\. Town, cen. Iraq, near the Euphrates 58 mi. (93 km.) S of Baghdad; pop. (1985e) 215,249; nearby is site of ancient Babylon.

Hill City. City, ⊗ of Graham co., NW cen. Kansas; pop. (1990c) 1835.

Hill Country. Hilly area, cen. Texas, comprising the E edge of Edwards Plateau; extends to Austin on the E.

Hil·le·gom \ˈhi-lə-ˌk̲ȯm\. Commune, South Holland prov., SW Netherlands, 8 mi. (13 km.) S of Haarlem; pop. (1992e) 19,784.

Hil·le·rød \ˈhē-lə-ˌrœt̲h̲\. Town, ⊗ of Frederiksborg co., N Sjælland, Denmark, 19 mi. (31 km.) NW of Copenhagen; pop. (1989e) 33,434; museum; tourism.

Hil·lers, Mount \ˈhi-lərz\. Peak, E Garfield co., S Utah; 10,650 ft. (3246 m.).

Hill·gard, Mount \ˈhil-ˌgärd\. Peak, Sevier co., cen. Utah; 11,527 ft. (3513 m.).

Hil·liard \ˈhil-yərd\. City, Franklin co., cen. Ohio, NW of Columbus; pop. (1990c) 11,796.

Hil·ling·don \ˈhi-liŋ-dən\. A borough of Greater London, SE England. See table at LONDON 4.

Hill·man Peak \ˈhil-mən\. Mountain, W Klamath co., S Oregon; 8156 ft. (2486 m.); highest point on rim of Crater Lake.

Hills·boro \ˈhilz-ˌbər-ō\. **1.** City, ⊗ of Montgomery co., S cen. Illinois, 48 mi. (77 km.) SSE of Springfield; pop. (1990c) 4400.
2. City, Marion co., E cen. Kansas; pop. (1990c) 2704; Tabor Coll. (1908).
3. Town, ⊗ of Jefferson co., E Missouri; pop. (1990c) 1625.
4. City, ⊗ of Traill co., E North Dakota; pop. (1990c) 1488.
5. City, ⊗ of Highland co., S Ohio, 32 mi. (52 km.) WSW of Chillicothe; pop. (1990c) 6235.
6. City, ⊗ of Washington co., NW Oregon, 15 mi. (24 km.) W of Portland; pop. (1990c) 37,520; electronics; settled 1842.
7. City, ⊗ of Hill co., NE cen. Texas, 33 mi. (53 km.) N of Waco; pop. (1990c) 7072.

Hills·bor·ough \ˈhilz-ˌbər-ō\. **1.** River, W Florida; flows SW into Tampa Bay.
2. Name of counties in two states of the U.S. See tables at FLORIDA and NEW HAMPSHIRE.
3. Residential town, San Mateo co., W California, 10 mi. (16 km.) S of San Francisco; pop. (1990c) 10,667.
4. Town, Hillsborough co., S New Hampshire, 18 mi. (29 km.) WSW of Concord; pop. (1990c) 4498; birthplace of Franklin Pierce, 14th president of the U.S., 1804.
5. Town, ⊗ of Orange co., N North Carolina, 13 mi. (21 km.) WNW of Durham; pop. (1990c) 4263; meeting place of Provincial Congress 1775 and of general assemblies 1778, 1780, 1783, 1784; center of disturbances 1768–71 by the Regulators, a group of residents who organized to fight taxes and

---

\ə\ **abut** \ə\ matches \ᵊ\ kitten, Fr table \ər\ **further** \a\ **ash** \ā\ **ace** \ä\ **cot, cart** \ȧ\ Fr bac \au̇\ **out** \b̲\ Span Avila \ch\ **chin** \e\ **bet** \ē\ **easy** \g\ **go** \i\ **hit** \ī\ **ice** \j\ **job** \k̲\ Ger **ich, Buch** \ⁿ\ Fr vin \ŋ\ **sing** \ō\ **go** \ȯ\ **all** \ȯ\ **law** \œ\ Fr **bœuf** \œ̄\ Fr **feu** \ȯi\ **boy** \th\ **thin** \t̲h̲\ **this** \ü\ **loot** \u̇\ **foot** \ue\ Ger **füllen** \ue̅\ Fr **rue** \y\ **yet** \ʸ\ Fr digne \ˈdēnʸ\, nuit \ˈnwʸē\ \yü\ **few** \yu̇\ **fury** \zh\ **vision**

regulate government; occupied by British under Gen. Charles Cornwallis 1781; raided by Loyalists 1781.

Hillsborough Bay. Inlet of Northumberland Strait, in S Prince Edward I., SE Canada.

Hills·dale \'hilz-ˌdāl\. **1.** County in S Michigan. See table at MICHIGAN.

2. City, ⊗ of Hillsdale co., S Michigan, 25 mi. (40 km.) SSW of Jackson; pop. (1990c) 8170; Hillsdale Coll. (1844).

3. Borough, Bergen co., NE corner of New Jersey, 9 mi. (15 km.) ENE of Paterson; pop. (1990c) 9750.

Hill·side \'hil-ˌsīd\. **1.** Village, Cook co., NE Illinois, WSW of Oak Park; pop. (1990c) 7672.

2. Township, Union co., NE New Jersey, 2 mi. (3 km.) N of Elizabeth; pop. (1990c) 21,044.

Hills·ville \'hilz-ˌvil\. Town, ⊗ of Carroll co., S Virginia; pop. (1990c) 2008.

Hill Tippera. See TRIPURA.

Hi·lo \'hē-lō\. City, ⊗ of Hawaii co., Hawaii, on **Hilo Bay** on E coast of Hawaii I.; pop. (1990c) 37,808; excellent harbor; exports sugar, fruits, orchids; tourist base for Mauna Kea and Mauna Loa and Kilauea volcanoes in Hawaii Volcanoes National Park; Univ. of Hawaii at Hilo (1970). American mission estab. early 1820s; damaged by tidal waves 1946 and 1960.

Hi·long·hi·long, Mount \'hē-ˌlòŋ-'hē-'lòŋ\. Mountain, NE Agusan del Norte prov., Mindanao, Philippines; 6599 ft. (2011 m.); highest point of Diuata Mts.

Hi·long·os \hē-'lòŋ-ōs\. Municipality on SW coast of Leyte I., Philippines, 62 mi. (100 km.) SSW of Tacloban; pop. (1980c) 43,744.

Hil·ton Head Island \'hilt-ᵊn-'hed\. Town, Beaufort co., S South Carolina, comprising an island in Atlantic Ocean S of mouth of Broad River; 42 sq. mi. (109 sq. km.); pop. (1990c) 23,694; resort; bridge to mainland completed 1956.

Hil·ver·sum \'hil-vər-səm\. Commune, North Holland prov., W Netherlands; pop. (1992e) 84,674; radio and television stations; electrical machinery, pharmaceutical products.

Hil·wān \hil-'wän, -'wan\ *or* **Hul·wān** \hu̇l-'wän\. Town on Nile River S of Cairo, Lower Egypt, opp. ruins of Memphis; cement; mineral baths.

Hi·ma·chal Pra·desh \hə-'mä-chəl-prə-'desh\. State, N India, in the Himalayas NW of Uttar Pradesh, bordering on Tibet, China; ✻ Simla; mountainous region, with highest peak ab. 22,000 ft. (6700 m.); wheat, corn, rice; estab. as a union territory 1948, reconstituted 1954 and 1966, made a state 1971. See table at INDIA.

Hi·ma·la·yas, the \ˌhi-mə-'lā-əz, hi-'mä-lə-yəz\ *or more correctly* **the Himalaya.** Mountain system, S Asia, bordering the Indian subcontinent on the N in a 1500-mile (2414-kilometer) long arc extending from Jammu and Kashmir in the W to Assam in the E and covering most of Nepal, Sikkim, Bhutan, and the S edge of Tibet; separated from the Karakoram Range in the NW by the Indus River and bounded on the N and E by the Brahmaputra River; divided into three main ranges: the **Great Himalayas** in the N, having an av. elev. of 20,000 ft. (6100 m.) and incl. Everest, 29,028 ft. (8848 m.), the **Lesser Himalayas** in the center, and the **Outer Himalayas** in the S, incl. Siwalik Range. Besides Everest, has numerous other high peaks incl. Kanchenjunga, Dhaulagiri, Nanga Parbat, Nanda Devi.

Hi·mal·chu·li \ˌhē-mäl-'chü-lē\. Peak in the Himalayas, Nepal, 28°25′N, 84°39′E; 25,801 ft. (7864 mi.).

Hi·ma·may·lan \ˌhē-mä-'mī-ˌlän\. Municipality, W Negros Occidental, Negros, Philippines, at S end of Guimaras Strait 40 mi. (64 km.) S of City of Bacolod; pop. (1980c) 70,467.

Hi·me·ji \hē-'mā-jē\. City, Hyōgo prefecture, W Honshū, Japan, 34 mi. (55 km.) WNW of Kōbe near N shore of Inland Sea; pop. (1990p) 454,360; textiles; 14th cent. castle (rebuilt 17th cent. and 1964).

Him·era \'hi-mə-rə\. Ancient Greek city on N coast of Sicily; home of Greek lyric poet Stesichorus; scene of battle in which Gelon of Siracusae defeated the Carthaginians 480 B.C.; destroyed by Carthaginian Gen. Hannibal 409 B.C. and a new city founded at Termini Imerese.

Hi·mi \'hē-mē\. City, Toyama prefecture, Honshū, Japan, 18 mi. (30 km.) NW of the city of Toyama; pop. (1990p) 60,768.

Ḥimṣ. See HOMS.

Hi·na·tuan \hē-'nä-ˌtwän\. Municipality, SE Surigao del Sur prov., Mindanao, Philippines, on coast 115 mi. (185 km.) SE of Surigao; pop. (1980c) 27,972.

Hinatuan Passage. Channel bet. Bucas Grande I. and mainland of NE Mindanao, Philippines; ab. 8 mi. (13 km.) wide; considered by some to include the channel bet. NE Mindanao and S Dinagat I.

Hin·chin·brook \'hin-chən-ˌbru̇k\. **1.** Island on E side of entrance to Prince William Sound, S Alaska; on its W side is Nuchek village.

2. Island on NE coast of Queensland, Australia, bet. Townsville and Cairns; constitutes **Hinchinbrook Island National Park**.

Hinck·ley \'hiŋ-klē\. Town, Leicestershire, cen. England, 23 mi. (37 km.) ENE of Birmingham; pop. (1981p) 55,273; hosiery.

Hinckley Lake *or* **Hinckley Reservoir.** Reservoir, NE cen. New York, on border of Herkimer and Oneida cos.

Hindenburg *or* **Hindenburg in Oberschlesien.** See ZABRZE.

Hin·den·burg Line \'hin-dən-ˌbərg\. A line of defensive fortifications estab. by Germans during WWI across NE France, extending S from near Lille, past Cambrai and St.-Quentin, turning E near Laon and reaching nearly to Metz; had many branch lines; scene of severe fighting esp. 1917.

Hin·dī·yah, Al \al-hin-'dē-yə\ *also* **Hin·di·ya** \hin-'dē-yə\. **1.** River in S cen. Iraq; leaves the Euphrates at **Al Hindīyah Barrage** (dam in the Euphrates ab. 45 mi. (70 km.) S of Baghdad) and after flowing SE past Babylon and Al Ḥillah returns to it lower in its course; flows through Shinafiya marsh region.

2. Town, Iraq, on E bank of main stream of the Euphrates ab. 10 mi. (16 km.) S of Al Hindīyah Barrage.

Hind·ley \'hind-lē\. Town, Greater Manchester, NW England, 14 mi. (23 km.) WNW of Manchester; pop. (1981p) 25,537.

Hind·man \'hīnd-mən\. City, ⊗ of Knott co., SE Kentucky; pop. (1990c) 798.

Hind·marsh, Lake \'hind-ˌmärsh\. Lake, W Victoria, SE Australia; 47 sq. mi. (122 sq. km.); receives Wimmera River.

Hin·dol \hin-'dōl\. Former Indian state, now part of Orissa state, NE India.

Hinds \'hīndz\. County in SW cen. Mississippi. See table at MISSISSIPPI.

Hin·du Kush \'hin-dü-'ku̇sh, -'kəsh\; *known in Alexander the Great's time as* **Cau·ca·sus In·di·cus** \'kò-kə-səs-'in-di-kəs\. Mountain range, cen. Asia, extending ab. 600 mi. (965 km.) along N Jammu and Kashmir border and W and SW into Afghanistan to the Koh-i-Baba Range W of Kabul; on E extends to the Pamirs and the Karakoram Range; watershed bet. Kabul River on S and tributaries of the Amu Dar'ya on N. In cen. part peaks above 20,000 ft. (6100 m.), highest point Tirich Mir 25,260 ft. (7699 m.); crossed by passes (up to 17,500 ft. or 5334 m.) from Chitral to Turkistan, one of most important being Baroghil Pass at 12,457 ft. (3797 m.).

Hindur. See NALAGARH.

Hin·du·stan \ˌhin-dü-'stan, -də-, -'stän\. A name for India, variously applied to: (1) The whole peninsula of India N of the Deccan (*q.v.*); *i.e.*, the region bounded on N by the Himalayas and on S by the Vindhya Mts. and Narmada River, comprising Ganges Valley from the Punjab to Assam. (2) A smaller area comprising the upper basin of the Ganges. (3) Historically, an occasional name for the Republic of India.

Hines·ville \'hīnz-ˌvil, -vəl\. City, ⊗ of Liberty co., SE Georgia; pop. (1990c) 21,603.

Hin·gan·ghat \'hiŋ-gən-ˌgät\. Town, NE Maharashtra state, cen. India, on tributary of Wardha River 50 mi. (81 km.) S of Nagpur; pop. (1991p) 78,709; has given its name to one of the best indigenous cotton staples of India.

Hing·ham \'hiŋ-əm\. Town, Plymouth co., SE Massachusetts, on Massachusetts Bay 11 mi. (18 km.) SE of Boston; pop. (1990c) 19,821; summer resort.

Hin·gol \ˈhiŋ-ˌgōl\. River, Pakistan; flows S into Arabian Sea; ab. 350 mi. (563 km.) long; its upper course also known as the **Nal** \ˈnəl\.

Hi·ni·ga·ran \ˌhē-nē-ˈgär-än\. Municipality, W Negros Occidental, Negros, Philippines, at S end of Guimaras Strait; pop. (1980c) 54,717.

Hin·lo·pen Strait \ˈhin-ˌlō-pən\. Channel, Arctic Ocean, bet. Spitsbergen I. and Northeast Land, Svalbard.

Hin·nom \ˈhi-nəm\. A valley near ancient Jerusalem; its identification uncertain, but believed to be the shallow wadi S of the city. In Old Testament times place where the refuse of the city was deposited and perpetual fires kept burning in worship of pagan god Moloch; hence, later, its Greek form **Ge·hen·na** \gi-ˈhe-nə\ became the New Testament word for "hell."

Hinn·øya \ˈhē-ˌnȯi-yə\ *or* **Hinn·øy** \-ˌnȯi\. Island, Norway, largest of the Vesterålen, in Norwegian Sea off NW coast; 848 sq. mi. (2196 sq. km.).

Hi·no \ˈhē-nō\. City, Tokyo prefecture, Honshū, Japan, 21 mi. (34 km.) W of the city of Tokyo; pop. (1990p) 165,935.

Hi·no·jo·sa del Du·que \ˌē-nō-ˈhō-sä-t͟hel-ˈt͟hü-kā\. Commune, Córdoba prov., S Spain, 48 mi. (77 km.) NNW of the city of Córdoba; pop. (1991c) 8141.

Hins·dale \ˈhinz-ˌdāl\. **1.** County in SW Colorado. See table at COLORADO.

2. Village, Cook and Du Page cos., NE Illinois, 9 mi. (14 km.) W of Chicago; pop. (1990c) 16,029.

3. Town, Cheshire co., SW corner of New Hampshire, on Ashuelot River near its junction with the Connecticut 14 mi. (23 km.) SSW of Keene; pop. (1990c) 3936.

Hinterpommern. See POMERANIA.

Hin·ter·rhein \ˌhin-tər-ˈrīn\. River in SE Switzerland; rises in glaciers on the Rheinwaldhorn and flows NE to join the Vorderrhein and form the Rhine River.

Hin·ton \ˈhint-ᵊn\. **1.** City, ⊗ of Summers co., S West Virginia, on New River 20 mi. (32 km.) ESE of Beckley; pop. (1990c) 3433.

2. Town, Alberta, Canada, 165 mi. (266 km.) E of Edmonton; pop. (1991c) 9046.

Hiogo. See HYŌGO.

Hippo *or* **Hippo Regius.** See ANNABA.

Hipponiates, Gulf of. See SANT'EUFEMIA, GULF OF.

Hipponium. See VIBO VALENTIA.

Hip·pos \ˈhi-pəs\. Greek town of the Decapolis (*q.v.*), ancient Palestine.

Hippo Zarytus. See BIZERTE.

Hi·ra \ˈhir-ə\ *or Arab.* **al–Ḥīrah** \ȧl-\. **1.** Ancient kingdom of the Lakhmid dynasty (3d cent. A.D. to 602) comprising lower Euphrates Valley and upper part of Persian Gulf, subordinate to the Sassanids of Persia.

2. Its chief town, 4 mi. (6 km.) SE of modern An Najaf, Iraq, captured by Muslims under Khālid ibn al-Walīd c. 633 and declined 7th cent.

Hi·ra·do \hē-ˈrä-dō\. Island off NW coast of Kyūshū, Japan; ab. 66 sq. mi. (171 sq. km.), 19.5 mi. (31 km.) long and 6 mi. (10 km.) wide; pop. (1990c) 26,864; chief town and harbor Hirado. Port opened to Portuguese c. 1550 and to British and Dutch 17th cent.

Hi·ra·ka·ta \ˌhē-rä-ˈkä-tä\. City, Ōsaka prefecture, Honshū, Japan; pop. (1990p) 390,790.

Hi·ram \ˈhī-rəm\. Village in Hiram township, Portage co., NE Ohio, ab. 30 mi. (48 km.) SE of Cleveland; pop. (1990c) 3218; Hiram Coll. (1850).

Hirata Gunto. See PARACEL ISLANDS.

Hi·ra·tsu·ka \hi-ˈrät-sə̇-ˌkä\. City, Kanagawa prefecture, SE Honshū, Japan; on N shore of Sagami Sea 18 mi. (29 km.) SW of Yokohama; pop. (1990p) 245,944; textiles.

Hi·ro·sa·ki \hē-ˈrȯ-sä-kē, ˌhē-rō-ˈsä-kē\. City, Aomori prefecture, N Honshū, Japan; in plain of the Iwaki River 23 mi. (37 km.) SW of the city of Aomori and near Mt. Iwaki; pop. (1990p) 174,710; center for fruit growing and manufacture of a special kind of lacquer; university (1949).

Hi·ro·shi·ma \ˌhē-rō-ˈshē-mä, hē-ˈrō-shē-mä\. **1.** Prefecture of Honshū, Japan; ✻ Hiroshima; rice, oranges, textiles; shipyards. See table at JAPAN.

2. City, its ✻, at W end of Inland Sea; pop. (1992e) 1,096,919; has rail, river, and canal connections; manufactures vehicles; shipbuilding; Hiroshima Univ. (1949). Founded 16th cent.; a military center from 1868; most of city destroyed Aug. 6, 1945 by explosion of first atomic bomb used in warfare (dropped by U.S. plane) which caused an estimated loss of 80,000 lives immediately and thousands more subsequently due to radiation exposure; memorials include the Peace Memorial Park and the Atomic Bomb Memorial Dome; city largely rebuilt since 1950. See also ITSUKU-SHIMA.

Hirschberg *or* **Hirschberg in Schlesien** *or* **Hirschberg im Riesengebirge.** See JELENIA GÓRA.

Hir·son \ir-ˈsōⁿ\. Commune, Aisne dept., N France, on Oise River 34 mi. (55 km.) NE of Laon.

Hi·sa·ka \ˈhē-sä-kä, hē-ˈsä-kä\. Island in Gotō Islands (*q.v.*), Japan.

Hi·sar *or* **His·sar** \hi-ˈsär\. Town, Haryana, N India, 100 mi. (161 km.) WNW of Delhi; founded 1356 by Sultan Fīrūz Shāh Tughluq; almost depopulated by famine 1783; occupied by Irish adventurer George Thomas 1797.

Ḥis·bān \ˈhis-bən, -ˌbän\; *anc.* **Hesh·bon** \ˈhesh-bən\. Town, Jordan, 13 mi. (21 km.) SW of Amman; mentioned numerous times in Old Testament.

Hispalis. See SEVILLE.

Hispania. See SPAIN.

Hispania Tarraconensis. See TARRACONENSIS.

His·pan·io·la \ˌhis-pən-ˈyō-lə\; *orig. Span.* **Es·pa·ño·la** \ˌes-ˌpä-ˈnyō-lä\; *formerly* **Hai·ti** \ˈhā-tē\. Island of the cen. West Indies, in N cen. Caribbean Sea E of Cuba and W of Puerto Rico; 29,371 sq. mi. (76,071 sq. km.); pop. (1990e) 13,032,000; divided bet. republic of Haiti on W and Dominican Republic on E.

History: Visited by explorer Christopher Columbus 1492; became center of Spanish rule in West Indies (see also *History* at WEST INDIES); indigenous population extirpated by the Spanish and replaced by African slaves; W part of island, occupied in 17th cent. by buccaneers and ceded to France by Spain 1697, came to be known as colony of St. Domingue, while E part (Santo Domingo) remained under the Spanish; slave insurrection late 18th cent. introduced period of conflict; entire island under former slave Toussaint-Louverture 1801–02; scene of struggle against domination of French 1802–03; independence declared 1804 under Jean-Jacques Dessalines and the island became republic of Haiti; divided again 1809–21 with Spanish ruling E part; entire island ruled by Haitian President Jean-Pierre Boyer from 1822 until E part revolted 1843 and formed the Dominican Republic 1844. For later history, see DOMINICAN REPUBLIC and HAITI.

His·par Glacier \his-ˈpär\. Glacier in Karakoram Range, in area controlled by Pakistan; 38 mi. (61 km.) long, 2 mi. (3 km.) wide near its terminus.

Hissar. See HISAR.

His·sar·lik \ˌhi-sər-ˈlik\. Site of ancient Troy (*q.v.*), Çanakkale prov., NW Turkey in Asia, 4 mi. (6 km.) SE of mouth of the Dardanelles.

His·sar Mountains \hi-ˈsär\. Mountain range in NW Tajikistan, a branch of the Alai Mts.

Histonium. See VASTO.

Hīt *or* **Hit** \ˈhit\ *anc.* **Is** \ˈis\. Town, W cen. Iraq, on W bank of the Euphrates at head of navigation ab. 90 mi. (145 km.) W of Baghdad; in ancient times source of bitumen used in construction of walls and buildings of Babylon.

Hi·ta·chi \hē-ˈtä-chē\. Coastal city, NE Ibaraki prefecture, Honshū, Japan, 83 mi. (134 km.) NE of Tokyo; pop. (1990p) 202,145; center of important industrial area; heavily bombed by Americans in WWII.

Hitch·cock \ˈhich-ˌkäk\. **1.** County in S Nebraska. See table at NEBRASKA.

2. City, Galveston co., SE Texas, NW of the city of Galveston; pop. (1990c) 5868.

Hitch·in \ˈhi-chən\. Town, Hertfordshire, SE England, on the Hiz River 32 mi. (51 km.) N of London; pop. (1981p) 30,317; engineering; flour, parchment.

Hither Pomerania. See POMERANIA.

Hit·ler Line \ˈhit-lər\. In WWII a German defense line, W Italy, from Terracina on W coast to Aquino in mountains W of Cassino; a support for the Gustav Line; taken by Allies May 1944.

Hit·ra \ˈhē-trä\; *formerly* **Hit·te·ren** \ˈhi-tə-rən\. Island in Norwegian Sea off W coast of Norway, WSW of entrance to Trondheim Fjord; 218 sq. mi. (566 sq. km.).

Hiu \ˈhē-ü\. Largest of the Torres Is. (*q.v.*), Vanuatu.

Hi·va Oa \ˌhē-və-ˈō-ə\. One of the Marquesas Is., French Polynesia, S Pacific Ocean; 23 mi. (37 km.) long; 77 sq. mi. (199 sq. km.); pop. (1988c) 1671; chief village Atuona, administrative center of the group. Of volcanic origin; has high cen. ridge, highest point Mt. Temetiu 4134 ft. (1260 m.); produces esp. copra; place where 19th cen. French artist Paul Gauguin is buried.

Hi·was·see \hī-ˈwä-sē\ *also* **Hi·a·was·see** \ˌhī-ə-ˈwä-sē\. River, SE United States; rises in NE Georgia, flows across W extremity of North Carolina and into SE Tennessee to empty into Tennessee River ab. 10 mi. (16 km.) SW of Decatur; ab. 150 mi. (240 km.) long; in its course are three great dams, Apalachia, Hiwassee, and Chatuge, of the Tennessee Valley Authority (*q.v.*).

Hiwassee Dam. See table at TENNESSEE VALLEY AUTHORITY.

Hjäl·ma·ren \ˈyel-mə-rən\. Lake in Örebro and Södermanland provs., S cen. Sweden, E of N Lake Vänern and N of Lake Vättern; 187 sq. mi. (484 sq. km.).

Hjør·ring \ˈyœr-iŋ\. City, Nordjylland co., NE Jutland, Denmark; pop. (1989e) 34,499; textiles; food processing.

Hlu·čín \ˈhlü-ˌchēn\ *or Ger.* **Hul·tschin** \ˈhu̇l-ˌchēn\. Town, E Czech Republic, ab. 6 mi. (10 km.) NW of Ostrava; pop. (1980p) 22,581.

Hlukhiv. See GLUKHOV.

Ho \ˈhō\. **1.** River, N China. See RUO.

2. Town, ✻ of Volta region, SE Ghana; pop. (1984c) 37,777.

Hoang Sa, Quan Dao. See PARACEL ISLANDS.

Ho·back Peak \ˈhō-bak\. Mountain, NW Sublette co., W Wyoming; 10,864 ft. (3311 m.).

Ho·bart \ˈhō-bərt\. **1.** City, Lake co., NW corner of Indiana, 8 mi. (13 km.) S of Lake Michigan; pop. (1990c) 21,822; settled 1849; incorp. 1921.

2. City, ⊗ of Kiowa co., SW Oklahoma, 31 mi. (50 km.) NNE of Altus; pop. (1990c) 4305.

Hobart \ˈhō-ˌbärt\. City, ✻ of Tasmania, Australia, in SE part on Derwent River 12 mi. (19 km.) from the sea, at base of Mt. Wellington; pop. (1991c) 47,106; deep sheltered harbor; electrolytic zinc, paper, textiles, food products; Univ. of Tasmania (1890). See RISDON. Founded in 1804 as **Hobart Town**; became a city 1842.

Hobbs \ˈhäbz\. City, Lea co., SE corner of New Mexico, near Texas border ab. 18 mi. (29 km.) N of Eunice; pop. (1990c) 29,115. Founded 1907, expanded following discovery of oil late 1920s; headquarters for oil-well supplies; New Mexico Junior Coll. (1965).

Hobbs Coast. Section of coast of West Antarctica, lying along N Marie Byrd Land, from 131° to 140°30′W.

Hob·do Gol \ˈhäb-dō-ˈgäl\ *or* **Kob·do** \ˈkäb-dō\. River in extreme W Mongolia; rises on N slope of Altai Shan, flows NE and SE to salt lakes Har Us Nuur and Har Nuur.

Hobe Sound \ˈhōb\. Unincorporated settlement, Martin co., E Florida, 12 mi. (19 km.) SE of Stuart; pop. (1990c) 11,507; grew rapidly in 1970s and 1980s.

Hob·kirk's Hill \ˈhäb-kərks\. Locality, South Carolina, 2 mi. (3 km.) N of Camden; battle Apr. 25, 1781 in which Americans, during their strategic retreat under Gen. Nathanael Greene, were defeated by British under Francis Rawdon-Hastings.

Ho·bo·ken \ˈhō-ˌbō-kən\. **1.** City, Hudson co., NE New Jersey, on Hudson River N of and adjoining Jersey City and opp. New York City (with which it is connected by ferries and tunnels); pop. (1990c) 33,397; railroad center, with long waterfront; electronic equipment, precision instruments, chemicals; shipbuilding. Stevens Institute of Technology (1870). Land purchased from Indians by Dutch 1630; purchased 1784 by American inventor John Stevens, who laid out town 1804; became resort, esp. for New Yorkers; incorp. as town 1849, as city 1855.

2. Former commune, N Belgium; a suburb that became part of Antwerp 1983.

Hoch·e·laga \ˌhä-shə-ˈla-gə\. Former Indian (Huron) village, E end of island (now Montreal I.) in St. Lawrence River, Canada, visited by French explorer Jacques Cartier 1535; it had disappeared when place was visited by French explorer Samuel de Champlain 1603.

Hoch·fei·ler \ˈhōk-ˌfī-lər\. Peak, highest point of the Zillertaler Alps, S Tirol, on Austria-Italy boundary; 11,513 ft. (3509 m.).

Hoch·heim \ˈhōk-ˌhīm\. Commune, Hesse, Germany, on the Main near its confluence with the Rhine; pop. (1980c) 15,280; noted for its production of a white wine, called *Hochheimer*, or *hock*.

Ho Chi Minh City \ˌhō-ˌchē-ˈmin\; *formerly* **Sai·gon** \sī-ˈgän, ˈsī-ˌgän\. City, S Vietnam, a commercial center on **Saigon River** on a branch of the Dong Nai; pop. (1989c) 2,899,753; laid out in French style with wide streets and numerous notable parks and public buildings; Univ. of Ho Chi Minh City (estab. 1954 as Univ. of Saigon).

History: Khmer village came under Annamese control in 17th cent.; captured by French 1859; 1862 Treaty of Saigon recognized French possession of Cochin China; chosen ✻ of South Vietnam after 1954 Geneva Convention; in early 1960s site of riots and demonstrations as government faced growing Communist force in the N; headquarters of U.S. and South Vietnamese forces in subsequent Vietnam War; attacked by Communists 1968; renamed for deceased leader of Vietnamese Communists after being taken by North Vietnam in 1975.

Ho Chi Minh Trail. Former trail system extending from North Vietnam to South Vietnam and cutting through E Laos and Cambodia; functioned as a major supply route for North Vietnamese forces from early 1960s to 1975 during Vietnam War.

Hoch·kirch \ˈhōk-ˌkirk\. Village, Saxony, E Germany, NW of Löbau; in Seven Years' War scene of victory 1758 of Austrians over Prussians under Frederick the Great.

Höch·städt \ˈhœk-ˌshtet\ *also* **Höchstädt an der Do·nau** \än-dər-ˈdō-ˌnau̇\. Town, Bavaria, Germany, on Danube NE of Ulm; scene of two battles in War of the Spanish Succession in 1703 and in 1704 (the latter often called the battle of Blenheim, *q.v.*).

Hoch·stuhl \ˈhōk-ˌshtül\. Mountain on border bet. Austria and Slovenia; 7341 ft. (2238 m.); highest point in the Karawanken Alps.

Hoch·vo·gel \ˈhōk-ˌfō-gel\. Peak in the Algäu Alps, on the border bet. S Germany and W Austria E of Lake Constance; 8505 ft. (2592 m.).

Hock·ing \ˈhä-kiŋ\. **1.** River, Ohio, rises in Fairfield co., S cen. Ohio, and flows SE into Ohio River below Parkersburg, West Virginia; ab. 80 mi. (130 km.) long.

2. County in S cen. Ohio. See table at OHIO.

Hock·ley \ˈhä-klē\. County in NW Texas. See table at TEXAS.

Hoddes·don \ˈhädz-dən\. Town, Hertfordshire, SE England, at confluence of Lea and Stort rivers 19 mi. (31 km.) N of London; pop. (1981p) 29,892.

Hodeida. See AL ḤUDAYDAH.

Hodge·man \ˈhäj-mən\. County in SW cen. Kansas. See table at KANSAS.

Hodg·en·ville \ˈhä-jən-ˌvil\. City, ⊗ of Larue co., cen. Kentucky, 47 mi. (76 km.) S of Louisville; pop. (1990c) 2721; gas wells; Abraham Lincoln, 16th U.S. president, born in a log cabin nearby Feb. 12, 1809.

Hód·me·ző·vá·sár·hely \ˈhōd-me-zœ-ˌvä-shär-ˌhā\. City, Csongrád co., SE Hungary; pop. (1991e) 52,200; textiles.

Hod·na, Chott el \ˈshät-el-ˈhȯd-nə\ *or Arab.* **Shatt al–Hodna** \ˌshät-ȧl-\. Marshy saline lake in NE Algeria.

Hodna Mountains. Range of the Little Atlas Mts. in NE Algeria.

Ho·do·nín \ˈhȯ-dȯn-ˌyēn\ *or Ger.* **Gö·ding** \ˈgœ-diŋ\. Town, E Czech Republic, across Morava River from Slovakia, 50 mi. (80 km.) N of Bratislava; pop. (1980p) 25,485.

Hoei. See HUY.

Hoeksche Waard. See BEIJERLAND.

Hoek van Hol·land \ˌhük-vän-ˈhȯ-länt\ *or Eng.* **Hook of Hol·land** \ˈhä-lənd\. **1.** Cape on SW coast of South Holland prov., SW Netherlands, N of mouth of Nieuwe Maas River. **2.** Seaport on the cape ab. 6 mi. (10 km.) NW of Rotterdam; belongs to Rotterdam.

Hoek van Mandar. See MANDAR, GULF OF.

Hoens·broek \ˈhünz-ˌbrük\. Commune, Limburg prov., SE Netherlands, NE of Maastricht; pop. (1981e) 22,441.

Hoet·jes Bay \ˈhü-chəs\. Village on N shore of Saldanha Bay, W Western Cape prov., Rep. of South Africa, 70 mi. (113 km.) NNW of Cape Town; harbor.

Hof \ˈhōf, ˈhȯf\. City, NE Bavaria, Germany, on Saale River 31 mi. (50 km.) NNE of Bayreuth; pop. (1992e) 52,859; railroad junction; manufactures textiles, machinery; brewing; first mentioned 1214; to Prussia 1792, to Bavaria 1810; after WWII, an important checkpoint bet. East and West Germany.

Ho–fei. See HEFEI.

Hoff·man Estates \ˈhäf-mən, ˌhȯf-\. Village, Cook co., NE Illinois, 15 mi. (24 km.) WNW of Chicago; pop. (1990c) 46,651.

Hoffman Island. Island off E coast of Staten I., New York, in Lower New York Bay; part of the borough of Staten I.

Hoff·mann, Mount \ˈhäf-mən, ˈhȯf-\. Peak in the Sierra Nevada, in E Tuolumne co., cen. California; 10,850 ft. (3307 m.).

Hoffmann Mountain. Peak in Adirondack Mts., Essex co., NE New York; ab. 3715 ft. (1130 m.).

Hō·fu \ˈhō-ˌfü\ *also* **Bō·fu** \ˈbō-\. City, Yamaguchi prefecture, Honshū, Japan, 56 mi. (90 km.) SW of Hiroshima; pop. (1990p) 117,639.

Hofuf. See AL HUFŪF.

Ho·gans·ville \ˈhō-gənz-ˌvil\. City, Troup co., W Georgia, 10 mi. (16 km.) NE of La Grange; pop. (1990c) 2976; incorp. 1870.

Hog·back Mountain \ˈhȯg-bak, ˈhäg-\. Peak in Banner co., W Nebraska; 5084 ft. (1550 m.).

Hogback Peak. Mountain in the Sierra Nevada, in E Fresno co., S cen. California; 10,500 ft. (3200 m.).

Hoggar Mountains. See AHAGGAR MOUNTAINS.

Hog Island \ˈhȯg, ˈhäg\. **1.** Island in N Lake Michigan, part of Charlevoix co., NW Michigan, NE of Beaver I.
2. Island in Delaware River below Philadelphia, Pennsylvania.
3. Island in Atlantic Ocean, N Northampton co., Virginia.

Hogland. See GOGLAND.

Hogolu. See CHUUK.

Hogue, La. See LA HOGUE.

Hohenfriedeberg. See DĄBROMIERZ.

Ho·hen·lim·burg \ˌhō-ən-ˈlim-ˌbu̇rk\. City, North Rhine-Westphalia, Germany, 40 mi. (64 km.) NE of Cologne; rolling mills; first mentioned 1243.

Ho·hen·lin·den \ˈhō-ən-ˌlin-dən, ˌhō-ən-ˈ\. Village, Bavaria, Germany, 20 mi. (32 km.) E of Munich; pop. (1980c) 2082; scene of battle Dec. 3, 1800 in which French under Gen. Jean-Victor-Marie Moreau defeated Austrians, a victory which together with that of French Emperor Napoléon at Marengo led to Peace of Lunéville 1801.

Hohenmauth. See VYSOKÉ MÝTO.

Hohensalza. See INOWROCŁAW.

Ho·hen·stau·fen \ˈhō-ən-ˌshtau̇-fən\. Mountain near Göppingen, cen. Baden-Württemberg, Germany; 2240 ft. (683 m.); contains ruins of ancestral castle of Hohenstaufen family.

Ho·hen·stein–Ernst·thal \ˈhō-ən-ˌshtīn-ˈernst-ˌtäl\. City, Saxony, E Germany, on N edge of the Erzgebirge 9 mi. (14 km.) W of Chemnitz; received city rights 1521.

Ho·hen·twiel \ˈhō-ən-ˌtfēl\. Conical mountain in S Baden-Württemberg, Germany, near Singen; 2260 ft. (689 m.).

Ho·hen·wald \ˈhō-ən-ˌwȯld\. Town, ⊗ of Lewis co., SW cen. Tennessee; pop. (1990c) 3760.

Ho·hen·zol·lern \ˈhō-ən-ˌtsȯ-lərn\. Historical region and province of Prussia, Germany, now part of Baden-Württemberg, Germany; castle on Mt. Zollern, near Hechingen. Formed in 1849 from territories of Hohenzollern-Hechingen and Hohenzollern-Sigmaringen which were derived from seat of Hohenzollern dynasty, of whom the Franconian branch were rulers of Prussia and emperors of Germany; ceded to Prussia by their rulers, members of (Swabian) line of Hohenzollerns; since 1952 part of Baden-Württemberg.

Ho·hes Licht \ˈhō-əs-ˈli<u>k</u>t\. Peak in the Algäu Alps (*q.v.*), on border bet. Bavaria, Germany and Tirol, Austria N of Lech Valley; 8706 ft. (2654 m.).

Hohe Tauern. See table at ALPS.

Ho·he Venn Mountains \ˈhō-ə-ˈfen\ *or Fr.* **Hautes Fagnes** \ōt-ˈfänʸ\. Range in Liège prov., E Belgium; highest peak Botrange 2277 ft. (694 m.).

Hoh·hot \ˈhə-ˈhȯt\ *or W.-G.* **Hu–ho–hao–t'e** \ˈhü-ˈhə-ˈhau̇-ˈtā\ *or* **Hu·he·hot** \ˈhü-ˌhə-ˈhȯt\; *Mongol.* **Ku·ku·kho·to** \ˌkü-kü-ˈ<u>k</u>ō-tō\; *formerly* **Kwei·sui** \ˈgwā-ˈswā\. Town, ✱ of Nei Monggol (Inner Mongolia), N China; pop. (1990c) 652,534; sugar; iron and steel; university (1957).

Hohokam Pima National Monument \hō-ˈhō-kəm-ˈpē-mə\. See UNITED STATES, *National Monuments.*

Ho–Ho–Kus \hō-ˈhō-kəs\. Borough, Bergen co., NE corner of New Jersey, on Hohokus River 7 mi. (11 km.) NNE of Paterson; pop. (1990c) 3935.

Ho Hu. See GE HU.

Hoi An \ˈhȯi-ˈän\; *formerly* **Fai·fo** \ˈfī-ˈfō\. Coastal town, 14 mi. (23 km.) S of Da Nang, cen. Vietnam.

Hoihow *or* **Hoï–Hao.** See HAIKOU.

Hoi·sing·ton \ˈhȯi-ziŋ-tən\. City, Barton co., cen. Kansas, 10 mi. (16 km.) N of Great Bend; pop. (1990c) 3182.

Hoje Tast·rup \ˈhȯi-ə-ˈtäs-tru̇p\. Town, Copenhagen co., Denmark; pop. (1989e) 44,521.

Ho–kang. See HEGANG.

Hoke \ˈhōk\. County in S North Carolina. See table at NORTH CAROLINA.

Ho·kiang \ˈhə-ˈjyäŋ\. Former province, E Manchuria, NE China, on the lower Songhua River; 50,816 sq. mi. (131,613 sq. km.); now part of Heilongjiang prov.

Ho·ki·anga Harbour *also* **Hokianga River** \ˌhō-kē-ˈäŋ-ə\. Broad inlet or harbor on W coast of N peninsula of North I., New Zealand, 125 mi. (201 km.) NW of Auckland.

Ho·ki·ti·ka \ˌhō-ki-ˈtē-kə, ˌhä-ki-ˈtik-ə\. Borough, W South I., New Zealand, 160 mi. (257 km.) SW of Nelson; pop. (1987e) 3420; gold and coal in vicinity.

Hok·kai·dō \hō-ˈkī-dō\; *formerly* **Ye·zo** *also* **Ye·so** \ˈye-zō\ *or* **Ezo** \ˈe-zō\. Northernmost of the four main islands of Japan, in Pacific Ocean off E coast of Asia, N of island of Honshū; separated from S Sakhalin on N by Sōya Strait, from Honshū on S by Tsugaru Strait, and from the Kuril Is. on NE by Nemuro Strait. Constitutes a region of Japan. Has several high peaks, esp. Asahi 7513 ft. (2290 m.), Horoshiri 6732 ft. (2052 m.), and Tokachi 6814 ft. (2077 m.); rivers include Ishikari, longest in Japan, and the Tokachi; fishing; produces rice, barley, oats, sugar beets, dairy products; potatoes; wood pulp; has substantial resources in coal. Chief cities Sapporo, Asahikawa, Hakodate. In early times inhabited by Ainus; major Japanese settlement began late 1860s; Seikan Tunnel completed 1988 connects Hokkaidō with Honshū by rail.
2. Administrative region and prefecture, N Japan, incl. Hokkaidō (see HOKKAIDŌ 1), adjacent small islands and (formerly) the Kuril Is. (Chishima Rettō); ✱ Sapporo. Since 1945 has not included the Kuril Is., which were transferred to U.S.S.R. following WWII. See table at JAPAN.

Hoko Shoto *or* **Hoko Gunto.** See PENGHU 1.

Hokou. Town, Jiangxi prov., China. See HUKOU.
Ho–k'ou. See HEKOU.
Hokow. See HEKOU 2.
Ho–lan Shan. See HELAN SHAN.
Hol·bæk \ˈhȯl-ˌbek\. Town, Vestsjælland co., NW Sjælland, Denmark, 33 mi. (53 km.) W of Copenhagen; pop. (1989e) 31,084; shipbuilding.
Hol·beach \ˈhōl-ˌbēch\. Market town, Parts of Holland, Lincolnshire, E England, 51 mi. (82 km.) ESE of Nottingham.
Hol·born Head *or* **Hol·burn Head** \ˈhäl-bərn, ˈhōl-\. Cape on NE coast of Scotland; lighthouse.
Hol·brook \ˈhōl-ˌbru̇k\. **1.** Town, ⊗ of Navajo co., NE Arizona; pop. (1990c) 4686; tourism; Northland Pioneer Coll. (1974).
2. Town, Norfolk co., E Massachusetts, 5 mi. (8 km.) N of Brockton; pop. (1990c) 11,041.
Hol·den \ˈhōl-dən\. Town, Worcester co., cen. Massachusetts, 8 mi. (13 km.) NNW of the city of Worcester; pop. (1990c) 14,628.
Hol·den·ville \ˈhōl-dən-ˌvil\. City, ⊗ of Hughes co., E cen. Oklahoma, 28 mi. (45 km.) NE of Ada; pop. (1990c) 4792.
Hol·der·ness. **1.** \ˈhōl-dər-nəs\. Town, Grafton co., W New Hampshire, on Squam Lake; pop. (1990c) 1694.
2. \ˌhōl-dər-ˈnes\. Peninsula in SE Humberside, N England, bet. Humber River and the North Sea; 309 sq. mi. (800 sq. km.); at S tip is Spurn Head.
Hol·drege \ˈhōl-drij\. City, ⊗ of Phelps co., S Nebraska, 24 mi. (39 km.) SW of Kearney; pop. (1990c) 5671.
Hol·guín \ȯl-ˈgēn\. **1.** Province of E Cuba. See table at CUBA.
2. Municipality, its ✱, in plateau region 65 mi. (105 km.) NW of Santiago de Cuba; pop. (1990c) 228,052; through its port, Gibara, exports tobacco and cattle products; founded c. 1523.
Hol·la \ˈhȯ-lə\. Peak, SW Ethiopia, NW of Lake Abaya; 12,093 ft. (3686 m.).
Hol·la·brunn \ˌhȯ-lə-ˈbrün\ *also* **Ober·hol·la·brunn** \ˈō-bər-\. Town, Lower Austria, Austria, N of Vienna; pop. (1991c) 10,570; scene of battle 1805 in which Russian Gen. Prince Pyotr Ivanovich Bagration successfully resisted greatly superior French force.
Hol·land \ˈhä-lənd\. **1.** Kingdom. See NETHERLANDS.
2. City, Allegan and Ottawa cos., W Michigan, on Lake Michigan 25 mi. (40 km.) WSW of Grand Rapids; pop. (1990c) 30,745; summer resort; poultry; Hope Coll. (1862); settled 1847.
3. County of Holy Roman Empire on North Sea coast, now in North and South Holland provs., Netherlands; estab. early 12th cent.; in 1247 its Count William II elected German king; united with Zeeland and Hainaut in 14th cent.; ceded to Burgundy (*q.v.*) by Countess Jacoba 1433; see NETHERLANDS.
Holland, The Parts of. See LINCOLNSHIRE 2.
Hol·lan·dale \ˈhä-lən-ˌdāl\. City, Washington co., W Mississippi, 21 mi. (34 km.) SE of Greenville; pop. (1990c) 3576.
Hollandia. See JAYAPURA.
Hol·landsch Diep \ˈhä-lənts-ˈdēp\. Estuary of the Maas (Meuse) River in SW Netherlands, on border bet. South Holland and North Brabant provs.
Holland Tunnel. Vehicular tunnel under Hudson River from Manhattan I., New York, to Jersey City, New Jersey; 8558 ft. (2608 m.) long; opened 1927.
Hol·li·days·burg \ˈhä-lə-ˌdāz-ˌbərg, -dēz-\. Borough, ⊗ of Blair co., S cen. Pennsylvania, 6 mi. (10 km.) S of Altoona; pop. (1990c) 5624; became railroad and canal terminus in 1830s; founded 1768.
Hol·li·days Cove \ˈhä-lə-dāz\. Former city in Brooke and Hancock cos., N West Virginia, 25 mi. (40 km.) NNE of Wheeling; since 1947 part of Weirton.
Hol·lins \ˈhä-linz\. Unincorporated settlement, Roanoke co., W cen. Virginia, just N of the city of Roanoke; Hollins Coll. (1842).
Hol·lis \ˈhä-lis\. **1.** Town, Hillsborough co., S New Hampshire, 16 mi. (26 km.) SSW of Manchester; pop. (1990c) 5705; apples and strawberries.
2. Residential neighborhood in Queens borough of New York City, Queens co., SE New York, on Long Island.
3. City, ⊗ of Harmon co., SW Oklahoma, 35 mi. (56 km.) W of Altus; pop. (1990c) 2584.
Hol·lis·ter \ˈhä-li-stər\. City, ⊗ of San Benito co., W California, 20 mi. (32 km.) E of Monterey Bay; pop. (1990c) 19,212.
Hol·lis·ton \ˈhä-li-stən\. Town, Middlesex co., E cen. Massachusetts, 18 mi. (29 km.) ESE of Worcester; pop. (1990c) 12,926.
Holl·man, Cape \ˈhōl-mən\. Cape at N end of Willaumez Penin., N New Britain, Bismarck Archipelago, Papua New Guinea.
Holloman Air Force Base. See ALAMOGORDO.
Hol·ly \ˈhä-lē\. Village, Oakland co., SE Michigan, 16 mi. (26 km.) S of Flint; pop. (1990c) 5595.
Holly Hill. City, Volusia co., E Florida, on Atlantic Ocean 5 mi. (8 km.) N of Daytona Beach; pop. (1990c) 11,141.
Holly Springs. City, ⊗ of Marshall co., N Mississippi, 54 mi. (87 km.) NW of Tupelo; pop. (1990c) 7261; ships cotton and dairy products; Rust Coll. (1866).
Hol·ly·wood \ˈhä-lē-ˌwu̇d\. **1.** District in city of Los Angeles, California, E of Beverly Hills; major center of U.S. motion-picture and television industries; became a district of Los Angeles 1910.
2. City, Broward co., SE Florida, on Atlantic Ocean 18 mi. (29 km.) N of Miami; pop. (1990c) 121,697; tourism; incorp. 1925.
Holmes \ˈhōmz, ˈhōlmz\. Name of counties in three states of the U.S. See tables at FLORIDA, MISSISSIPPI, OHIO.
Holmes, Mount. Peak in Yellowstone National Park, NW Wyoming; 10,336 ft. (3150 m.).
Holmes Beach. City, Manatee co., W cen. Florida, 17 mi. (27 km.) NW of Sarasota; pop. (1990c) 4810.
Holmes·burg \ˈhōmz-ˌbərg, ˈhōlmz-\. District of NE Philadelphia, Pennsylvania, near Delaware River; prison.
Holmes Reefs. Group of coral islets in W Coral Sea outside Great Barrier Reef, 16°27′S, 148°E.
Holm·firth \ˈhōm-ˌfərth\. Town, West Yorkshire, N England, 6 mi. (10 km.) S of Huddersfield; pop. (1981p) 21,839.
Holm·ön \ˈhȯl-ˌmœn\. Swedish island in Gulf of Bothnia off coast of Västerbotten prov., N Sweden.
Holm·sjön \ˈhȯlm-ˌshœn\. Lake, Västernorrland prov., E Sweden; drained by Ljungan River.
Hol·ni·cote Bay \ˈhäl-ni-ˌkōt\. Inlet of Solomon Sea, on coast of New Guinea I., Papua New Guinea.
Ho·lon \hō-ˈlōn\. Town, cen. Israel, a part of the Tel Aviv-Jaffa met. area; pop. (1992e) 161,800; textiles.
Hol·royd \ˈhäl-ˌrȯid\. City, E New South Wales, Australia, W of Sydney; pop. (1991c) 79,132.
Hol·ste·bro \ˌhōl-stə-ˈbrō\. Town, Ringkøbing co., W Jutland, Denmark, 24 mi. (39 km.) NE of the town of Ringkøbing; pop. (1989e) 38,439; tobacco processing.
Hol·stein \ˈhōl-ˌstīn, -ˌstēn\. The S part of the state of Schleswig-Holstein, Germany.
History: Part of German duchy of Saxony in Carolingian empire; became a county of the Holy Roman Empire 1111; formed personal union with Schleswig 1460; raised to a duchy 1474; became member of German Confederation 1815; with Schleswig (*q.v.*), object of conflict bet. German Confederation and Denmark 1848–50 and bet. Austria and Prussia in Austro-Prussian (Seven Weeks') War 1866; annexed to Prussia with Schleswig, forming prov. of Schleswig-Holstein (*q.v.*) 1866.
Hol·steins·borg \ˈhōl-ˌstīnz-ˌbȯrg\ *or native* **Si·si·miut** \ˈsi-sē-ˌmyüt\. Settlement on W coast of Greenland, just N of Arctic Circle; pop. (1991e) 4954; fishing.
Hol·ston \ˈhōl-stən\. River, E Tennessee; formed by junction of N and S forks in Sullivan co., flows SW to unite with French Broad River near Knoxville and form the Tennessee River; 140 mi. (225 km.) long; in its course are two great dams, Cherokee and South Holston, of the Tennessee Valley Authority (*q.v.*). See WATAUGA.
Holston High Knob *or* **Holston Mountain.** Peak, Carter and Sullivan cos., NE Tennessee; 4350 ft. (1326 m.).
Holt \ˈhōlt\. Name of counties in two states of the U.S. See tables at MISSOURI and NEBRASKA.

Hol·ton \'hōlt-ᵊn\. City, ⊗ of Jackson co., NE Kansas, 28 mi. (45 km.) N of Topeka; pop. (1990c) 3196.

Holt·ville \'hōlt-ˌvil\. City, Imperial co., SE corner of California, 10 mi. (16 km.) E of El Centro; pop. (1990c) 4820; ab. 10 ft. (3 m.) below sea level.

Holtz Bay \'hōlts\. Inlet, NE Attu I., Aleutian Is., Alaska; in WWII one of landing places of American forces May 11, 1943 (see also MASSACRE BAY).

Holy Cross, Mount of the. Peak in Sawatch Range, Eagle co., NW cen. Colorado; 14,005 ft. (4269 m.); features a cross-shaped fissure prominent when filled with snow.

Hol·y·head \'hä-lē-ˌhed\. **1.** Island in NE St. George's Channel, in Gwynedd, NW Wales, off W coast of island of Anglesey; 8 mi. (13 km.) long, 3.5 mi. (6 km.) wide; connected with Anglesey I. by a long causeway; mostly barren rock.
2. *or Welsh* **Caer Gy·bi** \'kīr-'gə-bē\. Seaport on N coast of Holyhead I., Wales; pop. (1981p) 10,467; seaside resort; harbor protected by breakwater more than a mile (1.6 kilometers) long; nearest British port to Dublin (61 mi. or 98 km.).

Holy Island *or* **Lin·dis·farne** \'lin-dəs-ˌfärn\. Peninsula, which becomes an island at high water, off NE coast of Northumberland, N England; 3 mi. (5 km.) long by 1.75 mi. (3 km.) wide; site of monastery founded 635 by St. Aidan where the Lindisfarne Gospels were produced; ruins of late 11th cent. priory; 16th cent. castle.

Holy Land. A name for Palestine (*q.v.*).

Holy Loch. Small inlet on W shore of Firth of Clyde, W Scotland, opp. mouth of Clyde River.

Hol·yoke \'hōl-ˌyōk\. **1.** Town, ⊗ of Phillips co., NE Colorado, 48 mi. (77 km.) E of Sterling; pop. (1990c) 1931.
2. City, Hampden co., SW Massachusetts, on Connecticut River 8 mi. (13 km.) N of Springfield; pop. (1990c) 43,704; paper; electronic equipment, fabricated steel; Holyoke Community Coll. (1946). Settled 1725 as part of Springfield; joined West Springfield 1774; incorp. as town 1850, as city 1873; volleyball invented here 1895; large power dam (see HOLYOKE DAM).

Holyoke Dam *or* **Had·ley Falls Dam** \'had-lē\. Dam at Hadley Falls across Connecticut River above Holyoke, SW Massachusetts; completed 1900.

Holy Roman Empire. A realm of primarily cen. Europe in medieval and modern periods; of varying extent with Germany as its chief component; originated 800 A.D. when Frankish King Charlemagne was crowned emperor of the West; revived with coronation 962 of Otto the Great; at its height in mid-11th cent. before emperors began great struggle with Papacy for dominance; under Hohenstaufens 1138–1254, imperial power absorbed by renewed struggle with popes over control of Italy; had no emperor 1250–73 (Great Interregnum) when German unity collapsed; under Rudolf of Hapsburg 1273–91 who consolidated dynastic monarchy (see AUSTRIA) at expense of imperial strength; Golden Bull of 1356 formally gave elector status to archbishops of Mainz, Trier, Cologne, king of Bohemia, count Palatine of Rhine, duke of Saxony, and margrave of Brandenburg and eliminated papal intervention in imperial elections; from 1438 emperor's crown almost hereditary in Hapsburg family; known as the Roman Empire of the German Nation from mid-15th cent.; weakened by Protestant Reformation; nearly dissolved after Thirty Years' War 1618–48; continued as loose association of states until formally dissolved during Napoleonic Wars 1806 (see GERMANY).

Hol·y·rood \'hä-lē-ˌrüd\. Royal palace, E Edinburgh, Scotland; residence of Mary, Queen of Scots, 1561–67; not much used by royalty since ascension of James VI to throne of England (as James I) 1603; official residence of the British monarch in Edinburgh; adjoining the palace are remains of abbey, founded 1128, which contains burial vault of Scottish kings.

Holy See. See VATICAN CITY.

Hol·y·well \'hä-lē-ˌwel, -wəl\ *or Welsh* **Tre·ffyn·non** \tre-'fə-nän\. Town, Clwyd co., NE Wales; pop. (1981p) 8905; diversified manufacturing; site of St. Winifred's Well, reputed to have burst forth on spot where her head fell when St. Winifred was beheaded in the 7th cent., now a place of pilgrimage.

Holz·min·den \'hȯlts-ˌmin-dən\. City, Lower Saxony, Germany, on Weser River 55 mi. (88 km.) SW of Brunswick; pop. (1980c) 22,218; founded c. 1200.

Homalig. See JOMALIG.

Ho·ma·lin \'hō-mə-ˌlin\. Town, NW Myanmar, on Chindwin River near Manipur border.

Homāyunshahr. See KHOMEYNISHAHR.

Hom·berg \'hȯm-ˌberk\ *also* **Homberg am Nie·der·rhein** \äm-ˌnē-dər-'rīn\. Town, North Rhine-Westphalia, Germany, on Rhine River opp. Duisburg; pop. (1980c) 41,847; coal mining; iron founding.

Homburg. See BAD HOMBURG.

Homel. See HOMYEL'.

Ho·mer \'hō-mər\. **1.** City, S Alaska, on Cook Inlet SW of Seward; pop. (1990c) 3660; seaport.
2. Town, ⊗ of Banks co., NE Georgia; pop. (1990c) 742.
3. Town, ⊗ of Claiborne parish, N Louisiana, 47 mi. (76 km.) ENE of Shreveport; pop. (1990c) 4152.
4. Village, Cortland co., cen. New York, 28 mi. (45 km.) S of Syracuse; pop. (1990c) 3476.

Ho·mer·ville \'hō-mər-ˌvil\. City, ⊗ of Clinch co., S Georgia; pop. (1990c) 2560; timber.

Home·stead \'hōm-ˌsted\. **1.** City, Miami-Dade co., SE Florida, 28 mi. (45 km.) SW of Miami; pop. (1990c) 26,866; trade center for region producing citrus fruits, vegetables; incorp. 1913; severely damaged by hurricane, Aug. 1992.
2. Borough, Allegheny co., SW Pennsylvania, on Monongahela River just ESE of Pittsburgh; pop. (1990c) 4179; machinery; settled 1871; incorp. 1880; scene of serious strike and ensuing violence 1892 at the (now closed) steel mill.

Homestead National Monument. See UNITED STATES, *National Monuments*.

Home·town \'hōm-ˌtau̇n\. City, Cook co., NE Illinois, SW suburb of Chicago; pop. (1990c) 4769.

Home·wood \'hōm-ˌwu̇d\. **1.** City, Jefferson co., cen. Alabama, 2 mi. (3 km.) SE of Birmingham; pop. (1990c) 22,922.
2. Village, Cook co., NE Illinois, 8 mi. (13 km.) S of Chicago; pop. (1990c) 19,278.

Hom·il·don Hill \'hä-mil-dən\ *or* **Hum·ble·don Hill** \'həm-bəl-dən\ *or* **Hum·ble·ton Hill** \-tən\. Small hill, N Northumberland, N England, SE of Flodden; scene of victory of Sir Henry Percy (Hotspur) and George Dunbar, earl of March, over the Scots 1402.

Ho·mon·hon \ˌhō-mən-'hȯn\ *or* **Jo·mon·jol** \ˌhō-mən-'hȯl\ *or* **Mal·hon** \mäl-'hȯn\. Island, S of Samar, Philippines, in entrance to Leyte Gulf; 40 sq. mi. (104 sq. km.); belongs to Guiuan munic. of Eastern Samar prov.

Homs \'hȯmz, 'hȯms\ *or* **Ḥimṣ** \'hims\; *anc.* **Em·e·sa** \'e-mə-sə\. City, W Syria, on the Orontes 85 mi. (137 km.) N of Damascus; pop. (1981p) 354,508; oil and sugar refineries; in fertile area with gardens and orchards; on ancient highway N from Egypt; nearby is battleground of Kadesh (*q.v.*).
History: As Emesa, devoted to worship of sun god and birthplace of Elagabalus, one of its priests who became Roman emperor 218 A.D.; scene of defeat of Queen Zenobia of Palmyra 272 by Emperor Aurelian; seized by Arabs 636 and renamed Hims; passed to Ottomans 16th cent.; held by Egyptians 1830s; in WWI taken by British and Arabs Oct. 15, 1918.

Homs. See AL KHUMS.

Ho·myel' \kȯ-'myel\ *or* **Go·mel** \gȯ-'mel, -'myel\ *or* **Ho·mel** \hȯ-\. **1.** Province of SE Belarus; 15,598 sq. mi. (40,399 sq. km.); pop. (1991e) 1,628,400; ✱ Homyel'; parts of W section swampy; potatoes, flax, timber.
2. City, SE Belarus, on the Sozh 140 mi. (225 km.) N of Kiev, Ukraine; pop. (1991e) 503,300; railroad junction; has river

connections with towns on the Dnieper. A historical and cultural center, first mentioned 1142; passed to Lithuania then Poland; passed to Russia 1772.

Hon. See HŪN.

Ho·nan \ˈhō-ˈnan\. **1.** Province, E cen. China. See HENAN. **2.** City, China. See LUOYANG.

Hon·da Rapids \ˈȯn-dä\. Rapids in Magdalena River in NW cen. Colombia, stopping navigation at that point.

Hon·do \ˈhän-dō\. **1.** City, ⊗ of Medina co., S cen. Texas, 37 mi. (60 km.) W of San Antonio; pop. (1990c) 6018.
2. Island of Japan. See HONSHŪ.
3. River, rising in N Guatemala and flowing NE into Chetumal Bay; ab. 150 mi. (240 km.) long; forms boundary bet. Belize and Mexico (Quintana Roo state).

Hon·du·ras \hän-ˈdu̇r-əs, -ˈdyu̇r-; ȯn-ˈdü-räs\. Republic, Central America, bounded on N by the Gulf of Honduras and the Caribbean Sea, on E by the Caribbean, on S by Nicaragua and the Gulf of Fonseca, on SW by El Salvador, and on W by Guatemala; 43,277 sq. mi. (112,087 sq. km.); pop. (1989e) 4,604,800; ✱ Tegucigalpa.

Physical features: Coastline ab. 400 mi. (645 km.) on the Caribbean and ab. 40 mi. (65 km.) on the Pacific (Gulf of Fonseca) bet. El Salvador and Nicaragua; most easterly point Cape Gracias a Dios; off N coast are Islas de la Bahía. Generally mountainous with many ranges much varied in extent and direction; highest in S above 10,000 ft. (3048 m.).

Chief rivers: Chamelecón and Ulúa in W, Aguán in N, Patuca in E, Choluteca in S; also in S, Coco (forming a large part of the border with Nicaragua); only large inland lake Yojoa in W with outlet to Ulúa River.

Chief products: Coffee, bananas, sugar, forest products; fish, livestock; cigars, textiles, cement; zinc, silver, lead; ab. 65 percent of labor force is engaged in agriculture.

Chief cities: Tegucigalpa, San Pedro Sula, La Ceiba, Choluteca, El Progreso.

Political divisions: Divided into the following 18 departments (for pronunciation of their names, see their individual entries):

NAME	AREA (sq. mi.)	AREA (sq. km.)	POP. (1991e)	CAPITAL
Atlántida	1,641	4,250	255,000	La Ceiba
Choluteca	1,625	4,209	309,000	Choluteca
Colón	3,426	8,873	164,000	Trujillo
Comayagua	2,006	5,196	257,000	Comayagua
Copán	1,236	3,201	226,000	Santa Rosa
Cortés	1,526	3,952	706,000	San Pedro Sula
El Paraíso	2,786	7,216	277,000	Yuscarán
Francisco Morazán	3,068	7,946	878,000	Tegucigalpa
Gracias a Dios	6,420	16,628	37,000	Puerto Lempira
Intibucá	1,186	3,072	130,000	La Esperanza
Islas de la Bahía	100	259	24,000	Roatán
La Paz	899	2,328	112,000	La Paz
Lempira	1,656	4,289	180,000	Gracias
Ocotepeque	648	1,678	77,000	Nueva Ocotepeque
Olancho	9,401	24,348	309,000	Juticalpa
Santa Bárbara	1,975	5,115	291,000	Santa Bárbara
Valle	604	1,564	121,000	Nacaome
Yoro	3,065	7,938	355,000	Yoro

History: Indigenous pre-Columbian population included part of Mayan civilization; reached by explorer Christopher Columbus 1502; Trujillo and Puerto Cortés founded c. 1524; war with Spain 1537–38; indigenous population enslaved and decimated; included in captaincy general of Guatemala after 1570; proclaimed independence 1821; part of United Provinces of Central America 1823–38; participant in several unsuccessful efforts to reunify Central America; received Bay Is. (Islas de la Bahía), former subject of dispute with Great Britain 1859; in 20th cent. scene of incessant civil war and of intervention of U.S. on several occasions; in WWI declared war on Germany 1918 and in WWII on Axis powers 1941; border with Nicaragua fixed 1961; fought brief border war with El Salvador 1969; adopted new constitution and civilian government elected 1982.

Honduras, British. See BELIZE.

Honduras, Cape *or Span.* **Ca·bo de Honduras** \ˈkä-bō-ˌthā-ȯn-ˈdü-räs\. Cape, N coast of Honduras, extending into Caribbean Sea.

Honduras, Gulf of. Inlet of Caribbean Sea, bet. S Belize, E Guatemala, and N Honduras.

Hon·ea Path \ˈhə-nē-ˌpath\. Town, Abbeville and Anderson cos., W South Carolina; pop. (1990c) 3841.

Hon·e·oye Lake \ˈhə-nē-ˌȯi\. Lake, W Ontario co., W New York; outlet from N end flows into Genesee River; ab. 5 mi. (8 km.) long; by some, considered one of the Finger Lakes.

Hones·dale \ˈhōnz-ˌdāl\. Borough, ⊗ of Wayne co., NE corner of Pennsylvania, 25 mi. (40 km.) ENE of Scranton; pop. (1990c) 4972; historically a shipping point for area coal mining; starting point of trial run of first locomotive in U.S. 1829.

Hon·ey Island *or* **Honey Island Swamp** \ˈhə-nē\. Swamp, SE Louisiana and SW Mississippi, in delta of Pearl River.

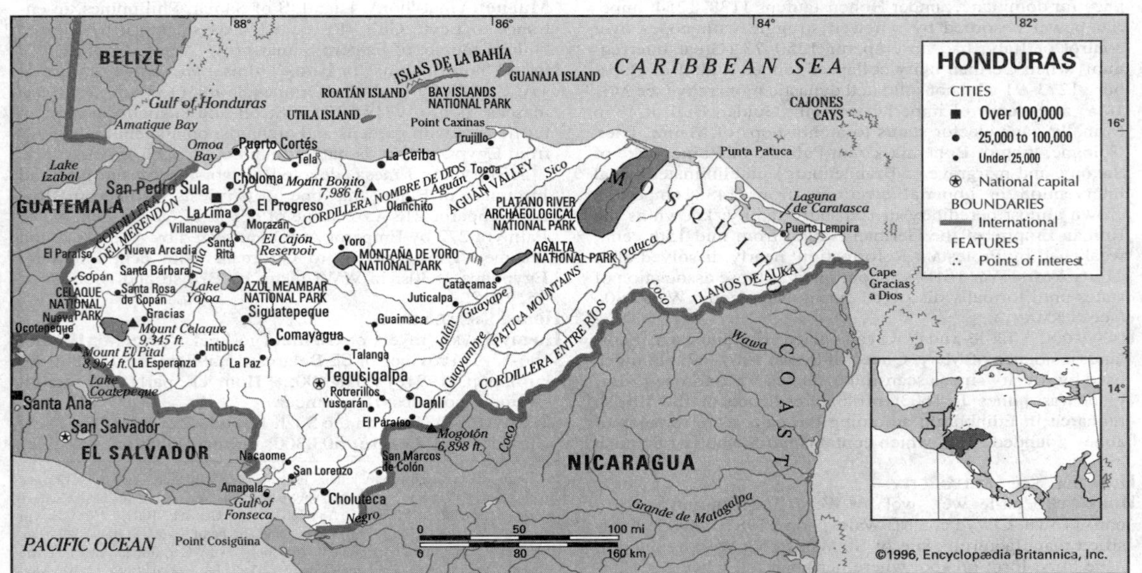

Honey Lake. Intermittent lake, SE Lassen co., NE California; ab. 20 mi. (32 km.) long; alt. 3949 ft. (1204 m.); no outlet.

Hon·fleur \ȯⁿ-ˈflœr\. Seaport, Calvados dept., NW France, on Seine estuary opp. Le Havre; pop. (1990c) 8346; tourism; founded in 11th cent.; frequently passed bet. France and England in Hundred Years' War 1337–1453 and not finally acquired by France until 1450; center for exploration in 16th and 17th cents.; in 19th cent. supplanted by Le Havre in commercial importance.

Hong. See RED 4.

Hon·ga River \ˈhäŋ-gə\. Inlet of Chesapeake Bay on SW shore of Dorchester co., SE Maryland.

Hong Gai \ˈhȯŋ-ˈgī\. Port city, NE Vietnam, on Gulf of Tonkin, ENE of Haiphong; pop. (1989c) 123,102.

Hong Kong \ˈhȯŋ-ˌkȯŋ, -ˈkȯŋ\ *also* **Hongkong.** Territory, SE China, formerly a British crown colony, E of mouth of the Zhu (Pearl) River ab. 90 mi. (145 km.) S of Guangzhou (Canton); 398 sq. mi. (1031 sq. km.); pop. (1986c) 5,395,997; ✻ Victoria. Comprises (a) **Hong Kong Island;** 29 sq. mi. (75 sq. km.); pop. (1991c) 1,214,253; irregular with broken ridge; highest point Victoria Peak 1805 ft. (550 m.) in NW; coast much indented; separated (1 mi. or 1.6 km. across) from Kowloon by spacious Hong Kong harbor and from mainland farther E by Lei Yue Mun Pass; on NW shore is city of Victoria (see VICTORIA 10). (b) **Kow·loon Peninsula** \ˌkau̇-ˌlün\, part of mainland opp. Hong Kong I.; 3 sq. mi. (8 sq. km.); chief town Kowloon (*q.v.*). (c) **New Territories,** enclave of Guangdong prov., China, comprising area N of Kowloon Penin. from Dapeng Wan on E to Deep Bay, inlet of Zhu River, on W; 366 sq. mi. (948 sq. km.); includes also Lan Tao and other islands. Territory an important center of world commerce and finance in the Far East; has one of the world's busiest ports; vegetables; electronic equipment, textiles, clothing, toys, plastic; shipbuilding; tourism; two universities.

History: Island occupied by British 1839, ceded to them by Chinese by Treaty of Nanking 1842; Kowloon Penin. ceded by China to British 1860; New Territories leased to Great Britain for 99 years 1898; bombed by Japanese, December 18–24, 1941 and surrendered Dec. 25; reoccupied by British forces Sept. 1945; joint declaration signed by Chinese and British 1984 calling for the return of Hong Kong to Chinese sovereignty 1997.

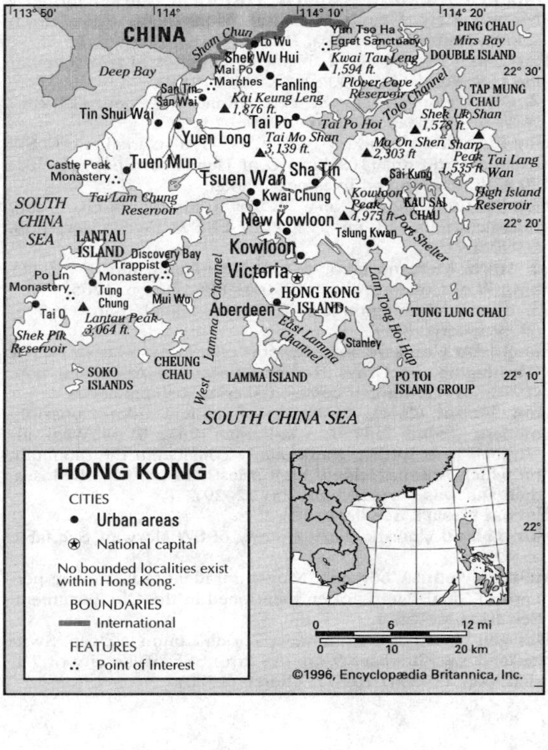

Hong·shui *or W.-G.* **Hung–shui** \ˈhu̇ŋ-ˈshwē\. River, S China; rises in E Yunnan, flows S and E forming part of boundary bet. Guizhou and Guangxi Zhuangzu, and flows through cen. Guangxi Zhuangzu; ab. 700 mi. (1125 km.) long; navigable for small vessels.

Hong·ze Hu *or W.-G.* **Hung–tse Hu** \ˈhu̇ŋ-ˈdzə-ˈhü\. Lake in Jiangsu prov., E China, at border of Anhui prov.; 502 sq. mi. (1300 sq. km.).

Ho·ni·a·ra \ˌhō-nē-ˈär-ə\. Town, ✻ of Solomon Is., on NW Guadalcanal I.; pop. (1990e) 35,288.

Hon·is·ter Hause \ˈhä-nis-tər-ˈhȯs\ *or* **Honister Pass.** Mountain pass, Cumberland, NW England, near Keswick; 1190 ft. (363 m.).

Hon·i·ton \ˈhä-ni-tən, ˈhə-\. Town, Devon, SW England, 16 mi. (26 km.) NE of Exeter; pop. (1981p) 6567; famous for its manufacture of Honiton lace.

Ho·no·ka·la Point \ˌhō-nō-ˈkä-lä\. Point on NE coast of Maui I., Hawaii.

Ho·no·ka·o·pe Bay \ˌhō-nō-kä-ˈō-pā\. Bay on NW coast of Hawaii I., bet. Keawaiki Bay and Kawaihae Bay.

Hon·o·lu·lu \ˌhä-nə-ˈlü-lü, ˌhō-nō-\. **1.** County, Hawaii, comprising Oahu I. and the small uninhabited islands of the Hawaiian group. See table at HAWAII.
2. Seaport city, ✻ of the state of Hawaii and ⊗ of Honolulu co., SE Oahu I., Hawaii; pop. (1990c) 365,272; has protected harbor; tourism; sugar processing, pineapple canning; its position in center of North Pacific Ocean (2090 naut. mi., 2404 statute mi., or 3867 km. from San Francisco; 4711 naut. mi., 5418 statute mi., or 8717 km. from Panama; 4483 naut. mi., 5155 statute mi., or 8295 km. via Suva from Sydney; 4767 naut. mi., 5482 statute mi., or 8821 km. from Manila; 3380 naut. mi., 3887 statute mi., or 6254 km. from Yokohama; 1304 statute mi. or 2098 km. by air from Midway) makes it a port of exceptional importance; at mouth of Nuuanu Valley with mountains immediately behind it (Punchbowl 500 ft. or 152 m. and Mt. Tantalus 2013 ft. or 614 m.) and farther to NE the Koolau Range with peaks above 3000 ft. or 914 m. (see NUUANU PALI); to SE is suburb of Waikiki with excellent beach; Iolani Palace, now a museum, completed 1882; Univ. of Hawaii (1907), Chaminade Univ. of Honolulu (1955), Hawaii Pacific Univ. (1965); Bishop Museum; state capitol. Harbor visited 1794 by British explorer Capt. William Brown; became trade center 19th cent.; declared ✻ of kingdom of Hawaii 1850; with Pearl Harbor, attacked by Japanese 1941; with Pearl Harbor served as a center for U.S. armed forces during WWII, Korean War, and Vietnam War.

Ho·no·pu Point \hō-ˈnō-pü\. Cape on NW coast of Lanai I., Hawaii.

Hon·shū \ˈhȯn-ˌshü\; *formerly also* **Hon·do** \-ˌdō\. Largest of the four chief islands of Japan; area with adjacent small islands 86,246 sq. mi. (223,377 sq. km.); pop. (1990p) 100,254,208; considered as the mainland of Japan. For additional information, see JAPAN.

Honto. See NEVEL'SK.

Hood \ˈhu̇d\. County in N cen. Texas. See table at TEXAS.

Hood, Mount. Peak in Cascade Range, in Clackamas and Hood River cos., NW Oregon; 11,235 ft. (3424 m.); highest mountain in Oregon.

Hood Canal. Navigable inlet of Puget Sound, W Washington; extends SW of Admiralty Inlet; ab. 80 mi. (130 km.) long, bet. 2 and 3 mi. (3 and 5 km.) wide.

Hood Island. See ESPAÑOLA 1.

Hoo·doo Peak \ˈhü-dü\. Mountain, W Park co., NW Wyoming; 10,522 ft. (3207 m.).

Hood River. 1. County in N Oregon. See table at OREGON.

2. City, its ⊗, on Columbia River ab. 17 mi. (27 km.) NW of the Dalles; pop. (1990c) 4632; ships apples, pears, cherries, and berries; fruit-packing plants; settled 1854.

Hoofd·dorp \ˈhōft-ˌdȯrp\ *also* **Haar·lem·mer·meer** \ˌhär-lə-mər-ˈmār\. Commune, North Holland prov., W Netherlands; pop. (1992e) 100,659; built on land reclaimed from the former **Haarlem Meer,** a branch of the Zuider Zee; in agricultural area.

Hoo·ge·veen \ˌhō-k̲ə-ˈvān\. Commune, Drenthe prov., NE Netherlands, 23 mi. (37 km.) NE of Zwolle; pop. (1992e) 46,456; 17th cent. church; museum; founded in 17th cent.

Hoo·ge·zand–Sap·pe·meer \ˌhō-k̲ə-ˈzänt-ˈsä-pə-ˌmār\. Commune, Groningen prov., NE Netherlands, on canal 9 mi. (15 km.) ESE of the city of Groningen; pop. (1981e) 35,247.

Hooghly. See HUGLI.

Hoogh·ly–Chin·su·ra \ˈhü-glē-ˈchin-sə-rə\ *or* **Hu·gli–Chun·cu·ra** \-ˈchəŋ-kə-rə\. Town (joint municipality), West Bengal, NE India, on Hugli River 22 mi. (35 km.) N of Calcutta; pop. (1991p) 142,388; trading post estab. by Portuguese 1537, by the English at Hooghly 1651, and by the Dutch at Chinsura 1656; towns united 1865.

Hook·er \ˈhu̇-kər\. County in W cen. Nebraska. See table at NEBRASKA.

Hooker Island. Island in Arctic Ocean, S cen. Franz Josef Land, Russia.

Hook Head \ˈhu̇k\. Cape on SE coast of Ireland, at E of entrance to Waterford Harbour.

Hook of Holland. See HOEK VAN HOLLAND.

Hooks \ˈhu̇ks\. Town, Bowie co., NE Texas, 16 mi. (26 km.) WNW of Texarkana; pop. (1990c) 2684.

Hook·sett \ˈhu̇k-sət\. Town, Merrimack co., S cen. New Hampshire, on Merrimack River 7 mi. (11 km.) S of Concord; pop. (1990c) 8767.

Hoo·per Island \ˈhü-pər\. Island, SW Dorchester co., Maryland, on E side of lower Chesapeake Bay.

Hooper Strait. Strait bet. Bloodsworth I. and mainland of Dorchester co., SE Maryland.

Hoopes·ton \ˈhüp-stən, ˈhu̇p-\. City, Vermilion co., E Illinois, 25 mi. (40 km.) N of Danville; pop. (1990c) 5871.

Hoorn \ˈhōrn\. Commune, North Holland prov., W Netherlands, on an inlet of IJsselmeer; pop. (1992e) 59,028; important agricultural market; has two gates from 16th cent. fortifications. Scene of Dutch naval victory over Spanish 1573. Birthplace (c. 1580) of mariner Willem C. Schouten, first to round Cape Horn (named after this town), and (c. 1603) of explorer Abel J. Tasman, discoverer of Tasmania.

Hoorn Islands. See FUTUNA ISLANDS.

Hoo·sac Mountains \ˈhü-sik\. A range of the Green Mts. in Berkshire co., W Massachusetts; highest peak Spruce Hill 1974 ft. (602 m.).

Hoosac Tunnel. Railroad tunnel, Berkshire co., W Massachusetts, in Hoosac Mts.; ab. 4.8 mi. (7.7 km.) long; completed 1875 after 24 years of work.

Hoo·sic \ˈhü-sik\. River, E United States; rises in N cen. Berkshire co., Massachusetts, flows N and NW across SW extremity of Vermont into New York, and empties into Hudson River 14 mi. (23 km.) N of Troy, Rensselaer co., E New York; ab. 70 mi. (115 km.) long.

Hoo·sick Falls \ˈhü-sik\. Village, Rensselaer co., E New York, on Hoosic River near Vermont border 21 mi. (34 km.) ENE of Troy; pop. (1990c) 3490; Bennington Battlefield (state park) nearby.

Hoo·sier Pass \ˈhü-zhər\. Mountain pass, Park and Summit cos., cen. Colorado, in Park Range of the Rocky Mts.; 11,541 ft. (3518 m.); contains a highway.

Hoo·ver \ˈhü-vər\. City, Jefferson co., Alabama; pop. (1990c) 39,788.

Hoover Dam. See UNITED STATES, *Dams and Reservoirs.*

Hop \ˈhäp\. River, E cen. Connecticut; rises in W Tolland co., flows SE into the Willimantic River near Willimantic.

Ho·pat·cong \hə-ˈpat-ˌkän, -ˌkäŋ\. Borough, Sussex co., N New Jersey, 14 mi. (23 km.) NW of Morristown; pop. (1990c) 15,586.

Hopatcong, Lake. Lake on boundary bet. Morris and Sussex cos., N New Jersey; ab. 8 mi. (13 km.) long; summer resort.

Hope \ˈhōp\. **1.** City, ⊗ of Hempstead co., SW Arkansas, 32 mi. (52 km.) NE of Texarkana; pop. (1990c) 9643; distributing point for truck-gardening and fruit-growing region; ⊗ since 1939; childhood home of President Bill Clinton.

2. Town, British Columbia, Canada, 75 mi. (121 km.) E of Vancouver; pop. (1991c) 3147; lumber.

Hope, Mount. Peak, Chaffee co., cen. Colorado; 13,943 ft. (4250 m.).

Hope, Point *or Inuit* **Tig·a·ra** \ˈti-gə-rə\. Cape and village, NW Alaska, on Arctic Ocean N of Bering Strait, 68°21′N, 166°50′W. Nearby is Ipiutak, site of ancient city that gives its name to the Ipiutak culture that flourished c. 100–700 A.D.

Hope·dale \ˈhōp-ˌdāl\. **1.** Town, Worcester co., cen. Massachusetts, 16 mi. (26 km.) ESE of the city of Worcester; pop. (1990c) 5666; location of a Utopian religious community 1841–56 estab. by Universalist minister Adin Ballou; incorp. as city 1886.

2. Community and harbor, E coast of Labrador, Newfoundland, Canada; pop. (1991c) 515.

Hopeh *also* **Hopei.** See HEBEI.

Hope Island. Island, Svalbard, Norway, in Barents Sea ab. 60 mi. (95 km.) SE of Edge I.; ab. 20 mi. (32 km.) long.

Hope Mills. Town, Cumberland co., North Carolina, S of Fayetteville; pop. (1990c) 8184.

Hopes Ad·vance, Cape \ˌhōps-əd-ˈvans\. Cape, N Ungava Penin., N Quebec, Canada, on Hudson Strait at W side of entrance to Ungava Bay.

Hope·town \ˈhōp-ˌtau̇n\. Town, Northern Cape prov., cen. Rep. of South Africa, on Orange River 70 mi. (113 km.) SSW of Kimberley.

Hope Town. Town on small island off E coast of Great Abaco I., Bahamas.

Hope·well \ˈhōp-ˌwel, -wəl\. **1.** City in Prince George co. but politically independent, SE Virginia, at confluence of James and Appomattox rivers 10 mi. (16 km.) NE of Petersburg; 7 sq. mi. (18 sq. km.); pop. (1990c) 23,101; manufactures textiles, chemicals; site of Union Gen. Ulysses S. Grant's headquarters 1864–65 during Civil War; incorp. 1916.

2. Parish, ⊗ of Albert co., SE New Brunswick, Canada; pop. (1991c) 757.

Hopewell Culture National Historical Park; *formerly* **Mound City Group National Monument.** See UNITED STATES, *National Historical Parks.*

Hop·kins \ˈhäp-kinz\. **1.** Name of counties in two states of the U.S. See tables at KENTUCKY and TEXAS.

2. City, Hennepin co., SE cen. Minnesota, 8 mi. (13 km.) WSW of Minneapolis; pop. (1980c) 15,336.

Hop·kins·ville \ˈhäp-kinz-ˌvil\. City, ⊗ of Christian co., SW Kentucky, 68 mi. (109 km.) S of Henderson; pop. (1990c) 29,809; tobacco and livestock market.

Hop·kin·ton \ˈhäp-kin-tən\. **1.** Town, Middlesex co., E cen. Massachusetts, 13 mi. (21 km.) ESE of Worcester; pop. (1990c) 9191.

2. Town, Merrimack co., S cen. New Hampshire, 7 mi. (11 km.) W of Concord; pop. (1990c) 4806; incorp. 1765.

3. Town, Washington co., S Rhode Island; pop. (1990c) 6873; incorp. 1757.

Ho·qui·am \ˈhō-kwē-əm\. Seaport city, Grays Harbor co., W Washington, on Grays Harbor adjacent to Aberdeen; pop. (1990c) 8972; lumber center; fisheries, fish canneries.

Hor, Mount \ˈhȯr\. Mountain of ancient Edom; possibly modern **Ja·bal Hā·rūn** \ˌja-bəl-hä-ˈrün\, E of Wadi al-ʻArabah in S Jordan; traditionally considered the mountain on which Aaron, Hebrew high priest and brother of Moses, died and was buried (*Num.* xx. 22–29).

Horbat Qesari. See CAESAREA 2.

Hor·da·land \ˈhȯr-də-ˌlän\. County of SW Norway. See table at NORWAY.

Ho·reb, Mount \ˈhōr-ˌeb\. Mountain, identity unknown, perhaps in Sinai Penin.; often mentioned in the Old Testament. See SINAI, MOUNT 1.

Hor·gen \ˈhȯr-gən\. Commune, Zürich canton, NE cen. Switzerland, on Zürichsee 9 mi. (15 km.) SSE of the city of Zürich; pop. (1980c) 16,577; church (1780).

Hor·i·con \ˈhȯr-ə-ˌkän\. City, Dodge co., SE cen. Wisconsin, 25 mi. (40 km.) S of Fond du Lac; pop. (1990c) 3873.

Horicon, Lake. See GEORGE, LAKE 2.

Horlivka. See GORLOVKA.

Hor·mi·gue·ros \ˌōr-mē-ˈgā-rōs\. Municipality, W Puerto Rico; on railroad line S of Mayagüez; pop. (1990c) 15,212.

Hor·moz *or* **Hor·muz** \ˈhȯr-ˌməz, hȯr-ˈmüz\; *mostly formerly* **Or·muz** \ˈȯr-ˌməz, ȯr-ˈmüz\. Island in Strait of Hormuz; belongs to Iran; under Portuguese control 1514–1622.

Hor·moz·gān \ˈhȯr-müz-ˌgän\. Province of S Iran. See table at IRAN.

Hormuz; *mostly formerly* **Ormuz;** *anc.* **Har·mo·zia** \här-ˈmō-zhə\. Town, ancient Persia, near modern Bandar ʻAbbās on Strait of Hormuz, S Iran. Original Arab mainland settlement became a major trade center by c. 1200; relocated to island c. 1300; taken by Portuguese 1514; retaken by Persian leader Shāh ʻAbbās I 1622; declined after removal of its trade to Bandar ʻAbbās on mainland.

Hormuz, Strait of; *mostly formerly* **Strait of Ormuz.** Strait bet. the N tip of Oman, SE Arabian Penin., and the S coast of Iran; connects the Persian Gulf with the Gulf of Oman; strategically important transport route for oil tankers.

Horn \ˈhȯrn\ *or* **North Cape.** Cape, NW Iceland, W of Húna Bay.

Horn, Cape *or Span.* **Ca·bo de Hor·nos** \ˈkä-b̲ō-t̲h̲ā-ˈȯr-nōs\. Cape, at S extremity of South America, 56°S, 67°16′W, on **Horn Island** of Wollaston group, S Tierra del Fuego Archipelago (*q.v.*), projecting S into Drake Passage; named Hoorn for the birthplace of Dutch mariner Willem C. Schouten who rounded it in 1616.

Hornád. See HERNÁD.

Hor·na Fjord \ˈhȯr-nä\. Inlet of Atlantic Ocean on SE coast of Iceland; good harbor.

Horn·a·van \ˈhür-ˌnä-vən\. Lake, Västerbotten prov., N Sweden; 89 sq. mi. (231 sq. km.); drained by Skellefte River.

Horn·cas·tle \ˈhȯrn-ˌka-səl\. Town, the Parts of Lindsey, Lincolnshire, E England; pop. (1981p) 4207; malting, tanning.

Hor·ne·len \hȯr-ˈnā-lən\. Island off SW coast of Norway, near entrance to Nord Fjord; shores rise abruptly to a height of ab. 3000 ft. (915 m.).

Hor·nell \hȯr-ˈnel\. City, Steuben co., S New York, 56 mi. (90 km.) S of Rochester; pop. (1990c) 9877; settled 1790.

Horn Island. **1.** Island, off SE Mississippi coast, bet. Mississippi Sound and Gulf of Mexico.

2. Small island off Cape York, N Queensland, Australia; airport.

3. Island, South America. See HORN, CAPE.

Horn Lake. City, De Soto co., NW corner of Mississippi; pop. (1990c) 9069.

Horn of Africa. Easternmost projection of Africa; variously used of Somalia, SE or all of Ethiopia, and sometimes Djibouti.

Hornos, Cabo de. See HORN, CAPE.

Horn Peak. Mountain, Custer and Saguache cos., S cen. Colorado; ab. 13,400 ft. (4085 m.).

Horns of Ḥaṭ·ṭīn \ˈk̲ä-ˌtēn, ˈhä-; k̲ä-ˈtēn\. Twin hills, N Israel, W of the Sea of Galilee; site of battle 1187 resulting in defeat of Christian armies led by Guy de Lusignan, king of Jerusalem, at the hands of Sultan Saladin's Muslim forces.

Horn·sund·tind \ˈhȯrn-sən-ˌtin\. Mountain, at S end of Spitsbergen I., near **Horn Sound** (*Norw.* **Horn·sund** \ˈhȯrn-ˌsu̇n\), inlet on SW coast.

Hör·num \ˈhœr-nəm\. S part of island of Sylt, Germany, off W coast of Schleswig-Holstein; sandy region.

Ho·ro·shi·ri \hō-ˈrō-shē-rē\. Mountain peak, Hidaka Mts., S Hokkaidō I., Japan; 6732 ft. (2052 m.).

Hor·qin You·yi Qian·qi \ˈhȯr-ˈchin-ˈyō-ˈyē-ˈchyan-ˈchē\ *or W.-G.* **Ko–erh–ch'in–yu–i–ch'ien–ch'i** \ˈkō-ˈər-ˈchin-ˈyue̅-ē-ˈchyen-ˈchē\; *locally* **Ulan Hot** \ˈü-lä-ˈhȯt\ *or W.-G.* **Wu–lan–hao–t'e** \ˈwü-ˈlän-ˈhau̇-ˈtə\; *formerly* **Wang·yeh·miao** \ˈwäŋ-ˈye-ˈmyau̇\. Town, NW Jilin, NE China, on a tributary of the Nen River 200 mi. (322 km.) NW of Changchun.

Hor·ry \ˈhȯr-ē\. Coastal county in E South Carolina. See table at SOUTH CAROLINA.

Horse·head Lake \ˈhȯrs-ˌhed\. Lake in cen. Kidder co., S cen. North Dakota.

Horse·heads \ˈhȯrs-ˌhedz\. Village, Chemung co., S New York, 5 mi. (8 km.) N of Elmira; pop. (1990c) 6802.

Hör·sel·ber·ge \ˈhœr-zəl-ˌber-gə\ *or* **Ve·nus·berg** \ˈvē-nəs-ˌbərg\. Mountains, Thuringia, cen. Germany, bet. Gotha and Eisenach; contains the cave in which, according to legend, Venus lived and lyric poet Tannhäuser visited.

Horse Mesa Dam \ˈhȯrs\. Dam across Salt River, Maricopa co., S cen. Arizona; height 300 ft. (91 m.); completed 1927; forms **Apache Lake** \ə-ˈpa-chē\.

Hor·sens \ˈhȯr-səns\. Seaport, Vejle co., E Jutland, Denmark, at head of **Horsens Fjord;** pop. (1989e) 54,940; ships dairy products; manufactures textiles, tobacco products.

Horse·shoe Bend National Military Park \ˈhȯrs-ˌshü\. See UNITED STATES, *National Historical Parks.*

Horseshoe Curve. Scenic curve of Pennsylvania Railroad, Pennsylvania, just W of Altoona; 2375 ft. (724 m.) long, and graded 91 ft. to the mile (17 m. to the kilometer); of exceptional engineering interest; completed 1852.

Horseshoe Falls. See NIAGARA FALLS.

Horseshoe Mountain. Peak, Park and Lake cos., cen. Colorado; 13,902 ft. (4237 m.).

Horse Trough \ˌtrȯf\. Peak, Union co., N Georgia; 4052 ft. (1235 m.).

Hor·sham \ˈhȯr-shəm\. **1.** City, W Victoria, SE Australia, 115 mi. (185 km.) W of Bendigo; pop. (1991c) 12,552.

2. Town, West Sussex, S England; pop. (1991p) 107,300; to NW is Field Place, birthplace of poet Percy Bysshe Shelley 1792; Christ's Hospital (transferred from London 1902).

Hor·ta \ˈȯr-tə\. **1.** Former district of Portugal, comprised Pico, Faial, Flores, and Corvo islands, Azores.

2. Seaport commune, Azores, Portugal, on SE coast of Faial I.; pop. (1991p) 15,155; radio station; exports wine, oranges; air base.

Hor·ten \ˈhȯrt-ᵊn\. Seaport, Vestfold co., SE Norway, on W side of Oslo Fjord; pop. (1980c) 13,185; naval museum.

Hor·ton \ˈhȯrt-ᵊn\. **1.** River, NW mainland part of Northwest Territories, Canada, E of Anderson River; flows NW into W side of Franklin Bay; 275 mi. (443 km.) long.

2. Parish, Berkshire, SE England, 3 mi. (5 km.) ESE of Windsor; residence 1632–38 of poet John Milton.

Hor·wich \ˈhȯr-ich, -ij\. Town, Greater Manchester, NW England, 15 mi. (24 km.) NW of Manchester; pop. (1981p) 17,970; cotton textiles.

Horyń. See GORYN.

Ho·ryu·ji \ˈhōr-yü-ˌjē\. Locality, Nara prefecture, W cen. Honshū, Japan, ab. 7 mi. (11 km.) SW of the city of Nara; site of oldest existing Buddhist shrine in Japan, built ab. 607 A.D.

Ho·shang·a·bad \hō-ˈshəŋ-ə-ˌbäd\. Town, cen. Madhya Pradesh, India, on Narmada River; pop. (1991p) 70,820; founded early 15th cent.

Ho·shi·ar·pur \ˌhō-shē-ˈär-pu̇r\. Town, cen. Punjab, NW India; pop. (1991p) 122,528; produces furniture.

Hos·pet \ˈhōsh-ˌpet\. Town, Karnataka, India, on Tungabhadra River 37 mi. (60 km.) W of Bellary; pop. (1991p) 96,499; ruins of Vijayanagar are nearby.

Hos·pi·ta·let \ˌōs-pē-tä-ˈlet\. City, Barcelona prov., NE Spain, SW suburb of the city of Barcelona; pop. (1991p) 269,241; steel, textiles; agricultural institute.

Hos·te \ˈōs-tā\. Island in Tierra del Fuego Archipelago (*q.v.*), Chile, S of W Tierra del Fuego I.; 90 mi. (145 km.) long, 50 mi. (81 km.) wide.

Ho·tan \ˈhō-ˈtan\ *or W.-G.* **Ho–t'ien** \ˈhō-ˈtyen\ *or conventional* **Kho·tan** \ˈkō-ˈtan\. **1.** River, W Xinjiang Uygur, W China; joins the Yarkant He to form the Tarim, but dry much of the year.

2. Town and oasis, SW Xinjiang Uygur, W China, 160 mi. (257 km.) SE of Shache; at foot of Kunlun Shan and on S highway and caravan route across Xinjiang Uygur; agricultural center producing cereals, cotton, fruits; some gold mining; silk, carpets; has been from earliest times on the Silk Road and the largest and most important oasis supply base on S edge of Taklimakan Desert; through it Buddhist culture introduced from India; has experienced many political changes, being ruled variously by Chinese (first cent. A.D.), Arabs (8th cent.), Uighurs (10th cent.), Mongols (13th cent.); Muslim rebellion of 19th cent. ultimately defeated; Chinese since 1878.

Hoth·am, Mount \ˈhä-thəm\. Mountain in the Darg Plateau, E Victoria, SE Australia, SW of Mt. Kosciusko; 6108 ft. (1862 m.).

Ho–t'ien. See HOTAN.

Hotin. See KHOTIN.

Hot Spring. County in SW cen. Arkansas. See table at ARKANSAS.

Hot Springs. **1.** County in NW cen. Wyoming. See table at WYOMING.

2. City, ⊗ of Garland co., W cen. Arkansas, in Ouachita Mts. 47 mi. (76 km.) WSW of Little Rock; pop. (1990c) 32,462; health and tourist resort noted for its 47 thermal springs. Settled 1807; made, with surrounding area, a U.S. Government reservation 1832, **Hot Springs National Park** 1921 (see UNITED STATES, *National Parks*).

3. City, New Mexico. See TRUTH OR CONSEQUENCES.

4. City, ⊗ of Fall River co., SW corner of South Dakota, in foothills of Black Hills 48 mi. (77 km.) S of Rapid City; pop. (1990c) 4325; health resort; thermal and mineral springs.

5. Village, Bath co., W Virginia, 5 mi. (8 km.) SW of Warm Springs; mineral springs.

Hot Springs Peak. Mountain, Humboldt co., NW Nevada; 6450 ft. (1966 m.).

Hot Sul·phur Springs \ˈsəl-fər\. Town, ⊗ of Grand co., N Colorado; pop. (1990c) 347.

Hotte, Mas·sif de la \mȧ-ˌsēf-də-lȧ-ˈȯt\ *also* **Massif du Sud** \dᵫ-ˈsᵫd\. Highland, Tiburon Penin., SW Haiti; highest point 7700 ft. (2347 m.).

Hot·ten·tot Point \ˈhät-ᵊn-ˌtät\. Cape on SW coast of Namibia, N of Lüderitz.

Hou·dan \ü-ˈdäⁿ\. Village, Yvelines dept., N France; has 15th–16th cent. church and keep of a 12th cent. castle.

Hou·deng–Goe·gnies \ü-ˌdeⁿ-gœ-ˈnyē\. Commune, Hainaut prov., SW Belgium, on a tributary of the Haine, E of Mons.

Houf·fa·lize \ˌü-fä-ˈlēz\. Village, Luxembourg prov., SE Belgium, 10 mi. (16 km.) N of Bastogne; pop. (1991c) 4248.

Hough·ton \ˈhō-tən\. **1.** County in NW Michigan. See table at MICHIGAN.

2. Village, ⊗ of Houghton co., NW Michigan, in Upper Penin., 70 mi. (113 km.) NW of Marquette; pop. (1990c) 7498; in copper-mining region; distribution center for Keweenaw Penin.; Michigan Technological Univ. (1885).

3. Village, Allegany co., SW New York, 65 mi. (105 km.) SE of Buffalo; pop. (1990c) 1740; Houghton Coll. (1883).

Houghton Lake. Lake in cen. Roscommon co., N cen. Michigan; 31 sq. mi. (80 sq. km.); 16 mi. (26 km.) long; largest inland lake in the state; source of Muskegon River.

Houghton–le–Spring \ˌhōt-ᵊn-lə-ˈspriŋ\. Town, Tyne and Wear, N England, 11 mi. (18 km.) SSE of Newcastle upon Tyne; pop. (1981p) 31,036; coal mining.

Hou·gou·mont \ˌü-gə-ˈmōⁿ\. Château on the battlefield of Waterloo, Belgium; held by British throughout the battle, June 18, 1815, against repeated attacks.

Hougue, La. See LA HOGUE.

Houilles \ˈüy\. Commune, Yvelines dept., N France, NW of Paris on Seine River; metalworking.

Houl·ton \ˈhōlt-ᵊn\. Town, ⊗ of Aroostook co., N Maine, on Canadian border 22 mi. (35 km.) N of Grand Lake; pop. (1990c) 6613; ships potatoes.

Hou·ma \ˈhō-mə, ˈhü-\. City, ⊗ of Terrebonne parish, SE Louisiana, 49 mi. (79 km.) WSW of New Orleans on the Intracoastal Waterway; pop. (1990c) 30,495; shrimp fisheries; sugar; oil; founded c. 1810; incorp. as city 1911.

Houns·low \ˈhau̇nz-ˌlō\. A borough of Greater London, SE England. See table at LONDON 4; includes **Hounslow Heath,** site of a Roman camp.

Hou·plines \ü-ˈplēn\. Commune, Nord dept., N France, on Belgian frontier just E of Armentières.

Hourn, Loch \ˈhu̇rn\. Inlet of Sound of Sleat, Highland region, on NW coast of Scotland; extends inland ab. 13 mi. (21 km.).

Hou·sa·ton·ic \ˌhü-sə-ˈtä-nik, ˌhü-zə-\. River, Berkshire co., W Massachusetts; formed by junction of E and W branches S of Pittsfield, and flowing S, across W Connecticut, into Long Island Sound at Stratford; 148 mi. (238 km.) long.

Hous·ton \ˈhyü-stən, ˈyü-, *in Georgia* ˈhau̇s-tən\. **1.** Name of counties in five states of the U.S. See tables at ALABAMA, GEORGIA, MINNESOTA, TENNESSEE, TEXAS.

2. Town, a ⊗ of Chickasaw co., NE Mississippi, 30 mi. (48 km.) SW of Tupelo; pop. (1990c) 3903.

3. City, ⊗ of Texas co., S Missouri, 42 mi. (68 km.) N of West Plains; pop. (1990c) 2118.

4. City and port of entry, ⊗ of Harris co., SE Texas, W of Galveston Bay; pop. (1990c) 1,630,553; connected with Gulf of Mexico by **Houston Ship Channel** (through Buffalo Bayou and Galveston Bay, ab. 50 mi. or 80 km. long, ab. 200 ft. or 60 m. wide, ab. 35 ft. or 10 m. deep); largest city in the state and its leading industrial center; ships esp. petroleum products, cotton, sulfur, lumber, rice; petroleum refining; manufactures chemicals, steel, cotton products, oil-well machinery; sulfur, salt deposits; Ellington Field Air National Guard Base, Johnson Space Center (estab. 1961); Astrodome (1965); museums; symphony orchestra; zoological gardens; planetarium; Rice Univ. (1891), Univ. of Houston (1927), Texas Southern Univ. (1947), Univ. of St. Thomas (1947), Houston Baptist Univ. (1960); city founded 1836; incorp. and became ⊗ 1837; ✻ of Republic of Texas 1837–39; port for Confederacy during Civil War; developed rapidly after completion of ship channel 1914; rapid pop. growth in 1940s and 1950s was partly the result of annexation.

Hout·man Abro·lhos \ˈhau̇t-mən-ə-ˈbrōl-ˌyüsh\ *also* **Houtman Rocks.** Rocky islets, Australia, in Indian Ocean ab. 80 mi. (130 km.) W of Geraldton, W Western Australia; seabird rookeries.

Hovd \ˈhȯv-də\ *also* **Kob·do** *or* **Khob·do** \ˈkȯb-dō\; *formerly* **Dzhir·ga·lan·tu** \ˌjir-gə-län-ˈtü\. Town, chief trading center of W Mongolia, SW of the Hobdo Gol at foot of Altai Shan ab. 260 mi. (420 km.) W of Uliastay; market for sheep and wool.

Hove \ˈhōv\. Town, East Sussex, S England, W suburb of Brighton on English Channel; pop. (1991p) 82,500.

Ho·ven·weep National Monument \ˈhō-vən-ˌwēp\. See UNITED STATES, *National Monuments.*

Hövs·göl Nuur \ˈhœfs-ˈgœl-ˈnür, ˈkœfs-\; *mostly formerly* **Ko·so Gol Nuur** *or* **Kos·so–gol Nuur** \ˈkȯ-sȯ-ˈgəl-ˈnür\. Lake, N Mongolia, near Russian border E of Tuva Rep.; elev. 5620 ft. (1713 m.).

How·ard \ˈhau̇-ərd\. **1.** Name of counties in seven states of the U.S. See tables at ARKANSAS, INDIANA, IOWA, MARYLAND, MISSOURI, NEBRASKA, TEXAS.

2. City, ⊗ of Elk co., SE Kansas; pop. (1990c) 815.

3. City, ⊗ of Miner co., E South Dakota; pop. (1990c) 1156.

4. Village, Brown co., E Wisconsin, 5 mi. (8 km.) NW of Green Bay; pop. (1990c) 9874.

Howe, Cape \ˈhau̇\. Extreme SE point of Australia, on border of New South Wales and Victoria.

Howe Caverns. Cavern system, Schoharie co., E cen. New York, W of Albany.

How·ell \ˈhau̇-əl\. **1.** County in S Missouri. See table at MISSOURI.

2. City, ⊗ of Livingston co., SE Michigan, 25 mi. (40 km.) NNW of Ann Arbor; pop. (1990c) 8184.

Howe Sound. Inlet of Strait of Georgia, Canada, extending N into British Columbia, N of Vancouver.

How·ick \ˈhau̇-ik\. **1.** Borough, North I., New Zealand, E of Auckland; pop. (1981c) 13,866.

2. Resort, KwaZulu-Natal prov., E Rep. of South Africa, NW of Pietermaritzburg; at the falls (364 ft. or 111 m. high) in the Mgeni River.

How·land Island \ˈhau̇-lənd\. Small island in cen. Pacific Ocean, near the Equator NW of Phoenix Is.; 1 sq. mi. (2.6 sq. km.); claimed by U.S. 1857; important as source of guano 1857–c. 1890; destination of aviator Amelia Earhart and navigator Fred Noonan when lost July 2, 1937; served as stopover for transpacific flights.

How·rah *or* **Hao·ra** \ˈhau̇-rə\. City, West Bengal state, NE India, on Hugli River opp. Calcutta; pop. (1991c) 950,435; important industrial community; iron and steel-rolling mills; jute and cotton mills, railroad workshops; Bengal engineering school; botanical gardens estab. 1786.

Hox·ie \ˈhäk-sē\. City, ⊗ of Sheridan co., NW Kansas; pop. (1990c) 1342.

Hox·ne \ˈhäk-sən—*sic*\. Village, N Suffolk, England; according to legend, scene of defeat of St. Edmund by the Danes c. 870.

Hoy \ˈhȯi\. One of the Orkney Is. (*q.v.*), off N coast of Scotland; 13 mi. (21 km.) long; its highest point (1564 ft. or 477 m.) is highest in the Orkneys.

Ho·ya \ˈhȯi-ä\. City, Tokyo prefecture, SE cen. Honshū, Japan; pop. (1990p) 95,148.

Hoy·ers·wer·da \ˌhȯi-ərs-ˈver-də\. City, Saxony, E Germany; pop. (1992e) 62,408; glass; received munic. rights 1371.

Hoy·lake \ˈhȯi-ˌlāk\. Resort town, Merseyside, NW England, on Irish Sea 9 mi. (15 km.) W of Liverpool; pop. (1981p) 32,914; famous golf course, scene of many championship matches.

Hoy·land Neth·er \ˈhȯi-lənd-ˈne-t͟hər\. Town, South Yorkshire, N England, near Barnsley; pop. (1981p) 15,390.

Hoy·ran, Lake \hȯi-ˈrän\ *or Turk.* **Hoyran Gö·lü** \ˈgœ̄-lü̅\. Lake (*gölü*) in W Turkey in Asia, S of Afyon; forms the N part of Eğridir Lake.

Hoy Sound \ˈhȯi\. Body of water bet. islands of Pomona (Mainland) on N and Hoy on S in the Orkney Is., off N coast of Scotland.

Hoyt Peak. Mountain, S Summit co., NE Utah; ab. 10,240 ft. (3120 m.).

Ho·zu \ˈhō-zü\. River, Honshū, Japan; joins Uji to form the Yodo River.

Hra·dec Krá·lo·vé \ˈhrä-dets-ˈkrä-lȯ-ˌve\ *or Ger.* **Kö·nig·grätz** \ˌkœ̄-nik̲s-ˈgrets\. Town, N cen. Czech Republic, on Labe (Elbe) River 60 mi. (97 km.) E of Prague; pop. (1991p) 99,889; near site of battle 1866 in which Prussians decisively defeated the Austrians in Austro-Prussian (Seven Weeks') War.

Hraz·dan \ˈhräz-dən\ *or* **Raz·dan** \ˈräz-\; *mostly formerly* **Zan·ga** \ˈzəŋ-gə\. River, Armenia; the outlet of Lake Sevan, flowing from its N end to the Araks S of Yerevan; 91 mi. (146 km.) long.

Hrod·na *or* **Hrod·no** \ˈk̲rȯd-nə\ *or* **Grod·no** \ˈgrȯd-\. **1.** Subdivision of Belarus, bounded on N by Lithuania and on W by Poland; 9652 sq. mi. (24,999 sq. km.); pop. (1991e) 1,188,700; ✻ Hrodna; sugar beets, tobacco, rye; livestock.
2. *or Lithuanian* **Gar·di·nas** \gär-ˈdē-näs\. City, ✻ of Hrodna subdivision, Belarus, on Neman River; pop. (1991e) 284,800; electrical equipment, textiles, leather, fertilizer.

History: First mentioned 1126; at various times in its history under Lithuanian, Russian, and Polish rule; sacked by Tatars 1241, by Teutonic Knights 1284 and 1391; ✻ of Lithuania in 14th cent.; site of congress 1793 which decided Second Partition of Poland; passed to Russia 1795; captured by Germans in WWI and WWII.

Hron \ˈhrȯn\ *or Hung.* **Ga·ram** \ˈgör-ˌöm\ *or Ger.* **Gran** \ˈgrän\. River, cen. Slovakia; flows W, then S into Danube River opp. Esztergom, Hungary; ab. 170 mi. (275 km.) long.

Hrvatska. See CROATIA.

Hsi. See XI.

Hsia–men. See XIAMEN.

Hsi–an. See XI'AN.

Hsiang. See XIANG.

Hsiang–fan. See XIANGFAN.

Hsiang–shan. See XIANGSHAN.

Hsiang–t'an. See XIANGTAN.

Hsiang–yün. See XIANGYUN.

Hsiao–hsiang–an Ling. See XIAO HINGGAN LING.

Hsien–yang. City, NE cen. China. See XIANYANG.

Hsikang. See SIKANG.

Hsin–chu *also* **Xin·chu** \ˈshin-ˈchü\. City, NW Taiwan, on coast of Taiwan Strait; pop. (1993e) 332,524.

Hsin·chuang \ˈshin-ˈchwäŋ\. City, N Taiwan, WSW of Taipei; pop. (1993e) 314,980.

Hsin–feng. See XINFENG.

Hsing·an \ˈshiŋ-ˈän\. One of nine former provinces of Manchuria, in NW part; 103,918 sq. mi. (269,148 sq. km.); created Sept. 1945; now part of Nei Monggol (Inner Mongolia).

Hsing–K'ai. See KHANKA.

Hsing–t'ai. See XINGTAI.

Hsin–hsiang. See XINXIANG.

Hsi–ning. See XINING.

Hsin·king \ˈshin-ˈkiŋ\. **1.** Former province (1932–45), S cen. Manchukuo, comprising the ✻ city Hsinking (Changchun); 169 sq. mi. (438 sq. km.).
2. City, Jilin, China. See CHANGCHUN.

Hsin–min. See XINMIN.

Hsin–p'u. See LIANYUNGANG.

Hsin·tien *or* **Hsin–tien** \ˈshin-ˈtyen\. Town, N Taiwan, SSE of Taipei; pop. (1993e) 240,558.

Hsin–yang. See XINYANG.

Hsi·paw \ˈsē-ˈpȯ\. **1.** One of the former Shan States, NE of Mandalay, E cen. Burma (Myanmar); 4591 sq. mi. (11,891 sq. km.).
2. Town, its ✻, ab. 90 mi. (145 km.) NE of Mandalay.

Hsi–tsang. See TIBET.

Hsüan–ch'eng. See XUANCHENG.

Hsüan–hua. See XUANHUA.

Hsü–ch'ang. See XUCHANG.

Hsü–chau. See YIBIN.

Hsü–chou. See XUZHOU.

Hsuchow. See XUCHANG.

Hua·cas Point \ˈwä-käs\. Cape on W cen. coast of Peru, S of Callao.

Hua·cho \ˈwä-chō\. Seaport, cen. Peru, 70 mi. (113 km.) N of Callao; pop. (1990e) 87,200; shipping point for cotton and sugar district.

Hua·chu·ca Peak \wä-ˈchü-kə\. Mountain, SW Cochise co., SE Arizona; 8406 ft. (2562 m.).

Hua·hi·ne \wä-ˈhē-nē\. Two islands of the Leeward Is. group of Society Is., French Polynesia, S Pacific Ocean, ab. 80 mi. (130 km.) WNW of Tahiti; combined length 7 mi. (11 km.) N to S; approx. width 4 mi. (6 km.); pop. (1988c) 4479; connected at low tide by an isthmus; produces copra; highest point 2331 ft. (711 m.).

Huai *also* **Hwai** \ˈhwī\. River, S Henan and W Anhui provs., E China; flows into the Hongze Hu (lake) in Jiangsu; over 600 mi. (965 km.) long; has many tributaries.

Huail·las \ˈwī-yäs\. Peak, W Bolivia, N of Lake Poopó; 18,045 ft. (5500 m.).

Huai·nan *or W.-G.* **Huai–nan** *also* **Hwai·nan** \ˈhwī-ˈnän\. Town, Anhui prov., E China, ab. 50 mi. (81 km.) NNW of Hefei; pop. (1990c) 703,934.

Huai·na Po·to·sí \ˈwī-nä-ˌpō-tō-ˈsē\. Andean mountain peak in Bolivia, 20 mi. (32 km.) N of La Paz; 20,340 ft. (6200 m.).

Huaina–Putina. See OMATE.

Huai–ning. See ANQING.

Hua–jung. See HUARONG.

Hu·a·la·lai \ˌhü-ä-lä-ˈlī\. Volcano, W Hawaii I., Hawaii; ab. 8275 ft. (2520 m.).

Hua·la·pai Peak \ˈwä-lə-ˌpī\ *also* **Hual·pai Peak** \ˈwäl-ˌpī\. Mountain in **Hualapai Mountains** (*also* **Hualpai Mountains**), S cen. Mohave co., W Arizona; 8417 ft. (2566 m.).

Hual·cán \wäl-ˈkän\. Peak in Cordillera Occidental, Peru; 21,000 ft. (6400 m.).

Hua–lien *or* **Hua·lien** *or* **Hua·lian** \ˈhwä-ˈlyen\. City, E coast of Taiwan; pop. (1993e) 107,090.

\ə\ **abut** \ᵊ\ **matches** \ᵊ\ **kitten, Fr table** \ər\ **further** \a\ **ash** \ā\ **ace** \ä\ **cot, cart** \à\ **Fr bac** \au̇\ **out** \b\ **Span Avila** \ch\ **chin** \e\ **bet** \ē\ **easy** \g\ **go** \i\ **hit** \ī\ **ice** \j\ **job** \k̲\ **Ger ich, Buch** \ⁿ\ **Fr vin** \ŋ\ **sing** \ō\ **go** \ö\ **all** \ȯ\ **law** \œ\ **Fr bœuf** \œ̄\ **Fr feu** \ȯi\ **boy** \th\ **thin** \t͟h\ **this** \ü\ **loot** \u̇\ **foot** \ue\ **Ger füllen** \ü̅\ **Fr rue** \y\ **yet** \ʸ\ **Fr digne** \ˈdēnʸ\, **nuit** \ˈnwʸē\ \yü\ **few** \yu̇\ **fury** \zh\ **vision**

Hual·la·ga \wä-'yä-gä\. River, W and N Peru; rises in Andes, flows N into Marañón River in N Peru; ab. 700 mi. (1125 km.) long.

Hualpai Mountains *and* **Hualpai Peak.** See HUALAPAI PEAK.

Hua·man·tla \wä-'mänt-lä\. Municipality, Tlaxcala state, Mexico, 80 mi. (129 km.) E of Mexico City; pop. (1990p) 51,995; grain, fruit.

Huam·bo \'wäm-bō\ *or Port.* **No·va Lis·boa** \'nȯ-və-lēzh-'vō-ə\. **1.** Province of W cen. Angola. See table at ANGOLA. **2.** Town, its ✻, in highlands; alt. 5580 ft. (1701 m.); founded by Portuguese 1912; damaged in war of independence 1960s–1975; captured by rebel forces in civil war 1993.

Hua·mi·na \wä-'mē-nä\. Peak, S Peru; 14,435 ft. (4400 m.).

Huan·ca·ve·li·ca \,wäŋ-kä-vä-'lē-kä\. Town, S Peru, 140 mi. (225 km.) SE of Lima; pop. (1990e) 25,800; alt. ab. 12,500 ft. (3810 m.); mining; founded by Spanish viceroy of Peru Francisco de Toledo 1572.

Huan·ca·yo \wäŋ-'kī-ō\. City, cen. Peru, on Mantaro River ab. 122 mi. (196 km.) E of Lima; met. area pop. (1990e) 207,600; alt. 10,958 ft. (3340 m.); university (1962); noted for its market.

Huan·doy \wän-'dȯi\. Peak, W Peru; 20,852 ft. (6356 m.).

Huang *or* **Hwang** \'hwäŋ\; *Eng.* **Yel·low** \'ye-lō\. River, N cen. and E China; rises in A'nyêmaqên Shan, SE Qinghai, at ab. 14,000 ft. (4270 m.); flows E and NE across Gansu, then N as E boundary of Ningxia Huizu; at 40°N makes a great bend flowing E across Hohhot, Nei Monggol (Inner Mongolia), then S bet. Shaanxi and Shanxi, receiving the Fen tributary from the E; in E Shaanxi receives the Wei and turns directly E through gorges along N Henan border; 2903 mi. (4671 km.) long; navigable as far as Lanzhou. Its lower course across the Great Plains has shifted many times through the centuries, vitally affecting 35,000,000 acres (14,175,000 hectares) of rich farmland; for more than 500 years before 1852 its outlet was Yellow Sea in Jiangsu; from 1852 to 1938 its course flowed NE from near Kaifeng across Shandong past Jinan to Bo Hai; in 1938 again diverted, this time by Chinese military action against the Japanese invaders, from near Zhengzhou in Henan SE across Henan and Anhui to unite with the Huai, passing through Hongze Hu (lake) to its old bed in Jiangsu and its new mouth 250 mi. (402 km.) farther S; in 1947 turned back to its old bed through Shandong. Large-scale construction of dam and reservoir system for flood control and power production begun 1955.

Huang Hai. See YELLOW SEA.

Huang·pu **1.** *or W.-G.* **Huang–p'u** *also* **Hwang Pu;** *formerly* **Whang·poo** \'hwäŋ-'pü\. River, S Jiangsu prov., E China; flows NE past Shanghai to enter mouth of the Chang at Wusong.

2. *or W.-G.* **Huang–pu** \'hwäŋ-'pü\ *also* **Wham·poa** \'hwäm-'pwä\. Seaport town, Guangdong, SE China, on island on S side of upper Zhu (Pearl) River in Xi Delta, 12 mi. (19 km.) below Guangzhou.

Huang·shi *or W.-G.* **Huang–shih** *also* **Hwang·shih** \'hwäŋ-'shē\. Town, Hubei prov., E cen. China, ab. 50 mi. (80 km.) ESE of Wuhan; pop. (1990c) 457,601.

Huá·nu·co \'wä-nü-,kō\. Town, cen. Peru, near Huallaga River ab. 170 mi. (275 km.) NE of Lima; pop. (1990c) 86,300; alt. 6273 ft. (1912 m.); university (1964); town founded 1539 by Spaniard Gómez Alvarado on the site of an Inca settlement now known as **Huánuco Vie·jo** \'vyā-hō\; later moved 35 mi. (56 km.) E to present location.

Hua·raz *or* **Hua·rás** \wä-'räs\. Town, W Peru, on Santa River 190 mi. (306 km.) N of Lima; pop. (1990e) 65,600; alt. 9932 ft. (3027 m.); silver, copper, coal; suffered severe earthquake damage 1970.

Hua·rong \'hwä-'rùŋ\ *or W.-G.* **Hua·jung** *also* **Hwa·jung** \'hwä-'jùŋ\. City, N Hunan, SE cen. China.

Huas·ca·rán \,wäs-kä-'rän\ *or* **Huas·cán** \wä-'skän\. Peak, W Peru; 22,205 ft. (6768 m.); highest mountain in Peru; lies within **Huascarán National Park** (estab. 1975).

Huas·co \'wäs-kō\. Port, Atacama prov., N cen. Chile, midway bet. Coquimbo and Caldera.

Hua Shan *also* **Hwa Shan** \'hwä-'shän\. Mountain in E Shaanxi prov., NE China; 6552 ft. (1997 m.).

Hua·ta·bam·po \,wä-tä-'bäm-pō\. Town, S Sonora state, NW Mexico, near coast; munic. pop. (1990p) 69,754.

Huau·chi·nan·go \,waù-chē-'näŋ-gō\. Town, Puebla state, SE cen. Mexico, 45 mi. (72 km.) E of Pachuca; munic. pop. (1991c) 69,968.

Huau·ra \'waù-rä\ *or* **Guau·ra** \'gwaù-\. River, cen. Peru; flows W into Pacific Ocean N of Lima; ab. 85 mi. (137 km.) long.

Huayhuash, Cordillera. See ANDES.

Hub·bard \'hə-bərd\. **1.** County in N cen. Minnesota. See table at MINNESOTA.

2. Village, Trumbull co., NE Ohio, 6 mi. (10 km.) NE of Youngstown; pop. (1990c) 8248.

Hubbard, Mount. Peak, NW North America, in Coast Mts., on boundary bet. Alaska and Yukon Terr., Canada, SE of Mt. Logan; 15,015 ft. (4576 m.).

Hubbard Glacier. Glacier, NW North America, in the St. Elias Mts., on border bet. Alaska and Yukon Terr., Canada; 71 mi. (114 km.) long, ab. 6 mi. (10 km.) wide near its terminus.

Hubbard Lake. Lake, N Alcona co., NE Michigan; ab. 10.5 sq. mi. (27 sq. km.); outlet N into Thunder Bay.

Hub·bard·ton \'hə-bər-tən\. Town, Rutland co., Vermont; pop. (1990c) 576; in American Revolution scene of battle July 7, 1777 in which British defeated Americans under Seth Warner.

Hu·bei *or W.-G.* **Hu·peh** *or* **Hu·pei** \'hü-'bā\. Province, E cen. China, bounded on N by Henan, on E by Anhui, on S by Jiangxi and Hunan, and on W by Sichuan and Shaanxi; ✻ Wuhan. In S crossed from W to E by the Chang River; contains Chang Gorges in W; in center crossed by the Han flowing SE to the Chang. Hilly with lakes and swamps in the two river valleys; bordered on N, W, and SW by mountain ranges 7000 to 10,000 ft. (2130 to 3050 m.). Products include rice, wheat, corn, tobacco, coal, iron ore, gypsum. Chief cities: Wuhan, Huangshi, Xiangfan, Yichang, Shashi, Shiyan. Part of first millennium B.C. kingdom ruled by Zhou dynasty; became part of Chinese empire during Han dynasty (206 B.C.–220 A.D.); with area of modern Hunan constituted prov. of Hukuang to mid-17th cent.; scene of beginning of Chinese Revolution 1911. See table at CHINA.

Hu·ber Heights \'hyü-bər\. City, Miami co., W Ohio, N of Dayton; pop. (1990c) 38,696.

Hu·ber·tus·burg \hü-'ber-təs-,bùrk, hyü-'bər-təs-,bərg\ *or* **Hu·berts·burg** \'hü-bərts-,bùrk, 'hyü-bərts-,bərg\. Castle near Oschatz, Saxony, E Germany; here on Feb. 15, 1763 treaty was signed ending the Seven Years' War.

Hub·li–Dhar·war \'hù-blē-där-'wär\. Municipality, NW Karnataka, India, 290 mi. (467 km.) SSE of Bombay; pop. (1991c) 648,298; joint municipality formed 1961.

Hu–chou. See WUXING.

Huck·nall \'hək-nəl\. Town, Nottinghamshire, N cen. England, 5 mi. (8 km.) NNW of Nottingham; pop. (1981p) 28,142; coal mines; burial place of poet Lord Byron at Newstead Abbey.

Ḥudaydah, Al. See AL ḤUDAYDAH.

Hud·ders·field \'hə-dərz-,fēld\. Town, West Yorkshire, N England, 24 mi. (39 km.) NE of Manchester; pop. (1981p) 123,888; has woolen mills.

Hud·dinge\'hù-diŋ-ə\. City, E Sweden, just S of Stockholm; munic. pop. (1994e) 75,537.

Hud·son \'həd-sən\. **1.** River, New York; rises in Essex co., in Adirondack Mts., E New York; flows S into Upper New York Bay, at its S end forming boundary bet. New York and New Jersey; has New York City at its mouth; 306 mi. (492 km.) long; navigable to Troy. Explored 1609 by English navigator Henry Hudson.

2. County in NE New Jersey. See table at NEW JERSEY.

3. Town, Middlesex co., NE Massachusetts, 15 mi. (24 km.) NE of Worcester; pop. (1990c) 17,233.

4. City, Lenawee co., S Michigan, 27 mi. (43 km.) S of Jackson; pop. (1990c) 2580.

5. Town, Hillsborough co., S New Hampshire, on Merrimack River opp. Nashua; pop. (1990c) 19,530; electronics.

6. City, ⊗ of Columbia co., SE New York, on E bank of Hudson River 28 mi. (45 km.) S of Albany; pop. (1990c) 8034;

American Museum of Fire Fighting. First permanently settled 1783; major ocean-trade center through early 19th cent.
7. Town, Caldwell co., W North Carolina, SE of Lenoir; pop. (1990c) 2819.
8. Village, Summit co., NE Ohio, 12 mi. (19 km.) NNE of Akron; pop. (1990c) 5159.
9. City, ⊗ of St. Croix co., W Wisconsin, on St. Croix River 15 mi. (24 km.) N of its confluence with Mississippi River; pop. (1990c) 6378.

Hudson Bay. Inland sea, E cen. Canada, bounded on N and NW by Nunavut, on SW by Manitoba, on S by Ontario, and on E by Quebec; 480,000 sq. mi. or 1,243,200 sq. km. (incl. James Bay, Hudson Strait, Ungava Bay); max. depth 2846 ft. (867 m.); connected with Atlantic Ocean by Hudson Strait and with Foxe Basin to N by Foxe Channel; on S has large shallow extension, James Bay; contains islands, largest Southampton I. in N, all of which are administratively a part of Nunavut; on its NW shore are two large inlets Wager Bay and Chesterfield Inlet. E coast navigated by Henry Hudson 1610; explored bet. 1612 and 1631 by British navigators Sir Thomas Button, Luke Foxe, and Thomas James; surrounding land, known as Rupert's Land (*q.v.*), controlled exclusively by Hudson's Bay Company 1821–69.

Hudson Falls. Village, ⊗ of Washington co., E New York, on Hudson River 40 mi. (64 km.) N of Troy; pop. (1990c) 7651; settled in 1760s; burned by British forces under Sir Guy Carleton 1780.

Hudson Strait. Strait bet. S Baffin I. and N Quebec, NE Canada, connecting Atlantic Ocean with Hudson Bay; 50 to 100 mi. (80 to 161 km.) wide, 450 mi. (724 km.) long; max. depth 2886 ft. (880 m.). Entered by English navigator Martin Frobisher 1578; navigated by Henry Hudson 1610.

Hud·son·ville \ˈhəd-sən-ˌvil\. City, Ottawa co., W Michigan, 15 mi. (24 km.) SW of Grand Rapids; pop. (1990c) 6170.

Hud·speth \ˈhəd-spəth\. County in W Texas. See table at TEXAS.

Hue *or* **Hué** \hü-ˈā, ˈwā\. City, cen. Vietnam; pop. (1989c) 211,718; in flat alluvial region surrounded by hills; a market town, trades esp. in rice; university (1957); former ✻ of Annam; an old city settled first by Chinese c. 200 B.C.; long contested over, when Vietnamese Nguyen dynasty took control 17th cent.; occupied by French 1883; imperial city, incl. palace built early 19th cent., suffered greatly in the Tet offensive of the Vietnam War 1968.

Hue·chu·cui·cui, Point \ˌwā-chü-ˈkwē-kwē\. Cape on NW tip of Chiloé I. off SW coast of Chile.

Hue·co Mountains \ˈwā-kō\. Range in S New Mexico and W Texas; highest point 6717 ft. (2047 m.).

Hue·hue·te·nan·go \ˌwā-ˌwā-tā-ˈnäŋ-gō\. **1.** Department of W Guatemala. See table at GUATEMALA.
2. Town, its ✻; pop. (1993e) 27,987; mining center (lead, silver, copper).

Hue·ju·tla \wā-ˈhü-tlä\. City, Hidalgo state, Mexico, 85 mi. (137 km.) NNE of Pachuca; munic. pop. (1990p) 85,136.

Huel·va \ˈwel-vä\. **1.** Province of SW Spain. See table at SPAIN.
2. Commune, its ✻, on Odiel River 10 mi. (16 km.) from the Atlantic Ocean and 53 mi. (85 km.) WSW of Seville; pop. (1991p) 141,041; fisheries, shipyards; copper, manganese, and iron mining. Roman aqueduct; monastery in which explorer Christopher Columbus resided for a time; large statue of Columbus. Founded by Carthaginians; colonized by Romans.

Hueneme. See PORT HUENEME.

Huér·cal–Ove·ra \ˈwer-käl-ō-ˈvā-rä\. Commune, Almería prov., SE Spain, 45 mi. (72 km.) NE of the seaport of Almería; pop. (1991c) 13,090.

Huer·fa·no \ˈȯr-fə-ˌnō, ˈwər-, ˈwer-\. **1.** River, S Colorado; flows E and NE from Sangre de Cristo Range into Arkansas River; ab. 90 mi. (145 km.) long.
2. County in S Colorado. See table at COLORADO.

Hues·ca \ˈwes-kä\. **1.** Province of NE Spain. See table at SPAIN.
2. *anc.* **Os·ca** \ˈäs-kə\. Commune, its ✻, 208 mi. (335 km.) NE of Madrid; pop. (1991c) 44,165; episcopal see; agricultural machinery, pottery; 14th–16th cent. cathedral; 12th–13th cent. church; episcopal palace and palace of kings of Aragon. Important Roman town; site of school founded by Roman general and politician Quintus Sertorius c. 76 B.C.; taken and fortified by Moors 8th cent.; recaptured 1096 by Peter I of Aragon; ✻ of kingdom of Aragon 1096–1118.

Hu·ey·town \ˈhyü-ē-ˌtau̇n\. City, Jefferson co., cen. Alabama, NW of Bessemer; pop. (1990c) 15,280.

Hufūf, Al. See AL HUFŪF.

Hug·gins, Mount \ˈhə-ginz\. Peak, Antarctica, 78°17′S, 162°28′E; 12,247 ft. (3733 m.).

Hughes \ˈhyüz\. **1.** River, W West Virginia; formed by confluence of forks on W boundary of Ritchie co., flows W into Little Kanawha River; ab. 15 mi. (24 km.) long.
2. Name of counties in two states of the U.S. See tables at OKLAHOMA and SOUTH DAKOTA.

Hughesovka. See DONETS'K 2.

Hugh·son \ˈhyü-sən\. City, Stanislaus co., cen. California, SE of Modesto; pop. (1990c) 3259.

Hugh Town \ˈhyü\. See SCILLY, ISLES OF.

Hu·gli *or* **Hoo·ghly** \ˈhü-glē\. Most westerly and commercially the most important channel of Ganges River in Ganges Delta (*q.v.*), West Bengal, NE India; ab. 120 mi. (195 km.) long from Santipur to Bay of Bengal; nearly 10 mi. (16 km.) wide at mouth; navigable to Calcutta; formed by confluence at Navadwip and Santipur of its headwaters, several distributaries of the Ganges, most important being the Bhagirathi, an old channel of the Ganges.

Hugli–Chuncura. See HOOGHLY-CHINSURA.

Hu·go \ˈhyü-gō\. **1.** Town, ⊗ of Lincoln co., E Colorado; pop. (1990c) 660.
2. City, Washington co., Minnesota; pop. (1990c) 4417.
3. City, ⊗ of Choctaw co., SE Oklahoma, 54 mi. (87 km.) E of Durant; pop. (1990c) 5978.

Hu·go·ton \ˈhyü-gō-tən\. City, ⊗ of Stevens co., SW Kansas; pop. (1990c) 3179.

Huhehot. See HOHHOT.

Hui–chou. See HUIZHOU.

Hui·la \ˈwē-lä\. Department of S cen. Colombia. See table at COLOMBIA.

Huí·la \ˈwē-lə\. Province of SW Angola. See table at ANGOLA.

Hui·la, Ne·va·do del \nā-ˈbä-t͟hō-t͟hēl-ˈwē-lä\. Volcano, W cen. Colombia, ab. 60 mi. (95 km.) NE of Popayán; 18,865 ft. (5750 m.).

Hui·li *or W.-G.* **Hui–li** *also* **Hwei·li** \ˈhwā-ˈlē\. Town, S Sichuan, S China.

Hui·man·guil·lo \ˌwē-mäŋ-ˈgē-yō\. Municipality, Tabasco state, Mexico, 35 mi. (56 km.) SW of Villahermosa; pop. (1990c) 21,536.

Huix·qui·lu·can \ˌwēs-kē-ˈlü-kän\. Municipality, México state, Mexico, 14 mi. (23 km.) W of Mexico City.

Huix·tla \ˈwēst-lä\. Town, S Chiapas state, SE Mexico, near Guatemalan border.

Hui·zen \ˈhȯiz-^{ə}n, ˈhīz-\. Commune, North Holland prov., W Netherlands, on the IJsselmeer; pop. (1992e) 42,031.

Hui·zhou *or W.-G.* **Hui–chou** \ˈhwē-ˈjō\; *formerly* **Wai·yeung** \ˈwī-ˈyu̇ŋ\. City, Guangdong prov., SE China, on Dong River 70 mi. (113 km.) E of Guangzhou (Canton); pop. (1990c) 161,023.

Hu·kawng *or* **Hu·kong** \ˈhü-ˈkȯŋ\. Valley, N Myanmar; lies in course of upper Chindwin River bet. Kumon Range and foothills of Patkai Range; 5586 sq. mi. (14,468 sq. km.). Scene of fierce fighting 1944 in WWII.

Hu·kou *or W.-G.* **Hu–k'ou** *also* **Hu·kow** \ˈhü-ˈkō, -ˈkau̇\ *or* **Ho·kou** \ˈhō-ˈkō, -ˈkau̇\. Town, N Jiangxi prov., SE China, on the Chang River ab. 140 mi. (225 km.) S of Wuhan, Hubei.

Hu·kuang *or* **Hu·kwang** \ˈhü-ˈgwäŋ\. Former political division of SE China, divided 17th cent. into modern provs. of Hubei and Hunan. See HUBEI.

\ə\ **abut** \ˈə\ **matches** \$^{ə}$\ **kitten**, Fr **table** \ər\ **further** \a\ **ash** \ā\ **ace** \ä\ **cot, cart** \ȧ\ Fr **bac** \au̇\ **out** \b\ Span **Avila** \ch\ **chin** \e\ **bet** \ē\ **easy** \g\ **go** \i\ **hit** \ī\ **ice** \j\ **job** \k\ Ger **ich, Buch** \$^{n}$\ Fr **vin** \ŋ\ **sing** \ō\ **go** \ȯ\ **all** \ȯ\ **law** \œ\ Fr **bœuf** \œ̄\ Fr **feu** \ȯi\ **boy** \th\ **thin** \t͟h\ **this** \ü\ **loot** \u̇\ **foot** \ue\ Ger **füllen** \ue̅\ Fr **rue** \y\ **yet** \$^{y}$\ Fr **digne** \ˈdēn^{y}\, **nuit** \ˈnw^{y}ē\ \yü\ **few** \yu̇\ **fury** \zh\ **vision**

Hu·lan *or W.-G.* **Hu–lan** \ˈhü-ˈlän\. Town, S Heilongjiang prov., NE China, on a tributary of the Songhua River ab. 20 mi. (32 km.) N of Harbin.

Hull \ˈhəl\. **1.** Town, Plymouth co., E Massachusetts, on point of peninsula in Massachusetts Bay 9 mi. (14 km.) ESE of Boston; pop. (1990c) 10,466.

2. Town, Portage co., cen. Wisconsin; pop. (1990c) 5559.

3. City, SW Quebec, Canada, on Ottawa River opp. Ottawa, Ontario, and at mouth of Gatineau River; pop. (1991c) 60,707; produces lumber, pulp, paper, and cement; mica mines in vicinity; Collège Marguerite d'Youville (1945); city founded c. 1800; incorp. 1875.

4. *or in full* **Kings·ton upon Hull** \ˈkiŋ-stən\. City, ⊗ of Humberside, N England, on the Humber where it is joined by the **Hull River** 157 mi. (253 km.) N of London; pop. (1991p) 242,200; an important seaport, forming outlet for products of nearby counties; manufactures chemicals, flour, pharmaceuticals, paper, iron and steel; shipbuilding; fisheries; Univ. of Hull (1954); Humber Bridge (completed 1981) has one of world's longest single spans. Passed to King Edward I c. 1293; its grammar school founded 1486; granted city rights 1897.

Hull Island. **1.** Island, Phoenix Is., Pacific Ocean. See ORONA.

2. Island, Austral Is., French Polynesia. See MARIA, ÎLES.

Hultschin. See HLUČÍN.

Hu·lu·dao *or W.-G.* **Hu–lu–tao** \ˈhü-ˈlü-ˈdau̇\. Town and seaport on Gulf of Liaodong, Liaoning prov., NE China.

Hulun. See HAILAR 2.

Hu·lun Bu·ir \ˈhü-ˌlün-ˈbwir\ *or W.-G.* **Hu–lun–pei–erh** \ˈhü-ˈlün-ˈbā-ˈər\; *formerly* **Bar·ga** \ˈbär-gə\. Region, NE China, W of the Da Hinggan Ling (Mts.).

Hu·lun Nur \hü-ˈlün-ˈnu̇r\; *formerly* **Ku·lun Nor** \kü-ˈlün-ˈnȯr\ *or* **Da·lai Nor** \ˈdä-ˌlī-ˈnȯr\. Lake, Heilongjiang, China; 425 sq. mi. (1101 sq. km.); receives Kerulen River; source of Argun River, a headstream of the Amur; ab. 40 mi. (64 km.) in circumference, alt. 4200 ft. (1280 m.).

Hu–lu–tao. See HULUDAO.

Hulwān. See HILWAN.

Hum. See *History* at BOSNIA AND HERZEGOVINA.

Hu·ma *or W.-G.* **Hu–ma** \ˈhü-ˈmä\ *or* **Hu–ma–erh** \ˈhü-ˈmä-ˈər\ *also* **Ku·ma·ra** \kü-ˈmär-ə\. River, Heilongjiang prov., N China; flows E into Amur River N of the Yilehuli Shan; 230 mi. (370 km.) long.

Hu·ma·cao \ˌüm-ə-ˈkau̇\. Town and municipality, E Puerto Rico; town near coast 28 mi. (45 km.) SE of San Juan; pop. (1990c) 21,306 (town), 55,203 (munic.); Univ. of Puerto Rico, Humacao Univ. Coll. (1962).

Hu·mans·dorp \ˈhü-məns-ˌdȯrp\. Town, near S coast of Eastern Cape prov., S Rep. of South Africa, W of Port Elizabeth.

Hum·ber \ˈhəm-bər\. **1.** River, W Newfoundland, Canada; flows SW to the Bay of Islands at Corner Brook; one branch flows from Grand Lake; 75 mi. (121 km.) long.

2. *anc.* **Abus** \ˈā-bəs\. Estuary on E coast of England, formed by confluence of Ouse and Trent rivers 8 mi. (13 km.) E of Goole; flows E and SE into North Sea; navigable for large vessels as far as Hull; spanned by Humber Bridge, one of longest suspension bridges in world (main span 4626 ft. or 1410 m.; completed 1981), near Hull.

Hum·ber·side \ˈhəm-bər-ˌsīd\. County, E England, comprising most of the former East Riding, Yorkshire, and N Lincolnshire. See table at ENGLAND.

Hum·ble \ˈhəm-bəl\. City, Harris co., SE Texas, just E of Houston Intercontinental Airport; pop. (1990c) 12,060.

Humbledon Hill *or* **Humbleton Hill.** See HOMILDON HILL.

Hum·boldt \ˈhəm-ˌbōlt\. **1.** River, N Nevada; rises in Elko co., flows W, NW and SW into Humboldt Lake; 290 mi. (467 km.) long.

2. Name of counties in three states of the U.S. See tables at CALIFORNIA, IOWA, NEVADA.

3. City, Humboldt co., NW cen. Iowa, 16 mi. (26 km.) N of Fort Dodge; pop. (1990c) 4438.

4. City, Gibson co., NW Tennessee, 15 mi. (24 km.) NNW of Jackson; pop. (1990c) 9651.

5. Town, S cen. Saskatchewan, Canada, 68 mi. (109 km.) E of Saskatoon; pop. (1991c) 4989.

Humboldt, Teluk. See YOS SUDARSO, TELUK.

Humboldt Bay. **1.** Inlet of Pacific Ocean on W cen. coast of Humboldt co., NW California.

2. *or* **Te·luk Humboldt** \ˈte-lu̇k\. Bay, Indonesia. See YOS SUDARSO, TELUK.

Humboldt Current. See PERU CURRENT.

Humboldt Glacier. Glacier, NW Greenland; 71 mi. (114 km.) long, 59 mi. (95 km.) wide near its terminus.

Humboldt Lake. Lake in S Pershing co., W Nevada; receives Humboldt River from the N; no outlet, but **Humboldt Sink,** an intermittent S extension, crosses into N Churchill co.

Humboldt Peak. Mountain, Custer co., S cen. Colorado; 14,064 ft. (4287 m.).

Humboldt Range. Range in cen. Pershing co., NW Nevada; in Great Basin.

Humboldt Salt Marsh. Marsh in NE Churchill co., W Nevada.

Humboldt Sink. See HUMBOLDT LAKE.

Hu·men·ne \ˈhü-ˌme-ne\. Town, E Slovakia; pop. (1989c) 35,449.

Hum·mels·town \ˈhə-məlz-ˌtau̇n\. Borough, Dauphin co., SE cen. Pennsylvania, 9 mi. (14 km.) E of Harrisburg; pop. (1990c) 3981.

Humphrey. See MANIHIKI.

Hum·phreys \ˈhəm-frēz\. Name of counties in two states of the U.S. See tables at MISSISSIPPI and TENNESSEE.

Humphreys, Mount. **1.** Peak in the Sierra Nevada, on boundary bet. Fresno and Inyo cos., SE cen. California; 13,986 ft. (4263 m.).

2. Peak in Yellowstone National Park, NW Wyoming; 11,050 ft. (3368 m.).

Humphreys Peak. Highest point in Arizona, in Coconino co.; ab. 12,633 ft. (3850 m.). See SAN FRANCISCO PEAKS.

Hu·mu·ya \ü-ˈmü-yä\. River of W Honduras; an important tributary of the Ulúa River.

Hun \ˈhu̇n\. **1.** River, NE China, mostly in Liaoning prov.; flows SW to the Liao near its mouth; ab. 240 mi. (385 km.) long.

2. River, N Shanxi prov., NE China. See YONGDING.

Hūn \ˈhün\ *also* **Hon** \ˈhōn\. Town, N cen. Libya, in oasis ab. 220 mi. (355 km.) SSE of Miṣrātah.

Hú·na Bay \ˈhü-nä\ *or Icel.* **Hú·na·flói** \ˈhü-nä-ˌflȯi\. Inlet of Arctic Ocean on NW cen. coast of Iceland.

Hu·nan \ˈhü-ˈnän\. Province, SE cen. China, bounded on N by Hubei prov., on E by Jiangxi, on S by Guangdong and Guangxi Zhuangzu, and on W by Guizhou and Sichuan; ✻ Changsha; lies S of the Chang River, which forms part of its boundary on NE; in NE is Dongting Hu into which flow Yuan, Xiang, and Zi rivers; along its W and SW borders is the Nan Ling mountain range (highest ab. 5000 ft. or 1524 m.); in E cen. part is Heng Shan, one of the traditionally sacred mountains of China (2953 ft. or 900 m.). Products include rice, beans, wheat, cotton, tea, fruit; embroidery; important mineral reserves (coal, antimony, tungsten, lead, zinc, manganese). Chief cities: Changsha, Hengyang, Xiangtan, Zhuzhou. Part of kingdom of Ch'u 3d cent. B.C.; passed to Ch'in dynasty and became cen. region of early kingdom of S China; became part of Chinese empire during Han dynasty (206 B.C.–220 A.D.); with area of modern Hubei constituted prov. of Hukuang to mid-17th cent.; invaded 1852 by Taiping rebels who failed to take Changsha; scene of much fighting in Sino-Japanese War 1939–41. See HUBEI; table at CHINA.

Hun·chun *or W.-G.* **Hun–ch'un** \ˈhu̇n-ˈchu̇n\. Town, Jilin prov., NE China, near Tumen River not far from its mouth and 40 mi. (64 km.) E of Yanji; near point where Russian, North Korean, and Chinese boundaries meet.

Hu·ne·doa·ra \ˌhü-nā-ˈdwär-ä\. **1.** County of W Romania. See table at ROMANIA.

2. Town, Hunedoara co., Romania, ab. 10 mi. (16 km.) S of Deva; pop. (1989c) 88,583; iron, steel, chemicals.

Hun·ga·ry \ˈhəŋ-gə-rē\ *or Hung.* **Ma·gyar·or·szág** \ˈmö-ˌjör-ˌȯr-ˌsäg\ *or Ger.* **Un·garn** \ˈu̇ŋ-ˌgärn\; *officially* **Republic of**

Hungary; *Hung.* **Ma·gyar Köz·tár·sa·ság** \ˈmö-ˌjör-ˈkœs-tär-shö-ˌshäg\. Republic, cen. Europe, bounded on N by Slovakia, on NE by Ukraine, on E and SE by Romania, on S by Yugoslavia, on SW by Croatia and Slovenia, and on W by Austria; 35,919 sq. mi. (93,030 sq. km.); pop. (1993e) 10,296,000; ✻ Budapest.

Physical features: Consists mainly of a plain, the Great Alföld, with fertile agricultural land; in N are S spurs of Carpathian Mts., highest point ab. 3330 ft. (1015 m.); bisected by the Danube flowing N to S; in W is Lake Balaton, largest lake in cen. Europe; in E is the Tisza, large tributary of the Danube, flowing across the Great Alföld N to S.

Chief products: Wheat, corn, barley, sugar beets, potatoes, sunflower seeds, grapes; livestock; bauxite, coal, manganese; manufacturing: textiles, motor vehicles, engines.

Chief cities: Budapest, Debrecen, Miskolc, Szeged, Pécs.

Political divisions: Divided into the following counties (for pronunciation of their names, see their individual entries):

NAME	AREA (sq. mi.)	AREA (sq. km.)	POP. (1992e)	CAPITAL
Bács-Kiskun	3,229	8,363	542,407	Kecskemét
Baranya	1,750	4,532	417,731	Pécs
Békés	2,189	5,670	406,861	Békéscsaba
Borsod-Abaúj-Zemplén	2,798	7,247	753,020	Miskolc
Budapest[1]	203	526	2,008,546	
Csongrád	1,645	4,260	438,364	Szeged
Fejér	1,689	4,374	422,516	Székesfehérvár
Győr-Moson-Sopron	1,549	4,012	426,911	Győr
Hajdú-Bihar	2,398	6,211	549,625	Debrecen
Heves	1,405	3,639	331,874	Eger
Jász-Nagykun-Szolnok	2,151	5,571	422,861	Szolnok
Komárom-Esztergom	869	2,251	313,677	Tatabánya
Nógrád	982	2,543	224,328	Salgótarján
Pest	2,468	6,392	953,750	Budapest
Somogy	2,349	6,084	342,085	Kaposvár
Szabolcs-Szatmár-Bereg	2,292	5,936	566,148	Nyíregyháza
Tolna	1,393	3,608	251,970	Szekszárd
Vas	1,290	3,341	274,756	Szombathely
Veszprém	2,003	5,188	378,499	Veszprém
Zala	1,268	3,284	303,898	Zalaegerszeg

[1] City with county rank. Area and pop. of Budapest not included in Pest figures.

History: Valleys of mid-Danube and of Tisza occupied by Magyars 9th cent. A.D.; Árpád ruling dynasty estab. late 9th cent.; Magyar westward advance defeated by German Emperor Otto I 955; first king, Stephen I (later St. Stephen) reigned c. 1000–1038 A.D. and Christianized realm; acquired Dalmatia, Slavonia, and Croatia in 11th cent.; Golden Bull issued by King Andrew II 1222 comparable to Magna Carta in limiting the power of the monarchy; invaded by Mongols 1241; after Árpád dynasty (997–1301) died out, crown became elective; ruled by Angevin kings 1308–82 and by Sigismund of Luxembourg 1387–1437; under military leader and regent János Hunyadi (d. 1456) resisted first wave of Turkish invasion; Hunyadi's son, Matthias Corvinus, elected king 1458, conquered Silesia, Moravia, Lusatia, and what is now Lower Austria (incl. Vienna) and made Hungary leading power of cen. Europe; broken by Turks at battle of Mohács 1526; in 16th cent., Transylvania (*q.v.*) became independent, and most of Hungary was divided bet. Turks (see OTTOMAN EMPIRE) and Austria (*q.v.*); recaptured Buda from Turks 1686; came under Hapsburgs 1687; with Slavonia and Transylvania, all Hungary except Banat ceded to Austrian crown 1699; Banat ceded to Austria 1718; movement for independence begun under Lajos Kossuth led to revolts in spring 1848, suppressed 1849; part of Dual Monarchy of Austria-Hungary (*q.v.*) 1867–1918; proclaimed independent republic 1918; soviet republic estab. under Béla Kun 1919; invaded by Romania 1919; monarchy with vacant throne estab. under regent Adm. Miklós Horthy 1920; lost about two thirds of territory by Treaty of Trianon 1920, incl. Slovakia, Ruthenia, W Hungary, Fiume, Croatia, Slavonia, Banat, Transylvania; received Sopron (*q.v.*) by plebiscite 1921; as sympathetic partner of the Axis powers during WWII, regained some of

the territory lost in 1920, but lost these regions again when Axis powers were defeated 1945; republic estab. 1946; People's Republic estab. 1949; joined Warsaw Pact 1955; popular anticommunist uprising suppressed by U.S.S.R. 1956; People's Republic abolished, Republic of Hungary estab., and border with Austria opened 1989.

Hungersteppe. See BETPAK-DALA.

Hun·gry Horse Dam *and* **Hungry Horse Reservoir** \ˈhəŋ-grē-ˈhȯrs\. See UNITED STATES, *Dams and Reservoirs.*

Hung–shui. See HONGSHUI.

Hung–t'ou. See LAN.

Hung–tse Hu. See HONGZE HU.

Huns·rück \ˈhu̇ns-ˌru̇k\. Mountainous region, North Rhine-Westphalia, Germany, bet. Moselle and Nahe rivers, extending SW from the Rhine to French border; highest peak 2677 ft. (816 m.).

Hunt \ˈhənt\. County in NE Texas. See table at TEXAS.

Hunt, Mount. Peak in S Grand Teton National Park, NW Wyoming; ab. 10,775 ft. (3285 m.).

Hun·te \ˈhu̇n-tə\. River, Lower Saxony, Germany; rises in hills E of Osnabrück and flows into Weser River near Bremen; 117 mi. (188 km.) long.

Hun·ter \ˈhən-tər\. Navigable river, E New South Wales, SE Australia; flows E to South Pacific Ocean at Newcastle; 287 mi. (462 km.) long.

Hunter, Cape. Cape on SW coast of Guadalcanal I., SE Solomon Is., W Pacific Ocean.

Hun·ter·don \ˈhən-tər-dən\. County in NW cen. New Jersey. See table at NEW JERSEY.

Hunter Island. **1.** Island off NW Tasmania, Australia. See HUNTER ISLANDS.

2. Island off W coast of British Columbia, Canada, opp. mouth of Dean Channel; 137 sq. mi. (355 sq. km.).

Hunter Islands. Group of islands off Cape Grim, the NW point of Tasmania, Australia; comprises Hunter, Three Hummock, and Robbins islands and many islets.

Hunter Mountain. Peak in Catskill Mts., Greene co., SE New York; 4040 ft. (1231 m.).

Hunter Peak. Mountain, E boundary of Idaho co., N cen. Idaho; 8742 ft. (2664 m.).

Hunt·er's Bay \ˈhən-tərz\. Inlet of Bay of Bengal on W coast of Myanmar, SE of Sittwe and E of Boronga Is.

Hunt·ers Creek Village \ˈhən-tərz\. City, Harris co., SE Texas, in an enclave surrounded by Houston; pop. (1990c) 3954.

Hunter's Hill. Municipality, E New South Wales, SE Australia, NW suburb of Sydney; pop. (1991c) 11,977.

Hunter's Island. Former island in Long Island Sound off E coast of the Bronx, New York City; attached to Bronx borough, made part of mainland by filled-in area.

Hunt·ers·ville \ˈhən-tərz-ˌvil\. Town, Mecklenburg co., S North Carolina, N of Charlotte; pop. (1990c) 3014.

Hun·ting·burg \ˈhən-tiŋ-ˌbərg\. City, Dubois co., SW Indiana, 38 mi. (61 km.) ENE of Evansville; pop. (1990c) 5242.

Hun·ting·don \ˈhən-tiŋ-dən\. **1.** County in S cen. Pennsylvania. See table at PENNSYLVANIA.

2. Borough, ⊗ of Huntingdon co., S cen. Pennsylvania, 22 mi. (35 km.) E of Altoona; pop. (1990c) 6843; Juniata Coll. (1876); borough platted 1767.

3. Town, ⊗ of Carroll co., W Tennessee; pop. (1990c) 4180.

4. *or* **Hunt·ing·don·shire** \-ˌshir, -shər\. Former county, England.

5. Town, Cambridgeshire, E cen. England, on the Great Ouse 58 mi. (93 km.) N of London; pop. (1991c) 2859; engineering works; birthplace of statesman and Parliamentarian commander Oliver Cromwell 1599.

Huntingdon and Peterborough. Former county in E cen. England; formed 1965 by amalgamation of counties of Huntingdon and Soke of Peterborough; went out of existence 1974.

Hun·ting·ton \ˈhən-tiŋ-tən\. **1.** County in NE Indiana. See table at INDIANA.

2. City, ⊗ of Huntington co., NE Indiana, 22 mi. (35 km.) SW of Fort Wayne; pop. (1990c) 16,389; limestone quarries; Huntington Coll. (1897).

3. Town, NW Suffolk co., SE New York, on N shore of Long Island; pop. (1990c) 191,474; includes the unincorporated settlements of Huntington (pop. 18,243) and **Huntington Station** (pop. 28,247); American Revolutionary hero Nathan Hale believed to have been captured near here by British 1776.

4. City, Cabell and Wayne cos., ⊗ of Cabell co., W West Virginia, on Ohio River ab. 50 mi. (80 km.) W of Charleston; pop. (1990c) 54,844; coal mines, gas wells; chemicals, nickel alloys; Marshall Univ. (1837).

Huntington Beach. City, Orange co., SW California, on Pacific Ocean 14 mi. (23 km.) SE of Long Beach; pop. (1990c) 181,519; oil wells and refineries; formerly a productive agricultural area; Golden West Coll. (1966); incorp. 1909; pop. increased tenfold in 1960s.

Huntington Lake. See SAN JOAQUIN 1.

Huntington Park. City, Los Angeles co., SW California, S and E of Los Angeles; pop. (1990c) 56,065; incorp. 1906.

Huntington Station. See HUNTINGTON 3.

Huntington Woods. Residential city, Oakland co., SE Michigan, 3 mi. (4.8 km.) N of Detroit; pop. (1990c) 6419.

Hunt Mountain. **1.** Peak in Blue Mts., Baker co., E Oregon; 8232 ft. (2509 m.).

2. Peak, E Big Horn co., N Wyoming; 10,162 ft. (3097 m.).

Hunts Peak \ˈhənts\. **1.** Mountain, Sangre de Cristo Mts., S Colorado, on boundary bet. Fremont and Saguache cos. S of Salida; 12,466 ft. (3800 m.).

2. Mountain, Colorado. See OURAY PEAK.

Hunts·ville \ˈhənts-ˌvil, -vəl\. **1.** City, ⊗ of Madison co., N Alabama, 23 mi. (37 km.) NE of Decatur; pop. (1990c) 159,789; aerospace industries, electronics, defense-related engineering, research, and technology; Marshall Space Flight Center is nearby; Oakwood Coll. (1896), Univ. of Alabama in Huntsville (1950). Settled 1805 around Big Spring (now in center of city); first settlement in Alabama to receive city charter 1811; site of Alabama constitutional convention and temporary ✱ 1819; burned by Union troops 1862.

2. City, ⊗ of Madison co., NW Arkansas; pop. (1990c) 1605.

3. City, ⊗ of Randolph co., N cen. Missouri, 7 mi. (11 km.) W of Moberly; pop. (1990c) 1567.

4. Town, ⊗ of Scott co., N Tennessee; pop. (1990c) 660.

5. City, ⊗ of Walker co., E Texas, 47 mi. (76 km.) E of Bryan; pop. (1990c) 27,925; lumber; Sam Houston State Univ. (1879); home and burial place of Gen. Sam Houston.

6. Town, Muskoka dist., SE Ontario, Canada, 20 mi. (32 km.) N of Bracebridge; pop. (1991c) 14,997; fishing and summer resort.

Hun·za \ˈhu̇n-zə\. River, Jammu and Kashmir, in region controlled by Pakistan; flows W from E Karakoram Range, then S to join the Gilgit at Gilgit; ab. 120 mi. (193 km.) long.

Hunza Kun·ji \ˈku̇n-jē\. Mountain in the Karakoram Range, in region of Jammu and Kashmir under Pakistani control; 25,543 ft. (7786 m.).

Hu·on \ˈhyü-ən\. **1.** River, S Tasmania, Australia; flows E and S through wide estuary to D'Entrecasteaux Channel; 100 mi. (161 km.) long; navigable to Huonville. The Huon pine (*Dacrydium franklinii*) is native to its banks.

2. Municipality, SE Tasmania, Australia. See HUONVILLE.

Huon Gulf. Large inlet of Solomon Sea on E coast of New Guinea I., Papua New Guinea, S of Huon Penin.; site of towns Lae, Salamaua, and Morobe.

Huon Islands. Small group of barren islands in E Coral Sea, 170 mi. (274 km.) NNW of New Caledonia; dependency of New Caledonia; guano deposits.

Huon Peninsula. Peninsula on E coast of New Guinea I., Papua New Guinea; bordered by Huon Gulf on S; scene of severe fighting bet. Japanese and Allied forces 1943.

Hu·on·ville \ˈhyü-ən-ˌvil\. Town in Huon municipality, SE Tasmania, Australia, at head of navigation on Huon River 17 mi. (27 km.) SW of Hobart; munic. pop. (1981c) 5200.

Hupeh *or* **Hupei** See HUBEI.

Hurd, Cape \ˈhərd\. Cape, SE Ontario, Canada, at end of Bruce Penin., on S side of channel connecting Georgian Bay and Lake Huron.

Hurghada. See AL GHURDAQAH.

Hur·ley \ˈhər-lē\. City, ⊗ of Iron co., N Wisconsin, on Michigan border 32 mi. (51 km.) ESE of Ashland; pop. (1990c) 1782; formerly important logging town, locale for American author Edna Ferber's *Come and Get It*.

Hur·ling·ham \ˈhər-liŋ-ˌham, ˌu̇r-liŋ-ˈän\. Town in Argentina, a W suburb of Buenos Aires.

Hu·ron \ˈhyu̇r-ˌän, -ən\. **1.** River, SE Michigan; flows from Oakland co. SW, then curves SE into Lake Erie at SE corner of Wayne co.; ab. 95 mi. (155 km.) long.
2. Name of counties in two states of the U.S. See tables at MICHIGAN and OHIO.
3. City, Fresno co., California; pop. (1990c) 4766.
4. City and resort, Erie co., N Ohio, on Lake Erie 8 mi. (13 km.) ESE of Sandusky; pop. (1990c) 7030.
5. City, ⊗ of Beadle co., E cen. South Dakota, 47 mi. (76 km.) N of Mitchell; pop. (1990c) 12,448; Huron Univ. (1883); city settled 1879; incorp. 1883.
6. County in SE Ontario, Canada. See table at ONTARIO.

Huron, Lake. Lake in U.S. and Canada, bounded on N and E by Ontario, Canada, and on S and W by Michigan, the U.S.-Canada boundary passing through it; ab. 206 mi. (331 km.) long; area 23,000 sq. mi. (59,570 sq. km.); greatest depth 750 ft. (229 m.); area of drainage basin ab. 74,800 sq. mi. (193,750 sq. km.); elev. 576 ft. (176 m.); 2d in size of the five Great Lakes (*q.v.*); at NW end connected through Straits of Mackinac with Lake Michigan, and through St. Marys River with Lake Superior, and at SE end through St. Clair River, Lake St. Clair, and Detroit River with Lake Erie. See GEORGIAN BAY; NORTH CHANNEL 1; SAGINAW BAY.

Huron Bay. Inlet of Lake Superior in NE Baraga co., Michigan, in NW Upper Penin.

Hur·ri·cane \ˈhər-ə-ˌkān\. **1.** City, Washington co., SW Utah; pop. (1990c) 3915.
2. City, Putnam co., W West Virginia, 25 mi. (40 km.) WNW of Charleston; pop. (1990c) 4461.

Hurricane Mountain. Peak in the Adirondack Mts., Essex co., NE New York; 3687 ft. (1124 m.).

Hurst \ˈhərst\. City, Tarrant co., N Texas, NE of Fort Worth; pop. (1990c) 33,574.

Hurstmonceux. See HERSTMONCEUX.

Hurst·ville \ˈhərst-ˌvil, -vəl\. City, E New South Wales, Australia, SW of Sydney; pop. (1991c) 63,757.

Hürth \ˈhu̇ert\. City, North Rhine-Westphalia, Germany; pop. (1992e) 51,287; motor vehicles; coal; truck farming.

Hu·ru·nui \ˌhu̇r-ə-ˈnü-ē\. River, NE South I., New Zealand; flows E into South Pacific Ocean N of Pegasus Bay; 86 mi. (138 km.) long.

Hú·sa·vík \ˈhü-sä-ˌvēk\. **1.** Point on NE coast of Iceland.
2. Town, NE Iceland; pop. (1992e) 2471.

Hu·şi \ˈhüsh\. City, NE Romania, near Prut River; pop. (1989c) 31,997; textiles; wine; in a tobacco- and grape-growing region; episcopal see; church founded 15th cent. by Stephen the Great, prince of Moldavia.

Hu·si·nec \ˈhü-sē-ˌnets\ *or Ger.* **Hu·si·netz** \ˈhü-zə-ˌnets\. Village, SW Czech Republic, ab. 20 mi. (32 km.) W of České Budějovice; birthplace of religious leader Jan Huss c. 1372.

Hus·kvar·na \ˈhüsk-ˌvär-nə\. Town, Jönköping prov., S Sweden, at S end of Lake Vättern E of Jönköping.

Hu·sum \ˈhü-zu̇m\. Seaport on W coast of Schleswig-Holstein, Germany; pop. (1980c) 24,327; ab. 2.5 mi. (4 km.) from the North Sea.

Huszt. See KHUST.

Hutch·ins \ˈhə-chənz\. City, Dallas co., NE Texas, just S of the city of Dallas; pop. (1990c) 2719.

Hutch·in·son \ˈhə-chən-sən\. **1.** Name of counties in two states of the U.S. See tables at SOUTH DAKOTA and TEXAS.
2. City, ⊗ of Reno co., cen. Kansas, on Arkansas River 42 mi. (68 km.) WNW of Wichita; pop. (1990c) 39,308; airplane parts; oil refining; oil wells; extensive salt mines; Hutchinson Community Coll. (1928).
3. City, McLeod co., S cen. Minnesota, 48 mi. (77 km.) S of St. Cloud; pop. (1990c) 11,523.

Hutchinson Island. Island, E cen. Florida, in Atlantic Ocean off coast of St. Lucie co.

Hüt·ten·tal \ˈhu̇et-ᵊn-ˌtäl\. City, North Rhine-Westphalia, Germany, just N of Siegen.

Huy \ˈwē\ *or Flem.* **Hoei** \ˈhwē\. Commune, Liège prov., E Belgium, on Meuse River ab. 15 mi. (24 km.) SW of the city of Liège; pop. (1991c) 18,197; papermills; metalworking; ruins of abbey of Neufmoustier founded c. 1100 by French ascetic Peter the Hermit, who preached the First Crusade.

Huy·ton–with–Ro·by \ˈhīt-ᵊn-wi<u>th</u>-ˈrō-bē, -with-\. Town, Merseyside, NW England, 7 mi. (11 km.) E of Liverpool; pop. (1981c) 61,808.

Huzhou. See WUXING.

Hva·ler \ˈhvä-lər\ *also* **Whale Islands** \ˈhwāl, ˈwāl\. Group of small islands in Oslo Fjord, SE Norway.

Hvan·na·dalsh·nú·kur \ˈhwä-nä-ˌdälsh-ˌnü-ku̇r\. Mountain, SE Iceland on S edge of Vatnajökull snowfield; at 6952 ft. (2119 m.), the highest in Iceland.

Hvar \ˈhvär\ *or Ital.* **Le·si·na** \ˈlā-zē-nä\; *anc.* **Phar·us** \ˈfar-əs\. **1.** Island, Croatia, in Adriatic Sea; 111 sq. mi. (287 sq. km.); pop. (1991p) 11,383; ✻ Hvar; honey, olives, wine; marble; fishing; tourism. Settled by Greeks early 4th cent. B.C.; occupied from 7th cent. A.D. by Slavs; annexed to Yugoslavia after WWI; became part of independent Croatia 1991.
2. Town and seaport, its ✻, at W end of the island; Franciscan monastery; 12th cent. cathedral; settled by Slavs 7th cent.

Hveen *or* **Hven.** See VEN.

Hvi·dov·re \ˈvē-ˌt͟hȯ-rə\. Commune, Sjælland I., Denmark; pop. (1989e) 48,987.

Hvítá River \ˈhwē-ˌtau̇\ *or* **White River** \ˈhwīt, ˈwīt\. River, cen. and SW Iceland; flows SW into Atlantic Ocean; 80 mi. (129 km.) long.

Hwai. See HUAI.

Hwainan. See HUAINAN.

Hwaiyin. See QINGJIANG.

Hwajung. See HUARONG.

Hwang. See HUANG.

Hwan·ge \ˈhwäŋ-gā\; *formerly* **Wan·kie** \ˈwäŋ-kē\. Town, W Zimbabwe, near Masvingo; pop. (1982c) 39,036; coal mines; coal-fired power station; to the S is the large **Hwange National Park,** extending to the Botswana border and containing abundant wildlife.

Hwang Hai. See YELLOW SEA.

Hwang Pu. See HUANGPU.

Hwangshih. See HUANGSHI.

Hwa Shan. See HUA SHAN.

Hweichow. See SHEXIAN.

Hweili. See HUILI.

Hwic·ce \ˈhwik-kā\. Ancient Anglo-Saxon kingdom, SW cen. England; probably included Worcestershire, S Warwickshire, and most of Gloucestershire; kingdom ultimately subsumed into Mercia.

Hy·a·lite Peak \ˈhī-ə-ˌlīt\. Mountain, S cen. Gallatin co., S Montana; 10,299 ft. (3139 m.).

Hy·an·nis \hī-ˈa-nəs\. **1.** Unincorporated settlement, S Barnstable co., SE Massachusetts; part of the town of Barnstable; pop. (1990c) 14,120; trading center for Cape Cod resort area.
2. Village, ⊗ of Grant co., W Nebraska; pop. (1990c) 210.

Hyannis Port. Harbor locale in the town of Barnstable, Barnstable co., SE Massachusetts, on Nantucket Sound; resort.

Hyar·gas Nuur \ˈhyär-gəs-ˈnu̇r\ *also* **Khir·gis Nur** \ˈkir-gis-ˈnu̇r\. Large lake, W Mongolia, NNE of Har Us Nuur.

Hy·atts·ville \ˈhī-əts-ˌvil\. City, Prince Georges co., S cen. Maryland, 7 mi. (11 km.) NE of Washington, D.C.; pop. (1990c) 13,864.

Hy·bla \ˈhī-blə\ *or* **Hybla Ma·jor** \ˈmā-jər\. Ancient town in Sicily, on S slope of Mt. Etna; considered by many scholars to be the modern Paternò.

Hybla Heraea. See RAGUSA 2.

Hy·da·burg \ˈhī-də-ˌbərg\. City, W coast of Prince of Wales I., SE Alaska, opp. N end of Dall I.; pop. (1990c) 384.

Hydaspes. See JHELUM.

Hyde \ˈhīd\. **1.** Name of counties in two states of the U.S. See tables at NORTH CAROLINA and SOUTH DAKOTA.
2. Town, Greater Manchester, NW England, on Tame River 9 mi. (14 km.) ESE of Manchester; pop. (1981p) 35,600; engineering; textile mills.

Hy·den \ˈhīd-ᵊn\. City, ⊗ of Leslie co., SE Kentucky; pop. (1990c) 375.

Hyde Park. **1.** Former town, Norfolk co., E Massachusetts; now a neighborhood of Boston, in S part.
2. Residential town, Dutchess co., SE New York, on E bank of Hudson River ab. 6 mi. (10 km.) N of Poughkeepsie; pop. (1990c) 21,230; settled 1741; Vanderbilt mansion, constructed 1896–98; Franklin D. Roosevelt Library (opened 1941); birthplace 1882 of Franklin Delano Roosevelt, 32d president of the U.S.
3. Village, ⊗ of Lamoille co., N Vermont; pop. (1990c) 457.
4. Park in W cen. London, England; area ab. 365 acres (150 hectares); recreation center; *Speaker's Corner* known for public speaking.

Hy·der·a·bad; *mostly formerly* **Hai·dar·a·bad** \ˈhī-də-rə-ˌbad, -ˌbäd\. **1.** *formerly often called* **Ni·zam's Dominions** \ni-ˈzämz, ˈnī-ˌzamz, nī-ˈzamz\. Former Indian state, its territory now divided among the states of Andhra Pradesh, Karnataka, and Maharashtra, S cen. India; bounded on N and NE by Berar, on S and SE by Tamil Nadu, and on W by Maharashtra; mountainous in some parts, has many fertile plains.
Chief rivers: Godavari, Wardha, Penganga, Krishna, and Tungabhadra.
History: In ancient kingdom of Golconda (*q.v.*); on overthrow of Golconda by Mogul Emperor ʻĀlamgīr (Aurangzeb) 1687, became part of Mogul Empire; ruled since 1713 by nizams, beginning with Asaf Jah, Mogul governor of the Deccan, who founded independent kingdom in 1724; after 1748 scene of rivalry over succession in which British and French supported different candidates; came under British protection 1798; refused to become part of India 1947 but yielded under threat of force 1948; reorganized and divided among the states of Andhra Pradesh, Mysore, and Bombay 1956.
2. Walled city, ✻ of Andhra Pradesh, India, on Musi River 310 mi. (499 km.) NNW of Madras; pop. (1991c) 3,145,939; paper, textiles, tobacco products; nizam's palace, the Char Minar (or Four Minarets), and several mosques and tombs; university (1918); was ✻ of Hyderabad state. Founded c. 1589 by ruler of Golconda; damaged during Mogul occupation; became ✻ of kingdom 1724; British cantonment estab. early 19th cent. at adjacent Secunderabad.
3. City, Sind, Pakistan, on E bank of Indus River 120 mi. (193 km.) N of its mouths and 90 mi. (145 km.) ENE of Karachi; pop. (1981p) 795,000; rail center; noted for handicrafts: silk, gold, and silver embroidery, lacquerware and enamelware; university (1947). Founded 1768 by Ghulam Shāh Kalhora; was ✻ of Sind until 1843 when it surrendered to the British.

Hy·dra \ˈhī-drə\ *or Gk.* **Ídhra** \ˈē-th̲rä\; *anc.* **Hyd·rea** \ˈhi-drē-ə\. **1.** Greek island in S Aegean Sea 4 mi. (6 km.) off E coast of Peloponnese; ab. 11 mi. (18 km.) long, area 20 sq. mi. (52 sq. km.); sponge fishing; refuge in 17th cent. for persecuted peoples from the mainland, who developed shipbuilding and commerce; fleets and patriotism of Hydriotes in War of Independence (1812–29) of great value to Greek cause.
2. Its chief town, port on N coast of island.

Hydraotes. See RAVI.

Hydruntum. See OTRANTO.

Hyères \ˈyer\. Commune, Var dept., SE France, near the Mediterranean 32 mi. (51 km.) S of Draguignan; pop. (1990c) 50,122; winter resort; orig. settled by Greeks; site of landing of King Louis IX on return from Seventh Crusade 1254.

Hyères Islands *or Fr.* **Îles d'Hyères** \ēl-ˈdyer\. French island group in the Mediterranean Sea off SE coast of France, SE of Toulon; group includes Port Cros, Île du Levant, and the fortified island of Porquerolles. Site of WWII Allied landing Aug. 1944.

Hyko Range. See HIKO RANGE.

Hy·met·tus \hī-ˈme-təs\. Mountain ridge just E and SE of Athens, Greece; highest point 3366 ft. (1026 m.); noted for ancient quarries of Kara marble.

Hynd·man Peak \ˈhīnd-mən\. Mountain, S Custer co., cen. Idaho; 12,078 ft. (3681 m.).

Hyō·go *or* **Hio·go** \ˈhyō-gō\. **1.** Prefecture, Honshū, Japan; ✻ Kōbe; textiles; lumbering. See table at JAPAN.
2. City, Japan. See KŌBE.

Hypanis. **1.** River, Russia in Europe. See KUBAN 1.
2. River, Ukraine. See BUG 2.

Hyphasis. See BEAS.

Hyrcania. See GORGĀN 1.

Hyrcanum Mare. See CASPIAN SEA.

Hy·rum \ˈhī-rəm\. City, Cache co., N Utah, 8 mi. (13 km.) S of Logan; pop. (1990c) 4829.

Hy·sham \ˈhī-shəm\. Town, ⊗ of Treasure co., SE cen. Montana; pop. (1990c) 361.

Hythe \ˈhīth̲\. Town, Kent, SE England, on Strait of Dover 10 mi. (16 km.) WSW of Dover; pop. (1981p) 12,723; one of the Cinque Ports (*q.v.*); summer resort.

Hy·vin·kää \ˈhü̅e-viŋ-ˌka\ *or Swed.* **Hy·vin·ge** \ˈhü̅e-viŋ-ə\. Town, Uusimaa prov., S Finland, ab. 30 mi. (48 km.) N of Helsinki; pop. (1989c) 39,992; textiles, rubber goods.

I

Iadera. See ZADAR.

Ia·lo·mi·ţa *also* **Ja·lo·mi·tsa** \ˈyä-lō-ˌmēt-sä\. **1.** *or* **Ia·lo·mi·tsa** \same\. River, SE Romania; rises in the Transylvanian Alps NW of Ploieşti and flows S and E into Danube River; 200 mi. (322 km.) long.

2. County of SE Romania. See table at ROMANIA.

Ialpug. See YALPUH.

Ial·y·sus \ī-ˈa-lə-səs\. Ancient city, N Rhodes, SE Aegean Sea; ruins just SW of the town of Rhodes.

Iao Valley \ē-ˈau̇\ *or* **Wai·lu·ku Valley** \wī-ˈlü-kü\. Canyon on slope of Mt. Puu Kukui, W Maui I., Hawaii; ab. 5 mi. (8 km.) long, 4000 ft. (1219 m.) deep.

Ia·pe·tus Ocean \ī-ˈya-pə-təs\. Former sea believed to have separated Laurentia and Baltica (*qq.v.*); believed to have closed by merger of these landmasses in mid-Paleozoic era and later reopened as Atlantic Ocean.

Ia·pyg·ia \ˌī-ə-ˈpi-jē-ə\. Ancient Greek name of SE Italy; the S part of the Salentina Penin.

Ia·şi \ˈyäsh\ *or Ger.* **Jas·sy** *also* **Yas·sy** \ˈyä-sē\. **1.** County of NE Romania. See table at ROMANIA.

2. Commercial city, its ⊗, on a tributary of Prut River; pop. (1989c) 330,195; chemicals, pharmaceutical products, textiles, machinery, plastics, clothing, furniture.

History: First mentioned late 14th or early 15th cent.; ✻ of Romania before 1861 when government was moved to Bucharest; suffered in various wars; burned by Tatars 1513, by Turks 1538, and by Russians 1686; Treaty of Jassy ending Russian Empress Catherine the Great's 2d war with Turkey signed here 1792; temporary ✻ of Romania in WWI; taken by U.S.S.R. Aug. 1944 in WWII.

Iaxartes. See SYR DAR'YA.

Iba \ˈē-bä\. **1.** Mountain, E Zambales prov., Luzon, Philippines; 5265 ft. (1605 m.).

2. Municipality, ✻ of Zambales prov., Philippines, on coast 85 mi. (137 km.) NW of Manila; pop. (1980c) 22,791; good anchorage at mouth of river.

Iba·dan \ˌē-bä-ˈdän; ē-ˈbäd-ᵊn, -ˈbad-\. City, ✻ of Oyo state, SW Nigeria, 89 mi. (143 km.) NNE of Lagos; pop. (1991e) 1,263,000; cigarettes, furniture, plastics; university (1948, university status 1962).

Iba·gué \ˌē-bä-ˈgā\. City, ✻ of Tolima dept., W cen. Colombia; pop. (1992e) 334,100; on high plain (alt. 4300 ft. or 1311 m.); university (1954); founded 1550.

Iba·jay \ˌē-bä-ˈhī\. Municipality, Panay, Philippines, on coast 43 mi. (69 km.) WNW of Roxas; pop. (1980c) 31,214.

Ibañeta, Puerto de. See RONCESVALLES.

Ibar \ˈē-ˌbär\. River, Serbia, S cen. Yugoslavia; rises in North Albanian Alps in Montenegro and flows N to the W branch of the Morava near Kraljevo; ab. 150 mi. (240 km.) long.

Iba·ra·ki \ˌē-bä-ˈrä-ke, i-ˈbä-rä-kē\. **1.** Prefecture, Honshū, Japan; ✻ Mito; tobacco, cereals, coal, copper. See table at JAPAN.

2. Town, Ōsaka prefecture, Honshū, Japan; pop. (1992e) 254,915.

Ibar·ra \ē-ˈbär-rä\. Town, ✻ of Imbabura prov., N Ecuador, 55 mi. (88 km.) NNE of Quito; pop. (1990c) 80,991; alt. 7340 ft. (2237 m.); founded late 16th or early 17th cent.; has suffered from volcanic eruptions of Imbabura and from earthquakes; nearby, Inca ruler Huayna Capac (whose son Atahuallpa was the last Inca king of Peru) won two decisive victories, adding to his realm a large part of Ecuador.

Ib·ben·bür·en \ˌib-ᵊn-ˈbue-rən\. City, North Rhine-Westphalia, Germany, 21 mi. (34 km.) N of Münster; pop. (1980c) 42,323; received charter 1721.

Ibe·ria \ī-ˈbir-ē-ə\. **1.** Parish in S Louisiana. See table at LOUISIANA.

2. See IBERIAN PENINSULA.

3. Ancient region S of the Caucasus Mts., approx. coextensive with modern Republic of Georgia; Iberians, as allies of the king of Pontus, Mithradates VI, were defeated by Pompey the Great, Roman general and statesman.

Ibe·ri·an Peninsula \ī-ˈbir-ē-ən\ *or* **Iberia.** Peninsula, SW Europe, occupied by Spain and Portugal; known as Hispania in Roman times.

Iberus. See EBRO.

Iber·ville. **1.** \ˈī-bər-ˌvil\. Parish in S Louisiana. See table at LOUISIANA.

2. \ˈē-bər-ˌvil, ˌē-ber-ˈvēl\. Town, Quebec, Canada, on Richelieu River 23 mi. (37 km.) SE of Montreal; pop. (1991c) 9352.

Ibi·cuí *or* **Ibi·cu·hy** \ˌē-bi-ˈkwē\. River, Rio Grande do Sul state, S Brazil; flows W to Uruguay River on Argentine boundary; ab. 300 mi. (480 km.) long.

Ibi·za *or Span.* **Ei·vis·sa** \ā-ˈvis-sä\ *also* **Ivi·za** \ē-ˈbē-zä\; *anc.* **Eb·u·sus** \ˈe-byu̇-səs\. **1.** Third largest island of Baleaic group, Baleares prov., Spain; in W Mediterranean SW of Majorca and ab. 80 mi. (129 km.) E of coast of Spain; 209 sq. mi. (541 sq. km.); agricultural products; tourism. See BALEARIC ISLANDS.

2. Seaport, its ✻, 80 mi. (129 km.) SW of Palma; munic. pop. (1991p) 27,886; exports salt.

Ibo \ˈē-bō, -bü\. **1.** Small island Mozambique, off NE coast.

2. Site, on Ibo I., of former ✻ of Cabo Delgado dist., N Mozambique.

Iboun·dji, Mount \ē-ˈbün-jē\. Mountain, S cen. Gabon; 5167 ft. (1575 m.); highest peak in Gabon.

Ib·rā' \ˈi-brə\. Inland town, Oman, WNW of Şūr.

Ica \ˈē-kä\. **1.** River, SW Peru; flows SW into Pacific Ocean; ab. 100 mi. (161 km.) long.

2. City, SW Peru, on Ica River 170 mi. (274 km.) SE of Lima; pop. (1990e) 152,300; cotton; vineyards; university (1961); original city founded 1563, twice destroyed by earthquakes.

Içá \ē-ˈsä\. Name of Putumayo River in Brazil.

Ica·cos Point \ē-ˈkä-kōs\. Tip of peninsula at SW corner of island of Trinidad, Trinidad and Tobago.

Iça·na *or in Colombia* **Isa·na** \ē-ˈsä-nä\. River, Colombia and Brazil; rises in E Colombia and flows E and SE into the Rio Negro, NW Brazil, above confluence of the Uaupés with the Rio Negro.

Icar·ia \ī-ˈkar-ē-ə, i-\. **1.** Island, Greece. See IKARIA.

2. Ancient town, Attica, Greece; on N slope of Mt. Pendelikón.

Icar·i·an Sea \ī-ˈkar-ē-ən, i-\ *or Lat.* **Icar·i·um Ma·re** \ī-ˈkar-ē-əm-ˈmā-rē, i-ˈkä-rē-u̇m-ˈmä-rā\. The part of the Aegean Sea bet. the islands of Patmos and Leros and the coast of Asia Minor. According to legend Icarus fell into the sea here while attempting to fly.

Ice Bay. See AMUNDSEN BAY.

Ice Fjord \ˈīs\. Inlet of Arctic Ocean, W coast of Spitsbergen, Norway; ab. 70 mi. (113 km.) long. See ADVENT BAY.

İçel \ˈē-chel\ *also* **Ichi·li** \ˈē-chi-ˌlē\. **1.** Province of Turkey in Asia; ✻ Mersin. See table at TURKEY.

2. City, Turkey. See MERSIN.

Ice·land \ˈīs-lənd, -ˌland\ *or Dan.* **Is·land** \ˈē-ˌslän\ *or Icelandic* **Ís·land** \ˈē-ˌslänt\. Island republic bet. North Atlantic and Arctic oceans, 155 mi. (249 km.) SE of Greenland and 570 mi. (917 km.) W of Norway; separated from Greenland by Denmark Strait and from Norway by Norwegian Sea; 39,702

\ə\ abut \ᵊ\ kitten, Fr table \ər\ further \a\ ash \ā\ ace \ä\ cot, cart \ȧ\ Fr bac \au̇\ out \b̲\ Span Avila \ch\ chin \e\ bet \ē\ easy \g\ go \i\ hit \ī\ ice \j\ job \k\ Ger ich, Buch \ⁿ\ Fr vin \ŋ\ sing \ō\ go \ȯ\ all \ȯ\ law \œ\ Fr bœuf \œ̄\ Fr feu \ȯi\ boy \th\ thin \th̲\ this \ü\ loot \u̇\ foot \ue\ Ger füllen \ue̅\ Fr rue \y\ yet \ʸ\ Fr digne \ˈdēnʸ\, nuit \ˈnwʸē\ \yü\ few \yu̇\ fury \zh\ vision

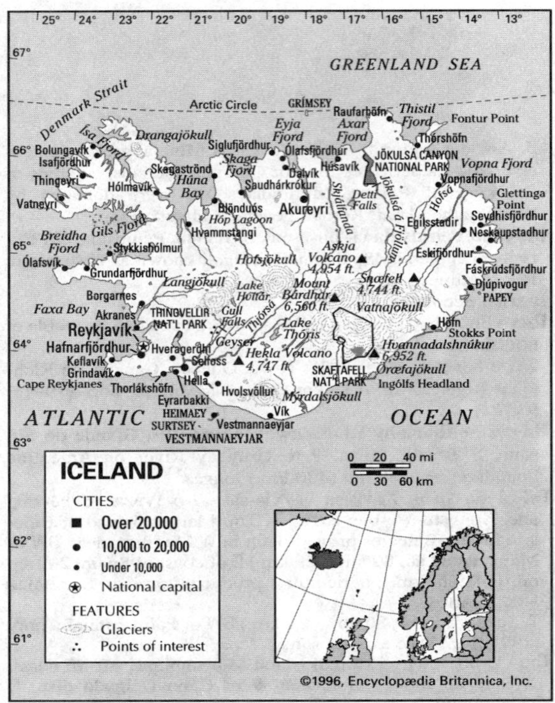

sq. mi. (102,828 sq. km.); pop. (1990c) 255,855; ✻ Reykjavík.

Physical features: Roughly oval with coastline ab. 3730 mi. (6002 km.) long; max. E to W length ab. 290 mi. (467 km.); indented by many long fjords; Faxa Bay on W coast and Húna Bay and Breidha Fjord on either side of base of large peninsula (av. alt. 2000 ft. or 610 m.) on NW; mostly tableland, esp. in SE where great snowfield of Vatnajökull (av. elev. 2000 to 3000 ft. or 610 to 914 m.) covers 3247 sq. mi. (8410 sq. km.); highest point Öraefajökull 6952 ft. (2119 m.); more than 100 volcanoes, which have created great lava fields, most noted Mt. Hekla 4747 ft. (1447 m.); 120 glaciers; lowland forms ab. one fourth of area and is only partly habitable and only ab. one seventh of land is productive; has suffered from destructive earthquakes; many small streams, lakes, and hot springs.

Chief products: Fishing and fish processing constitute the major industry; livestock raising; potatoes, turnips; greenhouse cultivation; hay; aluminum processing; cement; hydropower production.

Chief towns: Reykjavík, Kópavogur, Hafnarfjördhur, Akureyri.

History: Settled by Norwegians in 2d half of 9th cent. A.D. (date usually given as 874); founded the Althing (national assembly) 930; adopted Christianity c. 1000; united with Norway c. 1262, with Denmark 1380; by Act of Union 1918, became independent kingdom in personal union with Denmark; placed under British and American military occupation in WWII; British forces landed May 1940, American marines July 1941, both with permission; American North Atlantic naval base for rest of war. Proclaimed intention not to renew 1918 Act of Union with Denmark, the action being voted in plebiscite May 1944; independent republic proclaimed June 17, 1944; became a member of NATO 1949; signed defense agreement with U.S. 1951; extended its fishing limits from 4 to 12 mi. or 6 to 19 km. (1958), thereby precipitating serious dispute with Great Britain (settled 1961); joined European Free Trade Association 1970; further extensions of fishing limits to 50 mi. (80 km.) in 1972 and 200 mi. (322 km.) in 1975 provoked additional disputes with Great Britain; Vigdís Finnbogadóttir became world's first woman elected as chief of state 1980.

Ichal·ka·ran·ji \ˌi-chəl-ˈkər-ən-jē\. Town, Maharashtra, India; pop. (1991p) 214,835.

I–ch'ang. See YICHANG.

Ichi·ha·ra \ē-ˈchē-ˌhär-ä\. City, Chiba prefecture, Honshū, Japan; pop. (1990p) 257,717.

Ichi·ka·wa \ē-ˈchē-ˌkä-wä\. City, Chiba prefecture, Honshū, Japan; pop. (1990p) 436,597.

Ichili. See İÇEL.

Ichi·no·mi·ya \ˌē-chē-ˈnō-mē-ˌyä\. Town, Aichi prefecture, SE Honshū, Japan, ab. 11 mi. (18 km.) NNW of Nagoya; pop. (1990p) 262,434; textiles; 7th cent. Shinto shrine.

Ichinskaya Sopka. See SREDINNYY KHREBET.

Ichow. See LINYI.

I–ch'un. See YICHUN.

Ick·nield Way \ˈik-ˌnēld\ *or* **Icknield Street.** Ancient highway of S cen. England; thought to have extended W from Norfolk to Wiltshire or the S coast; one of the four great Roman roads of Britain (see ERMINE STREET, FOSSE WAY, and WATLING STREET).

Icod de los Vi·nos \ē-ˈkȯth-dā-lōs-ˈbē-nōs\ *or* **Icod.** Commune on NW Tenerife I., W Canary Is., in Santa Cruz de Tenerife prov., Spain, 28 mi. (45 km.) WSW of the seaport of Santa Cruz de Tenerife; pop. (1991c) 21,445.

Iconium. **1.** City, Turkey. See KONYA 2.
2. Seljuq sultanate, Asia Minor. See RUM.

Icosium. See ALGIERS 2.

Iculisma. See ANGOULÊME.

Icu·tú, Mount \ˌē-kü-ˈtü\. Peak, cen. Venezuela; ab. 11,000 ft. (3350 m.).

Icy Bay \ˈī-sē\. Inlet of Gulf of Alaska, SE Alaska, W of Yakutat Bay.

Icy Cape. Cape on NW coast of Alaska, ab. 161°31′W, 70°15′N.

Icy Strait. Strait, SE Alaska; joins Chatham Strait and Glacier Bay.

Ida \ˈī-də\. **1.** County in W Iowa. See table at IOWA.
2. *or mod.* **Kaz·da·ğı** \ˌkäz-ˈdī\. Famous mountain in NW Asia Minor, SE of site of ancient Troy and along N shore of Gulf of Adramyttium; actually a range (**Ida Mountains**), highest point 5797 ft. (1767 m.); in Homeric legend an abode of the gods.

Ida, Mount *or Gk.* **Ídhi Óros** \ˈē-t͟hē-ˈō-ˌrōs\ *also* **Mount Psil·to·rí·tis** \ˌpsēl-tō-ˈrē-tēs\. Highest mountain in Crete, Greece, in cen. part; 8058 ft. (2456 m.); in early times closely connected with worship of Zeus.

Ida·bel \ˈī-də-ˌbel\. City, ⊗ of McCurtain co., SE corner of Oklahoma; pop. (1990c) 6957.

Ida Grove. City, ⊗ of Ida co., W Iowa, 28 mi. (45 km.) S of Cherokee; pop. (1990c) 2357.

Ida·ho \ˈī-də-ˌhō\. **1.** A northwest state of U.S.A., bounded on N by British Columbia in Canada, on E by Montana and Wyoming, on S by Utah and Nevada, and on W by Oregon and Washington; 13th state in area, 83,557 sq. mi. or 216,413 sq. km. (land area 82,677 sq. mi. or 214,133 sq. km.); 42d state in population, (1990c) 1,006,749; ✻ Boise; 43d state admitted to Union (1890). See table of states at UNITED STATES.

Nickname: Gem State.

State flower: Syringa.

Motto: Esto Perpetua (Let It Be Perpetual).

Rivers: Snake, flowing from SE region W to Oregon border, then N forming boundary bet. Idaho and Oregon; Salmon, rising in cen. region, flowing N and then W across the state and emptying into the Snake.

Lakes: Pend Oreille and Coeur d'Alene in N, American Falls Reservoir in SE.

Highest peak: Borah Peak, 12,662 ft. (3859 m.), in Custer co.

Chief products: Potatoes, sugar beets, wheat; cattle; antimony, silver, phosphates, lead; manufacturing: wood products, chemicals, food products; fishing, hunting, and other forms of outdoor recreation.

IDAHO
CITIES
State capital
County seat
City
BOUNDARIES
International
State
County
FEATURES
Falls
Dams
0 40 80 mi
0 60 120 km
BRITISH COLUMBIA
CANADA
ALBERTA
WASHINGTON
OREGON
NEVADA
UTAH
WYOMING
MONTANA
BOUNDARY
BONNER
KOOTENAI
SHOSHONE
BENEWAH
LATAH
CLEARWATER
NEZ PERCE
LEWIS
IDAHO
ADAMS
VALLEY
LEMHI
WASHINGTON
PAYETTE
GEM
BOISE
CUSTER
CANYON
ADA
ELMORE
CAMAS
BLAINE
BUTTE
CLARK
FREMONT
JEFFERSON
MADISON
TETON
BONNEVILLE
BINGHAM
GOODING
LINCOLN
JEROME
MINIDOKA
POWER
BANNOCK
CARIBOU
OWYHEE
TWIN FALLS
CASSIA
ONEIDA
FRANKLIN
BEAR LAKE
ROCKY MOUNTAINS
CABINET MTS.
BITTERROOT RANGE
CLEARWATER MOUNTAINS
SALMON RIVER MTS.
SAWTOOTH RANGE
BEAVERHEAD MTS.
LEMHI RANGE
LOST RIVER RANGE
CENTENNIAL MTS.
SNAKE RIVER PLAIN
GRAND CANYON OF THE SNAKE R.
HELLS CANYON NATIONAL REC. AREA
SAWTOOTH NATIONAL REC. AREA
NEZ PERCE NATIONAL HISTORIC PARK
CRATERS OF THE MOON NATIONAL MONUMENT
National Reactor Testing Station
FORT HALL IND. RES.
DUCK VALLEY IND. RES.
YELLOWSTONE NATIONAL PARK
Helena
Boise
E. Sister Peak 6,867 ft.
Lolo Pass 5,187 ft.
Lost Trail Pass 6,992 ft.
Waugh Mtn. 8,882 ft.
Monument Peak 8,967 ft.
Mormon Mtn. 9,351 ft.
Twin Peaks 10,329 ft.
Cape Horn Mtn. 9,502 ft.
Castle Peak 11,821 ft.
Borah Peak 12,661 ft.
Lemhi Pass 7,999 ft.
7,658 ft.
Cache Peak 10,342 ft.
Continental Divide
Lake Koocanusa
Priest Lake
Lake Pend Oreille
Coeur d'Alene Lake
Hungry Horse Reservoir
Flathead Lake
Dworshak Reservoir
Cascade Reservoir
Arrowrock Reservoir
Anderson Ranch Reservoir
C.J. Strike Reservoir
Salmon Falls Creek Reservoir
Lake Walcott
American Falls Reservoir
Island Park Reservoir
Mud Lake
Palisades Reservoir
Grays Lake
Blackfoot Reservoir
Bear Lake
Jackson Lake
Shoshone Lake
Hebgen Lake
Hells Canyon Dam
Oxbow Dam
Brownlee Dam
Shoshone Falls
Bonners Ferry
Sandpoint
Priest River
Clark Fork
Spirit Lake
Rathdrum
Hayden
Post Falls
Coeur d'Alene
Kellogg
Osburn
Pinehurst
Wallace
Mullan
Avery
St. Maries
Potlatch
Moscow
Troy
Elk River
Genesee
Headquarters
Orofino
Pierce
Weippe
Lewiston
Lapwai
Craigmont
Nezperce
Kamiah
Kooskia
Cottonwood
Grangeville
Elk City
White Bird
Riggins
New Meadows
McCall
Council
Cambridge
Cascade
Warm Lake
Weiser
Payette
Fruitland
New Plymouth
Emmett
Garden Valley
Idaho City
Parma
Homedale
Garden City
Caldwell
Murphy
Mountain Home
Hammett
Glenns Ferry
Atlanta
Fairfield
Ketchum
Sun Valley
Hailey
Bellevue
Carey
Salmon
Baker
Cobalt
Challis
Clayton
Leadore
Mackay
Moore
Arco
Atomic City
Richfield
Shoshone
Gooding
Bliss
Wendell
Jerome
Buhl
Filer
Twin Falls
Kimberly
Rupert
Paul
Heyburn
Burley
Albion
Oakley
Almo
Riddle
Three Creek
Dubois
Ashton
St. Anthony
Rexburg
Driggs
Rigby
Idaho Falls
Iona
Ammon
Shelley
Blackfoot
Springfield
Aberdeen
Chubbuck
Pocatello
American Falls
Inkom
McCammon
Lava Hot Springs
Soda Springs
Grace
Georgetown
Downey
Montpelier
Paris
Malad City
Preston
Franklin
Pend Oreille R.
Spokane R.
Kootenai R.
Flathead R.
Clark Fork R.
St. Joe R.
N. Fork
Clearwater R.
Lochsa R.
Selway R.
Salmon R.
South Fork
Middle Fork
Snake R.
Payette R.
Boise R.
Big Wood R.
Big Lost R.
Bruneau R.
Owyhee R.
Bitterroot R.
Big Hole R.
Jefferson R.
Madison R.
Yellowstone R.
116°
114°
112°
48°
46°
44°
42°
©1996, Encyclopædia Britannica, Inc.

Chief cities: Boise, Pocatello, Idaho Falls, Nampa, Lewiston, Twin Falls.

Political divisions: Divided into the following 44 counties (for pronunciation of their names, see their individual entries):

NAME	AREA[1] (sq. mi.)	AREA[1] (sq. km.)	POP. (1990c)	CO. SEAT
Ada	1,043	2,701	205,775	Boise
Adams	1,371	3,551	3,254	Council
Bannock	1,122	2,906	66,026	Pocatello
Bear Lake	984	2,549	6,084	Paris
Benewah	788	2,041	7,937	St. Maries
Bingham	2,084	5,398	37,583	Blackfoot
Blaine	2,648	6,858	13,552	Hailey
Boise	1,910	4,947	3,509	Idaho City
Bonner	1,733	4,488	26,622	Sandpoint
Bonneville	1,836	4,755	72,207	Idaho Falls
Boundary[2]	1,275	3,302	8,332	Bonners Ferry
Butte	2,239	5,799	2,918	Arco
Camas	1,054	2,730	727	Fairfield
Canyon	578	1,497	90,076	Caldwell
Caribou	1,746	4,522	6,963	Soda Springs
Cassia	2,544	6,589	19,532	Burley
Clark	1,751	4,535	762	Dubois
Clearwater	2,521	6,529	8,505	Orofino
Custer	4,929	12,766	4,133	Challis
Elmore	3,048	7,894	21,205	Mountain Home
Franklin	664	1,720	9,232	Preston
Fremont	1,864	4,828	10,937	St. Anthony
Gem	555	1,437	11,844	Emmett
Gooding	720	1,865	11,633	Gooding
Idaho	8,516	22,056	13,783	Grangeville
Jefferson	1,096	2,839	16,543	Rigby
Jerome	595	1,541	15,138	Jerome
Kootenai	1,249	3,235	69,795	Coeur d'Alene
Latah	1,090	2,823	30,617	Moscow
Lemhi	4,580	11,862	6,899	Salmon
Lewis	476	1,233	3,516	Nezperce
Lincoln	1,203	3,116	3,308	Shoshone
Madison	473	1,225	23,674	Rexburg
Minidoka	750	1,943	19,361	Rupert
Nez Perce	844	2,186	33,754	Lewiston
Oneida	1,191	3,085	3,492	Malad City
Owyhee	7,641	19,790	8,392	Murphy
Payette	402	1,041	16,434	Payette
Power	1,413	3,660	7,086	American Falls
Shoshone	2,609	6,757	13,931	Wallace
Teton	457	1,184	3,439	Driggs
Twin Falls	1,947	5,043	53,580	Twin Falls
Valley	3,676	9,521	6,109	Cascade
Washington	1,462	3,787	8,550	Weiser
Yellowstone National Park (part)[3]	58	149		

[1] Area = land area.
[2] Northernmost county, bordering Canada (British Columbia) on N, Montana on E, Washington on NW.
[3] Main part of Yellowstone National Park is within Wyoming state boundaries (2930.8 sq. mi. or 7590.8 sq. km.), with adjacent strips in Montana (268.9 sq. mi. or 696.5 sq. km.) and Idaho (57.6 sq. mi. or 149.2 sq. km.). Total area with inland water 3419 sq. mi. (8855 sq. km.).

History: First inhabited by American Indians; explored by Lewis and Clark expedition 1805; part of Oregon Country (*q.v.*); ceded to U.S. by British 1846; included in Oregon Terr. (*q.v.*) 1848; became part of Washington Terr. (*q.v.*) in 1850s, and part of Idaho Terr. (*q.v.*) 1863; gold discovered 1860; crossed by Oregon Trail; admitted to Union July 3, 1890.

2. County in N cen. Idaho. See table at IDAHO.

Idaho City. Village, ⊗ of Boise co., W cen. Idaho; pop. (1990c) 322; founded 1862 during a gold rush; said to have had at one time a population of 30,000, which declined as mining claims were worked out.

Idaho Falls. City, ⊗ of Bonneville co., SE Idaho, on Snake River 50 mi. (80 km.) NNE of Pocatello; pop. (1990c) 43,929; tourism; Idaho National Engineering Laboratory tests nuclear reactors nearby.

Idaho Springs. Resort city, Clear Creek co., N cen. Colorado, 30 mi. (48 km.) W of Denver; pop. (1990c) 1834; thermal mineral springs.

Idaho Territory. Former territory, NW United States; region acquired by U.S. with Louisiana Purchase and Oregon Country (*qq.v.*); included in various territories of the U.S. bet. 1805 and 1863; organized as Idaho Terr. 1863, incl. present states of Idaho, Montana, and Wyoming; reduced to area of present state with loss of land to Montana 1864 and Wyoming 1868; Idaho admitted to the Union 1890.

Ida·li·um \ī-ˈdā-lē-əm\ *or mod.* **Da·li** \ˈdä-lē\. Village, E cen. Cyprus, on Yalias River; believed to be site of ancient temple; center of cult of Aphrodite.

Ida Mountains. See IDA 2.

Idar \ˈē-dər\. **1.** Former Indian state, now part of Gujarat state, W India; 1668 sq. mi. (4320 sq. km.); at one time in Mahi Kantha Agency; joined Union of Rajasthan June 26, 1947.

2. Town, its ✱, 55 mi. (88 km.) NNE of Ahmadabad.

Idar–Ober·stein \ˈē-där-ˈō-bər-ˌshtīn\. City, Rhineland-Palatinate, Germany, in Nahe River valley; pop. (1992e) 33,907; jewelry; formed 1933.

Idenburg. 1. Peaks, Indonesia. See PILIMSIT.

2. River, Indonesia. See TARITATU.

Id·fu \ˈid-ˌfü\ *or* **Ed·fu** \ˈed-\. Town on Nile River, Aswān governorate, Egypt; pop. (1986p) 45,737; ancient ruins; famous for its temple of Horus, almost wholly preserved, begun by Ptolemy III Euergetes 237 B.C. and not finally completed until 57 B.C.

Ídhi Óros. See IDA, MOUNT.

Ídhra. See HYDRA.

Idjen *or* **Ijen** \ē-ˈjen\. Old crater forming a plateau with many volcanoes on E end of Java, Indonesia; highest points Gunung Raung 10,932 ft. (3332 m.) and Gunung Merapi, an active volcano 9551 ft. (2911 m.).

Id·lib \ˈid-ˌlib\. Commercial town, NW Syria, 35 mi. (56 km.) SW of Aleppo; pop. (1992e) 77,000.

Id·ri·ja *or Ital.* **Id·ria** \ˈi-drē-ä, ˈē-drē-ä\. Commune, W Slovenia; formerly in Italy; 16th cent. castle; mercury deposits (discovered 1490); cinnabar.

Id·u·maea *or* **Id·u·mea** \ˌi-dyu̇-ˈmē-ə\. Name given by Greeks and Romans to the country of the Edomites (see EDOM) who, after being driven westward by the Nabataeans c. 300 B.C., settled in S Judaea.

Idu·ty·wa Reserve \i-ˈdü-tē-wə\. A district of former Transkei (*q.v.*), Rep. of South Africa; chief town **Idutywa.**

Ie·per \ˈē-pər\ *or Fr.* **Ypres** \ˈēprᵊ\. Commune, West Flanders prov., W Belgium; pop. (1991c) 35,235; famous as a commercial center in medieval times, esp. in the cloth-weaving industry; said to have a population of 200,000 in 13th cent., when the Cloth Hall (Les Halles) and cathedral of St. Martin were built; a border town, subject to many sieges, and therefore gradually declined; in WWI in one of most fiercely contested areas of entire war and scene of three great battles: Oct.–Nov. 1914, Apr.–May 1915, and July–Nov. 1917; completely destroyed but rebuilt.

Ie·rá·pe·tra \ˌē-e-ˈrä-pe-ˌträ\ *also* **Hie·rá·pe·tra** \ˌē-, ˌhē-\. Seaport town, Lasithion dept., E Crete, Greece.

Ier·ne \ī-ˈər-nē\. Ancient Greek name for Ireland.

Ie·si \ˈye-zē, ˈyā-\ *also* **Je·si** \ˈyā-zē\; *anc.* **Æsis** \ˈē-səs\. Commune, Ancona prov., Marche, cen. Italy, 16 mi. (26 km.) WSW of the seaport of Ancona; pop. (1989c) 40,336; episcopal see; birthplace of Holy Roman Emperor Frederick II 1194.

If \ˈēf\. Small island off S coast of France, 2 mi. (3 km.) from Marseille; site of famous fortress prison Château d'If, used by novelist Alexandre Dumas père as a setting for his *Le Comte de Monte Cristo.*

Ifa·lik \ˈē-fä-ˌlēk\. Island of the Caroline Is., W Pacific Ocean, ab. halfway bet. Chuuk and Yap.

Ife \ˈē-fā\. Town, Nigeria, 54 mi. (87 km.) E of Ibadan; pop. (1982e) 209,100; trades in cocoa; university (1961).

Iferten. See YVERDON.

If·ni \ˈif-nē, ˈēf-\. A former Spanish overseas province, on coast of SW Morocco; 579 sq. mi. (1500 sq. km.); ✱ Sidi Ifni; occupied nominally by Spain from 1860; boundaries fixed 1912 by treaty with France; Spanish occupation became effective 1934; territorial limits reduced by French government 1935; ceded to Morocco 1969.

Iforas, Adrar des. See ADRAR.

Ifu·gao \ˌē-fü-ˈgau̇\. Province, N cen. Luzon, Philippines; ✱ Lagawe; W and NW mountainous; E third sloping to Magat River on SE border thinly inhabited; under Spaniards region known as Kiangan; created a subprovince of Mountain Province 1908. See table at PHILIPPINES.

Igabrum. See CABRA.

Igidi, Erg. See ERG, AL-.

Igilgili. See DJIDJELLI.

Igilium. See GIGLIO.

Iglau. See JIHLAVA.

Igle·sias \ē-ˈglez-yäs\. Commune, Cagliari prov., S Sardinia, Italy, near W coast 32 mi. (51 km.) WNW of the seaport of Cagliari; pop. (1991p) 32,892.

Igló. See SPIŠSKÁ NOVÁ VES.

Igou·me·nít·sa \ˌē-gü-me-ˈnet-sä\ *also* **He·gou·me·nit·sa** \ˌhe-gü-mə-ˈnit-sə\. Town, ✱ of Thesprotia dept., Epirus, Greece; pop. (1991c) 6987.

Igridir. See EĞRİDİR.

Igua·çu \ˌē-gwə-ˈsü\ *or Span.* **Igua·zú** \ˌē-gwä-thü\. **1.** River and waterfall, S Brazil. See IGUAZÚ.
2. Territory of S Brazil 1943–46.

Igua·la \ē-ˈgwä-lä\. Town, Guerrero state, S Mexico, ab. 50 mi. (80 km.) SSW of Cuernavaca in silver-bearing district; munic. pop. (1990p) 101,170; Plan of Iguala, with the three guarantees: religion, independence, equality, proclaimed here Feb. 24, 1821 by Mexican soldier (later emperor) Agustín de Iturbide, but never implemented.

Igua·la·da \ˌē-gwä-ˈlä-thä\. City, Barcelona prov., NE Spain, 32 mi. (51 km.) WNW of the city of Barcelona; pop. (1991c) 31,855; textile mills, ironworks; ruins of ancient city walls; 12 mi. (19 km.) to the E is the Montserrat (*q.v.*) with its famous monastery.

Igua·tu \ˌē-gwə-ˈtü\. Municipality, Ceará state, NE Brazil, ab. 200 mi. (322 km.) S of Fortaleza, on railroad line from Fortaleza to Recife; pop. (1991p) 75,622.

Igua·zú *or* **Igua·çu** \ˌē-gwä-ˈsü\. River, S Brazil; flows W in Paraná state and empties into the Alto Paraná on border of NE Argentina, forming small sections of Argentina-Brazil boundary; 745 mi. (1199 km.) long; ab. 16 mi. (26 km.) from its junction with the Paraná are **Iguazú Falls**, ab. 2.5 mi. (4 km.) wide, composed of more than 20 cataracts averaging 200 ft. (61 m.) high and separated from each other by masses of rock- and tree-covered islands; discovered 1541 by Spanish explorer Álvar Núñez Cabeza de Vaca; formerly called **Vic·to·ria Falls** \vik-ˈtōr-ē-ə\.

Iguidi, Erg. See ERG, AL-.

Iguvium. See GUBBIO.

Ihing. See YIXING.

I–hsien. See YE XIAN.

I–hsing. See YIXING.

Ii·da \ˈē-dä\. City, Nagano prefecture, Honshū, Japan, 58 mi. (93 km.) NE of Nagoya; pop. (1990p) 91,859.

Ii·sal·mi \ˈē-ˌsäl-mē\. Commune, Kuopio prov., S cen. Finland, on railroad line 50 mi. (80 km.) N of the city of Kuopio; pop. (1980c) 22,500; founded 1891.

Ii–shi·ma \ē-ˈshē-mä\. Small island (*shima*) Japan, ab. 4 mi. (6 km.) off W coast of cen. Okinawa I., Ryukyu Is.; island and Japanese airfield at **Ii** \ˈē-ə\ village occupied by U.S. forces Apr. 1945; American war correspondent Ernie Pyle killed here Apr. 18, 1945.

Ii·zu·ka \ˈē-zu̇-kä\. City, Fukuoka prefecture, Kyūshū, Japan, 18 mi. (29 km.) E of the city of Fukuoka; pop. (1990p) 83,133.

IJ *or* **Y** \ˈā, ˈī\. Inland arm of the IJsselmeer, Netherlands; on its S side is Amsterdam.

Ije·bu–Ode \ē-ˈjā-bü-ˈō-dā\. Town, Nigeria, 45 mi. (72 km.) NE of Lagos; pop. (1991e) 138,000; timber; distribution point for cocoa, palm products, kola nuts.

Ijen. See IDJEN.

IJs·sel \ˈā-səl\; *Eng.* **Ijssel** *or* **Is·sel** *or* **Ys·sel** \ˈī-səl\; *anc.* **Sa·la** \ˈsa-lə, ˈsā-\. Navigable river, Netherlands, the N mouth of the Rhine; flows N out of Neder Rijn in E Netherlands to IJsselmeer; 70 mi. (113 km.) long; its ancient name applied to inhabitants along its banks, the *Salian* Franks.

IJs·sel·meer \ˈā-səl-ˌmer\; *Eng.* **Lake Ijs·sel** *or* **Lake Is·sel** *or* **Lake Ys·sel** \ˈī-səl\. The inner section of the former Zuider Zee (*q.v.*), Netherlands, reduced in size as result of reclamation of several polders; receives IJssel River.

IJs·sel·mon·de *also* **Ijsselmonde** \ˌā-səl-ˈmȯn-də\. Island in delta of the Meuse River, South Holland prov., SW Netherlands; diked since 13th cent.

Ika·ria \ˌē-kä-ˈrē-ä\ *or* **Ni·ka·ria** *also* **Ni·ca·ria** \ˌnē-kä-ˈrē-ä\ *or* **Ka·ri·ot** \ˌkär-ˈyōt\; *anc.* **Icar·ia** \ī-ˈkar-ē-ə, i-\. Island, Sámos dept., Greece, in Aegean Sea, ab. 13 mi. (21 km.) WSW of the island of Sámos; 99 sq. mi. (256 sq. km.); by some included among Southern Sporades (see SPORADES).

Ike·da \ē-ˈkā-dä\. City, Ōsaka prefecture, Honshū, Japan, 8 mi. (13 km.) NNW of the city of Ōsaka; pop. (1990p) 104,219; brewing, woodworking, manufacture of engines.

Ike·ja \ē-ˈkā-yä\. Town, ✱ of Lagos state, SW Nigeria; NNW of the seaport of Lagos; pop. (1983e) 60,370.

Iki \ˈē-kē\. Island in Tsushima Strait, bet. Tsushima and NW coast of Kyūshū, Japan; 53 sq. mi. (137 sq. km.); pop. (1980c) 41,035; administratively a part of Nagasaki prefecture; chief town Mushozu; overrun by Mongols in 13th cent.

Iki·re \i-ˈkē-rē\. Town, Nigeria, ab. 20 mi. (32 km.) E of Ibadan; pop. (1991e) 111,500.

Iki·run \ˌē-kē-ˈrün\. Town, Nigeria, just N of Oshogbo; pop. (1991e) 160,200.

Iko·ma \ē-ˈkō-mä\. City, Nara prefecture, W cen. Honshū, Japan; pop. (1990p) 99,598.

Iko·ro·du \ˌē-kō-rō-ˈdü\. Town, Nigeria, ab. 10 mi. (16 km.) NE of Lagos; pop. (1991e) 163,100.

Ila \ˈē-lä\. Town, Nigeria, ab. 90 mi. (145 km.) NE of Ibadan; pop. (1991e) 233,000.

Ila·gan \ē-ˈlä-gän\. Municipality, ✱ of Isabela prov., Luzon, Philippines, on Cagayan River; pop. (1980c) 79,336.

Īlām \ē-ˈläm\. **1.** Province (formerly a governorship) of W Iran. See table at IRAN.
2. City, its ✱; pop. (1986c) 89,035.

I–lan \ˈē-ˈlän\. **1.** City, NE China. See YILAN.
2. *formerly* **Gi–ran** \ˈgē-ˈrän\. Town, NE coast of Taiwan.

Iła·wa \ē-ˈwä-vä\ *or Ger.* **Deutsch–Ey·lau** \ˈdȯich-ˈī-ˌlau̇\. Town, Olsztyn prov., N Poland; pop. (1989e) 31,343; formerly in East Prussia, Germany.

Ila·we \ē-ˈlä-wā\. Town, Nigeria, ab. 80 mi. (130 km.) E of Ibadan.

Ile·bo \ē-ˈlā-bō\; *formerly* **Port Franc·qui** \ˌpōr-fräⁿ-ˈkē\. Town, Kasai Occidental administrative region, SW cen. Democractic Rep. of the Congo, bet. junction of the Kasai and Sankuru rivers.

Île–de–France *or* **Isle–de–France** \ˌēl-də-ˈfräⁿs\. **1.** Historical region of N cen. France; bounded anciently on N by Picardy, on E by Champagne, on S by Orléanais, and on W by Normandy; ✱ Paris; political center of old France; made a province in middle of 15th cent.
2. Region of N cen. France, roughly in S part of historical Île-de-France. See table at FRANCE.

Île de France. See MAURITIUS.

Île de la Ci·té \ˌēl-də-lȧ-sē-ˈtā\. Small island in Seine River, Paris, France, on which the city of Paris was first settled; Cathedral of Notre Dame, Palais de Justice, Ste.-Chapelle.

Île d'Orléans. **1.** District, Louisiana. See ORLEANS, ISLE OF.
2. Island, Quebec, Canada. See ORLEANS, ISLAND OF.

I–le–hu–li Shan. See YILEHULI SHAN.

Ilek \il-ˈyek\. River, W Asia; rises in W Kazakhstan and flows NW crossing border with Russia, forming a small section of Kazakhstan-Russia border, and crossing back into Kazakhstan where it joins the Ural; 373 mi. (600 km.) long.

Ilerda. See LÉRIDA 2.

Île Rouad. See ARWAD.

Île Rousse. See L'ÎLE ROUSSE.

Îles de Désolation. See KERGUELEN ISLANDS.

Îles de Loos. See LOS ISLANDS.

Îles des Saintes \ˌēl-dā-ˈseⁿt\ *also* **Les Saintes** \lā\. Island group in the French overseas dept. of Guadeloupe, West Indies, S of Basse-Terre I.; 5.5 sq. mi. (14 sq. km.).

\ə\ abut \ə\ matches \ᵊ\ kitten, Fr table \ər\ further \a\ ash \ā\ ace \ä\ cot, cart \ȧ\ Fr bac \au̇\ out \b̲\ Span Avila \ch\ chin \e\ bet \ē\ easy \g\ go \i\ hit \ī\ ice \j\ job \k̲\ Ger ich, Buch \ⁿ\ Fr vin \ŋ\ sing \ō\ go \ȯ\ all \ȯ\ law \œ\ Fr bœuf \œ̄\ Fr feu \ȯi\ boy \th\ thin \th̲\ this \ü\ loot \u̇\ foot \ue\ Ger füllen \ue̅\ Fr rue \y\ yet \ʸ\ Fr digne \ˈdēnʸ\, nuit \ˈnwʸē\ \yü\ few \yu̇\ fury \zh\ vision

Îles du Salut. See SAFETY ISLANDS.

Îles du Vent. See WINDWARD ISLANDS 2.

Ile·sha \ē-ˈlā-shä\. Town, Kwara state, Nigeria, ab. 15 mi. (24 km.) SE of Oshogbo; pop. (1991e) 333,900; distribution point for cacao.

Îles Loyauté. See LOYALTY ISLANDS.

Îles Marquises. See MARQUESAS ISLANDS.

Îles sous le Vent. See LEEWARD ISLANDS 2.

Iletsk *or* **Iletskaya Zashchita.** See SOL'-ILETSK.

Il·fov \ˈēl-fōv\. Former county of S Romania in area of Bucharest.

Il·fra·combe \ˈil-frə-ˌküm\. Town, Devon, SW England, on Bristol Channel 57 mi. (92 km.) N of Plymouth; pop. (1981p) 10,133; seaside resort.

Ilha Gran·de Bay \ˈēl-yə-ˈgrän-də\. Inlet of Atlantic Ocean on S coast of Rio de Janeiro state, SE Brazil.

Ilhas do Cabo Verde. See CAPE VERDE.

Ílha·vo \ˈēl-yə-vü\. Commune, Aveiro dist., NW Portugal, on coastal lagoon 3 mi. (5 km.) SW of the seaport of Aveiro; munic. pop. (1981p) 31,118.

Ilhé·us \il-ˈyā-u̇s\. City, SE coast of Bahia state, E Brazil, 140 mi. (225 km.) SSW of Salvador; munic. pop. (1991p) 223,352; exports timber, piassava, and large percentage of Brazil's cacao crop.

Ili \ˈē-ˈlē\. **1.** *or W.-G.* **I–li** \ˈē-ˈlē\. River, cen. Asia; flows from NW Xinjiang Uygur, W China into SW end of Lake Balkhash, Kazakhstan; ab. 800 mi. (1285 km.) long; formed in N ranges of the Tian Shan; in China flows through fertile valley, settled since early times; in Kazakhstan chief town on its banks is Kapchagay, above which it is navigable for ab. 280 mi. (450 km.) during rainy season.

2. Town, Kazakhstan. See KAPCHAGAY.

3. Former district, W cen. Asia, its E part now in Xinjiang Uygur; contested for by Russia and China late 19th cent.

Il·i·am·na Lake \ˌi-lē-ˈam-nə\. Lake, SW Alaska, W of Cook Inlet; at 1033 sq. mi. (2675 sq. km.), largest lake in Alaska.

Iliamna Volcano. Volcanic peak, SW Alaska, on W side of Cook Inlet; 10,016 ft. (3053 m.).

Ilici. See ELCHE.

Ili·gan \ē-ˈlē-ˌgän\. Chartered city, ✻ of Lanao del Norte prov., Mindanao, Philippines, on SE shore of Iligan Bay; pop. (1990p) 227,000; steel, fertilizer; chief port on N coast; hydroelectricity-generation plant nearby; scene of uprising in Philippine Revolution 1896.

Iligan Bay. Inlet of S Mindanao Sea, N coast of Mindanao, Philippines; 25 to 40 mi. (40 to 64 km.) wide; its SW arm is the long Panguil Bay.

Ilim \ē-ˈlēm\. River, S Russia in Asia; a tributary of the Angara, ab. 240 mi. (386 km.) long.

Ilin Island \i-ˈlēn\. Island off SW coast of Mindoro, Philippines; S of Mangarin Bay, 30 sq. mi. (78 sq. km.); in WWII, U.S. forces landed Dec. 1944.

Iliodhrómia. See ALÓNNISOS.

Il·i·on \ˈi-lē-ən\. Village, Herkimer co., NE cen. New York, on Mohawk River 11 mi. (18 km.) ESE of Utica; pop. (1990c) 8888; forms single community with Mohawk, Herkimer, and Frankfort; Herkimer County Community Coll. (1966).

Ilion. See TROY 8.

Ilio Point \i-ˈlē-ō\. Point, NW Molokai I., Hawaii, on Kaiwi Channel.

Il·i·pa \ˈi-lə-pə\. Ancient town, Baetica, S Hispania, N of the Baetis (Guadalquivir) River, near modern Seville; scene 206 B.C. of victory of Roman Gen. Scipio Africanus over the Carthaginians whose power in Spain was broken.

Ilis·sus \ī-ˈli-səs\ *or* **Ilis·sós** \ˌē-lē-ˈsōs\. Short river, Attica dept., E cen. Greece, S of Athens; flows into the Cephisus.

Ilium. See TROY 8.

Il·kes·ton \ˈil-kə-stən\. Town, Derbyshire, N cen. England, 8 mi. (13 km.) WNW of Nottingham; pop. (1981p) 33,031; hosiery.

Ilkhuri Alin. See YILEHULI SHAN.

Ilk·ley \ˈil-klē\. Town, West Yorkshire, N England; pop. (1981p) 24,082; health resort; Roman remains.

Ill \ˈil\. River, Vorarlberg, SW Austria, flowing NW into Rhine NW of Feldkirch; 45 mi. (72 km.) long.

Ill \ˈēl\. River, Haut-Rhin and Bas-Rhin depts., NE France; flows into Rhine; 129 mi. (208 km.) long.

Il·lam·pu \ē-ˈyäm-pü\. The lesser peak of Mt. Sorata, W Bolivia; 20,867 ft. (6360 m.). See ANCOHUMA.

Il·la·na Bay \ē-ˈyä-nä\. Inlet of Moro Gulf on W coast of Mindanao, Philippines; receives in SE the waters of the Rio Grande de Mindanao; ab. 45 mi. (72 km.) wide at mouth.

Il·la·war·ra \ˌi-lə-ˈwär-ə\. Division, SE New South Wales, SE Australia; extends along the coast over 100 mi. (160 km.) from ab. 30 mi. (48 km.) S of Sydney; pop. (1991c) 337,478; bet. its chief settlements, Kiama and Wollongong, is **Illawarra Lake,** a salt lagoon 9 mi. (14 km.) long and 3 mi. (5 km.) wide, connected with the sea by narrow channel.

Ille \ˈēl\. River, Ille-et-Vilaine dept., NW France, flowing S to the Vilaine at Rennes.

Il·le·cil·le·waet \ˌi-lə-ˈsi-lə-wət\. **1.** Glacier in Selkirk Mts. in Glacier National Park, British Columbia, Canada; its ice field drops 3600 ft. (1097 m.) into the valley.

2. River flowing from its foot into Columbia River near Revelstoke.

Ille–et–Vi·laine \ˈēl-ā-vē-ˈlen\. Department of NW France. See table at FRANCE.

Il·ler \ˈi-lər\. River, S Germany; rises in Algäu Alps and flows N through Bavaria and along boundary of Baden-Württemberg into the Danube near Ulm; 91 mi. (146 km.) long.

Illiberis. See ELNE.

Il·li·lou·ette Falls \ˌi-li-lu̇-ˈet\. Waterfall in Yosemite National Park, E cen. California; 370 ft. (113 m.) high.

Il·li·ma·ni \ˌē-yä-ˈmä-nē\. Mountain in W Bolivia, E of La Paz; its highest peak 21,201 ft. (6462 m.).

Il·li·ni·za \ˌē-lē-ˈnē-sä\. Peak in the Andes, Ecuador; 17,394 ft. (5302 m.).

Il·li·nois \ˌi-lə-ˈnȯi *also* -ˈnȯiz\. **1.** River, Arkansas and Oklahoma; rises in Benton co., Arkansas, flows W and NW, joining Arkansas River in Oklahoma; 145 mi. (233 km.) long.

2. Navigable river, Illinois; formed by confluence of Des Plaines and Kankakee rivers in Grundy co., SW of Joliet, NE Illinois, flows diagonally SW across Illinois to empty into the Mississippi in W Illinois; 273 mi. (439 km.) long; upper waters (Des Plaines River) connected by ship canal with Lake Michigan (see ILLINOIS WATERWAY).

3. A north central state of U.S.A., bounded on N by Wisconsin, on E by Lake Michigan and Indiana, on SE and S by Kentucky, on SW by Missouri, and on W by Missouri and Iowa; 24th state in area, 56,400 sq. mi. (146,076 sq. km.), not incl. 1526 sq. mi. (3952 sq. km.) of water of the Great Lakes (land area 55,875 sq. mi. or 144,716 sq. km.); 6th state in population, (1990c) 11,430,602; ✻ Springfield; 21st state admitted to Union (1818). See table of states at UNITED STATES.

Nickname: Prairie State.

State flower: Violet.

Motto: State Sovereignty—National Union.

Rivers: Mississippi, forming W boundary; Ohio, forming SE boundary; Wabash, forming lower section of E boundary; Illinois (see ILLINOIS 2).

Highest point: Charles Mound, 1235 ft. (376 m.), in Jo Daviess co.

Chief products: Corn, soybeans, dairy products; livestock; oil, coal; manufacturing: electrical and nonelectrical machinery, chemicals, metal products, food products; printing and publishing.

Chief cities: Chicago, Rockford, Peoria, Springfield, Aurora.

Political divisions: Divided into the following 102 counties (for pronunciation of their names, see their individual entries):

NAME	AREA[1] (sq. mi.)	AREA[1] (sq. km.)	POP. (1990c)	CO. SEAT
Adams	862	2,223	66,090	Quincy
Alexander	229	593	10,626	Cairo
Bond	383	992	14,991	Greenville
Boone	283	733	30,806	Belvidere
Brown	306	793	5,836	Mount Sterling
Bureau	866	2,243	35,688	Princeton
Calhoun	247	640	5,322	Hardin

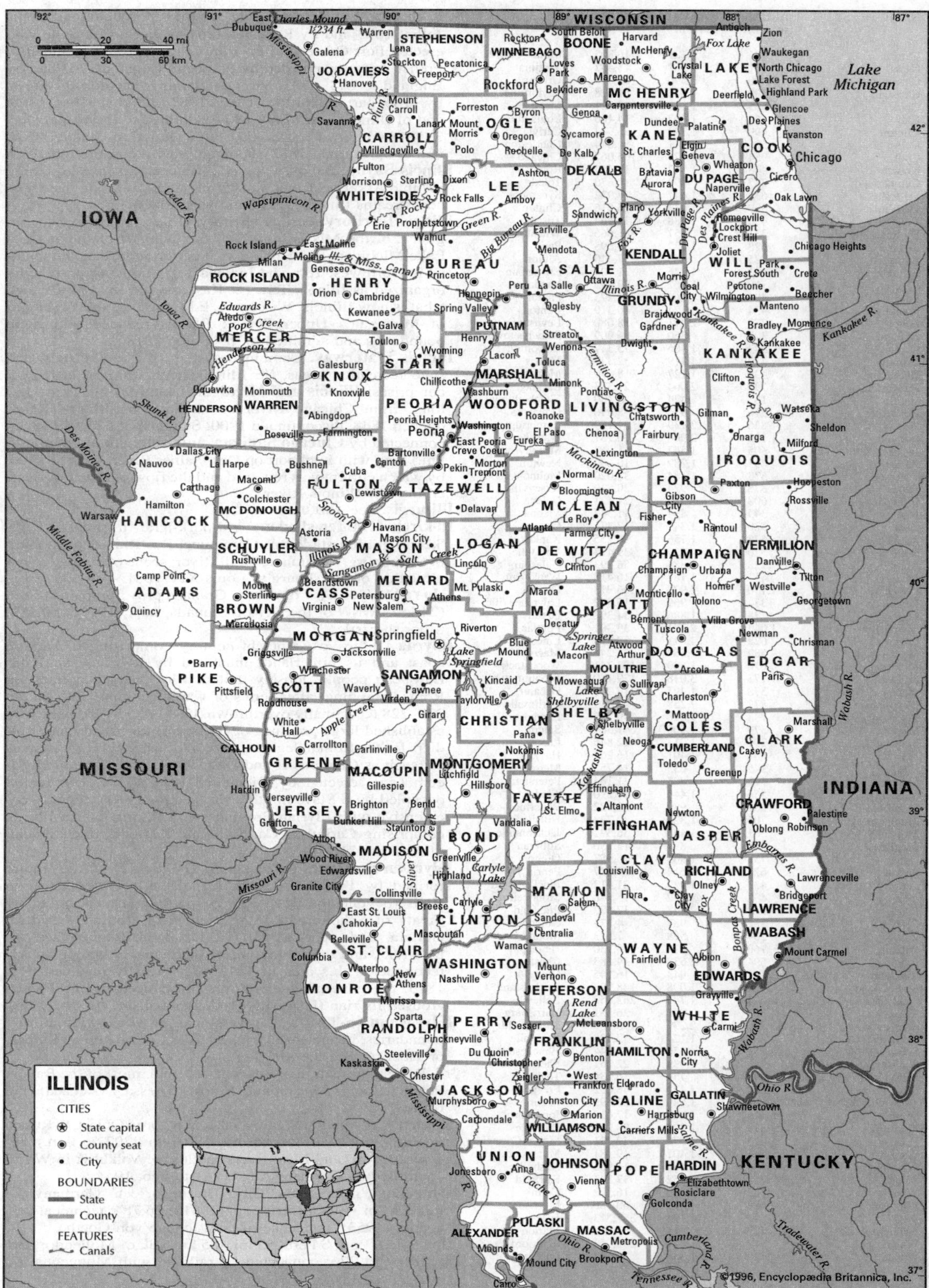
ILLINOIS
CITIES
State capital
County seat
City
BOUNDARIES
State
County
FEATURES
Canals
0 20 40 mi
0 30 60 km
92°
91°
90°
89°
88°
87°
42°
41°
40°
39°
38°
37°
WISCONSIN
IOWA
MISSOURI
INDIANA
KENTUCKY
Lake Michigan
East Dubuque
Charles Mound 1,234 ft.
Galena
Warren
Hanover
JO DAVIESS
STEPHENSON
Lena
Stockton
Pecatonica
Freeport
WINNEBAGO
Rockton
South Beloit
Loves Park
Rockford
BOONE
Belvidere
Harvard
McHenry
Woodstock
Marengo
MC HENRY
Crystal Lake
Antioch
Fox Lake
Zion
Waukegan
LAKE
North Chicago
Lake Forest
Highland Park
Deerfield
Glencoe
Des Plaines
Evanston
Chicago
Cicero
Oak Lawn
COOK
Palatine
Dundee
Carpentersville
Elgin
Geneva
Wheaton
DU PAGE
Naperville
Batavia
Aurora
St. Charles
KANE
Genoa
Sycamore
De Kalb
DE KALB
Mount Carroll
Savanna
Lanark
Mount Morris
Forreston
Byron
OGLE
Oregon
Polo
Rochelle
CARROLL
Milledgeville
Fulton
Morrison
Sterling
Dixon
Rock Falls
WHITESIDE
LEE
Ashton
Amboy
Erie
Prophetstown
Walnut
Sandwich
Plano
Yorkville
Romeoville
Lockport
Crest Hill
Joliet
WILL
Park Forest
Forest South
Chicago Heights
Crete
Peotone
Beecher
Manteno
Earlville
Mendota
KENDALL
East Moline
Rock Island
Moline
Milan
Ill. & Miss. Canal
Geneseo
BUREAU
Princeton
LA SALLE
Ottawa
Peru
La Salle
Oglesby
Morris
Coal City
Wilmington
GRUNDY
Braidwood
Gardner
ROCK ISLAND
HENRY
Orion
Cambridge
Kewanee
Galva
Hennepin
Spring Valley
PUTNAM
Henry
Aledo
MERCER
Toulon
Wyoming
STARK
Streator
Wenona
Dwight
Bradley
Momence
Kankakee
KANKAKEE
Galesburg
KNOX
Knoxville
Lacon
MARSHALL
Toluca
Minonk
Oquawka
HENDERSON
Monmouth
WARREN
Abingdon
Chillicothe
Washburn
PEORIA
Peoria Heights
Peoria
WOODFORD
Roanoke
Pontiac
LIVINGSTON
Chatsworth
Fairbury
Clifton
Gilman
Onarga
Watseka
Sheldon
Milford
IROQUOIS
Roseville
Farmington
Washington
East Peoria
Creve Coeur
Bartonville
Eureka
El Paso
Chenoa
Lexington
Dallas City
Nauvoo
La Harpe
Bushnell
Canton
Cuba
Pekin
Morton
Tremont
Carthage
Macomb
Colchester
FULTON
Lewistown
TAZEWELL
Normal
Bloomington
MC LEAN
Paxton
FORD
Gibson City
Hoopeston
Rossville
Hamilton
Warsaw
HANCOCK
MC DONOUGH
Delavan
Le Roy
Fisher
Rantoul
Havana
Mason City
MASON
Astoria
Atlanta
Farmer City
SCHUYLER
Rushville
LOGAN
Lincoln
DE WITT
Clinton
CHAMPAIGN
Champaign
Urbana
VERMILION
Danville
Tilton
Westville
Georgetown
Camp Point
ADAMS
Quincy
Mount Sterling
BROWN
Meredosia
Beardstown
CASS
Virginia
Petersburg
New Salem
MENARD
Athens
Mt. Pulaski
Maroa
MACON
Decatur
PIATT
Monticello
Tolono
Homer
Bement
Tuscola
Villa Grove
DOUGLAS
Atwood
Arthur
Newman
Chrisman
EDGAR
Paris
MORGAN
Springfield
Riverton
Jacksonville
Griggsville
Barry
PIKE
Pittsfield
Winchester
SCOTT
SANGAMON
Lake Springfield
Blue Mound
Springer Lake
Macon
MOULTRIE
Sullivan
Moweaqua
Lake Shelbyville
Arcola
Charleston
Mattoon
COLES
Waverly
Pawnee
Virden
Kincaid
Taylorville
Roodhouse
White Hall
Girard
CHRISTIAN
Pana
SHELBY
Shelbyville
Neoga
CUMBERLAND
Toledo
Greenup
CLARK
Marshall
Casey
CALHOUN
Carrollton
GREENE
Carlinville
MACOUPIN
Gillespie
Benld
MONTGOMERY
Nokomis
Litchfield
Hillsboro
FAYETTE
Vandalia
St. Elmo
Effingham
Altamont
EFFINGHAM
Newton
JASPER
CRAWFORD
Palestine
Robinson
Oblong
Hardin
Jerseyville
JERSEY
Grafton
Brighton
Bunker Hill
Staunton
BOND
Greenville
Alton
Wood River
Edwardsville
MADISON
Highland
Carlyle Lake
Granite City
Collinsville
CLAY
Louisville
Flora
Clay City
RICHLAND
Olney
LAWRENCE
Lawrenceville
Bridgeport
East St. Louis
Cahokia
Belleville
Breese
Carlyle
CLINTON
MARION
Salem
Sandoval
Centralia
Wamac
Mascoutah
ST. CLAIR
Columbia
Waterloo
WASHINGTON
Nashville
New Athens
MONROE
Marissa
Mount Vernon
JEFFERSON
WAYNE
Fairfield
Albion
EDWARDS
WABASH
Mount Carmel
Grayville
WHITE
Carmi
Sparta
RANDOLPH
Pinckneyville
PERRY
Sesser
Rend Lake
McLeansboro
FRANKLIN
Benton
HAMILTON
Norris City
Steeleville
Du Quoin
Christopher
Zeigler
Kaskaskia
Chester
JACKSON
Murphysboro
Carbondale
West Frankfort
Johnston City
Marion
WILLIAMSON
SALINE
Eldorado
Harrisburg
Carriers Mills
GALLATIN
Shawneetown
UNION
Jonesboro
Anna
JOHNSON
Vienna
POPE
HARDIN
Elizabethtown
Rosiclare
Golconda
PULASKI
ALEXANDER
Mounds
Mound City
MASSAC
Metropolis
Brookport
Cairo
Mississippi R.
Wapsipinicon R.
Cedar R.
Iowa R.
Skunk R.
Des Moines R.
Middle Fabius R.
Missouri R.
Edwards R.
Pope Creek
Henderson R.
Plum R.
Rock R.
Green R.
Big Bureau R.
Fox R.
Du Page R.
Des Plaines R.
Illinois R.
Kankakee R.
Vermilion R.
Iroquois R.
Mackinaw R.
Spoon R.
Sangamon R.
Salt Creek
Apple Creek
Silver Creek
Kaskaskia R.
Embarras R.
Fox R.
Bonpas Creek
Wabash R.
Ohio R.
Saline R.
Cache R.
Cumberland R.
Tennessee R.
Tradewater R.
©1996, Encyclopædia Britannica, Inc.

NAME	AREA[1] (sq. mi.)	AREA[1] (sq. km.)	POP. (1990c)	CO. SEAT
Carroll	456	1,181	16,805	Mount Carroll
Cass	371	961	13,437	Virginia
Champaign	1,000	2,590	173,025	Urbana
Christian	709	1,836	34,418	Taylorville
Clark	505	1,308	15,921	Marshall
Clay	464	1,202	14,460	Louisville
Clinton	499	1,292	33,944	Carlyle
Coles	506	1,311	51,644	Charleston
Cook	954	2,471	5,105,067	Chicago
Crawford	443	1,147	19,464	Robinson
Cumberland	347	899	10,670	Toledo
De Kalb	636	1,647	77,932	Sycamore
De Witt	399	1,033	16,516	Clinton
Douglas	420	1,088	19,464	Tuscola
Du Page	331	857	781,666	Wheaton
Edgar	628	1,627	19,595	Paris
Edwards	225	583	7,440	Albion
Effingham	481	1,246	31,704	Effingham
Fayette	719	1,862	20,893	Vandalia
Ford	488	1,264	14,275	Paxton
Franklin	434	1,124	40,319	Benton
Fulton	877	2,271	38,080	Lewistown
Gallatin	328	850	6,909	Shawneetown
Greene	543	1,406	15,317	Carrollton
Grundy	432	1,119	32,337	Morris
Hamilton	435	1,127	8,499	McLeansboro
Hancock	797	2,064	21,373	Carthage
Hardin	183	474	5,189	Elizabethtown
Henderson	376	974	8,096	Oquawka
Henry	826	2,139	51,159	Cambridge
Iroquois	1,122	2,906	30,787	Watseka
Jackson	605	1,567	61,067	Murphysboro
Jasper	495	1,282	10,609	Newton
Jefferson	573	1,484	37,020	Mount Vernon
Jersey	376	974	20,539	Jerseyville
Jo Daviess	608	1,575	21,821	Galena
Johnson	345	894	11,347	Vienna
Kane	520	1,347	317,471	Geneva
Kankakee	678	1,756	96,255	Kankakee
Kendall	320	829	39,413	Yorkville
Knox	728	1,886	56,393	Galesburg
Lake	457	1,184	516,418	Waukegan
La Salle	1,150	2,979	106,913	Ottawa
Lawrence	374	969	15,972	Lawrenceville
Lee	728	1,886	34,392	Dixon
Livingston	1,043	2,701	39,301	Pontiac
Logan	622	1,611	30,798	Lincoln
McDonough	582	1,507	35,244	Macomb
McHenry	610	1,580	183,241	Woodstock
McLean	1,173	3,038	129,180	Bloomington
Macon	578	1,497	117,206	Decatur
Macoupin	872	2,258	47,679	Carlinville
Madison	733	1,898	249,238	Edwardsville
Marion	579	1,500	41,561	Salem
Marshall	391	1,013	12,846	Lacon
Mason	541	1,401	16,269	Havana
Massac	245	635	14,752	Metropolis
Menard	312	808	11,164	Petersburg
Mercer	556	1,440	17,290	Aledo
Monroe	382	989	22,422	Waterloo
Montgomery	705	1,826	30,728	Hillsboro
Morgan	561	1,453	36,397	Jacksonville
Moultrie	345	894	13,930	Sullivan
Ogle	758	1,963	45,957	Oregon
Peoria	623	1,614	182,827	Peoria
Perry	439	1,137	21,412	Pinckneyville
Piatt	437	1,132	15,548	Monticello
Pike	828	2,145	17,577	Pittsfield
Pope	381	987	4,373	Golconda
Pulaski	204	528	7,523	Mound City
Putnam	160	414	5,730	Hennepin
Randolph	594	1,538	34,583	Chester
Richland	364	943	16,545	Olney
Rock Island	424	1,098	148,723	Rock Island
Saint Clair	673	1,743	262,852	Belleville
Saline	383	992	26,551	Harrisburg
Sangamon	879	2,277	178,386	Springfield
Schuyler	434	1,124	7,498	Rushville
Scott	251	650	5,644	Winchester
Shelby	772	1,999	22,261	Shelbyville
Stark	291	754	6,534	Toulon
Stephenson	568	1,471	48,052	Freeport
Tazewell	652	1,689	123,692	Pekin
Union	416	1,077	17,619	Jonesboro
Vermilion	899	2,328	88,257	Danville
Wabash	222	575	13,111	Mount Carmel
Warren	541	1,401	19,181	Monmouth
Washington	564	1,461	14,965	Nashville
Wayne	715	1,852	17,241	Fairfield
White	502	1,300	16,522	Carmi
Whiteside	687	1,779	60,186	Morrison
Will	847	2,194	357,313	Joliet
Williamson	429	1,111	57,733	Marion
Winnebago	519	1,344	252,913	Rockford
Woodford	528	1,368	32,653	Eureka

[1] Area = land area.

History: Explored by Père Jacques Marquette and Louis Jolliet 1673 and by René-Robert Cavelier de La Salle who erected Fort Crèvecœur on Illinois River 1680; included in French Louisiana; ceded by France to England 1763 and by England to U.S. 1783; Virginia claims to territory given up by 1786; part of Northwest Terr. 1787, of Indiana Terr. 1800, and of Illinois Terr. (*q.v.*) 1809; admitted to the Union Dec. 3, 1818 with ✻ at Kaskaskia (✻ transferred to Vandalia 1820 and to Springfield 1837); adopted present constitution 1970.

Illinois Bayou. Bayou, Pope co., NW cen. Arkansas, draining SW into Arkansas River; ab. 75 mi. (121 km.) long; has three headstreams (middle, east, and west forks).

Illinois Territory. Former territory, U.S.A.; comprised the region E of the Mississippi, N of the Ohio, W of Indiana and Lake Michigan, and S of Lake Superior and Canada; included in Northwest Terr. and Indiana Terr. (*qq.v.*) prior to being organized as Illinois Terr. (✻ Kaskaskia) Feb. 3, 1809 incl. what is now Illinois, Wisconsin, E Minnesota, and the W part of Michigan's Upper Penin.; Illinois reduced to present boundaries and admitted to the Union 1818.

Illinois Waterway. Combined system of rivers, canals, and state recreation areas, NE Illinois, with Chicago at N end; comprises: **Illinois and Michigan Canal** 96 mi. (154 km.) long, from Chicago River to La Salle on Illinois River, opened 1848, discontinued 1900; S branch of Chicago River, connected by **Chicago Sanitary and Ship Canal** 28 mi. (45 km.) long with Lockport on Des Plaines River, opened 1900, by which current was reversed and the flow of sewage directed into the Illinois River.

Illiturgis. See ANDÚJAR.

Ill·kirch–Graf·fen·sta·den \ˈil-ˌkirk-ˌgräf-ᵊn-ˈshtäd-ᵊn, ēl-ˈkĕrsh-ˌgrä-fen-stä-ˈden\. Commune, Bas-Rhin dept., suburb of Strasbourg, NE France, on Ill River; scene of signing of capitulation of Strasbourg to Louis XIV 1681.

Íl·lo·ra \ˈē-lyōr-ä\. Commune, Granada prov., S Spain, 15 mi. (24 km.) WNW of the city of Granada; pop. (1991c) 10,389; Moorish castle.

Il·lyr·ia \ə-ˈlir-ē-ə\. Ancient country comprising E Adriatic coast and its hinterland; inhabited by Illyrians, an Indo-European people, loosely united, who practiced piracy on Roman shipping; after series of wars beginning with one in 229–228 B.C., finally overthrown 35–33 B.C. by Romans who established large province of Illyricum; furnished many soldiers for the Roman legions, several of whom became emperor (such as Claudius II and Diocletian); prefecture of Illyricum (*q.v.*) erected by Diocletian (d. c. 313 A.D.); region occupied by S Slavs in 6th cent. (see BALKANS); roughly coextensive with Illyrian Provinces (*q.v.*); kingdom of Illyria, comprising Carinthia, Carniola, and Küstenland, a division of Austria 1816–49.

Il·lyr·i·an Provinces \ə-ˈlir-ē-ən\. The division of the empire formed by French Emperor Napoléon from the Austrian lands (beyond the Sava River) which France acquired by Treaty of Schönbrunn 1809; included Carinthia, Carniola, Gorizia, Istria, part of Croatia, Dalmatia, Ragusa (see DUBROVNIK), and the Ionian Is.; ✻ Ljubljana; although Austria reconquered this area in 1813 and formally regained it in 1815, the governmental reforms introduced by the French aroused Illyrian (later Yugoslav) nationalism.

Il·lyr·i·cum \ə-ˈlir-i-kəm\. **1.** Roman province with shifting boundaries, in ancient Illyria; estab. 9 A.D. by Roman Emperor Tiberius. See ILLYRIA.

2. Roman prefecture of 4th cent. A.D. incl. most of the Balkan Penin. (Dacia, Macedonia, Epirus, Thessaly, Achaea) and Crete.

Il'·men' \ˈilʸ-mənʸ\. Shallow lake, Novgorod Oblast, W Russia in Europe; 425 to 850 sq. mi. (1101 to 2202 sq. km.); receives Lovat' and Msta rivers; outlet the Volkhov; in WWII controlled by Germans Aug. 1941 to Feb. 1944.

Il·me·nau \ˈil-mə-ˌnau̇\. City, Thuringia, cen. Germany, 24 mi. (39 km.) S of Erfurt; pop. (1981c) 26,784; technical university (1953); residence of poet Johann von Goethe.

Ilo \ˈē-lō\. Port, S Peru, 53 mi. (85 km.) SE of Mollendo; pop. (1981p) 31,726; connected by railroad with Moquegua, 60 mi. (97 km.) N.

Ilo·bas·co \ˌē-lō-ˈbäs-kō\. City, El Salvador, 40 mi. (64 km.) NE of San Salvador; pop. (1987e) 67,214.

Ilo·bu \ē-ˈlō-bü\. Town, Nigeria; pop. (1991e) 175,600.

Ilo·cos \ē-ˈlō-kōs\. Region of the Philippines. See table at PHILIPPINES.

Ilocos Nor·te \ˈnȯr-tā\. Province, NW Luzon, Philippines; ✻ Laoag; coastline regular with few good harbors; on N coast are Bangui and Pasaleng bays and Cape Bojeador; in E is N end of Cordillera Central with highest point, Sicapoo (7716 ft. or 2352 m.), on SE boundary; plains and low hills along W coast; only large river the Laoag; plains inhabited mainly by Ilocanos, mountain region by Tinggian, Igorot, and Apayaos. See table at PHILIPPINES.

History: Region probably known to Chinese traders in pre-Spanish times; all NW Luzon known as Ilocos by Spaniards and created as a province by them; explored by Europeans as early as 1572; N part detached 1818 and created as Ilocos Norte prov.; revolted many times against Spanish injustices 16th–18th cents., and was active during 1898–99; civil government estab. Sept. 1901; region came under Japanese control Dec. 1941.

Ilocos Sur \ˈsu̇r\. Province, NW Luzon, Philippines, forming a narrow strip along coast of South China Sea widening at S end; ✻ Vigan; coastline fairly regular, but with frequent reefs; land comparatively level, except in SE; E boundary formed by coast range, a W part of Cordillera Central; highest point ab. 3600 ft. (1097 m.); only large river lower course of the Abra; little agriculture because of poor soil; best crop maguey; inhabitants mostly Ilocanos; fishing. See table at PHILIPPINES.

History: See ILOCOS NORTE; created a province 1818 but of much larger area incl. parts of Abra and La Union; contains several old towns antedating Spanish times; revolts against Spanish authority 17th–18th cents.; civil government estab. Sept. 1901; came under control of Japanese Dec. 1941.

Ilog \ˈē-ˌlȯg\. Municipality, SW Negros Occidental, Negros, Philippines, near coast on **Ilog River** (ab. 40 mi. or 64 km. long, flowing NNW from Negros Oriental) 45 mi. (72 km.) S of City of Bacolod; pop. (1980c) 38,956; an old town, settled 1584.

Ilo·i·lo \ˌē-lō-ˈē-lō\. **1.** Province, S and NE Panay I., Philippines; ✻ Iloilo; includes Guimaras I. (*q.v.*); one of most populous provinces of the archipelago; coastline quite irregular, esp. in E and SE, with many small islands; cen. and E parts level, NE hilly, W mountainous; largest stream the Jalaud; inhabitants Visayans. See table at PHILIPPINES.

History: Probably first settled on SW coast by Malay datos and their followers in pre-Spanish times; Spaniards made first visits about the time of Spanish explorer Miguel López de Legazpi 1565; region suffered in 16th and 17th cents. from Moro raids; grew rapidly in 19th cent.; given up to Revolutionary forces 1898; civil government estab. Apr. 1901.

2. *or officially* **City of Iloilo.** Chartered city, ✻ of Iloilo prov., Philippines, in SE part of Iloilo Strait; pop. (1990p) 311,000; noted for its manufacture of fabrics from pineapple leaves; commercial center; did not acquire a leading position until late 17th cent.; often raided by Moro pirates but because of prosperity of province declared a port for foreign trade 1855; suffered damage during Japanese occupation 1942–45.

Iloilo Strait. Channel bet. S Panay I. and N Guimaras I., Philippines; 1 to 5 mi. (1.6 to 8 km.) wide; at W end broadens out to ab. 25 mi. (40 km.) wide; Iloilo and Jordan are on it.

Ilo·pan·go, Lake \ˌē-lō-ˈpäŋ-gō\ *or Span.* **La·go de Ilopango** \ˈlä-gō-ˌthā-\. Volcanic lake, cen. El Salvador; 5.5 mi. (9 km.) long; has had islands intermittently.

i–Lora, Hamun–. See HAMUN-I-LORA.

Ilo·rin \ē-ˈlō-rēn\. Town, ✻ of Kwara state, Nigeria, ab. 170 mi. (274 km.) NE of Lagos; pop. (1991e) 420,000; surrounded by mud walls; trades esp. in palm oil; produces sugar; matches, woven products; ✻ of a Yoruba kingdom ab. 1800; overcome by Fulani c. 1825; came under British control 1897.

Ilva. See ELBA 2.

İl·yas·ba·ba \il-ˌyäs-bä-ˈbä\. S tip of Gallipoli Penin., Turkey in Europe.

Ima·ba·ri \ˌē-mä-ˈbä-rē, ē-ˈmä-bä-\ *also* **Ima·ha·ru** \ˌē-mä-ˈhä-rü, ē-ˈmä-hä-\. Town, Ehime prefecture, NW Shikoku, Japan; pop. (1990p) 123,114; port on Inland Sea.

Iman. See DAL'NERECHENSK.

Iman·dra \ˈē-ˌmən-drə\. Lake, W Kola Penin., Murmansk Oblast, N Russia in Europe; 340 sq. mi. (881 sq. km.); outlet flows S to Kandalaksha Gulf.

i–Mashkel, Hamun–. See HAMUN-I-MASHKEL.

Ima·tra \ˈi-mä-ˌträ\. Town, Kymi prov., SE Finland; pop. (1989c) 33,832; formed 1948.

Im·a·us \ˈi-mā-əs\. Ancient name of mountain range of W Himalayas.

Imaus Scyth·i·cus \ˈsi-thi-kəs\. The Tian Shan (Mts.).

Im·ba \ˈēm-bä\ *or Jp.* **Im·ba·nu·ma** \ēm-ˈbä-nu̇-mä\. Lake in SE Honshū, Japan, ab. 30 mi. (48 km.) E of Tokyo; ab. 44 mi. (71 km.) in circumference; 15 sq. mi. (39 sq. km.).

Im·ba·bu·ra \ˌēm-bä-ˈbü-rä\. **1.** Volcano, N Ecuador; 15,028 ft. (4581 m.).

2. Province of N Ecuador. See table at ECUADOR.

Imbros. See GÖKÇEADA.

Imeni Sverdlova Rudnik. See SVERDLOVS'K.

Im·e·ri·tia \ˌi-mə-ˈri-shə, -shē-ə\ *or* **Im·e·re·tia** \-ˈrē-\. District of W Republic of Georgia; formerly an independent kingdom, ✻ Kutaisi; became independent in early 15th cent.; in late 18th cent. threatened by Turks and occupied by them; signed treaty with Russia 1783 and forcibly incorp. into Russian empire by 1810.

Imi \ˈē-mē\. Town, SE cen. Ethiopia, on the Shabeelle.

Im·mac·u·la·ta \i-ˌmä-kyu̇-ˈlä-tə\. Locality, Chester co., SE Pennsylvania, ab. 25 mi. (40 km.) W of Philadelphia; Immaculata Coll. (1920).

Im·na·ha \im-ˈnȯ-hȯ, ˈim-nə-ˌhȯ\. River, NE Oregon; rises in S Wallowa co., and flows N into Snake River; ab. 75 mi. (121 km.) long; its gorge averages 5500 ft. (1676 m.) in depth for 40 mi. (64 km.), one of the deepest and narrowest in U.S.

Imo \ˈē-mō\. State of S Nigeria. See table at NIGERIA.

Imo·la \ˈē-mō-ˌlä\. Commune, Bologna prov., Emilia-Romagna, N Italy, on Santerno River 21 mi. (34 km.) SE of the commune of Bologna; pop. (1991p) 61,700; 12th cent. cathedral; former Franciscan monastery.

Imot·ski \ˈē-mȯt-skē\ *also* **Imo·schi** \ē-ˈmȯ-skē\. City, S Croatia, near border with Bosnia and Herzegovina, ab. 40 mi. (64 km.) ESE of Split.

Im·pe·ria \im-ˈpir-ē-ə, -ˈper-\. **1.** Province of Liguria, NW Italy. See table at ITALY.

2. Seaport, its ✻, on Ligurian Sea 60 mi. (97 km.) SW of Genoa; pop. (1991p) 40,171; formed 1923 by union of former communes Oneglia and Porto Maurizio; 18th cent. church; health resort.

Im·pe·ri·al \im-ˈpir-ē-əl\. **1.** County in SE corner of California. See table at CALIFORNIA.

2. City, Imperial co., SE corner of California, in Imperial Valley 5 mi. (8 km.) N of El Centro; pop. (1990c) 4113; headquarters of Imperial Irrigation District; 67 ft. (20 m.) below sea level; founded 1902.

3. City, ⊗ of Chase co., S Nebraska; pop. (1990c) 2007.

Imperial Beach. City, San Diego co., SW California, on San Diego Bay near Mexican border; pop. (1990c) 26,512; residential; has a military landing field.

Imperial Dam. Dam across Colorado River on S California-Arizona boundary, N of Yuma, Arizona; height 85 ft. (26 m.); completed 1938; impounds water for irrigation in **Imperial Reservoir** N of and adjoining Laguna Reservoir.

Imperial Valley. Valley in Imperial co., SE corner of California, and partly in Baja California, Mexico; mostly below sea level; formerly desert, uninhabited, a part of Colorado Desert; includes Salton Sea; first irrigation project completed

1901; region now watered by the All-American Canal, 80 mi. (129 km.) long, 200 ft. (61 m.) wide, which is fed by the Imperial Reservoir; truck farms; sugar beets, cotton, and alfalfa.

Imp·hal \ˈimp-ˌhəl\. City, ✱ of Manipur state, NE India, 400 mi. (644 km.) ENE of Calcutta; in **Imphal Plain** of cen. Manipur; pop. (1991p) 196,268; has military cantonment; object of Japanese attack and siege Mar.–June 1944.

Im·pru·ne·ta \ˌēm-prü-ˈnā-tä\. Commune, Firenze prov., Tuscany, cen. Italy, 6 mi. (10 km.) S of Florence; pop. (1981p) 14,720.

İmroz. See GÖKÇEADA.

Imus \ˈē-müs, -məs\. Municipality, Cavite prov., Luzon, Philippines, 7 mi. (11 km.) SE of City of Cavite; pop. (1980c) 59,103.

ʻImwas. See EMMAUS 3.

Ina·ban·ga \ˌē-nä-ˈbäŋ-gä\. Municipality on NW coast of Bohol I., Philippines, on Bohol Strait; pop. (1980c) 32,918.

In·ac·ces·si·ble \ˌin-ik-ˈse-sə-bel, ˌin-ˌak-\. Westernmost of the Tristan de Cunha Is., S Atlantic Ocean.

In·a·chus \ˈi-nə-kəs\ *or Gk.* **Ína·khos** \ˈē-nä-ˌkös\. River, a headstream of the Achelous in SE Epirus, NW Greece; ab. 75 mi. (121 km.) long.

In·a·du Knob \ˈi-nə-dü\. Peak, Cocke co., E Tennessee; 5941 ft. (1811 m.).

Ina·gua \i-ˈnäg-wə\. Either one of two islands of Bahamas: **Great Inagua** (50 mi. or 81 km. long and 25 mi. or 40 km. wide; lighthouse on its SW point) or **Little Inagua** (8 mi. or 13 km. long), both in Atlantic Ocean N of W Haiti; together constitute a district, 600 sq. mi. (1554 sq. km.).

Ínakhos. See INACHUS.

Ina·ri \ˈē-nä-rē, -ˌnär-ē\ *or Swed.* **Ena·re** \ˈā-nä-rē, -ˌnär-ē\. Town, Lappi prov., N Finland, on SW shore of Lake Inari; pop. (1980c) 6873.

Inari, Lake *or* **Lake Enare.** Lake, N Finland; 535 sq. mi. (1386 sq. km.); receives Ivalo River from the S; outlet into Arctic Ocean.

Ina·wa·shi·ro \ˌē-nä-ˈwä-shē-ˌrō\. Lake, Fukushima prefecture, N cen. Honshū, Japan, SW of Mt. Bandai; 40 sq. mi. (104 sq. km.); alt. 1920 ft. (585 m.).

Ina·za·wa \ē-ˈnä-zä-wä\. City, Aichi prefecture, Honshū, Japan, 9 mi. (15 km.) NW of Nagoya; pop. (1990p) 96,277.

In·ca \ˈiŋ-kä\. Commune, Baleares prov., Spain, N cen. Majorca I., 16 mi. (26 km.) ENE of Palma; pop. (1991c) 20,438.

Inca, Pa·so del \ˈpä-sō-thel-ˈēŋ-kä\. Pass in the Andes on border bet. La Rioja prov., NE Argentina, and cen. Atacama region, N cen. Chile; alt. 15,518 ft. (4730 m.).

In·ca·huá·si, Cerro de \ˈser-rō-thā-ˌēŋ-kä-ˈwä-sē\ *also* **Cerro de In·ca·guas·si** \-ˈgwä-sē\. Peak, NW Catamarca prov., NW Argentina, on border of Chile; 21,720 ft. (6620 m.).

Ince. See INCE-IN-MAKERFIELD.

In·ce, Cape \in-ˈje\ *or Turk.* **İn·ce·bu·run** \ən-ˌje-bü-ˈrün\. Cape (*burun*) on N coast of Turkey in Asia, projecting into Black Sea W of Sinop.

Ince–in–Ma·ker·field \ˈins … ˈmā-kər-ˌfēld\ *or* **Ince.** Town, Greater Manchester, NW England, 16 mi. (26 km.) WNW of Manchester; pop. (1981p) 14,498; engineering.

Inchcape Rock. See BELL ROCK.

Inch·colm \ˈinch-kəm\. Small island in Firth of Forth, E Scotland, NW of Leith; ruins of 12th cent. abbey.

Inch·keith \ˈinch-ˌkēth\. Small island in Firth of Forth, E Scotland, 4 mi. (6 km.) N of Leith; lighthouse.

In·ch'ŏn \ˈin-ˌchän\; *formerly* **Jin·sen** \ˈjin-ˌsen\ *or* **Che·mul·po** \jə-ˈmu̇l-pō\. Seaport city, South Korea, ab. 10 mi. (16 km.) WSW of Seoul; pop. (1985c) 1,386,911; iron and steel, glass, chemicals, lumber; opened 1883 as treaty port; has special city (provincial) status.

In·cline Village \ˈin-ˌklīn, ˈiŋ-\. Unincorporated settlement, S Washoe co., W Nevada, on NE shore of Lake Tahoe; Sierra Nevada Coll. (1969).

In·cu·dine, Mont L' \ˈmōⁿ-ˌleⁿ-kue-ˈdēn\. Mountain, S Corsica, ESE of Ajaccio; 7008 ft. (2136 km.).

In·dal \ˈēn-ˌdäl\ *or Swed.* **In·dals·älv** \-däl-ˌselv\. River (*älv*), N cen. Sweden; flows SE into Gulf of Bothnia; 261 mi. (420 m.) long.

In·dang \ēn-ˈdäŋ\. Municipality, Cavite prov., Luzon, Philippines; 21 mi. (34 km.) S of City of Cavite; pop. (1980c) 30,977.

In·daw \ˈin-ˌdȯ\. Town, Sagaing div., N cen. Myanmar, 140 mi. (225 km.) NW of Mandalay; taken by Allies Dec. 1944.

In·daw·gyi, Lake \ˌin-dȯ-ˈjē\. Lake, Kachin state, N Myanmar, ab. 60 mi. (97 km.) W of Myitkyina.

Indefatigable Island. Island, Galápagos Is., Ecuador. See SANTA CRUZ 6.

In·de·pend·ence \ˌin-də-ˈpen-dəns\. **1.** County in NE cen. Arkansas. See table at ARKANSAS.

2. Town, ⊗ of Inyo co., E California, 82 mi. (132 km.) E of Fresno.

3. City, ⊗ of Buchanan co., E Iowa, 25 mi. (40 km.) E of Waterloo; pop. (1990c) 5972.

4. City, ⊗ of Montgomery co., SE Kansas, 58 mi. (93 km.) WSW of Pittsburg; pop. (1990c) 9942; Independence Community Coll. (1925).

5. City, a ⊗ of Kenton co., N Kentucky; pop. (1990c) 10,444.

6. City, ⊗ of Jackson co., W Missouri, just E of Kansas City; pop. (1990c) 112,301; a suburb of Kansas City; home of Mormon colony 1831–33; now center of Reorganized Church of Jesus Christ of Latter-day Saints; starting point of Santa Fe and Oregon Trails during gold rush (1849); in Civil War briefly occupied twice by Confederate troops. Home of Harry S. Truman, 33d president of the U.S.; Harry S. Truman Library (dedicated 1957).

7. City, Cuyahoga co., N Ohio, 9 mi. (15 km.) S of Cleveland; pop. (1990c) 6500.

8. City, Polk co., NW Oregon, S of Salem; pop. (1990c) 4425.

9. Town, ⊗ of Grayson co., SW Virginia, WSW of Galax; pop. (1990c) 988.

Independence Mountains. Range, chiefly in W Elko co., in N Nevada.

Independence National Historical Park. See UNITED STATES, *National Historical Parks.*

Independence Pass. Mountain pass, Lake and Pitkin cos., W cen. Colorado, in Sawatch Range of the Rocky Mts.; elev. 12,095 ft. (3687 m.); traversed by a highway.

Independence Rock. Granite boulder in S Natrona co., cen. Wyoming, on N bank of Sweetwater River; 1950 ft. (594 m.) long, 850 ft. (259 m.) wide, 193 ft. (59 m.) high at N end; a landmark on the old Oregon Trail.

In·de·pen·den·cia \ˌēn-dā-pen-ˈden-sē-ä\. Province, SW Dominican Republic. See table at DOMINICAN REPUBLIC.

Inderagiri. See INDRAGIRI.

In·dex, Mount \ˈin-deks\. Mountain, King co., W Washington, in Cascade Mts. ENE of Seattle; 5979 ft. (1822 m.).

Index Peak. **1.** Mountain, Carbon co., S Montana; 11,977 ft. (3651 m.).

2. Mountain in the Absaroka Range, NW Wyoming near Montana border and just outside Yellowstone National Park; 11,500 ft. (3505 m.).

In·dia \ˈin-dē-ə\. **1.** Subcontinent, S Asia; ab. 1,704,300 sq. mi. (4,414,137 sq. km.).

Political divisions: Bangladesh, Bhutan, the Republic of India (see INDIA 2), Nepal, Pakistan, Sikkim (*qq.v.*).

History: Early cultures include that of the Indus civilization, an urban society that flourished in N India during the late 3d millennium B.C.; its decline may have been caused by arrival of Aryans, who invaded from Iranian plateau 2d millennium B.C. and spread to S and SE; developed important religious systems; Buddhism and Jainism, both founded 6th–5th cents. B.C.; Brahmanism, with its accompanying social caste system, evolved from the Vedic religion of Aryan invaders; invaded across Indus in NW (Punjab) by Macedonian King Alexander the Great c. 327–325 B.C. Northern part consolidated (with parts of modern Afghanistan) into an empire by Candragupta Maurya, founder of Maurya dynasty (c. 322–185 B.C.), whose grandson Aśoka (d. 232 B.C.) extended his empire by addition of kingdoms of Bengal and Orissa to include over two thirds of peninsula, all but extreme S part; N part again united by rulers of Gupta dynasty (fl. 320–480 A.D.); divided politically into states of varying size and power. Series of Muslim invasions begun ab. 1000

A.D. in N by the Afghan Maḥmūd of Ghaznī; earliest Muslim kingdom, Sultanate of Delhi, incl. N India and part of Coromandel Coast, founded 1206 by Quṭb-ud-Dīn Aybak but experienced decline following Turkic ruler Timur's invasion of 1398; a Muslim dynasty, the Bahmanī, flourished in the Deccan from 14th cent.; for chief contemporary Hindu kingdom in S, see VIJAYANAGAR; peninsula opened by Portuguese navigator Vasco da Gama's voyage 1497–98 to direct European trade, which Portuguese monopolized in 16th cent. and for which Dutch, English, and French competed in 17th cent. Gradually conquered 1526–1707 by Mogul emperors, of whom the first was Bābur (Ẓahīr-ud-Dīn Muḥammad) and the most famous Akbar (1556–1605), until their power was challenged in late 17th cent. by the Marathas, a Hindu people whose powerful confederacy was broken by Afghans at Panipat (*q.v.*) 1761; torn by dynastic conflicts with decline of Mogul power after 1707, thus opening way for European intervention and territorial acquisition.

Period of British control: Establishment of trading posts ("factories") in 17th cent. by rival British and French East India companies (chartered 1600 and 1664, respectively) led in 18th cent. to war bet. England and France culminating in British victory at Plassey 1757 (see CALCUTTA, DECCAN, FRENCH INDIA); ascendancy of British East India Company resulted in first extensive territorial acquisitions (Bengal and Bihar 1765, the Northern Circars 1766) but alleged misrule by company caused British parliament to pass Regulating Act 1773 and Prime Minister William Pitt's Act 1784 establishing "dual control" of company and crown; after wars with Mysore (see KARNATAKA) and Marathas, British acquired Malabar Coast 1792, Kanara 1799, Carnatic 1801, Orissa 1803, and Maratha lands (see PUNE); company's monopoly of trade abolished 1813; annexed Burma 1826–86, Sind 1843, Punjab 1849, Berar 1853, Nagpur 1854, Oudh 1856, and Baluchistan 1887 (*qq.v.*); by 1887 the parts of India not under direct British control were protected states, under native rulers, with varying degrees of dependence upon British; government modified (1861, 1909, 1919) in direction of limited self-rule. After WWI, scene of bitter struggle bet. British rulers and Indian nationalists, under Indian nationalist Mahatma Gandhi's leadership; eventual federation of all India the goal of Act of 1935 which separated Burma and Aden from India effective 1937. Areas under direct British control (i.e., **British India**) divided 1935 into 11 provinces each under a governor: Assam, Bengal, Bihar, Bombay, Central Provinces and Berar, Madras, North-West Frontier, Orissa, Punjab, Sind, United Provinces of Agra and Oudh and several other administrative units, each under a chief commissioner. British rule terminated with creation of sovereign states of India and Pakistan 1947 (see INDIA 2 and PAKISTAN).

2. *officially* **Republic of India** *also* **Indian Union** *or* **Union of India;** *Sanskrit* **Bha·rat** \ˈbər-ət\. Republic, S Asia, bounded on N by China, Nepal, Sikkim, and Bhutan, on E by Myanmar, Bangladesh, and the Bay of Bengal, on S by the Indian Ocean, and on W by the Arabian Sea and Pakistan; 1,195,063 sq. mi. (3,095,472 sq. km.); pop. (1993e) 896,567,000; ✱ New Delhi.

Physical features: May be divided into three well-defined regions: (a) Himalayan region in the N, (b) Gangetic Plain bet. foothills of the Himalayas and the Vindhya Mts., and (c) plateau region in the S and cen. part.

Chief mountains: The Himalayas (*q.v.*) in N, containing highest peaks in the world, and in NW the borders of the Hindu Kush, Safed Koh, and Sulaiman Range, this mountain barrier bet. India and the rest of Asia being crossed by several famous passes, esp. the Khyber (*q.v.*), Bolan (5900 ft. or 1798 m.), and Gumal (7500 ft. or 2286 m.); Vindhya Mts. bet. Ganges Valley and the Deccan (*q.v.*); Eastern and Western Ghats along E and W coasts; Nilgiri Hills in S.

Chief rivers: Ganges with its chief tributary, the Yamuna, in extensive river plain of the N; Indus system in NW with tributaries (Chenab, Jhelum, Sutlej, Beas, and Ravi); Brahmaputra in the NE flowing into the Ganges Delta; Narmada and Tapti in N Deccan; Godavari and Krishna in cen. Deccan.

Chief products: Rice, coffee, cotton, tea, wheat, jute, sugar; iron ore, coal, manganese, chromite, limestone, bauxite, mica; cut and polished diamonds, crude oil, textiles, processed foods, steel, machinery, transport equipment, cement, fertilizer, aluminum.

Chief cities: Bombay, Delhi, Calcutta, Madras, Bangalore, Hyderabad, Ahmadabad, Kanpur, Nagpur, Lucknow.

Political divisions: Divided into the following states and territories (for pronunciation of their names and other information, see their individual entries):

NAME	AREA (sq. mi.)	AREA (sq. km.)	POP. (1991p)	CAPITAL
States				
Andhra Pradesh	106,272	275,244	66,508,008	Hyderabad
Arunachal Pradesh	32,269	83,577	864,558	Itanagar
Assam	30,318	78,524	22,414,322	Dispur
Bihar	67,184	174,006	86,374,465	Patna
Goa	1,404	3,636	1,169,793	Panaji
Gujarat	72,236	187,091	41,309,582	Gandhinagar
Haryana	17,010	44,056	16,463,648	Chandigarh
Himachal Pradesh	21,490	55,659	5,170,877	Simla
Jammu and Kashmir[1]	53,665	138,992	7,718,700	Srinagar[2]
Karnataka	74,037	191,756	44,977,201	Bangalore
Kerala	15,007	38,868	29,098,518	Trivandrum
Madhya Pradesh	171,220	443,460	66,181,170	Bhopal
Maharashtra	118,637	307,270	78,937,187	Bombay
Manipur	8,628	22,346	1,837,149	Imphal
Meghalaya	8,665	22,442	1,774,778	Shillong
Mizoram	8,142	21,088	689,756	Aizawl
Nagaland	6,366	16,488	1,209,546	Kohima
Orissa	60,178	155,861	31,659,736	Bhubaneswar
Punjab	19,448	50,370	20,281,969	Chandigarh
Rajasthan	132,149	342,266	44,005,990	Jaipur
Sikkim	2,744	7,107	406,457	Gangtok
Tamil Nadu	50,180	129,966	55,858,946	Madras
Tripura	4,035	10,451	2,757,205	Agartala
Uttar Pradesh	113,655	294,366	139,112,287	Lucknow
West Bengal	33,852	87,677	68,077,965	Calcutta
Union Territories				
Andaman and Nicobar Islands	3,202	8,293	280,661	Port Blair
Chandigarh	44	114	642,015	Chandigarh
Dadra and Nagar Haveli	189	490	138,477	Silvassa
Daman and Diu	36	93	101,586	
Delhi	573	148	9,420,644	Delhi
Lakshadweep	11	28	51,707	Kavaratti
Pondicherry	183	474	807,785	Pondicherry

[1]Figures apply to India-controlled area only.
[2]Summer capital. Jammu is the winter capital.

History: For history of region prior to 1947, see INDIA 1. Estab. midnight of Aug. 14–15, 1947 by act of British parliament; military clashes with Pakistan over possession of Jammu and Kashmir 1947–49; inaugurated republic 1950; annexed remaining Portuguese territories 1961–62; military clashes with China 1959 and 1962, with Pakistan 1965 and 1971; its defeat of Pakistan (1971) decisive in establishment of Bangladesh; Sikkim voted April 15, 1975 to merge with India; in 1980s and early 1990s troubled by political instability, religious violence, terrorism, incl. the assassinations of Prime Ministers Indira Gandhi (1984), and later, her son, Rajiv Gandhi (1991) as he was campaigning, and tense relations with Pakistan.

India, Bas·sas da \ˌbä-ˈsäz-də-ēn-ˈdyä, ˈba-səz-də-ˈin-dē-ə\. Small uninhabited island group belonging to France, in cen. Mozambique Channel bet. SW Madagascar and SE Mozambique; administered by Réunion.

In·di·a·lan·tic \ˌin-dē-ə-ˈlan-tik\. City, Brevard co., E Florida, across Indian River lagoon from Melbourne; pop. (1990c) 2844.

In·di·ana \ˌin-dē-ˈa-nə\. **1.** A north central state of U.S.A., bounded on N by Michigan and Lake Michigan, on E by Ohio, on S by Kentucky, and on W by Illinois; 38th state in

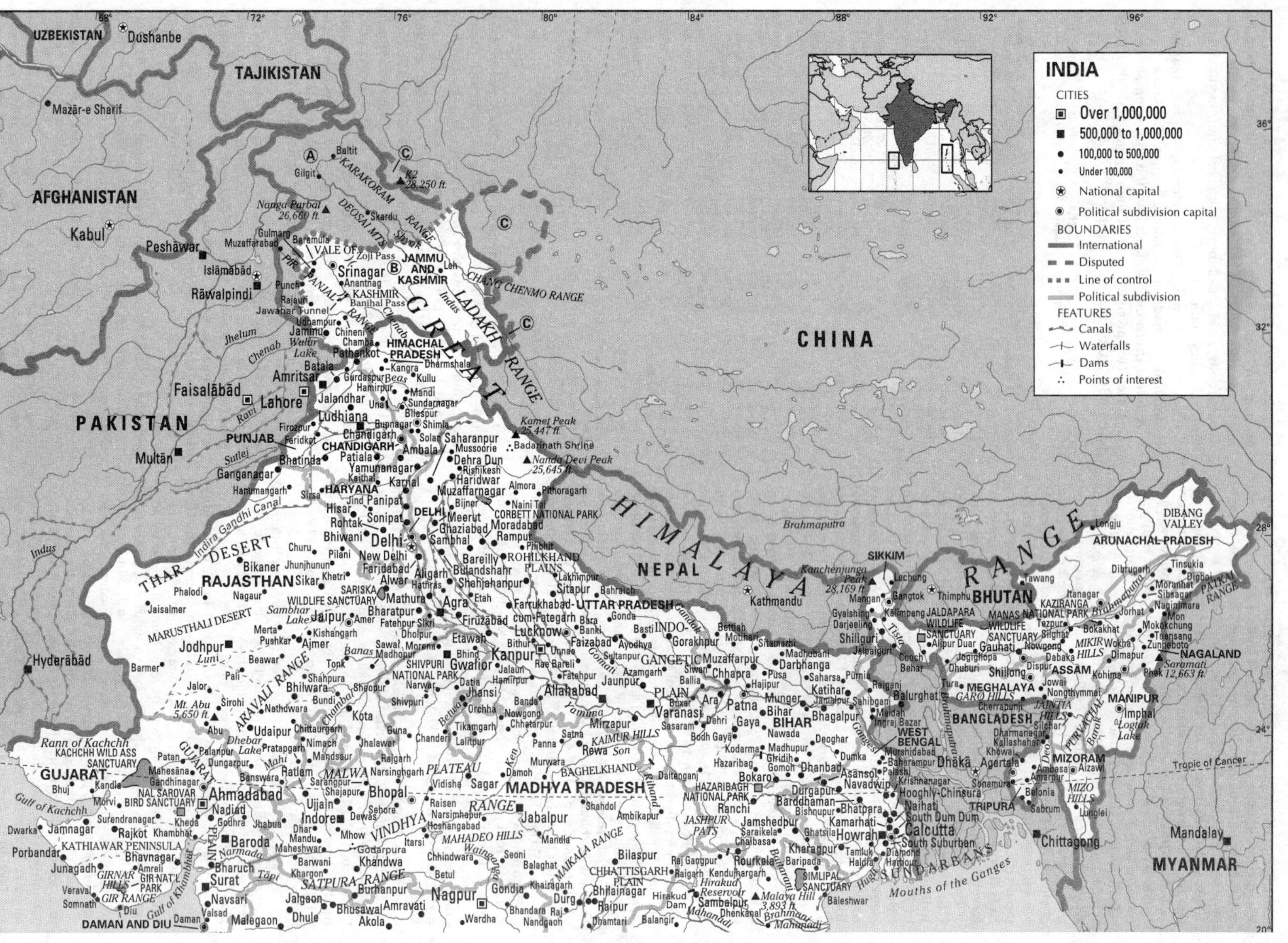
INDIA
CITIES
Over 1,000,000
500,000 to 1,000,000
100,000 to 500,000
Under 100,000
National capital
Political subdivision capital
BOUNDARIES
International
Disputed
Line of control
Political subdivision
FEATURES
Canals
Waterfalls
Dams
Points of interest
CHINA
PAKISTAN
AFGHANISTAN
TAJIKISTAN
UZBEKISTAN
NEPAL
BHUTAN
BANGLADESH
MYANMAR
SIKKIM
JAMMU AND KASHMIR
HIMACHAL PRADESH
PUNJAB
HARYANA
CHANDIGARH
DELHI
RAJASTHAN
UTTAR PRADESH
MADHYA PRADESH
BIHAR
WEST BENGAL
GUJARAT
DAMAN AND DIU
ARUNACHAL PRADESH
ASSAM
MEGHALAYA
NAGALAND
MANIPUR
MIZORAM
TRIPURA
GREAT HIMALAYA RANGE
THAR DESERT
Kabul
Islāmābād
Kathmandu
Thimphu
Dhaka
New Delhi
Delhi
Calcutta
Ahmadabad
Lahore
Tropic of Cancer
Mouths of the Ganges

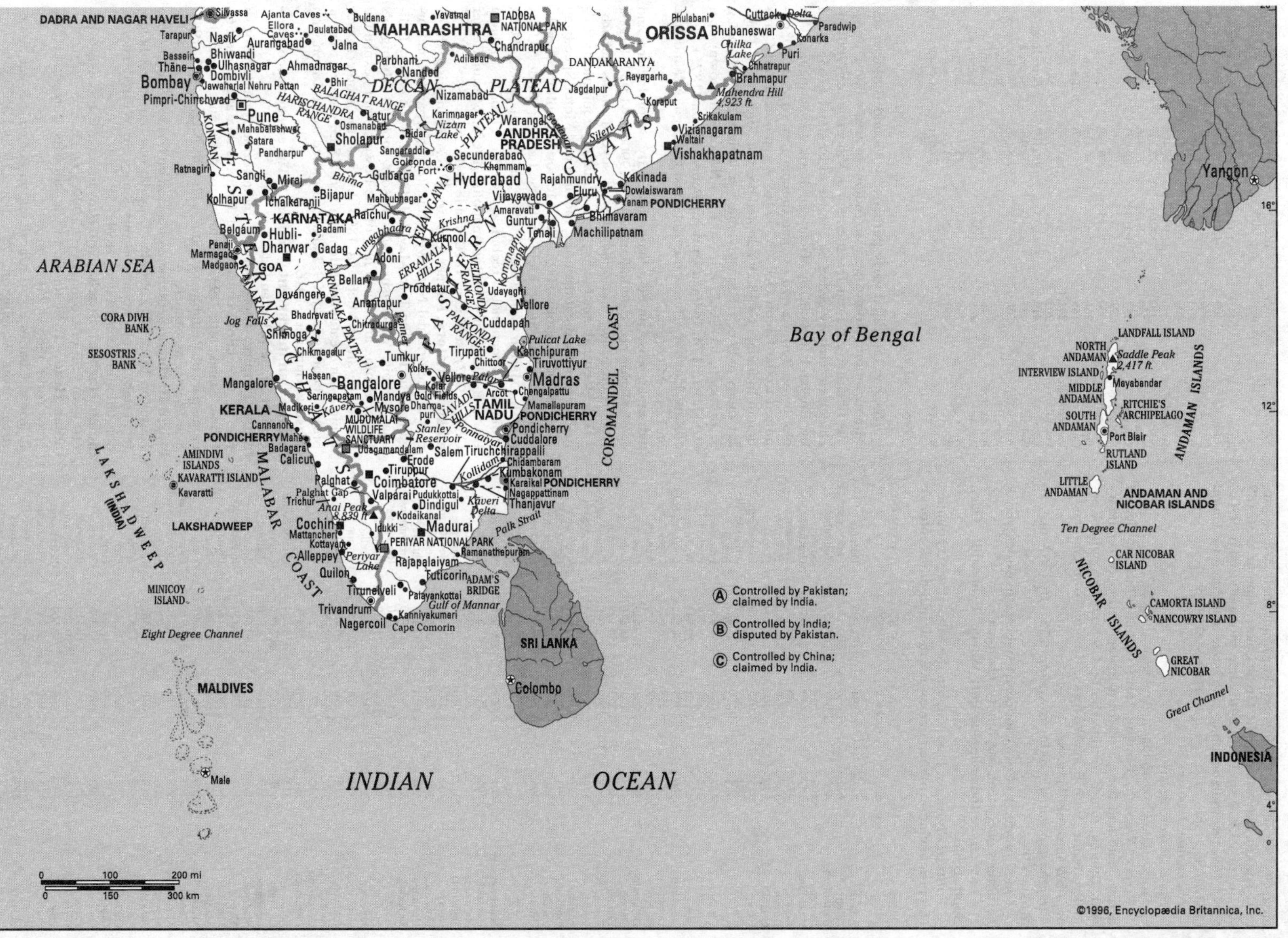

DADRA AND NAGAR HAVELI
MAHARASHTRA
ORISSA
ANDHRA PRADESH
KARNATAKA
GOA
KERALA
TAMIL NADU
PONDICHERRY
DECCAN PLATEAU
KARNATAKA PLATEAU
ARABIAN SEA
Bay of Bengal
INDIAN
OCEAN
COROMANDEL COAST
MALABAR COAST
KONKAN
Bombay
Pune
Sholapur
Hyderabad
Secunderabad
Bangalore
Mysore
Madras
Pondicherry
Madurai
Coimbatore
Cochin
Calicut
Mangalore
Trivandrum
Nagercoil
Cape Comorin
Vishakhapatnam
Bhubaneswar
Cuttack
Puri
Mahendra Hill 4,923 ft.
Anai Peak 8,839 ft.
PERIYAR NATIONAL PARK
MUDUMALAI WILDLIFE SANCTUARY
TADOBA NATIONAL PARK
Palk Strait
Gulf of Mannar
ADAM'S BRIDGE
SRI LANKA
Colombo
LAKSHADWEEP
LAKSHADWEEP (INDIA)
MINICOY ISLAND
Eight Degree Channel
MALDIVES
Male
CORA DIVH BANK
SESOSTRIS BANK
ANDAMAN ISLANDS
LANDFALL ISLAND
NORTH ANDAMAN
Saddle Peak 2,417 ft.
INTERVIEW ISLAND
MIDDLE ANDAMAN
SOUTH ANDAMAN
RITCHIE'S ARCHIPELAGO
Port Blair
RUTLAND ISLAND
LITTLE ANDAMAN
ANDAMAN AND NICOBAR ISLANDS
Ten Degree Channel
CAR NICOBAR ISLAND
NICOBAR ISLANDS
CAMORTA ISLAND
NANCOWRY ISLAND
GREAT NICOBAR
Great Channel
INDONESIA
Yangon
16°
12°
8°
4°
Ⓐ Controlled by Pakistan; claimed by India.
Ⓑ Controlled by India; disputed by Pakistan.
Ⓒ Controlled by China; claimed by India.
0 100 200 mi
0 150 300 km
©1996, Encyclopædia Britannica, Inc.

area, 36,291 sq. mi. (93,994 sq. km.), not incl. 228 sq. mi. (591 sq. km.) of water of the Great Lakes (land area 36,189 sq. mi. or 93,730 sq. km.); 14th state in population, (1990c) 5,544,159; ✱ Indianapolis; 19th state admitted to Union (1816). See table of states at UNITED STATES.

Nickname: Hoosier State.

State flower: Peony.

Motto: The Crossroads of America.

Rivers: Wabash, flowing from middle Ohio border W across state and then S to form lower section of boundary with Illinois; Ohio, forming SE and S boundary with Kentucky; White, with E and W forks, flowing from cen. and S area SW into the Wabash.

Highest point: Franklin township 1257 ft. (383 m.), in Wayne co.

Chief products: Corn, soybeans, wheat; livestock; coal, building stone; steel, machinery, chemicals.

Chief cities: Indianapolis, Fort Wayne, Evansville, Gary, South Bend.

Political divisions: Divided into the following 92 counties (for pronunciation of their names, see their individual entries):

NAME	AREA[1] (sq. mi.)	AREA[1] (sq. km.)	POP. (1990c)	CO. SEAT
Adams	345	894	31,095	Decatur
Allen	671	1,738	300,836	Fort Wayne
Bartholomew	402	1,041	63,657	Columbus
Benton	409	1,059	9,441	Fowler
Blackford	167	433	14,067	Hartford City
Boone	427	1,106	38,147	Lebanon
Brown	324	839	14,080	Nashville
Carroll	374	969	18,809	Delphi
Cass	415	1,075	38,413	Logansport
Clark	384	995	87,777	Jeffersonville
Clay	364	943	24,705	Brazil
Clinton	407	1,054	30,974	Frankfort
Crawford	312	808	9,914	English
Daviess	430	1,114	27,533	Washington
Dearborn	306	793	38,835	Lawrenceburg
Decatur	370	958	23,645	Greensburg
De Kalb	366	948	35,324	Auburn
Delaware	398	1,031	119,659	Muncie
Dubois	433	1,121	36,616	Jasper
Elkhart	468	1,212	156,198	Goshen
Fayette	215	557	26,015	Connersville
Floyd	149	386	64,404	New Albany
Fountain	397	1,028	17,808	Covington
Franklin	394	1,020	19,580	Brookville
Fulton	368	953	18,840	Rochester
Gibson	498	1,290	31,913	Princeton
Grant	421	1,090	74,169	Marion
Greene	549	1,422	30,410	Bloomfield
Hamilton	401	1,039	108,936	Noblesville
Hancock	305	790	45,527	Greenfield
Harrison	479	1,241	29,890	Corydon
Hendricks	417	1,080	75,717	Danville
Henry	400	1,036	48,139	New Castle
Howard	293	759	80,827	Kokomo
Huntington	390	1,010	35,427	Huntington
Jackson	520	1,347	37,730	Brownstown
Jasper	562	1,456	24,960	Rensselaer
Jay	386	1,000	21,512	Portland
Jefferson	366	948	29,797	Madison
Jennings	377	976	23,661	Vernon
Johnson	315	816	88,109	Franklin
Knox	517	1,339	39,884	Vincennes
Kosciusko	540	1,399	65,294	Warsaw
Lagrange	381	987	29,477	Lagrange
Lake	513	1,329	475,594	Crown Point
La Porte	607	1,572	107,066	La Porte
Lawrence	459	1,189	42,836	Bedford
Madison	453	1,173	130,669	Anderson
Marion	400	1,036	797,159	Indianapolis
Marshall	443	1,147	42,182	Plymouth
Martin	345	894	10,369	Shoals
Miami	380	984	36,897	Peru
Monroe	410	1,062	108,978	Bloomington
Montgomery	507	1,313	34,436	Crawfordsville
Morgan	406	1,052	55,920	Martinsville
Newton	413	1,070	13,551	Kentland
Noble	412	1,067	37,877	Albion
Ohio	87	225	5,315	Rising Sun
Orange	405	1,049	18,409	Paoli
Owen	390	1,010	17,281	Spencer
Parke	451	1,168	15,410	Rockville
Perry	384	995	19,107	Cannelton
Pike	335	868	12,509	Petersburg
Porter	425	1,101	128,932	Valparaiso
Posey	412	1,067	25,968	Mount Vernon
Pulaski	433	1,121	12,643	Winamac
Putnam	490	1,269	30,315	Greencastle
Randolph	457	1,184	27,148	Winchester
Ripley	442	1,145	24,616	Versailles
Rush	409	1,059	18,129	Rushville
Saint Joseph	466	1,207	247,052	South Bend
Scott	193	500	20,991	Scottsburg
Shelby	409	1,059	40,307	Shelbyville
Spencer	396	1,026	19,490	Rockport
Starke	310	803	22,747	Knox
Steuben	309	800	27,446	Angola
Sullivan	457	1,184	18,993	Sullivan
Switzerland	221	572	7,738	Vevay
Tippecanoe	500	1,295	130,598	Lafayette
Tipton	261	676	16,119	Tipton
Union	168	435	6,976	Liberty
Vanderburgh	241	624	165,058	Evansville
Vermillion	263	681	16,773	Newport
Vigo	415	1,075	106,107	Terre Haute
Wabash	421	1,090	35,069	Wabash
Warren	368	953	8,176	Williamsport
Warrick	391	1,013	44,920	Boonville
Washington	516	1,336	23,717	Salem
Wayne	405	1,049	71,951	Richmond
Wells	368	953	25,948	Bluffton
White	497	1,287	23,265	Monticello
Whitley	337	873	27,651	Columbia City

[1] Area = land area.

History: Inhabited early perhaps by Mound Builders; the Miami, among other American Indians in area when Europeans first arrived; French settlement at Vincennes c. 1700; included in territory ceded by France to England 1763; ceded by England to U.S. by Treaty of Paris 1783; included in Northwest Terr. (*q.v.*) 1787 and Indiana Terr. (*q.v.*) 1800; admitted to the Union Dec. 11, 1816; ✱ removed from Corydon to Indianapolis 1825; adopted present constitution 1851.

2. County in W cen. Pennsylvania. See table at PENNSYLVANIA.

3. Borough, its ⊗, 25 mi. (40 km.) NW of Johnstown; pop. (1990c) 15,174; Indiana Univ. of Pennsylvania (1875).

Indiana Harbor. Harbor district, East Chicago, NW Indiana, on Lake Michigan.

In·di·an·ap·o·lis \ˌin-dē-ə-ˈna-pə-lis\. City, ✱ of Indiana and ⊗ of Marion co., cen. Indiana; pop. (1990c) 741,952; largest city in the state; consolidated with several of its suburbs 1970; electrical machinery, transportation equipment; railroad center; medical facilities; Indianapolis Motor Speedway (site of Indianapolis 500); War Memorial (buildings, parkways, plazas); Stout Field military facility; Butler Univ. (1850), Marian Coll. (1851), Univ. of Indianapolis (1902), Indiana Vocational Technical Coll. (1963), Indiana Univ.–Purdue Univ. at Indianapolis (1969), Martin Center Coll. (1977); settled c. 1820; made ✱ 1825.

Indiana Territory. Former territory, U.S.A.; comprised the W part of the original Northwest Terr. (*q.v.*); separated and organized as Indiana Terr. May 7, 1800 incl. what is now Indiana, Illinois, Wisconsin, E Minnesota, most of Michigan's Upper Penin., and the W half of the Lower Penin.; expanded to include all of Michigan 1803, but lost the whole Lower Penin. with creation of Michigan Terr. 1805; reduced to near present boundaries 1809; Indiana admitted to the Union with present boundaries 1816.

In·di·an Countercurrent \ˈin-dē-ən\. The equatorial countercurrent in the N Indian Ocean.

Indian Empire. Those parts of India formerly under British rule or protection; consisted of British India and some 560 Indian States; after 1937 exclusive of Aden and Burma; became part of Republic of India midnight Aug. 14–15, 1947. See *History* at INDIA 1.

Indian Harbour. Settlement on island on N side of entrance to Hamilton Inlet, SE Labrador, Canada; one of earliest hospitals estab. by physician and missionary Sir Wilfred Thomason Grenfell located here 1894.

Indian Harbour Beach. City, Brevard co., E Florida, 6 mi. (10 km.) ESE of Cocoa; pop. (1990c) 6933.

Indian Head. **1.** Mountain in Catskill Mts., Greene co., SE New York; 3585 ft. (1093 m.).

2. Town, Charles co., S Maryland, on Potomac River downstream from Washington, D.C.; pop. (1990c) 3531; site of a U.S. naval facility.

INDIANA
CITIES
State capital
County seat
City
BOUNDARIES
State
County
FEATURES
Canals
Points of interest
MICHIGAN
Lake Michigan
ILLINOIS
OHIO
KENTUCKY
INDIANA DUNES NATIONAL LAKESHORE
GEORGE ROGERS CLARK NATIONAL HISTORICAL PARK
LINCOLN BOYHOOD NATIONAL MEMORIAL
Indianapolis
0 20 40 mi
0 30 60 km

Indian Head Park. Village, Cook co., NE Illinois, ab. 4.5 mi. (7.2 km.) W of Chicago; pop. (1990c) 3503.

Indian Hill, The Village of *or* **Indian Hill.** City, Hamilton co., SW Ohio, 12 mi. (19 km.) NE of Cincinnati; pop. (1990c) 5383.

Indian Lake. 1. Lake, E cen. Hamilton co., NE cen. New York; outlet N into Hudson River; ab. 7 mi. (11 km.) long.

2. Lake, NW Logan co., W Ohio.

Indian Ocean; *anc.* **Oce·a·nus In·di·cus** \ō-'sē-ə-nəs-'in-di-kəs\. Body of water E of Africa, S of Asia, W of Australia, and N of Antarctica; ab. 28,350,500 sq. mi. (73,427,795 sq. km.); greatest known depth 25,344 ft. (7725 m.).

In·di·a·no·la \ˌin-dē-ə-'nō-lə\. **1.** City, ⊗ of Warren co., S cen. Iowa, 16 mi. (26 km.) S of Des Moines; pop. (1990c) 11,350; Simpson Coll. (1860).

2. City, ⊗ of Sunflower co., W Mississippi, 23 mi. (37 km.) E of Greenville; pop. (1990c) 11,809; catfish processing.

Indian Peak. Mountain, W Park co., NW Wyoming; 10,923 ft. (3329 m.).

Indian River. 1. Lagoon, E Florida; runs parallel with the coast in Brevard, Indian River, and St. Lucie cos. S to St. Lucie Inlet in Martin co., connecting with the ocean at Indian River Inlet; 165 mi. (266 km.) long and of varying width; navigable for boats of shallow draft.

2. County on cen. E coast of Florida. See table at FLORIDA.

Indian River Bay. Inlet of Atlantic Ocean on SE coast of Sussex co., Delaware.

Indian River Inlet. Narrow strait leading from Atlantic Ocean through barrier reefs off E coast of St. Lucie co., E Florida.

Indian Rocks Beach. City, Pinellas co., W Florida; pop. (1990c) 3963.

Indian States. Various (formerly) semi-independent areas in India ruled by native princes; areas now part of India and Pakistan; formerly subject in varying degrees to British authority, but in Aug. 1947 made nominally independent states (see INDIA 1). There were more than 500 such states varying greatly in both area and population. Under British rule their systems of government varied, the larger states (such as Hyderabad, Gwalior, Baroda, Mysore, Cochin, Jammu and Kashmir, Travancore, Indore, Sikkim) were in direct relation with the governor-general through a resident, while many of the smaller states were grouped in Agencies (such as Central India, Eastern States, Rajputana, Punjab States, Gujarat, Western India, Kolhapur and Deccan, Madras States) administered by a resident assisted by political agents. Titles and remaining privileges of princes abolished by Indian government 1971.

Indian Subcontinent. Projecting landmass of S Asia; usu. considered as being S of the Himalayas and incl. the nations of India, Bangladesh, and Pakistan.

Indian Territory. Former territory in U.S.A., now in Oklahoma; 31,000 sq. mi. (80,290 sq. km.). See OKLAHOMA.

Indian Union. See INDIA 2.

In·dies \'in-dēz\. Usually, the East Indies; the plural form of *Indie* or *Indy*, applied orig. to India and adjacent lands and islands in the Far East; later applied by writers to lands discovered by Europeans in 15th and 16th cents. in the Western Hemisphere, and thought to be geographically the same region; later the two regions became known as East Indies and West Indies (*qq.v.*).

In·di·gir·ka \ˌin-də-'gir-kə\. River, NE Russia in Asia; rises on N slopes of Verkhoyansk Range, flows N, cutting a deep gorge through Cherskiy Range, to East Siberian Sea; 1112 mi. (1789 km.) long; drainage basin 139,150 sq. mi. (360,399 sq. km.); navigable but frozen much of the year.

In·dio \'in-dē-ˌō\. City, Riverside co., SE California, SE of San Bernardino; pop. (1990c) 36,793; founded 1876.

In·dis·pen·sa·ble Reefs \ˌin-dis-'pen-sə-bəl\. Reefs S of Rennell I., SE Solomon Is., W Pacific Ocean; ab. 11°S lat.

Indispensable Strait. Channel bet. NE Guadalcanal I. and SW Malaita I., SE Solomon Is., W Pacific Ocean; ab. 35 mi. (56 km.) wide.

In·do·chi·na *or* **In·do–Chi·na** \'in-dō-'chī-nə\; *formerly also* **Further India.** The SE peninsula of Asia, comprising Myanmar, Thailand, Laos, Cambodia, Vietnam, and West Malaysia. Since ancient times culturally subject to Indian (Hindu) and Chinese civilization; for history of important kingdoms, see ANNAM, MYANMAR, CAMBODIA, and THAILAND; after penetration by Europeans, E part controlled by French (see FRENCH INDOCHINA), center by Thai, and W and S part by British; in WWII occupied by Japanese 1940–45.

Indochina, French. See FRENCH INDOCHINA.

Indo–Gangetic Plain. See GANGETIC PLAIN.

In·do·ne·sia \ˌin-də-'nē-zhə, -shə\. **1.** Occasional name for the Malay Archipelago; refers generally to all regions inhabited by peoples related to the Malays proper.

2. *or in full* **Republic of Indonesia;** *formerly* **Netherlands Indies** *also* **Netherlands East Indies** *or* **Dutch East Indies;** *from 1949 to 1950* **United States of Indonesia.** Republic, SE Asia, an archipelago extending from long. 95°E to long. 141°E; 779,675 sq. mi. (2,019,358 sq. km.); pop. (1993e) 188,216,000; ✱ Jakarta. Constituent parts include: Bali, Bangka, Borneo (part), Ceram, Flores, Irian Jaya (the W part of New Guinea), Java, Lombok, Madura, Sulawesi, Sumatra, and Timor.

Chief products: Rice, corn, sugar, nutmeg, palm oil, timber, rubber, tea; tourism; natural gas, oil, tin, bauxite, coal, silver, copper.

Chief cities: Jakarta, Surabaja, Bandung, Medan, Cilacap, Palembang, Semarang.

Political divisions: Divided into the following provinces shown by island or island group (for pronunciation of their names, see their individual entries):

NAME	AREA (sq. mi.)	AREA (sq. km.)	POP. (1990c)	CAPITAL
Borneo				
Central Kalimantan	60,445	156,552	1,396,486	Palangkaraya
East Kalimantan	78,231	202,618	1,876,663	Samarinda
South Kalimantan	13,144	34,043	2,597,572	Banjarmasin
West Kalimantan	60,643	157,065	3,229,153	Pontianak
Java				
Central Java	13,207	34,206	28,520,643	Semarang
East Java	18,503	47,923	32,503,991	Surabaja
Jakarta[1]	228	590	8,259,266	Jakarta
West Java	17,876	46,299	35,384,352	Bandung
Yogyakarta[2]	1,193	3,090	2,913,054	Yogyakarta
Lesser Sunda Islands				
Bali	2,147	5,561	2,777,811	Denpasar
East Nusa Tenggara	18,485	47,876	3,268,644	Kupang
East Timor	5,763	14,926	747,750	Dili
West Nusa Tenggara	7,790	20,176	3,369,649	Mataram
Moluccas				
Maluku	28,766	74,504	1,857,790	Ambon
New Guinea				
Irian Jaya	162,927	421,981	1,648,708	Jayapura
Sulawesi				
Central Sulawesi	26,818	69,459	1,711,327	Palu
North Sulawesi	7,316	18,948	2,478,119	Manado
South-East Sulawesi	10,648	27,578	1,349,619	Kendari
South Sulawesi	27,993	72,502	6,981,646	Ujung Pandang
Sumatra				
Atjeh[2]	21,305	55,180	3,416,156	Banda Atjeh
Bengkulu	8,142	21,088	1,179,122	Bengkulu
Jambi	17,345	44,924	2,020,568	Jambi
Lampung	12,810	33,178	6,017,573	Tanjungkarang
North Sumatra	27,331	70,787	10,256,027	Medan
Riau	36,510	94,561	3,303,976	Pekanbaru
South Sumatra	39,880	103,289	6,313,074	Palembang
West Sumatra	19,219	49,777	4,000,207	Padang

[1] Capital territory.
[2] Special autonomous district.

History: First visited by Europeans 16th cent.; scene of activities of Dutch East India Company 17th and 18th cents.; increasingly dominated by Dutch as they built Batavia (*q.v.*) 1619, drove out English competitors 1623 (see AMBON 3), and captured Melaka on mainland 1641; company territory turned over c. 1798 to government of French-controlled Netherlands from which most of it was seized by British during Napoleonic Wars; restored to Netherlands 1816; legislative assembly estab. 1918; under Japanese control 1942–45 during WWII; retaken by Allies at end of war 1945; declared itself an independent republic 1945, not recognized by Netherlands; period 1945–49 marked by attempts of Dutch to reassert their control; establishment of United States of Indonesia (in nominal union with Netherlands) 1949; establishment of unitary republic (exclusive of W part of New

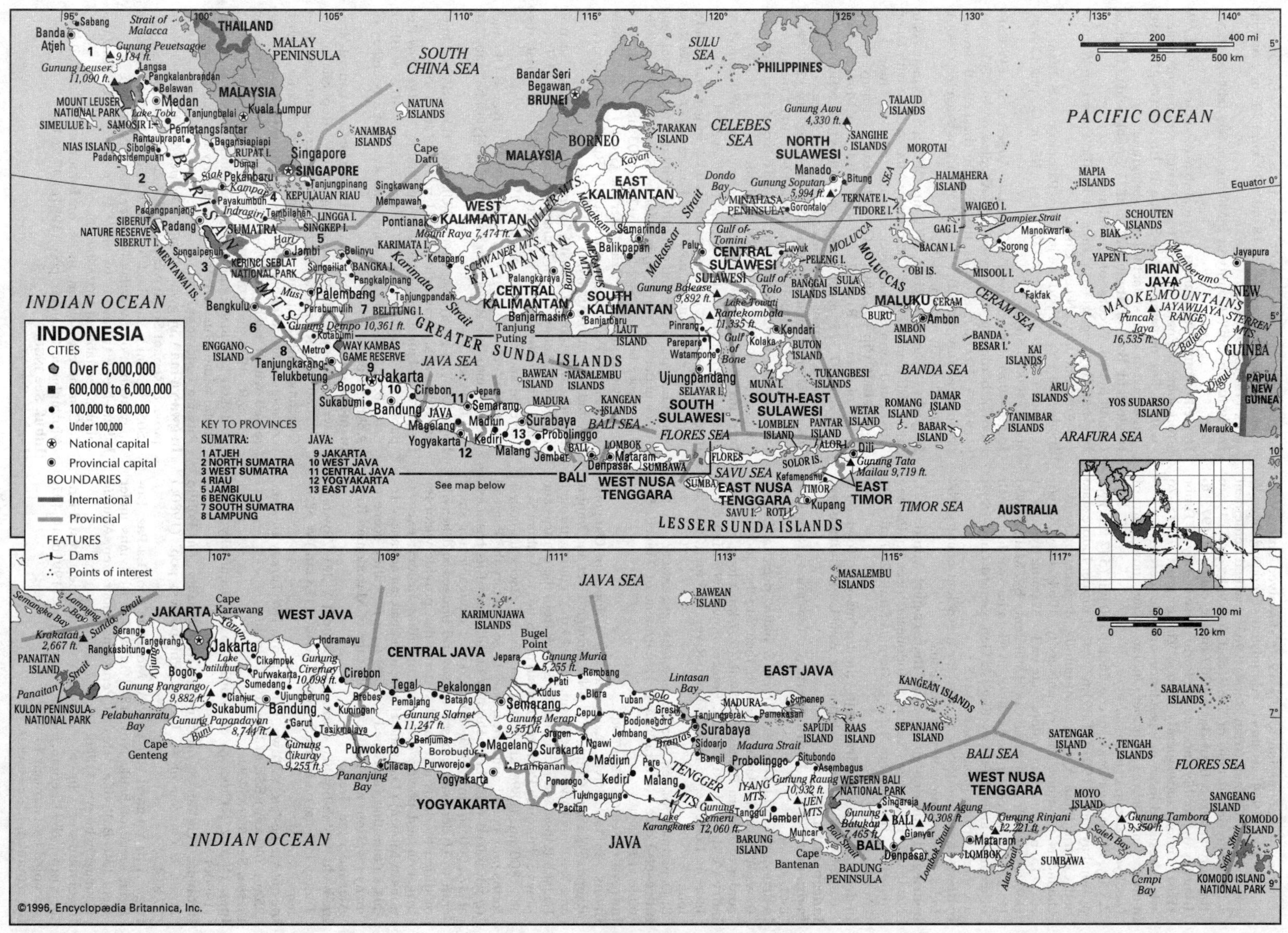
INDONESIA
CITIES
Over 6,000,000
600,000 to 6,000,000
100,000 to 600,000
Under 100,000
National capital
Provincial capital
BOUNDARIES
International
Provincial
FEATURES
Dams
Points of interest
KEY TO PROVINCES
SUMATRA:
1 ATJEH
2 NORTH SUMATRA
3 WEST SUMATRA
4 RIAU
5 JAMBI
6 BENGKULU
7 SOUTH SUMATRA
8 LAMPUNG
JAVA:
9 JAKARTA
10 WEST JAVA
11 CENTRAL JAVA
12 YOGYAKARTA
13 EAST JAVA
See map below
PACIFIC OCEAN
INDIAN OCEAN
SOUTH CHINA SEA
SULU SEA
CELEBES SEA
JAVA SEA
BANDA SEA
FLORES SEA
SAVU SEA
TIMOR SEA
ARAFURA SEA
CERAM SEA
BALI SEA
MOLUCCA SEA
GREATER SUNDA ISLANDS
LESSER SUNDA ISLANDS
THAILAND
MALAY PENINSULA
MALAYSIA
Kuala Lumpur
Singapore
SINGAPORE
Bandar Seri Begawan
BRUNEI
BORNEO
PHILIPPINES
AUSTRALIA
PAPUA NEW GUINEA
Equator 0°
Banda Atjeh
Sabang
Medan
Padang
Pekanbaru
Jambi
Palembang
Bengkulu
Tanjungkarang-Telukbetung
SUMATRA
BARISAN MTS.
Gunung Leuser 11,090 ft.
Gunung Peuetsagoe 9,184 ft.
Gunung Dempo 10,361 ft.
Lake Toba
MOUNT LEUSER NATIONAL PARK
SIBERUT NATURE RESERVE
KERINCI SEBLAT NATIONAL PARK
WAY KAMBAS GAME RESERVE
NIAS ISLAND
SIMEULUE I.
MENTAWAI IS.
ENGGANO ISLAND
BANGKA I.
BELITUNG I.
KEPULAUAN RIAU
LINGGA I.
SINGKEP I.
NATUNA ISLANDS
ANAMBAS ISLANDS
WEST KALIMANTAN
CENTRAL KALIMANTAN
SOUTH KALIMANTAN
EAST KALIMANTAN
KALIMANTAN
Pontianak
Palangkaraya
Banjarmasin
Balikpapan
Samarinda
Mount Raya 7,474 ft.
MULLER MTS.
SCHWANER MTS.
MERATUS MTS.
Karimata Strait
Makassar Strait
NORTH SULAWESI
CENTRAL SULAWESI
SOUTH SULAWESI
SOUTH-EAST SULAWESI
SULAWESI
Manado
Gorontalo
Palu
Kendari
Ujungpandang
Gunung Soputan 5,994 ft.
Gunung Awu 4,330 ft.
Gunung Balease 9,892 ft.
Rantekombola 11,335 ft.
MINAHASA PENINSULA
Gulf of Tomini
Gulf of Tolo
Gulf of Bone
MALUKU
MOLUCCAS
Ambon
HALMAHERA ISLAND
MOROTAI
TERNATE I.
TIDORE I.
BURU
CERAM
KAI ISLANDS
ARU ISLANDS
TANIMBAR ISLANDS
IRIAN JAYA
Jayapura
Merauke
MAOKE MOUNTAINS
JAYAWIJAYA RANGE
Puncak Jaya 16,535 ft.
STERREN MTS.
NEW GUINEA
BIAK
YAPEN I.
WAIGEO I.
MISOOL I.
Sorong
Manokwari
Fakfak
WEST NUSA TENGGARA
EAST NUSA TENGGARA
EAST TIMOR
Dili
Kupang
Mataram
Denpasar
LOMBOK
SUMBAWA
FLORES
SUMBA
TIMOR
BALI
Gunung Tata Mailau 9,719 ft.
JAKARTA
WEST JAVA
CENTRAL JAVA
YOGYAKARTA
EAST JAVA
JAVA
Jakarta
Bogor
Bandung
Sukabumi
Cirebon
Tegal
Pekalongan
Semarang
Magelang
Yogyakarta
Surakarta
Madiun
Kediri
Malang
Surabaya
Probolinggo
Jember
Purwokerto
Cilacap
Banyuwangi
Borobudur
Prambanan
Gunung Pangrango 9,882 ft.
Gunung Papandayan 8,744 ft.
Gunung Ciremay 10,098 ft.
Gunung Cikuray 9,255 ft.
Gunung Slamet 11,247 ft.
Gunung Merapi 9,551 ft.
Gunung Muria 5,255 ft.
Gunung Semeru 12,060 ft.
Gunung Raung 10,932 ft.
TENGGER MTS.
IYANG MTS.
IJEN MTS.
Krakatau 2,667 ft.
Sunda Strait
Madura Strait
Bali Strait
Lombok Strait
Alas Strait
Sape Strait
MADURA
KARIMUNJAWA ISLANDS
BAWEAN ISLAND
MASALEMBU ISLANDS
KANGEAN ISLANDS
KULON PENINSULA NATIONAL PARK
WESTERN BALI NATIONAL PARK
KOMODO ISLAND NATIONAL PARK
KOMODO ISLAND
Mount Agung 10,308 ft.
Gunung Batukau 7,465 ft.
Gunung Rinjani 12,221 ft.
Gunung Tambora 9,350 ft.
SUMBAWA
©1996, Encyclopædia Britannica, Inc.

Guinea) and admission to UN 1950; dissolved union with Netherlands 1954; assumed administrative control over W part of New Guinea (Irian Barat) 1963; reached settlement with Malaysia on status of Sabah and Sarawak (*qq.v.*) 1966; formally annexed Irian Barat 1969 (name changed 1973 to Irian Jaya); forcibly annexed the Portuguese colony of Timor (East Timor, subsequently Timor Timur prov.) 1975–76 which resulted in an independence struggle there.

In·dore \in-ˈdōr\. **1.** Former Indian state, now part of Madhya Pradesh, cen. India.
2. City, W Madhya Pradesh, cen. India, 340 mi. (547 km.) NE of Bombay; pop. (1991c) 1,091,674; ✻ of former Indore state and Central India Agency; cottonmills; engineering works; chemicals, furniture, hosiery; university (1964). City, founded 1715, became ✻ of Indore state under Maratha dynasty of Holkars which was estab. in 18th cent. by Malhār Rāo Holkar, an officer of the peshwa; in Maratha War lost much of territory after defeat by English Gen. Gerard Lake 1804; accepted British protectorate 1818.

In·do·scyth·ia \ˌin-dō-ˈsi-thē-ə, -thē-ə\. Ancient country, NW India, comprising valley of the Indus.

In·dra·gi·ri \ˌin-drə-ˈgir-ē\ *also* **In·de·ra·gi·ri** \ˌin-də-rə-\. Navigable river, cen. Sumatra, Indonesia; rises in Padang Highlands, flows E into N end of Berhala Strait; 250 mi. (402 km.) long.

In·dra·ma·yu *also* **In·dra·ma·ju** \ˌin-drə-ˈmä-yü\. Town on N coast of West Java prov., Indonesia, near **Cape Indramayu.**

Indraprastha. See DELHI 2.

In·dra·pu·ra *or Du.* **In·dra·poe·ra** \ˌin-drə-ˈpu̇r-ə\. See KERINCI.

In·dra·va·ti \in-ˈdrä-və-tē\. River, S India; rises in Orissa, flows W through Madhya Pradesh, then S to the Godavari on border of Andhra Pradesh; 315 mi. (507 km.) long.

Indre \ˈeⁿdrᵊ\. **1.** River, cen. France; flows NW in Indre and Indre-et-Loire depts. into the Loire River; 165 mi. (266 km.) long.
2. Department of cen. France. See table at FRANCE.

Indre–et–Loire \ˌeⁿd-rā-ˈlwär\. Department of France. See table at FRANCE.

Indreville. See CHÂTEAUROUX.

In·dus \ˈin-dəs\. River, Asia; rises on N slopes of Gangdisê Range, SW Tibet, China, flows NW through Tibet and Jammu and Kashmir (*q.v.*) ab. 680 mi. (1094 km.), cutting through Ladakh Range and receiving the Shyok from the E; turns and flows SW through Pakistan (Punjab and Sind) to Arabian Sea; ab. 1800 mi. (2896 km.) long; in several places its course forms provincial boundaries; only large tributary the Panjnad (*q.v.*); linked with the Jhelum by canal; area of its basin est. at 372,000 sq. mi. (963,480 sq. km.); navigable for small craft to Hyderabad; crossed by several bridges and heavily modified by dams and canal systems that provide water for irrigation and power. Important in Indian history: excavations at Mohenjo Daro and Harappa indicate an advanced Indus culture that flourished c. 2500 B.C.; its valley scene of many invasions and conflicts from time of Macedonian King Alexander the Great.

Ine·bo·lu \ē-ˈne-bȯ-ˌlü\; *formerly* **Ine·bo·li** \-ˌlē\. Town, N Turkey in Asia, on Black Sea coast 70 mi. (113 km.) W of Sinop.

İne·göl \ˌē-ne-ˈgœl\. Town, Bursa prov., NW Turkey in Asia, 25 mi. (40 km.) ESE of the city of Bursa.

Inessa. See BIANCAVILLA.

Inez \ˈī-ˌnez\. City, ⊗ of Martin co., E Kentucky; pop. (1990c) 511.

In·fan·ta \ēn-ˈfän-tä, in-ˈfan-tə\. Municipality on Polillo Strait, E Quezon prov., Luzon, Philippines; pop. (1980c) 27,814.

In·ga·vi *or* **Yn·ga·vi** \ēŋ-ˈgä-vē\. Mountain S of La Paz, Bolivia; scene of battle Nov. 1841 in which Bolivians under Gen. José Ballivián defeated Peruvians under Gen. Agustín Gamarra who was killed.

In·gel·mun·ster \ˈiŋ-gəl-ˌmœn-stər\. Commune, West Flanders prov., NW Belgium, E of Roeselare; pop. (1991c) 10,407; occupied by Germans in WWI.

Ingermanland. See INGRIA.

In·ger·soll \ˈiŋ-gər-ˌsȯl, -səl\. Town, Oxford co., SE Ontario, Canada, on Thames River 18 mi. (29 km.) NE of London; pop. (1991c) 9378.

Ing·ham \ˈiŋ-əm\. County in S Michigan. See table at MICHIGAN.

In·gle·bor·ough Mountain \ˈiŋ-gəl-ˌbər-ō, -bə-rə\. Peak, W Yorkshire, N England; 2373 ft. (723 m.); remains of ancient walled fort on summit; on S side is **Ingleborough Cave,** large cavern with stalactites and stalagmites.

In·gle·field Bay *or* **Inglefield Gulf** \ˈiŋ-gəl-ˌfēld\. Inlet of Smith Sound, W coast of Greenland.

In·gle·sa Bay \ēŋ-ˈglā-sä\. Inlet of Pacific Ocean on W coast of Atacama prov., N cen. Chile.

In·gle·side \ˈiŋ-gəl-ˌsīd\. City, San Patricio co., S Texas, on Corpus Christi Bay 15 mi. (24 km.) NE of Corpus Christi; pop. (1990c) 5696.

In·gle·wood \ˈiŋ-gəl-ˌwu̇d\. City, Los Angeles co., SW California, bordering the city of Los Angeles on the SW; pop. (1990c) 109,602; site of the Forum (basketball arena); Northrop Univ. (1942), Univ. of West Los Angeles (1966); founded 1873; incorp. 1908.

In·go·da \ˈiŋ-gə-də\. River, SW Chita Oblast, S Russia in Asia; flows NE from S end of Yablonovyy Mts. to unite with Onon River and form Shilka River; 360 mi. (579 km.) long.

In·gol·stadt \ˈiŋ-gəl-ˌshtät\. City, Bavaria, Germany, on left bank of Danube River 43 mi. (69 km.) N of Munich; pop. (1992e) 107,375; automobiles, machinery; oil refining; old ducal palace; ruins of 16th cent. Jesuit college; 15th cent. Gothic church. First mentioned 806; became city 1250; ✻ of a dukedom 1392; university founded here 1472 (transferred to Landshut 1802, to Munich 1826); 16th cent. fortifications destroyed by French 1800, later rebuilt.

In·gram \ˈiŋ-grəm\. Borough, Allegheny co., SW Pennsylvania, bordering W Pittsburgh; pop. (1990c) 3901.

In·gria \ˈiŋ-grē-ə\ *or* **In·ger·man·land** \ˈiŋ-gər-mən-ˌland\. District of early Russia, now in St. Petersburg Oblast, W Russia in Europe, S of E end of Gulf of Finland; for several centuries under Novgorod; fought for by Sweden and Russia in 17th cent.; became Swedish 1617 to 1703; its chief fort on the Neva captured by Czar Peter the Great 1703 who there founded St. Petersburg; permanently Russian by Treaty of Nystad (see UUSIKAUPUNKI) 1721.

In·grid Chris·ten·sen Coast \ˈiŋ-grəd-ˈkris-tən-sən\. Section of coast of Antarctica, on Indian Ocean, ab. 74° to 81°E, bet. Lars Christensen Coast and Luitpold and Astrid Coast; discovered and claimed by Norway 1935.

In·gul \in-ˈgül, iŋ-\ *or* **In·hul** \-ˈhül, -ˈkül\. River, S Ukraine; flows S into Bug River near its mouth, at Nykolayiv; ab. 220 mi. (354 km.) long.

In·gu·lets \ˌiŋ-gü-ˈlyets\. River, S Ukraine; flows S into Dnieper River near its mouth; ab. 341 mi. (549 km.) long.

In·gu·ri \in-ˈgu̇r-ē, iŋ-\ *or* **In·gur** \in-ˈgu̇r, iŋ-\. River, NW Republic of Georgia; flows SW from Caucasus Mts. to Black Sea; ab. 132 mi. (212 km.) long; forms part of E boundary of Abkhaz Rep.

In·gu·she·tia \ˌiŋ-gü-ˈshē-shə\ *or* **In·gu·she·ti·ya** \ˌiŋ-gü-ˈshe-tē-yə\ *or* **In·gush Republic** \in-ˈgüsh, iŋ-\. Republic, a subdivision, of S Russia in Europe, N of Caucasus Mts. and W of Chechnya; 1242 sq. mi. (3217 sq. km.); ✻ Nazran; Ingush constituted an autonomous oblast on its own before being joined with Chechnya 1934; Checheno-Ingush became an A.S.S.R. 1936 (see CHECHENO-INGUSH AUTONOMOUS SOVIET SOCIALIST REPUBLIC); union dissolved and Ingush became republic within Russia 1992; subsequently became member of Russian Federation.

In·gwa·vu·ma \ˌiŋ-gwä-ˈvü-mä\. District, NE KwaZulu-Natal prov., E Rep. of South Africa, in N Zululand; ab. 1950 sq. mi. (5051 sq. km.); acquired by Great Britain 1895; chief town Ingwavuma, on Swaziland border. See TONGALAND.

Inham·ba·ne \ˌē-nyäm-ˈbä-nā\. **1.** Province of SE Mozambique. See table at MOZAMBIQUE.
2. Commercial seaport, its ✻, on **Inhambane Bay**, inlet of Mozambique Channel; pop. (1991e) 47,764.

Inhul. See INGUL.

I–ning. See YINING.

Iní·ri·da \ē-ˈnē-rē-thä\. River, E Colombia; flows E and NE into Guaviare River near its confluence with the Orinoco on Venezuelan border.

Inisfail. See INNISFAIL 2.

Ini·sheer \ˌi-nə-ˈshir\. See ARAN ISLANDS.

In·ish·maan \ˌi-nish-ˈman, -ˈmän\. See ARAN ISLANDS.

In·ish·more \ˌi-nish-ˈmōr\ *also* **Ar·an·more** \ˌar-ən-ˈmōr\. Largest of the Aran Is., in Galway Bay, W Ireland; 9 mi. (15 km.) long; on it is Kilronan, chief town of the Aran Is.

In·ish·ow·en \ˌin-i-ˈshō-ən\. Peninsula on N coast of Ireland bet. Lough Swilly to the W and Lough Foyle to the E; cape on its E tip is **Inishowen Head.**

In·ish·tra·hull \ˌi-nish-trə-ˈhəl\. Island in co. Donegal, in Atlantic Ocean off N tip of Ireland; lighthouse.

In·ker·man \ˈiŋ-kər-mən\. Village, SW Crimea, Ukraine, near mouth of Chernaya River, just E of Sevastopol; scene of battle Nov. 5, 1854 during Crimean War in which English and French defeated Russians; in WWII occupied by Germans 1942–1944.

Ink·ster \ˈiŋk-stər\. City, Wayne co., SE Michigan, ab. 3 mi. (4.8 km.) WSW of Detroit; pop. (1990c) 30,772.

In·land Empire \ˈin-lənd\. Region in NW United States, bet. Cascade Range and Rocky Mts., incl. E Washington and NE Oregon, N Idaho, and extreme W Montana; lumbering, livestock raising, mining.

Inland Passage. See INSIDE PASSAGE.

Inland Sea *or Jp.* **Se·to–nai·kai** \ˈse-ˌtō-ˈnī-kī\ *also* **Seto no Uchi** \ˈse-tō-ˌnō-ˈü-chē\. Irregular-shaped body of water extending E and W bet. Honshū I. on N and Shikoku and Kyūshū islands on S, Japan; closed at E end by Awaji I.; connected with outer sea by four channels: Akashi Strait at NE, Naruto Strait at SE, Bungo Strait (formerly Hayasui) at SW, and Shimonoseki Strait at W end; noted for scenic beauty: contains ab. 300 islands and is bordered on N and S by mountain chains, 3000 to 6000 ft. (915 to 1830 m.) high; divided into five basins: Harima Sea, Bingo Sea, Mishima Sea, Iyo Sea, and Suō Sea; comparatively shallow and marked by strong tidal movements.

Inland Waterway. See ATLANTIC INTRACOASTAL WATERWAY and GULF INTRACOASTAL WATERWAY.

In·le, Lake \ˈin-lā\. Lake in cen. Myanmar, SW of Taunggyi.

Inn \ˈin\; *anc.* **Ae·nus** \ˈē-nəs\. River, Switzerland, Austria, and Germany; rises in lake in Rhaetian Alps, Graubünden, Switzerland, flows NE through Engadine valleys into Tirol, SW Austria; thence E past Innsbruck, then NE through Bavarian Alps to Bavaria, Germany, entering the Danube at Passau; 317 mi. (510 km.) long; in its lower course, boundary bet. Bavaria and Upper Austria, receives the Salzach. Extensively utilized as a source of hydroelectric power.

Inner City. See TATAR CITY.

Inner Hebrides. See HEBRIDES.

Inner Mongolia. See NEI MONGGOL.

Inner Rhodes. See APPENZELL.

Inner Sound. Body of water off NW coast of Scotland, bet. Raasay I. and Scottish mainland.

In·nis·fail. 1. \ˈi-nəs-ˌfāl\. Town, Alberta, Canada, 75 mi. (121 km.) N of Calgary; pop. (1991c) 5700.
2. *also* **In·is·fail** \ˈi-nish-ˌfȯl, ˈi-nəs-ˌfāl\. Poetic name of Ireland.

Inniskilling. See ENNISKILLEN.

In·no·ko \ˈi-nə-ˌkō\. River, W Alaska; flows SW, almost parallel to Yukon River which it enters at ab. 160°W; ab. 450 mi. (725 km.) long.

Inns·bruck \ˈins-ˌbrůk, ˈinz-\. City, ✻ of the Tirol, W Austria, on Inn River ab. 85 mi. (137 km.) SW of Salzburg; pop. (1991c) 118,112; tourist resort; textiles, food products; metalworking; university (c. 1677); made city 1239; in 1363 became residence of collateral line of Hapsburgs; ✻ of the Tirol from c. 1420; center of uprising of Tirolese peasants 1809; heavily damaged during WWII; headquarters of French zone of occupation 1945–55; site of Winter Olympic Games 1964, 1976.

In·ny \ˈi-nē\. River, NE cen. Ireland, flowing SW from Lough Sheelin into Lough Ree.

İnö·nü \ˈē-nœ̄-ˌnǖ\. Village, Bilecik prov., NW Turkey in Asia, on railroad line ab. 20 mi. (32 km.) WNW of Eskişehir; here Turkish Gen. İsmet Paşa twice defeated Greeks in war of 1919–22 and took name of village as last name (İsmet İnönü, president of Turkey 1938–50).

Ino·wroc·ław \ˌē-nȯ-ˈvrȯt-swäf\ *or Ger.* **Ho·hen·sal·za** \ˌhō-ən-ˈzält-sə\; *before 1905* **Ino·wraz·law** \ˌē-nȯ-ˈvrät-släf\. Commune, Bydgoszcz prov., N cen. Poland, ab. 25 mi. (40 km.) SSE of the city of Bydgoszcz; pop. (1989e) 76,627; health resort; salt mining nearby; machinery, chemicals.

In Sa·lah \ˌin-sə-ˈlä\. Oasis, cen. Algeria.

In·sein \ˈin-ˌsān\. Town, Myanmar, 10 mi. (16 km.) NW of Yangon.

Inside Passage *also* **Inland Passage.** Protected ship route from Seattle, Washington to Skagway, Alaska, following channels bet. the mainland and the many islands along the coast in this region; chief ports: Vancouver, Prince Rupert, Ketchikan, Wrangell, Juneau.

Insterburg. See CHERNYAKHOVSK.

In·sti·tute \ˈin-stə-ˌtüt, -ˌtyüt\. Village, Kanawha co., West Virginia, W of Charleston; West Virginia State Coll. (1891).

Insula. See LILLE.

In·ta \ˈēn-tə\. Town, Komi Rep., NW Russia in Europe, ab. 150 mi. (240 km.) SW of Vorkuta; pop. (1991e) 60,900; formed 1940.

Inter–American Highway. See PAN-AMERICAN HIGHWAY.

Interamna. See TERAMO 2.

Interamna Nahars. See TERNI 2.

Interior Highlands. A region in the interior of the U.S., incl. the Ouachita Mts. and the Ozark Plateau.

In·ter·la·ken \ˌin-tər-ˈlä-kən\. Commune, Bern canton, Switzerland, on Aare River bet. Thunersee and Brienzersee 26 mi. (42 km.) SE of the city of Bern; pop. (1988e) 5500; resort; textiles, watches; developed around a 12th cent. convent; valley region famous for view of the Jungfrau.

In·ter·loch·en \ˈin-tər-ˌlä-kən\. Village, Grand Traverse co., Michigan, on Green Lake in NW Lower Penin.; arts camp.

International Date Line. A hypothetical line coinciding approx. with the meridian 180° from Greenwich, England, fixed by international or general agreement as the place where each calendar day first begins. The day for any given locality commences when it is midnight at that place; hence, any given day, say Monday, first begins at midnight on the International Date Line, and following the midnight line begins continuously farther westward. It is thus Monday from the International Date Line westward to the midnight line and Sunday from the International Date Line eastward to the midnight line. Finally, as the midnight line reaches the International Date Line again, it is for the instant Monday over practically the whole world; then Tuesday begins, and so on. Thus for the greater part of the 24 hours Hawaii has the same day name as San Francisco, and Manila the same day name (one day later than the day of Hawaii) as Australia. Thus, when it is Monday noon, May 1, at San Francisco, it is 4 o'clock (standard time) or 14 minutes past 4 (local mean time) Tuesday morning, May 2, at Manila. A vessel crossing the International Date Line to the westward sets the date forward by one day, as from Sunday to Monday; if the line is crossed in going eastward, the date is set back. To avoid dividing places in close intercourse, the line is deflected bet. 48°N lat. and 75°N lat., so that all Asia lies to the W of it, all North America, incl. the Aleutian Is., to the E; and bet. 5°S lat. and 51°S lat. the line is deflected so that Chatham Is. and the Tonga group lie to the W.

In·ter·na·tion·al Falls \ˌin-tər-ˈna-shə-nəl\. City, ⊗ of Koochiching co., N Minnesota, on Rainy River near Rainy Lake; pop. (1990c) 8325; supply center for outdoor recreation area; paper mills, truck farms.

International Peace Garden. International park area, SW Manitoba, Canada and N North Dakota, near Whitewater Lake (Canada); 888 acres (360 hectares) in U.S.; estab. 1932 as sign of lasting friendship bet. U.S. and Canada.

International Zone. See TANGIER.

Internum, Mare. See MEDITERRANEAN SEA.

In·ti·bu·cá \ˌēn-tē-bü-ˈkä\. Department of W cen. Honduras. See table at HONDURAS.

In·tra·coast·al Waterway \ˌin-trə-ˈkōs-təl\. System of inland waterways E and SE United States; comprised of Atlantic Intracoastal Waterway and Gulf Intracoastal Waterway (*qq.v.*).

Inu·bo, Cape \ˈē-nü-ˌbō\ *or Jp.* **Inu·bō–sa·ki** \-ˈsä-kē\. Cape on SE coast of Honshū, Japan, in Chiba prefecture, E of Tokyo; lighthouse, 35°42′N, 140°53′E.

In·ú·til Bay \ē-ˈnü-tēl\ *or Eng.* **Use·less Bay** \ˈyüs-ləs\. Large inlet on NW coast of Tierra del Fuego I., Chile; opens into Strait of Magellan.

Inu·vik \ˈi-nü-ˌvik\. Region, NW mainland part of Canada; an administrative subdivision of Northwest Territories, in NW part of former Mackenzie dist.; area 152,129 sq. mi. (394,015 sq. km.); pop. (1991c) 8491.

In·ver·ar·ay \ˌin-və-ˈrar-ē\. Burgh, Strathclyde region, W Scotland; herring fishing; 18th cent. castle (ancestral seat of the dukes of Argyll) suffered damage in 1975 fire.

In·ver·car·gill \ˌin-vər-ˈkär-gil\. City, S South I., New Zealand, on estuary of Foveaux Strait 110 mi. (177 km.) WSW of Dunedin; pop. (1991p) 56,059; Bluff, its port; founded c. 1856.

In·ver·ell \ˌin-və-ˈrel\. Town, NE New South Wales, SE Australia, 280 mi. (451 km.) N of Sydney; pop. (1991c) 9736.

In·ver Grove Heights \ˈin-vər-ˈgrōv\. Village, Dakota co., SE Minnesota, ab. 2.5 mi. (4 km.) S of St. Paul; pop. (1990c) 22,477; residential suburb of St. Paul.

In·ver·ness \ˈin-vər-ˌnes\. **1.** City, ⊗ of Citrus co., W Florida Penin., just W of Lake Tsala Apopka; pop. (1990c) 5797.

2. Village, Cook co., NE Illinois, ab. 15.5 mi. (25 km.) NW of Chicago; pop. (1990c) 6503.

In·ver·ness \ˌin-vər-ˈnes\. **1.** County, on Cape Breton I., NE Nova Scotia, Canada. See table at NOVA SCOTIA.

2. *or* **Inverness–shire** \-ˌshir, -shər\. Former county, NW Scotland; ⊗ Inverness; included several of Inner and Outer Hebrides, as Harris, North Uist, South Uist, Skye, and Eigg; mountainous region, incl. Ben Nevis 4406 ft. (1343 m.), highest peak in British Isles.

3. Burgh, ⊗ of Highland region, NW Scotland, on the Ness River at NE terminus of Caledonian Canal; pop. (1991e) 63,090; tourism; chartered c. 1200.

In·ves·ti·ga·tor Strait \in-ˈves-tə-ˌgā-tər\. Channel bet. N Kangaroo I. and mainland, South Australia, Australia; forms SW entrance to Gulf St. Vincent.

In·wood \ˈin-wu̇d\. Unincorporated settlement, Nassau co., SE New York, on Long Island on E shore of Jamaica Bay; pop. (1990c) 7767.

In·yan·ga National Park \in-ˈyaŋ-gə-\. National park, E Zimbabwe, near Mozambique border.

In·yo \ˈin-yō\. County in E California. See table at CALIFORNIA.

Inyo Mountains. Range in W cen. Inyo co., E California.

Io·án·ni·na \yō-ˈä-nē-nä\. **1.** Department of Greece. See table at GREECE.

2. *also* **Yan·ni·na** *or Serb.* **Ja·ni·na** \ˈyä-nē-nä\. City, its ✱, N Epirus, NW Greece, near Albanian frontier on **Lake Ioánnina;** pop. (1991p) 56,496; university (1966); important in Byzantine times; captured by Turks 1430; in late 18th cent. became seat of Turkish brigand Ali Paşa, the Lion of Janina; to the Greeks 1913; during WWII occupied by Germans, 1941–44.

Io·la \ī-ˈō-lə\. City, ⊗ of Allen co., SE Kansas, on Neosho River; pop. (1990c) 6351; cement works; Allen County Community Coll. (1923).

Iol·cus \ī-ˈäl-kəs\. Ruined city, SE Thessaly, NE Greece, near modern Volos; legendary home of Jason, leader of the Argonauts, and port from which they set out.

Io·na \ī-ˈō-nə\. Island of the Inner Hebrides, Scotland, off SW tip of Mull I.; 6 sq. mi. (16 sq. km.); early center of the Celtic church; St. Columba and his disciples landed here from Ireland c. 563; burial place of early Scottish, Irish, and Norwegian kings, incl. Macbeth, the title character of William Shakespeare's tragedy.

Iô·na National Park \ē-ˈōn-ə\. National park, Angola; 6148 sq. mi. (15,923 sq. km.); abundant wildlife; estab. 1937.

Io·nia \ī-ˈō-nyə\. **1.** County in S cen. Michigan. See table at MICHIGAN.

2. City, its ⊗, 32 mi. (51 km.) E of Grand Rapids; pop. (1990c) 5935.

3. Ancient district on W coast of Asia Minor bordering on Aegean Sea and extending from a point near mouth of Hermus River S to the Halicarnassus Penin.; mountainous country 90 mi. (145 km.) long and 20 to 30 mi. (32 to 48 km.) wide; included some of islands of E Aegean Sea (such as Chios and Sámos); its hinterland was Lydia and Caria; received name from Ionians, a branch of ancient Greeks, who probably migrated from Greek mainland to Asia Minor c. 1000 B.C.; never a political unit, had religious league of **12 Ionian Cities** (N to S): Phocaea, Clazomenae, Erythrae, Teos, Lebedos, Colophon, Ephesus, Priene, Myus, Miletus, and the two island cities of Chios and Sámos; became subject to Lydia (*q.v.*) and later, to Persia c. 547 B.C.; produced architectural advances (Ionic order) and Ionic school of philosophy; revolt of Miletus (*q.v.*) brought on Greek wars with Persia; freed from Persia by Macedonian King Alexander the Great c. 334 B.C.; became part of the Roman prov. of Asia; ruined during the Turkish conquest of Asia Minor.

Io·ni·an Islands \ī-ˈō-nē-ən\; *anc.* **Hep·ta·ne·sus** \ˌhep-tə-ˈnē-səs\. Group of seven Greek islands in Ionian Sea: Corfu, Paxos, Levkás, Ithaca, Cephalonia, and Zákinthos off W coast of Greece, and Kíthira off S coast of Peloponnese; 868 sq. mi. (2248 sq. km.); pop. (1991p) 191,003; islands constitute an administrative region of Greece (see table at GREECE); generally mountainous; fruits, olive oil, grain, wine. Colonized by ancient Greeks; part of Roman and Byzantine empires; Corfu occupied by Venetians 1386–1797; taken by French 1797 but surrendered to Russian and Turkish forces 1799; organized as Septinsular Republic under Russian protection 1800–07; British protectorate 1815–64; ceded to Greece 1864.

Ionian Sea *or Lat.* **Ma·re Io·ni·um** \ˈmā-ˌrē-ī-ˈō-nē-əm, ˈmä-ˌrā-ē-ˈō-nē-u̇m\. Part of Mediterranean Sea bet. SE coast of Italy and W Greece, connected with Adriatic Sea by Strait of Otranto; along its E shore are the Ionian Is. and on NW is the Gulf of Taranto.

Io·ri·bai·wa \ˌyȯr-ē-ˈbī-wä\. Village, SE New Guinea I., Papua New Guinea, in mountains 30 mi. (48 km.) E of Port Moresby; in WWII Japanese advance from Buna and Gona stopped here by Australians Sept. 1942.

Ios \ˈē-ˌȯs, ˈī-ˌäs\. **1.** *or* **Nio** \ˈnē-ō\. Island in Aegean Sea, in S cen. Cyclades, Greece; 46 sq. mi. (119 sq. km.); belongs to Cyclades dept.

2. Town on W coast of island.

Ios·co \ī-ˈäs-kō\. County in NE Michigan. See table at MICHIGAN.

Ioshkar Ola. See YOSHKAR-OLA.

Io·wa \ˈī-ə-wə\. **1.** River, Iowa; formed by confluence of branches in N cen. Iowa and flowing SE into the Mississippi in SE Iowa; 291 mi. (468 km.) long.

2. A north central state of U.S.A., bounded on N by Minnesota, on E by Wisconsin and Illinois, on S by Missouri, and on W by Nebraska and South Dakota; 25th state in area, 56,275 sq. mi. or 145,752 sq. km. (land area 56,044 sq. mi. or 145,154 sq. km.); 30th state in population, (1990c) 2,776,755; ✱ Des Moines; 29th state admitted to Union (1846). See table of states at UNITED STATES.

Nickname: Hawkeye State.

State flower: Wild rose.

Motto: Our Liberties We Prize, and Our Rights We Will Maintain.

Rivers: Des Moines, flowing diagonally across state NW to SE, forming in its lower course the boundary with Missouri, and emptying into the Mississippi; Mississippi, forming E

IOWA
CITIES
State capital
County seat
City
BOUNDARIES
State
County
0 50 100 mi
0 75 150 km
MINNESOTA
WISCONSIN
ILLINOIS
MISSOURI
KANSAS
NEBRASKA
SOUTH DAKOTA
LYON
OSCEOLA
DICKINSON
EMMET
KOSSUTH
WINNEBAGO
WORTH
MITCHELL
HOWARD
WINNESHIEK
ALLAMAKEE
SIOUX
O'BRIEN
CLAY
PALO ALTO
HANCOCK
CERRO GORDO
FLOYD
CHICKASAW
FAYETTE
CLAYTON
PLYMOUTH
CHEROKEE
BUENA VISTA
POCAHONTAS
HUMBOLDT
WRIGHT
FRANKLIN
BUTLER
BREMER
BLACK HAWK
BUCHANAN
DELAWARE
DUBUQUE
WOODBURY
IDA
SAC
CALHOUN
WEBSTER
HAMILTON
HARDIN
GRUNDY
TAMA
BENTON
LINN
JONES
JACKSON
CLINTON
MONONA
CRAWFORD
CARROLL
GREENE
BOONE
STORY
MARSHALL
POWESHIEK
IOWA
JOHNSON
CEDAR
SCOTT
MUSCATINE
HARRISON
SHELBY
AUDUBON
GUTHRIE
DALLAS
POLK
JASPER
MAHASKA
KEOKUK
WASHINGTON
LOUISA
POTTAWATTAMIE
CASS
ADAIR
MADISON
WARREN
MARION
WAPELLO
JEFFERSON
HENRY
DES MOINES
MILLS
MONTGOMERY
ADAMS
UNION
CLARKE
LUCAS
MONROE
FREMONT
PAGE
TAYLOR
RINGGOLD
DECATUR
WAYNE
APPANOOSE
DAVIS
VAN BUREN
LEE
©1996, Encyclopædia Britannica, Inc.

boundary; Missouri, forming W boundary bet. Iowa and Nebraska; Big Sioux, forming W boundary bet. Iowa and South Dakota.

Highest point: Ocheyedan Mound 1670 ft. (509 m.), in Osceola co.

Chief products: Corn, soybeans, oats, hay; cattle, hogs; cement, food products, farm machinery, chemicals.

Chief cities: Des Moines, Cedar Rapids, Davenport, Sioux City, Waterloo.

Political divisions: Divided into the following 99 counties (for pronunciation of their names, see their individual entries):

NAME	AREA[1] (sq. mi.)	AREA[1] (sq. km.)	POP. (1990c)	CO. SEAT
Adair	569	1,474	8,409	Greenfield
Adams	426	1,103	4,866	Corning
Allamakee	636	1,647	13,855	Waukon
Appanoose	523	1,355	13,743	Centerville
Audubon	448	1,160	7,334	Audubon
Benton	718	1,860	22,429	Vinton
Black Hawk	568	1,471	123,798	Waterloo
Boone	573	1,484	25,186	Boone
Bremer	439	1,137	22,813	Waverly
Buchanan	568	1,471	20,844	Independence
Buena Vista	572	1,481	19,965	Storm Lake
Butler	582	1,507	15,731	Allison
Calhoun	571	1,479	11,508	Rockwell City
Carroll	574	1,487	21,423	Carroll
Cass	559	1,448	15,128	Atlantic
Cedar	585	1,515	17,381	Tipton
Cerro Gordo	575	1,489	46,733	Mason City
Cherokee	573	1,484	14,098	Cherokee
Chickasaw	505	1,308	13,295	New Hampton
Clarke	429	1,111	8,287	Osceola
Clay	570	1,476	17,585	Spencer
Clayton	779	2,018	19,054	Elkader
Clinton	693	1,795	51,040	Clinton
Crawford	716	1,854	16,775	Denison
Dallas	597	1,546	29,755	Adel
Davis	509	1,318	8,312	Bloomfield
Decatur	530	1,373	8,338	Leon
Delaware	572	1,481	18,035	Manchester
Des Moines	408	1,057	42,614	Burlington
Dickinson	380	984	14,909	Spirit Lake
Dubuque	612	1,585	86,403	Dubuque
Emmet	394	1,020	11,569	Estherville
Fayette	728	1,886	21,843	West Union
Floyd	503	1,303	17,058	Charles City
Franklin	586	1,518	11,364	Hampton
Fremont	524	1,357	8,226	Sidney
Greene	569	1,474	10,045	Jefferson
Grundy	501	1,298	12,029	Grundy Center
Guthrie	596	1,544	10,935	Guthrie Center
Hamilton	577	1,494	16,071	Webster City
Hancock	570	1,476	12,638	Garner
Hardin	574	1,487	19,094	Eldora
Harrison	696	1,803	14,730	Logan
Henry	440	1,140	19,226	Mount Pleasant
Howard	471	1,220	9,809	Cresco
Humboldt	435	1,127	10,756	Dakota City
Ida	431	1,116	8,365	Ida Grove
Iowa	584	1,513	14,630	Marengo
Jackson	644	1,668	19,950	Maquoketa
Jasper	734	1,901	34,795	Newton
Jefferson	436	1,129	16,310	Fairfield
Johnson	619	1,603	96,119	Iowa City
Jones	585	1,515	19,444	Anamosa
Keokuk	579	1,500	11,624	Sigourney
Kossuth	979	2,536	18,591	Algona
Lee	528	1,368	38,687	Keokuk and Fort Madison
Linn	717	1,857	168,767	Cedar Rapids
Louisa	403	1,044	11,592	Wapello
Lucas	434	1,124	9,070	Chariton
Lyon	588	1,523	11,952	Rock Rapids
Madison	564	1,461	12,483	Winterset
Mahaska	572	1,481	21,522	Oskaloosa
Marion	567	1,469	30,001	Knoxville
Marshall	574	1,487	38,276	Marshalltown
Mills	447	1,158	13,202	Glenwood
Mitchell	467	1,210	10,928	Osage
Monona	699	1,810	10,034	Onawa
Monroe	435	1,127	8,114	Albia
Montgomery	422	1,093	12,076	Red Oak
Muscatine	443	1,147	39,907	Muscatine
O'Brien	575	1,489	15,444	Primghar
Osceola	398	1,031	7,267	Sibley
Page	535	1,386	16,870	Clarinda
Palo Alto	561	1,453	10,669	Emmetsburg
Plymouth	863	2,235	23,388	Le Mars
Pocahontas	581	1,505	9,525	Pocahontas
Polk	594	1,538	327,140	Des Moines
Pottawattamie	963	2,494	82,628	Council Bluffs
Poweshiek	589	1,526	19,033	Montezuma
Ringgold	538	1,393	5,420	Mount Ayr
Sac	578	1,497	12,324	Sac City
Scott	454	1,176	150,979	Davenport
Shelby	587	1,520	13,230	Harlan
Sioux	766	1,984	29,903	Orange City
Story	568	1,471	74,252	Nevada
Tama	720	1,865	17,419	Toledo
Taylor	528	1,368	7,114	Bedford
Union	425	1,101	12,750	Creston
Van Buren	487	1,261	7,676	Keosauqua
Wapello	437	1,132	35,687	Ottumwa
Warren	572	1,481	36,033	Indianola
Washington	568	1,471	19,612	Washington
Wayne	532	1,378	7,067	Corydon
Webster	718	1,860	40,342	Fort Dodge
Winnebago	401	1,039	12,122	Forest City
Winneshiek	688	1,782	20,847	Decorah
Woodbury	871	2,256	98,276	Sioux City
Worth	400	1,036	7,991	Northwood
Wright	577	1,494	14,269	Clarion

[1] Area = land area.

History: Traces found of early inhabitation by Mound Builders, among others; French explorers Louis Jolliet and Jacques (Père) Marquette among first Europeans to visit 1673; became part of U.S. by Louisiana Purchase (*q.v.*) 1803; part of Louisiana Terr. 1805, of Missouri Terr. 1812, unorganized territory c. 1821–34, of Michigan Terr. 1834, of Wisconsin Terr. 1836, and of Iowa Terr. (*q.v.*) 1838; first permanent settlement made 1833 at Dubuque; held first constitutional convention 1844; present constitution dates from 1857. Admitted to Union Dec. 28, 1846; ✻ moved from Iowa City to Des Moines 1857.

3. Name of counties in two states of the U.S. See tables at IOWA and WISCONSIN.

Iowa City. City, ⊗ of Johnson co., E Iowa, 25 mi. (40 km.) S of Cedar Rapids; pop. (1990c) 59,738; medical and education center; Univ. of Iowa (1847); site selected 1839; ✻ of Iowa Territory (and later of Iowa state) to 1857.

Iowa Falls. City, Hardin co., N cen. Iowa, 37 mi. (60 km.) NW of Marshalltown; pop. (1990c) 5423; Ellsworth Community Coll. (1890).

Iowa Park. Town, Wichita co., N Texas, 10 mi. (16 km.) W of Wichita Falls; pop. (1990c) 6072.

Iowa Territory. Former territory, U.S.A.; comprised the region bet. the Mississippi and Missouri rivers, N of the state of Missouri and S of Canada; region acquired by the U.S. in the Louisiana Purchase (*q.v.*) and in 1818 border treaty with the British; included in Louisiana Terr., in Missouri Terr., unorganized territory c. 1821–34, in Michigan Terr., and in Wisconsin Terr. (*qq.v.*); organized as Iowa Terr. June 12, 1838 incl. what is now Iowa, W Minnesota, and E North and South Dakota; Iowa admitted to the Union with present boundaries 1846.

Ipa·me·ri \ˌē-pə-mi-ˈrē\. Municipality, Goiás state, cen. Brazil, 100 mi. (161 km.) SE of Goiânia; pop. (1980c) 20,409.

Ipek. See PEĆ.

Ipel' \ˈē-ˌpel\ *or Hung.* **Ipoly** \ˈē-ˌpȯi\ *or Ger.* **Ei·pel** \ˈī-pəl\. River, S Slovakia and N Hungary; flows SSW, forming section of boundary bet. Slovakia and Hungary, empties into Danube River 10 mi. (16 km.) below Esztergom, NW Hungary; 158 mi. (254 km.) long; in 1938–45 almost entirely within Hungary.

Ipia·les \ē-ˈpyä-lās\. Municipality, Nariño dept., SW Colombia; pop. (1985c) 46,226.

I–pin. See YIBIN.

Ipiranga. See YPIRANGA.

Ipoh \ˈē-pō\. City, ✻ of Perak state, Malaysia; pop. (1980c) 293,894; on railroad trunk line; commercial center of Kinta Valley tin-mining region; in WWII captured by Japanese Dec. 1941.

Ipoly. See IPEL'.

Ipsambul. See ABU SIMBEL.

Ipsara. See PSARÁ.

Ip·sus \ˈip-səs\. Ancient village in S Phrygia, Asia Minor, NW of modern Akşehir, Turkey; scene of a decisive battle 301

B.C. in Wars of the Diadochi in which Macedonian Gens. Lysimachus and Seleucus defeated Macedonian King Antigonus and his son Demetrius, precipitating the breakup of the Greco-Macedonian world; Antigonus was slain.

Ips·wich \ˈip-ˌswich\. **1.** Town, Essex co., NE corner of Massachusetts, 23 mi. (37 km.) E of Lowell; pop. (1990c) 11,873; electronic equipment.

2. City, ⊗ of Edmunds co., N South Dakota; pop. (1990c) 965.

3. Municipality, SE Queensland, Australia, 25 mi. (40 km.) SW of Brisbane; pop. (1991c) 73,299.

4. Town, ⊗ of Suffolk, E England, at head of Orwell estuary 64 mi. (103 km.) ENE of London; pop. (1991p) 115,500; farm machinery; port, shipping center; chartered 1200; birthplace of prelate and statesman Thomas Cardinal Wolsey.

Iqa·lu·it \ē-ˈkä-lü-it\; *formerly* **Fro·bish·er Bay** \ˈfrō-bi-shər\. Town, ✻ of Nunavut, Canada, on SE Baffin I.; pop. (1991c) 3552; airfield.

Iqui·que \ē-ˈkē-kā\. Seaport city, ✻ of Tarapacá region, N Chile, 130 mi. (209 km.) S of Peruvian border; pop. (1992p) 148,511; formerly ✻ of Tarapacá prov.; exports nitrates and fish meal; founded 16th cent.; partly destroyed by earthquakes 1868 and 1877, and by fire 1875; occupied by Chileans in war with Peru 1879; ceded to Chile by treaty 1883.

Iqui·tos \ē-ˈkē-tōs\. City and river port, NE Peru, on upper Amazon 1268 mi. (2040 km.) NE of Lima by overland route; pop. (1990e) 269,500; commercial outlet for NE Peru by way of the Amazon; university (1961); a Peruvian (not Indian) city, dating from c. 1863.

Irak. See IRAQ.

Irá·kli·on \ē-ˈrä-klē-ˌȯn\ *or Gk.* **Ira·klio** \ē-ˈrä-klē-ō\ *or* **He·rak·li·on** \hi-ˈra-klē-ən\. **1.** Department of Greece. See table at GREECE.

2. *also* **Hērákleion** *or Ital.* **Can·dia** \ˈkän-dē-ə, ˈkan-\; *anc.* **Her·ac·le·um** \ˌher-ə-ˈklē-əm\. Seaport city, ✻ of Crete before 1841 and since 1971 and ✻ of Iráklion dept., S Greece, on N shore of Crete; pop. (1991c) 117,167; exports include grapes, olives, wine, leather; episcopal see.

History: Founded by Saracens near site of ancient Knossos; occupied by Venetians (who knew it as Candia) 13th–17th cents.; after 20-year siege captured by Turks 1669; in modern times largest city in Crete; devastated 1941 during WWII, has since become important commercial and tourist center; major museum of Minoan culture.

Iran \i-ˈran, -ˈrän; ī-ˈran\; *formerly* **Per·sia** \ˈpər-zhə, -shə\. Islamic republic, SW Asia, bounded on N by Armenia, Azerbaijan, Turkmenistan, and the Caspian Sea, on E by Afghanistan and Pakistan, on S by the Gulf of Oman and the Persian Gulf, on W by Iraq, and on NW by Turkey; 635,932 sq. mi. (1,647,064 sq. km.); pop. (1992e) 59,570,000; ✻ Tehran.

Physical features: A region of plateaus and mountains, esp. Elburz Mts. in N along Caspian Sea; W end of the Hindu Kush in NE; and many ranges (Zagros Mts.) in W with peaks above 10,000 ft. (3048 m.); highest point Mt. Damāvand 18,934 ft. (5771 m.), in Elburz Mts.; E half occupied by greater part of Plateau of Iran (see IRAN, PLATEAU OF); only important island Qeshm in the Strait of Hormuz.

Chief rivers: Kārūn and Karkheh in W, Safīd in NW, and Atrek on N border.

Chief products: Oil, natural gas, iron ore, copper, coal; wheat, cotton, rice, barley, fruits, sugar beets; caviar; manufacturing: textiles, carpets, food products, cement.

Chief cities: Tehran, Rasht, Mashhad, Eşfahān, Tabrīz, Shīrāz.

Political divisions: Divided into 24 provinces (for pronunciation of their names, see their individual entries):

NAME	AREA (sq. mi.)	AREA (sq. km.)	POP. (1986c)	CAPITAL
Bakhtarān	9,121	23,623	1,462,965	Bakhtarān
Būshehr	9,792	25,361	612,183	Būshehr
Chahār Mahāll va Bakhtīarī	5,721	14,817	631,179	Shahr Kord
East Azerbaijan	25,421	65,840	4,114,084	Tabrīz
Eşfahān	40,852	105,807	3,294,916	Eşfahān
Fārs	51,465	133,294	3,193,769	Shīrāz
Gīlān	5,722	14,820	2,081,037	Rasht
Hamadān	7,508	19,446	1,505,826	Hamadān
Hormozgān	25,243	65,379	762,206	Bandar ʻAbbās
Īlām	7,369	19,086	382,091	Īlām
Kermān	71,690	185,677	1,622,958	Kermān
Khorāsān	121,887	315,687	5,280,605	Mashhad
Khūzestān	25,688	66,532	2,681,978	Ahvāz
Kohkīlūyeh va Boyer Ahmadī-ye Sardīr	5,289	13,698	411,828	Yāsūj
Kordestān	10,756	27,858	1,078,415	Sanandaj
Lorestān	11,027	28,560	1,367,029	Khorramābād
Markazi	11,402	29,531	1,082,109	Arāk
Māzandarān	18,010	46,646	3,419,346	Sārī
Semnān	35,345	91,544	417,035	Semnān
Sīstān va Balūchestān	70,066	181,471	1,197,059	Zāhedān
Tehran	10,896	28,221	8,712,087	Tehran
West Azerbaijan	16,856	43,657	1,971,677	Orūmīyeh
Yazd	24,704	63,983	574,028	Yazd
Zanjān	14,047	36,382	1,588,600	Zanjān

History: The name *Ariana*, in ancient Greek and Roman usage, was variously applied to the geographical region (the Plateau of Iran) and to SE parts, excluding Persis (modern Fārs); the plateau was the home of ancient civilizations of Elam, Media, and Persia; c. 2000 B.C., occupied by Iranian peoples among whom were Medes and Persians. Under King Cyrus the Great (c. 550–529 B.C.), orig. ruler of Anshan (*q.v.*), conquered Media, Lydia, Babylonia (*qq.v.*) and founded **Persian Empire** which extended from Indus River to Mediterranean and from Caucasus Mts. to Indian Ocean (later included Egypt); organized by Darius I against whom Greece began Persian Wars; conquered by Macedonian King Alexander the Great c. 331–327 B.C.; after an interlude of Seleucid and Parthian rule, Ardashīr I, the ruler of Fārs, founded neo-Persian Sassanid empire (c. 226–c. 641 A.D.); conquered by Muslim Arabs c. 633–c. 642; after Mongol conquest in 13th cent., formed separate Mongol dynasty, the Il-khans (13th–14th cents.); invaded by Turkic conqueror Timur late 14th cent.; modern Persia founded by Ṣafavid rulers (c. 1501–c. 1736), the greatest of whom was Shāh ʻAbbās I (c. 1588–c. 1629); held off Turks, but overcome by Afghans 1722 and lost territory to Russia; under Nāder Shāh (1736–47) invaded India, captured Bukhara and Khiva; ruled by Zand dynasty (1750–94); ruled by Qājār dynasty (c. 1794–1925); lost Caucasus (see CAUCASIA) to Russia in 19th cent.; secured constitution ending absolute rule 1906; Anglo-Russian rivalry over Persia settled in Anglo-Russian Entente 1907; in 1919, rejected agreement giving control to British; League of Nations member 1920; recognized as independent by U.S.S.R. 1921; deposed Qājār shahs and proclaimed Reza Shāh Pahlavi 1925; officially renamed Iran 1935; Reza Shāh Pahlavi abdicated to son Moḥammad Reza Pahlavi 1941; signed treaty of alliance with Great Britain and the U.S.S.R. 1942; declared war on Germany 1943; suppressed Communist regime (estab. with Soviet aid) in Azerbaijan 1946; initiated its first economic development plan 1949; nationalized oil industry 1951; dispute with Iraq over use of Shatt al Arab 1969; internal unrest forced shah to leave country 1979; empire abolished and Islamic republic estab. on return of Ayatollah Ruhollah Khomeini 1979 after 15 years of exile; fought eight-year war with Iraq following Iraqi invasion of Iran Sept. 1980; earthquake 1990 resulted in heavy casualties.

Iran, Plateau of. Plateau, extensive highland area in W Asia, comprising cen. and E Iran and W sections of Afghanistan and Pakistan; ab. 1,000,000 sq. mi. (2,590,000 sq. km.), of which ab. 600,000 sq. mi. (1,554,000 sq. km.) are in Iran; av. alt. 3000 to 5000 ft. (914 to 1524 m.); contains great salt deserts of Dasht-e-Lūt and Dasht-e-Kavīr.

Iran Mountains. Mountain range, Borneo, running N and S

along border bet. Malaysian state of Sarawak and Indonesian prov. of East Kalimantan; highest peak nearly 10,000 ft. (3048 m.).

Ira·pua·to \ˌē-rä-ˈpwä-tō\. City, Guanajuato state, cen. Mexico, ab. 35 mi. (55 km.) SE of León; munic. pop. (1990p) 362,471; trade center for area producing strawberries and other agricultural products.

Iraq \i-ˈräk, -ˈrak\ *also* **Irak** *or Arab.* **ʻIrāq.** Republic, SW Asia, bounded on N by Turkey, on E by Iran, on SE by Kuwait and Persian Gulf, on S by Saudi Arabia, and on W by Jordan and Syria; 168,927 sq. mi. (437,521 sq. km.); pop. (1992e) 18,838,000; ✻ Baghdad.

Physical features: Comprises for most part level country drained by Euphrates and Tigris rivers which unite ab. 120 mi. (193 km.) from Persian Gulf NNW of Basra to form the Shatt al Arab, and by tributaries of the Tigris from the E; includes most of Mesopotamia (*q.v.*); river region fertile with many lakes; wide desert region in W (part of Syrian Desert) and SW; mountainous in Kurdistan region of NE.

Chief products: Wheat, barley, rice, dates, cotton; sheep, cattle; oil, natural gas; manufacturing: textiles, construction materials.

Chief cities: Baghdad, Basra, Mosul, Kirkuk.

History: For history prior to 1921, see MESOPOTAMIA, BABYLONIA, and ASSYRIA. Kingdom estab. 1921 after WWI out of former Turkish territory; under British mandate 1920 until Oct. 1932 when it became independent under King Faisal I; semi-independent state in alliance with Great Britain 1922; a limited monarchy according to organic law 1924; awarded Mosul (*q.v.*) by League of Nations 1925; independence and sovereignty recognized in treaties with Great Britain 1927 and 1930, the full result of which was admission to League 1932; in treaty with Saudi Arabia (*q.v.*) 1936; occupied by British 1941 to prevent Nazi control; joined UN 1945; republic estab. following army coup July 1958 during which King Faisal II and Crown Prince ʻAbd al-Ilāh were assassinated; advanced claims to Kuwait (rejected by Great Britain) 1961; participated in Arab-Israeli War 1967; coup 1968 brought revolutionary Baʻth party to power; announced termination of (sporadic)

hostilities bet. central government and autonomy-seeking Kurds 1970, but fighting resumed 1974; Ba'thist Saddam Hussein became president 1979; invaded Iran Sept. 1980, provoking eight-year Iran–Iraq war; occupied and forcibly annexed Kuwait Aug. 1990; its subsequent failure to withdraw before UN deadline of Jan. 15, 1991 precipitated six-week offensive to liberate Kuwait, launched by alliance of international forces; after suffering heavy losses, accepted UN cease-fire terms Feb. 28, 1991.

'Iraq 'Ara·bi \i-ˈräk-ˈär-ä-bē\. Region, lower Mesopotamia; the Tigris-Euphrates Valley S of Baghdad, comprising Basra, Baghdad, and adjoining provinces in Iraq; nearly coextensive with ancient Babylonia.

'Iraq–i–'Ajam \i-ˈräk-ē-ˈä-jäm\ *or* **Iraq Aje·mi** \ˈä-ji-mē\. Region and former province in W cen. Iran; as province, a chief city was Sultanabad (Arāk).

Irawadi. See IRRAWADDY.

Ira·zú \ˌē-rä-ˈsü\. Volcano, cen. Costa Rica, near city of Cartago; 11,260 ft. (3,432 m.); notably active 1841, 1910, and 1963; only place on North American continent where on a clear day both the Atlantic and Pacific oceans can be seen.

Ir·bid \ˈir-bid\. Town, N Jordan, 42 mi. (68 km.) N of Amman; pop. (1990e) 314,680.

Irbīl. See ARBĪL.

Ir·bit \ir-ˈbēt\. Commercial town, Sverdlovs'k Oblast, W Russia in Asia, 110 mi. (177 km.) NE of Yekaterinburg; pop. (1991e) 51,300.

Ire·dell \ˈīr-ˌdel\. County in cen. North Carolina. See table at NORTH CAROLINA.

Ire·land \ˈīr-lənd\ *or Lat.* **Hi·ber·nia** \hī-ˈbər-nē-ə\ *also known as the* **Em·er·ald Isle** \ˈe-mə-rəld\ *and (in poetry)* **Er·in** \ˈer-in\. **1.** *or* **Ei·re** \ˈer-ə\; *from 1922 to 1937* **Irish Free State** \ˈī(ə)r-ish\ *or Gaelic* **Saor·stat Eir·eann** *or* **Saor·stát Éir·eann** \ˌsa(ə)r-ˌstȯt-ˈer-ən\. Republic occupying S, cen., and NW Ireland; 26,600 sq. mi. (68,894 sq. km.); pop. (1986c) 3,540,643; ✻ Dublin. Comprises most of the territory of the island of Ireland (for physical features, see IRELAND 2). Has many good harbors.

Chief products: Barley, wheat, oats, potatoes, sugar beets; livestock; zinc, lead, natural gas, gypsum; manufacturing:

\ə\ abut \ᵊ\ matches \ᵊ\ kitten, Fr table \ər\ further \a\ ash \ā\ ace \ä\ cot, cart \á\ Fr bac \au̇\ out \b\ Span Avila \ch\ chin \e\ bet \ē\ easy \g\ go \i\ hit \ī\ ice \j\ job \k\ Ger ich, Buch \ⁿ\ Fr vin \ŋ\ sing \ō\ go \ȯ\ all \ò\ law \œ\ Fr bœuf \œ̄\ Fr feu \ȯi\ boy \th\ thin \t͟h\ this \ü\ loot \u̇\ foot \ue\ Ger füllen \ue̅\ Fr rue \y\ yet \ʸ\ Fr digne \ˈdēnʸ\, nuit \ˈnwʸē\ \yü\ few \yu̇\ fury \zh\ vision

textiles, machinery, chemicals; brewing and distilling, engineering; tourism.

Chief settlements: Dublin, Cork, Limerick, Dun Laoghaire, Galway, Waterford.

Political divisions: Divided into the following 26 counties (listed according to province; for pronunciation of their names, see their individual entries):

NAME[1]	AREA (sq. mi.)	AREA (sq. km.)	POP. (1991c)	CAPITAL
Connacht				
Galway	2,293	5,939	129,511	Galway
Leitrim	589	1,526	25,301	Carrick on Shannon
Mayo	2,084	5,398	110,713	Castlebar
Roscommon	951	2,463	51,897	Roscommon
Sligo	693	1,795	54,756	Sligo
Leinster				
Carlow	346	896	40,942	Carlow
Dublin	356	922	546,915	Dublin
Kildare	654	1,694	122,656	Naas
Kilkenny	796	2,062	73,635	Kilkenny
Laoighis	664	1,720	52,314	Portlaoighise
Longford	403	1,044	30,296	Longford
Louth	317	821	90,724	Dundalk
Meath	903	2,339	105,370	Trim
Offaly	771	1,997	58,494	Tullamore
Westmeath	681	1,764	61,880	Mullingar
Wexford	908	2,352	102,069	Wexford
Wicklow	782	2,025	97,265	Wicklow
Munster				
Clare	1,231	3,188	90,918	Ennis
Cork	2,880	7,459	283,116	Cork
Kerry	1,815	4,701	121,894	Tralee
Limerick	1,037	2,686	109,873	Limerick
Tipperary[2]	1,643	4,255	132,772	Clonmel
Waterford	710	1,839	51,296	Waterford
Ulster[3]				
Cavan	730	1,891	52,796	Cavan
Donegal	1,865	4,830	128,117	Lifford
Monaghan	498	1,290	51,293	Monaghan

[1] In Irish idiom, *county* precedes the name, as in *county Cork, county Meath.*
[2] Divided for administrative purposes into North Riding and South Riding.
[3] Considered by many Irish to include also Northern Ireland.

History: For history before 1922, see IRELAND 2. As Irish Free State, estab. 1922, a dominion in the (British) Commonwealth of Nations, Northern Ireland (*q.v.*) having been formed 1920; adopted constitution 1922; settled boundary with Northern Ireland 1925; under Prime Minister Eamon De Valera gradually abandoned ties with British crown, in 1937 declaring Eire (its official new name) a sovereign, independent, democratic state; remained associated for certain purposes with Commonwealth of Nations; neutral throughout WWII; refused request of Great Britain and U.S. Mar. 1944 to expel Axis representatives; by Republic of Ireland Act 1948 declared itself completely independent with no allegiance to British crown or membership in Commonwealth of Nations; officially proclaimed the Republic of Ireland Apr. 18 (Easter Monday), 1949; member of UN 1955; signed treaty of accession to European Economic Community 1972; as result of continuing civil strife in Northern Ireland and terrorist activities of Irish extremists, joined with United Kingdom in several peace initiatives during 1970s, 1980s, and early 1990s.

2. Island, W of England and separated from it by St. George's Channel and the Irish Sea; area 32,052 sq. mi. (83,015 sq. km.); divided bet. the independent (republic of) Ireland, which occupies the 26 counties in the S, cen., and NW part, and Northern Ireland (forming part of the United Kingdom), which occupies the 26 districts in the NE part.

Physical features: Consists of cen. plain with lakes (*loughs*) in N, cen., and W parts, esp. Erne (chiefly in Northern Ireland), Neagh (entirely in Northern Ireland), Mask, Corrib, Conn, Ree, Derg, and the small and beautiful Lakes of Killarney in SW, and with groups of hills averaging 2000 to 3000 ft. (610 to 914 m.) on N, W, and S; highest point Carrantuohill 3414 ft. (1040 m.) in SW. Rivers include Shannon in cen. part, Bann and Lagan in Northern Ireland, Boyne and Liffey in E, Barrow, Nore, and Suir in SE, Blackwater and Lee in S. Coastline irregular; harbors include Belfast Lough (in Northern Ireland), Lough Foyle bet. Northern Ireland and the republic, Donegal Bay, Sligo Bay, Galway Bay, Dingle Bay, Bantry Bay, Dundalk Bay, and estuaries of the Shannon and Lee (Cork Harbour); numerous small islands, esp. Rathlin (in Northern Ireland), Achill, Aran Is., Valentia, and Fastnet.

History: Invaded by Celts c. 500 B.C.; governed as kingdoms of Ulster, Leinster, Connaught, Munster, and Meath, under which were numerous warring tribal kings; according to tradition, Christianized in 5th cent. A.D. by St. Patrick; Irish monasticism produced outstanding scholars and missionaries beginning 6th cent.; raided by Vikings (see CLONTARF) who founded various settlements, among them Dublin, Waterford, and Limerick; conquered 1169–71 by Norman lords and English King Henry II who established English rule over strip of coast around Dublin (later known as the Pale); Irish parliament restricted by Poynings' Law 1495; extent of Pale varied until English soldier and statesman Oliver Cromwell, after rebellion of 1641–42, subdued all of Ireland; colonized, esp. in N, by Scots and English; supported deposed British King James II at battle of the Boyne (*q.v.*) 1690; united legislatively with Great Britain, forming United Kingdom of Great Britain and Ireland (see UNITED KINGDOM) 1801; in 19th cent., "Irish Question" (incl. problems of status of Catholics, land, self-government—Home Rule after 1886) became a key issue of British politics; unsuccessfully attempted to throw off British rule by Easter Rebellion (Easter Monday, Apr. 24, 1916); S Ireland refused Home Rule as provided by Act of 1920, and, after civil war 1919–21, was granted dominion status as Irish Free State 1921 (estab. 1922); six counties of Ulster formed Northern Ireland 1920.

Ireland, Northern. Division of the United Kingdom of Great Britain and Northern Ireland, occupying NE section of the island of Ireland; 5452 sq. mi. (14,121 sq. km.); pop. (1981c) 1,543,000; ✻ Belfast. For physical features, see IRELAND 2.

Chief products: Barley, oats, potatoes; livestock; manufacturing: textiles, aircraft; shipbuilding.

Chief settlements: Belfast, Derry, Newtownabbey, Bangor.

Political divisions: Divided into the following districts (for pronunciation of their names, see individual entries):

NAME	AREA (sq. mi.)	AREA (sq. km.)	POP. (1991c)	DISTRICT SEAT
Antrim	217	562	44,322	Antrim
Ards	143	370	64,026	Newtownards
Armagh	260	673	51,331	Armagh
Ballymena	246	637	56,032	Ballymena
Ballymoney	162	420	23,984	Ballymoney
Banbridge	171	443	33,102	Banbridge
Belfast	54	140	283,746	Belfast
Carrickfergus	34	88	32,439	Carrickfergus
Castlereagh	33	85	60,649	Belfast
Coleraine	187	484	51,062	Coleraine
Cookstown	241	624	30,808	Cookstown
Craigavon	147	381	74,494	Craigavon
Derry	148	383	94,918	Derry
Down	250	648	57,511	Downpatrick
Dungannon	301	780	45,322	Dungannon
Fermanagh	724	1,875	54,062	Enniskillen
Larne	131	339	29,181	Larne
Limavady	226	585	29,201	Limavady
Lisburn	171	443	99,162	Lisburn
Magherafelt	221	572	35,874	Magherafelt
Moyle	191	495	14,617	Ballycastle
Newry and Mourne	345	894	82,288	Newry
Newtownabbey	58	150	73,832	Belfast
North Down	28	72	70,308	Bangor
Omagh	436	1,129	45,343	Omagh
Strabane	336	870	35,668	Strabane

Prior to 1974 divided into the following counties: Antrim, Armagh, Down, Fermanagh, Derry, Tyrone.

History: See ULSTER 2; accepted provisions of Government of Ireland Act 1920 which offered Home Rule to both northern and southern Ireland (see IRELAND 2); after long dispute, existing boundary with Irish Free State accepted 1925; scene of civil strife bet. Protestants and Catholics esp. since 1968; direct rule imposed by Britain, 1972; continuing civil violence and terrorist activities prompted several attempts by the United Kingdom and (republic of) Ireland at reconciliation during the 1970s, 1980s, and early 1990s. (see UNITED KINGDOM).

IRELAND
CITIES
Over 100,000
10,000 to 100,000
Under 10,000
Provincial capital
National capital
BOUNDARIES
International
Provincial
FEATURES
Canals
Dams
0 20 40 mi
0 30 60 km
ATLANTIC OCEAN
IRISH SEA
CELTIC SEA
North Channel
St. George's Channel
SCOTLAND (U.K.)
NORTHERN IRELAND (U.K.)
Belfast
Lough Neagh
Fair Head
Malin Head
Inishowen Head
Carndonagh
Lough Swilly
Buncrana
Lough Foyle
Londonderry
Tory Sound
Errigal Mountain 2,466 ft.
ARAN ISLAND
GLENVEAGH NATIONAL PARK
Letterkenny
Gweebarra Bay
DONEGAL
Lifford
BLUE STACK MOUNTAINS
Killybegs
Donegal
Donegal Bay
Ballyshannon
Bundoran
Erne
Belmullet
Ballycastle
Killala Bay
Sligo Bay
Sligo
Dromahair
Carrowmore Lake
SLIEVE GAMPH
SLIGO
Ballina
Ballymote
Blacksod Bay
Lough Conn
Lough Allen
Monaghan
MONAGHAN
Clones
Castleblayney
Belturbet
Dundalk
MAYO
ACHILL ISLAND
Newport
Swinford
LEITRIM
Carrick on Shannon
Boyle
Carrickmacross
Louth
Dundalk Bay
Cavan
CAVAN
LOUTH
Dunany Point
CLARE ISLAND
Clew Bay
Westport
Castlebar
Ballaghaderreen
Knock
ROSCOMMON
Castlerea
Ardee
Croagh Patrick 2,510 ft.
Baltinglass
Claremorris
LONGFORD
Longford
Ceanannus Mór
Drogheda
Lough Mask
Roscommon
Castlepollard
MEATH
Navan
Balbriggan
Skerries
CONNEMARA NATIONAL PARK
Ballinrobe
Ballymahon
WESTMEATH
Mullingar
Trim
Clifden
TWELVE BENS OF BENNEBEOLA
Tuam
Lough Corrib
Lough Ree
Kinnegad
Boyne
DUBLIN
Malahide
Swords
Slyne Head
CONNEMARA
Mount Bellew
Athlone
Kilcock
Clontarf
Howth
GALWAY
Ballinasloe
Clara
Edenderry
Maynooth
Celbridge
Lucan
Dublin
Blackrock
Dun Laoghaire
Galway
Athenry
Clonmacnoise
Grand Canal
Tullamore
BOG OF ALLEN
Liffey
Naas
OFFALY
Droichead Nua
Bray
Galway Bay
Loughrea
Shannon
Portarlington
Kildare
KILDARE
THE CURRAGH
Poulaphouca Reservoir
Greystones
ARAN ISLANDS
Ballyvaghan
Gort
Portumna
Birr
Mountmellick
Portlaoighise
WICKLOW
WICKLOW MTS.
Lugnaquillia Mountain 3,039 ft.
Wicklow
Lough Derg
Athy
Baltinglass
Ennistimon
CLARE
Ennis
LAOIGHIS
Abbeyleix
Roscrea
Barrow
Killaloe
Nenagh
Durrow
Carlow
Arklow
Tullow
TIPPERARY NORTH RIDING
Templemore
Donegal Point
Kilkee
Shannon
Thurles
CARLOW
Tara Hill 833 ft.
Gorey
Kilrush
Limerick
SILVERMINE MOUNTAINS
Kilkenny
Slaney
Bann
LIMERICK
KILKENNY
Cahore Point
Mouth of the Shannon
Listowel
Croom
Cashel
Thomastown
Callan
Enniscorthy
Newcastle
TIPPERARY SOUTH RIDING
Tipperary
Nore
WEXFORD
Abbeyfeale
Cahir
Clonmel
Carrick on Suir
New Ross
Wexford Bay
Brandon Mountain 3,125 ft.
Tralee
Charleville
GALTY MOUNTAINS
Suir
COMERAGH MTS.
Wexford
Rosslare
Castleisland
KNOCKMEALDOWN MOUNTAINS
Waterford
Tramore
GREAT BLASKET ISLAND
DINGLE PENINSULA
KERRY
Kanturk
Mallow
Fermoy
Dingle
Lough Leane
Blackwater
Lismore
WATERFORD
Dungarvan
Carnsore Point
SALTEE ISLANDS
Dingle Bay
KILLARNEY NATIONAL PARK
Killarney
Millstreet
Helvick Head
Carrantuohill 3,414 ft.
CORK
Cahersiveen
MACGILLYCUDDY'S REEKS
Kenmare
Blarney
Cork
Midleton
Youghal
Macroom
Ballincollig
Douglas
Passage West
Cloyne
Ballycotton
Cobh
Carrigaline
Crosshaven
CAHA MOUNTAINS
Bandon
Kinsale
Cork Harbour
Bandon
Castletownbere
Bantry
Bantry Bay
Clonakilty
Dursey Head
Seven Heads
Skibbereen
Mizen Head
CLEAR ISLAND
11° 10° 9° 8° 7° 6°
55° 54° 53° 52° 51°
©1996, Encyclopædia Britannica, Inc.

Ireland Island. One of the Bermuda Is., W of Grassy Bay and N of Great Sound.

Ireng \ˈē-reŋ\. River, Guyana; tributary of the Tacutú; flows S and forms section of boundary bet. W cen. Guyana and Brazil; 175 mi. (282 km.) long.

Ir·giz \ir-ˈgēs\. River, W cen. Kazakhstan; flowing SE into Chelkar-Tengiz; ab. 270 mi. (434 km.) long.

Iri. 1. River, of Greece. See EUROTAS.
2. \ˈē-ˈrē\. Town, North Chŏlla prov., South Korea, 14 mi. (23 km.) NW of Chŏnju; pop. (1985c) 192,269.

Irian. See NEW GUINEA.

Iri·an Ja·ya \ˈir-ē-ˌän-ˈjä-yä\ *or* **West Irian;** *chiefly formerly* **Irian Ba·rat** \ˈbä-ˌrät\ *or* **West New Guin·ea** \ˈgi-nē\; *formerly* **Dutch New Guinea** *or* **Neth·er·lands New Guinea** \ˈne-thər-ləndz\. A province of Indonesia, consisting of the W half of the island of New Guinea and adjacent islands off N and NW coasts; ✻ Jayapura. Traversed by Maoke Mts., highest peak Puncak Jaya 16,535 ft. (5040 m.). Coastline irregular, esp. in NW with indentations of Teluk Cenderawasih and Berau Bay. Has many rivers, Mamberamo largest in the N and Digul in the S, also large areas of swampland, esp. in the S. Some regions not extensively explored; chief settlements on N and NW coasts: Jayapura, Manokwari, Sorong, Fakfak. See table at INDONESIA.
History: First visited by Europeans in 16th cent.; coastal regions saw gradual extension of Dutch sovereignty in 18th cent.; in 1884 the meridian of 141°E agreed upon with British as frontier boundary and in 1885 defined as also the frontier of German New Guinea; this line slightly altered along course of Fly River by convention with Great Britain in 1895. In WWII the N coastal areas occupied by Japanese 1942 but mostly retaken by Allies 1944; remained under Dutch control when rest of the Netherlands Indies became independent 1949; relinquished to UN administration 1962 by the Dutch and transferred to Indonesia 1963.

Iri·ga \ē-ˈrē-gä\. **1.** Extinct volcano, S Camarines Sur prov., Luzon, Philippines; 4023 ft. (1226 m.).
2. Chartered city, S Camarines Sur prov., SW of Mt. Iriga; pop. (1990p) 74,000.

Irin·ga \ē-ˈriŋ-gä\. **1.** Administrative region of S cen. Tanzania. See table at TANZANIA.
2. Town, its ✻, 255 mi. (410 km.) SW of Dar es Salaam.

Iri·o·mo·te \ˌir-ē-ō-ˈmō-tā\. Island in Sakishima group, SW end of Ryukyu Is., Japan; 57 mi. (92 km.) in circumference.

Ir·i·on \ˈir-ē-ən\. County in W cen. Texas. See table at TEXAS.

Iri·ri \ˌir-ē-ˈrē\. River, cen. Pará state, N Brazil; rises in N Mato Grosso and flows N into Xingu River; ab. 570 mi. (917 km.) long.

Iris. See YEŞILIRMAK.

Irish Free State. See IRELAND 1.

Irish Sea \ˈī-rish\; *anc.* **Oce·a·nus Hi·ber·ni·cus** \ō-ˈsē-ə-nəs-hī-ˈbər-ni-kəs\. Sea bet. England and Ireland, connected with Atlantic Ocean on N through North Channel and on S through St. George's Channel; with St. George's Channel, extends 100 mi. (161 km.) N to S and 125 mi. (201 km.) E to W.

Ir·kutsk \ir-ˈkütsk, ər-\. City, ✻ of Irkutsk Oblast, Russia, on Angara River 45 mi. (72 km.) from SW shore of Lake Baikal; pop. (1992e) 639,000; one of chief cities on Trans-Siberian R.R.; cultural center; mica processing, timberworking; automobiles; hydroelectric plant; estab. 1652 as government station; grew because of trade with China and Amur Valley and connection with Lena goldfields and with fur trade; much damaged during Russian Civil War 1918–21.

Irkutsk Oblast \ˈō-bləst, -ˌblast\. Subdivision of S Russia in Asia; 296,486 sq. mi. (767,899 sq. km.); pop. (1992e) 2,872,000; ✻ Irkutsk; Lake Baikal forms a large part of its E border; principal streams the Angara, the upper headstreams of the Lena, the Lower Tunguska, and the Chuna, and the lower course of the Vitim; chiefly a mountain and plateau region with highest peaks in Sayan Mts. on SW boundary; most important resources mineral, esp. gold, coal, salt, iron ore, mica, but timber, fishing, and fur-bearing animals also valuable; large hydroelectric power plants; industrial centers Irkutsk and Cheremkhovo, both near or on the navigable Angara and the Trans-Siberian R.R., which traverses region from NW to SE; chief cities: Irkutsk, Angarsk, Cheremkhovo, Bratsk. Region began to be settled in latter half of 17th cent.; long used as place of banishment for political and other exiles; in 19th cent. received many voluntary settlers; became part of Eastern Siberia Region; scene of extensive fighting during Civil War 1918–21; reorganized as subdivision of U.S.S.R. 1937; rapid industrial development in 1960s.

Ir·lam \ˈər-ləm\. Town, Lancashire, NW England, at confluence of Mersey and Irwell rivers 7.5 mi. (12 km.) W of Manchester; pop. (1981p) 19,900.

Ir·mo \ˈər-mō\. Town, Lexington co., cen. South Carolina, ab. 10 mi. (16 km.) NW of Columbia; pop. (1990c) 11,280.

Iro, Cape \ˌē-rō\ *or Jp.* **Irō–Za·ki** \ˈē-ˈrō-ˈzä-kē\. Cape on SE coast of Honshū, Japan, bet. Suruga Bay and Sagami Sea.

Iron \ˈī-ərn\. Name of counties in four states of the U.S. See tables at MICHIGAN, MISSOURI, UTAH, WISCONSIN.

Iron Cur·tain \ˈī-ərn-ˈkərt-ᵊn\. The U.S.S.R. and its E European Communist dependencies—a term used after WWII to denote isolationism of the region.

Iron·dale \ˈī-ərn-ˌdāl\. City, Jefferson co., cen. Alabama, 3 mi. (5 km.) E of Birmingham; pop. (1990c) 9454.

Iron·de·quoit Bay \ir-ˈän-də-ˌkwoit, -kwät\. Inlet of Lake Ontario, W New York, E of Rochester.

Iron Gate *or* **Iron Gates** *or Rom.* **Por·ţi·le de Fier** \ˈpȯr-tsē-le-dā-ˈfyer\ *or Ger.* **Ei·ser·nes Tor** \ˈī-zər-nəs-ˈtōr\. Gorge, with rapids, in Danube River bet. Orşova and Drobeta-Turnu Severin, Romania, on Yugoslav boundary; 2 mi. (3 km.) long.

Iron Mountain. 1. Elevation, Polk co., cen. Florida Penin.; 325 ft. (99 m.); carillon tower.
2. Mountain, St. Francois co., E Missouri, ab. 12 mi. (19 km.) NE of Taum Sauk; 1077 ft. (328 m.).
3. Peak, Custer and Pennington cos., SW South Dakota; 5500 ft. (1676 m.).
4. City, ⊗ of Dickinson co., S Upper Penin. of Michigan, 48 mi. (77 km.) W of Escanaba; pop. (1990c) 8525; resort.

Iron Mountains. Ridge, part of Unaka Mts., extending along boundary bet. Smyth and Grayson cos. and bet. Grayson and Wythe cos., in Virginia, and SW into Tennessee; ab. 80 mi. (129 km.) long; highest peak ab. 4200 ft. (1280 m.).

Iron River. City, Iron co., SW Upper Penin. of Michigan; pop. (1990c) 2095; lake resort.

Iron·ton \ˈī-ərn-tən\. **1.** City, ⊗ of Iron co., SE Missouri; pop. (1990c) 1539.
2. City, ⊗ of Lawrence co., S Ohio, on Ohio River opp. Russell, Kentucky, 21 mi. (34 km.) SE of Portsmouth; pop. (1990c) 12,751; coke; limestone quarries; founded 1848.

Iron·wood \ˈī-ərn-ˌwu̇d\. City, Gogebic co., NW Upper Penin. of Michigan, on Wisconsin border 15 mi. (24 km.) SE of Lake Superior; pop. (1990c) 6849; resort; formerly mined iron deposits; Gogebic Community Coll. (1932).

Ir·o·quois \ˈir-ə-ˌkwȯi, -ˌkȯi\. **1.** River, Indiana and Illinois; rises in NW Indiana, and flows W across Illinois border, then N into Kankakee River in NE Illinois; ab. 120 mi. (193 km.) long.
2. County in E Illinois. See table at ILLINOIS.

Iroquois Falls. Town, Cochrane dist., E Ontario, Canada, 45 mi. (72 km.) NE of Timmins; on railroad line W of Lake Abitibi; pop. (1991c) 5999.

Iroquois Point. City, Honolulu co., Hawaii, at entrance to Pearl Harbor; pop. (1990c) 4188.

Irō–Zaki. See IRO, CAPE.

Ir·ra·wad·dy *also* **Ira·wa·di** \ˌir-ä-ˈwä-dē\. **1.** River, cen. Myanmar; formed by confluence of Mali and Nmai rivers just N of Myitkyina, flows S through cen. Myanmar into Bay of Bengal through several mouths, near Yangon; ab. 1300 mi. (2092 km.) long; has extensive delta; navigable to Bhamo; main tributary the Chindwin which joins it 60 mi. (96 km.) WSW of Mandalay; other branches the Shweli, Mu, and Myitnge; passes through three defiles where course is narrow and rapid; important towns on its banks: Myitkina, Bhamo, Mandalay, Myingyan, Pyè, and Henzada.
2. Division of Myanmar. See table at MYANMAR.

Ir·tysh \ir-ˈtəsh\ *or Kazakh* **Er·tis** \er-ˈtis\. River, NE Kazakhstan, and W part of Russia in Asia (Omsk Oblast); rises on W slopes of Altay Shan in N Xinjiang Uygur, flows W across Chinese border through Zaysan Lake and then NW to join Ob' River; ab. 2760 mi. (4440 km.) long; largest tributary of the Ob' and navigable for most of its course; Semey, Pavlodar, Omsk, and Tobol'sk are on its banks.

Iru·ma \ē-'rü-mä\. City, Saitama prefecture, Honshū, Japan, 25 mi. (40 km.) NW of Tokyo; pop. (1990p) 137,585.

Irún \ē-'rün\. Commune, Guipúzcoa prov., N Spain, on Bidassoa River 9 mi. (14 km.) E of San Sebastián near French border; pop. (1991p) 52,828; port of entry; medicinal springs.

Ir·vine \'ər-,vīn\. **1.** City, Orange co., SW California, just SE of Santa Ana; pop. (1990c) 110,330; Univ. of California, Irvine (1965), Christ Coll. Irvine (1972).
2. \'ər-vən\. City, ⊗ of Estill co., E Kentucky, 23 mi. (37 km.) SSE of Winchester; pop. (1990c) 2836.
3. \'ər-vən\. Burgh, Strathclyde region, SW Scotland, at an estuary of Firth of Clyde 11 mi. (18 km.) N of Ayr; pop. (1991e) 56,000; chemicals, glass products, electronics, pharmaceuticals; engineering.

Ir·ving \'ər-viŋ\. City, Dallas co., NE Texas, NW of Dallas; pop. (1990c) 155,037; Univ. of Dallas (1955), De Vry Institute of Technology (1969).

Ir·ving·ton \'ər-viŋ-tən\. **1.** Town, Essex co., NE New Jersey, WSW of and adjoining Newark; pop. (1990c) 61,018.
2. Village, Westchester co., SE New York, on Hudson River 22 mi. (35 km.) N of New York and 3 mi. (5 km.) S of Tarrytown; pop. (1990c) 6348; forms one community with Sleepy Hollow, Elmsford, and Tarrytown.

Ir·well \'ər-,wel, -wəl\. River, W England; flows in winding course S past Rochdale, Bury, and Manchester into the Mersey at Irlam; ab. 30 mi. (48 km.) long.

Ir·win \'ər-win\. **1.** County in S Georgia. See table at GEORGIA.
2. Borough, Westmoreland co., SW Pennsylvania, 18 mi. (29 km.) ESE of Pittsburgh; pop. (1990c) 4604.

Ir·win·ton \'ər-win-tən\. Town, ⊗ of Wilkinson co., cen. Georgia; pop. (1990c) 641.

Is. See HĪT.

Isabel. See SANTA ISABEL 4.

Is·a·bel, Mount \'i-zə-,bel\. Peak, N cen. Lincoln co., W Wyoming; 10,154 ft. (3095 m.).

Isa·be·la \,ē-sä-'bā-lä\. **1.** Cape, N Dominican Republic; settlement there (now in ruins) believed to have been founded by explorer Christopher Columbus c. 1493.
2. Province, NE Luzon, Philippines, in upper valley of Cagayan River; ✻ Ilagan; on E along Pacific coast is part of Sierra Madre Range; a major producer of tobacco and rice. See table at PHILIPPINES.
History: Province created 1856 out of lands belonging to Cagayan and Nueva Vizcaya; old towns centers of missionary activities in 17th cent.; civil government estab. 1901.
3. City, Philippines. See BASILAN 3.
4. Municipality, cen. Negros Occidental, Negros, Philippines, 37 mi. (60 km.) S of City of Bacolod; pop. (1980c) 39,704; communications center.
5. Municipality, NW Puerto Rico, on coast 10 mi. (16 km.) NE of Aguadilla; pop. (1990c) 39,147.

Isabela Island *also* **Al·be·marle Island** \'al-bə-,märl\. Island, largest of Galápagos Is.; in W part of the group, 0°30′S, 91°06′W, its N end crossed by Equator; 1650 sq. mi. (4274 sq. km.). See GALÁPAGOS ISLANDS.

Is·a·bel·la \,i-zə-'be-lə\. County in cen. Michigan. See table at MICHIGAN.

Isa·bel Se·gun·da \'ē-sä-,bel-sā-'gün-dä\ *or* **Vie·ques** \'byā-,kes\. Chief town of Vieques I., Puerto Rico; on N coast.

Isach·sen Peninsula \'ī-zik-sən, -zək-\. Peninsula in NW Ellef Ringnes I., N Nunavut, Canada; formerly thought to be an island.

Ísa·fjör·dhur \'ē-sä-,fyœr-thər\. Town at tip of peninsula of NW Iceland; pop. (1992e) 3496.

Isa·ha·ya \ē-'sä-hä-yä\. City, Nagasaki prefecture, Kyūshū, Japan, 15 mi. (24 km.) NW of the city of Nagasaki; pop. (1990p) 90,678.

Isana. See IÇANA.

Isan·ti \i-'san-tē\. County in E Minnesota. See table at MINNESOTA.

Isar \'ē-,zär\. River, Bavaria, Germany; rises in Tirol and flows through Munich and past Landshut NW into the Danube; 163 mi. (262 km.) long; not navigable.

Isar·co \ē-'zär-kō\. River, Trentino-Alto Adige, N Italy; flows into Adige River at Bolzano; ab. 70 mi. (113 km.) long.

Isa·rog \,ē-sä-'rȯg\. Volcanic mountain, E cen. Camarines Sur prov., Luzon, Philippines, on isthmus bet. Lagonoy Gulf and San Miguel Bay; 6448 ft. (1965 m.); base ab. 36 mi. (58 km.) in circumference; source of many streams.

Isau·ria \ī-'sȯr-ē-ə\. Ancient district in E Pisidia, Asia Minor (Turkey), on N slope of W Taurus Mts.; in first cent. B.C. boundaries were changed so that it included a part of W Cilicia; birthplace of Byzantine Emperor Zeno c. 466 A.D.

Isbarta. See ISPARTA.

Isca Dumnoniorum. See EXETER 6.

Isca Silurum. See CAERLEON.

Is·chia \'is-kē-ə\ *or* **Iso·la D'Ischia** \'ē-zō-lä-'dēs-kē-ä\; *anc.* **Ae·nar·ia** \ē-'nar-ē-ə\. Island, S Italy, in Tyrrhenian Sea bet. Gulf of Gaeta and Bay of Naples; 18 sq. mi. (47 sq. km.); administratively a part of Napoli prov., Campania; highest point the volcanic Monte Epomeo 2585 ft. (788 m.); summer resort, mineral springs; suffered greatly from volcanic eruptions and earthquakes, esp. the earthquake of 1883; chief town Ischia.

Ischl. See BAD ISCHL.

Ise \'ē-sā\. **1.** Old province, S coast of Honshū, Japan, now part of Mie prefecture.
2. *formerly* **Uji–ya·ma·da** \'ü-jē-yä-'mä-dä\. City, Mie prefecture, Honshū, Japan, at edge of a national park; pop. (1990p) 104,162; several Shinto shrines incl. the Grand Shrine of Ise, for centuries the mecca of pilgrims and of the emperor and high officials.

Ise Bay; *formerly* **Owa·ri Bay** \ō-'wär-ē\. Inlet of Pacific Ocean on S coast of Honshū, Japan, bet. Mie and Aichi prefectures.

Ise Fjord \'ē-sə\. Inlet of the Kattegat (arm of the North Sea), on N coast of Sjælland I., Denmark; extends S inland 20 mi. (32 km.); its E extension is Roskilde Fjord.

Iseghem. See IZEGEM.

Ise·ha·ra \,ē-sā-'hä-rä\. City, Kanagawa prefecture, Honshū, Japan; pop. (1990p) 89,568.

Isel·le \ē-'zel-lā\. Town, NE Piedmont, NW Italy, just NW of Domodossola; S terminus of Simplon Pass and Tunnel.

Iseo, Lake \ē-'zā-ō\ *or* **La·go d'Iseo** \'lä-gō-dē-'zā-ō\. Lake in Lombardy, N Italy, on border bet. Brescia and Bergamo provs.; 24 sq. mi. (62 sq. km.).

Iser. See JIZERA.

Ise·ran, Col de l' \'kȯl-də-,lēz-'räⁿ\. Mountain pass, Graian Alps, E Savoie dept., E France; 9084 ft. (2769 m.) high; highway, completed 1937.

Isère \ē-'zer\. **1.** River, SE France; rises on slopes of Graian Alps near border of Italy, flows W and SW into Rhone River 4 mi. (6 km.) NNW of Valence; 180 mi. (290 km.) long.
2. Department of France. See table at FRANCE.

Iser·lohn \,ē-zər-'lōn, 'ē-zər-,\. City, North Rhine-Westphalia, Germany, 15 mi. (24 km.) W of Arnsberg; pop. (1992e) 96,976; machinery; became city mid-13th cent.

Iser·nia \ē-'zer-nē-ä\; *anc.* **Æ·ser·nia** \ē-'zər-\. **1.** Province, Molise, cen. Italy. See table at ITALY.
2. Commune, its ✻, 22 mi. (35 km.) WNW of Campobasso; pop. (1989c) 21,623; cathedral; has ancient remains. Became Roman colony 3d cent. B.C.; took part in Social War c. 90 B.C.

Ise·sa·ki \,ē-sā-'sä-kē\. City, Gumma prefecture, Honshū, Japan, 55 m. (88 km.) NW of Tokyo; pop. (1990p) 115,939.

Ise·yin \ē-'sā-yin\. City, SW Nigeria, NNW of Ibadan; pop 1991e) 191,700.

Isfahan. See EŞFAHĀN 2.

Ish·a·woo·a Pass \ 'i-shə-wä\. Pass through Absaroka Range, SW Park co., NW Wyoming; 9870 ft. (3008 m.).

Ishi·ga·ki \ˌē-shē-'gä-kē\. Island in cen. part of Sakishima group, S Ryukyu Is., Japan.

Ishi·ka·ri River \ˌē-shē-'kä-rē\ *or Jp.* **Ishikari–ga·wa** \-'gä-wä\. River, W Hokkaidō I., Japan; flows W into **Ishikari Bay**; nearly 225 mi. (360 km.) long; 2d longest river in Japan.

Ishikari Dake. See ASAHI DAKE.

Ishi·ka·wa \ˌē-shē-'kä-wä\. Prefecture, Honshū, Japan; ✱ Kanazawa. See table at JAPAN.

Ishim \i-'shim\. **1.** River, N cen. Kazakhstan and W part of Russia in Asia (Tyumen' and Omsk oblasts); rises in cen. steppe region of Kazakhstan and flows N past Petropavlovsk to join the Irtysh at Ust-Ishim; ab. 1330 mi. (2140 km.) long. **2.** Town on lower Ishim River, Tyumen' Oblast, Russia, on railroad line 85 mi. (137 km.) N of Petropavlovsk; pop. (1991e) 65,900.

Ishim·bay \ˌē-shim-'bī\. Town, Bashkortostan (rep.), E Russia in Europe, ab. 90 mi. (145 km.) S of Ufa; pop. (1991e) 71,000.

Ishi·no·ma·ki \ˌē-shē-nō-'mä-kē\. Town, Miyagi prefecture, N Honshū on E coast, Japan; pop. (1990p) 121,980; fair harbor.

Ishinomaki Bay. Inlet of Pacific Ocean, Miyagi prefecture, NE coast of Honshū, Japan.

Ishi·zu·chi·no \ˌē-shē-'zü-chē-ˌnō\ *or Jp.* **Ishizuchino–mo·ri** \-'mō-rē\. Peak, W Shikoku I., Japan; 6500 ft. (1981 m.); highest peak on Shikoku.

Ish·pe·ming \'ish-pə-miŋ\. City, Marquette co., N Upper Penin. of Michigan, 15 mi. (24 km.) W of city of Marquette; pop. (1990c) 7200; National Ski Hall of Fame nearby.

Ishtib. See ŠTIP.

Isi·bo·ro \ˌē-sē-'bō-rō\. River, cen. Bolivia; flows NE ab. 130 mi. (210 km.) into the Sécure.

Isi·bo·ro–Se·cu·re National Park \ˌē-sē-'bō-rō-sā-'kü-rā\. National park, W cen. Bolivia, bet. the Isiboro and Sécure rivers; 4600 sq. mi. (11,914 sq. km.); tropical forest; estab. 1965.

Isi·gny \'ē-zē-'nyē\ *or in full* **Isigny–sur–Mer** \-sūr-'mer\. Village, NW Calvados dept., NW France, W of Bayeux and near Carentan; captured by U.S. forces in Normandy invasion of WWII, launched June 6, 1944.

Isin. See ISSIN.

Isis \'ī-səs\. Local name for upper course of the Thames River, in England.

Iskandarīyah, Al–. **1.** Governorate, Egypt. See *Alexandria* in table at EGYPT. **2.** Seaport, Egypt. See ALEXANDRIA 2.

Iskâr. See ISKŬR.

Iskelib. See İSKİLİP.

İs·ken·de·run *also* **Is·ken·de·ron** \ˌis-ˌken-də-'rün\; *formerly* **Al·ex·an·dret·ta** \ˌal-ig-zan-'dre-tə, ˌel-\ *or Fr.* **Alex·an·drette** \ˌá-lek-sä^{n}-'dret\. Seaport city on SE shore of Gulf of İskenderun (Alexandretta), Hatay, S Turkey in Asia ab. 60 mi. (96 km.) SE of Adana; pop. (1990c) 154,807; steel plant; chief town of former sanjak (district) of Alexandretta and of republic of Hatay; on branch railroad and on coastal highway S of site of Issus (battle 333 B.C.); founded by Macedonian King Alexander the Great and named by him to commemorate the battle; has good harbor; chief port of Aleppo and formerly outlet for overland trade from Persia, India, and points east until shipping routes estab. around Cape of Good Hope, and, later, opening of Suez Canal.

İskenderun, Gulf of *or Turk.* **İskenderun Kör·fe·zi** \ˌkœr-fe-'zē\; *formerly* **Gulf of Alexandretta.** Inlet of E Mediterranean Sea on S coast of Turkey near Syrian boundary; its E coast is province (former republic) of Hatay.

Is·ker \'ēs-kər\. **1.** River, Bulgaria. See ISKŬR. **2.** Ancient town in Siberia. See SIBIR.

İs·ki·lip *or* **Is·ke·lib** \ˌis-ki-'lēp, -'lip\. Town, Çorum prov., N cen. Turkey in Asia, near left bank of the Kızıl, 103 mi. (166 km.) NE of Ankara.

Is·ki·tim \ˌēs-kē-'tēm\. Town, Novosibirsk Oblast, S Russia in Asia, ab. 30 mi. (48 km.) SSE of the city of Novosibirsk; pop. (1991e) 68,700.

Is·kŭr *or* **Is·kâr** *also* **Is·ker** *or* **Iskr** \'is-kər\. River, NW cen. Bulgaria; rises in Rhodope Mts., flows N through Balkan Mts., into Danube River; 228 mi. (367 km.) long.

Is·la \'ī-lə\. River, Tayside region, E Scotland; flows S and SW to the Tay; 46 mi. (74 km.) long.

Is·la Cris·ti·na \'ēz-lä-krē-'stē-nä\. Seaport, Huelva prov., SW Spain, on the Mediterranean Sea 21 mi. (34 km.) W of the commune of Huelva; pop. (1991c) 16,524; tuna, sardines.

Isla de Aves. See AVES ISLAND.

Is·la de la Ju·ven·tud \'ēs-lä-thä-lä-ˌhü-ben-'tüth\. **1.** *or Eng.* **Isle of Youth** \'yüth\; *formerly* **Isle of Pines** \'pīnz\. Island, Cuba, in NW Caribbean Sea, S of W end; 1182 sq. mi. (3601 sq. km.); chief town Nueva Gerona. **2.** Special municipality of Cuba. See table at CUBA.

Isla de León. See LEÓN, ISLA DE.

Isla del Maíz Grande. See GREAT CORN ISLAND.

Isla del Maíz Pequeña. See LITTLE CORN ISLAND.

Isla de Pascua. See EASTER ISLAND.

Isla Grande de Tierra del Fuego. See TIERRA DEL FUEGO 2.

Is·lam·a·bad \is-'lä-mə-ˌbäd, iz-'la-mə-ˌbad\. City, ✱ of Pakistan, NE of Rawalpindi; pop. (1981c) 204,364; university; site chosen to succeed Karachi as national ✱ 1959; construction and moving took place early to mid-1960s; greater Islamabad constitutes an administrative subdivision apart from the provinces (see table at PAKISTAN).

Islamic Republic of Mauritania. See MAURITANIA 1.

Islamic Republic of Pakistan. See PAKISTAN.

Is·land \'ī-lənd\. County in NW Washington. See table at WASHINGTON.

Island *or* **Ísland.** See ICELAND.

Island Beach. Narrow sand spit off E coast of Ocean co., E New Jersey, enclosing Barnegat Bay.

Is·land·ia \ˌī-'lan-dē-ə\. Village, Suffolk co., SE New York, in cen. Long Island; pop. (1990c) 2769.

Island Lake. **1.** Village, McHenry and Lake cos., NE Illinois, NW of Chicago; pop. (1990c) 4449. **2.** Lake, E Manitoba, Canada; 550 sq. mi. (1424 sq. km.); outlet through Gods Lake and Hayes River to Hudson Bay.

Island No. 10. Former island in Mississippi River, in New Madrid co., SE Missouri; scene of Civil War engagements 1862; rejoined mainland with a shift in river's course.

Island Park. Village, Nassau co., SE New York, on Atlantic Ocean 20 mi. (32 km.) ESE of New York City; pop. (1990c) 4860.

Islands, Bay of. **1.** Inlet of Gulf of St. Lawrence, W Newfoundland, Canada; estuary of Humber River. **2.** Inlet of Pacific Ocean on NE coast of N extension of North I., New Zealand, W of Cape Brett.

Islands of the Four Mountains. Island group in E cen. Aleutian Is., Alaska, W of Umnak.

Islas Baleares. See BALEARIC ISLANDS.

Islas de Aves *or* **Islas Las Aves.** See AVES, ISLAS DE.

Islas Malvinas. See FALKLAND ISLANDS.

Islas Marías. See MARÍAS, ISLAS.

Islas Santanilla. See SWAN ISLANDS.

Is·lay \'ī-lə, -lā\. Most southerly island of the Inner Hebrides, off W coast of Scotland, in Strathclyde region; 234 sq. mi. (606 sq. km.); farming, fishing, whiskey distilling.

Isle \'ēl\. River, SW cen. France; rises in Haute-Vienne dept., flows SW into Dordogne River; 145 mi. (233 km.) long.

Isle au Haut \ˌī-lə-'hō, ˌē-\. Island at entrance to Penobscot Bay off S cen. Maine coast; included in Knox co.; half of it in Acadia National Park.

Isle–de–France. See ÎLE-DE-FRANCE.

Isle La Motte \ˌīl-lə-'mät\. Island in Lake Champlain, Grand Isle co., NW Vermont; ab. 6 mi. (10 km.) long; settled by French (Fort Ste. Anne) 1666; black-marble deposits.

Isle of Ely. See CAMBRIDGESHIRE AND ISLE OF ELY.

Isle of Man. See MAN, ISLE OF.

Isle of Palms \'pämz, 'pälmz\. City, Charleston co., South Carolina, on Isle of Palms barrier island, 7 mi. (11 km.) E of the city of Charleston; pop. (1990c) 3680.

Isle of Port·land \'pōrt-lənd\. Limestone peninsula, Dorset, S England, S of Weymouth; its connection with mainland is a stretch of shingle 200 yds. (183 m.) wide; its S tip is called **Portland Bill;** limestone quarries; 16th cent. castle, lighthouse; naval anchorage.

Isle of Wight \ˈwīt\. **1.** County in SE Virginia. See table at VIRGINIA.

2. Village, its ⊗, 17 mi. (27 km.) W of Newport News.

3. *anc.* **Vec·tis** \ˈvek-tis\. Island, England, in English Channel; has many seaside resorts incl. Ryde, Ventnor, Cowes.

4. Administrative county, S England, comprising the Isle of Wight; reorganized as administrative division 1974. See table at ENGLAND.

Isle of Youth. See ISLA DE LA JUVENTUD 1.

Isle Roy·ale \ˈī-ˈrȯi-əl\. Island in NW Lake Superior, N of, and a part of, Keweenaw co., N tip of Michigan's Upper Penin.; ab. 44 mi. (71 km.) long by 8 mi. (13 km.) wide; prehistoric copper mines still in evidence; with surrounding islands now constitutes **Isle Royale National Park** (see UNITED STATES, *National Parks*).

Isles Der·nieres \ˌēl-der-ˈnyer\. Small group of islands in Gulf of Mexico, in Terrebonne parish, SE Louisiana.

Isles of Scilly. See SCILLY, ISLES OF.

Isles of Shoals \ˈshōls\. Group of nine rocky islands, Maine and New Hampshire, 10 mi. (16 km.) SE of Portsmouth, New Hampshire; ab. 1 sq. mi. (2.6 sq. km.); most important Star and Appledore; resort.

Isles of the Sea. See GARVELLOCHS.

Is·le·ta \is-ˈle-tə\. American Indian village and pueblo, Bernalillo co., cen. New Mexico, on the Rio Grande in Isleta Indian Reservation, S of Albuquerque; pop. (1990c) 2915; inhabited chiefly by people whose ancestral language is Tanoan.

Is·ling·ton \ˈiz-liŋ-tən\. A borough of Greater London, SE England. See table at LONDON 4.

Islip \ˈī-sləp\. **1.** Unincorporated settlement, Suffolk co., SE New York, on Long Island on Great South Bay, ab. 10 mi. (16 km.) W of Patchogue; pop. (1990c) 18,924; formerly considered a resort.

2. Parish, Oxfordshire, cen. England, ab. 6 mi. (10 km.) N of Oxford; birthplace of King Edward the Confessor c. 1003.

Is·ly \ē-ˈslē\. Short river, NE Morocco.

Is·ma·il \ˌē-smä-ˈēl\. **1.** *or Russ.* **Iz·ma·il** \is-mə-ˈēl\. Former department, S Bessarabia, Romania, N of Danube Delta; 1626 sq. mi. (4211 sq. km.); now in Odessa subdivision, Ukraine.

2. City, its ✱. See IZMAIL 2.

Is·ma·i·lia *or* **Is·mâ·ʻi·lî·ya** \ˌiz-mā-ə-ˈlē-ə\ *or Arab.* **Al–Is·mā·ʻī·lī·yah** \ˌal-ˌis-mä-ē-ˈlē-ä\. **1.** Governorate of NE Egypt. See table at EGYPT.

2. Town, its ✱, on Lake Timsah; pop. (1991e) 247,000; halfway station on Suez Canal; founded 1863.

Ismailia Canal *or Arab.* **Tur·ʻat al–Ismā·ʻīlī·yah** \ˈtu̇r-ät-ˌal-ˌis-mä-ē-ˈlē-ä\. Canal extending from Nile River near Cairo, Egypt, to Suez Canal at Ismailia on Lake Timsah.

Ismid. See İZMİT.

Ismid, Gulf of. See İZMİT, GULF OF.

Is·na \ˈis-nə\ *or* **Es·na** \ˈes-\. Commercial town on Nile River, Upper Egypt, S of the ruins of Thebes; Ptolemaic and Coptic ruins.

Isola D'Ischia. See ISCHIA.

Isola Lunga. See DUGI OTOK.

Isole Borromeo. See BORROMEAN ISLANDS.

Isole Dahalach. See DAHLAK ARCHIPELAGO.

Isole Eolie. See LIPARI ISLANDS.

Isole Italiane dell'Egeo. See AEGEAN ISLANDS 2.

Ison·zo \ē-ˈzōnt-sō\ *or Serbo-Croat.* **So·ča** \ˈsō-chä\; *anc.* **Son·ti·us** \ˈsän-tē-əs, ˈsän-shē-əs\. River, Slovenia and Italy; rises in NW Slovenia, flows S into Gulf of Trieste near Monfalcone, NE Italy; 84 mi. (135 km.) long. In a long-contested area, where severe fighting occurred in WWI, esp. at Gorizia and Caporetto (Kobarid), and again in WWII.

Iso·to·ro Nāl \ˌē-sə-ˈtȯr-ō-ˈnəl\. Mountain in the Hindu Kush, on Afghanistan-Pakistan boundary; 24,273 ft. (7398 m.).

Ispahan. See EŞFAHAN.

İs·par·ta *also* **Is·bar·ta** \ə̇s-ˈpär-tä\. **1.** Province of Turkey in Asia. See table at TURKEY.

2. Town, its ✱, 110 mi. (117 km.) W of Konya; pop. (1990c) 112,117; carpets; attar of roses.

Is·ra·el \ˈiz-rē-əl, -rā-\. **1.** Ancient kingdom in Palestine; as first formed under King Saul c. 1020 B.C. comprised the lands in Canaan (*q.v.*) which in 12th cent. B.C. were occupied by Hebrew tribes, descended from the 12 sons of the patriarch Jacob (Israel), which had been led out of Egypt by the prophet and lawgiver Moses; consolidated by King David who began to rule c. 1000 B.C. and made Jerusalem his ✱ and under whom it included also Galilee and land E of the Jordan; became prosperous trading nation under his son Solomon who erected temple at Jerusalem; after death of Solomon kingdom divided, the 10 northern tribes seceding and forming in 10th cent. B.C. under Jeroboam the kingdom of Israel (*or* **Northern Kingdom**), while the two tribes in the S under Solomon's son Rehoboam formed kingdom of Judah (*q.v.*); Northern Kingdom (✱ first at Shechem, then Tirzah, finally at Samaria which was built by King Omri 9th cent. B.C.) weakened by rivalry with Judah and Damascus, finally overthrown by Assyrians, who under Sargon II captured Samaria 722 B.C.

2. *or officially* **State of Israel.** Republic, SW Asia, bounded on N by Lebanon, on E by Syria and Jordan, on SW by Egypt (Sinai Penin.), and on W by the Mediterranean Sea; 7992 sq. mi. (20,699 sq. km.); pop. (1983p) 4,037,620; ✱ Jerusalem; in extreme S has port on Gulf of Aqaba; hilly in N (highest peak Mt. Meron 3692 ft. or 1125 m.); coastal plain (max. width ab. 20 mi. or 32 km.) and Plain of Esdraelon, both below 300 ft. (91 m.); in S is Negev (*q.v.*).

Chief products: Citrus and other fruit, vegetables, potash, magnesium, copper, bromine, phosphate; manufacturing: textiles, chemicals, electrical goods; food processing, diamond cutting; tourism.

Chief towns: Jerusalem, Tel Aviv-Jaffa, Haifa.

Political divisions: For administrative purposes divided into the following six districts:

NAME	AREA (sq. mi.)	AREA (sq. km.)	POP. (1990e)	CAPITAL
Central	480	1,243	969,800	Ramla
Haifa	330	855	612,600	Haifa
Jerusalem[1]	215	557	556,000	Jerusalem
Northern	1,347	3,489	762,700	Nazareth
Southern	5,555	14,387	541,900	Beersheba
Tel Aviv	66	171	1,043,600	Tel Aviv-Jaffa

[1] Includes Jordanian sector of Jerusalem occupied by Israel 1967.

History: Estab. by decree of May 14, 1948, in the partition of Palestine bet. Jews and Arabs as recommended (1947) by a special committee of the UN. Its establishment intensified the state of civil war in Palestine (*q.v.*) bet. Arabs and Jews; invaded by Arab forces of neighboring countries, but later repulsed these attacks and gained additional territory in offensive actions; signed armistice agreements with Arab states retaining new city of Jerusalem but yielding to Egypt the coastal region around Gaza (*q.v.*); with Great Britain and France engaged in war (Sinai campaign) against Arab countries 1956; in the face of renewed Arab threats in 1967 occupied the immediately adjoining parts of Syria, the parts of Jordan W of the Jordan River, and the whole of the Sinai Penin. in a lightning campaign ("the six-day war") beginning June 5 and ending in a cease-fire but without withdrawal from occupied territories; following surprise attack by Egyptian and Syrian forces Oct. 1973 captured additional Syrian and Egyptian territory, but withdrew following cease-fire (May 1974); signed peace treaty with Egypt Mar. 1979 (last portion of occupied Sinai Penin. returned to Egypt 1982); invaded Lebanon 1982 (withdrawal of most troops by 1985); experienced widespread unrest in West Bank and Gaza Strip Dec. 1987, marking beginning of a continued Palestinian resistance movement ("intifada"); bombed by Iraq during Gulf War (Jan–Feb. 1991), but remained uninvolved at request of

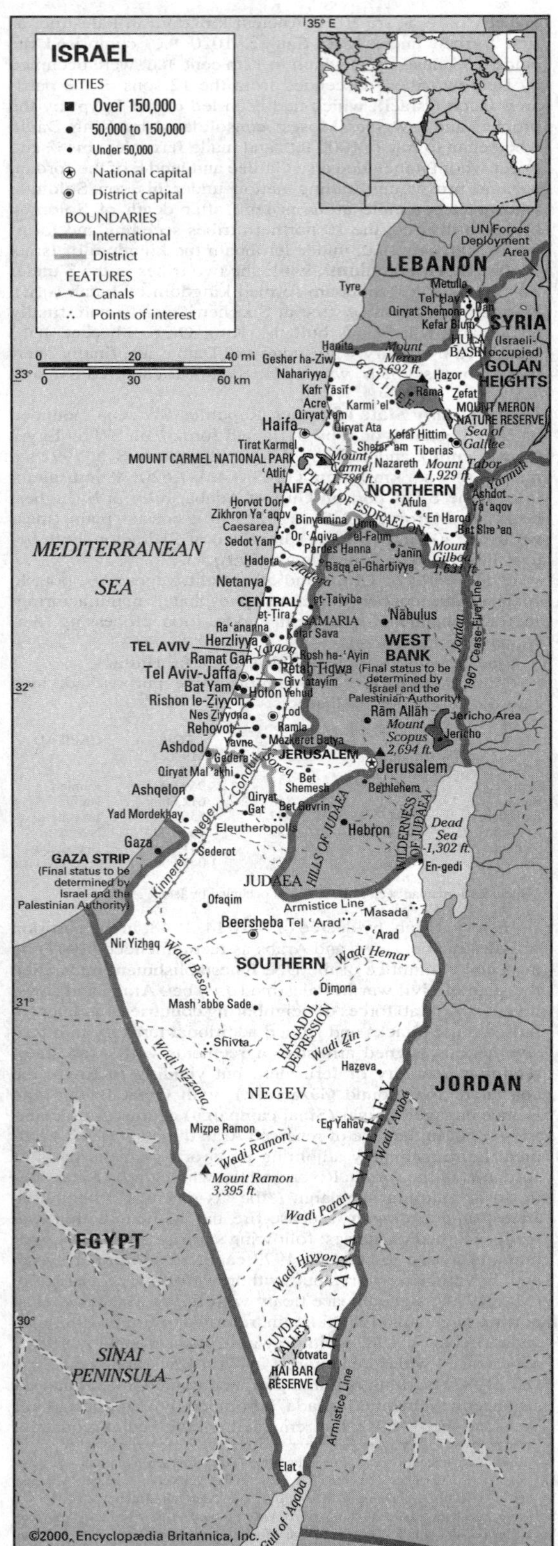

U.S.; signed peace agreement Sept. 1993 with Palestinian Liberation Organization providing for mutual recognition and for eventual Palestinian self-rule in West Bank and Gaza; talks initiated with Jordan toward normalizing relations 1994.

Issa. See VIS.

Is·sa·quah \ˈi-sə-ˌkwä\. City, King co., W cen. Washington, 15 mi. (24 km.) SE of Seattle; pop. (1990c) 7786.

Is·sa·que·na \ˌi-sə-ˈkwē-nə\. County in W Mississippi. See table at MISSISSIPPI.

Issel. See IJSSEL.

Issel, Lake. See IJSSELMEER.

Is·sin *or* **Is·in** \ˈis-ᵊn\. Archaeological site, a low mound with a large building on it, S Iraq, bet. Euphrates and Tigris rivers 60 mi. (96 km.) SE of Al Ḩillah; ancient city of Babylonia, of Semitic origin; part of Babylonian empire of King Hammurabi 18th cent. B.C.

Issiq Köl. See ISSYK-KUL.

Is·soire \ē-ˈswär\. Commune, Puy-de-Dôme dept., S cen. France, 18 mi. (29 km.) SSE of Clermont-Ferrand; 12th cent. Romanesque church.

Is·sus \ˈi-səs\. Ancient town, S Asia Minor, ab. 20 mi. (32 km.) N of modern İskenderun (Turkey), in a narrow coastal plain S of passes through Taurus Mts.; scene of two battles: (1) 333 B.C., Macedonian King Alexander the Great won victory over King Darius and the Persians, and (2) 194 A.D., Roman Emperor L. Septimius Severus defeated his rival Pescennius Niger.

Is·syk–Kul \ˌi-sik-ˈkəl\ *or* **Ysyk Köl** \ˌi-sik-ˈkœl\ *also* **Is·siq Köl** \-ˈkœl\. Lake (*kul*), NE Kyrgyzstan; a brackish lake lying in a basin at alt. 5279 ft. (1609 m.) bet. W spurs of the Tian Shan; 115 mi. (185 km.) long by 38 mi. (61 km.) wide; 2355 sq. mi. (6099 sq. km.); max. depth 2303 ft. (702 m.); mountain ranges to S and N have peaks 13,000 to 18,000 ft. (ab. 4000 to 5500 m.) high; sometimes receives waters from the Chu River at W end; in early times area inhabited by Usuns and Tocharians, later by Kirghiz peoples.

Is·sy–les–Mou·li·neaux \ē-ˌsē-lā-ˌmü-lē-ˈnō\ *or* **Issy.** Commune, Hauts-de-Seine dept., N France, SW suburb of Paris on Seine River; pop. (1990c) 46,734; aircraft, chemicals.

İs·tan·bul \is-ˈtän-ˌbül; ˌis-täm-ˈbül, -tam-, -tän-\; *formerly* **Con·stan·ti·no·ple** \ˌkän-ˌstant-ᵊn-ˈō-pəl\. **1.** Province of Turkey, on both sides of Bosporus, thus partly in Europe and partly in Asia. See table at TURKEY.

2. *anc.* **By·zan·ti·um** \bə-ˈzan-shəm, -shē-əm, -tē-əm\. City, its ✻, on both sides of the Bosporus; old part of city on W side of the Bosporus; pop. (1990c) 6,620,241; chief city and former ✻ of Turkey; major port and railroad junction; shipbuilding yards; textiles, leather goods, cement, pottery, glass; tourism; contains church of St. Sophia (later a mosque, now a museum), erected 532–562 in time of Emperor Justinian; university (1453), technical university (1944).

History: As ancient Byzantium founded c. 660 B.C. by Greeks from Megara perhaps, as legend has it, under Byzas; taken in reign (522–486) of Persian King Darius I (the Great) but recolonized by Greeks after 478 B.C.; rose to great importance as trading port; often contended for by various states (Sparta, Macedonia, Rome) in 750 years bet. Peloponnesian War and time of Roman Emperor Constantine the Great; captured by Roman Emperor L. Septimius Severus 196 A.D. Name changed 330 A.D. to Constantinople (*Lat. Constantinopolis, from Gk. Konstantinou polis* Constantine's city) by Constantine the Great, who chose its site for his new ✻ of Eastern Roman, or Byzantine, Empire (see BYZANTINE EMPIRE); official ✻ 395–1453; old city on Golden Horn, an arm of Bosporus, was greatly enlarged by Byzantine emperors and protected by walls; attacked many times; captured and sacked by Crusaders 1204; retaken by Byzantines 1261 under Emperor Michael VIII Palaeologus; captured 1453 by Turks under Ottoman Sultan Mehmed II; Muslim ✻ and seat of government (Sublime Porte) of Ottoman sultans from soon after the takeover to 1922, when, after its occupation by Allies 1918–23 and deposition of sultan 1922, Ankara became 1923 ✻ of new Turkish Republic. Following a decree of the Grand National Assembly Nov. 1928, the use of the

Latin alphabet became general and the name İstanbul was officially adopted 1930. For sections or suburbs of the city, see BEYOĞLU, GALATA, ÜSKÜDAR, and YEŞILKÖY.

Ister. See DANUBE.

Is·to, Mount \ˈis-tō\. Highest peak in Brooks Range, Alaska; ab. 9058 ft. (2761 m.).

Is·tok·po·ga, Lake \ˌis-täk-ˈpō-gə\. Lake in cen. Highlands co., cen. Florida Penin.

Istra. See ISTRIA.

Is·tran·ca \ēs-ˈträn-jä\ *or* **Yıl·dız** \ˈəl-ˌdəz\. Mountain range along Black Sea coast, Kirklareli and İstanbul provs., Turkey in Europe; highest point 3378 ft. (1030 m.).

Is·tria \ˈis-trē-ə\ *or* **Is·tra** \-trə\ *or* **Is·tri·an Peninsula** \-ən\. Peninsula, NE coast of Adriatic Sea, ab. 60 mi. (97 km.) long from Trieste at its base to its S point; 1220 sq. mi. (3160 sq. km.); Pula, its chief town, is near S end; Rijeka is just E of its E border; on SE is Gulf of Kvarnerić.

History: Inhabitants overthrown by Romans in 177 B.C.; united with duchy of Bavaria in 10th cent.; came to patriarchs of Aquileia and, in 13th cent., to Venice; N part was an Austrian crown land under the Hapsburgs, but S part was Venetian until 1797; part of Illyrian Provinces 1809–15; ceded by Austria 1919 and awarded to Italy, except for Fiume, 1920; after WWII E part claimed by Yugoslavia and all except region around Trieste (Free City of Trieste) assigned to it by treaty of 1947 (see TRIESTE 3); since breakup of Yugoslavia 1991 split bet. Croatia and at its base, Slovenia.

Isu·lan \ē-ˈsü-län\. Municipality, ✻ of Sultan Kudarat prov., SW Mindanao I., Philippines.

Ita·ba·ia·na \ˌē-tä-bä-ˈyä-nə\. Town, Paraíba state, E Brazil, on railroad line WSW of João Pessoa; munic. pop. (1991p) 64,354.

Ita·bi·ra \ˌē-tä-ˈbē-rə\; *formerly* **Pre·si·den·te Var·gas** \ˌprä-zi-ˈden-tē-ˈvär-gəs\. Town, Minas Gerais state, SE Brazil; munic. pop. (1991p) 85,294.

Ita·bu·na \ˌē-tä-ˈbü-nə\. City, SE Bahia state, E Brazil, W of Ilhéus; munic. pop. (1991p) 185,180.

Itai·pu \ē-ˈtī-pü\. Dam on Paraná River bet. Brazil and Paraguay; formally opened 1982; began operating 1984.

Ita·jaí \ˌē-tä-zhä-ˈē\. **1.** River, Santa Catarina state, S Brazil; flows E into Atlantic Ocean; 125 mi. (201 km.) long. **2.** Port at mouth of river; munic. pop. (1991p) 119,583.

Ita·ju·bá \ˌē-tä-zhu̇-ˈbä\. City, S Minas Gerais state, E Brazil, 110 mi. (177 km.) NE of São Paulo; munic. pop. (1991p) 74,617.

Italia. See ITALY.

Ita·lia ir·re·den·ta \ē-ˈtäl-yä-ˌer-rā-ˈden-tä\. Name given by Italians to lands near Italy (as Trentino, Trieste, Istria, Fiume, Dalmatia) once belonging to Italy and having a large Italian population, sought by Irredentists for reincorporation in Italy. Movement began c. 1878 and was esp. strong in the 1880s and in the years prior to WWI.

Italian East Africa *or Ital.* **Afri·ca Ori·en·ta·le Ita·li·a·na** \ˈä-frē-kä-ˌōr-ē-en-ˈtä-lā-ē-ˌtä-lē-ˈä-nä\. Former Italian possessions in East Africa, incl. Eritrea, Ethiopia, and Italian Somaliland (now part of Somalia).

Italian So·ma·li·land \sō-ˈmä-lē-ˌland\ *or Ital.* **So·ma·lia Ita·li·a·na** \sō-ˈmäl-yä-ē-ˌtä-lē-ˈä-nä\. Former Italian colony, E Africa, extending S from Ras (Cape) Asir to boundary of Kenya; 178,218 sq. mi. (461,585 sq. km.); ✻ Mogadishu.

History: Benadir coast granted to Italy by sultan of Zanzibar 1889; colony leased to a private company 1893–1905; incorp. as state in Italian East Africa 1936; invaded by British troops 1941; governed by the British after WWII until in 1950 it became a UN trust territory (Trust Terr. of Somalia) administered by Italy; united with former British Somaliland, it became (as Somalia) an independent republic 1960. See SOMALIA.

It·a·ly \ˈit-^{ə}l-ē\ *or Ital.* **Ita·lia** \ē-ˈtäl-yä\ *or Lat.* **Ital·ia** \i-ˈtal-yə, ē-ˈtäl-yä\. Republic in S Europe, comprising the boot-shaped peninsula (ab. 760 mi. or 1220 km. long and from 100 to 150 mi. or 160 to 240 km. wide) which extends S into the Mediterranean Sea, and the islands of Sicily and Sardinia (*qq.v.*), and a number of small islands, esp. Elba, Capri, Ischia, Capraia, and Lipari Is.; bounded on N by Switzerland, on NE by Slovenia, on E by the Adriatic and Ionian seas, on S and SW by the Tyrrhenian Sea (Mediterranean Sea), on W by the Ligurian Sea and on NW by France; 116,313 sq. mi. (301,251 sq. km.); pop. (1993e) 57,235,000; ✻ Rome.

Physical features: Peninsula traversed entire length by the Apennines (*q.v.*) and bordered on NW, N, and NE by various ranges of the Alps (*q.v.*); highest points on N border Mont Blanc 15,771 ft. (4807 m.) and Monte Rosa 15,203 ft. (4634 m.), in the Apennines Monte Corno 9560 ft. (2914 m.), and in Sicily Mt. Etna 10,902 ft. (3323 m.).

Rivers: Largest the Po, with its many tributaries forming a valley which constitutes the great plain of the N; other important streams the Tiber (Tevere) in cen. part, Arno, Volturno, and Liri in W, Adige in N, Piave and Tagliamento in NE, and Isonzo on NE border, and many shorter rivers on E side flowing to the Adriatic.

Lakes: Large lakes in N noted for their beauty: Maggiore, Como, Garda; Trasimeno in N cen. part, Bolsena and Bracciano in W cen. part; many lagoons at N end of the Adriatic near mouths of the Po.

Coastal features: E coastline fairly regular except for Gargano Promontory near the S; separated from Albania by Strait of Otranto; in SE large Gulf of Taranto forms the "heel" (Puglia) and the "toe" (Calabria) of Italy; S tip separated from Sicily by Strait of Messina; W coast indented by Gulfs of Sant' Eufemia, Salerno, and Gaeta, and Bay of Naples.

Chief products: Wheat, rice, olives, grapes, citrus fruit; fish; mercury, sulfur; manufacturing: chemicals, textiles, machinery, automobiles; food processing; tourism.

Chief cities: Rome, Milan, Naples, Turin, Palermo, Genoa, Bologna, Florence, Catania, Bari. Within its borders are two small sovereign states, San Marino and Vatican City (*qq.v.*).

Political divisions: Divided into 20 autonomous regions, which in turn are subdivided into a number of provinces (for pronunciation of their names, see their individual entries):

NAME	AREA (sq. mi.)	AREA (sq. km.)	POP. (1989c)	CAPITAL
Abruzzi	4,168	10,795	1,266,448	L'Aquila
Chieti	999	2,587	387,781	Chieti
L'Aquila	1,944	5,035	300,201	L'Aquila
Pescara	473	1,225	296,185	Pescara
Teramo	752	1,948	282,281	Teramo
Basilicata	3,857	9,990	623,175	Potenza
Matera	1,330	3,445	209,880	Matera
Potenza	2,527	6,545	413,295	Potenza
Calabria	5,822	15,079	2,152,539	Catanzaro
Catanzaro	2,026	5,247	775,801	Catanzaro
Cosenza	2,567	6,648	785,187	Cosenza
Reggio di Calabria	1,229	3,183	591,551	Reggio di Calabria
Campania	5,250	13,598	5,808,705	Naples
Avellino	1,082	2,802	452,673	Avellino
Benevento	796	2,062	299,876	Benevento
Caserta	1,019	2,639	824,623	Caserta
Napoli	452	1,171	3,160,907	Naples
Salerno	1,901	4,924	1,070,626	Salerno
Emilia-Romagna	8,543	22,126	3,921,597	Bologna
Bologna	1,429	3,701	911,715	Bologna
Ferrara	1,016	2,631	366,323	Ferrara
Forlì	1,124	2,911	609,943	Forlì
Modena	1,039	2,691	600,120	Modena
Parma	1,332	3,450	394,603	Parma
Piacenza	1,000	2,590	270,147	Piacenza
Ravenna	718	1,860	351,530	Ravenna
Reggio nell'Emilia	885	2,292	417,216	Reggio nell'Emilia
Friuli-Venezia Giulia	3,028	7,842	1,202,877	Trieste
Gorizia	180	466	139,266	Gorizia
Pordenone	889	2,302	275,486	Pordenone
Trieste	81	210	263,908	Trieste
Udine	1,878	4,864	524,217	Udine
Lazio	6,642	17,203	5,170,672	Rome
Frosinone	1,251	3,240	485,536	Frosinone
Latina	869	2,251	475,191	Latina
Rieti	1,061	2,748	146,431	Rieti
Roma	2,066	5,351	3,784,001	Rome
Viterbo	1,395	3,613	279,513	Viterbo

\ə\ **abut** \ə\ matches \$^{ə}$\ kitten, Fr table \ər\ **further** \a\ **ash** \ā\ **ace** \ä\ **cot, cart** \à\ Fr bac \au̇\ **out** \b\ Span Avila \ch\ **chin** \e\ **bet** \ē\ **easy** \g\ **go** \i\ **hit** \ī\ **ice** \j\ **job** \k\ Ger **ich, Buch** \$^{n}$\ Fr vin \ŋ\ **sing** \ō\ **go** \ö\ **all** \ȯ\ **law** \œ\ Fr bœuf \œ̄\ Fr **feu** \ȯi\ **boy** \th\ **thin** \t͟h\ **this** \ü\ **loot** \u̇\ **foot** \ue\ Ger füllen \ue̅\ Fr **rue** \y\ **yet** \$^{y}$\ Fr digne \ˈdēn^{y}\, nuit \ˈnw^{y}ē\ \yü\ **few** \yu̇\ **fury** \zh\ **vision**

NAME	AREA (sq. mi.)	AREA (sq. km.)	POP. (1989c)	CAPITAL
Liguria	2,089	5,410	1,727,212	Genoa
Genova	707	1,831	984,733	Genoa
Imperia	446	1,155	219,918	Imperia
La Spezia	340	881	232,174	La Spezia
Savona	596	1,544	290,387	Savona
Lombardy	9,202	23,833	8,911,995	Milan
Bergamo	1,065	2,758	924,804	Bergamo
Brescia	1,837	4,758	1,039,548	Brescia
Como	798	2,067	790,789	Como
Cremona	684	1,772	327,536	Cremona
Mantova	903	2,339	370,460	Mantova
Milano	1,067	2,764	3,986,838	Milan
Pavia	1,145	2,966	496,753	Pavia
Sondrio	1,240	3,212	176,485	Sondrio
Varese	463	1,199	798,782	Varese
Marche	3,742	9,692	1,430,726	Ancona
Ancona	748	1,937	437,669	Ancona
Ascoli Piceno	806	2,088	361,136	Ascoli Piceno
Macerata	1,071	2,774	295,516	Macerata
Pesaro e Urbino	1,117	2,893	336,405	Pesaro
Molise	1,713	4,437	335,348	Campobasso
Campobasso	1,123	2,908	241,202	Campobasso
Isernia	590	1,528	94,146	Isernia
Piedmont	9,807	25,400	4,357,559	Turin
Alessandria	1,375	3,561	445,139	Alessandria
Asti	583	1,510	209,420	Asti
Cuneo	2,665	6,902	546,396	Cuneo
Novara	1,388	3,595	500,653	Novara
Torino	2,637	6,830	2,275,390	Turin
Vercelli	1,159	3,002	380,561	Vercelli
Puglia	7,469	19,345	4,069,359	Bari
Bari	1,980	5,128	1,538,195	Bari
Brindisi	709	1,836	409,965	Brindisi
Foggia	2,774	7,185	703,734	Foggia
Lecce	1,065	2,758	815,599	Lecce
Taranto	941	2,437	601,866	Taranto
Sardinia	9,301	24,090	1,657,562	Cagliari
Cagliari	2,662	6,894	767,728	Cagliari
Nuoro	2,720	7,045	276,820	Nuoro
Oristano	1,016	2,631	160,028	Oristano
Sassari	2,903	7,519	452,986	Sassari
Sicily	9,925	25,706	5,172,785	Palermo
Agrigento	1,174	3,041	492,701	Agrigento
Caltanissetta	813	2,106	293,485	Caltanissetta
Catania	1,372	3,553	1,080,336	Catania
Enna	989	2,562	197,077	Enna
Messina	1,253	3,245	695,656	Messina
Palermo	1,937	5,017	1,268,047	Palermo
Ragusa	623	1,614	292,989	Ragusa
Siracusa	814	2,108	413,073	Siracusa
Trapani	950	2,460	439,421	Trapani
Trentino-Alto Adige	5,256	13,613	886,679	Trento
Bolzano	2,857	7,400	439,765	Bolzano
Trento	2,399	6,213	446,914	Trento
Tuscany	8,876	22,989	3,560,582	Florence
Arezzo	1,248	3,232	313,723	Arezzo
Firenze	1,498	3,880	1,192,967	Florence
Grosseto	1,736	4,496	219,808	Grosseto
Livorno	471	1,220	342,554	Livorno
Lucca	684	1,772	381,276	Lucca
Massa-Carrara	446	1,155	204,552	Massa
Pisa	945	2,448	387,724	Pisa
Pistoia	373	966	266,103	Pistoia
Siena	1,475	3,820	251,875	Siena
Umbria	3,265	8,456	820,316	Perugia
Perugia	2,446	6,335	595,089	Perugia
Terni	819	2,121	225,227	Terni
Valle d'Aosta	1,260	3,263	115,270	Aosta
Veneto	7,096	18,379	4,385,023	Venice
Belluno	1,420	3,678	214,495	Belluno
Padova	827	2,142	819,822	Padova
Rovigo	696	1,803	248,670	Rovigo
Treviso	956	2,476	738,905	Treviso
Venezia	950	2,460	831,645	Venice
Verona	1,196	3,098	787,722	Verona
Vicenza	1,051	2,722	743,764	Vicenza

History: For earlier history, see ETRURIA, ROME, and ROMAN EMPIRE; after barbarian invasions of 4th and 5th cents. A.D., Germanic kingdoms estab. by Ostrogoths and later by Lombards; S part remained longest under nominal Byzantine rule; in midst of disorder, Papacy at Rome founded its position as political arbiter of medieval Italy; part of Carolingian empire 774 and of Holy Roman Empire (*q.v.*) from 962; primarily in N Italy in course of struggle bet. papal and imperial authority (Guelph versus Ghibelline), the Italian communes such as Milan and Florence (*qq.v.*) obtained independence, built up petty states, and became commercial and political rivals; S Italy (see NAPLES and SICILY) ruled by foreign dynasties; c. 1000, Venice (*q.v.*) began its territorial expansion; experienced period of marked political disunity during late Middle Ages; in the vanguard of European cultural movements 14th–16th cents. with such leading figures as the poets Dante and Petrarch, the writer Giovanni Boccaccio, and the painter Giotto; scene of Italian Wars 16th cent.; a struggle for power bet. Hapsburg (imperial and Spanish) and Valois (French) forces; Hapsburg predominance temporarily broken and territorial consolidation effected by French Emperor Napoléon I who erected kingdom of Italy (included Venice and Cisalpine Republic) 1805 and finally incorp. in France Piedmont, Genoa, Parma, Lucca, Tuscany, and Papal States; from 1815–70, Italian unification movement (Risorgimento) sparked widespread revolutionary activity; most of Italy unified by 1861; unification completed with annexation of Venetia (1866) and Rome (1870); member of Triple Alliance 1882–1915; undertook colonial expansion (see ERITREA, ETHIOPIA, ADWA, ITALIAN SOMALILAND, LIBYA, and TRIPOLI); at war with Turkey 1911–12; entered WWI on side of Allies 1915; government seized by Fascists under Benito Mussolini in "March on Rome" 1922; annexed Fiume (see RIJEKA) 1924; abolished parliamentary institutions for rule by Fascist Grand Council 1928; made peace with Papacy (see VATICAN CITY) 1929; conquered Ethiopia 1935–36; occupied Albania (*q.v.*) 1939; became military and political ally of Germany 1939; entered WWII 1940; invaded by Allies 1943 and its Fascist government overthrown; German resistance strong in cen. part 1943–45 (battles of Salerno, Cassino, Anzio; Rome taken June 4, 1944); became republic June 1946; lost Dodecanese to Greece and territory on borders to France and Yugoslavia as provided for by treaty of Feb. 10, 1947; member of NATO 1949, UN 1955, and EEC 1958; completed process of setting up regional legislatures with limited autonomy 1970; since WWII has had rapid change of governments, but country has remained stable; severe earthquake S Italy 1980; in late 20th cent. began working with other European nations toward EC.

Ita·mi \ē-'tä-mē\. City, Hyogo prefecture, W Honshū, Japan; pop. (1990p) 186,132.

Ita·na·gar \,ē-tə-'nə-gər\. Town, ✻ of Arunachal Pradesh state, India.

Ita·ny \,ē-tä-'nē\. Upper tributary of Maroni River, N South America, forming section of boundary bet. French Guiana and Suriname.

Ita·pa·ri·ca \,ē-tä-pä-'rē-kə\. Island in Atlantic Ocean, off Bahia state, Brazil, at entrance to All Saints Bay.

Ita·pe·cu·ru \,ē-tä-,pā-kü-'rü\. River, Maranhão state, NE Brazil; flows N into São José Bay; ab. 450 mi. (724 km.) long.

Ita·pe·ru·na \,ē-tä-pē-'rü-nə\. City, Rio de Janeiro state, SE Brazil, 150 mi. (241 km.) NE of the city of Rio de Janeiro; munic. pop. (1991p) 78,015.

Ita·pe·ti·nin·ga \,ē-tä-,pā-tē-'niŋ-gə\. City, São Paulo state, SE Brazil, 85 mi. (137 km.) W of the city of São Paulo; munic. pop. (1991p) 105,049.

Ita·pi·cu·ru \,ē-tä-,pē-kü-'rü\. River, Bahia state, E Brazil; flows SE to Atlantic Ocean; ab. 250 mi. (402 km.) long.

Ita·pi·po·ca \,ē-tä-pē-'pō-kə\. Municipality, Ceará state, NE Brazil; pop. (1991p) 77,225.

Ita·pi·ra \,ē-tä-'pē-rə\. City, São Paulo state, SE Brazil, ab. 40 mi. (64 km.) NE of Campinas; munic. pop. (1991p) 56,505.

Ita·púa \,ē-tä-'pü-ä\. Department of SE Paraguay. See table at PARAGUAY.

Itar·si \i-'tär-sē\. Town, Madhya Pradesh, cen. India, SE of Bhopal; pop. (1991p) 78,700.

Itas·ca \ī-'tas-kə\. **1.** County in N Minnesota. See table at MINNESOTA.

2. Village, Du Page co., NE Illinois, ab. 3 mi. (4.8 km.) W of O'Hare International Airport; pop. (1990c) 6947.

Itasca, Lake. Lake in SE Clearwater co., N Minnesota; 2 sq. mi. (5 sq. km.); elev. 1475 ft. (450 m.); estab. as source of Mississippi River by Henry Schoolcraft in 1832; in **Itasca State Park** (35 sq. mi. or 91 sq. km.).

Ita·ta \ē-'tä-tä\. River, S cen. Chile, N of Concepción, flowing into Pacific Ocean; 110 mi. (177 km.) long.

Ita·ti·a·ia National Park \,ē-tä-'tyī-ə\. National park, oldest one in Brazil, on Serra da Mantiqueira, on border of Minas

ITALY
CITIES
Over 1,000,000
200,000 to 1,000,000
50,000 to 200,000
Under 50,000
Other localities
National capital
Regional capital
BOUNDARIES
International
Regional
FEATURES
Canals
Dams
Points of interest
GERMANY
AUSTRIA
SWITZERLAND
LIECHTENSTEIN
FRANCE
MONACO
SAN MARINO
VATICAN CITY
SLOVENIA
CROATIA
BOSNIA AND HERZEGOVINA
YUGOSLAVIA
ALGERIA
TUNISIA
MALTA
CORSICA (Fr.)
A L P S
A P E N N I N E S
A D R I A T I C S E A
LIGURIAN SEA
TYRRHENIAN SEA
IONIAN SEA
M E D I T E R R A N E A N S E A
Basel
Zürich
Bern
Vaduz
Innsbruck
Salzburg
Graz
Brenner Pass
Ljubljana
Zagreb
Geneva
Split
Sarajevo
Nice
Monaco
Annaba
Tunis
Tébessa
Safaqis
Valletta
TRENTINO-ALTO ADIGE
FRIULI-VENEZIA GIULIA
VALLE D'AOSTA
LOMBARDY
VENETO
PIEDMONT
LIGURIA
EMILIA-ROMAGNA
TUSCANY
MARCHE
UMBRIA
LATIUM
ABRUZZI
MOLISE
CAMPANIA
PUGLIA
BASILICATA
CALABRIA
SICILY
SARDINIA
RHAETIAN ALPS
DOLOMITES
GRAIAN ALPS
COTTIAN ALPS
MARITIME ALPS
LIGURIAN APENNINES
TUSCAN APENNINES
APUAN ALPS-APENNINES
UMBRIAN APENNINES
ABRUZZI
CAMPANIAN APENNINES
LUCANIAN APENNINES
CALABRIAN APENNINES
CILENTO MTS
KRAS PLATEAU
Mont Blanc 15,771 ft.
Monte Rosa 11,500 ft.
Lake Maggiore
Lake Como
Lake Garda
STELVIO NATIONAL PARK
ADAMELLO NATURE PARK
GRAN PARADISO NATIONAL PARK
TICINO VALLEY NATURE PARK
Merano
Bolzano
Trento
Belluno
Feltre
Udine
Cividale del Friuli
Gorizia
Monfalcone
Trieste
Pordenone
Portogruaro
Treviso
Venice
Gulf of Venice
Padua
Vicenza
Verona
Mantua
Montagnana
Rovigo
Adria
Aosta
Stresa
Varese
Como
Lecco
Bergamo
Biella
Legnano
Monza
Gorgonzola
Novara
Milan
Brescia
Vercelli
Vigevano
Voghera
Cremona
Piacenza
Dora Riparia
Rivoli
Turin
Moncalieri
Asti
Alessandria
Saluzzo
Alba
Novi Ligure
Fossano
Cuneo
Genoa
Savona
Chiavari
Portofino
Cadibona Pass
Imperia
San Remo
Ventimiglia
Gulf of Genoa
La Spezia
Parma
Reggio nell'Emilia
Modena
Ferrara
Argenta
Bologna
Lake Comacchio
Ravenna
Imola
Faenza
Forlì
Cesena
Massa
Viareggio
Pistoia
Prato
Florence
Pisa
Arno
Cascina
Empoli
Leghorn
Volterra
Larderello
Siena
Cortona
Arezzo
Sansepolcro
Urbino
San Marino
Pesaro
Senigallia
Iesi
Ancona
Mount Conero 1,876 ft.
Gubbio
Macerata
Chienti
Fermo
Lake Trasimeno
Perugia
Piombino
Grosseto
Mount Amiata 5,700 ft.
Orvieto
Terni
Ascoli Piceno
Teramo
Atri
Pescara
Chieti
Ortona
Lanciano
Vasto
Sulmona
Lake Bolsena
Tuscania
Viterbo
Rieti
Civita Castellana
L'Aquila
Tarquinia
Civitavecchia
Rome
Tiber
Vatican City
Tivoli
Avezzano
Marino
Anagni
Sora
Frosinone
Cassino
Cori
Latina
Fondi
Terracina
Monte Circeo 1,775 ft.
Agro Pontino
ABRUZZI NATIONAL PARK
Isernia
Campobasso
Fortore
Volturno
Liri
San Severo
Lake Varano
Manfredonia
Gulf of Manfredonia
Foggia
Cerignola
Barletta
Molfetta
Andria
Bari
Venosa
Altamura
Matera
Bradano
SALENTINA PENINSULA
Brindisi
Taranto
Lecce
Nardò
Otranto
Strait of Otranto
Gulf of Taranto
Benevento
Caserta
Aversa
Gulf of Gaeta
Naples
Portici
Avellino
Vesuvius 4,189 ft.
Torre del Greco
Castellammare di Stabia
Salerno
Gulf of Salerno
Potenza
Gulf of Policastro
POLLINO NATURE PARK
Monte Pollino 7,375 ft.
Crati
Cosenza
Crotone
Catanzaro
Vibo Valentia
Messina
Reggio di Calabria
Strait of Messina
CAPRI
ELBA ISLAND
PIANOSA ISLAND
GIGLIO ISLAND
MONTECRISTO ISLAND
PONZA ISLANDS
USTICA ISLAND
LIPARI ISLANDS
STROMBOLI ISLAND
FILICUDI ISLAND
ALICUDI ISLAND
SALINA ISLAND
LIPARI ISLAND
VULCANO ISLAND
ISOLE EGADI
PANTELLERIA ISLAND
PELAGIE ISLANDS
LINOSA ISLAND
LAMPIONE ISLAND
LAMPEDUSA ISLAND
Strait of Bonifacio
MADDALENA ISLAND
CAPRERA ISLAND
ASINARA ISLAND
Gulf of Asinara
Mount Limbara 4,456 ft.
Porto Torres
Sassari
Neptune's Cave
Nuoro
Bue Marino Cove
Mount Marmora 6,016 ft.
Oristano
Tirso
CAMPIDANO PLAIN
Iglesias
Carbonia
SAN PIETRO
SANT'ANTIOCO
Sarroch
Cagliari
Gulf of Cagliari
Cape Teulada
Palermo
Bagheria
Cefalù
Alcamo
Trapani
Segesta
Corleone
Marsala
Mazara del Vallo
Sciacca
Enna
Paternò
Bronte
Mount Etna 13,800 ft.
Catania
Gulf of Catania
PLAIN OF CATANIA
Caltanissetta
Salso
Agrigento
Piazza Armerina
Gela
Vittoria
Ragusa
Siracusa
Avola
Scicli
0 40 80 mi
0 60 120 km
©2000, Encyclopædia Britannica, Inc.

Gerais and Rio de Janeiro states; 46 sq. mi. (119 sq. km.); mountain range, lakes; estab. 1937.

It·a·wam·ba \ˌi-tə-ˈwäm-bə\. County in NE Mississippi. See table at MISSISSIPPI.

It·ba·yat \ēt-ˈbī-ˌät\. Island, largest of Batan Is., N Philippines; 33 sq. mi. (85 sq. km.).

Itch·en \ˈi-chin\. River, Hampshire, S England; empties into Southampton Water.

Iténez. See GUAPORÉ 1.

Ith·a·ca \ˈi-thi-kə\. **1.** City, ⊗ of Gratiot co., cen. Michigan, 24 mi. (39 km.) S of Mount Pleasant; pop. (1990c) 3009.

2. City, ⊗ of Tompkins co., S cen. New York, on S end of Cayuga Lake 29 mi. (47 km.) NE of Elmira; pop. (1990c) 29,541; salt; textiles; tourism; Cornell Univ. (1865), Ithaca Coll. (1892); settled 1789; became city 1888.

3. *or Gk.* **Ithá·ki** \ē-ˈthä-kē\. One of the Ionian Is., in the Ionian Sea off W coast of Greece and just NE of Cephalonia; 37 sq. mi. (96 sq. km.); with Cephalonia I. forms Cephalonia dept. (see table at GREECE). Consists of two mountain groups (highest point 2650 ft. or 808 m.) with narrow isthmus between; chief products olive oil, currants, and wine; generally identified in Greek mythology as home of the poet Homer's Odysseus; occupied by Germans 1941; suffered severe earthquake 1953; since rebuilt.

4. Chief town of Ithaca I., Greece; on E coast.

Ithome. See MESSENE 1.

Ito·gon \ē-ˈtō-ˌgän\. Municipality, Mountain prov., Luzon, Philippines; pop. (1980c) 47,605.

Itonamas. See SAN MIGUEL 1.

Itsu·ku–shi·ma \ˌēt-su̇-ˈku̇-shē-mä\. **1.** *also* **Mi·ya·ji·ma** \ˌmē-yä-ˈjē-mä\. Island in N inlet of the Inland Sea, Hiroshima prefecture, SW Honshū, Japan, ab. 12 mi. (19 km.) SW of the city of Hiroshima; ab. 5 mi. (8 km.) long by 2.5 mi. (4 km.) wide; highest point Mi-sen 1738 ft. (530 m.). One of the most scenic spots in Japan, has many noteworthy structures, incl. a Shinto shrine and torii, a Buddhist temple, and a pagoda. Of ancient origin.

2. Town on NW coast of island. See MIYAJIMA 2.

It·ta Be·na \ˌi-tə-ˈbē-nə\. Town, Leflore co., W Mississippi, 9 mi. (14 km.) W of Greenwood; pop. (1990c) 2377; Mississippi Valley State Univ. (1946).

Ittahad, Al–. See MADINAT ASH SHA'B.

It·toq·qor·toor·miit \ˌē-tȯk-kȯr-ˈtōr-ˌmēt\ *or* **Scores·by·sund** \ˈskōrz-bē-ˌsu̇n\. Settlement, E Greenland, at entrance to Scoresby Sound; area pop. (1993e) 527; estab. 1924.

Itu \ē-ˈtü\. City, São Paulo state, SE Brazil, on Tietê River 45 mi. (72 km.) NW of the city of São Paulo; munic. pop. (1991p) 106,872.

Itu·iu·ta·ba \ē-ˌtü-yü-ˈtä-bə\. Municipality, Minas Gerais state, E Brazil, 240 mi. (386 km.) SSW of Brasília; pop. (1991p) 84,584.

Itum·bi·a·ra \ˌē-tu̇m-ˈbyär-ə\. Municipality, Goiás state, central E Brazil, 120 mi. (193 km.) S of Goiânia; pop. (1991p) 79,457.

It·u·raea *or* **It·u·rea** \ˌi-tyu̇-ˈrē-ə\. Ancient country in NE part of Palestine, S of Damascus; part conquered and annexed to Judaea c. 106 B.C. by Aristobulus I; later in first cent. A.D. formed part of the domain of Philip the Tetrarch.

Itu·ri \ē-ˈtü-rē\. River, Democratic Rep. of the Congo; upper course of the Aruwimi (*q.v.*).

Itu·rup \ˌē-tü-ˈrüp\ *or Jp.* **Eto·ro·fu** \ˌe-tō-ˈrō-fü\ *also* **Ye·to·ro·fu** \ˌyā-\. Largest of the Kuril Is. (*q.v.*), Russia in Asia, at S end NE of Hokkaidō, Japan; 140 mi. (225 km.) long; 2587 sq. mi. (6700 sq. km.); chief town Kurilsk; occupied by U.S.S.R. (and now by Russia) since WWII; claimed by Japan.

Itu·zain·gó \ˌē-tü-sīŋ-ˈgō\. Town, NE Argentina, on Paraná River ab. 50 mi. (80 km.) W of Posadas; pop. (1980p) 8687; scene of battle 1827 in which Brazilian forces were decisively defeated by Argentine and Uruguayan forces under Carlos Maria de Alvear.

It·ze·hoe \ˈit-sə-ˌhō\. Seaport city, Schleswig-Holstein, Germany, 33 mi. (53 km.) NW of Hamburg; pop. (1980c) 33,613; commercial center; nets, machinery, cement; founded c. 810; became city 1238.

Iu·ka \ī-ˈyü-kə\. Town, ⊗ of Tishomingo co., NE corner of Mississippi, 20 mi. (32 km.) ESE of Corinth; pop. (1990c) 3122; resort; scene of battle Sept. 1862, when Union troops under Gen. William Stark Rosecrans successfully attacked a Confederate force under Gen. Sterling Price.

Ivaí \ˌē-vȧ-ˈē\. River, S Brazil; flows NW in Paraná state into Paraná River; 400 mi. (644 km.) long.

Ivangorod. See DĘBLIN.

Ivan·hoe \ˈī-vən-ˌhō\. Village, ⊗ of Lincoln co., SW Minnesota, 22 mi. (35 km.) W of Marshall; pop. (1990c) 751.

Iva·no–Fran·kivs'k \i-ˈvä-nȯ-fräŋ-ˈkifsk\. **1.** *formerly* **Sta·nis·lav Oblast** \ˌstȧ-ni-ˈsläf-ˈȯ-bləst, -ˌblast\. Administrative subdivision of Ukraine; 5367 sq. mi. (13,901 sq. km.); pop. (1991e) 1,442,900; ✻ Ivano-Frankivs'k; formerly part of Poland.

2. *formerly* **Sta·nis·lav** \ˌstȧ-ni-ˈsläf\ *or Pol.* **Sta·nis·ła·wów** \ˌstä-nē-ˈswä-vu̇f\ *or Ger.* **Sta·nis·lau** \ˈstä-nis-ˌlau̇\. City, ✻ of Ivano-Frankivs'k administrative subdivision, Ukraine; pop. (1991e) 226,000; furniture and other woodworking products, food products; engineering.

History: Long a center of fighting among many armies; in WWI scene of much fighting in 1915 and 1916 when it changed hands several times bet. Russians and Austrians; in July 1917 taken by Central Powers; occupied in WWII by U.S.S.R. 1939, by Germany 1941, and again by U.S.S.R. 1944.

Iva·nov Industrial Area \ˌē-vȧ-ˈnȯf\. Former subdivision of Russian S.F.S.R., U.S.S.R., in cen. part NE of Moscow; divided 1929 into Ivanovo Oblast and Yaroslavl' Oblast.

Iva·no·vo \ē-ˈvä-nə-və\; *before 1932* **Ivanovo Voz·ne·sensk** \ˌvəz-nə-ˈsensk\. City, ✻ of Ivanovo Oblast, cen. Russia in Europe, S of the Volga, ab. 145 mi. (233 km.) NE of Moscow; pop. (1992e) 480,000; textile factories, esp. cotton; textile machinery; formed 1871 by incorporating two villages, one of which was named Ivanovo; large worker population active in Revolutionary movement 1917–18.

Ivanovo Oblast \ˈȯ-bləst, -ˌblast\ *or* **Iva·nov·ska·ya Oblast'** \ˌē-və-ˈnȯf-skə-yə\. Subdivision of cen. Russia in Europe; 9228 sq. mi. (23,901 sq. km.); pop. (1992e) 1,312,000; ✻ Ivanovo; crossed by the Volga; N of the Volga is heavily forested, S of it is agricultural land; oats, potatoes; formerly part of Ivanov Industrial Area, in extensive plain of Volga, Oka, and Klyaz'ma rivers; created 1929.

Ivin·hei·ma \ˌē-vi-ˈnyā-mə\. River, S Mato Grosso state, SW Brazil; flows SE into Paraná River; ab. 200 mi. (320 km.) long.

Ivit·tuut \ˈē-vit-ˌtüt\ *or* **Ivig·tut** \ˈē-vig-ˌtüt\. Settlement on SW coast of Greenland; pop. (1991e) 4; important cryolite deposits now exhausted.

Iviza. See IBIZA.

Ivo·ry Coast \ˈī-və-rē\ *or* **Côte d'Ivoire;** *officially* **Republic of Côte d'Ivoire** \ˌkōt-dē-ˈvwär\. **1.** Republic, W Africa, bounded on N by Mali and Burkina Faso, on E by Ghana, on S by the Atlantic Ocean, and on W by Liberia and Guinea; 124,503 sq. mi. (322,463 sq. km.); pop. (1993e) 13,459,000; official ✻ Yamoussoukro; seat of government Abidjan.

Physical features: Coastline bordered with lagoons; coastal plain in the S part gradually slopes to plateau in cen. part; hilly in W and NW; highest peak Mt. Nimba 6069 ft. (1850 m.); watered by the Bandama and Sassandra rivers and upper tributaries of Volta and Niger.

Chief products: Corn, palm kernels, coffee, cocoa, rice, bananas, pineapples, rubber, timber; diamonds; fishing; manufacturing: textiles; food processing; sawmilling.

Chief towns: Abidjan, Bouaké, Daloa, Yamoussoukro, Korhogo.

History: Area inhabited by powerful native kingdoms before coming of Europeans; from early 19th cent. French had influence with native rulers of Ivory Coast; in 1889 formal French protectorate estab.; made a colony 1893; later included in reorganized French West Africa; received larger part of Upper Volta (now Burkina Faso *q.v.*) 1933; given territorial status by French Constitution of 1946; lost Upper Volta 1947; became an autonomous republic within the French Community 1958; achieved independence 1960; although

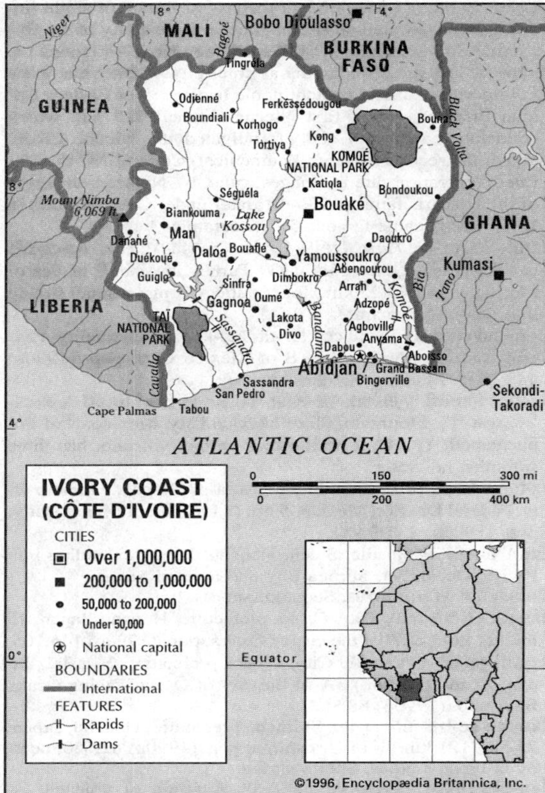

stable during early years of independence, country's economy and political structure subject to social unrest during late 20th cent.

2. Atlantic coast along Ivory Coast (republic), W of Ghana, ab. 2°30′W to 7°30′W long—so called because in early years much frequented by traders for ivory.

Ivrea \ē-'vrā-ä\; *anc.* **Ep·o·re·dia** \ˌe-pə-'rē-dē-ə\. Commune, Torino prov., Piedmont, NW Italy, 32 mi. (51 km.) ESE of Aosta; pop. (1991p) 24,546; textiles, typewriters; 11th cent. cathedral; 14th cent. castle; scene of action in French Emperor Napoléon's Italian campaign 1800.

Ivry–la–Ba·taille \ē-ˌvrē-là-bà-'tī\. Commune, Eure dept., N France, on Eure River 40 mi. (64 km.) W of Paris; scene of decisive victory of Huguenots under Henry IV over Catholics under Charles de Lorraine, duc de Mayenne, 1590.

Ivry–sur–Seine \ē-ˌvrē-sᵫr-'sān, -'sen\. Commune and river port, Val-de-Marne dept., N France, SE suburb of Paris on Seine River; pop. (1990c) 54,106; chemicals.

Ivy Lea. See THOUSAND ISLANDS 1.

Iwa·ki \ē-'wä-kē\. **1.** River, Aomori prefecture, N Honshū, Japan; flows N to Sea of Japan; ab. 50 mi. (80 km.) long.

2. *formerly* **Tai·ra** \'tī-rä\. City, Fukushima prefecture, Honshū, Japan; pop. (1990p) 355,817.

Iwaki, Mount *or Jp.* **Iwaki–yama** \-'yä-mä\. Peak, Aomori prefecture, N Honshū, Japan, NW of Hirosaki; 5330 ft. (1625 m.).

Iwa·ku·ni \ˌē-wä-'kü-nē\. City, Yamaguchi prefecture, Honshū, Japan; pop. (1990p) 109,534; international airport.

Iwa·mi·za·wa \ē-ˌwä-mē-'zä-wä\. Town, W Hokkaidō, Japan, 25 mi. (40 km.) ENE of Sapporo; pop. (1990p) 80,423; railroad junction; formerly, center for nearby coal mines.

Iwa·ta \ē-'wä-tä\. City, Shizuoka prefecture, Honshū, Japan, 8 mi. (12.8 km.) E of Hamamatsu; pop. (1990p) 83,521.

Iwa·te \ē-'wä-tā\. **1.** *or Jp.* **Iwa·te–ya·ma** \-'yä-mä\. Mountain, Iwate prefecture, N Honshū, Japan, just N of Morioka; 6694 ft. (2040 m.); a dormant volcano with ancient crater in which are shrines often visited by pilgrims.

2. Prefecture, Honshū, Japan; ✻ Morioka; rice; fishing; contains coastal and mountain national parks. See table at JAPAN.

Iwa·tsu·ki \ē-'wä-tsü-kē\. City, Saitama prefecture, Honshū, Japan; pop. (1990p) 106,462.

Iwo \'ē-wō\. City, SW Nigeria, on railroad line just NE of Ibadan; pop. (1991e) 319,500; cacao produced nearby.

Iwo Islands. See VOLCANO ISLANDS.

Iwo Ji·ma \'ē-wō-'jē-mä\ *or commonly shortened to* **Iwo** \'ē-wō\. Center island of the three in the Volcano Is., Japan; 660 naut. mi. (759 statute mi. or 1221 km.) S of Tokyo; small volcanic island 5.5 mi. (9 km.) long, max. width 2.5 mi. (4 km.), 8 sq. mi. (21 sq. km.). Scene of one of severest campaigns in U.S. history; bombed by U.S. planes Dec. 1944, Jan. and Feb. 1945; invaded by U.S. marines Feb. 19; Mt. Suribachi at S end seized Feb. 23; Motoyama airfields taken late Feb., and island finally completely taken by mid-Mar.; returned to Japan 1968.

Iwo Rettō. See VOLCANO ISLANDS.

Ix·elles \ēk-'sel\. Commune, Brabant prov., cen. Belgium, a suburb of Brussels; pop. (1991c) 72,610.

Ix·huat·lán de Ma·de·ro \ˌēs-wät-'län-t͟hā-mä-'t͟hā-rō\. Municipality, Veracruz state, Mexico, 55 mi. (88 km.) W of the city of Veracruz.

Ix·mi·quil·pan \ˌēs-mē-'kēl-ˌpän\. Municipality, Hidalgo state, Mexico, 44 mi. (71 km.) NW of Pachuca; pop. (1990p) 65,574; area first entered by Spanish 1530.

Ixtacalco. See IZTACALCO.

Ixtacihuatl. See IZTACCÍHUATL.

Ixtapalapa. See IZTAPALAPA.

Ix·tlán de Juá·rez \ēst-'län-t͟hā-'wä-rās\. Municipality, Oaxaca state, Mexico, 25 mi. (40 km.) NE of the city of Oaxaca.

Iyo Sea \'ē-yō\. Open body of water forming SW part of Inland Sea, Japan, bet. Shikoku and Kyūshū, Japan; connected with Pacific Ocean by Bungo Strait.

Iza·bal \ˌē-sä-'b͟äl\. Department of E Guatemala. See table at GUATEMALA.

Izabal, Lake *also* **Lake Yza·bal** \ˌē-sä-'b͟äl\; *formerly* **Dul·ce Gulf** \'dül-sā\. Lake, E Guatemala; drains through Dulce River (*q.v.*).

Izal·co \ē-'säl-kō\. **1.** Volcano, Sonsonate dept., El Salvador, ab. 10 mi. (16 km.) N of the city of Sonsonate; 7828 ft. (2386 m.); created 1770 by eruption from side of Santa Ana Volcano; has shown frequent activity.

2. City at foot of the volcano; pop. (1986e) 54,415.

Iz·ard \'i-zərd\. County in N Arkansas. See table at ARKANSAS.

Ize·gem \'ē-zə-k͟əm\; *formerly* **Ise·ghem** \'ē-sə-k͟əm\. Commune, West Flanders prov., NW Belgium, 25 mi. (40 km.) SW of Ghent; pop. (1991c) 26,462.

Izhevsk \'ē-ˌzhefsk\; *1985–87* **Us·ti·nov** \'ü-sti-ˌnȯf\. Town, ✻ of Udmurtia, E Russia in Europe; 175 mi. (282 km.) ENE of Kazan'; pop. (1992e) 651,000; on tributary of Kama River and on branch railroad; steel, armaments; founded 1760.

Izh·ma \'ēzh-mə, 'izh-\. Navigable river, N Russia in Europe; flows N in cen. Komi Rep.; ab. 180 mi. (290 km.) long; a W tributary of the Pechora.

Iz·ma·il \'iz-mē-əl, ˌis-mə-'ēl\ *or Rom.* **Is·ma·il** \ˌē-smä-'ēl, 'iz-mē-əl\. **1.** Former department, Romania. See ISMAIL 1.

2. *or* **Iz·may·il** \ˌē-smä-'ēl, 'iz-mē-əl\. City, Odessa administrative subdivision, Ukraine, on N side of Danube Delta ab. 45 mi. (72 km.) from Black Sea; pop. (1991e) 95,000; formerly a Turkish fort; occupied by Russia 1770 and 1790, and ceded to Russia 1812; since 1812 transferred several times: Moldavian 1856–78; Russian 1878–1918; Romanian 1918–40; Russian 1940–91, although from 1941 to 1944 held by Axis forces.

Izmail Oblast \ˈö-bləst, -ˌblast\. Former administrative subdivision, Ukrainian S.S.R., U.S.S.R., S part of former Bessarabia bordering on Black Sea SW of Odessa and on Danube Delta; chief towns Izmail, its ✻, and Belgorod-Dnestrovski; organized 1945; incorp. into what is now Odessa subdivision 1954.

İz·mir \iz-ˈmir\; *formerly* **Smyr·na** \ˈsmər-nə\. **1.** Province of Turkey in Asia. See table at TURKEY.

2. Seaport city, its ✻, at head of Gulf of İzmir; pop. (1990c) 1,757,414; Turkey's 3d largest city and its most important port in Asia; large harbor; exports include tobacco, carpets, and cotton; university (1955); connected by rail with Bandırma, İstanbul, Aydın, and through Konya with E Turkey.

History: Ancient Smyrna an Aeolian and later Ionian town; destroyed c. 600 B.C. by Alyattes, king of Lydia; new city built by Macedonian King Antigonus I in 4th cent. B.C. and improved by Macedonian Gen. Lysimachus; taken by Romans, it belonged mostly to Byzantine Empire; held for a time by Hospitallers prior to Turkish conquest in 15th cent.; occupied by Greeks 1919 and temporarily ceded to them 1920; recaptured by Turkish Nationalists 1922; nearly destroyed by fire Sept. 1922 and badly damaged by earthquakes 1928 and later.

İzmir, Gulf of; *formerly* **Gulf of Smyr·na** \ˈsmər-nə\; *anc.* **Si·nus Smyr·nae·us** \ˈsī-nəs-ˌsmər-ˈnē-əs\. Large irregular inlet of Aegean Sea, Turkey in Asia, N of the peninsula opp. Chios I.; extends inland ab. 40 mi. (64 km.); breadth at entrance 13 mi. (21 km.); city of İzmir is at its head.

İz·mit *or* **Is·mid** \iz-ˈmit\ *or* **Ko·ca·e·li** \kö-ˈjī-lē\; *anc.* **As·ta·cus** \ˈas-tə-kəs\; *later* **Nic·o·me·dia** \ˌni-kə-ˈmēd-ē-ə\. Town, ✻ of Kocaeli prov., NW Turkey in Asia, on Gulf of İzmit on railroad line 54 mi. (87 km.) ESE of İstanbul; pop. (1990c) 256,882; papermills; chemicals; oil refining; 16th cent. mosque; seat of a Greek metropolitan and an Armenian archbishop; founded by ancient Megarians as Astacus, but later destroyed by Macedonian Gen. Lysimachus; on neighboring site Nicomedia built c. 264 B.C. by Nicomedes I of Bithynia as his new ✻; important center later in Eastern Roman (Byzantine) Empire.

İzmit, Gulf of *or* **Gulf of Ismid.** Inlet of E Sea of Marmara on NW coast of Turkey in Asia.

İz·nik \iz-ˈnik\; *anc.* **Ni·caea** \nī-ˈsē-ə\ *or angl.* **Nice** \ˈnīs\. Village, Bursa prov., NW Turkey in Asia, at E end of İznik Lake, 39 mi. (63 km.) ENE of the city of Bursa; of slight importance but located on site of Nicaea, a great city of the Byzantine Empire; founded by Macedonian King Antigonus I c. 316 B.C.; rival of Nicomedia as chief city of Bithynia; grew in importance after Constantinople became ✻ of Eastern Roman Empire; seat of first Nicene Council 325 A.D. which condemned Arianism and promulgated the Nicene Creed, and of the second (seventh Ecumenical) Council 787 that defined veneration due to images; ruled by Nicaean emperors of the Lascaris family 1206–61; later under Ottoman rule; in 16th cent. became famous for its ceramics.

İznik Lake *or Turk.* **İznik Gö·lü** \gœ-ˈlue\; *anc.* **As·ca·nia** \as-ˈkā-nē-ə\. Lake (*gölü*), NW Turkey in Asia, E of Sea of Marmara; 14 mi. (23 km.) long; outlet through a small stream into Sea of Marmara.

Iz·ta·cal·co *or* **Ix·ta·cal·co** \ˌēs-tä-ˈkäl-kō\. Municipality, Federal District, Mexico, just S of Mexico City; pop. (1990p) 448,357; "Floating Gardens" nearby.

Iz·tac·cí·huatl \ˌēs-täk-ˈsē-ˌwät-ᵊl\ *or* **Ix·ta·ci·huatl** \ˌēs-tä-ˈsē-ˌwät-ᵊl\. Mountain, SE of Mexico City, Mexico, N of Popocatepétl; 17,343 ft. (5286 m.); extinct volcano, has three summits, no crater.

Iz·ta·pa·la·pa *or* **Ix·ta·pa·la·pa** \ˌēs-tä-pä-ˈlä-pä\. Municipality, Federal District, Mexico, 5 mi. (8 km.) SE of Mexico City; pop. (1990p) 1,490,981.

Izu \ˈē-zü\. Peninsula, S cen. Honshū, Japan, extending into Pacific Ocean bet. Suruga Bay and Sagami Sea.

Izúcar de Matamoros. See MATAMOROS 2.

Izu·mi \ē-ˈzü-mē\. City, Ōsaka prefecture, Honshū, Japan, 15 mi. (24 km.) SSW of the city of Ōsaka; pop. (1990p) 146,105.

Izumi–sa·no \-ˈsä-nō\. City, Ōsaka prefecture, Honshū, Japan, 22 mi. (35 km.) SW of the city of Ōsaka, facing Ōsaka Bay; pop. (1990p) 88,862.

Izu·mo \ē-ˈzü-mō\. City, Shimane prefecture, Honshū, Japan, 75 mi. (121 km.) N of Hiroshima; pop. (1990p) 82,680; nearby is Japan's oldest Shinto shrine.

Izu–shi·chi·tō \ˈē-zü-ˈshē-chē-ˌtō\. A group of volcanic islands, seven main ones, in Pacific Ocean off Izu Penin. on SE coast of Honshū, Japan, S of Yokohama.

Izyum \i-ˈzyüm\. Town, Kharkiv administrative subdivision, Ukraine, on Donets River 75 mi. (121 km.) SE of the city of Kharkiv; pop. (1991e) 65,000; held by Germans 1942–43.

J

Jabal. See JEBEL.
Jabal ad Durūz. See DRUZE, JEBEL.
Jabal ash–Shaykh. See HERMON, MOUNT.
Jabal at Tīh. See AL-TIH.
Jabal ʻAybāl. See EBAL, MOUNT.
Jabal Katrinah. See KATHERINA, GEBEL.
Jabal Mūsā. See MUSA, GEBEL.
Ja·bal·pur \ˈjə-bəl-ˌpu̇r\; *formerly* **Jub·bul·pore** \ˈjə-bəl-ˌpōr\. City, Madhya Pradesh, cen. India, near Narmada River 150 mi. (241 km.) NNE of Nagpur; pop. (1991p) 739,961; cement, textiles, armaments; university (1957); in region surrounded by rocky gorges and lakes; a trade and distribution point and rail junction; maintains large civil and military cantonment with government ordnance plants.
Jabbok. See ZARQA 1.
Ja·besh–gil·e·ad \ˈjā-besh-ˈgi-lē-əd\. Ancient town of Gilead, Palestine, in valley of the Jordan E of the river ab. 20 mi. (32 km.) S of the Sea of Galilee; in days of the Judges destroyed by tribe of Benjamin (*Judges* xxi. 8–15); besieged by Ammonites and siege relieved by King Saul (*1 Sam.* xi. 1–11).
Ja·blon·ec nad Ni·sou \ˈyä-blȯ-ˌnets-näd-ˈnē-sü\ *or Ger.* **Ga·blonz** \ˈgä-ˌblȯnts\. City, N Czech Republic, 55 mi. (88 km.) NE of Prague; pop. (1991p) 45,918; had large German population bet. WWI and WWII.
Ja·blo·ni·ca Pass \ˈyä-blȯ-ˌnyit-sä\ *also* **De·la·tyn Pass** \də-ˈlät-^{ə}n\ *or* **Ta·tar Pass** \ˈtä-tər\ *or* **Ya·blo·nit·sa Pass** \ˈyä-blȯ-ˌnyit-sä\. Pass through E Carpathian Mts., Ukraine, ab. 30 mi. (48 km.) SW of Kolomyya; through it passes railroad line to upper valley of the Tisza; used by Mongols (Tatars) in their invasion and conquest of Hungary 1241; scene of heavy fighting bet. Austrians and Russians Oct. 1914 to Feb. 1917; used by U.S.S.R. 1944 in its attack on Hungary.
Ja·boa·tão \ˌzhȧ-bwȧ-ˈtau̇^{n}\. City, Pernambuco state, E Brazil, a W suburb of Recife; munic. pop. (1991p) 482,434.
Ja·bor \ˈjä-ˌbȯr\. Port and chief village on Jaluit I., Marshall Is., W Pacific Ocean, at SE pass into the lagoon.
Ja·ca \ˈhä-kä\. Town, Huesca prov., N Spain, in S Pyrenees; pop. (1991p) 10,624; 11th cent. cathedral.
Ja·ca·reí \ˌzhȧ-kȧ-rē-ˈē\. Municipality, São Paulo state, SE Brazil, 50 mi. (80 km.) ENE of the city of São Paulo; pop. (1991p) 163,125.
Ja·ca·tra \ˌjä-kä-ˈträ\. **1.** Former town, Indonesia. See *History* at JAKARTA.
2. Japanese name for Batavia (now Jakarta) 1942–45.
Já·chy·mov \ˈyä-k̲ē-ˌmȯf\ *or Ger.* **Sankt Jo·a·chims·thal** \ˌzäŋkt-ˈyō-ə-kims-ˌtäl, ˌzäŋkt-yō-ˈäk-ims-\. Commune, NW Czech Republic, in Erzgebirge 12 mi. (19 km.) N of Karlovy Vary; pop. (1980c) 3503; famous 16th cent. silver-mining center; largely destroyed in Thirty Years' War.
Ja·cin·to City \jə-ˈsin-tō\. City, Harris co., SE Texas, an E suburb of Houston; pop. (1990c) 9343.
Jack \ˈjak\. County in N Texas. See table at TEXAS.
Jack·field \ˈjak-ˌfēld\. Village, Shropshire, W England, E of Much Wenlock; noted for its Jackfield ware, made in 18th cent., distinguished by its thick, brilliant black glaze applied over a common red clay.
Jacks·boro \ˈjaks-ˌbər-ō\. **1.** Village, ⊗ of Campbell co., N Tennessee; pop. (1990c) 1568.
2. City, ⊗ of Jack co., N Texas, 55 mi. (88 km.) NW of Fort Worth; pop. (1990c) 3350.
Jack·son \ˈjak-sən\. **1.** River, W Virginia; rises in Highland co., flows SW and then SE to unite with Cowpasture River in N Botetourt co. and form James River.
2. Name of a parish in N Louisiana and of counties in 23 states of the U.S. See tables at ALABAMA, ARKANSAS, COLORADO, FLORIDA, GEORGIA, ILLINOIS, INDIANA, IOWA, KANSAS, KENTUCKY, LOUISIANA, MICHIGAN, MINNESOTA, MISSISSIPPI, MISSOURI, NORTH CAROLINA, OHIO, OKLAHOMA, OREGON, SOUTH DAKOTA, TENNESSEE, TEXAS, WEST VIRGINIA, WISCONSIN.
3. City, Clarke co., SW Alabama, on Tombigbee River 50 mi. (80 km.) N of Mobile Bay; pop. (1990c) 5819.
4. City, ⊗ of Amador co., cen. California, 40 mi. (64 km.) ESE of Sacramento; pop. (1990c) 3545.
5. City, ⊗ of Butts co., cen. Georgia, 35 mi. (56 km.) NW of Macon; pop. (1990c) 4076.
6. City, ⊗ of Breathitt co., E Kentucky, 24 mi. (39 km.) NNW of Hazard; pop. (1990c) 2466; Lees Coll. (1883).
7. Town, East Feliciana parish, E Louisiana, 27 mi. (43 km.) N of Baton Rouge; pop. (1990c) 3891.
8. City, ⊗ of Jackson co., S Michigan, 34 mi. (55 km.) S of Lansing; pop. (1990c) 37,446; automobile and aircraft parts; Jackson Community Coll. (1928); settled 1829; scene of founding of the Republican party in a convention July 6, 1854.
9. City, ⊗ of Jackson co., S Minnesota, 25 mi. (40 km.) W of Fairmont; pop. (1990c) 3559.
10. City, ✻ of Mississippi and a ⊗ of Hinds co., SW cen. Mississippi, on Pearl River; pop. (1990c) 196,637; largest city in the state; railroad and distribution center. Jackson State Univ. (1877), Millsaps Coll. (1890), Belhaven Coll. (1883). Orig. a trading station known as Le Fleur's Bluff; selected as ✻ 1821; first session of legislature 1822; name changed to Jackson in honor of Andrew Jackson, 7th president of the U.S.; scene of secession convention Jan. 1861; captured by Union army under Gen. Ulysses S. Grant May 1863; reoccupied by Gen. William T. Sherman July 1863.
11. City, ⊗ of Cape Girardeau co., SE Missouri, 10 mi. (16 km.) NW of the city of Cape Girardeau; pop. (1990c) 9256.
12. Town, ⊗ of Northampton co., NE North Carolina; pop. (1990c) 592.
13. City, ⊗ of Jackson co., S Ohio, 25 mi. (40 km.) SE of Chillicothe; pop. (1990c) 6144.
14. City, ⊗ of Madison co., W Tennessee, on S fork of Forked Deer River 80 mi. (129 km.) ENE of Memphis; pop. (1990c) 48,949; textiles; Union Univ. (1823), Lambuth Univ. (1843), Lane Coll. (1882), Jackson State Community Coll. (1965); settled 1819; incorp. as town 1823, as city 1845.
15. Town, Washington co., SE Wisconsin; pop. (1990c) 3172.
16. Town, ⊗ of Teton co., NW Wyoming; pop. (1990c) 4472.
Jackson, Mount. **1.** Peak in Eagle co., NW cen. Colorado; 13,687 ft. (4172 m.).
2. Peak on Continental Divide in Glacier National Park, NW Montana; ab. 10,033 ft. (3058 m.).
3. Peak in S Coos co., E of Crawford Notch, N cen. New Hampshire, in the Presidential Range of the White Mts.; ab. 4012 ft. (1223 m.).
4. *formerly* **Mount Andrew Jackson.** Mountain at S end of Antarctic Penin., Antarctica, 71°23′S, 63°22′W; 13,745 ft. (4189 m.).
Jackson Heights. Residential section of N cen. Queens borough, New York City, New York.
Jackson Hole. Valley, NW Wyoming, E of Teton Range, in Grand Teton National Park; formerly an important hunting and trapping ground; now a major ski area.
Jackson Lake Dam. Dam across S fork of Snake River, Teton co., NW Wyoming; height 78 ft. (24 m.); forms **Jackson Lake** reservoir.
Jackson Peak. Mountain, S Teton co., NW Wyoming; 10,707 ft. (3263 m.).

Jack·son·ville \'jak-sən-ˌvil\. **1.** City, Calhoun co., NE Alabama; pop. (1990c) 10,283; Jacksonville State Univ. (1883).
2. City, Pulaski co., cen. Arkansas, 13 mi. (21 km.) NE of Little Rock; pop. (1990c) 29,101.
3. Seaport city, ⊗ of Duval co., NE Florida, near mouth of St. Johns River; pop. (1990c) 672,971; tourism; Edward Waters Coll. (1866), Jones Coll. (1918), Jacksonville Univ. (1934), Florida Community Coll. at Jacksonville (1963), Univ. of North Florida (1965); Jacksonville Naval Air Station; Mayport Naval Station nearby. Nearby, Fort Carolina National Memorial commemorating first French Huguenot settlement in America 1564, led by René de Laudonnière; resettled 1816; laid out and renamed 1822; incorp. 1832; base for Confederate blockade-runners during the Civil War; severely damaged by fire 1901; its rapid growth during 20th cent. has made it an important cultural, financial, commercial center in state; pop. more than doubled bet. 1960 and 1970.
4. City, ⊗ of Morgan co., W cen. Illinois, 30 mi. (48 km.) W of Springfield; pop. (1990c) 19,324; Illinois Coll. (1829), MacMurray Coll. (1846). Platted 1825.
5. City, ⊗ of Onslow co., SE North Carolina; pop. (1990c) 30,013; just S is Camp Lejeune Marine Corps Base.
6. City, Cherokee co., E Texas, 24 mi. (39 km.) ENE of Palestine; pop. (1990c) 12,765.

Jacksonville Beach. City, Duval co., NE Florida, on the Atlantic coast, 15 mi. (24 km.) E of Jacksonville; pop. (1990c) 17,839.

Jac·mel *also* **Jaque·mel** \zhȧk-'mel\. Seaport, S Haiti, on coast ab. 25 mi. (40 km.) SSW of Port-au-Prince.

Jacob. See NKAYI.

Ja·cob·a·bad \'jā-kə-bə-ˌbäd\. **1.** *formerly* **Upper Sind Frontier** \'sind\. District, N Sind, Pakistan; 2982 sq. mi. (7723 sq. km.); pop. (1981c) 1,012,476; ✻ Jacobabad.
2. Municipality, its ✻; pop. (1981c) 79,365.

Ja·co·na \hä-'kō-nä\. Municipality, Michoacán state, Mexico, 75 mi. (121 km.) WNW of Morelia.

Jacques Car·tier \ˌzhȧk-kär-'tyā\. River, S Quebec, Canada; flows S into St. Lawrence River 22 mi. (35 km.) WSW of Quebec City; ab. 70 mi. (113 km.) long.

Jacques–Cartier, Mount. Mountain, N Gaspé Penin., Quebec, Canada; 4160 ft. (1268 m.); highest point in Quebec.

Jac·qui·not Bay \ˌzhȧ-kē-'nō\. Large inlet of the Solomon Sea on S coast of New Britain I., Bismarck Archipelago, Papua New Guinea, near E end of the island.

Ja·cuí \zhȧ-'kwē\. River, Rio Grande do Sul state, S Brazil; flows S and E to Lagoa dos Patos; 280 mi. (451 km.) long.

Ja·dar \'yä-ˌdär\. Small river in NW Serbia, Yugoslavia, a tributary of Drina River; scene of battle Aug. 1914 in which the Serbs defeated the Austrians.

Ja·de Bay \'yä-də\ *or* **Ja·de·bu·sen** \ˌyä-də-'bü-zən\. Inlet of North Sea on N coast of Oldenburg region of Lower Saxony, NW Germany; on its W coast is Wilhelmshaven.

Jadida, El. See EL JADIDA.

Jadotville. See LIKASI.

Ja·én \hä-'ān\. **1.** Province of S Spain. See table at SPAIN.
2. Commune, its ✻, 178 mi. (286 km.) S of Madrid; pop. (1991p) 101,938; olive oil; 16th cent. cathedral; 13th cent. castle.

Jaf·fa \'yä-fə, 'jä-, 'ja-\ *or Arab.* **Ya·fa** \'yä-fə\ *or Heb.* **Ya·fo** \'yä-fō\; *anc.* **Jop·pa** \'jä-pə\. City, part of Tel Aviv-Jaffa (*q.v.*), Israel, 35 mi. (56 km.) NW of Jerusalem.
History: Ancient town, mentioned in biblical history (*2 Chron.* ii. 16); from 15th to 4th cents. B.C. conquered variously by Egyptians, Philistines, Israelites, Assyrians, Persians, and Macedonians (under Alexander the Great); ruled by Ptolemies (Macedonian rulers of Egypt) following Alexander's death 323 B.C.; taken from Syrians 2d cent. B.C.; destroyed by Roman Emperor Vespasian 68 A.D.; seat of early Christian bishopric; twice captured by Crusaders, but lost to Muslims 1196; destroyed 1345 by Egyptian sultan; captured by French Emperor Napoléon 1799; occupied by British 1917; center of post-WWII fighting bet. Arabs and Jews 1945–47 before Israeli independence 1948; incorp. with Tel Aviv 1950; served as a commercial seaport until 1965.

Jaff·na \'jäf-nə\. **1.** Peninsula, N extremity of Sri Lanka; ab. 50 mi. (80 km.) long.
2. Town on peninsula; pop. (1990c) 129,000; mangoes; good harbor; includes old Dutch fort and Hindu shrines. For centuries held by Tamil rajas until ousted by Portuguese 1617, who in turn were succeeded by Dutch 1658; became British 1795; was last Portuguese possession in Ceylon.

Jaf·frey \'ja-frē\; *formerly* **East Jaffrey**. Town in Cheshire co., SW New Hampshire; pop. (1990c) 5361; summer resort on S shoulder of Grand Monadnock.

Jagannath. See PURI.

Jag·dal·pur \'jəgd-ᵊl-ˌpu̇r\. Town in SE Madhya Pradesh, E India, 125 mi. (201 km.) NW of Vishakhapatnam; pop. (1991p) 65,544.

Jägerndorf. See KRNOV.

Ja·gers·fon·tein \'yä-kərs-ˌfän-ˌtān\. Town, SW Free State, E cen. Rep. of South Africa, 60 mi. (97 km.) SW of Bloemfontein; some of the world's largest diamonds were mined here.

Jag·ged Mountain \'ja-gəd\. Peak in San Juan co., SW Colorado; 13,829 ft. (4215 m.).

Ja·go·di·na \'yä-gō-ˌdē-nä\; *1946-93* **Sve·to·za·re·vo** \'sve-tō-ˌzä-re-ˌvō\. Town, E cen. Serbia, Yugoslavia; pop. (1991c) 37,326.

Jagst·hau·sen \'yäkst-ˌhau̇z-ᵊn\. Village, N Baden-Württemberg, Germany, NE of Heilbronn; pop. (1980c) 1452; birthplace of German knight Götz von Berlichingen 1480.

Ja·gua·rão \ˌzhȧg-wȧ-'rau̇ⁿ\. **1.** *or Span.* **Ya·gua·rón** \ˌyä-gwä-'rōn\. River, forming E section of boundary bet. Uruguay and S Brazil; empties into Lagoa Mirím; ab. 135 mi. (217 km.) long.
2. City, S Rio Grande do Sul state, S Brazil, near mouth of river; munic. pop. (1980c) 23,263.

Ja·gua·ri·be \ˌzhȧ-gwȧ-'rē-bē\. River, E Ceará state, NE Brazil; flows into Atlantic Ocean at Aracati; ab. 350 mi. (563 km.) long.

Ja·güey Gran·de \'hä-gwā-'grän-dā\. Municipality, Matanzas prov., W cen. Cuba, 45 mi. (72 km.) SE of the city of Matanzas; pop. (1981p) 43,417.

Ja·gun·gul, Mount \jə-'gəŋ-gəl\. Peak in Australian Alps, SE Australia; ab. 6762 ft. (2061 m.).

Jah·rom \yä-'rōm\. City, Fārs prov., SW Iran, ab. 90 mi. (145 km.) SE of Shīrāz; pop. (1986c) 77,174.

Jainat. See CHAINAT.

Jai·pur \'jī-ˌpu̇r\ *also* **Jey·pore** \'jā-ˌpōr\. **1.** Former Indian state, E Rajputana, NW India, now in Rajasthan state; 15,610 sq. mi. (40,430 sq. km.); ✻ Jaipur; hills and desert in N and W, fertile in E and S; founded in 12th cent. by Rajput chief; furnished famous generals to Mogul emperors; came under British protection 1818; was ruled by a maharaja.
2. City, ✻ of Rajasthan and ✻ of former Jaipur state, NW India; pop. (1991c) 1,458,183; commercial center; textiles, glass, enamel and metal work, jewelry, drugs; noted for walls and fortifications; city laid out in rectangular pattern with wide streets; has maharajah's palace with open-air observatories; founded 1727 by Maharajah Jai Singh II.

Jaipur Residency. Former division of Rajputana Agency, NW India, incl. Indian states of Alwar, Jaipur, Kishangarh, Shahpura, and Tonk. Since 1947 these states have either joined other groups or have been assimilated with administrative units of India.

Jai·sal·mer \'jī-səl-ˌmer\. **1.** Former Indian state, now a district of Rajasthan state, NW India; 14,847 sq. mi. (38,454 sq. km.); almost entirely a sandy waste, forming part of Thar, or Indian, Desert; has practically no crops, but some grazing; founded 1156 by a Rajput chief; entered into political relations with British 1818.
2. Town, its ✻, in desert 140 mi. (225 km.) WNW of Jodhpur; pop. (1991p) 38,813.

Jaj·ce \'yīt-se\. Town, N cen. Bosnia and Herzegovina, on Vrbas River. Held by Hungarians against Turks 1463–1526; finally surrendered to Turks 1528 and held by them until 1908 when Bosnia and Herzegovina was annexed by Austria-Hungary.

Ja·kar·ta *also* **Dja·kar·ta** \jə-'kär-tə\. Seaport city, ✻ of Indonesia, on NW coast of Java, on Jakarta Bay at mouth of Liwung River; pop. (1990c) 8,259,266; forms capital territory (see table at INDONESIA); largest city and principal port of Indonesia; iron foundries; financial center; exports include rubber, tea; several universities incl. the Univ. of Indonesia (1950).

History: Founded 1619 on site of Jacatra by Dutch merchant Jan Pieterszoon Coen naming it Batavia; became headquarters of Dutch East India Company; gradually extended control over neighboring sultanates and principalities; suffered severe earthquake 1699; defended by Allies 1942 but captured by Japanese; proclaimed ✻ of Indonesia 1949; one of the fastest growing cities in SE Asia.

Jakarta Bay *also* **Djakarta Bay;** *formerly* **Ba·ta·via Bay** \bə-ˈtā-vē-ə\. Inlet of Java Sea on NW coast of Java, Indonesia.

Jakko, Mount. See SIMLA.

Ja·kobs·havn \ˈyä-kəps-ˌhau̇n\. Settlement on Qeqertarsuup Tunua Bay, W coast of Greenland; pop. (1991e) 4135.

Jakobstad. See PIETARSAARI.

Jal \ˈjal\. City, Lea co., SE corner of New Mexico, 37 mi. (60 km.) S of Hobbs; pop. (1990c) 2156.

Ja·lāl·ā·bād *or* **Je·lal·a·bad** \jə-ˈlä-lə-ˌbäd\. Town, E Afghanistan, W of Khyber Pass and on Kabul River near its junction with the Chitral; pop. (1988e) 68,100; trade center; university (1963); in strategic location in river plain 70 mi. (113 km.) E of Kabul and 80 mi. (128 km.) W of Peshawar, Pakistan; also commands Kunar Valley N to Chitral, Pakistan; site chosen by Bābur (Ẓahīr-ud-Dīn Muḥammad) and town built c. 1560 by Akbar, both Mogul emperors; defended in First Afghan War by British 1841–42; large sections bombarded in decade-long civil war of 1980s.

Ja·lal–Abad *or* **Dzha·lal Abad** \jä-ˈläl-ä-ˌbäd\. Town, SW Kyrgyzstan, in upper Syr Dar'ya Valley on Uzbekistan border; pop. (1991e) 79,900.

Ja·lan·dhar \ˈjə-lən-dər\ *also* **Jul·lun·dur** \ˈjə-lən-dər\. City, Punjab, N India, ab. 46 mi. (74 km.) SE of Amritsar; pop. (1991c) 509,510; former ✻ of ancient kingdom of Jalandhar (*or* **Tri·gar·ta** \tri-ˈgər-tə\); came under Sikh jurisdiction early 19th cent.; came under British sovereignty 1846.

Ja·la·pa \hä-ˈlä-pä\. **1.** Department of SE Guatemala. See table at GUATEMALA.

2. Town, its ✻; munic. pop. (1993e) 26,568; alt. ab. 4500 ft. (1370 m.).

3. *or in full* **Jalapa En·rí·quez** \en-ˈrē-kās\; *formerly* **Xa·la·pa** \hä-\. City, ✻ of Veracruz state, Mexico; pop. (1990e) 279,451; alt. ab. 4670 ft. (1425 m.); processes coffee and tobacco; university (1944).

Ja·la·pa·har \ˌjə-lə-pə-ˈhär\. See DARJEELING.

Ja·laud \hä-ˈlau̇d\. River, NW and cen. Iloilo prov., Panay, Philippines; rises in mountains near Antique border, flows W and S to Iloilo Strait; ab. 60 mi. (97 km.) long.

Jal·gaon \ˈjäl-ˌgau̇n\. Town, N Maharashtra state, W India, 235 mi. (378 km.) NE of Bombay; pop. (1991p) 241,603; commercial center for cotton-growing area.

Ja·lin·go \jä-ˈliŋ-gō\. City, E Nigeria; ✻ of Taraba state.

Ja·lis·co \hä-ˈlēs-kō\. State of W cen. Mexico. See table at MEXICO.

Jal·na \ˈjäl-nə\. Town, N cen. Maharashtra state, S cen. India, ab. 35 mi. (56 km.) E of Aurangabad; pop. (1991p) 174,958.

Jalomitsa. See IALOMIȚA.

Ja·lón \hä-ˈlōn\. River, NE cen. Spain; flows NE into Ebro River 13 mi. (21 km.) above Saragossa; ab. 120 mi. (193 km.) long.

Ja·lo·sto·ti·tlán \hä-ˌlō-stō-tē-ˈtlän\. Municipality, Jalisco state, Mexico, 68 mi. (109 km.) NE of Guadalajara.

Jal·pa \ˈhäl-pä\. Municipality, Tabasco state, Mexico, 15 mi. (24 km.) NW of Villahermosa; pop. (1990p) 57,153.

Jal·pai·gu·ri \ˌjəl-pī-ˈgu̇r-ē\. **1.** District, formerly in Rajshahi div., N Bengal, NE British India, on Bhutan frontier; 3050 sq. mi. (7900 sq. km.); divided 1947 with SW portion assigned to East Pakistan (now Bangladesh), the remainder to West Bengal, India.

2. Town, in West Bengal, NE India, on Tista River; pop. (1991p) 67,495.

Jal·te·pec \ˌhäl-tā-ˈpek\. River on Isthmus of Tehuantepec, Mexico; rises in E Oaxaca state, flows NE into Bay of Campeche; 160 mi. (257 km.) long.

Jal·u·it \ˈjal-yu̇-it, ˈja-lu̇-\. One of the Marshall Is., in Ralik Chain, in W Pacific Ocean; atoll 38 mi. (61 km.) long by 21 mi. (34 km.) wide; has ab. 50 islets; harbor at Jabor, on SE side; in WWII strongly garrisoned by Japanese; taken by Allies 1944.

Ja·mai·ca \jə-ˈmā-kə\. **1.** Independent state, an island in the West Indies, 95 mi. (153 km.) S of Cuba; ab. 145 mi. (233 km.) long; 4471 sq. mi. (11,580 sq. km.); pop. (1993e) 2,464,000; ✻ Kingston; includes Morant Cays and Pedro Cays; mountainous with main ridge running E and W; highest point Blue Mt. Peak 7388 ft. (2252 m.) in Blue Mts. at E end; has many short streams; on coast are several bays with good anchorage, esp. Kingston harbor, Portland Bight, Montego Bay, Port Antonio.

Chief products: Sugar, bananas, coffee, cocoa, citrus fruit, rum; alumina, cement, gypsum, bauxite; tourism.

Chief towns: Kingston, Spanish Town, Montego Bay.

History: Inhabited by Arawaks when discovered by Christopher Columbus 1494; a Spanish colony 1509–1655; Santiago de la Vega founded bet. 1520–26 (see SPANISH TOWN); captured by English under naval officers William Penn and Robert Venables 1655; English possession formally recognized by Treaty of Madrid 1670; governed by representative council 1661–1866 when legislative council was substituted; Kingston built after Port Royal, a haven for buccaneers and center of island's flourishing slave trade, destroyed by earthquake 1692; until 19th cent., when slavery was abolished, prospered as a producer of sugar; put down several fugitive slave (Maroon) insurrections, notably in 1865; Kingston severely damaged by earthquake 1907; in WWII a fleet anchorage in Portland Bight leased to U.S. A British colony 1655–1958; a territory of West Indies Federation (see WEST INDIES 2) 1958–61; became independent nation within the Commonwealth 1962; joined Caribbean Free Trade Association 1968; in area subject to frequent hurricanes, suffered widespread damage from storms 1980, 1988.

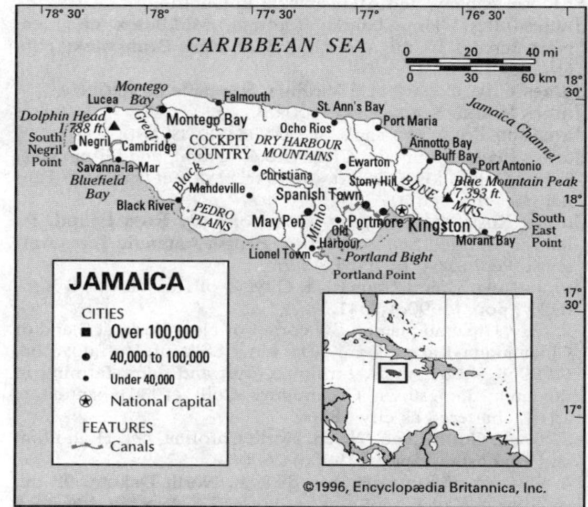

2. Former town, since 1898 part of borough of Queens in New York City, ⊗ of Queens co., SE New York, on Long Island; commercial center; St. John's Univ. (1870), York Coll. of the City Univ. of New York (1966); settled mid-17th cent.; became ⊗ 1683.

Jamaica Bay. Inlet of Atlantic Ocean at W end of Long Island, New York; ab. 20 sq. mi. (52 sq. km.); protected by the narrow peninsula on which Rockaway Beach is located.

Jamaica Plain. Former village in Suffolk co., Massachusetts, now a part of Boston; location of Arnold Arboretum.

Ja·mal·pur \jə-ˈmäl-ˌpu̇r\. Town, NE Bihar, NE India, near Ganges River 80 mi. (129 km.) E of Patna; pop. (1991p) 86,123.

Ja·may \hä-ˈmī\. Municipality, Jalisco state, Mexico, on NE shore of Lake Chapala.

Jambes \ˈzhäⁿb\. Commune, Namur prov., S Belgium, suburb of the commune of Namur.

Jam·bi *also* **Djam·bi** \ˈjäm-bē\. **1.** Province, S cen. Sumatra, Indonesia, extending nearly across the island from Barisan Mts. to South China Sea; ✱ Jambi; its low marshy area drained by Hari River; rubber, rice; fishing. See table at INDONESIA.

2. Town, its ✱, a river port on the Hari River ab. 60 mi. (97 km.) from its mouth; pop. (1990c) 340,066; university (1963); rubber processing; in 17th and 18th cents. ✱ of an influential sultanate.

Jambol. See YAMBOL.

Jam·bu·air \ˌjäm-bu̇-ˈīr\ *or Du.* **Di·a·mant** \ˈdē-ə-ˌmänt\ *or Eng.* **Di·a·mond** \ˈdī-mənd, ˈdī-ə-\. Cape on NE tip of Sumatra, Indonesia, at NW end of Strait of Malacca.

Jam·de·na *or* **Yam·de·na** \yäm-ˈdā-nä\. Largest of the Tanimbar group of islands in S Moluccas, E Malay Archipelago, Indonesia; 70 mi. (113 km.) long by 28 mi. (45 km.) wide; ab. 1100 sq. mi. (2849 sq. km.)

James \ˈjāmz\. **1.** River, North Dakota and South Dakota. See DAKOTA 1.

2. River, formed by confluence of Jackson and Cowpasture rivers in N Botetourt co., cen. Virginia; flows E into Chesapeake Bay through broad estuary at Hampton Roads; 340 mi. (547 km.) long; navigable to Richmond.

James Bay. S extension of Hudson Bay, Canada, bet. NE Ontario and W Quebec; ab. 280 mi. (451 km.) long and 150 mi. (241 km.) wide; contains Akimiski I. and several small islands; receives several large rivers, esp. the Fort George, Eastmain, Nottaway, and Harricanaw in Quebec, and the Moose, Albany, and Attawapiskat in Ontario.

James·burg \ˈjāmz-ˌbərg\. Borough, Middlesex co., cen. New Jersey, 10 mi. (16 km.) S of New Brunswick; pop. (1990c) 5294.

James City. County in E Virginia. See table at VIRGINIA.

James Island. See SAN SALVADOR 5.

Jame·son Bay \ˈjām-sən\. See JAN MAYEN ISLAND.

James Peak. Mountain, Clear Creek, Grand, and Gilpin cos., N cen. Colorado; 13,260 ft. (4042 m.); Moffat (railroad) Tunnel goes through it.

James Ross Island \ˈjāmz-ˈro̊s\; *formerly* **Ross Island.** Island in Weddell Sea, Antarctica, British Antarctic Terr., Antarctic Penin., 64°15′S, 57°45′W.

James·town \ˈjāmz-ˌtau̇n\. **1.** City, ⊗ of Russell co., S Kentucky; pop. (1990c) 1641.

2. City, Chautauqua co., SW corner of New York, at S end of Chautauqua Lake 57 mi. (92 km.) SSW of Buffalo; pop. (1990c) 34,681; tools, furniture; fruit and dairy farming in the area; Jamestown Community Coll. (1934); settled c. 1810; chartered as city 1886.

3. Town, Guilford co., N cen. North Carolina, bet. High Point and Greensboro; pop. (1990c) 2600.

4. City, ⊗ of Stutsman co., SE cen. North Dakota, 95 mi. (153 km.) W of Fargo; pop. (1990c) 15,571; grain, livestock farming; Jamestown Coll. (1883).

5. Residential town and summer resort, Newport co., SE Rhode Island, coextensive with Conanicut I., 3 mi. (5 km.) W of Newport; pop. (1990c) 4999.

6. City, ⊗ of Fentress co., N Tennessee; pop. (1990c) 1862.

7. Ruined village, James City co., E Virginia, on peninsula (now **Jamestown I.**) of James River almost opp. Williamsburg; in Colonial National Historical Park; first permanent English settlement in America, founded May 1607; ✱ of Virginia 1607–98; suffered famine ("Starving Time" 1609–10) and Indian attacks; meeting place of first legislative assembly in America 1619; almost entirely destroyed by colonial leader Nathaniel Bacon 1676, rebuilt, but again declined following removal of ✱ to Williamsburg; site of Jamestown Exposition (1907) celebrating tercentenary and of Jamestown Festival Park (1957).

8. Seaport town, ✱ of British island of St. Helena, S Atlantic Ocean; pop. (1991e) 1332.

James W. Ellsworth Land. See ELLSWORTH LAND.

Ja·mil·te·pec \hä-ˈmēl-tā-ˌpek, -ˌmēl-tā-ˈpek\. Municipality, Oaxaca state, Mexico, 95 mi. (153 km.) SW of the city of Oaxaca.

Jam·khan·di \jəm-ˈkən-dē\. **1.** Former Indian state in Deccan and Kolhapur States, W India, now part of Maharashtra state; 522 sq. mi. (1352 sq. km.); formerly in Southern Maratha States.

2. Town, its ✱, 68 mi. (109 km.) E of Kolhapur.

Jam·mu *also* **Jum·moo** \ˈjə-mü\. City, Jammu and Kashmir state, N India, on Tawi River (tributary of the Chenab) 95 mi. (153 km.) S of Srinagar; pop. (1981c) 206,135; university (1948); winter ✱ of state; has fort and a large palace of the (former) rajas; was seat of a Rajput dynasty, later acquired by the Sikhs.

Jammu and Kash·mir \ˈkash-ˌmir, ˈkazh-, kash-ˈ\ *or frequently* **Kashmir.** Former princely state, SW cen. Asia; now divided into two parts: (1) Indian state of Jammu and Kashmir; ✱ Srinagar (see table at INDIA); (2) area under Pakistani control; 32,358 sq. mi. (83,807 sq. km.); ✱ Muzaffarabad. Bounded on N by Afghanistan and China; mountainous, with several peaks over 20,000 ft. (6096 m.); major ranges: Karakoram, Ladakh, Pir Panjal; rice, corn, fruit, wool, wood carvings.

History: Became part of Mogul Empire (see INDIA) under Akbar 1586; in 2d half of 18th cent. included in Aḥmad Shāh Durrānī's Afghan empire; annexed to Sikh kingdom by its founder Ranjit Singh 1819; after Sikh Wars, held by raja of Jammu as part of British India 1846; scene of fighting bet. Indian and Pakistani forces 1947–49; princely state partitioned (1949) into two parts: NW area controlled by Pakistan, the remainder constituting a state of India; jurisdiction over whole territory claimed by both India and Pakistan since 1947; NE border areas in Indian territory occupied by China 1959; scene of fighting bet. India and China 1962; border regions scene of fighting bet. India and Pakistan 1965, 1971; experienced increase in secessionist-related violence in late 1980s and early 1990s.

Jam·na·gar \jäm-ˈnə-gər\; *formerly* **Na·va·na·gar** \ˌnä-və-ˈnə-gər\ *or* **Na·wa·na·gar.** City, Gujarat state, W India, on Gulf of Kachchh 310 mi. (499 km.) NW of Bombay; pop. (1991c) 350,544; cement, pottery, textiles, salt; dyeing, and gold embroidery; founded 1540; was ✱ of the former Navanagar state.

Jam·rud \jəm-ˈrüd\. Town, North-West Frontier prov., Pakistan, 9 mi. (15 km.) W of Peshawar; fort important as frontier outpost at mouth of Khyber Pass; scene of military operations at various times, esp. 1836–37, 1878–79, and 1897–98; former headquarters of Khyber Rifles; a British-led tribal militia (disbanded 1919).

Jam·shed·pur \ˈjäm-shed-ˌpu̇r\. City, SE Bihar, NE India, at confluence of Subarnarekha and Karkhai rivers 140 mi. (225 km.) W of Calcutta; pop. (1991c) 751,368; center of metal industry; blast furnaces, coke ovens, steel and iron works, railroad shops; developed around Tata steel mills, founded 1907.

Jämt·land \ˈyemt-ˌländ\. **1.** Old province of Sweden, in N cen. part bordering on Norway; ab. 20,000 sq. mi. (51,800 sq. km.); Östersund was only important town; acquired by treaty from Norway 1645 during reign of Queen Christina.

2. Province of W Sweden. See table at SWEDEN.

Ja·mu·na \ˈjə-mu̇-nə\. River, Bangladesh; main stream of Brahmaputra River from the Tista to the Ganges.

Jamundá. See NHAMUNDÁ.

Ja·murs·ba, Cape \jä-ˈmu̇rs-bä\; *formerly* **Cape of Good Hope.** Most northerly point of Doberai Penin., NW Irian Jaya, Indonesia.

Ja·nau·cu \zhä-ˈnau̇-kü\. Island in the mouth of the Amazon River, N of Caviana I., off NE coast of Pará state, Brazil.

Janes·ville \ˈjānz-ˌvil\. City, ⊗ of Rock co., S Wisconsin, 41 mi. (66 km.) SE of Madison; pop. (1990c) 52,133; automobiles, ink pens; Blackhawk Technical Coll. (1968); settled c. 1835; incorp. 1853.

Ja·nic·u·lum \jə-ˈni-kyə-ləm\ *also* **Mons Au·re·us** \ˈmänz-ˈȯr-ē-əs\. A hill on right bank of the Tiber River opp. the Seven Hills of Rome.

Janīn. See JENIN.

Janina. See IOÁNNINA 2.

Jänisjärvi. See YANISYARVI.

Ja·ni·uay \ˌhä-nē-ˈwī\. Municipality, Iloilo prov., Panay, Philippines, 19 mi. (31 km.) NNW of City of Iloilo; pop. (1980c) 40,120; one of oldest towns on the island.

Jan·ji·ra \ˈjən-ji-rə\. Former Indian state, Deccan and Kolhapur States, W India, now part of Maharashtra state, on coast 50 mi. (81 km.) S of the city of Bombay; 326 sq. mi. (844 sq. km.); ✻ Murud.

Jankovácz. See JÁNOSHALMA.

Jan May·en Island \ˈyän-ˈmī-ən\. Norwegian volcanic island in Arctic Ocean 300 mi. (483 km.) E of Greenland and 360 mi. (579 km.) NNE of Iceland, 71°N, 8°W; 33 mi. (53 km.) long and greatest width 10 mi. (16 km.); 144 sq. mi. (373 sq. km.); highest point extinct volcano of Beerenberg 7430 ft. (2265 m.); meteorological station at Jameson Bay; discovered by English navigator and explorer Henry Hudson 1607; often visited by explorers; annexed to Norway 1929.

Jannabatain. See AJNADAIN.

Já·nos·hal·ma \ˈyän-ōsh-ˌhöl-mö\ *also* **Jan·ko·vácz** \ˈyön-kō-ˌväts\. Commune, Bács-Kiskun co., S Hungary, 40 mi. (64 km.) W of Szeged; pop. (1980p) 12,534.

Jan Pie·ters·zoon Coen Peak \ˈyän-ˈpē-tər-sən-ˈkün\. Peak, E end of Maoke Mts., Irian Jaya, Indonesia; named after Jan Pieterszoon Coen, governor-general of Dutch possessions in the East 1617–23, 1627–29.

Ja·nuá·ria \zhȧ-ˈnwȧ-ryə\. Municipality, Minas Gerais state, E Brazil, ab. 300 mi. (483 km.) NNW of Belo Horizonte; pop. (1991p) 86,871.

Ja·nūb Sī·nā' \jä-ˈnüb-sē-ˈnä\. Governorate of Egypt, on Sinai Penin. See table at EGYPT.

Jao·ra \ˈjau̇r-ə\. **1.** Former Indian state, now part of Madhya Pradesh, cen. India; 601 sq. mi. (1557 sq. km.); founded 1808; its ruler had title of nabob.
2. Town, its ✻, 160 mi. (257 km.) ENE of Ahmadabad; pop. (1991p) 54,960.

Ja·pan \jə-ˈpan, ji-, ja-\; *Jp.* **Nip·pon** *also* **Nip·hon** \ni-ˈpän\ *or* **Ni·hon** \nē-ˈhȯn\. Independent state, consisting of an island chain in W Pacific Ocean, off E coast of Asia; 143,619 sq. mi. (371,973 sq. km.); pop. (1985c) 121,048,923; ✻ Tokyo.

Physical features: Comprises four main islands (Honshū, Shikoku, Kyūshū, and Hokkaidō). All islands mountainous, incl. many high peaks (7000 to 10,000 ft. or 2134 to 3048 m.) and volcanoes; highest peak Fuji 12,388 ft. (3776 m.), on S Honshū; lies in earthquake belt of W Pacific and has suffered from many destructive shocks, esp. Sept. 1923, Dec. 1946, and Jan. 1995; islands indented with many bays, affording fine harbors; most important water area Inland Sea (*q.v.*); off shores of large islands are many smaller islands (Sado, Awaji, Tsushima) and groups (Oki, Gotō, Izu Shichitō, Bonin, Volcano); rivers short and rapid and only a few partly navigable; many beautiful lakes (Biwa, Chuzenji, Inawashiro).

Chief products: Rice, vegetables, fruit, milk, tea; fishing; coal, copper, zinc; manufacturing: steel, chemicals, textiles, motor vehicles, electrical machinery, electronic equipment, optical and scientific instruments; shipbuilding.

Chief cities: Tokyo, Yokohama, Ōsaka, Nagoya, Sapporo, Kōbe, Kyōto, Fukuoka, Kawasaki, Hiroshima, Kitakyushu.

Political divisions: Administratively divided into the following regions and prefectures (for pronunciation of their names, see their individual entries):

NAME	AREA[1] (sq. mi.)	AREA[1] (sq. km.)	POP. (1990c)	CAPITAL
Chūbu				
Aichi	1,955	5,063	6,690,440	Nagoya
Fukui	1,617	4,188	823,595	Fukui
Gifu	4,092	10,598	2,066,579	Gifu
Ishikawa	1,620	4,196	1,164,627	Kanazawa
Nagano	5,244	13,582	2,156,656	Nagano
Niigata	4,855	12,574	2,474,602	Niigata
Shizuoka	300	777	3,670,891	Shizuoka
Toyama	1,642	4,253	1,120,182	Toyama
Yamanashi	1,723	4,462	852,980	Kōfu
Chūgoku				
Hiroshima	3,258	8,438	2,849,822	Hiroshima
Okayama	2,727	7,063	1,925,913	Okayama
Shimane	2,559	6,628	781,005	Matsue
Tottori	1,347	3,489	615,741	Tottori
Yamaguchi	2,347	6,079	1,572,645	Yamaguchi
Hokkaidō				
Hokkaidō	30,313	78,511	5,643,715	Sapporo
Kanto				
Chiba	1,950	5,050	5,555,467	Chiba
Gumma	2,452	6,351	1,966,287	Maebashi
Ibaraki	2,351	6,089	2,845,411	Mito
Kanagawa	917	2,375	7,980,421	Yokohama
Saitama	1,467	3,800	6,405,319	Urawa
Tochigi	2,479	6,421	1,935,186	Utsunomiya
Tokyo	783	2,028	11,854,987	Tokyo
Kinki				
Hyōgo	3,221	8,342	5,405,090	Kōbe
Kyōto	1,781	4,613	2,602,520	Kyōto
Mie	2,227	5,768	1,792,542	Tsu
Nara	1,425	3,691	1,375,478	Nara
Ōsaka	710	1,839	8,734,670	Ōsaka
Shiga	1,550	4,014	1,222,401	Ōtsu
Wakayama	1,821	4,716	1,074,321	Wakayama
Kyūshū				
Fukuoka	1,896	4,911	4,811,179	Fukuoka
Kagoshima	3,530	9,143	1,797,766	Kagoshima
Kumamoto	2,848	7,376	1,840,383	Kumamoto
Miyazaki	2,986	7,734	1,168,922	Miyazaki
Nagasaki	1,579	4,090	1,563,015	Nagasaki
Ōita	2,437	6,312	1,236,924	Ōita
Saga	929	2,406	877,865	Saga
Ryukyu Islands				
Okinawa	848	2,196	1,222,458	Naha
Shikoku				
Ehime	2,183	5,654	1,515,027	Matsuyama
Kagawa	719	1,862	1,023,434	Takamatsu
Kōchi	2,743	7,104	825,063	Kōchi
Tokushima	1,600	4,144	831,582	Tokushima
Tohoku				
Akita[2]	4,482	11,608	1,227,491	Akita
Aomori	3,712	9,614	1,482,935	Aomori
Fukushima	5,321	13,781	2,104,119	Fukushima
Iwate	5,898	15,276	1,416,960	Morioka
Miyagi	2,813	7,286	2,248,521	Sendai
Yamagata	3,600	9,324	1,258,404	Yamagata

[1] Area = land area.
[2] Gave its name to the Akita breed of dogs.

History: Inhabited by humans as early as 30,000 B.C.; later inhabitants included those of the prehistoric Jōmon (c. 5th millennium–c. 300 B.C.) and Yayoi (c. 200 B.C.–c. 200 A.D.) cultures; traditional history dates from 660 B.C., accession of Jimmu Tennō, ruler of Yamato (*q.v.*) and founder of the imperial line; written history began in 5th cent. A.D. after Japan entered contact with highly developed Chinese culture from which it adopted handwriting; Buddhism introduced c. 552; closely imitated Chinese institutions 6th–9th cents.; in 794, imperial ✻ moved to Heian-kyo (modern Kyōto) where it remained until 1869; from 9th–12th cents., court dominated by Fujiwara family; late 12th cent. powerful samurai family Taira defeated and, in 1192, Minamoto Yoritomo became shogun (military dictator) and founded first of the shogunates which controlled emperor 1192–1867; in Kamakura period 1192–1333, military feudalism, evolved since 9th cent., reached full development; invaded by Mongols 1274, 1281; in 15th cent. (Ashikaga shoguns c. 1338–c. 1573), general breakdown of feudalism occurred.

First visited by Europeans (Portuguese) 1542–43; Christianity introduced by St. Francis Xavier 1549–51; in late

16th cent. Japanese empire united and outlying provinces conquered by Oda Nobunaga, Toyotomi Hideyoshi, and Tokugawa Ieyasu (first of Tokugawa shoguns 1603–1867); edicts of successors of Ieyasu cut off Japanese contact with foreigners, incl. European traders and missionaries, except at Nagasaki (*q.v.*); in 1854, Commodore Matthew Perry, an American, secured first commercial treaty; Meiji era 1868–1912 began with emperor's resumption of direct rule 1868; rapidly adopted Occidental civilization, modified government (constitution of 1889) and extended foreign contacts; fought war with China over Korea (*q.v.*) 1894–95 (see SHIMONOSEKI); allied with Great Britain 1902; victorious in Russo-Japanese War 1904–05; annexed Korea 1910; made 21 demands on China 1915; for participation in WWI, secured former German possessions in Pacific, N of Equator.

Occupied Manchuria (*q.v.*) 1931–32, Shanghai 1932, and began war with China gradually taking over all large coastal cities and many interior areas 1937–45. Signed military alliance with Germany and Italy 1940; entered WWII Dec. 7, 1941 by surprise attack on Pearl Harbor, Hawaii; attacked Philippines Dec. 1941; occupied Manila Jan. 1942 and after long and severe fighting on Bataan Penin. overwhelmed smaller American and Filipino force Apr. 1942 and then took Corregidor. By Mar. 1942 had taken Hong Kong, Malay Penin., Siam (Thailand), invaded Burma (Myanmar), cutting Burma Road (*q.v.*), and seized Ambon, Borneo, Sumatra, and Java. Received first setback in naval and air battles of Coral Sea May 1942 and Midway June 1942; defeated on land and sea at Guadalcanal Aug. 1942–Feb. 1943; driven out of SE New Guinea (Territory of Papua) and out of Aleutians and defeated at Tarawa by end of 1943. Driven back in N Burma, defeated in Manipur, and by Aug. 1944 had lost Saipan, Tinian, Guam; lost Manila early 1945. Partly successful in China 1944–45 but with great losses of ships, planes, and material sources, unable to hold Iwo Jima Feb.–Mar. 1945 and Okinawa Apr.–June; many large cities devastated by carrier planes; Hiroshima Aug. 6 and Nagasaki Aug. 9 practically destroyed by atomic bombs; attacked by U.S.S.R. Aug. 8 in Manchuria; surrendered Aug. 14; mainland (first in Tokyo area) occupied by Allied troops in Sept.; adopted new constitution 1947; signed mutual security treaty with U.S. 1951; regained control over N Ryukyu Is. 1953; member of UN 1956; regained control over Bonin Is. 1968; 1960s marked by strong economic growth, giving Japan one of highest gross national products in the world; reversion of S Ryukyu Is. to Japanese control 1972; jurisdiction over Kuril Is. (*q.v.*) has remained in dispute bet. Japan and Russia since end of WWII; during 1980s experienced large trade surplus leading to increased tensions with U.S. in 1990s over trade policies; despite economic slowdown mid-1990s, remains one of world's most productive economies.

Japan, Sea of. Branch of W Pacific Ocean lying bet. Japan on E, and Primorskiy Kray, Russia in Asia, and Korean Penin. on W; 389,100 sq. mi. (1,007,769 sq. km.); max. depth 12,276 ft. (3742 m.); on N connects by Tatar Strait with Sea of Ōkhotsk; on NE by Sōya Strait bet. Sakhalin and Hokkaidō with Sea of Ōkhotsk; on E by Tsugaru Strait bet. Hokkaidō and Honshū with the Pacific; and on SW by Korea Strait bet. Korean Penin. and Japan with East China Sea. For naval battle fought here 1905, see TSUSHIMA STRAIT.

Japan Current *or Jp.* **Ku·ro·shio** \ˌku̇r-ō-ˈshē-ō\. A branch of the equatorial current of the Pacific Ocean, flowing along the E coast of Taiwan, thence NE along E coast of Honshū, Japan, and merging into the easterly drift of the North Pacific Ocean S of the Aleutian Is.; noticeable for its deep blue color (hence the name Kuroshio, which means "Black Current" in English); has influence on climate similar to that of the Gulf Stream (*q.v.*).

Jap·a·nese Alps \ˌja-pə-ˈnēz, -ˈnēs\. Mountains, Japan, in cen. Honshū; parts lie within two national parks.

Japan Trench. Ocean trench, NW Pacific Ocean, E of and approx. parallel to Honshū I., extending in a general N to S direction; subduction zone according to theory of plate tectonics.

Japara. See JEPARA.

Japara–Rembang. See DJAPARA-REMBANG.

Japen *or* **Jappen.** See YAPEN.

Ja·pu·rá \ˌzhä-pü-ˈrä\ *also* **Ya·pu·rá** \ˌyä-\. River, NW South America; rises in SW Colombia, where it is known as the **Caquetá**, and flows SE across Brazilian border into Amazon River; ab. 1750 mi. (2816 km.) long.

Jap·vo, Mount \ˈjəp-vō\. Mountain in S part of Naga Hills, NE India, on N boundary of Manipur; 9890 ft. (3014 m.); highest mountain in Naga Hills.

Jaquemel. See JACMEL.

Ja·rā·bu·lus \jȧ-ˈrä-bü-lu̇s\ *or* **Je·ra·blus** \je-ˈrä-blu̇s\. Town, N Syria, on the Euphrates, near Turkish border.

Ja·ra·ma \hä-ˈrä-mä\. River, cen. Spain; joins Henares River 10 mi. (16 km.) ESE of Madrid and empties into Tagus River a little below Aranjuez; 120 mi. (193 km.) long.

Ja·rash *or* **Je·rash** \ˈjer-ˌäsh\; *anc.* **Ger·a·sa** \ˈjer-ə-sə\. Town, N Jordan, ab. 20 mi. (32 km.) N of Amman; ancient Gerasa a city of the Decapolis; ruins.

Jarbah. See JERBA.

Jar·di·nes de la Rei·na \här-ˈdē-nā-ˌthä-lä-ˈrā-nä\. Chain of small islands in West Indies, extending NW to SE in Caribbean Sea S of cen. Cuba; belong to Cuba.

Jar·geau \zhär-ˈzhō\. Town, Loiret dept., N cen. France, on the Loire River 10 mi. (16 km.) E of Orléans; scene of victory of saint and national heroine Joan of Arc over the English 1429.

Ja·ri *or* **Ja·rí** *or* **Ja·ry** \zhȧ-ˈrē\. River, NE Brazil; rises in Tumuc-Humac Mts. and flows SSE from SW Suriname border into Amazon River near its mouth; 360 mi. (579 km.) long.

Jarīd, Shaṭṭ al–. See DJERID, CHOTT.

Jarlsberg. See VESTFOLD.

Jar·nac \zhär-ˈnȧk\. Commune, Charente dept., W France, on the Charente River 18 mi. (29 km.) W of Angoulême; scene of battle 1569 in which Catholics under duke of Anjou (later Henry III) defeated the Huguenots under Louis I, prince of Condé, and in which the prince was killed.

Ja·ro \ˈhä-ˌrō\. Municipality, Leyte prov., Leyte, Philippines, on E slope of mountains 15 mi. (24 km.) W of Tacloban; pop. (1980c) 29,739.

Jar·o·cin \yä-ˈrȯt-shin\. Commune, Kalisz prov., W cen. Poland; pop. (1989e) 24,683.

Ja·ro·sław \yä-ˈrȯ-ˌswäf\ *or Ger.* **Ja·ro·slau** \ˈyär-ə-ˌslau̇\ *or Russ.* **Ya·ro·slav** \ˈyär-ə-ˌsläf, -ˌsläv\. City, Przemyśl prov., SE Poland, on San River 28 mi. (45 km.) E of Rzeszów; pop. (1989e) 41,351; scene of German defeat by Russians 1914; occupied by Germans and Austrians 1915 and by Germans 1941.

Jar·rā·hī \jə-ˈrä-ˌhē\. River, SW cen. Iran; flows generally SW into head of Persian Gulf; ab. 165 mi. (266 km.) long; seaport of Bandar-e Khomeyni is at its mouth.

Jar·row \ˈjar-ō\. Town, Tyne and Wear, N England, 6 mi. (10 km.) E of Newcastle upon Tyne; pop. (1981c) 31,213; chemicals, iron and steel; ruins of 7th cent. monastery where Anglo-Saxon scholar and theologian the Venerable Bede spent most of his life.

Ja·ru·co \hä-ˈrü-kō\. Municipality, La Habana prov., W Cuba, 23 mi. (37 km.) ESE of Havana.

Jar·ven·paa \ˈyär-ven-ˌpä\. Town, Uusimaa prov., S Finland; pop. (1989c) 30,819.

Jar·vis Island *also* **Jer·vis Island** \ˈjär-vis\. Atoll, one of the Line Is. (*q.v.*) just S of Equator in cen. Pacific Ocean, 190 mi. (306 km.) SW of Christmas I.; 1.6 sq. mi. (4.1 sq. km.); worked by an American company for its guano 1857–79; annexed by Great Britain 1889; claimed by U.S. 1935.

Jary. See JARI.

Jash·pur \ˈjəsh-ˌpu̇r\. Former Indian state in Eastern States, NE India; now in Madhya Pradesh; 1955 sq. mi. (5064 sq. km.); ✻ **Jash·pur·na·gar** \-ˈnə-gər\.

Jasiołda. See YASELDA.

Jāsk \ˈjäsk\. Seaport, S Iran, on Gulf of Oman 140 mi. (225 km.) SE of Bandar ʻAbbās.

Ja·sło \ˈyä-swȯ\. Commune, Krosno prov., Poland, 30 mi. (48 km.) SE of Tarnów; pop. (1989e) 36,995.

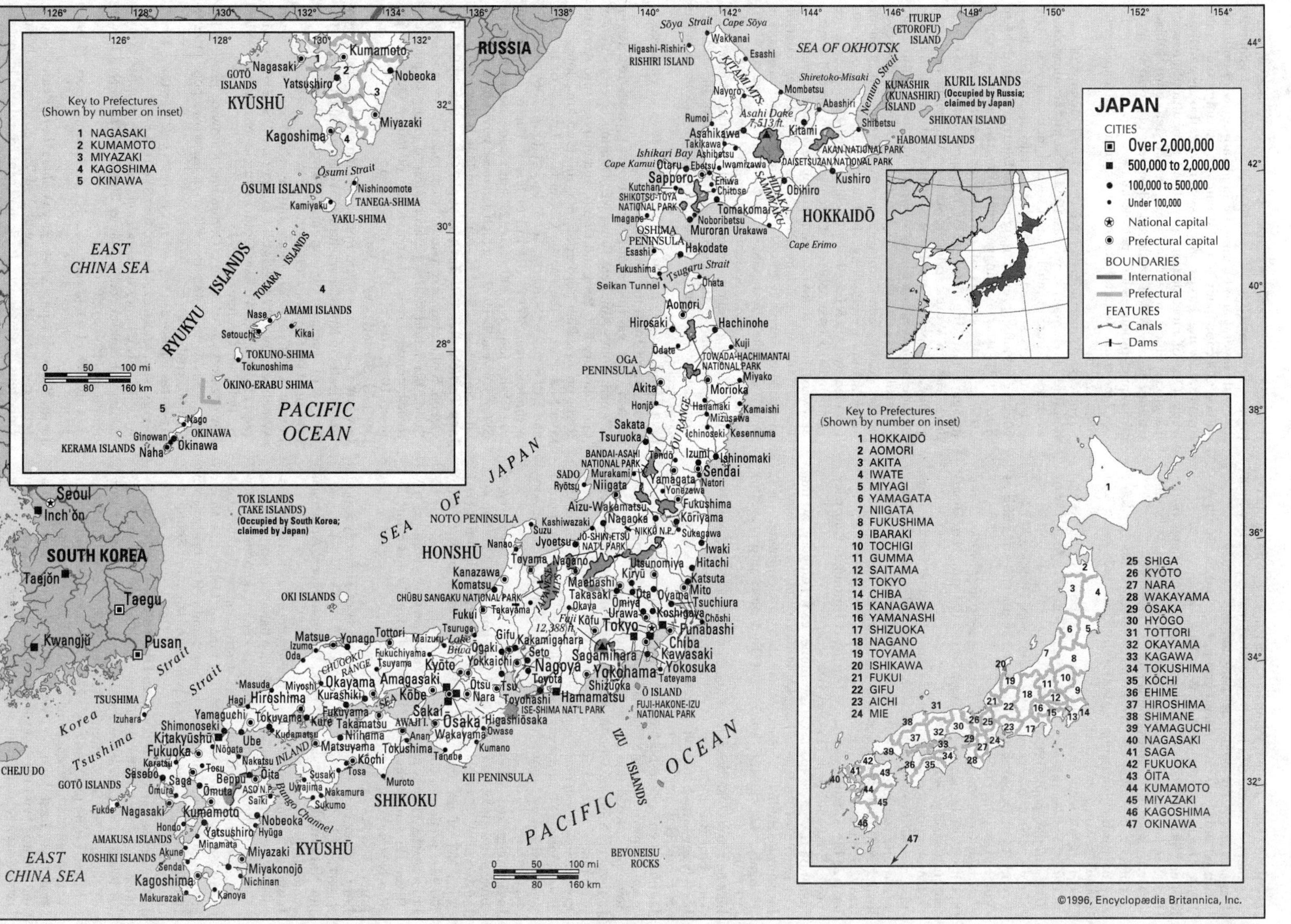

JAPAN
CITIES
Over 2,000,000
500,000 to 2,000,000
100,000 to 500,000
Under 100,000
National capital
Prefectural capital
BOUNDARIES
International
Prefectural
FEATURES
Canals
Dams
Key to Prefectures
(Shown by number on inset)
1 NAGASAKI
2 KUMAMOTO
3 MIYAZAKI
4 KAGOSHIMA
5 OKINAWA
EAST CHINA SEA
PACIFIC OCEAN
RYUKYU ISLANDS
TOKARA ISLANDS
AMAMI ISLANDS
ŌSUMI ISLANDS
TANEGA-SHIMA
YAKU-SHIMA
TOKUNO-SHIMA
ŌKINO-ERABU SHIMA
KERAMA ISLANDS
Ōsumi Strait
RUSSIA
SOUTH KOREA
SEA OF OKHOTSK
SEA OF JAPAN
HOKKAIDŌ
HONSHŪ
SHIKOKU
KYŪSHŪ
KURIL ISLANDS (Occupied by Russia; claimed by Japan)
TOK ISLANDS (TAKE ISLANDS) (Occupied by South Korea; claimed by Japan)
IZU ISLANDS
OKI ISLANDS
GOTŌ ISLANDS
Tokyo
Sapporo
Sendai
Yokohama
Nagoya
Kyōto
Ōsaka
Kōbe
Hiroshima
Kitakyūshū
Fukuoka
Seoul
Pusan
Key to Prefectures
(Shown by number on inset)
1 HOKKAIDŌ
2 AOMORI
3 AKITA
4 IWATE
5 MIYAGI
6 YAMAGATA
7 NIIGATA
8 FUKUSHIMA
9 IBARAKI
10 TOCHIGI
11 GUMMA
12 SAITAMA
13 TOKYO
14 CHIBA
15 KANAGAWA
16 YAMANASHI
17 SHIZUOKA
18 NAGANO
19 TOYAMA
20 ISHIKAWA
21 FUKUI
22 GIFU
23 AICHI
24 MIE
25 SHIGA
26 KYŌTO
27 NARA
28 WAKAYAMA
29 ŌSAKA
30 HYŌGO
31 TOTTORI
32 OKAYAMA
33 KAGAWA
34 TOKUSHIMA
35 KŌCHI
36 EHIME
37 HIROSHIMA
38 SHIMANE
39 YAMAGUCHI
40 NAGASAKI
41 SAGA
42 FUKUOKA
43 ŌITA
44 KUMAMOTO
45 MIYAZAKI
46 KAGOSHIMA
47 OKINAWA
©1996, Encyclopædia Britannica, Inc.

Jas·mund \ˈyäs-ˌmu̇nt\. Peninsula, NE Rügen I., NE Germany; in waters of Baltic Sea nearby occurred battle 1676 in which Danes under Adm. Niels Juel defeated the Swedes.

Ja·son Islands \ˈjās-ᵊn\. Island group, Falkland Is., South Atlantic Ocean, off NW coast of West Falkland.

Jas·per \ˈjas-pər\. **1.** Name of counties in eight states of the U.S. See tables at GEORGIA, ILLINOIS, INDIANA, IOWA, MISSISSIPPI, MISSOURI, SOUTH CAROLINA, TEXAS.

2. City, ⊗ of Walker co., NW cen. Alabama, 38 mi. (61 km.) NW of Birmingham; pop. (1990c) 13,553; coal; cattle and poultry raising; settled 1815.

3. City, ⊗ of Newton co., NW Arkansas; pop. (1990c) 332.

4. City, ⊗ of Hamilton co., N Florida, 79 mi. (127 km.) W of Jacksonville; pop. (1990c) 2099.

5. City, ⊗ of Pickens co., N Georgia; pop. (1990c) 1772.

6. City, ⊗ of Dubois co., SW Indiana, 36 mi. (58 km.) ESE of Vincennes; pop. (1990c) 10,030.

7. Town, ⊗ of Marion co., S Tennessee; pop. (1990c) 2780.

8. City, ⊗ of Jasper co., E Texas, 58 mi. (93 km.) N of Beaumont; pop. (1990c) 6959.

9. Unincorporated settlement in Jasper National Park, Alberta, Canada, on Athabaska River; alt. ab. 3470 ft. (1058 m.); resort and starting point for park excursions.

Jasper National Park. See CANADA, *National Parks.*

Jassy. See IAŞI.

Jas·trze·bie–Zdroj \yäs-ˈjā-bē-ˈzdrȯi\. Commune, Katowice prov., S Poland; pop. (1989e) 102,661.

Jász·a·pá·ti \ˈyä-sö-ˌpä-tē\. Commune, cen. Hungary, 50 mi. (81 km.) E of Budapest; pop. (1980p) 10,424.

Jász·á·rok·szál·lás \ˈyä-sä-rōk-ˌsä-läsh\. Commune, cen. Hungary, 42 mi. (68 km.) E of Budapest; pop. (1980p) 10,139.

Jász·be·rény \ˈyäz-be-ˌrān\. City, cen. Hungary, 37 mi. (60 km.) E of Budapest; pop. (1991e) 29,900.

Jász–Nagy·kun–Szol·nok \ˈyäs-ˈnȯj-ku̇n-ˈsȯl-nȯk\. County of E cen. Hungary. See table at HUNGARY.

Ja·ti·bo·ni·co \ˌhä-tē-bō-ˈnē-kō\. Municipality and town, Camagüey prov., E cen. Cuba; munic. pop. (1981p) 33,026; town on railroad line at Las Villas border.

Já·ti·va *or* **Xà·ti·va** \ˈhä-tē-ˌvä\; *anc.* **Se·ta·bis** \ˈse-tə-bəs\. Commune, Valencia prov., E Spain, 35 mi. (56 km.) S of the commune of Valencia; pop. (1991c) 24,461. Roman colony; noted during Middle Ages for production of paper; captured and fortified by Moors; reconquered by King James I of Aragon 1244.

Ja·ti·wan·gi *also* **Dja·ti·wan·gi** \ˌjä-tē-ˈwäŋ-gē\. Town, West Java prov., Indonesia, ab. 20 mi. (32 km.) W of Cirebon.

Jaú \zhȧ-ˈü\. City, São Paulo state, SE Brazil, 150 mi. (241 km.) NW of the city of São Paulo; munic. pop. (1991p) 90,961; processes coffee.

Jau·a·pe·ri \ˌzhau̇-ȧ-pe-ˈrē\ *also* **Yau·a·pe·ry** \ˌyau̇-ȧ-pe-ˈrē\. River, NE Amazonas state, N Brazil; flows SW and S into the Rio Negro; ab. 240 mi. (386 km.) long.

Jauer. See JAWOR.

Jau·ja \ˈhau̇-hä\. Town, cen. Peru, just N of Huancayo; pop. (1981p) 15,647.

Jau National Park. National Park, Brazil in N cen. Amazonas state; largest in Brazil.

Jaun·pur \ˈjau̇n-ˌpu̇r\. City, Uttar Pradesh, N India, on Gomati River 60 mi. (97 km.) ENE of Allahabad; pop. (1991p) 136,287; railroad and commercial center; known for perfumes; founded 11th cent.; after destruction by floods rebuilt 1359–64 by Fīrūz Shāh Tughluq, king of Delhi; has an old fort with gateway, notable mosques, and a fine bridge over the Gomati; ✻ 1394–1479 of princes of so-called Sharqi dynasty.

Ja·va \ˈjä-və, ˈja-\ *or Indonesian* **Dja·wa** \ˈjä-vä\. Island, Indonesia, in the Greater Sunda Is. group, SE of Sumatra and S of Borneo, bet. Java Sea and Indian Ocean; separated from SE Sumatra by Sunda Strait and from Bali on E by Bali Strait; 661 mi. (1064 km.) long by 124 mi. (200 km.) at widest part; with smaller adjacent islands comprises three provinces **Central Java, East Java,** and **West Java;** also contains the capital territory and the Yogyakarta special district (see table at INDONESIA). Mountainous with 20 or more peaks above 8000 ft. (2438 m.), mostly volcanic with about 13 active today; highest Semeru 12,060 ft. (3676 m.); N coastland generally low with several good harbors; S coast abrupt with only one harbor Cilacap; many short streams, most important Solo, Brantas, Liwung; has extensive system of railroads and highways. One of most densely populated agricultural areas on the globe; chief crops rice, sugar, coffee, tea, corn, rubber; fishing; before WWII produced 90 percent of world's supply of quinine; produces also petroleum.

Chief cities: Jakarta, Surabaya, Bandung, Cilacap, Semarang.

History: Archaeologists have discovered remains of early hominid (Java man) now classified with pithecanthropines; evidence of human inhabitation several thousand years B.C.; Indian traders arrived first cent. A.D., introducing Hinduism which gradually spread through area; Dharmavamsa, king of E Java 991–1007; Airlangga, ruler of united Javanese empire 1019–c. 1049, subject of Javanese epic *Arjunaivāha*; Kertanagara, last king 1268–92 of Tumapel (see SINGOSARI) in Java; Hayam Wuruk, ruler of state of Majapahit in E Java conquered Srivijaya empire of Sumatra and expanded rule to include almost all of Malay Archipelago during 14th cent.; Majapahit was conquered by Muslims and finally destroyed in 16th cent.; when Europeans arrived in 16th cent., Bantam and Mataram were leading Muslim states; Batavia (*q.v.*) was founded by Dutch East India Company 1619 which expelled English 1623 (see AMBON); Dutch gradually spread control eastward from Batavia; Bantam captured and annexed by Dutch 1808–09; held by British 1811–16; Dutch control, menaced by revolt 1825–30, afterwards became stronger; in WWII occupied by Japanese 1942–45; after close of WWII scene of strong Indonesian independence movement, resulting in the Linggadjati Agreement and the establishment 1950 of the Republic of Indonesia (*q.v.*); both politically and economically remains most important island in Indonesia in late 20th cent.

Java Head. Cape on extreme W end of Java at entrance to Sunda Strait from the Indian Ocean.

Ja·va·ri \ˌzhä-vä-ˈrē\ *or in Peru* **Ya·va·ri** \ˌyä-vä-ˈrē\. River, NW cen. South America; flows NE, forming large section of the boundary bet. Peru and Brazil, and empties into Amazon River on Brazilian border; ab. 600 mi. (965 km.) long.

Java Sea. Part of the Pacific Ocean N of Java, S of Borneo, and E of S end of Sumatra; lat. 3° to 7°S, long. 106° to 116°E; a shallow sea, 300 ft. (91 m.) or less in depth; ab. 600 mi. (965 km.) long by 200 mi. (322 km.) wide; scene of battle SW of Bawean I. 1942 in which Japanese naval forces defeated a combined U.S.-U.K.-Australian-Dutch fleet.

Java Trench; *formerly* **Java Trough.** Ocean trench, E Indian Ocean, S of and approx. parallel to Sumatra, Java, and Lesser Sunda Is.; subduction zone according to theory of plate tectonics; contains deepest known part of Indian Ocean, at approx. 10°S, 109°E, 25,344 ft. (7725 m.).

Jawf, Al. See AL JAWF.

Ja·whar \jə-ˈhwär, -ˈwär\. Former Indian state, W India; geographically in NW Maharashtra in Western Ghats, 75 mi. (121 km.) N of Bombay; 308 sq. mi. (798 sq. km.).

Jawlān, Al–. See GOLAN HEIGHTS.

Ja·wor \ˈyä-ˌvȯr\ *or Ger.* **Jau·er** \ˈyau̇-ər\. City, cen. Wrocław prov., SW Poland, 11 mi. (18 km.) SSE of Legnica; pop. (1989e) 24,241; late Gothic church; assigned to Poland by Potsdam Conference 1945.

Ja·worz·no \yä-ˈvȯzh-nȯ\. Commune, Katowice prov., S Poland, ab. 30 mi. (48 km.) WNW of Kraków; pop. (1989e) 99,050; coal.

Jax·ar·tes \jak-ˈsär-tēz\ *or* **Iax·ar·tes** \yak-ˈsär-tēz\. River, Kyrgyzstan and Kazakhstan. See SYR DAR'YA.

Jay \ˈjā\. **1.** County in E Indiana. See table at INDIANA.

2. Town, Franklin co., W Maine, 28 mi. (45 km.) N of Lewiston; pop. (1990c) 5080.

3. City, ⊗ of Delaware co., NE Oklahoma; pop. (1990c) 2220.

Ja·ya, Pun·cak \ˈpu̇n-ˌchäk-ˈjä-yə\ *also* **Dja·ja Peak** \ˈjä-yə\; *formerly* **Mount Su·kar·no** \su̇-ˈkär-nō\ *also* **Mount Car·stensz** \ˈkär-stens\. Peak in W cen. Irian Jaya, Indonesia, in the Sudirman Range; 16,535 ft. (5040 m.); highest mountain on New Guinea I.

Jayabum. See CHAIYAPHUM.

Jayanath. See CHAINAT.

Ja·ya·pu·ra *also* **Dja·ja·pu·ra** \ˌjä-yä-ˈpü-rä\; *formerly* **Hol·lan·dia** \hȯ-ˈlän-dē-ə\ *or* **Ko·ta·ba·ru** \ˌkō-tä-ˈbä-rü\ *or* **Su·kar·na·pu·ra** \sü-ˈkär-nä-ˌpü-rä\. Town, ✻ of Irian Jaya, Indonesia, on NE coast; good harbor; seized from Japanese by U.S. forces Apr. 1944; became headquarters of Gen. Douglas MacArthur.

Ja·ya·wi·ja·ya Range \ˌjä-yə-wi-ˈjä-yə\ *or* **Dja·ja·wi·dja·ja Range** \ˌjä-yə-wi-ˈjä-yə\ *or Indonesian* **Pe·gu·nun·gan Jayawijaya** \ˌpe-gü-ˈnüŋ-ˌgän\; *formerly* **Or·ange Range** \ˈȯr-inj, ˈär-, -ənj\. Mountain range, E cen. Irian Jaya, Indonesia, E of Sudirman Range and forming E end of Maoke Mts.; highest peak Trikora 15,585 ft. (4750 m.); source of the Digul and many other streams.

Jayhun. See AMU DARYA.

Jay Peak. Mountain, NW Orleans co., N Vermont; 3861 ft. (1177 m.); ski slopes.

Ja·yu·ya \hä-ˈyü-yä\. Municipality, cen. Puerto Rico, N of Ponce; pop. (1990c) 15,527.

Jazā'ir, Al–. See ALGIERS.

Jazā'ir, Farasān. See FARASĀN, JAZĀ'IR.

Jazā'ir Khurīyā Murīyā. See KHURĪYĀ MURĪYĀ, JAZĀ'IR.

Ja·zī·rah, Al \ˌal-jȧ-ˈzē-rə\. Region of upper Mesopotamia; in the Tigris-Euphrates Valley NW of Baghdad, Iraq; important as trading point in both ancient times and Middle Ages.

Jazīrah, Al–. See GEZIRA.

Jean·er·ette \ˌje-nə-ˈret\. City, Iberia parish, S Louisiana, 32 mi. (52 km.) SE of Lafayette; pop. (1990c) 6205.

Jean Laf·fite National Historical Park \ˌzhän-lə-ˈfēt\. See UNITED STATES, *National Historical Parks.*

Jean·nette \jə-ˈnet\. City, Westmoreland co., SW Pennsylvania, 22 mi. (35 km.) ESE of Pittsburgh; pop. (1990c) 11,221; settled 1888.

Jebeil. See JUBAYL.

Jeb·el \ˈje-bəl\; *Arab.* **Ja·bal** \ˈja-bȧl\ *also* **Ge·bel** \ˈje-bəl, ˈgȧ-bȧl\ *or French* **Dje·bel** \jä-ˈbel\. Forms from the Arabic word meaning "mountain, hill"; often used in place names in N Africa and SW Asia. For names of mountains containing this word, see the 2d element. So, for *Djebel Chélia,* see CHÉLIA, DJEBEL, and for *Jebel Sham,* see SHAM, JEBEL.

Jebel Au·lia \ˈaü-lē-ə\ *also* **Khaz·zān Ja·bal Al–Aw·li·yā** \kȧ-ˈzän-ˌjȧ-bəl-ȧl-ˌaü-lē-ˈȧ\. Site of storage dam across the White Nile, 27 mi. (43 km.) S of Khartoum in Sudan; completed 1937; holds back Nile flood waters July–Oct.

Jebel ed Druz \ed-ˈdrüz\ *or* **Jebel Druze** *or* **Djeb·el Druze** \ˌje-bəl-ˈdrüz\. **1.** Former subdivision of the Republic of Syria, SW Asia, E of the Sea of Galilee and bordering on N Jordan; 2700 sq. mi. (6993 sq. km.); ✻ As Suwaydā. Plateau and mountainous region; highest point Jebel Druze 5907 ft. (1801 m.); inhabited by Druzes, survivors of Muslim sect founded in 11th cent. A.D.; recognized 1921 as autonomous state within French mandate of Syria; led nationalist revolt in Syria against French 1925; incorp. into Syria (republic) 1942.

2. Mountain in this area. See DRUZE, JEBEL 1.

Jed·burgh \ˈjed-bə-rə\. Burgh, Borders region, SE Scotland; pop. (1981c) 4069; ruins of noted 12th cent. abbey; the proverbial Jedburgh justice (punishing first and trying afterwards) is so called from an early 17th cent. summary execution of a band of malefactors here.

Jedda *or* **Jeddah.** See JIDDA.

Jeff Da·vis \ˈjef-ˈdā-vis\. Name of counties in two states of the U.S. See tables at GEORGIA and TEXAS.

Jef·fer·son \ˈje-fər-sən\. **1.** River, SW Montana; formed by confluence of branches in NW Madison co., flows N and E to unite with Madison and Gallatin rivers and form Missouri River; 217 mi. (349 km.) long.

2. Name of parish in SE Louisiana and of counties in 25 states of the U.S. See tables at ALABAMA, ARKANSAS, COLORADO, FLORIDA, GEORGIA, IDAHO, ILLINOIS, INDIANA, IOWA, KANSAS, KENTUCKY, LOUISIANA, MISSISSIPPI, MISSOURI, MONTANA, NEBRASKA, NEW YORK, OHIO, OKLAHOMA, OREGON, PENNSYLVANIA, TENNESSEE, TEXAS, WASHINGTON, WEST VIRGINIA, WISCONSIN.

3. City, ⊗ of Jackson co., NE Georgia; pop. (1990c) 2763.

4. City, ⊗ of Greene co., W cen. Iowa, 33 mi. (53 km.) SSW of Fort Dodge; pop. (1990c) 4292.

5. Town, Coos co., N New Hampshire, in White Mts.; pop. (1990c) 965; summer resort.

6. Town, ⊗ of Ashe co., NW North Carolina; pop. (1990c) 1300.

7. Village, ⊗ of Ashtabula co., NE corner of Ohio, 8 mi. (13 km.) S of the city of Ashtabula; pop. (1990c) 3331.

8. Village, Madison co., SW cen. Ohio, 16 mi. (26 km.) W of Columbus; pop. (1990c) 4505.

9. Borough, Allegheny co., SW Pennsylvania, S of Pittsburgh; pop. (1990c) 9533.

10. City, ⊗ of Marion co., NE Texas, near W end of Caddo Lake 15 mi. (24 km.) N of Marshall; pop. (1990c) 2199; founded 1836 on route followed by Gen. Sam Houston, and, later, by frontiersman Davy Crockett.

11. City, ⊗ of Jefferson co., SE Wisconsin, 13 mi. (21 km.) S of Watertown; pop. (1990c) 6078; settled 1836.

Jefferson, Mount. **1.** Peak in Presidential Range of White Mts., in S Coos co., N New Hampshire; ab. 5715 ft. (1740 m.).

2. Peak, W Jefferson co., N cen. Oregon; 10,495 ft. (3199 m.).

Jefferson City. **1.** City, ✻ of Missouri and ⊗ of Cole co., cen. Missouri; pop. (1990c) 35,481; commercial center; electrical appliances; Lincoln Univ. (1866). Selected as ✻ 1821 and occupied as such 1826; incorp. as town 1825, as city 1839; occupied by Union troops June, 1861; state capitol built 1918.

2. City, Jefferson co., E Tennessee, WSW of Morristown; pop. (1990c) 5494; Carson-Newman Coll. (1851).

Jefferson Da·vis \ˈdā-vis\. Name of a parish in SW Louisiana and of a county in S Mississippi. See tables at LOUISIANA and MISSISSIPPI.

Jef·fer·son·town \ˈje-fər-sən-ˌtaün\. City, Jefferson co., N cen. Kentucky, E of Louisville; pop. (1990c) 23,221.

Jef·fer·son·ville \ˈje-fər-sən-ˌvil\. **1.** City, ⊗ of Twiggs co., cen. Georgia; pop. (1990c) 1545.

2. City, ⊗ of Clark co., S Indiana, on Ohio River across from Louisville, Kentucky; pop. (1990c) 21,841; steamboat museum.

Jehlam. See JHELUM.

Je·hol \jə-ˈhōl, ˈrō-ˈhō\. **1.** Region, NE China, N of the Great Wall; 74,278 sq. mi. (192,380 sq. km.); long considered a part of Nei Monggol (Inner Mongolia); later, the N part of Chihli prov., China Proper, from which it was separated 1928 to become a province of SW Manchuria; from 1933 to 1945 with reduced area a province of the newly estab. Japanese state of Manchukuo (*q.v.*) with ✻ at Chengde (Jehol); later a province of China; in 1955 divided among Nei Monggol (Inner Mongolia), Hebei, and Liaoning.

2. City, its ✻. See CHENGDE.

Je·hosh·a·phat \ji-ˈhä-shə-ˌfat, -sə-, -fət\. A common name of the valley of the Kidron (*q.v.*); mentioned in the Old Testament (*Joel* iii. 2, 12).

Je·jui Gua·zú \he-ˈhwē-gwä-ˈsü\. River in E cen. Paraguay, flowing W into Paraguay River.

Jek·yll Island \ˈjek-əl\. Island in Atlantic Ocean, off mainland of Glynn co., SE Georgia; 10 sq. mi. (26 sq. km.); formerly owned by the Jekyll Island Club, a group of influential businessmen incl. John D. Rockefeller and J.P. Morgan who maintained resort homes here; now a state park and resort.

Je·lai \ˈjä-ˌlī\. River, W headstream of the Pahang, NW Pahang state, Malaysia; joins the Tembeling to form the Pahang at 4°03′N.

Jelalabad. See JALĀLĀBĀD.

Je·le·nia Gó·ra \ye-'len-yä-'gü-rä\; *Ger.* **Hirsch·berg** \'hirsh-,berk\ *also* **Hirschberg in Schle·si·en** \in-'shlā-zē-ən\ *or* **Hirschberg im Rie·sen·ge·bir·ge** \im-'rēz-ᵊn-gə-,bir-gə\. **1.** Province, SW Poland. See table at POLAND.
2. City, its ✱, ab. 60 mi. (97 km.) WSW of Wrocław; pop. (1989e) 93,182; textiles; assigned to Poland by Potsdam Conference 1945.

Je·lep–la \'je-ləp-,lä\ *or Chin.* **Chih–lieh–p'u** \'jir-'lē-e-'pü\. Pass (*la*), on border of Sikkim, leading into Tibet, China, ab. 45 mi. (72 km.) NE of Darjeeling, India; alt. 14,390 ft. (4386 m.).

Jel·ga·va *also* **Yel·ga·va** \'yel-gə-və\ *or Ger.* **Mi·tau** \'mē-,taů\. City, S Latvia, on Lielupe River; pop. (1991e) 74,500; linen, refined sugar, and other food products.
History: Founded 1266 by Teutonic Knights; became ✱ of duchy of Courland 1561; fell under Russian rule 1795; headquarters Oct. 1919 of Bolshevik troops, who were expelled from the city by a combined Latvian and Lithuanian army; in WWII held by German forces 1941–44.

Jem, Al–. See AL-JEM.

Jem, El. See EL DJEM.

Je·mappes \zhə-'måp\. Commune, Hainaut prov., SW Belgium, just W of Mons; battlefield where the French under Gen. Charles-François Dumouriez defeated the Austrians 1792.

Jem·ber *also* **Djem·ber** \'jem-bər\. Town, East Java prov., Indonesia; pop. (1980c) 140,105; university (1964).

Je·mez Springs \'hā-mes\. Village, Sandoval co., NW cen. New Mexico; pop. (1990c) 413; S of it is the Jemez Indian Pueblo, estab. ab. 1700, on the **Jemez River** (tributary of the Rio Grande, ab. 50 mi. or 80 km. long); N of it is the **Jemez State Monument** with ruins of early mission.

Je·na \'jē-nə\. Town, ⊗ of La Salle parish, cen. Louisiana; pop. (1990c) 2626.

Je·na \'yā-nə\. City, Thuringia, E cen. Germany, on Saale River 25 mi. (40 km.) E of Erfurt; pop. (1992e) 100,967; chemicals, optical instruments (formerly a world center for lens making); university (1588); botanical garden; remains of old fortifications; 14th cent. town hall; 15th cent. church; first planetarium built here; first mentioned 9th cent.; became city 13th cent.; scene of famous victory of French Emperor Napoléon over Prussian and Saxon armies Oct. 14, 1806; original *Burschenschaft* (corporation of university students) organized here 1815; severely damaged in WWII, since rebuilt.

Jen·dou·ba \jen-'dü-bə\ *or* **Jun·du·bah** \jən-'dü-bə\. Town, NW Tunisia; pop. (1989e) 38,585.

Jenil. See GENIL.

Je·nin \je-'nēn\ *or* **Ja·nīn** \ja-\; *anc.* **En·gan·nim** \en-'ga-nəm, eŋ-\. Town at S end of Plain of Esdraelon, Jordan, in area occupied by Israel 1967; Israeli troops withdrawn late 1995.

Jen·kins \'jen-kinz\. **1.** County in E Georgia. See table at GEORGIA.
2. City, Letcher co., SE Kentucky, 22 mi. (35 km.) SSW of Pikeville; pop. (1990c) 2751.

Jen·kin·town \'jeŋ-kin-,taůn\. Residential borough, Montgomery co., SE Pennsylvania, 10 mi. (16 km.) N of Philadelphia; pop. (1990c) 4574; Manor Junior Coll. (1947).

Jenks \'jiŋks\. City, Tulsa co., NE Oklahoma; a S suburb of the city of Tulsa; pop. (1990c) 7493.

Jenné. See DJENNÉ.

Jen·nings \'je-niŋz\. **1.** County in SE Indiana. See table at INDIANA.
2. City, ⊗ of Jefferson Davis parish, SW Louisiana, 36 mi. (58 km.) E of Lake Charles; pop. (1990c) 11,305; rice; oil.
3. City, St. Louis co., E Missouri, 4 mi. (6 km.) N of the city of St. Louis; pop. (1990c) 15,905; residential suburb of St. Louis.

Je·pa·ra also **Ja·pa·ra** *or* **Dje·pa·ra** *or* **Dja·pa·ra** \jə-'pä-rä\. Coastal town, N cen. Java, Indonesia.

Je·quié \zhe-'kyā\. City, SE cen. Bahia state, E Brazil, 125 mi. (201 km.) SW of Salvador; munic. pop. (1991p) 135,497.

Je·qui·ti·nho·nha \,zhe-kē-tē-'nyō-nyə\. River, E Brazil; rises in cen. Minas Gerais state, flows NE and E through Bahia state into Atlantic Ocean; ab. 500 mi. (800 km.) long.

Jerablus. See JARĀBULUS.

Jerash. See JARASH.

Je·rauld \jə-'rȯld\. County in SE cen. South Dakota. See table at SOUTH DAKOTA.

Jer·ba *or* **Djer·ba** \'jər-bə, 'jer-\ *or* **Jar·bah** \'jer-bə\; *anc.* **Me·ninx** \'mē-ninks\. Island in cen. Mediterranean Sea, off SE coast of Tunisia, at S side of entrance to the Gulf of Gabès; 197 sq. mi. (510 sq. km.); a fertile island producing olives and dates; tourism; contains remains of ancient Roman civilization.

Je·ré·cua·ro \he-'rā-kwä-,rō\. Municipality, Guanajuato state, Mexico, 35 mi. (56 km.) SE of Celaya; pop. (1990p) 51,832.

Jé·ré·mie \,zhā-rā-'mē\. Seaport on NW Tiburon Penin., Haiti, 120 mi. (193 km.) W of Port-au-Prince.

Je·rez \hā-'reth\ *or in full* **Jerez de la Fron·te·ra** \,t͟hā-lä-frȯn-'tā-rä\; *formerly* **Xe·res** \'sher-ēz\ *or* **Xe·ra** \'sher-ä\. City, Cádiz prov., SW Spain, 13 mi. (21 km.) NE of the city of Cádiz; pop. (1991p) 182,939; commercial center; noted esp. for its sherry (named for the town); Roman colony; believed by some to be scene of famous battle of Moors under Ṭāriq ibn Ziyād with Visigoths under their king Roderick 711 (see BARBATE, RÍO); recaptured but lost by Spanish King Ferdinand III and finally taken 1264 by Alfonso X.

Je·rez de Gar·cía Sa·li·nas \hā-'res-t͟hā-gär-'sē-ä-sä-'lē-näs\. Town, Zacatecas state, cen. Mexico, W of the city of Zacatecas; munic. pop. (1990p) 58,001.

Jerez de los Ca·bal·le·ros \hā-'reth-,t͟hā-lōs-,kä-b͟ä-'lyā-rōs\. Commune, Badajoz prov., SW Spain, 37 mi. (60 km.) SSE of the city of Badajoz; pop. (1991c) 10,191; Moorish walls, gates, and fortress; birthplace of Spanish explorers Vasco Núñez de Balboa (1475) and Hernando de Soto (c. 1500); thought to have been founded by Phoenicians; reconquered from Moors 1229; enlarged and given to Knights Templars 1232.

Jer·i·cho \'jer-i-,kō\. **1.** Unincorporated settlement, Nassau co., SE New York, on Long Island; pop. (1990c) 13,141; residential.
2. Town, Chittenden co., Vermont; pop. (1990c) 4302.
3. *Arab.* **Arīhā** \ä-'rē-hä\. Village, Jordan, ab. 14 mi. (23 km.) ENE of Jerusalem, in area occupied by Israel 1967; 825 ft. (251 m.) below sea level. Site of an important ancient city, a stronghold commanding the valley of the lower Jordan; captured c. 1400 B.C. by Hebrew leader Joshua (*Josh.* vi). Later several times destroyed and rebuilt on a site at or near the modern village of Arīhā; captured by British Feb. 21, 1918 in WWI; under Israeli-Palestinian self-rule agreement, turned over to Palestinian rule May 1994.

Jerid, Chott el. See DJERID, CHOTT.

Jer·i·moth Hill \'jer-i-,mäth, -,mȯth\. Elevation, Providence co., Rhode Island, W of Providence on Connecticut border; 812 ft. (247 m.); highest point in the state.

Je·rome \jə-'rōm\. **1.** County in S Idaho. See table at IDAHO.
2. City, ⊗ of Jerome co., S Idaho, 14 mi. (23 km.) N of Twin Falls; pop. (1990c) 6529.

Jer·sey \'jər-zē\. **1.** New Jersey—a colloquial name.
2. County in W Illinois. See table at ILLINOIS.
3. One of the Channel Is., in the English Channel; 44.87 sq. mi. (116 sq. km.); pop. (1993e) 85,900; ✱ St. Helier; constitutes a bailiwick; potatoes; tourism; the fabric, upper-body garment, and cattle breed all took their names from the island.

Jersey Bay. Bay, SE end of St. Thomas I., Virgin Is. of the U.S., West Indies.

Jersey City. City and port, ⊗ of Hudson co., NE New Jersey, on Hudson River and Upper New York Bay, across from New York City; pop. (1990c) 228,537; railroad center; chemicals; the Colgate Clock (1924) features a 50-foot (15-meter) dial; St. Peter's Coll. (1872), New Jersey City Univ. (1927). Purchased from Indians by Dutch c. 1630 and settled before 1664, when it was taken by British; chartered as town 1668; scene of defeat of British by American Gen. "Light Horse Harry" Lee 1779; chartered as City of Jersey 1820, as Jersey City 1836; became ⊗ 1840; important station on Underground Railroad when southern slaves were fleeing north mid-19th cent.; scene of Black Tom explosion where U.S. munitions were blown up by German saboteurs 1916.

Jersey Shore. Borough, Lycoming co., N cen. Pennsylvania, on West Susquehanna River 13 mi. (21 km.) W of Williamsport; pop. (1990c) 4353.

Jer·sey·ville \ˈjər-zē-ˌvil\. Village, ⊗ of Jersey co., W Illinois, 60 mi. (97 km.) SW of Springfield; pop. (1990c) 7382.

Je·ru·sa·lem \jə-ˈrü-sə-ləm, -zə-ləm, -sləm\. **1.** Town, SE Virginia. See COURTLAND.

2. District of E cen. Israel. See table at ISRAEL.

3. *or Arab.* **Al–Quds** \äl-ˈküts\ *or Heb.* **Ye·ru·sha·lay·im** \ye-ˌrü-shä-ˈlī-im\; *anc.* **Hi·er·o·sol·y·ma** \ˌhī-ə-rō-ˈsä-lə-mə\. City, ✻ of Israel and ✻ of district of Jerusalem; situated on two rocky hills at alt. of 2500 ft. (762 m.), 35 mi. (56 km.) from the Mediterranean and ab. 13 mi. (20 km.) W of N end of Dead Sea; pop. (1992e) 544,200; connected by railroad with Tel Aviv-Jaffa on the coast and center of ancient highways N, E, S, and W; tourism. Holy city of Jews, Christians, and Muslims; called "City of David" and "City of the Great King" (*Ps.* xlviii. 2): see ZION 2; Hebrew Univ. (1925); numerous churches, synagogues, and mosques (3d holy city of Islam).

History: Mentioned in Tell el-ʻAmârna letters 14th cent. B.C.; fortress of Jebusites captured by King David c. 1000 B.C. and made the ✻ of kingdom of Israel, and later, of Judah (*qq.v.*); walls of city were built and the Temple founded by his son Solomon 10th cent. B.C.; destroyed by King Nebuchadrezzar of Babylon c. 586 B.C.; restored to Jews by Cyrus the Great, ruler of Persia (see IRAN) c. 538 B.C.; in mid-5th cent. B.C., Jewish leader Nehemiah rebuilt its walls; as city of Palestine (*q.v.*) ruled by Macedonian King Alexander the Great, Ptolemies, Seleucids, and by Romans who ruled it at the time Christianity was founded by Jesus; partly destroyed by Roman Emperor Titus 70 A.D. and by Emperor Hadrian in 135; rebuilt as Roman city, **Ae·lia Cap·i·to·li·na** \ˈē-lē-ə-ˌkap-ət-ᵊl-ˈīn-ə\; held by Persians 614–629; taken by Muslim Arabs c. 638; its capture c. 1077 by Seljuqs who mistreated Christian pilgrims was immediate cause of Crusades; captured by Crusaders who erected Latin kingdom of Jerusalem (1099–1187); after its fall into hands of Muslim Sultan Saladin 1187, its recovery was goal of several Crusades; changed hands several times bet. Turks and Egyptians 1244–1917; occupied by British in campaign against Turks Dec. 1917; old city taken over by Transjordan Arabs 1948; new city captured by Israeli forces 1948; on Feb. 1, 1949 declared by the provisional government of Israel to be part of the new state, and in 1950 made ✻; Jordanian part of city occupied by Israel 1967 and integrated with Israeli sector; officially annexed 1980; its status continues to be disputed by Arabs and Israelis.

Jer·vaulx \ˈjər-ˌvō\. Hamlet, North Riding, Yorkshire, N England; noted for ruins of its abbey, ab. 4 mi. (6 km.) SW, dating from 12th cent.

Jer·vis Bay \ˈjär-vis\. Inlet of South Pacific, on E coast of New South Wales, SE Australia; equidistant (ab. 90 mi. or 145 km.) SSW from Sydney and ENE from Canberra; 10 to 12 mi. (16 to 19 km.) long; 28 sq. mi. (73 sq. km.), incl. the harbor on S side of bay; a part of Australian Capital Terr. (*q.v.*).

Jervis Island. See JARVIS ISLAND.

Jesi. See IESI.

Jes·sa·mine \ˈje-sə-mən\. County in E cen. Kentucky. See table at KENTUCKY.

Jesselton. See KOTA KINABALU.

Jes·sore \je-ˈsōr\. **1.** Former district, SE Bengal, India; 2925 sq. mi. (7576 sq. km.); divided 1947 so that the greater portion of it was assigned to East Pakistan (now Bangladesh), the remainder to West Bengal, India.

2. Town, Bangladesh, on Ganges Delta, 90 mi. (145 km.) SW of Dhaka; pop. (1991p) 176,398; rice.

Jes·sup \ˈje-səp\. Borough, Lackawanna co., NE Pennsylvania, ab. 8 mi. (13 km.) NE of Scranton; pop. (1990c) 4605.

Jes·up \ˈje-səp\. City, ⊗ of Wayne co., SE Georgia, 40 mi. (64 km.) NE of Waycross; pop. (1990c) 8958.

Je·sus Island \ˈjē-zəs, -zəz\ *or Fr.* **Île Jé·sus** \ˌēl-zhā-ˈzüe\. Island in St. Lawrence River just W of Montreal I., Canada; 84 sq. mi. (218 sq. km.); separated from Montreal I. by Rivière des Prairies and from mainland by Rivière des Mille Îles; chief city Laval.

Je·thou \zhə-ˈtü\. Island Channel Is., England, in Guernsey bailiwick, S of Herm; 44 acres (18 hectares); uninhabited.

Jet·more \ˈjet-ˌmōr\. City, ⊗ of Hodgeman co., SW cen. Kansas; pop. (1990c) 850.

Jet·pur \ˈjet-ˌpu̇r\. Town, Gujarat state, W India, in cen. Kathiawar Penin., 240 mi. (386 km.) NW of Bombay; pop. (1991p) 73,556.

Jette \ˈzhet\. Commune, Brabant prov., cen. Belgium, a suburb of Brussels; pop. (1991c) 38,423.

Jeu·mont \zhœ-ˈmōⁿ\. Commune, Nord dept., N France, near Belgian frontier.

Jew·el Cave National Monument \ˈjü-əl\. See UNITED STATES, *National Monuments.*

Jew·ell \ˈjü-əl\. County in N Kansas. See table at KANSAS.

Jew·ett City \ˈjü-ət\. Borough in town of Griswold, Connecticut; pop. (1990c) 3349. See GRISWOLD.

Jewish Autonomous Oblast \ˈȯ-bləst, -ˌblast\ *or* **Ye·vrey·ska·ya Autonomous Oblast** \yi-ˈvrā-skə-yə\ *or* **Bi·ro·bi·dzhan** *or* **Bi·ro·bi·jan** \ˌbir-ō-bi-ˈjän\. Autonomous subdivision of SE Russia in Asia, on Amur River; 13,900 sq. mi. (36,001 sq. km.); ✻ Birobidzhan; territory set aside 1928 by Soviet government for colonization by Jews; made autonomous region 1934; majority of population non-Jewish.

Jeypore. See JAIPUR.

Jezairi–Bahri–Sefid. See ARCHIPELAGO.

Je·zio·rak \ye-ˈzhȯ-räk\; *formerly* **Lake Ge·se·rich** \ˈgā-zə-rik̲\. Lake, Olsztyn prov., N Poland; 12 sq. mi. (31 sq. km.); formerly in East Prussia, Germany.

Jeziret ibn Omar. See CİZRE.

Jez·re·el \ˈjez-rē-ˌel, -ˌrēl\ *or* **Yiz·ré·el** \ˌyiz-rā-ˈel\. Town, ancient Palestine, NW of Mt. Gilboa; a ✻ of Ahab, king of Israel (*1 Kings* xviii. 45); scene of death of his wife Jezebel (*2 Kings* ix. 30–35).

Jezreel, Valley of. See ESDRAELON, PLAIN OF.

Jha·bua \ˈjä-bwə\. Former Indian state, N cen. India, 80 mi. (129 km.) W of Indore; now part of Madhya Pradesh; 1265 sq. mi. (3276 sq. km.); ✻ Jhabua.

Jha·la·war \ˈjä-lə-ˌwär\. **1.** Former princely state, now a district of Rajasthan, NW India; 2405 sq. mi. (6229 sq. km.); pop. (1981c) 784,998.

2. *or* **Jhal·ra·pa·tan** \ˌjäl-rə-ˈpät-ᵊn\. Town, its ✻, in SE Rajputana, India, 160 mi. (257 km.) S of Jaipur.

Jhang Sa·dar \ˈjəŋ-ˈsə-dər\ *or* **Jhang–Ma·ghi·a·na** \-ˌmə-gē-ˈä-nə\. Town, Punjab, Pakistan, near left bank of Chenab River 120 mi. (193 km.) WSW of Lahore; pop. (1981c) 195,558; a joint municipality of which Maghiana is newer and more important part; trades in grain and cloth.

Jhan·si \ˈjän-sē\. City, Uttar Pradesh, India, 130 mi. (209 km.) S of Agra; pop. (1991c) 313,491; has military cantonment; rail junction; walled community with ancient Mogul fort, constructed 1613; city founded by Marathas 1732; ✻ of independent Maratha principality 1770–1853 when the last prince died without issue and sovereignty of British followed; scene of massacre during Indian mutiny 1857.

Jhe·lum *also* **Jeh·lam** \ˈjā-ləm\; *anc.* **Hy·das·pes** \hī-ˈdas-pēz\. **1.** River, India and Pakistan; rises in Himalayas in Jammu and Kashmir, India, flows NW through Vale of Kashmir, passing Srinagar, then SW out of India through Pir Panjal Range into Punjab, Pakistan, flowing S and uniting with the Chenab; ab. 450 mi. (725 km.) long; one of the "Five Rivers" of the Punjab; source of canals and irrigation systems in the Punjab; navigable except through the mountains.

2. Town, Punjab, Pakistan, on Jhelum River 105 mi. (169 km.) NNW of Lahore; pop. (1981c) 136,000.

Jhind. See JIND.

Jia·ling *or W.-G.* **Chia–ling** *also* **Kia·ling** \ˈjyä-ˈliŋ\. River, cen. China; rises in the Min Shan in Gansu and Sichuan provs. and flows S into the Chang at Chongqing; ab. 600 mi. (965 km.) long.

Jia·mu·si *or W.-G.* **Chia–mu–ssu** *or* **Kia·mu·sze** \ˈjyä-ˈmü-ˈsə\. City, Heilongjiang prov., China, on lower Songhua River 185 mi. (298 km.) NE of Harbin; pop. (1990c) 493,409.

Ji·'an *or W.-G.* **Chi–an** *or* **Ki·an** \ˈjē-ˈän\ *also* **Lu·ling** \ˈlü-ˈliŋ\. Town, S cen. Jiangxi prov., SE China on Gan River ab. 125 mi. (200 km.) SSW of Nanchang; pop. (1990c) 148,583; on great trade highway from Guangzhou N to Chang Valley.

Jiang·ling \ˈjyäŋ-ˈliŋ\ *or* **Jing·zhou** \ˈjiŋ-ˈjō\ *or W.-G.* **Chiang–ling** \ˈjyäŋ-ˈliŋ\ *or* **King–Chau** \ˈjiŋ-ˈjō\. Walled city on N bank of Chang, S Hubei prov., E cen. China, 2 mi. (3.2 km.) W of Shashi (*q.v.*); one of the oldest of Chinese cities, called by various names in different periods; once the ✻ of kingdom of Chu (8th–5th cent. B.C.); under the Manchus was a great garrison town; many temples.

Jiang·men *or W.-G.* **Chiang–men** \ˈjyäŋ-ˈmen\ *also* **Kong·moon** *or* **Kong–mun** \ˈku̇ŋ-ˈmu̇n\. Town, cen. Guangdong prov., SE China, in W part of Xi Delta, ab. 45 mi. (72 km.) above Macao; pop. (1990c) 230,587.

Jiang·su *or W.-G.* **Kiang·su** \ˈjyäŋ-ˈsü\. Province, E China, bounded on N by Shandong prov., on E by Yellow Sea and East China Sea, on S by Zhejiang, and on W by Anhui; ✻ Nanjing; one of smallest and most densely populated provinces of China, constituting for most part a deltaic plain, the mouth of the Chang; traversed also since 1938 by the Huang River following in part its old course of 1852 and by Da Yunhe (Grand Canal); covered with numerous lakes, largest Tai Hu; S part rich agriculturally; chief products: rice, cotton, wheat, tea; silk; fishing, pig and poultry raising; the leading industrial province; chief cities: Nanjing, Wuxi, Suzhou, Changzhou. Under Ming dynasty (1368–1644) a part of Nanking prov.; under Manchus E part of Kiang-nan; set up as separate province in 17th cent.; headquarters 1853–64 during Taiping Rebellion; occupied by Japanese forces 1937–1945; came under Communist control 1949; with growth of Shanghai (*q.v.*, now an independent municipality) increased rapidly in importance; became part of special economic zone 1984 in China's pursuit to encourage investment and trade. See table at CHINA.

Jiang·xi *or W.-G.* **Kiang·si** \ˈjyäŋ-ˈshē\. Province, SE China, bounded on N by Hubei and Anhui, on E by Zhejiang and Fujian, on S by Guangdong, and on W by Hunan; ✻ Nanchang; for the most part coincides with basin of Gan River; watered by many tributaries of the Gan, has very fertile soil; chief crops: rice, sweet potatoes, tobacco, cotton, peanuts, citrus fruits; fish. Hilly, esp. in S half; bordered by mountain ranges; coal mined at Pingxiang in W; tungsten also produced; for centuries has manufactured at Jingdezhen some of China's finest porcelain. Long a N and S corridor for migrations and communication, experienced rapid growth from 7th cent. with opening of Da Yunhe (Grand Canal); under the Mongol dynasty (1206–1368) included part of Guangdong; its present boundaries estab. under Ming dynasty; center of Communist movement 1927–34 and one of starting points of "Long March" (1934–35); came under Communist control 1949. See table at CHINA.

Jiang·yin *or W.-G.* **Chiang–yin** *or* **Kiang·yin** \ˈjyäŋ-ˈyin\. Town, S Jiangsu prov., E China, on the Chang 80 mi. (129 km.) NW of Shanghai; center of busy river traffic.

Jiao·xian *or W.-G.* **Chiao–hsien** *or* **Kiao·hsien** \ˈjyau̇-ˈshyen\; *formerly* **Kiao·chow** \ˈjyau̇-ˈjō\. Town, Shandong prov., NE China; NW of Jiaozhou Bay and ab. 25 mi. (40 km.) NW of Qingdao (45 mi. or 72 km. by rail), formerly a prosperous trading center.

Jiao Xian *or W.-G.* **Chiao Hsien** \ˈjyau̇-ˈshyen\ *or* **Kiao·chow** \ˈjyau̇-ˈjō\. Division of Shandong prov., NE China, surrounding **Jiao·zhou Bay** \ˈjyau̇-ˈjō\ (area 200 sq. mi. or 518 sq. km.); under German control 1898–1914; chief town Qingdao.

Jiao·zuo *or W.-G.* **Chiao–tso** \ˈjyau̇-ˈdzwȯ, -ˈdzwō\. Town, Henan prov., China, ab. 40 mi. (64 km.) NW of Zhengzhou; pop. (1990c) 409,100.

Jia·xing *or W.-G.* **Chia·hsing** *or* **Ka·shing** \ˈjyä-ˈshiŋ\. City, Zhejiang prov., E China, ab. 53 mi. (85 km.) SW of Shanghai.

Jiayuguan. See GREAT WALL.

Jibhalanta. See ULIASTAY.

Jibuti. See DJIBOUTI.

Ji·ca·rón \ˌhē-kä-ˈrōn\. Island, Panama, in Pacific Ocean off SW coast.

Ji·čín \ˈyē-ˌchēn\ *or Ger.* **Gitsch·in** \ˈgi-chēn, ˈyi-\. Town, N Czech Republic, ab. 45 mi. (72 km.) NE of Prague; pop. (1980p) 16,440; market center.

Jid·da *or* **Jiddah** \ˈji-də\ *or* **Jed·da** *or* **Jeddah** \ˈje-də\ *also* **Jud·dah** \ˈjə-də\. Port on Red Sea, Hejaz, W Saudi Arabia, 46 mi. (74 km.) W of Mecca and its seaport; pop. (1983e) 1,500,000; import center; former walled city, some walls preserved; ab. 400 years old; chief port for pilgrims to Mecca; resisted Wahhabi attacks in early 19th cent.; Turkish until June 1916 when it yielded to British and became part of the Hejaz; after yearlong siege surrendered Dec. 1925 to Ibn Sa'ūd, Muslim leader and founder of Saudi Arabia.

Ji·ga·wa \jē-ˈgä-wä\. State of Nigeria. See table at NIGERIA.

Ji·gua·ní \ˌhē-gwä-ˈnē\. Municipality and town, E Cuba, 48 mi. (77 km.) NW of Santiago de Cuba; munic. pop. (1981p) 51,969.

Jigüero, Point. See HIGÜERO, POINT.

Ji·güey Bay \hē-ˈgwā\. Bay on NW coast of Camagüey prov., E cen. Cuba, SW of Romano Cay.

Jih–k'a–tse. See XIGAZÊ.

Ji·hla·va \ˈyē-hlä-vä\ *or Ger.* **Iglau** \ˈē-ˌglau̇\. City, S cen. Czech Republic; pop. (1991p) 52,271; formerly-productive silver mines worked since the Middle Ages; textiles and tobacco products; compact, bringing some religious factional relief to Hussite Bohemia signed here 1436.

Jihun. See CEYHAN 1.

Jijelli. See DJIDJELLI.

Ji·lin \ˈje-ˈlin\ *or W.-G.* **Ki·rin** \ˈkē-rin\. **1.** Province, NE China; ✻ Changchun; produces corn and wheat; chief cities include Changchun, Jilin, Shuangliao, and Siping; formed 1945. See table at CHINA.

2. *also* **Chi–lin** \ˈchē-ˈlin\; *formerly* **Yung·ki** \ˈyu̇n-ˈkē\. City, Jilin prov., China; pop. (1990c) 1,036,858; produces chemicals; fortified 1673; seat of a Chinese military government during 18th–19th cents.; ✻ of Jilin prov. (see JILIN 1) until 1954.

Ji·ma \ˈjē-mə\ *or* **Jim·ma** *also* **Gim·ma** \ˈjim-mə\. Town, SW Ethiopia, ab. 170 mi. (275 km.) SW of Addis Ababa; pop. (1989e) 73,413.

Ji·ma·ní \ˌhē-mä-ˈnē\. Town, ✻ of Independencia prov., SW Dominican Republic; pop. (1981p) 7648.

Jim·bo·lia \zhēm-ˈbō-lyä\ *also* **Zsom·bo·lya** \ˈzhōm-bōl-yä\. Town, Timiş co., Romania, W of Timişoara near border of Yugoslavia; formerly belonged to Hungary; to Yugoslavia 1920; part of Romania since 1923.

Ji·me·nez \hē-ˈmā-nās\. Municipality, W Mindanao, Philippines, on W shore of Iligan Bay, 57 mi. (92 km.) W of Cagayan de Oro; pop. (1980c) 21,037.

Jim Hogg \ˈjim-ˈhȯg, ˈhäg\. County in S Texas. See table at TEXAS.

Jimma. See JIMA.

Jim Thorpe \ˈjim-ˈthȯrp\. Borough, Carbon co., E Pennsylvania, SSE of Wilkes-Barre; pop. (1990c) 5048; mountain resort; coal mines (now mostly abandoned); formed mid-1950s from former boroughs of Mauch Chunk and East Mauch Chunk to honor American athlete Jim Thorpe.

Jim Wells \ˈjim-ˈwelz\. County in S Texas. See table at TEXAS.

Ji·nan *or W.-G.* **Tsi·nan** \ˈjē-ˈnän\ *also* **Chi·nan** \ˈjē-\. City, ✻ of Shandong prov., NE China, in NW part of province on former course of the Huang ab. 225 mi. (360 km.) S of Beijing; railroad junction and center of small-boat traffic on rivers of region; produces textiles, vegetable oils, flour, iron and steel, chemicals; Shandong Univ. (1926). Dates at least from Chou period (c. 11th cent.–3d cent. B.C.); made ✻ of

Shandong under Ming dynasty (1368–1644); opened to foreign commerce 1904 and became railroad junction 1912; occupied by Japanese 1937–45 during Sino-Japanese War; entered by Communist forces 1948.

Jind *or* **Jhind** \ˈjind\. **1.** Former Indian state, one of the three Phulkian States, now in S Punjab and N Haryana states, India; 1299 sq. mi. (3364 sq. km.), in three separate tracts; ✻ Sangrur; founded by a Sikh raja 1763; loyal to British in Indian mutiny of 1857; rendered service to British government in other wars.

2. Town, Haryana, N India, 72 mi. (116 km.) NW of Delhi; pop. (1991p) 85,307.

Jind·ři·chův Hra·dec \ˈyēnd-zhē-ˌk̲üf-ˈhrä-ˌdets\ *or Ger.* **Neu·haus** \ˈnȯi-ˌhau̇s\. Town, S Czech Republic, 70 mi. (113 km.) SSE of Prague; pop. (1980p) 20,096.

Jing *or W.-G.* **Ching** \ˈjiŋ\ *or* **King** \ˈkiŋ\. River, rising in NE Gansu prov., N cen. China, and flowing SE to the Wei in cen. Shaanxi; ab. 200 mi. (320 km.) long.

Jing·de·zhen *or W.-G.* **Ching–te–chen** \ˈjiŋ-ˈdə-ˈjen\ *also* **King·teh·chen** \ˈkiŋ-ˈdə-ˈjen\; *formerly* **Fow·liang** \ˈfō-ˈlyäŋ\. Town, NE Jiangxi prov., SE China, near Anhui border 200 mi. (322 km.) ESE of Wuhan; pop. (1990c) 281,183; historically notable porcelain industry, estab. in Ch'ên dynasty (557–589 A.D.), became famous under the Sungs.

Jingzhou. See JIANGLING.

Jin·ja \ˈjin-jä\. Town, Uganda, on Lake Victoria just above Owen Falls Dam at beginning of Victoria Nile; pop. (1991p) 60,979; hydroelectric power; textiles.

Jinmen. See QUEMOY.

Ji·no·te·ga \ˌhē-nō-ˈtā-gä\. **1.** Department of W cen. Nicaragua. See table at NICARAGUA.

2. Town, its ✻, NNW of Matagalpa; pop. (1985e) 18,488.

Ji·no·te·pe \ˌhē-nō-ˈtā-pā\. Town, ✻ of Carazo dept., SW Nicaragua, 20 mi. (32 km.) S of Managua; munic. pop. (1985e) 23,538; coffee, rice, sugarcane, timber.

Jinsen. See INCH'ŎN.

Jin·sha *or W.-G.* **Kin·sha** \ˈjin-ˈshä\. Upper course of the Chang River, China, down to Yibin, junction point with the Min.

Jin·to·to·lo Channel \ˌhēn-tō-ˈtō-lō\. Passage bet. SW Masbate I. and NE Panay I., Philippines, connecting Visayan Sea with Sibuyan Sea; 20 mi. (32 km.) wide.

Jin·zhou *or W.-G.* **Chin–chou** *or* **Chin·chow** \ˈjin-ˈjō\; *formerly* **Chin·hsien** \ˈjin-ˈshyen\. Town, S Liaoning prov., NE China, at head of Bo Hai (gulf) on W side; pop. (1990c) 569,518; commercial center on Tianjin-Shenyang railroad line. Fighting here 1945 in Chinese Civil War.

Ji·pa·ra·ná; *formerly* **Gy–Pa·ra·ná** \ˌzhē-ˌpȧ-rȧ-ˈnä\. River, W cen. Brazil; rises in W Mato Grosso state, flows N and NW into Madeira River; ab. 500 mi. (800 km.) long (with longest headstream).

Ji·pi·ja·pa \ˌhē-pē-ˈhä-pä\. City, Manabí prov., W Ecuador, ab. 75 mi. (120 km.) NW of Guayaquil; traditionally noted for manufacture of Panama hats made of toquilla straw from the leaves of the jipijapa (*Carludovica palmata*).

Jiquipilco. See SAN JUAN JIQUIPILCO.

Jirjā. See GIRGA.

Jitomir. See ZHYTOMYR 2.

Jiu \ˈzhē-ü\. River, S Romania; flows SSE past Craiova into the Danube; ab. 200 mi. (320 km.) long.

Jiu·jiang *or W.-G.* **Chiu–chiang** *or* **Kiu·kiang** \ˈjyü-ˈjyäŋ\. City, N Jiangxi prov., SE China, N of Poyang Hu and on S bank of the Chang; pop. (1990c) 291,187; historically notable for tea shipments and pottery manufacture; now produces textiles, bricks, and tiles; designated a treaty port by Treaty of Tianjin 1858.

Jiu·quan \ˈjyü-ˈchwän\ *or* **Su·zhou** \ˈsü-ˈjō\ *or W.-G.* **Chiu–ch'üan** \ˈjyü-ˈchwän\ *or* **Su·chow** \ˈsü-ˈjō\ *also* **Kiu·chuan** \ˈjyü-ˈchwän\. Town, NW Gansu prov., N cen. China, on highway to Russia ab. 375 mi. (600 km.) NW of Lanzhou; center of fertile agricultural region; partially destroyed in Muslim uprising 1865–72.

Jiusanshui. See HEKOU.

Ji·wa·ni \ji-ˈwä-nē\ *also* **Ji·un·ri** \jē-ˈu̇n-rē\. Cape, SW Pakistan, extending into Arabian Sea.

Ji·xi *or W.-G.* **Chi–hsi** \ˈjē-ˈshə\. Town, SE Heilongjiang prov., China, ab. 210 mi. (340 km.) ESE of Harbin; pop. (1990c) 683,885.

Ji·yun *or W.-G.* **Chi–yün** \ˈjē-ˈyu̅e̅n, -ˈyün\. River, NE China, mostly in Tianjin munic.; empties into Bo Hai at Beitang.

Jīzah, Al. See GIZA.

Ji·ze·ra \ˈyē-ze-rä\ *or Ger.* **Iser** \ˈē-zər\. River, N Czech Republic; flows S into Labe (Elbe) River; 94 mi. (151 km.) long.

Jo. See RUO.

Jo·a·ça·ba \ˌzhō-ȧ-ˈsȧ-bə\; *formerly* **Cru·zei·ro** \krü-ˈzā-rü\. City, Santa Catarina state, S Brazil, on tributary of Uruguay River.

Joachimsthal, Sankt. See JÁCHYMOV.

João Pes·soa \ˌzhwau̇^{n}-pe-ˈsō-ə\; *formerly* **Pa·ra·í·ba** \ˌpȧr-ȧ-ˈē-bə\. City, ✻ of Paraíba state, E Brazil; munic. pop. (1991p) 497,214; ships cotton; university (1955); founded 1585.

Joazeiro. See JUÀZEIRO.

Job Peak \ˈjōb\. Mountain in cen. Churchill co., W Nevada; 8799 ft. (2682 m.).

Jo–ch'iang. See RUOQIANG.

Jo Da·viess \ˈjō-ˈdā-vis\. County in NW corner of Illinois. See table at ILLINOIS.

Jodh·pur \ˈjäd-pər, -ˌpu̇r\. **1.** *or* **Mar·war** \ˈmär-ˌwär\. Former Indian state, now part of Rajasthan state, NW India; 36,120 sq. mi. (93,551 sq. km.); ✻ Jodhpur; region borders on Thar Desert on W, touches Great Rann of Kachchh on SW; traversed by Luni River flowing SW; notable center for camel breeding.

2. City, Rajasthan, India, 235 mi. (378 km.) N of Ahmadabad; pop. (1991c) 666,279; textiles; university (1962); ruins of Mandor, former ✻ of princes of Marwar, 5 mi. (8 km.) N; a walled city, with large fort containing the maharaja's palace, founded 1459 by Rao Jodha; recognized English sovereignty 1818; the riding breeches called jodhpurs were named for the city.

Jod·rell Bank \ˈjä-drəl\. Locality, NE Cheshire, England, ab. 15 mi. (24 km.) SSW of Manchester; site of radio telescope maintained by Univ. of Manchester.

Jo·en·suu \ˈyȯ-en-ˌsü\. Commercial city, ✻ of Pohjois-Karjala prov., S Finland; pop. (1989c) 47,205; exports timber; founded 1848.

Jo·e·tsu \jō-ˈe-tsü\. City, Niigata prefecture, NW Honshū, Japan; pop. (1990p) 130,114.

Jof·fre, Mount \ˈzhä-fər\. Peak, SE British Columbia, Canada, on Alberta border SW of Calgary; 11,313 ft. (3448 m.).

Jog Falls \ˈjōg\ *or* **Falls of Ger·sop·pa** \jər-ˈsä-pə\. Cataract in small stream (Sharavati) ab. 18 mi. (29 km.) from its mouth, on border of NW Karnataka, India; 830 ft. (253 m.) high.

Jog·gins \ˈjä-ginz\. Site, Cumberland co., N Nova Scotia, Canada, on Chignecto Bay 17 mi. (27 km.) WSW of Amherst; source of fossils.

Jogjakarta. See YOGYAKARTA.

Jo·han·nes·burg \jō-ˈhä-nəs-ˌbərg, -ˈha-\. City, NE Rep. of South Africa, 300 mi. (483 km.) NW of Durban; pop. (1985c) 632,369; the republic's largest city and a leading industrial center; chemicals, textiles, leather products; engineering industries; gold mines; Univ. of Witwatersrand (1922), Rand Afrikaans Univ. (1966); has own observatory and also branch observatory of Leiden Univ.; founded 1886 after discovery of gold; occupied by British during Boer War 1900; created a city 1928.

Jo·han·nis·berg \yō-ˈhä-nis-ˌberk\. Village, Hesse, Germany, in the Rheingau on Rhine River; to the S lies its castle, built 18th cent. and given to Austrian statesman Prince Klemens von Metternich 1816; surrounded by vineyards yielding Johannisberger wine.

\ə\ **abut** \ˈə\ **matches** \ᵊ\ **kitten, Fr table** \ər\ **further** \a\ **ash** \ā\ **ace** \ä\ **cot, cart** \ȧ\ **Fr bac** \au̇\ **out** \b̲\ **Span Avila** \ch\ **chin** \e\ **bet** \ē\ **easy** \g\ **go** \i\ **hit** \ī\ **ice** \j\ **job** \k̲\ **Ger ich, Buch** \$^{n}$\ **Fr vin** \ŋ\ **sing** \ō\ **go** \ȯ\ **all** \ȯ\ **law** \œ\ **Fr bœuf** \œ̄\ **Fr feu** \ȯi\ **boy** \th\ **thin** \t̲h̲\ **this** \ü\ **loot** \u̇\ **foot** \ue\ **Ger füllen** \u̅e̅\ **Fr rue** \y\ **yet** \$^{y}$\ **Fr digne** \ˈdēn^{y}\, **nuit** \ˈnw^{y}ē\ \yü\ **few** \yu̇\ **fury** \zh\ **vision**

John Day \ˈjän-ˈdā\. **1.** River, N Oregon; rises in E Grant co. in E cen. part of state and flows W and N into Columbia River on boundary bet. Sherman and Gilliam cos.; 281 mi. (452 km.) long; principal tributaries the **South Fork** rising in N Harney co. and flowing N, and **Middle Fork** and **North Fork** which join in N Grant co. and flow SW; **John Day Fossil Beds National Monument** estab. 1975: see UNITED STATES, *National Monuments.*
2. City, Grant co., E cen. Oregon; pop. (1990c) 1836; tourism; timber, cattle.

John Day Dam. Dam across Columbia River bet. Washington and Oregon, roughly midway along the border.

John o'Groat's *or* **John o'Groats** *or* **John o'Groat's House** \ˈjän-ō-ˈgrōts\. Point on N coast of Caithness, N Scotland; popularly considered most northerly point of Great Britain (see DUNNET HEAD); named for 18th cent. Dutch settlers de Groats.

John·son \ˈjän-sən\. **1.** River, Alaska; 215 mi. (346 km.) long; tributary of the Kuskokwim (*q.v.*).
2. Name of counties in 12 states of the U.S. See tables at ARKANSAS, GEORGIA, ILLINOIS, INDIANA, IOWA, KANSAS, KENTUCKY, MISSOURI, NEBRASKA, TENNESSEE, TEXAS, WYOMING.
3. *or* **Johnson City.** City, ⊗ of Stanton co., SW Kansas; pop. (1990c) 1348.
4. Town, Lamoille co., N cen. Vermont; pop. (1990c) 3156; Johnson State Coll. (1828).

John·son·burg \ˈjän-sən-ˌbərg\. Borough, Elk co., NW cen. Pennsylvania, 25 mi. (40 km.) N of Du Bois; pop. (1990c) 3350.

Johnson City. **1.** Village, Broome co., S New York, 3 mi. (5 km.) W of Binghamton; pop. (1990c) 16,890; with Endicott and Binghamton, one of so-called Triple Cities.
2. City, Washington co., NE Tennessee, 20 mi. (32 km.) S of Virginia border; pop. (1990c) 49,381; alt. 1631 ft. (497 m.); tobacco; tourist center; East Tennessee State Univ. (1909); first settled in 1760s; incorp. 1869.
3. City, ⊗ of Blanco co., cen. Texas; pop. (1990c) 932; nearby, ranch of 36th U.S. president, Lyndon B. Johnson.

John·ston \ˈjän-stən, -sən\. **1.** Name of counties in two states of the U.S. See tables at NORTH CAROLINA and OKLAHOMA.
2. Town, Providence co., N Rhode Island, ab. 5 mi. (8 km.) SW of the city of Providence; pop. (1990c) 26,542; settled c. 1650; orig. part of Providence; became separate town 1759.
3. Town, Edgefield co., W South Carolina, 47 mi. (76 km.) SW of Columbia; pop. (1990c) 2688.
4. Coral atoll, cen. Pacific Ocean; ab. 700 mi. (1125 km.) SW of Honolulu, 16°45′N, 169°32′W; ab. 9 mi. (14 km.) long, 4 mi. (6 km.) wide; includes two small islets (**Johnston** and **Sand** \ˈsand\) and reef; belongs to the U.S.; not included in Hawaii statehood bill; discovered 1807 by British sea captain; claimed by the U.S. 1858; worked for guano; made part of U.S. defense system 1934; after WWII administered by U.S. Air Force; chemical-weapons disposal site.

Johnston City. City, Williamson co., S Illinois, 8 mi. (13 km.) N of Marion; pop. (1990c) 3706.

John·stone \ˈjän-stən\. Burgh, Strathclyde region, SW Scotland; pop. (1981p) 42,707; engineering works.

Johnstone, Lake. Lake, S Saskatchewan, Canada, ab. 20 mi. (32 km.) SW of Moose Jaw; 131 sq. mi. (339 sq. km.).

Johnstone Strait. Narrow passage, along N coast of Vancouver I., SW British Columbia, Canada, connecting Queen Charlotte Strait with Strait of Georgia; ab. 60 mi. (97 km.) long.

Johns·town \ˈjänz-ˌtau̇n\. **1.** City, ⊗ of Fulton co., E New York, 11 mi. (18 km.) WNW of Amsterdam; pop. (1990c) 9058; gloves; Fulton-Montgomery Community Coll. (1963); founded by British colonial administrator Sir William Johnson 1762. Birthplace of woman suffrage leader Elizabeth Cady Stanton 1815.
2. Village, Licking co., cen. Ohio, 21 mi. (34 km.) NE of Columbus; pop. (1990c) 3237.
3. City, Cambria co., SW cen. Pennsylvania, on Conemaugh River 60 mi. (97 km.) E of Pittsburgh; pop. (1990c) 28,134; steel; Christ the Saviour Seminary of Johnstown, Univ. of Pittsburgh at Johnstown (1927). Laid out 1800; scene of many disastrous floods, notably May 31, 1889, when South Fork Dam above city burst after heavy rains and more than 2200 people were drowned; floods again 1936, 1977.

Jo·hor *also* **Jo·hore** \jə-ˈhōr\. **1.** Short stream of SE Johor state, Malaysia, S Malay Penin., SE Asia; long and wide estuary.
2. A state of Malaysia, Malay Penin., SE Asia, lying between South China Sea and Strait of Malacca; ✱ Johor Baharu; two-thirds covered with jungle; mountainous in E cen. part (3300 ft. or 1006 m.) but highest point, Mt. Ophir 4186 ft. (1276 m.), is in NW near Melaka border; principal streams the Muar, Endau, and Johor; coastline ab. 250 mi. (400 km.) long with numerous small islands; separated from it to the S by Johore Strait is island of Singapore; rubber. See table at MALAYSIA.

History: A Muslim-ruled state founded after 1511 by former sultan of Melaka (*q.v.*); came under British influence in 19th cent.; ceded Singapore to British 1819; its relations with Great Britain estab. by treaties 1885 and 1914; occupied by Japanese Jan. 1942; became part of the independent Federation of Malaya 1957; became a state of Malaysia 1963; participated in national economic development plans late 20th cent.

Johor Ba·ha·ru *or* **Johore Ba·ha·ru** \ˈbä-hə-ˌrü\ *also* **Johore Bah·ru** \ˈbä-ˌrü\. Town, ✱ of Johor state, Malaysia, in S part on Johore Strait opp. Singapore I.; residence of sultan.

Johore Strait *or* **Johor Strait** *or Malay* **Se·lat Te·brau** \ˌsə-lät-te-ˈbrau̇\. Channel bet. Singapore I. and the mainland of Johor state, S Malay Penin.; crossed by causeway from Woodlands to Johor Baharu; ab. 0.75 mi. (1.2 km.) wide and 32 mi. (51 km.) long; large naval base at E end; scene of heavy fighting Feb. 1942 during WWII.

Joi·gny \zhwȧ-ˈnyē\; *anc.* **Jo·vi·ni·a·cum** \ˌjō-və-ˈnī-ə-kəm\. Commune, Yonne dept., NE cen. France, on Yonne River 15 mi. (24 km.) NNW of Auxerre; probably of Roman origin; seat of a countship in 10th cent.; unsuccessfully besieged by English 1429. Birthplace (1779) of French religious St. Madeleine-Sophie Barat, founder of Society of the Sacred Heart, and of French writer Marcel Aymé (1902).

Join·vi·le \zhwãⁿ-ˈvē-lē\; *formerly* **Join·vil·le** \-ˈvē-lē\. City, Santa Catarina state, S Brazil, 25 mi. (40 km.) inland from port of São Francisco do Sul; munic. pop. (1991p) 346,095.

Join·ville Island \ˈjȯin-vil\. Island in West Antarctica off tip of Antarctic Penin., British Antarctic Terr., at NW point of Weddell Sea, 63°15′S, 55°45′W; ab. 40 mi. (64 km.) wide by 20 mi. (32 km.) long.

Joinville–le–Pont \zhwȧⁿ-ˌvēl-lə-ˈpōⁿ\. Commune, Val-de-Marne dept., N France, ESE suburb of Paris.

Jo·ju·tla \hō-ˈhüt-lä\. Municipality, Morelos state, Mexico, 60 mi. (97 km.) S of Mexico City; thermal springs.

Jö·kul·sá á Brú \ˈyœ-kəl-ˌsau̇-au̇-ˈbrü\. River, E Iceland, flowing NE into Norwegian Sea.

Jökulsá á Fjöl·lum \au̇-ˈfyœt-lüm\. River, NE Iceland, flowing N into Arctic Ocean; 128 mi. (206 km.) long; 2d longest river in Iceland.

Jokyakarta. See YOGYAKARTA.

Joliba. See NIGER 2.

Jo·li·et \ˌjō-lē-ˈet, *chiefly by outsiders* ˌjä-\. City, ⊗ of Will co., NE Illinois, 35 mi. (56 km.) SW of Chicago; pop. (1990c) 76,836; state penitentiary; Coll. of St. Francis (1920), Joliet Junior Coll. (1902).

Jo·liette \ˌzhō-ˈlyet\. **1.** County in S Quebec, Canada. See table at QUEBEC.
2. City, its ⊗, 35 mi. (56 km.) N of Montreal; pop. (1991c) 17,396; educational, government, and service center; founded c. 1823 by a descendant of the explorer Louis Jolliet; incorp. 1863.

Jolla, La. See LA JOLLA.

Jo·lo \ˈhō-lō\ *also* **Su·lu** \ˈsü-lü\. **1.** Chief island, Sulu Archipelago, Philippines, SW of Basilan I.; 345 sq. mi. (894 sq. km.); pop. (1980c) 360,588; chief town Jolo; lies bet. Sulu Sea and Celebes Sea; of volcanic origin, crossed by three parallel mountain chains with several peaks, highest 2664 ft. (812 m.); good climate, fertile soil, agriculture well developed;

wooded. Inhabitants converted to Islam in 14th cent. See SULU ARCHIPELAGO 1.

2. Municipality, ✻ of Sulu prov., Philippines, on NW coast of Jolo I.; pop. (1980c) 52,429; port of entry with considerable trade with Zamboanga, Manila, and Singapore; ancient residence of Sulu sultans but most traces of Moro town now gone; present town begun by Spaniards c. 1878; during WWII taken by American troops Apr. 1945; severely damaged 1974 in fighting bet. members of Muslim independence movement and government troops.

Jo·ma·lig *or* **Ho·ma·lig** \hō-ˈmä-lig\. Island, E Polillo group, Philippines, at NE corner of Lamon Bay E of Luzon; 20 sq. mi. (52 sq. km.).

Jomanes. See YAMUNA.

Jomonjol. See HOMONHON.

Joms·borg \ˈyȯmz-ˌbȯrg\. Viking fortified settlement built c. 970 near Julin on Wolin I. at mouth of the Oder, Germany; destroyed by Danes 1098; site now in Poland.

Jones \ˈjōnz\. Name of counties in six states of the U.S. See tables at GEORGIA, IOWA, MISSISSIPPI, NORTH CAROLINA, SOUTH DAKOTA, TEXAS.

Jones, Mount. Mountain, Antarctica, 77°14′S, 142°11′W; 12,040 ft. (3700 m.).

Jones·boro \ˈjōnz-ˌbər-ō\. **1.** City, a ⊗ of Craighead co., NE Arkansas, 67 mi. (108 km.) NNW of Memphis, Tennessee; pop. (1990c) 46,535; trading center; cotton gins, rice mill; Arkansas State Univ. (1909); founded 1859; incorp. 1883.

2. City, ⊗ of Clayton co., NW cen. Georgia; pop. (1990c) 3635.

3. City, ⊗ of Union co., SW Illinois, 30 mi. (48 km.) SW of Marion; pop. (1990c) 1728.

4. Town, ⊗ of Jackson parish, N Louisiana, 41 mi. (66 km.) WSW of Monroe; pop. (1990c) 4305.

Jones·bor·ough \ˈjōnz-ˌbər-ō\ *also* **Jones·boro** *same*\. Town, ⊗ of Washington co., NE Tennessee, 7 mi. (11 km.) W of Johnson City; pop. (1990c) 3091; meeting place of constitutional convention and first legislative sessions of short-lived State of Franklin (created from land previously included in North Carolina) until 1785.

Jones Mountain. Peak, Hinsdale and San Juan cos., SW Colorado; 13,851 ft. (4222 m.).

Jones·port \ˈjōnz-ˌpōrt\. Town, Washington co., SE Maine, on Atlantic Ocean bet. Englishman and Pleasant bays; pop. (1990c) 1525; summer resort.

Jones Sound. Channel, Nunavut, Canada, bet. S Ellesmere I. and N Devon I.; ab. 40 mi. (64 km.) wide; opens into Baffin Bay; investigated by Norwegian explorer Otto Sverdrup 1898–1902.

Jones·ville \ˈjōnz-ˌvil\. **1.** Town, Catahoula parish, cen. Louisiana, 45 mi. (72 km.) ENE of Alexandria; pop. (1990c) 2720.

2. Town, ⊗ of Lee co., SW tip of Virginia; pop. (1990c) 927.

Jong·song \ˈjȯŋ-ˈsȯŋ\. Peak on boundary bet. Sikkim state, India, and Nepal; 24,472 ft. (7459 m.).

Jön·kö·ping \ˈyœn-ˌshœ-piŋ\. **1.** Province of S Sweden. See table at SWEDEN.

2. City, its ⊗, at S end of Lake Vättern; pop. (1993e) 309,867; paper, machinery; an old town, chartered 1284, important in early history of Sweden; destroyed by its citizens to deter encroaching Danes 1612 but soon rebuilt; place where treaty was signed 1809 bet. Sweden and Denmark.

Jon·quière \ˌzhōⁿ-ˈkyer\. Town, S Quebec, Canada, bet. the Saguenay River and Lake Kenogami; pop. (1991c) 57,933; pulp mills; aluminum; founded 1847.

Jop·lin \ˈjä-plin\. City, Jasper and Newton cos., SW Missouri, 72 mi. (116 km.) W of Springfield; pop. (1990c) 40,961; Missouri Southern State Coll. (1937), Ozark Christian Coll. (1942); settled c. 1838; chartered 1873; zinc mining spurred growth in 2d half of 19th cent.

Joppa. See JAFFA.

Jor·dan \ˈjȯrd-ᵊn\. **1.** *or officially* **Hash·em·ite Kingdom of Jordan** \ˈha-shə-ˌmīt\; *formerly* **Trans·jor·dan** \ˌtrans-, ˌtranz-\. Kingdom, SW Asia, bounded on N by Syria, on NE by Iraq, on E and S by Saudi Arabia, and on W by Israel; ab. 34,575 sq. mi. (89,549 sq. km.); pop. (1992e) 3,636,000; ✻ Amman; largely desert; region on W side of Jordan River is mountainous; has port on Gulf of Aqaba.

Chief products: Wheat, phosphates, fruits, olives, potash, vegetables; cement.

Chief towns: Amman, Zarqa, Irbid.

History: Created (as Transjordan) 1921 out of former Turkish territory and proclaimed an independent state 1923 under Emir Abdullah ibn al-Ḥusayn, but a mandate under British protection; mandate revoked 1946 and by treaty of Mar. 1946 became an independent kingdom; engaged in war with Israel 1948–49; at signing of armistice agreement with Israel Apr. 1949 held the cen. part of Palestine; adopted name of Jordan 1949; formally annexed Arab Palestine (area on W side of Jordan River) 1950; terminated special treaty relations with Great Britain 1957; participated in Arab-Israel War 1967, as a result of which its territory W of Jordan River came under Israeli military occupation; sided with Iraq in 1980s Iran-Iraq War; surrendered its claim to West Bank territory 1988 in support of Palestinian Liberation Organization; again sided with Iraq in 1991 Gulf War; signed peace accord with Israel 1994.

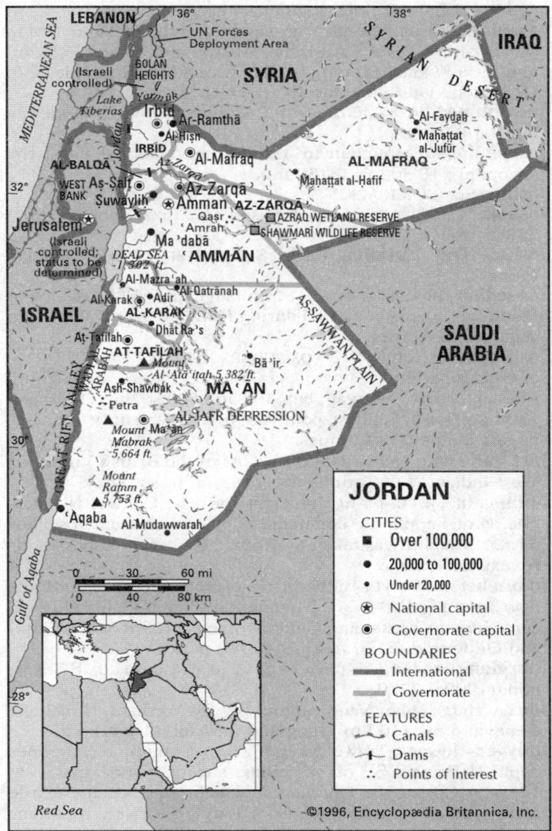

2. River, N cen. Utah, flows from Utah Lake N into Great Salt Lake; 60 mi. (97 km.) long.

3. City, Scott co., S Minnesota, SW of Minneapolis; pop. (1990c) 2909.

4. Town, ⊗ of Garfield co., Montana; pop. (1990c) 494.

5. River, SW Asia; rises in Syria, flows S through the Waters of Merom and Sea of Galilee to N end of the Dead Sea; ab. 200 mi. (320 km.) long; narrow and sluggish at its mouth; most of it S of Sea of Galilee lies in the great depression of the Ghor (ab. 65 mi. or 105 km. long); important source of irrigation water; not navigable; noted for associations with Old Testament and New Testament history.

Jordan \hȯr-ˈdän\. Municipality, N coast of Guimaras I., Philippines, on Iloilo Strait opp. City of Iloilo; pop. (1980c) 36,014.

Jor·dan, Mount \ˈjȯrd-ᵊn\. Peak in the Sierra Nevada, N Tulare co., S cen. California; 13,316 ft. (4059 m.).

Jor·ge Montt \ˈhȯr-hā-ˈmȯnt\. Island off SW coast of Chile, S of Hanover I.

Jos \ˈjȯs\. Town, ✱ of Plateau state, cen. Nigeria, ab. 143 mi. (230 km.) S of Kano; pop. (1991e) 182,100; in major tin-bearing area; has cool climate year-round.

Jo·se Pañ·ga·ni·ban \hō-ˈsā-ˌpäŋ-gä-nē-ˈbän\. Municipality on N coast of Camarines Norte prov., Luzon, Philippines, W of Paracale; pop. (1980c) 30,260.

Jo·seph \ˈjō-zef, -səf\. One of the Safety Is. (*q.v.*).

Joseph, Lake. Lake, NW Muskoka dist., SE Ontario, Canada, in the Muskoka Lake region, connected with Lake Muskoka (*q.v.*) and Lake Rosseau; summer resort.

Joseph Bo·na·parte Gulf \ˈbō-nə-ˌpärt\. Inlet of Timor Sea in NE corner of Western Australia, Australia; 225 mi. (362 km.) long E to W and 100 mi. (161 km.) long N to S; divides into Cambridge Gulf and Queens Channel.

Jo·se·phine \ˈjō-zə-ˌfēn, ˈjō-sə-\. County in SW Oregon. See table at OREGON.

Joseph Peak. Mountain in Yellowstone National Park, NW Wyoming; 10,300 ft. (3139 m.).

Joshin. See KIMCH'AEK.

Josh·ua \ˈjä-shə-wə\. City, Johnson co., Texas; pop. (1990c) 3828.

Joshua Tree National Park. See UNITED STATES, *National Parks*.

Jos·se·lin \zhȯ-ˈsleⁿ\. Town, Morbihan dept., NW France, W of Ploërmel; in area contested during Hundred Years' War; 16th cent. castle, homes.

Jos Sudarso, Teluk. See YOS SUDARSO, TELUK.

Jos·te·dals·bre·en \ˈyu̇s-tə-ˌdälz-ˌbrā-ən\. Plateau in Sogn og Fjordane co., W Norway; bet. 400 and 500 sq. mi. (1040 and 1300 sq. km.); highest point 6396 ft. (1950 m.); contains largest ice field in Europe.

Jost Van Dyke \ˌyōst-van-ˈdīk\. One of the British Virgin Is., West Indies, W of Tortola; ab. 3 sq. mi. (8 sq. km.).

Jo·tap·a·ta \jō-ˈtä-pə-tə\. Ancient fortress, Galilee, N Palestine, N of Sepphoris, commanded by Jewish Gen. Josephus 67 A.D. when it was taken by Roman Emperor Vespasian after extended siege.

Jo·tun·hei·men \ˈyōt-ᵊn-ˌhā-mən\ *or* **Jotunheim Mountains** *also* **Jo·tun·fjell** \-ˌfyel\. Mountain region in Oppland co., S cen. Norway, containing Galdhøpiggen (8100 ft. or 2469 m.) and Glittertind (8110 ft. or 2472 m.) peaks.

Jour·dan·ton \ˈjərd-ᵊn-tən\. City, ⊗ of Atascosa co., S Texas; pop. (1990c) 3220.

Joux \ˈzhü\. Lake, Vaud canton, SW Switzerland, N of Lake Geneva; 6 mi. (10 km.) long and 0.67 mi. (1 km.) wide.

Jouy–en–Jo·sas \ˈzhwē-ˌäⁿ-zhō-ˈzäs\. Commune, Yvelines dept., N France, SE of Versailles; site of workshop set up 1759 by Christophe Oberkampf which later became textile factory noted for manufacture of Jouy print cloth; museum.

Jo·vel·la·nos \ˌhō-vā-ˈyä-nōs\. Town and municipality, Matanzas prov., W cen. Cuba; transportation center 16 mi. (26 km.) S of Cárdenas.

Joviniacum. See JOIGNY.

Jo·yo \ˈjō-yō\. City, Kyōto prefecture, Honshū, Japan; pop. (1990p) 84,770.

Ju·ab \ˈjü-ab\. County in W Utah. See table at UTAH.

Jua·na·ca·tlán \ˌhwä-nä-kä-ˈtlän\. Falls in Río Santiago, Jalisco state, W cen. Mexico, near Guadalajara; 72 ft. (22 m.) high; used for waterpower.

Juana Dí·az \ˈhwä-nä-ˈt͟hē-ˌäs\. Municipality, S Puerto Rico; pop. (1990c) 45,198.

Juan de Fu·ca, Strait of *or* **Juan de Fuca Strait** \ˌhwän-də-ˈfyü-kə\. Strait bet. Vancouver I., Canada, and Clallam co., NW Washington; 100 mi. (161 km.) long and 15 to 20 mi. (24 to 32 km.) wide.

Juan de No·va \ˌhwän-də-ˈnō-və\. Small island belonging to France, in N cen. Mozambique Channel bet. NE cen. Mozambique and NW cen. Madagascar; administered by Réunion.

Juan Fer·nán·dez \ˌhwän-fer-ˈnän-dās\. Group of three islands, Más Afuera, Más a Tierra, and Santa Clara or Goat I., belonging to Chile, in S Pacific Ocean ab. 400 mi. (645 km.) W of Chile; 70 sq. mi. (181 sq. km.); Scottish sailor Alexander Selkirk, the original of English novelist Daniel Defoe's hero Robinson Crusoe, lived on Más a Tierra 1704–09.

Juan–les–Pins \ˌzhwäⁿ-lā-ˈpeⁿ\. Village, Alpes-Maritimes dept., SE France, on Cap d'Antibes SW of Antibes; coastal resort.

Juárez. See CIUDAD JUÁREZ.

Juà·zei·ro; *formerly* **Joa·zei·ro** \zhwȧ-ˈzā-rü\. City, N border of Bahia state, E Brazil, 275 mi. (442 km.) NW of Salvador; munic. pop. (1991p) 128,378.

Juàzeiro do Nor·te \dü-ˈnȯr-tē\. City, Ceará state, NE Brazil; munic. pop. (1991p) 173,304.

Ju·ba \ˈjü-bä\. **1.** River, E Africa. See JUBBA.
2. Town, S Sudan, on Bahr el Jebel (Nile) River; pop. (1990e) 320,000.

Ju·bail \ju̇-ˈbāl\ *or* **Al Ju·bayl** \ˌal-ju̇-ˈbāl, -ˈbīl\. Town, port of al-Hasa, E Nejd, Saudi Arabia, on Persian Gulf; has large oil refinery; cargo-port facilities; petrochemicals; large industrial city of the same name built nearby.

Ju·ba·land \ˈjü-bä-ˌland\ *or* **Trans–Ju·ba** \ˌtrans-, ˌtranz-\ *or Ital.* **Ol·tre Giu·ba** \ˈōl-trā-ˈjü-bä\. Region, SW Somalia, bet. Kenya border and the Jubba River; formerly a province of Kenya, ceded by Britain to Italy 1925; administered as separate colony until July 1, 1926 when it became part of Italian Somaliland.

Ju·bayl \ju̇-ˈbāl\; *Fr.* **Dje·beïl** *or* **Je·beil** \je-bāl\; *anc.* **Byb·los** \ˈbi-bləs\. Coast village, Lebanon, 20 mi. (32 km.) N of Beirut; as Byblos, a very old city of Phoenicia (the **Ge·bal** \ˈgē-bəl\ of the Bible, *Ezek.* xxvii. 9), seat of the worship of Adonis; an early Phoenician inscription has been found here and excavations have uncovered remains of temple, citadel, and tombs; exported papyrus to Egypt, hence the Greek *byblos* book, papyrus, and Eng. *Bible.*

Jubayl, Al. See JUBAIL.

Jub·ba *or* **Ju·ba** *or Ital.* **Giu·ba** \ˈjü-bä\. River, E Africa; ab. 1000 mi. (1600 km.) long; rises in several headstreams (Dawa, Genale, Wabē Gestro) in mountains of S cen. Ethiopia and flows S across SW Somalia into Indian Ocean just N of Kismaayo.

Ju·by, Cap *or* **Cape Juby** \ˈyü-bē\. Cape, SW coast of Morocco, E of Canary Is. See TARFAYA.

Jú·car \ˈhü-ˌkär\. River, E Spain; rises in N Cuenca prov., flows S, then turns E in N Albacete prov., and flows through cen. Valencia prov. into Mediterranean Sea 26 mi. (42 km.) S of Valencia; 309 mi. (497 km.) long.

Ju·chi·tán \ˌhü-chē-ˈtän\ *or officially* **Juchitán de Za·ra·go·za** \t͟hā-ˌsä-rä-ˈgō-sä\. Town, Oaxaca state, SE Mexico; pop. (1990p) 66,525; port on S side of Isthmus of Tehuantepec on Gulf of Tehuantepec; supply center for agricultural region.

Ju·daea *or* **Ju·dea** \jü-ˈdē-ə\. The S division of Palestine under Persian, Greek, and Roman rule, succeeding the kingdom of Judah (*q.v.*); bounded on N by Samaria, its N boundary extending approx. from N of Joppa to the Jordan ab. 13 mi. (21 km.) above the Dead Sea; on E bounded by the Jordan and Dead Sea, on SW by Sinai (Egypt), and on W by the Mediterranean; became Roman province after conquests of Gen. Pompey the Great; in late Roman years included Idumaea.

Ju·dah \ˈjü-də\. Ancient kingdom in S Palestine, bet. the Mediterranean and the Dead Sea; ✱ Jerusalem; the S kingdom of the Jews after N part of Israel (*q.v.*) had broken away c. 933 B.C.; passed under Babylonian rule c. 605 B.C.; kingdom came to an end with destruction of Jerusalem (*q.v.*) by Babylonian King Nebuchadrezzar 587–586 B.C. See JUDAEA.

Juddah. See JIDDA.

Judea. See JUDAEA.
Ju·dith \ˈjü-dith\. River, cen. Montana; flows NE and N through Judith Basin and Fergus cos. into the Missouri River; ab. 100 mi. (160 km.) long.
Judith, Point. SE point, Washington co., Rhode Island, at W side of entrance to Narragansett Bay; tourism.
Judith Basin. County in cen. Montana. See table at MONTANA.
Juf, Al–. See EL DJOUF.
Jufrah, Al. See AL JUFRAH.
Juggernaut. See PURI.
Jugoslavia *or* **Jugoslavija** *or* **Jugoslavija, Savezna Republika.** See YUGOSLAVIA.
Juhaynah. See GIHEINA.
Jui·gal·pa \hwē-ˈgäl-pä\. Town, ✽ of Chontales dept., S cen. Nicaragua, ab. 15 mi. (24 km.) from NE shore of Lake Nicaragua; munic. pop. (1985e) 25,625.
Juist \ˈyǖst, ˈyœist\. Narrow island, East Frisian Is., off NW coast of Germany, NE of Borkum; 9 mi. (14 km.) long.
Juiz de Fo·ra \ˈzhwēz-dē-ˈfȯr-ə\. City, S Minas Gerais state, E Brazil, on railroad line ab. 80 mi. (130 km.) N of Rio de Janeiro; munic. pop. (1991p) 385,756; textiles; university (1960).
Ju·juy \hü-ˈhwē\. **1.** Province of NW Argentina. See table at ARGENTINA.
2. *or in full* **San Sal·va·dor de Jujuy** \sän-ˈsäl-b̲ä-ˌt̲h̲ȯr-t̲h̲ā-\. Town, its ✽; pop. (1980c) 124,950; alt. ab. 4000 ft. (1220 m.).
Jules·burg \ˈjülz-ˌbərg\. Town, ⊗ of Sedgwick co., NE corner of Colorado, on South Platte River; pop. (1990c) 1295; railroad division point, founded 1881; the 4th and only remaining town of that name in vicinity.
Julfa. See DZHULʼFA.
Ju·lia·ca \hü-ˈlyä-kä\. Town, SE Peru, 189 mi. (304 km.) by rail NE of Arequipa; pop. (1981p) 88,978; alt. 12,550 ft. (3825 m.); railroad junction for Cuzco and Lake Titicaca.
Julia Joza. See TARIFA.
Julian Alps. See table at ALPS.
Juliana Top. See MANDALA.
Ju·li·a·ne·håb \ˌyü-lē-ˈä-nä-ˌhȯp\ *or* **Qa·qor·toq** \ˈkä-kȯr-ˌtȯk\. Settlement near S end of Greenland; pop. (1991e) 3127; radio station.
Jul·ian March \ˈjül-yən-ˈmärch\. The borderland region bet. W Slovenia and NE Italy traversed by Julian Alps and Isonzo River; Trieste and Istrian Penin. lie to the S.
Julia Traducta. See TARIFA.
Jü·lich \ˈyü-lik̲\. **1.** Region of W Germany bet. Cologne on the Rhine and Aachen (Aix-la-Chapelle); ab. 1600 sq. mi. (4140 sq. km.); chief town Jülich; county 11th to 14th cents.; became duchy 1356, united with duchy of Berg 1423; passed to dukes of Kleve 16th cent.; possession contested in 17th cent. by Netherlands and Saxony; held by German counts until 1801; held by France 1801–15; to Prussia 1815.
2. Town, North Rhine-Westphalia, W Germany, on the Ruhr River 16 mi. (26 km.) NE of Aachen; pop. (1980c) 30,449; chief town of county and duchy of Jülich; fortified in 17th cent. and several times captured; largely destroyed in WWII.
Ju·lier Pass \zhǖ-ˈlyā\. Mountain pass, SW of St. Moritz, in Rhaetian Alps, Graubünden canton, E Switzerland; alt. 7491 ft. (2283 m.).
Ju·lin \yü-ˈlēn\. Ancient Wendish trading town on S coast of Wolin I., off coast of Pomerania, Germany, identified with modern Wolin (*q.v.*), since 1945 in NW Poland, and called **Vi·ne·ta** \vē-ˈnā-tə\ by the Germans; in 10th and 11th cents. was important center for trade bet. Scandinavia, Saxony, and Russia; Viking fortress of Jomsborg was nearby.
Juliobona. See LILLEBONNE.
Juliomagus. See ANGERS.
Julische Alpen. See table at ALPS.
Jullundur. See JALANDHAR.
Ju·met \zhǖ-ˈmā\. Commune, Hainaut prov., SW Belgium, 25 mi. (40 km.) S of Brussels; glass-manufacturing center.
Jumhūrīyat as–Sūdān. See SUDAN 2.
Ju·mil·la \hü-ˈmē-lyä\. Commune, Murcia prov., SE Spain, 38 mi. (61 km.) NNW of the commune of Murcia; pop. (1991c) 20,092; vineyards, orchards; 15th cent. church; castle.
Jummoo. See JAMMU.
Jumna. See YAMUNA.
Jump \ˈjəmp\. River, NW cen. Wisconsin; rises in Price co., flows SW into Chippewa River in N Chippewa co.; ab. 100 mi. (160 km.) long.
Jump·off \ˈjəmp-ˌȯf\. Mountain, Sevier co., E Tennessee, in Great Smoky Mts.; 6100 ft. (1859 m.).
Jumporn. See CHUMPHON.
Ju·na·gadh \jü-ˈnä-gəd\ *or* **Ju·na·garh** \-gər\. **1.** Former Indian state, now part of Gujarat state, S cen. Kathiawar, W India; 3337 sq. mi. (8643 sq. km.); ruined temple of Somnath; entered into relations with British during early 19th cent.
2. Town, its ✽, 240 mi. (386 km.) NW of Bombay; pop. (1991p) 130,132; located at foot of sacred Girnar Hills (highest 3664 ft. or 1117 m.); has an old fort, Buddhist cave dwellings, temples, and other remains of early Hindu and Muslim times; college of arts.
Junaynah, Al. See AL JUNAYNAH.
Jun·cal \hüŋ-ˈkäl\. Peak in the Andes on boundary bet. Chile and Argentina just S of Mt. Aconcagua; 19,877 ft. (6059 m.).
Jun·cos \ˈhüŋ-kōs\. Municipality, E Puerto Rico, SE of San Juan; pop. (1990c) 30,612.
Junc·tion \ˈjəŋk-shən\. **1.** City, ⊗ of Kimble co., W cen. Texas, on Llano River 113 mi. (182 km.) W of Austin; pop. (1990c) 2654.
2. Town, ⊗ of Piute co., S cen. Utah, near confluence of two forks of Sevier River; pop. (1990c) 132.
Junction City. **1.** City, ⊗ of Geary co., NE cen. Kansas, 18 mi. (29 km.) SW of Manhattan at junction of Republican and Smoky Hill rivers; pop. (1990c) 20,604.
2. City, Lane co., W Oregon, 14 mi. (22 km.) NW of Eugene; pop. (1990c) 3670.
Junction Peak. Mountain in the Sierra Nevada, NE Tulare co., S cen. California; 13,625 ft. (4153 m.).
Jun·diaí \ˌzhün-dyȧ-ˈē\. City, SE São Paulo state, SE Brazil; munic. pop. (1991p) 312,517; railroad junction point 25 mi. (40 km.) NNW of the city of São Paulo.
Jundubah. See JENDOUBA.
Ju·neau \ˈjü-nō\. **1.** Division in SE Alaska. See table at ALASKA.
2. County in cen. Wisconsin. See table at WISCONSIN.
3. Seaport city, ✽ of Alaska, situated on Gastineau Channel, ab. 90 mi. (145 km.) NE of Sitka; pop. (1990c) 26,751; has vessel and airline connections with Seattle and Vancouver; formerly a trade center for a mining region; now a government and tourism center. Founded 1880; became ✽ 1900 and then seat of administration (transferred from Sitka) 1906; continued as ✽ of organized territory 1912 and of state 1959; munic. boundaries enlarged 1970, making it largest city in area (3108 sq. mi. or 8050 sq. km.) in U.S.
4. City, ⊗ of Dodge co., SE cen. Wisconsin; pop. (1990c) 2157.
Jungbunzlau. See MLADÁ BOLESLAV.
Jung·frau \ˈyu̇ŋ-ˌfrau̇\. Peak, SW cen. Switzerland, in Bernese Alps; 13,642 ft. (4158 m.); on border bet. Bern and Valais cantons S of Interlaken which is famous for its view of the Jungfrau.
Jung·gar \ˈju̇ŋ-ˌgär\ *or W.-G.* **Chun–ko–erh** \ˈchu̇n-kō-ˈər\ *or* **Dzun·gar·ia** \ju̇ŋ-ˈgar-ē-ə\ *or* **Dzun·gar·i·an Basin** \-ən\ *or* **Sun·gar·ia** \su̇ŋ-ˈgar-ē-ə\. Region, N Xinjiang Uygur, W China, N of the Tian Shan, a basin traversed by the Ili River. Before 14th cent. a Mongol kingdom; devastated by Turkic ruler Timur 1389; ruled by a western Mongol confederation until 1758–59 when it was conquered by Chinese.
Ju·ni·ata \ˌjü-nē-ˈa-tə\. **1.** River, S cen. Pennsylvania; formed by two branches in Huntingdon co., flows E through Mifflin, Juniata, and Perry cos. into Susquehanna River; ab. 150 mi. (240 km.) long.
2. County in S cen. Pennsylvania. See table at PENNSYLVANIA.

Ju·nín \hü-ˈnēn\. **1.** Town, Buenos Aires prov., E Argentina, on railroad line 150 mi. (241 km.) W of the city of Buenos Aires; pop. (1980c) 62,458.
2. *formerly* **Chin·chay·co·cha** \ˌchēn-chī-ˈkō-chä\. Lake, cen. Peru; ab. 25 mi. (40 km.) long and 8 to 10 mi. (13 to 16 km.) wide; alt. 12,225 ft. (3726 m.).
3. Town, W cen. Peru, 10 mi. (16 km.) SE of the S end of Junín Lake ab. 100 mi. (161 km.) NE of Lima; in wars of independence, scene of a decisive battle Aug. 6, 1824 in which Spaniards under the viceroy José de La Sernay Hinojosa and Gen. José de Canterac were defeated by South American liberators Simón Bolívar and Antonio José de Sucre.

Junkseylon. See PHUKET 1.

Ju·pi·ter \ˈjü-pi-tər\. Town, Palm Beach co., SE Florida, 15 mi. (24 km.) N of the resort town of Palm Beach; pop. (1990c) 24,986; lighthouse and adjoining museum; pop. more than doubled bet. 1980 and 1990.

Jupiter, Mount. Peak, Jefferson co., W Washington; ab. 5700 ft. (1740 m.).

Jupiter Inlet. Narrow strait leading from Atlantic Ocean through barrier reefs off NE coast of Palm Beach co., SE Florida.

Jupiter Island. Island in Atlantic Ocean, off coast of Martin co., SE Florida.

Jupiter Peak. Mountain, La Plata co., SW Colorado; 13,837 ft. (4218 m.).

Ju·qui·la \hü-ˈkē-lä\. Municipality, Oaxaca state, Mexico, 70 mi. (113 km.) SW of the city of Oaxaca.

Jur \ˈju̇r\. River, SW Sudan; flows N and NE to join with the Bahr el Arab to form the Bahr al-Ghazal; ab. 300 mi. (485 km.) long.

Ju·ra \ˈju̇r-ə\. **1.** Mountain range extending 143 mi. (230 km.) along boundary bet. France and Switzerland; highest peak Mt. Neige 5652 ft. (1723 m.), in Ain dept., France; the W slopes are source of the Doubs and Ain rivers of France.
2. Department of E France. See table at FRANCE.
3. Island of the Inner Hebrides, off W coast of Scotland; 24 mi. (39 km.) long; pop. (1981c) 239; nearly cut in two by Loch Tarbert (*q.v.*); in S are the Paps of Jura, highest point 2571 ft. (784 m.); administratively a part of Strathclyde region; fishing, agriculture.
4. Canton. Switzerland. See table at SWITZERLAND.

Jura, Sound of. Body of water off W coast of Scotland bet. island of Jura and Scottish mainland.

Jurjura. See DJURDJURA.

Ju·ruá \ˌzhu̇-ˈrwä\. River, NW cen. South America; rises in Andes Mts. in E cen. Peru, flows NE and empties into the Solimões, upper course of the Amazon, in NW Brazil; ab. 900 mi. (1450 km.) long; navigable length ab. 600 mi. (965 km.).

Ju·rue·na \ˌzhu̇-ˈrwā-nə\. River, W cen. Brazil; flows N in Mato Grosso state, receives the Arinos River from the E; forms part of boundary bet. Mato Grosso and Amazonas states; on border bet. Amazonas and Pará states is joined by the Teles Pires to form the Tapajós; ab. 600 mi. (965 km.) long.

Ju·ru·pa·ri \ˌzhu̇r-u̇-pȧ-ˈrē\. Small island in mouth of Amazon River, off NE coast of Pará state, Brazil.

Jus·tice \ˈjəs-tis\. Village, Cook co., NE Illinois, 4 mi. (6.4 km.) SW of Chicago Midway Airport; pop. (1990c) 11,137.

Justinianopolis. See KIRŞEHIR 2.

Justinopolis. See KOPER.

Ju·taí; *formerly* **Ju·ta·hy** \ˌzhü-tȧ-ˈē\. River, a S tributary of the Amazon in W Amazonas state, NW Brazil; flows NE and joins the Amazon above the Juruá; 400 mi. (644 km.) long.

Ju·tia·pa \ˌhü-ˈtyä-pä\. **1.** Department of SE Guatemala. See table at GUATEMALA.
2. Town, its ✻, 45 mi. (72 km.) SE of Guatemala City; pop. (1994e) 19,500.

Ju·ti·cal·pa \ˌhü-tē-ˈkäl-pä\. Town, ✻ of Olancho dept., E cen. Honduras, 70 mi. (113 km.) NE of Tegucigalpa; pop. (1989e) 20,600.

Jut·land \ˈjət-lənd\ *or Dan.* **Jyl·land** \ˈyu̅e̅-ˌlȧn\. Peninsula projecting N from Germany and extending bet. the North Sea and the Kattegat, comprising Danish mainland and N part of Schleswig-Holstein state, Germany, and mainland of Denmark. Politically the name applies only to the mainland of Denmark; incl. islands N of Limfjorden, 11,436 sq. mi. (29,619 sq. km.); has given its name to major naval battle fought off its W coast in North Sea May 31–June 1, 1916, bet. British and German fleets; although British losses were greater, the North Sea remained under British control.

Juvavum. See SALZBURG 2.

Juventud, Isla de la. See ISLA DE LA JUVENTUD.

Ju·vi·sy \ˌzhü-vē-ˈzē\ *or in full* **Juvisy–sur–Orge** \-su̅e̅r-ˈȯrzh\. Commune, Essone dept., N France, S of Paris; important railroad junction; observatory founded by astronomer Nicolas-Camille Flammarion early 1880s.

Jux·tla·hua·ca \ˌhüs-tlä-ˈwä-kä\. Municipality, Oaxaca state, Mexico, 90 mi. (145 km.) WNW of the city of Oaxaca.

Juzur Qarqannah. See KERKENNAH ISLANDS.

Jylland. See JUTLAND.

Jy·väs·ky·lä \ˈyu̅e̅-vas-ˌku̅e̅-la\. City, ✻ of Keski-Suomi prov., S cen. Finland, at N end of Lake Päijänne; pop. (1989c) 66,387; wood products; university (1966), among other educational institutions; founded 1837.

K

Ka·a·la \kä-'ä-lä\. Peak, Waianae Range, W Oahu I., Hawaii; ab. 4040 ft. (1230 m.); highest peak on Oahu.

Kaapprovinsie. See CAPE PROVINCE.

Kaapstad. See CAPE TOWN.

Kaap Valsch. See VALS, TANJUNG.

Kaa·ters·kill Creek \'kä-tərz-,kil, 'kò-, -tər-,skil\. Creek in Catskill Mts., New York; has waterfalls in its upper course; in lower course goes through a steep-sided, narrow ravine, **Kaaterskill Clove** \'klōv\.

Ka·ba·can \,kä-bä-'kän\. Municipality, cen. Mindanao, Philippines, N of marsh region on left bank of Pulangi River; pop. (1980c) 43,443; during WWII taken by American forces from Japanese 1945.

Ka·ba·e·na \,kä-bä-'ā-nä\. Island in N part of Flores Sea, off SE coast of Sulawesi, Malay Archipelago, Indonesia; part of South-East Sulawesi prov.

Ka·ba·le·ga Falls \,kä-bä-'lā-gä\ *or* **Ka·ba·re·ga Falls** \-'rā-\ *or* **Mur·chi·son Falls** \'mər-chə-sən\. Waterfall in the Victoria Nile, just upstream from Lake Albert, in Uganda; 130 ft. (40 m.) high.

Kabalega National Park. National park, NW Uganda; 1504 sq. mi. (3895 sq. km.); contains Kabalega Falls; estab. 1952.

Ka·ba·lo \kä-'bä-lō\. Town on Lualaba River (upper Congo), SE Democratic Rep. of the Congo; terminus of railroad line running 170 mi. (274 km.) to Kalemi on Lake Tanganyika.

Ka·ban·ka·lan \,kä-bäŋ-'kä-län\. Municipality, SW Negros, Philippines, on Ilog River 50 mi. (81 km.) S of City of Bacolod; pop. (1980c) 92,109.

Kab·ar·di·no–Bal·kar·i·a \,ka-bər-'dē-nō-,bòl-'kar-ē-ə, -,bal-\. Republic, in cen. part of N slopes of Caucasus Mts., S Russia in Europe, bounded on N by Stavropol' Kray, on E and SE by Alania, on S and W by Republic of Georgia; 4826 sq. mi. (12,499 sq. km.); pop. (1992e) 784,000; ❋ Nal'chik. Its component areas are **Ka·bar·dia** \kə-'bär-dē-ə\, mainly the N level part, and **Bal·kar·ia** \bòl-'kar-ē-ə, bal-\, the mountain area in the S. Chief river the Terek with many headstreams, all flowing NE. Chief mountains include some of the highest peaks of the Caucasus, such as Dykh Tau 17,070 ft. (5203 m.), Shkhara 17,063 ft. (5201 m.), and Koshtan Tau 16,899 ft. (5151 m.). Chief occupations agriculture (esp. cereals and wine grapes), raising of livestock, and mining; food processing. Area penetrated by Russians early 19th cent.; after Bolshevik Revolution became part of the Mountain Republic; two areas combined 1922 as one autonomous area; comprised **Kabardino–Balkarian A.S.S.R.** of the U.S.S.R. 1936–91; became a republic 1991.

Kabarega Falls. See KABALEGA FALLS.

Ka·bin·da \kä-'bin-dä\. Exclave and seaport of Angola. See CABINDA.

Ka·bou·dia, Cape \kə-'bü-dē-ə\. Cape on E coast of Tunisia.

Ka·bul \'kä-bəl, -,bùl; kə-'bül\. **1.** River, E Afghanistan and Pakistan; rises on S slopes of Koh-i-Baba Range W of Kabul; has several important tributaries incl. the Chitral from the N and the Swat in Pakistan; passes through gorges of Mohmand Hills N of Khyber Pass to the Indus near Campbellpore, Punjab, Pakistan; 435 mi. (700 km.) long.

2. City, ❋ of Afghanistan, on Kabul River at W end of its valley; met. area pop. (1988e) 1,424,400; largest city in Afghanistan; alt. above 1 mi. (1.6 km.); textiles, leather goods; university (1931), technical college (1967); commands strategic routes through mountain passes into Pakistan from the W; for centuries has been in path of great invasions of the peninsula—as of Macedonian King Alexander the Great, Muslim Sultan Maḥmūd of Ghaznī, Mongol conquerors Genghis Khan and Bābur, Nāder Shāh, king of Persia, and Aḥmad Shāh, Mogul emperor of India. For two centuries (1526–1738) included in the Mogul Empire; with Kandahār one of the two capitals under Aḥmad Shāh Durrāni (1747–73) and made only ❋ c. 1774 under his successor; in First Afghan War occupied by British, who partially destroyed it 1842 in retaliation for Afghan massacre of British; again occupied by British soldier Lord Frederick Sleigh Roberts 1879; after 1880 rebuilt and modernized by the emir 'Abdorraḥmān Khān; ruler's palace just outside the city; suffered damage during several years of factional fighting following 1989 withdrawal of Russian forces at close of Russia-Afghanistan War.

Ka·bu·ruang \,kä-bür-'wäŋ\. See TALAUD ISLANDS.

Kabūshīyah. See MEROË.

Ka·bwe \'kä-,bwā\; *formerly* **Bro·ken Hill** \'brō-kən\. Town, cen. Zambia, on railroad line ab. 70 mi. (115 km.) N of Lusaka; pop. (1990p) 166,519; mining (lead, zinc, vanadium); nearby was discovered (1921) the Broken Hill skull, remains of an extinct African hominid (Rhodesian man).

Ka·by·lia, Great *and* **Little Kabylia** \kə-'bī-lē-ə, -'bi-\. Two regions in N Algeria inhabited by Kabyles.

Kachchh, Gulf of \'kəch\ *or* **Gulf of Kutch** \'kəch\. Inlet of Arabian Sea, Gujarat, W India; at its head adjoins the Little Rann of Kachchh.

Kachchh, Rann of *or* **Rann of Kutch.** Large salt marsh, NW Gujarat, W India; the N section is the **Great Rann of Kachchh,** and the E section is the **Little Rann of Kachchh;** scene of a military clash bet. India and Pakistan 1965 (ab. 300 sq. mi. or 775 sq. km. awarded to Pakistan 1968) and 1971.

Kach·hi \'kä-chē\ *also* **Kach Gan·da·va** \,käch-gən-'dä-və\. Arid region, NE Baluchistan, Pakistan, a flat area E of mountains of N Kalat; ab. 5300 sq. mi. (13,730 sq. km.); outlet is through Jacobabad in Sind.

Ka·chin \kä-'chin\. State of N Myanmar. See table at MYANMAR.

Ka·cza·wa \kä-'chä-vä\ *or Ger.* **Katz·bach** \'käts-,bäk\ *also* **Ko·ca·ba** \kòt-'sä-bə\. River, SW Poland, flowing NE past Lignica into the Oder; scene of battle of Katzbach Aug. 1813.

Ka·dan Island \kä-'dän\; *formerly* **King Island** \'kiŋ\. Island, N Mergui Archipelago (*q.v.*), Myanmar.

Kadavu. See KANDAVU.

Ka·de·na \kä-'dā-nä\. Village, Japan, on W coast of Okinawa, near S end ab. 12 mi. (19 km.) N of Naha, Ryukyu Is.; pop. (1990p) 13,865; airport, taken in WWII by American forces Apr. 1945.

Ka·desh \'kā-,desh\. **1.** Ancient city in W Syria, on Orontes River ab. 15 mi. (24 km.) SW of modern Homs; in early times a kingdom, probably a survival of Hyksos power; seized by the Egyptian King Thutmose III, after Megiddo, c. 1471 B.C.; scene of indecisive battle bet. the Hittites and Ramses II of Egypt c. 1300 B.C.

2. City, ancient Palestine. See KADESH-BARNEA.

Kadesh–bar·nea \-'bär-nē-ə, -bär-'nē-ə\ *or* **Kadesh.** City, ancient Palestine, in the country of the Amalekites SW of the Dead Sea and on W edge of Wilderness of Zin; its location not exactly known; twice scene of encampments of Israelites (*Num. xiii.* 26; *xx.* 1; *xxxiii.* 36).

Kadesia. See KADISIYA.

Ka·di \'kə-dē\. Division of former Baroda state, W India, now in Gujarat state, N of Ahmadabad.

Kadievka. See STAKHANOV.

Ka·dı·köy \kä-'də-kœi\; *anc.* **Chal·ce·don** \'kal-sə-,dän, kal-'sēd-^{ə}n\. City, İstanbul prov., Turkey in Asia, a suburb and

---

\ə\ **abut** \ə\ matches \$^{ə}$\ kitten, Fr table \ər\ **further** \a\ **ash** \ā\ **ace**
\ä\ cot, cart \á\ Fr bac \aù\ **out** \b\ Span Avila \ch\ **chin** \e\ bet \ē\ **easy**
\g\ **go** \i\ hit \ī\ **ice** \j\ **job** \k\ Ger **ich**, **Buch** \$^{n}$\ Fr vin
\ŋ\ sing \ō\ **go** \ö\ **all** \ò\ **law** \œ\ Fr **bœuf** \ǣ\ Fr **feu** \òi\ **boy**
\th\ **thin** \th\ **this** \ü\ **loot** \ù\ **foot** \ue\ Ger **füllen** \ue\ Fr **rue**
\y\ **yet** \$^{y}$\ Fr digne \'dēn^{y}\, nuit \'nw^{y}ē\ \yü\ **few** \yù\ **fury** \zh\ vision

district of the city of İstanbul, opp. the city on E side of entrance to Bosporus and S of Üsküdar. Ancient Chalcedon founded 685 B.C. by Greeks of Megaris; later a city of Bithynia; became Roman 133 B.C.; under Byzantine Empire seat of Fourth Ecumenical Council 451 A.D. which condemned Eutychianism; suffered much in attacks by Persians and Turks, among others.

Ka·di·si·ya \ˌkä-dē-ˈsē-yə\ *or* **Ka·de·sia** \kə-ˈdē-zhə\ *or Arab.* **al–Qā·di·sī·yah** \ˌal-ˌkä-dē-ˈsē-yə\. Locality in medieval Persia (now in Iraq), on the Euphrates near Al Ḩillah and S of Baghdad; scene of battle c. 637 A.D. in which the caliph ʻUmar I defeated the Persian forces of Yazdegerd III, last of the Sassanids.

Kadiyevka. See STAKHANOV.

Ka·do·ka \kə-ˈdō-kə\. City, ⊗ of Jackson co., SW cen. South Dakota; pop. (1990c) 736.

Ka·do·ma \kä-ˈdō-mä\. City, Ōsaka prefecture, Honshū, Japan; pop. (1990p) 142,288.

Ka·do·ma \kä-ˈdō-mä\; *formerly* **Ga·too·ma** \gä-ˈtō-mä\. Town, cen. Zimbabwe, 85 mi. (137 km.) SW of Harare; pop. (1992p) 67,267; center of richest gold-mining region of Zimbabwe.

Ka·du·na \kä-ˈdü-nä\. **1.** River, cen. Nigeria, chief tributary of the Niger. The part near its source is seasonally intermittent.

2. State of N cen. Nigeria. See table at NIGERIA.

3. Town, its ✱; railway junction; textiles.

Ka·é·di \kä-ˈā-dē\. Town, S Mauritania, on Senegal River; pop. (1988c) 30,515.

Ka·e·na Point \kä-ˈā-nä\. **1.** Cape on NW coast of Lanai I., Hawaii.

2. Cape on extreme NW point of Oahu I., Hawaii.

Ka–erh. See GAR.

Kae·sŏng \ˈkä-ˌsȯŋ\ *or Jp.* **Kai·jo** \ˈkī-jō\. Town, North Korea; 2072 sq. mi. (5367 sq. km.); pop. (1987e) 331,000; one of oldest North Korean cities, many remains destroyed during Korean War; has had special administrative status since end of Korean War 1953.

Kaewieng. See KAVIENG.

Kaffa. See FEODOSIYA.

Kaf·frar·ia \kə-ˈfrar-ē-ə, ka-\. Region of Eastern Cape prov., Rep. of South Africa, from Great Kei River on S to KwaZulu-Natal prov. on N bet. the Drakensberg and the coast; largely equivalent to the main portion of former Transkei; inhabited by the Xhosas (Kaffirs), South African native Bantu people, who fought intermittently with British 1779–1878; British Kaffraria is the region to the SW roughly bet. the Great Kei and Fish rivers.

Kafirévs. See CAPHAREUS.

Kafiristan. See NURISTAN.

Ka·fir·ni·gan \ˌkə-fēr-nyi-ˈgän\. River, a N tributary of the Amu Dar'ya, in SW Tajikistan; flows SW near Uzbekistan border.

Kafr ash Shaykh \ˈkaf-rash-ˈshāk̲\ *or* **Kafr el Sheik** *or* **Kafr el Sheikh** \ˈkaf-rel-ˈshāk̲\. **1.** Governorate of Egypt. See table at EGYPT.

2. Town, its ✱, NNW of Tanta; pop. (1986c) 103,301.

Ka·fue \kä-ˈfü-ā\. River, Zambia; flows in winding course S, W, and E to the Zambezi River; ab. 600 mi. (965 km.) long.

Kafue National Park. National park, S cen. Zambia; 8650 sq. mi. (22,405 sq. km.); wide variety of wildlife, incl. antelope, elephant, rhinoceros, zebra.

Ka·ga·wa \kä-ˈgä-wä, ˈkä-gä-ˌwä\. Prefecture, Shikoku, Japan; ✱ Takamatsu. See table at JAPAN.

Ka·ge·ra \kä-ˈgā-rä\. **1.** River, NW Tanzania; flows N, along boundary of Rwanda; turns E along boundary of Uganda and empties into Lake Victoria; ab. 429 mi. (690 km.) long; known as the longest headstream of the Nile.

2. *formerly* **Zi·wa Ma·gha·ri·bi** \ˈzē-wä-ˌmä-gä-ˈrē-bē\; *Eng.* **West Lake** \ˈwest\. Administrative region of NW Tanzania. See table at TANZANIA.

Kagera National Park. National park, E Rwanda; 965 sq. mi. (2499 sq. km.), more than 9 percent of Rwanda's total area; antelope, zebra; estab. 1934.

Kâ·ği·tha·ne \ˌkä-yi-ˈtä-nā\. Town, İstanbul prov., NW Turkey in Europe.

Ka·go·shi·ma \ˌkä-gō-ˈshē-mä, kä-ˈgō-shē-\. **1.** Prefecture, Kyūshū, Japan; ✱ Kagoshima. See table at JAPAN.

2. Seaport city, its ✱, on W coast of **Kagoshima Bay,** a deep inlet on S coast of Kyūshū, Japan; pop. (1990p) 536,685; well-protected harbor; center of manufacture of Satsuma ware; textiles, metal goods; university (1949). An ancient place, long the castle city of a powerful daimyo of the Satsuma clan, esp. important at time of Meiji Restoration late 19th cent.; bombarded by British warships 1863; destroyed by fire during rebellion 1877; severely damaged by eruption of Ontake (on island in bay) 1914; in WWII heavily bombed by Allies 1945.

Ka·gul \kȧ-ˈgül\ *or Rom.* **Ca·hul** \kä-ˈhül\. Town, S Moldova, near Romanian border; before 1945 in Romania.

Ka·ha·ku·loa Head \kä-ˌhä-kü-ˈlō-ä\. Cape on NW coast of Maui I., Hawaii, on W side of Kahului Bay.

Ka·ha·la Point \kä-ˈhä-lä\. Cape on NE coast of Kauai I., Hawaii.

Ka·ha·na Bay \kä-ˈhä-nä\. Bay on NE coast of Oahu I., Hawaii.

Ka·ha·yan *also* **Ka·ha·jan** \kä-ˈhä-ˌyän\ *or* **Great Da·yak** \ˈdī-ˌäk\. River, S Borneo, Indonesia; rises in E end of Schwaner Mts. and flows S to Java Sea; ab. 225 mi. (360 km.) long.

Ka·hilt·na Glacier \kə-ˈhilt-nə\. Glacier in the Alaska Range, S Alaska, just S of Denali National Park; 47 mi. (76 km.) long, ab. 4 mi. (6 km.) wide near its terminus.

Kahlamba. See DRAKENSBERG.

Kah·len·berg \ˈkä-lən-ˌberk\. Elevation ab. 6 mi. (10 km.) NW of Vienna, Austria, in the Wienerwald; 1587 ft. (484 m.).

Ka·ho·ka \kə-ˈhō-kə\. City, ⊗ of Clark co., NE corner of Missouri, 54 mi. (87 km.) NNW of Hannibal; pop. (1990c) 2195.

Ka·ho·o·la·we \kä-ˌhō-ä-ˈlä-vā, -wā\. Island in S cen. Hawaii, W of S Maui I.; 45 sq. mi. (117 sq. km.); a part of Maui co.

Kah·ra·man·ma·raş \ˌkä-rä-ˌmän-ˈmä-ˌräsh\ *also* **Ma·raş** *or* **Ma·rash** \ˈmä-ˌräsh\. **1.** Province of Turkey in Asia. See table at TURKEY.

2. City, its ✱, at foot of E Taurus Mts. and near Ceyhan River 96 mi. (154 km.) NE of Adana; commercial center; exports carpets. A Hittite town c. 9th cent. B.C.; later under Romans; under Muslim control c. 700–1097 A.D., when it was captured by Crusaders; to Ottoman Turks early 16th cent.

Ka·hu·ku \kä-ˈhü-kü\. Unincorporated settlement, Honolulu co., Hawaii, near **Kahuku Point,** the N point of Oahu I.; pop. (1990c) 2063.

Ka·hu·lui \ˌkä-hü-ˈlü-ē\. Unincorporated settlement, Maui co., Hawaii, on **Kahului Bay** on N coast of Maui I.; pop. (1990c) 16,889; seaport, airport.

Ka·hu·zi–Bi·e·ga National Park \kä-ˈhü-zē-bē-ˈā-gä\. National park, E Democratic Rep. of the Congo, near Lake Kivu; 2317 sq. mi. (6001 sq. km.); mountainous with varied types of vegetation; chimpanzees, elephants, and noted for endangered gorillas; estab. 1970.

Kai·a·ka Bay \ˈkī-ä-ˌkä\. Bay on N coast of Oahu I., Hawaii, at base of Kaena Point.

Kai·a·poi \ˌkī-ə-ˈpȯi\. Borough, E South I., New Zealand, N of Christchurch at mouth of Waimakariri River; pop. (1981c) 4894.

Kai·bab Plateau \ˈkī-ˌbab\. Tableland in N Arizona and SW Utah, on N rim of Grand Canyon (*q.v.*); contains **Kaibab National Forest.**

Kai Besar. See KAI ISLANDS.

Kai·bi·to Plateau \kī-ˈbē-tō\. Tableland in NE Coconino co., N cen. Arizona.

Kaieiewaho. See KAUAI 1.

Kaieteur National Park \ˈkī-ə-ˌtu̇r\. National park, W cen. Guyana, along Potaro River in Pakaraima Mts.; estab. 1930; contains **Kaieteur Falls** which drops more than 740 ft. (225 m.); savanna; tapir and other wildlife.

Kai·feng *or W.-G.* **K'ai–feng** \ˈkī-ˈfəŋ\. City, N Henan prov., E cen. China, ab. 340 mi. (545 km.) NW of Nanjing; in Huang River valley and often menaced by floods. One of most historic cities of China, an early settlement site and junction point of routes to the E and S; ✻ of the empire in period of the Five Dynasties (907–960 A.D.) and, as **Pien–ching** \ˈbyen-ˈjiŋ\, under Northern Sung dynasty (960–1127); site of a Jewish colony which flourished esp. 12th–15th cents., as recorded on an inscription stone still in existence.

Kaiffa. See HAIFA.

Kai Islands \ˈkī\ *also* **Kei Islands** \ˈkā\ *or* **Ewab Islands** \ˈē-ˌwäb\. Island group of SE Moluccas, Indonesia, Malay Archipelago, SE of Ceram I. and W of Aru Is.; 572 sq. mi. (1482 sq. km.). Comprises **Kai Be·sar** \be-ˈsär\ *or* **Great Kai Island,** 290 sq. mi. (751 sq. km.), 50 mi. (81 km.) long, mountainous (volcanic), **Kai Ke·tjil** \kā-ˈchēl\ *or* **Little Kai Island,** and many small islets scattered over E end of Banda Sea. Inhabitants include many skilled boatbuilders.

Kaijo. See KAESŎNG.

Kai·kou·ra Range \kī-ˈku̇r-ä\. Mountain range in NE South I., New Zealand, N of Clarence River; elev. from 4000 ft. (1219 m.) to highest peak Tapuaenuku 9463 ft. (2884 m.).

Kai·las \kī-ˈläs\. **1.** Mountain range, SW Tibet, China. See GANGDISÊ.

2. Peak, SW Tibet, China. See KANGRINBOGÊ FENG.

Kai·lua \kī-ˈlü-ä\. **1.** Unincorporated settlement, Honolulu co., Hawaii, on Kailua Bay; pop. (1990c) 36,818.

2. *or* **Kailua–Ko·na** \-ˈkō-nä\. Unincorporated settlement, Hawaii co., Hawaii, on W coast of Hawaii I. N of Kealakekua; pop. (1990c) 9126; residence of early kings of the islands; landing place of first missionaries to Hawaii 1820.

Kailua Bay. Bay on E coast of Oahu I., Hawaii, N of Makapuu Point.

Kai·ma·na \kī-ˈmä-nä\. Town, S coast of Irian Jaya, Indonesia, 125 mi. (201 km.) SE of Fakfak; trading post.

Kai·ma·na·wa Mountains \kī-ˈmä-nä-wä\. Mountain range in cen. North I., New Zealand; highest peak 7534 ft. (2296 m.).

Kai·pa·ra Harbour \ˈkī-pə-rə\. Inlet of Pacific Ocean on W coast of N extension of North I., New Zealand, forming an excellent harbor.

Kai·ra \ˈkīr-ə\ *or* **Khe·da** \ˈkā-də\. Town, SE Gujarat, W India, 20 mi. (32 km.) S of Ahmadabad; pop. (1991p) 21,798; dates back to 5th cent.

Kair·ouan \ker-ˈwän\ *also* **al–Qay·ra·wān** \ˌal-kī-rä-ˈwän\. City, NE Tunisia, ab. 32 mi. (52 km.) WSW of Sousse; trades in leather goods and carpets; a holy city of the Muslims, has several mosques; founded 670 A.D. by Arab Gen. ʻUqbah ibn Nāfiʻ (Okba), to whom one of the mosques is dedicated; ✻ of the Aghlabid dynasty 800–909. In WWII occupied by Allies Apr. 1943.

Kais. See QEYS.

Kaisargarh. See TAKHT-I-SULAIMAN 1.

Kaisaria. See KAYSERİ.

Kaiserin Augusta. See SEPIK.

Kai·sers·lau·tern \ˌkī-zərz-ˈlau̇-tərn\. City, Rhineland-Palatinate, Germany, 43 mi. (69 km.) NW of Karlsruhe; pop. (1992e) 100,541; textiles, automobiles; first mentioned 882; became city 1276; scene of French victory over Prussians 1793; ✻ of French dept. of Donnersberg 1797–1814; passed to Bavaria 1816.

Kai·ser·stuhl \ˈkī-zər-ˌshtül\. Mountain group, SW Baden-Württemberg, Germany, NW of Freiburg; highest peak 1827 ft. (557 m.).

Kai·sers·werth \ˈkī-zərz-ˌvert\. Former town, Germany, 6 mi. (10 km.) below Düsseldorf on Rhine River; since 1929 a part of Düsseldorf; grew up around a Benedictine monastery built 710; scene of activities of German clergyman and philanthropist Theodor Fliedner, who became pastor here 1821 and opened refuge for discharged female convicts 1833 and later several other charitable institutions.

Kaiser Wilhelm Canal. See NORD-OSTSEE KANAL.

Kaiser Wilhelm II Land. See WILHELM II COAST.

Kaiser–Wilhelmsland. See NORTH-EAST NEW GUINEA.

Kaishu. See HAEJU.

Kai·thal \ˈkīt-ᵊl\. Town, Haryana state, NW India, 90 mi. (145 km.) NNW of Delhi; pop. (1991p) 71,096; an old town; connected with Hindu legends, esp. with the monkey-god Hanumān. Held by Sikhs 1767 to 1843 when it came under British influence.

Kai·wi \ˈkī-wē\. Channel bet. Oahu I. and Molokai I., Hawaii; 23 mi. (37 km.) wide.

Kai·yuan *or W.-G.* **K'ai–yüan** \ˈkī-ˈywän\. Town, E Liaoning prov., China, ab. halfway bet. Shenyang and Changchun; consists of walled town and new town around railroad station.

Kai·zu·ka \kī-ˈzü-kä\. City, Ōsaka prefecture, Honshū, Japan, 20 mi. (32 km.) SW of the city of Ōsaka; pop. (1990p) 79,236.

Ka·jaa·ni \ˈkä-ˌyä-nē\. City, Oulu prov., cen. Finland; pop. (1989c) 36,099; on rapids just SE of Oulujärvi; trade and transportation center; hydroelectric power; founded 1651.

Ka·jan \ˈkä-ˌyän\. River, E Borneo, Indonesia; rises in mountains of N cen. Borneo and flows E to Celebes Sea; ab. 250 mi. (400 km.) long.

Ka·jang \ˈkä-ˌyäŋ\. Town, E cen. Selangor, Malaysia, on W coast railroad line 10 mi. (16 km.) S of Kuala Lumpur.

Ka·je·li \kä-ˈyā-lē\. Village on bay on E coast of Buru I., Moluccas, Indonesia.

Ka·ka·du National Park \ˈkä-kə-ˌdü\. National park, N Northern Terr., Australia; erosion topography, birds and reptiles, aboriginal rock art; Australia's largest national park.

Ka·kam·bo·na \ˌkä-käm-ˈbō-nä\ *also* **Ko·kum·bo·na** \ˌkō-\. Coastal village, NW Guadalcanal I., SE Solomon Is., W Pacific Ocean, W of the Mataniko River; scene of severe fighting during WWII 1942–43, bet. Americans and Japanese.

Ka·ka·me·ga \ˌkä-kä-ˈmā-gä\. Town, ✻ of Western Prov., W Kenya.

Ka·ka·mi·ga·ha·ra \ˌkä-kä-ˌmē-gä-ˈhä-rä\. City, Gifu prefecture, W cen. Honshū, Japan; pop. (1990p) 129,682.

Ka·ki·na·da; *formerly* **Coc·a·na·da** \ˌkä-kə-ˈnä-də\. City, NE Andhra Pradesh, E India, on Bay of Bengal at N side of Godavari Delta, 300 mi. (483 km.) NNE of Madras; pop. (1991p) 279,875; harbor facilities maintained with difficulty because of alluvial soil; exports cotton.

Käkisalmi. See PRIOZERSK.

Ka·ko·ga·wa \ˌkä-kō-ˈgä-wä\. City, Hyōgo prefecture, Honshū, Japan; pop. (1990p) 239,803.

Kala, El. See EL KALA.

Kalaallit Nunaat. See GREENLAND.

Ka·la·ba·hi \ˌkä-lä-ˈbä-hē\. Chief town on Alor I., Lesser Sunda Is., Indonesia, at head of **Kalabahi Bay** at W end of island; excellent anchorage.

Ka·lach–na–Do·nu \kə-ˈläch-nə-ˈdȯ-nü\. Town, W cen. Volgograd Oblast, S Russia in Europe, on E bank of the Don at its nearest point to the Volga; head of navigation of the Don and W terminus of Volga-Don Canal.

Ka·la·dan \ˌkə-lə-ˈdən\. River, NE India and W Myanmar; flows S from Chin Hills to Bay of Bengal at Sittwe, Myanmar; ab. 300 mi. (485 km.) long; known as **Boi·nu** \ˈboi-(ˌ)nü\ in its upper course; one upper tributary rises in the Mizo Hills in Mizoram, India.

Ka Lae \kä-ˈlä-ā\ *or* **South Cape** *or* **South Point.** Cape on S extremity of Hawaii I.

Kalaeloa Point. See BARBERS POINT.

Ka·la·han·di \ˌkä-lə-ˈhän-dē\; *formerly* **Ka·rond** \kə-ˈrōnd\. Former Indian state, NE India, now part of Orissa state; 3559 sq. mi. (9218 sq. km.); ✻ Bhawanipatna.

Ka·la·ha·ri Desert \ˌka-lə-ˈhär-ē, kä-lä-ˈhä-rē\. Plateau and partly desert region, Botswana, W cen. Rep. of South Africa, and part of Namibia, N of the Orange River and S of Lake Ngami; area exceeds 100,000 sq. mi. (259,000 sq. km.); S portion traversed by dry river beds, as the Molopo and the Kuruman; av. elev. ab. 3000 ft. (915 m.); vegetation mostly grass, dense scrub in W and N; big game; first crossed by Scottish missionary and explorer David Livingstone and English hunter William C. Oswell 1849.

Kalahari Gems·bok National Park \ˈgemz-ˌbäk\. National park, N Northern Cape prov., Rep. of South Africa, bordering Namibia to the W and adjoining Gemsbok National Park, Botswana to the N and E; 3703 sq. mi. (9591 sq. km.); contains large herds of wildlife incl. lions, eland, hartebeests, wildebeests, leopards, cheetahs, hyenas, and springboks in addition to gemsboks; estab. 1931.

K'a–la–k'a–shih. See KARAKAX.

K'a–la–k'un–lun Shan K'ou. See KARAKORAM PASS.

Kalámai. See KALAMATA.

Kalamas. See THÝAMIS.

Kal·a·ma·ta \ˌkä-lä-ˈmä-tä, ˌka-\ *or* **Ka·lá·mai** \kä-ˈlä-me\. Commercial seaport city, ✻ of Messenia dept., SW Peloponnese, S Greece, at head of Gulf of Messenia; pop. (1981p) 41,998; nearby is site of ancient Pharae; 13th cent. castle remains from French Villehardouin family; occupied by Venetians during 15th cent. and again, during 17th cent.; intermittent occupation by Turks; sacked by Ottoman Gen. Ibrāhīm Pasha 1825; suffered severe earthquake damage Sept. 1986.

Kalamata, Gulf of. See MESSENIA, GULF OF.

Kal·a·ma·zoo \ˌka-lə-mə-ˈzü\. **1.** River, SW Michigan; rises in Hillsdale co., flows N, then W into Lake Michigan in Allegan co.; 200 mi. (320 km.) long.

2. County in SW Michigan. See table at MICHIGAN.

3. City, its ⊗, 47 mi. (76 km.) S of Grand Rapids; pop. (1990c) 80,277; diversified industry; Kalamazoo Coll. (1833), Western Michigan Univ. (1903), Kalamazoo Valley Community Coll. (1966); aviation history museum; first settlement 1829; incorp. as city c. 1884.

Ka·lam·bo Falls \kä-ˈläm-bō\. Falls in short river flowing into S part of Lake Tanganyika, on Tanzania-Zambia border; 726 ft. (221 m.) high.

Ka·lan \kä-ˈlän\. Town, ✻ of Tunceli prov., E cen. Turkey in Asia.

Ka·lat *or* **Khe·lat** *also* **Ke·lat** \kə-ˈlät\. **1.** Former Indian state, now part of Baluchistan, Pakistan; 72,503 sq. mi. (187,783 sq. km.); has rugged and barren mountains, but also wide, fertile valleys; in 1947 remained independent of newly formed Pakistan but joined the new state 1948.

2. Walled town with citadel, its ✻; 88 mi. (142 km.) SSW of Quetta; pop. (1981c) 11,037; alt. 6780 ft. (2067 m.); occupied by British 1839.

Ka·la·u·pa·pa \kä-ˌlä-ü-ˈpä-pä\. Village and leper settlement, Kalawao co., Hawaii, on N coast of Molokai I. on Kalaupapa Penin.; leper settlement one of best equipped in the world, covering 8576 acres (3473 hectares). See KALAWAO.

Kalaupapa National Historical Park. See UNITED STATES, *National Historical Parks.*

Kalaupapa Peninsula *also* **Ma·ka·na·lua Peninsula** \mä-ˌkä-nä-ˈlü-ä\. Promontory in center of N coast of Molokai I., Hawaii, in Kalawao co.

Ka·laus \kȧ-ˈlau̇s\. River, S Russia in Europe, largely in Stavropol' Kray; ab. 160 mi. (260 km.) long, flowing N to join the Eastern Manych.

Ka·la·wao \ˌkä-lä-ˈwau̇\. **1.** County in Hawaii; formerly comprised only of the Kalaupapa leper settlement and represented in state legislature as part of Maui co. See table at HAWAII.

2. Village, N Molokai, site of original leper settlement, where Belgian missionary Father Damien began his work 1873.

Kal·bar·ri National Park \kal-ˈbär-ē\. National park, W Western Australia, Australia, on the coast; 719 sq. mi. (1862 sq. km.); rocky gorges of the Murchison River.

Ka·le·mie \kä-ˈlā-mē\; *formerly* **Al·bert·ville** \ˌȧl-ber-ˈvēl, ˈal-bərt-ˌvil\. Port, Shaba administrative region, Democratic Rep. of the Congo, on W shore of Lake Tanganyika; pop. (1991e) 96,212; cotton cloth.

Kale–i Sultaniye. See ÇANAKKALE 2.

Ka·le·wa \kä-ˈlā-wə\. Town, W Myanmar, on Chindwin River 150 mi. (241 km.) NW of Mandalay; scene of fighting in WWII Japanese campaign against India.

Kalgan. See ZHANGJIAKOU.

Kal·goor·lie–Boul·der \kal-ˈgu̇r-lē-ˈbōl-dər\. Town, S Western Australia, Australia, 335 mi. (539 km.) ENE of Perth; pop. (1991c) 25,016; Western Australia School of Mines; gold (discovered late 19th cent.) and nickel (1966) are still mined.

Kalhu. See NIMRUD.

Ka·li \ˈkä-lē\. Upper course of Sarda River (*q.v.*), N India.

Ka·lia·kra, Nos \ˈnōs-käl-ˈyä-krä\ *or* **Cape Kaliakra.** Cape, NE Bulgaria, on the Black Sea, 43°21′N, 28°27′E.

Kalian Point. See CALIAN POINT.

Ka·li Bay \ˈkä-lē\. Inlet, W end of Manus I., Admiralty Is., W Pacific Ocean.

Ka·li·bo \kä-ˈlē-bō\; *formerly* **Ca·li·vo** \-vō\. Municipality, ✻ of Aklan prov., N Panay, Philippines, near coast 28 mi. (45 km.) WNW of Roxas; pop. (1990c) 51,387.

Kalimantan. See BORNEO.

Ka·li·man·tan, Central \ˌkä-lē-ˈmän-ˌtän, ˌka-lə-ˈman-ˌtan\ *or* **Kalimantan Ten·gah** \ˈteŋ-gə\. Province, Indonesia, on island of Borneo; mountainous in N; rivers include the Barito and Kahayan. See table at INDONESIA.

Kalimantan, East *or* **Kalimantan Ti·mur** \ˈtē-ˌmu̇r\. Province, Indonesia, on island of Borneo; mountainous in W; chief river Mahakam; produces oil. See table at INDONESIA.

Kalimantan, South *or* **Kalimantan Se·la·tan** \ˌsā-lä-ˈtän\. Province, Indonesia, on island of Borneo. See table at INDONESIA.

Kalimantan, West *or* **Kalimantan Ba·rat** \ˈbä-rät\. Province, Indonesia, on island of Borneo; mountainous in N and NE; chief river the Kapuas. See table at INDONESIA.

Ka·li Mas \ˌkä-lē-ˈmäs\. River, E Java, Indonesia; leaves the Brantas River (*q.v.*) near Mojokerto and flows NE and N through city of Surabaya to Surabaja Strait; a branch of the Brantas; ab. 35 mi. (56 km.) long.

Kā·lim·pang \ˈkä-lim-ˌpäŋ\ *or* **Ka·lim·pong** \ˈkä-lim-ˌpȯŋ\. Town, N West Bengal, NE India, ab. 8 mi. (13 km.) ENE of Darjeeling; pop. (1991p) 40,845; alt. 3933 ft. (1199 m.).

Ka·lin·ga \kə-ˈliŋ-gə\. Ancient and medieval kingdom, NE India.

Ka·lin·ga–Apa·yao \kä-ˈliŋ-gä-ä-ˈpä-ˌyau̇\. Province, N Luzon, Philippines; ✻ Tabuk; S part includes valley of Chico River; W and SW mountainous, with peaks ranging from 5000 to 8400 ft. (1524 to 2560 m.), has forests and much grass area; not well suited to agriculture. See table at PHILIPPINES.

Kalinin. See TVER' 2.

Ka·li·nin·grad \kə-ˈlē-nin-ˌgrȧt\ *or Ger.* **Kö·nigs·berg** \ˈkœ-niks-ˌberk, ˈkō-\. **1.** Seaport, ✻ of Kaliningrad Oblast, exclave of Russia, on Pregolya River near the Vislinski Zaliv 80 mi. (129 km.) ENE of Gdánsk, Poland; pop. (1992e) 411,000; connected with Gulf of Danzig by ship canal; paper, machinery, chemicals; 14th cent. Gothic cathedral, 17th cent. citadel, university (1544), all left in ruins by WWII; birthplace of German philosopher Immanuel Kant 1724 who taught at the university. Founded 1255; joined Hanseatic League 1340; in WWI besieged by Russians 1914; in WWII occupied by Soviet armies Apr. 1945 after long siege; assigned to U.S.S.R. by Potsdam Conference 1945; named Kaliningrad by U.S.S.R. 1946.

2. Town, Moscow Oblast, W cen. Russia in Europe, ab. 15 mi. (24 km.) NNE of the city of Moscow; pop. (1992e) 162,000.

Kaliningrad Oblast \ˈō-bləst, -ˌblast\ *or* **Ka·li·nin·grad·ska·ya Oblast'** \kə-ˌlē-nən-ˈgrȧt-skə-yə\. Subdivision of Russia, comprising an exclave around Kaliningrad (see KALININGRAD 1); 5830 sq. mi. (15,100 sq. km.); pop. (1992e) 894,000; ✻ Kaliningrad; includes cities of Sovetsk (Tilsit) and Chernyakhovsk (Insterburg); smallest oblast in Russia.

Kalinin Oblast. See TVER' OBLAST.

Kalininsk. See PETROZAVODSK.

Kal·i·spell \ˈka-lə-ˌspel, ˌka-lə-ˈ\. City, ⊗ of Flathead co., NW Montana, 8 mi. (13 km.) NW of N end of Flathead Lake; pop. (1990c) 11,917; lumber mill, aluminum plant; market center, tourist resort; Flathead Valley Community Coll. (1967).

Ka·lisz \ˈkä-lēsh\ *or Ger.* **Ka·lisch** \ˈkä-lish\. **1.** Province, W of cen. Poland. See table at POLAND.

2. Commune, its ✻, on Prosna River ab. 65 mi. (105 km.) SE of Poznań; pop. (1989e) 106,087; railroad junction; manufactures textiles and leather products.

History: Mentioned by Alexandrian astronomer Ptolemy

2d cent. A.D.; received town rights 1282; scene of Swedish defeat by combined army of Russians and Poles 1706; place where Prussia and Russia formed coalition against French Emperor Napoléon Feb. 28, 1813; occupied by Germans Aug. 1914 and greater part destroyed; restored to Poland 1919; again under Germans in WWII; to Poland again following WWII.

Ka·li·wun·gu *or Du.* **Ka·li·woen·goe** \ˌkä-lē-ˈwüŋ-gü\. Town, Central Java prov., Indonesia, just W of Semarang.

Ka·lix \ˈkä-lēks\. River, N Sweden; flows SE and S into head of Gulf of Bothnia; 267 mi. (430 km.) long; many rapids.

Kal·ka \ˈkäl-kä\ *or mod.* **Kal·mi·us** \ˈkal-mē-əs\. Short river, SE Ukraine, flows S into the Gulf of Taganrog; scene of victory of the Mongols over Russians 1223.

Kalka \ˈkäl-kə, ˈkal-\. Village, on border bet. Haryana and Himachal Pradesh, NW India; station on railroad line from Ambala to Simla.

Kalkandelen. See TETOVO.

Kal·kas·ka \kal-ˈkas-kə\. **1.** County in N Michigan. See table at MICHIGAN.
2. Village, ⊗ of Kalkaska co., N Michigan; pop. (1990c) 4269.

Kal·la·ve·si \ˈkäl-lä-ˌvā-sē\. Lake in S cen. Finland, 100 mi. (161 km.) E of Vaasa; W shore site of city of Kuopio.

Kal·li·théa *or* **Cal·li·thea** \ˌkä-lē-ˈthā-ä\. Commune, Greece, S suburb of Athens.

Kal·lo·ní, Gulf of \ˌkä-lö-ˈnē\ *or Gk.* **Kól·pos Kal·lo·nís** \ˈköl-ˌpös-ˌkä-lö-ˈnēs\. Long inlet of Aegean Sea in S Lesbos I., Aegean Is., Greece, widening out in center of island; town of **Kalloní** lies at head of it.

Kal·mar *also* **Cal·mar** \ˈkäl-ˌmär\. **1.** Province of SE Sweden. See table at SWEDEN.
2. Seaport, its ⊗, on Kalmarsund opp. Öland I.; pop. (1993e) 56,863; shipbuilding; automobiles, matches; Union of Kalmar, uniting Denmark, Sweden, and Norway into a single monarchy (1397–1523), was formed here.

Kal·mar·sund \ˈkäl-mär-ˌsu̇nd\. Body of water separating Öland I. in Baltic Sea from mainland of Sweden.

Kalmius. See KALKA.

Kal·myk·ia \kal-ˈmi-kē-ə\. Republic, S Russia in Europe, on NW shore of Caspian Sea and W of lower Volga; 29,305 sq. mi. (75,900 sq. km.); pop. (1993e) 322,000; ✱ Elista; largely steppe land, dry desert with hills along W border; no railroad except from Astrakhan S along the Caspian shore.
History: Region settled early 17th cent. by Kalmucks (Kalmyks), a nomadic, Buddhist people, W Mongols from cen. China, who became subject to Russia 1646 and later furnished men for some of Czar Peter the Great's armies; most of its present inhabitants descended from the western Kalmucks who were left behind when 300,000 of their people, fearing oppression, suddenly left 1771 to return to China and during a journey of great privations barely a third of them reached the destination; suffered heavily during civil war and famine after the Bolshevik Revolution 1917; estab. as an autonomous oblast 1920; made an autonomous republic 1935; after recapture of Volgograd (formerly Stalingrad) by Russians 1943, republic liquidated because of suspected Nazi collaboration; territory partitioned among Stavropol' Kray, Volgograd and Rostov oblasts, and the newly formed Astrakhan Oblast, which received most of it; reestablished as an autonomous oblast within Stavropol' Kray 1957, regaining status of autonomous republic 1958; comprised **Kal·myk A.S.S.R.** \ˈkal-mik\ of the U.S.S.R. before 1991; became a republic 1992 following breakup of Soviet Union, subsequently became member of Russian Federation.

Ka·lo·csa \ˈkö-lö-ˌchö\. City, S Hungary, near Danube River 70 mi. (113 km.) S of Budapest; pop. (1992e) 18,187; in an agricultural region; archbishopric founded 12th cent.; cathedral; frequently attacked by Turks in 16th cent.

Ka·lo·hi \kä-ˈlō-hē\. Channel bet. Molokai I. on N and Lanai I. on S, Hawaii; ab. 9 mi. (15 km.) wide.

Ka·lo·ko–Ho·no·ko·hau National Historical Park \kä-ˈlō-kō-ˌhō-nō-ˌkō-ˈhau̇\. See UNITED STATES, *National Historical Parks.*

Kal·pi \ˈkäl-pē\. Town, SW Uttar Pradesh, N India, on Yamuna River 45 mi. (72 km.) SW of Kanpur; founded 4th cent. A.D.; important in early wars; captured by British 1803; scene of British defeat of rebels 1858 during Indian mutiny.

Ka·lu·ga \kə-ˈlü-gə\. City, E Kaluga Oblast, Russia in Europe, ab. 90 mi. (145 km.) SW of Moscow; pop. (1992e) 347,000; on left bank of Oka River and on several railroad lines; smelting works, sawmills; manufactures machinery, railroad equipment. Dates back to 14th cent.; included in Moscow principality early 16th cent.; in early 17th cent. devastated by Cossacks, plague, and fire; in WWII held by Germans 1941.

Kaluga Oblast \ˈó-bləst, -ˌblast\ *or* **Ka·luzh·ska·ya Oblast'** \kə-ˈlüzh-skə-yə\. Subdivision of Russia in Europe, in black-earth area N of Ukraine; 11,544 sq. mi. (29,899 sq. km.); pop. (1992e) 1,081,000; ✱ Kaluga; crossed by Oka River; flax; livestock; region formerly part of Tula Oblast; estab. 1944.

Ka·lush \ˈkȧ-lu̇sh\ *or Pol.* **Ka·łusz** \ˈkä-ˌlu̇sh\. Town, Ivano-Frankivs'k subdivision, SW Ukraine, on a tributary of the Dniester 18 mi. (29 km.) WNW of the city of Ivano-Frankivs'k (formerly in Poland); pop. (1991e) 69,000; following WWI, located in Poland; following WWII, in U.S.S.R.

Ka·lu·ta·ra \ˈkə-lu̇-tə-rə, ˌkä-lə-ˈtär-ə\. Town, SW Sri Lanka, on Indian Ocean 26 mi. (42 km.) S of Colombo; pop. (1990e) 34,000.

Kaluwawa. See FERGUSSON.

Kal·yan \kəl-ˈyän\. Town, W Karnataka, W India, 33 mi. (53 km.) NE of Bombay; pop. (1991c) 1,014,557; important railroad-junction point; silk, bricks and tiles; a commercial center in 17th cent.

Kal·ya·ni \kəl-ˈyä-nē\. Town, N Mysore state, India, ab. 40 mi. (64 km.) N of Gulbarga; pop. (1991p) 56,056; formerly (10th to 12th cents.) seat of powerful Cālukya dynasty.

Ka·lym·nos \ˈkä-lēm-ˌnös\; *Ital.* **Ca·li·no** \kä-ˈlē-nō\ *or* **Ca·lim·no** \kä-ˈlēm-nō\; *anc.* **Ca·lym·na** \kə-ˈlim-nə\ *or* **Ca·lym·nos** \kə-ˈlim-nəs\. **1.** An island of the Dodecanese (*q.v.*), Greece, off end of Bodrum Penin. N of Kos I.; 49 sq. mi. (127 sq. km.).
2. *or* **Po·thea** \pō-ˈthē-ä\. Town, its ✱, on the S coast.

Kalyub. See QALYÛB.

Kalyubīya. See QALYUBĪYA.

Ka·ma \ˈkä-mə\. River in E Russia in Europe; rises in N border of Udmurtia, flows N in Vyatka Oblast, then E and S in Perm' Oblast along W slope of Middle Urals, then S in SE Udmurtia and WSW in Tatarstan to the Volga ab. 40 mi. (64 km.) below Kazan'; 1261 mi. (2029 km.) long; drainage basin 201,544 sq. mi. (521,999 sq. km.); largest tributary of the Volga; navigable for ab. 1000 mi. (1610 km.); important part of Russia's water transportation system; chief tributaries Belaya, Vyatka, and Chusovaya.

Ka·ma·ga·ya \ˌkä-mä-ˈgä-yä\. City, Chiba prefecture, SE Honshū, Japan; pop. (1990p) 95,052.

Ka·mai·ki Point \kä-ˈmī-kē\. Cape on SE coast of Lanai I., Hawaii.

Ka·maing \ˈkä-ˌmīŋ\. Town, N Myanmar, 20 mi. (32 km.) NW of Mogaung; taken by Chinese June 1944.

Ka·ma·kou \ˌkä-mä-ˈkō\. Mountain, E Molokai I., Hawaii; 4970 ft. (1515 m.).

Ka·ma·ku·ra \ˌkä-mä-ˈkü-rä\. Town, Kanagawa prefecture, SE Honshū, Japan, on Sagami Sea ab. 10 mi. (16 km.) S of Yokohama; pop. (1990p) 174,299; railroad junction and residential area; Kamakura Museum (contains national treasures), Kamakura Prefectural Museum of Modern Art.
History: Historically one of most important towns of Japan; probably founded in 7th cent. A.D.; selected by feudal military leader Minamoto Yoritomo as his residence and on his assumption of the shogunate 1192 became seat of government of Japan to remain so until downfall of Hojo rulers 1333 when it was nearly destroyed; during Minamoto shogu-

nate may have had population of close to a million; with rise of Edo (Tokyo) to power 1603 declined to a fishing village. Since the Meiji Restoration 1868 has become a favorite resort; site of Daibutsu, the great bronze image of Buddha, cast in 1252, ab. 50 ft. (15 m.) in height; has a shrine of Shinto war-god Hachiman (founded 1063) and several temples.

Ka·ma·ran *or* **Qa·ma·ran** \ˌka-ma-ˈran, ˌkä-mä-ˈrän\. Island in S Red Sea, off coast of Yemen, 45 mi. (72 km.) N of Al Ḩudaydah; 70 sq. mi. (181 sq. km.); fishing; formerly administered as part of British colony of Aden; since 1967 part of Yemen (People's Democratic Republic of Yemen before 1990 merger).

Kamar Bay. See QAMAR, GHUBBAT AL.

Ka·mar·ha·ti \ˌkä-mər-ˈhä-tē\. Town, West Bengal, NE India, on left bank of Hugli River 12 mi. (19 km.) N of Calcutta; pop. (1991p) 266,625.

Kambaeng Petch. See KAMPHAENG PHET.

Kambryk. See CAMBRAI.

Kam·chat·ka \kəm-ˈchät-kə, kam-ˈchat-kə\. **1.** Peninsula, NE Russia in Asia, extending S bet. Sea of Okhotsk and Bering Sea to a point (Cape Lopatka) 7 mi. (11 km.) from Shumshu, northernmost of Kuril Is.; 104,260 sq. mi. (270,033 sq. km.); 750 mi. (1207 km.) long, width varies from 80 to 300 mi. (129 to 483 km.); constitutes major portion of Kamchatka Oblast, within which is Koryak Autonomous Okrug; fishing; timber. Its mountain system, the **Kamchatka Mountains,** consists of two main ranges: (1) the Eastern Range, the shorter, along E coast, having many high volcanic peaks, incl. Klyuchevskaya Sopka 15,584 ft. (4750 m.), highest in Siberia; (2) the Sredinnyy Khrebet extending length of the peninsula, av. height 3000 ft. (914 m.). First visited by Russians late 17th cent.; explored in 18th cent.; developed slowly since 1850.

2. Chief river of the Kamchatka Penin.; rises in Sredinnyy Khrebet, flows N and E to Bering Sea; 478 mi. (769 km.) long.

Kamchatka Oblast \ˈo-bləst, -ˌblast\ *or* **Kam·chat·ska·ya Oblast'** \kəm-ˈchät-skə-yə\. A subdivision of Russia in Asia; 182,355 sq. mi. (472,299 sq. km.); pop. (1992e) 472,000; approx. coterminous with the peninsula (see KAMCHATKA 1).

Kam·chi·ya \ˈkäm-chē-ˌyä\. River in E Bulgaria; flows E into Black Sea S of Varna; ab. 110 mi. (177 km.) long.

Ka·men \ˈkä-mən\. **1.** City, North Rhine-Westphalia, Germany, 9 mi. (14 km.) NE of Dortmund; pop. (1980c) 44,017; received civic rights mid-13th cent.

2. City, Russia in Asia. See KAMEN'-NA-OBI.

Kamenets Podolski *or* **Kamenets–Podol'skiy** *or* **Kamenets Podolsky.** See KAM'YANETS'-PODIL'S'KYY.

Kamenets–Podolsky. See KHMEL'NYTS'KYY 1.

Ka·me·nic·ký Še·nov \ˈkä-me-ˌnēt-skē-ˈshe-ˌnȯf\. Commune, N Czech Republic, E of Labe (Elbe) River and ab. 20 mi. (32 km.) NE of Litoměřice.

Ka·me·njak, Cape \ˈkä-me-ˌnyäk\ *or Ital.* **Cape Pro·mon·to·re** \ˌprō-mən-ˈtȯr-ē\. S tip of Istria Penin., W Croatia.

Ka·men'–na–Obi *or* **Kamen–na–Obi** \ˈkä-mənʸ-nə-ˈō-bē\; *formerly* **Kamen.** Town, Altay Kray, S Russia in Asia, on Ob' River, ab. 110 mi. (177 km.) SW of Novosibirsk.

Kamensk. **1.** Town, Russia in Europe. See KAMENSK SHAKHTINSKIY.

2. Town, Russia in Asia. See KAMENSK URAL'SKIY.

Kamenskoye. See DNIPRODZERZHYNS'K.

Ka·mensk Shakh·tin·skiy *or* **Kamensk Shakh·tin·ski** \ˈkä-minsk-ˈshäk-tin-skē\; *formerly* **Kamensk.** Town, W Rostov Oblast, S Russia in Europe, on Donets River; pop. (1991e) 73,100; on railroad trunk-line; founded late 17th cent.; in WWII within German lines 1942–43.

Ka·mensk Ural'·skiy *or* **Kamensk–Ural·ski** \ˈkä-minsk-ü-ˈräl-skē\; *formerly* **Kamensk.** Town, N Sverdlovsk Oblast, W Russia in Asia, ab. 50 mi. (80 km.) SE of Yekaterinburg; pop. (1993e) 208,000.

Ka·menz \ˈkä-ˌments\. City, Saxony, E Germany, on the Schwarze Elster River; pop. (1992e) 209,000; Gothic churches; founded c. 1200; birthplace of dramatist and critic Gotthold Ephraim Lessing 1729.

Ka·me·o·ka \kä-ˈmā-ō-ˌkä\. City, Kyōto prefecture, Honshū, Japan; pop. (1990p) 85,283.

Kamerun. See CAMEROONS.

Ka·met \ˈkə-māt, kə-ˈmāt\. Peak in the Himalayas, Uttar Pradesh, N India, on India-China border; 25,447 ft. (7756 m.); ascended June 1931, at that time the highest peak ever climbed.

Ka·mien·na Gó·ra \kä-ˈmyen-nä-ˈgü-rä\ *or Ger.* **Lan·des·hut** \ˈlän-dəs-ˌhüt\ *also* **Landeshut in Schle·si·en** \in-ˈshlā-zē-ən\. City, SE Jelenà Góra prov., SW Poland, on Bóbr River 52 mi. (84 km.) WSW of Wrocław; pop. (1989e) 23,405. Scene of Prussian victory over Austrians 1745 and of Austrian victory over Prussians 1760; assigned to Poland by Potsdam Conference 1945.

Ka·mi·na \kä-ˈmē-nä\. Town, Shaba administrative region, Zaire, 190 mi. (306 km.) NW of Likasi; pop. (1991e) 82,160.

Kam·loops \ˈkam-ˌlüps\. City, S British Columbia, Canada, at confluence of N and S branches of Thompson River 160 mi. (257 km.) NE of Vancouver; pop. (1991c) 67,057; railroad divisional point; service and supply center in lumbering region; fruit canneries; outdoor recreation; copper deposits; founded c. 1810 as Fort Thompson.

Kammer, Lake *or* **Kammersee.** See ATTER, LAKE.

Kam·ou·ras·ka \ˌka-mu̇-ˈras-kə\. County, S Quebec, Canada. See table at QUEBEC.

Kam·pa·la \käm-ˈpä-lä\. City, * of Uganda, near Lake Victoria; pop. (1991p) 773,463; textiles; food processing; university (1922); by far the largest city in Uganda.

Kam·par \ˈkäm-ˌpär\. **1.** Town, S cen. Perak state, Malaysia, 20 mi. (32 km.) SE of Ipoh; on E coast railroad trunk line in Kinta Valley tin region.

2. River, cen. Sumatra, Indonesia; rises in Barisan Mts. N of Bukittingi, flows E into S end of Strait of Malacca; ab. 200 mi. (320 km.) long.

Kam·pen \ˈkäm-pən\. Commercial commune, Overijssel prov., E Netherlands, on IJssel River; pop. (1992e) 32,643; town hall; church of St. Nicholas; medieval ruins; formerly a member of Hanseatic League.

Kam·phaeng Phet *or* **Kam·baeng Petch** \käm-ˌpaŋ-ˈpet\. Town, W Thailand, on left bank of Ping River 65 mi. (105 km.) NW of Nakhon Sawan; pop. (1991e) 20,381.

Kamp–Lint·fort \kämp-ˈlint-fȯrt\; *formerly* **Lintfort.** Commune, North Rhine-Westphalia, Germany, WNW of Oberhausen; pop. (1980c) 37,961; coal mines.

Kampo. See CAMPO.

Kampong Cham. See KOMPONG CHAM.

Kâmpóng Saôm. See KOMPONG SOM.

Kam·pot \ˈkäm-ˈpōt\. Town and port, S Cambodia, 75 mi. (121 km.) SSW of Phnom Penh; center of pepper-producing area.

Kamp·tee *also* **Kam·thi** \ˈkämp-tē\. Town, NE Maharashtra state, India, on Wainganga River; part of munic. area of Nagpur; pop. (1991p) 78,586.

Kampuchea *or* **Kampuchea, Democratic.** See CAMBODIA.

Kam·sack \ˈkam-ˌsak\. Town, SE Saskatchewan, Canada, on Assiniboine River 35 mi. (56 km.) NE of Yorkton; pop. (1991c) 2323.

Kamthi. See KAMPTEE.

Kamuela. See WAIMEA 1.

Ka·mui, Cape \ˈkä-mu̇-ē\. Cape on W coast of Hokkaidō, Japan, W of entrance to Ishikari Bay.

Kam'·ya·nets'–Po·dil'·s'kyy *or Russ.* **Ka·me·nets–Po·dol'·skiy** \ˈkȧm-yə-nets-pə-ˈdilʸ-skyē\ *also* **Kamenets Po·dol·ski** *or* **Kamenets Po·dol·sky** \ˈkė-mi-nits-ˌpə-ˈdōlʸ-skē\. City, Ukraine; on a bluff on a small tributary of the Dniester 12 mi. (19 km.) N of Khotin; pop. (1991e) 105,000.

History: First mentioned 1196; destroyed by Mongols 1240; a major church city with cathedrals and monasteries dating from 14th cent.; became chief town of Podolia 1434; suffered much in 15th and 16th cents. from invasions of Tatars, Moldavians, and Turks; came under Turks 1672, restored to Poland 1699, and annexed to Russia 1793. In WWII held by Germans 1941–44.

Ka·my·shin \kə-ˈmə-shən\. Town, N Volgograd Oblast, S Russia in Europe, on the Volga opp. Nikolayevski ab. 110 mi.

(177 km.) NNE of the city of Volgograd; pop. (1992e) 125,000; river port; terminus of railroad from Tambov.

Kan. **1.** River, China. See GAN.
2. River, South Korea. See HAN 3.

Ka·nab \kə-ˈnab\. City, ⊗ of Kane co., S Utah; pop. (1990c) 3289.

Ka·na·bec \kə-ˈnā-bek, -ˈnȯ-\. County in E Minnesota. See table at MINNESOTA.

Kanab Plateau. Tableland, N Mohave co., NW Arizona, on NW border of Grand Canyon National Park; 6000 ft. (1830 m.) high.

Ka·na·ga \kə-ˈnä-gə\. One of the Andreanof Is. in Aleutian Is., SW Alaska, W of Adak I.

Ka·na·ga·wa \kä-ˈnä-gä-wä\. **1.** Prefecture, Honshū, Japan; ✻ Yokohama; fishing, horticulture. See table at JAPAN.
2. Subdivision of Yokohama, Kanagawa prefecture, Honshū, Japan; pop. (1990p) 205,533; formerly a town and important port, now incorp. with Yokohama; treaty signed here Mar. 31, 1854 bet. U.S. and Japan, opening two ports to trade. See URAGA.

Kanalit Mountains. See ACROCERAUNIA.

Ka·nan·ga \kä-ˈnäŋ-gä\; *formerly* **Lu·lu·a·bourg** \ˌlü-lwä-ˈbür\. Town, ✻ of Kasai-Occidental administrative region, S cen. Democratic Rep. of the Congo, on Lulua River 475 mi. (764 km.) ESE of Kinshasa; met. area pop. (1991e) 371,862; museum.

Kananur. See CANNANORE.

Ka·na·ra \ˈkä-nə-rə\; *formerly* **North Kanara.** Former district, now part of Karnataka state, W India; ✻ Karwar.

Kan·ash \kə-ˈnäsh\. Town, Chuvash Rep., cen. Russia in Europe, ab. 45 mi. (72 km.) SSE of Cheboksary; pop. (1991e) 56,100.

Ka·nata \kə-ˈna-tə\. City, SE Ontario, Canada, SW of Ottawa; pop. (1991c) 37,344.

Ka·na·wha \kə-ˈnȯ-wə, -ˈnȯ-ē, -ˈnȯi\. **1.** *or* **Great Kanawha.** Navigable river, W West Virginia; formed by junction of New and Gauley rivers in Fayette co., flows NW into the Ohio River; 97 mi. (156 km.) long.
2. County in W cen. West Virginia. See table at WEST VIRGINIA.

Ka·na·za·wa \kä-ˈnä-zä-wä, ˌkä-nä-ˈzä-\. Seaport city, ✻ of Ishikawa prefecture, W Honshū, Japan, near coast of Sea of Japan; pop. (1990p) 442,872; silk and other textiles, lacquerware, porcelain; university (1949); during 300 years of feudalism the seat of one of the most powerful of daimyos; scene of victory of Japanese Gen. Oda Nobunaga over rebellious priests c. 1575.

Kan·cha·na·bu·ri \ˌkän-bu̇-ˈrē—*sic*\. **1.** Province, SW Thailand; 7524 sq. mi. (19,497 sq. km.); pop. (1992e) 724,435; ✻ Kanchanaburi.
2. Town, its ✻, WNW of Bangkok on Mae Klong River; pop. (1991e) 38,828; site of bridge that was subject of the novel and film "The Bridge On The River Kwai"; Allied war cemetery; caves and waterfalls nearby.

Kan·chen·jun·ga \ˌkən-chən-ˈjəŋ-gə, -ˈju̇ŋ-\ *or* **Kang·chen·jun·ga** \ˌkəŋ-\ *also* **Kan·chan·jan·ga** \ˌkən\ *or* **Kin·chin·jun·ga** \ˌkin-chin-\. Peak in the Himalayas, on boundary bet. Nepal and Sikkim, India; 28,169 ft. (8586 m.); 3d highest mountain in the world; visible from Darjeeling, India; first climbed 1955.

Kan·chi·pu·ram \kän-ˈchē-pə-rəm\ *also* **Con·jee·ve·ram** \kən-ˈjē-və-rəm\. Town, NE Tamil Nadu, S India, 40 mi. (64 km.) WSW of Madras; pop. (1991p) 145,028; very ancient city with numerous temples—for Hindus, one of India's seven most sacred cities; ✻ of Pallava dynasty in early centuries A.D.; under sovereignty of Delhi c. 1310 and in realm of the Great Mogul mid-17th cent.; captured by British soldier and colonist Robert Clive mid-18th cent.

Kan–chou. See GANZHOU.

Kan·chra·pa·ra \ˌkänch-rə-ˈpär-ə\. Town, West Bengal, NE India; pop. (1991p) 100,059.

Kan·da·hār. See QANDAHĀR.

Kan·da·lak·sha \ˌkən-də-ˈlàk-shə\. Coast town, SW Murmansk Oblast, NW Russia in Europe, at head of Kandalaksha Gulf and on St. Petersburg-Murmansk railroad line; pop. (1991e) 54,300; settlement in area was known to Vikings.

Kandalaksha Gulf *or* **Kandalaksha Bay** *or Russ.* **Kan·da·laksh·skiy Za·liv** \ˌkən-də-ˈlàksh-kē-ˈzä-lyēf\. Inlet of NW White Sea on NW coast of Russia in Europe, S and SW of Kola Penin., Murmansk Oblast.

Kan·da·vu \kän-ˈdä-vü\ *or* **Ka·da·vu** \kä-ˈdä-vü\. Island, Fiji, in SW part of group, in SW Pacific Ocean; 32 mi. (51 km.) long, area 165 sq. mi. (427 sq. km.); almost cut in two by narrow isthmus at center; mountainous and fertile.

Kandavu Passage. Channel, Fiji, bet. Viti Levu I. on N and Kandavu I. on S; ab. 38 mi. (60 km.) wide.

Kan·der·steg \ˈkän-dər-ˌshtāk\. Town, S Bern canton, Switzerland, ab. 35 mi. (55 km.) SSE of the city of Bern; pop. (1980c) 959; resort, winter-sports center.

Kan·dı·ra \ˌkän-də-ˈrä\. Town, Kocaeli prov., NW Turkey in Asia, near Black Sea coast 25 mi. (40 km.) NW of Adapazarı.

Kan·di·yo·hi \ˌkan-də-ˈyō-hē\. County in SW cen. Minnesota. See table at MINNESOTA.

Kan·dy \ˈkan-dē\. Town, Sri Lanka, on Mahaweli River 60 mi. (97 km.) ENE of Colombo; pop. (1990e) 104,000; in midst of noted mountain and lake scenery; last ✻ of ancient kings of Ceylon (now Sri Lanka); contains Buddhist temples, incl. Dalada Maligawa, a sacred Buddhist temple said to house a tooth of the Buddha, palaces of ancient kingdoms, and crypts and tombs of ancient rulers and heroes; famous botanical gardens at Peradeniya, 3 mi. (5 km.) SW. Held briefly by Portuguese and Dutch before being taken over by British who gained permanent control by 1815.

Kane \ˈkān\. **1.** Name of counties in two states of the U.S. See tables at ILLINOIS and UTAH.
2. Borough, McKean co., N Pennsylvania, 23 mi. (37 km.) SSW of Bradford; pop. (1990c) 4590.

Kanea. See CANEA.

Kane Basin. Section of the channel bet. E Ellesmere I. and NW Greenland, N of Baffin Bay.

Ka·nem \ˈkä-ˌnem\. Former protected state of French Equatorial Africa, NE of Lake Chad, chief town Mao; a native state founded 9th cent.; became Muslim 11th cent. and reached height of its power 300 years later; with Bornu later formed a strong native empire until 19th cent.; for a time subject to Ouadaï; since 1958 part of Chad.

Ka·ne·o·he \ˌkä-nā-ˈō-hā\. City, Honolulu co., Hawaii, on **Kaneohe Bay,** wide inlet on E coast of Oahu I., N of Honolulu; pop. (1990c) 35,448; Hawaii Loa Coll. (1963).

Kanesh. See KANISH.

Kan·gar \ˈkäŋ-ˌgär\. Town, ✻ of Perlis state, Malaysia, near coast.

Kan·ga·roo Island \ˌkaŋ-gə-ˈrü\. Island, S of Yorke Penin. at entrance to Gulf St. Vincent, South Australia, Australia; 90 mi. (145 km.) long; 1970 sq. mi. (5102 sq. km.); pop. (1986c) 2044.

Kan·gā·var \ˌkäŋ-gä-ˈvär\. Town, W Iran, ab. 40 mi. (64 km.) SW of Hamadān; pop. (1986c) 38,453; on a main highway; in a fertile region at alt. of 6000 ft. (1829 m.).

Kangchenjunga. See KANCHENJUNGA.

Kang·ding \ˈkäŋ-ˈdiŋ\ *or* **Dar·do** \ˈdär-ˈdō\ *or W.-G.* **K'ang–ting** \ˈkäŋ-ˈdiŋ\; *formerly* **Ta·tsien·lu** \ˈdä-ˈjyen-ˈlü\. City, Sichuan prov., S China, 260 mi. (418 km.) W of Chongqing; alt. 8500 ft. (2591 m.); formerly a Chinese administrative center for Tibetan affairs; served as ✻ of former prov. of Sikang ab. 1928–1950.

Kang·e·an \ˈkäŋ-ā-ˌän\. **1.** Island group of Indonesia, in Java Sea 80 mi. (129 km.) E of Madura; 258 sq. mi. (668 sq. km.).
2. Largest island of the group; 188 sq. mi. (487 sq. km.).

Kang·hwa \ˈkäŋ-ˈhwä\. Island, South Korea, off its NW coast where the Han River flows into the Yellow Sea. Because of its location, the island has long been of strategic importance.

Kang·nŭng \ˈkäŋ-ˈnəŋ\. Town, Kangwŏn prov., South Korea, ab. 105 mi. (170 km.) ENE of Seoul; pop. (1985c) 132,897.

\ə\ **abut** \ə\ **matches** \ᵊ\ **kitten, Fr table** \ər\ **further** \a\ **ash** \ā\ **ace** \ä\ **cot, cart** \à\ **Fr bac** \au̇\ **out** \b̲\ **Span Avila** \ch\ **chin** \e\ **bet** \ē\ **easy** \g\ **go** \i\ **hit** \ī\ **ice** \j\ **job** \k̲\ **Ger ich, Buch** \ⁿ\ **Fr vin** \ŋ\ **sing** \ō\ **go** \ȯ\ **all** \ȯ\ **law** \œ\ **Fr bœuf** \œ̄\ **Fr feu** \ȯi\ **boy** \th\ **thin** \th̲\ **this** \ü\ **loot** \u̇\ **foot** \ue\ **Ger füllen** \ue̅\ **Fr rue** \y\ **yet** \ʸ\ **Fr digne** \ˈdēnʸ\, **nuit** \ˈnwʸē\ \yü\ **few** \yu̇\ **fury** \zh\ **vision**

Kan·gra \ˈkäŋ-grä\. Town, Himachal Pradesh, NW India, ab. 40 mi. (64 km.) ESE of Pathankot; pop. (1991p) 9019; important in early Indian history; ancient temple known for its wealth, sacked many times, often rebuilt; ruins of Rajpot fort.

Kang·rin·bo·qê Feng \ˈkäŋ-ˈrin-bō-chā-ˈfəŋ\ *or Eng.* **Kai·las** \ˈkī-ˌläs\. Peak in cen. part of Gangdisê Range, SW Tibet, China, 31°04′N, 81°19′E, N of Mapam Yumco and SE of Gar; 22,027 ft. (6714 m.); sacred to Hindus and before 1962 an important pilgrimage resort; famous in Sanskrit literature as Siva's paradise.

Kang–ti–ssu. See GANGDISÊ.

Kang·to \käŋ-ˈtō\. Mountain peak, E Himalayas, China, on border bet. Arunachal Pradesh, India and SE Tibet; 23,620 ft. (7199 m.).

Ka·Ngwa·ne \käŋ-ˈgwä-nā\. Former Swazi enclave in Transvaal, Rep. of South Africa, comprised of two separate parcels.

Kang·wŏn \ˈkäŋ-ˌwən\. Province of South Korea. See table at KOREA, SOUTH.

Kan·ha National Park \ˈkən-ˌhä\. National park, Madhya Pradesh, India; noted for its wildlife; estab. 1955.

Kanhsien. See GANZHOU.

Ka·ni \ˈkä-nē\. City, Gifu prefecture, W cen. Honshū, Japan; pop. (1990p) 80,012.

Kaniapiskau. See CANIAPISCAU.

Ka·ni·gu·ram \ˌkə-ni-ˈgu̇r-əm\. Chief town of the Wazirs, cen. South Waziristan, North-West Frontier prov., Pakistan, NE of Wana and ab. 80 mi. (130 km.) NW of Dera Ismail Khan.

Ka·nin Peninsula \ˈkä-nēn\. Peninsula projecting into Barents Sea on N coast of Nenets Autonomous Okrug, N Russia in Europe, having Cheshskaya Bay on E and entrance to White Sea on W; its NW extremity is **Kanin Point.**

Ka·nish \ˈkä-nish\ *or* **Ka·nesh** \-nesh\. Ancient city of E cen. Asia Minor, home of a branch of the Hittites; now the village of **Kul·te·pe** \ˌku̇l-tə-ˈpā\, an archaeological site NE of Kayseri and W of Erciyas; mines of area supplied silver to Assyria in very ancient times; Assyrian cuneiform tablets found in area during 20th cent. attest to life during 2d millennium B.C.

Kan·jut Sar \ˈkän-ju̇t-ˈsär\. Mountain in the Karakoram Range, in region of Jammu and Kashmir under Pakistani control; 25,461 ft. (7761 m.).

Kan·ka·kee \ˌkaŋ-kə-ˈkē\. **1.** River, Indiana and Illinois; rises in N Indiana and flows SW and W to unite with the Des Plaines in NE Illinois and form the Illinois River; 135 mi. (217 km.) long.

2. County in NE Illinois. See table at ILLINOIS.

3. City, ⊗ of Kankakee co., NE Illinois, 32 mi. (51 km.) SSE of Joliet; pop. (1990c) 27,575; Olivet Nazarene Univ. (1907), Kankakee Community Coll. (1966); has some houses designed by architect Frank Lloyd Wright.

Kan·kan \käⁿ-ˈkäⁿ\. Town, E Guinea; pop. (1983p) 88,760; terminus of railroad line from Conakry; highway junction point.

Kan·ker \ˈkäŋ-kər\. Former Indian state, now part of Madhya Pradesh, NE India; 1413 sq. mi. (3660 sq. km.).

Kanko. See HAMHŬNG.

Kan·maw Kyun \ˈkän-ˌmä-ˈkyün\; *formerly* **Kis·se·raing** \ˈki-sə-ˌrīŋ\ *or* **Ki·tha·reng** \ˈki-thə-ˌreŋ\. Island in E cen. Mergui Archipelago (*q.v.*), Myanmar.

Kan·nap·o·lis \kə-ˈna-pə-lis\. City, Cabarrus and Rowan cos., S cen. North Carolina, ab. 7 mi. (11 km.) N of Concord; pop. (1990c) 29,696.

Kan·nauj \kə-ˈnau̇j\. Town, SW cen. Uttar Pradesh, N India, on Ganges River 50 mi. (80 km.) NW of Kanpur; pop. (1991p) 59,650; noted for perfumes. An ancient city, famous in early times; mentioned by Alexandrian geographer Ptolemy; in 7th cent. reached height of its magnificence esp. as cultural center as ✻ of King Harsa's kingdom; captured by Maḥmūd of Ghaznī 1019 and came under Muslim sovereignty c. 1194; memorials of the Hindu age have completely disappeared.

Ka·no \ˈkä-nō\. **1.** State of N Nigeria. See table at NIGERIA.

2. Commercial city, its ✻, on railroad line in N cen. Nigeria 500 mi. (805 km.) NE of Lagos; pop. (1991e) 594,800; ships peanuts, leather and hides; textiles, food products; center of caravan routes; inhabitants chiefly Hausa, with a considerable number of Fulani. Known to Arab geographers in 12th cent.; figured prominently as center of Hausa state in wars with rival states 15th–16th cents.; early converted to Islam; conquered by Fulani c. 1800; visited by German explorer Heinrich Barth 1851 and 1854; captured by British 1903.

Ka·no·ya \kä-ˈnō-yä, ˈkä-nō-\. City, Kagoshima prefecture, S Kyūshū, Japan, on E side of Kagoshima Bay 22 mi. (35 km.) SE of the city of Kagoshima; pop. (1990p) 77,652.

Kan·pur \ˈkän-ˌpu̇r\ *or Eng.* **Cawn·pore** \ˈkȯn-ˌpōr\. City, S cen. Uttar Pradesh, N India, on right bank of Ganges River 245 mi. (394 km.) SE of Delhi; pop. (1991c) 1,879,420; important rail junction; most important industrial center of the state; leather goods, cotton goods; Indian Institute of Technology (1960). Garrisoned by British troops in late 18th cent. Known for the massacre by Indian leader Nana Sahib of British soldiers and European families during Indian mutiny July 1857.

Kanra. See HALLA.

Kan·san·shi \kän-ˈsän-shē\. Town, Zambia, 260 mi. (418 km.) NW of Lusaka near border with Democratic Rep. of the Congo.

Kan·sas \ˈkan-zəs, -səs\. **1.** *in Kansas usu. called* **Kaw** \ˈkȯ\. River, formed by confluence of Republican and Smoky Hill rivers at Junction City, Geary co., E Kansas; flows E into Missouri River at Kansas City.

2. A central state of U.S.A., bounded on N by Nebraska, on E by Missouri, on S by Oklahoma, and on W by Colorado; 14th state in area, ab. 82,277 sq. mi. (213,097 sq. km.); 32d state in population, (1990c) 2,477,574; ✻ Topeka; 34th state admitted to Union (1861). See table of states at UNITED STATES.

Nickname: Sunflower State.

State flower: Sunflower.

Motto: Ad Astra per Aspera (To the Stars Through Difficulties).

Rivers: In S the Arkansas, flowing from W border E to cen. area and then S across border into Oklahoma; in N, also flowing W to E, the Saline and Solomon rivers, tributaries of the Smoky Hill River which joins the Republican River from the N to form Kansas River (see KANSAS 1).

Highest point: Mt. Sunflower, 4039 ft. (1231 m.), on W border in Wallace co.

Chief products: Wheat, sorghum, corn; cattle; oil, salt; manufacturing: transportation equipment, machinery, chemicals.

Chief cities: Wichita, Kansas City, Topeka, Overland Park.

Political divisions: Divided into the following 105 counties (for pronunciation of their names, see their individual entries):

NAME	AREA[1] (sq. mi.)	AREA[1] (sq. km.)	POP. (1990c)	CO. SEAT
Allen	505	1,308	14,638	Iola
Anderson	577	1,494	7,803	Garnett
Atchison	427	1,106	16,932	Atchison
Barber	1,146	2,968	5,874	Medicine Lodge
Barton	894	2,315	29,382	Great Bend
Bourbon	639	1,655	14,966	Fort Scott
Brown	577	1,494	11,128	Hiawatha
Butler	1,442	3,735	50,580	El Dorado
Chase	774	2,005	3,021	Cottonwood Falls
Chautauqua	647	1,676	4,407	Sedan
Cherokee	587	1,520	21,374	Columbus
Cheyenne	1,027	2,660	3,243	Saint Francis
Clark	984	2,549	2,418	Ashland
Clay	658	1,704	9,158	Clay Center
Cloud	711	1,841	11,023	Concordia
Coffey	656	1,699	8,404	Burlington
Comanche	800	2,072	2,313	Coldwater
Cowley	1,136	2,942	36,915	Winfield
Crawford	598	1,549	35,568	Girard
Decatur	899	2,328	4,021	Oberlin
Dickinson	855	2,214	18,958	Abilene
Doniphan	388	1,005	8,134	Troy
Douglas	471	1,220	81,798	Lawrence
Edwards	617	1,598	3,787	Kinsley
Elk	647	1,676	3,327	Howard
Ellis	900	2,331	26,004	Hays
Ellsworth	717	1,857	7,586	Ellsworth
Finney	1,301	3,370	33,070	Garden City
Ford	1,091	2,826	27,463	Dodge City
Franklin	577	1,494	21,994	Ottawa

KANSAS

CITIES
- ⊛ State capital
- ◉ County seat
- • City

BOUNDARIES
- State
- County

FEATURES
- Dams
- Points of interest

0 30 60 mi
0 40 80 km

NAME	AREA[1] (sq. mi.)	AREA[1] (sq. km.)	POP. (1990c)	CO. SEAT
Geary	400	1,036	30,453	Junction City
Gove	1,070	2,771	3,231	Gove
Graham	891	2,308	3,543	Hill City
Grant	571	1,479	7,159	Ulysses
Gray	872	2,258	5,396	Cimarron
Greeley	783	2,028	1,774	Tribune
Greenwood	1,142	2,958	7,847	Eureka
Hamilton	992	2,569	2,388	Syracuse
Harper	801	2,075	7,124	Anthony
Harvey	540	1,399	31,028	Newton
Haskell	580	1,502	3,886	Sublette
Hodgeman	860	2,227	2,177	Jetmore
Jackson	656	1,699	11,525	Holton
Jefferson	550	1,425	15,905	Oskaloosa
Jewell	910	2,357	4,251	Mankato
Johnson	476	1,233	355,054	Olathe
Kearny	855	2,214	4,027	Lakin
Kingman	865	2,240	8,292	Kingman
Kiowa	720	1,865	3,660	Greensburg
Labette	654	1,694	23,693	Oswego
Lane	720	1,865	2,375	Dighton
Leavenworth	466	1,207	64,371	Leavenworth
Lincoln	726	1,880	3,653	Lincoln
Linn	606	1,570	8,254	Mound City
Logan	1,073	2,779	3,081	Oakley
Lyon	852	2,207	34,732	Emporia
McPherson	896	2,321	27,268	McPherson
Marion	959	2,484	12,888	Marion
Marshall	883	2,287	11,705	Marysville
Meade	979	2,536	4,247	Meade
Miami	592	1,533	23,466	Paola
Mitchell	716	1,854	7,203	Beloit
Montgomery	649	1,681	38,816	Independence
Morris	706	1,829	6,198	Council Grove
Morton	728	1,886	3,480	Elkhart
Nemaha	708	1,834	10,446	Seneca
Neosho	587	1,520	17,035	Erie
Ness	1,081	2,800	4,033	Ness City
Norton	880	2,279	5,947	Norton
Osage	720	1,865	15,248	Lyndon
Osborne	898	2,326	4,867	Osborne
Ottawa	723	1,873	5,634	Minneapolis
Pawnee	755	1,955	7,555	Larned
Phillips	897	2,323	6,590	Phillipsburg
Pottawatomie	820	2,124	16,128	Westmoreland
Pratt	729	1,888	9,702	Pratt
Rawlins	1,078	2,792	3,404	Atwood
Reno	1,262	3,269	62,389	Hutchinson
Republic	718	1,860	6,482	Belleville
Rice	725	1,878	10,610	Lyons
Riley	597	1,546	67,139	Manhattan
Rooks	886	2,295	6,039	Stockton
Rush	724	1,875	3,842	La Crosse
Russell	897	2,323	7,835	Russell
Saline	720	1,865	49,301	Salina
Scott	724	1,875	5,289	Scott City
Sedgwick	1,007	2,608	403,662	Wichita
Seward	646	1,673	18,743	Liberal
Shawnee	548	1,419	160,976	Topeka
Sheridan	893	2,313	3,043	Hoxie
Sherman	1,055	2,732	6,926	Goodland
Smith	893	2,313	5,078	Smith Center
Stafford	795	2,059	5,365	Saint John
Stanton	676	1,751	2,333	Johnson
Stevens	731	1,893	5,048	Hugoton
Sumner	1,186	3,072	25,841	Wellington
Thomas	1,070	2,771	8,258	Colby
Trego	901	2,334	3,694	Wakeeney
Wabaunsee	792	2,051	6,603	Alma
Wallace	911	2,359	1,821	Sharon Springs
Washington	891	2,308	7,073	Washington
Wichita	724	1,875	2,758	Leoti
Wilson	574	1,487	10,289	Fredonia
Woodson	504	1,305	4,116	Yates Center
Wyandotte	152	394	161,993	Kansas City

[1] Area = land area.

History: Before coming of Europeans, inhabited sparsely by both nomadic and settled American Indians, among them, the Kansa; probably entered by Spanish explorer Francisco de Coronado's expedition 1541; came to U.S. as part of Louisiana Purchase (*q.v.*) 1803; included in Louisiana Terr. 1805 and Missouri Terr. 1812; SW corner lost to Spanish in 1819 treaty; in unorganized territory c. 1821–54; regained SW corner with annexation of Texas 1845; by Kansas-Nebraska Act 1854, **Kansas Territory** organized, incl. Kansas and cen. portion of E Colorado; admitted to Union with present boundaries as free state Jan. 29, 1861.

Kansas City. 1. City, ⊗ of Wyandotte co., NE Kansas, at confluence of Kansas and Missouri rivers, separated from Kansas City, Missouri, by state line; pop. (1990c) 149,767; 2d largest city in state; railroad center; stockyards, packinghouses, and large grain-storage facilities; soap, flour milling, automobile assembly; ships corn, wheat, sorghum, oats; Kansas City Kansas Community Coll. (1923), Donnelley Coll. (1949). First settled by Wyandot Indians 1843; sold to federal government 1855; settled by non-Indians 1857; modern city formed 1886 by consolidation of a number of adjoining towns.

2. City, Clay, Platte, and Jackson cos., W Missouri, on S bank of Missouri River on Kansas-Missouri state line adjoining Kansas City, Kansas; pop. (1990c) 435,146; largest city in state; railroad, industrial, and commercial center; stockyards and packinghouses; food processing; auto assembly; Avila Coll. (1916), Kansas City Art Institute (1885), Rockhurst Coll. (1910), Penn Valley Community Coll. (1915), Univ. of Missouri–Kansas City (1929), DeVry Institute of Technology (1931), Calvary Bible Coll. (1932).

History: Permanent settlement dates from 1821 when trading post estab. within present boundaries of city by the Chouteaus, American fur traders; city grew out of settlements of Westport, founded 1833, and Westport Landing (on the river 4 mi. or 6.4 km. N), which became busy port for river traffic; **Town of Kansas,** laid out 1838, developed after 1846; name changed to **City of Kansas** 1853 and to Kansas City 1889.

Kansk \ˈkänsk\. City, S Krasnoyarsk Kray, S cen. Russia in Asia, on a tributary of the Yenisey and on Trans-Siberian R.R. 110 mi. (177 km.) E of the city of Krasnoyarsk; pop. (1992e) 110,000; near lignite and iron ore deposits; founded mid-17th cent. as military garrison.

Kansu. See GANSU.

Kan·tang \ˈkän-ˈtäŋ\. Village and port on W coast of Malay Penin., SW Thailand, 85 mi. (137 km.) SE of Phuket; port for Trang.

Kantara, El. See EL KANTARA.

Kan·ta·ra·wa·di \ˌkän-tə-rə-ˈwä-dē\. Former native state, E Karenni, E Burma (now Myanmar); 3161 sq. mi. (8187 sq. km.).

Kan·tish·na \kan-ˈtish-nə\. Village, S cen. Alaska, in N cen. part of Denali National Park.

Kan·to \ˈkän-tō\. Administrative region of Japan, in Honshū. For subdivisions, see table at JAPAN.

Kan·ton Island \ˌkan-ˈtän, ˈkan-ˌ\ *or esp. formerly* **Can·ton Island** *same or* ˈkant-ᵊn\. One of the Phoenix Is. (*q.v.*) of Kiribati, cen. Pacific Ocean, 2°48′S, 171°43′W, an atoll 8 mi. (13 km.) long by 4 mi. (6 km.) wide, enclosing large lagoon; has stunted vegetation, with coconut groves at S end; once afforded excellent base for seaplanes and airplanes. From 1939 was important aviation station under Anglo-American condominium on S route from Honolulu to New Caledonia; U.S. claim dropped 1983.

Ka·nu·ma \kä-ˈnü-mä\. City, Tochigi prefecture, Honshū, Japan, 8 mi. (13 km.) W of Utsunomiya; pop. (1990p) 90,044.

Kan·ye \ˈkän-yā\ *or* **Kan·ya** \-yä\. Town, SE Botswana, 70 mi. (113 km.) NNW of Mafiking; pop. (1991c) 31,354; ✻ of the Bangwaketsi people.

Kao–hsiung \ˈkau̇-ˈshyu̇ŋ, ˈgau̇-\; *Jp.* **Ta·kao** \tä-ˈkä-ō\ *or* **Ta·kow** \-ˈkau̇\. City, SW coast of Taiwan; munic. pop. (1993e) 1,405,860; Taiwan's leading port; petrochemicals, aluminum, textiles; fisheries.

Kao·ko·veld \ˈkau̇-kō-ˌfelt\. Mountain range, NW Namibia, parallel to coast just E of Namib Desert.

Kao·lack *or* **Kao·lak** \ˈkō-ˌlak, ˈkau̇-\. Town, W Senegal, on Saloum River, 95 mi. (153 km.) ESE of Dakar; pop. (1992e) 179,894.

Kaolan. See LANZHOU.

Kao Luang. See KHAO LUANG.

Kao–mi. See GAOMI.

Ka·paa \kä-ˈpä-ä\. City, E coast of Kauai I., Hawaii, N of Lihue; pop. (1990c) 8149.

Kapaonik. See KOPAONIK.

Kap·cha·gay \kȧp-ˈchä-ˌgī\; *formerly* **Ili** \ēl-ˈyē\. Town, SE Kazakhstan, on Ili River.

Ká·pe·la, Cape \ˈkä-pe-ˌlä\ *or Gk.* **Ák·ra Ka·pél·lo** \ˈä-krä-kä-ˈpe-lō\. S point of Kíthira, one of the Ionian Is. off the SE coast of Peloponnese, Greece.

Ka·pe·la, Great *and* **Little Kapela** \ˈkä-pe-lä\. Mountain ranges in Croatia, extending from NW to SE parallel with the coast; on E edge of the Kras Plateau; highest peak ab. 4600 ft. (1400 m.).

Kapéllo, Ákra. See KÁPELA, CAPE.

Ka·pen·gu·ria \ˌkä-pen-ˈgu̇r-ē-ə\. Town, Rift Valley prov., NW Kenya, SW of Lake Turkana.

Kap·fen·berg \ˈkäp-fən-ˌberk\. Commune, Styria, Austria, 25 mi. (40 km.) N of Graz; pop. (1991c) 23,380; resort; manufactures steel, paper; founded 12th cent.

Ka·pı·da·ğı \kä-ˌpə-ˈdau̇\; *anc.* **Cyz·i·cus** \ˈsi-zi-kəs\. Peninsula, triangular in shape, Balıkesir prov., NW Turkey in Asia, on S coast of the Sea of Marmara; in ancient times location of important Greek city.

Ka·pi·la·vas·tu \ˌkä-pi-lə-ˈvəs-tü\. Principality and town in ancient India; site ab. 27°28′N, 83°18′E; birthplace of Gautama Buddha, the Sakya Prince Siddhartha c. 563 B.C.

Ka·pi·ti Island \kä-ˈpē-tē\. Small island off SW coast of North I., New Zealand, at N end of Cook Strait; bird sanctuary.

Kap·lan \ˈka-plən\. Town, Vermilion parish, S Louisiana, 23 mi. (37 km.) SW of Lafayette; pop. (1990c) 4535.

Kaplan, Mount. Mountain, Antarctica, 84°33′S, 175°18′E; 13,878 ft. (4230 m.).

Kapoeas. See KAPUAS.

Ká·pol·na \ˈkä-pōl-ˌnȯ\. Town, cen. Hungary, SW of Eger; scene of battle 1849 in which Austrians under Field Marshal Alfred Windischgrätz defeated Hungarians under Polish commander Henryk Dembiński.

Ka·pos·vár \ˈkȯ-pōsh-ˌvär\. City, ⊗ of Somogy co., SW Hungary, 30 mi. (48 km.) S of Lake Balaton; pop. (1991e) 73,900; textiles.

Kap·pel \ˈkä-pəl\ *or in full* **Kappel am Al·bis** \äm-ˈäl-bis\. Village, Zürich canton, NE cen. Switzerland; pop. (1980c) 567; scene of battle (bet. Zürichers and the Catholic cantons) in which Swiss religious reformer Huldrych Zwingli was killed Oct. 11, 1531.

Kaproncza. See KOPRIVNICA.

Kap·su·kas \ˈkäp-sə-kəs\; *formerly* **Ma·ri·yam·po·lė** \ˌmär-i-ˈyäm-pō-ˌlā\. Town, Lithuania, ab. 30 mi. (48 km.) SW of Kaunas.

Ka·pu·as *or Du.* **Ka·poe·as** \ˈkä-pü-ˌwäs\. River, West Kalimantan prov., Borneo, Indonesia; rises in mountains of N cen. Borneo and flows W into South China Sea at Pontianak; ab. 450 mi. (724 km.) long; navigable for small vessels for over 300 mi. (483 km.).

Kapudzhikh. See KAPYDZHIK.

Ka·pur·tha·la \kə-ˈpu̇rt-ᵊl-ə\. **1.** Former Indian state, now part of Punjab state, NW India, on left bank of Beas River. **2.** City, its ✻; pop. (1991p) 63,083; founded 11th cent.

Kap·us·ka·sing \ˌka-pə-ˈskā-siŋ\. **1.** River, N cen. Ontario, Canada; flows N to the Mattagami; ab. 180 mi. (290 km.) long.
2. Town, Cochrane dist., E Ontario, Canada, 80 mi. (129 km.) NNW of Timmins; pop. (1991c) 10,344.

Ka·py·dzhik *also* **Ka·pu·dzhikh** \ˌkä-pə-ˈjik\. Mountain, SW Azerbaijan, 12,815 ft. (3906 m.).

Kap York. See YORK, CAPE 2.

Ka·ra \ˈkär-ə\. **1.** River in NW Iran. See QAREH SŪ.
2. River, N Russia, E of Yugorskiy Penin.; flows N from Ural Mts. into Kara Sea; 130 mi. (209 km.) long; in part forms boundary bet. the autonomous okrugs of Nenets (in Europe) and Yamalo-Nenets (in Asia).

Karabakh Mountain Area. See NAGORNO-KARABAKH.

Kara–Bo·gaz Gol \kə-ˈrȧ-bə-ˈgȧz-ˈgȯl\. Large shallow lake (*gol*), on coast of Turkmenistan; ab. 100 mi. (160 km.) long by 85 mi. (135 km.) wide; an inlet of E Caspian Sea until 1979 when a dike was built connecting the narrow strips of land on the W side.

Ka·ra·bük \ˌkä-rä-ˈbœk\. Town, Zonguldak prov., N Turkey in Asia; pop. (1990c) 105,373.

Kara Bu·run *or* **Ka·ra·bu·run** \ˌkä-rä-bü-ˈrün\. Name of several capes or points (Turk. *burun* cape) on the coast of Turkey in Asia, esp.: (1) on SW shore of Sea of Marmara; (2) on E shore of Gulf of Antalya, S Turkey; (3) on Black Sea coast just E of the Bosporus (Karadeniz Boğazı).

Ka·ra·ca·dağ \ˌkä-rä-jä-ˈdä\. Peak in SE Turkey in Asia, SW of Diyarbakır; 6070 ft. (1850 m.).

Ka·ra·chay–Cher·kes·sia \ˌkär-ə-ˈchī-chir-ˈke-syə\. Republic, an administrative subdivision of S Russia in Europe; 5444 sq. mi. (14,100 sq. km.); pop. (1992e) 431,000; ✻ Cherkessk; corn, wheat, millet; an autonomous oblast (**Ka·ra·chay·e·vo–Cher·kess** \-ˈchī-yə-ˌvō-chir-ˈkes\) of U.S.S.R. before 1991. For history and physical features, see CHERKESS AUTONOMOUS OBLAST and KARACHAYEV AUTONOMOUS OBLAST.

Ka·ra·cha·yev Autonomous Oblast \ˌkär-ə-ˈchä-yəf ... ˈȯ-bləst, -ˌblast\ *or* **Ka·ra·chai Autonomous Oblast** \ˌkär-ə-ˈchī\. Former autonomous oblast, Russian S.F.S.R., U.S.S.R., on N slope of Caucasus Mts. at W end, bounded on S by Georgian S.S.R. and on W by Krasnodar Kray; 3821 sq. mi. (9896 sq. km.); mountainous, along S boundary several peaks over 10,000 ft. (3050 m.); traversed by Kuban' River whose headstreams are in mountains in S part; its inhabitants include Russians and Karachayevs, a people who came from the Crimea c. 15th cent. and who with the Cherkess settled in upper Kuban' Valley. Part of Mountain Republic after the Bolshevik Revolution; united with the Cherkess Autonomous Oblast (forming Karachayevo-Cherkess Oblast) 1922–26; given separate administration 1926; abolished during WWII, N half incorp. in Stavropol' Kray and S half absorbed by Georgian S.S.R.; restored as Karachayevo-Cherkess Autonomous Oblast 1957; made a republic as Karachay-Cherkessia (*q.v.*) after breakup of U.S.S.R. 1991.

Karachayevo–Cherkess. See KARACHAY-CHERKESSIA.

Ka·ra·cha·yevsk \ˌkär-ə-ˈchī-efsk\ *or* **Klu·kho·ri** \klü-ˈkȯr-yi\; *formerly* **Mi·ko·yan Sha·khar** \ˈmi-kə-ˌyän-shə-ˈkär\. Town, Karachay-Cherkessia, S Russia in Europe, on right bank of Kuban' River 165 mi. (265 km.) SE of Krasnodar; served as ✻ of former Karachayev Autonomous Oblast, Russian S.F.S.R., U.S.S.R. From it the **Klu·khor Pass** \klü-ˈkȯr\ (8400 ft. or 2560 m.) leads through the Caucasus Mts. W of Mt. Elbrus to Sukhumi.

Ka·ra·chi \kə-ˈrä-chē\. City and seaport, ✻ of Sind, Pakistan, former ✻ of Pakistan, on arm of Arabian Sea just NW of the mouths of the Indus; met. area pop. (1981c) 5,208,132; principal seaport and largest city of Pakistan; trade and distribution center for extensive hinterland; exports grain, raw cotton, hides, skins, and raw wool; manufactures chemicals, textiles, plastics; shipbuilding; steel; university (1951); founded early 18th cent.; became British 1843 and development of city has taken place almost entirely since then.

Ka·ra·dag *or* **Ka·ra Dağ** \ˌkä-ˈrä-dä\. Name of several mountains (Turk. *dağ* mountain) in Turkey, esp.: (1) In S, peak near W end of Taurus Mts. and SE of Konya; 7451 ft. (2271 m.); and (2) in SE, peak in mountains of Kurdistan, SE of Lake Van; 11,910 ft. (3630 m.).

Karadeniz Boğazı. See BOSPORUS.

Karaferieh. See VEROIA.

Ka·ra·fu·to \ˌkä-rä-ˈfü-tō\. **1.** Japanese name of Sakhalin I. **2.** Former Japanese possession comprising S half of Sakhalin I., S of 50°N lat.; ab. 13,931 sq. mi. (36,081 sq. km.); following WWII to U.S.S.R. See SAKHALIN.

Karaganda. See QARAGHANDY.

Ka·ra·gin \kə-ˈrä-gən, -ˈra-\ *or* **Ka·ra·gin·skiy** *also* **Ka·ra·gin·ski** *or* **Ka·ra·gin·sky** \kə-ˈrä-gən-skē\. Island, W Bering Sea, E Russia in Asia, ab. 30 mi. (48 km.) off E coast of N Kamchatka Penin.; highest point 3140 ft. (957 m.); formerly in Khabarovsk Kray, now attached to Koryak Autonomous Okrug.

\ə\ **abut** \ə\ **matches** \ᵊ\ **kitten, Fr table** \ər\ **further** \a\ **ash** \ā\ **ace** \ä\ **cot, cart** \ȧ\ **Fr bac** \au̇\ **out** \b̶\ **Span Avila** \ch\ **chin** \e\ **bet** \ē\ **easy** \g\ **go** \i\ **hit** \ī\ **ice** \j\ **job** \k̲\ **Ger ich, Buch** \ⁿ\ **Fr vin** \ŋ\ **sing** \ō\ **go** \ȯ\ **all** \ȯ\ **law** \œ\ **Fr bœuf** \œ̄\ **Fr feu** \ȯi\ **boy** \th\ **thin** \t̲h̲\ **this** \ü\ **loot** \u̇\ **foot** \ue\ **Ger füllen** \ue̅\ **Fr rue** \y\ **yet** \ʸ\ **Fr digne** \ˈdēnʸ\, **nuit** \ˈnwʸē\ \yü\ **few** \yu̇\ **fury** \zh\ **vision**

Karahissar. See ŞEBINKARAHISAR.

Karaikal. See KARIKAL 2.

Ka·rai·ku·di *or* **Ka·raik·ku·di** \kə-'rī-kə-dē\. Town, Tamil Nadu, S India, 38 mi. (61 km.) ESE of Madurai; pop. (1991p) 71,599.

Ka·raj \kä-'räj\. Town, N Iran, ab. 22 mi. (35 km.) NW of Tehran; pop. (1986c) 275,100.

Karak, Al *also* **Karak.** See AL KARAK.

Ka·ra·kal·pak Autonomous Republic \ˌkə-rə-kål-'påk\. An autonomous region in NW part of Uzbekistan, SE of Aral Sea and N of the Khiva oasis along right bank of the Amu Dar'ya and in the delta; before 1991 comprised an A.S.S.R. of Uzbek S.S.R.; 63,938 sq. mi. (165,599 sq. km.); pop. (1991e) 1,273,800; ✻ Nukus; much of it desert (SW part of the Kyzyl Kum); cotton; cattle, karakul sheep. First became Russian latter part of 19th cent. as a part of Turkistan; comprised an A.S.S.R. of Uzbek S.S.R. 1936–91.

Ka·ra·kax \kä-'rä-'käsh\ *or W.-G.* **K'a–la–k'a–shih** \kä-'lä-'kä-shi\; *mostly formerly* **Ka·ra–kash** \kä-'rä-'käsh\. River, SW Xinjiang Uygur, W China; rises in Karakoram Range on Kashmir border, flows N and NE through E end of Kunlun Shan to join the Hotan below the city of Hotan.

Ka·ra·ke·long \ˌkä-rä-'kā-ˌlȯŋ\. Chief island of the Talaud Is., NE of Sulawesi, Indonesia; ab. 41 mi. (66 km.) long by 15 mi. (24 km.) wide; chief town Beo on W coast.

Karakhoto. See KHARA KHOTO.

Karaklis. See VANADZOR.

Karakol. See PRZHEVAL'SK.

Ka·ra·ko·ram Pass \ˌkä-rä-'kōr-äm\ *or Chin.* **Ka·ra·ko·rum Shan·kou** \ˌkä-rä-'kōr-u̇m-'shäŋ-kau̇\ *or W.-G.* **K'a–la–k'un–lun Shan K'ou** \'kä-lä-'kün-lün-'shän-kau̇\. Pass through Karakoram Range, Jammu and Kashmir, in region under Pakistani control, SE of K2; alt. 18,290 ft. (5575 m.); traditionally the chief route over the Himalayas bet. Jammu and Kashmir and China.

Karakoram Range *or* **Karakorum Range.** Mountain range, N Jammu and Kashmir, India and Pakistan; highest peak K2 28,250 ft. (8611 m.); has approx. 60 peaks at ab. 22,000 ft. (6700 m.).

Kar·a·ko·rum *also* **Qa·ra·qo·rum** \ˌkä-rä-'kōr-u̇m\ *or Mongolian* **Har Ho·rin** \'här-hō-'rin\. **1.** Ruins of ancient ✻ of Mongolia, on right bank of upper Orhon, 47°14′N, 102°50′E, 200 mi. (322 km.) WSW of Ulaanbaatar.

History: At first a Mongol camp, estab. by Genghis Khan as his ✻ early in 13th cent.; rebuilt and palace erected by Ögödei, his son and successor (1229–41); deserted by Kublai Khan for new ✻ at Khanbalik (Venetian traveler Marco Polo's Cambaluc, *mod.* Beijing) 1267; visited by Marco Polo c. 1275; later destroyed and by 16th cent. abandoned.

2. Ruins of earlier city, ✻ of Uighur kingdom 8th to 9th cents., 15 to 20 mi. (24 to 32 km.) NW on left bank of the Orhon.

Karakorum Shankou. See KARAKORAM PASS.

Ka·ra·kul *or* **Ka·ra Kul** *or* **Qa·ra Kul** \ˌkär-ə-'ku̇l\. Lake, Pamirs plateau, NE Gorno-Badakhshan subdivision, E Tajikistan; 140 sq. mi. (363 sq. km.); alt. 12,890 ft. (3929 m.).

Ka·ra–Kum *or* **Ka·ra·kum** \ˌkär-ə-'küm\ *or* **Ka·ra·ku·my** \-'kü-mē\. Desert area, S of Aral Sea; 115,830 sq. mi. (300,000 sq. km.); ab. 600 mi. (965 km.) long and 250 mi. (400 km.) wide; includes most of Turkmenistan, stretching from the Caspian Sea to the Amu Dar'ya on the E.

Ka·ra·kum·skiy Ka·nal \ˌkär-ə-'küm-skē-kə-'näl\ *or* **Ka·ra·kum Canal** \ˌkär-ə-'küm\. Irrigation canal, S Turkmenistan, from the Amu Dar'ya almost to the Caspian Sea.

Ka·ra·man \ˌkär-ə-'män\; *anc.* **La·ran·da** \lə-'ran-də\. **1.** Province of Turkey in Asia. See table at TURKEY.

2. Town, its ✻, on railroad line 62 mi. (100 km.) SE of Konya; renowned for its castle and mosques; early history obscure; became seat of Isaurian pirates; in 13th cent. made ✻ of an independent Armenian state, **Karaman** *or* **Kar·a·ma·nia (Ca·ra·man** *or* **Ca·ra·ma·nia)** \ˌkar-ə-'mā-nē-ə\, long at war with various Asian states, overcome by Ottoman Turks under Sultan Mehmed II 15th cent.

Ka·ra·mea Bight \ˌkä-rä-'mā-ə\. Wide gulf on NW coast of South I., New Zealand, bet. Kahurangi Point and Cape Foulwind.

Ka·rang \'kär-ˌäŋ\. Mountain, W Java, Indonesia, near Sunda Strait; 5833 ft. (1778 m.).

Ka·ran·ja \kə-'rən-jə\. Island on E side of entrance to Bombay Harbor, on W coast of India.

Ka·ra·pa·che·ta *also* **Ca·ra·pa·che·ta** \ˌkä-rä-pä-'chā-tä\. Peak, cen. Cochabamba dept., cen. Bolivia; 16,400 ft. (5000 m.).

Ka·ra Sea \'kär-ə\ *or Russ.* **Kar·skoye Mo·re** \'kär-skȯ-yə-'mȯr-ə\. Arm of Arctic Ocean extending E of Novaya Zemlya and off coasts of Taymyr, Yamolo-Nenets, and Nenets autonomous okrugs, N Russia; has many small islands; frozen much of the year.

Karashar. See YANQI.

Kara Strait *or Russ.* **Pro·liv Kar·ski·ye Vo·ro·ta** \'prȯ-lif-'kär-skē-yə-və-'rō-tə\. Strait connecting Kara Sea with Barents Sea, bet. Novaya Zemlya and Vaygach I., Nenets Autonomous Okrug, NE Russia in Europe; ab. 35 mi. (56 km.) wide.

Kara Su \ˌkä-rä-'sü\. See MESTA.

Ka·ra·su \ˌkä-rä-'sü\ *also* **Western Eu·phra·tes** \yu̇-'frā-tēz\. River, E Turkey in Asia, the main headstream of the Euphrates; rises N of Erzurum and flows W and S to unite with the Murat Nehri (or Eastern Euphrates) and continue as the Euphrates River (*q.v.*).

Karasubazar. See BELOGORSK.

Ka·ra·tsu \kä-'rät-sü\. Seaport city, Saga prefecture, NW Kyūshū, Japan; pop. (1990p) 79,206.

Ka·rau·li \kə-'rau̇-lē\. **1.** Former Indian state, now part of Rajasthan state, India; bordered on Jaipur on NW and was separated from Gwalior on SE by Chambal River; 1227 sq. mi. (3178 sq. km.). For a time under Mogul emperors and Marathas; taken under British protection 1817.

2. Town, its ✻, Rajasthan, 85 mi. (137 km.) SE of Jaipur.

Kara Usu Nur. See HAR US NUUR.

Karawanken. See table at ALPS.

Kar·ba·la *or* **Kar·ba·lā'** \'kär-bä-lä\ *also* **Ker·be·la** \'kər-bə-lə\. Town, cen. Iraq, 55 mi. (88 km.) SSW of Baghdad, on edge of the desert W of Al Hindīyah River; pop. (1985e) 184,574; holy city for Muslims of the Shiite branch, containing the shrine of Caliph Ḥasan, slain here in 680 A.D. and commemorated in the Muharram; active trade center.

Kar·cag \'kȯrt-ˌsȯg\. City, E Hungary, 35 mi. (56 km.) WSW of Debrecen; pop. (1991e) 24,300.

Karchi. See KHALKĒ.

Kar·di·tsa \kär-'dēt-sə\ *or Gk.* **Kar·dí·tsa** *or* **Kar·dhí·tsa** \kär-'thēt-sä\. **1.** Department of Greece. See table at GREECE.

2. Town, its ✻, W Thessaly, Greece; pop. (1991p) 30,451.

Ka·re·lia \kə-'rē-lē-ə, -'rēl-yə\. Republic, NW Russia in Europe, bounded on N by Murmansk Oblast, on E by White Sea and Arkhangel'sk Oblast, on S by Vologda and Leningrad oblasts, and on W by Finland; 66,564 sq. mi. (172,401 sq. km.); pop. (1992e) 800,000; ✻ Petrozavodsk; geologically similar to Finland with its low hills (highest ab. 1000 ft. or 1600 m.) and numerous lakes, marshes, and streams; includes practically all of Lake Onega and N part of Lake Ladoga, also other smaller lakes as Seg Ozero, Kunto, and Top. Forests its chief wealth; agriculture much restricted by cold climate and poor soil.

History: Karelians, one of the chief divisions of the Finns, first mentioned in history in 9th cent.; their folk tales and songs the source of the Finnish epic *Kalevala;* they formed in medieval times a strong independent state which in 17th cent. came under Swedish dominion and in 1721 was annexed by Russia; region constituted as **Karelian Autonomous Soviet Socialist Republic** 1923; territory much affected by Russian-Finnish War of 1939–40; after treaty of 1940 by which certain border areas of Finland (ab. 13,500 sq. mi. or 34,965 sq. km.) were transferred to the U.S.S.R., the **Ka·re·lo–Finn·ish Soviet Socialist Republic** \kə-'rē-lō-'finish\ was constituted in Mar., incorporating the new territory; part of this new union republic occupied during WWII by

Germans and Finns; abolished 1956 and Karelian A.S.S.R. reconstituted; became a republic of Russia 1991.

Ka·re·li·an Isthmus \kə-ˈrē-lē-ən, -ˈrēl-yən\ *or Russ.* **Ka·rel'·skiy Pe·re·she·yek** \kə-ˈrel^{y}-skē-ˌpir-ə-ˈshā-yik\. The strip of land bet. W shore of Lake Ladoga and the Gulf of Finland, W Russia in Europe; ab. 65 mi. (105 km.) wide; includes region around Vyborg which was formerly part of Finland; in WWII scene of fighting; taken by U.S.S.R. at end of war and added to Leningrad Oblast.

Karelo–Finnish Soviet Socialist Republic. See KARELIA.

Karel'skiy Peresheyek. See KARELIAN ISTHMUS.

Ka·ren \kə-ˈren\. State, S Myanmar; Karens in a state of sporadic rebellion against Myanmar government through late 20th cent. See table at MYANMAR.

Ka·ren·ni \kə-ˈre-nē\. Former district in E Burma (now Myanmar); 4519 sq. mi. (11,704 sq. km.); ✻ Loikaw; comprised a group of three feudatory states, Kantarawadi, Bawlake, and Kyebogyi; country of the Karens, a group of Indo-Chinese tribes; was not part of British Burma but administered by own chiefs under advice of commissioner of Federated Shan States. Proclaimed a state 1947; its area enlarged and name changed to Kayah 1952.

Karfreit. See KOBARID.

Kargilik *or* **Karghalik.** See YECHENG.

Kar·hu·la \ˈkär-hü-lä\. Town, Kymi prov., S Finland.

Ka·ri·ba Dam \kä-ˈrē-bä\. Dam in Kariba Gorge of Zambezi River, bet. SE Zambia and N Zimbabwe, SE of Lusaka; max. height 420 ft. (128 m.); completed Dec. 1958; forms **Lake Kariba** (175 mi. or 282 km. long; 2050 sq. mi. or 5310 sq. km.; max. depth 390 ft. or 119 m.), one of the world's largest artificial lakes.

Ka·ri·bib \ˌkär-ə-ˈbib\. Town, W cen. Namibia, 90 mi. (145 km.) WNW of Windhoek; pop. (1988e) 2000.

Ka·ri·kal \ˌkär-ə-ˈkäl\. **1.** Province of former French India, on Coromandel Coast E of Thanjavur 150 mi. (241 km.) S of Madras; 52 sq. mi. (135 sq. km.); received by French 1739; changed hands several times but was estab. as French 1817; reorganized 1947 as one of the five free cities of French India within the French Union; transferred to India 1954.

2. *or* **Ka·rai·kal** \ˈkä-ri-ˌkäl\. Seaport town, its ✻, 90 mi. (145 km.) S of Pondicherry, on a mouth of Kāveri River.

Ka·ri·ma·ta Islands \ˌkär-i-ˈmä-tə\. Group of islands of Indonesia, in South China Sea W of island of Borneo, on NE side of Karimata Strait; 86 sq. mi. (223 sq. km.); chief island **Karimata,** or **Great Karimata,** 70 sq. mi. (181 sq. km.); a part of West Kalimantan prov.

Karimata Strait. Passage bet. SW Borneo and Belitung I., connecting South China Sea and Java Sea; ab. 125 mi. (201 km.) wide.

Ka·rim·na·gar \kə-ˈrim-nə-gər\. Town, N Andhra Pradesh, S cen. India, 87 mi. (140 km.) NE of Hyderabad; pop. (1991p) 148,349.

Ka·ri·mun·ja·wa *also* **Ka·ri·mun·dja·wa** *or* **Ka·ri·mon Ja·va** \ˈkä-rē-ˌmün-ˈjä-və\ *or Du.* **Ka·ri·moen·djo·wo** \ˌkär-i-mün-ˈjō-vō\. Group of 27 islands, Indonesia, in Java Sea ab. 55 mi. (88 km.) N of Djepara, Java; 19 sq. mi. (49 sq. km.).

Kariot. See IKARIA.

Ka·ri·sim·bi \ˌkä-rē-ˈsim-bē\. Peak on boundary bet. Rwanda and Democratic Rep. of the Congo, NE of Lake Kivu; 14,787 ft. (4507 m.); a quiescent volcano; highest peak in the Virunga Mts.

Káristos. See CARYSTUS.

Ka·ri·ya \kä-ˈrē-yä\. City, Aichi prefecture, Honshū, Japan, 14 mi. (23 km.) SSE of Nagoya; pop. (1990p) 120,121.

Kar·kar \ˈkär-ˌkär\. **1.** Small island in Bismarck Archipelago, Papua New Guinea, W Pacific Ocean, off E coast of New Guinea I., N of Madang.

2. *or* **Qar·qar** \ˈkär-ˌkär\. Unidentified place in W part of ancient Syria, perhaps Apamea on the Orontes River; scene of indecisive battle 854 (or 853) B.C. bet. Shalmaneser III, king of Assyria, and King Ahab of Israel and his ally, Ben-hadad I of Damascus.

Kar·kheh *or* **Ker·kheh** \kər-ˈkā\; *anc.* **Cho·as·pes** \kō-ˈas-pēz\. River, W Iran; rises S of Mt. Alwand, flows SW to marshlands E of the Tigris in SE Iraq; 200 mi. (322 km.) long.

Kar·ki·nit Bay \kər-ˈkē-nət\. Inlet of Black Sea on NW coast of Crimea, Ukraine; indents the Perekop Isthmus.

Kār·li \ˈkär-lē\ *or* **Kar·la** \ˈkär-lə\. Site, W Maharashtra state, W India, ab. 32 mi. (51 km.) NW of Pune; nearby are celebrated caves containing Buddhist temples, some of the oldest and best preserved in India.

Karl–Marx–Stadt \kärl-ˈmärks-ˌshtät\. **1.** District of former East Germany.

2. *before 1953 and since 1990* **Chem·nitz** \ˈkem-ˌnits, -nəts\. City of E Germany. See CHEMNITZ.

Karlö \ˈkär-ˌlœ\. Island, N Gulf of Bothnia, W of Oulu, Finland.

Karlócza. See SREMSKI KARLOVCI.

Kar·lo·vac \ˈkär-lə-ˌväts\ *or Ger.* **Karl·stadt** \ˈkärl-ˌshtät\. City, Croatia, 30 mi. (48 km.) SW of Zagreb; pop. (1991c) 70,729; hydroelectric power plants; founded 1579.

Kar·lo·vo \ˈkär-lō-ˌvō\. Town, Plovdiv region, cen. Bulgaria, ab. 35 mi. (56 km.) N of the city of Plovdiv.

Kar·lo·vy Va·ry \ˈkär-lȯ-vē-ˈvär-ē\; *Ger.* **Karls·bad** *or* **Carls·bad** \ˈkärls-ˌbät\. Town, NW Czech Republic, on the Ohře, an Elbe tributary ab. 70 mi. (113 km.) W of Prague; pop. (1991p) 56,291; health resort; sulfur springs; scene of drawing up of the Carlsbad Decrees 1819 by ministers of the German states led by Austrian statesman Prince Klemens von Metternich, designed to suppress liberalism in German universities leading to revolutionary activities.

Karlowitz. See SREMSKI KARLOVCI.

Karlsbad. See KARLOVY VARY.

Karlsburg. See ALBA IULIA.

Karls·hamn \ˈkärls-ˌhämn, kärls-ˈ\. Town, Blekinge prov., S Sweden, on Baltic coast just W of Karlskrona; pop. (1989c) 31,410; received city charter 1664.

Karl·sko·ga \ˌkärl-ˈskü-gə\. City, Örebro prov., S cen. Sweden, 23 mi. (37 km.) W of the city of Örebro; pop. (1993e) 33,451; guns and explosives manufactured in the area.

Karls·kro·na \ˌkärl-ˈskrü-nə\. City, ✻ of Blekinge prov., S Sweden; munic. area pop. (1994e) 59,753; built on the mainland and five nearby islands in Baltic Sea; excellent fortified harbor, principal Swedish naval base; dry docks; fishing port; manufactures naval equipment; founded 1679.

Karls·ru·he *also* **Carls·ru·he** \ˈkärls-ˌrü-ə\. City, NW Baden-Württemberg, SW Germany, on the Rhine 35 mi. (56 km.) S of Mannheim; pop. (1992e) 278,579; machinery, bicycles and motorcycles, electrical equipment; technical college (1825), university (1865); ✻ of former state of Baden. Founded 1715 by Margrave Karl Wilhelm von Baden-Durlach; heavily damaged in WWII; since 1956 a nuclear-research center.

Karl·stad \ˈkärl-ˌstäd\. City, ✻ of Värmland prov., SW Sweden, on Lake Vänern; pop. (1993e) 77,290; wood products, machinery; founded 1584; destroyed by fire 1865; scene of signing of treaty 1905 ending union of Sweden and Norway.

Karlstadt. See KARLOVAC.

Kar·mah *or* **Ker·ma** \ˈkar-mə\. Town, N Sudan, on the Nile. Archaeological finds indicate surrounding area was ruled by strong Nilotic group during first half of 2d millennium B.C.

Karm·øy \ˈkär-ˌmœi\. Island in North Sea, a part of Rogaland co., SW Norway; 67 sq. mi. (174 sq. km.); 18 mi. (29 km.) long; pop. (1990c) 35,094.

Kar·nak \ˈkär-ˌnak\. Village on the right (E) bank of the Nile in Upper Egypt; N part (Luxor is S part) of site of ancient Thebes (*q.v.*); site of ruins of early temple of Amen, an ancient complex of temples and shrines; later temple complex begun in Middle Kingdom times, was greatly enlarged and embellished by, among others, Amenhotep III, Seti I, Ramses II; notable features include great hypostyle hall, pylons erected by various rulers, sphinx-lined avenues, and obelisks. Smaller temples to Mont (Egyptian war-god) and Mut (wife of Amen) are nearby.

Kar·nal \kər-ˈnäl\. Town, Punjab state, NW India, on Yamuna Canal 7 mi. (11 km.) from Yamuna River, 75 mi. (121 km.) N of New Delhi; pop. (1991p) 173,742; said to have been founded by Raja Karna, mythical champion of the Kauravas, integral figures in Hindu epic, the *Mahābhārata.* Scene of decisive battle 1739 in which Persian King Nāder Shāh defeated Mogul Emperor Muḥammad Shāh.

Karnali. See GHĀGHARA.

Kar·na·phu·li \ˌkär-nə-ˈpü-lē\. River, Bangladesh, flowing W into Bay of Bengal; navigable to Chittagong; dammed, creating large **Karnaphuli Reservoir.**

Kar·na·ta·ka \kär-ˈnä-tə-kə\; *formerly* **My·sore** \mī-ˈsōr\ *also* **Mai·sur** \mī-ˈsu̇r\. State, S India; ✻ Bangalore; occupies plateau region of Southern Deccan with hills in W; has many rivers incl. Krishna and Tungabhadra; rice, cotton, timber, gold; largest cities: Bangalore, Hubli-Dharwar, Mysore.

History: From early times for the most part ruled by Hindu dynasties; succeeded by Hindu rajas of Vijayanagar, who were overwhelmed 1565 by Muslims from the N; during period of Mysore Wars, army commander Hyder Ali usurped the throne 1761 and enlarged the country by force of arms, and his son Tipu Sultan ruled from his father's death 1782 until defeated and killed in battle 1799; administration taken over by British 1831; returned to native rule 1881; became part of India 1947. See table at INDIA.

Karnatik. See CARNATIC.

Karnes \ˈkärnz\. County in S Texas. See table at TEXAS.

Karnes City. Town, ⊗ of Karnes co., S Texas, 52 mi. (84 km.) SSE of San Antonio; pop. (1990c) 2916.

Kar Nicobar. See CAR NICOBAR.

Karnische Alpen. See table at ALPS.

Kärnten. See CARINTHIA.

Karnul. See KURNOOL.

Karolinen. See CAROLINE ISLANDS.

Karond. See KALAHANDI.

Ka·ron·ga \kä-ˈro̐ŋ-gä, -ˈräŋ-\. Town, Malawi, on NW Lake Malawi; pop. (1987c) 19,667; lake trading port.

Kar·oo *or* **Kar·roo** \kə-ˈrü\. An arid tableland region of the Rep. of South Africa; area in excess of 100,000 sq. mi. (259,000 sq. km.); divided into three parts: (1) **Great Karoo** *or* **Central Karoo,** in cen. Western Cape prov., ab. 300 mi. (485 km.) from E to W and from 2000 to 7000 ft. (610 to 2135 m.) above sea level, characterized by dry air and little rain, no grass, only vegetation being karroo bush (*Acacia horrida*); chief towns Beaufort West, Graaff Reinet, Aberdeen; (2) **Little Karoo** *or* **Southern Karoo,** along S coast of Western Cape prov., ab. 200 mi. (320 km.) long; 1000 to 2000 ft. (305 to 610 m.) alt., separated from Great Karoo by Groote Swartberge; some fertile sections; chief towns Worcester, Oudtshoorn, Robertson; and (3) **North Karoo** in Northern Cape prov., along Orange River; largely desert.

Kár·pa·thos \ˈkär-pä-ˌthös\ *also Ital.* **Scar·pan·to** \ˈskär-pän-ˌtō\; *anc.* **Car·pa·thus** \ˈkär-pə-thəs\ *or* **Car·pa·thos** \-ˌthäs\. An island of the Dodecanese (*q.v.*), Greece, bet. Rhodes and the E end of Crete; 117 sq. mi. (303 sq. km.); largest of the Dodecanese proper and next in size to Rhodes with which its history has long been closely connected; under Venetian rule 1306 to 1540 when it passed to the Turks; ceded to Italy 1912; returned to Greece following WWII.

Kárpathos Strait *also* **Scarpanto Strait** *or Gk.* **Ste·nón Kar·pa·thon** \ste-ˈnön-ˈkär-pä-ˌthön\. Channel in S Dodecanese, Greece, separating islands of Rhodes and Karpathos; ab. 30 mi. (48 km.) wide.

Karpaty, Bíle. See WHITE CARPATHIAN MOUNTAINS.

Kar·pe·ni·sion \ˌkär-pə-ˈnē-sē-ˌo̐n\ *also* **Car·pe·ni·si** \ˌkär-pe-ˈnē-sē\ *or Gk.* **Kar·pe·ní·si·on** \ˌkär-pe-ˈnē-sē-ˌön\. Town, ✻ of Eurytania dept., W Greece, at S end of Pindus Mts.; pop. (1981p) 5243; battle nearby Aug. 1823 with Turks, in which the Greek leader, Markos Botsaris, was killed.

Kar·pinsk \kär-ˈpinsk\. Town, Sverdlovsk Oblast, W Russia in Asia, ab. 20 mi. (32 km.) NW of Serov.

Kar·roo. See KAROO.

Kars *also* **Qars** \ˈkärs\. **1.** Province of Turkey in Asia; ✻ Kars; a mountainous region; after Middle Ages occupied or invaded by Turks, Kurds, Kabardinians, Circassians, and others; as a result of Russo-Turkish War 1877–78 transferred to Russia; returned to Turkey by treaty 1921. See table at TURKEY.

2. City, its ✻, 110 mi. (177 km.) NE of Erzurum; pop. (1990p) 79,496; woolen textiles, felt; built on a mountain spur, its citadel (built in 16th cent.) long a strong military post. Was ✻ of an independent Armenian principality in 9th and 10th cents.; captured by Seljuq Turks in 11th cent., by Mongols in 13th cent., and by Turkic ruler Timur in 1387; stormed and captured by Russians 1828, 1855, and 1878.

Kar·shi \ˈkär-shē\; *formerly* **Bek–Bu·di** \bek-ˈbü-dē\. Town, Kashka-Darya administrative subdivision, SE Uzbekistan; pop. (1991e) 168,000; transportation center; mosque. Possibly over 1,000 years old, was important stop on Samarkand-Afghanistan trade route.

Kar·ṣi·ya·ka \ˌkär-sē-yä-ˈkä\. District of the city of İzmir, Turkey; pop. (1990c) 424,196.

Karskiye Vorota, Proliv. See KARA STRAIT.

Karskoye More. See KARA SEA.

Karst. See KRAS.

Kar·ta·bo \kär-ˈtä-bō\. Village, Guyana, ab. 40 mi. (64 km.) SW of Georgetown on lower Essequibo River.

Kartala, Mount. See KARTHALA, MOUNT.

Kar·ta·ly \kər-ˈtä-lē\. Town, Chelyabinsk Oblast, W Russia in Asia.

Kar·tha·la, Mount \kär-ˈtä-lə\. Volcano, S Grande Comore I., Comoros, N Mozambique Channel, NW of Madagascar; 7746 ft. (2361 m.); several eruptions bet. mid-19th cent. and early 20th cent.

Kā·rūn \kä-ˈrün\. River, W Iran; flows W and S in Khūzestān prov. and empties into the Shatt al Arab at Khorramshahr at N end of Ābādān I.; 528 mi. (850 km.) long; has winding course through mountains, navigable in its lower course; chief tributary the Dez from the N.

Kar·vi·ná \ˈkär-vē-ˌnä\ *or Ger. and Pol.* **Kar·win** \ˈkär-ˌvēn\. City, E Czech Republic, just E of Ostrava; pop. (1991p) 68,368; in a coal-mining area; held by Poland 1938–45 with German occupation during WWII; to Czechoslovakia following WWII.

Kar·war \ˈkär-ˌwär\. Town, W Karnataka state, W India, on coast 50 mi. (80 km.) S of Panaji; pop. (1991p) 51,011.

Karwin. See KARVINÁ.

Kasaba. 1. Town, Cyprus. See KTIMA.

2. City, Turkey. See TURGUTLU.

Ka·sai *also* **Kas·sai** *or Port.* **Cas·sai** \kȧ-ˈsī\. River, SW Africa; rises in cen. Angola, flows E, then N, forming section of boundary bet. Angola and Democratic Rep. of the Congo; continues N and NW through S cen. and W Democratic Rep. of the Congo to empty into Congo River on border of Rep. of the Congo; 1338 mi. (2153 km.) long; chief S tributary of the Congo. See KWAMOUTH.

Kasai–Oc·ci·den·tal \-ˌōk-si-däⁿ-ˈtäl\. Administrative region of cen. Democratic Rep. of the Congo. See table at ZAIRE.

Kasai–Ori·en·tal \-ˌo̐r-ē-äⁿ-ˈtäl\. Administrative region of cen. Democratic Rep. of the Congo. See table at ZAIRE.

Ka·sa·ma \kä-ˈsä-mä\. Town, NE Zambia, 100 mi. (161 km.) S of S end of Lake Tanganyika; pop. (1980p) 38,093; distribution center for produce grown nearby.

Kasamansa. See CASAMANCE.

Kasan. Former political subdivision of U.S.S.R. and present-day city of Russia. See KAZAN'.

Ka·san·ga \kä-ˈsäŋ-gä\; *formerly* **Bis·marck·burg** \ˈbiz-ˌmärk-ˌbu̇rk, -ˌbərg\. Port at S end of Lake Tanganyika, SW Tanzania.

Ka·san·je \kä-ˈsän-jā\. Historical kingdom, in what is now Angola, c. 1600–1850; powerful enough to remain independent, it traded with Portuguese who had settled on coast.

Ka·sar, Cape \kä-ˈsär\. Cape on NE coast of Africa, extending into the Red Sea; marks N limit of Ethiopia.

Ka·sa·ri \ˈkä-sə-rē\. River, W Estonia; flows SW to an inlet of Baltic Sea; ab. 60 mi. (97 km.) long.

Kasbek. See KAZBEK.

Kaschau. See KOŠICE.

Kas·ganj \ˈkäs-ˌgənj\. Town, W Uttar Pradesh, N India, on affluent of Ganges River 100 mi. (161 km.) SE of Delhi; pop. (1991p) 75,610.

Kā·shān \kä-ˈshän\. City, cen. Iran, N of Eşfahān, on railroad line 65 mi. (105 km.) from Qom; pop. (1986c) 138,519; an old town formerly famous for its velvets and brocades and for its faience; now produces carpets.

Kashgar. 1. River, W China. See KAXGAR.
2. Town, Xinjiang Uygur, China. See KASHI.

Kashgaria. See CHINESE TURKISTAN.

Ka·shi *or W.-G.* **K'a–shih** \ˈkä-ˈshi\ *or Eng.* **Kash·gar** \ˈkäsh-ˌgär\. Chief commercial town of W Xinjiang Uygur, W China, on Kaxgar River; pop. (1990c) 174,570; in fertile region, but dependent on irrigation; alt. ab. 4000 ft. (1219 m.).

History: Occupied in 3d cent. B.C. by the Tocharians; later held by Chinese, Turks, and Mongols; conquered by Genghis Khan and Turkic ruler Timur; important center on trade route bet. China and cen. Asia; visited and described by Venetian traveler Marco Polo c. 1275; from 14th cent. to 1759 suffered many changes; Chinese since 1755 but at times under Russian influence; long a center of Muslim unrest; chief city of Chinese Turkistan (Kashgaria).

Ka·shi·ha·ra \kä-ˈshē-hä-rä, ˌkä-shē-ˈhä-rä\. City, Nara prefecture, Honshū, Japan, 20 mi. (32 km.) SE of Ōsaka; pop. (1990p) 115,556.

Kashing. See JIAXING.

Ka·shi·ra \kə-ˈshir-ə\. Town, Moscow Oblast, W cen. Russia in Europe, on Oka River 48 mi. (77 km.) NNE of Tula.

Ka·shi·wa \kä-ˈshē-wä\. City, Chiba prefecture, SE Honshū, Japan; pop. (1990p) 305,060.

Ka·shi·wa·ra \kä-ˈshē-wä-rä\. City, Ōsaka prefecture, Honshū, Japan; pop. (1990p) 76,819.

Ka·shi·wa·za·ki \ˌkä-shē-ˈwä-zä-kē\. City, Niigata prefecture, Honshū, Japan, 47 mi. (76 km.) SW of the city of Niigata; pop. (1990p) 88,309.

Kash·ka–Dar·ya \ˈkäsh-kə-dər-ˈyä\. Administrative subdivision of Uzbekistan; 10,965 sq. mi. (28,399 sq. km.); pop. (1991e) 1,697,700; before 1991 an oblast of the Uzbek S.S.R., U.S.S.R.

Kash·mir \ˈkash-ˌmir, ˈkazh-, kash-ˈ, kazh-ˈ\. Former princely state, Indian Subcontinent, now part of Jammu and Kashmir. See JAMMU AND KASHMIR.

Kashmir South. See SRINAGAR.

Ka–shun–no–erh. See GAXUN NUR.

Kasi. See VARANASI 2.

Ka·si·mov \kə-ˈsē-məf\. Town, Ryazan' Oblast, Russia in Europe, on Oka River 70 mi. (113 km.) ENE of the city of Ryazan'; founded 1152 and an important Tatar city 15th–17th cents.

Ka·si·ru·ta \ˌkä-sē-ˈrü-tä\. See BATJAN.

Kas·kas·kia \ka-ˈskas-kē-ə\. **1.** River, SW Illinois; rises in Champaign co., flows SW into Mississippi River in SW cen. Randolph co.; ab. 320 mi. (515 km.) long; partly navigable.
2. Village, Randolph co., SW Illinois, near junction of the Kaskaskia River with the Mississippi; pop. (1990c) 32; near site of oldest town in the West, founded 1703 as a Jesuit mission at an Indian village, passed to the British 1763; made ✻ of Illinois Terr. 1809, ✻ of state of Illinois 1818–20; severely damaged in floods 1844, 1881, and 1993.

Kas·ka·wulsh Glacier \ˈkas-kə-ˌwu̇lsh\. Glacier in the St. Elias Mts., SW Yukon, Canada; 40 mi. (64 km.) long, ab. 4 mi. (6 km.) wide near its terminus.

Kas·ki·nen \ˈkäs-kē-nen\ *or Swed.* **Kaskö** \ˈkäs-ˌkœ̄\. Seaport town, Vaasa prov., SW Finland, on small coastal island ab. 50 mi. (80 km.) S of Vaasa.

Ka·sos *or Gk.* **Ká·sos** \ˈkä-sös\ *or Ital.* **Ca·so** \ˈkä-sō\ *also* **Ca·sus** \ˈkā-səs\. An island of the Dodecanese (*q.v.*), Greece, SW of Karpathos and NE of E end of Crete; 27 sq. mi. (70 sq. km.).

Kasr, Al–. See AL-QASR.

Kassa. See KOŠICE.

Kassai. See KASAI.

Kas·sa·la \kä-ˈsä-lə, ˈkä-sə-\. **1.** Former province of NE Sudan; ✻ Kassala.
2. *or* **Kas·sa·lā** \-ˌlä\. Town, E Sudan, 250 mi. (402 km.) E of Khartoum near border of Eritrea; pop. (1983c) 141,429; fruit gardens; market and transportation center; built on a plain at ab. 1700 ft. (518 m.); founded by Egyptians as a fort 1840; held by Mahdists 1885–94; retaken by Italian force 1894 and restored to Egypt 1897; in WWII held briefly by Italians 1940–41.

Kas·sán·dra \kä-ˈsän-t͟hrä\; *anc.* **Pal·le·ne** \pə-ˈlē-nē\. SW peninsula of Chalcidice, projecting into Aegean Sea on NE coast of Greece, and forming part of E side of the Gulf of Salonika; on narrow isthmus at its base are ruins of ancient Potidaea.

Kas·sán·dra, Gulf of \kä-ˈsän-drä\ *or* **Kól·pos Kas·sán·dras** \ˈköl-ˌpös-kä-ˈsän-t͟hräs\ *or* **Tor·o·na·ic Gulf** \ˌtȯr-ə-ˈnā-ik\ *or* **Kólpos To·ro·naí·os** \ˌtō-rō-ˈne-ˌyös\. Inlet of N Aegean Sea, bet. the Sithonia and Kassándra penins. of Chalcidice, NE Greece. Ruins of ancient Olynthus (5th–4th cent. B.C.) are at its head.

Kas·sel *also* **Cas·sel** \ˈkäs-ᵊl\. City, Hesse, cen. Germany, on Fulda River 71 mi. (114 km.) WNW of Erfurt; pop. (1992e) 196,828; cultural and transportation center; locomotives, optical instruments, synthetic fabrics; palace of former elector of Hesse-Cassel; 14th cent. church; Karlsaue Park; ✻ of the former Hesse-Nassau prov.

History: Founded before 913 A.D.; became city in 12th cent.; captured by French in Seven Years' War; supplied mercenaries to aid British against American colonies; ✻ of kingdom of Westphalia 1807–13; passed to Prussia 1866; in WWII frequently bombed 1943–45, taken by Americans Apr. 1945; scene of discussions bet. Chancellor Willy Brandt of West Germany and Premier Willi Stoph of East Germany, May 1970, considering the status of the two states, one to another; home during early 1800s of philologists and folklorists Jacob and Wilhelm Grimm.

Kasserine *and* **Kasserine Pass.** See AL-QAŞRAYN.

Kas·ta·mo·nu \ˌkäs-tä-mō-ˈnü\ *or* **Kas·ta·mu·ni** \-mu̇-ˈnē\. **1.** Province of Turkey in Asia. See table at TURKEY.
2. Town, its ✻, on a tributary of the Kızıl Irmak 110 mi. (177 km.) NNE of Ankara; pop. (1990p) 52,363; near copper deposits, historically noted for its manufacture of copper utensils; became Turkish 1393.

Kas·tav \ˈkäs-ˌtäv\ *or Ital.* **Cas·tua** \ˈkäs-twä\. Commune, W Croatia, ab. 6 mi. (10 km.) W of Rijeka (Fiume) on the coast; Roman remains; on 1946 Italian border.

Kas·tel·lór·i·zon \ˌkäs-te-ˈlȯr-ē-ˌzȯn\ *or* **Me·gis·te** \me-ˈjis-tē\ *or* **Me·yis·ti** \mā-ˈyēs-tē\ *or angl.* **Ca·stel·lo·ri·zo** \ˌkäs-tə-ˈlȯr-ə-ˌzō\ *or Ital.* **Ca·stel·ros·so** \ˌkäs-tel-ˈrȯs-ō\. Island, Greece, in E Mediterranean Sea, 80 mi. (129 km.) E of Rhodes and 2 mi. (3 km.) off SW coast of Turkey in Asia; 9 sq. mi. (23 sq. km.); included in the Dodecanese, ceded by Turkey to Italy 1923; population entirely Greek; retroceded to Greece 1947.

Ka·sto·ria \ˌkäs-tō-ˈrē-ä\. **1.** Department of Greece. See table at GREECE.
2. Commune, ✻ of Kastoria dept., W Macedonia, N Greece, 20 mi. (32 km.) SSW of Florina on **Lake Kastoria** *or* **Lake Ka·sto·rí·as** \-ˈrē-ˌäs\ (20 sq. mi. or 52 sq. km.); pop. (1991p) 15,605.

Kastro. City, Greece. See MYTILENE 2.

Ká·stron \ˈkä-strön\; *mostly formerly* **Ka·stro** \ˈkäs-trō\. Seaport commune, on W coast of Lemnos I., Greece; ✻ of the island; in Lesbos dept.

Kastrop–Rauxel. See CASTROP-RAUXEL.

Ka·su·ga \kä-ˈsü-gä\. City, Fukuoka prefecture, N Kyūshū, Japan; pop. (1990p) 88,703.

Ka·su·gai \kä-ˈsü-gī\. City, Aichi prefecture, S Honshū, Japan; pop. (1990p) 266,599.

Ka·su·ka·be \kä-ˈsü-kä-bā\. City, Saitama prefecture, Honshū, Japan; pop. (1990p) 188,809.

Ka·su·mi·ga·u·ra *or* **Ka·su·mi·ga Ura** \ˌkä-sü-ˌmē-gä-'ü̇r-ä\. Lagoon, Ibaraki prefecture, SE Honshū, Japan, on lower course of the Tone River ab. 50 mi. (80 km.) NE of Tokyo; ab. 18 mi. (29 km.) long and 17 mi. (27 km.) wide at its broadest part; 73 sq. mi. (189 sq. km.); resort.

Ka·sun·gu \kä-'sü̇ŋ-gü\. Town, cen. Malawi, NW of Lilongwe; pop. (1993e) 13,892; tourism.

Kasungu National Park. National park, W Malawi, along the Zambia border; forested hills; elephants, antelope.

Ka·sur \kə-'sü̇r\. Town, Punjab, Pakistan, near Sutlej River 34 mi. (55 km.) SSE of Lahore; pop. (1981p) 228,000; settled comparatively late by a Pathan colony from beyond the Indus.

Kasvin. See QAZVĪN.

Ka·ta·gum \kə-'tä-gəm\. Region, N Nigeria; formerly an independent emirate, taken over by British 1903.

Ka·tah·din, Mount \kə-'täd-ᵊn\. Peak, E Piscataquis co., N cen. Maine; 5268 ft. (1606 m.); highest point in the state; N terminus of Appalachian National Scenic Trail.

Katanga. See SHABA.

Ka·tang·lad Mountains \kä-'täŋ-ˌläd\. Mountain group in N cen. Mindanao, Philippines; highest point ab. 9000 ft. (2743 m.).

Katar. See QATAR.

Katch·all \'ka-chəl\. One of the Nicobar Is. (*q.v.*).

Ka·te·rí·ni *or* **Ka·te·ri·ni** \ˌkä-te-'rē-nē\. Town, ✻ of Pieria dept., W cen. Macedonia, Greece, on W shore of Gulf of Salonika, SSW of Thessaloníki; pop. (1981p) 38,488; market town.

Kates Needle \'kāts\. Mountain on boundary bet. SE Alaska and W British Columbia, Canada; 10,002 ft. (3049 m.).

Ka·tha \kə-'thä\. Town, N cen. Myanmar, on right bank of the upper Irrawaddy 155 mi. (249 km.) N of Mandalay; port for river vessels; railroad terminus.

Katharinenstadt. See MARKS.

Kath·er·i·na, Geb·el \'je-bəl-ˌka-thə-'rē-nə\ *or* **Jab·al Kat·ri·nah** \ˌja-bəl-kə-'trē-nə\ *or* **Mount Cath·er·ine** \'kath-rən, 'ka-thə-\. Mountain, Egypt; 8652 ft. (2637 m.); highest part of Gebel Musa mountain group, Sinai Penin.

Kath·er·ine \'kath-rən, 'ka-thə-\. **1.** River, Northern Terr., Australia; 150 mi. (241 km.) long; intermittent near its source; upper course of the Daly River.
2. Town, N Northern Terr., Australia, on Katherine River and on railroad line ab. 170 mi. (274 km.) SE of Darwin; base for outdoor recreation.

Katherine Gorge National Park *or* **Nit·mi·luk National Park** \'nit-mi-ˌlu̇k\. National park, cen. N Northern Terr., Australia; estab. 1963; contains 13 gorges of the Katherine River; varied wildlife; aboriginal rock paintings; hiking trails.

Ka·thi·a·war \ˌkä-tē-ə-'wär\. Peninsula, W Gujarat state, W coast of India; 23,432 sq. mi. (60,689 sq. km.); bounded on N by Rann of Kachchh, on E by Gulf of Khambhat, and on S and W by Arabian Sea.
History: Peninsula first settled by Stone Age peoples, later (3d–2d millennium B.C.) by peoples of Harappan civilization; ruled by many great dynasties, among them the Mauryas (4th–2d cents. B.C.), Sakas (2d–5th cents. A.D.), Guptas (4th–5th cents.), Maitrakas (c. 8th cent.), Gurjara-Pratihāras (8th–9th cents.), Caulukyas (10th–13th cents.), and Vāghelās (13th cent.); came under Muslim rule 13th cent. (became part of Mogul Empire 16th cent.); taken by Marathas 18th cent.; accepted British protection by 1820; most of peninsula included in Saurāstra state 1948; became part of Gujarat state after partition of Bombay state 1960.

Kath·man·du *or* **Kat·man·du;** *mostly formerly* **Khat·man·du** \ˌkat-man-'dü, ˌkät-, -mən-\. City, ✻ of Nepal, in valley of Himalayas ab. 75 mi. (121 km.) from Indian frontier; pop. (1981p) 235,211; commercial and transportation center of Nepal; university (1958); founded 723 A.D.; captured by Gurkha kings 1768 and made ✻; severely damaged by earthquake 1934.

Ka·ti·har \'kə-tə-ˌhär\. Town, Bihar, NE India; pop. (1991p) 135,348.

Ka·ti·pu·nan \ˌkä-tə-pu̇-'nän\; *formerly* **Lu·bung·an** \lü-'bu̇ŋ-ˌän\. Municipality, W Mindanao, Philippines; pop. (1980c) 28,532; port on S side of passage bet. Sulu Sea and Mindanao Sea.

Kat·mai, Mount \'kat-ˌmī\. Volcano in **Katmai National Park and Preserve** (see UNITED STATES, *National Parks*), S Alaska, at N end of Alaska Penin. on Shelikof Strait; 6715 ft. (2047 m.); main crater one of largest in world; top of mountain blown off by great eruption of June 1912; region of importance to volcanologists because phenomena exist on scale of great magnitude. See VALLEY OF TEN THOUSAND SMOKES.

Katmandu. See KATHMANDU.

Ka·to·wi·ce \ˌkä-tō-'vēt-se\ *or Ger.* **Kat·to·witz** \'kä-tə-ˌvits\. **1.** Province of S Poland. See table at POLAND.
2. City, its ✻, 45 mi. (72 km.) WNW of Kraków; pop. (1989e) 367,041; Roman Catholic episcopal see; major railroad center; coal mining, metalworking; iron, zinc, chemicals, heavy machinery; university (1968). Founded in 16th cent.; became city 1865; to Poland c. 1921; in WWII occupied by Germans 1939–45.

Katrinah, Jabal. See KATHERINA, GEBEL.

Kat·rine, Loch \'ka-trən\. Lake in Central region, cen. Scotland, 5 mi. (8 km.) E of Loch Lomond; ab. 9.5 mi. (15 km.) long, 2 mi. (3 km.) wide; max. depth 495 ft. (151 m.); scene of poet and novelist Sir Walter Scott's *Lady of the Lake*. See ELLEN'S ISLE.

Ka·tri·ne·holm \kä-ˌtrē-nə-'hōlm\. Town, Södermanland prov., SE Sweden, 70 mi. (113 km.) WSW of Stockholm; pop. (1980p) 32,277.

Ka·tsi·na \'kät-sē-nä\. **1.** State of Nigeria. See table at NIGERIA.
2. Town, its ✻, 85 mi. (137 km.) NW of Kano; pop. (1991e) 182,400; commercial center; exports leather, cotton, peanuts; ✻ of ancient kingdom of **Katsina,** one of earliest of the Hausa states; ancient seat of learning; seized by the Fulani in early 19th cent.; taken over by British 1904; Muslim teachers college; hospital; ruins of wall that once surrounded the town.

Ka·tsu·ta \kät-'süt-ä\. City, Ibaraki prefecture, Honshū, Japan, 65 mi. (105 km.) NE of Tokyo; pop. (1990p) 109,826.

Kat·ta·kur·gan \kə-ˌtä-ku̇r-'gän\. Town, Samarqand administrative subdivision, Uzbekistan, ab. 40 mi. (64 km.) WNW of the city of Samarqand; pop. (1991e) 59,600.

Kat·te·gat *also* **Cat·te·gat** \'kä-tə-ˌgät, 'ka-ti-ˌgat\. Broad arm of North Sea, bet. Sweden on E and Jutland, Denmark, on W; max. width 88 mi. (142 km.); connected with North Sea through the Skagerrak and with Baltic Sea through Øresund, the Great Belt, and the Little Belt.

Kattowitz. See KATOWICE.

Ka·tun' *or* **Ka·tun** \kə-'tünʸ\. River, W and S Gorno-Altay Rep., S Russia in Asia; flows N, joins the Biya to form the Ob'; 386 mi. (621 km.) long.

Kat·wijk \'kät-ˌvīk, -ˌvāk\. Municipality, South Holland prov., SW Netherlands, at mouth of the Oude Rijn; pop. (1992e) 40,498; fishing; seaside resort 5 mi. (8 km.) NW of Leiden.

Ka·ty \'kā-tē\. City, Fort Bend, Harris, and Waller cos., SE Texas, 30 mi. (48 km.) W of Houston; pop. (1990c) 8005.

Katzbach. See KACZAWA.

Kat·zen·buck·el \'kät-sən-ˌbu̇-kəl\. Mountain, N Baden-Württemberg, Germany; 2054 ft. (626 m.); highest point in the Odenwald.

Kau·ai \kä-'wī\. **1.** *formerly* **Ka·i·e·i·e·wa·ho** \kä-ˌē-ā-ˌē-ā-'wä-hō\. Channel bet. the islands of Oahu and Kauai, Hawaii; 63 mi. (101 km.) wide.
2. Island in NW Hawaii, WNW of Oahu; 555 sq. mi. (1437 sq. km.); with Niihau forms Kauai co.; mountainous, its two chief peaks, Kawaikini and Waialeale, in the center; has several short streams, being the only island of the Hawaiian group that may be said to have rivers; its more important anchorages Nawiliwili, Hanalei, and Hanapepe bays; chief settlement Lihue; sugar and other agricultural products; has several parks and beaches.
3. County, NW Hawaii. See table at HAWAII.

Kauf·beu·ren \ˈkau̇f-ˈbȯi-rən\. City, Bavaria, Germany; pop. (1992e) 41,171; electronic instruments; breweries, glassworks; to Bavaria 1803.

Kauf·man \ˈkȯf-mən\. **1.** County in NE Texas. See table at TEXAS.

2. City, its ⊗, 30 mi. (48 km.) ESE of Dallas; pop. (1990c) 5238.

Kaufmann Peak. See LENIN PEAK.

Kau·i·ki Head \kau̇-ˈē-kē\. Cape and promontory on E end of Maui I., Hawaii.

Kau Kau Bay \ˈkau̇-ˌkau̇\. Bay on N side of E end of Guadalcanal I., SE Solomon Is., W Pacific Ocean.

Kau·kau·na \kȯ-ˈkȯ-nə\. City, Outagamie co., E Wisconsin; pop. (1990c) 11,982.

Kau·kau Veld \ˌkau̇-ˌkau̇-ˈfelt, -ˈvelt\. Barren region NW of the Kalahari Desert, S Africa, extending over NE Namibia and NW Botswana W of the Okavango Swamps.

Ka·u·la \kä-ˈü-lä\ *or* **Ta·hu·ra** \tä-ˈhu̇r-ä\. Small barren uninhabited rock in Pacific Ocean 23 mi. (37 km.) WSW of Niihau I., Hawaii; alt. 550 ft. (168 m.).

Kau·la·ka·hi \ˌkau̇-lä-ˈkä-hē\. Channel bet. islands of Niihau and Kauai, Hawaii.

Kaulun *or* **Kaulung.** See KOWLOON.

Kau·ma·la·pau \ˌkau̇-mä-ˈlä-ˌpau̇\. Village, Maui co., Hawaii, on W coast of Lanai I.; has the island's chief harbor.

Kau·na·ka·kai \ˌkau̇-nä-ˈkä-ˌkī\. Village, Maui co., Hawaii, on S coast of Molokai I.; pop. (1990c) 2658; largest settlement on Molokai.

Kau·nas \ˈkau̇-nəs, -ˌnäs\ *or Russ.* **Kov·no** \ˈkȯv-nō\ *or Pol.* **Kow·no** \ˈkȯv-ˌnȯ\. City, Lithuania, at confluence of Neris with Neman River; pop. (1992e) 433,600; transportation center; metal goods, textiles, machinery; several old buildings, esp. the Lithuanian-Gothic church of the ruler Vytautas (15th cent.).

History: Founded in 11th cent.; in medieval times often attacked and partially destroyed; to Russia at Third Partition of Poland 1795; in WWI captured by Germans 1915; ✻ of Lithuania 1920–40 after Poland's 2d seizure of the former ✻, Vilnius, Oct. 1920; in WWII occupied by U.S.S.R. 1940 and by Germans 1941–44.

Kau·ra Na·mo·da \ˈkau̇-rä-nä-ˈmō-dä\. Town, Sokoto state, N Nigeria, 100 mi. (161 km.) SE of the town of Sokoto; pop. (1991e) 58,460.

Kauriala. See GHĀGHARA.

Ka·va·jë \kä-ˈvä-yə\. Town, Durrës dist., W Albania, on coast ab. 10 mi. (16 km.) S of the seaport of Durrës.

Ka·vá·la *or* **Ka·vál·la** \kä-ˈvä-lä\. **1.** Department of Greece. See table at GREECE.

2. Seaport city, ✻ of Kavála dept., NE Macedonia, NE Greece, at head of **Gulf of Kavála** *or* **Gulf of Kavalla** *or Gk.* **Kól·pos Ka·vá·las** *or* **Kól·pos Ka·vál·las** \ˈköl-pös-kä-ˈvä-läs\ opp. Thásos I.; pop. (1991p) 58,576; exports tobacco; near site of ancient Neapolis where St. Paul landed on way to Philippi; center of revolution 1935. Birthplace of Egyptian rulers Muḥammad ʻAlī Pasha (1769) and his heir Ibrāhīm Pasha (1789) when it was part of Rumelia.

Ka·va·rat·ti Island \ˌkə-və-ˈrə-tē\. One of the Laccadive Is., Arabian Sea, ab. 230 mi. (370 km.) off the coast of Kerala, S India; its only town, **Kavaratti,** is the administrative center of the Indian territory of Lakshadweep.

Kā·ve·ri \ˈkä-və-rē\ *or* **Cau·ve·ry** \ˈkȯ-və-rē\. River, Karnataka, S India; rises in N Kerala, flows E and SE, and enters Bay of Bengal in a wide delta; 475 mi. (764 km.) long. On the border of Karnataka it forms island of Sivasamudram on either side of which are the **Kāveri Falls** (*or* **Cauvery Falls**), descending ab. 320 ft. (515 m.) and supplying waterpower. Navigable in short sections for small vessels only; source of extensive irrigation system; noted for its scenery; entire course, but esp. the sections at Seringapatam and Tiruchchirappalli, regarded as sacred.

Ka·vi·eng *or* **Kae·wi·eng** \ˌka-vē-ˈeŋ\. Town with good harbor on North Cape, NW tip of New Ireland, Bismarck Archipelago, Papua New Guinea, ab. 162 mi. (261 km.) NW of Rabaul; pop. (1990c) 6486; chief port on the island; shipping point esp. for coconut products; in WWII occupied by Japanese.

Kavīr, Dasht–e–. See DASHT-E-KAVIR.

Kavkaz. See CAUCASIA.

Kavkazski Khrebet. See CAUCASUS MOUNTAINS.

Ka·vo Mountains \ˈkä-vō\. Range extending along the length of the island of Guadalcanal, Solomon Is., W Pacific Ocean; highest peak 8028 ft. (2447 m.).

Kaw. See KANSAS 1.

Ka·wa·chi·na·ga·no \kä-ˌwä-chē-nä-ˈgä-nō\. City, Ōsaka prefecture, Honshū, Japan; pop. (1990p) 108,770.

Ka·wa·goe \kä-ˈwä-gō-ā\. City, Saitama prefecture, SE cen. Honshū, Japan, ab. 20 mi. (32 km.) NW of Tokyo; pop. (1990p) 304,860.

Ka·wa·gu·chi \ˌkä-wä-ˈgü-chē\. **1.** Lake in S Honshū, Japan, near Fuji; ab. 10 mi. (16 km.) in circumference; alt. 2700 ft. (823 m.).

2. City, Saitama prefecture, SE Honshū, Japan, just N of Tokyo; pop. (1990p) 438,667; textiles.

Ka·wai·hae \kä-ˌwī-ˈhī\. Bay, Hawaii co., Hawaii, on NW coast of Hawaii I.; commercial harbor, excellent beach.

Ka·wai·hoa, Cape \kä-ˌwī-ˈhō-ä\ *or* **Kawaihoa Point.** Cape on S end of Niihau I., Hawaii.

Kawaihoa Point. Promontory, Oahu, Hawaii. See KOKO HEAD.

Ka·wai·ki·ni \kä-ˌwī-ˈkē-nē\. Mountain, cen. Kauai I., Hawaii; 5170 ft. (1576 m.).

Ka·wa·ni·shi \kä-ˈwä-nē-shē, ˌkä-wä-ˈnē-shē\. City, Hyōgo prefecture, Honshū, Japan, 12 mi. (19 km.) NW of Ōsaka; pop. (1990p) 141,254.

Ka·war·dha \kə-ˈwär-də\. **1.** Former Indian state, now part of Madhya Pradesh, cen. India; 794 sq. mi. (2056 sq. km.).

2. Town, its ✻, 140 mi. (225 km.) NE of Nagpur.

Ka·war·tha Lakes \kə-ˈwȯr-thə\. A series of lakes in Peterborough and Victoria cos., SE Ontario, Canada, forming a chain E and W in region N of Peterborough and Lindsay; traversed by Trent Canal system.

Ka·wa·sa·ki \ˌkä-wä-ˈsä-kē\. City, Kanagawa prefecture, Honshū, Japan, a S suburb of Tokyo on W coast of Tokyo Bay; pop. (1990p) 1,173,606; major industrial center; shipbuilding, machinery, and chemicals; 12th cent. temple; almost completely destroyed in WWII, but since rebuilt.

Ka·we·ah Peaks \kə-ˈwē-ə\. Four mountains in the Sierra Nevada, in Tulare co., S cen. California: **Big Kaweah** 13,816 ft. (4211 m.), **Red Kaweah** 13,754 ft. (4192 m.), **Black Kaweah** 13,752 ft. (4192 m.), and **Gray Kaweah** 13,728 ft. (4184 m.).

Ka·we·li·koa Point \kä-ˌwā-lē-ˈkō-ä\. Cape on SE coast of Kauai I., Hawaii.

Ka·whia Harbor \ˈkä-fē-ä\. Inlet of Pacific Ocean, New Zealand, on NW cen. coast of North I.

Ka·wi \ˈkä-wē\. Mountain group, E Java, Indonesia; highest point 9968 ft. (3038 m.); includes Mt. Kelud and adjoins Mt. Ardjuno on the N.

Ka·wich Range \ˈkä-wich\. Range in S cen. Nye co., S Nevada; highest point **Kawich Peak** 9404 ft. (2866 m.).

Ka·wish·i·wi \kə-ˈwi-shə-wē\. River in N Lake co., NE Minnesota.

Kax·gar *or Eng.* **Kash·gar** \ˈkäsh-ˌgär\. River, W Xinjiang Uygur, W China; flows E toward Yarkant He; ab. 200 mi. (322 km.) long.

Kay \ˈkā\. County in N Oklahoma. See table at OKLAHOMA.

Ka·yah \ˈkī-ə\. State of E cen. Myanmar. See table at MYANMAR; see also KARENNI.

Kay·ak \ˈkī-ˌak\. Island off coast of SE Alaska, E of Prince William Sound; islet at its S end is Cape St. Elias.

Kayes \ˈkāz\. Town, SW Mali, on Senegal River; on railroad line from Dakar and Thiès in Senegal to Bamako and Koulikoro; pop. (1987p) 48,216.

Kay·nar·dzha \ˌkī-När-ˈjä\; *formerly* **Ku·chuk Kai·nar·ji** \kü-ˈchük-ˌkī-när-ˈjē\ *or Rom.* **Cai·nar·gea·va–Mi·că** \kī-ˌnär-jä-vä-ˈmē-kä\. Village, Bulgaria, a few miles SE of Silistra; scene of treaty 1774, terminating Russo-Turkish War, by which Russia gained: (1) territory on the Bug and Kuban' rivers and Kerch on the Crimean Penin. (see CRIMEA); (2) freedom for Russian shipping on Black Sea; (3) right of intervention in Danubian Principalities; (4) protection of Orthodox Christians in Ottoman Empire.

Kay·ser \ˈkī-zər\. Peak in SW Suriname; 3020 ft. (920 m.).

Kay·se·ri \ˈkī-se-rē\ *or* **Kai·sa·ria** \ˌkī-ˈsä-rē-ä\. **1.** Province of Turkey in Asia. See table at TURKEY.

2. *anc.* **Cae·sa·rea Maz·a·ca** \ˌsē-zə-ˈrē-ə-ˈma-zə-kə, ˌse-zə-, ˌse-sə-\ *or* **Mazaca.** City, its ✻, at foot of Erciyas; pop. (1990c) 421,362; textiles, carpets; for centuries an important trade center. Chief city of ancient Cappadocia; destroyed by Persians 3d cent. A.D.; center of Christianity in 4th cent.; attacked and held by Seljuqs (11th cent.), Mongols (13th cent.), Ottomans (16th cent.), among others.

Kays·ville \ˈkāz-ˌvil\. City, Davis co., N Utah, 18 mi. (29 km.) S of Ogden; pop. (1990c) 13,961.

Ka·zakh·stan *also* **Ka·zak·stan** \kə-ˌzäk-ˈstän, -ˌzäk-; ˌkä-zək-ˈstän, kə-ˌzak-ˈstan\; *Kazakh* **Qa·zaq·stan** \ˌkə-zək-ˈstán\; *officially* **Republic of Kazakhstan.** Country, W cen. Asia and W of the Ural extending into Europe; bounded on N by Russia, on E by China, on S by Kyrgyzstan, Uzbekistan, and Turkmenistan, on W by the Caspian Sea, and on NW by Russia; 1,048,300 sq. mi. (2,715,097 sq. km.); pop. (1993e) 17,186,000; ✻ Astana; comprised **Ka·zakh Soviet Socialist Republic** \kə-ˈzäk, kä-, -ˈzäk, -ˈzak\ 1936–91.

Physical features: Occupied in cen. part by great Kirgiz Steppe and in S by desert regions: in SW the Ustyurt Plateau and in SE the Muyun Kum desert region. Includes N half of Aral Sea, all of Lake Balkhash, and the smaller lakes Zaisan, Tengiz, and Chelkar Tengiz. In E, N of Lake Balkhash, plateau lands rise to the lofty Tian Shan and W Altay Shan on Chinese boundary. Chief rivers include the Syr Dar'ya in S, upper Irtysh in NE, the lower Ural in W; other important streams the Ishim, Tobol, Ili, and Emba.

Chief products: Wheat, fruit, tobacco; livestock; coal, tungsten, copper, zinc, chromium, oil (from fields along the NE Caspian); chemicals, textiles.

Chief settlements: Alma-Ata, Qaraghandy, Shymkent, Semey, Pavlodar.

History: Region came under the Mongols in 13th–14th cents.; gradually 18th–19th cents. came under Russian rule and formed large part of Russian Turkistan; an autonomous republic erected and named by the Kirghiz 1920; name changed to Kazakh A.S.S.R. 1925; admitted to U.S.S.R. as constituent republic 1936; declared independence 1991; ✻ moved 1997 from Alma-Ata to Aqmola (now Astana).

Ka·zan \kə-ˈzan\. River, Nunavut, cen. Canada; flows NNE through Yathkyed and other lakes to enter Baker Lake; 455 mi. (732 km.) long; one of main streams of the Barren Grounds.

Ka·zan' *or* **Ka·zan** \kə-ˈzánʸ, -ˈzän-yə\ *also* **Ka·san** \-ˈsän\. **1.** Former political subdivision in E Russia in Europe, now included in Mari El and Chuvash republics and Tatarstan, Russia in Europe.

2. City, ✻ of Tatarstan, cen. Russia in Europe, on short tributary 3 mi. (5 km.) from the Volga where it turns S 200 mi. (322 km.) E of Nizhniy Novgorod; pop. (1993e) 1,098,000; on Moscow-Yekaterinburg railroad line ab. 40 mi. (64 km.) above the junction of the Kama River with the Volga; a key city, commercially and industrially, of the Middle Volga Area; oil refining; leather goods, soap, furs, chemicals; many of its old buildings such as kremlin, cathedral, tower and monastery are still standing, although some were damaged during the Bolshevik Revolution; university (founded ab. 1804), many technical schools.

History: Original Kazan', not far from present city, under Black Bulgarian empire; converted to Islam in 10th cent.; conquered by Mongols of the Golden Horde in 13th cent.; made ✻ of independent khanate 15th cent.; captured by Czar Ivan the Terrible 1552; in 18th cent. main base for Russian expansion to S; burned by rebels under Cossack soldier Yemelyan I. Pugachov in revolt of 1773–74; rebuilt by Empress Catherine the Great; center of Tatar national movement Oct. 1917; captured by Czechs Aug. 1918; became ✻ of Tatar A.S.S.R. 1920; suffered during Bolshevik Revolution and subsequent famine 1921–22.

Ka·zan·lŭk \ˌkä-zän-ˈlək\ *or* **Ka·zan·lik** \-ˈlik\. Town, cen. Bulgaria, ab. 17 mi. (27 km.) NW of Stara Zagora; pop. (1991e) 65,184; taken by Russians 1878 in war with Turkey.

Kazan Rettō. See VOLCANO ISLANDS.

Kaz·bek *also* **Kas·bek** \kəz-ˈbyek\. Peak, cen. Caucasus Mts., bet. South Ossetia, Republic of Georgia, and Alania Rep., Russia; 16,558 ft. (5047 m.); an extinct volcano with steep slopes, towering above Daryal Pass; several glaciers; first climbed 1868; subject of many legends.

Kazdağı. See IDA 2.

Kā·ze·rūn \ˌkä-ze-ˈrün\. Town, Fārs prov., SW Iran, ab. 70 mi. (113 km.) W of Shīrāz; pop. (1986c) 73,367; produces cotton and rice.

Kāẓimīyah, Al. See AL KĀẒIMĪYAH.

Ka·zinc·bar·ci·ka \ˈkö-zēndz-ˌbört-sē-ˌkö\. Town, N Hungary; pop. (1991e) 44,800.

Kazvin. See QAZVĪN.

Kéa \ˈkā-ä\ *also* **Ke·os** \ˈkā-ös\ *or* **Tziá** \ˈtsyä, ˈchyä\; *anc.* **Ce·os** \ˈsē-äs\. Island, NW Cyclades, Greece, in Aegean Sea; ab. 13 mi. (21 km.) SE of Cape Sounion, the S point of Attica; belongs to Cyclades dept.; 12 mi. (19 km.) long, area 67 sq. mi. (174 sq. km.); honey, citrus fruits; chief town **Kéa.** Over the centuries ruled by Greeks, Italians, and Turks; birthplace of the Greek poets Simonides (c. 556 B.C.) and Bacchylides (5th cent. B.C.)

Ke·a·ho·le Point \ˌkā-ä-ˈhō-lā\. Cape on W coast of Hawaii I., Hawaii.

Ke·a·lai·ka·hi·ki \kā-ˌä-ˌlī-kä-ˈhē-kē\. Channel bet. Lanai I. and Kahoolawe I., Hawaii; ab. 20 mi. (32 km.) wide.

Ke·a·la·ke·kua \kā-ˌä-lä-kā-ˈkü-ä\. Unincorporated settlement, Hawaii co., Hawaii, on **Kealakekua Bay** on W coast of Hawaii I.; pop. (1990c) 1453; landing place of English explorer Capt. James Cook on his 2d visit to Hawaiian Is. Jan. 1779 and place where he was killed in quarrel with native inhabitants Feb. 14; a favorite place of anchorage for visiting foreign vessels in early years of kingdom; has monument to Cook.

Keans·burg \ˈkēnz-ˌbərg\. Borough, Monmouth co., E cen. New Jersey, on Raritan Bay; pop. (1990c) 11,069; port of call for pleasure craft.

Kear·ney \ˈkär-nē\. **1.** County in S Nebraska. See table at NEBRASKA.

2. City, ⊗ of Buffalo co., S cen. Nebraska, on Platte River 45 mi. (72 km.) WSW of Grand Island; pop. (1990c) 24,396; outdoor recreation; Univ. of Nebraska at Kearney (1903).

Kearn Peak \ˈkərn\. Mountain in the Sierra Nevada, E Tulare co., California.

Kearns \ˈkərnz\. Unincorporated settlement, Salt Lake co., N Utah, SW of Salt Lake City; pop. (1990c) 28,374.

Kear·ny \ˈkär-nē\. **1.** County in W Kansas. See table at KANSAS.

2. Town, Hudson co., NE New Jersey, bet. Passaic and Hackensack rivers at head of Newark Bay, 2 mi. (3 km.) N of Newark; pop. (1990c) 34,874.

Kear·sarge, Mount \ˈkir-ˌsärj\. Peak, Merrimack co., S cen. New Hampshire; ab. 2931 ft. (893 m.).

Kearsarge North; *mostly formerly* **Pe·quaw·ket** \pi-ˈkwȯ-kət, pē-\. Mountain, Carroll co., E New Hampshire; 3268 ft. (996 m.).

Ke·a·wai·ki Bay \ˌkā-ä-ˈwī-kē\. Bay on NW coast of Hawaii I., Hawaii, bet. Kiholo Bay and Honokaope Bay.

Keb·bi \ˈke-bē\. State of Nigeria. See table at NIGERIA.

Ké·bir, Oued al– \ˌwed-ȧl-kā-ˈbir\ *or* **Wa·di al–Ke·bir** \ˈwä-dē\. River, NE Algeria, flowing NNE through city of Constantine into Mediterranean Sea near Skikda; not navigable; in its upper course sometimes known as the **Rum·mel** \ˈrů-məl\ River.

Kebir, Tell el *or* **Kebîr, El Tell el.** See TEL EL KEBIR.

Kebir, Wadi al–. See GUADALQUIVIR.

Keb·ne·kai·se \ˌkeb-nə-ˈkī-sə, ˈkeb-nə-ˌ\. Peak in the Kjølen Mts., N Sweden; 6965 ft. (2123 m.); highest peak in Sweden.

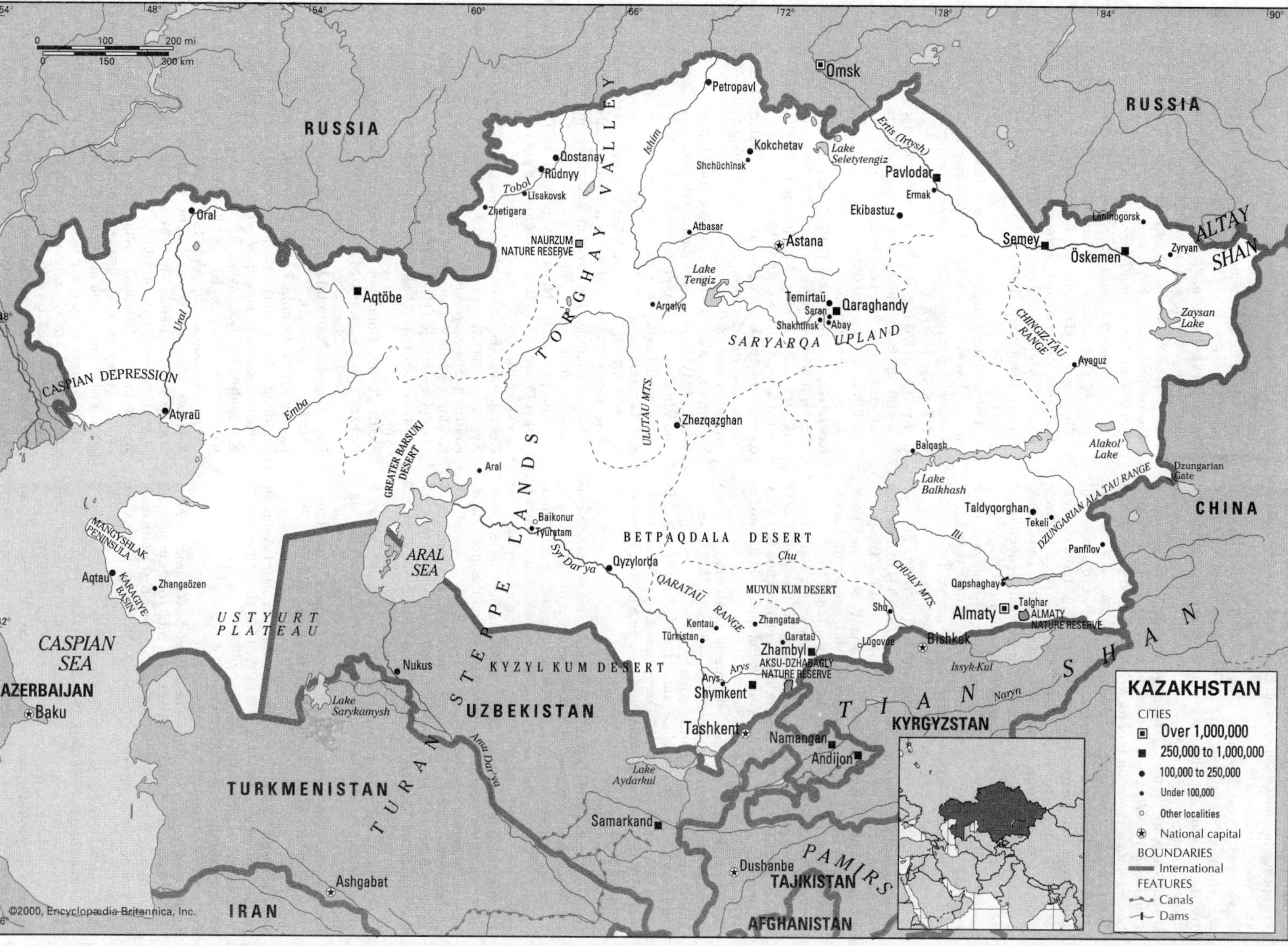
KAZAKHSTAN
CITIES
Over 1,000,000
250,000 to 1,000,000
100,000 to 250,000
Under 100,000
Other localities
National capital
BOUNDARIES
International
FEATURES
Canals
Dams
RUSSIA
CHINA
KYRGYZSTAN
UZBEKISTAN
TURKMENISTAN
TAJIKISTAN
AFGHANISTAN
IRAN
AZERBAIJAN
Omsk
Petropavl
Kokchetav
Shchūchīnsk
Astana
Pavlodar
Ermak
Ekibastuz
Semey
Öskemen
Leninogorsk
Zyryan
Ayaguz
Qaraghandy
Temirtaū
Saran
Abay
Shakhtinsk
Atbasar
Arqalyq
Zhezqazghan
Balqash
Taldyqorghan
Tekeli
Panfilov
Almaty
Talghar
Qapshaghay
Bishkek
Shū
Lugovoe
Qarataū
Zhambyl
Zhangatas
Kentau
Türkistan
Shymkent
Arys
Tashkent
Namangan
Andijon
Dushanbe
Samarkand
Qyzylorda
Baikonur
Tyuratam
Aral
Nukus
Ashgabat
Qostanay
Rūdnyy
Lisakovsk
Zhetigara
Aqtöbe
Oral
Atyraū
Zhangaözen
Aqtau
Baku
ALTAY SHAN
Zaysan Lake
Dzungarian Gate
Alakol' Lake
DZUNGARIAN ALA TAU RANGE
CHINGIZ-TAU RANGE
SARYARQA UPLAND
Lake Balkhash
Ili
Issyk-Kul
Naryn
TIAN SHAN
CHU-ILY MTS.
Chu
MUYUN KUM DESERT
BETPAQDALA DESERT
QARATAŪ RANGE
ULUTAU MTS.
Lake Tengiz
Ishim
Ertis (Irtysh)
Lake Seletytengiz
TORGHAY VALLEY
NAURZUM NATURE RESERVE
ALMATY NATURE RESERVE
AKSU-DZHABAGLY NATURE RESERVE
Tobol
Syr Dar'ya
TURAN STEPPE LANDS
KYZYL KUM DESERT
ARAL SEA
GREATER BARSUKI DESERT
Emba
Ural
CASPIAN DEPRESSION
USTYURT PLATEAU
Lake Sarykamysh
Amu Dar'ya
Lake Aydarkul
PAMIRS
MANGYSHLAK PENINSULA
KARAGIYE BASIN
CASPIAN SEA
0 100 200 mi
0 150 300 km
©2000, Encyclopædia Britannica, Inc.

Ke·bu·men *or Du.* **Ke·boe·men** \kə-'bü-mən\. Town, Central Java prov., Indonesia, on railroad line near S coast 50 mi. (80 km.) W of Yogyakarta.

Kecs·ke·mét \'kech-ke-ˌmāt\. City, ⊗ of Bács-Kiskun co., cen. Hungary, 52 mi. (84 km.) SE of Budapest; pop. (1991e) 108,000; market center for fruit-growing region; distilleries; leatherworking.

Ke·dah \'ke-də\. State of Malaysia; includes large island of Langkawi off NW coast; generally level with short streams; has mountain range on E border (3000 to 6100 ft. or 910 to 1860 m.); rice, rubber. See table at MALAYSIA.

History: In early centuries A.D. formed part of a powerful Indianized state; leased Penang to British East India Company 1786; subject to Siam 1821–1909, transferred to Great Britain 1909; overrun by Japanese Dec. 1941; part of Thailand 1943–45; became part of the independent Federation of Malaya 1957; became a state of Malaysia 1963.

Ke·dar·nath \kā-'där-ˌnät\. Peak in the Himalayas, Uttar Pradesh, N India, W of Badrinath; 22,770 ft. (6940 m.).

Ke·da·wung *or Du.* **Ke·da·woeng** \kə-'dä-ˌwu̇ŋ\. Town, West Java prov., Indonesia; suburb of Cirebon.

Ke·desh \'kē-ˌdesh\ *or* **Kedesh–naph·ta·li** \-'naf-tə-ˌlī\. Archaeological site, N Israel, ab. 23 mi. (37 km.) N of Tiberias; was a city of refuge, frequently mentioned in the Bible.

Kedg·es Strait *or* **Kedges Straits** \'ke-jəz\. Strait in Chesapeake Bay, Maryland, bet. South Marsh I. and Smith I., connecting Tangier Sound with Chesapeake Bay.

Ke·di·ri \kā-'dir-ē\. **1.** Former residency of the Netherlands Indies, now part of the Indonesian prov. of East Java; 2718 sq. mi. (7040 sq. km.); ✻ Kediri; fertile plain region in valley of Brantas River bet. the Wilis and Kelut mountain groups; in 11th–13th cents. part of a Hindu kingdom.

2. City, its ✻, East Java prov., Indonesia, on Brantas River 65 mi. (105 km.) SW of Surabaya; pop. (1990c) 235,602; distribution center of agricultural region.

Ked·le·ston \'ked-ᵊl-stən\. Locality, Derbyshire, N cen. England, 3.5 mi. (6 km.) NW of Derby; home of political leader and onetime viceroy of India Lord George Nathaniel Curzon.

Kedoe. See KEDU.

Kedron. See KIDRON.

Ke·du *or Du.* **Ke·doe** \'kā-ˌdü\. Former residency of the Netherlands Indies, now part of Indonesian prov. of Central Java; 1799 sq. mi. (4659 sq. km.); ✻ Magelang; bordered Banjumas on W, Semarang on N, and Yogyakarta and Surakarta principalities on E; area includes or is bordered by some of the highest mountains of Java; has no harbors on S coast; now one of most densely populated areas on the globe; agriculturally highly developed.

Kę·dzie·rzyn–Koź·le \ken-'je-zhēn-'ko̊zh-le\. Commune, Opole prov. S Poland; pop. (1989e) 71,677.

Kee·go Harbor \'kē-gō\. City, Oakland co., SE Michigan, 25 mi. (40 km.) NW of Detroit; pop. (1990c) 2932.

Keele \'kēl\. River, Northwest Territories, Canada; flows E from Mackenzie Mts. to Mackenzie River; 230 mi. (370 km.) long.

Keele Peak. Peak in Selwyn Mts., NW Canada, Yukon Terr. near boundary with Northwest Territories; 9751 ft. (2972 m.).

Kee·ler, Cape \'kē-lər\. Promontory on E coast of Antarctic Penin., Antarctica, 68°51′S, 63°13′W; 1700 ft. (518 m.) high; discovered 1928.

Keeling Islands. See COCOS ISLANDS.

Keelung. See CHI-LUNG.

Keene \'kēn\. **1.** City, ⊗ of Cheshire co., SW corner of New Hampshire, on Ashuelot River 40 mi. (64 km.) W of Manchester; pop. (1990c) 22,430; tourism; first permanent settlement 1750; incorp. as city 1873; Keene State Coll. (1909).

2. Town, New York. See KEENE VALLEY.

3. Resort village, New York. See KEENE VALLEY.

4. City, Johnson co., N cen. Texas, S of Fort Worth; pop. (1990c) 3944; Southwestern Adventist Coll. (1893).

Keene Valley. Village and resort, Essex co., NE New York, ab. 39 mi. (63 km.) SSW of Plattsburgh; ab. 3 mi. (5 km.) S of resort village of **Keene,** and with it included in **Keene** town (pop. [1990c] 908).

Keet·mans·hoop \'kāt-mäns-ˌhōp\. Town, S Namibia, 270 mi. (434 km.) SSE of Windhoek; pop. (1988e) 14,000; in sheep country.

Kee·wa·tin \kē-'wāt-ᵊn, -'wät-\. **1.** Former district, SE Northwest Territories (now Nunavut), Canada; included E part of mainland of N Canada NW of Hudson Bay and the islands in Hudson and James bays; area incl. water 228,160 sq. mi. (590,934 sq. km.); administered from Ottawa. Created 1876 when it included a much larger area (ab. 516,000 sq. mi. or 1,336,440 sq. km.); was several times reorganized with parts of it added to Manitoba and Ontario provs.

2. Region, cen. Canada, formerly an administrative subdivision of Northwest Territories, roughly equivalent to the former district; area 228,700 sq. mi. (592,335 sq. km.); pop. (1991c) 5834.

3. Town, Kenora dist., W Ontario, Canada, on N shore of Lake of the Woods at source of Winnipeg River across from Kenora; pop. (1991c) 2059; large power plant.

Kef, Le. See LE KEF.

Ke·fa \'kē-fə, kə-'fä\. Region of SW Ethiopia; 21,081 sq. mi. (54,600 sq. km.); chief town Jima; conquered by Muslims 16th cent., by Ethiopians 1897.

Kefallinía. See CEPHALONIA.

Kefe. See FEODOSIYA.

Kef·la·vík \'kyeb-lä-ˌvēk, 'kef-\. Town, SW Iceland, ab. 22 mi. (35 km.) WSW of Reykjavík on SW shore of Faxa Bay; pop. (1990c) 7520; fishing; location of **Keflavík Field,** international airport. See MEEKS FIELD.

Ke·gon–no–ta·ki \'kā-gōn-nō-'tä-kē\. Waterfall in Tochigi prefecture, cen. Honshū, Japan, near Nikkō; ab. 330 ft. (100 m.) high and 18 ft. (5 m.) wide.

Ke·gon·sa, Lake \ki-'gän-sə\. See FOUR LAKES.

Kehl \'kāl\. Commune, Baden-Württemberg, Germany, on the Rhine opp. Strasbourg, France; pop. (1980c) 29,924; first mentioned 1299.

Kei, Great. See GREAT KEI.

Keigh·ley \'kēth-lē\. Town, West Yorkshire, N England, in the Aire Valley 17 mi. (27 km.) WNW of Leeds; pop. (1981p) 57,451; manufactures woolen goods, spinning machinery, machine tools.

Kei·hin \'kā-'hēn\. Name given 1941 to the amalgamated Tokyo-Yokohama Harbor after completion of extensive improvements.

Kei Islands. See KAI ISLANDS.

Keijo. See SEOUL.

Keilberg. See KLÍNOVEC.

Kei·lor \'kē-lər\. City, Victoria, Australia, a NW suburb of Melbourne; pop. (1991c) 106,076.

Kei·te·le \'kā-te-le\. Lake, S cen. Finland; 174 sq. mi. (451 sq. km.).

Keith \'kēth\. County in W Nebraska. See table at NEBRASKA.

Kei·zer \'kī-zər\. City, Marion co., NW Oregon, N of Salem; pop. (1990c) 21,884.

Kej·im·ku·jik National Park \ˌke-jə-mə-'kü-jē\. See CANADA, *National Parks.*

Kejser Franz Josephs Fjord. See FRANZ JOSEF FJORD.

Ke·ka·ha \kā-'kä-hä\. Unincorporated settlement, on SW coast of Kauai I., Hawaii, W of Waimea; pop. (1990c) 3506.

Keksgolm. See PRIOZERSK.

Ke·lang \kə-'läŋ\ *or* **Klang** \'kläŋ\. Town, Selangor state, Malaysia, near coast; pop. (1980p) 284,941.

Ke·la·ni \'kā-lə-nē\ *or* **Kelani Gan·ga** \'gəŋ-gə\. River (*ganga*), W Sri Lanka; flows W to Indian Ocean near Colombo; ab. 90 mi. (145 km.) long.

Ke·lan·tan \kə-'län-ˌtän, kə-'lan-ˌtan\. **1.** River in Kelantan state, Malaysia; rises in the mountains on the SW border, flows NNE into the South China Sea; ab. 150 mi. (240 km.) long; navigable for much of its course; has many tributaries.

2. A state of Malaysia, bounded on N by Thailand, on NE by South China Sea, on E by Terengganu state, on S by Pahang, on W by Perak; level and fertile in N, hilly in S, with mountains on Pahang border (see TAHAN, GUNONG); almost entirely in basin of Kelantan River; rice, rubber, coconuts. See table at MALAYSIA.

History: In 14th cent. under Java, later under Melaka, and at end of 19th cent. under Siam; became a British dependency 1909; overrun by Japanese Dec. 1941; became part of the independent Federation of Malaya 1957; became a state of Malaysia 1963.

Ke·la·sa Strait \ke-ˈlä-sä\; *formerly* **Gas·par Strait** \ˈgas-pər\. Channel bet. Bangka and Belitung islands, Indonesia, E of S Sumatra; ab. 45 mi. (72 km.) wide.

Kelat. See KALAT.

Kel·heim \ˈkāl-ˌhīm\. Town, E Bavaria, Germany, on the Danube where the Altmühl joins it ab. 12 mi. (19 km.) SW of Regensburg; pop. (1980c) 14,165; founded c. 1200.

Kel·kit \ˈkel-kēt\. River in NE Turkey in Asia; flows generally W into the Yesil Irmak near its mouth; 232 mi. (373 km.) long.

Kel·ler \ˈke-lər\. City, Tarrant co., N Texas, a N suburb of Fort Worth; pop. (1990c) 13,683.

Kel·ler·wand \ˈke-lər-ˌvänt\ *or Ital.* **Mon·te Co·gli·ans** \ˈmȯn-tā-kōl-ˈyäns\. Mountain on border bet. Austria and Italy; 9217 ft. (2809 m.); highest peak in Carnic Alps.

Kel·leys Island \ˈke-lēz\. Island in Lake Erie, off NE coast of Ottawa co., N Ohio; a part of Erie co., Ohio.

Kel·logg \ˈke-ˌlȯg, -ˌläg\. City, Shoshone co., NE Idaho, 35 mi. (56 km.) ESE of Coeur d'Alene; pop. (1990c) 2591; former gold-, zinc-, and lead-mining center.

Kellogg, Mount. Peak, NE Pima co., S Arizona; 8385 ft. (2556 m.).

Kells. See CEANANNUS MÓR.

Kel·ly Air Force Base \ˈke-lē\. U.S. Air Force base, Bexar co., S Texas, just SW of San Antonio; estab. May 1917; Air Force matériel command depot.

Ke·low·na \ki-ˈlō-nə\. City, S British Columbia, Canada, on E shore of Okanagan Lake 60 mi. (77 km.) N of U.S. border; pop. (1991c) 75,950; wine; canneries; fruits; tourism.

Kel·so \ˈkel-sō\. **1.** City, ⊗ of Cowlitz co., SW Washington, on Cowlitz River just NE of Longview; pop. (1990c) 11,820; fishing; formerly a lumbering center.

2. Burgh, Borders region, SE Scotland, on the Tweed; pop. (1981p) 5609; ruined abbey; place where poet and novelist Sir Walter Scott attended school.

Keltsy. See KIELCE.

Ke·lud, Mount \kə-ˈlüd\ *or* **Gu·nung Kelud** \ˈgü-ˌnu̇ŋ\; *mostly formerly* **Mount Kelut** \kə-ˈlüt, ˈklüt\. Volcano, East Java prov., Java, Indonesia; 5679 ft. (1731 m.).

Kem' *or* **Kem** \ˈkem\. **1.** River, Karelia Rep., NW Russia in Europe; flows E to White Sea opp. Soloveskiye Ostrova; ab. 250 mi. (400 km.) long; outlet of Lake Kunto and other lakes of N cen. Karelia Rep.

2. Seaport town, NE Karelia Rep., NW Russia in Europe, on Kem' River ab. 10 mi. (16 km.) above its mouth, 185 mi. (298 km.) W of Arkhangel'sk; station on Murmansk R.R.

Kemarat. See KHEMMARAT.

Ke·me·ro·vo \ˈkye-mi-rə-və, -rō-və, -rə-ˌvō\. City, ✻ of Kemerovo Oblast, S Russia in Asia, in Kuznetsk Basin 125 mi. (201 km.) E of Novosibirsk; pop. (1992e) 521,000; industrial city on the Tom' River, a tributary of the Ob', above Tomsk; coal; coke, chemicals, fertilizers, machinery, plastics.

Kemerovo Oblast \ˈȯ-bləst, -ˌblast\ *or* **Ke·me·rov·ska·ya Oblast'** \ˌkye-mi-ˈrȯf-skə-yə\. Subdivision of S Russia in Asia; 36,873 sq. mi. (95,501 sq. km.); pop. (1992e) 3,181,000; ✻ Kemerovo; Kuznetsk Basin in cen. part; mountainous in S; watered by Tom' and Chulym rivers and their tributaries; coal, lead, zinc; iron and steel, chemicals; estab. 1943.

Ke·mi \ˈke-mē\. **1.** *or* **Ke·mi·jo·ki** \ˈke-mē-ˌyō-kē\. River in Oulu prov., N Finland; flows S into head of Gulf of Bothnia; ab. 300 mi. (480 km.) long.

2. Seaport, Lappi prov., N Finland, on Gulf of Bothnia; pop. (1989c) 25,565; sawmills; rail connections to the NE through Kemijärvi to Kandalaksha in Murmansk Oblast, NW Russia in Europe, and to the SE with Oulu; founded 1869.

Ke·mi·jär·vi \ˈke-mē-ˌyar-vē\. Lake in N cen. Finland, formed by expansion of Kemi River.

Kemiö. See KIMITO.

Kem·mel, Mont \ˌmō^{n}-ke-ˈmel\. Height, Belgium, 5 mi. (8 km.) SW of Ieper (Ypres); scene of heavy fighting in WWI, taken by Germans Apr. 1918 and recaptured by British Aug. 1918.

Kem·merer \ˈke-mər-ər\. Town, ⊗ of Lincoln co., SW Wyoming, 45 mi. (72 km.) NNE of Evanston; pop. (1990c) 3020.

Kemp, Lake. See BIG WICHITA DAM.

Kemp Coast; *formerly* **Kemp Land** \ˈkemp\. Section of coast of Antarctica W of Mac. Robertson Land, on shore of Indian Ocean.

Kem·pen \ˈkem-pən\. Commune, North Rhine-Westphalia, Germany, 40 mi. (64 km.) NW of Cologne; pop. (1980c) 30,169; birthplace of Dutch ecclesiastic and writer Thomas à Kempis 1379 or 1380; first mentioned c. 890.

Kem·per \ˈkem-pər\. County in E Mississippi. See table at MISSISSIPPI.

Kemp Land. See KEMP COAST.

Kemp·sey \ˈkemp-sē\. Town, E New South Wales, Australia, near the coast; pop. (1991c) 25,343; outdoor recreation.

Kemp·ston \ˈkemp-stən\. Town, Bedfordshire, SE cen. England, suburb of Bedford on the Ouse; pop. (1981p) 15,466.

Kemp·ten \ˈkemp-tən\. City, Bavaria, Germany, on Iller River 65 mi. (104 km.) WSW of Munich; pop. (1992e) 62,233; railroad center; dairy products, textiles, paper, beer; dates from Roman times; town made imperial city 1289; to Bavaria 1803.

Kemp·ton Park \ˈkemp-tən\. Town, Gauteng prov., Rep. of South Africa, suburb of Johannesburg.

Ken \ˈkān, ˈken\. River, N cen. India; flows N into S Uttar Pradesh to the Yamuna W of Allahabad; ab. 235 mi. (378 km.) long.

Kena. See QENA.

Ke·nad·sa \ˌkā-näd-ˈzä\. Town, NW Algeria, SW of Béchar; pop. (1987p) 9822; in area of coalfields.

Ke·nai \ˈkē-ˌnī\. City, S Alaska, on Cook Inlet on NW coast of Kenai Penin.; pop. (1990c) 6327; estab. 1791 by Russian fur traders; airfield, oil-related activities.

Kenai Mountains. Mountain range on Kenai Penin., S Alaska; highest peak Cooper Mt. 5269 ft. (1606 m.).

Kenai Peninsula. **1.** Peninsula, S Alaska, bet. Cook Inlet on W and Prince William Sound on E; ab. 160 mi. (257 km.) long by 130 mi. (209 km.) wide; location of Seward and Seldovia; **Kenai Fjords National Park** estab. 1980 (see UNITED STATES, *National Parks*).

2. Division in Alaska. See table at ALASKA.

Ke·nans·ville \ˈkē-nənz-ˌvil\. Town, ⊗ of Duplin co., SE North Carolina; pop. (1990c) 856.

Ken·dal \ˈkend-^{ə}l\. Town, Cumbria, NW England, on the Kent River 62 mi. (100 km.) NNW of Manchester; pop. (1981c) 23,550; has manufactured woolen goods since 14th cent.; also manufactures boots and shoes, paper. Ruins of a castle which was birthplace of Catherine Parr 1512, 6th wife of Henry VIII.

Ken·dall \ˈkend-^{ə}l\. Name of counties in two states of the U.S. See tables at ILLINOIS and TEXAS.

Ken·dall·ville \ˈkend-^{ə}l-ˌvil\. City, Noble co., NE Indiana, 27 mi. (43 km.) N of Fort Wayne; pop. (1990c) 7773.

Ken·da·ri \ken-ˈdär-ē\. Town and port, ✻ of South-East Sulawesi prov., Sulawesi, Indonesia, on E coast of the SE peninsula 240 mi. (386 km.) ENE of Ujung Pandang; pop. (1980c) 41,021; exports rattans, varnish resins, and gold and silver jewelry; in WWII occupied by Japanese 1942 and used as military base.

Ken·drick Peak \ˈken-drik\. Mountain, S cen. Coconino co., N cen. Arizona; 10,418 ft. (3175 m.).

Ken·e·dy \ˈke-nə-dē\. **1.** Coastal county in S Texas. See table at TEXAS.

\ə\ abut \ˈə\ matches \$^{ə}$\ kitten, Fr table \ər\ further \a\ ash \ā\ ace \ä\ cot, cart \å\ Fr bac \au̇\ out \b̲\ Span Avila \ch\ chin \e\ bet \ē\ easy \g\ go \i\ hit \ī\ ice \j\ job \k\ Ger ich, Buch \$^{n}$\ Fr vin \ŋ\ sing \ō\ go \ȯ\ all \ȯ\ law \œ\ Fr bœuf \œ̄\ Fr feu \ȯi\ boy \th\ thin \t̲h̲\ this \ü\ loot \u̇\ foot \ue\ Ger füllen \ue̅\ Fr rue \y\ yet \$^{y}$\ Fr digne \ˈdēn^{y}\, nuit \ˈnw^{y}ē\ \yü\ few \yu̇\ fury \zh\ vision

2. City, Karnes co., S Texas, 49 mi. (79 km.) W of Victoria; pop. (1990c) 3763.

Ke·ne·ma \ke-'ne-mə\. Town, SE Sierra Leone; pop. (1985p) 52,473; in area of timber production and diamond mining.

Kenesaw Mountain. See KENNESAW MOUNTAIN.

Keng·tung \'keŋ-'tůŋ\. **1.** Former state, E Burma (now Myanmar), 12,405 sq. mi. (32,129 sq. km.); was largest of Southern Shan States; ✻ Kengtung; since 1947 part of Shan State (see SHAN); **Kengtung Hills** in cen. part rise to above 6500 ft. (1980 m.).

2. Town, its ✻, on a tributary of the Mekong River and on main highway to Thailand 230 mi. (370 km.) ESE of Mandalay; pop. (1983c) 46,938.

Ken·horst \'ken-,hȯrst\. Borough, Berks co., SE Pennsylvania; pop. (1990c) 2918.

Kenia. See KENYA.

Ken·il·worth \'ken-ᵊl-,wərth\. **1.** Village, Cook co., NE Illinois, ab. 5 mi. (8 km.) N of Chicago; pop. (1990c) 2402.

2. Borough, Union co., NE New Jersey, 4 mi. (6 km.) W of Elizabeth; pop. (1990c) 7574.

3. Town, Warwickshire, cen. England; pop. (1981c) 19,337; ruins of major castle (celebrated by Scottish author Sir Walter Scott in his novel *Kenilworth*) founded by Geoffrey de Clinton c. 1120, and the property of Simon de Montfort, earl of Leicester, in 13th cent. and of Prince John of Gaunt in mid-14th cent., presented by Queen Elizabeth I to Robert Dudley, earl of Leicester, who entertained the queen there in 1575 (as described in Scott's novel), dismantled by Oliver Cromwell's Parliamentarian forces and abandoned 17th cent.

Ke·ni·tra \kə-'nē-trə\; *formerly* **Port Ly·au·tey** \,pȯr-lyō-'tā\. River port, NW Morocco, 10 mi. (16 km.) from the Atlantic Ocean, ab. 30 mi. (48 km.) NE of Rabat; pop. (1982c) 188,194; exports agricultural products and ores.

Ken·mare \ken-'mar\. Village, co. Kerry, SW Ireland; pop. (1986c) 1130; at head of **Kenmare River,** a deep narrow inlet of Atlantic Ocean N of Bantry Bay, 5 mi. (8 km.) wide at mouth.

Ken·more \'ken-,mōr\. Residential village, in town of Tonawanda, Erie co., W New York, on Niagara River 7 mi. (11 km.) N of Buffalo; pop. (1990c) 17,180; Sulpician Seminary of the Northwest (1930).

Ken·ne·bec \,ke-nə-'bek, 'ke-nə-,\. **1.** River, W cen. and S Maine; flows S from Moosehead Lake to Atlantic Ocean; ab. 150 mi. (240 km.) long; navigable for large vessels to Bath.

2. County in SW Maine. See table at MAINE.

3. Town, ⊗ of Lyman co., S cen. South Dakota; pop. (1990c) 284.

Ken·ne·bunk \'ke-nə-,bəŋk, ,ke-nə-'bəŋk, -nē-\. Town, York co., SW Maine, 8 mi. (13 km.) S of Biddeford; pop. (1990c) 8004; summer resort.

Ken·ne·bunk·port \,ke-nə-'bəŋk-,pōrt, -nē-\. Town, York co., SW Maine, on Atlantic Ocean 9 mi. (14 km.) S of Biddeford; pop. (1990c) 3356; summer resort.

Ken·ne·dale \'ke-nə-,dāl\. Town, Tarrant co., N Texas, 10 mi. (16 km.) SE of Fort Worth; pop. (1990c) 4096.

Kennedy, Cape. See CANAVERAL, CAPE.

Ken·ne·dy, Mount \'ke-nə-dē\. Peak in St. Elias Mts., SW Yukon, Canada; 13,905 ft. (4238 m.).

Kennedy Channel. Channel, NW coast of Greenland, bet. Washington Land and NE coast of Ellesmere I.; connects Kane and Hall basins; ab. 110 mi. (175 km.) long.

Ken·ner \'ke-nər\. City, Jefferson parish, SE Louisiana, on Mississippi River 12 mi. (19 km.) W of New Orleans; pop. (1990c) 72,033; site of New Orleans International Airport.

Ken·ne·saw \'ke-nə-,sȯ\. City, Cobb co., NW Georgia, 20 mi. (32 km.) NW of Atlanta; pop. (1990c) 8936.

Kennesaw Mountain *also* **Kenesaw Mountain.** Isolated peak in Cobb co., NW Georgia, near Atlanta; 1809 ft. (551 m.); scene of battle June 27, 1864 in which Union Gen. William T. Sherman made an unsuccessful frontal attack on Confederate troops in his campaign against Atlanta; set aside 1917 as Kennesaw Mountain Battlefield Site (648 acres or 262 hectares); now part of **Kennesaw Mountain National Battlefield Park**.

Ken·net \'ke-nət\. River, S England; flows ENE through Wiltshire and Berkshire into the Thames at Reading; 44 mi. (71 km.) long.

Ken·neth City \'ke-nəth\. Town, Pinellas co., W Florida; pop. (1990c) 4462.

Ken·nett \'ke-nət\. City, ⊗ of Dunklin co., SE Missouri, 22 mi. (35 km.) W of Caruthersville; pop. (1990c) 10,941.

Kennett Square. Borough, Chester co., SE Pennsylvania, 33 mi. (53 km.) WSW of Philadelphia; pop. (1990c) 5218.

Ken·ne·wick \'ke-nə-,wik\. City, Benton co., S Washington, on Columbia River 5 mi. (8 km.) W of its confluence with Snake River; pop. (1990c) 42,155; fruit orchards; dairy farming.

Ke·nog·a·mi \kə-'nä-gə-mē\. **1.** River, cen. Ontario, Canada; flows NE and N from its chief source, Long Lake, just N of Lake Superior, to the Albany River; ab. 200 mi. (322 km.) long.

2. Lake, S Quebec, Canada; receives the Chicoutimi River, which flows out of it NE into Saguenay River.

Ke·no·ra \kə-'nōr-ə\. **1.** District in W Ontario, Canada. See table at ONTARIO.

2. Town, administrative center of Kenora dist., W Ontario, Canada, on Winnipeg River just N of Lake of the Woods; pop. (1991c) 9782; flour, lumber, and paper mills; summer resort; railroad divisional point and commercial airfield. Settlement in area late 18th cent.; incorp. 1882 by Manitoba as **Rat Portage** \'rat-'pōr-tij, 'rä-pȯr-'täzh\; contested in boundary dispute bet. Manitoba and Ontario, 1883; subsequently, to Ontario; name changed c. 1904 to Kenora.

Ke·no·sha \kə-'nō-shə\. **1.** County in SE corner of Wisconsin. See table at WISCONSIN.

2. City, ⊗ of Kenosha co., SE corner of Wisconsin, on Lake Michigan 10 mi. (16 km.) S of Racine; pop. (1990c) 80,352; underwear, tools, metal products, hosiery; Carthage Coll. (1847; moved to Kenosha 1964), Univ. of Wisconsin–Parkside (1968); city founded 1835.

Ke·no·va \kə-'nō-və\. City, Wayne co., SW West Virginia, at mouth of Big Sandy River 8 mi. (13 km.) W of Huntington; pop. (1990c) 3748.

Ken·si·co Dam \'ken-zi-kō\. Dam across Bronx River, SE New York; completed 1916 to create **Kensico Reservoir** to supply in part the needs of New York City.

Ken·sing·ton \'ken-siŋ-tən, -ziŋ-\. Subdivision of town of Berlin, Connecticut. See BERLIN 1.

Ken·sing·ton and Chel·sea \'ken-ziŋ-tən...'chel-sē\. A borough of Greater London, SE England. See table at LONDON 4.

Kensington and Nor·wood \'nōr-,wůd\. Joint municipality, SE South Australia, Australia, E suburb of Adelaide; pop. (1991c) 8803.

Kent \'kent\. **1.** Name of counties in five states of the U.S. See tables at DELAWARE, MARYLAND, MICHIGAN, RHODE ISLAND, TEXAS.

2. Town, W Litchfield co., NW Connecticut, on New York border; pop. (1990c) 2918; resort and art colony; Kent School (coeducational preparatory school, 1906); town incorp. 1739.

3. City, Portage co., NE Ohio, on Cuyahoga River 8 mi. (13 km.) ENE of Akron; pop. (1990c) 28,835; meatpacking; plastics, machine parts; Kent State Univ. (1910). Four Vietnam War protesters were shot to death by National Guard troops at the university here May 4, 1970.

4. City, King co., W cen. Washington, 16 mi. (26 km.) S of Seattle; pop. (1990c) 37,960; residential; aerospace-related industry; plastics.

5. Counties in two provinces of Canada. See tables at NEW BRUNSWICK and ONTARIO.

6. River, Cumbria, NW England; flows S into Morecambe Bay; ab. 20 mi. (30 km.) long.

7. Former county, SE England.

History: Territory occupied by a people of Britain when Romans under Gen. Julius Caesar arrived mid-first cent. B.C.; settled by Anglo-Saxons, probably Jutes, 5th cent. A.D.; as a kingdom of Anglo-Saxon Heptarchy (*q.v.*) attained under King Aethelbehrt (560–616) supremacy S of the Humber; converted to Roman Christianity in 597 by St. Augustine, first archbishop of Canterbury; maintained its identity as subkingdom until 9th cent. although it was soon ruled by Mercia (*q.v.*) and later by Wessex (*q.v.*).

8. Administrative county, SE England, comprising the former county; agriculture (fruit, hops, barley, potatoes); sheep; dairying; fisheries; manufacturing (paper, cement); shipbuilding; chief settlements include Canterbury, Maidstone, Dover, Folkestone, Chatham, Ramsgate, Sheerness; estab. 1974. See table at ENGLAND.

Ken·tau \ˈken-ˌtau̇\. Town, South Kazakhstan region, Kazakhstan, ab. 100 mi. (160 km.) NW of Shymkent; pop. (1991e) 65,100; mining; formed 1955.

Kentei Mountains. See HENTIYN NURUU.

Kent Island. Island in upper Chesapeake Bay, W Queen Annes co., E Maryland; 15 mi. (24 km.) long; largest island in the bay; site of trading station estab. 1631 by Virginian William Claiborne.

Kent·land \ˈkent-lənd\. Town, ⊗ of Newton co., NW Indiana, 37 mi. (60 km.) NW of Lafayette; pop. (1990c) 1798.

Ken·ton \ˈkent-ᵊn\. **1.** County in N Kentucky. See table at KENTUCKY.

2. City, ⊗ of Hardin co., NW cen. Ohio, on the Scioto River 26 mi. (42 km.) E of Lima; pop. (1990c) 8356.

Kent Point. S tip of Kent I., Chesapeake Bay, Maryland.

Ken·tucky \kən-ˈtə-kē\. **1.** Navigable river, N cen. Kentucky; formed by confluence of forks in Lee co., flows NW into Ohio River in N Carroll co.; 259 mi. (417 km.) long.

2. An east central state of U.S.A., bounded on N by Illinois, Indiana, and Ohio, on E by West Virginia and Virginia, on S by Tennessee, and on W by Missouri; 37th state in area, 40,395 sq. mi. or 104,623 sq. km. (land area 39,851 sq. mi. or 103,214 sq. km.); 23d state in population, (1990c) 3,685,296; ✱ Frankfort; 15th state admitted to Union (1792). See table of states at UNITED STATES.

Nickname: Bluegrass State.

State flower: Goldenrod.

Motto: United We Stand, Divided We Fall.

Rivers: Ohio, forming N boundary of the state, and receiving in W the waters of the Tennessee and the Cumberland, and in N cen. region the waters of the Kentucky and the Licking.

Highest point: Black Mt., 4145 ft. (1263 m.), in Harlan co.

Chief products: Tobacco, corn, wheat; thoroughbred horses, cattle, hogs; oil, natural gas, coal; manufacturing: Kentucky bourbon whiskey, farm equipment, chemicals.

Chief cities: Louisville, Lexington, Owensboro, Covington, Bowling Green.

Political divisions: Divided into the following 120 counties (for pronunciation of their names, see their individual entries):

NAME	AREA[1] (sq. mi.)	AREA[1] (sq. km.)	POP. (1990c)	CO. SEAT(S)
Adair	393	1,018	15,360	Columbia
Allen	364	943	14,628	Scottsville
Anderson	206	534	14,571	Lawrenceburg
Ballard	259	671	7,902	Wickliffe
Barren	486	1,259	34,001	Glasgow
Bath	287	743	9,692	Owingsville
Bell	370	958	31,506	Pineville
Boone	249	645	57,589	Burlington
Bourbon[2]	300	777	19,236	Paris
Boyd	160	414	51,150	Catlettsburg
Boyle	183	474	25,641	Danville
Bracken	204	528	7,766	Brooksville
Breathitt	494	1,279	15,703	Jackson
Breckinridge	564	1,461	16,312	Hardinsburg
Bullitt	300	777	47,567	Shepherdsville
Butler	443	1,147	11,245	Morgantown
Caldwell	357	925	13,232	Princeton
Calloway	384	995	30,735	Murray
Campbell	149	386	83,866	Alexandria and Newport
Carlisle	195	505	5,238	Bardwell
Carroll	130	337	9,292	Carrollton
Carter	402	1,041	24,340	Grayson
Casey	435	1,127	14,211	Liberty
Christian	725	1,878	68,941	Hopkinsville
Clark	259	671	29,496	Winchester
Clay	474	1,228	21,746	Manchester
Clinton	190	492	9,135	Albany
Crittenden	365	945	9,196	Marion
Cumberland	310	803	6,784	Burkesville
Daviess	462	1,197	87,189	Owensboro
Edmonson[3]	304	787	10,357	Brownsville
Elliott	240	622	6,455	Sandy Hook
Estill	260	673	14,614	Irvine
Fayette[4]	280	725	225,366	Lexington
Fleming	350	907	12,292	Flemingsburg
Floyd	399	1,033	43,586	Prestonsburg
Franklin	211	546	43,781	Frankfort
Fulton	203	526	8,271	Hickman
Gallatin	100	259	5,393	Warsaw
Garrard	236	611	11,579	Lancaster
Grant	249	645	15,737	Williamstown
Graves	560	1,450	33,550	Mayfield
Grayson	512	1,326	21,050	Leitchfield
Green	282	730	10,371	Greensburg
Greenup	351	909	36,742	Greenup
Hancock	187	484	7,864	Hawesville
Hardin	616	1,595	89,240	Elizabethtown
Harlan	469	1,215	36,574	Harlan
Harrison	308	798	16,248	Cynthiana
Hart[3]	425	1,101	14,890	Munfordville
Henderson	433	1,121	43,044	Henderson
Henry	289	749	12,823	New Castle
Hickman	246	637	5,566	Clinton
Hopkins	553	1,432	46,126	Madisonville
Jackson	337	873	11,955	McKee
Jefferson	375	971	664,937	Louisville
Jessamine	177	458	30,508	Nicholasville
Johnson	264	684	23,248	Paintsville
Kenton	165	427	142,031	Independence
Knott	356	922	17,906	Hindman
Knox	373	966	29,676	Barbourville
Larue[5]	260	673	11,679	Hodgenville
Laurel	446	1,155	43,438	London
Lawrence	425	1,101	13,998	Louisa
Lee	210	544	7,422	Beattyville
Leslie	412	1,067	13,642	Hyden
Letcher	339	878	27,000	Whitesburg
Lewis	486	1,259	13,029	Vanceburg
Lincoln	340	881	20,045	Stanford
Livingston	312	808	9,062	Smithland
Logan	563	1,458	24,416	Russellville
Lyon	253	655	6,624	Eddyville
McCracken	250	648	62,879	Paducah
McCreary	408	1,057	15,603	Whitely City
McLean	257	666	9,628	Calhoun
Madison	446	1,155	57,508	Richmond
Magoffin	303	785	13,077	Salyersville
Marion	343	888	16,499	Lebanon
Marshall	303	785	27,205	Benton
Martin	231	598	12,526	Inez
Mason	238	616	16,666	Maysville
Meade	305	790	24,170	Brandenburg
Menifee	210	544	5,092	Frenchburg
Mercer	256	663	19,148	Harrodsburg
Metcalfe	296	767	8,963	Edmonton
Monroe	334	865	11,401	Tompkinsville
Montgomery	204	528	19,561	Mount Sterling
Morgan	369	956	11,648	West Liberty
Muhlenberg	481	1,246	31,318	Greenville
Nelson	437	1,132	29,710	Bardstown
Nicholas	204	528	6,725	Carlisle
Ohio	596	1,544	21,105	Hartford
Oldham	184	477	33,263	La Grange
Owen	351	909	9,035	Owenton
Owsley	197	510	5,036	Booneville
Pendleton	279	723	12,036	Falmouth
Perry	343	888	30,283	Hazard
Pike	786	2,036	72,583	Pikeville
Powell	173	448	11,686	Stanton
Pulaski	654	1,694	49,489	Somerset
Robertson	101	262	2,124	Mount Olivet
Rockcastle	311	805	14,803	Mount Vernon
Rowan	290	751	20,353	Morehead
Russell	238	616	14,716	Jamestown
Scott	284	736	23,867	Georgetown
Shelby	383	992	24,824	Shelbyville
Simpson	239	619	15,145	Franklin
Spencer	193	500	6,801	Taylorsville
Taylor	284	736	21,146	Campbellsville
Todd	376	974	10,940	Elkton
Trigg	459	1,189	10,361	Cadiz
Trimble	146	378	6,090	Bedford
Union	340	881	16,557	Morganfield
Warren	546	1,414	76,673	Bowling Green
Washington	307	795	10,441	Springfield
Wayne	440	1,140	17,468	Monticello
Webster	339	878	13,955	Dixon

\ə\ **abut** \ə̇\ matches \ᵊ\ kitten, Fr table \ər\ **further** \a\ **ash** \ā\ **ace** \ä\ **cot, cart** \ȧ\ Fr bac \au̇\ **out** \b̲\ Span Avila \ch\ **chin** \e\ **bet** \ē\ **easy** \g\ **go** \i\ **hit** \ī\ **ice** \j\ **job** \k̲\ Ger **ich, Buch** \ⁿ\ Fr **vin** \ŋ\ **sing** \ō\ **go** \ö\ **all** \ȯ\ **law** \œ\ Fr **bœuf** \œ̄\ Fr **feu** \ȯi\ **boy** \th\ **thin** \th̲\ **this** \ü\ **loot** \u̇\ **foot** \ue\ Ger **füllen** \ue̅\ Fr **rue** \y\ **yet** \ʸ\ Fr digne \ˈdēnʸ\, nuit \ˈnwʸē\ \yü\ **few** \yu̇\ **fury** \zh\ **vision**

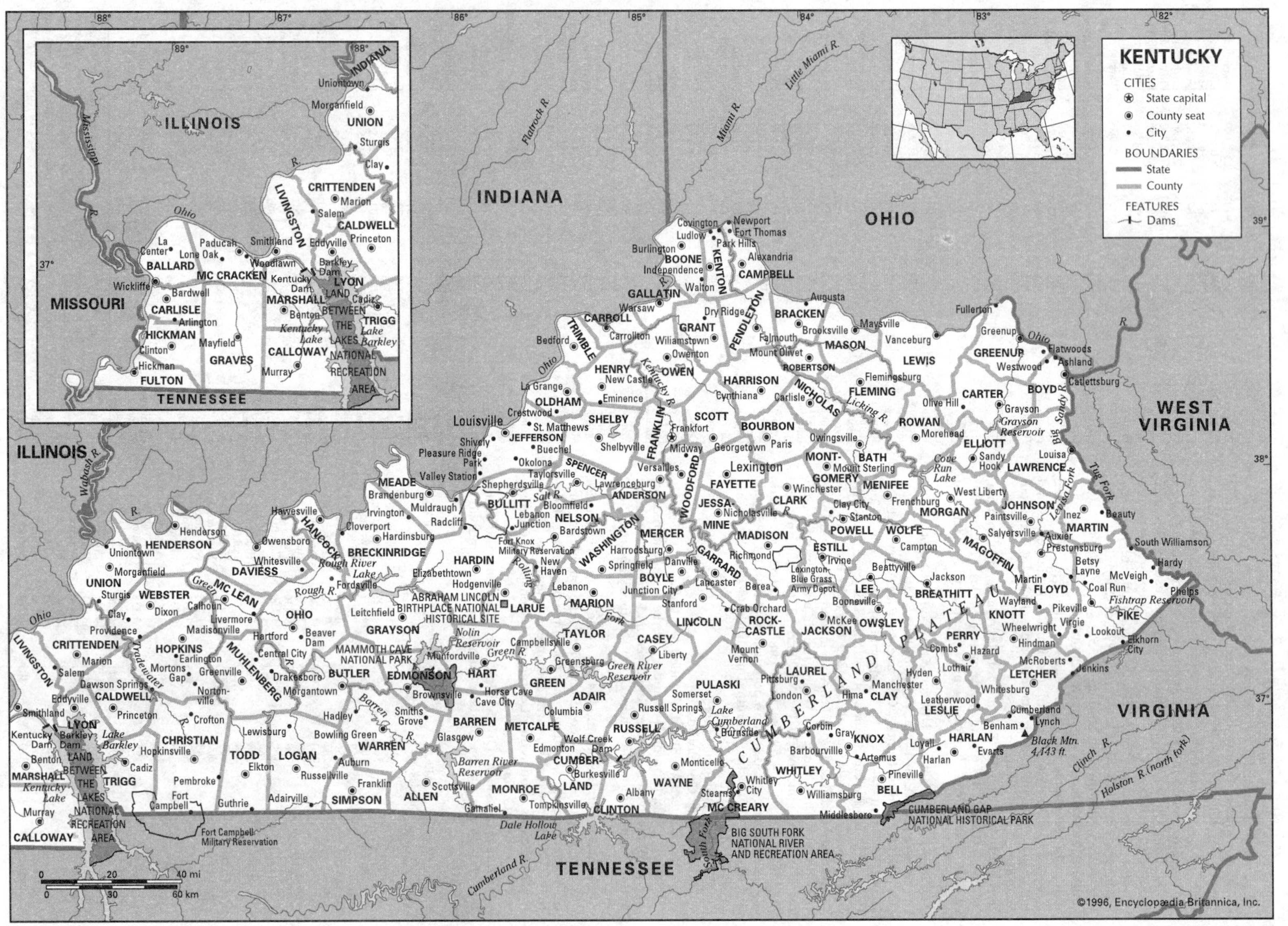
KENTUCKY
CITIES
State capital
County seat
City
BOUNDARIES
State
County
FEATURES
Dams
OHIO
INDIANA
ILLINOIS
MISSOURI
WEST VIRGINIA
VIRGINIA
TENNESSEE
Louisville
Lexington
Frankfort
Black Mtn. 4,143 ft.
CUMBERLAND PLATEAU
CUMBERLAND GAP NATIONAL HISTORICAL PARK
BIG SOUTH FORK NATIONAL RIVER AND RECREATION AREA
MAMMOTH CAVE NATIONAL PARK
ABRAHAM LINCOLN BIRTHPLACE NATIONAL HISTORICAL SITE
LAND BETWEEN THE LAKES NATIONAL RECREATION AREA
Fort Knox Military Reservation
Fort Campbell Military Reservation
JEFFERSON
FAYETTE
FRANKLIN
KENTON
BOONE
CAMPBELL
PIKE
HARLAN
BELL
WHITLEY
MC CREARY
WAYNE
CLINTON
MONROE
ALLEN
SIMPSON
LOGAN
TODD
CHRISTIAN
TRIGG
CALLOWAY
MARSHALL
LIVINGSTON
CRITTENDEN
UNION
HENDERSON
DAVIESS
HANCOCK
BRECKINRIDGE
MEADE
HARDIN
GRAYSON
EDMONSON
BUTLER
WARREN
BARREN
HART
OHIO
MC LEAN
MUHLENBERG
HOPKINS
WEBSTER
CALDWELL
LYON
BALLARD
MC CRACKEN
CARLISLE
HICKMAN
FULTON
GRAVES
0 20 40 mi
0 30 60 km
©1996, Encyclopædia Britannica, Inc.

NAME	AREA[1] (sq. mi.)	AREA[1] (sq. km.)	POP. (1990c)	CO. SEAT(S)
Whitley	459	1,189	33,326	Williamsburg
Wolfe	227	588	6,503	Campton
Woodford	193	500	19,955	Versailles

[1]Area = land area.
[2]The term *Bourbon whiskey* was orig. applied to corn whisky made in this county.
[3]Mammoth Cave National Park in Edmonson co. (E cen. and E; major portion of park, incl. Mammoth Cave itself) and Hart co. (W).
[4]Center of the "Bluegrass" region and of race-horse breeding; Lexington is now merged with Fayette co.
[5]Central portion contains Abraham Lincoln National Historical Park.

History: Inhabited by American Indian peoples before arrival of European explorers; entered by American explorer Thomas Walker 1750; included in territory ceded by French 1763; explored by expeditions under American pioneer Daniel Boone from 1769; first permanent English settlement at Boonesborough made by Transylvania Company 1775; because of its many Indian wars known as the "Dark and Bloody Ground"; organized as county of Virginia 1776; included in territory of U.S. by Treaty of Paris 1783; received consent of Virginia to statehood 1789; admitted to Union June 1, 1792; as border state during Civil War torn bet. North and South, providing troops to both sides; despite an attempt to be neutral, invaded by Confederate troops 1862; suffered skirmishes thereafter but remained in Union; adopted present constitution 1891.

Kentucky Dam. See table at TENNESSEE VALLEY AUTHORITY.

Kentucky Lake. Reservoir, W Kentucky and W Tennessee; created by Kentucky Dam in Tennessee River.

Kent·ville \ˈkent-ˌvil\. Town, ⊗ of Kings co., W Nova Scotia, Canada, 55 mi. (88 km.) NW of Halifax; pop. (1991c) 5506; settled c. 1760; near site of early Acadian settlements.

Kent·wood \ˈkent-ˌwu̇d\. City, Kent co., W Michigan, bordering Grand Rapids on the E and S; pop. (1990c) 37,826.

Ken·ya *also* **Ken·ia** \ˈken-yə, ˈkēn-\; *formerly* **East Africa Protectorate.** Republic, E Africa, bounded on NW by Sudan, on N by Ethiopia, on E by Somalia, on SE by the Indian Ocean, on S by Tanzania, and on W by Uganda; 224,960 sq. mi. (582,646 sq. km.); pop. (1993e) 28,113,000; ✱ Nairobi.

Physical features: Mountainous in W half, having two N to S ranges with the Great Rift Valley bet. them; highest peaks Mt. Kenya 17,058 ft. (5199 m.) in center, and Mt. Elgon 14,178 ft. (4321 m.) on Ugandan border. Lowland strip along coast extends gradually up into wide level plain which in the N is high and arid. Noted for its abundant wildlife. Rivers are Tana and Ewaso Ng'iro in the E and many short streams in the W flowing into lakes Victoria on SW and Turkana, a large long lake in NW; many small lakes in Great Rift Valley (*q.v.*).

Chief products: Coffee, cotton, wheat, sisal, corn, tea, rice, sugarcane, pyrethrum; soda ash, gold, limestone, diatomite, salt, fluorite ore; livestock raising; tourism (mostly related to wildlife safaris).

Chief towns: Nairobi, Mombasa, Kisumu, Nakuru.

Political divisions: Administratively divided into the Nairobi Area and seven provinces (for pronunciation of their names, see their individual entries):

NAME	AREA (sq. mi.)	AREA (sq. km.)	POP. (1990e)	CAPITAL
Nairobi	264	684	1,504,900	
Central	5,093	13,191	3,691,700	Nyeri
Coast	32,279	83,603	2,150,400	Mombasa
Eastern	61,734	159,891	4,367,900	Embu
North-Eastern	48,997	126,902	640,600	Garissa
Nyanza	6,240	16,162	4,322,700	Kisumu
Rift Valley	67,125	173,854	5,356,900	Nakuru
Western	3,228	8,360	2,836,700	Kakamega

History: Coast, long dominated by Arabs, seized 16th cent. by Portuguese, who were in turn expelled by Omanis; interior explored 19th cent. by Europeans and by Arab and Swahili traders; coastal strip belonging to ruler of Zanzibar (*q.v.*) leased 1887 to British East Africa Company (then Association) which later extended its holdings into the interior; boundaries with German East Africa (see TANZANIA) fixed

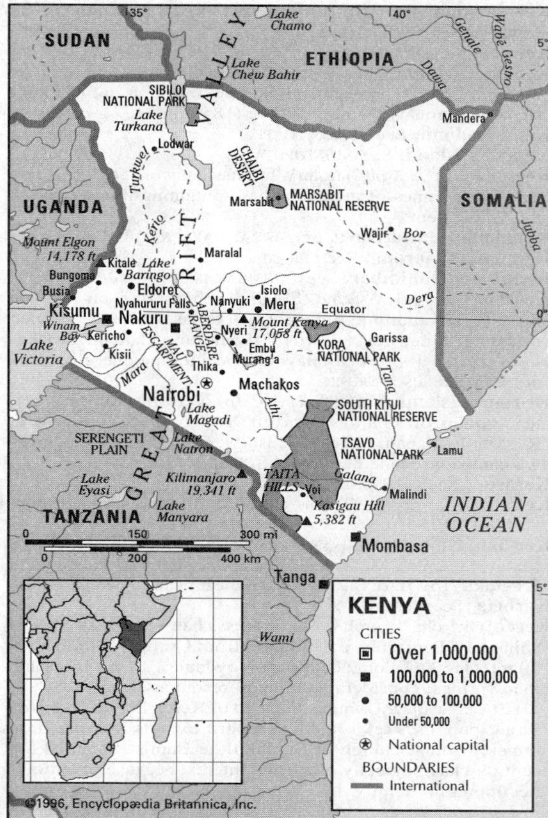

1886, 1890; region organized as British East Africa Protectorate 1895; except for the coastal strip (ab. 10 mi. or 16 km. wide, extending from S boundary to Tana River), which together with its islands was named Kenya Protectorate, region made British colony 1920; coastal strip to Kenya 1963 and along with colony became independent member of the Commonwealth 1963; established a republic 1964; formed (1967–77), with Tanzania and Uganda, the East African Community; suffered severe droughts latter part 20th cent.; multiparty system brought back 1991.

Kenya, Mount. Extinct volcano, cen. Kenya, near the Equator; 17,058 ft. (5199 m.); climbed 1899 by English geographer Sir Halford MacKinder.

Ken–zan–fu. See XI'AN.

Ke·o·kuk \ˈkē-ə-ˌkək\. **1.** County in SE cen. Iowa. See table at IOWA.

2. City, a ⊗ of Lee co., SE Iowa, on Mississippi River at extreme SE corner of state; pop. (1990c) 12,451; commercial center; rubber, die castings; diversified agriculture; site of **Keokuk Dam** (completed 1913 across Mississippi River, height 53 ft. or 16 m.), which impounds water, **Lake Keokuk,** for waterpower.

Ke·on·jhar \kā-ˈōn-jər\ *also* **Ke·un·jhar** \-ˈən-\. **1.** Former Indian state, now part of Orissa state, NE India; 3206 sq. mi. (8304 sq. km.).

2. Town, its ✱, 83 mi. (134 km.) N of Cuttack; pop. (1991p) 41,934.

Keos. See KÉA.

Ke·o·sau·qua \ˌkē-ə-ˈsȯ-kwə\. Town, ⊗ of Van Buren co., SE Iowa; pop. (1990c) 1020.
Keowee. See SENECA 2.
Kep·hart, Mount \ˈkep-ˌhärt\. Peak in Great Smoky Mts., on boundary bet. Tennessee and North Carolina 8 mi. (13 km.) NE of Clingmans Dome; 6100 ft. (1859 m.).
Kep i Rodonit. See RODONI, CAPE.
Keppel's Island. See NIUATOPUTAPU.
Ke·pu·lau·an \ˌkā-pü-ˈlau̇-än\. Indonesian word for "archipelago." For names of archipelagoes containing this word, see the 2d element.
Kepulauan Barat Daya. See BARAT DAYA, KEPULAUAN.
Kepulauan Gorong. See CERAM.
Kepulauan Tanimbar. See TANIMBAR ISLANDS.
Ke·ra·la \ˈker-ə-lə\. State, SW India, bordering on Arabian Sea; ✻ Trivandrum; rubber, tea, coffee, cashews, pepper, timber; fishing; major towns: Trivandrum, Calicut, Ernakulam; created 1956 for Malayalm-speaking people. See table at INDIA; see also COCHIN.
Ke·ra·ma Islands \ke-ˈrä-mä\ *or Jp.* **Kerama–Ret·tō** \-ˈret-tō\. Group of small islands off SW coast of Okinawa I., Ryukyu Is., Japan; largest Tokashiki; first landings in Okinawa campaign made here by U.S. forces Mar. 1945.
Kerasun. See GİRESUN.
Ke·ra·va \ˈke-rä-vä\. Town, Uusimaa prov., S Finland; pop. (1989c) 27,155.
Ker·bau, Gu·nong \ˈgü-ˌnȯŋ-ker-ˈbau̇\. Mountain (*gunong*) S Malaysia Penin., Malaysia, on boundary bet. NW Pahang and E Perak; 7159 ft. (2182 m.); 2d highest peak in Malay Penin.
Kerbela. See KARBALĀ'.
Kerch \ˈkerch, ˈkyerch\. **1.** *or Russ.* **Ker·chen·skiy** \ˈkyer-chin-skē\. Peninsula, extending E from Crimea, Ukraine; ab. 70 mi. (115 km.) long; consists of lowland with salt lakes and mud springs; considerable mineral resources.
2. City, E Crimea, Ukraine, at E end of Kerch Penin. on Kerch Strait; pop. (1991e) 178,000; seaport; exports iron ore; iron mines; fishing; church of St. John the Baptist, founded 8th cent.; archaeologically of special interest because of antiquities found in vicinity.
History: As ancient Greek colony of **Pan·ti·ca·pae·um** \ˌpan-tə-kə-ˈpē-əm\, founded by Milesians 6th cent. B.C.; with surrounding territory formed kingdom of the Cimmerian Bosporus (*q.v.*) which was later conquered by Pontus; held by Huns, Khazars, and other invaders of Crimea (*q.v.*); trading port held by Genoese from 14th to 15th cent. when Turks captured it; its conquest by Russia confirmed 1774; damaged in Crimean War. In WWII occupied by Germans.
Kerch Strait *or Russ.* **Ker·chen·skiy Pro·liv** \ˈkyer-chin-skē-prə-ˈlʸēf\; *formerly* **Ye·ni·ka·le Strait** \ˌye-nyi-kə-ˈlyä\; *anc.* **Cimmerian Bosporus** *or* **Bos·por·us Cim·me·ri·us** \ˈbäs-pə-rəs-sə-ˈmir-ē-əs\. Shallow strait connecting Sea of Azov with Black Sea; lies E of Kerch Penin.; 25 mi. (40 km.) long, 2 to 9 mi. (3 to 14 km.) wide.
Ke·rem·pe Cape \ˌker-em-ˈpā\ *or Turk.* **Kerempe Bu·run** \bu̇-ˈrün\. Cape on NW coast of Turkey in Asia, on the Black Sea bet. Zonguldak and Sinop.
Ke·ren *also* **Che·ren** \ˈke-ren\. Town, E cen. Eritrea; connected by rail with Asmara. Captured by British 1941.
Ker·gue·len Islands \ˈkər-gə-lən, ˌker-gā-ˈlen\ *also* **Des·o·la·tion Islands** \ˌde-sə-ˈlā-shən-, ˌde-zə-\ *or Fr.* **Îles de Dé·so·la·tion** \ˈēl-də-dā-zō-lä-ˈsyōⁿ\. French island group in S Indian Ocean, consisting of one major island, **Kerguelen** (2239 sq. mi. or 5799 sq. km.) and ab. 300 other islets (total area 2394 sq. mi. or 6200 sq. km.). Main island mountainous (highest point Mt. Ross 6430 ft. or 1960 m.) has irregular coastline and deep fjords with snowfields in central area and many lakes and pools in lower outer portion; Kerguelen cabbage (*Pringlea antiscorbutica*), a scurvy preventative, took its name from the islands. Discovered by French navigator Yves-Joseph de Kerguélen-Trémarec Feb. 1772; annexed by France 1893; became part of French Southern and Antarctic Territories 1955.
Ke·rin·ci *or* **Ke·rin·tji** *also* **Ko·rin·tji** \kə-ˈrin-chē\; *formerly* **In·dra·pu·ra** \ˌin-drə-ˈpu̇r-ə\. Volcanic peak, W cen. Sumatra, Indonesia, in Barisan Mts. 80 mi. (129 km.) SSE of Padang; 12,483 ft. (3805 m.); highest mountain in Sumatra.
Ke·rin·tji \ke-ˈrin-chē\ *or* **Ko·rin·tji** \kȯ-\. **1.** Lake in Barisan Mts., W Sumatra, Indonesia, 115 mi. (185 km.) SSE of Padang.
2. Volcanic peak, Sumatra, Indonesia. See KERINCI.
Ker·i·ya \ˌker-ē-ˈyä\ *or W.-G.* **K'o–li–ya** \ˈkə-ˈlē-ˈyä\ *also* **Kir·ia** \kir-ˈyä\. River, SW Xinjiang Uygur, W China; rises in Altun Shan and flows N into Taklamakan (desert).
Ker·ken·nah Islands \kər-ˈke-nə\ *or* **Iles Ker·ken·na** \ˈēl-ˌker-kā-ˈnȧ\ *or Arab.* **Ju·zur Qar·qan·nah** \ˌjə-zər-kär-ˈka-nə\; *anc.* **Cer·ci·na** \sər-ˈsī-nə\. Group of islands in cen. Mediterranean Sea, at N side of entrance to Gulf of Gabès and off E coast of Tunisia to which they belong; area 69 sq. mi. (179 sq. km.).
Kerkheh. See KARKHEH.
Ker·ki \ker-ˈkē\. Town, SE Turkmenistan, on left bank of Amu Dar'ya near Afghanistan border, 170 mi. (274 km.) SW of Samarqand.
Kerk·ra·de \ˈkerk-ˌrä-də\. Commune, Limburg prov., SE Netherlands, on German frontier 18 mi. (29 km.) E of Maastricht; pop. (1992e) 53,364; coal-mining center from 12th cent. to 1970s.
Kerkuk. See KIRKUK.
Kérkyra. See CORFU.
Kerma. See KARMAH.
Ker·mad·ec Islands \kər-ˈma-dək\. Island group in SW cen. Pacific Ocean, ab. 600 mi. (970 km.) NNW of New Zealand and ab. 500 mi. (800 km.) S of S Tonga; 13 sq. mi. (34 sq. km.); largest island Raoul, or Sunday I. Explored late 18th cent. by British and by French; annexed to New Zealand 1887.
Kermadec Trench. Ocean trench, SW Pacific Ocean, E of Kermadec Is., extending approx. from NE of Kermadec Is. to NE of North I., New Zealand; subduction zone according to theory of plate tectonics.
Ker·man \ˈker-mən\. City, Fresno co., S cen. California, 14 mi. (23 km.) W of the city of Fresno; pop. (1990c) 5448.
Ker·mān \kər-ˈmän, ker-\ *also* **Kir·man** \kər-, kir-\. **1.** *anc.* **Car·ma·nia** \kär-ˈmā-nē-ə, -nyə\. Province, SE Iran; ✻ Kermān; covers SW part of Plateau of Iran; ancient Carmania a subdivision of Ariana and a province of Persian Empire and of Macedonian King Alexander the Great's empire, bounded on N by Parthia, on E by Drangiana and Gedrosia, on S by water (*mod.* Persian Gulf and Gulf of Oman), and on W by Persis. See table at IRAN.
2. *anc.* **Car·ma·na** \kär-ˈmā-nə, -ˈma-, -ˈmä-\. City, its ✻, on road from Eşfahān and Yazd extending SE to Zāhedān; pop. (1986c) 257,284; manufactures shawls and carpets; among its several mosques one dates from 11th cent.; ruled by Sassanids 3d cent. A.D.; important under Şafavids 10th cent.
Kermānshāh. See BĀKHTARĀN 2.
Kermānshāhan. See BĀKHTARĀN 1.
Ker·mit \ˈkər-mit\. City, ⊗ of Winkler co., W Texas, 43 mi. (69 km.) NNE of Pecos; pop. (1990c) 6875.
Kern \ˈkərn\. **1.** River, S cen. California; rises in NE Tulare co., and flows SW through Bakersfield into Buena Vista Lake; 150 mi. (241 km.) long.
2. County in S California. See table at CALIFORNIA.
Ker·ners·ville \ˈkər-nərz-ˌvil\. Town, Forsyth co., N cen. North Carolina, 9 mi. (14 km.) E of Winston-Salem; pop. (1990c) 10,836.
Kern Peak \ˈkərn\. Mountain in the Sierra Nevada, E Tulare co., S cen. California; 11,510 ft. (3508 m.).
Kerns·town \ˈkərnz-ˌtau̇n\. Village, Frederick co., N Virginia, 4 mi. (6 km.) S of Winchester; battle Mar. 23, 1862 in which Union forces under Gen. Nathaniel Prentiss Banks defeated Gen. Thomas J. ("Stonewall") Jackson's Confederate troops.
Ké·ro·man \kā-rȯ-ˈmäⁿ\. Fishing port of Brittany, NW France, adjacent to Lorient; during WWII used by Germans as U-boat base; late 20th cent. base for French submarines.
Kerr \ˈkər\. County in SW cen. Texas. See table at TEXAS.
Kerr·ville \ˈkər-ˌvil, -vəl\. City, ⊗ of Kerr co., SW cen. Texas, 55 mi. (88 km.) NNW of San Antonio; pop. (1990c) 17,384; resort; Schreiner Coll. (1923).

Ker·ry \ˈker-ē\. County in Munster prov., SW Ireland; mountainous area, with many lakes (such as Lakes of Killarney); agriculture, dairy farming, fishing; exploitation of extensive peat bogs. See table at IRELAND.

Kerry Head. Cape on SW coast of Ireland, on S side of mouth of Shannon River.

Ker·shaw \kər-ˈshȯ\. County in N cen. South Carolina. See table at SOUTH CAROLINA.

Ker·u·len \ˈker-ə-ˌlen\. **1.** *or* **Her·len** \ˈhər-ˈlən\ *or W.-G.* **K'o–lu–lun** \ˈkō-ˈlü-ˈlu̇n\. River, NE Mongolia and NE China; rises in Hentiyn Nuruu, flows S then E to Hulun Nur in NW Manchuria; a headstream of the Amur; 785 mi. (1263 km.) long.
2. Town, Mongolia. See CHOYBALSAN.

Ke·she·na \kə-ˈshē-nə\. Unincorporated settlement, ⊗ of Menominee co., E cen. Wisconsin; pop. (1990c) 685.

Kes·ki–Suo·mi \ˈkes-kē-ˈswȯ-mē\. Province of S cen. Finland. See table at FINLAND.

Kes·sel Lo \ˈke-səl-lō\. Commune, Brabant prov., cen. Belgium, adjacent to Louvain 7 mi. (11 km.) E of Brussels.

Kes·te·ven, The Parts of \ke-ˈstē-vən\. See LINCOLNSHIRE 2.

Kes·wick \ˈke-zik\. Town, Cumbria, NW England, near N end of Derwent Water, 3.5 mi. (5.6 km.) S of Skiddaw; pop. (1981c) 5645; a major Lake District tourist center; home of poets Samuel Taylor Coleridge 1800–03 and Robert Southey 1803–43. Scene of first Keswick Convention, a religious revival movement 1875.

Keszt·hely \ˈkest-hā\. Commune, Veszprem co., W Hungary, at W end of Lake Balaton; pop. (1991e) 23,200.

Ket' \ˈket^{y}\ *or* **Ket** \ˈket\. Navigable river, S cen. Russia in Asia; rises N of the city of Krasnoyarsk in SW Krasnoyarsk Kray, flows W into Ob' River at Kolpashevo; 842 mi. (1355 km.) long.

Ke·ta *or* **Ki·ta** \ˈkē-tä\ *or* **Kwit·ta** \ˈkwi-tä\. Seaport, E Ghana, on **Keta Lagoon;** pop. (1984c) 12,595.

Ketch·i·kan \ˈke-chi-ˌkan\. Town and seaport on SW coast of Revillagigedo I., SE Alaska; pop. (1990c) 8263; pulp mill; salmon fishing; gold mining historically important.

Ketchikan Gateway. Division in Alaska. See table at ALASKA.

Ketch·um \ˈke-chəm\. Village, Blaine co., cen. Idaho, SE of Sawtooth Range; pop. (1990c) 2523; just N of it is Sun Valley (*q.v.*).

Ke·toi \ke-ˈtȯi\. One of the Kuril Is. (*q.v.*).

Kęt·rzyn \ˈkent-ˌchin\ *or Ger.* **Ra·sten·burg** \ˈräs-tən-ˌbu̇rk\. City, NE Olsztyn prov., N Poland, W of Lake Mamry; pop. (1989e) 30,046.

Ket·ter·ing \ˈke-tə-riŋ\. **1.** City, Montgomery co., SW Ohio, S of Dayton; pop. (1990c) 60,569; Kettering Coll. of Medical Arts (1967).
2. Town, Northamptonshire, cen. England, 50 mi. (80 km.) E of Birmingham; pop. (1991p) 75,200; boots and shoes.

Ket·tle \ˈket-^{ə}l\. River, British Columbia, Canada, and NE Washington; rises in British Columbia, flows S across Washington border, bends NE and enters British Columbia for a short distance, then turns S across border and joins Columbia River in E Ferry co., Washington; ab. 160 mi. (255 km.) long.

Kettle Dome. Peak in the Sierra Nevada, E Fresno co., S cen. California; 9452 ft. (2881 m.).

Kettle Peak. Mountain in the Sierra Nevada, N Tulare co., S cen. California; 10,038 ft. (3060 m.).

Kettle River Range. Range in N Ferry co., NE Washington, extending N into British Columbia, Canada.

Keu·ka Lake \ˈkyü-kə; kā-ˈyü-kə, kē-\. Lake in W New York; extends across boundary bet. Yates and Steuben cos.; 17.5 sq. mi. (45.3 sq. km.); ab. 18 mi. (29 km.) long and 1.5 mi. (2.4 km.) av. width; one of the Finger Lakes; outlet from N end into Seneca Lake; vineyards along its shores.

Keuka Park. Village, Yates co., W New York, on Keuka Lake; Keuka Coll. (1890).

Keunjhar. See KEONJHAR.

Ke·ve·laer \ˈkā-və-ˌlär\. Town, North Rhine-Westphalia, Germany, NW of Düsseldorf; pop. (1980c) 21,614.

Kew \ˈkyü\. **1.** Municipality, S Victoria, SE Australia, NE suburb of Melbourne; pop. (1991c) 27,291.
2. Parish, Greater London borough of Richmond upon Thames, SE England; Royal Botanic Gardens, originated in 1759 and became a national establishment 1841; Gardens have more than 25,000 varieties; area with adjoining pleasure grounds 288 acres (117 hectares).

Ke·wa·nee \ki-ˈwä-nē\. City, Henry co., NW Illinois, 38 mi. (61 km.) ESE of Rock Island; pop. (1990c) 12,969; boilers, work clothes, metal products, agricultural machinery.

Ke·wau·nee \ki-ˈwä-nē\. **1.** County in E Wisconsin. See table at WISCONSIN.
2. City, its ⊗, on Lake Michigan 25 mi. (40 km.) E of Green Bay (city); pop. (1990c) 2750.

Ke·wee·naw \ˈkē-wi-ˌnȯ\. County at N tip of Lower Penin. of Michigan. See table at MICHIGAN.

Keweenaw Bay. Inlet of Lake Superior, NW Upper Penin. of Michigan, SE of Keweenaw and upper Houghton cos. and extending S into Baraga co.

Keweenaw National Historical Park. See UNITED STATES, *National Historical Parks.*

Keweenaw Peninsula. Peninsula, NW part of Upper Penin. of Michigan, incl. Keweenaw co. and part of Houghton co., extending into Lake Superior; tip end is called **Keweenaw Point**. The **Keweenaw Waterway** crosses the peninsula from Keweenaw Bay, through Portage Lake to Lake Superior, shortening the route to Duluth, Minnesota.

Kew Gardens. Residential community, cen. Queens borough of New York City, Queens co., SE New York, on Long Island.

Kexholm. See PRIOZERSK.

Keya Pa·ha \ˈkē-ə-ˈpä-ˌhä\. **1.** River in Nebraska and South Dakota; 101 mi. (162 km.) long; tributary of the Niobrara.
2. County in N Nebraska. See table at NEBRASKA.

Key Bis·cayne \ˈkē-bis-ˈkān\. Island off coast of Miami-Dade co., SE Florida, bet. N Biscayne Bay and Atlantic Ocean; site of former vacation home of U.S. President Richard M. Nixon.

Key Lar·go \ˈlär-gō\. One of the larger of the Florida Keys, 30 mi. (48 km.) long, less than 2 mi. (3 km.) wide; traversed by the first island link of the Overseas Highway (see FLORIDA KEYS); diving and snorkeling.

Keyn·sham \ˈkān-shəm\. Town, Avon, England; pop. (1981p) 20,443.

Key·port \ˈkē-ˌpōrt\. **1.** Borough, Monmouth co., E cen. New Jersey, on Raritan Bay 7 mi. (11 km.) SSE of Perth Amboy; pop. (1990c) 7586.
2. Village, Kitsap co., W Washington, on arm of Puget Sound N of Bremerton; Naval Undersea Museum.

Key·ser \ˈkī-zər\. City, ⊗ of Mineral co., NE West Virginia, on N branch of the Potomac River; pop. (1990c) 5870; Potomac State Coll. of West Virginia Univ. (1901); supply point and battleground in Civil War.

Key·stone \ˈkē-ˌstōn\. City, McDowell co., S West Virginia, 8 mi. (13 km.) E of Welch; pop. (1990c) 627.

Keytes·ville \ˈkēts-ˌvil\. City, ⊗ of Chariton co., N cen. Missouri; pop. (1990c) 985.

Key Vaca \ˈva-kə\. See FLORIDA KEYS.

Key West \ˈwest\. City, ⊗ of Monroe co., SW corner of Florida, on **Key West Island** (less than 4 mi. or 6 km. long by 2 mi. or 3 km. wide at SW extremity of Florida Keys) 60 mi. (96 km.) SW of S tip of Florida; pop. (1990c) 24,832; southernmost city of the Lower 48 and S terminus of U.S. Route 1; tourism; winter resort; commercial and recreational fishing (formerly incl. turtles); cigar making; Fort Zachary Taylor; daily sunset gathering at Mallory Square Dock; Florida Keys Community Coll. (1965); Key West Naval Air Station estab. as a naval station 1822; city incorp. 1828, first in S Florida to do so; home at various times to American writers Ernest Hemingway, Elizabeth Bishop, and Tennessee Williams among others, and to naturalist John James Audubon.

\ə\ abut \ˈə\ matches \$^{ə}$\ kitten, Fr table \ər\ **further** \a\ ash \ā\ ace
\ä\ cot, cart \a̮\ Fr bac \au̇\ **out** \b\ Span Avila \ch\ **chin** \e\ bet \ē\ easy
\g\ go \i\ hit \ī\ ice \j\ job \k̲\ Ger **ich**, **Buch** \$^{n}$\ Fr vin
\ŋ\ sing \ō\ go \ö\ all \ȯ\ **law** \œ\ Fr bœuf \œ̄\ Fr feu \ȯi\ boy
\th\ **thin** \t̲h̲\ **this** \ü\ loot \u̇\ **foot** \ue\ Ger füllen \ue̅\ Fr **rue**
\y\ yet \$^{y}$\ Fr digne \ˈdēn^{y}\, nuit \ˈnw^{y}ē\ \yü\ **few** \yu̇\ fury \zh\ vision

Kha·ba·rovsk \k̲ə-'bär-əfsk\. City, ✻ of Khabarovsk Kray, SE Russia in Asia, on right bank of Amur River 29 mi. (47 km.) below Ussuri tributary; pop. (1992e) 615,000; junction station on Trans-Siberian R.R.; market for products of the Ussuri Valley; educational center; oil refining; ship repair; machinery, lumber, furniture; site of fort estab. 1652; settled by Russian colonists under Count N. Muravyov-Amursky 1858.

Khabarovsk Kray \'krī\. A territory of E Russia in Asia, along Sea of Okhotsk Coast, bounded on W and NW by Sakha Rep., on NE by Magadan Oblast, on E by Sea of Okhotsk, on SE by Primorskiy Kray, on S by China, and on SW by Amur Oblast; 318,378 sq. mi. (824,599 sq. km.); pop. (1992e) 1,855,000; ✻ Khabarovsk; includes the Jewish Autonomous Oblast.

Rivers: S part lies in basin of the lower Amur, which forms for ab. 700 mi. (1125 km.) the boundary with China; other rivers are the Zeya and Amgun, tributaries of the Amur, and the upper courses of the Maya and Kolyma.

Mountains: Traversed by numerous ranges, running generally NE and SW, esp. E end of the Stanovoi Mts.

Chief products: Potatoes, wheat, oats, corn; has great mineral resources, esp. in coal and iron, also manganese, molybdenum; steel industry at Komsomol'sk-na-Amure and other cities; oil refineries, mills and factories; fishing and agriculture.

Chief cities: Khabarovsk, Komsomolsk-na-Amure, Sovetskaya Gavan', Birobidzhan.

History: First settlements were estab. by Cossacks in latter half of 17th cent.; settlements along the Amur began in 19th cent. and Amur made the boundary by Treaty of Aigun 1858; Trans-Siberian R.R. completed c. 1915; much disorder in region 1917–20 but independent Far Eastern Republic set up 1920; estab. 1938. See FAR EASTERN REGION.

Khā·būr *also* **Kha·bour** \'k̲ä-,bu̇r\; *anc.* **Ha·bor** \'hā-,bȯr\. River, SE Turkey in Asia and NE Syria; rises in S slopes of Karacadağ and flows S into the Euphrates River just below the town of Dayr az Zawr; ab. 200 mi. (320 km.) long.

Kha·bu·ra \k̲ȧ-'bu̇r-ə\ *or* **Al–Khā·bū·rah** \ȧl-\. Coastal town, Oman, SE Arabian Penin., on Gulf of Oman ab. 100 mi. (160 km.) WNW of Masqat.

Kha·fa·je \'kä-fə-,yā\. Site of ancient Sumerian city, Mesopotamia, E Iraq, on E bank of Diyala River just E of Baghdad; has revealed archaeological objects, esp. building remains dating ab. 3d millennium B.C.

Khaibar. See KHYBER.

Khaifa. See HAIFA.

Khai·ra·garh \'kī-rə-,gär\. **1.** Former Indian state, now part of Madhya Pradesh, India; 931 sq. mi. (2411 sq. km.). **2.** Town, its ✻, 107 mi. (172 km.) E of Nagpur; pop. (1981p) 9812; music academy.

Khair·pur \'kīr-,pu̇r\. **1.** Former Indian state, now part of Sind, Pakistan, E of the Indus River; 5989 sq. mi. (15,512 sq. km.); loyal to British in Afghan campaigns of 19th cent. **2.** Town, its ✻, 15 mi. (24 km.) S of Sukkur; pop. (1981c) 61,447; textiles.

Kha·kas·sia \kə-'käs-yə, kə-'ka-zhə\. Republic of S Russia in Asia; 23,900 sq. mi. (61,901 sq. km.); pop. (1992e) 581,000; ✻ Abakan; mountainous; corn, wheat; lumbering; copper, coal, gold, and iron mines; formed as **Khakass Autonomous Oblast** 1930; became a republic 1991.

Khalépa. See HALEPA.

Kha·li·fat \'kə-li-fət\. Peak, N Baluchistan, Pakistan, E of Quetta; 11,434 ft. (3485 m.).

Khalīj at–Ṭīnah. See PELUSIUM.

Khalīj Surt. See SIDRA, GULF OF.

Khalīl, Al–. See HEBRON 4.

Khal·kē \'k̲äl-kē\ *also* **Kar·chi** \'kär-kē\ *or Ital.* **Cal·chi** \'käl-kē\. Island, Greece, in the Dodecanese (*q.v.*) W of Rhodes; 12 sq. mi. (31 sq. km.).

Khalkidhikí. See CHALCIDICE.

Khal·kís \k̲äl-'kēs\ *or* **Chal·cis** \'kal-səs\ *also* **Chal·kís** \k̲äl-'kēs\; *formerly* **Eu·ri·pus** \'e-vrē-pəs\. City, ✻ of Euboea dept., Greece, on Euboea I. on Evripos Strait; pop. (1991c) 51,482; important as a commercial center as early as 7th cent. B.C.; established colonies in Macedonia, Italy, Sicily; base for campaigns against Greece. Philosopher Aristotle died here 322 B.C. Became part of Greece 1830. See ERETRIA.

Kham·bhat \'kəm-bət\ *or* **Cam·bay** \kam-'bā\. Town, W India, in Gujarat, at N end of Gulf of Khambhat and at mouth of Mahi River 240 mi. (386 km.) N of Bombay; pop. (1991p) 76,724; ✻ of former state of Cambay. Mentioned by Venetian traveler Marco Polo in 1293 as one of India's two most important seaports; silting up of harbor in recent times has diverted former trade; has Jain ruins and remains of encircling wall. Held by Marathas during 18th cent.; ceded to British early 19th cent.

Khambhat, Gulf of *or* **Gulf of Cambay.** Inlet of Arabian Sea on W coast of India, SE of Kathiawar Penin.; gradually being filled with silt; receives Tāpi and Mahi rivers.

Kham·gaon \'käm-,gau̇n\. Town, N Maharashtra, cen. India, 166 mi. (267 km.) W of Nagpur; pop. (1991p) 73,705.

Kha·mīs Mus·hayṭ \kä-'mēs-mu̇s-'hīt, -'hāt\. City, S Saudi Arabia, in a mountainous agricultural area.

Kham·man \'kə-məm\. Town, N cen. Andhra Pradesh, India; pop. (1981c) 98,757.

Kham·seh *or* **Kham·se** \käm-'sā\. Former province, NW Iran; 10,825 sq. mi. (28,037 sq. km.); ✻ Zanjān.

Khā·na·qīn \,kä-nə-'kēn\. Town on E frontier of Iraq, 90 mi. (145 km.) NE of Baghdad on a tributary of the Diyala; in oil-producing region.

Khan Bagh·da·di \,k̲än-bəg-'dȧ-dē\ *or* **Khān al–Bagh·da·dī** \ȧl-\. Town, W cen. Iraq, on W bank of Euphrates 20 mi. (32 km.) NW of Hit; battle Mar. 1918 in WWI in which Turks were defeated by British.

Khan·ba·lik *or* **Khan·ba·liq** \,kän-bə-'lēk\. Mongol name of Kublai Khan's ✻ of China, transferred by him 1267 to the site of the earlier Yen, corresponding to the modern Beijing (*q.v.*); called **Cam·ba·luc** \'kam-bə-,lək\ by Venetian traveler Marco Polo who described it as a magnificent city; its Chinese name was **Ta–tu** \'dä-'dü\ ("great capital").

Khand·pa·ra \kənd-'pär-ə\. **1.** Former Indian state, now part of Orissa state, NE India; 229 sq. mi. (593 sq. km.). **2.** Town, its ✻, S of the Mahanadi and 50 mi. (80 km.) W of Cuttack.

Khand·wa \'kənd-wä\. Town, S Madhya Pradesh, India, 185 mi. (298 km.) WNW of Nagpur; pop. (1991p) 145,111; rail junction and cotton center.

Khanhhoa. See DIEN KHANH.

Khaniá. See CANEA.

Kha·ní·on, Kól·pos \'köl-,pös-k̲ä-'nē-,ön\ *or* **Ca·nea Bay** \kə-'nē-ə\. Inlet of Sea of Crete on N coast of Crete, Greece, at its W end; enclosed on E by Akroteri Penin.

Khan·ka \'kän-kə\ *or Pinyin* **Xing·kai** *or W.-G.* **Hsing–k'ai** \'shiŋ-'kī\. Lake, on boundary bet. China and Primorskiy Kray, SE Russia in Asia, N of Vladivostok; ab. S three quarters lies in Russian territory; 1700 sq. mi. (4400 sq. km.); 55 mi. (88 km.) long; max. depth 33 ft. (10 m.); unnavigable for large vessels; well stocked with fish; outlet is a W tributary of the Ussuri.

Khan·lar \kən-'lär\; *formerly* **Bi·bi Ei·bat** \bē-'bē-ā-'bät\. Locality, Apsheron Penin., Azerbaijan, 5 mi. (8 km.) W of Baku; has one of oldest and richest oil fields in Europe.

Khan–Ten·gri \'k̲ən-tyin-'grē\ *also* **Tengri Khan.** Mountain in the cen. Tian Shan, on boundary bet. Kyrgyzstan, and Xinjiang Uygur, China; 23,620 ft. (7199 m.).

Khan·ty–Man·si Autonomous Okrug \k̲ən-'tē-mən-'sē ...'ȯ-,krük\; *from 1930 to 1940* **Ostyak–Vo·gul National Okrug** \,əs-,tyȧk-və-'gül\. Administrative district, Tyumen' Oblast, W Russia in Asia; 201,969 sq. mi. (523,100 sq. km.); pop. (1992e) 1,305,000; ✻ **Khanty–Man·siysk** \-mən-'sēsk\, town at junction of the Ob' and Irtysh rivers; a large area of marshland traversed by Ob' and Irtysh rivers; oil and natural gas deposits; estab. 1930.

Khan Yun·is \k̲än-'yü-nis\. Frontier town, Gaza Strip, near coast and Egyptian border 5 mi. (8 km.) NE of Rafah and ab. 15 mi. (25 km.) SW of Gaza.

Khanzi. See GHANSI.

Khao Luang *or* **Kao Luang** \'kau̇-'lwäŋ\. Isolated peak, SW Thailand; in cen. Malay Penin. W of Nakhon Si Thammarat; 5860 ft. (1786 m.).

Kha·rag·pur \ˈkər-əg-ˌpu̇r\ *or* **Kha·rak·pur** \ˈkər-ək-\. City, West Bengal, NE India, on Kasai River 65 mi. (104 km.) W of Calcutta; pop. (1991p) 279,736; Indian Institute of Technology (1951).

Kha·ra Kho·to \ˌk̲är-ə-ˈkō-tō\ *or* **Ka·ra·kho·to** \ˌkär-ə-\. Ruined town, Nei Monggol (Inner Mongolia), N China, on E edge of an intermittent river valley and on S edge of Gobi Desert; discovered 1909, with its valuable library of 2500 volumes, by Russian scientist Pëtr Kozlov; formerly a great trade center, possibly the Etzina of Venetian traveler Marco Polo.

Khara Nur. See HAR NUUR.

Khara Usu Nur. See HAR US NUUR.

Kharbin. See HARBIN.

Kharg. See KHĀRK.

Khār·ga \ˈk̲är-gə, ˈkär-\. Valley and oasis in Egypt, 25°30′N, 30°35′E; chief town Al Khārijah.

Khārijah, Al *or* **Khârga, El.** See AL KHĀRIJAH.

Kha·rim·ko·tan \kə-ˌrēm-kə-ˈtän\ *or Jp.* **Ha·ri·mu·ko·tan** \ˌhär-ē-mu̇-ˈkō-ˌtän\. Small island of the Kuril Is., S of Onekotan; transferred to U.S.S.R. by Yalta agreement (1945).

Kharj, Al. See AL KHARJ.

Khārk \ˈk̲ärk\ *or* **Kharg** \ˈk̲arg\. Small island in NE Persian Gulf, off SW coast of Iran, NW of Būshehr; site of major oil-export terminal; important as last Dutch foothold in Persian Gulf, given up 1766 after destruction of factory by Persians; oil storage and shipment disrupted during war with Iraq 1980s.

Khar·kiv \ˈk̲är-kəf\ *or* **Khar·kov** \-kəf, -ˌko̐f\ **1.** Administrative subdivision of Ukraine; 12,124 sq. mi. (31,401 sq. km.); pop. (1991e) 3,194,800; ✽ Kharkiv; crossed by Donets River; wheat, corn, sugar beets, hemp.

2. City, ✽ of Kharkiv subdivision, Ukraine, on small tributaries of the Donets 400 mi. (644 km.) S of Moscow, Russia; pop. (1991e) 1,623,000; railroad, industrial, and cultural center; its proximity to the coal of the Donets Basin and the iron of Krivoi Rog has made it a center for manufacture of heavy metal products, incl. agricultural machinery, electrical equipment, turbines, locomotives, machine tools; university (founded 1805); several institutes; museums; cathedral.

History: Founded 1656 as an outpost fortress of Moscow; kept by Cossacks in allegiance to Russian czars during 17th cent.; increased rapidly in importance with development of the Donbas (Donets Basin); in WWI seized by Germans Apr. 1918; suffered considerably in civil war period until 1920; ✽ of new Ukrainian S.S.R., U.S.S.R. 1921–34; in WWII held by Germans 1941–1943.

Kharput. See HARPUT.

Khar·ta·phu \ˈkär-tə-ˌpü\. Peak in the Himalayas, NE of Mt. Everest; 23,800 ft. (7254 m.).

Khar·ti·chang·ri \ˌkär-tə-ˈchäŋ-rē\. Peak in the Himalayas, NE of Mt. Everest; 23,420 ft. (7138 m.).

Khar·toum *also* **Khar·tum** \k̲är-ˈtüm\. **1.** Former province of NE cen. Sudan; ✽ Khartoum.

2. City, ✽ of Sudan, at junction of White Nile and Blue Nile; pop. (1990e) 1,950,000; transportation and trade center; gum processing; cotton, textiles, glass; printing; university (1956), Industrial Research Institute (1965); founded under Egyptian ruler Muḥammad ʽAlī Pasha in early 1820s; leader of Anglo-Egyptian forces Charles "Chinese" Gordon killed and city captured by Sudanese religious and nationalist leader Muḥammad Aḥmad (known as "al-Mahdī") 1885; reoccupied by British led by Lord Kitchener 1898 and rebuilt.

Khartoum North *or* **North Khartoum.** Suburb of the city of Khartoum, Sudan; pop. (1983c) 341,146; textile mills; agricultural college (1954); under siege by al-Mahdī's army 1885.

Khart·syzsk \kərt-ˈsisk\. Town, Donets'k subdivision, Ukraine, ab. 17 mi. (27 km.) E of the city of Donetsk; pop. (1991e) 69,000.

Kha·ruf, Je·bel \ˌje-bəl-k̲ä-ˈrüf\. Mountain, on boundary bet. SW Israel and NE Sinai Penin.; 3301 ft. (1006 m.).

Kha·sav·yurt \ˌk̲ä-säv-ˈyu̇rt\. Town, NW Dagestan, S Russia in Europe, 45 mi. (72 km.) WNW of Makhachkala; on railroad line in hilly region; practically destroyed during civil war 1917–21.

Khashm al–Qir·bah \ˈk̲ash-ᵊm-ȧl-ˈkir-bə\ *or* **Khashm al–Gir·ba** \-ˈgir-bə\. Town, Sudan, ab. 230 mi. (370 km.) ESE of Khartoum; resettlement area for some evacuees from Wadi Halfa (*q.v.*), as a result of building of Aswān High Dam late 1960s.

Khasi Hills \ˈkä-sē\. Hill region, Meghalaya and Assam, NE India, bet. the Brahmaputra and Surma rivers; highest peak 6433 ft. (1961 m.).

Khasi States. Group of 25 former Indian states in Khasi Hills, now part of Assam and Meghalaya states, NE India; 3788 sq. mi. (9811 sq. km.); chief town Shillong; largest were Khyrim and Mylliem.

Khas·ko·vo \ˈk̲äs-kō-ˌvō\ *or* **Has·ko·vo** \ˈhäs-\. **1.** Region of S Bulgaria. See table at BULGARIA.

2. City, its ✽, 35 mi. (56 km.) S of Stara Zagora; pop. (1991e) 95,807; tobacco and other agricultural products; textiles.

Kha·tan·ga \k̲ə-ˈtäŋ-gə\. **1.** River, E Taymyr Autonomous Okrug, N Russia in Asia; rises in highlands N of Arctic Circle in NE Krasnoyarsk Kray, flows SE and N through broad estuary (**Khatanga Bay**) to Laptev Sea.

2. Town on right bank of Khatanga River ab. 150 mi. (240 km.) from its mouth.

Khatmandu. See KATHMANDU.

Kha·wak Pass \kə-ˈwək\. Pass in E Hindu Kush, Afghanistan; alt. 11,640 ft. (3548 m.).

Kha·zar·ia \kə-ˈzar-ē-ə\. Ancient region of SE Russia, inhabited 6th–10th cents. A.D. by the Khazars or Chozars, probably of Turkish origin. At first their home was in the Caucasus but later they controlled the lands bet. the Caucasus Mts. and the Volga and Don rivers and even beyond to the Dnieper River and Crimea and organized the trade routes bet. the Black Sea and the Caspian Sea; in 8th cent. the aristocracy embraced Judaism; conquered by Russians in 10th and 11th cents.

Khazzān Jabal Al–Awliyā. See JEBEL AULIA.

Kheda. See KAIRA.

Khelat. See KALAT.

Khem–Belder. See KYZYL.

Khem·ma·rat *or* **Ke·ma·rat** \ˈkā-mə-ˌrät\. Town on Mekong River, E Thailand.

Kher·son \k̲er-ˈso̐n\. **1.** Administrative subdivision of S Ukraine; borders on Black Sea and Sea of Azov and connects on S with Crimea; 10,927 sq. mi. (28,301 sq. km.); pop. (1991e) 1,258,700; ✽ Kherson; crossed by lower Dnieper River; agricultural region.

2. Seaport city, its ✽, on the Dnieper ab. 19 mi. (31 km.) from its mouth; pop. (1991e) 365,000; shipyards; has rail connection with Mykolayiv 35 mi. (56 km.) to the NW; harbor closed by ice Dec. to early Mar.; founded 1778 by Russian statesman Grigory Potemkin as a naval station and fortress; in WWII held by Germans.

Khe·ta \ˈk̲e-tə\. River, chief tributary of the Khatanga in Taymyr Autonomous Okrug, N Russia in Asia; flows N and NE; ab. 500 mi. (805 km.) long.

Khil·chi·pur \ˈkil-chi-ˌpu̇r\. Former state, cen. India, now part of Madhya Pradesh; 274 sq. mi. (710 sq. km.).

Khi·lok \k̲ē-ˈlo̐k\. River, SW Chita Oblast and S Buryatia Rep., S Russia in Asia; rises in Yablonovyy Mts., flows SW into Selenga River above Ulan Ude; 380 mi. (611 km.) long.

Khim·ki \ˈk̲ēm-kē\. Town, Moscow Oblast, W cen. Russia in Europe, ab. 10 mi. (16 km.) NW of the city of Moscow; pop. (1992e) 135,000.

Khing·an Mountains \ˈk̲iŋ-ˈän, ˈshiŋ-\. Two mountain ranges of E Asia: Da Hinggan Ling and Xiao Hinggan Ling (*qq.v.*).

Khí·os. See CHIOS.

Khir·bat Qum·ran *or* **Khir·bet Qumran** \kir-ˈbat-ku̇m-ˈrän\ *also* **Qumran**. Locality, West Bank near NW shore of the

\ə\ abut \ᵊ\ kitten, Fr table \ər\ further \a\ ash \ā\ ace \ä\ cot, cart \ȧ\ Fr bac \au̇\ out \b̲\ Span Avila \ch\ chin \e\ bet \ē\ easy \g\ go \i\ hit \ī\ ice \j\ job \k̲\ Ger ich, Buch \ⁿ\ Fr vin \ŋ\ sing \ō\ go \ö\ all \o̐\ law \œ\ Fr bœuf \œ̄\ Fr feu \o̐i\ boy \th\ thin \t̲h̲\ this \ü\ loot \u̇\ foot \ue\ Ger füllen \ue̅\ Fr rue \y\ yet \ʸ\ Fr digne \ˈdēnʸ\, nuit \ˈnwʸē\ \yü\ few \yu̇\ fury \zh\ vision

Dead Sea, in region occupied by Israel 1967; site of an ancient religious community (c. 100 B.C.–68 A.D.) of a Jewish sect, probably Essenes. Nearby is a series of caves in which since 1947 have been found manuscripts left by this group and known as the Dead Sea Scrolls.

Khirbat Saylūn. See SHILOH 2.

Khirbet Qumran. See KHIRBAT QUMRAN.

Khirgis Nur. See HYARGAS NUUR.

Khitai. See CATHAY.

Khiuma. See HIIUMAA.

Khi·va \ˈk̲ē-və\. **1.** *anc.* **Cho·ras·mia** \kȯ-ˈraz-mē-ə\; *later* **Khwā·rizm** \ˈk̲wä-ˌriz-ᵊm\. Former khanate, W Asia, on left bank of the lower Oxus (Amu Dar'ya); after its conquest by the Russians 1873 incorp. as subject territory in the empire; declared a republic 1920 and included in Uzbek and Turkmen S.S.R.s, U.S.S.R., 1924, now constituting Khorezm subdivision, Uzbekistan; lies S of Aral Sea and except for region along the Amu Dar'ya and oases is chiefly desert.
2. Town in oasis region W of lower Amu Dar'ya, NW Uzbekistan, pop. (1991e) 41,300; former ✱ of Khiva khanate and of Khorezm exclave (now Khorezm subdivision); flourished as early as 6th cent., but in later centuries suffered much from invasions; has a citadel and many mosques and Muslim schools.

Khmel'·nyt·s'kyy *or* **Khmel·nyt·sky** *also* **Khmel·nit·sky** *or Russ.* **Khmel'·nit·skiy** \k̲mel-ˈnit-skē\. **1.** *1937–54* **Ka·me·nets–Po·dol·sky** \ˈkȧ-mi-nits-pȧ-ˈdȯl-skē\. Administrative subdivision of Ukraine; 7954 sq. mi. (20,601 sq. km.); pop. (1991e) 1,520,600; ✱ Khmel'nyts'kyy; wheat, corn, tobacco; sugar refineries; formed 1937.
2. *formerly* **Pros·ku·rov** \prə-ˈsku̇r-əf\. Town, its ✱, 150 mi. (241 km.) WSW of Kiev; pop. (1991e) 245,000; food processing; engineering; founded 15th cent.

Khmer Republic. See CAMBODIA.

Khobdo. See HOVD.

Khodzhent. See KHUDZHAND.

Kho·jak Pass \ˈkō-jək\. Pass in a W ridge of the Sulaiman Mts., N Baluchistan, Pakistan, 30°51′N, 66°34′E; alt. ab. 7400 ft. (2255 m.).

Khojend. See KHUDZHAND.

Kholm \ˈk̲ȯlm\. **1.** Commune, Poland. See CHELM 2.
2. Town, NW Tver' Oblast, W Russia in Europe, on left bank of Lovat' River 60 mi. (97 km.) NE of Velikiye Luki; in WWII held by Germans 1941–44.

Khol·mo·go·ry \ˌk̲əl-mə-ˈgȯr-ē\. Town, Arkhangel'sk Oblast, N Russia in Europe, on left bank of Northern Dvina River 50 mi. (80 km.) SE of the city of Arkhangel'sk; long important as center for cattle raising and for shipping, but declined in time of Czar Peter the Great due to development of Arkhangel'sk.

Kholmsk \ˈk̲ȯlmsk\; *formerly* **Ma·o·ka** \mä-ˈō-kə\. Town, W coast of Sakhalin I., Sakhalin Oblast, E Russia in Asia, on Tatar Strait; connects with Yuzhno-Sakhalinsk by railroad and highway; Japanese until 1945.

Khomeyni, Bandar–e. See BANDAR-E KHOMEYNI.

Kho·mey·ni·shahr \ˈk̲ō-ˌmā-nē-ˌshär\ *or* **Ho·māy·un·shahr** \ˈhō-ˌmī-ən-ˌshär\. Town, Eşfahān prov., W cen. Iran, 6 mi. (10 km.) NW of the city of Eşfahān; pop. (1986c) 104,647.

Khoms. See AL KHUMS.

Khong \ˈkȯŋ\. Town and island in the Mekong River, S Laos, on the Cambodian boundary.

Khon Kaen \ˈkȯn-ˈkan\. Town, E cen. Thailand, on railroad line 100 mi. (161 km.) N of Nakhon Ratchasima; pop. (1991e) 131,478; university (1964).

Kho·per \k̲ə-ˈpyȯr\. River, SE Russia in Europe; rises in Penza Oblast and flows generally S through Saratov, Voronezh, and Volgograd oblasts into the Don; 626 mi. (1007 km.) long; navigable most of the year to Borisoglebsk.

Kho·rā·sān \ˌk̲ȯr-ä-ˈsän\ *also* **Khu·ra·san** \ˌku̇r-\ *or* **Kho·ras·san** \ˌk̲ȯr-\. Province, NE Iran, forms part of Plateau of Iran; ✱ Mashhad. See table at IRAN.
History: In early times under Arab rulers covered more area; its population comprises many different racial groups as a result of numerous invasions over the centuries; overrun by Muslims c. 650; scene of widespread unrest and revolts in 8th cent.; rise of Muslim religious leader Hāshim ibn Hākim, called al-Muqanna' ("The Veiled One") c. 774–779; conquered c. 1220 by Mongol ruler Genghis Khan and c. 1380 by Turkic ruler Timur.

Khorat. See NAKHON RATCHASIMA.

Kho·rezm *or* **Kho·resm** \k̲ə-ˈrez-ᵊm\. Administrative subdivision of Uzbekistan; 1737 sq. mi. (4499 sq. km.); pop. (1991e) 1,068,500; formerly an exclave of Uzbek S.S.R., U.S.S.R., now incorp. in Uzbekistan. See KHWARIZM.

Kho·rog \k̲ə-ˈrōg\. Town, ✱ of Gorno-Badakhshan subdivision, SE Tajikistan; pop. (1991e) 20,900.

Khor·ra·mā·bād \k̲ȯ-ˈrä-mä-ˌbäd\ *or* **Khur·ra·ma·bad** \k̲u̇-\. Town, ✱ of Lorestān prov., W Iran; pop. (1986c) 208,592; distribution center on highway running N from Persian Gulf ports through Ahvāz and Dezfūl to Arāk and Hamadān.

Khor·ram·shahr \ˌk̲ȯr-əm-ˈshä-hər\; *formerly* **Mo·ham·me·rah** \mə-ˈhȧ-mə-rə\. Town, ✱ of Khūzestān prov., W Iran, on the Kārūn at its junction with the Shatt al Arab, NNW of Ābādān; during WWII developed considerably as a trading port and oil-refining center; taken by Iraq 1980 during Iran-Iraq War; retaken by Iran 1982 having suffered severe damage; subsequently partially rebuilt.

Khors·a·bad \ˈk̲ȯr-sä-ˌbäd\. Village, N Iraq, ab. 12 mi. (19 km.) N of Mosul E of the Tigris; extensive ruins uncovered here are the ancient city Dur Sharrukin; palace and temple of Sargon II, king of Assyria 721–705 B.C.; list of Assyrian kings discovered here.

Khotan. See HOTAN.

Kho·tin \k̲ə-ˈtēn\ *or Rom.* **Ho·tin** \hȯ-ˈtēn\ *also* **Cho·cim** \ˈk̲ȯt-sēm\ *or* **Cho·tin** \k̲ə-ˈtēn\. Town, SW Ukraine, on right bank of the Dniester 30 mi. (48 km.) NE of Chernivitsi; formerly in Bessarabia; has some manufacturing and local trading activity but more important for its location, a former military post at a much-used crossing of the Dniester. In medieval times a Genoese colony; from 14th–20th cents. belonged variously to Moldavians, Poles, Russians, Turks, and Romanians; scene of Turkish defeat 1621 by Poles under Ruthenian soldier Jan Karol Chodkiewicz and again in 1673 by King John III Sobieski; seized by Russia 1739 and with Bessarabia incorp. in Russian empire 1812; under Romania 1918–40; held by Axis forces 1941–44.

Khrebet Cherskogo. See CHERSKIY RANGE.

Khroub, El. See EL KHROUB.

Khua Kem \ˈkü-ə-ˈkem\. See YENISEY.

Khu·dzhand \k̲u̇-ˈjȧnt\ *also* **Kho·dzhent** \k̲ō-ˈjent\; *1936–90* **Le·nin·a·bad** \li-ˌnē-nə-ˈbȧt\; *before 1936* **Kho·jend** \k̲ō-ˈjend\. Town, NW Tajikistan, on left bank of the Syr Dar'ya 90 mi. (145 km.) S of Tashkent, Uzbekistan; pop. (1991e) 164,500; one of oldest towns in cen. Asia; became Russian 1866; ✱ of former Leninabad Oblast.

Khulm \ˈk̲u̇lm\. See TASHKURGHĀN.

Khul·na \ˈku̇l-nə\. Town, SW Bangladesh, 77 mi. (124 km.) NE of Calcutta, India; pop. (1991p) 601,051; exports timber and forest products; shipbuilding.

Khums, Al. See AL KHUMS.

Khunsar. See KHVONSĀR.

Khūrān Strait. See CLARENCE STRAIT 3.

Khurasan. See KHORĀSĀN.

Khu·rī·yā Mu·rī·yā, Ja·zā·'ir \jä-ˈzä-ˌēr-k̲u̇-ˈrē-yä-mu̇-ˈrē-yä\ *or* **Ku·ria Mu·ria Islands** \ˈku̇r-ē-ə-ˈmu̇r-ē-ə\. Group of five rocky islets in the Arabian Sea off SW coast of Oman, bet. Capes Nus and Sharbatat, SE Arabian Penin.; 28 sq. mi. (73 sq. km.). Largest is Al Ḩallānīyah. Ceded by the sultan of Muscat and Oman (see OMAN) to Great Britain 1854 for a cable station; ceded by British to Oman 1967.

Khur·ja \ˈku̇r-jə\. Town, W Uttar Pradesh, N India, on Kali Nadi River 50 mi. (80 km.) SE of Delhi; pop. (1991p) 80,384; has a modern Jain temple.

Khurramabad. See KHORRAMĀBĀD.

Khust \ˈk̲üst\ *or Czech* **Chust** \ˈk̲üst\ *or Hung.* **Huszt** \ˈhu̇st\. Town, W Ukraine, in foothills of E Carpathian Mts.; before 1945 in Carpathian Ruthenia, E Czechoslovakia.

Khuwarizm. See KHWĀRIZM.

Khū·ze·stān \ˌk̲ü-zi-ˈstän, -ˈstan\; *formerly* **Ara·bi·stan** \ˌar-ə-bē-ˈstän, -ˈstan\; *anc.* **Su·si·ana** \ˌsü-zē-ˈa-nə, -ˈä-, -ˈā-\.

Province, SW Iran; ✻ Ahvāz; a fertile region, producing dates, melons, cotton, sorghum, vegetables; rich oil fields; its extent closely corresponds to the ancient country of Elam (*q.v.*) and to the later Susiana, a province of the Persian and Alexandrian empires, at the head of the gulf and bordered by Media on N, Persis on E, and Babylonia on W. Under Sassanid control early first millennium A.D.; to Arabs 7th cent.; Iraqi invasion June 1980 precipitated the Iran-Iraq War. See table at IRAN.

Khvon·sār \k̲vón-'sär\ *or* **Khun·sar** \k̲ün-'sär\. Town, W cen. Iran, ab. 80 mi. (130 km.) NW of Eşfahān and on highway from Eşfahān to Iraq.

Khvoy \'k̲vói\. Town, West Azerbaijan prov., NW Iran; pop. (1986c) 115,343; important trade and communications center in mountains N of Daryācheh-ye Orūmīyeh on highway from Tabrīz to Erzurum, Turkey; because of its nearness to borders of Turkey, Azerbaijan, and Armenia, strongly fortified, esp. since 19th cent.; has several times been object of fighting.

Khwā·rizm \'k̲wä-ˌriz-ᵊm\ *or* **Khwa·rezm** \-ˌrez-ᵊm\ *or* **Khwâ·razm** \-ˌraz-ᵊm\ *also* **Khu·wa·rizm** \k̲ü-'wä-ˌriz-ᵊm\. The region corresponding roughly with Chorasmia, a N province of ancient Persia; covered valley of lower Oxus River and extended across steppes W to Caspian Sea and E to Bukhara. In 11th–13th cents. ruled by Khwārezm-Shāh, a dynasty founded by a slave in service of Seljuq Sultan Malik-Shāh; became an empire by early 13th cent., extending conquests in Transoxiana and making Samarqand its ✻; overwhelmed c. 1220 by Mongols under Genghis Khan and again by Turkic ruler Timur 14th cent. Successfully repulsed all Russian military incursions until 1873, when it became a Russian protectorate. Approx. same region known as Khorezm (*q.v.*). See KHIVA.

Khy·ber \'kī-bər\ *also* **Khai·bar** \'kī-bər\. Former agency, North-West Frontier, India, 995 sq. mi. (2577 sq. km.); now part of Peshawar div., Pakistan.

Khyber Pass. Pass in Safed Koh Range and S of Mohmand Hills on border bet. Afghanistan and Pakistan, 10.5 mi. (17 km.) W of Peshawar (see JAMRUD); ab. 33 mi. (53 km.) long; ravine and watercourse, from 50 to 450 ft. (15 to 137 m.) wide, in places bet. cliffs (600 to 1000 ft. or 183 to 305 m. high) and mountains (1400 to 3000 ft. or 427 to 914 m. high); former British forts **Ali Mas·jid** \'ə-lē-'məs-jid\, in center of pass, and **Lan·di Ko·tal** \'lən-dē-'kō-ˌtəl\, at Afghan border (the highest point, ab. 3518 ft. or 1070 m.); has been traversed for centuries by armies and peoples invading India; scene of sharp fighting in Afghan Wars 1839–42 and 1878–80 and with Afridis; now a strategic military road.

Khy·rim \'kī-ˌrim\. See KHASI STATES.

Ki. See LHASA 1.

Kia \'kē-ä\. Settlement, NW end of Santa Isabel I., Solomon Is., W Pacific Ocean.

Kialing. See JIALING.

Ki·a·ma \kī-'a-mə\. Municipality, E New South Wales, Australia, on Pacific Ocean 50 mi. (80 km.) SSW of Sydney; pop. (1991c) 15,908; agriculture, coal mining.

Kiambone, Ras. See DICKS HEAD.

Ki·a·michi \ˌkī-ə-'mi-shē\. River, SE Oklahoma; rises in E Le Flore co., flows SW into Red River in SE Choctaw co.; ab. 165 mi. (265 km.) long.

Kiamusze. See JIAMUSI.

Kian. See JI'AN.

Kiang·an \'kyäŋ-'än\; *formerly* **Quiang·an** \'kyäŋ-\. Name under Spanish rule of Ifugao subprovince (now a full province), N cen. Luzon, Philippines.

Kiangmai. See CHIANG MAI.

Kiang–nan \'jyäŋ-'nän\. Province of China in Ming period. See ANHUI.

Kiang–ning. See NANJING.

Kiangsi. See JIANGXI.

Kiangsu. See JIANGSU.

Kiangtu. See YANGZHOU.

Kiangyin. See JIANGYIN.

Kiaochow. 1. Administrative division, China. See JIAO XIAN. **2.** Town, China. See JIAOXIAN.

Kiaohsien. See JIAOXIAN.

Kiating. See LESHAN.

Ki·a·wah Island \'kē-ə-wä, -wó\. Island in Atlantic Ocean, in Charleston co., South Carolina, ab. 15 mi. (25 km.) SW of the city of Charleston.

Kia·yu·kwan \'jyä-'yü̅-'gwän\. See GREAT WALL.

Ki·ba·we \kē-'bä-wā\. Municipality, Bukidnon prov., Mindanao, Philippines, 60 mi. (97 km.) ENE of Cotabato; pop. (1980c) 26,949.

Ki·bo \'kē-bō\. Highest peak of Kilimanjaro, Tanzania; the highest point in Africa; 19,341 ft. (5895 m.).

Kibris. See CYPRUS.

Kick·a·poo \'ki-kə-ˌpü\. River, SW Wisconsin; rises in Monroe co., flows S into Wisconsin River in S Crawford co.; ab. 100 mi. (160 km.) long.

Kick·ing Horse Pass \'ki-kiŋ-ˌhórs\. Mountain pass, Rocky Mts., Canada, on boundary bet. SE British Columbia and Banff National Park in Alberta.

Ki·da·pa·wan \ˌkē-dä-'pä-wän\. Municipality, ✻ of Cotabato prov., Mindanao, Philippines, 55 mi. (88 km.) ESE of the city of Cotabato; pop. (1980c) 54,864.

Kid·der \'ki-dər\. County in S cen. North Dakota. See table at NORTH DAKOTA.

Kid·der·min·ster \'ki-dər-ˌmin-stər\. Town, Hereford and Worcester, W cen. England, on the Stour 18 mi. (29 km.) WSW of Birmingham; pop. (1981p) 51,261; worsteds, metalware; Kidderminster carpets (manufactured since 1735).

Ki·de·po Valley National Park \kē-'dā-pō\. National park, northernmost Uganda, bordering on Sudan to the W; ab. 515 sq. mi. (1335 sq. km.); contains an isolated intermontane valley.

Kid·nap·pers, Cape \'kid-ˌna-pərz\. Cape on SE cen. coast of North I., New Zealand, forming S side of Hawke Bay.

Kid·ron \'ki-drən, 'kī-\ *also* **Ked·ron** \'ke-drən, 'kē-\. **1.** *or* **Je·hosh·a·phat** \ji-'hä-shə-ˌfat, -'hä-sə-\. Valley, in region of Jordan occupied by Israel 1967; source of the Kidron. **2.** Stream rising on E side of Jerusalem, separating it from Mount of Olives and flowing E to Dead Sea.

Kids·grove \'kidz-ˌgrōv\. Town, Staffordshire, W cen. England; pop. (1981p) 24,227.

Kid·wel·ly *or Welsh* **Cyd·weli** \kid-'we-lē\. Town, Dyfed co., S Wales, near coast of Carmarthen Bay; pop. (1981p) 3152; 13th cent. church and castle (original structure built c. 1100).

Kiel \'kēl\. **1.** City, Calumet and Manitowoc cos., E Wisconsin, 18 mi. (29 km.) NW of Sheboygan; pop. (1990c) 2910. **2.** Seaport city, ✻ of Schleswig-Holstein, Germany, at head of Kiel Harbor 40 mi. (64 km.) NW of Lübeck; pop. (1992e) 247,107; good harbor, 7 mi. (11 km.) long; shipbuilding, printing, fishing, brewing, engineering; university (1665).

History: Became city 1242; joined Hanseatic League 1284; part of kingdom of Denmark 1773; Peace of Kiel signed here 1814; passed to Prussia 1866; main base of German imperial fleet in WWI; scene of mutiny of German sailors which preceded German revolution of 1918; in WWII many times bombed and much damaged.

Kiel Bay *or Ger.* **Kie·ler Bucht** \'kē-lər-ˌbu̇k̲t\. Part of the Baltic Sea on the E coast of Schleswig-Holstein, Germany, extending E to Fehmarn I.; in SW is **Kiel Harbor** *or Ger.* **Kieler För·de** \ˌfœr-də\, the inlet at the head of which is the port of Kiel.

Kiel Canal. See NORD-OSTSEE KANAL.

Kiel·ce \'kyelt-se\ *or Russ.* **Kel·tsy** \'kelt-sē\. **1.** Province of SE Poland. See table at POLAND. **2.** City, its ✻, 90 mi. (145 km.) S of Warsaw; pop. (1989e) 212,901; railroad junction; episcopal see; agricultural center; copper mines; marble quarries; founded c. 1173; scene of battles bet. Russians and Germans 1914, 1915 in WWI; occupied by Germans in WWII; four concentration camps were here; recaptured by U.S.S.R. Jan. 1945.

Kieler Bucht *and* **Kieler Forde.** See KIEL BAY.

Kiel Harbor. See KIEL BAY.

Ki·e·ta \kē-'ā-tä\. Chief town of the Solomon Is., on E coast of Bougainville I. on Arawa Bay, W Pacific Ocean; trading center; had radio station when taken by Japanese Jan. 1942 in WWII.

Ki·ev *also* **Ki·yev** \'kē-if, -ef, -ev\; *Ukrain.* **Ky·yiv** \'ki-yē-ü\. **1.** Administrative subdivision of Ukraine; 11,197 sq. mi. (29,000 sq. km.); pop. (1991e) 4,581,400; ✻ Kiev; until 1991 an oblast of Ukrainian S.S.R., U.S.S.R.; crossed by Dnieper River; sugar beets, flax, potatoes; dairying.

2. City, its ✻, on right bank of the Dnieper 470 mi. (756 km.) SW of Moscow, Russia; pop. (1989p) 2,587,000; largest city in Ukraine and before 1991 3d largest in U.S.S.R.; important communications center; machinery, leatherwork, chemicals, textiles, footwear; wood processing; distributing point for a wide area, its trading activity having grown out of its former annual fair, the Kiev Contract Fair; university (1834); in its Old Town many old buildings famous in its long history, among them: the cathedral of St. Sophia (completed c. 1037), monastery of St. Michael (c. 1108), church of St. Andrew (c. 1753), and the Kiev-Pechersky Monastery, an ancient and sacred place of pilgrimage (founded 11th cent.).

History: One of the oldest cities in Europe and so long prominent that it is known to Russians as "the Mother of Cities." As the town of Kiev, 9th cent. A.D., became ✻ of a Varangian principality, Kievan Rus, under Prince Oleg (c. 879–912); center for trade down the Dnieper to Black Sea and on the route from Scandinavia to Constantinople; became seat of the metropolitan of Russian Christianity 988; its power and wealth declined in 12th cent.; became object of rivalry among other princes; captured by prince of Suzdal' 1169; overrun and ruined by Mongol invasion 1240; became part of Lithuania in 14th cent. and of Poland in 16th cent.; finally incorp. by Russia 1686. Proclaimed ✻ of independent Ukrainian republic 1918; held at various times 1918–20 by Bolsheviks, Germans, White Russians, and Poles; again made ✻ of Ukrainian S.S.R. 1934; in WWII occupied by Germans 1941–43, suffering extensive damage; nearby evacuations followed nuclear accident at Chernobyl Apr. 1986.

Kifisós. See CEPHISUS.

Kifissós Voiotikós. See CEPHISUS 2.

Ki·ga·li \kē-'gä-lē\. Town, ✻ of Rwanda, in cen. part E of Lake Kivu; pop. (1991c) 232,733.

Ki·go·ma \kē-'gō-mä\. **1.** Administrative region of W Tanzania. See table at TANZANIA.

2. Port, its ✻, on Lake Tanganyika 4 mi. (6 km.) N of Ujiji; terminus of railroad line from Dar es Salaam; ships timber, cotton, tobacco.

Ki·hei \kē-'hā-ē\. Unincorporated settlement, Maui I., Hawaii, on Maalaea Bay; pop. (1990c) 11,107.

Ki·ho·lo Bay \kē-'hō-lō\. Bay on W coast of Hawaii I., Hawaii, S of Keawaiki Bay.

Kii Channel \'kē, 'kē-ē\. Strait bet. E coast of Shikoku I. and S coast of Honshū I., Japan, and connecting Harima Sea and Ōsaka Bay (through Kitan Strait) with the Pacific Ocean; ab. 25 mi. (40 km.) wide.

Ki·kai·ga–shi·ma \kē-ˌkī-gä-'shē-mä\ *or* **Ki·kai Shi·ma** \'kē-kī-'shē-mä\ *or* **Kikai Ji·ma** \'jē-mä\. Island, NE Amami Is., N Ryukyu Is., Japan; 23 sq. mi. (60 sq. km.).

Ki·ke·pa Point \kē-'kā-pä\. Point, N end of Niihau I., Hawaii.

Ki·kin·da \'kē-kēn-dä\. Town, Serbia, NE Yugoslavia, ab. 70 mi. (113 km.) N of Belgrade.

Kikládhes. See CYCLADES.

Ki·koa Point \kē-'kō-ä\. Point on E coast of Lanai I., Hawaii, on Kealaikahiki Channel.

Ki·ko·ri \kē-'kōr-ē\. **1.** River, New Guinea I., in Papua New Guinea; flows SE to Gulf of Papua; ab. 200 mi. (320 km.) long.

2. Settlement in delta of Kikori River, Papua New Guinea, 7°35′S, 144°16′E at head of Gulf of Papua; has rainfall of ab. 230 inches (585 cm.) annually.

Ki·lau·ea \ˌkē-laủ-'wā-ä\. Crater, on E side of Mauna Loa, in Hawaii Volcanoes National Park, S cen. Hawaii I., Hawaii; 2 mi. (3 km.) wide and at an alt. of 4090 ft. (1247 m.); largest active crater in the world; began erupting 1983.

Kilauea Point. Point on N coast of Kauai I., Hawaii, 22°14′N, 159°24′W.

Kil·bran·nan Sound \kil-'bra-nən\ *or* **Kil·bren·nan Sound** \-'bre-\. Channel bet. Kintyre Penin. and Arran I., off SW coast of Scotland; ab. 14 mi. (23 km.) long and 4 mi. (6 km.) wide.

Kil·col·man \kil-'kəl-mən\. Castle N of Mallow, N co. Cork, SW Ireland; home of English poet Edmund Spenser; ruins.

Kil·dare \kil-'dar\. **1.** County, Leinster prov., E Ireland; ⊗ Naas; rivers Liffey, Boyne, Barrow; sheep and cattle raising, textile manufacture; oats, barley; agricultural machinery. See table at IRELAND.

2. Town, co. Kildare, E Ireland, 30 mi. (48 km.) SW of Dublin; pop. (1986c) 4268; Protestant cathedral; remains of 13th cent. castle; Curragh Plain is just E of it.

Kil·gore \'kil-ˌgōr\. City in Gregg and Rusk cos., NE Texas, 25 mi. (40 km.) E of Tyler; pop. (1990c) 11,066; large oil fields; Kilgore Coll. (1935); East Texas Oil Museum.

Ki·li \'kē-lē\. Island, Marshall Is., in the Ralik Chain; relocation site after atomic bomb tests on Bikini I. 1946.

Ki·lid Bahr \ki-'lēd-'bär\ *or Turk.* **Ki·lit·i·ba·hir** \ki-ˌlē-tē-bä-'hir\. Fortified town on Gallipoli Penin., Turkey in Europe, on W bank of Dardanelles nearly opp. Çanakkale.

Ki·li·fi \kē-'lē-fē\. Coastal town, E Kenya, ab. 40 mi. (64 km.) N of Mombasa.

Ki·lik Pass \'ki-lik\. Pass in range bet. E Hindu Kush and W Karakoram Range, Jammu and Kashmir, in area controlled by Pakistan, near Afghan border; alt. 15,600 ft. (4755 m.).

Kilimane. See QUELIMANE.

Kil·i·man·ja·ro \ˌki-lə-mən-'jär-ō\. **1.** *or* **Mount Kilimanjaro.** Mountain in NE Tanzania, near Kenya border; highest peak Kibo 19,341 ft. (5895 m.), the highest point in Africa, first climbed 1889; next highest peak Mawenzi 16,896 ft. (5150 m.), first climbed 1912; contained in **Kilimanjaro National Park;** 292 sq. mi. (756 sq. km.); estab. 1973.

2. Administrative region of NE Tanzania. See table at TANZANIA.

Ki·li·na·i·lau Islands \ˌkē-lē-'nī-ˌlaủ\. Group of islets N of Bougainville I., NW Solomon Is., W Pacific Ocean; part of Papua New Guinea.

Kil·in·di·ni \ˌkē-lin-'dē-nē\. Town on SW side of Mombasa I., off S coast of Kenya; **Kilindini Harbor,** the finest landlocked and sheltered harbor on E African coast, forms modern part of Mombasa harbor.

Ki·lis *or* **Kil·lis** \'kē-lēs\. Town, Gaziantep prov., S Turkey in Asia, 36 mi. (58 km.) N of Aleppo, Syria; pop. (1990p) 81,469; center of olive cultivation; silk and cotton.

Kilitibahir. See KILID BAHR.

Ki·li·ya \ˌkē-lē-'yä\ *or Rom.* **Chi·lia** \'kēl-yä\. **1.** River, the N branch of the Danube Delta, E Romania; borders Letea I. on N and marks boundary bet. Romania and Ukraine; ab. 65 mi. (105 km.) long.

2. *or Rom.* **Chilia–Nouă** \-'naủ-ə\. Town, Odessa subdivision, S Ukraine, on the Kiliya branch of the Danube Delta.

Kil·ken·ny \kil-'ke-nē\. **1.** County, Leinster prov., SE Ireland; ⊗ Kilkenny; rivers Suir, Nore, Barrow; brewing; agriculture. See table at IRELAND.

2. Town, its ⊗; pop. (1991p) 8513; coal mining, brewing; Coll. of St. John which had as students noted writers Jonathan Swift, William Congreve, George Farquhar, Bishop George Berkeley; 12th cent. castle and 13th cent. cathedral.

History: Site of many parliament meetings during 14th and 15th cents.; scene of parliament 1366 which passed statute to prevent further assimilation of the Anglo-Irish; scene of a meeting of Irish Catholic clergy and laity 1642 which tried to overcome the hostility bet. the old Irish and Anglo-Irish.

Kil·kís \kēl-'kēs\. **1.** Department of Greece. See table at GREECE.

2. Town, its ✻, W cen. Macedonia, N Greece, ab. 24 mi. (39 km.) N of Thessaloníki; pop. (1981p) 11,694.

Kil·lala Bay \ki-ˈla-lə\. Inlet of Atlantic Ocean on NW coast of Ireland, bet. cos. Sligo and Mayo; Moy River flows into it at its head.

Kil·lar·ney \ki-ˈlär-nē\. **1.** Town, SW Manitoba, Canada, 47 mi. (76 km.) SSE of Brandon; pop. (1991c) 2163; summer resort.

2. Town, co. Kerry, SW Ireland, near Lakes of Killarney; pop. (1991p) 7253; tourist center; ruins of ancient castles and two ancient abbeys nearby.

Killarney, Lakes of. Three lakes, co. Kerry, SW Ireland; lowest and largest (ab. 8 sq. mi. or 21 sq. km.) is Lough Leane; all are studded with islands and noted for their scenery; on Ross I. in Lough Leane is Ross Castle; other ruins nearby (see MUCKROSS).

Kil·la·ry Harbour \ˈki-lə-rē\. Inlet of Atlantic Ocean on W coast of Ireland, S of Clew Bay.

Kill Devil Hill. See KITTY HAWK.

Kil·leen \ki-ˈlēn\. City, Bell co., cen. Texas, N of Austin; pop. (1990c) 63,535; Fort Hood military installation located nearby; Central Texas Coll. (1967), Univ. of Central Texas (1973).

Kil·lie·cran·kie \ˌki-lē-ˈkraŋ-kē\. Mountain pass, Tayside region, cen. Scotland, in SE part of the Grampians; nearby occurred battle July 17, 1689 in which John Graham of Claverhouse, first viscount Dundee, defeated the rebelling Scots at the cost of his own life.

Kil·li·nek \ˈki-lə-ˌnek\ *or usu. formerly* **Kil·li·nik** \-ˌnik\. Small island off N tip of Labrador, Canada, S of E entrance to Hudson Strait; Port Burwell is on it and Cape Chidley is its N point; separated from mainland by McLelan Strait.

Kil·ling·ly \ˈki-liŋ-lē\. Town, E Windham co., NE corner of Connecticut, on Quinebaug River and Rhode Island border; pop. (1990c) 15,889; includes borough of Danielson (*q.v.*); settled 1693; incorp. 1708.

Kil·ling·ton Peak \ˈki-liŋ-tən\. Mountain, E cen. Rutland co., W Vermont; 4235 ft. (1291 m.); ski slopes.

Kil·ling·worth \ˈki-liŋ-ˌwərth\. Village, Northumberland, England, 6 mi. (10 km.) NE of Newcastle upon Tyne; place where inventor and founder of railways George Stephenson tried his first locomotive 1814.

Killíni. See CYLLENE.

Killinik. See KILLINEK.

Killis. See KILIS.

Kill Van Kull \ˈkil-van-ˈkəl\. Channel bet. New Jersey and Staten I., New York; connects Newark Bay with Upper New York Bay; spanned by Bayonne Bridge (steel arch; main span 1675 ft. or 511 m.; completed 1931).

Kilmain. See QUELIMANE.

Kil·mar·nock \kil-ˈmär-nək\. Burgh, Strathclyde region, SW Scotland, 12 mi. (19 km.) NE of Ayr; pop. (1981p) 52,080; carpets, woolens, whiskey, dairy products.

Kil·ro·nan \kil-ˈrō-nən\. Chief town in Aran Is., co. Galway, W Ireland, on Inishmore; pop. (1986c) 282; region noteworthy for ancient remains.

Kil·rush \kil-ˈrəsh\. Town, on Shannon estuary, SW coast of co. Clare, W Ireland; pop. (1991c) 2163; fishing, flagstone quarrying; on nearby Scattery I. are remains of several churches, a tower, and a castle.

Kil·syth \kil-ˈsīth\. Burgh, Strathclyde region, cen. Scotland; pop. (1981p) 10,446; scene of victory of James Graham, marquis of Montrose, and his Royalists over the Covenanters 1645.

Kil·wa \ˈkēl-wä\ *or in full* **Kilwa Ki·vin·je** \kē-ˈvin-jā\. Coastal town, SE Tanzania.

History: Probably founded 19th cent. by people from **Kilwa** *or* **Kilwa Ki·si·wa·ni** \ˌkē-sē-ˈwä-nē\ 25 mi. (40 km.) to the S, an older town on a small island off the coast which had been a leading trade center of coastal E Africa prior to Portuguese occupation 1505–12; became a center for slave and ivory trade; Germans, ruling from mid-1880s, laid out modern town.

Kil·win·ning \kil-ˈwi-niŋ\. Burgh, Strathclyde region, SW Scotland; pop. (1981p) 16,193; ruined abbey (founded c. 1140); according to tradition, birthplace of freemasonry (said to have been brought in by foreign craftsmen who built the abbey) in Scotland.

Kim·ball \ˈkim-bəl\. **1.** County in W Nebraska. See table at NEBRASKA.

2. City, its ⊗, 43 mi. (69 km.) S of Scottsbluff; pop. (1990c) 2574; ships potatoes and beans; oil wells; dairy farming.

Kimball, Mount. Mountain, N Wrangell Mts., SE Alaska, S of the Alaska Highway and E of the Richardson Highway; 10,350 ft. (3155 m.).

Kim·be \ˈkim-bē\. Port, N coast of cen. New Britain I., Papua New Guinea.

Kimbe Bay. Large inlet of Bismarck Sea on N coast of New Britain, Bismarck Archipelago, Papua New Guinea, bordered on W by Willaumez Penin.

Kim·ber·ley \ˈkim-bər-lē\. **1.** Town, British Columbia, Canada, 60 mi. (97 km.) ENE of Nelson; pop. (1991c) 6531; zinc and silver mining; tourism.

2. Town, Northern Cape prov., Rep. of South Africa, 86 mi. (138 km.) WNW of Bloemfontein, near Free State border; pop. (1985c) 149,667; world's diamond center with Kimberley, De Beers, and other famous mines nearby; commercial center; livestock. Founded 1871 shortly after discovery of diamonds in region; ✻ 1873–80 of Griqualand West before it became part of Cape Colony; besieged by Boers for four months during Boer War Oct. 1899–Feb. 1900. Scenery marked by immense pits and heaps of earth, the aftermath of mining operations. See BEACONSFIELD.

Kimberley Plateau *or* **The Kimberley** *also* **Kim·ber·leys** \ˈkim-bər-lēz\. Plateau region, N Western Australia, Australia, N of 19°30′S; ab. 133,140 sq. mi. (345,350 sq. km.); largest town, Broome; cattle.

Kim·ber·ly \ˈkim-bər-lē\. Village, Outagamie co., E Wisconsin, 4 mi. (6 km.) E of Appleton; pop. (1990c) 5406.

Kim·ble \ˈkim-bəl\. County in W cen. Texas. See table at TEXAS.

Kim·ch'aek \kēm-ˈchak\; *formerly* **Jo·shin** \jō-ˈshēn\ *also* **Song·jin** \səŋ-ˈjēn\. Seaport town, E North Korea, on the Sea of Japan.

Kí·mi *also* **Ký·mē** \ˈkē-mē\. Seaport commune, Euboea dept., Greece, on E coast of Euboea I.

Ki·mi·to \ˈkē-mē-ˌtō\ *or* **Ke·miö** \ˈkem-ē-ˈœ\. Finnish island in Gulf of Bothnia off SW Finland.

Ki·mi·tsu \kē-ˈmē-tsu̇\. City, Chiba prefecture, SE Honshū, Japan; pop. (1990p) 89,243.

Kímolos. See CIMOLUS.

Ki·movsk \kē-ˈmȯfsk\. Town, Tula Oblast, W cen. Russia in Europe, ab. 40 mi. (64 km.) ESE of the city of Tula.

Kimpolung. See CÎMPULUNG.

Kim·ry \ˈkēm-rē\. Town, SE Tver' Oblast, W cen. Russia in Europe, at NE end of reservoir, E of the city of Tver' and 75 mi. (121 km.) N of Moscow; pop. (1991e) 62,000; shoe and leather industry.

Kin. See KŬM.

Ki·na·ba·lu *or* **Ki·na·bu·lu** \ˌkē-nä-ˈbä-lü\; *formerly* **Ki·ni·ba·lu** \ˌkē-nē-\. Mountain in N cen. Sabah, East Malaysia, Malaysia; 13,455 ft. (4101 m.); highest peak on island of Borneo.

Kinabalu National Park. National park, Sabah, East Malaysia, Malaysia; includes Mt. Kinabalu; estab. 1964.

Ki·na·ba·tang·an \ˌkē-nä-bä-ˈtäŋ-ˌän\. River, Sabah, East Malaysia, Malaysia; flows E into the Sulu Sea; ab. 350 mi. (563 km.) long; navigable for ab. 200 mi. (320 km.).

Kinabulu. See KINABALU.

Kin·car·dine \kin-ˈkärd-ᵊn\. **1.** Resort town, Bruce co., SE Ontario, Canada, on E shore of Lake Huron 47 mi. (76 km.) SW of Owen Sound; pop. (1991c) 6585; fisheries; tourism.

2. *or* **Kin·car·dine·shire** \-ˌshir, -shər\; *formerly* **The Mearns** \ˈmərnz\. Former county, E Scotland; ⊗ Stonehaven.

\ə\ **abut** \ə\ matches \ᵊ\ kitten, Fr table \ər\ **further** \a\ **ash** \ā\ **ace** \ä\ cot, cart \á\ Fr bac \au̇\ **out** \b̲\ Span Avila \ch\ **chin** \e\ **bet** \ē\ **easy** \g\ **go** \i\ **hit** \ī\ **ice** \j\ **job** \k̲\ Ger **ich, Buch** \ⁿ\ Fr vin \ŋ\ **sing** \ō\ **go** \ȯ\ **all** \ȯ\ **law** \œ\ Fr **bœuf** \œ̄\ Fr **feu** \ȯi\ **boy** \th\ **thin** \t͟h\ **this** \ü\ **loot** \u̇\ **foot** \ue\ Ger **füllen** \ūe\ Fr **rue** \y\ **yet** \ʸ\ Fr digne \ˈdēnʸ\, nuit \ˈnwʸē\ \yü\ **few** \yu̇\ **fury** \zh\ **vision**

Kin·che·loe Point \ˈkin-chə-ˌlō\. Point on W coast of Tillamook co., NW Oregon.

Kinchinjunga. See KANCHENJUNGA.

Kin·der·hook \ˈkin-dər-ˌhu̇k\. Village, Columbia co., SE New York, E of Hudson River; pop. (1990c) 8112; birthplace of Martin Van Buren, 8th president of the U.S., 1782.

Kinder Scout. See PEAK DISTRICT.

Kin·ders·ley \ˈkin-dərz-lē\. Town, Saskatchewan, Canada, 115 mi. (185 km.) SW of Saskatoon; pop. (1991c) 4572.

Kin·dia \ˈkin-dē-ä\. Town, W Guinea, on railroad line 60 mi. (97 km.) NE of Conakry.

Kin·du \ˈkin-dü\. Town, ✱ of Maniema administrative region, E Democratic Rep. of the Congo, on upper Congo River.

Kin·eo, Mount \ˈki-nē-ˌō\. Peak on E shore of Moosehead Lake, NW cen. Maine; 1806 ft. (550 m.); composed of flint.

Ki·nesh·ma \ˈkē-nish-mə\. City on right bank of the Volga, N Ivanovo Oblast, cen. Russia in Europe, on railroad line 50 mi. (80 km.) NE of the city of Ivanovo; pop. (1992e) 104,000; chief river port of the region; textiles and chemicals.

King \ˈkiŋ\. **1.** Name of counties in two states of the U.S. See tables at TEXAS and WASHINGTON.
2. Name of several islands. See KING ISLAND.
3. City, Stokes co., N North Carolina; pop. (1990c) 4059.
4. Town, South Africa. See KING WILLIAM'S TOWN.

King. See JING.

King and Queen \ˈkwēn\. County in E Virginia. See table at VIRGINIA.

King and Queen Courthouse. Village, ⊗ of King and Queen co., E Virginia, 34 mi. (55 km.) ENE of Richmond.

King·bor·ough \ˈkiŋ-ˌbər-ō\. Municipality, Tasmania, Australia; pop. (1991c) 23,808.

King–chau. See JIANGLING.

King City. City, Monterey co., W California, on Salinas River 90 mi. (145 km.) SE of San Jose; pop. (1990c) 7634.

Kingdom of the Serbs, Croats, and Slovenes. See YUGOSLAVIA.

King Ed·ward VIII Falls \ˈe-dwərd-t͟hē-ˈāth\. Waterfall in a tributary of the Mazaruni River, W Guyana, in Pacaraima Mts., NW of Kaieteur Falls; 840 ft. (256 m.).

King Edward VII Land. See EDWARD VII PENINSULA.

King·fish·er \ˈkiŋ-ˌfi-shər\. **1.** County in cen. Oklahoma. See table at OKLAHOMA.
2. City, its ⊗, 36 mi. (58 km.) NW of Oklahoma City; pop. (1990c) 4095; grain farming.

Kingfisher Peak. Mountain, SW Park co., NW Wyoming; 11,100 ft. (3383 m.).

King Fred·er·ik VIII Land \ˌfre-də-rik-t͟hə-ˈāth\. Coastal region in NE Greenland.

King George \ˈjȯrj\. **1.** County in E Virginia. See table at VIRGINIA.
2. Village, its ⊗.

King George, Mount. **1.** Peak, SE British Columbia, Canada, near Alberta border; 11,226 ft. (3422 m.).
2. Peak in St. Elias Mts., SW Yukon, Canada, E of Mt. Logan; 12,300 ft. (3749 m.).

King George V Land. See GEORGE V COAST.

King George Island. See SOUTH SHETLAND ISLANDS.

King George Sound. Inlet of Indian Ocean, S coast of Western Australia, Australia; forms outer harbor of Albany.

Kin·gi·sepp \ˈkēŋ-gē-ˌsep\. **1.** Seaport, Estonia. See KURESSAARE.
2. *formerly* **Yam·burg** \ˈyäm-ˌbu̇rg\ *or* **Ya·ma** \ˈyä-mə\. Railroad town, NW St. Petersburg Oblast, W Russia in Europe, 20 mi. (32 km.) E of Narva, Estonia; one of oldest towns in Russia; founded as Yama in 9th cent. and important later in 14th cent. in Baltic wars; captured by anti-Bolshevik forces 1919 but retaken by Red Army; in 1944 after being under German control for three years retaken by U.S.S.R.

King Island. **1.** Steep rocky island at S end of Bering Strait off W coast of Seward Penin., Alaska, and ab. 65 mi. (105 km.) SE of the Diomede Is.; discovered by English explorer Capt. James Cook 1778.
2. Island, Australia, at W end of Bass Strait 50 mi. (80 km.) NW of Tasmania; ab. 42 mi. (68 km.) long; 424 sq. mi. (1098 sq. km.).
3. Island, Myanmar. See KADAN ISLAND.
4. Island off coast of British Columbia, Canada; 324 sq. mi. (839 sq. km.).

King·man \ˈkiŋ-mən\. **1.** County in S cen. Kansas. See table at KANSAS.
2. City, ⊗ of Mohave co., NW corner of Arizona, 65 mi. (105 km.) ESE of Boulder Dam; pop. (1990c) 12,722; historically in gold-mining area; livestock raising; tourism.
3. City, ⊗ of Kingman co., S cen. Kansas, 30 mi. (48 km.) SSW of Hutchinson; pop. (1990c) 3196.

Kingman Reef. Uninhabited reef in cen. Pacific at N end of Line Is., 920 mi. (1480 km.) S of Honolulu; triangular in shape, 9 mi. (14 km.) long by 5 mi. (8 km.) wide, enclosing a deep lagoon; discovered 1798; annexed by U.S. 1922.

King of Prussia. Unincorporated settlement, SE Pennsylvania, W of Philadelphia; pop. (1990c) 18,406.

King Peak. Peak in St. Elias Mts., Yukon Terr., Canada; 17,130 ft. (5221 m.).

Kings \ˈkiŋz\. **1.** River, NW Arkansas and SW Missouri; rises in SE Madison co., flows N across Missouri boundary and empties into White River; ab. 75 mi. (120 km.) long.
2. River, S cen. California; rises in E Fresno co., flows W and disappears in region formerly covered by Tulare Lake; upper canyon forms part of Kings Canyon National Park.
3. Name of counties in two states of the U.S. See tables at CALIFORNIA and NEW YORK.
4. Name of counties in three provinces of Canada. See tables at NEW BRUNSWICK, NOVA SCOTIA, PRINCE EDWARD ISLAND.

Kings, Valley of the. Defile, Thebes, SE cen. Egypt; site of ab. 60 tombs incl. that of Tutankhamen and other pharaohs who ruled bet. 1567 and c. 1085 B.C.

King's. See OFFALY.

Kings Bay. Inlet on NW coast of Spitsbergen I., Norway, S of Cross Bay.

Kings·burg \ˈkiŋz-bərg\. City, Fresno co., S cen. California, 20 mi. (32 km.) SE of the city of Fresno; pop. (1990c) 7205.

Kings·bury \ˈkiŋz-ˌber-ē\. County in E South Dakota. See table at SOUTH DAKOTA.

Kings Canyon National Park. See UNITED STATES, *National Parks.*

Kings·ford \ˈkiŋz-fərd\. City, Dickinson co., S Upper Penin. of Michigan, W of Iron Mountain; pop. (1990c) 5480.

Kings·land \ˈkiŋz-lənd\. City, Camden co., SE Georgia, 4 mi. (6 km.) N of the Florida border; pop. (1990c) 4699.

Kings·ley Dam \ˈkiŋz-lē\. Dam across North Platte River in W Nebraska, NNE of Ogallala; completed 1941.

King's Lynn \ˈkiŋz-ˈlin\ *or* **Lynn Re·gis** \ˈlin-ˈrē-jəs\ *or* **Lynn.** Town, Norfolk, E England, on the Ouse River near The Wash 90 mi. (145 km.) NNE of London; pop. (1981p) 33,340; formerly one of chief ports in England; sugar refining, fruit canning; fertilizers.

Kings·mill \ˈkiŋz-ˌmil\. **1.** Early name of Gilbert Is., W Pacific Ocean.
2. Island group comprising seven islands in S part of Gilbert Is. group, Kiribati, S of the Equator.

King's Mill. See MOLINO DEL REY.

Kings Mountain. **1.** Ridge in NW York co., N South Carolina, and SE Cleveland co., S North Carolina; the part in South Carolina is scene of an American victory over the British Oct. 7, 1780 and has been set aside as **Kings Mountain National Military Park** (see UNITED STATES, *National Historical Parks*).
2. City, Gaston and Cleveland cos., SW North Carolina, at foot of Kings Mt. W of Gastonia; pop. (1990c) 8763.

King Sound. Inlet, N Western Australia, Australia, SE of Cape Leveque; connected by Sunday Strait with Timor Sea; receives Fitzroy River.

Kings Peak. Peak in the Uinta Mts., Duchesne co., NE Utah; 13,528 ft. (4123 m.); highest point in Utah.

Kings Point. Village, Nassau co., near Great Neck, Long Island, New York; pop. (1990c) 4843; U.S. Merchant Marine Academy (1938).

Kings·port \ˈkiŋz-ˌpōrt\. City, Hawkins and Sullivan cos., NE Tennessee, on Holston River 22 mi. (35 km.) NW of Johnson

City; pop. (1990c) 36,365; books, paper, chemicals, plastics, glass, leather; settled c. 1761.

Kings·ton \ˈkiŋ-stən\. **1.** Town, Plymouth co., SE Massachusetts, on Plymouth Bay; pop. (1990c) 9045.

2. City, ⊗ of Caldwell co., NW Missouri; pop. (1990c) 539.

3. City, Rockingham co., SE New Hampshire, 19 mi. (31 km.) E of Manchester; pop. (1990c) 5591.

4. City, ⊗ of Ulster co., SE New York, on Hudson River 15 mi. (24 km.) N of Poughkeepsie; pop. (1990c) 23,095; resort in Catskill Mts. region; boatbuilding; computers, clothing; fruit farming. Estab. as Dutch trading post c. 1615; passed into English hands during 17th cent.; played important role in Revolution; meeting place of first state government, court, and legislature 1777; burned by British 1777; rebuilt, and incorp. as village 1805; chartered as city 1872.

5. Borough, Luzerne co., E Pennsylvania, 3 mi. (5 km.) N of Wilkes-Barre; pop. (1990c) 14,507; figured in "Wyoming Massacre" of 1778 in which troops led by American Loyalist John Butler attacked frontier outpost; incorp. 1857.

6. Unincorporated settlement in South Kingstown (*q.v.*), Washington co., S Rhode Island, 17 mi. (27 km.) NE of Westerly; pop. (1990c) 6504; ⊗ 1752–1900; Univ. of Rhode Island (1892).

7. Village, ⊗ of Roane co., E Tennessee; pop. (1990c) 4552; agriculture.

8. City, ⊗ of Frontenac co., SE Ontario, Canada, on NE shore of Lake Ontario near head of St. Lawrence River; pop. (1991c) 56,597; important transshipment point for Welland Canal and outlet for traffic on Rideau Canal; has locomotive works; shipbuilding; manufactures aluminum products, diesel engines, ceramics; International Hockey Hall of Fame; Queen's Univ. (1841) and Royal Military Coll. of Canada (1876). Site of Indian settlement when Fort Frontenac erected here by French 1673 and shortly thereafter destroyed by Iroquois Indians (later restored); destroyed again by British 1758; present city founded c. 1783 by Loyalist refugees; used as base for British naval force on Lake Ontario during War of 1812; ✻ of Canada 1841–44.

9. Seaport, ✻ of Jamaica, West Indies; pop. (1991p) 103,771; met. area pop. (1991p) 587,748; built on an excellent harbor; commercial center; oil refining, food processing; clothing; Univ. of the West Indies (1948, royal charter 1962); has numerous old buildings. Founded after earthquake had destroyed Port Royal 1692; became seat of government in 1872; has suffered much from fires, hurricanes, and earthquakes; almost destroyed by earthquake 1907; hit by powerful hurricane Sept. 1988.

Kingston upon Hull. See HULL 3.

Kingston upon Thames \ˈtemz\. A borough of Greater London, SE England. See table at LONDON 4.

Kings·town \ˈkiŋz-ˌtau̇n\. **1.** City, Ireland. See DUN LAOGHAIRE.

2. Seaport, ✻ of St. Vincent and the Grenadines, Windward Is., West Indies; on SW coast at head of **Kingstown Bay** at foot of the mountains; pop. (1991p) 15,670; has government buildings, cathedral church, and a botanical garden (estab. 1763), oldest institution of its kind in Western Hemisphere. It was to obtain breadfruit plants for this garden that English Capt. William Bligh made his famous voyage 1787 on the *Bounty* to Tahiti; a later voyage 1793 was successful in getting the plants.

King's Town. See NEWCASTLE 2.

Kings·tree \ˈkiŋz-ˌtrē\. Town, ⊗ of Williamsburg co., E South Carolina, on Black River 35 mi. (56 km.) S of Florence; pop. (1990c) 3858; settled 1732.

Kings·ville \ˈkiŋz-ˌvil, -vəl\. **1.** City, ⊗ of Kleberg co., S Texas, 34 mi. (55 km.) SW of Corpus Christi; pop. (1990c) 25,276; headquarters of King Ranch (ab. 2000 sq. mi. or 5180 sq. km.); natural gas; agriculture; livestock; Texas A & I Univ. (1925).

2. Town, Essex co., SE Ontario, Canada, on Lake Erie 25 mi. (40 km.) SE of Windsor; pop. (1991c) 5716; summer resort.

Kings·wood \ˈkiŋz-ˌwu̇d\. Village, Gloucestershire, SW cen. England, NE suburb of Bristol; pop. (1991p) 87,100.

Kingtehchen. See JINGDEZHEN.

King·us·sie \kiŋ-ˈyü-sē\. Burgh, Highland region, N cen. Scotland, on the Spey; pop. (1981p) 1178; health resort; across the river is **Ruth·ven** \ˈrəth-vən\, birthplace of James Macpherson 1736, self-alleged translator of *The Poems of Ossian.*

King Wil·helms Land \ˈvil-helmz\. Coastal region, NE Greenland.

King Wil·liam \ˈwil-yəm\. **1.** County in E Virginia. See table at VIRGINIA.

2. Village, its ⊗; Indian reservations nearby.

King William Island. Island, Nunavut, Canada, SW of Boothia Penin.; 4955 sq. mi. (12,833 sq. km.).

King William's Town *also* **King·wil·liams·town** *or* **King Williams Town** \kiŋ-ˈwil-yəmz-ˌtau̇n\; *sometimes locally* **King.** Town, S cen. Eastern Cape prov., S Rep. of South Africa, on Buffalo River; formerly surrounded on three sides by Ciseki; pop. (1985c) 16,123; textiles. Founded 1835; made ✻ of British Kaffraria 1847–65.

King·wood \ˈkiŋ-ˌwu̇d\. **1.** Unincorporated settlement, Harris co., SE Texas, a NE suburb of Houston; pop. (1990c) 37,397.

2. Town, ⊗ of Preston co., N West Virginia, 19 mi. (31 km.) SE of Morgantown; pop. (1990c) 3243.

Kinibalu. See KINABALU.

Kin·ki \ˈkin-kē\. Administrative region of Japan, in Honshū. For subdivisions, see table at JAPAN.

Kin·loch \ˈkin-ˌläk\. City, St. Louis co., E Missouri, NW of the city of St. Louis; pop. (1990c) 2702.

Kin·nairds Head \ki-ˈnardz\. Headland projecting into North Sea on NE coast of Scotland, NE Grampian region; lighthouse.

Kin·ne·lon \ˈkin-^{ə}l-ən\. Borough, Morris co., N New Jersey, 13 mi. (21 km.) NW of Paterson; pop. (1990c) 8470.

Kin·ney \ˈki-nē\. County in SW Texas. See table at TEXAS.

Kin·ross \kin-ˈrȯs\ *or* **Kin·ross–shire** \-ˌshir, -shər\. Former county, E cen. Scotland.

Kinsai. See HANGZHOU.

Kin·sale \kin-ˈsāl\. Town and seaport, S co. Cork, SW Ireland, at head of **Kinsale Harbour;** pop. (1991p) 1784; tourist center; fisheries; scene of short-lived landing of Spanish expeditionary force to assist Irish insurrectionaries 1601 and landing of British King James II and his French auxiliaries 1689.

Kinsale, Old Head of. Cape on S coast of Ireland, S of Kinsale; lighthouse. *Lusitania* sunk off coast 1915.

Kinsha. See JINSHA.

Kin·sha·sa \kin-ˈshä-sə\; *formerly* **Lé·o·pold·ville** \ˈlā-ə-ˌpōld-ˌvil, ˈlē-\. City, ✻ of Democratic Republic of the Congo, on W border, at outlet of Pool Malebo in the Congo River; 763 sq. mi. (1976 sq. km.); pop. (1991e) 3,804,000; constitutes an administrative region; commercial center of the republic; major river port; brewing; chemicals, textiles; university (1954); became ✻ of Belgian Congo (see ZAIRE 1) in 1920s and of independent republic 1960; renamed 1966.

Kins·ley \ˈkinz-lē\. City, ⊗ of Edwards co., SW cen. Kansas, 38 mi. (61 km.) ENE of Dodge City; pop. (1990c) 1875.

Kins·man Mountain \ˈkinz-mən\. Two peaks in Grafton co., New Hampshire, W of Franconia Notch; (north) 4275 ft. (1303 m.), (south) 4363 ft. (1330 m.).

Kin·ston \ˈkin-stən\. City, ⊗ of Lenoir co., E North Carolina; pop. (1990c) 25,295; lumber, fertilizer; truck farming; Lenoir Community Coll. (1960).

Kin·ta Valley \ˈkin-tä\. Area in SE Perak state, Malaysia; center of tin-producing region, one of the richest in the world; formed by the **Kinta River,** an E tributary of the Perak.

Kint·la Lake \ˈkint-lə\. Lake, Flathead co., NW Montana, in Glacier National Park; 6 mi. (10 km.) long; alt. 4000 ft. (1219 m.).

Kintla Peak. Mountain, Flathead co., NW Montana, in Glacier National Park; 10,110 ft. (3082 m.).

\ə\ **abut** \ə̇\ matches \$^{ə}$\ kitten, Fr table \ər\ **further** \a\ **ash** \ā\ **ace** \ä\ cot, cart \á\ Fr bac \au̇\ **out** \b̲\ Span Avila \ch\ **chin** \e\ **bet** \ē\ **easy** \g\ **go** \i\ **hit** \ī\ **ice** \j\ **job** \k̲\ Ger **ich, Buch** \$^{n}$\ Fr vin \ŋ\ **sing** \ō\ **go** \ȯ\ **all** \ȯ\ **law** \œ\ Fr **bœuf** \œ̄\ Fr **feu** \ȯi\ **boy** \th\ **thin** \t̲h̲\ **this** \ü\ **loot** \u̇\ **foot** \ue\ Ger **füllen** \ue̅\ Fr **rue** \y\ **yet** \$^{y}$\ Fr digne \ˈdēn^{y}\, nuit \ˈnw^{y}ē\ \yü\ **few** \yu̇\ **fury** \zh\ **vision**

Kin·tyre \kin-'tīr\ *or* **Can·tyre** \kan-\. Peninsula in Strathclyde region, extending S on coast of SW cen. Scotland, with the North Channel and the Atlantic Ocean on W and Kilbrannan Sound (an arm of the Firth of Clyde) on E; ab. 40 mi. (64 km.) long and 6.5 mi. (10 km.) av. width.

Kintyre, Mull of *or* **Mull of Cantyre.** Cape on S extremity of Kintyre Penin., off SW Scotland, projecting into North Channel; lighthouse.

Kin·yang Chhish \'kin-yäŋ-'chish\. Mountain in the Karakoram Range, in part of Jammu and Kashmir controlled by Pakistan; 25,762 ft. (7852 m.).

Kin·zua Dam \kin-'zü-ə\. Dam across Allegheny River, Warren co., N Pennsylvania; 234 ft. (71 m.) high; completed 1965; forms Allegheny Reservoir 27 mi. (43 km.) long extending into Cattaraugus co., New York.

Kioga. See KYOGA.

Ki·on·ga Triangle \kē-'öŋ-gä\. Area of NE Mozambique, surrounding the village of **Kionga** (now usu. spelled Quionga); occupied alternately by Portugal and Germany late 19th–early 20th cents.; transferred to Portugal 1919; became part of Mozambique at its independence 1975.

Kiōto. See KYŌTO.

Ki·o·wa \'kī-ə-,wä\. **1.** Name of counties in three states of the U.S. See tables at COLORADO, KANSAS, OKLAHOMA.
2. Town, ⊗ of Elbert co., E cen. Colorado; pop. (1990c) 275.

Kip·a·wa, Lac \,läk-'ki-pə-,wä\. Lake, SE of Lake Timiskaming in SW Quebec, Canada; 117 sq. mi. (303 sq. km.).

Ki·pe·do Valley National Park \ki-'pā-dō\. National park, NE Uganda, on Sudan border.

Kipp, Mount \'kip\. Peak in Glacier National Park, NW Montana; 8800 ft. (2682 m.).

Kip·pure \ki-'pyu̇r\. Mountain range on boundary bet. cos. Dublin and Wicklow, E Ireland; highest peak 2473 ft. (754 m.).

Ki·ra·ki·ra \,kir-ə-'kir-ə\. Settlement on N cen. coast of San Cristóbal I., SE Solomon Is., W Pacific Ocean.

Kir·by \'kər-bē\. City, Bexar co., S cen. Texas, bordering San Antonio on the E; pop. (1990c) 8326.

Kirch·heim un·ter Teck \'kir-,kīm-,u̇n-tər-'tek\. City, cen. Baden-Württemberg, Germany, 16 mi. (26 km.) ESE of Stuttgart; pop. (1980c) 32,136; first mentioned 960.

Ki·rensk \ki-'rensk\. Town, E cen. Irkutsk Oblast, S Russia in Asia, on right bank of Lena River.

Kir·ghiz *or* **Qir·ghiz** \kir-'gēz\. Former autonomous republic of the Russian S.F.S.R., U.S.S.R.; created 1920; renamed Kazakh A.S.S.R. 1925.

Kirghizia. See KYRGYZSTAN.

Kirgiz Range *or* **Kirghiz Range** *or* **Kirgizskiy Khrebet.** See KYRGYZ RANGE.

Kirgiz Soviet Socialist Republic *or* **Kirghiz Soviet Socialist Republic.** A constituent republic of the U.S.S.R., 1936–91; now independent as Kyrgyzstan (*q.v.*).

Kirgiz Steppe *or* **the Steppes.** Steppe region of cen. Kazakhstan.

Kiria. See KERIYA.

Ki·ri·bati \'kē-rē-bəs, -bäs, -bas—*sic*\. Island nation, W Pacific, SSE of the Marshall Is.; comprises Ocean I. and the Gilbert, Line, and Phoenix groups (*qq.v.*); 277 sq. mi. (717 sq. km.); pop. (1994e) 78,600; ✱ Bairiki on Tarawa; fish, copra.

Kı·rık·ka·le \kə̇-'rə-kä-le\. **1.** Province of Turkey in Asia. See table at TURKEY.
2. Town, its ✱, ab. 36 mi. (58 km.) ESE of Ankara; pop. (1990c) 185,431.

Ki·rin \'kē-'rin\. **1.** Province, NE China. See JILIN 1.
2. One of the three original provinces of Manchuria, China, in cen. and E part; 109,384 sq. mi. (283,305 sq. km.); ✱ Jilin. Under Japanese control 1932–45 it included the following provinces of Manchukuo: Kirin, Mutankiang (now Mudanjiang), parts of Sankiang, Pinkiang, and Chientao; much of its territory now part of Jilin prov.
3. Former province 1932–45, SE cen. Manchukuo; 34,284 sq. mi. (88,796 sq. km.); ✱ Jilin.
4. City, Jilin prov., China. See JILIN 2.

Ki·ri·shi·ma \,kē-rē-'shē-mä, kē-'rē-shē-mä\. Mountain in **Kirishima Range,** NE Kagoshima prefecture, S Kyūshū I., Japan; 5574 ft. (1699 m.); regarded as sacred because, according to legend, the god Ninigi descended on its E summit (Takachihodake) as the forerunner of Jimmu Tennō, the first Japanese sovereign.

Ki·riti·mati \kə-'ris-məs—*sic*\ *or* **Christ·mas Island** \'kris-məs\. One of the Line Is. (*q.v.*) of Kiribati, in cen. Pacific Ocean S of Hawaii and 160 mi. (257 km.) SE of Tabuaeran, ab. 1°57′N, 157°27′W; largest atoll in the Pacific, 234 sq. mi. (606 sq. km.), of which 94 sq. mi. (243 sq. km.) is land; pop. (1990c) 2537. Discovered by English mariner and explorer Capt. James Cook 1777; annexed by Great Britain 1888; included in colony of Gilbert and Ellice Is. 1919; British control disputed by U.S. from 1936; became part of independent Kiribati 1979; U.S. claim officially dropped 1983. See AMERICA ISLANDS.

Ki·ri·wi·na \,kir-ə-'wē-nə\. Largest of the Trobriand Is., W Solomon Sea, 50 mi. (80 km.) N of Fergusson I.; ab. 25 mi. (40 km.) long and bet. 3 and 6 mi. (5 and 10 km.) wide; chief town Losuia, near N end. Occupied by Allied forces 1943 and used as air base.

Kiriwina Islands. See TROBRIAND ISLANDS.

Kirjath–Arba. See HEBRON 4.

Kirk·bur·ton \kərk-'bərt-ᵊn\. Town, West Yorkshire, England; pop. (1981p) 21,387.

Kirk·by \'kər-bē\. Town, Merseyside, NW England; pop. (1981p) 50,898.

Kirkby in Ash·field \'ash-fēld\. Town, Nottinghamshire, N cen. England, 12 mi. (19 km.) NNW of Nottingham; pop. (1981p) 24,467.

Kirk·cal·dy \kə-'kȯ-dē, -'kä-\. Seaport burgh, Fife region, E Scotland, on the Firth of Forth 26 mi. (42 km.) N of Edinburgh; pop. (1981c) 46,520; linoleum, linen, malt, rope and twine, furniture; birthplace of economist Adam Smith 1723.

Kirk·cud·bright \kə-'kü-brē\. **1.** *or* **Kirk·cud·bright·shire** \-,shir, -shər\. Former county, S Scotland.
2. Burgh, S Dumfries and Galloway region, at head of Dee estuary 30 mi. (48 km.) SW of Dumfries; pop. (1981p) 3406; creamery; oil storage depot; 16th cent. ruined castle; ruins of Dundrennan Abbey nearby; at St. Mary's Isle poet Robert Burns first said the well-known grace "Some hae meat ... ".

Kir·kee \'kər-kē\. Town, suburb of Pune (*q.v.*), Maharashtra state, W India; pop. (1991p) 78,046; scene of British victory 1817 over Bājī Rāo II, the last peshwa of the Marathas.

Kir·ke·nes \'kir-kə-,nās\. Seaport town, Finnmark co., N Norway, at head of inlet on S side of Varanger Fjord near Finland border; iron ore; held by Germans as base during WWII.

Kirk·in·til·loch \,kər-kən-'ti-lək\. Burgh, Strathclyde region, W cen. Scotland, on Forth and Clyde Canal 8 mi. (13 km.) NE of Glasgow; pop. (1981p) 32,992.

Kırk Kılıse *or* **Kirk Kilisseh.** See KIRKLARELI 2.

Kirk·land \'kərk-lənd\. City, King co., W cen. Washington, on inlet of Puget Sound 8 mi. (13 km.) NE of Seattle; pop. (1990c) 40,052; residential; Northwest Coll. of the Assemblies of God (1934).

Kırk·lar·e·li \kə̇rk-'lär-e-'lē\. **1.** Province of Turkey in Europe, bordering on Black Sea on the E. See table at TURKEY.
2. *formerly* **Kırk Kı·lı·se** \kə̇rk-'kə̇-\ *or* **Kirk Ki·lis·seh** \kərk-'kē-li-,sā\. Town, its ✱, on highway and branch railroad line 35 mi. (56 km.) E of Edirne; pop. (1990p) 45,344; commercial center in agricultural region; has many mosques and Greek churches; has considerable trade with İstanbul. Scene of defeat of Turks by Bulgarians 1912.

Kirk·pat·rick, Mount \,kərk-'pa-trik\. Mountain, S Victoria Land, Antarctica, S of Mt. Markham, 166°19′E, 84°20′S; 14,855 ft. (4528 m.); the highest peak in Queen Alexandra Range.

Kirks·ville \'kərks-,vil\. City, ⊗ of Adair co., N Missouri, 55 mi. (88 km.) N of Moberly; pop. (1990c) 17,152; electrical appliances; Northeast Missouri State Univ. (1867).

Kir·kuk *or* **Kir·kūk** \kir-'kük\ *also* **Ker·kuk** \kər-\. Town, NE Iraq, 90 mi. (145 km.) SE of Mosul; pop. (1981e) 570,000; agricultural and market center; sheep raising; oil fields; inhabitants mainly Turkmeni; terminus of railroad line from Baghdad; has history of having been long since settled; one of first Arab areas where oil was found in 20th cent.; briefly seized by Arab forces 1941 but retaken by British during WWII; oil production interrupted during 1980s Iran-Iraq War.

Kirk·wall \ˈkərk-ˌwȯl, -wəl\. Burgh, ⊗ of Orkney administrative area, NE Scotland; on Pomona I. in the Orkney Is.; pop. (1981c) 6826; good harbor; exports dairy products; fisheries, boatbuilding; cathedral.

Kirk·wood \ˈkərk-ˌwu̇d\. City, St. Louis co., E Missouri, 13 mi. (21 km.) W of the city of St. Louis; pop. (1990c) 27,291; commercial and residential suburb of St. Louis.

Kirman. See KERMĀN.

Kirmanshah. See BĀKHTARĀN 2.

Kirmasti. See MUSTAFA KEMAL PAŞA.

Kir Moab *or* **Kir of Moab.** See AL-KARAK.

Kirov. See VYATKA 2.

Kirovabad. See GÄNCÄ.

Kirovakan. See VANADZOR.

Kirov Oblast. See VYATKA OBLAST.

Ki·ro·vo–Che·petsk \ˈkir-ə-ˌvō-chə-ˈpetsk\; *formerly* **Kiro·vo–Che·pet·ski** \-ˈpet-skē\. Town, Vyatka Oblast, E cen. Russia in Europe, ab. 20 mi. (32 km.) ESE of the city of Vyatka; pop. (1991e) 95,600.

Ki·ro·vo·hrad \ˌkē-rə-və-ˈhräd\ *or* **Ki·ro·vo·grad** \ˌkē-rə-və-ˈgrät, ki-ˈrō-və-ˌgrad\. **1.** Administrative subdivision of Ukraine, S of the Dnieper River; 9498 sq. mi. (24,600 sq. km.); pop. (1991e) 1,245,300; ✱ Kirovohrad; wheat, corn, sugar beets, sunflowers; livestock.

2. *formerly* **Zi·nov·ievsk** \zə-ˈnȯv-ˌyefsk\ *also* **Eli·sa·vet·grad** \i-ˌli-zə-ˈvet-ˌgrad\ *or* **Ye·li·za·vet·grad** \yi-\. City, its ✱, on Ingul River 155 mi. (249 km.) SE of Kiev; pop. (1991e) 278,000; agricultural center in the black-earth region; agricultural-machinery plants; founded as a fortress 1754 and named after Empress Elizabeth; after the 1917 Russian Revolution, renamed after Bolshevik leader G. E. Zinovyev, who was born here; again renamed 1936 after Soviet politician Sergey Kirov; held by Germans in WWII.

Ki·rovsk \ˈkē-ˌrȯfsk, -rəfsk\. Town, W cen. Murmansk Oblast, NW Russia in Europe, at base of Kola Penin.; pop. (1991e) 49,400; commercial town on railroad line 85 mi. (137 km.) S of the city of Murmansk and E of Lake Imandra.

Kir·rie·muir \ˌkir-ē-ˈmyu̇r\. Burgh, Tayside region, E Scotland; pop. (1981p) 5308; birthplace of writer Sir James M. Barrie 1860.

Kir·sa·nov \kir-ˈsä-nəf\. Town, E Tambov Oblast, S cen. Russia in Europe, on Tambov-Saratov railroad line.

Kır·şe·hir \ˌkər-she-ˈhir\. **1.** Province of Turkey in Asia. See table at TURKEY.

2. Town, its ✱, on highway N of the Kızıl Irmak; pop. (1990p) 74,546; noted for its carpets; important in Byzantine period; enlarged by Emperor Justinian; perhaps was ancient city of **Jus·tin·i·a·nop·o·lis** \jə-ˌsti-nē-ə-ˈnä-pə-lis\.

Kirte. See ALÇITEPE.

Kir·thar Range \ˈkir-tər\. Mountain range bet. Baluchistan and Sind, S Pakistan; highest peak ab. 7000 ft. (2135 m.).

Kirt·land \ˈkərt-lənd\. Village, Lake co., NE Ohio; pop. (1990c) 5881.

Kirun. See CHI-LUNG.

Ki·ru·na \ˈkē-rü-ˌnä\. Town, Norrbotten prov., N Sweden, SE of Torneälven Träsk, on railroad line bet. Narvik, Norway, and Luleå, Sweden; pop. (1993e) 26,217; a mining town near rich deposits of high iron content; geophysical institute.

Kir·yas Jo·el \ˈkir-ˌyäs-ˈjō-əl\. Village, Orange co., New York; pop. (1990c) 7437; estab. as an Orthodox Jewish community.

Kir·yū \ˈkēr-ˌyü\. Town, Gumma prefecture, Honshū, Japan, ab. 55 mi. (88 km.) NNW of Tokyo; pop. (1990p) 126,443; a center of the textile industry.

Kis–Alföld. See ALFÖLD, GREAT.

Ki·san·ga·ni \ˌkē-sän-ˈgä-nē\; *formerly* **Stan·ley·ville** \ˈstan-lē-ˌvil\. City, ✱ of Haut-Zaïre administrative region, Democratic Rep. of the Congo, on Congo River 750 mi. (1207 km.) NE of Kinshasa; pop. (1991e) 373,397; river port and commercial center; university (1963).

Ki·sar \kē-ˈsär\. Small island belonging to Indonesia; ab. 15 mi. (24 km.) N of E tip of Timor, S Malay Archipelago; 51 sq. mi. (132 sq. km.).

Ki·sa·ra·zu \ˌkē-sä-ˈrä-zü\. City, Chiba prefecture, Honshū, Japan, on Tokyo Bay 22 mi. (35 km.) SW of Tokyo; pop. (1990p) 123,434.

Ki·se·levsk \ˌkē-sil-ˈyȯfsk\. Town, Kemerovo Oblast, S cen. Russia in Asia, ab. 90 mi. (145 km.) SSE of the city of Kemerovo; pop. (1992e) 126,000.

Kish \ˈkish\. One of most important of the ancient cities of Sumer and Akkad; its ruins lie ab. 8 mi. (13 km.) E of site of Babylon (*q.v.*) and in early times was on the Euphrates whose course changed later; ruins are very extensive and different strata give valuable archaeological information of different eras: near the surface were found ruins of great temple of the time of Kings Nebuchadrezzar II and Nabonidus 605–539 B.C., below it the palace of Sargon I dating from 3d millennium B.C., and at lowest level remains of Sumerian culture of ab. 4th millennium B.C.; according to legend the ruling city after the Flood.

Ki·shan·garh *or* **Ki·shen·garh** \ki-ˈshən-gər\. **1.** Former Indian state, now part of Rajasthan, NW India; 837 sq. mi. (2168 sq. km.); made treaty with British government 1818; became member of Union of Rajasthan 1948.

2. Town, its ✱; pop. (1991p) 81,944; founded 1611.

Kishinev. See CHIŞINĂU.

Ki·shi·wa·da \ˌkē-shē-ˈwä-dä\. City, Ōsaka prefecture, Honshū, Japan; suburb of the city of Ōsaka; pop. (1990p) 188,553; textiles.

Kishm. See QESHM.

Kishon. See QISHON.

Kisimayo. See KISMAAYO.

Kis·ka \ˈkis-kə\. Island, most westerly and largest of Rat Is. group, W Aleutian Is., SW Alaska; 110 sq. mi. (285 sq. km.); mountainous, highest point above 4000 ft. (1292 m.); Kiska Harbor is on E coast; seized by Japanese 1942; reoccupied by Allied forces 1943.

Kis·ki·min·e·tas \ˌkis-ki-ˈmi-nə-təs\. River, SW Pennsylvania; flows NW into Allegheny River; ab. 20 mi. (32 km.) long; formed by confluence of Conemaugh River and Loyalhanna Creek in SW Indiana co.

Kis·kun·fé·legy·há·za \ˈkēsh-kün-ˈfā-lej-ˌhä-zö\ *or* **Fé·legy·há·za** \ˈfā-lej-ˌhä-zö\. City, cen. Hungary, 66 mi. (106 km.) SE of Budapest; pop. (1991e) 35,000; market center for livestock, tobacco, fruits, and wines; present town dates from 18th cent.

Kis·kun·ha·las \ˈkēsh-ku̇n-ˌhö-ˌlösh\ *or* **Ha·las** \ˈhö-ˌlösh\. City, S Hungary, 35 mi. (56 km.) NW of Szeged; pop. (1991e) 31,100; wine.

Kis·lo·vodsk \ˌkēs-lə-ˈvōtsk\. City, S Stavropol' Kray, S Russia in Europe, on a tributary of the Kuma; pop. (1992e) 118,000; in foothills of N Caucasus Mts. (alt. 2690 ft. or 820 m.) at end of branch railroad line ab. 15 mi. (24 km.) SW of Pyatigorsk; health resort; mineral springs; founded 1803. Birthplace of author Aleksandr Solzhenitsyn 1918.

Kis·maa·yo \kēs-ˈmä-yō\ *or* **Kis·ma·yu** \-ˈmä-yü\ *also* **Chi·si·ma·io** \ˌkē-zē-ˈmä-yō\ *or* **Ki·si·ma·yo** \ˌkē-sē-ˈmä-yō\ *or* **Kis·ma·yo** \ˌkēs-\. Seaport, S Somalia.

Ki·so \ˈkē-sō\. River, SW cen. Honshū, Japan; rises in Nagano prefecture and flows SW into the head of Ise Bay; 144 mi. (232 km.) long.

Kisseraing. See KANMAW KYUN.

Kis·si·dou·gou \ˌkē-sē-ˈdü-gü\. Town, Guinea, at an intersection of roads; pop. (1983p) 40,380.

Kis·sim·mee \ki-ˈsi-mē\. **1.** River, S cen. Florida; flows S from Tohopekaliga Lake through **Lake Kissimmee** (ab. 12 mi. or 19 km. long) into Lake Okeechobee; 140 mi. (225 km.) long; extensively channelized.

2. City, ⊗ of Osceola co., cen. Florida Penin., on Tohopekaliga Lake 18 mi. (29 km.) S of Orlando; pop. (1990c) 30,050; plastics; diversified agriculture; tourism.

Kissingen. See BAD KISSINGEN.

Kistna. See KRISHNA.

Ki·su·mu \kē-'sü-mü\; *formerly* **Port Flor·ence** \'flȯr-əns, 'flär-\. Town, ✱ of Nyanza prov., Kenya; pop. (1984e) 167,100; port on Homa Gulf, NE Lake Victoria.

Ki·ta \'kē-tä\. **1.** Seaport, Ghana. See KETA.

2. Town, W Mali, on Bamako-Dakar railroad line 100 mi. (161 km.) W of Bamako.

Ki·tai \ki-'tī\. See CATHAY.

Kita Iwo. See VOLCANO ISLANDS.

Ki·ta·ka·mi \kē-'tä-kä-mē\. River, Iwate and Miyagi prefectures, N Honshū, Japan; flows S into Ishinomaki Bay at Ishinomaki; 152 mi. (245 km.) long.

Ki·ta·kyū·shū \kē-'tä-ˌkyü-ˌshü\. Seaport city, Fukuoka prefecture, N Kyūshū, Japan; pop. (1990p) 1,026,467; formed 1963 by amalgamation of Kokura, Moji, Tobata, Wakamatsu, and Yawata; a major center of heavy industry; ships coal; shipbuilding, fishing; iron, steel, glass, textiles, chemicals, machinery, cement.

Ki·ta·le \kē-'tä-lā\. Town, W Kenya, near Ugandan border and just E of Mt. Elgon.

Ki·ta·mi \kē-'tä-mē\. City, Hokkaidō, Japan, 145 mi. (233 km.) NE of Sapporo; pop. (1990p) 107,247.

Ki·tan Strait \kē-'tän\; *formerly* **Yu·ra Strait** \yu̇-'rä\. Strait bet. S Honshū I., and SE Awaji I., Japan; connecting Ōsaka Bay with Kii Channel and the Pacific Ocean.

Kit Car·son \'kit-'kär-sən\. County in E Colorado. See table at COLORADO.

Kit Carson Mountain. Mountain, Saguache co., S Colorado; 14,165 ft. (4317 m.).

Kitch·e·ner \'ki-chə-nər\; *formerly* **Ber·lin** \bər-'lin\. City, ⊗ of Waterloo munic. region, SE Ontario, Canada, 62 mi. (100 km.) WSW of Toronto; pop. (1991c) 168,282, met. area pop. 356,421; rubber goods, furniture; meatpacking, distilling. First settled c. 1806 by Pennsylvania Dutch, then by Germans c. 1825; name changed from Berlin to Kitchener 1916 in honor of British field marshal Lord Kitchener.

Kithairón. See CITHAERON.

Kithareng. See KANMAW KYUN.

Kí·thi·ra *or* **Ky·the·ra** *or* **Ký·thi·ra** \'kē-thē-ˌrä\ *or Lat.* **Cy·the·ra** \si-'thir-ə\ *also Ital.* **Ce·ri·go** \chā-'rē-gō\. Southernmost island of the Ionian Is., Greece, in the Mediterranean Sea off SE coast of Peloponnese ab. 8 mi. (13 km.) S of Cape Malea; 107 sq. mi. (277 sq. km.); ✱ Kíthira. Rocky, but with fertile districts. In antiquity had temple of Aphrodite (Cytherea) who according to one legend emerged here from the sea. See PAPHOS.

Kíth·nos *or* **Kýth·nos** \'kēth-ˌnȯs\ *also* **Ther·mia** \ther-'myä\. Island, NW Cyclades, Aegean Sea; part of Cyclades dept., Greece; ab. 8 mi. (13 km.) SSE of Kéa; ab. 18 sq. mi. (47 sq. km.); chief town Kíthnos on NE coast; level and fertile; has thermal springs.

Ki·tik·me·ot \ki-'tik-mē-ət\. Region, N Canada, in Northwest Territories and Nunavut, consisting of Victoria and nearby islands and adjacent part of the mainland; area 243,898 sq. mi. (631,695 sq. km.); pop. (1991c) 4386; constituted an administrative subdivision of Northwest Territories prior to formation of Nunavut 1999.

Kit·i·mat \'ki-tə-ˌmat\. Seaport, W British Columbia, Canada, at head of Douglas Channel; pop. (1991c) 11,305.

Kit·sap \'kit-səp\. County in W Washington. See table at WASHINGTON.

Kit·tan·ning \kə-'ta-niŋ\. Borough, ⊗ of Armstrong co., W Pennsylvania, on Allegheny River 37 mi. (60 km.) NE of Pittsburgh; pop. (1990c) 5120.

Kit·ta·tin·ny Mountain *or* **Kittatinny Mountains** *or* **Kittatinny Ridge** \ˌki-tə-'ti-nē\. Ridge of the Appalachian Mts., SE New York, extending from Ulster co., SW through Sussex and Warren cos. in NW New Jersey, and into Pennsylvania where it forms boundary bet. Monroe, Carbon, and Schuylkill cos. on the NW and Northampton, Lehigh, and Berks cos. on the SE, and continuing SW to the Maryland border; av. height ab. 2000 ft. (610 m.); known as Shawangunk in New York and Blue Mt. in Pennsylvania.

Kit·tery \'ki-tə-rē\. Town, York co., SW Maine, across bay from Portsmouth, New Hampshire; pop. (1990c) 9372; site of Portsmouth Naval Shipyard (estab. 1800). See PORTSMOUTH 1.

Kittery Point. Extreme S point, York co., SW Maine.

Kittim. See CITIUM.

Kit·ti·tas \'ki-ti-təs\. County in cen. Washington. See table at WASHINGTON.

Kitt·son \'kit-sən\. County in NW corner of Minnesota. See table at MINNESOTA.

Kit·ty Hawk \'ki-tē-ˌhȯk\. Small village, Dare co., E North Carolina, on narrow sand barrier opp. Albemarle Sound; nearby is Kill Devil Hill (now a national memorial) where Wright brothers performed experiments, making first manned airplane flight in U.S. Dec. 17, 1903.

Kit·we \'kē-ˌtwä\. Town, Zambia, 180 mi. (290 km.) N of Lusaka; pop. (1990p) 338,207; copper mines.

Kitz·bühel \'kits-bu̅e̅-əl\. Resort town, Tirol, W Austria, 48 mi. (77 km.) ENE of Innsbruck; pop. (1991c) 8119; skiing; received charter 1271.

Kit·zing·en \'kit-siŋ-ən\. City, Bavaria, Germany, on Main River; pop. (1980c) 20,262.

Kiuchuan. See JIUQUAN.

Kiukiang. See JIUJIANG.

Kiungchow. See QIONGSHAN.

Kiūshū. See KYŪSHŪ.

Ki·vi·jär·vi \'kē-vē-ˌyar-vē\. Lake in Vaasa prov., SW cen. Finland.

Ki·vu \'kē-vü\; *or earlier* **Cos·ter·mans·ville** \'käs-tər-mənz-ˌvil\. Former province of E Democratic Rep. of the Congo; now divided into the administrative regions of Maniema, Nord-Kivu, and Sud-Kivu (see table at ZAIRE).

Kivu, Lake. Lake in cen. Africa, bet. Democratic Rep. of the Congo and Rwanda, N of Lake Tanganyika and S of Lake Edward; 1042 sq. mi. (2699 sq. km.); max. depth 1558 ft. (475 m.); alt. 4790 ft. (1460 m.); chief town on its shores Bukavu, Democratic Rep. of the Congo at S end; center of volcanic region: Karisimbi, Mikeno, Nyamlagira, and Nyiragongo, all above 10,000 ft. (3045 m.), nearby.

Kiyang. See QIYANG.

Kiyev. See KIEV.

Ki·zel \ki-'zel, kiz-'yel\. Town, Perm' Oblast, E Russia in Europe, ab. 90 mi. (145 km.) NE of the city of Perm'; pop. (1991e) 36,300.

Kizil. See KYZYL.

Kızıl Adalar. See KIZIL ISLANDS.

Kı·zıl Ir·mak \kə-'zəl-ēr-ˌmäk\; *anc.* **Ha·lys** \'hā-ləs\. River, cen. and N cen. Turkey in Asia; rises in the mountains E of Sıvas and flows in a great curve SW, W, N, and NE into the Black Sea bet. Samsun and Sinop; ab. 715 mi. (1150 km.) long; the largest river of Asia Minor; its main tributaries are the Delice from the E and the Gök from the W.

Kı·zıl Islands \kə-'zəl\ *or Turk.* **Kızıl Ada·lar** \ˌä-dä-'lär\ *or Eng.* **Princ·es Islands** \'prin-səz\; *anc.* **De·mo·ne·si In·su·lae** \ˌdē-mə-'nē-sī-'in-su̇-lē\. Nine small islands in E Sea of Marmara, near coast of Asia Minor ab. 15 mi. (24 km.) S of İstanbul and administratively part of İstanbul prov., Turkey; ab. 5.5 sq. mi. (14 sq. km.); pop. (1990p) 19,353; summer resort; in Byzantine times used as place of banishment; extensive Byzantine remains, incl. monasteries and convents.

Kizil Kum. See KYZYL KUM.

Kizil Uzen. See QEZEL OWZAN.

Kiz·lyar \ˌkiz-'lyär\. Town, E Dagestan, S Russia in Europe, at head of Terek Delta ab. 40 mi. (64 km.) from the Caspian Sea; on the Astrakhan-Makhachkala railroad line ab. 75 mi. (120 km.) NNW of the latter. An old town dating from 16th cent.

Ki·zu \'kē-zü\ *or* **Ki·zu·ga·wa** \ˌkē-zu̇-'gä-wä\. River, S Honshū, Japan, rising in Mie prefecture; a tributary of the Yodo, joining it S of Kyōto.

Kizugawa. **1.** River, Japan. See KIZU.

2. River mouth, Japan. See YODO 2.

Kizyl–Arvat. See GYZYLARBAT.

Kjöge Bugt. See KØGE BAY.

Kjø·len Mountains \ˈchœ-lən\ *or Swed.* **Kö·len** \ˈchœ-lən\. Range along boundary bet. NE Norway and NW Sweden; highest peak Kebnekaise 6965 ft. (2123 m.).

Kla·bat \ˈklä-ˌbät\. Volcanic peak, on NE tip of Sulawesi, Indonesia, just E of Manado; 6632 ft. (2021 m.).

Klabat Bay. Inlet of South China Sea, N coast of Bangka I., Indonesia.

Klad·no \ˈkläd-nȯ\. City, NW Czech Republic, 15 mi. (24 km.) W of Prague; pop. (1991p) 71,735; coal and iron mines; blast furnaces, rolling mills.

Kla·gen·furt \ˈklä-gən-ˌfu̇rt\. City, ✻ of Carinthia, Austria, near Slovenian border just N of Karawanken Mts. and 62 mi. (100 km.) WSW of Graz; pop. (1991c) 89,415; iron, woodworking products, leather; 16th cent. provincial assembly hall; became city 1279; at height of commercial importance in 18th cent.; occupied by Yugoslav troops 1919; center of plebiscite area in 1920 voting to join Austria. Birthplace of author Robert Musil 1880.

Klai·pė·da \ˈklī-pə-də\. **1.** *or Ger.* **Me·mel·ge·biet** \ˈmā-məl-gə-ˌbēt\ *or* **Me·mel·land** \-ˌland, -ˌlänt\. Former German territory, E coast of Baltic Sea, now part of Lithuania; 1092 sq. mi. (2828 sq. km.). For history, see KLAIPĖDA 2.

2. *or Ger.* **Me·mel** \ˈmā-məl\. Seaport city, Lithuania, on the Baltic Sea at the mouth of Neman River; pop. (1992e) 208,300; exports lumber, agricultural products, fish; manufactures wood pulp, textiles.

History: Settled c. 1200; destroyed 1252 by Teutonic Knights who rebuilt fort and changed name to **Me·mel·burg** \ˈmā-məl-ˌbu̇rk\; an important trading town in Hanseatic League; fought over by Swedes and Russians but mainly in Prussian control since 17th cent.; after 1919 administered by France under the League of Nations; seized by Lithuanians Jan. 1923 as their only good port; made part of autonomous territory, created by Memel Statute of 1924; seized by Germany 1939 and held until taken by Soviet armies Jan. 1945; made part of Lithuanian S.S.R., under Soviet control; since 1991 in independent Lithuania.

Klam·ath \ˈkla-məth\. **1.** River, S Oregon and NW California; rises in Lake Ewauna, Klamath co., S Oregon, flows SW across NW extremity of California into the Pacific Ocean; 250 mi. (402 km.) long.

2. County in S Oregon. See table at OREGON.

Klamath Falls. City, ⊗ of Klamath co., S Oregon, at S end of Upper Klamath Lake and on E slope of Cascade Range, 15 mi. (24 km.) N of California border; pop. (1990c) 17,737; lumber; grain and livestock farming; Oregon Institute of Technology (1947); settled c. 1867.

Klamath Lakes. Two lakes in Oregon and California which were formerly connected: **Upper Klamath Lake** in SW Klamath co., S Oregon, and **Lower Klamath Lake** formerly extending across the Oregon-California boundary, but now greatly reduced in size and wholly within Siskiyou co., California.

Klamath Mountains. Mountain range of the Coast Ranges in NW California, extending from Siskiyou co. N into Oregon; includes, in N part, the Siskiyou Mts.

Klang. See KELANG.

Klar \ˈklär\. River, SE cen. Norway and W Sweden; rises in SE cen. Norway, flows S across Swedish border into Lake Vänern; ab. 215 mi. (345 km.) long.

Kla·ten \ˈklä-tən\. Town, cen. Java prov., Indonesia, 20 mi. (32 km.) SW of Surakarta.

Kla·to·vy \ˈklä-tə-vē\ *or Ger.* **Klat·tau** \ˈklä-ˌtau̇\. Town, SW Czech Republic, ab. 70 mi. (115 km.) SW of Prague; pop. (1980p) 21,782; 16th cent. town hall; founded 13th cent.

Klausenburg. See CLUJ-NAPOCA.

Klau·sen Pass \ˈklau̇z-ᵊn\. Alpine pass, Uri canton, cen. Switzerland, E of Altdorf; 6390 ft. (1948 m.).

Klausthal–Zellerfeld. See CLAUSTHAL-ZELLERFELD.

Kle·berg \ˈklā-bərg\. **1.** Coastal county in S Texas. See table at TEXAS.

2. Former city, Dallas co., NE Texas, now part of the city of Dallas.

Kleine Mythe. See MYTHEN.

Kleine Scheidegg. See SCHEIDEGG.

Klerks·dorp \ˈklerks-ˌdȯrp\. Town, North-West prov., NE Rep. of South Africa, 10 mi. (16 km.) N of Vaal River and 100 mi. (161 km.) WSW of Johannesburg, formerly in Transvaal; pop. (1985c) 48,947; gold and uranium mining; lumber; beverages; machinery; grain; founded c. 1838, first Boer settlement in Transvaal.

Kle·ve *also* **Cle·ve** \ˈklā-və\ *or Eng.* **Cleves** \ˈklēvz\ *or Fr.* **Clèves** \klev\. City, North Rhine-Westphalia, Germany, near the Rhine River 66 mi. (106 km.) WSW of Münster; pop. (1992e) 46,450; tourism; footwear; old ducal castle Schwanenburg with Lohengrin legend association. Seat of old duchy of same name whose Duke John, a leader of German Protestantism, was father of Anne of Cleves (1515–57), 4th wife of English King Henry VIII; passed to elector of Brandenburg by treaty 1614 and later to Prussia; to France 1805; restored to Prussia by Congress of Vienna (1814–15); in WWII N anchor of German Siegfried Line, taken by Canadians Feb. 1945.

Klick·i·tat \ˈkli-kə-ˌtat\. **1.** River, S Washington; flows S in Yakima co. and through Klickitat co. into Columbia River.

2. County in S Washington. See table at WASHINGTON.

Klin \ˈklēn, ˈklin\. Town, Moscow Oblast, W cen. Russia in Europe, on Moscow-St. Petersburg R.R. 31 mi. (50 km.) NW of Moscow; pop. (1991e) 95,100; reached in German drive on Moscow Nov. 1941.

Klí·no·vec \ˈklē-nō-ˌvets\ *or Ger.* **Keil·berg** \ˈkīl-ˌberk\. Highest peak in the Erzgebirge, NW Czech Republic; 4080 ft. (1244 m.).

Klin·tsy \ˈklin-ˈsē\. Town, W Bryansk Oblast, W Russia in Europe, on railroad line ab. 85 mi. (137 km.) WSW of the city of Bryansk; pop. (1991e) 78,400.

Kłodz·ko \ˈklȯt-skȯ\ *or Ger.* **Glatz** \ˈgläts\. City, S cen. Wałbrzych prov., SW Poland, 52 mi. (84 km.) SSW of Wrocław; pop. (1989e) 30,294; tourist center; historic remains; varied manufactures. Long settled before fort built 10th cent.; contested over variously by Bohemia, Austria, Prussia; assigned to Poland by Potsdam Conference 1945.

Klöfa Jokull. See VATNAJÖKULL.

Klon·dike \ˈklän-ˌdīk\. District, cen. Yukon Terr., Canada, in Yukon River basin S of Ogilvie Mts.; ab. 800 sq. mi. (2070 sq. km.); lies on both sides of **Klondike River,** ab. 90 mi. (145 km.) long, a tributary of the Yukon flowing W to join it near Dawson; has very severe winter climate. Rich gold-bearing gravel occurs along the small creeks; gold discovered Aug. 1896 on Bonanza Creek, ab. 3 mi. (5 km.) from Dawson; news reached U.S. in summer of 1897 and was followed by rush 1897–99 of thousands, many traveling by way of Lynn Canal, Chilkoot and White passes, and the Yukon; peak of production reached in 1900; total production 1885 to 1929 was in the millions of dollars.

Klondike Gold Rush National Historical Park. See UNITED STATES, *National Historical Parks.*

Klo·ster·neu·burg \ˌklō-stər-ˈnȯi-ˌbu̇rk\. City, Lower Austria, Austria, on Danube River 17 mi. (27 km.) NW of Vienna; pop. (1991c) 24,442; wine; tourism.

Klos·ter–Ze·ven \ˌklōs-tər-ˈzā-vən, -ˈtsā-vən\. See ZEVEN.

Klu·a·ne Lake \klü-ˈō-nē, -ˈä-nē\. Lake, largest in Yukon Terr., Canada, in SW part along N slope of St. Elias Mts.; 184 sq. mi. (477 sq. km.); its outlet is **Kluane River,** ultimately discharging into White and Yukon rivers; the Alaska Highway extends along its S and W shores through the settlement of Burwash Landing.

Kluane National Park. See CANADA, *National Parks.*

Klu·ang \klu̇-ˈäŋ\. Town on railroad line, N Johor state, Malaysia; pop. (1980p) 184,831; airfield.

Klucz·bork \ˈklüj-bȯrk\; *Ger.* **Kreuz·burg** \ˈkrȯits-ˌbu̇rk\ *also* **Kreuzburg in Ober·schle·si·en** \in-ˈō-bər-ˌshlā-zē-ən\. Town, Opole prov., S Poland, 30 mi. (48 km.) NNE of the city

\ə\ **abut** \ə\ matches \ᵊ\ kitten, Fr table \ər\ **further** \a\ **ash** \ā\ **ace** \ä\ cot, cart \á\ Fr bac \au̇\ **out** \b̲\ Span Avila \ch\ **chin** \e\ **bet** \ē\ **easy** \g\ **go** \i\ **hit** \ī\ **ice** \j\ **job** \k̲\ Ger **ich, Buch** \ⁿ\ Fr **vin** \ŋ\ **sing** \ō\ **go** \ö\ **all** \ȯ\ **law** \œ\ Fr **bœuf** \œ̄\ Fr **feu** \ȯi\ **boy** \th\ **thin** \th̲\ **this** \ü\ **loot** \u̇\ **foot** \ue\ Ger **füllen** \ue̅\ Fr **rue** \y\ **yet** \ʸ\ Fr digne \ˈdēnʸ\, nuit \ˈnwʸē\ \yü\ **few** \yu̇\ **fury** \zh\ **vision**

of Opole; pop. (1989e) 26,137; formerly in Germany, assigned to Poland by Potsdam Conference 1945. Birthplace of German writer Gustav Freytag 1816.

Klukhori. See KARACHAYEVSK.

Klukhor Pass. See KARACHAYEVSK.

Klut·lan Glacier \ˈklüt-ˌlan\. Glacier in SW Yukon, Canada; 55 mi. (88 km.) long, ab. 4 mi. (6 km.) wide near its terminus.

Kly·az'·ma *or* **Kly·az·ma** \klē-ˈaz-mə\. River, cen. Russia in Europe; rises just N of Moscow, flows E to join the Oka near Nizhniy Novgorod; ab. 390 mi. (630 km.) long.

Klyu·chev·ska·ya Sop·ka \klē-ü-ˈchef-skə-yə-ˈsȯp-kə\. Volcano (*sopka*) in Eastern Range, Kamchatka Penin., E Russia in Asia; 15,580 ft. (4749 m.); highest mountain in Siberia.

Knä·red \ˈknar-ed\. Town, Halland prov., S Sweden, SE of Halmstad; scene of signing of peace bet. Sweden and Denmark Jan. 1613.

Knares·bor·ough \ˈnarz-bər-ō\. Town, North Yorkshire, N England; pop. (1981c) 13,379; market town; limestone quarries; ruins of ancient castle.

Knife \ˈnīf\. River, W North Dakota; rises in N Billings co., flows E into Missouri River at Stanton, in E Mercer co.; 165 mi. (265 km.) long.

Knight Inlet \ˈnīt\. Narrow inlet, SW British Columbia, Canada, opening into Queen Charlotte Strait; ab. 70 mi. (115 km.) long.

Knin \ˈknēn\. Town, E Croatia, 28 mi. (45 km.) NNE of Šibenik; pop. (1991c) 21,439.

Knit·tel·feld \ˈknit-ᵊl-ˌfelt\. City, Styria, Austria, on Mur River 30 mi. (48 km.) WNW of Graz; pop. (1991c) 13,023; founded c. 1224.

Knock \ˈnäk\. Town, co. Mayo, W Ireland; pop. (1986c) 332; shrine of the Virgin, visited by Pope John Paul II 1979.

Knock·a·doon Head \ˈnä-kə-ˌdün\. Cape on S coast of Ireland, S of entrance to Youghal Bay.

Knockanaffrin. See COMERAGH MOUNTAINS.

Knock·meal·down \näk-ˈmēl-ˌdau̇n\. Mountain range in S Ireland, on boundary bet. cos. Tipperary and Waterford; highest peak Knockmealdown 2609 ft. (795 m.).

Knos·sos *or* **Cnos·sus** *or* **Gnos·sus** \ˈnä-səs\. Royal city of ancient Crete, near the N coast of the island; ruins of its great palace are a few miles SE of Iráklion. Center of Cretan Bronze Age culture; probably fl. c. 2000–1400 B.C. and greatly influenced mainland Mycenaean culture. Seat of legendary King Minos (or line of kings of that name) and site of the labyrinth of Daedalus.

Knott \ˈnät\. County in SE Kentucky. See table at KENTUCKY.

Knot·ting·ley \ˈnä-tiŋ-lē\. Town, West Yorkshire, N England; pop. (1981p) 15,953.

Knowlton. See LAC BROME.

Knox \ˈnäks\. **1.** Name of counties in nine states of U.S. See tables at ILLINOIS, INDIANA, KENTUCKY, MAINE, MISSOURI, NEBRASKA, OHIO, TENNESSEE, TEXAS.

2. City, ⊗ of Starke co., NW Indiana, 33 mi. (53 km.) SW of South Bend; pop. (1990c) 3705.

3. City, Victoria, Australia, an E suburb of Melbourne; pop. (1991c) 121,982.

Knox Coast. Section of coast of Wilkes Land, Antarctica, on Indian Ocean, 66°30′S and 104°E to 109°E.

Knox·ville \ˈnäks-ˌvil, -vəl\. **1.** Town, ⊗ of Crawford co., cen. Georgia.

2. City, Knox co., W Illinois, 5 mi. (8 km.) ESE of Galesburg; pop. (1990c) 3243.

3. City, ⊗ of Marion co., S cen. Iowa, 32 mi. (51 km.) ESE of Des Moines; pop. (1990c) 8232.

4. City, ⊗ of Knox co., E Tennessee, on Tennessee River ab. 105 mi. (170 km.) NE of Chattanooga; pop. (1990c) 165,121; manufactures textiles, chemicals, plastics, foundry products; marble quarries; timber; tobacco; tourism; administrative center of Tennessee Valley Authority (1933 ff); site of World's Fair 1982; Univ. of Tennessee, Knoxville (1794), Knoxville Coll. (1863), Johnson Bible Coll. (1893). Settled c. 1786; became ⊗ 1792; served as first ✻ of Tennessee 1796–1812, again 1817–19; incorp. as city 1815; occupied by Union troops of Gen. Ambrose E. Burnside 1863, besieged by Confederate army under Gen. James Longstreet 1863.

Knud Ras·mus·sen Land \ˈknüd-ˈräs-ˌmu̇s-ᵊn, -ˈras-mə-sən\. Region, N and NW Greenland, bet. Baffin Bay and Lincoln Sea.

Knu·rów \ˈknü-rüf\. Town, Katowice prov., S Poland, ab. 14 mi. (23 km.) W of the city of Katowice; pop. (1989e) 35,969.

Knuts·ford \ˈnəts-fərd\. Town, Cheshire, NW England, near the Birken 13 mi. (21 km.) SSW of Manchester; pop. (1981p) 13,675; residential; the *Cranford* of novelist Elizabeth Cleghorn Gaskell.

Knys·na \ˈknis-nə\. Town, Western Cape prov., S Rep. of South Africa, 160 mi. (257 km.) W of Port Elizabeth; in forest region near the coast.

Ko *also* **Koh** \ˈkȯ, ˈkō\. Thai word for "island." For names beginning with this word, see the 2d element, as for **Ko Kut,** see KUT 2.

Ko·a·ni \kō-ˈä-nē\. Town, Zanzibar I., Tanzania, ✻ of Zanzibar South and Central region.

Ko·ba·rid \ˈkō-bə-ˌrēd\ *or Ger.* **Kar·freit** \ˈkär-ˌfrīt\ *or Ital.* **Ca·po·ret·to** \ˌkä-pō-ˈre-tō\. Village, Slovenia; in WWI campaign 1917, scene of a major defeat of Italian forces under Gen. Raffaele Cadorna who were driven back to the Piave by Austro-German forces under Gen. Otto von Below.

Kobdo. **1.** River, Mongolia. See HOBDO GOL.

2. Town, Mongolia. See HOVD.

Kō·be \ˈkō-bā\. Seaport and commercial city, ✻ of Hyōgo prefecture, S coast of W Honshū, Japan; pop. (1990p) 1,477,423; built partly along the N shore of Ōsaka Bay and partly on the hillsides; has close connections with city of Ōsaka ab. 20 mi. (32 km.) to the E; extensive port facilities; shipbuilding; manufacture of steel, rubber goods, textiles; Kōbe Univ. of Economics (1948); Kōbe Univ. (1949). Until the Meiji Restoration only a fishing village; developed rapidly, absorbing nearby Hyōgo, after latter was reopened to foreign trade 1868; in WWII severely bombed by Allied forces, entirely rebuilt since 1945; suffered severe earthquake Jan. 1995.

København. See COPENHAGEN.

Ko·blenz *or* **Co·blenz** \ˈkō-ˌblents\; *anc.* **Con·flu·en·tes** \ˌkän-flu̇-ˈen-tēz\. City, North Rhine-Westphalia, Germany, at confluence of Moselle and Rhine rivers 50 mi. (80 km.) SSE of Cologne; pop. (1992e) 109,046; trades in wine; furniture; tourism.

History: Orig. a Roman station; became city 13th cent.; besieged by French 1688; a place of refuge for French émigrés during Revolution; occupied by French 1794 and later made ✻ of French dept. of Rhin-et-Moselle; ceded to Prussia 1815; became ✻ of Rhine Province (Prussia) 1824; fortified; occupied by American troops 1919–23 and by French troops 1923–29; in WWII scene of battle Mar. 1945 in which it was taken by Americans. Birthplace of statesman and diplomatist Klemens von Metternich 1773.

Ko·buk \kō-ˈbu̇k\. River, NW Alaska, S of Baird Mts.; ab. 300 mi. (485 km.) long; flows W to Kotzebue Sound through **Kobuk Valley National Park** (see UNITED STATES, *National Parks*).

Koca. See XANTHUS 1.

Kocaba. See KACZAWA.

Kocabaş. See GRANICUS.

Ko·ca·e·li \ˌkȯ-ˈjä-e-ˌlē\. **1.** Province of Turkey in Asia. See table at TURKEY.

2. Town, NW Turkey in Asia. See İZMİT.

Koch Bihar. See COOCH BEHAR 2.

Ko·cher \ˈkȯ-ḵər\. River, Baden-Württemberg, Germany; flows into Neckar River 6 mi. (10 km.) N of Heilbronn; ab. 100 mi. (160 km.) long.

Kō·chi \ˈkō-chē\. **1.** Prefecture, Shikoku, Japan; ✻ Kōchi; agricultural machinery, paper, raw silk, dried fish. See table at JAPAN.

2. Seaport city, its ✻, on S coast of Shikoku I. on inlet of Tosa Bay; pop. (1990p) 317,090; fish processing; castle (orig. 17th cent.).

Koch Peak \ˈkäch\. Mountain, E Madison co., SW Montana; 11,286 ft. (3440 m.).

Kocs \'kōch\. Village, NW Hungary, SSE of Komárom; the coach (English word for a horse-drawn carriage derived from name of the village) said to have originated here.

Ko·dai·ka·nal *or* **Ko·daik·kā·nal** \kō-'dī-kä-ˌnal\. Town, Tamil Nadu, India, 50 mi. (80 km.) NW of Madurai; pop. (1991p) 27,461; health resort; government meteorological observatory, alt. ab. 7000 ft. (2135 m.).

Ko·dai·ra \kō-'dī-rä\. City, Honshū, Japan, E suburb of Tokyo; pop. (1990p) 164,021.

Ko·di·ak \'kō-dē-ˌak\. **1.** Island in Gulf of Alaska SE of Alaska Penin., S Alaska; 5363 sq. mi. (13,890 sq. km.); fishing, esp. for salmon, which is more abundant here than anywhere else in Alaska; Coast Guard station. Habitat of Kodiak bear. Site of first Russian colony in America (founded 1784); center of Russian fur trade through early 19th cent.

2. Former borough, S Alaska.

3. City, S Alaska, on NE coast of Kodiak I.; pop. (1990c) 6365; museum; incorp. 1940; founded at present site by Russian fur trader Aleksandr Baranov 1792.

Kodiak Island. Division in Alaska. See table at ALASKA.

Ko·dok \'kō-ˌdōk\; *formerly* **Fa·sho·da** \fə-'shō-də\. Town, SE Sudan, NE of Malakal; its seizure by a French force created serious international crisis 1898 almost causing war bet. Great Britain and France.

Koedoes. See KUDUS.

Koe·kel·berg \'kü-kəl-ˌberk\. Commune, Brabant prov., Belgium, suburb of Brussels; pop. (1981c) 16,643.

Koepang. See KUPANG.

K'o–erh–ch'in–yu–i–ch'ien–ch'i. See HORQIN YOUYI QIANQI.

Koesfeld. See COESFELD.

Koetai. See MAHAKAM.

Koetaradja. See BANDA ATJEH.

Koetoardjo. See KUTOARDJO.

Koett·litz Glacier \'ket-lits\. Glacier in the Royal Society Range, Antarctica; ab. 53 mi. (85 km.) long, 8 mi. (13 km.) wide near its terminus.

Ko·fo·ri·dua \ˌkō-ˌfō-rē-'dü-ä\. Town, ✻ of Eastern Region, S Ghana, on railroad line ab. 38 mi. (61 km.) N of Accra; pop. (1984c) 58,731.

Kō·fu \'kō-fü\. City, ✻ of Yamanashi prefecture, S cen. Honshū, Japan, 65 mi. (105 km.) W of Tokyo; pop. (1990p) 200,630; formerly center of silk industry; tourism; grapes; in feudal era a seat of several powerful lords.

Ko·ga \'kō-gä\. City, Ibaraki prefecture, Honshū, Japan, 37 mi. (60 km.) N of Tokyo; pop. (1990p) 58,227.

Ko·ga·nei \ˌkō-gä-'nā\. City, Tokyo prefecture, Honshū, Japan, 18 mi. (29 km.) W of the city of Tokyo; pop. (1990p) 105,888.

Kog·a·rah \'kä-gə-rə\. Municipality, E New South Wales, SE Australia, S suburb of Sydney, W of Botany Bay; pop. (1991c) 46,518.

Kø·ge \'kœ-gə\. Town, Roskilde co., Denmark; pop. (1989e) 36,211.

Kø·ge Bay *or* **Køge Bugt;** *mostly formerly* **Kjö·ge Bugt** \'kyœ-gə-'bu̇kt\. Bay on E cen. coast of Sjælland I., Denmark; scene of battle 1677 in which Danes under Adm. Niels Juel defeated superior Swedish naval force.

Ko·gi \'kō-gē\. State of Nigeria. See table at NIGERIA.

Ko·gur·yo \ˌkō-gu̇r-'yō\. Ancient kingdom, Korea. See *History* at KOREA.

Koh. 1. \'kō\ *or* **Kūh** \'kü\. Persian word for "mountain," or "mountain range." For names beginning with this word, see the 2d element.

2. Thai word for "island." See KO.

Ko·ha·la \kō-'hä-lä\ *or* **Kapa·au** \kä-'pä-ˌau̇\. Village, Hawaii co., Hawaii, near coast at N end of Hawaii I.; pop. (1990c) 1083. Birthplace of Kamehameha I c.1758, first to unite and to become king of the Hawaiian Is.

Kohala Mountains. Range in N end of Hawaii I., Hawaii; highest peak 5505 ft. (1678 m.).

Ko·hat \kō-'hät\. Town, North-West Frontier prov., Pakistan, on affluent of Indus River 37 mi. (60 km.) S of Peshawar; pop. (1981c) 77,604; former military base for S frontier of the Afridi people. Connected with Peshawar by **Kohat Pass** (ab. 13 mi. or 21 km. long and 1200 ft. or 366 m. to 1.25 mi. or 2 km. wide).

Ko·hi·ma \'kō-hē-mə\. Town, ✻ of Nagaland state, NE India; near N Manipur border and 30 mi. (48 km.) SE of the railroad line at Dimapur; pop. (1991p) 53,122; besieged unsuccessfully by Japanese during Manipur campaign Mar.–June 1944.

Koh–i–nuh. See ARARAT 2.

Koh·kī·lū·yeh va Bo·yer Ah·ma·dī–ye Sar·dīr \'kō-ˌkē-ˌlü-ye-ˌvä-'bȯi-ər-'äk-mä-ˌdē-ye-sär-'dēr\ *or* **Boyer Ahmadī–ye Sardīr va Kohkīlūyeh.** Province (formerly a governorship) of W cen. Iran. See table at IRAN.

Kohl·scheid \'kōl-ˌshīt\. Commune, North Rhine-Westphalia, Germany, N suburb of Aachen.

Koht·la–Jär·ve *or Russ.* **Kokht·la–Yar·ve** \'kōkt-lə-'yar-vā\. Town, Estonia, ab. 30 mi. (48 km.) W of Narva; pop. (1992e) 28,310.

Ko Hu. See GE HU.

Koil *or* **Koil–Aligarh.** See ALIGARH.

Koivisto *and* **Koivisto Island.** See PRIMORSK.

Kŏ·je–do \ˌkə-jā-'dō\. Island in Korea Strait, off SE coast of South Korea near Pusan; housed North Korean prisoners of war during Korean War.

Kokand. See QŪQON.

Kok·che·tav \ˌkək-chi-'täf\. **1.** Administrative subdivision of Kazakhstan, in N; 30,154 sq. mi. (78,099 sq. km.); pop. (1991e) 669,400; ✻ Kokchetav; dairying; gold.

2. Town, its ✻, 115 mi. (185 km.) S of Petropavlovsk; pop. (1991e) 143,300; railroad junction; food processing.

Kokhtla–Yarve. See KOHTLA-JÄRVE.

Kok·ko·la \'kȯ-kȯ-lä\. Seaport, Vaasa prov., W Finland, on Gulf of Bothnia 70 mi. (113 km.) NNE of the city of Vaasa; pop. (1989c) 34,566; founded 1620.

Ko·ko·da \kō-'kō-dä\. Settlement, New Guinea I., Papua New Guinea, WSW of Buna on E side of Owen Stanley Range; connected with Port Moresby by highway ab. 100 mi. (160 km.) long over the mountains; in WWII, involved in heavy fighting bet. Japanese and Allies 1942.

Ko·ko Head \'kō-kō\ *also* **Ka·wai·hoa Point** \ˌkä-wī-'hō-ä\. Promontory on SE coast of Oahu I., Hawaii, on E side of Maunalua Bay; 642 ft. (196 m.) high.

Ko·ko·le Point \kō-'kō-lā\. Cape on W coast of Kauai I., Hawaii.

Ko·ko·mo \'kō-kə-ˌmō\. City, ⊗ of Howard co., N cen. Indiana, 50 mi. (80 km.) N of Indianapolis; pop. (1990c) 44,962; automobile parts, glass, tool steel; Indiana Univ. at Kokomo (1945); city founded ab. 1843; home of inventor Elwood Haynes.

Koko Nor. See QINGHAI.

Ko·ko·po \'kō-kə-ˌpō\. Town, NE New Britain I., Bismarck Archipelago, Papua New Guinea, 14 mi. (23 km.) SE of Rabaul; formerly **Her·berts·hö·he** \'her-berts-ˌhœ-ə\, and former German ✻ of New Britain (Neu-Pommern).

Kok·so·ak \'käk-sə-ˌwak\. River, N Quebec, Canada; formed by confluence of Caniapiscau and Larch rivers, flows NE into S Ungava Bay; 110 mi. (177 km.) long.

Kok·stad \'kōk-ˌstät\. Town, S KwaZulu-Natal prov., Rep. of South Africa, 110 mi. (177 km.) SW of Durban; the chief town of Griqualand East (*q.v.*) in the Transkeian Territories; pleasant climate and high alt. (4500 ft. or 1372 m.).

Ko·ku·bun·ji \ˌkō-kü-'bün-jē\. City, Tokyo prefecture, Honshū, Japan, 15 mi. (24 km.) W of the city of Tokyo; pop. (1990p) 100,958.

Kokumbona. See KAKAMBONA.

Ko·ku·ra \'kō-kü-ˌrä, kō-'kü-rä\. See KITAKYŪSHŪ.

Ko Kut. See KUT 2.

Kol. See ALIGARH.

Ko·la \'kō-lə\. **1.** S tributary of the Tuloma River, W Murmansk Oblast, NW Russia in Europe, joining it at the town of Kola.

2. Town, Murmansk Oblast, NW Russia in Europe, ab. 12 mi. (19 km.) S of the city of Murmansk and at junction of Kola River with the Tuloma; one of oldest towns in extreme N of Russia.

Kola Bay *or Russ.* **Kol'·skiy Za·liv** \'kȯlʸ-skē-zə-'lʸēf\. Inlet of Barents Sea, NW Murmansk Oblast, NW Russia in Europe; ab. 22 mi. (35 km.) long; the city of Murmansk is at its head; receives Tuloma River.

Kola Peninsula *or Russ.* **Kol'·skiy Po·lu·o·strov** \'kȯlʸ-skē-ˌpȯ-lə-'ȯ-strəf\. Peninsula projecting E on NW coast of Russia in Europe bet. the White Sea and the Arctic Ocean (Barents Sea); forms Murmansk Oblast (*q.v.*).

Ko·lar \kō-'lär, 'kō-ˌ\. Town, E Karnataka, S India, 140 mi. (225 km.) W of Madras; pop. (1992e) 103,157; textiles.

Kolar Gold Fields. City, E Karnataka, S India, 145 mi. (233 km.) W of Madras; pop. (1991p) 156,398; gold mines.

Kolberg. See KOŁOBRZEG.

Kolchugino. See LENINSK-KUZNETSKI.

Kold·ing \'kȯ-leŋ\. Seaport, Vejle co., SE Jutland, Denmark, on inlet of Little Belt; pop. (1989e) 57,128; textiles, machinery, cement; 13th cent. castle; one of the oldest stone churches in Denmark (13th cent.). Dates back to 10th cent.; scene of two battles in Danish history: (1) 1644 victory over Swedes, and (2) Danish defeat in Schleswig-Holstein conflict 1849.

Ko·lea \ˌkō-lā-'ä\. Town, N Algeria, SW of Algiers; pop. (1987p) 33,115.

Kölen. See KJØLEN MOUNTAINS.

Kol·gu·yev \kəl-'gü-yəf\. Island in Barents Sea, Nenets Autonomous Okrug, N Russia in Europe, 50 mi. (80 km.) off the mainland, NE of Kanin Penin.; 2300 sq. mi. (5957 sq. km.); chiefly tundra; reindeer herding.

Kol·ha·pur \'kō-lə-ˌpu̇r\. **1.** Former Indian state, chief state of the Deccan and Kolhapur States, now part of SW Maharashtra, W India, in Western Ghats with E part sloping into plain of the Deccan; 3219 sq. mi. (8337 sq. km.); former ruling family traced descent from younger son of Śivājī, founder of Maratha power; invaded by British expeditions 18th cent.; came under British control early 19th cent.

2. City, Maharashtra, W India, 180 mi. (290 km.) SSE of Bombay; pop. (1991c) 406,370; trade center; university (1962); many old Buddhist temples.

Kolhapur and Deccan States. See DECCAN AND KOLHAPUR STATES.

Kolima. See KOLYMA.

Kolima Mountains. See KOLYMA MOUNTAINS.

Ko·lín \'kȯ-ˌlēn\ *or Ger.* **Ko·lin** \kō-'lēn\. Town, cen. Czech Republic, on Labe (Elbe) River E of Prague; pop. (1980p) 30,921; chemicals; nearby is battlefield where Prussian King Frederick the Great was defeated 1757 by Austrian forces of Field Marshal Daun during Seven Years' War.

Ko·li Point \'kō-lē\. Point on N coast of Guadalcanal I., Solomon Is., W Pacific Ocean, ab. 3 mi. (5 km.) E of Lunga Point; involved in Pacific campaign fighting during WWII.

K'o–li–ya. See KERIYA.

Kol·kas·rags \'kōl-kəs-ˌrägs\; *mostly formerly* **Do·mes·näs** \'du̇-məs-ˌnes\. Cape on NW coast of Latvia, on S side of entrance to Gulf of Riga.

Kollam. See QUILON.

Kölln \'kœln\. A c. 13th cent. Wendish village, W cen. Europe, which with village of Berlin united under name Berlin. See *History* at BERLIN.

Kolmar. See COLMAR.

Köln. See COLOGNE.

Ko·ło \'kȯ-wȯ\. Commune, E cen. Konin prov., Poland, on Warta River 44 mi. (71 km.) WNW of Łódź; pop. (1981p) 20,309.

Ko·loa \kō-'lō-ä\. Village, near S coast of Kauai I., Hawaii, SW of Lihue; pop. (1990c) 1791; had one of first sugar plantations in Hawaii (estab. 1835).

Koloa Bay. Bay on S coast of Kauai I., Hawaii, E of Lawai Bay.

Ko·łob·rzeg \kȯ-'wȯb-ˌzhek\ *or Ger.* **Kol·berg** \'kȯl-ˌberk\. City and port on Gulf of Pomerania, NW Koszalin prov., NW Poland, 25 mi. (40 km.) W of the city of Koszalin; pop. (1989e) 44,557; health and beach resort; fishing. Polish from 10th cent.; to Brandenburg 1648; member of Hanseatic League; captured by U.S.S.R. Mar. 1945; assigned to Poland by the Potsdam Conference 1945.

Ko·lom·bang·a·ra \ˌkō-lōm-'bäŋ-ä-rä\. Island off W end of New Georgia I., Solomon Is., W Pacific Ocean; circular shaped, ab. 17 mi. (27 km.) in diameter, with volcanic cone 5799 ft. (1768 m.); bet. it and New Georgia is Kula Gulf (naval battles July 1943); on S shore Japanese had airfield.

Kolomea. See KOLOMYYA.

Ko·lom·na \kə-'lȯm-nə\. City, Moscow Oblast, W cen. Russia in Europe, on railroad line near confluence of Moskva and Oka rivers 65 mi. (105 km.) SE of the city of Moscow; pop. (1992e) 164,000; diesel engines, rubber; first mentioned 1177; to Moscow early 14th cent.; sacked four times by Tatars.

Ko·lo·my·ya \ˌkə-lə-'mē-yə\ *or Pol.* **Ko·ło·my·ja** \ˌkȯ-wȯ-'mē-yä\ *or Ger.* **Ko·lo·mea** \ˌkō-lō-'mā-ə\. City, SW Ukraine, on Prut River 30 mi. (48 km.) SSE of Ivano-Frankivs'k, at E end of gateway through E Carpathian Mts. via Jablonica Pass; pop. (1991e) 66,000; connected by rail with Ivano-Frankivs'k and Chernivitsi; agricultural trade center; manufactures chemicals, textiles. Held by both Russians and Germans in WWII.

Ko·lo·nia \kō-'lō-nē-ə\. Town, Pohnpei I.; former ✻ of Federated States of Micronesia; pop. (1985c) 6169.

Ko·lon·jë \kə-'lȯn-yə\. **1.** *formerly* **Er·se·kë** \er-'se-kə\. District of SE Albania. See table at ALBANIA.

2. Town, Albania. See ERSEKË 2.

Kolozsvár. See CLUJ-NAPOCA.

Kol·pa·she·vo \kəl-'pä-shə-və\. Town, cen. Tomsk Oblast, SW cen. Russia in Asia, on right bank of the Ob' where the Ket' joins it.

Kólpos Kaválas *or* **Kólpos Kavállas.** See KAVÁLA 2.

Kólpos Merabéllou. See MIRABELLA BAY.

Kolski Poluostrov. See KOLA PENINSULA.

K'o–lu–lun. See KERULEN 1.

Kol·we·zi \kōl-'wā-zē\. Town, Shaba administrative region, Democratic Rep. of the Congo, 90 mi. (145 km.) WNW of Likasi; pop. (1991e) 544,497.

Ko·ly·ma *or* **Ko·li·ma** \ˌkä-lə-'mä\. River, E Russia in Asia; rises in Kolyma Mts. in Khabarovsk Kray, flows generally N and NE into Arctic Ocean; 1110 mi. (1786 km.) long; navigable to Verkhne-Kolymsk; gold diggings worked along its upper course; its chief tributaries the Omolon and Anyui.

Kolyma Mountains *or* **Kolima Mountains** *or Russ.* **Ko·lym·skiy Khre·bet** \kə-'lim-skē-kri-'byet\. Mountain range in NE Russia in Asia, N of the Sea of Okhotsk and nearly parallel to coastline.

Ko·ma·ga·ta·ke \kō-ˌmä-gä-'tä-kā\. Name of several mountain peaks in Japan: (1) Active volcano, SW shore of Uchiura Bay, SW Hokkaidō I.; 1183 ft. (361 m.); (2) Volcanic peak, W Kanagawa prefecture, SE Honshū, near Hakone; 4349 ft. (1326 m.); (3) Peak, S cen. Nagano prefecture, cen. Honshū; 9666 ft. (2946 m.); and (4) Peak, W Yamanashi prefecture, S cen. Honshū; 2966 ft. (904 m.).

Ko·ma·ki \kō-'mä-kē\. City, Aichi prefecture, Honshū, Japan, 8 mi. (13 km.) N of Nagoya; pop. (1990p) 124,441.

Ko·man·dor·ski·ye Os·tro·va \ˌkä-män-'dȯr-skē-yi-'ȯs-trə-və\ *or* **Ko·man·dor·ski Islands** \-'dȯr-skē\ *also* **Com·mand·er Islands** \kə-'man-dər\. Island group E of Kamchatka Penin., in SW Bering Sea; 850 sq. mi. (2202 sq. km.); administered as part of Khabarovsk Kray, Russia; chief islands Bering or Beringa (on which the Danish navigator Vitus Bering died 1741) and Medny; chief settlement Nikolskoye; former hunting ground for the fur seal, but by 1911 practically all animals slaughtered and during 20th cent. environmental protection efforts limited hunting; nearby waters scene of U.S. naval victory over Japanese 1943.

Ko·már·no \'kȯ-mär-ˌnȯ\ *or Ger.* **Ko·morn** \'kō-ˌmȯrn\ *or Hung.* **Ko·má·rom** \'kō-mä-ˌrōm\. Town, S Slovakia, at confluence of the Váh with the Danube opp. Komárom, Hungary; pop. (1991p) 37,370; commercial and shipping center; transferred from Hungary to Czechoslovakia 1920 by Treaty of Grand Trianon; birthplace of the Hungarian novelist Mór Jókai 1825.

Ko·má·rom \ˈkō-mä-ˌrōm\ *or Ger.* **Ko·morn** \ˈkō-ˌmȯrn\. City, NW Hungary, on Danube River 48 mi. (77 km.) WNW of Budapest; pop. (1980p) 19,955.

Komárom–Esztergom. County of NW Hungary. See table at HUNGARY.

Ko·ma·ti \kō-ˈmä-tē\. River, S Africa; rises in N Drakensberg, Mpumalanga prov., N Rep. of South Africa, flows E, curves through N Swaziland, turns N; joined by Crocodile River; ab. 1 mile (1.6 km.) below junction flows through a cleft 600 ft. (183 m.) deep at Komatipoort; crosses boundary bet. Rep. of South Africa and Mozambique and flows in a wide curve N then S, into Delagoa Bay; ab. 500 mi. (805 km.) long.

Ko·ma·ti·poort \kō-ˈmä-tē-ˌpȯrt\. Frontier railroad town, Mpumalanga prov., NE Rep. of South Africa, ab. 48 mi. (77 km.) NW of Maputo, Mozambique, on Komati River.

Ko·mat·su \kō-ˈmät-sü\. City, Ishikawa prefecture, Honshū, Japan, 15 mi. (24 km.) SW of Kanazawa; pop. (1990p) 106,072.

Komba. See GRANDE, RIO 1.

Ko·mi \ˈkō-mē\. Republic, NE Russia in Europe, W of the Northern Urals; 160,579 sq. mi. (415,900 sq. km.); pop. (1992e) 1,255,000; before 1991 comprised **Komi A.S.S.R.** and earlier **Zy·ri·an Autonomous Area** \ˈzir-ē-ən\; ✻ Syktyvkar. Mostly level country, with tundra in N, mountain slopes of Urals in E, and in NW a height of land not more than 1000 ft. (305 m.); lies chiefly in the basins of the Pechora and upper Vychegda rivers. Two thirds of area is covered by forests (largely spruce, pine, birch); has some agriculture: potatoes, rye, oats; livestock (cattle, reindeer); fur trapping; industries connected with lumbering; no railroads until early 1940s when 700 mi. (1126 km.) of Northern Pechora R.R. completed NE from Kotlas; extracts coal, oil, natural gas. An autonomous area created 1921; N strip along the Arctic transferred 1929 to Nenets National Okrug; reorganized 1936 as a republic; became republic within Russia 1991; subsequently became member of Russian Federation.

Ko·mi–Perm·yak Autonomous Okrug \ˈkō-mē-ˈperm-yak … ˈō-ˌkrük\ *also* **Komi–Perm·yat·skiy Autonomous Okrug** \-pər-ˈmyät-skē\. Administrative subdivision of Russia, W of the Ural Mts.; 12,703 sq. mi. (32,901 sq. km.); pop. (1992e) 160,000; ✻ Kudymkar; in basin of upper Kama River; lumbering; formed 1925 from area S of Komi A.S.S.R. (now Komi Rep.).

Kom·lo \ˈkōm-lō\. Town, Baranya co., S Hungary; pop. (1991e) 30,900.

Kommunarsk. See ALCHEVSK.

Kommunizma, Pik. See COMMUNISM PEAK.

Ko·mo·do \kə-ˈmō-dō\. Small island, E of Sumbawa I. and W of Flores I., in the Lesser Sunda Is., Indonesia; ab. 25 mi. (40 km.) long by 12 mi. (19 km.) wide; wild and rugged and little known until giant lizards (Komodo dragon, *Varanus komodoensis*) were discovered on it c. 1912.

Komorn. 1. Town, Slovakia. See KOMÁRNO.
2. City, Hungary. See KOMÁROM.

Komotau. See CHOMUTOV.

Ko·mo·ti·ní *also* **Ko·mo·ti·nē** \ˌkō-mō-tē-ˈnē\ *or Turk.* **Gü·mül·ji·na** \ˌgue-muel-yē-ˈnä\. City, ✻ of Rhodope dept., West Thrace, NE Greece, E of Xánthi; pop. (1991p) 40,522; market town; dates from Byzantine times.

Kom·pong Cham \ˈkäm-ˌpȯŋ-ˈchäm\ *also* **Kam·pong Cham** \ˈkäm-\. Town, SE Cambodia, ab. 39 mi. (63 km.) NE of Phnom Penh, near the Mekong River; pop. (1987c) 33,000.

Kompong Som \ˈsȯm\ *or* **Kompong Son** \ˈsȯn\ *also* **Kâm·póng Saôm** \ˈkäm-ˈpȯŋ-ˈsau̇m\; *formerly* **Si·ha·nouk·ville** \sē-ˈhä-nu̇k-ˌvil\. Port, S Cambodia; on **Kampong Som Bay** *Khmer* **Chhung Kampong Som** \ˈchu̇ŋ\; Cambodia's principal port.

Kom·so·mo·lets \ˌkäm-sə-ˈmȯ-ləts\. Northernmost of the large islands of the Severnaya Zemlya group, Taymyr Autonomous Okrug, N Russia in Asia; in Arctic Ocean, 80°30′N, 95°E.

Kom·so·mol'sk–na–Amure *or* **Kom·so·molsk–na–Amure** \ˌkäm-sə-ˈmȯlʸsk-nə-ə-ˈmu̇r-ə\. City, S Khabarovsk Kray, SE Russia in Asia, on left bank of Amur River 165 mi. (265 km.) NNE of the city of Khabarovsk; pop. (1992e) 319,000; an entirely new city when begun 1932 by volunteers of the Young Communist League (*Russ.* Komsomol—hence the name); has had very rapid growth, being now one of largest cities in Russia's Far East; on Trans-Siberian R.R. extension from Khabarovsk to Nikolayevsk-na-Amure and terminal of N transcontinental line (the BAM—Baikal-Amur-Magistral; *Eng.* Main Baikal-Amur Line); has major steelworks; shipyards; oil refineries, pulp and paper mills; heavy machinery; fishing.

Kŏ·mun–do \ˌkō-mən-ˈdō\ *or Eng.* **Ko·mun Island** \ˈkō-mən\; *formerly* **Port Ham·il·ton** \ˈha-məl-tən\. Island group off S South Korea; good harbor, occupied by Great Britain 1885–87.

Ko·na·hu·a·nui \ˌkō-nä-ˌhü-ä-ˈnü-ē\. Peak in Koolau Range, E Oahu I., Hawaii; 3105 ft. (946 m.).

Konakri. See CONAKRY.

Ko·nan \ˈkō-ˌnän, kō-ˈnän\. City, Aichi prefecture, Honshū, Japan, 11 mi. (18 km.) N of Nagoya; pop. (1990p) 93,836.

Konar. See CHITRAL 1.

Kong \ˈkȯŋ\. **1.** Region, E cen. Ivory Coast; home of a Mandingo people, a prominent kingdom esp. in 18th cent.
2. Town, Ivory Coast, on highway 100 mi. (161 km.) N of Bouaké.

Kön·gä·mä \ˈkœn-gœ-ˌmä\ *or* **Kön·kä·mä** \ˈkœn-kä-\. River in N extremity of Sweden, forming its extreme N boundary with Finland; flows SE to join the Muonio River.

Kong·ju \ˈgȯŋ-ˈjü\ *or Jp.* **Ko·shu** \ˈkō-shü\. Town, South Ch'ungch'ŏng prov., South Korea; in early Korean history a ✻ of the Paekche kingdom.

Kongmoon. See JIANGMEN.

Kong–mun. See JIANGMEN.

Kon·go \ˈkȯŋ-gō\. Former African kingdom in area of Congo River; probably existed before 14th cent.; visited by Portuguese late 15th cent. and trading ties were estab.; Christianity introduced and king converted; contacts with Portuguese and then Dutch resulted in conflicts, but kingdom maintained its importance into 18th cent.

Kongo–Central. See BAS-ZAÏRE.

Kon·go·lo \kȯŋ-ˈgō-lō\. Town on Lualaba River, N Shaba administrative region, Democratic Rep. of the Congo.

Kongo River. See CONGO 4.

Kongosan. See KŬMGANG MOUNTAINS.

Kongs·berg \ˈkȯŋs-ˌber\. Town, Buskerud co., S Norway, WSW of Oslo; pop. (1980c) 20,549; formerly a silver-mining center.

Kongs·weg·en \ˈkȯŋs-ˌvā-gən\. Glacier, Spitsbergen, Norway; 17 mi. (27 km.) long, ab. 2 mi. (3 km.) wide near its terminus.

Kon·gur \ˈku̇ŋ-ˈgu̇r\ *or W.-G.* **Kung–ko–erh** \ˈku̇ŋ-ˈgō-ˈər\ *or* **Kun·gur** \ˈku̇ŋ-ˈgu̇r\ *or* **Qun·gur** \ˈku̇ŋ-\. Mountain, W Xinjiang Uygur, China, SW of Kashi; 25,325 ft. (7719 m.).

Konieh *or* **Konia.** See KONYA.

Königgrätz. See HRADEC KRALOVÉ.

Königinhof. See DVŮR KRÁLOVÉ NAD LABEM.

Kö·nigs·berg \ˈkœ-niks-ˌberk, ˈkā-nigz-ˌbərg\. **1.** Former district, NW East Prussia prov., Prussia, Germany; 5076 sq. mi. (13,147 sq. km.); since 1946 the greater part of it has formed Kaliningrad Oblast, Russia.
2. City, Russia. See KALININGRAD.

Kö·nigs·see \ˈkœ-niks-ˌzā\. Small lake in extreme SE corner of Bavaria, Germany, located in E end of Bavarian Alps, S of Berchtesgaden; 5 mi. (8 km.) long by ab. 1 mi. (2 km.) wide.

Kö·nigs·win·ter \ˈkœ-niks-ˌvin-tər\. Town, S North Rhine-Westphalia, Germany, on the Rhine SE of Bonn; pop. (1992e) 35,487; summer resort.

Ko·nin \ˈkō-nēn\. **1.** Province, cen. Poland. See table at POLAND.
2. Commune, its ✻, on Warta River ab. 55 mi. (88 km.) ESE of Poznán; pop. (1989e) 79,658; aluminum; coal mines.

Koninginne Bay. See BAJUR BAY.

Kó·ni·tsa \ˈkō-nēt-sä\. Commune, Ioánnina dept., N Epirus, NW Greece, near Albanian border ab. 27 mi. (43 km.) N of the city of Ioánnina.

Konitz. See CHOJNICE.

Kö·niz \ˈkœ-nits\. Commune, Bern canton, W cen. Switzerland, SW suburb of the city of Bern; pop. (1991e) 36,101; old church and castle.

Könkämä. See KÖNGÄMÄ.

Kon·kan \ˈkäŋ-kən\. Coast region of Maharashtra state, W India; a humid, fertile plain; lacking in good harbors and made dangerous for shipping by violence of monsoon winds; coastal region marked by sand dunes.

Kon·kou·ré \ˌkȯŋ-kü-ˈrā\. River, Guinea; rises in Fouta Djallon, flows SW into Atlantic Ocean N of Conakry; 160 mi. (257 km.) long.

Ko·no·top \kə-nȧ-ˈtȯp\. City, W Sumy subdivision, NE Ukraine, 125 mi. (201 km.) NE of Kiev; pop. (1991e) 98,000; railroad junction point in rich farming area, on main line from Kiev to Moscow. In WWII occupied by Germans 1941–43.

Koń·skie \ˈkȯiⁿ-skye\. Commune, Kielce prov., SE cen. Poland, 18 mi. (29 km.) NNW of the city of Kielce; pop. (1981p) 18,855; iron ore deposits nearby.

Kon·stan·ti·nov·ka \kən-stȧn-ˈtē-nəf-kə\. City, Donets'k subdivision, E Ukraine, SW of Artemovsk, in the Dnieper bend; pop. (1991e) 108,000; large steel mills; glass.

Kon·stanz \ˈkȯn-ˌstänts\ *or Eng.* **Con·stance** \ˈkän-stəns\ *or less commonly* **Con·stanz** \ˈkȯn-ˌstänts\; *anc.* **Con·stan·tia** \kən-ˈstan-chē-ə\; *in Middle Ages sometimes called* **Kost·nitz** \ˈkȯst-ˌnits\. Lake port, Baden-Württemberg, Germany, on Lake Constance 75 mi. (121 km.) S of Stuttgart; pop. (1992e) 76,162; textiles, chemicals; university; 11th cent. church, grand-ducal residence, and the Kaufhaus (in which Council of Constance met). Thought to have been founded by Roman Emperor Constantius Chlorus c. 300 A.D.; seat of famous Council of Constance (partly ecumenical) 1414–18 in which three antipopes were deposed and the doctrines of religious leaders Jan Hus, John Wycliffe, and Jerome of Prague were condemned as heretical; annexed to Austria 1548, to Baden 1805.

Kon·ta·go·ra \ˌkȯn-tä-ˈgō-rä\. Town, W cen. Nigeria; at road junction; pop. (1991e) 50,450.

Kon·ya *also* **Kon·ieh** *or* **Kon·ia** \ˈkȯn-yä\. **1.** Province of Turkey in Asia. See table at TURKEY.
2. *anc.* **Ico·ni·um** \ī-ˈkō-nē-əm\. City, its ✻, on SW edge of cen. Turkish plateau; pop. (1990c) 513,346; carpets; textiles, leather; teacher-training college; university; several museums; declined in prosperity in 19th cent., but grew rapidly after coming of the railroad 1896; contains mosque of the Muslims known in the West as "whirling dervishes."

History: First settled as early as 3d millennium B.C.; at various times ruled by Hittites, Phrygians, Lydians, Persians, Macedonians, Seleucids, and Attalids; under Roman rule became ✻ of Lycaonia; visited by St. Paul on his first missionary journey; after its capture 11th cent. by Seljuq Turks became ✻ of Seljuq sultans of Rum; later seized by Crusaders; in 13th cent. a cultural center under Ala-ad-Din I; in 15th cent. a secondary city of Karaman; became part of Ottoman Empire 15th cent.

Koo·ca·nu·sa, Lake \ˌkü-kə-ˈnü-sə, -zə\. Reservoir in Kootenai River in Lincoln co., NW Montana, formed by Libby Dam (see UNITED STATES, *Dams and Reservoirs*).

Koo·chi·ching \ˈkü-chə-chiŋ\. County in N Minnesota. See table at MINNESOTA.

Koochiching Falls. Falls in the Rainy River, S Ontario, Canada, near Fort Frances and International Falls.

Ko·o·lau Range \ˌkō-ō-ˈlä-ü\. Mountain range extending along E side of Oahu I., Hawaii; highest peak 3150 ft. (960 m.).

Kooringa. See BURRA.

Koo·te·nai \ˈküt-ᵊn-ˌā, -ᵊn-ē\. **1.** County in N Idaho. See table at IDAHO.
2. River, Canada and U.S. See KOOTENAY.

Kootenai Mountain. Peak in Glacier National Park, NW Montana; 8542 ft. (2604 m.).

Koo·te·nay *also* **Ku·te·nai** *or in U.S. known as the* **Koo·te·nai** \ˈküt-ᵊn-ˌā, -ᵊn-ē\. River, SW Canada and NW United States; rises on W slopes of Rocky Mts. N of Kootenay National Park, SE British Columbia, flows S through the park into NW Montana where it turns W and N through Idaho; again crosses border into British Columbia and enters **Kootenay Lake** (65 mi. or 105 km. long, 168 sq. mi. or 435 sq. km.) at its S end; issues from W side of lake to flow W past Nelson to the Columbia River; 407 mi. or 655 km. long (of which 276 mi. or 444 km. is in Canada). Explored by Canadian fur trader David Thompson in 1807; 25-mile (40-kilometer) section bet. Kootenay Lake and Columbia River utilized for hydroelectric power production.

Kootenay National Park. See CANADA, *National Parks.*

Kopaïs. See COPAIS.

Ko·pao·nik \ˈkō-ˌpau̇-ˌnēk\ *or* **Ka·pao·nik** \ˈkä-\. Mountain range, cen. Yugoslavia, in cen. Serbia E of the Ibar River; highest peak Pančičev 6617 ft. (2017 m.).

Kopar. See KOPER.

Kó·pa·vo·gur \ˈkau̇-pä-ˌvȯ-gu̇ər\. Town, SW Iceland, S of Reykjavík; pop. (1990c) 16,211.

Köpenick. See CÖPENICK.

Ko·per \ˈkō-ˌpər\ *or* **Ko·par** \ˈkō-ˌpär\ *or Ital.* **Ca·po·di·stria** \ˌkä-pō-ˈdē-strē-ä\; *anc.* **Ægi·dia** \ē-ˈji-dē-ə\; *later* **Jus·tin·op·o·lis** \ˌjəs-tə-ˈnä-pə-lis\. Seaport, Istria, SW Slovenia, on Gulf of Trieste just SSW of Trieste, Italy; pop. (1991e) 78,300; cathedral; Venetian-influenced palaces. Before achieving independence 1478, belonged alternately to Venice and Genoa from 10th cent.; became ✻ of Istria; fell to Austria 1797–1805, 1814–1919, and to Italy 1919–47; to Yugoslavia 1954–91; became part of independent Slovenia 1991.

Ko·pet–Dag \kō-ˈpet-ˈdäg\ *or* **Kop·peh Dāgh** \kȯ-ˈpe-ˈdäg\. Mountain range bet. NE Iran and Turkmenistan, extending ab. 400 mi. (645 km.) NW to SE along border, E of S end of Caspian Sea; highest point 9650 ft. (2941 m.).

Ko·pe·ysk \kȧ-ˈpyāsk\. Town, Chelyabinsk Oblast, SW Russia in Asia, just SE of the city of Chelyabinsk; pop. (1991e) 78,300.

Kö·ping \ˈchœ-piŋ\. Town, Västmanland prov., E Sweden, at W end of Lake Mälaren; pop. (1989c) 26,318; textiles.

Kop·par·berg \ˈkȯ-par-ˌbar\; *formerly* **Dal·e·car·lia** \ˌdȧ-lə-ˈkär-lē-ə\. Province of cen. Sweden. See table at SWEDEN.

Koppeh Dāgh. See KOPET-DAG.

Kopreinitz. See KOPRIVNICA.

Köprili. See TITOV VELES.

Ko·priv·ni·ca \ˈkō-ˌprēv-nit-ˌsä\ *or Hung.* **Ka·pron·cza** \ˈkō-prōn-ˌtsö\ *or Ger.* **Ko·prei·nitz** \kō-ˈprī-nəts\. Town, N Croatia, S of the Drava and ab. 50 mi. (80 km.) NE of Zagreb; pop. (1991c) 27,795.

Kor \ˈkȯr\. River, SW cen. Iran; flows SW into Lake Bakhtegān; ab. 175 mi. (282 km.) long.

Korat. See NAKHON RATCHASIMA.

Kor·çë *or Gk.* **Ko·ry·tsa** \kō-ˈrēt-sä\ *or Ital.* **Co·riz·za** \kō-ˈrēt-sä\; *formerly* **Korr·çë** \ˈkȯr-chə\. **1.** District of SE Albania. See table at ALBANIA.
2. Town, its ✻, near Greek border; pop. (1990e) 65,300; industrial and commercial center in agricultural region; brewing; sugar processing; textiles, leather products. In WWII used in 1940 as advanced base by Italians in operations against Greece; captured by Greeks 1940 and later by Germans; returned to Albania 1944.

Kor·ču·la \ˈkȯr-chu̇-ˌlä\ *or Ital.* **Cur·zo·la** \ˈku̇rt-sō-ˌlä\. **1.** *anc.* **Cor·cy·ra Ni·gra** \kȯr-ˈsī-rə-ˈnī-grə, -ˈni-\. Croatian island in Adriatic Sea off Dalmatian coast; 105 sq. mi. (272 sq. km.); pop. (1991p) 19,582; olives, grapes, fishing.
2. Town on E end of the island; medieval monastery; orig. settled by Greeks; under Austrian rule 1815–1918; passed to newly-organized Yugoslavia after WWI; part of independent Croatia since 1991.

Kor·de·stān \ˌkȯr-də-ˈstän, -ˈstan\. Province of NW Iran. See table at IRAN.

Kor·do·fan \ˌkȯr-də-ˈfan\ *or* **Kur·du·fān** \ˌku̇r-du̇-ˈfän\. Former province of cen. Sudan; ✻ El Obeid.

Ko·rea \ˌkȯr-ē-ˈä\. Former Indian state, now part of Madhya Pradesh, India; 1647 sq. mi. (4266 sq. km.); ✻ Sonhat.

Ko·rea \kə-ˈrē-ə\; *Korean* **Cho·sŏn** \ˈchō-ˈsȯn\ *or* **Tae Han** \ˈta-ˈhän\; *Jp.* **Cho·sen** \ˈchō-ˈsen\. Former kingdom, a peninsula (**Korea Peninsula**) on E coast of Asia, since 1948 partitioned (along the 38th parallel) into two republics. See KOREA, NORTH and KOREA, SOUTH.

History: According to tradition, ancient kingdom of Chosŏn estab. in N part of peninsula probably by peoples from N China in 3d millennium B.C.; conquered and annexed by Chinese 108 B.C.; later developed into three independent kingdoms of Silla, Koguryŏ, and Paekche; introduced to Buddhism 4th cent. A.D. which Koreans later carried to Japan (*q.v.*); in period of predominance of kingdom of Silla c. 670–935, Chinese culture flourished; under Koryo dynasty (from 935), founders of a state in W cen. Korea, most of Korea united as one kingdom under Chinese suzerainty; invaded by Mongols 1231; kingdom of Chosŏn with ✻ at Seoul ruled by Yi dynasty 1392–1910; invaded twice by Japanese under warrior and statesman Toyotomi Hideyoshi 1592–98; from c. 1637, shut out foreign contacts; forced to grant treaty opening ports to Japan 1876; in period of internal disorder, forced to unite with Japan in resisting Chinese interference (Korea considered Chinese vassal), thus bringing on Chinese-Japanese War 1894–95; Russo-Japanese rivalry over Korea a cause of war 1904–05; after war became Japanese protectorate; formally annexed to Japan as province 1910; freed from Japanese control on defeat of Japan Aug. 1945; after the war divided at 38th parallel into two zones of occupation, Russian in N and American in S, in which were estab. (1948) respectively, North Korea (Democratic People's Republic of Korea; ✻ P'yŏngyang) and South Korea (Republic of Korea; ✻ Seoul); scene of warfare bet. North Korea and allied forces of UN 1950–53. For later history of area, see KOREA, NORTH and KOREA, SOUTH.

Korea, North; *officially* **Democratic People's Republic of Korea** *or Korean* **Cho·sŏn Min·ju·juŭi In'·min Kong·hwa·guk** \ˈchō-sȯn-ˈmin-jü-ˈjü-ē-ˈin-min-ˈkȯŋ-hwä-ˈgük\. Republic on E coast of Asia, bounded on N by China, on NE by Russia, on E by the Sea of Japan, on S by South Korea, and on W by the Yellow Sea and Korea Bay; 46,609 sq. mi. (120,717 sq. km.); pop. (1993e) 22,646,000; ✻ P'yŏngyang.

Physical features: Generally a mountainous region, esp. in N, with several peaks over 8000 ft. (2440 m.); relief less pronounced in W and SW; W coast has numerous estuaries and tidal flats.

Chief products: Rice, wheat, corn; fishing; iron ore, coal, copper, lead, zinc; manufacturing: iron and steel, chemicals, textiles, cement.

Chief cities: P'yŏngyang, Hamhŭng, Ch'ŏngjin.

History: For history prior to 1948, see KOREA. Communist republic estab. 1948 N of 38th parallel; invaded South Korea 1950, precipitating the Korean War (1950–53; armistice signed July 27, 1953); withdrawal of Chinese forces (allied with North Koreans during war) completed late 1950s; during the 1960s provoked numerous border incidents along the 38th parallel, and repeatedly called for a unified, Communist-controlled Korea; during 1980s and 1990s North Korea and South Korea began tentative talks to ease situation bet. the two countries.

Korea, South; *officially* **Republic of Korea** *or Korean* **Tae Han Min'·guk** \ta-ˈhän-min-ˈgük\. Republic, E Asia, bounded on N by North Korea, on E by the Sea of Japan, on S by the Korea Strait, and on W by the Yellow Sea; 38,022 sq. mi. (98,477 sq. km.); pop. (1993e) 44,042,000; ✻ Seoul.

Physical features: Mountainous in E and S cen. regions; numerous islands off S and SW coasts; best ports located on W coast, along which are found a number of alluvial plains.

Chief products: Rice, barley, wheat, vegetables, tobacco; coal, tungsten; livestock raising, fishing; manufacturing: textiles, clothing, footwear, chemicals, cement, steel, graphite, motor vehicles, electronics; shipbuilding.

Chief cities: Seoul, Pusan, Taegu, Inch'ŏn, Kwangju, Taejŏn.

Political divisions: Administrative divisions shown in the table below (for pronunciation of their names, see their individual entries):

NAME	AREA (sq. mi.)	AREA (sq. km.)	POP. (1990e)	CAPITAL
Provinces				
Cheju	706	1,828	507,000	Cheju
Kangwŏn	6,524	16,898	1,640,000	Ch'unch'ŏn
Kyŏnggi[1]	4,231	10,958	5,604,000	Suwŏn
North Chŏlla	3,108	8,050	2,093,000	Chŏnju
North Ch'ungch'ŏng	2,871	7,436	1,342,000	Ch'ŏngju
North Kyŏngsang	7,507	19,443	2,811,000	Taegu
South Chŏlla	4,561	11,813	2,465,000	Kwangju
South Ch'ungch'ŏng	3,211	8,316	1,942,000	Taejŏn
South Kyŏngsang[2]	4,545	10,722	3,639,000	Ch'ang-won
Special cities				
Inch'ŏn	121	313	1,682,000	
Kwangju	193	500	1,206,000	
Pusan	203	526	3,825,000	
Seoul	237	614	10,726,000	
Taegu	176	456	2,248,000	
Taejŏn	207	536	1,064,000	

[1]Excludes Seoul.
[2]Excludes Pusan.

History: For history prior to 1948, see KOREA. Estab. as an independent republic 1948; fought Korean War (with aid of UN forces) 1950–53; government unsettled during 1960s and 1970s; involved in countering border incidents with North Korea 1960s; continued to allow American troops to be stationed in country; during 1980s and 1990s South Korea and North Korea began tentative talks to ease situation bet. the two countries.

Korea Bay. NE arm of Yellow Sea bet. Liaodong Penin., China and North Korea; receives the Yalu River.

Korea Strait. Channel bet. South Korea and SW Japan; ab. 120 mi. (195 km.) wide; divided into Western Channel on NW and Tsushima Strait on SE by the island of Tsushima in its center; connects SW Sea of Japan with East China Sea.

Kor·ho·go \ˌkȯr-ˈhō-gō\. Town, N Ivory Coast, ab. 310 mi. (500 km.) NNW of Abidjan; pop. (1981e) 62,000.

Korinthiakós Kólpos. See CORINTH, GULF OF.

Kórinthos. See CORINTH 3.

Korinthou, Isthmos. See CORINTH, ISTHMUS OF.

Korintji. 1. Lake, Sumatra, Indonesia. See KERINTJI 1. **2.** Volcanic peak, Sumatra, Indonesia. See KERINCI.

Kō·ri·ya·ma \ˌkō-rē-ˈyä-mä\. City, Fukushima prefecture, N cen. Honshū, Japan, 25 mi. (40 km.) S of the city of Fukushima; pop. (1990p) 314,651; textiles, chemicals, and machinery.

Kor·ki·no \ˈkȯr-kē-nə\. Town, Chelyabinsk Oblast, SW Russia in Asia, ab. 20 mi. (32 km.) S of the city of Chelyabinsk; pop. (1991e) 44,800; coal mining.

Kor·la \ˈku̇r-ˈlä\ *or* **K'u-erh-le** \ˈkü-ˈər-ˈlē\ *also* **Kur·la** \ˈku̇r-ˈlä\. Town, cen. Xinjiang Uygur, W China.

Kor·ma·ki·ti, Cape \ˌkör-mä-ˈkē-tē\. Cape near cen. part of N coast of Cyprus, in E Mediterranean Sea.

Kor·man·tine *or* **Cor·man·tyne** \ˈkȯr-mən-ˌtīn\. Coastal village and remains of Dutch fort ab. 3 mi. (5 km.) W of Saltpond, Ghana; one of first W African ports used to take slaves to British West Indies.

Körmöczbánya. See KREMNICA.

Korn·west·heim \kȯrn-ˈvest-ˌhīm\. City, Baden-Württemberg, Germany; pop. (1980c) 27,037; church (1516).

Ko·ro \ˈkō-rō\. Island of the Lomai Viti group, Fiji (*q.v.*), SW Pacific Ocean, in cen. part S of Vanua Levu on NW border of Koro Sea; 58 sq. mi. (150 sq. km.).

Ko·ro·li Desert \kō-ˈrō-lē\. Desert area in N Kenya, E of S end of Lake Turkana.

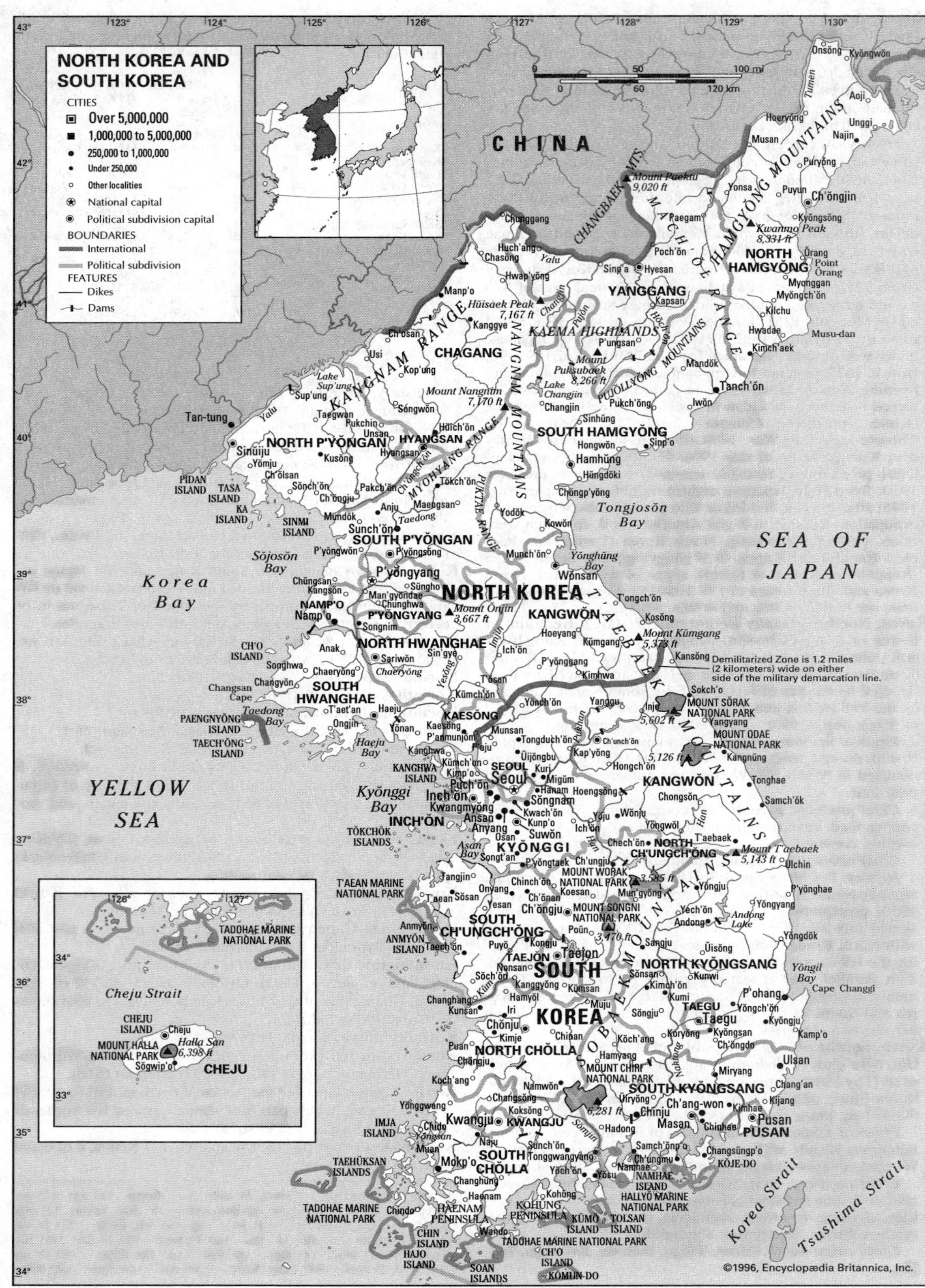
NORTH KOREA AND SOUTH KOREA
CITIES
Over 5,000,000
1,000,000 to 5,000,000
250,000 to 1,000,000
Under 250,000
Other localities
National capital
Political subdivision capital
BOUNDARIES
International
Political subdivision
FEATURES
Dikes
Dams
0 50 100 mi
0 60 120 km
CHINA
SEA OF JAPAN
Korea Bay
YELLOW SEA
NORTH KOREA
SOUTH KOREA
Demilitarized Zone is 1.2 miles (2 kilometers) wide on either side of the military demarcation line.
CHANGBAEK MTS.
Mount Paektu 9,020 ft
HAMGYŎNG MOUNTAINS
MACH'ŎL RANGE
Kwanmo Peak 8,331 ft
NORTH HAMGYŎNG
YANGGANG
KAEMA HIGHLANDS
Mount Puksubaek 8,266 ft
PUJŎLLYŎNG MOUNTAINS
CHAGANG
KANGNAM RANGE
Hŭisaek Peak 7,167 ft
NANGNIM MOUNTAINS
Mount Nangnim 7,170 ft
MYOHYANG RANGE
PUKTAE RANGE
SOUTH HAMGYŎNG
NORTH P'YŎNGAN
SOUTH P'YŎNGAN
P'YŎNGYANG
P'yŏngyang
Mount Ŏnjin 3,667 ft
NORTH HWANGHAE
SOUTH HWANGHAE
KANGWŎN
Mount Kŭmgang 5,373 ft
T'AEBAEK MOUNTAINS
KAESŎNG
SEOUL
Seoul
INCH'ŎN
Inch'ŏn
KYŎNGGI
KANGWŎN
MOUNT SŎRAK NATIONAL PARK
MOUNT ODAE NATIONAL PARK
Mount T'aebaek 5,143 ft
NORTH CH'UNGCH'ŎNG
SOUTH CH'UNGCH'ŎNG
MOUNT WORAK NATIONAL PARK
MOUNT SONGNI NATIONAL PARK
T'AEAN MARINE NATIONAL PARK
TAEJŎN
Taejŏn
SOBAEK MOUNTAINS
NORTH KYŎNGSANG
TAEGU
Taegu
NORTH CHŎLLA
MOUNT CHIRI NATIONAL PARK
SOUTH KYŎNGSANG
KWANGJU
Kwangju
SOUTH CHŎLLA
PUSAN
Pusan
Ulsan
Tongjosŏn Bay
Yŏnghŭng Bay
Sŏjosŏn Bay
Kyŏnggi Bay
Asan Bay
Yŏngil Bay
Korea Strait
Tsushima Strait
TADOHAE MARINE NATIONAL PARK
HALLYŎ MARINE NATIONAL PARK
HAENAM PENINSULA
KOHŬNG PENINSULA
KŎJE-DO
Cheju Strait
CHEJU ISLAND
Cheju
MOUNT HALLA NATIONAL PARK
Halla San 6,398 ft
Sŏgwip'o
CHEJU
Tan-tung
Sinŭiju
Hamhŭng
Ch'ŏngjin
Wŏnsan
Namp'o
Kaesŏng
Kwangmyŏng
Sŏngnam
Suwŏn
Anyang
Ansan
Ch'ŏngju
Chŏnju
Masan
Chinju
Mokp'o
Yŏsu
P'ohang
©1996, Encyclopædia Britannica, Inc.

Ko·rom·ba, Mount *or* **Mount Ku·ram·ba** \kə-ˈräm-bə\. Peak, W Viti Levu I., Fiji, SW Pacific Ocean; 3526 ft. (1075 m.).

Ko·ro·na·dal \ˌkō-rō-nä-ˈdäl\. Municipality, ✻ of South Cotabato, Mindanao, Philippines; pop. (1980c) 80,566.

Korónē, Gulf of. See MESSENIA, GULF OF.

Ko·ró·nia, Lake \kö-ˈrō-nē-ä\; *formerly* **Lake Lan·ka·da** \län-ˈgä-t͟hä\. Lake, N Chalcidice, Macedonia, NE Greece, W of Lake Bolbē and ENE of Thessaloníki.

Ko·ror *or* **Kor·ror** \ˈkȯr-ˌȯr\. Town on small island of same name off S tip of Babelthuap I., Palau, W Pacific Ocean; ✻ of Palau; has good harbor and was trading center under German regime; from 1921 to 1945 administrative ✻ of all Japanese mandated islands (called **Nan·yo** \ˈnän-ˌyō\ by the Japanese) in the Pacific.

Kö·rös \ˈkœr-ˌœsh\. River in E Hungary; formed by confluence of streams which rise in W Romania, flows SW into Tisza River at Csongrád; ab. 120 mi. (190 km.) long.

Koro Sea. Open sea in cen. area of Fiji, SW Pacific Ocean; Nanuku Passage on NE is shipping lane to the NE.

Ko·ro·sten' *or* **Ko·ro·sten** \ˌkōr-ə-ˈsten^{y}\. Town, NE Zhytomyr subdivision, W Ukraine, in steppe region 90 mi. (145 km.) WNW of Kiev; pop. (1991e) 68,000; a key railroad junction on the N to S line from Belarus to Berdichev and on the E to W line from Kiev to Kovel' and Lublin, Poland; scene of severe fighting late 1943 during Soviet advance W of Kiev; taken by Soviets Dec. 29, 1943.

Ko·ro·vin \kə-ˈrō-vin\. **1.** Volcano, N part of Atka I., Aleutians, SW Alaska; 4852 ft. (1479 m.).
2. Bay, inlet on N coast of Atka I., Alaska.

Korrçë. See KORÇË.

Korror. See KOROR.

Kor·sa·kov \ˈkȯr-sə-ˌkəf, -ˌkəv\ *or Jp.* **Oto·ma·ri** \ˌō-tō-ˈmä-rē\ *or* **Odo·ma·ri** \ˌō-dō-\. Seaport, S Sakhalin I., E Russia in Asia, on Aniva Bay; pop. (1991e) 45,300; formerly Japanese.

Kor·sør \kȯr-ˈsœr\. Seaport, Vestsjælland co., SW Sjælland, Denmark, 62 mi. (100 km.) WSW of Copenhagen; pop. (1981c) 20,850; trading center; fisheries.

Kor·sun'–Shev·chen·kov·skiy *or* **Kor·sun–Shev·chen·kov·ski** \ˈkȯr-sün^{y}-shəf-chen-ˈkȯf-skē\. Town, Cherkassy subdivision, N Ukraine, 80 mi. (129 km.) SSE of Kiev; on main railroad line of cen. Ukraine; scene of battle 1648 in which Bohdan Khmelnytsky, Cossack hetman, defeated the Poles; in WWII held by Germans 1941–44; taken by U.S.S.R. Feb. 1944.

Kort·rijk \ˈkȯrt-ˌrīk\ *or Fr.* **Cour·trai** \kůr-ˈtrā\. Commune, West Flanders prov., NW Belgium, on Leie (Lys) River 15 mi. (24 km.) NNE of Lille; pop. (1991c) 76,141; linens. In Middle Ages a populous commercial city of Flanders; scene of battle of the Golden Spurs 1302 in which Flemish defeated French.

Kor·yak Autonomous Okrug \kər-ˈyak ... ˈȯ-ˌkrük\ *also* **Kor·yak·skiy Autonomous Okrug** \kər-ˈyák-skē\. Administrative subdivision, NE Russia in Asia, borders Chukchi Autonomous Okrug on N and Khabarovsk Kray on SW; 116,409 sq. mi. (301,499 sq. km.); pop. (1992e) 39,000; ✻ Palana; comprises chiefly the mountainous region on coast of Bering Sea at the base, in the isthmus, and the NW third of Kamchatka Penin. and the region of the Penzhina basin NE of the Sea of Okhotsk; includes also Karagin I.; chief industry is fishing. Orig. a part of the Far Eastern Region; estab. 1930.

Kor·yak·ska·ya Sop·ka \kər-ˌyák-skə-yə-ˈsȯp-kə\. Volcano (*sopka*), at S end of Eastern Range, Kamchatka Penin., Khabarovsk Kray, E Russia in Asia; 11,342 ft. (3457 m.).

Koryakskiy Autonomous Okrug. See KORYAK AUTONOMOUS OKRUG.

Korytsa. See KORÇË.

Kos *or* **Cos** \ˈkös, ˈkäs\ *or Ital.* **Coo** \ˈkȯ-ˌō\. **1.** An island of the Dodecanese (*q.v.*), off end of Bodrum Penin., SW Turkey in Asia; 111 sq. mi. (287 sq. km.); pop. (1981c) 20,350; settled in very early times by Dorians; site of celebrated temple of Aesculapius; 14th cent. fortress; birthplace of physician Hippocrates c. 460 B.C.
2. Town on NE coast of the island; pop. (1981c) 11,851.

Ko·sa·la \ˈkō-sə-lə\. An ancient Aryan kingdom in N India (modern Oudh); ✻ Ajodhya (*q.v.*); now in Uttar Pradesh; a powerful state in time of Buddha.

Ko·ścian \ˈkosh-ˌchän\ *or Ger.* **Ko·sten** \ˈkȯ-stən\. Commune, N Leszno prov., W cen. Poland, 22 mi. (35 km.) SSW of Poznań; pop. (1989e) 23,840.

Kos·ci·us·ko \ˌkä-sē-ˈəs-ˌkō\. **1.** County in N Indiana. See table at INDIANA.
2. City, ⊗ of Attala co., cen. Mississippi, 46 mi. (74 km.) SE of Greenwood; pop. (1990c) 6986.

Kosciusko, Mount \ˌkä-zē-ˈəs-kō\. Mountain of Australian Alps, SE New South Wales, Australia; 7310 ft. (2228 m.); highest peak in mainland Australia; winter sports; in **Kosciusko National Park** (almost 2500 sq. mi. or 6480 sq. km.).

Ko·shi·ga·ya \kō-ˈshē-gä-yä, ˌkō-shē-ˈgä-yä\. Town, Saitama prefecture, Honshū, Japan, 16 mi. (26 km.) N of Tokyo; pop. (1990p) 285,280.

Ko·shi·ki Islands \ˈkō-shē-ˌkē\ *or Jp.* **Koshiki–Ret·tō** \ˈre-tō\. Group of small islands off SW coast of Kyūshū, Japan.

Koshk. See KUSHKA.

Kosh·ko·nong, Lake \ˈkäsh-kə-ˌnäŋ\. Lake, SW Jefferson co., SE Wisconsin; ab. 8 mi. (13 km.) long, 4 mi. (6 km.) wide; an expansion of Rock River.

Kosh·tan Tau \ˈkȯsh-tän-ˈtau̇\. Mountain in Caucasus Mts. near Dykh Tau, in S Kabardino-Balkaria Rep., S Russia in Europe; 16,875 ft. (5144 m.).

Ko·shu \ˈkō-ˌshü\. **1.** Town, South Chŏlla prov., South Korea. See KWANGJU.
2. Town, South Ch'ungch'ŏng prov., South Korea. See KONGJU.

Ko·si \ˈkō-sē\ *or* **Ku·si** \ˈkü-\. River, S Asia, in E Nepal and N India; formed by confluence of three streams in E Nepal, flows S across border into India and into the Ganges E of Bhagalpur; ab. 305 mi. (490 km.) long.

Kosi Bay. See KOSI LAKE.

Ko·ši·ce \ˈkȯ-shē-tse\ *or Hung.* **Kas·sa** \ˈkö-shö\ *or Ger.* **Ka·schau** \ˈkä-ˌshau̇\. City, SE Slovakia, on Hernád River 135 mi. (217 km.) NE of Budapest, Hungary; pop. (1991p) 234,840; commercial and market center; university (1959); 14th cent. Gothic cathedral. Chartered 13th cent.; became part of Czechoslovakia 1920; ceded to Hungary 1938 but returned to Czechoslovakia after 1945; part of independent Slovakia since 1992.

Ko·si Lake \ˈkō-sē\. Lake, NE KwaZulu-Natal prov., NE Rep. of South Africa, near coast, just S of border of Mozambique; in NE corner has an outlet by way of a short river, **Kosi River,** which flows NE into the Indian Ocean at **Kosi Bay.**

Köslin. See KOSZALIN.

Koso Gol Nuur. See HÖVSGÖL NUUR.

Ko·so·vo *or* **Kos·so·vo** \ˈkȯ-sȯ-ˌvȯ\ *or* **Kosovo Pol·je** \ˈpȯl-ye\. **1.** Elevated plain, S Yugoslavia, W of Priština, in Kosovo prov. Site of important battle in Balkan history June 1389 in which Serbs and their allies were defeated by Turks under Sultan Murad I; as a result Serbian empire was crushed and Serbia (*q.v.*) became vassal of Ottoman Empire; in a 2d battle Oct. 1448 Hungarian commander János Hunyadi was defeated by Sultan Murad II; in Nov. 1915 the scene of final defeat of Serbians by Bulgarian army in WWI.
2. Province, S Yugoslavia, in SW Serbia; 4203 sq. mi. (10,886 sq. km.); pop. (1991p) 1,954,747; formed under constitution of 1946.

Ko·sov·ska Mi·tro·vi·ca \ˈkȯ-sȯv-skä-ˈmē-trȯ-ˌvēt-sä\; *formerly* **Mitrovica.** Town, N cen. Kosovo, Serbia, Yugoslavia, 65 mi. (105 km.) NW of Skopje.

Kos·rae \ˈkȯs-ˌrī\ *also* **Ku·sa·ie** \kü-ˈsä-ye\. Island in E part of the Caroline Is., Federated States of Micronesia, W Pacific Ocean, 330 mi. (531 km.) ESE of Pohnpei I.; ab. 9 mi. (14 km.) long and 6 mi. (10 km.) wide; pop. (1980c) 5491; has

\ə\ abut \ᵊ\ matches \ᵊ\ kitten, Fr table \ər\ further \a\ ash \ā\ ace \ä\ cot, cart \à\ Fr bac \au̇\ out \b̶\ Span Avila \ch\ chin \e\ bet \ē\ easy \g\ go \i\ hit \ī\ ice \j\ job \k\ Ger ich, Buch \ⁿ\ Fr vin \ŋ\ sing \ō\ go \ö\ all \ȯ\ law \œ\ Fr bœuf \œ̄\ Fr feu \ȯi\ boy \th\ thin \t͟h\ this \ü\ loot \u̇\ foot \ue\ Ger füllen \ue̅\ Fr rue \y\ yet \$^{y}$\ Fr digne \ˈdēn^{y}\, nuit \ˈnw^{y}ē\ \yü\ few \yu̇\ fury \zh\ vision

several mountains (highest 2064 ft. or 629 m.) and two good harbors. Bombed by Americans but left in Japanese control 1942–44.

Kosseir. See QUSEIR.

Kosso–gol Nuur. See HÖVSGÖL NUUR.

Kossovo. See KOSOVO.

Kos·suth \kə-ˈsüth\. County in N Iowa. See table at IOWA.

Kosten. See KOŚCIAN.

Köstendil. See KYUSTENDIL.

Kos·ti \ˈkȯs-tē\ *or* **Kūs·tī** \ˈküs-\. Town, E Sudan, S of Ed Dueim; surrounding countryside scene of severe fighting Dec. 1989 bet. Arab Sobaha people and African Shilluks.

Kostnitz. See KONSTANZ.

Ko·stro·ma \kəs-trȧ-ˈmä\. **1.** River, cen. Russia in Europe; rises in NE corner of Kostroma Oblast, flows SSW to the Volga at the city of Kostroma; 250 mi. (402 km.) long; navigable for 200 mi. (322 km.).

2. City, SW Kostroma Oblast, cen. Russia in Europe, on left bank of the Volga where it is joined by the Kostroma, ab. 45 mi. (72 km.) ENE of Yaroslavl'; pop. (1992e) 282,000; flax-processing center; linen, textile machinery; 13th cent. cathedral; has suburbs on opp. side of the Volga. One of oldest towns in Russia, believed to have been founded 1152; in 13th cent. in Rostov-Suzdal' principality, later, in 14th cent., absorbed by Moscow principality; frequently plundered by Tatars.

Kostroma Oblast \ˈȯ-bləst, -ˌblast\ *or* **Ko·strom·ska·ya Oblast'** \kəs-ˈtrȯm-skə-yə\. Administrative subdivision of cen. Russia in Europe; 23,243 sq. mi. (60,199 sq. km.); pop. (1992e) 812,000; ✻ Kostroma; rye, oats, flax; lumbering; created during WWII out of E half of Yaroslavl' Oblast.

Kos·trzyn \ˈkȯs-chin\; *Ger.* **Kü·strin** *also* **Cü·strin** \kæ-ˈstrēn\. City, W Gorzów prov., W Poland, on the Oder at its confluence with the Warta; pop. (1981p) 14,302; 16th cent. castle in which Prussian King Frederick the Great was held prisoner 1730.

History: First mentioned 1232; later passed to Brandenburg; made seat of margravate 1535 and fortified; held by French 1806–14; fortifications expanded and improved in 19th cent.; in WWII an important German defense post taken by Soviet troops Mar. 1945 in campaign for Berlin; assigned to Poland by Potsdam Conference 1945.

Koswig. See COSWIG.

Ko·sza·lin \kȯ-ˈshä-ˌlēn\ *or Ger.* **Kös·lin** \ˌkœs-ˈlēn\. **1.** Province of N Poland. See table at POLAND.

2. City, its ✻, NW Poland, near Baltic Sea 88 mi. (142 km.) NE of Szczecin; pop. (1989e) 107,580; food processing; lumber, agricultural machinery. First mentioned 1214; became city 1266; to Brandenburg 1648; in WWII taken by U.S.S.R. Feb. 1945; assigned to Poland by Potsdam Conference 1945.

Kő·szeg \ˈkœ̄-seg\ *or* **Ko·szeg·szer·da·he·ly** \-ˌser-dä-ˈhā\. Town, W Hungary, N of Szombathely near Austrian border; pop. (1980p) 12,705; in fruit- and wine-producing region.

Ko·ta *also* **Ko·tah** \ˈkō-tə\. Town, SE Rajasthan, W cen. India, on right bank of Chambal River 120 mi. (193 km.) S of Jaipur; pop. (1991c) 537,371; textiles; contains old city walls, palaces, and temples.

Ko·ta Ba·ha·ru \ˈkō-tə-ˈbä-hä-ˌrü\ *also* **Kota Bah·ru** \ˈbä-rü\. Town, ✻ of Kelantan state, Malaysia, near coast at head of delta of Kelantan River; pop. (1980p) 281,161; one of the first places seized (Dec. 10, 1941) by Japanese in campaign against Singapore.

Kotabaru. See JAYAPURA.

Ko·tah \ˈkō-tə\. **1.** Former Indian state, now part of Rajasthan state, NW India; 5714 sq. mi. (14,799 sq. km.); drained by the Chambal and its tributaries; formed from Bundi state ab. 1625.

2. Town, Rajasthan, India. See KOTA.

Ko·ta Ki·na·ba·lu \ˈkō-tə-ˌki-nə-bü-ˈlü\; *formerly* **Jes·sel·ton** \ˈje-səl-tən\. Seaport town, ✻ of Sabah, Malaysia, on island of Borneo; pop. (1980p) 112,758; completely destroyed during WWII; subsequently rebuilt.

Ko·ta Ko·ta \ˌkō-tə-ˈkō-tə\. Town on W shore of Lake Malawi, Malawi.

Ko·tel'·nich *or* **Ko·tel·nich** \kȧ-ˈtyel^{y}-nich\. Railroad and commercial town, W Vyatka Oblast, E cen. Russia in Europe, on Vyatka River 50 mi. (80 km.) SW of the city of Vyatka.

Ko·tel·'nyy *or* **Ko·tel·ny** *or* **Ko·tel·ni** \kü-ˈtyel-nē, kō-ˈtel-nē\. Island in Arctic Ocean, largest of the New Siberian Is., Sakha Rep., Russia in Asia; in W part of group; 110 mi. (177 km.) long.

Kö·then *also* **Cö·then** \ˈkœt-^{ə}n\. City, Saxony-Anhalt, E cen. Germany, 12 mi. (19 km.) SW of Dessau; pop. (1992e) 32,642; railroad junction; textiles; sugar beets; 15th cent. church; city first mentioned 1115.

Kot·ka \ˈkȯt-kə\. Seaport, Kymi prov., SE Finland, on a small island in the Gulf of Finland E of Helsinki; pop. (1989c) 56,933; ships lumber; manufactures paper, cellulose; founded 1878.

Kot·las \ˈkȯt-ləs\. Town, SE Arkhangel'sk Oblast, N cen. Russia in Europe, on right bank of Northern Dvina; pop. (1991e) 68,900; a river and railroad junction point at head of Northern Dvina navigation; sawmills, pulp and paper plants.

Kot·lik \ˈkät-lik\. City, on the W coast of Alaska, on S shore of Norton Sound and at N end of the Yukon Delta; pop. (1990c) 461.

Kot·lin \ˈkȯt-lin\. Russian island at E end of Gulf of Finland. See KRONSHTADT.

Kotonu. See COTONOU.

Ko·tor \ˈkō-ˌtȯr\ *or* **Cat·ta·ro** \ˈkä-tə-ˌrō\. Seaport and commercial center, Montenegro, S Yugoslavia, on the **Gulf of Kotor,** an inlet of the Adriatic Sea; pop. (1991p) 22,496; since 1946 in Montenegro Rep., Yugoslavia; excellent harbor, formerly a base of Austro-Hungarian Navy; under ancient Roman rule; under Venetian rule 1420–1797; passed to Austria 1797, to France 1807–14, back to Austria 1814–1918, to Yugoslavia 1918.

Kotosho. See LAN.

Ko·tri \ˈkō-trē\. Town, S Sind, Pakistan, on right bank of the Indus opp. Hyderabad; pop. (1981c) 39,390; important railroad and river transportation center.

Kot·ta·gu·dem \ˌkä-tə-ˈgü-dəm\. Town, Andhra Pradesh, India, 139 mi. (224 km.) E of Hyderabad.

Kot·ta·yam \ˈkä-tə-yəm\. Town, W Kerala, S India, on inlet of Arabian Sea; pop. (1991p) 62,829; market and educational center; noted as site of an old Syrian Christian community.

Kottbus. See COTTBUS.

Kot·te \ˈkō-tā\. Town, Sri Lanka, ab. 7 mi. (11 km.) SE of Colombo; pop. (1990e) 109,000.

Kot·to \ˈkō-tō\. River, E Central African Rep.; flows S into Ubangi River on border of Democratic Rep. of the Congo; 400 mi. (644 km.) long.

Kot·ze·bue \ˈkät-sə-ˌbyü, -ˌbü\. City, NW Alaska, at tip of long neck of land (Baldwin Penin.) in Kotzebue Sound; pop. (1990c) 2751; airfield.

Kotzebue Sound. Large inlet, Chukchi Sea, NW Alaska, just NE of Bering Strait; 40 to 65 mi. (64 to 104 km.) wide; receives Noatak and Kobuk rivers.

Kouang–Tchéou–Wan. See KWANGCHOWAN.

Kou·chi·bou·guac National Park \kü-ˌshē-bü-ˈgwäk\. See CANADA, *National Parks.*

Kou·dou·gou \kü-ˈdü-gü\. Town, cen. Burkina Faso, ab. 55 mi. (88 km.) W of Ouagadougou; pop. (1985c) 51,926.

Kou·li·ko·ro \ˌkü-lē-ˈkō-rō\. Town, Mali, on the Niger River just NE of Bamako; pop. (1987p) 20,354.

Koulouri. See SALAMIS 2 and 3.

Koun·rad·ski \kün-ˈrät-skē\. Town, SE Qaraghandy subdivision, Kazakhstan; railroad terminus just N of Balkhash and N shore of Lake Balkhash.

Kountze \ˈkünts\. City, ⊗ of Hardin co., E Texas; pop. (1990c) 2056.

Kou·rou \kü-ˈrü\. Town, French Guiana, roughly midway along the coast; pop. (1990c) 6465; site of French space center.

Kou·rous·sa \kü-ˈrü-sə\. Town, E cen. Guinea, on railroad line from Conakry to Kankan and on upper Niger.

Koussi, Emi. See EMI KOUSSI.

Kou·vo·la \ˈkȯ-ü-ˌvō-ˌlä\. Town, ✻ of Kymi prov., S Finland;

pop. (1989c) 31,632; railroad junction point; town formed 1921.

Ko·vel' *or* **Ko·vel** \ˈkȯ-vil^{y}\ *or Pol.* **Ko·wel** \ˈkȯ-vel\. City, Volyn subdivision, NW Ukraine, 43 mi. (69 km.) NW of Lutsk; pop. (1991e) 52,000; formerly in Poland; in WWI captured by Austrians 1915; held by Germans in WWII until 1944.

Kovno. See KAUNAS.

Kov·rov \kəv-ˈrȯf, -ˈrȯv\. Town, Vladimir Oblast, cen. Russia in Europe, on Klyaz'ma River 150 mi. (241 km.) E of Moscow; pop. (1992e) 162,000; railroad junction; textiles, machinery.

Kov·zha \ˈkȯv-zhə\. Stream, Vologda Oblast, Russia in Europe; flows SSE to Lake Beloye; ab. 50 mi. (80 km.) long; forms part of the Volga-Baltic Waterway.

Koweit. See KUWAIT.

Kowel. See KOVEL'.

Ko·wie \ˈkō-vē\. Short river, Eastern Cape prov., S Rep. of South Africa; flows into Indian Ocean at Port Alfred.

Kow·loon \ˈkau̇-ˈlün\; *mostly formerly* **Kau·lun** \ˈkau̇-ˈlün\ *or* **Kau·lung** \ˈjyō-ˈlu̇ŋ\. **1.** Peninsula. See HONG KONG.
2. Town on W shore of Kowloon Penin., SE China, separated from Victoria on Hong Kong I. by Hong Kong harbor, 1 mi. (1.6 km.) wide at narrowest point; pop. (1991c) 1,975,265; extends N into leased New Territories (see HONG KONG) and includes Kowloon, **New Kowloon,** and **Kowloon City;** much of area is modern development; connected by rail with Guangzhou; important commercial center. Ceded to British 1860; British agreed 1984 to transfer to China in 1997.

Kowno. See KAUNAS.

Koy·u·kuk \ˈkȯi-ə-ˌkək\. River, W Alaska; flows SW from Brooks Range to Yukon River; ab. 500 mi. (800 km.) long.

Ko·zá·ni *also* **Ko·zá·nē** \kō-ˈzä-nē\. **1.** Department of Greece. See table at GREECE.
2. City, its ✱, ab. 65 mi. (105 km.) SW of Thessaloníki; pop. (1991p) 32,342; held by Germans in WWII 1941–44.

Kozhikode. See CALICUT.

Ko·zie·ni·ce \ˌkȯ-zhe-ˈnēt-se\. Town, Radom prov., SE cen. Poland, SE of Warsaw; pop. (1993e) 21,400.

Kozlov. See MICHURINSK.

Kpa·li·mé \ˌpä-lē-ˈmā\ *also* **Pa·li·mé** \ˌpä-\. Town, SW Togo, ab. 65 mi. (105 km.) NW of Lomé; pop. (1981c) 27,669.

Kra, Isthmus of \ˈkrä\. Narrow section in N cen. Malay Penin., in SW Thailand, 10°20′N, 99°E; ab. 40 mi. (64 km.) wide at its narrowest part; Pakchan River flows S in the isthmus forming S end of boundary bet. Lower Burma and Thailand; Ranong is Thai port at its mouth; range of hills at narrowest part ab. 2000 ft. (610 m.) high.

Kra·bi \ˈkrä-bē\. Town, SW Thailand, a port on W coast of Malay Penin. 40 mi. (64 km.) ENE of Phuket; pop. (1991e) 18,272.

Krâchéh. See KRATIE.

Kra·gerø \ˈkrä-gə-ˌrœ\. Seaport town, Telemark co., S Norway, 40 mi. (64 km.) NE of Arendal; pop. (1992e) 10,798.

Kra·gu·je·vac *or* **Kra·gu·ye·vats** \ˈkrä-gü-ye-ˌväts\. Town, Serbia, cen. Yugoslavia, 60 mi. (96 km.) SE of Belgrade; pop. (1991p) 178,881; automobile-assembly plant; ✱ of Serbia 1818–39, and a residence of Serbian princes to 1842; captured by Bulgarians and Germans 1915 in WWI; had iron foundry and ammunition factory and was formerly chief arsenal and garrison town of Serbia.

Krain. See CARNIOLA.

Kra·ka·tau \ˌkra-kə-ˈtau̇\ *or* **Kra·ka·toa** \-ˈtō-ə\ *also* **Kra·ka·tao** \-ˈtau̇\; *local Malay name* **Ra·ka·ta** \rə-ˈkä-tə\. Island volcano in center of Sunda Strait, bet. Sumatra and Java, Indonesia. Its eruption Aug. 26–28, 1883 was the most violent of modern times. Explosion caused tidal wave more than 100 ft. (30 m.) high, killing 36,000 people in Java and Sumatra; dust, ashes, and smoke rose to height of ab. 17 mi. (27 km.) and the sound of the explosion was heard in Australia, Philippines, and Japan; atmospheric effects encircling the globe caused strange sunrise and sunset conditions for months afterward; active during late 20th cent.

Kra·ków *or Eng.* **Cra·cow** \ˈkrä-ˌkau̇, ˈkra-, ˈkrā-, -kō, *Pol.* ˈkrä-ˌküf\ *or Ger.* **Kra·kau** \ˈkrä-ˌkau̇\. **1.** Province of S Poland. See table at POLAND.
2. City, its ✱, on Vistula River 156 mi. (251 km.) SSW of Warsaw; pop. (1989e) 748,356; metallurgical industries; chemicals; seat of Polish Academy of Science; university (1364), technical university (1945); several museums; 14th cent. Gothic cathedral.
History: Polish town, in 10th cent. part of territory under Boleslav I of Bohemia (*q.v.*); captured by Bolesław I of Poland c. 996; estab. as ✱ of Polish kingdom and an hereditary principality by Bolesław III (1102–38); invaded by Mongols 1241; received municipal rights (Magdeburg rights) 1257; made Polish ✱ by Władysław I Łokietek 1320 and remained ✱ until fire (1595) caused transfer of court to Warsaw (see WARSAW 2); captured by Swedes 1655, 1702; coronation and burial place of Polish kings to 18th cent.; taken by Austria in Third Partition of Poland 1795; included in French Emperor Napoléon's Grand Duchy of Warsaw 1809–15; independent buffer state, republic of Kraków, erected 1815; restored to Austria 1846; belonged to independent Poland after WWI; held by Germans in both WWI and WWII; taken by Russians 1945.

Kra·len·dijk \ˈkrä-lən-ˌdīk\. Chief town on Bonaire I., Netherlands Antilles, West Indies; on W coast.

Krá·lic·ká \ˈkrä-lit-ˌskä\ *or Ger.* **Kra·litz** \ˈkrä-lits\. Town, E cen. Czech Republic, just E of Prostějov; here was printed 1579–93 the Kralitz or Brothers' Bible, the most important Bohemian version.

Kra·lje·vo \ˈkräl-ye-ˌvō\. Town, Serbia, cen. Yugoslavia, at junction of Ibar River with W branch of the Morava; pop. (1991p) 124,309; 12th–13th cent. Zica and Studenica monasteries; Zica Monastery medieval site of coronation of Serbian kings.

Kra·ma·torsk \ˌkrä-mə-ˈtȯrsk\. City, N Donets subdivision, E Ukraine, in cen. Donets Basin on a tributary of the Donets ab. 25 mi. (40 km.) W of Artemovsk; pop. (1991e) 201,000; diversified heavy industry, incl. iron, steel, coke, cement, machinery; developed late 19th cent.; held by Germans from 1941 to Sept. 1943.

Kranj \ˈkrän-yə\. Town, N Slovenia, NW of Ljubljana.

Krapotkin. See KROPOTKIN.

Kras \ˈkräs\ *or Ger.* **Karst** \ˈkärst\ *or Ital.* **Car·so** \ˈkär-sō\. Mountain plateau, Italy and Slovenia, N of Trieste and E of the Isonzo River; scene of several battles in WWI incl. an 11th offensive Aug. 1917 in which the Italians were victors over the Austrians (but lost their gains Oct. 1917); treaty of 1947 put greater part in NW Yugoslavia.

Kras·li·ce \ˈkräs-lēt-ˌse\ *or Ger.* **Gras·litz** \ˈgräs-lits\. Town, NW Czech Republic, ab. 20 mi. (32 km.) NNE of Cheb.

Kraś·nik \ˈkräsh-nik\. Commune, Lublin prov., E Poland, 28 mi. (45 km.) SSW of the city of Lublin; pop. (1989e) 36,337; scene of Austrian defeat by Russians Aug. 1914.

Kras·no·ar·meysk *or* **Kras·no·ar·meisk** \ˌkräs-nō-ər-ˈmyāsk\. Town, Donets'k subdivision, Ukraine, ab. 30 mi. (48 km.) NW of the city of Donets'k; pop. (1991e) 73,000; coal mining.

Kras·no·dar \ˌkräs-nə-ˈdär\; *formerly* **Eka·te·ri·no·dar** \i-ˌkä-tə-ˈrē-nə-ˌdär\ *also* **Ye·ka·te·ri·no·dar** \yi-\. City, ✱ of Krasnodar Kray, S Russia in Europe, 160 mi. (257 km.) S of Rostov-na-Donu; pop. (1992e) 635,000; on right bank of Kuban' River and on railroad line from Rostov-na-Donu to Novorossiysk; food processing, oil refining; museum and art gallery. Founded c. 1794 as a small fort by Empress Catherine II; in WWII occupied by Germans 1942 and retaken 1943.

Krasnodar Kray *or* **Krasnodar Krai** \ˈkrī\. Territory of Russia in Europe, bounded on N by Rostov Oblast, on E by Stavropol' Kray and Karachay-Cherkessia, on SE by Abkhazia Rep. (in Republic of Georgia), on S and SW by Black Sea, and on W by Sea of Azov; 32,278 sq. mi. (83,600 sq. km.); pop. (1992e) 4,797,000; ✱ Krasnodar; separated from E

Crimea (Kerch Penin.) by Kerch Strait; includes Adygea Rep. and the lower and middle course of the Kuban' River. In S contains mountains and foothills of W Caucasus; constituted W part of the former North Caucasus region; much of it is fertile plain with marshland along the Azov shore; crossed by several railroad lines; essentially an agricultural region producing wheat, barley, rice, tobacco, sunflowers, vegetables, and sugar beets; has oil fields, and forests in S; cattle raising also important. Chief cities: Krasnodar, Sochi, Novorossiysk, Armavir. In medieval period under Tatar khanates; came under Russian control for the most part in 19th cent. See NORTH CAUCASUS. Territory created 1937; largely overrun by German armies 1942–43.

Kras·no·don \ˌkräs-nə-ˈdȯn\. Town, Luhans'k subdivision, Ukraine, ab. 30 mi. (48 km.) SE of the city of Luhans'k; pop. (1991e) 55,000; coal.

Kras·no·gorsk \ˈkräs-nō-ˌgȯrsk\. Town, Moscow Oblast, W cen. Russia in Europe, ab. 12 mi. (19 km.) W of the city of Moscow; pop. (1991e) 91,700.

Kras·no·grad \ˌkräs-nə-ˈgrät\ *or* **Kras·no·hrad** \-ˈhrät\. Town, Kharkiv subdivision, NE Ukraine, 55 mi. (88 km.) SW of the city of Kharkiv; railroad and highway junction point.

Krasnogvardeisk. See GATCHINA.

Krasnohrad. See KRASNOGRAD.

Kras·no·kamsk \ˌkräs-nō-ˈkämsk\. Town, Perm' Oblast, E Russia in Europe, ab. 20 mi. (32 km.) WNW of the city of Perm'; pop. (1991e) 57,800; formed 1929.

Krasnostav. See KRASNYSTAW.

Kras·no·tur'·insk *or* **Kras·no·tur·insk** \ˌkräs-nō-tu̇r-ˈyēnsk\. Town, Sverdlovsk Oblast, Russia in Asia, ab. 15 mi. (24 km.) NW of Serov; pop. (1991e) 67,200; aluminum.

Kras·nou·fimsk \ˌkräs-nō-ü-ˈfēmsk\. Town, Sverdlovsk Oblast, W Russia in Asia, ab. 110 mi. (177 km.) WSW of Yekaterinburg.

Kras·no·u·ral'sk *or* **Kras·no·u·ralsk** \ˌkräs-nō-yu̇-ˈrälʸsk\. Town, W Sverdlovsk Oblast, W Russia in Asia, 45 mi. (72 km.) N of Yekaterinburg, on E slope of Ural Mts.

Kras·no·vodsk \ˌkräs-nə-ˈvȯtsk\. Seaport town on **Krasnovodsk Gulf,** NW Turkmenistan; pop. (1991e) 59,500; across Caspian Sea from Baku; railroad terminus; exports petroleum products; dates from a fort built in 19th cent.

Kras·no·yarsk \ˌkräs-nə-ˈyärsk\. City, ✻ of Krasnoyarsk Kray, Russia in Asia, on left bank of upper Yenisey River and on Trans-Siberian R.R., 420 mi. (676 km.) E of Novosibirsk; pop. (1992e) 925,000; commercial and hydroelectric power center; metalworking, shipbuilding; heavy machinery, cement, lumber. Founded as a fort by Cossacks 1628; in later 17th cent. frequently attacked by Tatars and Kirghiz.

Krasnoyarsk Kray *or* **Krasnoyarsk Krai** \ˈkrī\. A territory of Russia in Asia, bounded on N by Arctic Ocean (Laptev and Kara seas), on E by Sakha Rep. and Irkutsk Oblast, on S by Tuva Rep., and on W by Kemerovo and Tomsk oblasts and the Khanty-Mansi and Yamalo-Nenets autonomous okrugs; 927,258 sq. mi. (2,401,598 sq. km.); pop. (1992e) 4,797,000; ✻ Krasnoyarsk. Includes Taymyr and Evenki autonomous okrugs and Taymyr Penin. In SW includes Khakassia which is politically independent; includes Yenisey River and the greater part of the valleys of its tributaries (see TUNGUSKA), and also the Khatanga River (in Taymyr Autonomous Okrug); largely tundra in the Taymyr and lower Yenisey region, hilly in cen. part, and quite mountainous in S, containing foothills of Sayan Mts. Crossed by the Trans-Siberian R.R., passing through Achinsk and Krasnoyarsk, also by a parallel trunk line farther S, reaching the rich mining and agricultural lands about Minusinsk. Great mineral wealth (gold, nickel, copper, iron ore, and uranium); timber. Chief settlements: Krasnoyarsk, Noril'sk, Achinsk, Kansk. Colonized by Russians from middle of 17th cent. but developed slowly; long a place of exile; after completion of Trans-Siberian R.R. (1891–98) from Moscow to Vladivostok, marked by rapid growth; made subdivision of Russian S.F.S.R. 1934; now a member of Russian Federation.

Kras·no·ye Se·lo \ˈkräs-nə-yə-si-ˈlȯ\. Former town, now a SSW section of the city of St. Petersburg, St. Petersburg Oblast, W Russia in Europe; taken in WWII by Germans Sept. 1941; incorp. into St. Petersburg (then Leningrad) 1973.

Krasny. See KYZYL.

Kras·ny Luch *or* **Kras·nyy Luch** \ˌkräs-nē-ˈlüch\. City, Luhans'k subdivision, Ukraine, in the Donets Basin; pop. (1991e) 113,000; coal mining.

Kras·ny·staw \kräs-ˈnis-ˌtäf\ *or Russ.* **Kras·no·stav** \ˌkräs-nə-ˈstäf, -ˈstäv\. Commune, SW Chełm prov., Poland, 32 mi. (51 km.) SE of Lublin; pop. (1981p) 17,257.

Krasny Su·lin *or* **Kras·nyy Su·lin** \ˌkräs-nē-sü-ˈlēn\. Town, Rostov Oblast, S Russia in Europe, ab. 15 mi. (24 km.) NNW of Shakhty.

Krat. See TRAT.

Kra·tie \krä-ˈtyā\ *or* **Krâ·chéh** \krä-ˈchā\. Commercial town on the Mekong, E Cambodia, 105 mi. (169 km.) NE of Phnom Penh; pop. (1987e) 14,000.

Kra·wang \krä-ˈwäŋ\. Town, West Java prov., Indonesia, on railroad line 35 mi. (56 km.) ESE of Jakarta.

Kre·feld \ˈkrā-ˌfelt\; *formerly* **Krefeld–Uer·ding·en** \-ˈᵫr-diŋ-ən\. City, W North Rhine-Westphalia, Germany, on Rhine River 19 mi. (31 km.) WSW of Essen; pop. (1992e) 245,772; machinery, clothing, textiles; printing, dyeing; granted city charter 1373; to Prussia 1702; bombed in WWII.

Kre·men·chug *or* **Kre·men·chuk** \ˌkri-min-ˈchük\. City, S Poltava subdivision, E cen. Ukraine, on the Dnieper 160 mi. (257 km.) SE of Kiev; pop. (1991e) 241,000; hydroelectric power station; steel castings, agricultural machinery; has rail connections N to Moscow and Kharkiv and S across the Dnieper with Kirovohrad by a long tubular bridge; many churches. Founded 1571; in the Bolshevik Revolution and succeeding civil war 1917–21, suffered much damage; in WWII seized by Germans 1941 but retaken in great Soviet drive late 1943.

Kre·me·nets \ˌkri-mi-ˈnyets\ *or Pol.* **Krze·mie·niec** \kshe-ˈmye-nyets\. City, W Ukraine, 47 mi. (76 km.) SSE of Luts'k; formerly in Poland.

Krem·lin–Bi·cê·tre \krem-ˌleⁿ-bē-ˈsetrᵊ\. Commune, Val-de-Marne dept., N France, a S suburb of Paris.

Krem·ni·ca \ˈkrem-nēt-ˌsä\ *or Ger.* **Krem·nitz** \ˈkrem-nits\ *or Hung.* **Kör·möcz·bá·nya** \ˌkœr-mœts-ˈbän-yö\. Commune, cen. Slovakia, NW of Zvolen; pop. (1980p) 7168.

Krems \ˈkrems, ˈkremz\ *or* **Krems an der Do·nau** \ˌän-dər-ˈdō-ˌnau̇\. City, Lower Austria, Austria, on Danube River 38 mi. (61 km.) WNW of Vienna; pop. (1991c) 22,766; metal goods; active trade in wine and fruit; first mentioned 995; chartered 12th cent.; many medieval buildings.

Kremsier. See KROMĚŘÍŽ.

Krētikòn Pélagos. See CRETE, SEA OF.

Kreuzburg *or* **Kreuzburg in Oberschlesien.** See KLUCZBORK.

Kreuz·ling·en \ˈkrȯits-liŋ-ən\. Commune, Thurgau canton, NE Switzerland, near W end of Lake Constance adjoining Konstanz; pop. (1980c) 16,101; 17th cent. church.

Kreuznach. See BAD KREUZNACH.

Kreuz·tal \ˈkrȯits-täl\. City, North Rhine-Westphalia, Germany, 41 mi. (66 km.) E of Cologne; pop. (1980c) 30,219; made city 1969.

Kri·bi \ˈkrē-bē\. Port, Cameroon, on the Bight of Biafra 80 mi. (129 km.) S of Douala; pop. (1987e) 18,973.

Kriens \ˈkrēns, ˈkrē-ens\. Commune, Lucerne canton, Switzerland; pop. (1989c) 22,237.

Kril'·on, Mys \ˈməs-krēl-ˈyȯn\ *or* **Cape Kril·on** \ˈkri-lən\ *or Jp.* **Ni·shi No·to·ro Mi·sa·ki** \ˈnē-shē-ˈnō-tō-rō-mē-ˈsä-kē\. Cape on SW extremity of Sakhalin I., E Russia in Asia, opp. N tip of Hokkaidō, Japan.

Krimmitschau. See CRIMMITSCHAU.

Krimm·ler Falls \ˈkrim-lər\. Falls in **Krimmler River,** an upper tributary of the Salzach flowing N from the Hohe Tauern, SW Austria; in three parts with total drop of 1250 ft. (381 m.).

Krio, Cape \krē-ˈō\. **1.** *or* **Cape Kri·ós** \krē-ˈōs\ *or Gk.* **Kri·oú Me·to·pon** \krē-ˈü-ˈme-tö-ˌpȯn\. SW point of the island of Crete, Greece, in E Mediterranean Sea.
2. Cape at W end of long narrow peninsula on SW coast of Turkey in Asia, S of Bodrum Penin.; site of ancient Cnidus.

Krish·na \'krish-nə\; *formerly* **Kist·na** \'kist-nə\. River of the Deccan, S India; rises near Mahabaleshwar in Maharashtra in the Western Ghats within 40 mi. (64 km.) of the Arabian Sea, flows SSE into Karnataka, continues E, flowing into Andhra Pradesh, then flows NE and SE into Bay of Bengal through several mouths S of Maghilipatnam; ab. 800 mi. (1285 km.) long.

Krish·na·na·gar \'krish-nə-ˌnə-gər\ *also* **Krish·na·gar** \'krish-nə-gər\. Town, West Bengal, NE India, on Hugli River 58 mi. (93 km.) N of Calcutta; pop. (1991p) 120,918; horticultural research station; contains former residence of the maharajas of Nadia.

Kristiania. See OSLO 2.

Kris·tian·sand *or* **Chris·tian·sand** \'kris-tē-ən-ˌsän\. Seaport, ⊗ of Vest-Agder co., SW Norway, on the Skagerrak SW of Oslo; pop. (1990c) 64,888; large ice-free port; shipbuilding, metalworking; fishing; 11th cent. church; 17th cent. Gothic cathedral; has resort beaches. Founded 1641; in WWII captured by Germans Apr. 9, 1940 after brief resistance in which German cruiser *Karlsruhe* was sunk.

Kris·tian·stad \'kris-tē-ən-ˌstäd\. **1.** Province of S Sweden. See table at SWEDEN.

2. Seaport, its ⊗; pop. (1993e) 72,789; trade center in agricultural region; flour mills, slaughterhouses; food processing; textiles; 17th cent. palace. Founded 1614 by Christian IV of Denmark; ceded to Sweden 1658; captured by Danes 1676, recaptured by Swedes 1678.

Kris·tian·sund *or* **Chris·tian·sund** \'kris-tē-ən-ˌsu̇n\. Seaport, Møre og Romsdal co., W Norway, WSW of Trondheim; pop. (1992e) 17,121; built on three small islands enclosing a harbor; base of large trawler fleet; exports fish; inhabited in prehistoric times; incorp. 1742.

Kris·ti·ne·hamn \ˌkris-tē-nə-'häm-ᵊn\. Lake port, Värmland prov., SW Sweden, on Lake Vänern; pop. (1993e) 25,954; machine factories; chartered 1642.

Krithia. See ALÇITEPE.

Kríti. See CRETE 3.

Krivoy Rog *also* **Krivoi Rog.** See KRYVYY RIH.

Krk \'kərk\ *or Ital.* **Ve·glia** \'vāl-yä\. **1.** Island at head of the Adriatic Sea, Croatia; 157 sq. mi. (407 sq. km.); wine and fruit; site of Krk Bridge, world's longest concrete-arch bridge (main span 1280 ft. or 390 m.; completed 1980).

2. Town on S coast of island; pop. (1991p) 15,850; 12th cent. cathedral; settled since ancient times, and successively under rule of Rome, Croatia, Venice, Austria 1797–1809, France 1809–13, Austria again 1813–1918; part of Yugoslavia 1920–91.

Kr·ka \'kər-kə\; *anc.* **Ti·ti·us** \'ti-shəs, -shē-əs\. River, Bosnia and Herzegovina; flows S into Adriatic Sea a little below Šibenik; 46 mi. (74 km.) long; has a long, wide estuary and is noted for several waterfalls bet. Knin and Šibenik.

Krkonoše. See RIESENGEBIRGE.

Kr·nov \'kər-ˌnȯf\ *or Ger.* **Jä·gern·dorf** \'yā-gərn-ˌdȯrf\. Town, NE Czech Republic, 30 mi. (48 km.) NW of Ostrava; pop. (1980p) 25,678; textile mills.

Kroja. See KRUJË.

Kro·le·vets \krə-li-'vyets\. Town, Sumy subdivision, Ukraine, ab. 23 mi. (37 km.) N of Konotop.

Kro·mě·říž \'krȯ-myer-ˌzhēsh\ *or Ger.* **Krem·sier** \'krem-ˌzir\. Town, E Czech Republic, on Morava River 35 mi. (56 km.) E of Brno; pop. (1991p) 28,926; commercial center; meeting place of Austrian Reichstag 1848–49 occasioned by revolt in Vienna.

Kro·no·berg \'krü-nü-ˌbar, -ˌbar-ē\. Province of S Sweden. See table at SWEDEN.

Kro·nots·ka·ya Sop·ka \krə-'nȯt-skə-yə-'sȯp-kə\. Volcano (*sopka*), in Eastern Range, Kamchatka Penin., Khabarovsk Kray, E Russia in Asia; 15,580 ft. (4749 m.).

Kro·nots·ki, Cape \krə-'nȯt-skē\ *or Russ.* **Mys Kro·nots·kiy** \'məs-krə-'nȯt-skē\. Point extending into Bering Sea, E coast of Kamchatka Penin., E Russia in Asia, at 54°45′N, 162°07′E.

Kron·shtadt \'krōn-ˌshtät\. Naval port on Kotlin I., E end of Gulf of Finland, NW St. Petersburg Oblast, W Russia in Europe, ab. 25 mi. (40 km.) W of the city of St. Petersburg; pop. (1991e) 45,300; has large harbor but blocked by ice for ab. five months yearly; important commercial harbor before deep channel to St. Petersburg constructed in late 19th cent. Fortress (*orig.* **Kron·slot** \'krȯn-ˌshlət\ *and later* **Kron·stadt** *or* **Kron·shtadt** \'krōn-ˌshtät\) founded by Peter the Great 1703; was strong defense point for Russian empire; scene of mutinies 1825, 1882, 1905; took active part in Bolshevik Revolution of 1917; in 1921 navy mutiny against Soviets was vigorously suppressed; in WWII played important role during siege of Leningrad (St. Petersburg).

Kronstadt. 1. City, Romania. See BRAŞOV 2.

2. Fortress, Russia. See KRONSHTADT.

Kroon·stad \'krōn-ˌstat\. Town, N Free State, E cen. Rep. of South Africa, 120 mi. (193 km.) NE of Bloemfontein; pop. (1985c) 22,886; center of rich farm district; railroad junction; clothing factory.

Kro·pot·kin *formerly* **Kra·pot·kin** \krə-'pät-kin\. Town, E Krasnodar Kray, S Russia in Europe, on Kuban' River 80 mi. (129 km.) ENE of the city of Krasnodar; pop. (1991e) 76,600; railroad junction; trade center.

Kros·no \'krȯs-nō\. **1.** Province, SE Poland. See table at POLAND.

2. Commune, its ✻; pop. (1992e) 50,100.

Kro·to·szyn *or Ger.* **Kro·to·schin** \krȯ-'tȯ-shin\. Commune, W Kalisz prov., W cen. Poland, 50 mi. (80 km.) SSE of Poznań; pop. (1981p) 24,279.

Kroub, El. See EL KHROUB.

Kru Coast \'krü\. That section of the SE coast of Liberia NW of Cape Palmas whose original inhabitants were called Krumen.

Kru·ger National Park \'krü-gər\. Park and game reserve, NE Rep. of South Africa, in E Northern and Mpumalanga provs., on Mozambique frontier; crossed by Olifants River; 200 mi. (322 km.) long by 40 mi. (64 km.) wide; 7523 sq. mi. (19,484 sq. km.); has large numbers of wild animals native to South Africa. Estab. 1926 by Act of Parliament; had its origin in President Paul Kruger's game sanctuary estab. 1898, which included country bet. Limpopo and Sabi rivers.

Kru·gers·dorp \'krü-gərz-ˌdȯrp\. Town, Gauteng prov., NE Rep. of South Africa, 20 mi. (32 km.) W of Johannesburg; pop. (1985c) 73,767; manganese and gold deposits in region. Founded 1887. The Pardekraal Monument marks site of 1880 proclamation for an independent Transvaal.

Kru·jë *also* **Kro·ja** \'krü-yə\ *or Ital.* **Cro·ia** \'krȯi-ä\. **1.** District of W Albania. See table at ALBANIA.

2. Town, its ✻.

Krung Thep. See BANGKOK.

Kru·še·vac \'krü-she-ˌväts\. Town, cen. Serbia, Yugoslavia, on W branch of the Morava ab. 95 mi. (155 km.) SE of Belgrade. In WWII occupied by Germans 1941.

Krušnéhory. See ERZGEBIRGE.

Kru·zof \'krü-ˌzȯf\. Small island in Alexander Archipelago, SE Alaska, W of Baranof I. and opp. Sitka; Mt. Edgecumbe at its S end.

Krym. See CRIMEA.

Krymsk \'krimsk\; *formerly* **Krym·ska·ya Sta·nit·sa** \'krim-skī-ə-stə-'nit-sə\. Town, Krasnodar Kray, S Russia in Europe, ab. 50 mi. (80 km.) WSW of the city of Krasnodar; pop. (1991e) 51,100.

Kry·vyy Rih \kri-'vi-'rik\ *or* **Kri·voy Rog** *also* **Kri·voi Rog** \kri-'vȯi-'rȯk\. City, Dnipropetrovs'k subdivision, SE cen. Ukraine; pop. (1991e) 724,000; railroad and industrial city, located in midst of rich iron mines and on W edge of the Donets Basin, a major coal-producing region; metallurgical plants, foundries, mills, and chemical works; cement, mining and drilling machinery. Village founded 17th cent.; rapid expansion followed exploitation of high-grade iron ore deposits beginning 1881–84; city and mines seized by Germans 1941; retaken by U.S.S.R. 1944.

Krzemieniec. See KREMENETS.

Ksar el Ke·bir \'ksär-el-ke-'bir\; *formerly also* **Al·ca·zar·qui·vir** \äl-'kä-zär-ki-'vir\. City, N Morocco, 60 mi. (96 km.) S of Tangier; pop. (1982c) 73,541; battle Aug. 4, 1578 in which King Sebastian of Portugal was defeated and slain by the Moors.

Ksour Mountains \'ksůr-\. Range of the Atlas Mts. in NW Algeria.

Ksto·vo \kə-'stȯ-və\. Town, Nizhegorod Oblast, cen. Russia in Europe, ab. 10 mi. (16 km.) SE of Nizhniy Novgorod; pop. (1991e) 65,300.

Kti·ma \kə-'tē-mə\ *or Turk.* **Ka·sa·ba** \kə-'sä-bə, ,kä-sə-'bä\ *or Gk.* **Ktē·ma** \'ktē-mə\. Town, W Cyprus, near the coast and just N of site of ancient Paphos.

K2 \'kā-'tü\ *also* **God·win Aus·ten** \'gȯ-dwin-'ȯs-tən, 'gä-, 'äs-\ *or* **Dap·sang** \,däp-'säŋ\. Peak, N Jammu and Kashmir, in region controlled by Pakistan; 28,250 ft. (8611 m.); highest mountain in Karakoram Range and 2d highest in the world; summit first reached 1954.

Kua·la Be·lait \'kwä-lə-bə-'līt, ků-'wä-\. Town, W Brunei, near border with Malaysia; pop. (1981c) 19,335.

Kuala Kang·sar \'kəŋ-sər\. Town, N cen. Perak state, Malaysia, on Perak River and W coast railroad line; pop. (1980c) 14,539.

Kuala Ku·bu Bha·ru \,kü-bü-'bär-ü\ *or* **Kuala Kubu Ba·ha·ru** \bə-'här-ü\. Town, NE Selangor state, W Malaysia, on main railroad line 25 mi. (40 km.) N of Kuala Lumpur; starting point of highway NE to Pahang state.

Kuala Li·pis \'lē-pəs\. Town, ✻ of Pahang state, in NW cen. Malaysia, on the cen. and E coast railroad line of Malay Penin. ab. 75 mi. (120 km.) N of Kuala Lumpur; pop. (1980c) 10,183.

Kuala Lum·pur \'lům-,půr, 'ləm-\. City, ✻ of Malaysia and ✻ of Kuala Lumpur Federal Terr., on main W coast railroad line ab. 200 mi. (320 km.) NW of Singapore (246 mi. or 396 km. by rail); pop. (1991p) 1,145,075; the most important Malay city on the peninsula; commercial center; tin mines nearby; university (1962). Founded as tin-mining camp 1857; became ✻ of Selangor 1880; underwent rebuilding and rapid expansion after 1882; ✻ of Federated Malay States 1895; occupied by Japanese in WWII 1942–45; made ✻ of Malaya 1957 and of Malaysia 1963.

Kuala Lumpur Federal Territory. Administrative subdivision of Malaysia. See table at MALAYSIA.

Kua–la–man–ta–t'a \'kwä-lä-män-'tä-tä\ *or* **Gur·la Man·dha·ta** \'gůr-lə-mänd-'hä-tə\. Peak in the Himalayas, in SW Tibet, China, near borders of Nepal and India; 25,355 ft. (7728 m.).

Kuala Pi·lah \'pē-lä\. Town, cen. Negeri Sembilan state, Malaysia; pop. (1980p) 68,671.

Kuala Se·lang·or \sə-'läŋ-,ȯr\. Coastal town on Strait of Malacca, NW Selangor state, Malaysia; pop. (1980p) 113,543.

Kuala Te·reng·ga·nu \tə-reŋ-'gä-nü\ *or* **Kuala Treng·ga·nu** \treŋ-\. Town, ✻ of Terengganu state, Malaysia, in NE part, at mouth of Terengganu River; pop. (1980c) 180,296.

Kuang–chou. See GUANGZHOU.

Kuang–hsi–chuang–tsu. See GUANGXI ZHUANGZU.

Kuang–hua. See GUANGHUA.

Kuang–te. See GUANGDE.

Kuan·tan \'kwän-,tän\. Coastal town, ✻ of Pahang state, Malaysia, N of the mouth of the Pahang River; pop. (1980c) 131,547; harbor at river mouth; was a key point on E coast seized by Japanese in their invasion of Malay Penin. Dec. 1941–Jan. 1942. British warships *Prince of Wales* and *Repulse* lost in naval battle Dec. 10, 1941 off this coast.

Kuba. See QUBA.

Ku·ban' *or* **Ku·ban** \kü-'banʸ, -'bän\. **1.** *anc.* **Hyp·a·nis** \'hi-pə-nəs\. River in region NW of Caucasus Mts., SE Europe; rises in the Caucasus in Republic of Georgia, flows N and NW into S Russia in Europe and forms a wide marshy delta with three mouths—two on the Sea of Azov and one on the Black Sea; 584 mi. (940 km.) long; navigable for less than 150 mi. (241 km.); its main headstream rises on slopes of Mt. Elbrus.

2. Former administrative unit of S Russia in Europe, along Kuban River and coast of Black Sea; now largely in Krasnodar Kray.

Ku·ben·sko·ye, Lake \'kü-bən-skə-yə\. Lake, W cen. Vologda Oblast, cen. Russia in Europe; ab. 40 mi. (64 km.) long; outlet the Sukhona River, a tributary of the Northern Dvina.

Kucha. See KUQA.

Kuchan. See QUCHAN.

K'u–ch'e. See KUQA.

Kuchengtze. See QITAI.

Ku·ching \'kü-chiŋ\; *formerly* **Sa·ra·wak** \sə-'rä-,wäk, -,wak\. Seaport, ✻ of Sarawak, East Malaysia, Malaysia, on Sarawak River ab. 10 mi. (16 km.) from its mouth; pop. (1980c) 72,555; trade center; founded 1839.

Kuchuk Kainarji. See KAYNARDZHA.

Küçük Menderes. 1. River in W Turkey in Asia. See CAŸSTER.

2. River in NW Turkey in Asia. See MENDERES 2.

Ku·da·ma·tsu \,kü-dä-'mät-sü\. City, Yamaguchi prefecture, SW Honshū, Japan, 53 mi. (85 km.) E of Shimonoseki on N shore of Inland Sea; pop. (1990c) 53,029.

Ku·dat \'kü-,dät\. Town, N Sabah, East Malaysia, Malaysia, on W side of Marudu Bay near N tip of island of Borneo; pop. (1980p) 41,872.

Ku·dus *or Du.* **Koe·does** \'kü-,düs\. Town, Central Java prov., Indonesia; pop. (1980c) 90,111.

Ku·dym·kar *or* **Ku·dim·kar** \kü-'dim-kər\. Town, ✻ of Komi-Permyak Autonomous Okrug, E Russia in Europe, on a tributary of the Kama River 100 mi. (161 km.) NW of Perm'; pop. (1991e) 33,800.

Kuei. See GUI.

Kuei–chou. See GUIZHOU.

Kuei–lin. See GUILIN.

Kuei–p'ing. See GUIPING.

Kuei–yang. See GUIYANG.

Kuenlun Shan. See KUNLUN SHAN.

K'u–erh–le. See KORLA.

Kufa, Al–. See AL-KUFA.

Kufow. See QUFU.

Kufra *or* **Kufrah, Al–.** See AL-KUFRAH.

Kuh. See KOH 1.

Kūh \'kü\. Persian for "mountain," and "mountain range." See 2d element.

Kūh–e Taftān *or* **Kuh–i–Taftan.** See TAFTĀN, KŪH-E-.

Kuh–i–Alwand. See ALWAND, MOUNT.

Kui·by·shev *or* **Kuy·by·shev** \'kü-ē-bə-shəf\. **1.** Town, W Novosibirsk Oblast, SW Russia in Asia, just N of the Trans-Siberian R.R. 190 mi. (306 km.) W of the city of Novosibirsk; pop. (1991e) 51,600.

2. City, Russia in Europe. See SAMARA.

Kuibyshevka. See BELOGORSK.

Kuibyshev Oblast. See SAMARA OBLAST.

Kui·to \'kwē-tü, -tō\. Town, ✻ of Bié prov., cen. Angola.

Ku·iu \'kü-yü\. Island, SE Alaska, W of Kupreanof I. and separated from Baranof I. by Chatham Strait.

Ku·jū \'kü-,jü\ *or* **Ku·ju·san** \-'sän\. Mountain, Ōita prefecture, NE Kyūshū, Japan; 5861 ft. (1786 m.).

Ku·kës \'kü-kəs\ *also* **Kuk·si** \'kůk-sē\. **1.** District of NE Albania. See table at ALBANIA.

2. Town, its ✻, on Drin River 25 mi. (40 km.) E of Pukë.

Kukong. See SHAOGUAN.

Kukukhoto. See HOHHOT.

Ku·kum \'kü-kəm\. Village on NW coast of Guadalcanal I., SE Solomon Is., W Pacific, just W of Lunga Point.

Kuku Nor. See QINGHAI 1.

Ku·la Gulf \'kü-lə\. Body of water, bet. NW New Georgia I. and Kolombangara I. in the Solomon Is., W Pacific Ocean; 17 mi. (27 km.) long, ab. 10 mi. (16 km.) wide; closed by small Arundel I. at SW.

Kula Kan·gri \kü-'lä-kän-'grē\. Mountain in the Himalayas, on Bhutan-Tibet boundary; 24,784 ft. (7554 m.).

Ku–lang \'kü-'läŋ\. See XIAMEN.

Kuldja. See YINING.

Ku·le·ba·ki \ˌkül-yə-ˈbä-kē\. Town, Nizhegorod Oblast, cen. Russia in Europe, ab. 85 mi. (135 km.) SW of Nizhniy Novgorod; pop. (1991e) 45,700.

Külek Boğazi. See CILICIAN GATES.

Ku·li·ko·vo \ˌku̇-li-ˈkȯ-və\. Plain in E Tula Oblast, SW cen. Russia in Europe, near source of the Don; battle Sept. 8, 1380 in which Dmitry Donskoi and Russian princes decisively defeated Mongol army, establishing a measure of Russian independence.

Kulja. See YINING.

Kulm. See CHEŁMNO.

Kulm·bach \ˈku̇lm-ˌbäk\. City, Bavaria, Germany, on Main River 13 mi. (21 km.) NNW of Bayreuth; pop. (1980c) 28,226; 15th cent. Gothic church; 17th cent. baroque monastery; 13th cent. Plassenburg (Hohenzollern fort) overlooks city; settled c. 10th cent. A.D.; passed to Prussia 1791, to Bavaria 1810.

Kulmsee. See CHEŁMŻA.

Kŭ·lob *or* **Ku·lyab** \kü-ˈlyȧp\. Town, SW Tajikistan, in mountains N of the Amu Dar'ya; pop. (1991e) 79,300.

Kulpa. See KUPA.

Kulp·mont \ˈkəlp-ˌmänt\. Borough, Northumberland co., E cen. Pennsylvania, 17 mi. (27 km.) WNW of Pottsville; pop. (1990c) 3233.

Kultepe. See KANISH.

Ku·lu \ˈkü-lü\. Valley, Himachal Pradesh, N India, in Himalayas SE of Chamba; forms mountain basin of upper Beas River; chief town Sultanpur (alt. 4584 ft. or 1397 m.); higher villages at 9000 ft. (2743 m.); in medieval times a Rajput principality.

Ku·lu·ma·dau \ˌkü-lü-ˈmä-ˌdau̇\. Village and chief settlement on Woodlark I. (*q.v.*), Papua New Guinea, in Solomon Sea.

Kulun Nor. See HULUN NUR.

Kulyab. See KŬLOB.

Kŭm \ˈku̇m\; *formerly* **Kin** \ˈkēn\. River, South Korea; flows SW into the Yellow Sea; 247 mi. (397 km.) long.

Ku·ma \ku̇-ˈmä\. River, S Russia in Europe; rises in Caucasus Mts., flows E to the Caspian Sea, reaching the sea only in flood season; ab. 360 mi. (580 km.) long.

Ku·ma·ga·ya \ku̇-ˈmä-gä-yä, ˌkü-mä-ˈgä-yä\. Town, Saitama prefecture, SE cen. Honshū, Japan, 35 mi. (56 km.) NW of Tokyo; pop. (1992e) 155,118.

Ku·ma·mo·to \ˌkü-mä-ˈmō-tō\. **1.** Prefecture, Kyūshū, Japan; ✻ Kumamoto. See table at JAPAN.
2. City, its ✻, on Shira River near its mouth on the W coast and in an extensive plain; pop. (1992e) 636,144; market center for agricultural region; food processing; textiles; founded in late 16th cent. at time of building of its great castle; confiscated 1632 and given to the daimyo Hosokawa, whose family retained town and castle until 1868. During feudal period the castle was one of strongest in all Japan; partly destroyed 1877, partly restored since.

Ku·ma·no Sea \ku̇-ˈmä-nō\. Inlet of W Pacific Ocean on S coast of Honshū, Japan, SW of Enshu Bight.

Ku·ma·no·vo \kü-ˈmä-nȯ-ˌvō\. Town, N Republic of Macedonia, 15 mi. (24 km.) NE of Skopje; pop. (1991p) 135,529; trade center, esp. in tobacco; battlefield 1912 where Serbians defeated the Turks.

Kumara. See HUMA.

Ku·ma·si \ku̇-ˈmä-sē, -ˈma-\; *formerly* **Coo·mas·sie** \-ˈma-\. City, ✻ of Ashanti region, Ghana, ab. 115 mi. (185 km.) NW of Accra; pop. (1988e) 385,192; connected by rail with Accra and Takoradi; commercial center; market town for cocoa-producing region; diversified handicrafts; university (1961). Chief town of tribe which in 18th cent. became leading Ashanti people and established Ashanti confederation or kingdom (see ASHANTI); captured by British late 19th cent.; experienced large growth in population during 20th cent.; remains the seat of Ashanti king.

Kumayri. See GYUMRI.

Kum·ba \ˈküm-bä\. Town, W Cameroon, NW of Douala; pop. (1987c) 70,280.

Kum·ba·ko·nam \ˌku̇m-bə-ˈkō-nəm\ *or* **Com·ba·co·num** \ˌkäm-bə-ˈkō-nəm\. City, SE Tamil Nadu, S India, 190 mi. (306 km.) SE of Madras; pop. (1991p) 139,449; has silk industry; a stronghold of Brahmanism, one of S India's most famed temple cities; every 12 years scene of festival held in the Mahamakam Tank (lake), attended by thousands of pilgrims. Once a ✻ of the Cōla kingdom.

Ku·me \ˈkü-mā\. Small island of Okinawa group, S Ryukyu Is., Japan, ab. 55 mi. (88 km.) W of Naha; seized by U.S. forces June 1945 in Okinawa campaign.

Kŭm·gang Mountains \ˈku̇m-ˌgäŋ\ *also* **Di·a·mond Mountains** \ˈdī-mənd, ˈdī-ə-\ *or Jp.* **Kon·go·san** \ˌkōn-gō-ˈsän\. Group of mountain peaks along cen. part of E coast of North Korea, S of Wŏnsan, covering area of ab. 75 sq. mi. (194 sq. km.); highest point 5373 ft. (1638 m.); remarkable for geological formation with many beautiful scenic wonders; notable as former center of Buddhist religion for centuries, with many temples.

Ku·mi \ˈkü-mē\. City, SE cen. South Korea, NW of Taegu; pop. (1985c) 142,094.

Kumilla. See COMILLA.

Kum Ka·le \ˈküm-kä-ˈlā\. Turkish fort on S side of Dardanelles at its W end, Turkey in Asia; scene of action in WWI when its guns were silenced by British fleet 1915.

Ku·mo \ˈkü-mō\. Town, E cen. Nigeria; pop. (1991e) 130,600.

Ku·mon Range \ˈkü-ˌmōn\. Mountain range in N Myanmar; source of Chindwin River.

Ku·mu·ka·hi, Cape \ˌkü-mü-ˈkä-hē\. Cape on E extremity of Hawaii I., Hawaii.

Ku·na Peak \ˈkü-nə\. Mountain in the Sierra Nevada, cen. California in Yosemite National Park; 12,951 ft. (3947 m.).

Ku·nar \kü-ˈnär\. See CHITRAL.

Ku·na·shir \ˌkü-nə-ˈshir\ *or Jp.* **Ku·na·shi·ri** \ku̇-ˈnä-shə-rē\. One of the Kuril Is. (*q.v.*), Russia in Asia; the 2d in size and the one nearest Hokkaidō, Japan.

Kun·dar \ˈku̇n-ˌdär\. River, Pakistan; flows NE into Gumal River, in its lower course forming a section of the Pakistan-Afghanistan boundary.

Kun·dūz \ku̇n-ˈdu̇z\. River, NE Afghanistan; flows N from Hindu Kush to Amu Dar'ya and forms in part W boundary of Badakhshān; ab. 250 mi. (400 km.) long.

Kuneitrah, El. See AL QUNAYTIRAH.

Kunene. See CUNENE.

Kunersdorf. See KUNOWICE.

Kü·nes \ˈkue̅-ˈnes\ *or W.-G.* **Kung–nai–ssu** \ˈku̇ŋ-ˈnī-ˈsə̇\. River, Xinjiang Uygur, China; joins the Tekes to form the Ili.

Kung·hit Island \ˈkəŋ-ˌhit\. S island of the Queen Charlotte Is. off W British Columbia, W Canada.

Kung–ko–erh *or* **Kungur.** See KONGUR.

Kung–nai–ssu. See KÜNES.

Kun·gur \ku̇n-ˈgu̇r\. Town, SE Perm' Oblast, E Russia in Europe, at foot of W slope of Ural Mts. on railroad line ab. 50 mi. (80 km.) SSE of the city of Perm'; pop. (1991e) 81,800; machinery; founded in 1648; because of its favorable location early became important in trade with Far East.

Kun·he·gyes \ˈku̇n-ˌhe-dyesh\. Commune, E Hungary, ab. 10 mi. (16 km.) NW of Karcag; pop. (1980p) 10,116.

Kunie. See PINS, ÎLE DES.

Kun·lun Shan *or W.-G.* **K'un–lun Shan** *also* **Kuen·lun Shan** *or* **Kwen·lun Shan** \ˈkün-ˈlün-ˈshän\. Mountain ranges (*shan*), W China; on N edge of Plateau of Tibet extending from Pamirs and Karakoram Range into Qinghai; highest peak 25,348 ft. (7726 m.); has many subsidiary ranges.

Kun·ming *or W.-G.* **K'un–ming** \ˈku̇n-ˈmiŋ\; *formerly* **Yun·nan** \ˈyü-ˈnän\. City, ✻ of Yunnan prov., S China, in E part of province 380 mi. (611 km.) SW of Chongqing, Sichuan; pop. (1990c) 1,127,411; chief city of SW China, advantageously situated on fertile plain at elev. of 6400 ft. (1951 m.) on N shore of a large lake (Dian Chi); trade and transportation center, linked by narrow-gauge railroad (opened 1910) to Hanoi, Vietnam; metalworking; electrical equipment, chemicals, textiles, copper; university (1934). An old city, settled c. 200 B.C.; visited by Venetian traveler Marco Polo 13th cent. A.D.; in WWII of great importance as transportation center, American air base, and Chinese military headquarters; frequently bombed by Japanese.

Ku·no·wi·ce \ˌkü-nȯ-ˈvēt-se\ *or Ger.* **Ku·ners·dorf** \ˈkü-nərs-ˌdȯrf\. Village, Zielona Góra prov., W Poland; battle of Kunersdorf fought here 1759, during Seven Years' War, in which Prussian King Frederick the Great was badly defeated by Russians and Austrians.

Kun·san \ˈku̇n-ˈsän\. Seaport, North Chŏlla prov., South Korea, on Yellow Sea; pop. (1990p) 218,216.

Kun·szent·már·ton \ˈku̇n-sent-ˌmär-tōn\. Commune, SE Hungary, on Körös River N of Csongrád; pop. (1980p) 11,103.

Kuo·la·yar·vi \ˈkwȯ-lä-ˌyär-vē\ *or Finnish* **Kuo·la·jär·vi** \-ˌyar-vē\. Town, NW Karelia Rep., NW Russia in Europe, in region ceded by Finland to U.S.S.R. 1940.

Kuo·pio \ˈkwȯ-pē-ˌȯ\. **1.** Province of S cen. Finland. See table at FINLAND.
2. City, its ✻, on W shore of Lake Kallavesi; pop. (1992e) 81,391; lumber center; winter sports center; chartered 1782.

Ku·pa \ˈkü-pə\ *or* **Kul·pa** \ˈku̇l-pə\. River, S Europe; flows E along Slovenia-Croatia border, through Croatia into Sava River; 184 mi. (296 km.) long.

Ku·pang *or Du.* **Koe·pang** \ˈkü-ˌpäŋ\. Town, ✻ of East Nusa Tenggara prov., Indonesia, SW end of Timor I. on **Kupang Bay;** pop. (1980c) 89,843; occupied by Dutch 17th cent.

Ku·pre·a·nof \ˌkü-prē-ˈa-ˌnȯf\. Island, E Alexander Archipelago, SE Alaska; chief town Kake.

Ku·pyansk \ku̇p-ˈyansk\. Town, E Kharkiv subdivision, NE Ukraine, on Oskol River 60 mi. (97 km.) E of the city of Kharkiv.

Ku·qa \ˈkü-ˈchə\ *or W.-G.* **K'u–ch'e** \ˈkü-ˈchə\; *angl.* **Ku·cha** \-ˈchə\. Town and oasis, W cen. Xinjiang Uygur, W China, S of the Tian Shan on early Silk Road (*q.v.*) and midway bet. Aksu and Yanqi on caravan route and highway; settled since ancient times; historically noted for its wealth and productiveness; in medieval times under the Uighurs.

Ku·ra \kə-ˈrä, ˈku̇r-ə\; *anc.* **Cy·rus** \ˈsī-rəs\. River, Turkey, Republic of Georgia, and Azerbaijan; rises in NE Turkey in Asia (where it is called **Ku·ru·çay** \ˌku̇r-u̇-ˈchī\) in mountains NW of Kars, flows N into Republic of Georgia, then ESE through Azerbaijan to the Caspian Sea S of Baku; 941 mi. (1514 km.) long. Has large reservoir in NW Azerbaijan and large delta, just above which it is joined by its largest tributary the Araks from the S; fed by many mountain streams and has rapid current in upper course; furnishes hydroelectric power at Tbilisi.

Kuramba, Mount. See KOROMBA, MOUNT.

Ku·ra·shi·ki \ku̇-ˈrä-shē-kē, ˌku̇r-ä-ˈshē-kē\. City, Okayama prefecture, Honshū, Japan, ab. 10 mi. (16 km.) WSW of the city of Okayama; pop. (1992e) 416,703.

Ku·ra·yo·shi \ˌku̇r-ä-ˈyō-shē\. City, Tottori prefecture, Honshū, Japan, 24 mi. (39 km.) W of the city of Tottori; pop. (1990c) 51,835.

Kur·di·stan \ˌku̇r-də-ˈstan, ˌkər-\. Mountainous region with indefinite boundaries forming a nonpolitical region in SE Turkey in Asia, and in adjoining areas of NW Iran, NE Iraq, and NE Syria; lies chiefly in Turkey S of Armenia and N of the Tigris, extending from the Euphrates on W to the mountains of Iran W of Hamadān and incl. Lake Van; ab. 74,000 sq. mi. (191,660 sq. km.); inhabited by Kurds; chief towns: Diyarbakır, Bitlis, and Van in Turkey, Mosul and Kirkuk in Iraq, and Kermānshāh in Iran. There are also many Kurds in Armenia. A Kurdish autonomous state was provided for in Treaty of Sèvres 1920 but terms never carried out.

Kurdufān. See KORDOFAN.

Kŭrd·zha·li \ˈku̇rd-zhä-lē\. Town, S Bulgaria; pop. (1991e) 61,287.

Ku·re \ˈkü-rā\. City, Hiroshima prefecture, SW Honshū, Japan, on N shore of Inland Sea at its W end, 12 mi. (19 km.) SE of the city of Hiroshima; pop. (1992e) 213,474; excellent natural harbor; shipbuilding; before WWII major Japanese naval dockyard; heavily bombed during 1945.

Kure Atoll *or* **Kure Island** *also* **Ocean Island.** Uninhabited islet of Leeward Is., Hawaiian Is., Hawaii, in cen. Pacific Ocean ab. 1500 mi. (2415 km.) NW of Niihau, 28°25′N, 178°25′W; 500 acres (202 hectares).

Ku·res·saa·re *or Russ.* **Ku·res·sa·re** \ˈku̇r-ə-ˌsä-rā\ *or Ger.* **Arens·burg** \ˈär-əns-ˌbu̇rk\. Seaport on S shore of Saaremaa I., W Estonia; in WWI held by Germans 1917–18 and by Bolsheviks 1918–19; in WWII held by Germans.

Kurg. See COORG.

Kur·gan \ku̇r-ˈgan, -ˈgän\. City, ✻ of Kurgan Oblast, SW Russia in Asia, on Trans-Siberian R.R. 140 mi. (225 km.) E of Chelyabinsk; pop. (1992e) 365,000; on the Tobol River in a rich agricultural plain E of the Urals; trade center for farm products; produces agricultural and other machinery. In a region long settled; its name in Russian means "tumulus " or "barrow " and it is so called from the many ancient burial mounds in the vicinity.

Kurgan Oblast \ˈȯ-bləst, -ˌblast\ *or* **Kur·gan·ska·ya Oblast'** \ku̇r-ˈgän-skə-yə\. Administrative subdivision of SW Russia in Asia; 27,413 sq. mi. (71,000 sq. km.); pop. (1992e) 1,115,000; ✻ Kurgan; wheat, oats, rye; dairying; estab. 1943 out of E half of Chelyabinsk Oblast; bounded on E and S by Kazakhstan.

Kurgan–Tyube See QŬRGHONTEPPA.

Kuria Muria Islands. See KHURĪYĀ MURĪYĀ, JAZĀ'IR.

Kurile Strait. See PERVYY KURIL'SKIY PROLIV.

Ku·ril Islands *or* **Ku·rile Islands** \ˈkyu̇r-ˌēl, ˈku̇r-; kyu̇-ˈrēl, ku̇-ˈ\ *also* **Ku·rils** *or* **Ku·riles** \-ˌēlz, -ˈrēlz\ *or Russ.* **Ku·ril·'ski·ye Ostro·va** \ku̇-ˈrēl-ski-yə-ˈȯs-trə-və\ *or Jp.* **Chi·shi·ma Ret·tō** \ˈchē-shē-mä-ˈre-tō\. Group of 56 islands off E coast of Asia, extending 750 mi. (1207 km.) N and S bet. S tip of Kamchatka Penin., E Russia in Asia, to NE coast of Hokkaidō, Japan; 6023 sq. mi. (15,600 sq. km.); administratively part of Sakhalin Oblast, Russia; a former province of Hokkaidō prefecture, Japan; fishing (esp. crab); vegetables. The nine most important islands, named from N to S, are Shumshu, Paramushir, Onekotan, Shiashkhotan, Shimushir, Urup, Iturup, Shikotan-tō (SE of Kunashir), and Kunashir, the last three being claimed by Japan. All islands of volcanic origin, some having active volcanoes today; highest point (on Atlasova I.) 7674 ft. (2339 m.); many peaks bet. 3000 and 6000 ft. (915 and 1830 m.); no notably good harbors; only a few islands inhabited. Islands visited 17th cent. by Dutch navigator Martin de Vries; N part of chain occupied by Russians in 18th cent.; given to Japan 1875 in exchange for Sakhalin I.; after end of WWII, returned to U.S.S.R. 1945.

Kuril Strait, First. See PERVYY KURIL'SKIY PROLIV.

Kuril Trench. Ocean trench, NW Pacific Ocean, extending approx. from E of Kamchatka Penin. to E of Hokkaidō I. in a general NE to SW direction; subduction zone according to theory of plate tectonics.

Ku–ring–gai \kə-ˈriŋ-ˌgī\. Municipality, E New South Wales, SE Australia, a N suburb of Sydney; pop. (1991c) 99,193.

Kurische Nehrung. See KURSKAYA KOSA.

Kurisches Haff. See KURSKIY ZALIV.

Kurla. See KORLA.

Kurland. See COURLAND.

Kurna. See AL QURNAH.

Kur·nool \kər-ˈnül\ *also* **Kar·nul** \kər-, kär-\. Town, W Andhra Pradesh, S India, on Tungabhadra River 240 mi. (386 km.) NW of Madras; pop. (1991p) 236,313; trade center; has remains of fort (c. 16th cent.).

Kuroshio. See JAPAN CURRENT.

Kur·ram \ˈku̇r-əm\. River, Pakistan; rises in the Safed Koh, flows E and SE to the Indus River W of Mianwali; ab. 200 mi. (320 km.) long.

Kursk \ˈku̇rsk\. City, ✻ of Kursk Oblast, Russia in Europe, in cen. part, on N bank of Seym River; pop. (1992e) 435,000; main railroad center of the region; food processing, distilling; electrical equipment; first mentioned 11th cent.; destroyed by Tatars c. 1240; rebuilt as frontier post 1586; in WWII suffered severe damage in German occupation 1941–43.

Kur·ska·ya Ko·sa \ˈku̇r-skī-yə-ˈkȯ-sə\ *or Ger.* **Kur·ische Nehr·ung** \ˈku̇r-i-shə-ˈner-u̇ŋ\ *or Eng.* **Cour·land Spit** \ˈku̇r-lənd\. Long spit of land separating the Kurskiy Zaliv from the Baltic Sea; 61 mi. (98 km.) long; formerly part of East Prussia, Germany, now in the Russian exclave of Kaliningrad.

Kur·skiy Za·liv \'kůr-skē-'zä-lif\ *or Ger.* **Kur·isch·es Haff** \'kůr-i-shəs-'häf\ *or Eng.* **Cour·land Lagoon** \'kůr-lənd\. Inlet of the Baltic Sea, Europe; S part in Kaliningrad Oblast, Russia, N part in Lithuania; ab. 625 sq. mi. (1620 sq. km.); formerly in East Prussia, Germany.

Kursk Oblast \'ó-bləst, -ˌblast\ *or* **Kur·ska·ya Oblast'** \'kůr-skə-yə\. Administrative subdivision of Russia in Europe, on Ukraine border; 11,506 sq. mi. (29,801 sq. km.); ✱ Kursk; crossed by Seym River; is source of Donets and tributaries of Donets and Dnieper. In N part of black-earth (chernozem) area, produces grain, sugar beets, potatoes; has forests in N; large-scale exploitation of extensive iron-ore deposits begun during 1950s. In WWII area scene of last major German offensive on Eastern Front, July 1943, incl. one of war's largest tank battles in which Russians defeated Germans.

Kuruçay. See KURA.

Ku·ruk·she·tra \ˌkůr-ůk-'shā-trə\. City, Haryana state, N India; pop. (1991p) 81,275; university (1956); city is place of Hindu pilgrimage.

Ku·ru·man \'kůr-ə-ˌmän\. Town, N Northern Cape prov., S Rep. of South Africa, just SE of the Kalahari Desert, ab. 120 mi. (195 km.) NW of Kimberley; pop. (1985c) 6931; mission station of Scotsman Robert Moffat c. 1825; nearby in a dolomite cave is a spring yielding more than 4 million gallons (15 million liters) of water a day; it is the source of the intermittent **Kuruman River** which formerly flowed W into the Molopo River but has disappeared over most of its lower course in S part of the Kalahari Desert (see also MOLOPO).

Ku·ru·me \'kü-rü-ˌmā, kü-'rü-mā\. City, Fukuoka prefecture, N Kyūshū, Japan, 55 mi. (89 km.) NE of Nagasaki; pop. (1992e) 231,825; textiles (incl. a blue-figured cotton fabric for which it is known); museum; shrine.

Ku·ru·ne·ga·la \ˌkůr-ə-'ne-gə-lə\. Town, W Sri Lanka, 52 mi. (84 km.) NE of Colombo; pop. (1990e) 28,000; trade and distribution center for important agricultural region growing rice, coconuts, and rubber.

Kur·ze·me \'kůr-zə-ˌmā\ *or* **Kur·land** \'kůr-lənd\. Former province, W Latvia, along coast of Baltic Sea and SW shore of Gulf of Riga; 5099 sq. mi. (13,206 sq. km.). Often a battlefield in WWI; ceded to Germany 1918; became a part of newly-organized Latvia 1918; Bolshevik forces driven out 1919. See COURLAND.

Kuş, Lake. See KUŞ GÖLÜ.

Kuş·a·da·sı *or* **Kush Ada·si** \ˌkü-shä-dä-'sə\. Seaport on Kuşadası Gulf, İzmir prov., W Turkey in Asia, 40 mi. (64 km.) S of İzmir and near ruins of Ephesus.

Kuşadası Gulf. Inlet of E Aegean Sea on W coast of Turkey in Asia, NE of island of Sámos; extends inland ab. 45 mi. (70 km.), av. width 20 mi. (32 km.).

Kusaie. See KOSRAE.

Kuş Gö·lü \'küsh-gœ̄-'lue\ *or Eng.* **Lake Kuş** \'küsh\; *formerly* **Lake Man·yas** \män-'yäs\. Lake, NW Turkey in Asia, S of Bandırma; 69 sq. mi. (179 sq. km.).

Kush. See CUSH.

Ku·shi·ro \'kü-shē-ˌrō, kü-'shē-rō\. Seaport, SE coast of Hokkaidō, Japan; pop. (1992e) 203,314; exports sulfur and lumber.

Kushk \'kůshk\. Town, NW Afghanistan, 40 mi. (64 km.) N of Herāt and N of Paropamisus mountain range; on the Kushka River ab. 30 mi. (48 km.) from the Turkmen frontier post of Kushka.

Kush·ka \'küsh-kə, 'kůsh-\. Military post and railhead, SE Turkmenistan, on Afghan border 66 mi. (106 km.) N of Herāt; on the **Kushka River** (Koshk in Afghanistan), 150 mi. (241 km.) long, a tributary of the Murgab.

Kush·va \'küsh-və, 'kůsh-\. Town, Sverdlovsk Oblast, W Russia in Asia, ab. 100 mi. (160 km.) NNW of Yekaterinburg; pop. (1991e) 43,300.

Kusi. See KOSI.

Kus·ko·kwim \'kəs-kə-ˌkwim\. River, SW Alaska, S of the Yukon; flows SW to **Kuskokwim Bay,** an inlet of Bering Sea; ab. 600 mi. (965 km.) long; its two upper tributaries rise in Alaska Range near Denali National Park.

Küs·nacht \'kues-ˌnäkt\. Commune, Zürich canton, Switzerland, on Zürichsee just SSE of the city of Zürich; pop. (1980c) 12,766.

Küss·nacht \'kues-ˌnäkt\ *or in full* **Küssnacht am Ri·gi** \äm-'rē-gē\. Village, Schwyz canton, Switzerland, at NE corner of Lake of Lucerne just E of Lucerne; pop. (1980c) 8091; nearby is scene, according to legend, of William Tell's shooting of Gessler.

Kustanai *or* **Kustanay.** See QOSTANAY.

Küstendil. See KYUSTENDIL.

Küstenja. See CONSTANȚA 2.

Kü·sten·land \'kues-tən-ˌlänt\ *or Eng.* **Coast·land** \'kōst-ˌland\. Former administrative district (province) of Austria, incl. the crown lands Istria and Görz and Gradisca, now divided bet. Slovenia, Croatia, and Italy.

Kūstī. See KOSTI.

Küstrin. See KOSTRZYN.

Kut \'küt\. **1.** City, Iraq. See AL KŪT.
2. *or* **Ko Kut** \kō\. Island, Thailand, in NE Gulf of Thailand off the country's SE coast.

Ku·ta \'kü-tə\. Coastal town, S Bali, Indonesia; a beach-centered tourist area since the 1970s.

Kü·tah·ya *or* **Ku·ta·iah** \kue-'tä-yä\. **1.** Province of W Turkey in Asia. See table at TURKEY.
2. Commerical town, its ✱, on railroad line 65 mi. (105 km.) SE of Bursa; pop. (1990c) 130,944; noted for ceramics.

Kutai. See MAHAKAM.

Ku·ta·i·si \ˌkü-tä-'ē-sē\ *or* **Ku·ta·is** \-'ēs\. City, W Republic of Georgia, on both banks of Rioni River ab. 65 mi. (105 km.) NE of Batumi; pop. (1991e) 238,200; major industrial center and important trading center; motor vehicles, mining machinery, textiles, silk, processed foods. Chief town, under the name **Aea** \'ē-ə\, of ancient Colchis; later ✱ of Imeritia; occupied by Russians early 19th cent.; suffered much in wars bet. Persians, Mongols, Turks, and Russians.

Kutaraja. See BANDA ATJEH.

Kutch \'kəch\. Former state, NW India; now in Gujarat; 17,060 sq. mi. (44,185 sq. km.); ✱ Bhuj; in N and E is the Rann of Kachchh.

Kutch, Gulf of. See KACHCHH, GULF OF.

Kutch, Rann of. See KACHCHH, RANN OF.

Kutenai. See KOOTENAY.

Kut·ná Ho·ra \'küt-nä-'hȯr-ä\ *or Ger.* **Kut·ten·berg** \'kůt-ᵊn-ˌberk\. Town, cen. Czech Republic, 45 mi. (72 km.) E of Prague; pop. (1991p) 21,541; 14th cent. Gothic cathedral; town developed near silver mines, worked from 13th cent.; suffered during severe fighting of the Hussite struggles 15th cent. and the Thirty Years' War 1618–48; the closing of the mines aided its decline.

Kut·no \'küt-nȯ\. Commune, Płock prov., cen. Poland, ab. 35 mi. (56 km.) NNW of Łódź; pop. (1989e) 49,863. Scene of German defeat of Russians 1914, in the battle for control of Łódź; in WWII scene of capture of Polish army by Germans Sept. 1939.

Ku·to·ar·djo *or Du.* **Koe·to·ar·djo** \ˌkü-tō-'är-ˌjō\. Town, Central Java prov., Indonesia, 30 mi. (48 km.) W of Yogyakarta.

Kuttenberg. See KUTNÁ HORA.

Kutz·town \'kůts-ˌtaůn\. Borough, Berks co., SE Pennsylvania, 15 mi. (24 km.) NE of Reading; pop. (1990c) 4704; Kutztown Univ. of Pennsylvania (1866); settled 1771.

Kuu·san·kos·ki \'kü-sän-ˌkōs-kē\. Town, Kymi prov., S Finland; pop. (1980c) 22,453.

Ku·wait *also* **Ku·weit** *or* **Ko·weit** \ků-'wāt, kü-, kyü-\. **1.** Independent state, NW coast of Persian Gulf, forming wedge of desert territory bet. Iraq and Saudi Arabia; 6880 sq. mi. (17,819 sq. km.); pop. (1985c) 1,697,301; ✱ Kuwait; an important oil-producing state; fisheries; construction materials.

Ruled by descendants of a dynasty founded in 18th cent.; independence under British protection recognized by Great Britain 1914; oil discovered 1938; became fully independent of Great Britain June 1961; joined UN 1963, Gulf Cooperation Council 1981; invaded and annexed by Iraq Aug. 1990; liberated by U.S.-led international coalition forces Jan.–Feb. 1991. See BŪBIYĀN and BAHRAIN.

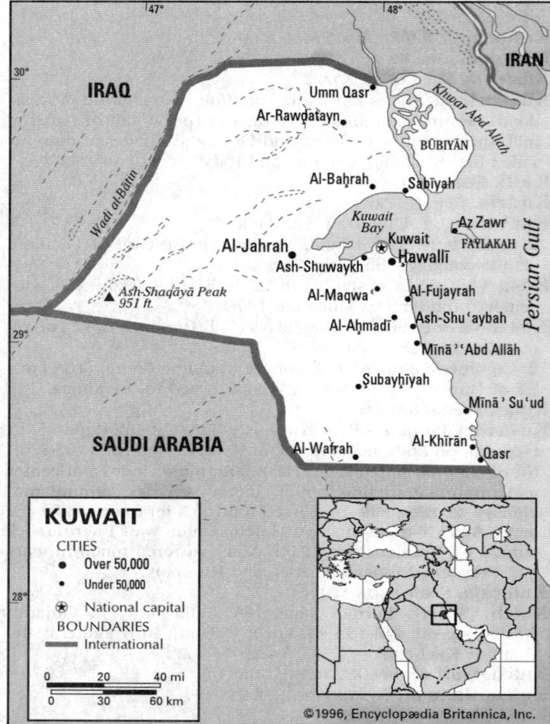

2. *or* **Kuwait City** *or* **Al–Kuwait** \ˌal-, ˌäl-\ *or* **Al Kuwayt** \-ˈwāt\. Seaport, ✻ of Kuwait, at head of Persian Gulf; pop. (1985c) 44,335; has good harbor and considerable trade; petrochemical plants; university (1966). Overrun and occupied by Iraq 1990; liberated by U.S.-led coalition of 29 countries 1991.

Ku·wa·na \kü-ˈwä-nä\. Coastal city, Mie prefecture, S Honshū, Japan, ab. 15 mi. (24 km.) SW of Nagoya near mouth of Kiso River; pop. (1990p) 97,911.

Kuweit. See KUWAIT.

Kuybyshev. See SAMARA 2.

Kuybyshevka–Vostochnaya. See BELOGORSK 1.

Kuybyshev Oblast. See SAMARA OBLAST.

Ku·yun·jik \ˌkü-yən-ˈjik\. Mound on E bank of the Tigris, N Iraq; the site at one time thought to be that of ancient Nineveh but turned out to be that of Nimrud (*q.v.*); discovered 1820, excavations carried out by British archaeologist Sir Austen Layard c. 1845.

Kuz·bas *or* **Kuz·bass** \ku̇z-ˈbas\. Short for Kuznetsk Basin (*q.v.*).

Ku·zey Ana·do·lu Dağ·la·ri \ˈkü-zā-ˌä-nä-ˌdō-lü-ˈdä-lä-rə\. Mountain range, N Turkey in Asia, along Black Sea coast from ab. 33°E long. to the border of the Republic of Georgia at 42°E; ab. 520 mi. (835 km.) long; has many peaks 9000 to 12,000 ft. (2745 to 3660 m.).

Kuz·netsk \ku̇z-ˈnyetsk\. City, E Penza Oblast, Russia in Europe, ab. 65 mi. (105 km.) E of the city of Penza; pop. (1992e) 101,000.

Kuznetsk Basin. Basin of Tom' River, cen. Kemerovo Oblast, S Russia in Asia, extending from Tomsk to Novokuznetsk; immense coal deposits around and S of Kemerovo; was converted into major independent industrial area based on discovery of rich iron ore deposits S of Novokuznetsk.

Kuznetsk Sibirski. See NOVOKUZNETSK.

Kvae·nang·en Fjord \ˈkvā-näŋ-ən\. Inlet of Arctic Ocean on NW coast of Norway.

Kval·øy \ˈkvä-ˌlȯi\. Island, Troms co., Norway, in Arctic Ocean off N coast; 284 sq. mi. (736 sq. km.). Tromsø is on islet bet. Kvaløy and mainland.

Kval·øya \ˈkvȧ-ˌlȯi-ə\ *or* **Kval·øy** \-ˌlȯi\. Island in Arctic Ocean, Finnmark co., Norway; chief town Hammerfest.

Kvar·ner \ˈkvär-ner\ *or Ital.* **Quar·ne·ro** \kwär-ˈner-ō\. Inlet of N Adriatic Sea, E side of Istria, Croatia; Cres I. is to the E and Rijeka at its head.

Kvar·ne·rić \ˈkvär-ne-rich\ *or Ital.* **Quar·ne·ro·lo** \ˌkwär-ne-ˈrō-lō\. Channel, NE Adriatic Sea, bet. Cres I. and Lošinj I. on W and Pag I. and Rab I. on E.

Kvi·tø·ya \ˈkvē-tȯi-ə\ *also* **White Island** *or* **Gil·lis Island** \ˈgi-lis\. Island of the Spitsbergen Archipelago (Svalbard), bet. NE Spitsbergen and Franz Josef Land; 102 sq. mi. (264 sq. km.).

Kwa \ˈkwä\. Name used for the Kasai River from the point where the Fimi enters it to its confluence with the Zaire.

Kwa·ja·lein \ˈkwä-jə-lən, -ˌlān\. Island (atoll) in cen. part of Ralik Chain, W Marshall Is., W Pacific, 2415 mi. (3886 km.) SW of Pearl Harbor, 9°05′N, 167°20′E; ab. 78 mi. (126 km.) long, with 18 islets and large anchorage in the lagoon; chief islets Kwajalein in SE and Roi and Namur in N. Strongly fortified during WWII by Japanese; taken Jan.–Feb. 1944 by Americans; site of missile testing facility.

Kwa·koe·gron \ˈkvä-ku̇-ˌgrȯn\. Town, N Suriname, 50 mi. (81 km.) SSW of Paramaribo on the Saramacca River.

Kwa·mouth \ˈkwä-ˌmau̇th\. Port, W Democratic Rep. of the Congo, at confluence of Kwa and Zaire rivers.

Kwa Nde·be·le \kwän-dā-ˈbā-lā\. Former self-governing black enclave of Transvaal, Rep. of South Africa.

Kwan·do \ˈkwän-dō\ *or Port.* **Cuan·do** \ˈkwän-dō\. River, S Africa; rises in cen. Angola, flows SE, forming S section of boundary bet. Angola and Zambia, continues E along NE boundary of Botswana, and empties into Zambezi River just above Victoria Falls; ab. 500 mi. (800 km.) long.

Kwang·cho·wan \ˈgwäŋ-ˈjō-ˈwän, ˈkwäŋ-\ *or* **Kwang·chow** \ˈgwäŋ-ˈjō\ *or Fr.* **Kouang–Tchéou–Wan** \ˌkwäŋ-cheu̇-ˈwän\. Former French leased territory, SW coast of Guangdong prov., SE China, on Zhanjiang Gang (**Kwangchowan Bay**) ab. 270 mi. (435 km.) W of Hong Kong; 325 sq. mi. (842 sq. km.). Narrow coastal area, two large islands and many small ones, and adjacent waters acquired by France 1898 by lease for 99 years; was attached to French Indochina but during WWII was held by Japanese; returned to China by France 1945.

Kwang·ju \ˈgwȯŋ-ˈjü\; *formerly* **Ko·shu** \ˈkō-ˈshü\. Town, SW South Korea; pop. (1985c) 905,896; serves as ✻ of South Chŏlla prov. and constitutes a special city (province) by itself. Rice, cotton; universities include Chosŏn Univ. (1946). An old city, long a trading center, now heavily industrialized; scene of 1980 confrontation bet. civilians and government forces during which many civilians were killed.

Kwang·myong \ˈkwäŋ-ˈmyu̇ŋ\. City, NW South Korea, just SW of Seoul; pop. (1985c) 219,611.

Kwan·go \ˈkwäŋ-gō\ *or Port.* **Cuan·go** \ˈkwäŋ-gō\. River, S cen. Africa; rises in cen. Angola, flows N, forming a section of boundary bet. Angola and Democratic Rep. of the Congo, and empties into Kasai River in W Democratic Rep. of the Congo ab. 100 mi. (160 km.) above its junction with the Congo River; ab. 300 mi. (485 km.) long.

Kwangsi Chuang *or* **Kwangsi.** Autonomous region of SE China. See GUANGXI ZHUANGZU.

Kwangteh. See GUANGDE.

Kwangtung. Province of SE China. See GUANGDONG.

Kwan·tung \ˈgwän-ˈdu̇ŋ, ˈkwän-, -ˈtu̇ŋ\ *or* **Kwantung Leased Territory** *also* **Kwan·to** \-ˈdȯ, -ˈtȯ\. Former territory, S part of Liaodong Penin., Liaoning prov., NE China; 1444 sq. mi. (3740 sq. km.); ✻ Dalian. Mountainous peninsula with two ports, Dalian and Lüshun. Leased to Russia by China 1898 under pressure; taken over by Japan 1905 by Treaty of Portsmouth and lease extended in 1915 to 99 years; again leased to U.S.S.R. by treaty 1945; returned to China by agreement 1954 and Soviet forces withdrawn 1955.

Kwanza. See CUANZA.

Kwa·ra \ˈkwä-rä\. State of W Nigeria. See table at NIGERIA.

Kwathlamba. See DRAKENSBERG.

Kwa·Zu·lu \kwä-ˈzü-lü\. Former group of noncontiguous black enclaves in Natal, Rep. of South Africa; set aside as a homeland for Zulus; became part of KwaZulu-Natal prov. 1994.

KwaZulu–Na·tal \-nä-ˈtäl\. Province of E Rep. of South Africa. See table at SOUTH AFRICA, REPUBLIC OF.

Kwei. See GUI.

Kwei·chow. **1.** Province of S China. See GUIZHOU. **2.** City, S Sichuan, China. See FENGJIE.

Kweichu. See GUIYANG.

Kweilin. See GUILIN.

Kweiping. See GUIPING.

Kweisui. See HOHHOT.

Kweiyang. See GUIYANG.

Kwe·kwe; *formerly* **Que Que** \ˈkwā-ˈkwā\. Town, cen. Zimbabwe, ab. 120 mi. (195 km.) SW of Harare; pop. (1982c) 47,976.

Kwenlun Shan. See KUNLUN SHAN.

Kwi·dzyn \ˈkfē-dzin\ *or Ger.* **Ma·ri·en·wer·der** \mä-ˈrē-ən-ˌver-dər\. Town, SW Elbląg prov., N Poland, ab. 45 mi. (72 km.) SSE of Gdańsk; pop. (1989e) 36,360. Founded 1233 by the Teutonic Knights; center of plebiscite 1920 by which people of town and vicinity voted to remain in East Prussia; in section of East Prussia assigned to Poland by Potsdam Conference 1945.

Kwi·na·na \kwi-ˈnä-nə\. Town, SW Western Australia, Australia, on coast, S of Perth; pop. (1993e) 18,998.

Kwitta. See KETA.

Kwo·ka \ˈkwō-kə\. Mountain, Arfak Range, NW Irian Jaya, Indonesia; 8042 ft. (2451 m.); highest point in the range.

Kworra. See NIGER 2.

Kyaik·ka·mi \ˈchīk-kä-mē\; *formerly* **Am·herst** \ˈa-mərst, ˈam-ˌhərst\. Seaport, Tenasserim division, Myanmar, on a peninsula, 30 mi. (48 km.) S of Moulmein; has good harbor. Founded by British after First Burmese War early 19th cent.

Kyaring. See GYARING.

Kyauk·pyu \ˈchau̇k-ˈpyü\. Town, Lower Burma, Myanmar, on Combermere Bay at N end of Ramree I.; pop. (1983c) 19,456.

Kyauk·se \ˈchau̇k-sā\. Town, Upper Burma, Myanmar, on railroad line 25 mi. (40 km.) S of Mandalay; pop. (1983c) 27,850.

Kyauk·taw \ˈchau̇k-tȯ\. Town, W Myanmar, on the Kaladan River N of Sittwe.

Kyi. See LHASA 1.

Ky·kots·mo·vi \ki-ˌkäts-ˈmō-vē\; *formerly* **Orai·bi** \ō-ˈrī-bē\. Hopi pueblo, Navajo co., NE Arizona, in Hopi Indian Reservation; on top of a mesa (alt. 6070 ft. or 1850 m.); one of the oldest (dating from ab. 1150 A.D.), and once the largest, of Hopi towns; a Spanish Franciscan mission in 17th cent.

Kyle \ˈkīl\. District of former Ayrshire, SW Scotland; celebrated in poetry of Robert Burns.

Kyle, Lake. Reservoir, SE cen. Zimbabwe; reedbuck, eland, white rhinoceros in area.

Kýmē. See KÍMI.

Ky·mi \ˈkü̅-mē\. Province of SE Finland. See table at FINLAND.

Ky·nance Cove \ˈkī-ˌnans\. Inlet of Atlantic Ocean off SW coast of England, 1.5 mi. (2.4 km.) W of Lizard Head.

Kynosura. See CYNOSURA.

Kyo·ga *or* **Kio·ga** \ˈkyō-gä\. Lake, S cen. Uganda; 1710 sq. mi. (4429 sq. km.); 50 mi. (81 sq. km.) long; max. depth 25 ft. (8 m.); Victoria Nile flows through it.

Kyō·ga, Cape \ˈkyō-gä\. Cape on N coast of W extension of Honshū I., Japan; W of Wakasa Bay.

Kyŏng·gi \ˈkyȯŋ-ˈgē\. Province of South Korea. See table at KOREA, SOUTH.

Kyŏng·ju \ˈkyȯŋ-ˈjü\. Town, North Kyŏngsang prov., South Korea, ab. 37 mi. (60 km.) E of Taegu; pop. (1985c) 127,544; tourism; served as ✻ during Silla dynasty 57 B.C.–935 A.D.; extensive historical remains of temples, shrines, palaces; surrounding area has many Buddhist shrines.

Kyongsong. See SEOUL.

Kyō·to *also* **Kiō·to** \ˈkyō-tō\. **1.** Prefecture, Honshū, Japan; ✻ Kyōto; numerous historic sites. See table at JAPAN. **2.** Manufacturing city, its ✻, W cen. Honshū; on a plain with mountain ranges on all sides except the S, 6 mi. (10 km.) W of S end of Lake Biwa and ab. 26 mi. (42 km.) NNE of Ōsaka; pop. (1990p) 1,461,140; center of Japanese art, having many factories producing porcelain, lacquerware, and brocades; part of the Ōsaka-Kōbe industrial area, manufacturing electrical equipment, textiles; Kyōto Univ. (1897); Kyōto Univ. of Technology (1949).

History: Residence for more than 1000 years of the imperial family; some palace buildings remain and there are many fine Buddhist temples and Shinto shrines. City founded as **Hei·an–kyo** \ˌhā-än-ˈkyō\ and estab. as ✻ of Japan in 794 by Emperor Kwammu; at times superseded as actual seat of government (see KAMAKURA), but remained the classical ✻ till 1869, when government was removed to Tokyo.

Kypros. See CYPRUS.

Ky·ra Pé·la·gos \ˈkē-rä-ˈpe-lä-ˌgȯs\. Island, Northern Sporades, in Euboea dept., Greece; in NW Aegean Sea NE of Alonēsos.

Ky·re·nia \ki-ˈrē-nyə, -nē-ə\ *or Turk.* **Gir·ne** \ˈgir-ne\. Seaport, N Cyprus, in cen. part of N coast; pop. (1987e) 7107.

Kyr·gyz Range \kir-ˈgēz, -ˈgēs\; *mostly formerly* **Kir·ghiz Range** *or* **Kir·giz Range** \kir-ˈgēz, -ˈgēs\; *earlier* **Alek·sandr Range** \ˌȧ-lik-ˈsȧn-dər\ *or* **Al·exan·der Range** \ˌa-lig-ˈzan-dər, ˌe-\; *Russ.* **Kir·giz·skiy Khre·bet** \kir-ˈgēs-kē-k̲ri-ˈbyėt\. Mountain range, N Kyrgyzstan, extending into S Kazakhstan; its highest peak, Semenov 15,994 ft. (4875 m.), is at E end; crossed by passes 6550 to 11,825 ft. (1995 to 3605 m.).

Kyr·gyz·stan \ˌkir-gi-ˈstan, -ˈstän; ˈkir-gi-ˌ\ *also* **Kir·ghi·zia** \kir-ˈgē-zhə, -zē-ə\. Independent republic, W cen. Asia, bounded on N by Kazakhstan, on E and SE by China, on SW by Tajikistan, and on W by Uzbekistan and Kazakhstan; 76,641 sq. mi. (198,500 sq. km.); pop. (1993e) 4,526,000;

comprised **Kir·ghiz Soviet Socialist Republic** *or* **Kirgiz Soviet Socialist Republic** \kir-ˈgēz, -ˈgēs\ 1936–91; ✻ Bishkek; entirely mountainous with Tian Shan Range along Chinese boundary and Alai Mts. in SW part, high peaks ranging from 16,000 to 23,620 (Khan-Tengri) ft. (4880 to 7200 m.); many glaciers and lakes at high altitudes (largest Issyk-Kul); its chief river, the Naryn, a tributary of the Syr Dar'ya, runs W in a high valley.

Chief products: Wheat, tobacco, sugar beets; livestock; coal; textiles, machinery.

Chief towns: Bishkek and Osh.

History: Region inhabited for many centuries by the Kirghiz, a people of Turkic speech; came under Russian control 19th cent.; rebelled 1916, resulting in long period of government repression; from 1924 nominally an autonomous area, which was made an autonomous republic 1926 and a constituent republic of the U.S.S.R. 1936; became independent 1991.

Kythera *or* **Kýthira.** See KÍTHIRA.

Kýthnos. See KÍTHNOS.

Kyū·shū *also* **Kiū·shū** \ˈkyü-ˌshü\. **1.** Southernmost of the four main islands of Japan, in Pacific Ocean off E coast of Asia, separated on N from SW Honshū by Shimonoseki Strait and on E from Shikoku by Bungo Strait; 16,205 sq. mi. (41,971 sq. km.); pop. (1990p) 13,296,054; a mountainous island with several famous volcanic peaks, ranging from 5000 to 6500 ft. (1525 to 1980 m.): Aso, Kujū, Kirishima, On-take. Its coastline irregular with good harbors; chief cities: Fukuoka, Kitakyūshū, Kumamoto, Kagoshima; was first part of Japanese empire opened to foreigners (see DESHIMA and HIRADO).

2. Administrative region of Japan consisting of the island of Kyūshū. For subdivisions, see table at JAPAN.

Kyu·sten·dil \ˌkyü-stən-ˈdil\ *or* **Kü·sten·dil** \ˌkǖ-sten-\ *also* **Kö·sten·dil** \ˌkœ̄-sten-\. City, W Bulgaria, 43 mi. (69 km.) SW of Sofia; pop. (1991e) 55,681; hot mineral springs; trades in fruit and tobacco. Evidence of Thracian settlement; later under Roman rule; in 14th cent. was seat of independent Macedonian principality.

Kyyiv. See KIEV.

Ky·zyl *or* **Ki·zil** \ki-ˈzil\ *or Russ.* **Kras·ny** \ˈkras-nē\; *formerly* **Khem–Bel·der** \ˈkem-ˈbel-dər\; *earlier* **Be·lots·arsk** \bi-ˈlòts-ˌärsk\. Town, ✻ of Tuva Rep., S Russia in Asia, in cen. part at junction of the Bei Kem and Khua Kem branches of the Yenisey (*q.v.*); pop. (1991e) 88,000.

Kyzyl Kum *or* **Qi·zil·kum** *also* **Ki·zil Kum** *or* **Qi·zil Qum** \ki-ˈzil-ˈküm\. Desert, Uzbekistan and Kazakhstan, SE of Aral Sea bet. Amu Dar'ya and the Syr Dar'ya rivers; covers 115,000 sq. mi. (297,850 sq. km.).

Ky·zyl–Ky·ya *or* **Ky·zyl–Ki·ya** \ki-ˈzil-kē-ˈyä\. City, Kyrgyzstan, at S edge of Fergana Valley; pop. (1991e) 49,400.

Kzyl–Orda. See QYZYLORDA.

L

Laagen. See LÅGEN.

La Al·bue·ra \läl-ˈbwā-rä\. Commune, Badajoz prov., SW Spain, 15 mi. (24 km.) SE of the city of Badajoz; pop. (1991c) 1784; scene of defeat 1811 of French under Marshal Nicolas-Jean de Dieu Soult by British, Portuguese, and Spanish under Viscount William Carr Beresford in Peninsular War.

La Al·ta·gra·cia \lä-ˌäl-tä-ˈgrä-syä\. Province, E Dominican Republic. See table at DOMINICAN REPUBLIC.

La Arau·ca·nía \lä-ˌär-ˌau̇-kä-ˈnē-ä\. Region of S cen. Chile. See table at CHILE.

La Asun·ción \lä-ˌsün-ˈsyōn\. Town, ✻ of Nueva Esparta state, Venezuela, located on E Margarita I., in Caribbean Sea off N coast of Venezuela; pop. (1990c) 16,552.

Laatokka. See LADOGA.

La·au Point \lä-ˈau̇\. Cape on SW Molokai I., Hawaii.

Laayoune. See AAIÚN, EL.

La Baie \lə-ˈbī\. Town, S Quebec, Canada, on the Saguenay; pop. (1991c) 20,995.

La·ba·le·kang \lä-ˌbä-lə-ˈkäŋ\. Volcano, S end of Lomblen I., Indonesia; 5394 ft. (1644 m.).

La Ban·da \lä-ˈbän-dä\. Town, Santiago del Estero prov., N Argentina; pop. (1980p) 46,994; NE suburb of the city of Santiago del Estero.

La Bar·ca \lä-ˈbär-kä\. Town, Jalisco state, W cen. Mexico, near E end of Lake Chapala.

La Bas·sée \lȧ-bȧ-ˈsā\. Commune, Nord dept., N France, 13 mi. (21 km.) SW of Lille; in WWI captured by Germans 1914; subjected to many attacks by British but not retaken until 1918.

La Baule–Es·cou·blac \lȧ-ˌbōl-ˌes-kü-ˈbläk\. Joint municipality, Loire-Atlantique dept., NW France; beach resort.

Labdah. See LEPTIS MAGNA.

Labe. See ELBE.

La·bé \lȧ-ˈbā\. Town, W cen. Guinea, 170 mi. (274 km.) NE of Conakry; chief town of the Fulani in the Fouta Djallon.

La Belle \lə-ˈbel\. City, ⊗ of Hendry co., S Florida; pop. (1990c) 2703.

La Belle–Al·liance \lȧ-ˌbel-ȧl-ˈyä^{n}s\. Hamlet in Belgium; battlefield of Waterloo (*q.v.*).

La·berge \lə-ˈberzh\. Lake, S Yukon, NW Canada, N of Whitehorse; 87 sq. mi. (225 sq. km.); Yukon River flows through it.

La·bette \lə-ˈbet\. County in SE Kansas. See table at KANSAS.

La Biche, Lac \ˌläk-lə-ˈbish\. Lake, E Alberta, Canada; 94 sq. mi. (244 sq. km.); outlet is short stream, **La Biche River,** a tributary of the Athabaska.

La·bin \ˈlä-ˌbēn\ *or Ital.* **Al·bo·na** \äl-ˈbō-nä\. Commune, W Croatia, on Istria Penin. 21 mi. (34 km.) NE of Pula.

La·binsk \lə-ˈbyinsk\; *formerly* **La·bin·ska·ya** \ˈlȧ-byin-skə-yə\. Town, SE Krasnodar Kray, S Russia in Europe, ab. 40 mi. (64 km.) ENE of Maykop; pop. (1991e) 60,100.

La·bo \lä-ˈbō\. Mountain, S Camarines Norte, Luzon, Philippines, at point where boundary bet. Quezon and Camarines Sur joins Camarines Norte border; 5066 ft. (1544 m.).

La Bo·ca \lä-ˈbō-kä\. Pacific coast seaport, Panama, near beginning of Panama Canal.

Lab·ra·dor \ˈla-brə-ˌdȯr\. **1.** Large peninsula, Canada, divided bet. Newfoundland and Quebec provs.; 625,000 sq. mi. (1,618,750 sq. km.). See NEW QUEBEC and UNGAVA.
2. Mainland section of Newfoundland prov., Canada, ab. one fifth of Labrador Penin.; 112,826 sq. mi. or 292,219 sq. km. (land area 102,631 sq. mi. or 265,814 sq. km.). Borders on Atlantic on E and on Quebec prov. on S and W; its N point, Cape Chidley on Killinek I. is at entrance to Hudson Strait. Only large river is the Churchill in the S, which enters Lake Melville; in it are Churchill Falls; the river and its tributaries drain several large lakes in SW part (Ashuanipi, Dyke, Lobstick, Michikamau). A plateau region, little explored, but its highest mountains are above 5000 ft. (1520 m.); along its S border (1000 to 2000 ft. or 305 to 610 m.) rise several streams of E Quebec flowing into the Gulf of St. Lawrence. Coast much indented with long fjords and lined with many small islands. Has good harbors: Battle Harbour, Cartwright, Hopedale, Nain; important iron ore deposits. Coast known to Norsemen as early as 10th cent.; visited by explorer in the employ of England, John Cabot (1498), by Portuguese navigator Gaspar Côrte-Real (1500), and by French explorer Jacques Cartier. Boundary with Canada, under dispute since 1809, settled by decision of Committee of British Privy Council Mar. 1927; became part of Canada 1949.

Labrador Current *also* **Arc·tic Current** \ˈärk-tik, ˈär-tik\. Ocean current flowing S along W Greenland and Labrador coasts and E of Newfoundland, Canada, uniting with Gulf Stream in the area of the Grand Bank; its cold waters meeting with the warm waters of the Gulf Stream cause the frequent fogs of this part of the North Atlantic.

Lá·brea \ˈlä-brē-ə\. Municipality, Amazonas state, W Brazil, on right bank of Purus River ab. 380 mi. (610 km.) SSW of Manaus; pop. (1980c) 21,716.

La Brea \lə-ˈbrā-ə\. **1.** Tar pits, Los Angeles, California from which Ice Age fossils have been recovered.
2. Village and port on S shore of Gulf of Paria, W Trinidad; location of Brighton Pier whence the pitch from Pitch Lake just S of the port is exported.

Lab·ro·foss \ˈlä-brə-ˌfȯs\. Waterfall in Lågen River, S Norway, 3 mi. (5 km.) below Kongsberg; 140 ft. (43 m.) high.

La·bu·an \lä-ˈbü-än\. Island, Malaysia, on N side of Brunei Bay, off NW coast of Borneo, 725 mi. (1167 km.) NE of Singapore; 38 sq. mi. (98 sq. km.); pop. (1980c) 12,219; constitutes with adjacent small islands a federal territory of Malaysia; ✻ Victoria, which has excellent harbor and is shipping and distributing point for parts of N Borneo; well cultivated.
History: Ceded 1846 to Great Britain by sultan of Brunei; for a time (1889–1905) administered by British North Borneo; transferred to Straits Settlements 1906 with which it was incorp. 1907 as part of Singapore; constituted a separate settlement 1912 under governor of Straits Settlements; seized by Japanese Dec. 1941; made part of colony of North Borneo (now Sabah) 1946; became part of Malaysia 1963; since 1984 comprises **Labuan Federal Territory.** See table at MALAYSIA.

La·buk \lä-ˈbu̇k\. River, E Sabah, Malaysia; flows ENE to **Labuk Bay,** large inlet of Sulu Sea; 210 mi. (338 km.) long.

Lab·y·rinth, The \ˈla-bə-ˌrinth\. Fortified position in Pas-de-Calais dept., N France, S of Neuville-St.-Vaast and near Vimy Ridge, during WWI scene of series of battles 1915.

La Calamine. See MORESNET.

La Calle. See EL KALA.

La Ca·na·da Flint·ridge \ˌlä-kən-ˈyä-də-ˈflint-rij\. City, Los Angeles co., SW California, NW of Pasadena; pop. (1990c) 19,378; residential; Descanso (flower) Gardens.

La Car·lo·ta \ˌlä-kär-ˈlō-tä\. Chartered city, W cen. Negros Occidental prov., Negros, Philippines, 18 mi. (29 km.) S of City of Bacolod; pop. (1980c) 45,812.

La Ca·ro·li·na \ˌlä-kä-rō-ˈlē-nä\. Commune, Jaén prov., S Spain, on S slope of the Sierra Morena 32 mi. (52 km.) N of the commune of Jaén; pop. (1991c) 15,071. Settled by Swabian colonists c. 1769 through efforts of Charles III to encourage exploitation of the Sierra Morena.

\ə\ **abut** \ə\ **matches** \$^{ə}$\ **kitten,** Fr **table** \ər\ **further** \a\ **ash** \ā\ **ace** \ä\ **cot, cart** \ȧ\ Fr **bac** \au̇\ **out** \b̲\ Span **Avila** \ch\ **chin** \e\ **bet** \ē\ **easy** \g\ **go** \i\ **hit** \ī\ **ice** \j\ **job** \k̲\ Ger **ich, Buch** \$^{n}$\ Fr **vin** \ŋ\ **sing** \ō\ **go** \ȯ\ **all** \ȯ\ **law** \œ\ Fr **bœuf** \œ̄\ Fr **feu** \ȯi\ **boy** \th\ **thin** \th̲\ **this** \ü\ **loot** \u̇\ **foot** \ue\ Ger **füllen** \ue̅\ Fr **rue** \y\ **yet** \$^{y}$\ Fr **digne** \ˈdēn^{y}\, **nuit** \ˈnw^{y}ē\ \yü\ **few** \yu̇\ **fury** \zh\ **vision**

La Cas·tel·la·na \lä-ˌkäs-te-ˈyä-nä\. Municipality, cen. Negros Occidental prov., Negros, Philippines, 24 mi. (39 km.) S of City of Bacolod; pop. (1980c) 44,684.

Lac Brome \läk-ˈbrōm\; *formerly* **Knowl·ton** \ˈnōlt-ᵊn\. Village, ⊗ of Brome-Missisquoi co., S Quebec, Canada; pop. (1991c) 4824; resort.

Lac·ca·dive Islands \ˈla-kə-ˌdiv\ *or* **Can·na·nore Islands** \ˈka-nə-ˌnōr\. Group of islands and coral reefs in Arabian Sea, Tamil Nadu prov. of India, 10°–12°20′N, 72°–74°E, 200 mi. (322 km.) off SW coast of India; the N group is sometimes called the **Amin·di·vi Islands** \ˌə-mən-ˈdē-vē\; since 1956 part of **Laccadive, Min·i·coy, and Amindivi Islands** \ˈmi-ni-ˌkȯi\ (now called **Lakshadweep**) territory of India. See LAKSHADWEEP.

Lac du Flam·beau \ˌläk-də-ˈflam-bō\. Lake in Vilas co., N Wisconsin; a source of Flambeau River.

Lacedaemon. See SPARTA 7.

La Cei·ba \lä-ˈsā-bä\. Caribbean seaport, ✻ of Atlántida dept., N Honduras; pop. (1989e) 71,600; bananas; soap, shoes.

La·cey \ˈlā-sē\. City, Thurston co., W Washington, 7 mi. (11 km.) E of Olympia; pop. (1990c) 19,279; St. Martin's Coll. (1895).

La·cha, Lake \ˈlä-chə\. Lake, SW Arkhangel'sk Oblast, Russia in Europe; ab. 141 sq. mi. (365 sq. km.); one of the sources of Onega River.

La Chaux–de–Fonds \lä-ˌshō-də-ˈfōⁿ\. Commune, Neuchâtel canton, W Switzerland, in Jura Mts. 31 mi. (50 km.) WNW of Bern; pop. (1989c) 36,107; watchmaking.

Lach Dera. See NG'IRO, EWASO.

La·chine \lə-ˈshēn\. City, Montreal I., S Quebec, Canada, on St. Lawrence River 8 mi. (13 km.) SW of Montreal; pop. (1991c) 35,266; electrical appliances; active as port, upper terminus of **Lachine Canal** (Lachine to Montreal, 9 mi. or 15 km., 5 locks, constructed 1821–24; opened 1825) around the **Lachine Rapids** (ab. 3 mi. or 5 km.) of the St. Lawrence, below Lake St. Louis and S of Montreal I. (now largely supplanted by 18 mi. or 29 km. long canal of St. Lawrence Seaway). First estab. as estate of French explorer René-Robert Cavelier, Sieur de La Salle c. 1668 and named (Fr. *La Chine* China) in mockery of his dream that it was a westward passage to China; settled 1675; destroyed by Iroquois 1689 and nearly all inhabitants massacred; remained important in fur trading; ultimately grew as transportation center.

La·chish \ˈlā-kish\. Ancient fortified city, W Judah, Palestine, W of Hebron; its ruins now marked by a mound, Tell ed-Duweir, ab. 16 mi. (26 km.) E of Gaza. An inhabited place probably as early as late 4th millennium B.C.; at time of Israelite conquest of Canaan overcome by Joshua; later besieged by Syrian King Sennacherib 701 B.C., and by King Nebuchadrezzar II of Babylon c. 589 B.C.

Lach·lan \ˈlä-klən\. River, tributary of Murrumbidgee, cen. New South Wales, SE Australia; 922 mi. (1484 km.) long; first river of Australian interior to be explored (1815–17); flows W from Blue Mts. but volume small in dry seasons.

La Chor·re·ra \ˌlä-chōr-ˈrā-rä\. Town, cen. Panama, 19 mi. (31 km.) W of Panama City; pop. (1990p) 44,110.

La·chute \lə-ˈshüt\. City, ⊗ of Argenteuil co., SW Quebec, Canada, 40 mi. (64 km.) WNW of Montreal; pop. (1991c) 11,730; receives waterpower from falls (Fr. *chute*) in North River.

Lacinium Promontorium. See COLONNE, CAPE.

La Cio·tat \lȧ-syō-ˈtä\; *anc.* **Cith·a·ris·ta** \ˌsi-thə-ˈris-tə\. Commune, Bouches-du-Rhône dept., SE France, on Mediterranean 12 mi. (19 km.) SE of Marseille; shipbuilding.

La Cisa. Mountain pass, Apennines. See table at APENNINES.

Lack·a·wan·na \ˌla-kə-ˈwä-nə\. **1.** County in NE Pennsylvania. See table at PENNSYLVANIA.
2. City, Erie co., W New York, on Lake Erie just S of Buffalo; pop. (1990c) 20,585; formerly an important steelmaking center.

La·clede \lə-ˈklēd\. County in S cen. Missouri. See table at MISSOURI.

Lac–Mégantic. See MEGANTIC 2.

Lacobriga. Seaport commune, S Portugal. See LAGOS.

La·combe \lə-ˈkōm\. Town, S cen. Alberta, Canada, 74 mi. (119 km.) S of Edmonton; pop. (1991c) 6934.

La Communauté. See FRENCH COMMUNITY.

La·con \ˈlā-kən\. City, ⊗ of Marshall co., N cen. Illinois, on Illinois River 25 mi. (40 km.) N of Peoria; pop. (1990c) 2442.

La Con·cep·ción \ˌlä-kȯn-ˌsep-ˈsyȯn\. Town, Chiriquí prov., W Panama, W of David; pop. (1980p) 10,460.

La Con·da·mi·ne \lä-ˌkȯn-dä-ˈmē-nā\. Commune, Monaco; pop. (1982c) 12,467; seaside resort.

La·co·nia \lə-ˈkō-nē-ə, -nyə\. **1.** City, ⊗ of Belknap co., cen. New Hampshire, 22 mi. (35 km.) N of Concord; pop. (1990c) 15,743; Lakes Paugus, Winnisquam, and Opechee S of city; year-round tourist center with facilities at nearby lakes, ski areas, and an automobile racetrack. Settled 1761 (long known as **Mer·e·dith Bridge** \ˈmer-ə-dəth\); incorp. as town 1855, as city 1893.
2. Tract of land of indefinite limits around Lake Champlain, extending N to the St. Lawrence; granted 1629 to English colonists, among them John Mason and Sir Fernando Gorges.
3. *or* **La·con·i·ca** \lə-ˈkä-ni-kə\. Ancient country, S Europe, occupying SE Peloponnese, Greece; ✻ Sparta. Its history is that of Sparta. See SPARTA 7.
4. *also* **La·ko·nia** \ˌlä-kō-ˈnē-ä\. Department of Greece, roughly equivalent to ancient Laconia. Bounded on N by Arcadia and Argolis, on E by Aegean Sea, on S by Mediterranean (Gulf of Laconia) and on W by Gulf of Messenia and the division of Messenia. Lofty Taíyetos Mts. are along its W coast and border, containing highest peak in the Peloponnese (7887 ft. or 2404 m.); Parnon Range is in the E. Drained by Eurotas River. Its two peninsulas on the S enclosing Gulf of Laconia are long rugged promontories terminating in Ákra Malea and Ákra Taínaron. Off Ákra Malea is Kíthira I., administered as one of the Ionian Is. Cen. part of river valley is fertile and productive but agriculture is restricted by general mountainous character. See table at GREECE.

Laconia, Gulf of *or Gk.* **La·ko·ni·kós Kól·pos** \lä-ˌkō-nē-ˈkōs-ˈkōl-ˌpōs\. Inlet of the Mediterranean Sea on the S coast of Peloponnese, S Greece, bet. Ákra Taínaron and Ákra Malea; 30 mi. (48 km.) long.

La Co·ru·ña \ˌlä-kō-ˈrü-nyä\. **1.** Province of NW Spain. See table at SPAIN.
2. *or Eng.* **Co·run·na** \kə-ˈrə-nə\. Seaport commune, its ✻, on Atlantic Ocean 127 mi. (204 km.) W of Oviedo; pop. (1991c) 246,953; trades in livestock, fruits, vegetables, sardines; manufactures cigars; lighthouse (Torre de Hércules) thought to have been built by Carthaginians.
History: Believed to antedate Roman times; reached height of prosperity in Middle Ages; part of caliphate of Córdoba; taken by English Prince John of Gaunt late 14th cent.; point of departure for Spanish Armada 1588; sacked by English mariner Sir Francis Drake 1589; scene of English naval victories over French 1747 and 1805; noted esp. for victory of English under Sir John Moore over French under Marshal Nicolas-Jean de Dieu Soult 1809; captured by French 1823 and by Carlists 1836.

Lacosta Island. See CAYO COSTA.

La Côte–de–Beau·pré \lə-ˌkōt-də-bō-ˈprā\. County, Quebec, Canada. See table at QUEBEC.

La Côte–de–Gas·pé \lə-ˌkōt-də-gȧs-ˈpā\. County, Quebec, Canada. See table at QUEBEC.

La Cour·neuve \lȧ-kür-ˈnœ̄v\. Commune, Seine-St.-Denis dept., N France; NNE suburb of Paris.

Lac qui Parle \ˌla-kē-ˈpärl\. **1.** Small lake, W Minnesota, an expansion of the Minnesota River; forms part of boundary bet. Lac qui Parle and Chippewa cos.
2. County in W Minnesota. See table at MINNESOTA.

La Cres·cent \lə-ˈkres-ᵊnt\. City, Houston co., Minnesota, 57 mi. (92 km.) ESE of Rochester; pop. (1990c) 4311.

La Crosse \lə-ˈkrȯs\. **1.** County in W Wisconsin. See table at WISCONSIN.
2. City, ⊗ of Rush co., cen. Kansas; pop. (1990c) 1427.
3. City, ⊗ of La Crosse co., W Wisconsin, at junction of Black and Mississippi rivers; pop. (1990c) 51,003; trade and shipping center of agricultural region; rubber footwear, beer, air-conditioning equipment; Viterbo Coll. (1890); Univ. of

Wisconsin–La Crosse (1909); settled c. 1841; chartered as city 1856.

Lac Saint–Jean. See SAINT JEAN, LAC.

Lac–Saint–Jean–Est. County, Quebec, Canada. See table at QUEBEC.

La Cumbre. See ANDES.

La·cus \ˈlā-kəs\. Latin meaning "lake"; used in classical names of bodies of water, as **Lacus Benacus** and **Lacus Avernus.** See the 2d element of these names or their anglicized form.

Lacus Asphaltites. See DEAD SEA.

Lac Vieux De·sert \läk-ˌvyüd-ə-ˈzar\. Lake on boundary bet. Vilas co., N Wisconsin, and Gogebic co., NW corner of Michigan's Upper Penin.; source of the Wisconsin River.

La·cy–Lake·view \ˈlā-sē-ˈlāk-ˌvyü\. City, McLennan co., cen. Texas, 7 mi. (11 km.) NW of Waco; pop. (1990c) 3617.

Lada, Te·luk \ˈte-lu̇k-ˈlä-dä\ *or Eng.* **La·da Bay** \ˈlä-də\; *formerly* **Pe·per Bay** \ˈpā-pər\. Inlet of Sunda Strait at W end of island of Java, Indonesia.

La·dakh *or* **La·dak** \lə-ˈdäk\. Region, Jammu and Kashmir (*q.v.*); 45,762 sq. mi. (118,524 sq. km.); ✱ Leh; contains W Himalayas (Ladakh Range) and Karakoram Range, also valley of upper Indus River. After cease-fire agreement 1949 S Ladakh to India, remainder to Pakistan; part of Indian sector occupied by Chinese 1959 and again 1962, with boundaries remaining in dispute.

Ladakh Range *or* **Ladak Range.** Mountain range in N India and N Pakistan, NE of Indus River; av. height 19,000 ft. (5791 m.).

La Digue \lə-ˈdēg\. See SEYCHELLES.

La·do Enclave \ˈlä-dō\. Former territory of Belgian Congo, on the W bank of the Nile N of Lake Albert, 15,000 sq. mi. (38,850 sq. km.); now in N Uganda and in SE Sudan; explored by Europeans mid-19th cent. and claimed for Great Britain 1894; leased to Belgium 1894–1910. Chief town was Lado, on the Nile just S of Mongalla, Sudan.

Lad·o·ga \ˈlȧ-də-gə\ *or Russ.* **La·dozh·sko·ye** \ˈlȧ-də-shkə-yə\ *or Finnish* **Laa·tok·ka** \ˈlä-tȯ-ˌkä\. Lake, W Russia in Europe; 6835 sq. mi. (17,703 sq. km.); 124 mi. (200 km.) long, 75 mi. (121 km.) wide; max. depth 738 ft. (225 m.); largest in Europe and 2d largest in Russia; formerly divided bet. U.S.S.R. and Finland; now entirely in Russia, divided bet. Karelia Rep. and St. Petersburg Oblast; fed by ab. 70 streams mostly in Finland and Karelia Rep. on N and W; on the S in Russia by the Volkhov and Syas', on the E by the Svir', the outlet of Lake Onega; its outlet is the Neva, from the SW corner through St. Petersburg to the Gulf of Finland; frozen from October to April; has abundance of fish and has canal system along its S and E shores. NW portion and adjacent lands taken by U.S.S.R. as result of treaty of 1940; S part held by Germans 1941–44 in WWII but regained 1944; during siege of Leningrad supplies brought to city across ice and water of lake.

La Dôle \lä-ˈdōl\. See DÔLE 2.

La Do·ra·da \ˌlä-t͟hō-ˈrä-t͟hä\. River port, Caldas dept., W cen. Colombia, on Magdalena River 613 mi. (986 km.) from Barranquilla and 109 mi. (175 km.) from Puerto Berrío.

La·dril·le·ro Gulf \ˌlä-t͟hrē-ˈyā-rō\. Inlet of Pacific Ocean W of Wellington I., off SW coast of Chile.

Ladrone. **1.** Islands, China Sea. See WANSHAN.
2. Islands, Pacific Ocean. See MARIANA ISLANDS.

La·drones \lə-ˈdrōnz, lä-ˈt͟hrō-nās\. Group of small islands in Pacific Ocean off extreme SW coast of Chiriquí prov., Panama.

La·due \lə-ˈdü, -ˈdyü\. City, St. Louis co., E Missouri, 10 mi. (16 km.) W of the city of St. Louis; pop. (1990c) 8847.

La Dumbéa. See DUMBÉA.

La·dy·brand \ˈlā-dē-ˌbrand\. Town, E Free State, E cen. Rep. of South Africa, on Caledon River 80 mi. (129 km.) E of Bloemfontein.

La·dy Lake \ˈlā-dē\. Town, Lake co., Florida, 45 mi. (72 km.) NW of Orlando; pop. (1990c) 8071.

La·dy·smith \ˈlā-dē-ˌsmith\. **1.** City, ⊗ of Rusk co., NW Wisconsin, at falls of Flambeau River 30 mi. (48 km.) E of the city of Rice Lake; pop. (1990c) 3938; Mount Senario Coll. (1962).
2. Town, SE Vancouver I., British Columbia, Canada, on Strait of Georgia 43 mi. (69 km.) NNW of Victoria; pop. (1991c) 4875; terminus of ferry from mainland and center of extensive logging industry. Incorp. 1904 and named after Ladysmith, Rep. of South Africa.
3. Town, W KwaZulu-Natal prov., E Rep. of South Africa, on a tributary of the Tugela River 115 mi. (185 km.) NW of Durban; pop. (1985c) 25,102; active center of trade with the NE provinces; railroad junction; food processing; textiles. Scene of famous siege of Boer War; occupied by British troops and invested by Boers Nov. 1899–Feb. 1900. See COLENSO.

Lae \ˈlä-ˌā\. Town on New Guinea I., Papua New Guinea, 6°45′S, 147°E, ab. 200 mi. (320 km.) N of Port Moresby; pop. (1990c) 80,655. Seized in WWII by Japanese 1942 and used as major supply base; frequently bombed by Allies 1942–43; occupied by Australians Sept. 1943.

Lae·ken \ˈlä-kə\. Former commune in Brabant prov., cen. Belgium, now part of Brussels; site of royal palace.

Læsø *also* **Læsö;** *mostly formerly* **Lessö** \ˈla-sœ̄\. Island forming a part of Denmark, lying in the upper Kattegat off NE coast of Jutland Penin.; 43 sq. mi. (111 sq. km.); pop. (1981c) 2685.

La Es·pe·ran·za \lä-ˌes-pā-ˈrän-sä\. Town, ✱ of Intibucá dept., SW Honduras.

La Estrada. See A ESTRADA.

La Estrelleta. Province, W Dominican Republic. See table at DOMINICAN REPUBLIC.

La·fay·ette \ˌlä-fē-ˈet, ˌlā-, ˌla-; lə-ˈfā-ət\. **1.** Name of a parish in S Louisiana and of counties in five states of the U.S. See tables at ARKANSAS, FLORIDA, LOUISIANA, MISSISSIPPI, MISSOURI, WISCONSIN.
2. City, ⊗ of Chambers co., E Alabama; pop. (1990c) 3151.
3. City, Contra Costa co., W California, 20 mi. (32 km.) NE of San Francisco; pop. (1990c) 23,501; residential.
4. City, Boulder co., N cen. Colorado, 18 mi. (29 km.) NNW of Denver; pop. (1990c) 14,548; grew rapidly in 1970s and 1980s.
5. City, ⊗ of Tippecanoe co., W cen. Indiana, on Wabash River 58 mi. (93 km.) NW of Indianapolis; pop. (1990c) 43,764; in agricultural region; market center for grain; manufactures electrical appliances, rubber and aluminum products, automobile parts, pharmaceuticals. The battlefield of Tippecanoe, in which Gen. William Henry Harrison defeated the Shawnee Indians 1811, is on the edge of the city.
6. City, ⊗ of Lafayette parish, S Louisiana, 55 mi. (88 km.) WSW of Baton Rouge; pop. (1990c) 94,440; market and distributing center for cotton, cottonseed oil, sugar; supply center for S Louisiana oil and natural-gas industry; Univ. of Southwestern Louisiana (1898); city settled late 18th cent.; laid out 1824; before WWII a predominantly French-speaking city.
7. City, ⊗ of Macon co., N Tennessee; pop. (1990c) 3641.
8. Town, Chippewa co., Wisconsin; pop. (1990c) 4448.

La Fay·ette \lə-ˈfet\. City, ⊗ of Walker co., NW Georgia, 18 mi. (29 km.) WSW of Dalton; pop. (1990c) 6313; scene of local engagements (1864) in the Civil War.

La·fay·ette, Mount \ˌlä-fē-ˈet\. Peak in Franconia Mts., in N Grafton co., N cen. New Hampshire; 5249 ft. (1600 m.).

Lafayette National Park. Former name (1919–29) of *Acadia National Park.* See UNITED STATES, *National Parks.*

La Fe·ria \lə-ˈfer-ē-ə\. City, Cameron co., S Texas, 25 mi. (40 km.) NW of Brownsville; pop. (1990c) 4360.

La Fer·té–Ber·nard \lä-fer-ˈtā-ber-ˈnär\. Commune, Sarthe dept., NW France, 27 mi. (43 km.) NE of Le Mans; 16th cent. church.

La Ferté–Mi·lon \-mē-ˈlōⁿ\. Commune, Aisne dept., N France, 47 mi. (76 km.) SW of Reims; birthplace of dramatist Jean Racine 1639; partially destroyed in WWI.

La·fia \lä-ˈfē-ä\. Town, cen. Nigeria; pop. (1991e) 108,100; trade center for agricultural produce.

La·fi·a·gi \ˌlä-fē-ˈä-gē\. Town, SW cen. Nigeria, on Niger River; pop. (1991e) 63,630.

La Flèche \lə-ˈflesh\. Commune, Sarthe dept., NW France, on Loir River 24 mi. (39 km.) SSW of Le Mans; 16th cent. castle (once a Jesuit college in which mathematician and philosopher René Descartes studied) now a military school.

La Fol·lette \lə-ˈfä-lət\. City, Campbell co., N Tennessee, 31 mi. (50 km.) NNW of Knoxville; pop. (1990c) 7192.

La·fourche \lə-ˈfüsh\. **1.** Bayou, SE Louisiana; an outlet of Mississippi River; ab. 150 mi. (240 km.) long.
2. Parish in SE Louisiana. See table at LOUISIANA.

La Futa. Mountain pass, Apennines. See table at APENNINES.

Lag·an \ˈla-gən\. River, E Northern Ireland; rises in Lisburn dist.; flows NNE into Belfast Lough at Belfast; ab. 35 mi. (56 km.) long.

La·gan \ˈlä-ˌgän\. River, S Sweden; flows S and W into the Kattegat S of Halmstad; 180 mi. (290 km.) long.

La Ga·renne–Co·lombes \ˌlä-gə-ˈren-kə-ˈlōⁿb\. Commune, Hauts-de-Seine dept., N France; NW suburb of Paris.

La·ga·ri·na \ˌlä-gä-ˈrē-nä\. Valley of the Adige River in Trentino-Alto Adige, NE Italy, E of Lake Garda; ab. 50 mi. (80 km.) long.

La·gar·to \lä-ˈgär-tü\. **1.** Municipality, Sergipe state, E Brazil, ab. 45 mi. (70 km.) W of Aracaju; pop. (1991p) 72,366.
2. River in cen. Panama, W of Panama Canal; flows NW into the Caribbean Sea.

La·gash \ˈlā-ˌgash\ *or* **Shir·pur·la** \shir-ˈpu̇r-lə\. Sumerian city and city-state in S Babylonia (its site now in Iraq), bet. the Euphrates and Tigris rivers ab. 31°30′N, 46°09′E. Flourished c. 3d millennium B.C., esp. under its ruler Gudea, c. 2150 B.C.; excavations have revealed ruins of palace, fountain, temple, and many inscribed tablets.

La·ga·we \lä-ˈgä-wā\. Municipality, ✻ of Ifugao prov., Luzon, Philippines; pop. (1980c) 15,075.

Lå·gen *or* **Laa·gen** \ˈlȯ-gən\ *or* **Nu·me·dals·lå·gen** \ˈnü-mə-ˌdäls-ˌlȯ-gən\. River, S Norway; flows S into Skagerrak at Larvik; 212 mi. (341 km.) long.

Lages. See LAJES.

Lag·gan, Loch \ˈla-gən\. Lake in Strathclyde region, cen. Scotland.

Laggan Bay. Inlet of Atlantic Ocean on S coast of Islay I., off W coast of Scotland.

La·ghou·at \lä-ˈgwät\. Oasis and commune, N cen. Algeria, in the Atlas Mts.; pop. (1987p) 67,214.

La Giudecca. See GIUDECCA.

La·go *Span.* ˈlä-gō, *Port.* ˈlä-gü\. Spanish, Portuguese, and Italian for "lake"; in such names as **Lago Puyehue, Lago Rupanco, Lago d'Orta,** see PUYEHUE, LAGO; RUPANCO, LAGO; ORTA, LAGO D'.

La·goa \lȧ-ˈgō-ə\. Portuguese for "lagoon" or "lake"; in such names as **Lagoa dos Patos,** see PATOS, LAGOA DOS.

La Goajira *or* **La Goagira.** See LA GUAJIRA.

La·go·noy \ˈlä-gō-ˌnȯi\. Municipality, E Camarines Sur prov., Luzon, Philippines, NE of Mt. Isarog and near head of Lagonoy Gulf; pop. (1980c) 34,717.

Lagonoy Gulf. Large inlet of the Pacific Ocean in SE Luzon, Philippines; its N and W shores formed by Camarines Sur prov. and its S shore by Albay prov. and the chain of four islands: San Miguel, Cagraray, Batan, and Rapu-Rapu; on the NE is Catanduanes I.

Lagoon Islands. See TUVALU.

La·gos \ˈlā-ˌgäs, ˈlä-gəs\. **1.** Island off low and marshy coast of SW Nigeria; 5 sq. mi. (13 sq. km.); named in 15th cent. by Portuguese explorers because of its many lagoons or lakes (*Port.* lagos).
2. State of SW Nigeria. See table at NIGERIA.
3. Seaport, former ✻ of Lagos state and of Nigeria, on Lagos I. (with section on mainland), at W end of a large lagoon, SW Nigeria; met. area pop. (1991e) 1,340,000; connected by rail with Kano in N; chief port of Nigeria; international airport; major trade and industrial center; brewing; textiles, soap; university (1962). Ceded to Britain 1861; governed from Sierra Leone 1866–74 and as part of Gold Coast to 1886, then separate colony; joined to protectorate of Southern Nigeria 1906; made ✻ of colony of Nigeria 1914; federal ✻ of independent Nigeria 1960–91.

La·gos \ˈlä-güsh\; *anc.* **Lac·o·bri·ga** \ˌla-kə-ˈbrī-gə\. Seaport commune, Faro dist., S Portugal, on Atlantic Ocean 41 mi. (66 km.) WNW of the commune of Faro; munic. pop. (1981p) 19,737; naval battle in **Lagos Bay** 1759, in which French fleet was defeated by English under Adm. Edward Boscawen.

La·gos de Mo·re·no \ˈlä-gōs-ˌthā-mō-ˈrā-nō\. Municipality, Jalisco state, Mexico, 25 mi. (40 km.) NW of León; pop. (1990p) 106,137.

Lagosta. See LASTOVO.

La Goulette. See HALQ AL-WADI.

La Grande \lə-ˈgrand\. City, ⊗ of Union co., NE Oregon, on Grande Ronde River at foot of Blue Mts. 40 mi. (64 km.) N of Baker City; pop. (1990c) 11,766; lumber; diversified agriculture; Eastern Oregon State Coll. (1929); first settled on old Oregon Trail 1861.

La·grange \lə-ˈgrānj\. **1.** County in N Indiana. See table at INDIANA.
2. Town, its ⊗, 40 mi. (64 km.) E of South Bend; pop. (1990c) 2382.

La Grange \lə-ˈgrānj\. **1.** City, ⊗ of Troup co., W Georgia, 40 mi. (64 km.) N of Columbus; pop. (1990c) 25,597; textiles; LaGrange Coll. (1831); incorp. 1828.
2. Village, Cook co., NE Illinois, 6 mi. (10 km.) W of Chicago; pop. (1990c) 15,362; suburb of Chicago.
3. City, ⊗ of Oldham co., N Kentucky; pop. (1990c) 3853.
4. Town, Lenoir co., E North Carolina, 13 mi. (21 km.) ESE of Goldsboro; pop. (1990c) 2805.
5. City, ⊗ of Fayette co., SE cen. Texas, on Colorado River 32 mi. (51 km.) WSW of Brenham; pop. (1990c) 3951.

La Grange Park. Village, Cook co., NE Illinois; pop. (1990c) 12,861; a W suburb of Chicago.

La Granja. See SAN ILDEFONSO 2.

La Gran Pie·dra \lä-ˌgrän-ˈpyā-thrä\. Peak near Santiago de Cuba, Cuba; 4100 ft. (1250 m.).

La Guai·ra \lä-ˈgwī-rä\. Seaport town in the Federal District, N Venezuela; port for Caracas; the leading seaport of Venezuela with good harbor and international airport; in direct line 8 mi. (13 km.) N of Caracas but 23 mi. (37 km.) by railroad in winding line up the mountains to the ✻ at 3020 ft. (920 m.); also connected by 10-mile (16-kilometer) road opened during 1950s. Founded 1577; during its early years was subject to attacks by pirates; destroyed by earthquake of 1812 and damaged during war for independence; American architect Thomas Ustick Walter was engineer for harbor 1840s.

La Gua·ji·ra *also* **La Goa·ji·ra** *or* **La Goa·gi·ra** \lä-gwä-ˈhē-rä\. Department of NE Colombia; forms a peninsula ab. 80 mi. (130 km.) long by 30 to 60 mi. (48 to 97 km.) wide bet. Gulf of Venezuela and the Caribbean; its N point is Point Gallinas. See table at COLOMBIA.

La·guna \lä-ˈgü-nä\. Spanish and Portuguese for "lake" or "lagoon"; in such names as **Laguna Blanca, Laguna del Perro, Laguna Madre,** see BLANCA, LAGUNA; PERRO, LAGUNA DEL; MADRE, LAGUNA.

Laguna. **1.** Indian pueblo, Valencia co., W New Mexico, in Laguna Indian Reservation, ab. 42 mi. (68 km.) W of Albuquerque; pop. (1990c) 3731.
2. Seaport city, Santa Catarina state, S Brazil, 60 mi. (97 km.) S of Florianópolis; munic. pop. (1980c) 39,528.
3. Province of irregular shape, S cen. Luzon, Philippines; ✻ Santa Cruz; on N and NE borders on Laguna de Bay and its NE portion N of the lake borders on Rizal prov.; bounded on E and SE by Quezon prov., on SW by Batangas, and on W by Cavite; mountainous in the NE and S parts; highest points Mt. Makiling 3650 ft. (1113 m.), and San Cristobal on the Quezon border ab. 4900 ft. (1495 m.); well watered by many short streams from the mountain ranges to the lake, some of which are remarkable for waterfalls (see PAGSANJAN), grottoes, or mineral springs. Its most notable physical feature the

Lake of Bay (Laguna de Bay), which abounds in fish. Produces coconuts, rice, sugarcane; fishing, tourism. Inhabitants mostly Tagalogs. See table at PHILIPPINES.

History: Region well populated when visited by Spaniards 16th cent.; invaded by British during Seven Years' War; active in 1896 revolt; civil government estab. July 1901.

Laguna, La. See LA LAGUNA.

Laguna Beach. City, Orange co., SW California, 27 mi. (43 km.) SE of Long Beach; pop. (1990c) 23,170; resort and artists' colony in rugged coastal area.

Laguna Dam. Dam across Colorado River on S California-Arizona boundary N of Yuma, Arizona.

Laguna de Bay. See BAY, LAGUNA DE.

Laguna de Flores. See PETÉN ITZA.

La·gu·na Ni·guel \lə-ˈgü-nə-nē-ˈgel\. City, Orange co., California; pop. (1990c) 44,400.

La Ha·ba·na \ˌlä-ä-ˈbä-nä\. **1.** Province of W Cuba. See table at CUBA.

2. Seaport, Cuba. See HAVANA 2.

La Habana, Ci·u·dad de \syü-ˈthäth-thā-\. Province of NW Cuba. See table at CUBA.

La Ha·bra \lə-ˈhä-brə\. City, Orange co., SW California, 19 mi. (31 km.) NE of Long Beach; pop. (1990c) 51,266; citrus.

La Ha·bra Heights \lə-ˈhä-brə\. City, Los Angeles co., California, 15 mi. (24 km.) E of the city of Los Angeles; pop. (1990c) 6226.

La·hai·na \lä-ˈhī-nä\. City, Maui co., Hawaii, on NW coast of Maui I. on Auau Channel; pop. (1990c) 9073; tourism; the channel at this point being known as **Lahaina Roadstead,** formerly an important anchorage of U.S. Pacific fleet; in 1840s rival of Honolulu as a leading town; in 19th cent. a place of residence of Hawaiian kings, an early mission station, and an important whaling station.

La Haute–Côte–Nord \là-ˌōt-ˌkōt-ˈnȯr\. County, Quebec, Canada. See table at QUEBEC.

La Haute–Ya·mas·ka \-yə-ˈmas-kə\. County, Quebec, Canada. See table at QUEBEC.

La Haye–du–Puits \lä-ˌā-dūē-ˈpwē\. Commune, Manche dept., NW France, on W side of Cotentin Penin. S of Cherbourg; during WWII captured by Americans July 1944.

La·ḩij *or* **La·hej** \ˈlä-həj\; *in the 1960s* **al–Haw·tah** \al-ˈhau̇-tə, -ˈhō-\. Town, Yemen, ab. 25 mi. (40 km.) NNW of Aden; former ✻ of a sultanate which was abolished in 1967.

La·hi·la·hi Point \ˌlä-hē-ˈlä-hē\. Cape on cen. W coast of Oahu I., Hawaii.

Lahn \ˈlän\. River, Hesse, Germany; flows S and SW into Rhine River 4 mi. (6 km.) SE of Koblenz; navigable to Giessen; 152 mi. (245 km.) long.

La Hogue \lə-ˈhōg\ *or* **La Hougue** \ˈhüg\. Roadstead off Point Barfleur on the E coast of Cotentin Penin., Manche dept., NW France; naval battle 1692 in which French under Comte Anne-Hilarion de Tourville were defeated by the combined English and Dutch fleets under Adm. Edward Russell.

La·hon·tan, Lake \lə-ˈhän-tən\. Prehistoric lake NW Nevada and NE California; formed during a pluvial period of the Pleistocene; chief remnants include Pyramid, Walker, and Winnemucca lakes and Carson Sink.

La·hore \lə-ˈhōr\. **1.** Former division of Punjab, NW British India; in 1947 divided bet. Pakistan and India.

2. City, ✻ of Punjab prov., Pakistan, near Ravi River; met. area pop. (1981c) 2,952,689; important rail junction and trade center; iron, steel, rubber, textiles, shoes, gold and silver handicrafts; Univ. of the Punjab (1882); Univ. of Engineering and Technology (1950). The modern city includes the old walled city, several suburbs, and a large cantonment; esp. notable among the fine architectural remains are the Fort and the mosque of Wazir Khan, several other mosques, the famous suburban Shalamar Gardens of Mogul leader Shāh Jahān laid out in 1637 with magnificent terraces and fountains, and the tomb of Sikh Prince Ranjit Singh.

History: An ancient city, but not prominent until the time of the Moguls; ✻ of Ghaznī and Ghurī sultans in 11th and 12th cents. and often the residence of the Great Mogul; under Emperor Akbar 1584–98 and under Jahāngīr 1622–27; became part of Sikh kingdom in 1760s and flourished anew under Ranjit Singh; conquered by British troops 1846, placed under British sovereignty 1849; to Pakistan 1947; made ✻ of reconstituted Punjab prov. 1970.

Lahr \ˈlär\. City, Baden-Württemberg, Germany, 22 mi. (35 km.) N of Freiburg; 13th cent. church. City first mentioned c. 1250; passed to Baden by Peace of Lunéville 1801.

Lah·ti \ˈlä-tē\. City, Häme prov., S Finland, NNE of Helsinki; pop. (1989c) 93,132; center of Finnish furniture industry; beer, clothing; founded 1878.

Lahu, Grand. See GRAND LAHOU.

Laibach. See LJUBLJANA.

Lai Chau \ˈlī-ˈchau̇\. City, NW Vietnam, NNE of Dien Bien Phu; area pop. (1992e) 485,700.

Laichow. See YE XIAN.

Laie \ˈlī-ā\. Town, Honolulu co., Hawaii, 25 mi. (40 km.) NW of the city of Honolulu; pop. (1990c) 5577; Brigham Young Univ.–Hawaii campus (1955).

Laigue, Fo·rêt de \fȯ-ˌrā-də-ˈlāg\. Woods near Compiègne, N France. See RETHONDES.

Laing's Nek \ˈlaŋz-ˈnek\ *also* **Langs Nek** \ˈlaŋz\. Mountain pass, cen. Drakensberg, E Rep. of South Africa; railroad bet. Durban and Pretoria goes through a tunnel here; scene 1881 of Boers' defeat of a British force which attempted to enter Transvaal.

Lainsitz. See LUŽNICE.

Lai·yang *or W.-G.* **Lai–yang** \ˈlī-ˈyäŋ\. City, E Shandong prov., NE China, 50 mi. (80 km.) SW of Yantai.

La·ja \ˈlä-hä\. **1.** Lake, cen. Chile, in the Andes.

2. River, S cen. Chile; flows W from Laja Lake into Bío-Bío River; ab. 150 mi. (240 km.) long; **Laja Falls** are a short distance from the city of Concepción.

Lajā, Al–. See AL-LAJĀ.

La Jacques–Car·tier \là-ˌzhäk-kär-ˈtyā\. County, Quebec, Canada. See table at QUEBEC.

La·jas \ˈlä-häs\. Municipality, SW Puerto Rico; pop. (1990c) 23,271; railroad junction point SE of Mayagüez.

La·jea·do \là-ˈzhyä-dü\. Municipality, Rio Grande do Sul, S Brazil, ab. 70 mi. (115 km.) NW of Pôrto Alegre; pop. (1991p) 63,890.

La·jem·me·rais \ˌlà-zhem-ˈrā\. County, Quebec, Canada. See table at QUEBEC.

La·jes *also* **La·ges** \ˈlä-zhis\. Municipality, Santa Catarina state, S Brazil; pop. (1991p) 137,169.

La·jes do Pi·co \ˈlä-zhis-dü-ˈpē-kü\. See PICO 3.

La Jol·la \lə-ˈhȯi-ə\. A NW section of San Diego, California; Univ. of California, San Diego (1959).

La Joya \lə-ˈhȯi-ə\. City, Hidalgo co., Texas, on the Rio Grande; pop. (1990c) 2604.

Lajta. See LEITHA.

La Jun·ta \lə-ˈhən-tə\. City, ⊗ of Otero co., SE Colorado, on the Arkansas River; pop. (1990c) 7637; sugar beets; cattle; Otero Junior Coll. (1941); city founded 1875.

Lake \ˈlāk\. **1.** Name of counties in 12 states of the U.S. See tables at CALIFORNIA, COLORADO, FLORIDA, ILLINOIS, INDIANA, MICHIGAN, MINNESOTA, MONTANA, OHIO, OREGON, SOUTH DAKOTA, TENNESSEE.

2. River, E cen. Tasmania, Australia; flows N to join the South Esk at Longford; ab. 35 mi. (55 km.) long.

Lake Al·fred \ˈal-frəd, -fərd\. City, Polk co., cen. Florida, 15 mi. (24 km.) E of Lakeland; pop. (1990c) 3622.

Lake An·des \ˈan-dēz\. City, ⊗ of Charles Mix co., S South Dakota; pop. (1990c) 846.

Lake and Peninsula. Division in Alaska. See table at ALASKA.

Lake Ar·thur \ˈär-thər\. Town, Jefferson Davis parish, SW Louisiana; pop. (1990c) 3194.

La·ke·ba \lä-ˈkā-bä\ *or* **La·kem·ba** \-ˈkem-\. **1.** Group of ab. 33 islands, S end of Lau Group, SE Fiji, SW Pacific Ocean.

2. Chief island of the Lakeba group, 18°10′S, 178°47′W; 12 sq. mi. (31 sq. km.); long a meeting place bet. Fijians and Tongans. Here first Wesleyan missionaries settled 1835.

Lake Bluff \ˈbləf\. Village, Lake co., NE corner of Illinois, on Lake Michigan 8 mi. (13 km.) S of Waukegan; pop. (1990c) 5513.

Lake Bue·na Vis·ta \ˈbwā-nə-ˈvis-tə\. City, Orange co., cen. Florida Penin., SW of the city of Orlando; pop. (1990c) 1776; Walt Disney World.

Lake But·ler \ˈbət-lər\. City, ⊗ of Union co., NE Florida; pop. (1990c) 2116.

Lake Charles \ˈchärlz\. City, ⊗ of Calcasieu parish, SW Louisiana, 13 mi. (21 km.) NNE of Calcasieu Lake; pop. (1990c) 70,580; ships rice; sulfur and oil deposits nearby; oil refineries; chemicals, rubber; McNeese State Univ. (1939); settled c. 1780.

Lake City. **1.** Town, a ⊗ of Craighead co., NE Arkansas; pop. (1990c) 1833.

2. Town, ⊗ of Hinsdale co., Colorado, 43 mi. (69 km.) SE of Montrose; pop. (1990c) 223; former mining center.

3. City, ⊗ of Columbia co., N Florida, 44 mi. (71 km.) NNW of Gainesville; pop. (1990c) 10,005; resort; lumber; Lake City Community Coll. (1947); headquarters for Ocala National Forest.

4. City, Clayton co., Georgia; pop. (1990c) 2733.

5. City, ⊗ of Missaukee co., NW cen. Michigan; pop. (1990c) 858.

6. City, Wabasha co., SE Minnesota, on Mississippi River 31 mi. (50 km.) NNE of Rochester; pop. (1990c) 4391.

7. Town, Florence co., E South Carolina, 22 mi. (35 km.) S of the city of Florence; pop. (1990c) 7153.

Lake Clark National Park \ˈklärk\. See UNITED STATES, *National Parks.*

Lake Dallas Dam. See GARZA DAM.

Lake District. Mountainous region in Cumbria, NW England; roughly coextensive with **Lake District National Park,** England's largest; contains many well-known lakes and peaks. Among the lakes are Bassenthwaite, Buttermere, Coniston Water, Crummock Water, Derwent Water, Ennerdale Water, Grasmere, Hawes Water, Loweswater, Rydal Water, Thirlmere, Ullswater, Wast Water, Windermere. A favorite resort of English poets, esp. since William Wordsworth's long residence here and his association with the other Lake Poets Robert Southey and Samuel Taylor Coleridge.

Lake El·si·nore *also* **Elsinore** \ˈel-sə-ˌnōr\. City, Riverside co., SE California, on Elsinore Lake 30 mi. (48 km.) S of San Bernardino; pop. (1990c) 18,285; mineral springs in vicinity; pop. more than tripled bet. 1980 and 1990.

Lake For·est \ˈfȯr-əst, ˈfär-\. City, Lake co., NE corner of Illinois, on Lake Michigan 10 mi. (16 km.) S of Waukegan; pop. (1990c) 17,836; residential; Lake Forest Coll. (1857), Barat Coll. (1858).

Lake Ge·ne·va \jə-ˈnē-və\. **1.** City and resort, Walworth co., S Wisconsin, on shore of Lake Geneva 30 mi. (48 km.) W of Kenosha; pop. (1990c) 5979.

2. Lake, Switzerland and France. See GENEVA, LAKE.

Lake George \ˈjȯrj\. Village, ⊗ of Warren co., E New York, on S end of Lake George 40 mi. (64 km.) NE of Amsterdam; pop. (1990c) 3211; recreation.

Lake Grove. Village, Suffolk co., SE New York, 7 mi. (11 km.) NE of Islip; pop. (1990c) 9612.

Lake Hav·a·su City \ˈha-və-ˌsü\. City, Mohave co., Arizona, on Lake Havasu; pop. (1990c) 24,363; site of reconstructed London Bridge.

Lake·hurst \ˈlāk-ˌhərst\. Borough, Ocean co., E New Jersey, 8 mi. (13 km.) NW of Toms River; pop. (1990c) 3078; estab. 1919; here the airship *Graf Zeppelin* started and finished 21-day around-the-world trip 1929 and the *Hindenburg* was destroyed by fire 1937.

Lake in the Hills. Village, McHenry co., N Illinois, 10 mi. (16 km.) N of Elgin; pop. (1990c) 5866.

Lake Jack·son \ˈjak-sən\. City, Brazoria co., SE Texas, S of Houston; pop. (1990c) 22,776; Brazosport Coll. (1968).

Lake·land \ˈlā-klənd\. **1.** City, Polk co., cen. Florida Penin., 30 mi. (48 km.) E of Tampa; pop. (1990c) 70,576; phosphate mining; citrus fruits; winter resort; Florida Southern Coll. (1885), Southeastern Coll. of the Assemblies of God (1935).

2. City, ⊗ of Lanier co., S Georgia, 20 mi. (32 km.) NE of Valdosta; pop. (1990c) 2467.

Lake Mac·quar·ie \mə-ˈkwär-ē\. City, E New South Wales, Australia; pop. (1991c) 162,026.

Lake Man·ya·ra National Park \män-ˈyär-ä\. National park, NE Tanzania; 123 sq. mi. (319 sq. km.); includes most of **Lake Manyara;** wide variety of wildlife; estab. 1960.

Lakemba. See LAKEBA.

Lake Mbu·ro National Park \əm-ˈbü-rō\. National park, S Uganda; plains and acacia grasslands surrounding **Lake Mburo.**

Lake Mills \ˈmilz\. City, Jefferson co., SE Wisconsin, 23 mi. (37 km.) E of Madison; pop. (1990c) 4143.

Lake·more \ˈlāk-ˌmōr\. Village, Summit co., NE Ohio, 8 mi. (13 km.) SE of Akron; pop. (1990c) 2684.

Lake Na·ku·ru National Park \nä-ˈkü-rü\. National park, Kenya, surrounding shallow alkaline **Lake Nakuru,** ab. 81 mi. (130 km.) NW of Nairobi; ab. 75 sq. mi. (195 sq. km.); habitat for flamingos and many other species of birds; estab. 1961.

Lake Nau·jan National Park \nau̇-ˈhän\. National park, Mindoro I., Philippines; contains marshlands with abundant birdlife surrounding Lake Naujan.

Lake of the Ozarks. See OZARKS, LAKE OF THE.

Lake of the Woods. **1.** Lake, SW Ontario and SE Manitoba, Canada and N Minnesota; 72 mi. (116 km.) long and from 10 to 60 mi. (16 to 97 km.) wide; area 1695 sq. mi. (4390 sq. km.), of which 642 sq. mi. (1663 sq. km.) are in U.S. territory; max. depth 69 ft. (21 m.); elev. 1060 ft. (323 m.); receives Rainy River from the SE and drains N into Lake Winnipeg.

2. County in N Minnesota. See table at MINNESOTA.

Lake Ori·on \ˈōr-ē-ən\. Village, Oakland co., SE Michigan, 10 mi. (16 km.) NNE of Pontiac; pop. (1990c) 3057.

Lake Os·wego \ä-ˈswē-gō\. City, Clackamas, Multnomah, and Washington cos., NW Oregon, 8 mi. (13 km.) S of Portland; pop. (1990c) 30,576; residential suburb of Portland.

Lake O'the Cherokees. See PENSACOLA DAM.

Lake Park. Town, Palm Beach co., SE Florida, 5 mi. (8 km.) N of Palm Beach; pop. (1990c) 6704.

Lake Plac·id \ˈpla-səd\. Village, Essex co., NE New York, in Adirondack Mts. on Mirror Lake, near Lake Placid (see PLACID, LAKE), 40 mi. (64 km.) SW of Plattsburg; pop. (1990c) 2485; summer and winter resort, scene of Winter Olympic Games 1932 and 1980; site of the exclusive Lake Placid Club, founded 1895 by librarian Melvil Dewey.

Lake Pleas·ant \ˈplez-ᵊnt\. Village and resort, ⊗ of Hamilton co., NE cen. New York, 50 mi. (80 km.) ENE of Utica; pop. (1990c) 887.

Lake·port \ˈlāk-ˌpōrt\. City, ⊗ of Lake co., W California, on W side of Clear Lake; pop. (1990c) 4390.

Lake Prov·i·dence \ˈprä-və-dəns\. Town, ⊗ of East Carroll parish, NE corner of Louisiana, on Mississippi River 60 mi. (97 km.) ENE of Monroe; pop. (1990c) 5380.

Lake·side Park \ˈlāk-ˌsīd\. City, Kenton co., N Kentucky, 5 mi. (8 km.) S of Cincinnati, Ohio; pop. (1990c) 3131.

Lake Sta·tion \ˈstā-shən\; *formerly* **East Gary** \ˈgar-ē\. City, Lake co., NW Indiana, 5 mi. (8 km.) S of Lake Michigan; pop. (1990c) 13,899.

Lake Suc·cess \sək-ˈses\. Village, Nassau co., SE New York, W Long Island, near N shore E of Flushing and ab. 4.5 mi. (7 km.) NW of Mineola; pop. (1990c) 2484; headquarters of UN 1946–51.

Lake·view \ˈlāk-ˌvyü\. Town, ⊗ of Lake co., S Oregon, 6 mi. (10 km.) N of Goose Lake; pop. (1990c) 2526; livestock raising.

Lake Village. City, ⊗ of Chicot co., SE corner of Arkansas, 80 mi. (129 km.) SSE of Pine Bluff; pop. (1990c) 2791.

Lake·ville \ˈlāk-ˌvil\. **1.** Subdivision of town of Salisbury, Connecticut; trade center; Hotchkiss School (preparatory school, 1891). See SALISBURY 1.

2. Town, Plymouth co., SE Massachusetts, 15 mi. (24 km.) S of Brockton; pop. (1990c) 7785.

3. Village, Dakota co., SE Minnesota, 26 mi. (42 km.) SE of Minneapolis; pop. (1990c) 24,854; grew rapidly in 1970s and 1980s.

Lake Wales \ˈwālz\. City, Polk co., cen. Florida Penin., 25 mi. (40 km.) ESE of Lakeland; pop. (1990c) 9670; winter resort; author Edward W. Bok's carillon tower and nature observatory are nearby.

Lake Washington Ship Canal. See WASHINGTON, LAKE.

Lake·wood \ˈlāk-ˌwu̇d\. **1.** City, Los Angeles co., SW coastal California, NE of Long Beach; pop. (1990c) 73,557.

2. City, Jefferson co., cen. Colorado, W of Denver; pop. (1990c) 126,481; residential; Colorado Christian Univ. (1914).

3. Unincorporated settlement, Ocean co., E New Jersey, 14 mi. (23 km.) SW of Asbury Park; pop. (1990c) 45,048; health resort in pine-forest and lake region; Georgian Court Coll. (1908); pop. nearly doubled in 1980s.

4. Village, Chautauqua co., SW corner of New York, on Chautauqua Lake 5 mi. (8 km.) W of Jamestown; pop. (1990c) 3564.

5. City, Cuyahoga co., N Ohio, on Lake Erie 5 mi. (8 km.) W of Cleveland; pop. (1990c) 59,718; residential suburb of Cleveland.

Lake Worth \ˈwərth\. **1.** Lagoon, SE Florida. See WORTH, LAKE.

2. City, Palm Beach co., SE Florida, on Lake Worth 6 mi. (10 km.) S of West Palm Beach; pop. (1990c) 28,564; winter resort; Palm Beach Community Coll. (1933); city incorp. 1913.

3. City, Tarrant co., N Texas, 13 mi. (21 km.) NW of Fort Worth; pop. (1990c) 4591.

Lake Zu·rich \ˈzu̇r-ik\. Village, Lake co., NE Illinois, 18 mi. (29 km.) SW of Waukegan; pop. (1990c) 14,947.

La·khim·pur \ˈlə-kəm-ˌpu̇r\. Town, E Uttar Pradesh, India, 75 mi. (121 km.) N of Lucknow; pop. (1991p) 79,549.

Lakhnauti. See GAUR.

Lakhon. See NAKHON PHANOM.

La·ki \ˈlä-kē\. Volcanic mountain, S Iceland, just SW of Vatnajökull; violent eruption in 1783.

La·kin \ˈlā-kən\. City, ⊗ of Kearny co., W Kansas; pop. (1990c) 2392.

Lakonia. See LACONIA 4.

Lakonikós Kólpos. See LACONIA, GULF OF.

La·kor \ˈlä-ko̊r\. Small island in E part of Leti Is., Indonesia; 10 mi. (16 km.) by 6 mi. (10 km.).

La·ko·ta \lə-ˈkō-tə\. City, ⊗ of Nelson co., E North Dakota; pop. (1990c) 898.

Lak·se Fjord \ˈläk-sə\. Inlet of Arctic Ocean on NE coast of Norway, bet. Porsangen Fjord and Tana Fjord.

Lak·se·våg \ˈläk-sə-ˌvo̊g\. Commune, Hordaland co., SW Norway.

Lak·shad·weep \lək-ˈshäd-ˌwēp\; *formerly* **Laccadive, Minicoy, and Amindivi Islands.** Union territory off SW coast of India; comprises more than 20 islands. See table at INDIA.

La La·gu·na \ˌlä-lä-ˈgü-nä\. Commune, NE Tenerife I., Santa Cruz de Tenerife prov. (W Canary Is.), Spain, 2 mi. (3 km.) NNW of the seaport of Santa Cruz de Tenerife; pop. (1991c) 110,895; former ✱; university (founded 18th cent.); 16th cent. cathedral; brandy, tobacco, leather.

Lā·leh Zār, Kūh–e \ˌkü-hə-ˌlä-lə-ˈzär\. Peak in Kermān prov., SE Iran, S of the city of Kermān; 14,347 ft. (4373 m.).

La Li·ber·tad \lä-ˌlē-ber-ˈtäth\. **1.** Department of SW El Salvador. See table at EL SALVADOR.

2. Seaport, its ✱, 23 mi. (37 km.) SSW of San Salvador; pop. (1987e) 33,321; beach resort; coffee, sugar.

3. Municipality, NE Negros Oriental prov., Negros, Philippines, on Tanon Strait, 51 mi. (82 km.) N of Dumaguete; pop. (1980c) 30,730.

La·lin \ˈlä-ˈlin\. River, NE China; flows NW and W into Songhua River, forming part of boundary bet. Jilin and Heilongjiang; ab. 200 mi. (320 km.) long.

La·lín \lä-ˈlēn\. Commune, Pontevedra prov., NW Spain, 28 mi. (45 km.) NE of the commune of Pontevedra; pop. (1991c) 20,360.

La Lí·nea \lä-ˈlē-nā-ä\ *or in full* **La Línea de la Concepción** \ˌt͟hā-lä-ˌko̊n-thep-ˈthyo̊n, -sep-ˈsyo̊n\. Commune, Cádiz prov., SW Spain, on Bay of Gibraltar and Gibraltar frontier 56 mi. (90 km.) SE of the city of Cádiz; pop. (1991p) 57,918.

La·lit·pur \lə-ˈlit-ˌpu̇r\ *or* **Pa·tan** \ˈpät-ᵊn\. Town, E cen. Nepal, adjoining Kathmandu on the S; pop. (1991p) 79,891; palace; Buddhist temples.

La Loche, Lac \ˈläk-lə-ˈlōsh\. Small lake, NW Saskatchewan, Canada; its immediate outlet a short stream to Churchill Lake. At its N end is **La Loche Portage,** ab. 12 mi. (19 km.) long, to Clearwater River, a headstream of the Athabaska and Mackenzie river system; used by hunters.

La·lo Point \ˈlä-lō\. Cape at S end of Tinian I., Mariana Is., W Pacific, 14°55′N, 140°38′E; last stand of Japanese on the island Aug. 1, 1944.

La Lou·vière \ˌlä-lü-ˈvyer\. Commune, Hainaut prov., SW Belgium, 27 mi. (43 km.) S of Brussels; pop. (1992e) 76,700.

La Mad·da·le·na \lä-ˌmä-dä-ˈlā-nä\. Seaport, Sassari prov., NW Sardinia, Italy, on Maddalena I. in Strait of Bonifacio 54 mi. (87 km.) NE of the commune of Sassari; pop. (1981p) 11,366.

La Ma·de·leine \lȧ-mȧd-ˈlen\. **1.** Rock shelter on the Vézère River above Les Eyzies (see EYZIES, LES), Dordogne dept., SW France; type station, from primitive implements and carvings found here, of the Magdalenian period representing the highest Paleolithic culture in Europe.

2. Commune, Nord dept., N France, NE suburb of Lille.

La Mag·da·le·na Con·tre·ras \lä-ˌmäg-t͟hä-ˈlā-nä-ko̊n-ˈträ-räs\. Town, N Federal District, cen. Mexico.

La Mal·baie \lä-mal-ˈbā\. Resort town, ⊗ of East Charlevoix co., S Quebec, Canada, at confluence of Malbaie and St. Lawrence rivers; pop. (1991c) 3968. Visited 1608 by French explorer Samuel de Champlain who gave it its name because of poor anchorage; settled early by Scots.

La Man·cha \lä-ˈmän-chä\. Region, S cen. Spain; comprises SE Ciudad Real, S Toledo, NW Albacete, and SW Cuenca provs.; formerly the southernmost division of New Castile; high (ab. 2000 ft. or 610 m.), level, arid, treeless plateau, producing some grain and wine; celebrated in Miguel de Cervantes' novel *Don Quijote de la Mancha.*

La Manche. See ENGLISH CHANNEL.

La·mar \lə-ˈmär\. **1.** Name of counties in four states of the U.S. See tables at ALABAMA, GEORGIA, MISSISSIPPI, TEXAS.

2. City, ⊗ of Prowers co., SE Colorado, on Arkansas River 50 mi. (80 km.) E of La Junta; pop. (1990c) 8343; Lamar Community Coll. (1937).

3. City, ⊗ of Barton co., SW Missouri, 32 mi. (51 km.) NNE of Joplin; pop. (1990c) 4168. Birthplace of Harry S Truman, 33d president of the U.S., 1884.

La·marck, Mount \lə-ˈmärk\. Peak in the Sierra Nevada, in E Fresno co., S cen. California; 13,302 ft. (4054 m.).

La Marque \lə-ˈmärk\. City, Galveston co., SE coastal Texas, SE of Houston; pop. (1990c) 14,120.

La·mas \ˈlä-mäs\. Town, N Peru, 45 mi. (72 km.) SE of Moyobamba; pop. (1981p) 11,206.

La Ma·ta·pé·dia \lə-ˌma-tə-ˈpē-dē-ə, -ˈpā-\. County, Quebec, Canada. See table at QUEBEC.

La Mau·ri·cie National Park \lə-ˌmo̊-rē-ˈsē\. See CANADA, *National Parks.*

Lamb \ˈlam\. County in NW Texas. See table at TEXAS.

Lambaesis. See TAZOULT-LAMBESE.

Lam·balle \läⁿ-ˈbȧl\. Commune, Côtes-du-Nord dept., NW France, ESE of St.-Brieuc; cathedral; ✱ of the counts of Penthièvre from 1134.

Lam·ba·ré \ˌläm-bä-ˈrā\. City, S Paraguay, SSE of Asunción; pop. (1992p) 99,681.

Lam·ba·ré·né \ˌläm-bä-ˈrā-ˈnā\. Town, W Gabon, on lower Ogooué River; hospital founded by French missionary physician Dr. Albert Schweitzer.

Lam·ba·ye·que \läm-bä-ˈyā-kā\. Town, NW Peru, near the coast just N of Chiclayo; pop. (1981p) 29,987.

\ə\ abut \ˈə\ matches \ᵊ\ kitten, Fr table \ər\ further \a\ ash \ā\ ace \ä\ cot, cart \ȧ\ Fr bac \au̇\ out \b̲\ Span Avila \ch\ chin \e\ bet \ē\ easy \g\ go \i\ hit \ī\ ice \j\ job \k̲\ Ger ich, Buch \ⁿ\ Fr vin \ŋ\ sing \ō\ go \ȯ\ all \o̊\ law \œ\ Fr bœuf \œ̄\ Fr feu \ȯi\ boy \th\ thin \t͟h\ this \ü\ loot \u̇\ foot \ue\ Ger füllen \ue̅\ Fr rue \y\ yet \ʸ\ Fr digne \ˈdēnʸ\, nuit \ˈnwʸē\ \yü\ few \yu̇\ fury \zh\ vision

Lambayong. See SULTAN SA BARONGIS.

Lam·ber·sart \ˌläⁿ-ˌber-ˈsär\. Commune, Nord dept., N France, NW suburb of Lille.

Lam·bert Glacier \ˈlam-bərt\. Glacier, S of Amery Ice Shelf, Antarctica; ab. 150 mi. (240 km.) long.

Lam·bert·ville \ˈlam-bərt-ˌvil\. City, Hunterdon co., NW cen. New Jersey, on Delaware River 14 mi. (23 km.) NNW of Trenton; pop. (1990c) 3927.

Lambèse *or* **Lambessa.** See TAZOULT-LAMBESE.

Lam·beth \ˈlam-bəth\. A borough of Greater London, SE England. See table at LONDON 4.

Lamb·ton \ˈlam-tən\. County in SE Ontario, Canada. See table at ONTARIO.

Lam·bu·nao \läm-ˈbü-ˌnau̇\. Municipality, Iloilo prov., Panay, Philippines, in foothills of W range 26 mi. (42 km.) NNW of City of Iloilo; pop. (1980c) 45,435.

La Meije. See MEIJE.

Lamèque, Île \ˌēl-lá-ˈmek\; *formerly* **Ship·pe·gan Island** \ˈshi-pə-gən\. Island off NE tip of New Brunswick, SE Canada.

La·me·sa \lə-ˈmē-sə\. City, ⊗ of Dawson co., NW Texas, 43 mi. (69 km.) NNW of Big Spring; pop. (1990c) 10,809.

La Me·sa \lə-ˈmā-sə\. Residential city, San Diego co., SW corner of California, 8 mi. (13 km.) E of the city of San Diego; pop. (1990c) 52,931; Coleman Coll. (1963).

La·me·zia Ter·me \lä-ˈmād-zyä-ˈter-mā\. Commune, Catanzaro prov., Calabria, S Italy; pop. (1989c) 68,985.

La·mía \lä-ˈmē-ä\; *or* **La·mia** \lə-ˈmē-ə\ *or* **Zi·tu·ni** \zē-ˈtü-nē\. Inland town, ✻ of Phthiotis dept., Greece, near head of Gulf of Maliakós; in ancient times in Malis and nearer the shoreline; pop. (1991p) 43,898. Macedonian Gen. Antipater besieged here by confederate Greeks under Leosthenes for several months (Lamian War, 4th cent. B.C.).

Lamia, Gulf of. See MALIAKÓS, GULF OF.

L'Amiante \lä-ˈmyänt\. County, Quebec, Canada. See table at QUEBEC.

La Mi·ra·da \ˌlä-mə-ˈrä-də\. City, Los Angeles co., SW California, 13 mi. (21 km.) SE of the city of Los Angeles; pop. (1990c) 40,452; Biola Univ. (1908).

La Mi·tis \lá-mē-ˈtē\. County, Quebec, Canada. See table at QUEBEC.

Lam·jung \läm-ˈju̇ŋ\. Mountain in the Himalayas, Nepal, ab. 90 mi. (145 km.) NW of Kathmandu; 26,041 ft. (7937 m.).

Lam·lash \lam-ˈlash\. Village, E coast of Arran I., Strathclyde region, SW Scotland; on **Lamlash Bay,** an inlet of the Firth of Clyde; fine harbor.

Lam·ma \ˈlä-ˈmä\ *or* **Pok Liu Chau** \ˈpȯk-ˈlyü-ˈjau̇\. Island, S part of New Territories, Hong Kong, just SW of Hong Kong I.

Lam·me Fjord \ˈlä-mə\. W extension of Ise Fjord on N coast of Sjælland, Denmark.

Lam·mer·muir Hills \ˈla-mər-ˌmyu̇r\ *or* **Lam·mer·moor Hills** \-ˌmu̇r\. Range of hills in Lothian and Borders regions, SE Scotland; highest point Lammer Law 1733 ft. (528 m.).

La·moille \lə-ˈmȯil\. **1.** River, NW Vermont; flows W through Lamoille and S Franklin cos., S and W into Lake Champlain in NW Chittenden co.; ab. 75 mi. (120 km.) long;

2. County in N Vermont. See table at VERMONT.

La·mon Bay \lä-ˈmȯn\. Large landlocked bay, an inlet of the Pacific on E coast of Luzon, Philippines, chiefly in Quezon prov., its SE shore in Camarines Norte; ab. 60 mi. (97 km.) each way, N to S and E to W; protected on N by the islands of Polillo, Patnanongan, and Jomalig and contains the large island of Alabat in the S.

La·mon·gan \lä-ˈmȯŋ-gän\. Town, East Java prov., Indonesia, on railroad line 25 mi. (40 km.) WNW of Surabaya.

La·mo·ni \lə-ˈmō-ˌnī\. Town, Decatur co., S Iowa, 68 mi. (109 km.) SSW of Des Moines; pop. (1990c) 2319; Graceland Coll. (1895).

La Mon·ja \lä-ˈmȯŋ-hä\. Rocky islet, outer part of entrance to Manila Bay, part of Corregidor Is., Philippines, nearly 3 mi. (5 km.) W of Corregidor I.

La Mont–Saint–Michel. See MONT-SAINT-MICHEL, LA.

La·motte Peak \lə-ˈmät\. Mountain, cen. Summit co., NE Utah; 12,723 ft. (3878 m.).

La Moure \lə-ˈmu̇r\. **1.** County in SE North Dakota. See table at NORTH DAKOTA.

2. City, its ⊗; pop. (1990c) 970.

Lam·pang \ˈläm-ˌpäŋ\. Town, NW Thailand, on left bank of Wang River and on railroad line 45 mi. (72 km.) SE of Chiang Mai; pop. (1991e) 44,509; connected by highway with Chiang Rai; commercial center; sugar refining.

Lam·pas·as \lam-ˈpa-səs\. **1.** County in cen. Texas. See table at TEXAS.

2. City, its ⊗, 45 mi. (72 km.) W of Temple; pop. (1990c) 6382.

Lam·pe·du·sa \ˌläm-pe-ˈdü-zä\; *anc.* **Lop·a·du·sa** \ˌlä-pə-ˈdü-sə, -ˈdyü-\. One of the Pelagie Is. in Mediterranean Sea, midway bet. Malta and Tunisia; 8 sq. mi. (21 sq. km.); pop. (1991p incl. Linosa) 5626; politically attached to Agrigento prov., SW Sicily, Italy; has one village, the port of Il Porto. Modern settlement dates from 18th cent.; in WWII capitulated after being heavily bombarded by Allied fleet 1943.

Lam·pert·heim \ˈläm-pərt-ˌhīm\. Commune, Hesse, Germany, near Rhine River 22 mi. (35 km.) SSW of Darmstadt; pop. (1980c) 31,449.

Lam·phun *or* **Lam·pun** \läm-ˈpün\. Town, NW Thailand, on railroad line 15 mi. (24 km.) S of Chiang Mai; pop. (1991e) 14,181; rice and tobacco produced in area.

Lam·pio·ne \läm-ˈpyō-nā\. See PELAGIE ISLANDS.

Lamp·sa·cus \ˈlamp-sə-kəs\; *mod.* **Lap·se·ki** \ˌläp-se-ˈkē\. Ancient Greek colony in Mysia on the Hellespont opp. Gelibolu; famous for its wine. Under Persia early in 5th cent. B.C.; ally of Athens 479 B.C., later of Rome. Home of Strato of Lampsacus, Greek Peripatetic philosopher.

Lam·pung \läm-ˈpu̇ŋ\. Province of Indonesia. See table at INDONESIA.

Lampung Bay *or* **Lam·pong Bay** \läm-ˈpȯŋ\ *or Du.* **Lam·poeng Bay** \-ˈpu̇ŋ\. Bay at the S end of the island of Sumatra, Indonesia, opening into Sunda Strait.

Lamta. See LEPTIS MINOR.

La·mu \ˈlä-mü\. **1.** Island off the E coast of Kenya, SW of Dicks Head and 150 mi. (240 km.) N of Mombasa.

2. Seaport on the island of Lamu.

3. Town, Rakhine state, W Myanmar, near coast.

Lan \ˈlän\ *or* **Hung–t'ou** \ˈhu̇ŋ-ˈtō\; *formerly* **Ko·to·sho** \ˈkō-tō-ˈshō\. Island in Pacific Ocean, ab. 40 mi. (64 km.) E of the S tip of Taiwan.

La·nai \lə-ˈnī\. Island in cen. Hawaii, W of Maui I.; 141 sq. mi. (365 sq. km.); part of Maui co., state of Hawaii; separated from Molokai on the N by Kalohi Channel, from Maui on the E by Auau Channel, and from Kahoolawe on the SE by Kealaikahiki Channel. Privately owned. Highest point 3369 ft. (1027 m.).

Lanai City. Unincorporated settlement, Maui co., Hawaii, in center of Lanai I.; pop. (1990c) 2400.

La·nal·hue, Lake \lä-ˈnäl-wā\. Lake in S Chile, 23 mi. (37 km.) SE of the port of Lebu on the Pacific Ocean.

La·nao, Lake \lä-ˈnau̇\. Lake in W Lanao del Sur prov., Mindanao, Philippines; 131 sq. mi. (339 sq. km.); 22 mi. (35 km.) long, max. width ab. 16 mi. (26 km.); largest lake on Mindanao; in plateau region N of range of active volcanoes; outlet is Agus River, flowing N to Iligan Bay.

Lanao del Nor·te \del-ˈnȯr-tā\. Province, Mindanao, Philippines; bounded on N by Iligan Bay; ✻ Iligan; estab. 1959. See table at PHILIPPINES.

Lanao del Sur \del-ˈsu̇r\. Province, Mindanao, Philippines; ✻ Marawi; contains Lake Lanao; estab. 1959. See table at PHILIPPINES.

Lan·ark \ˈla-nərk\. **1.** County in SE Ontario, Canada. See table at ONTARIO.

2. *or* **Lan·ark·shire** \-ˌshir, -shər\. Former county, S cen. Scotland; ⊗ Lanark; chief river Clyde; now part of Strathclyde region.

3. Burgh, Strathclyde region, S cen. Scotland, on the Clyde River 30 mi. (48 km.) SE of Glasgow; pop. (1981c) 9804. **New Lanark,** founded (1785) by English industrialist David Dale and manufacturer Richard Arkwright 1 mi. (1.6 km.) SW, was the scene of some of Welsh Socialist and philanthropist Robert Owen's social and industrial experiments.

Lan·bi Kyun \ˈlän-bē-ˈkyün\ *or Eng.* **Lanbi Island;** *formerly* **Sul·li·van Island** \ˈsə-lə-vən\ *or* **Sul·li·van's Island** \-vənz\. Island, S cen. Mergui Archipelago (*q.v.*), Myanmar.

Lancang. See MEKONG.

Lan·ca·shire \ˈlaŋ-kə-ˌshir, -shər\ *or* **Lan·cas·ter** \ˈlaŋ-kə-stər\. **1.** Former county, NW England; coal.
History: Region part of Anglo-Saxon kingdom of Northumbria and of the Danelaw; honor of Lancaster an important medieval fief; Lancastrian line of English kings the heirs of John of Gaunt, duke of Lancaster; esp. in Industrial Revolution in 18th cent. Lancashire became noted manufacturing center (see MANCHESTER 12 and LIVERPOOL 4).
2. Administrative county, NW England, comprising area included in the former county except N portion (now in Cumbria) and districts centering in Liverpool (now in Merseyside) and Manchester (now in Greater Manchester); textiles (esp. cotton), aircraft; vegetables; dairy farming. See table at ENGLAND.

Lan·cas·ter \ˈlaŋ-kə-stər; ˈlan-ˌkas-tər, ˈlaŋ-\. **1.** Name of counties in four states of the U.S. See tables at NEBRASKA, PENNSYLVANIA, SOUTH CAROLINA, VIRGINIA.
2. City, Los Angeles co., SW California, NE of the city of Los Angeles; pop. (1990c) 97,291; Antelope Valley Coll. (1929); city's pop. doubled bet. 1980 and 1990.
3. City, ⊗ of Garrard co., E cen. Kentucky, 13 mi. (21 km.) E of Danville; pop. (1990c) 3426.
4. Town, Worcester co., cen. Massachusetts, 10 mi. (16 km.) SE of Fitchburg; pop. (1990c) 6661; Atlantic Union Coll. (1882) nearby.
5. City, ⊗ of Schuyler co., N Missouri; pop. (1990c) 785.
6. Town, ⊗ of Coos co., N New Hampshire, on Connecticut River 18 mi. (29 km.) W of Berlin; pop. (1990c) 3522.
7. Village, Erie co., W New York, 11 mi. (18 km.) E of Buffalo; pop. (1990c) 11,940; residential suburb of Buffalo.
8. City, ⊗ of Fairfield co., S cen. Ohio, 27 mi. (43 km.) SE of Columbus; pop. (1990c) 34,507; trade center of dairying and livestock region; glass, machinery; founded 1800; incorp. 1831. Birthplace of army commander William T. Sherman 1820.
9. City, ⊗ of Lancaster co., SE Pennsylvania, 35 mi. (56 km.) ESE of Harrisburg; pop. (1990c) 55,551; trade center in region of diversified agriculture; cattle market; tourism; industrial products include watches, linoleum, electrical appliances; Franklin and Marshall Coll. (1787), Lancaster Theological Seminary (1825), Lancaster Bible Coll. (1933). Present town founded 1730; became gunmaking center; played important part in French and Indian War, and, later, in Revolution; site of one session of Continental Congress 1777; ✻ of Pennsylvania 1799–1812; became W terminus of Philadelphia and Lancaster turnpike 1794. Home to members of Pennsylvania Dutch sects, as the Amish.
10. City, ⊗ of Lancaster co., N South Carolina, 21 mi. (34 km.) SE of Rock Hill; pop. (1990c) 8914; textiles.
11. City, Dallas co., NE Texas, S of the city of Dallas; pop. (1990c) 22,117. Suffered heavy tornado damage April 25, 1994.
12. Village, ⊗ of Lancaster co., E Virginia.
13. City, ⊗ of Grant co., SW corner of Wisconsin, 13 mi. (21 km.) WNW of Platteville; pop. (1990c) 4192.
14. County, England. See LANCASHIRE.
15. City, ⊗ of former Lancashire co., England, on the Lune 46 mi. (74 km.) N of Liverpool; pop. (1991p) 125,600; textiles, linoleum, furniture; Univ. of Lancaster (1964); castle, Norman with traces of Roman construction; received first town charter 1193.

Lancaster Sound. Channel, bet. Devon I. and N Baffin I., Arctic Archipelago, Nunavut, N Canada; opens into NW Baffin Bay; ab. 50 mi. (80 km.) wide.

Lan–chou *or* **Lan–chow.** See LANZHOU.

Lan·cia·no \län-ˈchä-nō\. Commune, Chieti prov., Abruzzi, cen. Italy, 14 mi. (23 km.) ESE of the commune of Chieti; pop. (1991p) 34,062; cathedral; several churches.

Lan·cy \läⁿ-ˈsē\. Commune, Geneva canton, Switzerland; pop. (1989c) 23,435.

Lan·dau \ˈlän-ˌdau̇\ *also* **Landau in der Pfalz** \in-dər-ˈpfälts\. City, Bavaria, Germany, 18 mi. (29 km.) NW of Karlsruhe; pop. (1992e) 37,985; machinery, shoes, tobacco products; ships wine, cattle; 13th–15th cent. churches; founded before 13th cent.; made imperial city 1291; French 1680–1815.

Lan·deck \ˈlän-dek\. Town, W Tirol, SW Austria, on the Inn River ab. 40 mi. (64 km.) W of Innsbruck.

Land·er \ˈlan-dər\. **1.** County in cen. Nevada. See table at NEVADA.
2. City, ⊗ of Fremont co., cen. Wyoming, at SE corner of Shoshone Indian reservation; pop. (1990c) 7023; oil wells; uranium mines; livestock raising.

Lan·der·neau \ˌläⁿ-der-ˈnō\. Commune, Finistère dept., NW France, ENE of Brest; 16th cent. bridge.

Landes \ˈläⁿd\. Department of SW France. See table at FRANCE.

Landes, Les. See LES LANDES.

Landes de Lan·vaux \də-läⁿ-ˈvō\. Strip of rocky, desolate land, S Morbihan dept., Brittany, France, near coast; studded with megalithic monuments. See CARNAC.

Landeshut *or* **Landeshut in Schlesien.** See KAMIENNA GÓRA.

Landi Kotal. See KHYBER PASS.

Lands·berg \ˈlänts-ˌberk\. **1.** *also* **Landsberg am Lech** \äm-ˈlek\. Commune, Bavaria, Germany, on Lech River ab. 20 mi. (30 km.) S of Augsburg; pop. (1980c) 18,309.
2. *also* **Landsberg an der Warthe.** City, Poland. See GORZÓW WIELKOPOLSKI.

Land's End \ˈlandz-ˈend\; *anc.* **Bo·le·ri·um** \bə-ˈlir-ē-əm\. Cape, SW coast of Cornwall, SW England; westernmost land of England.

Lands·hut \ˈlänts-ˌhüt\. City, Bavaria, Germany, on Isar River NE of Munich; pop. (1992e) 59,670; machinery, electronic components, furniture, chocolate, beer, tobacco products; 13th–16th cent. castle; 14th cent. town hall; Gothic church; several museums. Became city 1279; residence of dukes of Lower Bavaria 1255–1340, and later (1392–1503) of dukes of Bavaria-Landshut; site of a university in early 19th cent.; scene of French Emperor Napoléon's defeat of Archduke Charles of Austria 1809.

Lands·kro·na \länts-ˈkrü-nə\. Seaport, Malmöhus prov., SW Sweden; pop. (1993e) 36,153; shipbuilding, metalworking, tanning, food processing; machinery, fertilizers; Swedes won naval victory off this port 1677 over the Danes.

Lane \ˈlān\. Name of counties in two states of the U.S. See tables at KANSAS and OREGON.

Lane Cove. Municipality, E New South Wales, Australia, NNW of Sydney; pop. (1991c) 28,954.

Lanes·bor·ough \ˈlānz-ˌbər-ō\. Town, Berkshire co., W Massachusetts, 6 mi. (10 km.) N of Pittsfield; pop. (1990c) 3032.

La·nett \lə-ˈnet\. City, Chambers co., E Alabama, on Georgia border 40 mi. (64 km.) E of Martin Lake; pop. (1990c) 8985.

Lan·ga·nes, Cape \ˈlau̇ŋ-gə-ˌnās\. Cape on NE extremity of Iceland.

Lan·ga·no, Lake \läŋ-ˈgä-nō\. Lake in cen. Ethiopia, S of Addis Ababa.

Lang–chung. See LANGZHONG.

Lang·dale Pikes \ˈlaŋ-ˌdāl\. Two mountain peaks, **Har·ri·son Stick·le** \ˈhar-ə-sən-ˈsti-kəl\ 2401 ft. (732 m.) and **Pike o' Stickle** \ˈpīk-ə-\ 2323 ft. (708 m.), in NW Westmorland, NW England, in the Lake District.

Lang·don \ˈlaŋ-dən\. City, ⊗ of Cavalier co., NE North Dakota, 49 mi. (79 km.) NNE of the city of Devils Lake; pop. (1990c) 2241.

Lang·e·land \ˈläŋ-ə-ˌlän\. Island, forming a part of Denmark, in Baltic Sea off SE coast of Fyn I. and bet. Fyn and Lolland; ab. 33 mi. (53 km.) long and 3 mi. (5 km.) wide; 110 sq. mi. (285 sq. km.); pop. (1991e) 15,022.

\ə\ abut \ᵊ\ kitten, Fr table \ər\ further \a\ ash \ā\ ace \ä\ cot, cart \å\ Fr bac \au̇\ out \b̲\ Span Avila \ch\ chin \e\ bet \ē\ easy \g\ go \i\ hit \ī\ ice \j\ job \k\ Ger ich, Buch \ⁿ\ Fr vin \ŋ\ sing \ō\ go \ȯ\ all \ȯ\ law \œ\ Fr bœuf \œ̄\ Fr feu \ȯi\ boy \th\ thin \t̲h̲\ this \ü\ loot \u̇\ foot \ue\ Ger füllen \ue̅\ Fr rue \y\ yet \ʸ\ Fr digne \ˈdēnʸ\, nuit \ˈnwʸē\ \yü\ few \yu̇\ fury \zh\ vision

Langeland Belt. Strait in the Baltic Sea, S of the Great Belt, and bet. Langeland I. and Lolland I., Denmark.
Lang·e·mark \ˈläŋ-ə-ˌmärk\. Commune, West Flanders prov., NW Belgium, 5 mi. (8 km.) NE of Ieper (Ypres); area pop. (1991c) 7364; destroyed during WWI and rebuilt since that time. First successful poison-gas attack said to have been made here Apr. 22, 1915; lost by Allies but recovered 1917.
Lang·en \ˈläŋ-ən\. City, Hesse, Germany, S of Frankfurt am Main; pop. (1980c) 28,826; became city 1883.
Langenbielau. See BIELAWA.
Lang·en·feld \ˈläŋ-ən-ˌfelt\. City, North Rhine-Westphalia, Germany, SE of Düsseldorf; pop. (1992e) 54,152.
Lang·en·ha·gen \ˌläŋ-ən-ˈhäg-^{ə}n\. City, Lower Saxony, Germany; pop. (1980c) 46,764; became city 1959.
Lang·en·sal·za \ˌläŋ-ən-ˈzält-sə\. City, Thuringia, cen. Germany, 19 mi. (31 km.) WNW of Erfurt. Joined to Prussia 1815; scene of battle in Austro-Prussian (Seven Days') War 1866, when the Prussians defeated the Hannoverians.
Lang·e·oog \ˈläŋ-ə-ˌōk\. Narrow island in cen. part of East Frisian Is., off NW coast of Germany, W of Spiekeroog; 9 mi. (15 km.) long.
Lang·ford, Mount \ˈlaŋ-fərd\. Peak in Yellowstone National Park, NW Wyoming; 10,600 ft. (3231 m.).
Lang·ka·wi, Pu·lau \ˈpü-ˌlau̇-läŋ-ˈkä-wē\. Island in Andaman Sea off NW coast of Kedah state, Malaysia; has peak 2890 ft. (881 m.).
Lan·glade \ˈlaŋ-ˌlād\. County in NE Wisconsin. See table at WISCONSIN.
Langlade. See MIQUELON ISLAND.
Langlade, Isthmus of \lä^{n}-ˈgläd\. Isthmus connecting the former islands of Great Miquelon and Little Miquelon (Langlade); 7 mi. (11 km.) long; has been created by the accumulation of sand on the reef bet. the two islands which were very close together and now comprise a single island (see MIQUELON ISLAND).
Lang·ley \ˌlaŋ-lē\. City, British Columbia, Canada, 25 mi. (40 km.) ESE of Vancouver; pop. (1991c) 19,765; diversified agriculture.
Langley, Mount. Peak in the Sierra Nevada, in E Tulare co., S cen. California; 14,028 ft. (4276 m.).
Lang·øy \ˈläŋ-ˌȯi\. Westernmost island of the Vesterålen, in the Norwegian Sea off NW coast of Norway; 332 sq. mi. (860 sq. km.).
Langreo. See SAMA DE LANGREO.
Langres \ˈlä^{n}gr^{ə}\; *anc.* **An·de·ma·tun·num** \ˌan-di-mə-ˈtə-nəm\; *later* **Lin·go·nes** \ˈliŋ-gə-ˌnēz\. Commune, Haute-Marne dept., NE France, ab. 38 mi. (61 km.) NNE of Dijon on a high part (ab. 1550 ft. or 470 m.) of **Langres Plateau;** pop. (1990c) 11,026; electrical equipment. In earlier times was important point strategically; 12th cent. cathedral and Gothic church of St. Martin; remains of Roman gate; medieval fortifications with later additions; birthplace of French encyclopedist Denis Diderot 1713.
Lang·side \ˈlaŋ-ˌsīd\. S suburb of Glasgow, Scotland; scene of the defeat of Mary, Queen of Scots, 1568.
Langs Nek. See LAING'S NEK.
Lang Son *or* **Lang·son** \ˈlaŋ-ˈsän\. Town, Vietnam, near Chinese frontier, 85 mi. (137 km.) NE of Hanoi; strategically important town on NE frontier; connected by rail with Hanoi. Occupied by French 1885; taken by Vietminh 1950 and became provisions center; overrun by Chinese 1979.
Langs Point \ˈlaŋz\. Elevation in Cheyenne co., W Nebraska; 4460 ft. (1359 km.).
Lang·ston \ˈlaŋ-stən\. Town, Logan co., cen. Oklahoma; pop. (1990c) 1471; Langston Univ. (1897); town founded 1890.
Lang Su·an *or* **Lang·su·an** \läŋ-ˈsü-ˌän\. Town, SW Thailand, on railroad line along E coast of Malay Penin. (on Isthmus of Kra) 55 mi. (89 km.) N of Surat Thani.
Langue·doc \lä^{n}g-ˈdȯk, lä^{n}ŋ-ˈdȯk, ˌlaŋ-gə-ˈdäk\. Historical region of S cen. France; bounded anciently on N by Auvergne and Lyonnais, on E by Dauphiné, Comtat Venaissin, and Provence, on SE by Mediterranean Sea, on S by Roussillon, on SW by Countship of Foix, on W by Gascony, and on NW by Guienne; capitals Toulouse and Montpellier; Cévennes Mts. in E.

History: Region without unity except that based on a common language (*Fr.* langue d'oc) and culture (oriented towards Provence, Italy, and Muslim Spain) until the Middle Ages when it was brought under influence of the counts of Toulouse; home of the Albigenses, exterminated in wars of religion in 13th cent.; region from Carcassonne to the Rhone passed to Louis IX of France 1229; W part left to counts of Toulouse until seized 1271 by Philip III; from 16th to 18th cents. scene of persecution of Protestants terminating in War of the Camisards 1702–05.
Languedoc–Rous·sil·lon \-ˌrü-sē-ˈyō^{n}\. Region of S France. See table at FRANCE.
Lang·zhong *or W.-G.* **Lang–chung** \ˈläŋ-ˈchu̇ŋ\; *formerly* **Pao·ning** \ˈpau̇-ˈniŋ\. City, N Sichuan prov., S cen. China, on right bank of the Jialing ab. 135 mi. (215 km.) N of Chongqing.
La·nier \lə-ˈnir\. County in S Georgia. See table at GEORGIA.
La·nín \lä-ˈnēn\. Volcanic peak on Argentina-Chile border, bet. SW Neuquén prov., W Argentina, and SE La Araucanía region, S cen. Chile; 12,388 ft. (3776 m.); Argentine part preserved in **Lanín National Park**.
Lankada, Lake. See KORÓNIA, LAKE.
Län·kä·rän \ˌlin-ka-ˈran\ *or* **Len·ko·ran** \ˌlin-kə-ˈrän^{y}\. Seaport town, SE Azerbaijan, on SW shore of Caspian Sea near Iranian border; pop. (1991e) 45,400; citrus fruit; first known mention 17th cent.; passed to Russia 1813.
Lan Na. See CHIANG MAI.
Lan·nion \lȧ-ˈnyō^{n}\. Town, Côtes-du-Nord dept., NW France, NW of St.-Brieuc; active port on a river that flows into the English Channel; ruins of 15th cent. castle of Tonquédec ab. 6 mi. (10 km.) to the SE.
La Nou·velle–Beauce \lȧ-nü-ˌvel-ˈbōs\. County, Quebec, Canada. See table at QUEBEC.
Lans·dale \ˈlanz-ˌdāl\. Borough, Montgomery co., SE Pennsylvania, 21 mi. (34 km.) N of Philadelphia; pop. (1990c) 16,362.
Lans·downe \ˈlanz-ˌdau̇n\. **1.** Residential borough, Delaware co., SE Pennsylvania, 5 mi. (8 km.) W of Philadelphia; pop. (1990c) 11,712; residential suburb of Philadelphia.
2. Cantonment and hill station, N Uttar Pradesh, N India, 120 mi. (193 km.) NE of Delhi.
L'Anse \ˈlans\. Township, ⊗ of Baraga co., Upper Penin., NW Michigan, on Lake Superior 52 mi. (84 km.) WNW of Marquette; pop. (1990c) 3818.
L'Anse aux Mead·ows \ˌlans-ō-ˈme-dōz\. Site, NE tip of Newfoundland I., Canada; has Norse ruins of what is believed to be the first European settlement in the New World.
Lans·ford \ˈlans-fərd, ˈlanz-\. Borough, Carbon co., E Pennsylvania, 28 mi. (45 km.) S of Wilkes-Barre; pop. (1990c) 4583.
Lan·sing \ˈlan-siŋ\. **1.** Village, Cook co., NE Illinois, on Indiana border 4 mi. (6.4 km.) S of Chicago's city limits; pop. (1990c) 28,086.
2. City, Leavenworth co., NE Kansas, just S of the city of Leavenworth; pop. (1990c) 7120.
3. City, ✻ of Michigan, in Clinton, Eaton, and Ingham cos., S Michigan, 50 mi. (81 km.) WSW of Flint; pop. (1990c) 127,321; automobile manufacturing, tools; Lansing Community Coll. (1957); settled c. 1840; made ✻ of Michigan 1847; site of first agricultural college in U.S., Michigan State Univ. (1855; now in East Lansing).
4. Village, Tompkins co., S cen. New York; pop. (1990c) 3281.
Lan·tana \lan-ˈta-nə\. Town, Palm Beach co., SE Florida, S of Lake Worth; pop. (1990c) 8392.
Lan Tau *also* **Lan Tao** \ˈlän-ˈdau̇\. Island, SW part of New Territories, Hong Kong, across E part of mouth of Zhu River W of Hong Kong I.; 58 sq. mi. (93 sq. km.); 16 mi. (26 km.) long.
Lan–ts'ang. See MEKONG.
La·nús \lä-ˈnüs\. City, Buenos Aires prov., E Argentina, a S suburb of the city of Buenos Aires; pop. (1991p) 466,755; part of Buenos Aires met. area.

La·nu·vi·um \lə-ˈnü-vē-əm, -ˈnyü-\; *modern* **La·nu·vio** \lə-ˈnü-vyō\; *formerly* **Ci·vi·ta La·vi·nia** \ˈchē-vē-tä-lä-ˈvēn-yä\. City in ancient Latium, Italy, near Albanus Mons, 20 mi. (32 km.) SE of Rome. Important in Roman times.

La·nu·za Bay \lä-ˈnü-zä\. Inlet of Pacific Ocean on E coast of Surigao del Sur prov., Mindanao, Philippines, ab. 13 mi. (21 km.) wide at entrance; Cauit Point marks its SE corner.

Lan·za·ro·te \ˌlän-zä-ˈrō-tā\. One of the Canary Is. (*q.v.*), in Las Palmas prov., Spain; 109 mi. (175 km.) NE of Grand Canary I. and easternmost island of the group; 323 sq. mi. (837 sq. km.); wine, vegetables; fisheries; bold and precipitous coast; basaltic cliffs; volcanic in origin; chief town Arrecife.

Lan·zhou *or W.-G.* **Lan–chou** \ˈlän-ˈjō\ *also* **Lan–chow** \ˈlän-ˈchau̇\ *or* \ˈchau̇-ˈlän\. City, ✱ of Gansu prov., N cen. China, on right bank of the Huang River and near the Great Wall; pop. (1990c) 1,194,640; oil refining; textiles, leather goods; several educational institutions. Settled as early as 6th cent. B.C.; came under the rule successively of several dynasties; an important trade center on Silk Road; a center of 19th cent. Muslim uprisings; subjected to severe bombing in WWII; following WWII grew as important industrial and cultural center.

La·oag \lä-ˈwäg\. **1.** River, largest of Ilocos Norte prov., Luzon, Philippines; has many tributaries in upper course spreading out fanwise in mountains to N and S; lower course flows W to South China Sea; ab. 60 mi. (95 km.) long. **2.** Chartered city, ✱ of Ilocos Norte prov., Luzon, Philippines, on right bank of Laoag River; pop. (1990p) 84,000; center of local commerce.

La·oang \lä-ˈwäŋ\. Municipality, NE coast of Northern Samar prov., on **Laoang Island** (12 sq. mi. or 31 sq. km.), Philippines, 57 mi. (92 km.) NNE of Catbalogan; pop. (1980c) 46,545.

Lao Cai *or* **Lao·kay** \ˈlau̇-ˈkī\. Border town, N Vietnam, on Red River 155 mi. (249 km.) NW of Hanoi, on railroad line leading from Hanoi into Yunnan prov., China. Only large town in region; strategically important, long subject to conflict bet. Chinese and Vietnamese; came under French control 1886.

Lao–chün–miao. See YUMEN.

La·od·i·cea \lā-ˌä-də-ˈsē-ə, ˌlā-ə-də-\. **1.** *or* **Laodicea ad Ma·re** \ad-ˈmā-rē\. Seaport, Syria. See LATAKIA 2. **2.** *or* **Laodicea ad Ly·cum** \ad-ˈlī-kəm\. Town, Turkey in Asia. See DENIZLI 2.

Laoet. See LAUT.

Laohekou *or* **Lao–ho–k'ou.** See GUANGHUA.

Laoigh, Ben. See BEN LUI.

Laoighis *or* **Laois** *or* **Leix** \ˈlāsh, ˈlēsh\; *formerly* **Queen's** \ˈkwēnz\. County, Leinster prov., cen. Ireland; ⊗ Portlaoighise; rivers Barrow, Nore. See table at IRELAND.

Laojunmiao. See YUMEN.

Laokay. See LAO CAI.

Laon \ˈläⁿ\; *anc.* **Lau·du·num** \lȯ-ˈdü-nəm, -ˈdyü-\. Commercial commune, ✱ of Aisne dept., N France, 77 mi. (124 km.) NE of Paris; pop. (1990c) 28,670; railroad center; sugar refining, metal founding; plastics; 12th cent. Gothic cathedral; old episcopal palace (now the palace of justice housing law courts); 12th cent. church; 13th cent. gates; to the SW is the abbey of Prémontré, founded 1120 by St. Norbert, founder of the Premonstratensians.

History: Probably ancient Bibrax; fortified by Romans; episcopal see 5th–18th cents.; checked invasions of Franks, Vandals, Huns, and others; gained charter 13th cent.; held successively by Burgundians, English, and French in Hundred Years' War; scene of French Emperor Napoléon's defeat by Prussian Field Marshal Gebhard Leberecht von Blücher 1814; occupied by Germans in Franco-Prussian War and both World Wars; taken by Americans Aug. 1944.

La Oro·ta·va \lä-ˌȯr-ō-ˈtä-vä\. Commune, N cen. Tenerife I., W Canary Is., Spain; pop. (1991p) 34,446; part of Santa Cruz de Tenerife prov.; includes **Puer·to Orotava** \ˈpwer-tō\, N cen. Tenerife I., 20 mi. (32 km.) WSW of the seaport of Santa Cruz de Tenerife, and **Vil·la Orotava** \ˈvē-yä, ˈb̲ēl-yä\, 4 mi. (6 km.) SE of Puerto Orotava; health resort.

La Oro·ya \ˌlä-ō-ˈrō-yä\. Town, cen. Peru, 80 mi. (129 km.) ESE of Lima; pop. (1981p) 33,594; alt. 12,180 ft. (3713 m.); lead refinery, large copper smelter.

Laos \ˈlau̇s, ˈlä-ōs, ˈlā-ˌäs, ˈlā-əs, ˈlau̇z\ *or officially* **Lao People's Democratic Republic** \ˈlau̇\. Republic, SE Asia, bounded on N by China and Vietnam, on E by Vietnam, on S by Cambodia, on W by Thailand, and on NW by Thailand and Myanmar; 91,428 sq. mi. (236,799 sq. km.); pop. (1993e) 4,533,000; ✱ Vientiane.

Physical features: In the NW occupies the valley of the Mekong but most of its N and S extent lies E of that river which forms large part of boundary with Thailand; mountainous, with peaks in the N above 9000 ft. (2740 m.) and in the S ab. 5000 ft. (1525 m.); thickly forested.

Chief products: Rice, corn, tobacco; fishing, tin mining; opium.

Chief towns: Vientiane, Savannakhet, Louangphrabang.

History: Much of area now known as Laos united as one kingdom 14th cent.; administrative seat moved from Louangphrabang to Vientiane c. 1563 due to hostilities with Burmese and Thais; disintegration of kingdom into several states (early 18th cent.) which gradually came under Thai control (Vientiane captured by Thais 1778, destroyed 1827); latter part of 19th cent. marked by Franco-Thai border clashes, resulting in establishment of French control over Laos beginning 1893; occupied by Japanese 1945, French control restored 1946; founding of Pathet Lao (a Communist organization) 1951; achieved total independence 1954; became a member of UN 1955; 1960s marked by civil strife involving Communist, neutralist, and rightist forces (ended by cease-fire 1973); Communist-controlled areas bombed by U.S. during fighting in Vietnam War. Became a republic Dec. 1975 following abdication of King Savang Vatthana; adopted new constitution 1991.

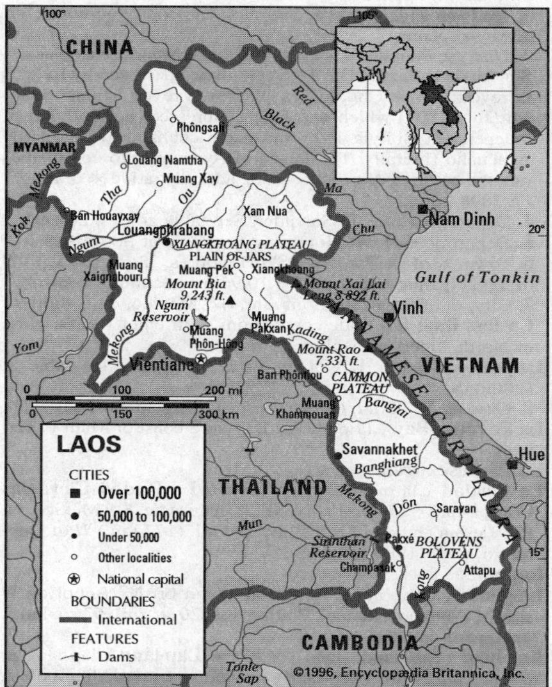

\ə\ **abut** \ə\ matches \ᵊ\ kitten, Fr table \ər\ **further** \a\ **ash** \ā\ **ace** \ä\ **cot, cart** \á\ Fr bac \au̇\ **out** \b\ Span Avila \ch\ **chin** \e\ **bet** \ē\ **easy** \g\ **go** \i\ **hit** \ī\ **ice** \j\ **job** \k̲\ Ger **ich**, Buch \ⁿ\ Fr vin \ŋ\ **sing** \ō\ **go** \ȯ\ **all** \ȯ\ **law** \œ\ Fr bœuf \œ̄\ Fr feu \ȯi\ **boy** \th\ **thin** \t̲h̲\ **this** \ü\ **loot** \u̇\ **foot** \ue\ Ger füllen \ue̅\ Fr rue \y\ **yet** \ʸ\ Fr digne \ˈdēnʸ\, nuit \ˈnwʸē\ \yü\ **few** \yu̇\ **fury** \zh\ **vision**

Lao·shan Wan \ˈlau̇-shän-ˈwän\ *or* **Lao–shan Bay** \ˈlau̇-ˈshän\. Bay overlooked by hills (**Lao Shan**), E Shandong, NE China, part of the Yellow Sea, ab. 20 mi. (32 km.) NE of Qingdao.

La·pac \lä-ˈpäk\. Island in Tapul group, cen. Sulu Archipelago, Philippines, just W of Siasi I.; 16 sq. mi. (41 sq. km.); forms part of Siasi municipality.

La Pal·lice \là-pà-ˈlēs\. Port, NW Charente-Maritime dept., W France, ab. 3 mi. (5 km.) W of La Rochelle; built to accommodate large vessels which cannot get into the harbor of La Rochelle; German submarine base during WWII.

La Pal·ma \lə-ˈpäl-mə\. **1.** City, Orange co., SW California, 16 mi. (26 km.) SE of Los Angeles; pop. (1990c) 15,392.
2. Town and port, ✻ of Darién prov., E Panama; pop. (1980p) 1634; on an inlet of Gulf of Panama 100 mi. (161 km.) SE of Panama (city).
3. *originally* **San Mi·guel de la Pal·ma** \ˌsän-mē-ˈgel-t͟hā-lä-ˈpäl-mä\. One of the Canary Is. (*q.v.*), in Santa Cruz de Tenerife prov., Spain, 53 mi. (85 km.) WNW of Tenerife I.; 280 sq. mi. (725 sq. km.); mountainous; chief town Santa Cruz de la Palma. Occupied by Spain late 15th cent.

La Pam·pa \lä-ˈpäm-pä\. Province of cen. Argentina; ✻ Santa Rosa. See table at ARGENTINA.

La Parida. See BOLÍVAR, CERRO.

La Paz \lə-ˈpaz\. County in SW Arizona. See table at ARIZONA.

La Paz \lä-ˈpäs, -ˈpäz\. **1.** Town, Entre Ríos prov., E Argentina, on left bank of the Paraná ab. 85 mi. (135 km.) NNE of the city of Paraná; pop. (1990e) 19,594.
2. Department of W Bolivia. See table at BOLIVIA.
3. *or in full* **La Paz de Aya·cu·cho** \t͟hā-ˌī-ä-ˈkü-chō\. City, administrative ✻ of Bolivia and ✻ of La Paz dept., E of Lake Titicaca; met. area pop. (1992p) 711,036; alt. 12,001 ft. (3658 m.); highest ✻ in the world, located in valley at foot of Illimani; principal industrial and distribution center of Bolivia; lead and silver; several churches; cathedral; museums; educational center.
History: Founded 1548 by Alonso de Mendoza as Nuestra Señora de la Paz; in late 18th cent. twice besieged by Indians in revolt; joined Chuquisaca (Sucre) in revolt against Spanish (July 1809) which was later suppressed; became part of independent Bolivia 1825 and name changed to La Paz de Ayacucho (literally, The Peace of Ayacucho) to commemorate the battle of Ayacucho; made administrative ✻ of republic 1898.
4. Department of S El Salvador. See table at EL SALVADOR.
5. Department of SW Honduras. See table at HONDURAS.
6. Town, ✻ of La Paz dept., SW Honduras, 33 mi. (53 km.) W of Tegucigalpa; pop. (1988p) 10,965; agricultural center.
7. City, ✻ of Baja California Sur, NW Mexico, on S shore of **La Paz Bay;** has trade connections with chief Pacific ports of North America; fishing; tourism.

La·peer \lə-ˈpir\. **1.** County in E Michigan. See table at MICHIGAN.
2. City, its ⊗, 20 mi. (32 km.) E of Flint; pop. (1990c) 7759.

La Pe·rouse Bay \ˌlä-pə-ˈrüs\. Bay on S coast of Maui I., Hawaii.

La Pérouse Strait. See SŌYA STRAIT.

La Pie·dad \ˌlä-pyā-ˈt͟häth\ *or in full* **La Piedad Ca·va·das** \kä-ˈbä-t͟häs\. Municipality, Michoacán state, SW Mexico, on Río Lerma and on railroad line 110 mi. (177 km.) W of Querétaro; pop. (1980c) 47,441.

Lapin. See LAPPI 2.

La·pi·nin \ˌlä-pi-ˈnēn\. Long flat island off NE Bohol on W side of Canigao Channel, Philippines; 20 sq. mi. (52 sq. km.); mangrove-covered.

Lap·land \ˈlap-ˌland, -lənd\ *or Norw.* **Lap·land** \ˈläp-län\ *or Swed.* **Lapp·land** \ˈläp-land\ *or Finnish* **Lap·pi** \ˈläp-pē\. A region extending over N Norway, N Sweden, N Finland, and the Kola Penin. in NW Russia in Europe, all above the Arctic Circle; total area ab. 150,000 sq. mi. (388,500 sq. km.), with larger parts in Sweden and Russia; pop. (1992e) 112,957; mountains, tundra, swamps, forests, and many lakes (Torneälven, Inari, Imandra) and rivers; chief industries fishing and reindeer herding; has several mining towns, esp. Kiruna and Gällivare in Sweden; timber. Lapps known from prehistoric times but have usually been held subject by other peoples (Swedes, Norwegians, Finns, or Russians).

La Pla·ta \lə-ˈpla-tə\. Town, ⊗ of Charles co., S Maryland; pop. (1990c) 5841; Charles County Community Coll. (1958).

La Pla·ta \lə-ˈpla-tə, -ˈplä-\. County in SW Colorado. See table at COLORADO.

La Pla·ta \lä-ˈplä-tä\. **1.** Seaport, ✻ of Buenos Aires prov., E Argentina, 35 mi. (56 km.) ESE of the city of Buenos Aires; pop. (1991p) 542,567; large artificial harbor; meatpacking, oil refining; chemical industries; university (1890); founded 1882 as the new ✻ of the province at village of Ensenada, now part of it; laid out like Washington, D.C.
2. River in E cen. Puerto Rico; flows N into Atlantic Ocean; ab. 35 mi. (55 km.) long.
3. *or* **Río de la Plata** \ˈrē-ō-ˌt͟hā-\ *or* **Bue·nos Ai·res** \ˈbwā-nȯs-ˈī-rās, ˈbwā-nəs-ˈar-ēz\. Viceroyalty in Spanish South America, estab. 1776, incl. modern Argentina, Uruguay, Paraguay, and Bolivia (then known as Upper Peru); ✻ Buenos Aires; unsuccessfully attacked by British 1806, 1807; divided into self-governing units during wars for independence of Latin American states c. 1813–28.

la Plata, Río de. See PLATA, RÍO DE LA.

La Pla·ta Mountains \lə-ˈpla-tə, -ˈplä-\. A range of the Rocky Mts. in SW Colorado; highest peak Hesperus Peak ab. 13,225 ft. (4030 m.).

La Plata Peak. Mountain in Chaffee co., cen. Colorado; 14,336 ft. (4370 m.).

La Po·ca·tière \lä-ˌpō-kə-ˈtyer\. Town, Kamouraska co., S Quebec, Canada, on St. Lawrence River 65 mi. (105 km.) NE of Quebec City; pop. (1991c) 4648.

La Pointe \lə-ˈpȯint\. Settlement on Madeline I., one of the Apostle Is. (*q.v.*), Wisconsin.

La·porte \lə-ˈpōrt\. Borough and mountain resort, ⊗ of Sullivan co., NE Pennsylvania; pop. (1990c) 213.

La Porte \lə-ˈpōrt\. **1.** County in N Indiana. See table at INDIANA.
2. City, ⊗ of La Porte co., N Indiana, 25 mi. (40 km.) W of South Bend; pop. (1990c) 21,507; radiators, steel castings; settled c. 1830; incorp. 1835.
3. City, Harris co., SE Texas, on Galveston Bay 20 mi. (32 km.) ESE of Houston; pop. (1990c) 27,910.

Lap·peen·ran·ta \ˈlä-ˌpen-ˌrän-tə\ *or Swed.* **Vill·man·strand** \ˈvil-mən-ˌstränd\. Town, Kymi prov., SE Finland, near border of Karelia Rep., NW Russia in Europe; pop. (1989c) 54,804; cement, machinery; chartered 1649.

Lap·pi \ˈlä-pē\. **1.** Region, Arctic. See LAPLAND.
2. *or* **La·pin** \ˈlä-pin\. Province of N Finland; the Finnish part of the region of Lapland. See table at FINLAND.

Lappland. See LAPLAND.

Lapp·mark \ˈläp-ˌmärk\. General name for the N districts of Sweden (see LAPLAND), inhabited by Lapps.

La·prai·rie *or* **La Prai·rie** \lə-ˈprer-ē\. Town, Quebec, Canada, on St. Lawrence River ab. 8 mi. (13 km.) SSE of Montreal across the river; pop. (1991c) 14,938; has an old fort which was attacked 1691 by New England troops; starting point of first railroad in British North America 1836.

Lapseki. See LAMPSACUS.

Lap·tev Sea \ˈlap-tif\ *or Russ.* **Mo·re Lap·te·vykh** \ˈmȯr-ə-ˈläp-tə-ˌvik\; *formerly* **Nor·den·skjöld Sea** \ˈnürd-ᵊn-ˌshœld\. Part of Arctic Ocean along N coast of Russia in Asia, bet. Severnaya Zemlya on W and New Siberian Is. on E.

La·puan \ˈläp-ˌwän\. River, Vaasa prov., W Finland; flows N into Gulf of Bothnia; ab. 100 mi. (160 km.) long.

La Puen·te \ˌlä-pu̇-ˈen-tē\. City, Los Angeles co., SW California, NNE of Long Beach; pop. (1990c) 36,955; residential; incorp. 1956.

La·pu–La·pu \ˌlä-pü-ˈlä-pü\; *formerly* **Opon** \ˈō-ˌpȯn\. Chartered city on NW coast of Mactan I., Cebu prov., Philippines; pop. (1990p) 146,000.

La Pun·til·la \ˌlä-pün-ˈtē-yä\. Cape on SW coast of Ecuador, the tip of Santa Elena Penin.

Lapurdum. See BAYONNE.

Lap·wai \ˈlap-ˌwī\. Village, Nez Perce co., W Idaho, ab. 12 mi. (19 km.) E of Lewiston on S tributary of the Clearwater River; pop. (1990c) 932; first white settlement in Idaho 1836; abandoned 1847 after "Whitman Massacre" (see WALLA WALLA); reopened 1871. Site of U.S. Indian agency.

La Quia·ca \lä-ˈkyä-kä\. Town, N Jujuy prov., NW Argentina, on border of Bolivia; alt. over 10,000 ft. (3050 m.); railroad terminus; on the Pan American Highway.

L'A·qui·la \ˈlä-kwē-lä\ *or* **Aqui·la** \ˈä-\ *or in full* **Aquila de·gli Abruz·zi** \ˌdāl-yē-ä-ˈbrüt-sē, -yē-ə-\. **1.** Province of Abruzzi, Italy. See table at ITALY.
2. Commune, ✻ of L'Aquila prov. and ✻ of Abruzzi autonomous region, cen. Italy, in valley of the Aterno 54 mi. (87 km.) NE of Rome; pop. (1991p) 66,863; summer resort; 2362 ft. (720 m.) above sea level; tourism; university (1952). Founded in mid-13th cent.; episcopal see 1257; part of kingdom of Italy 1860.

La·quin·horn \lä-ˈkvēn-ˌhȯrn\. Peak in the Pennine Alps, S Switzerland, S of Simplon Pass; 13,140 ft. (4005 m.).

La Quin·ta \lə-ˈkēn-tə\. City, Riverside co., S California; 15 mi. (24 km.) SE of Palm Springs; pop. (1990c) 11,215.

Lār \ˈlär\. Town, Persian Gulf prov., S Iran, 125 mi. (201 km.) WNW of Bandar 'Abbās; pop. (1986c) 37,924.

La·ra \ˈlä-rä\. State of NW Venezuela. See table at VENEZUELA.

La·ra·cha \lä-ˈrä-chä\. Commune, La Coruña prov., NW Spain, 11 mi. (18 km.) WSW of the commune of La Coruña.

La·rache \lə-ˈrȧsh\ *or Arab.* **Al–Araish** \ˌȧl-ȧ-ˈrīsh\; *anc.* **Lix·us** \ˈlik-səs\. Seaport, N Morocco, on Atlantic coast; pop. (1982c) 63,893; fishing; exports cork, timber, fruit, wool; nearby are ruins of Lixus, an ancient city held successively by Phoenicians, Carthaginians, and Romans; belonged to Spain 1610–89 and from 1912 to 1956.

Lar·a·mie \ˈlar-ə-mē\. **1.** River, N Colorado and SE Wyoming; rises in N Colorado, flows N across Wyoming border, turns NE and empties into North Platte River; 216 mi. (348 km.) long.
2. County in SE corner of Wyoming. See table at WYOMING.
3. City, ⊗ of Albany co., SE Wyoming, 45 mi. (72 km.) WNW of Cheyenne; pop. (1990c) 26,687; trade center in livestock-raising region; railroad shops; cement, lumber; tourism; Univ. of Wyoming (1886); city settled 1868; incorp. 1873.

Laramie Mountains. Range in SE Wyoming and N Colorado; highest point **Laramie Peak,** in Wyoming, 10,274 ft. (3132 m.).

Laranda. See KARAMAN.

La·ran·tu·ka *or Du.* **La·ran·toe·ka** \ˌlär-ən-ˈtü-kə\. Town and port on NE coast of Flores I., Lesser Sunda Is., Indonesia; seat of native state in early times; Portuguese missionaries settled early 17th cent.

La·rat \ˈlä-ˌrät\. Island in N part of Tanimbar Is., E Malay Archipelago, Indonesia; 20 mi. (32 km.) long by 7 mi. (11 km.) wide.

L'Ar·baa Na·ït Ira·then \ˌlär-bə-ˌnä-it-i-ˈrä-thən\; *formerly* **Fort–Na·tio·nal** \ˌfȯr-ˌnäs-yō-ˈnäl\. Commune, N Algeria, in hilly region ab. 64 mi. (103 km.) E of Algiers.

Larch \ˈlärch\. River, N Quebec, Canada; flows NE to unite with the Caniapiscau River and form the Koksoak River; 270 mi. (434 km.) long.

Larch·mont \ˈlärch-ˌmänt\. Residential village, Westchester co., SE New York, on Long Island Sound 20 mi. (32 km.) NE of New York City; pop. (1990c) 6181.

Larch Mountain. Peak, Multnomah co., NW Oregon; 4095 ft. (1248 m.).

La·re·do \lə-ˈrā-dō\. City and port of entry, ⊗ of Webb co., S Texas, on the Rio Grande opp. Nuevo Laredo, Mexico; pop. (1990c) 122,899; oil and gas wells; brick, clothing, electronic components; oil refining; tourism; Laredo Junior Coll. (1947), Laredo State Univ. (1969). Estab. by Spanish settlers 1755; occupied by Texas Rangers 1846 and by forces of Gen. Mirabeau Lamar 1847; chartered as city 1852; grew rapidly in 1970s and 1980s.

Laredo, Nuevo. See NUEVO LAREDO.

La·res \ˈlä-rās\. Municipality, W cen. Puerto Rico; pop. (1990c) 29,015.

Lar·go \ˈlär-gō\. City, Pinellas co., W cen. Florida, S of Clearwater; pop. (1990c) 65,674; citrus fruit.

Largo Cay. Island in N Caribbean Sea, E of Isle of Pines and S of W Cuba.

Largs \ˈlärgz\. Seaport burgh, Strathclyde region, SW Scotland; pop. (1981p) 9763; seaside resort; scene of victory of Scots King Alexander III over Haakon IV of Norway 1263.

Lar·i·mer \ˈlar-ə-mər\. County in N Colorado. See table at COLORADO.

La Rio·ja \ˌlä-rē-ˈō-hä\. **1.** Province of NW Argentina. See table at ARGENTINA.
2. Town, its ✻, in Andean region 90 mi. (145 km.) SW of Catamarca; pop. (1991p) 106,281; founded 1591; extensively damaged in 1894 earthquake.
3. Autonomous community, historical region, and province of N Spain; a wine-producing district along the upper Ebro. See table at SPAIN.

La·ris·sa \lə-ˈri-sə\ *or Gk.* **Lá·ri·sa** \ˈlä-rē-sä\. **1.** Department of Greece. See table at GREECE.
2. City, ✻ of Larissa dept., E Thessaly, Greece, on Piniós River ENE of Tríkala; pop. (1991p) 113,426; railroad and agricultural trading center. In ancient times ✻ of people living in Thessaly; supported Athens in Peloponnesian War; held by Turks from late 14th cent.; to Greece 1881; scene of severe fighting bet. Germans and army of Greeks and British Apr. 1941.

La·ri·stan \ˌlar-ə-ˈstan\. Region and former province, S Iran, on the Persian Gulf, now part of Fārs, Būshehr, and Hormozgān provs.; 21,020 sq. mi. (54,442 sq. km.); ✻ Bandar 'Abbās; mountains, arid upland, and swampy coastal strip.

Larius, Lacus. See COMO, LAKE.

La Ri·vière–du–Nord \lȧ-rē-ˌvyer-dꞓ̄-ˈnȯr\. County, Quebec, Canada. See table at QUEBEC.

Lark *or* **Larke** \ˈlärk\. River, Suffolk and Cambridgeshire, E England; flows ENE into the Ouse near Ely; ab. 26 mi. (42 km.) long.

Lar·ka·na *or* **Lar·kha·na** \lär-ˈkä-nə\. Town, Sind, Pakistan, near W bank of Indus River 200 mi. (322 km.) NNE of Karachi; pop. (1981c) 123,890; cotton, silk, leather, metalware.

Lark·spur \ˈlärk-ˌspər\. City, Marin co., W California, ab. 10 mi. (16 km.) NW of San Francisco; pop. (1990c) 11,070.

Larks·ville \ˈlärks-ˌvil\. Borough, Luzerne co., E Pennsylvania, 3 mi. (5 km.) W of Wilkes-Barre; pop. (1990c) 4700.

Lar·na·ca \ˈlär-nä-kä\. Seaport, SE Cyprus, on **Larnaca Bay** 23 mi. (37 km.) SE of Nicosia; met. area pop. (1989e) 60,900; on part of site of ancient Citium (*q.v.*).

Larne \ˈlärn\. **1.** District, E Northern Ireland. See table at IRELAND, NORTHERN.
2. Seaport, its ⊗, at head of Lough Larne, co. Antrim; pop. (1991c) 17,575; seaside resort; textiles, paper, cement; port facilities. Edward Bruce, brother of Robert the Bruce, king of Scotland, landed nearby 1315 on his journey to accept Irish throne.

Lar·ned \ˈlär-nəd\. City, ⊗ of Pawnee co., cen. Kansas, at confluence of Arkansas and Pawnee rivers 24 mi. (39 km.) SW of Great Bend; pop. (1990c) 4490; diversified agriculture.

La Ro·chelle \ˌlȧ-rȯ-ˈshel\; *anc.* **Ru·pel·la** \rü-ˈpe-lə\. Seaport, ✻ of Charente-Maritime dept., W France, on Bay of Biscay 124 mi. (200 km.) SW of Tours; aircraft, automobiles, chemicals; oil refining, fishing. In ancient times ✻ of Aunis; became chief Huguenot stronghold in 16th cent.; besieged by Armand-Jean du Plessis, Cardinal Richelieu 1627–28 and forced through famine to capitulate. See LA PALLICE.

La Roche–sur–Yon \lȧ-ˌrȯsh-ˌsu̅e̅r-ˈyōⁿ\. Commune, ✻ of Vendée dept., W France, 37 mi. (60 km.) S of Nantes; agricultural trade center. Founded by French Emperor Napoléon 1804 to serve as ✻ of Vendée dept.; called **Na·po·lé·on–**

Ven·dée \nä-ˌpō-lā-ˈōⁿ-väⁿ-ˈdā\ 1804–14, 1848–70, and **Bour·bon–Vendée** \ˌbür-ˌbōⁿ-\ 1814–48.

La Ro·da \lä-ˈrō-thä\. Commune, Albacete prov., SE Spain, 21 mi. (34 km.) NW of the commune of Albacete; pop. (1991c) 13,168.

La Ro·ma·na \ˌlä-rō-ˈmä-nä\. **1.** Province, E Dominican Republic. See table at DOMINICAN REPUBLIC.
2. Seaport, its ✻, 23 mi. (37 km.) E of San Pedro de Macorís; pop. (1986e) 101,350; sugar refining.

la Ronge, Lac. See RONGE, LAC LA.

Lar·rey Point \ˈlar-ē\. Cape on NW coast of Western Australia, Australia, at 19°58′S, 119°07′E.

Lar·sa \ˈlar-sə\; *bib.* **El·la·sar** \el-ˈlā-ˌsär\. Ancient city of S Babylonia, on left bank of the Euphrates bet. Erech and Ur. Known in biblical times (*Gen.* xiv. 1) and flourished in period of Sumerian decline c. 2000–c. 1760 B.C.

Lars Chris·ten·sen Coast \ˌlärz-ˈkris-tən-sən\. Section of coast of Antarctica, E of Mac. Robertson Land on the Indian Ocean, 69°30′S, 68°E; discovered by Norwegian whalers 1931.

Lar·sen Ice Shelf \ˈlärs-ᵊn\. Ice shelf in NW Weddell Sea, along E coast of Antarctic Penin., Antarctica, 68°30′S, 62°30′W; explored 1893.

La·rue \lə-ˈrü\. County in cen. Kentucky. See table at KENTUCKY.

Lar·vik \ˈlär-vik, -ˌvēk\. Seaport, Vestfold co., SE Norway, at head of **Larvik Fjord;** pop. (1990c) 38,019.

La–sa. See LHASA 1.

La Sa·gra \lä-ˈsä-grä\. Mountain in E Andalusia, Granada prov., S Spain; 7813 ft. (2381 m.).

La Salle \lə-ˈsal\. **1.** Name of a parish in cen. Louisiana and of counties in two states of the U.S. See tables at ILLINOIS, LOUISIANA, and TEXAS.
2. City, La Salle co., N Illinois, 13 mi. (21 km.) W of Ottawa; pop. (1990c) 9717.

LaSalle. City on S shore of Montreal I., S Quebec, Canada; pop. (1991c) 73,804; N terminus of railroad bridge.

La Sal Mountains \lə-ˈsal\. Mountain group of the Rocky Mts., Grand and San Juan cos., SE Utah; highest peak Mt. Peale 12,721 ft. (3877 m.).

Las An·i·mas \las-ˈa-nə-məs\. **1.** County in SE Colorado. See table at COLORADO.
2. City, ⊗ of Bent co., SE Colorado, on Arkansas River 20 mi. (32 km.) E of La Junta; pop. (1990c) 2481; agriculture.

La Sarre \lə-ˈsär\. Town, Abitibi co., SW Quebec, Canada; pop. (1991c) 8513.

Las Be·la \ləs-ˈbā-lə\. Former state, SE Baluchistan States, now part of Pakistan; 7043 sq. mi. (18,241 sq. km.); ✻ Bela; formerly under suzerainty of Kalat; Hab River formed most of E boundary with Sind; valley and delta of Porali River occupy cen. and W part.

La·scar \lä-ˈskär\. Volcano, Antofagasta region, Chile; 19,652 ft. (5990 m.).

Las Cas·ca·das \ˌläs-käs-ˈkä-thäs\. Village, cen. Panama, on W side of Panama Canal just NW of Gaillard Cut.

Las·caux Cave \lä-ˈskō\. See MONTIGNAC.

Las Charcas. See CHARCAS.

Las Conchas. See TIGRE 1.

Las Cru·ces \lä-ˈskrü-səs\. City, ⊗ of Dona Ana co., S New Mexico, near the Rio Grande 42 mi. (68 km.) NNW of El Paso, Texas; pop. (1990c) 62,126; in irrigated agricultural region; cotton, pecans. New Mexico State Univ. (1888) in nearby University Park.

La Selle \lə-ˈsel\. Mountain group in SE Haiti, Hispaniola I., West Indies; highest peak La Selle 8793 ft. (2680 m.).

La Se·re·na \ˌlä-sā-ˈrā-nä\. City, ✻ of Coquimbo region, cen. Chile, ab. 220 mi. (355 km.) N of Valparaíso; pop. (1982c) 83,283; beach resort; bishopric; several churches. Founded c. 1543; destroyed by Indians (1549) and rebuilt; sacked by English pirates 1680; scene of Chilean Declaration of Independence Feb. 12, 1818; heavily damaged by earthquake 1922.

Lasēthion. See LASITHION.

La Seu d'Ur·gell \lä-ˌsœ-dœr-ˈgel\ *or* **Seo de Ur·gel** \ˈsē-ō-ˌthā-ür-ˈhel\. Commune, Lérida prov., Catalonia, NE Spain, on Segre River 10 mi. (16 km.) SSW of Andorra; pop. (1991c) 10,374; founded early 9th cent.; late Romanesque cathedral. Its bishop is co-prince (with French president) of Andorra (*q.v.*).

La Seyne–sur–Mer \lə-ˌsān-sœr-ˈmer, -ˌsen-\. Seaport commune, Var dept., SE France, on Mediterranean Sea 4 mi. (6 km.) SW of Toulon; major shipbuilding center.

Las Guá·si·mas \läs-ˈgwä-sē-mäs\. Locality, E Cuba, ESE of Santiago de Cuba; scene of engagement 1898, won by Americans, which was preliminary to battle of El Caney and taking of Santiago during Spanish-American War.

Las He·ras \läs-ˈā-räs\. Town, Mendoza prov., W cen. Argentina, ab. 10 mi. (16 km.) N of the city of Mendoza.

La·shio \ˈlä-ˌshō\. Town, NE cen. Myanmar; pop. (1983c) 88,950; airport nearby.

Lash·kar \ˈləsh-kər\. City, Madhya Pradesh, N cen. India; formerly ✻ of Gwalior state; constitutes the new part of Gwalior town (see GWALIOR 3) and lies a few miles S of the old city; orig. founded as military campsite (Hindi *lashkar* "camp") early 19th cent.

Lash·kar Gāh \ˌləsh-kər-ˈgär\. Town, S cen. Afghanistan, on Helmand River, W of Qandahār.

La Sila. See *Calabrian Apennines* in table at APENNINES.

La·si·thi·on *or* **La·sē·thi·on** \lə-ˈsē-thē-ˌȯn\ *also* **Las·si·thi** \lə-ˈsē-thē\. Department of Greece. See table at GREECE.

Las Mar·ga·ri·tas \läs-ˌmär-gä-ˈrē-täs\. Municipality, Chiapas state, Mexico, 90 mi. (145 km.) SE of Tuxtla Gutiérrez.

Las Ma·rí·as \ˌläs-mä-ˈrē-äs\. Municipality, W Puerto Rico, ENE of Mayagüez; pop. (1990c) 9306.

Las Na·vas de To·lo·sa \läs-ˈnä-bäs-thā-tō-ˈlō-sä\. Village, Jaén prov., NE Andalusia, S Spain; scene of battle 1212 in which Alfonso VIII defeated the Moors.

La So·la·na \ˌlä-sō-ˈlä-nä\. Commune, Ciudad Real prov., S cen. Spain, 39 mi. (63 km.) ESE of the commune of Ciudad Real; pop. (1991c) 14,160.

La Soufrière. See SOUFRIÈRE 4.

Las Pal·mas \läs-ˈpäl-mäs\. **1.** Province of Spain. See table at SPAIN.
2. *or in full* **Las Palmas de Gran Ca·na·ria** \thä-ˌgrän-kä-ˈnär-yä\. Seaport city, ✻ of Las Palmas prov., Spain, in NE Grand Canary I., 57 mi. (92 km.) SE of Santa Cruz de Tenerife; pop. (1991p) 342,030; largest city and chief port of Canary Is.; exports sugar, tomatoes, bananas; tourism; governor's palace; 15th cent. cathedral; museums; year-round seaside resort; founded late 15th cent.; major growth since opening of port late 19th cent.

La Spe·zia \lä-ˈspet-syä\. **1.** Province of Liguria, NW Italy. See table at ITALY.
2. Fortified seaport, its ✻, on **Gulf of La Spezia** 51 mi. (82 km.) ESE of Genoa; pop. (1989c) 104,511; naval arsenal; largest harbor in Italy; became chief naval station of Italy after 1857; shipbuilding works; tourism. In WWII surrendered by Germans Apr. 1945.

Las Pie·dras \ˌläs-ˈpyā-thräs\. **1.** Municipality, E Puerto Rico, NW of Humacao; pop. (1990c) 27,896.
2. Town, Canelones dept., S Uruguay; pop. (1985c) 58,288.

Lassa. See LHASA 2.

Las·sen \ˈlas-ᵊn\. County in NE California. See table at CALIFORNIA.

Lassen Peak *also* **Mount Lassen.** Volcano, NE California, at S end of Cascade Range, in Shasta co., near border of Plumas co.; 10,457 ft. (3187 m.); cinder cone 6913 ft. (2107 m.); erupted 1914 and intermittently thereafter until 1921; principal feature in **Lassen Volcanic National Park** (see UNITED STATES, *National Parks*).

Las·si·gny \lä-sē-ˈnyē\. Village, Oise dept., N France, near Compiègne; scene of heavy fighting throughout WWI.

Lassithi. See LASITHION.

L'As·somp·tion \lə-ˈsəmp-shən, lə-ˌsōⁿp-ˈsyōⁿ\. **1.** River, chiefly in Joliette and L'Assomption cos., S Quebec, Canada; flows generally S; empties in St. Lawrence River opp. N end of Montreal I.; ab. 100 mi. (160 km.) long.
2. County, S Quebec, Canada. See table at QUEBEC.
3. Town, its ⊗, 23 mi. (37 km.) NNE of Montreal on L'Assomption River; pop. (1991c) 5706.

Lass·wade \la-ˈswād\. Village, Lothian region, SE Scotland, SE of Edinburgh; residence 1798–1804 of author Sir Walter Scott; English author Thomas De Quincey established his daughters here 1840 and lived with them at intervals until his death 1859.

Las Ta·blas \lä-ˈstä-bläs\. Town, ✻ of Los Santos prov., S Panama; pop. (1990p) 6731; near coast on W side of Gulf of Panama.

Last Mountain Lake \ˈlast\. Long narrow lake, S cen. Saskatchewan, Canada; S end ab. 20 mi. (32 km.) NW of Regina; 89 sq. mi. (231 sq. km.); discharges into Qu'Appelle River.

La·sto·vo \ˈlä-stō-ˌvō\ *or Ital.* **La·go·sta** \ˈlä-gōs-tä\. Island, Croatia, in Adriatic Sea off Dalmatian coast; 24 sq. mi. (62 sq. km.); formerly Italian.

La·stra a Si·gna \ˈläs-trä-ä-ˈsē-nyä\. Commune, Firenze prov., Tuscany, cen. Italy, on Arno River 8 mi. (13 km.) W of Florence; pop. (1981p) 16,356; church with 14th cent. frescoes; 14th cent. walls.

Las Tres Marias. See MARÍAS, ISLAS.

Las Tres Vír·ge·nes \ˌläs-ˈtrās-ˈvir-hā-ˌnās\. Mountain, E cen. Baja California, NW Mexico; 6547 ft. (1996 m.).

Las Tu·nas \ˌläs-ˈtü-näs\. Province of E Cuba. See table at CUBA.

Las Ve·gas \läs-ˈvā-gəs\. **1.** *often shortened to* **Vegas.** City, ⊗ of Clark co., SE corner of Nevada, 22 mi. (35 km.) NW of Boulder Dam; pop. (1990c) 258,295; alt. 2030 ft. (619 m.); distribution center for mining and stock-raising region; major tourist resort featuring legalized gaming and glitzy hotels; Univ. of Nevada, Las Vegas (1957); hot springs NW of city; housed offices for Hoover Dam (Boulder Dam) project until 1932. Occupied by Mormons 1855–57; bought by railroad for townsite and division point 1903; became ⊗ 1909, incorp. 1911; pop. grew rapidly in 1980s.
2. City, ⊗ of San Miguel co., NE cen. New Mexico, ab. 40 mi. (64 km.) E of Santa Fe; pop. (1990c) 14,753; formerly constituted two municipalities separated from each other by Gallinas River: **City of Las Vegas,** *sometimes called* **East Las Vegas** *or* **New Town,** and **Town of Las Vegas,** *sometimes called* **West Las Vegas** *or* **Old Town;** shipping point and supply depot in cattle and sheep country; lumber; dairy products; New Mexico Highlands Univ. (1893); health resort and hot springs nearby. Old Town settled on Santa Fe Trail by Spaniards 1823–33; taken for U.S. by Gen. Stephen W. Kearny 1846; seat of military operations until establishment nearby of Fort Union 1851.

Las Vil·las \läs-ˈvē-yäs\. Former province of W cen. Cuba.

Las·wa·ri \lə-ˈswär-ē\. Village, Rajasthan, NW India, in former Alwar state, 12 mi. (19 km.) E of the city of Alwar and ab. 78 mi. (126 km.) SSW of Delhi; scene of English Gen. Gerard Lake's defeat of Marathas 1803 in Second Maratha War.

La Syrie. See SYRIA 2.

La·ta·cun·ga \ˌlä-tä-ˈküŋ-gä\. City, ✻ of Cotopaxi prov., cen. Ecuador, 50 mi. (81 km.) S of Quito; pop. (1990c) 39,882; on plateau ab. 9150 ft. (2789 m.) above sea level; ab. 25 mi. (40 km.) S of the volcano Cotopaxi; has suffered repeatedly from eruptions and earthquakes; founded by Spanish 1534.

La·tah \ˈlā-ˌtä, lə-ˈtä\. County in NW Idaho. See table at IDAHO.

Lat·a·kia \ˌla-tə-ˈkē-ə\. **1.** Former republic, orig. a territory, now part of Syria; 1671 sq. mi. (4328 sq. km.); pop. (1992e) 738,000; ✻ Latakia; coastal region bet. N extension of Lebanon Mts. (Djebel Ansariya) and the Mediterranean Sea and opp. island of Cyprus; the Orontes forms part of its E boundary. Before WWI a part of Turkey; became a territory of the French mandate of Syria 1920; made a state 1922 and later an autonomous part of Syria; made an integral part of Syria 1942.
2. *or Fr.* **Lat·ta·quié** \là-tə-ˈkyā\; *anc.* **La·od·i·cea** \lā-ˌä-də-ˈsē-ə\ *or* **Laodicea ad Ma·re** \ad-ˈmā-rē, -ˈmär-ā\. Seaport, ✻ of Latakia, W Syria; pop. (1992e) 284,000; center of rich agricultural region; exports asphalt, cereals, pottery, tobacco; sponge fishing; in antiquity had several other names; captured by Norman leader Tancred 1103; became an important and wealthy city during the Crusades; taken by Muslim Sultan Saladin 1188; declined in importance but revived in 17th cent. by its cultivation of and trade in Latakia tobacco, which is still a major export.

La Tène \lä-ˈten, -ˈtān\. Shallows at E end of Lac de Neuchâtel, Switzerland; site of discovery of Iron Age remains; name now applied to a period of the Iron Age assumed to date from c. 500 B.C. to c. first cent. A.D.

La Teste \là-ˈtest\; *formerly* **La Teste–de–Buch** \-də-ˈbᵫsh\. Town, Gironde dept., SW France, SSE of Arcachon; ancient ✻ of the **Pays de Buch** \ˌpā-də-\, a territory ruled by a feudal lord.

La·thom and Burs·cough \ˈlā-t͟həm … ˈbər-skō\. Former urban district, Lancashire, NW England, NE of Liverpool; site of **Lathom House,** formerly seat of the Stanley family (earls of Derby) and object of siege by Parliamentarians Feb.–May 1644 when it was defended by the countess of Derby, Charlotte de la Trémoille.

La·thrup Village \ˈlā-thrəp\. City, Oakland co., SE Michigan; pop. (1990c) 4329.

La Thuile \lä-ˈtwēl\. Town, Valle d'Aosta, NW Italy; terminal of Little St. Bernard Pass; pop. (1981p) 723.

Lat·i·mer \ˈla-tə-mər\. County in E Oklahoma. See table at OKLAHOMA.

La·ti·na \lä-ˈtē-nä\; *formerly* **Lit·to·ria** \li-ˈtōr-ē-ə\. **1.** Province of Lazio, cen. Italy. See table at ITALY.
2. Commune, its ✻, 35 mi. (56 km.) SE of Rome; pop. (1991p) 105,543.

Latin America. 1. Spanish America (*q.v.*) and Brazil.
2. All of the Americas S of the U.S.

Latin Empire. Part of the Byzantine Empire ruled by the Crusaders 1204–61; ✻ Constantinople; included lands on W, N, and NE shores of the Aegean Sea (except Euboea) and around the Sea of Marmara. See BYZANTINE EMPIRE.

Latin Way *or Lat.* **Via La·ti·na** \ˈvī-ə-lə-ˈtī-nə\. Ancient Roman road running SE from Rome and joining the Appian Way near Capua.

La·ti·um \ˈlā-shē-əm\. **1.** Ancient country of Italy in cen. part of W coast on Tyrrhenian Sea, bounded by Etruria on NW and by Campania on SE; inhabited by Latins whose cities (incl. Ardea, Lavinium, Tusculum, and Alba Longa) had formed Latin League by 500 B.C.; dominated by Rome from 4th cent. B.C.; Latins revolted and Latin League dissolved after its defeat in Latin War 340–338 B.C.; after Social War c. 90–88 B.C. Latin cities received rights of Roman citizenship.
2. Autonomous region, Italy. See LAZIO.

La Tor·tu·ga \ˌlä-tȯr-ˈtü-gä\. Venezuelan island in the Caribbean Sea off N cen. coast of Venezuela, 55 mi. (88 km.) W of the island of Margarita; 85 sq. mi. (220 sq. km.).

La Tri·ni·dad \lä-ˌtrē-nē-ˈt͟häth\. Municipality, ✻ of Benguet prov., Luzon, Philippines, ab. 3 mi. (5 km.) N of City of Baguio; pop. (1980c) 28,713; at elev. of ab. 8000 ft. (2440 m.); has cool climate; vegetables of temperate zone raised in surrounding gardens.

La Tri·ni·té \lä-ˌtrē-nē-ˈtā\. Commune, E coast of Martinique, West Indies.

La·trobe \lə-ˈtrōb\. Borough, Westmoreland co., SW Pennsylvania, 26 mi. (42 km.) W of Johnstown; pop. (1990c) 9265; St. Vincent Coll. (1846).

La·trun \lə-ˈtrün\. Village in Israeli-occupied West Bank, on highway 15 mi. (24 km.) W of Jerusalem.

Lattaquié. See LATAKIA 2.

La·tu·kan, Mount \ˌlä-tü-ˈkän\. Active volcano, Lanao del Sur prov., Mindanao, Philippines, on Cotabato boundary; 7078 ft. (2157 m.).

La Tuque \là-ˈtᵫk\. Town, Champlain co., S Quebec, Canada, on St.-Maurice River 77 mi. (124 km.) N of Trois-Rivières; pop. (1991c) 10,003; resort; paper; hydroelectric power station.

La·tur \lä-ˈtu̇r\. Town, SE Maharashtra, S cen. India, 140 mi. (225 km.) NW of Hyderabad; pop. (1991p) 197,164.

Lat·via \ˈlat-vē-ə\ *or Lettish* **Lat·vi·ja** \ˈlät-vē-ˌyä\ *or Ger.* **Lett·land** \ˈlet-ˌlänt\. Republic, N Europe, bounded on N by Estonia, on E by Russia, on SE by Belarus and Poland, on S by Lithuania, and on W by the Baltic Sea; comprised **Lat·vi·an Soviet Socialist Republic** \ˈlät-vē-ən\ 1940–91; 24,595 sq. mi. (63,701 sq. km.); pop. (1993e) 2,596,000; ✻ Riga. N half of its W coast indented by Gulf of Riga, large inlet of Baltic Sea. A low-lying plain, with no part above 1000 ft. (305 m.). Chief river the Western Dvina, flowing from SE to Gulf of Riga near Riga; other streams the Venta, Lielupe, and Gauja.

Chief products: Flax, barley, potatoes, rye; livestock; paper, textiles, chemicals, clothing, electrical and transportation equipment.

Chief towns: Riga, Daugavpils, Liepāja.

History: See BALTIC PROVINCES, COURLAND, LIVONIA, and BALTIC STATES. Proclaimed an independent republic Nov. 1918; formed chiefly from Courland and Livonia (*qq.v.*); recognized by U.S.S.R. 1920; joined League of Nations 1921; ratified nonaggression treaty with U.S.S.R. 1932; established nationalist dictatorship 1934; signed mutual assistance treaty with U.S.S.R. and met German problem by repatriation 1939; annexed by U.S.S.R. Aug. 3, 1940; held by German army 1941–44; retaken by U.S.S.R. but incorporation in U.S.S.R. never recognized by U.S.; declared independence Aug. 1991; independence recognized by U.S.S.R. Sept. 1991.

Lauban. See LUBAN.

Lauch·ham·mer \ˈlau̇k-ˌhä-mər\. City, Brandenburg, E Germany, 30 mi. (48 km.) SW of Cottbus; pop. (1981c) 24,721; founded c. 1721.

Lau·der·dale \ˈlȯ-dər-ˌdāl\. **1.** Name of counties in three states of the U.S. See tables at ALABAMA, MISSISSIPPI, TENNESSEE.
2. Village, Ramsey co., E Minnesota; pop. (1990c) 2700.

Lauderdale–by–the–Sea. Town, Broward co., SE Florida; pop. (1990c) 2890.

Lauderdale Lakes. City, Broward co., SE Florida; pop. (1990c) 27,341; residential suburb of Fort Lauderdale; pop. more than doubled bet. 1970 and 1980.

Lau·der·hill \ˈlȯ-dər-ˌhil\. City, Broward co., SE Florida; pop. (1990c) 49,708; residential suburb of Fort Lauderdale; pop. quadrupled bet. 1970 and 1980.

Laudunum. See LAON.

Laudus. See SAINT-LÔ.

Lau·en·burg \ˈlau̇-ən-ˌbu̇rk\. **1.** Region, formerly a duchy, SE Schleswig-Holstein, Germany, E of Hamburg; 453 sq. mi. (1173 sq. km.); under German rulers 13th–17th cents.; during next two centuries to 1864 belonged for varying periods to France, Hannover, Prussia, and Denmark; became part of Prussia 1865 but retained its constitution and special privileges; entered North German Confederation 1866 and German Empire 1870; incorp. in Prussia 1876; ceased to be duchy 1918.
2. *also* **Lauenburg in Pom·mern** \in-ˈpȯ-mərn\. City, Poland. See LĘBORK.

Lauf·feld *or* **Lauf·feldt** \ˈlau̇-ˌfelt\ *also* **Law·feld** \ˈlȯ-ˌfeld\. Village in NE Belgium, just W of Maastricht, Netherlands; scene of victory of French Gen. Maurice of Saxony over Allies 1747 in War of Austrian Succession.

Lau Group \ˈlau̇\ *or* **Eastern Group.** Group of many small islands in E part of Fiji, SW Pacific Ocean; ab. 45 sq. mi. (117 sq. km.); comprises two main groups, Exploring Is. in N and Lakeba Is. in S.

Lauis. See LUGANO.

Laun. See LOUNY.

Laun·ces·ton \ˈlȯn-sə-stən, ˈlän-\; *originally* **Pat·er·so·nia** \ˌpa-tər-ˈsō-nyə\. City, NE Tasmania, Australia, at confluence of North Esk and South Esk rivers 40 mi. (64 km.) from Bass Strait; pop. (1991c) 62,504; hydroelectric power plant; seaport; exports agricultural produce and timber; textiles, aluminum, flour.

Launces·ton \ˈlȯn-stən, ˈlän-\; *anc.* **Dun·he·ved** \ˈdün-ˌhe-vəd\. Town, Cornwall, SW England, 52 mi. (84 km.) WSW of Exeter near the Tamar River; pop. (1981p) 6199; ruins (chiefly the circular keep) of old Norman castle.

La Union \ˌlä-ü-ˈnyȯn\. Narrow coastal province, NW Luzon, Philippines, along South China Sea; ✻ San Fernando. Well watered by many short streams. Has several good ports, esp. San Fernando. Inhabitants mainly Ilocanos. See table at PHILIPPINES. Region explored by Spanish as early as 1572; province created 1854; joined the Filipino revolutionary movement of 1896; civil government estab. Aug. 1901; invaded by Japanese 1941 in WWII.

La Unión \ˌlä-ü-ˈnyȯn\. **1.** Department of E El Salvador. See table at EL SALVADOR.

2. Town, its ✻, on Gulf of Fonseca; pop. (1987e) 58,829; major seaport of El Salvador.

3. Commune, Murcia prov., SE Spain, 28 mi. (45 km.) SE of the commune of Murcia; pop. (1991c) 13,940.

Lau·ra·sia \lȯ-ˈrā-zhə\. N subcontinent of Pangaea (*q.v.*) and later a separate supercontinent roughly comprising the current major landmasses of the Northern Hemisphere, except India, and believed to have formed in late Paleozoic era by merger of Asian landmasses with Laurussia (*q.v.*); part of Pangaea until separation from Gondwana in early Mesozoic era; fragmentation and separation into present landmasses believed to have continued throughout Mesozoic era and into Cenozoic era.

Lau·rel \ˈlȯr-əl, ˈlär-\. **1.** County in SE Kentucky. See table at KENTUCKY.

2. Town, Sussex co., S Delaware, 15 mi. (24 km.) SW of Georgetown; pop. (1990c) 3226.

3. Town, Prince Georges co., S cen. Maryland, 18 mi. (29 km.) NNE of Washington, D.C.; pop. (1990c) 19,438; Capitol Coll. (1964).

4. City, a ⊗ of Jones co., SE Mississippi, 53 mi. (85 km.) SW of Meridian; pop. (1990c) 18,827; oil refining; building board; Southeastern Baptist Coll. (1948); city founded c. 1882; incorp. c. 1890.

5. City, Yellowstone co., S cen. Montana, on Yellowstone River 17 mi. (27 km.) SW of Billings; pop. (1990c) 5686.

Lau·rel·dale \ˈlȯr-əl-ˌdāl, ˈlär-\. Borough, Berks co., SE Pennsylvania, 5 mi. (8 km.) N of Reading; pop. (1990c) 3726.

Laurel Hill. Ridge in SW Pennsylvania, extending along boundary bet. Somerset co. on E and Fayette and Westmoreland cos. on W, and N into Cambria and Indiana cos.

Laurel Mountain. Peak in E Preston co., N West Virginia; 2603 ft. (793 m.).

Lau·rens \ˈlȯr-ənz, ˈlär-\. **1.** Name of counties in two states of the U.S. See tables at GEORGIA and SOUTH CAROLINA.

2. City, ⊗ of Laurens co., NW South Carolina, 23 mi. (37 km.) NNE of Greenwood; pop. (1990c) 9694.

Lau·ren·tia \lȯ-ˈren-chē-ə\. Former landmass roughly comprising present-day North America, and believed to have merged with Baltica to form Laurussia (*qq.v.*) in mid-Paleozoic era; by subsequent merger and separation believed to have successively formed part of Pangaea and Laurasia (*qq.v.*).

Laurentian Plateau. See CANADIAN SHIELD.

Lau·ren·tian Mountains \lȯ-ˈren-chənz, -chē-ənz\ *also* **Lau·ren·tians** \-chənz, -chē-ənz\ *or* **Lau·ren·tides** \ˈlȯr-ən-ˌtīdz, ˈlär-, -ˌtēdz\. Range in Quebec prov., Canada, N of the St. Lawrence River on S edge of the Laurentian Plateau; highest point 3905 ft. (1190 m.).

Lau·rin·burg \ˈlȯr-ən-ˌbərg, ˈlär-\. City, ⊗ of Scotland co., S North Carolina, 39 mi. (63 km.) WSW of Fayetteville; pop. (1990c) 11,643; St. Andrews Presbyterian Coll. (1857).

Lau·ri·um \ˈlȯr-ē-əm, ˈlär-\ *or* **Lau·ri·on** \-ən\ *or Gk.* **Lá·vri·on** \ˈlä-vrē-ˌȯn\. Seaport, Greece, ab. 26 mi. (42 km.) SE of Athens; pop. (1991p) 10,551; near **Mount Laurium,** famous in ancient Greece for its silver mines, worked esp. during latter part of first millennium B.C.

Lau·rus·sia \lȯ-ˈrə-shə\. Former major landmass believed to have formed in mid-Paleozoic era by merger of Baltica and Laurentia (*qq.v.*); believed to have come into contact with Gondwana and merged with several Asian landmasses in late Paleozoic, thus forming N portion of Pangaea, called Laurasia (*qq.v.*).

Lau·sanne \lō-ˈzän, -ˈzan\. Commune, ✻ of Vaud canton, W Switzerland, on N shore of Lake Geneva 32 mi. (51 km.) NE of Geneva; pop. (1989c) 124,897; cultural center; metalworking; precision instruments, leather products, clothing; 13th cent. cathedral; medieval castle (former episcopal palace); university (founded as a theological institution 1537); headquarters of International Olympic Committee. Made episcopal see in late 6th cent.; Reformation introduced 1536 after conquest by the Bernese, who occupied city until 1798; made ✻ of Vaud canton 1803; treaties concluded here 1912, 1923; Lausanne Pact concluded here 1932 greatly reducing German WWI reparations.

Lausitz. See LUSATIA.

Lausitzer Neisse. See NEISSE.

Laut *or Du.* **Laoet** \ˈlau̇t\. Island in the Java Sea, off SE coast of Borneo, Indonesia; 796 sq. mi. (2062 sq. km.).

Lau·ter·brun·nen \ˈlau̇-tər-ˌbru̇-nən\. Valley in Bern canton, SW cen. Switzerland, S of Interlaken and NW of the Jungfrau; numerous waterfalls.

Laut Molucca. See MOLUCCA SEA.

Lau·to·ka \lau̇-ˈtō-kə\. Seaport, W coast of Viti Levu, Fiji, SW Pacific Ocean; pop. (1986c) 28,728; center of sugar industry.

Lau·wers Zee \ˈlau̇-vərs-ˌzā\. Inlet of North Sea on N coast of Netherlands, on border bet. Friesland and Groningen provs.

Lauzon. See LÉVIS-LAUZON.

La·va \ˈlä-vä\ *or Ger.* **Al·le** \ˈä-lə\ *or Pol.* **Ły·na** \ˈwə-nä\. River, Kaliningrad Oblast, Russia and NE Poland; a tributary of the Pregolya; 137 mi. (220 km.) long.

Lava, Mount \ˈlä-və, ˈla-\. Peak, Uinta co., SW Wyoming; 10,400 ft. (3170 m.).

Lava Beds National Monument. See UNITED STATES, *National Monuments.*

La·vaca \lə-ˈva-kə\. **1.** River, SE Texas; rises in Lavaca co., flows S into **Lavaca Bay** in Calhoun co., an arm of Matagorda Bay; ab. 100 mi. (160 km.) long.

2. County in SE cen. Texas. See table at TEXAS.

Lava Hot Springs. City, Bannock co., SE Idaho, 25 mi. (40 km.) SE of Pocatello; pop. (1990c) 420; hot mineral springs; interesting rock formations.

La·val \lə-ˈval, -ˈval\. **1.** County, S Quebec, Canada. See table at QUEBEC.

2. *or in full* **Ville de Laval** \ˌvēl-də-\. City, Laval co., S Quebec, Canada, on Jesus I. in St. Lawrence River, just N of Montreal; pop. (1991c) 314,398.

3. Commune, ✻ of Mayenne dept., NW France, 44 mi. (71 km.) E of Rennes; pop. (1990c) 53,479; textiles; castle with 12th cent. donjon; 15th cent. gate; 16th cent. castle (housing law courts). Founded before 9th cent. A.D.; royalist Vendeans defeated republicans here following French Revolution, but subsequently were defeated themselves.

La Val·lée–de–la–Ga·ti·neau \lȧ-vȧ-ˈlā-də-lȧ-ˌgȧ-tē-ˈnō\ County, Quebec, Canada. See table at QUEBEC.

La Vallée–du–Ri·che·lieu \-dū̅-rē-shəl-ˈyœ̅\. County, Quebec, Canada. See table at QUEBEC.

La·val·le·ja \ˌlä-vä-ˈyā-ä\; *formerly* **Mi·nas** \ˈmē-näs\. Department of S Uruguay. See table at URUGUAY.

La·van·saa·ri \ˈlä-vän-ˌsär-ē\. Small island in Gulf of Finland, E of Gogland.

La·va·pié, Point \ˌlä-vä-ˈpyā\. Cape on coast of Bío-Bío prov., S cen. Chile, S of Gulf of Arauco.

La·vaur \lȧ-ˈvȯr\. Commune, SW Tarn dept., S France; an old town of Languedoc, taken by French soldier Simon de Montfort 1211 during his campaign against the Albigenses; seat of bishopric until the Revolution.

La Ve·ga \lä-ˈb̠ā-gä\. **1.** Province, cen. Dominican Republic. See table at DOMINICAN REPUBLIC.

2. *or in full* **Con·cep·ción de la Vega** \ˌkȯn-sep-ˈsyȯn-ˌthā-lä-ˈb̠ā-gä\. Commune, its ✻; pop. (1989e) 189,000.

La Ven·ta \lä-ˈb̠en-tä\. Village, W Tabasco state, SE Mexico, near Tonalá River; on an island ab. 4 mi. (6 km.) wide surrounded by mangrove swamps on the coast; site of 20th cent.

\ə\ abut \ˈə\ matches \ᵊ\ kitten, Fr table \ər\ further \a\ ash \ā\ ace \ä\ cot, cart \ȧ\ Fr bac \au̇\ out \b̠\ Span Avila \ch\ chin \e\ bet \ē\ easy \g\ go \i\ hit \ī\ ice \j\ job \k̠\ Ger ich, Buch \ⁿ\ Fr vin \ŋ\ sing \ō\ go \ö\ all \ȯ\ law \œ\ Fr bœuf \œ̅\ Fr feu \ȯi\ boy \th\ thin \th̠\ this \ü\ loot \u̇\ foot \ue\ Ger füllen \ue̅\ Fr rue \y\ yet \ʸ\ Fr digne \ˈdēnʸ\, nuit \ˈnwʸē\ \yü\ few \yu̇\ fury \zh\ vision

excavations yielding artifacts of Olmec culture; among the finds were some excellent jade and several huge heads carved of basalt, representing "La Venta culture" of Olmecs flourishing c. 800 to 450 B.C.; most of finds have been removed to museum in Villahermosa.

La Verne \lə-ˈvərn\. City, Los Angeles co., SW California, 25 mi. (40 km.) E of the city of Los Angeles; pop. (1990c) 30,897; Univ. of La Verne (1891); pop. grew rapidly in 1970s.

La Ve·ta Pass \lə-ˈvē-tə\. Mountain pass, Costilla co., S Colorado, in Sangre de Cristo Range of the Rocky Mts.; ab. 9380 ft. (2860 m.).

Lavinia, Civita. See LANUVIUM.

La·vin·i·um \lə-ˈvi-nē-əm\. Ancient town in NW Latium, cen. Italy, near the coast 19 mi. (31 km.) S of Rome; sacred to Roman household gods the Penates and to Vesta; traditionally thought to have been founded by Aeneas from Troy and named for his wife Lavinia.

La Vis·ta \lə-ˈvis-tə\. City, Sarpy co., E Nebraska; pop. (1990c) 9840.

Lavongai. See NEW HANOVER 2.

La·vras \ˈlà-vràs\. City, S cen. Minas Gerais state, E Brazil, 150 mi. (241 km.) NW of Rio de Janeiro; munic. pop. (1991p) 65,858.

Lávrion. See LAURIUM.

La·wai Bay \lä-ˈwī\. Bay on S coast of Kauai I., Hawaii, bet. Koloa Bay and Wahiawa Bay.

Lawers, Ben. See BEN LAWERS.

Lawfeld. See LAUFFELD.

Lawk·sawk \ˈlȯk-ˌsȯk\. Former state, W Southern Shan States, now part of Shan State, E cen. Myanmar; 2365 sq. mi. (6125 sq. km.); chief town Lawksawk, 30 mi. (48 km.) N of Taunggyi.

Lawn·dale \ˈlȯn-ˌdāl, ˈlän-\. City, Los Angeles co., SW California, E of Manhattan Beach; pop. (1990c) 27,331.

Lawn·side \ˈlȯn-ˌsīd, ˈlän-\. Borough, Camden co., SW New Jersey, 7 mi. (11 km.) SSE of the city of Camden; pop. (1990c) 2841; incorp. 1926.

Lawoe. See LAWU.

Law·ra \ˈlȯr-ə\. Town, NW Ghana, near Burkina Faso border 160 mi. (257 km.) NW of Tamale.

Law·rence \ˈlȯr-əns, ˈlär-\. **1.** Name of counties in 11 states of the U.S. See tables at ALABAMA, ARKANSAS, ILLINOIS, INDIANA, KENTUCKY, MISSISSIPPI, MISSOURI, OHIO, PENNSYLVANIA, SOUTH DAKOTA, TENNESSEE.

2. Town, Marion co., cen. Indiana, NE of Indianapolis; pop. (1990c) 26,763; residential.

3. City, ⊗ of Douglas co., E Kansas, on Kansas River 25 mi. (40 km.) E of Topeka; pop. (1990c) 65,608; a residential and food-processing center; Univ. of Kansas (1866). Founded 1854 by New England Emigrant Aid Company to promote abolitionism; center of Free State activities in pre-Civil War years; scene of massacre by Confederate William Quantrill's guerrillas Aug. 21, 1863.

4. City, a ⊗ of Essex co., NE corner of Massachusetts, on Merrimack River 9 mi. (14 km.) ENE of Lowell; pop. (1990c) 70,207; textiles (esp. worsted cloth), machinery, paper, leather goods, clothing; incorp. as a city 1853.

5. Residential village, Nassau co., SE New York, on Long Island, 16 mi. (26 km.) ESE of New York City; pop. (1990c) 6513.

Law·rence·burg \ˈlȯr-əns-ˌbərg, ˈlär-\. **1.** City, ⊗ of Dearborn co., SE Indiana, on Ohio River 55 mi. (88 km.) SE of Shelbyville; pop. (1990c) 4375.

2. City, ⊗ of Anderson co., cen. Kentucky, 12 mi. (19 km.) S of Frankfort; pop. (1990c) 5911.

3. City, ⊗ of Lawrence co., S Tennessee, 31 mi. (50 km.) SSW of Columbia; pop. (1990c) 10,412.

Law·rence·ville \ˈlȯr-ən(t)s-ˌvil, ˈlär-, -vəl\. **1.** City, ⊗ of Gwinnett co., N Georgia, 26 mi. (42 km.) ENE of Atlanta; pop. (1990c) 16,848; became ⊗ 1821; grew rapidly in 1980s.

2. City, ⊗ of Lawrence co., SE Illinois, 55 mi. (88 km.) N of Evansville, Indiana; pop. (1990c) 4897.

3. Unincorporated settlement, Mercer co., W cen. New Jersey, ab. 6 mi. (10 km.) N of Trenton; pop. (1990c) 6446; Lawrenceville School (1810), Rider Coll. (1865); named in honor of naval hero Capt. James Lawrence (whose dying words "Don't give up the ship" became a motto).

4. Town, ⊗ of Brunswick co., S Virginia, SW of Petersburg; pop. (1990c) 1486; St. Paul's Coll. (1888).

Law·ton \ˈlȯt-ᵊn\. City, ⊗ of Comanche co., SW Oklahoma, 80 mi. (129 km.) SW of Oklahoma City; pop. (1990c) 80,561; farming; granite, limestone quarries nearby; oil wells; Cameron Univ. (1908); city founded 1901. Fort Sill (*q.v.*) 4 mi. (6 km.) N.

Law·ton·ka, Lake \lȯ-ˈtäŋ-kə\. Lake, Comanche co., SW Oklahoma; 2 sq. mi. (5 sq. km.); formed by dam (60 ft. or 18 m. high, 375 ft. or 114 m. long) across Medicine Bluff Creek; water supply for Fort Sill and Lawton to the S.

La·wu *or Du.* **La·woe** \ˈlä-wü\. Mountain, E cen. Java, Indonesia; 10,712 ft. (3265 m.).

La'youn. See AAIÚN, EL.

Lay·san \ˈlī-ˌsän\. Island of the Leeward Is., Hawaiian Is., cen. Pacific Ocean, ab. 750 mi. (1200 km.) NW of Niihau I., 25°50′N, 171°50′W; included in a bird reservation.

Lay·ton \ˈlāt-ᵊn\. City, Davis co., N Utah, N of Salt Lake City; pop. (1990c) 41,784; grew rapidly in 1980s.

La·zi \ˈlä-sē\. Municipality, S coast of Siquijor I., Siquijor prov., Philippines; pop. (1980c) 16,149; has good harbor.

La·zio \ˈlät-sē-ō\ *or* **La·tium** \ˈlā-shəm\. Autonomous region, cen. Italy; ✻ Rome; lies bet. Tyrrhenian Sea and Apennines and bet. Tuscany and Campania; includes the Campagna di Roma (*q.v.*) and the Pontine Marshes (see PONTINO, AGRO); watered chiefly by Tiber River. Estab. 1948. See table at ITALY.

Lea \ˈlē\. **1.** County in SE corner of New Mexico. See table at NEW MEXICO.

2. River, SE England; rises in Bedfordshire, flows SE through Hertfordshire and S bet. Essex and Greater London cos. into the Thames; 46 mi. (74 km.) long.

Lead \ˈlēd\. City, Lawrence co., W South Dakota, 33 mi. (53 km.) WNW of Rapid City; pop. (1990c) 3632.

Lead·bet·ter Point \ˈled-ˌbe-tər\. Point on NW coast of Pacific co., SW Washington, at S entrance to Willapa Bay.

Lead·ville \ˈled-ˌvil\. City, ⊗ of Lake co., cen. Colorado, in Rocky Mts. 75 mi. (121 km.) WSW of Denver; pop. (1990c) 2629; alt. 10,190 ft. (3106 m.); one of principal centers of 19th cent. American mining history; gold, silver, lead, zinc, copper, bismuth, manganese, and molybdenum were mined; founded c. 1860 as gold camp.

Leaf \ˈlēf\. **1.** River, SE Mississippi; rises in S Scott co., flows SE to unite with Chickasawhay River in N George co. and form the Pascagoula River; ab. 180 mi. (290 km.) long.

2. River, N Quebec prov., Canada; flows NE from Lake Minto into Ungava Bay; 300 mi. (483 km.) long.

League City \ˈlēg\. City, Galveston co., SE Texas, 25 mi. (40 km.) NW of the city of Galveston; pop. (1990c) 30,159; grew rapidly in 1980s.

League of Arab States. See ARAB LEAGUE.

Leake \ˈlēk\. County in cen. Mississippi. See table at MISSISSIPPI.

Leakes·ville \ˈlēks-ˌvil, -vəl\. Town, ⊗ of Greene co., SE Mississippi; pop. (1990c) 1129.

Lea·key \ˈlē-kē\. City, ⊗ of Real co., SW cen. Texas; pop. (1990c) 399.

Le·a·lui \ˌlē-ä-ˈlü-ē\. Town, Zambia, on E bank of Zambezi River.

Leam *or* **Leame** \ˈlēm\. River, cen. England; flows into the Avon near Warwick; 25 mi. (40 km.) long.

Lea·ming·ton \ˈlē-miŋ-tən\. Town, Essex co., SE Ontario, Canada, 30 mi. (48 km.) ESE of Windsor, near Lake Erie shore; pop. (1991c) 14,182.

Leam·ing·ton \ˈle-miŋ-tən\ *or officially* **Royal Leamington Spa.** Town, Warwickshire, cen. England, on the Leam River 2 mi. (3 km.) NE of Warwick; pop. (1981p) 42,953.

Leane, Lough \ˈläk-ˈlān\. Largest of the Lakes of Killarney (*q.v.*), SW Ireland.

Leath·er·head \ˈle-thər-ˌhed\. Town, Surrey, S England; pop. (1981p) 40,473.

Leav·en·worth \ˈle-vən-ˌwərth\. **1.** County in NE Kansas. See table at KANSAS.
2. City, its ⊗, on Missouri River 22 mi. (35 km.) NW of Kansas City; pop. (1990c) 38,495; railroad, trading, and industrial center; manufactures steel, flour; St. Mary Coll. (1923). Settled 1854 by proslavery emigrants from Missouri; oldest city in Kansas; federal penitentiary. See FORT LEAVENWORTH.
3. City, Chelan co., cen. Washington, on Wenatchee River 20 mi. (32 km.) NW of Wenatchee; pop. (1990c) 1692; outdoor recreation.

Leav·itt Peak \ˈle-vit\. Mountain in the Sierra Nevada, on boundary bet. Mono and Tuolumne cos., E cen. California; 11,570 ft. (3527 m.).

Lea·wood \ˈlē-ˌwu̇d\. City, Johnson co., E Kansas, S of Kansas City; pop. (1990c) 19,693.

Lebadea. See LEVÁDHIA.

Leb·a·non \ˈle-bə-nən, -ˌnän\. **1.** *or Fr.* **Li·ban** \lē-ˈbä^{n}\. Republic, at E end of Mediterranean Sea, bounded on N and E by Syria, on S by Israel, and on W by Mediterranean Sea; 3949 sq. mi. (10,228 sq. km.); pop. (1993e) 2,909,000; ✱ Beirut.

Physical features: Largely mountainous; Lebanon Mts. in cen. part; bounded on E by Anti-Lebanon Range; valley bet. the two ranges, known as Bekáa Valley (*anc.* Coele-Syria), watered by the Litani River in S and by the upper Orontes in N; Mt. Hermon on SE border.

Chief products: Fruit, vegetables, tobacco, olives.

Chief towns: Tripoli, Beirut, Zahlah.

History: In early history inhabited by Maronites, members of a Syrian Christian sect estab. in 7th cent. A.D., and by Muslims and Druzes; taken by Crusaders 11th cent.; in 1860, Maronites massacred by the Druzes (see JEBEL ED DRUZ); under pressure of European powers esp. France, **Mount Lebanon** estab. as autonomous government under Christian governor appointed by the Ottoman government 1861; as **Great Lebanon** (*Fr.* **Grand Liban** \grä^{n}-\) declared autonomous under French mandate 1920; reorganized as **Lebanese Republic** 1926 (see SYRIA 2); signed treaty of independence with France 1936 (not ratified by French government); under control of Vichy authorities 1940; passed under control of the British and Free French July 1941; declared independent 1941, but evacuation of French troops not completed until 1946; played minor role in Arab-Israeli War 1948–49; U.S. troops sent to Lebanon July 1958 (withdrawn Oct. 1958) following government's request for U.S. assistance during period of internal strife; suffered during civil war bet. religious factions 1975–90; Syrian troops intervened 1976 in an attempt to restore order; Israeli forces invaded 1982 to drive hostile forces from the south; scene of severe fighting during army revolts 1989 and 1990; experienced sporadic clashes with Israeli troops in south during early 1990s.

2. County in SE cen. Pennsylvania. See table at PENNSYLVANIA.
3. Agricultural town, N New London co., SE corner of Connecticut, 5 mi. (8 km.) S of Willimantic; pop. (1990c) 6041.
4. City, St. Clair co., SW Illinois, 20 mi. (32 km.) E of East St. Louis; pop. (1990c) 3688; McKendree Coll. (1828).
5. City, ⊗ of Boone co., cen. Indiana, 25 mi. (40 km.) NW of Indianapolis; pop. (1990c) 12,059.
6. City, E Smith co., N Kansas; pop. (1990c) 364; geographical center of the Lower 48 is ab. 4 mi. (6.4 km.) NW, at 39°49′N, 98°33′W.
7. City, ⊗ of Marion co., cen. Kentucky, 28 mi. (45 km.) W of Danville; pop. (1990c) 5695.
8. City, ⊗ of Laclede co., S cen. Missouri, 25 mi. (40 km.) S of E end of Lake of the Ozarks; pop. (1990c) 9983; boats; lake resort.
9. City, Grafton co., W New Hampshire, 19 mi. (31 km.) N of Claremont; pop. (1990c) 12,183.
10. Village, ⊗ of Warren co., SW Ohio, 18 mi. (29 km.) E of Hamilton; pop. (1990c) 10,453; prehistoric mounds and earthworks nearby.
11. City, Linn co., W Oregon, 20 mi. (32 km.) E of Corvallis; pop. (1990c) 10,950; fruit and berry farming.
12. City, ⊗ of Lebanon co., SE cen. Pennsylvania, 25 mi. (40 km.) E of Harrisburg; pop. (1990c) 24,800; iron and steel, textiles, chemicals. Laid out c. 1756.
13. City, ⊗ of Wilson co., N cen. Tennessee, 31 mi. (50 km.) E of Nashville; pop. (1990c) 15,208; flour, clocks; Cumberland Univ. of Tennessee (1842).
14. Town, ⊗ of Russell co., SW Virginia, NNE of Bristol; pop. (1990c) 3386.

Lebanon Mountains *or Arab.* **Ja·bal Lub·nān** \ˈja-bəl-ˌlüb-ˈnän\; *anc.* **Lib·a·nus** \ˈli-bə-nəs\. Mountain range in Lebanon, parallel with the Mediterranean coast; ab. 100 mi. (160 km.) long; highest peak Qurnet as Sauda 10,131 ft. (3088 m.) near N end.

Le Bar·do \le-ˈbär-dō\. Town, Tunisia, ab. 2 mi. (3 km.) NW of Tunis; pop. (1989e) 67,806.

Le Bas–Ri·che·lieu \lə-ˌbä-ˌrē-shəl-ˈyœ\. County, Quebec, Canada. See table at QUEBEC.

Lebda. See LEPTIS MAGNA.

Le Bec–Hel·louin \lə-ˈbek-el-ˈwe^{n}\. Commune, Eure dept., N France, ab. 25 mi. (40 km.) NW of Évreux; remains of the Benedictine abbey of Bec, founded 11th cent., which became famous under Italian prelate Lanfranc (prior 1045–62) and Scholastic philosopher Anselm (prior 1063–78, abbot 1078–93).

\ə\ **abut** \ə\ **matches** \ᵊ\ **kitten,** Fr **table** \ər\ **further** \a\ **ash** \ā\ **ace** \ä\ **cot, cart** \à\ Fr **bac** \au̇\ **out** \b\ Span **Avila** \ch\ **chin** \e\ **bet** \ē\ **easy** \g\ **go** \i\ **hit** \ī\ **ice** \j\ **job** \k\ Ger **ich, Buch** \$^{n}$\ Fr **vin** \ŋ\ **sing** \ō\ **go** \ȯ\ **all** \ȯ\ **law** \œ\ Fr **bœuf** \œ̄\ Fr **feu** \ȯi\ **boy** \th\ **thin** \t͟h\ **this** \ü\ **loot** \u̇\ **foot** \ue\ Ger **füllen** \u̅e\ Fr **rue** \y\ **yet** \$^{y}$\ Fr **digne** \ˈdēn^{y}\, **nuit** \ˈnw^{y}ē\ \yü\ **few** \yu̇\ **fury** \zh\ **vision**

Leb·e·dos \ˈle-bə-ˌdäs\. Ancient city, one of the 12 Ionian Cities, situated on coast of Asia Minor bet. Teos and Ephesus.

Le Blanc–Mes·nil \lə-ˌbläⁿ-mā-ˈnēl\. Commune, Seine-St.-Denis dept., N France, NE suburb of Paris.

Le·bong \lə-ˈbȯŋ\. See DARJEELING.

Lę·bork \ˈlem-ˌbȯrk\; *Ger.* **Lau·en·burg** \ˈlau̇-ən-ˌbu̇rk\ *also* **Lauenburg in Pom·mern** \in-ˈpȯ-mərn\. City, NE Słupsk prov., N Poland, ab. 40 mi. (65 km.) WNW of Gdańsk; pop. (1989e) 33,724; founded c. 1341; in WWII taken by U.S.S.R. Mar. 1945; assigned to Poland by Potsdam Conference 1945.

Le Bour·get \lə-bür-ˈzhā\. Commune, Seine-St.-Denis dept., N France, 6 mi. (10 km.) NE of Paris; formerly site of major airport (closed 1969), where American aviator Charles A. Lindbergh landed May 21, 1927 after first nonstop solo transatlantic flight.

Le Bous·cat \lə-bü-ˈskä\. Commune, Gironde dept., SW France, NNW suburb of Bordeaux.

Le·bo·wa \le-ˈbō-wə\. Former territory in N Transvaal, Rep. of South Africa; comprised several noncontiguous areas set aside for the N Sotho people.

Le·bri·ja \lā-ˈbrē-hä\; *older* **Le·bri·xa** \lā-ˈbrē-shä\ *or* **Ne·bri·ja** \nā-ˈbrē-hä\ *or* **Ne·bri·xa** \-shä\; *anc.* **Na·bris·sa** \nə-ˈbri-sə\ *or* **Ne·bris·sa** \nə-\. Commune, Sevilla prov., SW Spain, on Guadalquivir River 33 mi. (53 km.) S of Seville; pop. (1991c) 28,738; agricultural trading center; 12th cent. church. Settled by Phoenicians and later by Greeks; reconquered from Moors by Ferdinand III 1248 and Alfonso X 1264. Birthplace of humanist Elio Antonio de Nebrija (1444) and of navigator Juan Díaz de Solís (c. 1470).

Le·bu \ˈlā-bü\. Seaport, Bío-Bío region, S cen. Chile, ab. 60 mi. (100 km.) SW of Concepción; formerly ✻ of Arauco prov.

Le Can·net \ˌlə-kȧ-ˈnā\. Commune, Alpes-Maritimes dept., SE France, NNE suburb of Cannes.

Le Cap. See CAP HAITIEN.

Le Ca·teau \lə-kȧ-ˈtō\ *or in full* **Le Cateau–Cam·bré·sis** \-ˌkäⁿ-brā-ˈzē\. Commune, Nord dept., N France, 13 mi. (21 km.) ESE of Cambrai; peace agreement (Cateau-Cambrésis) 1559, bet. France, England, and Spain, confirmed French possession of Calais and surrendered French conquests in Italy; suffered much during religious conflicts of 16th cent. (1562–98), again during the Revolution; occupied by Germans WWI and WWII each time suffering greatly.

Le Ca·te·let \lə-kȧ-ˈtlā\. Village, Aisne dept., N France, 11 mi. (18 km.) N of St.-Quentin; battle WWI in 1918 when small force of U.S. troops was cut off; has American cemetery.

Lec·ce \ˈlā-chē, ˈle-\. **1.** Province of Puglia, SE Italy. See table at ITALY.

2. Commune, its ✻, near Adriatic Sea, ESE of Taranto; pop. (1991p) 100,233; textiles, pottery, canned foods; processes wine and olive oil; 12th cent. cathedral; Roman amphitheater; university (1959); made diocese 6th cent.; fortified by Aragonese 15th cent.

Lec·co \ˈlā-kō, ˈle-\. Commune, Como prov., Lombardy, N Italy, at S end of SE branch (**Lake Lecco**) of Lake Como at mouth of Adda River, 16 mi. (26 km.) ENE of the commune of Como; pop. (1991p) 45,859; metalworking.

Le Cen·ter \lə-ˈsen-tər\. Village, ⊗ of Le Sueur co., S Minnesota, 20 mi. (32 km.) NNE of Mankato; pop. (1990c) 2006.

Le Centre–de–la–Mau·ri·cie \lə-ˈsäⁿtrᵊ-də-lȧ-mō-rē-ˈsē\. County, Quebec, Canada. See table at QUEBEC.

Lech \ˈlek\; *anc.* **Li·cus** \ˈlī-kəs\. River, in Austria and Germany; rises in Vorarlberg, SW Austria, flows N through Tirol and S cen. Bavaria past Augsburg into the Danube; 155 mi. (249 km.) long.

Le Cham·bon–Feu·ge·rolles \lə-shäⁿ-ˈbōⁿ-fœzh-ˈrȯl\. Commune, Loire dept., SE cen. France, 4 mi. (6 km.) SW of St.-Étienne.

Le Châ·te·lard \lə-shät-ˈlär\. Commune, Vaud canton, W Switzerland, near E shore of Lake Geneva 15 mi. (24 km.) ESE of Lausanne. See MONTREUX.

Lech·feld \ˈlek-ˌfelt\. Field or plain on Lech River, Bavaria, Germany, S of Augsburg; scene of battle 955 in which king of Germany (later Holy Roman Emperor) Otto I defeated the Magyars.

Lech·lade \ˈlech-ˌlād\. Parish, Gloucestershire, SW cen. England, on the Thames; terminus of Thames and Severn Canal.

Le·comp·ton \li-ˈkämp-tən\. City, Douglas co., E Kansas; pop. (1990c) 619; scene of framing of the Lecompton Constitution 1857, a proslavery constitution for the state of Kansas which was overwhelmingly defeated by the voters.

Le Conte, Mount \lə-ˈkänt\. **1.** Mountain, Tulare co., S cen. California, on E boundary of Sequoia National Park; 13,960 ft. (4255 m.).

2. Peak, Sevier co., E Tennessee, in Great Smoky Mts.; 6593 ft. (2010 m.).

Le Crac. See AL-KARAK.

Le Creu·sot \lə-krœ-ˈzō\. Commune, Saône-et-Loire dept., E cen. France, 39 mi. (63 km.) NNW of Mâcon; steel; its modern development dates from the 1830s.

Lec·toure \lek-ˈtür\. Commune, N Gers dept., SW France; dates from pre-Roman times; ✻ of Armagnac from 1325; bishopric suppressed 1790; church (renovated 15th–17th cents.), formerly the cathedral.

Lectum, Cape. See BABA, CAPE.

Łę·czy·ca \wen-ˈshət-sä\ *or Russ.* **Len·chi·tsa** \lin-ˈchēt-sə\ *or Ger.* **Len·tschi·za** \len-ˈchēt-sə\. Commune, Płock prov., cen. Poland, on Bzura River 20 mi. (32 km.) NNW of Łódź; pop. (1981p) 15,678.

Ledang, Gunong. See OPHIR, MOUNT.

Ledi, Ben. See BEN LEDI.

Le·do \ˈlē-dō, ˈlā-\. Town, Arunachal Pradesh, NE India, ab. 35 mi. (56 km.) S of Sadiya; branch railhead of Bengal-Assam railroad and starting point of **Ledo Road,** strategic military highway begun during WWII in Dec. 1942 by U.S. Army engineers to connect with Burma Road (*q.v.*); road built under great difficulties across Patkai Range through Hukawng Valley to Mogaung, Myitkyina (Ledo to Myitkyina 262 mi. or 422 km.), and Bhamo in N Burma (Myanmar); name changed to Stilwell Road (*q.v.*) Jan. 1945.

Le Do·maine–du–Roy \lə-dȯ-ˈmen-dūe-ˈrwä\. County, Quebec, Canada. See table at QUEBEC.

Ledo Salinarius. See LONS-LE-SAUNIER.

Le·duc \lə-ˈdük\. Town, Alberta, Canada, 20 mi. (32 km.) S of Edmonton; pop. (1991c) 13,970; diversified agriculture.

Led·yard \ˈled-yərd, ˈle-jərd\. Town, New London co., SE Connecticut, E of Thames River 7 mi. (11 km.) NE of the city of New London; pop. (1990c) 14,913; American Indian-run casino; town incorp. 1836.

Lee \ˈlē\. **1.** Name of counties in 12 states of the U.S. See tables at ALABAMA, ARKANSAS, FLORIDA, GEORGIA, ILLINOIS, IOWA, KENTUCKY, MISSISSIPPI, NORTH CAROLINA, SOUTH CAROLINA, TEXAS, VIRGINIA.

2. Town, Berkshire co., W Massachusetts, 9 mi. (14 km.) S of Pittsfield; pop. (1990c) 5849.

3. River, SW Ireland; flows from W to E across co. Cork into Cork Harbour; ab. 50 mi. (80 km.) long.

Leech·burg \ˈlēch-ˌbərg\. Borough, Armstrong co., W Pennsylvania, 25 mi. (40 km.) ENE of Pittsburgh; pop. (1990c) 2504.

Leech Lake \ˈlēch\. Reservoir in N Cass co., N cen. Minnesota; 176 sq. mi. (456 sq. km.); ab. 20 mi. (32 km.) long and from 4 to 15 mi. (6 to 24 km.) wide; alt. 1297 ft. (395 m.); outlet E into Mississippi River; Minnesota's last armed conflict bet. Indians and the U.S. Army occurred nearby.

Leeds \ˈlēdz\. **1.** City, Jefferson, Shelby, and St. Clair cos., cen. Alabama, 15 mi. (24 km.) ENE of Birmingham; pop. (1990c) 9946.

2. City, West Yorkshire, N England, on the Aire 36 mi. (58 km.) ENE of Manchester; pop. (1991p) 674,400; major transportation, commercial, and industrial center; produces clothing, textiles, paper, leather goods, chemicals; Univ. of Leeds (1904); city incorp. 1626; early center of woolen industry but principal development took place from late 18th cent.

Leeds and Grenville. County, Ontario, Canada. See table at ONTARIO.

Leeds and Liverpool Canal. Canal, N England, bet. the cities of Leeds and Liverpool; part of a system of waterways that links the Irish Sea with the North Sea.

Leek \ˈlēk\. Town, Staffordshire, W cen. England; pop. (1981p) 19,739; market town; ruins of 13th cent. Cistercian abbey.

Lee·la·nau \ˈlē-lə-ˌnȯ\. County in NW Michigan. See table at MICHIGAN.

Leer \ˈler\ *also* **Leer in Ost·fries·land** \in-ˈȯst-ˈfrēs-ˌlänt\. City, Lower Saxony, Germany, near right bank of lower Ems River 34 mi. (55 km.) WNW of Oldenburg; pop. (1980c) 31,303.

Lees·burg \ˈlēz-ˌbərg\. **1.** City, Lake co., cen. Florida Penin., 36 mi. (58 km.) WNW of Orlando; pop. (1990c) 14,903; Lake-Sumter Community Coll. (1962).
2. City, ⊗ of Lee co., SW Georgia; pop. (1990c) 1452.
3. Town, ⊗ of Loudoun co., N Virginia, 38 mi. (61 km.) NW of Alexandria; pop. (1990c) 16,202; grew rapidly in 1980s.

Lees Ferry \ˈlēz\. Locality, N Coconino co., N Arizona, on Colorado River at head of Marble Canyon; ferry estab. 1872, only crossing of the Colorado River for many miles until construction of Navajo Bridge 5 mi. (8 km.) downstream; 467 ft. (142 m.) above the river; 616 ft. (188 m.) long; completed 1929.

Lee's Summit \ˈlēz\. City, Jackson co., W Missouri, 18 mi. (29 km.) SE of Kansas City; pop. (1990c) 46,418; grew rapidly in 1980s.

Lees·ville \ˈlēz-ˌvil\. Town, ⊗ of Vernon parish, W Louisiana, 53 mi. (85 km.) W of Alexandria; pop. (1990c) 7638; lumber.

Leeu·war·den \ˈlā-ˌvär-də\. Commune, ✱ of Friesland prov., N Netherlands, on the Ee River; pop. (1992e) 86,405; paper, dairy products; in 16th–18th cents. noted for its manufactures in gold and silver; Groote Kerk (church, built 15th cent.); Frisian museum; stadhouse; Oldehove tower; Kanselarij (chancellery).

Leeu·win, Cape \ˈlü-ən\. The extreme SW point of Australia.

Lee·ward Islands \ˈlē-wərd, ˈlü-ərd\. **1.** Chain of small islets, rocks, and shoals in cen. Pacific Ocean, extending 1250 mi. (2011 km.) WNW from main islands of the Hawaiian Is., ab. 162°W to 178°25′W; some composed of lava rock, some of coral and sand; all except Midway are uninhabited and seldom visited, and constitute a bird sanctuary, set aside 1909 by U.S. government; islets include Nihoa, Necker, Gardner Pinnacles, Laysan, Lisianski, Pearl and Hermes Atoll and Kure, or Ocean. Since discovery 1859 considered as belonging to the Hawaiian Is.; under the jurisdiction of Honolulu co.
2. *or Fr.* **Îles sous le Vent** \ˌēl-sü-lə-ˈvän\. W group of the Society Is., French Polynesia, S Pacific Ocean; 154 sq. mi. (399 sq. km.); pop. (1988c) 22,232; chief islands Huahine, Raïatéa, and Tahaa.
3. Geographically, the N chain of islands in the Lesser Antilles, E West Indies— so called because of their more sheltered position than the Windward Is. from the prevailing northeasterly winds. The chain extends from Dominica on the S to Virgin Is. on the N; administratively divided bet. the U.S. (St. Thomas, St. Croix, and St. John in the Virgin Is.), Netherlands (Saba, St. Eustatius, and S part of St. Martin), France (Guadeloupe, Marie-Galante, Désirade, Îles des Saintes, St.-Barthélemy, and N part of St. Martin) and United Kingdom (for geographical descriptions and history, see LEEWARD ISLANDS 4, entries for individual islands, and VIRGIN ISLANDS).
4. Former division of the West Indies Federation (formed 1958, dissolved 1962), consisting of: Anguilla, Antigua, Barbuda, Montserrat, Nevis, Redonda, St. Kitts, Sombrero.
History: First British settlement, on St. Christopher (see SAINT KITTS) 1623, followed by period of conflict with Spanish (17th cent.) and French (17th and 18th cents.); islands united under a common legislature early in 18th cent. and, after a lapse of this form of government, reunited under a common council 1871. For further details, see entries for individual islands.

Leeward Passage. Channel bet. Hans Lollik I. and N St. Thomas I., Virgin Is. of the U.S., West Indies.

Le Fjord–du–Sa·gue·nay \lə-ˌfyȯrd-säg-ˈnē\. County, Quebec, Canada. See table at QUEBEC.

Lefkás. See LEVKÁS.

Lefkosia. See NICOSIA 1.

Le·flore \lə-ˈflōr\. County in W Mississippi. See table at MISSISSIPPI.

Le Flore \lə-ˈflōr\. County in E Oklahoma. See table at OKLAHOMA.

Le·froy, Lake \lə-ˈfrȯi\. Lake, S Western Australia, Australia, N of Lake Cowan and near Boulder.

Le·gaz·pi *or* **Le·gas·pi** \lə-ˈgas-pē, -ˈgäs-\. Chartered city, ✱ of Albay prov., Philippines, at head of Albay Gulf, near S base of Mayon Volcano; pop. (1990c) 121,116; deepwater port; exports copra and Manila hemp; includes original municipalities of Legazpi on the coast and Albay ab. 2 mi. (3 km.) inland; two municipalities merged in 1907 and name of Albay changed to Legazpi 1925. Founded ab. 1636; partly destroyed by eruption of Mayon Volcano 1815; occupied by Japanese in WWII.

Leghorn. See LIVORNO.

Le·gio·no·wo \ˌle-gyȯ-ˈnȯ-vȯ\. Town, Warzawa prov., E cen. Poland; pop. (1989e) 50,681.

Le·gna·go \le-ˈnyä-gō\. Commune, Verona prov., Veneto, NE Italy, on Adige River 23 mi. (37 km.) SE of Venice; pop. (1989c) 26,518; connected by canal with Po River. Venetian and Austrian fortified stronghold.

Le·gna·no \le-ˈnyä-nō\. Commune, Milano prov., Lombardy, N Italy, 11 mi. (18 km.) NNW of Milan; pop. (1991p) 50,068; metalworking; candles, soap; Holy Roman Emperor Frederick Barbarossa defeated here 1176 by Lombard League.

Leg·ni·ca \leg-ˈnēt-sä\ *or Ger.* **Lieg·nitz** \ˈlēg-nits\. **1.** Province, SW Poland. See table at POLAND.
2. City, its ✱, 39 mi. (63 km.) WNW of Wrocław; pop. (1989e) 104,196; railroad junction; textile manufacturing, food processing, metalworking; 12th cent. castle. Received civic rights 1252; ✱ of duchy 1249–1675; to Prussia 1742; scene of victory of Prussian King Frederick the Great over Austrians Aug. 15, 1760; after WWII assigned to Poland by Potsdam Conference 1945.

Leg·nic·kie Po·le \leg-ˈnēts-kye-ˈpō-le\; *formerly* **Wahl·statt** \ˈväl-ˌshtät, ˈwäl-\. Village, Wrocław prov., SW Poland, suburb of Legnica; formerly in Prussia, Germany; scene of battle Apr. 9, 1241 in which forces of Mongol ruler Batu Khan defeated Henry, duke of Silesia.

Le Grand Andely. See LES ANDELYS.

Le Grand–Montrouge. See MONTROUGE.

Le Gra·nit \lə-grä-ˈnēt\. County, Quebec, Canada. See table at QUEBEC.

Le·guan \ˈlā-ˌgwän\. Island at mouth of the Essequibo River, off NE coast of Guyana.

Leh \ˈlā\. Town, E Jammu and Kashmir, N India; on N bank of Indus at alt. of 11,500 ft. (3505 m.), 160 mi. (257 km.) E of Srinagar; pop. (1981c) 8718.

Le Haut–Rich·e·lieu \lə-ˌō-ˌrē-shəl-ˈyœ̄\. County, Quebec, Canada. See table at QUEBEC.

Le Haut–Saint–Fran·çois \lə-ˌō-ˌsen-frän-ˈswä\. County, Quebec, Canada. See table at QUEBEC.

Le Haut–Saint–Lau·rent \lə-ˌō-ˌsen-lō-ˈrän\. County, Quebec, Canada. See table at QUEBEC.

Le Haut–Saint–Mau·rice \lə-ˌō-ˌsen-mō-ˈrēs\. County, Quebec, Canada. See table at QUEBEC.

Le Ha·vre \lə-ˈhävrᵊ, -ˈhäv\ *or Eng.* **Havre** \ˈhävrᵊ, ˈhä-vər, ˈha-vər\; *formerly* **Le Havre–de–Grâce** \lə-ˌhäv-rə-də-ˈgräs, -ˌhäv-də-ˈ\. Commercial seaport, Seine-Maritime dept., N France, on English Channel on N side of estuary of the Seine 110 mi. (177 km.) WNW of Paris; pop. (1990c) 197,219; major port for exports from Paris region and NW France; important industrial center; oil refining, shipbuilding; machinery; church of Notre Dame; museum; seaside resort adjacent on NW. Developed as port from 16th cent.; naval base under Emperor Napoléon I; major Allied base in WWI; in WWII occupied by Germans 1940–44 and suffered severe damage; city has largely been rebuilt.

Le·hi \ ˈlē-ˌhī\. City, Utah co., N cen. Utah, on Utah Lake 16 mi. (26 km.) NNW of Provo; pop. (1990c) 8475.

Le·high \ ˈlē-ˌhī\. **1.** River, E Pennsylvania; rises in S extremity of Wayne co., flows SW, then turns SE to empty into the Delaware River at Easton; ab. 100 mi. (160 km.) long.
2. County in E Pennsylvania. See table at PENNSYLVANIA.

Le·high·ton \lē-ˈhīt-ᵊn\. Borough, Carbon co., E Pennsylvania, on Lehigh River 21 mi. (34 km.) NW of Allentown; pop. (1990c) 5914. Settled by Moravians 1746; during French and Indian War destroyed 1755; resettled 1794; incorp. as borough 1866.

Leh·man Caves \ ˈlē-mən\. Caves, Whitepine co., E Nevada; formerly a national monument; since 1987 part of Great Basin National Park.

Lehr·te \ ˈler-tə\. City, Lower Saxony, Germany, 10 mi. (16 km.) E of Hannover; pop. (1980c) 38,371.

Le·hua \lā-ˈhü-ə\. Small barren uninhabited rock off N tip of Niihau I., NW Hawaii.

Lei \ ˈlā\. River, E Hunan, SE cen. China; flows W and N to the Xiang; ab. 200 mi. (320 km.) long.

Leices·ter \ ˈles-tər\. **1.** Town, Worcester co., cen. Massachusetts, 6 mi. (10 km.) W of the city of Worcester; pop. (1990c) 10,191; Becker Coll.–Leicester campus (1784).
2. County of England. See LEICESTERSHIRE.
3. City, ⊗ of Leicestershire, cen. England, on the Soar 35 mi. (56 km.) ENE of Birmingham; pop. (1991p) 270,600; railroad junction; hosiery, knitwear, footwear; Univ. of Leicester (1957); ruins of an ancient Norman castle, and of an abbey founded in 1143. Place where King Richard III spent the night before he was killed in the battle of Bosworth Field (1485), and to which his body was brought for burial.

Leices·ter·shire \ ˈles-tər-ˌshir, -shər\ *or* **Leices·ter** \ ˈles-tər\. **1.** Former county, cen. England.
2. Administrative county, cen. England, incl. former cos. of Leicestershire and Rutlandshire; rivers include the Soar and Wreak; grazing, agriculture, cheese, limestone, textiles, woolen hosiery. See table at ENGLAND.

Leich·hardt \ ˈlī-ˌkärt\. **1.** River, Queensland, Australia; flows N to Gulf of Carpentaria; ab. 300 mi. (485 km.) long.
2. Municipality, E New South Wales, Australia, a suburb of Sydney; pop. (1991c) 58,484.

Lei–chou Pan–tao. See LEIZHOU PENINSULA.

Lei·den *or* **Ley·den** \ ˈlīd-ᵊn, *Du. usu.* ˈlā-də\; *sometimes historically* **Lug·du·num Bat·a·vo·rum** \ˌləg-ˈdü-nəm-ˌba-tə-ˈvōr-əm, -ˈdyü-\. Commune, South Holland prov., SW Netherlands, on Oude Rijn River; pop. (1992e) 112,976; metalworking, printing, food processing; Univ. of Leiden (1575); residence of the Pilgrims for 11 years before they sailed 1620 for America; famous for its heroic defense May–Oct. 1574 against Spanish siege; home of the Elzevir family of printers. Birthplace (c. 1509) of Dutch religious leader Jon Beuckelson (known as John of Leiden), of several painters, among them Rembrandt (1606) and Jan Steen (c. 1626), and of Nobel Prize-winning physicist Johannes van der Waals (1837).

Leid·schen·dam \ˌlāt-sən-ˈdäm, ˌlīd-\. Commune, South Holland prov., Netherlands; pop. (1981e) 30,215.

Lei·dy, Mount \ ˈlī-dē\. Peak, E cen. Teton co., NW Wyoming; 10,317 ft. (3145 m.).

Leidy Peak. Mountain, N Uintah co., E Utah; 12,013 ft. (3662 m.).

Leie \ ˈlā-ə\ *or Fr.* **Lys** \ ˈlēs\. River in France and Belgium; flows NE, forming a section of the France-Belgium boundary and joining the Schelde River at Ghent; ab. 120 mi. (195 km.) long; navigable for ab. 100 mi. (160 km.).

Leigh \ ˈlē\. Town, Greater Manchester, NW England, 11 mi. (18 km.) W of Manchester; pop. (1981p) 45,341.

Leigh·ton \ ˈlāt-ᵊn\. Town, Bedfordshire, England; area pop. (1981p) 29,772.

Lei·kan·ger \ ˈlā-ˌkäŋ-ər\. Commune, ⊗ of Sogn og Fjordane co., Norway, on N side of Sogne Fjord; pop. (1990c) 2834.

Lei·ne \ ˈlī-nə\. River, cen. Germany; rises in the Eichsfeld and flows W and N past Göttingen and Hannover to the Aller; 119 mi. (191 km.) long; formerly crossed border of East Germany and West Germany.

Lein·ster \ ˈlen-stər\. Province, E Ireland; 7581 sq. mi. (19,635 sq. km.); includes cos. Carlow, Dublin, Kildare, Kilkenny, Laoighis, Longford, Louth, Meath, Offaly, Westmeath, Wexford, Wicklow. One of the early provinces of Ireland; its N part, Meath, made a separate kingdom in 2d cent. A.D.; remainder independent in 12th and 13th cents., and cos. Carlow and Wexford independent until 16th cent.

Leinster, Mount. Peak on boundary bet. cos. Carlow and Wexford, SE Ireland; 2610 ft. (796 m.).

Leip·zig \ ˈlīp-sik, -sig\. **1.** District of former East Germany.
2. *also* **Leip·sic** \ -sik\ *or Latin* **Lip·sia** \ ˈlip-sē-ə\. City, Saxony, E cen. Germany, at confluence of Weisse Elster, Pleisse, and Parthe rivers; formerly ✱ of Leipzig dist.; pop. (1992e) 503,191; railroad junction; important market for fur; publishing; chemicals, electrical products, textiles; Univ. of Leipzig (1409), formerly (1953–1990) Karl Marx Univ.; St. Thomas church (16th cent.; burial place of composer Johann Sebastian Bach); 18th cent. palace; before WWII center of German publishing industry; scene of annual trade fairs founded c. 1170.
History: First mentioned c. 11th cent.; chartered in 12th cent.; scene of famous religious debate bet. Martin Luther, Bodenstein von Karlstadt, and Johann Eck 1519; accepted Reformation 1539; in Thirty Years' War, two battles (sometimes called battles of Breitenfeld) won by Swedes nearby, 1631 and 1642; in 17th cent., supplanted Frankfurt am Main as center of German book trade; scene of "Battle of the Nations" (*Ger.* Völkerschlacht) Oct. 16–19, 1813, when French Emperor Napoléon's power in Germany was broken by the allies. In WWII taken by U.S. forces Apr. 1945; heavily damaged in WWII but much restored since; massive citizen demonstrations against Communism 1989 provided impetus toward change in government.

Lei·ria \lā-ˈrē-ə\. **1.** District of W cen. Portugal. See table at PORTUGAL.
2. Commune, its ✱, on Liz River 73 mi. (117 km.) NNE of Lisbon; pop. (1991p) 101,325; cathedral (1571); first Portuguese printing press 1466.

Leitch·field \ ˈlich-ˌfēld\. City, ⊗ of Grayson co., W cen. Kentucky; pop. (1990c) 4965.

Leith \ ˈlēth\. Former burgh, Midlothian co., SE Scotland, now united to Edinburgh; a seaport with several industries.

Lei·tha *or Hung.* **Laj·ta** \ ˈlī-tä\. River, E Austria; flows NE across Hungarian border and enters the Rába near its junction with the Danube; 112 mi. (180 km.) long; historically, formed section of boundary bet. Austria and Hungary until transfer of Burgenland to Austria 1922. See CISLEITHANIA.

Leith Hill. See NORTH DOWNS.

Leitmeritz. See LITOMĚŘICE.

Lei·trim \ ˈlē-trəm\. County, Connacht prov., N Ireland; ⊗ Carrick on Shannon; livestock grazing. See table at IRELAND.

Leix \ ˈlāsh, ˈlēsh\. County, Leinster prov., Ireland. See LAOIGHIS.

Lei·xõ·es \ˌlā-ˈshȯiⁿsh\. Seaport, NW Portugal, in parish of Matozinhos; artificial harbor, main port of Pôrto.

Lei Yue Mun *also* **Lei U Mun** *or* **Ly·e·mun Pass** \ ˈlā-ˈyüē-ˈmu̇n\. Strait bet. NE Hong Kong I. and mainland; 0.25 mi. (0.4 km.) wide.

Lei·zhou Peninsula \ ˈlā-ˈjō\ *or Pinyin* **Leizhou Ban·dao** \ ˈbän-ˈdau̇\ *or W.-G.* **Lei–chou Pan–tao** \ ˈlā-ˈjō-ˈbän-ˈdau̇\; *mostly formerly* **Lui·chow Peninsula** \ ˈlwē-ˈchau̇\. Peninsula of SW Guangdong prov., SE China, separated from Hainan I. by Hainan Strait; on its E coast is Kwangchowan, a former French leased territory, returned after WWII.

Lek \ ˈlek\. The N branch of the Lower Rhine in Netherlands, a continuation W of the Neder Rijn; unites with Merwede River to form the Nieuwe Maas.

Le Kef \lə-ˈkef\ *or* **Al–Kef** \al-\; *anc.* **Sic·ca Ve·ne·ria** \ ˈsi-kə-və-ˈnir-ē-ə\. Town, N Tunisia, ab. 90 mi. (145 km.) SSW of Tunis; built on a steep rock at a junction of main highways; a Carthaginian colony and later, a Roman colony; remains of Roman temple and baths.

le Krem·lin–Bi·cêtre \lə-krām-ˌleⁿ-bē-ˈsetrᵊ\. Suburb to the immediate S of Paris, France; site of early hospital founded 18th cent. for treatment of mentally disturbed.

Le·land \ˈlē-lənd\. **1.** Village, ⊗ of Leelanau co., NW Michigan.
2. City, Washington co., W Mississippi, 10 mi. (16 km.) E of Greenville; pop. (1990c) 6366.

Le·le \le-ˈlā\. Village and harbor on E coast of Kosrae I., E Caroline Is., Federated States of Micronesia, W Pacific Ocean.

Le·le·i·wi Point \ˌlā-lā-ˈē-wē\. Point on E coast of Hawaii I., Hawaii, S of Hilo Bay.

Le Locle \lə-ˈlȯkl^{ə}\. Commune, Neuchâtel canton, W Switzerland, on French border 5 mi. (8 km.) SW of La Chaux-de-Fonds; pop. (1980c) 12,039; watchmaking center.

Lelupe. See LIELUPE.

Le·ly·stad \ˈlā-lē-ˌstät\. Municipality, ✻ of Flevoland prov., cen. Netherlands, on IJsselmeer; pop. (1993e) 60,172.

Le Ma·do·nie \lā-ˌmä-dō-ˈnē-ā\. Mountain range in Palermo prov., NW cen. Sicily, Italy; highest peak 6491 ft. (1979 m.).

Le·ma·ha·bang \ˌle-mə-ˈhä-bäŋ\. Town, West Java prov., Indonesia, just SSE of Cirebon.

Le Maine. See MAINE 2.

Le Maire, Strait of \lə-ˈmer\. Strait, Isla de los Estados and SE Tierra del Fuego I., S Argentina; ab. 20 mi. (32 km.) wide.

Le·man \ˈlē-mən, ˈle-; lə-ˈman\. Name of Vaud canton, W Switzerland, under the Helvetic Republic 1798–1803.

Leman, Lake; *anc.* **Lemannus** *or* **Lemanus.** See GENEVA, LAKE.

Le Mans \lə-ˈmä^{n}\. City, ✻ of Sarthe dept., NW France, on Sarthe River 117 mi. (188 km.) SW of Paris; pop. (1990c) 148,465; railroad center; railroad shops; electrical equipment, tobacco products, textiles, plastics, motor vehicles; noted for its Grand Prix automobile race; 11th–12th cent. church; 11th–15th cent. cathedral; French defeated here by Prussians during Franco-Prussian War 1870–71 foreshadowing the fall of Paris. Birthplace of Henry II of England (1133), first king of the house of Plantagenet.

Le Mars \lə-ˈmärz\. City, ⊗ of Plymouth co., NW Iowa, 25 mi. (40 km.) NNE of Sioux City; pop. (1990c) 8454; Teikyo Westmar Univ. (1890).

Le Mas d'Azil \lə-ˌmȧs-də-ˈzēl\. Commune, N Ariège dept., S France, ab. 40 mi. (64 km.) SW of Toulouse; in 1887 nearby cave scene of discovery of prehistoric human remains representative of culture now called *Azilian* belonging to a period of the Stone Age.

Lem·bang \ˈlem-ˌbäŋ\. Village, W Java, Indonesia, N of Bandung at foot of Tangkubanperahu; alt. 4000 ft. (1219 m.).

Lemberg. See L'VIV.

Le·me·ry \ˌlā-mā-ˈrē\. Municipality, Batangas prov., Luzon, Philippines, near E shore of Balayan Bay; pop. (1980c) 42,783.

Lemessus. See LIMASSOL.

Lem·go \ˈlem-gō\. City, North Rhine-Westphalia, Germany, 44 mi. (71 km.) SW of Hannover; pop. (1980c) 39,864; founded c. 1200.

Lem·hi \ˈlem-ˌhī\. **1.** River, E cen. Idaho; rises in SE Lemhi co., flows N into Salmon River at Salmon; 75 mi. (121 km.) long.
2. County in E cen. Idaho. See table at IDAHO.

Lemhi Range. Range in E cen. Idaho, chiefly in Lemhi and Butte cos.; highest point ab. 11,020 ft. (3360 m.).

Lem·men·jo·ki National Park \ˈlem-men-ˌyȯ-kē\. National park, Finland; 149 sq. mi. (386 sq. km.); lakes; estab. 1956.

Lem·mon \ˈle-mən\. City, Perkins co., NW South Dakota, on North Dakota border 14 mi. (23 km.) N of Grand River; pop. (1990c) 1614; stock and grain farming.

Lemmon, Mount *also* **Mount Lem·on** \ˈle-mən\. Mountain, highest peak in Santa Catalina Mts., in NE corner of Pima co., S Arizona; 9157 ft. (2791 m.); ski area.

Lem·nos \ˈlem-ˌnäs, -nəs\ *or Gk.* **Lím·nos** \ˈlēm-ˌnȯs\. Island, Lesbos dept., Greece, in N Aegean Sea off W coast of Turkey in Asia; 177 sq. mi. (458 sq. km.); pop. (1981c) 15,721; ✻ Kástron; mountainous and fertile; harbor at Moudros on S coast; once noted for a medicinal earth (Lemnian bole or Lemnian earth) long sold in Europe as an astringent. Important in Greek mythology, esp. as sacred to Hephaestus, the god of fire and metalworking.

History: Occupied by pre-Hellenic people perhaps as early as 4th millennium B.C.; evidence of Greek inhabitation 8th cent. B.C.; held by Persians at beginning of 5th cent. B.C.; in Delian League and important part of Athenian empire; in Roman, Byzantine, and Ottoman empires; taken from Ottoman Empire by Greece 1913; base of British fleet in Dardanelles campaign of WWI.

Lem·on Grove \ˈle-mən\. City, San Diego co., S California, E of the city of San Diego; pop. (1990c) 23,984; residential.

Lemon Rock. See SKELLIGS.

Le·mont \lə-ˈmänt\. Village, Cook co., NE Illinois, on Illinois River 14 mi. (22 km.) WSW of Chicago; pop. (1990c) 7348.

Le·moore \lə-ˈmōr\. City, Kings co., SW cen. California, 29 mi. (47 km.) S of Fresno; pop. (1990c) 13,622; grew rapidly in 1970s and 1980s.

Le Mort Homme \lə-mȯr-ˈtȯm\ *or* **Dead Man's Hill.** Height ab. 6 mi. (10 km.) NW of Verdun, NE France; scene of violent battle during WWI (1916).

Le Moule \lə-ˈmül\. Seaport, Grande-Terre I., E part of island of Guadeloupe, West Indies; pop. (1982c) 15,227.

Le Mous·tier \lə-mü-ˈstyā\. Cave, Dordogne dept., SW France, on right bank of the Vézère above Les Eyzies (see EYZIES, LES); from important archaeological finds here, incl. a human skeleton and flint points, gives its name to the *Mousterian* period of Middle Paleolithic culture; tools often considered the work of Neanderthal man.

Lemovices. See LIMOGES.

Le·moyne \lə-ˈmȯin\. **1.** Residential borough, Cumberland co., S Pennsylvania, across Susquehanna River from Harrisburg; pop. (1990c) 3959.
2. \ *also* lə-ˈmwän\. Town, Quebec, Canada, ab. 3 mi. (5 km.) E of Montreal; pop. (1991c) 5412.

Lem·pa \ˈlem-pä\. River, El Salvador; flows through Lake Guija E and S into the Pacific Ocean; ab. 200 mi. (320 km.) long.

Lem·pi·ra \lem-ˈpē-rä\; *formerly* **Gra·cias** \ˈgrä-syä\. Department of W Honduras. See table at HONDURAS.

Lem·ro \ˈlem-ˈrō, ˈle-myō\. River, W Myanmar; rises in Chin Hills and flows S into Hunter's Bay, inlet of Bay of Bengal, E of Sittwe; 180 mi. (290 km.) long.

Le·na \ˈlē-nə, ˈlā-; ˈlye-nə\. River, E cen. Russia in Asia; rises on W slopes of Baikal Mts. W of Lake Baikal, flows NE in Irkutsk Oblast through wooded mountain ranges, then E forming part of S boundary of Sakha Rep.; from ab. 117°E flows in great bend E and N entirely within Sakha Rep. to enter Laptev Sea in delta 250 mi. (402 km.) wide at ab. 72°N; ab. 2700 mi. (4345 km.) long, with drainage basin estimated at more than 950,000 sq. mi. (2,460,500 sq. km.). Has many tributaries (estimated by some at 1000), chief of which on right are Vitim, Olekma, and Aldan, on left Vilyui; land along upper course and on tributaries rich in minerals, incl. gold and coal. In lower 1200 mi. (1930 km.) of course fall is slight and width is 4 to 20 mi. (6 to 32 km.). Delta first reached early 1630s; scene of death 1881 of members of expedition of American explorer George W. DeLong.

Le·na \ˈlā-nä\. Commune, Asturias prov., NW Spain, 13 mi. (21 km.) S of Oviedo; pop. (1991c) 14,135.

Len·a·wee \ˈle-nə-ˌwē\. County in S Michigan. See table at MICHIGAN.

Lenchitsa. See ŁĘCZYCA.

Len·çóis Ma·ra·nhen·ses National Park \lä^{n}-ˈsȯis-ˌmȧ-rȧ-ˈnyen-sis\. National park, NE Brazil, on the Atlantic coast; 598 sq. mi. (1549 sq. km.); dunes and lakes.

Len·di·na·ra \ˌlen-di-ˈnär-ə\. Commune, Rovigo prov., Veneto, NE Italy, 10 mi. (16 km.) W of the commune of Rovigo; pop. (1981p) 13,402.

Lendum. See LENS.

Le·nexa \lə-ˈnek-sə\. City, Johnson co., E Kansas, 10 mi. (16 km.) SW of Kansas City; pop. (1990c) 34,034; grew rapidly in 1970s and 1980s.

Lengeh, Bandar–e. See BANDAR–E LENGEH.

Len·ge·rich \ˈleŋ-ə-ˌrik\. City, North Rhine-Westphalia, Germany, 27 mi. (43 km.) N of Münster; pop. (1980c) 20,597.

Len·gua de Va·ca, Point \ˈleŋ-gwä-thā-ˈbä-kä\. Cape on W coast of Coquimbo region, cen. Chile, S of the city of Coquimbo.

Len·gwe National Park \ˈleŋ-gwā\. National park, S Malawi, containing antelope and other wildlife.

Leninabad. See KHUDZHAND.

Leninakan. See GYUMRI.

Leningrad. See SAINT PETERSBURG.

Leningrad Oblast. See SAINT PETERSBURG OBLAST.

Le·nin·o·gor \lə-ˈnē-nə-ˌgȯr\ *or* **Rid·der** \ˈri-dər\; *mostly formerly* **Le·nin·o·gorsk** \li-ˌnē-nə-ˈgȯrsk\. Town, East Kazakhstan subdivision, Kazakhstan, ab. 50 mi. (80 km.) NE of Öskemen; pop. (1991e) 69,500; lead and zinc mining.

Le·nin·o·gorsk \lə-ˈnē-nə-ˌgȯrsk\; *formerly* **No·va·ya Pi·smyan·ka** \ˈnȯ-və-yə-pēs-ˈmyäŋ-kə\. Town, Tatarstan, Russia in Europe, ab. 15 mi. (24 km.) WNW of Bugul'ma; pop. (1991e) 63,300.

Len·in Peak \ˈle-nin, ˈlyā-nēn\; *formerly* **Kauf·mann Peak** \ˈkau̇f-mən\. Mountain in Trans Alai Range, bet. Kyrgyzstan and Tajikistan; 23,405 ft. (7134 m.); was 2d highest peak in the U.S.S.R.

Len·insk \ˈlyā-nēnsk\. **1.** Town, St. Petersburg Oblast, Russia in Europe. See PETRODVORETS.

2. *formerly* **Pri·shib** \pri-ˈshib\. City, E Volgograd Oblast, S Russia in Europe, 35 mi. (56 km.) E of the city of Volgograd on an E arm of the lower Volga; near site of Sarai (*q.v.*).

3. Town, E Turkmenistan. See CHARDZHOU.

Len·insk–Kuz·nets·ki *or* **Len·insk–Kuz·nets·kiy** \-kůs-ˈnyet-skē\; *formerly* **Kol·chu·gi·no** \ˌkəl-ˈchü-gə-nə\. Mining town in center of Kuznetsk Basin, W Kemerovo Oblast, S Russia in Asia, on Tom' River 75 mi. (121 km.) NW of Novokuznetsk; pop. (1992e) 132,000; coal mining; mining machinery, chemicals, electric lights; coal mining begun on site 1912.

Lenkoran. See LÄNKÄRÄN.

Len·nox \ˈle-nəks\. Unincorporated settlement, Los Angeles co., SW California, SE of Santa Monica; pop. (1990c) 22,757.

Lennox and Ad·ding·ton \ˈa-diŋ-tən\. County in SE Ontario, Canada. See table at ONTARIO.

Lennox Hills. Range of hills in Central region, SW cen. Scotland; highest point **Earl's Seat** \ˈərlz\ 1894 ft. (577 m.).

Len·nox·ville \ˈle-nəks-ˌvil\. Town, Sherbrooke co., S Quebec, Canada, 4 mi. (6 km.) SSE of the city of Sherbrooke; pop. (1991c) 4046; Bishop's Univ. (1843).

Le·noir \lə-ˈnōr\. **1.** County in E North Carolina. See table at NORTH CAROLINA.

2. Town, ⊗ of Caldwell co., W North Carolina, near the Blue Ridge 38 mi. (61 km.) W of Statesville; pop. (1990c) 14,192.

Lenoir City. City, Loudon co., E Tennessee, on Tennessee River; pop. (1990c) 6147.

Le·nore Lake \lə-ˈnōr\. Lake, NW Grant co., cen. Washington; 8 mi. (13 km.) long.

Len·ox \ˈle-nəks\. Town, Berkshire co., W Massachusetts, 7 mi. (11 km.) S of Pittsfield; pop. (1990c) 5069; summer resort; estate incl. site of author Nathaniel Hawthorne's cottage (rebuilt) and Tanglewood, summer home of Boston Symphony Orchestra.

Lens \ˈläⁿs\; *anc.* **Len·ti·um** \ˈlen-chē-əm\ *or* **Len·dum** \ˈlen-dəm\. City, Pas-de-Calais dept., N France, 11 mi. (18 km.) NNE of Arras; pop. (1990c) 35,278; coal mining; chemicals. Scene of French victory over Spaniards during Thirty Years' War 1648; largely destroyed during both World Wars.

Lentia. See LINZ.

Len·ti·ni \len-ˈtē-nē\; *anc.* **Le·on·ti·ni** \ˌlē-ən-ˈtī-ˌnī\. Commune, Siracusa prov., SE Sicily, Italy, 22 mi. (35 km.) NW of the seaport of Siracusa; pop. (1989c) 29,780; one of the oldest Greek settlements in Sicily, founded 729 B.C. Birthplace of Sophist Gorgias c. 483 B.C.

Lentium. See LENS.

Lentschiza. See ŁĘCZYCA.

Le·o·ben \lā-ˈō-bən\. City, Styria, Austria, on Mur River 27 mi. (43 km.) NW of Graz; pop. (1991c) 28,897; manufactures metal goods; lignite mining; university of mining and metallurgy (1840); preliminary peace treaty bet. France and Austria signed here 1797.

Leobschütz. See GŁUBCZYCE.

Le·o·la \lē-ˈō-lə\. City, ⊗ of McPherson co., N South Dakota; pop. (1990c) 521.

Leom·in·ster. **1.** \ˈle-mən-stər\. City, Worcester co., cen. Massachusetts, 5 mi. (8 km.) SSE of Fitchburg; pop. (1990c) 38,145; plastics, paper products, furniture, chemicals. Part of Lancaster until 1740; chartered as city 1915. Birthplace of John Chapman (Johnny Appleseed) 1774.

2. \ˈlem-stər, ˈle-mən-stər\. Market town, Hereford and Worcester, W England, on the Lugg 40 mi. (64 km.) WSW of Birmingham; pop. (1991p) 39,000.

Le·on **1.** \lē-ən\. River, Texas; rises in Eastland co.; 185 mi. (298 km.) long.

2. \ˈlē-ən, ˈlē-ˌän\. Name of counties in two states of the U.S. See tables at FLORIDA and TEXAS.

3. \ˈlē-ən, ˈlē-ˌän\. City, ⊗ of Decatur co., S Iowa, 60 mi. (97 km.) S of Des Moines; pop. (1990c) 2047.

4. \lā-ˈōn\. Municipality, SW Iloilo prov., Panay, Philippines, 14 mi. (23 km.) WNW of City of Iloilo; pop. (1980c) 31,552.

Le·ón \lā-ˈōn\. **1.** Former name of Cotopaxi prov., Ecuador. See COTOPAXI 2.

2. Municipality, Guanajuato state, cen. Mexico, 32 mi. (51 km.) WNW of the city of Guanajuato; pop. (1990p) 872,453; tanneries, flour mills; leather goods, soap, gold and silver embroidery; founded 1576.

3. Department of W Nicaragua. See table at NICARAGUA.

4. City, ✻ of León dept. and 2d largest city in Nicaragua, on railroad line near Pacific coast ab. 50 mi. (80 km.) NW of Managua; cotton gins; cigars, leather products; exports sugar and cotton; university; several colonial churches; 18th cent. cathedral; city founded by Spanish explorer Fernández de Córdoba c. 1524 on the shore of Lake Managua; destroyed 1609 by violent eruption of Momotombo and earthquake, and rebuilt on its present site 1610; former ✻ of Nicaragua; has had long political and commercial rivalry with city of Granada. Burial place of poet Ruben Dario.

5. Historical region and ancient kingdom, NW Spain; bounded on N by Asturias, on E by Old Castile, on S by Extremadura, on SW by Portugal, and on NW by Galicia; comprises modern provs. of León, Salamanca, Zamora; 14,884 sq. mi. (38,550 sq. km.); traversed by Duero River and its affluents, the Esla and Tormes; cen. subtropical valley rises to severely cold mountain ranges on N and S borders; produces hops, flax, cereals; beech and chestnut timber; coal, iron mines; stock raising.

History: Independent Christian kingdom, ruled 910–914 by Garcia, son of Alfonso III of Asturias, after earlier Asturian reconquest of town of León from Moors in 8th cent.; ruled 999–1028 by Alfonso V; reconquest of León from Moors completed in 11th cent.; united with Castile 1037–1157, independent kingdom 1157–1230, and permanently reunited with Castile 1230; its chief city after union with Castile was Burgos.

6. Province of NW Spain. See table at SPAIN.

7. City, ✻ of León prov., NW Spain, 82 mi. (132 km.) NW of Valladolid; pop. (1991c) 144,021; tourist center; leather goods, iron, lumber; 13th cent. Gothic cathedral; 12th cent. convent; 11th cent. church of San Isidoro containing burial place of the early kings and queens of León and Castile. Ancient Roman military station; ✻ of medieval kingdom of León.

León, Is·la de \ˈēs-lä-ˌthā-lā-ˈōn\. **1.** Island, Cádiz prov., SW Spain; 10 mi. (16 km.) long and 2 mi. (3 km.) wide.

2. Seaport, Spain. See SAN FERNANDO 8.

Leon·ard Mur·ray, Mount \ˈle-nərd-ˈmər-ē\. Mountain, Papua New Guinea, cen. New Guinea I., NW of Kikori; 7808 ft. (2380 m.); source of several rivers.

Leon·ard·town \ˈle-nərd-ˌtau̇n\. Town, ⊗ of St. Marys co., S Maryland, on an inlet of the estuary of the Potomac River; pop. (1990c) 1475.
Le·on·berg \ˈlā-ȯn-ˌberk\. City, Baden-Württemberg, Germany, 8 mi. (13 km.) WNW of Stuttgart; pop. (1980c) 38,927; 14th cent. church; became city 1248; to Württemberg 1318.
Leon·ding \ˈlā-ȯn-ˌdiŋ\. Town, Upper Austria, Austria, WSW of Linz; pop. (1991c) 21,209.
Le·o·ne, Mon·te \ˈmȯn-tā-lā-ˈō-nā\. Highest peak of the Lepontine Alps, bet. Switzerland and Italy, on SW side of Simplon Pass. See table at ALPS.
Le·o·nia \lē-ˈō-nyə, -nē-ə\. Residential borough, Bergen co., NE New Jersey, 10 mi. (16 km.) N of Jersey City; pop. (1990c) 8365.
Le·o·nine City \ˈlē-ə-ˌnīn\. Historic section of Rome, Italy, W of the Tiber River; includes the Vatican.
Leontini. See LENTINI.
Le·on·top·o·lis \ˌlē-ən-ˈtä-pə-lis\. City of ancient Egypt, in Nile Delta 17 mi. (27 km.) N of Cairo; site of the Temple of Onias built c. 2d cent. B.C. by the Jewish high priest Onias IV.
Le·o·pold and As·trid Coast \ˈlē-ə-ˌpōld ... ˈas-trid\. Section of Antarctica coast on Indian Ocean, W of Wilkes Land, 67°10′S, 84°10′E.
Leopold Coast. See LUITPOLD COAST.
Le·o·polds·berg \ˈlē-ə-ˌpōldz-ˌbərg, ˈlā-ə-ˌpȯlts-ˌberk\. Elevation, Austria, ab. 5.5 mi. (9 km.) NW of Vienna, in the Wienerwald; 1388 ft. (423 m.).
Leopold II, Lake. See MAI-NDOMBE, LAC.
Léopoldville. See KINSHASA.
Le·o·ti \lē-ˈō-ˌtī\. City, ⊗ of Wichita co., W Kansas; pop. (1990c) 1738.
Le·pan·to \lē-ˈpän-tō\. See NÁVPAKTOS.
Lepanto, Gulf of. See CORINTH, GULF OF.
Lepanto Strait. Narrow channel connecting Gulfs of Patras and Corinth and separating N Peloponnese from cen. mainland of Greece. For battle of Lepanto, see NÁVPAKTOS.
Le Per·reux–sur–Marne \lə-pe-ˈrœ-sūr-ˈmärn\. Commune, Val de Marne dept., N France, ESE suburb of Paris on Marne River.
Le Petit Andely. See LES ANDELYS.
Le Pe·tit–Que·vil·ly \lə-pə-ˌtē-kə-vē-ˈyē\. Commune, Seine-Maritime dept., N France, WSW suburb of Rouen on Seine River; pop. (1990c) 22,718.
Le·pi·ni Mountains \lā-ˈpē-nē\ *or Ital.* **Mon·ti Lepini** \ˈmȯn-tē-lā-ˈpē-nē\; *anc.* **Vol·scian Mountains** \ˈvȯl-shən, ˈväl-\. Mountain range in SE Roma prov., Lazio, cen. Italy; highest peak 5039 ft. (1536 m.).
Le Ples·sis–Rob·in·son \lə-ple-ˈsē-rō-beⁿ-ˈsȯⁿ\. Commune, Hauts-de-Seine dept., France, S of Paris.
Lepontine Alps. See table at ALPS.
Le Port \lə-ˈpȯr\; *formerly* **Port–des–Ga·lets** \ˌpȯr-dā-gä-ˈlā\. Seaport on NW coast of the French island of Réunion in the Indian Ocean E of Madagascar; pop. (1990c) 29,190.
Le Prê·cheur \lə-prā-ˈshœr\. Coastal town, NW Martinique, West Indies; at foot of Mont Pelée whose eruption 1902 destroyed the town.
Le Pré–Saint–Ger·vais \lə-ˈprā-ˌseⁿ-zher-ˈvā\. Commune, Seine-St.-Denis dept., N France, NE suburb of Paris.
Lep·tis Mag·na \ˈlep-tis-ˈmag-nə\; *mod.* **Lab·dah** \ˈlab-də\ *also* **Leb·da** \ˈleb-də\. Ancient seaport in Roman Africa, now a suburb of Al Khums, Libya; founded by Phoenicians c. 6th cent. B.C.; one of three chief cities of Tripolis (see TRIPOLI 1); after Second Punic War under Masinissa, king of Numidia, from 202 B.C.; made a Roman colony by Emperor Trajan; birthplace 146 A.D. of Emperor Lucius Septimius Severus who was largely responsible for present plan of the city; some of best preserved Roman North African ruins, among them the forum, harbor, amphitheater, baths, and a basilica.
Leptis Mi·nor \ˈmī-nər\ *or* **Leptis Par·va** \pär-və\; *mod.* **Lam·ta** \ˈlam-tə\. Ancient town, Byzacium, N Africa, SE of Hadrumetum (modern Sousse, Tunisia); loyal to Rome from end of Second Punic War, prosperous under the Roman Empire.
Le Puglie. See PUGLIA.
Le Puy \lə-ˈpwē\; *formerly* **Le Puy–en–Ve·lay** \-äⁿ-və-ˈlā\; *medieval* **Ani·ci·um** \ə-ˈnish-(ē-)əm\ *or* **Po·di·um Ani·cen·sis** \ˈpō-dē-əm-ˌa-nə-ˈsen-sis\. City, ✱ of Haute-Loire dept., S cen. France, 65 mi. (105 km.) SE of Clermont-Ferrand; pop. (1990c) 23,434; in a mountainous volcanic region; has 12th cent. Romanesque cathedral and 10th cent. Gothic church. From 10th cent., a pilgrimage site.
Le Ques·noy \lə-kā-ˈnwä\. Commune, Nord dept., N France, 9 mi. (14 km.) SE of Valenciennes; occupied by Germans during both World Wars.
Lera. See LÉRINS, ÎLES DE.
L'Éra·ble \lā-ˈräblᵊ\. County, Quebec, Canada. See table at QUEBEC.
Le Rain·cy \lə-reⁿ-ˈsē\. Commune, Seine-St.-Denis dept., N France, NNE suburb of Paris.
Ler·ca·ra Frid·di \ler-ˈkä-rä-ˈfrē-dē\. Commune, Palermo prov., NW cen. Sicily, Italy, 29 mi. (47 km.) ESE of the seaport of Palermo; pop. (1981p) 9829.
Ler·do \ˈler-dō\. Town, Durango state, NW cen. Mexico, just S of Gómez Palacio; munic. pop. (1990p) 97,660.
Le·ri·be \lā-ˈrē-bā\. Town, N Lesotho; area pop. (1986c) 274,935.
Le·ri·ci \ˈlā-rē-ˌchē\. Seaport, La Spezia prov., Liguria, NW Italy, on Gulf of La Spezia 6 mi. (10 km.) SE of the seaport of La Spezia; pop. (1981p) 13,509; medieval castle.
Lé·ri·da \ˈlā-rē-t͟hä\. **1.** Province of NE Spain. See table at SPAIN.
2. *or* **Llei·da** \ˈyā-t͟hä\; *anc.* **Iler·da** \i-ˈlər-də\. Commune, its ✱, on Segre River 77 mi. (124 km.) E of Saragossa; pop. (1991p) 111,880; trades in wine, wool, leather, cattle, and fruit; two cathedrals; palaces. Scene of defeat of Roman statesman Pompey the Great's generals by Gen. Julius Caesar 49 B.C.; made episcopal see during Visigoth occupation; seat of medieval university; occupied by Moors early 8th cent.; captured by Ramón Berenguer IV of Aragon 1149 and by French 1707 and 1808; served as defensive position during 1930s Spanish Civil War.
Lerin. See FLORINA 2.
Lé·rins, Îles de \ˌāl-də-lā-ˈreⁿs\. Two islands, **Sainte–Mar·gue·rite** \ˌseⁿt-ˌmär-gə-ˈrēt\ (*anc.* **Le·ra** \ˈlir-ə\) and **Saint–Ho·no·rat** \seⁿ-ˌtä-nə-ˈrä\ (*anc.* **Le·ri·na** \lə-ˈrī-nə\), in the Mediterranean Sea off Cannes, Alpes-Maritimes dept., SE France.
Ler·ma, Río \ˌrē-ō-ˈler-mä\. The upper course of the Río Santiago, SW Mexico. See SANTIAGO, RÍO.
Ler·na \ˈlər-nə\ *or* **Ler·ne** \-nē\. Marsh and stream in ancient Argolis, E Peloponnese, S Greece, near Árgos; celebrated in Greek legend as the place where Hercules killed the Lernaean Hydra.
Le Roncole. See RONCOLE.
Le·ros \ˈler-ös\ *or Ital.* **Le·ro** \ˈler-ō\. An island of the Dodecanese (*q.v.*), Greece, N of Kalymnos; 28 sq. mi. (73 sq. km.).
Le Roy \li-ˈrȯi, ˈlē-ˌrȯi\. **1.** City, McLean co., cen. Illinois, 15 mi. (24 km.) SE of Bloomington; pop. (1990c) 2777.
2. Village, Genesee co., W New York, 24 mi. (39 km.) WSW of Rochester; pop. (1990c) 4974.
Ler·wick \ˈlər-wik\. Burgh, ⊗ of Shetland administrative area, Shetland Is., N Scotland; pop. (1981c) 7901; fishing; knitwear; services related to oil production; most northerly town in British Isles.
Les An·de·lys \ˌlā-zäⁿ-ˈdlē\. Commune, Eure dept., N France, on right bank of Seine River 20 mi. (32 km.) NE of Évreux; used for two small settlements, **Le Grand An·de·ly** \lə-ˌgräⁿ-täⁿ-ˈdlē\ and **Le Pe·tit Andely** \ləp-ˌtē-täⁿ-ˈdlē\; 13th cent. cathedral; ruins of Château Gaillard, built c. 1196 by English King Richard I (Cœur de Lion). Damaged during WWII.
Le Sars \lə-ˈsär\. Village, Pas-de-Calais dept., N France, just SW of Bapaume; scene of heavy fighting 1916, a phase of WWI battle of the Somme.

\ə\ abut \ᵊ\ kitten, Fr table \ər\ further \a\ ash \ā\ ace \ä\ cot, cart \ȧ\ Fr bac \au̇\ out \b̲\ Span Avila \ch\ chin \e\ bet \ē\ easy \g\ go \i\ hit \ī\ ice \j\ job \k̲\ Ger ich, Buch \ⁿ\ Fr vin \ŋ\ sing \ō\ go \ȯ\ all \ȯ\ law \œ\ Fr bœuf \œ̄\ Fr feu \ȯi\ boy \th\ thin \t͟h\ this \ü\ loot \u̇\ foot \ue\ Ger füllen \ue̅\ Fr rue \y\ yet \ʸ\ Fr digne \ˈdēnʸ\, nuit \ˈnwʸē\ \yü\ few \yu̇\ fury \zh\ vision

Le·sa·ti·ma \ˌle-sä-ˈtē-mä\ *also* **Sat·ti·ma** \sä-ˈtē-mä\. Peak, cen. Kenya, N of Nairobi, in Aberdare National Park; 13,104 ft. (3994 m.).

Les Basques \lā-ˈbȧsk\. County, Quebec, Canada. See table at QUEBEC.

Les Baux–de–Pro·vence \lā-ˌbō-də-prȯ-ˈvä^{n}s\; *formerly* **Les Beaux** \lā-ˈbō\. Commune, Bouches-du-Rhône dept., SE France, 9 mi. (14 km.) NE of Arles; pop. (1990c) 458; important in Middle Ages, now has many ruins; destroyed during 17th cent. religious wars; bauxite, which takes its name from the town, first discovered near here 1821.

Les·bos \ˈlez-ˌvōs; ˈlez-ˌbäs, -bəs\ *or* **Myt·i·le·ne** *also* **Mit·y·le·ne** *or Gk.* **Mi·ti·lí·ni** \ˌmē-tē-ˈlē-nē\. Island in E Aegean Sea off NW coast of Turkey in Asia, by some included among the Southern Sporades (see SPORADES); 630 sq. mi. (1632 sq. km.); pop. (1991e) 103,700; exports olives; fishing, livestock raising; grain, soap, hides; with Lemnos and Hagios Evstrátios, forms Lesbos dept., Northern Aegean region, Greece (see table at GREECE). Hilly, with highest point 3080 ft. (939 m.); cut from S into center by Gulf of Kalloni. Chief town Mytilene.

History: Evidence of inhabitation during Bronze Age; early first millennium B.C., peopled by Aeolians and became chief Aeolian settlement on Asian coast; active in commerce; in 7th cent. B.C. famous for its lyric poets, esp. Alcaeus and Sappho; declined in influence in 6th cent. B.C.; yielded to Persians; member of Delian League; frequently involved in wars before beginning of Christian era. Held by Byzantines, Seljuqs, Venetians, Genoese, and after 1462 by Turks; annexed by Greece 1913; held by Germans during WWII. See AEGEAN ISLANDS.

Les Chutes–de–la–Chau·dière \le-ˌshu̇t-də-lȧ-shō-ˈdyer\. County, Quebec, Canada. See table at QUEBEC.

Les Col·lines–de–l'Ou·ta·ouais \lā-kȯ-ˌlēn-də-lü-tə-ˈwā\. County, Quebec, Canada. See table at QUEBEC.

Les Combarelles. See EYZIES, LES.

Les Éparges \lā-zā-ˈpärzh\. Village, Meuse dept., NE France, 7 mi. (11 km.) SE of Verdun; scene of bitter fighting 1915 during WWI.

Les Etch·e·mins \lā-ze-chə-ˈme^{n}\. County, Quebec, Canada. See table at QUEBEC.

Les Eyzies. See EYZIES, LES.

Les Gonaïves. See GONAÏVES.

Lesh. See LEZHË.

Le·shan *or W.-G.* **Le–shan** \ˈlə-ˈshän\ *or* **Lo–shan** \ˈlȯ-\; *formerly* **Kia·ting** \ˈjyä-ˈdiŋ\. City, SW Sichuan prov., S cen. China, on right bank of Min River 77 mi. (124 km.) S of Chengdu; starting point for nearby pilgrimage sites incl. Emei Shan, ab. 30 mi. (48 km.) to the W.

Les Îles–de–la–Mad·e·leine \lā-ˌzēl-də-lȧ-mȧd-ˈlen\. Island group constituting a county of Quebec, Canada. See MAGDALEN ISLANDS and table at QUEBEC.

Lesina. See HVAR.

Le·si·na, La·go di \ˈlä-gō-dē-lā-ˈzē-nä\. Lagoon on N coast of Gargano Promontory, SE Italy.

Les Jar·dins–de–Na·pier·ville \lā-zhär-ˌdēn-də-ˈnȧ-pyer-ˌvēl\. County, Quebec, Canada. See table at QUEBEC.

Les·ko·vac *or* **Les·ko·vats** \ˈles-kȯ-ˌväts\. Town, Serbia, SE Yugoslavia, on S branch of the Morava River ab. 75 mi. (120 km.) NE of Skopje; manufactures furniture, soap, textiles.

Les Landes \lā-ˈlä^{n}d\. Sandy coastal region, Gironde and Landes depts., SW France, bet. the Gironde and the Adour; lagoons near the seashore; pine forests inland.

Les Lau·ren·tides \lā-ˌlō-rä^{n}-ˈtēd\. County, Quebec, Canada. See table at QUEBEC.

Les·lie \ˈles-lē\. County in SE Kentucky. See table at KENTUCKY.

Les Li·las \ˌlā-lē-ˈlä\. Commune, Seine-St.-Denis dept., N France, NW suburb of Paris.

Les Martigues. See MARTIGUES.

Les Mas·kou·tains \lā-ˌmȧ-skü-ˈten\. County, Quebec, Canada. See table at QUEBEC.

Les Mou·lins \lā-mü-ˈlen\. County, Quebec, Canada. See table at QUEBEC.

Les Mu·reaux \ˌlā-mu̅e̅-ˈrō\. Commune, Yvelines dept., N France, on the Seine WNW of Paris.

Le·so·tho \lə-ˈsō-tō, lə-ˈsü-tü\; *formerly* **Ba·su·to·land** \bə-ˈsü-tō-ˌland\. Kingdom, S Africa, an enclave lying within the Rep. of South Africa; 11,716 sq. mi. (30,344 sq. km.); pop. (1993e) 1,903,000; ✻ and only large town Maseru.

Physical features: Mountainous, with ab. 80 percent of land bet. 6000 and 11,000 ft. (1830 and 3350 m.) above sea level; has Drakensberg along E border; highest point Thabana Ntlenyana 11,425 ft. (3482 m.); main rivers Orange and Caledon, the latter constituting country's W border.

Chief products: Corn, wheat, peas, beans, sorghum; mohair; diamonds.

History: Before 1800 inhabited by native peoples (as the Sothos); in early 19th cent. many disputes with Boers; from c. 1830 area loosely organized and guided by Sotho Chief Mshweshwe; first received British protection 1843; annexed 1868 and made part of Cape Colony 1871; separated from Cape Colony and made a British colony 1884; achieved independence and adopted name Lesotho 1966.

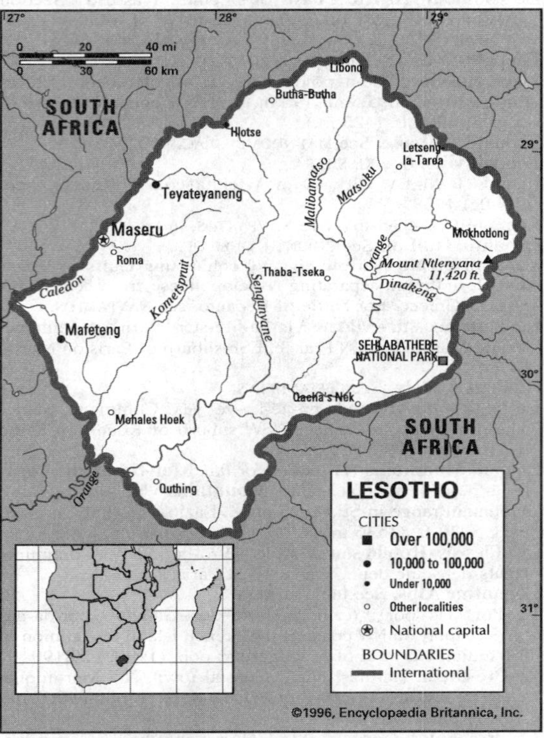

Les Pays–d'en–Haut \lā-ˌpe^{y}-dä^{n}-ˈō\. County, Quebec, Canada. See table at QUEBEC.

Les Planches \lā-ˈplä^{n}sh\. **1.** Town, Canada. See AMHERST 8. **2.** Commune, Vaud canton, W Switzerland, at E end of Lake Geneva. See MONTREUX.

Les Sa·bles–d'Olonne \lā-ˌsäb-lə-dō-ˈlōn\. Commune, Vendée dept., W France, on Bay of Biscay 21 mi. (34 km.) SW of La Roche-sur-Yon.

Les Saintes. See ÎLES DES SAINTES.

Les·say \le-ˈsā\. Village, Normandy, Manche dept., NW France, 12 mi. (19 km.) NNW of Coutances; 11th cent. church heavily damaged in WWII has been restored.

Les·se \ˈles, ˈle-sə\. River, SE Belgium; flows W through rocky gorges, partly underground, into Meuse River; 50 mi. (80 km.) long.

Lesser An·til·les \an-ˈti-lēz\. One of the three divisions of the West Indies (*q.v.*) comprising the islands stretching in an arc from Puerto Rico to the NE coast of South America and the islands N of Venezuela; includes Virgin Is., Leeward Is., Windward Is., and the islands of the Netherlands Antilles, and is generally considered to include Barbados, Trinidad, and Tobago.

Lesser Ar·me·nia \är-ˈmē-nē-ə, -nyə\. **1.** Former district, Asia Minor. See ARMENIA MINOR.
2. Kingdom, Cilicia. See LITTLE ARMENIA.
3. Region, Turkey. See CILICIA.

Lesser Himalayas. See HIMALAYAS, THE.

Lesser Khingan Mountains. See XIAO HINGGAN LING.

Lesser Slave Lake \ˈslāv\. Lake, cen. Alberta, Canada; 461 sq. mi. (1194 sq. km.); its outlet is **Lesser Slave River,** a tributary of the Athabaska.

Lesser Sunda Islands. See SUNDA ISLES.

Lesser Tunb. See TUNB.

Lesser Walachia. See OLTENIA.

Les·sines \le-ˈsēn\. Commune, Hainaut prov., SW Belgium, on Dender River 25 mi. (40 km.) SW of Brussels; pop. (1991c) 16,076.

Les·si·ni Mountains \le-ˈsē-nē\ *or Ital.* **Mon·ti Lessini** \ˈmȯn-tē\. Mountain group, SW Dolomites, NE Italy, E of Lake Garda; highest peak 5485 ft. (1672 m.).

Lessö. See LÆSØ.

Les Trois–Évê·chés \lā-ˈtrwä-zā-ve-ˈshā\. Ancient district in duchy of Lorraine; comprised the three bishoprics of Verdun, Toul, and Metz (the cities and some surrounding territory) which belonged to Germany in Middle Ages; taken by Henry II of France 1552; now included in Meuse, Moselle, and Meurthe-et-Moselle depts., NE France.

Le Sueur \lə-ˈsu̇r\. **1.** County in S Minnesota. See table at MINNESOTA.
2. City, Le Sueur co., S Minnesota, on Minnesota River 20 mi. (32 km.) N of Mankato; pop. (1990c) 3714.

Lesz·czy·ny \lesh-ˈchi-ni\. Commune, Katowice prov., S Poland, pop. (1989e) 29,893.

Lesz·no \ˈlesh-nȯ\ *or Ger.* **Lis·sa** \ˈli-sə\. **1.** Province, W Poland. See table at POLAND.
2. Commune, its ✻, 41 mi. (66 km.) SSW of Poznań; pop. (1989e) 57,589; grain market; machinery. Became city 1547; center of Moravians in Poland in 16th and 17th cents.; residence of Czech theologian and educator Jan Ámos Komenský (Comenius); burned by Poles 1656 in war with Sweden; ceded to Prussia 1793; returned to Poland 1919.

Letch·er \ˈle-chər\. County in SE Kentucky. See table at KENTUCKY.

Letch·worth \ˈlech-ˌwərth\. Town, Hertfordshire, SE England, 34 mi. (55 km.) N of London; pop. (1981c) 31,431; high technology; printing and publishing; first British garden city (1903).

Le·tea \ˈle-ˌtyä\ *also* **Lu·tea** \ˈlü-\. Marshy region, E Romania, on Black Sea coast forming an island bet. the Kiliya (on N) and Sulina branches of the Danube.

Le Teil \lə-ˈtā\. Town, Ardèche dept., SE France, on the Rhone 42 mi. (68 km.) NNW of Avignon.

Leth·bridge \ˈleth-ˌbrij\. City, S Alberta, Canada, on Oldman River 110 mi. (177 km.) SSE of Calgary; pop. (1991c) 60,974; center of irrigated farming region; Lethbridge Community Coll. (1957), Univ. of Lethbridge (1967); founded as a coal-mining settlement; named Lethbridge 1885. Fort Whoop-up, notorious for its whiskey trade in the early 1870s, was nearby.

Le·ti *or* **Let·ti** \ˈle-tē\. **1.** Island group, Moluccas, Indonesia, in S part NE of Timor; ab. 290 sq. mi. (465 sq. km.); comprises Leti, Moa, and Lakor islands and a few adjacent islets.
2. Westernmost island of Leti group ab. 25 mi. (40 km.) E of E point of Timor; 9 mi. (15 km.) long by 3 to 5 mi. (5 to 8 km.) wide.

Le·ti·cia \le-ˈtē-syä\. Town, ✻ of Amazonas dept., SE Colombia, on the Amazon River; pop. (1992e) 32,700; border town claimed by Peru and Colombia until Peru ceded it by treaty 1922; seized by Peruvian forces 1932; restored to Colombia by League of Nations, decision finally accepted by both countries 1934.

Let·mathe \ˈlet-ˌmä-tə\. City, North Rhine-Westphalia, Germany, 27 mi. (43 km.) ESE of Essen.

Let·pa·dan \ˌlet-pə-ˈdän\. Town, Pegu div., Myanmar, on railroad line 75 mi. (121 km.) NW of Yangon.

Le Tré·port \lə-trā-ˈpȯr\. Town, N Seine-Maritime dept., N France, on the English Channel 19 mi. (31 km.) NE of Dieppe; 16th cent. church; remains of 11th cent. abbey; important port in Middle Ages.

Let·sôk–aw Island \ˌlāt-sȯ-ˈkȯ\; *formerly* **Do·mel Island** \ˈdō-ˌmel\. Island, cen. Mergui Archipelago (*q.v.*), Myanmar.

Letti. See LETI.

Lettland. See LATVIA.

Leucadia *and* **Leucas.** See LEVKÁS.

Leucates. See DOUKATO, CAPE.

Leu·ca·yec \ˌleu̇-kä-ˈyek\. Island in N section of Chonos Archipelago, in Pacific Ocean off SW coast of Chile.

Leuc·tra \ˈlük-trə\. Ancient village in Boeotia, E cen. Greece, 10 mi. (16 km.) SW of Thebes; scene of battle 371 B.C. in which Thebans under Gen. Epaminondas defeated Spartans under King Cleombrotus I, breaking Spartan supremacy.

Leuk \ˈlȯik\. Town, Valais canton, SW cen. Switzerland, on the Rhone NE of Sion; pop. (1980c) 2983; hot mineral springs.

Leukas. See LEVKÁS.

Leu·ser, Mount \ˈlü-sər\ *also* **Mount Lo·ser** \ˈlō-sər\. Mountain, Indonesia, ab. 200 mi. (320 km.) from NW end of Sumatra, near coast; 11,090 ft. (3380 m.).

Leuthen. See LUTYNIA.

Leuven. See LOUVAIN.

Leuze \ˈlœz\ *or in full* **Leuze–en–Hai·naut** \-ˌäⁿ-e-ˈnō\. Commune, Hainaut prov., SW Belgium, 11 mi. (18 km.) E of Tournai; pop. (1991c) 12,869; scene of battle 1691 in which forces under Francois-Henri de Montmorency-Bouteville, duc de Luxembourg, defeated the army under Prince George Frederick of Waldeck.

Léva. See LEVICE.

Le·vá·dhia \le-ˈvä-t͟hē-ä\ *or* **Le·vá·deia** \le-ˈvä-t͟hē-ä\ *or* **Le·vad·ia** \li-ˈva-dē-ə\ *also* **Le·ba·dea** \ˌle-bə-ˈdē-ə\. Commune, ✻ of Boeotia dept., E Central Greece region, Greece, ab. 60 mi. (95 km.) NW of Athens; pop. (1981p) 17,697.

Le Val d'Ajol \lə-ˌväl-dä-ˈzhōl\. Commune, Vosges dept., NE France, comprising many hamlets in the Vosges Mts.

Le·val·lois–Per·ret \lə-ˌväl-ˌwä-pə-ˈrā\. Commune, Hauts-de-Seine dept., N France, NW suburb of Paris on Seine River; pop. (1990c) 47,788; automobiles.

Le Val–Saint–Fran·çois \lə-ˌväl-ˌseⁿ-fräⁿ-ˈswä\. County, Quebec, Canada. See table at QUEBEC.

Le·vang·er \le-ˈväŋ-ər\. Town, Nord-Trøndelag co., N cen. Norway, at head of Trondheim Fjord; pop. (1992c) 17,027.

Le·vant \lə-ˈvant, -ˈvänt\. Name given to the E shores of the Mediterranean Sea, bet. W Greece and W Egypt.

Le·vant, Île du \ˌēl-dü-lə-ˈväⁿ\. One of the Hyères Is. (*q.v.*).

Levante, Riviera di. See RIVIERA.

Levant States. See SYRIA 2.

Le Vauclin. See VAUCLIN.

Lev·el·land \ˈle-və-ˌland\. City, ⊗ of Hockley co., NW Texas, 26 mi. (42 km.) W of Lubbock; pop. (1990c) 13,986; South Plains Coll. (1958).

Le·ven \ˈlē-vən\. **1.** River, Strathclyde region, W Scotland; flows out of S end of Loch Lomond into Clyde River at Dumbarton; ab. 7 mi. (11 km.) long.
2. River, Tayside and Fife regions, E Scotland; flows E out of Loch Leven into Firth of Forth; 16 mi. (26 km.) long.
3. Seaport burgh, Fife region, E Scotland, on Firth of Forth at mouth of the Leven; pop. (1981p) 8591; lumber; seaside resort. Nearby is Largo, birthplace of Alexander Selkirk 1676, the sailor who was the prototype of English novelist Daniel Defoe's Robinson Crusoe.

Leven, Loch. **1.** Arm of Loch Linnhe, Highland region, W Scotland; 11 mi. (18 km.) long.

2. Lake in Tayside region, E cen. Scotland; max. depth 83 ft. (25 m.); has island on which are ruins of an ancient priory and another with the ruins of Lochleven Castle, where Mary, Queen of Scots, was held prisoner 1567–68.

Le·veque, Cape \lə-ˈvek\. Cape at N tip of Dampier Land on N coast of Western Australia, Australia.

Le·ver·ku·sen \ˌlā-vər-ˈküz-^{ə}n\. Industrial city, North Rhine-Westphalia, Germany, on Rhine River 16 mi. (26 km.) SE of Düsseldorf; pop. (1992e) 161,147; chemicals, textiles; formed 1930.

Le·vi·a·than Peak \li-ˈvī-ə-thən\. Mountain, San Juan co., SW Colorado; 13,528 ft. (4123 m.).

Le·vi·ce \ˈle-vit-ˌse\ *or Hung.* **Lé·va** \ˈlā-ˌvö\ *or Ger.* **Le·wenz** \ˈlā-ˌvents\. Town, S Slovakia, 75 mi. (121 km.) E of Bratislava; pop. (1980p) 26,132.

Le·vi·co \ˈlā-vē-ˌkō\ *or* **Levico Ter·me** \ˈter-mā\. Commune, S Trento prov., Trentino-Alto Adige, NE Italy, in the Dolomites just E of the commune of Trento; pop. (1981p) 5566.

Le·vin \lə-ˈvēn\. Borough, SW North I., New Zealand; pop. (1992e) 19,050.

Le·vi·sa Bay \lā-ˈvē-sä\. Bay in E Cuba, E of and adjoining Nipe Bay.

Levisa Fork \lə-ˈvī-sə\. River, E Kentucky; rises in NW Buchanan co., SW Virginia, flows N into Kentucky and unites with Tug Fork to form the Big Sandy River (*q.v.*); ab. 160 mi. (255 km.) long.

Lé·vis–Lau·zon \le-ˌvē-lō-ˈzō^{n}\. City, S Quebec, Canada, on right bank of St. Lawrence River opp. Quebec City; pop. (1991c) 39,452; shipbuilding; military fort.

History: Lévis, formerly Aubigny, renamed 1861; Lauzon, orig. named Pointe de Levy by French explorer Samuel de Champlain 1625, renamed 1867; site from which British Gen. James Wolfe undertook siege of Quebec 1759; cities united 1980s.

Lev·it·town \ˈle-vət-ˌtau̇n\. **1.** Unincorporated settlement, Nassau co., SE New York, on Long Island E of New York City; pop. (1990c) 53,286.

2. Urban township. See WILLINGBORO.

Lev·ka \ˈlef-kä\. Mountain, W cen. Crete, Greece, S of Canea; 8045 ft. (2452 m.); 2d highest peak in the island.

Lev·kás \lef-ˈkäs\ *also* **Lef·kás** \lef-\ *or* **Leu·cas** \ˈlü-kəs\; *anc.* **Leu·ca·dia** \lü-ˈkā-dē-ə\ *or Ital.* **San·ta Mau·ra** \ˈsän-tä-ˈmau̇-rä\. **1.** One of the Ionian Is., in the Ionian Sea off W coast of Greece, S of the entrance to Amvrakikós Kólpos; constitutes a department of Greece (see table at GREECE). Mountainous (highest ab. 3000 ft. or 910 m.), with little level ground; produces much olive oil, currants, and wine. S point is Cape Doukato (*q.v.*). Settled by Corinthians 7th cent. B.C.; has ancient cyclopean walls, remains of temple to Apollo Leukates, and several forts; by some scholars thought to be the Ithaca of the *Odyssey*, rather than nearby Ithaca itself.

2. Town, ✻ of Levkás dept., Ionian Is., Greece.

Levkosia. See NICOSIA 1.

Lé·vri·er Bay \ˌlā-vrē-ˈā\. Inlet of Atlantic Ocean on W coast of Mauritania, E of Cape Blanc.

Le·vu·ka \lä-ˈvü-kä\. Town, E coast of Ovalau I., W cen. Fiji, SW Pacific Ocean; pop. (1986c) 1186; ✻ of Fiji under British 1874–82.

Le·vy \ˈlē-vē\. Coastal county in NW Florida Penin. See table at FLORIDA.

Lewenz. See LEVICE.

Lew·es \ˈlü-əs\. **1.** Seaport town, Sussex co., S Delaware, on S end of Delaware Bay 15 mi. (24 km.) NW of Georgetown; pop. (1990c) 2295; settled 1631 by Dutch; bombarded by British during the War of 1812. Sheltered by Delaware Breakwater (built 19th cent.).

2. *or* **Upper Yukon.** River, S cen. Yukon, Canada; rises in Tagish and Atlin lakes on S border and flows NW through Lake Laberge to unite with Pelly River and form the Yukon River; 338 mi. (544 km.) long; considered the upper course of the Yukon; dammed for power production 1958.

3. Town, ⊗ of East Sussex, S England, on the Ouse 6 mi. (10 km.) N of English Channel and 43 mi. (69 km.) S of London; pop. (1981c) 14,772; beer; ruins of 11th cent. castle; scene of battle 1264 in which Simon de Montfort, earl of Leicester, defeated Henry III.

Lew·ey, Mount \ˈlü-ē\. Peak, Adirondack Mts., Hamilton co., NE cen. New York; 3740 ft. (1140 m.).

Lewey Lake Mountain. Peak in the Adirondack Mts., NE New York; 3903 ft. (1190 m.).

Lew·is \ˈlü-əs\. **1.** Early name of Snake River, Idaho.

2. River, SW Washington; rises in NE Skamania co., flows WSW into Columbia River forming boundary bet. Cowlitz and Clark cos.; ab. 80 mi. (130 km.) long.

3. Name of counties in seven states of the U.S. See tables at IDAHO, KENTUCKY, MISSOURI, NEW YORK, TENNESSEE, WASHINGTON, WEST VIRGINIA.

4. *or* **The Lews** \ˈlüz\. N section of the island of Lewis with Harris, in the Outer Hebrides off NW coast of Scotland; belongs to Western Isles region.

Lewis, Butt of. Headland on N tip of island of Lewis with Harris, in the Outer Hebrides off NW coast of Scotland; lighthouse.

Lewis and Clark \ˈklärk\. County in W cen. Montana. See table at MONTANA.

Lewis and Clark Caverns; *formerly* **Mor·ri·son Cave** \ˈmȯr-ə-sən, ˈmär-\. Limestone cave in SE Jefferson co., cen. Montana; preserved in a state park.

Lewis and Clark Lake *or* **Lewis & Clark Lake.** Reservoir in the Missouri River bet. SE South Dakota and NE Nebraska.

Lewis and Clark Range. See LEWIS RANGE.

Lewis and Harris. See LEWIS WITH HARRIS.

Lewis Bay. Inlet of Nantucket Sound on S coast of Barnstable co., Massachusetts.

Lew·is·burg \ˈlü-əs-ˌbərg\. **1.** Borough, ⊗ of Union co., cen. Pennsylvania, 21 mi. (34 km.) SSE of Williamsport; pop. (1990c) 5785; Bucknell Univ. (1846).

2. City, ⊗ of Marshall co., S cen. Tennessee, 18 mi. (29 km.) SE of Columbia; pop. (1990c) 9879.

3. City, ⊗ of Greenbrier co., SE West Virginia; pop. (1990c) 3598; West Virginia School of Osteopathic Medicine (1972).

Lew·i·sham \ˈlü-ə-shəm\. A borough of Greater London, SE England. See table at LONDON 4.

Lewis Lake. Lake in Yellowstone National Park, NW Wyoming, SW of Yellowstone Lake.

Lew·is·porte \ˈlü-əs-ˌpōrt\. Town, Newfoundland, Canada, 160 mi. (257 km.) NW of St. John's; pop. (1991c) 3848.

Lewis Range *or* **Lewis and Clark Range.** A range of the Rocky Mts., extending from NW of Helena, W Montana, along E side of Waterton-Glacier International Peace Park N into Alberta, Canada; highest peak Mt. Cleveland 10,448 ft. (3184 m.).

Lew·is·ton \ˈlü-ə-stən\. **1.** City, ⊗ of Nez Perce co., W Idaho, at confluence of Clearwater and Snake rivers across from Washington, 95 mi. (153 km.) SSE of Spokane; pop. (1990c) 28,082; pulp and paper mills; Lewis-Clark State Coll. (1893); first incorp. town in Idaho Terr., and first ✻ of the territory (1863–64).

2. City, Androscoggin co., SW Maine, on Androscoggin River opp. Auburn 30 mi. (48 km.) N of Portland; pop. (1990c) 39,757; textiles, footwear; Bates Coll. (1855); settled 1770; became city 1861.

3. Village, Niagara co., W New York, on Niagara River 7 mi. (11 km.) N of Niagara Falls; pop. (1990c) 3048; first nonnative settlement c. 1796; burned by British and Indians 1813.

Lew·is·town \ˈlü-əs-ˌtau̇n\. **1.** City, ⊗ of Fulton co., W cen. Illinois, 37 mi. (60 km.) SW of Peoria; pop. (1990c) 2572; prehistoric Indian burial mounds; home of writer Edgar Lee Masters.

2. City, ⊗ of Fergus co., cen. Montana, ESE of Great Falls; pop. (1990c) 6051; livestock raising.

3. Borough, ⊗ of Mifflin co., cen. Pennsylvania, 45 mi. (72 km.) WNW of Harrisburg; pop. (1990c) 9341; synthetic yarns, electronic equipment; laid out on site of earlier Shawnee village 1790.

Lew·is·ville \ˈlü-əs-ˌvil\. **1.** City, ⊗ of Lafayette co., SW Arkansas; pop. (1990c) 1424.

2. City, Denton co., N Texas, 15 mi. (24 km.) SSE of the city of Denton; pop. (1990c) 46,521; pop. has grown from 1373 in 1960.

Lew·is with Har·ris \ˌlü-əs-wit͟h-ˈhar-əs, -with-\ *or* **Lewis and Harris** \-ənd-\. Most northerly island of the Outer Hebrides, off NW coast of Scotland; 770 sq. mi. (1994 sq. km.); administratively part of Western Isles region. See LEWIS 4 and HARRIS 2.

Lews, The. See LEWIS 4.

Lex·ing·ton \ˈlek-siŋ-tən\. **1.** County in cen. South Carolina. See table at SOUTH CAROLINA.

2. City, ⊗ of Oglethorpe co., NE Georgia; pop. (1990c) 230.

3. City, ⊗ of and coextensive with Fayette co., NE cen. Kentucky, 23 mi. (37 km.) ESE of Frankfort; pop. (1990c) 225,366; tobacco market; raises thoroughbred horses; furniture; distilleries; Kentucky Horse Park; Transylvania Univ. (1780), oldest educational institution W of the Alleghenies, Univ. of Kentucky (1865); homes of politician Henry Clay, Confederate soldier John Hunt Morgan, and First Lady Mary Todd Lincoln are open to the public; Clay and Morgan, politician John Cabell Breckinridge, and novelist James Lane Allen are buried here. Founded 1779; chartered 1782; incorp. as city 1832. See *Fayette* in table at KENTUCKY.

4. Residential town, Middlesex co., NE Massachusetts, 10 mi. (16 km.) NW of Boston; pop. (1990c) 28,974; scene of battle Apr. 19, 1775 in which a force of minutemen resisted a British contingent marching to seize stores at Concord (see CONCORD 3), the opening engagement of the American Revolution.

5. City, ⊗ of Holmes co., W cen. Mississippi, 29 mi. (47 km.) S of Greenwood; pop. (1990c) 2227.

6. City, ⊗ of Lafayette co., W Missouri, on Missouri River 33 mi. (53 km.) E of Independence; pop. (1990c) 4860; coal mines, rock quarry; Wentworth Military Academy (1880); city laid out 1822; scene of Confederate victory Sept. 1861.

7. City, ⊗ of Dawson co., S cen. Nebraska, on Platte River 37 mi. (60 km.) W of Kearney; pop. (1990c) 6601; diversified agriculture.

8. City, ⊗ of Davidson co., cen. North Carolina, 19 mi. (31 km.) WSW of High Point; pop. (1990c) 16,581; Davidson County Community Coll. (1961).

9. Village, Richland co., N cen. Ohio, 8 mi. (13 km.) SW of Mansfield; pop. (1990c) 4124.

10. Town, ⊗ of Lexington co., cen. South Carolina; pop. (1990c) 3289.

11. City, ⊗ of Henderson co., W Tennessee, 26 mi. (42 km.) E of Jackson; pop. (1990c) 5810.

12. City, ⊗ of Rockbridge co. but politically independent of the county, W cen. Virginia, 30 mi. (48 km.) NW of Lynchburg; 2 sq. mi. (5 sq. km.); pop. (1990c) 6959; tourist center; market town in agricultural region; Washington and Lee Univ. (1749); Virginia Military Institute (1839); burial place of Confederate Generals Thomas ("Stonewall") Jackson and Robert E. Lee; became town 1777; rebuilt after fire 1796; bombarded June 10, 1864 during Civil War.

Leyden. See LEIDEN.

Ley·land \ˈlā-lənd\. Town, Lancashire, NW England, 22 mi. (35 km.) NNE of Liverpool; pop. (1981p) 26,567.

Ley·te \ˈlā-tē\. Island, one of the Visayan Is., E Philippines; separated from Samar on NE by very narrow San Juanico Strait; off its N end is Biliran I. and off S end Panaon I.; 121 mi. (195 km.) long from NW to SE, varies in width from 14 mi. (23 km.) at center to ab. 45 mi. (72 km.) in the N; 3090 sq. mi. (8003 sq. km.); pop. (1990c) 1,808,462. Constitutes with adjacent islands two provinces: **Leyte** (✻ Tacloban) and **Southern Leyte** (✻ Maasin). See table at PHILIPPINES.

Physical features: Of irregular shape, having many bays, some of which form good harbors. Mountainous, with long range N to S through the center, highest peak 4426 ft. (1349 m.); many peaks are extinct volcanoes; has many streams but few large ones.

Chief products: Rice, corn, sugar, and timber.

Chief towns: Tacloban, Ormoc.

History: Sighted 1521 by Portuguese navigator Ferdinand Magellan; under Spanish rule until late 19th cent.; under American rule first part 20th cent. In WWII occupied by Japanese 1942; invaded by Americans Oct. 20, 1944, prior to the battle of Leyte Gulf.

Leyte Gulf. Inlet of Pacific Ocean, E Philippines, E of Leyte and S of Samar; on S connects by Surigao Strait with Mindanao Sea. Offers good anchorage for large fleet; partially shut off from Pacific on E by Homonhon I.; during WWII, scene of major air-sea battle, in which Japanese were decisively defeated, Oct. 23–26, 1944.

Le·zhë \ˈlā-zhə\ *or* **Lesh** \ˈlāsh\. **1.** District of NW Albania. See table at ALBANIA.

2. *or Ital.* **Ales·sio** \ä-ˈles-syō\; *anc.* **Lis·sus** \ˈli-səs\. Town, its ✻, at mouth of Drin River; mausoleum of Skanderbeg (George Kastrioti), Albanian hero who led resistance against Turks 15th cent.

Lha·sa \ˈlä-sə, ˈla-\. **1.** *or W.-G.* **La–sa** \ˈlä-ˌsä\; *mostly formerly* **Ki** \ˈchē\ *or* **Kyi** \ˈchē\. River, SE Tibet, China; ab. 200 mi. (320 km.) long; N tributary of the upper Brahmaputra; the city of Lhasa is on its right bank.

2. *also* **Las·sa** \ˈlä-sə, ˈla-\. City, ✻ of Tibet (Xizang), China, in SE part ab. 250 mi. (400 km.) NE of Darjeeling, India; pop. (1990c) 106,885; alt. 11,830 ft. (3606 m.); located in a level plain on the Lhasa River; surrounded by hills, on one of which is the Potala, the great palace and former residence of the Dalai Lama (until 1959 the religious and political head of Tibet). Long the religious center of Tibet (sometimes known as the "forbidden city" because of its inaccessibility and the traditional hostility of its religious leaders towards outsiders), has many temples and monasteries, esp. Jokhang temple (7th cent.), and nearby Drepung and Sera monasteries. The *Lhasa apso* breed of dog takes its name from here.

History: Occupied by Chinese 1951; the Dalai Lama and numerous of his followers fled to India 1959 following the unsuccessful Tibetan revolt against Chinese rule; many of the monastic institutions were ransacked and closed by the Chinese in 1959, but have since been restored; Lhasa's considerable trade with India and Nepal, restricted after 1959 by sealed borders, has also been resumed. Martial law imposed 1989–90 following anti-Chinese demonstrations.

L'Hay–les–Roses \ˌlā-lā-ˈrōz\. Commune, Val-de-Marne dept., N France.

Lho·tse \ˈlōt-ˈsā\. Peak in the Himalayas, on Nepal-Tibet boundary, just S of Mt. Everest; 27,923 ft. (8511 m.).

Li \ˈlē\. **1.** *formerly* **Wu** \ˈwü\ *also* **Lin** \ˈlin\. River, N Hunan prov., SE cen. China, flows E to Dongting Hu; crosses cen. part of China's "rice bowl"; 251 mi. (404 km.) long.

2. Short river, NE Guangxi Zhuangzu, SE China; linked with the Xiang by Ling Canal.

Liakhov Islands. See LYAKHOVSKIYE OSTROVA.

Li·an·ga Bay \lē-ˈäŋ-gä\. Inlet of Pacific on SE coast of Surigao del Sur prov., Mindanao, Philippines; ab. 20 mi. (32 km.) wide at its mouth; at its head is the settlement of **Li-anga.**

Lian·yun·gang \ˈlyan-ˈyu̇en-ˈgäŋ\; *locally* **Xin·pu** \ˈshin-ˈpü\ *or W.-G.* **Lien–yün–kang** \ˈlyen-ˈyu̇en-ˈgäŋ\ *or* **Hsin–p'u** \ˈshēn-ˈpü\. City, Jiangsu prov., E China, ab. 120 mi. (195 km.) ENE of Xuzhou; pop. (1990c) 354,139.

Liao \ˈlyau̇\. River, NE China, chiefly in Liaoning prov. and Nei Monggol (Inner Mongolia); rises in S Nei Monggol, flows NE, then turns SW to the Gulf of Liaodong just below Yingkou; ab. 700 mi. (1125 km.) long; navigable for ab. 400 mi. (645 km.).

Liao·dong, Gulf of \ˈlyau̇-ˈdu̇ŋ\ *or Pinyin* **Liaodong Wan** \ˈwän\ *or W.-G.* **Liao–tung Wan** \ˈlyau̇-ˈdu̇ŋ-ˈwän\. N part of Bo Hai (the Gulf of Chihli), W of Liaodong Penin., NE China.

Liaodong Peninsula *or Pinyin* **Liaodong Ban·dao** \ˈbän-

\ə\ **abut** \ˈə\ **matches** \ᵊ\ **kitten, Fr table** \ər\ **further** \a\ **ash** \ā\ **ace** \ä\ **cot, cart** \ȧ\ **Fr bac** \au̇\ **out** \b̲\ **Span Avila** \ch\ **chin** \e\ **bet** \ē\ **easy** \g\ **go** \i\ **hit** \ī\ **ice** \j\ **job** \k\ **Ger ich, Buch** \ⁿ\ **Fr vin** \ŋ\ **sing** \ō\ **go** \ö\ **all** \ȯ\ **law** \œ\ **Fr bœuf** \œ̄\ **Fr feu** \ȯi\ **boy** \th\ **thin** \t͟h\ **this** \ü\ **loot** \u̇\ **foot** \ue\ **Ger füllen** \u̇e\ **Fr rue** \y\ **yet** \ʸ\ **Fr digne** \ˈdēnʸ\, **nuit** \ˈnwʸē\ \yü\ **few** \yu̇\ **fury** \zh\ **vision**

'daů\ *or W.-G.* **Liao–tung Pan–tao** \'lyaů-'dủŋ-'bän-'daů\. Peninsula, S part of Liaoning prov., NE China.

Liaodong Wan. See LIAODONG, GULF OF.

Liao·ning \'lyaů-'niŋ\; *formerly* **Feng·tien** \'fəŋ-'tyen\ *also* **Sheng·king** \'shəŋ-'jiŋ\. Province, NE China; ✱ Shenyang; soybeans, grain; coal, iron ore, petroleum. Under Japanese control 1932–45; contains important industrial areas. See table at CHINA.

Liao·peh \'lyaů-'bā\. Former prov., China; 40,498 sq. mi. (104,890 sq. km.); ✱ Szepingkai.

Liao–tung Pan–tao. See LIAODONG PENINSULA.

Liao–tung Wan. See LIAODONG, GULF OF.

Liao·yang *or W.-G.* **Liao–yang** \'lyaů-'yäŋ\. City, cen. E Liaoning prov., NE China, on a tributary of the Hun River 35 mi. (56 km.) S of Shenyang; pop. (1990c) 492,559; trade and market center for agricultural region producing soybeans and cotton; an ancient town, settled as early as 2d cent. B.C.; important as a district center under various dynasties incl. 17th cent. Manchus; site of battle 1904 in which Japanese defeated Russians during Russo-Japanese War.

Liaoyuan. See SHUANGLIAO.

Li·ard \'lē-ərd\. **1.** River, W Canada, rises in Stikine Mts. in SE Yukon, flows E across N British Columbia and turns N and NE to empty into Mackenzie River in SW Northwest Territories; 755 mi. (1215 km.) long. The Alaska Highway follows its N bank for a good distance in N British Columbia.
2. Trading post on the Liard. See FORT LIARD.

Li·ba·cao \ˌlē-bä-'kaů\. Municipality, Aklan prov., Panay, Philippines, on river at foot of the mountains 32 mi. (52 km.) WSW of Roxas; pop. (1980c) 21,683.

Liban. See LEBANON 1.

Libanus. See LEBANON MOUNTAINS.

Libau. See LIEPĀJA.

Lib·by \'li-bē\. City, ⊗ of Lincoln co., NW corner of Montana, on Kootenai River; pop. (1990c) 2532; silver mines.

Libby Dam. See UNITED STATES, *Dams and Reservoirs.*

Li·benge \lē-'bäⁿzh\. Town, NW Democratic Rep. of the Congo, on the Ubangi River ab. 50 mi. (80 km.) S of Bangui, Central African Rep.

Lib·e·ral \'li-bə-rəl\. City, ⊗ of Seward co., SW Kansas, on Oklahoma border 73 mi. (118 km.) SW of Dodge City; pop. (1990c) 16,573; Seward County Community Coll. (1967).

Liberalitas Julia. See ÉVORA 2.

Li·be·rec \'lē-be-ˌrets\ *or Ger.* **Rei·chen·berg** \'rī-kᵊn-ˌberk\. City, N Czech Republic; pop. (1989c) 104,158; cloth industry here dates from 16th cent.

Li·be·ria \lī-'bir-ē-ə\. **1.** Republic, W Africa, bounded on N by Guinea, on E by Ivory Coast, on S by the Atlantic Ocean, and on NW by Sierra Leone; ab. 43,000 sq. mi. (111,370 sq. km.); pop. (1984c) 2,101,628; ✱ Monrovia, the only large city.

Physical features: Coastline is marked by lagoons; its coast is known as the Grain Coast (*q.v.*) and the SE section is called the Kru Coast; its SE point on Ivory Coast border is marked by Cape Palmas; has no good natural harbors. A plateau country well watered and densely forested; highest point Mt. Wutivi 4528 ft. (1380 m.), in N; chief rivers Mano, St. Paul, St. John, Cestos, and Cavally.

Chief products: Rubber, palm kernels, rice, coffee, cassava, cocoa, timber; iron ore, diamonds; food processing.

History: American Colonization Society (founded 1816) began settlement of freed American slaves 1822 on land purchased from local tribes; colony named Liberia from the Latin word for "free"; estab. as Free and Independent Republic of Liberia July 26, 1847; suffered economic decline and government debt late 19th and early 20th cents.; granted concession of ab. one million acres to Firestone Company of U.S. for rubber plantation 1926; military coup Apr. 12, 1980 brought first indigenous African (or non-Americo-Liberian) to power; rebellion begun 1989 escalated into civil war 1990; some movement towards peace subsequently made but fighting among various factions continued well into 1990s.
2. Town, ✱ of Guanacaste prov., NW Costa Rica; pop. (1991e) 29,751.

Libertad, La. See LA LIBERTAD.

Li·ber·ta·dor Ge·ne·ral Ber·nar·do O'Hig·gins \ˌlē-ber-tä-'thòr-hā-nā-'räl-ber-'när-thō-ō-'ē-gēns\. Region of cen. Chile. See table at CHILE.

Lib·er·ty \'li-bər-tē\. **1.** Name of counties in four states of the U.S. See tables at FLORIDA, GEORGIA, MONTANA, TEXAS.
2. Town, ⊗ of Union co., E Indiana, 13 mi. (21 km.) S of Richmond; pop. (1990c) 910.
3. City, ⊗ of Casey co., cen. Kentucky; pop. (1990c) 1937.
4. Town, ⊗ of Amite co., SW Mississippi; pop. (1990c) 624.
5. City, ⊗ of Clay co., NW Missouri, 13 mi. (21 km.) NNE of Kansas City; pop. (1990c) 20,456; William Jewell Coll. (1849).
6. Village, Sullivan co., SE New York, 45 mi. (72 km.) W of Poughkeepsie; pop. (1990c) 4128.
7. Borough, Allegheny co., SW Pennsylvania, 11 mi. (18 km.) SE of Pittsburgh; pop. (1990c) 2744.
8. Town, Pickens co., NW South Carolina, in Blue Ridge foothills 18 mi. (29 km.) W of Greenville; pop. (1990c) 3228.
9. City, ⊗ of Liberty co., E Texas, on Trinity River ab. 40 mi. (64 km.) NE of Houston; pop. (1990c) 7733; hit with severe flooding Oct. 1994.

Liberty, Mount. Peak in Grafton co., New Hampshire; 4460 ft. (1359 m.).

Liberty Cap. Peak of Mount Rainier in Mount Rainier National Park, Washington, NW of the principal peak; 14,112 ft. (4301 m.).

Liberty Island; *formerly* **Bed·loe's Island** \'bed-lōz\ *or* **Bed·loe Island** \-lō\. Small island, New York, in Upper New York Bay; purchased by City of New York 1758 and c. 1800 ceded to U.S. government; location of Statue of Liberty.

Lib·er·ty·ville \'li-bər-tē-ˌvil\. Village, Lake co., NE corner of Illinois, 10 mi. (16 km.) SW of Waukegan; pop. (1990c) 19,174.

Libia. See LIBYA 2.

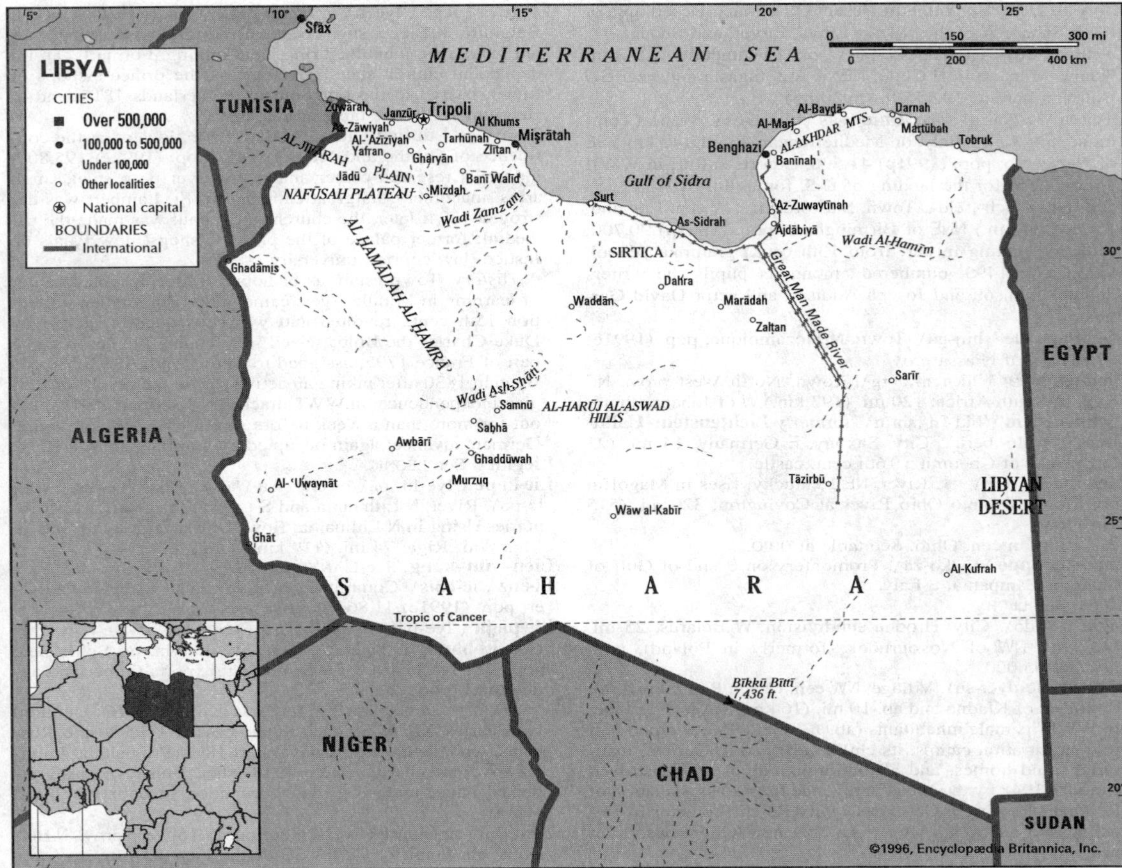

Libian Desert. See LIBYAN DESERT.

Lib·i·an Sa·ha·ra \ˈli-bē-ən-sə-ˈhar-ə, -ˈhär-\. Former (Italian) administrative and military territory, cen. and S Libya; 465,362 sq. mi. (1,205,288 sq. km.).

Lib·ma·nan \lēb-ˈmä-nän\. Municipality, W cen. Camarines Sur prov., Luzon, Philippines, on tributary of lower Bicol River 11 mi. (18 km.) NW of Naga; pop. (1980c) 68,413.

Li·bourne \lē-ˈbürn\. Commune, Gironde dept., SW France, on Dordogne River 17 mi. (27 km.) ENE of Bordeaux; pop. (1990c) 21,931; wines.

Li·brazhd \li-ˈbräsht\. **1.** District of E Albania. See table at ALBANIA.
2. Town, its ✱.

Li·bre·ville \ˈlē-brə-ˌvil\. Seaport town, ✱ of Gabon; pop. (1987e) 352,000; exports timber. Inhabited by indigenous peoples who in mid-19th cent. allowed French to settle freed slaves here; a chief city of former French Equatorial Africa.

Li·bur·nia \lī-ˈbər-nē-ə, -nyə\. District on the coast of the Adriatic Sea in ancient Illyria; included in modern Croatia; its inhabitants, the Liburni, noted for their nautical skill esp. in shipbuilding which later influenced Romans.

Lib·ya \ˈli-bē-ə\. **1.** Ancient Greek name for N Africa, outside of Egypt; later, for that part of Africa immediately W of Egypt which was afterwards divided into Marmarica and Cyrenaica and became part of the Roman colony of Africa.
2. *also* **Lib·ia** \ˈlē-byə\; *officially* **Socialist People's Lib·yan Arab Ja·ma·hi·ri·ya** \ˈli-bē-ən … ˌja-mə-hi-ˈrē-yə\. Republic, N Africa, bounded on N by the Mediterranean Sea, on E by Egypt, on SE by Sudan, on S by Chad and Niger, on W by Algeria, and on NW by Tunisia; 679,358 sq. mi. (1,759,537 sq. km.); pop. (1993e) 4,573,000; ✱ Tripoli.

Physical features: Largely desert, forming NE section of Sahara; agricultural areas developed along the coast, in the Barka Plateau, and in the oases; highland areas in N cen. part and along S border; in the interior are the Al Ḥamādah Al Ḥamrā' (desert in NW), Fezzan (desert and oases region in SW), Murzuq (dunes in SW), and the oases of Al Jufrah, Fezzan, Al-Kufrah, and Giarabub; coast is marked by wide indentation of Gulf of Sidra.

Chief export: Oil; other products: barley, wheat, dates, olives, fruits; livestock; gypsum, natural gas.

Chief towns: Tripoli, Benghazi.

History: For early history, see TRIPOLI 1, CYRENAICA, and FEZZAN. Occupied by Italians 1911, united as a colony under the name "Libya" 1934; scene of several extended campaigns in WWII; Axis forces expelled 1943; administered by British and French military governors 1943–51; achieved independence as a kingdom 1951; began exporting oil early 1960s; monarchy overthrown and republic estab. by military junta 1969; new government forced withdrawal of British and U.S. military installations, pursued policies oriented toward Arab unity, and supported the Palestine Liberation Organization and other revolutionary forces in the Middle East and Africa; attempted several unions with other Arab nations, none of which lasted; troops deployed in Chad intermittently throughout the 1970s and 1980s, defeated by Chadian forces 1987.

\ə\ abut \ə\ matches \ᵊ\ kitten, Fr table \ər\ further \a\ ash \ā\ ace \ä\ cot, cart \à\ Fr bac \aù\ out \b\ Span Avila \ch\ chin \e\ bet \ē\ easy \g\ go \i\ hit \ī\ ice \j\ job \k\ Ger ich, Buch \ⁿ\ Fr vin \ŋ\ sing \ō\ go \ȯ\ all \ò\ law \œ\ Fr bœuf \ᵫ\ Fr feu \ȯi\ boy \th\ thin \t͟h\ this \ü\ loot \u̇\ foot \ue\ Ger füllen \ᵫ\ Fr rue \y\ yet \ʸ\ Fr digne \ˈdēnʸ\, nuit \ˈnwʸē\ \yü\ few \yu̇\ fury \zh\ vision

Lib·y·an Desert *or* **Lib·i·an Desert** \ˈli-bē-ən\. Desert area of the E Sahara W of the Nile in Libya, Egypt, and Sudan.

Li·can·cá·bur \ˌlē-käŋ-ˈkä-bür\ *or* **Li·can·caur** \ˌlē-käŋ-ˈkau̇r\. Volcano in N Chile, NE of Antofagasta and near SW Bolivian border; 19,455 ft. (5930 m.).

Li·ca·ta \lē-ˈkä-tä\; *anc.* **Phin·ti·as** \ˈfin-tē-əs\. Seaport commune, SW Sicily, Italy, on Mediterranean 26 mi. (42 km.) SE of Agrigento; pop. (1991p) 41,596; exports sulfur; in WWII a beachhead for the landing of U.S. forces July 1943.

Lich·field \ˈlich-ˌfēld\. Town, Staffordshire, W cen. England, 15 mi. (24 km.) NNE of Birmingham; pop. (1991p) 90,700; cathedral, dating in part from 13th cent.; grammar school, founded c. 1495, numbered among its pupils the writers Samuel Johnson and Joseph Addison and actor David Garrick.

Li·chin·ga \lē-ˈshiŋ-gä\. Town, N Mozambique; pop. (1991e) 67,811; ✻ of Niassa prov.

Lich·ten·burg \ˈlik-tən-ˌbərg\. Town, North West prov., NE Rep. of South Africa, 120 mi. (193 km.) W of Johannesburg.

Lich·ten·stein \ˈlik-tᵊn-ˌshtīn\; *formerly* **Lichtenstein–Callnberg** \-ˈkäln-ˌberk\. City, Saxony, E Germany, 14 mi. (23 km.) WSW of Chemnitz; 16th cent. castle.

Lick·ing \ˈli-kiŋ\. **1.** River, NE Kentucky; rises in Magoffin co., flows NW into Ohio River at Covington; 320 mi. (515 km.) long.

2. County in cen. Ohio. See table at OHIO.

Li·co·sa, Cape \lē-ˈkō-zä\. Promontory on S end of Gulf of Salerno, Campania, S Italy.

Licus. See LECH.

Li·da \ˈlē-də\. City, Hrodna subdivision, W Belarus, 25 mi. (40 km.) NW of Novogrudok (formerly in Poland); pop. (1991e) 95,000.

Li·di·ce \ˈlē-dyēt-se\. Village, NW cen. Czech Republic, 4 mi. (6 km.) E of Kladno and ab. 10 mi. (16 km.) WNW of Prague; in WWII its male inhabitants (ab. 175) killed, its women sent to concentration camps, its children placed in German institutions and homes, and all buildings completely destroyed June 10, 1942 by the Nazis in revenge for the assassination of Reinhard Heydrich, German Deputy Reich Protector in Bohemia and Moravia. After the war a new village was built nearby.

Li·dingö \ˈlē-ˌdiŋ-œ̄\. City, Stockholm prov., SE Sweden, residential suburb NE of Stockholm; pop. (1989c) 38,615; made city 1926.

Lid·kö·ping \ˈlēd-ˌchœ̄-piŋ\. City, Skaraborg prov., Sweden, on Lake Vänern; pop. (1993e) 36,289; porcelain, matches.

Li·do \ˈlē-dō\ *or in full* **Lido di Ma·la·moc·co** \dē-ˌmä-lä-ˈmȯ-kō\. Island reef outside the Lagoon of Venice, Venezia prov., NE Italy, separating the lagoon from the Gulf of Venice; at N end of island is the town of Lido, formerly a fashionable resort.

Lidz·bark War·miń·ski \ˈlidz-ˌbärk-vär-ˈmin-skē\ *or Ger.* **Heils·berg** \ˈhīls-ˌberk\. Town, N cen. Olsztyn prov., N Poland, 25 mi. (40 km.) N of the city of Olsztyn on the Łyna River; pop. (1981p) 14,882; castle; founded in Middle Ages; ruled variously by Prussia and Poland; to Poland after WWII.

Liech·ten·stein \ˈlikt-ᵊn-ˌshtīn\; *officially* **Principality of Liechtenstein** *or Ger.* **Fürst·en·tum Liechtenstein** \ˈfu̇ərst-ᵊn-ˌtüm\. Independent principality, W Europe, on E bank of the Rhine bet. St. Gall and Graubünden cantons in NE Switzerland and prov. of Vorarlberg in W Austria; 62 sq. mi. (161 sq. km.); pop. (1990p) 28,877; ✻ Vaduz. Narrow strip of lowland along the Rhine; peaks of spur of Rhaetian Alps in S are above 8400 ft. (2560 m.).

Chief products: corn, wine; dairy products; manufacturing: textiles, pharmaceutical products, precision instruments, ceramics; tourism.

History: In 1719, counties of Schellenberg and Vaduz, in hands of branch of house of Liechtenstein, were erected as principality of Liechtenstein in the Holy Roman Empire; part of Confederation of the Rhine 1806; in German Confederation (see GERMANY) 1815–66; belonged to Austrian customs union before collapse of Hapsburg monarchy 1918; entered Swiss customs union 1924.

Liège *or* **Liége** \ˈlyezh\ *or Flem.* **Luik** \ˈlȯik\. **1.** Province, E Belgium; ✻ Liège; sugar beets, cereal grains; dairying; varied industries, manufacturing, coal mining. Formerly, an independent church state, governed by the prince-bishops of Liège; passed to the kingdom of Netherlands 1815; and to Belgium 1830. See table at BELGIUM.

2. *or Ger.* **Lüt·tich** \ˈlue-tik\. City, its ✻, located at the confluence of Ourthe and Meuse rivers; pop. (1992e) 195,800; industrial research center and major river port; steel, small arms, machinery. Its great cathedral of St. Lambert was destroyed 1794; later, the church of St. Paul was made the cathedral; former palace of the prince-bishops, now Palais de Justice (law courts); university (1817).

History: Town estab. as bishopric 8th cent.; noted center of learning in Middle Ages; came under Burgundian protection 15th cent., revolted and was subsequently sacked by Duke Charles the Bold; seized by French 1792 and became part of France 1795; assigned to Netherlands 1815; became Belgian 1830 after taking an active part in the revolt for Belgian independence; in WWI attacked by Germans 1914, held out for more than a week before surrendering thus delaying German advance; again occupied by Germans in WWII.

Liegnitz. See LEGNICA.

Lie·lu·pe \ˈlye-lü-ˌpä\ *or Ger.* **Aa** \ˈä\ *or Russ.* **Le·lu·pe** \ˈle-lə-pə\. River, N Lithuania and S Latvia; formed by two tributaries rising in N Lithuania, flows N past Jelgava to Gulf of Riga W of Riga; 74 mi. (119 km.) long.

Lien–yün–kang. See LIANYUNGANG.

Li·enz \ˈlē-ents\. Commune, Tirol, SW Austria, on Drava River; pop. (1991c) 11,864; tourist resort.

Lie·pā·ja \ˈlye-pä-ˌyä\ *or Russ.* **Li·ye·pa·ya** \lə-ˈye-pə-yə\ *or Ger.* **Li·bau** \ˈlē-ˌbau̇\. Seaport city, Latvia, on Baltic Sea; pop. (1991e) 114,900; steel; fishing; exports timber and agricultural produce.

History: Developed by Teutonic Knights 1263; captured by Charles XII of Sweden 1701; passed 1795 to the Russians, who developed its naval port 1893. Provisional Latvian government estab. here 1918 when Bolshevik army attacked Riga; under German occupation in both WWI and WWII.

Lier \ˈlir\ *or* **Lierre** \ˈlyer\. Commune, Antwerp prov., N Belgium, ab. 8 mi. (13 km.) SE of the city of Antwerp; pop. (1992e) 31,400; 15th–16th cent. High Gothic church.

Lies·tal \ˈlē-ˌstäl\. Commune, ✻ of Basel-Land demicanton, Basel canton, NW Switzerland, 8 mi. (13 km.) SE of the city of Basel; pop. (1989c) 12,453; chemicals, iron goods; 15th cent. town hall.

Lietuva. See LITHUANIA.

Lié·vin \lyā-ˈveⁿ\. Commune, Pas-de-Calais dept., N France, 9 mi. (15 km.) N of Arras; completely destroyed in WWI.

Lièvre \ˈlyevrᵊ\. River, SW Quebec, Canada; flows S into the Ottawa River below Hull; 205 mi. (330 km.) long; outlet of many lakes.

Lif·fey \ˈli-fē\. River, E Ireland; rises among the Wicklow Mts. in co. Wicklow, curves NW and NE into Dublin Bay (an inlet of the Irish Sea) at Dublin; 50 mi. (81 km.) long.

Lif·ford \ˈli-fərd\. Town, ⊗ of co. Donegal, N Ireland (republic); on Foyle River opp. Strabane in Northern Ireland.

Li·fou *or* **Li·fu** \lē-ˈfü\. Largest and most important island of the Loyalty Is., New Caledonia terr. (French), SW Pacific Ocean, ab. 60 mi. (97 km.) E of New Caledonia; 50 mi. (81 km.) long and 10 to 15 mi. (16 to 24 km.) wide; 650 sq. mi. (1684 sq. km.); pop. (1989p) 8726; irregular in shape and flat, with no hills or rivers; very fertile.

Li·fu·ka \lē-ˈfü-kä\. Island in NW part of Ha'apai group, Tonga, SW cen. Pacific Ocean; contains the only considerable village (Pangai) in the group.

Li·gao \lē-ˈgau̇\. Municipality, cen. Albay prov., Luzon, Philippines, on railroad line 16 mi. (26 km.) NW of Legazpi; pop. (1990c) 72,560; W of Mayon Volcano.

Liger. See LOIRE.

Light·house Point \ˈlīt-ˌhau̇s\. **1.** E tip of Franklin co., NW Florida, at W entrance to Apalachee Bay.

2. City, Broward co., SE Florida; residential suburb of Fort Lauderdale; pop. (1990c) 10,378.

Li·gny \lē-'nyē\. Commune, Namur prov., S Belgium, 14 mi. (23 km.) NW of the commune of Namur; battlefield where French Emperor Napoléon defeated the Prussians June 16, 1815 just before the battle of Waterloo.

Ligny–en–Bar·rois \-äⁿ-bär-'wä\. Commune, S Meuse dept., NE France, SE of Bar-le-Duc; 13th–17th cent. church; remains of ancient castle.

Lig·o·nier \ˌli-gə-'nir\. **1.** City, Noble co., NE Indiana, 35 mi. (56 km.) NW of Fort Wayne; pop. (1990c) 3443.
2. Borough, Westmoreland co., SW Pennsylvania, 19 mi. (31 km.) WSW of Johnstown; pop. (1990c) 1638; resort.

Li·gu·ria \lə-'gyůr-ē-ə\. **1.** Ancient region SW Europe, inhabited by Ligurians, a people of pre-Indo-European stock; the Ligurians were gradually subdued by Romans during 2d cent. B.C.
2. A strip of coast surrounding Genoa which in 1797 was erected as Ligurian Republic; annexed by France 1805–1815.
3. Autonomous region of NW Italy, on Ligurian Sea bet. France and Tuscany; ✱ Genoa; consists of extremely fertile coastal strip—the Italian Riviera—a major tourist center, and an inland mountainous region; produces wine, olives; shipbuilding, ironworks; chemicals, textiles. Estab. 1948; received limited autonomy 1970. See table at ITALY.

Ligurian Alps. See table at ALPS.

Ligurian Apennines *or Ital.* **Ligure, Appennino.** See table at APENNINES.

Li·gur·i·an Sea \lə-'gyůr-ē-ən\; *anc.* **Si·nus Li·gus·ti·cus** \'sī-nəs-lə-'gəs-ti-kəs\. Branch of Mediterranean Sea enclosed by the Italian autonomous regions of Liguria and Tuscany on N and E, and the French island of Corsica on the S; includes the Gulf of Genoa.

Li·hir \'lē-ˌhir\. Small island in the Bismarck Archipelago, W Pacific Ocean, off NE coast of New Ireland.

Li·hou \'lē-ˌhü\. One of the Channel Is., just W of Guernsey; 38 acres (15 hectares).

Lihou Reefs and Cays \'lē-hō\. Coral reefs in SW Coral Sea off NE Queensland, Australia; mark E limit of Great Barrier Reef formations.

Li·hue \lē-'hü-ā\. Unincorporated settlement, ⊗ of Kauai co., SE Kauai I., Hawaii; pop. (1990c) 5536; airport nearby.

Liim Fjord. See LIMFJORDEN.

Li·ka·si \lē-'kä-sē\; *formerly* **Ja·dot·ville** \ˌzhä-dō-'vēl\. City, SE Shaba administrative region, Democratic Rep. of the Congo; pop. (1991e) 279,839; copper-smelting center.

Likhvin. See CHEKALIN.

Li·ki·ep \'lē-kē-ˌep\. Island (atoll), cen. part of Ratak Chain, N cen. Marshall Is., W Pacific Ocean; has 44 islets.

Li·ko·ma \lē-'kō-mä\. Island in E cen. Lake Malawi, Malawi; Anglican cathedral.

Lilas, Les. See LES LILAS.

Lil·burn \'lil-bərn\. City, Gwinnett co., N Georgia, 15 mi. (24 km.) NE of Atlanta; pop. (1990c) 9301.

L'Île–d'Or·léans \ˌlēl-dȯr-lā-'äⁿ\. County, Quebec, Canada. See table at QUEBEC.

L'Île Rousse \lēl-'rüs\ *or* **Île Rousse** \ēl-'rüs\. Seaport, NW Corsica, France; founded 1758 by Corsican patriot Pasquale Paoli.

Lille \'lēl\; *formerly* **Lisle** \'lēl, 'līl\ *or sometimes* **L'Isle** \'lēl\; *Lat.* **In·su·la** \'in-sə-lə\ *or Flem.* **Rys·sel** \'rā-səl, 'rī-\. City, ✱ of Nord dept., N France, 130 mi. (209 km.) NNE of Paris; pop. (1990c) 178,301; textiles, iron, steel, machinery, chemicals; brewing, sugar refining; important railroad junction; 17th cent. citadel; 17th cent. exchange; university system evolved from university founded at Douai 1560.
History: Founded 11th cent.; changed hands frequently through Middle Ages; captured 1667 by Louis XIV of France; captured 1708 by John Churchill (duke of Marlborough) and Eugene, prince of Savoy; restored to France by Treaty of Utrecht 1713; in WWI under German occupation 1914–18 suffered population deportations; in WWII occupied by Germans and damaged by Allied bombs.

Lille·bonne \lēl-'bȯn\; *anc.* **Ju·li·o·bo·na** \ˌjü-lē-ə-'bō-nə\. Commune, Seine-Maritime dept., N France, near the mouth of the Seine; pop. (1990c) 9426; remains of Roman theater and castle of William the Conqueror, duke of Normandy and king of England.

Lil·le·ham·mer \'li-lə-ˌhä-mər\. Town, ⊗ of Oppland co., S cen. Norway, 85 mi. (137 km.) N of Oslo; pop. (1990c) 22,782; in valley of the Lågen at N end of Lake Mjøsa and on railroad line from Oslo to Trondheim; center of rich agricultural area; sawmills; tourist and winter-sports resort; open-air folk culture museum; site of Winter Olympic Games 1994.

Lil·lers \lē-'lär\. Commune, E cen. Pas-de-Calais dept., N France; 12th cent. church, restored.

Lil·le Vild·mo·se \'li-lə-'vil-ˌmō-sə\ *or* **Vildmose.** Swampy area, N Jutland Penin., Denmark, N of Limfjorden.

Lil·ling·ton \'li-liŋ-tən\. Town, ⊗ of Harnett co., cen. North Carolina; pop. (1990c) 2048.

Lil·loo·et \'li-lə-ˌwet\. River, SW British Columbia, Canada; rises in Coast Mts., flows SE through **Lillooet Lake** and Harrison Lake (87 sq. mi. or 225 sq. km.) into Fraser River E of Vancouver; ab. 150 mi. (240 km.) long.

Li·lon·gwe \li-'lȯŋ-gwā\. City, ✱ of Malawi, 50 mi. (80 km.) W of S end of Lake Malawi; pop. (1987c) 223,318; replaced Zomba as national ✱ 1975.

Lilybaeum. See MARSALA.

Lim \'lim, 'lēm\. River, S Europe; rises in North Albanian Alps in Montenegro, Yugoslavia and flows N into Drina River in Bosnia and Herzegovina; 136 mi. (219 km.) long.

Li·ma \'lī-mə\. **1.** City, ⊗ of Allen co., NW Ohio, 68 mi. (109 km.) SSW of Toledo; pop. (1990c) 45,549; motor vehicles, aircraft parts, machine tools, building machinery; Ohio State Univ.–Lima (1960); city founded 1831; incorp. 1842; in late 19th cent. center of N Ohio oil fields.
2. Town, Sheboygan co., E Wisconsin; pop. (1990c) 2715.

Li·ma \'lē-mä\. City, ✱ of Peru, on Rímac River ab. 8 mi. (13 km.) E from its port Callao; pop. (1990e) 5,825,900; alt. 512 ft. (156 m.); economic and cultural center of Peru; diversified industries, incl. textiles, cement, leather goods, processed foods, clothing, pharmaceuticals; oil refineries; cathedral (begun 16th cent.), government palace, and the National Univ. of San Marcos (founded 1551); remains from Inca and pre-Inca periods nearby (see PACHÁCAMAC). Founded by Spanish conquistador Francisco Pizarro 1535 and orig. called "City of the Kings" because its site was chosen on Jan. 6, the feast of the Wise Men or the Three Kings; became ✱ of viceroyalty of Peru (*q.v.*) and seat of audiencia; largely destroyed by earthquake 1746; occupied by Chilean forces 1881–83 during War of the Pacific; rapid pop. growth in 20th cent.

Li·ma, Point \'lē-mä\. Cape on E coast of Puerto Rico.

Li·man \'lē-ˌmän\. Mountain, highest point of Wilis mountain group, E cen. Java, Indonesia, SE of Madiun; 8409 ft. (2563 m.).

Li·ma Reservoir \'lī-mə\. Reservoir in Red Rock River, SE Beaverhead co., SW Montana.

Li·ma·sa·wa \ˌlē-mä-'sä-wä\. Long, narrow island ab. 2 mi. (3 km.) off S end of Leyte I., Philippines; 3 sq. mi. (7.7 sq. km.). Site of Portuguese explorer Ferdinand Magellan's landing and of first Mass celebrated in the Philippines Mar. 1521.

Li·mas·sol *or* **Li·ma·sol** \ˌlē-mä-'sȯl\; *anc.* **Le·mes·sus** \li-'me-səs\. Seaport, S Cyprus, on Akrotiri Bay; met. area pop. (1989e) 132,100; main port of Cyprus; tourist center; exports wine, asbestos, chrome; castle; site of Richard I of England's marriage to Berengaria of Navarre 1191.

Lim·a·vady \ˌli-mə-'va-dē\. **1.** District, NW Northern Ireland. See table at IRELAND, NORTHERN.
2. Town, its ⊗; pop. (1981c) 8015.

Li·may \lē-'mī\. River, SW cen. Argentina; flows NE out of Lake Nahuel Huapí in Andes on W boundary bet. Neuquén and Río Negro provs.; ab. 250 mi. (400 km.) long; unites with Neuquén River to form Río Negro.

\ə\ **abut** \ə\ **matches** \ᵊ\ **kitten, Fr table** \ər\ **further** \a\ **ash** \ā\ **ace** \ä\ **cot, cart** \å\ **Fr bac** \au̇\ **out** \b\ **Span Avila** \ch\ **chin** \e\ **bet** \ē\ **easy** \g\ **go** \i\ **hit** \ī\ **ice** \j\ **job** \k\ **Ger ich, Buch** \ⁿ\ **Fr vin** \ŋ\ **sing** \ō\ **go** \ȯ\ **all** \ȯ\ **law** \œ\ **Fr bœuf** \œ̄\ **Fr feu** \ȯi\ **boy** \th\ **thin** \t͟h\ **this** \ü\ **loot** \u̇\ **foot** \ue\ **Ger füllen** \u̅e\ **Fr rue** \y\ **yet** \ʸ\ **Fr digne** \'dēnʸ\, **nuit** \'nwʸē\ \yü\ **few** \yu̇\ **fury** \zh\ **vision**

Lim·bach–Ober·froh·na \ˈlim-ˌbäk-ˌō-bər-ˈfrō-nə\. City, Saxony, E Germany, 7 mi. (11 km.) W of Chemnitz; pop. (1981c) 23,165.

Lim·bang \ˈlim-ˌbäŋ\ *or* **Bru·nei** \ˈbrü-ˌnī\. Navigable river, NW Borneo; flows NW and N through N Sarawak into Brunei Bay near Bandar Seri Begawan; ab. 120 mi. (195 km.) long.

Limb·di \ˈlim-dē\. Former Indian state, NE Kathiawar, India, SE of Surendrangar; 344 sq. mi. (891 sq. km.).

Lim·be \ˈlim-bā\. **1.** *formerly* **Vic·to·ria** \vik-ˈtōr-ē-ə\. Seaport town, SW Cameroon, on Bight of Biafra; pop. (1987e) 42,511; port of Buea and chief trading town of former British Cameroons trust territory.

2. City, Malawi. See BLANTYRE.

Lim·bia·te \lēm-ˈbyä-tā\. Commune, Milano prov., Lombardy, N Italy; pop. (1989c) 32,406.

Lim·bo·to, Lake \lim-ˈbō-tō\. Small lake, cen. part of N peninsula of Sulawesi, Indonesia, just W of Gorontalo; resort with hot springs.

Lim·burg \ˈlim-ˌbərg\. **1.** Region of W Europe on E bank of the Meuse; orig. part of Lower Lorraine; united with duchy of Brabant to its W late 13th cent., subsequently coming under duchy of Burgundy and later Spain; N part passed to Netherlands 1648; S part conquered by French 1795; in 1815 became a province of new kingdom of Netherlands; later divided bet. Netherlands and Belgium (see LIMBURG 2 and 3).

2. *or Fr.* **Lim·bourg** \ˈlim-ˌbərg, leⁿ-ˈbür\. Province, NE Belgium; ✻ Hasselt; grains, sugar beets, fruit; dairying; coal mining. Limburger cheese orig. produced in this province near Liège. See table at BELGIUM.

3. Province, SE Netherlands; ✻ Maastricht; rye, wheat, sugar beets; poultry; dairy farming; chemicals. See table at NETHERLANDS.

Limburg an der Lahn \än-dər-ˈlän\. City, Hesse, Germany, on Lahn River 23 mi. (37 km.) NNW of Wiesbaden; pop. (1980c) 28,573; 13th cent. cathedral and castle.

Li·mei·ra \lē-ˈmā-rə\. Town, São Paulo state, SE Brazil, 80 mi. (129 km.) NW of the city of São Paulo; munic. pop. (1991p) 207,405; center of orange cultivation.

Lim·er·ick \ˈlim-rik, ˈli-mə-\ *or Gaelic* **Luim·neach** \ˈlim-nək\. **1.** County in Munster prov., SW Ireland; ⊗ Limerick; chief river Shannon; agriculture, livestock raising, dairy farming. See table at IRELAND.

2. City, its ⊗, seaport on the Shannon; pop. (1986c) 56,279; exports fish and farm products; flour mills, creameries, breweries; lacemaking, salmon fishing; castle erected under King John of England; 12th cent. cathedral. Important Norse settlement in 9th and 10th cents.; taken by Brian, later high king of Ireland, late 10th cent.; received charter 1197; object of many sieges, notably by supporters of English Parliamentarian leader Oliver Cromwell under his son-in-law Henry Ireton 1651 and, as the last important stronghold of the Jacobites, by William III and Gen. Godard van Reede-Ginkel (1690 and 1691 respectively).

Li·mes Ger·man·i·cus \ˈlī-mēz-jər-ˈma-ni-kəs\. Former fortified military road, W Europe, E of the Rhine and along NE border of Germania Superior; part of the Roman defense system against unconquered tribes to the N.

Lime·stone \ˈlīm-ˌstōn\. **1.** Name of counties in two states of the U.S. See tables at ALABAMA and TEXAS.

2. City, NE Kentucky. See MAYSVILLE.

3. Town, Aroostook co., N Maine, 18 mi. (29 km.) NNE of Presque Isle; pop. (1990c) 9922.

Lim·fjor·den \ˈlēm-ˌfyȯr-dən\ *or* **Lim Fjord** *also* **Liim Fjord** \ˈlēm, ˈlim\. Fjord in N section of Jutland, Denmark, extending from North Sea ENE across the peninsula to the Kattegat, and cutting off Vendsyssel-Thy; wide section (ab. 13 mi. or 21 km.) in center of fjord known as Løgstør Bredning.

Lim·it, Point \ˈli-mət\. Point of land, Cavite prov., S Luzon, Philippines, S of entrance to Manila Bay.

Lim·mat \ˈli-ˌmät\. River, Zürich and Aargau cantons, Switzerland; flows NW from NW end of Zürichsee to Aare River; ab. 87 mi. (140 km.) long; the city of Zürich is on the lake and on both sides of the river. See LINTH.

Lim·men Bight \ˈli-mən\. Bight and shallow bay in W part of Gulf of Carpentaria on E coast of Northern Terr., NE Australia, to the SW of Groote Eylandt.

Límni Vólvi. See BOLBĒ, LAKE.

Límnos. See LEMNOS.

Li·mo·ei·ro \lē-ˈmwā-rü\. City, NE Pernambuco state, E Brazil; 40 mi. (64 km.) NW of Recife; munic. pop. (1991p) 54,821.

Li·moges \lē-ˈmōzh\; *anc.* **Au·gus·to·ri·tum Lem·o·vi·cen·si·um** \ȯ-ˌgəs-tə-ˈrī-təm-ˌle-mə-vī-ˈsen-chē-əm\; *later* **Lem·o·vi·ces** \ˌle-mə-ˈvī-sēz\. City, ✻ of Limousin region and of Haute-Vienne dept., W cen. France, on Vienne River 110 mi. (177 km.) NE of Bordeaux; pop. (1990c) 136,407; chief seat of porcelain industry in France (begun 18th cent.); also produces leather goods, paper, textiles; as important center of enamel artwork, which flourished here in Middle Ages and beyond, produced series of artists noted for paintings in enamel; university (1808, suppressed 1840; reopened 1965); cathedral (begun 13th cent.); old fortified city walls converted into promenades. Gallic tribal ✻; two separate towns developed by 10th cent. (merged 1792); stormed and sacked by English under Edward the Black Prince 1370.

Li·mon \lē-ˈmōn\. Village near N coast of Leyte I., Philippines, ab 30 mi. (50 km.) W of Tacloban; in WWII scene of severe fighting during American invasion 1944.

Li·món \lē-ˈmōn\. **1.** Province of E cen. Costa Rica. See table at COSTA RICA.

2. City, Costa Rica. See PUERTO LIMÓN.

Li·mon Bay \lē-ˈmōn\ *or Span.* **Ba·hía de Limón** \bä-ˈē-ä-ˌthā-\. Inlet of the Caribbean Sea, at N end of Panama Canal.

Limonum. See POITIERS.

Li·mou·sin \ˌlē-mə-ˈzeⁿ, ˌli-mə-ˈzēn\. **1.** Historical region of cen. France; a plateau bounded anciently on N by Marche, on E by Auvergne, on S by Guienne, on W by Angoumois, and on NW by Poitou; ✻ Limoges.

History: Inhabited by ancient Gallic tribe of Lemovices; conquered by Romans; part of Aquitaine, it passed with Duchess Eleanor of Aquitaine to Henry II of England on her marriage to him 1152; subsequently fought over by England and France; in Hundred Years' War ceded to English 1360 but regained by French 1370–74; annexed to the French crown under Henry IV.

2. Region of France, roughly incl. the historical region. See table at FRANCE.

Lim·pio \ˈlim-pē-ˌō\. Town, a suburb of Asunción, in Central dept., S Paraguay; pop. (1992p) 26,282.

Lim·po·po \lim-ˈpō-pō\ *or* **Croc·o·dile** \ˈkrä-kə-ˌdīl\. River, SE Africa; rises near Johannesburg in Gauteng prov., Rep. of South Africa, flows N and NE, forming part of the boundary with Botswana and the entire boundary with Zimbabwe, turns SE across S Mozambique and empties into Indian Ocean; ab. 1100 mi. (1770 km.) long. Both its entire course and its headstream sometimes called the Crocodile.

Lin. See LI.

Li·na·pa·can \ˌlē-nä-ˈpä-kän\. Island, Palawan prov., Philippines, N of Palawan I. in the channel connecting Sulu Sea with South China Sea; 40 sq. mi. (104 sq. km.).

Linard, Piz. See SILVRETTA.

Li·na·res \lē-ˈnä-rās\. **1.** Former province of S cen. Chile.

2. City, Maule region, Chile, ab. 173 mi. (278 km.) S of Santiago; munic. pop. (1992c) 76,154; formerly ✻ of Linares prov.; trade and distribution center in agricultural region.

3. Town, Nuevo León state, NE Mexico, on railroad line 75 mi. (121 km.) SE of Monterrey; munic. pop. (1990p) 61,561.

4. Mining commune, Jaén prov., S Spain, 24 mi. (39 km.) N of the commune of Jaén; pop. (1991p) 58,039; center of lead mining; produces mining equipment and explosives.

Lin–ch'ing. See LINQING.

Lin·chuan *or W.-G.* **Lin–ch'uan** *also* **Lin·chwan** \ˈlin-ˈchwan\. City, E cen. Jiangxi prov., SE China, S of Poyang Lake and just SW of Fuzhou; pop. (1989e) 157,300.

Lin·coln \ˈliŋ-kən\. **1.** Name of a parish in N Louisiana and of counties in 23 states of the U.S. See tables at ARKANSAS, COLORADO, GEORGIA, IDAHO, KANSAS, KENTUCKY, LOUISIANA, MAINE, MINNESOTA, MISSISSIPPI, MISSOURI, MONTANA, NEBRASKA,

NEVADA, NEW MEXICO, NORTH CAROLINA, OKLAHOMA, OREGON, SOUTH DAKOTA, TENNESSEE, WASHINGTON, WEST VIRGINIA, WISCONSIN, WYOMING.

2. City, Talladega co., E cen. Alabama; pop. (1990c) 2941.

3. City, Placer co., E California, 25 mi. (40 km.) N of Sacramento; pop. (1990c) 7248.

4. City, ⊗ of Logan co., cen. Illinois, 30 mi. (48 km.) NNE of Springfield; pop. (1990c) 15,418; in agricultural region; glassware, clothing, electrical equipment; Lincoln Coll. (1865), Lincoln Christian Coll. (1944); city founded 1853.

5. *or* **Lincoln Center.** City, ⊗ of Lincoln co., cen. Kansas, on Saline River WNW of Salina; pop. (1990c) 1381.

6. Town, Penobscot co., E cen. Maine, 42 mi. (68 km.) N of Bangor; pop. (1990c) 5587.

7. Town, Middlesex co., NE Massachusetts, 13 mi. (21 km.) WNW of Boston; pop. (1990c) 7666.

8. City, ✻ of Nebraska and ✻ of Lancaster co., SE Nebraska, 52 mi. (84 km.) WSW of Omaha; pop. (1990c) 191,972; railroad junction and commercial center; produces agricultural machinery, pharmaceuticals, meat products; flour mills, grain elevators, railroad shops; Univ. of Nebraska, Lincoln (1869), Nebraska Wesleyan Univ. (1887), Union Coll. (1891). Orig. called Lancaster; chosen state ✻ 1867 and renamed after Abraham Lincoln; incorp. 1869; home of politician William Jennings Bryan late 19th and early 20th cents.

9. Town, Providence co., N Rhode Island, ab. 9 mi. (14 km.) SE of Woonsocket; pop. (1990c) 18,045; administrative center Lonsdale village (*q.v.*); taken from Smithfield and incorp. 1871; includes several villages.

10. Town, S Ontario, Canada, W of St. Catherines; pop. (1991c) 17,149.

11. Former county in England. See LINCOLNSHIRE 2.

12. County in England. See LINCOLNSHIRE 3.

13. *anc.* **Lin·dum** \ˈlin-dəm\. City, ⊗ of Lincolnshire, E England, on the Witham 39 mi. (63 km.) ESE of Sheffield; pop. (1991p) 81,900; market for agricultural area; machinery; cathedral, begun c. 1075; castle built by William I (the Conqueror) in 1068; site of early British, Roman, and Danish settlements.

Lincoln, Mount. **1.** Peak, Park co., cen. Colorado; 14,286 ft. (4354 m.); highest peak of Park Range of the Rocky Mts.

2. Peak in the Franconia Mts., N Grafton co., N cen. New Hampshire; 5108 ft. (1557 m.).

3. Peak in E Addison co., W Vermont; 4013 ft. (1223 m.).

Lincoln City. Coastal city, Lincoln co., Oregon, 57 mi. (92 km.) W of Salem; pop. (1990c) 5892.

Lincoln Heights. City, Hamilton co., SW Ohio, N of Cincinnati; pop. (1990c) 4805.

Lincoln Highway. Former highway from New York City to San Francisco, California; 3332 mi. (5361 km.) long; laid out 1913, completed 1927; later the name was used locally for sections of the route still in use.

Lincoln Park. **1.** Residential city, Wayne co., SE Michigan, S of Detroit; pop. (1990c) 41,832.

2. Borough, Morris co., N New Jersey, 7 mi. (11 km.) W of Paterson; pop. (1990c) 10,978.

Lincoln Sea. Part of Arctic Ocean N of Ellesmere I. and Greenland, 82° to 85°N; connects by Robeson and Kennedy channels with Kane Basin and Baffin Bay.

Lin·coln·shire \ˈliŋ-kən-ˌshir, -shər\. **1.** Village, Lake co., NE Illinois, 25 mi. (40 km.) NW of Chicago; pop. (1990c) 4931.

2. *or* **Lincoln.** Former county, E England; comprising three administrative counties: the Parts of Holland, 418 sq. mi. (1083 sq. km.); the Parts of Kesteven, 734 sq. mi. (1901 sq. km.); the Parts of Lindsey, 1510 sq. mi. (3911 sq. km.).

3. *or* **Lincoln.** Administrative county, E England, incl. most of former Lincolnshire; agriculture, tourism. See table at ENGLAND.

Lin·coln·ton \ˈliŋ-kən-tən\. **1.** Town, ⊗ of Lincoln co., E Georgia; pop. (1990c) 1476.

2. Town, ⊗ of Lincoln co., SW cen. North Carolina, 15 mi. (24 km.) NNW of Gastonia; pop. (1990c) 6847.

Lincoln Tunnel. Vehicular tunnel under the Hudson River from Manhattan I., New York City, to Weehawken, New Jersey; 8216 ft. (2504 m.) long; first tube opened 1937.

Lincoln Wolds. See WOLDS, THE.

Lin·coln·wood \ˈliŋ-kən-ˌwu̇d\. Village, Cook co., NE Illinois, N of Chicago; pop. (1990c) 11,365.

L'Incudine, Mont. See INCUDINE, MONT L'.

Lin·dau \ˈlin-ˌdau̇\ *also* **Lindau im Bo·den·see** \im-ˈbōd-ᵊn-ˌzā\. City, Bavaria, Germany, partly on island in Lake Constance 25 mi. (40 km.) ESE of Konstanz; pop. (1992e) 24,623; Renaissance town hall; 19th cent. Bavarian lion; resort.

Lin·den \ˈlin-dən\. **1.** Town, ⊗ of Marengo co., W Alabama; pop. (1990c) 2548.

2. City, Union co., NE New Jersey, just S of Elizabeth; pop. (1990c) 36,701; chemicals, paints, petroleum products.

3. Town, ⊗ of Perry co., W Tennessee; pop. (1990c) 1099.

4. Town, ⊗ of Cass co., NE Texas; pop. (1990c) 2375.

5. Town, N Guyana, on Demerara River ab. 50 mi. (80 km.) S of Georgetown; pop. (1985e) 35,000.

Linden Harbour. Inlet of Solomon Sea on S coast of New Britain I., Bismarck Archipelago, W Pacific Ocean, E of Gasmata; good harbor.

Lin·den·hurst \ˈlin-dən-ˌhərst\. **1.** Village, Lake co., NE Illinois, 10 mi. (16 km.) W of Waukegan; pop. (1990c) 8038.

2. Village, Suffolk co., SE New York, on Long Island, on Great South Bay 35 mi. (56 km.) E of New York City; pop. (1990c) 26,879.

Lin·den·wold \ˈlin-dən-ˌwōld\. Borough, Camden co., SW New Jersey, 12 mi. (19 km.) SSE of the city of Camden; pop. (1990c) 18,734.

Lin·des·nes \ˈlin-dəs-ˌnās\ *also* **The Naze** \ˈnāz\. Cape on S extremity of Norway, projecting into the North Sea.

Lin·di \ˈlin-dē\. **1.** River, NE Democratic Rep. of the Congo; rises W of Lake Edward, flows NW, then curves S; enters the Congo at Kisangani; ab. 375 mi. (605 km.) long.

2. Region of SE Tanzania; formerly part of Mtwara region. See table at TANZANIA.

3. Seaport, its ✻, at mouth of Lukuledi River.

Lindisfarne. See HOLY ISLAND.

Lin·don \ˈlind-ᵊn\. City, Utah co., Utah; pop. (1990c) 3818.

Lin·dos \ˈlēn-ˌdös\; *anc.* **Lin·dus** \ˈlin-dəs\. Town on E coast of Rhodes, Greece, off SW Turkey; Greek temple ruins; ancient city, began its importance first millennium B.C.; in Byzantine times taken by Knights of St. John.

Lind·say \ˈlin-zē\. **1.** City, Tulare co., S cen. California, 52 mi. (84 km.) SE of Fresno; pop. (1990c) 8338; once noted for olive production.

2. City, Garvin co., S cen. Oklahoma, on Washita River 27 mi. (43 km.) SE of Chickasha; pop. (1990c) 2947; oil wells.

3. Town, ⊗ of Victoria co., SE Ontario, Canada, on Scugog River 24 mi. (39 km.) W of Peterborough; pop. (1991c) 16,696; market center in agricultural region; summer resort; lumber.

Lindsay, Mount. Mountain in Macpherson Range bet. Queensland and New South Wales, Australia, near coast; 4064 ft. (1239 m.).

Linds·borg \ˈlinz-ˌbərg\. City, McPherson co., cen. Kansas, on Smoky Hill River 20 mi. (32 km.) S of Salina; pop. (1990c) 3576; Bethany Coll. (1881).

Lind·sey, Mount \ˈlin-zē\; *formerly* **Old Baldy Peak** \ˈbȯl-dē\. Mountain, Costilla co., Colorado; 14,042 ft. (4280 m.).

Lindsey, The Parts of. See LINCOLNSHIRE 2.

Lindum. See LINCOLN 13.

Lindus. See LINDOS.

Línea, La. See LA LÍNEA.

Line Islands \ˈlīn\. Group of islands in cen. Pacific Ocean S of the Hawaiian Is., N and S of the Equator, extending from Kingman Reef at 6°24′N, 162°22′W to Flint I., 11°26′S, 151°48′W; Jarvis, Kingman Reef, and Palmyra I. belong to U.S.; Teraina (Washington I.), Tabuaeran (Fanning I.), and Kiritimati (Christmas I.), N of the Equator, 158 sq. mi. (409 sq. km.), pop. (1990c) 4782, were formerly attached to British colony of Gilbert and Ellice Is. (abolished 1976); became part of Kiribati 1979, along with Malden, Starbuck, Caroline, Vostok, and Flint, S of the Equator, 40 sq. mi. (104 sq. km.).

Lin·fen *or W.-G.* **Lin–fen** \ˈlin-ˈfən\. Town, S cen. Shanxi prov., NE China, 140 mi. (225 km.) SSW of Taiyuan; pop. (1990c) 187,309.

Ling \ˈliŋ\. Canal, NE Guangxi Zhuangzu, China, connecting the Xiang and Li rivers.

Lin·ga·yen \ˌliŋ-gä-ˈyen\. Municipality, ✱ of Pangasinan prov., Luzon, Philippines, in N part, on S shore of Lingayen Gulf W of Dagupan (terminus of railroad line to Manila); pop. (1980c) 65,187; situated on an island in delta of the Agno.

Lingayen Gulf. Large inlet of South China Sea on NW coast of Luzon, Philippines; ab. 35 mi. (55 km.) long and 23 mi. (37 km.) across its entrance from Santiago I. to San Fernando Point; affords good anchorage for large number of vessels. Borders on La Union prov. on E and on Pangasinan on S and W and receives Agno River. Lingayen, Dagupan, San Fabian, and Sual are chief ports of Pangasinan on its shores. Scene during WWII of landing operations by Japanese Dec. 1941 and by Americans Jan. 1945.

Lingeh. See BANDAR-E LENGEH.

Ling·en \ˈliŋ-ən\ *also* **Lingen an der Ems** \ˌän-dər-ˈems, -ˈemz\. City, Lower Saxony, Germany, on Ems River 42 mi. (68 km.) NNW of Münster; pop. (1992e) 49,857; founded 13th cent.

Ling·ga \ˈliŋ-gə\. Chief island of the Lingga Archipelago, Indonesia; 40 mi. (64 km.) long; 360 sq. mi. (932 sq. km.).

Lingga Archipelago. Island group off the E coast of Sumatra, in Indonesia, S of Kepulauan Riau; 841 sq. mi. (2178 sq. km.). Comprises Lingga I. and Singkep I. and many small islands, mainly of coral growth and in shallow water; separated from Sumatra by Berhala Strait.

Ling·ga·dja·ti \ˌliŋ-gə-ˈjä-tē\. Town, N coast of Java, Indonesia, a suburb of Cirebon; agreement bet. Dutch and representatives of Republic of Indonesia initialed here Nov. 15, 1946, signaling preliminary Dutch recognition of independence of its former colony.

Ling·ling *or W.-G.* **Ling–ling** \ˈliŋ-ˈliŋ\. Town, S Hunan prov., SE cen. China, on Xiang River and on highway bet. Guilin to the SW and Hengyang to the NE.

Ling·mell \ˈliŋ-ˌmel\. Mountain, Cumberland co., NW England, 9 mi. (14 km.) SW of Keswick, in the Lake District; 2649 ft. (807 m.).

Lingones. See LANGRES.

Lin·gua·glos·sa \ˌlēŋ-gwä-ˈglȯ-sä\. Commune, Catania prov., E Sicily, Italy, just N of Mt. Etna; pop. (1981p) 5541.

Linguetta, Cape. See GJUHËZËS, CAPE.

Li·nha·res \lēn-ˈyär-ish\. Municipality, Espírito Santo state, E Brazil, ab. 70 mi. (115 km.) NNE of Vitória; pop. (1991p) 119,501.

Lin–i. See LINYI.

Lin·kö·ping \ˈlin-ˌchœ-piŋ\. City, ⊗ of Östergötland prov., SE Sweden, near S shore of Lake Roxen 110 mi. (177 km.) SW of Stockholm; pop. (1993e) 126,377; railroad junction; aircraft, automobiles, textiles; university (1967); 12th–15th cent. cathedral; 13th cent. castle; bishop's see estab. c. 1100; in 1598 the future Charles IX defeated Sigismund III Vasa nearby, assuring Protestant succession in Sweden.

Lin·lith·gow \lin-ˈlith-gō\. **1.** Former county in Scotland. See WEST LOTHIAN.

2. Burgh, NW Lothian region, SE Scotland; pop. (1981c) 9544; ruins of palace, residence of Scottish kings and birthplace of James V of Scotland (1512) and Mary, Queen of Scots (1542).

Linlithgowshire. See WEST LOTHIAN.

Linn \ˈlin\. **1.** Name of counties in four states of the U.S. See tables at IOWA, KANSAS, MISSOURI, OREGON.

2. City, ⊗ of Osage co., cen. Missouri, ESE of Jefferson City; pop. (1990c) 1148.

Lin·ne·us \ˈli-nē-əs\. City, ⊗ of Linn co., N Missouri; pop. (1990c) 364.

Linn·he, Loch \ˈli-nē\. Inlet of Atlantic Ocean on W coast of Scotland, extending NE 20 mi. (32 km.) from the head of the Firth of Lorn, bet. Highland and Strathclyde regions.

Li·no Lakes \ˈlī-nō\. Village, Anoka co., E Minnesota, 12 mi. (19 km.) N of St. Paul; pop. (1990c) 8807.

Li·no·sa \lē-ˈnō-sä\; *anc.* **Ae·gu·sa** \i-ˈgyü-sə\. One of the Pelagie Is. (*q.v.*), N of Lampedusa.

Lin·qing \ˈlin-ˈchiŋ\ *or W.-G.* **Lin–ch'ing** \-ˈchiŋ\; *mostly formerly* **Lin–tsing** \-ˈchiŋ\. City, W Shandong prov., NE China, on the Grand Canal (Da Yunhe) WNW of Jinan; pop. (1990c) 123,958.

Lins \ˈlēⁿs\. City, W cen. São Paulo state, SE Brazil, on railroad line 230 mi. (370 km.) WNW of the city of São Paulo; munic. pop. (1991p) 59,221; coffee.

Lintfort. See KAMP-LINTFORT.

Linth \ˈlint\. River, E cen. Switzerland; rises in S Glarus canton, flows N into W end of Lake Wallen; ab. 26 mi. (42 km.) long; as the **Linth Canal** it connects Lake Wallen with the Zürichsee; the Limmat, flowing from the Zürichsee to the Aare, is sometimes considered as the lower course of the Linth.

Lin·ton \ˈlint-ᵊn\. **1.** City, Greene co., SW Indiana, 32 mi. (51 km.) SSE of Terre Haute; pop. (1990c) 5814.

2. City, ⊗ of Emmons co., S North Dakota, 46 mi. (74 km.) SSE of Bismarck; pop. (1990c) 1410.

Lin–tsing. See LINQING.

Lin·wood \ˈlin-ˌwu̇d\. City, Atlantic co., SE New Jersey, 8 mi. (13 km.) W of Atlantic City; pop. (1990c) 6866.

Lin·yi \ˈlin-ˈyē, -ˈē\ *or W.-G.* **Lin–i** \ˈlin-ˈē, -ˈyē\; *formerly* **Ichow** \ˈē-ˈchau̇\. City, SW Shandong prov., NE China, NW of Jinan; pop. (1990c) 324,720.

Linyü–kuan. See SHANHAIGUAN.

Linz \ˈlints, ˈlinz\; *anc.* **Len·tia** \ˈlen-chē-ə\. City, ✱ of Upper Austria, Austria, on Danube River 95 mi. (153 km.) W of Vienna; pop. (1991c) 203,044; railroad junction; river port; steel, machinery, electrical equipment, tobacco products; university (opened 1966); cultural center, with two cathedrals, episcopal palace, town hall. Developed from Roman camp; important trade center by 13th cent. but without civic rights; suffered considerable damage in WWII.

Li·on, Gulf of \ˈlī-ən\ *or Fr.* **Golfe du Lion** \ˌgȯlf-dü̅-ˈlyōⁿ\; *anc.* **Si·nus Gal·li·cus** \ˈsī-nəs-ˈga-li-kəs\. Inlet of Mediterranean Sea on S coast of France, extending from peninsula of Giens, near Hyères, E of Marseille, to Cape Creus on NE coast of Spain.

Li·pa \lē-ˈpä\. Chartered city, E cen. Batangas prov., Luzon, Philippines, E of Lake Taal, 15 mi. (24 km.) N of the municipality of Batangas; pop. (1990p) 160,000; active inland trade center.

Lípa, Česká. See ČESKÁ LÍPA.

Lip·a·ri Islands \ˈli-pə-rē\ *or Ital.* **Iso·le Eo·lie** \ˈē-zō-ˌlā-ä-ˈō-lē-ˌā\; *anc.* **Ae·o·li·ae In·su·lae** \ē-ˈō-lē-ˌē-ˈin-sə-ˌlē\. Group of small volcanic islands in the SE Tyrrhenian Sea off N coast of Messina prov., Sicily, Italy; 44 sq. mi. (114 sq. km.); includes the islands of Salina, Vulcano, Stromboli, Panarea, and the chief island **Lipari** (*anc.* **Lip·a·ra** \ˈli-pə-rə\), 13 sq. mi. (34 sq. km.), on which is located the town of **Lipari.** According to legend, the island on which Aeolus kept the winds confined in caves was one of this group. Inhabited since Neolithic times; held successively by Greeks, Carthaginians, Romans, Saracens, Normans, and Aragonese.

Li·petsk \ˈli-ˌpitsk\. Town, ✱ of Lipetsk Oblast, Russia in Europe, 65 mi. (104 km.) N of Voronezh; pop. (1992e) 464,000; food processing; iron and steel works; tractors, chemicals, cement; founded by Czar Peter the Great as ironworking center early 18th cent.

Lipetsk Oblast \ˈō-bləst, -ˌblast\ *or* **Li·pet·ska·ya Oblast'** \ˈli-ˌpit-skə-yə-ˈō-bləstʸ\. Administrative subdivision of Russia in Europe; 9305 sq. mi. (24,100 sq. km.); pop. (1992e) 1,234,000; ✱ Lipetsk; rye, wheat.

Lip·no \ˈlēp-nȯ, ˈlip-\. Commune, Włocławek prov., N cen. Poland, 87 mi. (140 km.) NW of Warsaw; pop. (1981p) 12,645.

Lip·pe \'li-pə\. **1.** River, W Germany; rises in the Teutoburger Wald and flows W in North Rhine-Westphalia into Rhine River at Wesel; 147 mi. (236 km.) long.
2. Former German state, now part of North Rhine-Westphalia, Germany, bet. Teutoburger Wald and Weser River; 469 sq. mi. (1215 sq. km.); ✱ Detmold. Emerged as a lordship in medieval times; became a county 16th cent.; dynastic divisions 17th cent. resulted in two counties, Lippe and Schaumburg-Lippe (*q.v.*); Lippe became a principality 1720; joined Confederation of Rhine 1807 and German Confederation 1815; joined Weimar Republic 1918; incorp. 1947 in North Rhine-Westphalia state.

Lipp·stadt \'lip-ˌshtät\. City, North Rhine-Westphalia, Germany, on Lippe River 38 mi. (61 km.) SE of Münster; pop. (1992e) 63,028; textiles; several medieval churches; city founded c. 1168; during Middle Ages, member of Hanseatic League.

Lips·comb \'lip-skəm\. **1.** County in NW Texas. See table at TEXAS.
2. City, Jefferson co., cen. Alabama, 8 mi. (13 km.) SW of Birmingham; pop. (1990c) 2892.
3. Village, ⊗ of Lipscomb co., NW Texas.

Lipsia. See LEIPZIG 2.

Lip·sos \'lip-ˌsäs\ *or Gk.* **Lip·sós** \ˌlēp-'sȯs\; *Ital.* **Lis·so** \'lēs-sō\ *or* **Lip·so** \'lēp-sō\. An island of the Dodecanese (*q.v.*), Greece, N of Leros and E of Patmos; 7 sq. mi. (18 sq. km.).

Lip·tov·ský Mi·ku·láš \'lip-tȯv-skē-'mi-kü-ˌläsh\ *or Hung.* **Lip·tó·szent·mi·klós** \'lip-tō-sent-'mik-ˌlōsh\. Town, cen. N Slovakia, on the Váh River E of Ružomberok; pop. (1980p) 24,520.

Liqen i Shkodrës. See SCUTARI, LAKE.

Li·ra \'lē-rä\. Town, N Uganda, N of Lake Kyoga; pop. (1991p) 27,143.

Li·ri \'lē-rē\; *anc.* **Li·ris** \'lī-rəs\. River, cen. Italy; rises near Avezzano E of Rome, flows SE bet. parallel ranges of cen. Apennine Mts. and forms valley of the Liri; joined by the Sacco near Frosinone and farther E near Cassino by the Rapido after which it turns S to enter Gulf of Gaeta (Tyrrhenian Sea) near Minturno; ab. 100 mi. (160 km.) long; its lower course also known as the Garigliano. In WWII its valley invaded by Allies May 1944 as part of the Allied advance on Rome.

Lis. See LIZ.

Lis·boa \lēzh-'vō-ə\. **1.** District of W Portugal. See table at PORTUGAL.
2. City, Portugal. See LISBON 6.

Lis·bon \'liz-bən\. **1.** Town, New London co., SE Connecticut; pop. (1990c) 3790.
2. Town, Androscoggin co., SW Maine, 8 mi. (13 km.) SE of Lewiston; pop. (1990c) 9457.
3. Town, Grafton co., W New Hampshire, 9 mi. (14 km.) SW of Littleton; pop. (1990c) 1664; township includes **Sug·ar Hill** \ˌshu̇g-ər\, a hilltop settlement.
4. City, ⊗ of Ransom co., SE North Dakota, 38 mi. (61 km.) SSE of Valley City; pop. (1990c) 2177.
5. Village, ⊗ of Columbiana co., E Ohio, 23 mi. (37 km.) S of Youngstown; pop. (1990c) 3037. Site of Confederate Gen. John Hunt Morgan's surrender nearby 1863.
6. *or Port.* **Lis·boa** \lēzh-'vō-ə\; *anc.* **Olis·i·po** \ō-'li-sə-ˌpō\ *also* **Fe·lic·i·tas Ju·lia** \fə-'li-sə-tas-'jül-yə\. Seaport city, ✱ of Portugal and of Lisboa dist., W Portugal; pop. (1991p) 677,790; Portugal's leading seaport; exports olive oil, cork, wine, and fish; manufactures textiles, soap, flour, steel; oil refining; Univ. of Lisbon (1911), Technical Univ. of Lisbon (1930); built on terraced hills; cathedral; castle of St. George; monastery and Tower of Belém; birthplace of poet Luíz Vaz de Camões c. 1524.
History: Ancient settlement fell to Romans 205 B.C.; became Roman municipium under Gen. Julius Caesar; captured 5th cent. A.D. by Alans, Suevi, and Visigoths and 8th cent. by Moors; conquered 1147 by Crusaders under Afonso I, first king of Portugal; sacked by Castile in 14th cent. wars; during period of Portuguese voyages and colonial expansion, flourished as a leading European commercial center; began to lose prosperity at end of 16th cent.; held by Spain 1580–1640; devastated by earthquake 1755 with extreme loss of life; occupied by French 1807–08; shopping district dating back as early as 18th cent. destroyed by fire 1988. See PORTUGAL.

Lis·burn \'liz-bərn\. **1.** District, E Northern Ireland. See table at IRELAND, NORTHERN.
2. Town, its ⊗, on Lagan River 8 mi. (13 km.) SW of Belfast; pop. (1991c) 42,110; market town; a center of linen industry; 17th cent. Protestant cathedral.

Lis·burne, Cape \'liz-bərn\. Cape on NW coast of Alaska, on Chukchi Sea.

Lis·can·nor Bay \lis-'ka-nər\. Inlet of Atlantic Ocean on W coast of Ireland, S of Galway Bay.

Li·shui *or W.-G.* **Li–shui** \'lē-'shwē\; *formerly* **Chu·chow** \'chü-'jō\. City, S cen. Zhejiang prov., E China, ab. 55 mi. (88 km.) WNW of Wenzhou. Scene of fighting bet. Chinese and Japanese 1942.

Lis·i·an·ski \ˌlis-ē-'an-skē\. Islet of Leeward Is., Hawaiian Is., in cen. Pacific Ocean.

Li·si·chansk \ˌli-si-'chänsk\. Town, Luhansk subdivision, Ukraine, ab. 45 mi. (70 km.) WNW of the city of Luhansk, on the Donets River; pop. (1991e) 126,000.

Li·sieux \lēz-'yœ\; *anc.* **No·vi·om·a·gus** \ˌnō-vē-'ä-mə-gəs\. City, Calvados dept., NW France, 27 mi. (43 km.) E of Caen; pop. (1990c) 24,506; machinery; cathedral (begun 12th cent.); basilica (1929–54). Named for its ancient inhabitants, the Lexovii; taken by Romans; town often fought over during Hundred Years' War; long an episcopal see; heavily damaged in WWII. Shrine of St. Thérèse attracts numerous pilgrims.

Lis·kamm \'lis-ˌkäm\. Mountain in Alps, on Switzerland-Italy border; 14,852 ft. (4527 m.).

Lis·keard \lis-'kärd\. Town, Cornwall, SW England, WNW of Plymouth; pop. (1981p) 6316; nearby are prehistoric monuments.

Lis·ki \'lis-kē\; *1965–91* **Ge·or·giu–Dezh** \gi-'ȯr-gyə-'dezh\. Town, Voronezh Oblast, W Russia in Europe, ab. 50 mi. (80 km.) SSE of the city of Voronezh; pop. (1991e) 54,900.

Lisle \'līl\. **1.** Village, Du Page co., NE Illinois, ab. 5 mi. (8 km.) S of Wheaton; pop. (1990c) 19,512; Illinois Benedictine Coll. (1887); pop. more than doubled bet. 1970 and 1980.
2. *or* **L'Isle** \'lēl, 'līl\. City, France. See LILLE.

L'Is·let \lē-'lā, -'le\. County, S Quebec, Canada. See table at QUEBEC.

Lis·more \'liz-ˌmōr\. Town and river port, NE New South Wales, SE Australia, 100 mi. (161 km.) S of Brisbane; pop. (1991c) 41,389.

Lis·more \liz-'mōr\. **1.** Island at entrance to Loch Linnhe, Strathclyde region, W Scotland; 9.5 mi. (15.3 km.) long; parish church in restored cathedral.
2. Market town, co. Waterford, S Ireland; pop. (1986c) 703; castle built 1185.

Lissa. 1. Commune, Poland. See LESZNO.
2. Island, Croatia. See VIS.

Lis·se \'li-sə\. Municipality, South Holland prov., Netherlands, SW of Amsterdam's international airport; pop. (1993e) 21,536; bulb-growing center.

Lisso. See LIPSOS.

Lis·so·ne \lē-'sō-nā\. Commune, Milano prov., Lombardy, N Italy, 7 mi. (11 km.) N of Milan; pop. (1989c) 31,786.

Lissus. See LEZHË 2.

Lis·ter, Mount \'lis-tər\. Mountain, Antarctica, 78°04′S, 162°41′E; 13,205 ft. (4025 m.).

Lister og Mandals. See VEST-AGDER.

List Land \'list-ˌlänt\. N part of the island of Sylt, off W coast of Schleswig-Holstein, Germany.

Lis·tow·el \lis-'tō-əl\. **1.** Town, Perth co., SE Ontario, Canada, 26 mi. (42 km.) N of Stratford; pop. (1991c) 5404.
2. Market town, N co. Kerry, SW Ireland; pop. (1986c) 3494; remains of old castle.

Li·ta·ni \li-'tä-nē\ *or Arab.* **Nahr al–Lī·ta·nī** \ˌnär-al-li-'tä-nē\. River, S Lebanon; rises near Baalbek, flows S bet. the Lebanon and Anti-Lebanon mountain ranges, turns SW and empties into Mediterranean Sea 6 mi. (10 km.) N of Tyre; 90 mi. (145 km.) long.

Litch·field \'lich-ˌfēld\. **1.** County in NW Connecticut. See table at CONNECTICUT.
2. Town, cen. Litchfield co., NW Connecticut; pop. (1990c) 8365; summer resort; agriculture; manufactures electrical devices; incorp. 1719; important trading center and strategic military depot in Colonial and Revolutionary times; site of first law school in America (1784); birthplace of American Revolutionary soldier Ethan Allen (1738), clergyman Henry Ward Beecher (1813), and author Harriet Beecher Stowe (1811). Includes borough of Litchfield.
3. City, Montgomery co., S cen. Illinois, 45 mi. (72 km.) S of Springfield; pop. (1990c) 6883.
4. City, ⊗ of Meeker co., S cen. Minnesota, 35 mi. (56 km.) SSW of St. Cloud; pop. (1990c) 6041.

Lith·er·land \'li-thər-lənd\. Town, Merseyside, NW England, 4.5 mi. (7.2 km.) N of Liverpool; pop. (1981p) 21,946.

Lith·gow \'lith-gō\. Town, E New South Wales, SE Australia, 65 mi. (104 km.) WNW of Sydney; urban area pop. (1991c) 11,968; small-arms factory, textile factories; formerly a center of coal mining and ironworking; first steelworks estab. late 19th cent.; nearby is a restored zigzagging section of railway.

Lith·u·a·nia \ˌli-thə-'wā-nē-ə-, -thyə-, -nyə\ *or Lith.* **Lie·tu·va** \lye-'tü-vä\ *or Russ.* **Lit·va** \'lyēt-vä\. Republic, N Europe, bounded on N by Latvia, on E and SE by Belarus, on SW by Poland and Kaliningrad Oblast, Russia, and on W by Baltic Sea; comprised **Lith·u·a·ni·an Soviet Socialist Republic** \-nē-ən, -nyən\ 1940–91; 25,174 sq. mi. (65,201 sq. km.); pop. (1993e) 3,753,000; ✱ Vilnius. Mostly low-lying land with many lakes and swamps; highest point is not above 1000 ft. (305 m.); crossed in S part by Neman River; also drained in N by upper courses of Venta and Lielupe rivers; has ab. 60 mi. (100 km.) of coast on the Baltic; lacks good port.

Chief products: Dairy products, sugar beets, potatoes; livestock; food products, textiles, paper, machinery.

Chief towns: Vilnius, Kaunas, Klaipėda.

History: Region long occupied by pagan Lithuanians prior to uniting as a single state to oppose the Teutonic Knights 13th cent.; expanded 14th cent. by Grand Dukes Gediminas and Algirdas into large state that extended westward into Russia and as far S as the Black Sea; formed dynastic union with Poland (*q.v.*) 1386 when through marriage to Queen Jadwiga of Poland, the reigning grand duke of Lithuania became king of Poland as Władisław II Jagiełło; became predominantly Roman Catholic; merged with Poland by Union of Lublin 1569; acquired by Russia in Third Partition of Poland 1795; administered by Russia separately from Poland; joined Polish revolt 1863; demanded self-government 1905; occupied by Germans during WWI; proclaimed independent republic Feb. 16, 1918; recognized by U.S.S.R. 1920; seizure of Vilnius (*q.v.*) by Poland 1920 caused rupture of relations which lasted into the next decade; invaded Memel (Klaipėda) 1923; military coup d'état 1926; forced by Polish ultimatum to reestablish relations 1938; in 1939, Memel taken by Germany and Vilnius restored to Lithuania by U.S.S.R.; signed mutual assistance pact with U.S.S.R. which prepared way for annexation Aug. 3, 1940 as Lithuanian S.S.R.; overrun by German army 1941; recovered by U.S.S.R. 1944; independence from U.S.S.R. proclaimed by Lithuanian parliament Mar. 11, 1990; recognized by U.S.S.R. Sept. 6, 1991.

Lit·itz \'li-təts\. Borough, Lancaster co., SE Pennsylvania, 8 mi. (13 km.) N of the city of Lancaster; pop. (1990c) 8280; chocolate; founded by Moravians 1757.

Li·to·mě·ři·ce \'lē-tò-ˌmyer-zhit-ˌse\ *or Ger.* **Leit·me·ritz** \'līt-mə-ˌrits\. Town, N Czech Republic, on the Labe (Elbe) River

at head of vessel navigation, 35 mi. (56 km.) NNW of Prague; pop. (1980p) 23,835.

Lit·tle \ 'lit-ᵊl\. **1.** River, E North Carolina; rises in Wake co., flows SE into Neuse River near Goldsboro; 80 mi. (129 km.) long.

2. River, Oklahoma and Arkansas; rises in Le Flore co., SE Oklahoma, flows S, then E across Arkansas border to empty into Red River on SW boundary of Hempstead co., SW Arkansas; ab. 150 mi. (240 km.) long.

Little Abaco. See ABACO.

Little Alföld. See ALFÖLD, GREAT.

Little America. Settlement of the Byrd Antarctic Expedition (1929) near the outer edge of Ross Ice Shelf on Bay of Whales, Ross Sea, Antarctica; location of several bases used by American naval officer and explorer Richard E. Byrd and others on subsequent expeditions, incl. his 2d expedition (1933–35), his expedition of 1946–47, and the expedition of the International Geophysical Year 1957–58.

Little Andaman. One of the Andaman Is. (*q.v.*).

Little Ar·me·nia \ är-'mē-nē-ə, -nyə\ *or* **Lesser Armenia.** Medieval feudal kingdom, 12th–14th cents., of Armenians in Cilicia (*q.v.*); conquered by Mamluks 1375.

Little Atlas. See ATLAS MOUNTAINS.

Little Bahama Bank. See BAHAMA BANKS.

Little Bald \ 'bȯld\. Peak in Unicoi co., NE Tennessee; 5000 ft. (1525 m.).

Little Barrier Island. Small island off E coast of N extension of North I., New Zealand, in entrance to Hauraki Gulf.

Little Bear Peak \ 'bar\. Mountain, Costilla co., S Colorado; 14,037 ft. (4278 m.).

Little Belt. Strait bet. Fyn I. and the mainland of Denmark, connecting the Kattegat with the Baltic Sea; 30 mi. (48 km.) long, varies from ab. 2100 ft. to 18 mi. (640 m. to 30 km.) in width. See STORE STRAIT.

Little Belt Mountains. A range of the Rocky Mts. in cen. Montana, chiefly in Cascade and Judith Basin cos.

Little Big·horn \ 'big-ˌhȯrn\ *also* **Little Horn.** River, S Montana; rises in N Wyoming, flows N through Big Horn co., S Montana, into Bighorn River; ab. 80 mi. (130 km.) long; on its banks Gen. George Custer and his army command were defeated and slain by Indians June 25, 1876.

Little Bighorn Battlefield National Monument. See UNITED STATES, *National Monuments.*

Little Bitter Lake. See BITTER LAKES.

Little Blue. River, Nebraska and Kansas; rises in S Nebraska and flows SE across Kansas border into Big Blue River below Marysville, Marshall co., NE Kansas.

Lit·tle·bor·ough \ 'lit-ᵊl-ˌbər-ə, -ˌbər-ō\. Town, Greater Manchester, NW England, on the Roch 13 mi. (21 km.) NE of Manchester; pop. (1981p) 13,861.

Little Bras d'Or. See BRAS D'OR.

Little Bushman Land. See BUSHMAN LAND.

Little Canada. City, Ramsey co., Minnesota, 1 mi. (1.6 km.) N of St. Paul; pop. (1990c) 8971.

Little Car·pa·thi·an Mountains \ kär-'pā-thē-ən\ *also* **Little Carpathians** \ -ənz\ *or Czech* **Ma·lé Kar·paty** \ 'mä-lā-kär-'pä-tē\. Mountain range, a SW extension of the Carpathian Mts., Slovakia, N of Bratislava; highest point ab. 2500 ft. (760 m.).

Little Cayman. See CAYMAN ISLANDS.

Little Chief Mountain \ 'chēf\. Peak in Glacier National Park, NW Montana; 9552 ft. (2912 m.).

Little Chute \ 'shüt\. Village, Outagamie co., E Wisconsin, on rapids in Fox River 8 mi. (13 km.) E of Appleton; pop. (1990c) 9207.

Little Co·co \ 'kō-kō\. Small island of the Andaman Is., separated from North Andaman I. by Coco Channel.

Little Col·o·ra·do \ˌkä-lə-'ra-dō, -'rä-\. River, NE Arizona; rises in S Apache co., flows NW into the Colorado River on E edge of Grand Canyon National Park; 315 mi. (507 km.) long.

Little Comp·ton \ 'kämp-tən\. Town, Newport co., SE Rhode Island, 8 mi. (13 km.) E of the city of Newport; pop. (1990c) 3339.

Little Corn Island. See CORN ISLANDS.

Little Creek Peak. Mountain, E Iron co., SW Utah; 10,142 ft. (3091 m.).

Little Cumbrae Island. See CUMBRAES, THE.

Little Cuyahoga River. See CUYAHOGA 1.

Little Diomede. See DIOMEDE ISLANDS.

Little Dunmow. See DUNMOW.

Little Egg Harbor. Inlet of Barnegat Bay, on SE coast of Ocean co., E New Jersey.

Little Egg Inlet. Narrow strait, on extreme S tip of Ocean co., E New Jersey, leading from Atlantic Ocean into Great Bay.

Little Exuma. See EXUMA.

Little Falls. 1. City, ⊗ of Morrison co., cen. Minnesota, on Mississippi River; pop. (1990c) 6041.

2. Township, Passaic co., N New Jersey, on Passaic River 5 mi. (8 km.) SW of Paterson; pop. (1990c) 11,294.

3. City, Herkimer co., NE cen. New York, 20 mi. (32 km.) E of Utica; pop. (1990c) 5829. Settled c. 1725; incorp. as city 1895. The Mohawk River near here passes through **Little Falls Gorge** and falls ab. 45 ft. (14 m.) in 1 mi. (1.6 km.) of its course.

Little Ferry. Borough, Bergen co., NE New Jersey, on Hackensack River 9 mi. (15 km.) N of Jersey City; pop. (1990c) 9989.

Lit·tle·field \ 'lit-ᵊl-ˌfēld\. City, ⊗ of Lamb co., Texas, in Texas Panhandle, NW of Lubbock; pop. (1990c) 6489.

Little Fork. River, N Minnesota; rises in N cen. St. Louis co., flows NW into Rainy River on U.S.-Canada boundary; ab. 130 mi. (210 km.) long.

Lit·tle·hamp·ton \ 'lit-ᵊl-ˌhamp-tən\. Town, West Sussex, S England, on the coast at the mouth of the Arun River; pop. (1981p) 22,181; seaside resort.

Little Hay·stack Mountain \ 'hā-ˌstak\. Peak in the Adirondack Mts., Essex co., NE New York; 4700 ft. (1433 m.).

Little Horn. See LITTLE BIGHORN.

Little Inagua. See INAGUA.

Little Jay Peak \ 'jā\. Mountain, NW Orleans co., N Vermont; 3180 ft. (969 m.).

Little Kai Island. See KAI ISLANDS.

Little Ka·na·wha \ kə-'nȯ-wə, -'nȯ-ē\. River, cen. and W West Virginia; rises in S Upshur co., flows W and NW into Ohio River at Parkersburgh; ab. 160 mi. (255 km.) long; navigable by small boats for 48 mi. (77 km.).

Little Kapela. See KAPELA, GREAT.

Little Karoo. See KAROO.

Little Lake. Lake on boundary bet. Jefferson and Lafourche parishes, SE Louisiana.

Little Le·ver \ 'lē-vər\. Town, Greater Manchester, NW England, 3 mi. (5 km.) SE of Bolton; pop. (1981p) 11,439.

Little Loch Broom. See BROOM, LOCH.

Little Mi·ami \ mī-'a-mē\. River, Ohio; rises in Clark co., flows S to Ohio River just E of Cincinnati; ab. 140 mi. (225 km.) long.

Little Minch \ 'minch\. Strait off NW coast of Scotland, extending bet. Skye I. of the Inner Hebrides and the cen. islands of the Outer Hebrides; varies in width bet. 14 and 20 mi. (23 and 32 km.).

Little Miquelon. See MIQUELON ISLAND.

Little Mis·sou·ri \ mə-'zu̇r-ē, -'zu̇r-ə\. **1.** River, Arkansas; rises in Pike co. and flows SE into the Ouachita River; ab 150 mi. (240 km.) long.

2. River, NW United States; flows from NE Wyoming NE across SE corner of Montana and NW corner of South Dakota into North Dakota, and continuing N into McKenzie co., where it turns E to empty into Missouri River in NE Dunn co., W North Dakota; 560 mi. (901 km.) long.

Little Monadnock. See MONADNOCK, MOUNT.

Little Moose Mountain \ 'müs\. Peak in Adirondack Mts., Hamilton co., NE cen. New York; 3630 ft. (1106 m.).

Little Namaqualand. See NAMAQUALAND.

Little Neck Bay. Inlet of Long Island Sound, Queens borough, W Long Island; formerly source of littleneck clams, beds condemned 1909 because of pollution of the water.
Little Nemaha. See NEMAHA.
Little Nethe. See NETHE.
Little Nicobar. One of the Nicobar Is. (*q.v.*).
Little Paternosters. See BALABALAGAN ISLANDS.
Little Peconic Bay. See PECONIC BAY.
Little Pee Dee \ˈpē-ˌdē\. River, North Carolina and South Carolina; flows from Scotland co., S North Carolina, S across South Carolina border into Pee Dee River near its mouth; 145 mi. (233 km.) long.
Little Pow·der \ˈpaů-dər\. River, Wyoming and Montana; flows from cen. Campbell co., NE Wyoming, N into Powder River in Powder River co., SE Montana; 100 mi. (161 km.) long.
Little Quemoy. See QUEMOY.
Little Rann of Kachchh *or* **Little Rann of Kutch.** See KACHCHH, RANN OF.
Little Red. River, Arkansas; formed by two branches in Van Buren co., flows SE into the White River on E boundary of White co., E Arkansas; ab 120 mi. (195 km.) long.
Little River. **1.** Name of two rivers, United States. See LITTLE.
2. County in SW Arkansas. See table at ARKANSAS.
Lit·tle Rock \ˈlit-ᵊl-ˌräk\. City, ✻ of Arkansas and ⊗ of Pulaski co., cen. Arkansas, on S bank of the Arkansas River; pop. (1990c) 175,795; largest city in the state; clothing, lumber, sawmills; bauxite mines; center of farming region; Philander Smith Coll. (1868); Arkansas Baptist Coll. (1884), Univ. of Arkansas at Little Rock (1927). Founded 1821 and made territorial ✻ same year; chartered 1831; became state ✻ on admission of Arkansas to the Union 1836; in Civil War occupied by Union forces Sept. 1863; in 1957 federal troops sent to city to prevent interference by state authorities with school desegregation.
Little Ross \ˈrȯs\. Small island off S coast of Dumfries and Galloway region, S Scotland; E of entrance to Wigtown Bay; lighthouse.
Little Russia. Former area with indefinite boundaries incl. Carpathian Ruthenia (see ZAKARPATS'KA), E Poland, Ukraine, and W shores of Black Sea; inhabited chiefly by Ukrainians, who were also called Little Russians or Ruthenians.
Little Sa·ble Point \ˈsā-bəl\. Point on W coast of Oceana co., W Michigan, extending into Lake Michigan.
Little Saint Bernard. Mountain pass, in Alps. See table at ALPS.
Little Sal·ke·hatch·ie \ˌsȯl-kə-ˈha-chē\. River, South Carolina; rises in Bamberg co., flows SE to unite with Salkehatchie River and form Combahee River; ab 50 mi. (80 km.) long.
Little Sandy. River, NE Kentucky; rises in S Elliott co., flows NE into the Ohio River in NE Greenup co.; 45 mi. (72 km.) long.
Little Sark. See SARK 1.
Little Sa·tilla \sə-ˈti-lə\. River, SE Georgia; rises in Jeff Davis co., flows SE into Satilla River in Brantley co.; ab. 60 mi. (95 km.) long.
Little Scheidegg. See SCHEIDEGG.
Little Schütt. See SZIGETKÖZ.
Little Sil·ver \ˈsil-vər\. Borough, Monmouth co., E cen. New Jersey, SE of Perth Amboy; pop. (1990c) 5721.
Little Sioux \ˈsü\. River, Minnesota and Iowa; flows from Jackson co., S Minnesota, S into Missouri River in W Harrison co., W Iowa; 221 mi. (356 km.) long.
Little Skel·lig \ˈske-lig\. See SKELLIGS.
Lit·tles·town \ˈlitᵊlz-ˌtaůn\. Borough, Adams co., S Pennsylvania, near Maryland border 25 mi. (40 km.) SW of York; pop. (1990c) 2974.
Little Ten·nes·see \ˌte-nə-ˈsē, ˈte-nə-ˌsē\. River, S United States; rises near N boundary of Georgia and flows N through Macon co., SW North Carolina, N and W across Tennessee border, and into Tennessee River in Loudon co., E Tennessee; ab.150 mi. (240 km.) long. In its course in North Carolina near Tennessee border is Fontana Dam, one of the dams of the Tennessee Valley Authority (*q.v.*).
Little Tibet. See BALTISTAN.
Little To·ba·go \tə-ˈbā-gō\. Island in Atlantic Ocean off NE coast of Tobago; 1 sq. mi. (2.6 sq. km.).
Lit·tle·ton \ˈlit-ᵊl-tən\. **1.** City, ⊗ of Arapahoe co., NE cen. Colorado, 8 mi. (13 km.) S of Denver; pop. (1990c) 33,685; residential; Arapahoe Community Coll. (1965).
2. Town, Middlesex co., NE Massachusetts, 12 mi. (19 km.) SW of Lowell; pop. (1990c) 7051.
3. Town, Grafton co., W New Hampshire, 30 mi. (48 km.) WSW of Berlin; pop. (1990c) 5827; summer and winter resort; active in antislavery movement 19th cent.
Little Tra·verse Bay \ˈtra-vərs\. Inlet of Lake Michigan on SW coast of Emmet co., N Michigan.
Little Tupper Lake. See TUPPER LAKES.
Little Valley. Village, ⊗ of Cattaraugus co., SW New York; pop. (1990c) 1881.
Little Wa·bash \ˈwȯ-ˌbash\. River, Illinois; rises in Coles co., flows SE into the Wabash River 8 mi. (13 km.) from its mouth; ab. 200 mi. (320 km.) long.
Little Walachia. See OLTENIA.
Little Zab. See ZAB, LITTLE.
Little Zimbabwe. See ZIMBABWE.
Littoria. See LATINA.
Litva. See LITHUANIA.
Lit·ví·nov \lit-ˈvē-nȯf\. Town, NW Czech Republic, ab. 50 mi. (80 km.) NW of Prague; pop. (1991p) 29,085.
Litz·mann·stadt \ˈlits-män-ˌshtät\. German name of Łódź during WWII. See ŁÓDŹ 2.
Liu·gong *or W.-G.* **Liu–Kung** \ˈlyü-ˈgůŋ\. See WEI-HAI.
Li·vad·ia \li-ˈva-de-ə\ Suburb of Yalta, Crimea, Ukraine; health resort; former residence of czars, site of meeting of Allied heads of state 1945. See YALTA.
Li·ven·za \li-ˈvent-sä\. River, Veneto, NE Italy, N of Piave River; flows from the Alps SE into Adriatic Sea; 70 mi. (113 km.) long.
Live Oak \ˈlīv-ˌōk\. **1.** County in S Texas. See table at TEXAS.
2. City, Sutter co., N cen. California, 45 mi. (72 km.) N of Sacramento; pop. (1990c) 4320.
3. City, ⊗ of Suwannee co., N Florida, 62 mi. (100 km.) NW of Gainesville; pop. (1990c) 6332.
4. City, Bexar co., S cen. Texas; pop. (1990c) 10,023.
Liv·er·more \ˈli-vər-ˌmōr\. City, Alameda co., W California, 23 mi. (37 km.) E of San Francisco Bay; pop. (1990c) 56,741; wineries; Lawrence Livermore National (Research) Laboratory.
Livermore, Mount *also* **Baldy Peak** \ˈbȯl-dē\. Mountain, Jeff Davis co., W Texas, one of Davis Mts.; 8382 ft. (2555 m.).
Livermore Falls. Town, Androscoggin co., SW Maine, 26 mi. (42 km.) N of Lewiston; pop. (1990c) 3455.
Liv·er·pool \ˈli-vər-ˌpül\. **1.** Village, Onondaga co., cen. New York, 5 mi. (8 km.) N of Syracuse; pop. (1990c) 2624.
2. Municipality within the Sydney met. area, E New South Wales, SE Australia; pop. (1991c) 92,203.
3. Town, ⊗ of Queens co., SW Nova Scotia, Canada, on Atlantic Ocean 74 mi. (119 km.) SW of Halifax; pop. (1991c) 3113; paper, fisheries. Orig. settled by Indians who were followed by French colonizers; New Englanders arrived 1759, giving it its current name; base of operations for British privateers during American Revolution and War of 1812.
4. City, ⊗ of Merseyside, NW England, on estuary of the Mersey River; pop. (1991p) 448,300; port with extensive docks; formerly a major industrial center; the Anglican cathedral (begun 1904, completed 1978) is the largest in England; Roman Catholic cathedral (1967); town hall (1754); Univ. of Liverpool (1903); pop musicians the Beatles were born here. Received first charter 1207; developed rapidly as major Atlantic port from 18th cent.; known for its delftware and porcelain 18th cent.; suffered heavy damage from German bombing in WWII; declined in 2d half of 20th cent.
Liverpool Range. Mountains, NE New South Wales, SE Australia; extends W from Great Dividing Range, SW of New England Plateau; highest point Oxleys Peak 4500 ft. (1372 m.).

Liv·ing·ston \ˈli-viŋ-stən\. **1.** Name of a parish in SE Louisiana and of counties in five states of the U.S. See tables at ILLINOIS, KENTUCKY, LOUISIANA, MICHIGAN, MISSOURI, NEW YORK.
2. City, ⊗ of Sumter co., W Alabama; pop. (1990c) 3530; Livingston Univ. (1835).
3. City, Merced co., cen. California, 14 mi. (23 km.) NW of the city of Merced; pop. (1990c) 7317.
4. Village, ⊗ of Livingston parish, SE Louisiana, 27 mi. (43 km.) E of Baton Rouge; pop. (1990c) 999.
5. City, ⊗ of Park co., S Montana, 95 mi. (153 km.) SE of Helena; pop. (1990c) 6701; tourist center; livestock raising.
6. Township, Essex co., NE New Jersey, 9 mi. (15 km.) NW of Newark; pop. (1990c) 26,609.
7. Town, ⊗ of Overton co., N Tennessee, 20 mi. (32 km.) NNE of Cookeville; pop. (1990c) 3809.
8. Town, ⊗ of Polk co., E Texas, 45 mi. (72 km.) SSW of Lufkin; pop. (1990c) 5019.
9. Town, Lothian region, Scotland, WSW of Edinburgh; pop. (1991e) 43,300.

Li·ving·ston \ˈliv-iŋ-stən\. Port, Izabal dept., E Guatemala, on Amatique Bay 14 mi. (23 km.) NW of Puerto Barrios.

Liv·ing·stone \ˈli-viŋ-stən\. **1.** Island in center of Victoria Falls, Zambezi River, bet. Zambia and Zimbabwe.
2. Town, S Zambia, near Victoria Falls on Zambezi River 250 mi. (402 km.) WNW of Bulawayo; pop. (1990p) 82,218; automobile assembly; clothing; tourism; present site settled 1905; ✻ of Northern Rhodesia 1907–35; raided by South African army Apr. 25, 1987.

Livingstone Falls. Name of a number of rapids in Congo River (*q.v.*) bet. Matadi and Kinshasa; total drop 876 ft. (267 mi.).

Livingstone Mountains. Range on NE border of Lake Malawi, S Tanzania; highest point ab. 7000 ft. (2135 m.).

Livingston Island. Island, W end of South Shetland Is., British Antarctic Terr., on S side of Drake Passage, 62°36′S, 60°30′W; 37 mi. (60 km.) long by 5 to 19 mi. (8 to 31 km.) wide.

Liv·ny \ˈliv-nē\. Town, SE Orel Oblast, Russia in Europe, 28 mi. (45 km.) SW of Yelets; pop. (1991e) 52,600.

Li·vo·nia \lə-ˈvō-nyə\. City, Wayne co., SE Michigan, W of Detroit; pop. (1990c) 100,850; tools, paint; Madonna Coll. (1937), Schoolcraft Coll. (1961).

Li·vo·nia \li-ˈvō-nē-yə\ *or* **Liv·land** \ˈliv-ˌland, -lənd\. Region and former administrative unit E of the Baltic Sea, formerly in the Baltic Provinces of Russia, now included in Latvia and Estonia. Inhabited orig. by Livs, a Finno-Ugric people, and later included territory of their neighbors the Letts and Esths; in 13th cent. conquered and Christianized by Livonian Brothers of the Sword, who in 1237 united with Teutonic Knights; expansion and Christianization continued through 14th and 15th cents.; region disputed and divided by Poland, Sweden, and Russia in Livonian War 1558–82; Knights disbanded 1561 and grand master of former order became duke of Courland (*q.v.*); conquered by Sweden 1629; ceded to Russia 1721 (as result of Great Northern War); freed from Russia, N part became part of Estonia and S part joined to Latvia 1918.

Li·vor·no \lē-ˈvȯr-nō\. **1.** Province of Tuscany, Italy. See table at ITALY.
2. *or Eng.* **Leg·horn** \ˈleg-ˌhȯrn\. Seaport commune, ✻ of Livorno prov., Tuscany, cen. Italy, on Tyrrhenian Sea 160 mi. (257 km.) NW of Rome; pop. (1989c) 171,346; transportation center; shipbuilding, oil refining; chemicals, copper products; Italian naval academy; 16th cent. cathedral. Under Florentine rule 1421; harbor construction begun by Cosimo I de'Medici 16th cent.; became haven for refugees under Ferdinand I de'Medici; for two centuries most important harbor of Tuscany; joined Italy 1860; heavily damaged in WWII; since rebuilt.

Livramento. See SANTANA DO LIVRAMENTO.

Li·vry–Gar·gan \lē-ˈvrē-gär-ˈgäⁿ\. Commune, Seine-St.-Denis dept., N France, ENE suburb of Paris.

Li·wung \ˈlē-ˌwu̇ŋ\ *or Du.* **Tji·li·wong** \ˈchi-lē-ˌvȯŋ\. River, W Java, Indonesia; rises on N slopes of Gunung Pangrango and flows N to Jakarta Bay at Jakarta; ab. 50 mi. (80 km.) long.

Lixus. See LARACHE.

Liyepaya. See LIEPĀJA.

Liz *or* **Lis** \ˈlēsh\. River, cen. Portugal; flows N near Leira, then W into Atlantic Ocean.

Liz·ard, The \ˈli-zərd\. Peninsula, S Cornwall, SE England, extending S from the town of Helston and the Helford River; its S end is extreme S point of Great Britain, **Lizard Point** or **Lizard Head,** 49°56′N, 5°13′W (186 ft. or 57 m. high); lighthouse.

Ljubelj. See LOIBL.

Lju·blja·na *also* **Lyu·blya·na** \lē-ˌü-blē-ˈä-nə, lē-ˈü-blē-ə-ˌnä\ *or Ger.* **Lai·bach** \ˈlī-ˌbäk\; *anc.* **Emo·na** \i-ˈmō-nə\. City, ✻ of Slovenia, on Sava River ab. 75 mi. (120 km.) WNW of Zagreb, Croatia; pop. (1991p) 323,291; railroad and commercial center; manufactures textiles, footwear, soap, chemicals; university (1595); cathedral; museum; art gallery; medieval fortress.
History: Ancient city of Emona founded by Romans first cent. B.C.; left in ruins by barbarians 5th cent. A.D. Became part of Carinthia 12th cent.; came under rule of Hapsburgs 1277; ✻ of Illyrian Provinces 1809–13; ✻ of kingdom of Illyria 1816–49; meeting place 1821 of a congress of European powers (Congress of Laibach) which authorized Austria to use force to crush liberal revolutionary movements in Italy; suffered destructive earthquake 1895; to Yugoslavia 1918.

Ljung·an \ˈyu̇ŋ-ˌän\. River, Västernorrland prov., E Sweden; flows SE to the Gulf of Bothnia near Sundsvall; 217 mi. (349 km.) long.

Ljus·nan \ˈyu̅e̅s-ˌnän\. River, cen. Sweden; rises on Norwegian border and flows SE into the Gulf of Bothnia S of Söderhamn; 267 mi. (430 km.) long.

Llan·ber·is \hlan-ˈber-is\. Village and parish, Gwynedd co., NW Wales, S of Bangor near the foot of Mt. Snowdon; at entrance to the **Pass of Llanberis,** 1169 ft. (356 m.), narrow, rocky defile.

Llan·daff \ˈhlan-ˌdaf, hlan-ˈdäv\. Suburb of Cardiff, Glamorganshire, SE Wales; 12th cent. cathedral built on 6th cent. foundations.

Llan·do·ve·ry \hlan-ˈdə-və-rē\ *or Welsh* **Llan·ym·ddy·fri** \ˌhla-nəm-ˈthə-vrē\. Town, Dyfed co., S Wales, NE of Carmarthen; pop. (1981p) 1691; remains of Norman castle; public school, founded 1848.

Llan·drin·dod Wells \hlan-ˈdrin-ˌdäd-ˈwelz\. Town, Powys co., E Wales; pop. (1981c) 4329; mineral springs; health resort.

Llan·dud·no \hlan-ˈdid-nō, -ˈdəd-\. Seaside resort, NE Gwynedd co., NW Wales; pop. (1981c) 18,410; on the small peninsula terminating in Great Ormes Head.

Lla·nel·li *mostly formerly* **Lla·nel·ly** \hla-ˈne-hlē\. Town and commercial seaport, Dyfed co., S Wales; pop. (1991p) 73,500; tinplate mills, chemical plants.

Lla·ne·ra \lyä-ˈnār-ə, yä-\. Commune, Asturias prov., NW Spain, 6 mi. (10 km.) from Oviedo; pop. (1991c) 10,457.

Lla·nes \ˈlyä-nās, ˈyä-\. Seaport commune, Asturias prov., NW Spain, on Bay of Biscay 58 mi. (93 km.) ENE of Oviedo; pop. (1991c) 13,348; coastal trade; 15th cent. Gothic church.

Llan·fair \ˈhlan-ˌvīr\ *or* **Llan·fair·pwll·gwyn·gyll·go·ger·y·chwyrn·dro·bwll·llan·dy·sil·io·go·go·goch** \ˈhlan-ˌvīr-pu̇hl-ˈgwin-gihl-gō-ˌger-ək-ˌwərn-ˈdrō-bu̇hl-ˌhlan-də-ˈsil-yō-ˌgō-gō-ˈgōk\. Village, SE Anglesey I., NW Wales, on Menai Strait.

Llanfair–ym–Muallt. See BUILTH WELLS.

Llan·gef·ni \hlan-ˈgev-nē\. Town, Anglesey I., NW Wales; pop. (1981c) 4547.

Llan·gol·len \hlan-ˈgä-hlən, lan-ˈgä-lən\. Town, Clwyd co., N Wales; pop. (1981c) 3072; summer resort; 9th cent. cross;

13th cent. abbey; 14th cent. bridge; since 1946 home of the international musical eisteddfod (festival of the arts).

Llan·id·loes \hlan-ˈid-ˌlȯis\. Town, Powys co., cen. Wales, on the Severn; pop. (1981p) 2416; market center for an agricultural region; formerly a center for lead mining and woolens manufacture.

Llanilltud Fawr. See LLANTWIT MAJOR.

Llano \ˈla-nō\. **1.** River, cen. Texas; formed in Kimble co. by union of **North Llano** and **South Llano** rivers; flows E into Colorado River on E boundary of Llano co.; 100 mi. (161 km.) long.

2. County in cen. Texas. See table at TEXAS.

3. City, ⊗ of Llano co., cen. Texas, on Llano River 62 mi. (100 km.) NW of Austin; pop. (1990c) 2962.

Lla·no de la Mag·da·le·na \ˈyä-no-ˌt͟hā-lä-ˌmäg-dä-ˈlā-nä\. Extensive plain in SW Baja California, NW Mexico.

Llano Es·ta·ca·do \ˈla-nō-ˌes-tə-ˈkä-dō, ˈlä-\ *or* **Staked Plain** \ˈstākt\. Extensive plateau, W Texas and E & SE New Mexixo; by some, considered to extend into W Oklahoma; ab. 35,000 sq. mi. (90,650 sq. km.); grazing; wheat; oil and natural gas.

Lla·nos \ˈyä-nōs\. Vast plains in N South America; drained by the Orinoco River and its tributaries; ab. 225,000 sq. mi. or 582,750 sq. km. (approx. 125,000 sq. mi. or 323,750 sq. km. in Venezuela, 100,000 sq. mi. or 259,000 sq. km. in Colombia); cattle raising; sparsely populated.

Llan·qui·hue, Lake. \läŋ-ˈkē-wā\. Lake, S cen. Chile, just N of Puerto Montt; 22 mi. (35 km.) long by 15 mi. (24 km.) wide; ab. 240 sq. mi. (620 sq. km.).

Llan·tris·ant \hlan-ˈtri-sant\. Village, Mid Glamorgan co., S Wales; pop. (1981c) 31,639; site of the Royal Mint.

Llan·twit Ma·jor \ˈhlan-twit-ˈmā-jər\ *or Welsh* **Llan·ill·tud Fawr** \ˌhlan-ˈihl-tid-ˈvau̇r\. Town, South Glamorgan co., SE Wales, on Bristol Channel; pop. (1981c) 8981; site of former monastery, famous as a school, established c. 500 A.D. by St. Illtyd, a Celtic monk; parish church with remains of early Celtic cross; Roman ruins.

Llanymddyfri. See LLANDOVERY.

Lleida. See LÉRIDA 2.

Llerena, Point. See LLORONA, POINT.

Lleyn Peninsula *also* **The Lleyn** \ˈhlēn\. Headland extending SW into St. George's Channel from NW coast of Wales; 28 mi. (45 km.) long, av. width 7 mi. (11 km.); encloses Cardigan Bay on N.

Llo·bre·gat \ˌlyō-brē-ˈgät\. River, NE Spain; flows S into Mediterranean Sea 3 mi. (5 km.) S of Barcelona; 98 mi. (158 km.) long.

Llo·ro·na, Point \yō-ˈrō-nä\; *formerly* **Point Lle·re·na** \ye-ˈrā-nä, lye-\. Cape on W coast of Osa Penin., S Costa Rica.

Lloyd Harbor \ˈlȯid\. Village, Suffolk co., SE New York, 6 mi. (10 km.) E of Northport; pop. (1990c) 3343.

Lloyd·min·ster \ˈlȯid-ˌmin-stər\. City, on Alberta-Saskatchewan border, Canada, 82 mi. (132 km.) WNW of North Battleford, Saskatchewan; pop. (1991c) 17,283; gas and oil wells; grain farms; settled by British colonists 1903.

Llul·lail·la·co \ˌyü-ˌyī-ˈyä-kō\. Volcano in Andes, N Chile, just W of Argentine boundary; 22,057 ft. (6723 m.).

Llw·chwr \ˈhlü-ku̇r\ *or* **Lou·ghor** \ˈlə-kər\. Locality, West Glamorgan co., S Wales; pop. (1981p) 29,581.

Lo. **1.** River, E cen. China. See LUO.

2. Region, Nepal. See MUSTANG.

Loa \ˈlō-ə\. **1.** Town, ⊗ of Wayne co., S cen. Utah; pop. (1990c) 444.

2. River, Antofagasta region, N Chile; flows into the Pacific Ocean; ab. 275 mi. (445 km.) long.

Loanda. See LUANDA.

Lo·an·ge \lō-ˈäŋ-gā\ *or Port.* **Lu·an·gue** \lü-ˈäŋ-gə\. River in the Congo basin, S cen. Africa; rises in NE cen. Angola, flows N into Kasai River in SW Democratic Rep. of the Congo, forms boundary bet. Bandundu and Kasai-Occidental administrative regions; ab. 425 mi. (685 km.) long.

Lo·an·go \lō-ˈäŋ-gō\. **1.** Former kingdom in Africa, N of Congo River; along with ancient kingdom of Congo flourished 14th cent.

2. Seaport, S Rep. of the Congo, ab. 100 mi. (160 km.) N of the mouth of the Congo River.

Loangwa. See LUANGWA.

Lo·a·no \lō-ˈä-nō\. Commune, Savona prov., Liguria, NW Italy, on Italian Riviera; pop. (1981p) 12,233.

Lo·bam·ba \lō-ˈbäm-bə\. Settlement, legislative ✻ of Swaziland, in W cen. part, SE of Mbabane.

Lo·ba·tse \lō-ˈbät-sā\. Town, S Botswana, roughly halfway bet. Mmabatho, Rep. of South Africa to the S and Gaborone to the NNE; pop. (1991c) 26,052.

Lö·bau \ˈlœ-ˌbau̇\. City, Saxony, E Germany, 40 mi. (64 km.) E of Dresden; pop. (1981c) 17,186; textiles.

Lo·bi·to \lō-ˈbē-tō\. Seaport on **Lobito Bay,** W cen. Angola; airport; current city founded by Portuguese 1843.

Lob Nor. See LOP NUR.

Lo·bos \ˈlō-ˌbōs\. Island, Mexico, in Gulf of Mexico off coast of N Veracruz state.

Lobos, Cape. Cape on coast of W cen. Sonora state, Mexico, extending into the Gulf of California.

Lobos, Cay *or* **Lobos Cay.** Small island of S Bahamas, separated by Old Bahama Channel from NE cen. Cuba; lighthouse.

Lobos, Point. **1.** Point, San Francisco, California, on S side of entrance to Golden Gate.

2. Promontory, Monterey co., California, on Carmel Bay SW of Carmel; state park.

Lobos Islands *also* **Seal Islands** \ˈsēl\. Two groups of small islands in Pacific Ocean off N coast of Peru, incl. **Lobos de Tier·ra** \t͟hā-ˈtyer-rä\ and **Lobos de Afue·ra** \ˌt͟hā-ä-ˈfwā-rä\; guano deposits.

Lobositz. See LOVOSICE.

Lob·stick Lake \ˈläb-stik\. Large lake of irregular shape, W Labrador, Canada, SE of Dyke Lake; forms part of course of Churchill River.

Loburi. See LOP BURI.

Lo·car·no \lō-ˈkär-nō\ *or Ger.* **Lug·ga·rus** \lə-ˈgär-əs\. Commune, Ticino canton, SE cen. Switzerland, on N shore of Lake Maggiore 11 mi. (18 km.) W of Bellinzona; pop. (1990c) 14,430; resort; site of old castle of dukes of Milan (now museum); pilgrimage church (built 15th cent.).

History: First mentioned 8th cent. A.D.; passed to dukes of Milan 1342; taken by Swiss 1512; became part of canton of Ticino 1803; agreements reached here Oct. 16, 1925 which led to the signing (Dec. 1, 1925, London) of Locarno Pact, a series of treaties and arbitration conventions bet. Germany, Belgium, France, Great Britain, Italy, Poland, and Czechoslovakia designed to guarantee the continuation of peace and existing territorial boundaries.

Loch·a·ber \lä-ˈkä-bər\. Mountainous district in Highland region, NW Scotland, at W end of the Grampian Mts. and NE of Loch Linnhe; includes Ben Nevis.

Loch·ar Moss \ˈlä-kər-ˈmȯs\. Tract of moorland, Dumfries and Galloway region, S Scotland; ab. 10 mi. (16 km.) long.

Loches \ˈlōsh\. Town, Indre-et-Loire dept., W cen. France, 25 mi. (40 km.) SE of Tours; pop. (1990c) 7133; numerous medieval buildings incl. a château.

Loch·gel·ly \läk-ˈge-lē\. Burgh, Fife region, E Scotland, W of Kirkcaldy; pop. (1981p) 7308; collieries.

Loch·gilp·head \läk-ˈgilp-hed\. Burgh, Strathclyde region, W Scotland, at head of arm of Firth of Clyde; pop. (1981c) 2460.

Loch·ma·ben \läk-ˈmā-bən\. Town, Dumfries and Galloway region, S Scotland, 8 mi. (13 km.) NE of Dumfries; pop. (1981c) 1714; resort; ruins of castle associated with 14th cent. king of Scotland, Robert the Bruce.

Lochy, Loch \ˈlä-kē\. Lake, Highland region, N cen. Scotland; 10 mi. (16 km.) long; forms part of Caledonian Canal.

Locke, Mount \ˈläk\. Peak in Davis Mts., Jeff Davis co., W Texas; 6791 ft. (2070 m.); on its top McDonald Observatory, opened May 5, 1939.

Lock·hart \ˈläk-ˌhärt\. City, ⊗ of Caldwell co., S cen. Texas, 29 mi. (47 km.) S of Austin; pop. (1990c) 9205.

Lock Ha·ven \läk-ˈhā-vən\. City, ⊗ of Clinton co., cen. Pennsylvania, on W branch of Susquehanna River 25 mi. (40 km.) WSW of Williamsport; pop. (1990c) 9230; Lock Haven Univ. of Pennsylvania (1870); city settled 1769; lumber center in 19th cent.

Lock·land \ˈlä-klənd\. Village, Hamilton co., SW corner of Ohio, 9 mi. (15 km.) N of Cincinnati; pop. (1990c) 4357.

Lock·port \ˈläk-pōrt\. **1.** City, Will co., NE Illinois, ab. 20 mi. (32 km.) SW of Chicago; pop. (1990c) 9401; site of a lock and dam marking the end of the Chicago Sanitary and Ship Canal in the Illinois Waterway system; canal historical museum.

2. City, ⊗ of Niagara co., W New York, 20 mi. (32 km.) ENE of Niagara Falls; pop. (1990c) 24,426; on New York State Barge Canal; automobile parts, paper, textiles, brass and bronze products; incorp. as village 1829, as city 1865.

Locle, Le. See LE LOCLE.

Lo·cri \ˈlō-ˌkrī, ˈlä-\ *or* **Locri Epi·ze·phyr·ii** \ˌe-pi-zə-ˈfir-ē-ˌī\. Ancient city in Magna Graecia, on E coast of SW extremity of Italy; founded ab. 680 B.C.; adopted the Locrian code, said to be earliest written system of Greek legislation.

Lo·cris \ˈlō-kris, ˈlä-\. Region in cen. part of ancient Greece, comprising: **Eastern Locris,** divided into two parts: **Locris Ep·ic·ne·mid·ia** \ˌe-pik-nə-ˈmi-dē-ə\ along S shore of Gulf of Maliakós extending E from Pass of Thermopylae and bordering on Malis, Doris, and Phocis; separated by narrow strip of Phocis from **Locris Opun·tia** \ō-ˈpən-chə\ on Euboean Sea (*mod.* Atalante Channel) opp. Euboea, E of Phocis and N of Boeotia; chief town Opus. **Western Locris,** *or* **Locris Oz·o·lis** \ˈä-zə-lis\, mountainous region along N shore of strait joining Gulf of Patras and Gulf of Corinth, S of Aetolia and W of Phocis; chief town Amphissa. Locrians were probably early inhabitants of Greece, long subject to stronger neighboring states.

Loc·sin \lōk-ˈsin\. Municipality, E Albay prov., Luzon, Philippines, on railroad line 2 mi. (3 km.) W of Legazpi.

Lo·cust Mountain \ˈlō-kəst\. Ridge in Schuylkill co., E cen. Pennsylvania; contains rich coal deposits.

Lod \ˈlōd\ *also* **Lyd·da** \ˈli-də\. City, Israel, 23 mi. (37 km.) NW of Jerusalem; pop. (1992e) 45,500; aircraft.

History: The ancient city, in Judaea in the Plain of Sharon, had long history and is mentioned in several places in the Bible; scene of the apostle Peter's healing of the paralytic (*Acts* ix. 32); destroyed by Romans in the years leading up to 70 A.D.; rebuilt by Roman Emperor Hadrian and later became a bishopric; by some supposed to be birth and burial place of St. George, patron saint of England; captured by the Crusaders 1099; destroyed by Muslim Sultan Saladin 1191 and rebuilt by Richard I (the Lion-Hearted) of England. As a result of the town's capture by Israeli forces 1948 much of the former Arab population has been replaced by Jewish settlers.

Lo·dève \lō-ˈdev\; *anc.* **Lu·te·va** \lü-ˈtē-və\. Commune, N Hérault dept., S France, in S Cévennes; cathedral. A chief town of ancient territory of Septimania.

Lodge·pole Creek \ˈläj-pōl\. River, SE Wyoming and W Nebraska; flows E into South Platte River near Nebraska-Colorado boundary; 212 mi. (341 km.) long.

Lo·di \ˈlō-ˌdī\. **1.** City, San Joaquin co., cen. California, 12 mi. (19 km.) N of Stockton; pop. (1990c) 51,874; packs and ships fruit and vegetables; wine; vineyards and fruit orchards.

2. Borough, Bergen co., NE corner of New Jersey, 5 mi. (8 km.) SE of Paterson; pop. (1990c) 22,355; Felician Coll. (1923).

Lodi \ˈlȯ-dē\. Commune, Milano prov., Lombardy, N Italy, on Adda River 20 mi. (32 km.) SE of Milan; pop. (1991p) 42,170; center of dairy industry; ceramics, wrought iron; 12th cent. cathedral. Rebuilt on present site by Holy Roman Emperor Frederick I (Barbarossa) after destruction of nearby ancient settlement by the Milanese 12th cent.; scene of defeat of Austrians by French commander (later emperor) Napoléon Bonaparte May 10, 1796.

Lod·o·me·ria \ˌlä-də-ˈmir-ē-ə\. Principality of 12th and 13th cents. in Volhynia, E cen. Europe—also known as **Vlad·i·mir in Vol·hyn·ia** \ˈvla-də-ˌmir ... väl-ˈhin-ē-ə, vlə-ˈdē-ˌmir-\; joined with Galicia in 13th cent. to become part of Poland; in First Partition of Poland 1772 passed along with Galicia to Hapsburg empire. See VOLODYMYR-VOLYNS'KYY.

Lo·dore \lə-ˈdōr\. Waterfall in the Lake District, Cumberland, NW England, near head of Derwent Water.

Łódź \ˈwüch, ˈlōdz, ˈlädz\ *or Russ.* **Lodz** \ˈlȯts\. **1.** Province of cen. Poland. See table at POLAND.

2. *or Ger.* **Litz·mann·stadt** \ˈlits-mən-ˌshtät\. City, its ✻, ab. 75 mi. (120 km.) WSW of Warsaw; 83 sq. mi. (215 sq. km.); pop. (1989e) 851,690; textile center (esp. cotton); episcopal see; educational center; several museums; cinematography center. Birthplace of pianist Arthur Rubinstein 1887. Before WWI belonged to Russians, who in 19th cent. developed it from small village into large industrial city; in WWI occupied by Germans 1914; in WWII occupied by Germans 1939.

Loei *or* **Loey** \ˈlōi\. Town, N Thailand, 20 mi. (32 km.) S of the Mekong, 90 mi. (145 km.) E of Uttaradit; pop. (1991e) 21,240.

Loemadjang. See LUMAJANG.

Lo·fo·ten \ˈlō-ˌfōt-ᵊn\. Island group in Norwegian Sea, in Nordland co., off NW coast of Norway, SW of Vesterålen; 475 sq. mi. (1230 sq. km.); principal islands Austvågøy, Vestvågøy, Moskenes; valuable fisheries.

Lo·gan \ˈlō-gən\. **1.** Name of counties in 10 states of the U.S. See tables at ARKANSAS, COLORADO, ILLINOIS, KANSAS, KENTUCKY, NEBRASKA, NORTH DAKOTA, OHIO, OKLAHOMA, WEST VIRGINIA.

2. City, ⊗ of Harrison co., W Iowa, 25 mi. (40 km.) N of Council Bluffs; pop. (1990c) 1401.

3. City, ⊗ of Hocking co., S cen. Ohio, 16 mi. (26 km.) SE of Lancaster; pop. (1990c) 6725; founded 1816.

4. City, ⊗ of Cache co., N Utah, 36 mi. (58 km.) N of Ogden; pop. (1990c) 32,762; grain, sugar beets; dairy and livestock farming; Mormon tabernacle and Mormon temple; Utah State Univ. (1888); settled by Mormons c. 1855; incorp. 1886.

5. City, ⊗ of Logan co., SW West Virginia, 20 mi. (32 km.) NE of Williamson; pop. (1990c) 2206; coal mines.

Logan, Mount. **1.** Peak in N Mohave co., NW Arizona; 7866 ft. (2398 m.).

2. Peak in St. Elias Mts., SW Yukon Terr., Canada, near Alaskan boundary; 19,524 ft. (5951 m.); highest mountain in Canada.

Logan Mountain. Peak in Glacier National Park, NW Montana; 9252 ft. (2820 m.).

Lo·gans·port \ˈlō-gənz-ˌpōrt\. City, ⊗ of Cass co., N cen. Indiana, 22 mi. (35 km.) NNW of Kokomo; pop. (1990c) 16,812; settled c. 1828; incorp. 1838.

Lo·gan·ville \ˈlō-gən-ˌvil\. City, Walton co., N cen. Georgia, ENE of Atlanta; pop. (1990c) 3180.

Lo·gone \lō-ˈgōn\. River in NW equatorial part of Africa, bet. Chad and Cameroon; flows N into Chari River; 240 mi. (386 km.) long.

Lo·gro·ño \lə-ˈgrō-nyō\. Commune, ✻ of La Rioja prov., Spain, on Ebro River 155 mi. (249 km.) NNE of Madrid; pop. (1991p) 121,066; trade center for agricultural region; lumber, wine, textiles; several notable churches; remains of bridge (built 1138). A stop on old pilgrimage route to Santiago de Compostela; unsuccessfully besieged by French 1521; occupied by French during Peninsular War 1808–13.

Løg·stør Bred·ning \ˌlœg-stœr-ˈbred-niŋ\. Wide section in cen. part of Limfjorden, N Jutland, Denmark; ab. 13 mi. (21 km.) across.

Lo·ha·ru \lō-ˈhär-ü\. Former Indian state, now part of Haryana, NW India; 226 sq. mi. (585 sq. km.); ✻ Loharu.

Loheia *or* **Loheiya.** See AL LUḨAYYAH.

Löh·ne \ˈlœ̄-nə\. City, North Rhine-Westphalia, Germany; pop. (1980c) 37,147; made city 1969.

Loibl \ˈlȯi-bəl\ *or* **Lju·belj** \ˈlyü-bəl-yə\. Pass over the Karawanken Alps, connecting with highway Klagenfurt in Carinthia, Austria, and Ljubljana in cen. Slovenia; elev. 4487 ft. (1368 m.).

Loi·kaw \ˈlȯi-ˈkȯ\. Town, ✻ of Kayah state, E cen. Myanmar, on a tributary of the Salween ab. 70 mi. (115 km.) NE of Toungoo.

Loi·pyet Hills \ˈlȯi-ˌpyet\. Range of hills in N Myanmar, S of Kumon Range.

Loir \ˈlwär\. River, NW cen. France; rises in Eure-et-Loir dept., flows W into Sarthe River 5 mi. (8 km.) N of Angers; 193 mi. (311 km.) long.

Loire \ˈlwär\; *anc.* **Li·ger** \ˈlī-jər\. **1.** Longest river in France; rises in Ardèche dept., SE France, flows N and NW to Orléans, then turns W and flows through Blois, Tours, and Nantes and empties into Bay of Biscay by a wide estuary below St.-Nazaire; 634 mi. (1020 km.) long; navigable.
2. Department of France. See table at FRANCE.

Loire–At·lan·tique \-ȧt-läⁿ-ˈtēk\. Department of W France. See table at FRANCE.

Loi·ret \lwä-ˈrā\. Department of N cen. France. See table at FRANCE.

Loir–et–Cher \ˌlwär-ā-ˈsher\. Department of N cen. France. See table at FRANCE.

Lo·í·za \lō-ˈē-sä\; *formerly* **Ca·nó·va·nas** \kä-ˈnō-b̲ä-näs\. Municipality, NE Puerto Rico, ESE of San Juan; pop. (1990c) 29,307.

Lo·ja \ˈlȯ-hä\. **1.** Province of SW Ecuador. See table at ECUADOR.
2. City, its ✻, on Zamora River ab. 135 mi. (215 km.) SSE of Guayaquil; pop. (1990c) 94,305; in dairy-farming region; two universities; city founded mid-16th cent.
3. *earlier* **Lo·xa** \ˈlō-hä\. Commune, Granada prov., S Spain, on Genil River 21 mi. (34 km.) W of the city of Granada; pop. (1990c) 20,768; 16th cent. churches; Moorish citadel. As important strategic point in defense of Granada, strongly fortified by Moors; conquered by Ferdinand of Aragon and Isabella of Castile 15th cent.

Lo·ke·ren \ˈlō-kə-rə\. Commune, East Flanders prov., NW cen. Belgium, 23 mi. (37 km.) NW of Brussels; pop. (1992e) 35,100.

Lo·ko·ja \lō-ˈkō-jä\. Town, ✻ of Kogi state, Nigeria, on Niger River at mouth of Benue River; pop. (1991e) 50,340; founded c. 1860; formerly a regional ✻.

Lok·tak Lake \ˈläk-ˌtək\. Marshy lake, S Manipur state, NE India; ab. 25 sq. mi. (65 sq. km.); its outlet is the Manipur River.

Lol·land \ˈlȯ-län\. Island of Denmark, lying in Baltic Sea S of Sjælland and W of Falster; forms part of Storstrøm co.; 477 sq. mi. (1235 sq. km.); pop. (1989e) 73,564; sugar beets.

Lo·lo·bau \ˈlō-lō-ˌbau̇\. Small island, part of Papua New Guinea, in Bismarck Sea off N coast of E end of New Britain I., Bismarck Archipelago.

Lom \ˈlȯm\ *or* **Lom–Pa·lan·ka** \-pä-ˈläŋ-kä\. Town, Montana region, NW Bulgaria, on Danube River.

Lo·ma Lin·da \ˈlō-mə-ˈlin-də\. City, San Bernardino co., California, bordering on the S part of the city of San Bernardino; pop. (1990c) 17,400.

Lo·ma·lo·ma \ˌlō-mä-ˈlō-mä\. Chief town of the Exploring Isles, E Fiji, SW Pacific Ocean, on S shore of Vanua Mbalavu I.; has good harbor.

Lo·ma·mi \lō-ˈmä-mē\. River, Democratic Rep. of the Congo; rises in S cen. part, flows N parallel with and W of the Lualaba and the upper Congo and empties into the Congo below Kisangani; ab. 800 mi. (1285 km.) long.

Lo·mas de Za·mo·ra \ˈlō-ˌmäs-t̲hā-sä-ˈmō-rä\. City, Buenos Aires prov., E Argentina, part of Buenos Aires met. area; pop. (1991p) 572,769; chemical, electrical, and cement industries.

Lom·bard \ˈläm-ˌbärd\. Residential village, Du Page co., NE Illinois, 20 mi. (32 km.) W of Chicago; pop. (1990c) 39,408; National Coll. of Chiropractic (1906), DeVry Institute of Technology (1982).

Lom·bar·dy \ˈläm-ˌbär-dē, -bər-\ *or Ital.* **Lom·bar·dia** \ˌlȯm-bär-ˈdē-ä\. Autonomous region, N Italy, in Italian Alps bet. Piedmont and Trentino-Alto Adige and Veneto; for provincial divisions, see table at ITALY; ✻ Milan; contains numerous Alpine peaks, glaciers, and lakes; descends to fertile valley of Po River; important both agriculturally (wheat, rice, fruit; livestock) and industrially (automobiles, steel, chemicals, textiles).
History: Center of kingdom founded by Lombards, a German people who invaded Italy in 6th cent. A.D.; kingdom extended rule over much of Italy until it was crushed by Frankish King (later Holy Roman Emperor) Charlemagne 773–774; cities of Lombard plain formed 1167 Lombard League against Holy Roman Emperor Frederick I (Barbarossa) whom they defeated 1176 at Legnano; cities received independence by peace signed 1183; Lombard territory came to be scene of rise of duchy of Milan (*q.v.*) which became Spanish 1535; ceded to Austria 1713; became French 1796; restored to Austria as part of Lombardo-Venetian kingdom 1815; became part of Italy 1859 (see ITALY).

Lom·blen \läm-ˈblen\. Island of the Lesser Sunda Is., Indonesia, E of Flores I. and separated from Pantar I. by Alor Strait; 468 sq. mi. (1212 sq. km.); ab. 50 mi. (80 km.) long by 22 mi. (35 km.) wide, of irregular shape. Has numerous mountains, highest Labalekang 5394 ft. (1644 m.), an active volcano.

Lom·bok \ˈlȯm-ˌbȯk\. Island of the Lesser Sunda Is., West Nusa Tenggara prov., Indonesia; ab. 70 mi. (115 km.) long by 50 mi. (80 km.) at widest point; 1826 sq. mi. (4729 sq. km.); pop. (1980c) 1,957,128. Separated on W from Bali by Lombok Strait, and on E from Sumbawa by Alas Strait. Has two mountain ranges, one along N coast and the other along the S, with wide valley between; in N range is the volcano Rindjani 12,224 ft. (3726 m.), one of highest mountains in Indonesia. Mountain regions forest-clad and undeveloped, lowlands highly cultivated, producing rice and coffee; industry includes weaving and work in gold, silver, and iron. Its fauna and flora of great interest because the island is situated on Wallace's line (*q.v.*). Part of island under sultan of Makasar in 17th cent.; later subject to Bali; began relations with Dutch 1843 and came entirely under their control by 1894.

Lombok Strait. Channel bet. E Bali I. and W Lombok I., Indonesia, connecting W Flores Sea with the Indian Ocean; ab. 22 mi. (35 km.) wide; of interest to scientists as an important part of Wallace's line (*q.v.*).

Lo·mé \lō-ˈmā\. Seaport town, ✻ of Republic of Togo; pop. (1983e) 366,476; oil refinery; university (1965); ✻ of former French-mandated part of Togoland and of German protectorate of Togo; connected by rail with inland towns and with other coast towns.

Lo·me·la \lō-ˈmā-lä\. **1.** River, cen. Democratic Rep. of the Congo; flows NW into Tshuapa River; 290 mi. (467 km.) long.
2. Town, Kasai-Oriental administrative region, S cen. Democratic Rep. of the Congo, on the Lomela River ab. 180 mi. (290 km.) N of Lusambo; airport.

Lo·mi·ta \lō-ˈmē-tə\. City, Los Angeles co., SW California, SE of Torrance; pop. (1990c) 19,382; residential.

Lomme \ˈlȯm\. Commune, Nord dept., N France, WNW suburb of Lille.

Lom·mel \ˈlȯ-məl\. Commune, N Limburg prov., Belgium; pop. (1981c) 25,412.

Lomond, Ben. See BEN LOMOND.

Lo·mond, Loch \ˈlō-mənd\. Lake in Strathclyde and Central regions, S cen. Scotland; 27 sq. mi. (70 sq. km.); 24 mi. (39 km.) long by 0.75 to 5 mi. (1.2 to 8 km.) wide; largest lake in Scotland; surrounded by many mountains (incl. Ben Lomond and Ben Vorlich); S part expands and contains many islets; on its E shore near Ben Lomond is the region made famous by Rob Roy (1671–1734), Scottish outlaw of the clan Macgregor, popularized by author Sir Walter Scott.

Lo·mo·no·sov \lə-ˌmə-ˈnȯ-səf\; *formerly* **Ora·ni·en·baum** *also* **Ora·niy·en·baum** \ȯ-ˈrä-nē-ən-ˌbau̇m, ə-ˈrən-yin-\. Town, NW St. Petersburg Oblast, W Russia in Europe, on the Gulf of Finland opp. Kronshtadt; pop. (1991e) 42,000; two palaces; town founded c. 1710.

Lomonosov Ridge. Ridge, Arctic Ocean floor, extending from N of Greenland to N of New Siberian Is., passing near the North Pole, and roughly bisecting the Arctic Ocean.

Lom–Palanka. See LOM.

Lom·po·ba·tang \ˌlȯm-pō-ˈbä-ˌtäŋ\; *formerly* **Bon·thain** \bȯn-ˈtīn\. Peak, SW Sulawesi, Indonesia, E of Ujung Pandang; 9419 ft. (2871 m.).

Lom·poc \ˈläm-ˌpäk\. City, Santa Barbara co., SW California, near Pacific Ocean 45 mi. (72 km.) WNW of the city of Santa Barbara; pop. (1990c) 37,649; oil wells; founded 1874; Vandenberg Air Force Base (to the W).

Łom·ża \ˈwȯm-ˌzhä\ *or Russ.* **Lom·zha** \ˈlȯm-zhə\. **1.** Province, NE Poland. See table at POLAND.

2. City, its ✻, on the Narew River 80 mi. (129 km.) NE of Warsaw; pop. (1992e) 60,700; long a prosperous commercial town, esp. in 16th cent.; in 1795 came under Prussian rule, then Russian from early 19th cent. until end of WWI. In WWII taken by Russians 1939, but ceded back to Poland 1945; nearly destroyed 1944.

Lo·na·to \lō-ˈnä-tō\. Commune, Brescia prov., Lombardy, N Italy, ab. 15 mi. (24 km.) W of the commune of Brescia near S end of Lake Garda; pop. (1981p) 10,617; scene of an early victory of French commander (later emperor) Napoléon Bonaparte over the Austrians 1796.

Lon·don \ˈlən-dən\. **1.** City, ⊗ of Laurel co., SE Kentucky, 43 mi. (69 km.) NW of Middlesborough; pop. (1990c) 5757; Sue Bennett Coll. (1896).

2. City, ⊗ of Madison co., SW cen. Ohio, 23 mi. (37 km.) W of Columbus; pop. (1990c) 7807.

3. City, ⊗ of Middlesex co., SE Ontario, Canada, on Thames River 23 mi. (37 km.) N of Lake Erie; pop. (1991c) 303,165; railroad center; food products, diesel locomotives, textiles; Univ. of Western Ontario (1878). First settled 1826; incorp. as village 1840, town 1848, city 1855.

4. City, ✻ of the United Kingdom, lying in England on both sides of the Thames ab. 40 mi. (65 km.) from its mouth; 621.8 sq. mi. (1610 sq. km.); since 1965 comprises the **City of London,** *anc.* **Lon·din·i·um** \län-ˈdi-nē-əm, ˌlən-\, known as **The City** (the older part, now included in its financial district), and 32 other boroughs, which together are referred to as the met. county of **Greater London;** pop. (1989e) 6,756,400; a major political, industrial, cultural, financial, and transportation center (for further details, see table on page 664).

History: Roman town, Londinium, scene of revolt of Boudicca, queen of Iceni (see *History* at UNITED KINGDOM) 60 A.D.; its fortifications, which had been destroyed by Danes, restored by Alfred the Great 9th cent.; from Anglo-Saxon times, grew as trade center of England; received charter privileges from 11th cent.; city proper, governed by mayor (later "lord mayor") and aldermen of trade guilds, came to be the commercial center; Westminster the seat of English government; experienced rapid growth and increased power and wealth mid-16th through early 17th cents.; in Civil War (17th cent.) opposed to king; after the setbacks of severe plague 1665 and great fire 1666, continued to grow, eventually becoming for a while the most populous city and most important trade center of the world; site of conference leading to establishment of kingdom of Greece and separation of Belgium from Netherlands 1827–32; by act of 1888 London area placed under London County Council; site of Olympic Games 1908; in WWI raided by Germans; in WWII suffered esp. 1940–41 from bombings by German planes (Much of the city was destroyed and has subsequently been rebuilt.); site of meeting of first part of first session of UN 1946; Summer Olympic Games 1948; conference 1954 on termination of occupation regime in West Germany; administered by the Greater London Council, replacing the London County Council (1965–86).

Lon·don·der·ry \ˌlən-dən-ˈder-ē, ˈlən-dən-ˌder-ē\. Town, Rockingham co., SE New Hampshire, SSE of Manchester; pop. (1990c) 19,781.

Londonderry *or* **Der·ry** \ˈder-ē\. **1.** Former county, NW Northern Ireland.

2. District, NW Northern Ireland. See DERRY 3.

3. County borough and seaport, Northern Ireland. See DERRY 4.

Londonderry, Cape. Northernmost point of Western Australia, Australia, on Timor Sea; 13°45′S, 126°55′E.

Lon·dri·na \lōn-ˈdrē-nə\. Town, Paraná state, S Brazil; munic. pop. (1991p) 388,331.

Lone Grove \ˈlōn-ˈgrōv\. Town, Carter co., S Oklahoma, W of Ardmore; pop. (1990c) 4114.

Lone Mountain \ˈlōn\. **1.** Peak, SW Gallatin co., S Montana; 11,194 ft. (3412 m.).

2. Peak in E Esmeralda co., SW Nevada; 9114 ft. (2778 m.).

Lone Pine Peak \ˈlōn-ˌpīn\. Mountain in cen. Custer co., cen. Idaho; 9652 ft. (2942 m.).

Long \ˈlȯŋ\. County in SE Georgia. See table at GEORGIA.

Long, Loch. Inlet in Strathclyde region, W coast of Scotland, a N extension of Firth of Clyde; ab. 16 mi. (26 km.) long.

Lon·ga·ví \ˌlȯŋ-gä-ˈvē\. Peak, E Linares prov., S cen. Chile; 10,597 ft. (3230 m.).

Long Bay. **1.** Bay off S coast of North Carolina and NE coast of South Carolina, extending SW from Cape Fear.

2. Bay on W end of island of Jamaica, West Indies.

Long Beach. **1.** Narrow sandy island, SE Ocean co., E New Jersey.

2. City, Los Angeles co., SW California, on San Pedro Bay; pop. (1990c) 429,433; artificial harbor with modern facilities; shipbuilding, fishing; aircraft, chemicals, soap; oil and gas wells; *Queen Mary* ocean liner permanently berthed and open for tours; Long Beach City Coll. (1927), California State Univ., Long Beach (1949); incorp. as city 1897; major development took place after discovery of oil 1921; suffered substantial damage from earthquake 1933.

3. City, Harrison co., SE Mississippi, 5 mi. (8 km.) W of Gulfport; pop. (1990c) 15,804; grew rapidly in 1980s.

4. City, Nassau co., SE New York, on an island in Atlantic Ocean off S shore of Long Island 21 mi. (34 km.) ESE of New York City; pop. (1990c) 33,510; residential; seaside resort.

Long·ben·ton \lȯŋ-ˈbent-ᵊn\. Town, Tyne and Wear, N England, 3 mi. (5 km.) NE of Newcastle upon Tyne; pop. (1981p) 50,646.

Long·boat Key \ˈlȯŋ-bōt\. City, Manatee and Sarasota cos., W cen. Florida, on Gulf of Mexico 20 mi. (32 km.) NW of Sarasota; pop. (1990c) 5937.

Long Branch. City, Monmouth co., E cen. New Jersey, on Atlantic Ocean 21 mi. (34 km.) SE of Perth Amboy; pop. (1990c) 28,658; summer resort; clothing, boats, electronic equipment.

Long Cay; *formerly* **Fortune Island.** One of the SE Bahamas, SW of Crooked I.; 8 sq. mi. (21 sq. km.); pop. (1980c) 33; lighthouse.

Long·champ \lōⁿ-ˈshäⁿ\. See BOIS DE BOULOGNE.

Longchuan. See SHWELI.

Long Ea·ton \ˈēt-ᵊn\. Town, Derbyshire, N cen. England, 7 mi. (11 km.) WSW of Nottingham; pop. (1981p) 32,895.

Long·fel·low Peak \ˈlȯŋ-ˌfe-lō\. Mountain in Glacier National Park, NW Montana; ab. 8900 ft. (2715 m.).

Long·ford \ˈlȯŋ-fərd\. **1.** Town, N Tasmania, Australia, 15 mi. (24 km.) S of Launceston; pop. (1981c) 5621.

2. County, E cen. Ireland; ⊗ Longford; chief river Shannon; potatoes, oats; livestock raising, dairying. See table at IRELAND.

3. Town, ⊗ of co. Longford, Ireland; pop. (1991p) 6393; 17th cent. castle; 19th cent. cathedral.

Long Ga·bles \ˈlȯŋ-ˈgā-bəlz\. Mountain, Antarctica, 78°11′S, 86°14′W; 13,620 ft. (4151 m.).

Long Island. **1.** Island in Atlantic Ocean off SE coast of Maine, S of Mount Desert I.; included in Hancock co.

2. Island along SE approach to harbor of Boston, Massachusetts.

3. Island, SE New York, lying bet. Long Island Sound on N and Atlantic Ocean on S; 118.5 mi. (190.6 km.) long, 23 mi. (37 km.) at greatest width; 1723 sq. mi. (4462 sq. km.); comprises Suffolk, Nassau, Queens, and Kings cos. of New York

GREATER LONDON

NAME	AREA (sq. mi.)	AREA (sq. km.)	POP. (1991p)	BUILDINGS, LANDMARKS, AND ECONOMY
Barking and Dagenham	13.9	36.0	139,900	Ruins of Barking Abbey (c. 666 A.D.), Valence Manor House (1600); automobile manufacturing.
Barnet	34.5	89.4	283,000	Chipping Barnet Church (c. 1250).
Bexley	24.9	64.5	211,200	Ruins of Lessness Abbey (12th cent.), St. Mary's Church (13th cent.), Hall Place Manor (16th cent.); engineering; chemicals, food products.
Brent	17.1	44.3	226,100	Wembley Stadium (built 1924–25), venue of 1948 Summer Olympic Games.
Bromley	58.7	152.0	281,700	Chiefly residential.
Camden	8.4	21.8	170,500	British Museum, John Keats House and Museum, Gray's Inn, Lincoln's Inn, Telecom Tower (1964); railway stations: Euston (1849), King's Cross (1852), St. Pancras (1874).
Croydon	33.6	87.0	299,600	Palace used by archbishops of Canterbury (11th cent.); extensive shopping facilities; large concentration of offices.
Ealing	21.4	55.4	263,600	Engineering; chemicals.
Enfield	31.3	81.1	248,900	Manufacture of Enfield rifles, electronic equipment.
Greenwich	19.0	49.2	200,800	Site of the original Royal Observatory from which longitude is reckoned; Royal Navy Coll., National Maritime Museum.
Hackney	7.5	19.4	164,200	Parks include Victoria Park and Hackney Marshes.
Hammersmith and Fulham	6.2	16.0	136,500	St. Paul's School (1509), Wormwood Scrubs Prison (1874), White City Stadium, Fulham Palace (country residence of bishop of London), Olympia Exhibition Center; television studios.
Haringey	11.7	30.3	187,300	Chiefly residential; parks include Alexandra and Finsbury.
Harrow	19.6	50.8	194,300	St. Mary's Church (consecrated 1094), Harrow School (1571).
Havering	46.3	119.9	224,400	Chiefly residential.
Hillingdon	42.6	110.3	225,800	St. Dunstan's Church (14th cent.); Heathrow Airport; university (1966).
Hounslow	22.8	59.0	193,400	Hogarth House (17th cent.), Chiswick House (18th cent.).
Islington	5.8	15.0	155,200	Canonbury Tower, Armoury House (1735), Sadler's Wells.
Kensington and Chelsea	4.6	11.9	127,600	Kensington Palace which includes Nottingham House where Queen Victoria was born, Chelsea Royal Hospital (late 17th cent.), Victoria and Albert Museum.
Kingston upon Thames	14.5	37.6	130,600	Ceremonial stone used during coronations; aircraft, plastics.
Lambeth	10.5	27.2	220,100	Lambeth Palace (the Greater London residence of the archbishop of Canterbury), Royal Festival Hall, Queen Elizabeth Hall, National Theatre; Oval Cricket Ground.
Lewisham	13.4	34.7	215,300	Chiefly residential.
London, City of	1.0	2.6	4,000	Bank of England, Royal Exchange, Stock Exchange, St. Paul's Cathedral; financial center.
Merton	14.6	37.8	161,800	Wimbledon Common (site of Wimbledon Lawn Tennis Championships).
Newham	14.5	37.6	200,200	Royal Docks (now closed), railway yards.
Redbridge	21.8	56.5	220,600	Chiefly residential; contains part of Epping Forest.
Richmond upon Thames	21.2	55.0	154,600	Hampton Court Palace (residence of Henry VIII), Royal Botanic Gardens.
Southwark	11.5	29.8	196,500	Dulwich Coll. (c. 1619), Guy's (educational) Hospital (c. 1725), Imperial War Museum; Elephant and Castle traffic intersection.
Sutton	16.7	43.2	164,300	All Saints Church (12th cent., restored 1893).
Tower Hamlets	7.8	20.2	153,500	Christ Church (1723–29), Royal Mint (now closed); site of urban renewal in formerly busy docklands.
Waltham Forest	15.3	39.6	203,400	Chiefly residential.
Wandsworth	13.9	36.0	237,500	Battersea Park, Putney Heath; Battersea Coll. of Technology, Wandsworth Technical Coll.
Westminster, City of	8.3	21.5	181,500	Buckingham Palace, Houses of Parliament, Imperial Coll. of Science and Technology (1907), National and Tate galleries, Westminster Abbey, Madame Tussaud's Wax Museum.

state; borough of Brooklyn (Kings co.) at its SW extremity. At W end separated from the Bronx and Manhattan by East River and from Staten I. by the Narrows. Has 280 mi. (450 km.) of coastline indented by numerous inlets and bays, esp. Peconic and Gardiners bays at E end and Great South and Jamaica bays on S shore. Hilly along N shore; has many beaches along the S (Rockaway, Jones, Fire I., Coney I.). At its E end is Montauk Point with several large islands in adjacent waters (incl. Shelter, Gardiners, and Plum). Has grown to be major residential district for New York City; aircraft manufacturing and summer resort areas outside New York City; agriculture important in Suffolk co.

History: Orig. inhabited by Indians (mostly Delaware); included in grant to Plymouth Company; conventionally thought to have been conveyed to William Alexander, earl of Stirling, 1635; settled by Dutch (W end) and English (E end); became part of British colony of New York 1664; scene of battle of Long Island (at Brooklyn Heights) in Revolutionary War Aug. 27, 1776 in which Gen. William Howe defeated Americans under Gen. George Washington, who, however, successfully withdrew his forces across the river several days later.

4. Island in S end of Willapa Bay, Pacific co., SW Washington; 8 sq. mi. (21 sq. km.).

5. Island in SW Lake Superior, Wisconsin. See APOSTLE ISLANDS.

6. One of the SE Bahamas, SW of San Salvador; 230 sq. mi. (596 sq. km.); pop. (1980c) 3358.

7. British islands, North Atlantic Ocean. See BERMUDA.

8. Islands, Atlantic Ocean. See HEBRIDES.

9. Island in Bismarck Archipelago, Papua New Guinea, off NE coast of New Guinea, WNW of Umboi I. and separated from mainland by Vitiaz Strait; highest point 4278 ft. (1304 m.).

Long Island City. Former city, since 1898 part of Queens borough of New York City, on Long Island and East River, SE New York. Former village of Astoria now a part of it.

Long Island Sound. Body of water bet. S shore of Connecticut and N shore of Long Island, New York, connecting with East River on W and with Block Island Sound on E; 1299 sq. mi. (3364 sq. km.); 110 mi. (177 km.) long, from 10 to 25 mi. (16 to 40 km.) wide.

Long·ju·meau \ˌlō^{n}-zhūē-ˈmō\. Commune, Essonne dept., N France, ab. 11 mi. (18 km.) S of Paris; short-lived truce in Wars of Religion signed here 1568 bet. Catholics and Protestants.

Long Key. See FLORIDA KEYS.

Long·kou \ˈlu̇ŋ-ˈkō\ *or W.-G.* **Lung–k'ou** \ˈlu̇ŋ-ˈkō\. Port, Shandong prov., NE China, on N Shandong Penin. W of Yantai; pop. (1990c) 148,362.

Long Lake. **1.** Lake in NE Hamilton co., NE cen. New York; ab. 14 mi. (23 km.) long and 1 mi. (1.6 km.) wide; elev. 1615 ft. (492 m.); receives water from Raquette Lake to the SW and drains through Raquette River flowing N.

2. Lake extending across S boundary bet. Kidder and Burleigh cos., S cen. North Dakota.

Long·ling \ˈlu̇ŋ-ˈliŋ\ *or W.-G.* **Lung–ling** \ˈlu̇ŋ-ˈliŋ\. Town, W Yunnan prov., S China, bet. the Salween and Shweli rivers 85 mi. (137 km.) NE of Wandingzhen; 523 mi. (842 km.) by road from Kunming; alt. ab. 4500 ft. (1370 m.). Taken by Japanese 1942; recaptured by Chinese 1944.

Long·mead·ow \ˈlȯŋ-ˈme-dō\. Residential town, Hampden co., SW Massachusetts, on Connecticut River S of and adjoining Springfield; pop. (1990c) 15,467; Bay Path Coll. (1897).

Long·mont \ˈlȯŋ-ˌmänt\. City, Boulder co., N cen. Colorado, 30 mi. (48 km.) N of Denver; pop. (1990c) 51,555; manufactures campers; grows sugar beets; founded c. 1870.

Long Point. **1.** Cape on S side of tip of Cape Cod, Massachusetts.

2. Cape, S Norfolk co., SE Ontario, Canada, extending E into Lake Erie S of **Long Point Bay.**

Long Prairie. Village, ⊗ of Todd co., cen. Minnesota, 23 mi. (37 km.) ENE of Alexandria; pop. (1990c) 2786.

Long Range Mountains. Range of hills, W Newfoundland I., Canada; includes highest peak on island, 2672 ft. (814 m.).

Long·ships \ˈlȯŋ-ˌships\. Rocky islets, Cornwall, SW England, 1.25 mi. (2 km.) W of Land's End; lighthouse, 117 ft. (36 m.) high, visible 16 mi. (26 km.).

Longs Peak \ˈlȯŋz\. Mountain, Boulder co., N cen. Colorado, in Front Range; 14,255 ft. (4345 m.); highest peak in Rocky Mountain National Park. Named in honor of Stephen H. Long, American army officer and explorer, who discovered it 1820.

Long·ton \ˈlȯŋ-tən\. See POTTERIES, THE.

Lon·gueuil \lȯŋ-ˈgāl\. Residential city, S Quebec, Canada, on St. Lawrence River across from Montreal; pop. (1991c) 129,874.

Longue·val \lō^{n}g-ˈväl\. Village, Somme dept., N France, 7 mi. (11 km.) ENE of Albert; in territory gained by the British in the battle of the Somme July–Nov. 1916.

Long·view \ˈlȯŋ-ˌvyü\. **1.** City, ⊗ of Gregg co., NE Texas, 20 mi. (32 km.) W of Marshall; pop. (1990c) 70,311; steel, chemicals, oil-drilling machinery; oil and gas wells, oil refineries; LeTourneau Univ. (1946). Incorp. 1872; grew rapidly in the 1930s after discovery of oil.

2. City, Cowlitz co., SW Washington, at confluence of Cowlitz and Columbia rivers 37 mi. (60 km.) N of Vancouver; pop. (1990c) 31,499; center of lumber and pulp industry; seaport; Lower Columbia Coll. (1934); founded as planned city on site of old Monticello 1922; incorp. 1924; connected with Oregon by bridge.

Long View. Town, Burke and Catawba cos., W North Carolina, 41 mi. (66 km.) NW of Charlotte; pop. (1990c) 3229.

Long·wood \ˈlȯŋ-ˌwu̇d\. City, Seminole co., cen. Florida, 10 mi. (16 km.) N of Orlando; pop. (1990c) 13,316.

Long·wy \lō^{n}-ˈwē\. Commune, Meurthe-et-Moselle dept., NE France, 60 mi. (96 km.) N of Nancy; pop. (1990c) 15,647; iron mines. Fortified by French military engineer Sébastien Le Prestre de Vauban; battles 1815 and 1870; in WWI taken by Germans 1914.

Long Xuyen \lau̇ŋ-ˈswē-ən\. City, S Vietnam, on S side of Mekong Delta 100 mi. (161 km.) W of Ho Chi Minh City; pop. (1989c) 128,817.

Long·year·by·en \ˈlȯŋ-ˌyēr-ˌbūē-ən\ *or Eng.* **Long·year City** \ˈlȯŋ-ˈyir\. Village, Spitsbergen I., Norway, on Advent Bay, Ice Fjord; administrative center of Svalbard; coal deposits.

Long·zhou \ˈlu̇ŋ-ˈjō\ *or W.-G.* **Lung–chou** \ˈlu̇ŋ-ˈjō\. Town and port, SW Guangxi Zhuangzu, SE China, near Vietnamese border; made a treaty port 1889; during late 1930s a major trade center because of Japanese blockade of other Chinese ports.

Lon·ne·ker \ˈlō-nə-kər\. Commune, Overijssel prov., E Netherlands, suburb of Enschede 3 mi. (5 km.) to NE, near German border.

Lo·noke \ˈlō-ˌnōk\. **1.** County in cen. Arkansas. See table at ARKANSAS.

2. City, its ⊗, ab. 22 mi. (35 km.) ENE of Little Rock; pop. (1990c) 4022.

Lons·dale \ˈlänz-ˌdāl\. Village, Providence co., N Rhode Island, ab. 7 mi. (11 km.) SE of Woonsocket; seat of government for town of Lincoln.

Lons–le–Sau·nier \ˌlō^{n}-lə-sō-ˈnyā\; *anc.* **Le·do Sal·i·nar·i·us** \ˈlē-dō-ˌsa-lə-ˈnar-ē-əs\. Commune, ✱ of Jura dept., E France, 44 mi. (71 km.) NW of Geneva, Switzerland; pop. (1990c) 20,140; produces wines, optical equipment; warm saline springs (known since Roman times); salt mines in a W suburb; church, oldest part of which dates from 11th cent.

Loochoo Islands. See RYUKYU ISLANDS 1.

Loo·goo·tee \lə-ˈgō-tē\. Residential city, Martin co., SW Indiana, 33 mi. (53 km.) E of Vincennes; pop. (1990c) 2884.

Look·out, Cape \ˈlu̇k-ˌau̇t\. **1.** Cape, S tip of Core Banks off Carteret co., SE North Carolina; lighthouse.

2. Cape in Tillamook co., NW Oregon, S of Netarts Bay.

Lookout, Point. Point, SE tip of St. Marys co., S Maryland, on N side of mouth of Potomac River.

Lookout Mountain. **1.** Ridge in SE Tennessee, extending into Georgia and Alabama, near Chattanooga (*q.v.*); site of battle Nov. 24, 1863 in which Union troops under Gen. Joseph Hooker forced the withdrawal of the Confederates.
2. Residential and resort town, Hamilton co., SE Tennessee, on Lookout Mt. on Georgia border SW of Chattanooga; pop. (1990c) 1901; Covenant Coll. (1955).

Lookout Peak. **1.** Mountain in the Sierra Nevada, W Inyo co., S cen. California; 10,144 ft. (3092 m.).
2. Mountain, San Juan and San Miguel cos., SW Colorado; 13,660 ft. (4164 m.).
3. Mountain, Lawrence co., W South Dakota; 4887 ft. (1490 m.).

Loo·mis \ˈlü-məs\. Town, Placer co., E California; pop. (1990c) 5705.

Lo·on \lō-ˈȯn\. Municipality, W coast of Bohol I., Philippines, NNW of Tagbilaran; pop. (1980c) 35,643.

Loon op Zand \ˌlōn-ȯp-ˈzänt\. Commune, North Brabant prov., S Netherlands, 4 mi. (6 km.) N of Tilburg; pop. (1981e) 19,602.

Loop Head \ˈlüp\. Cape on W coast of Ireland, on N shore of mouth of the Shannon; lighthouse.

Loos \ˈlōs, ˈlȯs\. **1.** Commune, Nord dept., N France, 4 mi. (6 km.) W of Lille.
2. *or* **Loos–en–Go·helle** \-äⁿ-gō-ˈel\. Commune, Pas-de-Calais dept., N France, ab. 3 mi. (5 km.) NNW of Lens; in battle Sept. to Oct. 1915, part of Marshal Joseph-Jacques-Césaire Joffre's offensive in Champagne, village captured by British with heavy losses. Nearby are several British cemeteries.

Loos, Îles de. See LOS ISLANDS.

Lopadusa. See LAMPEDUSA.

Lopatino. See VOLZHSK.

Lo·pat·ka, Cape \lȧ-ˈpȧt-kə\. Cape on S extremity of Kamchatka Penin., Kamchatka Oblast, E Russia in Asia, projecting into Pervyy Kuril'skiy Proliv opp. Shumshu I.

Lop Bu·ri *or* **Lo·bu·ri** \ˈlȯp-bu̇-ˈrē\. City, SW cen. Thailand, 30 mi. (48 km.) N of Phra Nakhon Si Ayutthaya; pop. (1991e) 39,738.

Lo·pe·vi \lō-ˈpā-vē\. Volcano on island of same name, S cen. Vanuatu, SW Pacific Ocean; 4755 ft. (1449 m.).

Lo·pez, Cape \ˈlō-ˌpez\. Cape extending into Gulf of Guinea on W coast of Gabon, equatorial part of Africa.

Lopez Island. See SAN JUAN ISLANDS.

Lop Nur \ˈlȯp-ˈnu̇r\ *or W.-G.* **Lo–pu Po** \ˈlō-ˈpü-ˈpō\; *mostly formerly* **Lop Nor** \ˈlȯp-ˈnu̇r\ *or* **Lob Nor** \ˈlōb-\. Salt, marshy depression at E end of Tarim basin, Xinjiang Uygur, W China, N of the Altun Shan, 40°30′N, 90°30′E; receives the Tarim River but has no outflow; river has shifted channels at intervals, leading to changes in location. In region is major Chinese nuclear research and testing facility, test site of Chinese nuclear detonations since 1964.

Lo·po·ri \lō-ˈpōr-ē\. River, NW cen. Democratic Rep. of the Congo; flows NW and W nearly parallel with the Congo to join the Maringa and form the Lulonga; ab. 380 mi. (610 km.) long.

Lo–pu Po. See LOP NUR.

Lora, Hamun–i–. See HAMUN-I-LORA.

Lo·ra del Río \ˈlō-rä-t͟hel-ˈrē-ō\. Commune, Sevilla prov., SW Spain, 29 mi. (47 km.) NE of Seville; pop. (1991c) 18,551.

Lo·rain \lə-ˈrān, lȯ-\. **1.** County in N Ohio. See table at OHIO.
2. City and lake port, Lorain co., N Ohio, on Lake Erie 25 mi. (40 km.) W of Cleveland; pop. (1990c) 71,245; shipbuilding; steel, construction equipment; motor-vehicle assembly plants; settled 1807; orig. incorp. as Charleston 1836; later rechartered as Lorain.

Lo·ra·lai \ˈlȯr-ə-ˌlī\. Town, Baluchistan, Pakistan, 100 mi. (161 km.) E of Quetta; pop. (1981c) 13,900.

Lor·ca \ˈlȯr-kä\; *anc.* **Eli·o·cro·ca** \ˌē-lē-ə-ˈkrō-kə\. Commune, Murcia prov., SE Spain, 34 mi. (55 km.) SW of the commune of Murcia; pop. (1991p) 65,832; in grain- and livestock-farming region; Moorish castle.

Lorch \ˈlȯrk\. Town, E cen. Baden-Württemberg, Germany, 6 mi. (10 km.) N of Göppingen; pop. (1980c) 4647; 12th cent. church containing tombs of the Hohenstaufen dynastic family.

Lord Howe Island \ˈhau̇\. **1.** Island of volcanic origin in SW Pacific Ocean, off E coast of New South Wales, Australia, 436 mi. (702 km.) ENE of Sydney, 31°33′S, 159°05′E; 5 sq. mi. (13 sq. km.); belongs to New South Wales. Highest point 2871 ft. (875 m.); world's southernmost coral reef along its W coast; tourism. First sighted 1788; settled c. 1834.
2. Small island off S coast of Nendo I., Santa Cruz Is., SW Pacific Ocean, part of Solomon Is.

Lord Howe Islands. See ONTONG JAVA.

Lords·burg \ˈlȯrdz-ˌbərg\. City, ⊗ of Hidalgo co., SW corner of New Mexico, 38 mi. (61 km.) SW of Silver City; pop. (1990c) 2951.

Lords·town \ˈlȯrdz-ˌtau̇n\. Village, Trumbull co., NE Ohio; pop. (1990c) 3404.

Lo·re·lei \ˈlōr-ə-ˌlī\ *or Ger.* **Lur·lei** \ˈlu̇r-ˌlī\. Rock on right bank of Rhine, near Sankt Goarshausen, bet. Bingen and Koblenz, Germany; ab. 440 ft. (135 m.) above river; in German legend, said to be haunted by a siren (Lurlei) who by her beauty and singing enticed sailors to destruction on the reef below.

Lo·re·na \lü-ˈrā-nə\. City, São Paulo state, SE Brazil, 115 mi. (185 km.) NE of the city of São Paulo; munic. pop. (1991p) 65,443.

Lo·reng·au *also* **Lo·rung·au** \ˌlōr-əŋ-ˈau̇\. Seaport on E tip of Manus I., Admiralty Is., Bismarck Archipelago, Papua New Guinea; pop. (1990c) 4547.

Lo·ren·skog \ˈlō-rən-ˌskȯg\. Commune, Akershus co., SE Norway; pop. (1990c) 26,066.

Lo·re·stān \ˌlȯr-ə-ˈstän, ˈlȯr-ə-ˌstan\ *also* **Lu·ri·stan** \ˈlu̇r-ə-ˌstan, -ˌstän\. Province (formerly a governorship), W Iran; 12,116 sq. mi. (31,380 sq. km.); ✱ Khorramābād; mountainous region, incl. the Zagros Mts.; watered by the Karkheh and Kārūn. Parts, variously independent 12th–17th cents.; its inhabitants chiefly Lurs and Bakhtiaris.

Lo·re·to \lō-ˈrā-tō\. Region, NE Peru; includes territory N of Marañón River which was in dispute, claimed by both Peru and Ecuador (*qq.v.*), until settlement of 1942; forested region, watered by tributaries of the Amazon; separated from coastal departments by Andes; chief products rubber, Brazil nuts, skins and hides, hardwood.

Lo·rette·ville \lə-ˈret-ˌvil\. City, ⊗ of Quebec co., S Quebec, Canada, on St. Charles River 7 mi. (11 km.) WNW of Quebec City; pop. (1991c) 14,219; suburb of Quebec City, formerly site of a Huron village estab. 17th cent. Nearby in St. Charles River are **Falls of Lorette,** ab. 100 ft. (30 m.) high.

Lo·ret·to \lə-ˈre-tō\. Borough, Cambria co., SW cen. Pennsylvania, ab. 20 mi. (32 km.) NE of Johnstown; pop. (1990c) 1072; St. Francis Coll. (1847).

Lo·ri·an Swamp \ˈlōr-ē-ən\. Swamp, E Kenya; traversed by the Vasa Nyira River.

Lo·ri·ca \lō-ˈrē-kä\. Seaport town, Córdoba dept., N Colombia, at mouth of Sinú River.

Lo·rient; *formerly* **L'Ori·ent** \lȯr-ˈyäⁿ\. Fortified seaport commune, Morbihan dept., NW France, on the Bay of Biscay 29 mi. (47 km.) WNW of Vannes; pop. (1990c) 61,630; harbor 4 mi. (6 km.) from the sea formed by junction of Blavet and Scorff rivers; naval station and arsenal; shipbuilding, fishing and fish canning. French East India Company (Compagnie de l'Orient) estab. here 1664. Used as submarine base by Germans and frequently bombed and heavily damaged by Allied airplanes during WWII; taken by Allies May 1945; subsequently rebuilt. See KÉROMAN.

L'Ori·gnal \lȯr-ˈnel, lȯr-in-ˈyäl\. Village, ⊗ of Prescott and Russell co., SE Ontario, Canada, on Ottawa River 50 mi. (80 km.) ENE of Ottawa; pop. (1991c) 2164; has port facilities.

Lorn, Firth of *or* **Firth of Lorne** \ˈlȯrn\. Strait bet. Mull I. and mainland (Strathclyde region) of W Scotland.

Lör·rach \ˈlœr-ˌäk\. City, SW Baden-Württemberg, Germany, near Black Forest, 28 mi. (45 km.) SSW of Freiburg and on Swiss border near Basel; pop. (1980c) 41,355; received civic rights 1682.

Lor·raine \lə-ˈrān, lȯ-\; *anc.* **Lo·tha·rin·gia** \ˌlō-thə-ˈrin-jə\ *or Ger.* **Lo·thring·en** \ˈlō-triŋ-ən\. **1.** Medieval region, W Europe, in what is now NE France; in division of Carolingian empire by Treaty of Verdun 843 became part of realm (sometimes known as Middle Kingdom) of Emperor Lothair I; inherited by his son Lothair 855–869, becoming the kingdom of Lotharingia (Lat. *Lotharii regnum*); after Lothair's death contested by Germany and France, coming under German control 925.

2. Duchy, W Europe, orig. known as **Upper Lorraine** and later called simply **Lorraine,** formed by division of Lorraine (see LORRAINE 1) into two duchies 959: **Lower Lorraine,** bet. Rhine and Schelde rivers (later developing into separate duchies such as Brabant and Limburg) and Upper Lorraine, region of upper Meuse and Moselle rivers; ruled from 11th cent. continuously by one ducal family (united by marriage with rival dukes of Bar 1431); bishoprics (Les Trois-Évêchés) of Metz, Toul, and Verdun remained outside the dukes' control and in 1552 were seized by France; at times in the 17th cent. entire duchy held by French sovereigns; ruled 1737–66 by Stanisław I Leszczyński, dethroned king of Poland and father-in-law of Louis XV of France; permanently French from 1766; a province with its ✻ at Nancy until the French Revolution, when it was divided into departments; after Franco-Prussian War 1870–71 part of the Lorraine region was ceded to Germany as part of Alsace-Lorraine (*q.v.*).

3. Region of NE France. See table at FRANCE.

Lorungau. See LORENGAU.

Los Ala·mi·tos \lȯs-ˌa-lə-ˈmē-təs\. City, Orange co., SW California, E of Long Beach; pop. (1990c) 11,676.

Los Al·a·mos \lȯs-ˈa-lə-ˌmōs\. **1.** County in N cen. New Mexico. See table at NEW MEXICO.

2. Unincorporated settlement, Los Alamos co., New Mexico, ab. 35 mi. (55 km.) NW of Santa Fe, on a mesa in Jemez Mts.; pop. (1990c) 11,455; alt. ab. 7400 ft. (2255 m.); chosen 1942 as site for research and development of nuclear weapons, place where first atomic bombs were assembled; remains site of a major nuclear-research facility.

Los Aler·ces National Park \ˌlȯs-ä-ˈler-sās\. National park, Argentina, on S cen. Chile border; ab. 720 sq. mi. (1865 sq. km.); groves of tall ancient alerces trees, impressive Andean scenery.

Los Al·tos \lȯ-ˈsal-təs\. City, Santa Clara co., W California, SSE of Palo Alto; pop. (1990c) 26,303; residential.

Los An·des \lȯs-ˈän-dās\. **1.** See ANDES.

2. Former territory, NW Argentina, in the Andes; practically coextensive with the Puna de Atacama region.

3. City, Aconcagua prov., cen. Chile, ab. 40 mi. (65 km.) N of Santiago; pop. (1992c) 50,622; on Transandine R.R. 65 mi. (104 km.) E of Valparaíso (83 mi. or 134 km. by rail); alt. 2675 ft. (815 m.).

Los An·ge·les \lȯs-ˈan-jə-ləs, -ˈaŋ-gə-ləs, -ˌlēz\. **1.** County in SW California. See table at CALIFORNIA.

2. City, its ⊗, at its center ab. 15 mi. (25 km.) from the Pacific Ocean although extending to the coast in several places; pop. (1990c) 3,485,398, making it the largest city in the state and 2d largest in the U.S.; excellent harbor at San Pedro Bay ab. 25 mi. (40 km.) S of center of city; a major industrial center, producing aircraft and accessories, machinery, petroleum products, electronic equipment, glass, chemicals, cement; oil refining; ships oranges and dairy products; Hollywood, a district of Los Angeles, is a major center of the American motion-picture and television industry; tourist center. City area has absorbed many towns and villages and now surrounds several incorp. cities incl. Santa Monica, Culver City, West Hollywood, and Beverly Hills. Has numerous parks, recreational areas, and cultural facilities; several small structures of the early Spanish period. Site of Summer Olympic Games 1932 and 1984. Water supply brought from Colorado River by aqueduct (constructed early 20th cent.) 300 mi. (483 km.) long; suffers from earthquakes and air pollution. An important educational center: Univ. of Southern California (1880), Univ. of California at Los Angeles (1919), Occidental Coll. (1887), West Coast Univ. (1909), Loyola Marymount Univ. (1911), Southwestern Univ. School of Law (1911), Otis Art Institute of Parsons School of Design (1918), Mount St. Mary's Coll. (1925), Los Angeles City Coll. (1929), Pepperdine Univ. (1937), Center for Early Education (1939), Univ. of Judaism (1947), California State Univ. at Los Angeles (1947), Los Angeles Trade-Technical Coll. (1949), Columbia Coll.–Hollywood (1952). Founded 1781 by settlers from Mexico and named El Pueblo de la Reina de los Angeles; captured by U.S. forces without a fight 1846; incorp. 1850; growth accelerated by arrival of railroads (Southern Pacific in 1876, Sante Fe in 1885) and subsequent rate wars, discovery of nearby petroleum deposits in the 1890s, and improvement of the harbor early 20th cent. Suffered major earthquake 1994.

Los Án·ge·les \lȯs-ˈäŋ-hā-ˌlās\. City, Bío-Bío region, S cen. Chile, 58 mi. (93 km.) SE of Concepción in valley of Bío-Bío River; munic. pop. (1992c) 142,136; formerly ✻ of Bío-Bío prov.

Lo·san·ti·ville \lō-ˈsan-tə-ˌvil\. Original name of Cincinnati (*q.v.*), Ohio.

Los Ara·bos \lȯs-ä-ˈrä-b̲ōs\. Municipality, Matanzas prov., W cen. Cuba, on railroad line 38 mi. (61 km.) SE of Cárdenas; pop. (1981p) 24,880.

Los Ba·nos \lȯs-ˈba-nəs\. City, Merced co., cen. California, 60 mi. (96 km.) WNW of Fresno; pop. (1990c) 14,519.

Los Ba·ños \lȯs-ˈbä-nyōs\. Municipality, cen. Laguna prov., Luzon, Philippines, on S shore of Laguna de Bay 15 mi. (24 km.) SW of Santa Cruz, on provincial highway 34 mi. (55 km.) SE of Manila; pop. (1980c) 49,555; mineral springs; seat of Coll. of Agriculture of the Univ. of the Philippines. American air base early in WWII; Japanese concentration camp captured Feb. 23, 1945.

Los Dos Ca·mi·nos \lȯs-ˌt̲h̲ȯs-kä-ˈmē-nȯs\. City, N Venezuela, in the Caracas met. area; pop. (1990e) 76,559.

Loser, Mount. See LEUSER, MOUNT.

Los Estados, Isla de. See ESTADOS, ISLA DE LOS.

Los Gat·os \lȯs-ˈga-təs\. City, Santa Clara co., W California, 8 mi. (13 km.) SW of San Jose; pop. (1990c) 27,357.

Los Gla·ci·a·res National Park \ˌlȯs-glä-ˈsyä-rās\. National park, S Argentina on Chilean border; includes the W ends of Lake Argentino and Lake Viedma; glaciers; estab. 1937.

Lo–shan. See LESHAN.

Los Her·ma·nos \ˌlȯs-er-ˈmä-nȯs\. Group of small islands, Venezuela, in Caribbean Sea off NE cen. coast 50 mi. (80 km.) NNW of Margarita I.

Lo·šinj \ˈlō-ˌshēn-yə\ *or Ital.* **Lus·si·no** \lu̇-ˈsē-nō\. Small island in the Kvarnerić Channel, S of Cres I., W Croatia; 24 mi. (39 km.) long; 29 sq. mi. (75 sq. km.); formerly Italian.

Losinoostrovsk. See BABUSHKIN.

Los Islands \ˈlȯs\ *or* **Îles de Loos** \ˌēl-də-ˈlōs, -ˈlȯs\. Group of small islands off Conakry, Guinea; 6 sq. mi. (16 sq. km.); largest Tamara, with good harbor. Came into British possession 1818; ceded to France 1904; since 1958 part of independent Guinea.

Los La·gos \lȯs-ˈlä-g̲ōs\. Region of S cen. Chile. See table at CHILE.

Los Lu·nas \lȯs-ˈlü-näs\. Village, ⊗ of Valencia co., W New Mexico, on the Rio Grande 18 mi. (29 km.) S of Albuquerque; pop. (1990c) 6013.

Los Mo·chis \los-ˈmō-chēs\. City, Sinaloa state, W Mexico; pop. (1990c) 162,659.

Losoncz. See LUČENEC.

Los Pa·la·cios \ˌlȯs-pä-ˈläs-yȯs\. Municipality, Pinar del Río prov., W Cuba; pop. (1981p) 34,763.

Los Pa·tos \lȯs-ˈpä-tȯs\ *or* **Por·til·lo de los Patos** \pōr-ˈtē-yō-ˌt͟hā-lȯs-ˈpä-tȯs\. Mountain pass in the Andes, W Argentina, ab. 100 mi. (160 km.) N of Aconcagua; 11,700 ft. (3566 m.).

Los Ran·chos de Al·bu·quer·que \lȯs-ˈran-chōz-dē-ˈal-bə-ˌkər-kē\. Village, Bernalillo co., cen. New Mexico; pop. (1990c) 3955.

Los Re·yes \lȯs-ˈrā-es\. Town, Michoacán state, SW Mexico, 30 mi. (48 km.) WNW of Uruapan.

Los Rí·os \lȯs-ˈrē-ōs\. Province of W cen. Ecuador. See table at ECUADOR.

Los Ro·ques \lȯs-ˈrō-kes\. Group of small islands, Venezuela, in Caribbean Sea off N cen. coast of Venezuela.

Los San·tos \lȯs-ˈsän-tȯs\. Province of S cen. Panama. See table at PANAMA.

Los·ser \ˈlȯ-sər\. Commune, Overijssel prov., E Netherlands, 6 mi. (10 km.) NE of Enschede on German border; pop. (1981e) 21,792.

Los·sie·mouth \ˈlȯ-sē-ˌmau̇th\. Burgh, Grampian region, NE Scotland, on North Sea at mouth of **Los·sie River** \ˈlȯ-sē\ N of Elgin; pop. (1981c) 6848; port and seaside resort.

Lo Stato della Chiesa. See PAPAL STATES.

Lost City. See OVERTON 2.

Los Te·ques \lȯs-ˈtā-kes\. Town, ✻ of Miranda state, N Venezuela, ab. 15 mi. (25 km.) SW of Caracas; pop. (1990c) 140,617.

Los Tes·ti·gos \ˌlȯs-tes-ˈtē-ḡōs\. Group of small Venezuelan islands, in Caribbean Sea N of NE Venezuela.

Lost Mine Peak \ˈlȯst-ˈmīn\. Mountain, S Brewster co., W Texas; 7750 ft. (2362 m.).

Lost River Range. Range in E cen. Idaho, chiefly in Custer and Butte cos.

Lost·with·i·el \lȯs-ˈtwi-t͟hē-əl\. Town, Cornwall, SW England, 30 mi. (48 km.) W of Plymouth; borough pop. (1981c) 1998; castle (begun 11th cent.) of Restormel nearby; scene of battle 1644 in which Charles I defeated Robert Devereux, 3d earl of Essex.

Lo·su·ia \lȯ-ˈsü-yə\. Chief town of Trobriand Is. off SE New Guinea I., Papua New Guinea on W coast of Kiriwina I. near N end.

Lot \ˈlȯt, ˈlät\. **1.** *anc.* **Ol·tis** \ˈäl-təs, ˈȯl-\. Navigable river in S France; rises in Lozère dept. on slopes of the Lozère Mts.; flows W into Garonne River W of Agen; ab. 300 mi. (485 km.) long.
2. Department of S cen. France. See table at FRANCE.

Lo·ta \ˈlō-tä\. Seaport, Bío-Bío region, S cen. Chile, 21 mi. (34 km.) S of Concepción; pop. (1990e) 44,416; coal-mining center from 1852; copper smelters; nearby is Cousiño Park, containing plants and trees from all over the world; seaport founded 1662.

Lot·bi·nière \ˌlō-bi-ˈnyer\. County, S Quebec, Canada. See table at QUEBEC.

Lot–et–Ga·ronne \ˈlȯt-ā-gə-ˈrȯn\. Department of SW France. See table at FRANCE.

Lotharingia. See LORRAINE.

Lo·thi·an \ˈlō-t͟hē-ən\. **1.** Region of S Scotland; in early times extending from the Tweed River to the Firth of Forth; later divided into three counties, **The Lo·thi·ans** \-ənz\, East Lothian, Midlothian, and West Lothian.
2. Administrative region, S Scotland. See table at SCOTLAND.

Lothringen. See LORRAINE and *History* at ALSACE-LORRAINE.

Lothringen, Elsass–. See ALSACE–LORRAINE.

Löt·schen Pass \ˈlœ-chən\. Mountain pass in the Bernese Alps bet. Bern and Valais cantons, SW cen. Switzerland; 8823 ft. (2689 m.); under it is the **Lötsch·berg** \ˈlœch-ˌberk\ railroad tunnel, 9 mi. (14 km.) long, at an alt. of 4080 ft. (1244 m.).

Lötzen. See GIŻYCKO.

Loualaba. See LUALABA.

Louang·phra·bang \ˈlwäŋ-prä-ˈbäŋ\ *or* **Luang Pra·bang** \ˈlwäŋ-prä-\. Town, N Laos, on left bank of the Mekong; trade and market center; connected by highway with Vientiane; limit of navigation on the Mekong. Has numerous pagodas; former royal residence.

Lou·bo·mo \lü-ˈbō-mō\ *or* **Do·li·sie** \ˌdō-lē-ˈzē\. Town, S Rep. of the Congo, W of Brazzaville; pop. (1992e) 83,605.

Lou·don \ˈlau̇d-ᵊn\. **1.** County in E Tennessee. See table at TENNESSEE.
2. Town, Merrimack co., S cen. New Hampshire; pop. (1990c) 4114.
3. Town, ⊗ of Loudon co., Tennessee, on Tennessee River 30 mi. (48 km.) SW of Knoxville; pop. (1990c) 4026.

Loudon Hill. Locality, Strathclyde region, SW Scotland, E of Kilmarnock; scene of victory of Scottish King Robert the Bruce over the English 1307.

Lou·don·ville \ˈlau̇d-ᵊn-ˌvil\. **1.** Unincorporated settlement, Albany co., E New York, just N of the city of Albany; pop. (1990c) 10,822; Siena Coll. (1937).
2. Village, Ashland and Holmes cos., N cen. Ohio, 15 mi. (24 km.) SE of Mansfield; pop. (1990c) 2915.

Lou·doun \ˈlau̇d-ᵊn\. County in N Virginia. See table at VIRGINIA.

Lou·dun \lü-ˈdœⁿ\. Commune, NW Vienne dept., W cen. France, 40 mi. (64 km.) SW of Tours; a Protestant community, suffered much after revocation of the Edict of Nantes during Wars of Religion.

Lough·bor·ough \ˈləf-ˌbər-ə, -ˌbər-ō\. Town, Leicestershire, cen. England, 13 mi. (21 km.) SSW of Nottingham; pop. (1981c) 46,122; market center; electrical equipment, hosiery, pharmaceuticals, bell founding; Loughborough Univ. of Technology (1966); formerly a lacemaking center.

Loughor. See LLWCHWR.

Lough·rea \läk-ˈrā, läk-\. Market town, SE co. Galway, W Ireland, on N shore of Lough Rea 18 mi. (29 km.) SW of Ballinasloe; pop. (1986c) 3360; remains of castle and Carmelite friary; a cromlech (dolmen) is nearby.

Lou·i·sa \lü-ˈē-zə, *Iowa* -ˈī-\. **1.** Name of counties in two states of the U.S. See tables at IOWA and VIRGINIA.
2. City, ⊗ of Lawrence co., E Kentucky, on Big Sandy River 25 mi. (40 km.) S of Ashland; pop. (1990c) 1990.
3. Town, ⊗ of Louisa co., cen. Virginia; pop. (1990c) 1088.

Lou·is·bourg *also* **Lou·is·burg** \ˈlü-is-ˌbərg\. Town, Cape Breton co., E Nova Scotia, Canada, on Atlantic Ocean; pop. (1991c) 1147; anchorage for fishing fleet.
History: Founded by French 1713; strongly fortified in subsequent decades; during King George's War besieged and captured by New England colonials under Sir William Pepperell 1745; returned to the French by Treaty of Aix-la-Chapelle 1748; in Seven Years' War again taken by the English under Gen. Jeffrey Amherst and Adm. Edward Boscawen 1758; its fortifications destroyed soon after. Site of reconstructed fort now preserved as historic attraction.

Lou·is·burg \ˈlü-is-ˌbərg\. **1.** Town, ⊗ of Franklin co., N North Carolina, 30 mi. (48 km.) NE of Raleigh; pop. (1990c) 3037; Louisburg Coll. (1787).
2. Town, Nova Scotia, Canada. See LOUISBOURG.

Lou·ise, Lake \lu̇-ˈēz\. Lake near Banff, SW Alberta, Canada; 1.5 mi. by 0.75 mi. (2.4 km. by 1.2 km.); alt. 5670 ft. (1728 m.); in Banff National Park, at foot of high peaks; its outlet is short stream flowing into Bow River; region noted for its scenery.

Louise Island. Island, cen. Queen Charlotte Is. off W British Columbia, Canada, on Hecate Strait.

Lou·ise·ville \lu̇-ˈēz-ˌvil\. Town, ⊗ of Maskinongé co., S Quebec, Canada, on Lake St. Peter 20 mi. (32 km.) WSW of Trois Rivières; pop. (1990c) 8000.

Louis Gentil. See YOUSSOUFIA.

Lou·i·si·ade Archipelago \lu̇-ˌē-zē-ˈäd, -ˈad\. Island group in Solomon Sea SE of E end of New Guinea; ab. 600 sq. mi. (1555 sq. km.); pop. (1980c) 16,478; administratively part of Papua New Guinea; chief village, Bwagaoia, on E end of Misima I.; comprises large islands of Misima, Tagula, and Rossel, and many small islands and reefs; gold mines on Tagula I. Visited by Spanish navigator Luis Vaez de Torres 1606; in WWII used early in 1942 by Japanese as seaplane base; battle of Coral Sea fought nearby 1942.

Lou·i·si·ana \lu̇-ˌē-zē-ˈa-nə, ˌlü-ə-zē-, ˌlü-zē-\. **1.** A southern state of U.S.A., bounded on N by Arkansas, on E and SE by Mississippi and the Gulf of Mexico, on S by the Gulf of Mexico, and on W by Texas; 31st state in area, 48,523 sq. mi. (125,674 sq. km.); 21st state in population (1990c)

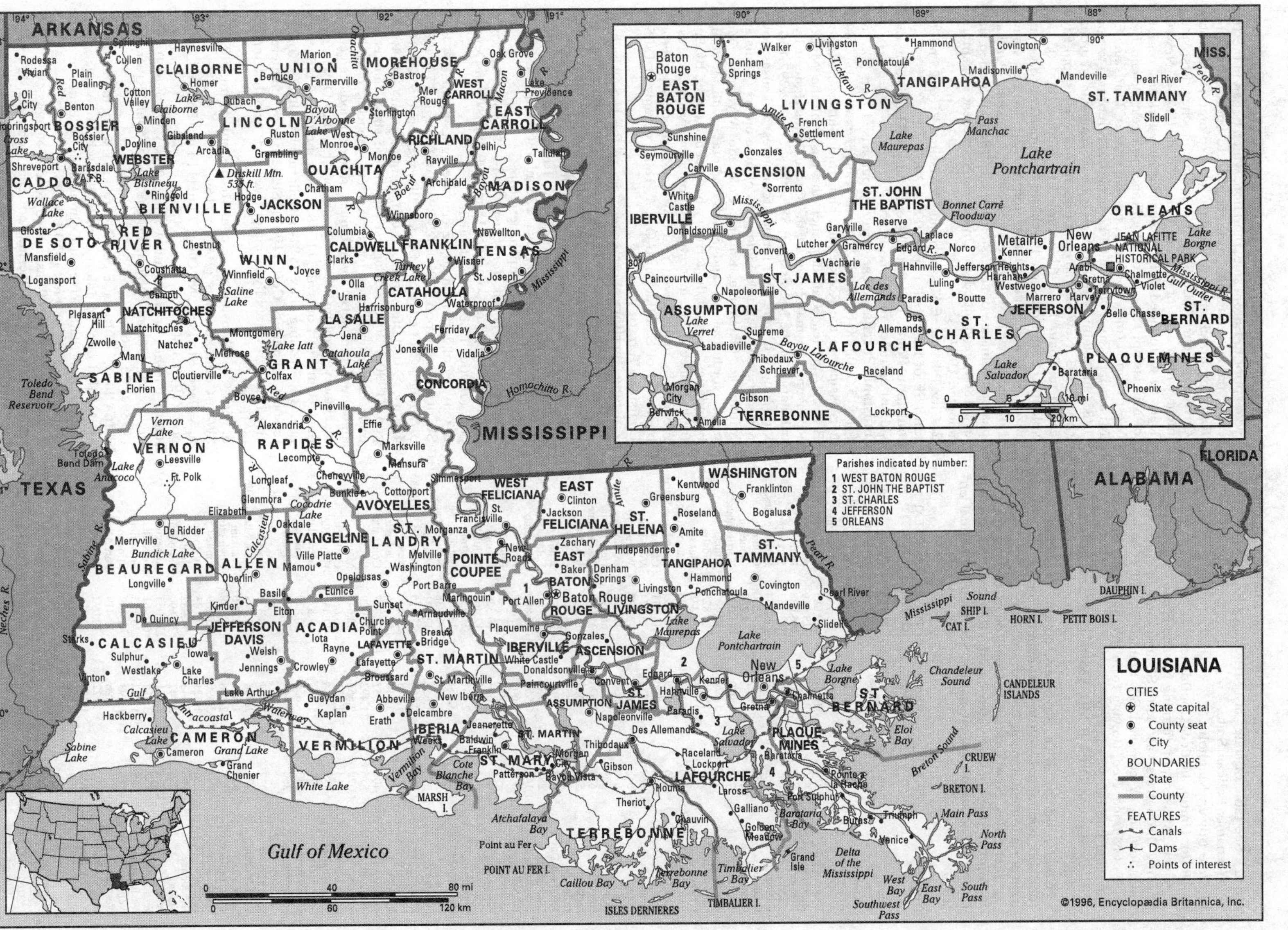

LOUISIANA
CITIES
State capital
County seat
City
BOUNDARIES
State
County
FEATURES
Canals
Dams
Points of interest
Parishes indicated by number:
1 WEST BATON ROUGE
2 ST. JOHN THE BAPTIST
3 ST. CHARLES
4 JEFFERSON
5 ORLEANS
ARKANSAS
MISSISSIPPI
TEXAS
ALABAMA
FLORIDA
MISS.
Gulf of Mexico
0 40 80 mi
0 60 120 km
0 8 16 mi
0 10 20 km

4,219,973; ✻ Baton Rouge; 18th state admitted to Union (1812). See table of states at UNITED STATES.

Nickname: Pelican State.

State flower: Magnolia.

Motto: Union, Justice, Confidence.

Rivers: Mississippi, forming NE and E cen. boundary and flowing through its vast delta SE into Gulf of Mexico; Sabine, forming W cen. and SW boundary, and flowing into Gulf of Mexico; Red, flowing from NW diagonally SE across state and into the Mississippi.

Highest point: Driskill Mt., 535 ft. (163 m.), in Bienville parish.

Chief products: Rice, soybeans, cotton, sugarcane; seafood; oil, natural gas, sulfur, salt; manufacturing: chemicals, transportation equipment, lumber; tourism.

Chief cities: New Orleans, Baton Rouge, Shreveport.

Political divisions: Divided into the following 64 parishes (for pronunciation of their names, see their individual entries):

NAME	AREA[1] (sq. mi.)	AREA[1] (sq. km.)	POP. (1990c)	PAR. SEAT
Acadia	663	1,717	55,882	Crowley
Allen	774	2,005	21,226	Oberlin
Ascension	301	780	58,214	Donaldsonville
Assumption	356	922	22,753	Napoleonville
Avoyelles	832	2,155	39,159	Marksville
Beauregard	1,184	3,067	30,083	De Ridder
Bienville	832	2,155	15,979	Arcadia
Bossier	849	2,199	86,088	Benton
Caddo	899	2,328	248,253	Shreveport
Calcasieu	1,105	2,862	168,134	Lake Charles
Caldwell	551	1,427	9,810	Columbia
Cameron	1,441	3,732	9,260	Cameron
Catahoula	742	1,922	11,065	Harrisonburg
Claiborne	763	1,976	17,405	Homer
Concordia	718	1,860	20,828	Vidalia
De Soto	904	2,341	25,346	Mansfield
East Baton Rouge	459	1,189	380,105	Baton Rouge
East Carroll	436	1,129	9,709	Lake Providence
East Feliciana	454	1,176	19,211	Clinton
Evangeline	669	1,733	33,274	Ville Platte
Franklin	648	1,678	22,387	Winnsboro
Grant	670	1,735	17,526	Colfax
Iberia	589	1,526	68,297	New Iberia
Iberville	627	1,624	31,049	Plaquemine
Jackson	582	1,507	15,705	Jonesboro
Jefferson	331	857	448,306	Gretna
Jefferson Davis	658	1,704	30,722	Jennings
Lafayette	283	733	164,762	Lafayette
Lafourche	1,141	2,955	85,860	Thibodaux
La Salle	643	1,665	13,662	Jena
Lincoln	469	1,215	41,745	Ruston
Livingston	654	1,694	70,526	Livingston
Madison	661	1,712	12,463	Tallulah
Morehouse	804	2,082	31,938	Bastrop
Natchitoches	1,295	3,354	36,689	Natchitoches
Orleans	205	531	496,938	New Orleans
Ouachita[2]	638	1,652	142,191	Monroe
Plaquemines	1,030	2,668	25,575	Pointe a la Hache
Pointe Coupee	563	1,458	22,540	New Roads
Rapides	1,318	3,414	131,556	Alexandria
Red River	406	1,052	9,387	Coushatta
Richland	576	1,492	20,629	Rayville
Sabine	1,029	2,665	22,646	Many
Saint Bernard	514	1,331	66,631	Chalmette
Saint Charles	288	746	42,437	Hahnville
Saint Helena	420	1,088	9,874	Greensburg
Saint James	253	655	20,879	Convent
Saint John the Baptist	250	648	39,996	Edgard
Saint Landry	932	2,414	80,331	Opelousas
Saint Martin[3]	736	1,906	43,978	Saint Martinville
Saint Mary	624	1,616	58,086	Franklin
Saint Tammany	925	2,396	144,508	Covington
Tangipahoa	807	2,090	85,709	Amite City
Tensas	626	1,621	7,103	St. Joseph
Terrebonne	1,368	3,543	96,982	Houma
Union	906	2,347	20,690	Farmerville
Vermilion	1,205	3,121	50,055	Abbeville
Vernon	1,357	3,515	61,961	Leesville
Washington	665	1,722	43,185	Franklinton
Webster	615	1,593	41,989	Minden
West Baton Rouge	203	526	19,419	Port Allen
West Carroll	356	922	12,093	Oak Grove
West Feliciana	405	1,049	12,915	St. Francisville
Winn	950	2,461	16,269	Winnfield

[1] Area = land area.
[2] Also called Washita.
[3] Area in SE separated from rest of parish by cen. part of Grand Lake and part of Iberia parish.

History: Inhabited by native peoples for thousands of years prior to European exploration, which began in the 16th cent.; name "Louisiana" orig. applied to entire Mississippi River basin, claimed for France by explorer René-Robert Cavelier, Sieur de La Salle 1682; Natchitoches, first settlement within area of present state, founded 1714; New Orleans (*q.v.*) founded 1718; except for New Orleans, region E of Mississippi River ceded by France to Great Britain 1763; West Florida (incl. portion of present state of Louisiana E of Mississippi River N of Lake Pontchartrain) returned to Spain 1783 and claimed by U.S. as part of Louisiana Purchase (*q.v.*) 1803; New Orleans and region W of Mississippi River ceded to Spain 1762–63; returned to France 1800–03, and sold to U.S. in Louisiana Purchase; Orleans Terr. (*q.v.*) organized 1804 and admitted to Union Apr. 30, 1812 as state of Louisiana, the first to be carved out of Louisiana Purchase; passed ordinance of secession Jan. 26, 1861; abolished slavery 1864; readmitted to Union 1868; present constitution adopted 1974.

2. City, Pike co., E Missouri, on Mississippi River 25 mi. (40 km.) SE of Hannibal; pop. (1990c) 3967.

Louisiana Point. Point at SW extremity of Louisiana, on E side of entrance to Sabine Pass.

Louisiana Purchase. The territory purchased Apr. 30, 1803 for $15,000,000 by the U.S. from France; extended from the Mississippi to the Rocky Mts. and from Gulf of Mexico to British America (Canada), incl. the basin of the Missouri River and the major part of the Great Plains drained by W tributaries of the Mississippi; 885,000 sq. mi. (2,292,150 sq. km.); out of it were later formed four states (Arkansas, Iowa, Missouri, and Nebraska) and parts of nine others (Louisiana, Minnesota, Oklahoma, Kansas, Colorado, Wyoming, Montana, North Dakota, and South Dakota); with ill-defined boundaries, most of the territory had been acquired by Spain from France 1762 in compensation for Spanish losses as French ally in the Seven Years' War and retroceded to France by Treaty of San Ildefonso Oct. 1, 1800; organized 1805 as Louisiana Terr. (*q.v.*).

Louisiana Territory. Former territory of the U.S. which included the entire area of the Louisiana Purchase except Orleans Terr. (*q.v.*); renamed Missouri Terr. 1812 upon admission of state of Louisiana to the Union.

Lou·is Trich·ardt \'lü-is-'tri-chərt\. Town, N cen. Northern prov., NE Rep. of South Africa, 225 mi. (362 km.) NE of Pretoria; on S slope of Soutpansberg Mts.

Lou·is·ville \'lü-is-ˌvil; *for 4 usu.* 'lü-i-ˌvil, -vəl\. **1.** Town, Boulder co., N cen. Colorado, 18 mi. (29 km.) NW of Denver; pop. (1990c) 12,361; residential.

2. City, ⊗ of Jefferson co., E cen. Georgia, 40 mi. (64 km.) SW of Augusta; pop. (1990c) 2429; ✻ of Georgia 1796–1807.

3. Village, ⊗ of Clay co., SE cen. Illinois; pop. (1990c) 1676.

4. City, ⊗ of Jefferson co., N cen. Kentucky, on Ohio River; pop. (1990c) 269,063; largest city in the state; market and trade center; produces food products, tobacco, chemicals, aluminum products, automobiles, rubber goods, electrical machinery; printing, distilling; site of Churchill Downs racetrack. Univ. of Louisville (1798; oldest municipal university in U.S.), Spalding Univ. (1814), Bellarmine Coll. (1950), Jefferson Community Coll. (1967). Settled 1778; chartered as city 1828; grew rapidly as major river port; heavily damaged by flood 1937.

5. City, ⊗ of Winston co., E cen. Mississippi, 45 mi. (72 km.) SW of Columbus; pop. (1990c) 7169.

6. Village, Stark co., NE Ohio, 7 mi. (11 km.) ENE of Canton; pop. (1990c) 8087.

Lou·ny \'lō-nē\ *or Ger.* **Laun** \'lau̇n\. Town, W Czech Republic, 35 mi. (56 km.) NW of Prague on the Ohře River; pop. (1989c) 26,046.

Loup \'lüp\. **1.** River, E cen. Nebraska; rises in three branches, North Loup, Middle Loup, and South Loup rivers, and flows E into Platte River at Columbus in SE Platte co.; incl. North Loup ab. 280 mi. (450 km.) long.

2. County in cen. Nebraska. See table at NEBRASKA.

Loup City. City, ⊗ of Sherman co., cen. Nebraska, 42 mi. (68 km.) NW of Grand Island; pop. (1990c) 1104.

Lourdes \ˈlu̇rd, ˈlu̇rdz\. Commune, Hautes-Pyrénées dept., SW France, on the Gave de Pau 11 mi. (18 km.) SSW of Tarbes; pop. (1990c) 16,581; one of chief shrines of pilgrimage in Europe, having become famous 1858 through reputed apparitions of the Virgin (Our Lady of Lourdes) to a peasant girl (Bernadette of Lourdes) in a grotto here; large underground basilica completed 1958.

Lou·ren·ço Mar·ques \lō-ˈren-sō-ˌmär-ˈkes\. **1.** Former district of Mozambique; 6480 sq. mi. (16,783 sq. km.); ✻ Maputo.
2. Seaport, Mozambique. See MAPUTO 3.

l'Ou·ta·ouais \ˌlü-tȧ-ˈwā\. County, Quebec, Canada. See table at QUEBEC.

Louth 1. \ˈlau̇th, ˈlau̇t͟h\. County, Leinster prov., NE Ireland; ⊗ Dundalk; rivers Dee, Boyne, Glyde; livestock raising, linen manufacture. See table at IRELAND.
2. \ˈlau̇th\. Town, Parts of Lindsey, Lincolnshire, E England, on the Lud 28 mi. (45 km.) SSE of Hull; pop. (1981p) 13,296; plastics, agricultural machinery.

Loutro. See PHOENIX 3.

Lou·vain \lü-ˈve^{n}\ *or Flem.* **Leu·ven** \ˈlœ̄-və\. Commune, Brabant prov., cen. Belgium, on the Dijle River 15 mi. (24 km.) E of Brussels; pop. (1992e) 85,200; brewing; has Gothic town hall and several fine churches. Probably dates from 9th cent.; became residence of counts (later dukes) of Brabant 11th cent.; at height of prosperity as center of textile industry 14th cent.; decreased in importance and ceased to be ✻ of Brabant because of civil wars 1379–83, but later became seat of learning; its university (founded c. 1425) had great library which was destroyed when town was captured and sacked by Germans 1914, and rebuilt after WWI by gifts from citizens of U.S. and other countries, only to be again destroyed and rebuilt as a result of WWII.

Louvière, La. See LA LOUVIÈRE.

Lou·viers \lü-ˈvyā\. Commune, Eure dept., N France, on Eure River 14 mi. (23 km.) N of Évreux.

Lo·vat' *or* **Lo·vat** \ˈlȯ-vȧt^{y}\. River, W Russia in Europe; flows N through Pskov Oblast and Novgorod Oblast into Lake Il'men'; 320 mi. (515 km.) long.

Lov·ćen \ˈlȯf-ˌchen\ *or* **Lov·chen** \-ˌchen\. Mountain, SW Montenegro, Yugoslavia, just W of Cetinje; 5735 ft. (1748 m.).

Love \ˈləv\. County in S Oklahoma. See table at OKLAHOMA.

Love Canal. Neighborhood of the city of Niagara Falls, New York; evacuated late 1970s due to toxic chemicals in the filled-in canal for which the neighborhood was named.

Lo·vech \lō-ˈvech\. **1.** Region of cen. Bulgaria. See table at BULGARIA.
2. Town, its ✻, 18 mi. (29 km.) S of Pleven; pop. (1991e) 51,669.

Love·land \ˈləv-lənd\. **1.** Commercial city, Larimer co., N Colorado, 12 mi. (19 km.) S of Fort Collins; pop. (1990c) 37,352; electronic equipment; sugar beets; founded 1877; an entry point to Rocky Mountain National Park.
2. City, Clermont, Hamilton, and Warren cos., SW Ohio, 16 mi. (26 km.) NE of Cincinnati; pop. (1990c) 9990.

Loveland Mountain. Peak in Park co., cen. Colorado; 13,624 ft. (4153 m.).

Loveland Pass. Mountain pass, Clear Creek and Summit cos., N cen. Colorado, in Front Range of the Rocky Mts.; 11,992 ft. (3655 m.).

Lov·ell \ˈlə-vəl\. Town, Big Horn co., N Wyoming, on Shoshone River 43 mi. (69 km.) NE of Cody; pop. (1990c) 2131.

Lovell Island *or* **Lov·ells Island** \ˈlə-vəlz\. Island in Boston Bay, off Boston, Massachusetts.

Love·lock \ˈləv-ˌläk\. City, ⊗ of Pershing co., NW Nevada; pop. (1990c) 2069.

Lo·ve·nia, Mount \lō-ˈvē-nē-ə\. Peak, E Summit co., NE Utah; 13,219 ft. (4029 m.).

Love Point \ˈləv\. Point at N end of Kent I. in upper Chesapeake Bay, Maryland.

Loves Park \ˈləvz\. City, Winnebago co., N Illinois, NE of Rockford; pop. (1990c) 15,462.

Lov·ing \ˈlə-viŋ\. County in W Texas. See table at TEXAS.

Lov·ing·ston \ˈlə-viŋ-stən\. Village, ⊗ of Nelson co., cen. Virginia.

Lov·ing·ton \ˈlə-viŋ-tən\. City, ⊗ of Lea co., SE corner of New Mexico, 23 mi. (37 km.) NNW of Hobbs; pop. (1990c) 9322.

Lo·vo·si·ce \ˈlȯ-vȯ-ˌsit-sə\ *or Ger.* **Lo·bo·sitz** \ˈlō-bə-ˌzits\. Town, NW Czech Republic, on Labe (Elbe) River; battle 1756 in which Prussian King Frederick the Great defeated the Austrians.

Low Archipelago. See TUAMOTU ARCHIPELAGO.

Low Countries. Name of region bordering on the North Sea, comprising modern Netherlands, Belgium, and Luxembourg.

Lowe, Mount \ˈlō\. Peak, Los Angeles co., SW California; ab. 5600 ft. (1705 m.).

Low·ell \ˈlō-əl\. **1.** Town, Lake co., NW Indiana, 20 mi. (32 km.) S of Hammond; pop. (1990c) 6430.
2. City, a ⊗ of Middlesex co., NE Massachusetts, 23 mi. (37 km.) NW of Boston on Merrimack River at Pawtucket Falls (32 ft. or 10 m.), its chief source of power; pop. (1990c) 103,439; formerly a major textile center; industries now include electronics and chemicals; incorp. as town 1826, as city 1836. Birthplace of artist James Abbott McNeill Whistler 1834; **Lowell National Historical Park** estab. 1978 (see UNITED STATES, *National Historical Parks*); Univ. of Massachusetts–Lowell (1894).
3. City, Kent co., W Michigan, 17 mi. (27 km.) E of Grand Rapids; pop. (1990c) 3983.
4. City, Gaston co., SW North Carolina; pop. (1990c) 2704.

Lowell, Lake. See DEER FLAT DAM.

Lö·wen·burg \ˈlœ̄v-ᵊn-ˌbu̇rk\. Peak of the Siebengebirge (*q.v.*), Germany; 1506 ft. (458 km.).

Lower Alsace. See *History* at ALSACE-LORRAINE.

Lower Andalusia. See ANDALUSIA 2.

Lower Apennines. Subsidiary ranges of the Apennines, situated in the triangular space bet. the Apennines proper and the W coast of Italy, incl.: (1) the Tuscan highland, bounded on the S by the lower Tiber; (2) the region of Maremma; (3) the Alban Hills and Lepini Mts. (bet. the Tiber and Garigliano rivers); (4) the S section from the Garigliano to the mountains of Castellammare di Stabia and Sorrento Penin., incl. Vesuvius.

Lower Arrow Lake. See ARROW LAKE.

Lower Austria *or Ger.* **Nie·der·ö·ster·reich** \ˌnē-dər-ˈœ̄-stə-ˌrī$\underline{k}$\; *from 1938 to 1945* **Lower Danube** *or Ger.* **Nie·der·do·nau** \ˌnē-dər-ˈdō-nau̇\. State, NE Austria; ✻ Sankt Pölten. Crossed by the Danube from W to E; bordered on NE by the Morava and has the Leitha forming part of boundary on SE. Hilly in N with higher mountains of E Alps on the S, crossed by the Semmering Pass. The city of Vienna forms a separate administrative unit in E part. Produces sugar beets, potatoes, wheat, rye, fruit; forestry, viticulture; livestock. Formerly an archduchy and crown land of Austrian Empire. See table at AUSTRIA.

Lower Avon. See AVON 8.

Lower Bann. See BANN.

Lower Burgundy. See BURGUNDY.

Lower Burma. See MYANMAR.

Lower Bur·rell \ˈbər-əl\. City, Westmoreland co., SW Pennsylvania, NE of Pittsburgh; pop. (1990c) 12,251.

Lower California. See BAJA CALIFORNIA.

Lower Canada. The S and E parts of Quebec prov., Canada, 1791 to 1841. See *History* at QUEBEC 1.

Lower Chateaugay Lake. See CHATEAUGAY LAKES.

Lower Danube. See LOWER AUSTRIA.

Lower Egypt. See EGYPT.

Lower Engadine. See ENGADINE.

Lower 48 *or* **lower 48** *also* **Lower For·ty–eight** \ˌfȯr-tē-ˈāt\. The continental states of the U.S. excluding Alaska.

Lower Gastein. See GASTEINER ACHE.

\ə\ abut \ᵊ\ matches \ᵊ\ kitten, Fr table \ər\ further \a\ ash \ā\ ace \ä\ cot, cart \ȧ\ Fr bac \au̇\ out \b̲\ Span Avila \ch\ chin \e\ bet \ē\ easy \g\ go \i\ hit \ī\ ice \j\ job \k̲\ Ger ich, Buch \$^{n}$\ Fr vin \ŋ\ sing \ō\ go \ȯ\ all \ȯ\ law \œ\ Fr bœuf \œ̄\ Fr feu \ȯi\ boy \th\ thin \t͟h\ this \ü\ loot \u̇\ foot \ue\ Ger füllen \ūe\ Fr rue \y\ yet \$^{y}$\ Fr digne \ˈdēn^{y}\, nuit \ˈnw^{y}ē\ \yü\ few \yu̇\ fury \zh\ vision

Lower Gle·nelg National Park \gle-ˈnelg\. National park, SW Victoria, Australia, along lower course of the Glenelg River; gorges.

Lower Goose Creek Reservoir. See OAKLEY DAM.

Lower Guinea. See GUINEA 1.

Lower Hutt \ˈhət\. City, suburb of Wellington, S North I., New Zealand; pop. (1991c) 94,540.

Lower Klamath Lake. See KLAMATH LAKES.

Lower Lorraine. See LORRAINE 2.

Lower Lough Erne. See ERNE.

Lower Mat·e·cum·be Key \ˌma-tə-ˈkəm-bē\. See FLORIDA KEYS.

Lower Mer·i·on \ˈmer-ē-ən\. Urban township, Montgomery co., SE Pennsylvania, NW of Philadelphia; pop. (1990c) 58,003.

Lower New York Bay. See NEW YORK BAY.

Lower Palatinate. See PALATINATE.

Lower Peninsula. S part of Michigan, S of Straits of Mackinac.

Lower Red Lake. See RED LAKE 1.

Lower Rhine *or Ger.* **Nie·der·rhein** \ˌnē-də-ˈrīn\ *or Du.* **Neder Rijn** \ˌnā-də-ˈrīn\. The section of the Rhine River bet. Bonn, Germany, and the North Sea; in Netherlands the general name for its various sections.

Lower Richardson Lake. See RICHARDSON LAKES.

Lower Saranac Lake. See SARANAC LAKES.

Lower Sax·o·ny \ˈsak-sə-nē\ *or Ger.* **Nie·der·sach·sen** \ˈnē-dər-ˌzäk-sən\. A state of Germany; ✻ Hannover; estab. 1946. See table at GERMANY.

Lower Silesia. See SILESIA.

Lower South·amp·ton \sau̇-ˈthamp-tən, sau̇th-ˈhamp-\. Urban township, Bucks co., SE Pennsylvania, NE of Philadelphia; pop. (1990c) 19,860.

Lower Suncook Lake. See SUNCOOK.

Lower Tunguska. See TUNGUSKA.

Lowes·toft \ˈlō-stȯft, ˈlō-is-\. Town, Suffolk, E England, on North Sea 23 mi. (37 km.) ESE of Norwich; pop. (1981c) 59,875; shipbuilding; fisheries; manufactures electrical equipment; seaside resort.

Lowes·water Lake \ˈlōz-ˌwȯ-tər\. Lake, Cumbria, NW England, 6 mi. (10 km.) SSE of Cockermouth; 1 mi. (2 km.) long.

Ło·wicz \ˈwȯ-vich\. Commune, NW Skierniewice prov., cen. Poland, 47 mi. (76 km.) WSW of Warsaw; pop. (1989e) 30,440.

Lowlands, The. See HIGHLANDS, THE.

Lowndes \ˈlau̇ndz\. Name of counties in three states of the U.S. See tables at ALABAMA, GEORGIA, MISSISSIPPI.

Low·ther Hill \ˈlau̇-t͟hər\. Mountain in the Lowther Hills, S Scotland; 2377 ft. (725 m.).

Lowther Hills *also* **The Low·thers** \ˈlau̇-t͟hərz\. Mountain range in S Scotland, along boundary bet. Strathclyde and Dumfries and Galloway regions; highest peak **Green Lowther** 2403 ft. (732 m.).

Low·ville \ˈlau̇-ˌvil\. Village, ⊗ of Lewis co., N cen. New York, 26 mi. (42 km.) ESE of Watertown; pop. (1990c) 3632.

Loxa. See LOJA 3.

Loy·al·han·na Creek \ˌlȯi-əl-ˈha-nə\. River, SW Pennsylvania; flows NW through Westmoreland co. to unite with Conemaugh River in SW Indiana co. and form Kiskiminetas River; ab. 40 mi. (64 km.) long.

Loy·al·ty Islands \ˈlȯi-əl-tē\ *or* **Loy·al·ties** \-tēz\ *or* **Îles Loy·au·té** \ˌēl-lwȧ-yō-ˈtā\. Island group in E part of New Caledonia, forming a chain 62 mi. (100 km.) E of New Caledonia and ab. 160 mi. (255 km.) SW of the S end of Vanuatu; 755 sq. mi. (1955 sq. km.); pop. (1989p) 17,912. Chief islands Lifou, Maré, and Uvéa. Mostly low coral upheavals; exports copra.

Lo–yang. See LUOYANG.

Lo·zère \lō-ˈzer\. **1.** Range in Cévennes Mts., S France; highest peak Pic de Finiels 5585 ft. (1702 m.).
2. Department of S France. See table at FRANCE.

Lu. See TUO.

Lu·a·la·ba \ˌlü-ä-ˈlä-bä\ *or Fr.* **Lou·a·la·ba** \lwȧ-lȧ-ˈbȧ\. River, SE Democratic Rep. of the Congo; flows N and joins the Luapula to form Congo River; ab. 400 mi. (645 km.) long to confluence with Luapula; from this point to Stanley Falls, 1000 mi. (1609 km.), the upper Congo is often called the Lualaba.

Lu·an; *mostly formerly* **Lwan** \lu̇-ˈwän\. River, Hebei prov., NE China; rises in E Nei Monggol (Inner Mongolia), flows N, then E, then SE to Bo Hai. Chengde is on its N bank; ab. 400 mi. (645 km.) long.

Lu–an. See CHANGZHI.

Lu·an·da \lu̇-ˈän-də\ *or* **Lo·an·da** \lō-\. **1.** Province of W Angola. See table at ANGOLA.
2. *also* **São Pau·lo de Lo·an·da** \sau̇ⁿm-ˈpau̇-lü-ˌdi-lu̇-ˈän-də\. Commercial city and seaport, ✻ of Angola and ✻ of Luanda prov., on Bay of Bengo; pop. (1990e) 1,544,400; exports ores and agricultural produce; oil refining; university (1962); founded by Portuguese official Paulo Dias de Novais 1576; made administrative center of Angola 1627; until 19th cent. was a center for export of slaves to Brazil.

Luang Pra·bang \ˈlwäŋ-prä-ˈbäŋ\. **1.** *or* **Luang·pra·bang** \ˈlwäŋ-prä-ˈbäŋ\. Former native Lao state (kingdom), N Laos, SE Asia; formerly under French protection; amalgamated with rest of Laos 1946.
2. Town, N Laos. See LOUANGPHRABANG.

Luangue. See LOANGE.

Lu·ang·wa \lü-ˈäŋ-wä\ *also* **Lo·ang·wa** \lō-ˈäŋ-wä\. River, E Zambia; flows SSW into Zambezi River, in its lower course forming a section of the W boundary of Mozambique; ab. 500 mi. (805 km.) long.

Lu·an·shya \lü-ˈän-shä\. Town, cen. Zambia; pop. (1990p) 146,275; copper mining; metalworking.

Lu·a·pu·la \ˌlü-ä-ˈpü-lä\. River, cen. Africa; outlet of Lake Bangweulu through the large swamp S of the lake, actually a continuation of the Chambeshi; flows N along boundary bet. NW Zambia and SE Democratic Rep. of the Congo through Lake Mweru and joins Lualaba to form Congo River.

Luar·ca \lü-ˈär-kä\. Seaport, Asturias prov., NW Spain, on Bay of Biscay 37 mi. (60 km.) WNW of Oviedo.

Lu·ba·an·tun \ˌlü-bä-ˈän-ˌtün\. Site of Mayan ruins, S Belize, 15 mi. (24 km.) NW of Punta Gorda.

Lu·bań \ˈlü-ˌbän\ *or Ger.* **Lau·ban** \ˈlau̇-ˌbän\. City, W Jelenia Góra prov., SW Poland, 38 mi. (61 km.) WSW of Legnica; pop. (1989e) 23,659; formerly in Germany, assigned to Poland 1945.

Lu·bang \lü-ˈbäŋ\. **1.** Group of islands, Philippines, off NW coast of Mindoro I. 46 mi. (74 km.) SW of entrance to Manila Bay and separated from Luzon by Verde Island Passage; 95 sq. mi. (246 sq. km.); chief town Lubang. Comprises Lubang I. and the small islands of Ambil, Golo, and Cabra.
2. Largest island of the group; 74 sq. mi. (192 sq. km.); 17 mi. (27 km.) long.
3. Municipality on N coast of the island; pop. (1980c) 15,293.

Lu·ban·go \lu̇-ˈbäŋ-gü\; *formerly* **Sá da Ban·dei·ra** \ˌsä-də-bän-ˈdā-rə\. Town, ✻ of Huíla prov., SW Angola, ab. 95 mi. (155 km.) ENE of Namibe; pop. (1984e) 105,000.

Lu·bao \lü-ˈbau̇\. Municipality, S Pampanga prov., Luzon, Philippines, on NW edge of Pampanga Delta 9 mi. (15 km.) SW of San Fernando; pop. (1980c) 77,502.

Lüb·be·nau \ˈlu̅e-bə-ˌnau̇\. City, Brandenburg, E Germany, on the Spree River 18 mi. (29 km.) NW of Cottbus.

Lub·bock \ˈlə-bək\. **1.** County in NW Texas. See table at TEXAS.
2. City, its ⊗; pop. (1990c) 186,206; major cotton market; cottonseed oil; oil wells; poultry farms; Texas Tech Univ. (1923); Lubbock Christian Coll. (1957); settled in 2d half of 19th cent.; struck by destructive tornado May 11, 1970.

Lu·bec \lü-ˈbek\. Town, Washington co., SE corner of Maine, on Passamaquoddy Bay across from Campobello I.; pop. (1990c) 1853; easternmost settlement in the Lower 48.

Lü·beck \ˈlu̅e-ˌbek\. City, Schleswig-Holstein, Germany, on two small streams connecting with Lübeck Bay 35 mi. (56 km.) NE of Hamburg; pop. (1992e) 215,999; formerly West Germany's most important Baltic port, exports salt, coal; shipbuilding, fish processing, iron and steel founding; 12th cent. cathedral; several 13th–14th cent. Gothic churches; impressive town hall.

History: Founded 1143 by Count Adolf II of Holstein on site of earlier Slavic settlement; refounded by Henry the Lion, duke of Saxony (see SAXONY) c. 1158; secured final privileges of free imperial city 1226; became leading center for medieval German trade in Baltic region and head of the Hanseatic League (*q.v.*); declined from 16th cent.; by Treaty of Lübeck 1629, Denmark withdrew from Thirty Years' War; briefly occupied by French in early 19th cent.; joined German Confederation 1815; lost its status as autonomous free state 1937 (see GERMANY). In WWII suffered major damage from Allied bombing.

Lübeck Bay. Inlet of SW Mecklenburg Bay, Germany, lying bet. Schleswig-Holstein and Mecklenburg-West Pomerania.

Lu·be·fu \lü-ˈbā-fü\. River, cen. Democratic Rep. of the Congo, in basin of the Congo; flows W into Sankuru River shortly before its junction with Kasai River; ab. 200 mi. (320 km.) long.

Lu·bi·lash \lü-ˈbē-ˌläsh\. River, the upper course of the Sankuru, S cen. Democratic Rep. of the Congo.

Lu·bin \ˈlü-bin\ *or Ger.* **Lü·ben** \ˈlue-bən\. Town, cen. Legnica prov., SW Poland, ab. 40 mi. (64 km.) WNW of Wrocław; pop. (1989e) 80,851; copper.

Lub·lin \ˈlü-blin, -ˌblēn\ *or Russ.* **Lyu·blin** \ˈlyü-blən\. **1.** Province of E Poland. See table at POLAND.

2. City, its ✻, 95 mi. (153 km.) SE of Warsaw; pop. (1989e) 349,672; automobiles, agricultural implements, sugar; food processing; brewing; Catholic Univ. of Lublin (1918), Marie Curie-Sklodowska Univ. (1944); castle; cathedral. Received town rights 1317; union of Poland and Lithuania signed here 1569; in WWII, site of the Nazi death camp Majdanek.

Lu·bli·niec \lü-ˈblē-nyets\. Commune, Częstochowa prov., S Poland; pop. (1989e) 25,492.

Lubnān, Jabal. See LEBANON MOUNTAINS.

Lub·ny \ˈlüb-nē\. Town, N Poltava subdivision, N cen. Ukraine, 110 mi. (177 km.) E of Kiev; pop. (1991e) 60,000.

Lub·sko \ˈlüp-skȯ\ *or Ger.* **Som·mer·feld** \ˈzȯm-ər-ˌfelt\. Town, S Zielona Góra prov., W Poland; pop. (1981p) 13,786.

Lu·bua·gan \lü-ˈbwä-gän\. Municipality, ✻ of Kalinga-Apayao prov., Luzon, Philippines; pop. (1980c) 8545.

Lu·bum·bashi \ˌlü-büm-ˈbä-shē\; *formerly* **Eli·sa·beth·ville** \i-ˈli-zə-bəth-ˌvil\. City, ✻ of Shaba administrative region, S Democratic Rep. of the Congo, near border with Zambia; pop. (1991e) 739,082; site of what was once one of the world's largest copper-mining and smelting operations; food processing; bricks, soap; university (1955); city founded 1910; center of Katanga province's secession movement during initial years of republic's independence (early 1960s).

Lubungan. See KATIPUNAN.

Luca. See LUCCA 2.

Lu·ca·la \lü-ˈkä-lə\. River, N Angola; ab. 130 mi. (210 km.) long.

Lu·ca·nia \lü-ˈkā-nyə, -ˈkä-\. **1.** Ancient district of S Italy incl. modern Basilicata and part of Salerno prov. in S Campania. Important Samnite area 4th cent. B.C.; to Rome 3d cent. B.C.

2. Autonomous region, Italy. See BASILICATA.

Lucania, Mount \lü-ˈkā-nē-ə, -nyə\. Peak in St. Elias Mts., SW Yukon Terr., Canada, N of Mt. Logan near Alaskan border; 17,147 ft. (5226 m.).

Lucanian Apennines *or Ital.* **Lucano, Appennino.** See table at APENNINES.

Lu·ca·pa \lü-ˈkä-pə\. Town, ✻ of Lunda Norte prov., NE Angola.

Lu·cas \ˈlü-kəs\. Name of counties in two states of the U.S. See tables at IOWA and OHIO.

Lu·ca·yas \lu̇-ˈkī-əs\. Early Spanish name of Bahamas (*q.v.*).

Luc·ban \lük-ˈbän\. Municipality, Quezon prov., Luzon, Philippines, near Laguna border 15 mi. (24 km.) NNW of Lucena; pop. (1980c) 25,826; in mountainous region.

Luc·ca \ˈlü-kä\. **1.** Province of Tuscany, cen. Italy. See table at ITALY.

2. *anc.* **Lu·ca** \ˈlü-kə\. Commune, its ✻, 38 mi. (61 km.) WNW of Florence; pop. (1991p) 86,188; road and rail center; market town in olive-growing region; silk, flour, paper, jute; 11th–c. 14th cent. cathedral; many notable churches and palaces; ancient Roman remains.

History: Ancient town most likely founded as Roman colony in 180 B.C. on site previously occupied by Ligurians; located at intersection of ancient travel routes; chief town in Tuscany before rise of Florence (*q.v.*); became free commune 12th cent. and more or less retained its freedom (with a few brief interruptions) over the next seven centuries; occupied by French 1799 and given as a principality to French Emperor Napoléon's sister Élisa 1805; awarded to member of Bourbon family c. 1815; reunited with Tuscany 1847 and thus became part of kingdom of Italy 1860.

Luce \ˈlüs\. County in E Upper Penin. of Michigan. See table at MICHIGAN.

Luce Bay. Inlet of Irish Sea on extreme SW coast of Scotland; enclosed by Mull of Galloway on W; 16 mi. (26 km.) long; 19 mi. (31 km.) wide at the mouth.

Luce·dale \ˈlüs-ˌdāl\. City, ⊗ of George co., SE Mississippi; pop. (1990c) 2592.

Lu·ce·na \lü-ˈsā-nä\. **1.** Chartered city, ✻ of Quezon prov., Luzon, Philippines, on N shore of Tayabas Bay 63 mi. (101 km.) SE of Manila; pop. (1990p) 151,000.

2. Commune, Córdoba prov., S Spain, 39 mi. (63 km.) SE of the city of Córdoba; pop. (1991p) 32,054; horse breeding; manufactures copper and zinc products, chemicals.

Lu·če·nec \ˈlü-che-nyets\ *or Hung.* **Lo·soncz** \ˈlō-ˌshōnts\. Town, S Slovakia, on the Ipel' 65 mi. (105 km.) NE of Budapest, Hungary; pop. (1980p) 26,399; textiles.

Lucentum. See ALICANTE 2.

Lu·ce·ra \lü-ˈchā-rä\. Commune, Foggia prov., Puglia, SE Italy, 12 mi. (19 km.) WNW of the commune of Foggia; pop. (1991p) 35,134; early 14th cent. cathedral; ruins of castle built by Holy Roman Emperor Frederick II 13th cent.

Lu·cerne \lü-ˈsərn\ *or Ger.* **Lu·zern** \lüt-ˈsern\. **1.** Canton, Switzerland. See *History* and table at SWITZERLAND.

2. Commune, its ✻, cen. Switzerland, on W shore of Lake of Lucerne 25 mi. (40 km.) SSW of Zürich; pop. (1989c) 59,932; rail and vessel connections; a major tourist center; medieval circular walls and watchtowers; medieval covered bridges; Renaissance town hall; 17th cent. cathedral; Jesuit church; many monuments, incl. esp. the famous Lion of Lucerne carved in rock. Developed around monastery of St. Leodegar (8th cent.); joined Swiss Confederation 1332; stronghold of Catholicism during Reformation; took part in short-lived civil Sonderbund War (see SWITZERLAND).

Lucerne, Lake of *or* **Lake of the Four Forest Cantons** *or Ger.* **Vier·wald·stät·ter See** \fir-ˈvält-ˌshte-tər-ˌzā\. Lake in cen. Switzerland, enclosed by Schwyz, Uri, Unterwalden, and Lucerne cantons; 24 mi. (39 km.) long and bet. 0.5 mi. (0.8 km.) and 2 mi. (3 km.) wide; 44 sq. mi. (114 sq. km.); max. depth 702 ft. (214 m.).

Lu–chiang. See LU-KANG.

Lu–chou. See LUZHOU.

Lu·chow \ˈlü-ˈjō\. **1.** City, Anhui, E China. See HEFEI.

2. City, Sichuan, S cen. China. See LUZHOU.

Luchu Islands. See RYUKYU ISLANDS 1.

Łuck. See ŁUTSK.

Luck·en·wal·de \ˌlu̇k-ᵊn-ˈväl-də\. City, Brandenburg, E Germany, 31 mi. (50 km.) SSW of Berlin; pop. (1981c) 27,409; paper; metalworking. Site of Cistercian monastery in Middle Ages; received charter 15th cent.

Luck·now \ˈlək-ˌnau̇\. City, ✻ of Uttar Pradesh, N India, on Gomati River 270 mi. (434 km.) ESE of Delhi; pop. (1991c) 1,619,115; important rail center with railroad workshops; paper factories; local handicrafts; university (1921). Has many notable old buildings incl. the Great Imambara (tomb) of Nabob Āṣaf-ud-Dawlah of Oudh; also the Residency where British were besieged throughout summer and fall during Indian mutiny of 1857. City gained prominence under Moguls after its capture in 1528 and again became important as ✻ of nabobs of Oudh 1775.

Lu·çon \lue-'sōn\. Commune, S Vendée dept., W France; connected with sea by canal ab. 8 mi. (13 km.) long; Armand-Jean du Plessis, cardinal and duc de Richelieu, was bishop here early 17th cent.

Lu·cre·cia, Point \lü-'krā-sē-ə\. Cape on N coast of E Cuba.

Lucus Augusti. See LUGO 3.

Lüda. See DALIAN.

Lü·den·scheid \'lued-ən-,shīt\. City, North Rhine-Westphalia, Germany, 37 mi. (60 km.) E of Düsseldorf; pop. (1992e) 79,922; manufactures aluminum, metal goods, plastics; settled 9th cent.; chartered 13th cent.; member of Hanseatic League; to Brandenburg in 17th cent.

Lü·de·ritz \'lue-də-rits\; *formerly* **An·gra Pe·que·na** \,aŋ-grə-pə-'kwē-nə\. Town, SW Namibia, on Atlantic Ocean 520 mi. (837 km.) NNW of Cape Town; pop. (1988e) 6000; well-sheltered harbor which is seaboard terminus for rail line; fishing; fish processing; founded 1883.

Lu·dhi·a·na \,lü-dē-'ä-nə\. Town, Punjab, NW India, near Sutlej River; pop. (1991c) 1,042,740; railroad junction; trade center; hosiery, textiles; agricultural university (1962); founded late 15th cent.

Lud·ing·ton \'lə-diŋ-tən\. City, ⊗ of Mason co., W Michigan, on Lake Michigan 51 mi. (82 km.) N of Muskegon; pop. (1990c) 8507; diversified light industry; lake port.

Lud·low \'ləd-lō\. **1.** City, Kenton co., N Kentucky, NW suburb of Covington; pop. (1990c) 4736.
2. Town, Hampden co., SW Massachusetts, 7 mi. (11 km.) NE of Springfield; pop. (1990c) 18,820; part of Springfield until 1775.
3. Town, Windsor co., E Vermont, on Black River 13 mi. (21 km.) WNW of Springfield; pop. (1990c) 1123.
4. Market town, Shropshire, W England, on the Teme 37 mi. (60 km.) WSW of Birmingham; pop. (1981c) 7580; tourist center; chartered 1189; here author Samuel Butler wrote *Hudibras,* and in Norman castle (built 11th cent.) poet John Milton's masque *Comus* was first performed (1634).

Ludlow, Mount. Peak, S cen. Vermont, on boundary bet. Windsor and Rutland cos.; 3372 ft. (1028 m.).

Lu·do·wici \,lü-də-'wi-sē\. City, ⊗ of Long co., SE Georgia; pop. (1990c) 1291.

Lud·vi·ka \'lüd-vi-kə\. Town, Kopparberg prov., Sweden; pop. (1980p) 31,695.

Lud·wigs·burg \'lüd-viks-,bu̇rk\. City, Baden-Württemberg, Germany, W of the Neckar River and 8 mi. (13 km.) N of Stuttgart; pop. (1992e) 83,913; machinery, iron and wire products, musical instruments, textiles; founded around 18th cent. castle; famous for its porcelain wares 1758–1824.

Lud·wigs·ha·fen am Rhein \,lüd-viks-'häf-ən-äm-'rīn\. City, SE Rhineland-Palatinate, Germany, on W bank of Rhine River opp. Mannheim; pop. (1992e) 165,368; important railroad junction and river port; tourist center; large chemical industry; steel; founded early 17th cent.; named by Louis I of Bavaria 1843; made city 1859; in WWII heavily damaged by Allied bombing.

Lu·e·bo \lü-'ā-bō\. Town, Kasai-Occidental administrative region, S cen. Democratic Rep. of the Congo, on Lulua River.

Lu·em·be \lü-'em-bā\. River in basin of the Congo, Angola and Democratic Rep. of the Congo; rises in NE Angola, flows N into Kasai River; ab. 350 mi. (560 km.) long.

Lue·na \'lwā-nə\ *or Port.* **Lu·so** \'lü-sü\. Town E cen. Angola, ✻ of Moxico prov.

Lu·feng *or W.-G.* **Lu–feng** \'lü-'fəŋ\. Town, cen. Yunnan, S China, 65 mi. (105 km.) W of Kunming.

Luf·kin \'ləf-kin\. City, ⊗ of Angelina co., E Texas, 115 mi. (185 km.) NE of Houston; pop. (1990c) 30,206; paper, lumber; oil-field equipment; diversified agriculture; Angelina Coll. (1968).

Lug. See LUGG.

Lu·ga \'lü-gə\. Town, W St. Petersburg Oblast, W Russia in Europe, 80 mi. (129 km.) S of the city of St. Petersburg on railroad line to Pskov.

Lugang. See LU-KANG.

Lu·ga·no \lü-'gä-nō\ *or Ger.* **Lau·is** \'lau̇-is\. Commune, Ticino canton, SE cen. Switzerland, on N shore of Lake Lugano; pop. (1990c) 26,530; episcopal see; tourist resort; manufactures chocolate, tobacco products; banking. First mentioned in 6th cent.; taken by Swiss Confederation 1512; an important town of former Swiss canton of Lugano, and from 1803 of Ticino canton.

Lugano, Lake; *Ital.* **La·go di Lugano** \'lä-gō-dē-\ *or* **Lago Ce·re·sio** \che-'res-yō\; *anc.* **La·cus Ce·re·si·us** \,lā-kəs-sə-'rē-zhē-əs\. Lake in S Ticino canton, S Switzerland and N Italy, bet. Lake Maggiore and Lake Como; ab. 19 sq. mi. (49 sq. km.); max. depth 945 ft. (288 m.).

Lugansk. See LUHANS'K.

Lu·gan·ville \,lü-gən-'vēl\ *or* **San·to** \'sän-tü, -tō\. Town, SE coast of Espíritu Santo I., Vanuatu; pop. (1991e) 6965.

Lu·gau \'lü-,gau̇\. City, Saxony, Germany, at N foot of Erzgebirge 10 mi. (16 km.) SW of Chemnitz.

Lug·du·nen·sis \,ləg-də-'nen-sis\. One of the administrative divisions of Gaul estab. by Roman Emperor Augustus 27 B.C. comprising the central part and named from its ✻, Lugdunum (Lyon).

Lugdunum. See LYON.

Lugdunum Batavorum. See LEIDEN.

Lu·gen·da \lü-'jen-də\. River, N Mozambique; flows out of Lake Chiuta NE into Ruvuma River.

Lugg *or* **Lug** \'ləg\. River, E Wales and W England; rises in Powys co., Wales, flows SE across English border into the Wye 5 mi. (8 km.) below Hereford; over 40 mi. (64 km.) long.

Luggarus. See LOCARNO.

Lugnaquillia *or* **Lugnaquilla.** See WICKLOW MOUNTAINS.

Lu·go \'lü-gō\. **1.** Commercial commune, Ravenna prov., Emilia-Romagna, N Italy, 15 mi. (24 km.) W of the commune of Ravenna; pop. (1991p) 32,174; trade center.
2. Province of NW Spain. See table at SPAIN.
3. *anc.* **Lu·cus Au·gus·ti** \'lü-kəs-ȯ-'gəs-tī\. Commune, ✻ of Lugo prov., NW Spain, on Miño River 48 mi. (77 km.) SE of La Coruña; pop. (1991p) 82,658; trade center, esp. in cattle and preserved meats; manufactures leather; ancient Roman walls; 12th cent. cathedral (with later additions); a former ✻ of Galicia; several times captured and plundered.

Lu·goj \'lü-gȯzh\. Commercial city, Timiş co., W Romania, ab. 35 mi. (55 km.) ESE of Timişoara on Timiş River; munic. pop. (1992p) 50,983; textiles.

Lu·gou·qiao \'lü-'gō-'chyau̇\ *or* **Wan·ping** \'wän-'piŋ\; *W.-G.* **Lu–kou–ch'iao** \'lü-'gō-'chyau̇\ *or* **Wan–p'ing** \'wän-'piŋ\. City, Beijing munic., NE China, on E bank of the Yongding 9 mi. (15 km.) SW of the city of Beijing; river crossed here by the Marco Polo Bridge (*q.v.*); scene July 7, 1937 of the clash bet. Chinese and Japanese troops which precipitated the Sino-Japanese War (1937–45).

Luguvallium *or* **Luguvallum.** See CARLISLE 6.

Lu·hans'k *or* **Lu·hansk** \lü-'hänsk\ *or* **Lu·gansk** \lü-'gänsk\; *1935–58 and 1970–89* **Vo·ro·shi·lov·grad** \,və-rə-shə-,lau̇-'grät\. **1.** Administrative subdivision of Ukraine; 10,309 sq. mi. (26,700 sq. km.); pop. (1991e) 2,871,000; ✻ Luhans'k.
2. City, its ✻, E Ukraine, on a tributary of the Donets 100 mi. (161 km.) N of Rostov-na-Donu; pop. (1991e) 504,000; center of coal-bearing region in Donets Basin. Founded c. 1795 when iron foundry opened; has grown rapidly since 1923; in WWII occupied by Germans.

Luḩayyah, Al. See AL LUḨAYYAH.

Lu·hit \'lü-,hit\. River, S Asia, rising in SW China and flowing SW into the Brahmaputra at the great bend in Arunachal Pradesh, NE India; Sadiya on its N bank near its mouth.

Luhsien. See LUZHOU.

Lui, Ben. See BEN LUI.

Luichow Peninsula. See LEIZHOU PENINSULA.

Luik. See LIÈGE 2.

Luimneach. See LIMERICK.

Lui·no \lü-'ē-nō\. Commune, Varese prov., Lombardy, N Italy, on E shore of Lake Maggiore 14 mi. (23 km.) NNW of the commune of Varese; pop. (1981p) 15,228; scene of battle bet. Italian patriot Giuseppe Garibaldi and Austrians 1848.

Lu·it·pold Coast \ˈlü-ət-ˌpōlt\; *formerly* **Le·o·pold Coast** \ˈlē-ə-ˌpōld\. Section of coast of Antarctica, ab. 78°38′S, 32°W, on SE coast of Weddell Sea, a part of Coats Land.

Lu·ján \lü-ˈhän\. **1.** Short river in NE Buenos Aires prov., E cen. Argentina; flows E into Río de la Plata.

2. Town, Buenos Aires prov., E cen. Argentina, ab. 40 mi. (64 km.) W of the city of Buenos Aires; pop. (1980c) 48,377; pilgrimage center.

Lu–kang \ˈlü-ˈkäŋ\ *or* **Lu–chiang** \-ˈchyäŋ\ *or Pinyin* **Lu·gang** \ˈlü-ˈgäŋ\. Seaport, W Taiwan, on cen. part of coast; pop. (1992e) 79,087.

Lu·kan·ga Swamp \lü-ˈkäŋ-gä\. Large marsh area in cen. Zambia, NW of Lusaka.

Lukchun. See TURPAN 1.

Lu·ke·nie \lü-ˈkā-nyē\. River, cen. Democratic Rep. of the Congo; flows W into Kasai River shortly before it joins the Congo; ab. 450 mi. (725 km.) long; in its lower course, after being joined by waters from Lac Mai-Ndombe, known as Fimi River.

Lu–kou–ch'iao. See LUGOUQIAO.

Łu·ków \ˈwü-ˌküf\. Commune, Siedlce prov., E Poland, 49 mi. (79 km.) N of Lublin; pop. (1989e) 30,706.

Lu·ku·ga \lü-ˈkü-gä\. River, E Democratic Rep. of the Congo; flows W from Lake Tanganyika into the Lualaba (upper course of the Congo); 200 mi. (322 km.) long.

Lule. See LULEÄLV.

Lu·leå \ˈlü-lə-ˌō\. Seaport, ⊗ of Norrbotten prov., N Sweden, on Gulf of Bothnia at mouth of Luleälv River; pop. (1993e) 68,924; exports iron ore, timber, wood pulp; founded 1621; moved to present site 1649.

Lu·le·älv \ˈlü-lə-ˌòlv\ *also* **Lu·le** \ˈlü-lə\. River in Norrbotten prov., Sweden; flows SE into the Gulf of Bothnia; 280 mi. (451 km.) long.

Lü·le·bur·gaz *or* **Lü·le Bur·gas** \ˌlue̅-lə-bu̇r-ˈgäz\. Town, S Kirklareli prov., Turkey in Europe, 86 mi. (138 km.) WNW of İstanbul; in the First Balkan War, scene of decisive battle 1912 in which Turks were defeated by Bulgarians.

Lu·ling. See JI'AN.

Luling \ˈlü-liŋ\. City, Caldwell co., S cen. Texas, 42 mi. (68 km.) S of Austin; pop. (1990c) 4661.

Lu·lon·ga \lü-ˈlòŋ-gä\. River in NW Democratic Rep. of the Congo; formed by junction of the Maringa and Lopori rivers, flows W into the Congo.

Lu·lua \lü-ˈlü-ä\. River, S Democratic Rep. of the Congo; flows N into Kasai River; ab. 550 mi. (885 km.) long.

Luluabourg. See KANANGA.

Lu·ma·jang *or* **Lu·ma·djang** *or Du.* **Loe·ma·djang** \ˌlü-mə-ˈjäŋ\. Town, East Java prov., Indonesia, in plain E of Mt. Semeru and S of Probolinggo; pop. (1980c) 58,495.

Lum·ber \ˈləm-bər\. River, rising near boundary bet. Montgomery and Moore cos., cen. North Carolina, and flowing SE across South Carolina border, then S into Little Pee Dee River; 125 mi. (201 km.) long.

Lum·ber·ton \ˈləm-bərt-ᵊn\. **1.** City, ⊗ of Robeson co., S North Carolina, S of Fayetteville; pop. (1990c) 18,601.

2. City, Hardin co., E Texas, N of Beaumont; pop. (1990c) 6640.

Lump·kin \ˈləmp-kən\. **1.** County in N Georgia. See table at GEORGIA.

2. City, ⊗ of Stewart co., W Georgia; pop. (1990c) 1250.

Lu·mut \lü-ˈmüt\. Port, Perak state, Malaysia, on the Strait of Malacca; pop. (1980c) 2988.

Lu·na \ˈlü-nə\. **1.** County in SW New Mexico. See table at NEW MEXICO.

2. *mod.* **Lu·ni** \ˈlü-nē\. Ancient town, Etruria, N Italy, on boundary bet. Etruria and Liguria; modern town site is W of Carrara, Tuscany; near the famous Carrara marble quarries. Excavation of Roman town ongoing. Gave its name to the district, **Lu·nig·i·a·na** \lu̇-ˌni-jē-ˈä-nə\.

Lund \ˈlu̇nd\. City, Malmöhus prov., SW Sweden; pop. (1993e) 92,027; packaging materials, textiles; printing; educational center with university (1666) and technical institute; cathedral. Made bishopric 11th cent. and archbishopric of Scandinavia 1103; reduced to bishopric 1536; passed to Sweden 1658; scene of signing of a treaty 1679 bet. Sweden and Denmark.

Lun·da Nor·te \ˈlün-də-ˈnòr-tē\. Province of NE Angola. See table at ANGOLA.

Lun·da Sul \ˈlün-də-ˈsül\. Province of NE Angola. See table at ANGOLA.

Lundenburg. See BŘECLAV.

Lundi. See SAVE.

Lun·dy Island \ˈlən-dē\. Island in Bristol Channel, 12 mi. (19 km.) off coast of NW Devon, SW England; ab. 4 mi. (6 km.) long by 0.5 mi. (0.8 km.) wide; ab. 2 sq. mi. (5 sq. km.); lighthouse; once a pirate stronghold. Prehistoric remains; also ruins of castle. Entire island maintained as a trust preserve.

Lun·dy's Lane \ˈlən-dēz\. Roadway near Niagara Falls, Ontario, Canada; in War of 1812, scene of indecisive battle July 25, 1814 in which Americans and British both lost heavily.

Lü·ne·burg \ˈlue̅-nə-ˌbu̇rk\. City, Lower Saxony, Germany, SE of Hamburg; pop. (1992e) 62,944; trade center; chemicals; woodworking and metalworking; saltworks (operating since 10th cent.); many notable buildings from Gothic and Renaissance periods. In medieval times a member of Hanseatic League; to Hannover 1705, to Prussia 1866; in WWII taken by Allies Apr. 1945.

Lü·ne·burg Heath \ˈlue̅-nə-ˌbu̇rk\ *or* **Lüneburg Hei·de** \ˈhī-də\ *or* **Lü·ne·bur·ger Heide** \-ˌbu̇r-gər\. Heath bet. the Elbe and Aller rivers, Germany; ab. 55 mi. (90 km.) long.

Lü·nen \ˈlue̅-nən\ *or in full* **Lünen an der Lip·pe** \-ˌän-dər-ˈli-pə\. City, N cen. North Rhine-Westphalia, Germany, on Lippe River 25 mi. (40 km.) S of Münster; pop. (1992e) 88,443; coal mining; aluminum, copper, iron; 18th cent. palace.

Lu·nen·burg \ˈlü-nən-ˌbərg\. **1.** County in S Virginia. See table at VIRGINIA.

2. Town, Worcester co., cen. Massachusetts, 4 mi. (6 km.) E of Fitchburg; pop. (1990c) 9117.

3. County, in S Nova Scotia, Canada. See table at NOVA SCOTIA.

4. Town, ⊗ of Lunenburg co., S Nova Scotia, Canada, on Atlantic Ocean 37 mi. (60 km.) SW of Halifax; pop. (1991c) 2781; fishing. Founded mid-18th cent. by Germans (from Lüneburg, Hannover) and Swiss on site of old village previously occupied by French and (earlier) by Indians.

Lu·né·ville \ˌlue̅-nā-ˈvēl\. City, Meurthe-et-Moselle dept., NE France, on Meurthe River 18 mi. (29 km.) SE of Nancy; pop. (1990c) 22,393; railway rolling stock, machinery, textiles, pottery; 18th cent. palace was residence of Stanisław I Leszczyński, former king of Poland and duke of Lorraine and Bar; Peace of Lunéville signed 1801 bet. Austria and France.

Lun·ga \ˈlu̇ŋ-gə\. Village at mouth of **Lunga River** on NW coast of Guadalcanal, SE Solomon Is., W Pacific Ocean, ab. 25 mi. (40 km.) E of Cape Esperance on **Lunga Point.** Just E of the river is a ridge of hills called **Lunga Ridge.** The area was the scene of severe fighting during WWII.

Lunga, Iso·la \ˈē-zò-lä-ˈlüŋ-gə\. See DUGI OTOK.

Lung–chou. See LONGZHOU.

Lung–ch'uan. See SHWELI.

Lung·ern, Lake of \ˈlu̇ŋ-ərn\. Small lake in cen. Switzerland, S of Lake of Sarnen; traversed by Aa River.

Lungki. See ZHANGZHOU.

Lung·kiang \ˈlu̇ŋ-ˈjyäŋ\. **1.** Former province (1932–45), N cen. Manchukuo; 25,904 sq. mi. (67,091 sq. km.).

2. City, China. See QIQIHAR.

Lung–k'ou. See LONGKOU.

Lung–ling. See LONGLING.

Lu·ni \ˈlü-nē\. **1.** River, NW India; rises on W slopes of Aravalli Range, flows SW in cen. and SW Rajputana to the Great Rann of Kachchh; ab. 330 mi. (530 km.) long.

2. Town in Italy. See LUNA 2.

Lunigiana. See LUNA 2.

Luo \ˈlwȯ\ *or W.-G.* **Lo** \ˈlō\. River, E cen. China; rises in E Shaanxi prov. and flows ab. 140 mi. (225 km.) ENE to the Huang E of Luoyang in N Henan.

Luo·yang \ˈlwȯ-ˈyäŋ\ *or W.-G.* **Lo–yang** \ˈlō-\; *formerly* **Ho·nan** \ˈhō-nän\. City, N Henan prov., E cen. China, ab. 120 mi. (195 km.) W of Kaifeng S of the Huang; pop. (1990c) 759,752; food products, agricultural machinery; in early history of China the ✻ of a number of dynasties.

Lupatia. See ALTAMURA.

Lu·peni \lü-ˈpen\. Town, Hunedoara co., W Romania; pop. (1989c) 32,402.

Lupin. See MANZHOULI.

Lup·ków \ˈlüp-ˌküf\. Pass in the East Beskids, Carpathian Mts., on highway from Sanok, Poland, to NE Slovakia; 2135 ft. (651 m.); scene of fighting bet. Russian and Austrian armies 1915.

Lu·que \ˈlü-kā\. City, Central dept., S Paraguay, 9 mi. (15 km.) E of Asunción; munic. pop. (1992p) 83,591; founded 1635; temporary ✻ of the republic during war against the Triple Alliance (Argentina, Brazil, and Uruguay) 1865–70.

Lu·quil·lo \lü-ˈkē-yō\. Municipality, NE Puerto Rico, on coast and on railroad line E of San Juan; pop. (1990c) 18,100.

Luquillo Mountains *or Span.* **Si·er·ra de Luquillo** \ˈsyer-rä-thā-\. Range in E Puerto Rico; highest peak El Yunque 3496 ft. (1066 m.).

Lu·ray \ˈlü-rā\. Town, ⊗ of Page co., N Virginia, in the Blue Ridge 30 mi. (48 km.) NE of Harrisonburg; pop. (1990c) 4587; **Luray Caverns** (discovered 1878) nearby are a major tourist attraction.

Lure \ˈlür\. Commune, E Haute-Saône dept., E France; abbey founded 7th cent.

Lur·gan \ˈlər-gən\. Town, Armagh dist., S Northern Ireland, 20 mi. (32 km.) SW of Belfast; pop. (1981c) 20,991; market town; linen manufacturing.

Luristan. See LORESTĀN.

Lurlei. See LORELEI.

Lu·sa·ka \lü-ˈsä-kä\. City, ✻ of Zambia; pop. (1990p) 982,362; center of a farming region; cement; Univ. of Zambia (1965).

Lu·sa·tia \lü-ˈsā-shə\ *or Ger.* **Lau·sitz** \ˈlaù-ˌzits\. Historical region, E Germany, bet. the Elbe and Oder rivers; in 10th cent. became part of the Holy Roman Empire; divided into upper and lower parts and during Middle Ages one or both parts variously absorbed by, among others, Brandenburg, Bohemia, and Saxony; partitioned bet. Saxony and Prussia 1815. Its inhabitants, Lusatians, orig. a Slavic tribe (the Sorbs, a group of the Wends).

Lushai Hills. See MIZO HILLS.

Lu·she·një \ˈlüsh-nyə\. **1.** District of W Albania. See table at ALBANIA.
2. Town, its ✻.

Lü·shun \ˈlue-ˈshün\ *or W.-G.* **Lü–shun** \ˈlue-\; *Jp.* **Ryo·jun** \ˈryō-ˌjün\; *traditionally* **Port Ar·thur** \ˈär-thər\. Seaport town at S end of Liaodong Penin., Liaoning prov., NE China, WSW of Dalian (*q.v.*), opp. N coast of Shandong; surrounded by hills on three sides, its harbor divided into two ports connected by a narrow channel.

History: Fortified port 15th–16th cents. under Ming dynasty; made headquarters of coastal defense unit 17th cent.; first visited by British c. 1860; made chief naval base by Chinese 1878; taken by Japanese in 1894 but returned to China following year; included in lease to Russia 1898, who built strong defenses around it. Captured by Japan 1905 after eight-month siege and later in year included in Kwantung Leased Terr. (*q.v.*); by 1945 treaty made a Sino-Soviet military base; Soviet forces withdrawn 1955.

Lu·si·gnan \ˌlue-zē-ˈnyäⁿ\. Commune, Vienne dept., W cen. France, 15 mi. (24 km.) SW of Poitiers; ancient town, original seat of Lusignan family, rulers of Cyprus 1192–1475, and of Jerusalem and Lesser Armenia.

Lu·si·ta·nia \ˌlü-sə-ˈtā-nē-ə, -nyə\. **1.** Region of W Hispania, corresponding approx. to the greater part of modern Portugal and the Spanish provs. of Salamanca and Cáceres; a province of the Roman Empire.
2. Country, Europe. See PORTUGAL.

Lusk \ˈləsk\. Town, ⊗ of Niobrara co., E Wyoming, 50 mi. (81 km.) N of Torrington; pop. (1990c) 1504.

Luso. See LUENA.

Lussino. See LOŠINJ.

Lus·te·nau \ˈlùs-tə-ˌnaù\. Town, Vorarlberg, W Austria; pop. (1991c) 18,484; noted for its embroidery.

Lusutfu. See USUTU.

Lut, Dasht–e–. See DASHT–E–LUT.

Lü–ta. See DALIAN.

Lutch·er \ˈlə-chər\. Town, St. James parish, SE Louisiana, on Mississippi River 40 mi. (64 km.) W of New Orleans; pop. (1990c) 3907.

Lutea. See LETEA.

Lutetia *or* **Lutetia Parisiorum.** See PARIS 10.

Luteva. See LODÈVE.

Lu·ton \ˈlüt-ᵊn\. Town, Bedfordshire, SE cen. England, on the Lea 28 mi. (45 km.) NNW of London; pop. (1991p) 167,300; hats, motor vehicles, ball bearings, electrical equipment; has notable church.

Luts'k *or* **Lutsk** \ˈlütsʸk\ *or Pol.* **Łuck** \ˈwütsk\. City, Volyn subdivision, NW Ukraine, on Styr River 125 mi. (201 km.) ESE of Lublin; pop. (1991e) 210,000. An important town of medieval Volhynia; taken from Poland by Russia 1791; in WWI center of Russian offensive operations 1916; became part of Poland after WWI; returned to U.S.S.R. as a result of WWII.

Lut·ter am Ba·ren·ber·ge \ˈlù-tər-äm-ˈbär-ən-ˌber-gə\. Town, Lower Saxony, Germany, 23 mi. (37 km.) SW of Brunswick; pop. (1980c) 2588; during Thirty Years' War scene of battle Aug. 1626 in which the forces of the Catholic League under Gen. Johann Tserclaes, Graf von Tilly defeated the Protestants under King Christian IV of Denmark and Norway.

Lüttich. See LIÈGE 2.

Lu·ty·nia \lü-ˈtin-yä\ *or Ger.* **Leu·then** \ˈlȯit-ᵊn\. Village, SW Poland, near Wrocław; scene of battle Dec. 5, 1757 in which Prussians under King Frederick the Great defeated the Austrians under Charles, prince of Lorraine during Seven Years' War.

Lüt·zel·burg \ˈlüt-səl-ˌbùrk\. Former German name of LUXEMBOURG.

Lüt·zen \ˈlœt-sən\. Commune, Saxony–Anhalt, Germany, SW of Leipzig; scene of two battles: (1) Nov. 16, 1632 during Thirty Years' War in which the Swedes under King Gustavus II Adolph defeated the Imperialists led by Austrian Gen. Albrecht von Wallenstein and in which Gustavus was killed; and (2) May 2, 1813 in which French Emperor Napoléon overcame the combined Russian and Prussian forces who retreated the following day (also called battle of Grossgörschen).

Lu·uk \lü-ˈük\. Municipality, E Jolo I., Philippines, 22 mi. (35 km.) ESE of Jolo; pop. (1980c) 19,669.

Lu·verne. 1. \lü-ˈvərn\. Town, ⊗ of Crenshaw co., S Alabama; pop. (1990c) 2555; agricultural trade center.
2. \lə-ˈvərn\. City, ⊗ of Rock co., SW corner of Minnesota, 30 mi. (48 km.) W of Worthington; pop. (1990c) 4382.

Lu·vua \lù-ˈvü-ä\. Name given to the Luapula River, cen. Africa, from Lake Mweru to its junction with the Lualaba (upper Congo River) in E Democratic Rep. of the Congo.

Lux·em·bourg *or* **Lux·em·burg** \ˈlùk-səm-ˌbùrk, ˈlək-səm-ˌbərg\. **1.** Medieval county and duchy, W Europe, now largely in the Grand Duchy of Luxembourg and the Belgian prov. of Luxembourg.
2. *or officially* **Grand Duchy of Luxembourg** *or Fr.* **Grand–Du·ché de Luxembourg** \gräⁿ-dü-ˈshā-də-luek-säⁿ-ˈbùrg\ *or Ger.* **Gross·herz·og·tum Lux·em·burg** \grōs-ˈhert-sōk-ˌtùm-ˈlùk-səm-ˌbùrk\. Grand duchy, W Europe, bounded on N and W by Belgium, on E by Germany, and on S by France; 999 sq. mi. (2587 sq. km.); pop. (1993e) 392,000; ✻ Luxembourg.

Physical features: Forms part of plateau of Ardennes; hilly and well-forested; watered by Sûre and Alzette rivers of the Moselle basin.

Chief products: Iron ore, wheat, potatoes; wine; livestock; manufacturing: iron and steel, chemicals.

Chief towns: Luxembourg and Esch-sur-Alzette.

History: Included in Roman Empire from c. 50 B.C.; later a part of Frankish kingdoms of Austrasia and of Charlemagne; county of Luxembourg (in Holy Roman Empire) emerged in 11th cent. A.D.; beginning with Henry VII (1308–13), house of Luxembourg produced four German emperors (see also BOHEMIA); raised to rank of duchy 1354; through Burgundian house which secured it 1451, duchy passed to Spanish and later, to Austrian Hapsburgs as part of the Netherlands (*q.v.*); occupied by French 1794 and incorp. into French First Republic; by Congress of Vienna 1815, Grand Duchy of Luxembourg estab. in personal union with the kingdom of Netherlands, while concurrently joining the German Confederation; after Belgian revolt, W half given to Belgium, but rest remained Grand Duchy of Luxembourg in personal union with Netherlands 1839; following dissolution 1866 of German Confederation and Franco-Prussian crisis of 1867, neutrality and independence of Luxembourg guaranteed in London conference and Prussian garrison of town of Luxembourg withdrawn; with accession of Adolph of Nassau as grand duke 1890, broke hereditary connection with Netherlands; neutrality violated and country occupied by Germany in WWI; concluded economic union with Belgium 1922; again occupied by Germans 1940–44 during WWII; formed Benelux customs union with Belgium and Netherlands 1947; member of NATO 1949, EEC 1958.

3. Province, SE Belgium; ✻ Arlon; rivers Ourthe, Semois; crossed by Forest of Ardennes; oats, rye, potatoes, wheat, tobacco; livestock; slate. See table at BELGIUM.

4. City, ✻ of Grand Duchy of Luxembourg; pop. (1991e) 75,377; on a rocky height with steep cliffs on three sides on the Alzette in S part; financial center; Gothic cathedral; grand-ducal palace; university (1958); tourism; fortifications, among the strongest in Europe, razed by treaty 1867; scene of discussions 1971 relating to British entry into the EEC.

Lu·xeuil \lu̅e̅k-ˈsœi\ *or in full* **Luxeuil–les–Bains** \-lā-ˈbeⁿ\. Commune, Haute-Saône dept., E France; thermal springs. Dates from pre-Roman times; often devastated, esp. by the Huns under Attila in 5th cent., by Saracens in 8th cent., and by Normans in 9th cent.; noted for its abbey, founded c. 590 by St. Columban, suppressed during the Revolution.

Lux·or \ˈlək-ˌsȯr, ˈlu̇k-\; *Arab.* **Al–Uq·sor** *or* **Al–Aq·sur** \a̐l-ˈu̇k-su̇r\ *or* **Al–Qu·sur** \a̐l-ˈku̇-su̇r\. Town on E bank of the Nile, Upper Egypt; pop. (1991e) 142,000; S part of site of ancient Thebes; tombs of kings; ruins of ancient temple built by King Amenhotep III (reigned c. 1417–1379 B.C.) and of other structures esp. by King Ramses II. See KARNAK.

Luzern. See LUCERNE.

Lu·zerne \lu̇-ˈzərn\. **1.** County in E Pennsylvania. See table at PENNSYLVANIA.

2. Borough, Luzerne co., E Pennsylvania, 3 mi. (5 km.) NNW of Wilkes-Barre; pop. (1990c) 3206.

Lu·zhou \ˈlü-ˈjō\ *or W.-G.* **Lu–chou** \-ˈjō\; *also* **Lu·chow** \-ˈjō, -ˈjau̇\; *formerly* **Lu·hsien** \ˈlü-ˈshyen\. City, S Sichuan prov., S cen. China, on N bank of the Chang ENE of Yibin and 146 mi. (235 km.) SSE of Chengdu; pop. (1990c) 262,892.

Luž·ni·ce \ˈlu̇zh-nyēt-se\ *or Ger.* **Lain·sitz** \ˈlīn-ˌzits\. River, W Czech Republic; rises in Austria, flows N to Tabor, then turns abruptly SW and empties into the Vltava; 129 mi. (208 km.) long.

Lu·zon \lü-ˈzȯn, -ˈzän\. Chief island of the Philippines, in N part; 41,765 sq. mi. (108,171 sq. km.); pop. (1980c) 23,900,796. Products include rice, sugar, coconuts; gold, copper, manganese. For history, see PHILIPPINES.

Physical features: Of irregular shape, coastline much indented forming many good anchorages, esp. Manila Bay, Lingayen Gulf, Lamon Bay, and Lagonoy Gulf. Has many islands and islets off its shores, esp. Babuyan Is. to the N, Catanduanes and Polillo off E coast. Principal mountain group, Cordillera Central, in NW; Sierra Madre Range along NE coast; highest peak Pulog 9606 ft.; (2928 m.); in S are active volcanoes Taal and Mayon. Chief rivers: Pampanga, Cagayan, Agno, Pasig; only large lakes Laguna de Bay and Taal.

Luzon Strait. Name sometimes given to wide passage bet. N Luzon, Philippines, and S Taiwan; connects the Pacific Ocean with the South China Sea and includes Bashi Channel, Balintang Channel, and Babuyan Channel.

Luz–Saint–Sau·veur \ˈlu̅e̅z-ˌseⁿ-sō-ˈvœr, ˈlu̅e̅s-\. Village, SW Hautes-Pyrénées dept., SW France; thermal springs; has 12th–14th cent. church built by Knights Templars.

Luz·za·ra \lüt-ˈsär-ä\. Commune, Reggio nell'Emilia prov., Emilia-Romagna, N Italy, 18 mi. (29 km.) N of the commune of Reggio nell'Emilia; pop. (1981p) 7929; scene of drawn battle 1702 bet. Austrian imperial army under Prince Eugene of Savoy and Spanish and French army.

L'viv *or* **Lviv** \lə-ˈvē-ü, -ˈvēf\ *or* **L'vov** *or* **Lvov** \lə-ˈvȯf, -ˈvȯv\. **1.** Administrative subdivision of Ukraine; 8417 sq. mi. (21,800 sq. km.); pop. (1991e) 2,764,400; ✻ L'viv; rye, wheat, sugar beets, corn, timber; oil and natural gas; formerly in Poland.

\ə\ **abut** \ə\ matches \ᵊ\ kitten, Fr table \ər\ **further** \a\ **ash** \ā\ **ace** \ä\ cot, cart \a̐\ Fr bac \au̇\ **out** \b̶\ Span Avila \ch\ **chin** \e\ **bet** \ē\ **easy** \g\ **go** \i\ **hit** \ī\ **ice** \j\ **job** \k\ Ger ich, Buch \ⁿ\ Fr vin \ŋ\ **sing** \ō\ **go** \ö\ **all** \ȯ\ **law** \œ\ Fr bœuf \œ̅\ Fr feu \ȯi\ **boy** \th\ **thin** \t͟h\ **this** \ü\ **loot** \u̇\ **foot** \ue\ Ger füllen \u̅e̅\ Fr **rue** \y\ **yet** \ʸ\ Fr digne \ˈdēnʸ\, nuit \ˈnwʸē\ \yü\ **few** \yu̇\ **fury** \zh\ **vision**

2. *or Pol.* **Lwów** \lə-ˈvüf, -ˈvüv\ *or Ger.* **Lem·berg** \ˈlem-berk\. Commercial city, its ❋, 115 mi. (185 km.) SW of Luts'k; pop. (1991e) 802,000; railroad junction; industrial center producing motor vehicles, agricultural machinery, foodstuffs; university (1661, renamed 1945); a center of Ukrainian culture.

History: Founded c. 1256 by Prince Daniel of Galicia; captured by Poles 1340; one of the great trading towns of medieval Europe; passed to Austria in First Partition of Poland 1772 and made ❋ of Austrian prov. of Galicia; scene of fighting in WWI, occupied by Russians 1914–15; occupied by Ukrainians 1918 who set up republic (Western Ukrainia); passed to Poland 1919; in WWII, occupied by Soviets 1939, by Germans 1941–44, retaken by U.S.S.R. July 1944; formally ceded by Poland 1945.

Lwan. See LUAN.

Lwów \lə-ˈvüf, -ˈvüv\. **1.** Former Polish department; 10,960 sq. mi. (28,386 sq. km.). After WWII greater part (E and cen.) transferred to Ukrainian S.S.R., U.S.S.R. (now Ukraine). Smaller W part now in Rzeszów prov., SE Poland.

2. City, Ukraine. See L'VIV.

Lya·khov·ski·ye Os·tro·va \lyȧ-ˈkȯf-skē-yə-ˈȯs-trə-və\ *also* **Lya·khov Islands** *or* **Lia·khov Islands** \lē-ˈä-kəf\. Two islands, **Bol'·shoy Lya·khov·skiy** \bōl-ˈshȯi-lyȧ-ˈkȯf-skē, bȯl-\ and **Ma·lyy Lya·khov·skiy** \ˈmä-lē-lē-ˈä-kəf-skē\, S of New Siberian Is., N Russia in Asia, E of Laptev Sea, belonging to Sakha Rep.; Bol'shoy Lyakhovskiy separated from mainland by Proliv Dmitriya Lapteva. The group considered by some to be a part of New Siberian Is. Has many remains of extinct mammoths. Discovered 1770 by a Russian merchant, Ivan Lyakhov.

Lyallpur. See FAISALABAD.

Lyc·a·bet·tus \ˌli-kə-ˈbe-təs, ˌlī-\ *or Gk.* **Ly·ka·bet·tos** \lē-ˈkä-ve-ˌtös\. Mountain in NE part of Athens, Greece; 909 ft. (277 m.).

Ly·cae·us \lī-ˈsē-əs\. Mountain in ancient Arcadia, Greece, NW of Megalopolis; on border bet. present depts. of Arcadia and Messenia; in Greek mythology sacred to Zeus.

Lyc·a·o·nia \ˌli-kā-ˈō-nē-ə, ˌlī-, -nyə\. Ancient district and Roman province, in S Asia Minor (Turkey), interior elevated region, in biblical times bounded on N by Galatia, on E by Cappadocia, on S by Cilicia, and on W by Pisidia and Phrygia, but its boundaries varied greatly; successively under Persia, Syria, and Rome. Its cities of Lystra, Iconium, and Derbe visited by St. Paul (*Acts* xiv).

Ly·ce·um \lī-ˈsē-əm\. A locality on the Ilissus in E part of ancient Athens, Greece, comprising an enclosure dedicated to Apollo and adorned with fountains and buildings erected by tyrant Peisistratus, statesman Pericles, and financier Lycurgus; frequented by philosophers for teaching, esp. Aristotle and his followers (Peripatetics).

Lychnidus. See OHRID.

Lychnitis. **1.** Lake, S Europe. See OHRID 1.

2. Lake, Armenia. See SEVAN.

Ly·cia \ˈli-shə, -shē-ə\. Ancient district in S Asia Minor (Turkey), bounded on NW by Caria and on NE by Pamphylia; a mountainous coastal region watered by the Xanthus; chief towns Myra and Patara. Settled in early times, came under Persia and Syria and in first cent. A.D. annexed by Rome; united c. 74 A.D. with Pamphylia and Pisidia to form a Roman province (**Lycia et Pam·phyl·ia** \-et-pam-ˈfi-lē-ə\).

Lyck. See EŁK.

Ly·com·ing \lī-ˈkō-miŋ\. County in N cen. Pennsylvania. See table at PENNSYLVANIA.

Lycoming Creek. River, N cen. Pennsylvania; rises in N Lycoming co., flows S and SW into the branch of Susquehanna River in S Lycoming co. near Williamsport; ab. 35 mi. (56 km.) long.

Lycopolis. See ASYŪT 2.

Lyc·o·rea \ˌli-kə-ˈrē-ə, ˌlī-\. **1.** Southernmost peak of Mt. Parnassus, Phocis, cen. Greece.

2. Ancient town at its foot.

Lyc·o·su·ra \ˌli-kə-ˈsu̇r-ə, ˌlī-\. Ancient city of S Arcadia, cen. Peloponnese, Greece, WSW of Megalopolis, said by geographer Pausanias to be the oldest city of Greece; some ruins remain.

Lydd \ˈlid\. Town, SE Kent, SE England, NW of Dungeness on coast of Strait of Dover; pop. (1981c) 4729; at military camp nearby, the explosive *lyddite* was first developed; received rights of Cinque Ports (*q.v.*) 12th cent.

Lydda. See LOD.

Ly·den·burg \ˈlīd-ᵊn-ˌbərg\. Town, NE Rep. of South Africa, 145 mi. (233 km.) ENE of Pretoria. Founded mid-19th cent. by Boers and made center of a district which they proclaimed a republic; became part of Utrecht dist. 1858 but remained in Transvaal when Utrecht (*q.v.*) was ceded to Natal 1903.

Lyd·ia \ˈli-dē-ə\. Ancient country in W part of Asia Minor, (Turkey); bounded on N by Mysia, on E by Phrygia, on S by Caria, and on W by the Aegean; ❋ Sardis; included the valleys of the Hermus and Caÿster; important towns Magnesia, Philadelphia, and Thyatira. Its early dynasties legendary, but during 7th–6th cents. B.C. it became a powerful and cultured kingdom, contributing notably to ancient economic progress, and credited with first use of coined money; conquered by Persians under Cyrus the Great 546 B.C., later passed to Syria and Pergamum, and under the Romans became a part of the prov. of Asia.

Lyemun Pass. See LEI YUE MUN.

Ly·ell, Mount \ˈlī-əl\. Peak in Sierra Nevada, near junction point of Madera, Mariposa, and Tuolumne cos., E cen. California, at edge of Yosemite National Park; 13,114 ft. (3997 m.).

Lyell Island. Island, cen. Queen Charlotte Is., off W British Columbia, Canada, on Hecate Strait.

Lykabettos. See LYCABETTUS.

Ly·man \ˈlī-mən\. **1.** County in S cen. South Dakota. See table at SOUTH DAKOTA.

2. Town, York co., SW Maine, W of Biddeford; pop. (1990c) 3390.

Lyme Bay \ˈlīm\. Widemouthed inlet of the English Channel on SW coast of England bet. Devon and Dorset cos.

Lyme Re·gis \ˈlīm-ˈrē-jəs\. Seaside resort, Dorset, S England, on Lyme Bay, at border of Devon; pop. (1981c) 3464; paleontological finds nearby; claimant to English throne James Scott, duke of Monmouth landed here with some of his rebels 1685.

Lym·ing·ton \ˈli-miŋ-tən\. Town and seaport, Hampshire, S England, on **Lymington River** near English Channel 6 mi. (10 km.) SW of the city of Southampton; pop. (1981p) 38,698; yachting center; received first charter 1150; had important saltworks from Middle Ages; Henry II landed here 1154 on the way to his coronation.

Lymm \ˈlim\. Town, Cheshire, NW England, 12 mi. (19 km.) SW of Manchester; pop. (1981p) 10,364.

Lympne \ˈlim\; *anc.* **Por·tus Le·ma·nis** \ˈpōr-təs-li-ˈmā-nəs\. Village, Kent, SE England, 2 mi. (3.2 km.) W of Hythe; castle.

Łyna. See LAVA.

Lyn·brook \ˈlin-ˌbru̇k\. Village, Nassau co., SE New York, on S shore of Long Island 18 mi. (29 km.) E of New York City; pop. (1990c) 19,208; chiefly residential.

Lynch·burg \ˈlinch-ˌbərg\. **1.** Town, ⊗ of Moore co., S Tennessee; pop. (1990c) 4721.

2. City, S cen. Virginia, in Campbell co. but politically independent, on James River in foothills of the Blue Ridge, 48 mi. (77 km.) ENE of Roanoke; 23 sq. mi. (60 sq. km.); pop. (1990c) 66,049; footwear; Virginia Theological Seminary and Coll. (1966), Central Virginia Community Coll. (1888), Randolph-Macon Woman's Coll. (1891), Lynchburg Coll. (1903), Liberty Univ. (1971); settled by Quakers 1757; incorp. as town 1805, as city 1852; Confederate supply base in Civil War, repulsed Union troops 1864.

Lynch·es \ˈlin-chəz\. River, North Carolina and South Carolina; rises in S North Carolina and flows SE into Pee Dee River on SE boundary of Florence co., South Carolina; 140 mi. (225 km.) long.

Lyn·den \ˈlin-dən\. City, Whatcom co., NW Washington, 14 mi. (23 km.) N of Bellingham; pop. (1990c) 5709.

Lynd·hurst \ˈlind-ˌhərst\. City, Cuyahoga co., N Ohio, 11 mi. (18 km.) E of Cleveland; pop. (1990c) 15,982; residential.

Lyn·don \ˈlin-dən\. **1.** City, ⊗ of Osage co., E Kansas; pop. (1990c) 964.

2. City, Jefferson co., N cen. Kentucky, E of Louisville; pop. (1990c) 8037.

3. Town, Caledonia co., NE Vermont; pop. (1990c) 5371.

Lyn·don B. John·son National Historical Park \ˈlin-dən-ˈbē-ˈjän-sən\. See UNITED STATES, *National Historical Parks.*

Lyn·don·ville \ˈlin-dən-ˌvil\. Village in town of Lyndon, NE Vermont; pop. (1990c) 1255; Lyndon State Coll. (1911).

Lyng·en \ˈlꟹŋ-ən, ˌlüŋ-\. Inlet of Arctic Ocean on NW coast of Norway, E of Tromsø.

Lynmouth. See LYNTON.

Lynn \ˈlin\. **1.** County in NW Texas. See table at TEXAS.

2. City, Essex co., NE corner of Massachusetts, on Lynn Harbor 10 mi. (16 km.) NE of Boston; pop. (1990c) 81,245; machinery; formerly the leading shoe-manufacturing center of the U.S. Orig. known as **Sau·gus** \ˈsȯ-gəs\; settled 1629; incorp. as town 1631; renamed 1637; incorp. as city 1850; manufacture of shoes began 1635, reached its height in 19th cent.

3. Town, England. See KING'S LYNN.

Lynn Canal. Deep fjord, SE Alaska, leading N from Juneau; 80 mi. (129 km.) long, 6 mi. (10 km.) wide; near its head divides into Chilkat Inlet on W and Chilkoot Inlet on E; Taiya Inlet, at entrance to which is Skagway, is an upper arm of Chilkoot Inlet. Important S gateway to Klondike region.

Lynn·field \ˈlin-ˌfēld\. Town, Essex co., NE corner of Massachusetts, 10 mi. (16 km.) NNE of Boston; pop. (1990c) 11,274.

Lynn Harbor. Inlet of Massachusetts Bay on S shore of Essex co., NE corner of Massachusetts; the city of Lynn is at its N end.

Lynn Haven. City, Bay co., NW Florida; pop. (1990c) 9298.

Lynn Regis. See KING'S LYNN.

Lynn·wood \ˈlin-ˌwu̇d\. City, Snohomish co., NW cen. Washington, on Puget Sound 15 mi. (24 km.) N of Seattle; pop. (1990c) 28,695; Edmonds Community Coll. (1967).

Lyn·ton \ˈlint-^{ə}n\. Resort, N Devon, SW England, NE of Barnstaple; pop. (1981p) 2037; on a cliff ab. 430 ft. (130 m.) high above **Lyn·mouth** \ˈlin-məth\, resort on shore of Bristol Channel; nearby is Doone Valley (*q.v.*).

Lyn·wood \ˈlin-ˌwu̇d\. **1.** City, Los Angeles co., SW California, bordering Watts neighborhood of Los Angeles; pop. (1990c) 61,945.

2. Village, Cook co., NE Illinois, on Indiana border, S of Chicago; pop. (1990c) 6535.

Ly·on \ˈlī-ən\. **1.** Name of counties in five states of the U.S. See tables at IOWA, KANSAS, KENTUCKY, MINNESOTA, NEVADA.

2. River in Tayside region, cen. Scotland; flows into the Tay River; 34 mi. (55 km.) long.

Ly·on \ˈlyȯ^{n}\ *or* **Ly·ons** \ˈlyȯ^{n}, ˈlī-ənz\; *anc.* **Lug·du·num** \lu̇g-ˈdü-nəm, ˌləg-\. City, ✻ of Rhône dept., E cen. France, at confluence of Rhone and Saône rivers; pop. (1990c) 422,444; railroad center; 13 bridges over Saône River, 11 bridges over Rhone River, extensive quays; major river port; for centuries served as important center of the silk industry. 12th–15th cent. Gothic cathedral (with four towers); 17th cent. hôtel de ville (city hall); 15th cent. archiepiscopal palace; a free Catholic university (1875); two public universities (1970) founded to replace the Université de Lyon (1809).

History: Founded 43 B.C.; became a principal city of Gaul and sometime residence of Roman emperors; Christianity first introduced to Gaul here 2d cent. A.D. (Irenaeus bishop of Lugdunum 177); sacked by Huns and Visigoths; held by Saracens 8th cent.; passed to kingdoms of Provence, then Arles; incorp. into Holy Roman Empire 1032; site of ecumenical church councils 1245, 1274; united to French crown early 14th cent.; attained great prosperity during 16th cent., but declined during Wars of Religion; suffered during French Revolution; site of several popular revolts in 19th cent.; occupied by Germans 1940–44, and was a center of the French resistance movement. Birthplace of Emperors Claudius I (10 B.C.) and Caracella (188 A.D.) and of physicist André-Marie Ampère (1775).

Lyonais. See LYONNAIS.

Lyon Mountain. Peak in the Adirondack Mts., Clinton co., NE corner of New York; 3880 ft. (1183 m.).

Ly·on·nais *or* **Ly·o·nais** \lyȯ-ˈnā, -ˈne\. Historical region of SE France; bounded anciently on N by Burgundy, on SE by Dauphiné, on S by Languedoc, on SW by Auvergne, and on NW by Bourbonnais; equivalent to modern depts. of Rhône and Loire; ✻ Lyon. Region joined to French crown 14th–16th cents. and made a province of France; became a department of France 1790, which was divided into the current departments 1793.

Ly·ons \ˈlī-ənz\. **1.** City, ⊗ of Toombs co., SE cen. Georgia, 72 mi. (116 km.) W of Savannah; pop. (1990c) 4502.

2. Residential village, Cook co., NE Illinois, 3 mi. (4.8 km.) W of Chicago; pop. (1990c) 9828; located at an old portage bet. the Des Plaines River and the Chicago River, which was used by early French explorers and by Indians.

3. City, ⊗ of Rice co., cen. Kansas, 27 mi. (43 km.) NNW of Hutchinson; pop. (1990c) 3688.

4. Village, ⊗ of Wayne co., W New York, 24 mi. (39 km.) WNW of Auburn; pop. (1990c) 4280.

5. Town, Walworth co., S Wisconsin; pop. (1990c) 2579.

Lyons. See LYON.

Lys. See LEIE.

Ly·saght, Mount \ˈlē-ˌsäkt\. Peak, Antarctica, 82°49′S, 161°19′E; 12,326 ft. (3757 m.).

Ły·sa Go·ra \ˈwi-sə-ˈgu̇r-ä\. Elevation, S cen. Poland, E of Kielce; 2005 ft. (611 m.).

Ly·se Fjord \ˈlꟹ-sə\. Inlet of North Sea on SW coast of Norway, E of Stavanger.

Lys·tra \ˈlis-trə\. Town in ancient Lycaonia, Asia Minor; its site is ab. 20 mi. (32 km.) SSW of Konya, Turkey in Asia; visited by St. Paul (*Acts* xiv. 6–21).

Lys'·va *or* **Lys·va** \ˈlis^{y}-və\. City, Perm' Oblast, E Russia in Europe, on railroad line 50 mi. (80 km.) E of the city of Perm'; pop. (1991e) 77,900.

Lyth·am St. Anne's \ˈli-thəm-sənt-ˈanz\. Seaside resort, Lancashire, NW England, on Irish Sea at mouth of the Ribble 22 mi. (35 km.) N of Liverpool; pop. (1981p) 39,707.

Lyt·tel·ton \ˈlit-^{ə}l-tən\; *formerly* **Port Coo·per** \-ˈküp-ər, -ˈku̇p-\. Borough, port, and suburb of Christchurch, E South I., New Zealand; pop. (1987e) 3190.

Lyu·ber·tsy \lyü-ˈbyert-sē\. Town, Moscow Oblast, W cen. Russia in Europe, ab. 13 mi. (21 km.) ESE of the city of Moscow; pop. (1992e) 164,000.

Lyublin. See LUBLIN.

Lyublyana. See LJUBLJANA.

\ə\ **abut** \ə\ matches \$^{ə}$\ kitten, Fr table \ər\ **further** \a\ **ash** \ā\ **ace**
\ä\ cot, cart \á\ Fr bac \au̇\ **out** \b\ Span Avila \ch\ **chin** \e\ **bet** \ē\ **easy**
\g\ **go** \i\ **hit** \ī\ **ice** \j\ **job** \k\ Ger **ich, Buch** \$^{n}$\ Fr **vin**
\ŋ\ **sing** \ō\ **go** \ö\ **all** \ȯ\ **law** \œ\ Fr **bœuf** \ꟹ\ Fr **feu** \ȯi\ **boy**
\th\ **thin** \t͟h\ **this** \ü\ **loot** \u̇\ **foot** \ue\ Ger **füllen** \ꟹ\ Fr **rue**
\y\ **yet** \$^{y}$\ Fr digne \ˈdēn^{y}\, nuit \ˈnw^{y}ē\ \yü\ **few** \yu̇\ **fury** \zh\ **vision**

M

M'-. Abbreviated form of MAC-. Names beginning with this prefix are all alphabetized as if spelled MAC-. M' was sometimes written M', primarily in pre-20th cent. British sources.

Maa·la·ea Bay \mä-ˌä-lä-ˈā-ä\. Bay on SW side of Maui I., Hawaii.

Ma·ʻān \mə-ˈän\. Town, SW Jordan, ab. 60 mi. (96 km.) SSE of the Dead Sea; pop. (1990e) 27,000; on railroad line S from Amman and on highway S to Aqaba; trade center.

Maarianhamina. See MARIEHAMN.

Maas. See MEUSE.

Maas·bree \ˈmäs-ˌbrā\. Commune, Limburg prov., SE Netherlands, W of the Meuse near Venlo; pop. (1981e) 10,916.

Maas·eik *also* **Maes·eyck** \ˈmä-ˌsīk\. Commune, Limburg prov., NE Belgium, on the Meuse River; pop. (1991c) 21,326; reputed birthplace of Flemish painters Hubert and Jan van Eyck late 14th cent.

Ma·a·sin \mä-ˈä-sēn\. Municipality, ❋ of Southern Leyte prov., SW coast of Leyte I., Philippines, 78 mi. (126 km.) SSW of Tacloban; pop. (1980c) 59,731; port.

Maas·sluis \mäs-ˈslœis, -ˈslīs\. Commune, South Holland prov., SW Netherlands; W of Rotterdam on the Nieuwe Maas; pop. (1992e) 33,232; fishing.

Maas·tricht *or* **Maes·tricht** \mä-ˈstrikt\. Commune, ❋ of Limburg prov., SE Netherlands, on Maas (Meuse) River near the Belgian frontier; pop. (1992e) 118,152; steel, chemicals, cement, paper, glass, pottery, cigars; grain and butter market; cathedral of St. Servatius, dating from 6th cent., oldest church in Netherlands; medieval Romanesque church. Founded on site of Roman town; its location as a border town has subjected it frequently to siege or capture in various wars; captured by Spanish 1579 during Dutch revolt, and many of its inhabitants massacred; occupied by French 1673, 1748, and 1794; withstood Belgian siege in 1830; occupied by Germans 1940–44; EC's Treaty of European Union signed here 1992.

Ma·ba·la·cat \ˌmä-bä-ˈlä-kät\. Municipality, Pampanga prov., Luzon, Philippines, on Manila-Dagupan railroad 15 mi. (24 km.) NNW of San Fernando; pop. (1980c) 80,966.

Ma·bi·ri, Cape \mä-ˈbē-rē\. Cape on E cen. Bougainville I., NW Solomon Is., Papua New Guinea, W Pacific Ocean.

Ma·cá, Mon·te \ˈmȯn-tā-mä-ˈkä\. Peak, S Chile, E of Melchor I. and NW of Puerto Aysén; 9710 ft. (2960 m.).

Ma·ca·be·be \ˌmä-kä-ˈbā-bā\. Municipality, Pampanga prov., Luzon, Philippines, on edge of Pampanga Delta 8 mi. (13 km.) S of San Fernando; pop. (1980c) 45,830.

Ma·caé \ˌmȧ-kȧ-ˈe\. Coastal city, Rio de Janeiro state, SE Brazil, 95 mi. (153 km.) ENE of the city of Rio de Janeiro; munic. pop. (1991p) 100,646.

Ma·ca·ja·lar Bay \ˌmä-kä-hä-ˈlär\. Inlet of S Mindanao Sea in Misamis Oriental prov., N Mindanao, Philippines; Cagayan de Oro is at its head; ab. 19 mi. (31 km.) across its mouth.

Mc·Al·es·ter \mə-ˈka-lə-stər\. City, ⊗ of Pittsburg co., SE Oklahoma, 50 mi. (80 km.) S of Okmulgee; pop. (1990c) 16,370; clothing manufacture; state penitentiary; U.S. Army ammunition plant; on site of trading post opened 1870.

Mc·Al·len \mə-ˈka-lən\. City, Hidalgo co., S Texas, 50 mi. (80 km.) WNW of Brownsville; pop. (1990c) 84,021; ships citrus fruits and vegetables; canneries; regional trade center; winter resort; founded c. 1905.

Ma·cao *or Port.* **Ma·cau** \mə-ˈkau̇\. **1.** Special administrative region, SE China, consisting of Macao Penin. (see MACAO 2), and the two small islands of Taipa and Colôane, ab. 40 mi. (64 km.) W of Hong Kong; 6 sq. mi. (16 sq. km.); pop. (1992e) 488,000; administrative center Macao (see MACAO 3); fishing; textiles, clothing, toys.

History: Visited by Portuguese traders 1513; settled by Portuguese 1557; declared Portuguese territory 1849, claim recognized by China in treaty 1887; status changed 1951 from colony to overseas territory of Portugal; by 1987 agreement, Macao returned to Chinese sovereignty in 1999.

2. Peninsula on the coast of SE China, W of mouth of Zhu River; ab. 2 sq. mi. (5 sq. km.); contains almost entire population of the special administrative region of Macao.

3. Town, administrative center of Macao (see MACAO 1), approx. coextensive with Macao Penin.; its harbor somewhat silted up; tourism. From 1717 until 19th cent., Macao and Canton (now Guangzhou) were the only Chinese ports open to European trade; for many years a haven for missionaries and traders; residence c. 1558–59 of the Portuguese poet Luis Vaz de Camões, who wrote part of *The Lusiad* here.

Ma·ca·pá \ˌmȧ-kȧ-ˈpä\. City, ❋ of Amapá state, N Brazil; port, N of Amazon Delta; munic. pop. (1991p) 179,609.

Ma·ca·rá \ˌmä-kä-ˈrä\. Town, Loja prov., SW Ecuador, on Peruvian border.

Ma·ca·re·na Mountains \ˌmä-kä-ˈrā-nä\ *or Span.* **Ser·ra·nía de la Macarena** \ˌser-rä-ˈnē-ä-ˌthā-lä-\. Mountain range, SE Colombia, ab. 200 mi. (320 km.) SE of Bogotá; ab. 150 mi. (240 km.) long; highest peak ab. 10,000 ft. (3050 m.).

Mc·Ar·thur \mə-ˈkär-thər\. Village, ⊗ of Vinton co., S Ohio, 26 mi. (42 km.) E of Chillicothe; pop. (1990c) 1541.

MacArthur. See ORMOC.

Ma·cas \ˈmä-käs\. Town, ❋ of Morona-Santiago prov., E Ecuador, on Santiago River 123 mi. (198 km.) E of Guayaquil; pop. (1990c) 8246.

Macassar. See UJUNG PANDANG.

Macau. See MACAO.

Mac·bride Head \mək-ˈbrīd\. Promontory extending into South Atlantic Ocean from NE coast of East Falkland I., Falkland Is.

Maccaluba. See ARAGONA.

Mc·Cau·ley Peak \mə-ˈkȯ-lē\. Mountain, La Plata co., SW Colorado; 13,558 ft. (4132 m.).

Mc·Clain \mə-ˈklān\. County in cen. Oklahoma. See table at OKLAHOMA.

Mc·Clel·lan–Kerr Ar·kan·sas River Navigation System \mə-ˈkle-lən-ˈkər-ˈär-kən-ˌsȯ\ *often shortened to* **Arkansas River Navigation System.** Waterway consisting of sections of the Verdigris, Arkansas, and White rivers, extending from Catoosa, Oklahoma (suburb of Tulsa) to junction of White and Mississippi rivers, Arkansas; 440 mi. (708 km.) long; 17 locks; dedicated 1971.

Mac·clen·ny \mə-ˈkle-nē\. Town, ⊗ of Baker co., NE Florida; pop. (1990c) 3966.

Mac·cles·field \ˈma-kəlz-ˌfēld\. Town, Cheshire, NW England, on the Bollin River 17 mi. (27 km.) S of Manchester; pop. (1991p) 147,000; formerly a major center of silk manufacture.

M'Clin·tock Channel \mə-ˈklin-tək\. Passage, Nunavut, Canada, bet. E Victoria I. and W Prince of Wales I.; 170 mi. (274 km.) long; 65 to 130 mi. (104 to 209 km.) wide.

McCluer Gulf. See BERAU BAY.

Mc·Clure, Lake \mə-ˈklu̇r\. See NEW EXCHEQUER DAM.

M'Clure Strait *or* **Mc·Clure Strait** \mə-ˈklu̇r\. Channel bet. Banks I. and Melville I., W Arctic Archipelago, Northwest Territories, Canada; opens on W into Arctic Ocean and on E into Viscount Melville Sound.

Mc·Clus·ky \mə-ˈkləs-kē\. City, ⊗ of Sheridan co., cen. North Dakota; pop. (1990c) 492.

Mc·Coll \mə-ˈkäl\. Town, Marlboro co., NE South Carolina, 10 mi. (16 km.) ENE of Bennettsville; pop. (1990c) 2685.

Mc·Comb \mə-ˈkōm\. City, Pike co., S Mississippi, 60 mi. (96 km.) ESE of Natchez; pop. (1990c) 11,591.

Mc·Cone \mə-ˈkōn\. County in E Montana. See table at MONTANA.

Mc·Con·nells·burg \mə-ˈkän-ᵊlz-ˌbərg\. Borough, ⊗ of Fulton co., S Pennsylvania; pop. (1990c) 1106; resort.

Mc·Con·nels·ville \mə-ˈkän-ᵊlz-ˌvil\. Village, ⊗ of Morgan co., SE Ohio, on Muskingum River 21 mi. (34 km.) SSE of Zanesville; pop. (1990c) 1804.

Mc·Cook \mə-ˈku̇k\. **1.** County in SE South Dakota. See table at SOUTH DAKOTA.
2. City, ⊗ of Red Willow co., S Nebraska, 65 mi. (104 km.) S of North Platte; pop. (1990c) 8112; McCook Community Coll. (1926).

Mc·Cor·mick \mə-ˈkȯr-mik\. **1.** County in W South Carolina. See table at SOUTH CAROLINA.
2. Town, its ⊗; pop. (1990c) 1659.

Mc·Crack·en \mə-ˈkra-kən\. County in W Kentucky. See table at KENTUCKY.

Mc·Crea·ry \mə-ˈkrir-ē\. County in SE Kentucky. See table at KENTUCKY.

Mc·Cul·loch \mə-ˈkə-lə\. County in cen. Texas. See table at TEXAS.

Mc·Cur·tain \mə-ˈkərt-ᵊn\. County in SE corner of Oklahoma. See table at OKLAHOMA.

Macdhui, Ben. See BEN MACDHUI.

Mc·Don·ald \mək-ˈdän-ᵊld\. **1.** County in SW corner of Missouri. See table at MISSOURI.
2. Village, Trumbull co., NE Ohio, 6 mi. (10 km.) NW of Youngstown; pop. (1990c) 3526.

Mac·don·ald, Lake \mək-ˈdän-ᵊld\. Lake in desert region of cen. Australia, on Tropic of Capricorn, on boundary bet. Western Australia and Northern Terr.

McDonald Islands. See HEARD ISLAND.

Mac·don·nell Ranges \mək-ˈdän-ᵊl\. A series of parallel ridges and valleys of hard folded Paleozoic rocks, running east and west, S Northern Terr., Australia; highest Mt. Ziel 5023 ft. (1531 m.).

Mc·Don·ough \mək-ˈdä-nə\. **1.** County in W Illinois. See table at ILLINOIS.
2. City, ⊗ of Henry co., NW cen. Georgia; pop. (1990c) 2929.

Mc·Dow·ell \mək-ˈdau̇-əl\. **1.** Name of counties in two states of the U.S. See tables at NORTH CAROLINA and WEST VIRGINIA.
2. Town, Highland co., W Virginia; scene of Confederate victory May 8, 1862, under Confederate Generals Thomas J. (Stonewall) Jackson and Edward Johnson.

Mc·Duf·fie \mək-ˈdə-fē\. County in E Georgia. See table at GEORGIA.

Mac·e·do·nia \ˌma-sə-ˈdō-nyə, -nē-ə\. **1.** Village, Summit co., NE Ohio, 18 mi. (29 km.) N of Akron; pop. (1990c) 7509.
2. A region in cen. Balkan Penin., NW of the Aegean Sea; ab. 25,700 sq. mi. (66,565 sq. km.); with somewhat indefinite boundaries but incl. Macedonia region of Greece, most of middle Vardar Valley in SE Republic of Macedonia (see MACEDONIA, REPUBLIC OF), and SW Bulgaria W of Mesta River.
3. *or* **Mac·e·don** \ˈma-səd-ᵊn, -sə-ˌdän\. Ancient country and kingdom in the Macedonia region; ✻ Pella. Ancient kingdom orig. located N of Thessaly and NW of Aegean Sea; under Philip II (359–336 B.C.), who developed the Macedonian phalanx, it came to include Thrace, Chalcidice, Thessaly, and others; attained final hegemony over Greece in battle of Chaeronea 338 B.C.; Macedonian empire, comprising Macedonia and countries conquered by Alexander the Great 336–323 B.C., reached from Macedonia beyond E boundaries of former Persian Empire into upper India, and S into Egypt; empire soon broke up (see IPSUS), and Macedonia sought to retain its power in Greece and Aegean Sea; decisively defeated 197 B.C. at Cynoscephalae (*q.v.*) by Rome after a series of wars; opposition to Rome finally suppressed and the empire ended when Perseus, last king of the Macedonians, was defeated at Pydna 168 B.C.; made a Roman province 148 B.C.; division of Byzantine Empire, lying W of Mesta River, when invaded and settled by Slavic peoples 6th cent. A.D.; included successively in medieval Bulgarian and Serbian empires; gradually came under Ottoman Empire 14th–15th cents. (Thessaloníki held out to 1430) which held it until 1912; with rise of Bulgarian nationalism esp. after 1878, the "Macedonian question," i.e., independence of Macedonia from Turkey, and rival Bulgarian, Serb, and Greek claims to Macedonia finally led to Balkan Wars 1912–13; as result of Second Balkan War 1913 most of Macedonia was partitioned bet. Serbia and Greece, largely to the exclusion of Bulgaria; during 1920s and 1930s, revolutionary activity in Macedonia threatened relations of Bulgaria with other Balkan powers; after WWII status of Macedonia an issue in Greek-Yugoslavian relations.
4. *or Gk.* **Ma·ke·do·nia** \ˌmä-ke-t͟hō-ˈnē-ä\. Region of modern Greece; includes all of N Greece except West Thrace; 12,304 sq. mi. (31,867 sq. km.); forms administrative region of Central Macedonia and parts of Eastern Macedonia and Thrace and Western Macedonia (see table at GREECE). Mountainous in W where it is drained by Aliákmon River; in E crossed by Vardar and Struma rivers; includes peninsula of Chalcidice. Chief towns: Thessaloníki, Kvála, Sérrai, and Drama.

Macedonia, Republic of. Republic, SE Europe, comprising former Yugoslav section of the region of Macedonia, bounded on N by Yugoslavia, on E by Bulgaria, on S by Greece, and on W by Albania; 9928 sq. mi. (25,714 sq. km.); pop. (1993e) 2,063,000; ✻ Skopje; a constituent republic of Yugoslavia 1946–91; declared independence from Yugoslavia Sept. 1991.
Chief products: Wheat, corn, tobacco; iron and steel.
Chief towns: Skopje and Tetovo.

Ma·ceió \ˌmȧ-sā-ˈō\. City, ✻ of Alagoas state, E Brazil, 130 mi. (209 km.) SSW of Recife; munic. pop. (1991p) 628,209; seaport, exporting sugar and cotton; other products include textiles, alcoholic beverages, and soap; university (1961); lighthouse in center of city; founded 1815; became city and ✻ 1839.

Ma·cen·ta \mä-ˈsen-tä\. Town, SE Guinea; pop. (1983p) 28,131.

Macequece. See VILA DA MANHIÇA.

Ma·ce·ra·ta \ˌmä-chä-ˈrä-tä\. **1.** Province of Marche, Italy. See table at ITALY.
2. Commune, its ✻, 110 mi. (177 km.) NNW of Rome; pop. (1989c) 43,527; brewing; bricks, musical instruments; university (1290); nearby ruins of Roman town destroyed 5th cent. by Visigoths; founded 11th cent.; birthplace of Jesuit missionary Matteo Ricci 1552.

Mc·Far·land \mək-ˈfär-lənd\. **1.** City, Kern co., S California, 23 mi. (37 km.) N of Bakersfield; pop. (1990c) 7005.
2. Village, Dane co., S Wisconsin, ESE of Madison; pop. (1990c) 5232.

Mc·Gehee \mə-ˈgē\. City, Desha co., SE Arkansas, 56 mi. (90 km.) SE of Pine Bluff; pop. (1990c) 4997.

Mac·gil·li·cud·dy's Reeks \mə-ˈgi-lə-ˌkə-dēz-ˈrēks\. Mountain range, co. Kerry, SW Ireland; highest peak Carrantuohill 3414 ft. (1040 m.), highest mountain in Ireland.

Mc·Greg·or \mə-ˈgre-gər\. City, McLennan co., cen. Texas, 13 mi. (21 km.) SSW of Waco; pop. (1990c) 4683.

Mc·Guire, Mount \mə-ˈgwīr\. Peak, NW Lemhi co., E cen. Idaho; 10,079 ft. (3072 m.).

Ma·cha·chi \mä-ˈchä-chē\. Resort town, Pichincha prov., N cen. Ecuador, in Andes at alt. 10,118 ft. (3084 m.), just S of Quito; mineral-water springs.

Ma·chae·rus \mə-ˈkir-əs\. Site, Jordan, E of Dead Sea, of fortified village of ancient Moab; the place where Jewish prophet John the Baptist was beheaded.

Ma·cha·la \mä-ˈchä-lä\. Town, ✻ of El Oro prov., SW Ecuador, 75 mi. (121 km.) S of Guayaquil; pop. (1990c) 144,197; distribution of cacao and coffee; its port is Puerto Bolívar.

Mc·Hen·ry \mə-ˈken-rē\. **1.** Name of counties in two states of the U.S. See tables at ILLINOIS and NORTH DAKOTA.
2. City, McHenry co., N Illinois, 23 mi. (37 km.) W of Waukegan; pop. (1990c) 16,177; in lake region; summer resort.

Ma·ches·ney Park \mə-ˈchez-nē\. Village, Winnebago co., N Illinois, on Rock River, N of Rockford; pop. (1990c) 19,033.

Ma·chi·as \mə-ˈchī-əs\. **1.** River, SE Maine; rises in NE Hancock co., flows SE across Washington co. into Machias Bay; ab. 70 mi. (113 km.) long.
2. Town, ⊗ of Washington co., SE corner of Maine, adjacent to Machias Bay 33 mi. (53 km.) S of Calais; pop. (1990c) 2569; Univ. of Maine at Machias (1909).

Machias Bay. Inlet of Atlantic Ocean on S coast of Washington co., SE Maine; receives Machias River on N.

Ma·chi·cha·co, Cape \ˌmä-chē-ˈchä-kō\. Cape extending into Bay of Biscay from Vizcaya prov., N coast of Spain, NE of Bilbao.

Ma·chi·da \mä-ˈchē-dä, ˈmä-chē-ˌdä\. City, Tokyo prefecture, Honshū, Japan; pop. (1992e) 355,843.

Ma·chi·li·pat·nam \ˌmə-shə-lē-ˈpət-nəm\ *or* **Ma·su·li·pat·nam** \ˌmə-sə-\ *or* **Ban·dar** \ˈbən-dər\. Seaport city, NE Andhra Pradesh, India, on Bay of Bengal on one of the mouths of Krishna River, 215 mi. (346 km.) NNE of Madras; pop. (1991p) 159,007; manufactures scientific instruments, carpets; educational center. British settlement estab. here 1611, earliest British settlement on Coromandel Coast; contested for during 17th–18th cents. by French, Dutch, and British; retaken by British 1759.

Ma–ch'ing–kang–jih. See MAQÊN GANGRI.

Machpelah, Cave of. See HEBRON 4.

Ma·chu Pic·chu \ˈmä-chü-ˈpēk-ˌchü\. Site of ancient Inca city on a mountain in the Andes, NW of Cuzco, Peru; ruins include a temple; citadel was surrounded by terraced gardens; discovered by American explorer Hiram Bingham 1911.

Ma·chyn·lleth \mə-ˈkən-hləth\. Town, W Powys co., Wales, on the Dyfi (Dovey) River; pop. (1981p) 2000; tourist resort.

Macias Nguema Biyogo. See BIOKO.

Ma·cie·jo·wi·ce \ˌmä-che-yȯ-ˈvēt-sä\. Commune, E Poland, near E bank of the Vistula 43 mi. (69 km.) SE of Warsaw; scene 1794 of Russian victory over rebelling Polish forces under Tadeusz Kościuszko who was wounded and captured.

Mc·In·tosh \ˈma-kən-ˌtäsh\. **1.** Name of counties in three states of the U.S. See tables at GEORGIA, NORTH DAKOTA, OKLAHOMA.
2. City, ⊗ of Corson co., N South Dakota; pop. (1990c) 302.

Mac·kay \mə-ˈkī\. Town, E Queensland, Australia, on Pacific Ocean within Great Barrier Reef 180 mi. (290 km.) NNW of Rockhampton; pop. (1991c) 23,052; extensive port facilities; in fertile agricultural region devoted largely to sugar and fruits.

Mackay, Lake. Lake in desert region of cen. Australia, on boundary bet. Western Australia and Northern Terr.

Mc·Kay Dam \mə-ˈkā\. Dam across **McKay Creek** (tributary of Umatilla River), S of Pendleton, Umatilla co., NE Oregon; height 165 ft. (50 m.); impounds water in **McKay Reservoir** for irrigation.

Mac·Kay Lake \mə-ˈkī, -ˈkā\. Lake, SE mainland portion of Northwest Territories, Canada; 250 sq. mi. (648 sq. km.); connected with Lake Aylmer.

Mc·Kean \mə-ˈkēn\. **1.** County in N Pennsylvania. See table at PENNSYLVANIA.
2. One of the smaller islands of the Phoenix Is. (*q.v.*) group, in W part, WSW of Kanton I., cen. Pacific Ocean, 3°36′S, 174°08′W; 1 sq. mi. (2.6 sq. km.).

Mc·Kee \mə-ˈkē\. City, ⊗ of Jackson co., SE Kentucky; pop. (1990c) 870.

Mc·Kees·port \mə-ˈkēz-ˌpōrt\. City, Allegheny co., SW Pennsylvania, at confluence of Youghiogheny and Monongahela rivers 10 mi. (16 km.) ESE of Pittsburgh; pop. (1990c) 26,016; coal mining and steel production have been historically important; Pennsylvania State Univ.–McKeesport campus (1947). Settled 1755; center of conflict during Whisky Rebellion 1794; incorp. as city 1890.

Mc·Kees Rocks \mə-ˈkēz\. Borough, Allegheny co., SW Pennsylvania, near Ohio River N and W of Pittsburgh; pop. (1990c) 7691. Settled 1764; incorp. 1892.

Mac·kel·lar, Mount \mə-ˈke-lər\. Mountain, Antarctica; 83°59′S, 166°39′E; 14,098 ft. (4297 m.).

Mc·Ken·zie \mə-ˈken-zē\. **1.** River, W Oregon; rises in SE Linn co., flows W into Willamette River near Eugene; 80 mi. (129 km.) long.
2. County in W North Dakota. See table at NORTH DAKOTA.
3. City, Carroll and Weakley cos., W Tennessee, pop. (1990c) 5168; Bethel Coll. (1842).

Mac·ken·zie \mə-ˈken-zē\. **1.** River, W mainland portion of Northwest Territories, Canada; flows NNW into Mackenzie Bay; ab. 1120 mi. (1800 km.) long; when considered as incl. Slave River, Peace River, and Finlay River, ab. 2635 mi. (4240 km.) long, 2d longest river in North America; navigable for greater part of its length (rapids in Slave River); its valley is rich in forests and mineral resources. Discovered and navigated by Scottish explorer Sir Alexander Mackenzie 1789. Trading posts of Hudson's Bay Company estab. along its course; these forts are now settlements, esp. Fort McPherson, Fort Good Hope, Fort Norman (now Tulita), Fort Simpson, and Fort Providence. Aklavik is chief settlement in delta and Fort Resolution on Great Slave Lake.
2. Former administrative district, cen. and W Northwest Territories, Canada; area incl. water 527,490 sq. mi. (1,366,199 sq. km.); included the greater part of N mainland of Canada bet. Yukon Terr. and Keewatin dist. and also most of the Mackenzie River valley, Great Bear Lake, Great Slave Lake, and many other lakes. Administered from Edmonton. Created 1895; boundaries redefined 1918; ceased to exist 1979. Extensive oil fields and uranium deposits.

McKenzie, Mount. Peak in the Adirondack Mts., Essex co., NE New York; 3872 ft. (1180 m.).

Mackenzie Bay. Widemouthed inlet of Beaufort Sea, N of Yukon Terr. and NW mainland portion of Northwest Territories, Canada; 100 mi. (161 km.) long, 120 mi. (193 km.) wide; receives Mackenzie River.

Mackenzie Mountains. Range in E Yukon Terr. and W mainland portion of Northwest Territories, Canada; highest point Keele Peak 9750 ft. (2972 m.). Watershed of tributaries of Mackenzie and Yukon rivers.

Mack·i·nac \ˈma-kə-ˌnȯ, -ˌnak\; *formerly* **Mich·i·li·mack·i·nac** \ˌmi-shə-lē-ˈma-kə-ˌnȯ, -ˌnak\. County in SE Upper Penin. of Michigan. See table at MICHIGAN.

Mackinac, Straits of. Straits connecting Lake Huron and Lake Michigan; 4 mi. (6 km.) wide at narrowest point; site of Mackinac Bridge (suspension; main span 3800 ft. or 1158 m.; completed 1957) connecting Michigan's Upper Penin. with Lower Penin.

Mackinac Island. Island in Straits of Mackinac, in Mackinac co., SE Upper Penin. of Michigan; coextensive with Mackinac Island city; 3 mi. (5 km.) long; pop. (1990c) 469; state park; resort.

Mack·i·naw \ˈma-kə-ˌnȯ\. River, cen. Illinois; flows W, from E McLean co. into the Illinois River a few miles below Pekin; ab. 100 mi. (160 km.) long.

Mc·Kin·ley \mə-ˈkin-lē\. County in NW New Mexico. See table at NEW MEXICO.

McKinley, Mount; *Russ.* **Bol·sha·ya** *also* **Bul·sha·ia** \bəl-ˈshī-ə\; *Athabascan* **De·na·li** \də-ˈnä-lē\. Mountain in Denali National Park, S cen. Alaska; 20,320 ft. (6194 m.); highest mountain in North America; first climbed 1913. See UNITED STATES, *National Parks* and CHURCHILL PEAKS.

McKinley Park. Unincorporated settlement, S cen. Alaska, SSW of Fairbanks, at NE end of Alaska Range; station on railroad line providing access to Denali National Park.

Mc·Kin·ney \mə-ˈki-nē\. City, ⊗ of Collin co., NE Texas, 30 mi. (48 km.) N of Dallas; pop. (1990c) 21,283.

Mc·Lean \mə-ˈklān\. Name of counties in three states of the U.S. See tables at ILLINOIS, KENTUCKY, NORTH DAKOTA.

Mc·Leans·boro \mə-ˈklānz-ˌbər-ō\. City, ⊗ of Hamilton co., SE Illinois, SE of Mount Vernon; pop. (1990c) 2677.

Mc·Lel·an Strait \mə-ˈkle-lən\. Strait separating Killinek I. from the mainland of Labrador, Canada.

Mc·Len·nan \mə-ˈkle-nən\. County in cen. Texas. See table at TEXAS.

Mc·Leod \mə-ˈklau̇d\. County in S cen. Minnesota. See table at MINNESOTA.

Macleod. See FORT MACLEOD.

Mac·leod, Lake \mə-ˈklau̇d\. Salt lake, extreme W Australia.

Mc·Lough·lin, Mount \mə-ˈglä-klən\; *formerly* **Mount Pitt** \ˈpit\. Peak, E Jackson co., SW Oregon; 9495 ft. (2894 m.).

McMillan, Lake *and* **McMillan Dam.** See CARLSBAD 2.

Mc·Minn \mək-ˈmin\. County in SE Tennessee. See table at TENNESSEE.

Mc·Minn·ville \mək-ˈmin-ˌvil, -vəl\. **1.** City, ⊗ of Yamhill co., NW Oregon, 21 mi. (34 km.) NNW of Salem; pop. (1990c) 17,894; Linfield Coll. (1849); settled 1844.

2. City, ⊗ of Warren co., cen. Tennessee, 53 mi. (85 km.) NW of Chattanooga; pop. (1990c) 11,194; settled c. 1800.

Mc·Mul·len \mək-ˈmə-lən\. County in S Texas. See table at TEXAS.

Mc·Mur·do Sound \mək-ˈmər-dō\. Inlet of SW Ross Sea, bet. James Ross I. and the coast of Victoria Land, Antarctica, 77°30′S, 165°E; site of a major research and exploration base.

McMurray. See FORT MCMURRAY.

Mc·Nairy \mək-ˈnar-ē\. County in SW Tennessee. See table at TENNESSEE.

Mc·Nary Dam \mək-ˈnar-ē\. Dam across Columbia River bet. Washington and Oregon in E part of stretch forming the state boundary.

Mac·Naugh·ton, Mount \mək-ˈnȯt-^{ə}n\. Peak in Adirondack Mts., Essex co., NE New York; 3976 ft. (1212 m.).

Mc·Neill Peak \mək-ˈnēl\. Mountain, Yakima co., S Washington; 6788 ft. (2069 m.).

Ma·comb \mə-ˈkōm\. **1.** County in SE Michigan. See table at MICHIGAN.

2. City, ⊗ of McDonough co., W Illinois, 37 mi. (60 km.) SSW of Galesburg; pop. (1990c) 19,952; Western Illinois Univ. (1899).

Macomb Mountain. Peak in the Adirondack Mts., Essex co., NE New York; 4371 ft. (1332 m.).

Ma·con \ˈmās-^{ə}n\; *orig.* **Ma·çon** \mä-ˈsō^{n}\. Bayou, NE Louisiana; rises near the Arkansas boundary and flows S to the Tensas River in SE Franklin parish; 150 mi. (241 km.) long; part of its course forms boundary bet. Madison and Richland parishes; navigable.

Macon \ˈmā-kən\. **1.** Name of counties in six states of U.S. See tables at ALABAMA, GEORGIA, ILLINOIS, MISSOURI, NORTH CAROLINA, TENNESSEE.

2. City, ⊗ of Bibb co., cen. Georgia, on Ocmulgee River 78 mi. (126 km.) SE of Atlanta; pop. (1990c) 106,612; processing and distributing center in an agricultural region; limestone; Mercer Univ. (1833), Wesleyan Coll. (1836), Macon Coll. (1968); Robins Air Force Base. Settled c. 1821; captured by Union forces in Civil War April 20, 1865; birthplace of poet Sidney Lanier 1842.

3. City, ⊗ of Noxubee co., E Mississippi, 28 mi. (45 km.) SSW of Columbus; pop. (1990c) 2256.

4. City, ⊗ of Macon co., N Missouri, 23 mi. (37 km.) N of Moberly; pop. (1990c) 5571.

Mâ·con \mä-ˈkō^{n}\; *anc.* **Ma·tis·co Ædu·o·rum** \mə-ˈtis-kō-ˌē-dyu̇-ˈwōr-əm\. City, ✱ of Saône-et-Loire dept., E cen. France, on Saône River 22 mi. (35 km.) WNW of Bourg; pop. (1990c) 38,508; railroad center; ships wine; remains of medieval cathedral. Episcopal see, 6th cent. until Revolution; Huguenot stronghold in 16th cent.; birthplace of poet Alphonse de Lamartine 1790.

Macoraba. See MECCA.

Ma·cou·pin \mə-ˈkü-pən\. County in SW cen. Illinois. See table at ILLINOIS.

Mc·Part·land Mountain \mək-ˈpärt-lənd\. Peak in Glacier National Park, NW Montana; 8400 ft. (2560 m.).

Mc·Pher·son \mək-ˈfərs-^{ə}n\. **1.** Name of counties in three states of the U.S. See tables at KANSAS, NEBRASKA, SOUTH DAKOTA.

2. City, ⊗ of McPherson co., cen. Kansas, 27 mi. (43 km.) NE of Hutchinson; pop. (1990c) 12,422; McPherson Coll. (1887), Central Coll. (1914).

3. Trading station, Canada. See FORT MCPHERSON.

Mac·pher·son Range. Short range of mountains forming E end of boundary bet. New South Wales and SE Queensland, Australia; highest peak 4449 ft. (1356 m.).

Mac·quar·ie \mə-ˈkwär-ē\. **1.** River, E cen. New South Wales, Australia; flows NNW from Blue Mts. to Darling River; 590 mi. (949 km.) long.

2. River, an E tributary of Lake River, E Tasmania, Australia; ab. 65 mi. (105 km.) long.

Macquarie Harbour. Large inlet of Indian Ocean on W coast of Tasmania, Australia; ab. 20 mi. (32 km.) long; receives Gordon River at S end. Cape Sorell is at W of entrance and town of Strahan is situated at N end.

Macquarie Island. Island, Australia, in S Pacific Ocean, 850 mi. (1368 km.) SE of Tasmania, 54°36′S, 158°55′E; 89 sq. mi. (231 sq. km.); crest of submarine mountain. Administered by Tasmania; nature reserve; home of seals and penguins. Discovered 1810; Australian research station estab. on island 1948.

Macquarie Ridge. Ridge, SW Pacific Ocean floor, extending approx. from SW of South I., New Zealand to S of Macquarie I. in a general NE to SW direction.

Mc·Rae \mə-ˈkrā\. City, ⊗ of Telfair co., S cen. Georgia, 78 mi. (126 km.) NE of Albany; pop. (1990c) 3007.

Mac. Rob·ert·son Land \mək-ˈrä-bərt-sən\. Section of Antarctica coast on Indian Ocean, 70°S, 59°40′ to 69°30′E; E of Enderby Land.

Mc·Sher·rys·town \mək-ˈsher-ēz-ˌtau̇n\. Borough, Adams co., S Pennsylvania, 12 mi. (19 km.) E of Gettysburg; pop. (1990c) 2769.

Mac·tan \mäk-ˈtän\. Island off E coast of Cebu prov., Philippines; 24 sq. mi. (62 sq. km.); pop. (1980c) 115,178; separated from Cebu I. by channel 1 mi. (1.6 km.) wide. Has mangrove swamps, coconut groves, and some cultivated area; chief town Lapu-Lapu. Here on Apr. 27, 1521, Portuguese explorer Ferdinand Magellan was killed in a war expedition on behalf of a native sovereign.

Mactaris. See MAKTHAR.

Ma·cun·gie \mə-ˈkən-jē\. Borough, Lehigh co., E Pennsylvania, SW of Allentown; pop. (1990c) 2597.

Ma·cu·ri·jes, Point \ˌmä-kä-ˈrē-hās\. Cape extending W from S coast of Camagüey prov., E cen. Cuba, S of the mouth of the San Pedro River.

Ma·cus·pa·na \ˌmä-kü-ˈspä-nä\. Municipality, Tabasco state, Mexico, 28 mi. (45 km.) SE of Villahermosa; pop. (1990p) 100,414.

Ma·cu·to \mä-ˈkü-tō\. Seaside resort on N coast of Venezuela, adjoining La Guaira.

Mad \ˈmad\. River, W cen. Ohio; flows S and SE, from Logan co., to Miami River at Dayton; 100 mi. (161 km.) long.

Ma'·da·bā *also* **Mad·e·ba** \ˈmȧ-də-ˌbä\; *anc.* **Med·e·ba** \ˈme-də-bə\. Town, N cen. Jordan, SSW of Amman; pop. (1990e) 64,530; ancient Moabite town; early (c. 6th cent.) mosaic map of Palestine found in Byzantine church here in 19th cent.

Mad·a·gas·car \ˌma-də-ˈgas-kər, -kär\. **1.** Island, W Indian Ocean off SE coast of Africa.

2. *formerly* **Mal·a·gasy Republic** \ˌma-lə-ˈga-sē\ *also* **Malgache Republic** \mȧl-ˈgȧsh\. Independent country occupying the island of Madagascar, Indian Ocean, separated from SE Africa by Mozambique Channel; 226,657 sq. mi. (587,042 sq. km.); pop. (1993e) 13,255,000; ✻ Antananarivo.

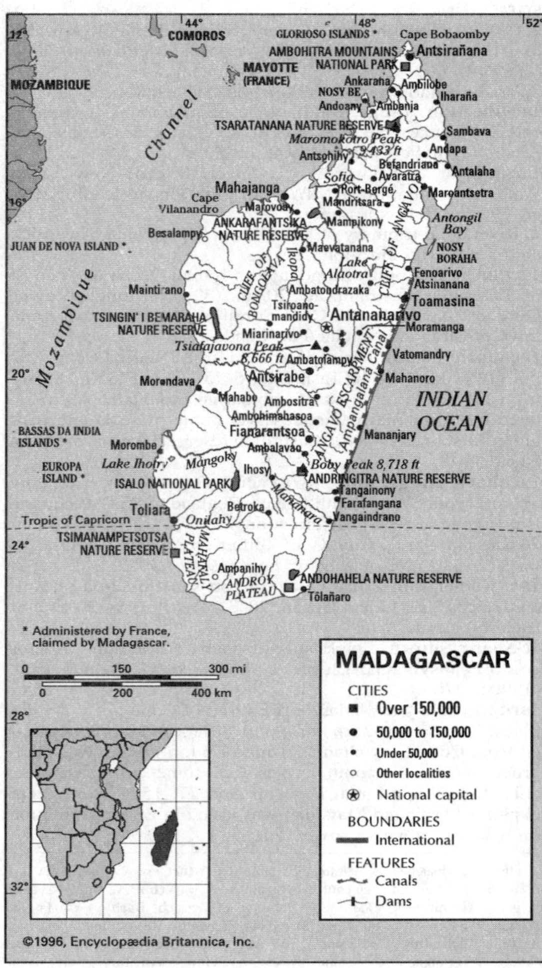

Physical features: Excluding Australia, the 4th largest island in the world; max. length 995 mi. (1601 km.), max. width 360 mi. (579 km.); plateaus and mountains cover the island; Ankaratra group (volcanic) in the center, and Tsaratanana Massif in the N (highest point 9449 ft. or 2880 m.). Has many short streams, most of them flowing E to W; among the more important are the Betsiboka and the Mangoky. Only large inlet is Antongil Bay on NE coast; numerous small islands along the coast, notably Ste.-Marie on the E and Nossi-Bé on NW.

Chief products: Rice, tobacco, coffee, sugar, cloves, vanilla, sisal, cotton, peanuts; livestock; graphite, mica, chromite; cement, soap, textiles, food products.

Chief towns: Antananarivo, Toamasina, Fianarantsoa, Mahajanga.

History: Natives of African and Indonesian descent arrived on island during first millennium A.D.; European discovery of island by Portuguese 1500; French stations maintained in 17th and 18th cents.; native kingdom expanded 18th cent.; with British assistance, came to rule most of Madagascar in 19th cent., and almost expelled Europeans before accession of a Christian ruler 1861; concluded treaty with France 1868; natives resisted French in war in 1883 and 1894–96; made French colony 1896 and gradually subdued; monarchy abolished by French 1897; in WWII aligned with Vichy France until occupied by British 1942; became an overseas territory within the French Union 1946; establishment of autonomous Malagasy Republic with membership in the French Community 1958; achieved independence 1960; adopted present constitution and name 1975.

Ma·dame Island \mə-ˈdam, ma-\. Island off S coast of Cape Breton I., Nova Scotia, Canada; belongs to Richmond co., Nova Scotia; the village of Arichat is on its S shore.

Ma·dang \ˈmä-ˌdäŋ\; *formerly* **Frie·drich–Wil·helms·ha·fen** \ˈfrē-drik-ˈvil-ˌhelmz-ˌhä-fən\. Seaport town, E New Guinea I., Papua New Guinea, on Astrolabe Bay; pop. (1990c) 27,057; good harbor; Japanese base in WWII, taken by Allies 1944.

Ma·da·ri·pur \mə-ˈdär-ē-ˌpu̇r\. Town, Bangladesh, on Ganges Delta; pop. (1991p) 46,842.

Ma·dau·ra \mə-ˈdȯr-ə\. Ancient city, Numidia, N Africa; near modern **Mdaou·rouch** \əm-ˈdau̇-ˌrüsh\, ab. 50 mi. (81 km.) NNW of Tebessa, Algeria; celebrated for its schools; birthplace of philosopher and writer Lucius Apuleius c. 124 A.D.; ruins of Roman colony, and of Byzantine fortress.

Mad·a·was·ka \ˌma-də-ˈwäs-kə\. **1.** Town, Aroostook co., N Maine, on St. John River 17 mi. (27 km.) ENE of Fort Kent; pop. (1990c) 4803.

2. River, SE Ontario, Canada; rises in lakes in Haliburton co. and flows SE and NE in Renfrew co. into the Ottawa River at Arnprior above Ottawa; 130 mi. (209 km.) long.

3. County in NW New Brunswick, Canada. See table at NEW BRUNSWICK.

Mad·da·le·na \ˌmä-dä-ˈlā-nä\. Island in Tyrrhenian Sea off extreme NE coast of Sardinia; pop. (1991p) 11,127; a commune of Sassari prov., Sardinia, Italy.

Maddalena, La. See LA MADDALENA.

Mad·da·lo·ni \ˌmä-dä-ˈlō-nē\. Commune, Caserta prov., Campania, S Italy, 15 mi. (24 km.) NNE of Naples; pop. (1989c) 37,059; aqueduct nearby.

Madeba. See MA'DABĀ.

Ma·dei·ra \mə-ˈdir-ə\. City, Hamilton co., SW corner of Ohio, NE suburb of Cincinnati; pop. (1990c) 9141.

Ma·dei·ra \mä-ˈdār-ə; mə-ˈdir-ə, -ˈder-\. **1.** River, W Brazil, formed by confluence of Bolivian rivers Mamoré and Beni at the Brazilian border; flows NE into Amazon below Manaus; 2013 mi. (3239 km.) long (with the Mamoré); most important tributary of Amazon.

2. Island group in E Atlantic Ocean off coast of Morocco, N of the Canary Is. and SE of the Azores, 32°30′N to 33°07′N and 16°13′W to 17°30′W; comprises two inhabited islands, Madeira and Porto Santo, and two groups of barren islets, the Desertas and Selvagens; ✻ Funchal on Madeira I.; constitutes an autonomous region of Portugal. See table at PORTUGAL.

History: Possibly known in ancient times, and probably known to Genoese by mid-14th cent.; rediscovered early 15th cent. by Portuguese navigator João Goncalves Zarco who founded Funchal 1421; British occupied Madeira for a short time in early 19th cent.

3. Largest island of the group ab. 440 mi. (708 km.) W of Morocco; ab. 34 mi. (55 km.) long and ab. 12 mi. (19 km.) wide; contains the group's ✻ Funchal; has deep ravines and rugged mountains, with highest Pico Ruivo 6106 ft. (1861 m.) in center of island; N coast is steep and very wild. Produces wine (*madeira*), sugar, bananas; fishing; tourism.

Ma·dei·ra Beach \mə-'dir-ə\. City, Pinellas co., W cen. Florida, on Boca Ciega Bay 5 mi. (8 km.) W of St. Petersburg; pop. (1990c) 4225.

Ma·dei·ra Falls \mä-'dār-ə\. Waterfall in the Madeira River, W Brazil, near junction of Mamoré and Beni rivers on the Bolivian border.

Mä·de·le·ga·bel \'med-ᵊl-ə-ˌgäb-əl\. Peak in the Algäu Alps, on the border bet. Bavaria, Germany and Tirol, Austria; 8689 ft. (2648 m.); 2d highest peak in Germany.

Madeleine, La. See LA MADELEINE.

Madeleine, Les Îles de la. See MAGDALEN ISLANDS.

Ma·de·leine, Ri·vière de la \rē-'vyer-də-lə-ˌmȧd-'len\. River, Gaspé Penin., SE Quebec, Canada; flows NE and N into St. Lawrence River; ab. 70 mi. (113 km.) long.

Mad·e·line Island \'mad-ᵊl-ən\. See APOSTLE ISLANDS.

Ma·de·ra \mə-'der-ə\. **1.** County in cen. California. See table at CALIFORNIA.

2. City, ⊗ of Madera co., cen. California, 20 mi. (32 km.) NW of Fresno; pop. (1990c) 29,281; founded 1876.

3. Volcano, Nicaragua; 4572 ft. (1394 m.); one of two peaks (see CONCEPCIÓN 3) on the island of Ometepe in Lake Nicaragua.

Madero, Ciudad. See CIUDAD MADERO.

Ma·dhav National Park \'mä-dəv\. National park, Madhya Pradesh, India; 61 sq. mi. (158 sq. km.); wildlife.

Madhumati. See GANGES DELTA.

Ma·dhya Bha·rat \'mä-dyə-'bär-ət\. Former state, cen. India; union of princely states, formed 1948; became part of Madhya Pradesh 1956.

Madhya Pra·desh \prə-'dāsh, -'desh\; *formerly* **Central Provinces and Be·rar** \bā-'rär\. State, cen. India; ✻ Bhopal; rice, wheat, corn, sugarcane, cotton; manganese, iron ore.

History: Area under Mogul Empire from 16th cent.; territory in Central Provinces conquered by Marathas in 18th cent. and ruled from Nagpur (*q.v.*); taken by British 19th cent.; Berar (*q.v.*) transferred to Central Provinces 1903; adopted present name 1950; present boundaries estab. 1956, incorporating former states of Bhopal, Madhya Bharat, and Vindhya Pradesh. See table at INDIA.

Ma·di·di \mä-'dē-dē\. River, NW Bolivia; flows NE into the Beni River; ab. 190 mi. (306 km.) long.

Ma·di·ke·ri \ˌmä-dē-'ker-ē\ *or* **Mer·ca·ra** \mer-'kä-rə\. Town, S Karnataka, India; pop. (1991p) 28,729.

Ma·dill \mə-'dil\. City, ⊗ of Marshall co., S Oklahoma, 22 mi. (35 km.) ESE of Ardmore; pop. (1990c) 3069.

Madīnah, Al–. See MEDINA 7.

Ma·dī·nat ash Sha'b \mȧ-'dē-ˌnət-ȧsh-'shȧb\; *formerly* **Al–It·ti·had** \ˌȧl-ˌi-ti-'hȧd\. Town, SW Yemen, ab. 10 mi. (16 km.) W of Aden; functioned as administrative ✻ of People's Democratic Republic of Yemen 1967.

Madioen. See MADIUN.

Mad·i·son \'ma-də-sən\. **1.** River, SW Montana; rises in S Gallatin co., flows W and N through Madison co. to unite with Jefferson and Gallatin rivers and form the Missouri River; ab. 180 mi. (290 km.) long.

2. Name of a parish in NE Louisiana and of counties in 19 states of the U.S. See tables at ALABAMA, ARKANSAS, FLORIDA, GEORGIA, IDAHO, ILLINOIS, INDIANA, IOWA, KENTUCKY, LOUISIANA, MISSISSIPPI, MISSOURI, MONTANA, NEBRASKA, NEW YORK, NORTH CAROLINA, OHIO, TENNESSEE, TEXAS, VIRGINIA.

3. City, Madison co., N Alabama, 7 mi. (11 km.) W of Huntsville; pop. (1990c) 14,904.

4. Town, SE New Haven co., S Connecticut, on Long Island Sound and Hammonasset River; pop. (1990c) 15,485.

5. City, ⊗ of Madison co., N Florida, 52 mi. (84 km.) E of Tallahassee; pop. (1990c) 3345.

6. City, ⊗ of Morgan co., N cen. Georgia, 25 mi. (40 km.) S of Athens; pop. (1990c) 3483.

7. City, Madison co., SW Illinois, 5 mi. (8 km.) N of East St. Louis; pop. (1990c) 4629.

8. City, ⊗ of Jefferson co., SE Indiana, on Ohio River 38 mi. (61 km.) NE of New Albany; pop. (1990c) 12,006.

9. Town, Somerset co., W Maine, on Kennebec River 20 mi. (32 km.) NW of Waterville; pop. (1990c) 4725.

10. City, ⊗ of Lac qui Parle co., W Minnesota, 22 mi. (35 km.) W of Montevideo; pop. (1990c) 1951.

11. City, Madison co., cen. Mississippi, N of Jackson; pop. (1990c) 7471.

12. City, ⊗ of Madison co., NE Nebraska, 14 mi. (23 km.) S of Norfolk; pop. (1990c) 2135.

13. Borough, Morris co., N New Jersey, 4 mi. (6 km.) SE of Morristown; pop. (1990c) 15,850; residential suburb; Drew Univ. (1866), Fairleigh Dickinson Univ. (1942); headquarters of Gen. Anthony Wayne during American Revolution.

14. City, ⊗ of Lake co., E South Dakota, 38 mi. (61 km.) NNW of Sioux Falls; pop. (1990c) 6257; summer resort; reconstructed 19th cent. prairie village nearby; Dakota State Univ. (1881).

15. Town, ⊗ of Madison co., N Virginia; pop. (1990c) 307.

16. City, ⊗ of Boone co., SW West Virginia; pop. (1990c) 3051.

17. City, ✻ of Wisconsin and ⊗ of Dane co., S Wisconsin, on isthmus bet. Lake Monona and Lake Mendota; pop. (1990c) 191,262; trade center for rich agricultural area; medical facilities; zoo; Univ. of Wisconsin–Madison (1848), Edgewood Coll. (1927); site chosen for ✻ of Wisconsin Terr. 1836; incorp. as village 1846, as city 1856.

Madison, Mount. Peak in the Presidential Range, White Mts., in S Coos co., N New Hampshire, N of Mt. Adams; 5363 ft. (1635 m.).

Madison Heights. City, Oakland co., SE Michigan, N suburb of Detroit; pop. (1990c) 32,196.

Mad·i·son·ville \'ma-də-sən-ˌvil\. **1.** City, ⊗ of Hopkins co., W Kentucky; pop. (1990c) 16,200.

2. Town, ⊗ of Monroe co., SE Tennessee; pop. (1990c) 3033; Hiwassee Coll. (1849).

3. City, ⊗ of Madison co., E cen. Texas, 33 mi. (53 km.) NE of Bryan; pop. (1990c) 3569.

Ma·di·un *or Du.* **Ma·di·oen** \ˌmä-dē-'ün\. **1.** Subdivision of the prov. of East Java, Java, Indonesia; 2348 sq. mi. (6081 sq. km.); ✻ Madiun. Region extends to S coast of island but has no port. Has fertile and well-watered plains in the N and lies bet. Mounts Lawu and Wilis. Produces rice, sugar, and teak; a residency of the former Netherlands Indies.

2. City, its ✻, on railroad line in cen. plain 90 mi. (145 km.) WSW of Surabaya; pop. (1990c) 170,242; repair shops of state railroads; scene of thwarted Communist rebellion 1948.

Madoera. See MADURA.

Madoera Strait. See MADURA STRAIT.

Mad·ra·ka, Cape \'ma-drə-kə\ *or Arab.* **Ras al–Mad·ra·kah** \ˌrȧs-ȧl-'mȧ-drȧ-kə\. Cape on E coast of Oman, SE Arabian Penin., extending into the Arabian Sea at 19°N, 57°52′E.

Mad·ras \'ma-drəs\. City, ⊗ of Jefferson co., N cen. Oregon; pop. (1990c) 3443.

Ma·dras \mə-'dras, -'dräs\. **1.** State, India. See TAMIL NADU.

2. *or* **Chen·nai** \'che-nī\. City, ✻ of Tamil Nadu state, India, on Coromandel Coast; pop. (1991c) 3,841,396; the main port on India's SE coast although harbor is wholly artificial; rail center; exports hides, cotton, magnesite; produces cotton textiles, railroad rolling stock; university (1857); technical institute (1959).

History: Founded c. 1640 by British East India Company; grew by process of accretion to original fort (**Fort Saint**

\ə\ abut \ᵊ\ kitten, Fr table \ər\ further \a\ ash \ā\ ace \ä\ cot, cart \ȧ\ Fr bac \au̇\ out \b̲\ Span Avila \ch\ chin \e\ bet \ē\ easy \g\ go \i\ hit \ī\ ice \j\ job \k̲\ Ger ich, Buch \ⁿ\ Fr vin \ŋ\ sing \ō\ go \ȯ\ all \ó\ law \œ\ Fr bœuf \œ̄\ Fr feu \ȯi\ boy \th\ thin \t̲h̲\ this \ü\ loot \u̇\ foot \ue\ Ger füllen \ue̅\ Fr rue \y\ yet \ʸ\ Fr digne \'dēnʸ\, nuit \'nwʸē\ \yü\ few \yu̇\ fury \zh\ vision

George \sānt-'jȯrj, sənt-\); captured by French 1746 but returned 1749 under terms of Treaty of Aix-la-Chapelle; besieged by French 1758–59 until relieved by English fleet; threatened by forces of Indian ruler Hyder Ali (Haidar Ali) 1769 and 1780; St. Thomé, now part of city, founded by Portuguese 16th cent., ceded to English 1749. Traditionally considered the burial place of the apostle St. Thomas.

Madras States. Former agency, S India, incl. five Indian states: Travancore, Cochin, Pudukkottai, Banganapalle, and Sandur; 10,757 sq. mi. (27,861 sq. km.).

Mad·re, La·gu·na \lə-'gü-nə-'mä-drē\. **1.** Long inlet of Gulf of Mexico bet. Padre I. and the mainland of S Texas, S of Corpus Christi.

2. Long narrow inlet of the Gulf of Mexico on coast of NE cen. Mexico, state of Tamaulipas.

Madre, María. See MARÍA MADRE.

Ma·dre de Dios \'mä-thrā-thā-'thyȯs\. River in Peru and Bolivia; rises in SE Peru, flows E across Bolivian border into Beni River in N Bolivia; 600 mi. (965 km.) long.

Madre de Dios Archipelago. Group of islands in S Pacific Ocean, off SW coast of Chile, N of Reina Adelaida Archipelago, and S of Wellington I.; 50°25′S, 75°05′W.

Ma·drid \mä-'thrēth, mə-'drid\. **1.** Autonomous community, historical region, and province of cen. Spain. See table at SPAIN.

2. City, ✻ of Spain and of Madrid autonomous community, historical region, and prov., cen. Spain, on Manzanares River; pop. (1991p) 2,909,792; principal transportation center of Spain; archiepiscopal see; commercial center for interior provinces; cultural center; important industrial city producing aircraft, electrical equipment, and leather goods; tourism; university (founded 1508 at Alcalá de Henares; transferred to Madrid 1836); formerly surrounded by 20-foot wall, three of the gates of which still remain; 18th cent. royal palace on site of old Moorish alcazar; numerous art galleries incl. esp. the Prado museum; national library; numerous parks, among them Buen Retiro gardens; several notable 17th and 18th cent. churches; bullring; El Escorial monastery and royal pantheon, often associated with Madrid, is 27 mi. (43 km.) NW of the city.

History: Moorish fortress from 10th cent.; taken from Moors by Alfonso VI of Castile c. 1083; made ✻ of Spain by Philip II 1561; occupied by French 1808–12 during Peninsular War; in Spanish Civil War held by Loyalists 1936–39, surrendered to Insurgents Mar. 1939.

Ma·driz \mä-'thrēs\. Department of NW cen. Nicaragua. See table at NICARAGUA.

Ma·dru·ga \mä-'thrü-gä\. Municipality, La Habana prov., W Cuba, 20 mi. (32 km.) WSW of Matanzas; pop. (1981p) 28,071.

Ma·du·ra *or Du.* **Ma·doe·ra** \mä-'dür-ə\. Island off NE coast of Java, Indonesia; a part of East Java prov.; 2113 sq. mi. (5473 sq. km.); pop. (1980c) 2,686,803; ✻ Pamekasan. Hilly, highest point 1545 ft. (471 m.). Chief economic activities include cattle breeding, fishing, and growing maize, cassava, and rice. Under Mataram from 1620s; Dutch influence estab. by end of 17th cent.; attached to Java as a residency 1885.

Ma·du·rai \,mä-də-'rī\ *or* **Mad·u·ra** \'ma-dyü-rə\. City, S Tamil Nadu, S India, 270 mi. (434 km.) SSW of Madras; pop. (1991c) 940,989; cotton cloth; tourism; university (1966). Noted for its great temple with colonnades and nine massive gate towers or gopuras adorned with elaborate carving and enclosing a quadrangle, the "Tank of the Golden Lilies"; also has several fine palaces. Was ✻ of old Pāndya dynasty from 5th cent. B.C. to end of 11th cent. A.D.; came under Vijayanagar kingdom in 14th cent.; under Nayak dynasty from mid-16th cent. to c. 1736 when taken by nabob of Carnatic; taken over by British East India Company 1801.

Ma·du·ra Strait *or Du.* **Ma·doe·ra Strait** \mä-'dür-ə\. Arm of the Java Sea, extending S of Madura I. and NE end of Java I., Indonesia; connects with Java Sea to the N by narrow Surabaja Strait W of Madura. Scene of battle Feb. 1942 in which *U.S.S. Marblehead* participated.

Maeander. See MENDERES 1.

Mae·ba·shi *also* **Ma·ye·bash·i** \,mä-yā-'bä-shē, mī-'bä-\. City, ✻ of Gumma prefecture, cen. Honshū, Japan; pop. (1990p) 286,261; in mountainous region with soil of volcanic origin favorable to the mulberry, hence noted as a center of growing silkworms and producing silk; university (1949).

Mae Hong Son *or* **Mae·hong·son** \'ma-'hȯŋ-'sȯn\ *also* **Mu·ai To** \'mü-'ī-'tō\. **1.** Province, NW Thailand; 5105 sq. mi. (13,222 sq. km.); pop. (1991e) 175,987; ✻ Mae Hong Son.

2. Town, its ✻, near Myanmar border 75 mi. (121 km.) NW of Chiang Mai; pop. (1991e) 6324.

Mae Klong *or* **Mae Khlong** \'mā-'klȯŋ\. River, W Thailand; rises at S end of Dawna Range, flows S and SSE to head of Gulf of Thailand; 250 mi. (402 km.) long.

Mael·strom \'māl-strəm, -,sträm\ *or Norw.* **Mal·strøm** \'mäl-,strœm\. Strong current in the Norwegian Sea, off the NW coast of Norway just S of Moskenes I.; under certain conditions of wind and tide forms a whirlpool; formerly exaggerated in accounts of its size and strength.

Mae·o·nia \mē-'ō-nē-ə\. Earlier name of Lydia, Asia Minor; later, a small district in NE Lydia.

Maeotis, Palus. See AZOV, SEA OF.

Maeseyck. See MAASEIK.

Maes·teg \mī-'steg\. Town, Mid Glamorgan co., S Wales, 12 mi. (19 km.) E of Swansea; pop. (1981p) 20,888; coal mining; apparel, automobile parts, cosmetics.

Maestra, Sierra. See SIERRA MAESTRA.

Maestricht. See MAASTRICHT.

Ma·é·wo \mä-'ā-wō, -vō\ *also* **Au·ro·ra** \ə-'rōr-ə, ȯ-\. Island, Vanuatu, SW Pacific Ocean, in NE part of the group 65 mi. (105 km.) E of Espíritu Santo I.; 29 mi. (47 km.) long and 4 mi. (6 km.) wide; 104 sq. mi. (269 sq. km.); pop. (1991e) 2362. Has long central range of mountains, thickly wooded.

Ma–fa–mu–ts'o. See MAPAM YUMCO.

Ma·fe·teng \'ma-fə-,teŋ\. Town, W Lesotho, ab. 38 mi. (61 km.) SSW of Maseru; area pop. (1986c) 206,423.

Ma·fia \'mä-fē-ə, 'ma-\. Island in the Indian Ocean off E coast of Tanzania, opp. mouth of Rufiji River, E Africa, ab. 90 mi. (145 km.) S of the N tip of Zanzibar; 170 sq. mi. (440 sq. km.); administratively a part of Tanzania.

Maf·i·keng \'ma-fə-kiŋ\. Town, ✻ of North-West prov., Rep. of South Africa, 160 mi. (257 km.) W of Pretoria; pop. (1980c) 6775; until 1965 seat of administration of Bechuanaland Protectorate (now Botswana). Trade and business center for region of dairy farming. Founded 1885. Starting point for the Jameson Raid, unsuccessful attempt to overthrow Transvaal's Boer government 1895; scene of famous siege 1899–1900 by Boers during Boer War.

Ma·fra \'ma-frə\. **1.** City, Santa Catarina state, S Brazil, on a headstream of the Iguaçu River 130 mi. (209 km.) NW of Florianópolis; munic. pop. (1980c) 40,673.

2. Commune, Lisboa dist., W Portugal, near Atlantic Ocean 16 mi. (26 km.) NNW of Lisbon; pop. (1991p) 44,340; monastery and palace containing a church and over 800 rooms, built in imitation of El Escorial, 1717–32.

Ma·ga·dan \,mə-gä-'dän\. Port, ✻ of Magadan Oblast E Russia in Asia, on N shore of Sea of Okhotsk; pop. (1992e) 152,000; fish canning; starting point of highways northward to head of navigation on the Kolyma.

Magadan Oblast \'ȯ-bləst, -,blast\ *or* **Ma·ga·dan·ska·ya Oblast'** \,mə-gə-'dän-skə-yə-'ȯ-bləstʸ\. Subdivision of NE Russia in Asia; 462,973 sq. mi. (1,199,100 sq. km.); pop. (1992e) 509,000; ✻ Magadan; mountainous region; formed 1953.

Ma·ga·dha \'mə-gə-də, 'mä-\. Ancient kingdom, India, incl. Bihar S of the Ganges; ✻ Pataliputra (*mod.* Patna); scene of many events in life of Siddhārtha Gautama Buddha, founder of Buddhism. A kingdom of early prominence c. 7th cent. B.C.; expanded under Bimbisāra 6th–5th cents. B.C.; became especially powerful, comprising most of Indian subcontinent, under the Maurya dynasty (c. 321–185 B.C.) founded by Candragupta Maurya and extended by Aśoka mid-3d cent. B.C., who strongly supported the spread of Buddhism; kingdom soon declined to obscurity until revived by the later Gupta dynasty 4th cent. A.D.; declined 5th cent.

Ma·ga·di \mä-ˈgä-dē\. Town, S cen. Kenya, 50 mi. (81 km.) SSW of Nairobi; terminus of railroad branch line.

Magadi, Lake. Lake, S Kenya, near Tanzanian border; 240 sq. mi. (622 sq. km.); ab. 30 mi. (48 km.) long; has large soda deposits. See NATRON, LAKE.

Ma·gal·la·nes \ˌmä-gä-ˈlyä-nās\. **1.** Former province of S Chile.
2. City, Chile. See PUNTA ARENAS.

Magallanes, Estrecho de. See MAGELLAN, STRAIT OF.

Magallanes y An·tár·ti·ca Chi·le·na \ē-ˌän-ˈtär-tē-kä-chē-ˈlā-nä\. Region of S Chile; estab. 1974. See table at CHILE.

Ma·gan·gué \mä-ˌgäŋ-ˈgā\. Town, Bolívar dept., N Colombia, at the junction of the Cauca and Magdalena rivers 90 mi. (145 km.) SE of Cartagena; munic. pop. (1985c) 52,154.

Ma·ga·noy \ˌmä-gä-ˈnȯi\. Municipality, ✻ of Maguindanao prov., Mindanao I., Philippines.

Ma·gat \mä-ˈgät\. River, an important left tributary of the upper Cagayan River, NE Luzon, Philippines; rises in Caraballo Mts. and flows generally NE to the Cagayan above Ilagan; ab. 90 mi. (145 km.) long.

Mag·a·zine Mountain \ˈma-gə-ˌzēn\. Peak, Logan co., NW cen. Arkansas, in Ouachita Mts.; 2753 ft. (839 m.); highest point in state.

Mag·da·la \ˈmag-də-lə\ *also* **Mig·dal** \mig-ˈdäl\ *or* **Maj·dal** \ˈmȧj-ˌdȧl\. Ancient town, Palestine, on the W shore of the Sea of Galilee; now an archaeological site just N of Tiberias, Israel. Considered home of Mary Magdalene (*Luke* viii. 2).

Mag·da·le·na \ˌmag-də-ˈlā-nə, ˌmäg-dä-ˈlā-nä\. **1.** Island, Chile, off SW coast of mainland, NE of Chonos Archipelago.
2. River, S cen. and N Colombia; rises on E slopes of Andes in S Colombia, flows N into the Caribbean Sea near Barranquilla (*q.v.*); 956 mi. (1538 km.) long; navigable for over 930 mi. (1496 km.); with its many tributaries provides ab. 2500 mi. (4025 km.) of navigable waterways.
3. Department of N Colombia. See table at COLOMBIA.
4. Island, Marquesas Is. See FATU HIVA.

Magdalena, María. See MARÍA MAGDALENA.

Magdalena Bay. Inlet of Pacific Ocean on SW coast of Baja California, Mexico.

Mag·da·len Islands \ˈmag-də-lən\ *or Fr.* **Les Îles de la Ma·de·leine** \lā-ˌzēl-də-lə-mȧd-ˈlen\. Island group, S cen. part of the Gulf of St. Lawrence, E Quebec, Canada; 102 sq. mi. (264 sq. km.); pop. (1991c) 13,991; comprises 13 islands (largest are Coffin, Amherst, Grindstone). About 50 mi. (81 km.) N of East Point, Prince Edward I. and ab. 100 mi. (160 km.) SW of Newfoundland. Most of inhabitants are Acadians; chief occupation fishing; discovered 1534 by French explorer Jacques Cartier.

Mag·de·burg \ˈmäg-də-ˌbu̇rk, ˈmag-də-ˌbərg\. **1.** District of former East Germany; 4450 sq. mi. (11,526 sq. km.); now largely in Saxony-Anhalt.
2. City, ✻ of Saxony-Anhalt state, E cen. Germany and formerly of Magdeburg dist., East Germany, on Elbe River 82 mi. (132 km.) WSW of Berlin; pop. (1992e) 275,238; most important inland port of E Germany; railroad junction; chemicals, textiles; sugar refineries; technical college (1953); 13th–16th cent. cathedral; 11th cent. church. First mentioned 805 A.D.; made archiepiscopal see 962; member of Hanseatic League for nearly 200 years; adopted Reformation 1524; sacked and burned during Thirty Years' War 1631; captured by French 1806; to Prussia 1814–15; heavily bombed by Allies in WWII. Birthplace of physicist Otto von Guericke (1602), composer Georg Telemann (1681), and American Revolutionary Gen. Baron von Steuben (1730).

Ma·ge·lang \ˌmä-gā-ˈläŋ\. City, Central Java prov., Indonesia, 37 mi. (60 km.) SSW of Semarang; pop. (1990c) 123,213; center for tourists visiting Borobudur temple (*q.v.*); almost in exact geographical center of Java on railroad line bet. Semarang on the N and Yogyakarta on the S; in fertile plain (alt. 1100 ft. or 335 m.) with high mountains on E and W.

Ma·gel·lan, Strait of \mə-ˈje-lən, *chiefly Brit.* -ˈge-\ *or Span.* **Es·tre·cho de Ma·gal·la·nes** \ā-ˈstrā-chō-t͟hā-ˌmä-gä-ˈlyä-nās\. Strait at S extremity of South America, passing in a winding course bet. the mainland and Tierra del Fuego Archipelago (*q.v.*); 350 mi. (563 km.) long; it connects the South Atlantic with the South Pacific, both its entrance and exit being 52°30′S. Dungeness Point (on N) and Cape Espíritu Santo (on S) mark entrance from the Atlantic; Cape Pilar at NW extremity of Desolación I. marks entrance from the Pacific. Punta Arenas (formerly Magallanes) is only town of importance on its course. Discovered 1520 by Portuguese explorer Ferdinand Magellan.

Ma·gens Bay \ˈmā-gənz\. Bay in N coast of St. Thomas I., Virgin Is. of the U.S., West Indies; known for its beautiful beach.

Ma·gen·ta \mä-ˈjen-tä\. Commune, Milano prov., Lombardy, N Italy, 14 mi. (23 km.) W of Milan; pop. (1991p) 22,916; scene of victory of French and Sardinian army over Austrian forces June 4, 1859; magenta dye named after this battle.

Ma·ger·øya \ˈmä-gə-ˌrȯi-yə\ *or* **Ma·ger·øy** \-ˌrȯi\. Island, Norway, in Arctic Ocean off N coast; 111 sq. mi. (288 sq. km.); its N tip is North Cape (*q.v.*).

Ma·gers·fon·tein \ˈmä-gərz-ˌfōn-ˌtān\. Battlefield, W Free State, E cen. Rep. of South Africa; battle Dec. 1899 in which Boers checked British advance toward Kimberly.

Ma·ge·tan \mä-ˈge-ˌtän\. Town, East Java prov., Indonesia, a few miles W of Madiun at foot of Mt. Lawu.

Mag·gia \ˈmä-jä\. River, Ticino canton, SE cen. Switzerland; rises in Lepontine Alps, flows SE into N end of Lake Maggiore near Locarno; ab. 35 mi. (56 km.) long; hydroelectric power stations.

Maggiorasca, Monte. Highest mountain in the Ligurian Apennines. See table at APENNINES.

Mag·gio·re, Lake \mä-ˈjō-rā\; *anc.* **Ver·ba·nus La·cus** \vər-ˈbā-nəs-ˈlā-kəs\. Lake, N Italy and S Switzerland; traversed (N to S) by Ticino River; Locarno, Ticino canton, Switzerland, is at N end; 40 mi. (64 km.) long and ab. 2 mi. (3 km.) wide; 81 sq. mi. (210 sq. km.); max. depth 1220 ft. (372 m.); has many resorts on its shores and is nearly surrounded by mountains of S Lepontine Alps. See BORROMEAN ISLANDS.

Magh·er·a·felt \ˌma-krə-ˈfelt, ˌma-hə-rə-\. **1.** District, cen. Northern Ireland; estab. 1974. See table at IRELAND, NORTHERN.
2. Town, its ⊗.

Maghiana. See JHANG-SADAR.

Ma·ghreb *also* **Ma·ghrib** \ˈmə-grəb\. Region of NW Africa and, during the Moorish occupation, Spain; used specifically of the Mediterranean coastal areas of Morocco, Algeria, Tunisia, and, sometimes, Libya, but often extended to refer to those countries in their entirety.

Ma·gi·cienne Bay \ˌmä-zhē-ˈsyen\. Inlet on SE coast of Saipan I., Mariana Is.

Ma·gil·li·gan Point \mə-ˈgi-li-gən\. Cape on N coast of Ireland, on E side of entrance to Lough Foyle.

Ma·gi·not Line \mȧ-zhē-ˈnō; ˌma-zhə-ˈnō, -jə-\. A system of defensive fortifications built 1930s by France to protect its eastern border—named after French Minister of War André Maginot (1877–1932); extended nearly 200 mi. (322 km.) from S of Belfort to the Belgian border; was position of major part of French army during first few months of WWII but yielded with little fighting after German invasion of Low Countries and collapse of French armies in 1940.

Mag·le·mo·se \ˈmag̅-lə-ˌmō-sə\. Locality on W coast of Sjælland, Denmark, NW of Slagelse; archaeological site yielding bone and stone implements.

Mag·na \ˈmag-nə\. Unincorporated settlement, Salt Lake co., N Utah, ab. 12 mi. (19 km.) WSW of Salt Lake City; pop. (1990c) 17,829.

Magna Grae·cia \ˈmag-nə-ˈgrē-shə\. Collective name for the seaport colonies of ancient Greece in S Italy; chief cities Tarentum (*mod.* Taranto), Sybaris, Crotona (*mod.* Crotone), Heraclea (*qq.v.*).

Mag·ne·sia \mag-ˈnē-zhə, -shə\. **1.** Narrow coastal district in ancient Thessaly, Greece, extending along the Aegean Sea from Peneus River S to and incl. the peninsula enclosing Pagasitikós Kólpos (Gulf of Pagasaí) on the E; according to tradition its inhabitants founded both cities of the same name in Asia Minor.

2. Department of Greece, approx. coextensive with ancient district. See table at GREECE.

3. *or* **Magnesia ad Mae·an·drum** \ˌad-mē-ˈan-drəm\. Ancient city, W Asia Minor, on the Maeander (Menderes) near its mouth, SE of Ephesus and just NE of modern Turkish town of Söke. Destroyed by Cimmerians c. 650 B.C. but rebuilt by Ionian colonists; site of temple to Artemis.

4. *or* **Magnesia ad Sipylum.** City, Turkey. See MANISA 2.

Mag·net·ic Island \mag-ˈne-tik\. Island, Australia, off the coast of Queensland, NE of Townsville and within the marine park of Great Barrier Reef.

Magnetic Pole. Either of two spots on Earth's surface toward which the compass needle points from any direction throughout adjacent regions (except in their immediate vicinity where the horizontal intensity is so small that the compass cannot be used to determine direction) and at which the needle dips vertically. The **North Magnetic Pole** was formerly located on W shore of Boothia Penin., Canada, at approx. 71°N, 96°W. (British Admiralty charts 70°40′N, 96°50′W), this location differing by nearly a degree from that found by Scottish explorer Sir James C. Ross in 1831; according to calculations made in 1984 it was located at 77°N, 102°18′W. The location of the **South Magnetic Pole** was calculated (1970) to be at 66°S, 139°06′E. Locations cannot be exactly fixed because of variations in positions due to several causes.

Mag·ni·to·gorsk \məg-ˌnē-tə-ˈgȯrsk\. City, SW Chelyabinsk Oblast, W Russia in Asia, on the left bank of the Ural River 160 mi. (257 km.) SSW of the city of Chelyabinsk; pop. (1992e) 441,000; site of one of the world's largest integrated metallurgical plants; also produces cement. For centuries a village on steppe E of the Urals, inhabited by Bashkirs and Kirghiz engaged in cattle raising; named **Mag·nit·na·ya** \məg-ˈnēt-nə-yə\ in early 18th cent. after discovery that two small mountains (Aider-Ly and Atach) nearby consisted of magnetized iron; began to be developed c. 1930 by the Soviet government; by 1933 had become a large city.

Mag·no·lia \mag-ˈnōl-yə\. **1.** City, ⊗ of Columbia co., SW Arkansas, 35 mi. (54 km.) W of El Dorado; pop. (1990c) 11,151; Southern Arkansas Univ. (1909).

2. City, ⊗ of Pike co., S Mississippi, 7 mi. (11 km.) S of McComb; pop. (1990c) 2245.

3. Borough, Camden co., SW New Jersey, 8 mi. (13 km.) SSE of the city of Camden; pop. (1990c) 4861.

Mago. See MANGO.

Ma·gof·fin \mə-ˈgä-fən\. County in E Kentucky. See table at KENTUCKY.

Ma·gog \ˈmā-ˌgäg\. City, S Quebec, Canada, on N end of Lake Memphremagog 17 mi. (27 km.) SW of Sherbrooke; pop. (1991c) 14,034; textiles; resort; founded c. 1776 by Loyalist emigrants from U.S.

Magosa. See FAMAGUSTA.

Ma·gra \ˈmä-grä\. River, NW Italy; rises near Cisa and marks approximately the line bet. the Ligurian and Tuscan Apennines; flows S into Ligurian Sea near La Spezia; ab. 40 mi. (64 km.) long.

Ma·gua·ri·nho, Cape \ˌmȧ-gwȧ-ˈrē-nyü\; *formerly* **Cape Ma·gua·rí** \ˌmȧ-gwȧ-ˈrē\. Cape on NE extremity of Marajó I. at the mouth of the Amazon River, NE Brazil.

Ma·guin·da·nao \mä-ˌgwin-dä-ˈnä-ˌō, -ˈnau̇\. Province, SW Mindanao, Philippines; ✻ Maganoy. See table at PHILIPPINES.

Maguntiacum. See MAINZ.

Ma·gwe \mə-ˈgwā\. **1.** Division of W cen. Myanmar. See table at MYANMAR.

2. Town, its ✻, on left bank of Irrawaddy 145 mi. (233 km.) SW of Mandalay; pop. (1983c) 54,881.

Magyar Köztársaság. See HUNGARY.

Magyarország. See HUNGARY.

Magyaróvár. See MOSONMAGYARÓVÁR.

Mah·ā·bād \ˌmä-hä-ˈbäd\; *formerly* **Sa·uj·bu·lagh** \sä-ˌüj-bü-ˈläg\. Town, West Azerbaijan prov., NW Iran; 20 mi. (32 km.) S of Daryācheh-ye Orūmīyeh; pop. (1986c) 75,238.

Ma·ha·ba·lesh·war \mə-ˌhä-bə-ˈlesh-wər\. Village and hill station, cen. Maharashtra, W India, ab. 90 mi. (145 km.) SE of Bombay; pop. (1991p) 10,564; on summit of a ridge of Western Ghats, alt. 4500 ft. (1372 m.); rainfall excessive, often 300 to 400 in. (750 to 1000 cm.) per year; near source of the Krishna River, sacred to the Hindus.

Ma·ha·jam·ba Bay \ˌmä-hə-jäm-bə-\. Inlet of Mozambique Channel, on NW coast of Madagascar.

Ma·ha·jan·ga \ˌmä-hä-ˈjäŋ-gä\ *also* **Ma·jun·ga** \mä-ˈjüŋ-gä\. Seaport town on Bombetoka Bay, NW coast of Madagascar; pop. (1990e) 121,967; sugar, soap, cement; base for French expeditionary force 1895.

Ma·ha·kam \mə-ˈhä-kəm\ *also* **Ku·tai** *or* **Koe·tai** \kü-ˈtī\. River, East Kalimantan prov., E Borneo, Indonesia; rises in mountains of cen. Borneo and flows ESE to Makassar Strait in wide delta ab. 1°S of the Equator; ab. 400 mi. (645 km.) long; navigable for most of its course; ab. 100 mi. (160 km.) from its mouth joined in a region of marsh and lakes by the Belajan and Telen. Samarinda is the port near its mouth.

Mahalla El Kubra, El. See EL MAHALLA EL KUBRA.

Mahamakam Tank. See KUMBAKONAM.

Ma·ha·na·di *also* **Ma·ha·nud·dy** \mə-ˈhä-nə-dē\. River, SE India; rises in mountains of S Madhya Pradesh, flows N, turns E, and flows S and E through Orissa to the Bay of Bengal through several mouths E of Cuttack; ab. 560 mi. (900 km.) long; its chief tributary is the Seonath. Has great volume in flood season; its waters source of irrigation system.

Ma·ha·noy City \ˌmä-hə-ˈnȯi\. Borough, Schuylkill co., E cen. Pennsylvania, 12 mi. (19 km.) NE of Pottsville; pop. (1990c) 5209.

Mahanoy Mountain. Ridge in Schuylkill and Northumberland cos., E cen. Pennsylvania; highest point 1745 ft. (532 m.); forms N boundary of Mahanoy coal basin and contains deposits of anthracite.

Mahanuddy. See MAHANADI.

Ma·ha·rash·tra \ˌmä-hə-ˈräsh-trə\. **1.** Region of W cen. India marking the original land of the Marathas; it lay S of the Narmada and extended from E of Nagpur westward to the coast bet. Daman and Goa; its chief cities were Pune and Satara.

2. State, W cen. India; comprises the Marathi-speaking SE portion of former Bombay state; bounded on W by the Arabian Sea; ✻ Bombay; rice, wheat, cotton, manganese; textiles, electrical engineering; largest cities: Bombay, Nagpur, Pune, Sholapur. Formed 1960; suffered large number of deaths in earthquake 1993. See GUJARAT 3 and table at INDIA.

Ma·ha·rès \ˌmä-hä-ˈres\. Coastal town, E Tunisia, on Gulf of Gabès SW of Sfax.

Ma·ha Sa·ra·kham *or* **Ma·ha·sa·ra·gam** \mə-ˈhä-sə-ˈrä-ˌkäm\ *also* **Ta·lat** \tä-ˈlät\. **1.** Province, E cen. Thailand; 2224 sq. mi. (5760 sq. km.); pop. (1991e) 909,429; ✻ Maha Sarakham.

2. Town, its ✻, 16 mi. (26 km.) NW of Roi Et; pop. (1991e) 36,483.

Ma·has·ka \mə-ˈhas-kə\. County in SE cen. Iowa. See table at IOWA.

Ma·ha·we·li \ˌma-hä-ˈwā-lē\ *or* **Ma·ha·ve·li–gan·ga** \ˌma-hä-ˈvä-lē-ˈgəŋ-gä\. Chief river (*ganga*) of Sri Lanka; flows N from S cen. part of the country to Bay of Bengal S of Trincomalee; 206 mi. (332 km.) long.

Mah·bub·na·gar \mə-ˈbüb-nə-gər\. Town, S Andhra Pradesh, S cen. India, 55 mi. (89 km.) SSW of Hyderabad; pop. (1991p) 116,775.

Mah·dia \mə-ˈdē-ə\. Seaport town, E Tunisia, SE of Sousse; pop. (1989e) 35,742; fishing; founded 912.

Ma·hé *or* **Ma·he** \mä-ˈā\. **1.** Chief island, Seychelles, Indian Ocean; 59 sq. mi. (153 sq. km.); pop. (1990e) 61,183; chief town Victoria; mountainous, highest point 2993 ft. (912 m.).

2. *formerly* **May·ya·li** \mī-ˈyä-lē\. Town, SW India, on Malabar Coast ab. 40 mi. (64 km.) N of Calicut; 23 sq. mi. (60 sq. km.); pop. (1991p) 10,437; formerly only French settlement on W coast of India. Occupied by French 1726; changed hands several times in French-English wars, restored to

France 1817; ceded to India 1954 and made part of territory of Pondicherry.

Ma·he·bourg \ˌmä-ā-ˈbu̇r\. Town on the SE coast of the island of Mauritius; pop. (1981c) 13,759.

Ma·he·sā·na \mə-ˌhā-ˈsä-nə\ *also* **Meh·sa·na** \mā-ˈsä-nə\. Town, Gujarat, W India, N of Ahmadabad; pop. (1991p) 109,540.

Ma·hi \ˈmä-hē\. River, W India; rises in NW Madhya Pradesh, flows NW and SW through S Rajputana and Gujarat into a wide estuary at the head of the Gulf of Khambhat, E of the mouth of the Sabarmati River; 350 mi. (563 km.) long.

Ma·hia Peninsula \ˈmä-hē-ə\. Peninsula projecting S from E cen. coast of North I., New Zealand, forming E side of Hawke Bay, 39°10′S, 177°54′E.

Ma·hi·lyow *or* **Mo·gi·lev** \mə-gi-ˈlyȯf\. **1.** Subdivision of Belarus, in E part; 11,197 sq. mi. (29,000 sq. km.); pop. (1991e) 1,269,400; ✱ Mahilyow; flax; dairying, timber.
2. City, its ✱, on both banks of the Dnieper, 112 mi. (180 km.) E of Minsk; pop. (1991e) 363,000; produces construction machinery, synthetic fibers, leather goods; has several old churches and an ancient tower built by the Tatars. Founded 13th cent.; control changed hands frequently bet. Lithuania, Poland, Sweden, and Russia; finally annexed to Russia 1772 in First Partition of Poland; near here Russian army under Prince Pyotr Ivanovich Bagration was defeated 1812 by French; in WWII occupied by Germans 1941–44.

Mah·no·men \mȯ-ˈnō-mən\. **1.** County in NW Minnesota. See table at MINNESOTA.
2. Village, its ⊗; pop. (1990c) 1154.

Ma·hom·et \mə-ˈhä-mət\. Village, Champaign co., E Illinois, NW of the city of Champaign; pop. (1990c) 3103.

Ma·hón \mä-ˈȯn\ *or Eng.* **Port Ma·hon** \mə-ˈhōn\; *anc.* **Por·tus Ma·go·nis** \ˈpōr-təs-mə-ˈgō-nəs\. Seaport, ✱ of Minorca I., Baleares prov., Spain, 89 mi. (143 km.) ENE of Palma; pop. (1991p) 21,564; good natural harbor, formerly of strategic importance. Founded by Carthaginians and named for Gen. Mago; held by Moors 8th–13th cents.; to kingdom of Aragon 13th cent.; sacked by Barbary pirate Barbarossa (Redbeard) 1535; occupied by English 1708–56 and 1763–82; by French 1756–62; captured by Spain 1782 and fully restored to Spain by Treaty of Amiens 1802.

Ma·hone Bay \mə-ˈhōn\. Inlet of Atlantic Ocean in Lunenburg co., S Nova Scotia, Canada; the city of Lunenburg is located at its S entrance.

Ma·ho·ning \mə-ˈhō-niŋ\. **1.** River, NE Ohio and Pennsylvania; rises in Columbiana co., E Ohio, flows NE then SE through Youngstown into Pennsylvania and joins Shenango River 4 mi. (6 km.) SW of New Castle to form Beaver River; ab. 95 mi. (155 km.) long.
2. County in NE Ohio. See table at OHIO.

Ma·ho·pac \ˈmā-ə-ˌpak\. Village, Putnam co., SE New York, on **Lake Mahopac**, ab. 12 mi. (19 km.) NE of Peekskill; pop. (1990c) 7755; center of a resort region.

Mah·ra \ˈmär-ə\. Former sultanate in E Ḥaḍramawt on S coast of Arabian Penin., now part of Yemen; mainly desert; chief town port of Qishn, 200 mi. (322 km.) ENE of Al Mukallā.

Mähren. See MORAVIA.

Mährisch–Ostrau. See OSTRAVA.

Mährisch–Schönberg. See ŠUMPERK.

Mah·to·me·di \ˌmät-ə-ˈmē-ˌdī\. Village, Washington co., E Minnesota; pop. (1990c) 5569.

Mai·ao \ˈmī-ˌau̇\ *also* **Tu·bai Ma·nu** \ˈtü-ˌbī-ˈmä-ˌnü\. Small island of the Society Is., most easterly of the Leeward Is., S Pacific Ocean, 45 mi. (72 km.) W of Mooréa; ab. 3 sq. mi. (8 sq. km.).

Mai·dan *or* **May·dān** \mī-ˈdan, mā-\. Town, NE Iraq, on upper Diyala near Iranian border, NNE of Baghdad.

Maid·en \ˈmād-ᵊn\. Town, Catawba co., W cen. North Carolina, 22 mi. (35 km.) N of Gastonia; pop. (1990c) 2574.

Maid·en·head \ˈmād-ᵊn-ˌhed\. Town, Berkshire, S England, on the Thames 27 mi. (43 km.) W of London; pop. (1981c) 60,461; engineering; pharmaceuticals; computer software; chartered 1582.

Maid·ens \ˈmād-ᵊnz\. Group of rocks, NE Northern Ireland, in the Irish Sea off E coast of Larne dist.; lighthouse.

Maid·stone \ˈmād-stən, -ˌstōn\. Town, ⊗ of Kent, SE England, on the Medway 30 mi. (48 km.) ESE of London; pop. (1991p) 133,200; papermaking, brewing; site of Roman station; received first charter 1549.

Maid·stone Lake \ˈmād-ˌstōn\. Lake in E Essex co., NE corner of Vermont.

Mai·du·gu·ri \mī-ˈdü-gə-rē\. Town, ✱ of Borno state, NE Nigeria; in Lake Chad region ab. 315 mi. (507 km.) E of Kano; pop. (1991e) 281,900; peanut processing.

Mai·har \ˈmī-hər\. **1.** Former Indian state, now part of Madhya Pradesh, E cen. India, 412 sq. mi. (1067 sq. km.).
2. Town, its ✱, NE Madhya Pradesh, ab. 95 mi. (155 km.) NNE of Jabalpur.

Mai·ka·la Range \ˈmī-kə-lə\. Mountain range in cen. India, extending NE to SW chiefly in NE Madhya Pradesh; highest point 3185 ft. (971 m.).

Maikop. See MAYKOP.

Mai·li \ˈmī-lē\. City, Honolulu co., Hawaii, 20 mi. (32 km.) WNW of the city of Honolulu; pop. (1990c) 6059.

Maimachin. See ALTANBULAG.

Mai·mā·na. See MEYMANEH.

Maimansingh. See MYMENSINGH.

Main \ˈmīn, ˈmān\; *anc.* **Moe·nus** \ˈmē-nəs\. **1.** River, S cen. Germany; rises in the Fichtelgebirge in N Bavaria, flows W into the Rhine opp. Mainz, passing through Wurzburg, Aschaffenburg, and Frankfurt in its course; 325 mi. (523 km.) long; navigable for ab. 240 mi. (385 km.).
2. River, NE Northern Ireland; flows into Lough Neagh; ab. 30 mi. (48 km.) long.

Main Barrier Range \ˈmān\ *also* **Stan·ley Range** \ˈstan-lē\. Mountain range, W New South Wales, SE Australia; highest point ab. 2000 ft. (610 m.); rich in lead, silver, and zinc ores.

Mai–Ndom·be, Lac \ˈmī-ən-ˈdȯm-bē\; *formerly* **Lake Leo·pold II** \ˈlē-ə-ˌpōld-t͟hə-ˈse-kənd\. Lake, W Democratic Rep. of the Congo; 900 to 3200 sq. mi. (2350 to 8300 sq. km.) according to the season; drains S into Fimi River and on into the Congo.

Maine \ˈmān\. A northeast state of U.S.A., bounded on N and E by Canadian province of New Brunswick, on S by Atlantic Ocean, on W by New Hampshire and Canadian province of Quebec; 39th state in area, 33,265 sq. mi. or 86,156 sq. km. (land area 30,933 sq. mi. or 80,116 sq. km.); 38th state in population, (1990c) 1,227,928; ✱ Augusta; 23d state admitted to Union (1820). See table of states at UNITED STATES.

Nickname: Pine Tree State.

State flower: White pine cone and tassel.

Motto: Dirigo (I Direct).

Rivers: St. Croix, forming lower section of E boundary; Penobscot, flowing from cen. area S to Atlantic Ocean; Kennebec, flowing from W cen. region S to Atlantic Ocean; Salmon Falls forming section of extreme SW boundary.

Lakes: Has ab. 1600; the largest Moosehead, Sebago, Chesuncook, Chamberlain, Grand, and the Rangeley Lakes.

Highest point: Mt. Katahdin, 5268 ft. (1606 m.), in Piscataquis co.

Chief products: Potatoes, blueberries, apples; poultry; gravel; tourism; fishing (esp. lobstering); manufacturing: food products, leather goods, paper, wood products.

Chief cities: Portland, Lewiston, Bangor, Auburn, South Portland, Augusta, Biddeford.

Political divisions: Divided into the following 16 counties (for pronunciation of their names, see their individual entries):

NAME	AREA[1] (sq. mi.)	AREA[1] (sq. km.)	POP. (1990c)	CO. SEAT
Androscoggin	474	1,228	105,259	Auburn
Aroostook	6,721	17,407	86,936	Houlton
Cumberland	879	2,277	243,135	Portland

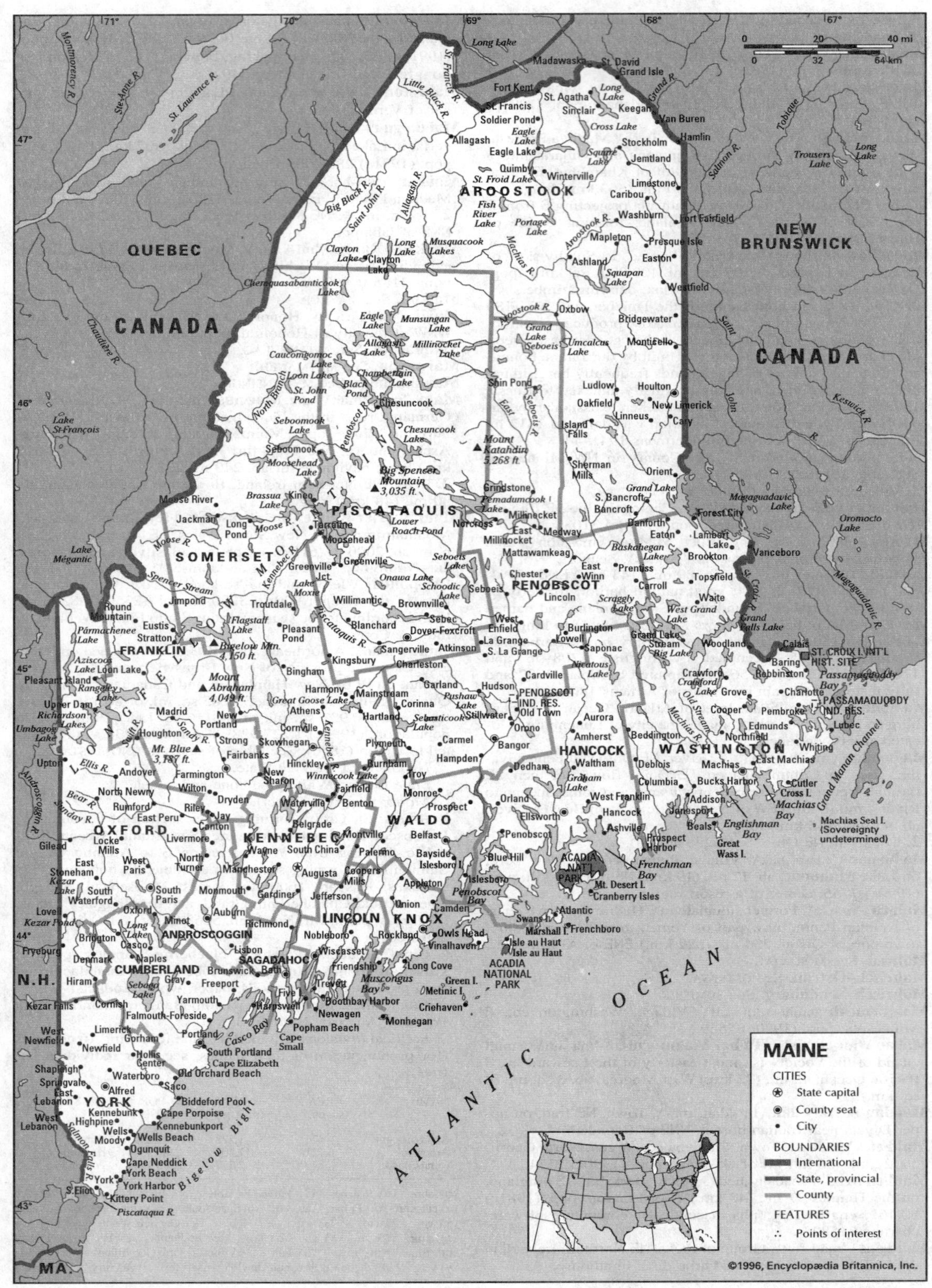
MAINE
CITIES
State capital
County seat
City
BOUNDARIES
International
State, provincial
County
FEATURES
Points of interest
0 20 40 mi
0 32 64 km
71°
70°
69°
68°
67°
47°
46°
45°
44°
43°
QUEBEC
CANADA
NEW BRUNSWICK
CANADA
N.H.
MA.
ATLANTIC OCEAN
LONGFELLOW MOUNTAINS
AROOSTOOK
PISCATAQUIS
SOMERSET
PENOBSCOT
FRANKLIN
OXFORD
KENNEBEC
WALDO
HANCOCK
WASHINGTON
ANDROSCOGGIN
CUMBERLAND
SAGADAHOC
LINCOLN
KNOX
YORK
Montmorency R.
Ste-Anne R.
St. Lawrence R.
Chaudière R.
Lake St-François
Lake Mégantic
Long Lake
Madawaska
St. David
Grand Isle
Fort Kent
St. Francis
St. Agatha
Long Lake
Sinclair
Keegan
Van Buren
Soldier Pond
Cross Lake
Hamlin
Eagle Lake
Allagash
Eagle Lake
Square Lake
Stockholm
Jemtland
Quimby
St. Froid Lake
Winterville
Limestone
Caribou
Fish River Lake
Portage Lake
Washburn
Fort Fairfield
Mapleton
Presque Isle
Ashland
Squapan Lake
Easton
Westfield
Oxbow
Bridgewater
Monticello
Umcalcus Lake
Grand Lake Seboeis
Shin Pond
Ludlow
Houlton
Oakfield
New Limerick
Linneus
Cary
Island Falls
Sherman Mills
Orient
Grand Lake
S. Bancroft
Bancroft
Forest City
Danforth
Eaton
Lambert Lake
Brookton
Vanceboro
Topsfield
Waite
Baskahegan Lake
Prentiss
Carroll
Scraggly Lake
West Grand Lake
Grand Falls Lake
Grand Lake Stream
Big Lake
Woodland
Calais
Baring
Robbinston
ST. CROIX I. INT'L HIST. SITE
Passamaquoddy Bay
Charlotte
PASSAMAQUODDY IND. RES.
Pembroke
Lubec
Crawford
Crawford Lake
Grove
Cooper
Edmunds
Whiting
Northfield
Beddington
Deblois
Machias
East Machias
Cutler
Cross I.
Machias Bay
Columbia
Bucks Harbor
Addison
Jonesport
Beals
Englishman Bay
Great Wass I.
Machias Seal I. (Sovereignty undetermined)
Grand Manan Channel
Prospect Harbor
Frenchman Bay
Little Black R.
St. Francis R.
Big Black R.
Saint John R.
Allagash R.
Clayton Lake
Clayton Lake
Long Lake
Musquacook Lakes
Aroostook R.
Machias R.
Chemquasabamticook Lake
Eagle Lake
Munsungan Lake
Allagash Lake
Millinocket Lake
Caucomgomoc Lake
Loon Lake
Chamberlain Lake
St. John Pond
Black Pond
Chesuncook
North Branch
Penobscot R.
Seboomook Lake
Chesuncook Lake
Mount Katahdin 5,268 ft.
Seboomook
Moosehead Lake
Big Spencer Mountain 3,035 ft.
Grindstone
Pemadumcook Lake
Millinocket
Medway
East Millinocket
Norcross
Moose River
Brassua Lake
Kineo
Jackman
Long Pond
Moose R.
Tarratine
Lower Roach Pond
Moosehead
Mattawamkeag
East Winn
Chester
Lincoln
Seboeis Lake
Seboeis
Schoodic Lake
Greenville Jct.
Greenville
Onawa Lake
Lake Moxie
Willimantic
Brownville
Sebec
Blanchard
Dover-Foxcroft
Kennebec R.
Piscataquis R.
Spencer Stream
Jimpond
Troutdale
Round Mountain
Eustis
Flagstaff Lake
Pleasant Pond
Stratton
Parmachenee Lake
Bigelow Mtn. 4,150 ft.
Kingsbury
Sangerville
Atkinson
West Enfield
La Grange
S. La Grange
Burlington
Lowell
Saponac
Nicatous Lake
Cardville
Hudson
PENOBSCOT IND. RES.
Old Town
Orono
Stillwater
Pushaw Lake
Charleston
Garland
Corinna
Mainstream
Hartland
Harmony
Great Goose Lake
Athens
Bingham
Aziscoos Lake
Loon Lake
Pleasant Island
Rangeley Lake
Mount Abraham 4,049 ft.
Upper Dam
Richardson Lakes
Umbagog Lake
Madrid
New Portland
Cornville
Kennebec R.
Skowhegan
Sebasticook Lake
Carmel
Bangor
Hampden
Aurora
Amherst
Dedham
Waltham
Graham Lake
Houghton
Sandy R.
Strong
Mt. Blue 3,187 ft.
Fairbanks
Plymouth
Upton
Ellis R.
Andover
Farmington
Wilton
New Sharon
Hinckley
Burnham
Winnecook Lake
Fairfield
Troy
Benton
Waterville
Monroe
Prospect
North Newry
Rumford
Bear R.
Sunday R.
East Peru
Riley
Dryden
Jay
Canton
Belgrade
Montville
Belfast
Orland
Ellsworth
West Franklin
Hancock
Ashville
Penobscot
Blue Hill
ACADIA NAT'L PARK
Mt. Desert I.
Cranberry Isles
Androscoggin R.
Gilead
Locke Mills
Livermore
Wayne
South China
Palermo
Bayside
Islesboro I.
Islesboro
East Stoneham
Kezar Lake
West Paris
North Turner
Manchester
Augusta
Coopers Mills
Appleton
Penobscot Bay
South Waterford
South Paris
Monmouth
Gardiner
Jefferson
Union
Camden
Atlantic
Swans I.
Marshall I.
Frenchboro
Lovell
Kezar Pond
Oxford
Auburn
Richmond
Long Lake
Mimot
Nobleboro
Rockland
Owls Head
Vinalhaven
Isle au Haut
Isle au Haut
Fryeburg
Bridgton
Casco
Lisbon
Wiscasset
Denmark
Naples
Brunswick
Bath
Friendship
Long Cove
ACADIA NATIONAL PARK
Hiram
Gray
Sebago Lake
Freeport
Trevett
Muscongus Bay
Green I.
Metinic I.
Kezar Falls
Cornish
Yarmouth
Five I.
Harpswell
Boothbay Harbor
Criehaven
Falmouth-Foreside
Newagen
Monhegan
West Newfield
Limerick
Gorham
Portland
Casco Bay
Popham Beach
Cape Small
Newfield
Hollis Center
South Portland
Cape Elizabeth
Shapleigh
Waterboro
Old Orchard Beach
Springvale
Alfred
Saco
East Lebanon
Biddeford Pool
Kennebunk
Cape Porpoise
West Lebanon
Highpine
Kennebunkport
Wells
Wells Beach
Moody
Ogunquit
Cape Neddick
York Beach
York
York Harbor
Bigelow Bight
Salmon Falls R.
S. Eliot
Kittery Point
Piscataqua R.
Tobique
Salmon R.
Trousers Lake
Long Lake
Saint John R.
Keswick R.
Magaguadavic Lake
Oromocto Lake
St. Croix R.
Magaguadavic R.
©1996, Encyclopædia Britannica, Inc.

NAME	AREA[1] (sq. mi.)	AREA[1] (sq. km.)	POP. (1990c)	CO. SEAT
Franklin	1,709	4,426	29,008	Farmington
Hancock[2]	1,537	3,981	46,948	Ellsworth
Kennebec	872	2,258	115,904	Augusta
Knox	369	956	36,310	Rockland
Lincoln	454	1,176	30,357	Wiscasset
Oxford	2,082	5,392	52,602	South Paris
Penobscot	3,390	8,780	146,601	Bangor
Piscataquis[3]	3,903	10,109	18,653	Dover-Foxcroft
Sagadahoc	257	666	33,535	Bath
Somerset[3]	3,894	10,085	49,767	Skowhegan
Waldo	737	1,909	33,018	Belfast
Washington	2,554	6,615	35,308	Machias
York	1,001	2,593	164,587	Alfred

[1] Area = land area.
[2] Includes Mount Desert I., containing Acadia National Park.
[3] Includes part of Moosehead Lake.

History: Evidence of prehistoric inhabitants; inhabited by Algonquians (esp. Penobscot and Passamaquoddy tribes) at time of European settlement; claimed and settled by both English and French; included in grant to Plymouth Company 1606; first settlement by English at mouth of the Sagadahoc (Kennebec) 1607 failed, but city of Saco and Monhegan I. were settled c. 1622; through series of grants, beginning in 1622, claimed by Massachusetts Bay Colony and English proprietor Sir Ferdinando Gorges; annexed to Massachusetts (1652) which bought out Gorges's claim 1677; N parts frequently attacked by French 17th–18th cents.; a district of Massachusetts until 1820; admitted to Union as free state as part of Missouri Compromise Mar. 15, 1820; boundary with Canada settled by treaty with Great Britain 1842.

Maine \ˈmen\. **1.** River, NW cen. France; formed by confluence of Sarthe and Mayenne rivers near Angers, flows S into Loire River; 8 mi. (13 km.) long.

2. *or* **Le Maine** \lə-\. Historical region of NW France; bounded anciently on N by Normandy, on E by Orléanais, on S by Touraine and Anjou, and on W by Brittany; ✻ Le Mans.

History: Region became hereditary countship in 10th cent. A.D.; united with countship of Anjou through marriage of heiress with count of Anjou 1126; became English when Henry Plantagenet became king of England as Henry II 1154; taken by French King Philip Augustus early 13th cent.; held alternately by English and French crowns; passed to house of Anjou; reverted to French crown 1481; made duchy under Louis XIV.

Maine–et–Loire \ˌmen-ā-ˈlwär\. Department of W France. See table at FRANCE.

Maing·kwan \ˈmīŋ-ˈkwän\. Town, N Myanmar, on upper Chindwin River, in Hukawng Valley; amber; during WWII occupied by Japanese 1942–44.

Ma·i·nit, Lake \mä-ˈē-nit\. Lake, NE Mindanao, Philippines; 67 sq. mi. (174 sq. km.); ab. 14 mi. (23 km.) long.

Main·land \ˈmān-ˌland, -lənd\. **1.** Chief island of Japan. See HONSHŪ.

2. Island, Orkney Is., Scotland. See POMONA 3.

3. Chief island of the Shetland Is., NE of N Scotland; ab. 225 sq. mi. (583 sq. km.); pop. (1981c) 14,279; chief town Lerwick.

Mainland China. See CHINA, MAINLAND.

Main Pass \ˈmān\. One of the channels at the mouth of the Mississippi River (*q.v.*), SE Louisiana.

Main·pu·ri \ˈmīn-pə-rē\. Town, W Uttar Pradesh, N India, 63 mi. (101 km.) E of Agra; pop. (1991p) 76,696.

Mainz \ˈmīnts\ *or Fr.* **Ma·yence** \mȧ-ˈyä^{n}s\. City, ✻ of Rhineland-Palatinate, W Germany, on Rhine at mouth of Main River 20 mi. (32 km.) WSW of Frankfurt am Main; pop. (1992e) 182,867; river port; center of Rhenish wine industry; chemicals, machinery; university (1477, closed 1816, reopened 1946); 11th cent. Romanesque cathedral; 17th cent. electoral palace; old citadel on site of Roman camp (see below); birthplace and residence of printer Johannes Gutenberg.

History: Settled near Roman fort **Mo·gon·ti·a·cum** \ˌmō-gän-ˈtī-ə-kəm\ (*also* **Ma·gun·ti·a·cum** \ˌmā-gən-\), founded by Roman Gen. Drusus Senior first cent. B.C.; made seat of archbishop 8th cent. A.D.; attained self-government and became in 13th cent. head of Rhenish League; archbishop made an imperial elector 14th cent.; city lost privileges after civil war 1462; occupied by French and Swedes during Thirty Years' War; held by French 1792–93 and 1797–1815; passed to Hesse-Darmstadt and became a German fortress; occupied by French 1918–30; in WWII was largely destroyed but has been rebuilt.

Ma·io *or* **Ma·yo** \ˈmī-ü\. One of the Cape Verde Is.; 104 sq. mi. (269 sq. km.); pop. (1990p) 4964; occupied by British until end of 18th cent.

Mai·po \ˈmī-pō\ *or* **Mai·pú** \mī-ˈpü\. **1.** River in Santiago prov., cen. Chile; flows W into Pacific Ocean. On its banks a few miles S of Santiago, in a battle Apr. 5, 1818, Argentinian soldier and statesman José de San Martín gained a victory over the Spanish forces that had been sent to regain Chile after its independence had been proclaimed (Feb. 12, 1818).

2. Volcano on Chile-Argentina boundary SE of Santiago, Chile; ab. 17,464 ft. (5323 m.).

Maipo, Pa·so de *or* **Paso de Maipú** \ˌpä-sō-t͟hā-mī-ˈpü\. Andean mountain pass on Argentina-Chile border, bet. W Mendoza prov., W Argentina, and E Santiago prov., cen. Chile; alt. ab. 11,316 ft. (3449 m.).

Mai·que·tía \ˌmī-kā-ˈtē-ä\. Coastal town and resort in Federal District, N Venezuela; pop. (1990e) 83,367; international airport.

Maire Strait, Le. See LE MAIRE, STRAIT OF.

Mai·sí, Cape *or* **Cape May·sí** \mī-ˈsē\. Cape at E extremity of Cuba, projecting into Windward Passage.

Mais·khāl Island \ˈmī-skäl\. Island, Bangladesh, ab. 80 mi. (129 km.) S of Chittagong, separated from the mainland by **Maiskhāl Channel**.

Mai·son·neuve \ˌmā-zȯ^{n}-ˈnœ̄v\. E residential section of the city of Montreal, S Quebec, Canada; on the St. Lawrence.

Mai·sons–Al·fort \mā-ˌzȯ^{n}-äl-ˈfȯr\. Commune, Val-de-Marne dept., N France, SE suburb of Paris on Marne River, S of Bois de Vincennes (park).

Maisons–La·fitte \mā-ˌzȯ^{n}-lȧ-ˈfēt\. Commune, Yvelines dept., N France, on Seine River 7 mi. (11 km.) NW of Paris; racecourse.

Maisur. See MYSORE.

Mait·land \ˈmāt-lənd\. **1.** City, Orange co., cen. Florida, 8 mi. (13 km.) N of Orlando; pop. (1990c) 9110.

2. City, E New South Wales, SE Australia, on Hunter River 20 mi. (32 km.) NW of Newcastle; pop. (1991c) 46,909; produces textiles, bricks; coal mines in vicinity.

Maíz Grande, Isla del *and* **Maíz Pequeña, Isla del.** See CORN ISLANDS.

Mai·zu·ru \ˈmī-zü-ˌrü\. City and seaport, Kyōto prefecture, N coast of SW Honshū, Japan, NNW of the city of Kyōto; pop. (1990p) 96,329; naval base, bombed in WWII.

Ma·ja \ˈmī-ä\. Island, West Kalimantan prov., Indonesia, off SW coast of Borneo.

Ma·ja·gua Bay \mä-ˈhä-gwä\. Bay in NE coast of Humacao municipality, E Puerto Rico.

Ma·ja·pa·hit \ˌmä-jä-ˈpä-hit\. Malay kingdom in the East Indies founded c. 1293 with its center in E Java and controlling most of Sumatra, coastal regions of Borneo and Celebes, and the Lesser Sunda Is.; finally overcome early 16th cent. by Muslims.

Ma·jāz al–Bāb \mə-ˈjaz-al-ˈbab\ *also* **Me·djez–el–Bab** \mə-ˈjez-el-ˈbab\. Town and road junction, N Tunisia, ab. 40 mi. (64 km.) WSW of the city of Tunis; scene of fighting 1942–43 in WWII.

Majdal. See MAGDALA.

Majdanek. See LUBLIN 2.

Ma·jor \ˈmā-jər\. County in NW Oklahoma. See table at OKLAHOMA.

Ma·jor·ca \mä-ˈjȯr-kə, mə-, -ˈyȯr-\ *or Span.* **Mal·lor·ca** \mä-ˈlyȯr-kä\; *anc.* **Bal·e·ar·is Ma·jor** \ˌbal-ē-ˈar-əs-ˈmā-jər\.

\ə\ abut \ə\ matches \ᵊ\ kitten, Fr table \ər\ further \a\ ash \ā\ ace \ä\ cot, cart \ȧ\ Fr bac \au̇\ out \b\ Span Avila \ch\ chin \e\ bet \ē\ easy \g\ go \i\ hit \ī\ ice \j\ job \k\ Ger ich, Buch \$^{n}$\ Fr vin \ŋ\ sing \ō\ go \ȯ\ all \ȯ\ law \œ\ Fr bœuf \œ̄\ Fr feu \ȯi\ boy \th\ thin \t͟h\ this \ü\ loot \u̇\ foot \ue\ Ger füllen \ue̅\ Fr rue \y\ yet \$^{y}$\ Fr digne \ˈdēn^{y}\, nuit \ˈnw^{y}ē\ \yü\ few \yu̇\ fury \zh\ vision

Largest island of the Balearic group, Baleares prov., Spain, in W Mediterranean 145 mi. (233 km.) E of Spanish coast; 1405 sq. mi. (3639 sq. km.); pop. (1981c) 561,215; ✱ Palma; irregularly shaped with deeply indented coastline, esp. in NE; extremely mountainous in NW, gently rolling and fertile in S and E; important tourist center; brandy.

History: See also BALEARIC ISLANDS; kingdom of Mallorca erected by James I of Aragon (1213–76), included Minorca, Ibiza, Roussillon, and Cerdaña; united to Aragon in mid-14th cent.; with Palma as port, was most prosperous of Balearic Is. until decline in trade in 15th cent.; in Spanish Civil War 1936–39, joined Nationalists and was a base of Italian aid against Loyalists.

Ma·ju·ba Hill \mä-ˈjü-bä\. Height in NW KwaZulu-Natal prov., Rep. of South Africa, ab. 75 mi. (120 km.) N of Ladysmith; scene of Boer victory over the British Feb. 27, 1881.

Ma·ju·li Island \ˈmä-jə-lē\. Island, formed by two channels of the Brahmaputra River in NE Assam, NE India; 485 sq. mi. (1256 sq. km.).

Majunga. See MAHAJANGA.

Ma·ju·ro \mä-ˈjü-rō\. Island (atoll) in S part of Ratak Chain, SE Marshall Is., W Pacific, 7°09′N, 171°12′E; pop. (1988c) 19,664; has 33 islets; contains ✱ of the group. In WWII taken by Allies 1944.

Ma·ka·ha \mä-ˈkä-hä\. Unincorporated settlement, Honolulu co., Hawaii, 25 mi. (40 km.) NW of the city of Honolulu; pop. (1990c) 7990.

Ma·ka·hu·e·na Point \mä-ˌkä-hü-ˈā-nä\. Cape on S coast of Kauai I., Hawaii.

Ma·ka·ki·lo City \ˌmä-kä-ˈkē-lō\. Unincorporated settlement, Honolulu co., Hawaii; pop. (1990c) 9828.

Makale. See MEKELE.

Ma·ka·lu \ˈmə-kə-ˌlü\. Peak in the Himalayas in NE Nepal; 27,824 ft. (8481 m.); first scaled 1955.

Makanalua Peninsula. See KALAUPAPA PENINSULA.

Makarikari. See MAKGADIKGADI PANS.

Ma·kar·ska \ˈmä-kär-ˌskä\. Town, Croatia, on Dalmatian coast ab. 35 mi. (56 km.) SE of Split; pop. (1991c) 13,718; destroyed by Avars 639 A.D.

Makasar *or* **Makassar.** See UJUNG PANDANG.

Ma·kas·sar Strait *also* **Ma·ka·sar Strait** \mə-ˈka-sər\ *or Indonesian* **Se·lat Makassar** *or* **Selat Makasar** \se-ˈlät\. Passage bet. E Borneo and W Sulawesi, Indonesia, connecting Sulawesi Sea on the N with Java Sea on the S; av. width 155 mi. (249 km.), narrowest (at N end) ab. 65 mi. (105 km.); length ab. 450 mi. (724 km.). Contains Balabalagan Is. in W cen. part and the large island of Laut at its SW corner. Forms a part of Wallace's line. Scene of naval and air battles bet. Japanese and Allied forces 1942.

Ma·ka·tea \ˌmä-kä-ˈtā-ä\. One of the islands of the Tuamotu Archipelago, French Polynesia, 140 mi. (225 km.) NNE of Tahiti, in the S Pacific; 8 sq. mi. (21 sq. km.); 5 mi. (8 km.) long by 3 mi. (5 km.) wide; pop. (1988c) 58; 15°50′S, 148°15′W; large phosphate deposits (see also OCEAN ISLAND) mined by British and French 1908–1966, until depleted.

Ma·ka·ti \ˌmä-kä-ˈtē\. Municipality, Rizal prov., Luzon, Philippines, on S bank of the Pasig 1 mi. (1.6 km.) E of E boundary of Manila; pop. (1990p) 452,000.

Ma·ka·tu·ring, Mount \ˌmä-kä-tu̇-ˈriŋ\. Active volcano, Mindanao, Philippines, S of Lake Lanao; 5720 ft. (1743 m.); eruption 1872.

Ma·ka·wao \ˌmä-kä-ˈwä-ō\. Unincorporated settlement, Maui co., Hawaii, cen. part of Maui I.; pop. (1990c) 5405.

Makedonia. See MACEDONIA 4.

Makeevka. See MAKEYEVKA.

Ma·ke·mo \mä-ˈkā-mō\. Island (atoll), NW cen. Tuamotu Archipelago, 125 mi. (201 km.) E of Fakarava, 16°35′S, 143°40′W.

Ma·ke·yev·ka *or* **Ma·ki·yiv·ka** *also* **Ma·ke·ev·ka** \mə-ˈkā-əf-kə\. City, cen. Donets'k, Ukraine, ab. 12 mi. (19 km.) NE of the city of Donets'k; pop. (1991e) 424,000; a major industrial center, one of the most important in the Donets Basin, esp. in steel production; also important coal-mining center.

Ma·kga·di·kga·di Pans \mä-ˌkä-dē-ˈkä-dē-ˈpanz\; *mostly formerly* **Ma·ka·ri·ka·ri** \mä-ˌkä-rē-ˈkä-rē\ *also* **Soa Salt Pan** \ˈsō-ä\. Large salt basin, NE Botswana; floods extensively during normal rainy seasons; inhabited by large number of flamingos.

Ma·khach·ka·la \mə-ˌkäch-kə-ˈlä\; *formerly* **Pe·trovsk** \pə-ˈtrȯfsk\. City, ✱ of Dagestan, S Russia in Europe, on W coast of Caspian Sea; pop. (1992e) 339,000; on railroad line from Astrakhan to Baku; transshipment point of oil from Grozny to the Volga; fishing, oil refining, textile and shoe manufacturing, brewing; university (1957); founded 1844; renamed 1921.

Makiling, Mount *or* **Mount Maquiling** \mä-ˈkē-liŋ\. Mountain, S Luzon, Philippines, SE of Manila; 3650 ft. (1112 m.).

Makin. See BUTARITARI.

Makira. See SAN CRISTÓBAL 7.

Ma·ki·ra Bay \mä-ˈkē-rä\. Widemouthed inlet on S coast at W end of San Cristóbal I., SE Solomon Is., W Pacific Ocean.

Makiyivka. See MAKEYEVKA.

Makkah. See MECCA.

Mak Khaeng, Ban. See UDON THANI.

Mak·nas·sy \mak-ˈna-sē\. Town, cen. Tunisia, ab. 65 mi. (104 km.) WSW of Sfax; scene of heavy fighting bet. Germans and Allies during WWII 1943.

Ma·kó \ˈmö-kō\. City, SE Hungary, on Mureşul River near Romanian border; pop. (1991e) 27,500; market town in agricultural and livestock-raising region; textiles. Birthplace of Joseph Pulitzer, American journalist, 1847.

Ma·kran *also* **Me·kran** \mə-ˈkrän\ *or Persian* **Mo·krān** \mō-ˈkrän\. Region of SW Asia, along Arabian Sea, in Sīstān va Balūchestān prov., SE Iran and Baluchistan prov., SW Pakistan; the Pakistani part is mountainous and arid except in fertile river valleys where dates are grown; the Iranian part comprises a former province with its ✱ at Jāsk.

Mak·thar *or* **Mak·tar** \ˈmak-tər\; *anc.* **Mac·ta·ris** \ˈmak-tə-ris\. Town, N Tunisia; remains of Roman colony include a triumphal arch, temples, and part of an aqueduct.

Makua. See UBANGI.

Makumma. See MORONA.

Ma·kung *or* **Ma-kung** \ˈmä-ˈgu̇ŋ\ *also* **P'eng-hu** \ˈpəŋ-ˈhü\. Town, Taiwan, on the island of P'eng-hu, largest of the P'eng-hu group, in Taiwan Strait; before WWII developed by Japan as a naval base; transferred to China 1945; now administratively part of Taiwan.

Ma·kur·di \mä-ˈku̇r-dē\. Town, ✱ of Benue state, Nigeria, on Benue River and on railroad line ab. 170 mi. (275 km.) N of Calabar; pop. (1991e) 108,600.

Ma·ku·shin \mə-ˈkü-shən\. Volcano, NE Unalaska I., SW Alaska, near Dutch Harbor; 6678 ft. (2035 m.).

Mak·war \ma-ˈkwär\. Village on Blue Nile, Sudan. See SENNAR 2.

Ma·la, Point \ˈmä-lä\. Cape, on E extremity of Azuero Penin. on S cen. Panama coast, at W entrance to the Gulf of Panama.

Mal·a·bar \ˈma-lə-ˌbär\. Former district, now part of Kerala, India; 5790 sq. mi. (14,996 sq. km.); ✱ Calicut; abolished 1956.

Malabar Coast. Region of SW coast of India, Karnataka and Kerala states, bet. Western Ghats and Arabian Sea.

Mal·a·ba·ta, Point \ˌma-lə-ˌbä-tə\. Point, N Morocco, E of Tangier.

Ma·la·bo \mä-ˈlä-bō\; *formerly* **San·ta Is·a·bel** \ˈsän-tä-ˈē-sä-ˌbel\. Town, ✱ of Equatorial Guinea; chief town on island of Bioko; pop. (1983c) 31,630.

Ma·la·bon \ˌmä-lä-ˈbȯn\. Municipality, NW Rizal prov., Luzon, Philippines, just N of Manila; pop. (1980c) 191,001.

Malaca. See MÁLAGA 3.

Malacca. See MELAKA.

Ma·lac·ca, Strait of \mə-ˈlä-kə, -ˈla-\; *mostly formerly* **Malacca Strait.** Channel bet. the S Malay Penin. and the island of Sumatra, connecting the Indian Ocean with the South China Sea; ab. 500 mi. (800 km.) long and varies in width from 40 mi. (64 km.) in the S to ab. 300 mi. (480 km.) in the N.

Ma·lad City \mə-ˈlad\. City, ⊗ of Oneida co., S Idaho; pop. (1990c) 1946.

Ma·la·de·ta \ˌmä-lä-ˈthā-tä\. Mountain range in the Pyrenees, in NE Spain near the French border; includes Pico de Aneto, 11,168 ft. (3404 m.), highest in the Pyrenees.

Ma·la·dzyech·na *or* **Mo·lo·dech·no** \ˌmə-lə-ˈdyech-nə\; *Pol.* **Mo·lo·decz·no** \ˌmȯ-lȯ-ˈdech-nō\. Town, Minsk administrative subdivision, NW Belarus, ab. 40 mi. (64 km.) NW of the city of Minsk; pop. (1991e) 93,500; formerly in Poland.

Má·la·ga \ˈmä-lä-gə, ˈma-lə-gə\. **1.** Town, Santander dept., N cen. Colombia, ab. 45 mi. (72 km.) SE of Bucaramanga.

2. Province of S Spain. See table at SPAIN.

3. *anc.* **Mal·a·ca** \ˈma-lə-kə\. Seaport city, ✻ of Málaga prov., S Spain, on Mediterranean 66 mi. (106 km.) NE of Gibraltar; pop. (1991p) 512,136; important Spanish Mediterranean port; beach resort; exports fruit and Malaga wine; produces foodstuffs, beer, textiles; 13th cent. citadel, called the Gibralfaro; cathedral begun 16th cent. on site of old Moorish mosque. Founded by Phoenicians 12th cent. B.C.; later held by Romans and Visigoths; taken by Moors 711 A.D.; fell to Spanish rulers Ferdinand and Isabella 1487; occupied by the French 1810–12. Birthplace of artist Pablo Picasso 1881.

Ma·la·ga·ra·si \mä-ˌlä-gä-ˈrä-sē\. River, W Tanzania; flows S and W into Lake Tanganyika; 250 mi. (402 km.) long.

Malagasy Republic. See MADAGASCAR.

Ma·lai·ta \mä-ˈlā-tä\. Long, narrow island in SE Solomon Is. in the SW Pacific Ocean, 50 mi. (80 km.) SE of Santa Isabel I. and NE of Guadalcanal; ab. 100 mi. (160 km.) long; area 1870 sq. mi. (4843 sq. km.); pop. (1986c) 80,032; chief village Auki. Formerly part of British Solomon Is. Protectorate; has many coastal villages. Interior not extensively explored; no good harbors; highest point 4275 ft. (1303 m.).

Ma·la·kal *or* **Ma·la·kāl** \ˌmä-lə-ˈkäl\. Town, SE Sudan, on right bank of White Nile 410 mi. (660 km.) S of Khartoum.

Ma·la·khov *also* **Ma·la·koff** \mȧ-ˈlȧ-kəf\. Fortification, SE part of Sevastopol', Crimea; captured by the French 1855 after a long siege; in WWII captured by the Germans 1942.

Mal·a·koff \ˈma-lə-ˌkȯf\ *also* **Malakoff–la–Tour** \ˌmȧ-lȧ-ˈkȯf-lə-ˈtür\. Commune, Hauts-de-Seine dept., N France, S suburb of Paris; pop. (1990c) 31,135; manufactures electrical equipment, pharmaceuticals.

Malakula. See MALEKULA.

Ma·la·lag \mä-ˈlä-läg\. Municipality, Davao del Sur prov., Mindanao, Philippines, ab. 40 mi. (64 km.) SSW of City of Davao; pop. (1980c) 44,690.

Ma·lan·court \ˌmȧ-läⁿ-ˈkür\. Village, Meuse dept., NE France, NW of Verdun; scene of battles Mar. 1916.

Ma·lang \mä-ˈläŋ\. **1.** Region, cen. East Java prov., Indonesia; 3413 sq. mi. (8840 sq. km.); pop. (1980c) 2,045,939; ✻ Malang. Has two ports on Madura Strait—Pasuruan and Probolinggo—but none on S coast. Comprises the mountain groups of Kawi on the W and Tengger on the E with fertile plains in between.

2. City, its ✻, 50 mi. (80 km.) S of Surabaya; pop. (1990c) 695,618; university (1957); scene of first session of Indonesian parliament Feb. 1947.

Ma·lan·je *also* **Ma·lan·ge** \mȧ-ˈläⁿ-zhē\. **1.** Province of N Angola. See table at ANGOLA.

2. Inland town, its ✻; pop. (1984e) 35,000; railroad terminus E of Luanda.

Ma·la Pas·cua, Point \ˌmä-lä-ˈpäs-kwä\. Cape on SE extremity of Puerto Rico.

Mä·lar·en \ˈmā-ˌlär-ən\ *also* **Ma·lar** \ˈmā-ˌlär\. Lake, SE Sweden; extends from the Baltic Sea 70 mi. (113 km.) inland; 440 sq. mi. (1140 sq. km.); the city of Stockholm is situated on both sides of the strait connecting the lake with the Baltic Sea.

Ma·lar·tic \ˌmȧ-lär-ˈtēk\. Town, SW Quebec, Canada; pop. (1991c) 4326.

Ma·la·si·qui \ˌmä-lä-ˈsē-kē\. Municipality, Pangasinan prov., Luzon, Philippines, on Manila-Dagupan railroad line 14 mi. (23 km.) SE of Lingayen; pop. (1980c) 70,905; on a branch of the Agno River.

Malaskirt. See MALAZGIRT.

Malaspina. See CANLAON 1.

Mal·a·spi·na Glacier \ˌma-lə-ˈspē-nə\. Glacier, S coast of Alaska, S from Mt. St. Elias to Yakutat Bay; ab. 90 mi. (145 km.) long; covers 1500 sq. mi. (3890 sq. km.) with front of ab. 60 mi. (96 km.) on the Pacific; more than 1000 ft. (300 m.) thick.

Ma·la·tya \ˌmä-ˈlä-tyä\. **1.** Province of Turkey in Asia. See table at TURKEY.

2. *anc.* **Mel·i·te·ne** \ˌme-lə-ˈtē-nē\. City, its ✻, on railroad line just W of the Euphrates ab. 112 mi. (180 km.) NE of Gaziantep; pop. (1990c) 281,776; distribution center for agricultural products; in region are many ruins of Hittite, Roman, and medieval settlements. As Melitene an important Roman military post; bet. 6th and 12th cents. as a frontier town changed hands many times and suffered much; became Turkish 12th cent.; incorp. into Ottoman Empire 16th cent. Birthplace of famous Syrian scholar Bar Hebraeus 1226.

Ma·la·wi *or* **Ma·la·ŵi** \mä-ˈlä-wē\; *formerly* **Ny·asa·land** \nī-ˈa-sə-ˌland, nē-\; *from 1893 to 1907* **British Central Africa Protectorate.** Republic, SE Africa, bounded on N and NE by Tanzania, on E, S, and SW by Mozambique, and on W by Zambia; 45,747 sq. mi. (118,485 sq. km.) incl. ab. 9350 sq. mi. (24,220 sq. km.) of water; pop. (1993e) 10,581,000; ✻ Lilongwe.

Physical features: Country is traversed by Great Rift Valley; Lake Malawi (*q.v.*) located in E; W of lake are elevated plateaus, ab. 5000 to 8000 ft. (1500 to 2450 m.) high; S part crossed by Shire River, outlet of Lake Malawi; highest point Mlanje Peak 9848 ft. (3002 m.), in S.

Chief exports: Tea, tobacco; other products: peanuts, sorghum, corn, rice, sugar; fishing; manufacturing: textiles, cement.

Chief towns: Blantyre and Lilongwe.

History: Inhabited from prehistoric times; two in-migrations of Bantu peoples occurred 1st–4th cents. and c. 14th cent.; a Maravi kingdom arose 15th cent. and encompassed present country by 17th cent., later declined; region visited by Scottish explorer and missionary David Livingstone

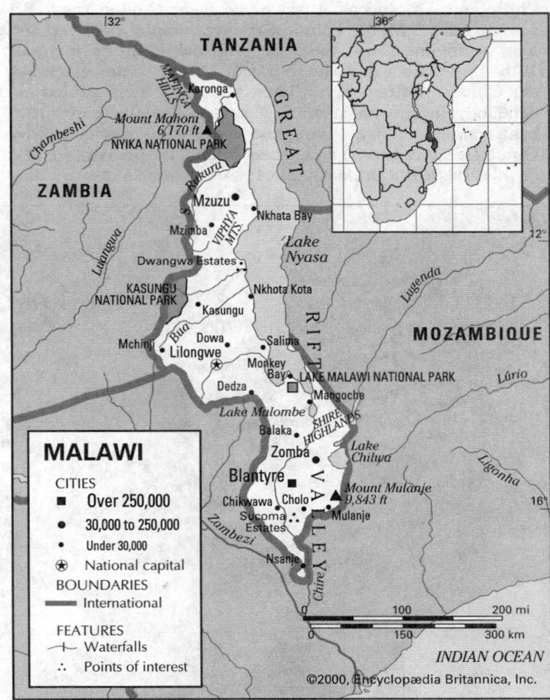

1859; became a British protectorate 1891; part of Federation of Rhodesia and Nyasaland 1953–63; achieved independence with membership in the Commonwealth 1964; became a republic 1966; accepted over 600,000 refugees from war in Mozambique in late 1980s.

Malawi, Lake *or* **Lake Nya·sa** *also* **Lake Nyas·sa** \ˈnyä-sä\. Lake in SE Africa, bounded on W and S by Malawi, on N and E by Tanzania, and on E by N Mozambique; ab. 360 mi. (580 km.) long, av. width 25 mi. (40 km.); 11,430 sq. mi. (29,604 sq. km.); max. depth 2226 ft. (679 m.); drains S into Zambezi River.

Malaya. See MALAY PENINSULA and MALAYA, FEDERATION OF.

Ma·laya, Federation of \mə-ˈlā-ə, mā-\. A former federation of the nine Malay States of the Malay Penin. (the former Federated Malay States of Negeri Sembilan, Pahang, Perak, and Selangor and the former Unfederated Malay States of Johor, Kedah, Kelantan, Perlis, and Terengganu) and two of the Straits Settlements (Melaka and Penang); ab. 60,000 sq. mi. (155,400 sq. km.); ✻ Kuala Lumpur. Comprised the larger part of British Malaya; set up 1946 as **Union of Malaya;** reorganized and estab. 1948 as the Federation of Malaya; achieved independence with membership in the Commonwealth 1957; became part of Federation of Malaysia Sept. 16, 1963. For physical features, see MALAY PENINSULA, MELAKA, PENANG, and the names of the various states.

Ma·lay Archipelago \mə-ˈlā, ˈmā-ˌlā\; *formerly* **Ma·lay·sia** \mə-ˈlā-zhə, -shə\. The largest island group in the world, off SE coast of Asia bet. the Pacific and Indian oceans. Major islands include: Borneo, Sulawesi, Java, Luzon, Mindanao, New Guinea, Sumatra.

History: S Malay Penin., Sumatra, cen. Java, and E Borneo were colonized from c. first cent. B.C. by Hindu Pallavas from SE India; later influenced by Buddhism; Sumatra, united under ruler of Śrivijaya, by 12th cent. ruled empire incl. Philippines, Moluccas, Borneo, W Java, Ceylon (now Sri Lanka), and S Malay Penin.; Śrivijaya empire declined and was supplanted by state of Majapahit in Java (*q.v.*) 13th–14th cents.; in early 15th cent., Malay states came under Chinese influence, but later, Muslim traders gained ascendancy in several states (see MELAKA); after early 16th cent. dominated by Portuguese who were succeeded by Dutch (see INDONESIA) and, on mainland, by British (see MALAYA, FEDERATION OF; MALAYSIA 1; SABAH; and SARAWAK); during WWII most of archipelago under Japanese control. Independence: Philippines 1946, Indonesia 1949, Federation of Malaya 1957.

Ma·lay·ba·lay \ˌmä-lī-ˈbä-ˌlī\. Municipality, ✻ of Bukidnon prov., Mindanao, Philippines; pop. (1980c) 60,779.

Malay Peninsula *also* **Ma·laya** \mə-ˈlā-ə, mā-\; *anc.* **Cher·so·ne·sus Au·rea** \ˌkər-sə-ˈnē-səs-ˈȯr-ē-ə\ *or Eng.* **Golden Cher·so·nese** \ˈkər-sə-ˌnēz, -ˌnēs\. Peninsula, SE Asia, comprising West Malaysia and SW part of Thailand; ab. 70,000 sq. mi. (181,300 sq. km.). Has range of mountains extending its entire length, dividing it on E and W unequally; highest peak Tahan 7186 ft. (2190 m.) on border bet. Kelantan and Pahang. Noted for wealth of its tin deposits.

Ma·lay·sia \mə-ˈlā-zhə, -shə\. **1.** Independent country, SE Asia, consisting of 11 states (**West Malaysia**) on the Malay Peninsula and two states (**East Malaysia**) on the island of Borneo; 128,727 sq. mi. (333,403 sq. km.); pop. (1993e) 19,077,000; ✻ Kuala Lumpur.

Chief products: Rubber, rice, timber, palm oil, cocoa, pineapples; natural gas, petroleum, tin, iron ore, bauxite; electronics.

Chief settlements: Kuala Lumpur, Ipoh, Penang, Johor Baharu.

Political divisions: Constituent states shown in table below (for pronunciation of their names, see their individual entries):

NAME	AREA (sq. mi.)	AREA (sq. km.)	POP. (1991p)	CAPITAL
East Malaysia				
Labuan Fed. Terr.	38	98	54,307	Victoria
Sabah	29,507	76,423	1,736,902	Kota Kinabalu
Sarawak	48,342	125,206	1,648,217	Kuching
West Malaysia				
Johor	7,360	19,062	2,074,297	Johor Baharu
Kedah	3,660	9,479	1,304,800	Alor Setar
Kelantan	5,780	14,970	1,181,680	Kota Baharu
Kuala Lumpur Fed. Terr.	94	243	1,145,075	Kuala Lumpur
Melaka	640	1,658	504,502	Melaka
Negeri Sembilan	2,590	6,708	691,200	Seremban
Pahang	13,920	36,053	1,036,724	Kuantan
Perak	8,030	20,798	1,880,016	Ipoh
Perlis	310	803	184,070	Kangar
Penang	400	1,036	1,065,075	George Town
Selangor	3,074	7,962	2,289,236	Shah Alam
Terengganu	5,000	12,950	770,931	Kuala Terengganu

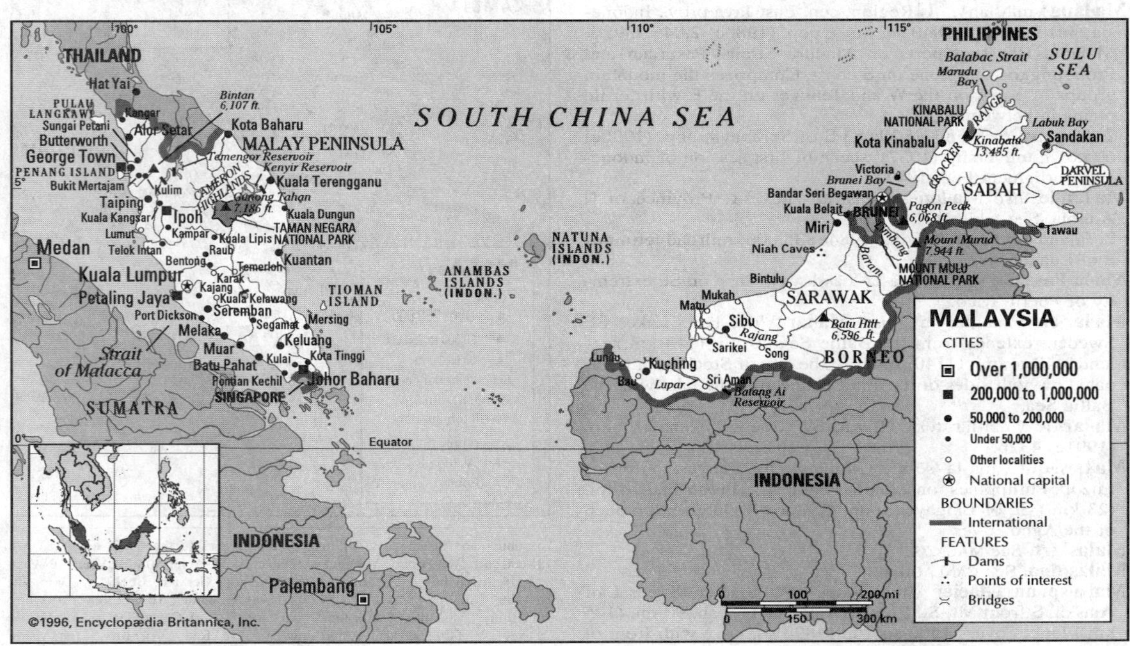

History: For history prior to 1963, see entries of individual states; see also MALAYA, FEDERATION OF and STRAITS SETTLEMENTS. Federation (consisting of Federation of Malaya, Sabah, Sarawak, and Singapore) estab. Sept. 16, 1963; period 1963–66 marked by hostilities with Indonesia; secession of Singapore from federation 1965; suspended constitution 1969–71.

2. Island group, Asia. See MALAY ARCHIPELAGO.

Malay States. The native states of the Malay Penin., SE Asia, esp. those formerly under British protection; formerly included, in cen. and N part of the peninsula, a group of semi-independent states inhabited chiefly by Malays and governed by Malay rulers; these states now part of Thailand; S states now part of Malaysia (*q.v.*).

Ma·laz·girt \ˌmä-ˌläz-ˈkirt\ *also* **Ma·las·kirt** \ˌmä-lə-ˈskirt\; *formerly* **Man·zi·kert** \ˈman-zə-ˌkert, -ˌkərt\. Ancient village, E Turkey, ab. 25 mi. (40 km.) NW of Lake Van. Scene 1071 of defeat and capture of Byzantine Emperor Romanus IV Diogenes by Seljuq Turks under Sultan Alp Arslan who thus crushed power of Byzantine Empire (*q.v.*) in Asia Minor.

Mal·baie \mål-ˈbā\. River, S Quebec, Canada; flows in wide curve, finally to the SE into the St. Lawrence River at La Malbaie; ab. 80 mi. (130 km.) long.

Malbaie, La. See LA MALBAIE.

Mal·bork \ˈmäl-ˌbȯrk\; *Ger.* **Ma·ri·en·burg** \mə-ˈrē-ən-ˌbu̇rk\ *also* **Marienburg in West·preus·sen** \in-vest-ˈprȯis-ᵊn\. City, Elbląg prov., N Poland, on Nogat River 25 mi. (40 km.) SE of Gdańsk; pop. (1992e) 40,000; 13th cent. castle; received town rights 1276; became seat of Grand Master of Teutonic Knights in 1309; to Poland 1457; to Prussia 1772; assigned to Poland by Potsdam Conference 1945.

Mal·den \ˈmȯl-dən\. **1.** City, Middlesex co., NE Massachusetts, ab. 3 mi. (5 km.) N of Boston; pop. (1990c) 53,884; settled 1640; incorp. as town 1649, as city 1881.

2. City, Dunklin co., SE Missouri, 28 mi. (45 km.) ESE of Poplar Bluff; pop. (1990c) 5123.

3. Island of the Line Is. in cen. Pacific Ocean S of Hawaii and 275 mi. (442 km.) SE of Jarvis I., 4°03′S, 154°59′W; 35 sq. mi. (91 sq. km.); yields guano; stone structures believed to be of Polynesian origin. In area once claimed by both Great Britain and U.S.; U.S. claim dropped 1983; now part of Kiribati.

Mal·dives \ˈmȯl-ˌdēvz, -ˌdīvz, *also* ˈmal-, -divz\; *mostly formerly* **Mal·dive Islands** \-ˌdēv, -ˌdīv, -div\. Republic, group of 19 clusters of coral islands (atolls) in Indian Ocean ab. 400 mi. (645 km.) SW of Sri Lanka; land area 115 sq. mi. (298 sq. km.); pop. (1985c) 181,453; chief island and ✻ Male.

Chief products: coconuts, millet, fish; tourism.

History: Settled by people of Asian origin; Islam introduced 12th cent.; under European control from 16th cent.; came under British protection in 19th cent.; became independent 1965; proclaimed itself a republic 1968; coup attempt 1988 put down by Indian troops.

Mal·don \ˈmȯl-dən\. Town, Essex, SE England, on Blackwater estuary 38 mi. (61 km.) ENE of London; pop. (1991p) 50,800; flour mills; scene of battle 991 A.D. bet. the East Saxons and the Danes, celebrated in an Old English poem.

Mal·do·na·do \ˌmäl-dō-ˈnä-dō\. **1.** Cape on SW extremity of Guerrero state, S Mexico.

2. Department of SE Uruguay. See table at URUGUAY.

3. Seaport town and resort, ✻ of Maldonado dept., S Uruguay, ab. 65 mi. (104 km.) E of Montevideo; pop. (1985c) 33,536.

Ma·le \ˈmä-lā\. Chief atoll and ✻ of Maldives, in cen. part; actually two groups of islets: **North Male,** 32 mi. (51 km.) by 23 mi. (37 km.), and **South Male,** 20 mi. (32 km.) by 12 mi. (19 km.); city pop. (1990c) 55,130.

Ma·lea, Cape \mä-ˈlē-ä\ *or Gk.* **Ák·ra Ma·lé·as** \ˈä-krä-mä-ˈlā-äs\. Cape at extremity of the E peninsula of Peloponnese, S Greece.

Ma·le·bo, Pool *or* **Malebo Pool** \mä-ˈlā-bō\; *formerly* **Stan·ley Pool** \ˈstan-lē\. Expansion of the Congo River, bet. Rep. of the Congo and Democratic Rep. of the Congo, 4°15′S, 15°25′E; Brazzaville and Kinshasa are situated on its NW and SW shore, respectively.

Ma·le·gaon \ˌmä-lə-ˈgau̇n\. Town, NW India, in Maharashtra 160 mi. (257 km.) NE of Bombay; pop. (1991p) 342,431; distribution center for agricultural produce.

Malé Karpaty. See LITTLE CARPATHIAN MOUNTAINS.

Mal·e·ku·la \ˌmä-lā-ˈkü-lä\ *or* **Ma·la·ku·la** \ˌmä-lä-\. An island of Vanuatu in the SW Pacific Ocean 25 mi. (40 km.) SE of Espíritu Santo; 2d in size of the group, ab. 50 mi. (80 km.) long by 23 mi. (37 km.) wide; 781 sq. mi. (2023 sq. km.); pop. (1991e) 19,289. Mountainous in cen. part, highest point Mt. Penot 2922 ft. (891 m.); several good harbors, esp. Port Sandwich in SE and Port Stanley in NE.

Má·le·me \ˈmä-le-mā\. Village on NW coast of Crete, in Canea dept., Greece; large airport here taken from British by airborne German force during WWII May 1941.

Ma·ler Kot·la *or* **Ma·ler·kot·la** \ˌmä-lər-ˈkōt-lə\. Town, Punjab state, NW India, 155 mi. (249 km.) NNW of Delhi; pop. (1991p) 88,587.

Ma·le·tsun·ya·ne \ˌmä-lā-tsü-ˈnyä-nā\. River, Lesotho; flows S into the Sinqu River, headstream of the Orange River; has notable waterfall **Maletsunyane Falls** which drops 630 ft. (192 m.).

Maleventum. See BENEVENTO 2.

Mal·fa \ˈmäl-fä\. See SALINA.

Malgache Republic. See MADAGASCAR 2.

Mal·heur \ma-ˈlu̇r\. **1.** River, E Oregon; rises in S Grant co., flows S, then turns NE into Snake River on NE boundary of Malheur co.

2. County in SE corner of Oregon. See table at OREGON.

Malheur Lake. Lake in cen. Harney co., SE Oregon.

Malhon. See HOMONHON.

Ma·li \ˈmä-lē\ *or* **Mali Kha** \-ˈkä\. River (*kha*), N Myanmar; ab. 200 mi. (320 km.) long; flows S from the slopes of the hills on N boundary and unites with Nmai to form the Irrawaddy River above Myitkyina.

Mali; *1958–60* **Su·da·nese Republic** \ˌsüd-ᵊn-ˈēz, -ˈēs\; *earlier* **French Su·dan** \sü-ˈdan, -ˈdän\. Republic, W Africa, bounded on N and NE by Algeria, on E and SE by Niger, on S by Burkina Faso and Ivory Coast, on SW by Guinea, on W by Senegal and Mauritania, and on NW by Mauritania; 478,652 sq. mi. (1,239,709 sq. km.); pop. (1993e) 8,646,000; ✻ Bamako.

Physical features: Generally flat; N region part of Sahara; crossed in S by upper Niger which flows through marshy region SW of Tombouctou.

Chief products: Sorghum, rice, millet, cotton, peanuts, corn; livestock; fishing; limestone; leather goods.

Chief town: Bamako; *others:* Ségou, Mopti, Sikasso.

History: Center of several medieval empires; last major empire fell to invasion from Morocco late 16th cent.; came under French control 19th cent.; territories of Senegambia and Niger formed into colony 1904, known as **Upper Senegal–Niger** until 1920; had status of a colony until reorganized as French overseas territory 1946; became autonomous republic within French Community 1958; joined Senegal in Mali Federation 1959–60; became an independent republic 1960; government overthrown by military coups 1968, 1991; border dispute with Burkina Faso 1985; adopted new constitution 1992.

Ma·li·a·kós, Gulf of \ˌmäl-yä-ˈkōs\; *formerly* **Gulf of La·mia** \lä-ˈmē-ä\; *anc.* **Ma·li·a·cus Si·nus** \mə-ˈlī-ə-kəs-ˈsī-nəs\. Inlet of Aegean Sea on E coast of Greece; a W extension of the Atalante Channel; on its S shore is the Pass of Thermopylae (*q.v.*).

Mal·i·bu \ˈma-lə-bü\. Coastal community, Los Angeles co., SW California, WNW of Santa Monica; Pepperdine Univ. (1937).

\ə\ **abut** \ᵊ\ matches \ᵊ\ kitten, Fr table \ər\ **further** \a\ **ash** \ā\ **ace** \ä\ cot, cart \å\ Fr bac \au̇\ **out** \b̶\ Span Avila \ch\ **chin** \e\ **bet** \ē\ **easy** \g\ **go** \i\ **hit** \ī\ **ice** \j\ **job** \k\ Ger **ich, Buch** \ⁿ\ Fr vin \ŋ\ **sing** \ō\ **go** \ȯ\ **all** \ȯ\ **law** \œ\ Fr bœuf \œ̄\ Fr **feu** \ȯi\ **boy** \th\ **thin** \t͟h\ **this** \ü\ **loot** \u̇\ **foot** \ue\ Ger **füllen** \ue̅\ Fr **rue** \y\ **yet** \ʸ\ Fr digne \ˈdēnʸ\, nuit \ˈnwʸē\ \yü\ **few** \yu̇\ **fury** \zh\ **vision**

Mali Federation. Federation of Senegal and Sudanese Republic (now Mali) 1959–60; ✻ Dakar.

Maligne, Isle. See SAINT-JOSEPH-D'ALMA.

Ma·ligne Lake \mə-ˈlēn\. Lake in E cen. part of Jasper National Park, SW Alberta, Canada; 18 sq. mi. (47 sq. km.); alt. ab. 5500 ft. (1680 m.); its outlet is **Maligne River,** tributary of the Athabaska. Largest glacier-fed lake in Canadian section of Rocky Mts.

Mali Island; *formerly* **Ta·voy Island** \tə-ˈvȯi\. Island in Andaman Sea off W coast of S Myanmar, S of Tavoy Point; northernmost island of the Mergui Archipelago.

Malik, Wadi al. See MILK, WADI EL.

Ma·lik–Si·ah, Kuh–i– *or* **Kūh–e Ma·lek Sī·āh** \ˈkü-hē-ˈmäl-lēk-sē-ˈyä\. Peak at junction of Iran-Afghanistan-Pakistan boundaries; 5390 ft. (1643 m.).

Ma·li·nao \mä-ˈlē-naů\. Municipality on NE coast of Albay prov., Luzon, Philippines, at entrance to Tabaco Bay 17 mi. (27 km.) N of Legazpi; pop. (1980c) 28,372; in hemp region.

Ma·lin·che \mä-ˈlēn-chā\ *or* **Ma·lin·tzi** \mä-ˈlin-tsē\. Mountain on Puebla-Tlaxcala border, Mexico; 14,636 ft. (4461 m.); native name is **Ma·tlal·cue·yatl** \ˌmä-ˌtläl-ˈkwā-ˌyät-ᵊl\.

Ma·lin·dang, Mount *or* **Gran Malindang** \ˌmä-lin-ˈdäŋ\. Mountain, S Misamis Occidental prov., Mindanao, Philippines, 16 mi. (26 km.) WNW of Ozamiz; 7954 ft. (2424 m.); highest point in province.

Ma·lin·di \mä-ˈlin-dē\. Seaport town, SE Kenya; early ✻ of Portuguese East Africa; reached 1498 by Portuguese navigator Vasco da Gama who erected a monument, still standing. Nearby are ruins of ancient **Gedi** \ˈge-dē\ (possibly of Persian origin) with mosque, tombs, palace, and encircling wall (ab. 6 mi. or 10 km.).

Malines. See MECHELEN.

Mal·in Head \ˈma-lən\. Cape on N coast of co. Donegal, N Ireland (republic); 55°23′N, 7°24′W, the northernmost point of Ireland.

Malintzi. See MALINCHE.

Ma·lis \ˈmā-ləs\. District of ancient Greece, S of Thessaly and Othrys Mts. and extending along N and W shores of Gulf of Maliakós. Its inhabitants were Dorians.

Ma·li·ta \mä-ˈlē-tä\. Municipality, Davao del Sur prov., Mindanao, Philippines, on SW coast of Davao Gulf 46 mi. (74 km.) S of City of Davao; pop. (1980c) 60,638.

Mal·la·wī \mə-ˈla-wē, -ˈlä-\. Town, Minya governorate, Egypt, on the Nile 43 mi. (69 km.) NNW of Asyūt; pop. (1986p) 99,062.

Mal·le·co \mä-ˈyā-ˌkō\. Former province of S cen. Chile.

Mal·lee, The \ˈma-lē\. Region of NW Victoria, Australia, along the Murray River; formerly covered with the dense brushwood or thicket formed by the eucalypts (esp. *Eucalyptus dumosa* and *E. oleosa*); covering 14,000,000 acres (5,670,000 hectares); now extensively cleared for farming.

Mal·lia \ˈma-lē-ə\. Ancient city in Crete, important at time of Knossos and Phaistos; site of a Minoan palace.

Mallorca. See MAJORCA.

Mal·low \ˈma-lō\. Town, N cen. co. Cork, SW Ireland, on Blackwater River; pop. (1986c) 6488; market town; tourism.

Mal·lus *or* **Mal·los** \ˈma-ləs\. Town, ancient Cilicia, near coast of modern Gulf of İskenderun; home of Crates of Mallus, Stoic philosopher of 2d cent. B.C.

Mal·mai·son \ˌmȧl-mā-ˈzō^{n}\. Château ab. 7 mi. (11 km.) W of Paris, France; built 1622; residence of French Emperor Napoléon I and Empress Josephine and later of Queen María Cristina de Borbón of Spain, and of the Empress Eugénie, wife of Napoléon III.

Malmasia. See MONEMVASÍA.

Mal·mé·dy \ˌmȧl-mā-ˈdē\. Commune, E Liège prov., E Belgium; pop. (1991c) 10,291; in WWII scene of heavy fighting 1944–45, and of "Malmédy Massacre," Dec. 1944, in which ab. 100 U.S. prisoners were shot by Germans. See EUPEN.

Malmes·bury \ˈmämz-bə-rē, ˈmälmz-\. Town, Wiltshire, S England; pop. (1981c) 3395; Anglo-Saxon scholar Aldhelm was the first abbot (c. 675) at the ancient abbey here, and English historian William of Malmesbury was a monk here in 12th cent.

Malmö \ˈmäl-ˌmœ\. Fortified seaport, ⊗ of Malmöhus prov., SW Sweden, on Øresund opp. Copenhagen, Denmark; pop. (1989c) 232,908; 3d largest city in Sweden; important port; exports grain, sugar, cement, clay; shipbuilding; food processing; textile manufacture; 15th–16th cent. fortress, now a museum; 16th cent. town hall; 14th cent. church; founded 12th cent.; under Danish rule until 1658, when conquered and made a part of Sweden by Charles X Gustav.

Malm·ö·hus \ˈmäl-mœ-ˌhüs\. Province of S Sweden. See table at SWEDEN.

Ma·lo \mä-ˈlō\. Island, Vanuatu, SW Pacific Ocean, S of Espíritu Santo; pop. (1991e) 2879.

Ma·lo·e·lap \ˌmä-lō-ā-ˈläp\. Island (atoll), cen. part of Ratak Chain, E Marshall Is., W Pacific Ocean, 8°45′N, 171°03′E; has 64 islets. Japanese air base during WWII, raided by U.S. Navy fleet 1942, but later bypassed in advance toward Japan.

Ma·lo–les–Bains \mȧ-ˌlō-lā-ˈbe^{n}\. Commune, Nord dept., N France, NE suburb of Dunkerque on North Sea; seaside resort.

Ma·lo·los \mä-ˈlō-lōs\. Municipality, ✻ of Bulacan prov., Luzon, Philippines; pop. (1980c) 95,699; trade center in agricultural region. Chosen as ✻ of Philippine Republic 1898; meeting place of the revolutionary congress; constitution of the republic framed here 1898 and proclaimed 1899; captured by U.S. forces later that year.

Ma·lone \mə-ˈlōn\. Village, ⊗ of Franklin co., NE New York, 45 mi. (72 km.) WNW of Plattsburg; pop. (1990c) 6777; port of entry near boundary bet. U.S. and Canada; hometown of William Wheeler, vice president under 19th president of the U.S. Rutherford B. Hayes; selected by Irish-American Fenians as base for invasion of Canada 1866.

Ma·lo·ya·ro·sla·vets \ˌmə-lə-ˌyir-ə-ˈslȧ-vits\. Town, Kaluga Oblast, W Russia in Europe, N of the city of Kaluga; scene of battle 1812 in which the Russians prevented French Emperor Napoléon's army from retreating southward; in WWII, an outer defense of Moscow, taken by Germans Oct. 1941, retaken in 1942.

Mal·pe·lo Island \mäl-ˈpā-lō\. Island, E Pacific Ocean, W of Buenaventura, Colombia, 3°59′N, 81°35′W; belongs to Colombia.

Mal·peque Bay \ˈmȯl-pek\; *formerly* **Rich·mond Bay** \ˈrich-mənd\. Inlet of Gulf of St. Lawrence, in NW cen. Prince Edward I., SE Canada.

Mal·pla·quet \ˌmȧl-plȧ-ˈkā\. Hamlet in Nord dept., N France; scene of battle Sept. 11, 1709 during War of Spanish Succession in which allies under John Churchill, first duke of Marlborough and Prince Eugene of Savoy forced retreat of French under Marshal Claude-Louis-Hector de Villars.

Malstrøm. See MAELSTROM.

Mal·ta \ˈmȯl-tə\. **1.** *also* **Mal·tese Islands** \ˈmȯl-tēz\. Independent state, consisting of three islands in the Mediterranean Sea, ab. 58 mi. (93 km.) S of Sicily, Italy; 122 sq. mi. (316 sq. km.); pop. (1993e) 362,000; ✻ Valletta; major island is Malta (*anc.* **Mel·i·ta** \me-ˈlē-tə\), 95 sq. mi. (246 sq. km.); smaller islands are Comino and Gozo; the coastlines are well-indented.

Chief products: Potatoes, tomatoes, citrus fruit; textiles, clothing; tourism.

Chief towns: Birkirkara and Qormi.

History: Prehistoric megalithic remains; Phoenician and Carthaginian colony; captured by Romans c. 218 B.C.; part of Byzantine holdings when overrun by Saracens 870 A.D.; taken by Norman kingdom of Sicily (*q.v.*) 1090; given to Knights of St. John (later, Knights of Malta) by Holy Roman Emperor Charles V (who was also Charles I, king of Spain) 1530; held out against Turkish siege 1565; occupied by French commander (later emperor) Napoléon Bonaparte 1798–1800; captured by British 1800 and retained by them in Treaty of Paris 1814; received dominion government 1921, but status reverted to that of crown colony 1933; bombed heavily by Italians and Germans in WWII; achieved independence 1964; member of UN 1965; became a republic within the Commonwealth by constitutional revision 1974; British military presence withdrawn 1979.

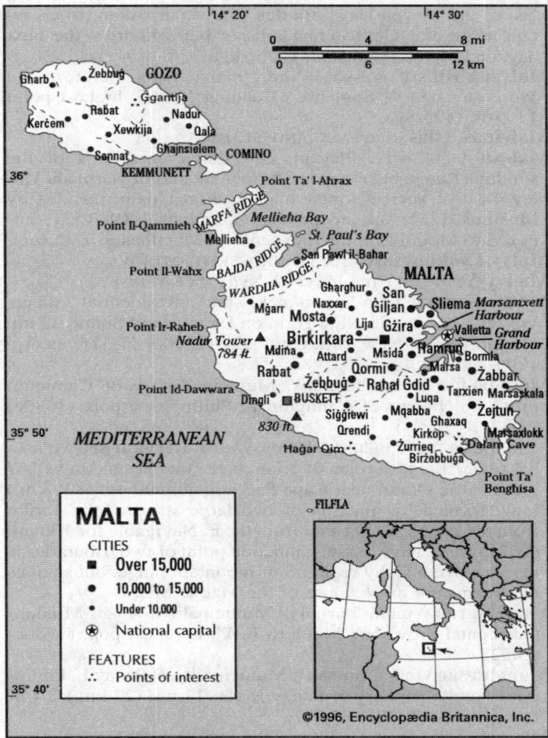

2. City, ⊗ of Phillips co., N Montana, 62 mi. (100 km.) WNW of Glasgow; pop. (1990c) 2340.

Malta Channel. Part of Mediterranean Sea constituting the passage bet. SE Sicily and Malta; ab. 58 mi. (93 km.) wide.

Malt·by \ˈmȯlt-bē\. Town, South Yorkshire, N England; pop. (1981p) 16,749; engineering; coal.

Maltese Islands. See MALTA 1.

Ma·lu·bi·ting \mä-ˌlü-bē-ˈtiŋ\. Mountain in the Karakoram Range, in region of Jammu and Kashmir controlled by Pakistan; 24,470 ft. (7458 m.).

Ma·łu·jo·wi·ce \ˌmä-wü-yō-ˈvēt-se\ *or Ger.* **Moll·witz** \ˈmȯl-ˌvits\. Village, SE Wrocław prov., SW Poland, just W of Brzeg; formerly in Silesia, Prussia, Germany; scene of battle of Mollwitz Apr. 10, 1741 during First Silesian War (War of Austrian Succession) in which Prussians defeated the Austrians.

Maluku. 1. Group of islands, E Indonesia. See MOLUCCAS. **2.** Province of Indonesia. See table at INDONESIA.

Malvasia, Napoli di. See MONEMVASÍA.

Mal·vern. 1. \ˈmal-vərn\. City, ⊗ of Hot Spring co., SW cen. Arkansas, 15 mi. (24 km.) SE of Hot Springs; pop. (1990c) 9256.
2. \ˈmal-vərn\. Borough, Chester co., SE Pennsylvania, 22 mi. (35 km.) WNW of Philadelphia; pop. (1990c) 2944.
3. \ˈmȯl-vərn\. Municipality, S Victoria, SE Australia; SE suburb of Melbourne; pop. (1991c) 41,340.

Malvern, Great. See GREAT MALVERN.

Mal·verne \ˈmal-vərn\. Village, Nassau co., Long Island, SE New York, 17 mi. (27 km.) E of New York City; pop. (1990c) 9054.

Mal·vern Hill \ˈmal-vərn\. Plateau on the James River, Virginia, 14 mi. (23 km.) SE of Richmond; battle July 1, 1862, last of the "Seven Days' Battles", in which Union troops repulsed several Confederate attacks but withdrew the next day, ending the Peninsular Campaign.

Malvern Hills \ˈmȯl-vərn, ˈmȯ-, ˈmäl-\. Hills, Hereford and Worcester co.; W England, extending N to S; highest point 1395 ft. (425 m.).

Malvinas, Islas. See FALKLAND ISLANDS.

Mal·wa \ˈmäl-wə\. Plateau, cen. India, mostly N of the Vindhya Range but extends S to include part of Narmada Valley. Seat of ancient kingdom with ✱ at Ujjain; invaded by Muslims 1235; an independent kingdom 1401–1531; annexed to Mogul Empire 16th cent.; to Marathas in 18th cent.

Malyy Lyakhovskiy. See LYAKHOVSKIYE OSTROVA.

Ma·lyy Ye·ni·sey \ˈmä-lē-ˌyi-nē-ˈsyā\. See YENISEY.

Ma·mar·o·neck \mə-ˈmar-ə-ˌnek, -nik\. Residential village, Westchester co., SE New York, on Long Island Sound 22 mi. (35 km.) NE of New York City; pop. (1990c) 17,325; incorp. 1895.

Mam·ba·jao \mäm-ˈbä-hau̇\. Municipality, ✱ of Camiguin prov., on N coast of Camiguin I., Philippines; pop. (1980c) 21,337.

Mam·be·ra·mo \ˌmäm-bā-ˈrä-mō\ *also* **Ta·ri·kai·kea** \ˌtär-ē-ˈkī-kē-ä\. Largest river of Irian Jaya, Indonesia; flows NW into Pacific Ocean near Cape Perkam; ab. 500 mi. (800 km.) long; formed by junction of two large streams, the Tariku from the W and the Taritatu from the E. Navigable for 100 mi. (161 km.) by large vessels; junction point of two tributaries is in extensive marshy region S of mountain range, but sources of streams are on N slopes of the Maoke Mts.

Mam·bu·rao \mäm-ˈbu̇r-au̇\. Municipality, ✱ of Mindoro Occidental prov., NW Mindoro I., Philippines; pop. (1980c) 15,523.

Mam·bu·sao \mäm-ˈbü-sau̇\. Municipality, N Panay I., Philippines, on W tributary of Panay River, 17 mi. (27 km.) SW of Roxas; pop. (1980c) 32,097.

Ma·metz \ˌmä-ˈmets\. Village, Somme dept., N France, 4 mi. (6 km.) SSE of Albert; battle July 1, 1916 during WWI in which British were victors.

Ma·mi·son Pass \ˌmə-mē-ˈsȯn\. Mountain pass over cen. Caucasus Mts., SE Europe, just S of Uilpata and on boundary bet. Alania Rep., Russia and South Ossetia, Republic of Georgia; alt. 9279 ft. (2828m.). Ossetian Military Road (built 1889) passes through it.

Mamlakah al–Maghribīyah, Al–. See MOROCCO 1.

Mam·moth \ˈma-məth\. Mountain in Grant co., E cen. Oregon; 6885 ft. (2098 m.).

Mammoth Cave. System of caves, SW cen. Kentucky, ab. 28 mi. (45 km.) ENE of Bowling Green; series of large irregular chambers in five levels (total length of chambers and passages over 300 mi. or 480 km.); shafts have been cut forming so-called pits or domes, as Bottomless Pit and Mammoth Dome which is 540 ft. (164 m.) long, 200 ft. (61 m.) wide, and 120 ft. (36 m.) high. Known to American Indians prior to discovery by white men c. 1799; source of saltpeter in War of 1812; Frozen Niagara (onyx cascades, gypsum flowers, stalactites and stalagmites) discovered 1923; new caverns remarkable for gypsum crystals and a 7000-foot (2130-meter) avenue discovered 1938; set aside as **Mammoth Cave National Park** (see UNITED STATES, *National Parks*).

Mammoth Hot Springs. Site, Yellowstone National Park, Wyoming; contains ab. 70 hot springs 60° to 175°F (15° to 80°C); remarkable for terraces of calcareous deposits covering ab. 200 acres (80 hectares). Administrative headquarters of Yellowstone National Park.

Mammoth Spring. Town, Fulton co., N Arkansas; pop. (1990c) 1097; site of one of largest springs in the world, source of hydroelectric power.

Ma·mo·ré \ˌmä-mō-ˈrā\. River, N cen. Bolivia; rises in W cen. Bolivia and is known as **Río Gran·de** \ˈrē-ō-ˈgrän-dā\ *or* **Gua·pay** \gwä-ˈpī\ in its upper course; flows SE, then turns NW and N through cen. Bolivia; forms section of boundary bet. NE Bolivia and Brazil; unites with Beni River to form Madeira River; ab. 1200 mi. (1930 km.) long; navigable for small craft.

Ma·mo·stang Kan·gri \ˈmä-mō-ˌstäŋ-ˈkäŋ-grē\. Mountain in the Karakoram Range, Jammu and Kashmir, India; 24,693 ft. (7526 m.).

Ma·mou \mə-ˈmü\. **1.** Town, Evangeline parish, S cen. Louisiana, 44 mi. (71 km.) S of Alexandria; pop. (1990c) 3483. **2.** Town, cen. Guinea, on Conakry-Kankan railroad line; pop. (1983p) 35,748.

Mam·ry \ˈmäm-rē\ *or Ger.* **Mau·er** \ˈmau̇-ər\. Lake, NW Suwałki prov., N Poland, NE of Olsztyn; ab. 40 sq. mi. (100 sq. km.); Węgorzewo is at its N end.

Mam Soul \mam-ˈsau̇l\. Peak, Highland region, N Scotland; ab. 3862 ft. (1177 m.).

Man \ˈmän\. Town, Ivory Coast, in mountainous area, 280 mi. (450 km.) NW of Abidjan; a center of Dan culture; noted for wooden masks.

Man, Calf of \ˌkaf...ˈman, ˌkȧf-\. Small island in the Irish Sea off SW coast of the Isle of Man.

Man, Isle of \ˈman\; *anc.* **Mo·na·pia** \mə-ˈnā-pē-ə\ *or* **Mo·na** \ˈmō-nə\. Island in the Irish Sea off NW coast of England; 221 sq. mi. (572 sq. km.); pop. (1986c) 64,282; ✱ Douglas; a crown possession; held by Norse (9th–13th cents.), Scots (13th–14th cents.), English (from 14th cent.); its language, Manx, now virtually extinct; has own legislature and laws; tourist center. The Manx breed of tailless cats is thought to have originated here.

Ma·na \mȧ-ˈnä\. **1.** River, cen. and N French Guiana; flows N into Atlantic Ocean near the Suriname boundary; 170 mi. (273 km.) long.
2. Coastal town, N French Guiana, at mouth of Mana River; pop. (1990c) 623.

Mana, Web·be \ˈwe-bā-ˈmä-nə\. River, S Ethiopia; flows SE; ab. 140 mi. (225 km.) long; a tributary of the Genale.

Ma·na·bí \ˌmä-nä-ˈbē\. Province of W Ecuador. See table at ECUADOR.

Ma·na·cor \ˌmä-nä-ˈkȯr\. Commune, Baleares prov., E Majorca I., Spain, 30 mi. (48 km.) E of Palma; pop. (1991c) 25,573; 13th cent. palace; resort, noted esp. for the underground lakes and caves nearby.

Ma·na·do *or* **Me·na·do** \mə-ˈnä-dō\. **1.** A residency of the former Netherlands Indies, now part of the prov. of North Sulawesi on Sulawesi, Indonesia; comprised the E peninsula, N half of cen. part of island, the long N peninsula (Minahasa), and adjacent island groups, esp. Banggai, Penju, Sangihe, and Talaud; 34,191 sq. mi. (88,555 sq. km.). Encloses on three sides the Gulf of Tomini. Mountainous, many peaks above 5000 ft. (1500 m.); highest Nokilalaki 10,860 ft. (3310 m.), in SW part (N cen. part of island); volcanic (Mt. Klabat) in extreme NE; no rivers of importance.

2. Commercial seaport, ✻ of North Sulawesi prov., Indonesia, at the NE end of Sulawesi (on Minahasa Penin.), on W slopes of Mt. Klabat; pop. (1990c) 318,796; university; good harbor; directly on sea routes from Hong Kong and Manila to Australia. Estab. by Dutch c. 1657; held by Japanese in WWII.

Ma·na·gua \mä-ˈnä-gwä\. **1.** Department of W Nicaragua. See table at NICARAGUA.

2. City, ✻ of Nicaragua, located on S shore of Lake Managua; munic. pop. (1985e) 682,111; alt. 200 ft. (61 m.); ✻ of Managua dept.; largest city and chief commercial center of Nicaragua; university; of minor importance during the Spanish era; made ✻ 1857; devastated by earthquakes in 1931 and 1972; scene of fighting 1978–79 during civil war.

Managua, Lake. Lake, W Nicaragua; drains S through Tipitapa River into Lake Nicaragua; 38 mi. (61 km.) long by 16 mi. (26 km.) wide; area 575 sq. mi. (1489 sq. km.).

Manahiki. See MANIHIKI.

Ma·na·ka·ra \ˌmä-nä-ˈkär-ə\. Coastal town, SE Madagascar; railroad terminus.

Ma·na·ma \mȧ-ˈnȧ-mə\ *or* **Al–Ma·na·mah** \ˌȧl-\. Seaport, ✻ of Bahrain, on N coast of Bahrain I. in Persian Gulf; pop. (1991c) 136,999; banking center; connected by causeway with Al Muharraq on adjacent island.

Manam Island. See VULCAN, MOUNT.

Ma·nan·ja·ry \ˌmä-nän-ˈzhär-ē\. Coastal town, E Madagascar, E of Fianarantsoa.

Ma·na·oag \mä-ˈnä-wäg\. Municipality, W Luzon, Philippines, 17 mi. (27 km.) E of Lingayen; pop. (1980c) 36,742.

Manáos. See MANAUS.

Ma·na·pia·ri \ˌmä-nä-ˈpyä-rē\. River, S cen. Venezuela; flows S into Ventuari River; ab. 100 mi. (160 km.) long.

Ma·na·pi·re \ˌmä-nä-ˈpē-rā\. River, N Venezuela; flows S into Orinoco River; 130 mi. (209 km.) long.

Ma·na·pla \mä-ˈnä-plä\. Municipality, N Negros, Philippines, on Guimaras Strait 24 mi. (39 km.) NNE of City of Bacolod; pop. (1980c) 40,524.

Ma·na·pou·ri Lake \ˌmä-nä-ˈpu̇r-ē\. Lake, SW South I., New Zealand; 48 sq. mi. (124 sq. km.); a source of the Waiau River.

Manar. See MANNAR.

Ma·nas \mə-ˈnäs\. River, E Bhutan; flows S across Indian border and into the Brahmaputra.

Manasarowar. See MAPAM YUMCO.

Man·a·squan \ˈma-nə-ˌskwän\. Borough, Monmouth co., E cen. New Jersey, on Atlantic Ocean 8 mi. (13 km.) S of Asbury Park; pop. (1990c) 5369; summer resort.

Ma·nas·sas \mə-ˈna-səs\. Independent city, ⊗ of Prince William co., NE Virginia, 25 mi. (40 km.) W of Alexandria; pop. (1990c) 27,957; battles of Bull Run (*q.v.*) (called Manassas by Confederates) fought here July 21, 1861 and Aug. 29–30, 1862.

Manassas Park. Independent city, Prince William co., NE Virginia, SW of Alexandria; pop. (1990c) 6734.

Ma·ná–Ta·rá, Cer·ro \ˈser-ō-mä-ˌnä-tä-ˈrä\. Peak, NW Venezuela, W of Lake Maracaibo; 12,240 ft. (3731 m.).

Man·a·tee \ˌma-nə-ˈtē, ˈma-nə-ˌtē\. County on W coast of Florida Penin. See table at FLORIDA.

Ma·na·tí \ˌmä-nä-ˈtē\. **1.** River, cen. and N cen. Puerto Rico; flows N into Atlantic Ocean; 25 mi. (40 km.) long.

2. Town and municipality, N Puerto Rico; pop. (1990c) 16,352 (town), 38,692 (munic.); town is on Manatí River and on railroad line 25 mi. (40 km.) W of San Juan.

Manatí, Point. Cape on SE coast of Las Villas prov., W cen. Cuba.

Ma·naus *or* **Ma·náos** \mȧ-ˈnau̇s\. City, ✻ of Amazonas state, W Brazil, on left bank of Rio Negro 12 mi. (19 km.) above its junction with the Amazon; munic. pop. (1991p) 1,010,558; trading port for products of the Amazon Basin, esp. rubber and forest products; oil refinery; tourism; 1000 mi. (1600 km.) from the mouth of the Amazon but accessible to ocean vessels; university (1965); cathedral; opera house; museum; notable botanical gardens; founded c. 1669; made provincial ✻ 1850; experienced extensive growth late 19th cent. because it had world's only supply of rubber; when rubber became available from other locations, economy rapidly declined; experienced economic growth again mid-20th cent. when it became duty-free area; now commercially important.

Ma·na·wa·tu \ˌmä-nä-ˈwä-tü\. River, SW North I., New Zealand; flows SW and W into Cook Strait; 113 mi. (182 km.) long.

Mancha, La. See LA MANCHA.

Manche \ˈmä^{n}sh\. Department of NW France. See table at FRANCE.

Manche, La. See ENGLISH CHANNEL.

Man·ches·ter \ˈman-ˌches-tər, -chə-stər\. **1.** Town, E Hartford co., N Connecticut; pop. (1990c) 51,618; Manchester Community Coll. (1963); settled 1672; incorp. 1823; important center of silk manufacture mid-19th cent. to mid-20th cent.

2. City, Meriwether and Talbot cos., W Georgia, 32 mi. (51 km.) NE of Columbus; pop. (1990c) 4104.

3. City, ⊗ of Delaware co., E Iowa, 35 mi. (56 km.) NNE of Cedar Rapids; pop. (1990c) 5137.

4. City, ⊗ of Clay co., SE Kentucky, 38 mi. (61 km.) N of Middlesborough; pop. (1990c) 1634.

5. Town, Essex co., Massachusetts. See MANCHESTER-BY-THE-SEA.

6. Village, St. Louis co., E Missouri, 16 mi. (26 km.) W of the city of St. Louis; pop. (1990c) 6542.

7. City, Hillsborough co., S New Hampshire, on Merrimack River 18 mi. (29 km.) N of Massachusetts border; pop. (1990c) 99,567; largest city in the state; supplied with power by Amoskeag Falls; state industrial school; St. Anselm Coll. (1889), New Hampshire Coll. (1932), Notre Dame Coll. (1950). Settled c. 1722; incorp. as **Der·ry·field** \ˈder-ē-ˌfēld\ 1751; renamed 1810; incorp. as city 1846; became major center of textile industry but diversified local industry after 1930s.

8. Village, Ontario co., W New York, 24 mi. (39 km.) ESE of Rochester; pop. (1990c) 9351; in Finger Lakes resort region.

9. City, Coffee co., Tennessee; pop. (1990c) 7709.

10. Village in Manchester town, a ⊗ of Bennington co., SW corner of Vermont, 21 mi. (34 km.) N of the town of Bennington; pop. (1990c) 3622 (town), 561 (village); summer resort (Big Equinox Mt. nearby); manufactures fishing rods and tackle; factory direct and outlet stores, mail-order houses.

11. Metropolitan district, ⊗ of Greater Manchester, NW England, on the Irwell 30 mi. (48 km.) ENE of Liverpool; pop. (1991p) 406,900; a major commercial and transportation center; produces textiles, electrical equipment, food products; engineering; important seaport, made accessible to ocean vessels by the Manchester Ship Canal (*q.v.*); cathedral (orig. a parish church, bishopric estab. 1847); Victoria Univ. of Manchester (1880); several technical institutes.

History: Woolen and linen manufacture introduced 14th cent., first cotton mill opened 1781; center of Puritanism 17th cent.; in 18th cent. strongly Jacobite; at beginning of 19th cent., without representation in parliament despite its growing size and importance as industrial city, became center of reform agitation initiated by the "Peterloo Massacre" Aug. 16, 1819, when a crowd of people, gathered on St. Peter's Fields to voice their grievances, was dispersed by cavalrymen, with several killed and many injured; became a city 1853; as an important textile center severely affected by cotton shortage during American Civil War; frequently bombed by Germans 1940–41. Birthplace of statesman David Lloyd George (1863).

Manchester–by–the–Sea *or* **Manchester.** Town, Essex co., NE Massachusetts, on Atlantic Ocean 21 mi. (34 km.) NE of Boston; pop. (1990c) 5286; summer resort.

\ə\ abut \ˊə\ matches \ᵊ\ kitten, Fr table \ər\ further \a\ ash \ā\ ace
\ä\ cot, cart \ȧ\ Fr bac \au̇\ out \b̲\ Span Avila \ch\ chin \e\ bet \ē\ easy
\g\ go \i\ hit \ī\ ice \j\ job \k̲\ Ger ich, Buch \$^{n}$\ Fr vin
\ŋ\ sing \ō\ go \ȯ\ all \ȯ\ law \œ\ Fr bœuf \œ̄\ Fr feu \ȯi\ boy
\th\ thin \th̲\ this \ü\ loot \u̇\ foot \ue\ Ger füllen \ue̅\ Fr rue
\y\ yet \$^{y}$\ Fr digne \ˈdēn^{y}\, nuit \ˈnw^{y}ē\ \yü\ few \yu̇\ fury \zh\ vision

Manchester Ship Canal. Canal, NW England, from Eastham, Merseyside, to Manchester; 35 mi. (56 km.) long; 28 ft. (8 m.) minimum depth; 120 ft. (37 m.) wide at the bottom; made Manchester a port accessible to large ocean vessels; commenced in 1887 and formally opened in 1894; rise of 60.5 ft. (18 m.) divided among five sets of locks; water supply provided from the Mersey and Irwell rivers.

Man–chou–li. See MANZHOULI.

Man·chu·kuo *or* **Man·chou·kuo** \ˈman-ˈchü-ˈkwō\ *also* **Man·chu·ti·kuo** \ˈmän-ˈchu̇-ˈtē-ˈkwō\. A former state of E Asia, 1932–45, set up under Japanese influence, comprising the three provinces of Manchuria (*q.v.*) and Jehol; approx. 482,440 sq. mi. (1,249,520 sq. km.); ✻ Hsinking (now Changchun). Set up as independent republic 1932 after Japanese occupation of Manchuria 1931; Jehol occupied by Japanese and added 1933; created an empire 1934 with puppet Manchu Emperor K'ang-te as nominal ruler; traditional provinces subdivided and reorganized 1934 into 18 provinces and the special municipality of Hsinking, but their boundaries were changed several times (for additional information, see MANCHURIA and JEHOL); dissolved 1945 at end of WWII.

Man·chu·ria \man-ˈchu̇r-ē-ə\. Region, comprising the three provinces of Liaoning, Jilin, and Heilongjiang (see table at CHINA), NE China, bounded on NW, N, and E by Russia in Asia (separated from it by the Amur and its tributaries, the Argun and Ussuri), on S by Hebei prov. (China), North Korea, and inlets of the Yellow Sea, and on W by Nei Monggol (Inner Mongolia). Its N two thirds is watered by the tributaries of the Amur, esp. the Songhua which covers with its tributaries all the cen. and N area; in the S is the Liao and on the North Korean border the Yalu. Much of its area is mountainous, of particular importance being the Da Hinggan Ling in the NW and the Changbai Shan on the North Korean border. In the S the wide Liaodong Penin. projects into Bo Hai (gulf), separating the Gulf of Liaodong on the W from Korea Bay. One of China's most important industrial regions; steel; coal, iron ore; soybeans, spring wheat, barley, oats.

History: Evidence of Stone Age inhabitants; included at various times in Chinese empire; under Khitans and other Mongol peoples to N and W of Manchuria; original home of Manchus who built a strong state under chieftain Nurhachi (d. 1626); conquered China, overthrowing Ming dynasty, and began Chinese Manchu (Ch'ing) dynasty (1644–1912); as result of Russian eastward advance from 17th cent., its N boundary came to be estab. at the Amur (*q.v.*); under loose Chinese control, coveted by Russia and Japan 19th and 20th cents.; occupied by Russians after Boxer Rebellion 1900; rivalry over Manchuria a partial cause of Russo-Japanese War 1904–05, most of which was fought there; after their defeat, Russians withdrew, leaving Japan in control of S Manchuria; Chinese civil administration set up 1907; increasingly the destination of Chinese immigration; adhered to Chinese Nationalist government 1928; annexed Jehol as a province 1928; after "Mukden Incident" 1931 (see *History* at SHENYANG), occupied by Japanese troops; despite protests of League of Nations, set up by Japan as puppet state of Manchukuo (*q.v.*) 1932, dissolved 1945 at end of WWII; occupied by Soviet troops 1945–46; scene of fighting bet. Chinese Nationalist and Communist troops 1946–48, came under complete control of Communists 1948; region utilized as a staging area for Chinese troops during Korean War 1950–53; administratively reorganized (incl. loss of Jehol) mid-1950s; several border incidents with Soviets 1960s.

Manchutikuo. See MANCHUKUO.

Man·cos \ˈmaŋ-kəs\. **1.** River, Montezuma co., SW Colorado; flows S and SE into San Juan River in NW New Mexico; ab. 60 mi. (96 km.) long; Mesa Verde National Park on W bank.

2. Town, Montezuma co., SW Colorado; pop. (1990c) 842; near Mesa Verde National Park.

Mand \ˈmänd\ *or* **Mund** \ˈmünd\. River, in SW Iran; flows W and SW into E cen. Persian Gulf S of Būshehr; ab. 300 mi. (480 km.) long.

Man·da \ˈmän-dä\. Town, S Tanzania, on good harbor on NE shore of Lake Malawi.

Man·da·la \män-ˈdä-lä\; *formerly* **Ju·li·a·na Top** \ˌyü-lē-ˈä-nə-ˈto̊p\. Peak, E end of Maoke Mts., Irian Jaya, Indonesia; 15,416 ft. (4699 m.).

Man·da·lay \ˌman-də-ˈlā\. **1.** Division of N Myanmar. See table at MYANMAR.

2. City, ✻ of Mandalay division, on Irrawaddy River, ab. 365 mi. (587 km.) N of Yangon; met. area pop. (1983c) 532,949; a trade center with railroad and river connections; many bazaars; religious center for Burmese Buddhists; at foot of Mandalay Hill are the 730 "pagodas" (*Kuthodaw*), stone tablets inscribed with Buddhist scriptures; university (1958). Its cantonment, a moated citadel known as Fort Dufferin, was old city built 1857–59 and containing palace, halls, and other buildings of King Thibaw; ✻ of kingdom of Burma 1860–85; occupied by Japanese 1942–45; largely destroyed in WWII.

Man·da·lu·yong \ˌmän-dä-lü-ˈyȯŋ\. Municipality, Luzon I., Philippines; pop. (1980c) 205,366.

Man·dan \ˈman-dən, -ˌdan\. City, ⊗ of Morton co., SW cen. North Dakota, across Missouri River from Bismarck; pop. (1990c) 15,177; tourism; incorp. 1881.

Manda National Park \ˈman-də\. National park, Chad; ab. 440 sq. mi. (1140 sq. km.); wildlife refuge (buffalo, elephant, giraffe, hippopotamus, hyena); estab. 1965.

Man·dar, Gulf of \ˈmän-ˌdär\. Inlet of Makassar Strait on SW coast of Sulawesi, Indonesia, N of Ujung Pandang; its NW point is **Tan·djung Ran·ga·sa** \ˈtän-ˌju̇ŋ-rän-ˈgä-sä\ *or Du.* **Hoek van Mandar** \ˈhük-vän-\.

Man·da·vi \ˈmən-də-vē\. See GOA 1.

Man·da·we \män-ˈdä-wē\. Chartered city, Cebu I., Philippines; pop. (1980c) 110,590.

Mandeb, Bab el. See BAB EL MANDEB.

Man·deure \mäⁿ-ˈdœr\. Commune, NE Doubs dept., E France; Roman remains.

Man·de·ville \ˈman-də-ˌvil\. **1.** Town, St. Tammany parish, SE Louisiana; pop. (1990c) 7083.

2. Town, S cen. Jamaica; pop. (1991p) 39,430.

Man·di \ˈmən-dē\. City, cen. Himachal Pradesh, N India, 45 mi. (72 km.) NNW of Simla; pop. (1991p) 23,208; trade center.

Man·din·ga \män-ˈdiŋ-gä\. Port, NE cen. Panama, on N shore of Gulf of San Blas.

Man·di·o·li \ˌmän-dē-ˈō-lē\. See BATJAN.

Mand·la \ˈmən-dlə\. Town, cen. Madhya Pradesh, India, ab. 40 mi. (64 km.) SE of Jabalpur; pop. (1991p) 38,390; road junction.

Man·dø \ˈmän-dœ\. Island, North Frisian Is., Denmark, S of Esbjerg.

Man·dor \ˈmən-ˌdȯr\. See JODHPUR 2.

Man·du·rah \ˈman-du̇-ˌrä\. City, SW Western Australia, Australia, ab. 35 mi. (56 km.) S of Perth; pop. (1993e) 34,194; a coastal resort.

Man·du·ria \män-ˈdür-ē-ä\. Commune, Taranto prov., Puglia, SE Italy, ESE of the seaport of Taranto; pop. (1989c) 32,737; cathedral; remains of pre-Roman walls.

Mand·vi \ˈmän-dvē\. Seaport town, Gujarat state, W India, on Gulf of Kachchh 210 mi. (338 km.) W of Ahmadabad.

Mand·ya \ˈmən-dyə\. Town, S Karnataka, S India; pop. (1991p) 119,970.

Man·fre·do·nia \ˌmän-frā-ˈdȯ-nyä\. Seaport, Foggia prov., Puglia, SE Italy, on Gulf of Manfredonia 22 mi. (35 km.) NE of the commune of Foggia; pop. (1989c) 58,920; tourism; cathedral; 13th cent. church; castle; built c. 1260 by King Manfred; destroyed by Turks 1620.

Manfredonia, Gulf of. Inlet of Adriatic Sea, in NE Puglia region, on SE coast of Italy.

Mang·a·ia \mäŋ-ˈī-ä\. Island in SE part of the Cook Is., in S Pacific Ocean 110 mi. (177 km.) ESE of Rarotonga, 21°55′S, 157°55′W; 20 sq. mi. (52 sq. km.); pop. (1986c) 1229; chief village Oneroa, on W side of island. Remarkable geologically as a fine example of a "makatea"—a broad uplifted coral reef surrounding an island.

Man·gal·dan \ˌmäŋ-gäl-ˈdän\. Municipality, W Luzon, Philippines, near coast on Dagupan-San Fernando railroad line; pop. (1980c) 50,434.

Man·ga·lia \mäŋ-ˈgä-lē-ä\. Town, Constanţa co., SE Romania; pop. (1989c) 40,668.

Man·ga·lore \ˈmäŋ-gə-ˌlȯr\. City, SW Karnataka, S India, on Malabar Coast 190 mi. (306 km.) W of Bangalore; pop. (1991p) 272,819; seaport, exporting coffee, sandalwood, nuts; manufactures textiles and roofing tiles; four colleges. Occupied by Portuguese 16th cent.; conquered by Hyder Ali of Mysore 1763; captured by British 1783 but the British garrison forced by Tipu Sultan to capitulate 1784; restored to British authority 1799.

Mang·a·re·va \mäŋ-ä-ˈrā-vä\. Chief island of the Gambier Is., French Polynesia, S Pacific Ocean; 5 mi. (8 km.) long; ab. 7 sq. mi. (18 sq. km.); has high central ridge covered with much vegetation.

Man·ga·rin Bay \ˌmäŋ-gä-ˈrēn\. Inlet on SW coast of Mindoro I., Philippines; San Jose is on its N shore.

Man·ga·ta·rem \ˌmäŋ-gä-ˈtä-rem\. Municipality, W Luzon, Philippines, near left bank of the Agno 16 mi. (26 km.) S of Lingayen; pop. (1980c) 40,582.

Man·ger·ton \ˈmaŋ-gərt-^{ə}n\. Mountain, cen. co. Kerry, SW Ireland; 2756 ft. (840 m.).

Mangishlak. See MANGYSHLAK.

Mang·ka·li·hat, Cape \ˌmäŋ-kä-lē-ˈhät\. Cape on E coast of the island of Borneo, East Kalimantan prov., Indonesia; projects into Celebes Sea at N entrance to Makassar Strait.

Man·gla Dam \ˈməŋ-glə\. Embankment dam on Jhelum River, N Pakistan; provides hydroelectric power.

Man·gla·res, Cape \ˈmäŋ-ˈglä-rās\ *or* **Cape Man·gles** \ˈmäŋ-glās\. Cape extending into Pacific Ocean at SW extremity of Colombia.

Man·go \ˈmäŋ-gō\ *or* **Ma·go** \ˈmä-gō\. Island, Fiji, SW Pacific Ocean, SW of Vanua Mbalavu I. in the Exploring Is.; ab. 3 mi. (5 km.) in diameter.

Man·go·chi *or* **Man·go·che** \mäŋ-ˈgō-chē\; *formerly* **Fort John·ston** \ˈjän-stən\. Town, S Malawi, 6 mi. (10 km.) from S end of Lake Malawi, ab. 65 mi. (105 km.) N of Zomba.

Man·go·ky \mäŋ-ˈgō-kē\. River, S cen. Madagascar; flows W into Mozambique Channel; ab. 350 mi. (560 km.) long.

Mang·o·le \mäŋ-ˈō-lā\. One of the Sula Is., Indonesia, E of Taliabu I. and N of Sanana; 63 mi. (101 km.) long by ab. 13 mi. (21 km.) wide; borders on Molucca Sea to the N.

Mang·o·nui \ˌmäŋ-ō-ˈnü-ē\. Village, on E coast of N extension of North I., New Zealand.

Man·gots·field \ˈmaŋ-gəts-ˌfēld\. Town, Avon co., SW cen. England; pop. (1981p) 23,046.

Man·grove Lagoon \ˈman-ˌgrōv, ˈmaŋ-\. Inlet of Jersey Bay in SE St. Thomas I., Virgin Is. of the U.S., West Indies.

Man·guei·ra, La·goa da \lȧ-ˈgō-ə-dȧ-mȧ^{n}-ˈgwā-rə\. Lake, S Rio Grande do Sul, S Brazil, along coast in strip of land bet. Lagoa Mirím and the Atlantic Ocean; 62 mi. (100 km.) long.

Man·gue·ni, Plateau of \ˌmäŋ-gā-ˈnē\. Elevated region, NE Niger, on Libyan border; 500 mi. (804 km.) E to W by 400 mi. (644 km.) N to S.

Man·gui·to \mäŋ-ˈgē-tō\. Municipality and town, Matanzas prov., W cen. Cuba, 35 mi. (56 km.) SE of Cárdenas.

Man·gum \ˈmaŋ-gəm\. City, ⊗ of Greer co., SW Oklahoma, 20 mi. (32 km.) NNW of Altus; pop. (1990c) 3344.

Man·gun·ça \mȧŋ-ˈgün-sə\. Island in Atlantic Ocean off N coast of Maranhão state, Brazil, at the entrance to Cabelo da Velha Bay.

Man·gysh·lak *also* **Man·gish·lak** \ˌmäŋ-gish-ˈläk\. Peninsula on the E coast of N Caspian Sea, SW Kazakhstan; oil-bearing region.

Man·has·set Bay \man-ˈha-sət\. Inlet of Long Island Sound on coast of Nassau co., Long Island, New York.

Man·hat·tan \man-ˈhat-^{ə}n, mən-\. **1.** Island at N end of New York Bay, bounded on N and NE by Spuyten Duyvil Creek and Harlem River, on E by East River, on S by New York Bay, and on W by Hudson River; 13.5 mi. (22 km.) long and 2.25 mi. (3.6 km.) wide; 23 sq. mi. (60 sq. km.); forms New York co. of New York state, and Manhattan borough (see MANHATTAN 2) of New York City. See *History* at NEW YORK 1 and 3.

2. Borough, SE New York, coextensive with New York co. (area 22 sq. mi. or 57 sq. km.) and Manhattan I., part of New York City bet. Hudson and East rivers; pop. (1990c) 1,487,536; separated from Long Island by East River and from mainland by Harlem River and Spuyten Duyvil Creek; includes islands: Roosevelt, Randall's, and Ward's, all in East River; chartered as one of five boroughs comprising city of New York 1898; contains main financial and commercial and important residential sections of the city. Columbia Univ. (chartered 1754 as King's College), New York Univ. (1831), City Coll. of the City Univ. of New York (founded as the Free Academy 1847), The Cooper Union for the Advancement of Science and Art (1859), Hunter Coll. of the City Univ. of New York (1870), Yeshiva Univ. (1886), Barnard Coll. (1889; affiliated with Columbia Univ.), Parsons School of Design (1896), The Juilliard School (1905), Pace Univ.–New York City (1906), Manhattan School of Music (1917), Bernard M. Baruch Coll. of the City Univ. of New York (1919), New School for Social Research (1919), Marymount Manhattan Coll. (1936), Laboratory Institute of Merchandising (1939), Fashion Institute of Technology (1944), School of Visual Arts (1947), Coll. of Insurance (1962), City Univ. of New York John Jay Coll. of Criminal Justice (1964), Touro Coll. (1971), Boricua Coll. (1974); New York Public Library; Metropolitan Museum of Art, American Museum of Natural History, Museum of Modern Art, Guggenheim Museum; Rockefeller Center (incl. Radio City Music Hall), Lincoln Center for the Performing Arts, Carnegie Hall; United Nations headquarters, Empire State Building, World Trade Center. Governed as part of New York City by a mayor and city council; has a borough president, with local and county functions conducted independently of central municipal government. See also NEW YORK 3.

3. City, ⊗ of Riley co., NE cen. Kansas, on Kansas River 50 mi. (80 km.) W of Topeka; pop. (1990c) 37,712; distribution point for agricultural products; Kansas State Univ. (1863), Manhattan Christian Coll. (1927); settled 1854; incorp. 1857.

Manhattan Beach. City, Los Angeles co., SW California, on Pacific Ocean 2 mi. (3.2 km.) S of Los Angeles International Airport; pop. (1990c) 32,063.

Man·heim \ˈman-ˌhīm\. Borough, Lancaster co., SE Pennsylvania, 10 mi. (16 km.) NNW of the city of Lancaster; pop. (1990c) 5011.

Manhiça. See VILA DA MANHIÇA.

Ma·ni·ca \mä-ˈnē-kä\. **1.** Province of W cen. Mozambique. See table at MOZAMBIQUE.

2. Town, Mozambique. See VILA DA MANHIÇA.

Manica and So·fa·la \sō-ˈfä-lä\. Former district, W and S cen. Mozambique; 50,137 sq. mi. (129,855 sq. km.); ✱ Beira.

Ma·ni·ca·land \-ˌland\. Territory in E Zimbabwe and W Mozambique; region has valuable goldfields, irrigated agricultural land.

Manich. See MANYCH.

Man·i·coua·gan \ˌma-nə-ˈkwä-gən\. **1.** River, SE Quebec, Canada; flows S into St. Lawrence River near its mouth; 285 mi. (459 km.) long; one branch flows through **Réservoir Manicouagan** (**Manicouagan Reservoir**); ab. 87 sq. mi. (225 sq. km.); river dammed in three places.

2. County, Quebec, Canada. See table at QUEBEC.

Ma·ni·e·ma \ˌmä-nē-ˈā-mä\. Administrative region of Democratic Rep. of the Congo. See table at ZAIRE.

Ma·ni·hi·ki \ˌmä-nē-ˈhē-kē\ *also* **Ma·na·hi·ki** \ˌmä-nä-\; *mostly formerly* **Hum·phrey** \ˈhəm-frē\. Chief island (atoll) of the Northern Cook Is., cen. Pacific Ocean, 650 mi. (1046 km.) N of Rarotonga; 2 sq. mi. (5 sq. km.); pop. (1986c) 508; chief villages Tukao on N end and Tauhunu on W coast; produces copra and pearl shell; U.S. claim dropped 1983.

Manihiki Islands. See NORTHERN COOK ISLANDS.

Maniitsoq. See SUKKERTOPPEN.

Ma·nila \mə-ˈni-lə\. **1.** City, Mississippi co., NE Arkansas; pop. (1990c) 2635.

\ə\ **abut** \ə̄\ **matches** \$^{ə}$\ **kitten, Fr table** \ər\ **further** \a\ **ash** \ā\ **ace**
\ä\ **cot, cart** \ȧ\ **Fr bac** \au̇\ **out** \b\ **Span Avila** \ch\ **chin** \e\ **bet** \ē\ **easy**
\g\ **go** \i\ **hit** \ī\ **ice** \j\ **job** \k̲\ **Ger ich, Buch** \$^{n}$\ **Fr vin**
\ŋ\ **sing** \ō\ **go** \ö\ **all** \ȯ\ **law** \œ\ **Fr bœuf** \œ̄\ **Fr feu** \ȯi\ **boy**
\th\ **thin** \th̲\ **this** \ü\ **loot** \u̇\ **foot** \ue\ **Ger füllen** \ue̅\ **Fr rue**
\y\ **yet** \$^{y}$\ **Fr digne** \ˈdēn^{y}\, **nuit** \ˈnw^{y}ē\ \yü\ **few** \yu̇\ **fury** \zh\ **vision**

2. Town, ⊗ of Daggett co., NE Utah; pop. (1990c) 207.

3. City, ✻ of the Republic of the Philippines on SW Luzon I.; pop. (1990p) 1,587,000; principal port and commercial, cultural, and industrial center of the Philippines; diversified industries include shipbuilding and food processing; produces textiles, chemicals; Far Eastern Univ. (1934) and other educational institutions; practically divided into two parts by the Pasig River; Intramuros or Walled City, the original Spanish fortified settlement, surrounded until WWII by a thick stone wall 25 ft. (7.6 m.) high and ab. 2.5 mi. (4 km.) in circumference.

History: Founded by Spanish explorer Miguel López de Legazpi 1571 on site of Muslim settlement; under early Spanish rule, became important commercial center; occupied by British 1762–63 during Seven Years' War; captured by U.S. forces 1898 during Spanish-American War, after defeat of the Spanish fleet (see MANILA BAY); occupied by Japanese 1942–45 in WWII, suffered much damage during recapture by U.S. forces; much of damage repaired during postwar expansion and modernization; damaged in earthquake 1968, flood 1972. See QUEZON CITY.

Manila Bay. Large inlet of South China Sea in W Luzon, Philippines; forms a landlocked sea of 770 sq. mi. (1994 sq. km.), 120 mi. (193 km.) in circumference, 30 mi. (48 km.) across from Manila to Corregidor I. and 36 mi. (58 km.) from the NW corner to Cavite shore. Its entrance is through North and South channels on either side of Corregidor I. Scene of a decisive naval battle of the Spanish-American War on May 1, 1898, when U.S. Commodore George Dewey's fleet destroyed the Spanish fleet off Cavite, with no U.S. losses. In WWII U.S. shipping bombed and destroyed 1941–42; Japanese vessels similarly attacked and destroyed by U.S. aircraft 1944–45; again under U.S. control 1945.

Ma·nin·djau \mä-ˈnin-ˌjau̇\. Crater lake in Barisan Mts., W Sumatra, Indonesia, W of Bukittinggi, ab. 11 mi. (18 km.) long by 6 mi. (10 km.) wide.

Ma·ni·pa Strait \mä-ˈnē-pä\. Channel bet. Buru and Ceram islands in the Moluccas, Indonesia, E Malay Archipelago; connects Ceram Sea with Banda Sea.

Ma·ni·pur \ˈmə-ni-ˌpu̇r\. **1.** River, W Myanmar; flows S out of Loktak Lake, S Manipur state, NE India and across border; bends E and N to empty into Chindwin River.

2. State, NE India, on Myanmar border; ✻ Imphal. Consists of wide valley with surrounding hills and mountains. Inhabited chiefly by Manipuris and Meithei. (See table at INDIA.) First relations with British 1762 treaty for help against Burmese invasions; came under British administration 19th cent.; invaded 1944 by Japanese (from Burma) who were driven out later that year; territory 1947–72; estab. as a state 1972.

Ma·ni·sa *or* **Ma·nis·sa** \ˈmä-nē-ˌsä\. **1.** Province of Turkey in Asia. See table at TURKEY.

2. *anc.* **Mag·ne·sia** \mag-ˈnē-zhə, -zhē-ə\. City, its ✻, 20 mi. (32 km.) NE of İzmir; pop. (1990c) 158,928; commercial center; on main railroad line E to Afyon; has buildings from Seljuq and early Osmanli period. Part of Nicaea (a fragment of Byzantine Empire) from 1204; later (1313) the ✻ of a Turkoman emirate; conquered by Sultan Bayezid I of Ottoman Empire, late 14th cent. Nearby are ruins of **Magnesia (ad Sip·y·lum)** \ad-ˈsi-pi-ləm\ where in 190 B.C. the Romans defeated Antiochus the Great, king of Syria.

Ma·nis·ses \mə-ˈni-sēz\. Native name for Block I. (*q.v.*).

Man·is·tee \ˌma-nə-ˈstē\. **1.** River, NW Michigan; rises in W Crawford co., flows SW into Lake Michigan at Manistee, in Manistee co.; 150 mi. (241 km.) long; navigable for a short distance.

2. County in NW Michigan. See table at MICHIGAN.

3. City, ⊗ of Manistee co., NW Michigan, on Lake Michigan at mouth of Manistee River 20 mi. (32 km.) N of Ludington; pop. (1990c) 6734; summer resort.

Man·is·tique \ˌma-nə-ˈstēk\. **1.** River, S Upper Penin. of Michigan; flows from Manistique Lake in SW Luce co. SW into N Lake Michigan at Manistique.

2. City, ⊗ of Schoolcraft co., S Upper Penin. of Michigan, on Lake Michigan at mouth of Manistique River, 43 mi. (69 km.) ENE of Escanaba; pop. (1990c) 3456; summer resort.

Manistique Lake. Lake in Luce and Mackinac cos., E Upper Penin. of Michigan; outlet, Manistique River.

Man·i·to·ba \ˌma-nə-ˈtō-bə\. Province, easternmost of the Prairie Provinces, cen. Canada, bounded on N by Nunavut, on NE by Hudson Bay, on E by Ontario, on S by U.S.A. (Minnesota and North Dakota), and on W by Saskatchewan; ✻ Winnipeg. See table at CANADA.

Physical features: Level country with many lakes and rivers, most draining to Hudson Bay. Has three large lakes—Winnipeg (larger than Lake Ontario), Winnipegosis, and Manitoba—in cen. part; these are fed by Red, Winnipeg, and Saskatchewan rivers and have the Nelson as their outlet; the Churchill and Seal are farther N. The port of Churchill is situated at mouth of Churchill River. Has one large national park (Riding Mountain), nine provincial parks.

Chief products: Wheat, barley; livestock raising; nickel, copper, gold, zinc; food products, electrical goods, transportation equipment; hydroelectric power.

Chief cities: Winnipeg is the province's only large city.

History: Region first visited by Europeans along the shore of Hudson Bay in early 17th cent.; Hudson's Bay Company post estab. at Port Nelson 1670; S part explored by Canadian explorer La Vérendrye and site of Winnipeg reached 1738; explored and fortified by both British and French; title to region surrendered by French in Treaty of Paris 1763; Red River Settlement (*q.v.*) founded by Thomas Douglas, 5th earl of Selkirk 1811; became part of Assiniboia region; acquired by Canada late 1860s; scene of Métis rebellion 1869–70; nucleus of province estab. 1870; enlarged 1881 and 1912; its growth accelerated by completion of railroads 1878–86.

Manitoba, Lake. Lake, S Manitoba, Canada, SW of Lake Winnipeg; ab. 1800 sq. mi. (4660 sq. km.); ab. 140 mi. (225 km.) long; outlet through Dauphin River to Lake Winnipeg.

Man·i·tou Island \ˈma-nə-ˌtü\. Island in Lake Superior, the NE extremity of Keweenaw co., off N tip of Upper Penin. of Michigan.

Manitou Island, North. Island in N Lake Michigan, in Leelanau co., NW Michigan.

Manitou Island, South. Island in N Lake Michigan, in Leelanau co., NW Michigan.

Man·i·tou·lin \ˌma-nə-ˈtü-lən\. District in S Ontario, Canada. See table at ONTARIO.

Manitoulin Island *also* **Grand Manitoulin.** Island, N Lake Huron, S Ontario, Canada; 80 mi. (129 km.) long; separated from the mainland by North Channel; with Cockburn and other small adjacent islands forms Manitoulin dist.

Man·i·tou Springs \ˈma-nə-tü\. Town, El Paso co., E cen. Colorado, at foot of Pikes Peak just W of Colorado Springs; pop. (1990c) 4535; tourist and health resort; mineral springs; Garden of the Gods and Cave of the Winds in vicinity.

Man·i·to·woc \ˈma-nə-tə-ˌwäk\. **1.** County in E Wisconsin. See table at WISCONSIN.

2. City and port of entry, its ⊗, E Wisconsin, on Lake Michigan 25 mi. (40 km.) N of Sheboygan; pop. (1990c) 32,520; processed foods; shipyards; Silver Lake Coll. (1869); fur-trading post 1795; settled c. 1835.

Man·i·wa·ki \ˌma-nə-ˈwȯ-kē\. Town, SW Quebec, Canada, on Gatineau River 67 mi. (108 km.) N of Hull; pop. (1991c) 4605.

Man·i·za·les \ˌmä-nē-ˈsä-lās\. City, ✻ of Caldas dept., W cen. Colombia, 110 mi. (177 km.) W of Bogotá; pop. (1992e) 327,100; important coffee-processing center in the Cordillera Central of the Andes; alt. 7064 ft. (2153 m.); has direct rail connection with Buenaventura; university (1943).

Manj·ra \ˈmənj-ˌrä\. River, cen. SE Maharashtra, S cen. India; rises on W border, flows SE, then turns N at border of Andhra Pradesh to join the Godavari NW of Nizamabad; ab. 385 mi. (619 km.) long.

Man·ju·yod \mäŋ-ˈhü-yȯd\. Municipality, E Negros, Philippines, on Tanon Strait near its S end, 28 mi. (45 km.) NNW of Dumaguete; pop. (1980c) 26,257.

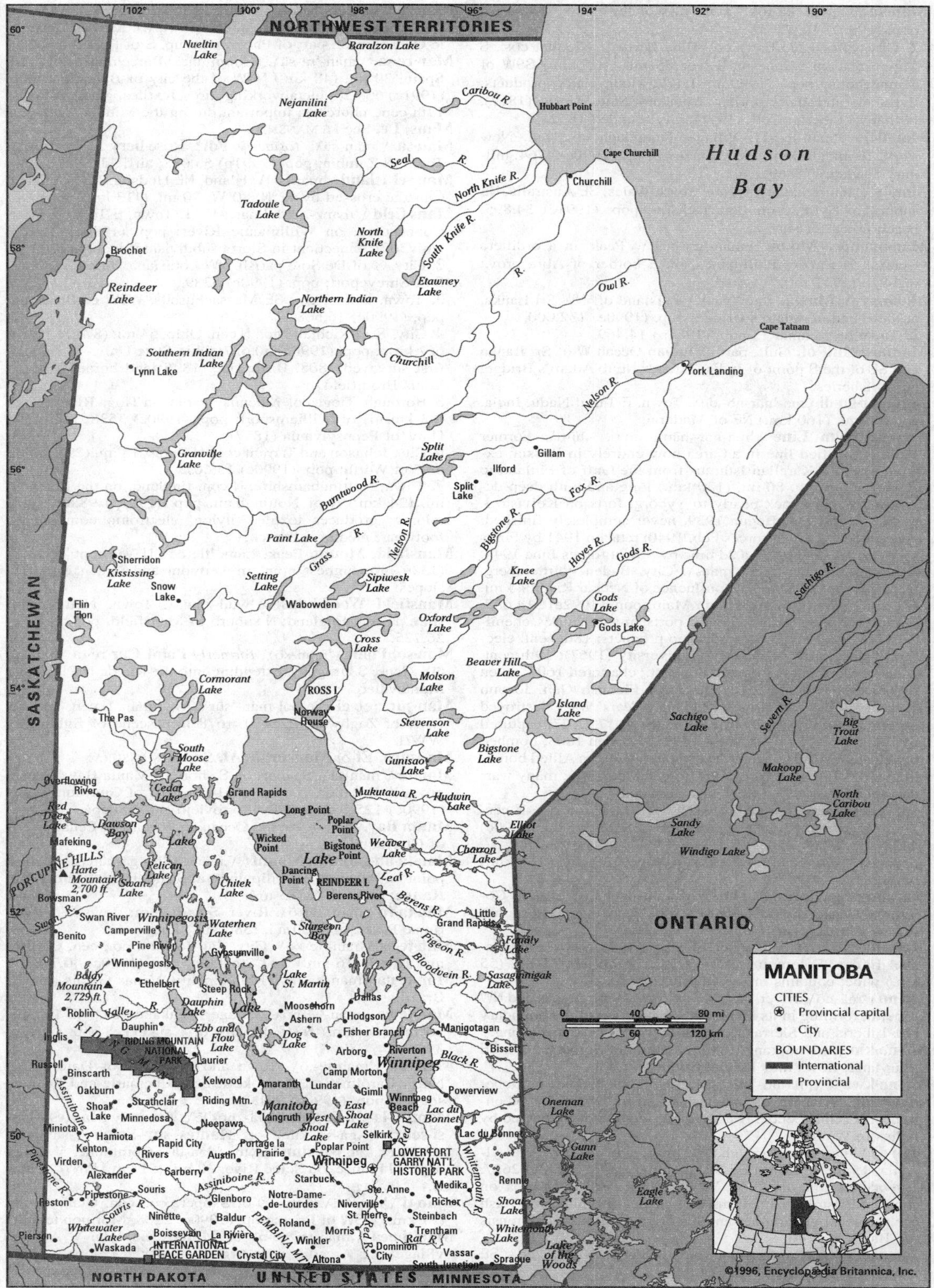
NORTHWEST TERRITORIES
Hudson Bay
SASKATCHEWAN
ONTARIO
NORTH DAKOTA
UNITED STATES
MINNESOTA
MANITOBA
CITIES
Provincial capital
City
BOUNDARIES
International
Provincial
0 40 80 mi
0 60 120 km
©1996, Encyclopædia Britannica, Inc.
Nueltin Lake
Baralzon Lake
Nejanilini Lake
Caribou R.
Hubbart Point
Seal R.
Cape Churchill
Churchill
North Knife R.
Tadoule Lake
North Knife Lake
South Knife R.
Brochet
Reindeer Lake
Etawney Lake
Northern Indian Lake
Owl R.
Cape Tatnam
Southern Indian Lake
Lynn Lake
Churchill
York Landing
Nelson R.
Gillam
Granville Lake
Split Lake
Ilford
Burntwood R.
Split Lake
Fox R.
Paint Lake
Grass R.
Nelson R.
Bigstone R.
Hayes R.
Gods R.
Sherridon
Kississing Lake
Setting Lake
Sipiwesk Lake
Knee Lake
Sachigo R.
Snow Lake
Wabowden
Gods Lake
Gods Lake
Flin Flon
Oxford Lake
Cross Lake
Beaver Hill Lake
Molson Lake
Cormorant Lake
ROSS I.
Island Lake
Sachigo Lake
Severn R.
Big Trout Lake
The Pas
Norway House
Stevenson Lake
South Moose Lake
Gunisao Lake
Bigstone Lake
Makoop Lake
Overflowing River
Cedar Lake
Grand Rapids
Mukutawa R.
Hudwin Lake
North Caribou Lake
Red Deer Lake
Dawson Bay
Long Point
Poplar Point
Sandy Lake
Mafeking
Wicked Point
Bigstone Point
Weaver Lake
Elliot Lake
Charron Lake
Windigo Lake
PORCUPINE HILLS
Harte Mountain 2,700 ft.
Pelican Lake
Lake
Dancing Point
REINDEER I.
Leaf R.
Swan Lake
Chitek Lake
Berens River
Berens R.
Bowsman
Swan R.
Swan River
Winnipegosis
Waterhen Lake
Little Grand Rapids
Benito
Camperville
Sturgeon Bay
Family Lake
Pine River
Gypsumville
Pigeon R.
Winnipegosis
Bloodvein R.
Sasaginnigak Lake
Baldy Mountain 2,729 ft.
Ethelbert
Lake St. Martin
Steep Rock
Dallas
Dauphin Lake
Lake
Moosehorn
Hodgson
Roblin
Valley R.
Ashern
Fisher Branch
Manigotagan
Dauphin
Ebb and Flow Lake
Dog Lake
Inglis
RIDING MOUNTAIN NATIONAL PARK
RIDING MTN.
Arborg
Riverton
Bissett
Black R.
Russell
Laurier
Winnipeg
Binscarth
Kelwood
Amaranth
Lundar
Camp Morton
Oakburn
Gimli
Powerview
Shoal Lake
Strathclair
Riding Mtn.
Manitoba
East Shoal Lake
Winnipeg Beach
Lac du Bonnet
Minnedosa
Langruth
West Shoal Lake
Oneman Lake
Miniota
Neepawa
Hamiota
Selkirk
Lac du Bonnet
Assiniboine R.
Kenton
Rapid City
Portage la Prairie
Poplar Point
Red R.
LOWER FORT GARRY NAT'L HISTORIC PARK
Gunn Lake
Rivers
Austin
Winnipeg
Whitemouth R.
Virden
Carberry
Alexander
Starbuck
Medika
Pipestone R.
Assiniboine R.
Ste. Anne
Rennie
Pipestone
Souris
Glenboro
Notre-Dame-de-Lourdes
Reston
Richer
Eagle Lake
Niverville
Souris R.
Ninette
Baldur
St. Pierre
Steinbach
Shoal Lake
Whitewater Lake
Roland
Trentham
Pierson
Boissevain
La Rivière
Morris
Whitemouth Lake
PEMBINA MTN.
Winkler
Waskada
INTERNATIONAL PEACE GARDEN
Red R.
Rat R.
Dominion City
Vassar
Crystal City
Altona
South Junction
Sprague
Lake of the Woods
60°
58°
56°
54°
52°
50°
102°
100°
98°
96°
94°
92°
90°

Man·ka·to \man-ˈkā-tō\. **1.** City, ⊗ of Jewell co., N Kansas; pop. (1990c) 1037.
2. City, ⊗ of Blue Earth co., Blue Earth & Nicollet cos., S Minnesota, on Minnesota River 65 mi. (105 km.) SSW of Minneapolis; pop. (1990c) 31,477; flour, dairy products; livestock and dairy farms; Mankato State Univ. (1867), Bethany Lutheran Coll. (1911); city founded 1852.

Man·li·us \ˈman-lē-əs\. Village, Onondaga co., cen. New York, 10 mi. (16 km.) E of Syracuse; pop. (1990c) 4764; military academy (1869).

Man·ly \ˈman-lē\. City, E New South Wales, SE Australia, NE suburb of Sydney on Port Jackson; pop. (1991c) 34,895; beach noted for surfing.

Man·ma·noc, Mount \män-ˈmä-nək\. Peak in Cordillera Central, N Luzon, Philippines, on E border of Abra prov.; 6334 ft. (1931 m.).

Man·nar *or* **Ma·nar** \mə-ˈnär\. **1.** Island off NW Sri Lanka, at the E end of Adam's Bridge; pop. (1990e) 132,000.
2. Town on Mannar I.; pop. (1981p) 14,469.

Mannar, Gulf of. Gulf, part of Indian Ocean W of Sri Lanka and SE of the S point of India; extends NE to Adam's Bridge; pearl fisheries.

Man·nar·gu·di \mə-ˈnär-gə-ˌdē\. Town, E Tamil Nadu, India, ab. 100 mi. (160 km.) NE of Madurai.

Man·ner·heim Line \ˈmä-nər-ˌhām, ˌma-, -ˌhīm\. Former Finnish fortified line in an area now entirely in Russia; extended across Karelian Isthmus from the Gulf of Finland to Lake Ladoga, ab. 80 mi. (130 km.) long and with deep defenses reaching back nearly to Vyborg; forts on Koivisto I. marked its W end. Begun 1939, never completely finished; penetrated by Soviet forces Feb. 1940; retaken 1941 by Finns and Germans but taken a 2d time by Soviet forces June 1944.

Mann·heim \ˈmän-ˌhīm, ˈman-\. City, Baden-Württemberg, Germany, on the Rhine at confluence of Neckar River, 44 mi. (71 km.) SSW of Frankfurt am Main; pop. (1992e) 314,685; one of Europe's largest inland ports; manufactures chemicals, electrical equipment, tobacco products; 18th cent. electoral palace, now occupied by university (1967); 19th cent. water tower. First mentioned 8th cent.; chartered 1607; taken by forces of Catholic League under Flemish Gen. Johann Tserclaes, Graf von Tilly 1622 (Thirty Years' War); destroyed by French 1689; seat of Rhine Palatinate 1720–77; captured by French 1795, by Austrians 1799; to Baden 1803; bombed by Allies in WWI; suffered heavy damage from Allied bombing in WWII; captured by U.S. forces Mar. 1945; many war-damaged historic buildings now restored.

Man·ning \ˈma-niŋ\. **1.** Town, ⊗ of Clarendon co., E cen. South Carolina, 17 mi. (27 km.) SSE of Sumter; pop. (1990c) 4428.
2. River, New South Wales, Australia; 139 mi. (224 km.) long.

Manning Provincial Park. Provincial park in S British Columbia, Canada, in Cascade Mts. E of Vancouver; 276 sq. mi. (715 sq. km.).

Manning Strait. Channel bet. SE Choiseul I. and NW Santa Isabel I., cen. Solomon Is., W Pacific Ocean; ab. 35 mi. (55 km.) wide; contains many small islands.

Ma·no \ˈmä-nō\. River, W Africa; flows SW through N and NW Liberia, forming in its lower course a section of the boundary bet. Liberia and Sierra Leone; ab. 200 mi. (320 km.) long.

Ma·no·kin \mə-ˈnō-kən\. River, W shore of Somerset co., SE Maryland; flows into Tangier Sound.

Ma·no·kwa·ri \ˌmä-nō-ˈkwär-ē\. Town, on NE coast of Doberai Penin., Irian Jaya, Indonesia, forming NW point of entrance to Teluk Cenderawasih; has good harbor; bypassed by Allies in WWII.

Man·or \ˈma-nər\. Borough, Westmoreland co., SW Pennsylvania, 15 mi. (24 km.) SE of Pittsburgh; pop. (1990c) 2627.

Man·or·bier \ˌma-nər-ˈbir\. Village, Dyfed co., SW Wales, on coast of Bristol Channel; ruins of castle, birthplace of Welsh ecclesiastical geographer and historian Giraldus Cambrensis (de Barri) c. 1146.

Man·or·ha·ven \ˈma-nər-ˌhā-vən\. Village, Nassau co., SE New York; pop. (1990c) 5672.

Man·ra \ˈmän-rə, ˈman-\; *formerly* **Syd·ney** \ˈsid-nē\. One of the smaller islands of the Phoenix Is. (*q.v.*), Kiribati, S Pacific Ocean, in SE part of Phoenix group, S of Enderbury I.

Man·re·sa \män-ˈrā-sä\. Commune, Barcelona prov., NE Spain, 30 mi. (48 km.) NNW of the city of Barcelona; pop. (1991c) 66,320; metalworking; tires, textiles, glass; 14th and 17th cent. churches; important during the Middle Ages.

Mans, Le. See LE MANS.

Man·sa \ˈmän-sä\; *formerly* **Fort Rose·bery** \ˈrōz-ˌber-ē\. Town, N Zambia; pop. (1991p) 55,088; airfield.

Man·sel Island \ˈman-səl\. Island, NE Hudson Bay, Nunavut, Canada; crossed by 62°N, 80°W; 70 mi. (113 km.) long.

Mans·field \ˈmanz-ˌfēld, ˈmans-\. **1.** Town, E Tolland co., N Connecticut, on Willimantic River; pop. (1990c) 21,103; Univ. of Connecticut in Storrs subdivision; incorp. 1702.
2. City, ⊗ of De Soto parish, NW Louisiana, 33 mi. (53 km.) S of Shreveport; pop. (1990c) 5389.
3. Town, Bristol co., SE Massachusetts, WSW of Brockton; pop. (1990c) 16,568.
4. City, ⊗ of Richland co., N cen. Ohio, 54 mi. (87 km.) WSW of Akron; pop. (1990c) 50,627; Ohio State Univ.–Mansfield; first surveyed 1808. Birthplace (1896) and home of writer Louis Bromfield.
5. Borough, Tioga co., N Pennsylvania, on Tioga River 39 mi. (63 km.) N of Williamsport; pop. (1990c) 3538; Mansfield Univ. of Pennsylvania (1857).
6. City, Johnson and Tarrant cos., N Texas, 18 mi. (29 km.) SE of Fort Worth; pop. (1990c) 15,607.
7. Town, Nottinghamshire, N cen. England, on the Maun 15 mi. (24 km.) N of Nottingham; pop. (1991p) 98,800; coal mining; produces textiles, nylon, electronic components, footwear; medieval church.

Mansfield, Mount. Peak, Lamoille co., N Vermont; 4393 ft. (1339 m.); highest point in Vermont and Green Mts.; ski slopes.

Mansfield Wood·house \ˈwu̇d-ˌhau̇s\. Town, Nottinghamshire, N cen. England; N suburb of Mansfield; pop. (1981p) 26,725.

Man·so, Point \ˈmän-sō\; *formerly* **Point Car·re·ta** \kär-ˈrā-tä\. Cape, S Uruguay, extending into the Rio de la Plata near Montevideo.

Man·ṣūr, Jeb·el \ˈje-bəl-man-ˈsür\. Mountain, N cen. Tunisia, WSW of Zaghwān; 2224 ft. (678 m.); scene of fighting in WWII.

Mansûra, El *or* **Manṣūrah, Al.** See EL MANSÛRA.

Man·ta \ˈmän-tä\. Seaport on S shore of Manta Bay, Manabí prov., W Ecuador, 100 mi. (161 km.) NW of Guayaquil; pop. (1990c) 125,505; port for Portoviejo and Jipijapa.

Manta Bay. Inlet of Pacific Ocean on W coast of Ecuador, NW of Guayaquil.

Man·ta·lin·ga·jan, Mount \ˌmän-tä-liŋ-ˈgä-hän\. Highest point on Palawan I., Philippines, at S end, in **Mantalingajan Range;** 6839 ft. (2085 m.).

Man·ta·ro \män-ˈtär-ō\. River, S cen. Peru; flows E to Apurímac River; ab. 360 mi. (580 km.) long.

Man·te·ca \man-ˈtē-kə\. City, San Joaquin co., cen. California, 10 mi. (16 km.) S of Stockton; pop. (1990c) 40,773.

Man·te·na \mȧn-ˈtā-nə\. Municipality, Minas Gerais state, E Brazil.

Man·te·no \man-ˈtē-nō\. Village, Kankakee co., NE Illinois, 10 mi. (16 km.) N of the city of Kankakee; pop. (1990c) 3488.

Man·teo \ˈman-tē-ˌō\. Town and resort, ⊗ of Dare co., E North Carolina, on Roanoke I. bet. Albemarle and Pamlico sounds; pop. (1990c) 991.

Mantes–la–Jo·lie \ˌmäⁿt-ˌlä-zhȯ-ˈlē\; *formerly* **Mantes–Gas·si·court** \-ˌgȧ-sē-ˈkür\ *or* **Mantes–sur–Seine** \-sūr-ˈsān, -ˈsen\ *or Lat.* **Me·dun·ta** \me-ˈdən-tä\. Commune, Yvelines dept., N France, on Seine River 32 mi. (51 km.) WNW of Paris.

Man·ti \ˈman-ˌtī\. City, ⊗ of Sanpete co., cen. Utah, 48 mi. (77 km.) WSW of Price; pop. (1990c) 2268; Mormon temple.

Man·ti·nea \ˌman-tə-ˈnē-ə\ *or* **Man·ti·neia** \-ˈnī-\. Ancient village in E Arcadia, near Argolis border, E Peloponnese, S Greece; scene of three battles: 418 B.C. in the Peloponnesian

War in which Agis II, king of Sparta, defeated the coalition of Athens, Argos, and Mantinea; 362 B.C. in which Spartans were defeated by Thebans under Epaminondas, who was killed; and 207 B.C. in which Spartans were defeated by Philopoemen, Greek general of the Achaean League.

Mantiqueira, Serra da. See SERRA DA MANTIQUEIRA.

Man·tor·ville \ˈman-tər-ˌvil\. Village, ⊗ of Dodge co., SE Minnesota, 13 mi. (21 km.) WNW of Rochester; pop. (1990c) 874.

Man·to·va \ˈmän-tō-vä\. **1.** Province of Lombardy, Italy. See table at ITALY.

2. *or Eng.* **Man·tua** \ˈmän-tü-ä\. Commune, ✻ of Mantova prov., Lombardy, N Italy, on Mincio River 80 mi. (129 km.) WSW of Venice; pop. (1991p) 52,948; tourism; buildings include cathedral (interior designed by Giulio Romano), several notable churches and palaces, ducal palace and castle of Gonzaga family, homes of artists Andrea Mantegna and Giulio Romano, Virgilian Academy of Sciences and Fine Arts.

History: Ancient town of Etruscan origin; later, a Roman town, near which the poet Virgil was born 70 B.C.; taken by Lombards (see LOMBARDY) 6th cent. A.D.; in 11th cent. belonged to Boniface, margrave of Canossa; became independent 1115; member of Lombard League; ruled by Gonzaga family 1328–1707; became duchy in 16th cent.; in War of Mantuan Succession 1627–31, France and German emperor backed rival claimants to duchy; to Austria 1708; taken in 1797 by future French Emperor Napoléon Bonaparte after a siege; duchy belonged to Cisalpine Republic 1797 and to kingdom of Italy 1805; restored to Austria 1814; one of the forts of the famous Quadrilateral by which Austria controlled N Italy; passed to kingdom of Italy 1866.

Man·tua \ˈmän-tü-ä\. **1.** Municipality, Pinar del Río prov., W Cuba, 37 mi. (60 km.) W of the city of Pinar del Río.

2. Commune, Italy. See MANTOVA 2.

Ma·nu·ae \ˌmä-nü-ˈwä-ā\. **1.** One of the Cook Is. (*q.v.*) in S Pacific Ocean, NNE of Rarotonga.

2. *also* **Scil·ly** \ˈsi-lē\. Group of islets forming an atoll, W Society Is., S Pacific Ocean, ab. 150 mi. (240 km.) W of Bora Bora.

Ma·nua Islands *also* **Ma·nu·ʻa Islands** \mä-ˈnü-ä\. Group of three islands, Tau (area 17 sq. mi. or 44 sq. km.), Ofu, and Olosega, in American Samoa, SW Pacific Ocean, 65 mi. (105 km.) E of the island of Tutuila; total area 22 sq. mi. (57 sq. km.); pop. (1990c) 1714; group constitutes an administrative district of American Samoa (*q.v.*).

Ma·nu·kau \ˈmä-nə-ˌkau̇\. City, North I., New Zealand, ab. 12 mi. (19 km.) SE of Auckland; pop. (1991c) 226,147.

Manukau Harbour. Inlet of Tasman Sea on NW coast of North I., New Zealand, forming an excellent harbor; suburbs of Auckland on its N shore.

Ma·nú National Park \mä-ˈnü\. Park, SE Peru, extending over a large area and a wide range of altitude.

Ma·nus \ˈmä-nüs\. **1.** Administrative district of Papua New Guinea, comprising the Admiralty Is. and adjacent islands; 800 sq. mi. (2072 sq. km.); ✻ Lorengau.

2. *also* **Ad·mi·ral·ty Island** \ˈad-mə-rəl-tē\. Largest of the Admiralty Is. and chief part of Manus prov., Papua New Guinea; ab. 50 mi. (80 km.) long and 17 mi. (27 km.) wide; area 600 sq. mi. (1554 sq. km.); terrain mountainous, and interior largely unexplored; has large harbor at Lorengau at its E tip. Held by Japanese 1942–44; former site of U.S. naval base. Taken over by Australia 1947.

Man·vel \ˈman-vəl\. City, Brazoria co., SE Texas, S of Houston; pop. (1990c) 3733.

Man·ville \ˈman-ˌvil\. Borough, Somerset co., N cen. New Jersey, 9 mi. (14 km.) WNW of New Brunswick; pop. (1990c) 10,567.

Many \ˈma-nē\. Town, ⊗ of Sabine parish, W Louisiana; pop. (1990c) 3112.

Manyara, Lake. Lake, NE cen. Tanzania. See LAKE MANYARA NATIONAL PARK.

Manyas Lake. See KUŞ, GÖLÜ.

Ma·nych *also* **Ma·nich** \ˈmä-nich\. **1.** Depression extending SE and NW from the lower Don to the lower Kuma River, S Russia in Europe; 330 mi. (531 km.) long; crosses S Rostov Oblast and forms S boundary of Astrakhan Oblast; usually a series of salt lakes but when flooded in spring season, two rivers are formed flowing in opposite directions from a high point ab. long. 44°E. The Kalaus River flows from the S to join the Eastern Manych River.

2. A lake in Manych depression, SW Astrakhan Oblast, S Russia in Europe.

3. *or* **Western Manych.** River in Manych depression, S Russia in Europe; 162 mi. (261 km.) long; a tributary of the lower Don, entering it near its mouth; receives the waters of Manych Lake during spring seasons. Another stream, the **Eastern Manych,** flows E at high water to the Kuma.

Man·zala, Lake \man-ˈzä-lə\ *or* **Bu·ḩay·rat Al Man·zi·lah** \bu̇-ˈhā-rät-al-ˈman-zi-lə\. Large lagoon, Egypt, SE of Damietta; N part of Suez Canal passes along its E edge. See TANIS.

Man·za·nar \ˈman-zə-ˌnär\. Locality, Inyo co., E California, ab. 12 mi. (19 km.) N of Owens Lake; during WWII a Japanese-American internment camp.

Man·za·na·res \ˌmän-thä-ˈnä-rās, -sä-\. **1.** River, Madrid prov., cen. Spain; flows past the city of Madrid into Jarama River, a tributary of the Tagus River; 50 mi. (80 km.) long.

2. Commune, Ciudad Real prov., S cen. Spain, on Manzanares River 30 mi. (48 km.) E of the commune of Ciudad Real; pop. (1991c) 17,916; wine; medieval castle.

Man·za·nil·lo \ˌmän-sä-ˈnē-yō\. **1.** Municipality and seaport, E Cuba, on Golfo de Guacanayabo; munic. pop. (1990e) 107,650; exports sugar, molasses, hardwood; mangrove swamps; founded 1784.

2. Seaport, Colima state, SW Mexico, on Manzanillo Bay 38 mi. (61 km.) WSW of the city of Colima; pop. (1990p) 92,168; major distribution center for W Mexico.

Manzanillo, Point. N extremity of Panama, extending into the Caribbean Sea NE of Colón.

Manzanillo Bay. **1.** Inlet of Caribbean Sea, Panama; separated from Limón Bay to the W by peninsula on which Colón is located.

2. Bay in N coast of the island of Hispaniola, West Indies, on boundary bet. Haiti and the Dominican Republic.

Man·zano Peak \man-ˈza-nō, -ˈzä-\. Mountain, W Torrance co., cen. New Mexico; 10,098 ft. (3078 m.); highest point in the **Manzano Mountains.**

Man·zhou·li *or W.-G.* **Man–chou–li** \ˈmän-ˈjō-ˈlē\; *formerly* **Lu·pin** \ˈlü-ˈpin\. Town, Nei Monggol (Inner Mongolia), N China, near border with Russia in Asia; pop. (1990c) 120,023.

Manzikert. See MALAZGIRT.

Manzilah, Buḩayrat Al. See MANZALA, LAKE.

Man·zi·ni \män-ˈzē-nē\; *formerly* **Bre·mers·dorp** \ˈbrā-mərs-ˌdȯrp\. Town, cen. Swaziland; pop. (1986c) 18,084; before 1902 ✻ of Swaziland.

Mao \ˈmau̇\. **1.** Town, W Chad, NE of Lake Chad; chief town of Kanem.

2. Town, ✻ of Valverde prov., Dominican Republic, ab. 42 mi. (68 km.) SE of Montecristi; pop. (1981c) 33,527.

Maoka. See KHOLMSK.

Mao·ke Mountains \ˈmau̇-kā\; *formerly* **Snow Mountains** *or Du.* **Sneeuw Ge·berg·te** \ˈsnā-ü-kə-ˈberk-tə\. Range of mountains, cen. Irian Jaya, Indonesia, running E and W from boundary of Papua New Guinea (141°E) to the narrow isthmus S of Teluk Cenderawasih, ab. 425 mi. (680 km.) long; comprises the subordinate ranges of Sudirman and Djajawidjaja (*qq.v.*). Highest point is Puncak Jaya 16,535 ft. (5040 m.) in Sudirman Range; has many peaks above 13,000 ft. (4000 m.).

Mao–wu–su. See MU US.

Ma·pam Yum·co \ˈmä-ˌpäm-ˈyu̇m-ˌkō\ *or* **Ma·na·sa·ro·war** \ˌmä-nä-sä-ˈrō-ˌwär\ *or W.-G.* **Ma–fa–mu–ts'o** \ˈmä-ˌfä-ˈmü-ˌtsō\. Lake in the Himalayas, SW Tibet, China, S of

\ə\ abut \ə\ matches \ᵊ\ kitten, Fr table \ər\ further \a\ ash \ā\ ace \ä\ cot, cart \å\ Fr bac \au̇\ out \b\ Span Avila \ch\ chin \e\ bet \ē\ easy \g\ go \i\ hit \ī\ ice \j\ job \k\ Ger ich, Buch \ⁿ\ Fr vin \ŋ\ sing \ō\ go \ȯ\ all \ò\ law \œ\ Fr bœuf \œ̄\ Fr feu \ȯi\ boy \th\ thin \t͟h\ this \ü\ loot \u̇\ foot \ue\ Ger füllen \ue̅\ Fr rue \y\ yet \ʸ\ Fr digne \ˈdēnʸ\, nuit \ˈnwʸē\ \yü\ few \yu̇\ fury \zh\ vision

Kanginboqê Feng (mountain); at 15,000 ft. (4575 m.) elev.; place of pilgrimage for Hindus.

Ma·pia \ˈmä-pē-ä\ *also* **Saint Da·vid** \ˈdā-vəd\. Group of three small islands and several islets in Pacific Ocean 150 mi. (241 km.) N of Numfoor I. off N coast of Irian Jaya, Indonesia, 134°20′E, 0°50′N; occupied by U.S. forces 1944.

Ma·pi·mí, Bol·són de \bȯl-ˈsȯn-dā-ˌmä-pē-ˈmē\. Rocky depression, N cen. plateau region, in Coahuila and Chihuahua states, Mexico; ab. 50,000 sq. mi. (129,500 sq. km.).

Maple Grove. Village, Hennepin co., SE cen. Minnesota, ab. 8 mi. (13 km.) NW of Minneapolis; pop. (1990c) 38,736.

Maple Heights. City, Cuyahoga co., N Ohio, 10 mi. (16 km.) SE of Cleveland; pop. (1990c) 27,089; residential suburb of Cleveland.

Maple Peak. Mountain, E Greenlee co., E Arizona; 8302 ft. (2530 m.).

Maple Shade. Urban township, Burlington co., S cen. New Jersey, ab. 7 mi. (11 km.) E of Camden; pop. (1990c) 19,211.

Ma·ple·wood \ˈmā-pəl-ˌwu̇d\. **1.** Village, Ramsey co., E Minnesota, N suburb of St. Paul; pop. (1990c) 30,954.

2. Residential city, St. Louis co., E Missouri, 7 mi. (11 km.) W of the city of St. Louis; pop. (1990c) 9962.

3. Township, Essex co., NE New Jersey, S of South Orange and 6 mi. (10 km.) W of Newark; pop. (1990c) 21,652.

Ma·po·cho \mä-ˈpō-ˌchō\. River, cen. Chile; flows into Maipo River 32 mi. (51 km.) SW of Santiago; ab. 75 mi. (121 km.) long.

Ma·pue·ra \mȧ-ˈpwā-rə\. River, N Brazil; rises near S border of Guyana; flows SE into Trombetas River NW of Lake Erepecu; 270 mi. (434 km.) long.

Ma·pu·to \mä-ˈpü-tō\. **1.** Navigable river, S Mozambique; flows E to Delagoa Bay; 50 mi. (80 km.) long; formed by the Usutu and Pongolo rivers.

2. Province of S Mozambique. See table at MOZAMBIQUE.

3. *formerly* **Lou·ren·ço Mar·ques** \lō-ˈrāⁿ-sü-ˈmȧr-kish\. Seaport, ✱ of Maputo prov. and ✱ of Mozambique, on Delagoa Bay; met. area pop. (1980c) 755,300; extensive port facilities; cement, furniture, footwear; university (1962); city incorp. 1887; became ✱ of Portuguese East Africa 1907.

Ma·qên Gangri \ˈmä-ˈchen-ˈgäŋ-ˈrē\ *or W.-G.* **Ma–ch'ing–kang–jih** \ˈmä-ˈchiŋ-ˈgäŋ-ˈjə̇\ *also* **Am·ne Ma·chin Shan** \ˈäm-ˈnā-ˈmä-ˈjin-ˈshän\. Mountain, Qinghai, W cen. China; 20,610 ft. (6282 m.); highest in the A'nyêmaqên Shan.

Ma·que·da Bay \mä-ˈkā-dä\. Inlet on W coast of Samar, Philippines, partly enclosed on W by Buad I.

Maquiling, Mount. See MAKILING, MOUNT.

Ma·quo·ke·ta \mə-ˈkō-kə-tə\. **1.** River, E cen. Iowa; rises in S Fayette co., NE Iowa, flows SE into Mississippi River in E Jackson co., E Iowa; ab. 150 mi. (240 km.) long.

2. City, ⊗ of Jackson co., E Iowa, 30 mi. (48 km.) S of Dubuque; pop. (1990c) 6111.

Mar, Serra do. See SERRA DO MAR.

Ma·ra \ˈmär-ä\. Administrative region of N Tanzania. See table at TANZANIA.

Ma·ra·cá \ˌmȧ-rȧ-ˈkä\. Island in Atlantic Ocean off NE coast of Pará state, Brazil.

Ma·ra·cai·bo \ˌmä-rä-ˈkī-bō, ˌmar-ə-\. City, ✱ of Zulia state, NW Venezuela, on W side of channel bet. Lake Maracaibo and the Gulf of Venezuela; pop. (1990p) 1,207,513; one of largest cities in Venezuela; handles most of the country's oil exports. Founded 1571; after c. 1669 a center for inland trade; major expansion took place entirely after discovery of oil 1917.

Maracaibo, Gulf of. See VENEZUELA, GULF OF.

Maracaibo, Lake. S extension of Gulf of Venezuela, in NW Venezuela; 5217 sq. mi. (13,512 sq. km.); 133 mi. (214 km.) long, 72 mi. (116 km.) wide; max. depth 115 ft. (35 m.); receives Catatumbo River from SW; in region of rich oil fields, some wells having been sunk in the lake.

Maracanda. See SAMARQAND 2.

Ma·ra·cay \ˌmä-rä-ˈkī\. City, ✱ of Aragua state, N Venezuela, on highway 50 mi. (80 km.) WSW of Caracas; pop. (1990p) 354,428; alt. 1500 ft. (460 m.); center of Venezuelan cattle industry; textiles; developed under dictatorship of Juan Vicente Gómez (1908–35), when it was the effective ✱ of Venezuela.

Ma·ra·dals·fos \ˈmä-rä-ˌdäls-ˌfȯs\. Waterfall, cen. Norway, just W of the Dovrefjell plateau; 650 ft. (198 m.).

Ma·ra·di \mä-ˈrä-dē\. Town, S Niger; pop. (1988c) 104,386.

Ma·rā·gheh \ˌmä-rä-ˈgä\ *also* **Ma·ra·gha** \-ˈgä\. Town, East Azerbaijan prov., NW Iran, ab. 18 mi. (29 km.) E of Daryācheh-ye Orūmīyeh; pop. (1986c) 100,679; nearby ruins of 13th cent. observatory. Seat of government of Hülegü, Mongol ruler who conquered the region in 13th cent.; scene of fighting bet. Russians and Turks in WWI.

Ma·rah \ˈmar-ə\. Locality on E coast of Gulf of Suez, Sinai Penin., NE Egypt, in region occupied by Israel 1967–79; first halting place of the Israelites after passing through the Red Sea and entering the wilderness; the waters were bitter (*Exod.* xv. 23–25).

Ma·rais \ma-ˈrā\. Marshy district in S Vendée dept., W France; once partly covered by the sea.

Mar·ais des Cygnes \ˈmer-də-ˌzēn\. River, E Kansas and Missouri; flows from S Wabaunsee co., Kansas E and SE to Osage River on boundary bet. Bates and Vernon cos., Missouri; ab. 150 mi. (240 km.) long. See OSAGE 1.

Ma·ra·jó \ˌmȧ-rȧ-ˈzhō\. Island in the Amazon Delta, NE Brazil, bet. the Amazon and Pará rivers; ab. 15,500 sq. mi. (40,150 sq. km.); W part low lying and often flooded; E part higher, largely savanna.

Marakesh. See MARRAKECH.

Ma·ra·mag \ˈmä-rä-ˌmäg\. Municipality, cen. Mindanao, Philippines, ab. 60 mi. (95 km.) SSE of Cagayan de Oro; pop. (1980c) 36,734.

Máramarossziget. See SIGHET MARMAȚIEI.

Ma·ra·ma·si·ke \ˌmä-rä-mä-ˈsē-kä\. Narrow island off SE coast of Malaita I., SE Solomon Is., W Pacific Ocean; ab. 32 mi. (51 km.) long.

Ma·ra·mureş \ˌmä-rä-ˈmu̇r-esh\. County of N Romania. See table at ROMANIA.

Ma·ra·nhão \ˌmȧ-rȧ-ˈnyau̇ⁿ\. **1.** Island off coast of NE Brazil. See SÃO LUÍS.

2. State, NE Brazil; ✱ São Luís; sugarcane, rice, cotton; oil. See table at BRAZIL.

Mar·a·noa \ˌmar-ə-ˈnō-ə\. River, SE Queensland, Australia; flows S and joins the Condamine to form the Culgoa; 200 mi. (322 km.) long.

Ma·ra·no di Na·po·li \mä-ˈrä-nō-dē-ˈnä-pō-lē\. Commune, Napoli prov., Campania, S Italy, 9 mi. (14 km.) NW of Naples; pop. (1989c) 47,352.

Ma·ra·ñón \ˌmä-rä-ˈnyōn\. River, Peru; rises in the Andes in W cen. Peru, flows NW to N Peru, bends E and joins the Ucayali River to form the Amazon River (*q.v.*); ab. 1000 mi. (1600 km.) long; navigable by shallow-draft vessels for ab. 500 mi. (800 km.).

Ma·ra·pi \ˌmȧ-rȧ-ˈpē\. River, N Brazil; rises in Tumuc-Humac Mts.; flows S to unite with Paru de Oeste.

Ma·raş. See KAHRAMANMARAŞ.

Mă·ră·şeş·ti \ˌmə-rə-ˈshest\. Commune, Vrancea co., Romania, N of Focşani; site of battlefront 1917 in WWI.

Mar·a·thon \ˈmar-ə-ˌthän, -thən\. **1.** County in cen. Wisconsin. See table at WISCONSIN.

2. Plain in E Attica dept., Greece, ab. 24 mi. (39 km.) NE of Athens; 5 mi. (8 km.) long, 2 mi. (3 km.) wide; borders on **Bay of Marathon** (*Gk.* **Ór·mos Ma·ra·thó·nos** \ˈȯr-ˌmȯs-ˌmä-rä-ˈthō-nȯs\), inlet of Aegean Sea, and ends in marsh at N.

3. Ancient town on this plain, probably located S of the modern town of **Ma·ra·thón** \ˌmä-rä-ˈthȯn\, Greece; scene of battle in 490 B.C., in which Athenian Gen. Miltiades and 10,000 Greeks (mostly Athenians) completely defeated a larger army of Persians under Datis and Artaphernes.

Marathus. See 'AMRIT.

Ma·ra·va·tío \mä-rä-vä-ˈtē-ō\. Municipality, Michoacán state, Mexico, 50 mi. (80 km.) NE of Morelia; pop. (1990p) 60,016.

Ma·ra·wi \mä-ˈrä-wē\; *formerly* **Dan·sa·lan** \ˌdän-sä-ˈlän\. Municipality, ✱ of Lanao del Sur prov., Mindanao I., Philippines; pop. (1990p) 92,000.

Ma·ra·wī \mä-ˈrä-wē\ *also* **Me·ro·we** \mā-ˈrä-wā\. Town, N Sudan, on the Nile River near the 4th of several cataracts.

Mar·bel·la \mär-ˈbā-lyä\. Commune, Málaga prov., S cen. Spain, on Mediterranean SW of the city of Málaga; pop. (1991c) 80,599.

Mar·ble Canyon \ˈmär-bəl\. Gorge along the Colorado River, N Arizona, extending from Lees Ferry (*q.v.*) S to the Little Colorado; often considered the upper part of Grand Canyon; set aside 1969 as **Marble Canyon National Monument** which was abolished 1975 and absorbed by Grand Canyon National Park.

Mar·ble·head \ˈmär-bəl-ˌhed, ˌmär-bəl-ˈhed\. Town, Essex co., NE Massachusetts, on Atlantic Ocean 15 mi. (24 km.) NE of Boston; pop. (1990c) 19,971; built on a rocky promontory (**Marblehead Neck**); noted as a resort and yachting center; fishing. Settled ab. 1629, until 1649 a part of Salem; important in early history of American navy, declining in importance after War of 1812.

Marble Hill. **1.** City, ⊗ of Bollinger co., SE Missouri; pop. (1990c) 1447.

2. Small section of Manhattan borough, New York City, on mainland N of Spuyten Duyvil Creek, bounded on N, W, and E by the Bronx.

Marble Point. Peak, Baker co., E Oregon; 6672 ft. (2034 m.).

Mar·burg \ˈmär-ˌbu̇rk, -ˌbərg\. **1.** *also* **Marburg an der Lahn** \än-dər-ˈlän\. City, Hesse, Germany, on Lahn River 46 mi. (74 km.) N of Frankfurt am Main; pop. (1992e) 75,331; pottery; tourism; university (1527, Europe's first Protestant university); 12th–14th cent. churches; 13th–15th cent. castle; founded in 12th cent.; associated with St. Elizabeth (d. 1231) and religious reformer Martin Luther (Colloquy of Marburg 1529); passed to Prussia 1866.

2. City, Yugoslavia. See MARIBOR.

Mar·ce·line \ˌmär-sə-ˈlēn\. City, Linn co., N Missouri, 35 mi. (56 km.) NW of Moberly; pop. (1990c) 2645.

March \ˈmärch\. **1.** River, Europe. See MORAVA 1.

2. Town, Cambridgeshire co., E England, on the Nene 52 mi. (84 km.) E of Leicester; pop. (1981p) 14,475.

Marche **1.** \ˈmärsh\ *or Lat.* **Mar·chia** \ˈmär-kē-ə\. Historical region of cen. France; bounded anciently on N by Touraine, on NE by Berry and Bourbonnais, on SE by Auvergne, S by Limousin, and on W by Poitou. Became countship in 10th cent.; in possession of Lusignan family in 13th cent.; acquired by dukes of Bourbon 14th cent.; confiscated by Francis I 1527; province of France until Revolution (1789).

2. *also* **March·es** \ˈmär-chəz\ *or* **The Marches.** Autonomous region of cent. Italy; lies bet. Adriatic Sea and Umbria, and bet. Emilia-Romagna and Abruzzi; ✻ Ancona; for provincial divisions, see table at ITALY; produces wine. Colonized by Rome 3d cent. B.C.; papal rule, nominal from 8th cent., solidified 14th–17th cents.; became part of Papal States (*q.v.*); occupied by French 1797–1815; to Italy 1860; received limited autonomy 1970.

Mar·che·na \mär-ˈchā-nä\ **1.** *also* **Bind·loe** \ˈbind-lō\. One of the Galápagos Is. (*q.v.*).

2. Commune, Sevilla prov., SW Spain, 32 mi. (51 km.) E of Seville; pop. (1991c) 17,221; sulfur baths.

March·feld \ˈmärk-ˌfelt\. Plain lying N of the Danube at Vienna, Austria, and W of the Morava; ab. 328 sq. mi. (850 sq. km.); scene of battle 1278 bet. Otakar II, king of Bohemia, and Holy Roman Emperor Rudolf I of Hapsburg, in which Otakar was defeated and killed; in Napoleonic Wars scene of battles of Aspern (*q.v.*), Essling, and Wagram (*q.v.*).

Marchia. See MARCHE 1.

Mar·chienne–au–Pont \mär-ˈshyen-ō-ˈpōⁿ\. Commune, Hainaut prov., SW Belgium, on the Sambre near Charleroi.

Mar Chi·qui·ta \ˌmär-chē-ˈkē-tä\. Salt lake, Córdoba prov., N cen. Argentina; 580 sq. mi. (1502 sq. km.), 45 mi. (72 km.) long.

March of Ancona. See *History* at ANCONA 2.

Mar·cia·ni·se \ˌmär-chä-ˈnē-zā\. Commune, Caserta prov., Campania, S Italy, N of Naples; pop. (1989c) 36,970.

Mar·ci·nelle \ˌmär-sē-ˈnel\. Commune, Hainaut prov., SW Belgium; suburb of S Charleroi.

Marcodurum. See DÜREN.

Mar·coing \mär-ˈkweⁿ\. Commune, Nord dept., N France, on the Schelde Canal near Cambrai; in WWI scene of heavy fighting 1917–18.

Mar·co Po·lo Bridge \ˈmär-kō-ˈpō-lō\. A marble bridge, with many arches, pillars, and sculptured lions, across the Yongding at Lugouqiao (*q.v.*), NE China, 9 mi. (14 km.) SW of Beijing; 900 ft. (275 m.) long; so named from Venetian traveler Marco Polo's description of it in his chronicle; a clash here July 1937 bet. Chinese and Japanese troops marked the start of the Sino-Japanese War (1937–45).

Marcq–en–Ba·rœul \ˌmärk-äⁿ-bȧ-ˈrœl\. Commune, Nord dept., N France, NNE suburb of Lille.

Mar·cus Hook \ˈmär-kəs\. Borough and port, Delaware co., SE Pennsylvania, on Delaware River 18 mi. (29 km.) WSW of Philadelphia; pop. (1990c) 2546.

Marcus Island *or Jp.* **Mi·na·mi–To·ri–Shi·ma** \mē-ˈnä-mē-ˈtȯr-ē-ˈshē-mä, -ˈtȯr-ē-shē-ˌmä\. Small, triangular-shaped island in W Pacific Ocean, NE of the Marianas and ab. 725 mi. (1170 km.) NW of Wake I., 24°18′N, 153°58′E; settlement on S coast. In WWII a Japanese air and naval base; frequently bombed by U.S. forces; administered by U.S. from 1945; returned to Japan 1968.

Mar·cy, Mount \ˈmär-sē\. Peak in the Adirondack Mts., NE New York; 5344 ft. (1629 m.); highest peak in the Adirondacks, and in New York state.

Mar·dan \ˈmär-ˌdan\. Town, Pakistan, 30 mi. (48 km.) NE of Peshawar; pop. (1981c) 147,977.

Mar del Pla·ta \ˌmär-del-ˈplä-tä\. Coastal city, Buenos Aires prov., E Argentina, S of the city of Buenos Aires; pop. (1980c) 407,024; tourism; major fishing port; fish canneries.

Mar·din \ˈmär-dēn\. **1.** Province of Turkey in Asia. See table at TURKEY.

2. Town, its ✻, on branch railroad line near Syrian border 53 mi. (85 km.) SE of Diyarbakır; pop. (1990p) 52,994; local trading center.

Ma·re \ˈmā-rē, ˈmä-rā\. Latin word meaning "sea"; used in classical names of bodies of water, such as **Mare Adriaticum,** and **Mare Ionium.** See the 2d element of these names, or its anglicized form.

Ma·ré \mä-ˈrā\. One of the Loyalty Is., at SE end of chain; 248 sq. mi. (642 sq. km.); ab. 22 mi. (35 km.) long and 10 mi. (16 km.) wide; pop. (1989c) 5646; low coral formation.

Ma·reb \mä-ˈreb\. River, E Africa; rises in N Ethiopia; flows NW, crosses W Eritrea into E Sudan, and during high-water seasons empties into the Atbara River; in its lower course, known as the **Gash** \ˈgash\ (*also* **Al–Qāsh** \ȧl-ˈkäsh\ in Sudan); ab. 300 mi. (480 km.) long.

Mare Cantabricum. See BISCAY, BAY OF.

Ma·ree, Loch \mə-ˈrē\. Lake, Highland region, N Scotland; 12.5 mi. (20 km.) long; max. depth 367 ft. (112 m.); connected with Loch Ewe by a short river.

Mare Germanicum. See NORTH SEA.

Mare Internum. See MEDITERRANEAN SEA.

Mare Island \ˈmar\. Island in E San Pablo Bay, W cen. California; separated from Vallejo by narrow **Mare Island Strait.** Site of what was once a major naval building and repair facility.

Ma·rem·ma \mä-ˈrem-mä\. Marshy region in W Italy, chiefly in Grosseto prov., SW Tuscany.

Ma·ren·go \mə-ˈreŋ-gō\. **1.** County in W Alabama. See table at ALABAMA.

2. City, McHenry co., N Illinois, 25 mi. (40 km.) E of Rockford; pop. (1990c) 4768.

3. Town, Crawford co., S Indiana; pop. (1990c) 856; nearby is **Marengo Cave,** a stalactite cave.

4. City, ⊗ of Iowa co., E cen. Iowa, 25 mi. (40 km.) WSW of Cedar Rapids; pop. (1990c) 2270.

\ə\ abut \ˈə\ matches \ᵊ\ kitten, Fr table \ər\ further \a\ ash \ā\ ace \ä\ cot, cart \ȧ\ Fr bac \au̇\ out \b\ Span Avila \ch\ chin \e\ bet \ē\ easy \g\ go \i\ hit \ī\ ice \j\ job \k\ Ger ich, Buch \ⁿ\ Fr vin \ŋ\ sing \ō\ go \ȯ\ all \ȯ\ law \œ\ Fr bœuf \œ̄\ Fr feu \ȯi\ boy \th\ thin \th\ this \ü\ loot \u̇\ foot \ue\ Ger füllen \ue̅\ Fr rue \y\ yet \ʸ\ Fr digne \ˈdēnʸ\, nuit \ˈnwʸē\ \yü\ few \yu̇\ fury \zh\ vision

5. Village, Alessandria prov., SE Piedmont, NW Italy; scene of battle June 14, 1800 in which the French under First Consul (later Emperor) Napoléon narrowly defeated the Austrians.

Mar·e·o·tis, Lake \ˌmar-ē-ˈō-tis\ *or Arab.* **Bu·ḫay·rat Mar·yūt** \bu̇-ˈhī-rät-mär-ˈyüt\. Lake in the Nile Delta, N Egypt, W of Rosetta Mouth of the Nile; Alexandria is situated on narrow strip of land bet. it and the Mediterranean Sea.

Mare Rubrum. See ERYTHRAEAN SEA.

Ma·res·cot, Mount \mə-ˈres-kət\. Peak, SE Santa Isabel I., E cen. Solomon Is., W Pacific Ocean; ab. 3900 ft. (1200 m.); highest point on the island.

Mare Suevicum. See BALTIC SEA.

Mar·eth \ˈmar-əth\. Town, SE Tunisia, SSE of Gabès; anchor point at N end of French defense line (**Mareth Line**), held by Germans 1942–43, penetrated by the British Mar. 27, 1943 during WWII.

Mare Tirreno. See TYRRHENIAN SEA.

Ma·ret·ti·mo \mä-ˈret-tē-mō\. Island, Italy, one of the Isole Egadi (*q.v.*) in the Mediterranean.

Mar·fa \ˈmär-fə\. City, ⊗ of Presidio co., W Texas, 40 mi. (64 km.) E of the Rio Grande; pop. (1990c) 2424; summer resort.

Mar·ga·nets \ˌmär-gə-ˈnets\. Town, Dnipropetrovs'k subdivision, Ukraine, ab. 60 mi. (97 km.) SSW of the city of Dnipropetrovs'k; pop. (1991e) 55,000.

Mar·ga·ri·ta \ˌmär-gä-ˈrē-tä\. Venezuelan island in the Caribbean Sea; 414 sq. mi. (1072 sq. km.); chief town Porlamar; tourism; forms major part of the Venezuelan state of Nueva Esparta (island group); discovered by explorer Christopher Columbus 1498; settled as center of pearl fishing; frequently raided by pirates; played prominent role in the wars of independence.

Mar·gate \ˈmär-ˌgāt\. City, Broward co., SE Florida; pop. (1990c) 42,985.

Mar·gate \ˈmär-ˌgāt, -gət\; *formerly* **Mer·gate** \ˈmər-gət\. Resort town, Kent, SE England, on coast of Isle of Thanet 65 mi. (105 km.) E of London; pop. (1981c) 54,980; suffered considerable damage in WWII.

Mar·gate City \ˈmär-gāt\. City, Atlantic co., SE New Jersey, on Atlantic Ocean 5 mi. (8 km.) SW of Atlantic City; pop. (1990c) 8431.

Margelan. See MARGILAN.

Margherita Peak. See RUWENZORI.

Mar·ghe·ri·ta di Sa·vo·ia \ˌmär-gā-ˈrē-tä-dē-sä-ˈvō-yä\; *before 1879* **Sa·li·ne di Bar·let·ta** \sä-ˈlē-nā-dē-bär-ˈlāt-tä\. Commune, Foggia prov., Puglia, SE Italy, on Adriatic Sea 31 mi. (50 km.) ESE of the commune of Foggia; pop. (1981p) 11,352.

Mar·gi·lan *also* **Mar·ge·lan** \ˌmär-gə-ˈlän\. Town, Fergana subdivision, E Uzbekistan, E of Qŭqon and adjoining the city of Fergana; pop. (1991e) 124,900; an old city; mosques and bazaars; important silk center. Known as **Old Margelan** 1876–1907 to distinguish it from **New Margelan,** now Fergana (*q.v.*).

Mar·go·sa·tu·big \ˌmär-gō-sä-ˈtü-big\. Municipality, W Mindanao, Philippines, on an inlet of Moro Gulf 87 mi. (140 km.) NE of City of Zamboanga.

Mar·gra·ten \ˈmär-ˌgrä-tə\. Locality, Netherlands; site of large temporary cemetery for U.S. soldiers killed in WWII.

Mar·gum \ˈmär-gəm\ *or* **Mar·gus** \-gəs\. Ancient town, Moesia Superior, at mouth of the Margus (*mod.* Morava) on the Danubius (Danube); scene of battle 285 A.D. bet. Roman Emperors Carinus and Diocletian which would have been a victory for Carinus had he not been murdered by one of his own officers.

Margus. **1.** River, Yugoslavia. See MORAVA 3.

2. Ancient town, Moesia. See MARGUM.

Maria, Îles \ˌēl-mȧr-ˈyȧ\ *or* **Ma·ria Island** \mə-ˈrē-ə\ *also* **Hull Island** \ˈhəl\. Group of islets comprising an atoll, NW Austral Is., French Polynesia, S Pacific Ocean.

Ma·ria–Chap·de·laine \mä-ˈrē-ə-ˌshap-də-ˈlen\. County, Quebec, Canada. See table at QUEBEC.

Ma·ría Cle·o·fás \mä-ˈrē-ä-ˌklā-ō-ˈfäs\. Island of the Islas Marías group (*q.v.*) in the Pacific Ocean off W coast of cen. Mexico.

Ma·ria Island \mə-ˈrī-ə\. **1.** Small island, W Gulf of Carpentaria, Australia, in Limmen Bight; 13 sq. mi. (34 sq. km.).

2. Island off SE coast of Tasmania, Australia, N of Tasman Penin.; ab. 37 sq. mi. (96 sq. km.); set aside as **Maria Island National Park.**

3. Island, NW Austral Is. See MARIA, ÎLES.

Ma·ría Ma·dre \mä-ˈrē-ä-ˈmä-drā\. Island of the Islas Marías group (*q.v.*) in Pacific Ocean off W coast of cen. Mexico.

María Mag·da·le·na \ˌmäg-dä-ˈlā-nä\. Island of the Islas Marías group (*q.v.*) in Pacific Ocean off W coast of cen. Mexico.

Ma·ri·ana Islands \ˌmar-ē-ˈa-nə\ *or commonly* **Marianas** \-nəz\; *formerly* **La·drone Islands** \lə-ˈdrōn\. Island group in W Pacific Ocean, ab. 1500 mi. (2400 km.) E of the Philippines and 1350 mi. (2170 km.) S of Honshū I., Japan; 12° to 21°N and 144° to 146°E; area 184 sq. mi. or 477 sq. km. (incl. Guam, 393 sq. mi. or 1018 sq. km.); pop. (1990p) 176,281; comprises 15 islands; Guam is an unincorporated U.S. territory, the remaining islands constitute part of the U.S. Commonwealth of the Northern Mariana Islands; major islands include: Saipan, Tinian, Rota, Pagan, Guguan, Agrihan, Aguijan.

History: Discovered by Portuguese navigator Ferdinand Magellan 1521; called *Islas de los Ladrones (Thieves Islands)* by ship's crew because natives pilfered articles from the boat; named *Las Marianas* 1668 in honor of Mariana of Austria, widow of Philip IV of Spain; sold (except for Guam) by Spain to Germany 1899, occupied by Japan 1914, and assigned as Japanese mandate 1919 after WWI; under Japanese were fortified to become "stationary island aircraft carriers." Saipan and Tinian (see also GUAM) attacked and captured by U.S. forces 1944; became part of Trust Territory of the Pacific Islands, assigned by UN to U.S. 1947; in 1978 the group (except Guam) became a commonwealth under U.S. sovereignty as the Northern Mariana Islands; UN trusteeship formally terminated 1990.

Ma·ria·nao \ˌmär-ē-ä-ˈnau̇\. Municipality and city, W Cuba; munic. pop. (1990e) 133,671; residential suburb of Havana; army base; founded early 18th century.

Mariana Trench. Ocean trench, W Pacific Ocean, extending from SE of Guam to NW of the Mariana Is.; max. depth (11°21′N, 142°12′E) 36,198 ft. (11,033 m.); deepest known depression on surface of earth.

Mar·i·an·na \ˌmar-ē-ˈa-nə\. **1.** City, ⊗ of Lee co., E Arkansas, 12 mi. (19 km.) W of Mississippi River SW of Memphis, Tennessee; pop. (1990c) 5910.

2. City, ⊗ of Jackson co., NW Florida, 62 mi. (100 km.) WNW of Tallahassee; pop. (1990c) 6292; Chipola Junior Coll. (1947).

Ma·rián·ské Láz·ně \ˈmär-yän-ˌske-ˈläz-nye\ *or Ger.* **Ma·ri·en·bad** \mə-ˈrē-ən-ˌbät, -ˌbad\. Town, W Czech Republic, ab. 20 mi. (32 km.) SSW of Karlovy Vary; pop. (1991p) 15,378; mineral springs; ab. 7 mi. (11 km.) E is the abbey of Tepl, founded 1193.

Ma·ri·as \mə-ˈrī-əs\. River, NW Montana; rises in Glacier co., NW Montana, flows E and SE into Missouri River in cen. Chouteau co., N cen. Montana; 210 mi. (338 km.) long.

Ma·rí·as, Islas \ˈēs-läs-mä-ˈrē-äs\ *or* **Islas Tres Marías** \-ˈtrās-\ *or* **Las Tres Marías** \ˌläs-\. Group of small islands, Pacific Ocean, off the state of Nayarit, W Mexico, comprising María Madre, María Magdalena, María Cleofás, and San Juanito.

Marías, Las. See LAS MARÍAS.

Marias Pass. Mountain pass, NW Montana, in Lewis Range of Continental Divide at SE corner of Glacier National Park; 5215 ft. (1590 m.); discovered 1889; railroad, highway.

Maria–Theresiopel. See SUBOTICA.

Ma·ri·a·to, Point \ˌmä-rē-ˈä-tō\. Cape on SW extremity of Azuero Penin., S Panama.

Ma·ría Tri·ni·dad Sán·chez \mä-ˈrē-ä-ˈtrē-nē-ˌthäth-ˈsän-chās\. Province, Dominican Republic. See table at DOMINICAN REPUBLIC.

Mari Autonomous Soviet Socialist Republic. See MARI EL.

Ma·ria van Die·men, Cape \mə-ˌrē-ə-van-ˈdē-mən\. Cape on NW extremity of North I., New Zealand.

Ma·r'ib \ˈmar-ib\. Ruins of ancient city of the Sabaeans, Yemen, 60 mi. (95 km.) ENE of Sanaa; a chief city of ancient Sheba; a major trading center; esp. famous for its great dam, constructed c. 7th cent. B.C. and destroyed in 6th cent. A.D., an event of importance in early Arab chronicles.

Ma·ri·bo \ˈmär-ē-ˌbō\. Town, Storstrøm co., Denmark, located on Lolland I.; pop. (1981c) 11,881.

Ma·ri·bor \ˈmär-ē-ˌbȯr\ *or Ger.* **Mar·burg** \ˈmär-ˌbu̇rk, -ˌbərg\. City, NE Slovenia, on Drava River near Austrian border ab. 65 mi. (105 km.) NE of Ljubljana; pop. (1991p) 153,053; diversified industry; hydroelectric power station; 12th cent. cathedral; 15th cent. castle; present town known from 12th cent.

Ma·ri·ca·ban \ˌmä-rē-kä-ˈbän\. Island off S Batangas prov., Luzon, Philippines; 12 sq. mi. (31 sq. km.), ab. 7 mi. (11 km.) long; in Verde Island Passage off the point that separates Balayan Bay from Batangas Bay. Its barrios belong to Bauan municipality.

Ma·ri·cao \ˌmä-rē-ˈkau̇\. Town and municipality, W Puerto Rico; munic. area pop. (1990c) 6206; town is inland on highway 11 mi. (18 km.) E of Mayagüez.

Ma·ri·co \mä-ˈrē-kō\. River, a headstream of the Limpopo, N North-West prov., Rep. of South Africa; flows N through fertile Marico Valley; ab. 130 mi. (210 km.) long; chief town Zeerust.

Mar·i·co·pa \ˌmar-ə-ˈkō-pə\. County in SW cen. Arizona. See table at ARIZONA.

Maricopa Mountains. Small range in SE Maricopa co., SW cen. Arizona.

Ma·rie Byrd Land \mə-ˈrē-ˈbərd\. Large section of Antarctica E of Ross Ice Shelf and Ross Sea and extending E to Ellsworth Land; ab. 73° to 85°S and 100° to 150°W; discovered by American explorer Richard E. Byrd 1929.

Ma·rie–Ga·lante \mȧ-ˈrē-gȧ-ˈlänt\. Island in E West Indies, a dependency of the French overseas territory of Guadeloupe SE of Basse-Terre; 58 sq. mi. (150 sq. km.); pop. (1990c) 13,463; ✱ Grand-Bourg; sugar; discovered by explorer Christopher Columbus 1493.

Ma·rie·hamn \mȧ-ˈrē-ə-ˌhämn\ *or* **Maa·ri·an·ha·mi·na** \ˈmä-rē-än-ˌhä-mē-nä\. Seaport, ✱ of Åland prov., Finland, on Åland I. in the Gulf of Bothnia; pop. (1989c) 10,067; founded 1861.

Ma·riel \ˌmär-ˈyel\. Municipality, Pinar del Río prov., W Cuba; pop. (1981p) 34,467; site 1980 of exodus of over 100,000 immigrants to U.S.

Ma·ri El *or* **Ma·riy El** \ˈmä-rē-ˈel\. Republic, cen. Russia in Europe; comprised **Mari Autonomous Soviet Socialist Republic** before 1991; 8958 sq. mi. (23,201 sq. km.); pop. (1992e) 762,000; ✱ Yoshkar-Ola; level country N of the Volga with lakes and peat bogs and large forest area. Few roads and only one railroad (branch from Kazan' to Yoshkar-Ola). The chief economic products are timber, corn, rye, flax, and potatoes. Populated by Russian and Finno-Ugric Mari peoples. Region annexed to Russia in 16th cent., but people were not assimilated. Created an autonomous oblast 1920, made an autonomous republic 1936 and a republic 1991.

Ma·rie·mont \mə-ˈrē-ˌmänt\. Village, Hamilton co., SW Ohio, 8 mi. (13 km.) NE of Cincinnati; pop. (1990c) 3118.

Marienbad. See MARIÁNSKÉ LÁZNĚ.

Marienburg *or* **Marienburg in Westpreussen.** See MALBORK.

Marienwerder. See KWIDZYŃ.

Mar·ies \ˈmar-ēz\. County in S cen. Missouri. See table at MISSOURI.

Ma·rie·stad \mȧ-ˈrē-ˌstäd\. Town, ⊗ of Skaraborg prov., S Sweden, on Lake Vänern; pop. (1989c) 24,617.

Mar·i·et·ta \ˌmar-ē-ˈe-tə\. **1.** Residential city, ⊗ of Cobb co., NW Georgia, 20 mi. (32 km.) NW of Atlanta; pop. (1990c) 44,129; Kennesaw State Coll. (1963); Southern Coll. of Technology (1948); naval air station; in Civil War held by Confederates for a time against Union Gen. William T. Sherman's advance on Atlanta, nearby Kennesaw Mt. (*q.v.*) scene of major battle 1864; has large national cemetery.

2. City, ⊗ of Washington co., SE Ohio, on Ohio River 45 mi. (72 km.) SE of Zanesville; pop. (1990c) 15,026; Marietta Coll. (1835), Washington State Community Coll. (1971); site of Mound Builders' earthworks; pioneer city in Northwest Terr. and oldest permanent settlement in Ohio (1788); developed as river port and shipbuilding center.

3. City, ⊗ of Love co., S Oklahoma, 17 mi. (27 km.) S of Ardmore; pop. (1990c) 2306; oil and gas deposits.

4. Borough, Lancaster co., SE Pennsylvania, on Susquehanna River W of the city of Lancaster; pop. (1990c) 2778.

Ma·rie·ville \mə-ˈrē-ˌvil\. Town, ⊗ of Rouville co., S Quebec, Canada, ESE of Montreal; pop. (1991c) 5164.

Ma·ri·glia·no \ˌmä-rē-ˈlyä-nō\. Commune, Napoli prov., Campania, S Italy, 11 mi. (18 km.) NE of Naples; pop. (1989c) 27,001; castle; damaged by eruptions of Vesuvius 1631 and 1793.

Ma·ri·gnane \ˌmä-rē-ˈnyän\. Town, Bouches-du-Rhône dept., SE France, ab. 12 mi. (19 km.) NW of Marseille.

Marignano. See MELEGNANO.

Marigot. See SAINT MARTIN.

Mariguana. See MAYAGUANA.

Mariinsk Waterway. See VOLGA-BALTIC WATERWAY.

Ma·ri·ki·na *also* **Ma·ri·qui·na** \ˌmär-ē-ˈkē-nä\. **1.** River, Luzon, Philippines; rises in Montalban reservoir system; flows into Pasig River near Pasig; ab. 30 mi. (48 km.) long.

2. Municipality, Luzon, Philippines, on Marikina River 5 mi. (8 km.) N of Pasig; pop. (1980c) 211,613.

Ma·rí·lia \mȧ-ˈrēl-yə\. City, W cen. São Paulo state, SE Brazil, 230 mi. (370 km.) NW of the city of São Paulo; munic. pop. (1991p) 151,760.

Ma·rin \mə-ˈrin\. Coastal county in W California. See table at CALIFORNIA

Ma·rín \mä-ˈrēn\. Seaport commune, Pontevedra prov., NW Spain, on inlet of Atlantic Ocean 6 mi. (10 km.) SSW of the commune of Pontevedra; pop. (1991c) 24,045..

Ma·ri·na \mə-ˈrē-nə\. City, Monterey co., California, on Monterey Bay; pop. (1990c) 26,436.

Ma·ri·na \mä-ˈrē-nä\. **1.** Waterfall in a tributary of the Essequibo River, W Guyana, in the Pacaraima Mts. NW of Kaieteur Falls; 500 ft. (152 m.).

2. Island, Vanuatu. See ESPÍRITU SANTO 1.

Ma·rin·du·que \ˌmä-rēn-ˈdü-kā\. Island and province, cen. Philippines, separated from coast of Luzon by Mompog Pass and Tayabas Bay; ✱ Boac. NW coast borders on Tayabas Bay and S coast on Sibuyan Sea. Covered with hills; chief town in addition to Boac is Santa Cruz. See table at PHILIPPINES.

Ma·rine City \mə-ˈrēn\. City, St. Clair co., SE Michigan, on St. Clair River 16 mi. (26 km.) S of Port Huron; pop. (1990c) 4556; summer resort.

Mar·i·nette \ˌmar-ə-ˈnet\. **1.** County in NE Wisconsin. See table at WISCONSIN.

2. City, its ⊗, on Green Bay 44 mi. (71 km.) NNE of the city of Green Bay; pop. (1990c) 11,843; trade center for recreational area.

Ma·rin·ga \mä-ˈriŋ-gä\. River, S cen. Africa; flows WNW in NW Democratic Rep. of the Congo and joins the Lopori River to form the Lulonga River; 270 mi. (434 km.) long.

Ma·rin·gá \ˌmȧ-rin-ˈgä\. Municipality, Paraná state, S Brazil, 220 mi. (354 km.) NW of Curitiba; pop. (1991p) 239,930.

Ma·ri·no \mä-ˈrē-nō\. Commune, Roma prov., Lazio, cen. Italy, 12 mi. (19 km.) SE of Rome; pop. (1991p) 30,409.

Mar·i·on \ˈmar-ē-ən\. **1.** Name of counties in 17 states of the U.S. See tables at ALABAMA, ARKANSAS, FLORIDA, GEORGIA, ILLINOIS, INDIANA, IOWA, KANSAS, KENTUCKY, MISSISSIPPI, MISSOURI, OHIO, OREGON, SOUTH CAROLINA, TENNESSEE, TEXAS, WEST VIRGINIA.

2. City, ⊗ of Perry co., W cen. Alabama, 45 mi. (72 km.) SSE of Tuscaloosa; pop. (1990c) 4211; Judson Coll. (1838), Marion Military Institute (1842).

3. City, ⊗ of Crittenden co., E Arkansas; pop. (1990c) 4391.

4. City, ⊗ of Williamson co., S Illinois, 45 mi. (72 km.) S of Mt. Vernon; pop. (1990c) 14,545; federal prison, coal deposits nearby.
5. City, ⊗ of Grant co., N cen. Indiana, 28 mi. (45 km.) NW of Muncie; pop. (1990c) 32,618; automobile parts, paper, wire; Indiana Wesleyan Univ. (1920).
6. City, Linn co., E Iowa, 7 mi. (11 km.) ENE of Cedar Rapids; pop. (1990c) 20,403.
7. City, ⊗ of Marion co., E cen. Kansas, 48 mi. (77 km.) NNE of Wichita; pop. (1990c) 1906.
8. City, ⊗ of Crittenden co., W Kentucky, 35 mi. (56 km.) ENE of Paducah; pop. (1990c) 3320; fluorite deposits.
9. Town, Plymouth co., SE Massachusetts, on Buzzards Bay 9 mi. (14 km.) ENE of New Bedford; pop. (1990c) 4496; summer resort.
10. Town, ⊗ of McDowell co., W North Carolina, 32 mi. (51 km.) E of Asheville; pop. (1990c) 4765; lake resort; McDowell Technical Coll. (1964).
11. City, ⊗ of Marion co., cen. Ohio, 43 mi. (69 km.) N of Columbus; pop. (1990c) 43,564; produces popping corn; Ohio State Univ.–Marion Campus (1957); settled c. 1821; incorp. as village 1830, as city 1890; home and burial place of Warren G. Harding, 29th president of the U.S., whose house is preserved as a museum.
12. Town, ⊗ of Marion co., E South Carolina, 24 mi. (39 km.) E of Florence; pop. (1990c) 7658; developed around site of courthouse 1800.
13. Town, ⊗ of Smyth co., SW Virginia, 42 mi. (68 km.) ENE of Bristol; pop. (1990c) 6630.
Marion, Lake. See SANTEE DAM.
Marion Reef. Circular coral atoll in Pacific off cen. part of Great Barrier Reef, Queensland, Australia, 19°10′S, 152°17′E.
Mar·i·po·sa \ˌmar-ə-ˈpō-sə, -zə\. **1.** County in cen. California. See table at CALIFORNIA.
2. Unincorporated settlement, its ⊗; pop. (1990c) 1152; historical museum displaying gold-rush artifacts.
Mariquina. See MARIKINA.
Ma·ris·cal Es·ti·gar·ri·bia \ˌmä-rē-ˈskäl-ˌes-tē-ˌgär-ˈrē-b̲ē-ä\. Town, NW Paraguay, in the Gran Chaco; dist. pop. (1985e) 6525; former ✻ of Boquerón dept.
Ma·ris·cal Mountain \ˈmar-ə-ˌskäl\. Peak in Big Bend National Park, S Brewster co., W Texas; 3940 ft. (1201 m.).
Ma·rí·ti·ma, Cor·dil·le·ra \ˌkȯr-t͟hē-ˈyä-rä-mä-ˈrē-tē-mä\. The Cordillera Occidental in Peru.
Maritima Avaticorum. See MARTIGUES.
Maritime Alps. See table at ALPS.
Maritime Atlas. See ATLAS MOUNTAINS.
Mar·i·time Province \ˈmar-ə-ˌtīm\. Former province of the U.S.S.R., comprising the coastal region of Siberia from Bering Strait to Vladivostok, with coastline of ab. 2300 mi. (3700 km.); the Russian Far East; organized after region became Russian by Peking Convention 1860; became a part of the Far Eastern Region (*q.v.*) 1920. See PRIMORSKIY KRAY.
Maritime Provinces *or often* **the Mar·i·times** \ˈmar-ə-ˌtīmz\. The provinces New Brunswick, Nova Scotia, and Prince Edward I. of Canada; sometimes thought to include Newfoundland.
Ma·ri·times, Alpes– \ˌalp-ˌmȧ-rē-ˈtēm\. Department, France. See table at FRANCE.
Maritime Territory. See PRIMORSKIY KRAY.
Ma·ri·tsa \mə-ˈrēt-sə\ *or Turk.* **Me·riç** \me-ˈrēch\ *or Gk.* **Év·ros** \ˈev-ˌrȯs\; *anc.* **He·brus** \ˈhē-brəs\. River, SE Europe; flows E in S Bulgaria, then turning S at Edirne, flows as the Meriç bet. Turkey in Europe and Greece to empty into the Aegean Sea; receives the Tundzha at Edirne; ab. 300 mi. (480 km.) long.
Ma·ri·u·pol' \mȧ-rē-ˈü-pəlʸ\; *1949–89* **Zhda·nov** \ˈzhdä-nəf\. City, Donets'k subdivision, Ukraine, on N shore of Sea of Azov 60 mi. (97 km.) W of Taganrog, at mouth of the Kalka; a major port, exports include steel; fishing. Site of ancient settlement; modern town founded 1779; in WWII held by Germans 1941–43.
Ma·ri·ve·les \ˌmä-rä-ˈvā-lās\. Municipality, Luzon, Philippines, WNW of Corregidor I., on **Mariveles Bay** (inlet of North Channel); pop. (1980c) 48,594; held by Japanese 1942–45.
Mariveles, Mount. Mountain, an extinct volcano, at S end of Zambales Mts. at S end of Bataan Penin., Luzon, Philippines; 4444 ft. (1355 m.); highest peak on Bataan.
Mariyampolė. See KAPSUKAS.
Mariy El. See MARI EL.
Marj, Al. See AL MARJ.
Mark \ˈmärk\. Medieval county, now part of North Rhine-Westphalia, Germany; belonged to Brandenburg in 17th cent.
Mar·ka·gunt Plateau \ˈmär-kə-ˌgənt\. Elevated region, SW Utah, in which is located Cedar Breaks National Monument (see UNITED STATES, *National Monuments*).
Mar·ka·zi \mär-ˈkä-zē\. Province, NW cen. Iran. See table at IRAN.
Marked Tree. City, Poinsett co., NE Arkansas, at confluence of St. Francis and Little rivers, 26 mi. (42 km.) SE of Jonesboro; pop. (1990c) 3100.
Mar·ken \ˈmär-kə\. Commune, North Holland prov., W Netherlands, in SW part of IJsselmeer off Monnikendam and ab. 10 mi. (16 km.) NE of Amsterdam; pop. (1981e) 2114; has seven small hamlets frequently visited by tourists; connected with mainland by dike carrying a highway.
Mar·ket Har·bor·ough \ˈmär-ket-ˈhär-bər-ō\. Town, Leicestershire, cen. England, on the Welland 15 mi. (24 km.) SE of Leicester; pop. (1981p) 15,934; textiles, electrical equipment, rubber goods.
Mark·ham \ˈmär-kəm\. **1.** Village, Cook co., NE Illinois, a S suburb of Chicago; pop. (1990c) 13,136.
2. Town, York munic. region, SE Ontario, Canada, 17 mi. (27 km.) NE of Toronto; pop. (1991c) 153,811.
3. River, E New Guinea I., Papua New Guinea; rises in mountains in NE, flows S and SE to Huon Gulf at Lae; an upper tributary is the Bulolo (*q.v.*); its valley scene of fighting 1943 during WWII bet. Japanese and Allies, and of severe earthquakes 1993.
Markham, Mount. Peak in Victoria Land, Antarctica, bet. Mt. Albert Markham and Mt. Kirkpatrick, 82°51′S, 161°21′E; 14,275 ft. (4351 m.).
Markirch. See SAINTE-MARIE-AUX-MINES.
Mark·klee·berg \ˈmär-klā-ˌberk\. City, Saxony, E Germany, 5 mi. (8 km.) S of Leipzig; pop. (1981c) 20,931.
Mark·lee·ville \ˈmär-klē-ˌvil\. Town, ⊗ of Alpine co., E California.
Marks \ˈmärks\. **1.** City, ⊗ of Quitman co., NW Mississippi; pop. (1990c) 1758.
2. *or Ger.* **Marx·stadt** \ˌmärks-ˌshtät\; *formerly* **Eka·te·ri·nen·stadt** \i-ˌkä-tə-ˈrē-nən-ˌshtät\ *also* **Ka·tha·ri·nen·stadt** \ˌkä-tə-ˈrē-nən-ˌshtät\ *or* **Ye·ka·te·ri·nen·shtadt** \yi-ˌkȧ-tə-\. Town, Saratov Oblast, Russia in Europe, on left bank of the Volga 35 mi. (56 km.) NNE of the city of Saratov; formerly in N Volga German Autonomous Socialist Republic. Founded 18th cent., and named after Empress Catherine the Great; later renamed in honor of German political philosopher Karl Marx.
Marks·ville \ˈmärks-ˌvil\. Town, ⊗ of Avoyelles parish, cen. Louisiana; pop. (1990c) 5526.
Marl \ˈmärl\. City, North Rhine-Westphalia, Germany, N of Gelsenkirchen; pop. (1992e) 91,864; first mentioned in 9th cent.; city chartered 1936.
Marl·boro \ˈmärl-ˌbər-ō\. **1.** County in NE South Carolina. See table at SOUTH CAROLINA.
2. City, Massachusetts. See MARLBOROUGH 2.
Marl·bor·ough \ˈmärl-ˌbər-ō\. **1.** Town, Hartford co., N Connecticut, 13 mi. (21 km.) SE of the city of Hartford; pop. (1990c) 5535.
2. *also* **Marl·boro.** City, Middlesex co., NE Massachusetts, 13 mi. (21 km.) ENE of Worcester; pop. (1990c) 31,813.
Mar·lin \ˈmar-lən\. City, ⊗ of Falls co., cen. Texas, 20 mi. (32 km.) SSE of Waco; pop. (1990c) 6386.
Mar·lin·ton \ˈmär-lən-tən\. Town, ⊗ of Pocahontas co., E cen. West Virginia; pop. (1990c) 1148.
Mar·low \ˈmär-lō\. **1.** City, Stephens co., S Oklahoma, 26 mi. (42 km.) E of Lawton; pop. (1990c) 4416.

2. Town, Buckinghamshire, SE cen. England, on the Thames 30 mi. (48 km.) W of London; pop. (1981c) 14,195.

Mar·ly–le–Roi \mär-ˌlē-lə-ˈrwä\. Suburb of Versailles, Yvelines dept., N France; 17th cent. church; castle ruins.

Mar·ma·ra \ˈmär-mə-rə\; *anc.* **Proc·on·ne·sus** \ˌprä-kə-ˈnē-səs\. Island, Turkey, in the Sea of Marmara; 11 mi. (18 km.) long; area 50 sq. mi. (130 sq. km.).

Marmara, Sea of *or Turk.* **Marmara De·ni·zi** \ˈmär-mä-ˌrä-ˌde-nē-ˈzē\; *anc.* **Pro·pon·tis** \prō-ˈpän-təs\. Sea in NW Turkey, bet. Europe and Asia; 175 mi. (282 km.) long; area 4429 sq. mi. (11,471 sq. km.); max. depth over 4000 ft. (1200 m.); connected with the Black Sea through the Bosporus, and with the Aegean Sea through the Dardanelles. Has several islands, esp. Marmara in the W and Kızıl Is. near İstanbul, a large promontory, Kapıdağı (Cyzicus), on the S coast, and two long inlets on the E.

Mar·mar·i·ca \mär-ˈmar-i-kə\. Desert plateau region of N Africa along the Mediterranean Sea bet. ancient Cyrenaica and Egypt; according to some geographers extended into NW Egypt nearly to Alexandria; in ancient times scene of conflict in many wars by Romans, Egyptians, Libyans, Arabs. In modern times the name was given by Italians to the NE section of Cyrenaica; scene of much fighting in WWII.

Mar Me·nor *or* **Mar·me·nor** \ˈmär-me-ˈnȯr\. Lagoon on SE coast of Spain, extending N from Cape of Palos ab. 14 mi. (23 km.); greatest width ab. 6 mi. (10 km.).

Mar·mo·la·da \ˌmär-mō-ˈlä-dä\. Highest peak in the Dolomites, NE Italy, bet. Veneto and Trentino-Alto Adige; 10,965 ft. (3342 m.).

Marmore, Cascata delle. See VELINO.

Marne \ˈmärn\ **1.** *anc.* **Mat·ro·na** \ˈma-trə-nə\. River, NE France; rises in NE cen. France, flows NW and W into Seine River at Charenton-le-Pont, near Paris; 326 mi. (525 km.) long; navigable for ab. 220 mi. (350 km.); scene of battles in WWI: Sept. 1914 in which the Allies succeeded in halting German advance on Paris; and July–Aug. 1918 in which last major German offensive of the war was halted, and the French and Americans made a successful counterattack, resulting in German defeat. Scene of heavy fighting in WWII. **2.** Department of NE France. See table at FRANCE.

Maroc. See MOROCCO 1.

Ma·ro·ni \mä-ˈrō-nē\ *or Du.* **Ma·ro·wij·ne** \ˌmär-ə-ˈvī-nə, -ˈvā-\. River, N South America; with its tributary, the Itany, forms boundary bet. Suriname and French Guiana; empties into Atlantic Ocean; ab. 450 mi. (720 km.) long.

Ma·roon Peak \mə-ˈrün\. Mountain, Pitkin co., W cen. Colorado; 14,156 ft. (4315 m.).

Maros. See MUREŞ 1.

Maros–Vásárhely. See TÎRGU MUREŞ.

Ma·roua \mä-ˈrü-ä\. Town, in cen. part of N Cameroon; pop. (1987c) 123,000; cotton.

Ma·ro·vo \mä-ˈrō-vō\. Lagoon, Solomon Is. See NEW GEORGIA.

Marowijne. See MARONI.

Mar·pi Point \ˈmär-pē\. N point of Saipan I., Northern Mariana Is., W Pacific Ocean.

Mar·ple \ˈmär-pəl\. **1.** Township, Delaware co., SE Pennsylvania, W suburb of Chester; pop. (1990c) 23,123. **2.** Town, Greater Manchester, NW England, on the Goyt 9 mi. (14 km.) SE of Manchester; pop. (1981p) 23,899.

Mar·que·sas Islands \mär-ˈkā-səz\ *or Fr.* **Îles Mar·quises** \ˌēl-mär-ˈkēz\. Group of 10 islands of French Polynesia, S Pacific Ocean, bet. ab. 8° to 11°S and 140°W, N of Tuamotu Archipelago and 2000 mi. (3200 km.) SSE of Honolulu; 480 sq. mi. (1243 sq. km.); pop. (1988c) 7358; ✱ Taiohae on Nuku Hiva I. The more important islands are in three groups: Nuku Hiva, Ua Pu, and Ua Huka in the center; Hiva Oa, Tahuata, and Fatu Hiva in the SE, and the small islands of Eïao and Hatutu in the NW. Rocky and mountainous islands of volcanic origin; highest point on Hiva Oa 4134 ft. (1260 m.); have fertile and well-watered valleys. First discovered by Spanish explorer Álvaro de Mendaña de Neira in 1595; rediscovered by English explorer Capt. James Cook 1774; taken by France 1842; French settlement not complete until after 1870.

Marquesas Keys. Small group of islands W of the SW end of Florida Keys, N of entrance to Gulf of Mexico, a part of Monroe co., Florida.

Mar·quette \mär-ˈket\. **1.** Name of counties in two states of the U.S. See tables at MICHIGAN and WISCONSIN. **2.** City, ⊗ of Marquette co., N Upper Penin. of Michigan, on Lake Superior; pop. (1990c) 21,977; ships iron ore; cathedral; historical museum, maritime museum; Northern Michigan Univ. (1899); founded 1849; incorp. as village 1859, city 1871.

Marquises, Îles. See MARQUESAS ISLANDS.

Mar·ra·kech *or* **Mar·ra·kesh** *also* **Ma·ra·kesh** \mə-ˈrä-kish, ˌmar-ə-ˈkesh\; *formerly* **Mo·roc·co** \mə-ˈrä-kō\. City, W cen. Morocco; pop. (1982c) 439,728; popular tourist resort; situated in N foothills of W end of the Grand Atlas; leather goods, carpets; many mosques, fountains; palace; souk. Founded 1062 by Yūsuf ibn Tāshufīn as African ✱ of Almoravids dynasty; in medieval period one of great cities of Islam; taken by French 1912; modern quarter developed by French after 1912.

Mar·rero \mə-ˈrer-ō\. Unincorporated settlement, Jefferson parish, SE Louisiana, across the Mississippi from New Orleans; pop. (1990c) 36,671.

Mar·rick·ville \ˈmar-ik-ˌvil\. Municipality, E New South Wales, SE Australia, S suburb of Sydney; pop. (1991c) 78,023.

Marruecos. See MOROCCO 1.

Mar·sa·la \mär-ˈsä-lä\; *anc.* **Lil·y·bae·um** \ˌli-li-ˈbē-əm\. Seaport, Trapani prov., Sicily, Italy, on Mediterranean 18 mi. (29 km.) S of the seaport of Trapani; pop. (1991p) 77,218; exports wine; cathedral; theater; walls; catacombs; Italian patriot Giusseppe Garibaldi and volunteer forces (Red Shirts) landed here 1860 during conquest of The Two Sicilies.

Marsa Matruh. See MATRUH.

Marsan. See MONT-DE-MARSAN.

Mars Diep \ˈmärz-ˈdēp\. Strait separating island of Texel from mainland of N North Holland prov., W Netherlands; ab. 2 mi. (3 km.) wide; outlet of Waddenzee to North Sea.

Mar·seille *or* **Mar·seilles** \mȧr-ˈsā\; *anc.* **Mas·si·lia** \mə-ˈsi-lē-ə\. Seaport, ✱ of Bouches-du-Rhône dept., SE France, on NE shore of Gulf of Lion 98 mi. (158 km.) WSW of Nice; pop. (1990c) 807,726; archiepiscopal see; military and naval station; major commercial seaport, exporting construction materials, food products, wine, metalwork; manufactures soap, sugar, building materials, chemicals; oil refining, shipbuilding; modern Byzantine cathedral (1893); Romanesque church of Notre Dame de la Garde; Renaissance-style Palais des Arts de Longchamps; mint.

History: Ancient Massilia colonized by Phocaeans (Ionian Greeks) c. 600 B.C.; developed trade up the Rhone Valley and in the Mediterranean; planted several colonies on Gallic and Spanish coasts; aided by Rome in conflict with Carthage; deprived of its colonies when it was annexed by Rome 49 B.C.; early seat of Christian bishopric; overrun by Visigoths, Ostrogoths, and Franks, 5th and 6th cents.; in 10th cent. belonged to Provence; in 13th cent. became independent, passed to Charles of Anjou, then back to Provence; passed to French crown 1481; rebelled against Louis XIV 1660; population halved by plague 1720; became important again in 19th cent. with development of French colonial empire and opening of Suez Canal; in WWII occupied by Germans Nov. 1942–Aug. 1944.

Mar·seilles. **1.** \mär-ˈsālz\. City, La Salle co., N Illinois, on Illinois River 8 mi. (13 km.) E of Ottawa; pop. (1990c) 4811. **2.** Seaport, SE France. See MARSEILLE.

Mar·shall \ˈmär-shəl\. **1.** Name of counties in 12 states of U.S. See tables at ALABAMA, ILLINOIS, INDIANA, IOWA, KANSAS, KENTUCKY, MINNESOTA, MISSISSIPPI, OKLAHOMA, SOUTH DAKOTA, TENNESSEE, WEST VIRGINIA.

2. City, ⊗ of Searcy co., N Arkansas; pop. (1990c) 1318.
3. City, ⊗ of Clark co., E Illinois, 53 mi. (85 km.) S of Danville; pop. (1990c) 3555.
4. City, ⊗ of Calhoun co., S Michigan, 12 mi. (19 km.) ESE of Battle Creek; pop. (1990c) 6891.
5. City, ⊗ of Lyon co., SW Minnesota, 35 mi. (56 km.) S of Montevideo; pop. (1990c) 12,023; Southwest State Univ. (1963).
6. City, ⊗ of Saline co., W cen. Missouri, 28 mi. (45 km.) N of Sedalia; pop. (1990c) 12,711; Missouri Valley Coll. (1888).
7. Town, ⊗ of Madison co., W North Carolina, 15 mi. (24 km.) NNW of Asheville; pop. (1990c) 809.
8. City, ⊗ of Harrison co., NE Texas, 54 mi. (87 km.) ENE of Tyler; pop. (1990c) 23,682; county historical museum; in resort region. Wiley Coll. (1873), East Texas Baptist Univ. (1912). Settled 1841 and named for Chief Justice John Marshall; incorp. as city 1848; served (in Texas) as temporary ✻ of (Union-held) Missouri in administration of Confederate affairs during the Civil War.
9. Coastal town, W Liberia, 30 mi. (48 km.) SE of Monrovia; port.

Marshall Islands *or officially* **Republic of the Marshall Islands.** Group of more than two dozen atolls and more than 867 reefs in W Pacific Ocean, E of the Caroline Is. and NNW of Kiribati, 5°30′ to 15°N and 161° to 172°E; comprise the Ratak and Ralik chains of islands; land area 70 sq. mi. (181 sq. km.), incl. lagoons 4500 sq. mi. (11,700 sq. km.); pop. (1983e) 52,000 inhabiting 24 of the islands; ✻ Majuro. The government is the biggest employer; coconut products, breadfruit.

History: Probably first sighted by Spanish 1529; claimed by Germany 1885 and all rights to islands purchased by Germany from Spain 1899; seized by Japan 1914 and granted to Japan as League of Nations mandate 1920; held with absolute sovereignty by Japan from 1935; invaded 1944 by U.S., which seized Kwajalein and Enewetak; became part of U.S. Trust Terr. of the Pacific Islands 1947; became internally self-governing republic 1979; became fully sovereign state 1986 with independent control over foreign policy except defense, which remains a U.S. responsibility.

Mar·shall·town \ˈmär-shəl-ˌtau̇n\. City, ⊗ of Marshall co., cen. Iowa, 48 mi. (77 km.) NE of Des Moines; pop. (1990c) 25,178; art gallery; Marshalltown Community Coll. (1927); settled 1851; incorp. 1863.

Marsh–Bil·lings National Historical Park \ˈmärsh-ˈbi-liŋz\. See UNITED STATES, *National Historical Parks.*

Marsh·field \ˈmärsh-ˌfēld\. **1.** Town, Plymouth co., SE Massachusetts, 15 mi. (24 km.) E of Brockton; pop. (1990c) 21,531; residence of statesman Daniel Webster during latter part of his life.
2. City, ⊗ of Webster co., S Missouri, 24 mi. (39 km.) ENE of Springfield; pop. (1990c) 4374.
3. City, Oregon. See COOS BAY 2.
4. City, Marathon and Wood cos., cen. Wisconsin, 25 mi. (40 km.) NW of Wisconsin Rapids; pop. (1990c) 19,291.

Mars Hill \ˈmärz\. **1.** Isolated mountain, Aroostook co., N Maine, near E Maine boundary; 1660 ft. (506 m.).
2. Town, Madison co., W North Carolina; pop. (1990c) 1611; Mars Hill Coll. (1856).

Mars' Hill. See AREOPAGUS.

Marsh Island \ˈmärsh\. Island off S coast of Louisiana, at entrance to Vermilion Bay; a game preserve.

Marsh Peak. Mountain in N Uintah co., E Utah; 12,219 ft. (3724 m.).

Marsivan. See MERZIFON.

Marske–by–the–Sea \ˈmärsk-\. Resort town, Cleveland, NE England, on North Sea coast.

Mars–la–Tour \ˌmärs-lə-ˈtür\. Village, Meurthe-et-Moselle dept., NE France, SW of Metz; with Vionville scene of battle in Franco-Prussian War Aug. 1870 in which Prussians blocked westward movement of French under Marshal Achille-François Bazaine and forced their withdrawal to Gravelotte and St.-Privat-la-Montagne (*qq.v.*).

Mars·ton Moor \ˈmär-stən\. Moor, N England, 7 mi. (11 km.) W of York, in English Civil War scene of battle July 2, 1644 in which Parliamentarians under Thomas Fairfax, Oliver Cromwell, and David Leslie defeated Royalists under Prince Rupert and George Goring, earl of Norwich.

Mar·ta \ˈmär-tä\. River, W cen. Italy; flows from Lake Bolsena into the N Tyrrhenian Sea; ab. 25 mi. (40 km.) long.

Mar·ta·ban \ˌmär-tə-ˈbän, -ˈban\. Town, Myanmar, at mouth of the Salween River opp. Moulmein.

Martaban, Gulf of. Inlet of Bay of Bengal on coast of Myanmar, bet. 16° and 17°N and 96° and 98°E; receives waters of the Salween River and the Sittang River.

Mar·ta·pu·ra *or Du.* **Mar·ta·poe·ra** \ˌmär-tə-ˈpu̇r-ə\. River, SE Borneo, Indonesia; ab. 100 mi. (160 km.) long; an E tributary of the Barito, joining it just below Banjarmasin.

Marthasville. See ATLANTA 1.

Mar·tha's Vine·yard \ˈmär-thəz-ˈvin-yərd\. Island in Atlantic Ocean off SW coast of Cape Cod, SE Massachusetts, bet. Elizabeth Is. to the W and Nantucket to the E; part of Dukes co.; 108 sq. mi. (280 sq. km.); ab. 20 mi. (32 km.) long, 2 to 10 mi. (3 to 16 km.) wide; summer resort; chief town Edgartown, on E coast.

Mar·tí \mär-ˈtē\. Municipality and town, Matanzas prov., W cen. Cuba, near N coast 19 mi. (31 km.) E of Cárdenas; munic. pop. (1981p) 23,295.

Mar·tigues \ˌmär-ˈtēg\ *or* **Les Martigues** \lā-\; *anc.* **Ma·rit·i·ma Avat·i·co·rum** \mə-ˈri-tə-mə-ə-ˌva-tə-ˈkōr-əm\. Commune, Bouches-du-Rhône dept., SE France, on Mediterranean 18 mi. (29 km.) NW of Marseille; pop. (1990c) 42,922. Probably site of Roman camp; town founded 13th cent.; important during Middle Ages; formerly important fishing port.

Mar·tin \ˈmärt-ᵊn\. **1.** Name of counties in six states of the U.S. See tables at FLORIDA, INDIANA, KENTUCKY, MINNESOTA, NORTH CAROLINA, TEXAS.
2. City, ⊗ of Bennett co., S South Dakota; pop. (1990c) 1151.
3. City, Weakley co., NW Tennessee, 31 mi. (50 km.) W of Paris; pop. (1990c) 8600; Univ. of Tennessee at Martin (1927).
4. \ˈmär-tēn\ Town, N cen. Slovakia; pop. (1991p) 58,338.

Mar·ti·na Fran·ca \mär-ˈtē-nä-ˈfräŋ-kä\. Commune, Taranto prov., Puglia, SE Italy, 17 mi. (27 km.) NNE of the seaport of Taranto; pop. (1991p) 45,186; 17th cent. baroque palace.

Martin Dam. Dam across Tallapoosa River, E cen. Alabama; height 168 ft. (51 m.); impounds water for power, forming **Martin Lake** in Elmore, Tallapoosa, and Coosa cos.

Mar·ti·nez \mär-ˈtē-nəs\. City, ⊗ of Contra Costa co., W California, on Suisun Bay 18 mi. (29 km.) NE of Oakland; pop. (1990c) 31,808; vertical lift bridge across Suisun Bay. The house that naturalist John Muir lived in is open to the public; town laid out 1849.

Mar·tí·nez de la Tor·re \mär-ˈtē-näs-t͟hā-lä-ˈtōr-rā\. Municipality, Veracruz state, Mexico, 87 mi. (140 km.) NW of the city of Veracruz; pop. (1990p) 102,722.

Mar·tin Gar·cía \mär-ˈtēn-gär-ˈsē-ä\. Island in the mouth of the Río de la Plata, off SW coast of Uruguay; claimed by both Argentina and Uruguay.

Mar·ti·nique \ˌmär-tə-ˈnēk\. Island, Windward Is., E West Indies; constituting an overseas department of France; 425 sq. mi. (1101 sq. km.); pop. (1993e) 377,000; ✻ Fort-de-France; mountainous, volcano of Mt. Pelée (*q.v.*) in N and Carbet (3929 ft. or 1198 m.) in NW cen. part; has many rivers; large inlet, Fort-de-France Bay, on N shore of which is the ✻ Fort-de-France. Exports sugar (chief industry), rum, bananas, pineapples, cement; tourism. Discovered by explorer Christopher Columbus 1502; settled by French 1635; passed to French crown 1674; attacked by Dutch and British in 17th cent.; captured by British 1762 but restored to France; again occupied by British 1794–1802 and 1809–1814; by French constitution of 1946 made an overseas department of France. Birthplace of Empress Josephine 1763.

Mar·tin·puich \ˌmär-teⁿ-ˈpwēsh\. Village, Pas-de-Calais dept., N France, 6 mi. (10 km.) NE of Albert; fell to Allies Sept. 1916.

Mar·tins·burg \ˈmärt-ᵊnz-ˌbərg\. City, ⊗ of Berkeley co., NE West Virginia, in E Panhandle; pop. (1990c) 14,073; ships fruit. Incorp. as town 1778, as city 1859; grew with arrival of railroad mid-19th cent.; during Civil War was valued for its location on railroad line and occupied alternately by both sides; railroad strike 1877 put down by federal troops.

Mar·tins Ferry \ˈmärt-ᵊnz\. City, Belmont co., E Ohio, on Ohio River 19 mi. (31 km.) S of Steubenville; pop. (1990c) 7990; birthplace of writer William Dean Howells 1837.

Mar·tins·ville \ˈmärt-ᵊnz-ˌvil\. **1.** City, ⊗ of Morgan co., cen. Indiana, 28 mi. (45 km.) SW of Indianapolis; pop. (1990c) 11,677; autumn resort.
2. City, ⊗ of Henry co., S Virginia, but politically independent, 32 mi. (51 km.) W of Danville; 10 sq. mi. (26 sq. km.); pop. (1990c) 16,162; natural history museum; founded 1793.

Mar·tos \ˈmär-tōs\. Commune, Jaén prov., S Spain, 14 mi. (23 km.) SW of the commune of Jaén; pop. (1991p) 20,900; textiles.

Mar·tre, Lac la \ˌläk-lə-ˈmär-trə\. Lake, cen. mainland part of Northwest Territories, Canada; 685 sq. mi. (1774 sq. km.); its outlet flows SE to Great Slave Lake.

Ma·ru·du Bay \mä-ˈrü-dü\. Inlet, N Sabah, Malaysia, S of Balabac Strait.

Ma·ru·ga·me \ˌmär-u̇-ˈgä-mā\. City, Kagawa prefecture, Shikoku I., Japan, on N coast on Inland Sea WSW of Takamatsu; pop. (1990p) 75,607.

Ma·ru·tea \ˌmä-rü-ˈtā-ä\. Large atoll of the Tuamotu Archipelago, French Polynesia, S Pacific Ocean, ab. 125 mi. (201 km.) E of Fakarava.

Mar·vine, Mount \ˈmär-vən\. Peak, Sevier co., cen. Utah; 11,600 ft. (3536 m.).

Marwar. See JODHPUR.

Marxstadt. See MARKS 2.

Ma·ry \mä-ˈrē\; *formerly* **Merv** \ˈmerv\. Town, Turkmenistan, in an oasis on Murgab River 180 mi. (290 km.) E of Ashkhabad; pop. (1991e) 94,900; center of cotton-producing region.
History: A town of great antiquity, in Hindu, Parsi, and Arab tradition believed to be the ancient Paradise, hence the original home (Mouru) of the Aryan families and hence of the human race; important town of several ancient kingdoms; under Arabs 7th–9th cents.; became center of Islamic learning; fell to Turks 11th cent.; destroyed by Mongols 1221; occupied by Russians 1884.

Mar·y·bor·ough \ˈmar-ē-ˌbər-ō\. **1.** Town, SE Queensland, Australia, on Mary River 140 mi. (225 km.) N of Brisbane; pop. (1981c) 21,530; timber.
2. Town, Ireland. See PORTLAOIGHISE.

Mary Es·ther \ˈmar-ē-ˈes-tər\. Town, Okaloosa co., NW Florida, 27 mi. (43 km.) E of Pensacola; pop. (1990c) 4139.

Mar·y·land \ˈmer-ə-lənd\. **1.** A middle Atlantic state of U.S.A., bounded on N by Pennsylvania, on E by Delaware and the Atlantic Ocean, on S by Virginia and West Virginia, and on W by West Virginia; 42d state in area, 10,460 sq. mi. or 27,091 sq. km. (land area 9837 sq. mi. or 25,478 sq. km.); 19th state in population, (1990c) 4,781,468; ✻ Annapolis; one of the original states of the Union, the 7th to ratify the U.S. Constitution (Apr. 28, 1788). See table of states at UNITED STATES.
Nickname: Old Line State.
State flower: Black-eyed Susan.
Motto: Fatti Maschii, Parole Femine (Manly Deeds, Womanly Words).
Rivers: Potomac, forming S boundary; Patuxent, flowing SE into Chesapeake Bay; Susquehanna, flowing across NE corner into headwaters of Chesapeake Bay.
Highest point: Backbone Mt., 3360 ft. (1024 m.), in Garrett co.
Chief products: Dairy products, food products, corn, tobacco; chickens and other livestock; fishing esp. for crabs; stone, sand and gravel; services; tourism; manufacturing: primary metals, transportation equipment, chemicals, electrical equipment.
Chief city: Baltimore.
Political divisions: Divided into the following 23 counties (for pronunciation of their names, see their individual entries):

NAME	AREA[1] (sq. mi.)	AREA[1] (sq. km.)	POP. (1990c)	CO. SEAT
Allegany	428	1,109	74,946	Cumberland
Anne Arundel	423	1,096	427,239	Annapolis
Baltimore[2]	598	1,549	692,134	Towson
Baltimore city[3]	75	194	736,014	
Calvert	217	562	51,372	Prince Frederick
Caroline	321	831	27,035	Denton
Carroll	456	1,181	123,372	Westminster
Cecil	362	938	71,347	Elkton
Charles	459	1,189	101,154	La Plata
Dorchester	594	1,538	30,236	Cambridge
Frederick	665	1,722	150,208	Frederick
Garrett	659	1,707	28,138	Oakland
Harford	453	1,173	182,132	Bel Air
Howard	251	650	187,328	Ellicott City
Kent	281	728	17,842	Chestertown
Montgomery	496	1,285	757,027	Rockville
Prince Georges	484	1,254	729,268	Upper Marlboro
Queen Annes	375	971	33,953	Centreville
Saint Marys	373	966	75,974	Leonardtown
Somerset	339	878	23,440	Princess Anne
Talbot	261	676	30,549	Easton
Washington	459	1,189	121,393	Hagerstown
Wicomico	381	987	74,339	Salisbury
Worcester	479	1,241	35,028	Snow Hill

[1] Area = land area.
[2] Exclusive of city of Baltimore which is administratively independent of the county.
[3] Administratively independent of Baltimore co. and has itself the status of a county.

History: Orig. inhabited by American Indians; English first visited early 17th cent.; granted to George Calvert (Lord Baltimore) as proprietary colony 1632; first American colony to achieve religious freedom; first settled at St. Marys 1634, which was its ✻ 1634–94; colony under rule of British crown 1689–1715; its long-standing boundary dispute with Pennsylvania settled by drawing of Mason-Dixon Line 1760s; first state constitution adopted 1776; adopted Articles of Confederation 1781; ceded territory for District of Columbia (*q.v.*); during Civil War remained in the Union, but was subjected to suspension of habeas corpus; invaded by Confederate forces 1862; abolished slavery 1864; adopted present constitution 1867. See BALTIMORE.
2. The southernmost county of Liberia; 1675 sq. mi. (4338 sq. km.); set up as an independent African state 1833 by freed black slaves from the U.S.; annexed to Liberia 1857.

Maryland Heights. City, St. Louis co., Missouri, on Missouri River; pop. (1990c) 25,407.

Mar·y·port \ˈmar-ē-ˌpōrt\. Town, Cumbria, NW England, on Solway Firth at mouth of the Ellen; pop. (1981p) 11,598.

Mar·ys·vale Peak \ˈmar-ēz-ˌvāl\. Mountain, Piute co., S cen. Utah; 10,943 ft. (3335 m.).

Mar·ys·ville \ˈmar-ēz-ˌvil\. **1.** City, ⊗ of Yuba co., N cen. California; pop. (1990c) 12,324; Yuba Coll. (1927).
2. City, ⊗ of Marshall co., NE Kansas, 45 mi. (72 km.) N of Manhattan on Big Blue River; pop. (1990c) 3359.
3. City, St. Clair co., SE Michigan, on St. Clair River 5 mi. (8 km.) S of Port Huron; pop. (1990c) 8515.
4. Village, ⊗ of Union co., W cen. Ohio; pop. (1990c) 9656.
5. Town, Snohomish co., NW cen. Washington, on Puget Sound 5 mi. (8 km.) N of Everett; pop. (1990c) 10,328.

Maryūt, Buḩayrat. See MAREOTIS, LAKE.

Mary·ville \ˈmar-i-vəl, -ˌvil\. **1.** Village, Madison co., Illinois, NE of East St. Louis; pop. (1990c) 2576.
2. City, ⊗ of Nodaway co., NW Missouri, 42 mi. (68 km.) N of St. Joseph; pop. (1990c) 10,663; Northwest Missouri State Univ. (1905).
3. City, ⊗ of Blount co., E Tennessee, near Great Smoky Mountains National Park 15 mi. (24 km.) S of Knoxville;

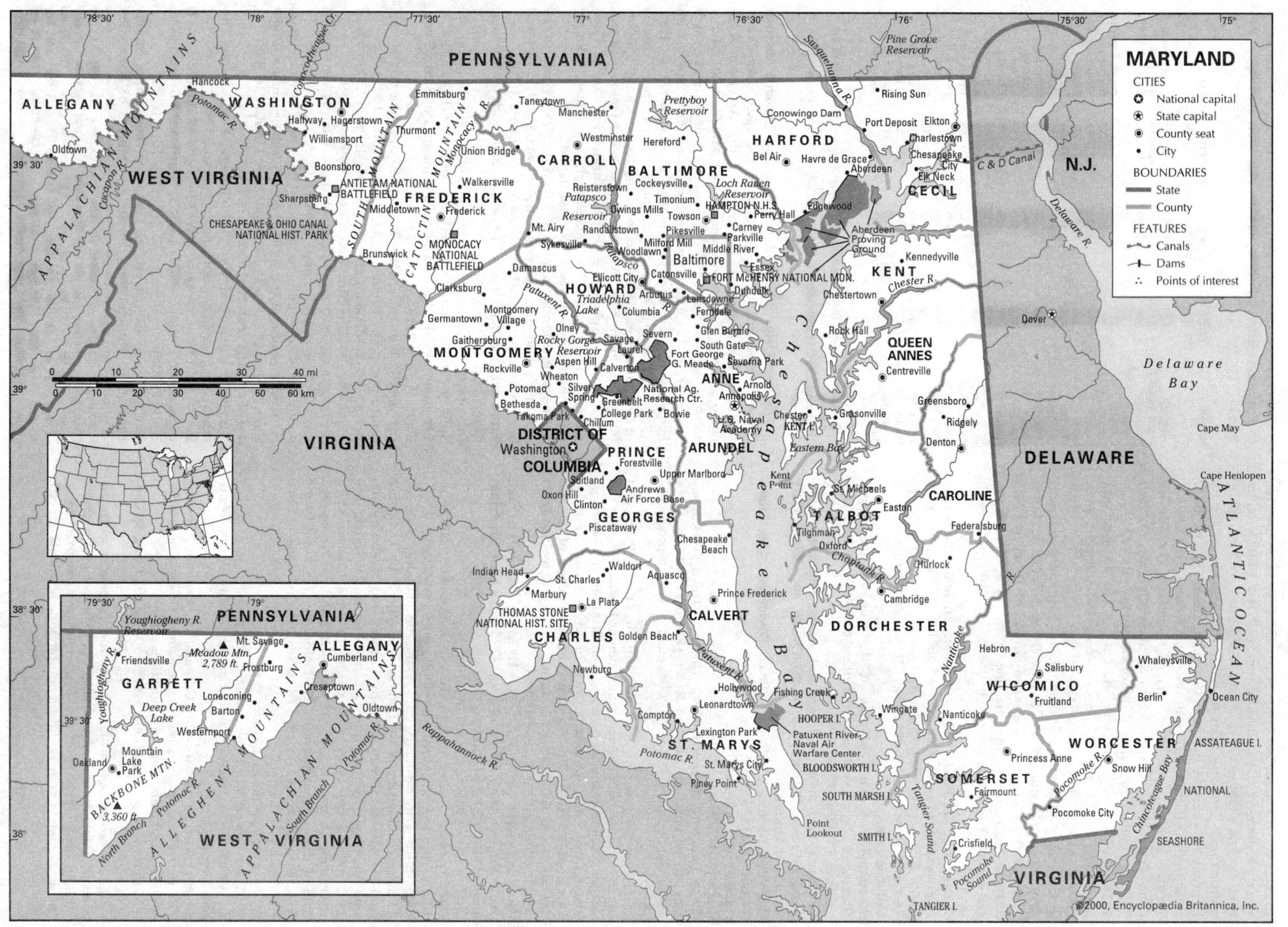

MARYLAND
CITIES
National capital
State capital
County seat
City
BOUNDARIES
State
County
FEATURES
Canals
Dams
Points of interest
PENNSYLVANIA
N.J.
DELAWARE
VIRGINIA
WEST VIRGINIA
DISTRICT OF COLUMBIA
ATLANTIC OCEAN
Delaware Bay
Chesapeake Bay
Cape May
Cape Henlopen
Delaware R.
C & D Canal
Dover
Susquehanna R.
Pine Grove Reservoir
Conowingo Dam
ALLEGANY
WASHINGTON
FREDERICK
CARROLL
BALTIMORE
HARFORD
CECIL
KENT
QUEEN ANNES
CAROLINE
TALBOT
DORCHESTER
WICOMICO
WORCESTER
SOMERSET
HOWARD
MONTGOMERY
PRINCE GEORGES
ANNE ARUNDEL
CALVERT
CHARLES
ST. MARYS
Baltimore
Washington
Hagerstown
Frederick
Salisbury
Ocean City
Easton
Cambridge
Towson
Bel Air
Elkton
Chestertown
Centreville
Denton
Rockville
Upper Marlboro
La Plata
Prince Frederick
Leonardtown
Princess Anne
Snow Hill
ASSATEAGUE I.
NATIONAL
SEASHORE
Chincoteague Bay
Tangier Sound
TANGIER I.
SMITH I.
SOUTH MARSH I.
BLOODSWORTH I.
HOOPER I.
Patuxent River Naval Air Warfare Center
Point Lookout
Potomac R.
Rappahannock R.
Patuxent R.
Choptank R.
Nanticoke R.
Pocomoke R.
Chester R.
Eastern Bay
Aberdeen Proving Ground
FORT McHENRY NATIONAL MON.
HAMPTON N.H.S.
MONOCACY NATIONAL BATTLEFIELD
ANTIETAM NATIONAL BATTLEFIELD
CHESAPEAKE & OHIO CANAL NATIONAL HIST. PARK
THOMAS STONE NATIONAL HIST. SITE
U.S. Naval Academy
Andrews Air Force Base
National Ag. Research Ctr.
CATOCTIN MOUNTAIN
SOUTH MOUNTAIN
APPALACHIAN MOUNTAINS
Loch Raven Reservoir
Prettyboy Reservoir
Triadelphia Lake
Rocky Gorge Reservoir
GARRETT
Cumberland
Oakland
Mountain Lake Park
Deep Creek Lake
BACKBONE MTN. 3,360 ft.
Meadow Mtn. 2,789 ft.
Youghiogheny R. Reservoir
ALLEGHENY MOUNTAINS
North Branch Potomac R.
South Branch Potomac R.
0 10 20 30 40 mi
0 10 20 30 40 50 60 km
©2000, Encyclopædia Britannica, Inc.

pop. (1990c) 19,208; Maryville Coll. (1819); schoolhouse where political leader Sam Houston once taught.

Marzūq. See MURZUQ.

Ma·sa·da \mə-ˈsä-də, -ˈsā-\. Fortified hill on W shore of Dead Sea at S end, SE Israel; fortifications constructed first cent. B.C.; in 72–73 A.D. scene of final stand of Jews against Romans (defenders killed themselves rather than surrender).

Más Afue·ra \ˌmäs-ä-ˈfwā-rä\ *or* **Ale·jan·dro Sel·kirk** \ˌä-lē-ˈkän-drō-ˈsel-ˌkirk\. An island of the Juan Fernández group, Chile. See JUAN FERNÁNDEZ.

Ma·san \ˈmä-ˌsän\; *formerly* **Ma·sam·po** \mä-ˈsäm-pō\. Seaport city, South Kyŏngsang prov., South Korea, at head of an inlet of Western Channel 26 mi. (42 km.) W of Pusan; pop. (1985c) 448,746; a commercial and industrial center.

Masandam, Ras. See MUSANDAM, CAPE.

Masanutton Mountain. See MASSANUTTEN MOUNTAIN.

Más a Tier·ra \ˌmäs-ä-ˈtyer-rä\ *or* **Ro·bin·son Cru·soe Island** \ˈrä-bin-sən-ˈkrü-ˌsō\. An island of the Juan Fernández group, Chile. See JUAN FERNÁNDEZ.

Ma·sa·ya \mä-ˈsä-yä\. **1.** Department of SW Nicaragua. See table at NICARAGUA.

2. Town, its ✻; pop. (1985e) 74,946; center of agricultural region; produces cigars, footwear.

Mas·ba·te \mäs-ˈbä-tā\. **1.** Island and province in Visayan Is., cen. Philippines, S of SE Luzon; ✻ Masbate. Formerly a subprovince of Sorsogon from which it is separated by Ticao Pass and Ticao I.; on the E borders on Samar Sea, on the S on Visayan Sea, and on the W on Sibuyan Sea; separated from NE Panay by Jintotolo Channel. Covered with mountains ranging from 1200 to 2000 ft. (370 to 610 m.). As province includes Burias I. and Ticao I. Produces hemp and rice. See table at PHILIPPINES.

History: Explored by Spaniards in latter half of 16th cent. and later under Spanish rule; after Spanish-American War, under Americans received civil government 1901; occupied by Japanese during WWII; retaken by Americans 1945.

2. Municipality, ✻ of Masbate prov., Philippines, on NE coast of Masbate I.; pop. (1980c) 52,944; port of entry.

Mas·ca·ra \ˈmas-kə-rə\ *also* **Mou·as·kar** \ˈmü-əs-kär\. Commune, NW Algeria, 60 mi. (97 km.) SE of Oran; pop. (1987p) 64,691; built on a mountain slope at alt. 1800 ft. (550 m.). Importance increased when it became headquarters of Abdelkader 1832; captured twice by French, 1835 and 1841, and considerably damaged.

Mas·ca·rene Islands \ˌmas-kə-ˈrēn\. Group of islands in the Indian Ocean, bet. 400 and 500 mi. (650 to 800 km.) E of Madagascar, comprising Réunion, Mauritius, and Rodrigues (*qq.v.*).

Mas·couche \mas-ˈküsh\. Town, S Quebec, Canada, N of Montreal; pop. (1991c) 25,828.

Mas·cou·tah \mas-ˈkü-tə\. City, St. Clair co., SW Illinois, 23 mi. (37 km.) ESE of East St. Louis; pop. (1990c) 5511.

Mas d'Azil, Le. See LE MAS D'AZIL.

Ma·se·ru \ˈma-zə-ˌrü\. Town, ✻ of Lesotho, on Caledon River near W border with Free State, Rep. of South Africa; area pop. (1986c) 311,829; diamond processing; tourism; alt. 4950 ft. (1509 m.); university; founded 1869 by Mshweshwe, chief of the Basotho.

Ma·sher·brum \ˈmə-shər-ˌbrüm\. Peak in the Karakoram Range of the Himalayas, N India, SW of K2; 25,660 ft. (7821 m.); scaled 1960.

Mash·had \mə-ˈshad\ *also* **Me·shed** \mə-ˈshed\. City, ✻ of Khorāsān prov., Iran; situated in the valley of a tributary of the Harī; pop. (1986c) 1,463,508; elev. ab. 3200 ft. (980 m.); in rich agricultural region; has for centuries been an important trade center and junction point on caravan routes and highways from India to Tehran and from N to S bet. Turkistan towns and Gulf of Oman. Has Shiite shrine to ʻAli ar-Riḍā and is place of annual pilgrimage. In 19th and 20th cents. important strategically because of its proximity to Russian and Afghan borders.

Mash·kel \mash-ˈkel\ *or Pers.* **Rūd–e Māsh·kid** \ˈrü-dē-mäsh-ˈkēd\. River in SE Iran and Pakistan; rises in SE Iran, flows in a curve E across Pakistan boundary, NE, and finally NW into Hamun-i-Mashkel.

Mashkel, Hamun–i–. See HAMUN–I–MASHKEL.

Ma·sho·na·land \mə-ˈshō-nə-ˌland\. Region, NE Zimbabwe; formerly a province, later divided into the provinces of **Northern Mashonaland** and **Southern Mashonaland** and 1981 redivided into **Mashonaland Central** (11,393 sq. mi. or 29,508 sq. km.; pop. [1982p] 563,407), **Mashonaland East** (10,353 sq. mi. or 26,814 sq. km.; pop. [1982p] 666,626), and **Mashonaland West** (21,520 sq. mi. or 55,737 sq. km.; pop. [1982p] 858,962); region is open plain and fertile tableland, inhabited by Shona (Mashona), a Bantu people; acquired by British South Africa Company 1890; became part of Southern Rhodesia 1923 and subsequently of Zimbabwe 1980.

Mash·pee \ˈmash-ˌpē\. Town, Barnstable co., Massachusetts; pop. (1990c) 7884.

Mash·riq *or* **Mash·req** \ˈmȧsh-rek\. Arabic name for the E Arab countries—used esp. of those countries not considered part of Maghreb.

Ma·si·a·ti \ˌmä-sē-ˈä-tē\. Peak in S cen. Venezuela, near Brazilian border; ab. 4900 ft. (1500 m.).

Masikesi. See VILA DA MANHIÇA.

Ma·sin·di \mä-ˈsin-dē\. Town, W cen. Uganda, E of Lake Albert.

Ma·sin·loc \ˌmä-sin-ˈlȯk\. Town on coast, W Luzon, Philippines, 16 mi. (26 km.) N of Iba; munic. pop. (1980c) 27,735; behind the town in foothills of W slope of Zambales Mts. are chromite deposits.

Ma·ṣī·rah \mə-ˈsir-ə\. Island in the Arabian Sea, off E coast of Oman, SE Arabian Penin., 150 mi. (241 km.) S of Ra's al Hadd; 44 mi. (71 km.) long; administratively attached to Oman.

Masis. See ARARAT 2.

Mas·jed So·ley·mān \ˈmȧs-jid-ˌsü-lā-ˈmän\. City, W Iran, in S Zagros Mts. ab. 60 mi. (100 km.) NE of Ahvāz and near Maidan-i-Naftun; pop. (1986c) 104,787; center of important oil field; has oil pipeline to Ahvāz.

Mask, Lough \läk-ˈmask, läk\. Lake, S co. Mayo, W Ireland; 32 sq. mi. (83 sq. km.).

Mas·ki·non·gé \ˌmäs-kē-nȯ^{n}-ˈzhā\. County, S Quebec, Canada. See table at QUEBEC.

Ma·son \ˈmās-ᵊn\. **1.** Name of counties in six states of the U.S. See tables at ILLINOIS, KENTUCKY, MICHIGAN, TEXAS, WASHINGTON, WEST VIRGINIA.

2. City, ⊗ of Ingham co., S Michigan, 12 mi. (19 km.) S of Lansing; pop. (1990c) 6768.

3. City, Warren co., SW Ohio, NNE of Cincinnati; pop. (1990c) 11,452.

4. City, ⊗ of Mason co., cen. Texas; pop. (1990c) 2041.

Mason City. **1.** Township, Mason co., cen. Illinois, 28 mi. (45 km.) N of Springfield; pop. (1990c) 2729.

2. City, ⊗ of Cerro Gordo co., N Iowa, 62 mi. (100 km.) NW of Waterloo; pop. (1990c) 29,040; in agricultural region; cement; meatpacking; North Iowa Area Community Coll. (1918); settled 1853; incorp. as city 1881.

3. Former town, Okanogan co., N Washington; consolidated with town of Coulee Dam 1943.

Mason–Dix·on Line \-ˈdik-sən\ *also* **Mason and Dixon Line.** The S boundary line of Pennsylvania, run (except for its westernmost 36 mi. or 58 km.) by two English surveyors, Charles Mason and Jeremiah Dixon, bet. 1763 and 1767 to settle an old boundary dispute bet. proprietors of Pennsylvania and Maryland; 1783–85 extended W and accepted as boundary bet. Virginia (now West Virginia) and Pennsylvania; became famous at time of Missouri Compromise 1820 as part of boundary bet. free and slave states; name later popularly applied to boundary bet. northern and southern states.

Ma·sons Island \ˈmās-ᵊnz\. Island in the harbor of Mystic, Connecticut, off SE coast of New London co.

\ə\ abut \ᵊ\ kitten, Fr table \ər\ further \a\ ash \ā\ ace \ä\ cot, cart \ȧ\ Fr bac \au̇\ out \b\ Span Avila \ch\ chin \e\ bet \ē\ easy \g\ go \i\ hit \ī\ ice \j\ job \k\ Ger ich, Buch \$^{n}$\ Fr vin \ŋ\ sing \ō\ go \ȯ\ all \ȯ\ law \œ\ Fr bœuf \œ̄\ Fr feu \ȯi\ boy \th\ thin \t͟h\ this \ü\ loot \u̇\ foot \ue\ Ger füllen \ūē\ Fr rue \y\ yet \$^{y}$\ Fr digne \ˈdēn^{y}\, nuit \ˈnw^{y}ē\ \yü\ few \yu̇\ fury \zh\ vision

Ma·son·town \ˈmās-ᵊn-ˌtau̇n\. Borough, Fayette co., SW Pennsylvania, on Monongahela River 11 mi. (18 km.) W of Uniontown; pop. (1990c) 3759.

Mas·qat \ˈməs-ˌkät\ *or* **Mus·cat** \ˈməs-ˌkät, -kət\. Seaport town, ✻ of Oman, SE Arabian Penin., on the S coast of the Gulf of Oman; pop. (1982e) 85,000; on a small peninsula with steep mountain range behind it; its N suburb Matrah is starting point for land routes.

History: Came under Persians 6th cent. B.C.; converted to Islam c. 630 A.D.; from early 16th cent. to 1622 an unimportant Portuguese port, but became their Arabian headquarters 1622–48 after loss of Hormuz; held by Persians 1650–1741; then became part of sultanate of Oman (*q.v.*).

Masqat and Oman. See OMAN.

Mas·sa \ˈmäs-sä\. Commune, ✻ of Massa-Carrara prov., Tuscany, Italy; pop. (1991p) 65,287; chemicals; resort.

Mas·sac \ˈma-ˌsak, -sək\. County in S Illinois. See table at ILLINOIS.

Mas·sa–Car·ra·ra \ˈmäs-sä-kä-ˈrär-ä\; *formerly* **Ap·ua·nia** \ä-ˈpwä-nyä\. Province of Tuscany, Italy. See table at ITALY.

Mas·sa·chu·setts \ˌma-sə-ˈchü-səts, -zəts\. A northeast state of U.S.A., bounded on N by Vermont and New Hampshire, on E by the Atlantic Ocean, on S by the Atlantic Ocean, Rhode Island, and Connecticut, and on W by New York; 45th state in area, 8284 sq. mi. or 21,456 sq. km. (land area 7824 sq. mi. or 20,264 sq. km.); 13th state in population, (1990c) 6,016,425; ✻ Boston; one of the original states of the Union, the 6th to ratify the U.S. Constitution (Feb. 6, 1788). See table of states at UNITED STATES.

Nickname: Bay State.

State flower: Mayflower.

Motto: Ense Petit Placidam Sub Libertate Quietem (By the Sword We Seek Peace, but Peace Only under Liberty).

Rivers: Connecticut, flowing N to S across W part of state; Taunton, in SE, flowing into arm of Narragansett Bay; Merrimack, in extreme NE, flowing into Atlantic Ocean.

Highest point: Mt. Greylock, 3491 ft. (1064 m.), in Berkshire co.

Chief products: Dairy products, cranberries and other fruit, vegetables; manufacturing: electronic equipment, electrical equipment; printing and publishing; tourism; education; fishing.

Chief cities: Boston, Worcester, Springfield.

Political divisions: Divided into the following 14 counties (for pronunciation of their names, see their individual entries):

NAME	AREA[1] (sq. mi.)	AREA[1] (sq. km.)	POP. (1990c)	CO. SEAT(s)
Barnstable[2]	393	1,018	186,605	Barnstable
Berkshire	941	2,437	139,352	Pittsfield
Bristol	554	1,435	506,325	Fall River, Taunton, and New Bedford
Dukes[3]	104	269	11,639	Edgartown
Essex	594	1,538	670,080	Salem, Newburyport, and Lawrence
Franklin	708	1,834	70,092	Greenfield
Hampden	622	1,611	456,310	Springfield
Hampshire	529	1,370	146,568	Northampton
Middlesex	825	2,137	1,398,468	Lowell and Cambridge
Nantucket[4]	46	119	6,012	Nantucket
Norfolk[5]	394	1,020	616,087	Dedham
Plymouth	654	1,694	435,276	Plymouth
Suffolk	56	145	663,906	Boston
Worcester	1,513	3,919	709,705	Worcester and Fitchburg

[1] Area = land area.
[2] Coextensive with Cape Cod (*q.v.*).
[3] Comprises Martha's Vineyard, Elizabeth Is., and other islands.
[4] Comprises Nantucket I. and a few islets.
[5] Comprises a main area whose NE corner borders Boston Bay and two smaller areas separated from main area: one on Massachusetts Bay and surrounded on landward side by Plymouth co., the other enclosed by Middlesex and Suffolk cos.

History: Perhaps explored by Norse c. 11th cent.; coast skirted by Florentine explorer Giovanni da Verrazano 1524; Cape Cod discovered by Englishman Bartholomew Gosnold 1602 who made first (temporary) European settlement within present limits of state; at time of European settlement, region inhabited by several Algonquin tribes; Plymouth (see PLYMOUTH 4) settled by Pilgrims 1620; Massachusetts Bay Colony, founded and governed by Massachusetts Bay Company 1629–84; Harvard Coll. founded 1636; joined New England Confederation 1643; acquired province of Maine 1652; after loss of first charter 1684, governed as part of Dominion of New England 1686; by its 2d charter 1691, received jurisdiction over Maine and Plymouth colonies; in 18th cent., gradually became a center of resistance to imperial colonial policy (see BOSTON 1); British troops withdrawn to Boston after colonial uprisings at Lexington and Concord 1775; battle of Bunker Hill 1775; British evacuated Boston 1776; gave up claims to W lands 1785–86; W Massachusetts scene of Shays' Rebellion, an uprising in protest of harsh government economic policies 1786–87; E Massachusetts early center of American cotton manufacture (see WALTHAM). Maine became separate state 1820.

Massachusetts Bay. Inlet of Atlantic Ocean on E coast of Massachusetts, extending from Cape Ann on the N to Cape Cod on the S; ab. 60 mi. (100 km.) long by 25 mi. (40 km.) wide; the city of Boston is situated at its W end.

Massachusetts Bay Colony. An early (17th cent.) English settlment in Massachusetts.

Mas·sa·cre Bay \ˈma-si-kər\. Inlet on SE coast of Attu I. in the Aleutians, Alaska; landing here of American troops during WWII led to capture of the island from Japanese 1943.

Mas·sa·fra \mä-ˈsä-frä\. Commune, Taranto prov., Puglia, SE Italy, 9 mi. (14 km.) NW of the seaport of Taranto; pop. (1989c) 30,231.

Mas·sa Ma·rit·ti·ma \ˈmäs-sä-mä-ˈrēt-tē-mä\. Commune, Grosseto prov., Tuscany, cen. Italy, 24 mi. (39 km.) NNW of the commune of Grosseto; pop. (1981p) 10,036; 13th cent. cathedral; in historically important mining region (copper, iron, lead, and silver).

Mas·sa·nut·ten Mountain *or* **Mas·a·nut·ton Mountain** \ˌma-sə-ˈnət-ᵊn\. Mountain ridge, N Virginia, in the Blue Ridge, bet. N and S forks of Shenandoah River.

Mas·sa·pe·qua \ˌma-sə-ˈpē-kwə\. Unincorporated settlement, Nassau co., SE New York, on S shore of Long Island, ab. 10 mi. (16 km.) SE of Mineola; pop. (1990c) 22,018.

Massapequa Park. Village, Nassau co., SE New York, on Long Island; pop. (1990c) 18,044.

Mas·sa·wa \mä-ˈsä-wä\ *or* **Mits·'i·wa** \mit-ˈsē-wä\ *also* **Mas·sa·ua** \mä-ˈsä-wä\. Seaport, Eritrea, on Massawa Channel, Red Sea; situated partly on an island; pop. (1989e) 16,579.

Massawa Channel *or* **Mits'iwa Channel.** Inlet of the Red Sea separating Dahlak Archipelago from mainland Eritrea.

Mas·se·na \mə-ˈsē-nə\. Village, St. Lawrence co., N New York, in town of Massena near St. Lawrence River; pop. (1990c) 11,719; nearby are two locks of the St. Lawrence Seaway and a hydroelectric power dam; museum.

Mas·sén·ya \mä-ˈsā-nyä\. Town, SW Chad, on a tributary of the Chari.

Mas·si·cault \ˌmȧ-sē-ˈkō\. Town, N Tunisia, ab. 12 mi. (19 km.) SW of Tunis on the road bet. Tunis and Majāz al-Bāb; taken from Germans by British May 1943 during WWII.

Mas·si·cus \ˈma-si-kəs\ *or Ital.* **Mas·si·co** \ˈmä-sē-ˌkō\. Mountain ridge, Caserta prov., Campania, Italy, NW of Capua near shore of Gulf of Gaeta.

Mas·sif Cen·tral \ma-ˈsēf-sä^{n}-ˈträl, sen-ˈ\. Plateau region, SE cen. France; 32,819 sq. mi. (85,001 sq. km.); highest point Puy de Sancy 6186 ft. (1885 m.) of the Monts Dore; centers in depts. of Cantal, Haute-Loire, and Aveyron; source of many streams, esp. Loire, Allier, Cher, and Creuse.

Massilia. See MARSEILLE.

Mas·sil·lon \ˈma-sə-lən, -ˌlän\. City, Stark co., NE Ohio, 8 mi. (13 km.) W of Canton; pop. (1990c) 31,007; Spring Hill, a house used by the Underground Railroad is open to the public; city founded 1826.

Mas·sive, Mount \ˈma-siv\. Mountain, Lake co., cen. Colorado, in Sawatch Range; 14,421 ft. (4396 m.); 2d highest mountain in Colorado.

Mas·sy \mȧ-ˈsē\. Commune, Essonne dept., N France, ab. 10 mi. (16 km.) SSE of Paris.

Mas·ter·ton \ˈmas-tər-tən\. Borough, S North I., New

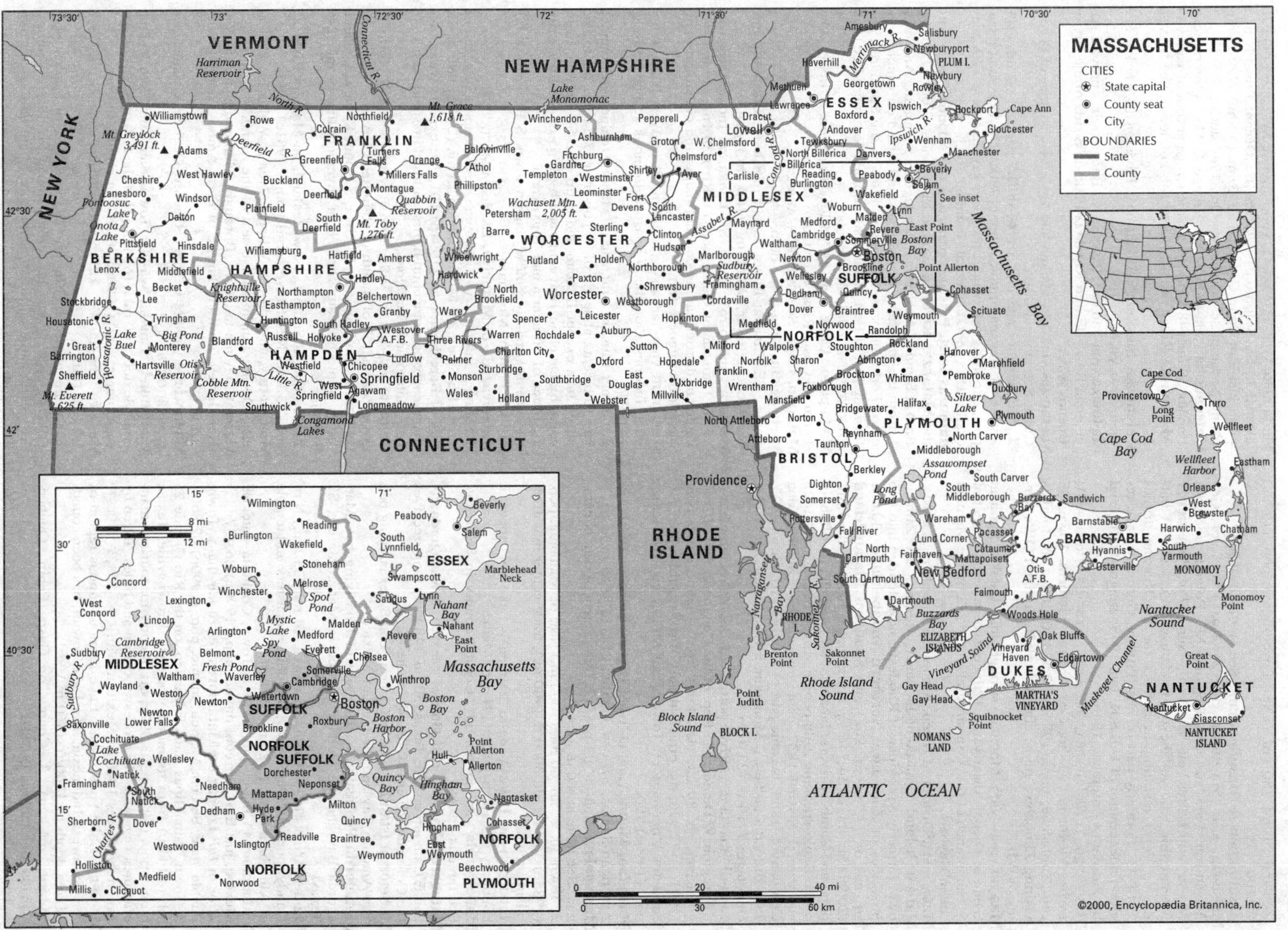
MASSACHUSETTS
CITIES
State capital
County seat
City
BOUNDARIES
State
County
VERMONT
NEW HAMPSHIRE
NEW YORK
CONNECTICUT
RHODE ISLAND
BERKSHIRE
FRANKLIN
HAMPSHIRE
HAMPDEN
WORCESTER
MIDDLESEX
ESSEX
SUFFOLK
NORFOLK
BRISTOL
PLYMOUTH
BARNSTABLE
DUKES
NANTUCKET
Boston
Springfield
Worcester
Lowell
New Bedford
Providence
Massachusetts Bay
Cape Cod Bay
Nantucket Sound
Rhode Island Sound
Block Island Sound
Buzzards Bay
ATLANTIC OCEAN
Quabbin Reservoir
Mt. Greylock 3,491 ft.
Mt. Grace 1,618 ft.
Mt. Toby 1,276 ft.
Wachusett Mtn. 2,005 ft.
Mt. Everett 2,625 ft.
Connecticut R.
MARTHA'S VINEYARD
NANTUCKET ISLAND
ELIZABETH ISLANDS
BLOCK I.
See inset
©2000, Encyclopædia Britannica, Inc.

Zealand, 50 mi. (80 km.) ENE of Wellington; pop. (1992e) 20,100.

Masulipatam *or* **Masulipatnam.** See MACHILIPATNAM.

Ma·su·ria *also* **Ma·zu·ria** \mə-'zu̇r-ē-ə, -'su̇r-\ *or Ger.* **Ma·su·ren** \mə-'zu̇r-ən\. Region, NE Poland; includes **Ma·su·ri·an Lakes** \mə-'zu̇r-ē-ən-, -'su̇r-\ (*Pol.* **Po·je·zier·ze Ma·zur·skie** \ˌpō-ye-'zhe-zhe-mä-'zür-skʸe\), scene of battles in WWI resulting in defeats for the Russian armies 1914–15. Formerly part of East Prussia, Germany; lake region under control of U.S.S.R. Jan. 1945; assigned to Poland by Potsdam Conference 1945.

Mas·vin·go \mäs-'viŋ-gō\; *formerly* **Nyan·da** \'nyän-dä\; *earlier* **Vic·tor·ia** \vik-'tōr-ē-ə\ *or* **Fort Victoria.** Town, SE cen. Zimbabwe; pop. (1982c) 30,523; facilities for tourists visiting Zimbabwe ruins; church built by Italian POWs during WWII.

Maş·yāf \mäs-'yäf\. Mountain stronghold, E Latakia, Syria, at S end of Djebel Ansariya; in 12th cent. became chief seat of Syrian branch of the Assassins; taken c. 1272 by the Mamlūk sultan Baybars.

Mat \'mät\. District of N cen. Albania. See table at ALBANIA.

Mat·a·be·le·land \ˌmä-tä-'bā-lā-ˌland\. Region, SW Zimbabwe; formerly a province of Rhodesia, now divided into two provinces of Zimbabwe: **Northern Matabeleland** (30,032 sq. mi. or 77,783 sq. km.) and **Southern Matabeleland** (20,983 sq. mi. or 54,346 sq. km.); region lies bet. the Limpopo and Zambezi rivers. Inhabited by Ndebele, an offshoot of the Bantu-speaking Zulu people, driven out of Natal 1823 and from Transvaal 1837; came under British South Africa Company c. 1889; became part of Southern Rhodesia 1923.

Mata Bia \ˌmä-tä-'bē-ä\. Mountain, E East Timor, Malay Archipelago; 7710 ft. (2350 m.).

Ma·ta·di \mä-'tä-dē\. River port, ✱ of Bas-Zaïre administrative region, W Democratic Rep. of the Congo, on Zaire (Congo) River, ab. 80 mi. (130 km.) from Atlantic coast; pop. (1991e) 172,926; the principal port of the republic.

Mat·a·dor \'ma-tə-ˌdōr\. Town, ⊗ of Motley co., NW Texas; pop. (1990c) 790.

Ma·ta·fao, Mount \ˌmä-tä-'fau̇\. Highest point on Tutuila I., American Samoa, SW cen. Pacific; 2141 ft. (653 m.).

Mat·a·gal·pa \ˌmä-tä-'gäl-pä\. **1.** Department of cen. Nicaragua. See table at NICARAGUA.
2. Town, its ✱, ab. 60 mi. (100 km.) NNE of Managua; pop. (1985e) 36,983; alt. 3000 ft. (900 m.); trade center in coffee-raising region.

Mat·a·gam·on Lake \ˌma-tə-'ga-mən\. Lake on upper E boundary of Piscataquis co., N cen. Maine.

Mat·a·gor·da \ˌma-tə-'gȯr-də\. Coastal county in SE Texas. See table at TEXAS.

Matagorda Bay. Inlet of Gulf of Mexico, S Matagorda co. and E Calhoun co., SE Texas; 30 mi. (48 km.) long; receives the Colorado River (of Texas) on the NE.

Matagorda Island. Island in Calhoun co., S Texas, lying bet. San Antonio Bay and the Gulf of Mexico.

Matagorda Peninsula. Narrow spit of land lying bet. Matagorda Bay and the Gulf of Mexico in Matagorda co., SE Texas.

Ma·ta·le \'mət-ᵊl-ˌä\. Town, Sri Lanka, 14 mi. (23 km.) N of Kandy; pop. (1990e) 31,000; Buddhist monastery and temple of Aluvihara 2 mi. (3.2 km.) distant.

Mat·a·mo·ros \ˌmä-tä-'mō-rōs\. **1.** Town, Coahuila state, NE Mexico, just E of Torreón; munic. pop. (1990p) 86,437.
2. *or in full* **Izú·car de Matamoros** \ē-'zü-kär-t͟hā-\. Town, Puebla state, SE cen. Mexico; munic. pop. (1990p) 62,860.
3. Town, Tamaulipas state, E Mexico, on the Rio Grande 25 mi. (40 km.) from its mouth and opp. Brownsville, Texas; munic. pop. (1990p) 303,392; port of entry for tourists; manufactures vegetable oil; processes cotton and hides. Taken by American forces 1846 in Mexican War.

Ma·ta·na, Lake \mä-'tä-nä\. Lake in mountainous region of cen. Sulawesi, Indonesia, near Lake Towuti; has been sounded to a depth of 1500 ft. (460 m.).

Ma·tane \mȧ-'tȧn\. **1.** County, on Gaspé Penin., Quebec, Canada. See table at QUEBEC.
2. Town, its ⊗, on St. Lawrence River; pop. (1991c) 12,756.

Ma·ta·ni·ko \mä-'tä-nē-ˌkō\. Short stream, NW coast of Guadalcanal I., SE Solomon Is., W Pacific Ocean; flows N to a point just E of Point Cruz and ab. 3 mi. (5 km.) W of Lunga Point. Scene of several battles Oct. 1942 during WWII.

Mat·a·nus·ka \ˌma-tə-'nüs-kə\. Village, S Alaska, on railroad line ab. 30 mi. (48 km.) NE of Anchorage at foot of valley of **Matanuska River** (ab. 90 mi. or 145 km. long). See PALMER 1.

Matanuska–Su·sit·na \-sü-'sit-nə\. Division in Alaska. See table at ALASKA.

Ma·tan·za \mä-'tan-sä\. River in NE Buenos Aires prov., E Argentina; flows NE into Río de la Plata on S side of the city of Buenos Aires.

Ma·tan·zas \mä-'tän-säs, mə-'tan-zəs\. **1.** Province of W cen. Cuba. See table at CUBA.
2. Municipality and city, its ✱, in NW part ab. 60 mi. (100 km.) E of Havana; munic. pop. (1990e) 113,724; major seaport, exporting esp. sugar; produces rayon, shoes; 17th cent. castle; 18th cent. cathedral; founded 1693.

Matanzas Inlet. Passage connecting the Atlantic Ocean with the **Matanzas River** (a lagoon, NE Florida, S of St. Augustine) at S end of Anastasia I.; the lagoon, separating Anastasia I. from the mainland, contains a small island on which is located Fort Matanzas, completed 1742 by the Spaniards, and forming part of Fort Matanzas National Monument (see UNITED STATES, *National Monuments*).

Ma·ta·pa·lo, Cape \ˌmä-tä-'pä-lō\. Cape on S tip of Osa Penin., S Costa Rica, W of Golfo Dulce.

Matapan, Cape. See TAÍNARON, ÁKRA.

Ma·ta·pé·dia \ˌma-tə-'pē-dē-ə, -'pā-\. River in W Gaspé Penin., SE Canada; flows SE out of **Lake Matapédia** into Restigouche River; ab. 60 mi. (100 km.) long.

Ma·ta·ra \'mä-tə-rə\. Town, Sri Lanka, on Indian Ocean 24 mi. (39 km.) E of Galle; pop. (1981p) 39,162; commercial center in district having coconut palms and cinnamon trees; has old Portuguese fort.

Ma·ta·ram \mə-'tär-əm\. **1.** Town, ✱ of West Nusa Tenggara, Indonesia, on the W coast of Lombok I.; pop. (1980c) 141,387.
2. Former Muslim sultanate in Malay Archipelago, founded late 16th cent.; at height of its power in 17th cent., controlled all of Java except Bantam and E tip, and SE Borneo; overcome by Dutch in 18th cent., and by 1755 divided bet. principalities of Surakarta and Yogyakarta.

Ma·ta·ra·ni \ˌmä-tä-'rä-nē\. Seaport town, S Peru, ab. 8 mi. (13 km.) NW of Mollendo.

Matarīya, Al– *or* **Matarīya, El.** See AL-MATARĪYA.

Ma·ta·ró \ˌmä-tä-'rō\. Commune and seaport, Barcelona prov., NE Spain, on Mediterranean 15 mi. (24 km.) NE of the city of Barcelona; pop. (1991p) 101,501; exports wine; produces soap; baroque church; first railroad in Spain built 1848 bet. Mataró and Barcelona.

Ma·ta·ta \mä-'tä-tä\. Village on Bay of Plenty, N North I., New Zealand, W of mouth of Rangitaiki River.

Ma·tau·ra \mə-'tau̇-rə\. **1.** River, S South I., New Zealand; flows S into Foveaux Strait E of Invercargill; 149 mi. (240 km.) long.
2. Borough, S South I., New Zealand, on Mataura River 27 mi. (43 km.) NE of Invercargill; pop. (1981c) 2345.

Ma·ta·u·tu \ˌmä-tä-'ü-tü\. Village, Uvéa I., Wallis Is., SW Pacific Ocean; administrative seat of the island.

Mat·a·wan \'ma-tə-ˌwän\. Borough, Monmouth co., E cen. New Jersey, 7 mi. (11 km.) S of Perth Amboy; pop. (1990c) 9270.

Ma·ta·wi·nie \ˌmä-tä-wē-'nē\. County, Quebec, Canada. See table at QUEBEC.

Ma·te·hua·la \ˌmä-tā-'wä-lä\. Town, San Luis Potosí state, cen. Mexico, 100 mi. (161 km.) N of the city of San Luis Potosí; munic. pop. (1990p) 70,283; in mining region.

Ma·te·ra \mä-'tā-rä\. **1.** Province of Basilicata, S Italy. See table at ITALY.
2. Commune, its ✱, 126 mi. (203 km.) ESE of Naples; pop. (1991p) 53,775; has numerous stone, cavelike dwellings; 13th cent. cathedral; castle; museum of antiquities and prehistoric artifacts.

Ma·te·se Mountains \mä-'tā-ze\. Plateau region of the Neapolitan Apennines. See table at APENNINES.

Má·té·szal·ka \'mä-tā-,söl-kö\. Commune, Szabolcs-Szatmár-Berg co., NE Hungary, 43 mi. (69 km.) NE of Debrecen; pop. (1980p) 17,709.

Ma·teur \,mä-'tœr\. Town, N Tunisia, ab. 10 mi. (16 km.) SSW of Menzel Bourguiba. Occupied by Germans Dec. 1942; taken by Americans May 1943 in battle for Bizerte.

Ma·the·ran \,mä-tə-'rän\. Hill station, cen. Maharashtra, W India, 30 mi. (48 km.) E of Bombay.

Math·ews \'ma-,thyüz\. **1.** County in E Virginia. See table at VIRGINIA.

2. Village, its ⊗.

Math·ew Town \'ma-,thyü\. Town on SW coast of Great Inagua I., Bahamas.

Ma·thi·as Point \mə-'thī-əs\. Point at NE tip of King George co., E Virginia, extending into Potomac River.

Math·is \'ma-thəs\. City, San Patricio co., S Texas, 33 mi. (53 km.) NW of Corpus Christi; pop. (1990c) 5423.

Ma·thu·ra \'mə-tə-rə\ *or* **Mut·tra** \'mə-trə\. City, W Uttar Pradesh, N India, on the right bank of the Yamuna River 30 mi. (48 km.) NW of Agra; pop. (1991p) 226,850; ancient city, one of the most important centers of Indian art (the Mathura school, sculptures in red sandstone, c. 2d cent. B.C. to 6th cent. A.D.), and revered by Hindus as birthplace of Krishna; in early Christian era a center of Buddhism and Jainism; has a mosque built by Mogul Emperor Aurangzeb (ʻĀlamgīr) and a museum of antiquities. Plundered by Muslim Sultan Maḥmūd of Ghaznī c. 1018 and sacked several times from early 16th cent. to mid-18th cent.; under British sovereignty 1803.

Ma·ti \'mä-tē\. Municipality, ✻ of Davao Oriental prov., Mindanao, Philippines; pop. (1980c) 78,178.

Matianus, Lake. See ORŪMĪYEH, DARYACHEH-YE.

Ma·tin·i·cus \mə-'ti-ni-kəs\. Island in Atlantic Ocean off S cen. coast of Maine.

Matisco Æduorum. See MÂCON.

Matlalcueyatl. See MALINCHE.

Mat·lock \'mat-,läk\. Town, ⊗ of Derbyshire, N cen. England, on the Derwent 19 mi. (31 km.) S of Sheffield; pop. (1981c) 13,867; tourist resort.

Mat·ma·ta \,mät-mä-'tä\. Town, SE Tunisia, ab. 27 mi. (43 km.) S of Gabès. Nearby **Matmata Hills** (highest 2000 ft. or 610 m.), noted for centuries for their cave dwellers; formed German defense in WWII until taken by Allies Mar. 1943.

Ma·to·bo National Park \mä-'tō-bō\; *formerly* **Ma·to·pos National Park** \-pōs\. National park, S Zimbabwe; 153 sq. mi. (396 sq. km.); Bushmen's cave paintings.

Ma·toch·kin Shar \'ma-təch-kin-'shär\. Channel bet. the two islands of Novaya Zemlya (*q.v.*), Russia; 3 mi. (5 km.) wide.

Ma·to Gros·so \'mä-tü-'grō-sü\; *formerly* **Mat·to Grosso. 1.** State, SW Brazil; ✻ Cuiabá; livestock raising; coffee, cotton, sugar. See table at BRAZIL.

2. Town on Guaporé River, Mato Grosso state, SW Brazil.

Mato Grosso, Pla·nal·to do \plȧ-'näl-tü-dü-\ *or* **Mato Grosso Plateau.** Highland in E cen. Mato Grosso state, SW Brazil; source of the Araguaia, Xingu, and Paraguay rivers, of headstreams of the Tapajós, and of many tributaries of the Alto Paraná.

Mato Grosso do Sul \dü-'sül\. State SW Brazil; ✻ Campo Grande; formed by division of Mato Grosso state 1979. See table at BRAZIL.

Ma·to·po Hills *or* **Ma·top·po Hills** \mä-'tō-pō\. Mountain group, S Zimbabwe, S of Bulawayo; tomb of colonial administrator Cecil Rhodes (see WORLD'S VIEW).

Matopos National Park. See MATOBO NATIONAL PARK.

Ma·to·zi·nhos \,mȧ-tü-'zē-nyüsh\. Parish, NW Portugal, NW of Pôrto on the coast; includes port of Leixões (*q.v.*).

Ma·ṭraḥ \'mä-trə\. Town, N Oman, on the Gulf of Oman; N suburb of Masqat and Oman's chief port; trade center for land routes into the interior.

Matrona. See MARNE.

Ma·truh \mə-'trü\. **1.** Governorate of NW Egypt. See table at EGYPT.

2. *or* **Mar·sa Matruh** *also* **Mer·sa Ma·trûh** \'mer-sə-mə-'trü\; *anc.* **Par·ae·to·ni·um** \,par-ē-'tō-nē-əm\. Town, its ✻, on coastal road, NW Egypt, E of Sīdī Barrānī, 150 mi. (241 km.) W of Alexandria; site of old Roman town; in WWII changed hands several times.

Ma·tsu *also* **Ma–tsu** \'mät-'sü\ *or Pinyin* **Ma·zu** \'mät-'sü\. Island, SE China, on coast ENE of Fuzhou; administered by Taiwan. See also QUEMOY.

Ma·tsu·ba·ra \,mät-sü-'bä-rä\. City, Ōsaka prefecture, Honshū, Japan, 12 mi. (19 km.) S of the city of Ōsaka; pop. (1990p) 135,921.

Mat·su·do \mät-'sü-dō\. City, Chiba prefecture, Japan, suburb of Tokyo; pop. (1990p) 456,211.

Ma·tsue *or* **Ma·tsu·ye** \mät-'sü-ā\. City, ✻ of Shimane prefecture, N coast of W Honshū, Japan; pop. (1990p) 142,931; tourist center.

Ma·tsu·mae \,mät-sü-'mī\; *formerly* **Fu·ku·ya·ma** \,fü-kü-'yä-mä\. Town at SW tip of Hokkaidō, Japan, on Tsugaru Strait; pop. (1990p) 13,546.

Ma·tsu·mo·to \,mät-sü-'mō-tō\. City, Nagano prefecture, cen. Honshū, Japan, 95 mi. (153 km.) NE of Nagoya; pop. (1990p) 200,723; chief commercial city of the prefecture; university (1949); prominent in feudal days.

Mat·su·sa·ka \,mät-sü-'sä-kä\ *or* **Ma·tsu·za·ka** \-'zä-kä\. Town, Mie prefecture, S Honshū, Japan, ab. 50 mi. (81 km.) SSW of Nagoya; pop. (1990p) 118,727.

Ma·tsu·shi·ma \,mät-sü-'shē-mä, mät-'sü-shi-mä\. Group of hundreds of small islands in **Matsushima Wan** \'wän\ (bay), Miyagi prefecture, N Honshū, Japan; composed of soft, porous, volcanic rock worn by waves into fantastic shapes.

Matsuwa. See MATUA.

Ma·tsu·ya·ma \,mät-sü-'yä-mä\. City, ✻ of Ehime prefecture, W Shikoku I., Japan, near Inland Sea; pop. (1990p) 443,317; cotton and synthetic textiles, chemicals, machinery; 17th cent. feudal castle.

Matsuye. See MATSUE.

Matsuzaka. See MATSUSAKA.

Mat·ta·gami \mə-'ta-gə-mē\. River, E Ontario, Canada; rises in Mattagami Lake and other lakes in Cochrane dist., flows N to join the Missinaibi and form the Moose River; 275 mi. (443 km.) long.

Mattagami Lake. 1. Lake in Cochrane dist., Ontario, Canada; a source of the Mattagami River.

2. Lake, Abitibi co., SW Quebec, Canada; with outlet N through Nottaway River into James Bay; ab. 91 sq. mi. (235 sq. km.).

Mat·ta·mus·keet Lake \,ma-tə-mə-'skēt\. Lake in SE Hyde co., E North Carolina.

Mat·tan·che·ri \mə-'tän-chə-rē\. Town, cen. Kerala state, S India, on Malabar Coast just S of Calicut; commercial center; 16th cent. palace; ancient Jewish community with magnificent 16th cent. synagogue.

Mat·ta·poi·sett \,ma-tə-'pȯi-sət\. Town, Plymouth co., SE Massachusetts, on Buzzards Bay 6 mi. (10 km.) E of New Bedford; pop. (1990c) 5850; summer resort.

Mat·ta·po·ni \,ma-tə-pə-'nī\. River, E Virginia; rises in Spotsylvania co., flows SE to unite with Pamunkey River at West Point and form York River; ab. 125 mi. (200 km.) long.

Mat·ta·wa \'ma-tə-,wä, -,wȯ\. **1.** River, SE Ontario, Canada; flows E out of Trout Lake into the Ottawa River; ab. 45 mi. (72 km.) long.

2. Town, Nipissing dist., SE Ontario, Canada, at confluence of Mattawa and Ottawa rivers 38 mi. (61 km.) E of North Bay; pop. (1991c) 2454; formerly a fur-trading post of the Hudson's Bay Company.

Mat·ta·wam·keag \,ma-tə-'wäm-,keg\. River, E Maine; formed by confluence of forks in S Aroostook co., flows SW into Penobscot River in E cen. Penobscot co.; ab. 50 mi. (80 km.) long.

Mat·ta·win \ˈma-tə-wən\. River, S Quebec, Canada; flows E into the St.-Maurice River; 100 mi. (161 km.) long.

Mat·tea·wan \ˈma-tə-ˌwän\. Former village, Dutchess co., SE New York; part of Beacon since 1913.

Mat·ter·horn \ˈma-tər-ˌhȯrn, ˈmä-\ *or Fr.* **Mont Cer·vin** \ˌmōⁿ-ser-ˈveⁿ\ *or Ital.* **Mon·te Cer·vi·no** \ˈmȯn-tā-cher-ˈvē-nō\. Peak in the Pennine Alps on the Switzerland-Italy border; 14,691 ft. (4478 m.); first scaled 1865.

Matterhorn Peak \ˈma-tər-ˌhȯrn\. Mountain, Hinsdale co., SW Colorado; ab. 14,015 ft. (4270 m.).

Mat·te·son \ˈmat-sən\. Village, Cook co., NE Illinois, S of Chicago; pop. (1990c) 11,378.

Mat·thews \ˈma-ˌthyüz\. Town, Mecklenburg co., S North Carolina, SSE of Charlotte; pop. (1990c) 13,651.

Matto Grosso. See MATO GROSSO.

Mat·toon \mə-ˈtün, ma-\. City, Coles co., E cen. Illinois, 40 mi. (64 km.) SE of Decatur; pop. (1990c) 18,441; Lake Land Coll. (1966); founded early 1850s at railroad junction.

Ma·tua \ˈmät-wä\ *or Jp.* **Ma·tsu·wa** \ˈmät-sü-ˌwä\. One of the Kuril Is., Russia, in cen. part of chain N of Rasshua; formerly under Japanese control.

Matupi, Mount. See TAVURVUR, MOUNT.

Ma·tu·rín \ˌmä-tü-ˈrēn\. Town, ✻ of Monagas state, NE Venezuela; pop. (1990p) 207,382.

Ma·tu·tum, Mount \mä-ˈtü-tüm\. Mountain, S Mindanao, Philippines; 7521 ft. (2292 m.).

Mauá \mau̇-ˈä\. Municipality, just SE of São Paulo, SE Brazil; pop. (1990e) 312,486.

Ma·u·ban \ˌmä-ü-ˈbän\. Municipality, S Quezon prov., Luzon, Philippines, near E coast of Lamon Bay 19 mi. (31 km.) NNE of Lucena; pop. (1980c) 37,814; important in coastal trade.

Mau·beuge \mō-ˈbœzh\. City, Nord dept., N France, on Sambre River near Belgian border 49 mi. (79 km.) SE of Lille; pop. (1990c) 35,225; manufactures steel goods. Built around monastery founded in 7th cent.; fell to France 1678; held by Germans in WWI; suffered heavy damage in WWII. Birthplace of painter Jan Mabuse (né Gossaert) c. 1478.

Mauch·berg \ˈmau̇k-ˌberg\. Peak, NE Rep. of South Africa; 8725 ft. (2659 m.).

Mauch Chunk \mȯ-ˈchəŋk\. Former borough, E Pennsylvania. See JIM THORPE.

Mauch·line \ˈmȯ-klin\. Town, Strathclyde region, SW Scotland, 8 mi. (13 km.) ESE of Kilmarnock; pop. (1981c) 3663; ab. 1 mi. (2 km.) N is **Moss·giel** \mȯs-ˈgēl\, the farm where poet Robert Burns lived with his brother 1784–88.

Mau·er \ˈmau̇-ər\. **1.** Village, Baden-Württemberg, Germany, SE of Heidelberg; Heidelberg jaw, the oldest human fragment ever found in Germany, found here 1907.

2. Lake, Poland. See MAMRY.

Maug \ˈmau̇g\. Small island, Northern Mariana Is., 140 mi. (225 km.) N of Pagan, 20°01′N, 145°13′E.

Mau·ga Si·li·si·li \ˈmau̇-gä-ˈsē-le-ˌsē-lē\ *or* **Mount Silisili.** Peak, center of Savai'i I., Samoa; 6095 ft. (1856 m.).

Maui \ˈmau̇-ē\. **1.** Island of S cen. state of Hawaii; 728 sq. mi. (1886 sq. km.); a part of the county of Maui; 2d largest island of the Hawaiian group; its E and W ends are high mountains with flat isthmus in center connecting them. In E is Haleakala National Park incl. Red Hill 10,023 ft. (3055 m.) and in W Puu Kukui 5787 ft. (1764 m.) and Eke Crater 4480 ft. (1366 m.). Maalaea Bay is large inlet on S coast and Lahaina Roadstead in Auau Channel on NW is anchorage. Chief settlements: Kahului, Kihei, Wailuku; tourism; ranching; sugar, pineapples.

2. County, Hawaii. See table at HAWAII.

Ma·u·ke \ˌmau̇-ˈkā\ *also* **Par·ry Island** \ˈpar-ē\. One of the Cook Is. in S Pacific Ocean, 150 mi. (241 km.) NE of Rarotonga; 7 sq. mi. (18 sq. km.); pop. (1986c) 692.

Maul·din \ˈmȯl-dən\. City, Greenville co., NW South Carolina, 7 mi. (11 km.) SE of Greenville; pop. (1990c) 11,587.

Mau·le \ˈmau̇-lā\. **1.** River, Maule region, S cen. Chile; flows into Pacific Ocean near the town of Constitución, S of Valparaíso; ab. 140 mi. (225 km.) long.

2. Former province of S cen. Chile.

3. Region of S cen. Chile. See table at CHILE.

Maul·lín \mau̇-ˈyēn\. River, Los Lagos region, S cen. Chile; flows out of Llanquihue Lake into the Pacific Ocean; waterfalls.

Maulmain. See MOULMEIN.

Mau·mee \mȯ-ˈmē, ˈmȯ-mē\. **1.** River, Indiana and Ohio; formed by confluence of St. Joseph and St. Marys rivers at Fort Wayne, Allen co., NE Indiana, flows E and NE into Lake Erie at Toledo, NW Ohio; ab. 175 mi. (280 km.) long. Navigable for 12 mi. (19 km.) from mouth.

2. Residential city, Lucas co., NW Ohio, 8 mi. (13 km.) SW of Toledo; pop. (1990c) 15,561; settled 1817 on site of Fort Miami (1764), where Gen. Anthony Wayne defeated a confederacy of Indian tribes 1794 at battle of Fallen Timbers.

Maumee Bay. Inlet of Lake Erie in NE Lucas co., NW Ohio, N of Toledo.

Mau·melle \ˈmau̇-ˌmel\. City, Pulaski co., cen. Arkansas, NNW of Little Rock; pop. (1990c) 6714.

Ma·un \mä-ˈün\. Town, N Botswana, NE of Lake Ngami; pop. (1991c) 26,768.

Mau·na·bo \mau̇-ˈnä-bō\. Municipality, SE Puerto Rico, on coast 14 mi. (23 km.) E of Guayama; pop. (1990c) 12,347.

Mau·na Kea \ˌmau̇-nä-ˈkā-ä\. Extinct volcano, N cen. Hawaii I., Hawaii; 13,796 ft. (4205 m.); highest peak in the state and from base to peak, highest island mountain in the world; site of astronomical observatory and several large telescopes.

Mauna Loa \ˈlō-ä\. **1.** Mountain, W Molokai I., Hawaii; 1382 ft. (421 m.).

2. Volcano, on S cen. Hawaii I., Hawaii, in Hawaii National Park; ab. 13,680 ft. (4170 m.); largest mountain in the world in cubic content; has erupted on average once every three to four years since 1830s; eruptions of summit crater, Mokuaweoweo, usually confined there; eruptions from side fissures and vents include significant 20th cent. lava flows of 1919, 1950, and 1984. See KILAUEA and MOKUAWEOWEO.

Mau·na·lua Bay \ˌmau̇-nä-ˈlü-ä\. Bay on SE coast of Oahu I., Hawaii, W of Koko Head.

Maunath Bhan·jan \ˈmau̇-nät-ˈbən-jən\. Town, E Uttar Pradesh, N India, on tributary of Ganges River 55 mi. (89 km.) NE of Varanasi.

Maung·daw \ˈmau̇ŋ-ˈdȯ\. Town, W Myanmar, on coast near Indian border 60 mi. (97 km.) NW of Sittwe.

Mau·per·tuis \ˌmō-per-ˈtwē\. Battlefield 7 mi. (11 km.) SE of Poitiers, France; where Edward, Prince of Wales (the Black Prince) defeated the French 1356. See POITOU.

Mau·pi·ti \mau̇-ˈpē-tē\. One of the Leeward Is., Society Is., S Pacific Ocean, ab. 30 mi. (48 km.) W of Bora Bora; 5 sq. mi. (13 sq. km.); ab. 6 mi. (10 km.) in circumference enclosing wide lagoon.

Mau·re·pas, Lake \ˌmōr-ə-ˈpä\. Lake in SE Louisiana; connected on the E, through a river ab. 2 mi. (3 km.) long, with Lake Pontchartrain.

Maures, Monts des \ˌmōⁿ-dā-ˈmōr\. Mountain massif, Var dept., SE France, on the Mediterranean coast at W end of the Riviera; highest point 2558 ft. (780 m.).

Mau·re·ta·nia *or* **Mau·ri·ta·nia** \ˌmȯr-ə-ˈtā-nē-ə, ˌmär-, -nyə\. Ancient country in N Africa, W of Numidia; included modern Morocco and part of Algeria.

History: Ancient region of North Africa, part of Carthaginian empire; Mauretanian kingdom received W part of Numidia (*q.v.*) after fall of Numidian King Jugurtha 106 B.C.; c. 25 B.C. Roman provs. of **Mauretania Cae·sar·i·en·sis** \si-ˌzar-ē-ˈen-səs\ (in the E) and **Mauretania Tin·gi·ta·na** \ˌtin-jə-ˈtā-nə, -ˈta-\ (in the W) were erected; became independent of Rome in 5th cent. A.D. only to be overrun by Vandals and later by Muslim Arabs; for later history, see BARBARY and MOROCCO.

Mau·rice \ˈmȯr-əs, ˈmär-\. River, SW New Jersey; flows S into **Maurice River Cove** of Delaware Bay; ab. 40 mi. (65 km.) long; formerly one of the nation's chief oystering centers.

Mau·ri·ta·nia \ˌmȯr-ə-ˈtā-nē-ə, ˌmär-, -nyə\. **1.** *or Fr.* **Mau·ri·ta·nie** \mȯ-rē-tȧ-ˈnē\ *or officially* **Islamic Republic of Mauritania.** Republic, W Africa, bounded on NW by Western Sahara, on N by Western Sahara and Algeria, on E and S by

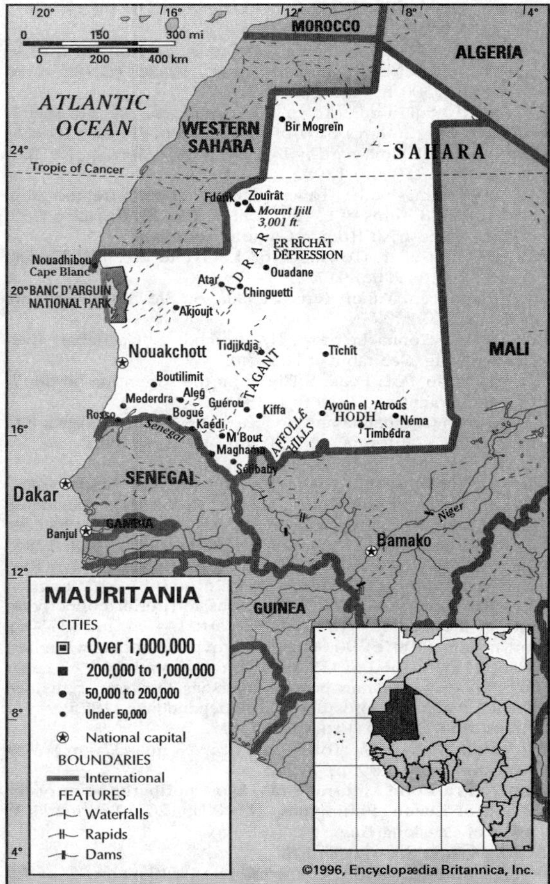

Mali, on SW by Senegal, and on W by the Atlantic Ocean; 397,955 sq. mi. (1,030,807 sq. km.); pop. (1993e) 2,171,000, with a large percentage being nomadic; ✻ Nouakchott.

Physical features: W extremity of Sahara covers most of territory; rich alluvial soils occur along Senegal River on SW boundary; mountainous plateaus in N and center have max. elev. of ab. 1500 ft. (460 m.).

Chief exports: Iron ore, copper, gum arabic; other products: millet, rice, dates; livestock raising, fish processing.

Chief town: Nouakchott.

History: Cradle of Berber Almorovid dynasty in 11th cent.; came under control of nomadic Arab tribes in 15th cent.; coast explored and opened by Portuguese in 15th cent.; coastal territory disputed by traders of different European nations; although recognized as in French sphere from 1817 Senegal treaty, it was not fully occupied until after 1900; made protectorate 1903 and part of French West Africa 1904, but conquered only gradually; made colony 1920; became French overseas territory 1946 and an autonomous republic of the French Community 1958; achieved independence 1960; became member of UN 1961; claims to Mauritanian territory withdrawn by Morocco 1969; held S Western Sahara 1975–79; suffered several coups since 1978; in late 1980s, hundreds of thousands of Mauritanians in Senegal and Senegalese in Mauritania returned to their home countries amid racial violence; adopted new constitution 1991 which allows for multiparty elections.

2. Ancient country, N Africa. See MAURETANIA.

Mau·ri·ti·us \mȯ-ˈri-shəs, -shē-əs\ *or officially* **Republic of Mauritius;** *formerly* **Île de France** \ˌēl-də-ˈfräⁿs\. Island of the Mascarene Is., in the Indian Ocean ab. 450 mi. (720 km.) E of Madagascar; 720 sq. mi. (1865 sq. km.); pop. (1993e) 1,103,000; with dependencies (island of Rodrigues and Agalega Is.) constitutes an independent state; ✻ Port Louis; mountainous, with fertile valleys and coastal plains; highest point Piton de la Rivière Noire in SW 2711 ft. (826 m.); chief industry is growing sugarcane; other products are tobacco, clothing, vegetables, molasses, tea; tourism.

History: Discovered by Portuguese early 16th cent.; occupied by Dutch 1598–1710; held by French 1715–1810; captured by British 1810 to protect shipping during wars with France; formally ceded to British 1814; became independent 1968; became republic 1992.

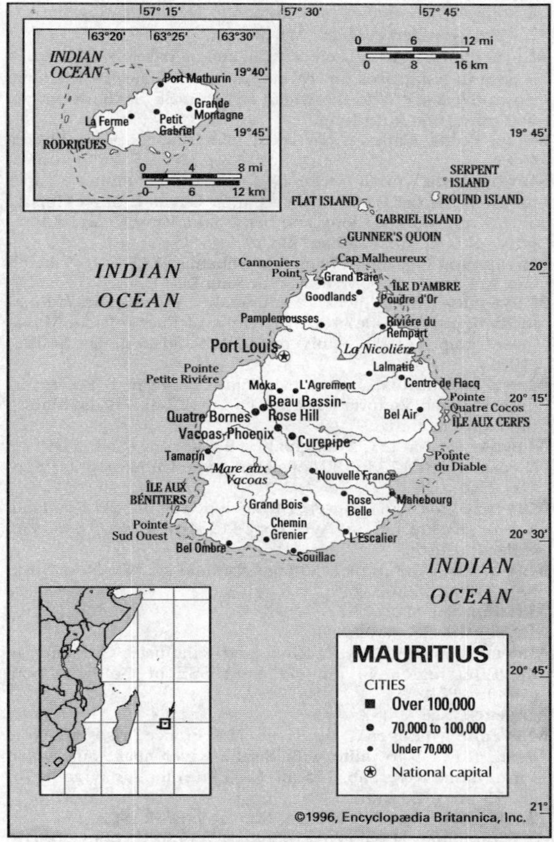

Mau·ry \ˈmȯr-ē\. County in W cen. Tennessee. See table at TENNESSEE.

Maus·ton \ˈmȯs-tən\. City, ⊗ of Juneau co., cen. Wisconsin, 35 mi. (56 km.) WNW of Portage; pop. (1990c) 3439.

Maut·hau·sen \ˈmau̇t-ˌhau̇-zən\. Village, Upper Austria, Austria, on the Danube opp. the mouth of the Enns; site of Nazi concentration camp during WWII.

Mauvaises Terres. See BADLANDS.

Mav·er·ick \ˈma-və-rik\. County in SW Texas. See table at TEXAS.

Maverick, Mount. Peak in Brewster co., W Texas; 3495 ft. (1065 m.).

Ma·wen·zi \mä-ˈwen-zē\. Second highest peak of Kilimanjaro, Tanzania; 16,896 ft. (5150 m.).

\ə\ **abut** \ˈə\ matches \ᵊ\ kitten, Fr table \ər\ **further** \a\ **ash** \ā\ **ace** \ä\ **cot, cart** \à\ Fr bac \au̇\ **out** \b\ Span Avila \ch\ **chin** \e\ **bet** \ē\ **easy** \g\ **go** \i\ **hit** \ī\ **ice** \j\ **job** \k\ Ger **ich, Buch** \ⁿ\ Fr vin \ŋ\ **sing** \ō\ **go** \ȯ\ **all** \ȯ\ **law** \œ\ Fr bœuf \œ̄\ Fr feu \ȯi\ **boy** \th\ **thin** \t͟h\ **this** \ü\ **loot** \u̇\ **foot** \ue\ Ger füllen \ue̅\ Fr rue \y\ **yet** \ʸ\ Fr digne \ˈdēnʸ\, nuit \ˈnwʸē\ \yü\ **few** \yu̇\ **fury** \zh\ **vision**

Maw·jib, Wa·di al– \ˈwä-dē-ȧl-ˈmau̇-jib\ *also* **Wadi al–Mo·jib** \-ˈmō-jib\; *anc.* **Ar·non** \ˈär-ˌnän\. River, W Jordan, flowing W into Dead Sea; in ancient times boundary (*Num.* xxi. 13–14) bet. Moab on S and country of Amorites on N; later, boundary bet. Moab and Palestine.

Maw·laik \ˈmȯ-ˌlīk\. Town, Sagaing division, Myanmar, on the Chindwin NE of Tiddim and 165 mi. (266 km.) NW of Mandalay.

Mawṣil, Al–. See MOSUL.

Má·xi·mo Gó·mez \ˈmäk-sē-mō-ˈgō-mās\. Town, Matanzas prov., W cen. Cuba, on railroad line 15 mi. (24 km.) SE of Cárdenas.

May, Cape \ˈmā\. **1.** Cape, S tip of Cape May co., at extreme S point of New Jersey, at entrance to Delaware Bay.
2. City, New Jersey. See CAPE MAY 3.

Ma·ya \ˈmī-ə\. River, chiefly in cen. Khabarovsk Kray, E Russia in Asia; rises on NW slopes of the Stanovoi Mts. and flows SW and NW to the Aldan River in SE Sakha Rep.; ab. 660 mi. (1060 km.) long.

Maya, Point. Cape on NW coast of Matanzas prov., W cen. Cuba.

May·a·gua·na \ˌmā-ä-ˈgwä-nä\; *formerly* **Mar·i·gua·na** \ˌmä-rē-\. One of the Bahamas in Atlantic Ocean E of Acklins I.; ab. 25 mi. (40 km.) long and bet. 3 and 5 mi. (5 and 8 km.) wide; 110 sq. mi. (285 sq. km.).

Mayaguana Passage. Channel in Bahamas, ESE of Crooked I. and Acklins I. and NW of Mayaguana I.

Ma·ya·güez \ˌmī-ä-ˈgwās\. Municipality and seaport, W Puerto Rico; pop. (1990c) 100,371; Univ. of Puerto Rico, Mayagüez Campus (1911), Universidad Adventista de las Antillas (1961).

Ma·ya Mountains \ˈmī-ä\. Mountain range in S Belize; its highest point, Victoria Peak 3681 ft. (1122 m.), is the highest mountain in Belize.

Ma·ya·rí \ˌmī-ä-ˈrē\. Municipality, E Cuba, near Nipe Bay on N coast 45 mi. (72 km.) N of Santiago de Cuba; pop. (1981p) 109,920.

May·bole \mā-ˈbōl\. Burgh, Strathclyde region, SW Scotland, 8 mi. (13 km.) S of Ayr; pop. (1981p) 4769; 18th cent. Culzean Castle.

May·brook \ˈmā-ˌbru̇k\. Village, Orange co., SE New York; pop. (1990c) 2802.

Maydān. See MAIDAN 2.

Mayebashi. See MAEBASHI.

May·en \ˈmī-ən\. City, N Rhineland-Palatinate, Germany, in the Eifel region 44 mi. (71 km.) SSE of Cologne; pop. (1980c) 21,033.

Mayence. See MAINZ.

Ma·yenne \mä-ˈyen\. **1.** River, NW France; rises in Orne dept., flows S to unite with Sarthe River near Angers and form Maine River; ab. 125 mi. (200 km.) long; navigable for ab. 75 mi. (120 km.).
2. Department of NW France. See table at FRANCE.
3. Commune, N Mayenne dept., NW France; pop. (1991e) 278,965; market town in agricultural region; cider making; center of conflict in 11th cent. campaigns of William the Conqueror, duke of Normandy and king of England, in 16th cent. Wars of Religion (it belonged to Guise family), and in 18th cent. Wars of the Vendée.

Mayes \ˈmāz\. County in NE Oklahoma. See table at OKLAHOMA.

May·fair \ˈmā-ˌfar\. A fashionable district in West End, London, England, in Westminster borough E of Hyde Park—so called from an annual fair formerly held there in May.

May·field \ˈmā-ˌfēld\. **1.** City, ⊗ of Graves co., SW Kentucky, 22 mi. (35 km.) S of Paducah; pop. (1990c) 9935.
2. Village, Cuyahoga co., N Ohio, ENE of Cleveland; pop. (1990c) 3462.

Mayfield Heights. City, Cuyahoga co., N Ohio, 13 mi. (21 km.) ENE of Cleveland; pop. (1990c) 19,847; residential suburb.

May·kop *also* **Mai·kop** \mī-ˈkȯp\. City, Adygea Rep., S Russia in Europe, 65 mi. (104 km.) SE of Krasnodar; pop. (1993e) 163,000; mineral springs and oil fields nearby. Founded 1857 as Russian fortress; occupied by the Germans during WWII 1942–43.

May·myo \ˈmā-ˌmyō\. Town, Myanmar, on railroad line 30 mi. (48 km.) ENE of Mandalay; pop. (1983c) 63,782; at an alt. of ab. 3500 ft. (1100 m.).

May·nard \ˈmā-nərd\. Town, Middlesex co., NE Massachusetts, 16 mi. (26 km.) SSW of Lowell; pop. (1990c) 10,325.

May·nard·ville \ˈmā-nərd-ˌvil\. City, ⊗ of Union co., NE Tennessee; pop. (1990c) 1298.

May·nooth \mā-ˈnüth\. Town, NE co. Kildare, E Ireland; pop. (1981c) 3388; ruins of c. 12th cent. castle; St. Patrick's Coll. (1795), noted Irish Roman Catholic seminary.

Mayo \ˈmā-ō\. **1.** Town, ⊗ of Lafayette co., NW Florida Penin.; pop. (1990c) 917.
2. Village, cen. Yukon Terr., Canada, on Stewart River; pop. (1991c) 243.
3. County, Connacht prov., NW Ireland; ⊗ Castlebar; livestock raising. See table at IRELAND.

Ma·yo \ˈmī-ō\. **1.** Peak, S Chile, on the Argentina border W of Lake Argentino; 7810 ft. (2381 m.).
2. River in Chihuahua and Sonora states, Mexico; flows into the Gulf of California; ab. 250 mi. (400 km.) long.

Mayo. See MAIO.

Ma·yon Volcano \mä-ˈyōn\ *or* **Mount Mayon.** Active volcano, SE Luzon, Philippines; 8077 ft. (2462 m.); considered one of the most perfect volcanic cones in the world; had destructive eruption 1814; recent eruptions 1947, 1968, 1984.

Ma·yor, Is·la \ˈēs-lä-mä-ˈyȯr\. Island, W of Guadalquivir River in a swamp S of Seville, Spain; 25 mi. (40 km.) long.

Ma·yotte \mä-ˈyȯt\. French overseas territorial collectivity; one of the Comoros (*q.v.*) in SE part; 144 sq. mi. (373 sq. km.); pop. (1991e) 90,000; chief town Mamoutzu; highest point 2165 ft. (660 m.). French colony from mid-19th cent.; in 20th cent. became part of overseas territory; remained French when Comoros declared independence (1975).

Mayoumba. See MAYUMBA.

May Pen \ˈmā-ˌpen\. Town, Jamaica, 23 mi. (37 km.) W of Kingston; pop. (1991p) 46,785.

May·ra·i·ra Point \ˌmī-rä-ˈē-rä\. Most northerly point of the island of Luzon, Philippines, 18°40′N, 120°50′E; marks W point of Pasaleng Bay.

Maysí, Cape. See MAISÍ, CAPE.

Mays Landing \ˈmāz\. Unincorporated settlement, ⊗ of Atlantic co., SE New Jersey, on Great Egg River 17 mi. (27 km.) WNW of Atlantic City; pop. (1990c) 2090; resort; Atlantic Community Coll. (1964).

Mays·ville \ˈmāz-ˌvil\. **1.** City, ⊗ of Mason co., NE Kentucky, on Ohio River 53 mi. (85 km.) SE of Covington; pop. (1990c) 7169; Maysville Community Coll. (1967); estab. 1787 as **Limestone.**
2. City, ⊗ of De Kalb co., NW Missouri; pop. (1990c) 1176.

Ma·yu \mä-ˈyü\. River, Myanmar; flows S into Bay of Bengal just N of Sittwe; ab. 70 mi. (110 km.) long; the narrow tongue of land extending S bet. it and the Bay of Bengal forms **Mayu Point** where during WWII there was fighting 1943–44 in Japanese attack on India.

Ma·yum·ba; *formerly* **Ma·youm·ba** \mä-ˈyüm-bä\. Seaport, S Gabon, at tip of a peninsula.

Mayu Range. Coastal range of the Arakan Yoma system, Myanmar, W of Mayu River and extending along Mayu Point; during WWII scene of severe fighting 1944.

May·ville \ˈmā-ˌvil\. **1.** Village and resort, ⊗ of Chautauqua co., SW corner of New York; pop. (1990c) 1636.
2. City, Traill co., E North Dakota; pop. (1990c) 2092; Mayville State Coll. (1889).
3. City, Dodge co., SE cen. Wisconsin, 22 mi. (35 km.) S of Fond du Lac; pop. (1990c) 4374.

May·wood \ˈmā-ˌwu̇d\. **1.** City, Los Angeles co., SW California, 5 mi. (8 km.) SE of the city of Los Angeles; pop. (1990c) 27,850.
2. Residential village, Cook co., NE Illinois, ab. 4 mi. (6 km.) W of Chicago; pop. (1990c) 27,139; incorp. 1881.
3. Borough, Bergen co., NE corner of New Jersey, 6 mi. (10 km.) ESE of Paterson; pop. (1990c) 9473.

Mayyali. See MAHÉ 2.

Mazaca. See KAYSERİ 2.
Mazagan. See EL JADIDA.
Ma·za·ma, Mount \mə-ˈzä-mə\. Prehistoric volcanic mountain of Cascade Mts., W Klamath co., S Oregon; its caldera now occupied by Crater Lake (*q.v.*).
Ma·za·met \ˌmä-zä-ˈmā\. Commune, Tarn dept., S France, 35 mi. (56 km.) SSE of Albi.
Mā·zan·da·rān \ˌmäz-ˌän-də-ˈrän\. Province of N Iran. See table at IRAN.
Ma·za·ra del Val·lo \mät-ˈsä-rä-del-ˈväl-lō\. Seaport, Trapani prov., NW Sicily, Italy; pop. (1991p) 45,912; cathedral; Norman church.
Ma·zār–e Sha·rīf \mȧ-ˈzär-ē-shȧ-ˈrēf\. City, N Afghanistan, in Balkh historical region, 190 mi. (306 km.) NW of Kabul; pop. (1988e) 130,600; trade center; ships lambskins and carpets; chief town of Afghan Turkistan, just E of ancient Balkh; mosque venerated by Shiite Muslims as the tomb of ʻAlī, son-in-law of Muḥammad.
Ma·zar·rón \ˌmä-thär-ˈrȯn, -sär-\. Commune, Murcia prov., SE Spain, 3 mi. (5 km.) from Mediterranean and 27 mi. (43 km.) S of the commune of Murcia; pop. (1991c) 14,591.
Maz·a·ru·ni \ˌma-zə-ˈrü-nē\. River, Guyana; joins the Cuyuni River, then flows NE into the Essequibo River near its mouth; ab. 350 mi. (560 km.) long.
Ma·za·te·nan·go \ˌmä-zä-tā-ˈnäŋ-gō\. Town, ✻ of Suchitepéquez dept., SW Guatemala; pop. (1993e) 41,367; in area producing coffee and sugar.
Ma·za·tlán \ˌmä-sä-ˈtlän\. Seaport, Sinaloa state, W Mexico; munic. pop. (1990p) 314,249; largest Mexican seaport on the Pacific coast; exports tobacco; large shrimp fleet; resort.
Ma·za·tzal Peak \ˌmä-sät-ˈsäl, -zət-\. Mountain in **Mazatzal Mountains,** on boundary bet. Gila and Yavapai cos., cen. Arizona; ab. 7894 ft. (2406 m.).
Ma·zoe \mä-ˈzō-ā\. Town, NE cen. Zimbabwe, 20 mi. (32 km.) N of Harare; pop. (1982p) 63,895; in fertile valley.
Ma·zo·via \mə-ˈzō-vē-ə\. Ancient principality, Poland, E of the Vistula; long semi-independent; in 14th–16th cents. sent many colonists into Masuria; completely united to Poland by 1526; from 16th cent. its ✻ was Warsaw, succeeding Płock; to Prussia in 18th cent. partitions of Poland, then held by Russia until restored to Poland in 1918; became the prov. of Warsaw; after 1945 divided bet. Warsaw and Białystok provs.
Mazu. See MATSU.
Mazuria *and* **Mazurskie, Pojezierze.** See MASURIA.
Ma·zyr *or* **Mo·zyr** \mə-ˈzir\. Town, Homyel' prov., Belarus, on Pripyat' River 75 mi. (121 km.) SW of city of Homyel'; pop. (1991e) 103,000; in WWII held by Germans 1941–44.
Mba \əm-ˈbä\ *or* **Ba** \ˈbä\. River, NW Viti Levu I., Fiji, SW Pacific Ocean.
Mba·ba·ne \əm-bä-ˈbä-nā\. Town, ✻ of Swaziland, 93 mi. (150 km.) WSW of Maputo, Mozambique; pop. (1986c) 38,290.
Mba·la \əm-ˈbä-lä\; *formerly* **Ab·er·corn** \ˈa-bər-ˌkȯrn\. Town, NE Zambia, 15 mi. (24 km.) SE of S end of Lake Tanganyika; alt. 5700 ft. (1737 m.); scene of surrender of last of German African forces Nov. 14, 1918.
Mba·le \əm-ˈbä-lā\. Town, Uganda, ab. 120 mi. (190 km.) NE of Kampala; pop. (1991p) 53,634; trade center.
Mban·da·ka \əm-bän-ˈdä-kä\; *formerly* **Co·quil·hat·ville** \kō-kē-ˈat-ˌvil, kō-ˈkē-ə-vil\. Town and port, ✻ of Équateur administrative region, Democratic Rep. of the Congo, on the Congo River where it is joined by the Ruki; pop. (1991e) 165,623.
M'banza Congo \əm-ˈbän-zä-ˈkäŋ-gō\; *formerly* **São Salvador do Congo** \ˌsau̇ⁿ-ˌsȧl-vȧ-ˈdȯr-dü-ˈkȯŋ-gü\. Town, ✻ of Zaire prov., N Angola; ✻ in 16th–18th cents. of kingdom of Congo.
Mbau \əm-ˈbau̇\. Town, former native ✻ of Viti Levu, Fiji, on small island off E coast N of the Rewa Delta.
Mbe·ya \əm-ˈbā-ä\. **1.** Administrative region of SW Tanzania. See table at TANZANIA.
2. Town, its ✻.
Mbi·ni \əm-ˈbē-nē\ *or* **Río Mu·ni** \ˈrē-ō-ˈmü-nē\. Mainland portion of Equatorial Guinea (*q.v.*), bounded on N by Cameroon, on E and S by Gabon, and on W by the Atlantic Ocean; 10,040 sq. mi. (26,004 sq. km.); chief town Bata.
Mbomou *also* **M'Bomu.** See BOMU.
Mbu·ji–Ma·yi \əm-ˈbü-jē-ˈmī-ē\; *formerly* **Ba·kwan·ga** \bä-ˈkwäŋ-gä\. Town, ✻ of Kasai-Oriental administrative region, Democratic Rep. of the Congo; pop. (1991e) 613,027; diamond mining.
Mbu·lu·zi \əm-bü-ˈlü-zē\ *or* **Umbeluzi** \ˌu̇m-be-\. River, SE Africa, in Swaziland and S Mozambique; flows E into Delgoa Bay; ab. 120 mi. (195 km.) long.
Mbu·ro, Lake \əm-ˈbü-rō\. Lake, SW Uganda; largest of several lakes in Lake Mburo National Park (*q.v.*).
Mc–. Abbreviated form of MAC-. Names beginning with this prefix are all alphabetized as if spelled MAC-.
Mdaourouch. See MADAURA.
Mdi·na \mə-ˈdē-nä\ *or* **Cit·tà Vec·chia** \chēt-ˈtä-ˈvek-kyä\ *also* **No·ta·bi·le** \ˌnō-ˈtä-bē-lā\. Fortified city, cen. Malta, 6 mi. (10 km.) W of Valletta; ✻ of the island until mid-16th cent.; cathedral; catacombs; ancient ruins.
Mead, Lake \ˈmēd\. Reservoir in Colorado River in Mohave co., NW Arizona, and Clark co., SE Nevada, formed by Hoover Dam (see UNITED STATES, *Dams and Reservoirs*); area 227 sq. mi. (588 sq. km.), length 115 mi. (185 km.), depth over 500 ft. (150 m.) near the dam; has capacity of over 31,250,000 acre-feet (38.5 billion cubic meters) of water, used for flood control, irrigation, and power.
Meade \ˈmēd\. **1.** Name of counties in three states of the U.S. See tables at KANSAS, KENTUCKY, SOUTH DAKOTA.
2. City, ⊗ of Meade co., SW Kansas, 37 mi. (60 km.) SSW of Dodge City; pop. (1990c) 1526.
Meade Peak. Mountain, Bear Lake co., SE Idaho; ab. 10,540 ft. (3210 m.).
Mead·ow \ˈme-dō\. River, S cen. West Virginia; flows NW from Greenbrier co. and forms boundary bet. Nicholas and Fayette cos. until it joins the Gauley River; ab. 50 mi. (80 km.) long.
Meadow Lake. Town, Saskatchewan, Canada, 135 mi. (217 km.) NW of Prince Albert; pop. (1991c) 4318; summer resort.
Mea·dow·lands, the \ˈme-dō-ˌlandz\. Area in Bergen and Hudson cos., NE New Jersey, traversed by Hackensack River; extensive tidal marshes, now partially drained; site of sports complex incl. football stadium, basketball arena, and racetrack.
Mead·ows \ˈme-dōz\. City, Fort Bend co., SE Texas, adjoining Houston on the SW; pop. (1990c) 4606.
Mead·ville \ˈmēd-ˌvil\. **1.** Town, ⊗ of Franklin co., SW Mississippi; pop. (1990c) 453.
2. City, ⊗ of Crawford co., NW Pennsylvania, 33 mi. (53 km.) S of Erie; pop. (1990c) 14,318; early center of zipper manufacture; Allegheny Coll. (1815); settled 1788; abolitionist John Brown operated a tannery nearby 1825–35.
Mea·ford \ˈmē-fərd\. Town and lake port, Grey co., SE Ontario, Canada, on Nottawasaga Bay 20 mi. (32 km.) E of Owen Sound; pop. (1991c) 4520.
Mea·gher \ˈmär\. County in cen. Montana. See table at MONTANA.
Me·a·rim \ˌmē-ȧ-ˈrēⁿ\. River, Maranhão state, SE Brazil; flows N to São Marcos Bay; chief tributaries the Pindaré and the Grajaú.
Mearns, The. See KINCARDINE 2.
Meath \ˈmēth, *by non-residents also* ˈmēth\. County, Leinster prov., E Ireland; rivers Boyne, Blackwater; principal economic activity is livestock raising. Ancient kingdom more extensive than present county; made county 13th cent. but status and boundaries not definitely estab. until early 17th cent. See table at IRELAND.
Meaux \ˈmō\. Commune, Seine-et-Marne dept., N France, 32 mi. (52 km.) NNE of Melun; pop. (1990c) 49,409; food prod-

ucts; ships wheat and sugar beets; chief town of Brie; episcopal see since 4th cent.; medieval cathedral; episcopal palace; prominent in 16th cent. Wars of Religion.

Meb·ane \'me-bən\. City, Alamance and Orange cos., N cen. North Carolina, 24 mi. (39 km.) WNW of Durham; pop. (1990c) 4754.

Mec·a·ti·na, Cape *or* **Cape Mec·ca·ti·na** \ˌme-kə-'tē-nə\. Point, SE Quebec, Canada, on Strait of Belle Isle.

Mec·ca *also* **Mek·ka** \'me-kə\ *or Arab.* **Mak·kah** \'mȧ-kə\; *anc.* **Mac·o·ra·ba** \ˌma-kə-'rā-bə\. City, ✻ of Hejaz, W Saudi Arabia; in a valley surrounded by low hills ab. 50 mi. (80 km.) from the coast; pop. (1980e) 550,000; Institute for Higher Education (1962); a holy city and chief pilgrimage destination of Islam; birthplace of Muḥammad, founder of Islam, c. 570 A.D.; contains the Great Mosque with the Kaaba and sacred Black Stone; its Red Sea port is Jidda; has large bazaars.

History: A place of religious pilgrimage before Muḥammad whose home it was until 622, when he was forced to flee to Medina (see MEDINA 7); sacked by Karmathians early 10th cent.; came under Ottoman Turks 1517; seat of amīr of Mecca who, in 1908, was Ḥusayn ibn ʻAlī; under Ḥusayn, declared independence from Turkey 1916 and became ✻ of kingdom of Hejaz (*q.v.*); in 1924 occupied by Wahhabis under Ibn Saʻūd who later erected kingdom of Saudi Arabia (*q.v.*).

Me·chan·ic Falls \mi-'ka-nik\. Town, Androscoggin co., SW Maine, on a river feeding into the Androscoggin, 10 mi. (16 km.) W of Lewiston; pop. (1990c) 2919.

Me·chan·ics·burg \mi-'ka-niks-ˌbərg\. Borough, Cumberland co., S Pennsylvania, 9 mi. (15 km.) WSW of Harrisburg; pop. (1990c) 9452; settled c. 1790.

Me·chan·ics·ville \mi-'ka-niks-ˌvil\. Unincorporated settlement in Hanover co., Virginia, ab. 7 mi. (11 km.) NE of Richmond; pop. (1990c) 22,027; battle June 26, 1862 in which Confederates under Gen. A. P. Hill and Gen. James Longstreet were repulsed with severe loss by Union forces; also known as the battle of **Beaver Dam Creek.**

Me·chan·ic·ville \mi-'ka-nik-ˌvil\. City, Saratoga co., E New York, on Hudson River 17 mi. (27 km.) N of Albany; pop. (1990c) 5249.

Me·chant, Lake \mi-'shän\. Lake in S Terrebonne parish, SE Louisiana; connected through Caillou Lake with Gulf of Mexico.

Me·che·len \'mā-k̲ə-lən\ *or Fr.* **Ma·lines** \mȧ-'lēn\ *or Eng.* **Mech·lin** \'me-klin\. Commune, Antwerp prov., N Belgium; pop. (1992e) 75,700; large vegetable market; furniture; formerly noted lacemaking center; 13th–15th cent. cathedral; Renaissance palace; enjoyed great prosperity in 15th and early 16th cents.

Mechili, Al–. See AL-MECHILI.

Meck·len·burg \'me-klən-ˌbərg\. **1.** Name of counties in two states of the U.S. See tables at NORTH CAROLINA and VIRGINIA.

2. \'mā-klən-ˌbu̇rk\. Former German state, now part of E Germany; 6068 sq. mi. (15,716 sq. km.); ✻ Schwerin; included also cities of Rostock and Neustrelitz.

History: Orig. Germanic territory which was occupied c. 7th cent. by Slavic peoples who were gradually driven back by German colonization completed under Henry the Lion, duke of Saxony and Bavaria, in 12th cent.; ruled briefly in 13th cent. by Waldemar II of Denmark; became duchy 1348; because of participation (in first part of Thirty Years' War) on Danish side, lost lands to Austrian Gen. Albrecht von Wallenstein c. 1629; received bishoprics of Schwerin and Ratzeburg 1648; in 1701 divided into duchies of **Meck·len·burg–Schwe·rin** \'me-klən-ˌbu̇rk-shfā-'rēn\ and **Mecklen·burg–Stre·litz** \-'shtrā-lits\; both became grand duchies 1815 and joined German Confederation; joined German Empire 1871; became republics in 1918; lost sovereign rights under Nazi government, and reunited into a single state 1934; to East Germany after WWII; divided into the districts of Rostock, Schwerin, and Neubrandenburg from 1952 to 1990 when Germany was once again united. See GERMANY.

Meck·len·burg Bay \'me-klən-ˌbu̇rk\ *or Ger.* **Meck·len·bur·ger Bucht** \'me-klən-ˌbu̇r-gər-'bu̇k̲t\. Inlet of SW Baltic Sea, in N Germany; includes Lübeck Bay; formerly bounded on W by West Germany and on S and E by East Germany.

Mecklenburg–West Pom·er·a·nia \-ˌpä-mə-'rā-nē-ə, -nyə\ *or Ger.* **Mecklenburg–Vor·pom·mern** \-'fōr-ˌpȯ-mərn\. State of NE Germany. See table at GERMANY.

Me·cos·ta \mi-'käs-tə, -'kȯs-\. County in cen. Michigan. See table at MICHIGAN.

Me·dan \mā-'dän\. Commercial city, ✻ of North Sumatra prov., NE Sumatra, Indonesia; pop. (1990c) 1,730,752; largest city of Sumatra; on small Deli River ab. 15 mi. (24 km.) from its mouth and from the port of Belawan; center of a rich agricultural region, shipping esp. rubber and tobacco; Islamic Univ. of North Sumatra, Univ. of North Sumatra.

Me·da·no·sa, Point \ˌmā-t̲h̲ä-'nō-sä\. Cape on N cen. coast of Santa Cruz prov., S Argentina.

Med·dy·bemps Lake \'me-dē-ˌbemps\. Lake in E cen. Washington co., E Maine.

Mé·déa \ˌmā-dā-'ä\. Town, N Algeria, S of Algiers; pop. (1987p) 85,195. Birthplace of French writer Jean Richepin 1849.

Medeba. See MA'DABĀ.

Me·del·lin \ˌmā-t̲h̲ā-'yēn, ˌmā-dā-'lēn\. Municipality on extreme NW coast of Cebu I., Philippines, at N end of Tanon Strait opp. Bantayan I.; pop. (1980c) 38,504.

Me·del·lín \ˌmā-thā-'yēn, ˌmed-ᵊl-'ēn\. **1.** City, ✻ of Antioquia dept., NW Colombia, NW of Bogotá; pop. (1992e) 1,581,400; 2d largest city in Colombia; coffee market; glassware, ceramics, foodstuffs, textiles, steel; educational center, with two universities and various colleges; founded 1675.

2. \ˌmā-t̲h̲äl-'yēn\. Village, Badajoz prov., Spain, on the Guadiana River; pop. (1991c) 2451; in ancient Extremadura; birthplace of Spanish conqueror of Mexico, Hernán Cortés 1485; ruined castle.

Med·field \'med-ˌfēld\. Town, Norfolk co., E Massachusetts, 17 mi. (27 km.) SW of Boston; pop. (1990c) 10,531; burned in King Philip's War 1675.

Med·ford \'med-fərd\. **1.** City, Middlesex co., NE Massachusetts, 5 mi. (8 km.) N of Boston; pop. (1990c) 57,407; Tufts Univ. (1852).

2. Town, ⊗ of Grant co., N Oklahoma; pop. (1990c) 1172.

3. City, ⊗ of Jackson co., SW Oregon, 60 mi. (97 km.) W of Klamath Falls; pop. (1990c) 46,951; alt. 1374 ft. (419 m.); pears; outdoor recreation; point of entry to Crater Lake National Park.

4. City, ⊗ of Taylor co., N Wisconsin, 32 mi. (52 km.) W of Merrill; pop. (1990c) 4283.

Medford Lakes. Borough, Burlington co., S cen. New Jersey, 18 mi. (29 km.) ESE of Camden; pop. (1990c) 4462.

Med·gi·dia \ˌmä-jē-'dē-ä\. Town, Constanța co., SE Romania, ab. 20 mi. (32 km.) WNW of the city of Constanța; pop. (1989c) 48,962; manufactures include building materials.

Me·dia \'mē-dē-ə\. **1.** Borough, ⊗ of Delaware co., SE Pennsylvania, 15 mi. (24 km.) W of Philadelphia; pop. (1990c) 5957.

2. Ancient country, S Asia, orig. the plateau region corresponding to NW part of modern Iran which was occupied by Medes, an Iranian people; in 8th cent. B.C. divided into small principalities; part of Assyrian empire to 626 B.C.; independent kingdom under King Cyaxares, aided Babylon in bringing about downfall of Assyria 612 B.C.; expanded territory to include part of Assyria, Armenia, and Cappadocia on W, to the Oxus River on NE, and Persia in S; conquered by Cyrus the Great, founder of Persian Empire 550 B.C. As a province of Persia it was bounded on N by the Elburz Mts., on NE by Hyrcania, on E by Parthia, on S by Persis and Susiana, on SW by Babylonia, on W by Assyria, and on NW by Armenia. Passed to Macedonian empire with the conquest of Persia by Macedonian King Alexander the Great, and upon his death it was divided into **Media At·ro·pa·te·ne** \ˌa-trō-pə-'tē-nē\ in the N (✻ Gazaca) and **Media Mag·na** \'mag-nə\ in the S (✻ Ecbatana, *mod.* Hamadān), which soon passed to Seleucids. See AZERBAIJAN 1.

Me·di·aş \ˌmä-dē-'äsh, 'mä-dē-ˌ\. Town, Sibiu co., cen. Romania; munic. pop. (1989c) 75,521; glass, leather goods, kitchenware, windowpanes, textiles, footwear; gas wells nearby.

Med·i·cal Lake \ˈme-di-kəl\. City, Spokane co., E Washington, 15 mi. (24 km.) WSW of the city of Spokane; pop. (1990c) 3664.

Me·di·ci·na \ˌmā-dē-ˈchē-nä\. Commune, Bologna prov., Emilia-Romagna, N Italy, 15 mi. (24 km.) E of the commune of Bologna; pop. (1981p) 12,605.

Med·i·cine Bow \ˈme-də-sən-ˌbō\. River, S Wyoming; formed by confluence of branches in E Carbon co., flows N and W into North Platte River; ab. 120 mi. (190 km.) long.

Medicine Bow Mountains. A range of the Rocky Mts., extending N and S in Colorado and Wyoming; highest point **Medicine Bow Peak** 12,013 ft. (3662 m.).

Medicine Creek. River, S cen. South Dakota; rises in E Jones co., flows E, then N into Missouri River on N boundary of Lyman co.; ab. 60 mi. (100 km.) long.

Medicine Hat. City, SE Alberta, Canada, on South Saskatchewan River 94 mi. (151 km.) ENE of Lethbridge; pop. (1991c) 43,625; railroad divisional point; river port; natural-gas wells; recreational facilities; Medicine Hat Coll. (1965); founded 1883.

Medicine Lake. Lake in S Sheridan co., NE Montana.

Medicine Lodge. City, ⊗ of Barber co., S Kansas, 64 mi. (103 km.) SW of Hutchinson; pop. (1990c) 2838.

Me·di·na \mə-ˈdē-nə\. **1.** River, S cen. Texas; flows through Bandera and Medina cos. to join the San Antonio River below San Antonio; 116 mi. (187 km.) long. See MEDINA DAM.
2. Name of counties in two states of the U.S. See tables at OHIO and TEXAS.
3. City, Hennepin co., Minnesota, 10 mi. (16 km.) W of Minneapolis; pop. (1990c) 3096.
4. Village, Orleans co., W New York, 41 mi. (66 km.) W of Rochester on New York State Barge Canal; pop. (1990c) 6686.
5. City, ⊗ of Medina co., N Ohio, 18 mi. (29 km.) WNW of Akron; pop. (1990c) 19,231.
6. City, King co., W cen. Washington, across Lake Washington E of Seattle; pop. (1990c) 2981.
7. *or Arab.* **Al–Ma·dī·nah** \ˌal-ma-ˈdē-nə\; *earlier* **Yath·rib** \ˈya-thrəb\. Inland city, E cen. Hejaz, W Saudi Arabia, 210 mi. (338 km.) N of Mecca; ab. 120 mi. (190 km.) from the Red Sea coast; pop. (1980e) 290,000; fruit, grain; Islamic Univ. (1962); its port is Yanbuʿ al Bahr. Second most important holy city of Islam, containing the tomb of Muḥammad; noted for its mosque enclosing the tomb and its palaces and fountains; the refuge of Muḥammad after his flight (hegira) from Mecca; date of his arrival Sept. 20, 622, later adopted as beginning of Muslim calendar. Was ✻ of the caliphate 622–661; after its sack by Umayyads 683 declined in influence; later came under Egyptians, Turks, and Wahhabis; city of the new kingdom of Hejaz 1919–24 when after a long siege it fell to Ibn Saʿūd, founder of Saudi Arabia.

Medina–Arkosh. See ARCOS DE LA FRONTERA.

Medina Dam. Dam across Medina River, bet. Bandera and Medina cos., S cen. Texas; height 178 ft. (54 m.); impounds water, **Medina Lake,** for irrigation.

Me·di·na del Cam·po \mā-ˈthē-nä-thel-ˈkäm-pō\. Commune, Valladolid prov., NW cen. Spain, 25 mi. (40 km.) SSW of the commune of Valladolid; pop. (1991c) 19,735.

Medina–Si·do·nia \-sē-ˈthō-nyä\. Commune, Cádiz prov., SW Spain, 19 mi. (31 km.) ESE of the city of Cádiz; pop. (1991c) 16,309; Gothic church; ancestral palace of dukes of Medina-Sidonia.

Mediolanum. 1. *or* **Mediolanum San·to·num** \san-ˈtō-nəm\. Ancient city, France. See SAINTES.
2. Ancient city, Italy. See MILAN.

Mediomatrica. See METZ.

Med·i·ter·ra·ne·an Sea \ˌme-də-tə-ˈrā-nē-ən, -nyən\; *anc.* **Ma·re In·ter·num** \ˈmä-rē-in-ˈter-nəm, ˈmär-ā\. Inland sea, enclosed by Europe on the W and N, Asia on the E, and Africa on the S; 969,100 sq. mi. (2,509,000 sq. km.); max. E to W extent 2300 mi. (3700 km.); max. depth 16,896 ft. (5150 m.); connected on W with the Atlantic Ocean by the Strait of Gibraltar, on SE with the Red Sea by the Suez Canal, and on NE with the Black Sea by the Dardanelles, Sea of Marmara, and Bosporus. Its main subdivisions are the Adriatic Sea, Aegean Sea, Tyrrhenian Sea, Ionian Sea, and Ligurian Sea; its chief islands Sicily, Sardinia, Corsica, Crete, Cyprus, Balearic Is., Dodecanese, Cyclades, Sporades, Ionian Is., Malta.

Me·di·um Lake \ˈmē-dē-əm\. Lake in Palo Alto co., N Iowa; ab. 4 mi. (6 km.) long.

Me·djer·da *or* **Me·jer·da** \mə-ˈjer-də\; *anc.* **Bag·ra·das** \ˈba-grə-ˌdas\. River, N Africa; rises in NE Algeria, flows E across N Tunisia into the Gulf of Tunis; 230 mi. (370 km.) long; fighting in WWII along its course 1943.

Medjerda Mountains. Range of the Little Atlas Mts. NE Algeria, extending across border into NW Tunisia; highest point ab. 3300 ft. (1000 m.).

Medjez–el–Bab. See MAJĀZ AL-BĀB.

Med·men·ham \ˈmed-nəm\. Village, S Buckinghamshire, SE cen. England; site of ruined Cistercian abbey, scene of revels of the Hell-fire Club or the secret society of the "Mad Monks of Medmenham" founded c. 1745 by profligate Sir Francis Dashwood.

Med·ny *or* **Med·nyy** \ˈmed-nē\. Island, Bering Sea. See KOMANDORSKIYE OSTROVA.

Medoacus Major. See BRENTA.

Mé·doc \mā-ˈdȯk\. District, NW Gironde dept., SW France, N of Bordeaux; ab. 50 mi. (80 km.) long, 6 to 7 mi. (10 to 11 km.) wide; noted for the wines produced in its vineyards.

Me·do·ra \mi-ˈdȯr-ə\. Village, ⊗ of Billings co., W North Dakota; pop. (1990c) 101.

Me·dūm \me-ˈdüm\. Locality, Egypt, bet. Memphis and El Faiyûm, ab. 40 mi. (64 km.) S of Cairo; site of step pyramid built by King Snefru (c. 2600 B.C.).

Medunta. See MANTES-LA-JOLIE.

Med·ve·di·tsa \med-ˈve-dət-sə\. Unnavigable river, S Russia in Europe, flows SSW to the Don River in Volgograd Oblast; ab. 425 mi. (680 km.) long.

Medvezhegorsk. See MEDVEZH'YEGORSK.

Medvezhi Ostrova. See BEAR ISLANDS.

Med·vezh'·ye·gorsk *or* **Med·vezh·e·gorsk** \mid-ˌvi-zhyi-ˈgȯrsk\. Town, S cen. Karelia Rep., NW Russia in Europe, at N end of Lake Onega; on Murmansk railroad line 80 mi. (129 km.) N of Petrozavodsk.

Med·way \ˈmed-ˌwā\. **1.** Town, Norfolk co., E Massachusetts, 22 mi. (35 km.) SW of Boston; pop. (1990c) 9931.
2. River, SE England; formed by confluence of branches in Kent, flows N into the Thames at Sheerness; 70 mi. (113 km.) long; its estuary extends W to Rochester.

Meeanee. See MIANI.

Mee·ker \ˈmē-kər\. **1.** County in S cen. Minnesota. See table at MINNESOTA.
2. Town, ⊗ of Rio Blanco co., NW Colorado; pop. (1990c) 2098.

Meeks Field \ˈmēks\. U.S. Army air base at Keflavík, SW Iceland; built during WWII, turned over to Iceland Oct. 1946 and renamed **Kef·la·vík Field** \ˈkye-blə-ˌvēk, ˈke-flə-\; now an international airport.

Meenen. See MENEN.

Mee·ra·ne \mā-ˈrä-nə\. City, Saxony, E Germany, 21 mi. (34 km.) W of Chemnitz; pop. (1981c) 22,646.

Meers·sen *or* **Mer·sen** \ˈmer-sən\. Commune, Limburg prov., SE Netherlands, just NNE of Maastricht; pop. (1981e) 20,270. Treaty signed here 870 A.D. bet. Holy Roman Emperor Charles the Bald and Louis the German, king of Germany, divided the kingdom of their nephew, Lothair II.

Mee·rut \ˈmā-rət, ˈmir-ət\. City, Uttar Pradesh, N India, on a tributary of the Ganges River 40 mi. (64 km.) NE of Delhi; pop. (1991c) 753,778; industrial center, producing textiles, chemicals, sugar, flour, and vegetable oils; an ancient town; important military cantonment, estab. early 19th cent. by

---

\ə\ abut \ˈə\ matches \ᵊ\ kitten, Fr table \ər\ further \a\ ash \ā\ ace \ä\ cot, cart \ȧ\ Fr bac \au̇\ out \b\ Span Avila \ch\ chin \e\ bet \ē\ easy \g\ go \i\ hit \ī\ ice \j\ job \k\ Ger ich, Buch \ⁿ\ Fr vin \ŋ\ sing \ō\ go \ȯ\ all \ȯ\ law \œ\ Fr bœuf \ᵫ\ Fr feu \ȯi\ boy \th\ thin \th\ this \ü\ loot \u̇\ foot \ue\ Ger füllen \ᵫ\ Fr rue \y\ yet \ʸ\ Fr digne \ˈdēnʸ\, nuit \ˈnwʸē\ \yü\ few \yu̇\ fury \zh\ vision

British; scene of first uprising of the Indian mutiny 1857 (see BARRACKPORE).

Me·ga \mə-'gä\. Town, S Ethiopia, on highway from Addis Ababa to Nairobi, Kenya.

Meg·a·lop·o·lis \,me-gə-'lä-pə-lis\. Highly urbanized region of the NE United States, stretching bet. the metropolitan areas of Boston on the NE to Washington, D.C. on the SW.

Meg·a·lóp·o·lis \,me-gā-'lö-pö-,lēs\. **1.** City, S Arcadia dept., cen. Peloponnese, Greece, just E of the Alpheus River. Founded c. 371 B.C. as Arcadian federal ✻ at suggestion of Theban general and statesman Epaminondas; its inhabitants were made up of persons taken from ab. 40 Arcadian towns; intended to be a defense against Sparta; usually an ally of Thebes and Macedon; joined Achaean League c. 234 B.C.; destroyed by Spartan King Cleomenes III c. 222 B.C.
2. Ancient city, Turkey. See SIVAS 2.

Me·gan·tic \mə-'gan-tik\ *or Fr.* **Mé·gan·tic** \mā-gäⁿ-'tēk\. **1.** Lake, S Quebec, Canada; ab. 10 sq. mi. (26 sq. km.); its outlet is the Chaudière.
2. *or* **Lac–Mégantic** \,läk-\. Town, S Quebec, Canada, on NE shore of Lake Megantic; pop. (1991c) 5838.

Meg·a·ra \'me-gə-rə\. **1.** Ancient city and state, N Africa. See CARTHAGE 8.
2. *or* **Mé·ga·ra** \'me-gə-rə\. Seaport city, Attica dept., Greece, on N coast of Saronic Gulf W of Athens; pop. (1981c) 17,719. Served as ✻ of ancient Megaris; flourished as maritime city under Dorians, establishing colonies on shores of Propontis and Euxine, most notably, Byzantium; ruined commercially in Peloponnesian War. Birthplace of Euclid, founder of the Megarian school of philosophy.

Megara Hy·blaea \hī-'blē-ə\. Ruins of town on E coast of Sicily, Italy, near Augusta and just NW of Siracusa; founded 8th cent. B.C. by Dorians from Megara.

Meg·a·ris \'me-gə-ris\. District in ancient Greece, bet. the Saronic Gulf and Gulf of Corinth; ab. 145 sq. mi. (375 sq. km.); ✻ Megara; formed E part of Isthmus of Corinth.

Me·gha·la·ya \,mā-gə-'lā-ə\. State, NE India; ✻ Shillong; potatoes, fruit, coal, limestone, corundum, clay, sandstone; formerly in Assam state, became a separate state 1972. See table at INDIA.

Megh·na \'māg-nə\. River, Bangladesh; formed by the Surma and its tributaries, flows S and is joined by the Padma (the merged Brahmaputra and Ganges) SE of Dhaka; ab. 125 mi. (200 km.) long; its wide lower course is the E mouth of the Ganges Delta (*q.v.*); navigable but dangerous at certain seasons because of the high tidal bore.

Me·gid·do \mi-'gi-dō\ *or* **Tel Megiddo** \,tel-\. City, ancient Palestine, now an archaeological site in Israel, on S side of Plain of Esdraelon ab. 15 mi. (24 km.) S of Haifa; modern excavations have shown that it was settled ab. 3500 B.C. A great battlefield of history (see ARMAGEDDON): c. 1468 B.C. Thutmose III of Egypt defeated Syrian army; ab. 609 B.C. Josiah, king of Judah, was killed by Necho II of Egypt; in WWI British Field Marshal Edmund Allenby defeated Turks 1918.

Megiste. See KASTELLÓRIZON.

Me·har·ry, Mount \mi-'har-ē\. Mountain, NW cen. Western Australia, Australia; 4098 ft. (1297 m.); highest in the state.

Me·he·dinţi \,mā-hā-'dēnts, -'dēn-tsē\. County of SW Romania. See table at ROMANIA.

Me·her·rin \mə-'her-ən\. River, S Virginia and NE North Carolina; flows E and SE from Virginia across state border to the Chowan River; 160 mi. (257 km.) long.

Meh Klong. See SAMUT SONGKHRAM.

Meh·sa·na. See MAHESĀNA.

Me·hun–sur–Yè·vre \mə-,œⁿ-sūr-'yevrᵊ\. Town, Cher dept., cen. France, NW of Bourges; ruins of 14th cent. castle where Charles VII was first crowned 1422 and died 1461.

Meiggs \'megz\. Peak, cen. Peru, NE of the city of Lima; 15,518 ft. (4730 m.).

Meigs \'megz\. Name of counties in two states of the U.S. See tables at OHIO and TENNESSEE.

Meije \'mezh\ *or* **La Meije** \lä-\. Mountain in the Dauphiné Alps, SE France, bet. Isère and Hautes-Alpes depts.; 13,081 ft. (3987 m.).

Meik·ti·la \'mek-tə-lə\. Town, Myanmar, on railroad line 75 mi. (121 km.) S of Mandalay; pop. (1983c) 96,496; a Buddhist center.

Mei·ning·en \'mī-niŋ-ən\. City, Thuringia, cen. Germany, near Werra River 40 mi. (64 km.) SW of Erfurt; pop. (1992e) 24,951; several museums; 16th–17th cent. castle; first mentioned 982; became city 1344; ✻ of duchy of Saxe-Meiningen 1680–1918.

Meis·sen \'mīs-ᵊn\. City, Saxony, E Germany, on the Elbe River 14 mi. (23 km.) NW of Dresden; pop. (1992e) 33,997; center of porcelain and ceramics manufacturing since early 18th cent.; 15th cent. castle; 13th–14th cent. Gothic cathedral.

Mejerda. See MEDJERDA.

Me·ji·ca·nos \,mā-hē-'kä-nōs\. Town, San Salvador dept., S El Salvador; pop. (1987e) 112,066.

Méjico. See MEXICO.

Me·jil·lo·nes \,mā-hē-'yō-nās\. Small port, Antofagasta region, N Chile, ab. 40 mi. (64 km.) N of the seaport of Antofagasta.

Mejillones del Sur, Bay of \t͟hel-'sür\. Inlet on N coast of Chile, 38 mi. (61 km.) N of Antofagasta.

Me·ke·le \'mā-kə-,lā\ *also* **Ma·ka·le** \'mä-kə-,lā\. Town, N Ethiopia, NE of Lake Tana; pop. (1989e) 76,400.

Mekili. See AL-MECHILI.

Mé·ki·nac \,mā-kē-'nak\. County, Quebec, Canada. See table at QUEBEC.

Mekka. See MECCA.

Meklong. See SAMUT SONGKHRAM.

Mek·nès \mek-'nes\ *or Span.* **Me·qui·nez** \,mā-kē-'nās\. City, N Morocco, 36 mi. (58 km.) WSW of Fès; a former ✻ of Morocco; pop. (1982c) 319,783; carpets. Founded 10th cent.; in Middle Ages a Berber citadel; for many years from 17th cent. was the residence of the Moroccan sultan; has large palace, mosques, gateway.

Me·kong \'mā-'kȯŋ, -'käŋ\ *or Tibetan* **Dza–chu** \'dzä-'chü\ *or Chin.* **Lancang** *or W.-G.* **Lan–ts'ang** \'län-'tsäŋ\. River, SE Asia; rises in Tanggula Range of E Tibet, China, flows SE through Yunnan prov., S China, and through E Indochina, forming the boundary bet. Laos and Myanmar and a large part of the boundary bet. Laos and Thailand; continues S through Cambodia and S Vietnam, where it empties into the South China Sea through several mouths; ab. 2600 mi. (4200 km.) long; receives the Yangbi from the E in cen. Yunnan. Navigable to Louangphrabang; the **Mekong Delta** forms a fertile rice-producing area. In Yunnan passes through deep gorges and lies bet. and close to the upper courses of the Nu and the Chang.

Mekran. See MAKRAN.

Me·la·ka *or* **Ma·lac·ca** \mä-'lä-kä\. **1.** State of Malaysia, on W coast of S Malay Penin., SE Asia, bounded on N by Negeri Sembilan, on E by Johor, on S and W by Strait of Malacca; ✻ Melaka; rice, rubber. British colony 1824; one of the Straits Settlements 1826; part of independent Federation of Malaya 1957; became a state of Malaysia 1963. See table at MALAYSIA.
2. Seaport municipality, its ✻, on Strait of Malacca 118 mi. (190 km.) by sea from Singapore; pop. (1980c) 250,635; coastal trade.

History: Founded c. 1400 by Malay Prince Paramesvara; taken for Portuguese by Afonso de Albuquerque 1511; early center of East Indian spice trade; its capture by Dutch (1641) secured Dutch predominance in Indies; held by British during French Revolution and Napoleonic Wars; returned to Dutch 1818; ceded to Great Britain in exchange for Bengkulu 1824; during WWII held by Japanese 1942–45.

Me·la·lap \mä-'lä-läp\. Town, SW cen. Sabah, Malaysia, on island of Borneo.

Mel·a·ne·sia \,me-lə-'nē-zhə, -shə\. Collective name for the islands in the SW Pacific Ocean NE of Australia and S of the Equator, incl. New Caledonia, Vanuatu, Solomon Is., Admiralty Is., Bismarck Archipelago, Fiji, and others; a subdivision of Oceania.

Mel·bourne \'mel-bərn\. **1.** City, ⊗ of Izard co., N Arkansas; pop. (1990c) 1562.

2. City, Brevard co., E Florida, on Indian River 58 mi. (93 km.) SE of Orlando; pop. (1990c) 59,646; electronic components; Florida Institute of Technology (1958).

3. City, ✻ of Victoria, SE Australia, at N end of Port Phillip Bay at mouth of the Yarra River; pop. (1991c) 60,476, met. area pop. (1991c) 2,761,995; good natural harbor; financial center; exports wool and food products; industries include motor vehicles, textiles, and electronics; Univ. of Melbourne (1853), Monash Univ. (1958), La Trobe Univ. (1964). Founded 1835 by settlers from Tasmania; made ✻ of Victoria when state estab. 1851; a center of the gold rush during the 1850s; temporary ✻ of Australia 1901–27; site of Summer Olympic Games 1956.

Melbourne Beach. Town, Brevard co., E Florida, on Indian River, E of Melbourne; pop. (1990c) 3021.

Mel·chor \mel-ˈchȯr\. Island in Chonos Archipelago, in Pacific Ocean off SW coast of Chile.

Meleda. See MLJET.

Me·le·gna·no \ˌmā-lā-ˈnyä-nō\; *formerly* **Ma·ri·gna·no** \ˌmä-rē-ˈnyä-nō\. Commune, Milano prov., Lombardy, N Italy, 10 mi. (16 km.) SE of Milan; pop. (1981p) 18,482. Scene of victory of French King Francis I over Swiss troops of duke of Milan 1515; French victory over Austrians 1859.

Melekess. See DIMITROVGRAD 2.

Mel·fi \ˈmel-fē\. Commune, Potenza prov., Basilicata, S Italy, 26 mi. (42 km.) NNW of the commune of Potenza; pop. (1991p) 15,751; 12th cent. cathedral; 13th cent. castle; of Roman origin; taken by Normans, and eventually passed to Italy 1861; suffered several destructive earthquakes, most notably in 1851.

Mel·fort \ˈmel-fərt\. Town, S cen. Saskatchewan, Canada, 55 mi. (89 km.) ESE of Prince Albert; pop. (1991c) 5628.

Melghir, Shatt al– *also* **Melghir, Shott.** See MELRHIR, CHOTT.

Mel·i·boea \ˌme-lə-ˈbē-ə\. Ancient town near the coast of Magnesia, Greece, bet. Mt. Pelion and Mt. Ossa.

Me·lil·la \mə-ˈlē-lyä\; *anc.* **Rus·ad·dir** \ˌrə-sə-ˈdir\. Presidio and commercial city of Spain, N coast of Morocco on Cape Tres Forcas in Er Rif region; pop. (1991p) 56,497; with Ceuta, comprises an autonomous community of Spain; ships iron ore. Conquered by Spain 1497; many times under siege; scene of revolt by Riffs 1921 under Berber leader Abd el-Krim; reoccupied 1926; scene of revolt of army officers which led to Spanish Civil War 1936.

Me·li·mo·yu, Mon·te \ˈmȯn-tā-ˌme-li-ˈmō-yü\. Peak, S Chile, E of Moraleda Channel; 7872 ft. (2399 m.).

Me·li·pil·la \ˌmā-lē-ˈpē-yä\. City, Santiago region, cen. Chile, 38 mi. (61 km.) SW of the city of Santiago; pop. (1992c) 80,086.

Melita. **1.** Independent state, Mediterranean Sea. See MALTA 1.

2. Island, Adriatic Sea. See MLJET.

Melitene. See MALATYA 2.

Me·li·to·pol' *or* **Me·li·to·pol** \ˌme-lə-ˈtȯ-pəl^{y}\. Town, S Zaporizhzhya subdivision, Ukraine, near NW shore of Sea of Azov 70 mi. (113 km.) S of the city of Zaporizhzhya; pop. (1991e) 177,000; center of agricultural region; diesel engines, clothing; settled late 18th cent.; in WWII occupied by Germans 1941–43.

Melk \ˈmelk\. Town, NE Austria, on Danube River, W of Vienna; pop. (1991c) 5139. Benedictine abbey, founded 1089, reconstructed in baroque style in 18th cent.; early medieval residence of Austrian rulers.

Mel·lette \mə-ˈlet\. County in S South Dakota. See table at SOUTH DAKOTA.

Měl·ník \ˈmyel-ˌnyēk\ *or Ger.* **Mel·nik** \ˈmel-nik\. Town, NW Czech Republic, 18 mi. (29 km.) N of Prague at junction of Elbe and Vltava rivers; pop. (1980p) 18,941; 14th cent. town hall.

Me·lo \ˈmā-lō\. City, ✻ of Cerro Largo dept., E Uruguay, 205 mi. (330 km.) NE of Montevideo; pop. (1985c) 42,615; distributing center for NE Uruguay.

Melodunum. See MELUN.

Me·lo·nes Dam \mə-ˈlō-nēz\. Dam across Stanislaus River, Tuolumne and Calaveras cos., N cen. California; height 225 ft. (69 m.); impounds water for irrigation.

Me·lo·ria \mə-ˈlōr-ē-ə\. Small island 4 mi. (6 km.) off Livorno, Italy; nearby waters site of two naval battles: 1241 in which Pisan fleet defeated Genoese and 1284 in which Genoese destroyed Pisan fleet.

Me·los \ˈmē-ˌläs\ *or Gk.* **Mí·los** \ˈmē-ˌlös\ *or Ital.* **Mi·lo** \ˈmē-lō\. **1.** An island of the Cyclades, Cyclades dept., Greece; 58 sq. mi. (150 sq. km); 14 mi. (23 km.) long; pop. (1981c) 4554; chief town Melos; formerly exported obsidian. Of volcanic origin, highest point 1854 ft. (565 m.); has large harbor on N which nearly divides the island. In early period occupied by Dorians; attacked and conquered 416 B.C. by Athenians and its people either killed or enslaved.

2. Ruined city on Melos, Greece; here the famous statue of Venus (Venus of Milo) was discovered 1820 and is now in the Louvre museum in Paris.

3. *formerly* **Pla·ka** \ˈplä-kä\. Chief town of island of Melos, Cyclades dept., Greece.

Mel·rhir, Chott \ˈshät-mel-ˈrir\ *or Arab.* **Shatt al–Mel·ghir** \ˈshät-ȧl-mel-ˈgir\ *also* **Shott Melghir** \ˈshät\. Marshy saline lake, N of Touggourt, NE Algeria; 80 to 100 mi. (130 to 160 km.) long.

Mel·rose \ˈmel-ˌrōz\. **1.** Residential city, Middlesex co., NE Massachusetts, 7 mi. (11 km.) N of Boston; pop. (1990c) 28,150.

2. City, Stearns co., cen. Minnesota, 30 mi. (48 km.) WNW of St. Cloud; pop. (1990c) 2561.

3. Burgh, cen. Borders region, SE Scotland; pop. (1981c) 2345; the "Kennaquhair" of poet and novelist Sir Walter Scott's *The Abbot* and *The Monastery.* Ruins of a Cistercian abbey, founded 1136 by David I, and partially destroyed and rebuilt several times.

Melrose Park. Village, Cook co., NE Illinois, 3.5 mi. (6 km.) W of Chicago and 3.5 mi. (6 km.) SE of O'Hare International Airport; pop. (1990c) 20,859; railroad yards.

Mel·tham \ˈmel-thəm\. Town, West Yorkshire, N England; pop. (1981p) 7395.

Mel·ton Hill Dam \ˈmelt-^{ə}n\. See table at TENNESSEE VALLEY AUTHORITY.

Melton Mow·bray \ˈmō-brā, -brē\. Town, Leicestershire, cen. England, 15 mi. (24 km.) NE of Leicester; pop. (1981p) 23,554; food products, pet food.

Me·lun \mə-ˈlœ̄^{n}\; *anc.* **Mel·o·du·num** \ˌme-lə-ˈdü-nəm, -ˈdyü-\. City, ✻ of Seine-et-Marne dept., N France, on Seine River 27 mi. (43 km.) SSE of Paris; pop. (1990c) 36,489; 11th cent. Romanesque church; fine château nearby. Conquered by Romans 53 B.C.; taken by Normans; royal residence under Capetians; taken by English under Henry V 1420 and retaken by French national heroine Joan of Arc 1430.

Mel·ville \ˈmel-ˌvil\. City, SE Saskatchewan, Canada, 26 mi. (42 km.) SW of Yorkton; pop. (1991c) 4905.

Melville, Cape. **1.** Cape, NE Queensland, Australia, on E coast of Cape York Penin., 14°11′S, 144°30′E; contained in **Cape Melville National Park.**

2. Cape, S Balabac I., SW Philippines.

Melville, Lake. Lake, SE Labrador, Canada; 1133 sq. mi. (2935 sq. km.); constitutes inner basin of Hamilton Inlet; at its SW corner receives the Churchill River.

Melville Bay. Large inlet of NE Baffin Bay on NW coast of Greenland, E of Cape York.

Melville Island. **1.** Island off NW coast of Northern Terr., Australia; 2400 sq. mi. (6200 sq. km.); separated from mainland by Clarence Strait.

2. Island in Queen Elizabeth Is., Northwest Territories & Nunavut, Canada, N of Victoria I.; 16,369 sq. mi. (42,396 sq. km.); 200 mi. (322 km.) long by 130 mi. (209 km.) wide.

Melville Peninsula. Peninsula, NE mainland part of Nunavut, Canada, bet. Committee Bay on the W and Foxe Basin on the E; separated from Baffin I. by Fury and Hecla Strait.

Melville Sound. See VISCOUNT MELVILLE SOUND.
Melville Water. See CLAREMONT 3.
Mel·vin·dale \'mel-vən-ˌdāl\. City, Wayne co., SE Michigan, WSW of Detroit; pop. (1990c) 11,216.
Me Ma·o·ya, Mount \ˌmā-mä-'ō-yə\. Peak, cen. New Caledonia, SW Pacific Ocean; 4728 ft. (1441 m.).
Mem·ba Bay \'mem-bä\. Inlet of Mozambique Channel on NE coast of Mozambique, N of Cape Loguno.
Memel. 1. River, Europe. See NEMAN.
2. City, Lithuania. See KLAIPĖDA 2.
Memelburg. See KLAIPĖDA 2.
Memelgebiet *or* **Memelland.** See KLAIPĖDA 1.
Mem·ming·en \'me-miŋ-ən\. City, Bavaria, Germany, 42 mi. (68 km.) SW of Augsburg; pop. (1992e) 39,864; 16th cent. town hall. First mentioned 12th cent.; became free imperial city 1286; passed to Bavaria 1803.
Mem·phis \'mem-fəs\. **1.** City, ⊗ of Scotland co., NE Missouri, 28 mi. (47 km.) NE of Kirksville; pop. (1990c) 2094.
2. City, ⊗ of Shelby co., SW corner of Tennessee, on Mississippi River 10 mi. (16 km.) N of Mississippi border; pop. (1990c) 610,337; cotton market; Graceland, singer Elvis Presley's mansion, is now open to the public; Rhodes Coll. (1848), LeMoyne-Owen Coll. (1862), Christian Brothers Univ. (1871), Memphis State Univ. (1912), Southern Coll. of Optometry (1932), Memphis Coll. of Arts (1936).
History: Former site of Chickasaw Indian settlement; forts erected by French, later by Spanish, and by U.S. in 1797; platted and settled in 1819; incorp. as town 1826, as city 1849; made port of customs 1850; became Confederate military center at beginning of Civil War 1861; temporary state ✻ 1862; captured by Union forces after the gunboat battle of Memphis 1862, and remained in Union control until after the war; suffered from yellow-fever epidemics 1867, 1873, and esp. 1878; became impoverished and surrendered charter to state 1879; rechartered as city 1893; civil rights leader Martin Luther King, Jr. assassinated here April 4, 1968.
3. City, ⊗ of Hall co., NW Texas, in the Panhandle 75 mi. (121 km.) SE of Amarillo; pop. (1990c) 2465.
4. Ancient city in Lower Egypt, its site now partly covered by village of **Mit Ra·hi·na** \'mēt-rə-'hē-nə\, ab. 14 mi. (23 km.) S of Cairo; traditionally the ✻ of Menes, first king of a united Egypt (c. 3100 B.C.) and of most of the rulers of the Old Kingdom; superseded by Heracleopolis during IXth and Xth dynasties and later by Thebes, but remained an important city; fell to Persians in 6th cent. B.C.; lost its importance after the conquest of Egypt by Macedonian King Alexander the Great. Sacred to the worship of Ptah. In its ruins are the great temple of Ptah, royal palaces, an extensive necropolis. Pyramids of Saqqara nearby and pyramids of Giza just to the N; in the Old Testament called **Noph** \'näf\ (*Isaiah* xix. 13; *Jer.* ii. 16, and elsewhere).
Mem·phré·ma·gog \ˌmem-frə-'mā-ˌgäg\. County, Quebec, Canada. See table at QUEBEC.
Mem·phre·ma·gog, Lake \ˌmem-frə-'mā-ˌgäg, -frē-\. Lake, extending across U.S.-Canada border from N Vermont into S Quebec; ab. 30 mi. (48 km.) long (7 mi. or 11 km. in Vermont) and from 1 to 4 mi. (2 to 6 km.) wide; its outlet flows into the St. Francis River, Quebec.
Me·na \'mē-nə\. City, ⊗ of Polk co., W Arkansas, in Ouachita Mts. 70 mi. (113 km.) W of Hot Springs; pop. (1990c) 5475.
Menado. See MANADO.
Men·ai Strait \'me-ˌnī\. Channel bet. Anglesey I. and the mainland, off NW coast of Wales; 14 mi. (23 km.) long, from 200 yards (180 m.) to 2 mi. (3 km.) wide; spanned by two bridges, tubular and suspension.
Me·nal·du·ma·deel \mā-'näl-dü-mä-ˌdāl\. Commune, Friesland prov., N Netherlands, just W of Leeuwarden; pop. (1981e) 13,280.
Me Nam *or* **Menam.** See CHAO PHRAYA.
Me·nands \mə-'nandz\. Village, Albany co., E New York, on Hudson River 2 mi. (3 km.) N of the city of Albany; pop. (1990c) 4333.
Me·nang·ka·bau \ˌmā-näŋ-'kä-ˌbau̇\. Former empire of cen. and W Sumatra, regarded as the original home of the Malay people; migrations to Malay Penin. and other parts of the Malay Archipelago began probably mid-12th cent. A.D.
Me·nard \mə-'närd\. **1.** Name of counties in two states of the U.S. See tables at ILLINOIS and TEXAS.
2. City, ⊗ of Menard co., W cen. Texas, 52 mi. (84 km.) SE of San Angelo; pop. (1990c) 1606; ruins of old Spanish mission (1757) nearby.
Me·nasha \mə-'na-shə\. City, Winnebago co., E Wisconsin, on Lake Winnebago and Fox River 5 mi. (8 km.) S of Appleton; pop. (1990c) 14,711; forms a continuous community with twin city of Neenah (*q.v.*); settled 1840s.
Mende \'mänd\; *anc.* **Mi·ma·tum** \mī-'mā-təm\. Commune, ✻ of Lozère dept., S France, 76 mi. (122 km.) NW of Avignon; pop. (1982c) 10,520; tourism; cathedral (14th cent., rebuilt 17th cent.). See CÉVENNES.
Men·den \'men-dən\. City, cen. North Rhine-Westphalia, Germany, ESE of Dortmund; pop. (1992e) 56,525.
Men·den·hall \'men-dən-ˌhȯl\. Town, ⊗ of Simpson co., S cen. Mississippi; pop. (1990c) 2463.
Men·de·res \ˌmen-de-'res\. **1.** *or in full* **Bü·yük Menderes** \bu̅e̅-'yu̅e̅k\; *anc.* **Mae·an·der** \mē-'an-dər\. River, W Turkey in Asia; rises in mountains W of Afyon and flows SW and W into Aegean Sea S of the island of Sámos; ab. 240 mi. (390 km.) long; notable in ancient legend for its wanderings. Near the mouth of the modern stream is the large Lake Bafa; fertile valley. The ancient Maeander flowed across N Caria and on or near its banks were the ancient cities of Laodicea, Magnesia, and Miletus.
2. *or in full* **Kü·çük Menderes** \ku̅e̅-'chu̅e̅k\; *anc.* **Scaman·der** \skə-'man-dər\. River, NW Turkey in Asia; rises in Kazdağı (Mt. Ida) and flows W and NW into the Dardanelles across the plain of ancient Troy; 60 mi. (97 km.) long. The ancient Scamander, flowing past Troy, in its lower course is supposed to have been E of the modern stream.
Men·des \'men-ˌdēz\. Archaeological site in Nile Delta, N Egypt, E of Damietta branch and just SE of El Mansûra; seat of veneration of Osiris, god of the underworld. Near here c. 373 B.C. Egyptians under Nectanebo I defeated the Persians.
Mend·ham \'men-dəm\. Borough, Morris co., N New Jersey, 8 mi. (13 km.) W of Morristown; pop. (1990c) 4890.
Men·dip Hills \'men-ˌdip\. Range of hills, NE Somerset, SW England; ab. 18 mi. (29 km.) long; highest elev. **Black Down** 1068 ft. (326 m.).
Men·do·ci·no \ˌmen-də-'sē-nō\. Coastal county in W California. See table at CALIFORNIA.
Mendocino, Cape. Cape on W coast of Humboldt co., NW California; extreme W point of California, 40°25′N, 124°25′W.
Men·don \'men-dən\. Town, Worcester co., cen. Massachusetts, 17 mi. (27 km.) SE of the city of Worcester; pop. (1990c) 4010.
Men·do·ta \men-'dō-tə\. **1.** City, Fresno co., S cen. California, 34 mi. (55 km.) W of the city of Fresno; pop. (1990c) 6821.
2. City, La Salle co., N Illinois, 20 mi. (32 km.) NW of Ottawa; pop. (1990c) 7018.
Mendota, Lake. See FOUR LAKES.
Mendota Heights. Village, Dakota co., SE Minnesota, S suburb of St. Paul; pop. (1990c) 9431.
Men·do·za \men-'dō-zə\. **1.** River, W Argentina; rises on slopes of Aconcagua Mt., flows E and N into Guanacache Marshes; ab. 200 mi. (320 km.) long.
2. Province of W Argentina. See table at ARGENTINA.
3. City, its ✻, ab. 60 mi. (100 km.) SE of Aconcagua; pop. (1991p) 121,696; center of grape culture; alt. 2320 ft. (707 m.); university (1939). Founded c. 1560; came under viceroyalty of La Plata 1776; headquarters of soldier and statesman José de San Martín in preparing for march across Andes to Chile 1817; destroyed by earthquake 1861, rebuilt.
Me·ne·men \ˌme-nə-'men\. Town, İzmir prov., W Turkey in Asia, 14 mi. (23 km.) NNW of the city of İzmir.
Me·nen *also* **Mee·nen** \'mā-nən\ *or Fr.* **Me·nin** \mə-'nan\. Commune, West Flanders prov., NW Belgium, on Leie River at French border; pop. (1991c) 32,645.
Menevia. See SAINT DAVID'S.
Men·fi \'men-fē\. Commune, Agrigento prov., SW Sicily, It-

aly, 40 mi. (64 km.) NW of the commune of Agrigento; pop. (1981p) 12,564.

Mêng Chiang \ˈməŋ-ˈjyäŋ\. Former Japanese buffer state, cen. W Asia, bet. Manchukuo and Outer Mongolia; comprising approx. the provs. of Chahar and Suiyuan of Nei Monggol (Inner Mongolia); ab. 220,000 sq. mi. (569,800 sq. km.); ✻ Hu-ho-hao-t'e; estab. 1937, collapsed with defeat of Japan 1945.

Meng·zi *or W.-G.* **Meng–tzu** \ˈməŋ-ˈdzə\. City and former treaty port, S Yunnan, S China, near Vietnamese border SSE of Kunming; on fertile plateau (alt. 4300 ft. or 1300 m.).

Men·i·fee \ˈme-nə-fē\. County in E Kentucky. See table at KENTUCKY.

Menin. See MENEN.

Me·nin·dee Lake \mə-ˈnin-dē\. Reservoir, W New South Wales, Australia, SE of Broken Hill; one of a series near the Darling River.

Meninx. See JERBA.

Men·lo Park \ˈmen-lō\. **1.** City, San Mateo co., W California, 23 mi. (37 km.) SE of San Francisco; pop. (1990c) 28,040; settled 1860s.
2. Unincorporated settlement, Middlesex co., cen. New Jersey, ab. 6 mi. (10 km.) SE of Plainfield; 129 ft. (39 m.) Edison Memorial Tower (topped by huge electric light bulb) on site of inventor Thomas Edison's laboratory where he invented incandescent light 1879.

Me·nom·i·nee \mə-ˈnä-mə-nē\. **1.** River, NE Wisconsin; formed by confluence of Michigamme and Brule rivers, flows SE on Wisconsin-Michigan boundary and empties into Green Bay; 125 mi. (201 km.) long; provides waterpower.
2. Name of counties in two states of the U.S. See tables at MICHIGAN and WISCONSIN.
3. City, Menominee co., Michigan, S tip of Upper Penin., on Green Bay; pop. (1990c) 9398; outdoor recreation; sawmills.

Menominee Range. Low range in Upper Penin., Michigan and NE Wisconsin; noted for iron ore.

Me·nom·o·nee Falls \mə-ˈnä-mə-nē\. Village, Waukesha co., SE Wisconsin, NNW of Milwaukee; pop. (1990c) 26,840.

Me·nom·o·nie \mə-ˈnä-mə-nē\. City, ⊗ of Dunn co., W Wisconsin, 21 mi. (34 km.) W of Eau Claire; pop. (1990c) 13,547; Univ. of Wisconsin–Stout (1893).

Me·nongue \mā-ˈnȯŋ\. Town, S cen. Angola, ✻ of Cuando-Cubango prov.

Menorca. See MINORCA.

Men·ta·na \mān-ˈtä-nä\. Commune, Roma prov., W Lazio, cen. Italy, NE of Rome; pop. (1989c) 30,100; scene of battle 1867 in which Italian patriot Giuseppe Garibaldi was defeated by combined papal and French troops, ending his campaign to capture Rome.

Men·ta·wai \men-ˈtä-ˌwī\. Island group of ab. 70 islands in the Indian Ocean off the W cen. coast of Sumatra, Indonesia; 2354 sq. mi. (6097 sq. km.); includes large islands of Siberut, Sipura, North Pagai, and South Pagai. Of volcanic origin and surrounded by reefs; inhabitants belong to very early indigenous peoples of Sumatra.

Men·teith, Loch \men-ˈtēth\. Small lake in Central region, cen. Scotland.

Men·ton \mäⁿ-ˈtōⁿ\ *or Ital.* **Men·to·ne** \men-ˈtō-nā\. Commune, Alpes-Maritimes dept., SE France, on Mediterranean Sea 12 mi. (19 km.) ENE of Nice; pop. (1990c) 29,474; famous resort. Under princes of Monaco from 14th cent. to 1848; independent republic 1848–60; to France 1860. Grimaldi (*q.v.*) caves nearby.

Men·tone \ˈmen-ˌtōn\. Village, ⊗ of Loving co., W Texas.

Men·tor \ˈmen-tər\. Village, Lake co., NE Ohio, near Lake Erie 22 mi. (35 km.) NE of Cleveland; pop. (1990c) 47,359; residential suburb of Cleveland; Lakeland Community Coll. (1967).

Mentor–on–the–Lake. Village, Lake co., NE Ohio, on Lake Erie 24 mi. (39 km.) NE of Cleveland; pop. (1990c) 8271.

Menufieh. See MINŪFĪYA.

Men·zel Bour·gui·ba \men-ˈzel-bu̇r-ˈgē-bə\; *formerly* **Fer·ry·ville** \ˈfer-ē-ˌvil\. Town, N Tunisia, on S shore of Lake Bizerte; during WWII occupied by U.S. troops 1943.

Meping. See PING.

Mep·pel \ˈme-pəl\. Commune, Drenthe prov., NE Netherlands, 14 mi. (23 km.) NNE of Zwolle; pop. (1992e) 24,139.

Mequinez. See MEKNES.

Meq·uon \ˈme-ˌkwän\. City, Ozaukee co., E Wisconsin, S of Sheboygan; pop. (1990c) 18,885; Concordia Univ. Wisconsin (1881).

Merabéllou, Kólpos. See MIRABELLO GULF.

Mer·a·mec \ˈmer-ə-ˌmak\. River, SE cen. Missouri; rises in Dent co., flows NE into Mississippi River below St. Louis; 174 mi. (280 km.) long.

Me·ra·no \mā-ˈrä-nō\ *or Ger.* **Me·ran** \mā-ˈrän\. Commune, Bolzano prov., Trentino-Alto Adige, NE Italy, on S slope of the Alps 17 mi. (27 km.) NW of the commune of Bolzano; pop. (1991p) 32,600; tourist and health resort; 15th cent. castle; 14th cent. church. Near site of first cent. A.D. military station *Castrum Maiense;* first mentioned 857 A.D.; ✻ of the Tirol 12th–15th cents.; under Austrian rule until ceded to Italy 1919 by Treaty of St.-Germain.

Me·ra·pi, Gu·nung \ˈgü-ˌnu̇ŋ-mə-ˈrä-pē\. **1.** Volcano, cen. Java, Indonesia, just N of Yogyakarta; 9551 ft. (2911 m.).
2. Volcanic peak in the Padang Highlands, W Sumatra, Indonesia, 40 mi. (64 km.) NE of Padang and near Bukittinggi; 9485 ft. (2891 m.); a peak of the Barisan Mts.; violent eruptions in 19th cent.

Me·rau·ke \mə-ˈrau̇-kə\. Seaport and chief town on S coast of Irian Jaya, Indonesia, at mouth of **Merauke River** (ab. 125 mi. or 200 km. long) 60 mi. (97 km.) from Papua New Guinea border; chief product copra.

Mer·ba·bu *or Du.* **Mer·ba·boe** \mər-ˈbä-bü\. Volcano, cen. Java, Indonesia, N of Yogyakarta; 10,308 ft. (3142 m.).

Mer·can Dağ·la·rı \mer-ˈjän-ˌdä-lä-ˈrē\. Mountain group, E cen. Turkey in Asia, S of Erzincan; highest peak 11,359 ft. (3462 m.).

Mercara See MADIKERI.

Mer·ca·to San Se·ve·ri·no \mer-ˈkä-tō-ˌsän-ˌsā-vā-ˈrē-nō\. Commune, Salerno prov., Campania, S Italy, 7 mi. (11 km.) N of the seaport of Salerno; pop. (1981p) 18,079.

Mer·ced \mər-ˈsed\. **1.** River, cen. California; rises in S Yosemite National Park, flows W through the 6-mile (10-kilometer) long Yosemite Valley (*q.v.*) and into the San Joaquin River; ab. 150 mi. (240 km.) long.
2. County in cen. California. See table at CALIFORNIA.
3. City, its ⊗, in valley of the San Joaquin and S of the Merced River 55 mi. (89 km.) NW of Fresno; pop. (1990c) 56,216; dairy products; diversified agriculture; tourism; Merced Coll. (1963).

Mer·ce·da·rio, Cer·ro \ˈser-rō-ˌmer-sā-ˈdär-ē-ˌō\. Peak, San Juan prov., W Argentina, near Chilean border; 22,211 ft. (6770 m.).

Mer·ce·des \mər-ˈsā-dēz\. City, Hidalgo co., S Texas, 20 mi. (32 km.) E of McAllen; pop. (1990c) 12,694.

Mer·ce·des \mer-ˈsā-t͟hās\. **1.** Town, Buenos Aires prov., E Argentina, 55 mi. (89 km.) W of the city of Buenos Aires; pop. (1980c) 50,992.
2. Town, cen. Corrientes prov., NE Argentina, 120 mi. (193 km.) SE of the city of Corrientes; pop. (1980p) 20,603.
3. City, San Luis prov., cen. Argentina, ab. 60 mi. (100 km.) E of the city of San Luis; pop. (1980p) 46,581.
4. City and river port, ✻ of Soriano dept., SW Uruguay, on Río Negro 155 mi. (249 km.) NW of Montevideo; pop. (1985c) 36,702; commercial center; tourism.

Mer·ced Peak \mər-ˈsed\. Mountain on S boundary of Yosemite National Park, E cen. California; 11,726 ft. (3574 m.).

Mer·cer \ˈmər-sər\. **1.** Name of counties in eight states of the U.S. See tables at ILLINOIS, KENTUCKY, MISSOURI, NEW JERSEY, NORTH DAKOTA, OHIO, PENNSYLVANIA, WEST VIRGINIA.
2. Borough, ⊗ of Mercer co., W Pennsylvania, 17 mi. (27 km.) NNE of New Castle; pop. (1990c) 2444.

3. Village, N North I., New Zealand, on Waikato River 32 mi. (52 km.) SSE of Auckland. Near here was old frontier bet. Maori and colonists; adjacent terrain scene of numerous encounters bet. Maoris and British troops 1863–64.

Mercer Island. City, King co., W cen. Washington, in Lake Washington 4 mi. (6 km.) E of Seattle; pop. (1990c) 20,816; residential suburb of Seattle.

Mer·cers·burg \ˈmər-sərz-ˌbərg\. Borough, Franklin co., S Pennsylvania, 17 mi. (27 km.) WSW of Chambersburg; pop. (1990c) 1640; Mercersburg Academy (1893); early home of James Buchanan, 15th president of the U.S., who was born nearby.

Mer·chant·ville \ˈmər-chənt-ˌvil\. Borough, Camden co., SW New Jersey, 3 mi. (5 km.) E of the city of Camden; pop. (1990c) 4095.

Mer·cia \ˈmər-shə, -shē-ə\. Ancient Anglian kingdom in cen. England, one of a group of seven Anglo-Saxon kingdoms, sometimes known as the Heptarchy (*q.v.*); in 7th cent. A.D. its pagan ruler overthrew Christian king of Northumbria (*q.v.*); leading member of Heptarchy in 8th cent., controlling most of S England; declined 9th cent. with rising power of Wessex (*q.v.*); in 9th cent. English Mercia separated by Watling Street from Danish Mercia to the NE in Danelaw; Danelaw reconquered in 10th cent.

Mer de Glace \ˌmer-də-ˈgläs\. Glacier, SE France, on N slope of Mont Blanc.

Mer·e·dith \ˈmer-ə-dith\. Town, Belknap co., cen. New Hampshire, on Lakes Winnipesaukee and Waukewan 9 mi. (15 km.) N of Laconia; pop. (1990c) 4837; lake resort.

Meredith Bridge. See LACONIA 1.

Me·re·va·ri \ˌmā-rā-ˈvä-rē\. River in SE cen. Venezuela; flows N into Caura River.

Mergate. See MARGATE.

Mer·gui \ˌmər-ˈgwē\. Seaport town, S Myanmar, on a coastal island; pop. (1983c) 88,600.

Mergui Archipelago. Group of more than 200 islands in Andaman Sea off coast of S Myanmar; bet. ab. lat. 9° and 13°N; largest is Mali I. at N end; among the other large islands (N to S) are Kadan, Thayawthadangyi, Daung, Saganthit, Bentinck, Kanmaw Kyun, Letsôkaw, and Lanbi. Sparsely inhabited, chiefly by Selungs and Burmans.

Meriç. See MARITSA.

Mé·ri·court \ˌmā-rē-ˈkür\. Commune, Pas-de-Calais dept., N France, 9 mi. (15 km.) from Arras; scene of fighting in WWI.

Me·ri·da \ˈmer-əd-ə\. Municipality on W side of Ormoc Bay, Leyte prov., NW coast of Leyte I., Philippines, SW of Ormoc and 42 mi. (68 km.) SW of Tacloban; pop. (1980c) 18,838.

Mé·ri·da \ˈmā-rē-thä\. **1.** City, ✻ of Yucatán state, SE Mexico; munic. pop. (1990p) 557,340; sisal industry; 16th cent. cathedral; university (1624, university status 1922); port is Progreso. Founded 1542 on the site of an ancient Mayan city.

2. *anc.* **Emer·i·ta Au·gus·ta** \i-ˈmer-i-tə-ȯ-ˈgəs-tə\. Commune, ✻ of Extremadura autonomous community in Badajoz prov., SW Spain, on Guadiana River 33 mi. (53 km.) ENE of the city of Badajoz; pop. (1991p) 47,982; textiles, leather, soap, cork, hats; noted esp. for its Roman ruins, incl. an amphitheater, bridge, aqueduct, circus, temple, arch by Emperor Trajan, and colonnaded theater. Roman colony founded 25 B.C.; became ✻ of prov. of Lusitania; passed to Visigoths, and later taken by Moors 713 A.D.; reconquered 1228 by Alfonso IX.

3. State of Venezuela. See table at VENEZUELA.

4. Town, ✻ of Mérida state, W Venezuela, in the Cordillera de Mérida ab. 30 mi. (48 km.) S of the S end of Lake Maracaibo on highway to Colombia; pop. (1990p) 167,992; textiles; cathedral; university (1785); founded 1558; suffers frequent earthquakes, severely damaged in those of 1812 and 1894.

Mérida, Cordillera de *and* **Mérida, Sierra Nevada de.** See CORDILLERA DE MÉRIDA.

Mer·i·den \ˈmer-əd-ᵊn\. **1.** City, New Haven co., S Connecticut, 17 mi. (27 km.) NE of the city of New Haven; pop. (1990c) 59,479; silverware. Settled 1661; incorp. as city 1867; consolidated 1922 with town (incorp. 1806) with which it is coextensive.

2. Village, Sullivan co., SW New Hampshire, ab. 12 mi. (19 km.) N of Claremont; bird sanctuary; first bird club in the U.S. was formed here in 1910.

Me·rid·i·an \mə-ˈri-dē-ən\. **1.** City, Ada co., SW Idaho, 10 mi. (16 km.) W of Boise; pop. (1990c) 9596.

2. City, ⊗ of Lauderdale co., E Mississippi, 16 mi. (26 km.) W of Alabama border; pop. (1990c) 41,036; Meridian Community Coll. (1937); late 19th cent. carousel; site first settled 1831; incorp. 1860; developed into important railroad junction; during Civil War became Confederate military camp; temporary state ✻ 1863; destroyed by Gen. William T. Sherman's Union troops 1864, but rebuilt after the war.

3. City, ⊗ of Bosque co., cen. Texas; pop. (1990c) 1390.

Mé·ri·gnac \ˌmā-rē-ˈnyak\. Commune, Gironde dept., SW France; suburb of Bordeaux; 13th cent. dungeon (Tour de Veyrines).

Me·ri·kar·via \ˈmer-ē-ˌkär-vē-ä\. Coastal town, Turku ja Pori prov., SW Finland, S of Kristiina; pop. (1980c) 4168.

Merín, Laguna. See MIRIM, LAGOA.

Mer·i·on·eth·shire \ˌmer-ē-ˈä-nəth-ˌshir, -shər\ *or* **Mer·i·on·eth** \ˌmer-ē-ˈä-nəth\. Former county, W Wales; ⊗ Dolgellau; hilly region; rivers Dyfi, Dee, Mawddach. In ancient times when a center of Welsh resistance to the English, Harlech (*q.v.*) was its ✻; slate industry became important in 18th cent. See GWYNEDD.

Mer·i·weth·er \ˈmer-ē-ˌwe-thər\. County in W Georgia. See table at GEORGIA.

Merk·sem \ˈmerk-səm\. Former commune, N Belgium; a N suburb that became part of Antwerp 1983.

Mer·kus, Cape \ˈmər-kəs\. Cape on SW coast of New Britain, Bismarck Archipelago, Papua New Guinea, near Arawe (*q.v.*).

Mer·lo \ˈmer-lō\. Town, Buenos Aires prov., E Argentina, ab. 20 mi. (32 km.) W of the city of Buenos Aires; part of Buenos Aires met. area; pop. (1991p) 390,031.

Mer·oë \ˈmer-ō-ˌwē\ *also* **Mer·o·we** \-ō-ˌwē\. Ancient city, NE Africa, on E bank of the Nile, 17°N; replaced Napata as ✻ of Nubian kingdom of Cush c. 6th cent. B.C., and of the later kingdom of Meroë (Meroitic kingdom) lasting until ab. 350 A.D.; its extensive ruins (temples, palaces, necropolis) are near modern **Ka·bū·shī·yah** \kə-ˈbü-shē-ə\, Sudan. The kingdom included the **Isle of Meroë;** *anc.* **Meroe In·su·la** \ˈin-sü-lə, -syü-\, the region bet. the Nile, the Blue Nile, and the Atbara rivers, notable as a great center of commerce and caravan trade and also for the language (Meroitic) of its inhabitants, some of which is written in hieroglyphics, and about which little is known.

Me·ron, Mount \mā-ˈrōn\. Mountain, N Israel; 3692 ft. (1125 m.); highest mountain in Israel.

Merowe. 1. Ancient city, Egypt. See MEROË.

2. Town, Sudan. See MARAWI.

Mer·ri·am \ˈmer-ē-əm\. City, Johnson co., E Kansas, suburb SSW of Kansas City; pop. (1990c) 11,821.

Mer·rick \ˈmer-ik\. **1.** County in E cen. Nebraska. See table at NEBRASKA.

2. Unincorporated settlement, Nassau co., SE New York, on Long Island; pop. (1990c) 23,042.

3. Peak, Dumfries and Galloway region, S Scotland; ab. 2768 ft. (844 m.).

Mer·rill \ˈmer-əl\. City, ⊗ of Lincoln co., N Wisconsin, on Wisconsin River 15 mi. (24 km.) N of Wausau; pop. (1990c) 9860.

Mer·rill·ville \ˈmer-əl-ˌvil\. Town, Lake co., NW Indiana, S of Gary; pop. (1990c) 27,257.

Mer·ri·mac \ˈmer-ə-ˌmak\. Town, Essex co., NE Massachusetts, NE of Lowell; pop. (1990c) 5166.

Mer·ri·mack \ˈmer-ə-ˌmak\. **1.** River, S New Hampshire and NE Massachusetts; formed by junction of Pemigewasset and Winnipesaukee rivers at Franklin, New Hampshire, flows S across Massachusetts border, then turns NE and empties into the Atlantic Ocean at Newburyport, NE Massachusetts; 110 mi. (177 km.) long.

2. County in S cen. New Hampshire. See table at NEW HAMPSHIRE.

3. Town, Hillsborough co., S New Hampshire; pop. (1990c) 22,156; electronics.

Mer·ri·man Dam \'mer-ə-mən\. See UNITED STATES, *Dams and Reservoirs.*

Mer·ritt, Mount \'mer-ət\. Peak in Glacier National Park, NW Montana; 9954 ft. (3034 m.).

Merritt Island. Island off E coast of Brevard co., E cen. Florida; ab. 40 mi. (64 km.) long and 6 mi. (10 km.) wide at N end; 93 sq. mi. (241 sq. km.); separated from the mainland by the Indian River and from Canaveral Penin. by Banana River; site of John F. Kennedy Space Center.

Mers–al–Kabir. See MERS EL-KÉBIR.

Mer·se·burg \'mer-zə-ˌbu̇rk\. City, Saxony-Anhalt E cen. Germany, on Saale River 18 mi. (29 km.) W of Leipzig; pop. (1992e) 42,245; a center of the chemical industry; also produces leather, beer, cellulose; medieval cathedral; 15th cent. castle. Important frontier fortification in Carolingian times; made episcopal see 968; made city 1188; residence 1656–1738 of dukes of Sachsen-Merseburg; passed to Prussia 1815 through Congress of Vienna; heavily bombed in WWII; taken by Allies 1945.

Mers el–Ké·bir \'mers-el-kə-'bir\ *or* **Mers–al–Ka·bir** \-ȧl-kȧ-'bir\. Town, NW Algeria, on coast just W of Oran; formerly a French naval base; in naval battle here 1940 several French warships were destroyed by the British to prevent German capture of them; base turned over to Algeria 1968.

Mersen. See MEERSSEN.

Mer·sey \'mər-zē\. **1.** River, N Tasmania, Australia; flows generally N to Bass Strait at Devonport; ab. 65 mi. (105 km.) long.

2. River, NW England; rises in SE Greater Manchester, flows NW and W through Cheshire and Merseyside into the Irish Sea through a large estuary that forms the harbor of Liverpool; 70 mi. (113 km.) long. See MANCHESTER SHIP CANAL. Road and railway tunnels pass under the river from Birkenhead to Liverpool.

Mer·sey·side \'mər-zē-ˌsīd\. Metropolitan county, NW England, incl. Liverpool, St. Helens, and Wirral; estab. 1974; lost its administrative function 1986. See table at ENGLAND.

Mer·sin \mer-'sēn\ *also* **İçel** \'ē-chel\. Seaport city, ✻ of İçel prov., S Turkey in Asia, 40 mi. (64 km.) WSW of Adana; pop. (1990c) 422,357; exports chiefly agricultural produce.

Mer·thyr Tyd·fil \'mər-thər-'tid-ˌvil\. Town, Mid Glamorgan co., S Wales; pop. (1991p) 59,300; engineering; chemicals; English inventor Richard Trevithick's steam locomotive built here, and the first to be tried on rails, successfully hauled a train of 10 tons of iron and 70 men on the Merthyr Tydfil-Pontypridd tramway 1804.

Mer·ton \'mərt-ᵊn\. A borough of Greater London, SE England. See table at LONDON 4. Ruins of an Augustinian priory founded in 1115, and scene 1236 of meeting of great council of barons who passed the Statutes of Merton defining several aspects of English law.

Mert·zon \'mərt-sən\. Town, ⊗ of Irion co., W cen. Texas; pop. (1990c) 778.

Me·ru, Mount \'mā-rü\. Peak, N Tanzania, W of Kilimanjaro; 14,954 ft. (4558 m.).

Meru National Park. National park, cen. Kenya; ab. 380 sq. mi. (985 sq. km.); grassland; zebras and other wildlife.

Merv. See MARY.

Mer·ville \mer-'vēl\. Town, Nord dept., N France, on the Leie 18 mi. (29 km.) W of Lille.

Mer·we·de \'mer-ˌvā-də\. The lower Meuse River below the Waal, in Netherlands, until its junction with the Lek to form as its right branch the Nieuwe Maas River. The section of the Merwede from Dordrecht to the Lek is sometimes called the Noord. See OUDE MAAS.

Mer·win, Lake \'mər-win\. Lake, SW Washington, formed behind dam (**Merwin Dam**) across Lewis River.

Mer·zi·fon \ˌmer-zē-'fȯn\ *or* **Mar·si·van** \ˌmär-sē-'vän\. Town, Amasya prov., N Turkey in Asia, 25 mi. (40 km.) NW of the city of Amasya; pop. (1990p) 40,227; 15th cent. mosque.

Mer·zig \'mert-sik\. Commercial commune, Saarland, Germany, on the Saar 21 mi. (34 km.) NW of Saarbrücken; pop. (1980c) 29,714.

Me·sa \'mā-sə\. **1.** County in W Colorado. See table at COLORADO.

2. City, Maricopa co., SW cen. Arizona, 15 mi. (24 km.) E of Phoenix; pop. (1990c) 288,091; Mesa Community Coll. (1965); fighter-plane museum, Mesa Southwest Museum; founded 1878 by Mormons.

Me·sa·bi Range \mə-'sä-bē\. Range in St. Louis and Itasca cos., NE Minnesota, ab. 100 mi. (160 km.) long; av. height 200 to 500 ft. (60 to 150 m.); highest point ab. 2000 ft. (600 m.); notable for its deposits of iron ore.

Me·sa·gne \mā-'sä-nyā\. Commune, Brindisi prov., Puglia, SE Italy, 8 mi. (13 km.) SW of the seaport of Brindisi; pop. (1989c) 30,957.

Mesarás, Kólpos. See MESSARA, BAY OF.

Mesa Verde National Park \'mā-sə-'ver-dē, 'vərd\. See UNITED STATES, *National Parks.*

Mes·ca·le·ro Ridge \ˌmes-kə-'ler-ō\. Ridge in SE New Mexico, extending from cen. Lea co. NW along the Lea-Chaves cos. boundary.

Mesembria. See NESEBÛR.

Mesen. See MESSINES.

Meshed. See MASHHAD.

Me·sil·la \mā-'sē-yə\. Town, Dona Ana co., S New Mexico, on the Rio Grande near Las Cruces; pop. (1990c) 1975; founded after end of Mexican War, it was in Mexican territory until Gadsden Purchase 1853 made it part of U.S.; occupied by Confederates 1862; the site of a trial of outlaw Billy the Kid (William Bonney).

Me·so·amer·i·ca \ˌme-zō-ə-'mər-i-kə, ˌmē-, -sō-\. Pre-Spanish culture area extending from Mexico to N Central America.

Me·so·la \mā-'zō-lä\. Commune, Ferrara prov., Emilia-Romagna, N Italy, in Po Delta 34 mi. (55 km.) ENE of the commune of Ferrara; pop. (1981p) 8217.

Me·so·lón·gi·on \ˌme-sō-'lȯŋ-gē-ˌȯn\ *or* **Mis·so·lon·ghi** \ˌmē-sō-'lȯŋ-gē\. Commercial city, ✻ of Aetolia and Acarnania dept., W Central Greece region, Greece, on N shore of Gulf of Patras; pop. (1991p) 12,674; ships fish. During Greek War of Independence, withstood first Turkish siege 1822–23, but fell in the second 1825–26. The poet Lord Byron died here 1824.

Mes·o·po·ta·mia \ˌme-sə-pə-'tā-mē-ə, -myə\. The region in SW Asia bet. the Tigris and Euphrates rivers, extending from the mountains of Asia Minor on the N to the Persian Gulf on the S. First so called after the time of Alexander the Great; in the Bible known as Paddan-Aram (*Gen.* xxv. 20). Its N part called by Arabs Al Jazīrah (see JAZĪRAH, AL); in modern usage region includes 'Iraq 'Arabi and whole Tigris-Euphrates Valley.

History: The fertility and location of the region made it seat of early civilizations of Sumer, Akkad, Babylonia, and Assyria (*qq.v.*) c. 4000–625 B.C.; part of Persian Empire from 538 B.C. until conquered by Macedonian King Alexander the Great c. 331 B.C.; prior to Arab conquest in mid-7th cent. A.D., formed part of Parthian, Roman, and Neo-Persian (Sassanid) empires; Basra, Al-Kufa, and later, Baghdad the centers of Arab control; after Mongol invasion 1258, importance of region as political and commercial center declined; taken by Ottoman Turks 16th–17th cents.; regained strategic value for Great Britain in 19th cent., and became scene of British Mesopotamian campaign against Turks 1914–18; became British mandate 1920; kingdom of Iraq (*q.v.*) estab. 1921.

Mes·quite \mə-'skēt, me-\. City, Dallas co., NE Texas, E of the city of Dallas; pop. (1990c) 101,484; Eastfield Coll. (1970).

Messana. See MESSINA 2.

Mes·sa·pia \mə-ˈsā-pē-ə\. In ancient geography, that part of SE Italy inhabited by the Messapii; later applied also to Calabria.

Mes·sa·ra, Bay of \ˌme-sä-ˈrä\ *or Gk.* **Kól·pos Me·sa·rás** \ˈköl-pös-ˌme-sä-ˈräs\. Inlet of Mediterranean Sea on S coast of Crete, near cen. part.

Mes·se·ne \me-ˈsā-nā, mə-ˈsē-nē\. **1.** *or Gk.* **Mes·sí·ní** \me-ˈsē-nē\. Commune, Messenia dept., SW Peloponnese, Greece. Ancient city founded c. 369 B.C. on site chosen by Theban Gen. Epaminondas as new ✻ of Messenia and as a check against Sparta. Its acropolis was the peak **Itho·me** \i-ˈthō-mē\ 2630 ft. (802 m.), and on it was a temple of Zeus. **2.** Seaport, Sicily, Italy. See MESSINA 2.

Mes·se·nia \mə-ˈsē-nē-ə, -nyə\. **1.** A division of ancient Greece in SW Peloponnese; bounded on N by Elis, on N and NE by Arcadia, on E by Laconia and Gulf of Messenia, and on S and W by Ionian Sea. Its S part forms westernmost point of peninsulas of Peloponnesus, terminating in Cape Gallo. One of the most fertile districts of Greece.

History: Dorians, first colonizers, united with original inhabitants to form strong people, but unable to resist Sparta; partly overcome by Spartans in First Messenian War c. 735–715 B.C., and reduced to helots; completely subjugated after revolt led by Aristomenes in Second Messenian War 7th cent. B.C.; revolted again in 464 B.C. (Third Messenian War) but many Messenians forced to leave their land c. 460 B.C.; freed from Sparta after the battle of Leuctra c. 371 B.C., and city of Messene (*q.v.*) founded; later, a member of the Achaean League and after 146 B.C. under Romans.

2. Department of Greece. See table at GREECE.

Messenia, Gulf of *or* **Mes·si·nia·kós Kól·pos** \ˌme-sē-nyä-ˈkös-ˈköl-pös\; *formerly* **Gulf of Ko·ró·nē** \kö-ˈrō-nē\ *or* **Gulf of Ka·la·ma·ta** \ˌkä-lä-ˈmä-tä\. Inlet of the Mediterranean Sea on SW coast of Peloponnese, S Greece; its E shore formed by Laconia.

Mes·si·na \me-ˈsē-nä\. **1.** Province of Sicily, Italy. See table at ITALY.

2. *anc.* **Zan·cle** \ˈzaŋ-ˌklē\; *later* **Mes·sa·na** \mə-ˈsä-nə\ *also* **Mes·se·ne** \mə-ˈsē-nē\. Seaport, ✻ of Messina prov., NE Sicily, Italy, on Strait of Messina; pop. (1991p) 272,461; trade and transportation center; chemicals; viceregal and archiepiscopal palaces; cathedral (possibly Byzantine, rebuilt by Normans 12th cent. and restored after earthquake of 1908); university (1548). Birthplace of painter Antonello da Messina c. 1430.

History: Founded 8th cent. B.C. by Greek colonists from Khalkís; destroyed by Carthaginians 397 B.C.; opposing factions in the city called for support (264 B.C.) from both Carthage and Rome, and after arriving first and securing peace, the Carthaginians were attacked and driven from the city by Romans, beginning the First Punic War; after the war became free city allied with Rome; captured by Saracens 9th cent. A.D.; taken by Normans 11th cent.; later passed to Spanish rule; suffered from plague 1743; destroyed by earthquakes 1783 and 1908; to Italy 1860; in WWII suffered heavy bombing damage, was evacuation port in German withdrawal from Sicily, and was occupied by Allied forces Aug. 1943.

3. Town, NE Rep. of South Africa; near S bank of Limpopo River and on one of main railroad lines to Zimbabwe; pop. (1985c) 4852; site of historically large copper deposits.

Messina, Strait of; *anc.* **Sic·u·lum Fre·tum** \ˈsi-kyu̇-ləm-ˈfrē-təm\. Channel bet. S Italy and NE island of Sicily; 2.5 to 12 mi. (4 to 19 km.) wide.

Mes·sines \me-ˈsēn\ *or* **Me·sen** \ˈmā-zən\. Commune in West Flanders prov., NW Belgium, near Ieper (Ypres); pop. (1991c) 1048. **Messines Ridge** dominates the surrounding terrain; scene of fighting throughout WWI incl. battles 1914, in which Germans seized the ridge, and 1917, in which it was retaken by the British.

Messíní. See MESSENE 1.

Messiniakós Kólpos. See MESSENIA, GULF OF.

Mes·ta \me-ˈstä\ *or Turk.* **Ka·ra Su** \ˌkä-rä-ˈsü\ *or in Greece* **Nés·tos** \ˈnes-ˌtös\. River, SW Bulgaria and NE Greece; flows from W end of Rhodope Mts. SE into N Aegean Sea opp. the island of Thásos; ab. 150 mi. (240 km.) long.

Mes·tre \ˈmes-trā\. Former town bordering on Lagoon of Venice, now a part of Venice, Italy, with industrial activity and port facilities.

Mes·u·ra·do, Cape \ˌme-sü-ˈrä-dō\. Cape on the W coast of Liberia, near Monrovia.

Me·ta \ˈmā-tä\. **1.** River, Colombia; rises in W cen. Colombia, flows NE and E forming a section of Colombia-Venezuela boundary, and empties into Orinoco River on the Colombia-Venezuela boundary; ab. 621 mi. (999 km.) long. **2.** Department of cen. Colombia. See table at COLOMBIA.

Meta In·cog·ni·ta \ˈmē-tə-in-ˈkäg-nə-tə\. Peninsula, S Baffin I., SE Nunavut, Canada; lies bet. Frobisher Bay and Hudson Strait.

Met·air·ie \ˈme-tə-rē\. Unincorporated settlement, Jefferson parish, SE Louisiana; pop. (1990c) 149,428.

Met·a·mora \ˈme-tə-ˌmȯr-ə\. Village, Woodford co., N cen. Illinois, NE of Peoria; pop. (1990c) 2520; restored courthouse used by Abraham Lincoln.

Met·a·pon·tum \ˌme-tə-ˈpän-təm\. Ancient Greek city, Lucania, S Italy, on NW shore of Gulf of Tarentum; founded by colonists from Crotona and Sybaris c. 700 B.C.; philosopher and mathematician Pythagoras died here c. 500 B.C.; location of Carthaginian Gen. Hannibal's headquarters after battle of Cannae. Ruins include two temples and some of the walls.

Mét·a·scouac \ˌme-tə-ˈskwak, ˌmā-tá-skü-ˈák\ *also* **Grand Lake Métascouac.** Lake, S Quebec, Canada.

Me·tau·ro \mä-ˈtau̇-rō\; *anc.* **Me·tau·rus** \-ˈtȯr-əs\. Small river in E cen. Italy; flows E into Adriatic Sea N of Ancona; its banks were scene of battle of Metaurus in Second Punic War 207 B.C. in which Roman consuls completely defeated the Carthaginians under Hasdrubal, ending his brother Hannibal's hope of conquest of Rome.

Met·calfe \ˈmet-ˌkaf, -kəf\. County in S Kentucky. See table at KENTUCKY.

Meteor Crater *also* **Coon Butte** \ˈkün\. Depression, SE Coconino co., Arizona, 20 mi. (32 km.) W of Winslow; 4000 ft. (1219 m.) in diameter, 600 ft. (183 m.) deep; encircled by a ridge 100 to 150 ft. (30 to 46 m.) high, containing loose pieces of rock and sand; many fragments of meteoric iron are found in the region; believed to be of meteoric origin; est. age 50,000 years.

Met·how \ˈmet-ˌhau̇\. River, N Washington; flows S in Okanogan co. into Columbia River; ab. 60 mi. (97 km.) long.

Me·thu·en \mə-ˈthü-ən\. Town, Essex co., NE corner of Massachusetts, 9 mi. (15 km.) NE of Lowell; pop. (1990c) 39,990; settled ab. 1642; was part of Haverhill until 1725.

Meth·ven \ˈmeth-vən\. Village, Tayside region, Scotland, ab. 7 mi. (11 km.) NW of Perth; pop. (1981p) 944; castle 1 mi. (1.6 km.) E; scene of battle 1306 in which English defeated Scottish King Robert the Bruce.

Me·tin·ic \mə-ˈti-nik\. Island in Atlantic Ocean off S cen. Maine coast.

Metis. See METZ.

Met·la·kat·la *also* **Met·la·kaht·la** \ˌmet-lə-ˈkat-lə\. Unincorporated settlement on Annette I., SE Alaska, S of Ketchikan, Revillagigedo I.; pop. (1990c) 1407. Settled 1887 by refugee Indians from British Columbia.

Me·to·hi·ja \me-ˈtō-hē-yä\. District, S Yugoslavia, forming part of Kosovo prov.

Me·trop·o·lis \mə-ˈträ-pə-lis\. City, ⊗ of Massac co., S Illinois, on Ohio River NW of Paducah, Kentucky; pop. (1990c) 6734.

Met·ter \ˈme-tər\. City, ⊗ of Candler co., E cen. Georgia, 16 mi. (26 km.) W of Statesboro; pop. (1990c) 3707.

Mett·mann \ˈmet-ˌmän\. City, North Rhine-Westphalia, Germany, E of Düsseldorf; pop. (1980c) 36,676.

Metu \ˈme-tü\. Town, SW Ethiopia; pop. (1980c) 11,974.

Me·tuch·en \mə-ˈtə-chən\. Borough, Middlesex co., cen. New Jersey, 5 mi. (8 km.) WNW of Perth Amboy; pop. (1990c) 12,804.

Metz \ˈmets, *Fr.* ˈmes\; *anc.* **Di·vo·du·rum** \ˌdī-və-ˈdu̇r-əm, -ˈdyu̇r-\ *or* **Divodurum Me·di·o·mat·ri·cum** \ˌmē-dē-ō-ˈma-tri-kəm\; *later* **Me·di·o·mat·ri·ca** \-tri-kə\ *also* **Me·tis** \mē-təs\. City, Moselle dept., NE France, on Moselle River 178 mi. (286 km.) ENE of Paris; pop. (1990c) 123,920; former ✻ of Moselle dept.; shoes, canned fruits and vegetables; brewing; 13th–16th cent. cathedral; church with 4th cent. foundations (oldest in France). Birthplace of poet Paul Verlaine 1844.

History: Of Gallic origin; fortified by Romans; sacked by Huns under Attila in 5th cent. A.D.; under Franks became ✻ of Austrasia; at height of prosperity as free imperial city in 13th cent.; accepted Reformation 16th cent. and accepted French protection from Holy Roman Empire; with Toul and Verdun (Les Trois-Évêchés, the three bishoprics) taken by French 1552; formally ceded to France 1648 under Treaty of Westphalia; during Franco-Prussian War, following battles of Mars-la-Tour and Gravelotte (*qq.v.*) and a lengthy siege, scene of surrender of French forces under Marshal Achille-François Bazaine in 1870; under German rule 1871–1918; reverted to France after WWI; in WWII heavily damaged in severe fighting, captured by Allies 1944.

Meu·don \ˌmœ̄-ˈdōⁿ\. Commune, Hauts-de-Seine dept., N France; SW suburb of Paris on Seine River; pop. (1990c) 46,173. The Forest of Meudon (*Fr.* Forêt de Meudon) formerly surrounded a famous château built by Louis XIV; later the wood became a holiday destination for Parisians.

Meurthe \ˈmœrt\. River, Vosges and Meurthe-et-Moselle depts., NE France; rises in Vosges Mts., flows NW into the Moselle near Nancy; 105 mi. (169 km.) long.

Meurthe–et–Mo·selle \-ā-mō-ˈzel\. Department of NE France. See table at FRANCE.

Meuse \ˈmœ̄z, ˈmyüz, ˈmərz, ˈmu̇z\ *or Du.* **Maas** \ˈmäs\; *anc.* **Mo·sa** \ˈmō-zə\. **1.** River, W Europe; rises in Haute-Marne dept., NE France, flows N across E Belgium, forming a section of the NE boundary of Belgium; enters Netherlands and as the Maas curves W uniting at Gorinchem with the Waal, entering the North Sea through Hollandsch Diep; 580 mi. (933 km.) long. It receives the tributaries Sambre and Ourthe in Belgium and in the Netherlands the Rur from Germany. The chief towns on its banks are Verdun, Sedan, and Mézières in France, Namur and Liège in Belgium, and Maastricht in Netherlands; Rotterdam is on the Nieuwe Maas in the Rhine Delta. Its valley, esp. in NE France, was scene of much severe fighting in WWI; held by Germans until 1918; in WWII overrun by German armies in 1940 and in 1945 its course SW of Liège was almost reached by Germans in Battle of the Bulge.

2. Department of NE France. See table at FRANCE.

Meu·sel·witz \ˈmȯi-zəl-ˌvits\. City, Thuringia, E Germany, 22 mi. (35 km.) S of Leipzig; first mentioned 1139.

Mewar. See UDAIPUR 2.

Me·war and Southern Raj·pu·ta·na States \mā-ˈwär … ˌräj-pə-ˈtä-nə\. A former group of states, S Rajputana, India, incl. Udaipur, Banswara, Dungarpur, Partabgarh, and Kushalgarh.

Mew Island \ˈmyü\. Island in North Channel, off E coast of Northern Ireland, at entrance to Belfast Lough; lighthouse.

Mex·bor·ough \ˈmeks-bər-ō\. Town, South Yorkshire, N England; pop. (1981p) 15,683.

Mexcala. See BALSAS.

Me·xia \mə-ˈhā-ə—*sic*\. City, Limestone co., E cen. Texas, 37 mi. (60 km.) ENE of Waco; pop. (1990c) 6933.

Me·xi·a·na \ˌmā-shē-ˈá-nə\. Island in the mouth of the Amazon River, Brazil; N of Marajó I., off Pará state.

Mex·i·cali \ˌmek-sē-ˈkä-lē\. Town, ✻ of Baja California, NW Mexico, adjacent to Calexico, California; munic. pop. (1990p) 602,390; cotton processing; university (1957).

Mex·i·can Plateau. Great central plateau in Mexico bet. the Sierra Madre Occidental and the Sierra Madre Oriental; includes Anáhuac, the valley in which Mexico City is located; elev. 5000 to 9000 ft. (1525 to 2743 m.) in states of Puebla and México, sloping to 3700 ft. (1128 m.) at El Paso on U.S. border; center of pre-Columbian Aztec civilization.

Mex·i·co \ˈmek-si-ˌkō\ *or Span.* **Mé·ji·co** \ˈme-hē-ˌkō\; *in Mexico* **Mé·xi·co** \ˈme-hē-ˌkō\ *or officially* **Es·ta·dos Uni·dos Me·xi·ca·nos** \ā-ˈstä-t͟hōs-ü-ˈnē-t͟hōs-ˌme-hē-ˈkä-nōs\. Republic, S North America, bounded on N by U.S., on W and S by the Pacific, on SE by Guatemala, Belize, and Caribbean Sea, and on E by Gulf of Mexico; separated from U.S. on NE boundary by the Río Bravo (Rio Grande in U.S.); 759,530 sq. mi. or 1,967,183 sq. km. (incl. uninhabited islands 761,600 sq. mi. or 1,972,544 sq. km.); pop. (1993e) 89,995,000; ✻ Mexico City.

Physical features: NW part (peninsula of Baja California) separated from rest of Mexico by Gulf of California; in SE is peninsula of Yucatán. Narrowest part, Isthmus of Tehuantepec 130 mi. (209 km.).

Chief mountains: Sierra Madre (S extension of Rocky Mts. system) dividing into mountain chains on E (Oriental) and W (Occidental) sides of central plateau (see ANÁHUAC), which has av. alt. of 6000 ft. (1800 m.) and occupies over 50 percent of country; highest point Citlaltépetl (volcano) 18,700 ft. (5700 m.) in cen. Veracruz state; other peaks Popocatépetl (volcano) 17,887 ft. (5452 m.), Iztaccíhuatl 17,343 ft. (5286 m.), Nevado de Toluca (volcano) 14,406 ft. (4391 m.), Malinche 14,636 ft. (4461 m.), and Colima (volcano) 13,993 ft. (4265 m.).

Chief rivers: Pánuco, Grijalva, Balsas, Santiago, Usumacinta, Conchos, Río Bravo (Rio Grande).

Chief lakes: Chapala, Cuitzeo, Pátzcuaro, Texcoco.

Chief products: Cotton, wheat, corn, beans, tomatoes, coffee, sugarcane, fruit, timber; livestock raising, fishing; silver, lead, zinc, copper, iron ore, sulfur, oil, gold, natural gas; manufacturing: textiles, steel, components for U.S. industries, motor vehicles; tourism.

Chief cities: Mexico City, Guadalajara, Netzahualcóyotl, Monterrey, Puebla, Ciudad Juárez, Léon.

Political divisions: Divided into the following 31 states and one federal district, (for pronunciation of their names, see their individual entries):

NAME	AREA (sq. mi.)	AREA (sq. km.)	POP. (1990c)	CAPITAL
Federal District	579	1,500	8,235,744	Mexico City
States				
Aguascalientes	2,158	5,589	719,659	Aguascalientes
Baja California[1]	27,071	70,114	1,660,855	Mexicali
Baja California Sur	28,447	73,678	317,764	La Paz
Campeche	21,666	56,115	535,185	Campeche
Chiapas	28,528	73,888	3,210,496	Tuxtla Gutiérrez
Chihuahua	95,400	247,086	2,441,873	Chihuahua
Coahuila	58,522	151,572	1,972,340	Saltillo
Colima	2,106	5,454	428,510	Colima
Durango	46,196	119,648	1,349,378	Durango
Guanajuato	11,810	30,588	3,982,593	Guanajuato
Guerrero	24,631	63,794	2,620,637	Chilpancingo
Hidalgo	8,103	20,987	1,888,366	Pachuca
Jalisco	30,941	80,137	5,302,689	Guadalajara
México	8,286	21,461	9,815,795	Toluca
Michoacán	23,114	59,865	3,548,199	Morelia
Morelos	1,908	4,942	1,195,059	Cuernavaca
Nayarit	10,664	27,620	824,543	Tepic
Nuevo León	24,925	64,556	3,098,736	Monterrey
Oaxaca	36,820	95,364	3,019,560	Oaxaca
Puebla	13,096	33,919	4,126,101	Puebla
Querétaro	4,544	11,769	1,051,235	Querétaro
Quintana Roo	16,228	42,030	493,277	Chetumal
San Luis Potosí	24,266	62,849	2,003,187	San Luis Potosí
Sinaloa	22,429	58,091	2,204,054	Culiacán
Sonora	71,403	184,934	1,823,606	Hermosillo
Tabasco	9,522	24,662	1,501,744	Villahermosa
Tamaulipas	30,822	79,829	2,249,581	Ciudad Victoria
Tlaxcala	1,511	3,913	761,277	Tlaxcala
Veracruz	28,114	72,815	6,228,239	Jalapa
Yucatán	16,749	43,380	1,362,940	Mérida
Zacatecas	28,973	75,040	1,276,323	Zacatecas

[1] Called Baja California Norte 1974–91.

History: Several pre-Columbian civilizations thrived here, incl. the Olmec, Maya, Toltec, and Aztec; at time of European contact, cen. and S part, from Gulf to Pacific, controlled

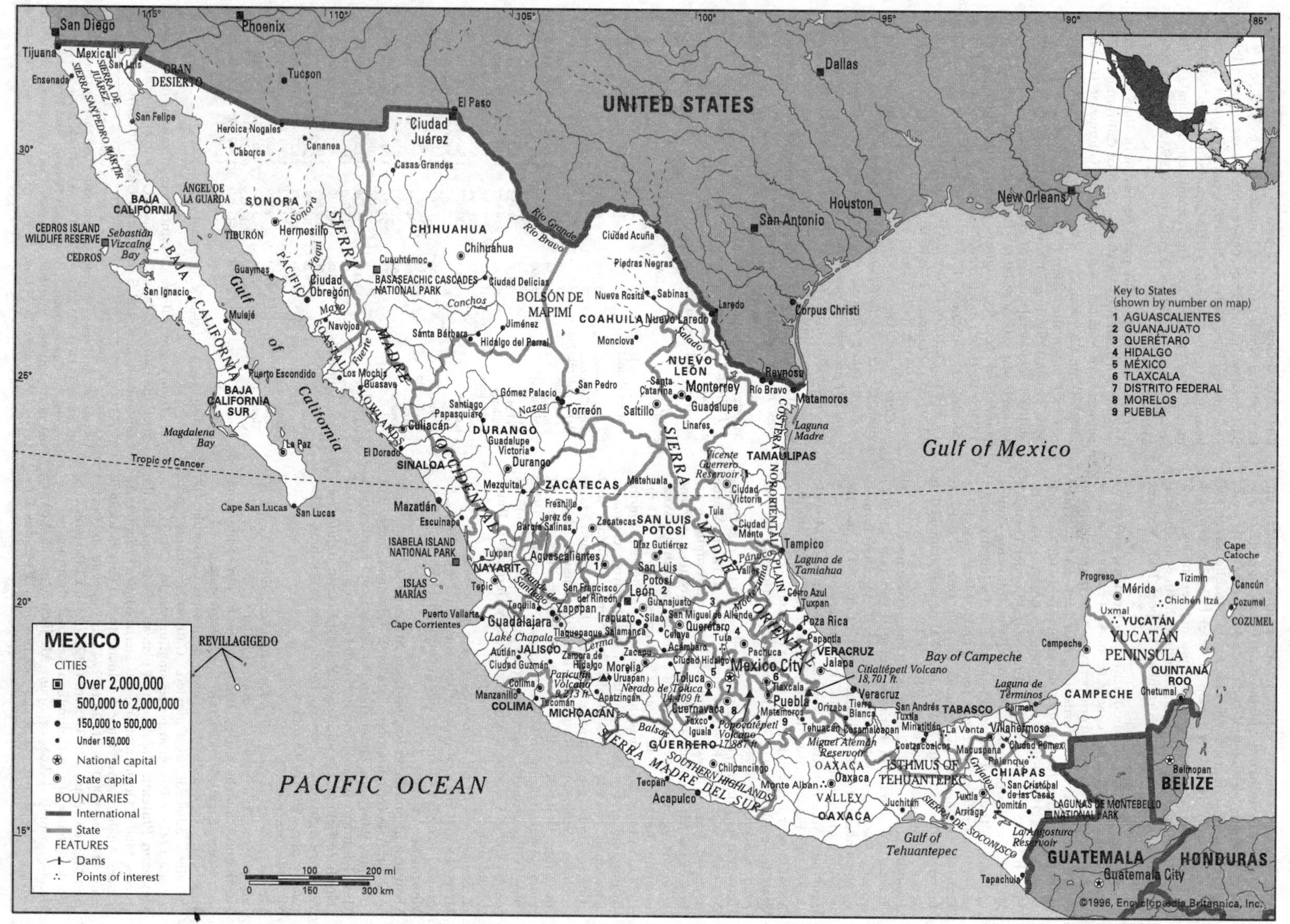
MEXICO
CITIES
Over 2,000,000
500,000 to 2,000,000
150,000 to 500,000
Under 150,000
National capital
State capital
BOUNDARIES
International
State
FEATURES
Dams
Points of interest
Key to States
(shown by number on map)
1 AGUASCALIENTES
2 GUANAJUATO
3 QUERÉTARO
4 HIDALGO
5 MÉXICO
6 TLAXCALA
7 DISTRITO FEDERAL
8 MORELOS
9 PUEBLA
UNITED STATES
Gulf of Mexico
PACIFIC OCEAN
Gulf of California
Bay of Campeche
Gulf of Tehuantepec
Tropic of Cancer
GUATEMALA
BELIZE
HONDURAS
YUCATÁN PENINSULA
SIERRA MADRE OCCIDENTAL
SIERRA MADRE ORIENTAL
SIERRA MADRE DEL SUR
SOUTHERN HIGHLANDS
ISTHMUS OF TEHUANTEPEC
BOLSÓN DE MAPIMÍ
GRAN DESIERTO
REVILLAGIGEDO
ISLAS MARÍAS
CEDROS ISLAND WILDLIFE RESERVE
BASASEACHIC CASCADES NATIONAL PARK
ISABELA ISLAND NATIONAL PARK
LAGUNAS DE MONTEBELLO NATIONAL PARK
BAJA CALIFORNIA
BAJA CALIFORNIA SUR
SONORA
CHIHUAHUA
COAHUILA
NUEVO LEÓN
TAMAULIPAS
SINALOA
DURANGO
ZACATECAS
SAN LUIS POTOSÍ
NAYARIT
JALISCO
COLIMA
MICHOACÁN
GUERRERO
OAXACA
VERACRUZ
TABASCO
CHIAPAS
CAMPECHE
YUCATÁN
QUINTANA ROO
Mexico City
Guadalajara
Monterrey
Tijuana
Mexicali
Ciudad Juárez
Puebla
León
Acapulco
Mérida
Cancún
Veracruz
Tampico
Chihuahua
Hermosillo
Mazatlán
La Paz
Oaxaca
Citlaltépetl Volcano 18,701 ft.
Popocatépetl Volcano 17,887 ft.
Nevado de Toluca 14,409 ft.
Paricutín Volcano 9,213 ft.
San Diego
Phoenix
Tucson
El Paso
San Antonio
Houston
Dallas
New Orleans
Corpus Christi
Río Grande
Río Bravo
0 100 200 mi
0 150 300 km
©1996, Encyclopædia Britannica, Inc.

by Aztecs, whose ✱, Tenochtitlán (*q.v.*), was founded 1325 A.D.; Yucatán (*q.v.*), home of Mayas, in decline by 15th cent.; Yucatán discovered by Spanish explorer Fernández de Córdoba 1517, and coast (to site of Veracruz) by Spanish explorer Juan de Grijalba 1518; Veracruz founded 1519 by Hernán Cortés, who conquered the country 1519–21 and established Mexico City, which became center of viceroyalty of New Spain; interior gradually subdued and Spanish authority extended N to California in 16th cent., though Texas and California not effectively occupied by Spanish until 18th cent. First rebellion against Spain 1810 a failure; after successful 2d revolt 1821, ruled by Emperor Agustín de Iturbide 1822–23; joined by Guatemala and other Central American states for brief period during 1822–23 (see CENTRAL AMERICA); established a federal republic 1824; defeated by Republic of Texas in its war for independence 1836; land disputes with U.S. led to war 1846–48; ceded to U.S. Upper California, New Mexico, and N parts of Mexico by Treaty of Guadalupe Hidalgo 1848 and Gadsden Purchase 1853; liberal reforms to the constitution led to civil war 1858–61; concerns over foreign debt repayment precipitated invasions by Spain, Great Britain, and France 1861; ruled by Emperor Maximilian who was supported by France 1864–67; when French support was withdrawn, republicans seized control again 1867; under dictatorship 1876–1911 of President Porfirio Díaz, whose overthrow inaugurated period of revolution; adopted revised constitution 1917; in policies of nationalization of resources, expropriation of church property and secularization of education, and subdivision of great estates, faced opposition of U.S. and Great Britain, Roman Catholicism, and Mexican Conservatives, respectively; foreign petroleum interests expropriated and oil industry nationalized 1938; declared war on Axis powers 1942; founding member of UN (1945) and Organization of American States (1948); resolved border dispute (see CHAMIZAL) with U.S. by treaty in 1960s; signed North American Free Trade Agreement with Canada and U.S. 1992, ratified by all three nations 1993.

Mexico \ˈmek-si-ˌkō\. **1.** Town, Oxford co., W Maine, 36 mi. (58 km.) NNW of Lewiston; pop. (1990c) 3344.

2. City, ⊗ of Audrain co., NE cen. Missouri, 29 mi. (47 km.) ENE of Columbia; pop. (1990c) 11,290; historically important production of clay products.

3. *or Span.* \ˈme-hē-ˌkō\. Municipality, Luzon, Philippines, on a tributary of the Pampanga River ab. 3 mi. (5 km.) NE of San Fernando; pop. (1980c) 53,491.

Mé·xi·co \ˈme-hē-ˌkō\. State of cen. Mexico. See table at MEXICO.

Mexico, Gulf of. Gulf on SE coast of North America; bounded on N by U.S., on E by U.S., Cuba, and Mexico, on S by Mexico, on W by Mexico and U.S.; ab. 600,000 sq. mi. (1,500,000 sq. km.); extends ab. 1000 mi. (1600 km.) E to W and ab. 775 mi. (1250 km.) N to S; max. depth 12,245 ft. (3732 m.) in SW cen. part; connects with Atlantic Ocean through Straits of Florida, and with Caribbean Sea through Strait of Yucatán; important source of fish, offshore oil, and natural gas.

Mexico, Valley of. Subdivision of the valley of Anáhuac (*q.v.*) in cen. Mexico; a vast oval basin ab. 50 mi. (80 km.) long by 40 mi. (65 km.) wide; total area 1758 sq. mi. (4553 sq. km.); mean elev. 7470 ft. (2277 m.).

Mexico City *or* **Mexico** *or officially* **Ciu·dad de Mé·xi·co, D.F.** \ˌsyü-ˈthäth-thā-ˈme-hē-ˌkō\. City, ✱ of Mexico and of the Federal District (Distrito Federal), located near S end of great central plateau and ab. 200 mi. (320 km.) WNW of Veracruz on the Gulf of Mexico; a few miles W of Lake Texcoco and NW of the Chalco and Xochimilco lakes; pop. (1990c) 9,815,795; alt. 7347 ft. (2239 m.); produces chemicals, cement; tourism. Regularly laid out with cathedral, national palace, and munic. building around a large square (Plaza Mayor) forming the political and commercial center. Has many churches, monasteries, museums; several universities and colleges incl. National Autonomous Univ. of Mexico (1551).

History: Before Spanish invasion, Mexico City was the site of the Aztec ✱ (Tenochtitlán); captured and razed by Spaniards under Hernán Cortés 1521; seat of the viceroyalty of New Spain throughout colonial period; captured by Mexican revolutionaries under Gen. Agustín de Iturbide 1821; captured by U.S. Gen. Winfield Scott 1847 in the Mexican War; held by the French 1863–67; greatly improved esp. during the presidency of Porfirio Díaz 1876–80, 1884–1911; site of Summer Olympic Games 1968; struck by devastating earthquake 1985; met. area experienced tremendous population growth in 20th cent.

Mey·ca·ua·yan \ˌmā-ˌkä-wä-ˈyän\. Municipality, Luzon, Philippines, on Manila-Dagupan railroad line 10 mi. (16 km.) N of Manila; pop. (1980c) 83,579.

Mey·ers·dale \ˈmī-ərz-ˌdāl\. Borough, Somerset co., S Pennsylvania, 35 mi. (56 km.) S of Johnstown; pop. (1990c) 2518.

Meyisti. See KASTELLÓRIZON.

Mey·ma·neh *or* **Mai·mā·na** \mā-ˈmä-nə\. Town, N Afghanistan; pop. (1988e) 45,100.

Mey·rin \me-ˈreⁿ\. Commune, Geneva canton, Switzerland; pop. (1989c) 20,165.

Mèze \ˈmez\. Seaport, Hérault dept., S France; near shore of the Étang de Thau opp. Sète.

Me·zen' *or* **Me·zen** \ˈmye-zənʸ\. **1.** River, N Russia in Europe; rises in W Komi Rep. and flows generally NW through cen. Arkhangel'sk Oblast into **Me·zen·ska·ya Gu·ba** \ˈmye-zənʸ-skə-yə-gü-ˈbä\ *or Eng.* **Gulf of Mezen** \ˈmāz-ᵊn\, an arm (ab. 50 mi. or 80 km. long) of the E White Sea; ab. 533 mi. (858 km.) long.

2. Town, Arkhangel'sk Oblast, N Russia in Europe, on right bank of Mezen' River near its mouth, ab. 130 mi. (210 km.) NE of city of Arkhangel'sk; a fishing and trading port.

Mé·zenc, Mount \mā-ˈzeⁿk\. Volcanic peak in the Cévennes Mts., S France, in Haute-Loire dept. near Ardèche border; 5755 ft. (1754 m.).

Mezenskaya Guba. See MEZEN' 1.

Mezh·du·re·chensk \ˌmezh-du̇r-ə-ˈchensk\. Town, Kemerovo Oblast, S Russia in Asia, ab. 140 mi. (225 km.) SE of the city of Kemerovo; pop. (1992e) 108,000.

Mézières, Charleville–. See CHARLEVILLE-MÉZIÈRES.

Mfumbiro. See VIRUNGA.

Mge·ni \əm-ˈgā-nē\ *or* **Um·ge·ni** \u̇m-\. River, S KwaZulu-Natal prov., E Rep. of South Africa; flows SE to Indian Ocean just N of Durban; ab. 100 mi. (160 km.) long; noted for its waterfall 311 ft. (95 m.) high at Howick, NW of Pietermaritzburg.

Mhow \ˈmau̇\. Town, Madhya Pradesh, cen. India, 13 mi. (21 km.) SSW of Indore; pop. with cantonment (1991p) 74,852.

Mia·gao \myä-ˈgau̇\. Municipality, S Panay, Philippines, on Iloilo Strait 22 mi. (35 km.) WSW of City of Iloilo; pop. (1980c) 45,816.

Mi·ami \mī-ˈa-mē\. **1.** *formerly* **Great Miami.** River, W Ohio; rises in Indian Lake, Logan co., and flows S into the Ohio River at the SW extremity of Ohio; 160 mi. (257 km.) long.

2. Name of counties in three states of the U.S. See tables at INDIANA, KANSAS, OHIO.

3. City, ⊗ of Miami-Dade co., SE Florida, on Biscayne Bay; southernmost large city in the continental U.S. at 25°46′N (see KEY WEST); pop. (1990c) 358,548; alt. 11 ft. (3 m.); center of a major winter resort area; a gateway to Central and South America; port handling cargo containers and world's largest number of cruise ship passengers; banking center; has a beach 7 mi. (11 km.) long; Florida Memorial Coll. (1879), Barry Univ. (1940), Miami Christian Univ. (1946), Miami-Dade Community Coll. (1960), St. Thomas Univ. (1961), Florida International Univ. (1965); occasionally hit by hurricanes incl. an esp. severe one in 1926. Permanent settlement began around Army post c. 1836 ff.; incorp. and reached by railroad 1896; major development as resort and residential city as well as transportation and commercial center after WWII; large influx of Cuban immigrants since 1959 with more recent immigration of Haitians and people from other Central and South American countries.

4. City, ⊗ of Ottawa co., NE corner of Oklahoma, 66 mi. (106 km.) E of Bartlesville; pop. (1990c) 13,142; Northeastern Oklahoma A&M Coll. (1919).

5. City, ⊗ of Roberts co., NW Texas; pop. (1990c) 675.

Miami Beach. City, Miami-Dade co., SE Florida, on island across Biscayne Bay from Miami; pop. (1990c) 92,639; popular resort and tourist center, connected with Miami by several causeways; art deco district; city incorp. 1915.

Mi·ami–Dade \ mī-ˌa-mē-ˈdād \. County in SE Florida. See table at FLORIDA.

Mi·am·is·burg \ mī-ˈa-mēz-ˌbərg \. City, Montgomery co., SW Ohio, on Miami River 10 mi. (16 km.) S of Dayton; pop. (1990c) 17,834; large American Indian burial mound.

Miami Shores. Village, Miami-Dade co., SE Florida, on Biscayne Bay 9 mi. (15 km.) N of Miami; pop. (1990c) 10,084.

Miami Springs. City, Miami-Dade co., SE Florida, NW suburb of Miami; pop. (1990c) 13,268.

Mī·ā·neh \ ˌmē-ä-ˈnā \. Town, East Azerbaijan, NW Iran, 90 mi. (145 km.) SE of Tabrīz; pop. (1986c) 65,959.

Mi·ang·as \ mē-ˈäŋ-äs \ *also* **Pal·mas** \ ˈpäl-mäs \. Small island, Indonesia, in the Malay Archipelago, ab. 60 mi. (97 km.) SE of Cape San Agustin, Mindanao; N of Talaud Is. and nearest point of Indonesia to Philippines.

Mi·a·ni *also* **Mee·a·nee** \ mē-ˈä-nē \. Village, cen. Sind, Pakistan, 6 mi. (10 km.) N of Hyderabad; scene of victory 1843 of Sir Charles Napier with small British force over mirs of Sind, which led to conquest and annexation of Sind.

Mi·an·us \ mī-ˈa-nəs \. Subdivision of town of Greenwich, Connecticut. See GREENWICH 1.

Mi·an·wa·li \ mē-ˈän-vä-lē \. Town, Punjab, Pakistan, on the Indus 105 mi. (169 km.) S of Peshawar; pop. (1981c) 59,159.

Mi·ca Peak \ ˈmī-kə \. Mountain in Kootenai co., N Idaho; 5250 ft. (1600 m.).

Mi Chai. See NONG KHAI.

Mi·cha·lov·ce \ ˈmē-ka̱-ˌlau̇t-se \ *or Hung.* **Nagy·mi·hály** \ ˈnäj-ˈmē-ˌhī \. Town, E Slovakia, 29 mi. (47 km.) E of Košice; pop. (1980p) 29,765.

Mich·i·gam·me \ ˌmi-shə-ˈga-mē, -ˈgä- \. River, W Upper Penin. of Michigan; rises in Baraga co., flows E and S until it joins the Brule to form the Menominee River on the Wisconsin-Michigan boundary.

Mich·i·gan \ ˈmi-shi-gən \. A north central state of U.S.A.; the Upper Penin. is bounded on N by Lake Superior, on E by Whitefish Bay and St. Marys River, on S by Lake Huron and Lake Michigan, and on SW and W by Wisconsin; the Lower Penin. is bounded on N by Lake Michigan and Lake Huron, on E by Lake Huron, Canadian prov. of Ontario, Lake St. Clair, and Lake Erie, on S by Ohio and Indiana, and on W by Lake Michigan; 23d state in area, 58,527 sq. mi. or 151,585 sq. km. (land area 56,954 sq. mi. or 147,511 sq. km.); in addition to this area has also 38,575 sq. mi. (99,909 sq. km.) of water of the Great Lakes; 8th state in population, (1990c) 9,295,297; ✻ Lansing; 26th state admitted to Union (1837). See table of states at UNITED STATES.

Nicknames: Wolverine State; Great Lakes State.

State flower: Apple blossom.

Motto: Si Quaeris Peninsulam Amoenam Circumspice (If You Seek a Beautiful Peninsula, Look Around You).

Rivers: Montreal, Brule, and Menominee, forming W and SW boundary of Upper Penin.; St. Clair, separating Michigan from Ontario bet. Lake Huron and Lake St. Clair; Detroit, separating Michigan from Ontario bet. Lake St. Clair and Lake Erie.

Chief products: Dairy products, fruit; iron ore, limestone, copper, natural gas; motor vehicles and parts (historically the primary center of the U.S. auto industry); tourism.

Chief cities: Detroit, Grand Rapids, Warren, Flint, Lansing, Sterling Heights, Ann Arbor, Livonia.

Political divisions: Divided into the following 83 counties (for pronunciation of their names, see their individual entries):

NAME	AREA[1] (sq. mi.)	AREA[1] (sq. km.)	POP. (1990c)	CO. SEAT
Alcona	670	1,735	10,145	Harrisville
Alger	905	2,344	8,972	Munising
Allegan	826	2,139	90,509	Allegan
Alpena	565	1,463	30,605	Alpena
Antrim	476	1,233	18,185	Bellaire
Arenac	367	951	14,931	Standish
Baraga	901	2,334	7,954	L'Anse
Barry	554	1,435	50,057	Hastings
Bay	447	1,158	111,723	Bay City
Benzie	316	818	12,200	Beulah
Berrien	580	1,502	161,378	St. Joseph
Branch	506	1,311	41,502	Coldwater
Calhoun	709	1,836	135,982	Marshall
Cass	491	1,272	49,477	Cassopolis
Charlevoix[2]	414	1,072	21,468	Charlevoix
Cheboygan	721	1,867	21,398	Cheboygan
Chippewa[2]	1,590	4,118	34,604	Sault Ste. Marie
Clare	571	1,479	24,952	Harrison
Clinton	572	1,481	57,883	St. Johns
Crawford	561	1,453	12,260	Grayling
Delta[2]	1,177	3,048	37,780	Escanaba
Dickinson	757	1,961	26,831	Iron Mountain
Eaton	577	1,494	92,879	Charlotte
Emmet	461	1,194	25,040	Petoskey
Genesee	642	1,663	430,459	Flint
Gladwin	503	1,303	21,896	Gladwin
Gogebic	1,107	2,867	18,052	Bessemer
Grand Traverse	462	1,197	64,273	Traverse City
Gratiot	566	1,466	38,982	Ithaca
Hillsdale	600	1,554	43,431	Hillsdale
Houghton	1,017	2,634	35,446	Houghton
Huron	819	2,121	34,951	Bad Axe
Ingham	559	1,448	281,912	Mason
Ionia	575	1,489	57,024	Ionia
Iosco	544	1,409	30,209	Tawas City
Iron	1,171	3,033	13,175	Crystal Falls
Isabella	572	1,481	54,624	Mount Pleasant
Jackson	698	1,808	149,756	Jackson
Kalamazoo	562	1,456	223,411	Kalamazoo
Kalkaska	566	1,466	13,497	Kalkaska
Kent	857	2,220	500,631	Grand Rapids
Keweenaw[3]	528	1,368	1,701	Eagle River
Lake	571	1,479	8,583	Baldwin
Lapeer	658	1,704	74,768	Lapeer
Leelanau[2]	345	894	16,527	Leland
Lenawee	753	1,950	91,476	Adrian
Livingston	572	1,481	115,645	Howell
Luce	906	2,347	5,763	Newberry
Mackinac[2]	1,014	2,626	10,674	St. Ignace
Macomb	480	1,243	717,400	Mount Clemens
Manistee	552	1,430	21,265	Manistee
Marquette	1,829	4,737	70,887	Marquette
Mason	490	1,269	25,537	Ludingston
Mecosta	560	1,450	37,308	Big Rapids
Menominee	1,038	2,688	24,920	Menominee
Midland	520	1,347	75,651	Midland
Missaukee	565	1,463	12,147	Lake City
Monroe	557	1,443	133,600	Monroe
Montcalm	712	1,844	53,059	Stanton
Montmorency	555	1,437	8,936	Atlanta
Muskegon	501	1,298	158,983	Muskegon
Newaygo	849	2,199	38,202	White Cloud
Oakland	867	2,246	1,083,592	Pontiac
Oceana	536	1,388	22,454	Hart
Ogemaw	571	1,479	18,681	West Branch
Ontonagon	1,316	3,408	8,854	Ontonagon
Osceola	581	1,505	20,146	Reed City
Oscoda	563	1,458	7,842	Mio
Otsego	527	1,365	17,957	Gaylord
Ottawa	563	1,458	187,768	Grand Haven
Presque Isle	648	1,678	13,743	Rogers City
Roscommon	521	1,349	19,776	Roscommon
Saginaw	814	2,108	211,946	Saginaw
Saint Clair	723	1,873	145,607	Port Huron
Saint Joseph	506	1,311	58,913	Centerville
Sanilac	961	2,489	39,928	Sandusky
Schoolcraft	1,181	3,059	8,302	Manistique
Shiawassee	540	1,399	69,770	Corunna
Tuscola	815	2,111	55,498	Caro
Van Buren	603	1,562	70,060	Paw Paw
Washtenaw	711	1,841	282,937	Ann Arbor
Wayne	605	1,567	2,111,687	Detroit
Wexford	559	1,448	26,360	Cadillac

[1] Area = land area.
[2] Includes islands.
[3] Includes Isle Royale, off Canadian shore NW of county proper.

History: Inhabited esp. by Algonquian tribes prior to arrival of Europeans; first European to visit the region was French adventurer Étienne Brulé in early 17th cent.; first settled at Sault Sainte Marie by French explorer and missionary Père Marquette 1668; military post of Detroit (*q.v.*) founded 1701; ceded to England 1763 following French and Indian

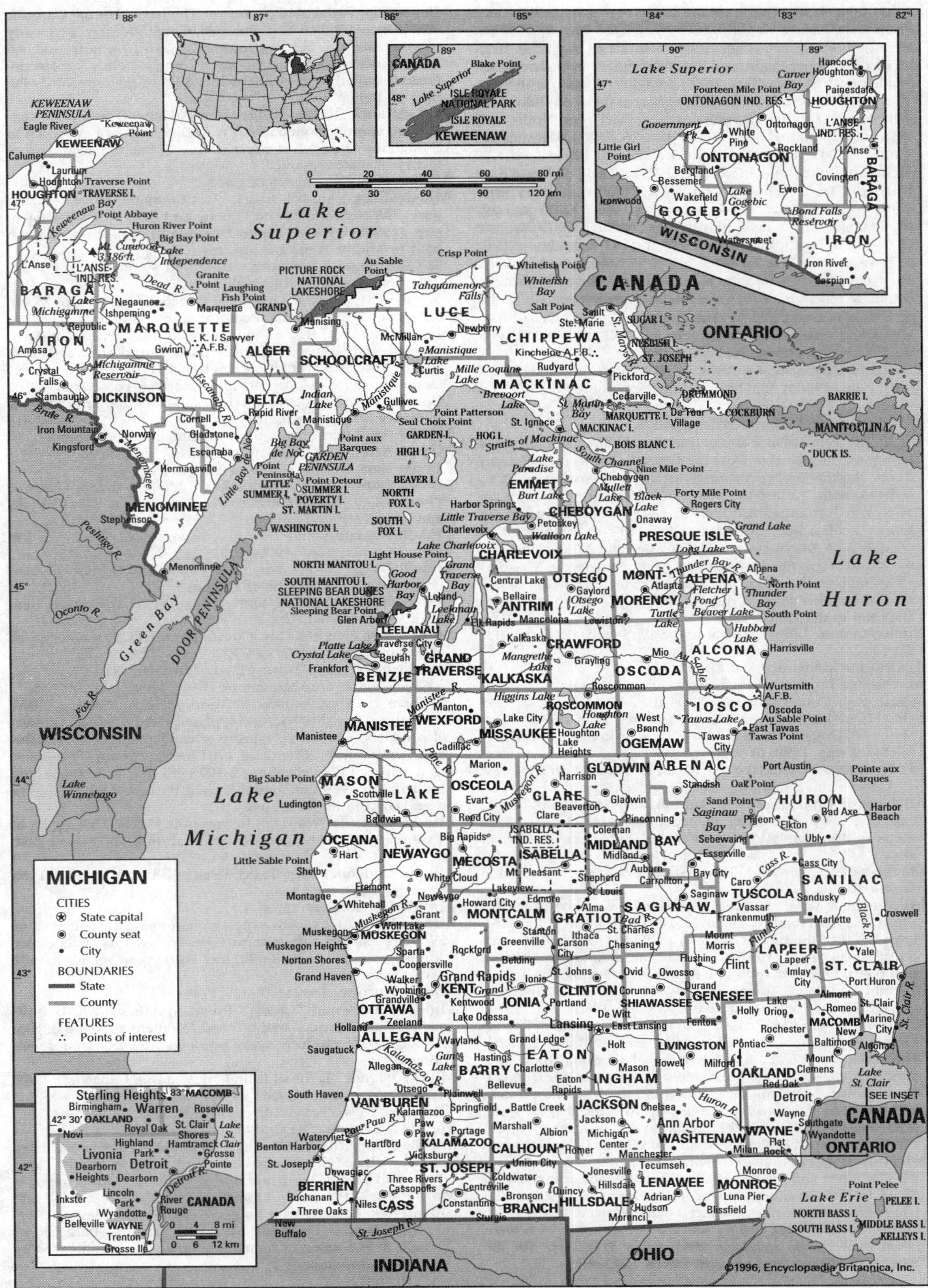

MICHIGAN
CITIES
State capital
County seat
City
BOUNDARIES
State
County
FEATURES
Points of interest
0 20 40 60 80 mi
0 30 60 90 120 km
Lake Superior
Lake Michigan
Lake Huron
Lake Erie
Lake St. Clair
CANADA
ONTARIO
WISCONSIN
INDIANA
OHIO
ISLE ROYALE NATIONAL PARK
ISLE ROYALE
KEWEENAW
Blake Point
KEWEENAW PENINSULA
Eagle River
Keweenaw Point
Calumet
Laurium
Houghton
Traverse Point
HOUGHTON
TRAVERSE I.
Keweenaw Bay
Point Abbaye
Huron River Point
Big Bay Point
Mt. Curwood 3,186 ft.
Lake Independence
L'Anse
L'ANSE IND. RES.
BARAGA
Dead R.
Granite Point
Laughing Fish Point
Negaunee
Ishpeming
Marquette
GRAND I.
Lake Michigamme
Republic
MARQUETTE
IRON
Amasa
K. I. Sawyer A.F.B.
Gwinn
Crystal Falls
Michigamme Reservoir
Stambaugh
DICKINSON
Brule R.
Iron Mountain
Kingsford
Norway
Cornell
Gladstone
Escanaba
Escanaba R.
Hermansville
Menominee R.
MENOMINEE
Stephenson
Menominee
Peshtigo R.
Oconto R.
Green Bay
DOOR PENINSULA
Fox R.
Lake Winnebago
PICTURE ROCK NATIONAL LAKESHORE
Au Sable Point
Munising
ALGER
DELTA
Rapid River
Indian Lake
Manistique
Big Bay de Noc
Little Bay de Noc
Point aux Barques
GARDEN PENINSULA
Point Peninsula
LITTLE SUMMER I.
SUMMER I.
Point Detour
POVERTY I.
ST. MARTIN I.
WASHINGTON I.
SCHOOLCRAFT
Manistique R.
Manistique Lake
Curtis
Gulliver
McMillan
LUCE
Newberry
Tahquamenon Falls
Crisp Point
Whitefish Point
Whitefish Bay
Salt Point
Sault Ste. Marie
CHIPPEWA
Kincheloe A.F.B.
Rudyard
Mille Coquins Lake
MACKINAC
Brevoort Lake
St. Martin Bay
St. Ignace
Point Patterson
Seul Choix Point
GARDEN I.
HOG I.
HIGH I.
Straits of Mackinac
MACKINAC I.
BOIS BLANC I.
SUGAR I.
NEEBISH I.
ST. JOSEPH I.
St. Marys R.
Pickford
Cedarville
DRUMMOND I.
MARQUETTE I.
De Tour Village
COCKBURN I.
BARRIE I.
MANITOULIN I.
DUCK IS.
South Channel
Nine Mile Point
Lake Paradise
Cheboygan
Mullett Lake
Black Lake
Forty Mile Point
Rogers City
BEAVER I.
NORTH FOX I.
SOUTH FOX I.
EMMET
Burt Lake
Harbor Springs
Little Traverse Bay
Petoskey
CHEBOYGAN
Onaway
Charlevoix
Walloon Lake
Lake Charlevoix
PRESQUE ISLE
Grand Lake
Long Lake
CHARLEVOIX
Light House Point
NORTH MANITOU I.
SOUTH MANITOU I.
SLEEPING BEAR DUNES NATIONAL LAKESHORE
Sleeping Bear Point
Glen Arbor
Good Harbor Bay
Grand Traverse Bay
Leland
Central Lake
Bellaire
Leelanau Lake
Elk Rapids
ANTRIM
Mancelona
OTSEGO
Gaylord
Otsego Lake
MONTMORENCY
Atlanta
Thunder Bay R.
ALPENA
Alpena
Fletcher Pond
Thunder Bay
North Point
South Point
Turtle Lake
Beaver Lake
Lewiston
LEELANAU
Traverse City
Platte Lake
Crystal Lake
Beulah
Frankfort
BENZIE
GRAND TRAVERSE
Kalkaska
Mangrethe Lake
KALKASKA
CRAWFORD
Grayling
Mio
OSCODA
Au Sable R.
ALCONA
Hubbard Lake
Harrisville
Manistee R.
Manton
WEXFORD
Cadillac
MANISTEE
Manistee
Higgins Lake
Lake City
MISSAUKEE
Roscommon
ROSCOMMON
Houghton Lake
Houghton Lake Heights
West Branch
OGEMAW
IOSCO
Tawas Lake
Tawas City
East Tawas
Tawas Point
Wurtsmith A.F.B.
Oscoda
Au Sable Point
Pine R.
Big Sable Point
MASON
Scottville
Ludington
LAKE
Baldwin
Marion
OSCEOLA
Evart
Reed City
Muskegon R.
Harrison
CLARE
Clare
GLADWIN
Gladwin
Beaverton
ARENAC
Standish
Oak Point
Port Austin
Pointe aux Barques
Sand Point
Saginaw Bay
Pigeon
Elkton
HURON
Bad Axe
Harbor Beach
Ubly
Pinconning
Coleman
OCEANA
Hart
Little Sable Point
Shelby
NEWAYGO
Big Rapids
MECOSTA
ISABELLA IND. RES.
ISABELLA
Mt. Pleasant
MIDLAND
Midland
BAY
Bay City
Sebewaing
Essexville
Auburn
Carrollton
Shepherd
White Cloud
Fremont
Newaygo
Lakeview
Montague
Whitehall
Muskegon R.
Howard City
Edmore
St. Louis
Alma
SAGINAW
Saginaw
Vassar
Frankenmuth
Caro
TUSCOLA
Cass R.
Cass City
SANILAC
Sandusky
Marlette
Croswell
Black R.
Grant
MONTCALM
Stanton
Greenville
GRATIOT
Ithaca
Bad R.
St. Charles
Chesaning
Wolf Lake
Muskegon
MUSKEGON
Muskegon Heights
Norton Shores
Grand Haven
Sparta
Rockford
Belding
Carson City
Mount Morris
Flint
Flint R.
LAPEER
Lapeer
Imlay City
ST. CLAIR
Yale
Port Huron
Coopersville
Walker
Grand Rapids
Wyoming
Grandville
KENT
Grand R.
Kentwood
Ionia
IONIA
St. Johns
CLINTON
Ovid
Owosso
Corunna
SHIAWASSEE
Durand
GENESEE
Fenton
Holly
Lake Orion
Rochester
Almont
Romeo
St. Clair
Marine City
St. Clair R.
MACOMB
New Baltimore
Algonac
Mount Clemens
OTTAWA
Zeeland
Holland
Lake Odessa
Portland
De Witt
Lansing
East Lansing
Grand Ledge
ALLEGAN
Saugatuck
Allegan
Kalamazoo R.
Wayland
Hastings
Gun Lake
BARRY
Charlotte
EATON
Eaton Rapids
Bellevue
Holt
Mason
INGHAM
LIVINGSTON
Howell
Pontiac
Milford
OAKLAND
Red Oak
Detroit
SEE INSET
Otsego
Plainwell
South Haven
VAN BUREN
Paw Paw R.
Kalamazoo
Paw Paw
Portage
KALAMAZOO
Springfield
Battle Creek
Marshall
Albion
CALHOUN
Homer
JACKSON
Jackson
Chelsea
Michigan Center
Ann Arbor
WASHTENAW
Manchester
Huron R.
Wayne
WAYNE
Southgate
Wyandotte
Flat Rock
Milan
Watervliet
Hartford
Benton Harbor
St. Joseph
Vicksburg
Dowagiac
Three Rivers
Cassopolis
ST. JOSEPH
Centreville
Coldwater
Union City
Jonesville
Hillsdale
Tecumseh
LENAWEE
Adrian
Hudson
Morenci
MONROE
Monroe
Luna Pier
Blissfield
Point Pelee
PELEE I.
NORTH BASS I.
SOUTH BASS I.
MIDDLE BASS I.
KELLEYS I.
BERRIEN
Buchanan
Three Oaks
Niles
CASS
Constantine
Sturgis
BRANCH
Bronson
Quincy
HILLSDALE
New Buffalo
St. Joseph R.
Lake Superior
Carver Bay
Hancock
Houghton
Fourteen Mile Point
ONTONAGON IND. RES.
Paynesdale
HOUGHTON
Government Pk.
White Pine
Ontonagon
L'ANSE IND. RES.
L'Anse
Little Girl Point
ONTONAGON
Rockland
BARAGA
Bergland
Bessemer
Covington
Wakefield
Lake Gogebic
Ewen
Ironwood
GOGEBIC
Bond Falls Reservoir
Watersmeet
IRON
WISCONSIN
Iron River
Caspian
Sterling Heights
MACOMB
Birmingham
Warren
Roseville
42° 30'
OAKLAND
Royal Oak
St. Clair Shores
Lake St. Clair
Novi
Highland Park
Hamtramck
Grosse Pointe
Livonia
Detroit
Dearborn Heights
Dearborn
Detroit R.
Inkster
Lincoln Park
River Rouge
CANADA
Wyandotte
Belleville
WAYNE
Trenton
Grosse Ile
0 4 8 mi
0 6 12 km
©1996, Encyclopædia Britannica, Inc.

War and to U.S. 1783; included in Northwest Terr. 1787 and in Indiana Terr. (*q.v.*) 1800, 1803; Michigan Terr. (*q.v.*) organized on the Lower Penin. 1805, boundaries extended 1818 to include Upper Penin. and beyond; Upper Penin. briefly included in Wisconsin Terr. 1836; boundary dispute with Ohio (Toledo War) settled by U.S. Congress in favor of Ohio, with Michigan receiving as compensation the Upper Penin. and statehood (admitted as free state Jan. 26, 1837); Lansing became ✻ 1847; adopted present constitution 1963.

Michigan, Lake. Lake in NE cen. U.S., bounded on N and E by Michigan, on S by Indiana, on SW by Illinois, on W by Wisconsin; ab. 307 mi. (494 km.) long; ab. 22,400 sq. mi. (58,000 sq. km.); area of drainage basin 67,900 sq. mi. (175,861 sq. km.); max. depth 923 ft. (281 m.); elev. 579 ft. (177 m.); 3d in size of the five Great Lakes (*q.v.*) and the only one wholly within the U.S.; at N end connected through Straits of Mackinac with Lake Huron; at its SW end is the city of Chicago; connected by means of the Chicago and Illinois rivers and connecting canals (see ILLINOIS WATERWAY) with the Mississippi River. See GREEN BAY.

Michigan City. City, La Porte co., N Indiana, on Lake Michigan; pop. (1990c) 33,822; lake port; outdoor recreation; museum.

Michigan Island. See APOSTLE ISLANDS.

Michigan Territory. Former territory, U.S.A.; comprised a region of variable size from the Great Lakes to the Missouri River; various parts previously included in Northwest Terr., Indiana Terr., Louisiana Terr., and Missouri Terr. (*qq.v.*); Michigan Terr. organized Jan. 11, 1805 including mainly the Lower Penin.; boundaries extended 1818 to include all of what is now Michigan and Wisconsin, and Minnesota E of the Mississippi; further extended all the way to the Missouri 1834; reduced to area of the present state 1836 with possession of Upper Penin. in dispute until 1837; Michigan (*q.v.*) admitted to the Union 1837.

Mich·i·ka·mau Lake \ˈmi-shi-kə-ˌmȯ\. See SMALLWOOD RESERVOIR.

Michilimackinac. See MACKINAC.

Mi·chin·má·hui·da \ˌmē-chēn-ˈmä-wē-t͟hä\. Peak, S cen. Chile, E of Corcovado Gulf; 8104 ft. (2470 m.).

Mich·i·pi·co·ten Bay \ˌmi-shə-pə-ˈkōt-ᵊn\. Inlet of Lake Superior, SE Ontario, Canada; on NE shore is township of **Michipicoten;** pop. (1991c) 4154.

Michipicoten Island. Island in NE Lake Superior off SW coast of Algoma co., S Ontario, Canada.

Mich·mash \ˈmik-ˌmash\ *or Arab.* **Mukh·mas** \ mu̇k-ˈmäs\. Locality, in West Bank region, occupied by Israel since 1967; scene of Jonathan's victory over the Philistines (*1 Samuel* xiv).

Mi·cho·a·cán \ˌmē-chō-ä-ˈkän\. State, SW Mexico. See table at MEXICO.

Mi·chu·rinsk \mə-ˈchu̇r-ənsk\; *formerly* **Koz·lov** \käz-ˈlȯf, -ˈlȯv\. City, W Tambov Oblast, Russia in Europe, 35 mi. (56 km.) WNW of the city of Tambov and ab. 115 mi. (185 km.) S of Ryazan'; pop. (1992e) 109,000; important railroad junction point. Founded 1636 as a frontier fort against the Tatars.

Mi·coud \mē-ˈkü\. Town, SE coast of St. Lucia, Windward Is., West Indies; administrative area pop. (1989e) 15,559.

Mi·cro·ne·sia \ˌmī-krə-ˈnē-zhə, -shə\. Islands of the W Pacific Ocean E of Philippines, widely scattered bet. 1° and 20°32′N and 131° and 177°E; a subdivision of Oceania; total area 1055 sq. mi. (2733 sq. km.). Includes the Marianas, Palau, the Caroline, Marshall, and Gilbert Is.; the Marianas, Palau, and many of the Caroline Is. are of volcanic origin, some with peaks of 1000 to 2500 ft. (300 to 750 m.); others of the Carolines, and all of the Marshall and Gilbert Is. are low coral atolls. Political divisions: Kiribati, Tuvalu, Guam, Nauru, the Carolines and the Marshalls. Some islands colonized by Spain in 17th cent., and most sold to Germany 1899; all the island groups were placed under Japanese mandate 1919–20, except Guam, Wake, Nauru, and the Gilbert Is., which were taken over by the Japanese 1941–42 in WWII but for the most part retaken by American forces 1943–45.

Micronesia, Federated States of. The islands of the Caroline group except Palau: Yap, Pohnpei, Chuuk, Kosrae, and many smaller islands; became internally self-governing and assumed independent control over foreign policy except defense (handled by the U.S.) 1986. Seat of government is Palikir on Pohnpei.

Mid–Atlantic Ridge. Ridge, cen. Atlantic Ocean floor, extending approx. from 55°N to W of Bouvet I. in a general N to S direction; a center of oceanic crust formation according to theory of plate tectonics.

Midbar Zin. See ZIN, WILDERNESS OF.

Mid·del·burg \ˈmid-ᵊl-ˌbərg\. **1.** Commune, ✻ of Zeeland prov., SW Netherlands, on Walcheren I. just N of Vlissingen; pop. (1992e) 39,828; market town; tourism; 16th cent. town hall; in Middle Ages a Hanse town.

2. Town, Eastern Cape prov., S Rep. of South Africa, 170 mi. (274 km.) N of Port Elizabeth.

3. Town, Mpumalanga prov., NE Rep. of South Africa, 75 mi. (121 km.) E of Pretoria; a coal-mining community.

Middle America. Region incl. Mexico and Central America; name sometimes used to include the islands of the Caribbean.

Middle America Trench. Ocean trench, E Pacific Ocean, extending approx. parallel to the American coast from W of Costa Rica to W of cen. Mexico; subduction zone according to theory of plate tectonics.

Middle Andaman. One of the Andaman Is. (*q.v.*).

Middle Atlas. See ATLAS MOUNTAINS.

Middle Bass Island. See BASS ISLAND.

Mid·dle·bor·ough *or* **Middleboro** \ˈmid-ᵊl-ˌbər-ō\. Town, Plymouth co., SE Massachusetts, 14 mi. (23 km.) S of Brockton; pop. (1990c) 17,867.

Mid·dle·bourne \ˈmid-ᵊl-ˌbȯrn\. Town, ⊗ of Tyler co., NW West Virginia; pop. (1990c) 922.

Mid·dle·burg \ˈmid-ᵊl-ˌbərg\. Borough, ⊗ of Snyder co., cen. Pennsylvania; pop. (1990c) 1422.

Mid·dle·burgh \ˈmid-ᵊl-ˌbərg\. Town, Schoharie co., E New York; pop. (1990c) 3296.

Middleburg Heights. City, Cuyahoga co., N Ohio, suburb S of Cleveland; pop. (1990c) 14,702.

Mid·dle·bury \ˈmid-ᵊl-ˌber-ē\. **1.** Town, NW New Haven co., S Connecticut, near Naugatuck River; pop. (1990c) 6145.

2. Town, ⊗ of Addison co., W Vermont, 30 mi. (48 km.) NNW of Rutland; pop. (1990c) 8034; plastics; dairy and agricultural products; education, tourism, financial services; Middlebury Coll. (1800). Chartered 1761 as New Hampshire grant; first settled 1773; abandoned 1778–83 due to Loyalist and Indian raids; Vermont's marble industry began with a quarry here 1803, no longer in use.

Middle Cascade. Waterfall in Yosemite Valley, California, in a tributary of the Merced River; total drop ab. 910 ft. (280 m.).

Middle Concho. River, Texas; rises in E Upton co. and flows E; 66 mi. (106 km.) long.

Middle Congo. See CONGO 3.

Middle East. An extensive region comprising the countries of SW Asia and NE Africa; term formerly used to include also Afghanistan, Pakistan, India, and Burma; an indefinite and unofficial term.

Middle Europe. See CENTRAL EUROPE.

Mid·dle·field \ˈmid-ᵊl-ˌfēld\. Town, Middlesex co., S Connecticut, bet. Meriden to the W and Middletown to the E; pop. (1990c) 3925; produce, dairy products; research and development.

Middle Island. **1.** Small island, SE Ontario, Canada, in Lake Erie, S of Pelee I.; Canada's most southerly point.

2. Island, New Zealand. See SOUTH ISLAND.

Middle Kingdom. See CHINA.

Middle Loup \ˈlüp\. River, cen. Nebraska; rises in S Cherry co., flows E and SE to unite with North Loup and South Loup rivers and form Loup River; ab. 220 mi. (350 km.) long.

Middle Park. Plateau in Grand co., N Colorado; bet. 60 and 70 mi. (100 and 110 km.) long; crossed by the Colorado River; with North Park, South Park, and San Luis Park (*qq.v.*) forms a N to S chain of high, level, grassy areas enclosed by snowcapped mountains.

Mid·dle·port \ˈmid-ᵊl-ˌpōrt\. Village, Meigs co., SE Ohio, on Ohio River 40 mi. (64 km.) SW of Marietta; pop. (1990c) 2725.

Middle Rhine. The English name sometimes used for the section of the Rhine River bet. Mainz and Bonn, Germany.

Middle River. Unincorporated settlement, Baltimore co., N Maryland, E suburb of the city of Baltimore; pop. (1990c) 24,616.

Middle Saranac Lake. See SARANAC LAKES.

Mid·dles·bor·ough *or* **Mid·dles·boro** \ˈmid-ᵊlz-ˌbər-ō\. City, Bell co., SE Kentucky, at Cumberland Gap on Tennessee border; pop. (1990c) 11,328.

Mid·dles·brough \ˈmid-ᵊlz-brə\. Town and port, ⊗ of Cleveland co., N England, at mouth of Tees River; pop. (1991p) 141,100; iron and steel, chemicals, fertilizer.

Mid·dle·sex \ˈmid-ᵊl-ˌseks\. **1.** Name of counties in four states of the U.S. See tables at CONNECTICUT, MASSACHUSETTS, NEW JERSEY, VIRGINIA.

2. Borough, Middlesex co., cen. New Jersey, 6 mi. (10 km.) N of New Brunswick; pop. (1990c) 13,055.

3. County in SE Ontario, Canada. See table at ONTARIO.

4. Former county, SE England; since 1965 part of Greater London.

Middle Te·ton \ˈtē-ˌtän\. Peak in cen. Grand Teton National Park, NW Wyoming; 12,804 ft. (3903 m.).

Mid·dle·ton \ˈmid-ᵊl-tən\. **1.** Town, Essex co., NE corner of Massachusetts, 15 mi. (24 km.) ESE of Lowell; pop. (1990c) 4921.

2. City, Dane co., S Wisconsin, 7 mi. (11 km.) W of Madison; pop. (1990c) 13,289.

3. Town, Greater Manchester, NW England, on the Irk 6 mi. (10 km.) NNE of Manchester; pop. (1981p) 51,696; chemicals.

Mid·dle·town \ˈmid-ᵊl-ˌtau̇n\. **1.** City, Middlesex co., S Connecticut, on Connecticut River 15 mi. (24 km.) S of Hartford; pop. (1990c) 42,762; arming and fusing devices, miniature power transmission belting; Wesleyan Univ. (1831), Middlesex Community Coll. (1966); settled 1650; town incorp. 1651, city 1784; town and city consolidated 1923; formerly ⊗ of Middlesex co. Leading shipping center in 18th and 19th cents.; site of pistol factory (from 1799) of Simeon North, first official pistol maker for U.S. government.

2. Town, New Castle co., N Delaware, 23 mi. (37 km.) SW of Wilmington; pop. (1990c) 3834.

3. City, Jefferson co., N cen. Kentucky, E of Louisville; pop. (1990c) 5016.

4. City, Orange co., SE New York, 23 mi. (37 km.) W of Newburgh; pop. (1990c) 24,160; Orange County Community Coll. (1950).

5. City, Butler co., SW Ohio, 11 mi. (18 km.) NE of Hamilton; pop. (1990c) 45,991; steel, paper products; Miami Univ.–Middletown campus (1966); founded 1802; incorp. as city 1883.

6. Borough, Dauphin co., SE cen. Pennsylvania, on Susquehanna River 9 mi. (15 km.) SE of Harrisburg; pop. (1990c) 9254; clothing; Pennsylvania State Univ. at Harrisburg, The Capital Coll. (1966).

7. Town and summer resort, Newport co., SE Rhode Island, on Narragansett Bay 5 mi. (8 km.) N of Newport; pop. (1990c) 19,460; center Middletown village; set off from Newport and incorp. as separate town 1743; pillaged by British fleet 1776.

8. Formerly separate community, N West Virginia. See FAIRMONT 3.

Middle Urals. See URAL MOUNTAINS.

Middle Vol·ga Area \ˈväl-gə, ˈvȯl-, ˈvōl-\. Former administrative region, Russian S.F.S.R., U.S.S.R., along the middle course of the Volga; ab. 92,000 sq. mi. (240,000 sq. km.); included part or most of Kuibyshev Oblast and the Tatar, Mari, Chuvash, and Mordovian A.S.S.R.s; ❋ Samara.

Middle West. See MIDWEST.

Mid·dle·wich \ˈmid-ᵊl-ˌwich\. Town, Cheshire, NW England, 21 mi. (34 km.) SSW of Manchester; pop. (1981p) 8170; salt.

Mid·field \ˈmid-ˌfēld\. City, Jefferson co., cen. Alabama, just SW of Birmingham; pop. (1990c) 5559.

Mid Glamorgan. County, S Wales. See table at WALES.

Mi·di \mē-ˈdē\. The south, esp. of France.

Midi, Dent du. See DENT DU MIDI.

Mid·i·an \ˈmi-dē-ən\. Ancient region of NW Arabian Penin., E of the Gulf of Aqaba and bordered by Edom on the NW; the Midianites of Old Testament times were frequently at war with the Israelites.

Mid–Indian Ridge. Ridge, cen. Indian Ocean floor, extending approx. from W of Maldives to ESE of Mascarene Is. in a general N to S direction; a center of oceanic crust formation according to theory of plate tectonics.

Midi–Pyrénées. Region of S France. See table at FRANCE.

Mid·land \ˈmid-lənd\. **1.** Name of counties in two states of the U.S. See tables at MICHIGAN and TEXAS.

2. City, ⊗ of Midland co., cen. Michigan, 18 mi. (29 km.) W of Bay City; pop. (1990c) 38,053; chemicals; Northwood Institute (1959); nature center; landscaped gardens; art museum.

3. Borough, Beaver co., W Pennsylvania, on Ohio River 29 mi. (47 km.) WNW of Pittsburgh; pop. (1990c) 3321.

4. City, ⊗ of Midland co., W Texas, 120 mi. (193 km.) SSW of Lubbock and approx. midway bet. Fort Worth and El Paso; pop. (1990c) 89,443; center of major oil-producing and cattle-raising region; petroleum museum; founded 1884; incorp. 1906.

5. *formerly* **Midland Junction.** Town, SW Western Australia, Australia, suburb of Perth on Swan River.

6. Town, Simcoe co., SE Ontario, Canada, on Georgian Bay 27 mi. (43 km.) NNW of Barrie; pop. (1991c) 13,865.

Midland Junction. See MIDLAND 5.

Midland Park. Borough, Bergen co., NE corner of New Jersey, 5 mi. (8 km.) N of Paterson; pop. (1990c) 7047.

Mid·lands, The \ˈmid-ləndz\. The central counties of England, esp. Derbyshire, Nottinghamshire, Leicestershire, Northamptonshire, Warwickshire, Staffordshire, and West Midlands; sometimes thought to include Lincolnshire, Hereford and Worcester, and Shropshire also; contains many large cities incl. Birmingham, Coventry, Leicester, Nottingham, Walsall, Stoke-on-Trent, Wolverhampton; suffered severely from German air raids in WWII.

Mid·lo·thi·an \mid-ˈlō-thē-ən\ **1.** Village, Cook co., NE Illinois, ab. 7 mi. (11 km.) S of Chicago; pop. (1990c) 14,372.

2. City, Ellis co., NE cen. Texas, SSW of Dallas; pop. (1990c) 5141.

3. \mid-ˈlō-t͟hē-ən\; *formerly* **Ed·in·burgh** \ˈed-ᵊn-ˌbər-ə\ *or* **Ed·in·burgh·shire** \-ˌshīr, -shər\. Former county, SE Scotland; ⊗ Edinburgh; rivers Esk, Almond, Tyne.

Mid·na·pore \ˈmid-nə-ˌpōr\ *or* **Mid·na·pur** \ˈmid-nə-ˌpu̇r\. Town, West Bengal, NE India, 68 mi. (109 km.) W of Calcutta; pop. (1991p) 125,098.

Mid·sa·yap \ˌmid-sä-ˈyäp\. Municipality, Mindanao, Philippines, on a N tributary of Mindanao River 20 mi. (32 km.) E of Cotabato; pop. (1980c) 66,952.

Mid·vale \ˈmid-ˌvāl\. City, Salt Lake co., N Utah, 11 mi. (18 km.) S of Salt Lake City; pop. (1990c) 11,886; incorp. 1909.

Mid·way \ˈmid-ˌwā\; *formerly* **Brooks Islands** \ˈbru̇ks\. Two small islands, Eastern I. and Sand I., parts of a low coral atoll in cen. Pacific Ocean under administration of the U.S.; 1134 naut. mi. (1304 mi. or 2098 km.) WNW of Honolulu, 28°13′N, 177°26′W; 2 sq. mi. (5 sq. km.); not incorp. in state of Hawaii. Discovered and claimed by U.S. 1859, formally annexed 1867; Sand I. made a submarine cable station 1905; transpacific commercial air station 1935; Navy air and submarine base completed 1941; in WWII attacked unsuccessfully by Japanese Dec. 1941 and Jan. 1942. Battle of Midway, one of the decisive naval battles and a turning point in the Pacific War, took place June 1942 in nearby waters; the invading Japanese forces were defeated, losing four carriers to one U.S. carrier sunk. Midway has a wildlife refuge, no commercial air service.

Midway–Hard·wick \ˈhärd-ˌwik\. Unincorporated settlement, Baldwin co., cen. Georgia; pop. (1990c) 4910.

Mid·west \mid-ˈwest\ *or* **Middle West.** Region of indefinite boundaries N cen. U.S. usu. thought to include area bet. Appalachian Mts. and Rocky Mts., around Great Lakes and in upper Mississippi Valley from Ohio on the E to North and South Dakota, Nebraska, and Kansas on the W; contains rich agricultural land.

Mid·west City. City, Oklahoma co., cen. Oklahoma, E suburb of Oklahoma City; pop. (1990c) 52,267; Rose State Coll. (1971).

Mid·ye \mid-ˈyā\. Town, Kırklareli prov., NE Turkey in Europe; port on the Black Sea 64 mi. (103 km.) NW of İstanbul.

Mie *also* **Mi·ye** \ˈmē-yā\. Prefecture, Honshū, Japan; ✻ Tsu; lumber; cement; lobster and shrimp fishing; tourism. See table at JAPAN.

Mi·e·lec \ˈmye-lets\. Town, Rzeszów prov., SE Poland, ab. 35 mi. (56 km.) NW of the commune of Rzeszów; pop. (1989e) 60,286.

Mier·cu·rea–Ciuc \ˈmyer-kür-yä-ˈchük\. Town, ⊗ of Harghita co., NE cen. Romania, ab. 50 mi. (80 km.) NNE of Braşov; pop. (1989c) 49,148; clothing; tourism.

Mie·res \ˈmyā-rās\ *or in full* **Mieres del Ca·mi·no** \ˌthel-kä-ˈmē-nō\. Commune, Asturias prov., NW Spain, 9 mi. (15 km.) SSE of Oviedo; pop. (1991p) 53,379; iron, coal, and sulfur mines nearby.

Mierzeja Wiślana. See VISLINSKI ZALIV.

Miff·lin \ˈmi-flən\. County in cen. Pennsylvania. See table at PENNSYLVANIA.

Miff·lin·burg \ˈmi-flən-ˌbərg\. Borough, Union co., cen. Pennsylvania, 24 mi. (39 km.) S of Williamsport; pop. (1990c) 3480.

Miff·lin·town \ˈmi-flən-ˌtau̇n\. Borough, ⊗ of Juniata co., S cen. Pennsylvania; in Appalachian Mts., 40 mi. (64 km.) NW of Harrisburg; pop. (1990c) 866.

Mifraz Shlomo. See SHARM AL-SHEIKH.

Migdal. See MAGDALA.

Migiurtinia. See MIJERTINS.

Mi·glia·ri·no \ˌmē-lyä-ˈrē-nō\. Commune, Ferrara prov., Emilia-Romagna, N Italy, 19 mi. (31 km.) ESE of the commune of Ferrara; pop. (1981p) 4340.

Mi·ha·ra \mē-ˈhär-ä\. City, Hiroshima prefecture, Honshū, Japan, 40 mi. (64 km.) E of the city of Hiroshima; pop. (1990c) 85,518.

Mi·ja·res \mē-ˈhä-rās\ *or* **Mil·la·res** \mē-ˈlyä-rās\. River, E Spain; flows SE, empties into Mediterranean Sea S of Castellón de la Plana; 97 mi. (156 km.) long.

Mij·er·tins \ˈmi-jərt-ᵊnz\ *or* **Mij·jar·ten** \ˈmi-jər-tən\ *or Ital.* **Mi·giur·ti·nia** \ˌmē-jür-ˈtē-nyä\. Region, NE Somalia; includes Cape Asir; formerly a sultanate.

Mi·ke·no \mē-ˈkā-nō\. Quiescent volcano, Rwanda, E of Lake Kivu; above 12,000 ft. (3660 m.).

Mikhaylovgrad. See MONTANA.

Mi·khay·lov·ka *or* **Mi·khai·lov·ka** \mi-ˈk̲ī-ləf-kə, -ləv-\. Town, Volgograd Oblast, S Russia in Europe, ab. 110 mi. (177 km.) NW of the city of Volgograd; pop. (1991e) 58,700.

Mi·ki \ˈmē-kē\. City, Hyōgo prefecture, W Honshū, Japan; pop. (1990p) 76,509.

Mik·ke·li \ˈmē-ke-lē\. **1.** Province of S Finland. See table at FINLAND.

2. *or Swed.* **Sankt Mi·chel** \säŋkt-mē-ˈshel\. City, its ✻; pop. (1989c) 31,785; commercial center; lumbering; chartered 1838.

Mi·ko·łów \mē-ˈkȯ-wüf\. Commune, Katowice prov., SW Poland, 7 mi. (11 km.) SSW of the city of Katowice; pop. (1989e) 37,072; near pre-WWII Polish boundary.

Mikonos *or* **Míkonos.** See MYKONOS.

Mikoyan Shakhar. See KARACHAYEVSK.

Mikrí Préspa. See PRESPA, LAKE.

Mi·ku·lov \ˈmē-kü-ˌlȯf\ *or Ger.* **Ni·kols·burg** \ˈnē-kȯls-ˌbu̇rk\. Commune, SE Czech Republic, ab. 30 mi. (48 km.) S of Brno; treaty of peace signed here 1621, bet. Holy Roman Emperor Ferdinand II and Gabriel Bethlen, prince of Transylvania; truce signed here July 26, 1866 bet. Austria and Prussia.

Mi·ku·mi National Park \mē-ˈkü-mē\. National park, E cen. Tanzania; ab.185 mi. (300 km.) WSW of Dar es Salaam; 1247 sq. mi. (3230 sq. km.); large variety of wildlife, incl. elephants, giraffes, lions, and zebras; estab. 1964.

Mi·la \ˈmē-lə\. Commune, NE Algeria, just NW of Constantine.

Mi·laca \mə-ˈla-kə\. Village, ⊗ of Mille Lacs co., E cen. Minnesota, 28 mi. (45 km.) ENE of St. Cloud; pop. (1990c) 2182.

Mi·la·gro \mē-ˈlä-grō\. Town, Guayas prov., W Ecuador, 25 mi. (40 km.) E of Guayaquil; pop. (1990c) 93,637.

Mi·la·gros \mē-ˈlä-grōs\. Municipality, S Masbate I. on Asid Gulf, Philippines; pop. (1980c) 28,496.

Mi·lam \ˈmī-ləm\. County in cen. Texas. See table at TEXAS.

Mi·lan \ˈmī-lən\. **1.** Village, Rock Island co., NW Illinois, 4 mi. (6 km.) S of the city of Rock Island; pop. (1990c) 5831.

2. Village, Monroe and Washtenaw cos., SE Michigan, 13 mi. (21 km.) S of Ann Arbor; pop. (1990c) 4040.

3. City, ⊗ of Sullivan co., N Missouri; pop. (1990c) 1767.

4. Town, Gibson co., NW Tennessee, 21 mi. (34 km.) N of Jackson; pop. (1990c) 7512.

Mi·lan \mə-ˈlan, -ˈlän\ *or Ital.* **Mi·la·no** \mē-ˈlä-nō\; *anc.* **Me·di·o·la·num** \ˌmē-dē-ō-ˈlä-nəm, ˌme-\. Commune, ✻ of Lombardy and of Milano prov., N Italy, 76 mi. (122 km.) NE of Genoa in a fertile plain bet. Adda and Ticino rivers; archiepiscopal see; principal financial center of Italy; produces textiles, chemicals, motor vehicles, clothing; numerous notable buildings, incl. white-marble cathedral (begun 1387, completed 1858, 3d largest in Europe), castle, amphitheater, triumphal arch, basilica of St. Ambrose (4th cent., restored), royal and archiepiscopal palaces, Brera palace (includes Brera art gallery), Ambrosian library (earliest public library in Europe), La Scala theater, Ospedale Maggiore (1456, first munic. hospital); 15th cent. monastery with Leonardo da Vinci's famous painting *Last Supper* on wall of its former refectory; Univ. of Milan (1924), technical institute (1863). See table at ITALY.

History: Ancient Gallic city captured by Romans 222 B.C.; in 4th cent. A.D. a chief city of Western Roman Empire from which Constantine the Great issued Edict of Milan 313 granting religious toleration for Christianity; seat of Archbishop Ambrose (d. 397); overrun by Huns (c. 450), and by Goths (539); under strong episcopal authority, it became semi-independent of the empire in 11th cent.; rebuilt after its destruction 1162 by Holy Roman Emperor Frederick I (Barbarossa); as member of Lombard League took lead in opposition to Frederick I (see LOMBARDY); independence granted 1183; ruled by the Visconti family from 13th cent. (as dukes of Milan 1395–1447) and under them expanded until the **Duchy of Milan** *or Ital.* **Du·ca·to di Milano** \dü-ˈkä-tō-dē-\ *also* **The Mil·a·nese** \ˌmi-lə-ˈnēz, -ˈnēs\ at its height included territory on both sides of middle Po River and shared with Venice control of N Italy incl. Genoa; under Sforza family 1447–1535 duchy became pawn in Hapsburg-French rivalry in Italian wars of 16th cent.; duchy passed to Spanish control 1535; ceded to Austria 1713 following War of Spanish Succession; under French rule 1796–1814; city became ✻ of Emperor Napoléon's Cisalpine Republic and kingdom of Italy (1805); as part of Lombardy 1815–59 duchy belonged to Austria again and was included in cession of Lombardy to Piedmont 1859; became part of Italy 1860; nucleus of the duchy now the prov. of Milano; in WWII city heavily damaged by bombing; entered by Allied forces Apr. 1945.

Mi·la·no \mē-ˈlä-nō\. **1.** Province of Lombardy, Italy. See table at ITALY.

2. Commune, Italy. See MILAN.

Mi·lâs \mē-ˈläs\; *mostly formerly* **Mi·las·sa** \mē-ˈlä-sä\; *anc.* **My·la·sa** \mī-ˈlā-sə\. Town, Muğla prov., SW Turkey in Asia, near coast; formerly famous for its rugs; ancient Mylasa was a flourishing city of Caria.

Mi·laz·zo \mē-ˈlät-sō\; *anc.* **My·lae** \ˈmī-ˌlē\. Seaport, Messina prov., NE Sicily, Italy, on Tyrrhenian Sea 17 mi. (27 km.) W of the seaport of Messina; pop. (1991p) 31,559; tourism; center of wine- and fruit-producing area; 13th cent. castle (now a prison); cathedral. Waters off ancient Mylae scene of naval victory of Roman Gen. Gaius Duilius over the Carthaginians 260 B.C. in First Punic War. Town scene of victory of Italian patriot Giuseppe Garibaldi over Bourbon forces 1860; suffered bombing damage in WWII.

Milazzo, Gulf of. Inlet of the Mediterranean Sea on N coast of Sicily, Italy; 16 mi. (26 km.) long.

Mil·bank \ˈmil-ˌbaŋk\. City, ⊗ of Grant co., NE South Dakota, 34 mi. (55 km.) NE of Watertown; pop. (1990c) 3879.

Mil·den·hall \ˈmil-dən-ˌhȯl\. Town, Suffolk, E England, 8 mi. (13 km.) NE of Newmarket; pop. (1981c) 11,971; 15th cent. wooden market cross; Roman artifacts found here.

Mil·du·ra \mil-ˈdu̇r-ə, -ˈdyu̇r-\. Town, NW Victoria, SE Australia, on Murray River 15 mi. (24 km.) above its junction with the Darling and ab. 300 mi. (480 km.) NW of Melbourne; pop. (1991p) 20,437.

Miles City \ˈmīlz\. City, ⊗ of Custer co., SE Montana, on Yellowstone River 140 mi. (225 km.) ENE of Billings; pop. (1990c) 8461; Miles Community Coll. (1939).

Mile·stone Mountain \ˈmīl-ˌstōn\. Peak, in the Sierra Nevada, N Tulare co., S cen. California; ab. 13,640 ft. (4160 m.).

Mi·let·to, Mon·te \ˈmȯn-tā-mē-ˈle-tō\. Mountain, S Italy; highest peak in Neapolitan Apennines. See table at APENNINES.

Mi·le·tus \mī-ˈlē-təs, mə-\. Ancient city, Turkey, near the mouth of the Menderes; now an archaeological site in the modern prov. of Aydın; one of the great cities of Asia Minor, on the coast of Caria and the southernmost and most important of the 12 Ionian Cities; had several harbors and a large trade; founded dozens of colonies esp. on the Black Sea; for a time was the rival of Lydia; after several years of Persian domination in Ionia, led failed Ionian revolt c. 500 B.C. but was overcome and occupied by Persia; later taken by Macedonian King Alexander the Great; in Roman times yielded in influence to Ephesus; c. 4th cent. A.D. its harbors became silted up, commerce declined, and the city was eventually abandoned; distinguished as a literary center.

Mile 26. See EIELSON AIR FORCE BASE.

Mil·ford \ˈmil-fərd\. **1.** City, SW New Haven co., S Connecticut, on Long Island Sound and Housatonic River; pop. (1990c) 49,938; founded 1639; incorp. as city 1959.
2. City, Kent and Sussex cos., cen. Delaware, 18 mi. (29 km.) S of Dover; pop. (1990c) 6040; produce distribution point.
3. Town, Worcester co., cen. Massachusetts, 16 mi. (26 km.) ESE of the city of Worcester; pop. (1990c) 25,355.
4. Village, Oakland co., SE Michigan, 17 mi. (27 km.) W of Pontiac; pop. (1990c) 5511; summer resort.
5. Town, Hillsborough co., S New Hampshire, 11 mi. (18 km.) WNW of Nashua; pop. (1990c) 11,795; metal castings; granite deposits.
6. Town, Otsego co., New York, on the Susquehanna River; pop. (1990c) 2845.
7. Village, Clermont and Hamilton cos., SW Ohio, 12 mi. (19 km.) ENE of Cincinnati; pop. (1990c) 5655.
8. Borough, ⊗ of Pike co., NE Pennsylvania, on Delaware River 47 mi. (76 km.) E of Scranton; pop. (1990c) 1064.

Milford Haven *or Welsh* **Ab·er·dau·gledd·yf** \ˌa-bər-ˈdī-ˌgle-t͟hər\. Town and seaport, Dyfed co., SW Wales; pop. (1981c) 13,927; oil refineries and dock facilities for tankers; excellent harbor on **Milford Haven** (large inlet of St. George's Channel); Henry Tudor (afterwards Henry VII) landed here from France 1485 to conduct his successful campaign for English throne.

Milford Sound. Inlet of Tasman Sea on SW coast of South I., New Zealand; noted for its scenery.

Milh, Cape \ˈmilk̲\ *or Arab.* **R'as al–Milh** \ˌrás-ˌál-\. Cape, NE Libya, near Egyptian border.

Milhau. See MILLAU.

Mi·li \ˈmē-lē\. Atoll at S end of Ratak Chain, SE Marshall Is., W Pacific Ocean, 6°08′N, 171°55′E; has 30 islets enclosing lagoon 23 mi. (37 km.) long; Japanese air base bombed by U.S. in WWII.

Mil·ia·na \mil-ˈyä-nä\. Commune, N Algeria, on railroad line 60 mi. (97 km.) WSW of Algiers; pop. (1987p) 27,183.

Mi·li·ane \mēl-ˈyän\. Small river flowing NE across N cen. Tunisia, and emptying into Mediterranean Sea just below and E of Tunis.

Milk \ˈmilk\. River, S Alberta, Canada, and N Montana; rises in Glacier co., NW Montana, flows NE across Canadian border and E along S Alberta, turns SE across Montana border and E along N Montana into Missouri River in S Valley co., NE Montana; 625 mi. (1006 km.) long.

Milk, Wa·di el \ˈwä-dē-el-ˈmilk\ *or* **Wadi al Ma·lik** \ál-ˈmä-lik\. Wadi, Sudan, extending from W cen. part of the country NE to the Nile.

Mil·lard \ˈmi-lərd\. County in W Utah. See table at UTAH.

Millares. See MIJARES.

Mil·lau *also* **Mi·lhau** \mē-ˈyō\; *anc.* **Æmil·i·a·num** \i-ˌmi-lē-ˈā-nəm, -ˈa-\. Commune, Aveyron dept., S France, 30 mi. (48 km.) SE of Rodez; pop. (1990c) 22,458; formerly a notable glovemaking center.

Mill·brae \ˈmil-ˌbrā\. City, San Mateo co., W California, NW of city of San Mateo; pop. (1990c) 20,412.

Mill·brook \ˈmil-ˌbru̇k\. City, Elmore co., SE cen. Alabama, N of Montgomery; pop. (1990c) 6050.

Mill·burn \ˈmil-bərn\. Unincorporated settlement, Essex co., NE New Jersey, W of Newark; pop. (1990c) 18,630.

Mill·bury \ˈmil-ˌber-ē\. Town, Worcester co., cen. Massachusetts, 5 mi. (8 km.) S of the city of Worcester; pop. (1990c) 12,228.

Mil·ledge·ville \ˈmi-lij-ˌvil\. City, ⊗ of Baldwin co., cen. Georgia, 30 mi. (48 km.) NE of Macon; pop. (1990c) 17,727; distribution center for agricultural products; served as ✻ of Georgia 1807–67; Georgia Military Coll. (1879), Georgia Coll. (1889); settled 1803.

Mille Îles, Ri·vière des \rē-ˌvyer-dā-mēl-ˈēl\. River, a part of the course of the St. Lawrence River, NW and N of Jesus I., S Quebec, Canada; flows NE from Lac des Deux Montagnes to junction with Rivière des Prairies; ab. 24 mi. (39 km.) long; separates Jesus I. from the mainland.

Mille Lacs \mil-ˈlak, ˈlaks\. **1.** Lake on boundary bet. Aitkin and Mille Lacs cos., E cen. Minnesota; ab. 16 mi. (26 km.) in diameter; 207 sq. mi. (536 sq. km.).
2. County in E cen. Minnesota. See table at MINNESOTA.
3. Lake, W Ontario, Canada, NW of Thunder Bay; 103 sq. mi. (267 sq. km.).

Mil·len \ˈmi-lən\. City, ⊗ of Jenkins co., E Georgia, 47 mi. (76 km.) S of Augusta; pop. (1990c) 3808.

Mil·ler \ˈmi-lər\. **1.** Name of counties in three states of the U.S. See tables at ARKANSAS, GEORGIA, MISSOURI.
2. City, ⊗ of Hand co., E cen. South Dakota; pop. (1990c) 1678.

Miller, Mount. Mountain, Antarctica, 83°20′S, 165°48′E; 13,648 ft. (4160 m.).

Mil·le·ro·vo \ˈmē-li-ˌrə-və\. Town, W Rostov Oblast, S Russia in Europe, on railroad line N of Kamensk Shakhtinskiy, ab. 60 mi. (97 km.) ENE of Luhans'k.

Miller Peak. Mountain in SW Cochise co., SE Arizona; 9466 ft. (2885 m.).

Mil·lers \ˈmi-lərz\. River, N Massachusetts; rises in S New Hampshire, flows S across Massachusetts border, then W into Connecticut River in cen. Franklin co., NW Massachusetts; ab. 60 mi. (97 km.) long.

Mil·lers·burg \ˈmi-lərz-ˌbərg\. **1.** Village, ⊗ of Holmes co., NE cen. Ohio, 20 mi. (32 km.) SE of Mansfield; pop. (1990c) 3051.
2. Borough, Dauphin co., SE cen. Pennsylvania, on Susquehanna River 20 mi. (32 km.) N of Harrisburg; pop. (1990c) 2729.

Mil·lers·ville \ˈmi-lərz-ˌvil\. Borough, Lancaster co., SE Pennsylvania, 4 mi. (6 km.) SW of the city of Lancaster; pop. (1990c) 8099; Millersville Univ. of Pennsylvania (1855).

Mil·li·gan College \ˈmi-li-gən\. Village (unincorporated), Carter co., NE Tennessee, just E of Johnson City; Milligan Coll. (1882).

Mil·ling·ton \ˈmi-liŋ-tən\. Town, Shelby co., SW corner of Tennessee, N of Memphis; pop. (1990c) 17,866.

Mil·li·nock·et \ˌmi-lə-ˈnä-kət\. Town, Penobscot co., E cen. Maine, 54 mi. (87 km.) SW of Houlton; pop. (1990c) 6956.

Millinocket Lake. 1. Lake on W boundary of Penobscot co., E cen. Maine, SE of Mt. Katahdin and just NE of Pemadumcook Lake with which it is connected by a short stream.
2. Small lake, NE Piscataquis co., N cen. Maine.

Mil·lis \ˈmi-ləs\. Town, Norfolk co., E Massachusetts, 20 mi. (32 km.) SW of Boston; pop. (1990c) 7613.

Mill·port \ˈmil-ˌpōrt\. Burgh, Strathclyde region, SW Scotland, at S end of Great Cumbrae I.; pop. (1981p) 1489; resort.

Mills \ˈmilz\. Name of counties in two states of the U.S. See tables at IOWA and TEXAS.

Mills, Fort. See FORT MILLS.

Mill Springs \ˈmil\. Village in Wayne co., S Kentucky, on Cumberland River; scene of battle Jan. 1862 in which Confederates were defeated.

Mill·stät·ter Lake \ˈmil-ˌshte-tər\ *or Ger.* **Millstätter See** \-ˌzā\. Lake (*See*), in cen. Carinthia, S Austria, in Drava Valley ab. 33 mi. (53 km.) W of Klagenfurt; 5 sq. mi. (13 sq. km.); ab. 7.5 mi. (12 km.) long; max. depth 462 ft. (141 m.); resort area.

Mill·town \ˈmil-ˌtau̇n\. Borough, Middlesex co., cen. New Jersey, 3 mi. (5 km.) S of New Brunswick; pop. (1990c) 6968.

Mill·vale \ˈmil-ˌvāl\. Borough, Allegheny co., SW Pennsylvania, on Allegheny River just N of Pittsburgh; pop. (1990c) 4341.

Mill Valley. City, Marin co., W California, NW of San Francisco; pop. (1990c) 13,038; near Mt. Tamalpais and Muir Woods National Monument.

Mill·ville \ˈmil-ˌvil\. City, Cumberland co., SW New Jersey, 10 mi. (16 km.) ESE of Bridgeton on Maurice River; pop. (1990c) 25,992; glass.

Milne Bay \ˈmiln\. Bay at SE extremity of New Guinea I., Papua New Guinea; Samarai is near its SE point; occupied by Japanese until mid-1942, and thereafter by Allies.

Mil·ner·ton \ˈmil-nər-tən\. Town, Western Cape prov., S Rep. of South Africa, on coast 5 mi. (8 km.) N of Cape Town of which it is a suburb.

Miln·ga·vie \mil-ˈgī\. Burgh, Strathclyde region, W cen. Scotland; residential suburb of Glasgow; pop. (1981c) 12,067.

Miln·row \ˈmiln-ˌrō\. Town, Greater Manchester, NW England, SE suburb of Rochdale; pop. (1981p) 11,759.

Mi·lo \ˈmī-lō\. **1.** Town, Piscataquis co., N cen. Maine, 35 mi. (56 km.) NNW of Bangor; pop. (1990c) 2600.
2. Island and city, Greece. See MELOS.

Mílos. See MELOS.

Mil·pa Al·ta \ˈmēl-pä-ˈäl-tä\. Municipality, Federal District, Mexico, 18 mi. (29 km.) SE of Mexico City.

Mil·pi·tas \mil-ˈpē-təs\. City, Santa Clara co., W California, S of Palo Alto; pop. (1990c) 50,686.

Mil·ton \ˈmilt-ᵊn\. **1.** Town, ⊗ of Santa Rosa co., NW Florida, 18 mi. (29 km.) NE of Pensacola; pop. (1990c) 7216.
2. Town, Norfolk co., E Massachusetts, 6 mi. (10 km.) S of Boston; pop. (1990c) 25,725; suburb of Boston with outdoor recreation area; Curry Coll. (1879); settled 1636; incorp. 1662.
3. Borough, Northumberland co., E cen. Pennsylvania, 19 mi. (31 km.) SSE of Williamsport; pop. (1990c) 6746.
4. Town, Chittenden co., Vermont, 10 mi. (16 km.) NNE of Burlington; pop. (1990c) 8404.
5. Town, King and Pierce cos., W cen. Washington, 7 mi. (11 km.) E of Tacoma; pop. (1990c) 4995.
6. Village, Rock co., S Wisconsin, 8 mi. (13 km.) NNE of Janesville; pop. (1990c) 4434.
7. Town, ⊗ of Halton munic. region, SE Ontario, Canada, 29 mi. (47 km.) WSW of Toronto; pop. (1991c) 32,075; in farm area.

Mil·ton–Free·water \ˈfrē-ˌwȯ-tər, -ˌwä-\. City, Umatilla co., NE Oregon, 28 mi. (45 km.) NE of Pendleton; pop. (1990c) 5533.

Milvian Bridge. See SAXA RUBRA.

Mil·wau·kee \mil-ˈwȯ-kē\. **1.** River, SE Wisconsin; rises in Fond du Lac co., flows into Lake Michigan at Milwaukee; 100 mi. (161 km.) long.
2. County in SE Wisconsin. See table at WISCONSIN.
3. City and lake port, its ⊗, on Lake Michigan; pop. (1990c) 628,088; largest city in the state; major lake port, shipping esp. grain; produces electrical machinery, beer. St. Francis Seminary (1856), Marquette Univ. (1857), Alverno Coll. (1887), Wisconsin Conservatory of Music (1899), Milwaukee School of Engineering (1903), Univ. of Wisconsin–Milwaukee (1956), Mount Mary Coll. (1913), Milwaukee Area Technical Coll. (1923), Cardinal Stritch Coll. (1937), Wisconsin Lutheran Coll. (1973), Milwaukee Institute of Art and Design (1974); zoo; museum. Platted 1835; settled 1836 ff.; incorp. 1846; major center of German immigration 1840–1900.

Mil·wau·kie \mil-ˈwȯ-kē\. City, Clackamas and Multnomah cos., NW Oregon, on Willamette River 7 mi. (11 km.) S of Portland; pop. (1990c) 18,692.

Mimatum. See MENDE.

Mim·bres \ˈmim-brəs\. Village, Grant co., SW New Mexico, on the Mimbres River, W of Mimbres Mts.; hot springs; pueblo ruins nearby.

Mimbres Mountains. Range in SW New Mexico, extending along boundary bet. Grant and Sierra cos.

Min \ˈmin\. **1.** River, Sichuan prov., S cen. China; flows SE through the Red Basin into the Chang at Yibin; ab. 350 mi. (560 km.) long; navigable for most of its course.
2. Navigable river, N cen. Fujian prov., SE China; flows SE into East China Sea near Fuzhou; ab. 250 mi. (400 km.) long.

Mi·na·ha·sa *also* **Mi·na·has·sa** \ˌmē-nä-ˈhä-sä\. Peninsula forming NE end of Sulawesi, Indonesia.

Mi·na·ma·ta \mē-ˈnä-mä-tä\. City, Kumamoto prefecture, Kyūshū, Japan; pop. (1990p) 34,595; "Minamata disease" first recognized here.

Mi·na·mi–Alps National Park \mē-ˈnä-mē\. National park, Honshū, Japan; 138 sq. mi. (357 sq. km.); mountainous area.

Minami Iwo. See VOLCANO ISLANDS.

Minami–Tori–Shima. See MARCUS ISLAND.

Mi·nas \ˈmē-näs\. **1.** Department, Uruguay. See LAVALLEJA.
2. Town, ✻ of Lavalleja dept., SE Uruguay; pop. (1985c) 34,661.

Minas Basin \ˈmī-nəs\. NE extension of the Bay of Fundy, in cen. Nova Scotia, Canada; connected by **Minas Channel** with the Bay of Fundy.

Minas de Rí·o·tin·to \ˈmē-näs-thā-ˌrē-ō-ˈtēn-tō\. Commune, Huelva prov., SW Spain, on Tinto River 36 mi. (58 km.) NE of the commune of Huelva; pop. (1991c) 5480.

Minas Ge·rais \ˈmē-nəs-zhē-ˈrīs\. State, E Brazil; ✻ Belo Horizonte; iron ore, manganese, diamonds, bauxite, nickel; cattle. See table at BRAZIL.

Mi·na·ti·tlán \ˌmē-nä-tē-ˈtlän\. Town, Veracruz state, E Mexico, head of navigation on the Coatzacoalcos River 24 mi. (39 km.) from its mouth; munic. pop. (1990p) 199,840; petroleum refinery.

Min·bu \ˈmin-ˈbü\. Town, Magwe div., Myanmar, on right bank of Irrawaddy opp. town of Magwe, ab. 145 mi. (233 km.) SW of Mandalay; pop. (1983c) 32,456; fishing; peanuts, oil.

Minch *also* **Minsh** \ˈminch\. Channel bet. the Outer Hebrides and the NW coast of Scotland; includes the North Minch and Little Minch (*qq.v.*).

Min·cio \ˈmēn-chō, ˈmin-chē-ˌō\; *anc.* **Min·ci·us** \ˈmin-shē-əs, -shəs, -sē-əs\. River, N Italy; issues from Lake Garda, flows S and E past Mantua and empties into Po River SE of Mantua; 115 mi. (185 km.) long; navigable up to Mantua.

Min·da·nao \ˌmin-də-ˈnä-ˌō, -ˈnau̇\. **1.** Island, S Philippines; 38,254 sq. mi. (99,078 sq. km.) incl. small adjacent islands; pop. (1990e) 13,966,000; Basilan I. in SW is largest island attached to it politically; other important islands are Dinagat, Siargao, Camiguin, Samal, and Bucas Grande. Separated from Visayan Is. to N by Mindanao Sea and bordered on E by Philippine Sea (part of Pacific), on S by Celebes Sea, and on W by Sulu Sea; for administrative subdivisions, see table at PHILIPPINES.

Physical features: Of irregular triangular shape, indented with many gulfs and bays. Mountainous with many peaks above 5000 ft. (1500 m.); highest Apo 9690 ft. (2954 m.) (highest in the archipelago). Has two great river systems, the Agusan in E and the Mindanao (with the Pulangi) in S and cen. parts.

Chief products: Corn, rice, coconuts, timber, coffee, abacá.

History: Islam spread throughout island 16th cent.; visited by Portuguese navigator and explorer Ferdinand Magellan 1521; although claimed by Spain, remained mostly independent of Spanish authority due to resistance of Muslim inhabitants (Moros); fully incorp. into civil government under Americans in early 20th cent.

2. *or* **Rio Gran·de de Mindanao** \ˌrē-ō-ˈgrän-dē-dā-\; *formerly* **Co·ta·ba·to** \ˌkō-tä-ˈbä-tō\. River, cen. Mindanao, Philippines; rises in NE Bukidnon prov., flows S and SW through cen. Cotabato prov. to Maguindanao prov., whence it flows WNW to Illana Bay; ab. 200 mi. (320 km.) long; known in its upper course as the Pulangi; navigable; with its many tributaries forms a wide fertile basin. Municipality of Cotabato is on N side of delta.

Mindanao Sea. Large interisland body of water, S Philippines, bordered on N by islands of Negros, Cebu, Bohol, and Leyte, and on S by Mindanao; ab. 70 mi. (110 km.) from N to S and 180 mi. (290 km.) from E to W; at W end opens into Sulu Sea and connects on NE with the Pacific by Surigao Strait and on N with Visayan Sea by Tanon Strait and with Camotes Sea by Bohol Strait and Canigao Channel. Contains the islands of Camiguin and Siquijor.

Min·de·lo \min-ˈde-lü\ *also* **Por·to Gran·de** \ˈpōr-tü-ˈgrän-dē\. Seaport town, NW São Vicente I., Cape Verde Is.; good harbor, a fueling stop for oceangoing vessels.

Min·den \ˈmin-dən\. **1.** City, ⊗ of Webster parish, NW Louisiana, 28 mi. (45 km.) E of Shreveport; pop. (1990c) 13,661; oil production in area.

2. City, ⊗ of Kearney co., S Nebraska, 16 mi. (26 km.) SSE of the city of Kearney; pop. (1990c) 2749.

3. Unincorporated settlement, ⊗ of Douglas co., W Nevada, 14 mi. (23 km.) S of Carson City; pop. (1990c) 1441.

4. *anc.* **Min·thun** \ˈmin-thən\. City, North Rhine-Westphalia, Germany, on Weser River 58 mi. (93 km.) ENE of Münster; pop. (1992e) 78,909; transportation center; textiles, glass, ceramics, furniture, machinery; 12th cent. churches; town hall with 13th cent. façade; 13th cent. early Gothic cathedral.

History: Founded in Roman times; bishopric founded here by Frankish King (later Holy Roman Emperor) Charlemagne in 8th cent.; member of Hanseatic League; besieged several times during Thirty Years' War; to Brandenburg 1648 by Peace of Westphalia; during Seven Years' War French decisively defeated near here by Hannoverian forces under Duke Ferdinand of Brunswick 1759; to kingdom of Westphalia 1807; to Prussia 1814; in WWII occupied by Allies 1945.

5. Settlement, SE Ontario, Canada; ⊗ of Haliburton co.

Min·do·ro \min-ˈdō-rō\. Island, cen. Philippines, SW of Luzon; touches South China Sea on W and Sulu Sea on S, separated from Luzon on N by Verde Island Passage, from Tablas and other islands on E by Tablas Strait, and from Calamian Group on SW by Mindoro Strait; ab. 80 mi. (130 km.) long by ab. 50 mi. (80 km.) wide; 3759 sq. mi. (9736 sq. km.); divided into two provinces, **Mindoro Oc·ci·den·tal** \ˌȯk-sē-ˌden-ˈtäl\ and **Mindoro Ori·en·tal** \ˌō-rē-ˌen-ˈtäl\ (see table at PHILIPPINES). Roughly of oval shape with long axis NW to SE; has fairly regular coastline with several good harbors; most important adjacent islands are Lubang Is. to NW, Semirara Is. to S, and Ilin I. off SW coast. Mountain range, with several high peaks, runs through center; highest are Halcon in N 8469 ft. (2581 m.) and Baco in the center 8163 ft. (2488 m.); coastal plains on E and W sides are wide and fertile. Numerous rivers with falls and rapids; known to Chinese before coming of Spaniards; first visited by Spaniards 1570; came under American control 1901; held by Japanese through WWII; invaded by Americans 1944; divided into two provinces 1950.

Mindoro Strait. Passage connecting South China Sea and N Sulu Sea, bet. SW Mindoro and Calamian Group, Philippines; ab. 50 mi. (80 km.) wide; much traveled by ships bet. Manila, Hong Kong, and other Asian ports on N and ports of S Philippines and Indonesia on S.

Mine·head \ˈmīn-ˌhed\. Seaside resort town, Somerset, SW England, on Bristol Channel 43 mi. (69 km.) WSW of Bristol; pop. (1981c) 11,211; chartered 1558.

Min·e·o·la \ˌmi-nē-ˈō-lə\. **1.** Village, ⊗ of Nassau co., SE New York, on Long Island 20 mi. (32 km.) E of New York City; pop. (1990c) 18,994; suburb of New York City.

2. City, Wood co., NE Texas, 23 mi. (37 km.) N of Tyler; pop. (1990c) 4321.

Mi·ner \ˈmī-nər\. County in E South Dakota. See table at SOUTH DAKOTA.

Min·er·al \ˈmi-nər-əl\. **1.** Name of counties in four states of the U.S. See tables at COLORADO, MONTANA, NEVADA, WEST VIRGINIA.

2. Locality, Tehama co., N cen. California; headquarters for Lassen Volcanic National Park.

Mi·ne·ral'·ny·ye Vo·dy *or* **Mi·ne·ral·ny·ye Vo·dy** \ˌmi-nə-ˈrälʸ-nē-ə-ˈvȯ-dē\. Town, Stavropol' Kray, S Russia in Europe, ab. 80 mi. (130 km.) SE of the city of Stavropol'; pop. (1991e) 72,500.

Mineral Point. City, Iowa co., SW Wisconsin, 17 mi. (27 km.) ENE of Platteville; pop. (1990c) 2428; lead and zinc mined in 1800s.

Mineral Wells. City, Palo Pinto and Parker cos., N cen. Texas, 42 mi. (68 km.) W of Fort Worth; pop. (1990c) 14,870.

Min·ers·ville \ˈmī-nərz-ˌvil\. Borough, Schuylkill co., E cen. Pennsylvania, 4 mi. (6 km.) WNW of Pottsville; pop. (1990c) 4877.

Mi·ner·va \mə-ˈnər-və\. Village, Carroll and Stark cos., E Ohio, 15 mi. (24 km.) ESE of Canton; pop. (1990c) 4318.

Mi·ner·vi·no Mur·ge \ˌmē-ner-ˈvē-nō-ˈmür-jā\. Commune, Bari prov., Puglia, SE Italy, 40 mi. (64 km.) W of the seaport of Bari; pop. (1981p) 11,888.

Min·gan Archipelago National Park \ˈmiŋ-gən\. See CANADA, *National Parks.*

Min·ga·nie–Côte–Nord–du–Golfe–Saint–Lau·rent \ˌmēn-gȧ-ˈnē-ˌkōt-ˌnȯrd-dᵫ-ˌgȯlf-seⁿ-lō-räⁿ\. County, Quebec, Canada. See table at QUEBEC.

Mingan Islands. Group of islands in Gulf of St. Lawrence, Canada, N of Anticosti I., near mouth of Romaine River; set aside as Mingan Archipelago National Park (see CANADA, *National Parks*).

Min·ge·chaur \ˌmēn-gi-ˈchyür\. City, N cen. Azerbaijan, on **Mingechaur Reservoir** in Kura River; pop. (1991e) 90,900.

Min·go \ˈmiŋ-gō\. County in SW West Virginia. See table at WEST VIRGINIA.

Mingo Junction. City, Jefferson co., E Ohio, on Ohio River 3 mi. (5 km.) S of Steubenville; pop. (1990c) 4297.

Min·gre·lia \min-ˈgrē-lē-ə, miŋ-\. Region and former principality now included in NW Republic of Georgia; lies within borders of ancient Colchis, partly in Caucasus Mts. and partly along Black Sea coast. Declared its independence early in 15th cent. but was subject to some extent to Persia and Turkey; came under Russian control early 19th cent.

Min·gu·lay \ˈmiŋ-ü-ˌlā\. See BARRA.

Mi·nho \ˈmē-nyü\ *or Span.* **Mi·ño** \ˈmē-nyō\; *anc.* **Min·i·us** \ˈmi-nē-əs\. River, Spain and Portugal; rises in N Lugo prov., NW Spain, flows S and SW, forming boundary bet. Portugal and Spain, and empties into Atlantic Ocean on the boundary S of Vigo; 171 mi. (275 km.) long.

Minhow. See FUZHOU.

Min·i·coy \ˈmi-ni-ˌkȯi\. Small island, S Laccadive Is., off SW coast of India; administratively part of the Indian union terr. of Lakshadweep.

Min·i·do·ka \ˌmi-nə-ˈdō-kə\. County in S Idaho. See table at IDAHO.

Minieh. See MINYA.

Minius. See MINHO.

Min·na \ˈmi-nə\. Town, ✱ of Niger state, Nigeria, on railroad line ab. 65 mi. (105 km.) N of the Niger River; pop. (1991e) 120,200.

Min·ne·ap·o·lis \ˌmi-nē-ˈa-pə-lis\. **1.** City, ⊗ of Ottawa co., NE cen. Kansas, on Solomon River 20 mi. (32 km.) N of Salina; pop. (1990c) 1983.

2. City, ⊗ of Hennepin co., SE cen. Minnesota, on Mississippi River at the Falls of St. Anthony (*q.v.*); pop. (1990c) 368,383; largest city in the state; railroad center and grain market; produces machinery, precision instruments, metal and paper products, food products; printing and publishing. Univ. of Minnesota, Twin Cities (1851), Augsburg Coll. (1869), Minneapolis Coll. of Art and Design (1886), North Central Bible Coll. (1930), St. Mary's Junior Coll. (1964), Minneapolis Community Coll. (1965); Walker Art Center. Site visited by French missionary Louis Hennepin c. 1680; included in area of Fort Snelling military reservation 1819; arose as two villages on opposite banks of the river 1830s–40s, later merged into one city; developed as center of lumber industry and later as center for milling flour; incorp. 1867; with St. Paul often referred to as the Twin Cities.

Min·ne·do·sa \ˌmi-nə-ˈdō-sə\. Town, SW Manitoba, Canada, 29 mi. (47 km.) N of Brandon; pop. (1991c) 2526; farm equipment.

Min·ne·ha·ha \ˌmi-nē-ˈhä-hä\. County in SE South Dakota. See table at SOUTH DAKOTA.

Minnehaha Creek. Small stream, Hennepin co., SE cen. Minnesota; outlet of Lake Minnetonka; flows through S part of Minneapolis (area set aside as a park); the falls, ab. 50 ft. (15 m.) high, celebrated by writer Henry Wadsworth Longfellow's use in his poem *Hiawatha,* occur just before the creek reaches the Mississippi River; natural flow of water small.

Min·ne·so·ta \ˌmi-nə-ˈsō-tə\. **1.** River, S Minnesota; flows out of Big Stone Lake on South Dakota-Minnesota boundary, bends SE, then NE to join the Mississippi River at St. Paul; 332 mi. (534 km.) long.

2. A north central state of U.S.A., bounded on N by Canadian provs. of Manitoba and Ontario, on E by Lake Superior and Wisconsin, on S by Iowa, and on W by South Dakota and North Dakota; 12th state in area, 84,068 sq. mi. or 217,736 sq. km. (land area 79,278 sq. mi. or 205,330 sq. km.), in addition to this area Minnesota has also 2212 sq. mi. (5729 sq. km.) of water of the Great Lakes; 20th state in population, (1990c) 4,375,099; ✱ St. Paul; 32d state admitted to Union (1858). See table of states at UNITED STATES.

Nicknames: Gopher State; North Star State.

State flower: Pink and white moccasin flower.

Motto: L'étoile du Nord (Star of the North).

Rivers: Mississippi, rising in N cen. region, flowing SE, and forming SE boundary of state; St. Croix, forming E cen. boundary and flowing into the Mississippi; Minnesota (see MINNESOTA 1).

Highest point: Eagle Mt., 2301 ft. (701 m.), in Cook co.

Chief products: Oats, corn, soybeans, sugar beets, wild rice; turkeys, hogs; dairy products; iron ore, granite, limestone; manufacturing: electronic equipment, pulp and paper products; food processing; tourism.

Chief cities: Minneapolis, St. Paul, Bloomington, Duluth, Rochester.

Political divisions: Divided into the following 87 counties (for pronunciation of their names, see their individual entries):

NAME	AREA[1] (sq. mi.)	AREA[1] (sq. km.)	POP. (1990c)	CO. SEAT
Aitkin[2]	1,831	4,742	12,425	Aitkin
Anoka	424	1,098	243,641	Anoka
Becker	1,297	3,359	27,881	Detroit Lakes
Beltrami	2,507	6,493	34,384	Bemidji
Benton	402	1,041	30,185	Foley
Big Stone	490	1,269	6,285	Ortonville
Blue Earth	737	1,909	54,044	Mankato
Brown	610	1,580	26,984	New Ulm
Carlton	862	2,233	29,259	Carlton
Carver	359	930	47,915	Chaska
Cass[3]	1,998	5,175	21,791	Walker
Chippewa	582	1,507	13,228	Montevideo
Chisago	419	1,085	30,521	Center City
Clay	1,045	2,707	50,422	Moorhead
Clearwater[4]	1,000	2,590	8,309	Bagley
Cook	1,346	3,486	3,868	Grand Marais
Cottonwood	636	1,647	12,694	Windom
Crow Wing	995	2,577	44,249	Brainerd
Dakota	576	1,492	275,227	Hastings
Dodge	435	1,127	15,731	Mantorville
Douglas	647	1,676	28,674	Alexandria
Faribault	711	1,841	16,937	Blue Earth
Fillmore	859	2,225	20,777	Preston
Freeborn	700	1,813	33,060	Albert Lea
Goodhue	753	1,950	40,690	Red Wing
Grant	546	1,414	6,246	Elbow Lake
Hennepin	567	1,469	1,032,431	Minneapolis
Houston	555	1,437	18,497	Caledonia
Hubbard	932	2,414	14,939	Park Rapids
Isanti	438	1,134	25,921	Cambridge
Itasca	2,633	6,819	40,863	Grand Rapids
Jackson	696	1,803	11,677	Jackson
Kanabec	524	1,357	12,802	Mora
Kandiyohi	783	2,028	38,761	Willmar
Kittson	1,123	2,909	5,767	Hallock
Koochiching	3,127	8,099	16,299	International Falls
Lac qui Parle	768	1,989	8,924	Madison
Lake	2,062	5,341	10,415	Two Harbors
Lake of the Woods[5]	1,311	3,395	4,076	Baudette
Le Sueur	440	1,140	23,239	Le Center
Lincoln	531	1,375	6,890	Ivanhoe
Lyon	709	1,836	24,789	Marshall
McLeod	488	1,264	32,030	Glencoe
Mahnomen	563	1,458	5,044	Mahnomen
Marshall	1,789	4,634	10,993	Warren
Martin	703	1,821	22,914	Fairmont
Meeker	619	1,603	20,846	Litchfield
Mille Lacs[2]	571	1,479	18,670	Milaca
Morrison	1,127	2,919	29,604	Little Falls
Mower	711	1,841	37,385	Austin
Murray	702	1,818	9,660	Slayton
Nicollet	432	1,119	28,076	St. Peter
Nobles	712	1,844	20,098	Worthington
Norman	885	2,292	7,975	Ada
Olmsted	656	1,699	106,470	Rochester
Otter Tail[6]	1,962	5,082	50,714	Fergus Falls
Pennington	622	1,611	13,306	Thief River Falls
Pine	1,414	3,662	21,264	Pine City
Pipestone	464	1,202	10,491	Pipestone
Polk	2,013	5,214	32,498	Crookston
Pope	669	1,733	10,745	Glenwood
Ramsey	155	401	485,765	St. Paul
Red Lake	432	1,119	4,525	Red Lake Falls
Redwood	874	2,264	17,254	Redwood Falls
Renville	979	2,536	17,673	Olivia
Rice	496	1,285	49,183	Faribault
Rock	485	1,256	9,806	Luverne
Roseau	1,676	4,341	15,026	Roseau
Saint Louis	6,092	15,778	198,213	Duluth
Scott	353	914	57,846	Shakopee
Sherburne	430	1,114	41,945	Elk River
Sibley	583	1,510	14,366	Gaylord
Stearns	1,342	3,476	118,791	St. Cloud
Steele	425	1,101	30,729	Owatonna
Stevens	558	1,445	10,634	Morris
Swift	739	1,914	10,724	Benson
Todd	942	2,440	23,363	Long Prairie
Traverse	568	1,471	4,463	Wheaton
Wabasha	522	1,352	19,744	Wabasha
Wadena	536	1,388	13,154	Wadena
Waseca	415	1,075	18,079	Waseca
Washington	386	1,000	145,896	Stillwater
Watonwan	433	1,121	11,682	St. James
Wilkin	752	1,948	7,516	Breckenridge
Winona	620	1,606	47,828	Winona
Wright	674	1,746	68,710	Buffalo
Yellow Medicine	753	1,950	11,684	Granite Falls

[1] Area = land area.
[2] Upper half of Mille Lacs Lake in Aitkin co., lower half in Mille Lacs co.
[3] Contains many lakes, incl. Leech Lake.
[4] Includes Lake Itasca, source of Mississippi River.
[5] Includes part of Lake of the Woods and a section of land on W shore of the lake N of the 49th parallel.
[6] Contains many lakes, incl. Otter Tail Lake.

History: Evidence of prehistoric habitation; at time of European arrival, inhabited by Algonquian Ojibwa and Siouan Dakota American Indian tribes; probably visited by French

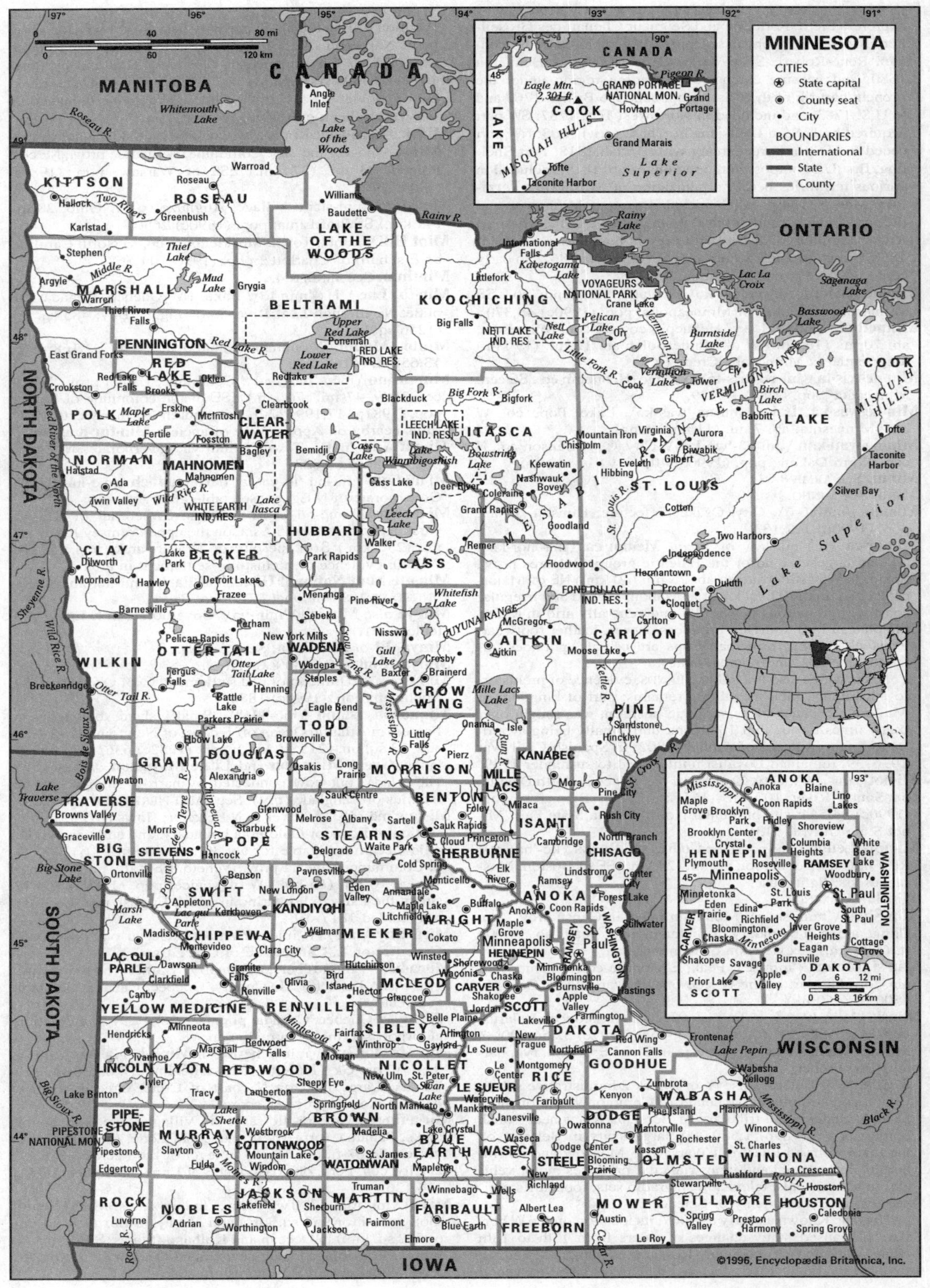
MINNESOTA
CITIES
State capital
County seat
City
BOUNDARIES
International
State
County
CANADA
MANITOBA
ONTARIO
NORTH DAKOTA
SOUTH DAKOTA
IOWA
WISCONSIN
Lake Superior
Minneapolis
St. Paul
Duluth
©1996, Encyclopædia Britannica, Inc.

explorers Pierre Radisson and Seigneur Chouart des Groseilliers 1654–60; Upper Mississippi Valley explored by Frenchmen René-Robert, Sieur de La Salle and Louis Hennepin 1680, and became extensive fur-trading region under the French; part NE of the Mississippi ceded to British 1763 and to U.S. 1783, and included in Northwest Terr. 1787; SW part acquired by U.S. in Louisiana Purchase (*q.v.*) 1803; NW part ceded to U.S. in border treaty with British 1818; Fort Snelling, first U.S. outpost in the region, estab. 1819; included in various territories before organization of **Minnesota Territory** Mar. 3, 1849, which included present Minnesota and the parts of North and South Dakota that lie E of the Missouri River; admitted to Union (with present boundaries) May 11, 1858; Sioux uprising occurred in S Minnesota 1862; an early center of the Grange movement 1867 ff.

Min·ne·ton·ka \ˌmi-nə-ˈtäŋ-kə\. Village, Hennepin co., SE Minnesota, W suburb of Minneapolis; pop. (1990c) 48,370.

Minnetonka, Lake. Lake, Hennepin co., SE cen. Minnesota, ab. 10 mi. (16 km.) W of Minneapolis; ab. 12 mi. (19 km.) long; outlet is Minnehaha Creek (*q.v.*).

Min·ne·tris·ta \ˌmi-nə-ˈtris-tə\. Village, Hennepin co., SE cen. Minnesota; pop. (1990c) 3439.

Min·ne·was·ka, Lake \ˌmi-nə-ˈwäs-kə\. Lake, Pope co., W cen. Minnesota; ab. 7 mi. (11 km.) long.

Min·ne·wau·kan \ˌmi-nə-ˈwȯ-kən\. City, ⊗ of Benson co., N cen. North Dakota; pop. (1990c) 401.

Minni. See ARMENIA 1.

Miño. See MINHO.

Mi·noo \ˈmē-nō-ō\. City, Osaka prefecture, Honshū, Japan; pop. (1990p) 122,133.

Mi·nor·ca \mi-ˈnȯr-kə\ *or Span.* **Me·nor·ca** \mā-ˈnȯr-kä\. Second largest island of the Balearic group, Baleares prov., Spain, in W Mediterranean ab. 25 mi. (40 km.) NE of Majorca; 271 sq. mi. (702 sq. km.); ✻ Mahón; rugged and irregular coast with numerous bays; hilly and generally arid in N, fertile plateau in S; tourism; produces cheese, leather footwear; livestock raising; principal crops are cereals, potatoes, almonds, melons, and pomegranates.

History: See also BALEARIC ISLANDS; evidence of prehistoric inhabitants, incl. megalithic remains; part of kingdom of Mallorca; because of its strategic position, was fought over many times throughout 18th cent. until finally being awarded to Spain in Peace of Amiens 1802; in Spanish Civil War 1936–39, remained Loyalist until forced to surrender 1939.

Mi·not \ˈmī-ˌnät\. City, ⊗ of Ward co., NW cen. North Dakota, on Souris River 100 mi. (161 km.) N of Bismarck; pop. (1990c) 34,544; site of annual North Dakota State Fair; Minot State Univ. (1913).

Mi·nots Ledge \ˈmī-nəts\ *or* **Co·has·set Rocks** \kō-ˈhas-ət\. Reef in Cohasset harbor, 15 mi. (24 km.) SE of Boston, Massachusetts; lighthouse.

Minsh. See MINCH.

Min Shan \ˈmin-ˈshän\. Mountain range in Gansu prov., cen. China, along N boundary of Sichuan prov.; peaks ab. 14,000 ft. (4300 m.); E extension of Kunlun Shan.

Min·si, Mount \ˈmin-sē\. Peak, E Monroe co., E Pennsylvania, forming part of the W side of Delaware Water Gap; ab. 1500 ft. (460 m.).

Minsk \ˈminsk\. **1.** Administrative subdivision of Belarus; 40,800 sq. mi. (105,672 sq. km.); pop. (1991e) 3,256,000; ✻ Minsk; swamps widespread, esp. in S and E; wheat, rye, barley, flax, timber.

2. City, ✻ of Belarus, also ✻ of Minsk administrative subdivision, and administrative center of Commonwealth of Independent States; on a tributary of Berezina River near Polish border; pop. (1989p) 1,589,000; largest city in Belarus; on the main railroad line from Warsaw to Moscow and an important commercial and industrial city; produces motor vehicles, machine tools, television and radio sets, foodstuffs; university (1921), Academy of Sciences.

History: Known as early as 1067, its location on the W border has caused many changes of rulers from 13th to 18th cents.—at times Lithuanian, Russian, Polish, or Swedish; ravaged by Tatars 1505; annexed by Russia 1793 in Second Partition of Poland; again partially destroyed by French Emperor Napoléon 1812; a key point in the Bolshevik Revolution of 1917 but occupied by Germans 1918 and by Poles 1919–20; in WWII again seized by Germans 1941 but retaken by Soviet forces 1944; although heavily damaged in WWII, has been extensively rebuilt.

Mińsk Ma·zo·wiec·ki \ˈmēⁿsk-ˌmä-zȯ-ˈvyet-skē\ *also* **No·wo–Mińsk** \ˈnȯ-vȯ-ˈmēⁿsk\. Commune, W Siedlce prov., NE cen. Poland, 23 mi. (37 km.) ESE of Warsaw; pop. (1989e) 34,097.

Min·ster \ˈmin-stər\. Village, Auglaize co., W Ohio, 28 mi. (45 km.) SSW of Lima; pop. (1990c) 2650.

Mint Hill \ˈmint\. Town, Mecklenburg co., S North Carolina, an E suburb of Charlotte; pop. (1990c) 11,567.

Minthun. See MINDEN 4.

Min·to, Lac \ˌlȧk-ˈmin-tō\. Lake, NW Quebec, Canada; has outlet NE through Leaf River into Ungava Bay; 485 sq. mi. (1256 sq. km.).

Minto, Mount. Mountain, Antarctica, 71°47′S, 168°45′E; 13,658 ft. (4163 m.).

Min·tur·no \mēn-ˈtür-(ˌ)nō\. Commune, Latina prov., Lazio, cen. Italy, 47 mi. (76 km.) ESE of the commune of Latina; pop. (1981p) 17,199; 12th cent. church (formerly cathedral); ruins nearby on Appian Way of ancient **Min·tur·nae** \-nē\.

Mi·nūf \mē-ˈnüf\. Town, Minūfīya governorate, N Egypt; pop. (1986p) 69,883.

Mi·nū·fī·ya \ˌmi-nü-ˈfē-yə\ *also* **Me·nu·fi·eh** \ˌme-nu̇-ˈfē-yə\. Governorate of N Egypt. See table at EGYPT.

Mi·nu·sinsk \ˌmē-nü-ˈsēnsk\. Town, SW corner of Krasnoyarsk Kray, S Russia in Asia, on the upper Yenisey River 160 mi. (257 km.) S of the city of Krasnoyarsk; pop. (1991e) 74,200; evidence of prehistoric settlement in area.

Min·ute Man National Historical Park \ˈmi-nət-ˌman\. See UNITED STATES, *National Historical Parks.*

Min·ya *also* **Min·ieh** \ˈmin-yə\. Governorate of N Egypt. See table at EGYPT.

Minya, El *or* **Al Minya.** See EL MINYA.

Minya Konka. See GONGGA SHAN.

Mio \ˈmī-ō\. Unincorporated settlement, ⊗ of Oscoda co., NE Michigan; pop. (1990c) 1886.

Mique·lon Island \mē-ˈklōⁿ\. Small island, belonging to France, in Atlantic Ocean off S coast of Newfoundland, Canada; 83 sq. mi. (215 sq. km.); pop. (1982c) 636; orig. two islands, **Great Miquelon** and **Little Miquelon** *or* **Lan·glade** \läⁿ-ˈglȧd\, but now connected by narrow shingle bar, the Isthmus of Langlade (*q.v.*). See SAINT-PIERRE AND MIQUELON.

Mi·ra \ˈmē-rä\. **1.** River in N Ecuador; flows NW, forming a section of Ecuador-Colombia boundary, and empties into Pacific Ocean; navigable for ab. 30 mi. (48 km.).

2. Commune, Venezia prov., Veneto, NE Italy, on Lagoon of Venice 10 mi. (16 km.) W of Venice; pop. (1989c) 36,877; site of the Palazzo Foscarino in which English poet Lord Byron resided 1817–19.

Mira Bay \ˈmī-rə\. Inlet of Atlantic Ocean on NE coast of Cape Breton I., Canada, SE of Glace Bay.

Mi·ra·bel \ˌmē-rä-ˈbel\; *formerly* **Sainte Scho·las·tique** \ˌseⁿt-ˌskȯ-lȧs-ˈtēk\. **1.** County, Quebec, Canada. See table at QUEBEC.

2. City, S Quebec, Canada; pop. (1991c) 17,971; international airport serving Montreal area.

Mir·a·bel·lo Gulf \ˌmir-ə-ˈbe-lō\ *or* **Mir·a·bel·la Bay** \ˌmir-ə-ˈbe-lə\ *or Gk.* **Kól·pos Me·ra·bél·lou** \ˈkȯl-ˌpȯs-ˌme-rä-ˈbe-lü\. Large inlet on N coast of Crete, Greece; town of Áyios Nikólaos on its W shore.

Mir·a·flo·res \ˌmē-rä-ˈflō-rās\. **1.** Village, lake, and double locks, Panama, formerly in the Canal Zone; the locks lower vessels 54.67 ft. (16.66 m.) to level of the Pacific.

2. City, cen. Peru, on coast, just S of Lima; area pop. (1990e) 114,126.

Mi·raj \mi-ˈrəj\. **1.** Two former Indian states: **Miraj Senior** (368 sq. mi. or 953 sq. km.) and **Miraj Junior** (194 sq. mi. or 502 sq. km.) in Deccan and Kolhapur States, S Bombay, W India. Miraj Junior joined new United Deccan State Aug. 26, 1947. Area now in S Maharashtra state.

2. Town, former ❋ of Miraj Senior state, near Krishna River 194 mi. (312 km.) SE of Bombay; pop. (1991p) 121,564.

Mi·ra·mar \'mir-ə-ˌmär\. **1.** City, Broward co., SE Florida S of Fort Lauderdale; pop. (1990c) 40,663.
2. *formerly* **Ge·ne·ral Al·va·ra·do** \ˌhā-nā-'räl-ˌäl-bä-'rä-thō\. Seaside resort, E Buenos Aires prov., E Argentina, S of Mar del Plata.

Mi·ra·mas \ˌmē-rá-'mä\. Town, Bouches-du-Rhône dept., S France; near shore of the Étang de Berre.

Mir·a·mi·chi Bay \ˌmir-ə-mə-'shē\. Inlet of Gulf of St. Lawrence, E Northumberland co., E New Brunswick, Canada; receives the **Miramichi River,** 135 mi. (217 km.) long, rising in Victoria co. and flowing from the SW, the main stream sometimes known as the **South West Miramichi.**

Mi·ran·da \mē-'rán-də\. **1.** River, S Mato Grosso state, SW Brazil; flows NW into the Paraguay River; 225 mi. (362 km.) long.
2. Municipality, S Mato Grosso state, SW Brazil, on railroad line and on right bank of Miranda River; pop. (1980c) 24,162.
3. State of N Venezuela. See table at VENEZUELA.

Miranda de Ebro \mē-'rän-dä-thā-'ā-brō\. Commune, Burgos prov., N cen. Spain, on the Ebro 36 mi. (58 km.) NE of the city of Burgos; pop. (1991p) 36,497.

Mi·ran·do·la \mē-'rän-dō-lä\. Commune, Modena prov., Emilia-Romagna, N Italy, 19 mi. (30 km.) NNE of the commune of Modena; pop. (1981p) 21,674.

Mi·ra·no \mē-'rä-nō\. Commune, Venezia prov., Veneto, NE Italy, 12 mi. (19 km.) WNW of Venice; pop. (1981p) 23,946.

Mir·di·të \mēr-'dē-tə\. District of N cen. Albania. See table at ALBANIA.

Mir·field \'mər-ˌfēld\. Town, West Yorkshire, N England; pop. (1981p) 18,686.

Mir·go·rod \'mir-gə-rət\. Town, cen. Poltava subdivision, E cen. Ukraine, on railroad line 50 mi. (80 km.) WNW of the city of Poltava.

Mi·ri \'mē-rē\. Seaport, NE Sarawak, Malaysia, on island of Borneo, S of Baram Point; pop. (1980c) 52,125.

Mi·rím, La·goa \lä-'gō-ä-mē-'rēm\ *or Eng.* **Lake Mirim** *or Span.* **La·gu·na Me·rín** \lä-'gü-nä-mā-'rēn\. Lake, E boundary of Uruguay, separating Uruguay from extreme S tip of Brazil; 108 mi. (174 km.) long.

Mīr·jā·veh \ˌmēr-jä-'ve\. Town, SE Iran, on railroad line ab. 120 mi. (190 km.) NE of Bampūr and near Pakistani border.

Mir·pur Khas \'mir-ˌpu̇r-'käs\. Town, S cen. Sind prov., Pakistan, ENE of Hyderabad; pop. (1981c) 124,371.

Mirs Bay. See DAPENG WAN.

Mir·za·pur \'mir-zə-ˌpu̇r\. City, SE Uttar Pradesh, N India, on right bank of Ganges River 45 mi. (72 km.) ESE of Allahabad; pop. (1991p) 169,368; trade center; carpets, brassware; sandstone; has mosques and Hindu temples. Now includes **Vindhyachal**, which has a shrine of Vindhyeshwari and is a center of pilgrimage.

Mi·sa·mis \mē-'sä-mēs, mi-'sä-məs\. In Spanish times the Philippine province along N coast of Mindanao, now divided into Misamis Occidental and Misamis Oriental.

Misamis Oc·ci·den·tal \ˌȯk-sē-den-'täl\. Province, N Mindanao, Philippines; ❋ Oroquieta; coastal area W of Iligan Bay; mountainous with highest peak Mt. Malindang 7954 ft. (2424 m.). Chief towns Ozamiz, Oroquieta, and Tangub. See table at PHILIPPINES.

Misamis Orien·tal \ˌȯr-ē-en-'täl\. Province, N Mindanao, Philippines; ❋ Cagayan de Oro; long coastal strip E of Iligan Bay and Camiguin I. in S cen. Mindanao Sea; contains two inlets Macajalar Bay and Gingoog Bay; has volcanic cone Hibokhibok 5620 ft. (1713 m.) on Camiguin I.; has fertile soil. See table at PHILIPPINES.

Mi·sant·la \mē-'sänt-lä\. City, Veracruz state, Mexico, 70 mi. (113 km.) NW of the city of Veracruz; munic. pop. (1990p) 58,144; commercial center; site of ancient ruins.

Mi·sa·to \mē-'sä-tō\. City, Saitama prefecture, Honshū, Japan; pop. (1990p) 128,377.

Misch·a·bel·hör·ner \'mish-ˌä-bəl-ˌhœr-nər\. Mountain group in the Pennine Alps, Valais canton, SW cen. Switzerland; highest peak the Dom 14,913 ft. (4545 m.).

Mis·cou Island \'mis-kü\. Island off NE tip of New Brunswick, Canada, S of entrance to Chaleur Bay; its N tip is **Miscou Point**.

Mi–sen \'mē-'sen\. See ITSUKU-SHIMA.

Mi·se·no \mē-'zā-nō, -'ze-\. Promontory, NW of the Bay of Naples and S of ruins of Cumae, Italy; at its base to the N is Porto di Miseno, site of ancient town of **Mi·se·num** \mī-'sē-nəm\, a naval base estab. by Romans under Roman Emperor Augustus, and important for several centuries.

Mis·ery, Mount \'mi-zə-rē\. Peak on the island of St. Kitts, St. Kitts-Nevis, West Indies; 3792 ft. (1156 m.).

Mish, Slieve. See SLIEVE MISH.

Mīshāb, Kūh–e \'kü-ə-mē-'shäb\. Mountain range in NW Iran, N of Daryācheh-ye Orūmīyeh; highest point 10,430 ft. (3179 m.).

Mi·shaum Point \mə-'shȯm\. S point of Bristol co., SE Massachusetts; extends into Buzzards Bay.

Mish·a·wa·ka \ˌmi-shə-'wȯ-kə, -'wä-\. City, St. Joseph co., N Indiana, SE of South Bend; pop. (1990c) 42,608; guided missiles, rubber goods, plastics; Bethel Coll. (1947).

Mi·shi·ma \mē-'shē-mä\. City, Shizuoka prefecture, Honshū, Japan, 31 mi. (50 km.) NE of the city of Shizuoka; pop. (1990p) 105,419.

Mi·sil·me·ri \ˌmē-sēl-'mā-rē\. Commune, Palermo prov., Sicily, Italy, 8 mi. (13 km.) SE of the seaport of Palermo; pop. (1981p) 15,809; castle.

Mi·si·ma \mē-'sē-mä\ *also* **Saint Ai·gnan** \ˌse^{n}-tā-'nyä^{n}\. Island in Louisiade Archipelago, administratively part of Papua New Guinea, 140 mi. (225 km.) E of Milne Bay; ab. 100 sq. mi. (260 sq. km.); ab. 25 mi. (40 km.) long and bet. 1 and 4 mi. (2 and 6 km.) wide; at E end is Bwagaoia, chief village of the group; mountainous, with some peaks above 3000 ft. (900 m.); formerly important gold producer.

Mi·sio·nes \mē-'syō-nās\. **1.** Province of N cen. Argentina, ❋ Posadas. See table at ARGENTINA.
2. Department of S Paraguay. See table at PARAGUAY.

Misiones, Sierra de. See SIERRA DE MISIONES.

Misis. See MOPSUESTIA.

Misithra. See MISTRA.

Miskish, Slieve. See SLIEVE MISKISH.

Miskito Coast. See MOSQUITO COAST.

Mis·kolc \'mish-ˌkōlts\. City, ⊗ of Borsod-Abaúj-Zemplén co., NE Hungary, 85 mi. (137 km.) NE of Budapest; pop. (1991e) 207,300; major industrial center, producing iron and steel, flour, textiles, wine; 13th cent. church. Invaded by Mongols 13th cent.; became free city 15th cent.

Mi·sool *or* **Mi·sol** \'mē-ˌsȯl\. Island, Indonesia, N of Ceram and just W of Doberai Penin. of W Irian Jaya; ab. 50 mi. (81 km.) long by 23 mi. (37 km.) wide; 672 sq. mi. (1741 sq. km.).

Misore Islands. See SCHOUTEN ISLANDS 1.

Mis·quah Hills \'mis-kwȯ\. Elevation, Cook co., NE corner of Minnesota; ab. 2230 ft. (680 m.).

Mişr. See EGYPT.

Mis·rā·tah \mēs-'rä-tə\ *also* **Mi·su·ra·ta** \ˌmē-sü-'rä-tə\. Coastal city, NW Libya, 125 mi. (201 km.) E of Tripoli; captured from Italians by British 1943 during WWII.

Mis·sau·kee \mi-'sȯ-kē\. County in NW cen. Michigan. See table at MICHIGAN.

Mis·si·nai·bi \ˌmi-sə-'nī-bē\. River, E cen. Ontario, Canada; rises in **Missinaibi Lake** and flows N and NE to join the Mattagami and form the Moose River; 265 mi. (426 km.) long.

Mis·sion \'mi-shən\. **1.** City, Johnson co., E Kansas, 4 mi. (6 km.) W of Kansas City; pop. (1990c) 9504; residential suburb of Kansas City.
2. City, Hidalgo co., S Texas, near the Rio Grande 5 mi. (8 km.) W of McAllen; pop. (1990c) 28,653; oil wells; packs and ships citrus fruits.

3. Municipality, SW British Columbia, Canada, on Fraser River and on railroad line 38 mi. (61 km.) E of Vancouver; pop. (1991c) 26,202; Seminary of Christ the King (1932).

Mis·sion·ary Ridge \ˈmi-shə-ˌner-ē\. Ridge, SE U.S., extending NE to SW in Hamilton co., Tennessee, and Dade co., Georgia; a section of this ridge near Chattanooga was the site of a Union victory Nov. 1863 in the Civil War.

Mission Hills. City, Johnson co., E Kansas; pop. (1990c) 3446.

Mission Range. A range of the Rocky Mts. chiefly in Lake and Missoula cos., W Montana; highest point 9900 ft. (3018 m.).

Mis·sion Vi·e·jo \ˈmish-ᵊn-vē-ˈā-hō\. City, Orange co., California, 10 mi. (16 km.) SE of Santa Ana; pop. (1990c) 72,820.

Mis·sis·quoi \mə-ˈsis-ˌkwȯi\. River, U.S. and Canada; rises in Orleans co., NW Vermont, flows N into Canada, then S into Franklin co., Vermont, and W into Lake Champlain; ab. 90 mi. (145 km.) long.

Mis·sis·sa·gi \ˌmi-sə-ˈsä-gē\. River, SE Ontario, Canada; flows SW and S into North Channel; ab. 130 mi. (210 km.) long.

Mississagi, Strait of. Strait bet. W Manitoulin I. and Cockburn I. in NE Lake Huron, SE Ontario, S Canada.

Mis·sis·sau·ga \ˌmi-sə-ˈsȯ-gə\. City, S Ontario, Canada, SW of Toronto; pop. (1991c) 463,388.

Mis·sis·sin·e·wa \ˌmi-si-ˈsi-nə-wə\. River in Ohio and Indiana, rises in Darke co., Ohio and flows W and NW through Marion, Indiana and into the Wabash at Peru.

Mis·sis·sip·pi \ˌmi-sə-ˈsi-pē\. **1.** Navigable river, cen. U.S.; rises in Lake Itasca, NW Minnesota, flows SE to form lower section of Minnesota-Wisconsin boundary, and the Iowa-Wisconsin and Iowa-Illinois boundaries, the Missouri-Illinois, Missouri-Kentucky, and Missouri-Tennessee boundaries, the Arkansas-Tennessee and Arkansas-Mississippi boundaries, and the N section of Louisiana-Mississippi boundary, then continuing SE into the Mississippi River delta and into the Gulf of Mexico through several mouths, known locally as the Passes—Main Pass, North Pass, South Pass, Southwest Pass; 2357 mi. (3792 km.) long or, if measured from headwaters of Missouri River, 3877 mi. (6238 km.) long; head of the Passes to the Gulf of Mexico 17 mi. (27 km.); drainage area ab. 1,235,000 sq. mi. (3,198,650 sq. km.).

History: Sighted and crossed by Spanish explorer Hernando de Soto 1540–41; upper reaches explored by French explorers Père Marquette and Louis Jolliet 1673; lower part traced by French explorer Rene-Robert, Sieur de La Salle who laid claim for French to entire Mississippi Valley (see LOUISIANA) 1682; after French cessions of 1762 and 1763, was boundary bet. Spanish on W and British on E; became W boundary of U.S. 1783, but its mouth was controlled by Spain which finally granted free navigation by treaty 1795; U.S. obtained control of W part of valley by Louisiana Purchase 1803; headwaters explored by American explorer Zebulon Pike 1805–06; after c. 1820, navigated by steamboats; during Civil War, gradually opened by Union forces until capture of Vicksburg 1863 destroyed Confederate hold on the river.

2. Southeastern state of U.S.A., bounded on N by Tennessee, on E by Alabama, on S by the Gulf of Mexico and Louisiana, and on W by Louisiana and Arkansas; 32d state in area, 47,689 sq. mi. (123,514 sq. km.); 31st state in population, (1990c) 2,573,216; ✱ Jackson; 20th state admitted to Union (1817). See table of states at UNITED STATES.

Nickname: Magnolia State.

State flower: Magnolia.

Motto: Virtute et Armis (By Valor and Arms).

Rivers: Mississippi, forming W boundary; Pearl, flowing SW and S and forming SW boundary bet. Mississippi and Louisiana; Big Black, flowing from N cen. area SW into the Mississippi; Tennessee, forming boundary in extreme NE area.

Highest point: Woodall Mt., 806 ft. (246 m.), in Tishomingo co.

Chief products: Cotton, soybeans, grains; livestock; petroleum, natural gas; manufacturing: chemicals, apparel, wood products.

Chief cities: Jackson, Biloxi, Greenville, Hattiesburg, Meridian, Gulfport.

Political divisions: Divided into the following 82 counties (for pronunciation of their names, see their individual entries):

NAME	AREA[1] (sq. mi.)	AREA[1] (sq. km.)	POP. (1990c)	CO. SEAT(S)
Adams	449	1,163	35,356	Natchez
Alcorn	405	1,049	31,772	Corinth
Amite	729	1,888	13,328	Liberty
Attala	724	1,875	18,481	Kosciusko
Benton	412	1,067	8,046	Ashland
Bolivar	923	2,391	41,875	Cleveland and Rosedale
Calhoun	575	1,489	14,908	Pittsboro
Carroll	637	1,650	9,237	Vaiden and Carrollton
Chickasaw	506	1,311	18,085	Houston and Okolona
Chocktaw	417	1,080	9,071	Ackerman
Claiborne	489	1,267	11,370	Port Gibson
Clarke	697	1,805	17,313	Quitman
Clay	414	1,072	21,120	West Point
Coahoma	569	1,474	31,665	Clarksdale
Copiah	780	2,020	27,592	Hazelhurst
Covington	416	1,077	16,527	Collins
De Soto	476	1,233	67,910	Hernando
Forrest	468	1,212	68,314	Hattiesburg
Franklin	568	1,471	8,377	Meadville
George	481	1,246	16,673	Lucedale
Greene	728	1,886	10,220	Leakesville
Grenada	431	1,116	21,555	Grenada
Hancock	482	1,248	31,760	Bay St. Louis
Harrison	585	1,515	165,365	Gulfport
Hinds	876	2,269	254,441	Jackson and Raymond
Holmes	769	1,992	21,604	Lexington
Humphreys	421	1,090	12,134	Belzoni
Issaquena	414	1,072	1,909	Mayersville
Itawamba	541	1,401	20,017	Fulton
Jackson	736	1,906	115,243	Pascagoula
Jasper	683	1,769	17,114	Bay Springs and Paulding
Jefferson	521	1,349	8,653	Fayette
Jefferson Davis	414	1,072	14,051	Prentiss
Jones	702	1,818	62,031	Ellisville and Laurel
Kemper	757	1,961	10,356	De Kalb
Lafayette	668	1,730	31,826	Oxford
Lamar	500	1,295	30,424	Purvis
Lauderdale	721	1,867	75,555	Meridian
Lawrence	433	1,121	12,458	Monticello
Leake	586	1,518	18,436	Carthage
Lee	455	1,178	65,581	Tupelo
Leflore	592	1,533	37,341	Greenwood
Lincoln	586	1,518	30,278	Brookhaven
Lowndes	548	1,419	59,308	Columbus
Madison	751	1,945	53,794	Canton
Marion	550	1,425	25,544	Columbia
Marshall	710	1,839	30,361	Holly Springs
Monroe	769	1,992	36,582	Aberdeen
Montgomery	403	1,044	12,388	Winona
Neshoba	568	1,471	24,800	Philadelphia
Newton	580	1,502	20,291	Decatur
Noxubee	695	1,800	12,604	Macon
Oktibbeha	454	1,176	38,375	Starkville
Panola	693	1,795	29,996	Sardis and Batesville
Pearl River	828	2,145	38,714	Poplarville
Perry	653	1,691	10,865	New Augusta
Pike	409	1,059	36,882	Magnolia
Pontotoc	501	1,298	22,237	Pontotoc
Prentiss	418	1,083	23,278	Booneville
Quitman	412	1,067	10,490	Marks
Rankin	800	2,072	87,161	Brandon
Scott	615	1,593	24,137	Forest
Sharkey	436	1,129	7,066	Rolling Fork
Simpson	587	1,520	23,953	Mendenhall
Smith	642	1,663	14,798	Raleigh
Stone	448	1,160	10,750	Wiggins
Sunflower	694	1,797	32,867	Indianola
Tallahatchie	644	1,668	15,210	Charleston and Sumner
Tate	405	1,049	21,432	Senatobia
Tippah	464	1,202	19,523	Ripley
Tishomingo	443	1,147	17,683	Iuka
Tunica	458	1,186	8,164	Tunica
Union	422	1,093	22,085	New Albany
Walthall	403	1,044	14,352	Tylertown
Warren	581	1,505	47,880	Vicksburg
Washington	734	1,901	67,935	Greenville
Wayne	827	2,142	19,517	Waynesboro
Webster	416	1,077	10,222	Walthall
Wilkinson	674	1,746	9,678	Woodville
Winston	606	1,570	19,443	Louisville

MISSISSIPPI
0 30 60 mi
0 40 80 km
CITIES
State capital
County seat
City
BOUNDARIES
State
County
FEATURES
Dams
Points of interest
TENNESSEE
ARKANSAS
LOUISIANA
ALABAMA
DE SOTO
MARSHALL
BENTON
TIPPAH
ALCORN
TISHOMINGO
PRENTISS
TATE
TUNICA
UNION
LAFAYETTE
PANOLA
COAHOMA
QUITMAN
LEE
ITAWAMBA
PONTOTOC
YALOBUSHA
MONROE
TALLAHATCHIE
CALHOUN
CHICKASAW
BOLIVAR
SUNFLOWER
GRENADA
WEBSTER
CLAY
LEFLORE
MONTGOMERY
CARROLL
CHOCTAW
OKTIBBEHA
LOWNDES
WASHINGTON
HUMPHREYS
HOLMES
ATTALA
WINSTON
NOXUBEE
SHARKEY
YAZOO
ISSAQUENA
MADISON
LEAKE
NESHOBA
KEMPER
WARREN
SCOTT
NEWTON
LAUDERDALE
HINDS
RANKIN
CLAIBORNE
COPIAH
SMITH
JASPER
CLARKE
SIMPSON
JEFFERSON
COVINGTON
JONES
WAYNE
ADAMS
FRANKLIN
LINCOLN
LAWRENCE
JEFFERSON DAVIS
WILKINSON
AMITE
PIKE
WALTHALL
MARION
FORREST
LAMAR
PERRY
GREENE
PEARL RIVER
STONE
GEORGE
HARRISON
JACKSON
HANCOCK
Jackson
Horn Lake
Olive Branch
Byhalia
Hernando
Holly Springs
Ashland
Corinth
Iuka
Woodall Mtn. 807 ft.
Arkabutla Lake
Arkabutla Dam
Coldwater
Senatobia
Ripley
Blue Mountain
Booneville
Wheeler
Baldwyn
Belmont
Tunica
Como
Sardis
Sardis Lake
Sardis Dam
Crenshaw
New Albany
BRICES CROSS ROADS NATIONAL BATTLEFIELD
TUPELO NATIONAL BATTLEFIELD
Tennessee-Tombigbee Waterway
Jonestown
Marks
Lambert
Batesville
Oxford
Pontotoc
Tupelo
Fulton
Clarksdale
Crowder
Verona
Plantersville
Shannon
Enid Lake
Water Valley
Tutwiler
Sumner
Charleston
Coffeeville
Bruce
Pittsboro
Okolona
Shelby
Rosedale
Webb
Mound Bayou
Merigold
Cleveland
Boyle
Drew
Ruleville
Grenada
Grenada Lake
Calhoun City
Houston
Aberdeen
Benoit
Shaw
Tie Plant
Duck Hill
Walthall
Eupora
Maben
West Point
Columbus
Sunflower
Greenwood
Carrollton
Itta Bena
Indianola
Moorhead
Winona
Starkville
Greenville
Leland
Inverness
Vaiden
Ackerman
Arcola
Isola
Belzoni
Tchula
Weir
Brooksville
Hollandale
Lexington
Ethel
Louisville
Midnight
Durant
Kosciusko
Columbus A.F.B.
Macon
Anquilla
Goodman
Noxapater
Shuqualak
Mayersville
Rolling Fork
Yazoo City
Pickens
MISSISSIPPI BAND OF CHOCTAW INDIANS
Scooba
Carthage
Philadelphia
De Kalb
Demopolis Lake
Bentonia
Lena
Canton
Sebastopol
Union
Lauderdale
Madison
Ross Barnett Reservoir
Okatibbee Reservoir
Ridgeland
Decatur
Vicksburg
VICKSBURG NATIONAL MILITARY PARK
Clinton
Tougaloo
Forest
Marion
Bolton
Brandon
Morton
Newton
Hickory
Meridian
Raymond
Pearl
Whitfield
Pelahatchie
Utica
Terry
Enterprise
Stonewall
Piney Woods
Quitman
Crystal Springs
Mendenhall
Raleigh
Paulding
Port Gibson
Bay Springs
Alcorn College
Magee
Heidelberg
Shubuta
Hazlehurst
Taylorsville
Fayette
Sandersville
Lake Bogue Homo
Wesson
Laurel
Waynesboro
Prentiss
Natchez
Brookhaven
Collins
Meadville
Monticello
Ellisville
Buckatunna
Catahoula Lake
Sumerall
State Line
Crosby
Summit
Morgantown
Petal
Richton
Hattiesburg
McComb
Columbia
New Augusta
Fernwood
Foxworth
Camp Shelby
Woodville
Liberty
Magnolia
Baeumont
Tylertown
McLain
Leakesville
Pervis
Centerville
Osyka
Brooklyn
Lumberton
Poplarville
Lucedale
Wiggins
McHenry
McNeill
Carriere
Picayune
Baton Rouge
Orange Grove
Ocean Springs
D'Iberville
Keesler A.F.B.
Gautier
Moss Point
Pascagoula
Stennis Space Center (N.A.S.A.)
Long Beach
Gulfport
Biloxi
Bay Saint Louis
Pass Christian
Waveland
GULF ISLANDS NATIONAL SEASHORE
ISLE AUX HERBES
Grants Pass
ROUND I.
Mississippi Sound
St. Louis Bay
CAT I.
SHIP I.
HORN I.
PETIT BOIS I.
DAUPHIN I.
Mobile Bay
Lake Maurepas
Lake Pontchartrain
Pickwick Lake
Mississippi R.
Arkansas R.
White R.
St. Francis R.
Coldwater R.
Little Tallahatchie R.
Tallahatchie R.
Sunflower R.
Yalobusha R.
Skuna R.
Deer Creek
Yazoo R.
Big Black R.
Tchula Lake R.
Yockanookany R.
Tallahaga Creek
Pearl R.
Strong R.
Bayou R.
Pierre R.
Leaf R.
Bowie Creek
Tallahala Creek
Thompson Creek
Chickasawhay R.
Black Creek
Pascagoula
Wolf R.
Homochitto R.
Bogue R.
Amite R.
Chitto R.
Tombigbee R.
Buttahatchee
Trim Cane Creek
Catalpa Creek
Noxubee R.
Sucarnoochee Creek
Okatibbee Creek
Saline R.
Bartholome
Bayou
Ouachita R.
Macon Bayou
Tensas
Red R.
92°
91°
90°
89°
88°
35°
34°
33°
32°
31°
30°
©1996, Encyclopædia Britannica, Inc.

NAME	AREA[1] (sq. mi.)	AREA[1] (sq. km.)	POP. (1990c)	CO. SEAT(S)
Yalobusha	488	1,264	12,033	Coffeeville and Water Valley
Yazoo	938	2,429	25,506	Yazoo City

[1] Area = land area.

History: Evidence of prehistoric inhabitants (Mound Builders); prior to European settlement inhabited by several tribes incl. the Choctaw, Natchez, and Chickasaw; became part of French-controlled Louisiana (*q.v.*); Biloxi settled by French colonist Pierre Le Moyne d'Iberville 1699; except for S part (British West Florida), region ceded to U.S. 1783; N section included in Terr. South of the Ohio River 1790; S part included in Mississippi Terr. (*q.v.*) 1798, which was expanded 1804 to include most of current state; W part of the territory admitted to the Union with its present boundaries Dec. 10, 1817 as state of Mississippi, but its southernmost strip of land not formally ceded by Spain until 1819; seceded Jan. 9, 1861; scene of important battles during Civil War; readmitted to Union Feb. 23, 1870; adopted present constitution 1890.

3. Name of counties in two states of the U.S. See tables at ARKANSAS and MISSOURI.

4. River, SE Ontario, Canada; flows NE and N through **Mississippi Lake** in Lanark co. into the Ottawa River; 105 mi. (169 km.) long.

Mississippi Sound. Inlet of Gulf of Mexico bet. mainland of S Mississippi and SW Alabama and an island chain off the coast; receives the Pascagoula River.

Mississippi Territory. Former territory, U.S.A.; comprised variable region E of the Mississippi, S of Tennessee, and W of Georgia; organized 1798 from a strip of land in what is now S Mississippi and S Alabama; expanded 1804 to include most of the land of the two modern states, except a strip along the S coast still claimed by Spain; Mississippi admitted to the Union with current boundaries 1817, but S strip not formally ceded to U.S. until 1819.

Missolonghi. See MESOLÓNGION.

Mis·sou·la \mə-ˈzü-lə\. **1.** County in W Montana. See table at MONTANA.

2. City, its ⊗, near confluence of Bitterroot River and Clark Fork; pop. (1990c) 42,918; lumber, paper pulp, dairy products; Univ. of Montana (1893). Began as trading settlement 1860s.

Mis·sou·ri \mə-ˈzu̇r-ē, -ˈzu̇r-ə\. **1.** River, cen. and NW cen. U.S.; formed by confluence of Jefferson, Madison, and Gallatin rivers in Gallatin co., S Montana; flows E to cen. North Dakota, then S across South Dakota to form E section of South Dakota-Nebraska boundary, and the Nebraska-Iowa and Nebraska-Missouri boundaries, and the N section of the Kansas-Missouri boundary, turns E across cen. Missouri and joins the Mississippi River ab. 10 mi. (16 km.) N of St. Louis; 2466 mi. (3968 km.) long (or 2683 mi. or 4317 km. incl. longest tributaries to ultimate source) to its junction with the Mississippi River. During high water, navigable by flat-bottomed boats nearly to Great Falls, Montana (*q.v.*). First explored by French traders; traced to its sources by American explorers Meriwether Lewis and William Clark 1804–06.

2. Central state of U.S.A., bounded on N by Iowa, on E by Illinois, Kentucky, and Tennessee, on S by Arkansas, on W by Oklahoma, Kansas, and Nebraska; 19th state in area, 69,697 sq. mi. (180,515 sq. km.); 15th state in population, (1990c) 5,117,073; ✻ Jefferson City; 24th state admitted to Union (1821). See table of states at UNITED STATES.

Nickname: Show Me State.

State flower: Hawthorn.

Motto: Salus Populi Suprema Lex Esto (Let the Welfare of the People Be the Supreme Law).

Rivers: Missouri (see MISSOURI 1); Mississippi, forming E boundary; Des Moines, forming boundary at extreme NE tip of state and emptying into the Mississippi.

Highest point: Taum Sauk Mt., 1772 ft. (540 m.), in Iron co.

Chief products: Soybeans, corn, wheat, cotton; livestock; cement, lead, iron ore, coal; manufacturing: transportation and aerospace equipment, chemicals, fabricated metal products.

Chief cities: Kansas City, St. Louis, Springfield, Independence.

Political divisions: Divided into the following 114 counties (for pronunciation of their names, see their individual entries):

NAME	AREA[1] (sq. mi.)	AREA[1] (sq. km.)	POP. (1990c)	CO. SEAT
Adair	572	1,481	24,577	Kirksville
Andrew	436	1,129	14,632	Savannah
Atchison	549	1,422	7,457	Rock Port
Audrain	692	1,792	23,599	Mexico
Barry	783	2,028	27,547	Cassville
Barton	594	1,538	11,312	Lamar
Bates	841	2,178	15,025	Butler
Benton	735	1,904	13,859	Warsaw
Bollinger	621	1,608	10,619	Marble Hill
Boone	685	1,774	112,379	Columbia
Buchanan	404	1,046	83,083	St. Joseph
Butler	715	1,852	38,765	Poplar Bluff
Caldwell	430	1,114	8,380	Kingston
Callaway	835	2,163	32,809	Fulton
Camden	640	1,658	27,495	Camdenton
Cape Girardeau	574	1,487	61,633	Jackson
Carroll	697	1,805	10,748	Carrollton
Carter	506	1,311	5,515	Van Buren
Cass	698	1,808	63,808	Harrisonville
Cedar	496	1,285	12,093	Stockton
Chariton	754	1,953	9,202	Keytesville
Christian	567	1,469	32,644	Ozark
Clark	506	1,311	7,547	Kahoka
Clay	412	1,067	153,411	Liberty
Clinton	420	1,088	16,595	Plattsburg
Cole	384	995	63,579	Jefferson City
Cooper	566	1,466	14,835	Boonville
Crawford	760	1,968	19,173	Steelville
Dade	504	1,305	7,449	Greenfield
Dallas	537	1,391	12,646	Buffalo
Daviess	563	1,458	7,865	Gallatin
De Kalb	423	1,096	9,967	Maysville
Dent	756	1,958	13,702	Salem
Douglas	809	2,095	11,876	Ava
Dunklin	543	1,406	33,112	Kennett
Franklin	934	2,419	80,603	Union
Gasconade	519	1,344	14,006	Hermann
Gentry	488	1,264	6,848	Albany
Greene	677	1,753	207,949	Springfield
Grundy	435	1,127	10,536	Trenton
Harrison	720	1,865	8,469	Bethany
Henry	734	1,901	20,044	Clinton
Hickory	397	1,028	7,335	Hermitage
Holt	458	1,186	6,034	Oregon
Howard	472	1,222	9,631	Fayette
Howell	920	2,383	31,447	West Plains
Iron	554	1,435	10,726	Ironton
Jackson	603	1,562	633,232	Independence
Jasper	642	1,663	90,465	Carthage
Jefferson	668	1,730	171,380	Hillsboro
Johnson	826	2,139	42,514	Warrensburg
Knox	512	1,326	4,482	Edina
Laclede	770	1,994	27,158	Lebanon
Lafayette	632	1,637	31,107	Lexington
Lawrence	619	1,603	30,236	Mount Vernon
Lewis	508	1,316	10,233	Monticello
Lincoln	625	1,619	28,892	Troy
Linn	622	1,611	13,885	Linneus
Livingston	530	1,373	14,592	Chillicothe
McDonald	540	1,399	16,938	Pineville
Macon	814	2,108	15,345	Macon
Madison	496	1,285	11,127	Fredericktown
Maries	525	1,360	7,976	Vienna
Marion	438	1,134	27,682	Palmyra
Mercer	455	1,178	3,723	Princeton
Miller	600	1,554	20,700	Tuscumbia
Mississippi	415	1,075	14,442	Charleston
Moniteau	419	1,085	12,298	California
Monroe	669	1,733	9,104	Paris
Montgomery	534	1,383	11,355	Montgomery City
Morgan	592	1,533	15,574	Versailles
New Madrid	679	1,759	20,928	New Madrid
Newton	629	1,629	44,445	Neosho
Nodaway	877	2,271	21,709	Maryville
Oregon	784	2,031	9,470	Alton
Osage	608	1,575	12,018	Linn
Ozark	732	1,896	8,598	Gainesville
Pemiscot	493	1,277	21,921	Caruthersville
Perry	471	1,220	16,648	Perryville
Pettis	679	1,759	35,437	Sedalia
Phelps	677	1,753	35,248	Rolla
Pike	681	1,764	15,969	Bowling Green
Platte	427	1,106	57,867	Platte City
Polk	642	1,663	21,826	Bolivar
Pulaski	551	1,427	41,307	Waynesville
Putnam	518	1,342	5,079	Unionville
Ralls	478	1,238	8,476	New London
Randolph	484	1,254	24,370	Huntsville
Ray	573	1,484	21,971	Richmond

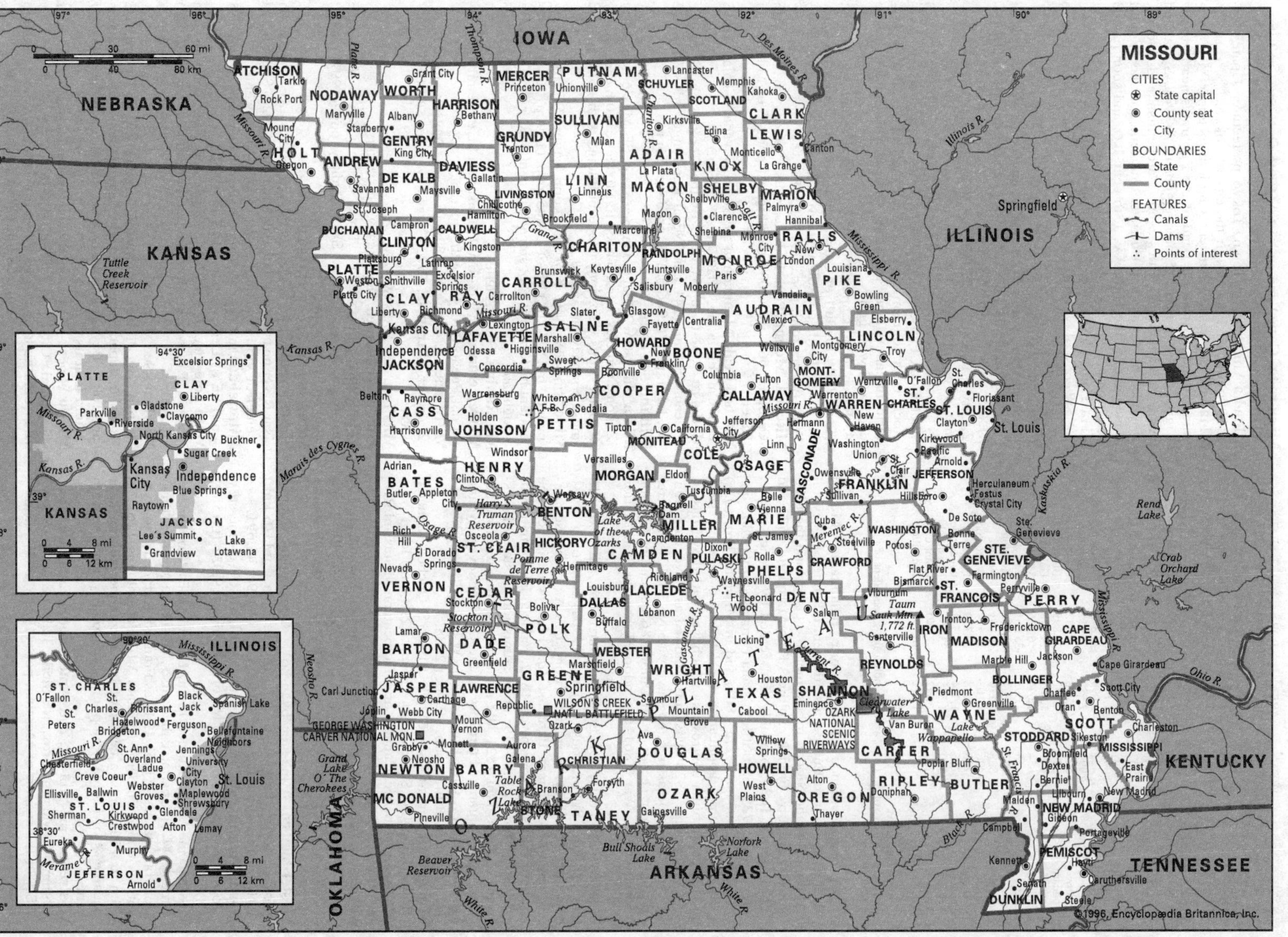

MISSOURI
CITIES
State capital
County seat
City
BOUNDARIES
State
County
FEATURES
Canals
Dams
Points of interest
IOWA
ILLINOIS
KENTUCKY
TENNESSEE
ARKANSAS
OKLAHOMA
KANSAS
NEBRASKA
ATCHISON
NODAWAY
WORTH
HARRISON
MERCER
PUTNAM
SCHUYLER
SCOTLAND
CLARK
HOLT
ANDREW
GENTRY
DAVIESS
GRUNDY
SULLIVAN
ADAIR
KNOX
LEWIS
BUCHANAN
DE KALB
CALDWELL
LIVINGSTON
LINN
MACON
SHELBY
MARION
PLATTE
CLINTON
CLAY
RAY
CARROLL
CHARITON
RANDOLPH
MONROE
RALLS
PIKE
AUDRAIN
LINCOLN
JACKSON
LAFAYETTE
SALINE
HOWARD
BOONE
CALLAWAY
MONT-GOMERY
WARREN
ST. CHARLES
ST. LOUIS
CASS
JOHNSON
PETTIS
COOPER
MONITEAU
COLE
OSAGE
GASCONADE
FRANKLIN
JEFFERSON
BATES
HENRY
BENTON
MORGAN
MILLER
MARIE
WASHINGTON
ST. FRANCOIS
STE. GENEVIEVE
PERRY
VERNON
ST. CLAIR
HICKORY
CAMDEN
PULASKI
PHELPS
CRAWFORD
IRON
MADISON
CAPE GIRARDEAU
BOLLINGER
CEDAR
POLK
DALLAS
LACLEDE
TEXAS
DENT
REYNOLDS
WAYNE
BARTON
DADE
GREENE
WEBSTER
WRIGHT
SHANNON
CARTER
BUTLER
STODDARD
SCOTT
MISSISSIPPI
JASPER
LAWRENCE
CHRISTIAN
DOUGLAS
HOWELL
OREGON
RIPLEY
NEW MADRID
NEWTON
BARRY
STONE
TANEY
OZARK
MC DONALD
DUNKLIN
PEMISCOT
OZARK PLATEAU
Springfield
Jefferson City
Kansas City
St. Louis
Independence
St. Joseph
Columbia
Cape Girardeau
Joplin
Mississippi R.
Missouri R.
Des Moines R.
Ohio R.
Lake of the Ozarks
Harry S. Truman Reservoir
Table Rock Lake
Bull Shoals Lake
Clearwater Lake
Lake Wappapello
Taum Sauk Mtn. 1,772 ft.
OZARK NATIONAL SCENIC RIVERWAYS
WILSON'S CREEK NAT'L BATTLEFIELD
GEORGE WASHINGTON CARVER NATIONAL MON.
©1996, Encyclopædia Britannica, Inc.
PLATTE
CLAY
JACKSON
KANSAS
ST. CHARLES
ST. LOUIS
JEFFERSON
ILLINOIS

NAME	AREA[1] (sq. mi.)	AREA[1] (sq. km.)	POP. (1990c)	CO. SEAT
Reynolds	817	2,116	6,661	Centerville
Ripley	639	1,655	12,303	Doniphan
Saint Charles	551	1,427	212,907	St. Charles
Saint Clair	697	1,805	8,457	Osceola
Sainte Genevieve	499	1,292	16,037	Sainte Genevieve
Saint Francois	457	1,184	48,904	Farmington
Saint Louis[2]	499	1,292	993,529	Clayton
Saint Louis city	61	158	396,685	
Saline	757	1,961	23,523	Marshall
Schuyler	306	793	4,236	Lancaster
Scotland	441	1,142	4,822	Memphis
Scott	421	1,090	39,376	Benton
Shannon	999	2,587	7,613	Eminence
Shelby	501	1,298	6,942	Shelbyville
Stoddard	823	2,132	28,895	Bloomfield
Stone	449	1,163	19,078	Galena
Sullivan	654	1,694	6,326	Milan
Taney	615	1,593	25,561	Forsyth
Texas	1,183	3,064	21,476	Houston
Vernon	838	2,170	19,041	Nevada
Warren	426	1,103	19,534	Warrenton
Washington	760	1,968	20,380	Potosi
Wayne	766	1,984	11,543	Greenville
Webster	590	1,528	23,753	Marshfield
Worth	267	692	2,440	Grant City
Wright	684	1,772	16,758	Hartville

[1]Area = land area.
[2]Exclusive of city of St. Louis, which is politically independent of the county.

History: Evidence of prehistoric inhabitants (Mound Builders); prior to European settlement inhabited by several Algonquian and Siouan tribes, incl. the Osage and the Missouri; visited by French explorers Père Marquette 1673 and Louis Jolliet 1683; probably first settled by French at Ste. Genevieve 1735; part of Louisiana Purchase (*q.v.*) 1803; included in Louisiana Terr. 1805, and in Missouri Terr. (*q.v.*) 1812; Missouri's application for admission as slave state 1817 caused bitter controversy which was settled by Missouri Compromise 1820 (Missouri admitted as slave state Aug. 10, 1821, Maine as free, no slavery above 36°30′—later repealed); did not secede from Union 1861; scene of fighting during Civil War 1861–64; adopted present constitution 1945.

Missouri City. City, Fort Bend and Harris cos., SE Texas, 15 mi. (24 km.) SW of Houston; pop. (1990c) 36,176.

Missouri Territory. Former territory, U.S.A.; comprised entire area of Louisiana Purchase (*q.v.*) less what is now the state of Louisiana; organized 1812; reduced by formation of Arkansas Terr. (*q.v.*) 1819; upon admission of state of Missouri to the Union 1821, the remainder of this territory became an unorganized territory of the U.S. for several years.

Missouri Valley. City, Harrison co., W Iowa, 20 mi. (32 km.) N of Council Bluffs; pop. (1990c) 2888.

Mis·tas·si·ni \ˌmis-tə-ˈsē-nē\. **1.** River, S Quebec, Canada; flows S into Lac St.-Jean; ab. 185 mi. (298 km.) long.
2. Town, S Quebec, Canada, opp. Dolbeau on Mistassini River 10 mi. (16 km.) N of Lac St.-Jean; pop. (1991c) 6842.

Mistassini, Lac \ˌlȧk-\. Lake, S cen. Quebec, Canada; ab. 100 mi. (160 km.) long and 12 mi. (19 km.) wide; 840 sq. mi. (2176 sq. km.); discharges through Rupert River into James Bay.

Mi·ster·bian·co \ˌmē-ster-ˈbyäŋ-kō\. Commune, Catania prov., E Sicily, Italy, on S slope of Mt. Etna 4 mi. (6 km.) WNW of the commune of Catania; pop. (1989c) 41,691.

Mi·sti, Vol·cán \vōl-ˈkän-ˈmē-stē\ *or* **El Misti** \el-ˈmē-stē\. Dormant volcano, S Peru, NE of Arequipa; 19,031 ft. (5801 m.).

Mi·stra \mē-ˈsträ\. Ruined town, Laconia, SE Peloponnese, Greece, W of Sparta; called also **Mi·si·thra** \ˌmi-sə-ˈthrä\ from famous castle built 1249 as Frankish fort; ceded to Byzantines under Emperor Michael VIII Palaeologus 1262; in 13th to 15th cents. a center of late-Byzantine culture; later became ✻ of Morea (Peloponnese); taken by Turks in 15th cent.

Mi·stret·ta \mē-ˈstrā-tä\; *anc.* **Ames·tra·tus** \ə-ˈmes-trə-təs\. Commune, Messina prov., NE Sicily, Italy, 68 mi. (109 km.) WSW of the seaport of Messina; pop. (1981p) 6337; castle.

Misurata. See MIŞRĀTAH.

Mi·su·ra·ta, Cape \ˌmē-sü-ˈrä-tə\. Cape on N coast of Libya, W of entrance to the Gulf of Sidra.

Mi·ta·ka \mē-ˈtä-kä\. Town, Tokyo prefecture, Japan; pop. (1990p) 165,555; suburb of the city of Tokyo.

Mi·tan·ni \mi-ˈta-nē\. Ancient kingdom of upper Mesopotamia, extending from the bend of the Euphrates nearly to the Tigris, covering parts of later regions of Assyria, Syria, and Armenia; among its cities were Carchemish and Aleppo. Founded by Aryans and Hurrians 15th cent. B.C.; lasted until conquered by the Hittites c. 13th cent. B.C. and soon passed to Assyria.

Mi·ta Point \ˈmē-tä\ *or Span.* **Pun·ta Mita** \ˈpün-tä\. Cape off SW coast of Nayarit state, Mexico, at N side of entrance to Banderas Bay.

Mitau. See JELGAVA.

Mitch·ell \ˈmi-chəl\. **1.** Name of counties in five states of the U.S. See tables at GEORGIA, IOWA, KANSAS, NORTH CAROLINA, TEXAS.
2. City, Lawrence co., S Indiana, 30 mi. (48 km.) S of Bloomington; pop. (1990c) 4669.
3. City, ⊗ of Davison co., SE South Dakota, 72 mi. (116 km.) W of Sioux Falls; pop. (1990c) 13,798; dairy products; livestock; corn; tourism; Dakota Wesleyan Univ. (1883); prehistoric Indian village; the Corn Palace, whimsical structure decorated with grains.
4. River, cen. Cape York Penin., Queensland, Australia; flows WNW to Gulf of Carpentaria; 300 mi. (483 km.) long.
5. Town, Perth co., SE Ontario, Canada, 13 mi. (21 km.) WNW of Stratford; pop. (1991c) 3382.

Mitchell, Mount. Peak in Black Mts., Yancey co., W North Carolina; 6684 ft. (2037 m.); highest point E of Mississippi River.

Mitchell Peak. Mountain in the Sierra Nevada, N Tulare co., S cen. California; ab. 10,365 ft. (3159 m.).

Mi·ti·a·ro \ˌmē-tē-ˈä-rō\. One of the Cook Is. in S Pacific Ocean, 150 mi. (241 km.) NE of Rarotonga; 8.5 sq. mi. (22 sq. km.); pop. (1986c) 273; produces copra.

Mitilíni. See MYTILENE.

Mi·tla \ˈmēt-lä\. Village, Oaxaca state, SE Mexico; an early Zapotec center; control passed to Mixtecs c. 10th cent.; many Zapotec ruins, esp. long stone buildings with columns and mosaic stonework walls.

Mi·to \ˈmē-tō\. City, ✻ of Ibaraki prefecture, SE Honshū, Japan, 60 mi. (97 km.) NE of Tokyo; pop. (1990p) 234,970; important historically, esp. since 17th cent. under the Tokugawa shogunate.

Mit Rahina. See MEMPHIS 4.

Mi·tre Peninsula \ˈmē-trā\. Peninsula at SE extremity of Tierra del Fuego I. off S South America.

Mitrovica. **1.** Town, Yugoslavia. See KOSOVSKA MITROVICA.
2. *or Ger.* **Mitrowitz.** Town, Yugoslavia. See SREMSKA MITROVICA.

Mits'iwa. See MASSAWA.

Mits'iwa Channel. See MASSAWA CHANNEL.

Mit·ta·gong \ˈmi-tə-ˌgäŋ\. Town, E New South Wales, SE Australia, 60 mi. (97 km.) SW of Sydney; pop. (1991c) 5666; coal and iron mines.

Mitteleuropa. See CENTRAL EUROPE.

Mit·ten·wald \ˈmit-ᵊn-ˌvält\. Village, Bavaria, Germany, on Isar River near border with Austria; pop. (1992e) 8436; noted center of violin making; resort, winter-sports center.

Mitt·wei·da \mit-ˈvī-də\. City, Saxony, E Germany, 34 mi. (55 km.) SE of Leipzig; pop. (1981c) 19,605.

Mi·tú \mē-ˈtü\. Town, ✻ of Vaupés dept., SE Colombia, on Vaupés River near Brazilian border; munic. pop. (1992e) 20,900.

Mitylene. See MYTILENE.

Mi·u·ra \mē-ˈü-ˌrä\. Peninsula, Kanagawa prefecture, SE Honshū, Japan, extending into Sagami Sea S of Yokohama and Tokyo Bay; Yokosuka is on its NE coast and the village of Miura is at its S tip.

Mix·co \ˈmēsh-kō\. City, S cen. Guatemala; a W suburb of Guatemala City; pop. (1994e) 413,002.

Mix·quia·hua·la \ˌmēs-kyä-ˈwä-lä\. Municipality, Hidalgo state, Mexico, 35 mi. (56 km.) W of Pachuca.

Mi·ya·gi \mē-ˈyä-gē\. Prefecture, Honshū, Japan, on E coast. See table at JAPAN.

Mi·ya·ji·ma \ˌmē-yä-ˈjē-mä\. **1.** Island, Japan. See ITSUKU-SHIMA 1.

2. *also* **Itsu·ku–shi·ma** \ˌēt-sü-ˈkü-shē-mä\. Town, NW coast of Itsuku-shima (island), SW Honshū, Japan.

Mi·ya·ko \mē-ˈyä-kō\. Small island in Sakishima group, S Ryukyu Is., Japan, 24°47′N, 125°20′E; 70 sq. mi. (181 sq. km.); largest in **Miyako Islands** group.

Mi·ya·ko·no·jō \mē-ˌyä-kō-nō-ˈjō\. Town, Miyazaki prefecture, SE Kyūshū, Japan; pop. (1990p) 130,155.

Mi·ya·za·ki \mē-ˈyä-ˌzä-kē\. **1.** Prefecture, Kyūshū, Japan; chemicals, wood pulp, charcoal. See table at JAPAN.

2. Seaport, its ✻, on SE coast of Kyūshū; pop. (1990p) 287,367; center of agricultural region; university (1949).

Miye. See MIE.

Miz·da \ˈmiz-də\. Oasis and caravan stop, NW Libya.

Miz·en Head \ˈmiz-ᵊn\. Cape on SW coast of Ireland bet. Long Island Bay and Dunmanus Bay; the southernmost point of Ireland, 51°27′N, 9°49′W.

Mi·zo Hills \ˈmē-ˌzō\ *formerly* **Lu·shai Hills** \ˈlü-ˌshī\. Hilly region, Mizoram, NE India; highest point ab. 7000 ft. (2140 m.); part of N Arakan Yoma system. Inhabited by Lushais, an Indo-Chinese people whose predatory raids 19th cent. made them troublesome in the region; brought under British control late 19th cent.

Mi·zo·ram \mi-ˈzȯr-əm\. State, NE India; inhabited by a loose affiliation of tribes known collectively as the Mizo (or Lushai). Estab. as a union territory 1972; became a state 1986. See table at INDIA.

Miz·pah \ˈmiz-ˌpä, -pə\. Name of several towns of ancient Palestine; literally "watchtower"; esp., the heap of stones erected in the mountains of Gilead N of the Jabbok by Hebrew patriarch Jacob and his father-in-law Laban (*Gen.* xxxi. 44–49).

Mjø·sa \ˈmœ̄-sä\. Lake in Oppland and Hedmark cos., SE Norway; 142 sq. mi. (368 sq. km.); 62 mi. (100 km.) long; largest lake in Norway.

Mko·a·ni \əm-kō-ˈä-nē\. Township on Pemba I., Tanzania.

Mko·ko·to·ni \əm-ˌkō-kō-ˈtō-nē\. Town, N coast of Zanzibar I., Tanzania; ✻ of Zanzibar North region.

Mla·dá Bo·le·slav \əm-ˈlä-dä-ˈbȯ-le-ˌsläf\ *or Ger.* **Jung·bunz·lau** \ˈyu̇ŋ-bu̇nt-ˌslau̇\. Town, N Czech Republic, 32 mi. (52 km.) NE of Prague; pop. (1991p) 44,471; 15th cent. cathedral; castle; railroad junction; motor vehicles; dates from the 10th cent.; an ecclesiastical center closely associated with the Bohemian Brethren.

Mlanje, Mount. See MULANJE, MOUNT.

Mła·wa \ˈmwä-vä\. Commune, Ciechanów prov., NE cen. Poland, on railroad line 65 mi. (105 km.) NNW of Warsaw; pop. (1989e) 28,804; scene of heavy fighting in WWI.

Mlil·wa·ne \əm-lil-ˈwä-nā\. Wildlife sanctuary, Swaziland; ab. 2 sq. mi. (5 sq. km.); habitat for numerous species incl. the white rhinoceros.

Mljet \mə-ˈlyet\ *or Ital.* **Me·le·da** \ˈme-lā-ˌdä\; *anc.* **Mel·i·ta** \ˈme-lə-tə\. Island in the Adriatic Sea off the lower Dalmatian coast; belongs to Bosnia and Herzegovina.

Mma·ba·tho \mä-ˈbä-tō\. Town, near Botswana border, North-West prov., Rep. of South Africa; ✻ of Bophuthatswana enclave 1977–93.

Moa \ˈmō-ä\. Largest of the Leti Is., Indonesia, ENE of Timor; ab. 25 mi. (40 km.) long by 9 mi. (15 km.) wide.

Mo·ab \ˈmō-ˌab\. **1.** City, ⊗ of Grand co., E Utah; pop. (1990c) 3971; tourism; Arches and Canyonlands national parks are nearby.

2. Ancient kingdom in Syria, E of the Dead Sea, now the SW part of Jordan; bounded on S by Edom and on N separated by the Arnon from the country of the Amorites. Moabites were closely related to the Israelites; sometimes at war with them, sometimes allied. An important source of information about Moab is the Moabite stone, discovered 1868 at Dibon (*q.v.*), which records the victories (9th cent. B.C.) of Mesha, king of Moab, esp. those over Israel (*2 Kings* iii.).

Moan·da *or* **Mouan·da** \ˈmwän-dä\. Town, SE Gabon; pop. (1985e) 45,500; one of the world's largest deposits of manganese is nearby.

Mobangi. See UBANGI.

Mo·ba·ra \mō-ˈbä-rä\. City, Chiba prefecture, SE Honshū, Japan; pop. (1990p) 83,437.

Mo·ber·ly \ˈmō-bər-lē\. City, ⊗ of Randolph co., N cen. Missouri, 34 mi. (55 km.) N of Columbia; pop. (1990c) 12,839; footwear, dairy products; coal deposits nearby; Moberly Area Community Coll. (1927).

Mo·bile \mō-ˈbēl, ˈmō-ˌbēl\. **1.** Navigable river, SW Alabama; formed by confluence of Tombigbee and Alabama rivers, flows S into Mobile Bay at Mobile; 38 mi. (61 km.) long.

2. County in SW Alabama; includes Dauphin I. See table at ALABAMA.

3. Commercial city and seaport, its ⊗, at mouth of Mobile River on N shore of Mobile Bay; pop. (1990c) 196,278; only seaport of Alabama, exporting cotton, coal, forest and agricultural products; manufactures textiles, paper, chemicals, aluminum, lumber; shipbuilding, food processing; restored historic houses; U.S.S. Alabama Battleship Memorial Park; U.S. Coast Guard facilities. Spring Hill Coll. (1830), Mobile Coll. (1961), Univ. of South Alabama (1963), S. D. Bishop State Junior Coll. (1965). French fort and settlement estab. nearby 1702, moved to present site 1711; was ✻ of French-controlled Louisiana until 1719; ceded to Britain 1763; occupied by U.S. 1813; incorp. as town 1814, as city 1819; during Civil War, Union won battle of Mobile Bay (*q.v.*) 1864; city taken by Union troops 1865.

Mobile Bay. Inlet of Gulf of Mexico, forming boundary bet. Baldwin co. on E and Mobile co. on W, SW Alabama; 30 mi. (48 km.) long, 10 to 12 mi. (16 to 19 km.) wide; receives the Mobile River on the N; scene of Civil War naval battle Aug. 1864 in which Union Adm. David Farragut ran a blockade of "torpedoes" (i.e., mines), dispersed the Confederate fleet, and secured surrender of the forts defending the bay.

Mobile Point. Point at SW extremity of Baldwin co., Alabama, at S entrance to Mobile Bay.

Mo·bridge \ˈmō-ˌbrij\. City, Walworth co., N South Dakota, on Missouri River 30 mi. (48 km.) S of North Dakota border; pop. (1990c) 3768; developed as retail and distribution center for farming and ranching area; tourism; pioneer museum.

Mobutu Sese Seko, Lake. See ALBERT, LAKE.

Mo·ca \ˈmō-kä\. **1.** Town and municipality, ✻ of Espaillat prov., N cen. Dominican Republic; pop. (1981c) 31,176; cacao.

2. Municipality, NW Puerto Rico; pop. (1990c) 32,926.

Mo·çam·bi·que \ˌmü-səm-ˈbē-kə\. **1.** Independent state; SE Africa. See MOZAMBIQUE 1.

2. *also* **Mo·zam·bique** \ˌmō-zəm-ˈbēk\. Seaport on small coral island (**Mozambique Island**) in Mozambique Channel off NE coast of Mozambique; ✻ of Ilha dist.; opp. the mainland town of Mossuril; has good harbor; population chiefly Muslims of mixed descent. Site of flourishing Arab town when visited by Portuguese navigator Vasco da Gama in 1498; settled and fortified by Portuguese 16th cent.; ✻ of Mozambique until 1907.

Moçâmedes. See NAMIBE.

Mo·ca·pra \mō-ˈkä-prä\. River, N Venezuela; flows S into Guárico River; ab. 100 mi. (160 km.) long.

Mo·cha \ˈmō-chä\. Island in Pacific Ocean off cen. Chile; administratively part of Bío-Bío region; 8 mi. (13 km.) long.

Mo·cha \ˈmō-kə\ *or* **Mo·kha** \ˈmō-k̲ə\ *or* **Al Mu·khā** \al-ˈmü-k̲ə\. Seaport, SW Yemen, SW Arabian Penin., on Tihama coastal plain; formerly noted for its export of coffee. From 15th cent. the most important port in Yemen; site of factories owned variously by Dutch, British, and French; with coming of Ottoman rule, disputes arose and gradually through 19th

\ə\ abut \ə\ matches \ᵊ\ kitten, Fr table \ər\ further \a\ ash \ā\ ace \ä\ cot, cart \ȧ\ Fr bac \au̇\ out \b\ Span Avila \ch\ chin \e\ bet \ē\ easy \g\ go \i\ hit \ī\ ice \j\ job \k̲\ Ger ich, Buch \ⁿ\ Fr vin \ŋ\ sing \ō\ go \ȯ\ all \ȯ\ law \œ\ Fr bœuf \œ̄\ Fr feu \ȯi\ boy \th\ thin \t̲h̲\ this \ü\ loot \u̇\ foot \ue\ Ger füllen \ue̅\ Fr rue \y\ yet \ʸ\ Fr digne \ˈdēnʸ\, nuit \ˈnwʸē\ \yü\ few \yu̇\ fury \zh\ vision

cent., Europeans moved facilities to Aden with resultant decline in Mocha's importance.

Moch·los \'mä-,kläs\ *or* **Mó·hlos** *or* **Mó·khlos** \'mö-,klös\. Ruins, E Crete, Greece, on N coast on Mirabella Bay; tombs; jewels and pottery found here.

Mo·cho Mountains \'mō-chō\. Range in S cen. Jamaica.

Mo·chu·di \mō-'chüd-ē\. Town, SE Botswana, on railroad line ab. 25 mi. (40 km.) NE of Gaborone; pop. (1991c) 25,542.

Mocks·ville \'mäks-vil\. Town, ⊗ of Davie co., cen. North Carolina; pop. (1990c) 3399.

Mo·co, Mount \'mō-kō\. Mountain, W Angola; 8397 ft. (2559 m.); highest mountain in Angola.

Mo·coa \mō-'kō-ä\. Town, ✻ of Putumayo dept., S Colombia, 45 mi. (72 km.) E of Pasto; munic. pop. (1992e) 29,100.

Mo·co·ri·to \,mō-kō-'rē-tō\. Municipality, Sinaloa state, Mexico, 60 mi. (97 km.) NE of Culiacán; pop. (1990p) 51,816.

Mo·dane \mȯ-'dän\. Town, SE Savoie dept., E France; terminus of Mont Cenis Pass and Tunnel (see table at ALPS).

Mod·der \'mȯ-dər\. River, Free State, Rep. of South Africa, a tributary of the Riet; ab. 180 mi. (290 km.) long; scene of battle 1899 in which British forces under Lieut. Gen. Paul Methuen defeated Boers under Gen. Piet Cronjé. See PAARDEBERG.

Mo·de·na \'mȯ-dā-nä\. **1.** Province of Emilia-Romagna, N Italy. See table at ITALY.

2. *anc.* **Mu·ti·na** \'myüt-ᵊn-ə\. Commune, its ✻, 207 mi. (333 km.) NNW of Rome; pop. (1989c) 176,857; archiepiscopal see; automobiles, machine tools, agricultural machinery, light alloys; metalworking, iron founding, tanning; 11th cent. Romanesque cathedral; 13th cent. campanile; 17th cent. ducal palace (now a military school); Palazzo dei Musei (art gallery and Estense library); university (1175).

History: Ancient Etruscan city; made Roman colony 183 B.C.; successfully defended against siege of Roman Gen. Mark Antony 44–43 B.C.; taken 311 A.D. by Roman Emperor Constantine the Great; to Este family 1288; made a duchy 1452; taken by French 1796 and made part of the Cisalpine Republic 1797 and of the Napoleonic kingdom of Italy 1805; lost by Este family on extinction of male line 1803 but reverted to descendant, Francis IV, 1815; to kingdom of Italy 1860.

Mo·des·to \mə-'des-tō\. City, ⊗ of Stanislaus co., cen. California, on Tuolumne River 25 mi. (40 km.) SE of Stockton; pop. (1990c) 164,730; processing and distribution center for productive agricultural area; wineries, fruit and nut orchards; Modesto Junior Coll. (1921); laid out 1870.

Mo·di·ca \'mȯ-dē-kä\; *anc.* **Mo·ty·ca** \'mō-ti-kə\. Commune, Ragusa prov., SE Sicily, Italy, 5 mi. (8 km.) SSE of the commune of Ragusa; pop. (1991p) 48,339; center of agricultural region; nearby grottoes contain ancient cave dwellings and ancient tombs. Site of prehistoric Sicilian settlement; devastated by earthquake 1692.

Modjokerto. See MOJOKERTO.

Mo·dlin \'mȯd-,lēn\; *Russ.* **No·vo·geor·gievsk** \,nȯ-və-gē-'ȯr-gē-ifsk\. Fortified commune, Warszawa dept., Poland, 20 mi. (32 km.) NW of Warsaw; founded as a fort built by French Emperor Napoléon 1807; to Russian Poland 1815; occupied by Poles during Polish Revolt 1830–31; taken by Germans 1915; again captured by Germans 1939.

Möd·ling \'mœd-liŋ\. City, Austria, 8 mi. (13 km.) SSW of Vienna; pop. (1991c) 20,290; metal goods, shoes; first mentioned 10th cent.; made city 1897.

Mo·doc \'mō-,däk\. County in NE corner of California. See table at CALIFORNIA.

Mo·du·gno \mō-'dü-nyō\. Commune, Bari prov., Puglia, SE Italy, 5 mi. (8 km.) SW of the seaport of Bari; pop. (1989c) 37,623; medieval church nearby.

Moearatewe. See MUARATEWE.

Moehne. See MÖHNE.

Moel Sych \'mȯil-'sik\. Peak, highest in the Berwyn Mts., N Wales; 2713 ft. (827 m.).

Moen. See WENO.

Möen. See MØN.

Moena. See MUNA.

Moengo \'müŋ-ō\. Town, NE Suriname, ab. 55 mi. (89 km.) ESE of Paramaribo; bauxite deposits.

Mo·en·ko·pi Plateau \,mō-ən-'kō-pē\. Tableland in E Coconino co., N cen. Arizona, along E boundary of the Painted Desert (*q.v.*).

Moenus. See MAIN.

Moer·dijk \mür-'dīk, -'dāk\. Village, North Brabant prov., S Netherlands, NW of Breda, on S bank of the Hollandsch Diep, here crossed by a long railroad bridge; captured by Germans May 1940.

Moe·ris, Lake \'mir-əs\. Large lake occupying Faiyûm Depression in El Faiyûm governorate, N Upper Egypt. See BIRKET QĀRŪN.

Moero, Lac. See MWERU, LAKE.

Moers *also* **Mörs** \'mœrs\. City, North Rhine-Westphalia, Germany, WNW of Duisburg; pop. (1992e) 105,322; chartered c. 1300; to Prussia early 18th cent.

Moesi. See MUSI 2.

Moe·sia \'mē-shə, -shē-ə\. Ancient country of SE Europe S of Danube River and extending from Drinus (Drina) River to the Euxine (Black Sea), inhabited by a Thracian people and included part of early Thrace. Invaded by Romans 75 B.C. but not conquered until c. 30 B.C.; made Roman province 15 A.D. and later divided into two provinces: **Moesia Superior** (Upper Moesia, i.e., Serbia) and **Moesia Inferior** (Lower Moesia, i.e., N Bulgaria); occupied by Goths in 4th cent. A.D. and by Slavs and Bulgarians in 7th cent.

Moeskroen. See MOUSCRON.

Mof·fat \'mä-fət\. County in NW corner of Colorado. See table at COLORADO.

Moffat Tunnel. Railroad tunnel through James Peak, Gilpin and Grand cos., N cen. Colorado, ab. 50 mi. (80 km.) NW of Denver; 6 mi. (10 km.) long.

Mo·ga·di·shu \,mō-gə-'dē-shü, -'di-\ *or* **Mog·a·di·scio** \,mō-gä-'dē-shō\ *also* **Mog·a·di·sho** \-shō\. Seaport, ✻ of Somalia; pop. (1985e) 700,000; the republic's principal port; 13th cent. mosque; 19th cent. palace, now a museum; university (1959). Founded 10th cent. by Arabs; became important trade center; passed to sultan of Zanzibar 1871; leased to Italians 1892, sold to them 1905 and became ✻ of Italian Somaliland; site of base for UN peacekeeping forces assisting famine relief efforts late 1992 to mid-1994.

Mogador. See ESSAOUIRA.

Mog·a·dore \'mä-gə-,dōr\. Village, Portage and Summit cos., NE Ohio, 7 mi. (11 km.) ESE of Akron; pop. (1990c) 4008.

Mo·ga·la·kwe·na \,mō-gä-lä-'kwē-nä\. River, Northern Transvaal, NE Rep. of South Africa; flows N into Limpopo River; 130 mi. (209 km.) long.

Mo·ga·mi \mō-'gä-mē\. River, Yamagata prefecture, N Honshū, Japan; flows N and NW into the Sea of Japan at Sakata; 134 mi. (216 km.) long.

Mo·gaung \'mō-'gau̇ŋ\. Town, N Myanmar, on railroad line 30 mi. (48 km.) W of Myitkyina, on **Mogaung River,** a tributary of the upper Irrawaddy; precious stones; valley scene of fighting during WWII bet. Japanese and Allied forces 1944.

Moghul Empire. See MOGUL EMPIRE.

Mo·gi das Cru·zes \mō-'zhē-dȧs-'krü-zēs\. City, São Paulo state, SE Brazil, on coast 30 mi. (48 km.) E of the city of São Paulo; pop. (1991p) 125,992; iron, steel.

Mogilev. See MAHILYOW.

Mo·gi·lev–Po·dol'·skiy *or* **Mo·gi·lev Po·dol·ski** \mə-gi-'lyȯf-,pə-'dȯl-skē\ *or mostly formerly* **Mo·hi·lev** \,mə-hi-'lyȯf\. Town, SW Vinnytsya subdivision, W Ukraine, on the Dniester 60 mi. (97 km.) S of the city of Vinnytsya; connected by rail with Zhmerynka; formerly more important as a trading center at a much used crossing of the Dniester on a main highway from Moldavia to Ukraine. Founded at end of 16th cent.; scene of much fighting bet. Cossacks, Poles, and Turks; suffered severely in WWI; in WWII held by Axis powers 1941–44.

Mo·gi Mi·rim \mō-'zhē-mi-'rēm\. City, E São Paulo state, SE Brazil, 80 mi. (129 km.) N of the city of São Paulo; munic. pop. (1991p) 64,746.

Mo·glia·no Ve·ne·to \mō-ˈlyä-nō-ˈve-nä-tō\. Commune, Treviso prov., Veneto, NE Italy 8 mi. (13 km.) S of the commune of Treviso; pop. (1989c) 25,260.

Mog·mog \ˈmäg-ˌmäg\. See ULITHI.

Mo·gok \ˈmō-ˌgōk\. Town, Myanmar, on highway E of the Irrawaddy 70 mi. (113 km.) NNE of Mandalay; formerly a major ruby-mining center.

Mo·gol·lon Mountains *also* **Mogollon Range** \ˌmə-gē-ˈōn, ˌmō-gə-ˈyōn\. Range in S Catron co., W New Mexico, extending across county boundary into Grant co.; highest point Whitewater Baldy ab. 10,895 ft. (3320 m.); also includes **Mogollon Baldy** ab. 10,770 ft. (3285 m.).

Mogollon Rim. Escarpment in S Coconino and S Navajo cos., Arizona.

Mogontiacum. See MAINZ.

Mo·guer \mō-ˈger\. Commune, S Huelva prov., SW Spain, E of the commune of Huelva; pop. (1991c) 11,905; explorer Christopher Columbus obtained some members of his crew from here. Birthplace of Nobel Prize recipient poet Juan Ramón Jiménez 1881.

Mo·gul Empire *or* **Mo·ghul Empire** \ˈmō-gəl\ *or* **Mu·ghal Empire** \ˈmü-\. Muslim empire throughout much of India, beginning with the rule of Bābur (Ẓahīr-ud-Dīn Muḥammad) 1526; lasted two centuries.

Mo·hács \ˈmō-ˌhäch\. City, Baranya co., S Hungary, on Danube River; pop. (1991e) 20,700; commercial center; battlefield 1526 where Turks completely defeated Hungarians; another battle took place in area 1687 in which Charles V, duke of Lorraine, defeated the Turks.

Mo·ha·les Hoek \mō-ˈhä-ləs-ˈhu̇k\. Town, SW Lesotho; area pop. (1986c) 174,998.

Mo·hall \ˈmō-ˌhȯl\. City, ⊗ of Renville co., N North Dakota; pop. (1990c) 931.

Mo·ham·ma·dia \mō-ˌä-mȧ-ˈdyä\; *formerly* **Per·ré·gaux** \ˌpe-rā-ˈgō\. Commune, NW Algeria, 40 mi. (64 km.) ESE of Oran.

Mo·ham·me·dia \mō-ˌä-mā-ˈdyä\; *formerly* **Fe·da·la** \fə-ˈdä-lə\. Town, Morocco, on coast 14 mi. (23 km.) NE of Casablanca; pop. (1982c) 105,120.

Mohammerah. See KHORRAMSHAHR.

Moharek. See AL MUHARRAQ.

Mo·ha·ve \mō-ˈhä-vē\. County in NW corner of Arizona. See table at ARIZONA.

Mohave Desert. See MOJAVE DESERT.

Mo·hawk \ˈmō-ˌhȯk\. **1.** River, largest tributary of the Hudson River, E cen. New York; formed by junction of E and W branches in Oneida co., flows S and E into Hudson River at Cohoes, above Troy; 148 mi. (238 km.) long; parallels the New York State Barge Canal. See LITTLE FALLS 3.
2. Village, Herkimer co., NE cen. New York, on Mohawk River 12 mi. (19 km.) ESE of Utica; pop. (1990c) 2986; forms single community with Frankfort, Ilion, and Herkimer.

Mo·hé·li \mō-ˈā-lē\ *or* **Mwa·li** \ˈmwä-lē\ *or mostly formerly* **Mo·hil·la** \mō-ˈhi-lə\. One of the Comoros (*q.v.*); 112 sq. mi. (290 sq. km.); pop. (1990e) 23,543; chief town Fomboni.

Mo·hen·jo Da·ro \mō-ˈhen-jō-ˈdär-ō\. Prehistoric city, S Sind, Pakistan, ab. 140 mi. (225 km.) NE of Karachi; a site of the Aeneolithic epoch of Indus Valley civilization, c. 2500–1600 B.C.; excavations have revealed a large, well-planned city, incl. a citadel, a large bathing pool, and a granary. See HARAPPA.

Mo·hi·can \mō-ˈhē-kən\. River, cen. Ohio; flows S to the Walhonding River; ab. 40 mi. (64 km.) long.

Mohilev. See MOGILEV-PODOL'SKIY.

Mohilla. See MOHÉLI.

Mohl, Mount \ˈmōl\. Mountain, Antarctica, 78°33′S, 85°05′W; 12,172 ft. (3710 m.).

Móhlos. See MOCHLOS.

Moh·mand Hills \mō-ˈmand\. Spur of Hindu Kush, cen. Asia, on border bet. Pakistan and E Afghanistan, just N of Khyber Pass in the Safed Koh; through gorges in the range passes the Kabul River.

Möh·ne *also* **Moeh·ne** \ˈmœ̄-nə\. River in North Rhine-Westphalia, Germany; flows W to the Ruhr at Neheim; ab 35 mi. (56 km.) long. In its lower course is great reservoir dam, damaged in aerial bombing 1943.

Moinkum. See MUYUN KUM.

Moi·sie \mwä-ˈzē\. River, SE Quebec, Canada; flows S from border of SW Labrador to the St. Lawrence at its mouth; 210 mi. (338 km.) long.

Mois·sac \mwȧ-ˈsäk\. Town, Tarn-et-Garonne dept., S France, on Tarn River; 15th cent. church with 12th cent. portal; 12th–13th cent. cloisters adjoining the church.

Mo·ja·ve Desert *or* **Mo·ha·ve Desert** \mō-ˈhä-vē\. Arid basin in S California, incl. parts of San Bernardino, Kern, and Los Angeles cos.; ab. 25,000 sq. mi. (64,750 sq. km.).

Mo·ji \ˈmō-jē\. See KITAKYŪSHŪ.

Mojib, Wadi al–. See MAWJIB, WADI AL-.

Mo·jo·ker·to *also* **Mo·djo·ker·to** \ˌmō-jō-ˈker-tō\. Town, East Java prov., Indonesia; on Brantas River; railroad junction point 20 mi. (32 km.) SW of Surabaya; pop. (1990c) 99,955; center of sugar industry. Nearby site of discovery of early human remains, probably of *Homo erectus*.

Mo·kai \ˈmō-ˌkī\. Village, N cen. North I., New Zealand, just N of Lake Taupo.

Mo·kau \ˈmō-ˌkau̇\. River, W North I., New Zealand; flows SW to North Taranaki Bight; 98 mi. (158 km.) long.

Mo·kel·um·ne \mō-ˈke-lə-mē, -ˈkä-\. River, cen. California; rises in the Sierra Nevada and flows into San Joaquin River ab. 20 mi. (32 km.) NW of Stockton; ab. 140 mi. (225 km.) long.

Mo·ke·na \mō-ˈkē-nə\. Village, Will co., NE Illinois, ab. 8 mi. (13 km.) E of Joliet; pop. (1990c) 6128.

Mokha. See MOCHA.

Mókhlos. See MOCHLOS.

Mok·mer \ˈmäk-mər\. Airfield on Biak I., Irian Jaya, Indonesia; captured by Americans June 1944. See BOSNIK.

Mok·ni·ne \ˈmȯk-nē-nē\. Coastal town, E Tunisia, SSE of Sousse.

Mok·p'o \ˈmäk-pō\. Seaport, South Chŏlla prov., South Korea; pop. (1985c) 236,085; textiles; fishing; opened to foreign trade late 19th cent.

Mokrān. See MAKRAN.

Mok·sha \ˈmȯk-shə\. River, cen. Russia in Europe; rises near Penza and flows N and W through Mordovinia to the Oka above Murom; 430 mi. (692 km.) long; navigable for much of its course.

Mo·ku·a·we·o·weo \mō-ˈkü-ä-ˌwā-ō-ˈwā-ō\. The summit crater of Mauna Loa in S cen. Hawaii I., Hawaii; 3.7 mi. (6 km.) in circumference, ab. 13,680 ft. (4170 m.) high.

Mol *formerly* **Moll** \ˈmȯl\. Commune, Antwerp prov., N Belgium, 30 mi. (48 km.) E of the city of Antwerp; pop. (1991c) 30,763; nuclear research.

Mo·la di Ba·ri \ˈmȯ-lä-dē-ˈbär-ē\. Commune, Bari prov., Puglia, SE Italy, on Adriatic Sea 12 mi. (19 km.) ESE of the seaport of Bari; pop. (1989c) 26,963; small harbor; 13th cent. castle and cathedral.

Mola di Gaeta. See FORMIA.

Mo·lal·la \mō-ˈla-lə\. City, Clackamas co., NW Oregon, ab. 27 mi. (43 km.) SSE of Portland; pop. (1990c) 3651.

Mold \ˈmōld\. Town, ⊗ of Clwyd co., NE Wales; pop. (1981c) 8505; in farming and coal-mining section; 15th cent. church; site of victory of native Christians under St. Germain of Auxerre over pagan Picts and Scots 430. Birthplace of Welsh novelist Daniel Owen 1836.

Moldau. **1.** River, Czech Republic. See VLTAVA.
2. Region, Romania. See MOLDAVIA.

Mol·da·via \mäl-ˈdā-vē-ə, mōl-, -vyə\ *or Rom.* **Mol·do·va** \mȯl-ˈdȯ-və\ *or Ger.* **Mol·dau** \ˈmȯl-ˌdau̇, ˈmōl-\. Former principality, SE cen. Europe, E of Transylvania and N of E Walachia; included Bessarabia and Bukovina; later a province of Romania, area 14,690 sq. mi. (38,047 sq. km.). Founded in 14th cent. of Vlach and Hungarian elements;

\ə\ abut \ᵊ\ matches \ᵊ\ kitten, Fr table \ər\ further \a\ ash \ā\ ace \ä\ cot, cart \ȧ\ Fr bac \au̇\ out \b\ Span Avila \ch\ chin \e\ bet \ē\ easy \g\ go \i\ hit \ī\ ice \j\ job \k\ Ger ich, Buch \ⁿ\ Fr vin \ŋ\ sing \ō\ go \ȯ\ all \ȯi\ law \œ\ Fr bœuf \œ̄\ Fr feu \ȯi\ boy \th\ thin \t͟h\ this \ü\ loot \u̇\ foot \ue\ Ger füllen \ue̅\ Fr rue \y\ yet \ʸ\ Fr digne \ˈdēnʸ\, nuit \ˈnwʸē\ \yü\ few \yu̇\ fury \zh\ vision

ruled by vaivodes (military governors) who were largely dependent on Hungarian or Polish control; came under rule of Ottoman Turks in 16th cent.; united briefly 1600 to Walachia by Michael the Brave (d. 1601); from early 18th cent. governed for Turks by Greek Phanariots; Bukovina annexed to Austria 1774 and Bessarabia (*q.v.*) to Russia; for history after 1774, see DANUBIAN PRINCIPALITIES.

Mol·da·vi·an Car·pa·thi·an Mountains \ mäl-ˈdā-vē-ən-kär-ˈpā-thē-ən, mōl-, -vyən\. Range in Romania, at SE end of the Carpathians, forming boundary bet. Moldavia and Transylvania.

Moldavian Republic. 1. Independent Bessarabia 1917. See BESSARABIA 2.

2. *or officially* **Moldavian Autonomous Soviet Socialist Republic.** Former autonomous republic, U.S.S.R.; 3200 sq. mi. (8288 sq. km.); ✱ Balta, later Tiraspol; a part of Ukrainian S.S.R. organized in 1924 from several districts of former Podol'sk government (Podolia) of the U.S.S.R. Plain country along E bank of Dniester, with fertile black soil. In 1940 merged with most of Bessarabia (*q.v.*) to form Moldavian S.S.R.

Moldavian Soviet Socialist Republic *or earlier* **Moldavian Federal Soviet Republic.** A constituent republic of the U.S.S.R. 1940–91; gained independence as Moldova (*q.v.*).

Mol·de \ ˈmȯl-də\. Town, ⊗ of Møre og Romsdal co., W Norway, on N shore of **Molde Fjord;** pop. (1990c) 22,125; fishing port; textiles.

Mol·do·va \ mȯl-ˈdȯ-və\. **1.** Former principality. See MOLDAVIA.

2. River, NE Romania; flows SE into the Siret River near Roman.

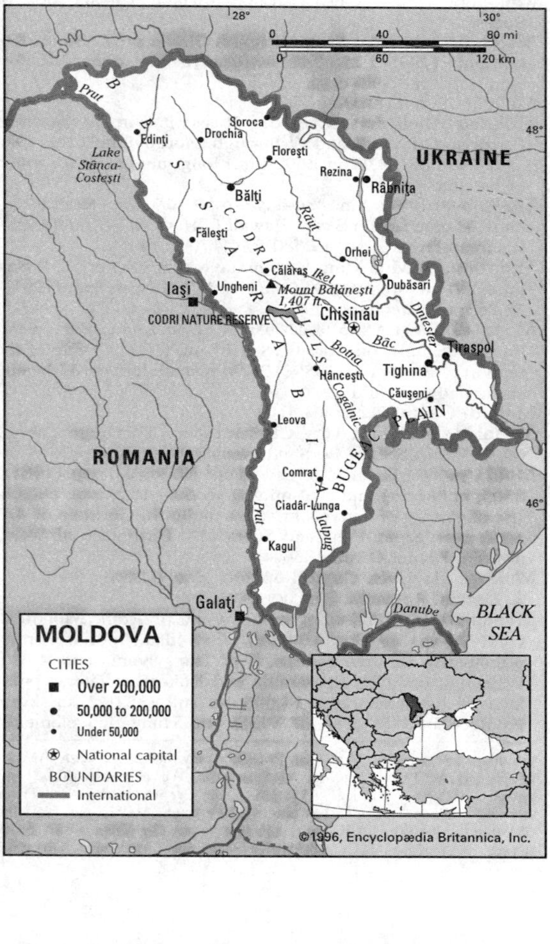

3. Republic, cen. Europe, bounded on N and NE by Ukraine, on SE by Black Sea, and on S and W by Romania; 13,012 sq. mi. (33,701 sq. km.); pop. (1993e) 4,362,000; ✱ Chişinău; cereals, fruits and vegetables, wine, sugar; formed a constituent republic of the U.S.S.R. before independence in 1991; Moldavian S.S.R. renamed Moldova 1990; declared independence from U.S.S.R. Aug. 27, 1991; joined Commonwealth of Independent States Dec. 1991; admitted to UN 1992; ethnic conflict erupted in Dniester River valley 1992.

Mol·do·ve·a·nu \ ˌmȯl-dȯ-ˈvyä-nu̇\. Mountain, cen. Romania; 8343 ft. (2543 m.); highest peak in Transylvanian Alps.

Mo·len·beek–Saint–Jean \ ˈmō-lən-ˌbāk-se^{n}-ˈzhä^{n}\. Commune, Brabant prov., cen. Belgium, a W suburb of Brussels; pop. (1991c) 68,759.

Mo·le·po·lo·le \ ˌmō-lā-pō-ˈlō-lā\. Town, SE Botswana, on SE edge of Kalahari Desert; pop. (1991c) 36,930.

Môle Saint–Ni·co·las \ ˈmōl-ˌse^{n}-ˌnē-kō-ˈlä\. Town, NW Haiti, near tip of peninsula just N of Cap à Foux; pop. (1982p) 1960; explorer Christopher Columbus landed here 1492.

Mo·lé·son \ ˌmō-lā-ˈzō^{n}\ *or* **Le Moléson** \ lə-\. Peak in the Alps, in Fribourg canton, W cen. Switzerland; 6567 ft. (2002 m.).

Mol·fet·ta \ mȯl-ˈfe-tä\. Seaport, Bari prov., Puglia, SE Italy, on Adriatic Sea 15 mi. (24 km.) WNW of the seaport of Bari; pop. (1991p) 66,658; fishing, boatbuilding; produces olive oil, foodstuffs; cement; 12th–13th cent. cathedral.

Mo·li·na de Se·gu·ra \ mō-ˈlē-nä-thā-sā-ˈgü-rä\. Commune, Murcia prov., SE Spain, on Segura River 8 mi. (13 km.) NNW of the commune of Murcia; pop. (1991c) 37,806.

Mo·line \ mō-ˈlēn\. City, Rock Island co., NW Illinois, on Mississippi River just above Rock Island; pop. (1990c) 43,202; historically notable for manufacture of agricultural implements; Black Hawk Coll. (1946); industrialist John Deere estab. his plow-making business here 1847.

Moline Acres. Village, St. Louis co., E Missouri; pop. (1990c) 2710.

Mo·li·nel·la \ ˌmō-lē-ˈnel-lä\. Commune, Emilia-Romagna, N Italy, 26 mi. (42 km.) ENE of Bologna; pop. (1981p) 12,192.

Mo·li·no del Rey \ mō-ˈlē-nō-del-ˈrā\ *or Eng.* **King's Mill.** Site in Mexico, SW of Mexico City; scene of battle Sept. 8, 1847 in which U.S. Gen. Winfield Scott defeated Mexican forces of Gen. Antonio López de Santa Anna.

Mo·li·se \ mō-ˈlē-zā\. Autonomous region, S cen. Italy; ✱ Campobasso (for provincial division, see table at ITALY); received limited autonomy 1970.

Molise, Abruzzi e. See ABRUZZI E MOLISE.

Moll. See MOL.

Molle, Ponte. See SAXA RUBRA.

Mol·len·do \ mō-ˈyen-(ˌ)dō\. Seaport town, S Peru; pop. (1990e) 27,900; former import and export center for S Peru and Bolivia; largely replaced as a port by that of Matarani (*q.v.*).

Mollwitz. See MAŁUJOWICE.

Möln·dal \ ˈmœln-ˌdäl\. City, Göteborg and Bohus prov., SW Sweden; pop. (1993e) 52,423; paper mills, margarine factories.

Molodechno *or* **Molodeczno.** See MALADZYECHNA.

Mo·lo·ga \ mə-ˈlȯ-gə\. River, Tver' and Vologda oblasts, Russia in Europe; flows into Volga River NW of Rybinsk; ab. 340 mi. (550 km.) long; lower course within the Rybinsk Reservoir.

Mo·lo·kai \ ˌmō-lō-ˈkī\. Island, Maui co., cen. Hawaii; ab. 40 mi. (65 km.) long by 7 mi. (11 km.) wide; 259 sq. mi. (671 sq. km.); chief settlement Kaunakakai; has mountains at either end (Mauna Loa 1381 ft. or 421 m. at W and Kamakou 4970 ft. or 1515 m. at E) with connecting saddle ab. 400 ft. (120 m.) high; on N coast is a leprosy-treatment center and Kalaupapa National Historical Park. See KALAWAO.

Mo·lo·po \ mō-ˈlō-pō\. Intermittent river, S Africa; forms S boundary of Botswana, joins Orange River in S near SE border of Namibia; lower course through Kalahari Desert. See KURUMAN.

Mo·los·sis \ mə-ˈlä-səs\ *or* **Mo·los·sia** \ -ˈlä-shə, -shē-ə\. District of ancient Epirus, NW Greece, extending along W bank of the Árakhthos; noted for its breed of large hounds. The

Molossians gradually became the most powerful people in Epirus; Olympias, Macedonian King Alexander the Great's mother, was Molossian.

Molotov. See PERM'.

Molotov, Mount. See MOSKVA-PEKIN.

Molotov Oblast. See PERM' OBLAST.

Molotovsk. See SEVERODVINSK.

Mo·luc·cas \mō-'lə-kəz\ *or* **Ma·lu·ku** \mä-'lü-kü\ *also* **Spice Islands** \'spīs\ *or Du.* **Mo·luk·ken** \mə-'lu̇-kən\. **1.** Group of islands, E Indonesia, bet. the island of Sulawesi and New Guinea; 32,307 sq. mi. (83,675 sq. km.); pop. (1990c) 1,857,790; comprises Maluku prov. of Indonesia; province includes the three large islands Halmahera, Ceram, Buru; several island groups, esp.: Sula, Bacan, Obi, Kai, Aru, Tanimbar, Banda, Babar, Leti; many smaller islands, as Morotai, Wetar, and the much smaller but important islands of Ambon, Ternate, and Tidore. Most of the islands are mountainous, many volcanic; dense forests with luxuriant vegetation; export sago, copra, forest products; formerly the major producers of spices (esp. nutmegs, mace, and cloves) which in 16th cent. were sought by Portuguese, Dutch, and English for world trade.

History: First visited by Portuguese c. 1512; in early 17th cent., captured by Dutch who thus were aided in securing virtual monopoly of spice trade; Ambon (*q.v.*) the early seat of Dutch control; held by British for several years late 18th and early 19th cents.; occupied by Japanese in WWII; after the war, included in East Indonesia (*q.v.*) prior to establishment of Republic of Indonesia. See also entries of separate islands.

2. Residency of the former Netherlands Indies, including the Moluccas and Netherlands New Guinea (now Irian Jaya); 191,632 sq. mi. (496,327 sq. km.); ✻ Ambon.

Mo·luc·ca Sea \mō-'lə-kə\ *or Indonesian* **Laut Ma·lu·ku** \'lau̇t-mä-'lü-ˌkü\ *or Du.* **Mo·luk·sche Zee** \mə-'lu̇k-sə-'zā\. Part of Pacific Ocean bet. NE Sulawesi on W and the Moluccas on E, Malay Archipelago; connected with the Pacific; by some extended to the S to include the Banggai and Sula Is. and the waters bet. SE Sulawesi and Buru I.

Molukken. See MOLUCCAS.

Mom·ba·sa \mōm-'bä-sä\. **1.** Island off the S coast of Kenya, 150 mi. (241 km.) N of Zanzibar at the mouth of a deep bay; 3 mi. (5 km.) long; 2.5 mi. (4 km.) wide; its chief harbor is Kilindini at SW end, connected by bridge with mainland.

2. Town, ✻ of Coast prov., Kenya, on the island of Mombasa; munic. area (incl. mainland segment) 27 sq. mi. (70 sq. km.); pop. (1984e) 425,600; chief port of Kenya; major agricultural market; exports coffee, fruits, vegetables; produces cement; tourism; remains of Portuguese buildings, esp. the 16th cent. fort.

History: Probably settled by Arabs in 11th cent.; visited by Portuguese navigator Vasco da Gama 1498; held by Portuguese most of 16th and 17th cents.; reverted to Arab control and passed in mid-19th cent. to sultan of Zanzibar (*q.v.*); passed to British control and became ✻ of East Africa Protectorate 1887–1907.

Momein. See TENGCHONG.

Mo·mence \mō-'mens\. City, Kankakee co., NE Illinois, 12 mi. (19 km.) E of the city of Kankakee; pop. (1990c) 2968.

Moming. See ZINAL ROTHORN.

Mo·mo·ste·nan·go \ˌmō-mō-stā-'näŋ-gō\. City, Totonicapán dept., W Guatemala; munic. pop. (1981c) 53,282.

Mo·mo·tom·bo \ˌmō-mō-'tȯm-bō\. Volcano, W Nicaragua, NW of Lake Managua; 4126 ft. (1258 m.); had violent eruption in 1609; also active in 1905.

Mom·pog Pass \mȯm-'pȯg\. Channel of interisland waters S of Luzon, Philippines, bet. mainland and Marinduque I.; ab. 37 mi. (60 km.) long by 12 mi. (19 km.) wide.

Mon \'mȯn\. State, SE Myanmar. See table at MYANMAR.

Møn \'mœn\; *formerly* **Mö·en** \'mœ-ən\. Island in Sjælland group, forming a part of Denmark, lying in the Baltic Sea E of S end of island of Sjælland and NE of Falster; 84 sq. mi. (218 sq. km.); pop. (1991e) 10,155; chief town Stege.

Môn. See ANGLESEY 1.

Mona. See MONA ISLAND and MAN, ISLE OF.

Mo·na·ca \mə-'nä-kə\. Borough, Beaver co., W Pennsylvania, on Ohio River 23 mi. (37 km.) NW of Pittsburgh; pop. (1990c) 6739; Community Coll. of Beaver County (1966); settled 1813.

Mon·a·co \'mä-nə-ˌkō, mə-'nä-kō\. **1.** Independent principality, SW Europe, on the Mediterranean Sea near the France-Italy border; an enclave of SE France; ab. 370 acres (150 hectares); pop. (1993e) 30,500; comprises communes of Monaco, La Condamine, Monte Carlo, and Fontvieille; tourism; has gambling casino.

History: Settled in ancient times; in hands of Grimaldi family from 13th cent. when it also became independent principality; annexed to France 1793–1814; under protection of Sardinia 1815–60; sold to France rights to towns of Menton and Roquebrune 1860; its sovereignty restored by Franco-Monégasque treaty 1861; constitutional monarchy since 1911; adopted new constitution 1962.

2. *or* **Mo·na·co–Ville** \ˌmō-nä-'kō-'vēl, 'mȯ-nä-ˌkō-\; *anc.* **Mo·noe·cus** \mə-'nē-kəs\. Commune, ✻ of the principality; pop. (1982c) 1234; situated on a rocky headland projecting into the Mediterranean; contains cathedral, palace, oceanographic museum.

Mo·nadh·li·ath Mountains \ˌmō-nə-'lē-ə\. Range of mountains, in Highland region, N cen. Scotland, NW of the Cairngorm Mts.; highest peak **Carn Mairg** \kärn-'marg\, 3087 ft. (941 m.).

Mo·nad·nock, Mount \mə-'nad-ˌnäk\. Peak, SE Cheshire co., SW New Hampshire; 3165 ft. (965 m.); often called **Grand Monadnock** to distinguish from **Little Monadnock** 1890 ft. (576 m.) nearby; popular with climbers.

Mo·na·gas \mō-'nä-gäs\. State of NE Venezuela. See table at VENEZUELA.

Mon·a·ghan \'mä-nə-hən, -ˌhan\. **1.** County, Ulster prov., NE Ireland; chief river Finn; potatoes, oats; livestock grazing. See table at IRELAND.

2. Town, its ⊗, NW of Dundalk; pop. (1991p) 5754; market town.

Mon·a·hans \'mä-nə-ˌhanz\. City, ⊗ of Ward co., W Texas, 33 mi. (53 km.) SW of Odessa; pop. (1990c) 8101.

Mo·na Island \'mō-nə\ *or* **Mona.** **1.** Island, Puerto Rico, West Indies; in S part of **Mona Passage** (80 mi. or 129 km. wide), bet. Hispaniola on W and Puerto Rico on E; ab. 6 mi. (10 km.) long and 4.5 mi. (7 km.) wide; 20 sq. mi. (52 sq. km.).

2. Island, Wales. See ANGLESEY 1.

Monapia. See MAN, ISLE OF.

Mo·nash·ee Mountains \mə-'na-shē\. Range in SE British Columbia, Canada, W of the Selkirk Mts. and bet. the Columbia River valley on the E and Shuswap and Okanagan lakes on the W; highest peak ab. 6000 ft. (1800 m.).

Mon·as·tir \ˌmä-nə-'stir\. **1.** *or* **al–Mu·na·stīr** \ˌal-ˌmü-nä-'stēr\; *anc.* **Rus·pi·na** \'rəs-pə-nə\. Seaport town, NE Tunisia, SSE of Sousse; site of Phoenician and Roman settlement; 2d cent. monastery/fortress.

2. City, Republic of Macedonia. See BITOLA.

Mon·ca·lie·ri \ˌmōŋ-kä-'lye-rē\. Commune, Torino prov., Piedmont, NW Italy, on Po River 7 mi. (11 km.) SSE of Turin; pop. (1991p) 58,433; 15th cent. royal palace.

Moncay. See MONG CAI.

Mon·ca·yo \mȯŋ-'kī-ō\. Peak, NE cen. Spain, ab. 55 mi. (88 km.) W of Saragossa, on the boundary bet. Aragon and Castilla y León; 2316 ft. (706 m.).

Mönch \'mœŋk\. Peak in the Bernese Alps, Bern canton, W cen. Switzerland; 13,445 ft. (4098 m.).

Mon·che·gorsk \ˌmən-chə-'gȯrsk\. Town, Murmansk Oblast, N Russia in Europe, ab. 70 mi. (115 km.) S of the city of Murmansk; pop. (1991e) 72,900.

Mön·chen·glad·bach \ˌmœn-kən-'glät-ˌbäk\; *before 1950* **Mün·chen–Glad·bach** \ˌmuen-kən-'glät-ˌbäk\. City, North

\ə\ abut \ˈə\ matches \ᵊ\ kitten, Fr table \ər\ further \a\ ash \ā\ ace \ä\ cot, cart \á\ Fr bac \au̇\ out \b\ Span Avila \ch\ chin \e\ bet \ē\ easy \g\ go \i\ hit \ī\ ice \j\ job \k\ Ger ich, Buch \ⁿ\ Fr vin \ŋ\ sing \ō\ go \ȯ\ all \ȯ\ law \œ\ Fr bœuf \œ̄\ Fr feu \ȯi\ boy \th\ thin \t͟h\ this \ü\ loot \u̇\ foot \ue\ Ger füllen \ue̅\ Fr rue \y\ yet \ʸ\ Fr digne \'dēnʸ\, nuit \'nwʸē\ \yü\ few \yu̇\ fury \zh\ vision

Rhine-Westphalia, Germany, 15 mi. (24 km.) WSW of Düsseldorf; pop. (1992e) 262,581; transportation center; major textile center; also produces machinery, iron, chemicals, paper, leather, petroleum products; 13th cent. church; developed around 10th cent. monastery; chartered 1336.

Mon·chy–le–Preux \mōⁿ-ˌshē-lə-ˈprœ\. Village, Pas-de-Calais dept., N France, 5 mi. (8 km.) E of Arras; held by Germans during most of WWI, taken by Allies 1917 and 1918.

Moncks Corner \ˈməŋks\. Town, ⊗ of Berkeley co., SE South Carolina; pop. (1990c) 5607; diversified agriculture.

Mon·clo·va \mōŋ-ˈklō-vä\. Town, Coahuila state, NE Mexico, 110 mi. (177 km.) N of Saltillo; munic. pop. (1990p) 178,023; alt. ab. 2000 ft. (610 m.); site of one of the largest steel mills in Latin America.

Mon·con·tour \ˌmōⁿ-kōⁿ-ˈtür\. Village, Vienne dept., W cen. France, 27 mi. (43 km.) NW of Poitiers; scene of battle 1569 in which Huguenots under Adm. Gaspard II de Coligny were defeated by forces of duke of Anjou, later King Henry III.

Monc·ton \ˈməŋk-tən\. City, Westmorland co., E New Brunswick, Canada, on Petitcodiac River at head of its estuary Chignecto Bay; pop. (1991c) 57,010; transportation center; fisheries; agriculture; educational and cultural center of French-Canadian population of New Brunswick; Coll. de l'Assomption (1832), Coll. St. Joseph (1864), Coll. Notre-Dame d'Acadie (1943), Séminaire Notre-Dame du Perpétuel Secours (1956), Univ. of Moncton (1963). Orig. settled by Acadian French; resettled by Germans from Pennsylvania 1763.

Mon·de·go \mōⁿ-ˈdā-gü\. River, cen. Portugal; flows SW into Atlantic Ocean at **Cape Mondego** 40°11′N, 8°55′W; 130 mi. (209 km.) long.

Mon·do·ñe·do \ˌmōn-dō-ˈnyā-t͟hō\. Commune, Lugo prov., N Spain; pop. (1991c) 5843; manufactures lace, leather, linen; 13th cent. cathedral.

Mon·do·vì \ˌmōn-dō-ˈvē\. Commune, Cuneo prov., Piedmont, NW Italy, 13 mi. (21 km.) ESE of the commune of Cuneo; pop. (1991p) 21,910; ceramic products; 18th cent. cathedral; founded 12th cent.; scene of French victory over Austrians 1796.

Mon·dra·go·ne \ˌmōn-drä-ˈgō-nā\. Commune, Caserta prov., Campania, S Italy, on Tyrrhenian Sea 27 mi. (43 km.) NW of Naples; pop. (1989c) 22,891.

Mon·em·va·sía *or* **Mon·em·ba·sia** \ˌmö-nem-vä-ˈsē-ä\ *or Ital.* **Na·po·li di Mal·va·sia** \ˈnä-pō-lē-di-ˌmäl-vä-ˈzē-ä\ *or medieval Latin* **Mal·ma·sia** \mal-ˈmā-zhə\. Village on small island off coast of SE Laconia dept., SE Peloponnese, Greece; an important commercial port and fortress in Middle Ages. Valued highly by Byzantine emperors; held by Venice c. 1463–1540 and 1690–1715; a Turkish possession 1540–1690 and 1715–1821; first town of Morea to be taken by Greeks in War of Independence; made seat of first national assembly 1821. Noted for export of wine known as malvasia.

Mo·nes·sen \mə-ˈnes-ᵊn\. City, Westmoreland co., SW Pennsylvania, on Monongahela River 20 mi. (32 km.) S of Pittsburgh; pop. (1990c) 9901.

Mo·nett \ˈmō-ˌnet\. City, Barry and Lawrence cos., SW Missouri, 35 mi. (56 km.) SE of Joplin; pop. (1990c) 6529.

Mon·fal·co·ne \ˌmōn-fäl-ˈkō-nā\. Commune, Friuli-Venezia Giulia, NE Italy, near mouth of Isonzo River 17 mi. (27 km.) NW of Trieste; pop. (1991p) 26,924; shipbuilding; manufactures chemicals; suffered heavy damage in WWI.

Monferrato. See MONTFERRAT.

Mon·for·te de Le·mos \mōn-ˈfōr-tā-t͟hā-ˈlā-mōs\. Commune, Lugo prov., NW Spain, 35 mi. (56 km.) S of the commune of Lugo; pop. (1991p) 20,318.

Mon·ga·la \mōŋ-ˈgä-lä\. River, S cen. Africa; flows SW from N Democratic Rep. of the Congo and empties into Congo River; ab. 400 mi. (640 km.) long (incl. its headstream, the Ebola).

Mong Cai *or* **Mon·cay** \ˈmōŋ-ˈkī\. Town, N Vietnam, on Gulf of Tonkin near border of China.

Monghyr. See MUNGER.

Mongibello. See ETNA.

Mon·go·lia \män-ˈgōl-yə, mäŋ-, -ˈgō-lē-ə\. **1.** Region, E cen. Asia; comprises independent Mongolia (Outer Mongolia), the Chinese autonomous region of Nei Monggol (Inner Mongolia), and Tuva Rep. of Russia; formerly considered a part of Outer China.

History: Region inhabited since early times by nomadic peoples; lacks historical clarity until 13th cent. A.D. when Genghis Khan (c. 1162–1227), the leader of one of the tribes, the Mongols, secured supremacy and began Mongol expansion; under Genghis and his successors, Mongol Empire, with its ✻ first at Karakorum and later at Beijing (called Khanbalik), stretched from China to the Danube in E Europe; chief successors of Mongol Empire after it broke up were khanate of the Golden Horde in Russia, Il-Khan dynasty in Persia, and Yüan dynasty in China (estab. by Kublai Khan, grandson of Genghis, 1279); in the 14th cent., Turkic ruler Timur established a short-lived empire in W Asia; Yüan dynasty supplanted by Ming dynasty in China 1368, shattering Mongol unity; in 17th cent. Manchus took control of China and began to incorporate S Mongols into China, forming the basis of a distinct Nei Monggol; later N Mongols also came under Chinese control; modern Mongolia loosely dependent upon China until Tannu Tuva (see TUVA REPUBLIC) became a republic 1911 and Outer Mongolia, under Russian auspices, declared its independence. (See MONGOLIA 2). Nei Monggol came under Chinese control, except Jehol (*q.v.*); in 1937 the two E provinces, Chahar and Suiyuan, were overrun by the Japanese, who formed them into the puppet buffer state of Mêng Chiang; following WWII Nei Monggol made an autonomous region of China (see NEI MONGGOL).

2. *also* **Outer Mongolia;** *formerly officially* **Mon·go·lian People's Republic** \-yən, -ən\. Republic, E cen. Asia, lying between China and Russia; 604,247 sq. mi. (1,565,000 sq. km.); pop. (1992e) 2,182,000; ✻ Ulaanbaatar.

Physical features: Mountainous in W part, with Altai Shan (some peaks over 10,000 ft. or 3000 m.) in SW and S, and Tannu-Ola on Tuva border in NW; in N cen. part are the Hentiyn Nuruu. The desert of Gobi (*q.v.*) covers a wide tract in cen. and SE part. Chief rivers the Selenga and its tributary, the Orhon, in N flowing into Lake Baikal, the Kerulen in E flowing into Hulun Nur in NW Manchuria, and the Hobdo Gol in extreme W flowing to the lakes Har Us Nuur and Har Nuur; other large lakes Ubsu-Nur near the Tuva border and Hövsgöl near border SW of Irkutsk.

Chief products: Wheat, potatoes, oats, barley; food products; pastoralism is an important factor in the economy; coal, oil, copper, gold, fluorspar.

History: For history prior to 1911, see MONGOLIA 1. Proclaimed itself an independent kingdom 1911, following collapse of Manchu dynasty in China; in treaties 1913 and 1915 estab. as an autonomous state under Chinese suzerainty; period 1919–21 marked by Chinese attempts to reassert their former sovereignty; Chinese forces expelled with aid of Soviet troops 1921; became a republic (Mongolian People's Republic) 1924; signed mutual assistance pact with U.S.S.R. 1936; E border scene of fighting bet. Soviet-Mongol and Japanese forces 1939; republic's independence officially recognized by China 1946; admitted to UN 1961; allied itself with the U.S.S.R. during the Sino-Soviet ideological dispute of the 1960s and 1970s; adopted new constitution and renamed Mongolia 1992.

Mongolia, Inner. See NEI MONGGOL.

Mon·gu \ˈmōŋ-gü\. Town, Zambia, 7 mi. (11 km.) SE of Lealui; pop. (1980p) 24,919.

Mon·he·gan \män-ˈhē-gən\. Island in Atlantic Ocean 9 mi. (14 km.) S of coast of Maine, in Lincoln co.; lobster fishing; art galleries; lighthouse built 1824; museum; settled c. 1622; during War of 1812 American brig *Enterprise* defeated and captured British brig *Boxer* in nearby waters 1813.

Mon·heim \ˈmōn-ˌhīm\. City, North Rhine-Westphalia, Germany; pop. (1980c) 40,559.

Mönh Sarĭdag. See MUNKU-SARDYK.

Mon·i·teau \ˈmä-nə-ˌtō\. County in cen. Missouri. See table at MISSOURI.

Mon·i·tor Peak \ˈmä-nə-tər\. Mountain, La Plata co., SW Colorado; 13,703 ft. (4177 m.).

Monitor Range. Range, cen. Nevada, chiefly in Nye co., extending N into Eureka co.

Monja, La. See LA MONJA.

Monk Bret·ton \ˈməŋk-ˈbret-^{ə}n\. Former urban district, South Yorkshire, N England, now part of Barnsley; has remains of Cluniac priory, founded c. 1157.

Mon·key Point \ˈməŋ-kē\ *or Span.* **Pun·ta Mi·co** \ˈpün-tä-ˈmē-kō\. Cape on SE coast of Nicaragua, extending into the Caribbean Sea.

Monk·wear·mouth \məŋk-ˈwir-məth\. Suburb of Sunderland (*q.v.*), Tyne and Wear co., N England; remains of 7th cent. monastery where Anglo-Saxon scholar and historian St. Bede studied.

Mon·mouth \ˈmän-məth, ˈmən-\. **1.** Coastal county in E cen. New Jersey. See table at NEW JERSEY.
2. City, ⊗ of Warren co., W Illinois, 15 mi. (24 km.) W of Galesburg; pop. (1990c) 9489; pottery, feed; Monmouth Coll. (1853); city estab. 1831; incorp. 1852. Birthplace of lawman Wyatt Earp 1848.
3. Town, Kennebec co., SW Maine, 12 mi. (19 km.) NE of Lewiston; pop. (1990c) 3353.
4. Town, Polk co., NW Oregon, ab. 13 mi. (21 km.) SW of Salem; pop. (1990c) 6288; fruit farms; Western Oregon State Coll. (1856).
5. Former county in Wales. See MONMOUTHSHIRE.
6. Town, NE Gwent, SE Wales, near junction of Monnow, Wye, and Trothy rivers 26 mi. (42 km.) N of Bristol; pop. (1991p) 75,000; market town; tourism; ruins of a 12th cent. castle in which Henry V was born 1387; received charter 1256.

Monmouth Court House. Borough (now called Freehold), New Jersey; scene in American Revolution of the battle of Monmouth June 28, 1778, and of the exploit of Mary McCauley ("Molly Pitcher") in taking her husband's place as artilleryman after he collapsed from heat exhaustion in the course of the engagement. See FREEHOLD.

Mon·mouth·shire \ˈmän-məth-ˌshir, ˈmən-, -shər\ *or* **Monmouth.** Former county, SE Wales, on the border of England; ⊗ Monmouth; rivers Wye, Usk, Ebbw, Rhymney; main towns included Newport, Abergavenny, Abetillery, Blaenavon, Caerlon. Frequently considered part of England, but for administrative purposes part of Wales. See GWENT.

Mon·ni·ken·dam \ˈmȯ-ni-kən-ˌdäm\. Commune, North Holland prov., W Netherlands; pop. (1981e) 9502; 14th cent. church.

Mo·no \ˈmō-nō\. **1.** County in E California. See table at CALIFORNIA.
2. River, Togo; 250 mi. (402 km.) long; lower course is boundary bet. Togo and Benin.
3. Island, largest of the Treasury Is. (*q.v.*), NW Solomon Is., W Pacific Ocean.

Mo·noc·a·cy \mə-ˈnä-kə-sē\. **1.** River, N Maryland; rises in Adams co., S Pennsylvania, crosses state boundary and flows S through Frederick co., N Maryland, into Potomac River.
2. Battlefield, Maryland, along river near city of Frederick; although Union forces under Gen. Lewis Wallace were routed July 9, 1864 by Gen. Jubal Anderson Early's Confederates, the delay allowed Union reinforcements to arrive in Washington and thus divert Early's planned attack on the city; set aside 1934 as Monocacy National Military Park, now called **Monocacy National Battlefield.** See UNITED STATES, *National Historical Parks.*

Monoecus. See MONACO 2.

Mono Lake. Lake, cen. Mono co., E California; elev. 6425 ft. (1958 m.); water strongly saline; no natural outlet; diversion of water from feeder streams 1940s to 1990s resulted in extensive receding of shoreline.

Mon·o·moy Point \ˈmä-nə-mȯi\. The S tip of a narrow island which comprised the largest part of a former peninsula extending S from Chatham on Cape Cod, Massachusetts; ab. 10 mi. (16 km.) long.

Mo·no·na \mə-ˈnō-nə\. **1.** County in W Iowa. See table at IOWA.

\ə\ abut \ə\ matches \$^{ə}$\ kitten, Fr table \ər\ further \a\ ash \ā\ ace \ä\ cot, cart \á\ Fr bac \aù\ out \b\ Span Avila \ch\ chin \e\ bet \ē\ easy \g\ go \i\ hit \ī\ ice \j\ job \k\ Ger ich, Buch \$^{n}$\ Fr vin \ŋ\ sing \ō\ go \ȯ\ all \ȯ\ law \œ\ Fr bœuf \œ̄\ Fr feu \ȯi\ boy \th\ thin \t͟h\ this \ü\ loot \u̇\ foot \ue\ Ger füllen \ue̅\ Fr rue \y\ yet \$^{y}$\ Fr digne \ˈdēn^{y}\, nuit \ˈnw^{y}ē\ \yü\ few \yu̇\ fury \zh\ vision

2. City, Dane co., S Wisconsin, SE of Madison; pop. (1990c) 8637.

Monona, Lake. See FOUR LAKES.

Mo·non·gah \mə-'näŋ-gə\. Town, Marion co., N West Virginia, 4 mi. (6 km.) SW of Fairmont; pop. (1990c) 1018; coal; scene of mine disaster 1907 in which 361 miners were killed.

Mo·non·ga·he·la \mə-ˌnän-gə-'hē-lə, -ˌnäŋ-, -'hā-\. **1.** River, N West Virginia and SW Pennsylvania; formed by junction of West Fork (rises in Lewis co.) and Tygart rivers in Marion co., N West Virginia, flows N across Pennsylvania border and unites with the Allegheny River to form the Ohio River at Pittsburgh; 128 mi. (206 km.) long; navigable for 60 mi. (97 km.).

2. City, Washington co., SW Pennsylvania, on Monongahela River 17 mi. (27 km.) S of Pittsburgh; pop. (1990c) 4928.

Mon·on·ga·lia \ˌmä-nən-'gā-lē-ə, -əŋ-, -lyə\. County in N West Virginia. See table at WEST VIRGINIA.

Mono Pass. Mountain pass in the Sierra Nevada, Mono co., E California; alt. 10,599 ft. (3231 m.).

Mo·no·po·li \mō-'nò-pō-lē\. Seaport, Bari prov., Puglia, SE Italy, on Adriatic 25 mi. (40 km.) ESE of the seaport of Bari; pop. (1989c) 47,326; 12th cent. cathedral; castle.

Mon·re·a·le \ˌmōn-rē-'ä-lā\. Commune, Palermo prov., NW cen. Sicily, Italy, 5 mi. (8 km.) SW of the seaport of Palermo; pop. (1991p) 25,537; trade center in fruit- and olive-growing region; 12th cent. cathedral with notable mosaics covering the walls.

Mon·roe \mən-'rō\. **1.** Name of counties in 17 states of the U.S. See tables at ALABAMA, ARKANSAS, FLORIDA, GEORGIA, ILLINOIS, INDIANA, IOWA, KENTUCKY, MICHIGAN, MISSISSIPPI, MISSOURI, NEW YORK, OHIO, PENNSYLVANIA, TENNESSEE, WEST VIRGINIA, WISCONSIN.

2. Town, E Fairfield co., SW Connecticut, on Housatonic River; pop. (1990c) 16,896.

3. City, ⊗ of Walton co., N cen. Georgia, 23 mi. (37 km.) SW of Athens; pop. (1990c) 9759.

4. City, ⊗ of Ouachita parish, N Louisiana, 100 mi. (161 km.) E of Shreveport; pop. (1990c) 54,909; chemicals, paper and paper products, lumber; gas wells; Northeast Louisiana Univ. (1931); founded 1785; incorp. 1820.

5. City, ⊗ of Monroe co., SE Michigan, on Lake Erie at mouth of Raisin River 35 mi. (56 km.) SW of Detroit; pop. (1990c) 22,902; paper, automobile parts; Monroe County Community Coll. (1964); settled 1780; in 1813 scene of "Raisin River Massacre" following defeat of Americans by British-Indian force under Col. H. Proctor during War of 1812; incorp. as city 1837.

6. Village in Monroe town, Orange co., SE New York, 15 mi. (24 km.) SW of Newburgh; pop. (1990c) 6672.

7. City, ⊗ of Union co., S North Carolina, 24 mi. (39 km.) SE of Charlotte; pop. (1990c) 16,127.

8. Village, Butler and Warren cos., SW Ohio, 27 mi. (43 km.) S of Dayton; pop. (1990c) 4490.

9. Town, Snohomish co., NW cen. Washington, 15 mi. (24 km.) ESE of Everett; pop. (1990c) 4278.

10. City, ⊗ of Green co., S Wisconsin, 30 mi. (48 km.) W of Beloit; pop. (1990c) 10,241; cheese.

Monroe, Lake. Lake on boundary bet. Volusia and Seminole cos., cen. Florida Penin.

Monroe, Mount. Peak in the White Mts., S Coos co., N New Hampshire, S of Mt. Washington; 5385 ft. (1641 m.).

Monroe City. City, Marion and Monroe cos., NE Missouri, 23 mi. (37 km.) W of Hannibal; pop. (1990c) 2701.

Monroe Peak. Mountain in SW Sevier co., cen. Utah; 11,226 ft. (3422 m.).

Mon·roe·ville \mən-'rō-ˌvil\. **1.** City, ⊗ of Monroe co., SW Alabama; pop. (1990c) 6993.

2. Borough, Allegheny co., SW Pennsylvania, E of Pittsburgh; pop. (1990c) 29,169; Community Coll. of Allegheny County, Boyce Campus (1966).

Mon·ro·via \mən-'rō-vē-ə\. **1.** City, Los Angeles co., SW California, 14 mi. (23 km.) ENE of the city of Los Angeles; pop. (1990c) 35,761; incorp. 1887.

2. Seaport, ✱ of Liberia, near the mouth of St. Paul River; pop. (1984c) 421,058; largest city in the country and its major seaport, with modern port facilities; pharmaceuticals, cement, paint; fish processing, oil refining; university. Founded as home for freed slaves 1822 by American Colonization Society; named after U.S. President James Monroe. Scene of civil war clashes beginning early 1990s.

Mons \'mōⁿs\ *or Flem.* **Ber·gen** \'ber-kə\. Commune, ✱ of Hainaut prov., SW Belgium; pop. (1992e) 92,300; trades in cloth and sugar; late Gothic cathedral and town hall; technical college (1837), State Univ. Center (1965). On site of Roman camp; made ✱ of Hainaut 804 by Holy Roman Emperor Charlemagne; became trading town with cloth market in 14th cent.; often besieged and occupied in wars of 16th–18th cents.; scene of the first engagement bet. British and German forces in WWI fought Aug. 23, 1914, and of another battle 1918.

Mons Aureus. See JANICULUM.

Mons Brisiacus. See BREISACH AM RHEIN.

Mon·schau \'mòn-ˌshau̇\; *formerly* **Mont·joie** \mōⁿ-'zhwä\. Town, North Rhine-Westphalia, Germany, SE of Aachen on French border; pop. (1980c) 10,993; 17th cent. church.

Mon·se·li·ce \mòn-'sā-lē-ˌchā\. Commune, Padova prov., Veneto, NE Italy, 13 mi. (21 km.) SSW of Padua; pop. (1981p) 17,552; 13th cent. cathedral.

Mon·se·ñor Nouel \mòn-'sā-nyòr-nō-'wel\. Province, Dominican Republic. See table at DOMINICAN REPUBLIC.

Mons Jo·vis \'mänz-'jō-vis\. See *Great Saint Bernard* Pass in table at ALPS.

Mons Lac·tar·i·us \'mänz-lak-'ter-ē-əs\. See ANGRI.

Mon·son \'mən-sən\. Town, Hampden co., SW Massachusetts, 14 mi. (23 km.) E of Springfield; pop. (1990c) 7776.

Mons Rubicus. See MONTROUGE.

Mon·ta·gna·na \ˌmòn-tä-'nyä-nä\. Commune, Padova prov., Veneto, NE Italy, 25 mi. (40 km.) SW of Padua; pop. (1981p) 10,036; largely intact medieval city walls with 24 towers; cathedral.

Mon·ta·gu \'män-tə-ˌgyü\. Town, W Western Cape prov., S Rep. of South Africa, 100 mi. (161 km.) E of Cape Town; has pleasant climate and thermal springs.

Mon·tague \män-'tāg\. **1.** County in N Texas. See table at TEXAS.

2. Unincorporated settlement, its ⊗.

Mon·ta·gue \'män-tə-ˌgyü\. Town, Franklin co., NW Massachusetts, SE of Greenfield; pop. (1990c) 8316.

Montague Island. Island on W side of entrance to Prince William Sound, S Alaska, E of Kenai Penin.; 50 mi. (80 km.) long and 8 mi. (13 km.) wide.

Mont·al·ban \ˌmòn-täl-'bän\. **1.** River, an upper tributary of the Marikina River, Luzon, Philippines; it and other streams have been developed into large reservoir furnishing water supply for Manila.

2. Municipality, Luzon, on Montalban River W of reservoir; pop. (1980c) 41,859.

Mont·al·ci·no \ˌmòn-täl-'chē-nō\. Commune, Siena prov., Tuscany, cen. Italy, 22 mi. (35 km.) SSE of the commune of Siena; pop. (1981p) 5529; cathedral; 14th cent. palace and art museum; 12th cent. abbey church.

Mont·al·to \mòn-'täl-tō\. Highest peak in the Aspromonte Ridge and Calabrian Apennines. See table at APENNINES.

Montalto Uf·fu·go \'ü-fü-gō\. Commune, Cosenza prov., Calabria, S Italy, 10 mi. (16 km.) NNW of the commune of Cosenza; pop. (1981p) 11,877.

Mon·tana \män-'ta-nə\. Northwestern state of U.S.A., bounded on N by Canadian provs. of British Columbia, Alberta, and Saskatchewan, on E by North Dakota and South Dakota, on S by Wyoming and Idaho, and on W by Idaho; 4th state in area, 147,046 sq. mi. or 380,849 sq. km. (land area 145,603 sq. mi. or 377,112 sq. km.); 44th state in population, (1990c) 799,065; ✱ Helena; 41st state admitted to Union (1889). See table of states at UNITED STATES.

Nickname: Treasure State.

State flower: Bitterroot.

Motto: Oro y Plata (Gold and Silver).

Rivers: Missouri, rising in S and flowing N then E across state; Yellowstone, rising in NW Wyoming and flowing

MONTANA
CITIES
State capital
County seat
City
BOUNDARIES
International
State and provincial
County
FEATURES
Dams
Points of interest
0 40 80 mi
0 60 120 km
BRITISH COLUMBIA
ALBERTA
CANADA
SASKATCHEWAN
NORTH DAKOTA
SOUTH DAKOTA
WYOMING
IDAHO
LINCOLN
FLATHEAD
GLACIER
TOOLE
LIBERTY
HILL
BLAINE
PHILLIPS
VALLEY
DANIELS
SHERIDAN
ROOSEVELT
RICHLAND
MC CONE
DAWSON
WIBAUX
PRAIRIE
GARFIELD
PETROLEUM
FERGUS
JUDITH BASIN
CHOUTEAU
PONDERA
TETON
CASCADE
LEWIS AND CLARK
POWELL
MISSOULA
MINERAL
SANDERS
LAKE
RAVALLI
GRANITE
DEER LODGE
SILVER BOW
JEFFERSON
BROADWATER
MEAGHER
WHEATLAND
GOLDEN VALLEY
MUSSELSHELL
TREASURE
ROSEBUD
CUSTER
FALLON
CARTER
POWDER RIVER
BIG HORN
YELLOWSTONE
STILLWATER
CARBON
SWEETGRASS
PARK
GALLATIN
MADISON
BEAVERHEAD
ROCKY MOUNTAINS
BITTERROOT RANGE
BEAVERHEAD MTS.
CENTENNIAL MTS.
BIGHORN MTS.
ABSAROKA RANGE
LITTLE BELT MTS.
BIG BELT MTS.
LEWIS AND CLARK RANGE
MISSION RANGE
CABINET MTS.
PURCELL MTS.
BEARPAW MTS.
BULL MTS.
TOOTH MTS.
GLACIER NATIONAL PARK
WATERTON-GLACIER INTERNATIONAL PEACE PARK
YELLOWSTONE NATIONAL PARK
BIGHORN CANYON NATIONAL RECREATION AREA
CUSTER BATTLEFIELD NATIONAL MONUMENT
BIG HOLE NATIONAL BATTLEFIELD
GRANTS-KOHRS RANCH NATIONAL HISTORIC SITE
BLACKFEET IND. RES.
FLATHEAD IND. RES.
ROCKY BOY'S IND. RES.
FORT BELKNAP IND. RES.
FORT PECK IND. RES.
CROW IND. RES.
TONGUE RIVER IND. RES.
Missouri R.
Yellowstone R.
Milk R.
Mussellshell R.
Fort Peck Lake
Flathead Lake
Helena
Mt. Stimson 10,165 ft.
Granite Peak 12,799 ft.
Crazy Peak 11,214 ft.
Electric Peak 10,992 ft.
Koch Peak 11,286 ft.
Lookout Pass 4,738 ft.
Lolo Pass 5,187 ft.
©1996, Encyclopædia Britannica, Inc.

through Yellowstone National Park across the boundary into Montana and then N and NE into the Missouri.

Highest point: Granite Peak, 12,799 ft. (3901 m.), in Park co.

Chief products: Wheat, barley, sugar beets, corn; livestock; copper, petroleum, phosphate rock; manufacturing: food processing; lumber, primary metals.

Chief cities: Billings, Great Falls, Missoula, Butte, Helena, Bozeman.

Political divisions: Divided into the following 56 counties (for pronunciation of their names, see their individual entries):

NAME	AREA[1] (sq. mi.)	AREA[1] (sq. km.)	POP. (1990c)	CO. SEAT
Beaverhead	5,560	14,400	8,424	Dillon
Big Horn	5,028	13,026	11,337	Hardin
Blaine	4,275	11,072	6,728	Chinook
Broadwater	1,193	3,090	3,318	Townsend
Carbon	2,067	5,354	8,080	Red Lodge
Carter	3,313	8,581	1,503	Ekalaka
Cascade	2,661	6,892	77,691	Great Falls
Chouteau	3,927	10,171	5,452	Fort Benton
Custer	3,756	9,728	11,697	Miles City
Daniels	1,443	3,737	2,266	Scobey
Dawson	2,370	6,138	9,505	Glendive
Deer Lodge[2]	740	1,917	10,278	Anaconda
Fallon	1,633	4,229	3,103	Baker
Fergus	4,242	10,987	12,083	Lewistown
Flathead[3,4]	5,137	13,305	59,218	Kalispell
Gallatin	2,517	6,519	50,463	Bozeman
Garfield[5]	4,455	11,538	1,589	Jordan
Glacier[3]	2,964	7,677	12,121	Cut Bank
Golden Valley	1,176	3,046	912	Ryegate
Granite	1,733	4,488	2,548	Philipsburg
Hill	2,927	7,581	17,654	Havre
Jefferson	1,652	4,279	7,939	Boulder
Judith Basin	1,880	4,869	2,282	Stanford
Lake[4]	1,494	3,869	21,041	Polson
Lewis and Clark	3,476	9,003	47,495	Helena
Liberty	1,439	3,727	2,295	Chester
Lincoln	3,714	9,619	17,481	Libby
McCone[5]	2,607	6,752	2,276	Circle
Madison	3,528	9,138	5,989	Virginia City
Meagher	2,354	6,097	1,819	White Sulphur Springs
Mineral	1,222	3,165	3,315	Superior
Missoula	2,612	6,765	78,687	Missoula
Musselshell	1,887	4,887	4,106	Roundup
Park	2,626	6,801	14,562	Livingston
Petroleum	1,655	4,286	519	Winnett
Phillips	5,213	13,502	5,163	Malta
Pondera	1,645	4,261	6,433	Conrad
Powder River	3,288	8,516	2,090	Broadus
Powell	2,336	6,050	6,620	Deer Lodge
Prairie	1,730	4,481	1,383	Terry
Ravalli	2,382	6,169	25,010	Hamilton
Richland	2,079	5,385	10,716	Sidney
Roosevelt	2,385	6,177	10,999	Wolf Point
Rosebud	5,037	13,046	10,505	Forsyth
Sanders	2,778	7,195	8,669	Thompson Falls
Sheridan	1,694	4,387	4,732	Plentywood
Silver Bow	715	1,852	33,941	Butte
Stillwater	1,794	4,646	6,536	Columbus
Sweet Grass	1,840	4,766	3,154	Big Timber
Teton	2,294	5,941	6,271	Choteau
Toole	1,950	5,051	5,046	Shelby
Treasure	985	2,551	874	Hysham
Valley[4]	4,974	12,883	8,239	Glasgow
Wheatland	1,420	3,678	2,246	Harlowton
Wibaux	890	2,305	1,191	Wibaux
Yellowstone	2,642	6,843	113,419	Billings
Yellowstone National Park (part)[6]	269	697	52	

[1] Area = land area.
[2] The county government was consolidated with that of its county seat (Anaconda) 1977.
[3] Glacier National Park occupies NE part of Flathead co. and NW part of Glacier co.
[4] Upper (smaller) part of Flathead Lake in Flathead co., lower part in Lake co.
[5] Fort Peck Reservoir on boundaries of Garfield co. (along both sides of its NE corner), McCone co. (upper W boundary), and Valley co. (cen. S boundary).
[6] Main part of Yellowstone National Park is within Wyoming state boundaries (3186 sq. mi. or 8252 sq. km.), with adjacent strips in Montana (232.9 sq. mi. or 603 sq. km.) and Idaho (49 sq. mi. or 127 sq. km.). Not a county.

History: Inhabited by several native tribes prior to European settlement, incl. Blackfoot, Cheyenne, Arapaho, and Flathead Indians; all except a small area in NW was part of Louisiana Purchase (*q.v.*) 1803; crossed by American explorers Meriwether Lewis and William Clark 1805–06; its boundary with Canada settled by treaties 1818 and 1846; part W of the Rocky Mts. acquired in Oregon Country (*q.v.*); parts included in various territories of the U.S. prior to organization of territory of Montana 1864; first crossed by rail (Northern Pacific) 1883; admitted to Union Nov. 8, 1889; adopted new state constitution 1972.

Mon·ta·ña \mȯn-ˈtä-nyä\. Forested region of the E slope of the Andes, esp. that of N Peru.

Mon·tar·gis \ˌmȯ^{n}-tär-ˈzhē\. Commune, Loiret dept., N cen. France, 38 mi. (61 km.) E of Orléans; remains of a castle which was long a royal residence; bronze statue of the "Dog of Montargis," which, according to legend, tracked down his master's murderer and vanquished him in a duel; unsuccessfully besieged by English 1427.

Mont·au·ban \ˌmȯn-tō-ˈbä^{n}\. **1.** Village, Somme dept., N France, 6 mi. (10 km.) E of Albert; scene of battle 1916, a part of the battle of the Somme.

2. City, ✻ of Tarn-et-Garonne dept., S France, on Tarn River 31 mi. (50 km.) N of Toulouse; pop. (1990c) 53,278; textiles, furniture; food processing; 17th–18th cent. cathedral; 17th cent. episcopal palace, now housing a museum; medieval bridge. Founded 1144; as Huguenot stronghold besieged repeatedly in 16th and 17th cents.; taken by Armand-Jean du Plessis, Cardinal Richelieu 1629. Birthplace of painter Jean-Auguste-Dominique Ingres 1780.

Mon·tauk Point \ˈmän-ˌtȯk\. Point on E extremity of Long Island, New York; lighthouse and museum; outdoor recreation.

Mont aux Sources. See AUX SOURCES, MONT.

Mont·bé·liard \ˌmȯ^{n}-bā-ˈlyär\. Commune, Doubs dept., E France, 43 mi. (69 km.) ENE of Besançon; pop. (1990c) 30,639; automobiles. Under dukes of Württemberg from 1397; given to France by Peace of Lunéville 1801; scene of battle 1871 bet. French and Prussians. Birthplace of naturalist George Cuvier 1769.

Mont Blanc. See BLANC, MONT.

Mont Blanc Tunnel. Vehicular tunnel, SW Europe. See BLANC, MONT.

Mont·bri·son \ˌmȯ^{n}-brē-ˈzȯ^{n}\. Town, Loire dept., SE cen. France; 13th–15th cent. church.

Mont·calm \mänt-ˈkälm\. **1.** County in cen. Michigan. See table at MICHIGAN.

2. County in S Quebec, Canada. See table at QUEBEC.

Mont·ceau–les–Mines \mȯ^{n}-ˌsō-lā-ˈmēn\. Commune, Saône-et-Loire dept., E cen. France.

Mont Cenis *or Ital.* **Monte Cenisio. 1.** See CENIS, MONT.

2. Alpine pass and tunnel. See table at ALPS.

Mont·clair \mänt-ˈklar\. **1.** City, San Bernardino co., SE California, NE of Pomona; pop. (1990c) 28,434.

2. Town, Essex co., NE New Jersey, 6 mi. (10 km.) NNW of Newark; pop. (1990c) 37,729; residential suburb of Newark and New York City; chemicals, paint, metalware; Montclair State Coll. (1908); settled 1666 as part of Newark; separated as part of Bloomfield 1812; separately incorp. 1868; art museum containing works of painter George Inness, who resided here.

Mont–de–Mar·san \ˌmȯ^{n}d-mär-ˈsä^{n}\. Commune, ✻ of Landes dept., SW France, 66 mi. (106 km.) S of Bordeaux; pop. (1990c) 31,864; food processing; founded 1141 as ✻ of viscountship of Marsan; passed to France 16th cent. after the Wars of Religion.

Mont·di·dier \ˌmȯ^{n}-dē-ˈdyā\. Commune, Somme dept., N France; devastated in battles 1918 in WWI.

Mont–Dore \mȯ^{n}-ˈdȯr\. **1.** Commune, Puy-de-Dôme dept., S cen. France, on the Dordogne near its source; thermal springs and baths, known since Roman times.

2. Coastal village, SW New Caledonia I., E of Nouméa; pop. (1989c) 16,370.

Mont·ea·gle \mänt-ˈē-gəl\. Town and summer resort, Grundy co., S cen. Tennessee, ab. 35 mi. (56 km.) NW of Chattanooga; pop. (1990c) 1138.

Mon·te·bel·lo \ˌmän-tə-ˈbe-lō\. Residential city, Los Angeles co., SW California, 8 mi. (13 km.) ESE of the city of Los Angeles; pop. (1990c) 59,564; incorp. 1920.

Montebello Islands *or* **Monte Bello Islands.** Group of small islands off NW coast of Western Australia, Australia.

Mon·te·bel·lu·na \ˌmȯn-tā-be-ˈlü-nä\. Commune, Treviso prov., Veneto, NE Italy, 13 mi. (21 km.) NW of the commune of Treviso; pop. (1989c) 24,922.

Mon·te·bourg \mȯ^{n}t-ˈbu̇r\. Town, SE coast of Cotentin Penin., Manche dept., NW France; beachhead estab. nearby June 1944 by Americans in Normandy campaign of WWII.

Mon·te Car·lo \ˌmȯn-tā-ˈkär-lō; ˌmän-ti-ˈkär-lō\. Commune, Monaco, on coast to the N of the principality's ✻; pop. (1990c) 14,702; tourist resort with casino and many hotels.

Mon·te Cas·si·no \ˈmȯn-tā-kä-ˈsē-nō\. Famous abbey in Frosinone prov., SE Lazio, cen. Italy, on a hill near Cassino; founded c. 529 A.D. by St. Benedict of Nursia, who died here; since 1866 a national monument. Rebuilt four times: after being sacked by the Lombards late 6th cent., destroyed by the Saracens late 9th cent., badly damaged by earthquake 1349, and destroyed by Allied bombing 1944 in WWII. See CASSINO.

Mon·te·ca·ti·ni–Ter·me \ˌmȯn-tā-kä-ˈtē-nē-ˈter-mā\. Commune, Pistoia prov., Tuscany, cen. Italy, 12 mi. (19 km.) SW of the commune of Pistoia; pop. (1981p) 21,505; thermal mineral springs and baths; health resort.

Mon·te·cor·vi·no \ˌmȯn-tā-kȯr-ˈvē-nō\ *or officially* **Montecorvino Ro·vel·la** \rō-ˈve-lä\. Commune, Campania, S Italy, 11 mi. (18 km.) E of Salerno; pop. (1981p) 19,068; scene of bitter fighting and heavy casualties 1943 in WWII.

Mon·te Cris·ti \ˈmȯn-tā-ˈkrēs-tē\. **1.** Province, NW Dominican Republic. See table at DOMINICAN REPUBLIC.
2. *or in full* **San Fer·nan·do de Monte Cristi** \ˌsän-fer-ˈnän-dō-t͟hā-\. Town, its ✻; pop. (1981c) 9265; rice, tobacco, bananas.

Mon·te·cris·to \ˌmȯn-tā-ˈkrēs-tō\. Italian island in Tyrrhenian Sea S of Elba; ab. 6 sq. mi. (16 sq. km.); state hunting preserve.

Monte Croce. See PLÖCKEN.

Mon·te·fia·sco·ne \ˌmȯn-tā-fyä-ˈskō-nā\. Commune, Viterbo prov., Lazio, cen. Italy, in volcanic region E of Lake Bolsena 10 mi. (16 km.) NNW of the commune of Viterbo; pop. (1981p) 12,436; 16th cent. cathedral; ruins of a castle; Romanesque church; noted for its muscatel wine.

Mon·te·frío \ˌmȯn-tā-ˈfrē-ō\. Commune, Granada prov., S Spain, 22 mi. (35 km.) WNW of the city of Granada; pop. (1991c) 8183.

Mon·te·go Bay \män-ˈtē-gō\. **1.** Inlet of the Caribbean, NW coast of Jamaica; the seaport of Montego Bay is on it.
2. Seaport, NW Jamaica, West Indies; pop. (1991p) 83,446; resort; has good harbor and export trade in fruit. Orig. site of large Arawak village, visited by explorer Christopher Columbus 1494.

Montego Bay Point. Cape on NW coast of the island of Jamaica, West Indies, just N of Montego Bay.

Monteleone di Calabria. See VIBO VALENTIA.

Mon·té·li·mar \mȯ^{n}-ˌtā-lē-ˈmär\; *anc.* **Acu·num Acu·sio** \ə-ˈkyü-nəm-ə-ˈkyü-shē-ˌō\; *later* **Mon·til·i·um Ad·he·ma·ri** \män-ˈti-lē-əm-ˌäd-hē-ˈmar-ī\. Commune, Drôme dept., SE France, on Rhone River 27 mi. (43 km.) SSW of Valence; pop. (1990c) 31,386; agricultural area; manufactures textiles, confectionery; medieval castle. Orig. a Gallo-Roman settlement; besieged and captured by Huguenots 16th cent.; in WWII seized by Allies 1944.

Mon·te Lir·io \ˈmȯn-tā-ˈlēr-ē-ˌō\. Town, at N end of island in Gatun Lake, Panama.

Mon·tel·lo \män-ˈte-lō\. **1.** City, ⊗ of Marquette co., cen. Wisconsin; pop. (1990c) 940.
2. *or Ital.* \mōn-ˈtel-lō\. Plateau, NE Italy, SW of Piave River and NE of Montebelluna, Veneto; scene of battles in WWI, esp. in June 1918, an Italian victory.

Mon·te·ne·gro \ˌmȯn-tā-ˈnā-grō, ˌmän-tə-ˈnē-grō\. **1.** *or Serbo-Croat.* **Cr·na Go·ra** \ˈtsər-nə-ˈgōr-ə\ *also* **Tser·na·go·ra** \ˌtsər-nə-ˈgōr-ə\. Former kingdom, SE Europe, now part of Yugoslavia; area (1918) 3733 sq. mi. (967 sq. km.); ✻ Cetinje; mountainous, well-forested region incl. ranges of the North Albanian Alps; highest peak Durmitor 8274 ft. (2522 m.) in cen. part; includes NW two thirds of Lake Scutari into which Morača River flows; other rivers are headstreams of the Drina and Ibar.
History: Originated after battle of Kosovo (*q.v.*) 1389, when defeated Serbs took refuge on "Black Mountain"; ruled by prince-bishops, through centuries of conflict, it never yielded to Turkish authority; ties with Russia began in 18th cent., and became an ally of Russia in its wars against Turkey; state became secular and modernized in 19th cent.; took part in war against Turkey 1876–78, and secured recognition of complete independence and additional territory 1878 (frontier disputes settled by 1880); kingdom proclaimed 1910; fought Turks in First and in Second Balkan Wars; for help to Serbia, received one half of sanjak (Turkish district) of Novi Pazar 1913; supported Serbia from start of WWI; invaded and occupied by Austro-Hungarian army 1915–18; voted union with Serbia, Croatia, and other Yugoslav territories to form Kingdom of the Serbs, Croats, and Slovenes 1918.
2. A constituent republic of Yugoslavia, in region of the former kingdom of Montenegro, bordering on Serbia, Bosnia and Herzegovina, Albania, and the Adriatic Sea; 5333 sq. mi. (13,812 sq. km.); pop. (1991p) 616,327; ✻ and largest city Podgorica; livestock raising; tobacco; bauxite; iron and steel; made a constituent republic in 1946 constitution; following secession of Slovenia, Croatia, Bosnia and Herzegovina, and Macedonia from Yugoslavia (*q.v.*), joined with Serbia to form new Federal Republic of Yugoslavia 1992.

Montenegro. Municipality, Brazil. See AMAPÁ 2.

Mon·te Pla·ta \ˈmȯn-tā-ˈplä-tä\. **1.** Province, Dominican Republic. See table at DOMINICAN REPUBLIC.
2. Commune, its ✻.

Mon·te·pul·cia·no \ˌmȯn-tā-pül-ˈchä-nō\. Commune, Tuscany, cen. Italy, 29 mi. (47 km.) SE of Siena; pop. (1981p) 14,087; 16th cent. cathedral; notable 16th cent. church; several Renaissance palaces. Site of ancient Etruscan town.

Mon·te·reau–faut–Yonne \mȯ^{n}-ˌtrō-fō-ˈyȯn\; *anc.* **Con·da·te** \kän-ˈdā-tē\. Town, Seine-et-Marne dept., N France, at confluence of Yonne and Seine rivers.

Mon·te·rey \ˌmän-tə-ˈrā\. **1.** Coastal county in California. See table at CALIFORNIA.
2. Commercial city, Monterey co., W California, at S end of Monterey Bay; pop. (1990c) 31,954; Presidio of Monterey; Monterey Naval Postgraduate School (1909); Monterey Peninsula Coll. (1947); Monterey Institute of International Studies (1955); aquarium, park preserving historic architecture. Area sighted 1542 by explorer Juan Rodríguez Cabrillo, explored 1602 by Spanish mariner Sebastián Vizcaíno; settled 1770 with founding of presidio and Franciscan mission; became social, military, and political center of Spanish California; ✻ of Spanish prov. of California 1775–1822, of Mexican prov. 1822–46; to U.S. 1846; site of first California constitutional convention 1849; incorp. 1850.
3. Town, Putnam co., N cen. Tennessee, 15 mi. (24 km.) E of Cookeville; pop. (1990c) 2559.
4. Town, ⊗ of Highland co., W Virginia; pop. (1990c) 222.
5. City, Mexico. See MONTERREY.

Monterey Bay. Inlet of Pacific Ocean in Santa Cruz and Monterey cos., W cen. California.

Monterey Park. Suburban residential city, Los Angeles co., SW California, just E of East Los Angeles; pop. (1990c) 60,738; East Los Angeles Coll. (1945).

Mon·te·ría \ˌmȯn-tā-ˈrē-ä\. City, ✻ of Córdoba dept., N Colombia, 120 mi. (193 km.) SSW of Cartagena; munic. pop. (1992e) 265,800; university (1966); cathedral.

Mon·te·ro·ton·do \ˌmȯn-tā-rō-ˈtün-dō\. Commune, Roma prov., Lazio, Italy; pop. (1989c) 29,090.

Mon·ter·rey \ˌmȯn-ter-ˈrā\ *or sometimes angl.* **Mon·te·rey** \ˌmän-tə-ˈrā\. City, ✻ of Nuevo León state, NE Mexico; pop. (1990p) 1,064,197; diversified industrial center, whose products include steel and beverages; several universities and an institute of technology; cathedral; García Caves (*q.v.*) nearby.

\ə\ **abut** \ᵊ\ **matches** \ᵊ\ **kitten, Fr table** \ər\ **further** \a\ **ash** \ā\ **ace**
\ä\ **cot, cart** \á\ **Fr bac** \au̇\ **out** \b̶\ **Span Avila** \ch\ **chin** \e\ **bet** \ē\ **easy**
\g\ **go** \i\ **hit** \ī\ **ice** \j\ **job** \k̲\ **Ger ich, Buch** \$^{n}$\ **Fr vin**
\ŋ\ **sing** \ō\ **go** \ȯ\ **all** \ȯ\ **law** \œ\ **Fr bœuf** \œ̄\ **Fr feu** \ȯi\ **boy**
\th\ **thin** \t͟h\ **this** \ü\ **loot** \u̇\ **foot** \ue\ **Ger füllen** \ue̅\ **Fr rue**
\y\ **yet** \$^{y}$\ **Fr digne** \ˈdēn^{y}\, **nuit** \ˈnw^{y}ē\ \yü\ **few** \yu̇\ **fury** \zh\ **vision**

Founded 1579; scene of battle in Mexican War 1846 in which city was taken by U.S. forces under Gen. Zachary Taylor; developed as center of metallurgical industry after 1882, when rail link with Laredo, Texas was estab.

Mon·te·sa·no \ˌmän-tə-ˈsā-nō\. City, ⊗ of Grays Harbor co., W Washington, on Chehalis River 11 mi. (18 km.) E of Aberdeen; pop. (1990c) 3064; lumber; dairy farming.

Mon·te Sant'An·ge·lo \ˈmȯn-tā-sän-ˈtän-jā-ˌlō\. Commune, Foggia prov., Puglia, SE Italy, 27 mi. (43 km.) NE of the commune of Foggia; pop. (1991p) 15,011; olive oil; tourism; rebuilt Norman castle; famous "sanctuary" of St. Michael, built 5th cent. over a grotto where the archangel Michael is said to have appeared, a pilgrimage site for centuries; 13th cent. campanile.

Mon·tes Cla·ros \ˈmōⁿ-tēsh-ˈklȧ-rüs\. City, N cen. Minas Gerais state, E Brazil, 225 mi. (362 km.) N of Belo Horizonte; munic. pop. (1991p) 247,286.

Mon·te Se·re·no \ˈmän-tə-sə-ˈrē-nō\. City, Santa Clara co., W California, 12 mi. (19 km.) SW of San Jose; pop. (1990c) 3287.

Mon·te·sil·va·no \ˌmȯn-tā-sēl-ˈvä-nō\. Commune, Pescara prov., Abruzzi, cen. Italy; pop. (1989c) 35,279.

Mon·te Tru·jil·lo \ˈmȯn-tā-trü-ˈhē-yō, -lyō\. See DUARTE, PICO.

Mon·te·val·lo \ˌmän-tə-ˈva-lō\. Town, Shelby co., cen. Alabama, 32 mi. (51 km.) S of Birmingham; pop. (1990c) 4239; Univ. of Montevallo (1896).

Mon·te·vid·eo \ˌmän-tə-ˈvi-dē-ˌō\. City, ⊗ of Chippewa co., SW cen. Minnesota, on Minnesota River 42 mi. (68 km.) SE of Big Stone Lake; pop. (1990c) 5499; agriculture.

Mon·te·vi·deo \ˌmȯn-tā-b̲ē-ˈt̲h̲ā-ō, ˌmän-tə-və-ˈdā-ō\. **1.** Department of S Uruguay. See table at URUGUAY.

2. Seaport city, ✻ of Uruguay, also ✻ of Montevideo dept., in S part on N shore of La Plata estuary 135 mi. (217 km.) E of Buenos Aires, Argentina; pop. (1985c) 1,251,647; political, industrial, commercial, and cultural center of Uruguay; exports wool and meat; produces textiles, wines, dairy products, soap, and clothing; meatpacking plants; tourism; Univ. of the Republic (1849); vocational university (1878); cathedral; several museums.

History: Settled by Spanish 1726 to counteract Portuguese influence in area; from 1807 to 1830 alternately occupied by British, Spanish, Argentine, Portuguese, and Brazilian forces; became ✻ of independent Uruguay 1830; underwent siege by combined Argentine-Uruguayan forces 1843–1851, in which British and French naval forces assisted defenders.

Mon·te Vis·ta \ˈmän-tə-ˈvis-tə\. City, Rio Grande co., S Colorado, in San Luis Park 15 mi. (24 km.) WNW of Alamosa; pop. (1990c) 4324; ships vegetables.

Mon·te·zu·ma \ˌmän-tə-ˈzü-mə\. **1.** County in SW corner of Colorado. See table at COLORADO.

2. City, Macon co., SW cen. Georgia, 45 mi. (72 km.) SW of the city of Macon; pop. (1990c) 4506.

3. Town, ⊗ of Poweshiek co., SE cen. Iowa; pop. (1990c) 1651.

Montezuma Castle National Monument. See UNITED STATES, *National Monuments.*

Montezuma Peak. Mountain, Archuleta co., S Colorado; 13,703 ft. (4177 m.).

Mont·fau·con \ˌmȯⁿ-fō-ˈkōⁿ\. Village, Meuse dept., NE France, 13 mi. (21 km.) NW of Verdun; American military cemetery with large memorial tower; held by Germans throughout WWI; taken 1918 by Americans in the Meuse-Argonne offensive.

Mont·fer·rand \ˌmȯⁿ-fə-ˈräⁿ\. Medieval city, now part of the city of Clermont-Ferrand (*q.v.*), Puy-de-Dôme dept., S cen. France.

Mont·fer·rat \ˌmōⁿ-fe-ˈrä\ *or Ital.* **Mon·fer·ra·to** \ˌmȯn-fer-ˈrä-tō\. Former marquisate and duchy in Italy, S of Po River, now mostly in Alessandria prov., SE Piedmont.

Mont·gom·ery \mənt-ˈgəm-rē, mänt-, -ˈgäm-\. **1.** Name of counties in 18 states of the U.S. See tables at ALABAMA, ARKANSAS, GEORGIA, ILLINOIS, INDIANA, IOWA, KANSAS, KENTUCKY, MARYLAND, MISSISSIPPI, MISSOURI, NEW YORK, NORTH CAROLINA, OHIO, PENNSYLVANIA, TENNESSEE, TEXAS, VIRGINIA.

2. Commercial city, ✻ of Alabama and ⊗ of Montgomery co., SE cen. Alabama, on Alabama River ab. 85 mi. (135 km.) SSE of Birmingham; pop. (1990c) 187,106; cotton, livestock, and lumber market; fertilizer factories. Huntingdon Coll. (1854), Alabama State Univ. (1874), Faulkner Univ. (1942), Auburn Univ. at Montgomery (1967); nearby is Maxwell Air Force Base with U.S. Air Force education center. Incorp. 1819; made state ✻ 1847; briefly served as first ✻ of the Confederacy 1861 until moved to Richmond, Virginia later that year; taken by Union army 1865. Scene of boycott against segregated buses 1950s and of civil rights demonstrations 1960s, some led by clergyman and reformer Martin Luther King, Jr.

3. Village, Kane and Kendall cos., NE Illinois, 41 mi. (66 km.) S of Aurora; pop. (1990c) 4267.

4. City, in Fayette and Kanawha cos., SW cen. West Virginia, on Kanawha River 22 mi. (35 km.) ESE of Charleston; pop. (1990c) 2449; coal; West Virginia Institute of Technology (1895).

5. Former county in Wales. See MONTGOMERYSHIRE.

6. *or Welsh* **Tre·fal·dwyn** \tre-ˈfäl-dwin\. Town, Powys, E Wales; pop. (1981c) 1035; cattle market.

Montgomery City. City, ⊗ of Montgomery co., E cen. Missouri, 46 mi. (74 km.) E of Columbia; pop. (1990c) 2281.

Mont·gom·er·y·shire \mənt-ˈgəm-rē-ˌshir, mänt-, -ˈgäm-, -shər\ *or* **Montgomery.** Former county, E Wales; ⊗ Welshpool; hilly region; rivers Dyfi, Severn, Vyrnwy. See POWYS.

Monti Albani. See ALBAN HILLS.

Mon·ti·cel·lo \ˌmän-tə-ˈse-lō\. **1.** City, ⊗ of Drew co., SE Arkansas; pop. (1990c) 8116; Univ of Arkansas at Monticello (1909).

2. Town, ⊗ of Jefferson co., N Florida, 28 mi. (45 km.) ENE of Tallahassee; pop. (1990c) 2573.

3. City, ⊗ of Jasper co., cen. Georgia, 32 mi. (51 km.) N of Macon; pop. (1990c) 2289.

4. City, Piatt co., cen. Illinois, 25 mi. (40 km.) NE of Decatur; pop. (1990c) 4549.

5. City, ⊗ of White co., NW Indiana, 25 mi. (40 km.) NNE of Lafayette on the Tippecanoe River bet. Shafer Lake and Freeman Lake (*qq.v.*); pop. (1990c) 5237; resort.

6. City, Jones co., E Iowa, 30 mi. (48 km.) ENE of Cedar Rapids; pop. (1990c) 3522.

7. City, ⊗ of Wayne co., S Kentucky, 22 mi. (35 km.) SW of Somerset; pop. (1990c) 5357.

8. City, Wright co., S cen. Minnesota; pop. (1990c) 4941.

9. Town, ⊗ of Lawrence co., S Mississippi; pop. (1990c) 1755.

10. Town, ⊗ of Lewis co., NE Missouri; pop. (1990c) 106.

11. Village, ⊗ of Sullivan co., SE New York, 42 mi. (68 km.) W of Poughkeepsie; pop. (1990c) 6597.

12. City, ⊗ of San Juan co., SE corner of Utah; pop. (1990c) 1806; founded by Mormons 1887; figured in San Juan River gold rush 1892.

13. \-ˈse-lō, -ˈche-lō \. Estate and residence of 3d U.S. President Thomas Jefferson, 3 mi. (5 km.) SE of Charlottesville, Virginia.

Mon·ti·chia·ri \ˌmȯn-tē-ˈkyä-rē\. Commune, Brescia prov., Lombardy, N Italy, SE of the commune of Brescia; pop. (1981p) 15,325.

Mon·tiel \mȯn-ˈtyel\. Town, SE Ciudad Real prov., SE cen. Spain; pop. (1991c) 1792; just NW is battlefield where Peter the Cruel, king of Castile and León, was defeated and killed 1369 by his half brother Henry of Trastámara, who then assumed the throne of Castile as Henry II.

Mon·ti·gnac \ˌmȯⁿ-tē-ˈny-ȧk\. Town, E Dordogne dept., SW cen. France; nearby is Lascaux Cave which contains impressive prehistoric cave paintings, discovered 1940, closed to public 1963 to halt deterioration.

Mon·ti·gnies–sur–Sam·bre \ˌmȯⁿ-tē-ˈnyē-su̅e̅r-ˈsäⁿbrᵊ\. Commune, Hainaut prov., SW Belgium, just E of Charleroi.

Mon·ti·gny–lès–Metz \ˌmȯⁿ-tē-ˈnyē-ˌlā-ˈmets, -ˈmes\ *sometimes shortened to* **Montigny.** Commune, Moselle dept., NE France, 5 mi. (8 km.) SSW of Metz; residential suburb of Metz.

Mon·ti·jo \mon-'tē-hō\. **1.** Pacific coast port, SW cen. Panama, near the head of the Gulf of Montijo.
2. Town, Setúbal dist., W Portugal, across Tagus River to the E of Lisbon; pop. (1991p) 23,407.
3. Town, Badajoz prov., W Spain, ab. 18 mi. (29 km.) ENE of the city of Badajoz; pop. (1991p) 23,407; scene of battle 1644 in which Portuguese defeated Spanish, who opposed reign of Portuguese King John IV.

Montijo, Gulf of. Inlet of Pacific Ocean on the SW coast of Panama, extending NE into Panama at the W base of Azuero Penin.

Montilium Adhemari. See MONTÉLIMAR.

Mon·ti·lla \mon-'tē-lyä, -yä\. Commune, Córdoba prov., S Spain, 22 mi. (35 km.) SSE of the city of Córdoba; pop. (1991p) 22,168; agricultural products; wine, esp. amontillado; nearby ducal palace; inhabited since Roman times.

Mon·ti·vil·liers \mōⁿ-,tē-vēl-'yā\. Town, Seine-Maritime dept., N France; clustered around former abbey, the remains of which form part of the church.

Montjoie. See MONSCHAU.

Mont Jo·li \,mōⁿ-zhō-'lē\. Town, Rimouski-Neigette co., S Quebec, Canada, 18 mi. (29 km.) ENE of Rimouski; pop. (1991c) 6265; starting point and terminal of automobile loop highway around Gaspé Penin.

Mont–Lau·ri·er \mōⁿ-'lór-ē-,ā\. Town, SW Quebec, Canada, on Lièvre River 77 mi. (124 km.) N of Ottawa; pop. (1991c) 7862; terminus of branch of Canadian Pacific Railway from Montreal.

Mont·lu·çon \,mōⁿ-lü-'sōⁿ\. City, Allier dept., cen. France, on Cher River 38 mi. (61 km.) WSW of Moulins; pop. (1990c) 46,660; chemicals, glass, rubber goods; 15th–16th cent. château of dukes of Bourbon, now a museum; 12th and 15th cent. churches.

Mont·ma·gny \,mōⁿ-mä-'nyē\. **1.** County, S Quebec, Canada. See table at QUEBEC.
2. City, its ⊗ on S bank of St. Lawrence River 34 mi. (55 km.) ENE of Quebec; pop. (1991c) 11,861; furniture, stoves; founded 1678; incorp. as city 1966.

Mont·mar·tre \mōⁿ-'märtrᵊ\. Section in N part of Paris, France, occupying a hill above the Seine River; highest point 420 ft. (128 m.). Has large cemetery; basilica of Sacré Coeur; an old town now within the city limits and noted for its cafés and nightlife; often figured in early battles and sieges.

Mont·mé·dy \,mōⁿ-mā-'dē\. Town, Meuse dept., NE France, near Belgian border 25 mi. (40 km.) N of Verdun; fortress town with citadel; captured from Spanish c. 1657 and retained by French in Treaty of the Pyrenees 1659; fortified under Louis XIV.

Mont·mo·ren·cy \,mänt-mə-'ren-sē\. **1.** County in NE Michigan. See table at MICHIGAN.
2. River, S Quebec, Canada; flows S into St. Lawrence River 6 mi. (10 km.) below Quebec; ab. 60 mi. (97 km.) long; rapid current; notable waterfalls, **Montmorency Falls** (251 ft. or 77 m. in one fall) which furnish light and power for Quebec City.
3. *Fr.* ,mōⁿ-mo-räⁿ-'sē\. Commune, Val-d'Oise dept., N France, 9 mi. (15 km.) N of Paris; 16th cent. Gothic church; museum of Rousseau. Formerly seat of Montmorency family; under Condé family (late 17th cent. ff.) and until the Revolution called **En·ghien** \äⁿ-'gäⁿ\; philosopher Jean-Jacques Rousseau resided here at one time.

Mon·to·ne \mon-'tō-nā\. River, N cen. Italy; flows NE into Adriatic Sea 6 mi. (10 km.) NE of Ravenna; 45 mi. (72 km.) long.

Mon·to·ro \mon-'tō-rō\. Commune, Córdoba prov., S Spain, on Guadalquivir River 22 mi. (35 km.) ENE of the city of Córdoba; pop. (1991c) 9681.

Mon·tour \män-'tůr\. **1.** County in E cen. Pennsylvania. See table at PENNSYLVANIA.
2. Town, Schuyler co., New York; pop. (1990c) 2528.

Montour Falls. Village, Schuyler co., SW cen. New York, near head of Seneca Lake, 16 mi. (26 km.) N of Elmira; pop. (1990c) 1845; contains Shequaga Falls, 156-foot (48-meter) waterfall.

Mon·tours·ville \män-'tůrz-,vil\. Residential borough, Lycoming co., N cen. Pennsylvania, 5 mi. (8 km.) E of Williamsport; pop. (1990c) 4983; settled 1807.

Mont·par·nasse \,mōⁿ-pȧr-'nȧs\. Quarter in S cen. Paris, France; since late 19th cent. a center of Parisian artistic, student, and bohemian life; many noted cafés. Has notable cemetery, laid out 1824, with tombs of several famous artists and writers.

Mont·pe·lier \mänt-'pēl-yər\. **1.** City, Bear Lake co., SE Idaho, 70 mi. (113 km.) SE of Pocatello; pop. (1990c) 2656; phosphate deposits.
2. Village, Williams co., NW corner of Ohio, on St. Joseph River 55 mi. (89 km.) W of Toledo; pop. (1990c) 4299.
3. City, ✻ of Vermont and ⊗ of Washington co., N cen. Vermont, on Winooski River; pop. (1990c) 8247; financial and service center; insurance; Vermont Coll. of Norwich Univ. (1834); city founded c. 1780; became ✻ 1805. Birthplace of Adm. George Dewey 1837.

Mont·pel·lier \,mōⁿ-pe-'lyā\. City, ✻ of Hérault dept., S France, near Mediterranean 77 mi. (124 km.) WNW of Marseille; pop. (1990c) 210,866; wine; textiles, chemicals, electronic components; notable structures include a château, citadel, 14th cent. cathedral, triumphal arch; university (1220); oldest botanical garden in France (1593). Founded c. 8th cent.; later held by Aragon and king of Majorca until it finally reverted to France in 14th cent.; Huguenot stronghold, captured 1622 by Louis XIII. Birthplace of the philosopher Auguste Comte 1798.

Mont·re·al \,män-trē-'ól, ,mən-\. **1.** River, N Wisconsin; rises in Iron co., flows NW and forms section of Wisconsin-Michigan boundary, empties into Lake Superior; ab. 40 mi. (64 km.) long.
2. *or Fr.* **Mont·ré·al** \mōⁿ-rā-'ȧl\. County, S Quebec, Canada. See table at QUEBEC.
3. *or Fr.* **Montréal.** City, ⊗ of Montreal co., on Montreal I., S Quebec, Canada, on the N bank of the St. Lawrence River; pop. (1991c) 1,017,666. Named from Mount Royal, the hill in its center. Canada's largest city and chief port of entry; its port is active terminal for both oceangoing and inland shipping; major railroad and transportation center of E Canada; manufactures electrical apparatus, aircraft, railway equipment, clothing; financial center; oil refineries; population predominantly of French extraction. Contains many churches (esp. St. James Cathedral and Notre Dame), religious institutions, libraries, museums, and many public parks; McGill Univ. (1821), Univ. de Montréal (1876), Loyola Coll. (1896), Univ. du Québec à Montréal (1969).

History: Occupied by Indian town of Hochelaga (*q.v.*) when visited by French explorer Jacques Cartier 1535; permanent settlement made by Sieur de Maisonneuve 1642 and given the name **Ville–Ma·rie de Montréal** \,vēl-mȧ-,rē-də-,mōⁿ-rā-'ȧl\; its residents constantly embroiled with the Iroquois; became center of fur trade and starting point for expeditions into the interior; last Canadian city held by the French, surrendering to the British in 1760; occupied briefly by American troops 1775–76; seat of Canadian government 1844–49; site of 1967 World's Fair (Expo '67); site of Summer Olympic Games 1976.

Montreal East *or Fr.* **Montréal–Est** \-'est\. Town, Montreal I., S Quebec, Canada, on St. Lawrence River 8 mi. (13 km.) N of the city of Montreal; pop. (1991c) 3767.

Montreal Island. Island in St. Lawrence River, Quebec, E Canada; site of the city of Montreal and its residential suburbs.

Montreal Lake. Lake, N cen. Saskatchewan, Canada; 137 sq. mi. (355 sq. km.); lower section is in Prince Albert National Park.

Montreal North *or Fr.* **Montréal–Nord** \ -ˈnȯr\. Town, Montreal I., S Quebec, Canada, on Rivière des Prairies 8 mi. (13 km.) N of the city of Montreal; pop. (1991c) 85,516.

Montreal West *or Fr.* **Montréal–Ouest** \ -ˈwest\. Residential town, Montreal I., S Quebec, Canada, 6 mi. (10 km.) SW of the city of Montreal; pop. (1991c) 5180.

Mon·treuil \mȯⁿ-ˈtrœi\ *also* **Montreuil–sous–Bois** \ -sü-ˈbwä\. Commune, Seine-St.-Denis dept., N France, E suburb of Paris; pop. (1990c) 95,038; 12th cent. church; manufactures chemicals, porcelain.

Mon·treux \ mȯⁿ-ˈtrœ\. Group of villages forming the communes of Le Châtelard and Les Planches in Vaud canton, W Switzerland; pop. (1990c) 20,060; a well-known resort at the E end of Lake Geneva. Here in 1936 an international conference met and agreed to return The Straits (*q.v.*) to Turkish military control.

Mon·trose \män-ˈtrōz, ˈmän-ˌ\. **1.** County in W Colorado. See table at COLORADO.

2. City, its ⊗, 57 mi. (92 km.) SE of Grand Junction; pop. (1990c) 8854; trade center for irrigated agricultural region; tourism; founded 1882.

3. Seaport burgh, Tayside region, E Scotland, at mouth of the South Esk; pop. (1981c) 12,323; fishing; services related to oil production; popular resort; scene of Scottish King John de Baliol's surrender 1296 to King Edward I of England.

Mon·tross \ män-ˈtrȯs, ˈmän-ˌtrȯs\. Town, ⊗ of Westmoreland co., E Virginia; pop. (1990c) 359.

Mont·rouge \mȯⁿ-ˈrüzh\ *also* **Le Grand–Montrouge** \ lə-ˌgräⁿ-\; *anc.* **Mons Ru·bi·cus** \ˈmänz-ˈrü-bi-kəs\. Commune, Hauts-de-Seine dept., N France, S suburb of Paris; pop. (1990c) 38,333; perfumery, precision instruments.

Mont Roy·al \ˌmȯⁿ-rwä-ˈyäl\. **1.** Height, Quebec, Canada. See ROYAL, MOUNT.

2. Town, Quebec, Canada. See MOUNT ROYAL.

Monts, Pointe de \ˌpweⁿt-də-ˈmȯⁿ\. Headland in Quebec, Canada, on the St. Lawrence River; 49°19′N, 67°23′W.

Mont–Saint–Amand. See SINT AMANDSBERG.

Mont–Saint–Hi·laire \ˌmȯⁿ-seⁿ-tē-ˈler\. Town, Rouville co., S Quebec, Canada, 18 mi. (29 km.) E of Montreal; pop. (1991c) 12,341.

Mont–Saint–Jean \ˌmȯⁿ-seⁿ-ˈzhäⁿ\. Village in Belgium S of the village of Waterloo and N of the battlefield where French Emperor Napoléon met defeat 1815.

Mont–Saint–Mar·tin \ˌmȯⁿ-seⁿ-mär-ˈteⁿ\. Town, Meurthe-et-Moselle dept., NE France, on the frontier near meeting point of Belgian-Luxembourgian-French boundaries.

Mont–Saint–Mi·chel, La \lä-ˌmȯⁿ-seⁿ-mē-ˈshel\. Fortified rock in **Mont–Saint–Michel Bay,** off the SW coast of Manche dept., NW France; pop. (1990c) 72; remarkable ancient abbey and town on the summit of the rock, a popular tourist attraction; the abbey, orig. built 8th cent., added to and rebuilt throughout the following centuries; fortified 13th cent.; remained in French possession throughout Hundred Years' War; was a prison c. 1790–1863.

Mont·ser·rat \ˌmȯnt-ser-ˈrät, ˌmänt-sə-ˈrat\. **1.** Mountain in Barcelona prov., NE Spain; 4054 ft. (1236 m.); jagged ridge, hence name (*Lat.* Mons Serratus); site of monastery dating from 9th cent.; present buildings, of more recent construction, contain famous wooden statue of Virgin and Child held to have been carved by St. Luke.

2. Island comprising a British crown colony, West Indies, 27 mi. (43 km.) SW of Antigua; 40 sq. mi. (104 sq. km.); pop. (1993e) 12,100; ✻ Plymouth. Entirely volcanic, with three groups of mountains, the highest Soufriére 3000 ft. (914 m.); mountains forested and intensively cultivated.

History: Discovered by explorer Christopher Columbus 1493; colonized by British and Irish 1632; held by French 1664–68 and 1782–83; part of Colony of Leeward Islands 1871–1956 and of West Indies (Federation) 1958–62; devastated by hurricane 1989.

Mon·tuo·sa \ mȯn-ˈtwō-sä\. Small island in Pacific Ocean, part of Veraguas prov., off SW coast of Panama; 7°28′N, 82°14′W.

Mont·vale \ˈmänt-ˌvāl\. Borough, Bergen co., NE New Jersey, 10 mi. (16 km.) NW of Paterson; pop. (1990c) 6946.

Mont Valérien. See VALÉRIEN, MONT.

Mont·ville \ˈmänt-ˌvil\. Town, cen. New London co., SE Connecticut, on Thames River; pop. (1990c) 16,673; paper products, aircraft parts, nuclear reactor components; incorp. 1786.

Mon·u·ment Peak \ˈmän-yə-mənt\. Mountain, N Adams co., W Idaho; 8956 ft. (2730 m.).

Monument Valley. Region in NE Arizona and SE Utah; a sandy plain from which rise monument-like buttes 1000 ft. (300 m.) high, also mesas and arches, all of red sandstone; to the W of the valley is Rainbow Bridge National Monument and to the N Natural Bridges National Monument (see UNITED STATES, *National Monuments*).

Monviso. See VISO, MOUNT.

Mon·ywa \ˈmōn-ywä\. Town, Sagaing div., Myanmar, on left bank of lower Chindwin River 55 mi. (89 km.) W of Mandalay; in WWII a Japanese communications center until captured by British 1945.

Mon·za \ˈmōnt-sä\. Commune, Milano prov., Lombardy, N Italy, 10 mi. (16 km.) NE of Milan; pop. (1991p) 121,151; felt hats and carpets, textiles, machinery, glass, plastics, furniture; famous auto-racing track; cathedral (founded 6th cent. by Lombard Queen Theodolinda; rebuilt 13th–14th cents.); among the cathedral's artifacts is the Crown of Lombardy, used in imperial coronations since the 14th cent.; 13th cent. town hall; palace of old Lombard kings. Site of a Roman town; ancient ✻ of Lombardy; scene of assassination of King Umberto I of Italy 1900.

Monze, Cape. See MUARI, RAS.

Moo·dy \ˈmü-dē\. **1.** County in E South Dakota. See table at SOUTH DAKOTA.

2. Town, St. Clair co., NE cen. Alabama, ENE of Birmingham; pop. (1990c) 4921.

Mooltan. See MULTAN.

Moon. See MUHU.

Moon, Mountains of the. See RUWENZORI, MOUNT.

Moo·nach·ie \mü-ˈna-chē\. Borough, Bergen co., NE corner of New Jersey, 8 mi. (13 km.) SE of Paterson; pop. (1990c) 2817.

Moor. See MÓR.

Moo·rab·bin \mu̇-ˈra-bin\. City, Victoria, Australia, a SE suburb of Melbourne; pop. (1991c) 94,161.

Moore \ˈmōr, ˈmu̇r\. **1.** Name of counties in three states of the U.S. See tables at NORTH CAROLINA, TENNESSEE, TEXAS.

2. City, Cleveland co., cen. Oklahoma, bordered on three sides by Oklahoma City; pop. (1990c) 40,318.

Moore, Lake. Dry lake in SW Salt Lake Region, Western Australia, Australia, NE of Perth.

Mo·o·rea \ˌmō-ō-ˈrā-ä\; *formerly* **Ei·meo** \ī-ˈmā-ō\. One of E group (Windward Is.) of the Society Is., French Polynesia, S Pacific Ocean, 12 mi. (19 km.) W of Papeete; 53 sq. mi. (137 sq. km.); pop. (1980p) 5788; mountainous, with highest peak 3975 ft. (1212 m.).

Moore·field \ˈmōr-ˌfēld, ˈmu̇r-\. **1.** River, E West Virginia; rises in SE Pendleton co., flows NE into S branch of Potomac River at Moorefield in Hardy co.; 50 mi. (81 km.) long.

2. Town, ⊗ of Hardy co., NE West Virginia; pop. (1990c) 2148.

Moore Haven. City, ⊗ of Glades co., S cen. Florida Penin.; pop. (1990c) 1432.

Moores Creek National Battlefield \ˈmōrz, ˈmu̇rz\. See UNITED STATES, *National Historical Parks.*

Moores·town \ˈmōrz-ˌtau̇n, ˈmu̇rz-\. Township, Burlington co., S cen. New Jersey, 9 mi. (15 km.) E of Camden; pop. (1990c) 16,116.

Moores·ville \ˈmōrz-ˌvil, ˈmu̇rz-\. **1.** Town, Morgan co., cen. Indiana, 15 mi. (24 km.) SW of Indianapolis; pop. (1990c) 5541.

2. Town, Iredell co., cen. North Carolina, 13 mi. (21 km.) S of Statesville; pop. (1990c) 9317.

Moor·foot Hills \ˈmōr-fu̇t, ˈmu̇r-\. Range of hills in Borders region and along the border of Lothian region, SE Scotland; highest peak **Black·hope Scar** \ˈblak-ˌhōp\, 2136 ft. (651 m.).

Moor·head \ˈmōr-ˌhed, ˈmu̇r-\. City, ⊗ of Clay co., W Minnesota, on Red River opposite Fargo, North Dakota; pop.

(1990c) 32,295; trade center of region producing potatoes, sugar beets, dairy products; Moorhead State Univ. (1885), Concordia Coll. (1891); founded 1871; incorp. as city 1881.

Moor·park \ˈmōr-ˌpärk, ˈmu̇r-\. City, Ventura co., SW California, NW of Los Angeles; pop. (1990c) 25,494.

Moos·burg \ˈmōs-ˌbu̇rk\. Town, Bavaria, Germany, on Isar River ab. 10 mi. (16 km.) WSW of Landshut; pop. (1980c) 13,236.

Moose \ˈmüs\. River, NE Ontario, Canada; flows NE into James Bay; 340 mi. (547 km.) long (to head of Mattagami); a wide stream, actually the estuary of the Abitibi, Mattagami, Missinaibi, and other rivers.

Moose·head Lake \ˈmüs-ˌhed\. Lake on boundary bet. Piscataquis and Somerset cos., NW cen. Maine; the state's largest at ab. 35 mi. (56 km.) long and 10 mi. (16 km.) wide; 117 sq. mi. (303 sq. km.); max. depth 246 ft. (75 m.); elev. ab. 1000 ft. (300 m.); outdoor recreation; resort.

Moose Jaw \ˈmüs-ˌjȯ\. City, S Saskatchewan, Canada, 43 mi. (69 km.) W of Regina; pop. (1991c) 33,593; stockyards, grain elevators, flour mills, slaughterhouses; founded 1882.

Moose Lake. Lake, W Manitoba, Canada; 525 sq. mi. (1360 sq. km.); has several outlets to Saskatchewan River and Cedar Lake.

Moose·look·me·gun·tic Lake \ˌmüs-lu̇k-mi-ˈgən-tik\. See RANGELEY LAKES.

Moose Mountain. Peak in Adirondack Mts., Essex co., NE New York; 3921 ft. (1195 m.).

Moose Peak. Mountain in W Flathead co., NW Montana; 7521 ft. (2292 m.).

Moo·sic \ˈmü-sik\. Borough, Lackawanna co., NE Pennsylvania, 5 mi. (8 km.) SW of Scranton; pop. (1990c) 5339.

Moo·si·lauke, Mount \ˈmü-sə-ˌlȯk\. Peak, cen. Grafton co., W New Hampshire; 4810 ft. (1466 m.).

Moo·sup \ˈmü-səp\. Subdivision of town of Plainfield, Connecticut; pop. (1990c) 3289. See PLAINFIELD 1.

Mop·su·es·tia \ˌmäp-su̇-ˈwes-chē-ə\ *or mod.* **Ya·ka·pi·nar** \ˌyä-kä-pə-ˈnär\ *or* **Mi·sis** \mē-ˈsēs\. Ancient city in Cilicia, Asia Minor, on the Pyramus (Ceyhan) River, now a village in Adana prov., S Turkey.

Mop·ti \ˈmȯp-tē\. Town on Niger River, Mali, on E edge of Niger depression area ab. 275 mi. (445 km.) NE of Bamako; pop. (1987p) 73,979.

Mo·que·gua \mō-ˈkā-gwä\. Town, S Peru, ab. 530 mi. (850 km.) SE of Lima; pop. (1990e) 31,500; grapes, olives; founded 1626.

Mór \ˈmōr\ *or Ger.* **Moor** \ˈmōr\. Commune, Fejér co., W Hungary, 43 mi. (69 km.) W of Budapest; pop. (1980p) 12,066.

Mo·ra \ˈmōr-ə\. **1.** County in NE New Mexico. See table at NEW MEXICO.

2. City, ⊗ of Kanabec co., E Minnesota, 47 mi. (76 km.) ENE of St. Cloud; pop. (1990c) 2905.

3. Village, ⊗ of Mora co., NE New Mexico, 40 mi. (64 km.) NE of Sante Fe.

4. Commune, Toledo prov., cen. Spain, 18 mi. (29 km.) SE of the commune of Toledo; pop. (1991c) 9302.

Mo·ra·ča \ˈmō-rä-ˌchä\. Small river in Montenegro, Yugoslavia, flowing S into Lake Scutari.

Mo·rad·a·bad \mə-ˈrä-də-ˌbäd, -ˈra-də-ˌbad\. City, Uttar Pradesh, N India, 90 mi. (145 km.) ENE of Delhi; pop. (1991c) 429,214; metalware, cotton textiles; 17th cent. fort and mosque; founded 1625 by Rustum Khan.

Mo·ra·ga \mə-ˈrä-gə\ *or* **Moraga Town.** City, Contra Costa co., W California, E of Oakland; pop. (1990c) 15,852; St. Mary's Coll. of California (1863).

Mo·raine \mə-ˈrān\. City, Montgomery co., SW Ohio, 5 mi. (8 km.) S of Dayton; pop. (1990c) 5989.

Mo·ra·le·da Channel \ˌmō-rä-ˈlā-t͟hä\. Passage off SW coast of Chile, bet. Chonos Archipelago and the Chilean mainland.

Mo·ra·man·ga \ˌmōr-ə-ˈmäŋ-gə\. Town, E cen. Madagascar, 45 mi. (72 km.) E of Tananarive; a railroad junction.

Mo·ran, Mount \mə-ˈran\. Peak in N Grand Teton National Park, NW Wyoming; 12,594 ft. (3839 m.).

Mo·rant Bay \mə-ˈrant\. Town and bay, SE coast of Jamaica, West Indies.

Morant Cays. Three small guano islands 33 mi. (53 km.) SE of Morant Bay, off SE coast of Jamaica; a dependency of Jamaica since 1882.

Morant Point. Cape at E end of Jamaica, West Indies.

Mor·ar, Loch \ˈmȯr-ər\. Lake in Highland region, on coast of W cen. Scotland, 1.5 mi. (2 km.) S of Lake Nevis; max. depth 1017 ft. (310 m.); deepest lake in Scotland.

Mo·rat \mȯ-ˈrä\ *or Ger.* **Mur·ten** \ˈmu̇rt-ᵊn\. Commune, Fribourg canton, Switzerland, on E shore of Lake of Morat; 13th cent. castle; 15th cent. town walls; 18th cent. church; scene of Swiss victory over Charles the Bold, duke of Burgundy June 22, 1476.

Morat, Lake of *or Ger.* **Mur·ten·see** \ˈmu̇rt-ᵊn-ˌzā\. Lake, Switzerland, 2 mi. (3 km.) SE of the Lac de Neuchâtel; ab. 9 sq. mi. (23 sq. km.).

Morata. See GOODENOUGH.

Mo·ra·tal·la \ˌmō-rä-ˈtä-lyä, -yä\. Commune, Murcia prov., SE Spain, 39 mi. (63 km.) WNW of the commune of Murcia; pop. (1991c) 8976.

Mo·ra·tu·wa \ˈmōr-ə-tu̇-wə\. Town, W Sri Lanka, on Indian Ocean 12 mi. (19 km.) S of Colombo; pop. (1990e) 170,000.

Mo·ra·va \ˈmȯ-rä-vä\. **1.** *or Ger.* **March** \ˈmär<u>k</u>\. River, W cen. Europe, flows SW and S, in Moravia, Czech Republic, forming a section of the boundary bet. Czech Republic and Slovakia and bet. Slovakia and Lower Austria; empties into Danube River 8 mi. (13 km.) W of Bratislava; 218 mi. (351 km.) long; navigable for 78 mi. (126 km.).

2. Region of Czech Republic. See MORAVIA.

3. *or* **Ve·li·ka Morava** \ˈve-lē-ˌkä\; *anc.* **Mar·gus** \ˈmär-gəs\. River in E cen. Yugoslavia, formed by confluence of S and W branches at a point 33 mi. (53 km.) NW of Niš; flows NNW into Danube River near Smederevo; 100 mi. (161 km.) long from point of confluence to the Danube; the W branch receives the Ibar from the S.

Mo·ra·via \mə-ˈrā-vē-ə\ *or Czech* **Mo·ra·va** \ˈmȯ-rä-vä\ *or Ger.* **Mäh·ren** \ˈmā-rən, ˈmer-\. Region, E Czech Republic.

History: Anciently inhabited by Celtic, then Germanic tribes; settled by Moravians, a Slavic people, from 6th–8th cents.; became tributary to Holy Roman Empire c. 843; introduced to Christianity by Sts. Cyril and Methodius; under Prince Svatopluk, Great Moravia (incl. Bohemia and other territories in cen. Europe) revolted against German emperor and became independent kingdom c. 870, but began to decline following Svatopluk's death in 894; conquered by Magyars (see HUNGARY) 906; in 10th cent. made part of Bohemian and briefly of Polish kingdoms; in 1029 reconquered by Bohemia (*q.v.*); in 1849 became a separate crown land of Austria, with ✻ at Brno; in 1918 organized as a province of Czechoslovakia; united with Silesia 1927 forming a province; all of Silesia and some areas in N and S Moravia became parts of German Sudetenland 1938, remainder of Moravia joined with Bohemia (1939–45) as German protectorate of Bohemia and Moravia (*q.v.*); pre-1938 boundaries restored to Czechoslovakia 1945; split among several provinces 1949; reorganized as two regions 1960; included in independent Czech Republic 1993.

Mo·ra·vi·an Gap *or* **Moravian Gate** \mə-ˈrā-vē-ən\. Mountain pass and ancient trade route for amber, E Czech Republic, along upper courses of Oder and Vistula rivers bet. SE Sudety and W Carpathian Mts. in area near border bet. former German Silesia, Poland, Czech Republic, and Slovakia; in modern history a strategic communications line.

Mo·rav·ska \ˈmȯr-äv-ˌskä\. Former county (1929–45), E Yugoslavia; 10,120 sq. mi. (26,211 sq. km.); ⊗ Niš.

Moravská Ostrava. See OSTRAVA.

Mo·ra·whan·nä \ˌmō-rä-ˈwä-nä\. Town and small port, extreme N Guyana, 150 mi. (241 km.) NW of Georgetown, on the Barima River near Venezuelan border; gold discovered in the vicinity c. 1889.

\ə\ abut \ə\ matches \ᵊ\ kitten, Fr table \ər\ further \a\ ash \ā\ ace \ä\ cot, cart \à\ Fr bac \au̇\ out \b\ Span Avila \ch\ chin \e\ bet \ē\ easy \g\ go \i\ hit \ī\ ice \j\ job \k\ Ger ich, Buch \ⁿ\ Fr vin \ŋ\ sing \ō\ go \ö\ all \ȯ\ law \œ\ Fr bœuf \œ̄\ Fr feu \ȯi\ boy \th\ thin \t͟h\ this \ü\ loot \u̇\ foot \ue\ Ger füllen \ue̅\ Fr rue \y\ yet \ʸ\ Fr digne \ˈdēnʸ\, nuit \ˈnwʸē\ \yü\ few \yu̇\ fury \zh\ vision

Mor·ay \'mər-ē\ *or* **El·gin** \'el-gən\ *or* **El·gin·shire** \-ˌshir, -shər\. Former county, NE Scotland; ⊗ Elgin; rivers Lossie, Spey, Findhorn.

Moray Firth. Deep inlet of the North Sea on NE coast of Scotland; extends inland 39 mi. (63 km.); the city of Inverness is near its head.

Mo·ra·zán \ˌmō-rä-'sän\. Department of NE El Salvador. See table at EL SALVADOR.

Morbi. See MORVI 2.

Mor·bi·han \ˌmȯr-bē-'äⁿ\. Department of NW France. See table at FRANCE.

Mor·den \'mȯrd-ᵊn\. Town, Manitoba, Canada, 70 mi. (113 km.) SW of Winnipeg; pop. (1991c) 5273; dairy products, pumps; diversified agriculture; grain elevators.

Mor·di·al·loc \ˌmȯr-dē-'a-lək\. City, S Victoria, SE Australia, SE suburb of Melbourne on E shore of Port Phillip Bay; pop. (1991c) 26,325.

Mord·vin·ia \mȯrd-'vi-nē-ə\ *or* **Mor·do·via** \mȯr-'dō-vē-ə\ *or* **Mor·do·vi·an Republic** \-vē-ən\. A constituent republic of Russia in Europe; 10,116 sq. mi. (26,200 sq. km.); pop. (1992e) 964,000; ✻ Saransk. Crossed by the Moksha River; in cen. plateau borders on the black-earth region, S and W of the middle part of the Volga; produces rye, wheat, millet, oats, corn, tobacco; livestock; beekeeping; crossed by Moscow-Samara railroad. Principal cities Saransk, Ruzayevka. Predominant ethnic strains Finno-Ugric and Slavic; chief nationalities Mordovian (or Mordvinian) and Russian. Formed as an autonomous oblast 1930; made **Mordovian A.S.S.R.** 1934; became republic within Russia 1991; subsequently became member of Russian Federation.

More, Ben. See BEN MORE.

Morea. See PELOPONNESE 1.

Mo·reau \'mōr-ō\. River, NW South Dakota; formed by confluence of N and S forks in SW Perkins co., flows E into Missouri River on E boundary of Dewey co.; 290 mi. (467 km.) long.

More·cambe and Hey·sham \'mōr-kəm … 'hā-shəm\. Town, Lancashire, NW England, on Morecambe Bay 46 mi. (74 km.) N of Liverpool; pop. (1981p) 41,187; seaside resort.

Morecambe Bay. Inlet of Irish Sea on NW coast of England; extends inland 18 mi. (29 km.) in N Lancashire.

Mo·ree \mō-'rē\. Municipality, NE New South Wales, SE Australia, on Gwydir River 315 mi. (507 km.) N of Sydney; center of grazing and agricultural district.

More·head \'mōr-ˌhed\. City, ⊗ of Rowan co., NE Kentucky, 37 mi. (60 km.) SSE of Maysville; pop. (1990c) 8357; Morehead State Univ. (1922).

Morehead City. Town and ocean port, Carteret co., SE North Carolina, on Atlantic Ocean 33 mi. (53 km.) SE of New Bern; pop. (1990c) 6046; resort and fishing center; has pier with large port facility (erected 1935–37).

More·house \'mōr-ˌhau̇s\. Parish in N Louisiana. See table at LOUISIANA.

More·land Hills \'mōr-lənd\. Village, Cuyahoga co., N Ohio, 15 mi. (24 km.) ESE of Cleveland; pop. (1990c) 3354.

Mo·re·lia \mō-'rāl-yä\. City, ✻ of Michoacán state, SW Mexico; munic. pop. (1990p) 489,756; center of agricultural region; 17th–18th cent. baroque cathedral; 18th cent. aqueduct; university. City founded 1541 as Valladolid; made state ✻ 1582; renamed 1828 after locally-born revolutionary leader J. M. Morelos y Pavón.

Mo·re·los \mō-'rā-lōs\. State of S cen. Mexico. See table at MEXICO.

Mo·re·na \'mō-rā-nə\. Town, N Madhya Pradesh, N cen. India, NW of Gwalior; pop. (1991p) 147,095.

Morena, Sierra. See SIERRA MORENA.

Mo·re·na Dam \mə-'rē-nə\. Dam across Cottonwood Creek, S San Diego co., SW California; height 279 ft. (85 m.); completed early 1930s; impounds water for water supply.

Mo·re·no \mō-'rā-nō\. Town, Buenos Aires prov., E Argentina, part of Buenos Aires met. area, to the W of the city.

Moreno Bay Inlet of Pacific Ocean in W Antofagasta prov., N Chile; location of the city of Antofagasta.

Moreno Glacier. Glacier in extreme S part of Andes, Santa Cruz prov., S Argentina; 31 mi. (50 km.) long, ab. 2 mi. (3 km.) wide near its terminus.

Mo·re·no Valley \mə-'rē-nō\. City, Riverside co., SE California, E of the city of Riverside; pop. (1990c) 118,779.

Mø·re og Roms·dal \'mœr-ȯ-'rüms-ˌdäl\. County of W Norway. See table at NORWAY.

Mores·by Island \'mōrz-bē\. Cen. island of the Queen Charlotte Is. off W British Columbia, Canada; 991 sq. mi. (2567 sq. km.).

Mo·res·net \ˌmȯ-res-'ne\. Former neutral territory bet. Belgium and Germany, near Aachen; since 1919 part of Liège prov., Belgium; 11 sq. mi. (29 sq. km.); comprises the communes of Moresnet, Neu-Moresnet, and La Calamine.

More·ton Bay \'mōrt-ᵊn\. Inlet of Pacific Ocean on SE coast of Queensland, Australia, at mouth of Brisbane River, enclosed on NE by **Moreton Island**; fishing.

Mo·rez \mō-'rā\. Town, SE Jura dept., E France; noted for manufacture of spectacles.

Mor·gan \'mȯr-gən\. **1.** Name of counties in 11 states of the U.S. See tables at ALABAMA, COLORADO, GEORGIA, ILLINOIS, INDIANA, KENTUCKY, MISSOURI, OHIO, TENNESSEE, UTAH, WEST VIRGINIA.
2. City, ⊗ of Calhoun co., SW Georgia; pop. (1990c) 252.
3. City, ⊗ of Morgan co., N Utah; pop. (1990c) 2023.

Morgan, Mount. **1.** Peak in Glacier National Park, NW Montana; 8710 ft. (2655 m.).
2. Peak in Australian Capital Terr., Australia; 6144 ft. (1873 m.).

Morgan City. City, St. Mary parish, S Louisiana, 53 mi. (85 km.) S of Baton Rouge; pop. (1990c) 14,531; offshore oil wells; shrimp fishing.

Mor·gan·field \'mȯr-gən-ˌfēld\. City, ⊗ of Union co., W Kentucky, 22 mi. (35 km.) WSW of Henderson; pop. (1990c) 3776; coal mines; agriculture.

Morgan Hill. City, Santa Clara co., W California, 17 mi. (27 km.) SE of San Jose; pop. (1990c) 23,928; canneries, feed mills; diversified agriculture.

Mor·gan·ton \'mȯr-gən-tən\. City, ⊗ of Burke co., W North Carolina, 15 mi. (24 km.) SSW of Lenoir; pop. (1990c) 15,085; clothing, furniture; Western Piedmont Community Coll. (1964).

Mor·gan·town \'mȯr-gən-ˌtau̇n\. **1.** City, ⊗ of Butler co., W cen. Kentucky; pop. (1990c) 2284.
2. City, ⊗ of Monongalia co., N West Virginia, on Monongahela River 15 mi. (24 km.) NE of Fairmont; pop. (1990c) 25,879; river port shipping coal and limestone; glass products, textiles, plumbing materials, chemicals; coal mines, limestone quarries; West Virginia Univ. (1867); settled 1767; incorp. as city 1905.

Mor·gar·ten \'mōr-ˌgärt-ᵊn\. Mountain slope in Zug canton, N cen. Switzerland, on the border of Schwyz canton, just SE of Lake of Aegeri; scene of battle Nov. 15, 1315 in which Swiss defeated greatly superior Austrian forces of Hapsburg Duke Leopold I.

Morges \'mȯrzh\. Commune, Vaud canton, W Switzerland, on Lake Geneva; pop. (1980c) 13,057; view of Mont Blanc; 13th cent. castle. Birthplace of Spanish novelist Cecilia Böhl de Faber (pseudonym: Fernán Caballero) 1796.

Morghāb. See MURGAB 1.

Mo·ri·ah \mə-'rī-ə\. **1.** Hilly area in S part of ancient Palestine on which Hebrew patriarch Abraham prepared to sacrifice his son Isaac (*Gen.* xxii. 2); its location is unidentified.
2. Hill in E part of Jerusalem, ancient Palestine, on which Solomon, king of Israel, built the Temple (*2 Chron.* iii. 1).

Moriah, Mount. Peak, SE Coos co., N New Hampshire, in E White Mts. N of Carter Notch; 3750 ft. (1143 m.).

Mo·ri·gu·chi \ˌmȯ-rē-'gü-chē\. Town, Ōsaka prefecture, Honshū, Japan; suburb of the city of Ōsaka; pop. (1990p) 157,365; textiles.

Mo·ring·en \'mōr-iŋ-ən\. Town, SE Lower Saxony, Germany, 12 mi. (19 km.) N of Göttingen; pop. (1980c) 7110; Nazi concentration camp in WWII.

Mo·ri·o·ka \ˌmōr-ē-'ō-kä\. City, ✻ of Iwate prefecture, N Honshū, Japan, on the Kitakami River; pop. (1990p)

235,440; commercial and cultural center; iron kettles; university; feudal castle.

Morlacca. See VELEBITSKI KANAL.

Mor·laix \mȯr-ˈle\. Commercial seaport, Finistère dept., NW France, on English Channel 42 mi. (68 km.) NNE of Quimper; pop. (1990c) 17,607.

Mor·ley \ˈmȯr-lē\. Town, West Yorkshire, N England, 5 mi. (8 km.) SW of Leeds; pop. (1981p) 44,134; textiles; engineering; coal mines.

Mor·mal Forest \mȯr-ˈmäl\. Wooded region, Nord dept., N France, SE of Valenciennes.

Mor·mon Flat Dam \ˈmȯr-mən\. Dam across Salt River below Horse Mesa Dam, E Maricopa co., S cen. Arizona; height 224 ft. (68 m.); completed 1925; impounds water for power, forming **Canyon Lake** 10 mi. (16 km.) long.

Mormon Lake. Lake, SE Coconino co., N cen. Arizona; 12 sq. mi. (31 sq. km.); did not exist before 1900; formed when underground drainage channels became filled with sediment.

Mormon Mountain. Peak, NE Valley co., W cen. Idaho; 9545 ft. (2909 m.).

Morne Diablotin *or* **Morne Diablatins.** See DIABLOTIN, MORNE.

Mor·ning·ton Island \ˈmȯr-niŋ-tən\. Island in Pacific Ocean off SW coast of Chile, W of S Wellington I.

Mo·ro \ˈmōr-ō\. City, ⊗ of Sherman co., N Oregon; pop. (1990c) 292.

Mo·ro·be \mō-ˈrō-bā\. **1.** Gold-bearing region, interior Papua New Guinea, on island of New Guinea, in the Bulolo Valley near the town of Wau; goldfield discovered c. early 1920s, and formerly mined extensively.

2. Seaport town, Papua New Guinea, on SE coast of Huon Gulf 95 mi. (153 km.) SSE of Lae; has good harbor.

Mo·roc·co \mə-ˈrä-kō\. **1.** *or Arab.* **Al–Mam·la·kah al–Ma·ghri·bī·yah** \äl-ˈmȧm-lȧ-kə-äl-ˌmȧ-grē-ˈbē-yə\ *or Fr.* **Ma·roc** \mȧ-ˈrȯk\ *or Span.* **Mar·rue·cos** \ˌmär-ˈrwā-kōs\. Kingdom, NW Africa, bounded on N by the Mediterranean Sea, on E and S by Algeria, on SW by Western Sahara, and on W by the Atlantic Ocean; 172,413 sq. mi. (446,550 sq. km.); pop. (1982c) 20,419,555; ✻ Rabat.

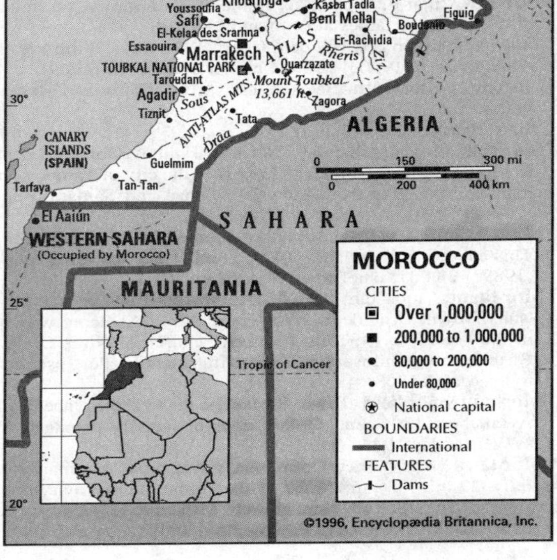

Physical features: Characterized by the great mountain range of Grand Atlas and its smaller subsidiary ranges (see ATLAS MOUNTAINS) stretching from SW to NE, the mountainous Er Rif belt along the Mediterranean, the wide fertile plain along the Atlantic, and the plain, partly desert, in the SE beyond the Atlas Range; highest point Toubkal 13,671 ft. (4167 m.). Rivers of the Atlantic plain are numerous but short; chief are the Moulouya in N and the Tensift; many short streams on SE slopes of the Atlas are lost in the Sahara.

Chief products: Wheat, corn, barley, citrus fruit, vegetables; wine; livestock raising, fishing; phosphates, iron ore, lead, copper, silver, manganese; tourism.

Chief cities: Casablanca, Rabat, Fès, Marrakech, Meknès.

History: Inhabited by Berbers from 2d millennium B.C.; loosely controlled Roman prov. of Mauretania (*q.v.*) underwent Muslim invasion 7th cent. A.D.; in 11th cent., independent kingdom founded under Almoravids, a Berber dynasty which conquered Spain and Portugal but was overthrown in 1147 by the Almohads; coastal towns attacked and occupied by Spanish and Portuguese 15th–16th cents. following expulsion of Moors from Iberian Penin.; Morocco invaded by Portuguese who were completely defeated 1578 (see KSAR EL KEBIR); as one of Barbary States (see BARBARY), engaged in piracy until early 19th cent.; engaged in hostilities with French from 1844 over Algerian boundary, and with Spain from 1859; control of Morocco became issue of European politics after Convention of Madrid (1880); with growth of internal disorder, independence question led to agreements bet. France and England (*Entente Cordiale* 1904, recognizing British authority in Egypt), Italy (recognizing Italian authority in Libya), and Spain, to the exclusion of Germany, stipulating French authority in Morocco, reserving the N Mediterranean coast for Spain; French rights in Morocco affirmed in crises with Germany 1905 and 1911 (see TANGIER, ALGECIRAS, and AGADIR); in 1912 **French Morocco** (a protectorate incl. most of Morocco; ab. 153,870 sq. mi. or 398,525 sq. km.; ✻ Rabat) and **Spanish Morocco** (a protectorate on the N coast; ab. 18,000 sq. mi. or 46,620 sq. km.; ✻ Tétouan) were estab.; Tangier (*q.v.*) made international zone 1923–56; war occurred in Er Rif region of Spanish zone 1921–26; Ifni under effective Spanish occupation 1934–69; signed accords with both France and Spain 1956 by which it received independence; joined UN 1956, Arab League 1958; upon Spain's withdrawal from Western Sahara (*q.v.*) 1975, Morocco occupied N two thirds of it 1976, remainder 1979; tense relations with Algeria concerning Western Sahara 1976–88; withdrew from Organization of African Unity 1984; entered into short-lived political union with Libya 1984–86.

2. City, one of traditional capitals of Morocco. See MARRAKECH.

MOROCCO

CITIES
- ⊡ Over 1,000,000
- ■ 200,000 to 1,000,000
- ● 80,000 to 200,000
- • Under 80,000
- ⊛ National capital

BOUNDARIES
- International

FEATURES
- Dams

©1996, Encyclopædia Britannica, Inc.

Mo·ro·co·ca·la \ˌmō-rō-kō-ˈkä-lä\. Peak, W Bolivia, E of N end of Lake Poopó; 17,054 ft. (5198 m.).

Mo·ro·go·ro \ˌmō-rō-ˈgō-rō\. **1.** Administrative region of SE Tanzania. See table at TANZANIA.

2. Town, its ✻, 105 mi. (169 km.) W of Dar es Salaam; tobacco, kapok, sugar; mica mines.

Mo·ro Gulf \ˈmōr-ō\. Large inlet in N part of Celebes Sea, SW of Mindanao, Philippines.

Mo·ro·land \ˈmōr-ō-ˌland\. Name sometimes given to islands in S of Philippines where the Moro people live, esp. Mindanao and the Sulu Archipelago.

Mo·ro·le·ón \ˌmō-rō-lā-ˈȯn\. Town, Guanajuato state, cen. Mexico, 60 mi. (97 km.) S of the city of Guanajuato; munic. pop. (1990p) 47,553.

Mo·rón \mō-ˈrȯn\. **1.** *or* **Seis de Sep·tiem·bre** \ˌsās-thā-sep-ˈtyām-brā\. City, Buenos Aires prov., E Argentina, 10 mi. (16 km.) SW of the city of Buenos Aires; pop. (1991p) 641,541; part of Buenos Aires met. area.

2. Town, W Camagüey prov., E cen. Cuba, on railroad line 68 mi. (109 km.) NW of the city of Camagüey; pop. (1990e) 48,718.

3. *or in full* **Morón de la Fron·te·ra** \ˌthā-lä-frōn-ˈtā-rä\. Commune, Sevilla prov., SW Spain, 35 mi. (56 km.) SE of Seville; pop. (1991c) 27,207; olive oil; cereal grains; cement; Gothic church; ruins of Moorish castle.

4. Town, Carabobo state, N Venezuela, on Caribbean coast, W of Caracas; pop. (1990e) 57,200.

Mo·ro·na \mō-ˈrō-nä\. River, Ecuador and Peru; rises in E Ecuador where it is called the **Ma·kum·ma** \mä-ˈkü-mä\, flows S across border into Peru; empties into Marañón River, headstream of the Amazon; ab. 260 mi. (418 km.) long.

Morona–San·ti·a·go \-ˌsän-tē-ˈä-gō\. Province of SE Ecuador. See table at ECUADOR.

Mo·ron·da·va \ˌmō-rōn-ˈdä-vä\. Coastal town, W Madagascar; airfield.

Morón de la Frontera. See MORÓN 3.

Mo·rong \ˈmō-ˌrōŋ\. **1.** Municipality on W coast of Bataan prov., Luzon, Philippines, 20 mi. (32 km.) W of Balanga on SE side of entrance to Subic Bay; pop. (1980c) 10,637.

2. Municipality, Rizal prov., Luzon, Philippines, near coast of Laguna de Bay 11 mi. (18 km.) ESE of Pasig; pop. (1980c) 24,858.

Mo·ro·ni \mō-ˈrō-nē\. Town, ✻ of Comoros, on Njazidja; pop. (1990e) 23,432.

Mo·ron·vil·liers \mō-ˌrōⁿ-vē-ˈlyā\. Heights in NE France, ab. 13 mi. (21 km.) E of Reims; held by Germans throughout WWI; scene of battles 1917; taken by Allies 1918.

Mo·ro Province \ˈmō-rō\. Former province of the Philippines under military government 1903–14; included most of Mindanao I., the Sulu Archipelago, and Palawan I.

Mo·ro·tai \ˌmō-rō-ˈtī\. Island, Indonesia, in the N Moluccas N of Halmahera; ab. 50 mi. (81 km.) long by 26 mi. (42 km.) wide; 695 sq. mi. (1800 sq. km.); highest point 4101 ft. (1250 m.). Site of Japanese base in WWII, taken by Allies 1944.

Mo·ro·vis \mō-ˈrō-vēs\. Municipality, N cen. Puerto Rico, SW of San Juan; pop. (1990c) 25,288.

Mor·peth \ˈmȯr-pəth\. Town, Northumberland, N England, on the Wansbeck 12 mi. (19 km.) N of Newcastle upon Tyne; pop. (1981c) 14,496; mineral water.

Mor·phou Bay \ˈmȯr-fü\. Inlet of Mediterranean on NW coast of Cyprus; Cape Kormakiti marks its N limit.

Mor·rill \ˈmȯr-əl\. County in W Nebraska. See table at NEBRASKA.

Mor·ril·ton \ˈmȯr-əl-tən\. City, ⊗ of Conway co., cen. Arkansas, near Arkansas River 40 mi. (64 km.) NW of Little Rock; pop. (1990c) 6551.

Mor·ris \ˈmȯr-əs\. **1.** Name of counties in three states of the U.S. See tables at KANSAS, NEW JERSEY, TEXAS.

2. City, ⊗ of Grundy co., NE Illinois, 20 mi. (32 km.) SW of Joliet; pop. (1990c) 10,270.

3. City, ⊗ of Stevens co., W Minnesota, 33 mi. (53 km.) SW of Alexandria; pop. (1990c) 5613; Univ. of Minnesota, Morris (1959).

Morris, Mount. Mountain, Antarctica, 78°19′S, 86°10′W; 12,500 ft. (3810 m.).

Mor·ris·burg \ˈmȯr-əs-ˌbərg\. Village, Stormont, Dundas and Glengarry co., SE Ontario, Canada, on St. Lawrence River 22 mi. (35 km.) WSW of Cornwall; pop. (1991c) 2429.

Morris Dam *and* **Morris Reservoir.** See UNITED STATES, *Dams and Reservoirs.*

Morris Island. Island at S entrance to the harbor of Charleston, South Carolina.

Mor·ris Jes·up, Cape \ˈmȯr-əs-ˈje-səp\. Cape, N Greenland, in Peary Land on Arctic Ocean; at 83°38′N, world's most northerly point of land.

Mor·ri·son \ˈmȯr-ə-sən\. **1.** County in cen. Minnesota. See table at MINNESOTA.

2. City, ⊗ of Whiteside co., NW Illinois, 40 mi. (64 km.) NE of Rock Island; pop. (1990c) 4363.

Morrison, Mount. See YÜ SHAN.

Morrison Cave. See LEWIS AND CLARK CAVERNS.

Morris Plains. Borough, Morris co., N New Jersey, 2 mi. (3 km.) N of Morristown; pop. (1990c) 5219.

Mor·ris Shep·pard Dam \ˈmȯr-əs-ˈshe-pərd\; *formerly* **Pos·sum King·dom Dam** \ˈpä-səm-ˈkiŋ-dəm\. Dam across Brazos River, Palo Pinto co., N cen. Texas; height 190 ft. (60 m.); completed 1941; impounds water for flood control and power.

Mor·ris·town \ˈmȯr-əs-ˌtau̇n\. **1.** Town, ⊗ of Morris co., N New Jersey, 17 mi. (27 km.) WNW of Newark; pop. (1990c) 16,189; residential; tourism; Coll. of St. Elizabeth (1899); Morristown National Historical Park (estab. 1933). Settled 1709–10; incorp. 1865; Gen. George Washington's headquarters 1776–77, 1779–80 during Revolutionary War; scene of electric telegraph experiments of Samuel Morse and Alfred Vail 1830s.

2. City, ⊗ of Hamblen co., NE Tennessee, 42 mi. (68 km.) ENE of Knoxville; pop. (1990c) 21,385; furniture, textiles; diversified agriculture. Frontiersman Davy Crockett lived here as a young boy.

3. Town, Lamoille co., N Vermont; pop. (1990c) 4733.

Morristown National Historical Park. See UNITED STATES, *National Historical Parks.*

Mor·ris·ville \ˈmȯr-əs-ˌvil\. **1.** Borough, Bucks co., SE Pennsylvania, on Delaware River across from Trenton, New Jersey; pop. (1990c) 9765.

2. Village, Lamoille co., N Vermont, on Lamoille River 20 mi. (32 km.) N of Montpelier; pop. (1990c) 1984.

Mor·ro \ˈmōr-ō\. River, Sierra Leone, tributary of the Mano.

Morro, Point. Cape extending into Pacific Ocean on W cen. coast of Atacama prov., N cen. Chile, S of Inglesa Bay.

Morro Bay. **1.** Inlet of the Pacific, San Luis Obispo co., California, NW of the city of San Luis Obispo; only landlocked harbor bet. San Francisco and Los Angeles.

2. City, San Luis Obispo co., SW California, on Pacific Ocean 80 mi. (129 km.) NW of Santa Barbara; pop. (1990c) 9664; beach resort.

Morro Castle. **1.** Fortification on E side of entrance to Havana harbor, Cuba; erected late 16th cent.; captured by English 1762.

2. Fort forming part of defenses of Santiago de Cuba, SE Cuba, on E side of entrance to harbor; bombarded 1898 by U.S. vessels during Spanish-American War.

Mor·ro·coy National Park \ˌmōr-rō-ˈkȯi\. National park, N Venezuela, comprising a Caribbean coastal strip and offshore cays and reefs; estab. 1974.

Mor·ros·quil·lo, Gulf of \ˌmōr-rōs-ˈkē-yō\. Inlet of Caribbean Sea on NW coast of Colombia, NE of the Gulf of Urabá.

Mor·row \ˈmär-ō, ˈmȯr-\. **1.** Name of counties in two states of the U.S. See tables at OHIO and OREGON.

2. City, Clayton co., NW cen. Georgia, 14 mi. (23 km.) S of Atlanta; pop. (1990c) 5168; Clayton State Coll. (1969).

Morrow Point Dam. See UNITED STATES, *Dams and Reservoirs.*

Mörs. See MOERS.

Mor·shansk \mər-ˈshänsk\. Town, N Tambov Oblast, S cen. Russia in Europe; 55 mi. (88 km.) N of the city of Tambov on main railroad line from Tula E to Penza and Samara; pop. (1991e) 50,500.

Mors Island \ˈmȯrs\. Island of Denmark, in Limfjorden, Thisted co., NW Jutland; 142 sq. mi. (368 sq. km.); pop. (1989e) 23,881; chief town Nykøbing.

Mor·tagne \mȯr-ˈtänʸ\ *or* **Mortagne–au–Per·che** \-ō-per-ˈshā\. Town, Orne dept., NW France, NE of Alençon; was ✻ of the Perche (*q.v.*); 15th–16th cent. church of Notre Dame. Birthplace of philosopher Émile-Auguste Chartier (pseudonym: Alain) 1868.

Mor·tain \mȯr-ˈteⁿ\. Town, S Manche dept., NW France, E of Avranches; 13th cent. Gothic church; heavily damaged in WWII battles 1944.

Mor·ta·ra \mȯr-ˈtä-rä\. Commune, Pavia prov., Lombardy, N Italy, 22 mi. (35 km.) WNW of the commune of Pavia; pop. (1981p) 14,648; 14th cent. church; 11th cent. convent; scene of Austrian victory over Piedmontese 1849.

Mor·te·ratsch, Piz \ˈpēts-ˌmȯr-tə-ˈräch\. Peak in the S part of the Rhaetian Alps N of Piz Bernina, Switzerland; 12,401 ft. (3780 m.); famous glacier.

Mort Homme, Le. See LE MORT HOMME.

Mor·ti·mer's Cross \ˈmȯrt-ə-mərz\. Village, Hereford and Worcester co., W England, ab. 5 mi. (8 km.) W of Leominster on the Lugg River; scene of battle Feb. 2, 1461 in Wars of the Roses in which Edward IV defeated the Lancastrians.

Mor·ton \ˈmȯrt-^{ə}n\. **1.** Name of counties in two states of the U.S. See tables at KANSAS and NORTH DAKOTA.

2. Village, Tazewell co., cen. Illinois, 10 mi. (16 km.) SE of Peoria; pop. (1990c) 13,799.

3. City, Scott co., cen. Mississippi, 32 mi. (52 km.) E of Jackson; pop. (1990c) 3212.

4. Borough, Delaware co., SE Pennsylvania, 9 mi. (15 km.) W of Philadelphia; pop. (1990c) 2851.

5. City, ⊗ of Cochran co., NW Texas; pop. (1990c) 2597.

Morton Grove. Village, Cook co., NE Illinois, 2 mi. (3.2 km.) N of Chicago; pop. (1990c) 22,408.

Mort·sel \mȯr-ˈsel\. Commune, Antwerp prov., N Belgium; pop. (1991c) 25,958; S suburb of the city of Antwerp.

Moruroa. See MURUROA.

Mor·van \mȯr-ˈvä^{n}\. Mountain range in E cen. France, in depts. of Nièvre, Yonne, Côte-d'Or, and Saône-et-Loire; highest peak Bois-du-Roi 2959 ft. (910 m.).

Mor·ven \ˈmȯr-vən\. **1.** Peak in Grampian region, NE cen. Scotland; 2862 ft. (872 m.).

2. Peak in Highland region, N Scotland; 2313 ft. (705 m.).

Mor·vi \ˈmȯr-vē\. **1.** Former Indian state, N Kathiawar, now part of Gujarat state, W India; 822 sq. mi. (2129 sq. km.).

2. *or* **Mor·bi** \-bē\. Town, its ✻, 40 mi. (64 km.) N of Rajkot.

Mor·well \ˈmȯr-ˌwel, ˈmär-, -wəl\. Town, Victoria, Australia, ESE of Melbourne; pop. (1991p) 17,763.

Mosa. See MEUSE.

Mos·ca Pass \ˈmäs-kə\. Mountain pass, Huerfano and Saguache cos., S Colorado, in Sangre de Cristo Range of the Rocky Mts.; 9700 ft. (2957 m.); road and trail; used since 1850, one of important passes on Arkansas River route to California and New Mexico.

Mos·cow \ˈmäs-ˌkō\. City, ⊗ of Latah co., NW Idaho, on Washington border 25 mi. (40 km.) N of Lewiston; pop. (1990c) 18,519; lumber; wheat, peas; Univ. of Idaho (1889).

Mos·cow \ˈmäs-ˌkau̇, -ˌkō\ *or Russ.* **Mos·kva** \mȧs-ˈkvȧ\. **1.** *also* **Mus·co·vy** \mə-ˈskō-vē, ˈməs-kō-\. Former principality, W cen. Russia in Europe; founded late 13th cent. by Daniel, son of Russian hero Alexander Nevsky, with fortified village of Moscow as its center; united with Vladimir principality in 14th cent.; its ruler became grand duke, who extended its power. For later history, see MOSCOW 2 and RUSSIA.

2. City, ✻ of Russia, also ✻ of Russian Rep., of Moscow Oblast, and before 1991 ✻ of U.S.S.R. and of Russian S.F.S.R.; on both sides of the Moskva River; pop. (1989p) 8,769,000; the largest city in Russia and its political, economic, transportation, and cultural center; an inland port on navigable waterway formed by the Moscow Canal and the Moskva River; important industrial center, producing motor vehicles, precision instruments, textiles, clothing, chemicals, footwear; food processing; publishing and motion-picture making center of Russia; tourism; site of Summer Olympic Games 1980. Most notable structure is the Kremlin (*Russ.* "citadel"), a large triangular fortress on the Moskva (first built in 12th cent. and built in present form 14th cent.), with Red Square to the E, until 1712 the residence of the ruler; Kremlin now houses sessions of parliament (in building completed 1961); Lenin Mausoleum is nearby. Numerous other notable buildings, incl. ab. 200 churches, several cathedrals, palaces, museums (incl. Tretyakov Gallery and Lenin Museum); Moscow Art Theater and Bolshoi Theater, the Moscow (formerly M.V. Lomonsov) State Univ. (1755, the largest in Russia) and many other higher educational institutions and scientific institutes; in SW is Gorki Park.

History: Site inhabited since Neolithic times, but first mentioned as village in Russian chronicles 1147; ✻ of principality of Moscow (see MOSCOW 1); burned and sacked several times by the Tatars 13th–15th cents.; became seat of metropolitan of Russian Orthodox Church 1326; incorp. principality of Vladmir 14th cent.; under Grand Duke Ivan III (1462–1505) overcame rival principalities, incl. chief rival Novgorod (*q.v.*), defeated Tatars, and invaded Lithuania. Grand Duke Ivan IV first to formally assume title of Czar of Russia (1547); ✻ of united Russia 1547–1712 (see SAINT PETERSBURG); in 1812 occupied by French under Emperor Napoléon; almost entirely destroyed by fire during the occupation. Became ✻ of U.S.S.R. 1918 and underwent major expansion as administrative center of country; in WWII the major objective of the German advance 1941, but was not taken; suffered considerable damage from German bombing; streets around Kremlin scene of both pro- and anti-reform demonstrations in early 1990s; streets occupied by military troops with tanks during failed coup Aug. 1991; scene of armed conflict Oct. 1993 bet. opposing government factions following dissolution of parliament by President Boris Yeltsin.

3. River, Russia. See MOSKVA 1.

Moscow Canal. Ship canal, W cen. Russia in Europe, connecting the Moskva River at Moscow with the Volga River to the N; opened 1937.

Moscow Oblast \ˈō-bləst, -ˌblast\ *or* **Mos·kov·ska·ya Oblast'** \məs-ˈkȧf-skə-yə-ˈō-bləst^{y}\. Subdivision of Russia in Europe; 18,147 sq. mi. (47,001 sq. km.); pop. (1991e) 15,721,600; ✻ and principal city Moscow. Traversed by the Moskva and in SE part by the Oka. Rolling country with considerable areas of forest; highly industrialized with excellent road and rail transportation; textiles, diesel locomotives, chemicals, cement; dairying; livestock raising; flax.

Mo·selle \mō-ˈzel\ *or Ger.* **Mo·sel** \ˈmō-zəl\; *anc.* **Mo·sel·la** \mō-ˈze-lə\. **1.** River, W Europe; rises in Vosges dept., NE France, flows N, forming part of the boundary bet. Germany and Grand Duchy of Luxembourg, turns NE and enters the Rhine at Koblenz; ab. 340 mi. (545 km.) long; navigable for most of its course. Chief tributaries the Orne and Sûre from left and the Meurth and Saar from right. Passes the cities of Nancy, Metz, Thionville in France and Trier in Germany.

2. Department of NE France. See table at FRANCE.

Mo·ses Lake \ˈmō-zəz, -zəs\. **1.** Lake, S cen. Grant co., cen. Washington; 16 mi. (26 km.) long; its lower extension, **Pot·holes Reservoir** \ˈpät-ˌhōlz\, formed by O'Sullivan Dam.

2. City, Grant co., cen. Washington, on E shore of Moses Lake; pop. (1990c) 11,235; Big Bend Community Coll. (1962).

Mo·shi \ˈmō-shē\. Town, ✻ of Kilimanjaro region, NE Tanzania, on S slope of Kilimanjaro.

Mosi–oa–Tunya. See VICTORIA FALLS 2.

Mos·kal'·vo *or* **Mos·kal·vo** \ˈmȯs-kəl^{y}-ˌvȯ\. Oil port on Gulf of Sakhalin, NW Sakhalin I., Sakhalin Oblast, E Russia in Asia; rail connection with Okha on E coast of island; icebound for six months.

Moskovskaya Oblast'. See MOSCOW OBLAST.

Mos·kva \mȧs-ˈkvȧ\ *or* **Mos·cow** \ˈmäs-ˌkau̇, -ˌkō\. **1.** River, Moscow Oblast, W cen. Russia in Europe; flows E through city of Moscow to join the Oka River just below Kolomna; 315 mi. (507 km.) long; navigable from Moscow.

2. Principality and city, Russia. See MOSCOW.

Mos·kva–Pe·kin \-ˈpā-kin\; *formerly* **Mount Mo·lo·tov** \ˈmä-lə-ˌtȯf, ˈmȯ-, ˈmō-, -tȯv\. Mountain, N cen. Tajikistan; 22,255 ft. (6783 m.).

Mos·man \ˈmäs-mən\. Municipality, E New South Wales, Australia, a NE suburb of Sydney; pop. (1991c) 25,353.

Mo·son·ma·gya·ró·vár \ˈmȯ-shȯn-ˌmö-dyö-ˌrō-vär\; *formerly* **Mag·ya·ró·vár** \ˈmö-dyö-ˌrō-vär\ *or Ger.* **Al·ten·burg** \ˈäl-tən-ˌbu̇rk\. Town, NW Hungary, ab. 22 mi. (35 km.) NW of Győr; pop. (1991e) 30,600.

Mos·que·ro \mäs-'ker-ō\. Village, ⊗ of Harding and San Miguel cos., NE New Mexico; pop. (1990c) 164.

Mos·qui·to Cays \mə-'skē-tō\. Group of small islands, Nicaragua, in Caribbean Sea off NE coast.

Mosquito Coast *or* **Mi·ski·to Coast** \mi-'skē-tō\. Region along coast of E Nicaragua and Honduras; ab. 40 mi. (64 km.) wide; a British protectorate 1655–1860 and later an autonomous Indian reserve; incorp. into Nicaragua 1894; N portion granted to Honduras 1960 by International Court of Justice. Chief town Bluefields. See SAN JUAN DEL NORTE.

Mosquito Gulf. *or Span.* **Mosquitos, Golfo de los** \'gȯl-fō-thā-,lȯs-mȯs-kē-tōs\. Widemouthed inlet of the Caribbean Sea on N coast of Panama, W of the Panama Canal.

Mosquito Peak. Mountain, Park and Lake cos., cen. Colorado; 13,784 ft. (4201 m.).

Mosquitos, Golfo de los. See MOSQUITO GULF.

Moss \'mȯs\. Seaport, Østfold co., SE Norway, on E side of Oslo Fjord; pop. (1990c) 24,657; seaside resort; shipbuilding yards, iron foundries; manufactures paper; scene Aug. 1814 of signing of agreement uniting Norway to Swedish crown (union dissolved 1905). See NORWAY.

Mos·sel·baai \,mȯ-səl-'bī\ *or angl.* **Mos·sel Bay** \'mȯ-səl\. Seaport on Mosselbaai (inlet of Indian Ocean), S Western Cape prov., S Rep. of South Africa, ab. 230 mi. (370 km.) E of Cape Town; harvests oysters and mussels—whence its name; summer resort. First visited by Portuguese navigator Bartolomeu Dias c. 1488; Portuguese hermitage erected here 1501.

Mossgiel. See MAUCHLINE.

Moss·ley \'mȯs-lē\. Town, Greater Manchester, NW England, on the Tame 10 mi. (16 km.) NE of Manchester; pop. (1981p) 10,224.

Mos·so·ró \,mō-sō-'rȯ\. City, NW Rio Grande do Norte state, NE Brazil, 150 mi. (241 km.) WNW of Natal; munic. pop. (1991p) 191,959; salt; chalk.

Moss Point \'mȯs\. City, Jackson co., SE corner of Mississippi, 20 mi. (32 km.) E of Biloxi; pop. (1990c) 17,837.

Mos·su·ril \,mȯ-sü-'rēl\. Coastal town, NE Mozambique, opp. Mozambique I.

Mos·sy·rock Dam \'mȯ-sē-räk\. See UNITED STATES, *Dams and Reservoirs.*

Most \'mȯst\ *or Ger.* **Brüx** \'brœks\. City, NW Czech Republic, ab. 48 mi. (77 km.) NW of Prague; pop. (1991p) 70,675; major lignite-mining center; also produces steel, chemicals, ceramics; has medieval churches; first mentioned 11th cent.; entire city relocated 1960s to allow expansion of coalfields.

Mos·ta·ga·nem \mȯ-,stä-gä-'nem\. City, N Algeria, 44 mi. (71 km.) ENE of Oran; pop. (1987p) 114,534; exports wine, fruits, and vegetables; 11th cent. citadel; garrisoned by the French 1833.

Mo·star \'mō-,stär\. Town, S cen. Bosnia and Herzegovina, on Neretva River ab. 50 mi. (80 km.) SW of Sarajevo; pop. (1991p) 126,067; formerly ✻ of Herzegovina and still its chief town; suffered much damage during ethnic fighting 1992–93, incl. destruction of 16th cent. arch bridge.

Mo·sul \mō-'sül, 'mō-səl\ *or Arab.* **Al–Maw·ṣil** \,al-maů-'sēl\. City, N Iraq, on the W bank of the Tigris 220 mi. (354 km.) NNW of Baghdad; pop. (1985e) 570,926; on the Turkey-Baghdad railroad and formerly an important town on caravan route from Iran across N Mesopotamia; a trading center for grain, wool, livestock, fruit; refines oil produced nearby; produces cement, sugar, textiles; has many historical buildings and numerous mosques, shrines, and churches; university (1967). Across the river from ruins of ancient Nineveh and other sites of ancient cities now partially excavated, such as Calah (*mod.* Nimrud) and Dur Sharrukin. An old Arabic town taken by Muslims 7th cent.; later under Mongols, Persians, and Turks; became part of Ottoman Empire c. 1534; occupied by British following WWI, but not officially included in British mandate of Iraq until awarded to it by decision of League of Nations 1925; formally ceded by Turks 1926.

Mo·ta·gua \mō-'tä-ḡwä\. River, S cen. Guatemala; flows E and NE into the Gulf of Honduras; ab. 340 mi. (550 km.) long.

Mo·ta·la \'mü-tä-,lä\. Town, Östergötland prov., SE Sweden, on NE shore of Lake Vättern 20 mi. (32 km.) WNW of Linköping; pop. (1993e) 42,264; summer resort; radio and television sets; incorp. 1881.

Mo·ta La·va \'mō-tä-'lä-vä\ *or* **Sad·dle** \'sad-ᵊl\ *or* **Va·lua** \'väl-wä\. Island, one of the Banks Is. in Vanuatu, W Pacific Ocean, NE of Vanua Lava, at 13°40′S, 167°40′E.

Moth·er, Mount \'mə-thər\ *or* **The Mother.** Volcano at NE tip of New Britain I., Bismarck Archipelago, Papua New Guinea, on a peninsula just E of and overshadowing Rabaul and Blanche Bay; its eruption and earthquakes in 1878 created Manam I. in the bay; in May 1937 Mt. Tavurvur (*q.v.*), a crater on its S slope, and Mt. Vulcan together caused great destruction at Rabaul and vicinity.

Mother Lode. Principal belt of gold-bearing quartz along the W foothills of the Sierra Nevada, California.

Mo·ti·ha·ri \,mō-tə-'hä-rē\. City, NW Bihar state, India; pop. (1991p) 77,440.

Mo·ti·ti Island \mō-'tē-tē\. Small island in the Bay of Plenty, off N cen. coast of North I., New Zealand.

Mot·ley \'mät-lē\. County in NW Texas. See table at TEXAS.

Mo·tril \mō-'trēl\. Commercial commune, Granada prov., S Spain, 2 mi. (3 km.) from Mediterranean and 31 mi. (50 km.) S of the city of Granada; pop. (1991c) 46,500.

Mott \'mät\. City, ⊗ of Hettinger co., SW North Dakota; pop. (1990c) 1019.

Mot·to·la \'mȯt-tō-lä\. Commune, Taranto prov., Puglia, SE Italy, 16 mi. (26 km.) NW of the seaport of Taranto; pop. (1981p) 15,889; 15th cent. cathedral.

Mo·tu–ari \,mō-tü-'är-ē\. Small island of Gambier Is., S Pacific Ocean, SW of Mangareva I.

Mo·tu·sa \mō-'tü-sä\. Chief village of Rotuma I., Fiji, SW Pacific Ocean.

Mo·tya \'mō-tē-ə\. Ruins of ancient Phoenician town on very small island, **San Pan·ta·leo** \,sän-,pän-tä-'lā-ō\ *or* **Pan·ta·le·o·ne** \-lā-'ō-nē\, off W coast of Sicily, Italy, just N of Marsala; attacked and taken from Carthaginians c. 397 B.C. by Dionysius the Elder, tyrant of Syracusae.

Motyca. See MODICA.

Mouanda. See MOANDA.

Mouaskar. See MASCARA.

Mou·choir Bank \'müsh-wär\. Bank in Atlantic Ocean off N coast of Hispaniola in the West Indies.

Mouchoir Passage. Channel in Atlantic Ocean, in N cen. West Indies SE of Turks Is. and NW of Mouchoir Bank.

Mou·dros *or* **Mu·dros** *or* **Moú·dhros** \'mü-,thrös, -,drös\. Town and seaport on S coast of Lemnos I. in N Aegean Sea; belongs to Lesbos dept., Greece; has fine harbor, a part of **Moudros Gulf.**

Mouhoun. See VOLTA, BLACK.

Moui·la \mwē-'lä\. Town, SW cen. Gabon; pop. (1985e) 37,500.

Moukden. See SHENYANG.

Moule, Le. See LE MOULE.

Mou·lins \mü-'lenⁿ\. City, ✻ of Allier dept., cen. France, on Allier River 58 mi. (93 km.) SE of Bourges; pop. (1990c) 23,353; shoes, beer, furniture; 15th cent. Gothic cathedral; 15th cent. campanile. Ancient ✻ of Bourbonnais.

Moul·mein \mül-'mān, mōl-, -'mīn\ *also* **Maul·main** \mȯl-'mīn\. Commercial city, ✻ of Mon state, Myanmar, at mouth of Salween on E shore of Gulf of Martaban; pop. (1983c) 219,961; formerly a shipbuilding center of great importance; now an important port with export trade in rice and teak.

Mou·lou·ya *or* **Mu·lu·ya** \mü-'lü-yä\ *or* **Mul·wi·ya** \mül-'wē-yä\; *anc.* **Mu·lu·cha** \'myü-lə-kə\. River, Morocco; rises in cen. Morocco, flows NE into Mediterranean Sea E of Melilla; 370 mi. (595 km.) long.

Moul·ton \'mōlt-ᵊn\. Town, ⊗ of Lawrence co., N Alabama; pop. (1990c) 3248.

Moul·trie \'mōl-trē\. **1.** County in cen. Illinois. See table at ILLINOIS.
2. City, ⊗ of Colquitt co., S Georgia, 35 mi. (56 km.) SE of Albany; pop. (1990c) 14,865.

Moultrie, Lake; *formerly* **Pi·nop·o·lis Reservoir** \ˌpī-ˈnä-pə-ləs\. Lake in Cooper River, SE South Carolina; formed 1941 upon completion of Pinopolis Dam.

Mound \ˈmau̇nd\. Village, Hennepin co., SE Minnesota, W of Minneapolis; pop. (1990c) 9634.

Mound City. **1.** City, ⊗ of Pulaski co., S Illinois, on Ohio River 8 mi. (13 km.) above its confluence with Mississippi River; pop. (1990c) 765.
2. City, ⊗ of Lion co., E Kansas; pop. (1990c) 789.
3. Town, ⊗ of Campbell co., N South Dakota; pop. (1990c) 89.

Mound City Group National Monument. Former national monument; redesignated Hopewell Culture National Historical Park 1992. See UNITED STATES, *National Historical Parks*.

Moun·dou \ˈmün-ˌdü\. Town, S Chad, ab. 241 mi. (388 km.) SSE of N'Djamena; pop. (1992e) 117,500.

Mounds View. Village, Ramsey co., E Minnesota, N suburb of Minneapolis; pop. (1990c) 12,541.

Mounds·ville \ˈmau̇ndz-ˌvil, -vəl\. City, ⊗ of Marshall co., N West Virginia, in N Panhandle on Ohio River 12 mi. (19 km.) S of Wheeling; pop. (1990c) 10,753; glassware; state penitentiary; coal deposits nearby. Named for Grave Creek Mound, a conical prehistoric Indian burial mound, ab. 900 ft. (270 m.) in circumference at the base and ab. 70 ft. (20 m.) high, which is in center of the city.

Mount, Cape \ˈmau̇nt\. Cape on SE coast of Liberia, a promontory 1000 ft. (305 m.) high.

Mount Abu. See ABU, MOUNT.

Moun·tain·air \ˌmau̇nt-ᵊn-ˈar\. Town and health resort, Torrance co., cen. New Mexico, 44 mi. (71 km.) SSE of Albuquerque; pop. (1990c) 926; pueblo ruins nearby.

Mountain Ash. Town, Mid Glamorgan co., S Wales; pop. (1981c) 23,547; historically noted for coal mining.

Mountain Brook. City, Jefferson co., cen. Alabama, E suburb of Birmingham; pop. (1990c) 19,810.

Mountain City. Town, ⊗ of Johnson co., NE corner of Tennessee; pop. (1990c) 2169.

Mountain Grove. City, Wright co., S Missouri, 38 mi. (61 km.) NW of West Plains; pop. (1990c) 4182.

Mountain Home. **1.** City, ⊗ of Baxter co., N Arkansas; pop. (1990c) 9027.
2. City, ⊗ of Elmore co., SW cen. Idaho; pop. (1990c) 7913.

Mountain Lakes. Residential borough, Morris co., N New Jersey, 7 mi. (11 km.) N of Morristown; pop. (1990c) 3847; spread out around eight artificial lakes.

Mountain Meadows. Valley in Iron and Washington cos., SW Utah; massacre of ab. 100 emigrants by local settlers inflamed by federal government policy occurred Sept. 1857 in Washington co., ab. 40 mi. (64 km.) SW of Cedar City.

Mountain Province. Province, N cen. Luzon, Philippines. See table at PHILIPPINES.

Mountain Republic. Former (c. 1921–27) administrative subdivision of Russia S.F.S.R., U.S.S.R., on N slopes of Caucasus Mts.; later replaced by Checheno-Ingush, Kabardino-Balkanian, and North Ossetian A.S.S.R.s and Karachayev Autonomous Oblast.

Moun·tain·side \ˈmau̇nt-ᵊn-ˌsīd\. Borough, Union co., NE New Jersey, 11 mi. (18 km.) SW of Newark; pop. (1990c) 6657.

Mountains of the Moon. See RUWENZORI, MOUNT.

Mountain View. **1.** City, ⊗ of Stone co., N Arkansas; pop. (1990c) 2439.
2. City, Santa Clara co., W California, 11 mi. (18 km.) NW of San Jose; pop. (1990c) 67,460; ships fruits; manufactures electronic equipment; settled 1852; incorp. 1902.

Mount Airy \ˈar-ē\. Town and summer resort, Surry co., N North Carolina, in foothills of the Blue Ridge 35 mi. (56 km.) NW of Winston-Salem; pop. (1990c) 7156.

Mount Al·bert \ˈal-bərt\. Borough, N North I., New Zealand, SW suburb of Auckland; pop. (1981c) 26,462.

Mount An·gel \ˈān-jəl\. City, Marion co., NW Oregon, 15 mi. (24 km.) NE of Salem; pop. (1990c) 2778.

Iount Apo National Park. See APO, MOUNT.

Iount Ar·ling·ton \ˈärl-iŋ-tən\. Borough, Morris co., N New ersey, on Lake Hopatcong; pop. (1990c) 3630.

Mount Ayr \ˈar\. Town, ⊗ of Ringgold co., S Iowa, 70 mi. (113 km.) SW of Des Moines; pop. (1990c) 1796.

Mount Car·mel \ˈkär-məl\. **1.** City, ⊗ of Wabash co., SE Illinois, on Wabash River 30 mi. (48 km.) SE of Olney; pop. (1990c) 8287; Wabash Valley Coll. (1961).
2. Borough, Northumberland co., E cen. Pennsylvania, 15 mi. (24 km.) WNW of Pottsville; pop. (1990c) 7196; estab. as a coal-mining town.
3. Town, Hawkins co., NE Tennessee; pop. (1990c) 4082.
4. Mountain, Israel. See CARMEL, MOUNT.

Mount Car·roll \ˈkar-əl\. City, ⊗ of Carroll co., NW Illinois; pop. (1990c) 1726.

Mount Clem·ens \ˈkle-mənz\. City, ⊗ of Macomb co., SE Michigan, 20 mi. (32 km.) NE of Detroit; pop. (1990c) 18,405; health resort with mineral springs.

Mount Des·ert \də-ˈzərt, ˈde-zərt\. Island, Hancock co., off SE Maine; 14 mi. (23 km.) long by 8 mi. (13 km.) wide; connected to mainland by bridge; summer resort; damaged by forest fire 1947; includes Acadia National Park (see UNITED STATES, *National Parks*).

Mount Do·ra \ˈdōr-ə\. Town, Lake co., cen. Florida Penin., 22 mi. (35 km.) NNW of Orlando; pop. (1990c) 7196.

Mount Edge·cumbe \ˈej-kəm\. Community on W coast of Baranof I., SE Alaska, SW of Juneau; incorp. into Sitka Sept. 1971.

Mount Ephra·im \ˈē-frē-əm, -frəm\. Borough, Camden co., SW New Jersey, 5 mi. (8 km.) S of the city of Camden; pop. (1990c) 4517.

Mount For·est \ˈfȯr-əst, ˈfär-\. Town, Wellington co., SE Ontario, Canada, 38 mi. (61 km.) NW of Guelph; pop. (1991c) 4266.

Mount Gam·bier \ˈgam-bir\. Town, SE corner of South Australia, Australia, near Victoria border 240 mi. (386 km.) SSE of Adelaide; pop. (1991c) 21,153; nearby is Mt. Gambier extinct volcano.

Mount Gil·e·ad \ˈgi-lē-əd\. Village, ⊗ of Morrow co., cen. Ohio, 16 mi. (26 km.) E of Marion; pop. (1990c) 2846.

Mount Heal·thy \ˈhel-thē\. City, Hamilton co., SW corner of Ohio, 9 mi. (14 km.) N of Cincinnati; pop. (1990c) 7580.

Mount Hol·ly \ˈhä-lē\. **1.** Township, ⊗ of Burlington co., S cen. New Jersey, 16 mi. (26 km.) S of Trenton; pop. (1990c) 10,639; site purchased by Quakers 1676; temporary ✻ of New Jersey 1779; occupied at times by British troops during Revolution; became ⊗ 1796.
2. Town, Gaston co., SW North Carolina, 10 mi. (16 km.) E of Gastonia; pop. (1990c) 7710.

Mount Hope Bay \ˈhōp\. NE arm of Narragansett Bay, E section in SE Massachusetts and W section in E Rhode Island; ab. 6 mi. (10 km.) long and 2 mi. (3 km.) wide; receives Taunton River at its NE extremity; city of Fall River, Massachusetts, on its NE shore.

Mount Ida \ˈī-də\. **1.** City, ⊗ of Montgomery co., W Arkansas; pop. (1990c) 775.
2. Mountain, Asia Minor. See IDA 2.
3. Mountain, Crete. See IDA, MOUNT.

Mount Isa \ˈī-zə\. Mining town, Queensland, Australia; pop. (1991c) 24,735; major producer of copper, lead, silver, and zinc.

Mount Joy \ˈjȯi\. Borough, Lancaster co., SE Pennsylvania, 12 mi. (19 km.) WNW of the city of Lancaster; pop. (1990c) 6398.

Mount Ken·ya National Park \ˈken-yə, ˈkēn-\. National park, cen. Kenya; 227 sq. mi. (588 sq. km.); heavily forested; contains Mt. Kenya.

Mount Kis·co \ˈkis-kō\. Village, Westchester co., SE New York, 36 mi. (58 km.) NNE of New York City; pop. (1990c) 9108; residential.

Mount·lake Terrace \ˈmau̇nt-lāk\. City, Snohomish co., NW Washington, S of Everett; pop. (1990c) 19,320.

\ə\ **abut** \ˈə\ matches \ᵊ\ kitten, Fr table \ər\ **further** \a\ **ash** \ā\ **ace** \ä\ **cot, cart** \ȧ\ Fr bac \au̇\ **out** \b\ Span Avila \ch\ **chin** \e\ **bet** \ē\ **easy** \g\ **go** \i\ **hit** \ī\ **ice** \j\ **job** \k̲\ Ger **ich, Buch** \ⁿ\ Fr vin \ŋ\ **sing** \ō\ **go** \ȯ\ **all** \ȯ\ **law** \œ\ Fr bœuf \œ̄\ Fr feu \ȯi\ **boy** \th\ **thin** \th̲\ **this** \ü\ **loot** \u̇\ **foot** \ue\ Ger füllen \ue̅\ Fr rue \y\ **yet** \ʸ\ Fr digne \ˈdēnʸ\, nuit \ˈnwʸē\ \yü\ **few** \yu̇\ **fury** \zh\ **vision**

Mount Lavinia. See DEHIWALA-MOUNT LAVINIA.

Mount Lebanon. See *History* at LEBANON.

Mount Marie. See PINE BLUFF.

Mount Mc·Kin·ley National Park \mə-'kin-lē\. See *Denali* at UNITED STATES, *National Parks*.

Mount Mor·ris \'mȯr-əs\. **1.** Village, Ogle co., N Illinois, 25 mi. (40 km.) SW of Rockford; pop. (1990c) 2919.
2. City, Genesee co., SE cen. Michigan, 8 mi. (13 km.) N of Flint; pop. (1990c) 3292.
3. Village in town of Mount Morris (pop. [1990c] 4633), Livingston co., W New York, 34 mi. (55 km.) SSW of Rochester; pop. (1990c) 3102.

Mount of the Holy Cross. See HOLY CROSS, MOUNT OF THE.

Mount Ol·ive \'ä-liv\. Town, Wayne and Duplin cos., E North Carolina, S of Goldsboro; pop. (1990c) 4582; Mount Olive Coll. (1951).

Mount Ol·i·ver \'ä-li-vər\. Borough, Allegheny co., SW Pennsylvania, surrounded by city of Pittsburgh; pop. (1990c) 4160.

Mount Ol·i·vet \'ä-li-vət\. City, ⊗ of Robertson co., NE Kentucky; pop. (1990c) 384.

Mount Olym·pus National Monument \ō-'lim-pəs\. Former U.S. national monument, NW Washington; 467 sq. mi. (1210 sq. km.); estab. 1909; included 1938 in Olympic National Park (see UNITED STATES, *National Parks*).

Mount Pearl \'pərl\. Town, Newfoundland, E Canada, SW of St. John's; pop. (1991c) 23,689.

Mount Penn \'pen\. Borough, Berks co., SE Pennsylvania, 3 mi. (5 km.) E of Reading; pop. (1990c) 2883.

Mount Pleas·ant \'plez-ᵊnt\. **1.** City, ⊗ of Henry co., SE Iowa, 28 mi. (45 km.) WNW of Burlington; pop. (1990c) 8027; Iowa Wesleyan Coll. (1842).
2. City, ⊗ of Isabella co., cen. Michigan, 46 mi. (74 km.) W of Bay City; pop. (1990c) 23,285; oil wells; Central Michigan Univ. (1892).
3. Borough, Westmoreland co., SW Pennsylvania, 21 mi. (34 km.) NNE of Uniontown; pop. (1990c) 4787; glassware.
4. Town, Charleston co., SE South Carolina, on Atlantic Ocean 5 mi. (8 km.) E of the city of Charleston; pop. (1990c) 30,108; resort.
5. Town, Maury co., W cen. Tennessee, 12 mi. (19 km.) WSW of Columbia; pop. (1990c) 4278.
6. City, ⊗ of Titus co., NE Texas, 48 mi. (77 km.) SE of Paris; pop. (1990c) 12,291.
7. Town, Racine co., SE Wisconsin; pop. (1990c) 20,084.

Mount Pros·pect \'präs-ˌpekt\. Village, Cook co., NE Illinois, ab. 7 mi. (11 km.) NW of Chicago; pop. (1990c) 53,170.

Mount·rail \'mau̇nt-ˌrāl\. County in NW North Dakota. See table at NORTH DAKOTA.

Mount Rai·nier \rə-'nir, rā-, 'rā-,\. City, Prince Georges co., S cen. Maryland, just NE of Washington, D.C.; pop. (1990c) 7954.

Mount Rainier National Park. See UNITED STATES, *National Parks*.

Mount Rev·el·stoke National Park \'re-vəl-ˌstōk\. See CANADA, *National Parks*.

Mount Roy·al \mau̇nt-'rȯi-əl\ *or* **Mont Royal** \ˌmōⁿ-rwȧ-'yȧl\. Town, Montreal I., S Quebec, Canada, NW of the height Mt. Royal; pop. (1991c) 18,212.

Mount Rushmore National Memorial. See RUSHMORE, MOUNT.

Mount Saint Helens National Volcanic Monument. See SAINT HELENS, MOUNT and UNITED STATES, *National Monuments*.

Mounts Bay \'mau̇nts\. Inlet of Atlantic Ocean on extreme SW tip of England, bet. Land's End on the W and Lizard Head on the E.

Mount Shas·ta \'shas-tə\. Town, Siskiyou co., N California, at foot of Mt. Shasta, ab. 100 mi. (160 km.) NE of Eureka; pop. (1990c) 3460; resort.

Mount Ster·ling \'stər-liŋ\. **1.** City, ⊗ of Brown co., W Illinois, 34 mi. (55 km.) E of Quincy; pop. (1990c) 1922.
2. City, ⊗ of Montgomery co., E Kentucky, 15 mi. (24 km.) ENE of Winchester; pop. (1990c) 5362; prehistoric mounds nearby; city captured by Confederates 1863.

Mount Un·ion \'yü-nyən\. Borough, Huntingdon co., S cen. Pennsylvania, on Juniata River 24 mi. (39 km.) SW of Lewistown; pop. (1990c) 2878.

Mount Ver·non \'vər-nən\. **1.** City, ⊗ of Montgomery co., SE cen. Georgia; pop. (1990c) 1914; Brewton-Parker Coll. (1904).
2. City, ⊗ of Jefferson co., S Illinois, 20 mi. (32 km.) SE of Centralia; pop. (1990c) 16,988; diversified agriculture; settled 1819; incorp. as city 1872.
3. City, ⊗ of Posey co., SW corner of Indiana, on Ohio River 18 mi. (29 km.) W of Evansville; pop. (1990c) 7217.
4. City, Linn co., E Iowa, 13 mi. (21 km.) E of Cedar Rapids; pop. (1990c) 3657; Cornell Coll. (1853).
5. City, ⊗ of Rockcastle co., SE cen. Kentucky; pop. (1990c) 2654.
6. City, ⊗ of Lawrence co., SW Missouri, 32 mi. (51 km.) WSW of Springfield; pop. (1990c) 3726.
7. City, Westchester co., SE New York; residential suburb on Bronx River adjacent to New York City; pop. (1990c) 67,153; electronic components; Revolutionary War battles fought in area; developed 1850 ff. as refuge from high rents of New York City; incorp. as city 1892.
8. City, ⊗ of Knox co., cen. Ohio, 25 mi. (40 km.) S of Mansfield; pop. (1990c) 14,550; diesel engines, glass; livestock and dairy farms.
9. Town, ⊗ of Franklin co., NE Texas; pop. (1990c) 2219.
10. Home and burial place of George Washington, first U.S. president, in Fairfax co., Virginia, on Potomac River ab. 15 mi. (24 km.) below Washington, D.C.; acquired by Washington 1752; has been restored and is maintained by Mount Vernon Ladies' Association of the Union which bought it c. 1860.
11. City, ⊗ of Skagit co., NW Washington, on Skagit River 25 mi. (40 km.) S of Bellingham; pop. (1990c) 17,647; Skagit Valley Coll. (1926).

Mount Wash·ing·ton \'wȯ-shiŋ-tən, 'wä-\. City, Bullitt co., Kentucky, 16 mi. (26 km.) SSE of Louisville; pop. (1990c) 5226.

Mount Wel·ling·ton \'we-liŋ-tən\. Borough, North I., New Zealand, a suburb of Auckland; pop. (1981c) 19,528.

Mourne \'mōrn\. River, N Ireland (island); flows NNW in W Northern Ireland to unite with the Finn on the Ireland (republic) border; 10 mi. (16 km.) long.

Mourne Mountains. Range in SE Northern Ireland, bet. Dundrum Bay and Carlingford Lough; highest peak Slieve Donard 2796 ft. (852 m.).

Mous·cron \müs-'krōⁿ, mü-\ *or Flemish* **Moes·kroen** \müs-'krün\. Commune, West Flanders prov., NW Belgium, just S of Kortrijk.

Mouse. See SOURIS.

Moustier, Le. See LE MOUSTIER.

Mow·er \'mau̇-ər\. County in S Minnesota. See table at MINNESOTA.

Mo·xi·co \'mō-shē-kü\. Province of E Angola. See table at ANGOLA.

Moy \'mȯi\. River, NW Ireland; rises in co. Sligo, curves SW, W, and N through co. Mayo into Killala Bay; 40 mi. (64 km.) long.

Mo·ya·le \mō-'yä-lā\. Town, N Kenya, near Ethiopian border; British base in attack on Italian East Africa 1941 during WWII.

Moyen Atlas. See ATLAS MOUNTAINS.

Mo·yeu·vre–Grande \mwȧ-ˌyœ̄v-rə-'grȧⁿd\. Commune Moselle dept., NE France, on Orne River 11 mi. (18 km NNW of Metz.

Moyle \'mȯil\. District of N Northern Ireland. See table at LAND, NORTHERN.

Mo·yo·bam·ba \ˌmȯi-ō-'bäm-bä\. Town, N Peru, on River 420 mi. (676 km.) N of Lima; pop. (1990e) manufactures Panama hats.

Moy·tu·ra \mȯi-'tu̇r-ə\. Two localities in Ireland with legends of the Firbolg: **Northern Moytura,** Connacht, and **Southern Moytura,** near Cong Mask and Lough Corrib; both areas marked by historic remains; both were scenes of defeat of

Moyun Kum. See MUYUN KUM.

Mo·zam·bique \ˌmō-zäm-ˈbēk\. **1.** *or Port.* **Mo·çam·bi·que** \ˌmü-sȧm-ˈbē-kə\; *formerly* **Portuguese East Africa.** Republic, SE Africa, bounded on N by Tanzania, on E by the Indian Ocean (Mozambique Channel), on S by Rep. of South Africa and Swaziland, and on W by Zimbabwe, Zambia, and Malawi; 297,846 sq. mi. (771,421 sq. km.); pop. (1993e) 15,243,000; ✻ Maputo.

Physical features: Mountainous in N (highest peak 7936 ft. or 2419 m.) and along Zimbabwe border (ab. 9000 ft. or 2700 m.). Crossed in cen. part by lower course (ab. 480 mi. or 770 km.) of Zambezi River flowing SE into Mozambique Channel at Chinde; other important rivers the Limpopo in S, Save in S cen. part, Lugenda in N, and many shorter streams in NE; coastal plain extensive; N boundary marked by Ruvuma River and Cape Delgado.

Chief products: Corn, cashew nuts, sugar, tea, copra, cotton; coal, bauxite; shrimp.

Political divisions: Divided into the city of Maputo and the following 10 provinces (for pronunciation of their names, see their individual entries):

NAME	AREA (sq. mi.)	AREA (sq. km.)	POP. (1991e)	CAPITAL
Maputo (city)	232	601	931,591	
Provinces				
Cabo Delgado	31,902	82,626	1,202,221	Pemba
Gaza	29,231	75,708	1,401,485	Xai-Xai
Inhambane	26,492	68,614	1,156,958	Inhambane
Manica	23,807	61,660	609,512	Chimoio
Maputo	9,944	25,755	840,757	Maputo
Nampula	31,508	81,606	2,841,416	Nampula
Niassa	49,828	129,054	686,650	Lichinga
Sofala	26,262	68,018	1,427,493	Beira
Tete	38,890	100,725	734,561	Tete
Zambézia	40,544	105,009	2,619,281	Quelimane

History: Inhabited from prehistoric times; settled by Bantu peoples c. 3d cent. A.D.; major trade civilization developed in Middle Ages; Arab traders occupied coastal region from ab. 14th cent.; occupied by Portuguese traders from early in 16th cent.; in 1875, the disputed Delagoa Bay (*q.v.*) region awarded to Portugal; after efforts of Portuguese explorers to expand to interior, British secured agreement which defined its boundaries with British South and East Africa 1891; boundary with German East Africa determined 1894; until 1942 was in two parts: (1) territory under direct Portuguese administration, and (2) territory under administration of several trading companies, esp. the Mozambique Company (chartered 1891) whose charter expired 1942, the territory reverting to the Portuguese government; became an overseas province of Portugal 1951; outbreak of fighting bet. Portuguese forces and Mozambique Liberation Front (Frelimo), anti-Portuguese nationalists, 1964; after a decade of civil war, granted independence June, 1975 as People's Republic of Mozambique, a single-party Marxist-style state under Frelimo control; gave refuge and support to exiled nationalist forces from Rhodesia (mid-1970s) and South Africa (until 1984); faced armed insurgency (supported for a time by the governments of Rhodesia and South Africa) 1970s–80s; adopted new constitution 1990 as Republic of Mozambique, ending Marxist collectivism and introducing privatization, a market economy, and multiparty government; signed peace treaty with rebels 1992.

2. Seaport, Mozambique. See MOÇAMBIQUE 2.

Mozambique Channel. Strait bet. Madagascar and the SE African mainland (Mozambique); ab. 950 mi. (1530 km.) long; 250 mi. (402 km.) wide at narrowest (central) part and ab. 625 mi. (1000 km.) at widest.

Mozambique Current. A warm ocean current flowing from the Indian Ocean S through Mozambique Channel, becoming the Agulhas Current (*q.v.*) along the coast of the Rep. of South Africa.

Mozambique Island. See MOÇAMBIQUE 2.

Moz·dok \mȧz-ˈdȯk\. Town, Alania, S Russia in Europe, on Terek River 55 mi. (88 km.) WNW of Grozny, Chechnya.

Mo·zhaisk *or* **Mo·zhaysk** \mə-ˈzhīsk\. Village, Moscow Oblast, W cen. Russia in Europe, on railroad line 65 mi. (105 km.) W of the city of Moscow. Taken by Germans Oct. 1941 in the advance on Moscow; regained by Soviet forces in winter counteroffensive 1941–42.

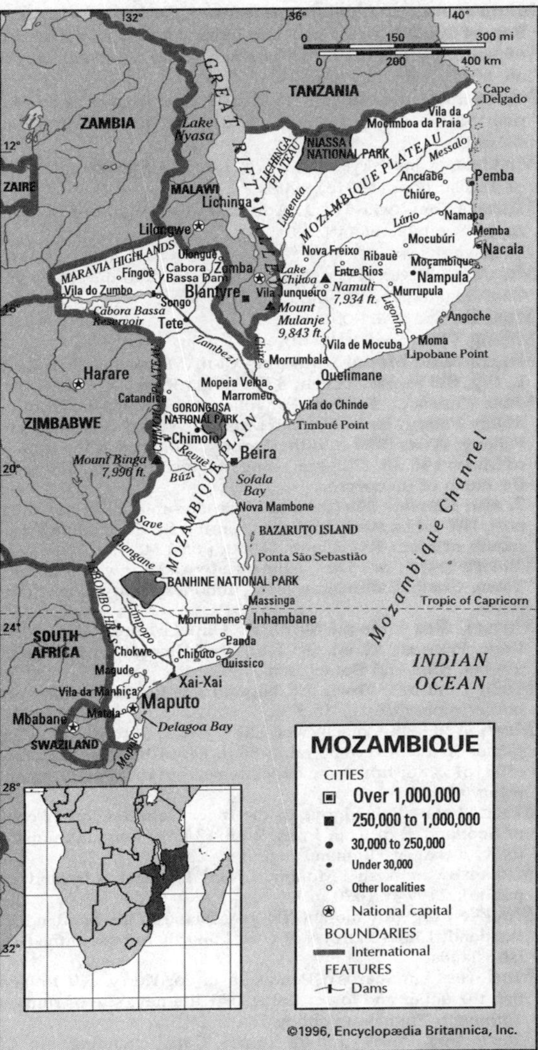

Mozyr. See MAZYR.

Mpon·da \əm-ˈpȯn-dä\. Town, S Malawi, at S end of Lake Malawi.

Mpu·ma·lan·ga \əm-ˌpü-mä-ˈläŋ-gä\; *formerly* **Eastern Trans·vaal** \trans-ˈväl, tranz-\. Province of NE Rep. of South Africa. See table at SOUTH AFRICA, REPUBLIC OF.

M'Si·la \əm-sē-ˈlä\. Town, N cen. Algeria in area of salt lakes; pop. (1987p) 65,805.

Msta \əm-ˈstä\. River, cen. Novgorod Oblast, W Russia in Europe; flows NW and W into N end of Lake Ilmen; 275 mi. (442 km.) long; navigable and connected by canals with the Volga through the Tvertsa at Vyshni Volochek.

Msus \əm-ˈsüs\. Village in desert, NE Libya, 68 mi. (109 km.) SE of Benghazi; during WWII British tank brigades destroyed here by German forces 1941–42.

Mtam·vu·na *also* **Um·tam·vu·na** \əm-ˌtäm-ˈvü-nä\. River, E Rep. of South Africa; flows into Indian Ocean and marks part of boundary bet. Eastern Cape and KwaZulu-Natal provs.; ab. 50 mi. (80 km.) long.

Mta·ta *also* **Um·ta·ta** \əm-ˈtä-tä\. River, E Rep. of South Africa; 50 mi. (81 km.) long; divides Tembuland from Pondoland.

Mtskhe·ta \əmt-ˈskye-tə\. Town, Republic of Georgia, NNW of Tbilisi; pop. (1991e) 9900.

Mtwa·ra \əm-ˈtwär-ä\. **1.** Administrative region of SE Tanzania. See table at TANZANIA.
2. Town, its ✻.

Mu \ˈmü\. River, N cen. Myanmar; flows S to the Irrawaddy W of Sagaing;ab. 170 mi. (275 km.) long.

Muai To. See MAE HONG SON.

Muang Thai. See THAILAND.

Mua·ni·va·tu, Mount \ˌmwä-nē-ˈvä-tü\. Peak, cen. Viti Levu I., Fiji, SW Pacific Ocean; 3708 ft. (1130 m.).

Muar \ˈmwär\. **1.** River, NW Johor state, Malaysia, S end of Malay Penin.; its headstreams rise in Negeri Sembilan and Pahang; flows SSW into the Strait of Malacca at the seaport of Muar; 140 mi. (225 km.) long; navigable for small vessels for much of its course.
2. *also* **Ban·dar Ma·ha·ra·ni** \ˈbən-dər-ˌmä-hə-ˈrä-nē\. Seaport, NW Johor state, Malaysia; on the Strait of Malacca, at mouth of Muar River; pop. (1980c) 65,151.

Mu·a·ra·te·we *or Du.* **Moe·a·ra·te·we** \ˌmwä-rä-ˈtā-wā\. Town, South Kalimantan prov., Indonesia, on upper Barito River.

Mu·a·ri, Ras \ˈräs-mu̇-ˈär-ē\ *or* **Cape Mon·ze** \ˈmȯn-zā\. Cape, Pakistan, 22 mi. (35 km.) W of Karachi on the boundary bet. Sind and Baluchistan.

Mu·bi \ˈmü-bē\. Town, NE Nigeria not far from Cameroon border; pop. (1991e) 56,570.

Much Wen·lock \ˈməch-ˈwen-ˌläk\. Town, Shropshire, W England, on the Severn 30 mi. (48 km.) W of Birmingham; pop. (1981c) 2486; limestone deposits nearby; ruins of 11th cent. priory church.

Muck \ˈmək\. Island, one of the Inner Hebrides, off W coast of Scotland, S of Rum I.; ab. 2 mi. (3 km.) long; administratively a part of Highland region.

Muck·ish \ˈmə-kish\. Mountain, N co. Donegal, N Ireland (republic); 2197 ft. (670 m.).

Muck·le Flug·ga \ˈmə-kəl-ˈflə-gə\. Island in the Shetland Is., Scotland; 1 mi. (2 km.) N of Unst I.; northernmost of the British islands.

Muck·ross \ˌmə-ˈkrȯs\. Peninsula in co. Kerry, SW Ireland, bet. the upper and lower Lakes of Killarney; site of ruins of 15th cent. Franciscan abbey.

Mu·cu·ri·pe, Point \ˌmü-ku̇-ˈrē-pē\. Cape extending into Atlantic Ocean on coast of Ceará state, NE Brazil, 5 mi. (8 km.) E of Fortaleza.

Mu·dan *or W.-G.* **Mu–tan** \ˈmü-ˈdän\. River, Jilin and Heilongjiang provs., NE China; flows NE and N from Jilin prov. to join the Songhua at Yilan, Heilongjiang; ab. 310 mi. (500 km.) long.

Mu·dan·jiang *or W.-G.* **Mu–tan–chiang** \ˈmü-ˈdän-ˈjyäŋ\. City, Heilongjiang prov., NE China, on Mudan River ab. 160 mi. (260 km.) SE of Harbin; pop. (1990c) 571,705.

Mu·dan·ya \mu̇-ˈdän-yä\. Town on Gemlik Gulf, an inlet of the Sea of Marmara, Bursa prov., NW Turkey in Asia; port serving Bursa.

Mud·dus National Park \ˈmu̇-du̇s\. National park, N Sweden; 195 sq. mi. (505 sq. km.); coniferous woodland, bogs.

Mud·dy \ˈmə-dē\. River, SE Nevada; rises in Lincoln co., flows S into Virgin River; ab. 80 mi. (130 km.) long.

Muddy Bog·gy Creek \ˈbȯ-gē\. River, SE Oklahoma; rises in Pontotoc co., flows SE into Red River in S Choctaw co.; ab. 100 mi. (160 km.) long.

Muddy Pass. Mountain pass, Jackson and Grand cos., N Colorado, in Park Range of the Rocky Mts.; 8772 ft. (2674 m.); traversed by highway.

Mud Flat \ˈməd\. Intermittent lake, W Nevada, N of Pyramid Lake.

Mu·dhol \ˈmu̇-ˌdȯl\. **1.** Former Indian state, now part of Karnataka state, W India; 350 sq. mi. (907 sq. km.).
2. Town, its ✻, 70 mi. (113 km.) SE of Kolhapur.

Mud·ki \ˈmu̇d-kē\. Village, Punjab state, NW India, 18 mi. (29 km.) SE of Firozpur; scene of British victory over Sikhs 1845.

Mud Mountain Dam. See UNITED STATES, *Dams and Reservoirs.*

Mudros. See MOUDROS.

Mu·fu·li·ra \ˌmü-fü-ˈlē-rä\. Town, Zambia, 21 mi. (34 km.) NNE of Kitwe and not far from the border with Democratic Rep. of the Congo; pop. (1990p) 152,944.

Mufumbiro. See VIRUNGA.

Mug·gia \ˈmü-ˌjä\. Seaport, Trieste prov., Fruili-Venezia Giulia, NE Italy, on bay in Gulf of Trieste at N end of Adriatic Sea 4 mi. (6 km.) SW of the seaport of Trieste; pop. (1981p) 13,875; 15th cent. cathedral; medieval basilica.

Mughal Empire. See MOGUL EMPIRE.

Muğ·la *or* **Mugh·la** \ˈmü-lä\. **1.** Province of SW Turkey in Asia. See table at TURKEY.
2. Town, its ✻, near coast; pop. (1990p) 35,850; center of medieval Turkish emirate.

Mu·gna·no di Na·po·li \mü-ˈnyä-nō-dē-ˈnä-pō-lē\. Commune, Napoli prov., Campania, S Italy, pop. (1989c) 24,509.

Mu·gu, Point \mə-ˈgü\. Cape, Ventura co., SW California, SE of Oxnard; site of a military base with a missile test center.

Mu·ham·mad, Ra's \ˌräs-mu̇-ˈka̱-mȧd\. Cape, S end of Sinai Penin., NE Egypt, extending S into Red Sea.

Muharraq, Al *or* **Muharraq.** See AL MUHARRAQ.

Mühl·berg \ˈmᵫl-ˌberk\. Town, Brandenburg, E Germany, on the Elbe ab. 37 mi. (60 km.) E of Leipzig; scene of battle 1547 in which John Frederick, elector of Saxony was defeated and captured by Holy Roman Emperor Charles V; in WWII taken by U.S.S.R. 1945.

Mühl·dorf \ˈmᵫl-ˌdȯrf\. Town, Bavaria, Germany, on the Inn River 45 mi. (72 km.) E of Munich; pop. (1980c) 14,598.

Muh·len·berg \ˈmyü-lən-ˌbərg\. County in W Kentucky. See table at KENTUCKY.

Muh·len·fels Point \ˈmyü-lən-ˌfelz\. Cape on S coast of St. Thomas I., Virgin Is. of U.S., West Indies.

Mühl·hau·sen in Thü·ring·en \ˈmᵫl-ˌhau̇-zᵊn-in-ˈtᵫr-iŋ-ən\; *sometimes shortened to* **Mühlhausen.** City, Thuringia, cen. Germany, 29 mi. (47 km.) NW of Erfurt; pop. (1992e) 39,667; textiles, leather, wood products; 13th cent. church; 14th cent. church; medieval town walls; 13th cent. town hall. First mentioned 775 A.D.; became city c. 1200; a site from which religious reformer Thomas Münzer once preached and where he was executed 1525; to Prussia 1802, to kingdom of Westphalia 1807, again to Prussia 1815.

Mühl·heim am Main \ˈmᵫ-ˌhīm-äm-ˈmīn\. City, Hesse, Germany, 8 mi. (13 km.) E of Frankfurt am Main; pop. (1980c) 24,490.

Mu·hu \ˈmü-hü\ *or Ger.* **Moon** \ˈmōn\ *or Russ.* **Mu·khu** \ˈmü-ku̱\. Island, Estonia, in Baltic Sea bet. Saaremaa I. and the mainland; 80 sq. mi. (207 sq. km.).

Mui Bai Bung \ˈmü-ē-ˈbī-ˈbu̇ŋ\ *or* **Ca Mau Peninsula** \ˈkä-ˈmau̇\ *or* **Mui Cau Mau** \ˈmü-ē-ˈkau̇-ˈmau̇\; *formerly* **Cam·bo·dia Point** \kam-ˈbō-dē-ə\. Cape, S end of Vietnam; extends W into South China Sea and marks the SE corner of Gulf of Thailand.

Muichdhui, Ben. See BEN MACDHUI.

Muil·rea *or* **Mweel·rea** \mwēl-ˈrā\. Mountain in SW co. Mayo, W Ireland; highest point 2688 ft. (819 m.).

Muir, Mount \ˈmyu̇r\. Peak in the Sierra Nevada, E Tulare co., S cen. California; 14,015 ft. (4272 m.).

Muir Glacier. Glacier in Glacier Bay National Park, SE Alaska; crossed by 59°N, 136°W; covers ab. 350 sq. mi. (910 sq. km.). See UNITED STATES, *National Parks.*

Muir Pass. Mountain pass, Fresno co., S cen. California; in N part of Kings Canyon National Park on the John Muir Trail which extends from Yosemite National Park to Sequoia National Park; 12,059 ft. (3676 m.).

Muir Woods National Monument. See UNITED STATES, *National Monuments.*

Mui·zen·berg \ˈmȯiz-ᵊn-ˌberk̲\. Community, SW Western Cape prov., S Rep. of South Africa, on NW shore of False Bay; now included in municipality of Cape Town; summer resort facilities; cottage in which British colonial administrator and financier Cecil Rhodes died 1902.

Mu·je·res \mü-ˈhā-rās\. An island belonging to Mexico in the Caribbean Sea off NE coast of Yucatán Penin.

Mu·ka·che·ve *or* **Mu·ka·che·vo** \ˌmü-kə-ˈchō-və\ *or Czech* **Mu·ka·če·vo** \ˈmu̇-kä-ˌche-vȯ\ *or Hung.* **Mun·kács** \ˈmu̇ŋ-käch\. Town, Zakarpatska subdivision, W Ukraine; pop. (1991e) 88,000. Ancient Hungarian fortress town; became part of Carpathian Ruthenia, Czechoslovakia 1920 following WWI; ceded to Hungary 1938, to U.S.S.R. 1945.

Mu·kah \ˈmü-kä\. Coastal town, W Sarawak, Malaysia, on island of Borneo just NE of the Rajang Delta; pop. (1980p) 35,831.

Mukalla. See AL MUKALLĀ.

Mukden. See SHENYANG.

Mukhā, Al. See MOCHA.

Mukhaylá, Al *or* **Mukaylī, Al.** See AL-MECHILI.

Mukhmas. See MICHMASH.

Mukhu. See MUHU.

Mu·ko–Ji·ma \ˈmü-kō-ˈjē-mä\ *or* **Mu·ko–shi·ma** \ˈshē-mä\. One of the Bonin Is., Japan.

Mu·la \ˈmü-lä\. Commune, Murcia prov., SE Spain, 18 mi. (29 km.) WNW of the commune of Murcia; pop. (1991c) 13,053; ruins of ancient castle.

Mulahacen. See MULHACÉN.

Mu·lan·je, Mount \mə-ˈlän-jā\ *also* **Mount Mlan·je** \mə-ˈlän-\. Mountain, S Malawi; 9843 ft. (3000 m.); highest peak in **Mulanje Mountains** and in Malawi.

Mul·ber·ry \ˈməl-ˌber-ē\. City, Polk co., cen. Florida Penin., 12 mi. (19 km.) S of Lakeland; pop. (1990c) 2988.

Mul·de \ˈmu̇l-də\. River, E Germany; rises in the Erzgebirge and flows N past Chemnitz into Elbe River near Dessau; ab. 155 mi. (250 km.) long.

Mule Ear Peaks. Mountain, S Brewster co., W Texas; 3880 ft. (1183 m.).

Mule·shoe \ˈmyül-ˌshü\. City, ⊗ of Bailey co., NW Texas; pop. (1990c) 4571.

Mul·grave \ˈməl-ˌgrāv\. Island in Torres Strait, N of Queensland, Australia, adjacent to Banks I. and N of Thursday I.

Mul·ha·cén \ˌmü-lä-ˈthān, -ˈsān\ *also* **Mu·la·ha·cen** \mü-ˌlä-ä-\ *or* **Mu·ley–Ha·cén** \mü-ˌlā-ä-\. Peak in the Sierra Nevada, Granada prov., S Spain; 11,407 ft. (3477 m.); highest peak in Europe outside of the Alps and Caucasus.

Mül·heim an der Ruhr \ˈmuel-ˌhīm-ˌän-dər-ˈrür\. City, North Rhine-Westphalia, Germany, on Ruhr River near its mouth 7 mi. (11 km.) WSW of Essen; pop. (1992e) 177,042; iron and steel foundries, tube and rolling mills, machine shops; 11th cent. church; first mentioned 1093; chartered 1808; to Prussia 1815; bombed by Allies in WWII, and taken 1945.

Mul·house \mue̅-ˈlüz\ *or Ger.* **Mül·hau·sen** \muel-ˈhau̇z-ᵊn\. Commune, Haut-Rhin dept., NE France, on Ill River 22 mi. (35 km.) S of Colmar; pop. (1990c) 109,905; fertilizers, chemicals, textiles, machinery; 16th cent. town hall; fabric museum. First mentioned 9th cent. A.D.; imperial free city 1308; allied with Swiss 16th–18th cents.; joined French First Republic 1798; under German rule 1871–1918 and 1940–44.

Mu·li·a·ma \ˌmü-lē-ˈä-mə\. Village on E coast of New Ireland, Bismarck Archipelago, Papua New Guinea; has good harbor.

Mu·ling \ˈmü-ˈliŋ\. River, Heilongjiang prov., NE China; flows NE into Ussuri River; 260 mi. (418 km.) long.

Mull \ˈməl\. Island of the Inner Hebrides, off W coast of Scotland; ab. 27 mi. (43 km.) long by 20 mi. (32 km.) wide max.; pop. (1981c) 2605; chief town Tobermory; stock farms, granite quarries; highest point 3185 ft. (971 m.); administratively a part of Strathclyde region.

Mull, Ross of \ˈrȯs\. Long SW peninsula of the island of Mull, off W coast of Scotland.

Mull, Sound of. Body of water bet. the NE coast of island of Mull and the Scottish mainland.

Mul·lagh·more \ˌmə-lə-ˈmōr\. Promontory extending N into Donegal Bay, NW Ireland, 13 mi. (21 km.) N of Sligo.

Mul·lan Road \ˈmə-lən\. Wagon trail, NW United States, from Fort Benton, Montana, at head of navigation of Missouri River, across Bitterroot Range to Walla Walla, Washington; built 1859–62 under direction of Lt. John Mullan; helped to open rich mining region.

Mul·len \ˈmə-lən\. Village, ⊗ of Hooker co., W cen. Nebraska; pop. (1990c) 554.

Mul·ler Mountains \ˈmə-lər\. Range in cen. island of Borneo, Indonesia, running N and S bet. provs. of West, South, and East Kalimantan; av. height ab. 4000 to 5000 ft. (1200 to 1500 m.); highest point 7349 ft. (2240 m.); source of many of the streams of the island.

Mul·let \ˈmə-lət\. Peninsula in co. Mayo, on W coast of Ireland, S of Erris Head, enclosing Blacksod Bay on the W, and connected with the mainland by a narrow isthmus at the NE.

Mul·lett Lake \ˈmə-lət\. Lake in N Cheboygan co., N Michigan; outlet N into Straits of Mackinac.

Mul·li·ca \ˈmə-li-kə\. River, S New Jersey; flows from W Burlington co. SE into Great Bay; ab. 40 mi. (64 km.) long.

Mul·lin·gar \ˌmə-lən-ˈgär\. Town, ⊗ of co. Westmeath, N cen. Ireland; pop. (1986c) 8077.

Mul·lins \ˈmə-lənz\. City, Marion co., E South Carolina, 32 mi. (52 km.) E of Florence; pop. (1990c) 5910; annual tobacco market.

Mull of Galloway. See GALLOWAY, MULL OF.

Mull of Kintyre. See KINTYRE, MULL OF.

Mull of Oa. See OA, MULL OF.

Mul·roy Bay \məl-ˈrȯi\. Inlet of Atlantic Ocean on N coast of co. Donegal, N Ireland (republic), W of Lough Swilly.

Mul·tan *also* **Mool·tan** \mu̇l-ˈtän\. City, Punjab, Pakistan, near Chenab River 200 mi. (322 km.) WSW of Lahore; pop. (1981c) 742,000; major industrial center, with cotton gins, textile mills, foundries, glass factory, flour mills, and various cottage industries incl. pottery and camelskin work. Includes surrounding wall and fort enclosing shrines of two Muslim saints and an ancient Hindu temple; large military cantonment. An ancient city; taken by Macedonian King Alexander the Great 4th cent. B.C.; fell to Muslim control 8th cent. A.D.; seized by Muslim Sultan Maḥmūd of Ghaznī (*q.v.*) early 11th cent.; under sultans of Delhi 13th cent. ff., Mogul Empire 16th–18th cents., Afghans 1779–1818, and Sikhs 1818–1849; under British sovereignty 1849–1947.

Mult·no·mah \məlt-ˈnō-mə\. County in NW Oregon. See table at OREGON.

Multnomah Falls. Waterfall, Multnomah co., NW Oregon, E of Portland, in a small tributary of the Columbia River which rises near summit of Larch Mt., 4095 ft. (1248 m.) high; height of falls 620 ft. (189 m.).

Mulucha *or* **Muluya.** See MOULOUYA.

Mul·vane \məl-ˈvān\. City, Sedgwick and Sumner cos., S Kansas, 16 mi. (26 km.) SSE of Wichita; pop. (1990c) 4674.

Mulvius, Pons. See SAXA RUBRA.

Mulwiya. See MOULOUYA.

Mumbai. See BOMBAY 2.

Mun \ˈmün\. River, E Thailand; rises in hills NE of Bangkok, flows E into the Mekong River on the border of Laos; ab. 350 mi. (560 km.) long; receives large tributary, the Chi, ab. 50 mi. (81 km.) from its mouth. Largest town on its banks is Nakhon Ratchasima; navigable in wet season.

Mu·na *or Du.* **Moe·na** \ˈmü-nə\. Island off SE coast of Sulawesi, Indonesia; 63 mi. (101 km.) long by 35 mi. (56 km.) wide; 1124 sq. mi. (2911 sq. km.).

Munastīr, al–. See MONASTIR 1.

München. See MUNICH.

München–Gladbach. See MÖNCHENGLADBACH.

Mun·cie \ˈmən-sē\. City, ⊗ of Delaware co., E cen. Indiana, 50 mi. (81 km.) ENE of Indianapolis; pop. (1990c) 71,035; trade center; furniture, electrical equipment; Ball State Univ. (1918); region inhabited by Munsee Indians until land passed

---

\ə\ abut \ᵊ\ matches \ᵊ\ kitten, Fr table \ər\ further \a\ ash \ā\ ace \ä\ cot, cart \å\ Fr bac \au̇\ out \b̲\ Span Avila \ch\ chin \e\ bet \ē\ easy \g\ go \i\ hit \ī\ ice \j\ job \k̲\ Ger ich, Buch \ⁿ\ Fr vin \ŋ\ sing \ō\ go \ȯ\ all \ò\ law \œ\ Fr bœuf \œ̄\ Fr feu \ȯi\ boy \th\ thin \th̲\ this \ü\ loot \u̇\ foot \ue\ Ger füllen \ue̅\ Fr rue \y\ yet \ʸ\ Fr digne \ˈdēnʸ\, nuit \ˈnwʸē\ \yü\ few \yu̇\ fury \zh\ vision

to U.S. government 1818 by treaty; founded 1827; incorp. as town 1847, as city 1865.

Mun·cy \ˈmən-sē\. Borough, Lycoming co., N cen. Pennsylvania, 13 mi. (21 km.) E of Williamsport; pop. (1990c) 2702.

Mund. See MAND.

Mun·da 1. \ˈmün-də, ˈmən-\. Settlement on S side of NW end of New Georgia I., cen. Solomon Is., W Pacific Ocean. Site of Japanese air base 1942–43; taken by U.S. forces 1943.

2. \ˈmən-də\. Ancient town, S Baetica, S Spain; scene of Roman Gen. Julius Caesar's victory 45 B.C. over Roman Gen. Pompey the Great's sons, Gnaeus and Sextus.

Mun·de·lein \ˈmən-də-ˌlīn\. Village, Lake co., NE Illinois, NW of Chicago; pop. (1990c) 21,215.

Mün·den \ˈmuen-dən\ *also* **Han·no·versch–Münden** \hä-ˈnō-vərsh-\. City, S Lower Saxony, Germany, at confluence of Werra and Fulda rivers 10 mi. (16 km.) NE of Kassel; pop. (1980c) 25,539; summer resort; river port; medieval castle; 14th–15th cent. stone bridge; 17th cent. Renaissance town hall.

Mun·ford·ville \ˈmən-fərd-ˌvil\. City, ⊗ of Hart co., cen. Kentucky; pop. (1990c) 1556.

Mun·ger \ˈməŋ-gir\ *or* **Mon·ghyr** \ˈməŋ-gir\. Town, NE cen. Bihar, NE India, on right bank of the Ganges 235 mi. (378 km.) NNW of Calcutta; pop. (1991p) 150,042; cigarettes, swords, firearms; has remains of old Mogul fort.

Mun·hall \ˈmən-ˌhȯl\. Borough, Allegheny co., SW Pennsylvania, on Monongahela River 7 mi. (11 km.) E of Pittsburgh; pop. (1990c) 13,158; steel products.

Mu·ni \ˈmü-nē\. River, Equatorial Guinea; 50 mi. (81 km.) long; empties into Corisco Bay.

Mu·nich \ˈmyü-nik\ *or Ger.* **Mün·chen** \ˈmuen-kən\. City, ✻ of Bavaria, Germany, on Isar River; pop. (1992e) 1,229,052; trade, cultural, and industrial center; manufactures precision instruments, optical equipment, motor vehicles, chemicals, cigarettes; wholesale vegetable market; noted center of brewing industry. Numerous notable buildings, incl. 12th cent. Peterskirche (restored), three 14th cent. town gates, 15th cent. cathedral, 15th cent. town hall, 16th cent. Michaelkirche (Renaissance), 17th cent. palace, 19th cent. Glyptothek Museum, many 18th cent. palaces and town houses; noted university (founded at Ingolstadt 1472; transferred to Landshut, then to Munich 1826), technical university (1868).

History: Founded c. 1158 at the site of an ancient monastery; became ✻ of Bavaria under Wittelsbach family, who made their residence here from 1255; occupied by Swedes 1632 during Thirty Years' War; held by Austria 1705 and 1742–44; site of attempted revolt by German politican Adolf Hitler ("Beer Hall Putsch") Nov. 8–9, 1923 and of early activities of Nazi party; scene 1938 of four-power conference (Germany, Italy, Great Britain, France) and signing of Munich Pact leading to partition of Czechoslovakia; in WWII suffered considerable damage from Allied bombing; occupied by Allied forces ab. May 1, 1945; site of Summer Olympic Games 1972.

Municipality of Murrysville. See MURRYSVILLE.

Mu·ni·sing \ˈmyü-nə-ˌsiŋ\. City, ⊗ of Alger co., N Upper Penin. of Michigan, on Lake Superior 37 mi. (60 km.) E of Marquette; pop. (1990c) 2783.

Munkács. See MUKACHEVE.

Mun·ku–Sar·dyk \ˈmu̇ŋ-kü-ˈsär-dik\ *or* **Mönh Sa·rĭ·dag** \ˈməŋ-ˌsär-i-ˈdäg\. Highest peak in the Sayan Mts., on boundary bet. Buryatia Rep., S Russia in Asia and Mongolia, at the N end of Hövsgöl; 11,451 ft. (3490 m.).

Mu·ñoz \mü-ˈnyōs\. Municipality, Nueva Ecija prov., Luzon, Philippines, ab. 16 mi. (26 km.) N of Cabanatuan; pop. (1980c) 43,211.

Mun·roe Falls \mən-ˈrō, ˈmən-rō\. Village, Summit co., Ohio, 7 mi. (11 km.) NE of Akron; pop. (1990c) 5359.

Mun·sey Park \ˈmən-sē\. Village, Nassau co., SE New York; pop. (1990c) 2692.

Mun·ster \ˈmən-stər\. **1.** Town, Lake co., NW corner of Indiana, 10 mi. (16 km.) S of Lake Michigan; pop. (1990c) 19,949.

2. Province, S Ireland; 9315 sq. mi. (24,126 sq. km.); includes cos. Clare, Cork, Kerry, Limerick, Tipperary (North Riding and South Riding), Waterford.

3. \mēⁿs-ˈter\. Town, Haut-Rhin dept., E France; noted for the cheese to which it gives its name (Muenster cheese).

Mün·ster \ˈmuen-stər\ *also* **Münster in West·fa·len** \in-vest-ˈfä-lən\. City, North Rhine-Westphalia, Germany, near the Dortmund-Ems Canal 78 mi. (126 km.) NNE of Cologne; pop. (1992e) 264,181; railroad junction; machinery; restored 13th cent. cathedral; 14th cent. town hall; 18th cent. palace, now housing a university (founded late 18th cent., received university status 1902). Grew up in 12th cent. around a monastery or minster (Ger. *münster*); member of Hanseatic League from 13th cent.; fell to Anabaptists 1532–35; Treaty of Westphalia signed here 1648, ending Thirty Years' War; in WWII suffered heavy damage; taken by Allies Apr. 1945.

Mun·te·nia \mün-ˈtā-nē-ä\ *or* **Greater Wa·la·chia** \wə-ˈlā-kē-ə\. Region, S Romania, E part of Walachia; 20,267 sq. mi. (52,492 sq. km.); formerly a province.

Mun·tok \ˈmün-ˌtu̇k\. Seaport, NW Bangka I., Indonesia.

Muong·sing \ˈmwȯŋ-ˈsiŋ\. Town, NW Laos, SE Asia, near Chinese border just E of the Mekong River.

Muo·nio \ˈmwȯ-nē-ˌō\. River, NW Finland; flows S into Torneälven River, forming a section of the boundary bet. Finland and Sweden; ab. 200 mi. (320 km.) long.

Mu·pa National Park \ˈmü-pä\. National park, S Angola; 2548 sq. mi. (6599 sq. km.); wildlife refuge (antelope, black rhinoceros, elephant, zebra).

Muqaiyir. See UR.

Mur \ˈmür\ *or Serbo-Croat.* **Mu·ra** \ˈmü-rä\. River, S cen. Europe; rises in Austria in E end of Hohe Tauern and flows E in Salzburg, E and NE across Styria, turns S and SE forming small part of Austria-Slovenia border, running across NE Slovenia, and forming parts of Slovenia-Croatia and Croatia-Hungary borders before emptying into Drava River 25 mi. (40 km.) E of Varaždin, Croatia; 279 mi. (449 km.) long.

Mu·ran·g'a \mü-ˈräŋ-gä\; *formerly* **Fort Hall** \ˈhȯl\. Town, S cen. Kenya, on Tana River; alt. 4410 ft. (1344 m.).

Mu·ra·no \mü-ˈrä-nō\. N suburb of Venice, Italy, on five small islands in the Lagoon of Venice; noted for its medieval basilica and for the manufacture of Venetian glass since late 13th cent.

Mu·rat·dağı \mu̇-ˌrät-ˈdä-ē\. Peak, W Turkey in Asia, W of Afyon; 7583 ft. (2311 m.).

Mu·rat Neh·ri \ˈmü-rät-ˈnā-rē\ *also* **Eastern Eu·phra·tes** \yü-ˈfrā-tēz\; *anc.* **Ar·sa·ni·as** \är-ˈsā-nē-əs\. One of the two headstreams of the Euphrates River, in NE Turkey in Asia; rises in the mountains SW of Mt. Ararat and flows W to unite with the Karasu and form the Euphrates River.

Mur·chi·son \ˈmər-chə-sən\. River, W Western Australia, Australia; flows W to Indian Ocean; 440 mi. (708 km.) long.

Murchison Falls. 1. See KABALEGA FALLS.

2. Waterfall in the Shire River, Malawi, 15°54′S, 34°44′E.

Mur·cia \ˈmər-shə\. **1.** Region and ancient kingdom, SE Spain; bounded on N and NW by New Castile, on SW by Andalusia, on S by Mediterranean, and on E by Valencia; comprises modern autonomous community and prov. of Murcia; watered by the Segura and its affluents; climate varies from subtropical to temperate and its arid regions require irrigation for agricultural exploitation; produces principally citrus fruit, esparto, and olives; zinc and lead mines; fishing. See table at SPAIN.

History: Center of Carthaginian colonization in Spain; conquered by Moors in 8th cent.; came under rule of Umayyad Caliphate of Córdoba 9th–11th cents.; briefly became nominally independent late 9th to early 10th cents.; became independent Moorish kingdom in 11th cent. following overthrow of Umayyad Caliphate; came under rule of Almoravids late 11th cent., then Almohads 12th cent.; submitted to Castilian rule mid-13th cent.; Muslim uprising suppressed 1264 by Christian forces.

2. Autonomous community and province of SE Spain. See table at SPAIN.

3. Commune, ✻ of Murcia autonomous community, historical region, and province, SE Spain, on Segura River 47 mi.

(76 km.) SW of Alicante; pop. (1991p) 318,838; agricultural market; manufactures silk, textiles, flour, aluminum products, leather goods, hats; university (1915); 14th–16th cent. Gothic-Romanesque cathedral, restored 18th cent.; 18th cent. episcopal palace; Moorish granary; city walls. First settled by Romans; refounded by Moors 9th cent.; reconquered from Moors in 13th cent.; ✻ of ancient kingdom of Murcia. Birthplace of Islamic mystic, philosopher, and writer Ibn al-ʿArabī 1165.

Mur·cié·la·gos, Gulf of \mür-ˈsyā-lä-gōs\; *formerly* **Cu·le·bra Gulf** \kü-ˈlā-brä\. Inlet of Pacific Ocean on NW coast of Costa Rica.

Mur·do \ˈmər-dō\. City, ⊗ of Jones co., S cen. South Dakota; pop. (1990c) 679.

Mu·reş \ˈmü-resh\. **1.** *also* **Mu·re·şul** \ˈmü-re-ˌshül\ *or Hung.* **Ma·ros** \ˈmär-ósh\. River, Hungary and Romania; rises in the Carpathian Mts., flows W across N Romania, continues W across Hungarian border and into Tisza River opp. Szeged; ab. 450 mi. (725 km.) long; navigable for small boats for over 200 mi. (322 km.).
2. County of N cen. Romania. See table at ROMANIA.

Mur·frees·boro \ˈmər-frēz-ˌbər-ō\. **1.** City, ⊗ of Pike co., SW Arkansas; pop. (1990c) 1542.
2. Town, Hertford co., NE North Carolina, 50 mi. (81 km.) WNW of Elizabeth City; pop. (1990c) 2580; Chowan Coll. (1848).
3. Commercial city, ⊗ of Rutherford co., cen. Tennessee, on W fork of Stones River 33 mi. (53 km.) SE of Nashville; pop. (1990c) 44,922; raising horses; dairy products; Middle Tennessee State Univ. (1909). Founded and made county seat 1811, ✻ of Tennessee 1819–25; during Civil War site of battle (also called battle of Stones River, *q.v.*), Dec. 31, 1862–Jan. 2, 1863 in which Union forces under Maj. Gen. William Starke Rosecrans won a strategic victory over Confederates under Gen. Braxton Bragg.

Mur·gab \múr-ˈgäb\. **1.** *in Afghanistan* **Mor·ghāb** *or* **Mur·ghab** \múr-ˈgäb\. River, NW Afghanistan and SE Turkmenistan; rises in W slopes of the Hindu Kush and flows W and NW until lost in the sands of the Kara-Kum Desert beyond Mary; ab. 600 mi. (965 km.) long.
2. *or* **Mur·ghak** \múr-ˈgäk\. River, Tajikistan; flows W in Pamirs.

Murgh \ˈmúrg\. Pass, NE Afghanistan, N of Kabul, in the Hindu Kush; 7480 ft. (2280 m.).

Mur·ghab \múr-ˈgäb, -ˈgäp\. **1.** River, NW Afghanistan and SE Turkmenistan. See MURGAB 1.
2. Plain, ancient Persia. See PASARGADAE.

Murghak. See MURGAB 2.

Mu·riaé \ˌmúr-yá-ˈā\. City, SE Minas Gerais state, E Brazil, 75 mi. (121 km.) NE of Juiz de Fora; munic. pop. (1991p) 84,507.

Mü·ritz, Lake \ˈmue-rits\. Lake, Mecklenburg-West Pomerania, NE Germany, W of Neustrelitz; 44 sq. mi. (114 sq. km.); largest natural lake in Germany.

Mur·man Coast \múr-ˈman, -ˈmän\ *or* **Mur·mansk Coast** \múr-ˈmansk, -ˈmänsk\ *also earlier* **Nor·man Coast** \ˈnór-mən\. The N coast of Kola Penin., Murmansk Oblast, NW Russia in Europe; ab. 165 mi. (266 km.) long from 36°E to 41°E; generally ice-free because of warm easterly ocean current; has many inlets and good harbors and in many places cliffs 300 to 1000 ft. (90 to 300 m.).

Mur·mansk \múr-ˈmansk, -ˈmänsk\. City, ✻ of Murmansk Oblast, NW Russia in Europe; in NW part on Kola Bay, ab. 22 mi. (35 km.) from the ocean; pop. (1992e) 468,000; largest city in the world N of the Arctic Circle; ice-free port; naval base; shipyards, fish canneries, sawmills; base for Russia's most important fishing fleet. Founded 1915 as supply port during WWI; occupied by British, French, and American expeditionary forces during intervention against Communists 1918; in WWII a major supply base, the main port for the Anglo-American convoys.

Murmansk Oblast \ˈó-bləst, -ˌblast\ *or* **Mur·man·ska·ya Oblast'** \ˈmúr-mən-skə-yə-ˈó-bləstʸ\. Subdivision of Russia in Europe, nearly coextensive with Kola Penin.; 55,946 sq. mi. (144,900 sq. km.); pop. (1992e) 1,148,000; ✻ Murmansk. A plateau with av. elev. of 600 to 700 ft. (183 to 213 m.), highest point 3906 ft. (1191 m.); a tundra region of many lakes (largest Imandra), small rivers, morasses; chief river the Tuloma, in the NW. Among the inhabitants are a large number of Lapps; main occupation fishing; its shore controlled 1918–19 by British; since 1944 has included in the NW Petsamo (Pechenga) and surrounding territory acquired from Finland (see PECHENGA).

Mu·ro Lu·ca·no \ˈmü-rō-lü-ˈkä-nō\. Commune, Potenza prov., W Basilicata, S Italy; pop. (1981p) 7110; cathedral; castle, scene of imprisonment and death of Joan I, queen of Naples 1382.

Mu·rom \ˈmü-rəm\. Town, SE Vladimir Oblast, cen. Russia in Europe, on the Oka 90 mi. (145 km.) SW of Nizhniy Novgorod; pop. (1992e) 127,000; textiles, lumber; one of oldest Russian cities, first mentioned 862; to Moscow 1393.

Mu·ro·ran \mü-ˈrō-rän\. Seaport, SW Hokkaidō, Japan, on N side of Uchiura Bay; pop. (1990p) 117,852; ships coal, wood pulp, lumber; iron and steel center of N Japan; oil refining.

Mu·ros \ˈmü-rōs\. Commune, La Coruña prov., NW Spain, on inlet of Atlantic Ocean 49 mi. (79 km.) SW of the commune of La Coruña; pop. (1991c) 11,255.

Mu·ro·to, Cape \mü-ˈrō-tō\. Cape on SE coast of Shikoku I., Japan.

Mur·phy \ˈmər-fē\. **1.** Town, ⊗ of Owyhee co., SW corner of Idaho.
2. Town and mountain resort, ⊗ of Cherokee co., W tip of North Carolina, 5 mi. (8 km.) W of Georgia border and 16 mi. (26 km.) E of Tennessee border; pop. (1990c) 1575.

Mur·phys·boro \ˈmər-fēz-ˌbər-ō\. City, ⊗ of Jackson co., SW Illinois, 24 mi. (39 km.) W of Marion; pop. (1990c) 9176. Birthplace nearby of soldier and politician John A. Logan 1826.

Mur·ray \ˈmər-ē\. **1.** Name of counties in three states of the U.S. See tables at GEORGIA, MINNESOTA, OKLAHOMA.
2. City, ⊗ of Calloway co., SW Kentucky, 22 mi. (35 km.) ESE of Mayfield; pop. (1990c) 14,439; Murray State Univ. (1922).
3. City, Salt Lake co., N Utah, on Jordan River 8 mi. (13 km.) S of Salt Lake City; pop. (1990c) 31,282; suburb of Salt Lake City.
4. Major river of Australia. Rises near Mt. Kosciusko, E Victoria, flows NW as boundary bet. Victoria and New South Wales into SE South Australia where it turns S and flows into Encounter Bay through Lake Alexandrina (*q.v.*); 1609 mi. (2589 km.) long; to the source of the Darling (*q.v.*) 2310 mi. (3717 km.); at ab. 142°E it receives the Darling from the N and farther E at 143°13′E the Murrumbidgee. In the dry season often shallow; in the wet season navigable to Albury for smaller vessels; sandbars at its mouth prevent entrance of large vessels.

Murray, Lake. **1.** Lake extending across boundary bet. Carter and Love cos., S Oklahoma.
2. Artificial lake, NW cen. South Carolina, in Saluda River, W of Columbia.
3. Large lake in swamp and lake region bet. Fly and Strickland rivers, New Guinea I., Papua New Guinea.

Murray Bridge. Town, SE South Australia, Australia, on Murray River near its mouth 40 mi. (64 km.) WSW of Adelaide; pop. (1991c) 12,725.

Mur·rum·bidg·ee \ˌmər-əm-ˈbi-jē\. River, S New South Wales, SE Australia; flows W from Great Dividing Range near Canberra to join Murray River at ab. 143°E; 981 mi. (1578 km.) long; navigable for small vessels for ab. 500 mi. (800 km.) in rainy season.

Mur·rys·ville \ˈmər-ēz-ˌvil\ *or* **Municipality of Murrysville.** Borough, Westmoreland co., SW Pennsylvania, E of Pittsburgh; pop. (1990c) 17,240.

Mur·shid·a·bad \ˈmu̇r-shi-də-ˌbäd\. Town, West Bengal, NE India, on left bank of the Bhagirathi (old channel of the Ganges); pop. (1991p) 30,339; founded 16th cent.; made ❋ of Bengal 1704; Nabob Sirāj-ud-Dawlah fled here and was captured and executed here following his defeat at Plassey (*q.v.*) 1757; contains fine 19th cent. palace of the nabobs of Bengal.

Murten. See MORAT.

Murtensee. See MORAT, LAKE OF.

Murua. See WOODLARK.

Mu·rud \ˈmu̇r-u̇d\. Seaport town, E Maharashtra, W India, 45 mi. (72 km.) S of Bombay.

Mu·ru·roa \ˌmü-rü-ˈrō-ä\ *or* **Mo·ru·roa** \ˌmō-\. Atoll in S Tuamotu Archipelago, French Polynesia, S Pacific Ocean; French nuclear test site since 1960s.

Murviedro. See SAGUNTO.

Mur·wa·ra \mu̇r-ˈwä-rə\. Town, cen. Madhya Pradesh, India, on the Son River ab. 200 mi. (320 km.) NNE of Nagpur; pop. (1991p) 163,390.

Mürz \ˈmuε̄rts\. River, Styria, SE Austria; rises in N Styria and flows SW to the Mur at Bruck; ab. 45 mi. (72 km.) long.

Mur·zuq \mu̇r-ˈzük, mür-\ *or* **Mur·zuk** \-ˈzük\ *or* **Mar·zūq** \mär-ˈzük\ *also* **Mur·zuch** \ˈmu̇r-ˌzu̇k\. Town, Fezzan, SW Libya.

Muş *or* **Mush** \ˈmüsh\. **1.** Province of E Turkey in Asia. See table at TURKEY.
2. Town, its ❋, 45 mi. (72 km.) W of Lake Van; pop. (1990p) 42,334.

Mu·sa, Geb·el \ˈje-bəl-ˈmü-sə\ *or* **Ja·bal Mūsā** \ˈja-bəl\ *also* **Mount Si·nai** \ˈsī-ˌnī, ˈsī-nē-ˌī\. Mountain, S Sinai Penin., Egypt; 7497 ft. (2285 m.); traditionally identified with biblical Mt. Sinai. At its base, 6th cent. St. Catherine's monastery, commissioned by Justinian of Constantinople, has fine library; in it biblical scholar Konstantin von Tischendorf in 1844 found one of oldest Greek biblical manuscripts known, the *Codex Sinaiticus,* which was sold to British Museum by U.S.S.R. in 1933.

Musa, Jeb·el \ˈje-bəl-ˈmü-sə\; *anc.* **Ab·i·la** *or* **Ab·y·la** \ˈa-bə-lə\. Mountain, Ceuta, NW Africa, opp. Gibraltar; 2775 ft. (846 m.). See PILLARS OF HERCULES.

Mu·sa·la \ˌmü-sä-ˈlä\. Highest peak in the Rhodope Mts., in the Rila Mts., SW Bulgaria, SSE of Sofia; 9596 ft. (2925 m.).

Mu·san·dam, Cape \mə-ˈsan-dəm\ *or Arab.* **Ra's Ma·san·dam** \ˈräs-mə-ˈsan-dəm\. Cape, N Oman, extending N into the Strait of Hormuz, at tip of **Musandam Peninsula** which extends into NE United Arab Emirates.

Mu·sa·shi·no \mü-ˈsä-shē-ˌnō\. City, Tokyo prefecture, Honshū, Japan; pop. (1990p) 139,069; suburb of the city of Tokyo.

Muscat. See MASQAT.

Muscat and Oman. See OMAN.

Mus·ca·tine \ˌməs-kə-ˈtēn\. **1.** County in E Iowa. See table at IOWA.
2. City, its ⊗, on Mississippi River 25 mi. (40 km.) W of Davenport; pop. (1990c) 22,881; buttons, canned foods; Muscatine Community Coll. (1929); founded 1833; incorp. 1851.

Mus·cle Shoals \ˈmə-səl\. **1.** Former rapids extending ab. 37 mi. (60 km.) in Tennessee River, in Lauderdale co., N Alabama; now submerged under at least 9 ft. (3 m.) of water by completion of Wilson Dam at W end and Wheeler Dam at E end. See TENNESSEE 1.
2. City, Colbert co., NW Alabama, near Wilson Dam 3 mi. (5 km.) S of Tennessee River; pop. (1990c) 9611; developed at site of Tennessee Valley Authority construction base.

Mus·co·gee \məs-ˈkō-gē\. County in W Georgia. See table at GEORGIA.

Mus·co·net·cong \ˌməs-kə-ˈnet-ˌkäŋ\. River, N New Jersey; flows from Lake Hopatcong SW to Delaware River at SW extremity of Warren co.; 50 mi. (81 km.) long.

Mus·con·gus Bay \mə-ˈskäŋ-gəs\. Inlet of Atlantic Ocean on SW coast of Knox co., S Maine.

Muscovy. See MOSCOW 1.

Mus·grave Ranges \ˈməs-grāv\. Mountain ranges along boundary bet. South Australia and Northern Terr., Australia; highest point Mt. Woodroffe 4724 ft. (1440 m.).

Mush. See MUŞ.

Mu–shih–t'a–ko. See MUZTAGATA.

Mu·shin \ˈmü-ˌshin\. Town, Lagos state, SW Nigeria; pop. (1991e) 294,100; textiles.

Mu·sho·zu \mü-ˈshō-zü\. See IKI.

Mu·si \ˈmü-sē\. **1.** River, Andhra Pradesh, S cen. India; flows E and then S into Krishna River.
2. *or Du.* **Moe·si** \ˈmü-sē\. River, S Sumatra, Indonesia; rises in Barisan Mts. NE of Bengkulu, flows E and NE to Bangka Strait; ab. 325 mi. (523 km.) long; has many tributaries; Palembang on it 56 mi. (90 km.) from its mouth.

Mu·sic Pass \ˈmyü-zik\. Mountain pass, Huerfano and Saguache cos., S Colorado, in the Sangre de Cristo Range of the Rocky Mts.; 11,800 ft. (3597 m.); was used by travelers on Arkansas River route to California and New Mexico in late 19th cent.; trail.

Musigny. See CHAMBOLLE-MUSIGNY.

Mus·keg Bay \ˈməs-keg\. Inlet of Lake of the Woods, in NE Roseau co., N Minnesota.

Mus·ke·get Channel \mə-ˈskē-gət\. Strait bet. Martha's Vineyard on the W and Muskeget I., Tuckernuck I., and Nantucket on the E, in SE Massachusetts; connects Nantucket Sound with the Atlantic Ocean.

Muskeget Island. Island in Atlantic Ocean at E entrance of Muskeget Channel S of Cape Cod, SE Massachusetts; a part of Nantucket co.

Mus·ke·go \məs-ˈkē-gō\. City, Waukesha co., SE Wisconsin, 16 mi. (26 km.) SW of Milwaukee; pop. (1990c) 16,813.

Mus·ke·gon \mə-ˈskē-gən\. **1.** River, W cen. Michigan; rises in Houghton Lake, Roscommon co., flows SW into Lake Michigan at Muskegon, in Muskegon co.; 200 mi. (322 km.) long; navigable for a short distance.
2. County in W Michigan. See table at MICHIGAN.
3. City, its ⊗, on Lake Michigan at mouth of Muskegon River 35 mi. (56 km.) WNW of Grand Rapids; pop. (1990c) 40,283; lake port and railroad center; furniture; tourism; Muskegon Community Coll. (1926); trading post founded on site 1812; city incorp. 1869; in late 19th cent. a major lumbering and lumber-shipping center.

Muskegon Heights. City, Muskegon co., W Michigan, S suburb of the city of Muskegon; pop. (1990c) 13,176.

Mus·kin·gum \mə-ˈskiŋ-əm, -gəm\. **1.** River, E Ohio; formed by confluence of Tuscarawas and Walhonding rivers in Coshocton co., E cen. Ohio, flows S and SE into Ohio River at Marietta, Washington co.; ab. 120 mi. (195 km.) long; navigable for 90 mi. (145 km.).
2. County in SE cen. Ohio. See table at OHIO.

Mus·ko·gee \mə-ˈskō-gē\. **1.** County in E Oklahoma. See table at OKLAHOMA.
2. City, its ⊗, on Arkansas River 47 mi. (76 km.) SE of Tulsa; pop. (1990c) 37,708; steel, glass; oil wells and refineries; founded 1872; was headquarters for agency of Five Civilized Tribes; incorp. 1898.

Mus·ko·ka \mə-ˈskō-kə\. District, SE Ontario, Canada. See table at ONTARIO.

Muskoka, Lake. Lake, Muskoka dist., SE Ontario, Canada; 54 sq. mi. (140 sq. km.); with Lakes Rosseau and Joseph and several hundred small lakes forms **Muskoka Lake Region,** noted for its scenery, its hunting and fishing, and as a summer resort. Outlet is **Muskoka River,** ab. 100 mi. (160 km.) long, with two headstreams rising in lakes of Haliburton co. and Muskoka dist. and flowing SW through Lake Muskoka to Georgian Bay. Bracebridge is on it.

Mus·li·mi·ya *or* **Mus·li·mī·yah** \ˌmu̇s-lē-ˈmē-ə\. Town, NW Syria, ab. 8 mi. (13 km.) N of Aleppo; junction on railroad lines NW to Adana in Turkey and NE to Nusaybin in Turkey.

Mus·lim Min·da·nao \ˈməz-ləm-ˌmin-dä-ˈnau̇, ˈmu̇s-, ˈmu̇z-\. Autonomous region of the Philippines. See table at PHILIPPINES.

Mu·so·ma \mü-ˈsō-mä\. Town, ❋ of Mara region, N Tanzania.

Mus·sau \mü-ˈsau̇\. **1.** Island group in Bismarck Archipelago, Papua New Guinea. See SAINT MATTHIAS GROUP.

2. Island, W Pacific Ocean, N Bismarck Archipelago, in St. Matthias Group NNW of New Hanover; ab. 20 mi. (32 km.) long by 10 mi. (16 km.) wide; largest island in the group.

Mus·sel·shell \ˈmə-səl-ˌshel\. 1. River, cen. Montana; rises in Meagher co., flows E, then N into Missouri River in NW Garfield co; 300 mi. (483 km.) long.

2. County in cen. Montana. See table at MONTANA.

Mus·so·me·li \ˌmü-sō-ˈme-lē\. Commune, Caltanissetta prov., cen. Sicily, Italy, 18 mi. (29 km.) WNW of the commune of Caltanissetta; pop. (1981p) 11,261; castle ruins.

Mus·soo·rie \mə-ˈsu̇r-ē\. Hill station, N Uttar Pradesh, N India, 135 mi. (217 km.) NNE of Delhi; pop. (1991p) 29,326; summer resort; alt. ab. 6600 ft. (2010 m.).

Mus·ta·fa·ke·mal·pa·şa \ˌmu̇s-tä-ˈfä-ke-ˈmäl-pä-ˈshä\ *sometimes shortened to* **Mus·ta·fa·pa·şa** \-ˈfä-pä-ˈshä\; *formerly* **Kir·mas·ti** \ˌkir-mä-ˈstē\. Town, W Bursa prov., NW Turkey in Asia, 37 mi. (60 km.) WSW of the city of Bursa.

Mus·tagh Range \mü-ˈstäg, -ˈstä\. Former name of Karakoram Range (*q.v.*).

Mu·stang \mu̇-ˈstäŋ\; *locally* **Lo** \ˈlō\. Historical kingdom, N Nepal, in remote area bounded on N, W, and E by Tibet; largest settlement Mustang.

Mus·tang \ˈməs-ˌtaŋ\. City, Canadian co., cen. Oklahoma, surrounded by Oklahoma City; pop. (1990c) 10,434.

Mus·tang Island \ˈməs-taŋ\. Island in Nueces co., S Texas, bet. Corpus Christi Bay and the Gulf of Mexico; one of the chain of islands along the Texas coast incl. St. Joseph I. and Padre I. (*qq.v.*).

Mus·ters, Lake \ˈməs-tərz, ˈmü-ˌsterz\. Lake in S Chubut prov., S cen. Argentina, W of San Jorge Gulf.

Mu·su–dan \ˈmü-ˈsu̇-ˈdän\; *formerly* **Bu·sui·tan** \ˌbu̇-swē-ˈtän\. Cape on E coast of North Korea extending into the Sea of Japan, 40°50′N, 129°43′E.

Mu–tan. See MUDAN.

Mu–tan–chiang. See MUDANJIANG.

Mu·ta·re \mü-ˈtä-rā\; *formerly* **Um·ta·li** \u̇m-ˈtä-lē\. Town, E Zimbabwe, on Mozambique border 130 mi. (210 km.) ESE of Harare; pop. (1982c) 75,358; distribution and trade center for mining and agricultural area; gold found in area; soil particularly adapted to tobacco.

Mutina. See MODENA 2.

Mu·tsu Bay \ˈmüt-sü\. Large bay in Aomori prefecture, N extremity of Honshū, Japan.

Mut·tenz \ˈmu̇-tents\. Commune, N Switzerland, SE of Basel; pop. (1980c) 16,911; castle ruins; medieval church.

Mut·ton·town \ˈmət-ᵊn-ˌtau̇n\. Village, Nassau co., Long Island, SE New York; pop. (1990c) 3024.

Muttra. See MATHURA.

Mu-tzu-t'a-ko. See MUZTAG.

Mu Us \ˈmü-ˈu̇s\ *or W.-G.* **Mao–wu–su** \ˈmau̇-ˈü-ˈsü\ *or* **Or·dos** \ˈȯr-dəs\. Desert region, N China, S of the Huang in Nei Monggol (Inner Mongolia) and Shaanxi; highest point ab. 5950 ft. (1815 m.).

Mu·yun Kum \ˈmü-yu̇n-ˈku̇m\ *also* **Mo·yun Kum** \ˈmō-\ *or* **Moin·kum** \ˈmoin-ˌku̇m\. Sandy desert region, S Kazakhstan, N of the Syr Dar'ya River.

Mu·zaf·fa·ra·bad \mu̇-ˌzə-fər-ə-ˈbäd\. Town, ✻ of section of Jammu and Kashmir controlled by Pakistan, ab. 50 mi. (80 km.) NNE of Islamabad. See JAMMU AND KASHMIR.

Mu·zaf·far·na·gar \mu̇-ˈzə-fər-ˌnə-gər\. Town, NW Uttar Pradesh, N India, 63 mi. (101 km.) NNE of Delhi; pop. (1991p) 240,057; trades in wheat and sugar; founded 17th cent.

Mu·zaf·far·pur \mə-ˈzä-fər-ˌpu̇r\. Town, NW Bihar, NE India, 35 mi. (56 km.) N of Patna; pop. (1991p) 240,450; university (1952).

Mu·zon, Cape \ˈmü-ˌzän\. S point of Dall I. on Dixon Entrance, SE Alaska.

Muz·tag \ˌmüz-ˈtäg, mü-ˈstäg\ *or W.-G.* **Mu-tzu-t'a-ko** \ˈmü-ˈdzü-ˈtä-ˈkō\ *also* **Ulugh Muz·tagh** \ˈü-ˌlu̇g-müz-ˈtäg, -mü-ˈstäg\. Mountain peak, W China, on border bet. S Xinjiang Uygur and N Tibet, 36°25′N, 87°25′E; 25,338 ft. (7723 m.); highest in Kunlun Shan.

Muz·tag·ata \mu̇z-ˌtäg-ä-ˈtä\; *mostly formerly* **Muz·tagh Ata** \mu̇z-ˈtäg-ä-ˈtä, mu̇z-ˈtä\ *or W.-G.* **Mu–shih–t'a–ko** \ˈmu̇-ˈshə-ˈtä-ˈkō\. Mountain, W Xinjiang Uygur, W China, near border of Tajikistan, and ab. 75 mi. (121 km.) SW of Kashi; 24,757 ft. (7546 m.).

Muz·tagh Tow·er \müs-ˈtäg, -ˈtä\. Mountain in the Karakoram Range, in region of Jammu and Kashmir controlled by Pakistan; 23,882 ft. (7279 m.).

Mwali. See MOHÉLI.

Mwan·za \ˈmwän-zä\. 1. Administrative region of N Tanzania. See table at TANZANIA.

2. Town, its ✻, on S shore of Lake Victoria; lake port and railroad terminus.

Mweelrea. See MUILREA.

Mwe·ru, Lake \ˈmwā-rü\ *or* **Lac Moe·ro** \ˌlȧk-mwā-ˈrō\. Lake, cen. Africa, on boundary bet. SE Zaire and Zambia, W of S tip of Lake Tanganyika; 76 mi. (122 km.) long; 1770 sq. mi. (4584 sq. km.); max. depth 84 ft. (26 m.); the Luapula, a headstream of the Congo River, flows through it.

Mya, Wa·di \ˈwä-dē-ˈmyȧ\. Dry river course in NE cen. Algeria, S of Chott Melrhir.

Myan·mar \ˈmyän-ˌmär\ *or* **Bur·ma** \ˈbər-mə\. Republic, SE Asia, bounded on N by India and China, on E by China, Laos, and Thailand, on S by Thailand and the Andaman Sea, and on W by the Bay of Bengal, Bangladesh, and India; extends from lat. 10° to ab. 28°30′N and long. 92° to 101°E, constituting NW section of Indochina Penin.; total area 261,789 sq. mi. (678,034 sq. km.); pop. (1994e) 45,573,000; ✻ Yangon (Rangoon). Often divided into **Lower Burma** (the coastal region—Arakan, Irrawaddy, Pegu, and Tenasserim divisions) and **Upper Burma** (the N or inland part—Magwe, Mandalay, and Sagaing divisions). An agricultural country. Inhabitants chiefly Burman groups; others include Shan and Karen peoples.

Physical features: Mountainous along border with India and Bangladesh in N part, and in Shan State; other important ranges are the Arakan Yoma, Pegu Yoma, and Dawna and Bilauktaung ranges. Basin of the Irrawaddy, with its tributaries Chindwin, Shweli, Myitnge, occupies most of country; Salween and Sittang are the main streams of E part. Long coastline and numerous islands provide several good harbors.

Chief products: Rice, pulses, beans, peanuts, corn, sugarcane; oil, silver, lead, zinc; timber; textiles.

Political divisions: Divided into seven administrative divisions and seven states (for pronunciation of the names, see their individual entries):

NAME	AREA (sq. mi.)	AREA (sq. km.)	CAPITAL
Divisions			
Irrawaddy	13,567	35,138	Bassein
Magwe	17,305	44,820	Magwe
Mandalay	14,295	37,024	Mandalay
Pegu	15,214	39,404	Pegu
Sagaing	36,535	94,626	Sagaing
Tenasserim	16,735	43,344	Tavoy
Yangon	3,927	10,171	Yangon
States			
Chin	13,907	36,019	Haka
Kachin	34,379	89,042	Myitkyina
Karen	11,731	30,383	Pa-an
Kayah	4,530	11,733	Loikaw
Mon	4,748	12,297	Moulmein
Rakhine	14,200	36,778	Sittwe
Shan	60,155	155,801	Taunggyi

History: Area long inhabited and after first cent. A.D., Mon and Pyu states dominant; first united in 11th cent. under a Burmese dynasty led by King Anawrahta at Pagan which was overthrown by Mongols in 13th cent.; Toungoo dynasty arose assisted by Portuguese who first traded there 16th cent.; short-lived Dutch and English factories were founded in 17th cent.; modern Burmese state founded in 18th cent. by King Alaungpaya and his successors who conquered Arakan, Tenasserim coast, Manipur, Assam, and eventually came into

conflict with the English East India Company; fought three wars with British: First (1824), Second (1852), and Third (1885); as result of First Burmese War, by Treaty of Yandabu (*q.v.*) British acquired Assam, Arakan, Tenasserim, and Pegu; after Second Burmese War, Rangoon (see YANGON) retained by British and Lower Burma formed 1862; as result of Third Burmese War, Upper Burma formed 1886, incl. Mandalay (*q.v.*), a kingdom founded by native dynasty in 19th cent.; subsequently became a province of British India; separated from India and made crown colony in 1937. In WWII overcome by Japanese 1942; retaken by Allies 1945; granted independence by pact signed with Great Britain, effective Jan. 4, 1948; settled border disputes with China 1960; civilian government overthrown 1962; during 1980s civilian unrest led to rioting which was brutally put down by military; military government installed 1988; name changed to Union of Myanmar 1989.

Myaung·mya \ˈmyau̇ŋ-ˈmyä\. Town, SW Myanmar, in Irrawaddy Delta, 22 mi. (35 km.) SE of Vasi.

Myc·a·le \ˈmi-kə-lē\. Ancient name of promontory in the S of Ionia (NW Caria) on the coast of Asia Minor; a religious center with temple to Poseidon on N shore. Battle fought 479 B.C. on the shore of this promontory was a contest for the Persian ships and was a Greek victory.

My·ce·nae \mī-ˈsē-nē\. Ruined city, NE Peloponnese, Greece, ab. 7 mi. (11 km.) N of Árgos. One of the most ancient cities of Greece; a natural rock citadel on N edge of Argive plain.

History: Flourished during Bronze Age; on basis of Minoan or Cretan culture (see CRETE), built a distinctive art and civilization known as Mycenaean (more accurately Late Helladic c. 1600–1100 B.C., corresponding to Late Minoan); at height of its supremacy in Aegean area c. 1400 B.C.; declined c. 1100 B.C. before invasion of Greeks (Dorians) from north, but sporadically inhabited until Roman times; scene of German archaeologist Heinrich Schliemann's great discoveries c. 1876, incl. "Treasury of Atreus," which revealed existence of Bronze Age civilization in Aegean; ruins include famous Lion Gate, acropolis, palace, granary, and several royal beehive tombs and shaft grave tombs. Legendary ✱ of King Agamemnon.

My·ers·town \ˈmī-ərz-ˌtau̇n\. Borough, Lebanon co., SE cen. Pennsylvania, 22 mi. (35 km.) W of Reading; pop. (1990c) 3236.

Myin·gyan \ˈmyin-ˈjän\. Town, cen. Myanmar, on the left bank of the Irrawaddy River at its confluence with the Chindwin 60 mi. (97 km.) WSW of Mandalay; pop. (1983c) 77,060; river port.

Myit·kyi·na \ˌmyit-chē-ˈnä\. Town, ✱ of Kachin state, N Myanmar, on left bank of upper Irrawaddy near Chinese border 260 mi. (418 km.) NNE of Mandalay; pop. (1983c) 56,427; most important town in N Myanmar N of Bhamo with which it is connected by the upper defile of the Irrawaddy; on the Stilwell Road; terminus of railroad from Yangon; ships teak. Captured in WWII by the Japanese 1942 and used as air base until retaken by Allied forces Aug. 1944.

Myit·nge \ˈmyit-gā\. River, NE Myanmar; flows SW and W to the Irrawaddy River just S of Mandalay; ab. 250 mi. (400 km.) long.

My·ko·la·yiv \ˌmē-kə-ˈlä-yif\ *or* **Ni·ko·la·yev** \ˌnē-kə-ˈlä-yif\. **1.** Administrative subdivision, of Ukraine; 9537 sq. mi. (24,701 sq. km.); pop. (1991e) 1,342,400; ✱ Mykolayiv; borders on Black Sea and contains lower course of Bug River. **2.** *also* **Ver·no·le·ninsk** \ˌvər-nə-ˈlye-ninsk\. City and seaport, its ✱, at confluence of Bug and Ingul rivers 70 mi. (113 km.) NE of Odessa. Founded ab. 1789; captured by Germans Aug. 1941 and naval base destroyed; retaken by U.S.S.R. Mar. 13, 1944.

Myk·o·nos \ˈmi-kə-ˌnäs, -nəs\ *also* **Mi·ko·nos** *or* **Mí·ko·nos** \ˈmē-kə-ˌnōs\ *or Gk.* **Mý·ko·nos** \ˈmē-kō-ˌnōs\. Island, NE Cyclades, Aegean Sea, in Cyclades dept., Greece, SE of Tínos; 35 sq. mi. (91 sq. km.); chief village Mykonos; island of Delos is off its SW coast.

Mylae. See MILAZZO.

Mylasa. See MILÂS.

Myl·liem \mil-ˈlēm\. See KHASI STATES.

My·men·singh *also* **Mai·man·singh** \ˌmī-mən-ˈsiŋ\; *formerly* **Na·sir·a·bad** \nə-ˈsir-ə-ˌbäd\. City, N cen. Bangladesh; pop. (1991p) 198,662; agricultural college.

My·nydd·is·lw·yn \mə-ˌnith-ˈis-lə-wən\. Locality, Gwent co., SE Wales, 28 mi. (45 km.) WNW of Bristol, England; pop. (1981p) 15,547.

My·nydd Ta·rw \mə-ˈnith-ˈtär-ü\. Peak in the Berwyn Mts., N Wales; 2230 ft. (680 m.).

Mynyw. See SAINT DAVID'S.

My·ra \ˈmī-rə\. One of the chief cities of ancient Lycia, S Asia Minor, on the coast; earliest ruins date to c. 5th cent. B.C.; later came under Roman control; as a prisoner, St. Paul changed ships here on his way to Rome; St. Nicholas was bishop of city 4th cent. A.D.; declined following Arab raids, which began in 7th cent.; ancient ruins include an acropolis, a theater, and several rock tombs hewn to resemble houses.

Mýr·dals·jö·kull \ˈmēr-ˌdäl-ˌsyœ̄-ˌkœd-ᵊl\. Glacier in S Iceland.

My·ri·na \mə-ˈrī-nə\. Ancient town of Aeolis, NW Asia Minor, on the coast; necropolis excavations here have uncovered many small terra-cotta figures.

Myr·tle Beach \ˈmərt-ᵊl\. City, Horry co., E South Carolina, on Atlantic Ocean 13 mi. (21 km.) SE of Conway; pop. (1990c) 24,848; seaside resort with fishing and golf.

Myrtle Creek. City, Douglas co., SW Oregon, 67 mi. (108 km.) S of Eugene; pop. (1990c) 3063.

Myrtle Point. City, Coos co., SW Oregon, 41 mi. (66 km.) SW of Roseburg; pop. (1990c) 2712.

Mys Chelyuskin. See CHELYUSKIN, CAPE.

Mys Dezhneva. See DEZHNEVA, MYS.

My·sia \ˈmi-shē-ə\. Ancient country in NW Asia Minor; bounded on N by Propontis, on E by Bithynia and Phrygia (E boundary varied with the fortunes of the kingdoms on that side), on S by Lydia, and on W by the Aegean; included regions of the Troad in the NW and Aeolis along SW coast; chief cities Pergamum and Cyzicus. Ruled in turn by Lydia, Persia, Macedon, Syria, and Pergamum (*q.v.*); became part of Roman prov. of Asia 129 B.C.

Mys·ki \ˈmis-kē\. Town, Kemerovo Oblast, S Russia in Asia, ab. 30 mi. (48 km.) E of Novokuznetsk.

Mys·ło·wi·ce \ˌmēs-wȯ-ˈvēt-se\ *or Ger.* **Mys·lo·witz** \ˈmœs-lō-ˌvits\. Industrial commune, Katowice prov., S Poland, 8 mi. (13 km.) ESE of the city of Katowice; pop. (1989e) 92,475;passed from Germany to Poland following WWI.

Mys Olyutorskiye. See OLYUTORSKIY, MYS.

My·sore \mī-ˈsōr\ *or* **Mai·sur** \mī-ˈsu̇r\. **1.** State, S India. See KARNATAKA.
2. City, S Karnataka, S India, S of Kāveri River 85 mi. (137 km.) SW of Bangalore; pop. (1991c) 606,755; important industrial city, producing textiles, rice, sandalwood oil, chemicals, leather goods, coffee, and cigarettes; numerous notable buildings, incl. former maharaja's palace; university (1916). Site occupied before 3d cent. B.C.; one of the capitals of Muslim state which emerged late 16th cent.; occupied by British 1831.

Mys Tarkhankut. See TARKHANKUT, CAPE.

Mys·tic \ˈmis-tik\. **1.** Short river rising in **Mystic Lakes** (two connected lakes), Middlesex co., NE Massachusetts; flows SE into Boston Harbor N of Charlestown; navigable as far as Medford.
2. Subdivision of town of Stonington, Connecticut, at mouth of Mystic River (short stream flowing S to Long Island Sound); pop. (1990c) 2618; restored 19th cent. seaport; aquarium. See STONINGTON.

Mys Yelizavety. See YELIZAVETY, MYS.

Mysz·kow \ˈmēsh-küf\. Commune, Częstochowa prov., S Poland, on Warta River; pop. (1989e) 33,107.

My·then \ˈmēt-ᵊn\. Twin peaks, Schwyz canton, E cen. Switzerland, near the commune of Schwyz; **Gros·se My·the** \ˈgrō-sə-ˈmē-tə\, 6229 ft. (1898 m.), and **Klei·ne Mythe** \ˈklī-nə\, 5955 ft. (1815 m.).

My Tho \ˈmē-ˈtō\. Town, S Vietnam, in the Mekong Delta 45 mi. (72 km.) SSW of Ho Chi Minh City; terminus of railroad from Ho Chi Minh City; former French port.

Myt·i·le·ne *also* **Mi·ty·le·ne** \ˌmit-ᵊl-ˈē-nē\ *or Gk.* **Mi·ti·lí·ni** \ˌmē-tē-ˈlē-nē\. **1.** Island. See LESBOS.
2. *formerly* **Ka·stro** \ˈkäs-trō\. City, ✻ of Lesbos dept., Aegean Is., Greece; pop. (1991p) 25,440; two harbors; chief town on Lesbos I.; remains of 14th cent. castle, ancient theater, and acropolis; a town of ancient origins and importance.

My·tish·chi \mə̇-ˈtish-chē\. Town, Moscow Oblast, W cen. Russia in Europe, ab. 10 mi. (16 km.) NNE of the city of Moscow; pop. (1992e) 154,000; textiles, transportation equipment.

Mýto Vysoké. See VYSOKÉ MÝTO.

My·us \ˈmī-əs\. Ancient city near the mouth of the Maeander (Menderes) and just ENE of Miletus, Asia Minor. One of the 12 Ionian Cities; declined due to silting of harbor, and eventually abandoned.

Mzi·mku·lu *or* **Umzi·mku·lu** \əm-zēm-ˈkü-lü\. River, S KwaZulu-Natal prov., E Rep. of South Africa; flows SE into Indian Ocean at Port Shepstone; ab. 125 mi. (200 km.) long.

Mzi·mvu·bu *or* **Umzi·mvu·bu** \əm-zēm-ˈvü-bü\. River, E Eastern Cape prov., S Rep. of South Africa; flows SE through Transkei and into Indian Ocean at Port St. Johns; ab. 300 mi. (485 km.) long.

Mzu·zu \əm-ˈzü-ˌzü\. Town, N Malawi; pop. (1987c) 44,217.

\ə\ **abut** \ə̇\ matches \ᵊ\ kitten, Fr table \ər\ **further** \a\ **ash** \ā\ **ace** \ä\ cot, cart \à\ Fr bac \au̇\ **out** \b̶\ Span Avila \ch\ **chin** \e\ **bet** \ē\ **easy** \g\ **go** \i\ **hit** \ī\ **ice** \j\ **job** \k̲\ Ger **ich**, **Buch** \ⁿ\ Fr vin \ŋ\ **sing** \ō\ **go** \ȯ\ **all** \ȯ\ **law** \œ\ Fr bœuf \œ̄\ Fr feu \ȯi\ **boy** \th\ **thin** \t̲h̲\ **this** \ü\ **loot** \u̇\ **foot** \ue\ Ger füllen \ue̅\ Fr rue \y\ **yet** \ʸ\ Fr digne \ˈdēnʸ\, nuit \ˈnwʸē\ \yü\ **few** \yu̇\ **fury** \zh\ **vision**

N

Naab *or* **Nab** \'näp\. River, E Bavaria, Germany; rises in the Fichtelgebirge and flows S to join the Danube above Regensburg; 90 mi. (145 km.) long.

Naald·wijk \'nält-,vīk, -,vāk\. Commune, South Holland prov., SW Netherlands, near mouth of the Meuse 9 mi. (15 km.) SSW of The Hague; pop. (1981e) 25,875.

Na·a·le·hu \,nä-ä-'lā-hü\. Village, Hawaii co., Hawaii, on S coast of Hawaii I. NE of Ka Lae; pop. (1990c) 1027.

Naar·den \'när-də\. Commune, North Holland prov., W Netherlands, ab. 12 mi. (19 km.) ESE of Amsterdam on S shore of Zuider Zee; pop. (1981e) 16,419.

Naas \'nās\. Town, ⊗ of co. Kildare, E Ireland; pop. (1991p) 11,140; notable foxhunting center; once seat of kings of Leinster.

Nab. See NAAB.

Na·bad·wip. See NAVADWIP.

Naband. See NĀY BAND.

Nabaṭīyah at Taḥtā, An. See AN NABAṬĪYAH AT TAḤTĀ.

Nab·be·ru, Lake \,na-bə-'rü\. Intermittent lake on W edge of Gibson Desert, along Canning Stock Route, cen. Western Australia, Australia.

Na·be·rezh·nye Chel·ny *or* **Na·be·rezh·ny·ye Chel·ny** \nə-bir-'yezh-ni-yə-chil-'nē\; *1982–88* **Brezh·nev** \'bryezh-nif\; *before 1930* **Chel·ny.** City, Tatarstan (republic), E Russia in Europe, on Kama River; pop. (1992e) 514,000.

Na·bes·na Glacier \nə-'bez-nə\. Glacier in the Wrangell Mts., S Alaska; 54 mi. (87 km.) long, ab. 2 mi. (3 km.) wide near its terminus.

Na·beul \na-'bœl\ *or Arab.* **Nā·bul** \'nä-bu̇l\; *anc.* **Ne·ap·o·lis** \nē-'a-pə-lis\. Coastal town, NE Tunisia, at S end of base of Cape Bon Penin.; pop. (1989e) 48,070; ancient Phoenician town destroyed by Romans 2d cent. B.C., later rebuilt as Roman colony.

Na·bha \'nä-bə\. **1.** Former Indian state, now part of Punjab state, NW India; 947 sq. mi. (2453 sq. km.); one of the Sikh states of the Phulkian group; established its independence 1763.
2. Town, its ✻, 37 mi. (60 km.) W of Ambala; pop. (1991p) 54,079.

Nablus. See NĀBULUS.

Nabrissa. See LEBRIJA.

Na·bua \'nä-bwä\. Municipality, Camarines Sur prov., Luzon, Philippines, 5 mi. (8 km.) W of Iriga; pop. (1980c) 53,295.

Nabūl. See NABEUL.

Nāb·u·lus \'nä-bu̇-lu̇s\; *or* **Nab·lus** \'na-bləs, 'nä-\; *anc.* **She·chem** \'shē-kəm, -,kem\; *later* **Ne·ap·o·lis** \nē-'a-pə-lis\. Town, W Jordan, 30 mi. (48 km.) N of Jerusalem in a valley bet. Mts. Ebal and Gerizim; pop. (1987e) 106,944. Long thought to be ancient Shechem which actually was close by in hill country of Ephraim; important in early biblical period; home of Hebrew patriarch Jacob; site of Jacob's well and tomb of his son Joseph; scene of King Jeroboam's rebellion and, as chief city of Samaria, became his ✻ of Israel 10th cent. B.C.; fell into decay following Assyrian conquest of Israel 8th cent. B.C.; refounded near the site of earlier town and renamed Neapolis by Roman Emperor Vespasian first cent. A.D.; occupied by Christians and suffered damage in Crusades 11th–12th cents.; included in British mandate of Palestine 1923–48; taken by Arabs 1949 in Arab-Israeli War and passed to Jordan; part of territory occupied by Israel in 1967; Israeli troops withdrawn late 1995.

Na·ca·o·me \,nä-kä-'ō-mā\. Town, ✻ of Valle dept., S Honduras, 22 mi. (35 km.) NNE of Amapala; pop. (1988p) 9785.

Nacham. See NA SAM.

Nach·es \'na-,chēz\. River, S cen. Washington; flows SE through N Yakima co. into Yakima River at Yakima; ab. 60 mi. (100 km.) long.

Na·chi \'nä-chē\. Waterfall, S Honshū, Japan, SE of Ōsaka; at 427 ft. (130 m.), highest in Japan.

Ná·chod \'nä-,ku̇t\. Town, N Czech Republic, on Polish border ab. 75 mi. (120 km.) NE of Prague; pop. (1980p) 19,892; battlefield June 1866 where Prussians defeated Austrians in Austro-Prussian War.

Na·ci·mien·to Peak \,nä-si-'myen-tō\. Mountain, S Rio Arriba co., N New Mexico; ab. 10,045 ft. (3060 m.).

Nac·ka \'nä-kə\. Town, Sweden, suburb of Stockholm; pop. (1993e) 66,098.

Nac·og·do·ches \,na-kə-'dō-chəz\. **1.** County in E Texas. See table at TEXAS.
2. City, its ⊗; pop. (1990c) 30,872; Stephen F. Austin State Univ. (1923); developed from Spanish mission estab. 1716; scene of rebellions 1826 and 1832 against Mexican authority, quickly suppressed; active in Texas Revolution 1836.

Nadezhdinsk. See SEROV.

Nadi. See NANDI.

Na·dia \'nə-dē-ə\. **1.** Former district, Bengal, NE India; 2879 sq. mi. (7457 sq. km.); ✻ Krishnanagar; divided 1947 bet. West Bengal, India, and East Pakistan (now Bangladesh).
2. Town, West Bengal, India. See NAVADWIP.

Na·di·ad \,nə-dē-'äd\. Town, N Gujarat state, India, on tributary of Sabarmati River 30 mi. (48 km.) SE of Ahmadabad; pop. (1991p) 166,852.

Na·dor \nə-'dȯr\. Town, N Morocco, on coast ab. 10 mi. (16 km.) S of Melilla; pop. (1982c) 62,040; center of sheep-herding region.

Nad·vir·na \näd-'vir-nə\ *or* **Nad·vor·na·ya** \nad-'vȯr-nə-yə\ *or Pol.* **Nad·wór·na** \näd-'vu̇r-nä\. Commune, S cen. Ivano-Frankivs'k subdivision, Ukraine; scene of battles 1915 bet. Austrians and Russians in WWI.

Nad·zab \'näd-,zäb\. Village, New Guinea I., Papua New Guinea, 19 mi. (31 km.) NW of Lae; Japanese airport in WWII seized by American paratroopers Sept. 1943.

Næst·ved \'nest-,veth\. City, Storstrøm prov., SE Sjælland, Denmark; pop. (1989e) 45,182; railroad center.

Nafa. See NAHA.

Na·fa·da \nä-'fä-dä\. Town, NE Nigeria, NE of Bauchi.

Nä·fels \'nef-ᵊls\. Village, Glarus canton, Switzerland; pop. (1980c) 3766; scene of battle 1388 in which Swiss Confederation defeated Austrians.

Nafplio. See NAUPLIA.

Naft–e–Shāh \,näf-tē-'shä\. Oil field, W Iran, at border W of Kermānshāh; adjoins Naft Khaneh oil field of E Iraq.

Naft Kha·neh \,näft-kä-'nā\. Oil field, E Iraq, on Iranian border NE of Baghdad.

Nafud *or* **Nafūd, An.** See AN NAFŪD.

Na·ga \'nä-gä\. **1.** Municipality, Cebu prov., on E coast of Cebu I., Philippines; pop. (1980c) 45,831; coastal trade.
2. *formerly* **Nue·va Ca·ce·res** \'nwā-vä-'kä-sā-rās\. Chartered city, Camarines Sur, Luzon, Philippines, on Bicol River ab. 5 mi. (8 km.) S of San Miguel Bay; pop. (1990p) 115,000; university (1954); visited and settled by Spaniards 16th cent.; Spanish town of Nueva Caceres founded on its site.

Na·ga Hills \'nä-gə, nə-'gä\. Hill region, India and Myanmar, incl. Naga and Patkai hills; part of N Arakan Yoma system. See BARAIL RANGE. Highest point 9890 ft. (3015 m.). Primarily inhabited by Nagas; subdued by British 19th cent.

Na·ga·land \'nä-gə-,land\. State, NE India; ✻ Kohima; rice; became a state 1963. See table at INDIA.

Na·ga·no \'nä-gä-,nō, nä-'gä-\. **1.** Prefecture, Honshū, Japan; ✻ Nagano; sericulture; hydroelectric power. See table at JAPAN.
2. City, its ✻, ab. 100 mi. (160 km.) NW of Tokyo; pop. (1992e) 350,673; commercial center; silk; has Buddhist temple founded in 7th cent. A.D. and developed as major shrine; site of Winter Olympic Games 1998.

Na·ga·o·ka \ˌnä-gä-ˈō-kä, nä-ˈgä-ō-ˌkä\. City, Niigata prefecture, NW Honshū, Japan, 35 mi. (56 km.) S of the city of Niigata; pop. (1990p) 185,938; chemicals; important in feudal times; declined on downfall of the Tokugawa family 19th cent.; later regained prosperity with discovery of oil fields in vicinity.
Na·gao·ka·kyo \nä-ˈgä-ō-ˌkä-kyō\. City, Kyōto prefecture, Honshū, Japan; pop. (1990p) 77,193.
Nagaon. See NOWGONG.
Na·ga·pat·ti·nam \ˌna-gə-ˈpə-tə-nəm\ *or* **Ne·ga·pa·tam** \ˌne-gə-ˈpə-təm\ *or* **Ne·ga·pat·ti·nam** \ˌne-gə-ˈpə-tə-nəm\. Seaport town, SE Tamil Nadu, S India, on Coromandel Coast 160 mi. (257 km.) S of Madras; pop. (1991p) 86,155. Forms joint municipality with **Na·gore** \nə-ˈgȯr\, a port ab. 5 mi. (8 km.) N. Site of Portuguese colony 16th–17th cents.; occupied by Dutch 1660–1781, then by British.
Na·ga·ra \nä-ˈgä-rä\. Tributary of the Kiso River in SW cen. Honshū, Japan; flows past Gifu.
Nagara. For towns in Thailand having Nagara as first element, see those beginning NAKHON.
Na·ga·re·ya·ma \ˌnä-gä-ˈrā-yä-mä\. City, Chiba prefecture, SE Honshū, Japan; pop. (1990p) 140,059.
Na·ga·sa·ki \ˌnä-gä-ˈsä-kē, ˌna-gə-ˈsa-kē\. **1.** Prefecture, Kyūshū, Japan; ✻ Nagasaki; coal mining, fishing. See table at JAPAN.
2. Seaport and commercial city, its ✻, at head of inlet ab. 3 mi. (5 km.) long; pop. (1992e) 442,373; major economic activity is shipbuilding; fishing port.
History: Unimportant before arrival of first Portuguese ships mid-16th cent.; thereafter principal center of contact with foreigners and of Japanese Christianity; made an imperial city by Japanese warrior and statesman Toyotomi Hideyoshi 1587; a port of call for Spanish, Dutch, and Portuguese ships; after measures taken to exclude foreigners from contact with Japan, was only port in Japan kept open to foreign (Dutch and Chinese) trade 1639–1859 (see DESHIMA); fully reopened to foreign trade 1859; important into 20th cent. as industrial center and coaling station but later declined; in WWII inner city destroyed by atomic bomb Aug. 9, 1945, with ab. 40,000 persons killed; rebuilt since 1945.
Na·ga·to \nä-ˈgä-tō\. Old province at SW tip of Honshū, Japan, now part of Yamaguchi prefecture.
Nagb Al–Halfāyah. See HALFAYA PASS.
Nag·car·lan \ˌnäg-kär-ˈlän\. Municipality, SE cen. Laguna prov., Luzon, Philippines, 45 mi. (72 km.) SE of Manila; pop. (1980c) 30,637.
Na·ger·coil \ˈnä-gər-ˌkȯil\. City, S Tamil Nadu, India, 10 mi. (16 km.) N of Cape Comorin, extreme S tip of India; pop. (1991p) 189,482.
Na·gi·na \ˈnä-gi-nə\. Town, Uttar Pradesh, N India, on tributary of Ramganga River 95 mi. (153 km.) NE of Delhi; pop. (1991p) 58,494.
Na·god \nə-ˈgōd\. **1.** Former Indian state, now part of Madhya Pradesh state, cen. India; 532 sq. mi. (1378 sq. km.). **2.** Town, its ✻, 100 mi. (161 km.) SW of Allahabad.
Nagore. See NAGAPATTINAM.
Na·gor·no–Ka·ra·bakh \nə-ˈgȯr-nə-ˈkär-ə-ˌbäk\ *also Eng.* **Karabakh Mountain Area.** Republic, comprising a subdivision within Azerbaijan; 1699 sq. mi. (4400 sq. km.); pop. (1991e) 193,300; ✻ Xankändı: chief nationalities Armenian and Turkic; a mountainous forested area, well watered by short tributaries of the Kura; wheat, corn; livestock; annexed from Persia by Russia early 19th cent.; ethnic demonstrations 1988; before 1991 comprised an autonomous oblast of the the U.S.S.R.
Na·go·ya \nä-ˈgȯi-ä\. City, ✻ of Aichi prefecture, S Honshū, Japan, ab. 75 mi. (120 km.) E of Kyōto at head of Ise Bay; pop. (1990p) 2,154,664; industrial center, producing textiles, watches, bicycles, sewing machines, machine tools, chemicals, and ceramics; university; technical institute; 17th cent. castle, destroyed in WWII, rebuilt 1959; Buddhist temple; important Shinto shrine, first founded 3d cent. Modern town estab. with construction of castle 1612; port facilities opened 1907; heavily bombed in WWII.
Nag·pur \ˈnäg-ˌpu̇r\. City, Maharashtra, cen. India, 265 mi. (426 km.) N of Hyderabad; pop. (1991c) 1,624,752; textiles, iron goods, pharmaceuticals; oranges. Founded 18th cent. by Gond prince; passed to Marathas after 1743; to British 1853.
Na·gua \ˈnä-gwä\. Town, ✻ of María Trinidad Sánchez prov., Dominican Republic; pop. (1981p) 57,998.
Na·gua·bo \nä-ˈgwä-bō\. Municipality, E Puerto Rico near coast NE of Humacao; pop. (1990c) 22,620.
Na·gui·li·an \ˌnä-gē-ˈlē-än\. Municipality, La Union prov., Luzon, Philippines, 9 mi. (14 km.) SE of San Fernando; pop. (1980c) 29,304.
Nagybánya. See BAIA MARE.
Nagybecskerek. See ZRENJANIN.
Nagyenyed. See AIUD.
Nagy·ka·ni·zsa \ˈnöj-ˌkö-nē-ˌzhö\. City, SW Hungary, ab. 65 mi. (105 km.) WNW of Pécs; pop. (1991e) 55,400; grain, livestock; held by Turks in 17th cent.
Nagykároly. See CAREI.
Nagy·kö·rös \ˈnöj-ˌkœr-ˌœsh\. City, cen. Hungary, 47 mi. (76 km.) SE of Budapest; pop. (1991e) 26,200; market center in grape-growing section.
Nagymihály. See MICHALOVCE.
Nagyszalonta. See SALONTA.
Nagyszentmiklós. See SÎNNICOLAU MARE.
Nagyszombat. See TRNAVA.
Nagyvárad. See ORADEA.
Na·ha \ˈnä-hä\ *or* **Na·wa** \ˈnä-wä\ *also* **Na·fa** \ˈnä-fä\. Seaport, ✻ of Okinawa prefecture, Ryukyu Is., Japan, on W coast of S Okinawa I.; pop. (1990p) 304,896; commercial center of the Ryukyu Is.; university; nearby castle ruins; largely destroyed in WWII, taken by U.S. forces June 1945 after long battle.
Na·han \ˈnä-hən\. **1.** Former state, India. See SIRMUR.
2. Town, Himachal Pradesh, N India, 35 mi. (56 km.) ENE of Ambala; pop. (1991p) 21,867; ✻ of former Sirmur state.
Nahanni, South. See SOUTH NAHANNI.
Na·han·ni National Park \nä-ˈhä-nē\. See CANADA, *National Parks.*
Na·hant \nə-ˈhänt, -ˈhant\. Town, Essex co., NE corner of Massachusetts, 9 mi. (14 km.) ENE of Boston on a long narrow peninsula extending S from Lynn into Massachusetts Bay; pop. (1990c) 3828.
Nahant Bay. Inlet of Massachusetts Bay on S shore of Essex co., NE corner of Massachusetts, separated from Lynn Harbor by the peninsula on which Nahant is situated.
Na·hā·vand \ˌnä-hə-ˈvand\ *also* **Ne·ha·vend** \ˌnē-hə-ˈvend\. Town, W Iran, 42 mi. (68 km.) S of Hamadān; pop. (1986c) 52,265; battle here and nearby c. 641 A.D. in which the Persians under Yazdegerd III were completely defeated by the Arabs, marking the de facto end of the Persian Empire.
Nahawend. See NEHAVEND.
Na·he \ˈnä-ə\. River, Saarland and Rhineland-Palatinate, W Germany; flows NE into Rhine River at Bingen on SE border of the Hunsrück; 72 mi. (116 km.) long.
Nahr. Arabic word meaning "river"; for names incl. this word, see the 2d element.
Nahr Al–ʿĀṣī. See ORONTES 2.
Nahr al–Līṭanī. See LITANI.
Nah·ra·wān \ˌnä-rə-ˈwän\ *or* **Nahr·wan** \när-ˈwän\. Ancient canal, E of the Tigris River near Baghdad, E Iraq; ab. 60 mi. (95 km.) long.
Nahud, En. See EN NAHUD.
Na·huel Hua·pí, Lake \nä-ˈwel-wä-ˈpē\. Lake in Andes, in S Neuquén prov., SW Argentina, on boundary of Río Negro prov., near Chilean border; alt. 2516 ft. (767 m.); area 212 sq. mi. (549 sq. km.); depth nearly 1000 ft. (300 m.) in places; source of Limay River; surrounded by mountains, Monte Tronador to SW; one of best-known of Argentine resorts; in **Nahuel Huapí National Park**.

\ə\ **abut** \ˈə\ **matches** \ᵊ\ **kitten**, Fr table \ər\ **further** \a\ **ash** \ā\ **ace** \ä\ **cot, cart** \å\ Fr bac \au̇\ **out** \b\ Span Avila \ch\ **chin** \e\ **bet** \ē\ **easy** \g\ **go** \i\ **hit** \ī\ **ice** \j\ **job** \k\ Ger **ich**, **Buch** \ⁿ\ Fr **vin** \ŋ\ **sing** \ō\ **go** \ȯ\ **all** \ȯ\ **law** \œ\ Fr **bœuf** \œ̄\ Fr **feu** \ȯi\ **boy** \th\ **thin** \t͟h\ **this** \ü\ **loot** \u̇\ **foot** \ue\ Ger **füllen** \ue̅\ Fr **rue** \y\ **yet** \ʸ\ Fr digne \ˈdēnʸ\, nuit \ˈnwʸē\ \yü\ **few** \yu̇\ **fury** \zh\ **vision**

Na·hun·ta \nā-ˈhən-tə\. City, ⊗ of Brantley co., SE Georgia; pop. (1990c) 1049.

Na·ic \ˈnä-ēk\. Municipality, N coast of Cavite prov., Luzon, Philippines, ab. 25 mi. (40 km.) SW of Manila; pop. (1980c) 38,243.

Nai·ha·ti \nī-ˈhä-tē\. Town, West Bengal, NE India, on Hugli River 23 mi. (37 km.) N of Calcutta; pop. (1991p) 132,032.

Nā'īn *or* **Nain** \ˈnīn\. Town, cen. Iran, 75 mi. (121 km.) E of Eşfahān; highway junction point.

Nain \ˈnān, ˈnā-in\ *or* **Nein** \ˈnān, ˈnen\. Village, Galilee (*q.v.*), 5 mi. (8 km.) SSE of Nazareth (*Luke* vii. 11–17).

Nai·ni Tāl \ˈnī-nē-ˈtäl\. Town and hill station, NE Uttar Pradesh, N India, 148 mi. (238 km.) NE of Delhi; pop. (1991p) 29,831; alt. 6400 ft. (1951 m.); popular resort; summer ✱ of Uttar Pradesh; suffered from severe landslide 1880.

Nairn \ˈnarn\. **1.** Small river in Highland region, NE Scotland; flows NE into Moray Firth; 38 mi. (61 km.) long. **2.** *or* **Nairn·shire** \-shi(ə)r, -shər\. Former county, NE Scotland, S of Moray Firth; ⊗ Nairn; rivers Nairn, Findhorn. **3.** Burgh, Highland region, on Moray Firth at mouth of the Nairn; pop. (1991e) 10,420; seaside resort.

Nai·ro·bi \nī-ˈrō-bē\. City, ✱ of Kenya, forming an extraprovincial division, S cen. Kenya; pop. (1990e) 1,504,000; the republic's principal commercial and industrial city; food products, soft drinks, cigarettes, furniture; railway repair shops; three universities; cathedral; Nairobi National Park game reserve nearby. City founded c. 1899 as site of railroad workshops; became seat of government of British East Africa 1905; was made municipality 1919, city 1950; remained ✱ upon independence, with its area greatly expanded by constitution of 1963.

Nairobi National Park. National park, Kenya, ab. 15 mi. (25 km.) S of Nairobi; 45 sq. mi. (117 sq. km.); noted for its wildlife, incl. rhinos and giraffe; estab. 1946.

Nais·saar \ˈnī-ˌsär\ *or Russ.* **Nais·sar** \-sər\. Island, Estonia, in Gulf of Finland, ab. 12 mi. (19 km.) off Tallinn; ab. 5 mi. (8 km.) long.

Naissus *or* **Naïssus.** See NIŠ.

Nai·va·sha \nī-ˈvä-shä\. Town on Lake Naivasha, SW cen. Kenya, ab. 40 mi. (65 km.) NW of Nairobi.

Naivasha, Lake. Lake, SW cen. Kenya, in the Great Rift Valley (*q.v.*); 12 mi. (19 km.) long by 9 mi. (14 km.) wide; 108 sq. mi. (280 sq. km.); alt. 6135 ft. (1870 m.); has no known outlet.

Najaf, An. See AN NAJAF.

Na·ja·fā·bād \nə-ˌjä-fə-ˈbäd\. Town, Eşfahān prov., W cen. Iran, ab. 15 mi. (24 km.) W of the city of Eşfahān; pop. (1986c) 129,058.

Na·ja·sa \nä-ˈhä-sä\. River, SE Camagüey prov., E cen. Cuba; flows S into Caribbean Sea; ab. 50 mi. (80 km.) long.

Najd. See NEJD.

Ná·je·ra \ˈnä-hā-rä\. Commune, Logroño prov., N Spain, W of the commune of Logroño; scene of victory of Edward, Prince of Wales, (the Black Prince) over claimant to Castilian throne Henry II (of Trastámara) 1367 in his campaign for Peter the Cruel, Henry's half brother; also called battle of Navarrete.

Na·jib·a·bad \nə-ˈjē-bə-ˌbäd\. Town, NW Uttar Pradesh, N India, E of Ganges River 98 mi. (158 km.) NE of Delhi; pop. (1991p) 66,842; founded in middle of 18th cent. by Rohillas (Afghans).

Na·jin \ˈnä-ˈjēn\. City, NE North Korea; pop. (1987e) 89,000.

Na·ka·dō·ri \nä-ˈkä-ˌdō-rē; ˌnä-kä-ˈdō-rē\. Island in Gotō Is. (*q.v.*), Japan.

Na·ka·gu·su·ku Bay \nä-ˌkä-gü-ˈsü-kü, ˌnä-kä\ *also* **Buck·ner Bay** \ˈbək-nər\. Inlet of the Pacific Ocean in SE coast of Okinawa I., Ryukyu Is., Japan; Japanese naval base in WWII.

Na·ka·le·le Point \ˌnä-kä-ˈlā-lā\. Point on N coast of Maui I., Hawaii, near W end on Pailolo Channel.

Na·kan·be \nä-ˈkän-bā\; *formerly* **White Vol·ta** \ˈvȯl-tə, ˈväl-\ *or Fr.* **Vol·ta Blanche** \ˌvȯl-ˌtȧ-ˈblä^{n}sh\. The White Volta River in Burkina Faso—so called since 1986.

Na·ka·no Shi·ma \nä-ˈkä-nō-ˈshē-mä, ˌnä-kä-ˈnō-shē-mä\. Volcanic island, Tokara Is., in N Ryukyu Is., Japan; 3125 ft. (953 m.) high.

Na·ka·tsu \nä-ˈkät-sü\. Seaport town, Ōita prefecture, NE Kyūshū, Japan, 27 mi. (43 km.) SSE of Kitakyūshū on S shore of Suō Sea; pop. (1990p) 66,383; birthplace of educator, journalist, and author Yukichi Fukuzawa 1835.

Nakel. See NAKŁO NAD NOTECIĄ.

Nakhichevan. See NAXÇIVAN 2.

Nakhichevan Autonomous Soviet Socialist Republic. See NAXÇIVAN 1.

Na·khod·ka \nə-ˈkȯt-kə\. Seaport town, S Primorsky Kray, SE Russia in Asia, 55 mi. (88 km.) ESE of Vladivostok; pop. (1992e) 166,000; commercial and fishing port.

Na·khon Na·yok \ˌnä-ˌkȯn-ˈnä-ˌyək\ *also* **Na·ga·ra Nayok** \ˌnä-ˌkon-ˈnä-ˌyək—*sic*\. Town, S Thailand, on a tributary of the Chao Phraya and on highway to Cambodia 60 mi. (97 km.) NE of Bangkok; pop. (1991e) 12,155.

Na·khon Pa·thom \ˌnä-ˌkȯn-pä-ˈtəm\. Town, SW Thailand, ab. 38 mi. (60 km.) WNW of Bangkok; pop. (1991e) 43,878. An ancient town and religious center, some artifacts date to 6th cent. A.D.; site of important temple with tallest Buddhist monument in the world, ab. 410 ft. (125 m.) high.

Na·khon Pha·nom \ˌnä-ˌkȯn-pä-ˈnəm\ *also* **La·khon** \ˈlä-ˌkȯn\. Town, NE Thailand, on Mekong River; pop. (1991e) 33,192; nearby Buddhist shrine; site of major air base used by U.S. Air Force during Vietnam War mid-1960s to mid-1970s.

Na·khon Rat·cha·si·ma \ˌnä-ˌkȯn-ˌrä-chə-ˈsē-mä\ *also* **Kho·rat** *or* **Ko·rat** \kō-ˈrät\. Town, S Thailand, on Mun River 110 mi. (177 km.) E of Phra Nakhon Si Ayutthaya; pop. (1991e) 202,503; railroad junction point; distribution and trade center for E part of Thailand; an ancient town; nearby 11th cent. Khmer ruins; U.S. Air Force used nearby air base during Vietnam War.

Na·khon Sa·wan \ˌnä-ˌkȯn-sä-ˈwän\ *also* **Na·ga·ra Svar·ga** \ˌnä-ˌkȯn-sä-ˈwän—*sic*\. Commercial town, W Thailand, on the Chao Phraya where it is formed by confluence of Nan and Ping rivers; pop. (1991e) 108,569.

Na·khon Si Tham·ma·rat \ˈnä-ˌkȯn-ˌsē-ˌtä-mə-ˈrät\ *also* **Na·ga·ra Sri·dhar·ma·raj** \ˈnä-ˌkȯn-ˌsē-ˌtä-mə-ˈrät—*sic*\. Seaport town, SW Thailand, on E coast of Malay Penin. 100 mi. (161 km.) N of Songkhla; pop. (1991e) 74,219; one of Thailand's oldest towns, was a main town of early empires of the region; noted for its niello work in silver.

Na·kło nad No·te·cią \ˈnä-kwȯ-näd-nȯ-ˈte-chȯ\ *or Ger.* **Na·kel** \ˈnä-kəl\. Commune, W Bydgoszcz prov., N cen. Poland, 20 mi. (32 km.) W of the city of Bydgoszcz on Noteć River; pop. (1989e) 20,121.

Nak·nek Lake \ˈnak-ˌnek\; *formerly* **Lake Co·ville** \ˈkō-ˌvil\. Lake, SW Alaska, near base of Alaska Penin.; lies entirely within Katmai National Park.

Naksh–i–Rus·tam \ˌnäk-shē-rü-ˈstäm\. See PERSEPOLIS.

Nak·skov \ˈnäk-ˌskau̇\. Seaport, Storstrøm co., on W coast of Lolland I., Denmark; pop. (1988c) 15,268; sugar refineries, shipbuilding yards; St. Nicholas church, dating from the 15th cent.

Na·ku·ru \nä-ˈkü-rü\. Town, ✱ of Rift Valley prov., W cen. Kenya; pop. (1984e) 101,700; just S of the town is **Lake Nakuru** in Lake Nakuru National Park.

Nal. See HINGOL.

Na·la·garh \ˈnä-lə-ˌgär\ *or* **Hin·dur** \ˈhin-dər\. Former Indian state, now part of Himachal Pradesh state, NW India, W of Simla; 276 sq. mi. (715 sq. km.); the town of Nalagarh near Himachal Pradesh's W border was its ✱.

Nal'·chik *or* **Nal·chik** \ˈnäl^y-chik\. Town, ✱ of Kabardino-Balkaria Rep., S Russia in Europe, 63 mi. (101 km.) NW of Ordzhonikidze; pop. (1992e) 242,000; railroad terminus; health resort situated in a mountain valley; footwear, clothing, furniture, processed foods; university; founded as fortress c. 1818; briefly held by Germans in WWII 1942–43.

Nal·gon·da \nəl-ˈgän-də\. Town, cen. Andhra Pradesh, India, 55 mi. (88 km.) ESE of Hyderabad; pop. (1991p) 84,674.

Nam *or* **'Nam** \ˈnäm, ˈnam\. Colloquial for VIETNAM.

Na·mak, Dar·yā·cheh–ye \där-ˈyä-chə-yə-nə-ˈmäk\. Salt lake and swamp (*darya*), NW cen. Iran, S of Tehran.

Na·mak·zār \ˌnä-mäk-ˈzär\. Swampy lake, SW Asia, across Iran-Afghanistan border.

Namaland. See NAMAQUALAND.

Na·man·gan \ˌnä-mäŋ-ˈgän\. **1.** Administrative subdivision, E Uzbekistan; 3012 sq. mi. (7801 sq. km.); pop. (1991e) 1,557,800; ✻ Namangan; estab. 1941; before 1991 comprised an oblast of the U.S.S.R.

2. Town, its ✻, in the Fergana Valley NE of Qŭqon; pop. (1991e) 319,200; textiles, foodstuffs; annexed by Russia 1876; earthquake 1927.

Na·ma·qua·land \nä-ˈmä-kwä-ˌland\ *or* **Na·ma·land** \ˈnä-mä-ˌland\. Coastal region, SW Africa, extending from ab. 23°S to 31°S and from ab. 80 to 350 mi. (130 to 560 km.) inland; divided by Orange River into **Great Namaqualand** to the N (in Namibia) and **Little Namaqualand** to the S (in Northern Cape prov., Rep. of South Africa); sandy plains and bare hills; rich in copper.

Na·ma·ta·nai \ˌnä-mə-tə-ˈnī\. Village on NE coast of New Ireland, Bismarck Archipelago, W Pacific Ocean; good harbor.

Nam·cha Bar·wa \ˈnäm-chə-ˈbär-wä\. Peak at E end of the Himalayas, SE Tibet, China, in the bend of the Brahmaputra; 25,445 ft. (7756 m.).

Nam Co \ˈnäm-ˈchō\ *W.-G.* **Na–mu–ts'o** \ˈnä-mə̇-ˈtsō\ *also* **Nam Tsho** \ˈnäm-ˈchō\; *Eng.* **Na·mu Lake** \ˈnä-mü\ *or mostly formerly* **Ten·gri Nor** \ˈteŋ-grē-ˈnȯr\. Salt lake, E cen. Tibet, W China, 30°42′N, 90°30′E; 50 mi. (80 km.) long and 25 mi. (40 km.) wide at its greatest extent; alt. 15,186 ft. (4629 m.); hot springs nearby on the NW.

Nam Dinh \ˈnäm-ˈdēn\. Town, N Vietnam, in Red River Delta 45 mi. (72 km.) SE of Hanoi; a trade center; connected by rail with Hanoi.

Nam·e·ka·gon \ˌna-mə-ˈkä-gən\. River, NW Wisconsin; flows out of **Namekagon Lake,** S Bayfield co., SW and W into St. Croix River in Burnett co; ab. 75 mi. (120 km.) long.

Namen. See NAMUR.

Namh·kam \ˈnäm-ˌkäm\. Town, Shan State, Myanmar, on Shweli River near Chinese border. Held by Japanese 1942–45.

Namhoi. See FOSHAN.

Na·mib Desert \ˈnä-mib\. Arid region, along entire length of coast of Namibia; ab. 800 mi. (1300 km.) long by 30 to 100 mi. (50 to 160 km.) wide; traversed by rail lines linking Walvis Bay and Lüderitz with Rep. of South Africa.

Na·mi·be \nä-ˈmē-bā\; *formerly* **Mo·çâ·me·des** \mü-ˈsȧ-mə-dish\. **1.** Province of SW Angola. See table at ANGOLA.

2. Seaport, its ✻; pop. (1987e) 77,000.

Na·mib·i·a \nə-ˈmi-bē-ə\; *1915–68* **South–West Africa;** *earlier* **German Southwest Africa.** Independent state, SW Africa, bounded on N by Angola and Zambia, on E by Botswana and Rep. of South Africa, on S by Rep. of South Africa, and on W by the Atlantic Ocean; 318,321 sq. mi. (824,451 sq. km.); pop. (1992e) 1,511,600; ✻ Windhoek.

Physical features: Greater part is plateau 3000 to 4000 ft. (914 to 1219 m.); highest point 8153 ft. (2485 m.) near Windhoek. Namib Desert extends along the coast; in N is extensive depression with salt pans, esp. Etosha Pan. The Cunene and Okavango rivers form part of boundary on N with Angola, and the Orange River forms boundary with Rep. of South Africa.

Chief products: Diamonds, copper, zinc, lead, salt; karakul sheep; fishing, food processing.

Chief towns: Windhoek, Oshakati, Rehoboth.

History: Long inhabited by indigenous peoples, among them, the San and later, the Khoikhoi; explored by Portuguese late 15th cent.; visited variously by British and Germans mid-19th cent.; annexed by Germany 1885, becoming German Southwest Africa; widespread unrest among esp. Khoikhoi and Herreros early 20th cent. led to their brutal suppression by Germans; captured in WWI by forces from Union (now Rep.) of South Africa, which after the war received it as mandate from League of Nations; renamed Southwest Africa; following WWII, South Africa refused to give up mandate, moving to incorporate area in spite of international opposition; UN resolution lifted mandate status 1966; UN recognized change of name to Namibia 1968; South Africa continued to challenge UN resolution throughout 1970s and 1980s; through long negotiations involving many factions and interests, agreement finally reached and Namibia achieved independence 1990.

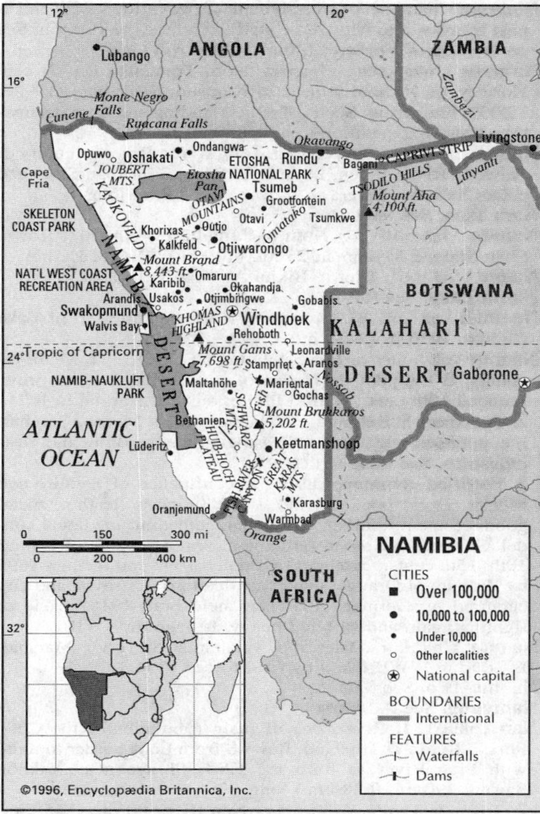

Nam·lea \ˈnäm-lā-ˌä\. Village on bay on E coast of Buru I., Indonesia.

Namnetes. See NANTES.

Nam·ni Pass \ˈnäm-nē\. Mountain pass on N border of Myanmar; 15,300 ft. (4663 m.); leads from upper valley of Nmai River to China.

Nam·oi \ˈna-ˌmȯi\. River, NW New South Wales, SE Australia; flows into Darling River; 526 mi. (846 km.) long.

Na·mo·nui·to \ˌnä-mō-ˈnwē-tō\. Atoll group in cen. Caroline Is. in W Pacific Ocean, 8°46′N, 150°02′E, NW of Chuuk.

Namosi Peak. See VUIMASIA.

Nam·pa \ˈnam-pə\. City, Canyon co., SW Idaho, 18 mi. (29 km.) W of Boise; pop. (1990c) 28,365; railroad center; milk processing, vegetable-seed production; Northwest Nazarene Coll. (1913); founded c. 1886.

Nam Pawn \ˈnäm-ˌpȯn\. River, Myanmar; flows S out of Shan State and empties into Salween River; ab. 160 mi. (260 km.) long.

Nam·p'o \ˈnäm-ˈpō\; *formerly* **Chin·nam·po** \ˈchēn-ˈnäm-ˈpō\. City, North Korea, on the W coast 25 mi. (40 km.) SW of P'yŏngyang; opened to foreign trade 1897.

Nam·pu·la \näm-ˈpü-lä\. **1.** Province of E Mozambique. See table at MOZAMBIQUE.

2. Town, its ✻; on highway and railroad line.

Nam–quan. See NA SAM.

\ə\ **abut** \ə̇\ matches \ᵊ\ kitten, Fr table \ər\ **further** \a\ **ash** \ā\ **ace** \ä\ **cot, cart** \ȧ\ Fr bac \au̇\ **out** \b\ Span Avila \ch\ **chin** \e\ **bet** \ē\ **easy** \g\ **go** \i\ **hit** \ī\ **ice** \j\ **job** \k\ Ger **ich, Buch** \ⁿ\ Fr vin \ŋ\ **sing** \ō\ **go** \ȯ\ **all** \ȯ\ **law** \œ\ Fr **bœuf** \œ̄\ Fr **feu** \ȯi\ **boy** \th\ **thin** \t͟h\ **this** \ü\ **loot** \u̇\ **foot** \ue\ Ger **füllen** \ue̅\ Fr **rue** \y\ **yet** \ʸ\ Fr digne \ˈdēnʸ\, nuit \ˈnwʸē\ \yü\ **few** \yu̇\ **fury** \zh\ **vision**

Nam·sen \ˈnäm-sən\. River, N cen. Norway; flows SSW and W past Namsos into **Namsen Fjord,** an inlet of Norwegian Sea on W coast of Norway; 130 mi. (209 km.) long.

Nams·os \ˈnäm-ˌsōs\. Seaport, Nord-Trøndelag co., N cen. Norway, on N shore at head of Namsen Fjord; pop. (1992e) 12,059; lumbering. Scene of Allied landing and brief occupation 1940 in expedition to aid Norway.

Nam Teng \ˈnäm-ˈteŋ\ *or Eng.* **Teng River.** River, tributary of Salween River, E cen. Myanmar; flows S in Shan State and enters Salween River; ab. 225 mi. (360 km.) long.

Nam Tsho. See NAM CO.

Nam·tu \ˈnäm-tü\ *or* **Namtu–Pang·hai** \-ˈpäŋ-ˌhī\. Town, Shan State, E Myanmar, 25 mi. (40 km.) WNW of Lashio.

Na·mu \ˈnä-mü\. Islet in Bikini Atoll, 8°N, 168°10′E.

Namu Lake. See NAM CO.

Na·mu·li \nä-ˈmü-lē\. Mountain, N Mozambique, E of Lake Chilwa; 7936 ft. (2419 m.).

Na·mur \nä-ˈmu̇r\ *or Flem.* **Na·men** \ˈnä-mən\. **1.** Medieval county, S Belgium, in N part of present-day Namur prov.; founded 10th cent.; sold to Philip, duke of Burgundy 1421.
2. Province, S Belgium; ✻ Namur; rivers Meuse, Sambre; rye, potatoes, sugar beets; livestock; metalworking and glass industries. See table at BELGIUM.
3. Fortified commune, its ✻, at confluence of Sambre and Meuse rivers; pop. (1992e) 104,200; glass, leather, metal goods, cement; tourism; 18th cent. cathedral; medieval citadel. Site of pre-Roman settlement; seat of counts of Namur 10th–15th cents.; captured by French 1692 and retaken 1695 by William of Orange; outer fortifications destroyed and city captured by Germans 1914 and held until 1918; scene of fighting again and suffered heavy damage in WWII.

Na·mur \ˈnä-mür\. Islet of Kwajalein Atoll (*q.v.*), Marshall Is.; during WWII taken by U.S. forces 1944.

Na–mu–ts'o. See NAM CO.

Namyung. See NANXIONG.

Nan \ˈnän\. **1.** River, one of main tributaries of the Chao Phraya River, W Thailand; flows S from Laos border to unite with Ping River to form the Chao Phraya near Nakhon Sawan; 390 mi. (628 km.) long.
2. Town, N Thailand, on upper Nan River 90 mi. (145 km.) NNE of Uttaradit; pop. (1991e) 22,457.

Na·nai·mo \nə-ˈnī-mō\. City, SE Vancouver I., British Columbia, Canada, on Strait of Georgia 38 mi. (61 km.) W of Vancouver; pop. (1991c) 60,129; harbor; center of lumbering region; wood pulp; tourism; home port of fishing fleet. Site of trading post estab. by Hudson's Bay Company mid-19th cent.

Na·na·ku·li \ˌnä-nä-ˈkü-lē\. City, Honolulu co., Hawaii, 18 mi. (29 km.) W of the city of Honolulu; pop. (1990c) 9575.

Na·nam \ˈnä-ˈnäm\; *formerly* **Ra·nan** \ˈrä-ˈnän\. Coastal town, North Korea, WSW of port of Ch'ongjin.

Na·nao \ˈnä-ˌnau̇\. Town, Ishikawa prefecture, W coast of Honshū, Japan, on E side of Noto Penin.; pop. (1990p) 50,101; seaport.

Nance \ˈnans\. County in E cen. Nebraska. See table at NEBRASKA.

Nan·chang *or W.-G.* **Nan–ch'ang** \ˈnän-ˈchäŋ\. Old walled city, ✻ of Jiangxi prov., SE China, on right bank of Gan River just SW of Poyang Hu; pop. (1990c) 1,086,124; trades in rice, tea, cotton, hemp; textiles, paper, agricultural machinery. An ancient town, originating c. 2d cent. A.D.; scene of Communist revolutionary activity 1927; in WWII occupied by Japanese 1939–45.

Nancheng. See HANZHONG.

Nan–ching. See NANJING.

Nan·cow·ry *or* **Nan·kau·ri** \nan-ˈkau̇r-ē\. **1.** Island, cen. group of Nicobar Is., Bay of Bengal, India; 19 sq. mi. (49 sq. km.).
2. Town at S end of island; good harbor.

Nan·cy \nän-ˈsē, ˈnan-sē\. City, ✻ of Meurthe-et-Moselle dept., NE France, on Meurthe River 178 mi. (286 km.) E of Paris; pop. (1990c) 102,410; transportation center; episcopal see; center of iron-mining region; produces machinery, clothing, steel, ironware; 18th cent. cathedral; ducal palace (now a museum); university.
History: Site of castle and small town 11th cent.; fortified and made ✻ of ancient Lorraine from 12th cent.; scene of battle in which Charles the Bold, duke of Burgundy, was defeated and slain by René II, duke of Lorraine, 1477; residence (c. 1736–66) of Stanisław Leszczyński, duke of Lorraine and Bar, former king of Poland; passed to French crown 1766; important railroad center in WWI; unsuccessfully attacked by Germans 1914; received only slight damage in WWII and was retaken by Allies 1944.

Nan·da De·vi \ˈnən-də-ˈdā-vē\. Peak in the Himalayas, Uttar Pradesh, N India; 25,645 ft. (7817 m.).

Nan·da·rua \ˌnän-dä-ˈrü-ä\. Peak, cen. Kenya; ab. 12,900 ft. (3930 m.).

Nan·ded \ˈnän-ˌded\ *also* **Nander** \-ˌder\. Town, SE Maharashtra, S cen. India, on Godavari River 140 mi. (225 km.) NNW of Hyderabad; pop. (1991p) 274,626; market town; cotton processing.

Nand·gaon \ˈnänd-ˌgau̇n\. Former Indian state, Eastern States Agency, NE India, N of Bastar; 872 sq. mi. (2258 sq. km.); ✻ Raj Nandgaon.

Nan·di *or* **Na·di** \ˈnän-dē\. **1.** Small river on Viti Levu I., Fiji, W Pacific Ocean; flows W into **Nandi Bay,** inlet of Pacific Ocean.
2. Village, Fiji, on W Viti Levu I. at mouth of Nandi River; international airport.

Nandi Drug *or* **Nan·di·droog** \ˈnən-di-ˌdru̇g\. Fortified hill, E Karnataka, S India, 31 mi. (50 km.) N of Bangalore; 4813 ft. (1467 m.); fort constructed by Indian rulers Hyder Ali and Tipu Sultan; taken by storm 1791 by British under Lord Charles Cornwallis.

Nan·dyal \nən-ˈdyäl\. Town, W Andhra Pradesh, S India, on tributary of Penner River 125 mi. (201 km.) S of Hyderabad; pop. (1991p) 120,171.

Nangal Dam. See BHAKRA DAM.

Nan·ga Par·bat \ˈnəŋ-gə-ˈpər-bət\. Peak in the W Himalayas, in region of Jammu and Kashmir under Pakistani control; 26,660 ft. (8126 m.); first scaled 1953.

Nang·tud, Mount \näŋ-ˈtüd\. Mountain, W Panay, Philippines, in cen. part of range bet. Antique and Capiz provs.; 6724 ft. (2049 m.).

Nan–hsiung. See NANXIONG.

Naniwa. See ŌSAKA 2.

Nan·jing *or W.-G.* **Nan–ching** \ˈnän-ˈjiŋ\ *or* **Nan·king** \ˈnan-ˈkiŋ, ˈnän-\; *formerly* **Chian–ning** \ˈjyäŋ-ˈniŋ\ *or* **Kiang-ning** \ˈjyäŋ-ˈniŋ\. Commercial city, ✻ of Jiangsu prov., E China, on S bank of the Chang 150 mi. (241 km.) NW of Shanghai and ab. 200 mi. (320 km.) above it by river; pop. (1990c) 2,090,204; ✻ of China 1928–37 and 1946–49; fertilizers, steel, textiles, motor vehicles; university and several colleges.
History: Site inhabited for thousands of years; site of settlements under various names that served as capitals of several dynasties from c. 3d cent. A.D.; present city founded 1368 in Ming dynasty; was ✻ of empire under Mings 1368–1421; taken by British in Opium War 1842; scene of treaty signed 1842 which ceded Hong Kong to Great Britain and opened five treaty ports; covered wide extent and was surrounded by high walls; contained imperial tombs and notable buildings, esp. the porcelain tower (begun 1413); largely destroyed by Taiping rebels who held city as their headquarters 1853–64; declared a treaty port 1858 but not opened until 1899; chosen 1928 by the Kuomintang as ✻; the ✻ removed to Chongqing 1937 upon occupation of the city by the Japanese (1937–45); became ✻ again 1946–49; occupied by Communist forces 1949; became ✻ of Jiangsu prov. 1952.

Nan·kai \ˈnän-ˈkī\. Island in Western Channel, off S coast of South Korea.

Nan·kai·do \nän-ˈkī-dō\. Former division of Japan incl. Shikoku and Awaji islands and Kii prov. on Honshū.

Nankauri. See NANCOWRY.

Nanking. See NANJING.

Nan·kou·zhen *or W.-G.* **Nan–k'ou–chen** \ˈnän-ˈkō-ˈjen\; *also* **Nan–k'ou** *or* **Nan·kow** \ˈnän-ˈkō\. Town, Beijing municipality, NE China, ab. 25 mi. (40 km.) NW of the city of Beijing;

nearby to the E in Shisanling (*q.v.*) are Ming Tombs. **Nan–k'ou Pass** is 5 to 12 mi. (8 to 19 km.) NW of Nankouzhen through hills and gate in Great Wall; highest point ab. 1900 ft. (580 m.); four railroad tunnels.

Nan Ling \ˈnän-ˈliŋ\ *or* **Nan Shan** \ˈnän-ˈshän\. Mountain system in S China, roughly separating Guangdong prov. and Guangxi Zhuangzu from Hunan and Guizhou provs.

Nan·ning *or W.-G.* **Nan–ning** \ˈnän-ˈniŋ\; *1913–45* **Yung–ning** \ˈyu̇ŋ-ˈniŋ\. City, ✻ of Guangxi Zhuangzu, SE China, ab. 330 mi. (530 km.) W of Guangzhou; pop. (1990c) 721,877; in region producing sugarcane and fruits; notable stalactite cave nearby; a former treaty port, opened to foreign trade 1907; supply base for Communist forces during anti-French campaign in Indochina (ending 1954), and again during the Vietnam War 1960s–70s.

Nan·ping *or W.-G.* **Nan–p'ing** \ˈnän-ˈpiŋ\; *formerly* **Yen-ping** \ˈyen-ˈpiŋ\. City on Min River, N cen. Fujian prov., SE China, 85 mi. (137 km.) WNW of Fuzhou.

Nansei Islands. See RYUKYU ISLANDS 1.

Nan·se·mond \ˈnan-sə-mənd\. **1.** Short stream in Nansemond co., SE Virginia; flows NNE into Hampton Roads.
2. Former county in Virginia. See SUFFOLK 2.

Nan·sen Sound \ˈnan-sən\. Strait bet. W Grant Land, Ellesmere I. and Axel Heiberg I., Canada.

Nan Shan. **1.** Mountain range, cen. China. See QILIAN SHAN.
2. Mountain range, S China. See NAN LING.

Nan·ta·ha·la \ˌnan-tə-ˈhā-lə, -lē\. River, W North Carolina; rises near Georgia-North Carolina boundary and flows N through Nantahala National Forest into Little Tennesee River in Swain co.; noted for scenery, the deep Nantahala Gorge, and whitewater rafting.

Nan–t'ai \ˈnän-ˈtī\. Island in Min River, opposite the city of Fuzhou, Fujian prov., SE China; formerly site of a foreign settlement.

Nan·tai \ˈnän-ˈtī\ *or* **Nan·tai–zan** \-ˈzän\. Peak, N cen. Honshū, Japan, NNE of Lake Chuzenji; 8150 ft. (2484 m.); has extinct crater 1000 ft. (305 m.) in diameter.

Nan·tas·ket Beach \nan-ˈtas-kət\. Beach area in Plymouth co., Massachusetts, on Massachusetts Bay, 10 mi. (16 km.) SE of Boston; formerly a popular summer resort.

Nan·terre \näⁿ-ˈter\. Commune, ✻ of Hauts-de-Seine dept., N France, W suburb of Paris; pop. (1990c) 86,627; automobiles, electrical equipment, perfume; Univ. of Paris. Birthplace of the Revolutionary leader François Hanriot 1759.

Nantes \ˈnäⁿt, ˈnants\ *or Breton* **Naoned;** *anc.* **Con·di·vin·cum** \ˌkän-di-ˈviŋ-kəm\; *later* **Nam·ne·tes** \nam-ˈnē-tēz\. City, ✻ of Loire-Atlantique dept., NW France, on Loire River 107 mi. (172 km.) W of Tours; pop. (1990c) 252,029; connected by ship canal with St.-Nazaire; seaport; industrial center, producing aircraft parts, fertilizers, paint; shipbuilding and repairing, sugar processing, food canning; university (1962); cathedral, 13th cent. Gothic church, ducal castle. Birthplace of writer Jules Verne 1828.
History: ✻ of ancient Namnetes before Roman conquest of Gaul; passed to Romans; unsuccessfully besieged by Huns 5th cent. A.D.; captured by Normans in 9th cent.; held by dukes of Brittany 10th cent. ff.; passed to France 1499 on marriage of Duchess Anne of Brittany to Louis XII; famous Edict of Nantes issued by Henry IV Apr. 13, 1598; scene of noyades (mass drownings) during French Revolution; American supply channel in WWI; heavily damaged by Allied bombing in WWII, taken by Americans Aug. 1944.

Nan·ti·coke \ˈnan-ti-ˌkōk\. **1.** River, SE Maryland; rises in S cen. Delaware, flows SW into Chesapeake Bay, SE Maryland; 63 mi. (101 km.) long.
2. City, Luzerne co., E Pennsylvania, on Susquehanna River 8 mi. (13 km.) W of Wilkes-Barre; pop. (1990c) 12,267.
3. City, Haldimand-Norfolk munic. region, S Ontario, Canada, on N shore of Lake Erie; pop. (1991c) 22,727.

Nan·tong *or W.-G.* **Nan–t'ung** \ˈnän-ˈtu̇ŋ\; *formerly* **Tung-chow** \ˈtu̇ŋ-ˈjō\. Seaport city, SE Jiangsu prov., E China, on N side of Chang estuary 65 mi. (105 km.) NW of Shanghai; pop. (1990c) 343,341. Site of important textile industrial reforms carried out by reformer Chang Chien late 19th–early 20th cents.

Nan·tuck·et \nan-ˈtə-kət\. **1.** Island, Atlantic Ocean S of Cape Cod, Massachusetts, constituting with adjoining islands Nantucket co., SE Massachusetts; area 57 sq. mi. (148 sq. km.); summer resort. Birthplace of first American woman astronomer Maria Mitchell 1818.
2. County in SE Massachusetts. See table at MASSACHUSETTS.
3. Town, ⊗ of Nantucket co., SE Massachusetts, on Nantucket Sound in N cen. Nantucket I.; pop. (1990c) 6012; former whaling center.

Nantucket Sound. Body of water bet. S coast of Cape Cod and Nantucket I., SE Massachusetts, connecting with Atlantic Ocean on the E and Vineyard Sound on the W.

Nan–t'ung. See NANTONG.

Nant·wich \ˈnant-ˌwich\. Town, Cheshire, NW England, on the Weaver 30 mi. (48 km.) SE of Liverpool; pop. (1981c) 12,023; clothing; health resort; 14th cent. church.

Nan·ty Glo *also* **Nan·ty–Glo** \ˈnan-tē-ˈglō\. Borough, Cambria co., SW cen. Pennsylvania, 11 mi. (18 km.) NNE of Johnstown; pop. (1990c) 3190.

Na·nu·ku Passage \nä-ˈnü-kü\. Channel bet. Taveuni I. on the W and islets of N Lau group on the E, NE Fiji, SW Pacific Ocean; ab. 30 mi. (48 km.) wide; leads out of Koro Sea and at its NE end is an islet used as a navigational guide.

Na·nu·mea \ˌnä-nü-ˈmā-ä\. Island (atoll), N end of Tuvalu, W Pacific Ocean; 6 mi. (10 km.) long; two islets with no sheltered anchorage; occupied by U.S. forces 1943.

Na·nu·sa Islands \nä-ˈnü-sä\. See TALAUD ISLANDS.

Nan·xiong *or W.-G.* **Nan–hsiung** \ˈnän-ˈshyu̇ŋ\; *also* **Nam·yung** \ˈnäm-ˈyu̇ŋ\. Town, N Guangdong prov., SE China, ab. 150 mi. (240 km.) NE of Guangzhou (Canton).

Nan·yang *or W.-G.* **Nan–yang** \ˈnän-ˈyäŋ\. City, SW Henan prov., E cen. China, ab. 150 mi. (240 km.) SW of Kaifeng. Important trade center under various names from first millennium B.C. into first millennium A.D.; revived in importance with coming of Mongols c. 1300; a commercial center late 20th cent.

Nan·yo \ˈnän-ˈyō\. **1.** Japanese name of the South Sea Mandated Territories (*q.v.*), the islands in the Pacific that were under Japanese mandate after WWI (see JAPAN).
2. Town, its ✻. See KOROR.

Nao, Cape \ˈnau̇\ *or Span.* **Ca·bo de la Nao** \ˈkä-b̲ō-ˌt̲hā-lä-\. Cape on E coast of Spain, 47 mi. (76 km.) NE of Alicante, 38°44′N, 0°14′E.

Nao·gaon \ˈnau̇-ˌgau̇n\. City, W Bangladesh; pop. (1991p) 109,156.

Naoned. See NANTES.

Naos \ˈnau̇s\. Small island, Panama, in the Bay of Panama, just off SE end of Panama Canal.

Napa \ˈna-pə\. **1.** County in W cen. California. See table at CALIFORNIA.
2. City, its ⊗, on Napa River 10 mi. (16 km.) N of San Pablo Bay; pop. (1990c) 61,842; leather; **Napa Valley** vineyards are a major source of wine; Napa Valley Coll. (1941); city founded c. 1848; incorp. 1872.

Nap·a·nee \ˈna-pə-ˌnē\. Town, ⊗ of Lennox and Addington co., SE Ontario, Canada, 25 mi. (40 km.) W of Kingston at E end of Bay of Quinte; pop. (1991c) 5179.

Nap·a·ta \ˈna-pə-tə\. Town, ancient Egypt, below the 4th of several cataracts near modern Marawī; ruins in the area include pyramids and temples; ✻ of Nubian kingdom of Cush 8th–6th cents. B.C.

Nap·a·tree Point \ˈna-pə-ˌtrē\. SW extremity of Washington co., S Rhode Island, on the Connecticut border.

Na·per·ville \ˈnā-pər-ˌvil\. City, Du Page co., NE Illinois, ab. 17 mi. (27 km.) W of Chicago; pop. (1990c) 85,351; 19th cent. village museum; North Central Coll. (1861).

Na·pi·er \ˈnā-pē-ər\. City, E North I., New Zealand, on Hawke Bay 170 mi. (274 km.) NE of Wellington; pop. (1991c) 51,645; exports fruit, wool, frozen meats, dairy products.

Na·pi·er·ville \ˈnā-pē-ər-ˌvil\. Village, S Quebec, Canada, 24 mi. (39 km.) SSE of Montreal near New York state border; pop. (1991c) 2909.

Na·pi·li Bay \nä-ˈpē-lē\. Inlet of Pailolo Channel on NW coast of Maui I., Hawaii.

Na·ples \ˈnā-pəlz\. **1.** City, Collier co., SW Florida, on Gulf of Mexico 35 mi. (56 km.) S of Fort Myers; pop. (1990c) 19,505; resort.

2. Village, Ontario co., W New York, 24 mi. (39 km.) NNE of Hornell; pop. (1990c) 2559; vineyards.

3. Former kingdom comprising S mainland Italy, S of the former Papal States.

History: Region held by Romans, Byzantines, Saracens; conquered by Normans 11th cent. and incorp. into their kingdom of Sicily; passed to Hohenstaufens 12th cent.; taken by French Duke Charles of Anjou c. 1268; when Sicily passed to Aragonese 1282, the separate kingdom of Naples arose and remained in Angevin hands; crown reunited to that of Sicily under Alfonso V of Aragon 1442–58, but separated again upon his death; rival French and Spanish claims to the crown of Naples in the late 15th cent. led to armed conflict, brief French occupation, temporary partition of the kingdom, and finally to Spanish conquest of the kingdom in 1503, by which it was rejoined with Sicily; ceded 1713 to Austrian Hapsburgs by Treaty of Utrecht; conquered (along with Sicily) 1734 by Spanish Bourbons who reestablished the Kingdom of The Two Sicilies; held (excluding Sicily) by Napoleonic forces as Parthenopean Republic (1799) and Kingdom of Naples (1806–15), after which Bourbons were restored; see SICILIES, THE TWO for later history.

4. *or Ital.* **Na·po·li** \ˈnä-pō-lē\; *anc.* **Ne·ap·o·lis** \nē-ˈa-pə-lis\. Seaport, ✻ of Campania, also ✻ of Napoli prov., S Italy, on N side of Bay of Naples 117 mi. (188 km.) SE of Rome; pop. (1991p) 1,054,601; commercial and cultural center of S Italy; archiepiscopal see; major port activities; diversified industries, incl. textiles, steel, aircraft parts; shipbuilding, oil refining; tourism; near heights of Posilipo and Vesuvius; five medieval castles (among them St. Elmo); Roman poet Virgil's tomb; 13th cent. Gothic cathedral; church of the Holy Apostles (said to have been founded by Roman Emperor Constantine the Great), church of St. Paul (1817–31; in imitation of Pantheon at Rome), and numerous other notable churches; the royal palace; the Galleria Umberto I, and a national museum containing artifacts of ancient Pompeii and Herculaneum; university (1224); zoological station, and marine aquarium and laboratory; naval and military station, arsenal.

History: Founded near site of ancient Parthenope (hence its ancient name *Neapolis,* i.e., "new city") c. 600 B.C. by refugees from an ancient Greek colony; conquered by Romans in 4th cent. B.C.; included successively in realms of Byzantines and Saracens; conquered by Norman ruler of Sicily in 11th cent.; through 19th cent. served alternately as ✻ of Kingdom of The Two Sicilies (see SICILIES, THE TWO) and of Kingdom of Naples (see NAPLES 3); occupied by French 1495 and 1501–03; ✻ of French Emperor Napoléon's Parthenopean Republic 1799 and Neapolitan kingdom 1806–15; city entered by Italian patriot Giuseppe Garibaldi's expedition Sept. 7, 1860; in WWII heavily damaged by Allied and German bombing; occupied by Allies 1943; extensive reconstruction since 1945; suffered severe earthquake devastation Nov. 1980.

Naples, Bay of. Inlet of Tyrrhenian Sea on SW coast of Italy, S of Gulf of Gaeta and N of Gulf of Salerno; 22 mi. (35 km.) long.

Na·po \ˈnä-pō\. **1.** Province of NE Ecuador. See table at ECUADOR.

2. River, NW South America; rises near Cotopaxi Mt. in N cen. Ecuador, flows E and SE across Peruvian border, and empties into Amazon River; ab. 700 mi. (1100 km.) long.

Napoca. See CLUJ-NAPOCA.

Na·po·le·on \nə-ˈpōl-yən, -ˈpō-lē-ən\. **1.** City, ⊗ of Logan co., S North Dakota; pop. (1990c) 930.

2. City, ⊗ of Henry co., NW Ohio, 35 mi. (56 km.) WSW of Toledo; pop. (1990c) 8884.

Napoléon–Vendée. See LA ROCHE-SUR-YON.

Na·po·le·on·ville \nə-ˈpōl-yən-ˌvil, -ˈpō-lē-ən-\. Town, ⊗ of Assumption parish, SE Louisiana; pop. (1990c) 802.

Napoletano, Appennino. See table at APENNINES.

Na·po·li \ˈnä-pō-lē\. **1.** Province of Campania, Italy. See table at ITALY.

2. City, Italy. See NAPLES 4.

Napoli di Malvasia. See MONEMVASÍA.

Na·po–Pa·sta·za \ˈnä-pō-pä-ˈstä-sä\. Former province, E Ecuador, E of the Andes and N of the Pastaza River; ✻ Tena; formed 1925; with the prov. of Santiago-Zamora, constituted the El Oriente (*q.v.*) of Ecuador; 33,237 sq. mi. (86,084 sq. km.); divided into Napo and Pastaza provs. 1960.

Nap·pa·nee \ˈna-pə-ˌnē\. City, Kosciusko and Elkhart cos., N Indiana, 20 mi. (32 km.) SE of South Bend; pop. (1990c) 5510; mint, onions; many Amish farmers in the area.

Na·qâ·da \nə-ˈkä-də\. Village, containing archaeological site, on left bank of the Nile, cen. Egypt, just N of Karnak; excavations by British archaeologist Sir Flinders Petrie 1895 revealed prehistoric burial grounds.

Naqura, En *or* **Nāqūrah, An.** See EN NAQURA.

Nar. See NERA.

Na·ra \ˈnä-rä\. **1.** Prefecture, W cen. Honshū, Japan; ✻ Nara. See table at JAPAN.

2. City, its ✻, 26 mi. (42 km.) E of Ōsaka, on the slope of a range of hills; pop. (1990p) 349,356; major tourist center; university (1949); has extensive park, the largest in Japan, in which are temples, shrines, a museum, and a great image of Buddha slightly larger than that at Kamakura (*q.v.*); nearby is Japan's oldest extant temple. The oldest permanent ✻ of Japan 710–784; chief Buddhist center of early Japan and when ✻ several times larger than today; suffered rapid decline after court removed to Nagaoka (784), but several 8th cent. buildings (such as temples) survive.

Nara Canal. Water channel, E Sind, Pakistan, probably a former bed of the Indus; ab. 250 mi. (400 km.) long; has been transformed into an irrigation canal system with 631 mi. (1015 km.) of canals; main channel is E of the Indus and flows N across the desert, crossing Khaipur and entering the Indus at Sukkur.

Na·rada Falls \nə-ˈra-də\. Waterfall, Mount Rainier National Park, W cen. Washington; 168 ft. (51 m.) high.

Naradhivas. See NARATHIWAT.

Narainganj. See NARAYANGANJ.

Na·ran·ji·to \ˌnär-ˌäŋ-ˈhē-tō\. Municipality, NE cen. Puerto Rico; pop. (1990c) 27,914; highway SW of San Juan.

Na·ran·jo \nä-ˈräŋ-hō\. Site of early Maya city near Tikal, N Guatemala.

Na·ra·shi·no \ˌnä-rä-ˈshē-nō, nä-ˈrä-shē-ˌnō\. City, Chiba prefecture, Honshū, Japan, 16 mi. (26 km.) E of Tokyo; pop. (1990p) 151,472.

Na·ra·thi·wat \ˌnär-ə-tē-ˈwät\ *or* **Na·ra·dhi·vas** \ˌnär-ə-tē-ˈwät—*sic*\. Town, SW Thailand, seaport on Gulf of Thailand on E coast of Malay Penin. 100 mi. (161 km.) SE of Pattani; pop. (1991e) 40,469.

Nā·rā·yan·ganj \nə-ˈrä-yən-ˌgənj\ *also* **Na·rain·ganj** \nä-ˈrīn-ˌgənj\. Town, SE Bangladesh, on Meghna River 12 mi. (19 km.) E of Dhaka; met. area pop. (1991p) 288,008; jute and hide market; river port; textiles, glass, leather goods.

Narbada. See NARMADA.

Nar·berth \ˈnär-bərth\. Residential borough, Montgomery co., SE Pennsylvania, ab. 3 mi. (5 km.) of Philadelphia; pop. (1990c) 4278.

Narbo Martius. See NARBONNE.

Nar·bo·nen·sis \ˌnär-bə-ˈnen-sis\ *or* **Gal·lia Narbonensis** \ˈga-lē-ə\. Part of ancient Gallia (see GAUL); under Emperor Augustus made a Roman province (orig. called Provincia); in SE part bet. the Alps and Cévennes, extending up the Rhone River as far as Vienna (Vienne) and W as far as Tolosa (Toulouse); chief town Narbo Martius (Narbonne).

Nar·bonne \nȧr-ˈbȯn; när-ˈbän, -ˈbən\; *anc.* **Nar·bo Mar·ti·us** \ˌnär-bō-ˈmär-shē-əs\. Commune, Aude dept., S France, near Mediterranean 31 mi. (50 km.) E of Carcassonne; pop. (1990c) 47,086; trades in wine; honey; sulfur refining, distilling, barrel making; 13th–14th cent. cathedral (unfinished);

town hall (formerly fortified archiepiscopal palace); museums.

History: Said to be first Roman colony of Gaul (founded 118 B.C.), later became ❋ of Gallia Narbonensis (see GAUL); taken by Visigoths 5th cent., Saracens 719, Franks under King Pépin the Short 759; prosperous manufacturing city 11th and 12th cents.; port silted up 14th cent.; passed to French crown 16th cent.; archiepiscopal see suppressed 1790.

Narborough Island. See FERNANDINA 2.

Nar·dò \när-ˈdō\; *anc.* **Ne·re·tum** \nə-ˈrē-təm\. Commune, Lecce prov., Puglia, SE Italy, on E shore of Gulf of Taranto 12 mi. (19 km.) SW of the commune of Lecce; pop. (1991p) 31,066; 13th cent. cathedral; baroque church.

Narenta. See NERETVA.

Na·rew \ˈnär-ˌef, -ˌev\ *or Russ.* **Na·rev** \ˈnȧ-rif\. River, NE Poland; rises SE of Białystok, flows generally W and SW into Bug River near its confluence with the Vistula; 296 mi. (476 km.) long; its banks were scenes of fighting in WWI and WWII.

Na·rin·da Bay \nä-ˈrin-dä\. Inlet of Mozambique Channel on NW coast of Madagascar.

Na·ri·ño \nä-ˈrē-nyō\. Department of S Colombia. See table at COLOMBIA.

Na·ri·ta \nä-ˈrē-tä\. City, Chiba prefecture, SE Honshū, Japan; pop. (1990p) 86,708; international airport serving Tokyo.

Nar·ma·da \nər-ˈmə-də\ *also* **Nar·ba·da** \nər-ˈbə-də\ *or* **Ner·bud·da** \nər-\. River, cen. India; rises in the Maikala Range, Madhya Pradesh, flows W bet. the Vindhya Mts. and the Satpura Range, into the Gulf of Khambhat; 801 mi. (1289 km.) long; forms traditional boundary bet. Hindustan and the Deccan; only the Ganges is more sacred to the Hindus; navigable only in its lower course.

Nar·naul \nər-ˈnau̇l\. Town, Haryana state, NW India, 80 mi. (129 km.) WSW of Delhi; pop. (1991p) 51,880.

Nar·ni \ˈnär-nē\; *anc.* **Nar·nia** \ˈnär-nē-ə\. Commune, Terni prov., Umbria, cen. Italy, on Nera River 8 mi. (13 km.) SW of the commune of Terni; pop. (1989c) 20,630; episcopal see; town built on a rock 787 ft. (240 m.) high; 12th cent. cathedral; palaces of 12th and 14th cents.

Na·ro \ˈnä-rō\. Commune, Agrigento prov., SW Sicily, Italy, 12 mi. (19 km.) E of the commune of Agrigento; pop. (1981p) 10,704; ruins of castle and walls; early Christian necropolis nearby.

Naro. River, S Europe. See NERETVA.

Na·roch' *or* **Na·roch** \nə-ˈrȯchʸ\ *or Pol.* **Na·rocz** \ˈnä-ˌrȯch\. Small lake, N Belarus; 8 mi. (13 km.) long; ab. 32 sq. mi. (83 sq. km.); scene of battle on its shores in WWI.

Na·rod·na·ya, Mount \nä-ˈrȯd-nə-yə\. Mountain in N Ural Mts., Russia; 6214 ft. (1894 m.); highest peak in Ural Mts.

Naro–Fo·minsk \ˈnȧ-rə-fə-ˈminsk\. Town, SW Moscow Oblast, W Russia in Europe, 40 mi. (64 km.) SW of the city of Moscow; pop. (1991e) 58,800; held for a few months 1941–42 by Germans in WWII.

Na·rón \nä-ˈrȯn\. Commune, La Coruña prov., NW Spain, near Atlantic Ocean 17 mi. (27 km.) NE of the commune of La Coruña; pop. (1991c) 31,594.

Narova. See NARVA 1.

Nar·ra·bri \ˈnar-ə-ˌbrē\. Town, NE New South Wales, Australia; pop. (1991c) 14,653; base for outdoor recreation.

Nar·ra·gan·sett \ˌnar-ə-ˈgan-sət\. Town and summer resort, Washington co., S Rhode Island, at entrance to Narragansett Bay 9 mi. (14 km.) WSW of Newport; pop. (1990c) 14,985; includes the unincorporated summer resort of **Narragansett Pier** (pop. [1990c] 3721); at its S tip is **Port Judith**. Settled 1675; scene of engagement bet. colonists and Narraganset Indians 1675; set aside 1888 as special district in South Kingstown; incorp. as separate town 1901.

Narragansett Bay. Inlet of Atlantic Ocean, in SE Rhode Island; 28 mi. (45 km.) long; contains a number of islands incl. Rhode I., Prudence I., and Conanicut I.; the city of Providence is at its N extremity and the city of Newport is on Rhode I. at the E side of the entrance to the bay.

Nar·ro·gin \ˈnar-ə-jən\. Town, SW Western Australia, Australia, 110 mi. (177 km.) SE of Perth; pop. (1991c) 4638.

Nar·rows, The \ˈnar-ōz\. **1.** Strait bet. W end of Long Island and Staten I., SE New York, and connecting Upper New York Bay with Lower New York Bay; min. width 1.25 mi. (2 km.); spanned by Verrazano-Narrows Bridge (suspension; main span 4260 ft. or 1298 m.; completed 1964).

2. Narrowest part of the Dardanelles, ab. 10 mi. (16 km.) from the Aegean Sea; ab. 0.75 mi. (1.2 km.) wide.

3. Narrow channel in Virgin Is., West Indies, bet. N St. John I. (U.S.) and SW Tortola (British).

Narrows Dam *or* **Yad·kin Dam** \ˈyad-kin\. Dam across narrows of Yadkin River bet. Stanly and Montgomery cos., S cen. North Carolina; height 216 ft. (66 m.); impounds water, **Ba·din Lake** \ˈbā-dən\, for power.

Nar·sars·su·ak \när-ˈsär-ˌswäk\. Village at head of a fjord on SW coast near S tip of Greenland, ab. 90 mi. (145 km.) E of Ivigtut; airport.

Nar·simh·a·pur \ˈnär-si-mə-ˌpu̇r\ *also* **Nar·singh·pur** \ˈnär-siŋ-ˌpu̇r\. Town, cen. Madhya Pradesh, cen. India, on railroad line 50 mi. (80 km.) WSW of Jabalpur; pop. (1991p) 41,025.

Nar·singh·di \ˈnər-siŋ-ˌdē\. City, E cen. Bangladesh, NE of Dhaka; pop. (1991p) 100,120.

Nar·singh·garh \ˈnär-siŋ-ˌgär\. **1.** Former Indian state, now part of Madhya Pradesh, India; 731 sq. mi. (1893 sq. km.); founded as a Rajput state 17th cent.

2. Town, its ❋, ab. 38 mi. (61 km.) NW of Bhopal; pop. (1991p) 22,157.

Nar·singh·pur \ˈnär-siŋ-ˌpu̇r\. **1.** Former Indian state, now part of Orissa, NE India, N of Mahanadi River, W of Cuttack; 204 sq. mi. (528 sq. km.).

2. Town, Madhya Pradesh, India. See NARSIMHAPUR.

Na·ru \ˈnä-rü\. Island in Gotō Is. (*q.v.*), Japan.

Na·ru·to Strait \ˌnä-rü-ˈtō\. Strait bet. NE Shikoku I. and Awaji I., Japan, connecting the Inland Sea with Kii Channel and the Pacific Ocean; 1 mi. (2 km.) wide; remarkable for great velocity (7 to 11 knots) of its tides, esp. in the spring.

Nar·va \ˈnär-vä\. **1.** *or Russ.* **Na·ro·va** \ˈnär-ə-və\. River, NE Estonia; the outlet of Lake Peipus, flowing N past city of Narva (8 mi. or 13 km. from its mouth) to the Gulf of Finland; ab. 48 mi. (77 km.) long; navigable to Narva but has falls just above city (20 ft. or 6 m.), site of hydroelectric power plant.

2. City, NE Estonia, on Narva River ab. 8 mi. (13 km.) from its mouth in Gulf of Finland; pop. (1992e) 82,927; chief industrial center of Estonia; cotton and jute mills. Its port and a summer resort on the Gulf of Finland is **Narva–Jõe·suu** \-ˈyȯ-en-ˌsü\.

History: Founded 1223 by Danes; a seat of the Livonian (Teutonic) Knights and member of the Hanseatic League; seized by Russia 1558; captured by Swedes 1581; scene of battle Nov. 30, 1700 in which Swedes under Charles XII defeated Czar Peter the Great of Russia; recaptured by Russians 1704; scene of battles in WWI; became part of independent Estonia 1919; in WWII occupied by Germans 1941–44; included in U.S.S.R. 1944–91.

Nar·va·can \ˌnär-vä-ˈkän\. Municipality, Ilocos Sur prov., Luzon, Philippines, on main highway 13 mi. (21 km.) SSE of Vigan; pop. (1980c) 30,682.

Nar·vik \ˈnär-vik, -ˌvēk\. Seaport, Nordland co., N Norway, on a peninsula in Ofoten Fjord opp. the Lofoten; pop. (1992e) 18,736; ice-free harbor; exports iron ore; terminus of railroad line from Sweden. Occupied by Germans Apr. 1940, and scene of important offshore naval battles; briefly retaken by Allies May–June 1940.

Nar·'yan–Mar *or* **Nar·yan–Mar** \nərʸ-ˈyän-ˈmär\. Village, ❋ of Nenets Autonomous Okrug, NE Russia in Europe, on right shore of Pechora Delta, ab. 60 mi. (97 km.) from the sea.

\ə\ **abut** \ə̇\ matches \ᵊ\ kitten, Fr table \ər\ **further** \a\ **ash** \ā\ **ace**
\ä\ cot, cart \ȧ\ Fr bac \au̇\ **out** \b̲\ Span Avila \ch\ **chin** \e\ bet \ē\ **easy**
\g\ **go** \i\ hit \ī\ **ice** \j\ **job** \k̲\ Ger **ich**, Buch \ⁿ\ Fr vin
\ŋ\ sing \ō\ **go** \ö\ **all** \ȯ\ **law** \œ\ Fr **bœuf** \œ̄\ Fr **feu** \ȯi\ **boy**
\th\ **thin** \t̲h̲\ **this** \ü\ **loot** \u̇\ **foot** \ue\ Ger **füllen** \ue̅\ Fr **rue**
\y\ **yet** \ʸ\ Fr digne \ˈdēnʸ\, nuit \ˈnwʸē\ \yü\ **few** \yu̇\ **fury** \zh\ vision

Na·ryn \nə-ˈrin\. Town, cen. Kyrgyzstan, on **Naryn River,** an upper tributary of the Syr Dar'ya; pop. (1991e) 44,500; in mountainous region at ab. 6800 ft. (2100 m.).

Na Sam \ˈnä-ˌsäm\ *also* **Na·cham** \ˈnä-ˌchäm\ *or* **Nam–quan** \ˈnäm-ˌkwän\. Town, N Vietnam, just NW of Lang Son, terminus of railroad line from Hanoi; on Chinese frontier opp. Pingxiang in Guangxi Zhuangzu.

Nasca. See NAZCA.

Nase·by \ˈnāz-bē\. Parish, Northamptonshire, cen. England, 12 mi. (19 km.) ENE of Rugby; scene of battle June 14, 1645 in which Thomas Fairfax and Oliver Cromwell's Parliamentarian army disastrously defeated Charles I and Prince Rupert's Royalist forces, ending all chance of success for Royalist cause.

Nash \ˈnash\. County in NE North Carolina. See table at NORTH CAROLINA.

Nash·a·we·na Island \ˌna-shə-ˈwē-nə\. Island in S part of Elizabeth Is., Dukes co., SE Massachusetts.

Nashborough. See NASHVILLE 6.

Nāshik. See NASIK.

Nash·ua \ˈna-shu̇-wə, -ˌwā\. **1.** River, NE cen. Massachusetts and SE New Hampshire; flows N from Wachusett Reservoir, Worcester co., cen. Massachusetts, across the state border into Merrimack River at Nashua, New Hampshire; ab. 80 mi. (130 km.) long.

2. City, ⊗ of Hillsborough co., S New Hampshire, on Merrimack River 15 mi. (24 km.) S of Manchester; pop. (1990c) 79,662; electronics, office machines; Rivier Coll. (1933), Daniel Webster Coll. (1965); settled c. 1655; chartered as city 1853.

Nash·ville \ˈnash-ˌvil, -vəl\. **1.** City, ⊗ of Howard co., SW Arkansas, 37 mi. (60 km.) N of Texarkana; pop. (1990c) 4639.

2. City, ⊗ of Berrien co., S Georgia, 26 mi. (42 km.) N of Valdosta; pop. (1990c) 4782.

3. City, ⊗ of Washington co., SW Illinois, 20 mi. (32 km.) SW of Centralia; pop. (1990c) 3202.

4. Town, ⊗ of Brown co., S cen. Indiana, 17 mi. (27 km.) W of Columbus; pop. (1990c) 873.

5. Town, ⊗ of Nash co., NE North Carolina; pop. (1990c) 3617.

6. City, ✻ of Tennessee and ⊗ of Davidson co., N cen. Tennessee, on Cumberland River; pop. (1990c) 510,784; financial and commercial center; shoes, glass and rubber products; printing and publishing; important center of recording industry. Fisk Univ. (1866), Vanderbilt Univ. (1872), Meharry Medical Coll. (1876), David Lipscomb Univ. (1891), Trevecca Nazarene Coll. (1901), Tennessee State Univ. (1912), American Baptist Coll. (1924), Free Will Baptist Bible Coll. (1942), Belmont Univ. (1951), Aquinas Junior Coll. (1961); Greek Revival capitol (1855); replica of Greek Parthenon (1897); the Hermitage (home of Andrew Jackson, 7th U.S. president) is nearby.

History: Founded 1779 as **Nash·bor·ough** \ˈnash-ˌbər-ō\; incorp. as town 1784 and renamed Nashville; chartered as city 1806; became permanent ✻ of state 1843; scene of Nashville (Southern) Convention 1850; captured and held in Civil War by Union Army from Feb. 1862; scene of battle of Nashville Dec. 15–16, 1864 in which Union forces under Gen. George Henry Thomas decisively defeated Confederates under Gen. John Bell Hood.

Nä·si·jär·vi \ˈna-sē-ˌyar-vē\. Lake, SW Finland; the city of Tampere is situated on its S shore.

Na·sik \ˈnä-sik\ *or* **Nā·shik** \ˈnä-shik\. Town, cen. Maharashtra, W India, on Godavari River 100 mi. (161 km.) NE of Bombay; pop. (1991c) 656,925; brass and copper ware; renowned pilgrimage city of the Hindus; nearby cavern temples and cloisters of Buddhists dating from ab. 2000 years ago.

Nasira, En. See NAZARETH 2.

Na·sir·a·bad \nə-ˈsir-ə-ˌbäd\. See MYMENSINGH.

Nāsirīyah, An *or* **Nasiriya, An.** See AN NĀSIRĪYAH.

Na·so Point \ˈnä-sō\. SW point of Panay I., Philippines, at S end of Antique prov.

Nasratabad. See ZĀBOL.

Nass \ˈnas\. River, W British Columbia, Canada; flows SW through the Coast Mts. into Pacific Ocean (Dixon Entrance) 30 mi. (48 km.) N of Prince Rupert; 236 mi. (380 km.) long.

Nas·sau \ˈna-ˌsȯ\. **1.** Name of counties in two states of the U.S. See tables at FLORIDA and NEW YORK.

2. City, ✻ of Bahamas, on NE coast of New Providence I.; pop. (1990c) 172,196; exports include sisal, tomatoes, sponges; good harbor; popular winter resort; cathedral; three forts. Settled in 17th cent.; rendezvous of pirates in 18th cent.; city laid out 1729; forts built 17th–18th cents. to ward off attacks by Spaniards; a base for Confederate blockade-runners during U.S. Civil War.

3. \ *Ger.* ˈnä-ˌsau̇\. Region, W cen. Germany; former duchy, later Wiesbaden government dist. of Hesse-Nassau prov., Prussia, now in W Hesse and NE Rhineland-Palatinate states; chief city Wiesbaden; a thickly-forested and hilly territory N and E of the Rhine, crossed by the Lahn River and Taunus Mts. Title "Count of Nassau" first assumed 12th cent.; joined Confederation of the Rhine and raised to duchy 1806; annexed by Prussia 1866.

4. Island (atoll), Northern Cook Is., W cen. Pacific Ocean; pop. (1986) 119.

Nassau Bay. City, Harris co., SE Texas, SE of Houston; pop. (1990c) 4320; Lyndon B. Johnson Space Center is nearby.

Nas·sau Gulf \ˈnä-ˌsau̇\. Gulf in S Tierra del Fuego Archipelago (*q.v.*), extreme S Chile, bet. Navarino I. on N and Wollaston I. on S.

Nassau Range. See SUDIRMAN RANGE.

Nas·ser, Lake \ˈnä-sər, ˈna-\ *or in Sudan* **Lake Nu·bia** \ˈnü-bē-ə, ˈnyü-\. Lake, S Egypt and N Sudan; ab. 300 mi. (483 km.) long; formed in 1960s as a result of construction of Aswān High Dam; lake has flooded a number of archaeological sites, incl. Abu Simbel (*q.v.*).

Näss·jö \ˈne-ˌshœ\. Town, Jönköping prov., S Sweden, ab. 20 mi. (32 km.) SE of the city of Jönköping; pop. (1980p) 31,694.

Na·su \ˈnä-sü\ *or* **Na·su·da·ke** \ˌnä-sü-ˈdä-kā\. Volcanic peak on border bet. Fukushima and Tochigi prefectures, N cen. Honshū, Japan, NE of Nikkō; 6289 ft. (1917 m.).

Na·sug·bu \ˌnä-süg-ˈbü\. Municipality on W coast of Batangas prov., Luzon, Philippines, on South China Sea S of entrance to Manila Bay; pop. (1980c) 59,405; in WWII, U.S. forces landed here 1945.

Na·tal \nə-ˈtäl\. **1.** Seaport city, ✻ of Rio Grande do Norte state, NE Brazil; munic. pop. (1991p) 606,541; port and naval base; ships cotton, hides, and sugar; airport developed during WWII for flights to Africa; 16th cent. fort; cathedral; university (1958). Founded by Portuguese 1597; occupied by Dutch 1633–54.

2. Province, E Rep. of South Africa. See KWAZULU–NATAL.

Natanya. See NETANYA.

Na·tash·quan *or* **Na·tash·kwan** \nə-ˈtash-kwən\. River, S Labrador and E Quebec, Canada; flows S to the St. Lawrence opp. E end of Anticosti I.; 241 mi. (388 km.) long.

Nat·chaug \nə-ˈchȯg\. River, NE Connecticut; rises in NW Windham co., flows S and joins the Willimantic to form the Shetucket River at Willimantic.

Natch·ez \ˈna-chəz\. City, ⊗ of Adams co., SW Mississippi, on Mississippi River; pop. (1990c) 19,460; trade center; tires, wood pulp, paper products.

History: Region orig. inhabited by Natchez Indians; fortified settlement founded by French 1716; ceded to England 1763; seized by Spain 1779; yielded to U.S. 1798; ✻ of Mississippi Terr. 1798–1802; incorp. as city 1803; bombarded by Federal gunboat 1863 during Civil War and occupied by Union forces 1863–65.

Natchez National Historical Park. See UNITED STATES, *National Historical Parks.*

Natchez Trace. Old road, SE U.S., from Nashville, Tennessee, to Natchez, Mississippi; over 500 mi. (800 km.) long; orig. followed Indian trails; wagon road constructed early 19th cent. and used by traders, travelers, settlers, and as a post road.

Natch·i·toches \ˈna-kə-ˌtäsh\. **1.** Parish in NW cen. Louisiana. See table at LOUISIANA.

2. City, its ⊗, 52 mi. (84 km.) NW of Alexandria; pop. (1990c) 16,609; Northwestern State Univ. of Louisiana (1884).

Na·te·wa Bay *and* **Natewa Peninsula** \nä-ˈtā-wə\. See VANUA LEVU.

Nath·dwa·ra \nät-ˈdvä-rə\. Town, Rajasthan state, W cen. India, NNE of Udaipur; pop. (1991p) 30,855; Hindu pilgrimage site.

Na·thia Ga·li \ˈnä-tē-ə-ˈgäl-ē\. Town in North-West Frontier prov., Pakistan, in hills 38 mi. (61 km.) NNE of Rawalpindi; former summer ✻ of the province.

Na·tib, Mount \nä-ˈtēb\. Mountain, Zambales Range, cen. Bataan prov., Luzon, Philippines; 4111 ft. (1253 m.).

Na·tick \ˈnā-tik\. Town, Middlesex co., NE Massachusetts, 15 mi. (24 km.) WSW of Boston; pop. (1990c) 30,510; founded c. 1651 by clergyman John Eliot, "Apostle of the Indians," as first of his Praying Towns; later settled by colonial Americans as a farming community.

National Capital. Region of the Philippines. See table at PHILIPPINES.

Na·tion·al City \ˈnash-ən-ᵊl\. City, San Diego co., SW corner of California, on San Diego Bay 5 mi. (8 km.) S of the city of San Diego; pop. (1990c) 54,249.

National District. Administrative subdivision of the Dominican Republic. See table at DOMINICAN REPUBLIC.

National Park. Borough, Gloucester co., SW New Jersey, on Delaware River 6 mi. (10 km.) SSW of Camden; pop. (1990c) 3413.

National Road. See CUMBERLAND ROAD.

NATO. See NORTH ATLANTIC TREATY ORGANIZATION.

Natoena Islands. See NATUNA ISLANDS.

Na·tron, Lake \ˈnā-trən\. Lake, N Tanzania, near Kenyan border; ab. 35 mi. (56 km.) long by 15 mi. (24 km.) wide; large soda deposits. See MAGADI, LAKE and NATRON LAKES.

Na·tro·na \nə-ˈtrō-nə\. County in cen. Wyoming. See table at WYOMING.

Natron Lakes. Seven soda lakes (Arabic *naṭrūn* "native sodium carbonate") in **Wa·di an–Na·ṭrūn** \ˈwä-dē-ȧn-nä-ˈtrün\, a valley below sea level in N Egypt, 60 mi. (97 km.) WNW of Cairo.

Na·tu La \ˌnä-tü-ˈlä\. Pass (*la*) over the Himalayas in SE Sikkim state, India, E of Gangtok; alt. 14,199 ft. (4328 m.).

Na·tu·na Islands *or Du.* **Na·toe·na Islands** \nə-ˈtü-nə\. Island groups, **Natuna Be·sar Islands** \be-ˈsär\ and **Bun·gu·ran Se·la·tan Islands** \ˌbüŋ-gür-ˈän-sə-ˈlä-tən\, of Indonesia, in the South China Sea E of S Malay Penin. and W of Borneo; area of Natuna Besar Is., incl. Natuna Besar *or* **Great Natoena** (40 mi. or 64 km. by 30 mi. or 48 km.), 727 sq. mi. (1883 sq. km.); area of Bunguran Selatan Is., 89 sq. mi. (231 sq. km.); total area, 815 sq. mi. (2111 sq. km.).

Natural Bridge. Village in S Rockbridge co., W cen. Virginia, 16 mi. (26 km.) S of Lexington; site of a natural bridge of limestone (over Cedar Creek) 215 ft. (66 m.) high, 50 to 150 ft. (15 to 45 m.) wide, with a 90-foot (27-meter) span.

Natural Bridges National Monument. See UNITED STATES, *National Monuments.*

Nat·u·ral·iste, Cape \ˈna-chə-rə-list\. Cape, SW Western Australia, Australia, on W side of Geographe Bay.

Nauchampatepetl. See COFRE DE PEROTE.

Nau·cra·tis \ˈnȯ-krə-tis\. Greek city of ancient Egypt, in the Nile Delta, W of Rosetta branch. Founded 7th cent. B.C.; for a time was sole Greek trading station in Egypt; declined after founding of Alexandria.

Nau·ga·tuck \ˈnȯ-gə-ˌtək\. **1.** River, W Connecticut; rises in N Litchfield co., flows S through W New Haven co. into the Housatonic River at Derby; 65 mi. (105 km.) long; formerly an important source of waterpower for industrial plants. **2.** Town, New Haven co., S Connecticut, on Naugatuck River 5 mi. (8 km.) S of Waterbury; pop. (1990c) 30,625; chemicals; incorp. 1893.

Nauheim. See BAD NAUHEIM.

Nau·jan \naü-ˈhän\. Municipality, NE coast of Mindoro I., Mindoro Oriental prov., Philippines, just N of **Lake Naujan** 13 mi. (21 km.) SE of Calapan; pop. (1980c) 61,216.

Nau·lo·chus \ˈnȯ-lə-kəs\. Ancient port and Roman naval station, on N coast of Sicily at its E end E of Mylae; in naval battle 36 B.C. Roman fleet under Agrippa defeated fleet of Sextus Pompeius Magnus.

Naum·burg \ˈnaüm-ˌbürk\ *also* **Naumburg an der Saa·le** \ˌän-dər-ˈzä-lə\. Manufacturing city, Saxony-Anhalt, E cen. Germany, on the Saale River 28 mi. (45 km.) SW of Halle; 12th cent. cathedral; 16th cent. late-Gothic town hall. City founded c. 1000; became episcopal see c. 1028; received city rights 1142; member of Hanseatic League 15th cent.; passed to Saxony 1564, to Prussia 1815.

Naupactus. See NÁVPAKTOS.

Nau·plia \ˈnȯ-plē-ə\ *or* **Nau·pli·on** \-plē-ən\ *also* **Naf·plio** \ˈnäf-plē-ō\ *or Gk.* **Náv·pli·on** \ˈnäf-plē-ön\. Seaport city, ✻ of Argolis dept., NE Peloponnese, Greece, on Gulf of Argolis ab. 25 mi. (40 km.) SSW of Corinth; pop. (1991p) 11,453. Traces of Neolithic settlement found nearby; an ancient pre-Roman city, was a port of Árgos from 7th cent. B.C.; became important commercial center in Middle Ages under Byzantines; captured 13th cent. by Franks; passed to Venetians in 14th cent.; held by Turks 1540–1686, Venice 1686–1715, Turks 1715–1822; after liberated in Greek War of Independence, served as first ✻ of independent Greece 1829–34; an evacuation point of the British 1941 in WWII.

Nauplia, Gulf of. See ARGOLIS, GULF OF.

Nauplion. See NAUPLIA.

Na·u·ru \nä-ˈü-rü\; *formerly* **Pleas·ant Island** \ˈplez-ᵊnt\. Island republic in W Pacific Ocean, W of the Gilbert Is.; area 8.5 sq. mi. (22 sq. km.); highest point 225 ft. (69 m.); pop. (1993e) 10,000; government offices in Yaren dist.; phosphate deposits.

History: Inhabited by Pacific islanders when discovered by British 1798; annexed by Germany 1888; occupied by Australia 1914 and placed under British mandate (administered by Australia) 1919; occupied by Japanese in WWII; became a joint Australian, British, and New Zealand trust territory 1947; became an independent republic 1968.

Nausari. See NAVSARI.

Nau·shon Island \nȯ-ˈshän\. Island, largest of the Elizabeth Is., in Dukes co., SE Massachusetts; 7 mi. (11 km.) long.

Nau·voo \nȯ-ˈvü, ˈnȯ-vü\. City, Hancock co., W Illinois, on Mississippi River 45 mi. (72 km.) N of Quincy; pop. (1990c) 1108. Original town settled and renamed by Mormons under Joseph Smith 1839; became prosperous city of 20,000 people under Smith's leadership; abandoned by Mormons who migrated to Utah 1846 after Smith was killed by a mob in nearby Carthage (*q.v.*) 1844; made site of Utopian communistic society estab. 1849 by group of French Icarians under leadership of Étienne Cabet, settlement breaking up 1856 because of internal factional disagreements.

Na·va·cer·ra·da, Puer·to de \ˈpwer-tō-t͟hā-ˌnä-bä-t͟här-ˈrä-t͟hä\. Mountain pass in the Sierra de Guadarrama, cen. Spain; 6053 ft. (1845 m.)

Na·vad·wip \ˌnə-vəd-ˈvēp, -ˈwip\ *or* **Na·bad·wip** \-bəd-\; *formerly* **Na·dia** \ˈnə-dyə\. Town, West Bengal, India, on Bhagirathi River ab. 60 mi. (95 km.) N of Calcutta; pop. (1991p) 156,117; founded 1063; notable Hindu educational center.

Na·va·jo \ˈnä-və-ˌhō, ˈna-\. County in NE Arizona. See table at ARIZONA.

Navajo Dam *and* **Navajo Reservoir.** See UNITED STATES, *Dams and Reservoirs.*

Navajo Mountain. Solitary peak, San Juan co., SE Utah, near Rainbow Bridge National Monument; 10,388 ft. (3166 m.).

Navajo National Monument. See UNITED STATES, *National Monuments.*

Navajo Peak. Mountain in Boulder and Grand cos., N cen. Colorado; 13,406 ft. (4086 m.).

Nav·an \ˈna-vən\ *or* **An Uaimh** \än-ˈü-əv\. Town, cen. co. Meath, E Ireland, at confluence of Blackwater and Boyne rivers 16 mi. (26 km.) SW of Drogheda; pop. (1991p) 3411; lead and zinc mines.

Na·va·na·gar *or* **Na·wa·na·gar** \ˌnə-və-ˈnə-gər\. **1.** Former Indian state, now part of Gujarat state, W India; 3791 sq. mi. (9819 sq. km.); ✻ Jamnagar, on S shore of Gulf of Kachchh. **2.** City, India. See JAMNAGAR.

Nav·a·rin, Cape \ˌnə-və-ˈrēn\. Point, Chukot Autonomous Okrug, Magadan Oblast, NE Russia in Asia; extends into Bering Sea just S of Gulf of Anadyr.

Na·va·ri·no \ˌnä-vä-ˈrē-nō\. **1.** Island in Tierra del Fuego Archipelago (*q.v.*), Chile, S of E Tierra del Fuego I.
2. *or Ital.* **Py·los** \ˈpē-ˌlòs\. Seaport in SW Peloponnese, Greece; nearby ruins of ancient Mycenaean city; modern town arose in Middle Ages. In Peloponnesian War, scene of Athenian land and naval victory over Spartans 425 B.C.; from 16th cent. A.D. alternately held by Turks and Venetians; scene of naval battle fought in nearby waters Oct. 20, 1827 in which British, French, and Russian fleets under Sir Edward Codrington soundly defeated Turkish and Egyptian fleet.

Na·var·ra \nä-ˈbär-rä\. Autonomous community and province of N Spain. See table at SPAIN.

Na·varre \nə-ˈvär\ *or Span.* **Na·var·ra** \nä-ˈbär-rä\ *or Fr.* **Na·varre** \nà-ˈvàr\. Ancient kingdom, N Spain; bordered on N by France, on E and S by Aragon, on SW by Old Castile, and on NW by Basque Country; now forms modern Spanish autonomous community and prov. of Navarra and W part of French dept. of Pyrénées-Atlantiques; in Pyrenees and Cantabrian Mts.; watered by Ebro, Bidassoa, Arga, and Aragon rivers.
History: In early times inhabited by Vascones, progenitors of the Basques and Gascons; region conquered by Romans, and subsequently, by Visigoths, and gained early importance through famous mountain pass of Roncesvalles (*q.v.*); conquered by Frankish King (later Holy Roman Emperor) Charlemagne 778; became independent kingdom 10th cent.; under Sancho III (reigned 1000–1035), united by marriage with crown of Castile, this domain being divided upon his death into three kingdoms of Navarre, Aragon, and Castile; annexed to Aragon 1076; appanage of France 1234–1328; S part conquered by Ferdinand II of Aragon 1512 and incorp. with Castile 1515; N part (now in dept. of Pyrénées-Atlantiques, France) united to French crown when Henry of Navarre became Henry IV of Bourbon, king of France 1589.

Na·var·re·te \ˌnä-vär-ˈrā-tā\. Commune, La Rioja prov., N Spain, bet. Logroño and Nájera (*q.v.*); pop. (1991c) 2021.

Na·var·ro \nə-ˈvar-ō\. County in NE cen. Texas. See table at TEXAS.

Navas de Tolosa, Las. See LAS NAVAS DE TOLOSA.

Nav·a·so·ta \ˌna-və-ˈsō-tə\. **1.** River, E Texas; flows S into Brazos River at point where Brazos, Grimes, and Washington cos. meet; 125 mi. (201 km.) long.
2. City, Grimes co., E cen. Texas, 26 mi. (42 km.) SSE of Bryan; pop. (1990c) 6296.

Na·vas·sa \nə-ˈva-sə\. Island in Caribbean Sea bet. Jamaica and Hispaniola; 2 mi. (3 km.) long; belongs to U.S.

Nav·e·sink River \ˈna-və-ˌsiŋk\. Estuary, NE Monmouth co., E cen. New Jersey, N of Shrewsbury River; forms an inlet about 5 mi. (8 km.) long; barred from flowing directly into the Atlantic Ocean by the peninsula at the N end of which is Sandy Hook extending into Lower New York Bay.

Navigators Islands. See SAMOA.

Na·voi *or* **Na·woiy** \ˈnà-ˌvòi\. City, Uzbekistan, NE of Bukhara and WNW of Samarqand; pop. (1991e) 111,600.

Na·vo·joa \ˌnä-vä-ˈhō-ä\. Town, S Sonora state, NW Mexico; munic. pop. (1990p) 122,390; on coastal railroad line.

Na·vo·tas \nä-ˈvō-tä\. Municipality, Rizal prov., Luzon, Philippines, on coast of Manila Bay adjacent to Malabon just N of Manila; pop. (1990p) 186,000.

Náv·pak·tos \ˈnäf-ˌpäk-tös\ *or Ital.* **Le·pan·to** \ˈle-pän-ˌtō\; *anc.* **Nau·pac·tus** \nò-ˈpak-təs\. Seaport in Aetolia and Acarnania dept., Greece, on the strait connecting the Gulfs of Corinth and Patras; captured by Athens 5th cent. B.C. and made new home of exiled Messenians after Third Messenian War; served as important Athenian naval base during Peloponnesian Wars, and nearby waters were scene 429 B.C. of naval battles in which Athenian fleet defeated a superior Peloponnesian fleet; site of peace treaty 217 B.C. bet. Aetolians and Philip V of Macedon; in 16th cent. known as Lepanto and noted for naval battle in nearby strait Oct. 7, 1571, in which Turkish fleet was decisively defeated by combined fleets of Holy League under Don John of Austria.

Návplion. See NAUPLIA.

Na·vron·go \nä-ˈvròŋ-gō\. Town, N Ghana, near Burkina Faso border and 100 mi. (161 km.) N of Tamale.

Nav·sa·ri \nəv-ˈsär-ē\ *also* **Nau·sa·ri** \naù-\. Town, Gujarat, W India, near Gulf of Khambhat 135 mi. (217 km.) N of Bombay; pop. (1991p) 125,980.

Nawa. See NAHA.

Na·wab·ganj \nə-ˈwäb-ˌgənj\. **1.** City, W Bangladesh, on the Ganges; pop. (1991p) 131,260.
2. Town, E Uttar Pradesh, N India, 17 mi. (27 km.) E of Lucknow; pop. (1991p) 131,260; scene of victory by British officer Sir James Hope Grant June 12, 1858 during the Indian mutiny.

Na·wab·shah \nə-ˈwäb-ˌshä\. Town, cen. Sind, Pakistan, ab. 60 mi. (95 km.) N of Hyderabad; munic. pop. (1981c) 102,139.

Na·wa·da \nə-ˈvä-də\. Town, cen. Bihar state, E India, E of Gaya; pop. (1991p) 53,075.

Nawanagar. See NAVANAGAR.

Na·wi·li·wi·li Bay \nä-ˌwē-lē-ˈwē-lē\. Bay on SE coast of Kauai I., Hawaii, S of Ninini Point.

Nax·çi·van *or* **Na·khi·che·van** \ˌnə-k̲ē-chi-ˈvän\; *anc* **Nax·ua·na** \näk-ˈswä-nä\. **1.** Autonomous republic of Azerbaijan, an exclave separated from the rest of the country by Armenia, bordering also Iran and in small part Turkey; 2124 sq. mi. (5501 sq. km.); pop. (1991e) 305,700; ✻ Naxçivan. An agricultural area on a high plateau in bend of Araks River; produces wheat and cotton; vineyards, fruit orchards; silkworm breeding, cattle raising. Republic estab. 1924; before 1991 comprised an A.S.S.R. of the U.S.S.R.
2. Town, its ✻, on Araks River 85 mi. (137 km.) SE of Yerevan, Armenia; pop. (1991e) 61,700; wine, furniture; according to Armenian tradition founded by Old Testament patriarch Noah. Ancient trading center; passed from Persia to Russia 1828.

Nax·os \ˈnak-säs, -ˌsäs\. **1.** *or Gk.* **Ná·xos** \ˈnäk-ˌsös\. Largest island of the Cyclades, Aegean Sea, E of Paros, in Cyclades dept., Greece; ab. 22 mi. (35 km.) long by 16 mi. (26 km.) wide; area 165 sq. mi. (427 sq. km.); pop. (1981c) 14,037; chief town Naxos (on NW coast); wine. In mythology, the island where Theseus abandoned Ariadne after she helped him escape from the labyrinth; famous as an early center for worship of Dionysus; seized and sacked by Persians 490 B.C.; member of Delian League, but upon failed revolt against the League 471 B.C. was made directly subject to Athens; seat of a medieval Venetian duchy 1207–1566 (see AEGEAN ISLANDS); held by Turks 1566–1830; since War of Independence has belonged to Greece.
2. Oldest colony of ancient Greece in Sicily, founded c. 735 B.C. by Chalcidians; opposed Syracuse in 5th cent. B.C. and was destroyed by Dionysius the Elder, tyrant of Syracusae, 403 B.C.; its ruins excavated in hills near Taormina on E coast.

Naxuana. See NAXÇIVAN.

Na·ya·garh \nə-ˈyä-gər\. **1.** Former Indian state, now part of Orissa state, NE India; 562 sq. mi. (1456 sq. km.).
2. Town, its ✻, 55 mi. (89 km.) WSW of Cuttack.

Na·ya·rit \ˌnī-ä-ˈrēt\. State of W Mexico. See table at MEXICO.

Nāy Band \ˈnī-ˈbänd\ *or* **Na·band** \nä-ˈbänd\. Cape on SW coast of Iran, projecting into E cen. Persian Gulf.

Na·zan Bay \nə-ˈzan\. Inlet, SE Atka I., Andreanof Is., Aleutian Is., SW Alaska.

Na·za·ré \ˌnà-zà-ˈrā\; *formerly* **Na·za·reth** \ˌnà-zà-ˈret\. City, Bahia state, E Brazil, near coast 35 mi. (56 km.) W of Salvador; munic. pop. (1991p) 15,058.

Naz·a·reth \ˈna-zə-rəth\. **1.** Borough, Northampton co., E Pennsylvania, 13 mi. (21 km.) NE of Allentown; pop. (1990c) 5713; settled by Moravians c. 1740.

2. *or Heb.* **Na·ze·rat** \ˌnä-zə-ˈrät\ *or Arab.* **En Na·si·ra** \en-ˈnä-sē-ˌrä\. Town, ✱ of Northern District, N Israel, ab. 18 mi. (30 km.) SE of Haifa; pop. (1992e) 49,800; textiles, tourism; numerous churches; junction point of highways from Haifa and Jerusalem NE to Tiberias on the Sea of Galilee and on N edge of Plain of Esdraelon. Home of Joseph and Mary and of Jesus in his childhood; site of St. Mary's Well; captured several times during the Crusades; its Christian inhabitants massacred by Mamlūk (Egyptian) Sultan Baybars I 1263; taken by Turks 1517; occupied by British 1918; captured by Israeli forces 1948.

Naz·ca *also* **Nas·ca** \ˈnäs-kä\. Archaeological site of pre-Inca culture, SW Peru, at town of Nazca, 85 mi. (137 km.) SE of Ica on Pan American Highway; nearby Nazca lines: geometric shapes and animal pictures, up to hundreds of feet in length, scratched into the earth's surface, of pre-Inca (Nazca) origin and unknown purpose, and best seen from the air.

Na·ze \ˈnä-zā\. Chief town of Amami Is., Japan, on N coast of Amami-Ō-shima.

Naze, The \ˈnāz\. **1.** Headland on E coast of Essex, SE England, 5 mi. (8 km.) S of Harwich.

2. Cape, Norway. See LINDESNES.

Nazerat. See NAZARETH 2.

Na·zil·li \ˌnä-zē-ˈlē\. Town, Aydın prov., SW Turkey in Asia, on railroad line and on N bank of Menderes River 26 mi. (42 km.) E of the town of Aydın.

Nazinon. See VOLTA, RED.

Naz·ran' *or* **Naz·ran** \ˈnáz-rənʸ\. Town, Ingushetia, Russia, WSW of Grozny, Chechnya.

Naz·ret *or* **Naz·rēt** \ˈnäz-ret\. Town, cen. Ethiopia, SE of Addis Ababa; pop. (1989e) 94,184.

Nda·la·tan·do *or* **N'da·la·tan·do** \ᵊn-ˌdä-lä-ˈtän-dō\; *formerly* **Vi·la Sa·la·zar** \ˈvē-lə-ˌsa-lə-ˈzär, ˌsä-\. Town, NW Angola, 160 mi. (257 km.) ESE of Luanda; ✱ of Cuanza Norte prov.

Ndeni See NENDO.

Ndi·ke·va, Mount \ᵊn-dē-ˈkā-vä\; *formerly* **Mount Thur·ston** \ˈthər-stən\. Peak, E Vanua Levu I., Fiji, SW Pacific Ocean; 3134 ft. (955 m.); highest point on the island.

N'Dja·me·na \ᵊn-jä-ˈmā-nä\; *formerly* **Fort–La·my** \ˌfȯr-lə-ˈmē\. City, ✱ of Chad, on Chari River in SW part of the country; pop. (1992e) 687,800; has the nation's only university (founded 1971).

Ndo·la \ᵊn-ˈdō-lä\. Town, N Zambia, ab. 170 mi. (275 km.) N of Lusaka; pop. (1990p) 376,311; cement; center of copper-mining region.

Ndon·go \ᵊn-ˈdȯŋ-gō\. Historic African kingdom arising c. 1500 in what is now Angola; established trade with Portuguese 16th cent., but when Portuguese tried to take over, fighting ensued, lasting nearly 100 years; ultimately absorbed into Angola c. 1670.

Ndre·ke·ti \ᵊn-drā-ˈke-tē\ *or* **Dre·ke·ti** \drā-ˈke-tē\. Chief river of Vanua Levu I., Fiji, SW Pacific Ocean.

Neagh, Lough \läk-ˈnā\. Lake, E cen. Northern Ireland; 18 mi. (29 km.) long by 15 mi. (24 km.) wide; 153 sq. mi. (396 sq. km.); largest lake in British Isles.

Ne·ah Bay \ˈnē-ə\. Unincorporated settlement, NW Clallam co., NW Washington, on inlet of Strait of Juan de Fuca; pop. (1990c) 916, most of whom are American Indians; headquarters of Makah Indian Reservation; site 1791 of earliest European settlement (Spanish, lasted five months) in the state of Washington.

Neamţ \ˈnyämts\. County of NE Romania. See table at ROMANIA.

Ne·an·der·thal \nā-ˈän-dər-ˌtäl, nē-ˈan-dər-ˌthȯl\. Valley just E of Düsseldorf, in North Rhine-Westphalia, Germany, where parts of a skeleton of a Middle Paleolithic hominid (*Homo sapiens neanderthalensis*) were first discovered 1856.

Ne·ap·o·lis \nē-ˈa-pə-lis\. **1.** Ancient city, Macedonia, NE Greece, the port where St. Paul landed on his way to Philippi on his 2d missionary journey (*Acts* xvi. 11). Its site is near the modern Kavála.

2. Ancient city, Italy. See NAPLES 4.

3. Town, Jordan. See NĀBULUS.

4. Town, Tunisia. See NABEUL.

Neapolitan Apennines. See table at APENNINES.

Near East. **1.** The Ottoman Empire at its greatest extent—a former usage.

2. General term used of the countries of SW Asia and frequently extended to include NE Africa; sometimes used interchangeably with Middle East (*q.v.*), which has become the more commonly used term. See also EAST, THE 1 and FAR EAST.

Near Islands. Island group, farthest W of the Aleutian Is., SW Alaska, 52°40′N, 173°30′E; E of International Date Line; includes Attu (*q.v.*), the chief island, and Agattu, and Semichi Is.; during WWII occupied by Japanese 1942–43.

Neath \ˈnēth\. **1.** *or Welsh* **Nedd** \ˈneth\. River, S Wales; flows S into Bristol Channel E of Gower Penin.; 25 mi. (40 km.) long.

2. *or Welsh* **Cas·tell–nedd** \ˌkas-tehl-ˈneth\. Town, West Glamorgan co., SE Wales, on the Neath River; pop. (1991p) 64,100; iron, steel, tinplate, chemicals; ruins of Neath Abbey, founded 1130.

Ne·bit–Dag \nyi-ˈbēt-ˈdäk\; *formerly* **Nef·te·dag** \ˌnyif-ti-ˈdäk\. Town, Turkmenistan, ab. 80 mi. (130 km.) SE of Krasnovodsk; pop. (1991e) 89,100.

Nebo. See PISGAH, MOUNT 2.

Ne·bo, Mount \ˈnē-bō\. Peak, E Juab co., W Utah; 11,877 ft. (3620 m.).

Ne·bras·ka \nə-ˈbras-kə\. A central state of U.S.A., bounded on N by South Dakota, on E by Iowa and a corner of Missouri, on S by Kansas and Colorado, and on W by Wyoming; 15th state in area, 77,355 sq. mi. (200,349 sq. km.); 36th state in population, (1990c) 1,578,385; ✱ Lincoln; 37th state admitted to Union (1867). See table of states at UNITED STATES.

Nickname: Cornhusker State.

State flower: Goldenrod.

Motto: Equality Before the Law.

Rivers: Missouri, forming E boundary; North Platte and South Platte, uniting in SW cen. area to form the Platte, flowing E into the Missouri.

Highest point: Johnson Township, 5426 ft. (1654 m.), in Kimball co.

Chief products: Corn, wheat; livestock; oil; food processing; manufacturing: machinery, fabricated metal products.

Chief cities: Omaha and Lincoln.

Political divisions: Divided into the following 93 counties (for pronunciation of their names, see their individual entries):

NAME	AREA[1] (sq. mi.)	AREA[1] (sq. km.)	POP. (1990c)	CO. SEAT
Adams	562	1,456	29,625	Hastings
Antelope	853	2,209	7,965	Neligh
Arthur	704	1,823	462	Arthur
Banner	738	1,911	852	Harrisburg
Blaine	710	1,839	675	Brewster
Boone	683	1,769	6,667	Albion
Box Butte	1,065	2,758	13,130	Alliance
Boyd	538	1,393	2,835	Butte
Brown	1,216	3,149	3,657	Ainsworth
Buffalo	949	2,458	37,447	Kearney
Burt	483	1,251	7,868	Tekamah
Butler	582	1,507	8,601	David City
Cass	557	1,443	21,318	Plattsmouth
Cedar	742	1,922	10,131	Hartington
Chase	890	2,305	4,381	Imperial
Cherry	5,971	15,465	6,307	Valentine
Cheyenne	1,186	3,072	9,494	Sidney
Clay	570	1,476	7,123	Clay Center
Colfax	406	1,052	9,139	Schuyler
Cuming	571	1,479	10,117	West Point
Custer	2,558	6,625	12,270	Broken Bow
Dakota	255	660	16,742	Dakota City
Dawes	1,386	3,590	9,021	Chadron
Dawson	975	2,525	19,940	Lexington
Deuel	436	1,129	2,237	Chappell

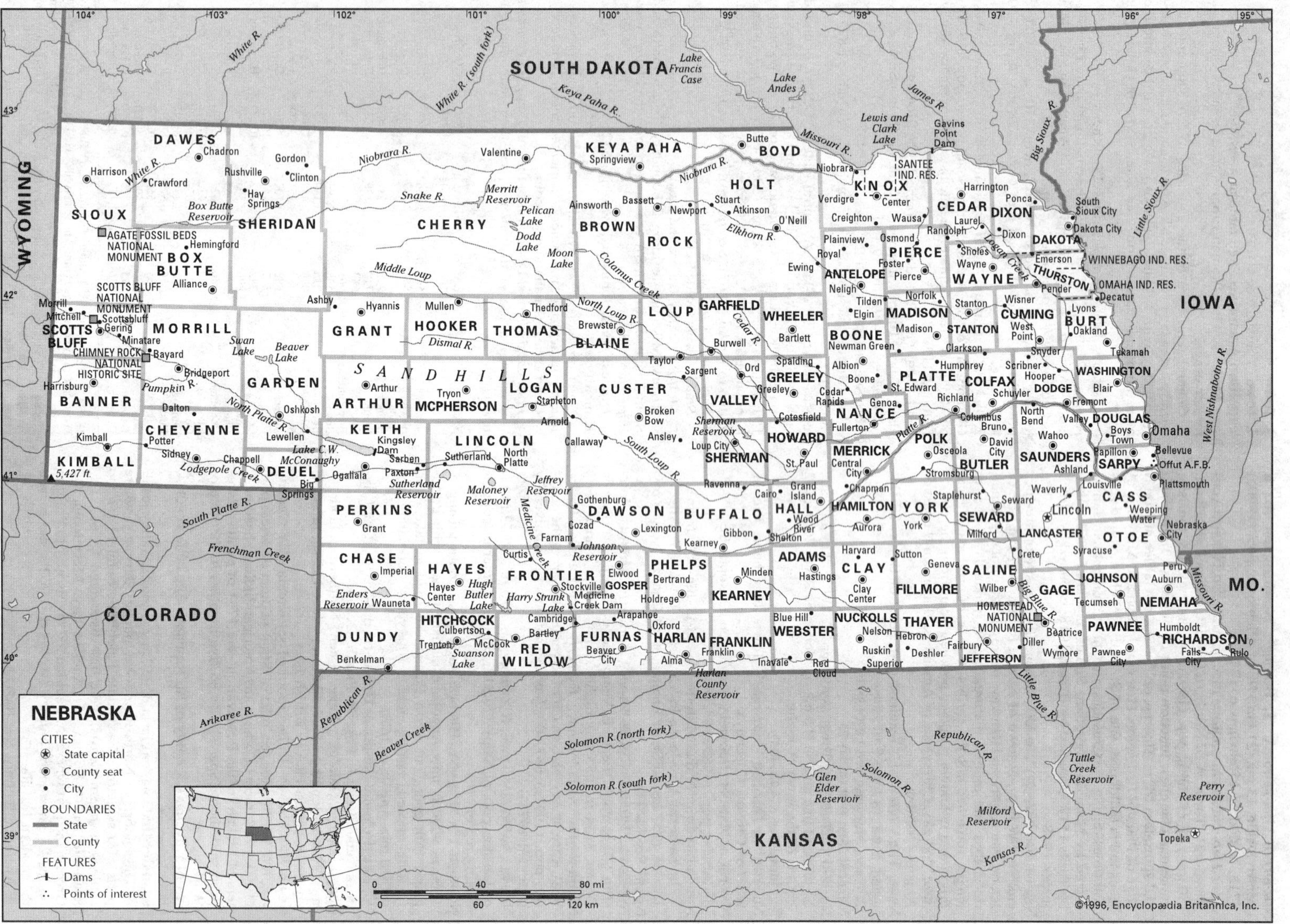
NEBRASKA
CITIES
State capital
County seat
City
BOUNDARIES
State
County
FEATURES
Dams
Points of interest
0 40 80 mi
0 60 120 km
SOUTH DAKOTA
WYOMING
IOWA
MO.
KANSAS
COLORADO
DAWES
SIOUX
BOX BUTTE
SHERIDAN
CHERRY
KEYA PAHA
BROWN
ROCK
BOYD
HOLT
KNOX
CEDAR
DIXON
DAKOTA
THURSTON
WAYNE
PIERCE
ANTELOPE
SCOTTS BLUFF
MORRILL
GRANT
HOOKER
THOMAS
BLAINE
LOUP
GARFIELD
WHEELER
BOONE
MADISON
STANTON
CUMING
BURT
BANNER
GARDEN
ARTHUR
MCPHERSON
LOGAN
CUSTER
VALLEY
GREELEY
PLATTE
COLFAX
DODGE
WASHINGTON
KIMBALL
CHEYENNE
DEUEL
KEITH
LINCOLN
SHERMAN
HOWARD
NANCE
MERRICK
POLK
BUTLER
SAUNDERS
DOUGLAS
SARPY
PERKINS
DAWSON
BUFFALO
HALL
HAMILTON
YORK
SEWARD
LANCASTER
CASS
OTOE
CHASE
HAYES
FRONTIER
GOSPER
PHELPS
KEARNEY
ADAMS
CLAY
FILLMORE
SALINE
GAGE
JOHNSON
NEMAHA
DUNDY
HITCHCOCK
RED WILLOW
FURNAS
HARLAN
FRANKLIN
WEBSTER
NUCKOLLS
THAYER
JEFFERSON
PAWNEE
RICHARDSON
SANDHILLS
Lincoln
Omaha
©1996, Encyclopædia Britannica, Inc.

NAME	AREA[1] (sq. mi.)	AREA[1] (sq. km.)	POP. (1990c)	CO. SEAT
Dixon	475	1,230	6,143	Ponca
Dodge	528	1,368	34,500	Fremont
Douglas	335	868	416,444	Omaha
Dundy	921	2,385	2,582	Benkelman
Fillmore	577	1,494	7,103	Geneva
Franklin	578	1,497	3,938	Franklin
Frontier	962	2,492	3,101	Stockville
Furnas	722	1,870	5,553	Beaver City
Gage	858	2,222	22,794	Beatrice
Garden	1,678	4,346	2,460	Oshkosh
Garfield	569	1,474	2,141	Burwell
Gosper	464	1,202	1,928	Elwood
Grant	764	1,979	769	Hyannis
Greeley	570	1,476	3,006	Greeley
Hall	537	1,391	48,925	Grand Island
Hamilton	542	1,404	8,862	Aurora
Harlan	556	1,440	3,810	Alma
Hayes	711	1,841	1,222	Hayes Center
Hitchcock	712	1,844	3,750	Trenton
Holt	2,405	6,229	12,599	O'Neill
Hooker	722	1,870	793	Mullen
Howard	564	1,461	6,055	St. Paul
Jefferson	577	1,494	8,759	Fairbury
Johnson	377	976	4,673	Tecumseh
Kearney	512	1,326	6,629	Minden
Keith	1,035	2,681	8,584	Ogallala
Keya Paha	768	1,989	1,029	Springview
Kimball	953	2,468	4,108	Kimball
Knox	1,107	2,867	9,534	Center
Lancaster	845	2,189	213,641	Lincoln
Lincoln	2,522	6,532	32,508	North Platte
Logan	570	1,476	878	Stapleton
Loup	574	1,487	683	Taylor
McPherson	856	2,217	546	Tryon
Madison	572	1,481	32,655	Madison
Merrick	480	1,243	8,042	Central City
Morrill	1,402	3,631	5,423	Bridgeport
Nance	439	1,137	4,275	Fullerton
Nemaha	400	1,036	7,980	Auburn
Nuckolls	579	1,500	5,786	Nelson
Otoe	619	1,603	14,252	Nebraska City
Pawnee	433	1,121	3,317	Pawnee City
Perkins	885	2,292	3,367	Grant
Phelps	544	1,409	9,715	Holdrege
Pierce	573	1,484	7,827	Pierce
Platte	667	1,728	29,820	Columbus
Polk	432	1,119	5,675	Osceola
Red Willow	716	1,854	11,705	McCook
Richardson	550	1,425	9,937	Falls City
Rock	1,009	2,613	2,019	Bassett
Saline	575	1,489	12,715	Wilber
Sarpy	239	619	102,583	Papillion
Saunders	759	1,966	18,285	Wahoo
Scotts Bluff	726	1,880	36,025	Gering
Seward	571	1,479	15,450	Seward
Sheridan	2,462	6,377	6,750	Rushville
Sherman	571	1,479	3,718	Loup City
Sioux	2,063	5,343	1,549	Harrison
Stanton	431	1,116	6,244	Stanton
Thayer	577	1,494	6,635	Hebron
Thomas	716	1,854	851	Thedford
Thurston	388	1,005	6,936	Pender
Valley	569	1,474	5,169	Ord
Washington	386	1,000	16,607	Blair
Wayne	443	1,147	9,364	Wayne
Webster	575	1,489	4,279	Red Cloud
Wheeler	576	1,492	948	Bartlett
York	577	1,494	14,428	York

[1]Area = land area.

History: Part of Louisiana Purchase (*q.v.*) 1803, of Louisiana Terr. 1805, and of Missouri Terr. 1812; part of unorganized U.S. territory c. 1821–54; part of Nebraska Terr. (*q.v.*) organized 1854 as result of Kansas-Nebraska Act; territory reduced to area of present state by 1863; held first constitutional convention 1866; admitted to Union Mar. 1, 1867; established one-house legislature, the nation's only one, 1937.

Nebraska City. City, ⊗ of Otoe co., SE Nebraska, on Missouri River 41 mi. (66 km.) S of Omaha; pop. (1990c) 6547; home of J. Sterling Morton, the originator of Arbor Day, his residence now in a state park.

Nebraska Territory. Former territory, U.S.A.; comprised a region of variable size bet. the Rocky Mts. and the Missouri River, and bet. 40°N and Canada; acquired by U.S. in Louisiana Purchase (*q.v.*) 1803; included in Louisiana Terr., Missouri Terr. (*qq.v.*), and unorganized U.S. territory prior to 1854; Nebraska Terr. organized under Kansas-Nebraska Act May 30, 1854 encompassing all U.S. land bet. the Missouri River and the Rocky Mts. and north of 40°N, and incl. what is now Nebraska, NE Colorado, most of Wyoming and Montana, and W North and South Dakota; reduced to area of Nebraska and SE Wyoming 1861 with formation of Dakota Terr. (*q.v.*) and territory of Colorado; reduced to area of present state 1863 with formation of Idaho Terr. (*q.v.*); Nebraska admitted to the Union 1867.

Nebrija *or* **Nebrixa** *or* **Nebrissa.** See LEBRIJA.

Ne·ca·xa \nā-ˈkä-hä\. River, cen. Mexico, in Puebla and Veracruz states (known as the **Te·co·lu·tla** \ˌtā-kō-ˈlüt-lä\ in Veracruz); has falls 540 ft. (165 m.) high.

Ne·chako \ni-ˈcha-kō\. River, cen. British Columbia, Canada; flows N and E into Fraser River; 287 mi. (462 km.) long.

Nech·es \ˈne-chəz\. River, E Texas; rises in Van Zandt co., NE Texas, runs S and SE into Sabine Lake; 416 mi. (669 km.) long. See SABINE-NECHES WATERWAY.

Neck·ar \ˈne-kär\. River, SW Germany; rises in the Black Forest, S Baden-Württemberg, flows N and W into the Rhine at Mannheim; 228 mi. (367 km.) long; navigable up to Bad Cannstatt, near Stuttgart.

Neck·er \ˈne-kər\. Island of Leeward Is. group, Hawaii, in cen. Pacific Ocean ab. 300 mi. (480 km.) NW of Niihau I., 164°42′W, 23°35′N.

Ne·co·chea \ˌnā-kō-ˈchā-ä\. Seaport town, Buenos Aires prov., E Argentina, 265 mi. (426 km.) directly S of city of Buenos Aires; pop. (1980p) 50,939; beach resort.

Nedd. See NEATH 1.

Ne·der·land. 1. \ˈnā-dər-ˌlänt\. Kingdom, W Europe. See NETHERLANDS.

2. \ˈnē-dər-ˌland\. City, Jefferson co., SE Texas, near Beaumont; pop. (1990c) 16,192.

Ne·der Rijn \ˈnā-dər-ˈrīn\. The Lower Rhine in Netherlands; from it the IJssel flows N into IJsselmeer, and the Lek River continues W into the Nieuwe Maas and the North Sea.

Nedjed. See NEJD.

Nee·bish Island \ˈnē-bish\. Island in Chippewa co., E Upper Penin., Michigan, in St. Marys River, S of Sault Sainte Marie.

Need·ham \ˈnē-dəm\. Town, Norfolk co., E Massachusetts, 10 mi. (16 km.) WSW of Boston; pop. (1990c) 27,557.

Nee·dle Mountain \ˈnēd-^{ə}l\. Peak, S Park co., NW Wyoming, in the Absaroka Range; 12,130 ft. (3697 m.).

Nee·dles \ˈnēd-^{ə}lz\. City, San Bernardino co., SE California, on Colorado River; pop. (1990c) 5191.

Needles, The. Three pointed limestone rocks in the English Channel just W of the Isle of Wight; lighthouse.

Ñe·em·bu·cú \ˌnā-em-bü-ˈkü\. Department of SW Paraguay. See table at PARAGUAY.

Nee·nah \ˈnē-nə\. City, Winnebago co., E Wisconsin, on Lake Winnebago 7 mi. (11 km.) S of Appleton; pop. (1990c) 23,219; forms one community with its twin city, Menasha (*q.v.*); papermaking; settled 1835.

Nee·pa·wa \ˈnē-pə-ˌwȯ, -ˌwä\. Town, SW Manitoba, Canada, 35 mi. (56 km.) NE of Brandon; pop. (1991c) 3258.

Neer·win·den \ˈner-ˌvin-dən\. Village, Liège prov., E Belgium, 22 mi. (35 km.) NW of the city of Liège; scene of two battles: July 1693, when the forces of the Grand Alliance under William III of England were defeated by French under Marshal Francois-Henri de Montmorency-Bouteville, duc de Luxembourg; Mar. 1793, when the French under Gen. Charles-Francois Dumouriez were defeated and subsequently forced to withdraw to France by Austrians.

Nef·ta \ˈnef-tə\. Town, W Tunisia, on W shore of Chott Djerid.

Neftedag. See NEBIT-DAG.

Nefud. See AN NAFŪD.

Negapatam *or* **Negapattinam.** See NAGAPATTINAM.

Ne·gau·nee \ni-ˈgȯ-nē\. City, Marquette co., Upper Penin., Michigan, W of the city of Marquette; pop. (1990c) 4741.

Ne·ge·ri Sem·bi·lan \ˈnā-gə-rē-səm-ˈbē-lən\ *also* **Ne·gri Sem·bilan** \nə-ˈgrē\. A state of Malaysia, SE Asia, bounded on N and NE by Pahang, on SE by Johor, on S by Melaka, on SW by the Strait of Malacca, and on W by Selangor; ✻ Seremban; rubber, rice, tin. See table at MALAYSIA.

History: Confederation of nine states (united 1889); came under British protection 1874–88; under Japanese control in WWII; became part of the independent Federation of Malaya 1957; became a state of Malaysia 1963.

Neg·ev \ˈne-ˌgev\ *or* **Ha·Negev** \hä-\ *or* **Neg·eb** \-ˌgeb\. Desert region, S Israel; ab. 4700 sq. mi. (12,200 sq. km.); max. elev. ab. 3300 ft. (1000 m.); largest town Beersheba; includes several irrigated areas producing fruit and vegetables; potash, bromine, copper; assigned to Israel in partition of Palestine 1948; scene of clashes bet. Israeli and Egyptian forces 1948–49; site of many planned Israeli settlements.

Ne·goi·u \ne-ˈgȯi-ˌü\ *or* **Ne·goi·ul** \ne-ˈgȯi-ˌül\. Mountain, cen. Romania; 8317 ft. (2535 m.); 2d highest peak in Transylvanian Alps.

Ne·gom·bo \nā-ˈgȯm-bō\. Seaport, Sri Lanka, 19 mi. (31 km.) N of Colombo; pop. (1990e) 64,000; fishing port. Ruled by Portuguese 16th–17th cents., then by Dutch c. 1644–1796; taken by English 1796.

Negra, Cumbre. See CUMBRE NEGRA.

Ne·grais, Cape \nə-ˈgrīs\. Headland, Myanmar, projecting into Bay of Bengal SSW of city of Vasi; 16°N, 94°10′E.

Ne·gra Point \ˈnā-grä, ˈne-\. Headland on NW coast of Ilocos Norte prov., Luzon, Philippines, bet. Cape Bojeador on W and Mayraira Point on E; marks W side of Bangui Bay.

Negri Sembilan. See NEGERI SEMBILAN.

Ne·gro, Cape \ˈnā-grō, ˈne-\. Point, N Morocco, NE of Tétouan.

Negro, Mount. Peak in cen. Panama, in the Tabasara Mts.; 4429 ft. (1350 m.).

Ne·gro, Rio \ˈrē-ō-ˈnā-grō, ˈne-\. **1.** River, S Mato Grosso state, Brazil; flows SW and W through extensive marshland into Paraguay River.

2. *or Span.* **Río Ne·gro** \ˈrē-ü-ˈnā-grü\. River, NW South America; rises in E Colombia, where it is known as the **Guai·nía** \gwī-ˈnē-ə\; flows E to the Venezuela boundary, and then S forming a section of the Colombia-Venezuela boundary; crosses into Brazil and continues SE into Amazon River at Manaus; is joined also to the Orinoco River through the Casiquiare River; ab. 1400 mi. (2250 km.) long.

3. *or Span.* **Río Negro.** River, cen. Uruguay; rises in S Brazil, flows SW across Uruguay into the Uruguay River; 434 mi. (698 km.) long.

Negro, Río \ˈrē-ō-ˈnā-grō, ˈne-\. River, Río Negro prov., S cen. Argentina; formed by confluence of Neuquén and Limay rivers, flows E into Atlantic Ocean N of Gulf of San Matías; ab. 400 mi. (640 km.) long.

Negro Mountain. See DAVIS, MOUNT.

Negroponte. See EUBOEA.

Ne·gros \ˈnā-ˌgrōs, ˈne-\. Island, one of the Visayan Is., cen. Philippines; 5278 sq. mi. (13,670 sq. km.); pop. (1980c, with adjacent small islands) 2,749,700; 4th in size in the archipelago, 134 mi. (216 km.) long; sugar, rice, coconuts; tobacco, timber; divided into two provinces, Negros Occidental and Negros Oriental (*qq.v.*). Largest cities are Bacolod and San Carlos. In WWII held by Japanese until invaded and captured by U.S. forces 1945.

Negros Oc·ci·den·tal \ˌȯk-sē-den-ˈtäl\. Province, N and W Negros I., Philippines; ✻ Bacolod. Has fairly regular coastline, with few good harbors; broad coastal plains in N and W; separated on E from Negros Oriental by S part of the mountain range which crosses center of the island N to S; highest peak Canlaon volcano 8070 ft. (2460 m.) on boundary; many small streams. See table at PHILIPPINES.

Negros Orien·tal \ˌōr-ē-en-ˈtäl\. Province, E and SE Negros I., cen. Philippines; ✻ Dumaguete; includes Siquijor I. Separated on NW from Negros Occidental by mountain range which in S curves toward coast W of Dumaguete; highest point Cuernos of Negros 6101 ft. (1860 m.); except for narrow coastal strip entire province mountainous or plateau. See table at PHILIPPINES.

Ne·ha·vend \ˌnā-hä-ˈvend\ *also* **Na·ha·wend** \ˌnā-hä-ˈvend\. **1.** Former province, W Iran; ✻ Borūjerd.

2. Town, Iran. See NAHĀVAND.

Ne·heim–Hüs·ten \ˈnā-hīm-ˈhūe-stən\. City, North Rhine-Westphalia, Germany, in the Ruhr dist. 23 mi. (37 km.) ESE of Dortmund.

Nei·a·fu \nā-ˈä-fü\. Town and port on Vava'u I., N Tonga, SW cen. Pacific Ocean; pop. (1986c) 3879; has completely landlocked harbor at head of sound.

Nei·ba *or* **Ney·ba** \ˈnā-bä\. Commune, ✻ of Bahoruco prov., SW Dominican Republic; munic. pop. (1981p) 28,049.

Nei–chiang. See NEIJIANG.

Neige, Mount *or* **Crête de la Neige** \ˌkred-lä-ˈnāzh, -ˈnezh\. Peak, Ain dept., E France; 5652 ft. (1723 m.); highest peak in the Jura Mts.

Neiges, Pi·ton des \pē-ˌtōⁿ-dā-ˈnāzh, -ˈnezh\. Peak, cen. Réunion I., Indian Ocean; 10,069 ft. (3069 m.).

Nei·jiang *or W.-G.* **Nei–chiang** \ˈnā-ˈjyäŋ\. Town, Sichuan prov., S cen. China, ab. 90 mi. (145 km.) SE of Chengdu; pop. (1990c) 256,012.

Neills·ville \ˈnēlz-ˌvil\. City, ⊗ of Clark co., W cen. Wisconsin, 21 mi. (34 km.) WSW of Marshfield; pop. (1990c) 2680.

Nei Mong·gol \ˈnā-ˈmu̇ŋ-ˈgȯl\ *or* **Nei Mon·gol** \-ˈmu̇ŋ-ˈgȯl\ *or* **Nei Meng·gu** \-ˈməŋ-ˈgü\ *or Eng.* **Inner Mongolia.** Autonomous region, N China, bounded on N by Mongolia (republic); ✻ Hohhot; its N portion lies within the Gobi Desert; its S border partly marked by the Great Wall; known as Inner Mongolia since 1644. See table at CHINA.

Nein. See NAIN.

Neis·se \ˈnī-sə\. **1.** *also* **Lau·sit·zer Neisse** \ˈlau̇-zit-sər\ *or Pol.* **Ny·sa Łu·życ·ka** \ˈnə̇-sä-wü-ˈzhə̇t-skä\. River, W cen. Europe; rises near Liberec, N Czech Republic, flows N past Görlitz, Germany, and joins the Oder 21 mi. (34 km.) SSE of Frankfurt; 159 mi. (256 km.) long; from the Czech border to its junction with the Oder forms, by decision of the Potsdam Conference 1945, part of the Germany-Poland boundary. See POLAND.

2. River and city, Poland. See NYSA.

Neist Point \ˈnēst\. Cape on W coast of island of Skye in the Inner Hebrides, off NW Scotland.

Nei·va \ˈnā-vä\. **1.** Peak in Cordillera Oriental, cen. Colombia, SE of city of Neiva; 12,000 ft. (3660 m.).

2. City, ✻ of Huila dept., S cen. Colombia, on the Magdalena River 150 mi. (241 km.) SSW of Bogotá; munic. pop. (1992e) 232,600; produces cattle, coffee, Panama hats. Birthplace of lawyer and author José Eustacio Rivera 1889.

Nejd \ˈnejd\ *or* **Najd** \ˈnajd\ *also* **Ne·djed** \ˈne-jəd\. Region, cen. Saudi Arabia; ab. 447,000 sq. mi. (1,158,000 sq. km.).

History: Consolidated mid-18th cent. by Wahhabi movement; captured from rival family c. 1905 by Ibn Sa'ūd who by 1925 had accepted British protection (1915), overthrown Turkish suzerainty, and expanded realm over much of the Arabian Penin., incl. Hejaz (*q.v.*); united with Hejaz as a dual kingdom 1926; independence recognized by Great Britain 1927, and other European nations soon followed suit; became a single kingdom under the name of Saudi Arabia (*q.v.*) 1932.

Nek·'em·tē *or* **Nek·em·te** \ne-ˈkem-tē\. Town, W cen. Ethiopia, W of Addis Ababa; pop. (1989e) 34,993.

Ne·koo·sa \ni-ˈkü-sə\. City, Wood co., cen. Wisconsin, on Wisconsin River; pop. (1990c) 2557.

Ne·ligh \ˈnē-lē\. City, ⊗ of Antelope co., NE Nebraska, on Elkhorn River 35 mi. (56 km.) WNW of Norfolk; pop. (1990c) 1742.

Nel·lore \ne-ˈlōr\. Town, S Andhra Pradesh, S India, on Penner River near its mouth 95 mi. (153 km.) N of Madras; pop. (1991p) 316,445; one of the chief ports of the Coromandel Coast.

Nel·son \ˈnel-sən\. **1.** Name of counties in three states of the U.S. See tables at KENTUCKY, NORTH DAKOTA, VIRGINIA.

2. City, ⊗ of Nuckolls co., S Nebraska; pop. (1990c) 627.

3. River, N cen. Manitoba, cen. Canada; flows out of N Lake Winnipeg through several lakes NE into Hudson Bay at Port Nelson; 400 mi. (644 km.) long; area of drainage basin 444,000 sq. mi. (1,149,960 sq. km.); considered as incl. its headstreams, the Saskatchewan and Bow rivers, 1660 mi. (2671 km.) long; navigable for part of its course. Its mouth

discovered 1612 and a post of Hudson's Bay Company established there c. 1670; long used as a route inland for fur traders.
4. City, SE British Columbia, Canada, on W arm of Kootenay Lake 33 mi. (53 km.) NE of Trail; pop. (1991c) 8760; supply center for extensive mining district; lumbering; founded c. 1887.
5. Town, Lancashire, NW England, 28 mi. (45 km.) W of Leeds; pop. (1992e) 47,800.
6. City, N South I., New Zealand, at head of Tasman Bay 75 mi. (121 km.) W of Wellington; pop. (1991c) 37,943; center of fruit- and vegetable-producing area; has large and well-sheltered harbor; founded c. 1841.

Nelson Lakes National Park. National park, cen. N part of South I., New Zealand; ab. 395 sq. mi. (1025 sq. km.); remote lakes surrounded by mountains; estab. 1956.

Nelson Reservoir. Reservoir in NE cen. Phillips co., N Montana, in area of outdoor recreation.

Nel·son·ville \\'nel-sən-ˌvil\\. City, Athens co., SE Ohio, on Hocking River 25 mi. (40 km.) SE of Lancaster; pop. (1990c) 4563.

Nel·spruit \\'nel-ˌsprȯit\\. Town, Mpumalanga prov., Rep. of South Africa, on Crocodile River.

Nem·a·ha \\'ne-mə-ˌhȯ, 'nē-\\. **1.** Two rivers, SE Nebraska: (1) **Great Nemaha** *or* **Big Nemaha,** flows from Lancaster co. SE to Missouri River near SE corner of the state; ab. 150 mi. (240 km.) long; (2) **Little Nemaha,** N of the Great Nemaha, flows SE into the Missouri in SE Nemaha co.; ab. 90 mi. (145 km.) long.
2. Names of counties in two states of the U.S. See tables at KANSAS and NEBRASKA.

Ne·man \\'ne-mən\\ *also* **Nye·man** \\'nye-mən\\ *or Pol.* **Nie·men** \\'nye-mən\\ *or Lith.* **Ne·mu·nas** \\'ne-mü-ˌnäs\\. River, cen. Europe; rises in cen. Belarus, S of Minsk, flows W, then N into Lithuania, and W bet. Lithuania and Kaliningrad Oblast, Russia into Kurskiy Zaliv; 582 mi. (936 km.) long and navigable for most of its length; was known as the **Me·mel** \\'mā-məl\\ River in former East Prussia, and as the **Russ** \\'rüs\\ 22 mi. (35 km.) from its mouth; connected by canal with the Pripyat'. Area scene of numerous battles bet. Russian and German forces in WWI, esp. in the region of the bend bet. Hrodna, Belarus, and Kaunas (Kovno), Lithuania.

Nemausus. See NÎMES.

Nem·by \\'nām-bē\\. Town, Central dept., S Paraguay, SE of Asunción; pop. (1992p) 27,206.

Ne·mea \\'nē-mē-ə\\. **1.** Valley in N Argolis, ancient Greece; site of ancient and present towns of Nemea; in Greek mythology scene of the slaying of the Nemean lion by Hercules, the first of his famous labors; had temple of Zeus in whose honor the biennial Nemean games, inaugurated 573 B.C., were held; scene of battle 394 B.C. in which Spartans defeated coalition forces in Corinthian War. Ruins include the temple, a stadium, and a theater.
2. Town, Corinth dept., NE Peloponnese, Greece, ab. 15 mi. (24 km.) WSW of the city of Corinth.

Německý Brod. See HAVLÍČKŮV BROD.

Ne·men·cha Mountains \\nə-'men-chə\\. Range of the Atlas Mts., NE Algeria, extending to border of Tunisia.

Nemetocenna. See ARRAS.

Ne·mi, Lake \\'nā-mē, 'ne-\\; *anc.* **Nem·o·ren·sis La·cus** \\ˌne-mə-'ren-səs-'lā-kəs\\. Lake in the Alban Hills, SE of Lake Albano, Italy; 0.67 sq. mi. (1.7 sq. km.); nearby in ancient times were a grove and temple dedicated to Diana; two ships from first cent. A.D. raised c. 1930, burned 1944 by retreating Germans.

Ne·mours \\nə-'mür\\. Town, Seine-et-Marne dept., N France, S of Melun; pop. (1990c) 12,115; seat from 14th cent. of dukedom held at various times by the houses of Savoy and Orléans.

Nemunas. See NEMAN.

Ne·mu·ro \\'nā-mü-ˌrō\\. Town, E Hokkaidō, Japan, at S end of Nemuro Strait; pop. (1990c) 36,914.

Nemuro Strait. Strait off E Hokkaidō, Japan, separating Kunashir I., Russia, from Hokkaidō.

Nen \\'nən\\. **1.** *formerly* **Non·ni** \\'nən-'nē\\. River, NE China; rises on E slopes of Da Hinggan Ling in N Heilongjiang prov., flows S, forms part of border bet. Heilongjiang and Jilin provs., and joins the Songhua; ab. 740 mi. (1190 km.) long; waters the fertile N section of Manchurian plain.
2. River, England. See NENE.

Ne·nagh \\'nē-nä, 'nē-nək\\. Town, co. Tipperary, S Ireland, near **Nenagh River;** pop. (1991p) 5531; trade center of agricultural area; ruins of castle erected in 13th cent., dismantled in 17th cent.

Ne·nana \\nē-'na-nə\\. City, E cen. Alaska, on S bank of Tanana River 50 mi. (81 km.) WSW of Fairbanks; pop. (1990c) 393; estab. 1916 as railroad construction base; site of popular annual sweepstakes for guessing the day and time of ice breakup on the river.

Nen·do \\'nen-dō\\ *also* **Nde·ni** \\ən-'dā-nē\\ *formerly* **San·ta Cruz** \\'san-tə-'krüz\\. Chief island of the Santa Cruz Is., SW Pacific Ocean, 250 mi. (402 km.) E of S Solomon Is.; 215 sq. mi. (557 sq. km.); has good harbor at Graciosa Bay.

Nene \\'nēn, 'nen\\ *or* **Nen** \\'nen\\. River, cen. and E England; rises in N Northamptonshire, flows NE into the North Sea through the Wash; 90 mi. (145 km.) long.

Ne·nets Autonomous Okrug \\ne-'nəts ... 'ȯ-ˌkrük\\. Administrative district, part of Arkhangel'sk Oblast, N Russia in Europe, the tundra coast N of Komi Rep.; 68,224 sq. mi. (176,700 sq. km.); pop. (1992e) 54,900; ✱ Nar'yan-Mar; reindeer herding, fishing; oil; estab. 1929 as Nenets National Okrug, a district for Nenets (Samoyeds); status and name changed 1977.

Neocaesarea. See NIKSAR.

Ne·o·de·sha \\nē-ˌō-də-'shā, -'ō-də-ˌshā\\. City, Wilson co., SE Kansas, 13 mi. (21 km.) N of Independence; pop. (1990c) 2837.

Ne·o·sho \\nē-'ō-shō, -shə\\. **1.** *in Oklahoma called* **Grand** \\'grand\\. River, SE Kansas and NE Oklahoma; rises in Morris co., E cen. Kansas, flows SE and S into Arkansas River in N Muskogee co., E Oklahoma; 460 mi. (740 km.) long.
2. County in SE Kansas. See table at KANSAS.
3. City, ⊗ of Newton co., SW Missouri, 16 mi. (26 km.) SSE of Joplin; pop. (1990c) 9254; trade center in agricultural region; fish hatchery; lead deposit nearby. Birthplace of artist Thomas Hart Benton 1889.

Ne·pal \\'nā-ˌpäl, nə-'pȯl, -'päl\\. Kingdom on NE border of India, bounded on N by Tibet, China, and on E, S, and W by India; 54,362 sq. mi. (140,798 sq. km.); pop. (1993e) 20,220,000; ✱ Kathmandu.

Physical features: The S portion is level cultivated and forest land (Terai), the cen. and N parts are occupied by great Himalaya ranges; highest peaks Everest, Kanchenjunga, Dhaulagiri, Gauri Sankar, and many others above 20,000 ft. (6100 m.); rivers flow southward and are upper tributaries of the Ganges system.

Chief products: Rice, corn, wheat, potatoes, millet, jute, oilseed, sugarcane; carpets; tourism.

Chief cities: Kathmandu, Biratnagar, Lalitpur, Pokhara.

History: Region's history has ancient roots; developed under early Buddhist influence; dynastic rule dates to c. 4th cent. A.D.; the numerous principalities of the region conquered 1769 by Gurkha ruler Prithvi Narayan Shah and consolidated into a single kingdom; border wars 18th–19th cents. with China, Tibet, and British India resulted in present boundaries by mid-19th cent.; independence recognized by Great Britain 1923; democratic constitution of 1959 replaced 1962 with constitutional monarchy which banned opposition political parties and left most of ruling authority with the king; new constitution 1990 restricted royal authority, stated basic human and civil rights, and accepted democratically elected multiparty bicameral parliamentary government.

Ne·pal·ganj \\'nā-päl-ˌgənj\\. Town, SW Nepal, near border with Uttar Pradesh, India; pop. (1981c) 34,015.

\\ə\\ **abut** \\ə\\ **matches** \\ᵊ\\ **kitten**, Fr **table** \\ər\\ **further** \\a\\ **ash** \\ā\\ **ace** \\ä\\ **cot, cart** \\à\\ Fr **bac** \\aü\\ **out** \\b\\ Span **Avila** \\ch\\ **chin** \\e\\ **bet** \\ē\\ **easy** \\g\\ **go** \\i\\ **hit** \\ī\\ **ice** \\j\\ **job** \\k\\ Ger **ich, Buch** \\ⁿ\\ Fr **vin** \\ŋ\\ **sing** \\ō\\ **go** \\ö\\ **all** \\ȯ\\ **law** \\œ\\ Fr **bœuf** \\œ̄\\ Fr **feu** \\ȯi\\ **boy** \\th\\ **thin** \\th\\ **this** \\ü\\ **loot** \\u̇\\ **foot** \\ue\\ Ger **füllen** \\ūē\\ Fr **rue** \\y\\ **yet** \\ʸ\\ Fr **digne** \\'dēnʸ\\, **nuit** \\'nwʸē\\ \\yü\\ **few** \\yu̇\\ **fury** \\zh\\ **vision**

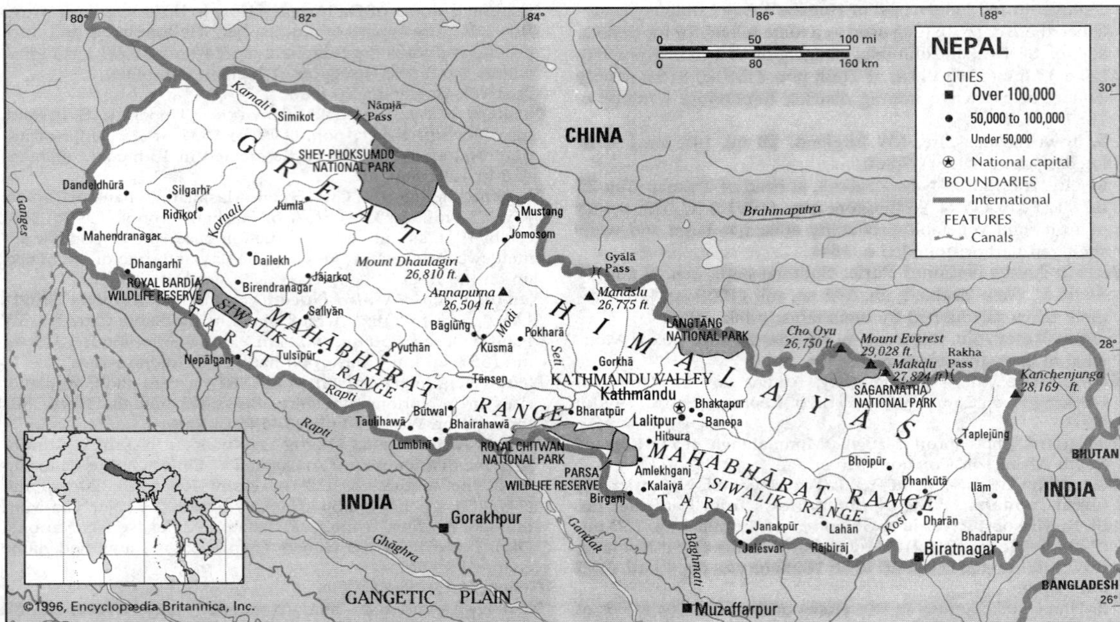

Ne·paug \ˈnē-ˌpȯg\. River, NW Connecticut; rises in NE Litchfield co., flows SE into Farmington River.

Nepaug Reservoir. Reservoir in Nepaug River, Litchfield and Hartford cos., N Connecticut; water supply for Hartford.

Ne·pe·an \ni-ˈpē-ən\. City, SE Ontario, Canada, just SW of Ottawa; pop. (1991c) 107,627.

Ne·phi \ˈnē-ˌfī\. City, ⊗ of Juab co., W Utah, 38 mi. (61 km.) S of Provo; pop. (1990c) 3515; settled 1852; suffered in Indian raids; peace bet. Mormon leader Brigham Young and Chief Walker made nearby 1854.

Neph·in \ˈne-fən\. Mountain, cen. co. Mayo, Connaught, NW Ireland; 2646 ft. (807 m.).

Neph·in·beg \ˌne-fən-ˈbeg\. Mountain, W co. Mayo, Connaught, NW Ireland; 2065 ft. (629 m.).

Nepigon, Lake. See NIPIGON, LAKE.

Ne·pis·i·guit Bay *or* **Ni·pis·i·guit Bay** \nə-ˈpi-zə-gwit\. S extension of Chaleur Bay, extending into N Gloucester co., NE New Brunswick, SE Canada; receives the **Nepisiguit River** (*or* **Nipisiguit River**), ab. 75 mi. (120 km.) long, which rises in NW Northumberland co. and flows E and N.

Nepissing, Lake. See NIPISSING, LAKE.

Nep·tune \ˈnep-ˌtün, -ˌtyün\. Urban township, Monmouth co., E cen. New Jersey, WSW of Asbury Park; pop. (1990c) 28,148.

Neptune City. Borough, Monmouth co., E New Jersey, SW of Asbury Park; pop. (1990c) 4997.

Ne·ra \ˈner-ä\; *anc.* **Nar** \ˈnär\. River, cen. Italy; flows out of the Apennines SW into Tiber River; 80 mi. (129 km.) long.

Né·rac \nā-ˈrȧk\. Town, S Lot-et-Garonne dept., SW France, on the Baïse River; center of Protestant activities during 16th cent.; peace bet. Catholics and Huguenots signed here 1579; headquarters of Henry of Navarre (later King Henry IV) 1580; taken by Louis XIII 1621 and subsequently ruined.

Nerbudda. See NARMADA.

Ner·chinsk \ˈner-ˌchintsk\. Town, S cen. Chita Oblast, S Russia in Asia, near N bank of Shilka River ab. 135 mi. (215 km.) E of the city of Chita. Founded as a fort 1654; for two centuries one of Russian outposts in Far East; Treaty of Nerchinsk 1689 with China, the first treaty concluded with that country by any European power, estab. boundaries bet. the two countries, delayed Russia's advance in Amur Valley, and was basis of relations with China until 1858.

Neretum. See NARDÒ.

Ne·ret·va \ˈner-et-ˌvä\ *or Ital.* **Na·ren·ta** \nä-ˈren-tä\; *anc.* **Na·ro** \ˈnar-ō\. River, S Europe; rises E of Mostar, Bosnia and Herzegovina, flows NNW, and ab. 28 mi. (45 km.) N of Mostar, turns S; flows past Mostar into Adriatic Sea in SE Croatia; 135 mi. (217 km.) long; navigable for small vessels.

Ne·ris \ne-ˈris; *Russ.* nir-ˈyēs\ *or Pol.* **Wi·lja** \ˈvēl-yä\; *formerly* **Vi·li·ya** \ˈvē-li-yə\. River, NE Poland and E Lithuania; rises on E border of Poland and flows W into Neman River at Kaunas, Lithuania; 317 mi. (510 km.) long.

Nerium Promontorium. See FINISTERRE, CAPE.

Ne·ro·ne, Mon·te \ˈmōn-tā-nā-ˈrō-nā\. Highest mountain in the Umbrian Apennines. See table at APENNINES.

Ne·se·bûr \ne-ˈse-bər\; *formerly* **Me·sem·bria** \mə-ˈsem-brē-ə\. Town, E Bulgaria, on Black Sea, NE of Burgas; pop. (1988e) 15,947; resort. Settled as Mesembria by Greeks 6th cent. B.C.; remained important trading center up to Roman times; revived in importance during Byzantine era; once the site of ab. 40 churches, those remaining mostly in ruins.

Ne·sho·ba \nə-ˈshō-bə\. County in E cen. Mississippi. See table at MISSISSIPPI.

Nesis. See NISIDA.

Nesle \ˈnel\. Town, Somme dept., N France, 7 mi. (11 km.) WNW of Ham; taken and briefly occupied by Germans 1918 during WWI.

Nes·que·hon·ing \ˌnes-kwə-ˈhō-niŋ\. Borough, Carbon co., E Pennsylvania, 28 mi. (45 km.) S of Wilkes-Barre; pop. (1990c) 3364.

Ness \ˈnes\. **1.** County in W cen. Kansas. See table at KANSAS.
2. River, Highland region, NW Scotland; flows NE out of Loch Ness into Moray Firth below Inverness; 7 mi. (11 km.) long.

Ness, Loch. Lake in Highland region, NW Scotland; from NE to SW, 23 mi. (37 km.) long; forms part of Caledonian Canal. Remains of two fortresses on its shores; reports of an aquatic monster here date back centuries, but remain unproven.

Ness City. City, ⊗ of Ness co., W cen. Kansas; pop. (1990c) 1724.

Nes·ton \ˈnes-tən\; *formerly* **Neston and Park·gate** \ˈpärk-ˌgāt\. Town, Cheshire, NW England, on the Dee Estuary 10 mi. (16 km.) S of Liverpool; pop. (1981p) 18,415.

Néstos. See MESTA.

Nes·vizh \ˈnās-vish\ *or Pol.* **Nieś·wież** \ˈnyesh-ˌvyesh\. Town, W Belarus, 44 mi. (71 km.) SE of Novogrudok; formerly in Poland; old castle of Polish-Lithuanian princes of Radziwill.

Ne·tan·ya *also* **Na·tan·ya** \nə-ˈtä-nyä\ Coastal city, Israel, ab. 35 mi. (55 km.) SSW of Haifa; pop. (1993e) 141,800; important center of diamond cutting and polishing; also produces textiles and rubber goods; founded c. 1928.

Ne·tarts Bay \nē-ˈtärts, ˈnē-ˌ\. Inlet on coast of Tillamook co., NW Oregon.

Net·cong \ˈnet-ˌkȯŋ\. Borough, Morris co., N New Jersey, 14 mi. (23 km.) WNW of Morristown; pop. (1990c) 3311.

Nethe \ˈnet\. River in Belgium; formed by the confluence of the **Great Nethe** and **Little Nethe** near Lier; flows WSW in Antwerp prov. to unite with the Dijle NW of Mechelen and form the Rupel River.

Neth·er·lands \ˈne-t͟hər-ləndz\ *or Du.* **Ne·der·land** \ˈnā-dər-ˌlänt\ *also* **Hol·land** \ˈhä-lənd\ *or* **the Netherlands** *or* **The Netherlands.** Kingdom, NW Europe, bounded on W and N by the North Sea, on E by Germany, and on S by Belgium; 16,033 sq. mi. (41,525 sq. km.), incl. 419 sq. mi. (1085 sq. km.) of reclaimed land from the IJsselmeer; pop. (1990e) 15,009,000; de jure ✻ Amsterdam, court residence and de facto ✻ The Hague.

Physical features: Part of the plain of NW Europe with nearly a quarter of its area below sea level and max. elev. ab. 1635 ft. (500 m.); protected along part of the coast by dikes. All S part lies in plain and delta of the Neder Rijn and Maas

\ə\ abut \ˀ\ matches \ᵊ\ kitten, Fr table \ər\ further \a\ ash \ā\ ace \ä\ cot, cart \à\ Fr bac \au̇\ out \b\ Span Avila \ch\ chin \e\ bet \ē\ easy \g\ go \i\ hit \ī\ ice \j\ job \k\ Ger ich, Buch \ⁿ\ Fr vin \ŋ\ sing \ō\ go \ȯ\ all \ȯ\ law \œ\ Fr bœuf \œ̄\ Fr feu \ȯi\ boy \th\ thin \t͟h\ this \ü\ loot \u̇\ foot \ue\ Ger füllen \ue̅\ Fr rue \y\ yet \ʸ\ Fr digne \ˈdēnʸ\, nuit \ˈnwʸē\ \yü\ few \yu̇\ fury \zh\ vision

(Meuse) rivers; N cen. part formerly occupied by large shallow inlet of North Sea, the Zuider Zee (*q.v.*), ab. 80 mi. (130 km.) long, now partly reclaimed and separated from North Sea by dike from W Friesland prov. to Wieringermeer. Off N coast and enclosing large area of water is chain of West Frisian Is. (see FRISIAN ISLANDS) connecting on E with German East Frisian Is.; in SW (Zeeland prov.) are other large islands in combined delta of Schelde and Maas. Covered by many canals and canalized rivers connecting larger cities.

Chief products: Wheat, barley, potatoes, sugar beets; horticulture; natural gas; chemicals, petroleum products, steel, electrical equipment; food processing.

Chief cities: Amsterdam, Rotterdam, The Hague, Utrecht.

Political divisions: Divided into the following 12 provinces (for pronunciation of their names, see their individual entries):

NAME	AREA (sq. mi.)	AREA (sq. km.)	POP. (1993e)	CAPITAL
Drenthe	1,037	2,686	448,256	Assen
Flevoland	549	1,422	243,441	Lelystad
Friesland	1,464	3,792	603,998	Leeuwarden
Gelderland	1,981	5,131	1,839,883	Arnhem
Groningen	934	2,419	555,397	Groningen
Limburg	853	2,209	1,119,942	Maastricht
North Brabant	1,971	5,105	2,243,546	's Hertogenbosch
North Holland	1,124	2,911	2,440,165	Haarlem
Overijssel	1,518	3,932	1,039,083	Zwolle
South Holland	1,259	3,261	3,295,522	The Hague
Utrecht	538	1,393	1,047,035	Utrecht
Zeeland	1,043	2,701	361,195	Middelburg

History: Evidence throughout region of Paleolithic inhabitants; region subjected to early Celtic, Germanic, and Roman influences; came under Franks, was included in Holy Roman Emperor Charlemagne's empire, and became part of medieval kingdom of Lotharingia (see LORRAINE); split up into several counties and duchies (see BRABANT, FLANDERS, and HOLLAND 3) which were first united in 14th–15th cents. under dukes of Burgundy (*q.v.*); passed 15th cent. by marriage to Hapsburgs, who later (16th cent.) inherited Spanish crown; in 1568 began revolt against repressive policies of Fernando Álvarez de Toledo, duke of Alva (sent to govern by Philip II of Spain); the seven N Protestant provinces, Holland, Zeeland, Utrecht, Gelderland, Groningen, Friesland, and Overijssel (the United Provinces) formed Union of Utrecht 1579 and declared independence from Spain 1581 (see BELGIUM for history of Spanish Netherlands, the provinces remaining loyal to Spain); after 80 years of war, independence finally recognized by Spain 1648; in 17th cent. became leading commercial nation of Europe (see AMSTERDAM 2), expanded greatly its overseas territory (see CURAÇAO, INDONESIA, and NEW NETHERLAND); engaged in numerous important wars of commercial and political rivalry, with the English 1652–54, 1665–67, and 1672–74, and with France 1672–78, 1689–97, and 1702–13; its ruler, William III, and his wife, Mary II, became corulers of England 1689; overrun by French 1794; organized as Batavian Republic 1795–1806 and as kingdom of Holland 1806–10, both under French control, then incorp. directly into French First Empire 1810–13 under Emperor Napoléon; in 1814, received constitution, later revised; its ruler given sovereignty over present Belgium and Luxembourg (1815–30) until revolt of Belgium (*q.v.*) 1830; neutral in WWI; declared neutrality in WWII, but occupied by German forces 1940–45; recognized independence of Netherlands Indies (Indonesia) 1949; became a member of NATO 1949; joined EEC 1958; in 1962 relinquished control over Irian Jaya (*q.v.*).

Netherlands An·til·les \ an-ˈti-lēz\; *formerly* **Cu·ra·çao** \ˌkůr-ə-ˈsō, ˌkyůr-, -ˈsaů\. An integral part of the Netherlands realm, consisting of several islands in the West Indies: Curaçao, Bonaire, and formerly Aruba off the coast of Venezuela, and St. Martin (S section), St. Eustatius, and Saba at N end of Leeward Is.; 371 sq. mi. (961 sq. km.); pop. (1990c) 190,566; ✻ Willemstad (on Curaçao); tourism; petroleum refining; textiles; colonial status abolished and domestic autonomy granted by Netherlands government 1954; Aruba was separated from the group 1986.

Netherlands East Indies. See INDONESIA 2.

Netherlands Guiana. See SURINAME 2.

Netherlands Indies. See INDONESIA 2.

Netherlands New Guinea. See IRIAN JAYA.

Netherlands Timor. See TIMOR, NETHERLANDS.

Neth·er Prov·i·dence \ˈne-t͟hər-ˈprä-vi-dəns, -ˌdens\. Urban township, Delaware co., SE Pennsylvania; pop. (1990c) 13,229.

Nether Stow·ey \ˈstō-ē\. Village, Somerset, SW England, 7 mi. (11 km.) WNW of Bridgwater, N of the Quantock Hills; residence 1796–98 of poet Samuel Taylor Coleridge who wrote *The Rime of the Ancient Mariner* here.

Néthou, Pic de. See ANETO, PICO DE.

Net·ley \ˈnet-lē\. Village, Hampshire, S England, 3 mi. (5 km.) SE of Southampton; ruins of Cistercian abbey founded 13th cent. by Henry III.

Net·ti·ling Lake *or* **Net·til·ling Lake** \ˈne-chə-liŋ\. Lake in S cen. Baffin I., E Nunavut, Canada; largest lake on the island at 1956 sq. mi. (5066 sq. km.); 67 mi. (108 km.) long; its primary feeder stream flows N from Amadjuak lake; empties into Foxe Basin.

Net·tu·no \net-ˈtü-nō\. Commune, Roma prov., Lazio, cen. Italy, on Tyrrhenian Sea 31 mi. (50 km.) SSE of Rome; pop. (1989c) 34,653; in WWII site of American landing Jan. 1944 at same time as adjoining Anzio (*q.v.*).

Netum. See NOTO.

Netzahualcóyotl. See NEZAHUALCÓYOTL.

Netze. See NOTEĆ.

Neu·bran·den·burg \nȯi-ˈbrän-dən-ˌbůrk\ *or* **New Brandenburg.** **1.** District, of former East Germany.

2. City, Mecklenburg-West Pomerania, NE Germany, 74 mi. (119 km.) E of Schwerin; pop. (1992e) 87,879; formerly ✻ of Neubrandenburg dist., East Germany; machinery, chemicals, paper; 14th cent. city walls; founded 1248; to Mecklenburg 1292.

Neubreisach. See NEUF-BRISACH.

Neu·burg \ˈnȯi-ˌbůrk\. Town, Bavaria, Germany, on the Danube ab. 11 mi. (18 km.) W of Ingolstadt; pop. (1980c) 24,097; ceded by Bavaria to the Palatinate c. 1507; was ✻ of a small principality 16th–18th cents.; reunited with Bavaria 1777.

Neu·châ·tel \ˌnœ-shä-ˈtel; ˌnü-shə-ˈtel, ˌnyü-\. **1.** Canton, W Switzerland, in the Jura Mts.; ✻ Neuchâtel; watered by numerous tributaries of the Rhine. (See table at SWITZERLAND.) Independent principality 11th cent.; under French family of Longueville 1504–1707; to Prussia 1707–1806, France 1806–14; reverted to Prussia 1814; joined Swiss Confederation 1815 as only canton with monarchical government (monarchy suppressed 1848); Prussian claims renounced 1857.

2. Commune, its ✻, on W shore of Lac de Neuchâtel 25 mi. (40 km.) W of Bern; pop. (1989c) 32,757; watches, electronics, chocolate, tobacco products; ancient castle; 12th cent. church; university (1838).

Neuchâtel, Lac de \ˌlák-də-\ *or Eng.* **Lake of Neuchâtel** *or* **Lake Neuchâtel.** Lake, W Switzerland, on S border of Neuchâtel canton; 84 sq. mi. (218 sq. km.); max. depth 502 ft. (153 m.); largest lake entirely within Switzerland.

Neuenahr–Ahrweiler, Bad. See BAD NEUENAHR-AHRWEILER.

Neuf–Bri·sach \ˌnœ-brē-ˈzäk\ *or Ger.* **Neu·brei·sach** \ˌnȯi-ˈbrī-zäk\. Town, NE Haut-Rhin dept., NE France, near German frontier ESE of Colmar; fortress founded under Louis XIV 1699.

Neuf·châ·teau \ˌnœ-shä-ˈtō\. Town, NW Vosges dept., NE France, ab. 35 mi. (56 km.) NW of Épinal; ruins of castle dating from Middle Ages.

Neuf·châ·tel \ˌnœ-shä-ˈtel\ *or* **Neufchâtel en Bray** \äⁿ-ˈbrā\. Town, E Seine-Maritime dept., N France, ab. 25 mi. (40 km.) NE of Rouen; chief town of Bray region; famous for its cheese.

Neuhaus. See JINDŘICHŮV HRADEC.

Neuhäusel. See NOVÉ ZÁMKY.

Neu·hof \ˈnȯi-ˌhōf\. Farm, Aargau canton, Switzerland,

where educational reformer Johann Heinrich Pestalozzi established his first school for poor children c. 1776–80.

Neuil·ly–Plai·sance \nœ-'yē-ple-'zäⁿs\. Commune, Seine-St.-Denis dept., N France, E suburb of Paris.

Neuilly–sur–Marne \-sür-'märn\. Commune, Seine-St.-Denis dept., N France, E suburb of Paris on Marne River.

Neuilly–sur–Seine \-sür-'sān, -'sen\. Commune, Hauts-de-Seine dept., N France, a NW suburb of Paris near Bois de Boulogne; automotive industry; Treaty of Neuilly signed here Nov. 27, 1919 bet. Allies and Bulgaria after WWI.

Neu–Isen·burg \nȯi-'ēz-ᵊn-,bu̇rk\. City, S Hesse, Germany, 5 mi. (8 km.) S of Frankfurt am Main; pop. (1980c) 35,816; made city 1894.

Neumarkt. See NOWY TARG.

Neu–Mecklenburg. See NEW IRELAND.

Neu·mün·ster \nȯi-'mᵫn-stər\. City, Schleswig-Holstein, Germany, SSW of Kiel; pop. (1992e) 81,175; important railroad junction; manufactures textiles, machinery, paper. Founded c. 12th cent.; became city 1870.

Neun·kir·chen \'nȯin-,kir-kən\. **1.** *or in full* **Neunkirchen am Stein·feld** \äm-'shtīn-,felt\. City, Lower Austria, Austria, 35 mi. (56 km.) SSW of Vienna; pop. (1991c) 10,334; became city 1920.

2. City, Saarland, Germany, ab. 12 mi. (19 km.) NE of Saarbrücken; pop. (1992e) 51,743; iron; coal mining in region.

Neu–Pommern. See NEW BRITAIN 2.

Ne·u·quén \neu̇-'kān\. **1.** River, cen. W Argentina; rises in W Neuquén prov., flows E to join Limay River on border of Río Negro prov. and form the Río Negro (river); 320 mi. (515 km.) long.

2. Province, W Argentina; on Chilean border, its W part mountainous, E part level; forests and fertile valleys in W; in S is Lake Nahuel Huapí (*q.v.*). See table at ARGENTINA.

3. Town, its ✱, on Neuquén River; pop. (1980p) 90,037.

Neurode. See NOWA RUDA.

Neu·rup·pin \,nȯi-ru̇-'pēn\. Manufacturing city, Brandenburg, Germany, 40 mi. (64 km.) NNW of Berlin; pop. (1981c) 25,635; 13th cent. Gothic church; became city 1256; almost completely destroyed by fire 1787. Birthplace of writer Theodor Fontane (1819) and of architect Karl Friedrich Schinkel (1781).

Neusalz an der Oder. See NOWA SÓL.

Neusandez. See NOWY SĄCZ.

Neusatz. See NOVI SAD.

Neuse \'nüs, 'nyüs\. River, E cen. North Carolina; formed by junction of streams in Durham co., NE cen. North Carolina, flows SE into Pamlico Sound, E North Carolina; 275 mi. (442 km.) long; navigable to New Bern.

Neu·sie·dler Lake \'nȯi-,zēd-lər\ *or Hung.* **Fer·tő tó** \'fer-tœ-'tō\ *or Ger.* **Neusiedler See** \'zā\. Shallow lake, E Austria and NW Hungary; 123 sq. mi. (319 sq. km.); 23 mi. (37 km.) long; formerly entirely within Hungary, but in 1922 N two thirds transferred with Burgenland to Austria.

Neusohl. See BANSKÁ BYSTRICA.

Neuss \'nȯis\. **1.** *anc.* **No·vae·si·um** \nō-'vē-zhəm, -zē-əm\. City, W North Rhine-Westphalia, Germany, 5 mi. (8 km.) W of Düsseldorf; pop. (1992e) 147,663; railroad junction; manufactures paper goods, agricultural machinery, chemicals, food products. Ancient Roman camp; besieged by Charles the Bold, duke of Burgundy, 1474–75; destroyed by Alessandro Farnese, duke of Parma 1586; taken by French during French Revolutionary Wars; passed to Prussia c. 1815; in WWII taken by Allies Mar. 1945.

2. Commune in Switzerland. See NYON.

Neustadt. See PRUDNIK.

Neu·stadt an der Wein·stras·se \'nȯi-,shtät-än-dər-'vīn-,shträ-sə\; *formerly* **Neustadt an der Haardt** \'härt\; *anc.* **No·va Civ·i·tas** \'nō-və-'si-və-təs\; *later* **Nie·wen·stat** \'nē-vən-,shtät\. City, Rhineland-Palatinate, Germany, 18 mi. (29 km.) SW of Mannheim; pop. (1992e) 52,687; 14th cent. Gothic church; 18th cent. city hall; manufactures metal goods, textiles, paper; trades in wines. Founded early 13th cent.; chartered 1275.

Neustadt in Oberschlesien. See PRUDNIK.

Neustettin. See SZCZECINEK.

Neu·stre·litz \nȯi-'shtrā-lits\. City, Mecklenburg-West Pomerania, Germany, 61 mi. (98 km.) NNW of Berlin; pop. (1981c) 27,132; railroad junction; 18th cent. grand-ducal palace; founded 1733; was ✱ of former grand duchy (later sovereign state) of Mecklenburg-Strelitz.

Neus·tria \'nü-strē-ə, 'nyü-\. The W part of the dominions of the Franks after the conquest by Clovis in 6th cent., comprising then the NW part of modern France bet. the Meuse, the Loire, and the Atlantic Ocean. See AUSTRASIA. Later, c. 11th cent., the name was applied to Normandy.

Neutitschein. See NOVÝ JIČÍN.

Neutra. See NITRA.

Neutral Zone. A formerly recognized diamond-shaped area of no sovereignty, bet. N Saudi Arabia and SE Iraq, just W of Kuwait, now divided roughly in half bet. Saudi Arabia and Iraq.

Neu–Ulm \nȯi-'u̇lm\. City, Bavaria, Germany, on right bank of Danube River 2 mi. (3 km.) SE of Ulm; pop. (1980c) 47,415; leather goods.

Neuve–Cha·pelle \,nœv-shȧ-'pel\. Town, Pas-de-Calais dept., N France, 7 mi. (11 km.) NE of Béthune; scene of fighting throughout WWI, esp. battle Mar. 1915, in which the British captured the town but failed in their larger objective of taking the ridge to the E.

Neuve–Église \,nœ-vā-'glēz\ *or Flem.* **Nieuw·ker·ke** \,nē-ü-'ker-kə\. Village, West Flanders prov., NW Belgium, S of Ieper (Ypres); scene of heavy fighting 1918 in WWI.

Neu·ville–Saint–Vaast \nœ-,vēl-seⁿ-'väst\. Commune, Pas-de-Calais dept., N France, 4 mi. (6 km.) N of Arras; much fighting here and in the area throughout WWI.

Neu·wied \nȯi-'vēt\. City, North Rhine-Palatinate, Germany, on the Rhine 7 mi. (11 km.) NNW of Koblenz; pop. (1992e) 63,318; river port; manufactures cement, rolled metal; 18th cent. castle; excavations of large Roman camp nearby; founded 1653.

Neuzen. See TERNEUZEN.

Ne·va \nye-'vä; 'nā-və, 'nē-\. Navigable river, NW St. Petersburg Oblast, W Russia in Europe; flows from SW corner of Lake Ladoga into the Gulf of Finland through several mouths; ab. 40 mi. (65 km.) long; connected by canals and other waterways with the White Sea in the N and the Volga and Caspian Sea in the SE (see VOLGA-BALTIC WATERWAY); usu. frozen Nov. to Apr.; St. Petersburg (*q.v.*) is in its delta. Its banks the scene of a battle 1240 in which Alexander Nevsky, prince of Novgorod, defeated Swedes.

Ne·va·da \nə-'va-də, -'vä-\. **1.** A western state of U.S.A., bounded on N by Oregon and Idaho, on E by Utah and Arizona, and on SW and W by California; 7th state in area, 110,561 sq. mi. (286,353 sq. km.); 39th state in population, (1990c) 1,201,833; ✱ Carson City; 36th state admitted to Union (1864). See table of states at UNITED STATES.

Nickname: Silver State.

State flower: Sagebrush.

Motto: All For Our Country.

Rivers: Humboldt, rising in NE area, flowing W then SW and emptying into Humboldt Lake; Colorado River, forming extreme SE boundary.

Other physical features: Lakes include Pyramid and Winnemucca in W, and Walker in SW; many dry lakes (as Mud Flat) and marshy salt regions (Carson Sink and Humboldt Salt Marsh in W cen. part); Black Rock Desert in NW.

Highest point: Boundary Peak, 13,140 ft. (4005 m.) in Esmeralda co. on California-Nevada boundary.

Chief economic activities: Legalized gambling, tourism; products: wheat; livestock; gold, barite, mercury; copper historically important; manufacturing: lumber and wood products, chemicals.

Chief settlements: Las Vegas, Reno, Paradise (unincorporated).

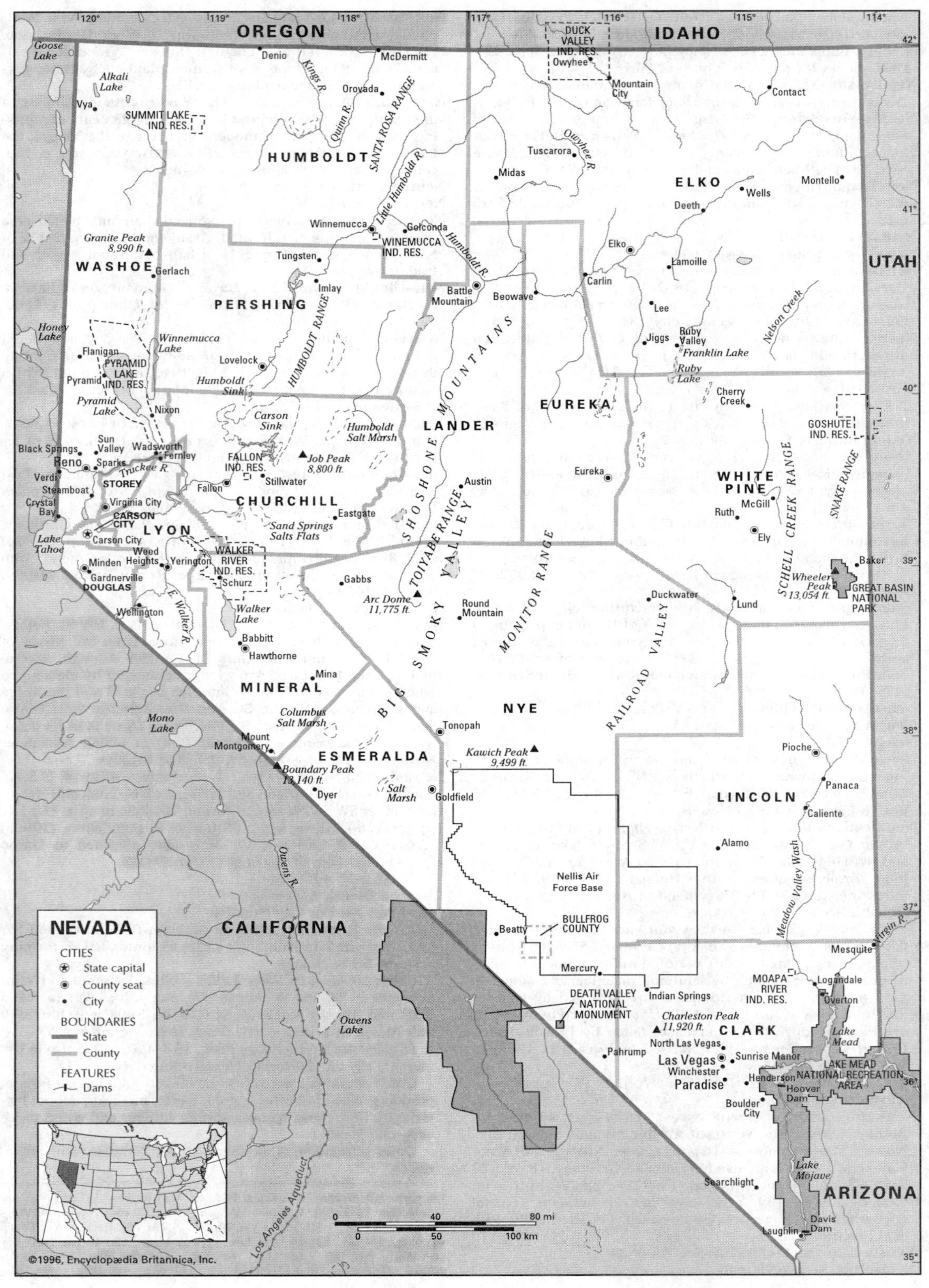
OREGON
IDAHO
UTAH
ARIZONA
CALIFORNIA
NEVADA
CITIES
State capital
County seat
City
BOUNDARIES
State
County
FEATURES
Dams
HUMBOLDT
ELKO
WASHOE
PERSHING
LANDER
EUREKA
WHITE PINE
CHURCHILL
STOREY
CARSON CITY
LYON
DOUGLAS
MINERAL
ESMERALDA
NYE
LINCOLN
CLARK
Goose Lake
Alkali Lake
Vya
SUMMIT LAKE IND. RES.
Denio
McDermitt
Orovada
Kings R.
Quinn R.
SANTA ROSA RANGE
Little Humboldt R.
DUCK VALLEY IND. RES.
Owyhee
Mountain City
Contact
Owyhee R.
Tuscarora
Midas
Montello
Wells
Deeth
Winnemucca
Golconda
WINEMUCCA IND. RES.
Humboldt R.
Granite Peak 8,990 ft.
Gerlach
Tungsten
Imlay
Elko
Lamoille
Carlin
Battle Mountain
Beowave
Lee
Nelson Creek
Honey Lake
Winnemucca Lake
Flanigan
PYRAMID LAKE IND. RES.
Pyramid
Pyramid Lake
Lovelock
HUMBOLDT RANGE
Humboldt Sink
SHOSHONE MOUNTAINS
Jiggs
Ruby Valley
Franklin Lake
Ruby Lake
Cherry Creek
GOSHUTE IND. RES.
Nixon
Carson Sink
Humboldt Salt Marsh
Black Springs
Sun Valley
Wadsworth
Reno
Sparks
Fernley
Truckee R.
FALLON IND. RES.
Job Peak 8,800 ft.
Stillwater
Verdi
Steamboat
Fallon
Austin
Eureka
SCHELL CREEK RANGE
SNAKE RANGE
Crystal Bay
Virginia City
Eastgate
TOIYABE RANGE
McGill
Ruth
Ely
Lake Tahoe
Carson City
Sand Springs Salts Flats
Minden
Weed Heights
Yerington
WALKER RIVER IND. RES.
Schurz
Gardnerville
Gabbs
Arc Dome 11,775 ft.
MONITOR RANGE
Baker
Wheeler Peak 13,054 ft.
GREAT BASIN NATIONAL PARK
Duckwater
Round Mountain
Lund
Wellington
E. Walker R.
Walker Lake
SMOKY VALLEY
Babbitt
Hawthorne
RAILROAD VALLEY
Mina
BIG
Columbus Salt Marsh
Mono Lake
Tonopah
Mount Montgomery
Kawich Peak 9,499 ft.
Pioche
Boundary Peak 13,140 ft.
Dyer
Salt Marsh
Goldfield
Panaca
Caliente
Owens R.
Alamo
Nellis Air Force Base
Meadow Valley Wash
Virgin R.
Beatty
BULLFROG COUNTY
Mesquite
Mercury
MOAPA RIVER IND. RES.
Logandale
Overton
DEATH VALLEY NATIONAL MONUMENT
Indian Springs
Charleston Peak 11,920 ft.
Owens Lake
Lake Mead
North Las Vegas
Pahrump
Las Vegas
Sunrise Manor
Winchester
Paradise
Henderson
LAKE MEAD NATIONAL RECREATION AREA
Hoover Dam
Boulder City
Lake Mojave
Searchlight
Los Angeles Aqueduct
Davis Dam
Laughlin
0
40
80 mi
0
50
100 km
120°
119°
118°
117°
116°
115°
114°
42°
41°
40°
39°
38°
37°
36°
35°

Political divisions: Divided into the following 16 counties and one independent city (for pronunciation of their names, see their individual entries):

NAME	AREA[1] (sq. mi.)	AREA[1] (sq. km.)	POP. (1990c)	CO. SEAT
Churchill	4,883	12,647	17,938	Fallon
Clark	7,874	20,394	741,459	Las Vegas
Douglas	723	1,873	27,637	Minden
Elko	17,162	44,450	33,530	Elko
Esmeralda	3,570	9,246	1,344	Goldfield
Eureka	4,182	10,831	1,547	Eureka
Humboldt	9,702	25,128	12,844	Winnemucca
Lander	5,621	14,558	6,266	Battle Mountain
Lincoln	10,649	27,581	3,775	Pioche
Lyon	2,010	5,206	20,001	Yerington
Mineral	3,765	9,751	6,475	Hawthorne
Nye[2]	18,064	46,786	17,781	Tonopah
Pershing	6,001	15,543	4,336	Lovelock
Storey	262	679	2,526	Virginia City
Washoe	6,375	16,511	254,667	Reno
White Pine	8,904	23,061	9,264	Ely
Carson City[3]	141	365	40,443	

[1] Area = land area.
[2] The small, unpopulated co. of Bullfrog (*q.v.*) was carved out of S Nye co. (E of Death Valley National Monument) 1987.
[3] Independent city.

History: Evidence of prehistoric inhabitants in the region (since ab. 20,000 years ago) includes projectile points, rock art, and dwelling remains; some Anasazi sites in SE; at time of European contact (c. 18th cent.) region inhabited by several Indian tribes incl. Shoshoni and Paiute; some exploration by Spanish (18th cent.), fur traders (1820s), and others; major exploration and mapping by John C. Frémont and Kit Carson 1843–45; included in region ceded by Mexico to U.S. 1848; included in Utah Terr. 1850–61; first permanent settlement made c. 1850 at Mormon Station (now Genoa); settlement increased after discovery of Comstock Lode 1859 (see VIRGINIA CITY 2); organized as **Territory of Nevada** 1861; admitted to Union as state Oct. 31, 1864; enlarged slightly 1866 to present boundaries.

2. Name of counties in two states of the U.S. See tables at ARKANSAS and CALIFORNIA.

Ne·va·da \nə-'vā-də\. **1.** City, ⊗ of Story co., cen. Iowa, 30 mi. (48 km.) N of Des Moines; pop. (1990c) 6009.

2. City, ⊗ of Vernon co., W Missouri, 53 mi. (85 km.) N of Joplin; pop. (1990c) 8597.

Ne·va·da \nā-'vä-t͟hä\. Mountain in the Andes, on Argentina-Chile border; 20,023 ft. (6103 m.).

Nevada, Sierra. See SIERRA NEVADA.

Ne·vada City \nə-'va-də, -'vä-\. City, ⊗ of Nevada co., E California, 45 mi. (72 km.) W of Lake Tahoe; pop. (1990c) 2855; gold mining.

Nevada de Cocuy, Sierra. See SIERRA NEVADA DE COCUY.

Nevada de Mérida, Sierra. See CORDILLERA DE MÉRIDA.

Nevada de Santa Marta, Sierra. See SIERRA NEVADA DE SANTA MARTA.

Nevada Fall *also* **Nevada Falls** \nə-'va-də, -'vä-\. Waterfall in Yosemite National Park, E cen. California; 594 ft. (181 m.).

Ne·va·do \nə-'vä-dō\. For names of mountains beginning with this element see the distinguishing element.

Ne·va·do del Ru·iz \nā-'vä-t͟hō-t͟hel-'rwēs\. Volcano, W cen. Colombia; mudflows from the Nov. 1985 eruption devastated the nearby town of Armero.

Ne·vel'sk *or* **Ne·velsk** \nye-'velʸsk\ *or Jp.* **Hon·to** \'hȯn-tō, 'hōn-\. Town, SW coast of Sakhalin I., SE Russia in Asia.

Ne·vers \nə-'ver\; *anc.* **No·vi·o·du·num** \ˌnō-vē-ō-'dü-nəm, -'dyü-\. Commune, ✻ of Nièvre dept., cen. France, at confluence of Nièvre and Loire rivers 38 mi. (61 km.) ESE of Bourges; pop. (1990c) 43,889; famous for manufacture of faience, introduced from Italy in 16th cent.; episcopal see since 6th cent.; 11th cent. Romanesque church; 13th–16th cent. cathedral (restored); 15th cent. courthouse (former ducal palace); was ✻ of former duchy and prov. of Nivernais.

Ne·ves \'ne-vis\. City, Rio de Janeiro state, SE Brazil, NE of city of Rio de Janeiro; pop. (1991p) 151,067.

Ne·vi·ges \'nā-vi-gəs\. City, North Rhine-Westphalia, Germany, 21 mi. (34 km.) NE of Düsseldorf.

Nev·ille's Cross \'ne-vilz\. Parish, Durham co., N England, near Durham; site of battle Oct. 17, 1346 in which invading Scots under King David Bruce were defeated, and the king taken prisoner, by English forces of Edward III.

Ne·vin·no·myssk \nye-ˌvi-nə-'misk\. Town, Stavropol' Kray, S Russia in Europe, ab. 30 mi. (48 km.) S of the city of Stavropol'; pop. (1992e) 125,000.

Ne·vis \'nē-vis, 'ne-\. Island in E West Indies, part of St. Kitts-Nevis, Leeward Is.; 36 sq. mi. (93 sq. km.); chief town Charlestown; tourism; formerly produced sugarcane; birthplace of American politician Alexander Hamilton 1755. Separated from St. Kitts on NW by narrow strait 2 mi. (3 km.) wide; comprised of a volcanic cone, rising to **Nevis Peak** at a height of 3232 ft. (985 m.). Discovered by Christopher Columbus 1493; colonized by English 1628; held for short time by French 18th cent. See SAINT KITTS-NEVIS.

Nevis, Ben. See BEN NEVIS.

Nevis, Loch. Inlet of the Sound of Sleat on W coast of Highland region, NW Scotland; extends inland ab. 14 mi. (23 km.).

Nev·şe·hir \'nev-shə-ˌhir\ *or* **Nev·shehr** \'nev-ˌsher\. **1.** Province of Turkey in Asia. See table at TURKEY.

2. Town, its ✻, 40 mi. (64 km.) W of Kayseri; pop. (1990p) 52,514.

New \'nü, 'nyü\. **1.** River, SE North Carolina; rises in N Onslow co., flows S into **New River Inlet** and Atlantic Ocean; ab. 35 mi. (55 km.) long.

2. River, SW Virginia and S West Virginia; formed by junction of N and S forks in Ashe co., NW North Carolina; flows N across state of Virginia into West Virginia and joins Gauley River to form Kanawha River in N Fayette co., S cen. West Virginia; ab. 320 mi. (515 km.) long; spanned by longest steel-arch bridge in world (main span 1700 ft. or 518 m.; completed 1977), near Fayetteville, West Virginia.

3. Artificial stream, Hertfordshire and Greater London, SE England; commences near Ware, flows S into reservoirs at Haringey and Hackney; 36 mi. (58 km.) long.

New Al·ba·ny \'ȯl-bə-nē\. **1.** City, ⊗ of Floyd co., S Indiana, on Ohio River across from Louisville, Kentucky; pop. (1990c) 36,322; wood products; former shipbuilding center in steamboat era (mid-19th cent.); Indiana Univ. Southeast (1941); incorp. as city 1839.

2. City, ⊗ of Union co., N Mississippi, 24 mi. (39 km.) NW of Tupelo; pop. (1990c) 6775.

New Am·ster·dam \'am-stər-ˌdam\. **1.** The Dutch city on Manhattan I. which became the city of New York; ✻ of New Netherland colony; founded c. 1625 by Dutch West India Co.; taken by English 1664 and renamed New York. See NEW YORK 1 and NEW YORK 3.

2. \'äm-stər-ˌdäm\. Town, NE Guyana, on E bank of Berbice River near its mouth; ab. 55 mi. (88 km.) SE of Georgetown; pop. (1985e) 25,000.

3. Island, Indian Ocean. See AMSTERDAM 3.

New Archangel. See SITKA 2.

New·ark \'nü-ərk, 'nyü-, *esp 2 and 5* 'nü-ˌärk\. **1.** City, Alameda co., W California, SE of San Francisco; pop. (1990c) 37,861.

2. City, New Castle co., N Delaware, 12 mi. (19 km.) WSW of Wilmington; pop. (1990c) 25,098; paper products, automobile parts; Univ. of Delaware (1743); settled late 17th cent.

3. City and port of entry, ⊗ of Essex co., NE New Jersey, on Passaic River and Newark Bay 9 mi. (14 km.) W of New York City; pop. (1990c) 275,221; transportation center, connected to New York City by tunnel; insurance and financial center; manufactures electrical equipment, chemicals, machinery; international airport serving the New York met. area; New Jersey Institute of Technology (1881), Rutgers Coll. of Nursing (1956), Essex County Coll. (1968), Univ. of Medicine

\ə\ **abut** \ə̇\ matches \ᵊ\ kitten, Fr table \ər\ **further** \a\ **ash** \ā\ **ace**
\ä\ cot, cart \ȧ\ Fr bac \au̇\ **out** \b̲\ Span Avila \ch\ **chin** \e\ bet \ē\ **easy**
\g\ **go** \i\ hit \ī\ ice \j\ **job** \k̲\ Ger **ich**, Bu**ch** \ⁿ\ Fr vin
\ŋ\ sing \ō\ **go** \ö\ **all** \ȯ\ **law** \œ\ Fr **bœuf** \œ̄\ Fr **feu** \ȯi\ **boy**
\th\ **thin** \t͟h\ **this** \ü\ **loot** \u̇\ **foot** \ue\ Ger **füllen** \ue̅\ Fr **rue**
\y\ **yet** \ʸ\ Fr digne \'dēnʸ\, nuit \'nwʸē\ \yü\ **few** \yu̇\ **fury** \zh\ **vision**

and Dentistry of New Jersey (1970). Birthplace of Vice President Aaron Burr (1756) and writer Stephen Crane (1871).

History: First settled by Puritans 1666; site of Coll. of New Jersey (later Princeton Univ.) 1748–56; Gen. George Washington's supply base on retreat across state 1776; incorp. as city 1836; scene of major civil disturbance 1967.

4. Village, Wayne co., W New York, 29 mi. (47 km.) ESE of Rochester; pop. (1990c) 9849.

5. City, ⊗ of Licking co., cen. Ohio, 30 mi. (48 km.) E of Columbus; pop. (1990c) 44,389; glass, aluminum products, automobile parts, plastics; Ohio State Univ.–Newark (1957), Central Ohio Technical Coll. (1971); several earthworks of prehistoric Mound Builders in vicinity.

6. Town, Nottinghamshire, England. See NEWARK-ON-TRENT.

Newark Bay. A bay in NE New Jersey, SE of Newark; separated from Lower New York Bay on S by Staten I. and connected with Upper New York Bay through Kill Van Kull; receives on the N the Passaic and Hackensack rivers.

Newark–on–Trent \-ˌän-ˈtrent, -ˌȯn-\ *or* **Newark.** Town, Nottinghamshire, N cen. England, 20 mi. (32 km.) ENE of Nottingham; pop. (1981p) 24,091; market town; ball bearings, limestone; brewing. On the ancient Fosse Way; has remains of castle of 12th–15th cents. which was besieged three times during English Civil War.

New Au·gus·ta \ȯ-ˈgəs-tə, ə-\. Town, ⊗ of Perry co., SE Mississippi; pop. (1990c) 668.

Ne·way·go \ni-ˈwā-gō\. County in W Michigan. See table at MICHIGAN.

New Bal·ti·more \ˈbȯl-tə-ˌmōr\. City, Macomb and St. Clair cos., SE Michigan, on Lake St. Clair; pop. (1990c) 5798.

New Barbados. See HACKENSACK 2.

New Bed·ford \ˈbed-fərd\. City, a ⊗ of Bristol co., SE Massachusetts, on **New Bedford Harbor** on W side of Buzzards Bay, 50 mi. (80 km.) S of Boston; pop. (1990c) 99,922; first settled c. 1652; separate village estab. 1760 and early became shipping and whaling center; a leading U.S. whaling port in 19th cent.; incorp. as city 1847; textile and apparel industries spurred growth in early 20th cent.

New·berg \ˈnü-ˌbərg, ˈnyü-\. City, Yamhill co., NW Oregon, 21 mi. (34 km.) SW of Portland; pop. (1990c) 13,086; fruit and nut packing; George Fox Coll. (1891); restored boyhood home of President Herbert Hoover; city founded c. 1869 as first Quaker settlement W of the Rocky Mts.

New Ber·lin \ˈbər-lin\. City, Waukesha co., SE Wisconsin, W of Milwaukee; pop. (1990c) 33,592.

New·bern \ˈnü-bərn, ˈnyü-\. Town, Dyer co., NW Tennessee, 10 mi. (16 km.) NE of Dyersburg; pop. (1990c) 2515.

New Bern \ˈnü-ˌbərn, ˈnyü-, -ˈbərn\. City and port, ⊗ of Craven co., SE North Carolina, at confluence of Neuse and Trent rivers; pop. (1990c) 17,363; commercial center in farming and resort area; Tryon Palace (constructed 1767–70, restored 1950s) was colonial capitol and governor's mansion until 1774. Settled by Swiss and Germans 1710; incorp. and made ⊗ 1723; early colonial ✻; seat of royal governors 1770–74; site of first provincial congress (in opposition to the British) 1774; in Civil War a fortified port of the Confederacy, captured by Union forces under Gen. Ambrose Burnside 1862 and held by Union throughout the war.

New·ber·ry \ˈnü-ˌber-ē, -bə-rē, ˈnyü-\. **1.** County in NW cen. South Carolina. See table at SOUTH CAROLINA.

2. Village, ⊗ of Luce co., Michigan, in Upper Peninsula, 58 mi. (93 km.) W of Sault Sainte Marie; pop. (1990c) 1873.

3. Town, ⊗ of Newberry co., NW cen. South Carolina, 32 mi. (51 km.) ENE of Greenwood; pop. (1990c) 10,542; Newberry Coll. (1856).

New·big·gin by the Sea \nü-ˈbig-ᵊn, nyü-, ˈnü-ˌbig-, ˈnyü-\. Resort town, Northumberland, N England, on the North Sea 17 mi. (27 km.) NNE of Newcastle upon Tyne; pop. (1981p) 12,132.

New Bloom·field \ˈblüm-ˌfēld\. Borough, ⊗ of Perry co., S cen. Pennsylvania.

New Bos·ton \ˈbȯ-stən\. **1.** Town, Hillsborough co., cen. S New Hampshire; pop. (1990c) 3214.

2. City, Scioto co., S Ohio, on Ohio River 4 mi. (6 km.) E of Portsmouth; pop. (1990c) 2717.

3. Town, Bowie co., NE Texas, 24 mi. (39 km.) W of Texarkana; pop. (1990c) 5057.

New Brandenburg. See NEUBRANDENBURG.

New Braun·fels \ˈbrau̇n-fəlz\. City, ⊗ of Comal co., S cen. Texas, on Guadalupe River 32 mi. (51 km.) NE of San Antonio; pop. (1990c) 27,334; textiles, hosiery, flour; diversified agriculture.

Newbridge. See ABERCARN.

New Brigh·ton \ˈbrīt-ᵊn\. **1.** Village, Ramsey co., SE cen. Minnesota, N of Minneapolis; pop. (1990c) 22,207.

2. Residential neighborhood, N Staten I., New York City, on Kill Van Kull.

3. Borough, Beaver co., W Pennsylvania, on Beaver River just S of Beaver Falls and 19 mi. (47 km.) S of New Castle; pop. (1990c) 6854; settled around a blockhouse erected 1789.

New Brit·ain \ˈbrit-ᵊn\. **1.** City, Hartford co., N Connecticut, 9 mi. (14 km.) SW of the city of Hartford; pop. (1990c) 75,491; tools, hardware, ball bearings; Central Connecticut State Univ. (1849). Settled 1687; incorp. 1870; consolidated 1905 with the town (incorp. 1850) with which it is coextensive.

2. *formerly* **Neu–Pom·mern** \nȯi-ˈpȯ-mərn\. Largest island in the Bismarck Archipelago, administratively part of Papua New Guinea; 14,160 sq. mi. (36,674 sq. km.); pop. (1989e) 263,500; divided into two districts: **East New Britain** (✻ Rabaul) and **West New Britain** (✻ Kimbe); crescent-shaped with several volcanoes, esp. at E end; highest peak Mt. Sinewit 7999 ft. (2438 m.), sudden violent eruption May 1937 (see VULCAN, MOUNT and TAVURVUR, MOUNT). Has many good harbors, esp. Blanche Bay, Talasea, Jacquinot Bay, Linden Harbour. Chief islands off coast, belonging to the two districts, are Lolobau, Witu Is., Umboi, Long, and Duke of York Is. Rich in tropical vegetation; coconuts and cocoa of value commercially.

History: Visited and named by English explorer William Dampier 1700; made part of German protectorate 1884 (see KOKOPO); occupied during WWI by Australians, and after the war made a part of Australian mandate; invaded by Japanese Jan. 1942 and held until taken by U.S. forces 1944; part of UN trust territory under Australian administration until 1975.

New Bruns·wick \-ˈbrənz-(ˌ)wik\. **1.** City, ⊗ of Middlesex co., cen. New Jersey, at head of navigation on Raritan River 9 mi. (14 km.) W of Perth Amboy; pop. (1990c) 41,711; automobile parts, pharmaceuticals and surgical supplies, machinery, chemicals, leather goods; Rutgers, The State Univ. of New Jersey (1766), New Brunswick Theological Seminary (1784), Rutgers–Douglass Coll. (1918), Rutgers–Livingston Coll. (1969), Rutgers–Mason Gross School of the Arts (1976). Birthplace of poet Joyce Kilmer 1886.

History: Settled by English colonists 1681; granted town charter 1736, incorp. as city 1784; alternately headquarters for American and British troops in Revolutionary War; entered by Gen. George Washington's retreating army 1776; starting point for Washington's march to Yorktown 1781.

2. Province, one of the Maritime Provinces, E Canada, bounded by Quebec prov. on N, by the Gulf of St. Lawrence and Northumberland Strait (separating it from Prince Edward I.) on E, on S by Bay of Fundy, and on W by Maine; on SE connected with Nova Scotia by Isthmus of Chignecto; ✻ Fredericton. See table at CANADA.

Physical features: Highest point of land Mt. Carleton 2690 ft. (820 m.); larger part lies within basin of St. John River; other rivers the St. Croix (on Maine border), Miramichi, Restigouche, and Nepisiguit.

Chief products: Potatoes, dairy products, fish; timber; coal, gypsum, zinc.

Chief cities: St. John, Moncton, Fredericton.

Political divisions: Divided into the following 15 counties (for pronunciation of their names, see their individual entries):

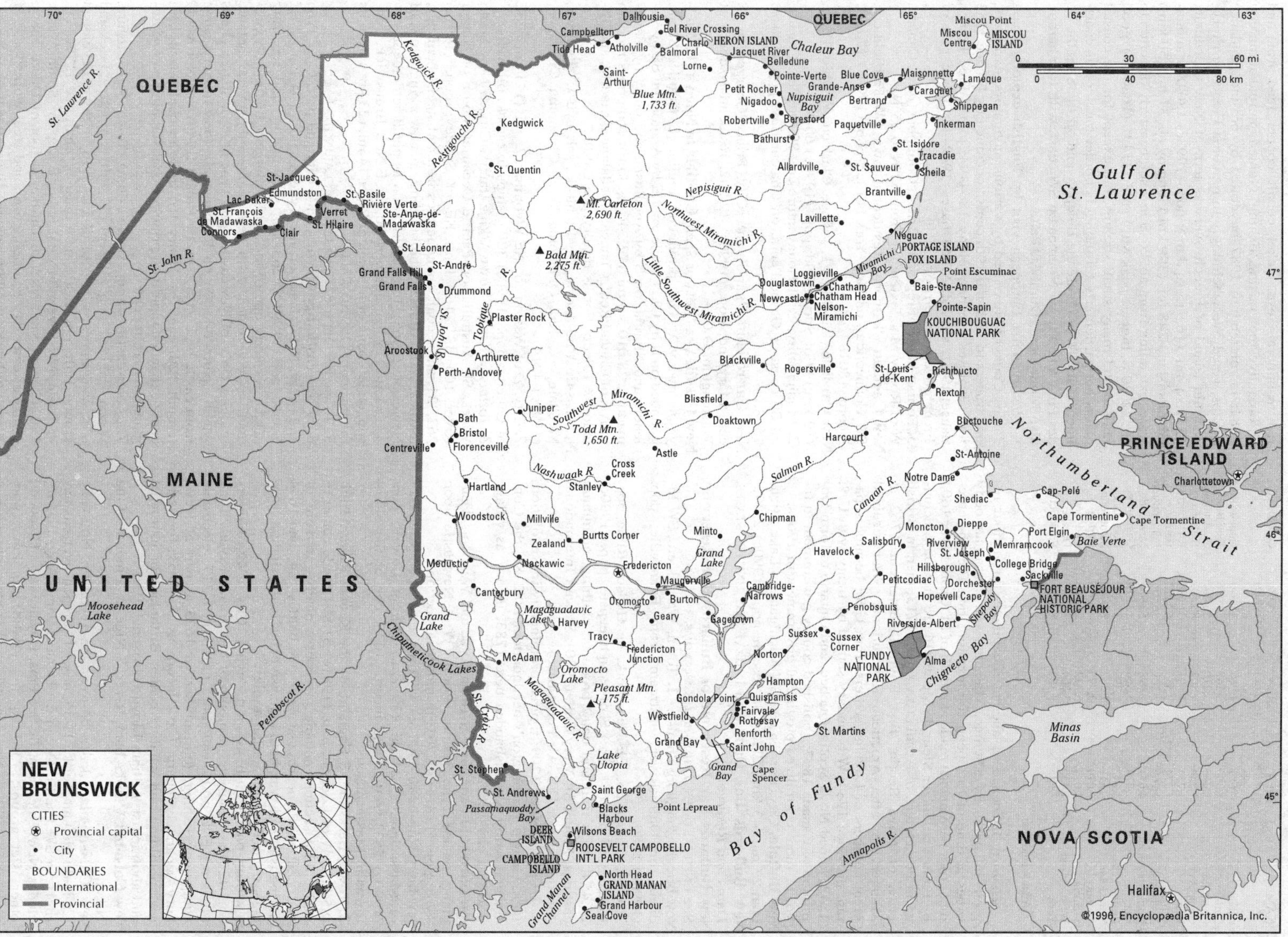
NEW BRUNSWICK
CITIES
Provincial capital
City
BOUNDARIES
International
Provincial
0 30 60 mi
0 40 80 km
©1996, Encyclopædia Britannica, Inc.
QUEBEC
MAINE
UNITED STATES
NOVA SCOTIA
PRINCE EDWARD ISLAND
Gulf of St. Lawrence
Chaleur Bay
Northumberland Strait
Bay of Fundy
Minas Basin
Chignecto Bay
Shepody Bay
Baie Verte
Passamaquoddy Bay
Grand Manan Channel
Miramichi Bay
Nepisiguit Bay
Grand Bay
Chiputneticook Lakes
Grand Lake
Moosehead Lake
Magaguadavic Lake
Oromocto Lake
Lake Utopia
St. John R.
St. Croix R.
Restigouche R.
Kedgwick R.
Tobique R.
Miramichi R.
Northwest Miramichi R.
Little Southwest Miramichi R.
Southwest Miramichi R.
Nashwaak R.
Salmon R.
Canaan R.
Magaguadavic R.
Nepisiguit R.
Penobscot R.
Annapolis R.
St. Lawrence R.
Mt. Carleton 2,690 ft.
Bald Mtn. 2,275 ft.
Blue Mtn. 1,733 ft.
Todd Mtn. 1,650 ft.
Pleasant Mtn. 1,175 ft.
FUNDY NATIONAL PARK
KOUCHIBOUGUAC NATIONAL PARK
FORT BEAUSÉJOUR NATIONAL HISTORIC PARK
ROOSEVELT CAMPOBELLO INT'L PARK
MISCOU ISLAND
HERON ISLAND
PORTAGE ISLAND
FOX ISLAND
DEER ISLAND
CAMPOBELLO ISLAND
GRAND MANAN ISLAND
Miscou Point
Miscou Centre
Dalhousie
Eel River Crossing
Campbellton
Tide Head
Atholville
Charlo
Balmoral
Saint-Arthur
Lorne
Jacquet River
Belledune
Pointe-Verte
Petit Rocher
Nigadoo
Beresford
Robertville
Bathurst
Grande-Anse
Blue Cove
Maisonnette
Caraquet
Lamèque
Shippegan
Bertrand
Paquetville
Inkerman
St. Isidore
Tracadie
Sheila
Allardville
St. Sauveur
Brantville
Lavillette
Neguac
Point Escuminac
Baie-Ste-Anne
Pointe-Sapin
Loggieville
Douglastown
Chatham
Chatham Head
Newcastle
Nelson-Miramichi
Kedgwick
St. Quentin
St-Jacques
Edmundston
Lac Baker
St. François de Madawaska
Connors
Clair
Verret
St. Hilaire
St. Basile
Rivière Verte
Ste-Anne-de-Madawaska
St. Léonard
St-André
Grand Falls Hill
Grand Falls
Drummond
Plaster Rock
Aroostook
Arthurette
Perth-Andover
Blackville
Rogersville
St-Louis-de-Kent
Richibucto
Rexton
Blissfield
Doaktown
Juniper
Bath
Bristol
Florenceville
Centreville
Astle
Harcourt
Buctouche
St-Antoine
Notre Dame
Shediac
Cap-Pelé
Cape Tormentine
Charlottetown
Cross Creek
Stanley
Hartland
Woodstock
Millville
Zealand
Burtts Corner
Chipman
Minto
Moncton
Dieppe
Riverview
St. Joseph
Memramcook
Port Elgin
College Bridge
Sackville
Salisbury
Havelock
Hillsborough
Petitcodiac
Dorchester
Hopewell Cape
Meductic
Nackawic
Fredericton
Maugerville
Canterbury
Oromocto
Burton
Geary
Cambridge-Narrows
Gagetown
Penobsquis
Riverside-Albert
Harvey
Tracy
Fredericton Junction
Sussex
Sussex Corner
Alma
Norton
McAdam
Hampton
Gondola Point
Quispamsis
Fairvale
Rothesay
Renforth
Westfield
Grand Bay
Saint John
St. Martins
Cape Spencer
St. Stephen
St. Andrews
Saint George
Blacks Harbour
Point Lepreau
Wilsons Beach
North Head
Grand Harbour
Seal Cove
Halifax

NAME	AREA[1] (sq. mi.)	AREA[1] (sq. km.)	POP. (1991c)	CO. SEAT
Albert	681	1,764	25,640	Hopewell
Carleton	1,300	3,367	26,026	Woodstock
Charlotte	1,243	3,219	26,607	St. Andrews
Gloucester	1,854	4,802	88,101	Bathurst
Kent	1,734	4,491	31,694	Richibucto
Kings	1,374	3,559	62,122	Hampton
Madawaska	1,262	3,269	36,554	Edmundston
Northumberland	4,671	12,098	52,983	Newcastle
Queens	1,373	3,556	12,519	Gagetown
Restigouche	3,242	8,397	38,760	Dalhousie
Saint John	611	1,582	81,462	Saint John
Sunbury	1,079	2,795	23,575	Burton
Victoria	2,074	5,372	20,786	Andover
Westmorland	1,430	3,704	114,745	Dorchester
York	3,545	9,182	82,326	Fredericton

[1]Area = land area.

History: Evidence of ancient inhabitants throughout region; inhabited by Micmac, Malecite, and Passamaquoddy tribes at time of European colonization; first French settlement (not permanent) made at mouth of St. Croix River 1604 by French colonizer Sieur de Monts (Pierre du Gua); included in French terr. of Acadia (*q.v.*) until 1713, then in British prov. of Nova Scotia; first English settlement 1762 at Maugerville; after American Revolutionary War received great numbers of Loyalist settlers from U.S.; became separate province 1784; W boundary settled by treaty with U.S. 1842; joined Nova Scotia, Quebec, and Ontario to form Dominion of Canada 1867; abolished county government in favor of more centralized provincial government in 1960s.

New Buffalo. City, Berrien co., SW Michigan, on Lake Michigan 27 mi. (43 km.) SW of St. Joseph; pop. (1990c) 2317.

New Bull·ards Bar Dam \ˈbu̇-lərdz\. See UNITED STATES, *Dams and Reservoirs.*

New Bullards Bar Reservoir *or* **Bullards Bar Reservoir.** See UNITED STATES, *Dams and Reservoirs.*

New·burgh \ˈnü-ˌbərg, ˈnyü-\. **1.** Town, Warrick co., SW Indiana, on Ohio River, upstream from Evansville; pop. (1990c) 2880.

2. City, Orange co., SE New York, on Hudson River opp. Beacon; 15 mi. (24 km.) S of Poughkeepsie; pop. (1990c) 26,454; ships fruit and dairy products; clothing, aluminum castings; Mount St. Mary Coll. (1930); Stewart International Airport (former U.S. Air Force base).

History: Settled 1709; figured prominently in Revolution; Gen. George Washington's headquarters 1782–83; the Continental Army was disbanded here 1783; incorp. as village 1800, as city 1865.

New·burn \ˈnü-bərn, ˈnyü-\. Town, Tyne and Wear co., N England, on the Tyne 5.5 mi. (9 km.) W of Newcastle upon Tyne; pop. (1981c) 43,701; in industrial section.

New·bury \ˈnü-bə-rē, ˈnyü-\. **1.** Town, Essex co., NE corner of Massachusetts, 24 mi. (39 km.) ENE of Lowell; pop. (1990c) 5623; settled and incorp. 1635, one of the oldest towns in Massachusetts.

2. Town, Berkshire, S England, on the Kennet River 53 mi. (85 km.) W of London; pop. (1981c) 31,894; trade center in agricultural section; notable racecourse nearby; remains of 14th cent. castle nearby; scene of two battles 1643 and 1644 in English Civil War, both indecisive, but to the slight advantage of the Parliamentarian armies.

New·bury·port \ˈnü-bə-rē-ˌpōrt, ˈnyü-\. City, a ⊗ of Essex co., NE Massachusetts, at mouth of Merrimack River 25 mi. (40 km.) ENE of Lowell; pop. (1990c) 16,317; electronic equipment; fishing; tourism; settled 1635 as part of Newbury; separately incorp. 1764; incorp. as city 1851; formerly a shipbuilding and whaling center. Birthplace of journalist and abolitionist William Lloyd Garrison 1805.

New Cal·a·bar \ˈka-lə-ˌbär\. River, S Nigeria, a mouth of the Niger.

New Cal·e·do·nia \ˌka-lə-ˈdō-nyə, -nē-ə\ *or Fr.* **Nou·velle Ca·lé·do·nie** \nü-ˈvel-kȧ-lā-dȯ-ˈnē\. **1.** French overseas territory in SW Pacific Ocean E of Queensland, Australia; includes New Caledonia, Île des Pins, Loyalty Is., and several other islet groups; 7367 sq. mi. (19,081 sq. km.); pop. (1994e) 183,100; ✻ Nouméa; principal crops copra, coffee; rich in minerals, esp. nickel, cobalt, copper, lead, iron, and chrome; livestock raising, fishing; granted internal autonomy 1984; in referendum 1987 boycotted by pro-independence groups, voted overwhelmingly to remain a French territory.

2. Main island of French overseas terr. of New Caledonia; 6531 sq. mi. (16,915 sq. km.); pop. (1993e) 180,000; mountainous island 248 mi. (399 km.) long by ab. 31 mi. (50 km.) wide, extending from ab. 20°S in a southeasterly direction to ab. 22°20′S; highest peak Mt. Panié 5314 ft. (1620 m.); good rainfall and many small streams, but except for the coastal plains not particularly fertile; reefs border much of its coastline; off its NW point are the Belep Is. and off the S tip the Île des Pins. Chief town Nouméa on SW coast, with fine harbor, also Mont-Dore, Dumbéa, Païta.

History: First European visit by English explorer Capt. James Cook 1774; visited by various navigators, explorers, and traders in 18th and 19th cents.; occupied by France 1853 and set up as a penal colony 1864–94; joined Free French cause 1940; site of Allied bases 1942–44; made part of French overseas territory 1946.

3. Former name of region in British Columbia (*q.v.*), Canada, W of Rocky Mts., extending from 52°N to 55°N.

New Ca·naan \ˈkā-nən\. Residential town, SW Fairfield co., SW Connecticut, on New York border; pop. (1990c) 17,864; incorp. 1801.

New Car·lisle \kär-ˈlīl\. **1.** Village, Clark co., W Ohio, 12 mi. (19 km.) W of Springfield; pop. (1990c) 6049.

2. Municipality, ⊗ of Bonaventure co., SE Quebec, Canada, on SE coast of Gaspé Penin. on Chaleur Bay; pop. (1991c) 1568.

New Car·roll·ton \ˈkar-əl-tən\. City, Prince Georges co., S cen. Maryland; pop. (1990c) 12,502; residential suburb of Washington, D.C.

New Cas·tile \ka-ˈstēl\ *or Span.* **Cas·til·la la Nue·va** \kä-ˈstēl-yä-ˌlä-ˈnwā-vä\. Old provincial region, S Castile, Spain; bounded on N by Old Castile, on NE by Aragon, on SE by Valencia and Murcia, on S by Andalusia, and on W by Extremadura; 28,010 sq. mi. (72,546 sq. km.); comprises modern provs. of Ciudad Real, Cuenca, Guadalajara, Madrid, and Toledo; ✻ Toledo. For its history, see CASTILE.

New·cas·tle \ˈnü-ˌka-səl, ˈnyü-; nü-ˈka-səl, nyü-\. **1.** Town, McClain co., cen. Oklahoma, S of Oklahoma City; pop. (1990c) 4214.

2. City, ⊗ of Weston co., NE Wyoming, 75 mi. (121 km.) ESE of Gillette; pop. (1990c) 3003; ships livestock; oil wells.

3. *formerly* **King's Town** \ˈkiŋz-ˌtau̇n\. City, E New South Wales, SE Australia, on Pacific Ocean at mouth of Hunter River 100 mi. (161 km.) NE of Sydney; pop. (1991c) 262,331; ships coal; manufactures iron and steel, chemicals, textiles, and fertilizers; shipbuilding, metalworking; Univ. of Newcastle (1965); founded c. 1804 as penal settlement.

4. Town, ⊗ of Northumberland co., E New Brunswick, Canada, on left bank of Miramichi River 14 mi. (23 km.) from its mouth; pop. (1991c) 5711.

5. Town, SE Ontario, Canada. See CLARINGTON.

6. *or* **Newcastle upon Tyne** \ˈtīn\. City and port, ⊗ of Tyne and Wear, N England, on the Tyne 83 mi. (134 km.) N of Leeds; pop. (1991p) 263,000; shipbuilding and repairing center, formerly one of the world's largest; historically productive coal mines; 14th cent. cathedral; several notable bridges; Univ. of Newcastle upon Tyne (1963). Station (**Pons Ae·lii** \ˈpänz-ˈē-lē-ˌī\) on Roman wall; took modern name from castle built 11th cent. by Robert II, duke of Normandy (rebuilt 12th cent. by Henry II); trade in coal began 13th cent.; expanded rapidly as principal coal-shipping port of England after 16th cent.

7. *or* **Newcastle–under–Lyme** \-ˈlīm\. Town, Staffordshire, W cen. England; pop. (1991p) 117,400; computers; brick and tile; coal mines; Univ. of Keele (1962); town developed around 12th cent. castle, now in ruins; chartered 1173.

8. Town, NW Kwazulu-Natal prov., E Rep. of South Africa, 150 mi. (241 km.) NNW of Durban at foot of Drakensberg; center of extensive coalfields; iron and steel works; base of British military operations against Boers in war of 1880–81.

New Cas·tle \ˈnü-ˌka-səl, ˈnyü-\. **1.** County in N Delaware. See table at DELAWARE.

2. City, New Castle co., N Delaware, on Delaware River 5 mi. (8 km.) S of Wilmington; pop. (1990c) 4837; steel castings; Wilmington Coll. (1967).

3. City, ⊗ of Henry co., E cen. Indiana, 18 mi. (29 km.) S of Muncie; pop. (1990c) 17,753; automobile parts; rose nurseries; founded c. 1820; nearby farm was birthplace of aviation pioneer Wilbur Wright 1867.

4. City, ⊗ of Henry co., N Kentucky, ab. 35 mi. (56 km.) NE of Louisville; pop. (1990c) 893.

5. Town, Rockingham co., SE New Hampshire, on an island at mouth of Piscataqua River, just E of Portsmouth; pop. (1990c) 840; was seat of early government functions in New Hampshire.

6. City, ⊗ of Lawrence co., W Pennsylvania, on the Shenango River 44 mi. (71 km.) NNW of Pittsburgh; pop. (1990c) 28,334; steel products, pottery, chemicals; coal mines; settled c. 1798; incorp. as borough 1825, as city 1869.

7. Town, ⊗ of Craig co., W Virginia, ab. 55 mi. (88 km.) W of Lynchburg; pop. (1990c) 152.

Newchwang. See YINGKOU 1.

New City. Unincorporated settlement, ⊗ of Rockland co., SE New York; pop. (1990c) 33,673; residential.

New·com·ers·town \ˈnü-ˌkə-mərz-ˌtau̇n, ˈnyü-\. Village, Tuscarawas co., E Ohio, 30 mi. (48 km.) NE of Zanesville; pop. (1990c) 4012.

New Con·cord \ˈkäŋ-kərd\. Village, Muskingum co., SE cen. Ohio, 14 mi. (23 km.) E of Zanesville; pop. (1990c) 2086; Muskingum Coll. (1837).

New Cor·dell \kȯr-ˈdel\. City, ⊗ of Washita co., W Oklahoma; pop. (1990c) 2903.

New Croton Dam *and* **New Croton Reservoir.** See UNITED STATES, *Dams and Reservoirs.*

New Cum·ber·land \ˈkəm-bər-lənd\. **1.** Borough, Cumberland co., S Pennsylvania, on Susquehanna River 3 mi. (5 km.) S of Harrisburg; pop. (1990c) 7665; settled c. 1810.

2. City, ⊗ of Hancock co., N tip of West Virginia Panhandle, on Ohio River 31 mi. (50 km.) NNE of Wheeling; pop. (1990c) 1363.

New Del·hi \ˈde-lē\. City, ✱ of India, in Delhi terr., on Yamuna River S of Old Delhi; pop. (1991p) 294,149. Constructed 1912–29; formally opened 1931. See DELHI 2.

New Dorp \ˌdȯrp\. Section of Staten Island, borough of New York City. See STATEN ISLAND 2.

New Ea·gle \ˈē-gəl\. Borough, Washington co., SW Pennsylvania, on Monongahela River 16 mi. (26 km.) S of Pittsburgh; pop. (1990c) 2172.

New Echo·ta \i-ˈkō-tə\. Indian town, NW Georgia, in Gordon co. NE of Calhoun; site reconstructed and open to tourists; chosen by the Cherokee as their ✱ 1819; by 1828 had a newspaper; given up by the Cherokee in treaty 1835 surrendering all their lands E of the Mississippi River to the U.S.

New El·len·ton \ˈe-lən-tən\. Town, Aiken co., W South Carolina, 49 mi. (79 km.) SW of Columbia; pop. (1990c) 2515.

New En·gland \ˈiŋ-glənd *also* ˈiŋ-lənd\. **1.** Northeast section of the U.S., comprising the states of Connecticut, Maine, Massachusetts, New Hampshire, Rhode Island, and Vermont; total area 66,667 sq. mi. (172,668 sq. km.); pop. (1990c) 13,206,943.

History: Name first applied to the area by Capt. John Smith who explored the coast 1614; Council for New England, incorp. 1620 with English soldier and proprietor Sir Ferdinando Gorges as president, was granted territory from sea to sea bet. 40th and 48th parallels; its jurisdiction came to be ignored by colonies, esp. Massachusetts Bay which was governed by Massachusetts Bay Company with a charter directly from the king; Council surrendered its charter 1635. The New England Confederation (1643–84) was formed by the colonies of Massachusetts Bay, Plymouth, Connecticut, and New Haven largely for defense esp. against the Indians; the Confederation fell apart upon revocation 1684 of the charter of Massachusetts Bay Colony, its strongest member. The Dominion of New England formed by English government in 1686 made into one province, under rule of Sir Edmund Andros, the colonies of New Hampshire, Massachusetts (incl. Maine), Rhode Island, and Connecticut; New York and New Jersey added in 1688; Andros overthrown 1689 and colonies resumed separate existences. For later history, see individual states.

2. Mountain range and plateau, NE New South Wales, SE Australia; ab. 200 mi. (320 km.) long by 75 mi. (120 km.) broad; part of the Great Dividing Range; highest peak Ben Lomond 4877 ft. (1487 m.); contains **New England National Park** (115 sq. mi. or 298 sq. km.) featuring tropical forest; residents of the region have repeatedly considered separation from New South Wales.

New·en·ham, Cape \ˈnü-ən-ˌham, ˈnyü-\. Cape on SW coast of Alaska bet. Kuskokwim Bay and Bristol Bay, 58°37′N, 162°12′W.

New Ex·che·quer Dam \ˈeks-ˌche-kər\. See UNITED STATES, *Dams and Reservoirs.*

New Fair·field \ˈfar-ˌfēld\. Town, Fairfield co., SW Connecticut, 20 mi. (32 km.) WSW of Waterbury; pop. (1990c) 12,911.

New·fane \ˈnü-ˌfān, ˈnyü-; nü-ˈfān, nyü-\. Residential village, ⊗ of Windham co., SE corner of Vermont; pop. (1990c) 1555.

Newfield. See BRIDGEPORT 3.

New Forest. District in SW Hampshire, S England, bet. the Avon and Southampton Water; 130 sq. mi. (337 sq. km.); partly under private ownership and cultivated, the remainder, partly bog and heath and administered as a state park; highest point Lewis Hills 2672 ft. (814 m.); set apart 1079 by King William the Conqueror as a hunting ground.

New·found Gap \ˈnü-ˌfau̇nd, ˈnyü-\. Pass through Great Smoky Mts. bet. Tennessee and North Carolina in cen. Great Smoky Mountains National Park; alt. 5048 ft. (1539 m.).

Newfound Lake. Lake in SE Grafton co., cen. New Hampshire; 6 mi. (10 km.) long by ab. 2.5 mi. (4 km.) wide.

New·found·land \ˈnü-fənd-lənd, ˈnyü-, -ˌland; nü-ˈfau̇nd-lənd, nyü-\. **1.** Island in Atlantic Ocean, off E coast of Canada, constituting with Labrador on the mainland a province of Canada; 43,359 sq. mi. (112,300 sq. km.).

Physical features: In general a plateau (highest point in Long Range Mts., 2672 ft. or 814 m., ab. 25 mi. or 40 km. WSW of Corner Brook); triangular in form with Cape Bauld at the N, Cape Race at SE, and Cape Ray at SW; coasts much indented, esp. in the E and S; separated on N from mainland (Labrador) by the Strait of Belle Isle; has many islands along coasts, esp. Belle Isle, Groais, Bell, and Fogo in the N and the French islands of St.-Pierre and Miquelon off S coast; largest rivers the Exploits, Humber, and Gander; chief lakes Grand, Red Indian, and Gander.

Chief products: Fish, lumber; copper.

2. Province of Canada, consisting of island of Newfoundland (see NEWFOUNDLAND 1) and Labrador (*q.v.*); ✱ St. John's. See table at CANADA.

Chief settlements: St. John's, Wabana, Mount Pearl, Corner Brook, all of which are on Newfoundland I.

History: Evidence of prehistoric inhabitants throughout region; coastal areas probably explored and briefly settled c. 10th cent. by Norsemen; region inhabited by various natives at time of European settlement, esp. Beothuk (on the island) and Naskapi and Inuit (in Labrador) peoples; discovery of the island 1497 by Italian explorer John Cabot (under English patent) resulted at once in visits of fishermen from countries of W Europe; English ownership formally proclaimed in 1583 by Sir Humphrey Gilbert who established first colony at St. John's; several unsuccessful attempts at colonization followed, esp. by John Guy 1610 and Sir George Calvert 1621–29 (see FERRYLAND); possession actively disputed by France and England, with English settlements along E coast offset by French settlements along W

\ə\ **abut** \ə\ matches \ᵊ\ kitten, Fr table \ər\ **further** \a\ **ash** \ā\ **ace** \ä\ cot, cart \à\ Fr bac \au̇\ **out** \b\ Span Avila \ch\ **chin** \e\ **bet** \ē\ **easy** \g\ **go** \i\ **hit** \ī\ **ice** \j\ **job** \k\ Ger **ich**, Buch \ⁿ\ Fr vin \ŋ\ **sing** \ō\ **go** \ȯ\ **all** \ȯ\ **law** \œ\ Fr **bœuf** \œ̄\ Fr **feu** \ȯi\ **boy** \th\ **thin** \t͟h\ **this** \ü\ **loot** \u̇\ **foot** \ue\ Ger **füllen** \ue̅\ Fr **rue** \y\ **yet** \ʸ\ Fr digne \ˈdēnʸ\, nuit \ˈnwʸē\ \yü\ **few** \yu̇\ **fury** \zh\ **vision**

NEWFOUNDLAND
CITIES
Provincial capital
City
BOUNDARIES
Provincial
FEATURES
Falls
Dams
0 50 100 mi
0 70 140 km
LABRADOR SEA
ATLANTIC OCEAN
Ungava Bay
QUEBEC
LABRADOR
NEWFOUNDLAND
Gulf of St. Lawrence
AKPATOK ISLAND (N.W. TERR.)
BUTTON ISLANDS
KILLINEK ISLAND
Cape Chidley
TORNGAT MTS.
NORTH AULATSIVIK ISLAND
Cirque Mtn. 5,160 ft.
Saglek Bay
R. George
COD ISLAND
OKAK ISLANDS
Fraser R.
SOUTH AULATSIVIK ISLAND
Nain
TUNUNGAYUALOK ISLAND
Davis Inlet
Hopedale
Makkovik
Schefferville
Cape Harrison
Canairiktok R.
Menihek Lakes
Esker
Smallwood Reservoir
Rigolet
Groswater Bay
GEORGE ISLAND
2,895 ft.
Churchill Falls
North R.
HUNTINGDON ISLAND
Lake Melville
3,700 ft.
Cartwright
Sandwich Bay
Table Bay
North West River
Happy Valley-Goose Bay
MEALY MTS.
ISLAND OF PONDS
Labrador City
Wabush
Lac Joseph
Churchill R.
Eagle R.
HAWKE ISLAND
STONY ISLAND
Atikonak Lake
Gilbert R.
Alexis R.
Square Islands
Ashuanipi Lake
Embar
Minipi Lake
1,920 ft.
Port Hope Simpson
Fox Harbour
Mary's Harbour
Battle Harbour
R. St-Paul
St. Lewis R.
Henley Harbour
BELLE ISLE
R. Moisie
R. du Petit Mécatina
West St. Modeste
L'Anse-au-Loup
Forteau
Strait of Belle Isle
Cook's Harbour
St. Anthony
Flowers Cove
Hare Bay
R. Romaine
Ten Mile Lake
GROAIS ISLAND
ST. JOHN ISLAND
Roddickton
GREY ISLANDS
Lac Musquaro
Englee
BELL ISLAND
Canada Bay
Ingornachoix Bay
LONG RANGE MTS.
Harbour Deep
Daniel's Harbour
White Bay
Fleur De Lys
Baie Verte
Cape St. John
La Scie
Cow Head
GROS MORNE NATIONAL PARK
Seal Cove
Nippers Harbour
Notre Dame Bay
Fogo
Joe Batt's Arm
FOGO ISLAND
Hamilton Sound
Bonne Bay
Gros Morne 2,644 ft.
King's Point
Carmanville
ANTICOSTI ISLAND (QUEBEC)
Trout River
Norris Pt.
Springdale
Robert's Arm
Upper Trout River Pond
Sandy Lake
Botwood
Lewisporte
Wesleyville
Bay of Islands
Deer Lake
Howley
Windsor
Bishop's Falls
Gander
Greenspond
Lark Harbour
Cox's Cove
Badger
Gander Lake
Hare Bay
Bonavista Bay
Bonavista
Corner Brook
PORT AU PORT PENINSULA
Lourdes
Grand Lake
TERRA NOVA NATIONAL PARK
Catalina
Stephenville
Port Blandford
Trinity
Cape St. George
St. George's Bay
Stephenville Crossing
Meelpaeg Reservoir
Mt. Sylvester 1,250 ft.
Bay de Verde
Grates Point
Trinity Bay
Round Pond
Conception Bay
Carbonear
Cape Anguille
Milltown
St. Alban's
Harbour Grace
St. John's
Bay Roberts
Wabana
Terrenceville
Holyrood
Cape Ray
Burgeo
François
Harbour Breton
Belleoram
Channel-Port aux Basques
Rose Blanche
Ramea
Hermitage Bay
AVALON PENINSULA
Cape Broyle
Placentia Bay
Placentia
Garnish
BURIN PEN.
Ferryland
MAGDALEN ISLANDS (QUEBEC)
Grand Bank
Marystown
Renews
Cabot Strait
Fortune
Burin
Branch
St. Mary's
NEW BRUNSWICK
MIQUELON (FRANCE)
Lamaline
St. Lawrence
Cape Pine
Cape Race
PRINCE EDWARD ISLAND
NOVA SCOTIA
©1996, Encyclopædia Britannica, Inc.
65°
60°
55°
50°

coast of the island; by Treaty of Utrecht 1713 became English, but fishing rights retained by France (see FRENCH SHORE); assigned first (seasonal) governor 1729; by treaties of 1763 was confirmed under British sovereignty and was granted coast of Labrador; controversies over fishing rights continued through 19th cent.; received representative government 1832 and responsible government 1855; W boundary of Labrador set 1927; colonial government reestablished 1934; became a province of Canada 1949.

New France \ˈfrans\. The possessions of France in North America from the time of the first claim of land for France by explorer Jacques Cartier 1534, but esp. from 1627 (when the "Company of New France" was founded by statesman Armand Jean du Plessis, Cardinal Richelieu) to 1763 Treaty of Paris. Strengthened by French politician Jean-Baptiste Colbert's new Company of the West, founded 1664; its boundaries expanded beyond the lower St. Lawrence to cover the Great Lakes and all the Mississippi Valley, the result esp. of the work of the great French explorers Samuel de Champlain, Père Jacques Marquette, René-Robert Cavelier, Sieur de La Salle, Louis Hennepin, Daniel Dulhut (Duluth), Louis Jolliet, Jean Nicolet, and others; in 1689 began the long period of rivalry in Europe bet. England and France directly affecting their possessions in the Western Hemisphere through four wars, known in Europe as the War of the Grand Alliance (1688–97), the War of the Spanish Succession (1701–14), the War of the Austrian Succession (1740–48), and the Seven Years' War (1756–63), whose counterparts in America were known collectively as the French and Indian Wars: King William's War (1689–97) resulting in the temporary French gain of the territory around Hudson Bay, Queen Anne's War (1702–13) resulting in the loss to England of Acadia, Newfoundland, and the territory around Hudson Bay, King George's War (1744–48), and the French and Indian War (1754–63) resulting in the cession of Canada and the territory E of the Mississippi River to England and of the territory W of the Mississippi River to Spain, France retaining only the islands of St.-Pierre and Miquelon.

New Geor·gia \ˈjȯr-jə\. **1.** Group of islands, cen. Solomon Is., incl. New Georgia I. and Vella Lavella, Ganongga, Kolombangara, Rendova, and Vangunu islands; administrative center on Gizo I.; formerly part of British Solomon Is. protectorate.

2. Chief island of the group, 40 mi. (64 km.) S of Choiseul I.; ab. 50 mi. (80 km.) long, 10 to 12 mi. (16 to 18 km.) wide; highest point 3300 ft. (1000 m.); in SE enclosed by Vangunu I. and reefs is Marovo Lagoon, one of largest in world; along W coast E of Munda is Roviana Lagoon. During WWII, occupied by Japanese 1942 and fortified, esp. at Munda on NW coast; used as base for attacks on Guadalcanal; captured by Americans 1943. See KULA GULF.

New Georgia Sound. See SLOT, THE.

New Gla·rus \ˈglar-əs\. Village, Green co., S Wisconsin, SW of Madison; pop. (1990c) 1899; site of a recreated Swiss village.

New Glas·gow \ˈglas-ˌgō, ˈglaz-\. Town, Pictou co., N Nova Scotia, Canada, near Pictou Harbor 37 mi. (60 km.) NE of Truro; pop. (1991c) 9905; heavy machinery, boilers; pulp and steel mills.

New Glouces·ter \ˈgläs-tər, ˈglȯs-\. Town, Cumberland co., SW Maine, 20 mi. (32 km.) N of Portland; pop. (1990c) 3916.

New Goa. See PANAJI.

New Gra·na·da \grə-ˈnä-də, -ˈnā-\ *or Span.* **Nue·va Gra·na·da** \ˈnwā-vä-grä-ˈnä-t͟hä\. **1.** Spanish viceroyalty in NW South America; region conquered and named by Spaniards 1537–38 under Gonzalo Jiménez de Quesada; subject to viceroyalty of Peru until organized as separate viceroyalty (temporarily 1717, permanently 1740) which included what is now Colombia, Panama, Venezuela, and Ecuador; freed from Spanish rule 1810–19. See GRAN COLOMBIA.

2. Former nation, consisting of present-day Colombia and Panama; constituent of Gran Colombia (*q.v.*) 1819–30; independent country 1830–58; reorganized as Grenadine Confederation 1858 (see COLOMBIA).

New·grange \nü-ˈgrānj, nyü-\. The principal tumulus of the Brugh na Boinne (*q.v.*), co. Meath, NE Ireland, on N bank of the Boyne; the mound, surrounded by remains of a stone circle, has a domed chamber.

New Guin·ea \ˈgi-nē\ *also* **Pap·ua** \ˈpa-pyu̇-wə\ *or Indonesian* **Iri·an** \ˌir-ē-ˈän\ *or Du.* **Nieuw Gui·nee** \ˈnyᵫ-gi-ˈnā\. Island of E Malay Archipelago, in W Pacific Ocean N of Australia; 2d largest island in the world; 341,631 sq. mi. (884,824 sq. km.); pop. over 5,000,000; administratively divided into Irian Jaya prov., Indonesia, on the W and the independent country of Papua New Guinea on the E. Evidence of prehistoric inhabitants; first sighted by Europeans in 16th cent.; in 19th cent. W half claimed by Dutch, NE section by Germans, SE section by British. For later history, see IRIAN JAYA, TRUST TERRITORY OF NEW GUINEA, and PAPUA, TERRITORY OF.

New Guinea, British. See PAPUA, TERRITORY OF.

New Guinea, Dutch. See IRIAN JAYA.

New Guinea, Trust Territory of. Former territory comprising the NE section of New Guinea I. (North-East New Guinea) together with Bougainville, Buka, and adjacent small islands, and the Bismarck Archipelago; 92,160 sq. mi. (238,694 sq. km.); ✱ Port Moresby; as **German New Guinea,** controlled by Germans 1884–1914; in WWI occupied by Australians who were later given a League of Nations mandate to govern the renamed **Territory of New Guinea;** administratively united with Terr. of Papua to form Papua New Guinea 1949. See NORTH-EAST NEW GUINEA and BISMARCK ARCHIPELAGO.

New Gulf *or Span.* **Gol·fo Nue·vo** \ˈgȯl-fō-ˈnwā-vō\. Inlet, NE Chubut prov., S cen. Argentina, S of Valdés Penin.

New·ham \ˈnü-əm, ˈnyü-\. A borough of Greater London, SE England. See table at LONDON 4.

New Hamp·shire \ˈhamp-shər, -ˌshir\. A northeastern state of U.S.A., bounded on N by Canadian prov. of Quebec, on E by Maine and (in the extreme SE) the Atlantic Ocean, on S by Massachusetts, and on W by Vermont; 44th state in area, 9279 sq. mi. (24,033 sq. km.); 40th state in population, (1990c) 1,109,252; ✱ Concord; an original state of the Union, the 9th to ratify the U.S. Constitution (June 21, 1788). See table of states at UNITED STATES.

Nickname: Granite State.

State flower: Purple lilac.

Motto: Live Free Or Die.

Rivers: Connecticut, forming boundary with Vermont; Salmon Falls and Piscataqua, forming SE boundary; Saco, flowing SE across the border into Maine; Merrimack, flowing from S cen. area S across border into Massachusetts.

Mountains: White Mts. in N cen. part, incl. highest point in New England, Mt. Washington 6288 ft. (1917 m.), in Coos co.

Chief products: Dairy products, apples, maple syrup, vegetables, nursery plants; tourism; electrical products, electronic equipment, paper products, leather goods; once an important center of granite quarrying.

Chief cities: Manchester, Nashua, Concord.

Political divisions: Divided into the following 10 counties (for pronunciation of their names, see their individual entries):

NAME	AREA[1] (sq. mi.)	AREA[1] (sq. km.)	POP. (1990c)	CO. SEAT
Belknap[2]	400	1,036	49,216	Laconia
Carroll[2]	938	2,429	35,410	Ossipee
Cheshire	715	1,852	70,121	Keene
Coos	1,820	4,714	34,828	Lancaster
Grafton	1,732	4,486	74,929	Woodsville
Hillsborough	893	2,313	336,073	Nashua
Merrimack	930	2,409	120,005	Concord
Rockingham	691	1,790	245,845	Exeter

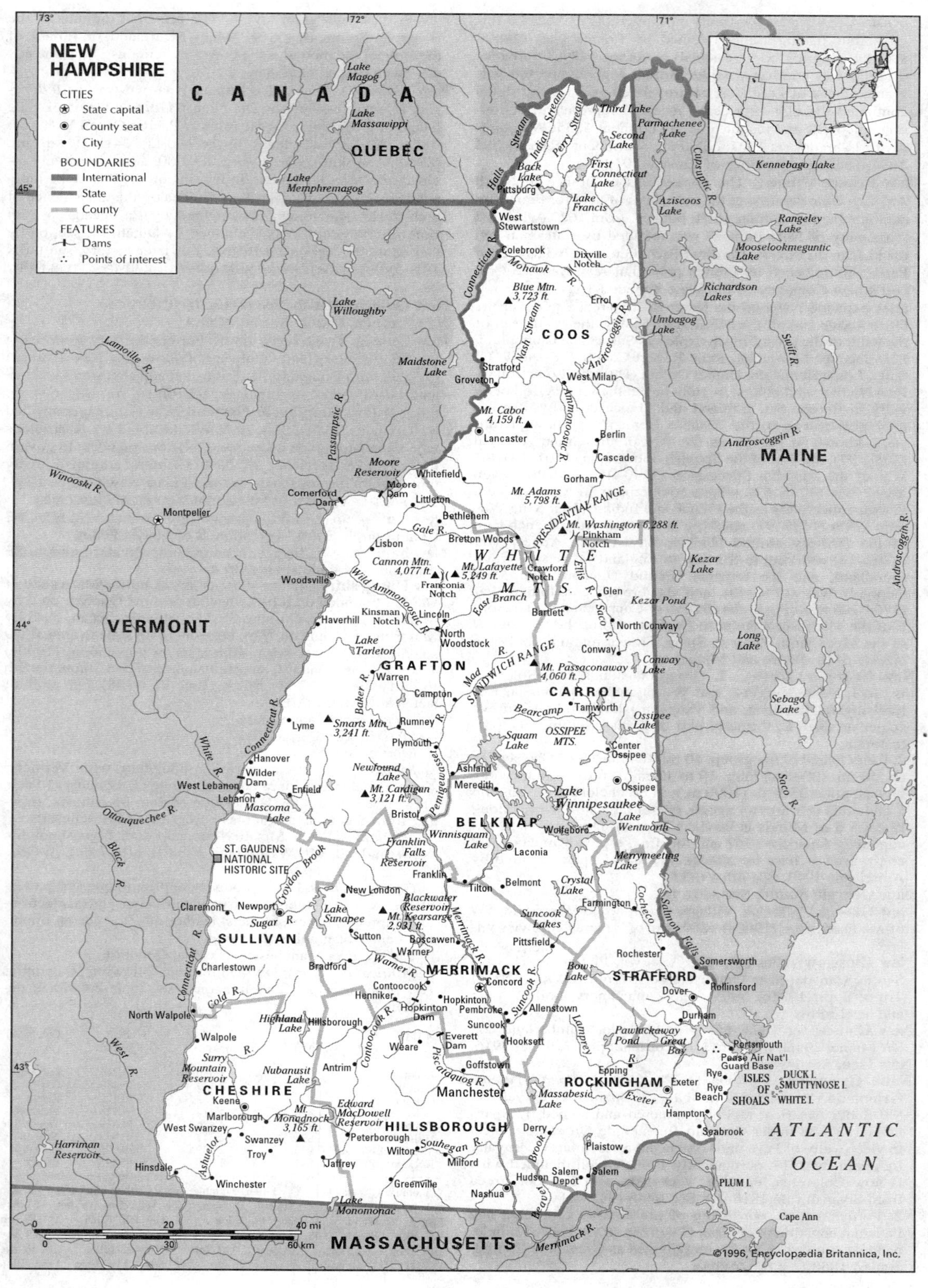

NEW HAMPSHIRE
CITIES
State capital
County seat
City
BOUNDARIES
International
State
County
FEATURES
Dams
Points of interest
CANADA
QUEBEC
VERMONT
MAINE
MASSACHUSETTS
ATLANTIC OCEAN
COOS
GRAFTON
CARROLL
BELKNAP
SULLIVAN
MERRIMACK
STRAFFORD
CHESHIRE
HILLSBOROUGH
ROCKINGHAM
WHITE MTS.
PRESIDENTIAL RANGE
SANDWICH RANGE
OSSIPEE MTS.
Montpelier
Concord
Manchester
Nashua
Portsmouth
Mt. Washington 6,288 ft.
Mt. Adams 5,798 ft.
Mt. Lafayette 5,249 ft.
Mt. Cabot 4,159 ft.
Cannon Mtn. 4,077 ft.
Mt. Passaconaway 4,060 ft.
Blue Mtn. 3,723 ft.
Smarts Mtn. 3,241 ft.
Mt. Monadnock 3,165 ft.
Mt. Cardigan 3,121 ft.
Mt. Kearsarge 2,931 ft.
Lake Winnipesaukee
ST. GAUDENS NATIONAL HISTORIC SITE
ISLES OF SHOALS
0 20 40 mi
0 30 60 km
©1996, Encyclopædia Britannica, Inc.

NAME	AREA[1] (sq. mi.)	AREA[1] (sq. km.)	POP. (1990c)	CO. SEAT
Strafford	376	974	104,233	Dover
Sullivan	539	1,396	38,592	Newport

[1]Area = land area.
[2]Includes part of Lake Winnipesaukee (larger part in Belknap co.).

History: Prior to European settlement, inhabited by numerous Algonquin tribes, esp. of the Pennacook confederacy; coast explored by several English explorers early 17th cent.; area E of the Merrimack River included in grant to John Mason and Sir Ferdinando Gorges 1622 and in New Hampshire grant to Mason 1629; first settled by English near Portsmouth 1623; controlled by Massachusetts 1641–79; made a separate royal province 1679 but under same governor as Massachusetts 1699–1741; area of Vermont (*q.v.*) settled under New Hampshire jurisdiction, which New York disputed; area of Vermont awarded 1764 by royal order to jurisdiction of New York (final claims to area not relinquished by New Hampshire until 1782); first colony to declare independence from Great Britain 1776; adopted first constitution 1776, present constitution 1784 which later was frequently amended; Dartmouth College case decided 1819 in U.S. Supreme Court, confirming right of private corporations against excessive state regulation.

New Hamp·ton \ˈhamp-tən\. City, ⊗ of Chickasaw co., NE Iowa, 37 mi. (60 km.) N of Waterloo; pop. (1990c) 3660.

New Han·o·ver \ˈha-ˌnō-vər, ˈha-nə-\. **1.** Coastal county in SE North Carolina. See table at NORTH CAROLINA.

2. *or* **La·von·gai** \lə-ˈvȯŋ-ˌgī\. Island in the Bismarck Archipelago, W Pacific Ocean, NW of New Ireland; 460 sq. mi. (1191 sq. km.); mountainous, with highest point 3150 ft. (960 m.).

New Har·mo·ny \ˈhär-mə-nē\. Town, Posey co., SW corner of Indiana, on Wabash River 23 mi. (37 km.) WNW of Evansville; pop. (1990c) 846; Mound Builder sites nearby. Founded (as Harmonie) 1814 by Harmony Society under German religious leader George Rapp; sold out 1825 to Welsh Socialist Robert Owen, who renamed it New Harmony and estab. a utopian communistic colony; became a center for scientific and cultural pursuits and for education reform in 19th cent.; internal dissensions caused failure of the colony by 1828, but the town survived.

New Hart·ford \ˈhärt-fərd\. Town, E Litchfield co., NW Connecticut, on Farmington River; pop. (1990c) 5769.

New·ha·ven \nü-ˈhā-vən, nyü-; ˈnü-ˌhā-vən, ˈnyü-\. Port, East Sussex, S England, on seacoast at mouth of the Ouse 55 mi. (88 km.) S of London; pop. (1981c) 9834; boatbuilding; popular cross-channel port.

New Ha·ven \ˈhā-vən\. **1.** Coastal county in S Connecticut. See table at CONNECTICUT.

2. City, New Haven co., S Connecticut, on New Haven Harbor 36 mi. (58 km.) SSW of Hartford; pop. (1990c) 130,474; firearms, aircraft parts, rubber goods, clocks; Yale Univ. (founded 1701, moved to New Haven 1716), Southern Connecticut State Univ. (1893), Albertus Magnus Coll. (1925); South Central Community Coll. (1968). Birthplace of inventor Charles Goodyear 1800.

History: Settled 1638 (named Quinnipiac) by Puritans under John Davenport and Theophilus Eaton, the latter civil governor of New Haven Colony 1639–58; given present name 1640; colony came to include nearby settlements of Branford, Guilford, Milford, Southold, and Stamford; united to Connecticut Colony 1664; with Hartford, joint ✱ of Connecticut 1701–1875; sacked by Loyalists 1779 during American Revolution; incorp. 1784; important maritime trade port in late 18th and early 19th cents.; became important manufacturing center, a number of its residents, among them Eli Whitney (mass production of muskets with interchangeable parts), Charles Goodyear (vulcanization of rubber), and Samuel F. B. Morse (telegraph), making significant contributions to industrial technology.

3. City, Allen co., NE Indiana, 7 mi. (11 km.) E of Fort Wayne; pop. (1990c) 9320.

New Haven Harbor. Inlet of Long Island Sound, on S shore of New Haven co., Connecticut; receives Quinnipiac, Mill, and West rivers.

New Hebrides. See VANUATU.

New Hol·land \ˈhä-lənd\. Borough, Lancaster co., SE Pennsylvania, 15 mi. (24 km.) ENE of city of Lancaster; pop. (1990c) 4484.

New Hol·stein \ˈhōl-ˌstēn, -ˌstīn\. City, Calumet co., E Wisconsin, 20 mi. (32 km.) NE of Fond du Lac; pop. (1990c) 3342.

New Hope \ˈnü-ˌhōp, ˈnyü-\. **1.** Village, Hennepin co., SE cen. Minnesota; pop. (1990c) 21,853; residential suburb of Minneapolis.

2. Borough, Bucks co., SE Pennsylvania; pop. (1990c) 1400; artists colony.

New Hyde Park \ˈhīd\. Village, Nassau co., SE New York, on Long Island 17 mi. (27 km.) E of New York City; pop. (1990c) 9728.

New Ibe·ria \ī-ˈbir-ē-ə\. City, ⊗ of Iberia parish, S Louisiana, 20 mi. (32 km.) SSE of Lafayette; pop. (1990c) 31,828; sugarcane; salt; oil-related industries; settled 18th cent. by Spanish and French; occupied by Union forces 1863.

New·ing·ton \ˈnü-iŋ-tən, ˈnyü-\. Suburban residential town, S Hartford co., N Connecticut, SW of Hartford; pop. (1990c) 29,208; Newington Children's Hospital; settled 1670; incorp. 1871.

New Ire·land \ˈīr-lənd\; *formerly* **Neu–Meck·len·burg** \nȯi-ˈme-klən-ˌbərg, -ˌbu̇rk\. Island in the Bismarck Archipelago, W Pacific Ocean; 3340 sq. mi. (8651 sq. km.); ab. 200 mi. (320 km.) long; not volcanic, terrain largely mountainous, with peaks bet. 4000 and 7000 ft. (1200 to 2100 m.); highest Mt. Lambel 7054 ft. (2150 m.); chief port Kavieng, at NW end, 162 mi. (261 km.) NW of Rabaul; harbors also at Namatanai on NE coast, and Muliama on E coast. Most important adjacent island is New Hanover on NW; others are St. Mathias Group, Tabar Is., Lihir I., Dyaul I., and Tanga I. European discovery by Dutch navigators Jakob Le Maire and Willem Schouten 1616, but little known of it before 1884 when it became part of German protectorate; after WWI became part of Australian mandate (Trust Terr. of New Guinea); occupied by Japanese 1942–44 in WWII.

New Jer·sey \ˈjər-zē\. An eastern state of U.S.A., bounded on N by New York, on E by New York and the Atlantic Ocean, on S by Atlantic Ocean and Delaware Bay, on SW by Delaware Bay and Delaware, and on W by Pennsylvania; 46th state in area, 7787 sq. mi. (20,168 sq. km.); 9th state in population, (1990c) 7,730,188; ✱ Trenton; an original state of the Union, the 3d to ratify the U.S. Constitution Dec. 18, 1787. See table of states at UNITED STATES.

Nickname: Garden State.

State flower: Violet.

Motto: Liberty and Prosperity.

Rivers: Hudson, forming NE boundary; Delaware, forming W boundary.

Highest point: High Point, 1803 ft. (550 m.), in Sussex co.

Chief products: Corn, cranberries, peppers, tomatoes, nursery plants; manufacturing: chemicals, electronic equipment, apparel, electrical machinery; corporate research and development.

Chief cities: Newark, Jersey City, Paterson, Elizabeth.

Political divisions: Divided into the following 21 counties (for pronunciation of their names, see their individual entries):

NAME	AREA[1] (sq. mi.)	AREA[1] (sq. km.)	POP. (1990c)	CO. SEAT
Atlantic	569	1,474	224,327	Mays Landing
Bergen	234	606	825,380	Hackensack
Burlington[2]	819	2,121	395,066	Mount Holly

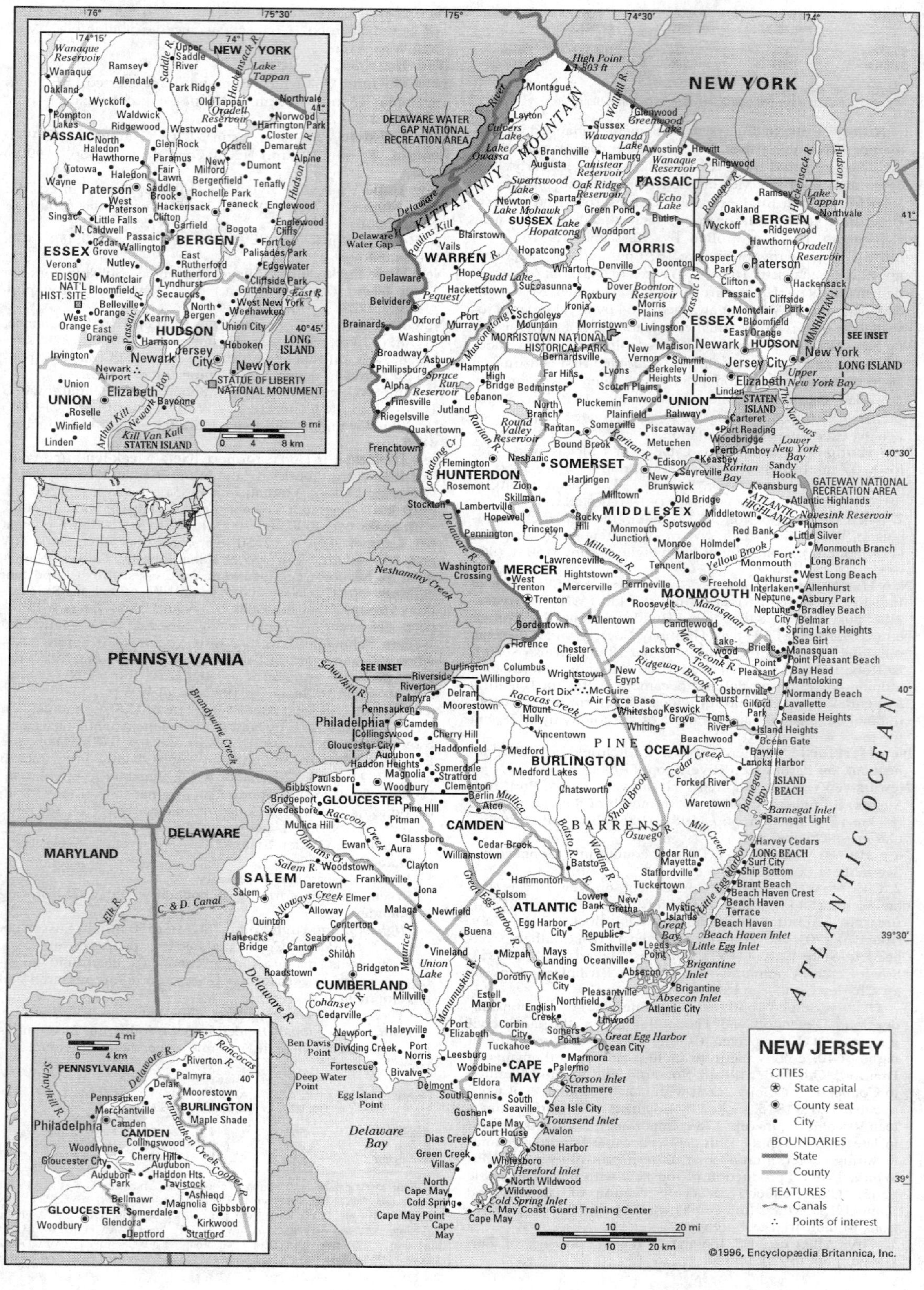
NEW JERSEY
CITIES
State capital
County seat
City
BOUNDARIES
State
County
FEATURES
Canals
Points of interest
0 10 20 mi
0 10 20 km
©1996, Encyclopædia Britannica, Inc.
NEW YORK
PENNSYLVANIA
DELAWARE
MARYLAND
ATLANTIC OCEAN
Delaware Bay
SUSSEX
PASSAIC
BERGEN
MORRIS
WARREN
ESSEX
HUDSON
UNION
HUNTERDON
SOMERSET
MIDDLESEX
MERCER
MONMOUTH
BURLINGTON
OCEAN
CAMDEN
GLOUCESTER
SALEM
ATLANTIC
CUMBERLAND
CAPE MAY
PINE BARRENS
KITTATINNY MOUNTAIN
DELAWARE WATER GAP NATIONAL RECREATION AREA
MORRISTOWN NATIONAL HISTORICAL PARK
GATEWAY NATIONAL RECREATION AREA
High Point 1,803 ft
Trenton
Newark
Jersey City
Paterson
Elizabeth
Camden
Atlantic City
Philadelphia
New York
SEE INSET
STATUE OF LIBERTY NATIONAL MONUMENT
EDISON NAT'L HIST. SITE
STATEN ISLAND
LONG ISLAND

NAME	AREA[1] (sq. mi.)	AREA[1] (sq. km.)	POP. (1990c)	CO. SEAT
Camden	221	572	502,824	Camden
Cape May	267	692	95,089	Cape May Courthouse
Cumberland	500	1,295	138,053	Bridgeton
Essex	130	337	778,206	Newark
Gloucester	329	852	230,082	Woodbury
Hudson	47	122	553,099	Jersey City
Hunterdon	434	1,124	107,776	Flemington
Mercer	228	591	325,824	Trenton
Middlesex	312	808	671,780	New Brunswick
Monmouth	476	1,233	553,124	Freehold
Morris	468	1,212	421,353	Morristown
Ocean[2,3]	642	1,663	433,203	Toms River
Passaic	193	500	453,060	Paterson
Salem	365	945	65,294	Salem
Somerset	307	795	240,279	Somerville
Sussex	527	1,365	130,943	Newton
Union	103	267	493,819	Elizabeth
Warren	362	938	91,607	Belvidere

[1]Area = land area.
[2]Fort Dix military reservation in NE Burlington co. and NW Ocean co.
[3]Includes Barnegat Bay, extending almost full length of its coastline.

History: Prior to European colonization, region inhabited esp. by Delaware tribes; sighted by Florentine navigator Giovanni da Verrazano 1524 and English navigator Henry Hudson 1609; first settled by Dutch and along Delaware River by Swedes; ceded to English as part of New Netherland 1664 and given the Latin name of Nova Caesarea; its E and N part (East Jersey) became a proprietary colony regranted by duke of York to Sir George Carteret and was sold to William Penn and associates 1682; its W and S part (West Jersey), or the lower counties on Delaware River, held by William Penn 1676–1702; became royal province 1702; governed by governor of New York until 1738; declared independence from England and adopted first state constitution 1776; scene of numerous battles during the Revolutionary War, esp. the important battles at Trenton, Princeton, and Monmouth; delegates to Constitutional Convention 1787 forwarded New Jersey Plan for small states; Trenton became state ✱ 1790; adopted new state constitution 1844 which included several democratic reforms; present constitution adopted 1947; casino gambling legalized 1976.

New Ken·sing·ton \ˈken-ziŋ-tən, ˈken-siŋ-\. City, Westmoreland co., SW Pennsylvania, on Allegheny River 16 mi. (26 km.) ENE of Pittsburgh; pop. (1990c) 15,894; New Kensington campus of Pennsylvania State Univ. (1958); city estab. 1891 on site of a Revolutionary War fort.

New Kent \ˈkent\. **1.** County in E Virginia. See table at VIRGINIA.
2. Village, its ⊗.

New·kirk \ˈnü-ˌkərk, ˈnyü-\. City, ⊗ of Kay co., N Oklahoma, 14 mi. (23 km.) N of Ponca City; pop. (1990c) 2168.

New Kowloon. See KOWLOON 2.

New Lanark. See LANARK 3.

New·land \ˈnü-lənd, ˈnyü-\. Town and resort, ⊗ of Avery co., W North Carolina; pop. (1990c) 642.

New Leb·a·non \ˈle-bə-nən\. Village, Montgomery co., SW Ohio, 11 mi. (18 km.) W of Dayton; pop. (1990c) 4323.

New Len·ox \ˈle-nəks\. Village, Will co., NE Illinois, 6 mi. (10 km.) E of Joliet; pop. (1990c) 9627.

New Lex·ing·ton \ˈlek-siŋ-tən\. Village, ⊗ of Perry co., SE cen. Ohio, 19 mi. (31 km.) SSW of Zanesville; pop. (1990c) 5117.

New Lis·keard \lis-ˈkärd\. Town, Timiskaming dist., SE Ontario, Canada, 85 mi. (137 km.) N of North Bay, near N end of Lake Timiskaming and N of Cobalt; pop. (1991c) 5431; summer resort; dairy products.

New Lon·don \ˈlən-dən\. **1.** County in SE Connecticut. See table at CONNECTICUT.
2. City, New London co., SE Connecticut, on Long Island Sound at mouth of Thames River 43 mi. (69 km.) E of New Haven; pop. (1990c) 28,540; manufactures clothing. U.S. Coast Guard Academy (1876), Connecticut Coll. (1911), Mitchell Coll. (1938). Founded 1646; incorp. 1784; a privateers' port during the Revolutionary War, was attacked, captured, and burned by British under American traitor Benedict Arnold 1781; became major whaling port during 19th cent. City and town coextensive.
3. City, ⊗ of Ralls co., NE Missouri, 8 mi. (13 km.) S of Hannibal; pop. (1990c) 988.
4. Town, Merrimack co., cen. New Hampshire, 40 mi. (64 km.) NW of Concord; pop. (1990c) 3180; Colby-Sawyer Coll. (1837).
5. Village, Huron co., N Ohio, 23 mi. (37 km.) N of Mansfield; pop. (1990c) 2642.
6. City, Outagamie and Waupaca cos., E Wisconsin, 18 mi. (29 km.) NW of Appleton; pop. (1990c) 6658; lumber.

New Lynn \ˈlin\. Borough, North I., New Zealand; pop. (1981c) 10,445.

New Mad·rid \ˈma-drid\. **1.** County in SE Missouri. See table at MISSOURI.
2. City, its ⊗, on Mississippi River 28 mi. (45 km.) N of Caruthersville; pop. (1990c) 3350; suffered from major earthquakes 1811–12 which created Reelfoot Lake (*q.v.*) in Tennessee; during the Civil War, occupied by Confederate troops 1861 until taken by Union forces.

New·man \ˈnü-mən, ˈnyü-\. City, Stanislaus co., cen. California, 21 mi. (34 km.) S of Modesto; pop. (1990c) 4151.

New Margelan. See FERGANA 2.

New·mar·ket \ˈnü-ˌmär-kət, ˈnyü-\. **1.** Town, Rockingham co., SE New Hampshire, 9 mi. (14 km.) W of Portsmouth; pop. (1990c) 7157.
2. Town, ⊗ of York munic. region, SE Ontario, Canada, 30 mi. (48 km.) N of Toronto; pop. (1991c) 45,474.
3. Town, Suffolk, England, near Cambridgeshire-Suffolk boundary; pop. (1981c) 16,129; horse-racing center.

New Mar·ket \ˈnü-ˌmär-kət, ˈnyü-\. Town, S Shenandoah co., N Virginia; pop. (1990c) 1435; scene in Civil War of victory of Confederates under Gen. John Cabell Breckinridge over Union forces under Gen. Franz Sigel May 1864.

New Mar·tins·ville \ˈmärt-ᵊnz-ˌvil\. City, ⊗ of Wetzel co., N West Virginia, on Ohio River; pop. (1990c) 6705.

New Mex·i·co \ˈmek-si-ˌkō\. A southwestern state of U.S.A., bounded on N by Colorado, on E by Oklahoma and Texas, on S by Texas and the Mexican state of Chihuahua, and on W by Arizona; 5th state in area, 121,593 sq. mi. (314,926 sq. km.); 37th state in population, (1990c) 1,515,069; ✱ Santa Fe; 47th state admitted to Union (1912). See table of states at UNITED STATES.

Nickname: Land of Enchantment.

State flower: Yucca.

Motto: Crescit Eundo (It Grows as It Goes).

Rivers: Rio Grande, bisecting state from N to S and forming for a short distance a boundary on the S with Texas; Pecos, rising in N cen. area and flowing SE across border into Texas.

Mountains: In W crossed from N to S by Continental Divide; in S many small isolated ranges; in N the Sangre de Cristo Mts. incl. Wheeler Peak 13,161 ft. (4011 m.), highest point in state.

Chief products: Livestock; oil, natural gas, potash, copper, uranium; manufacturing: food processing; chemical and petroleum products.

Chief cities: Albuquerque, Las Cruces, Santa Fe.

Political divisions: Divided into the following 33 counties (for pronunciation of their names, see their individual entries):

NAME	AREA[1] (sq. mi.)	AREA[1] (sq. km.)	POP. (1990c)	CO. SEAT
Bernalillo	1,169	3,028	480,577	Albuquerque
Catron	6,897	17,863	2,563	Reserve
Chaves	6,092	15,778	57,849	Roswell
Cibola[2]	4,581	11,865	23,794	Grants
Colfax	3,764	9,749	12,925	Raton
Curry	1,403	3,634	42,207	Clovis

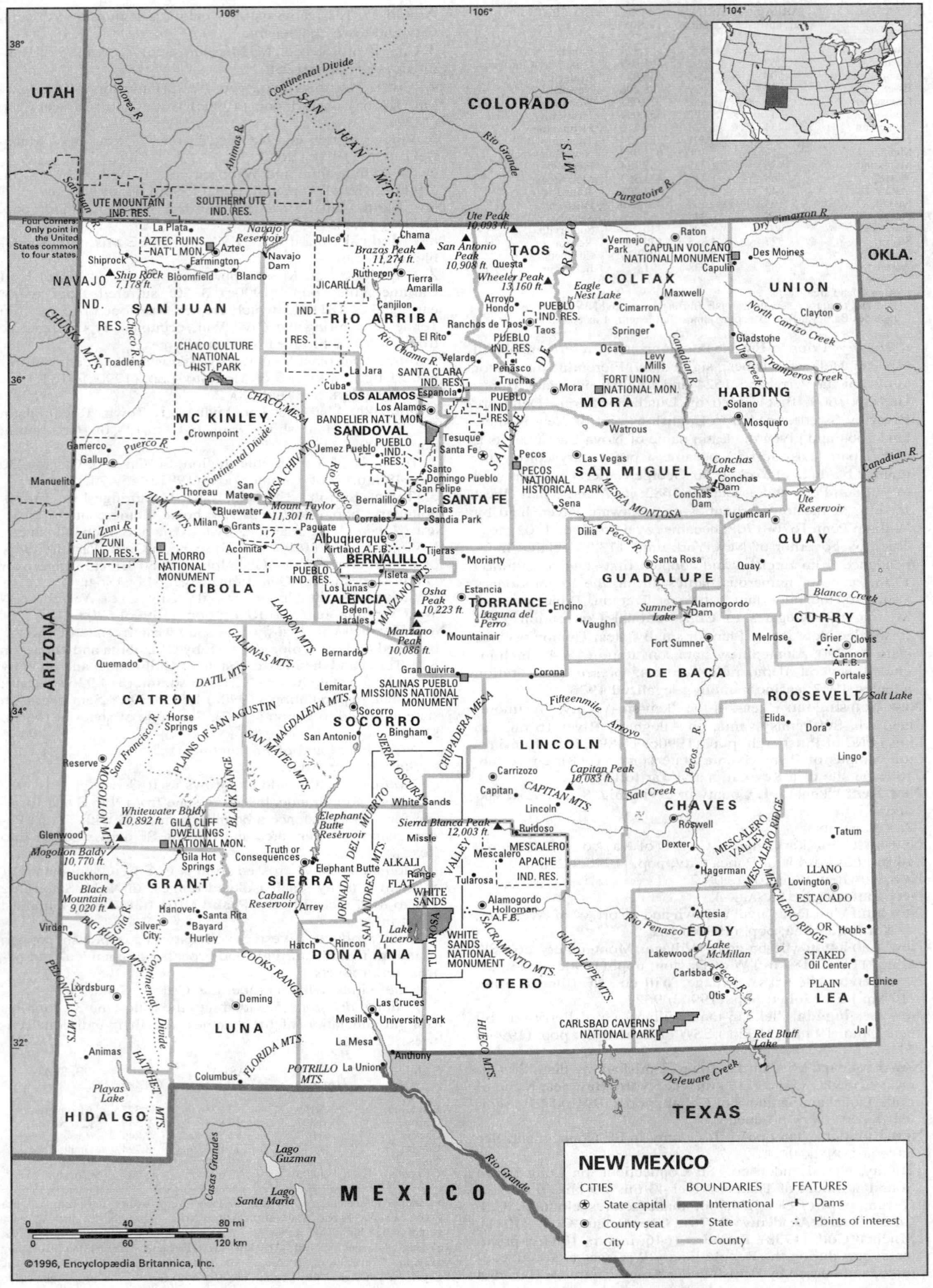
NEW MEXICO
CITIES
State capital
County seat
City
BOUNDARIES
International
State
County
FEATURES
Dams
Points of interest
0 40 80 mi
0 60 120 km
©1996, Encyclopædia Britannica, Inc.
108°
106°
104°
38°
36°
34°
32°
UTAH
COLORADO
OKLA.
ARIZONA
TEXAS
MEXICO
Four Corners: Only point in the United States common to four states.
UTE MOUNTAIN IND. RES.
SOUTHERN UTE IND. RES.
Continental Divide
SAN JUAN MTS.
SANGRE DE CRISTO MTS.
Dolores R.
Animas R.
San Juan R.
Rio Grande
Purgatoire R.
Dry Cimarron R.
La Plata
AZTEC RUINS NAT'L MON.
Aztec
Navajo Reservoir
Navajo Dam
Farmington
Shiprock
Ship Rock 7,178 ft.
Bloomfield
Blanco
Dulce
Chama
Brazos Peak 11,274 ft.
San Antonio Peak 10,908 ft.
Ute Peak 10,093 ft.
Rutheron
Tierra Amarilla
JICARILLA IND. RES.
Canjilon
RIO ARRIBA
El Rito
TAOS
Questa
Wheeler Peak 13,160 ft.
Eagle Nest Lake
Arroyo Hondo
Ranchos de Taos
Taos
PUEBLO IND. RES.
Vermejo Park
Raton
CAPULIN VOLCANO NATIONAL MONUMENT
Capulin
Des Moines
COLFAX
Maxwell
Cimarron
Springer
UNION
Clayton
North Carrizo Creek
Gladstone
Tramperos Creek
Ute Creek
Canadian R.
NAVAJO IND. RES.
SAN JUAN
CHUSKA MTS.
Chaco R.
CHACO CULTURE NATIONAL HIST. PARK
Toadlena
La Jara
Cuba
Rio Chama R.
Velarde
SANTA CLARA IND. RES.
Espanola
Peñasco
Truchas
PUEBLO IND. RES.
Ocate
Levy Mills
FORT UNION NATIONAL MON.
Mora
MORA
HARDING
Solano
Mosquero
Watrous
LOS ALAMOS
Los Alamos
BANDELIER NAT'L MON.
SANDOVAL
CHACO MESA
MC KINLEY
Crownpoint
Gamerco
Gallup
Puerco R.
Manuelito
Continental Divide
MESA CHIVATO
Jemez Pueblo
PUEBLO IND. RES.
Tesuque
Santa Fe
Pecos
PECOS NATIONAL HISTORICAL PARK
Las Vegas
SAN MIGUEL
Conchas Lake
Conchas Dam
Canadian R.
Santo Domingo Pueblo
San Felipe
SANTA FE
Sena
MESEA MONTOSA
Ute Reservoir
Tucumcari
Rio Puerco
Thoreau
San Mateo
Mount Taylor 11,301 ft.
Bluewater
Milan
Grants
ZUNI MTS.
Zuni R.
Zuni
ZUNI IND. RES.
EL MORRO NATIONAL MONUMENT
Acomita
Paguate
Bernalillo
Corrales
Placitas
Sandia Park
Albuquerque
Kirtland A.F.B.
BERNALILLO
Tijeras
Moriarty
Dilia
Pecos R.
Santa Rosa
QUAY
Quay
GUADALUPE
Blanco Creek
CIBOLA
PUEBLO IND. RES.
Isleta
Los Lunas
VALENCIA
Belen
Jarales
MANZANO MTS.
Osha Peak 10,223 ft.
Estancia
TORRANCE
Encino
Laguna del Perro
Manzano Peak 10,086 ft.
Mountainair
Sumner Lake
Alamogordo Dam
Vaughn
CURRY
Fort Sumner
Melrose
Grier
Clovis
Cannon A.F.B.
LADRON MTS.
GALLINAS MTS.
Bernardo
Quemado
DATIL MTS.
Gran Quivira
SALINAS PUEBLO MISSIONS NATIONAL MONUMENT
Corona
DE BACA
Portales
CATRON
Lemitar
MAGDALENA MTS.
Socorro
SOCORRO
CHUPADERA MESA
Fifteenmile Arroyo
ROOSEVELT
Salt Lake
Elida
Dora
Horse Springs
PLAINS OF SAN AGUSTIN
San Antonio
Bingham
SAN MATEO MTS.
SIERRA OSCURA
LINCOLN
Lingo
Reserve
San Francisco R.
MOGOLLON MTS.
BLACK RANGE
Carrizozo
Capitan Peak 10,083 ft.
Capitan
CAPITAN MTS.
Salt Creek
Lincoln
CHAVES
White Sands
Whitewater Baldy 10,892 ft.
GILA CLIFF DWELLINGS NATIONAL MON.
Glenwood
Mogollon Baldy 10,770 ft.
Elephant Butte Reservoir
JORNADA DEL MUERTO
Missle
Sierra Blanca Peak 12,003 ft.
Ruidoso
MESCALERO APACHE IND. RES.
Mescalero
Roswell
MESCALERO VALLEY
MESCALERO RIDGE
Tatum
Dexter
Gila Hot Springs
Truth or Consequences
Elephant Butte
SAN ANDRES MTS.
ALKALI FLAT
Range
TULAROSA VALLEY
Tularosa
Hagerman
LLANO ESTACADO
Lovington
Buckhorn
Black Mountain 9,020 ft.
GRANT
SIERRA
Caballo Reservoir
Arrey
WHITE SANDS
Alamogordo
Holloman A.F.B.
Hanover
Santa Rita
Bayard
Hurley
Silver City
Gila R.
BIG BURRO MTS.
Virden
Hatch
Rincon
DONA ANA
Lake Lucero
WHITE SANDS NATIONAL MONUMENT
SACRAMENTO MTS.
GUADALUPE MTS.
Rio Penasco
Artesia
EDDY
Lake McMillan
Lakewood
Hobbs
STAKED PLAIN
Oil Center
Eunice
LEA
Carlsbad
Pecos R.
Otis
OTERO
COOKS RANGE
Lordsburg
PELONCILLO MTS.
Continental Divide
Deming
LUNA
Las Cruces
Mesilla
University Park
La Mesa
FLORIDA MTS.
HUECO MTS.
CARLSBAD CAVERNS NATIONAL PARK
Red Bluff Lake
Jal
Animas
HATCHET MTS.
Anthony
La Union
POTRILLO MTS.
Columbus
Delaware Creek
Playas Lake
HIDALGO
Casas Grandes
Lago Guzman
Lago Santa Maria
Rio Grande

NAME	AREA[1] (sq. mi.)	AREA[1] (sq. km.)	POP. (1990c)	CO. SEAT
De Baca	2,356	6,102	2,252	Fort Sumner
Dona Ana	3,804	9,852	135,510	Las Cruces
Eddy[3]	4,167	10,793	48,605	Carlsbad
Grant	3,970	10,282	27,676	Silver City
Guadalupe	2,998	7,765	4,156	Santa Rosa
Harding	2,134	5,527	987	Mosquero
Hidalgo	3,447	8,928	5,958	Lordsburg
Lea	4,393	11,378	55,765	Lovington
Lincoln	4,858	12,582	12,219	Carrizozo
Los Alamos[4]	108	280	18,115	Los Alamos
Luna	2,957	7,659	18,110	Deming
McKinley	5,454	14,126	60,686	Gallup
Mora	1,940	5,025	4,264	Mora
Otero	6,638	17,192	51,928	Alamogordo
Quay	2,882	7,464	10,823	Tucumcari
Rio Arriba	5,853	15,159	34,365	Tierra Amarilla
Roosevelt	2,454	6,356	16,702	Portales
Sandoval	3,714	9,619	63,319	Bernalillo
San Juan	5,516	14,286	91,605	Aztec
San Miguel	4,741	12,279	25,743	Las Vegas
Santa Fe	1,905	4,934	98,928	Santa Fe
Sierra	4,166	10,790	9,912	Truth or Consequences
Socorro	6,603	17,102	14,764	Socorro
Taos	2,256	5,843	23,118	Taos
Torrance	3,346	8,666	10,285	Estancia
Union	3,816	9,883	4,124	Clayton
Valencia[2]	1,075	2,784	45,235	Los Lunas

[1] Area = land area.
[2] The W part of Valencia co. became the county of Cibola in 1981.
[3] Carlsbad Caverns (national park) in SW part of county.
[4] Organized from parts of Sandoval and Santa Fe cos. 1949.

History: Evidence of prehistoric inhabitants, esp. Mogollon and Anasazi peoples; at time of European arrival inhabited mainly by Pueblo tribes (such as the Zuni) and Athabascan tribes (such as the Apache and the Navajo); first European visitor to area was missionary Marcos de Niza sent from Mexico (New Spain) 1539; explored by Spanish explorer Francisco Vásquez de Coronado's expedition 1540–42; Spanish settlement begun by explorer Juan de Oñate 1598; Santa Fe (*q.v.*) founded in 1609–10; governed by Mexico after 1821; part E of Rio Grande included in annexation of Texas 1845; rest ceded to U.S. by Mexico 1848 (Treaty of Guadalupe Hidalgo) except for S strip which was included in Gadsden Purchase 1853; first bid for statehood 1850 denied in favor of organization of New Mexico Territory (*q.v.*); territory reduced to area of present state by 1863; held several constitutional conventions before finally being admitted to Union as state Jan. 6, 1912.

New Mexico Territory. Former territory, U.S.A.; comprised the region of the SW U.S. bet. California and Texas; acquired from Mexico 1845–53; territory organized Sept. 9, 1850, incl. most of what is now New Mexico and Arizona, the S tip of Nevada, and a portion of S Colorado; territory expanded with addition of S strip of Arizona and New Mexico from Gadsden Purchase (*q.v.*) 1853; lost its small possessions in Nevada and Colorado 1861; reduced to area of present state 1863 upon formation of the separate territory of Arizona; New Mexico admitted to the Union 1912.

New Mi·ami \mī-'a-mē\. Village, Butler co., SW Ohio, 24 mi. (39 km.) N of Cincinnati; pop. (1990c) 2555.

New Mil·ford \'mil-fərd\. **1.** Town, Litchfield co., NW Connecticut; pop. (1990c) 23,629; settled 1707; incorp. 1712; was home of politician Roger Sherman, signer of Declaration of Independence, Articles of Confederation, and U.S. Constitution.

2. Borough, Bergen co., NE corner of New Jersey, 8 mi. (13 km.) ENE of Paterson; pop. (1990c) 15,990.

New·nan \'nü-nən, 'nyü-\. City, ⊗ of Coweta co., W Georgia, 35 mi. (56 km.) SW of Atlanta; pop. (1990c) 12,497.

New Neth·er·land \'ne-t͟hər-lənd\. Dutch colony in North America c. 1613–64, occupying lands bordering the Hudson River and later the lower Delaware River; conquered by English 1664 and split into New Jersey and New York (after its proprietor, duke of York); ✻ New Amsterdam. See NEW YORK 1.

New Nor·folk \'nȯr-fək\. Town, SE Tasmania, Australia, on Derwent River 20 mi. (32 km.) NNW of Hobart; pop. (1981c) 9617.

New Or·ange \'ȯr-inj, 'är-\. Name given New York City 1673–74 when reconquered by the Dutch.

New Or·le·ans \nü-'ȯr-lənz, ˌnü-ȯr-'lēnz, 'nȯr-lənz; nü-'ȯr-lē-ənz, -lyənz\. City, ⊗ of Orleans parish, SE Louisiana, bet. the Mississippi River and Lake Pontchartrain; pop. (1990c) 496,938; largest city in the state; transportation center; major deepwater port, exporting agricultural products, oil, and petrochemicals; cotton market; produces clothing, chemicals; shipbuilding, oil refining. Notable tourist center, principal attractions include the annual Mardi Gras celebration and the French Quarter (Vieux Carré). Tulane Univ. (1834), Loyola Univ. (1912), Our Lady of Holy Cross Coll. (1916), Delgado Community Coll. (1921), Notre Dame Seminary Graduate School of Theology (1923), Xavier Univ. of Louisiana (1925), Dillard Univ. (1930), Louisiana State Univ. Medical Center (1931), Univ. of New Orleans (1958).

History: Founded 1718 by French colonist Sieur de Bienville (Jean-Baptiste Le Moyne), and made ✻ of the colony a few years later; ceded to Spain 1763; ceded back to France 1803 and then sold to U.S. 1803 by French First Consul (later Emperor) Napoléon Bonaparte; incorp. 1805; ✻ of Louisiana 1812–49; on Jan. 8, 1815, scene of victory of U.S. troops under Gen. Andrew Jackson over British during War of 1812; captured by Union naval force under Adm. David Glasgow Farragut 1862, and occupied by Union troops under Gen. Benjamin F. Butler.

New Paltz \'nü-ˌpȯlts, 'nyü-\. Village, Ulster co., SE New York, 10 mi. (16 km.) W of Poughkeepsie; pop. (1990c) 5463; State Univ. of New York Coll. at New Paltz (1828).

New Phil·a·del·phia \ˌfi-lə-'del-fyə, -fē-ə\. City, ⊗ of Tuscarawas co., E Ohio, 20 mi. (32 km.) S of Canton; pop. (1990c) 15,698; tools, ceramics, machinery.

New Plym·outh \'pli-məth\. **1.** Early name (The Colony of New Plymouth) of Plymouth, Massachusetts, 1620–91. See PLYMOUTH 4.

2. Urban area, W North I., New Zealand, on Tasman Sea 160 mi. (257 km.) N of Wellington; pop. (1992e) 48,700; dairy products; founded 1841.

New·port \'nü-ˌpōrt, 'nyü-\. **1.** County in SE Rhode Island. See table at RHODE ISLAND.

2. City, ⊗ of Jackson co., NE Arkansas, on White River 38 mi. (61 km.) SW of Jonesboro; pop. (1990c) 7459.

3. Town, ⊗ of Vermillion co., W Indiana; pop. (1990c) 627.

4. City, a ⊗ of Campbell co., N Kentucky, on Ohio River just E of Covington; pop. (1990c) 18,871; steel; founded 1790; incorp. as city 1835.

5. Town, Penobscot co., E cen. Maine, 25 mi. (40 km.) W of Bangor; pop. (1990c) 3036.

6. Village, Washington co., E Minnesota, 6 mi. (10 km.) SSE of St. Paul; pop. (1990c) 3720.

7. Town, ⊗ of Sullivan co., SW New Hampshire, 8 mi. (13 km.) E of Claremont; pop. (1990c) 6110.

8. City, ⊗ of Lincoln co., W Oregon, on Pacific Ocean 41 mi. (66 km.) W of Corvallis; pop. (1990c) 8437; fisheries; seashore resort.

9. Borough, Perry co., S cen. Pennsylvania, 21 mi. (34 km.) NW of Harrisburg; pop. (1990c) 1568; settled 1789.

10. City and port of entry, ⊗ of Newport co., SE Rhode Island, on S end of Rhode I. (island) at mouth of Narragansett Bay; pop. (1990c) 28,227; naval education and training facilities incl. U.S. Naval Undersea Warfare Center, U.S. Naval War Coll. (1885), and U.S. Surface Warfare Officers School; tourism. Formerly a fashionable summer resort; several mansions incl. The Breakers built 1895 for industrialist Cornelius Vanderbilt, now open to guided tours; Tennis Hall of Fame; Touro synagogue, built 1763 (oldest in U.S.); Fort Adams, used for defense of Narragansett Bay 1799–1945; Salve Regina Univ. (1934).

History: Settled 1639 by religious refugees from Massachusetts Bay Colony; united with Portsmouth 1640; joined "Incorporation of Providence Plantations" (chartered 1644), separated 1651–54; haven for religious refugees (incl. Quakers and Jews); held by British 1776–79; nearby waters scene of naval action bet. French and British fleets 1778; headquarters of French commander John-Baptiste-Donatien de Vimeur, comte de Rochambeau and troops 1780–81; with Providence, was joint ✻ of Rhode Island until 1900.
11. Town, ⊗ of Cocke co., E Tennessee, 18 mi. (29 km.) SSE of Morristown; pop. (1990c) 7123.
12. City, ⊗ of Orleans co., N Vermont, on S end of Lake Memphremagog; pop. (1990c) 4434; sportswear; lake resort.
13. City, ⊗ of Pend Oreille co., NE corner of Washington, on Idaho border; pop. (1990c) 1691.
14. Town, ⊗ of Isle of Wight, S England, in English Channel 10 mi. (16 km.) WSW of Portsmouth; pop. (1981c) 20,324.
15. Town, Gwent co., SE Wales, on the Usk 20 mi. (32 km.) WNW of Bristol, England; pop. (1991p) 129,900; large modern port; manufactures steel, aluminum, chemicals, electronics; chartered in 14th cent.; Chartist riots 1839.

Newport Beach. Coastal city, Orange co., SW California, on Pacific Ocean 18 mi. (29 km.) SE of Long Beach; pop. (1990c) 66,643; residential and resort community; electronic components; a leading yachting center; incorp. 1906.

Newport News \ˈnüz, ˈnyüz\. Independent city, SE Virginia, at mouth of James River at entrance to Hampton Roads 11 mi. (18 km.) NNW of Norfolk; area 75 sq. mi. (194 sq. km.); pop. (1990c) 170,045; with Norfolk and Portsmouth constitutes Port of Hampton Roads (see HAMPTON ROADS). Major seaport with modern facilities, handling coal, bulk liquids, and general cargo; one of the major shipbuilding centers of the U.S.; textiles, paper products, electronic equipment; Christopher Newport Univ. (1960); Mariner's Museum (1930). Settled c. 1621; during the Civil War, in nearby waters of Hampton Roads, the Confederate ironclad *Virginia* (née *Merrimac*) destroyed in battle the Union ships *Cumberland* and *Congress*, Mar. 8, 1862, one day before engaging the Union ironclad *Monitor;* laid out as city 1882; incorp. 1896; important embarkation point in both World Wars; absorbed city of Warwick (former Warwick co.) 1958.

New Port Rich·ey \ˈri-chē\. City, Pasco co., W cen. Florida, 20 mi. (32 km.) NW of Tampa; pop. (1990c) 14,044.

New Prague \ˈprāg\. City, Le Sueur and Scott cos., S Minnesota, 22 mi. (35 km.) NW of Faribault; pop. (1990c) 3569.

New Prov·i·dence \ˈprä-və-dəns, -ˌdens\. **1.** Borough, Union co., NE New Jersey, 8 mi. (13 km.) SSE of Morristown; pop. (1990c) 11,439.
2. One of the Bahamas, in the Atlantic Ocean bet. Andros I. on the W and Eleuthera I. on the E; area 80 sq. mi. (207 sq. km.); pop. (1990c) 172,196; contains city of Nassau, ✻ of Bahamas; settled by British 17th cent.; site of British air base in WWII.

New·quay \ˈnü-ˌkē, ˈnyü-\. Town, Cornwall, SW England, on Atlantic Ocean 42 mi. (68 km.) W of Plymouth; pop. (1981p) 16,050; seaside resort.

New Que·bec \kwi-ˈbek, ke-\ *or Fr.* **Nou·veau–Qué·bec** \nü-ˌvō-kā-ˈbek\. District, N and E Quebec, Canada, comprising the region N of Eastmain River and bet. Hudson Bay on the W and Labrador on the E, touching Hudson Strait and Ungava Bay on the N; area about 300,000 sq. mi. (777,000 sq. km.); includes Ungava Penin. in the N. Established from part of the earlier, larger region of New Quebec which was organized 1912 from former region of Ungava (*q.v.*), divided 1927 bet. Quebec prov. and Labrador (Newfoundland).

New Quebec Crater. See NOUVEAU-QUÉBEC, CRATÈRE DU.

New Republic. Republic (1884–88) formed by Boers from part of Zululand; now in KwaZulu-Natal prov., Rep. of South Africa.

New Rich·mond \ˈrich-mənd\. **1.** Village, Clermont co., SW Ohio, on Ohio River SE of Cincinnati; pop. (1990c) 2408.
2. City, St. Croix co., W Wisconsin, 35 mi. (56 km.) WNW of Menomonie; pop. (1990c) 5106.

New River. **1.** River, South I., New Zealand. See ORETI.
2. Name of several rivers. See NEW.

New River Inlet. See NEW 1.

New Roads. Town, ⊗ of Pointe Coupee parish, SE cen. Louisiana, on Mississippi River; pop. (1990c) 5303.

New Ro·chelle \rə-ˈshel\. City, Westchester co., SE New York on Long Island Sound; pop. (1990c) 67,265; Coll. of New Rochelle (1904), Iona Coll. (1940); settled 1688 by Huguenots; incorp. as city 1899.

New Rock·ford \ˈräk-fərd\. City, ⊗ of Eddy co., E cen. North Dakota, SSW of Devils Lake (city); pop. (1990c) 1604.

New Rom·ney \ˈräm-nē\. Town, Kent, SE England, in Romney Marsh district; pop. (1981c) 4547; one of the original Cinque Ports (*q.v.*), the sea has since receded.

New Ross \ˈrȯs\. Town, SW co. Wexford, SE Ireland, on Barrow River; pop. (1991p) 5021; former site of ancient abbey.

New Russia *or Russ.* **No·vo·ros·si·ya** \ˌnə-və-rə-ˈsē-yə\. A former region (18th and 19th cents.) of cen. and S Ukraine; included the territory around modern Dnipropetrovs'k, Kherson, Odessa, and Crimea; ab. 75,000 sq. mi. (194,000 sq. km.).

New·ry \ˈnü-rē, ˈnyü-\. **1.** Short canalized stream, SE Northern Ireland; flows S bet. Armagh and Banbridge dists. and through Newry and Mourne into Carlingford Lough.
2. Urban district, ⊗ of Newry and Mourne dist., SE Northern Ireland, 38 mi. (61 km.) SW of Belfast, on Newry River; pop. (1981c) 19,426; has canal connections with Carlingford Lough, Bann River, and Lough Neagh; granite quarrying.

Newry and Mourne \ˈmȯrn\. District of Northern Ireland. See table at IRELAND, NORTHERN.

New Sa·lem \ˈsā-ləm\. See PETERSBURG 2.

New Sarum. See SALISBURY 6.

New Scone. See SCONE 2.

New Shore·ham \ˈshōr-əm\. Town, coextensive with Block Island (village), Washington co., SE Rhode Island; pop. (1990c) 836; legal name of Block Island, but seldom used.

New Shrewsbury. See TINTON FALLS.

New Si·be·ri·a Island \sī-ˈbir-ē-ə\ *or Russ.* **Os·trov No·va·ya Si·bir'** \ˈȯs-trəf-ˈnə-və-yə-si-ˈbir\. Large island in E part of New Siberian Is., N Russia in Asia; 90 mi. (145 km.) long by 40 mi. (64 km.) wide.

New Siberian Islands *or Russ.* **No·vo·si·bir·ski·ye Ostro·va** \ˌnə-və-si-ˈbir-ski-yə-ˌə-strə-ˈvä\. Island group in Arctic Ocean bet. Laptev Sea and East Siberian Sea, a part of Sakha Rep., N Russia in Asia; chief islands Kotel'nyy, Faddeyevski, and New Siberia I.; the Lyakhovskiye Ostrova (*q.v.*) are by some included in the group. First sighted in 18th cent.; site of permanent scientific stations since c. 1927.

New Smyr·na Beach \ˈsmər-nə\. City, Volusia co., E Florida, on Atlantic Ocean 15 mi. (24 km.) S of Daytona Beach; pop. (1990c) 16,543; bathing, boating, and fishing resort; nearby Indian mounds; site of Indian village and Spanish mission (1696); colonized 1767–76, then abandoned; resettled c. 1803; known as New Smyrna until 1937.

New South Wales. State, SE Australia; ✻ Sydney. See table at AUSTRALIA.

Physical features: S section of Great Dividing Range (Eastern Highlands) covers E third of state; highest point (at S end) Mt. Kosciusko 7310 ft. (2228 m.); nearly all of state drained by the Darling and its tributaries and the Murray (with Murrumbidgee and Lachlan rivers); Port Jackson, harbor of Sydney, one of finest in world; also good harbors at Newcastle and Jervis Bay.

Chief products: Wheat, oats, corn, rice, grapes; coal, silver, lead, zinc; livestock raising; iron and steel, chemicals, textiles; food processing.

Chief urban centers: Sydney, Newcastle, Wollongong.

History: Inhabited from prehistoric times; visited, named, and claimed for Britain by Capt. James Cook 1770; first settled at Botany Bay 1788 by marines and convicts, but soon transferred to Port Jackson (later Sydney); colony included all of continent except Western Australia; interior explored and settled throughout 19th cent.; Tasmania (1825), South Australia (1836), Victoria (1851), Queensland (1859), and Northern Terr. (1863) set up as separate colonies; New Zealand under nominal jurisdiction of New South Wales until chartered as separate colony 1840; granted representative government 1842, responsible government 1856; became part of Commonwealth of Australia 1901; ceded area of Australian Capital Terr. (*q.v.*) 1911–17.

New Spain. Former Spanish viceroyalty (1535–1821) in North America, incl. SW United States, Mexico, Central America N of Panama, much of the West Indies, and also the Philippines in the W Pacific Ocean. Mexico City was the seat of government.

New Sweden. Swedish colony on the Delaware River, cen. E North America; extended from site of Trenton, New Jersey, to mouth of the river, mostly on W side of the river; founded 1638 when Fort Christina (on site of Wilmington) was built; taken by the Dutch 1655.

New Territories. That part of Hong Kong leased to Great Britain by China 1898 for 99 years; comprises the area N of Kowloon Penin. and several islands, the largest being Lan Tau.

New·ton \ˈnüt-ᵊn, ˈnyüt-\. **1.** Name of counties in six states of the U.S. See tables at ARKANSAS, GEORGIA, INDIANA, MISSISSIPPI, MISSOURI, TEXAS.

2. City, ⊗ of Baker co., SW Georgia; pop. (1990c) 703.

3. City, ⊗ of Jasper co., SE cen. Illinois, 20 mi. (32 km.) N of Olney; pop. (1990c) 3154.

4. City, ⊗ of Jasper co., S cen. Iowa, 30 mi. (48 km.) E of Des Moines; pop. (1990c) 14,789; construction machinery, dairy products.

5. City, ⊗ of Harvey co., SE cen. Kansas, 35 mi. (56 km.) E of Hutchinson; pop. (1990c) 16,700; railroad shops; grain, farms.

6. Residential city, Middlesex co., NE Massachusetts, W of Boston; pop. (1990c) 82,585; includes 14 villages, among them **Newton Corner, Newton Center, Newton Highlands, Newton Upper Falls, Newton Lower Falls, West Newton, New·ton·ville** \ˈnüt-ᵊn-ˌvil, ˈnyüt-\; Andover Newton Theological School (1825), Lasell Coll. (1851), Mount Ida Coll. (1899) in Newton Center.

7. City, Newton co., E cen. Mississippi, 30 mi. (48 km.) W of Meridian; pop. (1990c) 3701.

8. Town, Rockingham co., New Hampshire; pop. (1990c) 3473.

9. Town, ⊗ of Sussex co., N corner of New Jersey, 23 mi. (37 km.) NW of Morristown; pop. (1990c) 7521.

10. Town, ⊗ of Catawba co., W cen. North Carolina, 20 mi. (32 km.) WSW of Statesville; pop. (1990c) 9304.

11. City, ⊗ of Newton co., E Texas; pop. (1990c) 1885.

Newton, Mount. Peak, E Spitsbergen, Norway; 5617 ft. (1712 m.); highest point on the island.

Newton Ab·bot \ˈa-bət\. Market town, Devon, SW England, on estuary of the Teign 15 mi. (24 km.) S of Exeter; pop. (1981c) 20,979; William of Orange proclaimed king here as William III in 1688.

Newton Centre *and* **Newton Corner.** See NEWTON 6.

Newton Falls. City, Trumbull co., NE Ohio, on Mahoning River 17 mi. (27 km.) WNW of Youngstown; pop. (1990c) 4866.

Newton Highlands. See NEWTON 6.

Newton–le–Wil·lows \-lə-ˈwi-lōz\ *also* **Newton in Ma·ker·field** \ˈmā-kər-ˌfēld\. Village, Merseyside, NW England, 15 mi. (24 km.) W of Manchester; pop. (1981p) 19,723; paper, glass.

Newton Lower Falls *and* **Newton Upper Falls** *and* **Newtonville.** See NEWTON 6.

New·town \ˈnü-ˌtau̇n, ˈnyü-\. **1.** Town, N cen. Fairfield co., SW Connecticut, on Housatonic River; pop. (1990c) 20,779.

2. Former town, Queens co., SE New York, on Long Island; settled mid-17th cent.; since 1898 part of Queens borough in New York City.

3. City, New York. See ELMIRA.

4. Borough, Bucks co., SE Pennsylvania, 22 mi. (35 km.) NE of Philadelphia; pop. (1990c) 2565; Bucks County Community Coll. (1965).

5. Town, Powys co., E Wales; terminus of Montgomery Canal.

New Town. See LAS VEGAS 2.

New·town·abbey \ˌnüt-ᵊn-ˈa-bē, ˌnyüt-\. **1.** District, E Northern Ireland. See table at IRELAND, NORTHERN.

2. Town, Newtownabbey dist., Northern Ireland, just N of Belfast; pop. (1990e) 72,900; textiles; was constituted 1958.

New·town·ards \ˌnüt-ᵊn-ˈärdz, ˌnyüt-\. Town, ⊗ of Ards dist., SE Northern Ireland, 9 mi. (14 km.) E of Belfast at N end of Strangford Lough; pop. (1981c) 20,531; linen, hosiery; engineering; on site of 13th cent. Dominican priory; NE of the town are ruins of an abbey said to have been founded by St. Finian in 6th cent.

Newtown But·ler \ˌnüt-ᵊn-ˈbət-lər, ˌnyüt-\. Village, Fermanagh dist., SW Northern Ireland, 16 mi. (26 km.) SE of Enniskillen; site of a battle 1689 in which Enniskillen Protestants defeated Jacobite force.

New Towne \ˈnü-ˌtau̇n, ˈnyü-\. See CAMBRIDGE 3.

New·town St. Bos·wells \ˈnüt-ᵊn-sənt-ˈbäz-wəlz, ˈnyüt-\. Town, ⊗ of Borders region, SE Scotland.

New Ulm \ˈəlm\. City, ⊗ of Brown co., S Minnesota, on Minnesota River 24 mi. (39 km.) WNW of Mankato; pop. (1990c) 13,132; Dr. Martin Luther Coll. (1884); founded 1854 by Germans; successfully defended twice during the Sioux uprising 1862.

New Urgench. See URGANCH.

New Utrecht. See *History* at BROOKLYN 3.

New Valley. Governorate of Egypt. See table at EGYPT.

New Wa·ter·ford \ˈwȯ-tər-fərd, ˈwä-\. Town, Cape Breton co., E Nova Scotia, Canada, on Atlantic Ocean 8 mi. (13 km.) N of Sydney; pop. (1991c) 7695.

New West·min·ster \ˈwest-ˌmin-stər\. City, SW British Columbia, Canada, on Fraser River 12 mi. (18 km.) ESE of Vancouver and 16 mi. (26 km.) from river's mouth; pop. (1991c) 43,586; suburb of Vancouver; ships timber; processes lumber, vegetables, salmon; ✻ of British Columbia 1859–66.

New Whatcom. See BELLINGHAM 2.

New White·land \ˈhwīt-lənd, ˈwīt-\. Town, Johnson co., cen. Indiana, 6 mi. (10 km.) N of Franklin; pop. (1990c) 4097.

New Wil·ming·ton \ˈwil-miŋ-tən\. Borough, Lawrence co., W Pennsylvania, 8 mi. (13 km.) N of New Castle; pop. (1990c) 2706; Westminster Coll. (1852).

New Windsor. See WINDSOR 10.

New World. The land of the Western Hemisphere; term first used by Pietro Martire d'Anghiera (Peter Martyr), Italian historian, author of *De Rebus Oceanicis et Orbe Novo* (published posthumously in 1530) giving first account of discovery of America.

New York \ˈyȯrk\. **1.** A middle Atlantic state of U.S.A., bounded on N by Lake Ontario and the Canadian provs. of Ontario and Quebec, on E by Vermont, Massachusetts, and Connecticut, on S by Atlantic Ocean, New Jersey, and Pennsylvania, and on W by Pennsylvania, Lake Erie, and the Canadian prov. of Ontario; 30th state in area, 49,576 sq. mi. (128,402 sq. km.), in addition to this area New York has also 4376 sq. mi. (11,334 sq. km.) of water of the Great Lakes; 2d state in population, (1990c) 17,990,456; ✻ Albany; an original state of the Union, the 11th to ratify the U.S. Constitution (July 26, 1788). See table of states at UNITED STATES.

Nickname: Empire State.

State flower: Rose.

Motto: Excelsior (Ever Upward).

Rivers: Hudson, in E area, flowing into Atlantic Ocean at New York City, and in the S forming boundary bet. New York and New Jersey; St. Lawrence, forming N boundary bet. New York and Canadian prov. of Ontario; Delaware, forming section of S boundary bet. New York and Pennsylvania; Niagara, forming W boundary bet. New York and Canadian prov. of Ontario.

Mountains: Adirondacks (in NE) and Catskills (in E). Highest point Mt. Marcy, 5344 ft. (1629 m.), in Essex co. in the Adirondacks.

\ə\ abut \ˈə\ matches \ᵊ\ kitten, Fr table \ər\ further \a\ ash \ā\ ace \ä\ cot, cart \ȧ\ Fr bac \au̇\ out \b̬\ Span Avila \ch\ chin \e\ bet \ē\ easy \g\ go \i\ hit \ī\ ice \j\ job \k\ Ger ich, Buch \$^{n}$\ Fr vin \ŋ\ sing \ō\ go \ȯ\ all \ȯ\ law \œ\ Fr bœuf \œ̄\ Fr feu \ȯi\ boy \th\ thin \t͟h\ this \ü\ loot \u̇\ foot \ue\ Ger füllen \ue̅\ Fr rue \y\ yet \$^{y}$\ Fr digne \ˈdēn^{y}\, nuit \ˈnw^{y}ē\ \yü\ few \yu̇\ fury \zh\ vision

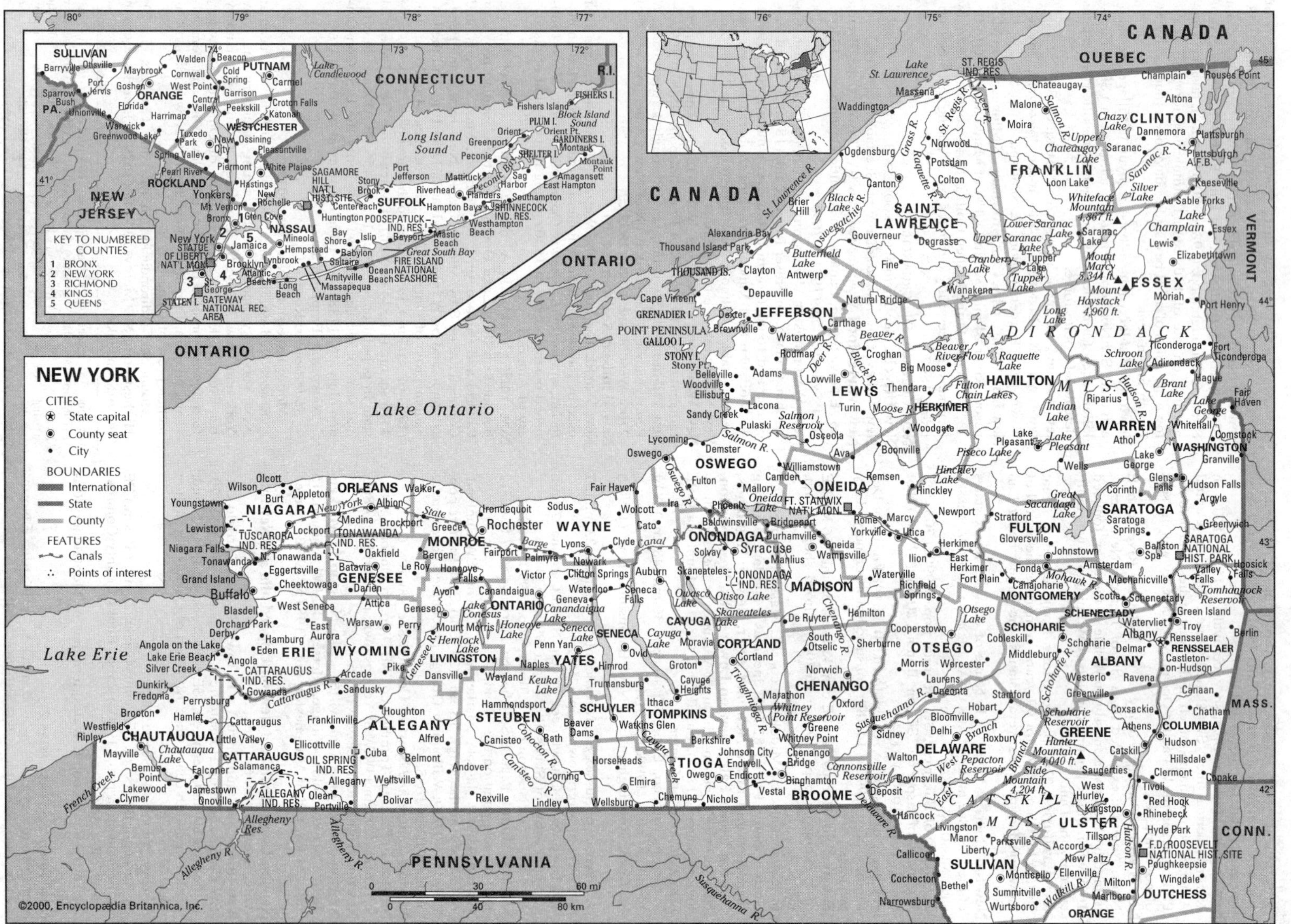
NEW YORK
CITIES
State capital
County seat
City
BOUNDARIES
International
State
County
FEATURES
Canals
Points of interest
KEY TO NUMBERED COUNTIES
1 BRONX
2 NEW YORK
3 RICHMOND
4 KINGS
5 QUEENS
CANADA
QUEBEC
VERMONT
MASS.
CONN.
R.I.
PA.
PENNSYLVANIA
NEW JERSEY
CONNECTICUT
ONTARIO
Lake Ontario
Lake Erie
Long Island Sound
ADIRONDACK MTS.
CATSKILL MTS.
0 30 60 mi
0 40 80 km
©2000, Encyclopædia Britannica, Inc.

Chief products: Vegetables, fruit; dairy products; zinc, gravel, salt; apparel, primary metals, electrical machinery, chemicals; finance, printing and publishing, food processing.

Chief cities: New York City, Buffalo, Rochester, Yonkers, Syracuse, Albany.

Political divisions: Divided into the following 62 counties (for pronunciation of their names, see their individual entries):

NAME	AREA[1] (sq. mi.)	AREA[1] (sq. km.)	POP. (1990c)	CO. SEAT(S)
Albany	526	1,362	292,594	Albany
Allegany	1,047	2,712	50,470	Belmont
Bronx[2]	41	106	1,203,789	Bronx *or* the Bronx
Broome	714	1,849	212,160	Binghamton
Cattaraugus	1,334	3,455	84,234	Little Valley
Cayuga	698	1,808	82,313	Auburn
Chautauqua	1,081	2,800	141,895	Mayville
Chemung	415	1,075	95,195	Elmira
Chenango	909	2,354	51,768	Norwich
Clinton	1,059	2,743	85,969	Plattsburg
Columbia	645	1,671	62,982	Hudson
Cortland	502	1,300	48,963	Cortland
Delaware	1,458	3,776	47,225	Delhi
Dutchess	814	2,108	259,462	Poughkeepsie
Erie	1,058	2,740	968,532	Buffalo
Essex	1,823	4,722	37,152	Elizabethtown
Franklin	1,674	4,336	46,540	Malone
Fulton	498	1,290	54,191	Johnstown
Genesee	501	1,298	60,060	Batavia
Greene	654	1,694	44,739	Catskill
Hamilton	1,735	4,494	5,279	Lake Pleasant
Herkimer	1,435	3,717	65,797	Herkimer
Jefferson	1,294	3,351	110,943	Watertown
Kings[2]	70	181	2,300,664	Brooklyn
Lewis	1,291	3,344	26,796	Lowville
Livingston	638	1,652	62,372	Geneseo
Madison	661	1,712	69,120	Wampsville
Monroe	675	1,748	713,968	Rochester
Montgomery	408	1,057	51,981	Fonda
Nassau	289	749	1,287,348	Mineola
New York[2]	23	60	1,487,536	New York
Niagara	532	1,378	220,756	Lockport
Oneida	1,224	3,170	250,836	Rome, Utica
Onondaga	747	1,935	468,973	Syracuse
Ontario[3]	651	1,686	95,101	Canandaigua
Orange	833	2,157	307,647	Goshen
Orleans	396	1,026	41,846	Albion
Oswego	964	2,497	121,771	Oswego, Pulaski
Otsego[4]	1,013	2,624	60,517	Cooperstown
Putnam	232	601	83,941	Carmel
Queens[2]	108	280	1,951,598	Jamaica
Rensselaer	665	1,722	154,429	Troy
Richmond[2]	58	150	378,977	Saint George
Rockland	176	456	265,475	New City
St. Lawrence	2,768	7,169	111,974	Canton
Saratoga	818	2,119	181,276	Ballston Spa
Schenectady	207	536	149,285	Schenectady
Schoharie	624	1,616	31,859	Schoharie
Schuyler[5]	330	855	18,662	Watkins Glen
Seneca	338	875	33,683	Ovid, Waterloo
Steuben	1,410	3,652	99,088	Bath
Suffolk	929	2,406	1,321,864	Riverhead
Sullivan	980	2,538	69,277	Monticello
Tioga	524	1,357	52,337	Owego
Tompkins[6]	482	1,248	94,097	Ithaca
Ulster	1,141	2,955	165,304	Kingston
Warren	887	2,297	59,209	Lake George
Washington	836	2,165	59,330	Hudson Falls
Wayne	606	1,570	89,123	Lyons
Westchester	443	1,147	874,866	White Plains
Wyoming	598	1,549	42,507	Warsaw
Yates	343	888	22,810	Penn Yan

[1] Area = land area.
[2] Each of these five counties is coextensive with one of the five boroughs of New York City and two of them are also coextensive with two islands, as follows: Bronx co. coextensive with Bronx borough, Kings co. (occupying W corner of Long Island) with Brooklyn borough, New York co. with Manhattan borough and with Manhattan I., Queens co. (on W part of Long Island) with Queens borough, Richmond co. with Richmond borough and with Staten I.
[3] Includes most of Canandaigua Lake (cen.).
[4] Includes Otsego Lake in N cen. part.
[5] Includes S part of Seneca Lake.
[6] Includes S part of Cayuga Lake.

History: Prior to European colonization inhabited by Algonquins (Mahican, Wappinger) and Iroquois (Mohawk, Oneida, Onondaga, Cayuga, and Seneca); New York Bay visited by Florentine navigator Giovanni da Verrazano 1524; explored 1609 by English navigator Henry Hudson (Hudson River) and French explorer Samuel de Champlain (N New York to Lake Champlain); Dutch trading posts, estab. on Manhattan I. and at Fort Nassau, were taken over by Dutch West India Company under which early colonization occurred (see FORT ORANGE and NEW AMSTERDAM); opened 1629 to patroon colonization for several years; formed part of Dutch colony of New Netherland (*q.v.*), surrendered without resistance to English 1664 and renamed New York after its proprietor, duke of York; briefly recaptured by Dutch 1673–74; scene of much fighting during French and Indian War, in which the Iroquois Confederacy became allied with the British; after ratifying Declaration of Independence, held first state constitutional convention 1776, adopted first state constitution 1777; scene of numerous engagements of the American Revolution incl. Ticonderoga, Long Island, White Plains, Saratoga, and Kingston (*qq.v.*), and also of Benedict Arnold's treason at West Point; ratified U.S. Constitution 1788; state ✻ moved 1797 from New York City to Albany; Canadian frontier scene of several engagements during War of 1812; opening of Erie Canal 1825 spurred development of W New York; adopted present constitution 1894.

2. County in SE New York. See table at NEW YORK 1.

3. *or* **New York City.** City, SE New York, at mouth of the Hudson River; pop. (1990c) 7,322,564; largest city in the U.S. and important seaport; comprises five boroughs coextensive with five counties: Bronx (Bronx co.), Brooklyn (Kings co.), Manhattan (New York co.), Queens (Queens co.), and Staten Island (Richmond co.); extensive harbor facilities (port has ab. 755 mi. or 1215 km. of developed frontage); the world's foremost financial center (New York Stock Exchange and American Stock Exchange are located here, as are the headquarters of many major corporations); UN headquarters; holds a leading position in the retail and wholesale trades, entertainment, media, fashion, art, and the service industries; manufactured products include: apparel, fabricated metal products, leather goods; printing and publishing, graphic arts, food processing; tourism. For educational institutions and other notable features, see the entries of the individual boroughs.

History: Site of a trading post estab. at S end of Manhattan I. by Dutch 1610; fortified and colonized under name New Amsterdam (*q.v.*) by Dutch West India Company; island purchased from Indians by Peter Minuit for Dutch West India Company 1626 for ab. $24 worth of trinkets; settlements extended to Breuckelen (Brooklyn), New Harlem, Bronx, and Staaten Eylandt (Staten I.); surrendered without a struggle to British and named New York 1664 in honor of the king's brother, the duke of York; Dutch regained control and held it for a short time as New Orange 1673–74; new city charter granted 1686; scene of Leisler Rebellion 1689–91; after the British parliament passed the Stamp Act 1765, Stamp Act Congress met in City Hall and drew up a declaration of colonists' rights, incl. assertion of no taxation without representation; on July 9, 1776 Gen. George Washington caused the Declaration of Independence to be read to the assembled army; after the battle of Long Island Aug. 27, 1776, Washington retreated to Manhattan, then to White Plains; city held by British to the end of the Revolutionary War; ✻ of state 1784–97, of U.S. 1789–90; George Washington inaugurated first president of the U.S. in a building (Federal Hall) on Wall Street; sharp increase in commerce and industry followed the opening of the Erie Canal (1825); suffered disastrous fire 1835; opposed the Civil War at its outbreak 1861, and was scene of serious draft riots 1863; expanded rapidly after Civil War, developing transportation and communication systems; Tweed Ring political scandal exposed 1871; by legislative act of 1896 the five boroughs were merged into a single city Jan. 1, 1898. For further details, see MANHATTAN 2, BRONX 3, BROOKLYN 3, QUEENS 2, and STATEN ISLAND 2.

New York Bay. Inlet of Atlantic Ocean at mouth of Hudson River, in SE New York; it consists of **Upper New York Bay** and **Lower New York Bay,** connected by the Narrows; Manhattan I. lies at its NE end.

New York City. See NEW YORK 3.

New York Mills. Village, Oneida co., cen. New York, 5 mi. (8 km.) E of Utica; pop. (1990c) 3534.

New York State Barge Canal. Canal system, New York, connecting Lake Erie at Buffalo with the Hudson River opp. Troy, near mouth of the Mohawk River (*q.v.*); length 522 mi. (840 km.); branches connect the main waterway, Erie Canal (*q.v.*), with Lake Ontario (see OSWEGO CANAL) and Lake Champlain (see CHAMPLAIN CANAL); natural waterways are used extensively, esp. the Oswego, Seneca (see CAYUGA LAKE and SENECA LAKE), and Clyde rivers and Oneida Lake.

New Zea·land \ˈzē-lənd\. Independent state, consisting of several islands in SW Pacific Ocean; lat. 34°50′ to 47°S and long. 166° to 178°50′E; 103,736 sq. mi. (268,676 sq. km.); pop. (1986c) 3,307,084; ✻ Wellington; major islands include: North I., South I., Stewart I., and Chatham Is.

Chief products: Meat, fish, wool, dairy products; timber; coal, gold, limestone, iron sand; natural gas; manufacturing: machinery, paper products, textiles; food processing.

Chief cities: Auckland (on North I.) and Christchurch (on South I.).

North Island: Mountainous, in cen. part has several ranges with volcanoes Mt. Ruapehu 9175 ft. (2797 m.), Ngauruhoe 7515 ft. (2291 m.), and Tongariro 6516 ft. (1986 m.), all in Tongariro National Park; on W coast is Mt. Egmont 8260 ft. (2518 m.); in center is Lake Taupo in midst of remarkable hot-springs country; chief rivers: Waikato, Rangitaiki, Wanganui, Rangitikei; irregular coastline, excellent harbors.

South Island: Mountainous, with Southern Alps (highest peak Mt. Cook 12,349 ft. or 3764 m.) extending almost its entire length and incl. many glaciers and lakes; largest lakes: Wakatipu, Wanaka, Te Anau; chief rivers: Wairau, Rangitata, Waitaki, Clutha; coastline irregular.

History: Settled by Polynesians, probably by 1000 A.D.; first European sighting by Dutch explorer Abel Tasman 1642; visited by English explorer Capt. James Cook 1769 who circumnavigated and charted the two main islands; first European settlements made esp. by whalers and missionaries; first colonized in 1840 at Wellington by New Zealand Company; nominally under jurisdiction of colony of New South Wales until by Treaty of Waitangi 1840 native leaders ceded sovereignty to British who proclaimed New Zealand a crown colony; wars over land bet. colonists and Maori natives 1840s and 1860s; in new constitution 1852, organized as six provinces; transferred ✻ from Auckland to Wellington 1865; provincial governments abolished 1876; annexed Kermadec Is. 1887 and Niue and Cook Is. 1901; colonial status formally terminated 1907, became Dominion of New Zealand; administered Western Samoa 1919–62; participated in WWI and WWII; added Tokelau 1948; adopted unicameral government 1950; entered into defense alliance with Australia and U.S. (ANZUS treaty) 1951, excluded 1986 after refusing to allow nuclear-armed or nuclear-powered U.S. warships into New Zealand ports; granted internal self-government to Cook Is. 1965, to Niue 1974.

Ne·ya·ga·wa \ˌnā-yä-ˈgä-wä, nā-ˈyä-gä-wä\. City, Ōsaka prefecture, Honshū, Japan, suburb of the city of Ōsaka; pop. (1990p) 256,521.

Neyba. See NEIBA.

Ney·rīz \nā-ˈrēz\ *or* **Ni·riz** \nē-ˈrēz\. Town, Fārs prov., SW Iran; on the old trade route from Kermān to Shīrāz.

Ney·shā·būr \ˌnā-shä-ˈbür\ *or* **Ni·sha·pur** \ˌnē-shə-ˈpu̇r\. Town, Khorāsān prov., NE Iran, ab. 40 mi. (64 km.) W of Mashhad; pop. (1986c) 109,258; market town; cotton, cereal grains, pottery, carpets; turquoise mines nearby; birthplace and burial place of the Persian poets Omar Khayyám and Farīd od-Dīn ʻAṭṭār. Traditionally thought to have been founded by Shāpūr I in 3d cent. A.D.; royal residence until mid-5th cent.; declined but again flourished beginning in 9th cent.; destroyed three times in 13th cent., twice by earthquakes and once by the Mongols.

Ne·za·hual·có·yotl \nā-ˌsä-wäl-ˈkō-ˌyō-tᵊl\ *or* **Ne·tza·hual·có·yotl** \-ˌtsä-\. City, Mexico state, Mexico, a suburb of Mexico City; pop. (1990c) 1,255,456.

Ne·zhin *also* **Nye·zhin** \ˈnye-zhin\. Town, cen. Chernihiv subdivision, N Ukraine, 70 mi. (113 km.) NE of Kiev; pop. (1991e) 82,000; rail junction point on the main Kiev-Moscow line; an old town dating from 11th cent.

Nezib. See NIZIP.

Nez·perce \ˈnez-ˈpərs\. City, ⊗ of Lewis co., W Idaho; pop. (1990c) 453.

Nez Perce \ˈnez-ˈpərs\. **1.** Mountain, cen. Grand Teton National Park, NW Wyoming; 11,901 ft. (3627 m.).
2. County in W Idaho. See table at IDAHO.

Nez Perce National Historical Park. See UNITED STATES, *National Historical Parks.*

Ngaliema, Mount. See RUWENZORI, MOUNT.

Nga·mi \əŋ-ˈgä-mē\. Lake, NW Botswana, N of Kalahari Desert and S of Okavango Basin; discovered by Scottish missionary and explorer David Livingstone 1849.

Ngan·juk *or* **Nagan·djuk** \əŋ-ˈgän-ˌjük\. Town, East Java prov., Indonesia, ab. 25 mi. (40 km.) E of Madiun.

Ngang·long Kan·gri \ˈgäŋ-ˌlȯŋ-ˈkäŋ-grē\ *or W.-G.* **Ang–lung–kang–jih** \ˈäŋ-ˈlüŋ-ˈgäŋ-ˈji\ *or* **A–ling Mountains** \ˈä-ˌliŋ\. Mountain range, W Tibet, China; highest peak 24,000 ft. (7315 m.) near its W end.

Ngan–king. See ANQING.

Ngaoun·dé·ré \əŋ-ˌgau̇n-dā-ˈrā\. Town, N cen. Cameroon; pop. (1987e) 61,925.

Nga·ru·ro·ro \əŋ-ˌgä-rü-ˈrō-rō\. River, E cen. North I., New Zealand; flows S and E into Hawke Bay below Napier; 96 mi. (155 km.) long.

Nga·tik \əŋ-ˈgä-tik\. Atoll, Senyavin Is. group, E Caroline Is., Federated States of Micronesia, W Pacific Ocean, ab. 90 mi. (145 km.) SSW of Pohnpei, 5°51′N, 157°16′E.

Ngau. See GAU.

Ngau·ru·hoe \əŋ-ˌgau̇-rü-ˈhō-ā\. Volcano, Tongariro National Park, cen. North I., New Zealand; 7515 ft. (2291 m.).

Nga·wi \əŋ-ˈgä-wē\. Town, East Java prov., Indonesia, ab. 17 mi. (27 km.) NW of Madiun on the Solo River; pop. (1980c) 56,597.

Nge·se·bus \əŋ-ˈgā-sā-ˌbu̇s\. Small island just N of Peleliu, Palau Is., W Pacific Ocean.

Ngga·to·kae \əŋ-ˈgä-tu̇-ˌkī\; *formerly* **Ga·tu·kai** \ˈgä-tu̇-ˌkī\. Small island of the New Georgia Is., cen. Solomon Is., W Pacific Ocean, off SE coast of Vangunu I.

Nggela Sule Ailan. See FLORIDA ISLAND.

Ng'i·ro, Ewa·so \ā-ˈwä-sōŋ-ˈgē-rō\ *also* **Ewaso Nyi·ro** \-sōn-ˈyē-rō\. River, Kenya; flows NE 350 mi. (563 km.) into Lorian Swamp in E part of country; issues from the swamp as **Lach De·ra** \ˈläk-ˈder-ə\ and in certain seasons empties into the Jubba River in S Somalia.

Ngoo Linh \əŋ-ˈgü-ˈlin\. Mountain, cen. Vietnam, ab. 70 mi. (115 km.) S of Da Nang; 8521 ft. (2597 m.).

Ngo·ron·go·ro Crater \əŋ-ˌgōr-oŋ-ˈgō-rō\. Extinct volcanic crater, N cen. Tanzania in **Ngorongoro Conservation Area** (estab. 1956) noted for its abundant wildlife.

Ngo·zi \əŋ-ˈgō-zē\. Town, N Burundi, NE of Bujumbura; pop. (1990c) 74,218.

Nguiu \əŋ-ˈgwē-ü\. Town, Bathurst I., Australia; the island's chief settlement.

Ngunza. See SUMBE.

Ngur·do·to Crater \əŋ-gür-ˈdō-tō\. Extinct volcanic crater, Arusha National Park, N Tanzania.

Ngu·ru \əŋ-ˈgü-rü\. Town, N Nigeria; pop. (1991e) 87,660.

Nha·mun·dá \ˌnyȧ-mün-ˈdä\ *also* **Ja·mun·dá** \zhȧ-\ *or* **Ya·mun·dá** \ˌyä-\. River, N Brazil; rises near Guyana boundary, flows S into Amazon River, forming section of boundary bet. Pará and Amazonas states.

Nha Trang \ˈnyä-ˈträŋ\. Seaport town, S Vietnam, ab. 50 mi. (80 km.) N of Phan Rang; pop. (1989c) 216,430; Pasteur Institute (1895); remains of ancient Cham temple nearby.

Nhka·ta Bay \əŋ-ˈkä-tä\. Town, W cen. shore of Lake Malawi, Malawi; an administrative center with best anchorage on W side of lake.

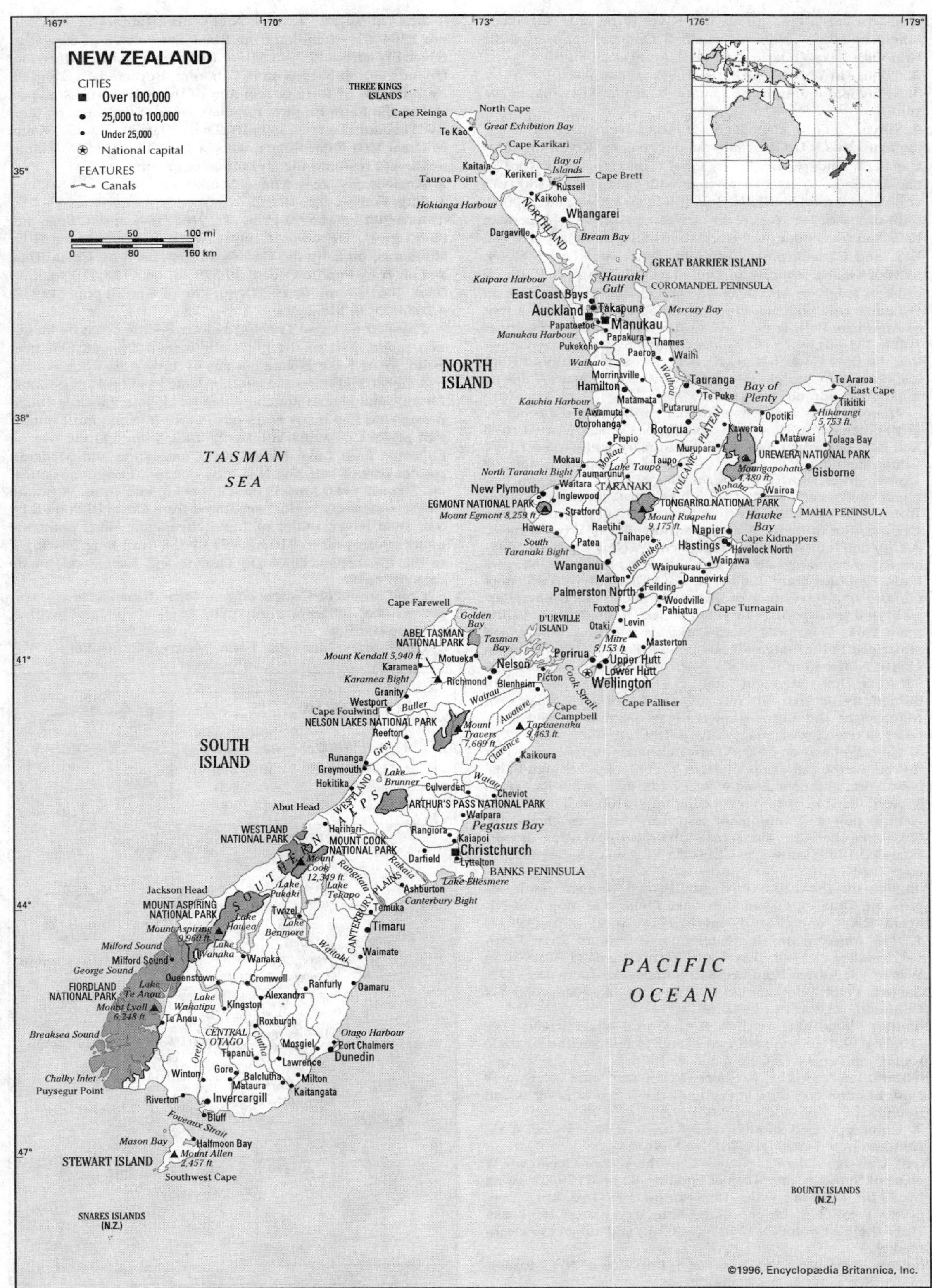

NEW ZEALAND
CITIES
Over 100,000
25,000 to 100,000
Under 25,000
National capital
FEATURES
Canals
0 50 100 mi
0 80 160 km
TASMAN SEA
PACIFIC OCEAN
NORTH ISLAND
SOUTH ISLAND
STEWART ISLAND
THREE KINGS ISLANDS
Cape Reinga
North Cape
Great Exhibition Bay
Te Kao
Cape Karikari
Kaitaia
Kerikeri
Bay of Islands
Russell
Cape Brett
Tauroa Point
Kaikohe
Hokianga Harbour
NORTHLAND
Whangarei
Dargaville
Bream Bay
GREAT BARRIER ISLAND
Kaipara Harbour
Hauraki Gulf
COROMANDEL PENINSULA
East Coast Bays
Auckland
Takapuna
Mercury Bay
Manukau
Papatoetoe
Manukau Harbour
Papakura
Pukekohe
Thames
Paeroa
Waihi
Waikato
Waihou
Morrinsville
Hamilton
Tauranga
Te Puke
Bay of Plenty
Te Araroa
East Cape
Tikitiki
Kawhia Harbour
Matamata
Putaruru
Te Awamutu
Otorohanga
Rotorua
Kawerau
Opotiki
Hikurangi 5,753 ft.
Matawai
Tolaga Bay
Piopio
Murupara
VOLCANIC PLATEAU
UREWERA NATIONAL PARK
Mokau
Mokau
Taupo
Lake Taupo
Maungapohatu 4,480 ft.
Gisborne
North Taranaki Bight
Taumarunui
Waitara
TARANAKI
New Plymouth
Inglewood
Mohaka
Wairoa
EGMONT NATIONAL PARK
TONGARIRO NATIONAL PARK
MAHIA PENINSULA
Mount Egmont 8,259 ft.
Stratford
Mount Ruapehu 9,175 ft.
Hawke Bay
Hawera
Raetihi
Napier
Taihape
Patea
Hastings
Cape Kidnappers
Havelock North
South Taranaki Bight
Rangitikei
Wanganui
Waipukurau
Waipawa
Marton
Dannevirke
Palmerston North
Feilding
Foxton
Woodville
Pahiatua
Cape Turnagain
Cape Farewell
Golden Bay
D'URVILLE ISLAND
Otaki
Levin
ABEL TASMAN NATIONAL PARK
Tasman Bay
Mitre 5,153 ft.
Masterton
Mount Kendall 5,940 ft.
Motueka
Nelson
Porirua
Upper Hutt
Karamea
Lower Hutt
Wellington
Karamea Bight
Richmond
Blenheim
Picton
Cook Strait
Granity
Wairau
Westport
Buller
Cape Campbell
Cape Palliser
Cape Foulwind
Awatere
NELSON LAKES NATIONAL PARK
Mount Travers 7,669 ft.
Tapuaenuku 9,463 ft.
Reefton
Clarence
Kaikoura
Grey
Runanga
Greymouth
Lake Brunner
Hokitika
WESTLAND
Culverden
Waiau
Cheviot
Abut Head
ARTHUR'S PASS NATIONAL PARK
Harihari
Waipara
Pegasus Bay
WESTLAND NATIONAL PARK
Rangiora
Kaiapoi
MOUNT COOK NATIONAL PARK
Christchurch
Darfield
Lyttelton
Mount Cook 12,349 ft.
Rangitata
Rakaia
BANKS PENINSULA
Lake Ellesmere
SOUTHERN ALPS
CANTERBURY PLAINS
Jackson Head
Lake Pukaki
Lake Tekapo
Ashburton
Canterbury Bight
MOUNT ASPIRING NATIONAL PARK
Temuka
Lake Hawea
Twizel
Lake Benmore
Timaru
Mount Aspiring 9,960 ft.
Milford Sound
Lake Wanaka
Waitaki
Waimate
Milford Sound
Wanaka
George Sound
Queenstown
Cromwell
Ranfurly
FIORDLAND NATIONAL PARK
Lake Te Anau
Oamaru
Lake Wakatipu
Alexandra
Mount Lyall 6,248 ft.
Kingston
Te Anau
Roxburgh
Breaksea Sound
CENTRAL OTAGO
Otago Harbour
Port Chalmers
Oreti
Clutha
Mosgiel
Tapanui
Dunedin
Lawrence
Gore
Chalky Inlet
Winton
Balclutha
Milton
Puysegur Point
Mataura
Kaitangata
Riverton
Invercargill
Bluff
Foveaux Strait
Mason Bay
Halfmoon Bay
Mount Allen 2,457 ft.
Southwest Cape
SNARES ISLANDS (N.Z.)
BOUNTY ISLANDS (N.Z.)
167°
170°
173°
176°
179°
35°
38°
41°
44°
47°

Ni·ag·a·ra \nī-'a-grə, -gə-rə\. **1.** River forming U.S.-Canada boundary bet. W New York and S Ontario; connects Lake Erie with Lake Ontario. See NIAGARA FALLS.

2. County in W New York. See table at NEW YORK.

3. Municipal region in SE Ontario, Canada. See table at ONTARIO.

4. Town, Ontario, Canada. See NIAGARA-ON-THE-LAKE.

Niagara Falls. **1.** Great falls of the Niagara River, on U.S.-Canada boundary, divided by Goat I. into Horseshoe (or Canadian) Falls, 158 ft. (48 m.) high with crest 2600 ft. (800 m.) wide, and American Falls, 167 ft. (51 m.) high and 1000 ft. (300 m.) wide; ab. 6 percent of water passes over American Falls and remainder over Horseshoe Falls. Boundary line bet. U.S. and Canada passes through center of Niagara River, leaving Goat I. entirely in United States. Prospect Point on brink of ledge on American side and Queen Victoria Park on Canadian side both afford excellent views of the falls; at foot of American Falls is the Cave of the Winds, a rocky chamber 100 ft. (31 m.) by 75 ft. (23 m.), formed by erosion. River below the falls flows bet. high cliffs, forming Whirlpool Rapids; crossed by bridges bet. the two cities of Niagara Falls; an important hydroelectric center.

History: Falls well known to many tribes of Indians before any settlement of Europeans in U.S. or Canada; visited 1678 and later described by French missionary and explorer Pére Louis Hennepin; in center of region of trading posts and frontier forts 18th cent. and in War of 1812 of several engagements (see LUNDY'S LANE, QUEENSTON, CHIPPEWA); water from American Falls diverted temporarily 1969, permitting examination of bedrock and determination of erosion rates.

2. City and tourist resort, Niagara co., W New York, on Niagara River extending above and below the falls opp. Niagara Falls, Ontario, and 17 mi. (27 km.) NNW of Buffalo; pop. (1990c) 61,840. Center of electrochemical, electrometallurgical and aerospace industries; paper; Niagara Reservation State Park, Whirlpool State Park, Cave of the Winds, and American Falls; Niagara Falls power plant (developed from 1890); Niagara Univ. (1856). Site of early French, then British forts; first settlement estab. c. 1805; fort and settlement burned by British in War of 1812; former villages of Manchester and Suspension Bridge consolidated and chartered as one city of Niagara Falls 1892.

3. City, Welland co., SE Ontario, Canada, on Niagara River just below the falls; pop. (1991c) 75,399; opp. Niagara Falls, New York, and connected with it by bridges; from its Queen Victoria Park is finest view of the falls. Hub of large hydroelectric power development; tourism; produces chemicals, fertilizers, cereals, abrasives, silverware, sporting goods. Founded 1853; known as **Clif·ton** \'klif-tən\ 1856–1881; incorp. 1904.

Niagara–on–the–Lake *or* **Niagara.** Town, Niagara munic. region, SE Ontario, Canada, on Lake Ontario at mouth of Niagara River opp. Fort Niagara, New York; pop. (1991c) 12,945; tourism; site of annual George Bernard Shaw Festival; founded c. 1784; first ✻ of Upper Canada (1792–96); in War of 1812 town occupied and burned by Americans 1813.

Niagara Peak. Mountain, Hinsdale and San Juan cos., SW Colorado; 13,800 ft. (4200 m.).

Nia·mey \'nyä-mā\. City, ✻ of Niger, on Niger River; pop. (1988c) 392,165; commercial center at intersection of trade routes; university (1971); made ✻ 1926.

Ni·an·tic \nī-'an-tik\. **1.** Short stream and wide inlet, in W New London co., SE Connecticut; flows S into Long Island Sound.

2. Unincorporated subdivision of town of East Lyme, Connecticut; pop. (1990c) 3048. See EAST LYME.

Ni·as \'nē-əs\. Island, Indonesia, in the Indian Ocean off W coast of Sumatra, just N of the Equator; 80 mi. (129 km.) long by 30 mi. (48 km.) wide; 1569 sq. mi. (4064 sq. km.); pop. (1980c) 468,375; chief village Gunungsitoli on NE coast. Hilly (highest point 2907 ft. or 886 m.) and subject to earthquakes.

Ni·as·sa *or* **Ny·as·sa** \nē-'a-sə, nī-\. Province of NW Mozambique. See table at MOZAMBIQUE.

Ni·caea \nī-'sē-ə\. **1.** *angl.* **Nice** \'nīs\. Empire in Asia Minor 1204–61; extending from Black Sea coast E of Sangarius River SW across W Asia Minor to Miletus and the Maeander (Menderes); ✻ Nicaea on its N border. Bordered on E and SE by sultanate of Rum or Iconium of the Seljuq Turks and on NW by the Latin Empire. Its rulers were of the Lascaris family: Theodore I and II, John III (Ducas Vatatzes), John IV, and Michael VIII Palaeologus, who in 1261 liberated Constantinople and restored the Byzantine emperors.

2. Ancient city, Asia Minor. See İZNİK.

3. City, France. See NICE 2.

Nic·a·ra·gua \,ni-kə-'rä-gwə, *esp. Brit* -'ra-gyů-wə, *Span* ,nē-kä-'rä-ḡwä\. Republic, Central America, bounded on N by Honduras, on E by the Caribbean Sea, on S by Costa Rica, and on W by Pacific Ocean; 49,579 sq. mi. (128,410 sq. km.) (incl. 4061 sq. mi. or 10,518 sq. km. of water); pop. (1993e) 4,265,000; ✻ Managua.

Physical features: Traversed along Pacific coast by mountain range, part of the great continental axis; in SW, near Brito, W of Lake Nicaragua cut by lowest gap bet. Alaska and Tierra del Fuego and hence selected as W part of possible future canal bet. Atlantic and Pacific oceans; range is volcanic and has had many eruptions in recent years; most important peaks Cosigüina Volcán, Momotombo, and the two on Ometepe I. in Lake Nicaragua (Concepción and Madera); greater part of cen. and N is hilly country. Longer coastline, ab. 300 mi. (480 km.) is on Caribbean, known as Mosquito Coast, a swampy region; separated from Costa Rica on S by San Juan River, outlet of Lake Nicaragua; on E coast are many streams 60 to 210 mi. (97 to 338 km.) long flowing E to the Caribbean, chief are Grande and Escondido; many cays off coast.

Chief products: Coffee, cotton, sugar, bananas, beans, sorghum, rice, tobacco, corn; fish; gold; chemicals, textiles; food processing.

Chief cities: Managua, León, Masaya, Chinandega.

Political divisions: Divided into the following 16 departments (for pronunciation of their names, see their individual entries):

NAME	AREA[1] (sq. mi.)	AREA[1] (sq. km.)	POP. (1990e)	CAPITAL
Boaco	1,924	4,983	117,900	Boaco
Carazo	398	1,031	150,000	Jinotepe
Chinandega	1,800	4,662	330,500	Chinandega
Chontales	1,910	4,947	129,600	Juigalpa
Estelí	849	2,199	169,100	Estelí
Granada	372	963	162,600	Granada
Jinotega	3,697	9,575	175,600	Jinotega
León	2,021	5,234	344,500	León
Madriz	679	1,759	88,700	Somoto
Managua	1,403	3,634	1,026,100	Managua
Masaya	210	544	230,800	Masaya
Matagalpa	2,623	6,794	322,300	Matagalpa
Nueva Segovia	1,290	3,341	122,100	Ocotal
Río San Juan	2,876	7,449	52,200	San Carlos
Rivas	830	2,150	149,800	Rivas
Zelaya	22,816	59,093	298,900	Bluefields

[1] Area = land area.

History: Inhabited for thousands of years, most notably by the Mayan civilization; coast discovered by Christopher Columbus 1502; region explored and Lake Nicaragua discovered by Spanish 1522; colonization begun when Granada and León founded by Spanish explorer Francisco Fernández de Córdoba 1524; governed under Spanish as part of captaincy general of Guatemala; declared itself independent of Spain 1821, briefly part of Mexico, then part of United Provinces of Central America until complete independence achieved 1938 (see SAN JUAN DEL NORTE for dispute with Great Britain); invaded by several expeditions of American filibuster William Walker 1855–60; Managua made ✻ 1857; Mosquito Coast (*q.v.*) ceded by Britain 1860, remained autonomous until 1890s; to prevent competition with Panama Canal, U.S. gained exclusive canal-building rights in Nicaragua in Bryan-Chamorro Treaty 1916, annulled 1970; U.S. intervened in political affairs by maintaining nearly continuous troop presence 1912–33; ruled by dictatorial Somoza dynasty 1936–79; founding member of Central American Common Market 1960; government control taken by Sandinistas 1979 following popular revolt; Sandinistas opposed by contras, armed insurgents backed by the U.S., 1981 ff.; present constitution adopted 1987; organized opposition coalition defeated Sandinistas in 1990 elections.

Nicaragua, Lake *or Span.* **La·go de Ni·ca·ra·gua** \ˈlä-gō-ˌthā-ˌnē-kä-ˈrä-gwä\. Lake in S Nicaragua; 102 mi. (164 km.) long; area ab. 3100 sq. mi. (8000 sq. km.); max. depth 230 ft. (70 m.) largest lake in Central America and largest body of freshwater bet. U.S. and Peru; connected with Lake Managua by Tipitapa River; source of San Juan River; discovered by Spanish 1522.

Nicaria. See IKARIA.

Nic·a·tous Lake \ˈni-kə-ˌtau̇s\. Lake in N Hancock co., E cen. Maine.

Nice \ˈnēs\. **1.** Countship, historical region of SE France, bounded anciently on N by Dauphiné, on E and S by Savoy, and on W by Provence; equivalent to E part of modern dept. of Alpes-Maritimes; ✻ Nice.

2. *or Ital.* **Niz·za** \ˈnēt-sä\; *anc.* **Ni·caea** \nī-ˈsē-ə\. Seaport, ✻ of Alpes-Maritimes dept., SE France, on Mediterranean 98 mi. (158 km.) ENE of Marseille; pop. (1990c) 345,674; ships olive oil, fruits, flowers; produces perfume, soap; 17th cent. cathedral; observatory; university (1965). The leading resort city of the French Riviera.

History: Founded by colony of Phocaeans from ancient Massilia (Marseille); became subject to Rome in 2d cent. B.C.; with surrounding territory (countship of Nice) became subject to counts of Provence and, in 1388, to house of Savoy; sacked by Turks 1543; captured several times by French; held by France 1792–1814; ceded to France by Sardinian house of Savoy 1860. Birthplace of rococo painter Charles-André (Carle) Van Loo (1705), English physicist and chemist Henry Cavendish (1731), French Napoleonic Gen. André Masséna (1758), Italian nationalist leader Giuseppe Garibaldi (1807), and bacteriologist Albert-Léon-Charles Calmette (1863), codeveloper of tuberculosis vaccine.

3. Empire, Asia Minor. See NICAEA.

4. Ancient city, Asia Minor. See İZNİK.

Nicephorium. See AR RAQQAH.

Nice·ville \ˈnīs-ˌvil\. City, Okaloosa co., NW Florida, 38 mi. (61 km.) ENE of Pensacola; pop. (1990c) 10,507; Okaloosa-Walton Community Coll. (1963).

Ni·che·li·no \ˌnē-ke-ˈlē-nō\. Commune, Torino prov., Piedmont, NW Italy, S of Turin; pop. (1989c) 45,660.

Nich·o·las \ˈni-kə-ləs\. Name of counties in two states of the U.S. See tables at KENTUCKY and WEST VIRGINIA.

Nicholas Channel. Channel in the W West Indies, N of W Cuba and S of Cay Sal Bank.

Nicholas II Land. See SEVERNAYA ZEMLYA.

Nich·o·las·ville \ˈni-kə-ləs-ˌvil\. City, ⊗ of Jessamine co., E cen. Kentucky, 12 mi. (19 km.) SSW of Lexington; pop. (1990c) 13,603.

Nich·ols Hills \ˈni-kəlz\. City, Oklahoma co., cen. Oklahoma, an enclave of Oklahoma City; pop. (1990c) 4020.

Nicholson Viaduct. See TUNKHANNOCK.

Nick·a·jack Dam \ˈni-kə-ˌjak\. See table at TENNESSEE VALLEY AUTHORITY.

Nick·el Cent·re \ˈni-kəl-ˈsen-tər\. Town, Sudbury munic. region, SE Ontario, Canada; pop. (1991c) 12,332.

Nick·e·rie \ˈni-kə-rē, ni-ˈkar-ē-ə\. **1.** River, NW Suriname; flows NNW into Atlantic Ocean near border of Guyana; ab. 200 mi. (320 km.) long.

2. Coastal town, Suriname. See NIEUW NICKERIE.

Nicobar, Kar. See CAR NICOBAR.

Nic·o·bar Islands \ˈni-kə-ˌbär\ *or* **Nic·o·bars** \-ˌbärz\. Island group, India, in Bay of Bengal, NW of Sumatra, forming S part of Andaman and Nicobar Is. terr.; 740 sq. mi. (1917 sq. km.); pop. (1981c) 30,454. Comprises three groups of islands; chief islands: Great Nicobar, Camorta, Nancowry, Car Nicobar, Teressa, and Little Nicobar. Occupied by British 1869 and used as penal colony; occupied by Japanese in WWII 1942–45.

Ni·co·lás Ro·me·ro \ˌnē-kō-ˈläs-rō-ˈmā-rō\. Municipality, México state, Mexico, 18 mi. (29 km.) NW of Mexico City.

Ni·co·let \ˌnē-kō-ˈlā\. Town, S Quebec, Canada, on S shore of Lake St. Peter 10 mi. (16 km.) S of Trois-Rivières; pop. (1991c) 4789; cathedral.

Ni·co·let–Ya·mas·ka \ˌnē-kō-ˈlā-ˌyä-ˈmäs-kä\. County, Quebec, Canada. See table at QUEBEC.

Nic·ol·let \ˈni-kə-ˌlet\. County in S Minnesota. See table at MINNESOTA.

Nic·olls Town \ˈni-kəlz\. Town, N coast of Andros I., Bahamas.

Ni·co·ma Park \nə-ˈkō-mə\. City, Oklahoma co., cen. Oklahoma, on E side of Oklahoma City; pop. (1990c) 2353.

Nicomedia. See İZMİT.

Ni·cop·o·lis \nə-ˈkä-pə-lis, nī-\. **1.** Town, Bulgaria. See NIKOPOL 1.

2. City in ancient Epirus, NW Greece; its ruins are ab. 3 mi. (5 km.) N of Preveza on the peninsula bet. the Ionian Sea and the Amvrakikós Kólpos. Ruins include walls, basilica, Roman theater, aqueduct. Founded 31 B.C. by Octavian (later Emperor Augustus) to commemorate his victory at Actium; became ✻ of Epirus and Acarnania; famous for its buildings and games (Actian Games); destroyed in 4th cent. A.D., but rebuilt; finally destroyed by Bulgarians 11th cent. See PREVEZA.

Nic·o·sia \ˌni-kə-ˈsē-ə, *Gk* ˌnē-kō-ˈsē-ä\. **1.** *or* **Lef·ko·sia** *also* **Lev·ko·sia** \ˌlef-kō-ˈsē-ə\. City, ✻ of Cyprus, W of Famagusta (its port) in cen. part of island; met. area pop. (1989e) 168,800; archiepiscopal see; textiles, flour, clothing, footwear, beverages; 14th cent. cathedral (now a mosque);

founded before 7th cent. B.C.; ✻ of island from 10th cent. A.D.; fortified by Lusignan kings; sacked by Genoese (14th cent.) and Mamlūks (15th cent.); passed to Venetians 1489, to Turks 1571, to British 1878; UN buffer zone in N section of city has separated Greek and Turkish sectors since 1974.
2. Commune, Enna prov., cen. Sicily, Italy, 15 mi. (24 km.) NNE of the commune of Enna; pop. (1981p) 15,239; episcopal see; 14th cent. cathedral; ruins of medieval castle; taken by Allies July 1943 in WWII.

Ni·co·ya \nē-ˈkō-yä\. Town on Nicoya Penin., NW Costa Rica.

Nicoya, Gulf of. Inlet of Pacific Ocean on NW cen. coast of Costa Rica, E of Nicoya Penin.

Nicoya Peninsula. Peninsula extending SE from NW Costa Rica, bet. Gulf of Nicoya and the Pacific Ocean.

Nictheroy. See NITERÓI.

Ni·da \ˈnē-dä\. River, S Poland, NE of Kraków; a tributary of the Vistula flowing E and S; 111 mi. (179 km.) long.

Nidaros. See TRONDHEIM.

Nidwalden. See UNTERWALDEN.

Niederdonau. See LOWER AUSTRIA.

Nie·de·re Tau·ern \ˈnē-dər-ə-ˈtau̇-ərn\. Mountain range in S Austria bet. valleys of the Mur and Enns; highest point 9393 ft. (2863 m.); a range of the E Alps.

Niederösterreich. See LOWER AUSTRIA.

Niederrhein. See LOWER RHINE.

Niedersachsen. See LOWER SAXONY.

Niederschlesien. See SILESIA.

Niel \ˈnyel\. Commune, Antwerp prov., N Belgium, just S of the city of Antwerp; pop. (1991c) 7807.

Niemen. See NEMAN.

Nien·burg an der We·ser \ˈnēn-ˌbu̇rk-än-dər-ˈvā-zər\. City, Lower Saxony, Germany, on Weser River 28 mi. (45 km.) NW of Hannover; pop. (1980c) 29,884.

Nieśwież. See NESVIZH.

Nieuport. See NIEUWPOORT.

Nieuwe Maas \ˈnyü-wə-ˈmäs\. A right branch of the Merwede River after it unites with the Lek River in Netherlands; empties into North Sea at the Hoek van Holland; one of the mouths of the Meuse (Maas) River.

Nieuw Guinee. See NEW GUINEA.

Nieuwkerke. See NEUVE-ÉGLISE.

Nieuw Nick·e·rie \nyü-ˈni-kə-rē, ˌnyü-ni-ˈkar-ē-ə\. Coastal town, NW Suriname, on Nickerie River near its mouth 122 mi. (196 km.) W of Paramaribo; pop. (1980c) 7700.

Nieuw·poort *or* **Nieu·port** \ˈnyü-ˌpōrt\. Commune, West Flanders prov., NW Belgium, on the Yser 10 mi. (16 km.) SW of Oostende; pop. (1991c) 9572; medieval town, fortified 12th cent. as a new port for Ieper (Ypres); scene of several battles or sieges in various European wars since 14th cent., esp. in 1600 when Dutch defeated Spaniards; a center of fighting throughout WWI, region intentionally flooded 1914 to halt German advance.

Nieuw·veld \ˈnyü-ˌfelt\. Mountain range, Western Cape prov., extending into Northern Cape prov., Rep. of South Africa; highest point 6276 ft. (1913 m.).

Nièvre \ˈnyevrᵉ\. Department of cen. France. See table at FRANCE.

Niewenstat. See NEUSTADT AN DER WEINSTRASSE.

Niğ·de \nē-ˈdā\. **1.** Province of Turkey in Asia. See table at TURKEY.
2. Town, its ✻, on railroad line 75 mi. (121 km.) NNW of Adana; pop. (1990p) 54,822; several medieval buildings, esp. mosques; important town of Seljuq sultanate of Rum 11th–14th cents.; came under Ottomans mid-15th cent.

Ni·gel \ˈnī-jəl\. Town, Gauteng prov., Rep. of South Africa, SE of Johannesburg.

Ni·ger \ˈnī-jər\. **1.** Republic, W Africa, bounded on N by Algeria and Libya, on E by Chad, on S by Nigeria, on SW by Benin and Burkina Faso, and on W by Mali; 459,073 sq. mi. (1,188,999 sq. km.); pop. (1993e) 8,516,000; ✻ Niamey.

Physical features: The republic is landlocked, and is characterized by savanna in S and desert in cen. and N; traversed in SW by Niger River; Aïr (*q.v.*), a mountainous region, is located in the N cen. part of the country.

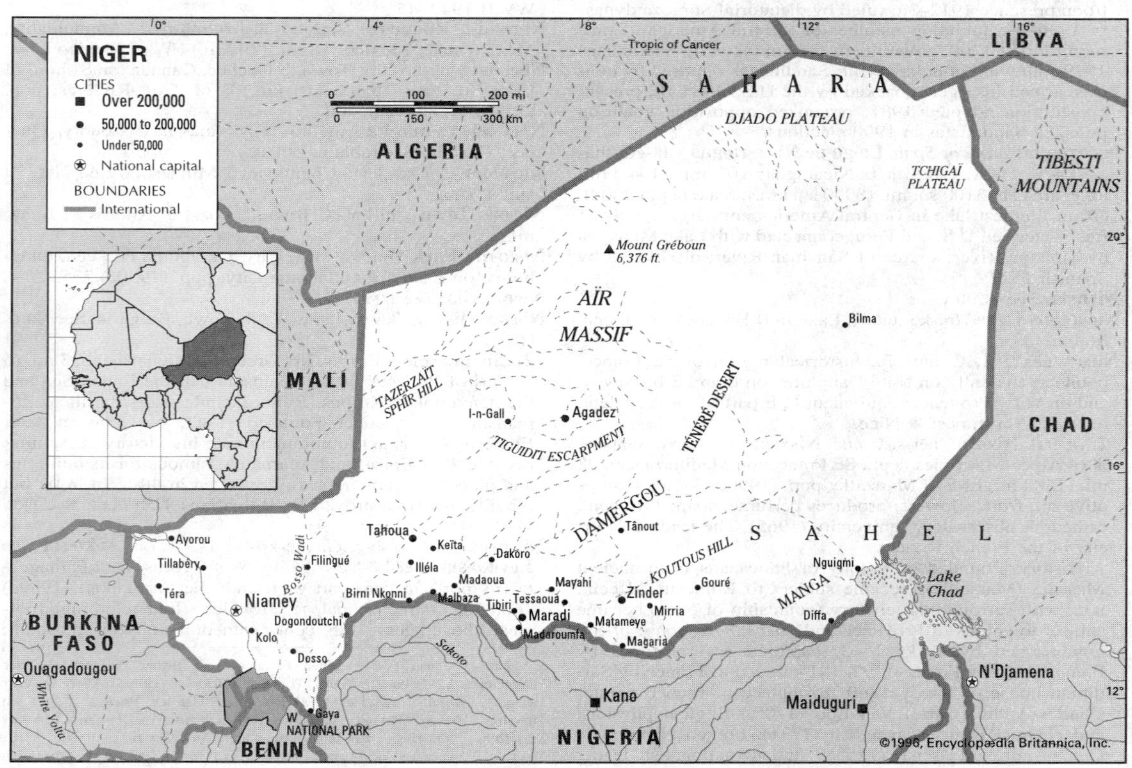

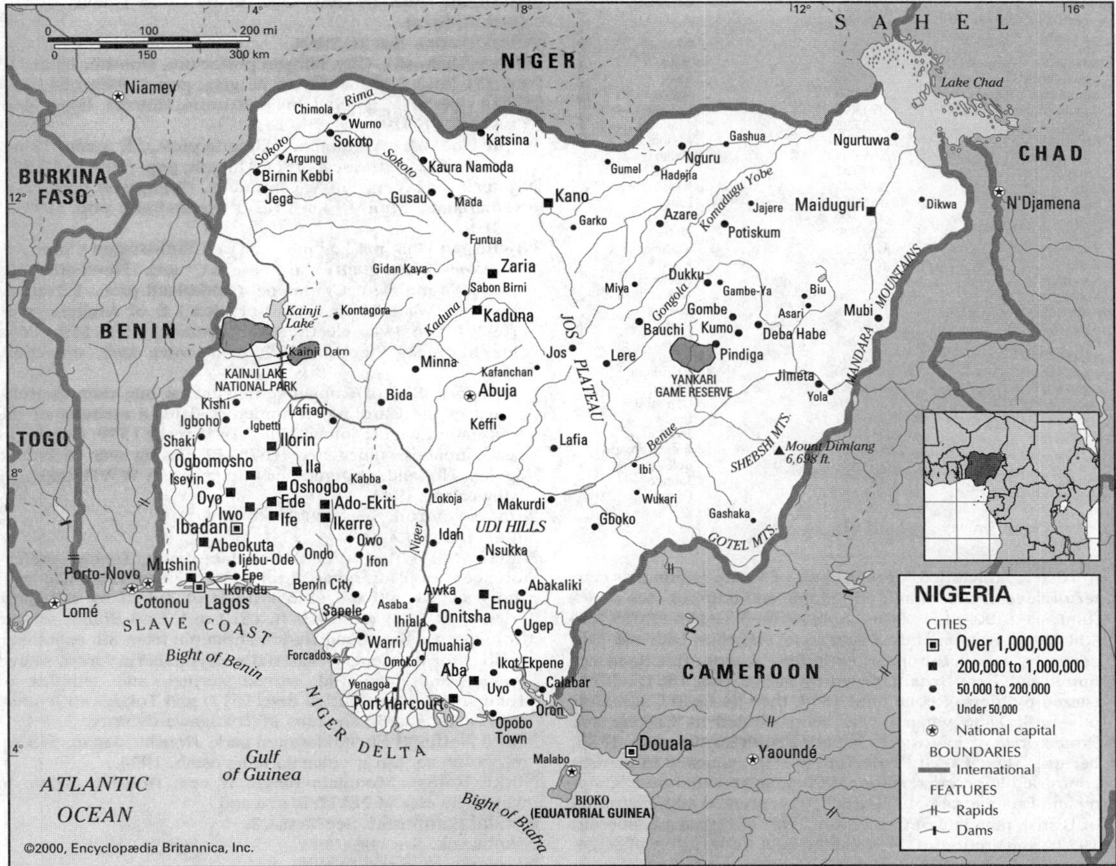

Chief products: Peanuts, cotton, rice; livestock; uranium.

Chief towns: Niamey, Zinder, Maradi.

History: Evidence of Neolithic inhabitants; area subject to several kingdoms over time incl. Kanem, Songhai, and Bornu (*qq.v.*); first explored by Europeans in late 18th cent.; became part of French sphere of influence in latter part of 19th cent.; formally constituted as part of French West Africa 1904; S boundary demarcated by Anglo-French accords of 1899 and 1904; placed under military jurisdiction until it became a colony within French West Africa 1922; became an overseas territory of France 1946; became an autonomous republic within the French Community 1958; achieved independence 1960; military coup 1974; present constitution 1992; first multiparty elections 1993.

2. River, W Africa; rises in Guinea near Sierra Leone border, flows in a great curve in W Africa, first NE then E and finally SE across border into Nigeria, continues S into Gulf of Guinea; 2600 mi. (4183 km.) long; known by many native names, esp. **Jol·i·ba** \ˈjäl-ə-bə\ and **Kwor·ra** \ˈkwȯr-ə, ˈkwär-\; estimated area of basin 584,000 sq. mi. (1,513,000 sq. km.). Above Tombouctou, Mali, passes through swampy, treeless region with many lakes; its middle course navigable for ab. 1000 mi. (1600 km.) above Ansongo and in Nigeria but rapids and bars prevent continuous navigation; in Nigeria receives from the E its only large tributary, the Benue (*q.v.*); has very extensive delta (14,000 sq. mi. or 36,000 sq. km.) with unhealthy climate; principal mouths are the Bonny, Brass, New Calabar, Forcados (now the main channel), and Nun; historically of importance in shipping palm oil, hence the name **Oil Rivers** for its delta region; dammed in various places (such as Kainji Dam, Nigeria) for power production. First explored by Scottish explorer Mungo Park 1796–97 and 1805–06.

3. State of W cen. Nigeria. See table at NIGERIA.

Ni·ge·ria \nī-ˈjir-ē-ə\ *or officially* **Federal Republic of Nigeria.** Republic, W Africa, bounded on NW and N by Niger, on NE by Lake Chad, on E by Cameroon, on S by the Gulf of Guinea, and on W by Benin; 356,669 sq. mi. (923,773 sq. km.); pop. (1991c) 88,514,501 (most populous country in Africa); ✻ Abuja.

Physical features: Coastal plain from 10 to 60 mi. (16 to 97 km.) wide is characterized by mangrove swamps; in cen. is Jos Plateau (with max. elev. over 6000 ft. or 1800 m.) and in E is mountain range; extreme N is semidesert; chief rivers: Niger, Benue, Kaduna.

Chief product: Oil.

Other products: Cacao, groundnuts, yams, cassava, rice, corn, millet, food products, cocoa, cotton, rubber, timber, tobacco; livestock; gas, tin, coal, columbite, limestone, lead, zinc; automobile assembly.

Chief cities: Lagos, Ibadan, Ogbomosho, Kano, Oshogbo, Ilorin.

Political divisions: Divided into the Federal Capital Territory (Abuja) and the following 30 states (for pronunciation of their names, see their individual entries):

NAME	POP. (1991c)	CAPITAL
Abia	2,297,978	Umuahia
Adamawa	2,124,049	Yola
Akwa Ibom	2,359,736	Uyo
Anambra	2,767,903	Awka
Bauchi	4,294,413	Bauchi
Benue	2,780,398	Makurdi
Borno	2,596,589	Maiduguri
Cross River	1,865,604	Calabar
Delta	2,570,181	Asaba
Edo	2,159,848	Benin City
Enugu	3,161,295	Enugu
Imo	2,485,499	Owerri
Jigawa	2,829,929	Dutse
Kaduna	3,969,252	Kaduna
Kano	5,632,040	Kano
Katsina	3,878,344	Katsina
Kebbi	2,062,226	Birnin Kebbi
Kogi	2,099,046	Lokoja
Kwara	1,566,469	Ilorin
Lagos	5,685,781	Ikeja
Niger	2,482,367	Minna
Ogun	2,338,570	Abeokuta
Ondo	3,884,485	Akure
Osun	2,203,016	Oshogbo
Oyo	3,488,789	Ibadan
Plateau	3,283,704	Jos
Rivers	3,983,857	Port Harcourt
Sokoto	4,392,391	Sokoto
Taraba	1,480,590	Jalingo
Yobe	1,411,481	Damaturu
Federal Capital Territory (Abuja)	378,671	

History: Inhabited for thousands of years; region was center of several precolonial kingdoms and empires (see SONGHAI EMPIRE, BORNU, YORUBALAND, BENIN 3, HAUSA STATES, and SOKOTO 1). Region of the Niger (*q.v.*) visited in 18th and 19th cents. by many European explorers; Lagos, first land acquired by Great Britain, ceded by native king 1861; administered by Sierra Leone until 1874, then by Gold Coast Colony until 1886 when it was reconstituted as Colony and Protectorate of Lagos; **Oil Rivers Protectorate** estab. 1885; became **Niger Coast Protectorate** 1893; annexed to British-controlled Nigerian territory 1900; amalgamated into "Colony and Protectorate of Nigeria" 1914; granted administration of British mandate of Cameroons (part of German Kamerun) 1922; constitution of 1954 established **Federation of Nigeria,** which included part of the British mandate of Cameroons; achieved independence 1960; in 1961 plebiscite, N part of British mandate of Cameroons voted for union with Nigeria; became a republic 1963; military coups 1966, 1975, 1983, 1985 have resulted in military-run governments 1966–79 and beginning 1983; civil war bet. central government and Eastern Region (see BIAFRA) 1967–70; new constitution ratified 1978, effective under civilian government 1979–83; new constitution promulgated 1989; ✻ moved 1991 from Lagos to Abuja; national assembly elections 1992; presidential elections 1993, annulled by military regime; transitional government (to civilian rule) estab. 1993, then abolished by military regime which reassumed control and restored the 1978 constitution.

Night·in·gale \ˈnīt-ᵊn-ˌgāl, -iŋ-\. Most southerly island in Tristan da Cunha group in S Atlantic; 1 mi. (1.6 km.) long.

Ni·hoa \ni-ˈhō-ə\. Islet of Hawaii, one of the Leeward Is. in cen. Pacific Ocean, ab. 125 mi. (200 km.) NW of Niihau I.; 0.5 sq. mi. (1.3 sq. km.); included in a wildlife refuge.

Nihon. See JAPAN.

Ni·i·ga·ta \nē-ˈgä-tä\. **1.** Prefecture, Honshū, Japan. See table at JAPAN.
2. City and seaport, its ✻, on NW coast of Honshū, 160 mi. (257 km.) NNW of Tokyo at mouth of Shinano River; pop. (1990p) 486,087; leading port on Sea of Japan; chemicals, textiles, machinery; university (1949).

Nii·ha·ma \ˈnē-hä-mä\. City, Ehime prefecture, Shikoku, Japan; pop. (1990p) 129,151.

Ni·i·hau \ˈnē-ˌhau̇\. Island in NW Hawaii, W of Kauai I., from which it is separated by Kaulakahi Channel; 72 sq. mi. (187 sq. km.); with Kauai forms Kauai co.; partly a tableland 1300 ft. (400 m.) high, partly low coral formation; chief village Puuwai; privately owned since 1864.

Nii–shi·ma \ˈnē-shē-mä\. One of the seven islands of Izu-shichitō (*q.v.*).

Niitakayama. See YÜ SHAN.

Ni·it·su \ˈnēt-ˌsü\. City, Niigata prefecture, Honshū, Japan, 13 mi. (21 km.) S of the city of Niigata; pop. (1990p) 64,005.

Ni·i·za \ˈnē-zä\. City, Saitama prefecture, Honshū, Japan; pop. (1990p) 138,919.

Ní·jar \ˈnē-ˌhär\. Commune, Almería prov., SE Spain, 18 mi. (29 km.) ENE of the seaport of Almería; pop. (1991c) 12,554.

Nij·kerk \ˈnā-ˌkerk, ˈnī-\. Commune, Gelderland prov., cen. Netherlands, 5 mi. (8 km.) NE of Amersfoort; pop. (1981e) 24,101.

Nij·me·gen \ˈnā-ˌmā-kə, ˈnī-, -gən\ *or* **Nim·we·gen** \ˈnim-ˌvā-gən\ *or* **Ni·me·guen** \ˈnī-ˌmā-gən\; *anc.* **No·vi·om·a·gus** \ˌnō-vē-ˈä-mə-gəs\. Commune, Gelderland prov., E Netherlands, on Waal River 12 mi. (19 km.) S of Arnhem; pop. (1992e) 146,344; electrical equipment; 15th–16th cent. church of St. Stephen; 16th cent. town hall; university (1923).

History: Site of Roman settlement; at one time the residence of the Carolingian emperors; later a member of the Hanseatic League; joined Union of Utrecht 1579; a series of peace treaties signed here 1678–79 closing war of France against Holland; suffered heavy damage in WWII, taken by Allies Sept. 1944.

Nijni Novgorod. See NIZHNIY NOVGOROD.

Nikaria. See IKARIA.

Nik·kō \ˈnik-kō\. City and mountain resort, Tochigi prefecture, cen. Honshū, Japan, 7 mi. (11 km.) E of Lake Chuzenji (*q.v.*) and ab. 90 mi. (145 km.) N of Tokyo by rail; pop. (1990c) 20,128; alt. 2000 ft. (610 m.). Had Shinto temple from earliest times and Buddhist temple from 8th cent.; esp. famous for its scenery, waterfalls, cryptomeria forest, sacred bridge, and memorial carved shrines and temples of Tokugawa Ieyasu (buried here 1617) and Tokugawa Iemitsu (1651), 1st and 3d shoguns of Tokugawa dynasty.

Nikkō National Park. National park, Honshū, Japan; 543 sq. mi. (1406 sq. km.); volcanic area; estab. 1934.

Nikkō Range. Mountain range, W cen. Honshū, Japan, in which the city of Nikkō is situated.

Nikolainkaupunki. See VAASA 2.

Nikolaevsk. See PUGACHEV.

Nikolayev. See MYKOLAYIV.

Nikolayevsk. See PUGACHEV.

Ni·ko·la·yevsk–na–Amu·re \ˌnē-kə-ˈlä-yifsk-nə-ə-ˈmu̇r-ə\. Seaport town, E Khabarovsk Kray, E Russia in Asia, near mouth of the Amur 400 mi. (644 km.) NE of the city of Khabarovsk; pop. (1991e) 36,500; ship repairing, fishing; founded 1850.

Nikolsburg. See MIKULOV.

Ni·kol·sko·ye \ni-ˈkȯl-skə-yə\. See KOMANDORSKIYE OSTROVA.

Nikolsk–Ussuriiski *or* **Nikols'k–Ussuriyskiy.** See USSURIYSK.

Ni·ko·pol \ni-ˈkȯ-pōl\. *anc.* **Ni·cop·o·lis** \ni-ˈkä-pə-lis, nī-\. Commercial town, N Bulgaria, on Danube River 23 mi. (37 km.) NE of Pleven; pop. (1988e) 16,897; scene of many battles, esp. 1396 in which Christian forces of King Sigismund of Hungary, supported by French, English, and German forces, were defeated by Ottoman Turks under Sultan Bayezid I; taken by Russians 1877.

Ni·ko·pol' *or* **Ni·ko·pol** \ˈnē-kə-pəlʸ\. Town, S Dnepropetrovs'k subdivision, E cen. Ukraine, on right bank of the Dnieper 55 mi. (89 km.) SE of Krivoi Rog; pop. (1991e) 159,000; center of manganese-mining area; steel tubes, electric cranes, beer. From early times a strategic crossing point of the Dnieper, scene of many conflicts; founded in 1630s; in WWII held by Germans 1941–44.

Nik·sar \nik-ˈsär\; *anc.* **Neo·cae·sa·rea** \ˌnē-ō-ˌsē-zə-ˈrē-ə, -ˌse-\. Town, Tokat prov., N cen. Turkey in Asia, on Kelkit River 33 mi. (54 km.) NE of the town of Tokat. One of the principal cities of ancient Pontus.

Nik·šić \ˈnik-ˌshich\. Town, Montenegro, S Yugoslavia, ab. 27 mi. (43 km.) SE of Podgorica; pop. (1991p) 75,025; on N to S trade route; has Roman remains, incl. a bridge; held by Turks 15th–19th cents.

Ni·ku·ma·ro·ro \ˌnē-kü-mä-ˈrō-rō\; *formerly* **Gard·ner** \ˈgärd-nər\. One of the Phoenix Is. (*q.v.*), cen. Pacific Ocean, 4°40′S, 174°32′W; ab. 2 mi. (3.2 km.) long; coconuts.

Ni·ku·nau \ˈnē-kə-ˌnau̇\ *or* **Nu·ku·nau** \ˈnü-\ *also* **By·ron** \ˈbī-rən\. Island (atoll), SE Gilbert Is., Kiribati, SW Pacific Ocean; 8 mi. (13 km.) by 1.5 mi. (2 km.); has several villages; discovered by English navigator and explorer John Byron 1765.

Nile \ˈnīl\ *or Lat.* **Ni·lus** \ˈnī-ləs\; *Arab.* **Al–Bahr** \al-ˈbär\ *also* **Bahr en Nīl** \an-ˈnēl\. River in E and NE Africa; flows generally N from E Africa through Uganda, Sudan, and Egypt; the longest river in the world; ab. 4160 mi. (6693 km.) from its remotest headstream, the Luvironza, and 3473 mi. (5588 km.) from Lake Victoria, to the Mediterranean; basin drained estimated at more than 1.1 million sq. mi. (2.8 million sq. km.). Its headwaters (longest, Kagera, *q.v.*) drain uplands of N Tanzania, SW Kenya, and country NE of Congo Basin into Lake Victoria. Nile proper, **Vic·to·ria Nile** \vik-ˈtōr-ē-ə\ *or* **Som·er·set Nile** \ˈsə-mər-sət, -ˌset\, ab. 300 mi. (480 km.), leaves N Lake Victoria (alt. ab. 3720 ft. or 1130 m.) near Jinja (its flow controlled by the Owen Falls Dam), 30 mi. (48 km.) N of the Equator, flows N to and through Kyoga Lake, then NW over Kabalega Falls (118 ft. or 36 m.) into NE corner of Lake Albert (*q.v.*); leaves N end (alt. c. 2200 ft. or 670 m.) of Lake Albert and flows N through NW Uganda (**Al·bert Nile** \ˈal-bərt\); crosses into Sudan where it is called Bahr el Jebel in the swamp (sudd) region; at Lake No (9°29′N) joined by W tributary Bahr al-Ghazal, and takes name of **White Nile** (*or Arab.* **Bahr al–Ab·yad** \ˌbär-al-ˈab-yäd\); flows E to confluence, 1652 mi. (2658 km.) from Owen Falls Dam, with Sobat (from highlands of SW Ethiopia), then 520 mi. (837 km.) N through Sudan to Khartoum; here joined by **Blue Nile** (*or Arab.* **Bahr al–Az·raq** \ˌbär-al-ˈaz-ˌräk\), 850 mi. (1368 km.) long, which rises in the mountains of Ethiopia, flows into Lake Tana, then (as the **Ab·bai** *or* **Abai** *or* **Abay** \ä-ˈbī\) by a wide SE to NW bend enters Sudan and flows N to join White Nile at Khartoum; then combined stream flows 200 mi. (322 km.) to Atbara, where it is joined by the Atbara River, which rises near Lake Tana; then, without any tributaries to its mouth, in great southwest S-shaped bend crosses into Egypt ab. 3 mi. (5 km.) N of Wadi Halfa and flows N ab. 400 mi. (640 km.) to the Mediterranean; 12 mi. (19 km.) below Cairo enters delta (120 mi. or 193 km. wide), which in ancient times had seven branches but now has two principal mouths, each ab. 146 mi. (235 km.) long: Rosetta (on W) entering sea just E of Alexandria, and Damietta (on E) just W of Port Said. Generally navigable from sea to Kabalega Falls, except in low season along stretch of ab. 900 mi. (1400 km.) that contains its six so-called cataracts (actually rapids): the first just above Aswān (*q.v.*) 24°N, the only one in Egypt proper, where early Mediterranean civilization ended; the 2d (now under water) in N Sudan, just W of Wadi Halfa ab. 21°50′N, marking roughly the N limits of ancient Cush; the 3d in ancient Nubia ab. 47 mi. (76 km.) below Dongola 19°50′N (700 mi. or 1100 km. by river below Khartoum); the 4th in the great bend of the Nile just above Marawī ab. 18°36′N, obstructed by granite and basalt ridges, the most difficult of all to navigate; the 5th ab. 40 mi. (64 km.) below Berber at ab. 18°30′N; the 6th in the desert ab. 55 mi. (89 km.) below Khartoum 16°10′N. Three large dams: Aswān High Dam, Gebel Aulia (20 mi. or 32 km. S of Khartoum), and Makwar (near Sennar on Blue Nile). Extent bet. Aswān High Dam and ab. 20°40′N forms Lake Nasser; in Egypt lined with famous structures and ruins of ancient dynasties, incl. Luxor and Karnak (site of ancient Thebes), Memphis, Giza, Cairo, and Dendera (*qq.v.*); formation of Lake Nasser in 1960s caused the flooding of numerous other archaeological sites, incl. Philae and Abu Simbel (*qq.v.*). Its source a matter of mystery and legend for centuries, believed to be in "Mountains of the Moon" (probably Mt. Ruwenzori). Along its course notable discoveries have been made by European explorers: Spanish missionary Pedro Páez Xaramillo, who visited Lake Tana early 17th cent.; Scottish explorer James Bruce, who rediscovered source of Blue Nile and traced its course 1768–73; various Egyptian expeditions bet. 1820 and 1842 explored White Nile as far S as Gondokoro (ab. 5°N); English explorer John Hanning Speke, who first determined Lake Victoria (*q.v.*) as main reservoir of Nile 1858; Speke and British soldier J. A. Grant, who further explored the lake 1860–62 by reaching Nile outlet at Ripon Falls (now flooded due to construction of Owen Falls Dam); English explorer Sir Samuel Baker, who in two journeys 1861–62 and 1863–65 discovered Lake Albert and Kabalega Falls. Battle of the Nile fought at Abū Qīr Bay 1798, in which British fleet under Adm. Horatio Nelson defeated French fleet.

Niles \ˈnīlz\. **1.** Village, Cook co., NE Illinois, just N of Chicago; pop. (1990c) 28,284; residential.
2. City, Berrien co., SW Michigan, 48 mi. (79 km.) SW of Kalamazoo; pop. (1990c) 12,458; previously held by France, England, and Spain; became stagecoach stop in 1830s. Birthplace of writer Ring Lardner 1885.
3. City, Trumbull co., NE Ohio, on Mahoning River 8 mi. (13 km.) NNW of Youngstown; pop. (1990c) 21,128; birthplace 1843 of William McKinley, 25th president of the U.S.

Niles Center. See SKOKIE.

Nil·gi·ri \ˈnil-gə-rē\. **1.** Former Indian state, now part of Orissa state, India, near coast of Bay of Bengal; 263 sq. mi. (681 sq. km.).
2. Town, its ✻, 125 mi. (201 km.) SW of Calcutta.

Nilgiri Hills *or* **Nil·gi·ris** \ˈnil-gə-rēz\. Plateau, Tamil Nadu state, India; av. alt. 6500 ft. (1980 m.); highest point **Mt. Do·da Bet·ta** \ˈdō-də-ˈbe-tə\. Indigenous peoples include the Badaga.

Ni·ló·po·lis \nē-ˈlȯ-pu̇-lēs\. City, Rio de Janeiro state, SE Brazil, NW of the city of Rio de Janeiro; munic. pop. (1991p) 157,819.

Nil·sen Plateau \ˈnil-sən\; *formerly* **Thor·vald Nilsen Mountains** \ˈtȯr-vald\. Mountain group, Queen Maud Mts., Ross Dependency, Antarctica, 86°20′S, 158°W; highest peaks over 13,000 ft. (4000 m.); discovered by Norwegian explorer Roald Amundsen 1911.

Nilus. See NILE.

Ni·mach \ˈnē-məch\. Town, Madhya Pradesh state, W cen. India; pop. (1991p) 81,397.

Nim·ba, Mount \ˈnim-bə\. Mountain, W Ivory Coast, on Guinea border; 6069 ft. (1850 m.); highest peak in Ivory Coast.

Nimburg. See NYMBURK.

Nimeguen. See NIJMEGEN.

Nîmes *or older* **Nismes** \ˈnēm\; *anc.* **Ne·mau·sus** \ni-ˈmȯ-səs\. City, ✻ of Gard dept., S France, 64 mi. (103 km.) NW of Marseille; pop. (1990c) 133,607; textiles, brandy, footwear; trades in wine and grain; 11th cent. cathedral (on site of former temple of Apollo); noted esp. for its ancient Roman buildings and monuments, among which are a Corinthian temple (Maison Carrée) restored 1789 and converted into a museum 1823, a large amphitheater (Les Arènes) used as a fortress by Visigoths, remains of an ancient tower (Tour Magne), and, nearby, ruins of a major aqueduct (Pont du Gard). Roman colony founded by Emperor Augustus on site of Gallic settlement; held by Romans for five centuries and one of the principal cities of Roman Gaul; sacked by Vandals and Visigoths 5th cent.; occupied by Saracens 8th cent.; passed to French crown 13th cent.; Protestant stronghold in 16th cent. Birthplace of writer Alphonse Daudet 1840.

Nimfaíon, Ákra. See NYMPHAION, CAPE.

Nim·rud \ˈnim-ˌrüd\; *bib.* **Ca·lah** \ˈkā-lə\ *also* **Kah·lu** \ˈkä-ˌlü\. Ancient city, a ✻ of Assyria, on E bank of Tigris River ab. 20 mi. (32 km.) SSE of modern Mosul, Iraq. Shalmaneser I made it his ✻ 13th cent. B.C.; under Ashurnasirpal II (883–859 B.C.) replaced Nineveh as ✻ and remained royal residence for 150 years. Archaeological excavations

19th–20th cents. uncovered ruins of several buildings, yielding, among other artifacts, ivory carvings from first millennium B.C.

Ni·mu·le \ˈnē-mü-ˌlā\. Town, S Sudan, on border with Uganda, ab. 90 mi. (145 km.) SSE of Juba.

Nimwegen. See NIJMEGEN.

Nine Point Mesa. Elevation, cen. Brewster co., W Texas; 5551 ft. (1692 m.).

Ninety East Ridge. Ridge, cen. Indian Ocean floor, extending approx. from SW of Andaman Is. to NE of Amsterdam I. in a general N to S direction at approx. 90°E.

Ninety Mile Beach. Straight stretch of flat coastal land, Gippsland, SE Victoria, SE Australia.

Nin·e·veh \ˈni-nə-və\; *anc.* **Ni·nus** \ˈnī-nəs\. Ancient city, a ✻ of Assyria; its ruins on the Tigris River, orig. covered by the mound Kuyunjik opp. Mosul, N Iraq. One of the greatest cities of antiquity; excavations, begun by Sir Austen Henry Layard 1845, have revealed palaces, a library, many other buildings, city walls, and numerous gates. One of the oldest cities of ancient Assyria; greatest development took place under Kings Sennacherib and Ashurbanipal (7th cent. B.C.); captured and destroyed by Nabopolassar of Babylonia and his allies (Scythians and Medes) 612 B.C.

Nin·fas, Point \ˈnim-ˌfäs\. Cape on NE coast of Chubut prov., S Argentina, at S entrance to New Gulf.

Ning·'an *or W.-G.* **Ning–an** \ˈniŋ-ˈän\; *formerly* **Ning·u·ta** \ˈniŋ-ˈü-ˈtä\. Town, Heilongjiang prov., NE China, 150 mi. (241 km.) ENE of Jilin (city).

Ning·bo *or W.-G.* **Ning–po** \ˈniŋ-ˈbō\; *formerly* **Ning·hsien** \ˈniŋ-ˈshyen\. City, NE Zhejiang prov., E China, ab. 90 mi. (145 km.) ESE of Hangzhou on S side of Hangzhou Bay and on small stream ab. 13 mi. (21 km.) from its mouth; pop. (1990c) 552,540; textiles, canned foods; ships cotton and fish. Area inhabited for thousands of years; present site occupied since c. 8th cent. A.D.; site of Portuguese trading station in 16th cent.; made a treaty port by Treaty of Nanking 1842; designated "open" city 1984 to stimulate foreign investment.

Ning·sia *or* **Ning·hsia** \ˈniŋ-ˈshyä\. Former province, W Nei Monggol (Inner Mongolia), N China; bounded on N by Mongolia; 106,115 sq. mi. (274,838 sq. km.); constituted 1928; merged 1954 with Gansu; in 1956 most of its territory merged with Nei Monggol, the remainder being reconstituted 1958 as Ningxia Huizu (*q.v.*).

Ninguta. See NING'AN.

Ning·xia Hui·zu \ˈniŋ-ˈshyä-ˈhwē-ˈzü\ *or* **Ning·xia Hui** \ˈhwē\; *often shortened to* **Ningxia;** *W.-G.* **Ning·sia Hui·su** \ˈniŋ-ˈshyä-ˈhwē-ˈsü\ *or* **Ningsia Hui** \ˈhwē\; *shortened to* **Ningsia.** Autonomous region, N China; ✻ Yinchuan; Great Wall runs along part of its NE boundary; rice, wheat; livestock; formed 1958. See table at CHINA.

Ningyuan. See YINING.

Ni·ni·go Group \ˈnē-nē-ˌgō\. See NORTHWESTERN ISLANDS.

Ni·ni·ni Point \nē-ˈnē-nē\. Point on SE coast of Kauai I., Hawaii, just N of Nawiliwili Bay; airport nearby.

Ni·nove \nē-ˈnȯv\. Commune, East Flanders prov., NW cen. Belgium, on the Dender W of Brussels; pop. (1991c) 33,489.

Ninus. See NINEVEH.

Nio. See IOS 1.

Ni·o·brara \ˌnī-ə-ˈbrar-ə\. **1.** River, Wyoming and Nebraska; flows from Niobrara co., E Wyoming, E across N Nebraska and into Missouri River in N cen. Knox co., NE Nebraska; 431 mi. (694 km.) long.

2. County in E Wyoming. See table at WYOMING.

Nio·ko·lo–Ko·ba National Park \nyō-ˈkō-lō-ˈkō-bä\. National park, S Senegal; 3525 sq. mi. (9130 sq. km.); wildlife incl. lions; estab. 1954.

Ni·o·ro du Sa·hel \ˈnyōr-ō-dü-sä-ˈel\. Town, Mali, 200 mi. (322 km.) NW of Bamako and not far from border with Mauritania.

Niort \ˈnyȯr\. City, ✻ of Deux-Sèvres dept., W France, 83 mi. (134 km.) SE of Nantes; pop. (1990c) 58,660; market town; leather goods; 15th cent. Gothic-Renaissance church; keep of castle built 12th cent. by England's Henry II and Richard I; celebrated public garden and nursery gardens. Intermittently held by England until finally passing to France 1373; became Protestant stronghold in 16th cent. Wars of Religion.

Nip·a·win \ˈni-pə-ˌwin\. Town, Saskatchewan, Canada, 75 mi. (121 km.) ENE of Prince Albert; pop. (1991c) 5419.

Ni·pe Bay \ˈnē-pā\. Bay on N coast of E Cuba.

Niphon. See JAPAN.

Nip·i·gon, Lake \ˈni-pi-ˌgän\ *also* **Lake Nep·i·gon** \ˈne-\. Lake, Thunder Bay dist., Ontario, Canada, ab. 35 mi. (56 km.) N of Lake Superior; 1870 sq. mi. (4843 sq. km.); 72 mi. (116 km.) long; max. depth 540 ft. (165 m.); its outlet is **Nipigon River,** ab. 40 mi. (64 km.) long, flowing S to **Nipigon Bay** in Lake Superior. Has many wooded islands and steep shores; outdoor recreation.

Nipisiguit Bay *and* **Nipisiguit River.** See NEPISIGUIT BAY.

Nip·is·sing \ˈni-pə-ˌsiŋ\. District, Ontario, Canada. See table at ONTARIO.

Nipissing, Lake *also* **Lake Nep·is·sing** \ˈne-\. Lake, Nipissing dist., SE Ontario, Canada, NE of Georgian Bay; 350 sq. mi. (907 sq. km.); its outlet is French River, flowing W to Georgian Bay. Contains many islands; once considered as link in route of possible canal from Ottawa River to Georgian Bay. Part of route of early (17th–18th cent.) French explorers and traders to the West.

Nip·ple·top \ˈni-pəl-ˌtäp\. Peak in the Adirondack Mts., Essex co., NE New York; 4620 ft. (1408 m.).

Nippon. See JAPAN.

Nip·pur \ni-ˈpu̇r\. Ancient Sumerian and Babylonian city; its ruins lie in SE Iraq ab. 100 mi. (160 km.) SE of site of Babylon; was orig. on the Euphrates River whose course later changed. Dates to at least the 3d millennium B.C.; was center of worship of the important Sumerian god Enlil; excavations have revealed temples, a ziggurat, and thousands of clay tablets which are a primary source of modern knowledge of ancient Sumerian civilization; ruins also include later Parthian relics.

Ni·que·ro \nē-ˈkā-rō\. Municipality, E Cuba, on S shore of Golfo de Guacanayabo 37 mi. (60 km.) SW of Manzanillo; pop. (1981p) 37,934.

Niriz. **1.** Town, Iran. See NEYRĪZ.

2. Lake, Iran. See BAKHTIGĀN.

Niš *or* **Nish** \ˈnēsh\; *anc.* **Na·is·sus** *or* **Na·ïs·sus** \nā-ˈi-səs\ *or* **Nis·sa** \ˈni-sə\. City, Serbia, E Yugoslavia, on Nišava River, ab. 125 mi. (200 km.) SE of Belgrade; pop. (1991p) 247,898; railroad junction and commercial center; textiles, electronic equipment, tobacco products; railroad workshops; university (1965); birthplace of Roman Emperor Constantine the Great. Held at various periods by Bulgarians, Hungarians, and Turks (for ab. 300 years); passed to Serbia 1878 and was ✻ of Serbia until 1901; taken by Germans 1915 and Apr. 1941; taken by U.S.S.R. 1944.

Ni·saea \nī-ˈsē-ə\. Plain, ancient Media, just SW of Caspian Sea; famous for its (*Nisaean*) breed of large fine horses used by Persians c. 5th cent. B.C.

Ni·ša·va *or* **Ni·sha·va** \ˈnē-shä-ˌvä\. River, W Bulgaria and E Yugoslavia; flows out of Bulgaria NW into Morava River 8 mi. (13 km.) W of Niš; total length 135 mi. (217 km.), of which 93 mi. (150 km.) is in Yugoslavia.

Ni·sce·mi \nē-ˈshā-mē, -ˈshe-\. Commune, Caltanissetta prov., cen. Sicily, Italy, 30 mi. (48 km.) SE of the commune of Caltanissetta; pop. (1989c) 26,973.

Nish. See NIŠ.

Nishapur. See NEYSHĀBŪR.

Nishava. See NIŠAVA.

Ni·shi·no·mi·ya \ˌnē-shē-ˈnō-mē-ˌyä\. City, Hyōgo prefecture, W Honshū, Japan, ab. 11 mi. (18 km.) E of Kōbe on N shore of Ōsaka Bay; pop. (1990p) 426,919; chemicals, rubber, cosmetics, machinery; sake breweries.

Nishi Notoro Misaki. See KRIL'ON, MYS.

Ni·shio \nē-ˈshē-ō, ˈnē-shē-ˌō\. City, Aichi prefecture, Honshū, Japan, 25 mi. (40 km.) SSE of Nagoya; pop. (1990p) 95,198.

Nish·na·bot·na \ˌnish-nə-ˈbät-nə\. River, W Iowa and Missouri; formed by confluence of **East Nishnabotna** (ab. 160 mi. or 260 km. long) and **West Nishnabotna** (ab. 160 mi. or 260 km. long), flows S across Missouri border and into Missouri River in Atchison co., NW Missouri; 40 mi. (64 km.) long.

Nisibin *or* **Nisibis.** See NUYSAYBİN.

Ni·si·da \ˈnē-zē-ˌdä\; *anc.* **Ne·sis** \ˈnē-səs\. Island in the Bay of Naples, S Italy, SE of Pozzuoli.

Ní·si·ros *also* **Ní·sy·ros** \ˈnē-sē-ˌrös\; *Ital.* **Ni·si·ro** \-ˌrō\. Island, Greece, one of the Dodecanese (*q.v.*), S of Kos; 14 sq. mi. (36 sq. km.).

Nismes. See NÎMES.

Nis·qual·ly \nə-ˈskwä-lē\. River, W cen. Washington; flows NW from **Nisqually Glacier** on S slope of Mt. Rainier, forming boundary bet. Pierce and Thurston cos., and empties into **Nisqually Reach,** inlet at S end of Puget Sound; ab. 70 mi. (110 km.) long.

Nissa. See NIŠ.

Nis·san \ni-ˈsän\. Main island of Green Is. group, W Pacific Ocean, E of SE New Ireland; belongs to Papua New Guinea. Taken by Allies in WWII 1944.

Nissan \ˈni-ˌsän\. River, S Sweden; flows SW into the Kattegat at Halmstad.

Nistru. See DNIESTER.

Nísyros. See NÍSIROS.

Ni·te·rói \ˌnē-tā-ˈrȯi\; *formerly* **Nic·the·roy** \ˌnē-tā-ˈrȯi\. City, ✻ of Rio de Janeiro state, SE Brazil, on SE shore of Guanabara Bay opp. the city of Rio de Janeiro, of which it is a suburb; munic. pop. (1991p) 416,123; textiles, matches, pharmaceuticals; shipbuilding and repairing, food processing; university (1960). Founded 1671; ✻ of state 1835–1975; made city 1836.

Nith \ˈnith\. River, SW Scotland; rises in Strathclyde region, flows SE into Solway Firth 10 mi. (16 km.) S of Dumfries; 79 mi. (127 km.) long.

Nitmiluk National Park. See KATHERINE GORGE NATIONAL PARK.

Ni·tra \ˈnyē-trä\ *or Hung.* **Nyi·tra** \ˈnyi-trö\ *or Ger.* **Neu·tra** \ˈnȯi-trə\. **1.** River, Slovakia; flows S into Váh River just above Komárno on the Hungarian border; ab. 110 mi. (180 km.) long.
2. Town, W Slovakia, on Nitra River; pop. (1991p) 89,888; in agricultural region; site of oldest church in the country, estab. c. 830.

Ni·tro \ˈnī-trō\. City, Kanawha and Putnam cos., SW West Virginia, on Kanawha River 13 mi. (23 km.) WNW of Charleston; pop. (1990c) 6851; developed around explosives plant erected by U.S. government 1918; incorp. 1932.

Nit·ta·ny Valley \ˈnit-ᵊn-ē\. Fertile valley in Centre and Clinton cos., cen. Pennsylvania; ab. 30 mi. (48 km.) long by 4 mi. (6 km.) wide.

Ni·u·a·fo·'ou *also* **Ni·u·a·foo** \nē-ˈü-ä-ˌfō-ō\. Island in extreme N part of Tonga, SW cen. Pacific Ocean, 400 mi. (644 km.) N of Tongatabu; 15°34′S, 175°40′W; area 6 sq. mi. (16 sq. km.); pop. (1986p) 763.

Ni·u·a·to·pu·ta·pu \nē-ˌü-ä-ˌtō-pü-ˈtä-pü\; *formerly* **Ni·u·a·to·bu·ta·bu** \-bü-ˈtä-bü\ *or* **Kep·pel's Island** \ˈke-pəlz\. Island in N part of Tonga, SW cen. Pacific Ocean, ab. 150 mi. (240 km.) N of Vava'u group; 5 sq. mi. (13 sq. km.); pop. (1980p) 1650.

Niuchwang. See YINGKOU 1.

Ni·ue \nē-ˈü-ā\ *also* **Sav·age Island** \ˈsa-vij\. Island in S cen. Pacific Ocean E of Tonga and 350 mi. (563 km.) SSE of Samoa, 19°02′S, 169°52′W; 100 sq. mi. (259 sq. km.); pop. (1991p) 2244; ✻ and chief port Alofi, on W coast; bananas, copra. A New Zealand dependency, with respect to defense and foreign affairs, having achieved internal self-government in 1974. Inhabited when discovered by English explorer Capt. James Cook 1774; annexed to New Zealand 1901.

Nive \ˈnēv\. River, Pyrénées-Atlantiques dept., SW France; flows W to the Adour along base of W Pyrenees; ab. 50 mi. (80 km.) long.

Ni·velles \nē-ˈvel\. Commune, Brabant prov., cen. Belgium; pop. (1991c) 23,217; manufactures machinery; convent dating from 7th cent.; 11th cent. Romanesque church of St. Gertrude.

Ni·ver·nais \ˌnē-vər-ˈnā\. Historical region of cen. France; bounded anciently on N, E, and SE by Burgundy, on S and SW by Bourbonnais, on W by Berry, and on NW by Orléanais; ✻ Nevers. Orig. part of Burgundian kingdom; became county c. 10th cent.; made duchy 1539; held by various families over the centuries; purchased from Gonzaga family by Cardinal Jules Mazarin 1659; French province until Revolution.

Nivernais, Ca·nal du \kə-ˈnál-dᵫ-\. Canal, Yonne and Nièvre depts., cen. France; connects Loire River at Decize with the Seine by way of the Seine's tributary, the Yonne, which it follows above Auxerre; 45 mi. (72 km.) long.

Ni·zam·a·bad \ni-ˈzä-mə-ˌbäd, nī-ˈza-mə-ˌbad\. Town, NW Andhra Pradesh, S cen. India, 100 mi. (161 km.) N of Hyderabad; pop. (1991p) 240,924.

Nizam's Dominions. See HYDERABAD 1.

Ni·zhe·go·rod \ˈni-zhə-gə-rət\ *or* **Nizhniy Novgorod** *or* **Nizh·ni Nov·go·rod** *or* **Nizhny Novgorod** \ˈnizh-nē-ˈnȯv-gə-rət\; *formerly* **Gor·ki** *or* **Gor'·kii** *or* **Gor'·kiy** *or* **Gor·ky** \ˈgȯr-kē\ *or* **Gor'·kov·ska·ya** \gȯr-ˈkȯf-skə-yə\. Oblast, cen. Russia in Europe; 28,880 sq. mi. (74,799 sq. km.); pop. (1992e) 3,704,000; ✻ Nizhniy Novgorod; crossed by the Volga; N part along the Vetluga covered with pine forests; S part fertile black-earth area.

Nizh·ne·kamsk \ˈnizh-nē-ˌkämsk\. City, Tatarstan, E Russia in Europe, on Kama River; pop. (1992e) 199,000.

Nizh·ne·u·dinsk \ˌnizh-nē-ů-ˈdinsk\. Town, W Irkutsk Oblast, S Russia in Asia, on the upper Chuna River and on the Trans-Siberian R.R.

Nizh·ne·var·tovsk \ˌnizh-nē-ˈvär-təfsk\. City, Tyumen' Oblast, W Russia in Asia, on the Ob'; pop. (1992e) 243,000.

Nizh·ni Nov·go·rod \ˈnizh-nē-ˈnȯv-gə-rət\. **1.** Old province of Russia. see NIZHNIY NOVGOROD.
2. Oblast, Russia. See NIZHEGOROD.
3. City, Russia. See NIZHNIY NOVGOROD 1.

Nizhni Tagil See NIZHNIY TAGIL.

Nizh·niy Nov·go·rod *or* **Nizh·ni Nov·go·rod** *or* **Nizh·ny Nov·go·rod** \ˈnizh-nē-ˈnȯv-gə-rət\ **1.** *also* **Nij·ni Novgorod.** Old province of Russia, somewhat larger than the modern oblast of Nizhegorod.
2. Oblast, Russia. See NIZHEGOROD.
3. *1932–90* **Gor·ki** *or* **Gor'·kii** *or* **Gor'·kiy** *or* **Gor·ky** \ˈgȯr-kē\. City, ✻ of Nizhegorod Oblast, cen. Russia in Europe, on S bank of the Volga at its confluence with the Oka 250 mi. (402 km.) E of Moscow; pop. (1993e) 1,433,000; one of Russia's major industrial cities; 16th cent. kremlin; 17th cent. church and palace; university (c. 1918). Founded 1221 by Prince Yuri Vsevolodovich; annexed to Moscow 1392; strategically important in Russian conquest of the Volga through mid-16th cent.; famous for annual fair 1817–1930; birthplace of writer Maksim Gorky 1868 for whom the city was renamed 1932–90; under Soviet regime was place of internal exile for Russian physicist and political dissident Andrei Sakharov 1980–84.

Nizhniy Ta·gil *or* **Nizhni Ta·gil** \tə-ˈgil\. City, W Sverdlovsk Oblast, W Russia in Asia, on E slopes of Ural Mts. 80 mi. (129 km.) N of Yekaterinburg; pop. (1992e) 437,000; metallurgy; foundries, chemical factories; city founded 1725.

Nizhnyaya Tunguska. See TUNGUSKA.

Nizhny Novgorod 1. Oblast, Russia. See NIZHEGOROD.
2. City, Russia. See NIZHNIY NOVGOROD.

Ni·zip \nə-ˈzēp\; *formerly* **Ni·zib** *or* **Ne·zib** \nə-ˈzēb\. Town, Gaziantep prov., S Turkey in Asia, ab. 22 mi. (35 km.) E of the town of Gaziantep; scene of battle June 24, 1839, in which Egyptian army under Ibrāhīm Pasha completely defeated Turkish (Ottoman) forces.

Niz·wa, Kuh–i– \ˈkü-hē-nēz-ˈwä\. Mountain in E Elburz Mts., N Iran, ab. 55 mi. (89 km.) SSE of Bābol; 13,051 ft. (3978 m.).

Nizza. See NICE 2.

Niz·za Mon·fer·ra·to \ˈnēt-sä-ˌmōn-fer-ˈrä-tō\. Commune, Asti prov., SE Piedmont, NW Italy, ab. 15 mi. (24 km.) SE of the commune of Asti; pop. (1981p) 10,254.

Njazidja. See GRANDE COMORE.

Njommelsaska. See HARSPRÅNGET.

Nkaw·kaw \əŋ-ˈkȯ-ˌkȯ\. Town, Eastern Region, Ghana, ab. 60 mi. (97 km.) ESE of Kumasi; pop. (1984c) 31,785.

Nka·yi \əŋ-ˈkä-yē\; *formerly* **Ja·cob** \ˈjā-kəb\. Town, S Rep. of the Congo, ab. 137 mi. (220 km.) W of Brazzaville; pop. (1992e) 42,465.

Nkong·sam·ba \əŋ-kȯŋ-ˈsäm-bä\. Town, W Cameroon, ab. 133 mi. (214 km.) NW of Yaoundé; pop. (1987e) 112,454.

Nmai River \nə-ˈmī\ *or* **Nmai Hka** \ˈkä\. River, Myanmar; flows S from SE corner of Tibet, China, to unite with the Mali and form the Irrawaddy; ab. 300 mi. (480 km.) long.

No. See THEBES 1.

No, Lake \ˈnō\. Lake in S cen. Sudan, where Bahr el Jebel and Bahr al-Ghazal join to form the White Nile (see NILE); max. area 40 sq. mi. (104 sq. km.).

No·ailles \nȯ-ˈī\. Commune, Corrèze dept., cen. France, S of Brive-la-Gaillarde; castle from which famous Noailles family took its name.

No·a·tak \nō-ˈä-tək\. **1.** River, NW Alaska; flows W bet. Brooks Range and Baird Mts., then S to Kotzebue Sound; ab. 400 mi. (640 km.) long. Its basin was proclaimed a national monument 1978; redesignated a national preserve 1980.
2. Unincorporated settlement, Alaska, on right bank of the Noatak near its mouth, ab. 55 mi. (89 km.) N of Kotzebue; pop. (1990c) 333.

No·be·o·ka \ˌnō-bē-ˈō-kä\. City, Miyazaki prefecture, E coast of Kyūshū, Japan; pop. (1990p) 130,615.

Nob Hill \ˈnäb\. Hill and surrounding neighborhood in SW San Francisco, California; in early days a fashionable residential section.

No·ble \ˈnō-bəl\. **1.** Name of counties in three states of the U.S. See tables at INDIANA, OHIO, OKLAHOMA.
2. Town, Cleveland co., cen. Oklahoma, on the Canadian River, SE of Oklahoma City; pop. (1990c) 4710.

No·bles \ˈnō-bəlz\. County in SW Minnesota. See table at MINNESOTA.

No·bles·ville \ˈnō-bəlz-ˌvil\. City, ⊗ of Hamilton co., cen. Indiana, 20 mi. (32 km.) NNE of Indianapolis; pop. (1990c) 17,655.

Noc, Big Bay de \ˌbā-də-ˈnäk\. N extension of Green Bay on S coast of Delta co., S Upper Penin. of Michigan, just E of **Little Bay de Noc.**

No·ce·ra In·fe·ri·o·re \nō-ˈchā-rä-in-ˌfā-rē-ˈō-rā\; *anc.* **Nu·ce·ria Al·fa·ter·na** \nü-ˈsir-ē-ə-ˌal-fə-ˈtər-nə\. Commune, Salerno prov., Campania, S Italy, 8 mi. (13 km.) NW of the seaport of Salerno; pop. (1989c) 48,262; lumber, textiles; castle ruins; commune destroyed 216 B.C. by Carthaginian Gen. Hannibal, rebuilt by Roman Emperor Augustus.

Nocera Su·pe·ri·o·re \sü-ˌpā-rē-ˈō-rā\. Commune, Salerno prov., Campania, S Italy, 5 mi. (8 km.) NW of the seaport of Salerno; pop. (1989c) 22,860; 4th cent. round church.

No·chix·tlán \ˌnō-chēs-ˈtlän\. Municipality, Oaxaca state, Mexico, 45 mi. (72 km.) NW of the city of Oaxaca.

No·ci \ˈnō-chē\. Commune, Bari prov., Puglia, SE Italy, 27 mi. (43 km.) SE of the seaport of Bari; pop. (1981p) 18,058.

No·co·na \nə-ˈkō-nə\. City, Montague co., N Texas, 42 mi. (68 km.) E of Wichita Falls; pop. (1990c) 2870.

No·da \ˈnō-dä\. City, Chiba prefecture, Honshū, Japan, 22 mi. (35 km.) N of Tokyo; pop. (1990p) 114,476.

Nod·a·way \ˈnä-də-ˌwā\. **1.** River, Iowa and Missouri; rises in Cass co., SW Iowa, and flows S into Missouri River in W Andrew co., NW Missouri; ab. 150 mi. (240 km.) long.
2. County in NW Missouri. See table at MISSOURI.

No·el Kempff Mer·ca·do National Park \nō-ˈel-ˈkempf-mer-ˈkä-t͟hō\. National park, Bolivia, near the Brazilian border; wildlife.

Noemfoor. See NUMFOOR.

Nœux–les–Mines \ˌnœ̄-lā-ˈmēn\. Commune, Pas-de-Calais dept., N France, 14 mi. (23 km.) NNW of Arras; on front lines in WWI.

No·fil·ia \nō-ˈfil-yə\ *also* **En Nofilia** \ˌen-\. Town, N Libya, near S cen. coast of the Gulf of Sidra.

No·gal·es \nō-ˈgä-ləs\. **1.** City, ⊗ of Santa Cruz co., S Arizona, on Mexican border 60 mi. (97 km.) S of Tucson and immediately adjacent to Mexican town of the same name; pop. (1990c) 19,489; regional trade; tourism. Settled c. 1880; incorp. 1893; scene of skirmishes bet. U.S. National Guard and forces of Mexican bandit Francisco (Pancho) Villa 1916.
2. Town, Sonora state, NW Mexico, on the U.S. frontier adjacent to Nogales, Arizona (see NOGALES 1); munic. pop. (1990p) 107,119; port of entry; trades in cattle and minerals.
3. Town, Veracruz state, E Mexico.

No·gal Peak \nō-ˈgal\. Mountain in the Sierra Blanca, S cen. New Mexico; 9983 ft. (3043 m.).

No·gat \ˈnȯ-ˌgät\. E branch of the lower Vistula, Poland; flows NE out of the main stream into Vilinski Zaliv; ab. 33 mi. (53 km.) long. Bet. WWI and WWII formed boundary bet. East Prussia and Free City of Danzig.

Nō·ga·ta \nō-ˈgä-tä\. Town, Fukuoka prefecture, N Kyūshū, Japan; pop. (1990p) 62,532.

No·gent–le–Ro·trou \nȯ-ˌzhäⁿl-rȯ-ˈtrü\. Town, W Eure-et-Loir dept., N cen. France; 17th cent. tomb of Maximilien de Béthune, duc de Sully.

Nogent–sur–Marne \-sœ̄r-ˈmärn\. Commune, Val-de-Marne dept., N France, ESE suburb of Paris on Marne River.

Nogent–sur–Seine \-ˈsān, -ˈsen\. Town, NW Aube dept., NE France; ab. 4 mi. (6 km.) SE is a farm on site of the Paraclete (*Fr.* Abbaye du Paraclet), the abbey which philosopher and theologian Peter Abélard founded for religious Héloïse c. 1123.

No·ginsk \nō-ˈginsk\; *formerly* **Bo·go·rodsk** \ˌbə-gə-ˈrȯtsk\. City, Moscow Oblast, W cen. Russia in Europe, on spur of main railroad line 35 mi. (56 km.) E of the city of Moscow; pop. (1992e) 122,000; textiles; city founded 16th cent.

No·go·yá \ˌnō-gō-ˈyä\. Town, Entre Ríos prov., E Argentina, 60 mi. (97 km.) SE of Paraná; pop. (1980p) 15,862.

Nó·grád \ˈnō-ˌgräd\. County of N Hungary. See table at HUNGARY.

No·gue·ra Pal·la·re·sa \nō-ˈgā-rä-ˌpäl-yä-ˈrā-sä\. River in NE Spain; flows out of the Pyrenees into Segre River 20 mi. (32 km.) NE of Lérida.

Noguera Ri·ba·gor·za·na \ˌrē-b̲ä-gȯr-ˈsä-nä\ *or* **Noguera Ri·va·go·ran·zo** \-ˌrē-b̲ä-gō-ˈrän-sō\. River in NE Spain; flows out of the Pyrenees into Segre River 15 mi. (24 km.) N of Lérida.

No·hi·li Point \nō-ˈhē-lē\. Point on W coast of Kauai I., Hawaii.

Noia *or* **Noya** \ˈnȯi-ä\. Seaport commune, La Coruña prov., NW Spain, 45 mi. (72 km.) SSW of the commune of La Coruña; pop. (1991c) 14,893.

Noire \ˈnwär\. French name of Black River, Indochina.

Noir·mou·tier, Île de \ˌēl-dən-ˌwär-mü-ˈtyā\. Island in Bay of Biscay off NW coast of Vendée dept., W France; ab. 12 mi. (19 km.) long and 1 to 4 mi. (2 to 6 km.) wide; belongs to Vendée dept.; site of monastery founded c. 680; chief town **Noirmoutier,** in NE part of the island.

Noi·sy–le–Grand \nwä-ˌzē-lə-ˈgräⁿ\. Commune, Seine-St.-Denis dept., N France, ab. 9 mi. (15 km.) E of Paris.

Noisy–le–Sec \nwä-ˌzēl-ˈsek\. Commune, Seine-St.-Denis dept., N France, ENE suburb of Paris.

No·ji·ma, Cape \nō-ˈjē-mä\. Cape, S tip of Chiba prefecture, SE Honshū, Japan, marking SE point of Sagami Sea.

No·ji·ri \ˈnō-jē-rē\. Lake on N border of Nagano prefecture, cen. Honshū, Japan; ab. 8.5 mi. (14 km.) in circumference.

No·kia \ˈnō-kē-ä\. Town, Häme prov., S Finland, W of Tampere; pop (1989c) 25,807.

No·ki·la·la·ki \ˌnō-kē-lə-ˈlä-kē\. Mountain, NW cen. Sulawesi, Indonesia, SE of Donggala; 10,860 ft. (3255 m.).

No·ko·mis \nə-ˈkō-məs\. City, Montgomery co., S cen. Illinois, 38 mi. (61 km.) SE of Springfield; pop. (1990c) 2534.

No·la \ˈnō-lä\. Commune, Napoli prov., Campania, S Italy, 16 mi. (26 km.) ENE of Naples; pop. (1991p) 32,573; in agricultural region; cathedral (remodeled in 14th cent.); seminary; Franciscan convent. Founded before 5th cent. B.C.; inhabited by Oscans, Etruscans, Samnites, and others before passing to

Rome 313 B.C.; site of battles bet. Romans and Carthaginian Gen. Hannibal c. 216 B.C.; place where Roman Emperor Augustus died 14 A.D.; sacked by Vandals 455. Birthplace of philosopher Giordano Bruno 1548.

No·lan \ˈnō-lən\. County in NW Texas. See table at TEXAS.

Nol·i·chucky \ˌnä-lə-ˈchə-kē\. River, North Carolina and Tennessee; rises in the Blue Ridge, W North Carolina, and flows NW into French Broad River in Tennessee; ab. 150 mi. (240 km.) long.

No Mans Land \ˈnō-ˌmanz-ˌland\. Small island in Atlantic Ocean in Dukes co., SE Massachusetts, SW of Martha's Vineyard.

Nom·bre de Dios \ˈnóm-brā-thā-ˈthē-ōs\. Spanish port and early settlement on the N coast of Panama, just NE of Portobelo; founded early 16th cent.; became important in 16th cent. as port of destination for cargo fleets from Spain; later declined; some archaeological work has been carried out.

Nome \ˈnōm\. **1.** Division in Alaska. See table at ALASKA. **2.** City on S side of Seward Penin., W Alaska, 14 mi. (23 km.) W of Cape Nome and ab. 100 mi. (160 km.) E of Bering Strait; pop. (1990c) 3500; tourism, fur trapping; intermittent gold-mining center. Founded c. 1898 as gold-mining camp and later a center of the great Alaskan gold rush 1899–1903.

Nome, Cape. Cape, W Alaska, on S side of Seward Penin., ab. 64°30′N, 165°W.

No·mo, Cape \ˈnō-mō\ *or Jp.* **Nomo Za·ki** \ˈzä-kē\. Cape, W Kyūshū, Japan, jutting into East China Sea SW of Nagasaki.

No·moi Islands \ˈnō-mȯi\. Atoll group in S Caroline Is. in W Pacific Ocean, SE of Chuuk; 5°27′N, 153°40′E.

No·nan·to·la \nō-ˈnän-tō-lä\. Commune, Modena prov., Emilia-Romagna, N Italy, 6 mi. (10 km.) NE of the commune of Modena; pop. (1981p) 10,339; 8th cent. abbey.

Nondaburi. See NONTHABURI.

Nong Khai \ˈnȯŋ-ˈkī\ *or* **Nong·ka·ya** \ˈnȯŋ-ˈkī—*sic*\ *also* **Mi Chai** \ˈmē-ˈchī\. Town, NE Thailand, on right bank of the Mekong; pop. (1991e) 23,284; since 1994 linked by bridge to Vientiane, Laos.

Nonni. See NEN 1.

No·no·u·ti \ˌnō-nō-ˈü-tē\. Island (atoll) in cen. part of Kiribati, just S of the Equator, W Pacific Ocean; 24 mi. (39 km.) long by 10 mi. (16 km.) wide; good anchorage.

Non·such Island \ˈnən-səch\. Small island in the Bermuda group, E of Castle Harbour.

Non·tha·bu·ri \ˌnən-bu̇-ˈrē—*sic*\ *also* **Non·da·bu·ri** \ˌnən-bu̇-ˈrē—*sic*\. Town, S Thailand, a N suburb of Bangkok on left bank of the lower Chao Phraya; pop. (1991e) 264,201.

Noon·mark \ˈnün-ˌmärk\. Peak in the Adirondack Mts., Essex co., NE New York; 3552 ft. (1083 m.).

Noord \ˈnōrt\. Name sometimes given to the Merwede River (*q.v.*) bet. Dordrecht and its confluence with the Lek, W Netherlands.

Noord–Brabant. See NORTH BRABANT.

Noord–Holland. See NORTH HOLLAND.

Noord·wijk \ˈnōrt-ˌvīk, -ˌvāk\. Commune, South Holland prov., SW Netherlands, on coast 12 mi. (19 km.) N of The Hague; pop. (1981e) 24,034.

Noord Zee Kanaal. See NORTH SEA CANAL.

Noot·ka Sound \ˈnu̇t-kə, ˈnüt-\. Inlet of Pacific Ocean in W Vancouver I., SW British Columbia, Canada, 49°33′N, 126°38′W; it forms a good harbor with three arms, one of which is a narrow channel separating **Nootka Island** (203 sq. mi. or 526 sq. km.) from Vancouver I. Visited by English explorer Capt. James Cook 1778; seizure of British ships by Spanish 1789 led to breach bet. England and Spain which was settled by Nootka Convention 1790.

Noph. See MEMPHIS 4.

No·ra \ˈnȯr-ə\. Ancient city, S Sardinia; settled first by Phoenicians, taken later by Romans; extensive ruins of both.

No·ran·da \nə-ˈran-də\. City, Témiscamingue co., SW Quebec, Canada; pop. (1986c) 8870; copper and gold mines in area; has developed in close association with the city of Rouyn.

Nor·cia \ˈnȯr-ˌchä\ *also* **Nur·sia** \ˈnu̇r-sē-ə\. Commune, Perugia prov., Umbria, cen. Italy, 41 mi. (66 km.) ESE of the commune of Perugia; pop. (1981p) 4756; cathedral; 6th cent. church; 14th cent. walls; birthplace of St. Benedict c. 480.

Nor·co \ˈnōr-kō\. City, Riverside co., SE California, 45 mi. (72 km.) W of Palm Springs; pop. (1990c) 23,302.

Nor·cross \ˈnȯr-ˌkrȯs\. City, Gwinnett co., N Georgia, 15 mi. (24 km.) NE of Atlanta; pop. (1990c) 5947.

Nord \ˈnȯr\. Department of N France. See table at FRANCE.

Nordalbingia. See DITHMARSCHEN.

Nor·den \ˈnȯrd-ᵊn\. Seaport city, NW Lower Saxony, Germany, on North Sea 16 mi. (27 km.) N of Emden, E of estuary of the Ems; pop. (1980c) 24,384; one of the oldest towns in Ostfriesland.

Nordenskjöld Sea. See LAPTEV SEA.

Nor·der·ney \ˌnȯr-dər-ˈnī\. Island, Lower Saxony, Germany, in cen. part of East Frisian Is. in the North Sea; 9 sq. mi. (23 sq. km.); pop. (1991e) 6215; resort.

Nord Fjord \ˈnōr-ˈfyōr\. Inlet of Norwegian Sea on SW cen. coast of Norway.

Nord·hau·sen \ˈnȯrt-ˌhau̇-zᵊn\. City, Thuringia, cen. Germany, at S foot of Harz Mts. 36 mi. (58 km.) NNW of Erfurt; pop. (1992e) 45,794; drilling equipment, tobacco; distilling; Gothic cathedral; 17th cent. town hall. First mentioned 927 A.D.; free imperial city 13th–19th cents.; to Prussia 1803; in Napoleonic kingdom of Westphalia 1807–13; to Prussia 1813.

Nord·horn \ˈnȯrt-ˌhȯrn\. Town, Lower Saxony, Germany, ab. 44 mi. (71 km.) NW of Münster; pop. (1992e) 49,869; textiles.

Nord·jyl·land \ˈnȯrd-ˌyᵫ-lȧn\. County, N Jutland, Denmark. See table at DENMARK.

Nordkapp. See NORTH CAPE 4.

Nord–Ki·vu \ˈnȯrd-ˈkē-vü\. Administrative region of Democratic Rep. of the Congo. See table at ZAIRE.

Nord–Kval·øy \ˈnȯrd-ˈkvȧ-ˌlȯi\ *or Eng.* **North Kval·oy** \ˈkvä-ˌlȯi\. Island in Arctic Ocean, Troms co., Norway NNE of Kvaløy I.; 127 sq. mi. (329 sq. km.).

Nord·kyn, Cape \ˈnür-ˌk̲ᵫn\. Cape on NE coast of Norway, 45 mi. (72 km.) E of North Cape (*q.v.*); northernmost point of European mainland, 70°55′N, 27°45′E.

Nord·land \ˈnōr-län\. County of W Norway. See table at NORWAY.

Nörd·ling·en \ˈnœrt-liŋ-ən\. Commune, Bavaria, Germany; pop. (1992e) 19,091; medieval town walls; annual site of Germany's oldest horse race. Founded c. 9th cent.; free imperial city 13th cent.; scene of two battles in Thirty Years' War: (1) in 1634, in which Swedish army was defeated by imperial forces; (2) in 1645, in which Germans were defeated by the French.

Nordost Landet. See NORTH EAST LAND.

Nord–Ost·see Ka·nal \ˌnȯrt-ˌȯst-ˌzā-kə-ˈnäl\ *or* **Kiel Canal** \ˈkēl\; *formerly* **Kai·ser Wil·helm Canal** \ˈkī-zər-ˈvil-ˌhelm\. Canal in Germany, extending from the Baltic Sea to the North Sea, NE to SW across Schleswig-Holstein; 61 mi. (98 km.) long, from city of Kiel past Rendsburg to Brunsbüttelkoog at the mouth of the Elbe; constructed 1887–95; enlarged 1914; surface width 338 ft. (103 m.), bottom width 144 ft. (44 m.), depth 37 ft. (11 m.); has no locks except those at either end, necessary because of tides; bombed in WWII; today one of world's busiest canals.

Nord–Pas–de–Ca·lais \ˌnȯr-ˌpȧd-kȧ-ˈlā\. Region of northernmost France. See table at FRANCE.

Nordrhein–Westfalen. See NORTH RHINE-WESTPHALIA.

Nord Slesvig. See SOUTH JUTLAND.

Nord·strand \ˈnȯrt-ˌshtränt\. One of the Halligen Is. in S part of North Frisian Is. off W coast of Schleswig-Holstein, N Germany; area 19 sq. mi. (49 sq. km.).

Nord–Trøn·de·lag \ˈnür-ˌtrœn-də-ˌläg\. County of cen. Norway. See table at NORWAY.

Nord·vik \ˈnȯrd-ˌvik\. **1.** Bay, a large inlet of Laptev Sea, N Russia in Asia; just E of mouth of Khatanga River, NW Sakha Rep.

2. Village on E bank of Khatanga River at its mouth.

Nore \ˈnōr\. River, SE Ireland; rises in N co. Tipperary, flows SE through co. Kilkenny into the Barrow River near its mouth; 70 mi. (113 km.) long.

Nore, The. Sandbank in center of the estuary of the Thames River in SE England, 3 mi. (5 km.) NE of Sheerness; at its E end is **Nore Light.** Generally taken as the dividing line bet. the river and its wide estuary; 48 mi. (77 km.) below London Bridge.

Nor·folk \ˈnȯr-fək, *U.S. also* -ˌfȯk, -fō(l)k\. **1.** Coastal county in E Massachusetts. See table at MASSACHUSETTS.

2. Town, Norfolk co., E Massachusetts, 21 mi. (34 km.) SW of Boston; pop. (1990c) 9270.

3. City, Madison co., NE Nebraska, 54 mi. (87 km.) NW of Fremont; pop. (1990c) 21,476; livestock; Northeast Community Coll. (1973).

4. *also* \ˈnȯ-fək\ Independent city, SE Virginia, on Elizabeth River just S of Hampton Roads; 50 sq. mi. (130 sq. km.); pop. (1990c) 261,229; with Newport News and Portsmouth comprises Port of Hampton Roads; exports coal, grain, tobacco, timber, vegetables; major shipbuilding center, produces automobiles; Old Dominion Univ. (1930), Norfolk State Univ. (1935), Virginia Wesleyan Coll. (1961); major military facilities.

History: Founded 1682; incorp. as borough 1736; during American Revolution, taken from Loyalists by Americans 1775, bombarded by British 1776, and destroyed by fires 1776; incorp. as city 1845; yellow-fever epidemic 1855; in Civil War evacuated by Federal troops 1861, but reoccupied 1862 until end of the war.

5. Former county, E England.

6. Administrative county, E England, incl. the former county; rivers Ouse, Bure, Yare, Waveney, Nene; wheat, barley, oats, sugar beets; livestock and poultry farming; tourism; main towns include Norwich, Great Yarmouth, King's Lynn, Thetford. See table at ENGLAND.

Norfolk Broads. See BROADS, THE.

Norfolk Island. Island in S Pacific Ocean, an external territory of Australia; midway bet. New Caledonia and N New Zealand, and 930 mi. (1496 km.) ENE of Sydney, Australia; 13 sq. mi. (34 sq. km.); pop. (1991c) 1912; highest point 1043 ft. (318 m.); tourism; collectible postage stamps. Discovered by English explorer Capt. James Cook 1774 and used as a British penal colony 1788–1814 and 1825–55; inhabitants of Pitcairn I. (*q.v.*) moved here 1856; made federal territory 1913; present government system dates to 1979.

Norge. See NORWAY.

Noric Alps. See table at ALPS.

Nor·i·cum \ˈnȯr-i-kəm\. Ancient kingdom and Roman province, W cen. Europe S of Danube River, comprising the modern Lower and Upper Austria, the greater part of Carinthia, Styria, and Salzburg, and a small part of Bavaria; to the N across the Danube was Germania, on the E Pannonia, on the S Pannonia and Italy, and on the W Raetia and Vindelicia. A mountainous country (E Alps) with rich iron mines worked by the Romans. The Celtic inhabitants were conquered by Emperor Augustus c. 15 B.C.

No·ri·ku·ra \ˈnō-rē-kü-ˌrä\. Mountain peak, Gifu prefecture, W cen. Honshū, Japan; 9918 ft. (3023 m.).

No·ril'sk *or* **No·rilsk** \nə-ˈrēlsk\. Town, Krasnoyarsk Kray, N Russia in Asia, ab. 50 mi. (80 km.) ESE of Dudinka; pop. (1992e) 165,000; mining center (copper, platinum, nickel).

Norische Alpen. See table at ALPS.

Nor·mal \ˈnȯr-məl\. **1.** Village, Madison co., N Alabama, 4 mi. (6 km.) N of Huntsville; Alabama Agricultural and Mechanical Univ. (1875).

2. Town, McLean co., cen. Illinois, 5 mi. (8 km.) N of Bloomington; pop. (1990c) 40,023; residential; dairy and livestock farms; Illinois State Univ. (1857).

Nor·man \ˈnȯr-mən\. **1.** County in NW Minnesota. See table at MINNESOTA.

2. City, ⊗ of Cleveland co., cen. Oklahoma, bordering Oklahoma City on the S; pop. (1990c) 80,071; center of farming region; oil wells; Univ. of Oklahoma (1890); settled 1889.

3. River, N Queensland, Australia; flows NW into Gulf of Carpentaria; 190 mi. (306 km.) long.

4. Small island, British Virgin Is., West Indies, S of Tortola I.

Norman, Cape. Cape, N tip of Newfoundland, Canada, at NE entrance to the Strait of Belle Isle.

Nor·man·by \ˈnȯr-mən-bē\. One of the D'Entrecasteaux Is., Papua New Guinea; off SE point of New Guinea I., 3 mi. (5 km.) SSE of Fergusson I.; ab. 45 mi. (70 km.) long and from 12 to 15 mi. (19 to 24 km.) wide; ab. 4000 sq. mi. (10,360 sq. km.); separated from East Cape of New Guinea by Goschen Strait; cen. mountain range (highest point 3600 ft. or 1097 m.); good harbor; produces copra.

Norman Coast. See MURMAN COAST.

Nor·man·dy \ˈnȯr-mən-dē\. **1.** City, St. Louis co., E Missouri, 4 mi. (6 km.) NW of the city of St. Louis; pop. (1990c) 4480.

2. *or Fr.* **Nor·man·die** \nȯr-mäⁿ-ˈdē\. Historical region of NW France; bounded anciently on W and N by English Channel, on NE by Picardy, on E by Île-de-France, on S by Maine, and on SW by Brittany; ✻ Rouen; watered by Seine, Orne, and Eure rivers; includes Cotentin Penin.

History: Evidence of Paleolithic inhabitants; Celtic inhabitants conquered by Romans c. 56 B.C., became part of prov. of Lugdunensis; part of kingdom of Neustria after Frankish conquest 5th cent. A.D.; invaded by Norsemen (whence its name) in middle of 9th cent.; region ceded to conquerors under Rollo, first duke of Normandy, by Charles III of France 911; united with English kingdom after Norman conquest of England 1066 by William, duke of Normandy; conquered by French under King Philip Augustus 1204; retaken by English 15th cent. until finally restored to France 1450, after which it became a province of France; province was divided after French Revolution into several departments; region was scene in WWII of Allied invasion of German-occupied France June 6, 1944.

Normandy Park. City, King co., W cen. Washington, 10 mi. (16 km.) S of Seattle; pop. (1990c) 6709.

Nor·man·ton \ˈnȯr-mən-tən\. **1.** Town, N Queensland, Australia, on Norman River 23 mi. (37 km.) from Gulf of Carpentaria.

2. Town, West Yorkshire, N England; pop. (1981p) 17,256.

Nor·man Wells \ˈnȯr-mən\. Unincorporated settlement, W mainland part of Northwest Territories, Canada, on right bank of the Mackenzie River, 50 mi. (81 km.) NW of Tulita; developed as distribution center for oil from nearby fields.

No·ro·ton \nȯ-ˈrōt-ᵊn\ *and* **Noroton Heights.** Subdivisions of town of Darien, Connecticut. See DARIEN.

Norr·bot·ten \ˈnȯr-ˌbȯt-ᵊn\. Province of N Sweden. See table at SWEDEN.

Nor·ridge \ˈnȯr-ij, ˈnär-\. Village, Cook co., NE Illinois, W suburb of Chicago; pop. (1990c) 14,459; lost pop. in 1970s and again in 1980s.

Nor·ridge·wock \ˈnȯr-ij-ˌwäk, ˈnär-\. Town, Somerset co., W Maine, on Kennebec River 13 mi. (21 km.) NW of Waterville; pop. (1990c) 3105; near site of an Abnaki Indian village, visited by French Jesuit missionaries 17th and 18th cents., destroyed by English 1724.

Nor·ris, Mount \ˈnȯr-əs, ˈnär-\. Peak, Yellowstone National Park, NW Wyoming; 9936 ft. (3029 m.).

Norris Lake; *formerly* **Clinch–Pow·ell Reservoir** \ˈklinch-ˈpau̇-əl\. Lake, N cen. Tennessee; formed by **Norris Dam,** one of the dams of the Tennessee Valley Authority (*q.v.*). See CLINCH 1.

Nor·ris·town \ˈnȯr-əs-ˌtau̇n, ˈnär-\. Borough, ⊗ of Montgomery co., SE Pennsylvania, on Schuylkill River 4 mi. (6 km.) E of Valley Forge and 17 mi. (27 km.) NW of Philadelphia; pop. (1990c) 30,749; machinery, rubber products, chemicals, plastics; founded 1704; incorp. 1812.

Norr·kö·ping \ˈnȯr-ˌshœ-piŋ\. Seaport, Östergötland prov., SE Sweden, SW of Stockholm, at mouth of a river (draining Lake Vättern) at head of a long inlet of **Norrköping Bay;**

pop. (1993e) 120,798; major industrial center, producing textiles, paper, and chemicals; Bronze Age rock carvings nearby; founded c. 1350; chartered 1384; burned by Russians 1719.

Norr·land \ˈnȯr-ˌländ\. N part of Sweden, comprising Gävleborg, Västernorrland, Jämtland, Västerbotten, and Norrbotten; land area 93,858 sq. mi. (243,092 sq. km.); pop. (1992e) 1,204,803; heavily forested.

Nor·te, Ca·bo \ˈkä-bü-ˈnȯr-tē\ *also* **Cabo Ra·so** \ˈrä-zü\. Cape, extending into Atlantic Ocean on coast of Amapá state, N Brazil, N of the mouth of the Amazon.

Nor·te de San·tan·der \ˈnȯr-ˌtā-thā-ˌsän-tän-ˈder\. Department of N Colombia. See table at COLOMBIA.

North \ˈnȯrth\. River, estuary of Hudson River bet. New York and New Jersey; flows into Upper New York Bay; crossed by bridge (George Washington, at 179th Street, New York City).

North, Cape. Cape at N tip of Cape Breton I., on S side of Cabot Strait at entrance to the Gulf of St. Lawrence, SE Canada.

North Ad·ams \ˈa-dəmz\. City, Berkshire co., NW Massachusetts; pop. (1990c) 16,797; paper products; North Adams State Coll. (1894).

North Africa. A term often used to include the countries of N Africa except for Egypt: Morocco, Algeria, Tunisia, and Libya; used esp. by Rome of its colonies (see AFRICA, ROMAN), and in modern times in WWII during the campaign 1942–43 in which the Allies defeated all German and Italian forces in Africa.

North Al·ba·nian Alps \al-ˈbā-nē-ən, -nyən, ȯl-\ *or Serbo-Croat.* **Pro·kle·ti·je** \prō-ˈkle-tē-ˌyā\ *or Albanian* **Bjesh·kët e Ne·mu·na** \ˈbyesh-kət-ā-nə-ˈmü-nə\. Mountain range, S Europe, running generally W to E in N Albania and S Yugoslavia (Montenegro); av. height 6500 to 8500 ft. (2000 to 2600 m.); highest point 8835 ft. or 2693 m. (in Albania).

North·al·ler·ton \nȯr-ˈtha-lər-tən\. Town, ⊗ of North Yorkshire, N England; pop. (1981c) 9556; scene of Battle of the Standard Aug. 22, 1138 in which English forces defeated Scottish supporters of Holy Roman Empress Matilda under King David I of Scotland, her uncle.

Nor·tham. 1. \ˈnȯr-thəm\. Town, SW Western Australia, Australia, on Avon River 47 mi. (76 km.) E of Perth; pop. (1981c) 6791.

2. \ˈnȯr-thəm\. Town, Devon, SW England, on the Torridge 47 mi. (76 km.) N of Plymouth; pop. (1981p) 8715.

North America. Continent in Western Hemisphere; 3d in size at 9,361,791 sq. mi. (24,247,039 sq. km.); generally considered to include island of Greenland in NE.

Boundaries: On N, Arctic Ocean (Beaufort Sea on NW); large bodies of water in N Canada: Viscount Melville Sound, Foxe Basin, Hudson Bay and Hudson Strait; on NE, Baffin Bay and Davis Strait; most northerly point (on mainland) tip of Boothia Penin. 70°30′N, most northerly point on islands Cape Morris Jesup, N Greenland, 83°38′N; many large islands in N, belonging to Canada: Baffin, Ellesmere, Victoria, Banks, Southampton, Parry Is. On E, North Atlantic Ocean (chief inlets: Gulf of St. Lawrence, Bay of Fundy, Chesapeake Bay); most easterly point (continental) SE coast of Labrador, Canada, ab. 55°42′W; islands: Newfoundland, Anticosti, Prince Edward, Cape Breton, Long, Bermuda Is. On SE, Gulf of Mexico and Caribbean Sea; for islands see WEST INDIES. On S, Pacific Ocean (chief inlets: Gulf of Panama, Gulf of California); most southerly point SE Panama 7°15′N. On W, North Pacific Ocean (chief subdivisions: Gulf of Alaska, Bering Sea); most westerly point (continental) Cape Prince of Wales, Alaska, 168°05′W; separated from Asia by Bering Strait; most important islands: Vancouver, Queen Charlotte Is., islands of SE Alaska, Aleutian Is., Nunivak, and St. Lawrence.

Topographic features: Greatest mountain ranges along Pacific coast (esp. Rocky Mts.) extending from Alaska into Mexico and Central America; Great Plains E of Rocky Mts. extending from Arctic Ocean to Gulf of Mexico; lowlands in center around Hudson Bay and in Mississippi Valley; highlands in E (Canadian Shield and Appalachian Mts.); low coastal plain along Atlantic; high ice-covered plateau in Greenland; highest point Mt. McKinley, Alaska, 20,320 ft. (6194 m.); lowest Badwater in Death Valley, California, 282 ft. (86 m.) below sea level.

Rivers: Yukon (Canada and Alaska), Mackenzie, Saskatchewan and Nelson (Canada), St. Lawrence and Columbia (Canada and U.S.), Mississippi-Missouri system, Colorado (in SW), Penobscot, Connecticut, Hudson, Delaware, Susquehanna, Potomac, James, Cape Fear, Savannah (Atlantic seaboard, U.S.), Apalachicola, Mobile, Pearl, Sabine, Brazos, Colorado (Texas), to Gulf of Mexico; San Joaquin and Sacramento (W coast), Rio Grande (U.S. and Mexico), Pánuco, Balsas, Grijalva (Mexico).

Lakes: Great Bear, Great Slave, Winnipeg (Canada); Great Lakes (Superior, Huron, Erie, Ontario—in Canada and U.S.) and Michigan (U.S.), Great Salt Lake (U.S.).

Political divisions: Canada, United States, Mexico, Central America (*q.v.*) adjoining South America in extreme S, and West Indies off SE coast enclosing Caribbean Sea. Central America, Mexico, and the West Indies are sometimes known as Middle America.

North·amp·ton \nȯr-ˈthamp-tən, nȯrth-ˈhamp-\. **1.** Name of counties in three states of the U.S. See tables at NORTH CAROLINA, PENNSYLVANIA, VIRGINIA.

2. City, ⊗ of Hampshire co., W Massachusetts, on Connecticut River 15 mi. (24 km.) N of Springfield; pop. (1990c) 29,289; optical instruments; Smith Coll. (1871), Clark School for the Deaf; city founded 1654; incorp. as city 1883; home of Calvin Coolidge, 30th president of the U.S.

3. Borough, Northampton co., E Pennsylvania, on Lehigh River 6 mi. (10 km.) N of Allentown; pop. (1990c) 8717.

4. Town, ⊗ of Northamptonshire, cen. England, on the Nene 60 mi. (97 km.) NNW of London; pop. (1981p) 145,421; footwear, leather, automobile parts, electronic components; site of an early Saxon settlement; became Norman stronghold; a meeting place of parliaments 12th–14th cents.; site of battle 1460 during Wars of the Roses in which Henry VI was defeated and captured by Yorkists; castle and walls razed under Charles II (17th cent.) as penalty for supporting the Parliamentarian side in the English Civil War.

North·amp·ton·shire \nȯr-ˈthamp-tən-ˌshir, nȯrth-ˈhamp-, -shər\ *or* **Northampton. 1.** Former county, cen. England.

2. Administrative county, cen. England, approx. equivalent to the former county; food processing; iron deposits; main towns include Northampton, Corby, Kettering, Wellingborough. See table at ENGLAND.

North Andaman. One of the Andaman Is. (*q.v.*), India, Bay of Bengal.

North An·do·ver \ˈan-ˌdō-vər\. Town, Essex co., NE Massachusetts, 10 mi. (16 km.) ENE of Lowell; pop. (1990c) 22,792; Merrimack Coll. (1947).

North An·na \ˈa-nə\. River, E cen. Virginia; flows SE to unite with South Anna River in N Hanover co. and form Pamunkey River; just above the junction battle occurred May 1864 in which the Union forces under Gen. Ulysses S. Grant failed to dislodge Gen. Robert E. Lee's Confederate forces who were covering Richmond to the S.

North Ar·ling·ton \ˈär-liŋ-tən\. Borough, Bergen co., NE New Jersey, on Passaic River 7 mi. (11 km.) W of Manhattan borough, New York City; pop. (1990c) 13,790.

North Atlantic Current *or* **North Atlantic Drift.** A warm ocean current in the Atlantic Ocean flowing NE toward NW Europe where it modifies the climate and mixes with cold polar water to produce good fishing grounds.

North Atlantic Ocean. See ATLANTIC OCEAN.

North Atlantic Treaty Organization *or abbr.* **NATO** \ˈnā-tō\.Military alliance, consisting of Belgium, Canada, Czech Republic, Denmark, France, Germany, Greece, Hungary, Iceland, Italy, Luxembourg, Netherlands, Norway, Poland, Portugal, Spain, Turkey, United Kingdom, and United States; headquarters Brussels, Belgium; purpose is to promote the

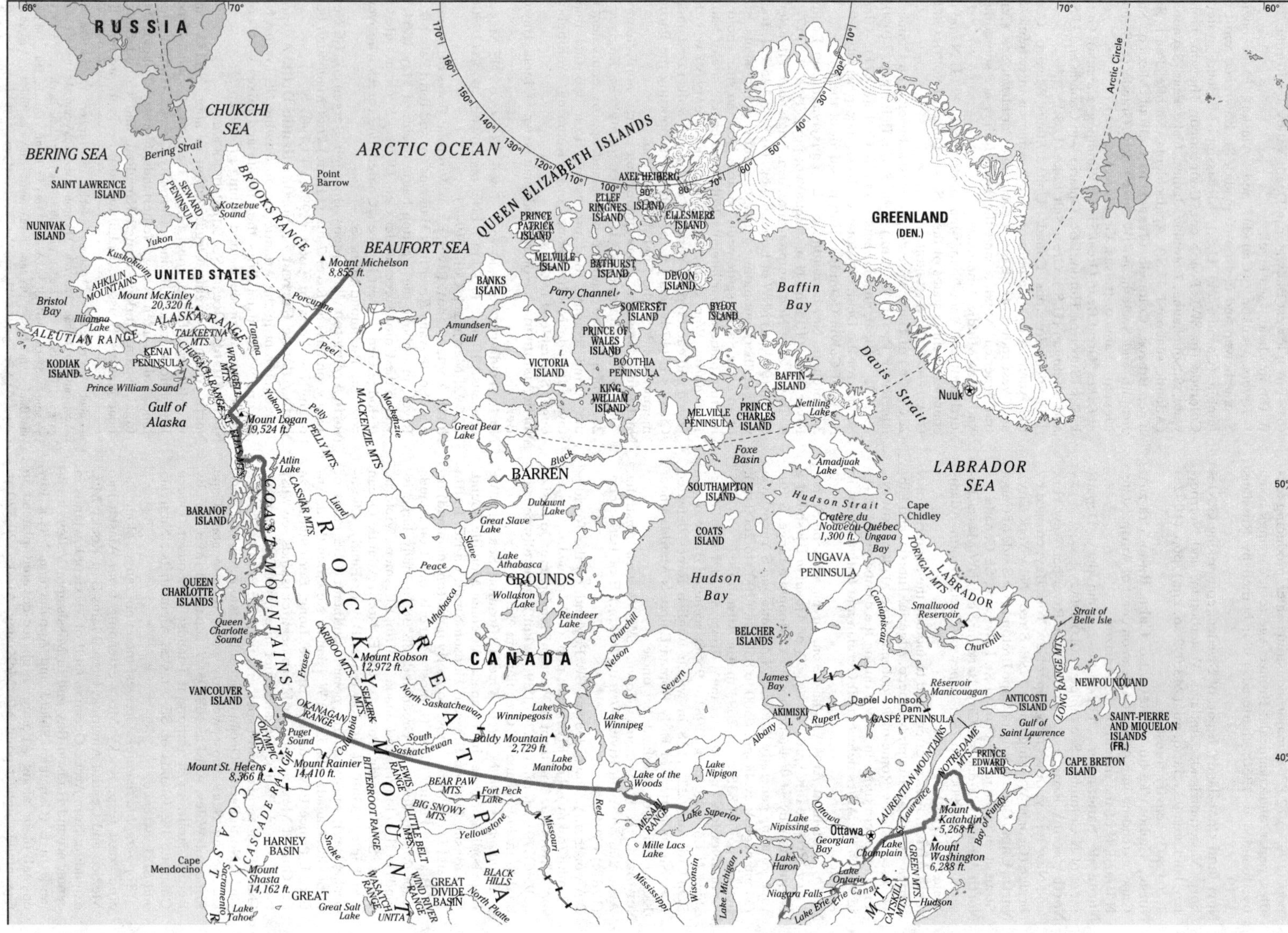

RUSSIA
CHUKCHI SEA
BERING SEA
Bering Strait
SAINT LAWRENCE ISLAND
NUNIVAK ISLAND
SEWARD PENINSULA
Kotzebue Sound
BROOKS RANGE
Point Barrow
ARCTIC OCEAN
QUEEN ELIZABETH ISLANDS
AXEL HEIBERG ISLAND
ELLEF RINGNES ISLAND
ELLESMERE ISLAND
PRINCE PATRICK ISLAND
MELVILLE ISLAND
BATHURST ISLAND
DEVON ISLAND
GREENLAND (DEN.)
Arctic Circle
BEAUFORT SEA
Mount Michelson 8,855 ft.
UNITED STATES
Yukon
Kuskokwim
AHKLUN MOUNTAINS
Mount McKinley 20,320 ft.
Bristol Bay
Iliamna Lake
ALASKA RANGE
ALEUTIAN RANGE
TALKEETNA MTS.
KENAI PENINSULA
CHUGACH RANGE
WRANGELL MTS.
KODIAK ISLAND
Prince William Sound
Gulf of Alaska
Tanana
Porcupine
Peel
BANKS ISLAND
Parry Channel
Amundsen Gulf
VICTORIA ISLAND
SOMERSET ISLAND
PRINCE OF WALES ISLAND
BOOTHIA PENINSULA
KING WILLIAM ISLAND
BYLOT ISLAND
Baffin Bay
BAFFIN ISLAND
Davis Strait
Nuuk
MELVILLE PENINSULA
PRINCE CHARLES ISLAND
Nettilling Lake
Mount Logan 19,524 ft.
ST. ELIAS MTS.
Yukon
Pelly
PELLY MTS.
MACKENZIE MTS
Mackenzie
Great Bear Lake
Black
BARREN
Foxe Basin
Amadjuak Lake
LABRADOR SEA
Atlin Lake
CASSIAR MTS.
Liard
BARANOF ISLAND
COAST MOUNTAINS
Dubawnt Lake
Great Slave Lake
Slave
SOUTHAMPTON ISLAND
Hudson Strait
Cratère du Nouveau-Québec 1,300 ft.
Ungava Bay
Cape Chidley
COATS ISLAND
Peace
Lake Athabasca
GROUNDS
Wollaston Lake
Athabasca
Hudson Bay
UNGAVA PENINSULA
TORNGAT MTS
LABRADOR
QUEEN CHARLOTTE ISLANDS
Queen Charlotte Sound
ROCKY MOUNTAINS
GREAT PLA
Reindeer Lake
Churchill
Caniapiscau
Smallwood Reservoir
Strait of Belle Isle
BELCHER ISLANDS
Churchill
Fraser
CARIBOO MTS.
Mount Robson 12,972 ft.
CANADA
Nelson
Severn
James Bay
LONG RANGE MTS.
NEWFOUNDLAND
Réservoir Manicouagan
VANCOUVER ISLAND
SELKIRK MTS.
North Saskatchewan
Lake Winnipegosis
Lake Winnipeg
AKIMISKI I.
Rupert
Daniel Johnson Dam
GASPÉ PENINSULA
ANTICOSTI ISLAND
Gulf of Saint Lawrence
SAINT-PIERRE AND MIQUELON ISLANDS (FR.)
OKANAGAN RANGE
Columbia
Puget Sound
OLYMPIC MTS.
South Saskatchewan
Baldy Mountain 2,729 ft.
Albany
Lake Manitoba
Mount St. Helens 8,366 ft.
Mount Rainier 14,410 ft.
LEWIS RANGE
BITTERROOT RANGE
Lake of the Woods
Lake Nipigon
LAURENTIAN MOUNTAINS
NOTRE-DAME MTS.
PRINCE EDWARD ISLAND
CAPE BRETON ISLAND
BEAR PAW MTS.
Fort Peck Lake
Red
BIG SNOWY MTS.
Missouri
MESABI RANGE
Lake Superior
Ottawa
St. Lawrence
Mount Katahdin 5,268 ft.
Bay of Fundy
CASCADE RANGE
HARNEY BASIN
Snake
LITTLE BELT MTS.
Yellowstone
Lake Nipissing
Ottawa
Georgian Bay
Lake Champlain
Mount Washington 6,288 ft.
Cape Mendocino
Sacramento
Mount Shasta 14,162 ft.
COAST R
Lake Tahoe
GREAT
Great Salt Lake
WASATCH RANGE
UINTA
WIND RIVER RANGE
GREAT DIVIDE BASIN
BLACK HILLS
North Platte
Mille Lacs Lake
Mississippi
Wisconsin
Lake Michigan
Lake Huron
Lake Ontario
Niagara Falls
Lake Erie
Erie Canal
CATSKILL MTS.
GREEN MTS.
Hudson

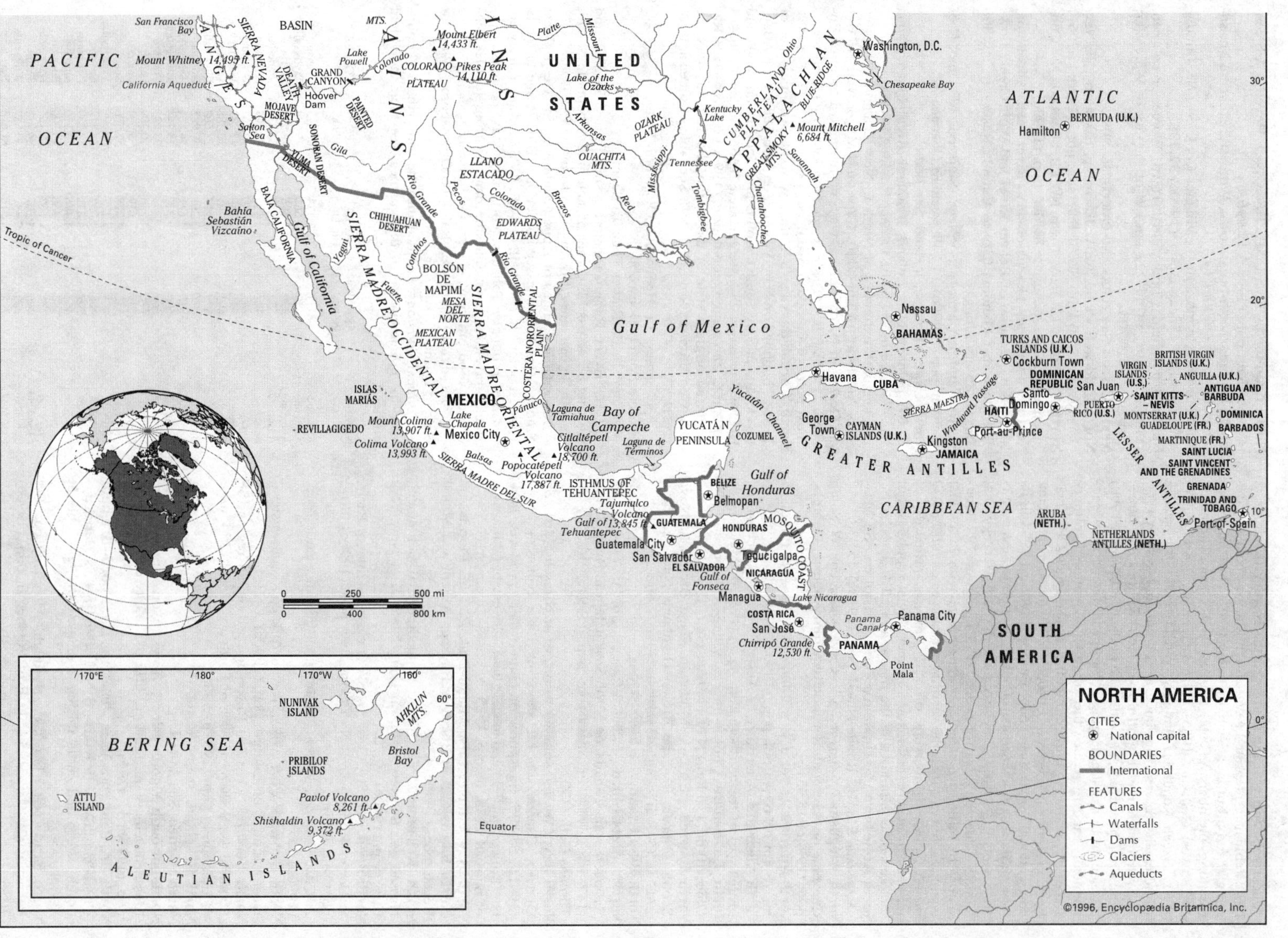
NORTH AMERICA
CITIES
National capital
BOUNDARIES
International
FEATURES
Canals
Waterfalls
Dams
Glaciers
Aqueducts
©1996, Encyclopædia Britannica, Inc.
PACIFIC
OCEAN
ATLANTIC
OCEAN
UNITED
STATES
MEXICO
Gulf of Mexico
CARIBBEAN SEA
GREATER ANTILLES
LESSER ANTILLES
SOUTH
AMERICA
San Francisco Bay
Mount Whitney 14,495 ft.
California Aqueduct
SIERRA NEVADA
BASIN
MTS.
DEATH VALLEY
MOJAVE DESERT
Salton Sea
GRAND CANYON
Hoover Dam
Lake Powell
Colorado
PAINTED DESERT
COLORADO PLATEAU
Mount Elbert 14,433 ft.
Pikes Peak 14,110 ft.
Platte
Missouri
Lake of the Ozarks
Arkansas
OZARK PLATEAU
OUACHITA MTS.
Red
Mississippi
Tennessee
Tombigbee
Kentucky Lake
Chattahoochee
Savannah
Ohio
CUMBERLAND PLATEAU
APPALACHIAN
BLUE RIDGE
GREAT SMOKY MTS.
Mount Mitchell 6,684 ft.
Washington, D.C.
Chesapeake Bay
Hamilton
BERMUDA (U.K.)
Gila
YUMA DESERT
SONORAN DESERT
Rio Grande
Pecos
LLANO ESTACADO
Colorado
Brazos
EDWARDS PLATEAU
Bahía Sebastián Vizcaíno
BAJA CALIFORNIA
Gulf of California
Tropic of Cancer
CHIHUAHUAN DESERT
Yaqui
Conchos
Fuerte
BOLSÓN DE MAPIMÍ
MESA DEL NORTE
MEXICAN PLATEAU
SIERRA MADRE OCCIDENTAL
SIERRA MADRE ORIENTAL
COSTERA NORORIENTAL PLAIN
ISLAS MARÍAS
REVILLAGIGEDO
Mount Colima 13,907 ft.
Colima Volcano 13,993 ft.
Lake Chapala
Mexico City
Balsas
SIERRA MADRE DEL SUR
Popocatépetl Volcano 17,887 ft.
Citlaltépetl Volcano 18,700 ft.
Pánuco
Laguna de Tamiahua
Bay of Campeche
Laguna de Términos
ISTHMUS OF TEHUANTEPEC
Tajumulco Volcano 13,845 ft.
Gulf of Tehuantepec
YUCATÁN PENINSULA
COZUMEL
Yucatán Channel
BELIZE
Belmopan
Gulf of Honduras
GUATEMALA
Guatemala City
San Salvador
EL SALVADOR
Gulf of Fonseca
HONDURAS
Tegucigalpa
MOSQUITO COAST
NICARAGUA
Managua
Lake Nicaragua
COSTA RICA
San José
Chirripó Grande 12,530 ft.
Panama Canal
Panama City
PANAMA
Point Mala
Nassau
BAHAMAS
Havana
CUBA
SIERRA MAESTRA
George Town
CAYMAN ISLANDS (U.K.)
Kingston
JAMAICA
Windward Passage
HAITI
Port-au-Prince
DOMINICAN REPUBLIC
Santo Domingo
TURKS AND CAICOS ISLANDS (U.K.)
Cockburn Town
PUERTO RICO (U.S.)
San Juan
VIRGIN ISLANDS (U.S.)
BRITISH VIRGIN ISLANDS (U.K.)
ANGUILLA (U.K.)
SAINT KITTS – NEVIS
ANTIGUA AND BARBUDA
MONTSERRAT (U.K.)
GUADELOUPE (FR.)
DOMINICA
MARTINIQUE (FR.)
BARBADOS
SAINT LUCIA
SAINT VINCENT AND THE GRENADINES
GRENADA
TRINIDAD AND TOBAGO
Port-of-Spain
ARUBA (NETH.)
NETHERLANDS ANTILLES (NETH.)
Equator
30°
20°
10°
0°
0 250 500 mi
0 400 800 km
BERING SEA
170°E
180°
170°W
160°
60°
NUNIVAK ISLAND
AHKLUN MTS.
Bristol Bay
PRIBILOF ISLANDS
ATTU ISLAND
Pavlof Volcano 8,261 ft.
Shishaldin Volcano 9,372 ft.
ALEUTIAN ISLANDS

collective security of the nations of the North Atlantic area; has established integrated naval and military commands covering W and S Europe. Estab. by treaty 1949, all members are founding members except: Turkey and Greece admitted 1952, West Germany 1955 (unified Germany 1991), Spain 1982, Czech Republic, Hungary, and Poland 1999; France withdrew its forces from integrated command system 1966 and required removal of all non-French facilities and forces from French territory; since the end of the Cold War (c. 1990) has sought to assist emerging E European democracies economically, and to reduce the size of conventional military forces maintained in Europe; member states signed CFE treaty (Conventional Forces in Europe) 1990 aimed at reducing conventional forces throughout Europe; involved 1994 in its first military action since its founding, shot down several aircraft violating no-fly zone over Bosnia and Herzegovina; launched "partnerships for peace" (PFP) program 1994 consisting of military cooperation agreements with individual countries, but not incl. the security guarantees of full NATO membership; membership of PFP consists primarily of former Soviet bloc nations and former Soviet republics, but includes other countries of the region as well.

North At·tle·boro \ˈat-ᵊl-ˌbər-ō\. Town, Bristol co., SE Massachusetts, E of NE Rhode Island; pop. (1990c) 25,038.

North Au·gus·ta \ȯ-ˈgəs-tə, ə-\. City, Aiken co., W South Carolina, on Savannah River across from Augusta, Georgia; pop. (1990c) 15,351.

North Au·ro·ra \ə-ˈrȯr-ə, ȯ-\. Village, Kane co., NE Illinois, 4 mi. (6 km.) N of Aurora; pop. (1990c) 5940.

North Australia. A territory of Australia 1927–31; consisted of that part of the Northern Terr. (*q.v.*) N of 20°S lat.

North Bal·ti·more \ˈbȯl-tə-ˌmōr\. Village, Wood co., NW Ohio, 10 mi. (16 km.) N of Findlay; pop. (1990c) 3139.

North Bar·ren \ˈbar-ən\. Mountain, Cape Breton I., Nova Scotia, Canada, in Cape Breton Highlands National Park; 1747 ft. (533 m.); highest peak in Nova Scotia.

North Bass Island. See BASS ISLAND.

North Bat·tle·ford \ˈbat-ᵊl-fərd, -ˌfōrd\. City, W Saskatchewan, Canada, on North Saskatchewan River 85 mi. (137 km.) WNW of Saskatoon; pop. (1991c) 14,350; St. Thomas Coll. (1932).

North Bay. City and summer resort, ⊗ of Nipissing dist., SE Ontario, Canada, on NE shore of Lake Nipissing; pop. (1991c) 55,405; transportation center; dairy products, lumber; military airfield and missile base; city estab. with arrival of railroad 1882; incorp. 1925.

North Bay Village. City, Miami-Dade co., SE Florida, on **North Bay Island** in Biscayne Bay bet. Miami and Miami Beach; pop. (1990c) 5383.

North Bell·more \ˈbel-ˌmōr\. Unincorporated settlement, Nassau co., SE New York, on Long Island E of New York City; pop. (1990c) 19,707.

North Bend. **1.** City, Coos co., SW Oregon, on inlet of Pacific Ocean 4 mi. (6 km.) N of Coos Bay; pop. (1990c) 9614; plywood; fishing.

2. City, King co., W cen. Washington, ESE of Seattle; pop. (1990c) 2578.

North Ber·wick \ˈbər-ˌwik\. Town, York co., southwesternmost Maine, S of Sanford; pop. (1990c) 3793.

North Ber·wick \ˈber-ik\. Resort town, Lothian region, SE Scotland, on S shore of Firth of Forth ab. 22 mi. (35 km.) E of Edinburgh; pop. (1981p) 5388.

North Beveland. See BEVELAND.

North Borneo. See SABAH.

North·bor·ough \ˈnȯrth-ˌbər-ō\. Town, Worcester co., cen. Massachusetts, 9 mi. (15 km.) ENE of the city of Worcester; pop. (1990c) 11,929.

North Bra·bant \brə-ˈbant, -ˈbänt\ *or Du.* **Noord–Bra·bant** \ˈnōrt-ˈbrä-ˌbänt\. Province, S Netherlands; ✻ 's Hertogenbosch; sheep and cattle raising. See BRABANT and table at NETHERLANDS.

North Brad·dock \ˈbra-dək\. Borough, Allegheny co., SW Pennsylvania, 9 mi. (15 km.) E of Pittsburgh; pop. (1990c) 7036.

North Bran·ford \ˈbran-fərd\. Town, New Haven co., S cen. Connecticut; pop. (1990c) 12,996.

North·bridge \ˈnȯrth-brij\. Town, Worcester co., cen. Massachusetts; pop. (1990c) 13,371.

North·brook \ˈnȯrth-ˌbru̇k\. Village, Cook co., NE Illinois, NW suburb of Chicago; pop. (1990c) 32,308.

North Brook·field \ˈbru̇k-ˌfēld\. Town, Worcester co., cen. Massachusetts, 14 mi. (23 km.) W of the city of Worcester; pop. (1990c) 4708.

North Caicos. See TURKS AND CAICOS ISLANDS.

North Cald·well \ˈkäld-ˌwel\. Township, Essex co., NE New Jersey, 6 mi. (10 km.) SW of Paterson; pop. (1990c) 6706.

North Ca·naan \ˈkā-nən\. Town, NW Litchfield co., NW Connecticut, on Massachusetts border; pop. (1990c) 3284.

North Ca·na·di·an \kə-ˈnā-dē-ən\. River, cen. Oklahoma; formed by junction of Beaver River and Wolf Creek, flows ESE through Oklahoma City to Eufaula Reservoir; ab. 800 mi. (1285 km.) long.

North Can·ton \ˈkant-ᵊn\. Village, Stark co., NE Ohio, N of Canton; pop. (1990c) 14,748; vacuum cleaners.

North Cape. **1.** Cape, Iceland. See HORN.

2. NW point of New Ireland, Bismarck Archipelago, Papua New Guinea in W Pacific Ocean; Kavieng is on it.

3. Cape on N extremity of North I., New Zealand.

4. *or* **Nord·kapp** \ˈnür-ˌkäp\. Cape on N Magerøya I. in Arctic Ocean off N coast of Norway; northernmost point of Europe, 71°10′20″N, 25°48′E; Cape Nordkyn (*q.v.*) is northernmost point of European mainland.

North Car·o·li·na \ˌkar-ə-ˈlī-nə\. A south Atlantic state of U.S.A., bounded on N by Virginia, on E and SE by the Atlantic Ocean, on S by South Carolina and Georgia, and on W and NW by Tennessee; 28th state in area, 52,669 sq. mi. (136,413 sq. km.); 10th state in population, (1990c) 6,628,637; ✻ Raleigh; an original state of the Union, the 12th to ratify the U.S. Constitution (Nov. 21, 1789). See table of states at UNITED STATES.

Nicknames: Tar Heel State; Old North State.

State flower: Dogwood.

Motto: To Be Rather Than To Seem.

Chief rivers: Roanoke, entering state from S Virginia and flowing SE across NE corner of state into Albemarle Sound; Yadkin, in cen. area, flowing S to form the Pee Dee.

Mountains: Ranges of Appalachian Mts. in W esp. Great Smoky Mts. on Tennessee border, and Blue Ridge to the E. Highest point Mt. Mitchell, 6684 ft. (2037 m.), in Yancey co.

Chief products: Tobacco, corn, soybeans, peanuts; livestock; gravel, feldspar; tourism; manufacturing: textiles, cigarettes, food products, chemicals, furniture.

Chief cities: Charlotte, Raleigh, Greensboro, Winston-Salem, Durham.

Political divisions: Divided into the following 100 counties (for pronunciation of their names, see their individual entries):

NAME	AREA[1] (sq. mi.)	AREA[1] (sq. km.)	POP. (1990c)	CO. SEAT
Alamance	434	1,124	108,213	Graham
Alexander	255	660	27,544	Taylorsville
Alleghany	230	596	9,590	Sparta
Anson	533	1,380	23,474	Wadesboro
Ashe	427	1,106	22,209	Jefferson
Avery	247	640	14,867	Newland
Beaufort	831	2,152	42,283	Washington
Bertie	693	1,795	20,388	Windsor
Bladen	879	2,277	28,663	Elizabethtown
Brunswick[2]	873	2,261	50,985	Bolivia
Buncombe[3]	645	1,671	174,821	Asheville
Burke	506	1,311	75,744	Morganton
Cabarrus	360	932	98,935	Concord
Caldwell	476	1,233	70,709	Lenoir
Camden	239	619	5,904	Camden
Carteret[4,5]	532	1,378	52,556	Beaufort
Caswell	435	1,127	20,693	Yanceyville
Catawba	406	1,052	118,412	Newton
Chatham	707	1,831	38,759	Pittsboro
Cherokee	454	1,176	20,170	Murphy
Chowan	180	466	13,506	Edenton
Clay	213	552	7,155	Hayesville
Cleveland	466	1,207	84,714	Shelby
Columbus	939	2,432	49,587	Whiteville
Craven	725	1,878	81,613	New Bern

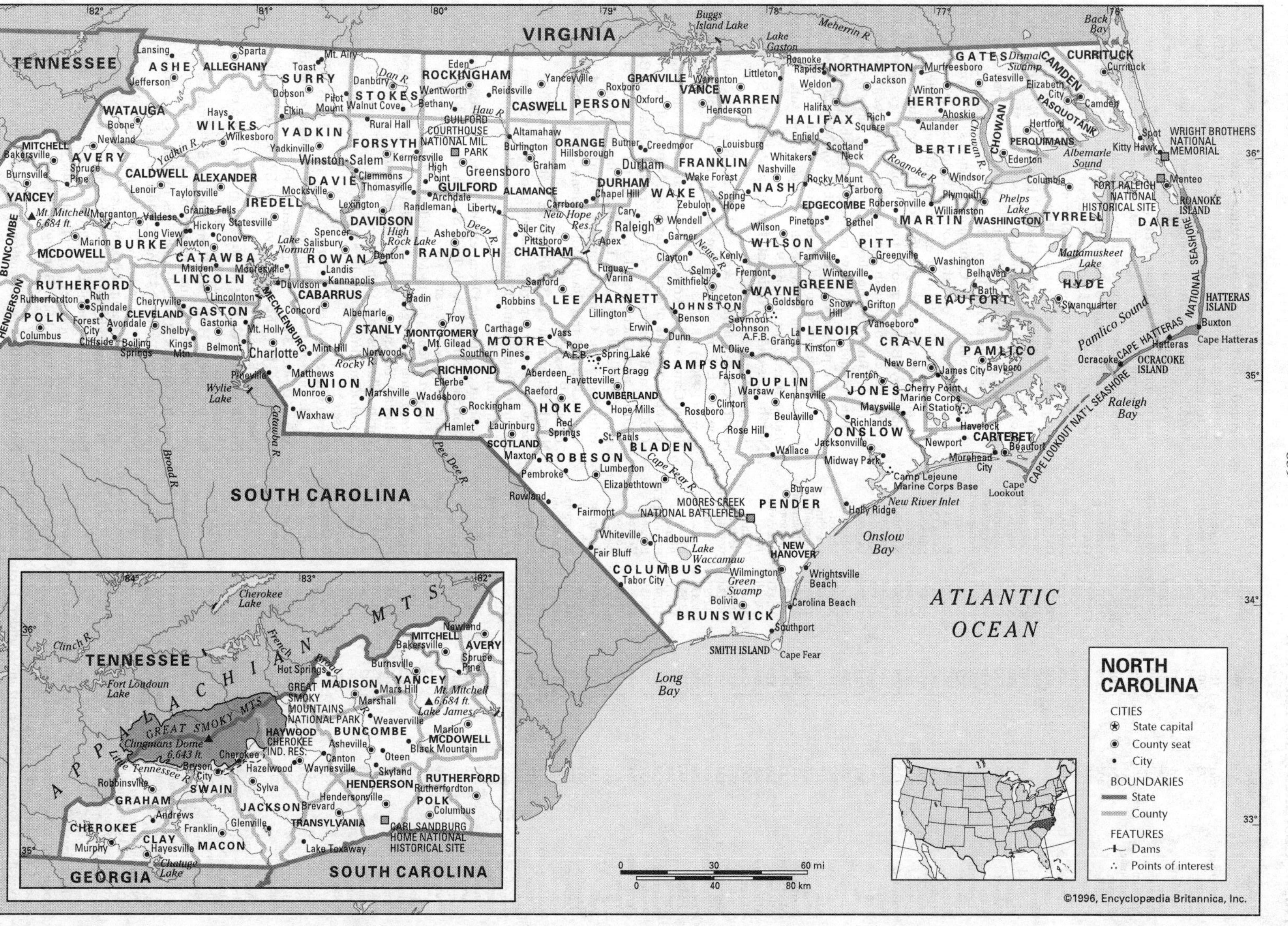
NORTH CAROLINA
CITIES
State capital
County seat
City
BOUNDARIES
State
County
FEATURES
Dams
Points of interest
VIRGINIA
TENNESSEE
SOUTH CAROLINA
GEORGIA
ATLANTIC OCEAN
Onslow Bay
Long Bay
Raleigh Bay
Pamlico Sound
Albemarle Sound
CAPE HATTERAS NATIONAL SEASHORE
CAPE LOOKOUT NAT'L SEASHORE
WRIGHT BROTHERS NATIONAL MEMORIAL
FORT RALEIGH NATIONAL HISTORICAL SITE
GUILFORD COURTHOUSE NATIONAL MIL. PARK
MOORES CREEK NATIONAL BATTLEFIELD
CARL SANDBURG HOME NATIONAL HISTORICAL SITE
GREAT SMOKY MOUNTAINS NATIONAL PARK
APPALACHIAN MTS
Mt. Mitchell 6,684 ft.
Clingmans Dome 6,643 ft.
0 30 60 mi
0 40 80 km
©1996, Encyclopædia Britannica, Inc.

NAME	AREA[1] (sq. mi.)	AREA[1] (sq. km.)	POP. (1990c)	CO. SEAT
Cumberland	661	1,712	274,566	Fayetteville
Currituck	273	707	13,736	Currituck
Dare[5,6]	388	1,005	22,746	Manteo
Davidson	546	1,414	126,677	Lexington
Davie	264	684	27,859	Mocksville
Duplin	822	2,129	39,995	Kenansville
Durham	299	774	181,835	Durham
Edgecombe	511	1,323	56,558	Tarboro
Forsyth	424	1,098	265,878	Winston-Salem
Franklin	494	1,279	36,414	Louisburg
Gaston	358	927	175,093	Gastonia
Gates	343	888	9,305	Gatesville
Graham	289	749	7,196	Robbinsville
Granville	542	1,404	38,345	Oxford
Greene	269	697	15,384	Snow Hill
Guilford	651	1,686	347,420	Greensboro
Halifax	722	1,870	55,516	Halifax
Harnett	606	1,570	67,822	Lillington
Haywood[7]	543	1,406	46,942	Waynesville
Henderson	382	989	69,285	Hendersonville
Hertford	356	922	22,523	Winton
Hoke	381	987	22,856	Raeford
Hyde[5]	634	1,642	5,411	Swan Quarter
Iredell	591	1,531	92,931	Statesville
Jackson[7]	496	1,285	26,846	Sylva
Johnston	795	2,059	81,306	Smithfield
Jones	467	1,210	9,414	Trenton
Lee	255	660	41,374	Sanford
Lenoir	391	1,013	57,274	Kinston
Lincoln	308	798	50,319	Lincolnton
McDowell	442	1,145	35,681	Marion
Macon	517	1,339	23,499	Franklin
Madison	456	1,181	16,953	Marshall
Martin	481	1,246	25,078	Williamston
Mecklenburg	542	1,404	511,433	Charlotte
Mitchell	220	570	14,433	Bakersville
Montgomery	488	1,264	23,346	Troy
Moore	705	1,826	59,013	Carthage
Nash	552	1,430	76,677	Nashville
New Hanover	194	502	120,284	Wilmington
Northhampton	539	1,396	20,798	Jackson
Onslow	756	1,958	149,838	Jacksonville
Orange	398	1,031	93,851	Hillsboro
Pamlico	341	883	11,372	Bayboro
Pasquotank	229	593	31,298	Elizabeth City
Pender	857	2,220	28,855	Burgaw
Perquimans	261	676	10,447	Hertford
Person	400	1,036	30,180	Roxboro
Pitt	656	1,699	107,924	Greenville
Polk	234	606	14,416	Columbus
Randolph	801	2,075	106,546	Asheboro
Richmond	477	1,235	44,518	Rockingham
Robeson	944	2,445	105,179	Lumberton
Rockingham	572	1,481	86,064	Wentworth
Rowan	517	1,339	110,605	Salisbury
Rutherford	566	1,466	56,918	Rutherfordton
Sampson	963	2,494	47,297	Clinton
Scotland	317	821	33,754	Laurinburg
Stanly	399	1,033	51,765	Albemarle
Stokes	459	1,189	37,233	Danbury
Surry	537	1,391	61,704	Dobson
Swain[7]	530	1,373	11,268	Bryson City
Transylvania	379	982	25,520	Brevard
Tyrrell	399	1,033	3,856	Columbia
Union	643	1,665	84,211	Monroe
Vance	249	645	38,892	Henderson
Wake	864	2,238	423,380	Raleigh
Warren	443	1,147	17,265	Warrenton
Washington	336	870	13,997	Plymouth
Watauga	320	829	36,952	Boone
Wayne	555	1,437	104,666	Goldsboro
Wilkes	765	1,981	59,393	Wilkesboro
Wilson	373	966	66,061	Wilson
Yadkin	335	868	30,488	Yadkinville
Yancey	311	805	15,419	Burnsville

[1] Area = land area.
[2] Includes Cape Fear, on Smith I. off SE corner.
[3] This county name is source of colloquial common noun *buncombe*.
[4] Includes offshore islands from which it is separated by Core Sound (on E) and Bogue Sound (on S).
[5] Cape Hatteras National Seashore Park comprises most of chain of islands (enclosing Pamlico Sound on ocean side) belonging to Dare, Hyde, and Carteret cos., with Cape Hatteras itself on island SE of and belonging to Dare co.
[6] Kitty Hawk (*q.v.*), scene of first airplane flight in U.S. (1903), on sand barrier NE of and belonging to Dare co.
[7] Great Smoky Mountains National Park occupies most of N and E part of Swain co., N section of Jackson co., and NW section of Haywood co. (as well as adjacent section of Tennessee).

History: Inhabited by several Algonquian, Siouan, and Iroquoian tribes prior to European contact, esp. the Cherokee, Catawba, and Tuscarora; coast explored by Florentine navigator Giovanni da Verrazano (under French employ) 1524, and others; first English settlement in the New World estab. 1585 at Roanoke I. (*q.v.*); region of Albemarle Sound settled mid-17th cent. by Virginia colonists; formed a part of Carolina grant given 1663 (expanded 1665) by King Charles II to eight noblemen of his court (see CAROLINA); governed largely separately from South Carolina from late 17th cent., and officially separated 1712; became a royal province after the proprietors sold their rights to the crown 1729; Regulator movement (1768–71) against excessive taxation and government corruption suppressed by colonial forces at Alamance (*q.v.*) 1771; reports of Mecklenburg Declaration, a statement of rights and of independence from Britain drawn up May 1775 by the citizens of Mecklenburg co., now considered spurious by most; first Revolutionary battle in the state occurred at "Moores Creek Bridge" Feb. 27, 1776, in which a Loyalist force was defeated in the so-called "Lexington and Concord of the South"; Provincial Congress adopted Apr. 12, 1776 the Halifax resolution that authorized the delegates for North Carolina to the Continental Congress "to concur with the delegates of the other colonies in declaring independency"—the first explicit sanction of independence by an American colony; adopted state constitution 1776; invaded by British troops under Lord Charles Cornwallis 1780; the end of British control of the colony began with the battle at Guilford Courthouse (*q.v.*) 1781; gave up claim to western lands 1790, now part of Tennessee (see FRANKLIN, STATE OF); passed ordinance of secession May 20, 1861; secession ordinance annulled and slavery abolished 1865; new state constitution 1868; readmitted to Union July 11, 1868; latest state constitution 1971.

North Cas·cades National Park \ka-ˈskādz\. See UNITED STATES, *National Parks*.

North Cat·a·sau·qua \ˌka-tə-ˈsȯ-kwə\. Borough, Northampton co., E Pennsylvania, on Lehigh River N of Allentown; pop. (1990c) 2867.

North Cau·ca·sus \ˈkȯ-kə-səs\. Extensive region, S Russia in Europe; consists of Krasnodar Kray, Stavropol' Kray, Rostov Oblast, and the republics of Dagestan, Kabardino-Balkaria, Alania, and Chechnya; 137,105 sq. mi. (355,102 sq. km.); pop. (1993e) 16,511,000. Inhabitants include many different ethnic groups. Consists largely of earlier Terr. of the Don Cossacks, and the Stavropol', Kuban', and Terek provs. of czarist Russia.

North Channel. **1.** Strait in NE Lake Huron, SE Ontario prov., Canada; separates Manitoulin and Cockburn islands, both in Ontario and Drummond I., Michigan from the Canadian mainland.
2. Strait of Atlantic Ocean extending bet. NE Ireland and SW Scotland; connects with Irish Sea on the S; 14 mi. (23 km.) wide at its widest part.
3. N part of entrance to Manila Bay, Philippines, bet. Bataan Penin. and Corregidor I.; 3.5 mi. (6 km.) wide; called **Bo·ca Chi·ca** \ˈbō-kä-ˈchē-kä\ by the Spaniards.

North Charles·ton \ˈchärl-stən\. City, Charleston co., SE South Carolina; pop. (1990c) 70,218; naval and air force bases.

North Chi·ca·go \shə-ˈkä-gō, -ˈkȯ-\. City, Lake co., NE corner of Illinois, on Lake Michigan 5 mi. (8 km.) S of Waukegan; pop. (1990c) 34,978; pharmaceuticals.

North Chŏl·la \ˈchȯ-lə\. Province of SW South Korea. See table at KOREA, SOUTH.

North Ch'ung·ch'ŏng \ˈchu̇ŋ-ˈchȯŋ\. Province of cen. South Korea. See table at KOREA, SOUTH.

North College Hill. City, Hamilton co., SW corner of Ohio, 9 mi. (15 km.) N of Cincinnati; pop. (1990c) 11,002.

North Concho. River, Texas; rises in Gaines co., flows SE to join Concho River; 137 mi. (220 km.) long.

North Con·way \ˈkän-wā\. Unincorporated settlement, Carroll co., E New Hampshire, on Saco River ab. 6 mi. (10 km.) N of Conway; pop. (1990c) 2032; summer and winter resort.

North·cote **1.** \ˈnȯrth-kət\. City, S Victoria, SE Australia, N suburb of Melbourne; pop. (1991c) 46,547.
2. \ˈnȯrth-kət, -ˌkōt\. Borough, North I., New Zealand; pop. (1981c) 10,061.

North Country. An occasional name for the N part of England.

North Da·ko·ta \də-ˈkō-tə\. A northwestern state of U.S.A., bounded on N by Canadian provs. of Saskatchewan and Manitoba, on E by Minnesota, on S by South Dakota, and on W by Montana; 17th state in area, 70,665 sq. mi. (183,022 sq. km.); 47th state in population, (1990c) 638,800; ✻ Bismarck; 39th state admitted to Union (1889); geographical center of North America is in Pierce co. See table of states at UNITED STATES.

Nickname: Flickertail State.

State flower: Wild prairie rose.

Motto: Liberty and Union, Now and Forever, One and Inseparable.

Rivers: Missouri, entering state at upper W border and flowing E, then SE, across S border into South Dakota; Red, forming E boundary.

Highest point: White Butte, 3506 ft. (1069 m.), in Slope co.

Chief products: Wheat, barley, flaxseed, oats; livestock; oil, coal; food processing.

Chief cities: Fargo, Grand Forks, Bismarck, Minot.

Political divisions: Divided into the following 53 counties (for pronunciation of their names, see their individual entries):

NAME	AREA[1] (sq. mi.)	AREA[1] (sq. km.)	POP. (1990c)	CO. SEAT
Adams	989	2,562	3,174	Hettinger
Barnes	1,479	3,831	12,545	Valley City
Benson	1,403	3,634	7,198	Minnewaukan
Billings	1,139	2,950	1,108	Medora
Bottineau	1,677	4,343	8,011	Bottineau
Bowman	1,170	3,030	3,596	Bowman
Burke	1,119	2,898	3,002	Bowbells
Burleigh	1,625	4,209	60,131	Bismarck
Cass	1,749	4,530	102,874	Fargo
Cavalier	1,512	3,916	6,064	Langdon
Dickey	1,143	2,960	6,107	Ellendale
Divide	1,300	3,367	2,899	Crosby
Dunn	2,992	7,749	4,005	Manning
Eddy	635	1,645	2,951	New Rockford
Emmons	1,503	3,893	4,830	Linton
Foster	645	1,671	3,983	Carrington
Golden Valley	1,014	2,626	2,108	Beach
Grand Forks	1,438	3,724	70,683	Grand Forks
Grant	1,666	4,315	3,549	Carson
Griggs	710	1,839	3,303	Cooperstown
Hettinger	1,134	2,937	3,445	Mott
Kidder	1,358	3,517	3,332	Steele
La Moure	1,136	2,942	5,383	La Moure
Logan	1,001	2,593	2,847	Napoleon
McHenry	1,871	4,846	6,528	Towner
McIntosh	992	2,569	4,021	Ashley
McKenzie	2,735	7,084	6,383	Watford City
McLean	2,065	5,348	10,457	Washburn
Mercer	1,042	2,699	9,808	Stanton
Morton	1,920	4,973	23,700	Mandan
Mountrail	1,819	4,711	7,021	Stanley
Nelson	995	2,577	4,410	Lakota
Oliver	721	1,867	2,381	Center
Pembina	1,124	2,911	9,238	Cavalier
Pierce	1,038	2,688	5,052	Rugby
Ramsey	1,248	3,232	12,681	Devils Lake
Ransom	861	2,230	5,921	Lisbon
Renville	886	2,295	3,160	Mohall
Richland	1,449	3,753	18,148	Wahpeton
Rolette	913	2,365	12,772	Rolla
Sargent	853	2,209	4,549	Forman
Sheridan	989	2,562	2,148	McClusky
Sioux	1,103	2,857	3,761	Fort Yates
Slope	1,225	3,173	907	Amidon
Stark	1,316	3,408	22,832	Dickinson
Steele	710	1,839	2,420	Finley
Stutsman	2,264	5,864	22,241	Jamestown
Towner	1,043	2,701	3,627	Cando
Traill	861	2,230	8,752	Hillsboro
Walsh	1,286	3,331	13,840	Grafton
Ward	2,044	5,294	57,921	Minot
Wells	1,299	3,364	5,864	Fessenden
Williams	2,064	5,346	21,129	Williston

[1] Area = land area.

History: Evidence of prehistoric inhabitants throughout the state; at time of European contact was inhabited by native Algonquian (Cheyenne and Ojibwa), Caddoan (Arikara), and esp. Siouan (Assiniboin, Dakota, Hidatsa, and Mandan) peoples; for intervening history, see DAKOTA TERRITORY; N part of Dakota Terr. (organized 1861); separated from South Dakota and admitted to Union as state Nov. 2, 1889; constitution passed 1889.

North Devon Island. See DEVON ISLAND.

North Dome. **1.** Peak in the Sierra Nevada, E Fresno co., S cen. California; 8657 ft. (2639 m.).
2. Peak in the Catskill Mts., Greene co., SE New York; 3593 ft. (1095 m.).

North Down. District, E Northern Ireland, on Belfast Lough. See table at IRELAND, NORTHERN.

North Downs. Range of low hills in S cen. England, extending from W to E; highest point Leith Hill 965 ft. (294 m.).

North East. **1.** Town, Cecil co., NE Maryland; pop. (1990c) 1913; Cecil Community Coll. (1968).
2. Borough, Erie co., NW Pennsylvania, on Lake Erie 16 mi. (26 km.) ENE of the city of Erie; pop. (1990c) 4617.

North East Cape Fear \ˈfir\. River, SE North Carolina; rises in Sampson co., flows E and S into Cape Fear River near its mouth; ab. 130 mi. (210 km.) long.

North–Eastern. Province of NE Kenya. See table at KENYA.

North East Frontier Agency. See ARUNACHAL PRADESH.

North East Land *or Norw.* **Nord·ost Land·et** \ˌnȯrt-ˈōst-ˈlän-dət\. An island of Svalbard, NE of Spitsbergen, Norway; 6400 sq. mi. (16,600 sq. km.); ice cap. See SPITSBERGEN.

North–East New Guinea; *earlier* **Kai·ser–Wil·helms·land** \ˈkī-zər-ˈvil-ˌhelms-ˌlänt\. Historic name for NE part of mainland of New Guinea I., part of Papua New Guinea; bounded on N by Pacific Ocean, on NE by Bismarck Sea, on E by Vitiaz Strait and Solomon Sea, on S by the former Terr. of Papua, and on W by Irian Jaya, Indonesia; 69,700 sq. mi. (180,500 sq. km.); entire cen. region very mountainous; with many peaks 9000 to 15,000 ft. (2700 to 4600 m.); highest peak Mt. Wilhelm 14,762 ft. (4499 m.); much of it remote. Largest river the Sepik in NW. In Bulolo Valley in SE are goldfields (see MOROBE). Separated on E from Long I. and Umboi I. and New Britain by Vitiaz Strait and on E coast marked by Huon Penin. and Huon Gulf. Along the coast are several good harbors: Morobe, Salamaua, Saidor, Madang, Wewak, and Aitape. For history, see NEW GUINEA and NEW GUINEA, TRUST TERRITORY OF.

Northeast Passage. A passage by sea along N coast of Europe and Asia bet. the Atlantic and Pacific oceans; parts explored since 15th cent. by many, incl. Dutch navigator Willem Barents and English navigator Henry Hudson; first traversed by Swedish explorer Baron Nils Nordenskiöld 1878–79. See ARCTIC, THE.

Northeast Pol·der \ˈpōl-dər\. See ZUIDER ZEE.

North East Providence Channel. See PROVIDENCE CHANNEL, NORTH WEST.

North Emporia. See EMPORIA 2.

North·ern \ˈnȯr-t͟hərn\; *1993–95* **Northern Trans·vaal** \trans-ˈväl, tranz-\. Province of NE Rep. of South Africa. See table at SOUTH AFRICA, REPUBLIC OF.

Northern Ae·ge·an \i-ˈjē-ən\. Region of Greece; 1481 sq. mi. (3836 sq. km.); pop. (1991c) 198,241. For subdivisions, see table at GREECE.

Northern Cape. Province of W Rep. of South Africa. See table at SOUTH AFRICA, REPUBLIC OF.

Northern Caucasia. See CISCAUCASIA.

Northern Cir·cars \sər-ˈkärz\. A historic name formerly used for the region now in NE Andhra Pradesh, E India, along the coast bet. the Krishna River and Orissa; ✻ Eluru; ceded to Great Britain 1766 by the nizam of Hyderabad.

Northern Cook Islands \ˈku̇k\ *or* **Ma·ni·hi·ki Islands** \ˌmä-nē-ˈhē-kē\. Group of seven islands in cen. Pacific Ocean in Cook Is. (*q.v.*); ab. 9 sq. mi. (23 sq. km.); pop. (1986c) 2247; administered by New Zealand.

Northern District. District of N Israel. See table at ISRAEL.

Northern Donets. See DONETS.

Northern Dvina. See DVINA, NORTHERN.

\ə\ **abut** \ə\ matches \ᵊ\ kitten, Fr table \ər\ **further** \a\ **ash** \ā\ **ace** \ä\ cot, cart \à\ Fr bac \au̇\ **out** \b\ Span Avila \ch\ **chin** \e\ bet \ē\ **easy** \g\ **go** \i\ **hit** \ī\ **ice** \j\ **job** \k\ Ger **ich**, **Buch** \ⁿ\ Fr vin \ŋ\ **sing** \ō\ **go** \ȯ\ **all** \ȯ\ **law** \œ\ Fr **bœuf** \œ̄\ Fr **feu** \ȯi\ **boy** \th\ **thin** \t͟h\ **this** \ü\ **loot** \u̇\ **foot** \ue\ Ger füllen \u̅e\ Fr **rue** \y\ yet \ʸ\ Fr digne \ˈdēnʸ\, nuit \ˈnwʸē\ \yü\ **few** \yu̇\ fury \zh\ vision

NORTH DAKOTA
CITIES
State capital
County seat
City
BOUNDARIES
State
County
FEATURES
Dams
Historical sites
CANADA
SASKATCHEWAN
MANITOBA
MINNESOTA
SOUTH DAKOTA
MONTANA
INTERNATIONAL PEACE GARDEN
TURTLE MTN. IND. RES.
FT. TOTTEN IND. RES.
FORT BERTHOLD IND. RES.
STANDING ROCK IND. RES.
SISSETON IND. RES.
KNIFE RIVER INDIAN VILLAGES NATIONAL HIST. SITE
FORT UNION TRADING POST NATIONAL HISTORICAL SITE
THEO. ROOSEVELT NATIONAL PARK (NORTH UNIT)
THEO. ROOSEVELT NATIONAL PARK (SOUTH UNIT)
THEO. ROOSEVELT NATIONAL PARK (ELKHORN RANCH)
Geographical Center of North America
COTEAU DU MISSOURI
BADLANDS
DIVIDE
BURKE
RENVILLE
BOTTINEAU
ROLETTE
TOWNER
CAVALIER
PEMBINA
WILLIAMS
MOUNTRAIL
WARD
MC HENRY
PIERCE
BENSON
RAMSEY
WALSH
NELSON
GRAND FORKS
MC KENZIE
MC LEAN
SHERIDAN
WELLS
EDDY
FOSTER
GRIGGS
STEELE
TRAILL
DUNN
MERCER
OLIVER
BURLEIGH
KIDDER
STUTSMAN
BARNES
CASS
BILLINGS
GOLDEN VALLEY
STARK
MORTON
GRANT
SIOUX
EMMONS
LOGAN
LA MOURE
RANSOM
RICHLAND
SLOPE
HETTINGER
ADAMS
BOWMAN
MC INTOSH
DICKEY
SARGENT
Bismarck
Fargo
Grand Forks
Minot
Williston
Dickinson
Jamestown
Mandan
Devils Lake
Valley City
Wahpeton
Lake Sakakawea
Lake Oahe
Missouri R.
Souris R.
Red River of the North
Sheyenne R.
James R.
Pembina R.
Heart R.
Cannonball R.
Little Missouri R.
Yellowstone R.
White Butte 3,506 ft.
Garrison Dam
0 10 20 30 40 mi
0 10 20 30 40 50 60 km
©1996, Encyclopædia Britannica, Inc.

Northern Highlands. Elevated plateau region of N Scotland, N part of the Highlands (see SCOTLAND) in Highland region; highest points Beinn Dearg 3547 ft. (1996 m.) and Ben More 3273 ft. (998 m.).

Northern Ireland. See IRELAND, NORTHERN.

Northern Kingdom. See ISRAEL 1.

Northern Land. See SEVERNAYA ZEMLYA.

Northern Mariana Islands *or* **Northern Marianas.** The Mariana Is. except for Guam; 184 sq. mi. (477 sq. km.); pop. (1993e) 45,400; seat of government is on Saipan; for earlier history, see MARIANA ISLANDS; became Commonwealth of the Northern Mariana Islands under U.S. sovereignty 1978; trusteeship officially ended by UN 1990.

Northern Mashonaland. See MASHONALAND.

Northern Matabeleland. See MATABELELAND.

Northern Min·da·nao \ˌmin-dä-'naů\. Region of the Philippines. See table at PHILIPPINES.

Northern Moytura. See MOYTURA.

Northern Neck. Region in N colonial Virginia bet. the Rappahannock and Potomac rivers.

Northern Region. Administrative region of N Ghana. See table at GHANA.

Northern Rhodesia. See ZAMBIA.

Northern Sa·mar \'sä-ˌmär\. Province, N Samar, Philippines; ✱ Catarman. See table at PHILIPPINES.

Northern Sporades. See SPORADES.

Northern Territories. 1. Former British protectorate, W Africa, now part of Ghana; 37,723 sq. mi. (97,703 sq. km.); with N section of Togoland mandate, 41,063 sq. mi. (106,353 sq. km.). Plateau in W part, plain traversed by the Volta in cen. and E parts. Chief towns Tamale, Yendi, Savelugu. Organized as protectorate and attached to Gold Coast c. 1901; protectorate terminated 1957, and became part of Ghana; partitioned into Northern Region and Upper Region 1960.
2. Japan's name for the southernmost islands in the Kuril chain: Kunashir, Shikotan, Iturup, and some smaller islands; in Sea of Okhotsk; administered by Russia, but claimed by Japan.

Northern Territory. Territory, N part of Australia, bounded on S by 26th parallel of S lat., on W and E respectively by 129th and 138th meridians E long., and on N by Timor and Arafura seas and Gulf of Carpentaria; ✱ Darwin. Most of interior is tableland rising gradually to ab. 1700 ft. (500 m.); good grazing land in N but sandy in S; Macdonnell Ranges in S with highest point Mt. Ziel 5023 ft. (1531 m.), Simpson Desert in SE, and region of Arnhem Land in N. See table at AUSTRALIA.
Chief rivers: Victoria, Daly, and Roper. Adjacent islands Bathurst, Melville, and Groote Eylandt.
Chief products: Copper, iron ore, manganese, bauxite, gold, uranium; cattle; tourism.
Major towns: Darwin and Alice Springs.
History: Inhabited by aborigines for thousands of years; coast explored by Dutch 17th cent., surveyed by English mariner Matthew Flinders early 19th cent.; included 1825 as a part of New South Wales; annexed 1863 to South Australia and entered Commonwealth 1901 as part of South Australia; transferred to direct control of the Commonwealth 1911; divided 1927 into North Australia and Central Australia but by act of 1931 original Northern Terr. reestablished; N parts bombed by Japanese in WWII, and occupied by Allied troops throughout the war; self-government within Commonwealth of Australia granted 1978.

Northern Transvaal. See *Northern* in table at SOUTH AFRICA, REPUBLIC OF.

Northern Yukon National Park. See CANADA, *National Parks.*

North Esk \'esk\. **1.** River, NE Tasmania, Australia; flows E to join South Esk at Launceston to form the Tamar; ab. 45 mi. (70 km.) long.
2. Small river in E cen. Scotland, N of the South Esk; flows SE into North Sea near Montrose.
3. River, Scotland. See ESK 3.

North·field \'nȯrth-ˌfēld\. **1.** Village, Cook co., NE Illinois, 8 mi. (13 km.) N of Chicago; pop. (1990c) 4635; residential.
2. Town, Franklin co., NW Massachusetts; pop. (1990c) 2838; Northfield Mount Hermon School formed 1971 by merger of Northfield Seminary (1879) and Mount Hermon School for Boys (1881).
3. City, Rice co., S Minnesota; pop. (1990c) 14,684; Carleton Coll. (1866), St. Olaf Coll. (1874).
4. Town, Merrimack co., S cen. New Hampshire, 13 mi. (21 km.) N of Concord; pop. (1990c) 4263. See TILTON 2.
5. City, Atlantic co., SE New Jersey, 6 mi. (10 km.) W of Atlantic City; pop. (1990c) 7305.
6. Village, Summit co., NE Ohio; pop. (1990c) 3624.
7. Town, Washington co., N cen. Vermont, 10 mi. (16 km.) S of Montpelier; pop. (1990c) 5610; Norwich Univ. (1819).

North·fleet \'nȯrth-ˌflēt\. Town, Kent, SE England, on the Thames 20 mi. (32 km.) E of London; pop. (1981p) 26,250.

North Flin·ders Range \'flin-dərz\. Mountain range, E South Australia, Australia, E of Lake Torrens; highest peak St. Mary Peak 3838 ft. (1170 m.).

North Fond du Lac \'fän-d^{ə}l-ˌak, 'fän-jə-ˌlak\. Village, Fond du Lac co., E Wisconsin, on Lake Winnebago; pop. (1990c) 4292.

North Foreland. See FORELAND, NORTH.

North Fox Island. See FOX ISLANDS 2.

North Fremantle. See FREMANTLE.

North Frisian Islands. See FRISIAN ISLANDS.

North·glenn \'nȯrth-ˌglen\. City, Adams co., NE cen. Colorado; pop. (1990c) 27,195; residential suburb of Denver.

North Hale·don \'hāl-dən\. Borough, Passaic co., N New Jersey, 4 mi. (6 km.) N of Paterson; pop. (1990c) 7987.

North Hamp·ton \'hamp-tən\. Town, Rockingham co., SE New Hampshire; pop. (1990c) 3637.

North Haven. 1. Island in entrance to Penobscot Bay, off S cen. Maine coast.
2. Suburban residential town, cen. New Haven co., S Connecticut, on Quinnipiac River; pop. (1990c) 22,247.

North Head. 1. Promontory, SW Washington, N side of mouth of Columbia River near Cape Disappointment.
2. Promontory on N side of entrance to Port Jackson, the harbor of Sydney, Australia.

North Hemp·stead \'hemp-ˌsted, -stəd\. Town, Nassau co., SE New York, on Long Island, E of New York City; pop. (1990c) 211,393.

North He·ro \'hē-rō, -'hir-ō\. Town, ⊗ of Grand Isle co., NW corner of Vermont, on **North Hero Island** in Lake Champlain 10 mi. (16 km.) W of St. Albans; pop. (1990c) 502.

North High·lands \'hī-ləndz\. Unincorporated settlement, Sacramento co., N cen. California, NE of the city of Sacramento; pop. (1990c) 42,105; residential.

North Hills. Village, Nassau co., Long Island, New York; pop. (1990c) 3453.

North Holland *or Du.* **Noord–Hol·land** \nōrt-'hȯ-länt\. Province, W Netherlands; ✱ Haarlem; dairy farming, tulip growing; chemical and metallurgical industries; tourism. See table at NETHERLANDS.

North Holland Canal. Canal, extending N from Amsterdam, Netherlands, through North Holland prov. to Den Helder; 50 mi. (81 km.) long; built 1819–25.

North Hsing·an \'shiŋ-'än\. Former province (1932–45), NW Manchukuo; 61,489 sq. mi. (159,257 sq. km.); ✱ Hailar.

North Island. 1. Island, SE coast of Georgetown co., South Carolina; in Atlantic Ocean off Winyah Bay.
2. Northernmost of the two main islands of New Zealand (*q.v.*); 44,297 sq. mi. (114,729 sq. km.); pop. (1991c) 2,553,413.

North Kanara. See KANARA.

North Kansas City. City, Clay co., NW Missouri, N suburb of Kansas City; pop. (1990c) 4130.

North Karoo. See KAROO.

\ə\ **abut** \ə̇\ matches \$^{ə}$\ kitten, Fr table \ər\ **further** \a\ **ash** \ā\ **ace**
\ä\ cot, cart \ȧ\ Fr bac \aů\ **out** \b̲\ Span Avila \ch\ **chin** \e\ bet \ē\ **easy**
\g\ **go** \i\ hit \ī\ **ice** \j\ **job** \k̲\ Ger **ich**, Buch \$^{n}$\ Fr vin
\ŋ\ sing \ō\ **go** \ö\ **all** \ȯ\ **law** \œ\ Fr bœuf \œ̄\ Fr **feu** \ȯi\ **boy**
\th\ **thin** \th̲\ **this** \ü\ **loot** \ů\ **foot** \ue\ Ger füllen \ue̅\ Fr **rue**
\y\ **yet** \$^{y}$\ Fr digne \'dēn^{y}\, nuit \'nw^{y}ē\ \yü\ **few** \yů\ **fury** \zh\ **vision**

North Kazakhstan. Administrative subdivision of Kazakhstan; 17,104 sq. mi. (44,299 sq. km.); ✻ Petropavlovsk.

North Khartoum. See KHARTOUM NORTH.

North Kings·town \ˈkiŋz-tau̇n\. Town, Washington co., S Rhode Island, on Narragansett Bay; pop. (1990c) 23,786; residential; machine tools; administrative center is the village of Wickford. Formerly part of Kings Towne (Kingstown), incorp. 1674 and divided into North Kingstown and South Kingstown 1723. Birthplace of painter Gilbert Stuart 1755.

North Korea. See KOREA, NORTH.

North Kvaloy. See NORD-KVALOY.

North Kyŏng·sang \ˈkyəŋ-ˈsäŋ\. Province of South Korea. See table at KOREA, SOUTH.

North·lake \ˈnȯrth-ˌlāk\. City, Cook and Du Page cos., NE Illinois, suburb of Chicago; pop. (1990c) 12,505.

North Land. See SEVERNAYA ZEMLYA.

North Las Vegas \läs-ˈvā-gəs\. City, Clark co., SE Nevada, N suburb of Las Vegas; pop. (1990c) 47,707; warehousing and distribution; Community Coll. of Southern Nevada (1971).

North Lau·der·dale \ˈlȯ-dər-ˌdāl\. City, Broward co., Florida, NW of Fort Lauderdale; pop. (1990c) 26,506.

North Little Rock; *formerly* **Ar·gen·ta** \är-ˈjen-tə\. City, Pulaski co., cen. Arkansas, on N bank of Arkansas River opp. Little Rock; pop. (1990c) 61,741; Shorter Coll. (1884).

North Llano. See LLANO.

North Loup \ˈlüp\. River, Nebraska; flows from cen. Cherry co., N Nebraska, SE to unite with Middle Loup and South Loup rivers and form the Loup River; 212 mi. (341 km.) long.

North Magnetic Pole. See MAGNETIC POLE.

North Male. See MALE.

North Man·ches·ter \ˈman-ˌches-tər, -chə-stər\. Town, Wabash co., N Indiana, 33 mi. (53 km.) W of Fort Wayne; pop. (1990c) 6383; Manchester Coll. (1889).

North Man·ka·to \man-ˈkā-tō\. City, Nicollet co., S Minnesota, across Minnesota River from Mankato; pop. (1990c) 10,164.

North Ma·roon Peak \mə-ˈrün\. Mountain, Pitkin co., W cen. Colorado; 14,014 ft. (4272 m.).

North Mi·ami \mī-ˈa-mē, -mə\. City, Miami-Dade co., SE Florida; suburb of Miami on Biscayne Bay; pop. (1990c) 49,998.

North Miami Beach. City, Miami-Dade co., SE Florida, N of Miami Beach; pop. (1990c) 35,359; Southeastern Univ. of Health Sciences (1979).

North Minch \ˈminch\. Strait bet. the mainland of NW Scotland and the island of Lewis with Harris in the Outer Hebrides; varies in width bet. 24 and 45 mi. (39 and 72 km.).

North Mus·ke·gon \mə-ˈskē-gən\. City, Muskegon co., W Michigan; N suburb of the city of Muskegon; pop. (1990c) 3919.

North Myr·tle Beach \ˈmərt-ᵊl\. City, Horry co., E South Carolina; pop. (1990c) 8636.

North Ne·gril Point \nə-ˈgril\. Cape on W end of Jamaica, West Indies, N of entrance to Long Bay.

North New·ton \ˈnüt-ᵊn\. City, Harvey co., SE cen. Kansas; pop. (1990c) 1262; Bethel Coll. (1887).

North Og·den \ˈȯg-dən, ˈäg-\. City, Weber co., N Utah, 14 mi. (23 km.) N of Ogden; pop. (1990c) 11,668; grew rapidly in 1970s.

North Olm·sted \ˈōm-ˌsted\. City, Cuyahoga co., N Ohio, 13 mi. (21 km.) WSW of Cleveland; pop. (1990c) 34,204.

North Ossetia. See ALANIA.

North Os·se·tian A.S.S.R. \ä-ˈsē-shən, -shē-ən\. Autonomous republic, SE Russian S.F.S.R. of U.S.S.R. 1936–91; became North Ossetia Rep. of Russia 1991; name later changed to Alania (*q.v.*).

North Ossetiya. See ALANIA.

North Pacific Ocean. See PACIFIC OCEAN.

North Pagai. See PAGAI.

North Palisade. See PALISADE, NORTH.

North Palm Beach. Village, Palm Beach co., SE Florida, 7 mi. (11 km.) N of the resort town of Palm Beach; pop. (1990c) 11,343.

North Park. Elevated tract, Jackson co., N Colorado, bet. Medicine Bow Mts. and Park Range; contains headwaters of the North Platte. See SOUTH PARK.

North Pass. One of the channels at the mouth of the Mississippi River (*q.v.*).

North Plainfield. Borough, Somerset co., N cen. New Jersey, 9 mi. (15 km.) N of New Brunswick; pop. (1990c) 18,820.

North Platte \ˈplat\. **1.** River in Colorado, Wyoming, and Nebraska; rises in Jackson co., N Colorado, flows N across Wyoming border into cen. Wyoming, turns E and SE across Nebraska border through W cen. Nebraska to unite with South Platte River in Lincoln co., SW cen. Nebraska, and form the Platte River; 680 mi. (1094 km.) long.

2. City, ⊗ of Lincoln co., Nebraska, at confluence of North Platte and South Platte rivers; pop. (1990c) 22,605; railroad shops, Mid-Plains Community Coll. (1965). Nearby ranch was home of William F. Cody (Buffalo Bill).

North Point. **1.** Point on E coast of Alpena co., NE Michigan, at N entrance to Thunder Bay.

2. Cape at N tip of W end of Prince Edward I., SE Canada, extending into the Gulf of St. Lawrence.

North Polar Regions. See POLAR REGIONS.

North Pole. The N extremity of Earth's axis, at 90°N lat. and the N center from which start all meridians of long.; the point from which the only direction is S. The area around it (North Polar Regions: see POLAR REGIONS) is entirely water (Arctic Ocean), usually ice-covered. First reached by expedition of American Adm. Robert E. Peary April 6, 1909, though this claim is now in dispute; reached several times since. See MAGNETIC POLE.

North·port \ˈnȯrth-ˌpȯrt\. **1.** City, Tuscaloosa co., W cen. Alabama, 3 mi. (5 km.) N of the city of Tuscaloosa; pop. (1990c) 17,366; grew rapidly in 1970s and 1980s.

2. Village in town of Huntington, Suffolk co., SE New York, on N coast of Long Island; pop. (1990c) 7572.

North Port. City, Sarasota co., SW Florida, 35 mi. (56 km.) NW of Cape Coral; pop. (1990c) 11,973; has grown rapidly since 1960.

North Providence. Town, Providence co., N Rhode Island; NW suburb of the city of Providence; pop. (1990c) 32,090.

North Read·ing \ˈre-diŋ\. Town, Middlesex co., NE Massachusetts, 13 mi. (21 km.) ESE of Lowell; pop. (1990c) 12,002.

North Rhine–West·pha·lia \ˈrīn-west-ˈfāl-yə, -ˈfā-lē-ə\ *or Ger.* **Nord·rhein–West·fa·len** \nȯrt-ˈrīn-vest-ˈfä-lən\. A state of W Germany; ✻ Düsseldorf; iron and steel; chemicals, textiles, machinery; oil refining, coal mining; formed 1946; added Lippe 1947. See table at GERMANY.

North Rich·land Hills \ˈrich-lənd\. City, Tarrant co., N Texas, NE of Fort Worth; pop. (1990c) 45,895; has grown rapidly since 1960.

North·ridge \ˈnȯrth-ˌrij\. Neighborhood of Los Angeles, California, in the NW part of the city; California State Univ., Northridge (1958); epicenter of earthquake Jan. 17, 1994.

North Ridge·ville \ˈrij-ˌvil\. City, Lorain co., N Ohio, ab. 5 mi. (8 km.) NE of Elyria; pop. (1990c) 21,564; residential.

North Riding. **1.** Former administrative county, England. See YORKSHIRE.

2. Subdivision of co. Tipperary, Ireland. See TIPPERARY.

North River. See NORTH.

North Riv·er·side \ˈri-vər-ˌsīd\. Village, Cook co., NE Illinois, W suburb of Chicago; pop. (1990c) 6005.

North Ron·ald·say \ˈrän-ᵊld-ˌsā\ *or* **North Ron·ald·shay** \-ˌshā\. Northernmost of the Orkney Is. (*q.v.*) off N coast of Scotland.

North Roy·al·ton \ˈrȯi-əl-tən\. City, Cuyahoga co., N Ohio, 13 mi. (21 km.) S of Cleveland; pop. (1990c) 23,197.

North Saint Paul. Village, Ramsey co., E Minnesota, 7 mi. (11 km.) NE of St. Paul; pop. (1990c) 12,376.

North Salt Lake. City, Davis co., N Utah, just N of Salt Lake City; pop. (1990c) 6474.

North Saskatchewan. See SASKATCHEWAN 1.

North Scit·u·ate \ˈsi-chə-wət\. Village, Providence co., N Rhode Island, NW of Cranston; administrative center of Scituate.

Norths Coast \ˈnȯrths\. Section of coast of East Antarctica, 67°S, bet. 125°E and 130°E; part of Wilkes Land and Australian claim.

North Sea *also* **German Ocean;** *anc.* **Ma·re Ger·man·i·cum** \ˈmä-rē-jər-ˈma-ni-kəm, ˈmä-ˌrā-\. Arm of the Atlantic Ocean extending bet. the European continent on the S and E and Great Britain on the W; ab. 600 mi. (970 km.) long and 350 mi. (560 km.) wide; ab. 220,000 sq. mi. (570,000 sq. km.); av. depth 308 ft. (94 m.); important fisheries; site of extensive oil and natural-gas fields; explosion and fire at a British oil production platform resulted in the deaths of more than 160 workers July 6, 1988.

North Sea Canal *or* **Amsterdam Ship Canal** *or Du.* **Noord Zee Ka·naal** \ˈnōrt-ˈzā-kə-ˈnäl\. Canal, Netherlands, from Amsterdam to North Sea at IJmuiden; 17 mi. (27 km.) long; constructed 1865–76; restored importance of Amsterdam as commercial port.

North Sheep Mountain \ˈshēp\. Peak, Park and Summit cos., cen. Colorado; 13,600 ft. (4145 m.).

North Slope. 1. *also* **Arctic Slope.** Coastal region, N Alaska, bet. Brooks Range and the Arctic Ocean; extensive oil reserves discovered 1968; connected to Valdez by Trans-Alaska Pipeline 1977.

2. Division in Alaska. See table at ALASKA.

North Smith·field \ˈsmith-ˌfēld\. Town, Providence co., N Rhode Island, near Woonsocket; pop. (1990c) 10,497; its administrative center is Slatersville.

North Ston·ing·ton \ˈstō-niŋ-tən\. Town, New London co., SE Connecticut, 14 mi. (23 km.) NE of the city of New London; pop. (1990c) 4884.

North Stradbroke. See STRADBROKE.

North Stradbroke Island. Island off W coast of Australia, just W of Brisbane.

North Su·la·we·si \ˌsü-lə-ˈwā-sē\. Province of Indonesia, on Sulawesi. See SULAWESI and table at INDONESIA.

North Su·ma·tra \su̇-ˈmä-trə\. Province of Indonesia, on Sumatra. See SUMATRA and table at INDONESIA.

North Sydney. 1. Municipality, E New South Wales, SE Australia; N suburb of Sydney on N side of Port Jackson; pop. (1991c) 50,446; connected with Sydney by Sydney Harbour Bridge (steel arch; main span 1650 ft. or 503 m.; completed 1932).

2. Town, Cape Breton co., E Nova Scotia, Canada; on W side of Sydney Harbor 4 mi. (6 km.) SW of entrance; pop. (1991c) 7260.

North Syracuse. Village, Onondaga co., cen. New York, 8 mi. (13 km.) NNE of Syracuse; pop. (1990c) 7363.

North Ta·ra·na·ki Bight \ˌtär-ə-ˈnä-kē\. Gulf N of W bulge on W coast of North I., New Zealand.

North Tarryall Peak. See TARRYALL PEAK, NORTH.

North Tarrytown. See SLEEPY HOLLOW 2.

North Thompson. See THOMPSON 2.

North To·na·wan·da \ˌtä-nə-ˈwän-də\. City and port of entry, Niagara co., W New York, 10 mi. (16 km.) E of Niagara Falls; pop. (1990c) 34,989.

North Twin Mountain. See TWIN MOUNTAINS.

North Tyne. See TYNE 1.

North Uist \ˈyü-əst\. Island of the Outer Hebrides, off NW coast of Scotland; separated by Little Minch from Skye; pop. (1981c) 1454; administratively part of Western Isles region.

North·um·ber·land \nȯr-ˈthəm-bər-lənd\. **1.** Name of counties in two states of the U.S. See tables at PENNSYLVANIA and VIRGINIA.

2. Borough, Northumberland co., E cen. Pennsylvania, on Susquehanna River 28 mi. (45 km.) SSE of Williamsport; pop. (1990c) 3860. Home of English clergyman and chemist Joseph Priestley 1794–1804.

3. Counties in two provinces of Canada. See tables at NEW BRUNSWICK and ONTARIO.

4. Former county, N England, on the border of Scotland; important settlements: Newcastle upon Tyne, Tynemouth, Berwick-upon-Tweed, Alnwick, Morpeth, Hexham.

5. Administrative county, N England, incl. all of the former county except SE portion now in metropolitan co. of Tyne and Wear; includes Holy I. or Lindisfarne, the Farne Is., and Coquet Isle; chief rivers: Tyne, Tweed, Till, Coquet. See table at ENGLAND.

Northumberland, Cape. Cape on Indian Ocean, SE corner of South Australia, Australia, 38°05′S.

Northumberland Isles *or* **Northumberland Islands.** Group of islands off E coast of Queensland, Australia, enclosing Broad Sound.

Northumberland National Park. Park, Northumberland, N England, on Scottish border; ab. 400 sq. mi. (1035 sq. km.); estab. 1956.

Northumberland Strait. Channel off E New Brunswick and N Nova Scotia, Canada, bet. Prince Edward I. and the SE Canadian mainland; ab. 180 mi. (290 km.) long and 12 to 30 mi. (19 to 48 km.) wide.

North·um·bria \nȯr-ˈthəm-brē-ə\. Anglo-Saxon kingdom of Britain, bet. the Humber River and the Firth of Forth; formed by 7th cent. consolidation of Anglian kingdoms of Deira and Bernicia (*qq.v.*); expanded during 7th cent. and became the leading kingdom of the Heptarchy (*q.v.*); accepted Roman and Celtic Christianity until Synod of Whitby in 664 which determined the English Church's adherence to Rome; S part ruled by Danes 9th–10th cents.; acknowledged supremacy of Wessex (*q.v.*) in 10th cent.

North Ump·qua \ˈəmp-kwə\. River, SW Oregon; rises in E Douglas co., flows E uniting with South Umpqua River ab. 8 mi. (13 km.) NW of Roseburg to form Umpqua River; ab. 85 mi. (135 km.) long.

North·vale \ˈnȯrth-ˌvāl\. Borough, Bergen co., NE New Jersey, 12 mi. (19 km.) NE of Paterson; pop. (1990c) 4563.

North Valley Stream. Unincorporated settlement, Nassau co., SE New York, in cen. Long Island; pop. (1990c) 14,574.

North Vancouver. Residential city, S British Columbia, Canada, on Burrard Inlet across from Vancouver; pop. (1991c) 38,436; sawmills, shipyards.

North Ver·non \ˈvər-nən\. City, Jennings co., SE Indiana, 36 mi. (58 km.) S of Shelbyville; pop. (1990c) 5311.

North Ver·sailles \vər-ˈsālz\. Urban township, Allegheny co., SW Pennsylvania, SE of Pittsburgh; pop. (1990c) 12,302.

North Vietnam. See VIETNAM, NORTH.

North·ville \ˈnȯrth-ˌvil\. City, Oakland and Wayne cos., SE Michigan, 23 mi. (37 km.) WNW of Detroit; pop. (1990c) 6226.

North Wales \ˈwālz\. Borough, Montgomery co., SE Pennsylvania, 18 mi. (29 km.) N of Philadelphia; pop. (1990c) 3802.

North Waziristan. See WAZIRISTAN.

North West. Province, N Rep. of South Africa, bounded on N by Botswana, on NE by Northern prov., on E by Gauteng prov., on SE by Free State, and on SW by Northern Cape prov.; ✻ Mafikeng; created 1994. See table at SOUTH AFRICA, REPUBLIC OF.

Northwest Angle. The part of Lake of the Woods co., N Minnesota, which is on NW shore of Lake of the Woods N of the 49th parallel; ab. 130 sq. mi. (340 sq. km.); belongs to U.S. instead of Canada because of inadequate survey at time of Treaty of 1783.

Northwest Arctic. Division in Alaska. See table at ALASKA.

North West Cape. Point, W Western Australia, Australia, at entrance to Exmouth Gulf, 21°45′S, 114°10′E.

Northwestern Islands. Widely scattered island groups N of New Guinea I. in the Admiralty Is.; belong to Papua New Guinea; Hermit Is. and Ninigo Group are the most important.

North–West Frontier. Province, Pakistan, bounded on W and N by Afghanistan; ✻ Peshawar. Mountainous area beyond the Indus, the country of the Pashtuns. On its W border are Sulaiman Mts. in S, Safed Koh, and ranges of Hindu Kush; highest peaks Tirich Mir in NW Chitral 26,115 ft. (7960 m.), Himalaya peaks in Hazara dist. 10,000 to 16,700 ft. (3000 to 5100 m.), Sikaram on Afghanistan border in the Safed Koh

15,619 ft. (4761 m.), and Takht-i-Sulaiman in the Sulaiman Mts. 11,289 ft. (3441 m.). Rivers are W tributaries of the Indus (Kabul, Kurram, Gumal). Important mountain passes are the Khyber and Gumal (*qq.v.*). Has small area under cultivation; chief crops wheat, corn. Chief settlements Peshawar, Mardan. See table at PAKISTAN.

History: Region came successively under Persians (c. 5th cent. B.C.), Macedonians, Kushans, Afghans, and others; for centuries region has been home of the Pashtuns, Muslims of Indo-Iranian origin, who were partially subjugated by Moguls (16th–17th cents.) and later (19th cent.) by Sikhs; at end of Second Sikh War trans-Indus districts annexed by British 1849; province created and separated from Punjab 1901 under present name; made autonomous province within British India 1937; by referendum became part of Pakistan 1947; provincial status abolished 1955, restored 1970; inundated with Afghan refugees 1980s.

Northwest Passage. A passage by sea bet. the Atlantic and Pacific oceans along the N coast of America; the lengthy search for a navigable route led to discovery of St. Lawrence River by Jacques Cartier 1534–35, of Frobisher Bay by Sir Martin Frobisher 1576, and of Davis Strait by John Davis 1587, and of Hudson River and Hudson Bay by Henry Hudson 1609–11; other explorers of the area included John Cabot, Sir Francis Drake, Capt. James Cook, Sir William Parry, Sir John Franklin, and Sir Robert McClure who discovered the route during his unsuccessful search (1850–54) for Franklin; the first to navigate the passage was the Norwegian explorer Roald Amundsen (1903–06). See ARCTIC, THE.

North West Providence Channel. See PROVIDENCE CHANNEL, NORTH WEST.

North–West Provinces. Former province of British India. See AGRA 1.

North West Region. Name occasionally used for the NW part of Western Australia, Australia; a plateau along coast extending S from Indian Ocean to Murchison River.

Northwest Territories. Federally administered division of Canada, consisting of the mainland N of 60°N bet. Yukon Terr. and Nunavut and that portion of the Arctic Archipelago N of 70° N and W of 110° W; ✱ Yellowknife. See table at CANADA.

Physical features: large area ranging from mountains to islands and incl. many lakes and rivers; av. elev. of peaks in Mackenzie Mts. on Yukon Terr. border is 7000 ft. or 2100 m. (highest point Mt. Sir James MacBrien 9062 ft. or 2762 m.), but most of the region is comparatively low. The Mackenzie River and its tributaries and the lakes drained by them (esp. Great Bear and Great Slave lakes) fill more than two thirds of the mainland area.

Chief minerals: Lead, gold, zinc, silver; oil.

History: Region inhabited by several native peoples prior to European exploration; mainland explored by English explorer Samuel Hearne, Scottish explorer Sir Alexander Mackenzie, and others; territory W of Prince Rupert's Land part of Hudson's Bay Company lands 1821–69; transferred to Canada 1869 by acquisition of territorial rights of Hudson's Bay Company; Yukon Terr. formed from W part 1898; Ungava Penin. transferred to Quebec 1912; Nunavut formed from E part 1999.

Northwest Territory. Region, North America, around the Great Lakes and bet. the Ohio and Mississippi rivers, comprising what was earlier known as the **Old Northwest,** a territory of ab. 248,000 sq. mi. (642,000 sq. km.) awarded to U.S. by Treaty of Paris 1783. As the first national territory of the U.S. estab. by Congress July 13, 1787, officially known as the **Territory Northwest of the River Ohio,** it included present states of Ohio, Indiana, Illinois, Michigan, Wisconsin, and part of Minnesota (*qq.v.*). Parts claimed by several seaboard states but relinquished late 18th cent. except Western Reserve (*q.v.*); government framework outlined by Ordinance of 1787; first settlement at Marietta 1788; region divided 1800, forming the Indiana Terr. (*q.v.*) and reducing the Northwest Terr. to Ohio and parts of Michigan and Minnesota; ceased to exist upon admission of Ohio to the Union 1803.

North·wich \ˈnȯrth-wich\. Town, Cheshire, NW England, 19 mi. (31 km.) SSW of Manchester; pop. (1981c) 17,195; formerly an important center of England's salt industry.

North Wild·wood \ˈwīld-ˌwu̇d\. City and seaside resort, Cape May co., S New Jersey, on Atlantic Ocean 32 mi. (52 km.) SW of Atlantic City; pop. (1990c) 5017. See WILDWOODS, THE.

North Wilkes·boro \ˈwilks-ˌbər-ō\. Town, Wilkes co., NW cen. North Carolina, 30 mi. (48 km.) NW of Statesville; pop. (1990c) 3384.

North·wood \ˈnȯrth-ˌwu̇d\. **1.** Town, ⊗ of Worth co., N Iowa, 20 mi. (32 km.) N of Mason City; pop. (1990c) 1940.
2. City, Wood co., NW Ohio; pop. (1990c) 5506.

North·woods \ˈnȯrth-ˌwu̇dz\. City, St. Louis co., E Missouri, a N suburb of the city of St. Louis; pop. (1990c) 5106.

North Yemen. See YEMEN ARAB REPUBLIC.

North York \ˈyȯrk\. City, Toronto met. municipality, Ontario, Canada, N of the city of Toronto; pop. (1991c) 562,564.

North York Moors National Park \ˈmȯrz, ˈmu̇rz\. Park, North Yorkshire and Cleveland, NE England; ab. 555 sq. mi. (1435 sq. km.); includes moorlands and North Sea coast beaches; estab. 1952.

North Yorkshire. Administrative county, N England, approx. equivalent to the former North Riding, Yorkshire. See table at ENGLAND.

Nor·ton \ˈnȯrt-ᵊn\. **1.** County in N Kansas. See table at KANSAS.
2. City, ⊗ of Norton co., N Kansas, 120 mi. (193 km.) NW of Great Bend; pop. (1990c) 3017.
3. Town, Bristol co., SE Massachusetts, 11 mi. (18 km.) SW of Brockton; pop. (1990c) 14,265; Wheaton Coll. (1834).
4. City, Summit co., NE Ohio; pop. (1990c) 11,477.
5. City, SW Virginia, 35 mi. (56 km.) NW of Bristol; 3 sq. mi. (8 km.); pop. (1990c) 4247; in Wise co. but politically independent.

Norton Peak. Mountain, NW Blaine co., S cen. Idaho; 10,200 ft. (3109 m.).

Norton Shores. City, Muskegon co., W Michigan, on Lake Michigan 7 mi. (11 km.) S of the city of Muskegon; pop. (1990c) 21,755.

Norton Sound. Large inlet of NE Bering Sea, in W Alaska, bet. Seward Penin. and mouths of the Yukon; ab. 200 mi. (320 km.) long.

Nor·um·be·ga \ˌnȯr-əm-ˈbē-gə, ˌnär-\. Name applied by 16th and 17th cent. mapmakers to undefined region along E coast of North America incl. by narrowest definition only the area around the mouth of the Penobscot River and by broadest definition the entire coast from Nova Scotia to Florida.

Nor·ve·gia Cape \nȯr-ˈvē-jə, -jē-ə\. Cape on Princess Martha Coast, Queen Maud Land, Antarctica, 71°25′S, 12°18′W.

Nor·walk \ˈnȯr-ˌwȯk\. **1.** River, SW Connecticut; rises in cen. Fairfield co., flows S into Long Island Sound at South Norwalk.
2. City, Los Angeles co., SW California, SE of the city of Los Angeles; pop. (1990c) 94,279; Cerritos Coll. (1955).
3. City, SW Fairfield co., SW Connecticut, on Long Island Sound; pop. (1990c) 78,331; apparel, electronic equipment; Norwalk Community Coll. (1961), Norwalk State Technical Coll. (1961); traversed by Norwalk River; settled c. 1650; incorp. 1651; town and city of Norwalk (incorp. 1893) consolidated and made coextensive 1913 and expanded to include surrounding towns and municipalities, among them South Norwalk (*q.v.*); during American Revolution burned by British 1779.
4. City, Warren co., S cen. Iowa, S of Des Moines; pop. (1990c) 5726.
5. City, ⊗ of Huron co., N Ohio, 15 mi. (24 km.) S of Sandusky; pop. (1990c) 14,731; manufactures furniture; founded c. 1816.

Nor·way \ˈnȯr-ˌwā\. **1.** *or Norw.* **Nor·ge** \ˈnȯr-gə\. Kingdom, NW Europe, occupying W part of Scandinavia, bounded on the W by the Atlantic Ocean and the North Sea, on the N by the Arctic Ocean, on the NE by Russia and Finland, on the E by Sweden, and on the S by Skagerrak; 154,790 sq. mi. (400,906 sq. km.); pop. (1993e) 4,308,000; ✱ Oslo.

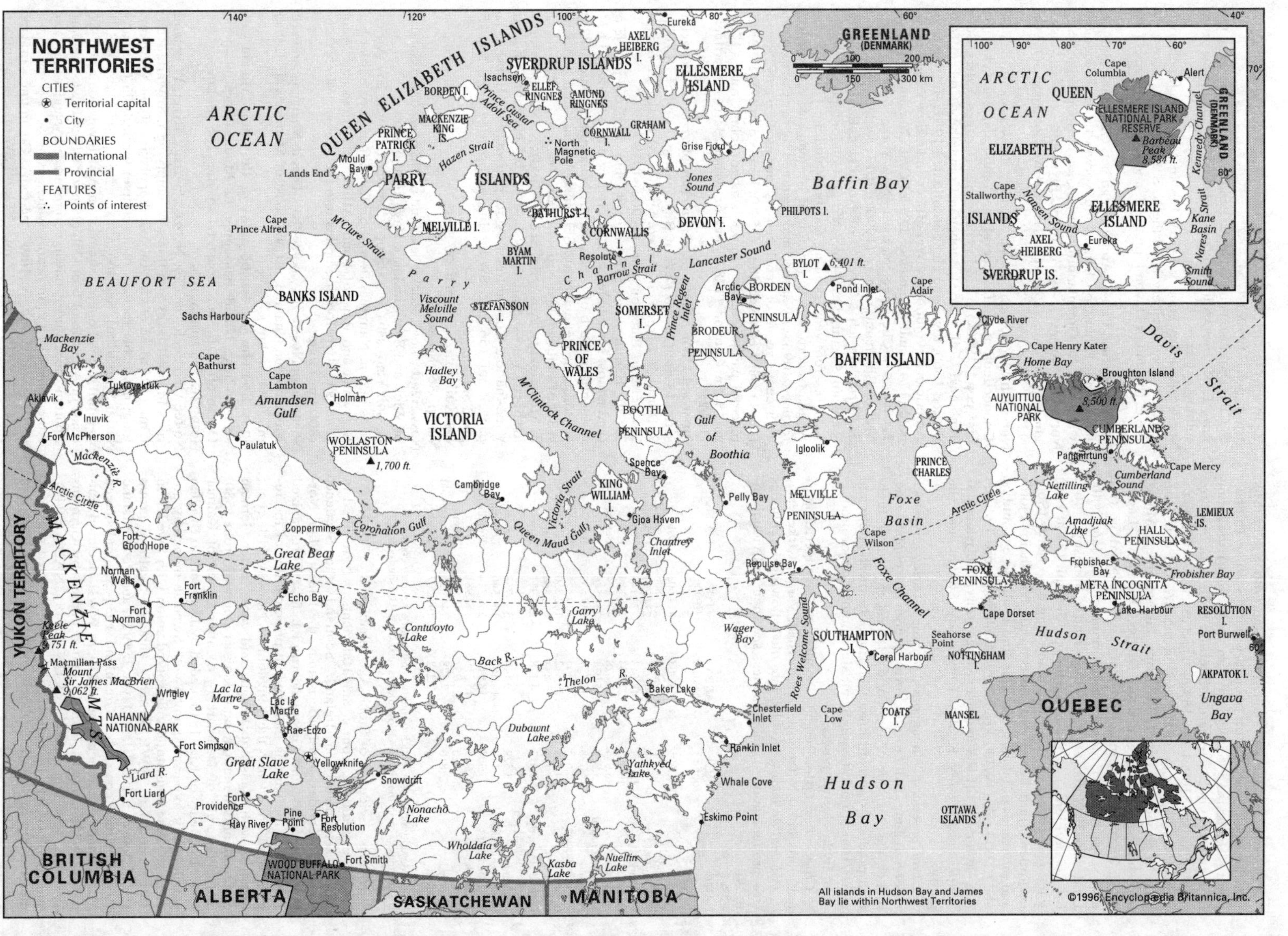

NORTHWEST TERRITORIES
CITIES
Territorial capital
City
BOUNDARIES
International
Provincial
FEATURES
Points of interest
ARCTIC OCEAN
QUEEN ELIZABETH ISLANDS
SVERDRUP ISLANDS
PARRY ISLANDS
BEAUFORT SEA
BANKS ISLAND
VICTORIA ISLAND
BAFFIN ISLAND
Baffin Bay
Davis Strait
Foxe Basin
Foxe Channel
Hudson Strait
Hudson Bay
Ungava Bay
GREENLAND (DENMARK)
QUEBEC
BRITISH COLUMBIA
ALBERTA
SASKATCHEWAN
MANITOBA
YUKON TERRITORY
MACKENZIE MTS.
Great Bear Lake
Great Slave Lake
Yellowknife
WOOD BUFFALO NATIONAL PARK
NAHANNI NATIONAL PARK
AUYUITTUQ NATIONAL PARK
ELLESMERE ISLAND NATIONAL PARK RESERVE
Barbeau Peak 8,584 ft.
All islands in Hudson Bay and James Bay lie within Northwest Territories
©1996 Encyclopædia Britannica, Inc.

Physical features: A mountainous land with Kjølen Mts. forming the N part of the boundary with Sweden (highest point Kebnekaise 6965 ft. or 2123 m., in Sweden), the Jotunheimen group in S cen. part (Glittertind 8110 ft. or 2472 m., Galdhøpiggen 8100 ft. or 2469 m.), and extensive plateau regions called *fjells* or *vidde,* esp. in the SW and cen. parts (Hardangervidda, Dovrefjell); many lakes (largest Mjøsa) and short streams; largest rivers Glåma, Dramselva, Lågen, Tana. Northernmost mainland point is Cape Nordkyn (see also NORTH CAPE 4), most southerly point of mainland is the Lindesnes 58°N, most westerly the island of Steinsøy 5°46′E off Sogne Fjord. Coastline is approx. 1500 mi. (2400 km.) long, but is very irregular with many long deep fjords (Sognefjorden, Hardanger Fjord, Oslo Fjord, Trondheim Fjord) and thousands of islands; est. shoreline of all these would be ab. 12,000 mi. (19,300 km.); largest island groups Lofoten and Vesterålen off NW and many large individual islands as Senja, Nord-Kvaløy, Kvaløy, Ringvassøy, Sørøya, and Magerøya.

Chief products: Wheat, oats, potatoes, barley; livestock raising, fishing, fish farming; forestry; iron ore, copper, zinc, nickel, gas, oil (one of the world's largest exporters); high-tech products; tourism; manufacturing: chemicals, pulp and paper, transportation equipment, aluminum; a major producer of hydroelectric power.

Chief cities: Oslo, Bergen, Trondheim, Stavanger; important ports in far N Tromsø, Hammerfest, Vardø, Kirkenes.

Political divisions: Divided into the following 19 counties (for pronunciation of their names, see their individual entries):

NAME	AREA (sq. mi.)	AREA (sq. km.)	POP. (1990c)	CO. SEAT
Akershus	1,895	4,908	414,503	Oslo
Aust-Agder	3,556	9,210	96,880	Arendal
Buskerud	5,765	14,931	224,701	Drammen
Finnmark	18,783	48,648	74,148	Vadsø
Hedmark	10,557	27,343	186,884	Hamar
Hordaland[1]	6,034	15,628	409,124	Bergen
Møre og Romsdal	5,820	15,074	238,346	Molde
Nordland	14,798	38,327	239,532	Bodø
Nord-Trøndelag	8,673	22,463	126,858	Steinkjer
Oppland	9,773	25,312	182,350	Lillehammer
Oslo[2]	175	453	458,364	Oslo
Østfold (formerly Smaalenenes)	1,613	4,178	237,981	Sarpsborg
Rogaland	3,529	9,140	335,753	Stavanger
Sogn og Fjordane	7,168	18,565	106,540	Leikanger
Sør-Trøndelag	7,304	18,917	250,344	Trondheim
Telemark	5,913	15,315	162,981	Skien
Troms	10,020	25,952	146,594	Tromsø
Vest-Agder	2,810	7,278	144,026	Kristiansand
Vestfold	854	2,212	197,207	Tønsberg

[1] Includes city of Bergen, which formerly constituted a separate county.
[2] Coextensive with the city of Oslo which is also ⊗ of Akershus co.

History: Evidence of Stone Age inhabitants c. 7000 B.C.; Viking expeditions from c. 8th–10th cents. A.D. resulted in Norse settlements on Ireland, Scotland, the Shetland, Orkney, Hebrides, and Faroe islands, the Isle of Man, Normandy, Iceland, and Greenland (*qq.v.*); first Christianized 10th cent.; the various independent principalities of the region were united into the Kingdom of Norway 11th cent.; lost war with Hanseatic League and came under German commercial domination; same king as Denmark from 1380, and under rule of Denmark (*q.v.*) after Union of Kalmar 1397; by Treaty of Kiel 1814, ceded by Denmark to Sweden which held it in personal union with Swedish monarchy under a separate constitution; dissolved union with Sweden in 1905; neutral in WWI; formally annexed Svalbard group 1925, Bouvet I. 1928, Jan Mayen I. 1929, and Peter I Island 1931; claimed coast of E Greenland 1931–33, and Queen Maud Land (Antarctica) since 1939; in WWII, declared neutrality 1939, but was invaded and occupied by Germans 1940–45; founding member of UN (1945), NATO (1949), and EFTA (1960); by national referenda, rejected proffered membership in European Community 1972 and European Union 1994.

2. Town, Oxford co., W Maine, 18 mi. (29 km.) WNW of Lewiston; pop. (1990c) 4754.

3. City, Dickinson co., S Upper Penin. of Michigan, 8 mi. (13 km.) E of Iron Mountain; pop. (1990c) 2910; former iron-mining center.

Nor·we·gian Bay \nȯr-ˈwē-jən\. Bay in Arctic Archipelago, N Canada; Axel Heiberg is on the N, S end of Ellesmere I. on the E, NW end of Devon I. on the S, and Amund Ringnes I. on the W.

Norwegian Sea. Part of Arctic Ocean bet. Greenland and Iceland on the W and Spitsbergen and Norway on the E; includes waters off NE Greenland formerly known as Greenland Sea.

Nor·well \ˈnȯr-ˌwel, -wəl\. Town, Plymouth co., SE Massachusetts, 12 mi. (19 km.) ENE of Brockton; pop. (1990c) 9279.

Nor·wich \ˈnȯr-ˌwich; ˈnär-\. **1.** City, New London co., SE Connecticut, at confluence of the Yantic and Shetucket rivers; pop. (1990c) 37,391; chemicals; Thames Valley State Technical Coll. (1963), Mohegan Community Coll. (1970). Settled 1660; town and city consolidated 1952. Birthplace of American Revolutionary War officer and traitor Benedict Arnold (1741) and of educator Daniel Coit Gilman (1831).

2. City, ⊗ of Chenango co., S cen. New York, 36 mi. (58 km.) NNE of Binghamton; pop. (1990c) 7613; settled 1788.

3. *Brit.* ˈnȯr-ich\. City, ⊗ of Norfolk, E England, on the Wensum 97 mi. (156 km.) NE of London; pop. (1991p) 120,700; footwear; printing and bookbinding; Univ. of East Anglia (incorp. 1964); remains of Norman castle; cathedral, founded 1096; city sacked and occupied by the Danes in the 11th cent.; scene of rebel activity during Peasants' Revolt (1381) and Ket's Rebellion (1549); bombed in WWII. Birthplace of painters of the Norwich school John Crome (1768) and John Cotman (1782) and of writer Harriet Martineau (1802).

Nor·wood \ˈnȯr-ˌwu̇d\. **1.** Town, Norfolk co., E Massachusetts, 13 mi. (21 km.) SW of Boston; pop. (1990c) 28,700.

2. Borough, Bergen co., NE corner of New Jersey, 12 mi. (19 km.) ENE of Paterson; pop. (1990c) 4858.

3. City, Hamilton co., SW corner of Ohio, 5 mi. (8 km.) NE of (and almost surrounded by) Cincinnati; pop. (1990c) 23,674; residential suburb of Cincinnati; Athenaeum of Ohio (1829).

4. Borough, Delaware co., SE Pennsylvania, 9 mi. (15 km.) WSW of Philadelphia; pop. (1990c) 6162.

5. Municipality, Australia. See KENSINGTON AND NORWOOD.

No·shi·ro \ˈnō-shē-ˌrō, nō-ˈshē-rō\ *or* **No·shi·ro·mi·na·to** \-mē-ˈnä-tō\. Coastal town, Akita prefecture, N Honshū, Japan, 35 mi. (56 km.) SW of Hirosaki; pop. (1990p) 55,915; good anchorage.

Nos Kaliakra. See KALIAKRA, NOS.

Nosop. See NOSSOB.

Noss Head \ˈnȯs\. Rocky headland on NE coast of Scotland, N of Wick and S of Sinclair's Bay; lighthouse.

Nos·sob \ˈnō-ˌsäb\ *or* **No·sop** \ˈnō-ˌsäp\. River, SW Africa; rises in cen. Namibia, flows SSE forming part of border bet. Botswana and Rep. of South Africa, and flows into Auob River shortly before it empties into the Molopo; ab. 500 mi. (800 km.) long.

No·sy Be *or* **Nos·si-Bé** \ˌnȯ-sē-ˈbā\. Island, Madagascar, in NE Mozambique Channel, off NW coast of Madagascar; 129 sq. mi. (334 sq. km.).

No·sy Bo·ra·ha \nȯ-ˈsē-ˌbō-rä-ˈä\ *or* **Île Sainte Ma·rie** \ˌēl-saⁿt-mə-ˈrē\. Island belonging to Madagascar, in Indian Ocean off its NE cen. coast; 64 sq. mi. (166 sq. km.).

Notabile. See MDINA.

No·teć \ˈnȯ-ˌtech\ *or Ger.* **Net·ze** \ˈnet-sə\. River, W Poland; rises in small lakes and flows W, emptying into Warta River 6 mi. (10 km.) E of Gorzów Wielkopolski; 230 mi. (370 km.) long; navigable for part of its course; formerly in Germany.

Nótiai Sporádhes. See SPORADES.

No·ti·um \ˈnō-shē-əm, -shəm\. Ancient town, Ionia, on SW coast of Asia Minor S of Colophon for which it was the port; Spartan fleet under naval commander Lysander defeated Athenians 407 B.C. in nearby waters.

No·to \ˈnȯ-tō\; *anc.* **Ne·tum** \ˈnē-təm\. Commune, Siracusa prov., SE Sicily, Italy, 17 mi. (27 km.) SW of seaport of Sir-

ARCTIC OCEAN
NORWEGIAN SEA
North Cape
MAGERØYA ISLAND
Honningsvåg
Kjøllefjord
Kongs Fjord
Båtsfjord
Vardø
SØR ISLAND
Hammerfest
Porsangen Fjord
Vadsø
Varanger Fjord
STABBURS VALLEY NATIONAL PARK
Lakselv
Kirkenes
Bjørnevatn
VANNA ISLAND
RINGVASSØY ISLAND
Alta
Tana
Skjervøy
FINNMARK
KVALØY ISLAND
Karasjok
Reisa
Lake Inari
Tromsø
FINNMARK PLATEAU
SENJA
TROMS
Kautokeino
Finnsnes
VESTERÅLEN
And Fjord
ØVRE DIVIDAL NATIONAL PARK
ØVRE ANARJÅKKA NATIONAL PARK
RUSSIA
Harstad
HINNØYA ISLAND
LOFOTEN ISLANDS
Svolvær
Narvik
Vest Fjord
Nordfold
Mosken Marine Channel
Folda Fjord
RAGO NATIONAL PARK
Bodø
Fauske
NORDLAND
Arctic Circle
Mount Semske 5,022 ft.
DUNDERLANDS VALLEY
Mo
Sandnessjøen
Mosjøen
Hornavan
VEGA
Brønnøysund
Lake Røs
BØRGEFJELL NATIONAL PARK
Oulu
Lake Oulu
VIKNA
NORD-TRØNDELAG
Namsos
Folda Fjord
Gulf of Bothnia
Fro Sound
GRESSÅMOEN NATIONAL PARK
FRØYA ISLAND
Trondheim Fjord
Steinkjer
Brekkstad
Levanger
Stjørdalshalsen
FINLAND
Trondheim
Romsdals Fjord
Kristiansund
Orkanger
Surnadalsøra
SØR-TRØNDELAG
Molde
Ålesund
Mardals Falls
Berkåk
SWEDEN
Hareid
Åndalsnes
Ørstavik
DOVREFJELL
MØRE OG ROMSDAL
DOVRE MOUNTAINS NATIONAL PARK
Måløy
FEMUNDSMARKA NATIONAL PARK
Lake Päijänne
Seven Sisters
GUDBRANDSDALEN
RONDANE MTS.
Florø
Galdhøpiggen 8,100 ft.
RONDANE NATIONAL PARK
SOGN OG FJORDANE
JOTUNHEIMEN
Høyanger
Sogne Fjord
Lågen
HEDMARK
JOTUNHEIM NATIONAL PARK
Hermansverk
Lillehammer
Tampere
Store Jukleggi 6,301 ft.
OPPLAND
Alversund
Dale
Glåma
Elverum
Vossavangen
Brumunddal
Bergen
HORDALAND
BUSKERUD
Gol
Gjøvik
Hamar
Toka Gorge
HARDANGER PLATEAU NATIONAL PARK
Fana
Mjøsa
Vantaa
Osøyri
Espoo
Helsinki
HARDANGER-VIDDA
Eidsvoll
Turku
Leirvik
Lågen
Hardanger Fjord
Uskedal
Hønefoss
Kongsvinger
Sauda
Rjukan
Kolsås
Årnes
Gulf of Finland
Haugesund
Drammen
Oslo
Uppsala
Askim
ROGALAND
TELEMARK
Ski
Tallinn
ESTONIA
KARMØY ISLAND
Notodden
Moss
Västerås
Bokn Fjord
Tønsberg
RJUVEN UPLAND
Stockholm
Stavanger
Skien
Sarpsborg
Vänern
Otra
Oslo Fjord
Fredrikstad
Porsgrunn
Örebro
Nærbø
Sandnes
Sira
Sandefjord
JÆREN PLAIN
Evje
VEST-AGDER
AUST-AGDER
Risør
Flekkefjord
Grimstad
Arendal
Norrköping
BALTIC SEA
Farsund
Lyngdal
Lillesand
Linköping
Lindesnes
Mandal
Kristiansand
Vättern
Skagerrak
Göteborg
Key to Provinces (Shown by number on map)
1 VESTFOLD
2 OSLO
3 AKERSHUS
4 ØSTFOLD
Ålborg
DENMARK
Århus
NORWAY
CITIES
Over 75,000
25,000 to 75,000
Under 25,000
National capital
Provincial capital
BOUNDARIES
International
Provincial
FEATURES
Canals
Waterfalls
0 100 200 mi
0 100 200 300 km
3° 0° 3° 6° 9° 12° 15° 18° 21° 24° 27° 30° 33°
71° 68° 65° 62° 59° 56°
©1996, Encyclopædia Britannica, Inc.

acusa; pop. (1991p) 21,344; cathedral; commune founded 1703 SE of older town which was destroyed 1693 by earthquake.

Not·od·den \ˈnō-ˌtȯd-^{ə}n\. Town, Telemark co., S Norway; pop. (1992e) 12,374; hydroelectric power plant.

No·to Peninsula \ˈnō-tō\ *or Jp.* **Noto Hantō.** Headland, Honshū, Japan, projecting N into Sea of Japan, its E coast enclosing Toyama Bay; largely in Ishikawa prefecture.

No·tre Dame \ˈnō-tər-ˈdām, ˈnō-trə-, -ˈdäm\. Locality, St. Joseph co., N Indiana, just N of South Bend; Univ. of Notre Dame (1842), St. Mary's Coll. (1844), Holy Cross Coll. (1966).

Notre Dame Bay. Inlet of Atlantic Ocean on N coast of Newfoundland, Canada.

Notre Dame des Vertus. See AUBERVILLIERS.

Notre Dame du Lac \dü-ˈläk\. Town, ⊗ of Témiscouata co., S Quebec, Canada, on SW shore of Lake Témiscouata near New Brunswick border; pop. (1991c) 2133.

Not·ta·wa·sa·ga Bay \ˌnä-tə-wə-ˈsȯ-gə\. Inlet in S part of Georgian Bay, Lake Huron, extending into Grey and Simcoe cos., SE Ontario prov., Canada.

Not·ta·way \ˈnä-tə-ˌwā\. River, Abitibi co., SW Quebec, Canada; flows NW into SE part of James Bay; 400 mi. (644 km.) long; outlet of Lake Mattagami and other lakes.

Notte·ly \ˈnät-lē\. Stream, NE Georgia and SW North Carolina; flows N from Blue Ridge in Union co., Georgia, to join the Hiwassee in Cherokee co., North Carolina; ab. 40 mi. (64 km.) long; in its course in Georgia is **Nottely Dam.** (See table at TENNESSEE VALLEY AUTHORITY).

Nøt·ter·øy \ˈnœ-tə-ˌrȯi\. Island in Oslo Fjord, SE Norway; 17 sq. mi. (44 sq. km.); chief town Tønsberg.

Not·ting·ham \ˈnä-tiŋ-əm\. **1.** Town, Rockingham co., SE New Hampshire 20 mi. (32 km.) NE of Manchester; pop. (1990c) 2939.

2. County in England. See NOTTINGHAMSHIRE.

3. City, ⊗ of Nottinghamshire, N cen. England, on the Trent 47 mi. (76 km.) NE of Birmingham; pop. (1991p) 261,500; pharmaceuticals, tobacco products; textile mills; lace manufacture; castle, on site of earlier Norman castle, houses art museum; cathedral; Univ. of Nottingham (founded 1881, incorp. 1948). Original Saxon town held by Danes 9th cent.; scene of three parliaments in 14th cent.; place where Charles I raised his standard 1642 and began the English Civil War. Birthplace 1829 of William Booth, founder of Salvation Army.

Nottingham Island. Small island at W end of Hudson Strait, Arctic Archipelago, S Nunavut, Canada.

Not·ting·ham·shire \ˈnä-tiŋ-əm-ˌshir, -shər\ *or* **Nottingham** *or* **Notts** \ˈnäts\. **1.** Former county, N cen. England.

2. Administrative county, N cen. England, incl. most of the former county; chief river the Trent; grains; livestock; limestone, gypsum; major towns include Nottingham, Newark-on-Trent, Mansfield, Worksop. See table at ENGLAND.

Not·ting Hill \ˈnä-tiŋ\. District, W London, England, in Kensington and Chelsea borough.

Not·to·way \ˈnä-tə-ˌwā\. **1.** River, S Virginia; flows from Lunenburg co. SE across North Carolina border to unite with the Blackwater River and form the Chowan River, NE North Carolina; 175 mi. (282 km.) long.

2. County in S cen. Virginia. See table at VIRGINIA.

3. Village, its ⊗.

Notts. See NOTTINGHAMSHIRE.

Nouad·hi·bou \ˌnwä-dē-ˈbü\; *formerly* **Port–Étienne** \ˌpȯr-tā-ˈtyen\. Seaport town at Cape Blanc, NW Mauritania, pop. (1988c) 59,198; fisheries; exports iron ore.

Nouak·chott \nü-ˈäk-ˌshät\. City, ✻ of Mauritania; near coast in SW part of the country; pop. (1988c) 393,325; university; a small village until development as ✻ began 1958.

Nou Island \ˈnü\. Section of Nouméa, New Caledonia, SW Pacific Ocean; an island before land reclamation connected it to the town.

Noulos, Pic. See ALBÈRES, MONTS.

Nou·méa \nü-ˈmā-ə\; *formerly* **Port–de–France** \ˌpȯr-də-ˈfrä^{n}s\. Town, ✻ of New Caledonia terr., on SW coast of New Caledonia I., SW Pacific Ocean; pop. (1989c) 65,110; has large, landlocked harbor, formed partly by Nou Island, ab. 4 mi. (6 km.) long, with seaplane base, just opp. the town; site of U.S. air base in WWII.

Noup Head \ˈnüp\. Promontory on NW coast of Westray I., Orkney Is., off N coast of Scotland; lighthouse.

Nouveau–Québec. See NEW QUEBEC.

Nou·veau–Qué·bec, Cra·tère du \krȧ-ˈter-dᵫ-nü-ˌvō-kā-ˈbek\ *or Eng.* **New Que·bec Crater** \kwi-ˈbek\; *formerly* **Chubb Crater** \ˈchəb\. Circular depression, N Quebec, Canada; 1300 ft. (400 m.) deep; has a diameter of ab. 2 mi. (3 km.).

Nouvelle Calédonie. See NEW CALEDONIA 1 and 2.

No·va Cae·sa·rea \ˈnō-və-ˌsē-zə-ˈrē-ə; ˌse-sə-, ˌse-zə-\. Latin name for the colony of New Jersey upon its creation 1664.

Nova Civitas. See NEUSTADT AN DER WEINSTRASSE.

Novaesium. See NEUSS 1.

Nova Fri·bur·go \ˌnȯ-və-frē-ˈbür-gü\. City, Rio de Janeiro state, SE Brazil, on railroad line 65 mi. (105 km.) NE of the city of Rio de Janeiro; munic. pop. (1991p) 111,020.

No·va Go·ri·ca \ˈnȯ-və-ˈgȯ-rēt-sä\. Settlement, W Slovenia, on border adjacent to Gorizia, Italy of which it was formerly a part; pop. (1992e) 14,862.

No·va Igua·çu \ˈnȯ-və-ˌē-gwä-ˈsü\. City, Rio de Janeiro state, SE Brazil, NW of the city of Rio de Janeiro; munic. pop. (1991p) 1,286,337.

No·va Li·ma \ˈnȯ-və-ˈlē-mə\. City, Minas Gerais state, E Brazil; S suburb of Belo Horizonte; munic. pop. (1991p) 52,202.

Nova Lisboa. See HUAMBO 2.

No·va·ra \nō-ˈvä-rä\. **1.** Province of Piedmont, NW Italy. See table at ITALY.

2. *anc.* **No·var·ia** \nō-ˈvar-ē-ə\. Commune, its ✻, 28 mi. (45 km.) W of Milan; pop. (1991p) 102,473; medieval cathedral (rebuilt 19th cent.), 16th cent. church of San Gaudenzio; ruins of old castle; episcopal palace; manufactures silks, cottons; important trade in rice and grain. Important city in Middle Ages; scene of battles 1513, 1821, and famous Austrian victory over Piedmontese under King Charles Albert of Sardinia-Piedmont 1849.

No·va Sco·tia \ˌnō-və-ˈskō-shə\. Province, E Canada, one of the Maritime Provinces; ✻ Halifax.

Physical features: Comprises peninsula ab. 375 mi. (605 km.) long by 50 to 100 mi. (80 to 160 km.) wide, joined to continent by isthmus of Chignecto; includes Cape Breton I. (*q.v.*) on NE, separated from it by Strait (or Gut) of Canso; separated on N from Prince Edward I. by Northumberland Strait, and on W from New Brunswick by Bay of Fundy; highest peak North Barren 1747 ft. (533 m.).

Chief products: Coal, gypsum, barite; agricultural products; fishing.

Chief cities: Halifax and Dartmouth.

Political divisions: Divided into the following 18 counties (for pronunciation of their names, see their individual entries):

NAME	AREA[1] (sq. mi.)	AREA[1] (sq. km.)	POP. (1991c)	CO. SEAT
Annapolis	1,285	3,328	23,641	Annapolis Royal
Antigonish	541	1,401	19,226	Antigonish
Cape Breton	972	2,517	120,098	Sydney
Colchester	1,451	3,758	47,683	Truro
Cumberland	1,683	4,359	34,284	Amherst
Digby	970	2,512	21,250	Digby
Guysborough	1,611	4,172	11,724	Guysborough
Halifax	2,063	5,343	330,846	Halifax
Hants	1,229	3,183	37,843	Windsor
Inverness	1,409	3,649	21,620	Port Hood
Kings	842	2,181	56,317	Kentville
Lunenburg	1,169	3,028	47,634	Lunenburg
Pictou	1,124	2,911	49,651	Pictou
Queens	983	2,546	12,923	Liverpool
Richmond	489	1,267	11,260	Arichat
Shelburne	979	2,536	17,343	Shelburne
Victoria	1,105	2,862	8,708	Baddeck
Yarmouth	838	2,170	27,891	Yarmouth

[1] Area = land area.

History: Coast may have been reached by Norsemen 11th cent.; inhabited by Micmacs prior to European settlement; coast probably explored by John Cabot 1497; first permanent

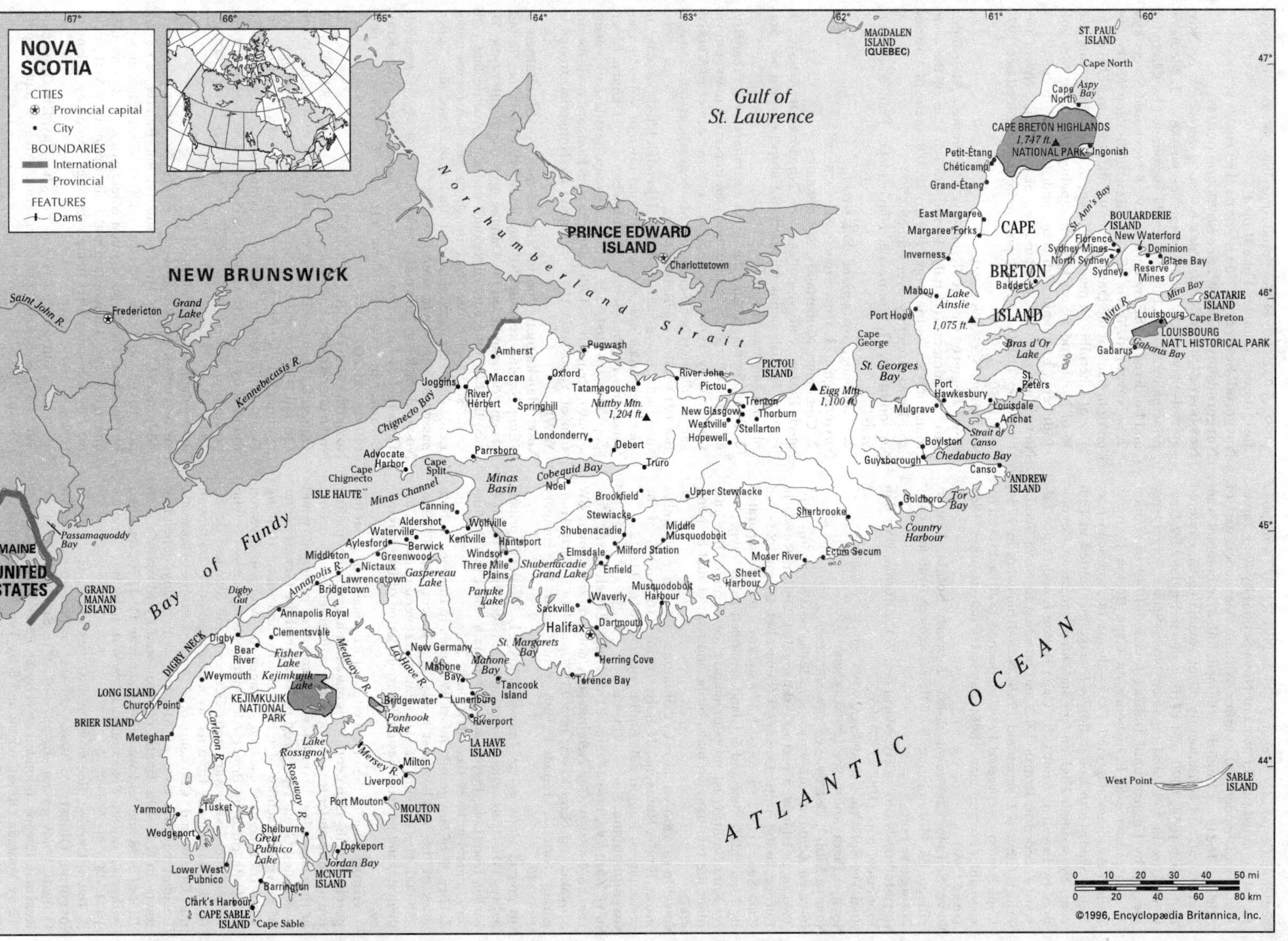
NOVA SCOTIA
CITIES
Provincial capital
City
BOUNDARIES
International
Provincial
FEATURES
Dams
NEW BRUNSWICK
MAINE
UNITED STATES
Fredericton
Grand Lake
Saint John R.
Kennebecasis R.
Passamaquoddy Bay
GRAND MANAN ISLAND
Bay of Fundy
Chignecto Bay
ISLE HAUTE
Minas Channel
Minas Basin
Cobequid Bay
Northumberland Strait
PRINCE EDWARD ISLAND
Charlottetown
Gulf of St. Lawrence
MAGDALEN ISLAND (QUEBEC)
ST. PAUL ISLAND
Cape North
Cape North
Aspy Bay
CAPE BRETON HIGHLANDS
1,747 ft.
NATIONAL PARK
Ingonish
Petit-Étang
Chéticamp
Grand-Étang
East Margaree
Margaree Forks
Inverness
CAPE BRETON ISLAND
St. Ann's Bay
BOULARDERIE ISLAND
Florence
New Waterford
Sydney Mines
Dominion
North Sydney
Glace Bay
Sydney
Reserve Mines
Baddeck
Mabou
Lake Ainslie
Port Hood
1,075 ft.
Mira R.
Mira Bay
SCATARIE ISLAND
Louisbourg
Cape Breton
LOUISBOURG NAT'L HISTORICAL PARK
Gabarus
Gabarus Bay
Bras d'Or Lake
Cape George
St. Georges Bay
Port Hawkesbury
St. Peters
Louisdale
Arichat
Mulgrave
Strait of Canso
Boylston
Chedabucto Bay
Guysborough
Canso
ANDREW ISLAND
Goldboro
Tor Bay
Country Harbour
Eigg Mtn. 1,100 ft.
PICTOU ISLAND
River John
Pictou
Trenton
New Glasgow
Thorburn
Westville
Stellarton
Hopewell
Pugwash
Amherst
Oxford
Tatamagouche
Maccan
Joggins
River Hébert
Springhill
Nuttby Mtn. 1,204 ft.
Londonderry
Debert
Parrsboro
Truro
Advocate Harbor
Cape Chignecto
Cape Split
Noel
Brookfield
Upper Stewiacke
Sherbrooke
Canning
Aldershot
Wolfville
Stewiacke
Middle Musquodoboit
Waterville
Kentville
Hantsport
Shubenacadie
Aylesford
Berwick
Elmsdale
Milford Station
Moser River
Ecum Secum
Middleton
Greenwood
Windsor
Three Mile Plains
Shubenacadie Grand Lake
Enfield
Sheet Harbour
Nictaux
Lawrencetown
Gaspereau Lake
Annapolis R.
Bridgetown
Digby Gut
Panuke Lake
Musquodoboit Harbour
Waverly
Sackville
Annapolis Royal
Halifax
Dartmouth
DIGBY NECK
Digby
Clementsvale
Bear River
Fisher Lake
Medway R.
La Have R.
New Germany
St. Margarets Bay
Mahone Bay
Mahone Bay
Herring Cove
Weymouth
Kejimkujik Lake
Tancook Island
Terence Bay
LONG ISLAND
Church Point
KEJIMKUJIK NATIONAL PARK
Bridgewater
Lunenburg
BRIER ISLAND
Riverport
Meteghan
Carleton R.
Ponhook Lake
LA HAVE ISLAND
Lake Rossignol
Mersey R.
Milton
Liverpool
Roseway R.
Port Mouton
MOUTON ISLAND
Yarmouth
Tusket
Wedgeport
Shelburne
Great Pubnico Lake
Lockeport
Jordan Bay
Lower West Pubnico
MCNUTT ISLAND
Barrington
Clark's Harbour
CAPE SABLE ISLAND
Cape Sable
ATLANTIC OCEAN
West Point
SABLE ISLAND
67°
66°
65°
64°
63°
62°
61°
60°
47°
46°
45°
44°
0 10 20 30 40 50 mi
0 20 40 60 80 km
©1996, Encyclopædia Britannica, Inc.

settlement estab. by French 1605 at Port Royal (Annapolis Royal); granted (under name of Nova Scotia) by King James I to Scottish poet and courtier William Alexander, earl of Stirling, 1621, but English settlement failed; in colonial wars Port Royal, and consequently all of Acadia (*q.v.*), captured by English 1654, 1690, and 1710; ceded to England by Treaty of Utrecht 1713 and renamed Nova Scotia; largely neglected by English until Halifax founded 1749 to counter French presence at Louisbourg on Cape Breton I.; many French Acadians deported 1755—theme of American poet Henry Wadsworth Longfellow's *Evangeline;* settled in 18th cent. by Scottish Highlanders and, after American Revolution, by Loyalists from U.S.; Cape Breton I. and Prince Edward I. ceded to British 1763 and attached to Nova Scotia; Prince Edward I. separated 1769, New Brunswick in 1784; Cape Breton I. separated 1784, reattached 1820; achieved responsible government 1848; entered Confederation 1867 (see CANADA).

No·va So·fa·la \ˌnȯ-və-sü-ˈfä-lə\; *formerly* **Sofala.** Seaport village, SE Mozambique, S of Beira; ancient Arab and early Portuguese port.

No·va·to \nō-ˈvä-tō\. City, Marin co., W California, N of San Francisco; pop. (1990c) 47,585.

Nová Ves Spišská. See SPIŠSKÁ NOVÁ VES.

Novaya Pismyanka. See LENINOGORSK.

Novaya Sibir', Ostrov. See NEW SIBERIA ISLAND.

No·va·ya Zem·lya \ˌnō-və-yə-ˌzem-lē-ˈä, ˈnȯ-və-yə-zim-ˈlyä\. Two large islands, a part of Arkhangel'sk Oblast, Russia in Europe, in the Arctic Ocean off N coast bet. Barents Sea and Kara Sea; 31,382 sq. mi. (81,279 sq. km.); islands separated by Matochkin Shar and S island separated from Vaygach I. by Kara Strait; N island permanently ice-covered; has little plant life but many animals, birds, and fish; visited by hunters.

No·vel·la·ra \ˌnō-vä-ˈlä-rä\. Commune, Reggio nell'Emilia prov., Emilia-Romagna, N Italy, 10 mi. (16 km.) N of the commune of Reggio nell'Emilia; pop. (1981p) 11,312.

Novempopulana. See AQUITANIA.

No·vé Zám·ky \ˈnȯ-ve-ˈzäm-kē\ *or Hung.* **Ér·sek·új·vár** \ˈer-she-ˌkü-ē-vär\ *or Ger.* **Neu·häu·sel** \ˈnȯi-ˌhȯi-zəl\. Town, SW Slovakia, on Nitra River; pop. (1980p) 34,147. Early Hungarian fortress, founded 16th cent.; held by Hungary 1938–45.

Nov·go·rod \ˈnȯv-gə-rət, ˈnäv-gə-ˌräd\. **1.** Medieval principality, 11th–15th cents., covering extensive region of all N Russia from Lake Peipus and Lithuania to the Urals. Its history centers in its ✻ (see NOVGOROD 2).

2. City, ✻ of Novgorod Oblast, W Russia in Europe, on both sides of the Volkhov just N of Lake Ilmen; pop. (1992e) 235,000. Has kremlin of 11th cent. and several churches, cathedrals, and monasteries dating from period of its supremacy.

History: One of the oldest cities of Russia and of great importance 11th–15th cents. Originated as a Varangian trading town; came under Rurik who became its grand prince c. 862; at first dependent upon Kiev; became ✻ of principality and was called **Great Novgorod** *or* **Novgorod the Great;** center of Novgorod school of medieval icon and mural painting 12th–16th cents.; escaped ravages of Mongol invasion 1237–40; ruled by Prince Alexander Nevsky 1238–63 who fought successful wars with Germans and Swedes; developed economically from its favorable location by trade with the Orient and Constantinople and with the Hanseatic League; became rival of Moscow, with many dependent towns in N Russia; finally overpowered by Moscow's Ivan III 1471–78 and laid waste by Czar Ivan IV 1570; declined with rise of St. Petersburg; in WWII held by Germans 1941–44.

3. Town, Ukraine. See NOVHOROD-SIVERS'KYY 2.

Novgorod Oblast \ˈō-bləst, -ˌblast\ *or* **Nov·go·rod·ska·ya Oblast'** \ˈnȯv-gə-ˌrət-skə-yə-ˈō-bləstʸ\. Subdivision of W Russia in Europe, bounded on N by St. Petersburg Oblast, on NE by Vologda Oblast, on SE and S by Tver' Oblast, and on W by Pskov Oblast; 21,351 sq. mi. (55,299 sq. km.); pop. (1992e) 752,000; ✻ Novgorod; dairying; potatoes, oats, rye, flax, timber; includes Lake Il'men'.

Novgorod–Severskyy. See NOVHOROD-SIVERS'KYY.

Novgorodskaya Oblast'. See NOVGOROD OBLAST.

Nov·ho·rod–Si·vers'·kyy \ˈnȯv-hə-rət-ˈsi-ver-skyē\ *or* **Nov·go·rod–Se·ver·skyy** \ˈnȯv-gə-rət-ˈse-vyir-skē\. **1.** Medieval principality, E cen. Europe, nearly surrounded by Chernihiv and bordered on SE by Pereyaslav; ✻ Novhorod-Sivers'kyy. **2.** *or* **Novgorod.** Town, NE Chernihiv subdivision, N Ukraine, on right bank of the Desna River 95 mi. (153 km.) ENE of the city of Chernihiv; a medieval town; in 11th–13th cents. was ✻ of Novhorod-Sivers'kyy principality; passed to Mongols 13th cent., Lithuania 14th cent., and Russia 17th cent.

No·vi \ˈnō-ˌvī\. City, Oakland co., SE Michigan, NW of Detroit; pop. (1990c) 32,998; pop. more than doubled bet. 1970 and 1980.

Novibazar. See NOVI PAZAR.

No·vi Li·gu·re \ˈnȯ-vē-ˈlē-gu̇r-ā\. Commune, Alessandria prov., Piedmont, NW Italy, 14 mi. (23 km.) SE of the commune of Alessandria; pop. (1991p) 29,788; scene of Austrian and Russian victory over French 1799.

Noviodunum. 1. Commune, Nièvre dept., France. See NEVERS.

2. Commune, Switzerland. See NYON.

Noviomagus. 1. City, France. See LISIEUX.

2. Commune, Netherlands. See NIJMEGEN.

No·vi Pa·zar \ˈnō-vē-pə-ˈzär\ *or* **No·vi·ba·zar** \-bə-\. **1.** Former Turkish sanjak (district), S Europe, divided bet. Serbia and Montenegro in 1913.

2. Town, Serbia, S Yugoslavia, on a tributary of the Ibar River; pop. (1991p) 85,583; formerly an important market town. Captured by Turks in 15th cent.; became center of Turkish sanjak (district) bet. Serbia and Montenegro; assigned to Serbia 1913 following Balkan Wars.

No·vi Sad \ˈnȯ-vē-ˈsäd\ *or Hung.* **Új·vi·dék** \ˈü-ē-ˌvē-ˌdāk\ *or Ger.* **Neu·satz** \ˈnȯi-ˌzäts\. City, chief town of Vojvodina autonomous region, Serbia, N Yugoslavia, on Danube River; pop. (1991p) 264,533; porcelain, soap, textiles; university (1960); founded in 17th cent.; part of Hungary until formation of Yugoslavia 1918; occupied by Hungarian troops in WWII.

No·vi Slan·ka·men \ˈnȯ-vē-ˈsläŋ-kä-men\ *or* **Slankamen** *or Hung.* **Sza·lán·ke·mén** \ˈsö-läŋ-ˌke-mān\. Commune, Serbia, N cen. Yugoslavia, on the Danube opp. the mouth of the Tisza; held by Ottoman Turks until ceded to Austria late 17th cent.; scene of battle 1691 in which Austrian forces under Louis William I, margrave of Baden, defeated the Turks; passed to Yugoslavia after WWI.

No·vo·al·taisk *or* **No·vo·al·taysk** \ˌnō-və-ȧl-ˈtīsk\; *formerly* **Ches·no·kov·ka** \ˌches-nə-ˈkȯf-kə, -ˈkȯv-\. City, Altay Kray, S Russia in Asia, ab. 10 mi. (16 km.) E of Barnaul; pop. (1991e) 55,200.

Novoarkhangel'sk. See SITKA 2.

No·vo·cher·kassk \ˌnō-və-chər-ˈkȧsk\. City, SW Rostov Oblast, S Russia in Europe, on a delta arm of the Don 25 mi. (40 km.) NE of Rostov-na-Donu; pop. (1992e) 188,000; a commercial city on the main railroad line from Rostov-na-Donu to Voronezh; electric locomotives, machine tools; founded by Don Cossacks in 1805 as their ✻; a center of opposition to Bolsheviks 1917–20; in WWII held by Germans 1942–43.

Novogeorgievsk. See MODLIN.

No·vo·gru·dok \ˌnə-və-ˈgrü-dək\ *or Pol.* **No·wo·gró·dek** \ˌnō-vō-ˈgrü-ˌdek\. Town, Hrodna subdivision, Belarus, S of Neman River and 77 mi. (124 km.) SSE of Vilnius; has mosque; birthplace of Polish poet Adam Mickiewicz 1798. Variously under Russian, Lithuanian, and Polish rule; in WWII occupied by Germans; after being recovered, ceded by Poland to U.S.S.R. 1945.

No·vo Ham·bur·go \ˈnō-vü-ȧm-ˈbür-gü\. City, Rio Grande do Sul state, S Brazil, just N of Pôrto Alegre; munic. pop. (1991p) 200,879.

Novokazalinsk. See ZHANGAQAZALY.

No·vo·kui·by·shevsk *or* **No·vo·kuy·by·shevsk** \ˌnə-və-ˈkwē-bə-ˌshefsk, -ˈkü-ē-bə-\. Town, Samara Oblast, E Russia in Europe, ab. 10 mi. (16 km.) SW of the city of Samara; pop. (1992e) 113,000.

No·vo·kuz·netsk \ˌnȯ-və-küz-ˈnyetsk\ *or* **Kuz·netsk Si·bir·ski** \küz-ˈnyetsk-sə-ˈbir-skē\; *formerly* **Sta·linsk** \ˈstäl-yinsk\. City, S Kemerovo Oblast, S Russia in Asia, at head of navigation of Tom' River 190 mi. (306 km.) SE of Novosibirsk; pop. (1992e) 600,000; coal mining; iron and steel, aluminum, chemicals; at S end of Kuznetsk Basin; first settled 1617 and until 20th cent. a small town.

No·vo·mos·kovsk \ˌnȯ-və-mä-ˈskȯfsk\; *formerly* **Bob·ri·ki** \ˈbȯ-bri-kē\ *also* **Sta·li·no·gorsk** \ˌstə-lē-nȯ-ˈgȯrsk\. City, Tula Oblast, W Russia in Europe, ab. 35 mi. (56 km.) ESE of the city of Tula; pop. (1992e) 145,000; chemicals; coal mining; founded 1930.

No·vo·mos·kovs'k *or* **No·vo·mos·kovsk** \ˌnȯ-və-ˌməs-ˈkȯfs^{y}k\. Town, E cen. Ukraine, 16 mi. (26 km.) NE of Dnepropetrovs'k, on a tributary of the Dnieper; pop. (1991e) 77,000.

Novonikolaevsk. See NOVOSIBIRSK.

Novoradomsk. See RADOMSKO.

Novo Redondo. See SUMBE.

No·vo·ros·siysk \ˌnə-və-rə-ˈsēsk\. Seaport city, W Krasnodar Kray, S Russia in Europe, on Black Sea coast ab. 65 mi. (105 km.) WSW of the city of Krasnodar; pop. (1992e) 190,000; naval base; shipbuilding yards; cement; formerly a Turkish town, became Russian in 1829; in Russian Civil War it was held by White Russians 1919–20; in WWII held by Germans 1942–43.

Novorossiya. See NEW RUSSIA.

No·vo·shakh·tinsk \ˌnȯ-vä-ˈshäk-tēnsk\. Town, Rostov Oblast, S Russia in Europe, ab. 40 mi. (64 km.) NNE of Rostov-na-Donu; pop. (1992e) 107,000; coal mining.

No·vo·si·birsk \ˌnō-vō-si-ˈbirsk\; *formerly* **No·vo·ni·ko·la·evsk** \-ni-kə-ˈlī-əfsk, -əvsk\. City, ✱ of Novosibirsk Oblast, S Russia in Asia, ab. 390 mi. (630 km.) E of Omsk, on the navigable Ob' River and N terminus on the Trans-Siberian R.R. of the Turk-Sib line S to Barnaul, Semey, and Alma-Ata; pop. (1992e) 1,442,000; important industrial center, producing mining equipment, hydraulic presses, chemicals; steel mill; center for scientific research; university (1959). Developed 1893 ff. with construction of Trans-Siberian R.R.; became regional ✱, then ✱ of Novosibirsk Oblast c. 1937; in WWII many industrial plants removed to this area.

Novosibirskiye Ostrova. See NEW SIBERIAN ISLANDS.

Novosibirsk Oblast \ˈō-bləst, -ˌblast\ *or* **No·vo·si·bir·ska·ya Oblast'** \ˌnō-vō-si-ˈbir-skə-yə-ˈō-bləst^{y}\. Subdivision of S Russia in Asia, bounded on N by Tomsk Oblast, on E by Kemerovo Oblast, on S by Altay Kray, on SW by Kazakhstan, and on W by Omsk Oblast; 68,803 sq. mi. (178,200 sq. km.); pop. (1992e) 2,803,000; ✱ Novosibirsk; lies in basin of middle Ob' River with flat steppe and taiga land in N and cen. parts and hilly region in SE; in the SW is Lake Chany; spring wheat, oats, barley, flax; borders on the Kuznetsk Basin (*q.v.*), one of the major industrial areas of Russia; crossed by the Trans-Siberian R.R. Organized as new subdivision of the Russian S.F.S.R. c. 1937; reduced in size 1940s.

No·vo·troitsk \ˌnȯ-və-ˈtrō-itsk\. Town, Orenburg Oblast, E Russia in Europe, ab. 10 mi. (16 km.) W of Orsk; pop. (1992e) 107,000.

Novo Urgench. See URGANCH.

No·vo·zyb·kov \ˌnȯ-və-ˈzip-kəf\. Town, SW Bryansk Oblast, W Russia in Europe, on railroad line ab. 45 mi. (72 km.) E of Homyel'.

No·vý Ji·čín \ˈnȯ-vē-ˈyē-ˌchēn\ *or Ger.* **Neu·tit·schein** \ˈnȯi-ti-ˌchīn\. Town, E Czech Republic, 21 mi. (34 km.) SSW of Ostrava; pop. (1980p) 31,506; tobacco.

Novyy Margelan. See FERGANA 2.

No·wa Ru·da \ˈnȯ-vä-ˈrü-dä\ *or Ger.* **Neu·ro·de** \nȯi-ˈrō-də\. Town, W Wałbrzych prov., SW Poland, SE of the city of Wałbrzych; pop. (1989e) 27,616; founded 14th cent.; formerly in Silesia, Prussia, and Germany (*qq.v.*); to Poland 1945.

No·wa Sól *or* **No·wa·sól** \ˈnȯ-və-ˈsül\ *or Ger.* **Neu·salz an der Oder** \ˈnȯi-ˌzälts-ˌän-dər-ˈō-dər\. City, Zielona Góra prov., SW Poland, on the Odra (Oder); pop. (1989e) 43,113; railroad junction; river port; manufactures textiles; formerly in Silesia, Prussia, and Germany (*q.q.v.*); to Poland 1945.

No·wa·ta \nō-ˈwä-tə\. **1.** County in NE Oklahoma. See table at OKLAHOMA.

2. City, its ⊗, 20 mi. (32 km.) E of Bartlesville; pop. (1990c) 3896.

Nowawes. See BABELSBERG.

Nowe Tychy. See TYCHY.

Now·gong \ˈnau̇-ˌgȯŋ\ *or* **Na·gaon** \ˈnä-ˌgau̇n\. **1.** Town, Assam, NE India, 56 mi. (90 km.) E of Gauhati; pop. (1991p) 93,324.

2. Town, Madhya Pradesh, India, 175 mi. (282 km.) W of Allahabad; pop. (1991p) 21,517; under British, ✱ of former Bundelkhand Agency.

Nowogródek. See NOVOGRUDOK.

Nowo–Mińsk. See MIŃSK MAZOWIECKI.

Now·she·ra \nau̇-ˈsher-ə\. Town, North-West Frontier prov., Pakistan, 20 mi. (32 km.) E of Peshawar on the Kabul River; pop. (1981p) with cantonment 151,000.

No·wy Dwor Ma·zo·wiec·ki \ˈnȯ-vė-ˈdvür-ˌmä-zȯ-ˈvyet-skē\. Commune, Warszawa prov., NE cen. Poland, NW of Warsaw; pop. (1989e) 26,796.

No·wy Sącz \ˈnȯ-vė-ˈsȯ^{n}ch\ *or Ger.* **Neu·san·dez** \nȯi-ˈzän-dets\. **1.** Province, S Poland. See table at POLAND.

2. Commune, its ✱, on upper Dunajec River in N foothills of Carpathian Mts., 46 mi. (74 km.) SE of Kraków; pop. (1989e) 76,738; manufactures textiles, chemicals; on highway leading S through the Carpathians and across Slovakia to Košice.

No·wy Targ \ˈnȯ-vė-ˈtärk\ *or Ger.* **Neu·markt** \ˈnȯi-ˌmärkt\. Commune, Nowy Sącz prov., Poland, on upper Dunajec River 45 mi. (72 km.) S of Kraków; pop. (1989e) 32,213; at foot of Tatra Mts.

Nox·u·bee \ˈnäk-shə-bē\. **1.** *or* **Oka·nox·u·bee** \ˌō-kə-\. River, E cen. Mississippi and W cen. Alabama; rises in Oktibbeha co., NE cen. Mississippi, flows SE across border of Alabama into Tombigbee River, W of Eutaw, Greene co., W cen. Alabama; ab. 140 mi. (225 km.) long.

2. County in E Mississippi. See table at MISSISSIPPI.

Noya. See NOIA.

Noy·il \ˈnȯi-əl\. River, Tamil Nadu, S cen. India; flows E into Kāveri River; ab. 95 mi. (153 km.) long.

Noy·on \nwä-ˈyō^{n}\. Town, Oise dept., N France; pop. (1990c) 14,628; 12th cent. cathedral, mostly rebuilt after WWI; birthplace 1509 of religious reformer John Calvin whose home is now a museum; bishopric from 6th cent.; scene of crowning of Charlemagne 768 as king of Neustria, and of election of Hugh Capet as king of France 987; often scene of conflict, during Hundred Years' War, in 16th cent., and during WWI and WWII; occupied by Germans in both World Wars.

Nsa·wam \ən-ˌsä-ˈwäm\. Town, Eastern Region, Ghana, ab. 20 mi. (32 km.) NNW of Accra; pop. (1984c) 20,439.

Nsuk·ka \ən-ˈsu̇k-kä\. Town, S cen. Nigeria; pop. (1991e) 52,780; Univ. of Nigeria (1960).

Ntem \ən-ˈtem\; *formerly* **Cam·po** *or* **Kam·po** \ˈkäm-pō\. River, W Africa in Equatorial Guinea (Mbini) and Cameroon; empties into Gulf of Guinea at Campo, Cameroon.

Nu. See SALWEEN.

Nu·ba Mountains \ˈnü-bə\. Group of hills, cen. Sudan; highest peak 4344 ft. (1324 m.).

Nu·bia \ˈnü-bē-ə, ˈnyü-\. Region in Nile Valley, NE Africa, N of ab. 16°N, extending northward to include Aswān and before completion of the Aswān Dam incl. the first of several cataracts of the Nile, but its boundaries indefinite; now included in Sudan and Egypt; mostly desert and includes the Nubian Desert in NE.

History: In ancient times for ab. 1800 years subject to Egypt as a part of Ethiopia; culture and nation of Cush (*q.v.*)

\ə\ abut \ə̇\ matches \ᵊ\ kitten, Fr table \ər\ further \a\ ash \ā\ ace
\ä\ cot, cart \á\ Fr bac \au̇\ out \b\ Span Avila \ch\ chin \e\ bet \ē\ easy
\g\ go \i\ hit \ī\ ice \j\ job \k\ Ger ich, Buch \$^{n}$\ Fr vin
\ŋ\ sing \ō\ go \ȯ\ all \ȯ\ law \œ\ Fr bœuf \œ̄\ Fr feu \ȯi\ boy
\th\ thin \t͟h\ this \ü\ loot \u̇\ foot \ue\ Ger füllen \ue̅\ Fr rue
\y\ yet \$^{y}$\ Fr digne \ˈdēn^{y}\, nuit \ˈnw^{y}ē\ \yü\ few \yu̇\ fury \zh\ vision

was centered in S Nubia; from 6th cent. A.D. was center of a powerful kingdom, with ✻ Dongola which was conquered by Arabs in 14th cent.; region conquered by Egypt 1820–22; see SUDAN for additional history; construction of Aswān High Dam during 1960s left much of region flooded.

Nubia, Lake. See NASSER, LAKE.

Nu·bi·an Desert \ˈnü-bē-ən, ˈnyü-\. Desert area in NE Sudan, E of the Nile River.

Nuceria Alfaterna. See NOCERA INFERIORE.

Nu Chiang. See SALWEEN.

Nuck·olls \ˈnə-kəlz\. County in S Nebraska. See table at NEBRASKA.

Nu·e·ces \nü-ˈā-səs, ˈnyü-\. **1.** River, S Texas; rises near border of Edwards and Real cos., flows S and SE into **Nueces Bay,** at head of Corpus Christi Bay; 315 mi. (507 km.) long. **2.** Coastal county in S Texas. See table at TEXAS.

Nues·tra Se·ño·ra Bay \ˈnwās-trä-sā-ˈnyō-rä\. Inlet of Pacific Ocean on SW coast of Antofagasta region, N Chile.

Nuestra Señora de la Asunción. See ASUNCIÓN 2.

Nueva Caceres. See NAGA 2.

Nue·va Eci·ja \ˈnwā-vä-ˈā-sē-hä\. Province, cen. Luzon, Philippines, in cen. plain; ✻ Palayan; W two thirds lies in level fertile country watered by the Pampanga and its many tributaries; the SE is hilly and in the NE are the foothills of the Caraballo Mts. Produces rice, also corn, sugarcane, and tobacco. See table at PHILIPPINES.

Nue·va Es·par·ta \ˈnwā-vä-es-ˈpär-tä\. State of Venezuela, comprising an island group in the Caribbean Sea, off N coast of Venezuelan mainland; ✻ La Asunción; chief island Margarita. See table at VENEZUELA.

Nue·va Ge·ro·na \ˈnwā-vä-he-ˈrō-nä\. Barrio in Isla de la Juventud municipality, La Habana prov., W Cuba.

Nueva Granada. See NEW GRANADA.

Nue·va Lo·ja \ˈnwā-vä-ˈlō-hä\. Town, ✻ of Sucumbíos prov., Ecuador.

Nueva Oco·te·pe·que \ˈnwā-vä-ō-ˌkō-tā-ˈpā-kā\; *formerly* **Ocotepeque.** Town, ✻ of Ocotepeque dept., Honduras; pop. (1988p) 6667.

Nue·va Pal·mi·ra \ˈnwā-vä-päl-ˈmē-rä\. River port, Colonia dept., SW Uruguay, on Uruguay River.

Nue·va Paz \ˈnwā-vä-ˈpäs\. Municipality, E La Habana prov., W Cuba, 47 mi. (76 km.) SE of Havana; pop. (1981p) 20,118.

Nue·va Ro·si·ta \ˈnwā-vä-rō-ˈsē-tä\. Municipality, Coahuila state, NE Mexico; pop. (1980c) 33,121.

Nue·va San Sal·va·dor \ˈnwā-vä-sän-ˈsäl-vä-ˌt͟hȯr\; *formerly* **San·ta Te·cla** \ˈsän-tä-ˈtā-klä\. City, ✻ of La Libertad dept., SW El Salvador, 8 mi. (13 km.) W of San Salvador; pop. (1992c) 116,575; coffee-growing center.

Nue·va Se·go·via \ˈnwā-vä-sē-ˈgō-vyä\. Department of NW Nicaragua. See table at NICARAGUA.

Nue·va Viz·ca·ya \ˈnwā-vä-vēs-ˈkī-ä\. Province, N cen. Luzon, Philippines; ✻ Bayombong; a hilly and plateau area, much of it above 2000 ft. (610 m.); in cen. and S parts are the Caraballo Mts. and in the E foothills of the Sierra Madre; in the NE is the upper Cagayan Valley and through the W and N flows the Magat. Contains much forest and fertile land; produces rice and vegetables. See table at PHILIPPINES.

Nue·vi·tas \nwā-ˈvē-ˌtäs\. Municipality and town, NE Camagüey prov., E cen. Cuba; munic. pop. (1990e) 41,391; on a fine harbor, **Nuevitas Bay;** chromium ore mined nearby.

Nuevo, Golfo. See NEW GULF.

Nue·vo Ca·sas Gran·des \ˈnwā-vō-ˈkä-säs-ˈgrän-dās\. Municipality, Chihuahua state, Mexico, 140 mi. (225 km.) SSW of Ciudad Juárez.

Nue·vo La·re·do \ˈnwā-vō-lä-ˈrā-t͟hō\. Municipality, Tamaulipas state, E Mexico, on the Rio Grande opp. Laredo, Texas; pop. (1990p) 217,912; in cattle district.

Nue·vo Le·ón \ˈnwā-vō-lā-ˈōn\. State of NE Mexico. See table at MEXICO.

Nu·gi·ma \nü-ˈgē-mä\. Chief village of New Hanover I., Bismarck Archipelago, Papua New Guinea, on NW coast.

Nûgs·su·aq \ˈnüg-sü-ˌäk\. Peninsula on W coast of Greenland in cen. part just N of Qeqertarsuag I.

Nuhūd, An. See EN NAHUD.

Nukahiva. See NUKU HIVA.

Nukha. See SHEKI.

Nu·ku·ʼa·lo·fa \ˌnü-kü-ä-ˈlō-fä\. Seaport on N coast of Tongatapu I., ✻ of Tonga, SW Pacific Ocean; pop. (1986c) 21,383; 19th cent. palace and chapel.

Nu·ku·fe·tau \ˌnü-kü-fe-ˈtau̇\. Island (atoll), cen. Tuvalu, W Pacific Ocean, NW of Funafuti I., comprising islets in a reef 24 mi. (39 km.) in circuit.

Nu·ku Hi·va *also* **Nu·ka·hi·va** \ˌnü-kü-ˈhē-vä\. Largest of the Marquesas Is., French Polynesia, S Pacific Ocean; ab. 60 sq. mi. (155 sq. km.); has high ridge (highest point 3888 ft. or 1185 m.) and plateau in center; coastline of 70 mi. (113 km.) with several indentations; pop. (1988c) 2100; best harbor is Anaho Bay on N.

Nu·ku·lae·lae *or* **Nu·ku·lai·lai** \ˌnü-kü-ˈlī-ˌlī\. Island (atoll) at S end of Tuvalu, W Pacific Ocean; ab. 6.5 mi. (11 km.) long.

Nukunau. See NIKUNAU.

Nu·ku·no·no *or* **Nu·ku No·no** \ˌnü-kü-ˈnō-nō\ *also* **Duke of Clar·ence** \-ˈklar-ən(t)s\. Island of the Tokelau group, cen. Pacific, N of Samoa.

Nu·kus \nü-ˈküs\. Town, ✻ of Karakalpak Autonomous Rep., Uzbekistan, on Amu Dar'ya at head of delta; pop. (1991e) 179,600; food products; replaced Turtkul' as ✻ 1939.

Nu·la·to \nu̇-ˈlä-tō\. City, W cen. Alaska, on right bank of the Yukon 220 mi. (354 km.) E of Nome; pop. (1990c) 359; estab. as Russian blockhouse 1838; garrison massacred in Athabascan uprising 1851.

Null·ar·bor National Park \ˈnəl-ə-ˌbȯr-, ˈnəl-ˌär-bər-\. National park, SW South Australia, Australia, in Nullarbor Plain; steep coastal cliffs, caves; saltbush, wombats.

Nullarbor Plain. Plain along coast of SW South Australia and SE Western Australia, Australia, from E end of Great Australian Bight; extends inland almost to 30°S; traversed by railway containing world's longest stretch of straight track and highway at its edge completed 1976; explored and crossed by English explorer Edward John Eyre 1841.

Nu·man \ˈnü-män\. Port, E Nigeria on Benue River.

Nu·man·tia \nu̇-ˈman-chə, nyu̇-\. Ancient city of Spain, on the Duero River near modern Soria; center of Celtiberian resistance to Rome in wars throughout 2d cent. B.C.; resisted several sieges and attacks, but was finally taken by Romans under Scipio the Younger 133 B.C., marking the end of organized resistance to Rome in Spain.

Nu·ma·zu \nü-ˈmä-zü\. Town, Shizuoka prefecture, S coast of cen. Honshū, Japan, on NE shore of Suruga Bay across from the city of Shizuoka; pop. (1990p) 211,731.

Numedalslågen. See LÅGEN.

Num·foor *or Du.* **Noem·foor** \ˈnüm-ˌfōr\. Island, W Schouten Is., on W side of entrance to Teluk Cenderawasih, N Irian Jaya, Indonesia, 45 mi. (72 km.) W of Biak; roughly circular; 14 mi. (23 km.) long, 12 mi. (19 km.) wide; generally flat. Had Japanese airfields in WWII, taken by Allies 1944.

Nu·mid·ia \nu̇-ˈmi-dē-ə, nyu̇-\. Ancient country in North Africa; its territory approx. coextensive with modern Algeria. In Second Punic War (218–201 B.C.) its two great tribes divided, one in support of the Romans, the other of the Carthaginians; after 206 B.C. Masinissa, son of a tribal chieftain, changed sides and supported Romans, and upon Roman victory became king of all Numidia 201 B.C.; suffered in civil war and war with Rome 111–106 B.C.; became Roman province 46 B.C.; its ✻ was Cirta and its most important city Hippo, the see of St. Augustine (see ANNABA); flourished until invasion by Vandals c. 428 A.D.

Nun \ˈnün\ *or* **Nun Entrance.** One of the mouths of the Niger River, S Nigeria.

Nu·na·vut \nü-ˈnä-vüt; ˈnü-nə-vu̇t, -vüt\. Territory, N Canada, consisting of the mainland N of 60° N bet. Northwest Territories and Hudson Bay, the islands in Hudson, James, and Ungava bays, the E & S parts of Victoria I., the E parts of Melville I. and Borden I., and all of the Arctic Archipelago E of 110° W; formed from Northwest Territories 1999. See table at CANADA .

Nun·a·wa·ding \ˈnə-nə-wə-ˌdiŋ\. City, Victoria, Australia, an E suburb of Melbourne; pop. (1991c) 91,468.

Nun·ea·ton \ˌnə-ˈnēt-ᵊn\. Town, Warwickshire, cen. England, 20 mi. (32 km.) E of Birmingham; textile mills; electronics; formerly significant coal mines nearby.

Nu·ni·vak \ˈnü-nə-ˌvak\. Alaskan island, 2d largest in Bering Sea, in E part; 1625 sq. mi. (4209 sq. km.); separated from mainland of SW Alaska and Nelson I. by Etolin Strait; crossed by 167°W; usually fogbound. Has been made a game and bird reservation.

Nun·kiang \ˈnu̇n-ˈjyäŋ\. One of the nine former provinces of Manchuria, in N cen. part; 23,912 sq. mi. (61,932 sq. km.); created 1946.

Nuo·ro \ˈnü-ō-rō\. **1.** Province of E Sardinia, Italy. See table at ITALY.
2. Commune, its ✱, 75 mi. (121 km.) NNE of Cagliari; pop. (1991p) 37,487; cathedral; evidence of prehistoric inhabitants in the area.

Nuremberg. See NÜRNBERG.

Nu·ri·stan *or* **Nū·re·stān** \ˌnü-ri-ˈstan\; *formerly* **Kaf·i·ri·stan** \ˌka-fə-ri-ˈstan\. Mountainous area, E Afghanistan, S of Hindu Kush; ab. 5000 sq. mi. (13,000 sq. km.); inhabited by a small remnant of a very early Iranian people, conquered by Afghanistan 1890s.

Nur·mes \ˈnu̇r-məs\. Town, SE cen. Finland; at N end of Lake Pielinen ab. 60 mi. (95 km.) NE of Kuopio; pop. (1980c) 11,576.

Nur Mountains \ˈnu̇r\; *formerly* **Al·ma Dağ** \ˈäl-mä-ˈdä\; *anc.* **Ama·nus** \ə-ˈmā-nəs\. Mountains, S Turkey in Asia, part of Taurus Mts.; S end is in Hatay prov.

Nürn·berg \ˈnuern-ˌberk, ˈnərn-ˌbərg\ *or angl.* **Nu·rem·berg** \ˈnu̇r-əm-ˌbərg, ˈnyu̇r-\. Commercial and manufacturing city, Bavaria, Germany, on Pegnitz River 92 mi. (148 km.) NNW of Munich; pop. (1992e) 497,496; metal production; business machines, electrical equipment, motor vehicles, toys, pharmaceuticals; brewing; famous for its medieval aspect; medieval city walls; 11th cent. royal palace; town hall; national museum (founded 1852) in 14th cent. Carthusian monastery; numerous old churches; annual international toy fair. Founded in 11th cent.; made free imperial city early 13th cent.; became one of greatest and wealthiest of all German free imperial cities; adopted Reformation 1525; center of German culture in 16th cent.; to Bavaria 1806; first German railway (Nürnberg to Fürth) opened 1835; after 1933 made annual meeting place of Chancellor Adolf Hitler's National Socialist (Nazi) party; Nürnberg Laws promulgated here 1935 deprived Jews of citizenship and other rights; much of city destroyed in bombings of WWII; taken by Americans Apr. 21, 1945; scene of Allied trials of German war criminals (Nuremberg trials) 1945–46. Birthplace of geographer Martin Behaim (1436), sculptor Adam Kraft (1455), painter and engraver Albrecht Dürer (1471), and poet Hans Sachs (1494).

Nursia. See NORCIA.

Nür·ting·en \ˈnuer-tiŋ-ən\. City, Baden-Württemberg, Germany, 14 mi. (23 km.) SE of Stuttgart; pop. (1980c) 35,680; became city 13th cent.

Nur·u·hak Da·ği \ˌnü-rü-ˈhäk-dä-ˈē\. Peak in E cen. Turkey in Asia, NE of Maraş; 10,138 ft. (3090 m.).

Nus, Cape \ˈnüs\ *or Arab.* **Ras Nus** \räs\. Cape on S coast of Oman, SE Arabian Penin.

Nu·say·bin \ˌnü-sī-ˈbēn\ *or* **Ni·si·bin** \ˌnē-sē-ˈbēn\; *anc.* **Nis·i·bis** \ˈni-sə-bəs\. Town, Mardin prov., SE Turkey in Asia, on railroad line on the border of Syria; a frontier fortress, in early times important on the trade routes; residence of Armenian kings c. 2d cent. B.C. to c. 2d cent. A.D.; a key point for both Romans and Parthians; scene of Egyptian victory over the Turks 1839.

Nut·ley \ˈnət-lē\. Town, Essex co., NE New Jersey, 6 mi. (10 km.) N of Newark; pop. (1990c) 27,099; pharmaceuticals; residential suburb.

Nu·u·a·nu \ˌnü-ü-ˈä-nü\. Valley, SE Oahu I., Hawaii, incl. part of the city of Honolulu.

Nuuanu Pa·li \ˈpä-lē\. Cliff and mountain pass, at head of Nuuanu Valley, 6 mi. (10 km.) from Honolulu; alt. 1207 ft. (368 m.); famous as a scenic spot. Here in 1795 Kamehameha I completed his conquest of the island of Oahu.

Nuuk \ˈnük\ *or* **Godt·håb** *also* **Godt·haab** \ˈgȯt-ˌhȯp\. Town, ✱ of Greenland, on SW coast; pop. (1991e) 12,181; fish processing; scientific stations; oldest Danish settlement in Greenland, founded 1721; 10th cent. Norse settlement was located in area.

Nu·wa·ra Eli·ya \ˌnü-və-rə-ˈā-lē-ə\. Town, S cen. Sri Lanka; pop. (1990e) 26,000; on elevated plateau at ab. 6000 ft. (1800 m.) alt.; health resort.

Nu·zi \ˈnü-zē\. Archaeological site just SW of Kirkuk, NE Iraq; relics found here include pottery and thousands of clay tablets, one with map of c. 2500 B.C.

Ny·ack \ˈnī-ˌak\. Residential village, Rockland co., SE New York, on W shore of Hudson River 25 mi. (40 km.) N of New York City; pop. (1990c) 6558; tourism; Nyack Coll. (1882); settled 1684.

Nyain·qên·tang·lha *or W.-G.* **Nyen·chen·tang·lha** \ˈnyen-ˈchen-ˈtäŋ-ˈglä\. Mountain range, S Tibet, China, parallel with the Himalayas and N of the Brahmaputra (Dihang) River; ab. 600 mi. (965 km.) long; highest point 23,250 ft. (7087 m.), 60 mi. (97 km.) NW of Lhasa.

Nya·la \ˈnyä-lä\. City, W Sudan; pop. (1983c) 111,693; has an airport and road connections to distant settlements.

Nya·mu·la·gi·ra \nyä-mü-lä-ˈgē-rä\ *or* **Nya·mu·ra·gi·ra** \-rä-\. Volcano in the Virunga Mts., E Democratic Rep. of the Congo; 10,026 ft. (3056 m.); erupted 1938.

Nyanda. See MASVINGO.

Nyan·za \ˈnyän-zä; nē-ˈan-zə, nī-\. Province of SW Kenya. See table at KENYA.

Nyasa, Lake. See MALAWI, LAKE.

Nyasaland. See MALAWI.

Nyassa. See NIASSA.

Nyassa, Lake. See MALAWI, LAKE.

Ny·borg \ˈnue-ˌbȯr\. Seaport, Fyn co., Denmark, on Fyn I.; pop. (1981c) 18,619; seaside resort.

Ny·bro \ˈnue-ˌbrü\. Town, Kalmar prov., SE Sweden, ab. 16 mi. (26 km.) WNW of the seaport of Kalmar; pop. (1989c) 20,855.

Nye \ˈnī\. County in cen. and S Nevada. See table at NEVADA.

Nyeman. See NEMAN.

Nyenchentanglha. See NYAINQÊNTANGLHA.

Nye·ri \ˈnye-rē\. Town, ✱ of Central prov., SW cen. Kenya, N of Nairobi; pop. (1983e) 39,200.

Nyezhin. See NEZHIN.

Nyi·ka National Park \ˈnyē-kä\. National park, N Malawi; incl. most of **Nyika Plateau,** highest peak over 6500 ft. (2000 m.); wildlife habitat (eland, leopard, lion, zebra), grassland; estab. 1965.

Nyi·ra·gon·go \ˌnyē-rä-ˈgȯŋ-gō\. Volcano, E Democratic Rep. of the Congo, at N end of Lake Kivu; 11,400 ft. (3475 m.).

Nyí·regy·há·za \ˈnē-ˌrej-ˌhä-zö\. City, ⊗ of Szabolcs-Szatmár-Bereg co., NE Hungary, E of the Tisza, 30 mi. (48 km.) N of Debrecen; pop. (1991e) 120,600; distribution center for tobacco, potatoes, and vegetables.

Nyi·ri Desert \ˈnyē-rē\. Desert area, S Kenya, on border of Tanzania just NW of Kilimanjaro.

Nyiro, Ewaso. See NG'IRO, EWASO.

Nyitra. See NITRA.

Nyitrabánya. See HANDLOVÁ.

Ny·kø·bing \ˈnue-ˌkœ-biŋ\. **1.** *or* **Nykøbing Fal·ster** \ˈfäl-stər\. Seaport, ⊗ of Storstrøm prov., on W coast of Falster I., Denmark; pop. (1989e) 25,168; sugar refineries; tobacco products.
2. Town, Viborg co., NW Jutland Penin., Denmark, on E coast of Mors I.

Ny·kö·ping \ˈnue-ˌchœ-piŋ\. Seaport, ⊗ of Södermanland co., SE Sweden, on the Baltic Sea; pop. (1993e) 48,093; textile mills, furniture factories.

Nyland. See *Uusimaa* in table at FINLAND.

Nym·burk *or Ger.* **Nim·burg** \ˈnim-ˌbu̇rk\. Town, N cen. Czech Republic, on the Labe (Elbe) E of Prague; pop. (1980p) 14,033.

Nym·phai·on, Cape \nim-ˈfī-ən\ *or* **Cape Nym·phae·um** \-ˈfē-əm\ *or Gk.* **Ákra Nim·faí·on** \ˈä-krä-nēm-ˈfā-ön\. Cape at SE end of Acte Penin., Chalcidice, NE Greece, extending into Aegean Sea; in a storm off this point the Persian fleet of Darius the Great in an expedition against Greece was wrecked 492 B.C.

Nym·phen·burg \ˈnim-fən-ˌbu̇rk\. Former village, now part of Munich, Bavaria, Germany; site of 17th cent. palace and famous porcelain factory founded in 18th cent.; secret treaty signed here 1741, forming an alliance against Austria (War of the Austrian Succession) which finally included France, Bavaria, Spain, Saxony, and Prussia.

Nyon \ˈnyōⁿ\ *or Ger.* **Neuss** \ˈnȯis\; *anc.* **No·vi·o·du·num** \ˌnō-vē-ō-ˈdü-nəm, -ˈdyü-\. Commune, Vaud canton, W Switzerland, on W shore of Lake Geneva 13 mi. (21 km.) N of Geneva; pop. (1980c) 12,842; 16th cent. castle.

Nyong \ˈnyȯŋ\. River, Cameroon; flows W into Bight of Biafra; ab. 400 mi. (640 km.) long.

Ny·sa \ˈni-sə\; *Ger.* **Neis·se** \ˈnī-sə\. **1.** *Ger. also* **Glat·zer Neisse** \ˈglät-sər\. River, SW Poland; rises on Czech Republic border, and flows NE joining the Odra (Oder) 15 mi. (24 km.) NW of Opole; ab. 120 mi. (190 km.) long. **2.** City, Opole prov., S Poland, on the Nysa River 47 mi. (76 km.) SSE of Wrocław; pop. (1989e) 46,912; formerly in Silesia, Germany; churches of 15th and 17th cents.; 15th cent. tower. Medieval origins; was ✻ of a Silesian principality; in War of Austrian Succession, captured by Prussia 1741, formally ceded by Austria 1742; withstood Austrian siege 1758; occupied by French 1807–08; assigned to Poland after WWII by Potsdam Conference 1945.

Nysa Łużycka. See NEISSE 1.

Nys·sa \ˈni-sə\. City, Malheur co., SE corner of Oregon, on Snake River 12 mi. (19 km.) S of its confluence with Malheur River; pop. (1990c) 2629.

Nystad. See UUSIKAUPUNKI.

Nyu·do, Cape \ˈnyü-dō\. Cape, Akita prefecture, NW coast of Honshū, Japan; 40°N, 139°42′E.

Nzé·ré·ko·ré \ən-ˌzā-rā-kȯ-ˈrā\. Town, SE Guinea; pop. (1983p) 55,356; has road connections with Liberia and Ivory Coast.

Nzwani. See ANJOUAN.

Oa, Mull of \ˌməl-əv-ˈō\. Cape on S tip of Islay I. in the Inner Hebrides, off W coast of Scotland.

Oad·by \ˈōd-bē\. Town, Leicestershire, cen. England, ab. 4 mi. (6 km.) SE of Leicester; pop. (1981p) 18,669.

Oahe Dam *and* **Oahe, Lake** \ō-ˈwä-hē\. See UNITED STATES, *Dams and Reservoirs*.

Oa·hu \ō-ˈwä-hü\. Island, Hawaii, included in Honolulu co.; 3d in size and most important of the Hawaiian Is.; ab. 600 sq. mi. (1555 sq. km.). Geologically once two great volcanoes; erosion has left them as two mountain ranges—the Koolau (highest Konahuanui 3105 ft. or 946 m.) along NE coast parallel with the Waianae (highest Kaala 4040 ft. or 1231 m.) along the SW coast with plateau 800 to 1000 ft. (245 to 305 m.) bet.; Honolulu and Pearl Harbor on S coast. Mountains very rugged (see NUUANU PALI); cen. plateau under wide cultivation. Early kings of Oahu overcome by Kamehameha I 1795; royal residence and influence gradually transferred from Hawaii I. to Oahu in first half of 19th cent.

Oak \ˈōk\. One of the Apostle Is. (*q.v.*).

Oak Brook. Village, Du Page co., NE Illinois, 10 mi. (16 km.) W of Chicago; pop. (1990c) 9178.

Oak Creek. City, Milwaukee co., SE Wisconsin, SSE of the city of Milwaukee; pop. (1990c) 19,513.

Oak·dale \ˈōk-ˌdāl\. **1.** City, Stanislaus co., cen. California, 23 mi. (37 km.) ESE of Stockton; pop. (1990c) 11,961.
2. City, Allen parish, SW Louisiana, 37 mi. (60 km.) SSW of Alexandria; pop. (1990c) 6832.
3. Village, Washington co., E Minnesota; pop. (1990c) 18,374; residential suburb of St. Paul.

Oak·en·gates \ˈō-kən-ˌgāts\. Town, Shropshire, W England, 28 mi. (45 km.) WNW of Birmingham; pop. (1981p) 17,663.

Oak Forest. Village, Cook co., NE Illinois, 5 mi. (8 km.) SSW of Chicago; pop. (1990c) 26,203; residential.

Oak Grove. **1.** Town, ⊗ of West Carroll parish, NE Louisiana, 52 mi. (84 km.) ENE of Monroe; pop. (1990c) 2863.
2. City, Franklin co., E Missouri; pop. (1990c) 4565.

Oak·ham \ˈō-kəm\. Market town, Leicestershire, E cen. England, 19 mi. (31 km.) ENE of Leicester; pop. (1981c) 8035; remains of Norman castle.

Oak Harbor. **1.** Village, Ottawa co., N Ohio, 20 mi. (32 km.) ESE of Toledo; pop. (1990c) 2637.
2. City, Island co., NW Washington, 50 mi. (80 km.) NNW of Seattle; pop. (1990c) 17,176.

Oak Hill. **1.** City, Davidson co., N cen. Tennessee; pop. (1990c) 4301.
2. City, Fayette co., S cen. West Virginia, 14 mi. (23 km.) N of Beckley; pop. (1990c) 6812.

Oak·land \ˈō-klənd\. **1.** County in SE Michigan. See table at MICHIGAN.
2. City, ⊗ of Alameda co., W California, on E side of San Francisco Bay nearly opp. the Golden Gate; pop. (1990c) 372,242; seaport producing automobiles, electronic equipment, fabricated-steel items, chemicals; food processing; connected with San Francisco by Bay Bridge (combination; main span 2310 ft. or 704 m.; total length 8.2 mi. or 13.2 km.; completed 1936). Mills Coll. (1852), Holy Names Coll. (1868), California Coll. of Arts and Crafts (1907), Laney Coll. (1927), Patten Coll. (1944). In area settled by Spanish 1820; incorp. as city under present name 1854; grew rapidly into industrial center in the first half of the 20th cent.; suffered damage and loss of life in 1989 earthquake.
3. Town, Kennebec co., SW Maine, 5 mi. (8 km.) W of Waterville; pop. (1990c) 5595.
4. Town, ⊗ of Garrett co., NW corner of Maryland, 52 mi. (84 km.) WSW of Cumberland; pop. (1990c) 1741.
5. Borough, Bergen co., NE New Jersey, NNW of Paterson; pop. (1990c) 11,997.

Oakland City. Residential city, Gibson co., SW Indiana, 28 mi. (45 km.) NNE of Evansville; pop. (1980c) 3301; Oakland City Coll. (1885).

Oakland Park. City, Broward co., SE Florida, N of Fort Lauderdale; pop. (1990c) 26,326.

Oak Lawn. Village, Cook co., NE Illinois, just W of the S part of Chicago; pop. (1990c) 56,182.

Oak·leigh \ˈō-klē\. Town, SE suburb of Melbourne, S Victoria, SE Australia; pop. (1991c) 55,151.

Oak·ley \ˈō-klē\. City, Logan and Thomas cos., NW Kansas; ⊗ of Logan co.; pop. (1990c) 2045.

Oakley Dam. Dam across Goose Creek, S Cassia co., S Idaho; height 145 ft. (44 m.); impounds water for irrigation, forming **Lower Goose Creek Reservoir**.

Oak·lyn \ˈō-klən\. Residential borough, Camden co., SW New Jersey, 3 mi. (5 km.) SSE of the city of Camden; pop. (1990c) 4430.

Oak·mont \ˈōk-ˌmänt\. Borough, Allegheny co., SW Pennsylvania, on Allegheny River 11 mi. (18 km.) ENE of Pittsburgh; pop. (1990c) 6961.

Oak Park. **1.** Residential village, Cook co., NE Illinois, bordering Chicago on the W; pop. (1990c) 53,648; has notable examples of Frank Lloyd Wright architecture; settled 1833; incorp. 1901.
2. City, Oakland co., SE Michigan, just N of Detroit; pop. (1990c) 30,462.

Oak·ridge \ˈōk-ˌrij\. City, Lane co., W Oregon, 42 mi. (68 km.) SE of Eugene; pop. (1990c) 3063.

Oak Ridge. City, Anderson and Roane cos., E Tennessee, 17 mi. (27 km.) W of Knoxville; area 58,800 acres (23,814 hectares); pop. (1990c) 27,310; community originated during WWII as a vast nuclear research and development complex, estab. by U.S. government in conjunction with the Manhattan Project; incorp. as city 1959; Oak Ridge National Laboratory (estab. 1943 as Clinton Engineer Works, later called Clinton National Laboratory until 1948); Oak Ridge Institute of Nuclear Studies, estab. 1948; produces radioactive isotopes and U-235.

Oak·ville \ˈōk-ˌvil\. Town, Halton munic. region, SE Ontario, Canada, on Lake Ontario 22 mi. (35 km.) SW of Toronto; pop. (1991c) 114,670; automobiles; pop. grew rapidly in 1980s esp. in 2d half.

Oak·wood \ˈōk-ˌwu̇d\. **1.** Village, Cuyahoga co., N Ohio, 15 mi. (24 km.) SE of Cleveland; pop. (1990c) 3392.
2. City, Montgomery co., SW Ohio, 3 mi. (5 km.) S of Dayton; pop. (1990c) 8957.

Oam·a·ru \ˈä-mə-ˌrü\. Borough, E South I., New Zealand, on Pacific Ocean 55 mi. (88 km.) NNE of Dunedin; pop. (1992e) 13,750; has port facilities; limestone quarries.

Oaracta. See QESHM 1.

Oas \ō-ˈäs\. Municipality, N cen. Albany prov., Luzon, Philippines, 18 mi. (29 km.) NW of Legazpi; pop. (1990c) 53,061.

OAS. See ORGANIZATION OF AMERICAN STATES.

Oasis Butte \ō-ˈā-səs-ˈbyüt\. Isolated peak in W Klamath co., S Oregon, NW of Crater Lake; 5685 ft. (1733 m.).

Oates Coast \ˈōts\. Part of Antarctica W of the N part of Victoria Land, ab. 70°S, 160°E, S of Balleny Is.

OAU. See ORGANIZATION OF AFRICAN UNITY.

Oa·xa·ca \wä-ˈhä-kä\. **1.** State of SE Mexico. See table at MEXICO.
2. *or in full* **Oaxaca de Juá·rez** \thā-ˈwä-rās\. City, its ✱; munic. pop. (1990p) 212,943; alt. 5070 ft. (1545 m.); noted

handicrafts market (glazed pottery, leather goods, wool and cotton textiles) and 16th cent. buildings; university (1827); founded 1486 as Aztec garrison post; conquered by Spanish 1521; home of Presidents Benito Juárez and Porfirio Díaz.

Ob' \ˈōbʸ\ *or* **Ob** \ˈäb, ˈōb\. River, W Russia in Asia; flows into the Gulf of Ob; ab. 2287 mi. (3680 km.) long (with Irtysh 3461 mi. or 5569 km.); its basin has an area of ab. 1,131,000 sq. mi. (2,929,290 sq. km.). Its headstreams are the Biya and Katun', rising in the Altay Shan; its middle course is through extensive swampland, frozen much of the year; its main tributaries on the right are the Tom', Chulym, and Ket', and on the left the Irtysh; chief towns on its banks Novosibirsk and Barnaul; important source of hydroelectric power and one of the major transportation routes of Siberia.

Ob, Gulf of *or* **Gulf of Ob'** *or Russ.* **Ob·ska·ya Gu·ba** \ˈōbʸ-skə-yə-gü-ˈbä\. Inlet of Arctic Ocean, E of Yamal Penin., NW Russia in Asia; ab. 550 mi. (885 km.) long by 50 mi. (80 km.) wide; represents drowned lower course of the Ob'.

Oba. See AOBA.

Oban \ˈō-bən\. Seaport burgh, Strathclyde region, W Scotland, on the Firth of Lorn; pop. (1981p) 8134; cathedral; tourist resort. Nearby are ruins of Dunstaffnage Castle; figures in Sir Walter Scott's novel *Lord of the Isles*.

Ob·bia \ˈō-byä\. Coastal town, E Somalia, on road bet. Mogadishu and Eil.

Obeid, El. See EL OBEID.

Ob·e·lisk \ˈä-bə-ˌlisk, -ləsk\. Peak, E Fresno co., in the Sierra Nevada, S cen. California; 9707 ft. (2959 m.).

Ober·alp \ˈō-bə-ˌrälp\. Small lake in the Alps, SW Uri canton, cen. Switzerland, NE of Andermatt; alt. 6654 ft. (2028 m.). Near the lake is **Oberalp Pass,** alt. 6704 ft. (2043 m.), on the boundary bet. Uri and Graubünden cantons.

Ober·alp·stock \ˌō-bə-ˈrälp-ˌshtȯk\. Peak, Uri and Graubünden cantons, E cen. Switzerland; 10,915 ft. (3327 m.).

Ober·am·mer·gau \ō-bə-ˈrä-mər-ˌgau̇\. Village, Bavaria, Germany, 42 mi. (68 km.) SSW of Munich; pop. (1980c) 4906; wood carving; famous for its Passion play, presented every 10th year (with a few exceptions) since the 17th cent. Play first given as a result of vow by villagers because of deliverance from the plague.

Oberdonau. See UPPER AUSTRIA.

Oberelsass. See *History* at ALSACE-LORRAINE.

Ober–Ga·bel·horn \ˌō-bər-ˈgä-bəl-ˌhȯrn\. Peak in the Pennine Alps, Valais canton, SW Switzerland; 13,365 ft. (4074 m.).

Ober·hau·sen \ˈō-bər-ˌhau̇-zən\. City, North Rhine-Westphalia, Germany, in the Ruhr Valley 7 mi. (11 km.) WNW of Essen; pop. (1992e) 224,559; railroad junction; manufactures iron and steel, wire, glass, chemicals; railroad workshops, dyeworks, zinc smelters, sugar refineries; coal mining; 14th and 16th cent. castles; became city 1874; incorp. neighboring towns of Sterkrade and Osterfeld 1929.

Oberhollabrunn. See HOLLABRUNN.

Ober·land \ˈō-bər-ˌland, -ˌlänt\. In German-speaking lands, a mountainous region; esp. notable in Switzerland, the **Ber·nese Oberland** \bər-ˈnēz, -ˈnēs\ (*Ger.* **Ber·ner Ober·land** \ˈber-nər\) incl. Bern canton S of Thunersee, and parts of Uri canton and former Unterwalden canton; in general usage equivalent to the Bernese Alps. See table at ALPS.

Ober·lin \ˈō-bər-lən\. **1.** City, ⊗ of Decatur co., NW Kansas, 75 mi. (121 km.) ENE of Goodland; pop. (1990c) 2197.
2. City, ⊗ of Allen parish, SW Louisiana; pop. (1990c) 1808.
3. Residential city, Lorain co., N Ohio, 30 mi. (48 km.) WSW of Cleveland; pop. (1990c) 8191; antislavery center before Civil War; Oberlin Coll. (1833).

Oberlin Mountain. Peak in Glacier National Park, NW Montana; 8100 ft. (2469 m.).

Oberösterreich. See UPPER AUSTRIA.

Oberrhein. See UPPER RHINE.

Oberschlesien. See SILESIA.

Ober·ur·sel \ˌō-bər-ˈu̇r-səl\. City, Hesse, Germany, 8 mi. (13 km.) NW of Frankfurt am Main; pop. (1980c) 38,979.

Óbi·dos; *mostly formerly* **Oby·dos** \ˈō-bi-ˌdüs\. Town, Pará state, N Brazil, on left bank of the Amazon where the Trombetas joins it, 500 mi. (805 km.) above Belém; center of district producing sugar, coffee, cacao, and tobacco; orig. a fortified town.

Obi·hi·ro \ˌō-bē-ˈhē-rō\. City, Hokkaidō, Japan, ab. 95 mi. (155 km.) E of Sapporo; pop. (1990p) 167,389.

Obi Islands \ˈō-bē\. Island group of the N cen. Moluccas, Indonesia, in Malay Archipelago S of Bacan and Halmahera; highest point 5285 ft. (1611 m.); densely forested. Chief island **Obi** *or* **Obi·ra** \ō-ˈbir-ə\ (*formerly* **Om·bi·rah** \ōm-\), 951 sq. mi. (2463 sq. km.).

Obi·on \ō-ˈbī-ən\. **1.** River, NW Tennessee; formed by confluence of N and S forks in E Obion co., flows SW into Forked Deer River near its junction with the Mississippi in S Dyer co; 70 mi. (113 km.) long.
2. County in NW Tennessee. See table at TENNESSEE.

Obi·ra \ō-ˈbir-ə\. See OBI ISLANDS.

Obiralovka. See ZHELEZNODOROZHNYY.

Obla·tos, Bar·ran·ca de \bä-ˌräŋ-kä-ˌthā-ō-ˈblä-tōs\. Gorge of the Río Santiago, W cen. Mexico, 5 mi. (8 km.) SW of Guadalajara in Jalisco state.

Ob·ninsk \ˈōb-ninsk\. Town, Kaluga Oblast, W Russia in Europe; pop. (1992e) 105,000.

Obock *or* **Obok** \ō-ˈbȯk\. Seaport village, Djibouti, N side of the Gulf of Tadjoura, nearly opp. Djibouti (city); historically important as the point of entrance of the French into this region; acquired 1862; seat of government transferred to Djibouti (city) 1892.

O'·Bri·en \ō-ˈbrī-ən\. County in NW Iowa. See table at IOWA.

Obringa. See AARE.

Observatory Peak. See OGDEN, MOUNT.

Ob·sid·ian Cliff \əb-ˈsi-dē-ən\. Cliff of black volcanic glass in Yellowstone National Park, NW Wyoming; elev. ab. 7350 ft. (2240 m.).

Obskaya Guba. See OB, GULF OF.

Obua·si \ō-ˈbwä-sē\. Town, S Ghana, ab. 35 mi. (56 km.) S of Kumasi; pop. (1984c) 60,617.

Óbuda. See BUDAPEST.

Obwalden. See UNTERWALDEN.

Obydos. See ÓBIDOS.

Ocala \ō-ˈka-lə\. Commercial city, ⊗ of Marion co., N cen. Florida Penin., 35 mi. (56 km.) S of Gainesville; pop. (1990c) 42,045; packs fruit and vegetables; horse raising; citrus and truck farms; Central Florida Community Coll. (1958).

Oca·ña \ō-ˈkä-nyä\. City, Norte de Santander dept., N Colombia, 60 mi. (97 km.) NW of Cúcuta; munic. pop. (1985c) 50,784; in the Cordillera Oriental at alt. of 3820 ft. (1164 m.).

Oc·ci·den·tal \ˌȯk-sē-then-ˈtäl\. Administrative region of W Paraguay; 98,480 sq. mi. (255,063 sq. km.); pop. (1990e) 65,800. For subdivisions, see table at PARAGUAY.

Occidental Misamis. See MISAMIS OCCIDENTAL.

Occidental Negros. See NEGROS OCCIDENTAL.

Oc·cum \ˈä-kəm\. Subdivision of city of Norwich, Connecticut. See NORWICH 1.

Ocean \ˈō-shən\. Coastal county in E New Jersey. See table at NEW JERSEY.

Oce·ana \ˌō-shē-ˈa-nə\. County in W Michigan. See table at MICHIGAN.

Ocean Cape. Cape, SE Alaska, on S side of entrance to Yakutat Bay.

Ocean City. **1.** Resort town, Worcester co., SE Maryland, on a 10-mile (16-kilometer) long barrier island; pop. (1990c) 5146.
2. City, Cape May co., S New Jersey, on Atlantic Ocean 10 mi. (16 km.) SW of Atlantic City; pop. (1990c) 15,512; seaside resort.

Ocean Grove. Unincorporated settlement and summer resort, Monmouth co., E cen. New Jersey, on Atlantic coast ab. 1 mi. (2 km.) S of and adjoining Asbury Park; pop. (1990c) 4818; founded c. 1869 for camp meetings and religious conferences; large auditorium; no industries allowed.

Oce·an·ia \ˌō-shē-ˈa-nē-ə, -ˈā-\ *also* **Oce·an·i·ca** \-ˈa-ni-kə\. **1.** Collective name for the lands of the Pacific Ocean and esp. of the cen. and S Pacific, incl. Micronesia, Melanesia, and Polynesia, and sometimes Australia, New Zealand, and the Malay Archipelago.

2. French overseas territory, South Pacific Ocean. See FRENCH POLYNESIA.

Ocean Island. 1. Island, Kiribati. See BANABA.

2. Islet, Leeward Is. See KURE ATOLL.

Ocean Pond. See OLUSTEE.

Ocean·port \'ō-shən-,pōrt\. Borough, Monmouth co., E cen. New Jersey, 6 mi. (10 km.) N of Asbury Park; pop. (1990c) 6146.

Ocean·side \'ō-shən-,sīd\. Residential city, San Diego co., SW corner of California, on Gulf of Santa Catalina 45 mi. (72 km.) N of the city of San Diego; pop. (1990c) 128,398; seaside resort; truck farms; Mira Costa Coll. (1934); Camp Pendleton, U.S. Marine Corps base, just to N. Incorp. 1888.

Ocean Springs. Town, Jackson co., SE corner of Mississippi, across inlet from Biloxi; pop. (1990c) 14,658; seaside resort.

Oceanus Atlanticus. See ATLANTIC OCEAN.

Oceanus Indicus. See INDIAN OCEAN.

Ocha. See ÓKHI ÓROS.

Ocha·kiv *or* **Ocha·kov** \ə-'chä-kəf\. Seaport town, S Ukraine, on the Black Sea bet. Odessa and Kherson.

Oche·ye·dan Mound \ō-'chēd-^{ə}n\. Hill in Osceola co., NW Iowa; 1670 ft. (509 m.); highest peak in Iowa.

Ochiai. See DOLINSK.

Ochil Hills \'ō-kəl, 'ä-\. Range of hills, S Tayside region, cen. Scotland; highest peak **Ben Cleuch** \ben-'klük\ 2363 ft. (720 m.).

Och·il·tree \'ä-kəl-,trē\. County in NW Texas. See table at TEXAS.

Och·lock·o·nee \ä-'klä-kə-nē\. River, S Georgia and NW Florida; rises in Worth co., S Georgia, flows SW across NW Florida into Gulf of Mexico; ab. 135 mi. (215 km.) long.

Ocho Ri·os \'ō-chō-'rē-ōs\. Seaport, N Jamaica, NW of Kingston; resort.

Ochrida. See OHRID 1.

Ocil·la \ō-'si-lə\. **1.** River, Florida. See AUCILLA.

2. City, ⊗ of Irwin co., S Georgia; pop. (1990c) 3182.

Oc·mul·gee \ōk-'məl-gē\. River, cen. Georgia; formed by junction of Yellow and South rivers in Newton co., flows S and SE to join the Oconee in S Montgomery co. and form the Altamaha River; 255 mi. (410 km.) long.

Ocmulgee National Monument. See UNITED STATES, *National Monuments*.

Ocoa Bay \ō-'kō-ə\. Bay in S coast of the Dominican Republic, Hispaniola I., West Indies.

Oco·ee \ō-'kō-ē\. **1.** River, NE Georgia and SE Tennessee; rises in S Fannin co., Georgia, flows N and NW to Hiwassee River in Polk co., Tennessee; ab. 70 mi. (115 km.) long; whitewater rafting; called **Toc·coa** \tə-'kō-ə\ in Georgia. In its course in N Georgia is the Blue Ridge Dam and in Tennessee are three dams, **Ocoee No. 1, Ocoee No. 2,** and **Ocoee No. 3** (see table at TENNESSEE VALLEY AUTHORITY).

2. City, Orange co., cen. Florida, 10 mi. (16 km.) W of Orlando; pop. (1990c) 12,778.

Oco·nee \ō-'kō-nē\. **1.** River, cen. Georgia; rises in Hall co., N Georgia, flows S and SE to join the Ocmulgee and form the Altamaha River in S Montgomery co., SE cen. Georgia; ab. 250 mi. (400 km.) long.

2. Name of counties in two states in the U.S. See tables at GEORGIA and SOUTH CAROLINA.

Ocon·o·mo·woc \ə-'kä-nə-mə-,wȯk\. City, Waukesha co., SE Wisconsin, 13 mi. (21 km.) ESE of Watertown; pop. (1990c) 10,993; summer resort.

Ocon·to \ō-'kän-tō\. **1.** River, NE Wisconsin; rises in SE Forest co., flows S and E into Green Bay at Oconto; ab. 130 mi. (210 km.) long.

2. County in NE Wisconsin. See table at WISCONSIN.

3. City, its ⊗, on Green Bay at mouth of Oconto River 18 mi. (29 km.) SSW of Marinette; pop. (1990c) 4474; sawmills; summer resort.

Oconto Falls. City, Oconto co., NE Wisconsin, 27 mi. (43 km.) N of Green Bay (city); pop. (1990c) 2584.

Oco·sin·go \,ō-kō-'sēŋ-gō\. Municipality, Chiapas state, Mexico, 70 mi. (113 km.) E of Tuxtla Gutiérrez; munic. pop. (1990p) 120,697.

Oco·tal \,ō-kō-'täl\. Town, ✻ of Nueva Segovia dept., NW Nicaragua, near Honduras border; pop. (1985e) 19,097.

Oco·te·pe·que \ō-,kō-tā-'pā-kā\. **1.** Department of W Honduras. See table at HONDURAS.

2. Town, Honduras. See NUEVA OCOTEPEQUE.

Oco·tlán \,ō-kō-'tlän\. Town, Jalisco state, W cen. Mexico, at NE corner of Lake Chapala; munic. pop. (1990p) 69,559.

Ocra·coke Island \'ō-krə-,kōk\. Island off cen. North Carolina coast, in chain of narrow sandy islands lying bet. Pamlico Sound and Atlantic Ocean; 9 sq. mi. (23 sq. km.); Hatteras Inlet NE of it and **Ocracoke Inlet** SW of it connect the sound with the ocean.

Ocriculum. See OTRICOLI.

October Revolution Island *or Russ.* **Ostrov Ok·tya·br'·skoy Re·vo·lyu·tsii** \'ȯ-strəf-ək-'tyä-bər-,skȯi-,re-vəl-'yüt-sē\. Cen. island of the Severnaya Zemlya group, Arctic Ocean, Taymyr Autonomous Okrug, N Russia in Asia.

Ocu·ma·re del Tuy \,ō-kü-'mä-rā-thel-'twē\ *or* **Ocumare.** Town, Miranda state, N Venezuela, 30 mi. (48 km.) S of Caracas.

Ocus·si *or* **Oku·si** \ō-'kü-sē\. Former military station of the Portuguese on N coast of Timor I., Indonesia, in the former exclave of Oé-Cusse.

Oda \'ō-də\. Town, Eastern Region, Ghana, ab. 60 mi. (95 km.) WNW of Accra; pop. (1982e) 22,675.

Oda·wa·ra \,ō-dä-'wä-rä\. Town, Kanagawa prefecture, SE Honshū, Japan, on Sagami Sea 50 mi. (80 km.) SW of Tokyo; pop. (1990p) 193,415.

Öde·miş \,œ-de-'mēsh\. Town, SE İzmir prov., W Turkey in Asia, 45 mi. (72 km.) ESE of the city of İzmir.

Ödenburg. See SOPRON.

Oden·daals·rus \,ō-dən-däls-'rəs\. Town, Free State, Rep. of South Africa, 38 mi. (61 km.) SW of Kroonstad; pop. (1985c) 8819; largely developed after discovery of important goldfield in vicinity 1946.

Oden·se \'ō-dən-sə, -thən-, *locally* 'ü-ən-zə\. City, ⊗ of Fyn co., N cen. Fyn I., Denmark; pop. (1989e) 174,948; 3d largest settlement of Denmark; machinery, textiles, electrical equipment; shipbuilding; 14th cent. cathedral; 18th cent. palace; university (1964). First mentioned c. 1000 A.D.; birthplace of author Hans Christian Andersen 1805.

Oden·wald \'ōd-^{ə}n-,vält\. Mountainous region, S Germany in the states of Hesse, Baden-Württemberg, and Bavaria bet. the Neckar and Main rivers; ab. 50 mi. (80 km.) long by 25 mi. (40 km.) wide; highest point the Katzenbuckel 2057 ft. (627 m.).

Oder \'ō-dər\ *or Czech and Polish* **Odra** \'ȯ-drä\; *anc.* **Vi·ad·ua** \vī-'a-jə-wə\. River, cen. Europe; rises in the mountains of E Czech Republic; flows N through W Poland to join the Neisse 21 mi. (34 km.) SSE of Frankfurt, Germany, where it forms the boundary bet. Poland and Germany, thence N into the Baltic Sea, passing through Opole, Wrocław, Frankfurt, and Szczecin in its course; 567 mi. (912 km.) long; navigable for most of its length; chief tributaries on the left Nysa, Kaczawa, Bóbr, and Neisse; on the right Warta. Partially internationalized under terms of the Treaty of Versailles 1919. In WWII much fighting along its course in early part of 1945; by Potsdam Conference 1945, its upper course, formerly in Silesia, placed in Poland, and its lower course from confluence with the Neisse made boundary bet. Germany and Poland.

Oder–Neis·se Line \-'nī-sə\. Boundary line bet. Germany (formerly East Germany) and Poland; adopted at the Potsdam Conference 1945; formed by the Neisse River from the Sudety Mts. to its junction with the Oder S of Frankfurt and the Oder thence N to the Zalew Szczeciński.

Oder·zo \ō-'dert-sō\; *anc.* **Op·i·ter·gi·um** \,ō-pə-'tər-jē-əm\. Commune, Treviso prov., NE Veneto, NE Italy, 15 mi. (24 km.) NE of the commune of Treviso; pop. (1981p) 16,297; 14th cent. cathedral; Roman museum.

Odes·sa \ō-'de-sə\. **1.** City, Lafayette co., W Missouri, 28 mi. (45 km.) E of Independence; pop. (1990c) 3695.
2. City, ⊗ of Ector co., W Texas; pop. (1990c) 89,699; center of major oil field; manufactures oil-drilling equipment, chemicals; carbon black mining; Odessa Coll. (1946), Univ. of Texas of the Permian Basin (1969); founded 1886; incorp. 1927.
3. *or* **Odesa.** Administrative subdivision of Ukraine; 12,857 sq. mi. (33,300 sq. km.); pop. (1991c) 2,635,300; ✻ Odessa; on NW shore of Black Sea; bordered on S by the lower Dniester; grain, sunflowers; vineyards; livestock raising; industry is centered in Odessa (city).
4. *or* **Odesa.** City, ✻ of Odessa subdivision, Ukraine, 25 mi. (40 km.) NE of the mouth of the Dniester on **Odessa Bay;** pop. (1991e) 1,101,000; major seaport and industrial center; base of a fishing fleet and formerly of the Soviet Antarctic whaling fleet; produces machine tools, agricultural machinery, construction equipment, fertilizer, foodstuffs; shipbuilding and repairing, oil refining; university (1865). Covers a series of terraced hills; port is icebound an average of three months per year.
History: Present city founded around Tatar fortress 14th cent.; passed to Turkey 1764 and to Russia 1791; made naval base and port 1794; given name Odessa 1795; rapid expansion as grain-exporting port during 19th cent.; center of revolutionary activity 1905 (incl. mutiny aboard battleship *Potemkin*); in WWII occupied by Axis forces 1941–44 and suffered extensive damage.

Odessus. See VARNA 2.

Odiel \ō-'dyel\. River, Huelva prov., SW Spain; flows S and joins the Tinto below Huelva; combined streams flow into the Mediterranean; ab. 60 mi. (97 km.) long.

Odien·né \ō-'dye-nā\. Town, NW Ivory Coast, in a savanna region; pop. (1988c) 28,052.

Odin·tso·vo \,ə-dyin-'tsȯ-və\. Town, Moscow Oblast, W cen. Russia in Europe, 14 mi. (23 km.) WSW of the city of Moscow; pop. (1992e) 129,000.

Odioñ·gan \ō-'dyȯn-gän\. Municipality on W coast of Tablas I., Romblon prov., Philippines, on Tablas Strait; pop. (1980c) 27,188.

Od·i·shaw, Mount \'ō-də-,shȯ\. Mountain, Antarctica, 84°42′S, 174°54′E; 13,008 ft. (3965 m.).

Odomari. See KORSAKOV.

Odon \ȯ-'dōⁿ\. Short stream of Normandy, NW France; a W tributary of the Orne, entering it at Caen; in WWII severe fighting on its banks in battle of Normandy June–July 1944.

Odoorn \ō-'dōrn\. Commune, Drenthe prov., NE Netherlands, near German border; pop. (1981e) 12,143.

Odor·hei·ul Se·cuiesc \,ō-dōr-'kā-ül-'sā-,kwēsh\. Town, Harghita co., NE cen. Romania; pop. (1989c) 42,501.

Odra. See ODER.

Od·za·la National Park \ōd-'zä-lä\. National park, W Rep. of the Congo; 424 sq. mi. (1098 sq. km.); varied wildlife; estab. 1940.

Oea. See TRIPOLI 4.

Oé–Cus·se \wā-'kü-sē\. A wedge-shaped region on N coast of East Timor, Indonesia; formed an exclave of former Portuguese Timor; ab. 950 sq. mi. (2460 sq. km.).

Oedanes. See BRAHMAPUTRA.

Oeleëheuë. See ULEELHEUE.

Oels *or* **Oels in Schlesien.** See OLEŚNICA.

Oel·wein \'ōl-,wīn\. City, Fayette co., NE Iowa, 25 mi. (40 km.) ENE of Waterloo; pop. (1990c) 6493.

Oe·no·tria \ē-'nō-trē-ə\. Ancient region, S Italy; comprised Bruttium (*mod.* Calabria) and Lucania (*mod.* Basilicata); the name probably first applied by Greeks.

Oer–Er·ken·schwick \'œr-'er-kən-,shfik\. Town, North Rhine-Westphalia, Germany, NE suburb of Recklinghausen; pop. (1980c) 27,329.

O–erh–ku–na. See ARGUN.

Oesel. See SAAREMAA.

Oe·ta \'ē-tə\. Mountain chain in Phthiotis and Phocis depts., cen. Greece; highest point 7060 ft. (2152 m.). Forms an E spur of the Pindus Mts. and terminates on E at Pass of Thermopylae on Gulf of Maliakós; in ancient times was on E border of Aetolia. In legend, scene of death of Hercules.

O'·Fal·lon \ō-'fa-lən\. **1.** City, St. Clair co., SW Illinois, 15 mi. (24 km.) E of East St. Louis; pop. (1990c) 16,073.
2. City, St. Charles co., E Missouri, 30 mi. (48 km.) NW of St. Louis; pop. (1990c) 18,698; pop. more than doubled bet. 1980 and 1990.

Ofan·to \'ȯ-fän-,tō\; *anc.* **Au·fi·dus** \'ȯ-fə-dəs\. River, SE Italy; flows E through Avellino prov., Campania, into the Adriatic Sea 4 mi. (6 km.) NW of Barletta, Puglia; 103 mi. (166 km.) long.

Of·fa \'ȯ-fä\. Town, Kwara state, SW Nigeria, ab. 30 mi. (48 km.) SSE of Ilorin; pop. (1991e) 174,500.

Of·fa·ly \'ȯ-fə-lē, 'ä-\; *formerly* **King's** \'kiŋz\. County, E cen. Ireland, in W Leinster prov.; ⊗ Tullamore; rivers Shannon, Brosna, Barrow, Boyne; wheat, barley; livestock raising. See table at IRELAND.

Of·fa's Dyke \'ȯ-fəz\. Remains of an entrenchment extending from the Wye River to the Dee River in England and Wales; built by Offa (d. 796), king of the Mercians, along W border of Mercia as a fortification against the Welsh.

Of·fen·bach \'ȯ-fən-,bäk\ *also* **Offenbach am Main** \äm-'mīn\. City, Germany, on left bank of Main River just E of Frankfurt am Main; pop. (1992e) 115,790; center of tanning and leather-goods industry; machinery, electrical equipment, chemicals, textiles; castle. First mentioned c. 977; annexed to Hesse 1816; rebuilt after heavy damage in WWII.

Of·fen·burg \'ȯ-fən-,bu̇rk\. Manufacturing city, Baden-Württemberg, Germany, at foot of the Black Forest 33 mi. (53 km.) N of Freiburg; pop. (1992e) 53,873; structural steel, electrical equipment, textiles; printing, tourism; became imperial free city 1289.

Of·fi·da \ȯf-'fē-dä\. Commune, Ascoli Piceno prov., S Marche, cen. Italy; pop. (1981p) 5475; 14th cent. church.

Ofot·en Fjord \'ō-fə-tən-,fyōr\ *or* **Ofot·fjord** \'ō-fōt-,fyōr, 'ō-fu̇t-,fyōr\. NE extension of Vestfjorden on NW coast of Norway; site of port of Narvik.

Ofu \'ō-fü\. Westernmost island of the Manua Is. (*q.v.*) in American Samoa; 3 sq. mi. (8 sq. km.); separated from Olosega (2 sq. mi. or 5 sq. km.) on the E by so narrow a channel that the two islands appear to be one. Both islands mountainous; highest point on Ofu 1587 ft. (484 m.), on Olosega 2092 ft. (638 m.).

Oga·den \ō-'gä-den\. Region, E Ethiopia; in the triangular wedge that juts into Somalia; a dry, barren, and sparsely populated plain; conquered by Menelik II late 19th cent.; invaded by Italy 1935 and made part of Italian East Africa; recovered by Ethiopia in WWII; invaded by Somalia 1977, recovered 1978.

Ōga·ki \ō-'gä-kē\. Town, Gifu prefecture, W cen. Honshū, Japan, just W of Gifu and 20 mi. (32 km.) NW of Nagoya; pop. (1990p) 148,281; castle.

Ogal·la·la \,ō-gə-'lä-lə\. City, ⊗ of Keith co., W Nebraska, on South Platte River; pop. (1990c) 5095.

Ogasawara Islands *or* **Ogasawara–guntō.** See BONIN ISLANDS.

Og·bo·mo·sho \ōg-bō-'mō-shō\. City, SW Nigeria, 50 mi. (80 km.) NNE of Ibadan; pop. (1991e) 644,200; trade center and road junction; ships foodstuffs, tobacco, and livestock; founded mid-17th cent.; center of resistance to Fulani invasions of early 19th cent.

Og·den \'ȯg-dən, 'äg-\. City, ⊗ of Weber co., N Utah, 33 mi. (53 km.) N of Salt Lake City; pop. (1990c) 63,909; alt. 4259 ft. (1298 m.); railroad center; clothing, jet engines, packing plants, stockyards; tourism; Weber State Univ. (1889); Hill Air Force Base; settled c. 1845; incorp. 1851.

Ogden, Mount; *formerly* **Observatory Peak.** Mountain in Morgan and Weber cos., N Utah, just E of Ogden in Wasatch Range; 9572 ft. (2918 m.).

Og·dens·burg \'ȯg-dənz-,bərg, 'äg-\. **1.** Borough, Sussex co., N New Jersey; pop. (1990c) 2722.
2. City, St. Lawrence co., N New York, on St. Lawrence River 55 mi. (88 km.) NNE of Watertown; pop. (1990c) 13,521; resort; office supplies; Wadhams Hall (college, 1924).

History: Settled 1749; site purchased late 18th cent. by Col. Samuel Ogden; incorp. as village 1817; chartered as city 1868; at **Heu·vel·ton** \'hyü-vəl-tən\, just SE of the city, Prime Minister Mackenzie King and President Franklin D. Roosevelt met Aug. 17–18, 1940 to formulate the "Ogdensburg Agreement" establishing a joint U.S.-Canadian board for studying problems of the defense of North America.

Ogee·chee \ō-'gē-chē\. River, E Georgia; rises in Green co., flows SE into Atlantic Ocean on border of Bryan and Chatham cos.; ab. 250 mi. (400 km.) long.

Oge·maw \'ō-gə-ˌmȯ\. County in NE Michigan. See table at MICHIGAN.

Ogi·da·ki Mountain \ˌō-gə-'dä-kē\. Mountain, S Ontario, Canada; 2183 ft. (665 m.); highest peak in the province.

Ogil·vie Mountains \'ō-gəl-vē\. Range, cen. Yukon Terr., Canada; av. height ab. 4000 ft. (1220 m.); highest point 7189 ft. (2191 m.).

Ogle \'ō-gəl\. County in N Illinois. See table at ILLINOIS.

Ogles·by \'ō-gəlz-bē\. City, La Salle co., N Illinois; pop. (1990c) 3619; Illinois Valley Community Coll. (1924).

Ogle·thorpe \'ō-gəl-ˌthȯrp\. **1.** County in NE Georgia. See table at GEORGIA.
2. City, ⊗ of Macon co., SW cen. Georgia; pop. (1990c) 1302.

Oglethorpe, Mount. Mountain, Pickens co., N Georgia; 3290 ft. (1003 m.); at S end of Blue Ridge.

Oglio \'ȯl-yō\; *anc.* **Ol·li·us** \'ä-lē-əs\. River, N Italy; rises in the Rhaetian Alps, flows SE through Lake Iseo and into Po River 10 mi. (16 km.) SW of Mantua; 175 mi. (282 km.) long.

Ogo·ja \ō-'gō-jä\. Town, SE Nigeria; pop. (1982e) 22,020.

Ogo·ki \ō-'gō-kē\. River, a S tributary of the Albany, in cen. Ontario, Canada; rises in chain of lakes and flows NE and E; ab. 300 mi. (485 km.) long.

Ogo·oué *or* **Ogo·we** \ˌō-gō-'wā\. River, Gabon; flows W into Atlantic Ocean S of Cape Lopez; 683 mi. (1099 km.) long; navigable for ab. 250 mi. (400 km.).

Ogu·lin \'ō-gü-lēn\. Commune, Croatia, 40 mi. (64 km.) E of Rijeka; pop. (1991c) 16,732.

Ogun \ō-'gün, 'ō-ˌgün\. State of SW Nigeria. See table at NIGERIA.

Ohau, Lake \'ō-ˌhau̇\. Lake, S cen. South I., New Zealand; 23 sq. mi. (60 sq. km.); from its S end issues the **Ohau River,** one of the headstreams of the Waitaki River.

O'·Hig·gins \ō-'hig-ənz, ō-'ē-gēns\. Peak, S Chile, W of Lake San Martín; 9545 ft. (2909 m.).

Ohio \ō-'hī-ō\. **1.** Navigable river in Pennsylvania, Ohio, Indiana, and Illinois; formed by confluence of Allegheny and Monongahela rivers at Pittsburgh, SW Pennsylvania, flows W and SW to form Ohio-West Virginia, Ohio-Kentucky, Indiana-Kentucky, and Illinois-Kentucky boundaries; empties into Mississippi River at Cairo, S extremity of Illinois; 975 mi. (1569 km.) long; area of its basin 203,900 sq. mi. (528,101 sq. km.).
2. A north central state of U.S.A., bounded on N by Michigan and Lake Erie, on E by Pennsylvania and Ohio River, on S by Ohio River, and on W by Indiana; 35th state in area, 41,222 sq. mi. (106,765 sq. km.); in addition to this area Ohio has also 3457 sq. mi. (8954 sq. km.) of water of the Great Lakes; 7th state in population, (1990c) 10,847,115; ✱ Columbus; 17th state admitted to Union (1803). See table of states at UNITED STATES.

Nickname: Buckeye State.

State flower: Scarlet carnation.

Rivers: Ohio (SE and S boundary) and its tributaries the Muskingum, Scioto, and Miami; Maumee and Sandusky flowing to Lake Erie.

Highest point: Campbell Hill, 1550 ft. (472 m.), in Logan co.

Chief products: Corn, soybeans, oats; livestock; natural gas, coal; manufacturing: iron and steel, rubber products, machinery.

Chief cities: Columbus, Cleveland, Cincinnati, Toledo, Akron, Dayton.

Political divisions: Divided into the following 88 counties (for pronunciation of their names, see their individual entries):

NAME	AREA[1] (sq. mi.)	AREA[1] (sq. km.)	POP. (1990c)	CO. SEAT
Adams	587	1,520	25,371	West Union
Allen	410	1,062	109,755	Lima
Ashland	424	1,098	47,507	Ashland
Ashtabula	700	1,813	99,821	Jefferson
Athens	504	1,305	59,549	Athens
Auglaize	400	1,036	44,585	Wapakoneta
Belmont	534	1,383	71,074	Saint Clairsville
Brown	490	1,269	34,966	Georgetown
Butler	471	1,220	291,479	Hamilton
Carroll	390	1,010	26,521	Carrollton
Champaign	432	1,119	36,019	Urbana
Clark	402	1,041	147,548	Springfield
Clermont	458	1,186	150,187	Batavia
Clinton	410	1,062	35,415	Wilmington
Columbiana	534	1,383	108,276	Lisbon
Coshocton	562	1,456	35,427	Coshocton
Crawford	404	1,046	47,870	Bucyrus
Cuyahoga	456	1,181	1,412,140	Cleveland
Darke	605	1,567	53,619	Greenville
Defiance	412	1,067	39,350	Defiance
Delaware	450	1,166	66,929	Delaware
Erie	264	684	76,779	Sandusky
Fairfield	505	1,308	103,461	Lancaster
Fayette	406	1,052	27,466	Washington Court House
Franklin	538	1,393	961,437	Columbus
Fulton	407	1,054	38,498	Wauseon
Gallia	471	1,220	30,954	Gallipolis
Geauga	407	1,054	81,129	Chardon
Greene	415	1,075	136,731	Xenia
Guernsey	528	1,368	39,024	Cambridge
Hamilton	414	1,072	866,228	Cincinnati
Hancock	532	1,378	65,536	Findlay
Hardin	467	1,210	31,111	Kenton
Harrison	401	1,039	16,085	Cadiz
Henry	416	1,077	29,108	Napoleon
Highland	549	1,422	35,728	Hillsboro
Hocking	421	1,090	25,533	Logan
Holmes	424	1,098	32,849	Millersburg
Huron	497	1,287	56,240	Norwalk
Jackson	419	1,085	30,230	Jackson
Jefferson	411	1,064	80,298	Steubenville
Knox	531	1,375	47,473	Mount Vernon
Lake	231	598	215,499	Painesville
Lawrence	456	1,181	61,834	Ironton
Licking	686	1,777	128,300	Newark
Logan	460	1,191	42,310	Bellefontaine
Lorain	495	1,282	271,126	Elyria
Lucas	343	888	462,361	Toledo
Madison	464	1,202	37,068	London
Mahoning	415	1,075	264,806	Youngstown
Marion	405	1,049	64,274	Marion
Medina	425	1,101	122,354	Medina
Meigs	436	1,129	22,987	Pomeroy
Mercer	454	1,176	39,443	Celina
Miami	407	1,054	93,182	Troy
Monroe	456	1,181	15,497	Woodsfield
Montgomery	459	1,189	573,809	Dayton
Morgan	420	1,088	14,194	McConnelsville
Morrow	403	1,044	27,749	Mount Gilead
Muskingum	667	1,728	82,068	Zanesville
Noble	398	1,031	11,336	Caldwell
Ottawa	258	668	40,029	Port Clinton
Paulding	417	1,080	20,488	Paulding
Perry	410	1,062	31,557	New Lexington
Pickaway	507	1,313	48,255	Circleville
Pike	443	1,147	24,249	Waverly
Portage	495	1,282	142,585	Ravenna
Preble	428	1,109	40,113	Eaton
Putnam	486	1,259	33,819	Ottawa
Richland	496	1,285	126,137	Mansfield
Ross	687	1,779	69,330	Chillicothe
Sandusky	409	1,059	61,963	Fremont
Scioto	608	1,575	80,327	Portsmouth
Seneca	551	1,427	59,733	Tiffin
Shelby	408	1,057	44,915	Sidney
Stark	576	1,492	367,585	Canton
Summit	410	1,062	514,990	Akron
Trumbull	615	1,593	227,813	Warren
Tuscarawas	569	1,474	84,090	New Philadelphia
Union	434	1,124	31,969	Marysville
Van Wert	409	1,059	30,464	Van Wert
Vinton	411	1,064	11,098	McArthur
Warren	408	1,057	113,909	Lebanon
Washington	641	1,660	62,254	Marietta

\ə\ **abut** \ə\ matches \ᵊ\ kitten, Fr table \ər\ **further** \a\ **ash** \ā\ **ace** \ä\ cot, cart \à\ Fr bac \au̇\ **out** \b\ Span Avila \ch\ **chin** \e\ **bet** \ē\ **easy** \g\ **go** \i\ **hit** \ī\ **ice** \j\ **job** \k\ Ger i**ch**, Bu**ch** \ⁿ\ Fr vin \ŋ\ **sing** \ō\ **go** \ȯ\ **all** \ò\ **law** \œ\ Fr bœuf \œ̄\ Fr feu \ȯi\ **boy** \th\ **thin** \t͟h\ **this** \ü\ **loot** \u̇\ **foot** \ue\ Ger füllen \ūe\ Fr rue \y\ **yet** \ʸ\ Fr digne \'dēnʸ\, nuit \'nwʸē\ \yü\ **few** \yu̇\ **fury** \zh\ **vision**

OHIO
CITIES
State capital
County seat
City
BOUNDARIES
International
State
County
FEATURES
Points of interest
0 20 40 mi
0 30 60 km
CANADA
MICHIGAN
ONTARIO
Lake St. Clair
Lake Erie
PENNSYLVANIA
WEST VIRGINIA
KENTUCKY
INDIANA
Detroit R.
Huron R.
Maumee Bay
Point Pelee
PELEE I.
WEST SISTER I.
NORTH BASS I.
MIDDLE BASS I.
SOUTH BASS I.
PERRY'S VICTORY AND INT'L PEACE MEMORIAL
KELLEYS I.
Sandusky Bay
Point Aux Pins
SEE INSET
Pymatuning Reservoir
Mosquito Creek Reservoir
Berlin Reservoir
Indian Lake
Lake St. Marys
Campbell Hill 1,550 ft.
Hoover Reservoir
Buckeye Lake
Dillon Reservoir
Clear Fork Reservoir
Atwood Reservoir
Leesville Reservoir
Tappan Reservoir
Clendening Reservoir
Piedmont Reservoir
Salt Fork Lake
Senecaville Reservoir
Rocky Fork Lake
HOPEWELL CULTURE NATIONAL HISTORICAL PARK
BLENNERHASSETT I.
Ohio R.
Scioto R.
Muskingum R.
Tuscarawas R.
Hocking R.
Great Miami R.
Big Sandy R.
Licking R.
Columbus
Cleveland
Toledo
Cincinnati
Dayton
Akron
WILLIAMS
FULTON
LUCAS
OTTAWA
WOOD
SANDUSKY
ERIE
HURON
LORAIN
CUYAHOGA
LAKE
GEAUGA
ASHTABULA
TRUMBULL
PORTAGE
SUMMIT
MEDINA
MAHONING
COLUMBIANA
STARK
WAYNE
ASHLAND
RICHLAND
CRAWFORD
SENECA
HANCOCK
HENRY
DEFIANCE
PAULDING
PUTNAM
VAN WERT
ALLEN
HARDIN
WYANDOT
MARION
MORROW
KNOX
HOLMES
TUSCARAWAS
CARROLL
JEFFERSON
HARRISON
BELMONT
GUERNSEY
COSHOCTON
MUSKINGUM
LICKING
DELAWARE
UNION
LOGAN
AUGLAIZE
MERCER
SHELBY
DARKE
MIAMI
CHAMPAIGN
CLARK
MADISON
FRANKLIN
FAIRFIELD
PERRY
MORGAN
NOBLE
MONROE
WASHINGTON
ATHENS
HOCKING
VINTON
MEIGS
GALLIA
JACKSON
LAWRENCE
SCIOTO
PIKE
ROSS
PICKAWAY
FAYETTE
GREENE
MONTGOMERY
PREBLE
BUTLER
WARREN
CLINTON
HIGHLAND
ADAMS
BROWN
CLERMONT
HAMILTON
Lake Erie
CUYAHOGA
LAKE
MEDINA
SUMMIT
LORAIN
Cleveland Hopkins Munic. Airport
HAMILTON
WARREN
CLERMONT
KENTUCKY
WILLIAM H. TAFT NAT'L HIST. SITE
©1996, Encyclopædia Britannica, Inc.

NAME	AREA[1] (sq. mi.)	AREA[1] (sq. km.)	POP. (1990c)	CO. SEAT
Wayne	561	1,453	101,461	Wooster
Williams	421	1,090	36,956	Bryan
Wood	619	1,603	113,269	Bowling Green
Wyandot	406	1,052	22,254	Upper Sandusky

[1] Area = land area.

History: Has many earthwork mounds of prehistoric Mound Builders; inhabited by various Indian tribes (incl. Miami, Shawnee, Delaware, and Wyandot) when Europeans began settling the area; claimed by both France and Britain in colonial times; ceded to Britain 1763 following French and Indian War; became part of U.S. by Treaty of Paris 1783 following American Revolution; included 1787 in Northwest Terr. (*q.v.*); first permanent white settlement at Marietta 1788; W boundary with Indian lands determined by Maj. Gen. Anthony Wayne's defeat of Indians 1794 at Fallen Timbers and by Treaty of Greenville 1795; Western Reserve (*q.v.*) incorp. 1800; first constitution 1802; unofficially entered Union Feb. 19, 1803. In 1953, by resolution of U.S. Congress, Mar. 1, 1803 declared official day of admission to Union.

3. Name of counties in three states of the U.S. See tables at INDIANA, KENTUCKY, WEST VIRGINIA.

Ohi·o·ville \ō-ˈhī-ə-ˌvil\. Borough, Beaver co., W Pennsylvania, 23 mi. (37 km.) SSW of New Castle; pop. (1990c) 3865.

Ohlau. See OŁAWA.

Ohoo·pee \ō-ˈhü-pē\. River, Georgia; rises in Washington co., flows SE to Altamaha River in S Tattnall co.; 125 mi. (201 km.) long.

Ohře \ˈȯr-zhe\ *or Ger.* **Eger** \ˈā-gər\. River, E Germany and NW Czech Republic; rises in NE Bavaria, flows ENE across Czech Republic, into the Elbe at Litoměřice; 193 mi. (311 km.) long.

Ohrid \ˈō-ˌkrēd\; *anc.* **Lych·ni·dus** \ˈlik-nə-dəs\. **1.** *or* **Okhri·da** \ō-ˈkrē-də\ *also* **Ochri·da** \-ˈkrēd-ä\ *or* **Lych·ni·tis** \lik-ˈnī-təs\. Lake, S Europe, in Republic of Macedonia and Albania; 25 mi. (40 km.) long.

2. Town on the lake, Republic of Macedonia; pop. (1991p) 65,531; tourism, fishing; several notable medieval churches; remains of citadel.

Oich, Loch \ˈȯik\. Lake, cen. Highland region, NW cen. Scotland; 4 mi. (6 km.) long; max. depth 154 ft. (47 m.); part of the chain of lakes incorp. into the Caledonian Canal; drains NE into Loch Ness.

Oil City \ˈȯil\. City, Venango co., NW Pennsylvania, on Allegheny River at mouth of Oil Creek, 52 mi. (84 km.) SSE of Erie; pop. (1990c) 11,949; engines; formerly a major oil-processing center; founded 1860; incorp. as city 1871.

Oil Creek. River, NW Pennsylvania; flows S through E Crawford co. and N Venango co., enters Allegheny River at Oil City; ab. 50 mi. (80 km.) long.

Oil Rivers. The delta of the Niger River, S Nigeria; of indefinite boundaries. See NIGER 2.

Oil Rivers Protectorate. See *History* at NIGERIA.

Oi·mya·kon *or* **Oy·mya·kon** *also* **Oi·me·kon** \ˌī-myə-ˈkȯn\. Town, SE Sakha Rep., E Russia in Asia, on the upper Indigirka River in mountain range S of the Cherskiy Range, 63°28′N, 142°49′E; weather station; one of the coldest places in Siberia; has had temperature of −79°F (−62°C).

Oirot Tura. See GORNO-ALTAYSK.

Oise \ˈwäz\. **1.** River, N France; formed by confluence of two streams, one rising near Chimay in Belgium and the other near Rocroi in France; flows SW into Seine River at Conflans-Ste.-Honorine; 188 mi. (302 km.) long; navigable for ab. 80 mi. (130 km.).

2. Department of N France. See table at FRANCE.

Ōi·ta \ˈō-ē-ˌtä, ō-ˈē-tä\. **1.** Prefecture, NE Kyūshū, Japan; ✻ Ōita; tobacco, citrus fruit; cattle. See table at JAPAN.

2. Seaport city, its ✻, 65 mi. (105 km.) SE of Moji on Beppu Bay; pop. (1992e) 417,051; ships tobacco and citrus fruit; commercial center; textiles, cement; university (1949). In 16th cent. a castle city that controlled nearly all Kyūshū.

Ojai \ˈō-hī\. Residential and resort city, Ventura co., SW California, in a valley of the Sierra Madre Range, 23 mi. (37 km.) E of Santa Barbara; pop. (1990c) 7613.

Ojo de Lie·bre, La·gu·na \lä-ˈgü-nä-ˈō-hō- thā-ˈlye-brā\. Inlet of Sebastián Vizcaíno Bay on coast of W cen. Baja California, Mexico.

Ojos del Sa·la·do, Cer·ro \ˈser-rō-ˈō-hōs-thel-sä-ˈlä-thō\. Mountain, NW Catamarca prov., NW Argentina, near border of Chile; 22,664 ft. (6908 m.).

Oka \ō-ˈkä\. **1.** River, cen. Irkutsk Oblast, S cen. Russia in Asia; flows N from the Sayan Mts. to the Angara River; 530 mi. (853 km.) long.

2. River, cen. Russia in Europe; rises in N part of Kursk Oblast, flows N and NE with several bends through Orel and Kaluga oblasts, to the Volga at Nizhniy Novgorod; 919 mi. (1479 km.) long. The largest right (W) tributary of the Volga; navigable for most of its length; important artery for lumber and grain trade; main tributaries the Klyaz'ma, Moksha, and Moskva.

Oka–Ako·ko \ˈō-kä-ä-ˈkō-kō\. Town, SW Nigeria; pop. (1991e) 126,400.

Oka·lo·a·coo·chee Slough \ˌō-kə-ˌlō-ə-ˈkü-chē\. The NW section of the Everglades, S Florida, N of Big Cypress Swamp.

Oka·loo·sa \ˌō-kə-ˈlü-sə\. Coastal county in NW Florida. See table at FLORIDA.

Oka·na·gan Lake \ˌō-kə-ˈnä-gən\. Long narrow lake, S British Columbia, Canada; 136 sq. mi. (352 sq. km.); ab. 60 mi. (97 km.) long; its outlet is the Okanagan River, called the Okanogan (*q.v.*) in the U.S.

Oka·nog·an \ˌō-kə-ˈnä-gən\. **1.** County in N Washington. See table at WASHINGTON.

2. Town, its ⊗, on Okanogan River; pop. (1990c) 2370; in farming and lumbering area.

3. *or in Canada* **Oka·na·gan** \-ˈnä-gən\. River, British Columbia, Canada, and N Washington; rises in Okanagan Lake, British Columbia, flows S across Washington border and into Columbia River on S boundary of Okanogan co.; ab. 300 mi. (485 km.) long.

Okanoxubee. See NOXUBEE 1.

Oka·ra \ō-ˈkä-rə\. City, Punjab, E Pakistan, SW of Lahore; pop. (1981c) 153,483.

Oka·van·go \ˌō-kä-ˈväŋ-gō\ *or in Angola* **Cu·ban·go** \kü-ˈbäŋ-gō\. River, SW cen. Africa; rises in cen. Angola; flows S and then E, forming a section of the boundary bet. Angola and Namibia; crosses Caprivi Strip and empties into **Okavango Swamps** *or* **Okavango Delta,** a large marsh N of Lake Ngami in N Botswana; ab. 1000 mi. (1610 km.) long.

Oka·ya \ō-ˈkä-yä\. City, Nagano prefecture, Honshū, Japan, 12 mi. (19 km.) SSE of Matsumoto; pop. (1990p) 59,854.

Oka·ya·ma \ˌō-kä-ˈyä-mä\. **1.** Prefecture, W Honshū, Japan; ✻ Okayama; rice, grapes, peaches. See table at JAPAN.

2. Seaport city, its ✻, on N side of Inland Sea 75 mi. (121 km.) W of Kōbe; pop. (1992e) 601,094; market center; manufactures rubber products, machinery; university (1949); former castle town of Ikeda clan.

Oka·za·ki \ō-ˈkä-zä-kē, ˌō-kä-ˈzä-kē\. Town, Aichi prefecture, S Honshū, Japan, 21 mi. (34 km.) SE of Nagoya; pop. (1990p) 306,821; textiles; birthplace 1543 of Ieyasu, founder of the Tokugawa shogunate.

Okee·cho·bee \ˌō-kə-ˈchō-bē\. **1.** County in SE cen. Florida. See table at FLORIDA.

2. City, its ⊗, 2 mi. (3 km.) N of Lake Okeechobee; pop. (1990c) 4943.

Okeechobee, Lake. Lake in S cen. Florida; largest lake in S United States; ab. 40 mi. (65 km.) long by 25 mi. (40 km.) wide; greatest depth ab. 20 ft. (6 m.); elev. 19 ft. (5.8 m.) above sea level; receives Kissimmee River from N and drains to the sea through the Everglades.

Okeechobee Waterway *or* **Cross–Florida Waterway.** System of waterways, S Florida, linking the Atlantic coast at Stuart with the Gulf of Mexico at the mouth of the Caloosahatchee River by way of St. Lucie Canal and Lake Okeechobee; also forms a link bet. Atlantic Intracoastal Waterway and Gulf Intracoastal Waterway.

Oke·fe·no·kee Swamp *also* **Oke·fi·no·kee Swamp** \ˌō-kə-fə-ˈnō-kē\. Swamp, SE Georgia and NE Florida; area 660 sq. mi. (1709 sq. km.).

Oke·mah \ō-ˈkē-mə\. City, ⊗ of Okfuskee co., E cen. Oklahoma, 25 mi. (40 km.) WSW of Okmulgee; pop. (1990c) 3085.

Oker \ˈō-kər\. Stream, N cen. Germany; flows N from Harz Mts. to the Aller; ab. 65 mi. (105 km.) long.

Ok·fus·kee \ōk-ˈfəs-kē\. County in E cen. Oklahoma. See table at OKLAHOMA.

Okha \ə-ˈkä\. Town and port on NE coast of N Sakhalin I., Sakhalin Oblast, E Russia in Asia; important port open year round; has railroad connection with W coast of Sakhalin.

Ókhi Óros \ˈō-kē-ˈör-ˌös\; *anc.* **Ocha** \ˈō-kə\. Peak, S Euboea I., Greece; 4839 ft. (1475 m.).

Okhotsk \ə-ˈkótsk\. Town on NW coast of Sea of Okhotsk, Khabarovsk Kray, E Russia in Asia, 440 mi. (708 km.) N of Nikolayevsk-na-Amure; port closed by ice for more than half the year; founded 1649, one of the earliest settlements of Russia's Far East.

Okhotsk, Sea of. Inlet of Pacific Ocean on coast of Khabarovsk Kray, E Russia in Asia, W of Kamchatka Penin. and the Kuril Is.; 613,838 sq. mi. (1,589,840 sq. km.); av. depth 3192 ft. (973 m.), max. depth 11,069 ft. (3374 m.); has Sakhalin I. in SW; main traffic outlets Tatar Strait, Sōya Strait, and Pervyy Kuril'skiy Proliv.

Okhrida. See OHRID 1.

Oki·e·ra·bu \ˌō-kē-ā-ˈrä-bü\. Island, S Amami Is., Ryukyu Is., Japan, just N of Okinawa.

Oki Islands \ˈō-kē\ *also* **Oki Gun·tō** \ˈgün-ˌtō\. Group of islands in SE Sea of Japan, 44 mi. (71 km.) off W coast of island of Honshū; 131 sq. mi. (339 sq. km.); belongs to Shimane prefecture. Largest island Dōgo, on SE coast of which is Saigō, the chief port, with good harbor.

Oki·na·wa \ˌō-kē-ˈnä-wä, ˌō-kə-ˈnaù-ə\. **1.** Island group in center of chain of Ryukyu Is.; comprises Okinawa and small islands of Ii-shima, Iheya, Kume, and Kerama Is.; placed under U.S. control after WWII; returned to Japan 1972.
2. Only large island in group, bet. East China Sea and Pacific Ocean, 26°39′N, 128°E; ab. 70 mi. (115 km.) long; excluding adjacent islands, 454 sq. mi. (1176 sq. km.); entirely of coral formation; largest settlement Naha at S end. Of vital importance in WWII; scene of severe fighting bet. Americans and Japanese Mar.–June 1945; after bombarding the island for several days, U.S. army and marine troops landed Apr. 1; island soon overrun except for S tip and area around Naha; this part not completely conquered until June 21 (see also YONABARU); campaign costly but made possible the establishment of Allied air bases close to Japanese mainland.
3. Prefecture of Japan, comprising the S part of the Ryukyu Is. (Okinawa and Sakishima groups); ✻ Naha. See table at JAPAN.
4. City, Okinawa prefecture, on Okinawa island, Japan; pop. (1990p) 105,852.

Oki·no–shi·ma \ō-ˈkē-nō-ˌshē-mä\. Small island off SW Shikoku, Japan, on E side of Bungo Strait, 32°44′N, 132°33′E; belongs to Kōchi prefecture.

Okla·ho·ma \ˌō-klə-ˈhō-mə\. **1.** A southwest central state of U.S.A., bounded on N by Colorado and Kansas, on E by Missouri and Arkansas, on S by Texas, and on W by Texas and New Mexico; 18th state in area, 69,956 sq. mi. (181,186 sq. km.); 28th state in population, (1990c) 3,145,585; ✻ Oklahoma City; 46th state admitted to Union (1907). See table of states at UNITED STATES.

Nickname: Sooner State.

State flower: Mistletoe.

Motto: Labor Omnia Vincit (Labor Conquers All).

Rivers: Red, forming S boundary; Canadian, flowing across cen. region to empty into the Arkansas near E cen. border; Arkansas, flowing diagonally NW to SE across NE quarter of state.

Mountains: Highest point Black Mesa, 4973 ft. (1516 m.) in Cimarron co. in the Panhandle; Wichita Mts. in SW; W part of Ouachita Mts. in SE.

Chief products: Wheat, cotton, sorghum; beef cattle; gas and petroleum; food processing; fabricated-metal products.

Chief cities: Oklahoma City, Tulsa.

Political divisions: Divided into the following 77 counties (for pronunciation of their names, see their individual entries):

NAME	AREA[1] (sq. mi.)	AREA[1] (sq. km.)	POP. (1990c)	CO. SEAT
Adair	570	1,476	18,421	Stilwell
Alfalfa	868	2,248	6,416	Cherokee
Atoka	991	2,567	12,778	Atoka
Beaver	1,790	4,636	6,023	Beaver
Beckham	907	2,349	18,812	Sayre
Blaine	917	2,375	11,470	Watonga
Bryan	889	2,303	32,089	Durant
Caddo	1,275	3,302	29,550	Anadarko
Canadian[2]	897	2,323	74,409	El Reno
Carter	830	2,150	42,919	Ardmore
Cherokee	756	1,958	34,049	Tahlequah
Choctaw	781	2,023	15,302	Hugo
Cimarron	1,843	4,773	3,301	Boise City
Cleveland	541	1,401	174,253	Norman
Coal	526	1,362	5,780	Coalgate
Comanche[2]	1,087	2,815	111,486	Lawton
Cotton	651	1,686	6,651	Walters
Craig	764	1,979	14,104	Vinita
Creek	936	2,424	60,915	Sapulpa
Custer	1,001	2,593	26,897	Arapaho
Delaware	707	1,831	28,070	Jay
Dewey	1,018	2,637	5,551	Taloga
Ellis	1,242	3,217	4,497	Arnett
Garfield	1,054	2,730	56,735	Enid
Garvin	814	2,108	26,605	Pauls Valley
Grady	1,096	2,839	41,747	Chickasha
Grant	1,007	2,608	5,689	Medford
Greer	633	1,639	6,559	Mangum
Harmon	545	1,412	3,793	Hollis
Harper	1,041	2,696	4,063	Buffalo
Haskell	602	1,559	10,940	Stigler
Hughes	807	2,090	13,023	Holdenville
Jackson	810	2,098	28,764	Altus
Jefferson	780	2,020	7,010	Waurika
Johnston	638	1,652	10,032	Tishomingo
Kay	950	2,461	48,056	Newkirk
Kingfisher	904	2,341	13,212	Kingfisher
Kiowa	1,027	2,660	11,347	Hobart
Latimer	737	1,909	10,333	Wilburton
Le Flore	1,560	4,040	43,270	Poteau
Lincoln	973	2,520	29,216	Chandler
Logan	751	1,945	29,011	Guthrie
Love	513	1,329	8,157	Marietta
McClain	573	1,484	22,795	Purcell
McCurtain	1,849	4,789	33,433	Idabel
McIntosh	608	1,575	16,779	Eufaula
Major	963	2,494	8,055	Fairview
Marshall	366	948	10,829	Madill
Mayes	678	1,756	33,366	Pryor Creek
Murray	428	1,109	12,042	Sulphur
Muskogee	818	2,119	68,078	Muskogee
Noble	743	1,924	11,045	Perry
Nowata	577	1,494	9,992	Nowata
Okfuskee	637	1,650	11,551	Okemah
Oklahoma	705	1,826	599,611	Oklahoma City
Okmulgee	700	1,813	36,490	Okmulgee
Osage	2,272	5,884	41,645	Pawhuska
Ottawa	464	1,202	30,561	Miami
Pawnee	561	1,453	15,575	Pawnee
Payne	694	1,797	61,507	Stillwater
Pittsburg	1,241	3,214	40,581	McAlester
Pontotoc	714	1,849	34,119	Ada
Pottawatomie	794	2,056	58,760	Shawanee
Pushmataha	1,423	3,686	10,997	Antlers
Roger Mills	1,140	2,953	4,147	Cheyenne
Rogers	712	1,844	55,170	Claremore
Seminole	630	1,632	25,412	Wewoka
Sequoyah	696	1,803	33,828	Sallisaw
Stephens	891	2,308	42,299	Duncan
Texas	2,062	5,341	16,419	Guymon
Tillman	901	2,334	10,384	Frederick
Tulsa	573	1,484	503,341	Tulsa
Wagoner	563	1,458	47,883	Wagoner
Washington	424	1,098	48,066	Bartlesville
Washita	1,009	2,613	11,441	New Cordell
Woods	1,298	3,362	9,103	Alva
Woodward	1,251	3,240	18,976	Woodward

[1] Area = land area.
[2] Contains Fort Sill military reservation in cen. part.

OKLAHOMA
CITIES
State capital
County seat
City
BOUNDARIES
State
County
FEATURES
Dams
Points of interest
KANSAS
MISSOURI
ARKANSAS
TEXAS
COLORADO
NEW MEXICO
BEAVER
HARPER
WOODS
ALFALFA
GRANT
KAY
OSAGE
WASHINGTON
NOWATA
CRAIG
OTTAWA
DELAWARE
MAYES
ROGERS
TULSA
PAWNEE
NOBLE
GARFIELD
MAJOR
WOODWARD
ELLIS
DEWEY
BLAINE
KINGFISHER
LOGAN
PAYNE
CREEK
WAGONER
CHEROKEE
ADAIR
SEQUOYAH
MUSKOGEE
OKMULGEE
LINCOLN
OKLAHOMA
CANADIAN
CUSTER
ROGER MILLS
BECKHAM
WASHITA
CADDO
GRADY
MCCLAIN
CLEVELAND
POTTAWATOMIE
SEMINOLE
OKFUSKEE
MCINTOSH
HASKELL
LE FLORE
LATIMER
PITTSBURG
HUGHES
PONTOTOC
COAL
ATOKA
PUSHMATAHA
MCCURTAIN
CHOCTAW
BRYAN
MARSHALL
JOHNSTON
MURRAY
GARVIN
CARTER
LOVE
JEFFERSON
STEPHENS
COTTON
COMANCHE
TILLMAN
KIOWA
JACKSON
GREER
HARMON
CIMARRON
OUACHITA MTS.
WICHITA MTS.
CHICKASAW NATIONAL RECREATIONAL AREA
OSAGE IND. RES.
Oklahoma City
Tulsa
Lawton
Norman
Enid
Muskogee
Ardmore
Stillwater
Bartlesville
Shawnee
Ponca City
Durant
McAlester
Guymon
Boise City
Black Mesa 4,973 ft.
Lake Texoma
Denison Dam
Keystone Reservoir
Eufaula Reservoir
Robert S. Kerr Reservoir
Tenkiller Ferry Reservoir
Grand Lake O' The Cherokees
Canton Lake
Fort Supply Reservoir
Foss Reservoir
Fort Cobb Reservoir
Altus Reservoir
Lake Murray
Lake Dallas
Arkansas R.
Canadian R.
North Canadian R.
Cimarron R.
Red R.
North Fork Red R.
Salt Fork
Prairie Dog Town Fork
Beaver R.
Kiamichi R.
Little R.
0 30 60 mi
0 40 80 km
©1996, Encyclopædia Britannica, Inc.

History: Except for Panhandle, formed part of Louisiana Purchase (*q.v.*) 1803; S part nominally included in Arkansas Terr. 1819–28; settled by Indians as unorganized Indian Terr. c. 1820–40, esp. following the 1830 Indian Removal Act and subsequent forced migration of tribes from the East; part opened to white settlement 1889; W part organized as **Oklahoma Territory** 1890; rest gradually opened to whites; on Nov. 16, 1907, Indian Terr. and Oklahoma Terr. were merged and admitted to Union as state.

2. County in cen. Oklahoma. See table at OKLAHOMA.

Oklahoma City. City, ✻ of Oklahoma and ⊗ of Oklahoma co., cen. Oklahoma; pop. (1990c) 444,719; largest city in the state and its principal commercial, financial, industrial, and transportation center; packinghouses; manufactures aircraft, oil-drilling equipment, steel products; oil wells and refineries; botanical conservatory; zoo; state museum of history; National Cowboy Hall of Fame; Tinker Air Force Base. Oklahoma City Univ. (1904), Oklahoma Christian Univ. of Science and Arts (1950), Oklahoma State Univ. Technical Institute (1961). Settled during Oklahoma land rush Apr. 1889; incorp. 1890; made state ✻ 1910; rapid expansion following discovery of petroleum in region 1928; federal building bombed with large loss of life 1995.

Oklahoma Panhandle. The NW projection of land in Oklahoma; comprises the counties of Beaver, Cimarron, and Texas.

Ok·la·wa·ha \ˌäk-lə-ˈwȯ-hȯ\. River, N cen. Florida Penin.; rises in Lake co., flows N and E through Marion and Putnam cos. into St. Johns River; ab. 60 mi. (95 km.) long.

Ok·mul·gee \ōk-ˈməl-gē\. **1.** County in E cen. Oklahoma. See table at OKLAHOMA.

2. City, its ⊗, 37 mi. (60 km.) S of Tulsa; pop. (1990c) 13,441; glass; oil and gas wells; ✻ of the Creek Nation 1868–1907.

Oko·bo·ji \ˌō-kə-ˈbō-jē\. Two lakes, **East Okoboji** and **West Okoboji,** in cen. Dickinson co., NW Iowa; ab. 6 mi. (10 km.) long, area ab. 6 sq. mi. (16 sq. km.).

Oko·bo·jo Creek \ˌō-kə-ˈbō-jō\. River, cen. South Dakota; rises in Potter co., flows SW into Missouri River in SW Sully co.; ab. 75 mi. (120 km.) long.

Oko·lo·na \ˌō-kə-ˈlō-nə\. City, a ⊗ of Chickasaw co., NE Mississippi, 18 mi. (29 km.) S of Tupelo; pop. (1990c) 3267.

Ok·tib·be·ha \äk-ˈti-bə-ˌhȯ\. County in NE cen. Mississippi. See table at MISSISSIPPI.

Ok·tyabr'·skiy *or* **Ok·tyabr·skiy** *or* **Ok·tyabr·ski** \ək-ˈtyä-bər^{y}-skē\. Town, Bashkortostan, E Russia in Europe, ab. 100 mi. (160 km.) WSW of Ufa; pop. (1992e) 107,000.

Oktyabr'skoy Revolyutsii, Ostrov. See OCTOBER REVOLUTION ISLAND.

Oku·shi·ri \ō-ˈkü-shi-rē\. Island in the Sea of Japan off SW coast of Hokkaidō, Japan; 56 sq. mi. (145 sq. km.); struck by powerful earthquake July 1993.

Okusi. See OCUSSI.

Ólafs·vík \ˈō-ləfs-ˌvēk\. Town, W Iceland, on coast of peninsula S of Breidha Fjord; pop. (1980c) 1180.

Olan·cho \ō-ˈlän-chō\. Department of E cen. Honduras. See table at HONDURAS.

Öland \ˈœ-ˌländ\. Island in Baltic Sea off SE coast of Sweden, in Kalmar prov. and separated from the mainland by Kalmarsund; 85 mi. (137 km.) long; area 519 sq. mi. (1344 sq. km.); pop. (1992e) 25,382; chief town Borgholm, on W coast; fishing. Mentioned early (8th cent.) in Scandinavian history; often a battleground in Northern wars.

Ola·the \ō-ˈlā-thə\. City, ⊗ of Johnson co., E Kansas, 20 mi. (32 km.) SW of Kansas City; pop. (1990c) 63,352; footwear; Mid-America Nazarene Coll. (1968).

Ola·var·ría \ō-ˌlä-vär-ˈrē-ä\. Town, Buenos Aires prov., Argentina, ab. 160 mi. (255 km.) NNE of Bahía Blanca; pop. (1980p) 63,686.

Oła·wa \ȯ-ˈwä-vä\ *or Ger.* **Oh·lau** \ˈō-ˌlau̇\. City, E Wrocław prov., SW Poland, on left bank of the Oder 18 mi. (29 km.) SE of the city of Wrocław; pop. (1989e) 31,180; medieval church. In WWII, taken Feb. 1945 by Soviet troops; assigned to Poland by Potsdam Conference 1945.

Öl·berg \ˈœl-ˌberk\. Highest peak in the Siebengebirge (*q.v.*), Germany; 1509 ft. (460 m.).

Ol·bern·hau \ˈȯl-bərn-ˌhau̇\. City, Saxony, Germany, in the Erzgebirge 21 mi. (34 km.) SE of Chemnitz.

Ol·bia \ˈȯl-byä\. **1.** *formerly* **Ter·ra·no·va Pau·sa·nia** \ˌter-ä-ˈnȯ-vä-pau̇-ˈzä-nyä\. Commune, Sassari prov., Sardinia, Italy, on NE coast of Sardinia 50 mi. (81 km.) NE of the commune of Sassari; pop. (1991p) 40,600; harbor; medieval church.

2. Ancient town on N coast of Black Sea, S Sarmatia, at mouth of the Hypanis; colonized by settlers from Miletus; important trading center 6th cent. B.C.

Olcinium. See ULCINJ.

Old Ba·ha·ma Channel \bə-ˈhä-mə, -ˈhā-\. Channel in W West Indies, N of E cen. Cuba and SE of Santaren Channel.

Old Baldy Peak. See LINDSEY, MOUNT.

Old Cas·tile \ka-ˈstēl\ *or Span.* **Cas·til·la la Vie·ja** \kä-ˈstēl-yä-lä-ˈvyā-hä\. Old provincial region, N Castile, Spain; 25,523 sq. mi. (66,105 sq. km.); bounded on N by Bay of Biscay, on NE by Basque Country and Navarre, on SE by Aragon, on S by New Castile, on W by León, and on NW by Asturias; comprises modern provs. of Ávila, Burgos, Cantabria, La Rioja, Palencia, Segovia, Soria, and Valladolid; ✻ Burgos. For history, see CASTILE.

Old Clump Hill \ˈkləmp\. Mountain in Delaware co., S New York, in the Catskills near Roxbury (*q.v.*); site of "Woodchuck Lodge" where American naturalist John Burroughs spent his last years.

Old Deer. See DEER, OLD.

Old Delhi. See DELHI 2.

Ol·den·burg \ˈōl-dən-ˌbərg\. **1.** Former German state, since 1946 part of Lower Saxony, Germany; 2083 sq. mi. (5395 sq. km.); ✻ Oldenburg.

History: Held by counts of Oldenburg from c. 1100; after Count Christian of Oldenburg became king of Denmark 1448, held by his brother and descendants until extinction of that line 1667, then passed to Denmark; to the bishop of Lübeck late 18th cent., who was then given the ducal title by the Holy Roman emperor; became grand duchy early 19th cent.; took Prussia's side in Austro-Prussian War 1866; joined German Empire 1871; last grand duke abdicated 1918.

2. City, Lower Saxony, Germany, on Hunte River 80 mi. (129 km.) W of Bremen; pop. (1992e) 145,161; river port; railroad and road junction; important meatpacking center; shipbuilding, glassmaking; 13th cent. church; former grand-ducal palace (now museum). First mentioned 1108; made city 1345; in WWII occupied by Allied forces May 1945.

Ol·den·zaal \ˈȯl-dən-ˌzäl\. Commune, Overijssel prov., E Netherlands, 38 mi. (61 km.) ESE of Zwolle near German border; pop. (1981e) 28,753.

Old Faithful. Geyser in Yellowstone National Park, NW Wyoming, erupts regularly at intervals averaging ab. 70 minutes.

Old Flet·ton \ˈflet-^{ə}n\. Town, Cambridgeshire, E cen. England, S suburb of Peterborough 72 mi. (116 km.) N of London; pop. (1981p) 13,657.

Old Forge \ˈfōrj\. Borough, Lackawanna co., NE Pennsylvania, 6 mi. (10 km.) SW of Scranton; pop. (1990c) 8834.

Old Goa. See GOA 2.

Old Greenwich. Subdivision of town of Greenwich, Connecticut. See GREENWICH 1.

Old·ham \ˈōl-dəm\. **1.** Name of counties in two states of the U.S. See tables at KENTUCKY and TEXAS.

2. City, Greater Manchester, NW England, on the Medlock 6 mi. (10 km.) NE of Manchester; pop. (1991p) 211,400; textiles, textile machinery.

Old Harbour Bay. See PORTLAND BIGHT.

Old House Point. Cape on S coast of the island of Jamaica, West Indies, on W side of entrance to Kingston harbor.

Old Lyme \ˈlīm\. Residential town and summer resort, SW New London co., SE Connecticut, at mouth of Connecticut River on left bank; pop. (1990c) 6535; settled c. 1665; incorp. 1885; noted for numerous old homes of architectural interest.

Old·man \ˈōld-mən\. River, S Alberta, Canada; rises in Rocky Mts. near the British Columbia border and flows E to unite with the Bow and form the South Saskatchewan River;

ab. 200 mi. (320 km.) long; receives tributaries Belly and St. Mary from the S.

Old Man of Coniston. See CONISTON FELLS.

Old Margelan. See MARGILAN.

Old Northwest. See NORTHWEST TERRITORY.

Old Or·chard Beach \ˈȯr-chərd\. Town, York co., SW Maine, on Atlantic Ocean 6 mi. (10 km.) ENE of Biddeford; pop. (1990c) 7789; summer resort.

Old Point Com·fort \ˈkəm-fərt\. Point, Hampton, SE Virginia, on N shore of Hampton Roads.

Old Road Town. Town, E coast of St. Kitts, WNW of Basseterre.

Old Ryazan. See RYAZAN 2.

Olds \ˈōldz\. Town, Alberta, Canada, 50 mi. (81 km.) N of Calgary; pop. (1991c) 5542.

Old Sar·um \ˈsar-əm\ *or Latin* **Sor·bi·o·du·num** \ˌsȯr-bē-ə-ˈdü-nəm, -ˈdyü-\. Extinct borough and city in Wiltshire, England, 2 mi. (3 km.) N of Salisbury; fortified by Iron Age Britons and held in turn by Romans, Saxons, and Normans; extensive ruins remain: large mound and traces of the cathedral (consecrated 1092) which was razed 1331 to furnish materials for use in Salisbury Cathedral. Became seat of bishopric c. 1075 (liturgical *Sarum use* formulated by Osmund, bishop 1078–99); see transferred to New Sarum (Salisbury) 1220; became one of the rotten boroughs (until 1833).

Old Say·brook \ˈsā-ˌbrůk\. Town, SE Middlesex co., S Connecticut, on Long Island Sound, on W bank of Connecticut River opp. Old Lyme; (1990c) 9552; settled by Dutch 1623; Puritan settlement estab. 1635; incorp. 1854.

Old Scab Mountain \ˈskab\. Peak, Yakima co., S Washington; 6642 ft. (2025 m.).

Old Scone. See SCONE 2.

Olds·mar \ˈōldz-ˌmär\. City, Pinellas co., Florida, W of Tampa and N of St. Petersburg; pop. (1990c) 8361.

Old Tap·pan \ˈta-pən\. Borough, Bergen co., NE New Jersey, 11 mi. (18 km.) NE of Paterson; pop. (1990c) 4254.

Old Town. **1.** City, Penobscot co., E cen. Maine, on Penobscot River 11 mi. (18 km.) NNE of Bangor; pop. (1990c) 8317; canoes, wood pulp.

2. Formerly separate urban community, New Mexico. See LAS VEGAS 2.

Ol·du·vai Gorge \ˈōl-də-ˌwā, -ˌvā\. Ravine, N Tanzania, 150 mi. (241 km.) WNW of Kilimanjaro; site of rich fossil beds where numerous hominid fossils have been found.

Old West·bury \ˈwest-bər-ē\. Village, Nassau co., New York, on W cen. Long Island SE of Roslyn; pop. (1990c) 3897; New York Institute of Technology (1955), State Univ. of New York Coll. at Old Westbury (1966).

Ole·an \ˈō-lē-ˌan, ˌō-lē-ˈ\. City, Cattaraugus co., SW New York, on Allegheny River; pop. (1990c) 16,946.

O'Lea·ry Peak \ō-ˈlir-ē\. Mountain, cen. Coconino co., N cen. Arizona; 8925 ft. (2720 m.).

Olek·ma \ə-ˈlyȯk-mə\. River, cen. Russia in Asia; rises in Yablonovyy Mts., flows N to the Lena River; 794 mi. (1278 km.) long.

Ole·nek \ə-li-ˈnyȯk\. River, NW Sakha Rep., N Russia in Asia; rises at W end of Vilyuisk Mts., flows generally NE into Laptev Sea W of the Lena; ab. 1500 mi. (2415 km.) long.

Olé·ron, Île d' \ˌēl-dȯ-lā-ˈrōⁿ\; *anc.* **Uli·a·rus** \yů-ˈlī-ə-rəs\. Island in E Bay of Biscay, off W coast of Charente-Maritime dept., W France; 66 sq. mi. (171 sq. km.); tourism; chief towns St.-Pierre, in center of island, and Le Château, port at SE end. Noted for its association with the Laws of Oléron, a medieval (12th cent.) code of maritime laws named for island; the code forms the basis of modern maritime law; island connected to mainland by bridge since 1966.

Oleś·ni·ca \ˌȯ-lesh-ˈnēt-sə\; *Ger.* **Oels** \ˈœls\ *or* **Oels in Schle·si·en** \in-ˈshlā-zē-ən\. City, E Wrocław prov., SW Poland, 17 mi. (27 km.) ENE of the city of Wrocław; pop. (1989e) 37,830; assigned to Poland by Potsdam Conference 1945.

Ole·vu·ga \ˌō-lə-ˈvü-gə\. Small island off W end of Florida I., SE Solomon Is., W Pacific Ocean.

Olhão \ōl-ˈyaůⁿ\. Commune, Faro dist., S Portugal, on Atlantic Ocean 5 mi. (8 km.) ENE of the commune of Faro; pop. (1991p) 36,777.

Ol·i·fants \ˈä-lə-fənts\. **1.** River, extreme SW Africa, in Western Cape prov., Rep. of South Africa; flows WNW into Atlantic Ocean ab. 31°42′S, 18°12′E.

2. River, SE Africa; rises in NE Rep. of South Africa, flows NNE across Mozambique border into Limpopo River; ab. 350 mi. (565 km.) long.

3. River, S Rep. of South Africa; ab. 115 mi. (185 km.) long; joins Gamka River to form the Gourits River.

4. River, Namibia. See ELEPHANT 2.

Oli·mar \ˌō-li-ˈmär\. River, E Uruguay; flows E into Lagoa Mirim.

Olím·pia \ō-ˈlēm-pē-ə\. City, N São Paulo state, SE Brazil, 240 mi. (386 km.) NW of the city of São Paulo; munic. pop. (1980c) 31,781.

Olin·da \ō-ˈlin-də\. City, Pernambuco state, E Brazil, N suburb of Recife; munic. pop. (1991p) 340,673; notable 16th and 17th cent. buildings; city founded by Portuguese 1537 as colonial ✳; occupied by Dutch 1630–1654.

Olisipo. See LISBON 6.

Oli·va. **1.** *also* **Oli·wa** \ō-ˈlē-vä\. Former commune, now a part of the city of Gdańsk, Gdańsk prov., N Poland, in NW near the coast. Peace treaty signed here 1660 by which the war with Sweden (1655–60) was ended, N Livonia was ceded to Sweden, and John II Casimir Vasa of Poland relinquished claim to Swedish throne.

2. \ō-ˈlē-b̲ä\. Commune, Valencia prov., E Spain, on Mediterranean Sea 43 mi. (69 km.) SSE of Valencia; pop. (1991c) 20,289; in region producing citrus fruit.

Oliva de la Fron·te·ra \ō-ˈlē-b̲ä-t̲h̲ā-lä-frōn-ˈtā-rä\; *formerly* **Oliva de Je·rez** \t̲h̲ā-he-ˈrās\. Commune, Badajoz prov., SW Spain, near Portuguese border 38 mi. (61 km.) S of the city of Badajoz; pop. (1991c) 6588.

Oli·va·res \ˌō-lē-ˈvä-rās\. Peak, W San Juan prov., W Argentina near Chilean border; 20,512 ft. (6252 m.).

Ol·ive Branch \ˈä-liv-ˌbranch\. City, DeSoto co., NW Mississippi, SE of Memphis, Tennessee; pop. (1990c) 3567.

Olive Bridge Dam. See ASHOKAN DAM.

Oli·ven·za \ˌō-lē-ˈvān-sä\. Fortified commune, Badajoz prov., SW Spain, near Portuguese border 15 mi. (24 km.) SW of the city of Badajoz; pop. (1991c) 10,176.

Ol·i·ver \ˈä-lə-vər\. **1.** County in W cen. North Dakota. See table at NORTH DAKOTA.

2. Locality, Fayette co., SW Pennsylvania, ab. 2 mi. (3 km.) N of Uniontown; pop. (1990c) 3271.

Oliver Springs. Town, Anderson, Morgan, and Roane cos., E Tennessee, 23 mi. (37 km.) NW of Knoxville; pop. (1990c) 3433.

Ol·ives, Mount of \ˈä-livz\ *or* **Ol·i·vet** \ˈä-lə-ˌvet, ˌä-lə-ˈ\. **1.** Ridge, Jordan, in region occupied by Israel 1967, running N and S on E side of Jerusalem; separated from the city by the valley of the Kidron. At its W foot, outside the city walls, is the Garden of Gethsemane; on its E slope the village of Al-ʽAyzarīyah (Bethany). Mentioned in various biblical stories.

2. A section of this ridge containing its three culminating heights; highest point 2737 ft. (834 m.).

Oli·vet **1.** \ˌä-lə-ˈvet\. City, S Eaton co., S Michigan, 11 mi. (18 km.) SW of Charlotte; pop. (1990c) 1604; Olivet Coll. (1844).

2. \ˈō-lə-ˌvet\. Town, ⊗ of Hutchinson co., SE South Dakota; pop. (1990c) 74.

Ol·i·vette \ˈä-lə-ˌvet\. City, St. Louis co., E cen. Missouri, W of the city of St. Louis; pop. (1990c) 7573.

Oliv·ia \ō-ˈli-vē-ə\. City, ⊗ of Renville co., SW cen. Minnesota, 36 mi. (58 km.) ESE of Montevideo; pop. (1990c) 2623.

Oliwa. Former commune, Poland. See OLIVA 1.

\ə\ abut \ə\ matches \ᵊ\ kitten, Fr table \ər\ further \a\ ash \ā\ ace \ä\ cot, cart \å\ Fr bac \aů\ out \b̲\ Span Avila \ch\ chin \e\ bet \ē\ easy \g\ go \i\ hit \ī\ ice \j\ job \k̲\ Ger ich, Buch \ⁿ\ Fr vin \ŋ\ sing \ō\ go \ö\ all \ȯ\ law \œ\ Fr bœuf \œ̄\ Fr feu \ȯi\ boy \th\ thin \t̲h̲\ this \ü\ loot \ů\ foot \ue\ Ger füllen \ue̅\ Fr rue \y\ yet \ʸ\ Fr digne \ˈdēnʸ\, nuit \ˈnwʸē\ \yü\ few \yů\ fury \zh\ vision

Ol·kusz \ˈọl-ˌküsh\. Commune, E Katowice prov., S Poland, 19 mi. (31 km.) E of Sosnowiec; pop. (1989e) 40,768; lead mines noted in Middle Ages.

Ol·la·güe \ō-ˈyä-gwā\ *or* **Oya·hue** \ō-ˈyä-wā\. **1.** Volcano, NE Antofagasta region, N Chile, near the Bolivian border; 19,250 ft. (5867 m.).
2. Town, NE Antofagasta region, N Chile, at the Bolivian border N of Ollagüe peak; railroad junction; on the highway from Antofagasta to Uyuni, Bolivia.

Ollius. See OGLIO.

Olmaliq. See ALMALYK.

Olm·sted \ˈäm-ˌsted, ˈōm-\. County in SE Minnesota. See table at MINNESOTA.

Olmsted Falls. City, Cuyahoga co., N Ohio, 12 mi. (19 km.) SW of Cleveland; pop. (1990c) 6741.

Olmütz. See OLOMOUC.

Ol·ney \ˈäl-nē\. **1.** City, ⊗ of Richland co., SE Illinois, 54 mi. (87 km.) NE of Mount Vernon; pop. (1990c) 8664; Olney Central Coll. (1963).
2. City, Young co., N Texas, 40 mi. (64 km.) S of Wichita Falls; pop. (1990c) 3519.
3. Town, N Buckinghamshire, SE cen. England, ab. 59 mi. (95 km.) NNW of London; residence 1767–86 of English poet William Cowper who assisted John Newton, curate of Olney, in composition of *Olney Hymns* 1779.

Olo·mouc \ˈọ-lọ-ˌmōts\ *or Ger.* **Ol·mütz** \ˈọl-müts\. City, E Czech Republic, on Morava River ab. 40 mi. (65 km.) NE of Brno; pop. (1991p) 105,690; brewing, sugar refining, malting, food processing; steel; university (1573); several fountains; c. 14th cent. Gothic cathedral; 15th cent. town hall.
History: Possibly originated as Roman fort; made bishopric c. 1063; ceded to Hungary 1478 and ✻ of Moravia until c. 1640; destroyed by Swedes 1642; an Austrian stronghold 18th cent., unsuccessfully besieged by Prussians 1758; scene of Conference of Olmütz 1850, at which Prussia yielded to Austrian demands that it abstain from seeking leadership among the German states.

Olo·nets \ə-lə-ˈnyets\. **1.** *formerly* **Au·nus** \ˈaụ-nụs\. Isthmus, NW Russia in Europe, extending bet. Lake Ladoga and Lake Onega; during WWII overrun by Soviet army 1944.
2. Town, S Karelia Rep., NW Russia in Europe, near E shore of Lake Ladoga 112 mi. (180 km.) NE of St. Petersburg.

Olon·ga·po \ō-ˌlọŋ-gä-ˈpō\. Chartered city, Zambales prov., Luzon, Philippines, on NE coast of Subic Bay near Bataan border; pop. (1990p) 192,000; good harbor, formerly site of U.S. naval facility. Occupied by Japanese WWII.

Olonos. See ERYMANTHUS.

Olo·ron–Sainte–Ma·rie \ọ-lọ-ˌrōⁿ-seⁿt-mȧ-ˈrē\. City, Pyrénées-Atlantiques dept., SW France, 13 mi. (21 km.) SW of Pau; former cathedral; episcopal see to 1790.

Olo·se·ga \ˌō-lə-ˈsā-gə\. One of the Manua Is. in American Samoa. See OFU.

Olot \ō-ˈlọt\. Commune, Gerona prov., NE Spain, 17 mi. (27 km.) NW of the commune of Gerona; pop. (1991c) 26,713.

Ol·son Mountain \ˈōl-sən\. Peak in Glacier National Park, NW Montana; 7800 ft. (2377 m.).

Olsz·tyn \ˈọlsh-tən\. **1.** Province of N Poland. See table at POLAND.
2. *or Ger.* **Al·len·stein** \ˈä-lən-ˌshtīn\. City, its ✻, on Łyna River 80 mi. (129 km.) SE of Gdańsk; pop. (1989e) 161,238; transportation and market center in agricultural region; 14th cent. castle. Received town rights 1353; to Poland 1466; to Prussia 1772; awarded to Germany by plebiscite 1920; assigned to Poland by Potsdam Conference 1945.

Olt \ˈọlt\. **1.** River, S Romania; rises in E Transylvania, flows S, cutting through the Transylvanian Alps; enters the Danube River opp. Nikopol; 308 mi. (496 km.) long.
2. County of S Romania. See table at ROMANIA.

Ol·ten \ˈọlt-ᵊn\. Commune, Solothurn canton, NW Switzerland, on Aare River 7 mi. (11 km.) WSW of Aarau; pop. (1980c) 18,991.

Ol·te·nia \ọl-ˈtē-nē-ə\ *or* **Little Wa·la·chia** *also* **Lesser Walachia** \wä-ˈlā-kē-ə\. Region, S Romania, W division of Walachia; 9294 sq. mi. (24,072 sq. km.); formerly a province.

Ol·te·ni·ţa *or* **Ol·te·ni·tza** \ōl-ˈtā-nēt-sä\; *anc.* **Con·stan·ti·o·la** \ˌkän-stan-tē-ˈō-lə\. City, Ilfov co., S Romania, on Argeş River at its confluence with the Danube; pop. (1989c) 32,025; battle 1853 in which Turks under Omer Pasha defeated the Russians.

Oltis. See LOT 1.

Oltre Giuba. See JUBALAND.

O–luan Pi \ˈō-ˈlwän-ˈpē\ *or Eng.* **Cape O–lu·an** \ˈō-lü-ˌän\. Cape at S end of Taiwan, on Bashi Channel.

Olus·tee \ō-ˈləs-tē\. Village, Baker co., NE Florida, 45 mi. (72 km.) SW of Jacksonville; battle Feb. 20, 1864 in which Confederates decisively defeated Union forces.

Olu·tan·ga \ˌō-lü-ˈtäŋ-gä\. Island in N Moro Gulf, S Zamboanga del Sur prov., Mindanao, Philippines; 78 sq. mi. (202 sq. km.); low island covered with mangroves.

Ol·ve·ra \ōl-ˈb̲ā-rä\. Commune, Cádiz prov., SW Spain, 62 mi. (100 km.) ENE of the city of Cádiz; pop. (1991c) 9091.

Olviopol. See PERVOMAYSK 1.

Olym·pia \ō-ˈlim-pē-ə\. **1.** City and port of entry, ✻ of Washington and ⊗ of Thurston co., W Washington, at S extremity of Puget Sound 60 mi. (97 km.) SSW of Seattle; pop. (1990c) 33,840; ships forest products and agricultural produce; center of oyster culture; Evergreen State Coll. (1967). Settled 1840s; ✻ of Washington Terr. 1853; chartered as city 1859.
2. Plain and sanctuary, ancient Elis, NW Peloponnese, S Greece, on N bank of the Alpheus River; a center of religious worship of Greece, with notable festival (*Olympian* games) celebrated every 4th year in honor of Zeus. These are traditionally thought to have begun in 776 B.C., the year that came to be adopted as the primary date in Greek chronology (the calendar was based on four-year periods known as *Olympiads*); games were chiefly athletic contests. Here in the temple of Zeus was the statue of Olympian Zeus by Phidias (one of the Seven Wonders of the Ancient World); excavation has disclosed ruins of many temples, the stadium, and other ancient buildings.

Olympia Fields. Village, Cook co., NE Illinois, 13 mi. (21 km.) S of Chicago; pop. (1990c) 4248.

Olym·pic Mountains \ō-ˈlim-pik\. Mountain group, part of the Coast Ranges, chiefly in Jefferson and Clallam cos., in NW Washington in the Olympic Penin.; chief peaks Mt. Olympus 7965 ft. (2428 m.) and Mt. Constance 7743 ft. (2360 m.); part of **Olympic National Park** (see UNITED STATES, *National Parks*).

Olympic Peninsula. Peninsular part of W Washington bounded on W by Pacific Ocean, on N by Juan de Fuca Strait, and on E by Puget Sound.

Olym·pus \ō-ˈlim-pəs, *Greek* ˈọ-lēm-ˌbọs\. Mountain range in Thessaly, NE Greece, near coast of Gulf of Salonika; highest peak 9570 ft. (2917 m.); in ancient Greek mythology, the home of the gods.

Olympus, Mount. **1.** Peak in Olympic Mts., Jefferson co., NW Washington; 7965 ft. (2428 m.).
2. *formerly* **Mount Tro·o·dos** \ˈtrō-ō-ˌthọs\. Mountain, W cen. Cyprus; 6403 ft. (1962 m.); highest peak in Cyprus.
3. Mountain, Turkey in Asia. See ULU DAĞ.

Olyn·thus \ō-ˈlin-thəs\. Town in ancient Macedonia, NE Greece; its site is on the Chalcidice Penin. at the head of the Gulf of Kassándra and bet. Sithonia and Pallene penins. An important ancient Greek city; from late 5th cent. B.C., head of a strong confederacy of Greek towns known as the Chalcidian League (dissolved by Sparta 379 B.C., but soon reestablished); besieged by Philip II of Macedon, and despite appeals to Athens and orations of Demosthenes (*Olynthiac* orations), overcome and destroyed by Philip 348 B.C.; ruins have been excavated.

Oly·phant \ˈọ-li-fənt, ˈō-\. Borough, Lackawanna co., NE Pennsylvania; pop. (1990c) 5222.

Ol·yu·tor·skiy, Mys \ˈmis-ˌəl-yə-ˈtọr-skē\. Point at NE base of Kamchatka Penin. extending into Bering Sea, in Koryak Autonomous Okrug, E Russia in Asia.

Om' *or* **Om** \ˈọmʸ\. River, SW Russia in Asia; flows W in Novosibirsk and Omsk oblasts to join the Irtysh at Omsk; ab. 450 mi. (725 km.) long.

Ōma, Cape \ˈō-mä\. Cape on N extremity of Honshū, Japan, projecting into Tsugaru Strait.

Omagh \ˈō-mä, -mə\. **1.** District, W cen. Northern Ireland. See table at IRELAND, NORTHERN.
2. Town, its ⊗; pop. (1990e) 45,800; dairy products.

Oma·ha \ˈō-mə-ˌhȯ, -ˌhä\. City, ⊗ of Douglas co., E Nebraska, on the Missouri River 15 mi. (24 km.) N of its confluence with Platte River; pop. (1990c) 335,795; largest city in the state; major livestock and grain market; railroad and insurance center; produces railroad equipment, agricultural machinery, electronic components; oil refineries, packing plants; Offutt Air Force Base, headquarters of U.S.A.F. Strategic Air Command. Univ. of Nebraska Medical Center (1869), Creighton Univ. (1878), Univ. of Nebraska at Omaha (1908), Coll. of St. Mary (1923), Grace Coll. of the Bible (1943), Metropolitan Community Coll. (1974).
History: Fur-trading post estab. in vicinity during War of 1812; Mormon encampment 1846–47; first permanent settlement 1854; incorp. 1857; ✱ of Nebraska Terr. 1855–67 and E terminus of first transcontinental railroad.

Omaha Beach. West cen. part of Normandy beaches, NW France, NW of Bayeux and NE of Isigny and on either side of the Vire River at the village of St.-Laurent-sur-Mer, in WWII landing place of part of American army in invasion of France June 6, 1944, and scene of intense fighting.

Omak \ˈō-ˌmak\. City, Okanogan co., N Washington, on Okanogan River; pop. (1990c) 4117; apples.

Omak Lake. Alkaline lake in S Okanogan co., N Washington.

Oman \ō-ˈmän, -ˈman\; *formerly* **Mus·cat and Oman** \ˈməs-ˌkat, -kət\ *also* **Mas·qat and Oman** \ˈməs-ˌkat, -kət\. Sultanate, SE Arabian Penin., bounded on N by Gulf of Oman, on E and S by the Arabian Sea, on SW by Yemen, on W by Saudi Arabia, and on NW by Saudi Arabia and United Arab Emirates; 82,000 sq. mi. (212,380 sq. km.); pop. (1990e) 2,000,000; ✱ Masqat.
Physical features: Mountainous in N, highest peak Jebel Sham, 9927 ft. (3026 m.); to the W borders on the Rub ʾal-Khali Desert region; coastline ab. 1000 mi. (1610 km.) long; includes Khurīyā Murīyā Jazāʾir and a small exclave extending into the Strait of Hormuz.
Chief products: Oil; also produces natural gas; dates, cereals, limes; fishing.
History: Engaged in sea trade in ancient times; converted to Islam 7th cent. A.D.; ruled by imams of the Ibādī sect from c. 750 until the establishment of a dynasty of kings 1154, maintaining relative independence from Abbasid caliphate at Baghdad; imam authority revived mid-15th cent.; Portuguese captured Masqat and controlled coastal region c. 1507–1650; following conflicts with Persia, Al Bū Saʿīd dynasty (still in power) founded mid-18th cent. by Ahmad ibn Saʿīd; realm expanded 18th and 19th cents. to include parts of E Africa and Baluchistan; ✱ of sultanate was Zanzibar (*q.v.*) for short time mid-19th cent.; African lands separated and ruled independently after 1856; signed first treaty with British late 18th cent. and after decline of Oman's importance late 19th cent. became virtually dependent on British government, which supported the dynasty against the insurrections of imam-led interior tribes; sultan recognized limited authority of imam over interior tribes in treaty 1920; renewed conflict bet. sultanate and imamate in 1950s again suppressed with British aid; ceded last of its colonial holdings, Gwador (*q.v.*), to Pakistan 1958; oil discovered in commercial quantities 1964; ruling sultan deposed 1970 by his son, who began modernization; in 1971 joined Arab League and UN; in 1981 helped found Gulf Cooperation Council; cooperated with allied coalition against Iraq in Persian Gulf War 1991.

Oman, Gulf of. An arm of the Arabian Sea, extending bet. N Oman, SE Arabian Penin., and the SE coast of Iran; ab. 340 mi. (545 km.) long by 230 mi. (370 km.) wide at mouth.

Oma·na·go \ˌō-mä-ˈnä-gō\. Peak in the Nikkō Range, N cen. Honshū, Japan, N of Lake Chuzenji; 7546 ft. (2300 m.).

Oma·ru·ru \ˌō-mä-ˈrü-rü\. Town, W cen. Namibia, on **Omaruru River** 110 mi. (177 km.) NW of Windhoek.

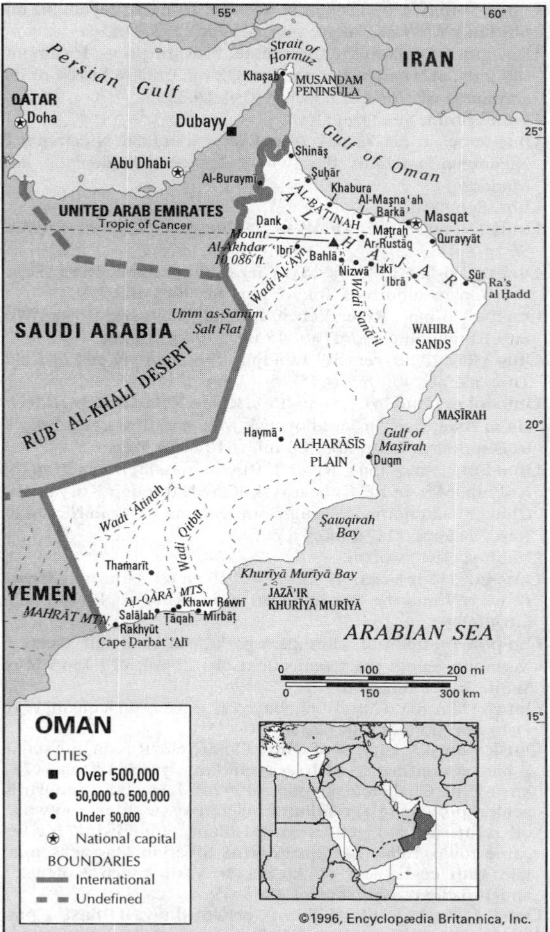

Oma·te \ō-ˈmä-tā\ *or* **Huai·na–Pu·ti·na** \ˌwī-nä-pü-ˈtē-nä\. Volcano in Andes in Peru, SE of Arequipa.

Ombai. See ALOR.

Om·bai Strait \ˈȯm-ˌbī\. Strait, extending in a curve bet. Alor I. on N and W, Timor on S, and Wetar I. on E; 17 mi. (27 km.) wide; connects Banda Sea with E end of Savu Sea, Lesser Sunda Is., Indonesia.

Ombirah. See OBI ISLANDS.

Om·bro·ne \ȯm-ˈbrō-nā\; *anc.* **Um·bro** \ˈəm-brō\. River, NW cen. Italy; flows S and SW through Tuscany and into the N Tyrrhenian Sea 10 mi. (16 km.) S of Grosseto; ab. 100 mi. (160 km.) long.

Om·dur·man \ˌäm-dər-ˈman\ *or Arab.* **Umm Dur·mān** \ˌōm-du̇r-ˈmän\. City, NE cen. Sudan, on left bank of White Nile opp. Khartoum; pop. (1983c) 526,287; commercial center, trading in hides, textiles, and livestock; furniture, pottery, leather goods; handicrafts; university (1912, university status 1965); ✱ of nationalist leader Muḥammad Aḥmad (known as "al-Mahdī") and his successor ʿAbd Allāh 1885–98; scene of Anglo-Egyptian victory over ʿAbd Allāh's forces 1898, but continued to grow as important cultural center.

Ōme \'ō-mā\. City, Tokyo prefecture, Honshū, Japan, 30 mi. (48 km.) WNW of Tokyo; pop. (1990p) 125,945.

Ome·gna \ō-'mā-nyä\. Commune, Novara prov., Piedmont, NW Italy, at N end of Lago d'Orta 32 mi. (52 km.) NNW of the commune of Novara; pop. (1981p) 16,319.

O–mei Shan. See EMEI SHAN.

Ome·te·pe \ˌō-mā-'tā-pā\. Island, largest in Lake Nicaragua, S Nicaragua; contains the twin volcanoes Concepción and Madera.

Omi. See BIWA.

Omiš \'ō-mēsh\ *or* **Al·mis·sa** \äl-'mē-sə\. Seaport, Croatia, SE of Split.

Ōmi·ya \ō-'mē-ä, 'ō-mē-ˌä\. City, Saitama prefecture, Honshū, Japan, suburb of Tokyo; pop. (1990p) 403,779.

Om·me \'ò-mə\. River, W cen. Jutland, Denmark; flows WNW into Ringkøbing Fjord; ab. 45 mi. (70 km.) long.

Omo \'ō-mō\. River, SW Ethiopia; flows into N end of Lake Turkana; ab. 400 mi. (645 km.) long.

Omo·loi *or* **Omo·loy** \ˌə-mə-'lòi\. River, N Sakha Rep., N Russia in Asia; rises in Verkhoyansk Mts. and flows generally N to Buorkhaya Gulf; ab. 380 mi. (610 km.) long.

Omo·lon \ˌə-mə-'lòn\. River, E Russia in Asia; flows from the Kolyma Mts. in NE Khabarovsk Kray N through Koryak and Chukchi autonomous okrugs into Kolyma River in NE Sakha Rep.; 715 mi. (1150 km.) long.

Omoloy. See OMOLOI.

Omo·no \'ō-mō-ˌnō, ō-'mō-nō\. River, N Honshū, Japan; flows NW into the Sea of Japan near Akita; ab. 80 mi. (130 km.) long.

Om·pom·pa·noo·suc \äm-ˌpäm-pə-'nü-sək\. Small river, E Vermont; enters the Connecticut ab. 17 mi. (27 km.) N of White River Junction.

Om·ro \'äm-rō\. City, Winnebago co., E cen. Wisconsin, W of Oshkosh; pop. (1990c) 2836.

Omsk \'òmsk\. City, ✻ of Omsk Oblast, SW Russia in Asia, in S part at confluence of Irtysh and Om' rivers 480 mi. (772 km.) E of Chelyabinsk; pop. (1992e) 1,169,000; industrial center, producing agricultural machinery, textiles, footwear; oil refineries and petrochemical plants; founded 1716; became town 1804; headquarters of Siberian Cossacks until late 19th cent.; seat of Aleksandr Vasiliyevich Kolchak's anti-Bolshevik government 1918–19.

Omsk Oblast \'ò-bləst, -ˌblast\ *or* **Om·ska·ya Oblast'** \'òm-skə-yə-'ò-bləstʸ\. Administrative subdivision of SW Russia in Asia; 53,861 sq. mi. (139,500 sq. km.); pop. (1992e) 2,170,000; ✻ Omsk. Lies in basin of middle Irtysh River; cereals, flax, sunflowers; livestock; crossed in cen. part by two trunk railroad lines. Region developed rapidly from late 19th cent.; created an oblast of Russian S.F.S.R. 1934.

Ōmu·ra \'ō-mü-ˌrä, ō-'mü-rä\. Town, Nagasaki prefecture, NW Kyūshū, Japan, on **Ōmura Bay** (inlet of East China Sea) 12 mi. (19 km.) NNE of the city of Nagasaki; pop. (1990p) 73,437.

Omu·ram·ba Oma·ta·ko \ˌō-mü-'räm-bä-ˌō-mä-'tä-kō\. Riverbed, NE Namibia; extends from mountains in N cen. part NE to the Okavango River; dry through most of its lower course.

Ōmu·ta \'ō-mü-ˌtä, ō-'mü-tä\. City, Fukuoka prefecture, NW Kyūshū, Japan, on Shimabara Bay 22 mi. (35 km.) NW of Kumamoto; pop. (1990p) 150,461; coal mining; zinc, alloy steel, brick, chemicals; heavily bombed in WWII.

On. See HELIOPOLIS 1.

On·a·las·ka \ˌä-nə-'las-kə\. City, La Crosse co., W Wisconsin, 5 mi. (8 km.) N of the city of La Crosse; pop. (1990c) 11,284.

On·a·wa \'ä-nə-ˌwä, -wə\. City, ⊗ of Monona co., W Iowa, 36 mi. (58 km.) SSE of Sioux City; pop. (1990c) 2936.

On·dji·va \òn-'jē-və\. Town, ✻ of Cunene prov., S Angola.

On·do \'òn-dō\. **1.** State of SW Nigeria. See table at NIGERIA.
2. Town, Ondo state, SW Nigeria, 105 mi. (169 km.) NE of Lagos; pop. (1991e) 149,700.

One·ga \ˌə-'nye-gə\. **1.** Bay at SW end of the White Sea extending into the coast of N Russia in Europe; receives Onega River.
2. River, W part of Arkhangel'sk Oblast, N Russia in Europe; flows from Lakes Vozhe and Lacha N to Onega Bay; ab. 250 mi. (400 km.) long; navigable for ab. 100 mi. (160 km.).
3. Town, W Arkhangel'sk Oblast, N Russia in Europe, at head of Onega bay and on right bank of Onega River at its mouth, 90 mi. (145 km.) S of Arkhangel'sk.

Onega, Lake *or Russ.* **Onezh·sko·ye Oze·ro** \ə-'nyesh-skə-yə-'ò-zyir-ə\. Lake in S Karelia Rep., Russia; 3710 sq. mi. (9609 sq. km.); 145 mi. (233 km.) long by 50 mi. (81 km.) wide; max. depth 328 ft. (100 m.); 2d largest lake in Europe. Its S shore and the canal along it from the Svir' to the Vytegra (see VOLGA-BALTIC WATERWAY) lie in Vologda Oblast. Its outlet is the Svir', flowing from SW corner to Lake Ladoga; main affluents Vodla, Vytegra, and Andoma, on the E; has numerous long arms or inlets and many islands along its N shore; frozen over ab. one half the year; has fisheries.

One·hunga \ˌō-nē-'hüŋ-gə\. Borough, N North I., New Zealand, S suburb of Auckland on Manukau Harbor; pop. (1981c) 15,386.

Onei·da \ō-'nī-də\. **1.** River, cen. New York; flows from Oneida Lake, forming section of boundary bet. Onondaga and Oswego cos.; joins Seneca River to form Oswego River; 16 mi. (26 km.) long.
2. Name of counties in three states of the U.S. See tables at IDAHO, NEW YORK, WISCONSIN.
3. City, Madison co., cen. New York, 5 mi. (8 km.) SE of Oneida Lake, 13 mi. (21 km.) WSW of Rome; pop. (1990c) 10,850; silverware, wood products; founded c. 1830; 1848 ff. site of utopian community; reorganized c. 1880 as business corporation to produce Oneida silverware.
4. Town, Scott co., N Tennessee, 46 mi. (74 km.) NW of Knoxville; pop. (1990c) 3502.

Oneida Lake. Lake in cen. New York, bounded by Oswego, Oneida, Madison, and Onondaga cos.; 80 sq. mi. (207 sq. km.); ab. 22 mi. (35 km.) long and 6 mi. (10 km.) wide at its greatest extent; part of New York State Barge Canal system.

O'Neill \ō-'nēl\. City, ⊗ of Holt co., N Nebraska, on Elkhorn River 74 mi. (119 km.) WNW of Norfolk; pop. (1990c) 3852.

On·e·ko·tan \ˌä-nə-kə-'tän, ˌōn-\. One of the Kuril Is. (*q.v.*), SW of Paramushir, E Russia in Asia.

One·on·ta \ˌō-nē-'än-tə\. **1.** City, ⊗ of Blount co., N cen. Alabama; pop. (1990c) 4844.
2. City, Otsego co., cen. New York, on Susquehanna River 45 mi. (72 km.) S of Utica; pop. (1990c) 13,954; clothing; Hartwick Coll. (1797), State Univ. of New York Coll. at Oneonta (1889).

One Tree Hill \'wən-ˌtrē\. Borough, N North I., New Zealand, suburb of Auckland; pop. (1981c) 11,078.

Onezhskoye Ozero. See ONEGA, LAKE.

Oni·da \ō-'nī-də\. City, ⊗ of Sully co., cen. South Dakota; pop. (1990c) 761.

Onion. See WINOOSKI 1.

Onit·sha \ō-'nē-chä\. Town, S Nigeria, on Niger River ab. 135 mi. (215 km.) from its mouth; pop. (1991e) 328,300; commercial and market center; ships palm products.

Ono·jo \ō-'nō-jä\. City, Fukuoka prefecture, N Kyūshū, Japan; pop. (1990p) 75,217.

Ono·mi·chi \ˌō-nō-'mē-chē\. City on the Inland Sea, Hiroshima prefecture, SW Honshū, Japan, 45 mi. (72 km.) W of Okayama; pop. (1990p) 97,104; several notable Buddhist temples.

Onon \'ō-ˌnän\. River, NE Mongolia and SW Chita Oblast, S Russia in Asia; flows NE to unite with Ingoda River and form the Shilka River; 592 mi. (953 km.) long.

On·on·da·ga \ˌä-nən-'dä-gə\. County in cen. New York. See table at NEW YORK.

Onondaga, Lake. Lake, Onondaga co., cen. New York; 5 mi. (8 km.) long by 1 mi. (1.6 km.) wide.

Ons·low \'änz-lō\. Coastal county in SE North Carolina. See table at NORTH CAROLINA.

Onslow Bay. Bay off SE coast of North Carolina bet. Cape Lookout and Cape Fear.

On·ta·ke \ōn-'tä-kā\. Peak, E border of Gifu prefecture, cen. Honshū, Japan; 10,049 ft. (3063 m.); 2d only to Fuji as the most sacred peak in Japan; annually climbed by thousands of pilgrims.

On–ta·ke \ō̄n-'tä-kā\ *or* **Sa·ku·ra·ji·ma** \sä-ˌkü-rä-'jē-mä\. Volcano on a peninsula in Kagoshima Bay, S Kyūshū, Japan; 3668 ft. (1118 m.); was on an island until destructive eruption in 1914.

On·tar·io \än-'tar-ē-ˌō\. **1.** County in W New York. See table at NEW YORK.

2. City, San Bernardino co., SE California, 20 mi. (32 km.) W of city of San Bernardino; pop. (1990c) 133,179; aircraft parts, plastics, electrical equipment; settled 1882; incorp. as city 1891.

3. Town, Wayne co., W New York, ab. 17 mi. (27 km.) NE of Rochester; pop. (1990c) 8560.

4. Village, Richland co., N cen. Ohio, 8 mi. (13 km.) W of Mansfield; pop. (1990c) 4026.

5. City, Malheur co., E Oregon, on Snake River just S of its confluence with Malheur River; pop. (1990c) 9392; diversified agriculture; Treasure Valley Community Coll. (1962).

6. Province, Canada, bounded on N by Hudson Bay and James Bay, on E by Quebec prov., on S by U.S., and on W by Manitoba prov.; ✻ Toronto. See table at CANADA.

Physical features: SE part is large peninsula bet. Ottawa River on NE and St. Lawrence River and Lakes Ontario and Erie on S, Lake Huron and Georgian Bay on W. Largely a level region with generally fertile soils; highest point Ogidaki Mt. 2183 ft. (665 m.). Largest lakes of N and W part Lakes Nipigon, Eagle, Seul, St. Joseph, Rainy, and Abitibi; Lake of the Woods belongs in part to U.S.; in SE part Lakes Nipissing, Simcoe, Muskoka, and Kawartha chain are most important. Bordered on SE by Ottawa and St. Lawrence rivers; in most populated (SE) part chief rivers the Thames, Grand, Rideau, and Trent, and N of Lakes Huron and Superior are Moose, Albany, Attawapiskat, English, and Severn.

Chief products: Grains, vegetables, tobacco; dairy farms; livestock; nickel, gold, copper, iron ore; manufacturing: iron and steel, motor vehicles, aircraft, electrical equipment; food processing.

Chief cities: Toronto, North York, Scarborough, Mississauga, Hamilton, Ottawa, Etobicoke, London.

Political divisions: Divided into the following counties, districts, municipal regions, and metropolitan municipality (for pronunciation of their names, see their individual entries):

NAME	AREA[1] (sq. mi.)	AREA[1] (sq. km.)	POP. (1991c)	CO. SEAT
Counties				
Brant	421	1,090	110,806	Brantford
Bruce	1,650	4,274	65,268	Paisley
Dufferin	557	1,443	39,897	Orangeville
Elgin	720	1,865	75,423	Saint Thomas
Essex	707	1,831	327,365	Windsor
Frontenac	1,599	4,141	129,089	Kingston
Grey	1,708	4,424	84,071	Owen Sound
Haliburton	1,486	3,849	14,421	Minden
Hastings	2,323	6,017	116,434	Belleville
Huron	1,295	3,354	59,065	Goderich
Kent	918	2,378	109,943	Chatham
Lambton	1,124	2,911	128,943	Sarnia
Lanark	1,138	2,947	54,803	Perth
Leeds and Grenville	1,309	3,390	90,235	Brockville
Lennox and Addington	1,170	3,030	37,243	Napanee
Middlesex	1,240	3,212	372,274	London
Northumberland	734	1,901	78,224	Cobourg
Oxford	765	1,981	92,888	Woodstock
Perth	840	2,176	69,976	Stratford
Peterborough	1,415	3,665	119,992	Peterborough
Prescott and Russell	773	2,003	67,183	L'Orignal
Prince Edward	390	1,010	23,763	Picton
Renfrew	3,009	7,793	91,685	Pembroke
Simcoe	1,663	4,307	288,684	Barrie
Stormont, Dundas and Glengarry	1,275	3,302	107,841	Cornwall
Victoria	1,348	3,491	63,332	Lindsay
Wellington	1,019	2,639	159,609	Guelph
Districts				
Algoma	19,320	50,039	127,269	Sault Sainte Marie
Cochrane	52,237	135,294	93,917	Cochrane
Kenora	153,220	396,840	58,748	Kenora
Manitoulin	1,588	4,113	11,192	Gore Bay
Muskoka	1,585	4,105	48,005	Bracebridge
Nipissing	7,560	19,580	84,723	North Bay
Parry Sound	4,336	11,230	38,423	Parry Sound
Rainy River	7,276	18,845	22,997	Fort Frances
Sudbury	18,058	46,770	26,178	Sudbury
Thunder Bay	52,471	135,900	158,810	Thunder Bay
Timiskaming	5,896	15,271	38,983	Haileybury
Municipal Regions				
Durham	1,482	3,838	409,070	Whitby
Haldimand-Norfolk	1,112	2,880	98,707	Simcoe
Halton[2]	363	940	313,136	Milton
Hamilton-Wentworth[3]	458	1,186	451,665	Hamilton
Niagara	719	1,862	393,936	St. Catherines
Ottawa-Carleton	947	2,453	678,147	Ottawa
Peel	469	1,215	732,798	Brampton
Sudbury	1,003	2,598	161,210	Sudbury
Waterloo[2]	516	1,336	377,762	Kitchener
York[2]	882	2,284	504,981	Newmarket
Metropolitan Municipality				
Toronto	242	627	2,275,771	Toronto

[1] Area = land area.
[2] Formerly a county.
[3] Formerly Wentworth co.

History: Prior to arrival of Europeans, inhabited by various Iroquoian and Algonquian tribes; in 17th cent. visited by French explorers (first by Étienne Brulé 1610–11) and missionaries; passed to British 1763 following French and Indian War; in 1774 became part of prov. of Quebec (*q.v.*); received many Loyalist settlers from U.S. during and after American Revolution; present S boundary estab. 1783; at division of Quebec prov. 1791 became known as Upper Canada; scene of many battles of War of 1812 incl. one in which Shawnee Chief Tecumseh was killed 1813; scene of unsuccessful uprising 1837; reunited with Lower Canada 1841 until 1867, when (as Ontario) it became one of four provinces of the new Dominion of Canada; boundaries later extended.

Ontario, Lake; *early Fr. name* **Lac Fron·te·nac** \ˌlȧk-frōⁿt-'nȧk\. Lake, easternmost and smallest of the Great Lakes (*q.v.*), U.S. and Canada; bounded on E and S by New York, and on S, W, and N by Canadian prov. of Ontario; 193 mi. (311 km.) long; area 7600 sq. mi. (19,684 sq. km.); greatest depth 778 ft. (237 m.); elev. 245 ft. (75 m.); the U.S.-Canada boundary passes through the lake; connected on SW by Niagara River and Welland Canal with Lake Erie; outlet on NE St. Lawrence River. See OSWEGO CANAL.

On·ti·nyent \ˌȯn-tē-'nyent\ *or* **On·te·nien·te** \ˌȯn-tā-'nyen-tā\. Commune, Valencia prov., E Spain, 48 mi. (77 km.) SSW of the commune of Valencia; pop. (1991c) 29,888.

On·to·na·gon \ˌän-tə-'nȯ-gən, -'nä-\. **1.** County in NW Upper Penin. of Michigan. See table at MICHIGAN.

2. Township, its ⊗, on Lake Superior 50 mi. (81 km.) ENE of Ironwood; pop. (1990c) 3238; resort.

On·tong Ja·va \'än-tȯŋ-'jä-və, -'ja-\; *formerly* **Lord Howe Islands** \'hau̇\. Island group comprising a coral atoll and several islets in the Solomon Is., W Pacific Ocean, 160 mi. (257 km.) NE of Santa Isabel, 5°20′S, 159°30′E.

Oodeypore. See UDAIPUR.

O'o·kiep \ō-'kēp\. Village, Northern Cape prov., W Rep. of South Africa, connected by rail with Port Nolloth.

Oos–Londen. See EAST LONDON.

Oos·ta·nau·la \ˌü-stə-'nȯ-lə\. Navigable river, NW Georgia; formed by confluence of Conasauga and Coosawattee rivers in NW extremity of Georgia, flows S to unite with the Etowah near Rome and form the Coosa River.

Oost·en·de \ō-'sten-də\ *or Fr.* **Os·tende** \ȯ-'stäⁿd\ *or Eng.* **Ost·end** \ä-'stend, 'äs-ˌtend\. Commune, seaport, and seaside resort, West Flanders prov., NW Belgium; pop. (1991c) 68,500; leading fishing port of Belgium and one of busiest passenger ports in Europe; oyster beds; shipbuilding; soap,

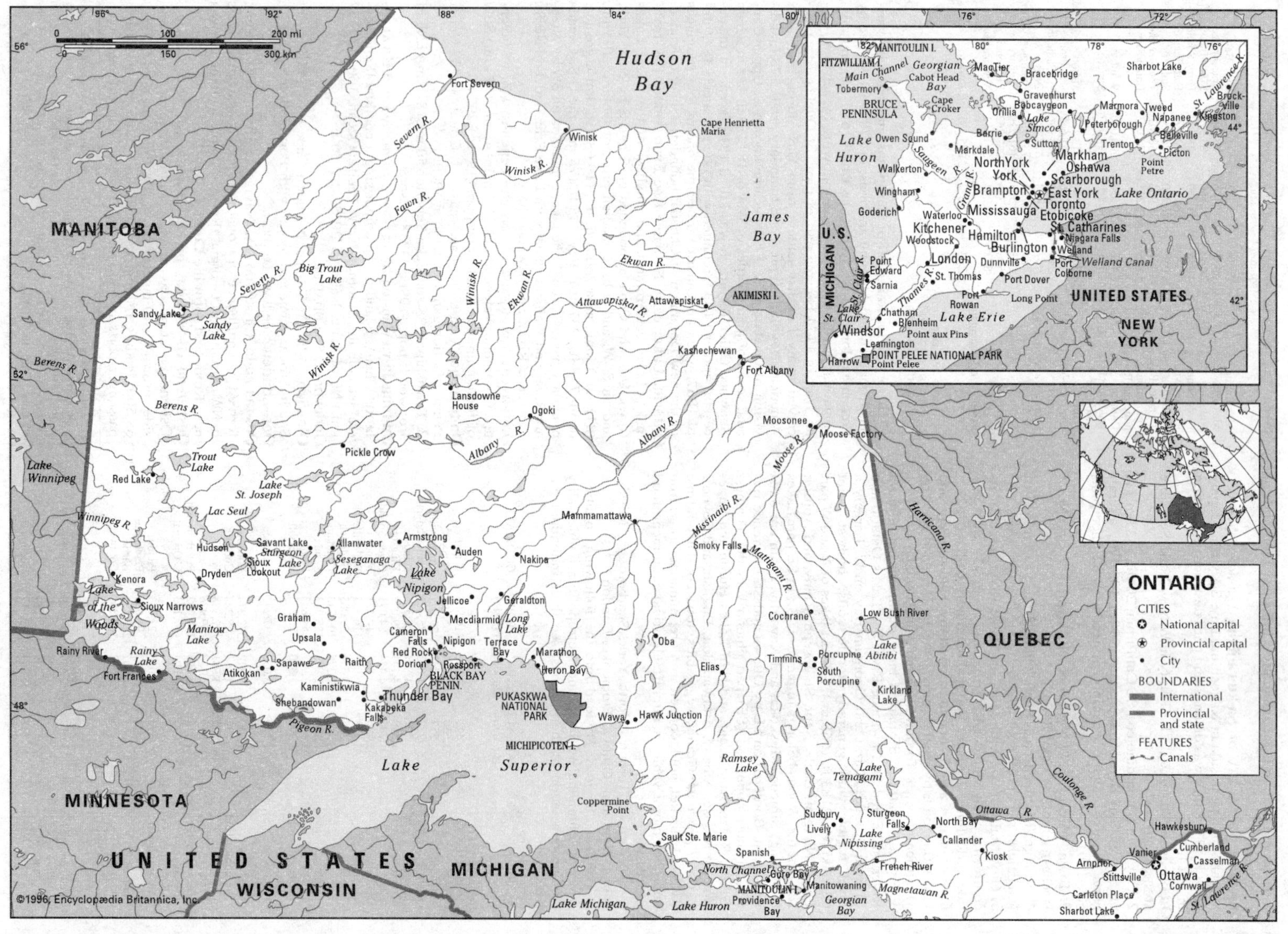

ONTARIO
CITIES
National capital
Provincial capital
City
BOUNDARIES
International
Provincial and state
FEATURES
Canals
Hudson Bay
James Bay
MANITOBA
QUEBEC
UNITED STATES
MINNESOTA
WISCONSIN
MICHIGAN
NEW YORK
Lake Superior
Lake Huron
Lake Michigan
Lake Ontario
Lake Erie
Georgian Bay
Lake Nipigon
Lake of the Woods
Lake Winnipeg
Lake Nipissing
Lake Simcoe
Lake St. Clair
AKIMISKI I.
MANITOULIN I.
MICHIPICOTEN I.
BRUCE PENINSULA
PUKASKWA NATIONAL PARK
POINT PELEE NATIONAL PARK
Ottawa
Toronto
Thunder Bay
Sudbury
Sault Ste. Marie
Kenora
Windsor
London
Hamilton
Kingston
Fort Severn
Winisk
Moosonee
Moose Factory
Fort Albany
Attawapiskat
Timmins
Cochrane
North Bay
Red Lake
Fort Frances
Rainy River
Dryden
Sioux Lookout
Geraldton
Marathon
Wawa
Hawk Junction
Kirkland Lake
Hawkesbury
Cornwall
Arnprior
Mississauga
Brampton
Kitchener
Niagara Falls
St. Catharines
Oshawa
Peterborough
Belleville
Sarnia
Barrie
Owen Sound
200 mi
300 km
©1996, Encyclopædia Britannica, Inc.

tobacco. May date from 9th cent.; suffered extended siege early 17th cent. in war bet. Dutch and Spanish; developed as resort 1830 ff.; in WWI occupied by the Germans 1914 and used as submarine base; raided 1918 by British naval force which succeeded in temporarily blocking the harbor by sinking vessel across its mouth; in WWII captured by Canadians Sept. 1944.

Oos·ter·hout \ˈō-stər-ˌhau̇t\. Commune, North Brabant prov., S Netherlands, just NE of Breda; pop. (1992e) 49,036.

Oo·ster·schel·de \ˌō-stər-ˈsḵel-də\ *or Eng.* **Eastern Schel·de** *or* **East Schelde** \ˈskel-də\. Inlet of the North Sea on SW coast of Netherlands, at mouth of Schelde River, N of Walcheren, North Beveland, and South Beveland islands.

Oost·stel·ling·werf \ˌōst-ˌste-liŋ-ˈverf\. Commune, Friesland prov., N Netherlands, W of Assen; pop. (1981e) 24,355.

Ootacamund. See UDAGAMANDALAM.

Opa–locka \ˌō-pə-ˈlä-kə\. City, Miami-Dade co., SE Florida, NW of Miami; pop. (1990c) 15,283.

Opa·ti·ja \ȯ-ˈpä-tē-yə\. Resort town, W Croatia, on Istria; pop. (1991c) 13,566.

Opa·va \ˈȯ-pä-vä\. **1.** *or Ger.* **Op·pa** \ˈȯ-pə\. River, Czech Republic; flows into Oder River at Ostrava; 70 mi. (113 km.) long.

2. *or Ger.* **Trop·pau** \ˈtrȯ-ˌpau̇\. City, E Czech Republic, on a tributary of the Oder on the Polish border ab. 15 mi. (24 km.) WNW of Ostrava; pop. (1991p) 63,601; textiles; former ✻ of Austrian Silesia; scene of Congress of Troppau, Oct. 1820, when Russia, Prussia, and Austria adopted principle of armed intervention to suppress European liberal movements, Great Britain and France dissenting.

OPEC. See ORGANIZATION OF THE PETROLEUM EXPORTING COUNTRIES.

Ope·li·ka \ˌō-pə-ˈlī-kə\. City, ⊗ of Lee co., E Alabama, 57 mi. (92 km.) ENE of Montgomery; pop. (1990c) 22,122; lumber, textiles, tires; dairy farms; settled c. 1835.

Op·e·lou·sas \ˌä-pə-ˈlü-səs\. City, ⊗ of St. Landry parish, S cen. Louisiana, 22 mi. (35 km.) N of Lafayette; pop. (1990c) 18,151; diversified agriculture; during Civil War became ✻ of the state for a short time after Union forces occupied Baton Rouge.

Opeq·uon \ō-ˈpe-kən\. Village and creek, Frederick co., N Virginia, just E of Winchester; scene of Union victory Sept. 1864, more often known as the battle of Winchester. See WINCHESTER 8.

Ophir \ˈō-fər\. Ancient country of unknown location, perhaps in Arabian Penin. or East Africa; rich in gold as mentioned several times in Old Testament.

Ophir, Mount. 1. *or Malay* **Gu·nong Le·dang** \ˈgü-ˌnȯŋ-ˈlā-ˌdäŋ\. Mountain, NW Johor state, W Malaysia, near Melaka border; 4186 ft. (1276 m.); highest peak in state.

2. Peak, Sumatra, Indonesia. See TALAKMAU, MOUNT.

Ophiusa. See FORMENTERA.

Opin·a·ca *or* **Opin·a·ka** \ō-ˈpi-nə-ˌkȯ\. River, W and cen. Quebec, Canada; ab. 280 mi. (450 km.) long.

Opis \ˈō-pəs\. Ruins of ancient Assyrian city on W bank of the Tigris, E Iraq, ab. 43 mi. (69 km.) N of Baghdad; scene of battle c. 539 B.C. in which Persian King Cyrus the Great defeated the Babylonians.

Opitergium. See ODERZO.

Op·la·den \ˈȯp-ˌläd-ᵊn\. City, North Rhine-Westphalia, Germany, on Wupper River just S of Solingen; became city 1858.

Opo·le \ȯ-ˈpȯ-le\. **1.** Province of S Poland. See table at POLAND.

2. *or Ger.* **Op·peln** \ˈȯ-pəln\. City, its ✻, on the Oder River 52 mi. (84 km.) SE of Wrocław; pop. (1989e) 127,653; railroad junction and river port; cement; cast iron foundry. Was ✻ of independent Piast principality of Oppeln 1202–1327; to Bohemia 1327 and Prussia 1742; in WWII occupied by U.S.S.R. Jan. 1945; assigned to Poland by Potsdam Conference 1945.

Opon. See LAPU-LAPU.

Oporto. See PORTO.

Opp \ˈäp\. City, Covington co., S Alabama, 50 mi. (80 km.) W of Dothan; pop. (1990c) 6985.

Oppa. See OPAVA 1.

Oppeln. See OPOLE 2.

Op·pen·heim \ˈä-pən-ˌhīm, ˈȯ-\. Town, Hesse, Germany, on the Rhine 20 mi. (32 km.) S of Mainz; pop. (1980c) 4621; 13th–15th cent. church; wine museum. In WWII American army crossed the Rhine here in advance on Frankfurt 1945.

Oppidum Ubiorum. See COLOGNE.

Opp·land \ˈȯp-ˌlän\. County of S cen. Norway. See table at NORWAY.

Op·por·tu·ni·ty \ˌä-pər-ˈtü-nə-tē, -ˈtyü-\. Unincorporated settlement, Spokane co., E Washington, E of the city of Spokane; pop. (1990c) 22,326.

Op·py \ȯ-ˈpē\. Village, Pas-de-Calais dept., N France, 6 mi. (10 km.) NE of Albert; scene of fighting 1917–18.

Op·ster·land \ˈȯp-stər-ˌlänt\. Commune, Friesland prov., N Netherlands; pop. (1981e) 26,140.

Opus \ˈō-pəs\. Ancient town, ✻ of Locris Opuntia (Eastern Locris), E cen. Greece, on coast of Euboean Sea.

Oqair \ō-ˈkīr, -ˈkar\ *or* **Al–ʻUqayr** \ˌal-u̇-ˈkīr, -ˈkar\. Coastal town, E Nejd, Saudi Arabia, NE of Al Hufūf and opp. Qatar.

Oquaw·ka \ō-ˈkwȯ-kə\. Village, ⊗ of Henderson co., W Illinois, on Mississippi River W of Galesburg; pop. (1990c) 2100.

Oquirrh Mountains \ˈō-kər\. Mountain range in Utah, S of Great Salt Lake.

Ora·dea \ȯ-ˈrä-dyä\ *or* **Oradea Ma·re** \ˈmä-re\ *or Hung.* **Nagy·vá·rad** \ˈnöj-ˌvär-öd\ *or Ger.* **Gross·war·dein** \ˌgrōs-vär-ˈdīn\. City, ⊗ of Bihor co., NW Romania, on Körös River near Hungarian border; pop. (1989c) 225,416; machine tools, chemicals, mining equipment, textiles, woodworking articles, footwear, processed foods; Greek Catholic and Roman Catholic cathedrals; cultural center. A very old town; bishopric founded by Lászlo I c. 1080; destroyed by Tatars 1241; held by Turks 1660–92; after WWI ceded by Hungary to Romania; again held by Hungary during WWII.

Ora·dell \ˈōr-ə-ˌdel\. Borough, Bergen co., NE corner of New Jersey, 8 mi. (13 km.) ENE of Paterson; pop. (1990c) 8024.

Öræ·fa·jö·kull \ˈœ-rī-ˌvä-yœ̄-ˌkœd-ᵊl\. Highest peak in Iceland, near SE coast of the island; 6952 ft. (2119 m.).

Orai \ō-ˈrī\. Town, SW Uttar Pradesh, N India, 65 mi. (105 km.) SW of Kanpur; pop. (1991p) 98,640.

Oraibi. See KYKOTSMOVI.

Oral \ȯ-ˈral\ *or* **Uralsk** *or* **Ural'sk** \ü-ˈralsk, yu̇-ˈralsk\. Town, W Kazakhstan, on Ural River at its lower bend near Orenburg Oblast, Russia in Europe; pop. (1991e) 214,000; trade center in an agricultural area.

Oran \ȯ-ˈrän\. Seaport city, NW Algeria, 210 mi. (338 km.) WSW of Algiers; pop. (1987p) 628,558; ships wine, cereals, fruit and vegetables; produces textiles, iron, footwear, glass, cigarettes; food processing; distinguished by a great variety of architectural styles; university (1965).

History: Founded 10th cent.; important seaport 15th cent.; held by Spanish 1509–1708, Turks 1708–1732, and Spanish 1732–c. 1790; devastated by earthquake 1790, after which it again came under Turkish control; occupied by French 1831; in WWII, captured by Allied forces Nov. 1942.

Or·ange \ˈȯr-inj, ˈär-, -ənj\. **1.** Name of counties in eight states of the U.S. See tables at CALIFORNIA, FLORIDA, INDIANA, NEW YORK, NORTH CAROLINA, TEXAS, VERMONT, VIRGINIA.

2. City, Orange co., SW California, 22 mi. (35 km.) E of Long Beach; pop. (1990c) 110,658; ships citrus fruit; electronic components; Chapman Univ. (1861). Founded as **Rich·land** \ˈrich-lənd\ 1868; renamed 1875; incorp. 1888.

3. Town, SW New Haven co., S Connecticut, E of the Housatonic River; pop. (1990c) 12,830; commercial center.

4. Town, Franklin co., NW Massachusetts, 14 mi. (23 km.) E of Greenfield; pop. (1990c) 7312; incorp. 1810.

5. City, Essex co., NE New Jersey, 4 mi. (6 km.) WNW of the main part of and adjoining a small part of Newark; pop. (1990c) 29,925; residential; business machines, clothing,

pharmaceuticals; separated from Newark 1806 and from East, South, and West Orange 1861–63; incorp. as city 1872.
6. Village, Cuyahoga co., N Ohio; pop. (1990c) 2810; birthplace of James A. Garfield, 20th president of the U.S., 1831.
7. City and port of entry, ⊗ of Orange co., Texas, on Sabine River 22 mi. (35 km.) E of Beaumont; pop. (1990c) 19,381; chemicals, pulp and paper; shipbuilding; gas and oil wells; Lamar Univ.–Orange campus (1969); city founded c. 1836.
8. Town, ⊗ of Orange co., N cen. Virginia, 27 mi. (43 km.) NE of Charlottesville; pop. (1990c) 2582.
9. River, S Africa; flows W, forming S boundary of Free State; continues W across Northern Cape prov., in its lower course forming the boundary bet. Rep. of South Africa and Namibia; empties into Atlantic Ocean at Alexander Bay; ab. 1300 mi. (2090 km.) long; numerous dams constructed along its course as part of major hydroelectric power and irrigation project.
10. Town, E New South Wales, SE Australia, in Blue Mts. 130 mi. (209 km.) WNW of Sydney; pop. (1991c) 32,910; in fruit-growing district.

Orange \ȯ-ˈräⁿzh\; *anc.* **Arau·sio** \ə-ˈrō-zhē-ˌō\. City, ✻ of Vaucluse dept., SE France, 17 mi. (27 km.) N of Avignon; pop. (1990c) 28,136; preserves; tourist resort; extensive Roman ruins include a triumphal arch and a theater.
History: Scene of defeat of Romans by the Cimbri and the Teutons 105 B.C.; prosperous under Roman Emperor Augustus; devastated by Alemanni and Visigoths 5th cent. A.D.; long an episcopal see; ✻ of former principality; in 16th cent., became possession of house of Nassau whence it passed to house of princes who were styled princes of Orange-Nassau, and of whom William, afterward William III of England, was one; town captured by Louis XIV of France 17th cent., but title continued to be held by a branch of the Orange-Nassau family, who are now the royal line of the Netherlands.

Orange, Cape. Cape on N coast of Brazil, near the French Guiana border.

Orange Bay. Bay on W end of island of Jamaica, West Indies.

Or·ange·burg \ˈȯr-inj-ˌbərg, ˈär-, -ənj-\. **1.** County in S cen. South Carolina. See table at SOUTH CAROLINA.
2. City, its ⊗, 35 mi. (56 km.) SSE of Columbia; pop. (1990c) 13,739; textiles, chemicals; Claflin Coll. (1869), South Carolina State Coll. (1896).

Orange City. City, ⊗ of Sioux co., NW Iowa, 38 mi. (61 km.) NNE of Sioux City; pop. (1990c) 4940; Northwestern Coll. (1882).

Orange Cove. City, Fresno co., S cen. California, 27 mi. (43 km.) SE of the city of Fresno; pop. (1990c) 5604.

Orange Free State. See FREE STATE.

Orange Lake. Lake, SE corner of Alachua co., N Florida Penin.; ab. 14 mi. (23 km.) long.

Orange Park. Town, Clay co., NE Florida, just S of Jacksonville; pop. (1990c) 9488.

Orange Range. See JAYAWIJAYA RANGE.

Orange River. See ORANGE 9.

Orange River Colony *and* **Orange River Sovereignty.** See FREE STATE.

Orange Town. Town, St. Eustatius I., Netherlands Antilles, West Indies.

Or·ange·ville \ˈȯr-inj-ˌvil, ˈär-, -ənj-\. Town, ⊗ of Dufferin co., SE Ontario, Canada, 43 mi. (69 km.) WNW of Toronto; pop. (1991c) 17,921.

Orange Walk. **1.** Administrative district, NW Belize. See table at BELIZE.
2. Town, its ✻; pop. (1990p) 10,410.

Oran·go \ȯ-ˈräŋ-ˌgü\. See BIJAGÓS, ARQUIPÉLAGO DOS.

Oranienbaum *or* **Oraniyenbaum.** See LOMONOSOV.

Ora·ni·en·burg \ō-ˈrä-nē-ən-ˌbu̇rk\. City, Brandenburg, Germany, on Havel River N of Berlin; pop. (1981c) 25,793. Mentioned in 12th cent. under name of Bötzow; in WWII site nearby of concentration camp, now Sachsenhausen memorial.

Oran·je \ō-ˈrän-yə\. Peak, SE Suriname; 2428 ft. (740 m.).

Oran·je·stad \ō-ˈrän-yə-ˌstät\. Chief town, Aruba I., Netherlands Antilles; on W coast; pop. (1991c) 20,046.

Oras \ȯ-ˈräs\. Municipality, Eastern Samar prov., Philippines, 45 mi. (72 km.) NE of Catbalogan; pop. (1980c) 27,031; has harbor on **Oras Bay,** on Pacific coast.

Ora·va \ˈȯr-ä-vä\ *or Pol.* **Ora·wa** \ȯ-ˈrä-vä\. Area, constituting a former county of Hungary (*Hung.* **Ar·va** \ˈär-ˌvȯ\); divided 1920 bet. Poland and Czechoslovakia; now mostly in Slovakia.

Or·be·tel·lo \ˌȯr-bā-ˈtel-lō\. Commune, Grosseto prov., Tuscany, cen. Italy, on Tyrrhenian Sea 23 mi. (37 km.) S of the commune of Grosseto; pop. (1981p) 14,749; Etruscan ruins; cathedral.

Ór·bi·go \ˈȯr-ˈbē-gō\. River, NW Spain; rises in N León prov., flows S into Esla River; 67 mi. (108 km.) long.

Orcadas del Sur. See SOUTH ORKNEY ISLANDS.

Orcades. See ORKNEY ISLANDS.

Or·cas Island \ˈȯr-kəs\. See SAN JUAN ISLANDS.

Or·chard Park \ˈȯr-chərd\. Village, Erie co., W New York, 10 mi. (16 km.) SSE of Buffalo; pop. (1990c) 3280.

Orch·ha \ˈȯr-chə\ *or* **Or·cha** \ˈȯr-chə\. **1.** Former Indian state, now part of Madhya Pradesh; 1999 sq. mi. (5177 sq. km.); ✻ Orchha and later Tikamgarh.
2. Town, Madhya Pradesh, cen. India; palaces; temples; 17th cent. fort; served as ✻ of Orchha state to 1783; declined after transfer of ✻ to Tikamgarh.

Or·chil·la \ȯr-ˈchē-yä\ *or* **Or·chi·la** \-ˈchē-lä\. Venezuelan island, Caribbean Sea N of N cen. Venezuela, 80 mi. (129 km.) NW of La Tortuga; ab. 8 mi. (13 km.) long.

Or·chom·e·nus \ȯr-ˈkä-mə-nəs\. **1.** Ancient town, E Arcadia, cen. Peloponnese, S Greece, ab. 9 mi. (14 km.) NNW of Mantinea.
2. City in NW Boeotia, ancient Greece, 7 mi. (11 km.) NE of Levádhia on N bank of the Cephisus; now an archaeological site. A city of prehistoric period settled by the Minyae; wealthy and powerful in Mycenaean times, but in later historic times generally subject to power of Thebes; frequently attacked and finally destroyed by Thebes 4th cent. B.C.; scene of battle 85 B.C. in which Roman Gen. Sulla destroyed an army of Mithradates VI, king of Pontus.

Ord \ˈȯrd\. **1.** City, ⊗ of Valley co., cen. Nebraska, 57 mi. (92 km.) NNW of Grand Island; pop. (1990c) 2481.
2. River, NE Western Australia, Australia; flows N to Joseph Bonaparte Gulf near Wyndham; ab. 200 mi. (320 km.) long; in its course is the artificial Lake Argyle, created 1971.

Ord, Mount. Peak, N Brewster co., W Texas; ab. 6800 ft. (2075 m.).

Ordos. See MU US.

Ord Peak. Mountain, SW Apache co., E Arizona; 10,860 ft. (3310 m.).

Or·du \ˈȯr-dü\. **1.** Province of Turkey in Asia. See table at TURKEY.
2. *anc.* **Cot·y·o·ra** \ˌkä-tē-ˈȯr-ə\. Town, its ✻, on the Black Sea 80 mi. (129 km.) E of Samsun; pop. (1990c) 102,107; ships hazelnuts. Ancient Greek Cotyora was founded c. 500 B.C.; point of embarkation for the survivors of Greek historian Xenophon's "Ten Thousand" (retreating Greek soldiers) after the battle of Cunaxa (*q.v.*).

Ord·way \ˈȯrd-ˌwā\. Town, ⊗ of Crowley co., E Colorado, near Arkansas River; pop. (1990c) 1025.

Ordzhonikidze. **1.** City, S Russia in Europe. See VLADIKAVKAZ.
2. City, Ukraine. See YENAKIYEVE.

Ordzhonikidzegrad. See BEZHITSA.

Ordzhonikidze Kray. See STAVROPOL' KRAY.

Öre·bro \ˌœ̄-rə-ˈbrü\. **1.** Province of S cen. Sweden. See table at SWEDEN.
2. City, its ⊗, on E shore of Lake Hjälmaren 100 mi. (161 km.) W of Stockholm; pop. (1993e) 123,188; footwear, baked goods; road junction; college (1967); 16th cent. castle (restored); 13th cent. church. Dates from 11th cent.; site of many important diets or assemblies, incl. National Diet of 1810 at which French Marshal Jean-Baptiste-Jules Bernadotte (later Charles XIV John) was elected crown prince of Sweden.

Or·e·gon \ˈȯr-i-gən, ˈär-, *chiefly by outsiders* -ˌgän\. **1.** Earlier name of Columbia River. See COLUMBIA 1.
2. A northwestern state of U.S.A., bounded on N by Washing-

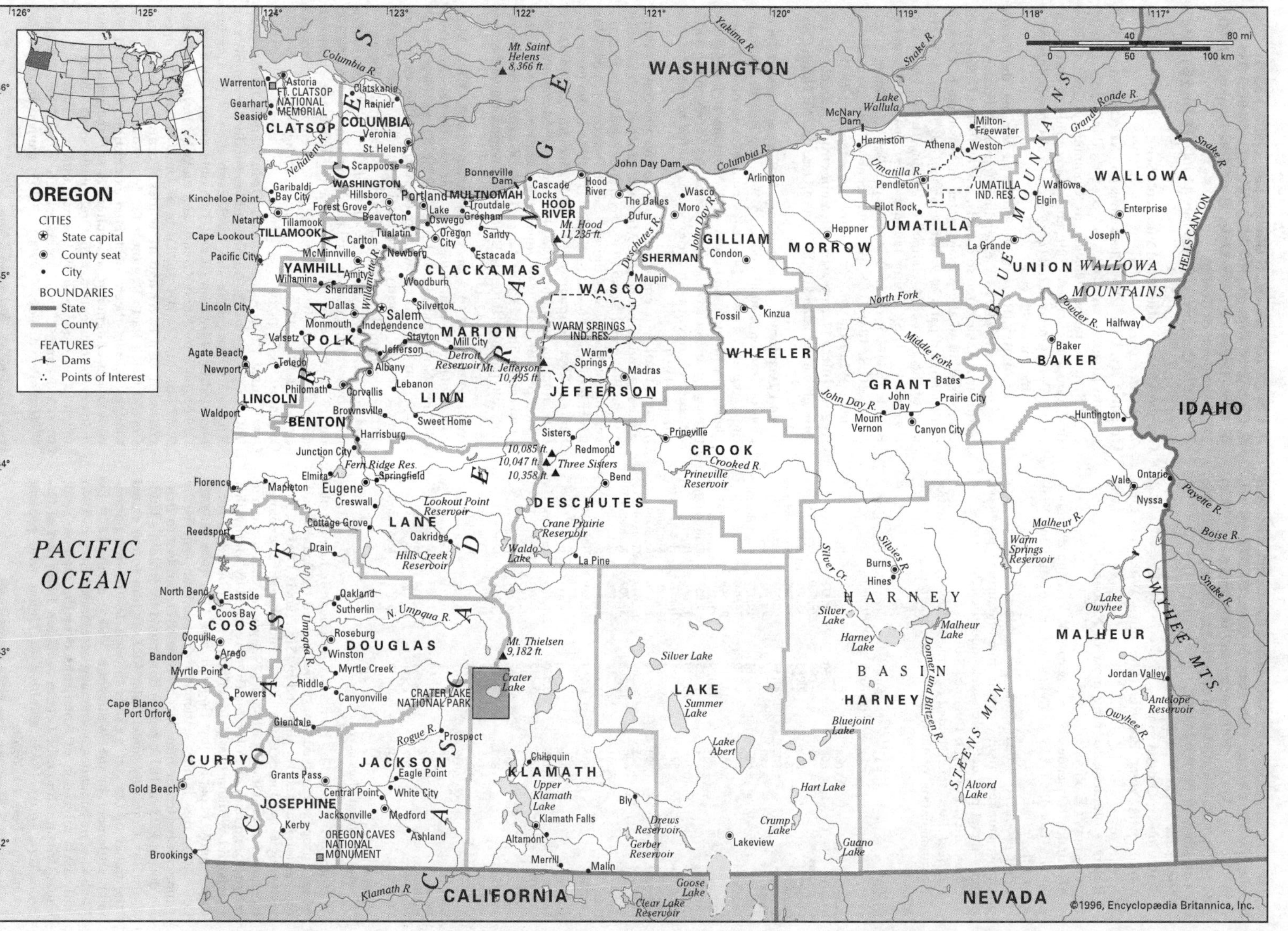
OREGON
CITIES
State capital
County seat
City
BOUNDARIES
State
County
FEATURES
Dams
Points of Interest
0
40
80 mi
0
50
100 km
126°
125°
124°
123°
122°
121°
120°
119°
118°
117°
46°
45°
44°
43°
42°
WASHINGTON
IDAHO
CALIFORNIA
NEVADA
PACIFIC OCEAN
COAST RANGE
CASCADE RANGE
BLUE MOUNTAINS
WALLOWA MOUNTAINS
OWYHEE MTS.
STEENS MTN.
HARNEY BASIN
HELLS CANYON
CLATSOP
COLUMBIA
TILLAMOOK
WASHINGTON
MULTNOMAH
HOOD RIVER
YAMHILL
CLACKAMAS
POLK
MARION
LINCOLN
BENTON
LINN
LANE
DOUGLAS
COOS
CURRY
JOSEPHINE
JACKSON
KLAMATH
DESCHUTES
JEFFERSON
WASCO
SHERMAN
GILLIAM
MORROW
UMATILLA
UNION
WALLOWA
BAKER
GRANT
WHEELER
CROOK
LAKE
HARNEY
MALHEUR
Warrenton
Astoria
FT. CLATSOP NATIONAL MEMORIAL
Gearhart
Seaside
Clatskanie
Rainier
Vernonia
St. Helens
Scappoose
Garibaldi
Bay City
Kincheloe Point
Netarts
Tillamook
Cape Lookout
Pacific City
Hillsboro
Forest Grove
Beaverton
Portland
Lake Oswego
Troutdale
Gresham
Oregon City
Sandy
Estacada
Tualatin
Carlton
Newberg
McMinnville
Amity
Willamina
Sheridan
Woodburn
Silverton
Salem
Dallas
Monmouth
Independence
Stayton
Mill City
Valsetz
Jefferson
Detroit Reservoir
Mt. Jefferson 10,495 ft.
Lincoln City
Agate Beach
Newport
Toledo
Albany
Lebanon
Philomath
Corvallis
Waldport
Brownsville
Sweet Home
Harrisburg
Junction City
Fern Ridge Res.
Elmira
Springfield
Florence
Mapleton
Eugene
Creswall
Lookout Point Reservoir
Cottage Grove
Oakridge
Reedsport
Drain
Hills Creek Reservoir
North Bend
Eastside
Coos Bay
Oakland
Sutherlin
N. Umpqua R.
Coquille
Arago
Roseburg
Winston
Umpqua R.
Bandon
Myrtle Point
Myrtle Creek
Riddle
Powers
Canyonville
CRATER LAKE NATIONAL PARK
Crater Lake
Mt. Thielsen 9,182 ft.
Cape Blanco
Port Orford
Glendale
Rogue R.
Prospect
Grants Pass
Eagle Point
Gold Beach
Central Point
White City
Jacksonville
Medford
Kerby
OREGON CAVES NATIONAL MONUMENT
Ashland
Brookings
Klamath R.
Columbia R.
Nehalem R.
Willamette R.
Mt. Saint Helens 8,366 ft.
Bonneville Dam
Cascade Locks
Hood River
Mt. Hood 11,235 ft.
John Day Dam
The Dalles
Dufur
Wasco
Moro
Deschutes R.
John Day R.
Maupin
WARM SPRINGS IND. RES.
Warm Springs
Madras
Sisters
Redmond
10,085 ft.
10,047 ft.
10,358 ft.
Three Sisters
Bend
Crane Prairie Reservoir
Waldo Lake
La Pine
Chiloquin
Upper Klamath Lake
Klamath Falls
Altamont
Merrill
Malin
Bly
Drews Reservoir
Gerber Reservoir
Goose Lake
Clear Lake Reservoir
Lakeview
Crump Lake
Hart Lake
Guano Lake
Lake Abert
Summer Lake
Silver Lake
Bluejoint Lake
Yakima R.
Snake R.
Lake Wallula
McNary Dam
Arlington
Condon
Fossil
Kinzua
Heppner
Hermiston
Umatilla R.
Pendleton
Athena
Milton-Freewater
Weston
UMATILLA IND. RES.
Pilot Rock
Grande Ronde R.
Wallowa
Elgin
Enterprise
Joseph
La Grande
North Fork
Powder R.
Halfway
Baker
Middle Fork
Bates
Prairie City
John Day
Mount Vernon
Canyon City
Huntington
Prineville
Crooked R.
Prineville Reservoir
Ontario
Vale
Nyssa
Payette R.
Boise R.
Malheur R.
Warm Springs Reservoir
Silver Cr.
Silvies R.
Burns
Hines
Silver Lake
Harney Lake
Malheur Lake
Donner und Blitzen R.
Alvord Lake
Lake Owyhee
Jordan Valley
Antelope Reservoir
Owyhee R.
©1996, Encyclopædia Britannica, Inc.

ton, on E by Idaho, on S by Nevada and California, and on W by the Pacific Ocean; 10th state in area, 97,073 sq. mi. (251,419 sq. km.); 29th state in population, (1990c) 2,842,321; ✻ Salem; 33d state admitted to Union (1859). See table of states at UNITED STATES.

Nickname: Beaver State.

State flower: Oregon grape.

Motto: Alis Volat Propriis (She Flies With Her Own Wings).

Rivers: Columbia, forming most of N boundary; Snake, forming upper E boundary.

Mountains: Cascade Range, across W cen. part; highest point Mt. Hood, 11,235 ft. (3424 m.); Blue Mts. and Wallowa Mts. in NE.

Chief products: Wheat, fruit, vegetables; livestock; dairy products; lumber; fish; gravel; manufacturing: plywood; primary-metal products; high-tech industries; tourism.

Chief cities: Portland, Eugene, Salem.

Political divisions: Divided into the following 36 counties (for pronunciation of their names, see their individual entries):

NAME	AREA[1] (sq. mi.)	AREA[1] (sq. km.)	POP. (1990c)	CO. SEAT
Baker	3,068	7,946	15,317	Baker
Benton	668	1,730	70,811	Corvallis
Clackamas	1,884	4,880	278,850	Oregon City
Clatsop	805	2,085	33,301	Astoria
Columbia	640	1,658	37,557	Saint Helens
Coos	1,604	4,154	60,273	Coquille
Crook	2,980	7,718	14,111	Prineville
Curry	1,627	4,214	19,327	Gold Beach
Deschutes	3,031	7,850	74,958	Bend
Douglas	5,063	13,113	94,649	Roseburg
Gilliam	1,208	3,129	1,717	Condon
Grant	4,531	11,735	7,853	Canyon City
Harney	10,166	26,330	7,060	Burns
Hood River	523	1,355	16,903	Hood River
Jackson	2,812	7,283	146,389	Medford
Jefferson	1,793	4,644	13,676	Madras
Josephine	1,625	4,209	62,649	Grants Pass
Klamath[2]	5,970	15,462	57,702	Klamath Falls
Lake	8,231	21,318	7,186	Lakeview
Lane	4,562	11,816	282,912	Eugene
Lincoln	986	2,554	38,889	Newport
Linn	2,291	5,934	91,227	Albany
Malheur	9,861	25,540	26,038	Vale
Marion	1,166	3,020	228,483	Salem
Morrow	2,060	5,335	7,625	Heppner
Multnomah	423	1,096	583,887	Portland
Polk	736	1,906	49,541	Dallas
Sherman	830	2,150	1,918	Moro
Tillamook	1,115	2,889	21,570	Tillamook
Umatilla	3,227	8,358	59,249	Pendleton
Union	2,032	5,263	23,598	La Grande
Wallowa	3,178	8,231	6,911	Enterprise
Wasco	2,382	6,169	21,683	The Dalles
Washington	716	1,854	311,554	Hillsboro
Wheeler	1,707	4,421	1,396	Fossil
Yamhill	711	1,841	65,551	McMinnville

[1] Area = land area.
[2] Crater Lake National Park in W part.

History: Inhabited by numerous American Indian peoples when Europeans arrived; coast first sighted by Spanish sailors; region claimed for England by Sir Francis Drake 1579; visited by Capt. James Cook 1778; Columbia River explored by Capt. Robert Gray of Boston 1792, giving U.S. a claim to the region; mouth of Columbia River reached by Meriwether Lewis and William Clark's overland expedition 1805; for a time jointly occupied by England and U.S. (see OREGON COUNTRY); first white settlement founded at Astoria by American fur trader John Jacob Astor 1811, but lost to British during War of 1812; region dominated by Britain's Hudson's Bay Company under John McLoughlin (often called "the father of Oregon") 1820s through 1840s; first permanent settlement in the Willamette Valley estab. 1834 by Methodist missionaries; settlement accelerated from c. 1843 with mass migration of Americans over the Oregon Trail; Great Britain relinquished claim to region 1846; part of Oregon Terr. (*q.v.*) 1848; admitted to Union with present boundaries Feb. 14, 1859.

3. County in S Missouri. See table at MISSOURI.

4. City, ⊗ of Ogle co., N Illinois; pop. (1990c) 3891.

5. City, ⊗ of Holt co., NW Missouri; pop. (1990c) 935.

6. City, Lucas co., NW Ohio, E of Toledo; pop. (1990c) 18,334; suburb of Toledo.

7. Village, Dane co., S Wisconsin, 11 mi. (18 km.) S of Madison; pop. (1990c) 4519.

Oregon Caves National Monument. See UNITED STATES, *National Monuments.*

Oregon City. City, ⊗ of Clackamas co., NW Oregon, on Willamette River 11 mi. (18 km.) S of Portland; pop. (1990c) 14,698; fruit farms; Clackamas Community Coll. (1966); first Europeans settled 1829; grew with influx of settlers arriving along Oregon Trail (*q.v.*); first ✻ of Oregon Terr. for a short time mid-19th cent.

Oregon Country. Region, W North America, bet. the Pacific coast and the Rocky Mts. extending from the N border of California to Alaska, often so called c. 1818–46; the U.S. portion comprised all of the present states of Washington, Oregon, and Idaho and parts of W Montana and Wyoming; at beginning of the 19th cent. claimed by Spain, Russia, Great Britain, and the U.S.; claims withdrawn by Spain 1819 and by Russia 1824–25; divided at 49th parallel bet. Great Britain and the U.S. 1846; U.S. portion, scene of mission estab. by Marcus Whitman 1836, organized as a territory 1848.

Oregon Inlet. Narrow strait leading from Atlantic Ocean through barrier island off E coast of Dare co., NE North Carolina.

Oregon Territory. Former territory, U.S.A.; comprised the region of Oregon Country ceded to U.S. by British 1846; territory organized Aug. 14, 1848 incl. what is now Oregon, Idaho, Washington, and parts of W Montana and Wyoming; reduced to area of Oregon, S Idaho, and W Wyoming 1853; reduced to present boundaries and admitted to the Union as Oregon 1859.

Oregon Trail. An emigrant route to the Oregon Country; started at Independence, W Missouri; crossed Nebraska following Platte and North Platte rivers; crossed Wyoming, traversing the Rocky Mts. through South Pass (*q.v.*) in the Wind River Range; followed Snake River across Idaho to the Columbia River; terminus was in the Willamette-Columbia river region; ab. 2000 mi. (3220 km.) long, used esp. mid-19th cent.; part of trail was covered by explorers Meriwether Lewis and William Clark during 1804–06 expedition; despite difficult passage through Blue Mts., wagon travel became very heavy c. 1842–60.

Ore·kho·vo–Zu·ye·vo \ˌər-ˈye-k̲ə-və-ˈzü-yə-və\. City, Moscow Oblast, W cen. Russia in Europe, on the Moscow-Nizhniy Novgorod railroad line and the Klyaz'ma River 58 mi. (93 km.) E of Moscow; pop. (1992e) 136,000; a center of cotton textile industry; chemicals, plastics; peat; formed 1917 by consolidation of neighboring industrial villages.

Orel \ȯ-ˈrel, ȯr-ˈyȯl\. City, ✻ of Orel Oblast, Russia in Europe, on left bank of Oka River and on main railroad line 205 mi. (330 km.) S of Moscow; weaving machines, footwear, automobile parts, beer. Founded 1564; occupied by Germans in WWII 1941–43, suffering heavy damage.

Orellana. See AMAZON.

Orel Oblast \ˈȯ-bləst, -ˌblast\ *or* **Or·lov·ska·ya Oblast'** \ər-ˈlȯf-skə-yə-ˈȯ-bləstʸ\. Administrative subdivision of SW cen. Russia in Europe, in the black-earth area N of Ukraine, bounded on N by Kaluga and Tula oblasts, on E by Lipetsk Oblast, on S by Kursk Oblast, and on W by Bryansk Oblast; 9537 sq. mi. (24,701 sq. km.); ✻ Orel. Watered by upper course of Oka River and tributaries. Formerly a part of the Central Black Earth Region, a fertile agricultural region. Although there has been substantial exhaustion of the soil and consequent emigration, agriculture is still the main pursuit; industry is concentrated in Orel. Formed as oblast 1937; much of province held by German armies in WWII.

Orem \ˈōr-əm\. City, Utah co., N cen. Utah, 7 mi. (11 km.) NNW of Provo; pop. (1990c) 67,561; canned food. Settled 1861.

Ore Mountains. See ERZGEBIRGE.

Oren·burg \ˈōr-ən-ˌbərg\; *formerly* **Chka·lov** \ˈchkȧ-ləf\. City, ✻ of Orenburg Oblast, E Russia in Europe, on Ural River; on railroad line from Samara to Tashkent, Uzbekistan; pop. (1992e) 557,000; engineering industries; clothing; first estab. as a fort moved here from Orsk (*q.v.*) 1743; a point of severe fighting after Bolshevik Revolution of 1917; ✻ of Kirghiz Autonomous Rep. (now Kyrgyzstan) 1920–24; name changed 1938 in honor of V. P. Chkalov, Russian aviator; again renamed Orenburg 1957.

Orenburg Oblast \ˈȯ-bləst, -ˌblast\ *or* **Oren·burg·ska·ya Oblast'** \ˈȯr-ən-ˌbərg-skə-yə-ˈȯ-bləstʸ\; *formerly* **Chka·lov Oblast** \ˈchkȧ-ləf\ *or* **Chka·lov·ska·ya Oblast'** \ˈchkȧ-ləf-skə-yə-ˈȯ-bləstʸ\. Administrative subdivision of E Russia in Europe; 47,876 sq. mi. (123,999 sq. km.); pop. (1992e) 2,204,000; ✻ Orenburg; corn, wheat, millet.

Oren·se \ȯ-ˈren-sā\. **1.** Province of NW Spain. See table at SPAIN.
2. Commune, its ✻, on Miño River 250 mi. (402 km.) NW of Madrid; pop. (1991p) 101,623; flour, lumber, iron goods; hot springs; 13th cent. cathedral; notable 13th cent. bridge; ✻ of the Suevi under the Visigoths; destroyed by Moors 8th cent.; rebuilt 9th cent.

Øre·sund \ˈœ̄-rə-ˌsən\ *or Eng.* **The Sound.** Strait bet. Sjælland I., Denmark, and S Sweden, connecting the Kattegat with the Baltic Sea; width at its narrowest section 3.5 mi. (6 km.).

Ore·ti \ō-ˈrā-tē\ *also* **New River.** River, S South I., New Zealand; flows S into Foveaux Strait; 126 mi. (203 km.) long.

Orfani, Gulf of *or* **Orfanou, Kolpos.** See STRYMONIC GULF.

Orford, Cape \ˈȯr-fərd\. Point on S coast of New Britain I., Bismarck Archipelago, Papua New Guinea, near E end of island, and extending into Solomon Sea.

Orford Ness \ˈnes\. Headland on SE coast of England, ENE of Ipswich; lighthouse.

Organization of African Unity *or abbr.* **OAU.** Political organization, consisting of independent African states; headquarters Addis Ababa, Ethiopia; purpose is to promote cooperation in various fields. Since its establishment in 1963, has mediated various conflicts and border disputes bet. its members and intervened in several civil wars; membership has increased from 32 to more than 50 nations since founding, although one original member, Morocco, withdrew in 1984.

Organization of American States *or abbr.* **OAS.** Political organization, consisting of Antigua and Barbuda, Argentina, Bahamas, Barbados, Belize, Bolivia, Brazil, Canada, Chile, Colombia, Costa Rica, Cuba (in name only), Dominica, Dominican Republic, Ecuador, El Salvador, Grenada, Guatemala, Guyana, Haiti, Honduras, Jamaica, Mexico, Nicaragua, Panama, Paraguay, Peru, Saint Kitts and Nevis, Saint Lucia, Saint Vincent and the Grenadines, Suriname, Trinidad and Tobago, United States of America, Uruguay, and Venezuela; headquarters Washington, D.C.; purpose is to promote political, social, and economic cooperation and advancement among the members; estab. 1948 by charter which came into effect 1951. Has acted as consultative or mediating body in several cases of conflict within the region; Cuba excluded from participation 1962.

Organization of the Pe·tro·le·um Ex·port·ing Countries \pə-ˈtrō-lē-əm-ek-ˈspōr-tiŋ, -ˈek-ˌspōr-\ *or abbr.* **OPEC** \ˈō-ˌpek\. Organization, consisting of Algeria, Gabon, Indonesia, Iran, Iraq, Kuwait, Libya, Nigeria, Qatar, Saudi Arabia, United Arab Emirates, and Venezuela; headquarters Vienna, Austria; purpose is to coordinate petroleum policies among the members; estab. 1960; Ecuador joined 1973, withdrew 1993.

Organ Mountains \ˈȯr-gən\. **1.** Range in S Dona Ana co., S New Mexico, extending S across border into Texas.
2. Range in Rio de Janeiro state, SE Brazil. See SERRA DOS ORGÃOS.

Órganos, Sierra de los. See SIERRA DE LOS ÓRGANOS.

Or·gan Pipe Cactus National Monument \ˈȯr-gən-ˌpīp\. See UNITED STATES, *National Monuments.*

Orgãos, Serra dos. See SERRA DOS ORGÃOS.

Or·hei \ȯr-ˈhā\; *Russ.* **Or·ge·yev** \ˈȯr-gē-əf\. Town, cen. Moldova, on tributary of Dniester 23 mi. (37 km.) N of Chişinău.

Or·hon \ˈȯr-ˌk̲ȯn, -ˌhȯn\ *or* **Or·khon** \ˈȯr-ˌk̲ȯn\. River, N Mongolia; flows NE from N edge of the Gobi and joins the Selenga just W of Altanbulag at the border; 698 mi. (1123 km.) long; ruins of Karakorum are near its banks.

Oria \ˈȯr-yä\. Commune, Brindisi prov., Puglia, SE Italy, 16 mi. (26 km.) SW of the seaport of Brindisi; pop. (1981p) 14,789; cathedral; 13th cent. castle.

Ori·ent, The \ˈōr-ē-ənt, -ē-ˌent\. The East; generally, Eastern countries. In ancient times, the countries E of the Mediterranean; today the countries of Asia generally, esp. the countries of E Asia; the Far East. See EAST, THE 1.

Ori·en·tal \ˌȯr-yen-ˈtäl\. Administrative region of E Paraguay; 63,982 sq. mi. (165,713 sq. km.); pop. (1990e) 4,213,700. For subdivisions, see table at PARAGUAY.

Orientale. See HAUT-ZAÏRE.

Oriental Misamis. See MISAMIS ORIENTAL.

Oriental Negros. See NEGROS ORIENTAL.

Ori·en·te \ˌōr-ē-ˈen-tā\ *or* **Oriente, El** \ˌel-\. Region of Ecuador. See EL ORIENTE.

Ori·en·te, Is·las de \ˈēs-läs-dē-ȯr-ˈyen-tē\. Early Portuguese name of the Philippines—literally "Eastern Islands," because lying to the E within the new lands assigned to Portugal by Treaty of Tordesillas (*q.v.*) 1494.

Orient Point. Point at NE extremity of Long Island, Suffolk co., SE New York, at N entrance to Gardiners Bay.

Ori·hue·la \ˌōr-ē-ˈwā-lä\. City, Alicante prov., SE Spain, on Segura River 30 mi. (48 km.) SW of the seaport of Alicante; pop. (1991p) 48,013; citrus fruit, potatoes, cotton, hemp, cereals, almonds; 14th cent. cathedral; 14th cent. church; formerly had a university. Dates from ancient times; held by Moors 713–1264; earthquake 1829.

Oril·lia \ō-ˈril-yə\. Town, Simcoe co., SE Ontario, Canada, where Lake Couchiching and Lake Simcoe join 21 mi. (34 km.) NE of Barrie; pop. (1991c) 25,925; summer resort. Monument to French explorer Samuel de Champlain erected 1925.

Orin·da \ə-ˈrin-də\. City, Contra Costa co., W California, NE of Oakland; pop. (1990c) 16,642; John F. Kennedy Univ. (1964).

Ori·no·co \ˌōr-ē-ˈnō-kō\. River, Venezuela; rises in Serra Parima Mts. in S Venezuela, flows W, then N, forming a section of the Colombia-Venezuela boundary; turns E in cen. Venezuela and empties through a wide delta into the Atlantic Ocean; 1281 mi. (2061 km.) long. In S Venezuela connects with Rio Negro of the Amazon system through the Casiquiare; has many tributaries, esp. the Guaviare, Vichada, and Meta, rising in and flowing E in Colombia, the Apure in W Venezuela, and the Caura and Caroní in SE Venezuela. Navigable in many sections for small vessels but is obstructed by rapids ab. 100 mi. (161 km.) from its mouth.

Orion \ōr-ˈyōn, ȯr-ˈyȯn\. Municipality, Bataan prov., Luzon, Philippines, SSE of Balanga; pop. (1980c) 28,049.

Oris·ka·ny \ȯ-ˈris-kə-nē\. Village, Oneida co., cen. New York, on Mohawk River 7 mi. (11 km.) WNW of Utica; pop. (1990c) 1450; Oriskany Battlefield, scene of Revolutionary War battle Aug. 6, 1777, to W of village; Americans marching to relieve Fort Stanwix (known also as Fort Schuyler) were ambushed by British and Indians but were not driven from the field; losses on both sides severe; American Gen. Nicholas Herkimer received a fatal wound.

Oris·sa \ȯ-ˈri-sə\. State, E coast of India; ✻ Bhubaneswar; rice, timber; chromite, iron ore, manganese; fishing; largest cities: Bhubaneswar, Cuttack. See table at INDIA.

History: Part of a powerful ancient and medieval kingdom known as Kalinga; stronghold of Hinduism prior to being conquered by Afghans and passing to Mongol Empire 16th cent.; most of region came under Marathas 18th cent.; conquered by British 1803; until 1912 a part of Bengal; 1912–36 a subdivision of Bihar and Orissa; constituted separate province 1936; greatly increased in area with the absorption of various princely states following India's independence 1947; became a state 1950.

Orissa Feudatory States. Indian states formerly in Eastern States Agency; now in E India. See EASTERN STATES 3.

Ori·sta·no \ˌō-rē-ˈstä-nō\. **1.** Province of S Sardinia, Italy. See table at ITALY.

2. Commune, its ✻, on Gulf of Oristano 54 mi. (87 km.) NW of Cagliari; pop. (1991p) 30,793; 13th cent. cathedral (rebuilt 18th cent.); Phoenician and Roman ruins nearby.

Oristano, Gulf of. Inlet of Mediterranean Sea on W cen. coast of Sardinia; 10 mi. (16 km.) long; receives Tirso River.

Ori·ve·si \ˈō-rē-ˌve-sē\. Lake, Kuopio prov., SE Finland.

Ori·za·ba \ˌō-rē-ˈsä-b̲ä\. **1.** *or* **Ci·tlal·té·petl** \sē-ˌtläl-ˈtā-ˌpet-ᵊl\. Volcanic peak in cen. Veracruz state, Mexico; 18,700 ft. (5700 m.); highest point in Mexico.

2. City, Veracruz state, E Mexico, 65 mi. (105 km.) WSW of the city of Veracruz; munic. pop. (1990p) 113,516; alt. 4211 ft. (1284 m.); textiles, tobacco products, sugar, beer; tourism; many notable buildings; an Aztec garrison post; Spanish settled during 16th cent.; chartered as city 1774; suffered severe earthquake 1973.

Orkhon. See ORHON.

Ork·ney \ˈȯrk-nē\. Administrative area, N Scotland, comprising the Orkney Is. See table at SCOTLAND.

Orkney Islands *or* **Ork·neys** \-nēz\; *anc.* **Or·ca·des** \ˈȯr-kə-ˌdēz\. Archipelago off NE coast of Scotland, constituting Orkney administrative area; 376 sq. mi. (974 sq. km.); pop. (1991e) 19,570; ✻ Kirkwall, on Pomona I.; chief islands are Pomona (or Mainland), Hoy, South Ronaldsay, North Ronaldsay, Sanday, Stronsay, Shapinsay, and Rousay; separated from Caithness co. on the mainland by Pentland Firth; islands are low (highest point 880 ft. or 268 m. on Pomona) and irregular in shape; in S bet. Pomona, Hoy, and South Ronaldsay is Scapa Flow; chief occupation agriculture (fertile soil produces fine pasturage for cattle and sheep). Inhabited since prehistoric times; a Norse dependency from 9th cent.; annexed by Scotland 1472; major British naval base in both World Wars (see SCAPA FLOW).

Or·land \ˈōr-lənd\. City, Glenn co., N California, 16 mi. (26 km.) N of Willows; pop. (1990c) 5052.

Or·lan·do \ȯr-ˈlan-(ˌ)dō\. City, ⊗ of Orange co., cen. Florida Penin., 78 mi. (126 km.) NE of Tampa; pop. (1990c) 164,693; center of citrus-fruit region and truck-farming region; electronic and aerospace components; tourism; Orlando Coll. (1918), Univ. of Central Florida (1963), Valencia Community Coll. (1967); Sea World of Florida, Universal Studios Florida; Walt Disney World (amusement park) is ab. 6 mi. (10 km.) to SW.

Orlando, Cape. Point on N coast of Sicily, Italy, near E end.

Orland Park. Village, Cook co., NE Illinois, ab. 8 mi. (13 km.) SW of Chicago; pop. (1990c) 35,720.

Orlau. See ORLOVÁ.

Or·lé·a·nais \ˌȯr-lā-á-ˈne\. Historical region of N cen. France, bounded anciently on N by Île-de-France, on E by Champagne, Burgundy, and Nivernais, on S by Berry, on SW by Touraine, and on W by Maine; ✻ Orléans; watered by Loir, Loire, and Cher rivers; provincial appanage of younger members of ruling house of France.

Or·le·ans *La.* ˈȯr-lē-ənz, -lənz; *N.Y.* ˈȯr-ˌlēnz; *Vt.* ȯr-ˈlēnz\. Name of a parish in SE Louisiana and of counties in two states of the U.S. See tables at LOUISIANA, NEW YORK, VERMONT.

Or·leans \ȯr-ˈlēnz\. Town, Barnstable co., SE Massachusetts, on inlet of Atlantic Ocean 18 mi. (29 km.) ENE of the town of Barnstable; pop. (1990c) 5838; summer resort.

Or·lé·ans \ˌȯr-lā-ˈäⁿ\; *anc.* **Au·re·li·a·num** \ȯ-ˌrē-lē-ˈā-nəm\. Commune, ✻ of Loiret dept., N cen. France, on Loire River 70 mi. (113 km.) SSW of Paris; pop. (1990c) 107,965; important railroad junction; produces wine, vinegar, textiles, automobile parts; flower nurseries; in fruit- and vegetable-growing region; 17th–19th cent. cathedral; 16th cent. church; 16th cent. town hall; 17th cent. prefecture; equestrian statue of French national heroine Joan of Arc; museums; university (1962).

History: Conquered by Roman Gen. Julius Caesar 52 B.C.; a major cultural center in early Middle Ages; center of a royal duchy created by Philip VI in 1344; during the Hundred Years' War, English siege relieved 1429 by Joan of Arc, also called the Maid of Orléans; Huguenot headquarters during Wars of Religion 16th cent.; occupied by the Prussians 1870; during WWII, heavily damaged 1940 and 1944.

Or·le·ans, Island of \ˈȯr-lē-ənz\ *or Fr.* **Île d'Or·lé·ans** \ˌēl-ˌdȯr-lā-ˈäⁿ\. Island in St. Lawrence River, E Canada, 4 mi. (6 km.) downstream from the city of Quebec, Quebec; 21 mi. (34 km.) long; 72 sq. mi. (186 sq. km.); chief town Sainte Famille. Named for duc d'Orléans by French explorer Jacques Cartier; settled mid-17th cent.

Or·le·ans, Isle of \ˈȯr-lē-ənz, ˈȯr-lənz\ *or Fr.* **Île d'Or·lé·ans** \ēl-ˌdȯr-lā-ˈäⁿ\. Name used historically for district around New Orleans, Louisiana, S of Lake Pontchartrain and E of the Mississippi; ab. 2800 sq. mi. (7250 sq. km.); ceded by France to Spain in Treaty of Paris 1763.

Orleans Territory. Former territory, U.S.A.; approx. comprised, and later became, the state of Louisiana; organized 1804, although SW portion claimed by Spain until formally ceded by treaty 1819; Louisiana admitted to the Union 1812.

Or·lo·vá \ˈȯr-lȯ-ˌvä\ *or Pol.* **Or·ło·wa** \ȯr-ˈwȯ-vä\ *or Ger.* **Or·lau** \ˈȯr-ˌlau̇\. Town, E Czech Republic, just E of Ostrava near border with Poland; pop. (1989c) 37,558; coal mining.

Orlovskaya Oblast'. See OREL OBLAST.

Or·ly \ȯr-ˈlē\. Commune, Val-de-Marne dept., N France, S suburb of Paris; site of an international airport.

Or·ma·ra \ȯr-ˈmär-ə\. Headland and town, S coast of Baluchistan, Pakistan, ab. 150 mi. (240 km.) W of Karachi.

Or·moc \ȯr-ˈmäk, -ˈmȯk\ *or* **Mac·Ar·thur** \mə-ˈkär-thər\. Chartered city, Leyte prov., on W coast of Leyte I., Philippines, on **Ormoc Bay,** an inlet of Camotes Sea; pop. (1990p) 129,000. In WWII developed by Japanese as military base; captured by U.S. troops Dec. 1944 after severe fighting.

Or·mond Beach \ˈȯr-mənd\. City, Volusia co., E Florida, on Atlantic Ocean 7 mi. (11 km.) N of Daytona Beach; pop. (1990c) 29,721.

Ormond by–the–Sea. Community, Volusia co., E Florida; pop. (1990c) 8157.

Órmos Marathónos. See MARATHON 2.

Orms·by \ˈȯrmz-bē\. Former county in W Nevada, surrounding Carson City; abolished 1969.

Orms·kirk \ˈȯrmz-ˌkərk\. Town, Lancashire, NW England, 11 mi. (18 km.) NNE of Liverpool; pop. (1981p) 27,753; textiles.

Ormuz. **1.** Island, Iran. See HORMOZ.

2. Ancient town, Iran. See HORMUZ.

Ormuz, Strait of. See HORMUZ, STRAIT OF.

Orne \ˈȯrn\. **1.** River, NW France; flows N in Orne and Calvados depts. past Caen into the English Channel; ab. 95 mi. (155 km.) long; its bridges seized by Allies on invasion of Normandy June 6, 1944.

2. Department of NW France. See table at FRANCE.

Ornes \ˈȯrn\. Village, Meuse dept., NE France, 8 mi. (13 km.) NE of Verdun; destroyed during WWI.

Örn·skölds·vik \œrn-ˌshœlds-ˈvēk\. City, Västernorrland prov., E Sweden, on Gulf of Bothnia; pop. (1994e) 58,832.

Oro, El. See EL ORO.

Oro Bay \ˈōr-ō\. Small inlet of Dyke Ackland Bay on New Guinea I., Papua New Guinea, 20 mi. (32 km.) S of Buna; in WWII site of an Allied base, often raided by Japanese during 1943.

Oro·co·vis \ˌōr-ō-ˈkō-bēs\. Municipality, cen. Puerto Rico, SW of San Juan; pop. (1990c) 21,158.

Oro·fi·no \ˌȯr-ə-ˈfē-nō\. City, ⊗ of Clearwater co., NE Idaho, 40 mi. (64 km.) E of Lewiston; pop. (1990c) 2868; lumbering, diversified agriculture.

Oro·he·na, Mount \ˌōr-ə-ˈhā-nə\. Peak in center of the island of Tahiti, French Polynesia, S Pacific Ocean; 7352 ft. (2241 m.); a double peak, steep and thickly forested.

Orolaunum. See ARLON.

Oro·moc·to \ˌȯr-ə-ˈmäk-tō\. Town, Sunbury co., S cen. New Brunswick, Canada, 45 mi. (72 km.) NW of St. John; pop. (1991c) 9325.

Oro·na \ə-ˈrō-nə\; *formerly* **Hull** \ˈhəl\. One of the smaller islands of the Phoenix Is. (*q.v.*), Kiribati, in S part, cen. Pacific Ocean, 4°29′S, 172°10′W, SSW of Kanton I.

Oro·no \ˈōr-ə-ˌnō\. **1.** Town, Penobscot co., E cen. Maine, on Penobscot River 8 mi. (13 km.) NNE of Bangor; pop. (1990c) 10,573; Univ. of Maine (1865).
2. Village, Hennepin co., SE cen. Minnesota, W of Minneapolis; pop. (1990c) 7285.

Oron·say \ˈōr-ən-ˌzā, -ˌsā\. Small island of the Inner Hebrides near Colonsay, off W coast of Scotland; administratively a part of Strathclyde region.

Oron·tes \ō-ˈrän-tēz\. **1.** Mountain, Iran. See ALWAND, MOUNT.
2. *or Arab.* **Nahr Al–ʿĀṣī** \ˈnä-hər-ȧl-ˈä-sē\ *or Turk.* **Asi Neh·ri** \ˌä-sē-ˈner-ē\. Unnavigable river, W Syria; rises in the Bekaa Valley of Lebanon near Baalbek and flows N to the W of the Anti-Lebanon Mts. past the cities of Homs and Hamāh, then turns W and SW through Hatay, S Turkey in Asia, past Antakya into the Mediterranean Sea at Samandağ 40 mi. (64 km.) N of Latakia; 355 mi. (571 km.) long; receives tributary Afrine from the N.

Oropeza. See COCHABAMBA 2.

Oro·pus \ō-ˈrō-pəs\. Ancient town of Boeotia, E cen. Greece, on the coast opp. Eretria; occasionally seized by Athenians, becoming part of Attica.

Oro·quie·ta \ˌōr-ə-kē-ˈā-tə\. Municipality, ✻ of Misamis Occidental prov., Mindanao, Philippines, on NW shore of Iligan Bay; pop. (1990p) 53,000.

Oro·sei, Gulf of \ˌōr-ə-ˈzā\. Widemouthed inlet of Tyrrhenian Sea on E cen. coast of the island of Sardinia.

Oros·há·za \ˈō-rōsh-ˌhä-zō\. Commune, SE Hungary, 32 mi. (51 km.) NE of Szeged; pop. (1991e) 34,800; market center for grain, wine, and livestock.

Orotava, La. See LA OROTAVA.

Oro·te \ō-ˈrō-tē\. Peninsula, W coast of Guam, W Pacific Ocean; ab. 4 mi. (6 km.) long by 0.5 to 1 mi. (0.8 to 1.6 km.) wide; forms S side of Apra Harbor.

Oro·ville \ˈōr-ō-ˌvil\. **1.** City, ⊗ of Butte co., N California, on Feather River 66 mi. (106 km.) N of Sacramento; pop. (1990c) 11,960.
2. Town, Okanogan co., N Washington, on Okanogan River and Osoyoos Lake 5 mi. (8 km.) S of Canadian border; pop. (1990c) 1505.

Oroville Dam *and* **Oroville Reservoir.** See UNITED STATES, *Dams and Reservoirs.*

Oroya, La. See LA OROYA.

Or·re·fors \ˌȯr-ə-ˈfȯrz, -ˈfȯsh\. Town, Kronoberg prov., SE Sweden, ab. 26 mi. (42 km.) NW of Kalmar; famous crystal-glass factory.

Or·rell \ˈȯr-əl\. Town, Greater Manchester co., NW England, 16 mi. (26 km.) NE of Liverpool; pop. (1981p) 12,699.

Or·ring·ton \ˈȯr-iŋ-tən\. Town, Penobscot co., E cen. Maine, on Penobscot River 7 mi. (11 km.) SSW of Bangor; pop. (1990c) 3309.

Orrs Island \ˈōrz\. Island in Casco Bay in Cumberland co., off E coast of SW Maine.

Orr·ville \ˈōr-ˌvil\. City, Wayne co., NE cen. Ohio, 20 mi. (32 km.) SSW of Akron; pop. (1990c) 7712.

Orsera. See ANDERMATT.

Or·sha \ˈȯr-shə\. Town, Vitsyebsk subdivision, Belarus, on right bank of the Dnieper 122 mi. (196 km.) NE of Minsk; pop. (1991e) 125,300; railroad junction; textiles (esp. linen), machinery, processed foods. First mentioned 1067; a trade center in W Poland until annexed by Russia 1772; occupied by Germans in WWII 1941–44.

Orsk \ˈȯrsk\. Town, E Orenburg Oblast, E Russia in Europe, on railroad line 155 mi. (249 km.) E of Orenburg; pop. (1992e) 273,000; railroad center; produces nickel, heavy machinery, chemicals; oil refineries, meatpacking plants; nickel refining; founded 1735 as fortress of Orenburg (*q.v.*) which was moved downriver to present site 1743.

Orsona. See OSUNA.

Or·ta, La·go d' \ˈlä-gō-ˈdȯr-tä\. Lake, NW Italy, ab. 8 mi. (13 km.) long and 0.8 mi. (1.3 km.) wide; 7 sq. mi. (18 sq. km.).

Orta No·va \ˈnō-vä\. Commune, Foggia prov., Puglia, SE Italy, 11 mi. (18 km.) SE of the commune of Foggia; pop. (1981p) 14,391.

Or·te·gal, Cape \ˌȯr-tē-ˈgäl\. Cape on NW coast of Spain, projecting from N coast of La Coruña prov.

Ortelsburg. See SZCZYTNO.

Or·thez \ȯr-ˈtez\. Town, N Pyrénées-Atlantiques dept., SW France, on the Gave de Pau ab. 25 mi. (40 km.) NW of Pau; 13th–14th cent. bridge; ✻ of Béarn to 15th cent.; British under Arthur Wellesley, duke of Wellington, defeated the French under Nicolas-Jean de Dieu Soult nearby 1814.

Or·ti·guei·ra \ˌȯr-tē-ˈgā-rä\. Seaport commune, La Coruña prov., NW Spain, on inlet of Bay of Biscay 35 mi. (56 km.) NE of the commune of La Coruña; pop. (1991c) 9925; coasting trade.

Ort·ler \ˈȯrt-lər\ *or Ital.* **Ort·les** \ˈȯrt-ˌlās\. Mountain range of E Alps, bet. Trentino-Alto Adige and NE Lombardy, N Italy; highest peak **Ortles** *or* **Ort·ler·spit·ze** \ˈȯrt-lər-ˌshpit-sə\, 12,792 ft. (3899 m.).

Or·tón \ȯr-ˈtōn\. River, Peru and Bolivia; rises in SE Peru, flows E across N Bolivia into Beni River shortly before it joins the Mamoré River; ab. 340 mi. (545 km.) long.

Or·to·na \ȯr-ˈtō-nä\. Commune, Chieti prov., Abruzzi, cen. Italy, on the Adriatic 13 mi. (21 km.) E of the commune of Chieti; pop. (1991p) 21,999; fishing; ships grapes; cathedral; 15th cent. castle. A town of the Frentani clan; came under Rome 4th cent. B.C.; to Naples in 18th cent.; in WWII occupied by Allies Dec. 1943.

Or·ton·ville \ˈȯrt-ᵊn-ˌvil\. City, ⊗ of Big Stone co., W Minnesota, at S end of Big Stone Lake on South Dakota border; pop. (1990c) 2326.

Or·tyg·ia \ȯr-ˈti-jē-ə\. Name from ancient times of an island adjacent to the SE coast of Sicily, Italy, and separated from the mainland by a narrow canal; a part of the city of Siracusa. See SIRACUSA 2.

Oruba. See ARUBA.

Orū·mī·yeh \u̇-ˌrü-ˈmē-yə\ *also* **Ur·mia** \ˈu̇r-mē-ə\; *1926–80* **Re·zā·ʼī·yeh** *or* **Ri·za·i·yeh** \ˌre-zä-ˈē-yə\. City, ✻ of West Azerbaijan prov. (see AZERBAIJAN 1), NW Iran; pop. (1986c) 300,746; in region producing fruit and tobacco; reputed birthplace of religious leader Zoroaster c. 628 B.C.

Orū·mī·yeh, Dar·yā·cheh·ye \ˌdär-yä-ˈche-ye-u̇-ˌrü-ˈmē-yə\; *formerly* **Daryācheh-ye Re·zā·ʼī·yeh** \ˌre-zä-ˈē-yə\; *Eng.* **Lake Ur·mia** \ˈu̇r-mē-ə\ *also* **Lake Uru·mi·yah** \u̇-ˌrü-mē-ˈya\; *anc.* **Lake Ma·ti·a·nus** \ˌma-tē-ˈā-nəs, -ˈa-\. Shallow saline lake, NW Iran, E of the city of Orūmīyeh and W of Tabrīz; area 1815 sq. mi. (4701 sq. km.); ab. 90 mi. (145 km.) long; max. depth 49 ft. (15 m.). Shāhī I. is in N cen. part and a group of smaller islands in S cen. part; Sharafkhāneh on NE shore is lake's only port.

Oru·ro \ō-ˈrü-rō\. **1.** Department of W Bolivia. See table at BOLIVIA.
2. City, its ✻, 120 mi. (193 km.) SSE of La Paz; pop. (1992p) 183,194; alt. 12,160 ft. (3706 m.); tin, copper; technical university (1892); founded c. 1600; an important silver-mining center until 19th cent.

Orust \ˈü-ˌrüst\. Swedish island in the Kattegat, off SW coast of Sweden SW of Lake Vänern and 28 mi. (45 km.) NW of Göteborg; ab. 14 mi. (23 km.) long and 10 mi. (16 km.) wide; 133 sq. mi. (344 sq. km.).

Or·vie·to \ȯr-ˈvyā-tō\; *in Middle Ages* **Urbs Ve·tus** \ˈərbz-ˈvē-təs\. Commune, Terni prov., Umbria, cen. Italy, 29 mi. (47 km.) WNW of the commune of Terni; pop. (1991p) 21,302; tourism; ceramics, wine; cathedral (begun 1290) noted esp. for its fine facade and its interior artworks; papal palace (now a museum); 16th cent. well; Etruscan necropolis.

\ə\ **abut** \ᵊ\ matches \ᵊ\ kitten, Fr table \ər\ **further** \a\ **ash** \ā\ **ace** \ä\ **cot, cart** \ȧ\ Fr bac \au̇\ **out** \b̲\ Span Avila \ch\ **chin** \e\ **bet** \ē\ **easy** \g\ **go** \i\ **hit** \ī\ **ice** \j\ **job** \k̲\ Ger **ich, Buch** \ⁿ\ Fr vin \ŋ\ **sing** \ō\ **go** \ȯ\ **all** \ō\ **law** \œ\ Fr bœuf \œ̄\ Fr **feu** \ȯi\ **boy** \th\ **thin** \t͟h\ **this** \ü\ **loot** \u̇\ **foot** \ue\ Ger füllen \ue̅\ Fr **rue** \y\ **yet** \ʸ\ Fr digne \ˈdēnʸ\, nuit \ˈnwʸē\ \yü\ **few** \yu̇\ **fury** \zh\ **vision**

Orvieto is a probable site of the ancient Etruscan city **Volsinii** \väl-ˈsin-ē-ˌī\.

Or·well \ˈȯr-ˌwel, -wəl\. River, Suffolk, E England, extending 10 mi. (16 km.) SE from Ipswich to the Stour.

Or·wigs·burg \ˈȯr-wigz-ˌbərg\. Borough, Schuylkill co., E cen. Pennsylvania, 7 mi. (11 km.) ESE of Pottsville; pop. (1990c) 2780.

Oryokko. See YALU.

Osage \ō-ˈsāj, ˈō-ˌsāj\. **1.** River, W Missouri; largest tributary of the Missouri River; formed by junction of Marais des Cygnes and Little Osage rivers on border of Bates and Vernon cos., flows E and NE through Lake of the Ozarks formed by Bagnell Dam, and enters the Missouri River just E of Jefferson City; ab. 500 mi. (800 km.) long. The Osage is sometimes considered as incl. the Marais des Cygnes.
2. Name of counties in three states of the U.S. See tables at KANSAS, MISSOURI, OKLAHOMA.
3. City, ⊗ of Mitchell co., N Iowa, 24 mi. (39 km.) ENE of Mason City; pop. (1990c) 3439.

Osage City. City, Osage co., E Kansas, 25 mi. (40 km.) NE of Emporia; pop. (1990c) 2689.

Ō·sa·ka \ō-ˈsä-kä, ˈō-sä-ˌkä\. **1.** Prefecture, Honshū, Japan; ✱ Ōsaka; highly urbanized. See table at JAPAN.
2. Seaport city, its ✱, on NE shore of Ōsaka Bay; pop. (1990p) 2,623,831; a major commercial and industrial center; textiles, iron and steel, electrical equipment, chemicals; printing and publishing; university (1931); castle (orig. built 16th cent., restored). Intersected by canals and channels of the Yodo River; connected with Amagasaki by Ōsaka Port Bridge (cantilever; main span 1673 ft. or 510 m.; completed 1974).
History: A long-established city and port; formerly known as **Na·ni·wa** \ˈnä-nē-ˌwä, nä-ˈnē-wä\; made castle town by warrior and statesman Toyotomi Hideyoshi 16th cent.; leading commercial city of Japan during feudal era; developed as leading industrial city of Japan from late 19th cent.; badly damaged by American bombing WWII. Has close connections with port of Kōbe (*q.v.*).

Ōsaka Bay. Inlet of Pacific Ocean on S coast of Honshū, Japan, E of Awaji I. which separates it from the Inland Sea; connected with the ocean by Kitan Strait and Kii Channel; site of ports of Ōsaka and Kōbe.

Osam. See OSŬM.

Osa Peninsula \ˈō-sä\. Peninsula on S coast of Costa Rica bet. the Golfo Dulce, Coronado Bay, and the Pacific Ocean.

Osa·sco \ō-ˈsäs-ˌkü\. Municipality, São Paulo state, SE Brazil, 9 mi. (14 km.) WNW of the city of São Paulo; pop. (1991p) 563,419.

Osa·wat·o·mie \ˌō-sə-ˈwä-tə-mē\. City, Miami co., E Kansas, 45 mi. (72 km.) SSW of Kansas City; pop. (1990c) 4590; a station on the Underground Railroad in pre-Civil War days; site of the cabin in which abolitionist John Brown (known as "Old Brown of Osawatomie") lived 1856 and scene of the bloody fight (Aug. 1856) bet. Brown and his sympathizers and a group of proslavery adherents.

Os·born \ˈäz-bərn\. Former village, Greene co., SW Ohio, 10 mi. (16 km.) NE of Dayton. See FAIRBORN.

Os·borne \ˈäz-bərn\. **1.** County in N cen. Kansas. See table at KANSAS.
2. City, its ⊗, on Solomon River 59 mi. (95 km.) W of Concordia; pop. (1990c) 1778.

Osca. See HUESCA 2.

Os·ce·o·la \ˌō-sē-ˈō-lə, ˌä-\. **1.** Name of counties in three states of the U.S. See tables at FLORIDA, IOWA, MICHIGAN.
2. City, a ⊗ of Mississippi co., NE Arkansas, on Mississippi River 16 mi. (26 km.) S of Blytheville; pop. (1990c) 8930.
3. City, ⊗ of Clarke co., S Iowa, 39 mi. (63 km.) SSW of Des Moines; pop. (1990c) 4164.
4. City, ⊗ of St. Clair co., W Missouri; pop. (1990c) 755.
5. City, ⊗ of Polk co., E Nebraska; pop. (1990c) 879.

Osceola, Mount. Mountain, N Grafton co., N cen. New Hampshire; 4326 ft. (1319 m.).

Oschatz \ˈō-ˌshäts, ˈō-\. City, Saxony, E Germany, 31 mi. (50 km.) SE of Leipzig; pop. (1981c) 19,278.

Oschers·le·ben \ˈō-shərs-ˌlā-bən\. City, Saxony-Anhalt, cen. Germany, 20 mi. (32 km.) WSW of Magdeburg. First mentioned 1235; bombed by Americans in WWII.

Os·co·da \äs-ˈkō-də\. **1.** County in NE Michigan. See table at MICHIGAN.
2. Unincorporated settlement, NE Iosco co., NE Michigan, on Lake Huron at mouth of Au Sable River; pop. (1990c) 1061; resort; outdoor recreation.

Ose·ras \ō-ˈsā-räs\. Peak in Cordillera Oriental, W cen. Colombia, S of Bogotá; 11,480 ft. (3499 m.).

Osetia *or* **Osetiya.** See OSSETIA.

Osh \ˈōsh\. Town, S Kyrgyzstan, on Uzbekistan border ab. 30 mi. (48 km.) SE of Andizhan, Uzbekistan; pop. (1991e) 238,200; at E end of fertile Fergana Valley; center of agricultural region; silk and cotton mills; food processing. The rock Takht-i-Sulaiman (Solomon's Throne), famous in Muslim legends, is W of the town center. Osh was scene of ethnic massacres bet. Uzbeks and Kyrgyz 1990.

Osha·ka·ti \ˌō-shä-ˈkä-tē\. Town, N Namibia, in Ovamboland; pop. (1991c) 35,077.

Osha Peak \ˈō-shə\. Mountain, W Torrance co., cen. New Mexico; 10,223 ft. (3116 m.).

O'Shaugh·nes·sy Dam \ō-ˈshȯ-nə-sē\. See UNITED STATES, *Dams and Reservoirs.*

Osh·a·wa \ˈä-shə-wə, -ˌwä, -ˌwȯ\. City, Durham munic. region, SE Ontario, Canada, on Lake Ontario 33 mi. (53 km.) ENE of Toronto; pop. (1991c) 129,344; motor vehicles and parts, foundry products, glass, textiles, pharmaceuticals, plastics, furniture; founded 1795; incorp. as town 1879, as city 1924.

Oshima. See AMAMI.

Ō–shi·ma \ō-ˈshē-mä, ˈō-shē-ˌmä\ *also* **Vries Island** \ˈvrēs\. Largest island of the Izu-shichitō island group, Japan; ab. 35 sq. mi. (91 sq. km.); has active volcano Mihara 2477 ft. (755 m.), subject to frequent eruptions. Site of Ō-shima Bridge (continuous truss; main span 1066 ft. or 325 m.; completed 1976).

Osh·kosh \ˈäsh-ˌkäsh\. **1.** City, ⊗ of Garden co., W Nebraska; pop. (1990c) 986.
2. City, ⊗ of Winnebago co., E Wisconsin, on W shore of Lake Winnebago; pop. (1990c) 55,006; clothing, wood products, machinery; summer resort; Univ. of Wisconsin–Oshkosh (1871). Settled 1836; incorp. as city 1853; a major lumbering center in latter half of 19th cent.

Osho·gbo \ō-ˈshōg-bō\. City, ✱ of Osun state, Nigeria, on railroad line ab. 50 mi. (80 km.) NE of Ibadan; pop. (1991e) 420,800; trading center; dyeing, weaving, cotton ginning; settled from Ibokun in precolonial era; from mid-19th cent. to 1951 paid tribute to Ibadan.

Osi·jek \ˈō-sē-ˌyek\. City, Croatia, on the Drava River ab. 130 mi. (210 km.) ESE of Zagreb; pop. (1991c) 129,792; ships agricultural produce, livestock; textiles, shoes, sugar. Settled by Romans and soon after became bishopric; under Turks 1526–1687.

Osi·mo \ˈō-zē-ˌmō\. Commune, Ancona prov., Marche, cen. Italy, 9 mi. (15 km.) SSW of the seaport of Ancona; pop. (1989c) 27,743; musical instruments; episcopal see; ancient Roman walls; cathedral.

Osin·ni·ki \ə-ˈsēn-yi-kē\. Town, Kemerovo Oblast, S Russia in Asia, ab. 15 mi. (24 km.) SE of Novokuznetsk; pop. (1991e) 63,200.

Osipenko. See BERDYANSK.

Os·ka·loo·sa \ˌäs-kə-ˈlü-sə\. **1.** City, ⊗ of Mahaska co., SE cen. Iowa, 55 mi. (89 km.) ESE of Des Moines; pop. (1990c) 10,632; coal mining formerly significant; William Penn Coll. (1873).
2. City, ⊗ of Jefferson co., NE Kansas; pop. (1990c) 1074.

Os·kars·hamn \ˌōs-kərs-ˈhäm-ᵊn\. Coastal town, Kalmar prov., SE Sweden; pop. (1989c) 27,232.

Ös·ke·men \ˈœs-ki-ˌmin\ *or* **Ust–Ka·me·no·gorsk** \ˈu̇st-kə-ˌmi-nə-ˈgȯrsk\. Town, ✱ of East Kazakhstan subdivision, E Kazakhstan, on Irtysh River; pop. (1991e) 332,900; on a branch of the Turkistan-Siberian R.R.

Oskol \ˌə-ˈskȯl\. River, E cen. Europe; rises near Stary Oskol in Kursk Oblast, Russia in Europe and flows S into Donets River in E Ukraine; 285 mi. (459 km.) long.

Os·lo \ˈäz-lō, ˈäs-, *Norwegian* ˈüs-lü\. **1.** County of SE Norway. See OSLO 2 and table at NORWAY.

2. *formerly* **Chris·ti·a·nia** *or* **Kris·ti·a·nia** \ˌkris-chē-ˈa-nē-ə, ˌkris-tē-, -ˈä-\. City, ✻ of Norway, also ⊗ of Akershus co., SE Norway, at N end of **Oslo Fjord** (inlet of the Skaggerrak, extending inland 80 mi. or 129 km.) and itself constituting a county (area 175 sq. mi. or 423 sq. km.); pop. (1990c) 458,364; largest city in Norway and its principal commercial, industrial, and transportation center; seaport, shipping wood products, chemicals; produces electronic equipment, metal goods, chemicals; shipyards. Has numerous notable buildings, incl. royal palace (1848), national theater (1899), Akershus fortress (c. 1300), numerous museums, 17th cent. cathedral, and various government buildings; extensive system of parks; university (1811) and college of architecture (1965); site of Winter Olympic Games 1952.

History: Founded by King Harald III (Haardraade) c. 1050; destroyed by fire 1624 and rebuilt as Christiania on present site; captured by Swedes 1716; named Oslo 1925; occupied by Germans in WWII 1940–45.

Os·man·a·bad \ä-ˈsmä-nə-ˌbäd\. Town, SE Maharashtra, S cen. India, ab. 35 mi. (55 km.) NNE of Sholapur; pop. (1991p) 67,980.

Os·na·brück \ˌȯs-nə-ˈbrœk\. Manufacturing city, Lower Saxony, Germany, 30 mi. (48 km.) NE of Münster; pop. (1992e) 165,143; road and rail junction; steel, machinery, automobile parts, paper, chemicals, textiles; 13th cent. cathedral and 13th–14th cent. church; 15th–16th cent. town hall. Episcopal see founded here c. 785 by Frankish King (later Holy Roman Emperor) Charlemagne; made city 1171; member Hanseatic League; accepted Reformation 1543; negotiations leading to Peace of Westphalia (1648) held here 1644 ff.; see secularized and passed to Hannover 1803, diocese reestablished 1858. Substantially damaged in In WWII.

Oso, Mount \ˈō-sō\. Peak, La Plata co., SW Colorado; 13,706 ft. (4178 m.).

Osorhei. See TÎRGUMUREŞ.

Osó·rio \ü-ˈzȯr-yü\. Municipality, Rio Grande do Sul state, S Brazil, ab. 55 mi. (90 km.) E of Pôrto Alegre.

Osor·no \ō-ˈsȯr-nō\. **1.** Volcanic peak, S cen. Chile, on E shore of Lake Llanquihue; 8730 ft. (2661 m.).

2. Former province of S cen. Chile.

3. City, Los Lagos region, S cen. Chile, ab. 240 mi. (385 km.) S of Concepción; pop. (1982c) 95,286; formerly ✻ of Osorno prov.; tourism; lumber, dairy products; meatpacking plants; ships cattle; founded 1553; destroyed by Araucanian Indians 1602 and repopulated 1796; experienced an influx of German immigrants in 2d half of 19th cent.

Oso·wiec \ȯ-ˈsȯ-vyets\ *or Russ.* **Oso·vets** \ə-ˈsȯ-vyəts\. Village and fortress, Białystok prov., NE Poland, 32 mi. (52 km.) NW of the city of Białystok.

Oso·yoos Lake \ə-ˈsü-yəs\. Narrow lake, extending across international border bet. British Columbia, Canada and the state of Washington (Okanogan co.); ab. 15 mi. (24 km.) long.

Os·prey Reef \ˈäs-prē, -ˌprā\. Coral reef island in W Coral Sea, 130 mi. (209 km.) E of Cape Melville, off NE coast of Queensland, Australia.

Os·ro·e·ne *or* **Os·rho·e·ne** \ˌäz-rə-ˈwē-nē\. Ancient kingdom, NW Mesopotamia, E of the Euphrates; ✻ Edessa; founded 2d cent. B.C.; allied for varying periods to Parthia or Rome; kingdom abolished by Roman Emperor Caracalla 216 A.D.

Oss \ˈȯs\. Commune, North Brabant prov., S Netherlands, S of the Maas (Meuse) and ab. 11 mi. (18 km.) ENE of 's Hertogenbosch; pop. (1992e) 52,132; meat products, pharmaceuticals, metalware; granted civic rights 1399.

Os·sa, Mount \ˈä-sə\. **1.** Mountain, Tasmania, Australia; 5305 ft. (1617 m.); highest peak in Tasmania.

2. Peak, E Thessaly, NE Greece, NE of Larissa near the coast; 6489 ft. (1978 m.).

Os·sa·baw Island \ˈä-sə-ˌbȯ\. Island in Atlantic Ocean off S mainland of Chatham co., SE Georgia.

Os·seo \ˈä-sē-ˌō\. Village, Hennepin co., SE cen. Minnesota, 8 mi. (13 km.) NW of Minneapolis; pop. (1990c) 2704.

Os·se·tia *also* **Ose·tia** \ä-ˈsē-shə\ *or* **Os·se·ti·ya** *or* **Ose·ti·ya** \ä-ˈse-tē-ə\. Region of the cen. Caucasus, SE Europe; divided into Alania Rep., Russia (formerly North Ossetian A.S.S.R., U.S.S.R.) and South Ossetia, Republic of Georgia (formerly South Ossetian Autonomous Oblast, Georgian S.S.R., U.S.S.R.).

Os·sett \ˈä-sət\. Town, West Yorkshire, N England, 9 mi. (15 km.) S of Leeds; pop. (1981p) 20,416.

Os·si·ning \ˈȯ-sə-ˌniŋ\. Village, Westchester co., SE New York, on E bank of Hudson River overlooking Tappan Zee, 30 mi. (48 km.) N of New York City; pop. (1990c) 22,582; pharmaceuticals, furniture; residential; Ossining Correctional Facility (Sing Sing, 1824). Incorp. as village of **Sing Sing** \ˈsiŋ-ˌsiŋ\ 1813; name changed 1901.

Os·si·pee \ˈä-sə-pē\. **1.** River, E New Hampshire and SW Maine; flows out of Ossipee Lake E across Maine border into Saco River.

2. Town, ⊗ of Carroll co., E New Hampshire, 21 mi. (34 km.) ENE of Laconia; pop. (1990c) 3309.

Ossipee Lake. Lake, E cen. Carroll co., E New Hampshire; outlet, Ossipee River, flowing E into Saco River; ab. 8 mi. (13 km.) long.

Os·so·ry \ˈä-sə-rē\. Ancient kingdom, SW Leinster, Ireland.

Os·tash·kov \əs-ˈtȧsh-kəf\. Town, W Tver' Oblast, W Russia in Europe, on S shore of Lake Seliger at source of the Volga, 100 mi. (161 km.) WNW of the city of Tver'.

Oste \ˈō-stə\. River, N Germany; flows N in Lower Saxony to the estuary of the Elbe River 13 mi. (21 km.) SE of Cuxhaven; 99 mi. (159 km.) long.

Ost·el·bi·en \ˈȯst-ˈel-bē-ən\. Literally, the region E of the Elbe in Germany, comprising before WWII the state of Mecklenburg and the Prussian provs. of Brandenburg, Pomerania, Silesia, and East Prussia.

Ostende *or* **Ostend.** See OOSTENDE.

Os·ten·so, Mount \ˈäs-tən-ˌsō\. Mountain, Antarctica, 78°19′S, 86°14′W; 13,710 ft (4179 m.).

Øs·ter·dal \ˈœ-stər-ˌdäl\. Valley, Norway, parallel to Swedish border and equivalent generally to the course of the Glåma River; traversed by Norway's easternmost railroad from Oslo N through Elverum, Røros, and Støren to Trondheim.

Öster Dal. See DAL.

Ös·ter·göt·land \ˌœ-stər-ˈyœt-ˌländ\. Province of SE Sweden. See table at SWEDEN.

Øs·terø \ˈœ-stər-ˌœ\. One of the Faeroe Is. (*q.v.*), North Atlantic Ocean, E of Strømø; 111 sq. mi. (288 sq. km.).

Oste·ro·de \ˌȯs-tə-ˈrō-də\. **1.** *or in full* **Osterode am Harz** \äm-ˈhärts\. City, Lower Saxony, cen. Germany; pop. (1992e) 27,163.

2. *or* **Osterode in Ost·preus·sen** \in-ˈȯst-ˌprȯis-ᵊn\. City, Poland. See OSTRÓDA.

Os·ter·øy \ˈüs-tə-ˌrȯi\. Island in a fjord N of Bergen on SW coast of Norway; 127 sq. mi. (329 sq. km.).

Österreich. See AUSTRIA.

Ös·ter·sund \ˈœ-stər-ˌsənd\. City, ⊗ of Jämtland prov., W Sweden, on Lake Storsjön; pop. (1993e) 59,019; manufactures machinery and furniture.

Øst·fold \ˈœst-ˌfȯl\. County of SE Norway. See table at NORWAY.

Ost·fries·land \ȯst-ˈfrē-ˌslänt\ *or* **East Fries·land** \ˈfrēz-lənd, ˈfrēs-ˌland\. Region on the coast of the North Sea, NW Germany, in Lower Saxony; includes the East Frisian Is. (see FRISIAN ISLANDS).

Os·tia \ˈäs-tē-ə\. Village at the mouth of the Tiber River, Lazio, Italy, just E of the ancient town of same name, the port of Rome, which according to legend was founded by King Ancus Marcius 7th cent. B.C., although archaeological findings suggest it was probably founded 4th cent. B.C.; reached height of prosperity 2d cent. A.D.; declined thereafter; new town estab. at modern site by Pope Gregory IV 9th cent.; extensive ruins of ancient town include dwellings, baths, temples, and a theater.

Os·ti·an Way \ˈäs-tē-ən\ *or Lat.* **Via Os·ti·en·sis** \ˈvī-ə-ˌäs-tē-ˈen-səs\. Ancient road, Italy, from Rome to Ostia following the Tiber River; modern road takes nearly the same course, utilizing the ancient bridges.

Ost·land \ˈȯst-ˌlänt\. Name under Nazi regime for proposed German colony in E Europe, usu. thought to comprise Estonian, Latvian, Lithuanian, and Belorussian S.S.R.'s, U.S.S.R.

Ostmark. See *History* at AUSTRIA.

Ostpreussen. See EAST PRUSSIA.

Ostrasia. See AUSTRASIA.

Ostra·va \ˈȯ-strə-və\; *formerly* **Mo·rav·ská Ostrava** \ˈmȯr-əf-skə\ *or Ger.* **Mäh·risch–Os·trau** \ˈmā-rish-ˈȯ-ˌstrau̇\. City, NE Czech Republic, near confluence of Opava and Oder rivers near Moravian Gap; pop. (1991p) 327,553; manufacturing center; blast furnaces.

Os·tró·da \ȯ-ˈstrü-də\; *Ger.* **Oste·ro·de** \ˌȯ-stə-ˈrō-də\ *or in full* **Osterode in Ost·preus·sen** \in-ˈȯst-ˈprȯis-ᵊn\. City, Olsztyn prov., N Poland, 19 mi. (31 km.) WSW of the city of Olsztyn; pop. (1989e) 33,850; railroad junction; assigned to Poland by Potsdam Conference 1945.

Ostrog \ə-ˈstrȯk\ *or Pol.* **Ostróg** \ˈȯ-ˌstrük\. Town, W Ukraine, 59 mi. (95 km.) SE of Luts'k on upper Goryn River; formerly in Poland. Founded in 9th cent.; first complete Bible in Slavonic printed here 1581.

Os·tro·gozhsk \ˌəs-trə-ˈgȯshk\. Town, W cen. Voronezh Oblast, Russia in Asia; 60 mi. (97 km.) S of the city of Voronezh.

Ostro·łę·ka \ˌȯ-strō-ˈweⁿ-kä\ *or Russ.* **Ostro·len·ka** \ˌəs-trəl-ˈyeŋ-kə\. **1.** Province, E cen. Poland. See table at POLAND. **2.** Commune, its ✻, on Narew River 62 mi. (100 km.) NNE of Warsaw; pop. (1989e) 49,566. Dates to 14th cent.; medieval trading center; Poles defeated by Russians here May 26, 1831.

Ostrov \ˈȯs-trȯf\. **1.** Island, Slovakia. See GREAT SCHÜTT. **2.** Town, Pskov Oblast, W Russia in Europe, ab. 30 mi. (48 km.) S of Pskov on the Velikaya River; railroad and commercial town on Latvian border.

Ostrov Dikson. See DICKSON ISLAND.

Ostrov Novaya Sibir'. See NEW SIBERIA ISLAND.

Ostrov Oktyabr'skoy Revolyutsii. See OCTOBER REVOLUTION ISLAND.

Ostrov Vrangelya. See WRANGEL ISLAND.

Ostro·wiec Swię·to·krzy·ski \ȯ-ˈstrȯ-ˌvyets-shfyen-tȯk-ˈshis-kē\ *or* **Ostrowiec.** Industrial commune, Kielce prov., SE cen. Poland, on a tributary of the Vistula 33 mi. (53 km.) ENE of the city of Kielce; pop. (1989e) 77,472; construction materials, iron and steel.

Ostrów Wiel·ko·pol·ski \ˈȯ-ˌstrüf-ˌvyel-kȯ-ˈpȯl-skē\ *or* **Ostrów** *or Ger.* **Ostro·wo** \ȯs-ˈtrō-vō\. Commune, Poznań prov., W cen. Poland, 62 mi. (100 km.) SE of the city of Poznań; pop. (1989e) 72,311; railroad junction; machine tools, lumber, ceramics; mentioned in 13th cent.; became town in 18th cent.; to Prussia 1793 and to Poland after WWI.

Ostsee. See BALTIC SEA.

Osttirol. See EAST TIROL.

Ostu·ni \ō-ˈstü-nē\. Commune, Brindisi prov., Puglia, SE Italy, 21 mi. (34 km.) WNW of the seaport of Brindisi; pop. (1989c) 32,175; 15th cent. cathedral.

Östvågöy. See AUSTVÅGØY.

Ostyak–Vogul National Okrug. See KHANTY-MANSI AUTONOMOUS OKRUG.

Osŭm \ˈȯ-su̇m\ *or* **Osam** \ˈȯ-ˌsäm\. River, N Bulgaria; flows N into Danube River just above Nikopol; 195 mi. (314 km.) long.

Osu·mi Islands \ˈō-sü-ˌmē, ō-ˈsü-mē\ *or Jp.* **Ōsumi Gun·tō** \ˈgu̇n-tō\. Group of islands just S of Kyūshū, Japan, part of Kagoshima prefecture; chief islands Tanega-Shima and Yaku Shima; separated from S tip of Kyūshū by **Osumi Strait** *or* **Van Die·men Strait** \van-ˈdē-mən\ *or Jp.* **Ōsumi Kai·kyō** \ˈkī-kyō\.

Osun \ˈō-ˌsün\. State of Nigeria. See table at NIGERIA.

Osu·na \ō-ˈsü-nä\; *anc.* **Ur·so** \ˈər-sō\; *later* **Or·so·na** \ȯr-ˈsō-nə\. Commune, Sevilla prov., SW Spain, 52 mi. (84 km.) ESE of Seville; pop. (1991p) 16,638; flour, lime, olive oil; in agricultural region; 16th cent. collegiate church; former university (founded 1549, suppressed 1820). Ancient Roman garrison; reconquered from Moors 1240 by Ferdinand III.

Os·wald·twis·tle \ˈäz-wəld-ˌtwi-səl\. Town, Lancashire, NW England, on Leeds and Liverpool Canal 19 mi. (31 km.) NNE of Manchester; pop. (1981p) 14,519.

Os·we·gatch·ie \ˌäs-wi-ˈgä-chē\. River, N New York; rises in N Herkimer co., flows NW and NE into St. Lawrence River at Ogdensburg; ab. 150 mi. (240 km.) long.

Os·we·go \ä-ˈswē-gō\. **1.** River, cen. New York; formed by junction of Seneca and Oneida rivers, Onondaga co., flows N into Lake Ontario at Oswego, Oswego co.; 23 mi. (37 km.) long; canalized (the Oswego Canal) and part of the New York State Barge Canal system.

2. County in cen. New York. See table at NEW YORK.

3. Village, Kendall co., Illinois; pop. (1990c) 3876.

4. City, ⊗ of Labette co., SE Kansas, 30 mi. (48 km.) SW of Pittsburg; pop. (1990c) 1870.

5. City, a ⊗ of Oswego co., cen. New York, on Lake Ontario at mouth of Oswego River 33 mi. (53 km.) NNW of Syracuse; pop. (1990c) 19,195; most easterly Great Lakes port and on New York State Barge Canal; center of hydroelectric power for cen. New York; aluminum, paper products; State Univ. of New York Coll. at Oswego (1861). Mary Edwards Walker, women's rights advocate and physician, born nearby 1832.

History: Founded as English trading post 1722; a contested fortress in Seven Years' War and War of 1812; incorp. as village 1828, as city 1848; became important lake port 1917 after completion of New York State Barge Canal and international port 1959 with completion of St. Lawrence Seaway.

Oswego Canal. Canal, New York, connecting Lake Ontario at Oswego with the Erie Canal at Syracuse; part of the New York State Barge Canal system. See SYRACUSE 2.

Os·wes·try \ˈäz-wə-strē\. Town, Shropshire, W England, near Welsh border 55 mi. (89 km.) WNW of Birmingham; pop. (1991p) 33,600; market town.

Oś·wię·cim \ȯsh-ˈfyen-chēm\ *or Ger.* **Ausch·witz** \ˈau̇sh-ˌvits\. Commune, N Bielsko Biała prov., S Poland, 33 mi. (53 km.) W of Kraków; pop. (1989e) 45,282; railroad junction; chemicals. During WWII with nearby Birkenau site of one of the largest of the German concentration camps, in which from 1 million to 2.5 million or more persons were exterminated.

Ōta \ˈō-ˌtä\. City, Gumma prefecture, Honshū, Japan, 47 mi. (76 km.) NE of Tokyo; pop. (1990p) 139,801.

Ota·go Harbour \ō-ˈtä-gō\. Bay, inlet of Pacific Ocean on SE coast of South I., New Zealand, ab. 11 mi. (18 km.) long with **Otago Peninsula** on its E side, Dunedin at its head (SW), and Port Chalmers on its W shore.

Otaheite. See TAHITI.

Ota·hu·hu \ˌō-tə-ˈhü\. Borough, N North I., New Zealand, SE suburb of Auckland; pop. (1981c) 10,298.

Ota·ru \ō-ˈtä-rü\. City, Hokkaidō prefecture, Japan, on W coast of Hokkaidō ab. 22 mi. (35 km.) WNW of Sapporo; pop. (1990p) 163,215; industrial and commercial center of W Hokkaidō; harbor on **Ishi·ka·ri Bay** \ˌē-shē-ˈkär-ē\, inlet of Sea of Japan.

Ota·va·lo \ˌō-tä-ˈvä-lō\. Town, Imbabura prov., N Ecuador, ab. 42 mi. (68 km.) NNE of Quito; pop. (1990c) 21,548; has a notable market; manufactures cotton and woolen cloth, ponchos, carpets. Orig. a settlement of the Otavalo Indians; came under Spanish control 16th cent.; destroyed by earthquake 1868.

Otdykh. See ZHUKOVSKIY.

Otea. See GREAT BARRIER ISLAND.

Otero \ō-ˈter-ō\. Name of counties in two states of the U.S. See tables at COLORADO and NEW MEXICO.

Othel·lo \ō-ˈthe-lō\. City, Adams co., E Washington, 100 mi. (161 km.) SW of Spokane; pop. (1990c) 4638.

Othonoí. See FANO.

Oth·rys \ˈä-thrəs, ˈō-\ *or* **Óth·ris** \ˈö-thrēs\. Mountain range in E cen. Greece; highest point 5663 ft. (1726 m.); forms S barrier of Thessalian plain.

Oti·ra Gorge \ō-ˈtir-ə\. Narrow cleft in Southern Alps, cen. South I., New Zealand; traversed by highway (Arthur's Pass) and railroad (through **Otira Tunnel**), connecting Christchurch with Greymouth; at W end is the village of Otira.

Ot·ley \ˈät-lē\. Town, West Yorkshire, N England; pop. (1981p) 13,806; woolens, leather.

Otoe \ˈō-tō\. County in SE Nebraska. See table at NEBRASKA.

Oton \ō-ˈtōn\. Municipality, Iloilo prov., Panay, Philippines, on Iloilo Strait 6 mi. (10 km.) W of City of Iloilo; pop. (1980c) 41,044.

Oton·a·bee \ō-ˈtä-nə-bē\. Short stream, a part of Trent River, Peterborough co., SE Ontario, Canada; forms part of Trent Canal system; Peterborough is on it.

Ot·ra \ˈü-trə\. River, S Norway; flows S into the Skagerrak at Kristiansand; 150 mi. (241 km.) long.

Otrad·ny *or* **Otrad·nyy** \ə-ˈträd-nē\. Town, Samara Oblast, E Russia in Europe, ab. 50 mi. (80 km.) ENE of the city of Samara.

Otran·to \ˈō-trän-tō, ō-ˈtran-tō\; *anc.* **Hy·drun·tum** \hī-ˈdrən-təm\. Town, Lecce prov., SE tip of Puglia, S Italy; pop. (1991p) 5152; linked to Greece by ferry; archiepiscopal see; orig. settled by Greeks; important port in Roman times; later declined, but revived in Byzantine times; destroyed by Turks 1480. During WWII an important supply base. English author Horace Walpole's novel *Castle of Otranto* set here.

Otranto, Cape. Cape on SE coast of Italy, on W side of the Strait of Otranto.

Otranto, Strait of. Strait bet. SE Italy and W Albania, connecting the Adriatic Sea with the Ionian Sea; ab. 47 mi. (76 km.) wide.

Otri·co·li \ō-ˈtrē-kō-ˌlē\. Commune, Terni prov., S Umbria, cen. Italy, on the Tiber River and on the Flaminian Way; pop. (1981p) 1789; remains of ancient **Ocric·u·lum** \ō-ˈkri-kyə-ləm\.

Ot·se·go \ät-ˈsē-gō\. **1.** Name of counties in two states of the U.S. See tables at MICHIGAN and NEW YORK.
2. City, Allegan co., SW Michigan, 13 mi. (21 km.) N of Kalamazoo; pop. (1990c) 3937.

Otsego Lake. Lake in N cen. Otsego co., cen. New York; ab. 9 mi. (15 km.) long and an av. of 1 mi. (2 km.) wide; elev. 1193 ft. (364 m.); the village of Cooperstown lies at S end; main source of Susquehanna River. Noted for its association with the novels (Leatherstocking series) of James Fenimore Cooper.

Ōtsu \ˈōt-sü\. City, ✻ of Shiga prefecture, W cen. Honshū, Japan, ab. 10 mi. (16 km.) from Kyōto on SW shore of Lake Biwa; pop. (1990p) 260,004; 7th cent. Mii-dera temple.

Ot·ta·wa \ˈä-tə-wə, -ˌwä, -ˌwȯ\. **1.** Name of counties in four states of the U.S. See tables at KANSAS, MICHIGAN, OHIO, OKLAHOMA.
2. City, ⊗ of La Salle co., N Illinois, on Illinois River 40 mi. (64 km.) WSW of Joliet; pop. (1990c) 17,451; glass; coal mines; diversified agriculture; incorp. as town 1837, as city 1853; scene of first Lincoln-Douglas debate Aug. 21, 1858.
3. City, ⊗ of Franklin co., E Kansas, 37 mi. (60 km.) SE of Topeka; pop. (1990c) 10,667; dairy products; poultry; Ottawa Univ. (1865).
4. Township, ⊗ of Putnam co., NW Ohio, 20 mi. (32 km.) N of Lima; pop. (1990c) 7589.
5. Town, Waukesha co., SE Wisconsin; pop. (1990c) 2988.
6. River, SE Ontario and S Quebec, Canada; forms lower section of boundary bet. Ontario and Quebec, and continues E across S Quebec (bet. Deux-Montagnes and Vaudreuil-Soulanges cos.) to empty into the St. Lawrence River (Lac des Deux-Montagnes) at Montreal I.; 696 mi. (1120 km.) long. Known to Algonquin Indians; among Europeans who later explored was Samuel de Champlain 1613; long a transportation route for explorers, missionaries, and traders.
7. City, ✻ of Canada, also ⊗ of Ottawa-Carleton munic. region, SE Ontario, on right bank of Ottawa River and on Rideau Canal 100 mi. (161 km.) W of Montreal; pop. (1991c) 313,987; national government; watches and clocks; paper and pulp mills. Univ. of Ottawa (1848), Carleton Univ. (1942). Numerous public buildings, incl. those of the national government (rebuilt after fire 1916) and headquarters of several educational and cultural organizations.
History: Area home to American Indians when site reached by French explorer Samuel de Champlain 1613; settlement developed with construction of Rideau Canal 1826 ff.; orig. named **By·town** \ˈbī-ˌtau̇n\; incorp. as city under present name 1855; selected by Queen Victoria as ✻ 1857.

Ottawa–Carle·ton \-ˈkär-əl-tən, -ˈkärlt-ᵊn\. Municipal region, SE Ontario, Canada. See table at ONTARIO.

Ottawa Hills. Village, Lucas co., NW Ohio, 4 mi. (6 km.) W of Toledo; pop. (1990c) 4543.

Ottawa Islands. Group of small islands in E Hudson Bay, S Nunavut, Canada, off coast of N Quebec.

Ot·ter \ˈä-tər\. River, SW cen. Virginia; flows S through Bedford co., turns SE and empties into Roanoke River in S Campbell co.; ab. 40 mi. (65 km.) long.

Otter, Peaks of. Two summits in the Blue Ridge, in Bedford and Botetourt cos., W cen. Virginia; height of Southwest Peak 3875 ft. (1181 m.), and of Flat Top 4001 ft. (1220 m.).

Ot·ter·burn \ˈä-tər-ˌbərn\. Parish, N cen. Northumberland, N England; scene of battle 1388 in which English led by Hotspur (Sir Henry Percy) were defeated by the Scots under James Douglas; Douglas was killed and Hotspur captured; celebrated by the English in the ballad *Chevy Chase* and in the old Scottish ballad *The Ballad of Otterburn.*

Otter Creek. **1.** River, cen. Utah, flowing N from Piute co. into Sevier River in N Sevier co.
2. River, W Vermont; rises in N Bennington co., flows N into Lake Champlain in NW Addison co.; ab. 100 mi. (160 km.) long.

Otter Creek Reservoir. Reservoir in Otter Creek, SE Piute co., S cen. Utah.

Otter Tail. **1.** River, W Minnesota; flows from Otter Tail Lake in cen. Otter Tail co., W cen. Minnesota, W, then S, and again W to unite with Bois de Sioux River at Breckenridge, W Minnesota, and form Red River (or Red River of the North); ab. 150 mi. (240 km.) long.
2. County in W cen. Minnesota. See table at MINNESOTA.

Otter Tail Lake. Lake, cen. Otter Tail co., W cen. Minnesota; ab. 12 mi. (19 km.) long; largest of numerous glacial lakes in the area.

Ot·tery Saint Mary \ˈä-tə-rē\. Town, Devon, SW England; pop. (1981p) 7069; notable 13th–14th cent. church; birthplace of poet and critic Samuel Taylor Coleridge 1772.

Ot·to·man Empire \ˈä-tə-mən\ *also* **Turk·ish Empire** \ˈtər-kish\. Former sultanate in Europe, Asia, and Africa, incl. at greatest extent Syria, Egypt, Iraq, Barbary States, Balkan States, Palestine, part of Arabia, and part of Russia and Hungary; ✻ Constantinople.
History: Originated under Osman I c. 1300 as one of the small states that developed among the Turkish tribes in Anatolia (previously from cen. Asia) following the defeat of the Seljuqs by the Mongols; beginning with Osman's son Orhan (c. 1324–60), an empire was organized on both sides of the Straits (see DARDANELLES); by end of 15th cent., it had liquidated Byzantine Empire (*q.v.*) and included the Balkan region, the rest of Anatolia, and Crimea; overthrew Mamlūks early 16th cent. and secured Syria and Egypt; at its height under Süleyman the Magnificent (1520–66) who expanded the empire into Hungary, N Africa, and Mesopotamia; although Crete, Cyprus, Arabian coasts, and Caucasus territory were later added to Ottoman holdings, the power of the empire began to decline in late 16th cent.; by series of exhausting wars with Poland, Austria, and Russia in 17th and 18th cents., Turks were expelled from Hungary and N shores of Black Sea; in 19th cent., because of internal corruption, the

steady southward advance of Russia (*q.v.*), and successful revolts in the Balkans, the weakened Ottoman Empire came to be known as "Sick Man of Europe" and the problem of preventing too rapid a dissolution of the empire in face of Russian advance became the "Eastern Question" of European diplomacy; Great Britain and France joined with the Turks against Russia in the Crimean War 1854–56. (See EGYPT, TUNIS, and TRIPOLI 1 for loss of African holdings.) Most of the last important European territory lost in the Balkan Wars 1912–13; as one of Central Powers in WWI, was an important area of conflict (see GALLIPOLI PENINSULA and MESOPOTAMIA); sultan accepted Treaty of Sèvres (1920) which greatly reduced the extent of the remaining empire and outraged the new nationalist government at Ankara (see TURKEY); sultanate abolished 1922 and Republic of Turkey proclaimed 1923.

Ot·tum·wa \ä-ˈtəm-wə, ə-ˈtəm-\. City, ⊗ of Wapello co., SE Iowa, on Des Moines River 75 mi. (121 km.) SE of Des Moines; pop. (1990c) 24,488; meatpacking, dairy products, agricultural machinery; Indian Hills Community Coll. (1966).

Otum·ba \ō-ˈtüm-bä\. Town, NE México state, cen. Mexico; battle July 7, 1520 fought on **Plain of Otumba** in which conquistador Hernán Cortés and Spaniards, retreating from Mexico, decisively defeated a large Aztec army.

Otvazhny. See ZHIGULEVSK.

Ot·way, Cape \ˈät-wā\. Cape, S Victoria, SE Australia, 70 mi. (113 km.) SW of entrance to Port Phillip Bay; site of **Otway National Park.**

Otway Water *or* **Otway Bay.** Wide inlet, Magallanes region, S Chile, bet. Brunswick Penin. on the SE and Riesco I. on the NW, connecting by a narrow passage on the SW with the Strait of Magellan.

Ot·wock \ˈót-ˌvótsk\. Commune, Warszawa prov., NE cen. Poland, ab. 15 mi. (24 km.) SE of Warsaw; pop. (1989e) 44,692.

Ötz·tal Alps \ˈœts-ˌtäl\ *also* **Oetz·ta·ler Alp·en** \ˈœts-ˌtä-lər-ˈäl-pən\ *or Ital.* **Al·pi Ve·nos·te** \ˈäl-pē-ve-ˈnós-tē\. Mountain range of the E Alps, in S Tirol, Austria, and N Trentino-Alto Adige, Italy; highest peak Wildspitze 12,382 ft. (3774 m.); many glaciers. Named from a valley (**Ötztal**) and S tributary of the Inn in Tirol, Austria.

Ou \ˈō\; *mostly formerly* **Wu** \ˈwü\. River, Zhejiang prov., E China; rises on SW border of province and flows E to East China Sea at Wenzhou; 285 mi. (458 km.) long.

Ouach·i·ta; *mostly formerly* **Wash·i·ta** \ˈwä-shə-ˌtó\. **1.** River, SW Arkansas and E Louisiana; rises in Polk co., W Arkansas, flows E and then SE across Louisiana border and S to the Black River in Catahoula parish; 605 mi. (974 km.) long; navigable 350 mi. (491 km.).

2. Name of a parish in N Louisiana and of a county in S Arkansas. See tables at ARKANSAS and LOUISIANA.

Ouachita Mountains. Range, W cen. Arkansas and E Oklahoma, a S continuation of Ozark Plateau; highest peak 2660 ft. (811 m.).

Ouadaï. See WADAI.

Oua·dane *or* **Oua·dan** \wȧ-ˈdȧn\ *also* **Wa·dan** \wä-ˈdȧn\. Oasis settlement, W cen. Mauritania.

Ouaddaï. See WADAI.

Oua·ga·dou·gou *also* **Wa·ga·du·gu** \ˌwä-gä-ˈdü-gü\. City, ✱ of Burkina Faso; pop. (1985e) 366,000; railroad terminus; ships peanuts; handicrafts; university. Government functions transferred here from Bobo-Dioulasso in 1947.

Oua·hi·gou·ya \wī-ˈgü-yä\. Town, Burkina Faso, 100 mi. (161 km.) NW of Ouagadougou. Attacked by Malian troops in border war Dec. 25, 1985.

Ouarg·la \ˈwär-glä\ *or* **Warg·la** \ˈwär-glä\ *also* **Warq·la** \ˈwór-klä, ˈwär-\. Town and oasis, NE Algeria, ab. 90 mi. (145 km.) SW of Touggourt; pop. (1987p) 81,721.

Ouar·se·nis Mas·sif \ˌwär-sə-ˈnē-ma-ˈsēf\. Highland region in NE Algeria; highest peak 6512 ft. (1985 m.).

Oubangui. See UBANGI.

Oubangui–Chari *or* **Oubangui–Chari–Tchad.** See CENTRAL AFRICAN REPUBLIC.

Ouche \ˈüsh\. River, Côte-d'Or dept., E France; flows into Saône River; ab. 60 mi. (95 km.) long.

Ou·chy \ü-ˈshē\. Village, Vaud canton, on Lake Geneva in SW Switzerland; the port of Lausanne.

Ou·de Maas \ˈau̇-də-ˌmäs, ˈau̇-ə-\. Left branch of the Merwede River in Netherlands, flowing into the North Sea just S of the Nieuwe Maas River; it leaves the Merwede near Dordrecht.

Ou·de·naar·de \ˌau̇d-ᵊn-ˈär-də\ *or Fr.* **Au·de·narde** \ˌō-də-ˈnärd\. Commune, East Flanders prov., NW cen. Belgium, on Schelde River 31 mi. (50 km.) W of Brussels; pop. (1991c) 27,162; railroad junction; notable for its churches and late-Gothic hôtel de ville; scene of defeat 1708 of French under Louis-Joseph de Bourbon, duke of Vendôme, by Prince Eugene of Savoy and John Churchill, duke of Marlborough, during War of the Spanish Succession.

Oudergem. See AUDERGHEM.

Oude Rijn \ˈau̇-də-ˌrīn, ˈau̇-ə-\. Branch of the Lek River in Netherlands; flows N out of the Lek and then W to the North Sea at Katwijk; passes Utrecht and Leiden in its course.

Oudh *also* **Audh** \ˈau̇d\. A former province of British India, now the NE portion of Uttar Pradesh state, India; 24,071 sq. mi. (62,344 sq. km.). Received its name from Ajodhya (*q.v.*), sacred city of the Hindus and early ✱ of the ancient kingdom of Kosala, which was nearly coextensive with modern Oudh. Overrun by Muslim invaders late 12th cent.; became part of Mogul Empire 16th cent.; annexed to British dominions 1856 (one of the causes of the Indian mutiny 1857); united with Agra under one administrator 1877 (name later changed to United Provinces of Agra and Oudh, and after India's independence in 1947 to Uttar Pradesh).

Oudjda. See OUJDA.

Oudts·hoorn \ˈōts-ˌhórn\. Town, SE cen. Western Cape prov., S Rep. of South Africa, near Olifants River 220 mi. (354 km.) E of Cape Town; in Little Karoo; pop. (1985c) 34,124; ostrich farming; in fertile area watered by irrigation. Cango Caves, noted for stalactite and stalagmite formations, nearby.

Oued, El *or* **Oued, Al–.** See EL OUED.

Oued Zem \wed-ˈzem\. City, W cen. Morocco, 110 mi. (177 km.) E of El Jadida; pop. (1982c) 58,744.

Oued–Zé·na·ti \ˌwed-zā-nə-ˈtē\. Commune, NE Algeria, ab. 50 mi. (80 km.) E of Constantine.

Oues·sant, Île d' \ˌēl-dwe-ˈsäⁿ\ *or Eng.* **Ushant** \ˈəsh-ᵊnt\; *anc.* **Uxan·tis** \ək-ˈsan-tis\. Island off tip of Brittany, NW France; 6 sq. mi. (16 sq. km.); 4.5 mi. (7 km.) long; lighthouse; scene of naval battles 1778 and 1794 bet. French and English.

Ouez·zane \we-ˈzȧn\ *or Arab.* **Waz·zan** *also* **Wa·zan** \wȧ-ˈzȧn\. City, N Morocco, 60 mi. (97 km.) NW of Fès; pop. (1982c) 40,485; Muslim pilgrimage center.

Ou·grée \ü-ˈgrā\. Commune, Liège prov., E Belgium, on Meuse River; S suburb of the city of Liège.

Oui·dah *or* **Wi·da** \ˈwē-də\ *or Eng.* **Whyd·ah** \ˈhwi-də\. Seaport town, S Benin, on lagoon 23 mi. (37 km.) W of Cotonou; important in 18th and 19th cents. as a slave-trade port.

Ouj·da *or* **Oudj·da** \üj-ˈdä\ *or Arab.* **Uj·da** \ˈüj-də\. Commercial city, NE Morocco, near the Algerian border; pop. (1982c) 260,082; railroad junction; founded 944; occupied by French 1907.

Ou·lan·ka National Park \ˈō-läŋ-kə\. National park, E Finland, just S of the Arctic Circle; 41 sq. mi. (106 sq. km.); wilderness region; estab. 1956.

Ouled–Naïl Mountains \ü-ˈled-ˈnīl, -ˈnāl\. Range of the Atlas Mts. in N cen. Algeria.

Oul·lins \ü-ˈleⁿ\. Commune, Rhône dept., E cen. France, SSW suburb of Lyon.

Ou·lu \ˈau̇-lü\. **1.** Province of N cen. Finland. See table at FINLAND.

2. *or Swed.* **Ule·å·borg** \ˈü-le-ō-ˌbórʸ, -ˌbór-ē\. Seaport, its ✱, on Gulf of Bothnia and at mouth of Oulu River; pop. (1989c) 100,281; pulp and flour mills, shipyards, foundries; university (1958); castle built 1590; 19th cent. cathedral; founded early 17th cent.; destroyed by fire 1822, subsequently rebuilt; became major industrial center 19th cent.

Ou·lu·jär·vi \ˈau̇-lü-ˌyar-vē\. Lake in cen. Finland; drains NW through **Oulu River** (65 mi. or 105 km. long) into NE Gulf of Bothnia.

Oum er Rbia \ˌüm-er-ˈbē-ə\. River, cen. Morocco; flows NW into Atlantic Ocean at El Jadida; 345 mi. (555 km.) long.

Ou·nas \ˈau̇-ˌnäs\. River, NW Finland; flows S into Kemi River; 210 mi. (338 km.) long.

Our \ˈür\. River, forming section of NE boundary bet. Germany and the Grand Duchy of Luxembourg; flows S into Sûre River E of Diekirch; 50 mi. (89 km.) long.

Ou·ray \ü-ˈrā\. **1.** County in SW Colorado. See table at COLORADO.
2. City, its ⊗; pop. (1990c) 644; mining formerly significant; hot springs.

Ouray Peak *also* **Hunts Peak** \ˈhənts\. Mountain, Chaffee co., cen. Colorado; 13,955 ft. (4254 m.).

Ourcq \ˈürk\. River, Aisne dept., N France; 50 mi. (81 km.) long; part of the water supply for Paris; WWI battles fought in vicinity.

Ou·ri·que \ō-ˈrē-kə\. Commune, Beja dist., S Portugal, 31 mi. (50 km.) SSW of the commune of Beja; pop. (1981p) 7693; Alfonso I defeated the Moors nearby 1139.

Ou·ro Fi·no \ˈō-rü-ˈfē-nü\. City, SW Minas Gerais state, E Brazil, 100 mi. (161 km.) N of São Paulo; munic. pop. (1980c) 22,438.

Ouro Prê·to \ˈprā-tü\. Town, Minas Gerais state, E Brazil, 40 mi. (64 km.) SE of Belo Horizonte; munic. pop. (1991p) 62,483; tourism; noted for its baroque colonial architecture; national monument; several churches; many works by Brazilian sculptor and architect Aleijadinho (Antonio Lisboa) found here; founded as gold-mining settlement c. 1700; a center of Brazilian gold production during 18th cent.; former ✻ of Minas Gerais, to 1897.

Ourthe \ˈürt\. River, SE Belgium; flows N in Luxembourg and Liège provs. into the Meuse; ab. 100 mi. (160 km.) long.

Ouse \ˈüz\. **1.** *or* **Great Ouse.** River, cen. and E England; rises in Northamptonshire, flows in a winding course E and NE into the Wash below King's Lynn; 156 mi. (251 km.) long.
2. River, NE England; formed by confluence of the Swale and Ure rivers in North Yorkshire, flows SE to unite with the Trent River and form the Humber; 45 mi. (72 km.) long; navigable as far as York.
3. River, West Sussex, S England; 30 mi. (48 km.) long.

Ou·ta·gam·ie \ˌau̇-tə-ˈga-mē\. County in E Wisconsin. See table at WISCONSIN.

Ou·tardes \ü-ˈtärd\. River, S cen. Quebec, Canada; rises in Lake Pletipi and flows S to the St. Lawrence; 270 mi. (434 km.) long.

Out·back \ˈau̇t-ˌbak\. Name given to those parts of Australia that are isolated, rural, and usu. inland.

Outer Banks. Chain of narrow islands and peninsulas off the North Carolina mainland stretching from the Virginia border to Cape Lookout; ab. 175 mi. (280 km.) long; most are connected by road; contains beaches, recreational areas, several lighthouses.

Outer City. See CHINESE CITY.

Outer Hebrides. See HEBRIDES.

Outer Himalayas. See HIMALAYAS, THE.

Outer Island. See APOSTLE ISLANDS.

Outer Mongolia. See MONGOLIA.

Outer Provinces *or Du.* **Bui·ten·ge·wes·ten** \ˈbȯit-ᵊn-k̲ə-ˌvestən\. Those parts of the former Netherlands Indies outside of Java and Madura; comprised Sumatra, Borneo, Celebes, Moluccas, and Lesser Sunda Is.; 684,064 sq. mi. (1,771,726 sq. km.). See INDONESIA 2.

Outer Rhodes. See APPENZELL.

Outer San·ta Bar·ba·ra Channel \ˈsan-tə-ˈbär-brə\. Strait bet. Santa Catalina I. and San Clemente I. off NW coast of San Diego co., S California.

Ou·tes \ˈō-tās\. Commune, La Coruña prov., NW Spain, 44 mi. (71 km.) SW of the commune of La Coruña; pop. (1991c) 9273.

Ou·tre·mont \ˈü-trə-ˌmänt, *Fr.* ˌü-trə-ˈmōⁿ\. Residential city, an independent municipality adjoining Montreal, S Quebec, Canada, lying N of Mount Royal in cen. part of Montreal I.; pop. (1991c) 22,935; Coll. Jésus-Marie d'Outremont (1933).

Ouvéa *or* **Uvéa** \ü-ˈvā-ä\ *also* **Uea** \ü-ˈwā-ä\. Northernmost island of the chain of the Loyalty Is., E of New Caledonia and NW of Lifou; 51 sq. mi. (132 sq. km.); pop. (1989p) 3540; low, narrow island ab. 30 mi. (48 km.) long with large lagoon on W side.

Ova·lau \ˌō-vä-ˈlau̇\. Island in the Lomai Viti group, Fiji, SW Pacific Ocean, ab. 12 mi. (19 km.) off E coast of Viti Levu; 40 sq. mi. (104 sq. km.); chief town Levuka, ✻ of Fiji 1874–82.

Oval·le \ō-ˈvī-ˌā\. City, Coquimbo region, cen. Chile, 200 mi. (322 km.) N of Santiago.

Ov·am·bo·land \ō-ˈvam-bō-ˌland\ *also* **Am·bo·land** \ˈam-bō-ˌland\. The region in the N part of Namibia inhabited by the Ovambo.

Ovar \ō-ˈvär\. Commune, Aveiro dist., NW Portugal, near Atlantic Ocean N of the seaport of Aveiro; pop. (1981p) 45,272; port.

Overflakkee. See GOEREE.

Over·ijs·sel \ˌō-vər-ˈā-səl, -ˈī-səl\. Province, E Netherlands; ✻ Zwolle; livestock raising, dairy farming, textile weaving. See table at NETHERLANDS.

Over·land \ˈō-vər-lənd\. City, St. Louis co., E Missouri, 10 mi. (16 km.) WNW of the city of St. Louis; pop. (1990c) 17,987.

Overland Park. City, Johnson co., NE Kansas, S of Kansas City; pop. (1990c) 111,790; Johnson County Community Coll. (1967).

Overland Track. See CRADLE MOUNTAIN-LAKE SAINT CLAIR NATIONAL PARK.

Over·lea \ˈō-vər-ˌlē\. Unincorporated settlement, Baltimore co., N Maryland, NE of the city of Baltimore; pop. (1990c) 12,137.

Overseas Highway. See FLORIDA KEYS.

Over·ton \ˈō-vər-tən\. **1.** County in N Tennessee. See table at TENNESSEE.
2. Town, Clark co., SE Nevada, ab. 48 mi. (77 km.) NE of Las Vegas; nearby museum houses relics of ancient Indian village of **Lost City** ab. 5 mi. (8 km.) S, now covered by Lake Mead.

Ovid \ˈō-vid\. Village, a ⊗ of Seneca co., W cen. New York; pop. (1990c) 660.

Ovie·do \ˌō-ˈvy-ā-t̲h̲ō\. **1.** Province of NW Spain. See ASTURIAS.
2. *anc.* **As·tu·ri·as** \a-ˈstu̇r-ē-əs, -ˈstyu̇r-\. City, ✻ of Asturias autonomous community and prov., NW Spain, 230 mi. (370 km.) NNW of Madrid; pop. (1991p) 194,919; center of mining region; cathedral (begun 14th cent.); two 9th cent. churches; convent; university (1608). Founded 8th cent.; bishopric 812; ✻ of Asturias kingdom 9th cent.; sacked by French 1809 and badly damaged in Spanish Civil War 1936–39.

Ovie·do \ō-ˈvē-dō\. City, Seminole co., cen. Florida, NE of Orlando; pop. (1990c) 11,114.

Ovilava. See WELS.

Ovoca. See AVOCA 2.

Owari Bay. See ISE BAY.

Owas·co Lake \ō-ˈwäs-kō\. Lake, Cayuga co., cen. New York; ab. 11 mi. (18 km.) long by 1 mi. (1.6 km.) wide; one of the Finger Lakes (*q.v.*); N end outlet flows into Seneca River.

Owas·so \ō-ˈwä-sō\. City, Tulsa co., NE Oklahoma, 2 mi. (3.2 km.) N of the city of Tulsa; pop. (1990c) 11,151.

Owa·ton·na \ˌō-wə-ˈtä-nə\. City, ⊗ of Steele co., S Minnesota, 15 mi. (24 km.) S of Faribault; pop. (1990c) 19,386; dairy products; dairy and truck farms.

Owe·go \ō-ˈwē-gō\. Village, ⊗ of Tioga co., S New York, on Susquehanna River 20 mi. (32 km.) W of Binghamton; pop. (1990c) 4442.

Ow·en \ˈō-ən\. Name of counties in two states of the U.S. See tables at INDIANA and KENTUCKY.

\ə\ abut \ᵊ\ kitten, Fr table \ər\ further \a\ ash \ā\ ace \ä\ cot, cart \à\ Fr bac \au̇\ out \b̲\ Span Avila \ch\ chin \e\ bet \ē\ easy \g\ go \i\ hit \ī\ ice \j\ job \k̲\ Ger ich, Buch \ⁿ\ Fr vin \ŋ\ sing \ō\ go \ȯ\ law \œ\ Fr bœuf \œ̄\ Fr feu \ȯi\ boy \th\ thin \t̲h̲\ this \ü\ loot \u̇\ foot \ue\ Ger füllen \ue̅\ Fr rue \y\ yet \ʸ\ Fr digne \dēnʸ\, nuit \nwʸē\ \yü\ few \yu̇\ fury \zh\ vision

Owen, Mount. Peak, cen. Grand Teton National Park, NW Wyoming; 12,922 ft. (3939 m.).

Owen·do \ˌō-wen-ˈdō\. Deepwater port, NW Gabon; serves as port for Libreville which is ab. 10 mi. (16 km.) NNW.

Owen Falls. Former waterfall in the Victoria Nile in Uganda; 65 ft. (20 m.) high; submerged by **Owen Falls Dam.**

Ow·ens \ˈō-ənz\. River, E California; rises in W Mono co., flows S; ab. 120 mi. (195 km.) long; now diverted from Owens Lake (*q.v.*) into Los Angeles Aqueduct to supply water to city of Los Angeles.

Ow·ens·boro \ˈō-ənz-ˌbər-ō\. City, ⊗ of Daviess co., NW Kentucky, on Ohio River 85 mi. (137 km.) WSW of Louisville; pop. (1990c) 53,549; grain and tobacco market; chemicals, electrical equipment, steel, whiskey, cigars; oil wells; Kentucky Wesleyan Coll. (1858), Brescia Coll. (1874). Settled c. 1800; raided by Confederate guerrillas during Civil War 1864.

Owens Lake. Intermittent lake in cen. Inyo co., E California; formerly held waters forming body ab. 18 mi. (29 km.) long by 10 mi. (16 km.) wide and fed by Owens River; water now taken by Los Angeles Aqueduct to Los Angeles.

Owen Sound. **1.** Inlet of SW Georgian Bay, SE Ontario, Canada.
2. City, ⊗ of Grey co., SE Ontario, Canada, on Owen Sound 105 mi. (169 km.) NW of Toronto; pop. (1991c) 21,674; port; tourist resort.

Owen Stan·ley Range \ˈstan-lē\. Mountain range extending SE and NW on New Guinea I., Papua New Guinea; ab. 600 mi. (965 km.) long; highest peak Mt. Victoria 13,363 ft. (4073 m.).

Ow·en·ton \ˈō-ən-tən\. City, ⊗ of Owen co., N Kentucky; pop. (1990c) 1306.

Ower·ri \ō-ˈwer-ē\. Town, ✱ of Imo state, S Nigeria; pop. (1983e) 35,010.

Ow·ings·ville \ˈō-iŋz-ˌvil\. City, ⊗ of Bath co., NE Kentucky; pop. (1990c) 1491.

Owl Creek \ˈau̇l\. See BELLE FOURCHE.

Owl Creek Mountains. Range of the Rocky Mts. in NW cen. Wyoming, extending along boundary bet. Hot Springs and Fremont cos.; highest peak ab. 9600 ft. (2925 m.).

Owls Head \ˈau̇lz\. Point of land, S Maine, jutting out from mainland in E Knox co., into Penobscot Bay, SE of Rockland.

Owo \ˈō-wō\. Town, SW cen. Nigeria, 30 mi. (48 km.) NE of Ibadan; pop. (1991e) 161,900.

Owos·so \ō-ˈwä-sō\. City, Shiawassee co., S cen. Michigan, 26 mi. (42 km.) W of Flint; pop. (1990c) 16,322.

Ows·ley \ˈau̇z-lē\. County in E Kentucky. See table at KENTUCKY.

Owy·hee \ō-ˈwī-hē, -ˈwī-ē\. **1.** River, SE Oregon; formed by junction of forks in Owyhee co., SW corner of Idaho, flows NW across Oregon boundary, N through Malheur co., and empties into Snake River; ab. 300 mi. (480 km.) long.
2. County in SW corner of Idaho. See table at IDAHO.

Owyhee Dam *and* **Lake Owyhee.** See UNITED STATES, *Dams and Reservoirs.*

Ox·ford \ˈäks-fərd\. **1.** County in W Maine. See table at MAINE.
2. City, Calhoun co., NE Alabama, S of Anniston; pop. (1990c) 9362.
3. Town, New Haven co., S Connecticut, 10 mi. (16 km.) W of the city of New Haven; pop. (1990c) 8685.
4. Town, Oxford co., Maine; pop. (1990c) 3705.
5. Town, Worcester co., cen. Massachusetts, 10 mi. (16 km.) SSW of the city of Worcester; pop. (1990c) 12,588.
6. Village, Oakland co., SE Michigan, 14 mi. (23 km.) N of Pontiac; pop. (1990c) 2929.
7. City, ⊗ of Lafayette co., N Mississippi, 46 mi. (74 km.) WNW of Tupelo; pop. (1990c) 9984; sawmills; dairy and poultry farms; Univ. of Mississippi (1844) nearby. Home of author William Faulkner for much of his life.
8. City, ⊗ of Granville co., N North Carolina, 30 mi. (48 km.) NNE of Durham; pop. (1990c) 7913.
9. Township, Butler co., SW Ohio, 12 mi. (19 km.) NW of Hamilton; pop. (1990c) 23,092; residential; Miami Univ. (1809).
10. Borough, Chester co., SE Pennsylvania, 25 mi. (40 km.) SE of Lancaster; pop. (1990c) 3769.
11. County in SE Ontario, Canada. See table at ONTARIO.
12. County in England. See OXFORDSHIRE.
13. *or Lat.* **Ox·o·nia** \äk-ˈsō-nē-ə\. City, ⊗ of Oxfordshire, cen. England, on the Thames 52 mi. (84 km.) WNW of London; pop. (1991p) 109,000; motor vehicles, steel stampings; printing and binding; cathedral (chapel of Christ Church Coll.); Univ. of Oxford (12th cent.). First mentioned 912; meeting place of 13th cent. parliament resulting in government reform agreed to by Henry III; Royalist stronghold in Civil War.

Ox·ford·shire \ˈäks-fərd-ˌshir, -shər\ *or* **Oxford** *or* **Ox·on** \ˈäk-ˌsän, -sən\. **1.** Former county, cen. England.
2. Administrative county, cen. England, approx. equivalent to the former county; rivers the Thames and its tributaries; grain; livestock; manufacturing: farm machinery, automobiles, paper, blankets; main towns include Oxford, Banbury, Abingdon, Henley-on-Thames. See table at ENGLAND.

Oxianus Lacus. See ARAL SEA.

Ox·leys Peak \ˈäk-slēz\. Highest mountain in Liverpool Range, NE New South Wales, SE Australia; 4500 ft. (1372 m.).

Ox·nard \ˈäks-ˌnärd\. City, Ventura co., SW California, near coast of Santa Barbara Channel 30 mi. (48 km.) WNW of Los Angeles; pop. (1990c) 142,216; oil refining, sugar processing; in agricultural region; Oxnard Coll. (1975); pop. almost tripled bet. 1960 and 1980.

Oxon. See OXFORDSHIRE.

Oxonia. See OXFORD 13.

Oxus. See AMU DARYA.

Ox·y·rhyn·chus \ˌäk-si-ˈriŋ-kəs\ *or Arab.* **Al–Bah·na·sā** \äl-ˈbà-nə-ˌsä\ *also* **Beh·ne·sa** \ˈbe-nə-sə\. Archaeological site, Egypt, on heights above Bahr Yûsef, W bank of Nile ab. 54 mi. (87 km.) S of El Faiyûm. Large finds of ancient papyri discovered here in late 19th cent. and early 20th cent.; of note were fragments containing Jesus' sayings, probably dating from 3d cent. A.D.

Oya·hue \ō-ˈyä-wā\. **1.** Volcanic peak, SW Bolivia; 19,225 ft. (5860 m.).
2. Volcano, Chile. See OLLAGÜE.

Oya·ma \ō-ˈyä-mä\. **1.** Peak, Japan. See DAI-SEN.
2. City, Tokyo prefecture, Honshū, Japan, 44 mi. (71 km.) N of the city of Tokyo; pop. (1990p) 142,263.

Oya·pock \ˌo-yä-ˈpȯk\. **1.** *or* **Oya·pok** \-ˈpȯk\. River, N South America; rises in the Tumuc-Humac Mts. in S French Guiana, flows NE, forming boundary bet. N Brazil and French Guiana, into the Atlantic Ocean through a wide mouth, **Oyapock Bay;** ab. 260 mi. (420 km.) long.
2. Port, French Guiana, on the Oyapock River N of St. Georges.

Øy·e·ren \ˈȯi-ə-rən\. Lake in SE Norway, E of Oslo; 34 sq. mi. (88 sq. km.); traversed by the Glåma River.

Oymyakon. See OIMYAKON.

Oyo \ˈō-yō\. **1.** State of SW Nigeria. See table at NIGERIA.
2. Town, Oyo state, Nigeria, ab. 32 mi. (51 km.) N of Ibadan; pop. (1991e) 226,300; in agricultural region; handicrafts; St. Andrew's Coll. (1897).

Ōyo·do \ˈō-yō-ˌdō\. River in SE Kyūshū, Japan; flows E into Pacific Ocean at Miyazaki.

Oyon·nax \ˌō-yō-ˈnäks\. Commune, Ain dept., E France, 12 mi. (19 km.) E of Bourg.

Oyrot Autonomous Oblast. See GORNO-ALTAY.

Oys·ter Bay \ˈȯi-stər\. **1.** Inlet of Long Island Sound, Nassau co., SE New York, N shore of Long Island.
2. Village, Nassau co., SE New York, on Long Island, on inlet of Long Island Sound; pop. (1990c) 6687; residential suburb of New York City; known for summer White House (1901–09) of Theodore Roosevelt (Sagamore Hill) which is actually in nearby village of **Cove Neck** \ˈkōv\ (pop. 332); arboretum; Roosevelt's grave in Young's Memorial Cemetery. Oyster Bay village is a part of **Oyster Bay** town (pop. 292,657), which also includes the village of **Oyster Bay Cove** (pop. 2109).

Oza·miz \ō-ˈsä-mēs\. Chartered city, W Mindanao, Philippines; pop. (1990p) 92,000.

Ozark \ˈō-ˌzärk\. **1.** County in S Missouri. See table at MISSOURI.

2. City, ⊗ of Dale co., SE Alabama; pop. (1990c) 12,922.

3. City, a ⊗ of Franklin co., NW Arkansas, on Arkansas River; pop. (1990c) 3330.

4. City, ⊗ of Christian co., SW Missouri; pop. (1990c) 4243.

Ozark Plateau *or* **Ozark Mountains.** Eroded tableland, S cen. U.S., extending from the Missouri River in E Missouri to the Arkansas River in NE Oklahoma and NW Arkansas; bet. 1500 and 2500 ft. (460 and 760 m.) high; approx. 50,000 sq. mi. (129,500 sq. km.).

Ozarks, Lake of the \ˈō-ˌzärks\. Reservoir, S cen. Missouri, formed by Bagnell Dam in the Osage River; ab. 125 mi. (200 km.) long.

Ozau·kee \ō-ˈzȯ-kē\. County in E Wisconsin. See table at WISCONSIN.

Ózd \ˈōzd\. Town, N Hungary, ab. 25 mi. (40 km.) WNW of Miskolc; pop. (1991e) 38,300.

Ozero Baykal. See BAIKAL, LAKE.

Ozero El'ton. See ELTON, LAKE.

Ozette, Lake \ō-ˈzet\. Lake, W Clallam co., NW Washington.

Ozie·ri \ȯt-ˈsyā-rē\. Commune, Sassari prov., NW Sardinia, Italy, 25 mi. (40 km.) ESE of the commune of Sassari; pop. (1981p) 11,036; cathedral; prehistoric burial places nearby.

Ozo·na \ō-ˈzō-nə\. Town, ⊗ of Crockett co., W Texas, 70 mi. (113 km.) SW of San Angelo; pop. (1990c) 3181; only town in Crockett co.

\ə\ abut \ə\ matches \ᵊ\ kitten, Fr table \ər\ further \a\ ash \ā\ ace \ä\ cot, cart \å\ Fr bac \au̇\ out \b\ Span Avila \ch\ chin \e\ bet \ē\ easy \g\ go \i\ hit \ī\ ice \j\ job \k\ Ger ich, Buch \ⁿ\ Fr vin \ŋ\ sing \ō\ go \ȯ\ all \ȯ\ law \œ\ Fr bœuf \œ̄\ Fr feu \ȯi\ boy \th\ thin \t͟h\ this \ü\ loot \u̇\ foot \ue\ Ger füllen \ue̅\ Fr rue \y\ yet \ʸ\ Fr digne \ˈdēnʸ\, nuit \ˈnwʸē\ \yü\ few \yu̇\ fury \zh\ vision

P

Paa·ma \pä-'mä\. Island, Vanuatu, SW Pacific Ocean; pop. (1991e) 1696.

Paamiut. See FREDERIKSHÅB.

Pa–an \'bä-än\. Town, ✱ of Karen state, cen. Myanmar.

Paar·de·berg \'pär-də-,berk\. Battlefield, W Free State, E cen. Rep. of South Africa, on the Modder River 23 mi. (37 km.) SE of Kimberley; scene of Boer Gen. Piet Cronjé's surrender to British Army's Lord (Frederick) Roberts Feb. 1900.

Paarl \'pärl\. Town, SW Western Cape prov., S Rep. of South Africa, 30 mi. (48 km.) ENE of Cape Town on Great Berg River; pop. (1985c) 63,671; has extensive fruit orchards and vineyards; produces wine; settled c. 1690 by Huguenot settlers.

Pab·bay \'pa-bā\. **1.** Island, Scotland, in Outer Hebrides SW of island of Lewis with Harris.

2. Island, Scotland, in Outer Hebrides S of Barra I.

Pab·bi·ring Archipelago \pä-'bir-iŋ\; *formerly* **Sper·mun·de Archipelago** \spər-'mu̇n-də\. Group of small low islands, SE Makassar Strait, off SW coast of Sulawesi, Malay Archipelago, Indonesia.

Pa·bia·ni·ce *or* **Pa·bja·ni·ce** \,pä-byä-'nēt-se\. Commune, Łódź prov., cen. Poland, on railroad line 10 mi. (16 km.) SSW of the city of Łódź; pop. (1989e) 74,824; textiles. Taken by Germans in 1914 and 1939.

Pab·na \'pəb-,nä\. Town, Bangladesh, near Ganges River ab. 72 mi. (116 km.) WNW of Dhaka; munic. pop. (1991p) 113,146; rice.

Pa·bok \pa-'bo̊k\. County, Quebec, Canada. See table at QUEBEC.

Pac·a·rai·ma Mountains \,pä-kä-'rī-mä\; *in Brazil* **Serra Pacaraima;** *in Venezuela* **Sierra Pacaraima;** *in Guyana* **Pakaraima Mountains.** Mountain range, N South America, along a section of Brazil-Venezuela boundary with a NE extension into Guyana; highest peak Mt. Roraima 9219 ft. (2810 m.).

Pa·cas·ma·yo \,pä-käs-'mä-yō\. Seaport, NW Peru, ab. 65 mi. (105 km.) NW of Salaverry and 360 mi. (579 km.) NW of Callao.

Pa·ca·ya \pä-'kī-ä\. River in Loreto region, NE Peru; a W tributary of the Ucayali River. ab. 100 mi. (160 km.) long.

Pa·cha·ca·mac \pä-'chä-kä-,mäk\. Site of a pre-Incan city, ab. 20 mi. (32 km.) SE of Lima, Peru; famous for remains of ancient temple to the god Pachacamac, the later Incan Temple of the Sun, and ruins of the surrounding city; sacked by Spanish soldiers under Francisco Pizarro c. 1523; site now occupied by the village of La Mamacoma.

Pa·cha·cha·ca \,pä-chä-'chä-kä\. Short stream, SE Peru, a tributary of the Apurímac near Abancay.

Pach·aug Pond \'pa-cho̊g\. Lake in NE cen. New London co., SE Connecticut; outlet, **Pachaug River,** flowing NW into Quinebaug River.

Pa·chi·no \pä-'kē-nō\. Coastal commune, Siracusa prov., SE Sicily, Italy, near SE tip of Sicily 26 mi. (42 km.) SSW of seaport of Siracusa; pop. (1981p) 21,157.

Pa·chi·tea \,pä-chē-'tā-ä\. River, Peru; flows from the Andes into Ucayali River; ab. 220 mi. (355 km.) long.

Pa·chu·ca \pä-'chü-kä\ *or in full* **Pachuca de So·to** \thā-'sō-tō\. City, ✱ of Hidalgo state, cen. Mexico, 50 mi. (80 km.) N of Mexico City; munic. pop. (1990p) 179,440; alt. 8150 ft. (2484 m.); silver mines, smelters, ore-reduction plants; university; 16th cent. Franciscan convent. Spanish settlement founded 1534; silver mines date from Aztec period.

Pachynus Promontorium. See PASSERO, CAPE.

Pa·cif·ic \pə-'si-fik\. **1.** Coastal county in SW corner of Washington. See table at WASHINGTON.

2. City, Franklin and St. Louis cos., E Missouri, 33 mi. (53 km.) W of St. Louis; pop. (1990c) 4350; paper products, building materials; agriculture.

Pa·cif·i·ca \pə-'si-fi-kə\. City, San Mateo co., W California, on Pacific coast S of San Francisco; pop. (1990c) 37,670; residential; formed 1957 by consolidation of several communities.

Pacific–Antarctic Ridge. Ridge, S Pacific Ocean floor, extending generally E from S of Macquarie I. to approx. 120°W long.; a center of oceanic crust formation according to theory of plate tectonics.

Pacific Grove. Residential and resort city, Monterey co., W California, at S end of Monterey Bay; pop. (1990c) 16,117; annual stopover point for migrating monarch butterflies.

Pacific Islands. The islands of the Pacific Ocean, divided into Micronesia, Melanesia, and Polynesia (incl. New Zealand). See OCEANIA.

Pacific Islands, Trust Territory of the. Former U.S. trust territory, comprising the Northern Mariana Is. (until 1978), the Federated States of Micronesia (until 1991), the Marshall Is. (until 1991), and Palau (until 1994).

Pacific Ocean. Body of water extending from the Arctic circle to the Equator (**North Pacific Ocean**) and from the Equator to the Antarctic Regions (**South Pacific Ocean**), and from W North America and W South America to Australia, the Malay Archipelago, and E Asia; area ab. 70,000,000 sq. mi. (181,300,000 sq. km.); max. depth 36,198 ft. (11,033 m.) at 11°21′N, 142°12′E (Mariana Trench).

Pacific Rim. The countries bordering on or located in the Pacific Ocean and esp. those in Asia having rapidly developing economies.

Pacific Rim National Park. See CANADA, *National Parks.*

Pa·ci·jan \pä-'sē-,hän\. Island, westernmost of Camotes Is., Philippines; 34 sq. mi. (88 sq. km.); coextensive with San Francisco municipality.

Pa·coi·ma \pə-'ko̊i-mə\. Short river, Los Angeles co., SW California, N of the city of Los Angeles; dammed to form **Pacoima Reservoir**.

Pacoima Dam. See UNITED STATES, *Dams and Reservoirs.*

Pacsan, Mount. See SICAPOO, MOUNT.

Pac·to·lus \pak-'tō-ləs\. River in Lydia, Asia Minor; a tributary of the Hermus (*mod.* Gediz) entering it near Sardis; historically yielded gold-bearing sand.

Padalung. See PHATTALUNG.

Pa·dang \'pä-,däŋ\. **1.** Island in Strait of Malacca, off coast of Sumatra at 1°10′N, 102°21′E.

2. Seaport city, ✱ of West Sumatra prov., Sumatra I., Indonesia, 575 mi. (925 km.) NW of Jakarta ab. 1°S of the Equator; pop. (1990c) 631,543; major port at Telukbajur ab. 5 mi. (8 km.) to S, shipping rubber, copra, tea, coffee; university. Estab. as Dutch factory early 17th cent.; fortified 1667; held by British intermittently late 18th–early 19th cents.; in WWII occupied by Japanese 1942–45.

Pa·dang·pan·jang *or* **Pa·dang·pan·djang** \,pä-daŋ-'pän-,jäŋ\. Town, W Sumatra, Indonesia; junction point for railroads to Padang and Bukittinggi.

Paddan–Aram. See MESOPOTAMIA.

Pa·den City \'pā-dən\. Town, NW West Virginia, in Tyler and Wetzel cos., on Ohio River 24 mi. (39 km.) SSW of Moundsville; pop. (1990c) 2862.

Pa·der·born \'pä-dər-,bo̊rn\. City, North Rhine-Westphalia, Germany, 50 mi. (80 km.) ESE of Münster; pop. (1992e) 125,730; rail and road junction; cement, iron products; 11th–13th cent. cathedral; 17th cent. town hall; baroque 17th cent. Franciscan church. Meeting place of Frankish King Charlemagne and Pope Leo III 799 (leading to foundation of Holy Roman Empire); came under prince-bishops c. 1100; to Prussia 1803.

Pa·de·ria \pə-'der-ē-ə\. Town, S Nepal, near boundary of Uttar Pradesh, N India, 47 mi. (76 km.) N of Gorakhpur.

Pa·der·no Du·gna·no \pä-'der-nō-dü-'nyä-nō\. Commune, Milano prov., Lombardy, N Italy, N of Milan; pop. (1989c) 43,760.

Pad·je·lan·ta National Park \ˌpä-dyə-'län-tə\. National park, N Sweden, on Norwegian border; 788 sq. mi. (2041 sq. km.); important botanical area; estab. 1962.

Padma. See GANGES DELTA.

Pa·do·va \'pä-dō-vä\. **1.** Province of Italy. See table at ITALY. **2.** Commune, Italy. See PADUA.

Pad·re Island \'pä-drē, -drā\. Barrier island, off the mainland of Kleberg, Kenedy, Willacy, and Cameron cos., S Texas, lying bet. Laguna Madre and the Gulf of Mexico; 113 mi. (182 km.) long and up to 3 mi. (4.8 km.) wide; contains a recreational preserve; notable variety of birds, excellent fishing, nice beaches.

Pad·stow \'pad-ˌstō\. Town near N coast of Cornwall, SW England, NW of Bodmin; tourism.

Pad·ua \'pa-dyü-wə\ *or Ital.* **Pa·do·va** \'pä-dō-vä\; *anc.* **Pa·ta·vi·um** \pə-'tā-vē-əm\. Commune, ✻ of Padova prov., Veneto, NE Italy, 22 mi. (35 km.) W of Venice; pop. (1991p) 215,025; railroad junction and commercial center; produces agricultural machinery, motorcycles, textiles, chemicals; tourism; numerous notable buildings, incl. the 16th cent. cathedral with Romanesque baptistery, 13th cent. basilica, 13th–14th cent. Palazzo della Ragione, other medieval and Renaissance buildings with frescoes by Giotto, Mantegna, and Titian, botanical gardens (1545, the oldest in Europe), and museums. Univ. of Padua (1222) the 2d oldest in Italy, formerly noted for faculties of law and medicine; had among faculty Italian mathematician and astronomer Galileo and anatomist Fallopio, among students Italian poets Dante, Petrarch, and Tasso.

History: First mentioned 302 B.C.; prospered as Roman city; under Lombard rule 7th–8th cents.; under Carrara family 1318–1405; to Venice 1405 and shared its later history; in WWII heavily damaged by bombing; occupied by Allies 1945. Birthplace of Roman historian Livy (59 B.C.) and of painter Andrea Mantegna (1431).

Pa·du·cah \pə-'dü-kə\. **1.** City, ⊗ of McCracken co., W Kentucky, on Ohio River just below its confluence with Tennessee River; pop. (1990c) 27,256; tobacco, livestock, coal, and strawberry market; Paducah Community Coll. (1932); settled 1827; chartered as city 1856.

2. Town, ⊗ of Cottle co., NW Texas, 87 mi. (140 km.) ENE of Lubbock; pop. (1990c) 1788.

Padus. See PO.

Paek·che \'pak-ˌchə\. Ancient kingdom, Korea. See *History* at KOREA.

Pae·o·nia \pē-'ō-nē-ə\. Ancient district N of Macedonia in what is now N part of Republic of Macedonia; conquered by Philip II of Macedon mid-4th cent. B.C.; chief town Stobi (*q.v.*).

Paes·tum \'pes-təm, 'pēs-\. Ancient city, W Lucania (now Basilicata), S Italy, on the Gulf of Salerno (*anc.* Bay of Paestum); founded 6th cent. B.C. by Greek colonists from Sybaris who called it **Pos·ei·do·nia** \ˌpō-sī-'dō-nē-ə\; taken by Lucanians 4th cent. B.C. and by Romans 273 B.C.; destroyed by Arabs c. 871 A.D.; well-preserved ruins include portions of three Doric temples and almost the entire walls.

Paestum, Bay of. See SALERNO, GULF OF.

Pag \'päg\ *or Ital.* **Pa·go** \'pä-gō\. **1.** Island of Croatia, in the Adriatic Sea off N Dalmatian coast; 111 sq. mi. (287 sq. km.). **2.** Town on E coast of the island.

Pa·ga·di·an \ˌpä-gä-'dē-än\. Chartered city, ✻ of Zamboanga del Sur prov., Mindanao, Philippines, on NW shore of Illana Bay; pop. (1990p) 107,000.

Pa·gai *or* **Pa·gaï** *or* **Pa·gi** \'pä-ˌgī\ *or* **Pa·geh** \'pä-gā\. Two islands in Indian Ocean, S part of Mentawai Is. off W coast of Sumatra, Indonesia; **North Pagai** *or* **Pagai Uta·ra** \ü-'tär-ä\, ab. 25 mi. (40 km.) long by 17 mi. (27 km.) wide, and **South Pagai** *or* **Pagai Se·la·tan** \ˌse-lä-'tän\, ab. 42 mi. (68 km.) long by 13 mi. (21 km.) wide.

Pa·ga·lu \pä-'gä-lü\ *or* **An·no·bón** \ˌä-nō-'bon\. Small mountainous island in Gulf of Guinea, part of Equatorial Guinea, 120 mi. (193 km.) SW of São Tomé; 4 mi. (6.4 km.) long; 7 sq. mi. (18 sq. km.); pop. (1983c) 2120; a Spanish possession 1778–1968.

Pa·ga·lun·gan \ˌpä-gä-'lüŋ-ˌgän\. Town, Mindanao, Philippines; ✻ of former Cotabato prov.

Pa·gan \pə-'gän\. **1.** Ruined town, Myanmar, extending 8 mi. (13 km.) along left bank of Irrawaddy 92 mi. (148 km.) SW of Mandalay; founded c. 849 and ✻ of a powerful dynasty 11th–13th cents.; conquered by Mongols 1287. Contains thousands of ancient Buddhist pagodas and shrines; 1975 earthquake caused much damage.

2. Island, Northern Mariana Islands, W Pacific Ocean; 18°17′N, 145°46′E; 8 mi. (13 km.) long by 2.5 mi. (4 km.) wide.

Pa·ga·ni \pä-'gä-nē\. Commune, Salerno prov., Campania, S Italy, 9 mi. (14 km.) NW of the seaport of Salerno; pop. (1989c) 33,053.

Pa·ga·si·ti·kós Kól·pos \ˌpä-gä-ˌsē-tē-'kös-'köl-ˌpös\ *or* **Gulf of Pa·ga·saí** \ˌpä-gä-'sī\; *mostly formerly* **Gulf of Vo·lo** \'vō-ˌlō\ *or* **Gulf of Vo·los** \'vō-ˌlös, -ˌläs\; *anc.* **Si·nus Pag·a·sae·us** \'si-nəs-ˌpa-gə-'sē-əs\. Inlet of the Aegean Sea, E Thessaly, E coast of Greece; shut in on E by a peninsula.

Page \'pāj\. **1.** Name of counties of two states in the U.S. See tables at IOWA and VIRGINIA.

2. City, Coconino co., N Arizona, S of Lake Powell; pop. (1990c) 6598; estab. 1958 for workers constructing Glen Canyon Dam.

Page·dale \'pāj-ˌdāl\. City, St. Louis co., E Missouri; pop. (1990c) 3771; residential suburb of the city of St. Louis.

Pageh *or* **Pagi.** See PAGAI.

Page·land \'pāj-lənd\. Town, Chesterfield co., NE South Carolina, close to the North Carolina border; pop. (1990c) 2666.

Pago. See PAG.

Pa·go·da Mountain \pə-ˌgō-də\. Peak, Boulder co., N cen. Colorado; 13,491 ft. (4112 m.).

Pagoda Point. Point on SW coast of Myanmar, adjacent to Cape Negrais on W side of mouth of Bassein River.

Pa·go Pa·go; *formerly also* **Pango·pango** \'päŋ-ō-'päŋ-ō, 'pä-gō-'pä-gō\. Village, ✻ of American Samoa, on Tutuila I., SW Pacific Ocean, at head of long inlet forming **Pago Pago Harbor,** one of the best harbors in the South Pacific; pop. (1990c) 3519. Site chosen by Commander Richard W. Meade 1872 and treaty signed 1878 for U.S. use as a naval and coaling station; made ✻ of American Samoa 1899; ceased as naval base 1951.

Pa·go·sa Peak \pə-'gō-sə\. Mountain, Mineral co., S Colorado, in San Juan Mts.; 12,674 ft. (3863 m.).

Pagosa Springs. Town, ⊗ of Archuleta co., S Colorado, 50 mi. (80 km.) E of Durango; pop. (1990c) 1207; hot springs.

Pag·san·jan \ˌpäg-säŋ-'hän\. Municipality, Luzon, Philippines, 3 mi. (4.8 km.) E of Santa Cruz; pop. (1980c) 19,489; on **Pagsanjan River** and noted for its gorge and waterfall, also known as **Bo·to·can** \ˌbō-tō-'kän\, ab. 200 ft. (61 m.) drop.

Pa·ha·la \pä-'hä-lä\. Town, Hawaii co., Hawaii, S part of Hawaii I. near coast; pop. (1990c) 1520; S point of access to Hawaii National Park.

Pa·hang \pä-'haŋ\. **1.** River in Pahang state, Malaysia, Malay Penin.; formed in NW part of the state by confluence of the Jelai and Tembeling rivers; flows S and E to South China Sea; 285 mi. (459 km.) long; navigable for boats for ab. 250 mi. (400 km.).

2. A state of Malaysia, E coast of Malay Penin., bounded on N by Kelantan and Terengganu, on E by South China Sea, on S by Johor, on SW by Negeri Sembilan, and on W by Selangor and Perak; ✻ Kuantan. Mountainous, with many peaks above 3000 ft. (914 m.); has the two highest mountains of the peninsula on its border: on the NW, Kerbau 7159 ft. (2182 m.) and on the N, Tahan 7186 ft. (2190 m.); most of its area lies

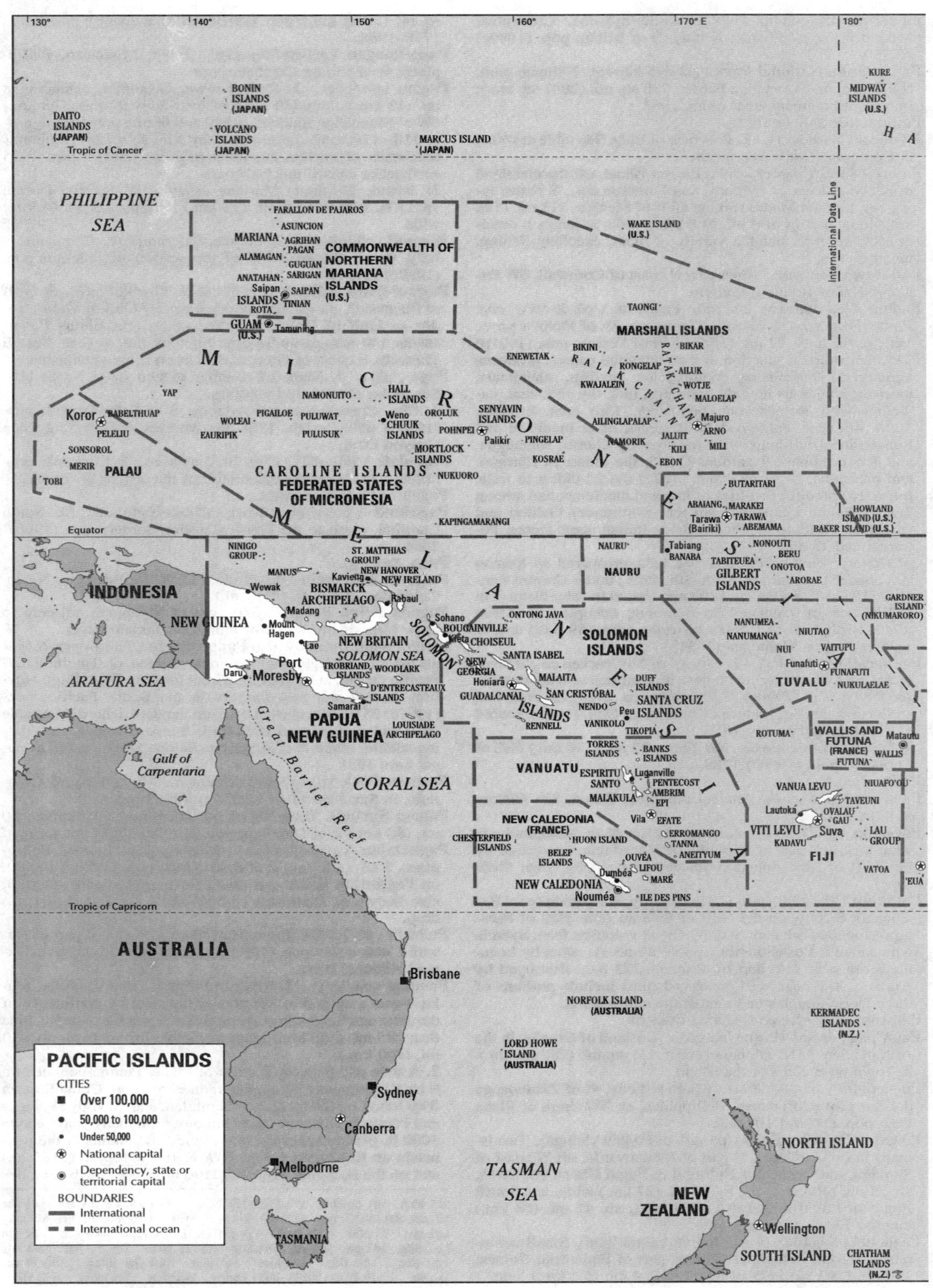

PACIFIC ISLANDS
CITIES
Over 100,000
50,000 to 100,000
Under 50,000
National capital
Dependency, state or territorial capital
BOUNDARIES
International
International ocean
PHILIPPINE SEA
DAITO ISLANDS (JAPAN)
BONIN ISLANDS (JAPAN)
VOLCANO ISLANDS (JAPAN)
MARCUS ISLAND (JAPAN)
Tropic of Cancer
KURE
MIDWAY ISLANDS (U.S.)
International Date Line
WAKE ISLAND (U.S.)
COMMONWEALTH OF NORTHERN MARIANA ISLANDS (U.S.)
FARALLON DE PAJAROS
ASUNCION
MARIANA
AGRIHAN
PAGAN
ALAMAGAN
GUGUAN
SARIGAN
ANATAHAN
Saipan
SAIPAN
ISLANDS
TINIAN
ROTA
GUAM (U.S.)
Tamuning
MICRONESIA
MARSHALL ISLANDS
TAONGI
BIKINI
BIKAR
ENEWETAK
RONGELAP
AILUK
RALIK CHAIN
RATAK CHAIN
KWAJALEIN
WOTJE
MALOELAP
AILINGLAPALAP
Majuro
ARNO
JALUIT
NAMORIK
KILI
MILI
EBON
YAP
Koror
BABELTHUAP
PELELIU
SONSOROL
MERIR
PALAU
TOBI
WOLEAI
EAURIPIK
PIGAILOE
PULUWAT
PULUSUK
NAMONUITO
HALL ISLANDS
Weno
CHUUK ISLANDS
OROLUK
SENYAVIN ISLANDS
POHNPEI
Palikir
PINGELAP
MORTLOCK ISLANDS
KOSRAE
NUKUORO
CAROLINE ISLANDS
FEDERATED STATES OF MICRONESIA
KAPINGAMARANGI
Equator
BUTARITARI
ABAIANG
MARAKEI
Tarawa (Bairiki)
TARAWA
ABEMAMA
HOWLAND ISLAND (U.S.)
BAKER ISLAND (U.S.)
NAURU
Tabiang
BANABA
NONOUTI
BERU
TABITEUEA
ONOTOA
ARORAE
GILBERT ISLANDS
NINIGO GROUP
ST. MATTHIAS GROUP
MANUS
NEW HANOVER
Kavieng
NEW IRELAND
INDONESIA
Wewak
BISMARCK ARCHIPELAGO
Rabaul
Madang
NEW GUINEA
Mount Hagen
Lae
NEW BRITAIN
SOLOMON SEA
Sohano
BOUGAINVILLE
Kieta
SOLOMON
CHOISEUL
SANTA ISABEL
NEW GEORGIA
Honiara
MALAITA
GUADALCANAL
ISLANDS
SAN CRISTÓBAL
RENNELL
ONTONG JAVA
SOLOMON ISLANDS
MELANESIA
DUFF ISLANDS
SANTA CRUZ ISLANDS
NENDO
Peu
VANIKOLO
TIKOPIA
GARDNER ISLAND (NIKUMARORO)
NANUMEA
NANUMANGA
NIUTAO
NUI
VAITUPU
Funafuti
FUNAFUTI
TUVALU
NUKULAELAE
ROTUMA
WALLIS AND FUTUNA (FRANCE)
Mata'utu
WALLIS
FUTUNA
Daru
Port Moresby
ARAFURA SEA
TROBRIAND ISLANDS
WOODLARK
D'ENTRECASTEAUX ISLANDS
Samarai
PAPUA NEW GUINEA
LOUISIADE ARCHIPELAGO
Great Barrier Reef
Gulf of Carpentaria
CORAL SEA
TORRES ISLANDS
BANKS ISLANDS
VANUATU
ESPIRITU SANTO
Luganville
PENTECOST
AMBRIM
MALAKULA
EPI
Vila
EFATE
ERROMANGO
TANNA
ANEITYUM
NEW CALEDONIA (FRANCE)
CHESTERFIELD ISLANDS
HUON ISLAND
BELEP ISLANDS
OUVÉA
LIFOU
Dumbéa
MARÉ
NEW CALEDONIA
Nouméa
ILE DES PINS
NIUAFO'OU
VANUA LEVU
TAVEUNI
Lautoka
OVALAU
GAU
VITI LEVU
Suva
LAU GROUP
KADAVU
FIJI
VATOA
'EUA
Tropic of Capricorn
AUSTRALIA
Brisbane
NORFOLK ISLAND (AUSTRALIA)
KERMADEC ISLANDS (N.Z.)
LORD HOWE ISLAND (AUSTRALIA)
Sydney
Canberra
Melbourne
TASMAN SEA
NORTH ISLAND
NEW ZEALAND
Wellington
SOUTH ISLAND
TASMANIA
CHATHAM ISLANDS (N.Z.)
130°
140°
150°
160°
170° E
180°

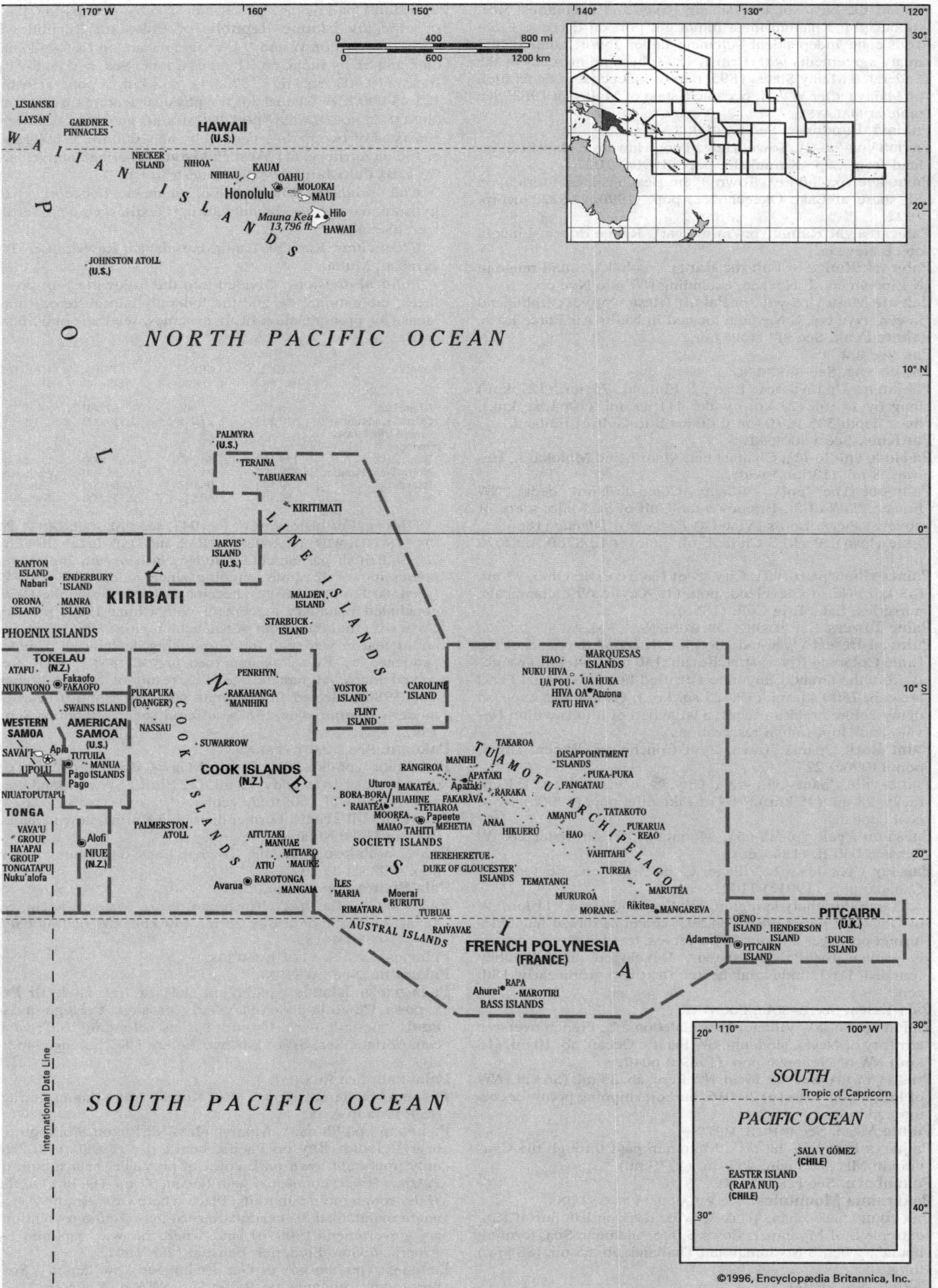
170° W
160°
150°
140°
130°
120°
0
400
800 mi
600
1200 km
30°
20°
LISIANSKI
LAYSAN
GARDNER PINNACLES
HAWAII (U.S.)
NECKER ISLAND
NIHOA
NIIHAU
KAUAI
OAHU
Honolulu
MOLOKAI
MAUI
Hilo
Mauna Kea 13,796 ft
HAWAII
JOHNSTON ATOLL (U.S.)
HAWAIIAN ISLANDS
NORTH PACIFIC OCEAN
10° N
PALMYRA (U.S.)
TERAINA
TABUAERAN
KIRITIMATI
0°
JARVIS ISLAND (U.S.)
LINE ISLANDS
KANTON ISLAND
Nabari
ENDERBURY ISLAND
KIRIBATI
ORONA ISLAND
MANRA ISLAND
MALDEN ISLAND
STARBUCK ISLAND
PHOENIX ISLANDS
TOKELAU (N.Z.)
ATAFU
Fakaofo
FAKAOFO
NUKUNONO
PENRHYN
PUKAPUKA (DANGER)
RAKAHANGA
MANIHIKI
VOSTOK ISLAND
CAROLINE ISLAND
FLINT ISLAND
EIAO
MARQUESAS ISLANDS
NUKU HIVA
UA HUKA
UA POU
HIVA OA
Atuona
FATU HIVA
10° S
SWAINS ISLAND
WESTERN SAMOA
AMERICAN SAMOA (U.S.)
SAVAI'I
Apia
TUTUILA
UPOLU
MANUA ISLANDS
Pago Pago
NASSAU
SUWARROW
COOK ISLANDS (N.Z.)
COOK ISLANDS
NIUATOPUTAPU
TONGA
VAVA'U GROUP
HA'APAI GROUP
TONGATAPU
Nuku'alofa
Alofi
NIUE (N.Z.)
PALMERSTON ATOLL
AITUTAKI
MANUAE
MITIARO
ATIU
MAUKE
Avarua
RAROTONGA
MANGAIA
POLYNESIA
TAKAROA
MANIHI
RANGIROA
APATAKI
Apataki
DISAPPOINTMENT ISLANDS
PUKA-PUKA
FANGATAU
TUAMOTU ARCHIPELAGO
Uturoa
MAKATEA
BORA-BORA
HUAHINE
FAKARAVA
RARAKA
RAIATEA
TETIAROA
MOOREA
Papeete
MAIAO
TAHITI
MEHETIA
ANAA
HIKUERU
AMANU
TATAKOTO
HAO
PUKARUA
REAO
SOCIETY ISLANDS
VAHITAHI
20°
HEREHERETUE
DUKE OF GLOUCESTER ISLANDS
TEMATANGI
TUREIA
MURUROA
MARUTEA
ÎLES MARIA
Moerai
RURUTU
RIMATARA
TUBUAI
MORANE
Rikitea
MANGAREVA
RAIVAVAE
AUSTRAL ISLANDS
OENO ISLAND
HENDERSON ISLAND
PITCAIRN (U.K.)
DUCIE ISLAND
Adamstown
PITCAIRN ISLAND
FRENCH POLYNESIA (FRANCE)
RAPA
Ahurei
MAROTIRI
BASS ISLANDS
SOUTH PACIFIC OCEAN
International Date Line
110°
100° W
30°
20°
SOUTH
Tropic of Capricorn
PACIFIC OCEAN
SALA Y GÓMEZ (CHILE)
EASTER ISLAND (RAPA NUI) (CHILE)
30°
40°
©1996, Encyclopædia Britannica, Inc.

within the basin of the Pahang River and tributaries; rice, rubber, tin; Kuantan most important port on E coast. From 16th cent. independent sultanate under Johor; entered into treaty agreements with British 1887; became member of the Federated Malay States 1895, part of independent Federation of Malaya after WWII; became a state of Malaysia 1963. See table at MALAYSIA.

Pahlavī, Bandar–e. See BANDAR-E ANZALI.

Pa·hoa \pä-'hō-ä\. Town, Hawaii co., Hawaii, E Hawaii I., inland from Cape Kumukahi; pop. (1990c) 1027.

Pa·ho·kee \pə-'hō-kē\. Town, Palm Beach co., SE Florida, on SE shore of Lake Okeechobee; pop. (1990c) 6822; incorp. 1922.

Pah·ran·a·gat Range \pə-'ra-nə-ˌgat\. Range in cen. Lincoln co., E Nevada.

Pah·rock Range *or* **Pah·roc Range** \pə-'räk\. Small range in N Lincoln co., E Nevada, extending NW into Nye co.

Pah·ute Mesa \'pä-yüt\ *or* **Pai·ute Mesa** \'pī-yüt\. Tableland in cen. Nye co., S Nevada, located in Nellis Air Force Base.

Pahute Peak. See BIG MOUNTAIN.

Pai. See BAI.

Pai–ch'eng. See BAICHENG.

Päi·jan·ne \'pā-ˌya-ne\. Lake, S Finland; 75 mi. (121 km.) long by 14 mi. (23 km.) wide; 411 sq. mi. (1064 sq. km.); max. depth 305 ft. (93 m.); drains S to Gulf of Finland.

Pai Khoi. See YUGORSKIY.

Pa·i·lo·lo \pī-'lō-lō\. Channel bet. Maui I. and Molokai I., Hawaii; 8 mi. (13 km.) wide.

Paim·pol \pe^{n}-'pȯl\. Village, Côtes-du-Nord dept., NW France, NNW of St.-Brieuc on the Gulf of St.-Malo; scene of novelist Pierre Loti's (Viaud's) *Pêcheur d'Islande* (1866).

Paine \'pān\. Peak, S Chile, E of Hanover I.; 8760 ft. (2670 m.).

Paines·ville \'pānz-ˌvil\. City, ⊗ of Lake co., NE Ohio, 27 mi. (43 km.) NE of Cleveland; pop. (1990c) 15,699; chemicals; nurseries; Lake Erie Coll. (1856).

Paine Towers. See TORRES DEL PAINE NATIONAL PARK.

Paint·ed Desert \'pān-təd\. Region, N cen. Arizona, E of the Little Colorado River; stretches ab. 150 mi. (240 km.) roughly from the Grand Canyon to Petrified Forest National Park; area ab. 7500 sq. mi. (19,425 sq. km.); erosion has exposed many-colored rock surfaces; a large part of it falls within Navajo and Hopi Indian reservations.

Paint Rock \'pānt\. Town, ⊗ of Concho co., W cen. Texas; pop. (1990c) 227.

Paints·ville \'pānts-ˌvil, -vəl\. City, ⊗ of Johnson co., E Kentucky, 28 mi. (45 km.) NNW of Pikeville; pop. (1990c) 4354; coal deposits.

Pai·sa·no Peak \pī-'sä-nō\. Mountain, NW Brewster co., W Texas; 6050 ft. (1844 m.).

Pais·ley \'pāz-lē\. **1.** Village, ⊗ of Bruce co., SE Ontario, Canada; pop. (1991c) 1102.
2. Burgh, Strathclyde region, SW Scotland, 7 mi. (11 km.) W of Glasgow; pop. (1981c) 84,593; center of thread manufacturing; produces chemicals, preserves, textiles, flour; formerly known for Paisley shawls. Developed around abbey founded 1163; industrial center (textiles) from early 18th cent.

País Vasco. See BASQUE COUNTRY.

Pa·ï·ta \pä-'ē-tä\. Village, New Caledonia I., French overseas territory of New Caledonia, SW Pacific Ocean, ab. 10 mi. (16 km.) NW of Nouméa; pop. (1989c) 6049.

Pai·ta \'pī-tä\. Seaport town, NW Peru, ab. 35 mi. (56 km.) NW of Piura; pop. (1981p) 20,016; harbor; shipping point for cotton and hides.

Paiute Mesa. See PAHUTE MESA.

Pa·ja·res Pass \pä-'hä-rās\. Mountain pass through the Cantabrian Mts., N Spain; 4524 ft. (1379 m.).

Pakanbaru. See PEKANBARU.

Pakaraima Mountains. See PACARAIMA MOUNTAINS.

Pak·chan \'päk-ˌchän, 'pau̇k-\. Wide river on Isthmus of Kra, extreme S of Myanmar; flows S into Andaman Sea, forming boundary bet. S Myanmar and Thailand; ab. 55 mi. (88 km.) long.

Pakhoi. See BEIHAI.

Pak·i·stan \'pa-ki-ˌstan, 'pä-ki-ˌstän, *chiefly Brit* ˌpä-ki-'stän\ *or officially* **Islamic Republic of Pakistan.** Republic, S Asia, bounded on W and N by Afghanistan, on NE by China, on E and SE by India, on S by the Arabian Sea, and on SW by Iran; 310,403 sq. mi. (803,944 sq. km.); pop. (1994e) 131,434,000; ✱ Islamabad; for physical features, see BALUCHISTAN 2, NORTH-WEST FRONTIER, PUNJAB, and SIND. Formerly consisted of two parts separated by ab. 1000 mi. (1600 km.) of Indian territory: (1) **West Pakistan,** described above, and (2) **East Pakistan,** now Bangladesh (*q.v.*).

Chief products: Wheat, cotton, sugarcane, rice, corn; coal, gypsum, natural gas; manufacturing: textiles, cement, fertilizer, chemicals.

Chief cities: Karachi, Lahor, Faisalabad, Rawalpindi, Hyderabad, Multan.

Political divisions: Divided into the following four provinces, the national ✱, and the federally administered tribal areas (for pronunciation of their names, see their individual entries):

NAME	AREA (sq. mi.)	AREA (sq. km.)	POP. (1983e)	CAPITAL
Islamabad	350	906	359,000	
federally administered tribal areas	10,509	27,218	2,329,000	
Provinces				
Baluchistan	133,107	344,747	4,611,000	Quetta
North-West Frontier	28,773	74,522	11,658,000	Peshawar
Punjab	79,542	206,014	50,460,000	Lahore
Sind	54,407	140,914	20,312,000	Karachi

History: For history prior to 1947, see BALUCHISTAN 2, INDIA 1, NORTH-WEST FRONTIER, PUNJAB, and SIND. Estab. 1947 by act of British parliament; military clashes with India over possession of Kashmir ongoing since independence 1947 (see JAMMU AND KASHMIR); became an Islamic republic 1956; concluded boundary agreement with China 1963; military clash with India (in Rann of Kachchh region) 1965; civil war and defeat in war with India following declaration of independence by East Pakistan (see BANGLADESH) 1971. Received many Afghan refugees as result of Soviet-Afghan War 1980s; elected first woman (Benazir Bhutto) head of modern Islamic state 1988; suffered severe flooding Sept. 1992.

Paknam. See SAMUT PRAKAN.

Pa·kok·ku \pä-'kȯ-kü\. Town, Magwe div., Myanmar, on right bank of Irrawaddy 75 mi. (121 km.) SW of Mandalay; pop. (1983c) 71,860; trade center.

Pakokku Hill Tracts. Former district in Burma, now included in Chin Hills, Myanmar.

Pak·xé *or* **Pak·se** \'päk-'sā\. Town, S Laos, on Mekong River; pop. (1985c) 47,232.

Pala Bianca. See WEISSKUGEL.

Pa·la·cios \pə-'la-shəz\. Town and resort, Matagorda co., SE Texas, on Matagorda Bay 25 mi. (40 km.) SW of Bay City; pop. (1990c) 4418.

Palacios, Los. See LOS PALACIOS.

Palaestina. See PALESTINE.

Pa·la·gru·ža Islands \ˌpä-lä-'grü-zhä\ *or Ital.* **Iso·le di Pe·la·go·sa** \'ē-zō-lā-dē-ˌpä-lä-'gō-sä\ *or angl.* **Pel·a·go·sa Islands** \ˌpe-lə-'gō-sə\. Group of islets belonging to Croatia, cen. Adriatic Sea, SW of Lastovo; before 1947 belonged to Italy.

Palakkad. See PALGHAT.

Pa·la·na \pä-'lä-nə\. Town, ✱ of Koryak Autonomous Okrug, NE Russia in Asia.

Pa·la·nan \pä-'lä-nän\. Municipality, NE Luzon, Philippines, near **Palanan Bay** on Pacific coast; pop. (1980c) 10,295; only important town on E coast of province, near mouth of Palanan River; connected with Ilagan, 37 mi. (60 km.) to the W, by rough mountain trails. Place where Gen. Emilio Aguinaldo maintained his headquarters of the Filipino revolutionary government 1900–01 and where he was captured by American Gen. Frederick Funston Mar. 1901.

Pa·lan·ga \pə-'läŋ-gə\ *or Ger.* **Po·lang·en** \pō-'läŋ-ən\. Seaport town, Lithuania, on Baltic Sea, NNW of Klaipėda.

Pa·lang·ka·ra·ya \pä-ˈläŋ-kä-ˈrä-jä\. Town, ✱ of Central Kalimantan prov., Borneo, Indonesia; pop. (1990c) 112,562.

Pa·lan·pur \ˈpä-lən-ˌpu̇r\. **1.** Former Indian state, now part of Gujarat state, NW India; 1794 sq. mi. (4646 sq. km.). **2.** Town, its ✱, 77 mi. (124 km.) N of Ahmadabad; pop. (1991p) 80,620.

Palantia. See PALENCIA 2.

Pa·la·oa Point \ˌpä-lä-ˈō-ä\. Southernmost point of Lanai I., Hawaii, on Kealaikahiki Channel.

Pa·la·pag \pä-ˈlä-päg\. Municipality and port, NE coast of Samar, Philippines, opp. Batag I.; munic. pop. (1980c) 23,115.

Pa·la·pye \pä-ˈlä-pyā\. Town, E Botswana, E of Serowe on a tributary of the Limpopo River and ab. 100 mi. (160 km.) S of Francistown; pop. (1991c) 17,362; a former ✱ of a subgroup of the Tswana people.

Pa·lar \pä-ˈlär\. River, SE India; rises in E Karnataka near Kolar, flows ESE into Bay of Bengal; 230 mi. (370 km.) long.

Pa·la·san \pä-ˈlä-sän\. Island in Polillo group off E Luzon, Philippines, bet. E coast of Polillo I. and Patnanongan I.; 6 sq. mi. (16 sq. km.).

Palāshi. See PLASSEY.

Pa·lat·i·nate \pə-ˈlat-ᵊn-ət\ *or Ger.* **Pfalz** \ˈpfälts\. Historical region, now part of Germany; once under the jurisdiction of the counts palatine, who in 14th cent. became electors of the Holy Roman Empire; in two parts: **Lower Palatinate** *or* **Rhine Palatinate,** on both sides of the Rhine in the area S of the Main River; and **Upper Palatinate** some distance to the east in E Bavaria around Amberg and Regensberg.

Pal·a·tine \ˈpa-lə-ˌtīn\. **1.** Village, Cook co., NE Illinois, ab. 15 mi. (25 km.) NW of Chicago; pop. (1990c) 39,253; residential; William Rainey Harper Coll. (1965). **2.** Formerly separate community, N West Virginia. See FAIRMONT 3. **3.** One of the Seven Hills of Rome, Italy. See SEVEN HILLS.

Pa·lat·ka \pə-ˈlat-kə\. City, ⊗ of Putnam co., NE Florida Penin., on St. Johns River 28 mi. (45 km.) SW of St. Augustine; pop. (1990c) 10,201; lumber; St. Johns River Community Coll. (1958).

Pa·lau \pə-ˈlau̇\ *or* **Be·lau** \bə-ˈlau̇\; *formerly usu.* **Pe·lew** \pə-ˈlü\. Republic, a group of ab. 100 islands and islets, generally considered a W part of the Caroline Is., W Pacific Ocean, 1060 mi. (1706 km.) SE of Manila and ab. the same distance SW of Saipan; 191 sq. mi. (495 sq. km.); pop. (1993e) 16,200; ✱ Koror; chief island Babelthuap; other islands Urukthapel, Peleliu, Angaur, Eli Malk, and Koror.

History: Under Spanish regime administered as part of the Caroline Is.; sold to Germany 1899; seized by Japan 1914; mandated to Japan 1919. In WWII taken by Allies 1944

\ə\ **abut** \ə̇\ matches \ᵊ\ kitten, Fr table \ər\ **further** \a\ **ash** \ā\ **ace** \ä\ cot, cart \á\ Fr bac \au̇\ **out** \b\ Span Avila \ch\ **chin** \e\ **bet** \ē\ **easy** \g\ **go** \i\ **hit** \ī\ **ice** \j\ **job** \k\ Ger **ich**, Buch \ⁿ\ Fr vin \ŋ\ **sing** \ō\ **go** \ȯ\ **all** \ȯ\ **law** \œ\ Fr **bœuf** \œ̄\ Fr **feu** \ȯi\ **boy** \th\ **thin** \t͟h\ **this** \ü\ **loot** \u̇\ **foot** \ue\ Ger **füllen** \u̅e\ Fr **rue** \y\ **yet** \ʸ\ Fr digne \ˈdēnʸ\, nuit \ˈnwʸē\ \yü\ **few** \yu̇\ **fury** \zh\ **vision**

(heaviest fighting on Peleliu); became part of U.S. Trust Terr. of the Pacific Islands 1947; constitution adopted 1980; became independent 1994, with U.S. responsible for foreign policy and defense.

Pa·la·ui \pä-ˈlä-wē\. Island off NE point of Luzon, Philippines; 10 sq. mi. (26 sq. km.); its N tip is Cape Engaño; lighthouse.

Pa·la·uig \pä-ˈlä-wig\. Municipality, W Luzon, Philippines, on coast at **Palauig Point,** 15°26′N, 119°53′E, 10 mi. (16 km.) N of Iba; pop. (1980c) 17,176.

Pa·la·wan \pä-ˈlä-wän\; *formerly* **Pa·ra·gua** \pä-ˈrä-gwä\. Island, SW Philippines; with adjacent islands (Calamian, Cuyo, and Cagayan groups and Linapacan I., Dumaran I., Balabac I., and Cagayan Sulu I.) constitutes a province, 5571 sq. mi. (14,429 sq. km.); ✻ Puerto Princesa. The province extends from Mindoro Strait SW to Balabac Strait, which separates it from N Borneo, and separates Sulu Sea from South China Sea. The island has a chain of mountains running nearly the entire length; highest Mt. Mantalingajan 6839 ft. (2085 m.); has lowland at N end and narrow plain along the coasts; chief products rice, corn, sweet potatoes, and coconuts; fishing. Forests provide valuable woods and island is rich in mineral resources. Inhabitants are Visayans in the N, Moros and Palawans in the S, and the Bataks and Tagbanuas in the interior. There are no large towns; the most important places include Puerto Princesa, Cuyo, Culion, and Coron. See table at PHILIPPINES.

History: Archaeological evidence suggests island has been long inhabited; native peoples converted to Islam in 15th cent.; when Spanish friars arrived early 17th cent. belonged to sultan of Borneo; Spain established garrisons in the N early 18th cent. and soon thereafter sultan ceded island to Spain. Spanish rule ended after Spanish-American War; U.S. troops occupied island and civil government estab. under name of Paragua 1902. Occupied by American forces in WWII.

Pa·la·yan \ˌpä-ˈlä-yän\. City, ✻ of Nueva Ecija prov., Luzon, Philippines; pop. (1980c) 14,959.

Pa·laz·zo·lo Acre·i·de \ˌpä-lät-ˈtsō-lō-ä-ˈkrā-ē-dā\. Commune, Siracusa prov., SE Sicily, Italy, 22 mi. (35 km.) W of seaport of Siracusa; pop. (1991p) 8973; site of ancient Acrae nearby.

Pal·dis·ki \ˈpäl-dē-skē\; *formerly* **Bal·tis·ki** \ˈbäl-tē-skē\ *or Eng.* **Bal·tic Port** \ˈbȯl-tik\. Seaport, NW Estonia, at S of entrance to Gulf of Finland 26 mi. (42 km.) W of Tallinn.

Pa·lem·bang \ˌpä-lem-ˈbäŋ\. **1.** Residency of the former Netherlands Indies, now part of the Indonesian prov. of South Sumatra; 33,333 sq. mi. (86,332 sq. km.); ✻ Palembang; was a sultanate prior to 1825.

2. City and river port, ✻ of South Sumatra prov., Indonesia, on both banks of the Musi River 56 mi. (90 km.) from its mouth; pop. (1990c) 1,141,036; port for seagoing vessels, exporting rubber and oil; fertilizer, textiles; oil refinery; university (c. 1960); 18th cent. mosque and several tombs of sultans. Was ✻ of a Buddhist kingdom beginning 7th cent. A.D.; Dutch established trading post 1617 and fort 1659; under intermittent British rule early 19th cent.; sultanate abolished by Dutch 1825; in WWII occupied by Japanese 1942–45.

Pa·len·cia \pä-ˈlen-thyä\. **1.** Province of N Spain. See table at SPAIN.

2. *anc.* **Pa·lan·tia** \pə-ˈlan-shə, -shē-ə\. City, its ✻, on Carrión River 28 mi. (45 km.) NE of Valladolid; pop. (1991p) 77,772; transportation center in region raising grain, flax, and sheep; produces woolen goods; 14th–16th cent. cathedral rich in works of art and two 13th cent. churches. Ancient Celtiberian settlement; occupied by Romans; later held by Goths and Moors; recaptured by Spanish in 10th cent.; seat of Castilian kings 12th–13th cents.; scene of Castilian soldier-hero Rodrigo Díaz de Vivar's (El Cid's) marriage to Jimena 1074; made episcopal see 11th cent.; site of first university in Spain, founded by Alfonso VIII c. 1208.

Pa·len·que \pä-ˈleŋ-kā\. Village in N Chiapas state, S Mexico; munic. pop. (1990p) 63,015; ruins of an ancient Mayan city nearby; among buildings archaeologically investigated is a temple with crypt (found 1952) of 7th cent. A.D. ruler.

Pa·ler·mo \pä-ˈler-mō\. **1.** Province of Sicily, Italy. See table at ITALY.

2. *anc.* **Pan·or·mus** *or* **Pan·hor·mus** \pa-ˈnȯr-məs\. Seaport, ✻ of Sicily, also ✻ of Palermo prov., on **Bay of Palermo** 265 mi. (426 km.) SE of Rome; pop. (1991p) 697,162; shipbuilding center; ships fruit, glass; tourism; 12th–15th cent. cathedral containing tombs of Roger II and the Holy Roman Emperor Frederick II; 12th cent. Arab-Norman churches; royal palace containing notable 12th cent. Palatine Chapel; baroque palaces; national museum and library; army base; university.

History: Founded by Phoenicians 8th cent. B.C.; passed to Carthaginians; taken by Romans 254 B.C. as a free town; ruled by Ostrogoths; part of Byzantine Empire; prospered under Arabs 832–1071; taken 1072 by Roger the Norman (who assumed countship as Roger I) and reached greatest prosperity as ✻ of Norman kingdom of Sicily; revolted against French and abuses of Charles of Anjou 1282 (the famous Sicilian Vespers), passing to Aragon, Savoy, and later to the Bourbon house of Naples; revolt against Bourbon rule 1848; liberated by Italian patriot Giuseppe Garibaldi 1860 and made part of the kingdom of Italy 1861; heavily bombed during WWII and captured by Allied forces 1943.

Pal·es·tine. **1.** \ˈpa-lə-ˌstīn\ *or Lat.* **Pal·aes·ti·na** \ˌpa-lə-ˈstē-nə, -ˈstī-\; *bib.* **Ca·naan** \ˈkā-nən\. Region, SW Asia, at E end of Mediterranean Sea; approx. coextensive with Israel and that part of Jordan lying W of the Jordan River; 10,160 sq. mi. (26,314 sq. km.).The Holy Land (*Zech.* ii. 12) of the Jewish, Christian, and Islamic religions. Ancient Palestine was somewhat larger and included Bashan and Gilead E of the Jordan.

History: From very early times, Palestine influenced by invasion from S (Egypt) and from N and E (Amorites); Canaanite culture estab. by time of arrival of Hyksos 17th cent. B.C.; conquered by Egypt 16th–15th cents. B.C. (see MEGIDDO); invaded by Philistines who established kingdom on coast and by Hebrews (Israelites) c. 12th cent. B.C.; for Hebrew kingdoms of Palestine, see ISRAEL 1, JUDAH, and JERUSALEM 3; from 8th cent. B.C., Palestine became successively part of Assyrian, Chaldean, and Persian empires; under Alexander the Great and his successors the Ptolemies and Seleucids from 4th cent. B.C.; conquered by Roman Gen. Pompey the Great c. 64 B.C.; part of Roman prov. of Syria during lifetime of Jesus; conquered by Arabs 7th cent. and except for Crusaders' Kingdom of Jerusalem in 12th cent. was subsequently ruled by various Muslim dynasties; under Ottoman Empire 1516–1917; conquered by British under Gen. Edmund Allenby 1917; assigned as British mandate (1920) which became effective 1923; as result of Balfour Declaration 1917, expressing British support for establishment of national home for Jews in Palestine, received many Jewish immigrants; with reversal of British policy 1939 and increase in number of Jewish immigrants in years immediately before and after WWII, became scene of increasing conflicts bet. Jews and Arabs and opposition of Jews to British control; 1947 UN proposal for partition into Arab state and Jewish state of Israel followed by fighting bet. Arab and Israeli forces 1948–49; boundaries of Israel determined and remaining lands divided bet. Jordan and Egypt 1949; after Arab-Israeli War of 1967 entire territory of former mandate under Israeli administration. Eruptions of violence bet. Palestine Liberation Organization, formed 1964, and Israel continued despite international mediation attempts; peace accord providing for Israeli withdrawal from Gaza Strip and Jericho and limited Palestinian self-rule in West Bank signed by Israel and PLO 1993.

2. \ˈpa-lə-ˌstēn\. City, ⊗ of Anderson co., E Texas, 82 mi. (132 km.) E of Waco; pop. (1990c) 18,042.

Pa·les·tri·na \ˌpä-le-ˈstrē-nä\; *anc.* **Prae·nes·te** \prē-ˈnes-tē\. Commune, Roma prov., Lazio, cen. Italy, 20 mi. (32 km.) ESE of Rome; pop. (1981p) 13,295; a very ancient city, founded before 8th cent. B.C.; allied with Rome before becoming part of Roman Empire; destroyed by Roman Gen. Sulla's forces 82 B.C.; rebuilt and became famous for oracle

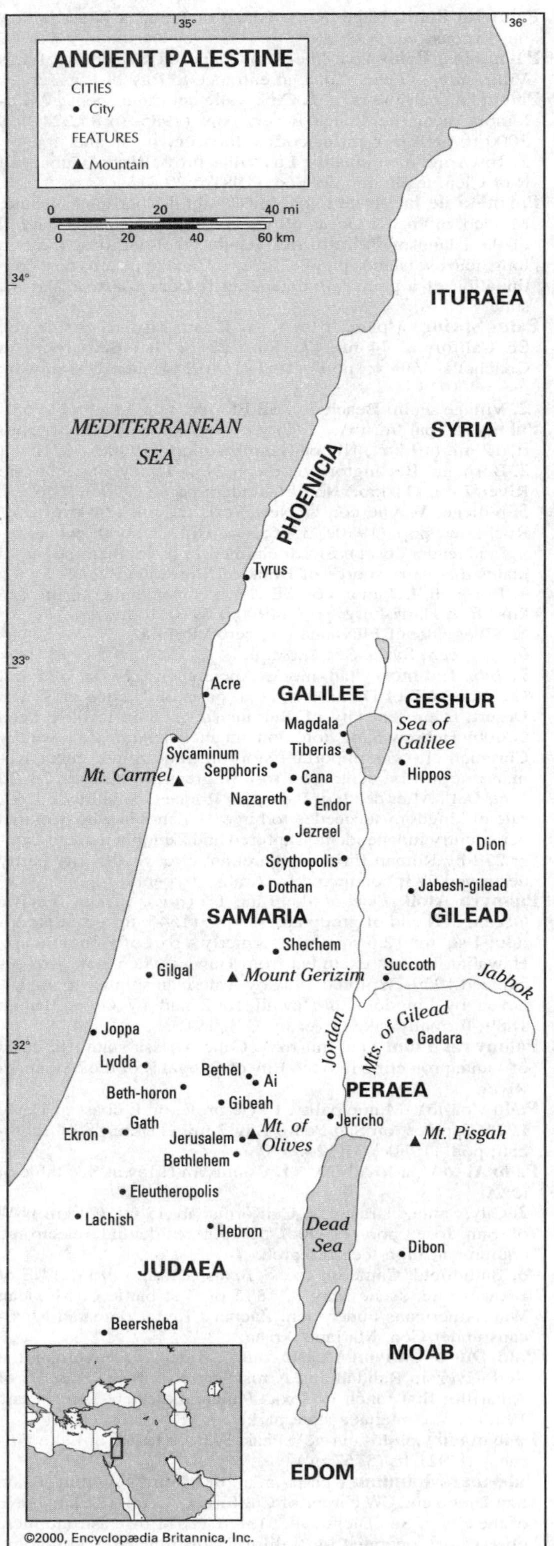

of goddess Fortuna and as a summer resort for wealthy Romans. Modern town birthplace of composer Giovanni Pierluigi da Palestrina c. 1525.

Pa·let·wa \pə-ˈlet-wä\. Town, W Myanmar, on the Kaladan River 85 mi. (137 km.) N of Sittwe.

Pal·ghat \ˈpäl-ˌgät\ *or* **Pal·ak·kad** \ˈpä-lə-kəd\ *also* **Pul·i·cat** \ˈpə-li-kət\. Town, cen. Kerala, S India, on Ponnani River 112 mi. (180 km.) WNW of Madurai; pop. (1991p) 122,964; trade center; Government Victoria Coll.

Palghat Gap. Pass through the Western Ghats, S India, S of the Nilgiri Hills; 20 mi. (32 km.) wide.

Pal·grave Point \ˈpal-grāv, ˈpȯl-\. Cape on coast of Namibia.

Pali, Nuuanu. See NUUANU PALI.

Pa·li·kir \ˌpä-lē-ˈkir\. Locality, ✻ of Federated States of Micronesia, on Pohnpei.

Pa–li–k'un. See BARKOL.

Palimé. See KPALIMÉ.

Pa·li·nu·ro \ˌpä-lē-ˈnü-rō\; *anc.* **Pal·i·nu·rus** \ˌpa-lə-ˈnu̇r-əs, -ˈnyu̇r-\. Cape on W coast of Italy, 40°02′N, 15°16′E.

Pa–lin–yu–ch'i. See BAIRIN YOUQI.

Pal·i·sade, Middle \ˌpa-lə-ˈsād\. Peak in the Sierra Nevada, in E Fresno co., S cen. California; 14,040 ft. (4279 m.).

Palisade, North. Peak in the Sierra Nevada, in E Fresno co., S cen. California, on NE edge of Kings Canyon National Park; 14,242 ft. (4341 m.).

Pal·i·sades \ˌpa-lə-ˈsādz\. A line of high cliffs of traprock on W bank of Hudson River in SE New York and NE New Jersey; ab. 15 mi. (24 km.) long.

Palisades Interstate Park. A chain of parks in New Jersey and New York extending from Fort Lee, New Jersey, opp. New York City, to Newburgh, New York, and incl. Bear Mt.; total area ab. 70 sq. mi. (181 sq. km.); river frontage 22 mi. (35 km.), incl. 13 mi. (21 km.) of the Palisades.

Palisades Park. Residential borough, Bergen co., NE corner of New Jersey, 9 mi. (14 km.) N of Jersey City; pop. (1990c) 14,536; site of former notable amusement park.

Pa·li·ta·na \ˌpä-lə-ˈtä-nə\. **1.** Former Indian state, SE Kathiawar Penin., now part of Gujarat state, W India; 300 sq. mi. (777 sq. km.).

2. Town, its ✻, 70 mi. (113 km.) WNW of Surat. Nearby is sacred hill of **Sa·trun·ja·ya** \sə-ˈtru̇n-jə-yə\ covered with Jain temples.

Palk Bay \ˈpȯk, ˈpȯlk\. Bay on extreme NW coast of Sri Lanka.

Palk Strait. Channel bet. N Sri Lanka and SE India, N of Adam's Bridge; 40 mi. (64 km.) wide.

Pal La·ha·ra \ˌpäl-lə-ˈhär-ə\. Former Indian state, now part of Orissa state, NE India, ab. 80 mi. (129 km.) NW of Cuttack; 450 sq. mi. (1166 sq. km.); ✻ Pal Lahara.

Pal·las \ˈpa-ləs\. Hamlet in co. Longford, N cen. Ireland, E of Lough Ree; possibly birthplace of author Oliver Goldsmith 1730.

Pal·las–Ou·nas·tun·tu·ri National Park \ˈpäl-les-ˈō-näs-ˌtün-tü-rē\. National park, NW Finland; 193 sq. mi. (500 sq. km.); arctic region; estab. 1938.

Pallene. See KASSÁNDRA.

Pallice, La. See LA PALLICE.

Pal·li·ser, Cape \ˈpa-lə-sər\. Cape on S extremity of North I., New Zealand, at the E entrance to Cook Strait.

Palliser Bay. Bay on S coast of North I., New Zealand, an inlet of Cook Strait W of Cape Palliser.

Palliser Islands. Former name of the W islands of the Tuamotu Archipelago (*q.v.*).

Pal·ma \ˈpäl-mä\ *or in full* **Palma de Mal·lor·ca** \t͟hā-mä-ˈyȯr-kä, mäl-\. Commune, ✻ of Baleares autonomous community and prov., Spain, and ✻ of Majorca I., on **Bay of Palma;** pop. (1991p) 296,754; chief port of Balearic Is.; trades in agricultural produce, wine; manufactures textiles, footwear, basketwork, embroidery; tourism; Gothic cathedral; Moorish palace (the Almudaina); 14th cent. castle; 16th cent. town hall; residence of Majorcan kings; birthplace and burial place of 13th–14th cent. Catalan mystic and poet Ramon Llull. Captured from Moors by James I of Aragon 1229.

Palma, La. See LA PALMA.

Palma di Mon·te·chia·ro \ˈpäl-mä-dē-ˈmòn-tā-ˈkyä-rō\. Commune, Agrigento prov., SW Sicily, Italy, near Mediterranean Sea 14 mi. (23 km.) SE of the commune of Agrigento; pop. (1989c) 25,159.

Palmas. **1.** Town, ✻ of Tocantins state, cen. Brazil.
2. Island, Malay Archipelago. See MIANGAS.

Pal·mas, Cape \ˈpäl-məs\. Cape, S tip of Liberia; extends into Atlantic Ocean.

Palmas, Golfo di. Gulf on SW coast of the island of Sardinia, Italy.

Pal·mas, Las \läs-ˈpäl-mäs\. **1.** Province of Spain, in Canary Is. See table at SPAIN.
2. City, Grand Canary I., Spain. See LAS PALMAS 2.

Palmas Al·tas \ˈpäl-mäs-ˈäl-täs\. Cape on N coast of Puerto Rico.

Palma So·ria·no \ˈpäl-mä-sōr-ˈyä-nō\. Municipality, E Cuba, 18 mi. (29 km.) NW of Santiago de Cuba; pop. (1990e) 77,677.

Palm Bay \ˈpäm, ˈpälm\. Town, Brevard co., E Florida, on Indian River Inlet 24 mi. (39 km.) SSE of Cocoa; pop. (1990c) 62,632; pop. tripled in 1980s.

Palm Beach. **1.** Coastal county in SE Florida. See table at FLORIDA.
2. Resort town, Palm Beach co., SE Florida, at N end of island separating Lake Worth (lagoon) from the Atlantic; pop. (1990c) 9814; incorp. 1911.

Palm Beach Gardens. City, Palm Beach co., SE Florida; pop. (1990c) 22,965.

Palm·dale \ˈpäm-ˌdāl\. City, Los Angeles co., SW California, NE of the city of Los Angeles; pop. (1990c) 68,946; 1990 pop. is more than five times that of 1980.

Palm Desert \ˈpäm, ˈpälm\. City, Riverside co., S California, 60 mi. (96 km.) SE of San Bernardino; pop. (1990c) 23,252.

Pal·mei·ra das Mis·sões \pȧl-ˈmā-rə-däs-mē-ˈsȯⁿs\. Municipality, Rio Grande do Sul state, S Brazil, 190 mi. (306 km.) NW of Pôrto Alegre; pop. (1991p) 52,946.

Pal·mei·ri·nhas, Ponta das \ˌpäl-mə-ˈrē-nyəsh\. Cape, Angola, on NW coast S of Luanda.

Palm·er \ˈpä-mər, ˈpäl-\. **1.** City, SE Alaska, 6 mi. (10 km.) NE of Matanuska in the Matanuska Valley; pop. (1990c) 2866; an important agricultural area.
2. Town, Hampden co., SW Massachusetts, ENE of Springfield; pop. (1990c) 12,054.

Palmer Archipelago; *formerly* **Antarctic Archipelago.** Island group in the South Atlantic Ocean bet. South America and Antarctica, 53°W to 78°W, NW of Weddell Sea; includes Anvers I., Brabant I., and other small islands off NW coast of Antarctic Penin.; part of British Antarctic Terr.

Palmer Land. Part of the Antarctic Penin., British Antarctic Terr.; constitutes the broad S half of the peninsula; thought to contain mineral deposits.

Palmer Peninsula. See ANTARCTIC PENINSULA.

Palmerston. See DARWIN.

Pal·mer·ston \ˈpä-mər-stən, ˈpäl-\ *or* **Ava·rau** \ˌä-vä-ˈrau̇\. Island (atoll) in cen. Pacific Ocean 270 mi. (434 km.) NW of Rarotonga in the Cook Is.; 1 sq. mi. (3 sq. km.); pop. (1986c) 66; administered by New Zealand.

Palmerston, Cape. Headland, Queensland, NE Australia, SE of Mackay, 21°32′S, 149°29′E.

Palmerston North. City, S North I., New Zealand, 80 mi. (129 km.) NE of Wellington; pop. (1991c) 70,318; textiles, electrical equipment, pharmaceuticals; in dairy-farming region; Massey Univ. (c. 1964).

Palm·er·ton \ˈpä-mər-tən, ˈpäl-\. Borough, Carbon co., E Pennsylvania, on Lehigh River 17 mi. (27 km.) NNW of Allentown; pop. (1990c) 5394.

Pal·met·to \pal-ˈme-tō\. City, Manatee co., W Florida Penin., at lower end of Tampa Bay; pop. (1990c) 9268.

Palmetto Point. Cape on the island of Jamaica, West Indies, on NE coast.

Pal·mil·las, Point \päl-ˈmē-yäs\. Cape on SW coast of Las Villas prov., W cen. Cuba, at entrance to Bay of Pigs.

Pal·mi·ra \päl-ˈmē-rä\. **1.** City, Valle del Cauca dept., W Colombia, near the Cauca River; pop. (1985c) 185,224; alt. 3000 ft. (914 m.); raises coffee, tobacco, sugarcane.
2. Town and municipality, Las Villas prov., W cen. Cuba, just N of Cienfuegos; munic. pop. (1981p) 29,815.

Pal·mi·ta de la Vir·gen \päl-ˈmē-tä-ˌthā-lä-ˈbēr-hān\. Island, Mexico, in Pacific Ocean off the coast of SW Sinaloa state, N of the island of **Palmito del Ver·de** \thel-ˈver-dā\; the two long, narrow islands parallel the coast and appear to be a continuation of a peninsula extending N from coast of Nayarit state.

Palm Springs \ˈpäm, ˈpälm\. **1.** Resort city, Riverside co., SE California, 44 mi. (71 km.) SE of San Bernardino in Coachella Valley; pop. (1990c) 40,144; aerial tramway; incorp. 1938.
2. Village, Palm Beach co., SE Florida; pop. (1990c) 9763.

Pal·my·ra \pal-ˈmī-rə\. **1.** City, ⊗ of Marion co., NE Missouri, 12 mi. (19 km.) NW of Hannibal; pop. (1990c) 3371.
2. Borough, Burlington co., S cen. New Jersey, on Delaware River 7 mi. (11 km.) NE of Camden; pop. (1990c) 7056.
3. Village, Wayne co., W New York, 21 mi. (34 km.) E of Rochester; pop. (1990c) 3566; near Hill Cumorah, where religious leader Joseph Smith claimed to have unearthed gold plates that were source of Book of Mormon (1827).
4. Borough, Lebanon co., SE cen. Pennsylvania, 16 mi. (26 km.) E of Harrisburg; pop. (1990c) 6910; footwear.
5. Village, ⊗ of Fluvanna co., cen. Virginia.
6. City, cen. Syria. See TADMUR.
7. *bib.* **Tad·mor** \ˈtad-ˌmȯr\. Ancient city, Syria, 135 mi. (217 km.) NE of Damascus, at an oasis on N edge of Syrian Desert, at present city of Tadmur (*q.v.*). Said to have been built by Hebrew King Solomon; an ancient Aramaic town; by Christian era was important stop on trade route; under Roman rule in first cent. A.D.; rose to great prominence 2d–3d cents. A.D. After death of Palmyran Prince Odenathus, c. 267, rule of kingdom succeeded to his wife Zenobia who declared her country independent. Captured and Zenobia made prisoner 272 by Roman Emperor Aurelian; after revolt, city partly destroyed 273; conquered by Arabs 7th cent.

Palmyra Atoll. One of the Line Is. (*q.v.*), in cen. Pacific Ocean; at N end of group ab. 960 mi. (1545 km.) S of Honolulu; 1 sq. mi. (2.6 sq. km.); formerly a part of Honolulu co., Hawaiian Is., but excluded from Hawaii when state was organized 1959. Explored 1802 by American ship *Palmyra;* annexed by kingdom of Hawaii 1862 and by Great Britain 1889; formally taken over by U.S. 1912.

Pal·my·ras Point \pal-ˈmī-rəz\. Cape, Orissa state, NE coast of India, projecting into the Bay of Bengal N of the Mahanadi River.

Pa·lo \ˈpä-lō\. Municipality, Leyte prov., on E coast of Leyte I., Philippines, on San Pedro Bay 7 mi. (11 km.) S of Tacloban; pop. (1980c) 31,124.

Pa·lo Al·to \ˈpa-lō-ˈal-tō\. **1.** County in N Iowa. See table at IOWA.
2. City, Santa Clara co., W California, ab. 13 mi. (21 km.) NW of San Jose; pop. (1990c) 55,900; residential; electronic equipment; high-tech research.
3. Battlefield, Cameron co., S Texas, 12 mi. (19 km.) NE of Brownsville; scene May 8, 1846 of first battle of Mexican War; Americans under Gen. Zachary Taylor defeated Mexicans under Gen. Mariano Arista.

Palo Du·ro Canyon \ˈpa-lō-ˈdu̇r-ō, ˈdȯr-ə\. Canyon of the Red River, in Randall and Armstrong cos., NW Texas, SE of Amarillo; first ranch in Texas Panhandle estab. here in late 19th cent.; contains a state park.

Pa·lo·ma·ni \ˌpä-lō-ˈmä-nē\. Peak, W Bolivia, NE of Lake Titicaca; 18,921 ft. (5767 m.).

Pal·o·mar Mountain \ˈpa-lə-ˌmär\ *or* **Mount Palomar.** Peak, San Diego co., SW corner of California, 45 mi. (72 km.) NNE of the city of San Diego; ab. 6138 ft. (1871 m.); astronomical observatory operated by California Institute of Technology;

instruments include the giant 200-inch (5-meter) Hale telescope.

Pa·lo·mas Mountains \pə-'lō-məs\. Small range in E Yuma co., SW Arizona.

Pa·lom·pon \ˌpä-lȯm-'pȯn\. Municipality, Leyte prov., on NW coast of Leyte I., Philippines, 15 mi. (24 km.) W of Ormoc; scene of one of final operations of Leyte campaign against Japanese late Dec. 1944.

Palo Pin·to \'pa-lō-'pin-tō, 'pā-\. **1.** County in N cen. Texas. See table at TEXAS.

2. Village, its ⊗; deposits of petrified wood nearby.

Pa·lo·po \pä-'lō-pō\. Seaport, Sulawesi, Indonesia, on NW shore of Gulf of Bone.

Pa·los \'pä-lōs\ *or officially* **Palos de la Fron·te·ra** \ˌthā-lä-frȯn-'tā-rä\. Former seaport, Huelva prov., SW Spain, on Rió Tinto; pop. (1991c) 6750; explorer Christopher Columbus sailed from here Aug. 3, 1492; harbor now silted up.

Palos, Cape of. Cape, Spain, on SE coast E of Cartagena.

Pa·los Heights \'pā-ləs\. City, Cook co., NE Illinois, ab. 4 mi. (6 km.) WSW of Chicago; pop. (1990c) 11,478; Trinity Christian Coll. (1959).

Palos Hills. City, Cook co., NE Illinois, ab. 5 mi. (8 km.) W of Chicago; pop. (1990c) 17,803; Moraine Valley Community Coll. (1967).

Palos Park. Village, Cook co., NE Illinois, ab. 5 mi. (8 km.) WSW of Chicago; pop. (1990c) 4199.

Pa·los Ver·des Estates \'pa-ləs-'vər-dēz\. City, Los Angeles co., SW California, S of the city of Los Angeles; pop. (1990c) 13,512; residential.

Pa·louse *or* **Pe·louse** \pə-'lüs\. **1.** River, NW Idaho and SE Washington; rises in Latah co., NW Idaho, flows W across Washington border, turns S and empties into Snake River on E border of Franklin co.; ab. 140 mi. (225 km.) long.

2. *or* **Palouse Hills.** Fertile hilly region, SE Washington and NW Idaho, N of Snake and Clearwater rivers; wheat growing.

Palpana, Cerro. See CERRO PALPANA.

Palti, Lake. See YAMZHO YUMCO.

Pa·lu \'pä-lü\. Town, ✻ of Central Sulawesi prov., Sulawesi, Indonesia; pop. (1980c) 99,530.

Pa·lu·an Bay \pä-'lü-än\. Inlet of South China Sea in NW coast of Mindoro, Philippines; Americans secured anchorage here and seized town of **Paluan** Jan. 8, 1945 in WWII.

Pa·lus \'pā-ləs\. Latin, "lowland seasonally covered with water," "shallow sea," as in: (1) **Palus Maeotis.** See AZOV, SEA OF. (2) **Palus Tattaeus.** Tuz Lake (*q.v.*) in Turkey. (3) **Palus Labeatis.** See SCUTARI, LAKE. (4) **Palus Tritonis.** See DJERID, CHOTT. (5) **Palus Acherusia.** See FUSARO.

Pal·wal \'pəl-wəl\. Town, Haryana, NW India, ab. 35 mi. (55 km.) S of Delhi; a place of great antiquity, of importance in Indo-Aryan traditions, esp. in the Pandava kingdom.

Pam·ban Channel \'päm-bən\. Shallow channel in Bay of Bengal off S Indian coast separating Rameswaram I. from the mainland and connecting the Gulf of Mannar with Palk Strait.

Pa·me·ka·san \ˌpä-mā-kä-'sän\. Town, S Madura I., Indonesia, ab. 55 mi. (88 km.) E of Surabaya.

Pa·miers \pä-'myā\. Commune, Ariège dept., S France, on Ariège River 10 mi. (16 km.) N of Foix.

Pa·mirs \pə-'mirz\ *also* **Pa·mir** \-'mir\. High-altitude region of cen. Asia, mostly in Tajikistan, partly on borders of Xinjiang Uygur, China, Jammu and Kashmir, India, and Afghanistan. Many peaks above 20,000 ft. (6100 m.); highest in Tajikistan and formerly highest in U.S.S.R., Communism Peak 24,590 ft. (7495 m.); highest in China Kongur 25,325 ft. (7719 m.); many glaciers. Central mountain knot from which extend great ranges: Tian Shan to N, Kunlun Shan and Karakoram to E, and Hindu Kush to W.

Pam·li·co \'pam-li-ˌkō\. **1.** River bisecting Beaufort co., E North Carolina; actually the estuary of the Tar River (*q.v.*); at its head is Washington, the ⊗.

2. Coastal county in E North Carolina. See table at NORTH CAROLINA.

Pamlico Sound. Passage of the Atlantic Ocean bet. E North Carolina mainland and islands off the coast; 80 mi. (129 km.) long and 8 to 30 mi. (13 to 48 km.) wide; receives the Pamlico River on the W, and the Neuse River on the SW.

Pam·pa \'pam-pə\. City, ⊗ of Gray co., NW Texas, in the Panhandle 52 mi. (84 km.) ENE of Amarillo; pop. (1990c) 19,959; carbon black, chemicals, clothing; oil and gas deposits; livestock and grain farms.

Pampa, La. See LA PAMPA.

Pam·pan·ga \päm-'päŋ-gä\. **1.** *or* **Rio Gran·de de Pampanga** \'rē-ō-'grän-dā-ˌthā-\. River, cen. Luzon, Philippines; rises in Caraballo Mts. on N border of Nueva Ecija prov., flows S into Pampanga and enters N Manila Bay in a wide swampy delta in Pampanga and Bulacan provs.; 120 mi. (193 km.) long. Navigable for smaller vessels. Has many tributaries in fertile plain; main branch is the Chico.

2. Province, cen. Luzon, Philippines; ✻ San Fernando. Lies in S part of cen. Luzon, plain watered by lower Pampanga River and tributaries. Mountains on the W boundary are part of the Zambales Range; on the border is Pinatubo which erupted in 1991–92; in the NE is isolated volcanic peak of Mt. Arayat 3867 ft. (1179 m.), but province as a whole is level. Chief occupation agriculture; fishing also important. Entire E part is covered by Candaba swamp and the delta of the Pampanga is an extensive mangrove swamp; many streams afford easy transportation. Largest city Angeles. See table at PHILIPPINES.

History: In pre-Spanish times home of Pampangans, who had many prosperous settlements; overcome by Spanish explorer Miguel de Legazpi and his followers c. 1571; civil government estab. by U.S. Feb. 1901; relinquished by Americans to Japanese Dec. 1941, but recovered Jan.–Feb. 1945.

Pampanga Chico. See CHICO 4.

Pam·pas \'pam-pəz, -pəs\. Plains of South America extending for nearly 1000 mi. (1600 km.) from the lower Paraná River to S cen. Argentina, SSW of Buenos Aires; area in Argentina ab. 294,000 sq. mi. (761,460 sq. km.); dry in W, well watered in E; livestock raising.

Pam·pas del Sa·cra·men·to \'päm-päs-thel-ˌsä-krä-'men-tō\. Plains in NE Peru, chiefly in S Loreto region.

Pampeluna. See PAMPLONA 2.

Pam·phyl·ia \pam-'fi-lē-ə, -'fil-yə\. Ancient region and Roman province in S Asia Minor, a narrow territory on the coast S of Pisidia and bet. Lycia and Cilicia; chief settlements Perga, Aspendus, Side. Subject in turn to all the empires that controlled Asia Minor; came under Roman rule c. 2d cent. B.C. and then included Pisidia; united with Lycia (*q.v.*) first cent. A.D. to form a Roman province.

Pam·plo·na \päm-'plō-nä\. **1.** City, Norte de Santander dept., N Colombia, ab. 40 mi. (64 km.) NE of Bucaramanga; pop. (1985c) 35,058.

2. *formerly* **Pam·pe·lu·na** \ˌpäm-pā-'lü-nä\; *anc.* **Pom·pae·lo** \päm-'pē-lō\. City, ✻ of Navarra autonomous community and prov., N Spain, 196 mi. (315 km.) NNE of Madrid; pop. (1991p) 179,251; center of agricultural region; manufactures kitchenware, paper, chemicals, rope, pottery, wineskins; distilling, flour milling; university (1952); 14th–15th cent. cathedral; July festival honoring St. Fermin, when bulls run through the city streets, described by American writer Ernest Hemingway in his novel *The Sun Also Rises.* Ancient Basque city; believed to have been built by Roman Gen. Pompey the Great 75 B.C.; taken by Visigoths, Franks, Moors 5th cent. A.D.; captured from Moors by Frankish King (later Holy Roman Emperor) Charlemagne 778; became ✻ of kingdom of Navarre; on union of Navarre and Castile, made viceroyalty 1515; fortified by Spanish King Philip II 1571; captured by French 1808 during Peninsular War and retaken by British under Arthur Wellesley (later duke of Wellington) 1813.

Pa·mun·key \pə-'məŋ-kē\. River, E Virginia; formed by confluence of North Anna and South Anna rivers in NE Hanover co., flows SE and unites with Mattaponi River at West Point to form York River; ab. 80 mi. (130 km.) long.

Pa·na \ˈpā-nə\. City, Christian co., cen. Illinois, 30 mi. (48 km.) S of Decatur; pop. (1990c) 7081.

Pa·na·bo \pä-ˈnä-bō\. Municipality, Davao del Norte prov., Mindanao, Philippines, ab. 15 mi. (24 km.) NNE of Davao; pop. (1980c) 71,098.

Pa·na·du·ra \ˌpə-nə-ˈdu̇r-ə\. Seaport, W Sri Lanka, on Indian Ocean 16 mi. (26 km.) S of Colombo.

Pa·nai·tan \pə-ˈnīt-ən\ *or Du.* **Prin·sen** \ˈprin-sən\. Island, Indonesia, at S end of Sunda Strait off the SW tip of Java; 47 sq. mi. (122 sq. km.).

Pa·na·ji \pä-ˈnä-jē\ *also* **Pan·gim** *or* **Pan·jim** \ˈpän-ˈzhim\ *or* **New Goa** \ˈgō-ə\. Town and seaport, ✻ of the Indian state of Goa, W India, on Arabian Sea at mouth of Mandavi River; pop. (1991p) 42,915; ✻ of former union terr. of Goa, Daman, and Diu. Replaced Old Goa as residence of the Portuguese viceroy 1759 and as ✻ of Portuguese India 1843.

Pan·a·ma \ˈpa-nə-ˌmä, -ˌmȯ\ *or Span.* **Pa·na·má** \ˌpä-nä-ˈmä\. **1.** *or officially* **Re·pú·bli·ca de Panamá** \rā-ˈpü-blē-kä-t͟hā-\. Republic, S Central America, occupying the Isthmus of Panama (*q.v.*); bounded on N by the Caribbean Sea, on E by Colombia, on S by the Pacific Ocean, and on W by Costa Rica; 33,659 sq. mi. or 87,177 sq. km. (incl. 4451 sq. mi. or 11,528 sq. km. of water); pop. (1993e) 2,563,000; ✻ Panama.

Physical features: Has coastline of ab. 760 mi. (1225 km.) on Pacific side and 470 mi. (760 km.) on the Atlantic; traversed by two parallel ranges with valleys and plains in between; highest point is in W, near Costa Rica boundary: Chiriquí volcano 11,400 ft. (3475 m.); in cen. part and in the E (Serranía del Darién) av. height is ab. 3000 ft. (900 m.). Most important rivers the Chagres, Chepo, Tuira, and only large lake is Gatun in the former Canal Zone (*q.v.*). Pacific coast indented by large Gulf of Panama containing several islands (incl. Pearl Is.); on W side is Azuero Penin., and W of that is island of Coiba; on N coast are Mosquito Gulf and the Gulf of San Blas. Has fertile soil and well-forested mountain slopes.

Chief products: Bananas, timber, corn, rice, fish, shrimp, sugar, coffee; manufacturing: apparel, cement; food processing.

Political divisions: Divided into the following nine provinces and one special territory (for pronunciation of their names, see their individual entries):

NAME	AREA[1] (sq. mi.)	AREA[1] (sq. km.)	POP. (1990c)	CAPITAL
Provinces				
Bocas del Toro	3,443	8,917	92,731	Bocas del Toro
Chiriquí	3,381	8,757	368,023	David
Coclé	1,944	5,035	172,165	Penonomé
Colón	2,882	7,464	167,873	Colón
Darién	6,488	16,804	43,032	La Palma
Herrera	937	2,427	93,360	Chitré
Los Santos	1,493	3,867	76,604	Las Tablas
Panama	4,360	11,292	1,064,221	Panama
Veraguas	4,280	11,085	202,904	Santiago
Special Territory				
Comarca de San Blas	910	2,357	34,134	El Porvenir

[1]Area = land area.

History: Inhabited by American Indian groups when explorer Christopher Columbus arrived 1502; Spanish explorer Vasco Nuñez de Balboa established first successful colony at Darién 1510 and discovered Pacific Ocean 1513; city of Panama founded 1519; Portobelo the Atlantic port for important Spanish trade across the isthmus; in viceroyalty of Peru before 18th cent.; in viceroyalty of New Granada, later part of Colombia (*q.v.*); in early 20th cent., projects for a canal across Panama were the subject of negotiations with U.S.; in 1903, Panama revolted from Colombia and was recognized by U.S. to whom it ceded Canal Zone; rejected (1970) the unratified Panama-U.S. treaty of 1967 dealing with the future status of the Canal Zone; Canal Zone returned to Panama 1979; invasion of Panama by U.S. troops 1989 to overthrow de facto ruler Gen. Manuel Noriega.

2. Province of E cen. Panama. See table at PANAMA.

3. *or* **Panama City.** City, ✻ of the Republic of Panama and of Panama prov.; pop. (1990p) 411,549; commercial and transportation center of the republic; Univ. of Panama (1935), Santa Maria Univ. (1965). Old city founded 1519 and completely destroyed by British buccaneer Henry Morgan 1671; soon rebuilt on present site ab. 7 mi. (11 km.) W; center of revolt against Colombia 1903 and made ✻ the same year.

Panama, Gulf of *or Span.* **Gol·fo de Pa·na·má** \ˈgȯl-fō-ˌt͟hā-ˌpä-nä-ˈmä\. Large inlet of Pacific Ocean on S coast of Panama; the inner part (N of the Pearl Is.) on which the city of Panama is located is called the **Bay of Panama** *or Span.* **Ba·hía de Panamá** \bä-ˈē-ä-ˌt͟hā-ˌpä-nä-ˈmä\.

Panama, Isthmus of; *formerly* **Isthmus of Dar·i·en** \ˌdar-ē-ˈēn\. The link in Central America bet. North America and South America, separating the Atlantic and Pacific oceans; 420 mi. (676 km.) long; forms the Republic of Panama. Sometimes, in a restricted use, the name Isthmus of Panama is reserved for the crossing from Panama to Colón, the course of the Panama Canal, and the name Isthmus of Darien is reserved for the narrow crossing (46 mi. or 74 km.) nearest the mainland of South America, and the name Isthmus of San Blas for the narrowest part (31 mi. or 50 km.) S of the Gulf

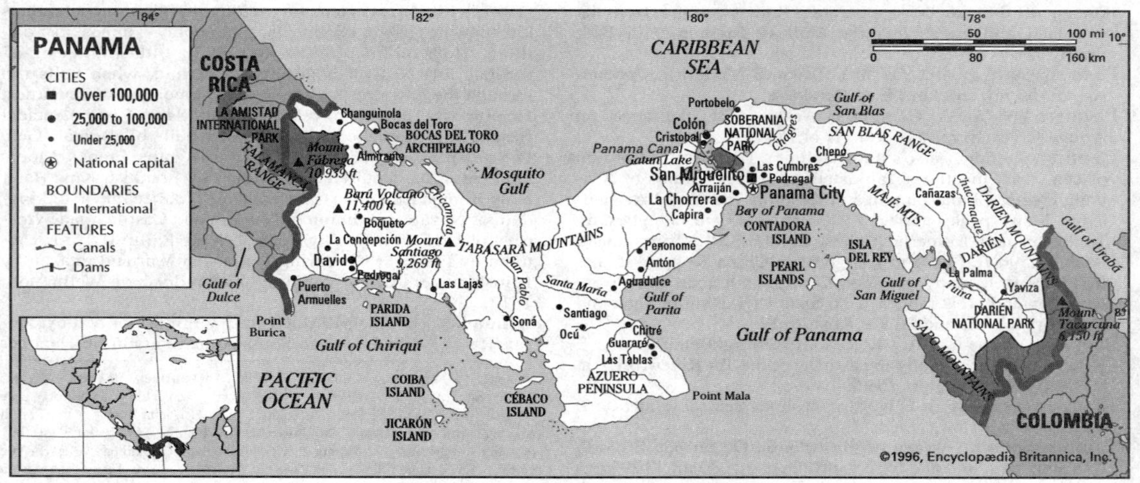

of San Blas. Isthmus also crossed by Panama R.R., in general course parallel to the canal from Colón to Panama City, completed 1855, 46.5 mi. (75 km.) long.

Panama Canal. Ship canal, Panama, extending across the Isthmus of Panama from Colón on the Caribbean Sea to Balboa on the Bay of Panama, the inner part of the Gulf of Panama, and the Pacific Ocean; length 40.3 mi. (65 km.) from shore to shore and 50.7 mi. (81.5 km.) from deepwater to deepwater; min. width 300 ft. (91 m.); min. depth 41 ft. (12 m.); highest elev. above sea level 85 ft. (26 m.). The Atlantic entrance to the Canal is 27 mi. (43 km.) W of the Pacific entrance.

History: First attempt at construction of a canal undertaken by French under diplomat Ferdinand de Lesseps 1879–89; concession granted to U.S. by Panama (see CANAL ZONE) under Hay-Bunau-Varilla Treaty 1903; U.S. purchased holdings of bankrupt French company and construction of canal begun early 1904; canal opened to traffic Aug. 15, 1914; construction to widen canal completed 1970 and further widening initiated 1991. During U.S. invasion of Panama, canal closed for first time in its history Dec. 1989; 1977 treaty provides for control of canal by Panama beginning 2000.

Panama Canal Zone. See CANAL ZONE.

Panama City. 1. City, ⊗ of Bay co., NW Florida, on Gulf of Mexico 30 mi. (48 km.) W of Apalachicola River; pop. (1990c) 34,378; fish, paper, chemicals; Gulf Coast Community Coll. (1957); Tyndall Air Force Base. Formed 1909 by merger of village of Panama City with adjoining villages.

2. City, Republic of Panama. See PANAMA 3.

Pan–American Highway. International highway system in the Americas, extending from the U.S.-Canada border to Santiago, Chile; complete except for a small stretch in area of Panama-Colombia border; section from Nuevo Laredo, Mexico to Panama City is sometimes called the **Inter–American Highway**.

Pan·a·mint Mountains \ˈpa-nə-ˌmint, -mənt\. Mountain range, Inyo co., E California, W of Death Valley; highest peak Telescope Peak 11,049 ft. (3368 m.).

Pa·na·on \ˌpä-nä-ˈōn\. Island, SE of Leyte I., Philippines, on W side of S end of Surigao Strait; 78 sq. mi. (202 sq. km.), 20 mi. (32 km.) long by 6 mi. (10 km.) wide; chief town Liloan at N end.

Pa·nar·ea *or* **Pa·nar·ia** \pə-ˈner-ē-ə\; *anc.* **Eu·on·y·mus** \yü-ˈä-ni-məs\. One of the Lipari Is. (*q.v.*) in the Tyrrhenian Sea NE of Sicily, Italy.

Pa·na·ro \pä-ˈnä-rō\; *anc.* **Scul·ten·na** \ˌskəl-ˈte-nə\. River, N Italy; rises on slopes of Monte Cimone; flows N and NE into Po River; 103 mi. (166 km.) long.

Pa·nay \pə-ˈnī\. **1.** Island, one of the Visayan Is., cen. Philippines; bounded on N by Sibuyan Sea, on NE by Visayan Sea, on E by Guimaras Strait, on S by Panay Gulf, and on W by Sulu Sea; 4749 sq. mi. (12,300 sq. km.), 6th in size in Philippines; pop. (1980c) 2,595,314; chief city Iloilo. Comprises four provinces of Aklan, Antique, Capiz, and Iloilo. In WWII occupied by Allies 1945.

2. River, E and cen. Capiz prov., Panay, Philippines; rises in mountains of SW Capiz, flows NE and N to Sibuyan Sea at Roxas; ab. 50 mi. (80 km.) long. Has four large tributaries; navigable for small vessels for a considerable distance.

3. Municipality, Capiz prov., Panay, Philippines, 3 mi. (5 km.) SE of Roxas; pop. (1980c) 31,650; old town, first Spanish settlement (1569) on Panay I. and 2d in the Philippines.

Panay Gulf. Large inlet of NE Sulu Sea, Philippines, formed by S Panay I., Guimaras I., and SW Negros I.; ab. 45 mi. (72 km.) across from Naso Point to Negros coast; connects by Guimaras Strait with Visayan Sea.

Pan·cake Range \ˈpan-ˌkāk\. Range in NE Nye co., SE cen. Nevada, extending N into White Pine co.

Pan·če·vo \ˈpän-che-ˌvȯ\ *or Hung.* **Pan·cso·va** \ˈpön-chō-ˌvö\. City, N cen. Serbia, Yugoslavia, on Danube River opp. Belgrade; town dates back to medieval times; old church with traditional Serbian art.

Pan–ch'iao \ˈpän-ˈchyau̇\. City, N Taiwan, SW of Taipei; pop. (1993e) 543,982.

Pan·či·čev \ˌpän-chē-ˈchef, -ˈchev\. See KOPAONIK.

Pan·dan \pän-ˈdän\. Municipality, Antique prov., Panay, Philippines, on bend of W coast 66 mi. (106 km.) N of San Jose de Buenavista; pop. (1980c) 20,396.

Pan de Azú·car \ˌpän-dā-ä-ˈsü-ˌkär\. **1.** Small island in Pacific Ocean off NW coast of Atacama prov., Chile.

2. Peak in the cen. Andes, in Venezuela, NE of Mérida; 15,978 ft. (4870 m.).

Panderma. See BANDIRMA.

Pan·dhar·pur \ˈpən-dər-ˌpu̇r\. Town, SE Maharashtra, W India, on Bhima River 185 mi. (298 km.) ESE of Bombay; pop. (1991p) 79,798; favorite place of pilgrimage in the Deccan, with celebrated temple to Vishnu.

Pan·do \ˈpän-dō\. **1.** *formerly* **Colonial Territories** *or Span.* **Co·lo·nias** \kō-ˈlō-nyäs\. Department of NW Bolivia. See table at BOLIVIA.

2. Town, Canelones dept., S Uruguay, just NE of Montevideo.

Pando, Mount. Peak in the Cordillera de Talamanca, W Panama; 8097 ft. (2468 m.).

Pan·do·sia \pan-ˈdō-shə, -shē-ə\. Ancient town, S Italy, W of Heraclea; site of battle c. 330 B.C. in which Alexander I of Epirus was killed.

Pan·dya \ˈpən-dyə\. Early kingdom of extreme S India; estab. by 4th cent. B.C.; struggled for dominance with other Tamil kingdoms, esp. Chola; subdued by Pallavas 6th–8th cents. and Cholas 11th–12th cents.; became dominant Tamil power 12th–14th cents. At height reached as far N as Nellore and included Kerala in the W, but in general occupied SE tip of Indian Penin. S of Pudukottai; ✱ Madurai.

Paneas. See BĀNIYĀS 2.

Pa·ne·vė·žys *or Russ.* **Pa·ne·ve·zhis** \ˌpä-nye-ve-ˈzhēs\. City, Lithuania, 55 mi. (88 km.) NNE of Kaunas on Daugavpils-Šiauliai railroad line; pop. (1992e) 132,300; flour milling, sugar refining.

Pan·gaea \pan-ˈjē-ə\. Supercontinent which comprised most of the major landmasses of the world, and consisted of the N and S subcontinents of Laurasia and Gondwana (*qq.v.*) respectively; believed to have formed in late Paleozoic era by merger of Laurussia and Gondwana and subsequent accretion of Asian landmasses; surrounded by worldwide ocean, Panthalassa; Laurasia believed to have separated from Gondwana in early-Mesozoic era, and throughout Mesozoic and into Cenozoic these supercontinents fragmented further into the continents present today.

Pan·gae·us, Mount \pan-ˈjē-əs\ *or Gk.* **Pan·gaí·on Óros** \päŋ-ˈge-ön-ˈö-rös\. Mountain range, NE Greece, N of Strymonic Gulf; in ancient times noted for gold and silver mines.

Pan·ga·ni \päŋ-ˈgä-nē\. **1.** River, NE Tanzania; flows from Kilimanjaro SE into Indian Ocean opp. the island of Zanzibar; ab. 250 mi. (400 km.) long. Called **Ru·vu** \ˈrü-vü\ in its lower course.

2. Coastal town at mouth of Pangani (or Ruvu) River, NE Tanzania.

Pan·ga·si·nan \ˌpäŋ-gä-sē-ˈnän\. Province, N cen. Luzon, Philippines; bounded on N by Lingayen Gulf, and on W by South China Sea; ✱ Lingayen. Cen. part is broad level plain of the Agno River; in the E has low mountains, the foothills of the Cordillera Central, and in NW on peninsula is somewhat hilly. Chief river the Bued in the N flowing into SE corner of Lingayen Gulf, which is the notable feature of the coastline. On NW shore of the gulf are Cabarruyan I. and Santiago I.; Cape Bolinao is NW point of the peninsula and Dasol Bay is on SW coast. Agriculturally one of richest provinces of the Philippines; main products rice, corn, sugarcane, tobacco, and coconuts. Inhabitants include mainly Pangasinans and Ilocanos. See table at PHILIPPINES.

History: Native peoples, the Pangasians, established trade with China; explored 1572 by Spaniards and soon visited by missionaries; created a province 1611; Chinese made attempt to establish fort on Lingayen Gulf but were overcome and forced to flee 16th cent.; experienced rapid economic growth during latter half of 19th cent.; civil government estab. Feb. 1901. In Dec. 1941 scene of early Japanese landings; Americans landed Jan. 1945 in reconquest of Philippines in WWII.

Pangerango, Gunung. See PANGRANGO.

Panggong. See PANGONG.

Panggong Tso. See PANGONG TSO.

Pangim. See PANAJI.

Pang·kah, Cape \ˈpäŋ-kä\. Cape on NE coast of Java I., Indonesia, on W side of entrance to Surabaja Strait.

Pang·ka·lan·bran·dan \ˌpäŋ-kä-ˌlän-ˈbrän-dän\ *or* **Pang·ka·lan·be·ran·dan** \-bə-ˈrän-dän\. Town, N Sumatra, Indonesia, near N end of Strait of Malacca 40 mi. (64 km.) NNW of Medan; pop. (1980c) 58,198.

Pang·kal·pi·nang \ˌpäŋ-käl-pē-ˈnäŋ\. Town, Indonesia, on NE coast of Bangka I.; pop. (1990c) 113,163; port.

Pang·kor \ˈpäŋ-ˌkȯr\. Small island, Malaysia, in Strait of Malacca, off W coast of S Malay Penin.; formerly belonged to Perak. Ceded to British 1826; returned to Perak 1935.

Pang–kung Hu. See PANGONG TSO.

Pan·glao \päŋ-ˈglau̇\. Low flat island off SW Bohol I., Philippines, separated from it by a narrow strait; 35 sq. mi. (91 sq. km.); munic. pop. (1980c) 14,547.

Pang–nga. See PHANGNGA 2.

Pan·gong \ˈpən-ˌgȯŋ\ *or* **Pang·gong** \ˈpəŋ-ˌgȯŋ\. Mountain range, S cen. Asia, SW and S of Pangong Lake; highest peak 22,060 ft. (6724 m.).

Pan·gong Tso *also* **Pang·gong Tso** \ˈbäŋ-ˈgu̇ŋ-ˈtsō\; *Eng.* **Pan·gong Lake** \ˈpan-ˌgȯŋ\; *Pinyin* **Ban·gong Co** \ˈbäŋ-ˈgu̇ŋ-ˈtsō\; *W.-G.* **Pang–kung Hu** \ˈbäŋ-ˈgu̇ŋ-ˈhü\. Long narrow lake, India and China, extending across border bet. Jammu and Kashmir and Tibet; ab. 100 mi. (160 km.) long; elev. 14,000 ft. (4267 m.).

Pangopango. See PAGO PAGO.

Pang–pu. See BENGBU.

Pang·rango, Gu·nung \ˈgü-nu̇ŋ-ˌpäŋ-ˈräŋ-ō\; *formerly* **Gunung Pang·e·rango** \ˌpäŋ-ə-ˈräŋ-ō\. Extinct volcano, W Java I., Indonesia, SE of Bogor; 9882 ft. (3012 m.); twin peak of Gunung Gede.

Pan·guil Bay \päŋ-ˈgēl\. Narrow inlet at SW corner of Iligan Bay, N coast of Mindanao, Philippines; lies bet. Misamis Occidental and Lanao del Norte provs.; ab. 23 mi. (37 km.) long; Ozamiz is the port on N side of its entrance.

Pan·guitch \ˈpan-gwich\. City, ⊗ of Garfield co., S Utah, on Sevier River; pop. (1990c) 1444.

Pang·u·ta·ran \ˌpäŋ-ü-ˈtä-rän\. **1.** Island group, N Sulu Archipelago, Philippines, NW of Jolo; ab. 96 sq. mi. (249 sq. km.); coextensive with Pangutaran munic. dist. Includes Pangutaran I., Panducan I., and ab. 12 small islands and islets. Heavily wooded; fishing.

2. Largest island of the Pangutaran Is.; 37 sq. mi. (96 sq. km.).

3. Town on E side of Pangutaran I.

Pan·han·dle \ˈpan-ˌhan-dᵊl\. Town, ⊗ of Carson co., NW Texas; pop. (1990c) 2353.

Panhandle, the. Any of several projections of land like the handle of a pan; esp. Alaska Panhandle, Florida Panhandle, Oklahoma Panhandle, Texas Panhandle (*qq.v.*).

Panhormus. See PALERMO 2.

Pa·nié, Mount \pȧ-ˈnyā\. Highest peak on the island of New Caledonia, SW Pacific Ocean, near NE coast; 5341 ft. (1628 m.).

Pa·ni·ha·ti \ˌpä-nə-ˈhä-tē\. Town, West Bengal, India, 10 mi. (16 km.) N of Calcutta; pop. (1991p) 275,359.

Pa·ni·pat \ˈpä-nē-pət\. Town, Haryana, NW India, near Yamuna River 53 mi. (85 km.) N of Delhi; pop. (1991p) 191,010; market town; cotton textiles; of great antiquity, dating back to legendary period; scene of three battles: Mogul Emperor Bābur (Zahīr-ud-Dīn-Muḥammad) conquered Afghan Sultan Ibrāhīm Lodī of Delhi 1526; Mogul Emperor Akbar routed army of Hindu Gen. Hēmū 1556; Afghan ruler Aḥmad Shāh Durrāni overcame the Maratha army 1761. Came under British rule 1803.

Pa·ni·qui \pä-ˈnē-kē\. Municipality, Tarlac prov., Luzon, Philippines, on a tributary of the Agno and on the Manila-Dagupan railroad line 13 mi. (21 km.) N of the municipality of Tarlac; pop. (1980c) 55,006.

Pa·ni·zos \pä-ˈnē-sōs\ *or* **Pa·ni·zo** \pä-ˈnē-sō\. Peak, S Potosí dept., SW Bolivia; 18,025 ft. (5494 m.).

Panj \ˈpänj\ *or* **Pan·ja** \ˈpän-jə\ *also* **Pyandzh** \ˈpyänj\. River on Afghanistan-Tajikistan boundary; ab. 400 mi. (645 km.) long; a headstream of the Amu Dar'ya.

Panjāb. See PUNJAB.

Panj·deh \ˈpanj-ˌdā\ *or* **Penj·deh** \ˈpenj-\. Village, Turkmenistan, on E bank of Kushka River near its junction with the Murgab; scene Mar. 1885 of clash bet. Russian and Afghan forces over a part of boundary in dispute; incident nearly caused war bet. Great Britain and Russia, but compromise reached June 1886.

Panjim. See PANAJI.

Panj·ko·ra \pənj-ˈkōr-ə\. River, North-West Frontier prov., Pakistan; rises in the Hindu Kush and flows S to join the Swat River N of Peshawar.

Panj·nad \pənj-ˈnäd\. River in Pakistan; the combined flow of the Sutlej and Chenab rivers, joining the Indus at ab. 29°N; ab. 50 mi. (80 km.) long. Three other streams, the Beas, Ravi, and Jhelum, rivers of the Punjab region, join the Sutlej and Chenab farther up in their courses.

Pan·kow \ˈpäŋ-kō\. Formerly, a district of East Berlin, East Germany; seat of East German government.

P'an·mun·jŏm \ˈpän-ˈmu̇n-ˈjȯm\. Village, cen. Korea, in the demilitarized zone separating North Korea and South Korea; site 1951–53 of Korean War truce talks; now a site for international discussions.

Pan·na \ˈpə-nə\. **1.** Former Indian state, now part of Madhya Pradesh, India.

2. Town, its ✻; now in Madhya Pradesh, N of Jabalpur; pop. (1991p) 38,073.

Pan·no·nia \pə-ˈnō-nē-ə\. Roman province incl. territory now mostly in Hungary, but extending into Austria, Slovenia, Croatia, and Vojvodina; S and W of the Danube, E of Noricum, and N of Dalmatia. Original inhabitants probably Illyrians; conquered by Rome beginning 35 B.C.; at beginning of 2d cent. A.D. divided into Pannonia Superior and Pannonia Inferior.

Pa·no·la \pə-ˈnō-lə\. Name of counties in two states of the U.S. See tables at MISSISSIPPI and TEXAS.

Panopolis. See AKHMĪM.

Pa·nor·mos \pä-ˈnȯr-mōs\. **1.** Small seaport on Mykonos I., Cyclades, Greece.

2. Seaport, Tínos I., Cyclades, Greece.

Panormus. See PALERMO 2.

Pan·si·pit \pän-ˈsē-pət\. Stream, Batangas prov., S Luzon, Philippines; flows out of Lake Taal SSW to Balayan Bay; ab. 8 mi. (13 km.) long; towns of Taal and Lemery on it.

Pan·ta·nal \ˌpȧn-tȧ-ˈnäl\. Region of swamps and marshland, S Mato Grosso state, SW Brazil, extending ab. 100 mi. (160 km.) along E bank of upper Paraguay River; traversed by several tributaries of the Paraguay incl. the São Lourenço and the Taquari.

Pan·tar \ˌpän-ˈtär\. Island of the Alor group, Lesser Sunda Is., Indonesia, E of Lomblen I., W of Alor I., and 60 mi. (96 km.) NW of Timor; 30 mi. (48 km.) long by 13 mi. (21 km.) wide. Mountainous, with rugged coast; highest point 4450 ft. (1356 m.). Separated on W from Lomblen by Alor Strait and on E from Alor by narrow **Pantar Strait** (ab. 8 mi. or 13 km. wide).

Pan·tel·le·ria \pan-ˈte-lə-ˈrē-ə\; *anc.* **Cos·sy·ra** *or* **Co·sy·ra** \kə-ˈsī-rə\. Italian island in the Mediterranean Sea E of NE Tunisia and ab. 70 mi. (115 km.) SW of Sicily; 32 sq. mi. (83 sq. km.); pop. (1991p) 7316; remains of prehistoric tombs. In Roman times a place of banishment; in WWII a heavily fortified base, which suffered intense air and naval attack by Allies 1943.

Pan·thal·as·sa \pan-ˈtha-lə-sə, -thə-ˈla-sə\. Former worldwide ocean, esp. the one surrounding Pangaea (*q.v.*).

Pan·ther Mountain \ˈpan-thər\. **1.** Peak in the Adirondack Mts., Hamilton co., NE cen. New York; 3865 ft. (1178 m.).

2. Peak in the Catskill Mts., Ulster co., SE New York; 3760 ft. (1146 m.).

Panther Peak. 1. Mountain in the Adirondack Mts., Essex co., NE New York; 4448 ft. (1356 m.).

2. Mountain, S Brewster co., W Texas; 6405 ft. (1952 m.).

Panticapaeum. See KERCH 2.

Pan·ti·co·sa \ˌpän-tē-ˈkō-sä\. Village, Huesca prov., NE Spain, in the Pyrenees near French border; pop. (1991c) 589.

Pan·tin \pä^{n}-ˈte^{n}\. Commune, Seine-St.-Denis dept., N France, NE suburb of Paris.

Pan·tu·kan \pän-ˈtü-ˌkän\. Municipality, cen. Davao del Norte, Mindanao, Philippines, on NE shore of Davao Gulf opp. N end of Samal I.; pop. (1980c) 30,281.

Pá·nu·co \ˈpä-nü-ˌkō\. **1.** River, cen. Mexico; rises in Hidalgo state, flows NE into the Gulf of Mexico 7 mi. (11 km.) below Tampico;ab. 100 mi. (160 km.) long.

2. Town, Veracruz state, E Mexico, 25 mi. (40 km.) WSW of Tampico; munic. pop. (1990c) 29,817.

Pao–an. See SHENZHEN.

Pao–chi. See BAOJI.

Pão de Açú·car \ˌpaů^{n}-dē-á-ˈsü-kər\ *or Eng.* **Sug·ar·loaf Mountain** \ˈshů-gər-ˌlōf\. Rocky peak in Rio de Janeiro city on W side of entrance to Guanabara Bay, SE Brazil; 1296 ft. (395 m.); connected by cable car; view of city from its summit.

Paoki. See BAOJI.

Paoking. See SHAOYANG.

Pa·o·la \pā-ˈō-lə\. City, ⊗ of Miami co., E Kansas, 40 mi. (64 km.) SSW of Kansas City; pop. (1990c) 4698.

Pa·o·la \ˈpä-ō-lä\. Commune, Cosenza prov., Calabria, S Italy, on Tyrrhenian Sea 12 mi. (19 km.) WNW of the commune of Cosenza; pop. (1981p) 15,372; 15th cent. monastery.

Pa·o·li \pā-ˈō-lē\. Town, ⊗ of Orange co., S Indiana, 22 mi. (35 km.) S of Bedford; pop. (1990c) 5624.

Paoning. See LANGZHONG.

Pao–shan. See BAOSHAN.

Pao–ting. See BAODING.

Pao–t'ou. See BAOTOU.

Pá·pa \ˈpä-pö\. City, Veszprém co., W Hungary, 80 mi. (129 km.) W of Budapest; pop. (1991e) 34,100; tobacco products, textiles; 18th cent. castle.

Pap·a·go Sa·gua·ro \ˈpa-pə-ˌgō-sə-ˈwä-rō, -ˈgwä-\. Former national monument, Maricopa co., SW cen. Arizona; 2050 acres (830 hectares); giant saguaros.

Pa·pa·i·kou \pä-ˌpä-ē-ˈkō-ü\. Town, Hawaii co., Hawaii, on E coast of Hawaii I. N of Hilo; pop. (1990c) 1634.

Pa·pa·ku·ra \ˌpa-pə-ˈkůr-ə\. Borough, North I., New Zealand; pop. (1991c) 36,553.

Papal States *also* **States of the Church** *or Ital.* **Lo Sta·to del·la Chie·sa** \lō-ˈstät-ō-ˌdel-ə-kē-ˈez-ə, -ˈāz-\. Temporal domain of the pope, cen. Italy, 754–1870; 16,000 sq. mi. (41,440 sq. km.); ✻ Rome, during periods when actually under control of Papacy.

History: Temporal power of medieval Papacy based upon Donation of Pépin 754 A.D., by which king of Franks promised to pope lands in cen. Italy, conquered from Lombards but formerly Byzantine; acquired duchy of Benevento mid-11th cent.; strengthened and expanded by Pope Innocent III (d. 1216) who controlled Ravenna, Romagna, Spoleto, the Pentapolis, and for a time, much of Tuscany; from 1274 to 1791 included Comtat Venaissin in S France; during residence of pope at Avignon (*q.v.*) 1309–77, under rule of virtually independent lords; boundaries until 19th cent. were reestablished by Pope Julius II (1503–13); invaded by French 1796; territorial status altered during Napoleonic Wars; divided bet. France and kingdom of Italy 1809; restored to papacy 1815; in 1860, Romagna, Marche, and Umbria joined Piedmont; Rome annexed to kingdom of Italy 1870; temporal authority in Vatican City (*q.v.*) granted to pope 1929.

Pa·pan·da·yan, Gu·nung \ˈgü-nůŋ-ˌpä-pän-ˈdä-yän\ *or* **Papan·da·jan.** Volcanic peak, W Java, Indonesia, ab. 12 mi. (19 km.) SW of Garut; 8744 ft. (2665 m.). Frequently climbed by tourists for view of Garut plain; major eruption 1772.

Pa·pan·tla de Olar·te \pä-ˈpän-tlä-ˌthā-ō-ˈlär-tā\. Town, Veracruz state, E Mexico, ab. 70 mi. (110 km.) NNW of Jalapa; munic. pop. (1990p) 158,160; vanilla plantations; nearby is ruined city, with Pyramid of the Niches (4th–7th cents.) and Building of the Columns with carvings depicting human figures and hieroglyphs.

Pa·pas \ˈpä-päs\; *anc.* **Arax·us** \ə-ˈrak-səs\. Cape on NW coast of Peloponnese, S Greece, 20 mi. (32 km.) W of Patras.

Pa·pa Stour \ˈpä-pə-ˈstůr\. One of the Shetland Is., N Scotland; 2.75 mi. (4.4 km.) long.

Pa·pa·toe·toe \ˌpa-pə-toi-ˈtoi\. City, North I., New Zealand; pop. (1981c) 21,700.

Pa·pa·wai Point \ˈpä-pä-ˌwī, -ˌvī\. Point on SW coast of Maui I., Hawaii, NW of Maalaea Bay.

Pa·pe·e·te \ˌpä-pā-ˈā-tā, pä-ˈpe-tē\. Seaport, ✻ of French Polynesia, also ✻ of Society Is., on NW coast of the island of Tahiti, Society Is., W Pacific Ocean; pop. (1988c) 23,555; commercial town, center for Pacific Rim trade.

Paph·la·go·nia \ˌpa-flə-ˈgō-nē-ə, -nyə\. Ancient country and Roman province in N Asia Minor, on the Black Sea, and bounded on the E by Pontus, on the S by Galatia, and on the W by Bithynia. A mountainous country, one of the oldest nations of Asia Minor; had several Greek settlements, incl. Sinope (see SINOP 2), along coast; subject to Macedonian King Alexander the Great and kingdoms of Bithynia and Pontus; to Rome c. 65 B.C.

Pa·phos \ˈpä-ˌfōs, ˈpā-ˌfäs\. Coastal town, SW Cyprus; met. area pop. (1989e) 27,800.

History: The old town of Paphos was probably founded by Greeks in the Mycenaean period; its site is ab. 26 mi. (42 km.) W of Limassol and 1 mi. (1.6 km.) inland; long famous as the seat of worship of Aphrodite who is said by one legend to have landed here after her birth among the waves; suffered greatly from earthquakes and several times rebuilt. New Paphos (the present town), on the coast 10 mi. (16 km.) WNW of old Paphos, superseded the older town after the Ptolemaic conquest of Cyprus c. 300 B.C. and Roman occupation 58 B.C. and became important Roman administrative city. Destroyed by Arabs 960 A.D. and rebuilt in modern times; still has many Roman remains. After Turkish occupation of Cyprus 1974, thousands of Greek Cypriot refugees settled in Paphos.

Pa·pil·lion \pə-ˈpil-yən\. City, ⊗ of Sarpy co., E Nebraska; pop. (1990c) 10,372.

Pa·pi·neau \ˌpa-pi-ˈnō\. County, SW Quebec, Canada. See table at QUEBEC.

Pa·pi·neau·ville \ˌpa-pi-ˈnō-ˌvil\. Village, ⊗ of Papineau co., SW Quebec, Canada, on Ottawa River, 35 mi. (56 km.) ENE of Ottawa; pop. (1991c) 1637.

Paps of Ju·ra \ˈpaps ... ˈjůr-ə\. Three mountains on Jura I., in the Inner Hebrides, off W coast of Scotland; highest peak 2571 ft. (784 m.).

Papua. See NEW GUINEA.

Papua, Gulf of \ˈpa-pyů-wə\. Large gulf on SE coast of New Guinea I., Papua New Guinea, an inlet of the Coral Sea; Port Moresby lies at the E entrance; Kikori River enters at N and Fly River at SW.

Papua, Territory of; *earlier* **British New Guinea** \ˈgi-nē\. Former territory comprising the SE section of New Guinea I.; 90,540 sq. mi. or 234,499 sq. km. (mainland 87,786 sq. mi. or 227,366 sq. km.); ✻ Port Moresby. Included also the D'Entrecasteaux, Trobriand, and Woodlark Is. and the Louisiade Archipelago off E coast.

History: Visited in 16th cent. by Portuguese and Spanish navigators; region annexed by Queensland 1883 and became British protectorate 1884; annexed by Great Britain 1888 as British New Guinea. Administration passed to Australia 1905 and name changed to Terr. of Papua; invaded by Japanese forces during WWII; administratively united with Trust Terr. of New Guinea to form Papua New Guinea 1949.

Papua New Guinea; *formerly* **Territory of Papua and New Guinea.** Country, W Pacific Ocean, comprising the E part of New Guinea, the island of Bougainville, and the Bismarck Archipelago; 178,260 sq. mi. (461,693 sq. km.); pop. (1993e) 3,918,000; ✻ Port Moresby; has high mountain ranges in NW part and the high Owen Stanley Range in SE; highest point Mt. Victoria, 13,363 ft. (4073 m.), NE of Port Moresby. Coastline indented at S by large Gulf of Papua, with shores low and swampy at deltas of many rivers, esp. the Fly, Kikori, and Purari; on E are several bays: Holnicote, Dyke Ackland, Collingwood, Goodenough, and Milne. East Cape marks most easterly point of New Guinea at 151°E. Rich in resources but largely undeveloped. Until 1975 an Australian-administered territory, consisting of the Terr. of Papua and the Trust Terr. of New Guinea (*qq.v.*); became independent 1975.

Chief products: Coffee, cocoa, copra, palm oil, tea; copper, oil, silver.

Chief towns: Port Moresby and Lae.

Pa·que·tá \ˌpä-kā-ˈtä\. Island in Guanabara Bay NE of the city of Rio de Janeiro, Brazil.

Pa·rá \pȧ-ˈrä\. **1.** Name given to the navigable E mouth of the Amazon River in Brazil; flows S and E of Marajó I.; receives Tocantins River from the S; ab. 200 mi. (320 km.) long; 40 mi. (64 km.) wide at its mouth.

2. State, N Brazil; ✻ Belém; jute, nuts. See table at BRAZIL.

3. Seaport city, Brazil. See BELÉM.

Pa·ra·bia·go \ˌpä-rä-ˈbyä-gō\. Commune, Milano prov., Lombardy, N Italy, 14 mi. (23 km.) NW of Milan; pop. (1989c) 22,667.

Pa·ra·ca·le \ˌpä-rä-ˈkä-lā\. Municipality on an inlet of the N coast of Camarines Norte, Luzon, Philippines, ab. 16 mi. (26 km.) NW of Daet; pop. (1980c) 25,308; the Spaniards worked gold and coal mines here for two centuries.

Pa·ra·cas Peninsula \pä-ˈrä-käs\. Peninsula extending from W cen. coast of Peru, S of Lima.

Pa·ra·cel Islands \ˌpar-ə-ˈsel\ *or Chin.* **Xi·sha Qun·dao** \ˈshē-ˌshä-ˈchu̇n-ˈdau̇\ *or Vietnamese* **Quan Dao Hoang Sa** \ˈkwän-ˈdau̇-ˈhwäŋ-ˈsä\ *or Jp.* **Hi·ra·ta Gun·to** \hē-ˈrä-tä-ˈgün-tō\. Group of small islands and reefs in the South China Sea at 16°30′N, 112°15′E. Controlled by French Indochina before WWII; occupied by Japan 1939; subsequently claimed by China and Vietnam.

Pa·ra·ćin \ˈpä-rä-ˌchēn\. Commune, cen. Serbia, Yugoslavia, ab. 75 mi. (120 km.) SE of Belgrade.

Par·a·clete \ˈpar-ə-ˌklet\. See NOGENT-SUR-SEINE.

Par·a·dise \ˈpar-ə-ˌdīs, -ˌdīz\. **1.** Urban community, Butte co., N California, N of Sacramento; pop. (1990c) 25,401.

2. Unincorporated settlement, Clark co., S Nevada, just S of Las Vegas; pop. (1990c) 124,682.

Paradise Valley. Town, Maricopa co., SW cen. Arizona; pop. (1990c) 11,671.

Paradiso, Gran. See GRAN PARADISO.

Paraetonium. See MAṬRŪḤ 2.

Par·a·gould \ˈpar-ə-ˌgüld\. City, ⊗ of Greene co., NE Arkansas, 20 mi. (32 km.) NE of Jonesboro; pop. (1990c) 18,540.

Pa·ra·gua \pä-ˈrä-gwä\. **1.** *or* **Pi·ra·gua** \pē-\. River, E Bolivia; flows NW into Guaporé River; ab. 230 mi. (370 km.) long.

2. Island, Philippines. See PALAWAN.

3. River, E Venezuela; ab. 300 mi. (485 km.) long; a tributary of the Caroní.

Pa·ra·gua·çu *or* **Pa·ra·guas·sú** \ˌpä-rä-gwȧ-ˈsü\. River, Bahia state, E Brazil; flows E to All Saints Bay; ab. 300 mi. (485 km.) long.

Pa·ra·gua·ná Peninsula \ˌpä-rä-gwä-ˈnä\. Peninsula extending from NW coast of Venezuela, enclosing Gulf of Venezuela from the E.

Pa·ra·gua·rí \ˌpä-rä-gwä-ˈrē\. **1.** Department of S cen. Paraguay. See table at PARAGUAY.

2. Town, its ✻, 35 mi. (56 km.) SE of Asunción; pop. (1992p)

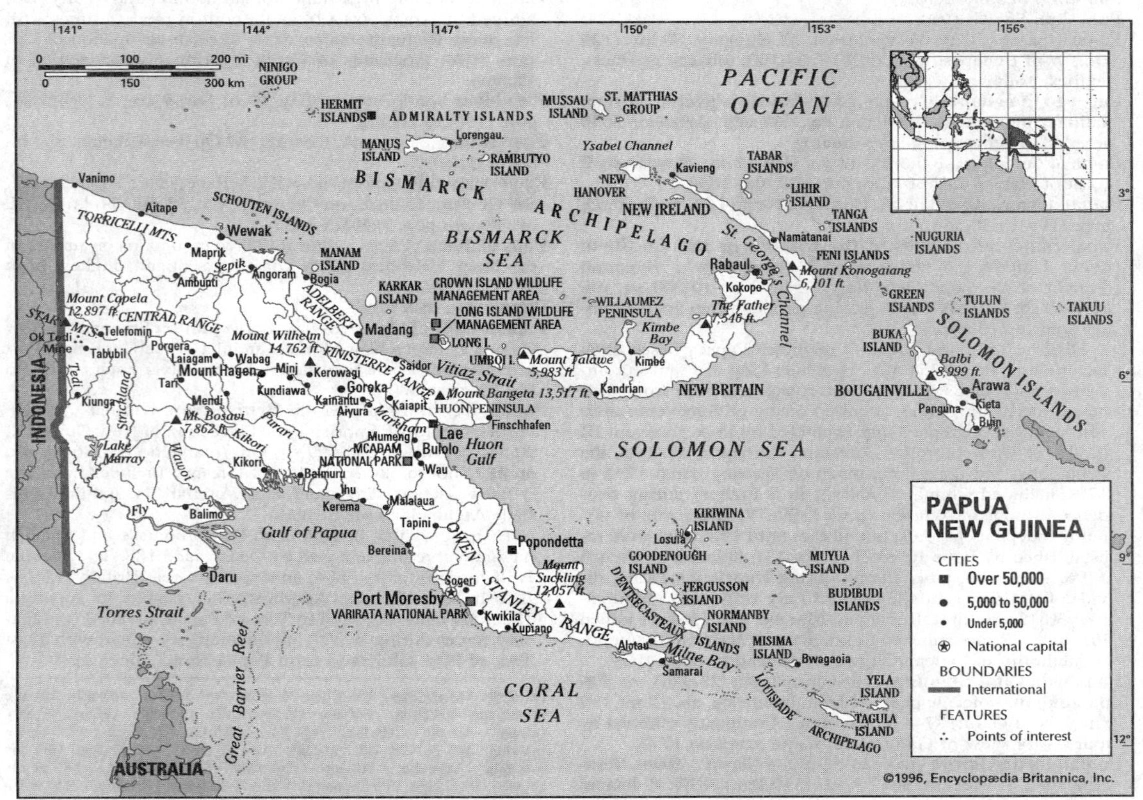

7279; trade center in agricultural region; founded 1775; in wars of independence scene of victory over Argentine army 1811.

Paraguassú. See PARAGUAÇU.

Par·a·guay \ˌpä-rä-ˈgwī; ˈpar-ə-ˌgwī, -ˌgwā\. **1.** Republic, cen. South America, bounded on N and NW by Bolivia, on NE and E by Brazil, and on SE, S, and W by Argentina; 157,043 sq. mi. (406,741 sq. km.); pop. (1993e) 4,643,000; ✻ Asunción.

Physical features: Landlocked republic, divided by the Paraguay River into an E (Oriental) section, 61,693 sq. mi. (159,785 sq. km.), and a W (Occidental) section, 95,350 sq. mi. (246,957 sq. km.), the W section incl. that part of the Gran Chaco (*q.v.*) which was added to Paraguay 1938; country is mostly low-wooded plains, with much swampland; in E are densely forested low ridges; highest point not much over 2200 ft. (670 m.).

Chief rivers: Paraguay (see PARAGUAY 2), the Alto Paraná on E border, and the Pilcomayo which is W tributary of the Paraguay and which forms a section of the boundary with Argentina.

Lakes: Only large one Lake Ypoá, ab. 100 sq. mi. (260 sq. km.), in S near Paraguay River.

Chief products: Meat, corn, sugarcane, soybeans, vegetable oils, yerba maté, tobacco; cotton, timber; cement, textiles.

Political divisions: Divided into the following two regions comprising 17 departments and the city of Asunción (for pronunciation of their names, see their individual entries):

\ə\ abut \ə\ matches \ᵊ\ kitten, Fr table \ər\ further \a\ ash \ā\ ace \ä\ cot, cart \à\ Fr bac \au̇\ out \b\ Span Avila \ch\ chin \e\ bet \ē\ easy \g\ go \i\ hit \ī\ ice \j\ job \k\ Ger ich, Buch \ⁿ\ Fr vin \ŋ\ sing \ō\ go \ȯ\ all \ȯ\ law \œ\ Fr bœuf \œ̄\ Fr feu \ȯi\ boy \th\ thin \th\ this \ü\ loot \u̇\ foot \ue\ Ger füllen \ue̅\ Fr rue \y\ yet \ʸ\ Fr digne \ˈdēnʸ\, nuit \ˈnwʸē\ \yü\ few \yu̇\ fury \zh\ vision

NAME	AREA (sq. mi.)	AREA (sq. km.)	POP. (1992c)	CAPITAL
Occidental				
Alto Paraguay	31,795	82,349	11,816	Fuerte Olimpo
Boquerón	35,393	91,668	91,669	Filadelfia
Presidente Hayes	28,150	72,908	72,907	Pozo Colorado
Oriental				
Alto Paraná	5,751	14,895	403,858	Ciudad del Este
Amambay	4,994	12,934	97,158	Pedro Juan Caballero
Caaguazú	4,430	11,474	383,319	Coronel Oviedo
Caazapá	3,666	9,495	128,550	Caazapá
Canendiyú	5,663	14,667	96,826	Salto del Guairá
Central	952	2,466	864,540	Asunción
Concepción	6,970	18,052	166,946	Concepción
Cordillera	1,910	4,947	206,097	Caacupé
Guairá	1,485	3,846	162,244	Villarrica
Itapúa	6,380	16,524	375,748	Encarnación
Misiones	3,690	9,557	88,624	San Juan Bautista
Ñeembucú	4,690	12,147	69,884	Pilar
Paraguarí	3,361	8,705	203,012	Paraguarí
San Pedro	7,723	20,002	277,110	San Pedro
city of Asunción	45	116	502,426	

History: First European settlements in area around Asunción by Spain early 16th cent.; Jesuit missions in south among Guarani Indians from beginning of 17th cent. until expulsion of Jesuits 1767; a part of viceroyalty of La Plata (*q.v.*), it achieved independence from Spain 1811; governed by José de Francia as dictator 1814–40, by Carlos A. López as president with dictatorial powers 1844–62, and by the latter's son Francisco Solano López 1862–70, who provoked a disastrous war with Brazil, Argentina, and Uruguay 1865–70 by which Paraguay lost more than half of its population; after long dispute with Bolivia over the Gran Chaco region, fought Chaco War 1932–35; peace treaty signed 1938; adopted new constitution 1940 which, however, was set aside on establishment of absolute rule under Higinio Morínigo the same year; ousted Morínigo 1948; scene of six revolts 1948–49; Gen. Alfredo Stroessner, who assumed power in military coup 1954, deposed in coup 1989.

2. River, S cen. South America; rises in Mato Grosso state, SW Brazil, where its upper tributaries form small sections of boundary with Bolivia; flows S to form boundary bet. Brazil and NE Paraguay and, after crossing cen. Paraguay, a section of boundary bet. SW Paraguay and Argentina; empties into the Paraná at SW corner of Paraguay; 1584 mi. (2549 km.) long; navigable for larger vessels to Concepción, for small craft for almost its entire length.

Pa·ra·í·ba \ˌpä-rä-ˈē-bə\; *formerly* **Pa·ra·hi·ba** *or* **Pa·ra·hy·ba** \ˌpä-rä-ˈē-bə\. **1.** Either of two rivers of Brazil: (a) **Paraíba** *or* **Paraíba do Nor·te** \dü-ˈnȯr-tē\, in Paraíba state; flows NE and E into Atlantic Ocean; ab. 180 mi. (290 km.) long; (b) **Paraíba** *or* **Paraíba do Sul** \dü-ˈsül\, in E São Paulo and Rio de Janeiro states; flows SW, then turns NE to traverse half the length of Rio de Janeiro state and empty into Atlantic Ocean near Campos; ab. 600 mi. (965 km.) long; called **Pa·ra·hi·tin·ga** \ˌpä-rä-ē-ˈtiŋ-gə\ in its upper course.
2. State, NE Brazil; ✻ João Pessoa; cotton, sisal, oiticica oil. See table at BRAZIL.
3. City, Brazil. See JOÃO PESSOA.

Pa·raí·so \ˌpär-ä-ˈē-sō\. Municipality, Tabasco state, Mexico, 35 mi. (56 km.) NW of Villahermosa; pop. (1990p) 57,553; diversified agriculture.

Paraíso, El. See EL PARAÍSO.

Pa·ra·kou \ˌpä-rä-ˈkü\. Town, E cen. Benin, ab. 200 mi. (320 km.) N of Porto Novo; pop. (1982e) 65,945.

Pa·ra·mar·i·bo \ˌpä-rä-ˈmä-rē-bō, ˌpar-ə-ˈmar-ə-ˌbō\. Seaport city, ✻ of Suriname, on the Suriname River ab. 13 mi. (21 km.) from its mouth; pop. (1990e) 200,000; port limited to vessels drawing less than 20 ft. (6 m.) of water; only large town of Suriname. Orig. an Indian village that became site of French garrison; made ✻ of first permanent European settlement, organized by British Lord Francis William Willoughby of Parham 1651.

Par·a·mount \ˈpar-ə-ˌmau̇nt\. City, Los Angeles co., SW California, SE of the city of Los Angeles; pop. (1990c) 47,669; residential.

Pa·ram·us \pə-ˈra-məs\. Borough, Bergen co., NE corner of New Jersey, 6 mi. (10 km.) NE of Paterson; pop. (1990c) 25,067; Bergen Community Coll. (1965).

Pa·ra·mu·shir \ˌpär-ə-mu̇-ˈshir\. Large island at N end of Kuril Is., E Russia in Asia; separated by narrow channel from Shumshu, the northernmost island of the chain; highest point 5958 ft. (1816 m.); chief town Severo-Kuril'sk at N end. Bombed by U.S. in WWII; became part of U.S.S.R. 1945 (see KURIL ISLANDS).

Pa·ran, Wilderness of \ˈpar-ən\. Desert region of indefinite location; probably in Sinai Penin., Egypt; here according to the biblical account the Israelites camped after they left Mt. Sinai (*Num.* xii. 12).

Pa·ra·ná \ˌpä-rä-ˈnä\. **1.** River, SE cen. South America; formed by confluence of Rio Grande and Paranaíba River in S cen. Brazil; flows S (sometimes known as **Al·to Paraná** \ˈäl-tō\) and forms SE and S boundary of Paraguay; continues S through NE Argentina (as **Paraná**) and empties into Río de la Plata; ab. 3030 mi. (4875 km.) long; its chief tributaries are: in Brazil (on left bank) Tietê, Paranapanema, Ivaí, Piquiri, Iguaçu, (on right bank) Verde, Pardo, Ivinheima; in Argentina, Salado and Gualeguay; completion of Itaipu Dam bet. Paraguay and Brazil early 1980s created a large reservoir and submerged Sete Quedas Cataract.
2. City, ✻ of Entre Ríos prov., E Argentina, on left bank of Paraná River 80 mi. (129 km.) N of Rosario; pop. (1991p) 277,338; river port for small oceangoing vessels; in livestock and grain-farming region; founded as Bajada de Santa Fe 1730; ✻ of Argentina 1853–62.
3. River, E Goiás state, cen. Brazil; ab. 250 mi. (400 km.) long; a headstream of the Tocantins.
4. State, S Brazil; ✻ Curitiba; coffee. See table at BRAZIL.

Pa·ra·na·guá \ˌpä-rä-nä-ˈgwä\. Town, chief port of Paraná state, S Brazil; munic. pop. (1991p) 107,583; exports coffee, sugar, Paraguay tea; founded c. 1600.

Pa·ra·na·í·ba \ˌpä-rä-nä-ˈē-bə\; *formerly* **Pa·ra·na·hi·ba** \ˌpä-rä-nä-ˈē-bə\. One of the headstreams of Paraná River, Brazil; rises in W cen. Minas Gerais state; flows W and SW to unite with Rio Grande and form Paraná River; 500 mi. (805 km.) long.

Pa·ra·na·pa·ne·ma \ˌpä-rä-nä-pä-ˈnā-mə\. River, SE Brazil; rises in SE São Paulo state, flows W, forming part of boundary bet. São Paulo and Paraná states, and empties into Paraná River; ab. 500 mi. (805 km.) long.

Pa·ra·ña·que \ˌpä-rä-ˈnyä-kā\. Municipality, SW Rizal prov., Luzon, Philippines, on SE shore of Manila Bay ab. 4 mi. (6 km.) S of Manila; pop. (1990p) 300,000; residential.

Pa·ra·na·vaí \ˌpä-rä-nä-ˈvī\. Municipality, Paraná state, S Brazil, 260 mi. (418 km.) NW of Curitiba; pop. (1991p) 71,169.

Pa·rang \ˈpär-äŋ\. **1.** Municipality, SW coast of Jolo I., Sulu prov., Philippines; pop. (1980c) 22,304.
2. Municipality, N Maguindanao prov., SW Mindanao, Philippines, on Illana Bay NNE of Cotabato; pop. (1980c) 46,003.

Pa·ran·ga·ba \ˌpä-rän-ˈgä-bə\. City, N Ceará state, NE Brazil, just SW of Fortaleza; pop. (1991p) 267,679.

Parapanisus. See PAROPAMISUS 2.

Pa·ras·nath, Mount \pə-ˈrəs-nät\ *also* **Parasnath Hill.** Eminence, E Bihar, NE India, 50 mi. (81 km.) E of Hazaribagh; 4481 ft. (1366 m.); sacred spot and place of pilgrimage of Jains.

Pa·ray–le–Mo·nial \pä-ˌrā-lə-mō-ˈnyäl\. Commune, Saône-et-Loire dept., E cen. France, ab. 55 mi. (90 km.) NNW of Lyon. Became famous place of pilgrimage from visions of 17th cent. nun, Marguerite Marie Alacoque (canonized 1920), origin of the cult of Sacred Heart of Jesus; has notable Romanesque basilica of the Sacred Heart and convent of the Visitation.

Par·ba·ti \ˈpär-bə-tē\. River, cen. India; flows N through W Madhya Pradesh and SE Rajasthan, forming in its course sections of the E Rajasthan boundary, and empties into Chambal River on that boundary; ab. 270 mi. (435 km.) long.

Par·bha·ni \ˈpər-bə-nē\. Town, SE Maharashtra, India, 100 mi. (161 km.) ESE of Aurangabad; pop. (1991p) 190,235.

Par·chim \ˈpär-ˌkim\. Commune, Mecklenburg-West Pomerania, N Germany, 23 mi. (37 km.) SE of Schwerin; pop. (1981c) 23,186; founded c. 1210; had prosperous trade in 14th cent. but lost it in Thirty Years' War; birthplace of Prussian Field Marshal Helmuth von Moltke 1800.

Par·do \ˈpär-dü\. **1.** River, E Brazil; rises in N Minas Gerais state, flows NE and E into Atlantic Ocean; ab. 400 mi. (644 km.) long.
2. River, S Brazil; rises in SW Minas Gerais state, flows NW to Rio Grande in São Paulo state; ab. 300 mi. (485 km.) long.
3. River, S Mato Grosso state, SW Brazil; flows SE into Paraná River; ab. 230 mi. (370 km.) long.

Par·du·bi·ce \ˈpär-dü-ˌbēt-se\ *or Ger.* **Par·du·bitz** \ˈpär-dü-ˌbits\. Town, N cen. Czech Republic, on Elbe River 60 mi. (97 km.) E of Prague; pop. (1991p) 94,857; brewing, sugar processing, oil refining; historical town, with 16th cent. gates, 13th cent. cathedral, 16th cent. castle.

Parecis, Serra dos. See SERRA DOS PARECIS.

Pa·re Mountains \ˈpä-rā\. Range, NE Tanzania; N of N end of the range is Kilimanjaro.

Parenzo. See POREČ.

Pa·re·pa·re \pä-ˌrā-pä-ˈrā\. Seaport town, Sulawesi, Indonesia, on W coast of SW peninsula 80 mi. (129 km.) N of Ujung Pandang; pop. (1990c) 84,199.

Par·ham Harbour \ˈpar-əm\. Inlet on N coast of Antigua I., Leeward Is., West Indies; in WWII site of U.S. seaplane base. See ANTIGUA.

Pa·ria \pə-ˈrē-ə\. River, S Utah and N Arizona; rises in S Garfield co., flows S across Arizona border and into Colorado River at Lees Ferry; ab. 65 mi. (105 km.) long.

Pa·ria, Gulf of \pä-ˈrē-ä\. Inlet of Atlantic Ocean lying bet. the W coast of the island of Trinidad and the Venezuelan mainland; enclosed on the N by **Paria Peninsula,** extending E from NE coast of Venezuela. See DRAGON'S MOUTH and SERPENT'S MOUTH.

Pa·ria Plateau \pə-ˈrē-ə\. Tableland, N Coconino co., N Arizona; elev. 6000 to 7300 ft. (1830 to 2225 m.).

Pa·ri·cu·tín \pä-ˈrē-kü-ˌtēn\. **1.** Former village, Michoacán state, Mexico, 200 mi. (322 km.) W of Mexico City.
2. Volcano on site of former village of Paricutín; ab. 9100 ft. (2775 m.) above sea level; started Feb. 20, 1943 in a cornfield; ceased activity 1952.

Pa·ri·da \pä-ˈrē-t͟hä\. Island at entrance to Charco Azul Bay on extreme SW Panama.

Parida, La. See BOLÍVAR, CERRO.

Pa·ri·ka \pä-ˈrē-kä\. Town, N Guyana, on E bank of Essequibo River at its mouth, 20 mi. (32 km.) W of Georgetown.

Parikía. See PAROS 2.

Pa·ri·ma \pà-ˈrē-mə\. River, headstream of the Uraricoera, NW Brazil; rises in the Serra Parima and flows N; ab. 50 mi. (80 km.) long.

Pa·ri·ma, Ser·ra \ˈser-rä-pä-ˈrē-mä\ *or in Venezuela* **Si·er·ra Parima** \ˈsyer-rä\. Mountain range, N South America, extending N and S along a section of the Venezuela-Brazil boundary; ab. 200 mi. (320 km.) long; highest peak ab. 5000 ft. (1525 m.); source of the Orinoco River.

Pa·ri·ñas, Point \pä-ˈrē-nyäs\. Extreme W point of South America, in NW Peru at 4°40′S, 81°20′W.

Parion. See PARIUM.

Par·is \ˈpar-əs\. **1.** City, a ⊗ of Logan co., W Arkansas, 42 mi. (68 km.) SSE of Fort Smith; pop. (1990c) 3674.
2. City, ⊗ of Bear Lake co., SE Idaho; pop. (1990c) 581.
3. City, ⊗ of Edgar co., E Illinois, 38 mi. (61 km.) S of Danville; pop. (1990c) 8987.
4. City, ⊗ of Bourbon co., NE Kentucky, 19 mi. (31 km.) NE of Lexington; pop. (1990c) 8730; ships livestock.
5. Town, Oxford co., W Maine, 18 mi. (29 km.) NW of Lewiston; pop. (1990c) 4492.
6. City, ⊗ of Monroe co., NE Missouri; pop. (1990c) 1486.
7. City, ⊗ of Henry co., NW Tennessee; pop. (1990c) 9332; clay pits.
8. City, ⊗ of Lamar co., NE Texas, 90 mi. (145 km.) NE of Dallas; pop. (1990c) 24,699; commercial center; ships cotton and livestock; Paris Junior Coll. (1924); settled early 1840s; incorp. as town 1874, as city 1905.
9. Town, Brant co., SE Ontario, Canada, 7 mi. (11 km.) WNW of Brantford; pop. (1991c) 8600.
10. *Fr.* pà-ˈrē\; *anc.* **Lu·te·tia** \lü-ˈtē-shə, -shē-ə\ *or* **Lutetia Pa·ris·i·o·rum** \pə-ˌri-zē-ˈōr-əm\ *or later* **Pa·ris·ii** \pə-ˈri-zē-ˌī\. City and river port, ✻ of France, also ✻ of Ville-de-Paris dept., on both banks of Seine River 110 mi. (177 km.) ESE of Le Havre and 107 mi. (172 km.) from the English Channel; pop. (1990c) 2,175,200; financial, commercial, transportation, artistic, and intellectual center of France; automobiles, chemicals, electrical equipment, pharmaceuticals, leather products, jewelry; motion-picture and publishing industries; major tourist center; an international fashion center; served by numerous boulevards (many following the course of former city walls), incl. Boulevard de Sébastopol, Rue St.-Michel, Rue de Rivoli, Avenue des Champs-Élysées, Avenue de la Grande Armée, Boulevard St.-Germain, Rue Royal, Rue du Faubourg St.-Honoré; city centers around Île de la Cité, an island in Seine River; famed Latin Quarter, inhabited chiefly by students, lies S of Seine; public squares and parks include the Tuileries Gardens, Place de la Concorde (containing sculptured fountains and obelisk from Luxor), Place Charles de Gaulle (formerly Place de l'Étoile, with world's largest triumphal arch), Luxembourg Gardens, Jardin des Plantes, Places de la République, d'Iéna, de la Vendôme, des Innocents (containing a fountain), and des États-Unis, and the Champ de Mars (in which is located the 984-foot or 300-meter Eiffel Tower); world-famous buildings include the Palais de Justice, 12th cent. Cathedral of Notre Dame, Louvre (containing an outstanding art collection), Luxembourg Palace, Tribunal de Commerce, Ste.-Chapelle, L'Opéra, Palais de l'Élysée (residence of president of France), Bibliothèque Nationale, Panthéon, church of La Madeleine, basilica of Sacré-Coeur, Hôtel des Invalides, church of St.-Germain-des-Prés, Bourse, Centre Georges-Pompidou (Centre Beaubourg), Musée d'Orsay, La Défense, La Villette (science museum), and Opéra-Bastille; educational institutions include the 12th cent. Univ. of Paris (one of oldest in Europe), reorganized 1970 as Universities of Paris I-XIII of which the Sorbonne is a part, the Institut de France, Collège de France, Institut Pasteur, and the famous Observatoire; noted Père-Lachaise Cemetery.
History: Pre-Roman settlement on island in Seine; captured 52 B.C. and fortified by Romans; made bishopric in 3d cent. A.D.; came to Clovis, king of the Franks, after victory of 486; seat of a Carolingian count; withstood severe siege by Vikings 885–887; after accession to French throne of Hugh Capet 987, definitely estab. as ✻ of France; Univ. of Paris developed in 12th cent. and was chartered c. 1200; held by English 1419–36; scene of leading events of French Revolution 1789–99; entered by allies after Emperor Napoléon's defeat 1814; besieged and taken by Germans 1870–71; the following important treaties were signed here: 1763 (concluding Seven Years' War), 1783 (War of American Independence), 1814 and 1815 (Napoleonic Wars), 1856 (Crimean War), 1898 (Spanish-American War); Declaration of Paris signed here 1856; scene of peace conference at end of WWI 1919; site of Olympic Games 1900 and Summer Olympic Games 1924; occupied by Germans June 1940; liberated by Allies Aug. 1944. In 1968 scene of widespread leftist student and worker strikes and demonstrations; scene of U.S.-North Vietnam peace talks on Vietnam War 1968–73. See FRANCE.

Pa·ri·ta, Gulf of \pä-ˈrē-tä\ *or Span.* **Golfo de Parita** \ˈgòl-fō-ˌt͟hā\. Inlet of the Gulf of Panama on the W, extending into W cen. Panama at the base of Azuero Penin.

Pa·rit Bun·tar \ˈpä-rēt-ˈbùn-ˌtär\. Town, NW Perak, Malaysia, ab. 50 mi. (80 km.) NW of Ipoh.

Par·i·um \ˈpar-ē-əm\ *or* **Par·i·on** \-ē-ən\. Town in ancient Mysia, Asia Minor, on the SW shore of the Propontis (Sea of Marmara).

Park. Name of counties in three states of the U.S. See tables at COLORADO, MONTANA, WYOMING.

Park City. **1.** City, Lake co., NE Illinois, 5 mi. (8 km.) W of Waukegan; pop. (1990c) 4677.

2. City, Sedgwick co., S cen. Kansas, N of Wichita; pop. (1990c) 5050.

3. City, Summit co., NE Utah, 22 mi. (35 km.) ESE of Salt Lake City; pop. (1990c) 4468; tourist and ski resort.

Parke \ˈpärk\. County in W Indiana. See table at INDIANA.

Parke Peak. Mountain, Glacier National Park, NW Montana; ab. 9100 ft. (2775 m.).

Par·ker \ˈpär-kər\. **1.** County in N cen. Texas. See table at TEXAS.

2. Town, ⊗ of La Paz co., SW Arizona; pop. (1990c) 2897.

3. Town, Douglas co., cen. Colorado, SE of Denver; pop. (1990c) 5450.

4. City, Bay co., NW Florida; pop. (1990c) 4598.

5. City, ⊗ of Turner co., SE South Dakota; pop. (1990c) 984.

Parker Dam. Dam across Colorado River bet. San Bernardino co., California and La Paz co., Arizona; completed 1938 to form Lake Havasu.

Parker Peak. **1.** Mountain, Fall River co., SW corner of South Dakota; 4849 ft. (1478 m.).

2. Mountain, Yellowstone National Park, NW Wyoming; 10,203 ft. (3110 m.).

Par·kers·burg \ˈpär-kərz-ˌbərg\. City, ⊗ of Wood co., W West Virginia, at confluence of Ohio and Little Kanawha rivers; pop. (1990c) 33,862; river port; metal products, synthetic textiles, plastic products; Ohio Valley Coll. (1960).

Parkes \ˈpärks\. Town, E cen. New South Wales, SE Australia, 180 mi. (290 km.) WNW of Sydney; pop. (1991c) 13,953; site of large radio telescope and space-tracking station.

Parkes·burg \ˈpärks-ˌbərg\. Borough, Chester co., SE Pennsylvania, 22 mi. (35 km.) E of Lancaster; pop. (1990c) 2981.

Park Falls. City, Price co., N Wisconsin, 50 mi. (81 km.) SSE of Ashland; pop. (1990c) 3104.

Park Forest. Village, Cook and Wills cos., NE Illinois, S of Chicago; pop. (1990c) 24,656; residential.

Park Hills. City, Kenton co., N Kentucky, just S of Covington; pop. (1990c) 3321.

Park·land \ˈpär-klənd\. **1.** City, Broward co., SE Florida, N of Coral Springs; pop. (1990c) 3558.

2. Unincorporated settlement, Pierce co., W cen. Washington, ab. 6 mi. (10 km.) S of Tacoma; pop. (1990c) 20,882; residential; Pacific Lutheran Univ. (1890).

Park Range. A range of the Rocky Mts. in N Colorado; highest peak Mt. Lincoln 14,286 ft. (4354 m.).

Park Rapids. City, ⊗ of Hubbard co., N cen. Minnesota, 40 mi. (64 km.) S of Bemidji; pop. (1990c) 2863.

Park Ridge. **1.** City, Cook co., NE Illinois, N suburb of Chicago; pop. (1990c) 36,175; residential.

2. Borough, Bergen co., NE corner of New Jersey, on New York border 12 mi. (19 km.) NE of Paterson; pop. (1990c) 8102.

Park·ville \ˈpärk-ˌvil\. **1.** Unincorporated settlement, Baltimore co., cen. Maryland, NE of the city of Baltimore; pop. (1990c) 31,617; residential.

2. City, S Platte co., NW Missouri, 9 mi. (15 km.) NW of Kansas City; pop. (1990c) 2402; Park Coll. (1875).

Par·lier \ˈpär-lər\. City, Fresno co., S cen. California; pop. (1990c) 7938.

Par·ma \ˈpär-mə\. City, Cuyahoga co., N Ohio, 8 mi. (13 km.) S of Cleveland; pop. (1990c) 87,876; residential suburb of Cleveland; automobile parts, tools and dies; incorp. as city 1932.

Parma \ˈpär-mä\. **1.** Province of Emilia-Romagna, Italy. See table at ITALY.

2. Commune, its ✱, 75 mi. (121 km.) SE of Milan; pop. (1991p) 168,905; rail and road junction; in agricultural region; produces Parmesan cheese, alcohol, fertilizers, and glass; 12th cent. cathedral; 13th cent. Romanesque baptistery; late 16th cent. Palazzo della Pilotta (restored after war damage 1944), containing art gallery, museum, library; 16th cent. monastery; university (11th cent., reorganized in 1601 by Ranuccio Farnese, duke of Parma).

History: Founded by Romans 183 B.C.; important Roman road junction; made bishopric 4th cent. A.D.; under successive local lords before passing as part of Duchy of Parma and Piacenza to Farnese family, then to Austrians; after 1815 held by Marie Louise, wife of French Emperor Napoléon I; became part of kingdom of Italy 1861; during WWII heavily damaged by Allied bombing 1944; birthplace of conductor Arturo Toscanini 1867.

Parma Heights. City, Cuyahoga co., N Ohio, S suburb of Cleveland; pop. (1990c) 21,448.

Par·mer \ˈpär-mər\. County in NW Texas. See table at TEXAS.

Par·na·í·ba \ˌpär-nə-ˈē-bə\; *formerly* **Par·na·hy·ba** \-ˈē-bə\. **1.** River, NE Brazil; flows NE, forming boundary bet. Piauí and Maranhão states, and empties into Atlantic Ocean; ab. 600 mi. (965 km.) long.

2. Port, N Piauí state, NE Brazil, 11 mi. (18 km.) from mouth of the Parnaíba River; munic. pop. (1991p) 127,986; commercial center; exports cotton and sugar; founded 1761.

Par·nas·sus \pär-ˈna-səs\. Former borough, Westmoreland co., SW Pennsylvania, on Allegheny River ab. 17 mi. (27 km.) ENE of Pittsburgh; consolidated with New Kensington (*q.v.*) 1931.

Parnassus, Mount *or Gk.* **Par·nas·sós Óros** \ˌpär-nä-ˈsös-ˈör-ˌös\. Mountain, cen. Greece, N of Gulf of Corinth; 8061 ft. (2457 m.); in Greek mythology sacred to Apollo and the Muses, esp. the **Cas·ta·lian Spring** \ka-ˈstāl-yən\, just above Delphi which lay at its foot to the S. **Co·ry·cian Cave** \kə-ˈri-shən, -shē-ən\, a stalactite grotto 350 ft. (107 m.) long and ab. 200 ft. (60 m.) wide, is bet. Delphi and the summit on a plateau.

Par·nes \ˈpär-ˌnēz\ *or Gk.* **Pár·nis** \ˈpär-nēs\. Mountain, E cen. Greece, 16 mi. (26 km.) N of Athens; 4636 ft. (1413 m.); an E extension of Mt. Cithaeron.

Par·non \ˈpär-ˌnän\ *or Gk.* **Pár·non Óros** \ˈpär-nön-ˈör-ös\. Mountain range, E Laconia, SE Peloponnese, S Greece; highest peak 6348 ft. (1935 m.); shuts in the valley of the Eurotas on the E.

Pär·nu *or* **Par·nu** \ˈper-nü\ *or Russ.* **Pyar·nu** \ˈpyer-\; *formerly* **Per·nov** \ˈper-nəf\ *or Ger.* **Per·nau** \ˈper-ˌnau̇\. **1.** Bay on SW coast of Estonia, an inlet of the N part of the Gulf of Riga.

2. River, cen. Estonia; flows SW into Pärnu Bay; ab. 80 mi. (130 km.) long.

3. Seaport, Estonia, near mouth of Pärnu River on Pärnu Bay; pop. (1992e) 52,596; lumber, textiles; seaside resort. Founded c. 1251; held by Poland from 1561 and by Sweden from 1629; to Russia 1710–1918.

Pa·ro \ˈpä-rō\. Town, W Bhutan, SW of Thimphu; pop. (1982e) 3000.

Par·o·pa·mi·sus \ˌpar-ə-pə-ˈmī-səs\. **1.** Mountain range, NW Afghanistan, at W end of the Hindu Kush, N of Herāt and the Harī; highest point 11,772 ft. (3588 m.).

2. *or* **Pa·ra·pa·ni·sus** \ˌpar-ə-pə-ˈnī-səs\. Ancient name of Hindu Kush (*q.v.*) range, cen. W Asia.

Pá·ros \ˈpär-ˌös\ *or* **Par·os** \ˈpar-ˌäs\. **1.** Island, cen. Cyclades, Greece, in the Aegean Sea 6 mi. (10 km.) W of Naxos; 75 sq. mi. (194 sq. km.); pop. (1981c) 7881; ✱ Paros; formed by a mountain 2451 ft. (747 m.) high, from which has been obtained a fine white marble, widely used in ancient times by sculptors. Colonized by Ionians and itself founder of colonies in Thásos, Illyria, and along the shores of the Sea of Marmara; sided with Persians in Greco-Persian Wars; not historically important after 4th cent. B.C.; site of discovery 1627 of a marble fragment, part of the *Parian Chronicle,* giving an outline of Greek history from before 1000 B.C. to c. 354 B.C., one of the Arundel marbles now at Oxford Univ., England.

2. *also* **Pa·ri·kía** \ˌpä-rē-ˈkē-ä\. Town, its ✱, on W coast.

Par·ot·tee Point \ˌpar-ət-ē\. Cape on SW coast of the island of Jamaica, West Indies.

Par·o·wan \ˌpar-ə-ˈwan, ˈpar-ə-wən\. City, ⊗ of Iron co., SW Utah, 17 mi. (27 km.) NE of Cedar City; pop. (1990c) 1873; settled 1851.

Par·ral \pär-ˈräl\ *or in full* **Hi·dal·go del Parral** \ē-ˈthäl-gō-thel-\. City, Chihuahua state, N Mexico, 115 mi. (185 km.) S of the city of Chihuahua; munic. pop. (1990p) 90,703; alt. 6200 ft. (1890 m.); gold, silver, lead, and zinc mines nearby.

Par·ra·mat·ta \ˌpar-ə-ˈma-tə\. **1.** River, E New South Wales, SE Australia; 18 mi. (29 km.) long; actually the tidal estuary of a small creek forming W arm of Port Jackson; spanned by Gladesville Bridge (concrete arch; main span 1000 ft. or 305 m.; completed 1964) near Sydney.

2. Municipality on Parramatta River, SE Australia; a W suburb of Sydney; pop. (1991c) 132,798; textiles, flour; founded 1790; incorp. 1861.

Par·ra·more Island \ˈpar-ə-ˌmōr\. Island in Atlantic Ocean off SE coast of Accomac co., Virginia.

Par·ret \ˈpar-ət\. River, Dorset and Somerset cos., SW England; flows NW into Bristol Channel; 35 mi. (56 km.) long.

Par·ris Island \ˈpar-əs\. Island of the Sea Is. chain in Beaufort co., S South Carolina, S of Port Royal I.; since 1915 a U.S. Marine Corps training station.

Parrs·boro \ˈpärz-ˌbər-ō\. Town, Cumberland co., N Nova Scotia, Canada, on N shore of Minas Basin 31 mi. (50 km.) S of Amherst; pop. (1991c) 1634; summer resort; ships coal. In a region rich for geological studies, contains one of the world's largest fossil discoveries incl. footprints of prehistoric animals and plant fossils.

Par·ry, Cape \ˈpar-ē\. Point extending from N coast of Northwest Territories, Canada, into Amundsen Gulf on E side of Franklin Bay, 70°08′N, 124°24′W.

Parry Island. See MAUKE.

Parry Islands. Group of islands in Queen Elizabeth group, Northwest Territories & Nunavut, Canada, N of Viscount Melville Sound; includes Prince Patrick I., Melville I., Bathurst I., Borden I., and Cornwallis I.

Parry Sound. 1. District, SE Ontario, Canada. See table at ONTARIO.

2. Town, its ⊗; port at center of E shore of Georgian Bay; pop. (1991c) 6125; summer resort.

Par·sip·pa·ny–Troy Hills \pär-ˈsi-pə-nē-ˈtrȯi\. Township, Morris co., N New Jersey, 6 mi. (10 km.) NE of Morristown; pop. (1990c) 48,478.

Pars·nip \ˈpär-snip\. River, E cen. British Columbia, Canada; rises near the bend of the Fraser and flows N to unite with Finlay River and form Peace River; 145 mi. (233 km.) long.

Par·son Bald \ˈpärs-ᵊn\. Peak, Blount co., E Tennessee; 4760 ft. (1451 m.).

Par·sons \ˈpärs-ᵊnz\. **1.** City, Labette co., SE Kansas, 33 mi. (53 km.) W of Pittsburg; pop. (1990c) 11,924; Labette Community Coll. (1923).

2. City, ⊗ of Tucker co., NE West Virginia, 16 mi. (26 km.) NNE of Elkins; pop. (1990c) 1453.

Parsons Peak. Mountain in the Sierra Nevada, near E end of boundary bet. Mariposa and Tuolumne cos., cen. California; 12,120 ft. (3694 m.).

Parsonstown. See BIRR.

Par·tab·garh \pər-ˈtäb-ˌgär\. Former Indian state, now part of Rajasthan state, NW India; 873 sq. mi. (2261 sq. km.).

Par·tan·na \pär-ˈtä-nä\. Commune, Trapani prov., NW Sicily, Italy, 29 mi. (47 km.) SE of the seaport of Trapani; pop. (1981p) 11,768.

Partenkirchen. See GARMISCH-PARTENKIRCHEN.

Par·the·nay \ˌpär-tə-ˈnā\. Town, cen. Deux-Sèvres dept., W France, 27 mi. (43 km.) NNE of Niort; 13th cent. ramparts; 15th cent. houses; several medieval churches.

Par·then·o·pe \pär-ˈthe-nə-pē\. Ancient town, S Italy, on site of Naples (*q.v.*), the place where, according to legend, the Siren Parthenope was cast ashore. The **Par·then·o·pe·an Republic** \pär-ˌthe-nə-ˈpē-ən\ was a short-lived republic Jan.–June 1799 erected at Naples by Napoléon's French Revolutionary army under Gen. Jean Championnet.

Par·thia \ˈpär-thē-ə\. Ancient country in W Asia, nearly coextensive with modern Khorāsān prov., NE Iran; a subdivision of Ariana, SE of Hyrcania; formed a province of the Persian Empire and later of the empire of Macedonian King Alexander the Great; on dissolution of Seleucid Empire c. 250 B.C., new Parthian kingdom founded by Arsaces, first of the Arsacidae, a dynasty of ab. 30 kings which ruled until overthrown by Ardashīr c. 226 A.D., the first Sassanid ruler of Persia (see IRAN). Kingdom at its height, known as Parthian empire (*Lat.* **Reg·num Par·tho·rum** \ˈreg-nəm-pär-ˈthōr-əm\) at beginning of first cent. B.C., included all regions bet. Euphrates and Indus rivers and bet. Amu Dar'ya and Arabian Sea; weakened by internal disorder and then advances from Rome. The Parthians were famous as horsemen and archers. Best known cities were Hecatompylos, Seleucia, and Ctesiphon whose ruins are now in Iraq.

Par·ti·ni·co \ˌpär-tē-ˈnē-kō\. Commune, Palermo prov., Sicily, Italy, 15 mi. (24 km.) WSW of the seaport of Palermo; pop. (1989c) 29,520.

Par·ti·zansk \ˌpȧr-tʸē-ˈzȧnsk\; *formerly* **Su·chan** \sü-ˈchan\. Town, S Primorskiy Kray, SE Russia in Asia, near coast 60 mi. (97 km.) E of Vladivostok; pop. (1991e) 50,000; coal deposits in area.

Par·ti·zan·ske \ˈpär-ti-ˌzän-ske\. Town, W cen. Slovakia; pop. (1989c) 26,678.

Parts of Holland *and* **Parts of Kesteven** *and* **Parts of Lindsey.** See LINCOLNSHIRE 2.

Pa·ru *or* **Pa·rú** \pȧ-ˈrü\. River, N Brazil; rises in the Tumuc-Humac Mts., flows SE into the Amazon; ab. 370 mi. (595 km.) long.

Paru de Oes·te \dē-ˈwesh-tə\; *formerly* **Ere·pe·cu·rú** \ˌer-ē-ˌpe-kü-ˈrü\. River, N Brazil; flows S into Trombetas River just before it empties into the Amazon; ab. 250 mi. (400 km.) long.

Pa·rys \pə-ˈrīs\. Town, N Free State, E cen. Rep. of South Africa, on Vaal River 60 mi. (97 km.) SW of Johannesburg; pop. (1985c) 31,608; resort.

Pas, The \ˈpä\. Town, W Manitoba, Canada, on Saskatchewan River; pop. (1991c) 6166.

Pa·sa·cao \ˌpä-sä-ˈkaù\. Municipality, Camarines Sur prov., Luzon, Philippines, 12 mi. (19 km.) SW of Naga and its port on Ragay Gulf; pop. (1980c) 25,303.

Pas·a·de·na \ˌpa-sə-ˈdē-nə\. **1.** Suburban residential city, Los Angeles co., SW California, just NE of the city of Los Angeles; pop. (1990c) 131,591; precision instruments; California Institute of Technology (1891), Pasadena City Coll. (1924), Art Center Coll. of Design (1930), Pacific Oaks Coll. (1945), Fuller Theological Seminary (1947); site of college football's Rose Bowl and of annual New Year's Day Tournament of Roses (flower festival inaugurated 1890). Founded 1874; incorp. as city 1886.

2. City, Harris co., SE Texas, just E of Houston; pop. (1990c) 119,363; chemicals; oil refining; residential; Texas Chiropractic Coll. (1908), San Jacinto Coll.–Central Campus (1961); founded 1895; incorp. 1929; site of Mexican Gen. Antonio López de Santa Anna's capture (Apr. 22, 1836) after battle of San Jacinto (*q.v.*) NE of city.

Pa·sa·do, Cape \pä-ˈsä-t͟hō\. Cape extending into Pacific Ocean on W cen. coast of Ecuador.

Pa·sa·je \pä-ˈsä-hā\. Town, El Oro prov., SW Ecuador, 80 mi. (129 km.) S of Guayaquil.

Pa·sa·leng Bay \pä-ˈsä-leŋ\. Inlet of South China Sea (Babuyan Channel), NE Ilocos Norte prov., Luzon, Philippines, E of Mayraira Point; ab. 11 mi. (18 km.) wide at mouth.

Pa·sar·ga·dae \pə-ˈsär-gə-ˌdē\. Ruined city of ancient Persia, ab. 30 mi. (48 km.) NE of later Persepolis and 60 mi. (96 km.) NE of modern Shīrāz, Iran; ✱ of Cyrus the Great, founder of the Achaemenian dynasty; said to have been founded by him on the site of his victory over Astyages, last king of Media, 550 B.C. Its ruins today comprise bases of several large buildings and the tomb of Cyrus. Surrendered to Macedonian King Alexander the Great c. 336 B.C.

Pa·say \ˈpä-ˌsī\. Chartered city, Rizal prov., Luzon, Philippines, on E shore of Manila Bay 1 mi. (2 km.) S of S boundary of Manila; pop. (1990p) 354,000.

Pas·ca·gou·la \ˌpas-kə-ˈgü-lə\. **1.** Navigable river, SE Mississippi; formed by confluence of Leaf and Chickasawhay rivers in N George co., SE Mississippi, flows S into Mississippi Sound.
2. City, ⊗ of Jackson co., SE corner of Mississippi, on Mississippi Sound 18 mi. (29 km.) E of Biloxi; pop. (1990c) 25,899; coastal resort and fishing center; shipbuilding.

Paş·cani \päsh-ˈkänʸ\. Town, Iaşi co., NE Romania; pop. (1986c) 36,420.

Pas·co \ˈpas-kō\. **1.** Coastal county in W cen. Florida Penin., Florida. See table at FLORIDA.
2. City, ⊗ of Franklin co., SE Washington, on the Columbia River; pop. (1990c) 20,337; Columbia Basin Coll. (1955); developed as supply center during WWII for Richland (*q.v.*) and Hanford sites of industrial plants of the Manhattan Project which produced the first atomic bombs.

Pasco, Cerro de. See CERRO DE PASCO.

Pas·coag \ˈpas-ˌkōg\. Unincorporated settlement, Providence co., N Rhode Island, ab. 18 mi. (29 km.) NW of the city of Providence; pop. (1990c) 5011.

Pascua, Isla de. See EASTER ISLAND.

Pas–de–Ca·lais \ˌpäd-kȧ-ˈlā\. Department of N France. See table at FRANCE.

Pas de Calais. See DOVER, STRAIT OF.

Pa·se·walk \ˈpä-zə-ˌvälk\. City, Mecklenburg-West Pomerania, NE Germany, 24 mi. (39 km.) WNW of Szczecin, Poland; pop. (1981c) 15,527.

Pa·sig \ˈpä-sig\. **1.** Stream, cen. Luzon, Philippines; the outlet of Laguna de Bay flowing NNW in Rizal prov. and city of Manila; 14 mi. (23 km.) long; navigable for small vessels.
2. Municipality, ✻ of Rizal prov., Luzon, Philippines, on N bank of Pasig River near its source and 5 mi. (8 km.) from E boundary of city of Manila; pop. (1980c) 268,570; important market town.

Paš·man \ˈpäsh-ˌmän\. Island in Adriatic Sea off coast of Croatia, S of Zadar, bet. Dugi Otok I. and mainland; ab. 34 sq. mi. (88 sq. km.).

Pas·ni \ˈpəs-nē\. Seaport town, Baluchistan, Pakistan, 75 mi. (121 km.) E of Gwadar; pop. (1981p) 18,000.

Pa·so \ˈpä-sō, ˈpa-\. Spanish term meaning "pass." For names of mountain passes beginning with this element see the distinguishing element (e.g., **Paso de Maipo.** See MAIPO, PASO DE).

Pasoeroean. See PASURUAN.

Paso Ro·bles \ˈpa-sō-ˈrō-bəlz\ *or officially* **El Paso de Robles** \el-ˈpa-sō-də-\. City, San Luis Obispo co., SW California, on the Salinas 24 mi. (39 km.) N of the city of San Luis Obispo; pop. (1990c) 18,583; grew rapidly in 1980s.

Pas·quo·tank \ˈpas-kwō-ˌtaŋk\. County in NE North Carolina. See table at NORTH CAROLINA.

Pas·sa·con·a·way, Mount \ˌpa-sə-ˈkä-nə-ˌwā\. Mountain, S Grafton co., W New Hampshire; 4060 ft. (1238 m.); highest point in the Sandwich Range, S White Mts.

Pas·sage Island \ˈpa-sij\. Small island off NE tip of Isle Royale, NW Lake Superior, a part of Keweenaw co., N tip of Upper Penin. of Michigan.

Pas·sa·ic \pə-ˈsā-ik\. **1.** River, NE New Jersey; rises near Morristown, SE Morris co., flows S, E, and N on the Morris co. line, E across Passaic co., turns S at Paterson, where occur the **Great Falls of the Passaic** 70 ft. (21 m.) high; follows the line of the Essex co. boundary into Newark Bay; ab. 80 mi. (130 km.) long; navigable 11 mi. (18 km.).
2. County in N New Jersey. See table at NEW JERSEY.
3. City, Passaic co., N New Jersey, on Passaic River 4 mi. (6 km.) S of Paterson; pop. (1990c) 58,041; chemicals, pharmaceuticals, clothing, electronic components. Settled by Dutch 1678; incorp. as city 1873; in American Revolution, occupied by Gen. George Washington's troops before retreat from British under Gen. Charles Cornwallis 1776.

Pas·sa·ma·quod·dy Bay \ˌpa-sə-mə-ˈkwä-dē\. Inlet of SW Bay of Fundy, SW New Brunswick, Canada, bet. SW New Brunswick and SE Maine, at the mouth of the St. Croix River; Deer I. and Campobello I. in S part of it.

Passaro, Cape. See PASSERO, CAPE.

Passarowitz. See POŽAREVAC.

Pas·sau \ˈpä-ˌsau̇\. City, Bavaria, Germany, at confluence of Danube, Inn, and Ilz rivers 93 mi. (150 km.) ENE of Munich; pop. (1992e) 50,665; railroad junction and commercial center; 17th cent. cathedral with one of the world's largest pipe organs; 13th–16th cent. fortress; 14th cent. town hall. Of ancient Celtic origin; treaty signed here 1552 settling religious differences bet. Holy Roman Emperor Charles V and German states. During WWII captured by Allies May 2, 1945.

Pass·chen·dae·le \ˈpäs-ᵊn-ˌdä-lə\. Small commune, West Flanders prov., NW Belgium; scene of heavy fighting in WWI.

Pass Chris·ti·an \ˈpas-ˈkris-chən\. City, Harrison co., SE Mississippi, on Gulf of Mexico 11 mi. (18 km.) W of Gulfport; pop. (1990c) 5557; resort.

Pas·se·ro, Cape *also* **Cape Pas·sa·ro** \ˈpä-sə-rō\; *anc.* **Pa·chy·nus Prom·on·to·ri·um** \pə-ˈkī-nəs-ˌprä-mən-ˈtōr-ē-əm\. Cape projecting into Mediterranean Sea at SE point of the island of Sicily, Italy. Naval battle 1718 nearby in which British Adm. George Byng destroyed Spanish fleet; in WWII landing place of British forces in invasion of Sicily July 1943.

Passes, The. See MISSISSIPPI 1.

Pas·si \ˈpä-sē\. Municipality, Iloilo prov., Panay, Philippines, on Jalaud River and on railroad line 29 mi. (47 km.) N of City of Iloilo; pop. (1980c) 47,988.

Pas·so Fun·do \ˈpä-sü-ˈfün-dü\. City, N Rio Grande do Sul state, S Brazil, 150 mi. (241 km.) NW of Pôrto Alegre; munic. pop. (1991p) 147,215.

Pas·sos \ˈpä-süs\. City, SW Minas Gerais state, E Brazil, 180 mi. (290 km.) SW of Belo Horizonte; munic. pop. (1991p) 84,515.

Pas·sump·sic \pə-ˈsəmp-sik\. River, NE Vermont; rises in N Caledonia co., flows S into Connecticut River.

Pa·sta·za \pä-ˈstä-sä\. **1.** River, Ecuador and Peru; rises in cen. Ecuador and flows S into Peru to empty into Marañón River, headstream of the Amazon; ab. 400 mi. (645 km.) long.
2. Province of E Ecuador. See table at ECUADOR.

Pas·to \ˈpäs-tō\. **1.** Volcano, Colombia. See GALERAS.
2. City, ✻ of Nariño dept., SW Colombia, on high plateau (8400 ft. or 2560 m.) E of Galeras volcano; pop. (1992e) 303,400; commercial center; hats; founded 1539.

Pas·to·ra Peak \pa-ˈstōr-ə\. Mountain, NE Apache co., NE Arizona; 9412 ft. (2869 m.).

Pa·stra·na \pä-ˈsträ-nä\. Municipality, N cen. Leyte prov., Philippines, 14 mi. (23 km.) SW of Tacloban; pop. (1980c) 10,854.

Pa·su·bio \pä-ˈsü-bē-ˌō\. Peak, Veneto, NE Italy, SE of Rovereto; 7323 ft. (2232 m.).

Pa·su·ru·an *or Du.* **Pa·soe·roe·an** \ˌpä-su̇-rü-ˈän\. Seaport city, East Java prov., Indonesia, at SW corner of Madura Strait; ab. 30 mi. (48 km.) S of Surabaya; pop. (1990c) 134,019; shipbuilding, rice milling.

Pat·a·go·nia \ˌpa-tə-ˈgō-nyə, -nē-ə\. Region of South America, mostly in Argentina, S of the Limay and Río Negro rivers, or ab. 39°S, extending to the Strait of Magellan, ab. 1000 mi. (1610 km.); a barren tableland bet. the Andes and Atlantic Ocean; ab. 311,000 sq. mi. (805,490 sq. km.). Crossed by the Chubut, Deseado, and Chico rivers flowing E to the Atlantic; its Atlantic coastline indented by the Gulf of San Matías and San Jorge Gulf. Orig. inhabited by Tehuelche Indians; coast explored by Spanish 16th cent. and by English 18th cent.; divided 1881 bet. Chile (Magallanes prov.) and Argentina (provs. of Río Negro, Chubut, and Santa Cruz).

Pataliputra. See PATNA 3.

Patalung. See PHATTHALUNG.

Pa·tam·bán, Cer·ro de \ˈser-rō-t͟hā-ˌpä-täm-ˈbän\. Mountain, W Michoacán state, SW Mexico, NW of Uruapan; 12,303 ft. (3750 m.).

Pa·tan \ˈpä-tən\. **1.** *or* **Pat·tan** \ˈpä-tən\. Town, Gujarat, W India, on Sarasvati River 65 mi. (105 km.) NNW of Ahmadabad; pop. (1991p) 96,109; has numerous Jain temples with valuable Jain manuscripts. Occupies site of **An·hil·wa·ra** \ˌən-hil-ˈwär-ə\ ancient ✻ of kingdom of Gujarat, captured 1024 by Muslim Sultan Maḥmūd of Ghaznī.

2. Town, India. See LALITPUR.

Pa·ta·ni \pä-'tä-nē\. Former Malay state in the Malay Penin. under Siamese protection, included among the Malay States (*q.v.*).

Patan Somnath. See SOMNATH.

Pa·taps·co \pə-'tap-skō\. River, N cen. Maryland; rises in Carroll co., N Maryland, flows SE into Chesapeake Bay; ab. 80 mi. (130 km.) long; the city of Baltimore lies on a navigable estuary of this river; estuary spanned by Francis Scott Key Bridge (continuous truss; main span 1200 ft. or 366 m.; completed 1977).

Pat·a·ra \'pa-tə-rə\. One of the chief cities of ancient Lycia, S Asia Minor, on the coast just E of the mouth of the Xanthus.

Patavium. See PADUA.

Pa·tay \pȧ-'tā\. Town, Loiret dept., N cen. France, NW of Orléans; scene of defeat of English under Sir John Fastolf and John Talbot, earl of Shrewsbury, by saint and national heroine Joan of Arc 1429, just after siege of Orléans had been lifted.

Patch·ogue \'pa-,chòg\. Village, Suffolk co., SE New York, on S shore of Long Island, on Great South Bay 53 mi. (86 km.) E of New York City; pop. (1990c) 11,060.

Pa·ter·nò \,pä-ter-'nō\. Commune, Catania prov., E Sicily, Italy, on SW slope of Mt. Etna 12 mi. (19 km.) WNW of the commune of Catania; pop. (1991p) 44,197; 11th cent. castle. Taken during WWII by British Aug. 1943 in Sicily campaign. See HYBLA.

Pat·er·son \'pa-tər-sən\. City, ⊗ of Passaic co., N New Jersey, on Passaic River 14 mi. (23 km.) N of Newark; pop. (1990c) 140,891; manufactures clothing, chemicals, machine tools, plastics; formerly the principal American silk-manufacturing center; Passaic County Community Coll. (1968). Founded 1791 as industrial settlement of Society for Establishing Useful Manufactures (S.U.M.), formed by American statesman Alexander Hamilton as part of plan to encourage development of independent American industry; in 19th cent. a center of cotton-textile and locomotive manufacturing; received city charter 1851.

Patersonia. See LAUNCESTON.

Pa·than·kot \pə-'tän-kōt\. Town, Punjab, India, ab. 65 mi. (105 km.) NE of Amritsar; pop. (1991p) 142,862.

Path·find·er Dam \'path-,fīn-dər\. Dam across N Platte River in E cen. Wyoming; completed 1913.

Path·ros \'pa-thrəs\. A biblical name for Upper Egypt (*Isa.* xi. 11, *Jer.* xliv. 1, 15).

Pa·thum Tha·ni \pä-'tüm-tä-'nē\ *or* **Pra·thum Thani** \prä-'tüm\ *or* **Pa·tum·dha·ni** \pä-,tüm-dä-'nē\. Town, cen. Thailand, on the Chao Phraya a few miles N of Bangkok; pop. (1991e) 16,660.

Pa·ti \'pä-tē\. Town, Central Java prov., Indonesia, 15 mi. (24 km.) E of Kudus; pop. (1980c) 53,408.

Pa·tía \pä-'tē-ä\. River, SW Colombia; flows WNW into Pacific Ocean; ab. 200 mi. (320 km.) long.

Pa·ti·a·la \,pə-tē-'ä-lə\ *or* **Put·ti·a·la** \,pə-\. **1.** Former Indian state, now part of Punjab state, NW India; 5942 sq. mi. (15,390 sq. km.); chief of the three Phulkian states of the Punjab; founded by a Sikh chieftain c. 1763; came under British control 1849.

2. City, its ✻, 130 mi. (209 km.) NNW of Delhi; pop. (1991p) 253,341; cotton gins, distilleries; university (1962).

Pa·til·las \pä-'tē-yäs\. Municipality, SE Puerto Rico, near coast just E of Guayama; pop. (1990c) 19,633.

Pat·kai Range *or* **Patkai Hills** \'pät-kī\. Hill region extending NE to SW along the border bet. NE India and NW Myanmar; commonly included with the Naga Hills on the SW. Av. height 8000 to 9000 ft. (2440 to 2740 m.). Forms watershed bet. Brahmaputra and Chindwin rivers. See NAGA HILLS.

Pat·mos \'pat-məs\ *or Gk.* **Pát·mos** \'pät-mös\ *or Ital.* **Pat·mo** \'pät-mō\. **1.** An island of the Dodecanese (*q.v.*), Greece, ab. 28 mi. (45 km.) SSW of Sámos; 13 sq. mi. (34 sq. km.); scene of St. John the Apostle's exile (c. 95 A.D.) where he is supposed to have written the Book of Revelation.

2. Town, S end of the island.

Pat·na \'pət-nə\. **1.** Former Indian state, now part of Orissa state, NE India, 170 mi. (274 km.) W of Cuttack; 2530 sq. mi. (6553 sq. km.); ✻ Bolangir.

2. City, ✻ of Bihar state, NE India, on right bank of Ganges River 290 mi. (467 km.) NW of Calcutta; pop. (1991c) 1,099,647; road and rail junction; university (1917); 16th cent. mosque. Extends along river for ab. 12 mi. (19 km.); to W lies new section, Bankipur, and to W and SW of Bankipur is modern ✻ area with government buildings.

History: Founded 5th cent. B.C. as **Pa·ta·li·pu·tra** \,pä-tə-li-'pü-trə\; ✻ of Magadha kingdom and of later Mauryan dynasty; fell into ruins after 4th cent. A.D.; revived 16th cent. as ✻ under Afghan Emperor Shēr Shāh, who ruled the Mogul Empire; passed to British c. 1764; lost economic importance as river port with construction of railroads.

Pat·na·non·gan \,pät-nə-'nòŋ-gän\. Island in Polillo group off E Luzon, Philippines, E of the island of Polillo; 34 sq. mi. (88 sq. km.); in Quezon prov.

Pat·noñ·gon \,pät-nòŋ-'gòn\. Municipality, Antique prov., on W coast of Panay, Philippines, 12 mi. (19 km.) N of San Jose de Buenavista; pop. (1980c) 24,262.

Pa·to·ka \pə-'tō-kə\. River, SW Indiana; rises in Orange co., flows W into Wabash River; 138 mi. (222 km.) long.

Pa·tos \'pä-tüs\ *or* **Patos de Mi·nas** \dē-'mē-nəs\. City, W cen. Minas Gerais state, E Brazil, 190 mi. (306 km.) NW of Belo Horizonte; munic. pop. (1991p) 102,698.

Patos \'pä-tōs\. **1.** Island on W side of Dragon's Mouth, strait bet. NW Trinidad and tip of Paria Penin., NE coast of Venezuela; ab. 200 acres (81 hectares); claim to it ceded to Venezuela by Great Britain 1942, ending 150-year dispute.

2. City, W cen. Paraíba state, NE Brazil; pop. (1991p) 76,378.

Patos, La·goa dos \lȧ-'gō-ə-düs-'pä-tüs\. Lagoon, E Rio Grande do Sul state, S Brazil; has Pôrto Alegre at its N end and the port of Rio Grande at its S end where it has an outlet to the Atlantic Ocean; 124 mi. (200 km.) long by 37 mi. (60 km.) wide; separated from the ocean by a sandy peninsula ab. 15 mi. (24 km.) wide.

Patos, Lago de los. See PORONGOS, LAGUNA DE.

Patos, Los. See LOS PATOS.

Patos de Minas. See PATOS.

Pátrai, Gulf of *or* **Patraïkós Kólpos.** See PATRAS, GULF OF.

Pa·tras \'pa-trəs\ *or Gk.* **Pá·trai** \'pä-tre\; *anc.* **Pa·trae** \'pä-trē, 'pä-,trī\. Seaport city, ✻ of Achaea dept., NW Peloponnese, Greece, on Gulf of Patras; pop. (1981p) 140,878; ships fruit, wine, brandy, olive oil; medieval castle. Had military importance 3d cent. B.C.; estab. as commercial center by Romans first cent A.D.; ruled by Venetians and Turks 15th–19th cents.; place where Greek War of Independence began 1821; in WWII occupied by Axis powers 1941–44.

Patras, Gulf of *or* **Gulf of Pátrai** *or Gk.* **Pa·traïkós Kól·pos** \pä-,trä-ē-'kös-'köl-pös\; *anc.* **Si·nus Cal·y·do·ni·us** \'sī-nəs-,ka-lə-'dō-nē-əs\. Inlet of the Ionian Sea on W coast of Greece, joined by narrow strait (Lepanto Strait) to the Gulf of Corinth N of Peloponnese.

Pa·tria, Lake \'pä-trē-ä\. Small lake, 13 mi. (21 km.) NW of Naples, Italy.

Pat·rick \'pa-trik\. County in S Virginia. See table at VIRGINIA.

Patrimony of Saint Peter. See ROME, DUCHY OF.

Pattan. See PATAN 1.

Pat·ta·ni *also* **Pa·ta·ni** \pä-'tä-nē\. Seaport town, SW Thailand, on E coast of Malay Penin. 50 mi. (81 km.) ESE of Songkhla; pop. (1991e) 41,509; ships tin.

Pat·ten \'pat-ᵊn\. Town, Penobscot co., E cen. Maine, 31 mi. (50 km.) WSW of Houlton; pop. (1990c) 1256; base for hunting and fishing.

Pat·ter·son \'pa-tər-sən\. **1.** City, Stanislaus co., cen. California, 12 mi. (19 km.) SW of Modesto; pop. (1990c) 8626.

2. City, St. Mary parish, S Louisiana, 60 mi. (97 km.) SE of Lafayette; pop. (1990c) 4736.

Pat·ti \ˈpä-tē\. Commune, Messina prov., NE Sicily, Italy, on N coast of Sicily 33 mi. (53 km.) W of the seaport of Messina; pop. (1981p) 12,322; episcopal see; small harbor.

Pa·tu·ca \pä-ˈtü-kä\. River, S cen. and E Honduras; rises in several headstreams in mountains of cen. Honduras, flows NE into the Caribbean Sea; ab. 300 mi. (480 km.) long.

Pa·tu·ca, Pun·ta \ˈpün-tä-pä-ˈtü-kä\ *also* **Patuca Point** *or* **Point Patuca.** Cape on NE coast of Honduras, at the mouth of the Patuca River.

Pa·tux·ent \pə-ˈtək-sənt\. River, cen. Maryland; rises in SW Carroll co., flows S and SE into Chesapeake Bay bet. Calvert and St. Marys cos., S Maryland; ab. 100 mi. (160 km.) long.

Patuxent River Naval Air Warfare Center. See CEDAR POINT 2.

Pátz·cua·ro \ˈpäts-kwä-rō\. Town, N cen. Michoacán state, SW Mexico; munic. pop. (1990p) 66,704; on S shore of **Lake Pátzcuaro,** ab. 30 mi. (48 km.) in circumference, alt. 6706 ft. (2044 m.).

Pat·zi·cía \ˌpät-sē-ˈsē-ä\. Town, Chimaltenango dept., S cen. Guatemala; pop. (1981c) 12,294.

Pat·zún \pät-ˈsün\. Town, Chimaltenango dept., S cen. Guatemala, E of Lake Atitlán; pop. (1981c) 23,489.

Pau \ˈpō\. Commune, ✻ of Pyrénées-Atlantiques dept., SW France, on right bank of the Gave de Pau 109 mi. (175 km.) S of Bordeaux; pop. (1990c) 83,928; produces chemicals, footwear; winter-sports center; 12th–15th cent. castle. During 16th cent. important French cultural center under patronage of Margaret of Angoulême; birthplace of Henry IV of France (1553) and Jean-Baptiste Bernadotte (1763), who became Charles XIV John, king of Sweden; former ✻ of Béarn.

Pau, Gave de \ˌgäv-də-ˈpō\. River, S France; a mountain stream (*gave*), rises in S Hautes-Pyrénées dept., flows NW into the Adour on boundary bet. Pyrénées-Atlantiques and Landes depts.; Lourdes and Pau are on it. See also GAVARNIE.

Pau·car·tam·bo \ˌpau̇-kär-ˈtäm-bō\. Town, SE Peru, on **Paucartambo River** (*or* **Ya·ve·ro River** \yä-ˈvā-rō\, ab. 180 mi. or 290 km. long) which flows NNW into the Urubamba; pop. (1981p) 9390.

Pauil·lac \pō-ˈyäk\. Commune, Gironde dept., SW France, on Gironde River ab. 25 mi. (40 km.) NW of Bordeaux; in the Médoc; noted for its vineyards.

Paul·ding \ˈpȯl-diŋ\. **1.** Name of counties in two states of the U.S. See tables at GEORGIA and OHIO.

2. Town, a ⊗ of Jasper co., SE cen. Mississippi.

3. Village, ⊗ of Paulding co., NW Ohio, 37 mi. (60 km.) NW of Lima; pop. (1990c) 2605.

Pau·lis·ta \pau̇-ˈlēs-tə\. City, Pernambuco state, E Brazil; munic. pop. (1991p) 211,024.

Pau·lo Afon·so \ˈpau̇-lü-ə-ˈfōⁿ-sü\. **1.** Series of three waterfalls in the São Francisco River, Brazil, ab. 190 mi. (305 km.) from its mouth bet. Alagoas and Bahia states; total height of falls ab. 275 ft. (85 m.).

2. City, NE Bahia state, E Brazil, near Paulo Afonso Waterfalls; pop. (1991p) 74,326.

Pauls·boro \ˈpȯlz-ˌbər-ō\. Borough, Gloucester co., SW New Jersey, 10 mi. (16 km.) SSW of Camden; pop. (1990c) 6577.

Pauls Valley \ˈpȯlz\. City, ⊗ of Garvin co., S cen. Oklahoma; pop. (1990c) 6150.

Paumotu. See TUAMOTU ARCHIPELAGO.

Paung·de \ˈpau̇ŋ-ˈdā\. Town, S cen. Myanmar, ab. 30 mi. (48 km.) SE of Prome.

Pau·ri \ˈpau̇-rē\. Town in N Uttar Pradesh, N India; nearby are some of the highest peaks of the Himalayas: Kamet, Trisul, Badrinath, and Nanda Devi.

Pau·te \ˈpau̇-tā\. River, SE Ecuador; ab. 110 mi. (175 km.) long; unites with Zamora River to form Santiago River.

Pau·to \ˈpau̇-tō\. River, NE cen. Colombia; flows SE into Meta River; ab. 120 mi. (193 km.) long.

Pa·via \pä-ˈvē-ä\. **1.** Province of Lombardy, Italy. See table at ITALY.

2. *anc.* **Ti·ci·num** \tə-ˈsī-nəm\. Commune, its ✻, on Ticino River 19 mi. (31 km.) S of Milan; pop. (1991p) 76,418; manufactures sewing machines, foundry products, chemicals; 14th cent. Visconti castle; cathedral (begun 15th cent.), 12th cent. church of St. Michael, 12th cent. church of St. Peter containing the remains of St. Augustine of Hippo; university (1361); 5 mi. (8 km.) N is Certosa de Pavia, 14th cent. Carthusian monastery with notable Gothic church.

History: Orig. a Roman municipality; sacked by Huns and Goths 5th cent. A.D.; came under the Visconti family c. 1359 and became a leading Italian city-state; in 1525 scene of a decisive victory by Holy Roman Emperor Charles V over the French under Francis I, who was captured.

Pa·vil·ion Dome \pə-ˈvil-yən\. Peak in the Sierra Nevada, E Fresno co., S cen. California; 11,355 ft. (3461 m.).

Pav·lo·dar \ˌpȧv-lə-ˈdär\. **1.** Administrative subdivision of Kazakhstan; 49,228 sq. mi. (127,501 sq. km.); pop. (1991e) 956,900; ✻ Pavlodar; wheat, millet; coal, gold, salt, copper; an oblast of Kazakh S.S.R. 1938–91.

2. Town, its ✻, on right bank of Irtysh River 180 mi. (290 km.) NW of Semey; pop. (1991e) 342,500; food processing; oil refinery; in a rich agricultural region and on the railroad line ab. halfway bet. Astana and Barnaul, Russia.

Pav·lof \ˈpav-ˌlȯf\. Volcano, SW Alaska Penin., Alaska; on W shore of **Pavlof Bay,** inlet ab. 50 mi. (80 km.) long on S coast of peninsula; 8261 ft. (2518 m.); several eruptions mid 1970s to mid 1980s.

Pav·lo·hrad \ˌpə-vlə-ˈkrät\ *or Russ.* **Pav·lo·grad** \-ˈgrät\. Town, Dnipropetrovs'k subdivision, E cen. Ukraine, ab. 37 mi. (60 km.) E of the city of Dnipropetrovs'k; pop. (1991e) 134,000.

Pav·lo·vo \ˈpȧ-vlə-və\. Town, Nizhegorod Oblast, cen. Russia in Europe, ab. 40 mi. (64 km.) SW of Nizhniy Novgorod; pop. (1991e) 72,200.

Pa·vlovsk \ˈpȧv-ləfsk\; *formerly* **Slutsk** \ˈslütsk\. Town, St. Petersburg Oblast, W Russia in Europe, near Pushkin and ab. 15 mi. (24 km.) S of the city of St. Petersburg; pop. (1991e) 25,400; former royal palace and park.

Pa·vlov·ski Po·sad *or* **Pa·vlov·skiy Po·sad** \ˌpȧv-ləf-skē-pə-ˈsȧt\. Town, Moscow Oblast, W cen. Russia in Europe, on the Klyaz'ma River just E of the city of Moscow; pop. (1991e) 70,900.

Paw·ca·tuck \ˈpȯ-kə-ˌtək\. River, SW Rhode Island; forms S section of Rhode Island-Connecticut boundary.

Paw·hus·ka \pȯ-ˈhəs-kə\. City, ⊗ of Osage co., N Oklahoma, 22 mi. (35 km.) W of Bartlesville; pop. (1990c) 3825; tribal ✻ of Osage Indians; oil.

Paw·nee \pȯ-ˈnē\. **1.** River, W cen. Kansas; rises in N Gray co., SW Kansas, flows N and E into Arkansas River at Larned, in Pawnee co., cen. Kansas; ab. 110 mi. (175 km.) long.

2. Name of counties in three states of the U.S. See tables at KANSAS, NEBRASKA, OKLAHOMA.

3. Village, Sangamon co., Illinois; pop. (1990c) 2775.

4. City, ⊗ of Pawnee co., N Oklahoma, 30 mi. (48 km.) SSE of Ponca City; pop. (1990c) 2197; site of Pawnee Agency estab. 1876; opened for settlement 1893.

Pawnee City. City, ⊗ of Pawnee co., SE Nebraska, 35 mi. (56 km.) ESE of Beatrice; pop. (1990c) 1008.

Paw Paw \ˈpȯ-ˌpȯ\. Village, ⊗ of Van Buren co., SW Michigan, 17 mi. (27 km.) WSW of Kalamazoo; pop. (1990c) 3169; vineyards.

Paw·tuck·et \pə-ˈtə-kət, pȯ-\. City, Providence co., N Rhode Island, 4 mi. (6 km.) NE of Providence on both sides of Blackstone River at Pawtucket Falls; pop. (1990c) 72,644; historically a center of the textile industry. Settled 1671; site of first successful water-powered cotton mill in U.S. (now open to the public), built 1793 by Samuel Slater, who reproduced from memory English inventor Sir Richard Arkwright's invention; incorp. as city 1885.

Pawtucket Falls. **1.** City, Massachusetts. See LOWELL 2.

2. Waterfall, Rhode Island. See PAWTUCKET.

Paw·tux·et \pȯ-ˈtək-sət, pə-\. River, Rhode Island; flows from Scituate Reservoir E into Providence River; ab. 28 mi. (45 km.) long.

Pax Augusta. See BADAJOZ 2.

Pax Julia. See BEJA 2.

Pax·os \ˈpak-səs\ *or Gk.* **Pa·xoí** \päk-ˈsē\. One of the Ionian Is., in the Ionian Sea S of Corfu, with which it forms Corfu dept. of Greece; 7 sq. mi. (18 sq. km.); pop. (1981c) 2247; chief village Gaïon.

Pax·ton \ˈpaks-tən\. **1.** City, ⊗ of Ford co., NE cen. Illinois, 25 mi. (40 km.) N of Champaign; pop. (1990c) 4289.
2. Town, Worcester co., cen. Massachusetts, 6 mi. (10 km.) NW of the city of Worcester; pop. (1990c) 4047; Anna Maria Coll. (1946).

Pa·ya·cha·ta \ˌpä-yä-ˈchä-tä\. Peak in N Tarapacá region, N Chile; 20,767 ft. (6330 m.).

Pay·erne \pe-ˈyern\ *or Ger.* **Pe·ter·ling·en** \ˈpā-tər-ˌliŋ-ən\. Commune, Vaud canton, Switzerland, ab. 10 mi. (16 km.) W of Fribourg; pop. (1980c) 6713; 11th cent. abbey church.

Pay·ette \pā-ˈet\. **1.** River, W Idaho; N fork rises in NW corner of Valley co., N of the two **Payette Lakes;** flows S and in Boise co. is joined by S fork which flows W across Boise co.; combined stream turns W and WNW and empties into Snake River at Payette on Oregon border; total length with N fork is 110 mi. (177 km.), with S fork is ab. 70 mi. (110 km.).
2. County in SW Idaho. See table at IDAHO.
3. City, ⊗ of Payette co., SW Idaho, on Snake River across from Oregon; pop. (1990c) 5592.

Payne \ˈpān\. County in N cen. Oklahoma. See table at OKLAHOMA.

Payne Lake. Lake, Ungava Penin., N Quebec, Canada; 230 sq. mi. (596 sq. km.); has outlet (**Payne River**) E into Ungava Bay.

Pay·san·dú \ˌpī-sän-ˈdü\. **1.** Department of W Uruguay. See table at URUGUAY.
2. City and port, its ✻, on E bank of Uruguay River 210 mi. (338 km.) NW of Montevideo; pop. (1985c) 76,191; meatpacking; flour mills, breweries, tanneries; founded 1772.

Pays de Buch. See LA TESTE.

Pays de Gex. See GEX.

Pays de la Loire \ˌpād-lə-ˈlwär\. Region of W France. See table at FRANCE.

Pays de Waes. See WAES.

Pay·son \ˈpā-sən\. City, Utah co., N cen. Utah, 15 mi. (24 km.) S of Provo; pop. (1990c) 9510.

Pa·yún \pä-ˈyün\. Peak, SW Mendoza prov., W Argentina; 12,073 ft. (3680 m.).

Paz, La. See LA PAZ.

Pa·zar·dzhik \ˈpä-zär-ˌjēk\; *formerly* **Ta·tar Pazardzhik** \ˈtä-tär\. City, SW Bulgaria; pop. (1991e) 87,227.

Pa·zin \ˈpä-ˌzēn\ *or Ital.* **Pi·si·no** \pē-ˈzē-nō\. Commune, S cen. Istria Penin., W Croatia, 27 mi. (43 km.) NE of Pula; 13th cent. cathedral; before 1947 belonged to Italy.

Pea \ˈpē\. River, Alabama; rises in Bullock co., flows S and empties into the Choctawhatchee in Geneva co., near the Florida border; ab. 100 mi. (160 km.) long.

Pea·body \ˈpē-bə-dē, -ˌbä-\. City, Essex co., NE corner of Massachusetts, 13 mi. (21 km.) SE of Lowell; pop. (1990c) 47,039; leather products; orig. part of Salem and then of Danvers (*qq.v.*); made town as South Danvers 1855; renamed 1868; incorp. as city 1916.

Peabody, Mount. Peak in Glacier National Park, NW Montana; 9200 ft. (2800 m.).

Peace \ˈpēs\. **1.** River, W cen. Florida; rises in Polk co., cen. Florida Penin., flows S and SW into Charlotte Harbor, Charlotte co., on SW coast; ab. 85 mi. (135 km.) long.
2. River, W Canada; formed by confluence of Finlay and Parsnip rivers in E cen. British Columbia, flows E across border of Alberta, turns NE and joins the Slave River just N of its outlet from Lake Athabaska; 1195 mi. (1923 km.) long (to head of Finlay). Explored by Scotsman Alexander Mackenzie 1792–93.

Peace River. **1.** Rivers, Florida and Canada. See PEACE.
2. Town, W Alberta, Canada, on the right bank of Peace River where it is joined by the Smoky; pop. (1991c) 6717; road and railroad center.

Peach \ˈpēch\. County in cen. Georgia. See table at GEORGIA.

Peach·tree City \ˈpēch-ˌtrē\. City, Fayette co., NW Georgia; pop. (1990c) 19,027.

Peach Tree Creek. Creek in Georgia, flowing into the Chattahoochee River near Atlanta; scene of battle July 1864 in which the Confederates failed to drive back Union Gen. William T. Sherman's forces advancing on Atlanta; Confederate Gen. John Bell Hood's first engagement after replacing Gen. Joseph Johnston.

Peak District \ˈpēk\. Plateau region in N Derbyshire, N cen. England, at S end of the Pennine Chain; highest point **Kin·der Scout** \ˈkin-dər-ˌskau̇t\ 2088 ft. (636 m.); region of wild moors, cultivated valleys, and hills with craggy summits; included in **Peak District National Park** (ab. 540 sq. mi. or 1400 sq. km.) which extends into the surrounding counties and is popular with hikers.

Peak Ridge. Mountain in the Adirondack Mts., NE New York; 4375 ft. (1334 m.).

Peale \ˈpēl\. Small island, N part of Wake I. group, North Pacific Ocean, bordering the lagoon on the N; airport.

Peale, Mount. Peak in N San Juan co., SE Utah; 12,721 ft. (3877 m.); highest in La Sal Mts.

Pea Ridge \ˈpē\. City in Benton co., NW Arkansas; pop. (1990c) 1620; scene of battle Mar. 1862 in which Union forces under Gen. Samuel R. Curtis defeated Confederates under Gen. Earl Van Dorn; site of **Pea Ridge National Military Park** (see UNITED STATES, *National Historical Parks*).

Pear·is·burg \ˈper-is-ˌbərg\. Town, ⊗ of Giles co., W Virginia; pop. (1990c) 2064.

Pearl \ˈpərl\. **1.** River, cen. and S cen. Mississippi; rises in Neshoba co., flows SW, then S into the Gulf of Mexico, forming in the S section the Louisiana-Mississippi boundary; ab. 410 mi. (660 km.) long.
2. City, Rankin co., Mississippi, E of Jackson; pop. (1990c) 19,588.
3. River, SE China. See ZHU.

Pear·land \ˈpar-ˌland, -lənd\. Village, Brazoria co., SE Texas, ab. 3 mi. (5 km.) S of Houston; pop. (1990c) 18,697.

Pearl and Her·mes Atoll \ˈpərl ... ˈhər-mēz\ *or* **Pearl and Hermes Reef.** Atoll in Hawaii consisting of 12 islets, in cen. Pacific Ocean ab. 1000 mi. (1600 km.) NW of Niihau I.; part of Leeward Is.; bird reservation.

Pearl Cays *or Span.* **Ca·yos de Per·las** \ˈkī-ōs-t͟hā-ˈper-läs\. Group of small islands in Caribbean Sea near the coast of SE cen. Nicaragua, outside of Perlas Lagoon.

Pearl City. Unincorporated settlement, Honolulu co., S Oahu I., Hawaii, on Pearl Harbor; pop. (1990c) 30,993; suffered damage in Japanese attack on Pearl Harbor Dec. 7, 1941.

Pearl Harbor. Inlet on S coast of the island of Oahu, Hawaii, 6 mi. (10 km.) W of Honolulu, forming a landlocked harbor used by U.S. as a naval station and base; connected with Pacific Ocean. By treaty of 1887 Hawaii granted U.S. exclusive right to use Pearl Harbor as coaling and repair station; not so used until after 1908 when Congress authorized establishment of naval station; dry dock completed 1919; attacked without warning by Japanese Air Force Sunday morning Dec. 7, 1941, precipitating U.S. entry into WWII.

Pearl Islands. **1.** Island group, Caribbean Sea. See PEARL CAYS.
2. *or Span.* **Ar·chi·pié·la·go de las Per·las** \ˌär-chē-ˈpyā-lä-gō-ˌt͟hā-läs-ˈper-läs\. Group of islands, Panama, in the Gulf of Panama; 450 sq. mi. (1166 sq. km.); historically notable pearl fisheries.

Pearl Lagoon. See PERLAS LAGOON.

Pearl Point. See PERLAS, PUNTA DE.

Pearl River. **1.** River in Mississippi. See PEARL 1.
2. County in S Mississippi. See table at MISSISSIPPI.
3. Unincorporated settlement, Rockland co., SE New York, near New Jersey border ab. 12 mi. (19 km.) NE of Paterson, New Jersey; pop. (1990c) 15,314.

Pear·sall \ˈpir-ˌsȯl\. City, ⊗ of Frio co., S Texas, 43 mi. (69 km.) ESE of Uvalde; pop. (1990c) 6924.

Pear·son \ˈpir-sən\. City, ⊗ of Atkinson co., S Georgia; pop. (1990c) 1714.

Pea·ry Land \ˈpir-ē\ *also* **Pea·ry·land** \-ˌland\. Region of N Greenland on Arctic Ocean, forming a mountainous peninsula, 82° to 84°N; does not have the ice cap that covers most of Greenland. Its N cape, Morris Jesup, is one of the most northerly points of land; penetrated by several fjords; highest point 6300 ft. (1920 m.). First visited 1881–82; charted by American polar explorer Robert Peary 1900.

Peb·ble Island \ˈpe-bəl\. Island off N coast of West Falkland, Falkland Is.

Peć *or* **Pech** *also* **Petch** \ˈpech\ *or Turk.* **Ipek** \i-ˈpek\. Town, Serbia, S Yugoslavia, ab. 75 mi. (120 km.) NW of Skopje, Republic of Macedonia; pop. (1981c) 111,071; trades in agricultural products; in the Middle Ages, seat of the patriarchs of the Serbian Orthodox Church.

Pe·chen·ga \pe-ˈcheŋ-gä\ *or Finn.* **Pet·sa·mo** \ˈpet-sä-ˌmō\. **1.** Territory, NW Russia in Europe, extending nearly to Varanger Fjord, Norway, forming a narrow strip 135 mi. (217 km.) long from N to S bordering on W Murmansk Oblast; 3860 sq. mi. (9997 sq. km.); ceded by U.S.S.R. to Finland 1920; occupied by Germans 1940–44; ceded back to U.S.S.R. by Finnish-Soviet armistice 1944.

2. Village in Murmansk Oblast, Russia in Europe, in extreme NW part on narrow inlet of Arctic Ocean, 60 mi. (97 km.) W of the city of Murmansk; center of copper-mining region; used by Finnish-German forces as a naval and aviation base in WWII. Belonged to Finland 1920–44.

Pe·cho·ra \pi-ˈchȯ-rə\. River, NE Russia in Europe, chiefly in Komi Rep.; rises in Middle Ural Mts. in N Perm' Oblast, flows N, W, and N in great bend into Pechorskaya Guba; 1112 mi. (1789 km.) long; its main tributaries the Tsil'ma and Izhma on the W and the Usa on the E; both the main stream and its tributaries are navigable for most of their courses; has extensive delta; coalfields in its basin.

Pechora Bay. See PECHORSKAYA GUBA.

Pechora Sea. See PECHORSKOYE MORE.

Pe·chor·ska·ya Gu·ba \pi-ˈchȯr-skə-yə-ˈgü-bə\; *or Eng.* **Pe·cho·ra Bay** \pi-ˈchȯ-rə\. Inlet of Pechorskoye More, NE coast of Nenets Autonomous Okrug, N Russia in Europe; ab. 40 mi. (65 km.) long; receives Pechora River from the S.

Pechorskoye Mo·re \pi-ˈchȯr-skə-yə-ˈmȯr-yə\; *or Eng.* **Pechora Sea.** Sea, a SE extension of Barents Sea, bet. Novaya Zemlya and Nenets Autonomous Okrug, N Russia in Europe.

Pe·con·ic Bay \pi-ˈkä-nik\. Inlet at E end of Long Island, New York, SW of Gardiners Bay; divided into **Great Peconic Bay** on the W and **Little Peconic Bay** on the E; receives the **Peconic River.**

Pe·cos \ˈpā-kəs\. **1.** *or* **Rio Pecos** \ˈrē-ō\. River, E New Mexico and W Texas; rises in W Mora co., New Mexico, flows SE across Texas border and empties into Rio Grande in S Val Verde co., SW Texas; 500 mi. (805 km.) long.

2. County in W Texas. See table at TEXAS.

3. City, ⊗ of Reeves co., W Texas, near Pecos River 40 mi. (64 km.) S of New Mexico border; pop. (1990c) 12,069; oil wells; cantaloupes.

Pecos National Historic Park; *formerly* **Pecos National Monument.** See UNITED STATES, *National Historic Parks.*

Pécs \ˈpāch\ *or Ger.* **Fünf·kir·chen** \ˈfœnf-ˌkir-kən\. City, ⊗ of Baranya co., S Hungary, 106 mi. (171 km.) W of Budapest; 56 sq. mi. (145 sq. km.); pop. (1991e) 179,000; wine, leather goods; center of coal-mining region; 11th cent. cathedral; university (1922). A settlement of Celtic tribes and Romans; made bishopric 1009; occupied by Turks 1543–1686.

Ped·docks Island \ˈpe-dəks\. Island in S area of Boston Bay, E Massachusetts, off N tip of penin. on which the town of Hull is situated; contains the remains of a fort.

Pedee. See PEE DEE.

Ped·er·nal·es \ˌpərd-ᵊn-ˈa-ləs, ˌpe-dər-ˈna-ləs\. River, cen. Texas; rises in Kimble co. and flows E to Colorado River NW of Austin; 106 mi. (171 km.) long.

Pe·der·na·les \ˌpā-der-ˈnä-lās\. **1.** Province, SW Dominican Republic. See table at DOMINICAN REPUBLIC.

2. Town, its ✻; pop. (1981p) 11,571.

Pe·di·e·os *or* **Pe·dhi·e·os** \ˌpē-t͟hē-ˈā-ˌȯs\; *anc.* **Ped·i·ae·us** \ˌpe-dē-ˈē-əs\. River on the island of Cyprus; flows E to Famagusta Bay; ab. 60 mi. (95 km.) long.

Pedras, Point. See COQUEIROS, POINT.

Pe·dre·gal \ˌpā-t͟hrā-ˈgäl\. **1.** River, SE Mexico; rises in W Chiapas state, flows N to the Tonalá in Tabasco state; ab. 50 mi. (80 km.) long.

2. Pacific coast port, W Panama; port for David.

Pe·dro Bank \ˈpe-drō\. Shoal in NW Caribbean Sea, S of Jamaica; includes the Pedro Cays.

Pe·dro Be·tan·court \ˈpā-t͟hrō-ˌbā-täŋ-ˈkür\. Municipality, Matanzas prov., W cen. Cuba, SE of the city of Matanzas; pop. (1981p) 30,253.

Pe·dro Cays \ˈpe-drō\. Four small guano islands ab. 45 mi. (72 km.) SW of Jamaica; a dependency of Jamaica from 1882.

Pe·dro Juan Ca·bal·le·ro \ˈpā-t͟hrō-ˈhwän-ˌkä-bä-ˈyā-rō\. Town, ✻ of Amambay dept., E Paraguay, on Brazilian border 125 mi. (201 km.) ENE of Concepción; pop. (1992p) 53,601.

Pe·dro Mi·guel \ˈpā-t͟hrō-mē-ˈgel\. Town, cen. Panama at the Pedro Miguel Locks in the Panama Canal, just NW of Miraflores.

Pedro Miguel Locks. Locks in the Panama Canal, NW of Miraflores Lake and NW of the city of Panama; lowers vessels 31 ft. (9 m.) to level of Miraflores Lake.

Pedro Point \ˈpe-drō\. Cape on NW tip of the island of Jamaica, West Indies.

Pee·bles \ˈpē-bəlz\. **1.** *or* **Pee·bles·shire** \ˈpē-bəl-ˌshir, -shər\ *or* **Tweed·dale** \ˈtwēd-ˌdāl\. Former county, SE Scotland; ⊗ Peebles; its chief river the Tweed.

2. Market town, W Borders region, SE Scotland, on the Tweed; pop. (1981c) 6692; woolen textiles.

Pee Dee *also* **Pe·dee** \ˈpē-ˌdē\ *or in South Carolina often* **Great Pee Dee.** River, North Carolina and South Carolina; formed by junction of Yadkin and Uharie rivers in Montgomery co., S cen. North Carolina, flows SE into South Carolina and into Winyah Bay; 233 mi. (375 km.) long.

Peek·a·moose Mountain \ˈpē-kə-ˌmüs\. Peak in the Catskill Mts., Ulster co., SE New York; 3843 ft. (1171 m.).

Peeks·kill \ˈpēk-ˌskil\. City, Westchester co., SE New York, on Hudson River 39 mi. (63 km.) N of New York City; pop. (1990c) 19,536. In American Revolution strategically important; burned by British 1777.

Peel \ˈpēl\. **1.** River, NW Canada; rises in W Yukon Terr., flows E and then N into Mackenzie River in extreme NW mainland part of Northwest Territories; 425 mi. (684 km.) long (to head of Ogilvie).

2. Municipal region in SE Ontario, Canada. See table at ONTARIO.

3. Coastal town, W Isle of Man, England; pop. (1991c) 3829; fishing center and seaside resort; ancient chapel dedicated to St. Patrick, who is believed to have founded first church in Isle of Man; ruins of castle and cathedral.

Peel \ˈpāl\. Marsh area, North Brabant and Limburg provs., S Netherlands; 60 sq. mi. (155 sq. km.).

Peel Sound \ˈpēl\. Passage bet. Prince of Wales I. and Somerset I., cen. Arctic Archipelago, Nunavut, Canada.

Pee·ne \ˈpā-nə\. Navigable river, NE Germany; flows E into Peene estuary which flows N to S bet. Zalew Szczeciński and the Baltic Sea; 70 mi. (113 km.) long.

Pee·ne·mün·de \ˌpā-nə-ˈmœn-də\. Village on small island at mouth of Peene estuary, NE Germany, at W end of Usedom I. and NW of Zalew Szczeciński; in WWII the principal German research and testing facility for rockets and missiles; severely bombed by British Aug. 18, 1943; captured by Soviet troops Apr. 1945.

Peg·a·sus Bay \ˈpe-gə-səs\. Inlet of Pacific Ocean on NE cen. coast of South I., New Zealand, N of Banks Penin.; receives the Waimakariri River from the W.

Peg·nitz \ˈpāg-nəts\. River, Bavaria, Germany; flows S and W through Nürnberg to unite with the Rednitz at Fürth and form the Regnitz River; 53 mi. (85 km.) long.

Pe·gu \pe-ˈgü\. **1.** River, Pegu division, Myanmar; ab. 150 mi. (240 km.) long; tributary of the Yangon River.

2. Division of Myanmar. See table at MYANMAR.

3. Town, ✱ of Pegu division, 47 mi. (76 km.) NE of Yangon and on railroad line from Yangon to Toungoo and to Martaban; pop. (1983c) 150,528; ships rice; has numerous pagodas, incl. the notable Shwemawdaw (288 ft. or 88 m. high), and reclining figure of Buddha.

History: Possibly first settled 6th cent. A.D.; estab. as ✱ of Mon kingdom c. 825; later ✱ of Burmese Toungoo dynasty; Mons briefly restored 1740 to 1757, when city mostly destroyed by Burmese King Alaungpya; annexed by British 1852; occupied by Japanese 1942–45.

Pegunungan Jayawijaya. See JAYAWIJAYA RANGE.

Pe·gu Yo·ma \pe-'gü-'yō-mə\. Mountain range, Myanmar, extending N and S bet. the Irrawaddy and the Sittang rivers; ab. 270 mi. (435 km.) long; highest point Mt. Popa 4981 ft. (1518 m.) at N end.

Pehanchen. See BEI'AN.

Pehtaiho. See BEIDAIHE.

Pehtang. See BEITANG.

Pei \'bā\. **1.** River, Hebei prov., China. See BAI.

2. River, Guangdong prov., China. See BEI.

Pei–an *or* **Pei·an** \'bā-'än\. **1.** Former province (1932–45), N cen. Manchukuo; 27,596 sq. mi. (71,474 sq. km.).

2. Town, NE China. See BEI'AN.

Pei–erh Hu. See BUIR NUR.

Pei–hai. See BEIHAI.

Pei·ne \'pī-nə\. City, Lower Saxony, Germany, 17 mi. (27 km.) NE of Hildesheim; pop. (1980c) 47,591; founded c. 1220.

Pei–piao. See BEIPIAO.

Peiping. See BEIJING.

Pei·pus, Lake \'pī-pəs\ *or Estonian* **Peip·si Järv** \'pāp-sē-'yarv\ *or Russ.* **Chud·sko·ye Oze·ro** \'chüt-skə-yə-'ö-zyə-rə\. Lake, N cen. Europe, bet. E Estonia and W Pskov Oblast, Russia; 60 mi. (97 km.) long and 31 mi. (50 km.) wide; 1390 sq. mi. (3600 sq. km.). Its outlet is the Narva flowing N to Gulf of Finland; receives from the S the Velikaya and from the W the Ema. Its S extension is sometimes called Lake Pskov (*q.v.*). Estonia-Russia boundary line runs nearly in center except at N end, where entire N shore and Narva River are in Estonia. Teutonic Knights defeated by Alexander Nevsky, prince of Novgorod, on ice of the lake 1242, greatly reducing Teutonic threat to Russian lands.

Peiraeus. See PIRAEUS.

Pei–tai–ho. See BEIDAIHE.

Pei–t'ang. See BEITANG.

Pei·war Pass \'pā-wär\. Mountain pass, W end of Safed Koh Range from NW Pakistan into Afghanistan, SE of Kabul, in the Kurram Valley; scene of defeat of Afghans by Lord (Frederick) Roberts during Second Afghan War (1878–80).

Pe·ka·long·an \pə-ˌkä-'lòŋ-ˌän\. **1.** Regency, Central Java prov., Indonesia; 2176 sq. mi. (5636 sq. km.); pop. (1990c) 227,535; ✱ Pekalongan; bounded on N by Java Sea; has considerable area of flat fertile land along the coast with mountain range along S border; chief crop sugar; much rice and some indigo and kapok grown.

2. City, its ✱, on N coast and on railroad line 55 mi. (88 km.) W of Semarang; pop. (1990c) 242,874; exports sugar; textiles, batiks; fort built 1753.

Pe·kan \pə-'kän\. Seaport town on S side of the Pahang River near its mouth, E Pahang state, Malaysia; pop. (1980p) 59,891; sultan's residence and until 1898 the ✱.

Pe·kan·ba·ru \pə-'kän-ˌbä-ˌrü\ *or* **Pa·kan·ba·ru** \pə-\. Town, ✱ of Riau prov., Sumatra, Indonesia, 130 mi. (209 km.) NE of Padang; pop. (1990c) 398,694.

Pe·kin \'pē-kən, -ˌkin\. City, ⊗ of Tazewell co., cen. Illinois, on Illinois River 10 mi. (16 km.) S of Peoria; pop. (1990c) 32,254; river port and railroad center, shipping livestock, grain, and coal; produces aluminum and brass castings, alcohol, barrels, corn products; settled 1824; incorp. 1839.

Peking. See BEIJING.

Pe·la·bu·han·ra·tu Bay \ˌpe-lə-ˌbü-hän-'rä-tü\ *or Du.* **Wijn·koops–Baai** \'vīn-kōps-'bī, 'vān-\ *or Eng.* **Wyn·koops Bay** \'wīn-küps\. Inlet of the Indian Ocean, S side of the W end of Java, Indonesia.

Pe·la·gi Islands \pe-'lä-jē\ *also* **Pe·la·gi·an Islands** \pə-'lā-jən, -jē-ən\ *or Ital.* **Iso·le Pe·la·gie** \'ē-zò-lā-pā-'lä-jā\. Three barren Italian islands, Lampedusa, Linosa, and Lampione (uninhabited), in the Mediterranean Sea S of Sicily, Italy, and bet. Malta and Tunisia; politically attached to Agrigento prov., Italy. Taken by Allies 1943.

Pelagosa Islands *or* **Pelagosa, Isole di.** See PALAGRUŽA ISLANDS.

Pe·lée, Mount \pə-'lā\ *or Fr.* **Mon·tagne Pelée** \mōⁿ-'tänʸ, -'tä-nyə\. Volcano, N Martinique I., West Indies; 4583 ft. (1397 m.); erupted 1902, destroying St. Pierre and killing more than 30,000 persons, incl. all the town's inhabitants.

Pe·lee, Point *or* **Pelee Point** \'pē-lē\. Headland, Essex co., SE Ontario, Canada, projecting into Lake Erie; has remarkable beaches and flora; estab. 1918 as a national park (see CANADA, *National Parks*). **Pelee Island** is 8 mi. (13 km.) to the S in Lake Erie.

Pel·e·liu \'pe-lel-yü, ˌpe-lə-'lē-ü\. Island at S end of Palau Is., W Pacific Ocean, bet. Angaur and Eil Malk; ab. 5 mi. (8 km.) long by 2 mi. (3 km.) wide; chief village Ngardololok. Many islets and reefs off its N shore. Captured by U.S. forces after severe fighting during WWII Sept. and Oct. 1944.

Pe·leng \'pā-ˌleŋ\. Largest island in the Banggai Archipelago, off the E coast of Sulawesi, Malay Archipelago, Indonesia; ab. 53 mi. (85 km.) long by 32 mi. (51 km.) wide; 929 sq. mi. (2406 sq. km.).

Peleng Strait. Passage bet. E peninsula of Sulawesi and Peleng I. of the Banggai Archipelago, connecting the Gulf of Tolo with the Molucca Sea.

Pelew. See PALAU.

Pel·ham \'pe-ləm\. **1.** City, Shelby co., N cen. Alabama, 15 mi. (24 km.) S of Birmingham; pop. (1990c) 9765.

2. City, Mitchell co., SW Georgia, 32 mi. (51 km.) S of Albany; pop. (1990c) 3869; incorp. 1881.

3. Town, Hillsborough co., S New Hampshire, 9 mi. (14 km.) E of Nashua; pop. (1990c) 9408.

4. Village in Pelham town, Westchester co., SE New York, 17 mi. (27 km.) NE of New York City; pop. (1990c) 6413 (village), 11,903 (town).

5. Town, SE Ontario, Canada, SW of Niagara Falls; pop. (1991c) 13,328.

Pelham Manor. Village in Pelham town, Westchester co., SE New York, on Long Island Sound 17 mi. (27 km.) NE of New York City; pop. (1990c) 5443; suburb of New York City.

Pel·i·can Island \'pe-li-kən\. Island in Atlantic Ocean, off NE coast of Volusia co., E Florida.

Pelican Point. Cape on W cen. coast of Namibia, enclosing Walvis Bay.

Pe·li·on, Mount \'pē-lē-ən\ *or Gk.* **Pí·li·on Óros** \'pē-lē-ˌòn-'ör-ˌòs\. Peak, S Larissa dept., E Thessaly, NE Greece, near Volos; 5089 ft. (1551 m.). In Greek mythology the home of Chiron the centaur; also figured in the war against the gods waged by the giants Otus and Ephialtes, who piled Mt. Pelion on top of Mt. Ossa in an attempt to scale the heavens.

Pe·lje·šac \'pel-ye-ˌshäts\ *or Ital.* **Sab·bion·cel·lo** \ˌsä-byōn-'chel-lō\. Peninsula on coast of S Croatia, projecting NW into the Adriatic Sea E of Korčula I.; 43 mi. (69 km.) long.

Pel·kum \'pel-ˌküm\. City, North Rhine-Westphalia, Germany, 14 mi. (23 km.) N of Dortmund.

Pel·la \'pe-lə\. **1.** City, Marion co., S cen. Iowa, 17 mi. (27 km.) WNW of Oskaloosa; pop. (1990c) 9270; Central Coll. (1853).

2. Department of Central Macedonia, Greece. See table at GREECE.

3. Ruins of ancient city 24 mi. (39 km.) WNW of Thessaloníki, Greece; ancient ✱ of Macedonia and birthplace of King Alexander the Great 356 B.C.

Pell City \'pel\. City, ⊗ of St. Clair co., NE cen. Alabama; pop. (1990c) 8118.

\ə\ abut \ˈə\ matches \ᵊ\ kitten, Fr table \ər\ further \a\ ash \ā\ ace \ä\ cot, cart \à\ Fr bac \aù\ out \b\ Span Avila \ch\ chin \e\ bet \ē\ easy \g\ go \i\ hit \ī\ ice \j\ job \k\ Ger ich, Buch \ⁿ\ Fr vin \ŋ\ sing \ō\ go \ò\ all \òi\ law \œ\ Fr bœuf \œ̄\ Fr feu \òi\ boy \th\ thin \th\ this \ü\ loot \ù\ foot \ue\ Ger füllen \ue̅\ Fr rue \y\ yet \ʸ\ Fr digne \'dēnʸ\, nuit \'nwʸē\ \yü\ few \yù\ fury \zh\ vision

Pel·les·tri·na \ˌpe-les-ˈtrē-nä\. Island in S Lagoon of Venice, Italy; 9 mi. (14 km.) long; a part of the seaport of Venice.

Pell·worm \ˈpel-ˌvȯrm\. One of the Halligen Is., in S part of North Frisian Is. off W coast of Schleswig-Holstein, NW Germany, W of Nordstrand; area 14 sq. mi. (36 sq. km.).

Pel·ly \ˈpe-lē\. **1.** Former city, Harris co., SE Texas, on Galveston Bay; now part of Baytown.

2. River, S cen. Yukon Terr., Canada; rises in Mackenzie Mts. and flows W to unite with Lewes River and form Yukon River; 330 mi. (531 km.) long.

Pelly, Lake. Lake, NE mainland part of Nunavut, Canada; 331 sq. mi. (857 sq. km.); connects with Garry Lake.

Pelly Bay. Bay, inlet of Gulf of Boothia, in NE mainland part of Nunavut, Canada, W of Simpson Penin.

Pe·lon·cil·lo Mountains \ˌpe-lən-ˈsē-yō\. Range, SW Hidalgo co., in extreme SW New Mexico, and extending across border into Arizona.

Pel·o·pon·nese \ˈpe-lə-pə-ˌnēz, -ˌnēs\ *or* **Pel·o·pon·ne·sus** \ˌpe-lə-pə-ˈnē-səs\ *or* **Pel·o·pon·ne·sos** \-səs\. Peninsula, forming S part of the mainland of Greece; ancient subdivisions: Achaea, Arcadia, Argolis, Elis, Laconia, Messenia, and Sicyonia; chief cities Corinth and Sparta; under the Romans was larger part of the prov. of Achaea 146 B.C.–c. 4th cent. A.D.; since early 13th cent. when it was under the Latin Empire often called **Mo·rea** \ˈmōr-ē-ə\.

Pel·o·pón·ni·sos \ˌpe-lō-ˈpō-nē-ˌsōs\. Administrative region of modern Greece, coextensive with Peloponnese Penin.; 8603 sq. mi. (22,282 sq. km.); pop. (1991p) 1,077,022. See table at GREECE.

Pelorus. See FARO, CAPE.

Pe·lo·tas \pä-ˈlȯ-tȧs\. City, SE Rio Grande do Sul state, S Brazil, at S end of Lagoa dos Patos 29 mi. (47 km.) NNW of Rio Grande; munic. pop. (1991p) 289,484; ships meat products, rice; produces flour, leather goods, footwear, soap; university (1883), Catholic university (1960).

Pelouse. See PALOUSE.

Pel·to, Lake \ˈpel-tō\. Inlet of Gulf of Mexico in S Terrebonne parish, SE Louisiana.

Pe·lu·si·ac Branch \pə-ˈlü-sē-ˌak, -shē-\. Ancient E arm of the Nile River, E of the Phatnitic (Damietta) mouth, now filled up.

Pe·lu·si·um \pə-ˈlü-shē-əm\. Ancient city of Egypt, on Pelusiac Branch of the Nile. Here Persian King Cambyses II defeated the Egyptians under Psamtik III 525 B.C.; ruins dating from Roman times are in Plain of Tina E of Suez Canal and ab. 22 mi. (35 km.) SE of Port Said, on **Bay of Pelusium** (*or Arab.* **Kha·līj aṭ–Ṭī·nah** \kä-ˈlēj-ȧt-tē-nə\), an inlet of the Mediterranean.

Pel·voux \pel-ˈvü\. Mountain group, SE France, in the Dauphiné Alps in Hautes-Alpes and Isère depts.; contains Barre des Écrins 13,461 ft. (4103 m.), highest peak of the Dauphiné Alps; **Mont Pelvoux** 12,920 ft. (3938 m.), just SE of Barre des Écrins, was for a long time considered the highest point.

Pem·a·dum·cook Lake \ˌpe-mə-ˈdəm-ku̇k\. Lake on boundary bet. Penobscot and Piscataquis cos., N cen. Maine; connected with Millinocket Lake on the NE; traversed NW to SE by W branch of the Penobscot River.

Pe·ma·lang \ˌpä-mə-ˈläŋ\. Town, Central Java prov., Indonesia, on railroad line near coast bet. Pekalongan and Tegal.

Pem·a·quid Point \ˈpe-mə-kwid\. Point, S Lincoln co., S Maine; lighthouse.

Pe·ma·tang·sian·tar \ˌpə-mə-ˌtäŋ-syän-ˈtär\. Town, NE Sumatra, Indonesia, 23 mi. (37 km.) NE of Lake Toba; pop. (1990c) 219,328.

Pem·ba \ˈpem-bä\. **1.** Island, Tanzania, in Indian Ocean off NE coast of mainland, N of island of Zanzibar; 379 sq. mi. (982 sq. km.); pop. (1988p) 265,039; ✻ Wete; administratively divided into **Pemba North** and **Pemba South** (see table at TANZANIA); included with island of Zanzibar in the former Zanzibar sultanate.

2. *formerly* **Por·to Amé·lia** \ˈpōr-tü-ȧ-ˈmel-yə\ *or* **Port Ame·lia** \ə-ˈmēl-yə\. Seaport town, ✻ of Cabo Delgado prov., NE Mozambique, on Pemba Bay; pop. (1980p) 3629.

Pemba Bay. Inlet of Mozambique Channel on NE coast of Mozambique; constitutes harbor for seaport of Porto Amélia.

Pem·bi·na \ˈpem-bə-nə, -ˌnȯ\. **1.** County in NE corner of North Dakota. See table at NORTH DAKOTA.

2. City, Pembina co., NE North Dakota, ab. 22 mi. (35 km.) NE of Cavalier; pop. (1990c) 642; site of earliest trading post (1797–98) and center of European settlement in North Dakota.

3. River, cen. Alberta, Canada; rises near E border of Jasper National Park and flows NE and N into the Athabaska; ab. 210 mi. (338 km.) long.

Pem·broke \ˈpem-ˌbrōk, -ˌbru̇k\. **1.** City, ⊗ of Bryan co., SE Georgia, 31 mi. (50 km.) W of Savannah; pop. (1990c) 1503.

2. Town, Plymouth co., SE Massachusetts, 10 mi. (16 km.) E of Brockton; pop. (1990c) 14,544.

3. Town, Merrimack co., S cen. New Hampshire, on Merrimack River 6 mi. (10 km.) SE of Concord; pop. (1990c) 6561.

4. Town, Robeson co., S North Carolina, ab. 12 mi. (19 km.) NW of Lumberton; pop. (1990c) 2241; Pembroke State Univ. (1887).

5. Town, ⊗ of Renfrew co., SE Ontario, Canada, on Allumette Lake across from Allumette I.; pop. (1991c) 13,997; fishing resort; lumber. Site of limit of French navigator Samuel de Champlain's exploration of the Ottawa River 1613, where he was persuaded to turn back.

6. Former county in Wales. See PEMBROKESHIRE.

7. Market town, SW Dyfed co., SW Wales; pop. (1981c) 15,576; tourist center; 11th cent. castle (birthplace of Henry VII 1457); had large naval dockyard 1814–1926.

Pembroke Park. Town, Broward co., SE Florida; pop. (1990c) 4933.

Pembroke Pines. City, Broward co., SE Florida; pop. (1990c) 65,452; residential suburb of Fort Lauderdale; population has more than quadrupled in size since 1970.

Pem·broke·shire \ˈpem-bru̇k-ˌshir, -brōk-, -shər\ *or* **Pembroke.** Former county, SW Wales; surrounded on three sides by rugged coastline. See DYFED.

Pembrokeshire Coast National Park. National park, Dyfed co., SW Wales.

Pem·i·ge·was·set \ˌpe-mi-jə-ˈwä-sət\. River, cen. New Hampshire; rises in N Grafton co., flows S through Franconia Notch, unites with Winnipesaukee River at Franklin to form the Merrimack River; 70 mi. (113 km.) long; the **Pemigewasset Wilderness** is the region bet. Franconia Notch and Crawford Notch (Saco River) to the E containing many peaks of the White Mts., several over 4000 ft. (1219 m.).

Pem·i·scot \ˈpe-mi-ˌskät, -ˌskō\. County in SE corner of Missouri. See table at MISSOURI.

Pen \ˈpen\. Ancient village, Wessex, S England; probably at present-day village of **Penselwood** in W Somerset, S of Frome; scene of defeat of Canute the Great of Denmark by Edmund II of England 1016.

Peña de Cerredo. See CERREDO, TORRE DE.

Pe·ña·la·ra \ˌpä-nyä-ˈlä-rä\. Highest peak in the Sierra de Guadarrama, N Madrid prov., cen. Spain; 7972 ft. (2430 m.).

Pe·nang \pə-ˈnaŋ\. **1.** *or* **Pi·nang** \pə-\; *formerly* **Prince of Wales Island.** Island, Malaysia, 2.5 mi. (4 km.) off W coast of the Malay Penin., forming part of the Malaysian state of Penang (see PENANG 2); 108 sq. mi. (280 sq. km.).

2. *or* **Pu·lau Pi·nang** \ˈpü-ˌlau̇\. A state of Malaysia, on the Malay Penin.; ✻ George Town; rice, rubber. See table at MALAYSIA.

History: Penang I. the first British settlement in Malaya, acquired 1786 by cession to East India Company from sultan of Kedah; Province Wellesley (adjacent area on mainland) added 1800; Penang settlement made separate presidency 1805 combined with Melaka and Singapore to form Straits Settlements (*q.v.*) 1826, for which it was seat of government 1826–32; occupied by Japanese during WWII; became state of Federation of Malaya 1957 and of Malaysia 1963.

3. See GEORGE TOWN 4.

Pen Ar·gyl \pen-ˈär-jel\. Borough, Northampton co., E Pennsylvania, 22 mi. (35 km.) NE of Allentown; pop. (1990c) 3492.

Pe·ñar·ro·ya–Pue·blo·nue·vo \ˌpā-nyär-ˈrō-yä-ˌpwā-b̲lō-ˈnwā-b̲ō\. Commune, Córdoba prov., S Spain, 40 mi. (64 km.) NW of the city of Córdoba; pop. (1991c) 14,035; iron and lead.

Pen·arth \pe-ˈnärth\. Seaport, South Glamorgan co., S Wales; pop. (1981c) 20,558; seaside resort and residential suburb of Cardiff.

Pe·ñas, Cape \ˈpā-nyäs\ *or Span.* **Ca·bo de Peñas** \ˈkä-b̲ō-t̲h̲ā-\. **1.** Cape on NW coast of Spain, projecting into Bay of Biscay from Asturias prov.

2. Cape on E cen. coast of Tierra del Fuego I., off S South America, at 53°51′S, 67°33′W.

Pe·nas, Gulf of \ˈpā-nyäs\. Inlet of S Pacific Ocean on SW coast of Chile, S of Taitao Penin.

Pen·brook \ˈpen-ˌbru̇k\. Borough, Dauphin co., SE cen. Pennsylvania, 3 mi. (5 km.) NE of Harrisburg; pop. (1990c) 2791.

Pen–ch'i. See BENXI.

Pen·de·li·kón \ˌpen-de-lē-ˈkön\ *or* **Pen·te·li·kon** \ˌpen-de-\ *also* **Pen·tel·i·cus** \pen-ˈte-li-kəs\. Mountain, E cen. Greece, in Central Greece region, 10 mi. (16 km.) NE of Athens; 3639 ft. (1109 m.); has long been a source of excellent marble.

Pen·dem·bu \pen-ˈdem-bü\. Town, SE Sierra Leone, near border of Liberia; terminus of railroad line (227 mi. or 365 km. long) from Freetown.

Pen·der \ˈpen-dər\. **1.** Coastal county in SE North Carolina. See table at NORTH CAROLINA.

2. Village, ⊗ of Thurston co., NE Nebraska; pop. (1990c) 1208.

Pen·dle·ton \ˈpend-ᵊl-tən\. **1.** Name of counties in two states of the U.S. See tables at KENTUCKY and WEST VIRGINIA.

2. City, ⊗ of Umatilla co., NE Oregon, on Umatilla River ab. 42 mi. (68 km.) NW of La Grande; pop. (1990c) 15,126; diversified agriculture; Blue Mountain Community Coll. (1962); center of E Oregon cattle country in 1870s and 1880s.

Pend Oreille \ˌpän-də-ˈrā\. **1.** River, N Idaho and NE Washington, outlet of Pend Oreille Lake; flows W and N into Columbia River in British Columbia near Washington boundary; ab. 100 mi. (160 km.) long.

2. County in NE corner of Washington. See table at WASHINGTON.

Pend Oreille, Mount. Peak, Bonner co., N Idaho; 6754 ft. (2059 m.).

Pend Oreille Lake. Lake, cen. Bonner co., N Idaho; an expansion of Clark Fork River.

Pe·ne·do \pī-ˈnā-dü\. City, Alagoas state, E Brazil, on the São Francisco near its mouth 70 mi. (113 km.) SW of Maceió; munic. pop. (1991p) 52,228.

Penedos de São Pedro e São Paulo. See SAINT PETER AND SAINT PAUL ROCKS.

Pen·e·tan·gui·shene \ˌpe-nə-ˈtaŋ-gwə-ˌshēn\. Town, Simcoe co., SE Ontario, Canada, on an inlet of Georgian Bay 29 mi. (47 km.) NNW of Barrie; pop. (1991c) 6643; summer resort; formerly Canada's naval station on the Great Lakes; visited by French explorer Samuel de Champlain 1615.

Peneus. See PINIÓS.

Pen·field \ˈpen-ˌfēld\. Town, Monroe co., W New York, ab. 7 mi. (11 km.) SE of Rochester; pop. (1990c) 30,219.

Pen·gan·ga \pen-ˈgəŋ-gə, peŋ-\. River, cen. India; flows E to the Wardha River; ab. 200 mi. (322 km.) long.

Penggaram, Bandar. See BATU PAHAT.

P'eng–hu \ˈpəŋ-ˈhü\. **1.** *Eng.* **Pes·ca·do·res** \ˌpes-kə-ˈdōr-ēz, -ˈdōr-əs\; *Jp.* **Ho·ko** \ˌhō-kō\. Group of ab. 48 islands in Taiwan Strait bet. Taiwan and the mainland of China, separated from Taiwan by **P'eng–hu Shui–tao** \ˈshwē-ˈtau̇\ *or* **Penghu Channel** (30 mi. or 48 km. wide); 49 sq. mi. (127 sq. km.); largest island Penghu, on which is chief town Penghu. Ceded to Japan by China 1895; retroceded 1945; since 1949 held by Taiwan government.

2. Island, chief of the Penghu group.

3. Town, P'eng–hu I. See MAKUNG.

Peng·lai *or W.-G.* **P'eng–lai** \ˈpəŋ-ˈlī\; *formerly* **Teng·chow** \ˈdeŋ-ˈjō\. Town on N coast of Shandong Penin., Shandong prov., NE China, on Bo Hai; has good harbor.

Peng–pu. See BENGBU.

Pen·guin \ˈpen-gwən, ˈpeŋ-\. Municipality and seaport on N coast of Tasmania, Australia, 10 mi. (16 km.) E of Burnie; munic. pop. (1981c) 5097.

Pengunungan Jayawijaya. See JAYAWIJAYA RANGE.

Pengwern. See SHREWSBURY 5.

Pen–hsi. See BENXI.

Pe·nig \ˈpā-nik̲\. Town, Saxony, E Germany, ab. 30 mi. (48 km.) SE of Leipzig.

Pen·i·kese Island \ˌpe-nə-ˈkēs\. Small island at S end of Buzzards Bay, Massachusetts, N of Cuttyhunk I.; site of former school of natural history, estab. 1873 by American naturalist Louis Agassiz.

Peninsula, Point. Point, N New York, extending into Lake Ontario NW of Sackets Harbor.

Peninsula, The. **1.** A district in SE Virginia, bet. the York and James rivers; Fort Monroe is at its SE tip; Richmond, to the NW, was Union objective in an unsuccessful campaign Apr.–July 1862 during the Civil War; Union Gen. George McClellan was opposed by Confederates led by Gen. Joseph Johnston and after Fair Oaks (*q.v.*) by Gen. Robert E. Lee who took the offensive at Mechanicsville June 26. See also GAINES' MILL and MALVERN HILL.

2. The Iberian Peninsula, incl. Spain and Portugal; scene of 5th phase of Napoleonic Wars, the Peninsular War 1808–14, in which the British, Portuguese, and Spanish successfully opposed French Emperor Napoléon's forces and British Gen. Arthur Wellesley earned for himself the title of duke of Wellington; chief battles at La Coruña, Talavera de la Reina, and Vitoria (*qq.v.*).

Península de Guajira. See GUAJIRA PENINSULA.

Peninsula Point. Point at S tip of peninsula forming E side of Little Bay de Noc, Delta co., S Michigan on Upper Penin., jutting into Green Bay.

Pen·ja·mo \ˈpen-hä-ˌmō\. Municipality, SW Guanajuato state, cen. Mexico, 50 mi. (80 km.) SW of the city of Guanajuato; pop. (1990p) 137,450.

Penjdeh. See PANJDEH.

Pen·ju Islands \ˈpen-ˌjü\; *formerly* **Tur·tle Islands** \ˈtərt-ᵊl\. Group of islands, in E part of the Gulf of Tomini, off NE coast of Sulawesi, Indonesia; extend nearly 80 mi. (130 km.) E and W; chief islands Batudaka (largest), Talatakoh, and Togian.

Pen·maen·mawr \ˌpen-mīn-ˈmau̇r\. Resort, Gwynedd co., NW Wales. on coast near NE entrance to Menai Strait; pop. (1981p) 3903.

Pen·march \peⁿ-ˈmär\. Village, Finistère dept., NW France, 18 mi. (29 km.) SW of Quimper on a small peninsula which ends in **Point Penmarch;** a flourishing seaport 14th–16th cents.

Pen·ne \ˈpā-nā\; *anc.* **Pin·na** \ˈpi-nə\. Commune, Pescara prov., Abruzzi, cen. Italy, 15 mi. (24 km.) W of the seaport of Pescara; pop. (1981p) 11,634; cathedral.

Pen·nell, Mount \pə-ˈnel\. Peak, E Garfield co., S Utah; 11,371 ft. (3466 m.).

Pen·ner \ˈpe-nər\. River, SE cen. India; rises in SE Karnataka, flows N and E through S Andhra Pradesh to Bay of Bengal 15 mi. (24 km.) N of Nellore; ab. 350 mi. (565 km.) long.

Penn Hills \ˈpen\. Urban township, Allegheny co., SW Pennsylvania, E suburb of Pittsburgh; pop. (1990c) 51,479.

Pennine Alps. See table at ALPS.

Pen·nine Chain \ˈpe-ˌnīn\ *or* **Pen·nines** \-ˌnīnz\. Mountain range extending S from the Scottish border to Derbyshire and Staffordshire in cen. England; highest peak **Cross Fell** \ˈkrȯs-ˈfel\ 2930 ft. (893 m.).

Pen·ning·ton \ˈpe-niŋ-tən\. Name of counties in two states of the U.S. See tables at MINNESOTA and SOUTH DAKOTA.

Penn·sau·ken \pen-ˈsȯ-kən\. Township, Camden co., SW New Jersey, just E of the city of Camden; pop. (1990c) 34,738.

Penns Grove \ˈpenz\. Borough, Salem co., SW New Jersey, on Delaware River opp. Wilmington, Delaware, and 24 mi. (39 km.) SW of Camden; pop. (1990c) 5228.

Penn·syl·va·nia \ˌpen-səl-ˈvā-nyə, -nē-ə, *rapid* -sə-ˈvā-\. A middle Atlantic state of U.S.A., bounded on N by New York, on E by New York and New Jersey, on S by Delaware, Maryland, and West Virginia, and on W by West Virginia and Ohio; 33d state in area, 45,333 sq. mi. (117,412 sq. km.), not incl. 735 sq. mi. (1904 sq. km.) of water of the Great Lakes; 5th state in population, (1990c) 11,881,643; ✱ Harrisburg; one of the original states of the Union, the 2d to ratify the U.S. Constitution (1787). See table of states at UNITED STATES.

Nickname: Keystone State.

State flower: Mountain laurel.

Motto: Virtue, Liberty, and Independence.

Rivers: Delaware, forming E boundary; Susquehanna, flowing N to S through E cen. region; Monongahela in W and SW region, uniting at Pittsburgh with Allegheny River to form the Ohio River; Juniata, in S cen. region, flowing E into the Susquehanna; the Schuylkill in the SE flowing through Philadelphia to the Delaware.

Highest point: Mt. Davis, 3213 ft. (979 m.), in Somerset co.

Chief products: Corn, wheat, oats; dairy products, coal, iron ore; manufacturing: iron and steel; electrical machinery, apparel, chemicals, transportation equipment.

Chief cities: Philadelphia, Pittsburgh, Erie, Allentown.

Political divisions: Divided into the following 67 counties (for pronunciation of their names, see their individual entries):

NAME	AREA[1] (sq. mi.)	AREA[1] (sq. km.)	POP. (1990c)	CO. SEAT
Adams	526	1,362	78,274	Gettysburg
Allegheny	728	1,886	1,336,449	Pittsburgh
Armstrong	658	1,704	73,478	Kittanning
Beaver	440	1,140	186,093	Beaver
Bedford	1,018	2,637	47,919	Bedford
Berks	862	2,233	336,523	Reading
Blair	531	1,375	130,542	Hollidaysburg
Bradford	1,148	2,973	60,967	Towanda
Bucks	614	1,590	541,174	Doylestown
Butler	794	2,056	152,013	Butler
Cambria	695	1,800	163,029	Ebensburg
Cameron	401	1,039	5,913	Emporium
Carbon	405	1,049	56,846	Jim Thorpe
Centre	1,115	2,888	123,786	Bellefonte
Chester	761	1,971	376,396	West Chester
Clarion	597	1,546	41,699	Clarion
Clearfield	1,144	2,963	78,097	Clearfield
Clinton	902	2,336	37,182	Lock Haven
Columbia	484	1,254	63,202	Bloomsburg
Crawford	1,012	2,621	86,169	Meadville
Cumberland	555	1,437	195,257	Carlisle
Dauphin	518	1,342	237,813	Harrisburg
Delaware	184	477	547,651	Media
Elk	807	2,090	34,878	Ridgway
Erie	813	2,106	275,572	Erie
Fayette	802	2,077	145,351	Uniontown
Forest	419	1,085	4,802	Tionesta
Franklin	754	1,953	121,082	Chambersburg
Fulton	435	1,127	13,837	McConnellsburg
Greene	578	1,497	39,550	Waynesburg
Huntingdon	894	2,315	44,164	Huntingdon
Indiana	825	2,137	89,994	Indiana
Jefferson	652	1,689	46,083	Brookville
Juniata	386	1,000	20,625	Mifflintown
Lackawanna	454	1,176	219,039	Scranton
Lancaster	946	2,450	422,822	Lancaster
Lawrence	367	951	96,246	New Castle
Lebanon	363	940	113,744	Lebanon
Lehigh	348	901	291,130	Allentown
Luzerne	888	2,300	328,149	Wilkes-Barre
Lycoming	1,216	3,149	118,710	Williamsport
McKean	997	2,582	47,131	Smethport
Mercer	681	1,764	121,003	Mercer
Mifflin	431	1,116	46,197	Lewistown
Monroe	611	1,582	95,709	Stroudsburg
Montgomery	496	1,285	678,111	Norristown
Montour	130	337	17,735	Danville
Northampton	376	974	247,105	Easton
Northumberland	453	1,173	96,771	Sunbury
Perry	551	1,427	41,172	New Bloomfield
Philadelphia[2]	129	334	1,585,577	Philadelphia
Pike	542	1,404	27,966	Milford
Potter	1,092	2,828	16,717	Coudersport
Schuylkill	784	2,031	152,585	Pottsville
Snyder	327	847	36,680	Middleburg
Somerset	1,085	2,810	78,218	Somerset
Sullivan	478	1,238	6,104	Laporte
Susquehanna	835	2,163	40,380	Montrose
Tioga	1,150	2,979	41,126	Wellsboro
Union	318	824	36,176	Lewisburg
Venango	678	1,756	59,381	Franklin
Warren	916	2,372	45,050	Warren
Washington	857	2,220	204,584	Washington
Wayne	743	1,924	39,944	Honesdale
Westmoreland	1,024	2,652	370,321	Greensburg
Wyoming	398	1,031	28,076	Tunkhannock
York	909	2,354	339,574	York

[1] Area = land area.
[2] Coextensive with Philadelphia city since annexation by city in 1854 of remaining part of county.

History: French adventurer Étienne Brulé probably first European to visit this area 1615–16, inhabited principally by Delaware, Susquehanna, and Shawnee tribes; first European settlement made by Swedes on Tinicum I. (*q.v.*) 1643; rights to land granted by British crown to William Penn, who established Quaker colony 1682; first hospital in U.S. established in Philadelphia 1751; Pennsylvania-Maryland boundary line determined 1763–67 (see MASON-DIXON LINE); Declaration of Independence pronounced in Philadelphia 1776; delegation headed by Benjamin Franklin represented Pennsylvania in Constitutional Convention in Philadelphia 1787; ratified U.S. Constitution Dec. 12, 1787; flood disaster at Johnstown (*q.v.*) May 31, 1889.

Penn Yan \ˈpen-ˈyan\. Village, ⊗ of Yates co., W New York, at outlet of Keuka Lake 30 mi. (48 km.) SW of Auburn; pop. (1990c) 5248; site of American religious leader Jemima Wilkinson's Jerusalem colony 1789–1819.

Pe·nob·scot \pə-ˈnäb-skət, -ˌskät\. **1.** River, cen. Maine; flows S into Penobscot Bay; 101 mi. (163 km.) long; navigable to Bangor (60 mi. or 97 km.); formed by confluence in N cen. Penobscot co. of E branch, from the N, and W branch, 112 mi. (180 km.) long, which is formed by junction of headstreams in Somerset co., W Maine, and flows generally SE, through three lakes (Seboomook, Chesuncook, and Pemadumcook).

2. County in E cen. Maine. See table at MAINE.

Penobscot Bay. Inlet of Atlantic Ocean, SW Hancock co., SE Waldo co., and E Knox co., S Maine, receiving the Penobscot River on the N, and containing a number of islands incl. Deer I., North Haven I., Vinalhaven I., Isle au Haut; 30 mi. (48 km.) long.

Pe·ñón de Vé·lez de la Go·me·ra \pā-ˈnyōn-t͟hā-ˈvā-lās-ˌt͟hā-lä-gō-ˈmā-rä\. Small island off N coast of Morocco, ab. 75 mi. (121 km.) SE of Ceuta; a presidio of Spain.

Pe·no·no·mé \ˌpā-nō-nō-ˈmā\. Town, ✱ of Coclé prov., cen. Panama; pop. (1990p) 12,134.

Pe·not, Mount \pə-ˈnō\. Mountain, cen. Malekula I., Vanuatu, SW Pacific; 2922 ft. (891 m.); highest point on the island.

Pen·rhyn \ˈpen-ˌrin\ *or* **Ton·ga·re·va** \ˌtäŋ-gə-ˈrā-və\. Island (atoll), Northern Cook Is., cen. Pacific Ocean; land area ab. 4 sq. mi. (10 sq. km.), with lagoon area of 108 sq. mi. (280 sq. km.); pop. (1986c) 497; chief village Omoka; administratively part of Cook Is.

Pen·rith \ˈpen-rith\. **1.** Town, Cumbria, NW England, on the Eamont 16 mi. (26 km.) SSE of Carlisle; pop. (1981c) 12,290; tourist resort on the edge of the Lake District; trade center in agricultural section; ruins of 14th cent. castle.

2. City, E New South Wales, Australia; pop. (1991c) 149,630.

Pen·sa·cola \ˌpen-sə-ˈkō-lə\. City, ⊗ of Escambia co., NW Florida, on Gulf of Mexico 10 mi. (16 km.) E of Alabama border; pop. (1990c) 58,165; chemicals, lumber, naval stores; Pensacola Junior Coll. (1948), Univ. of West Florida (1963); U.S. Naval Air Station (contains Naval Aviation Depot). First European attempt at settlement by Spanish 1559–61; new Spanish settlement estab. 1698; to England 1763; reverted to Spain 1783; captured by U.S. forces under Gen. Andrew Jackson 1814 and passed to U.S. 1821; in Civil War abandoned by Confederate forces 1862.

Pensacola Bay. Inlet of Gulf of Mexico on S coast of Santa Rosa and Escambia cos., NW Florida, receiving the Escambia

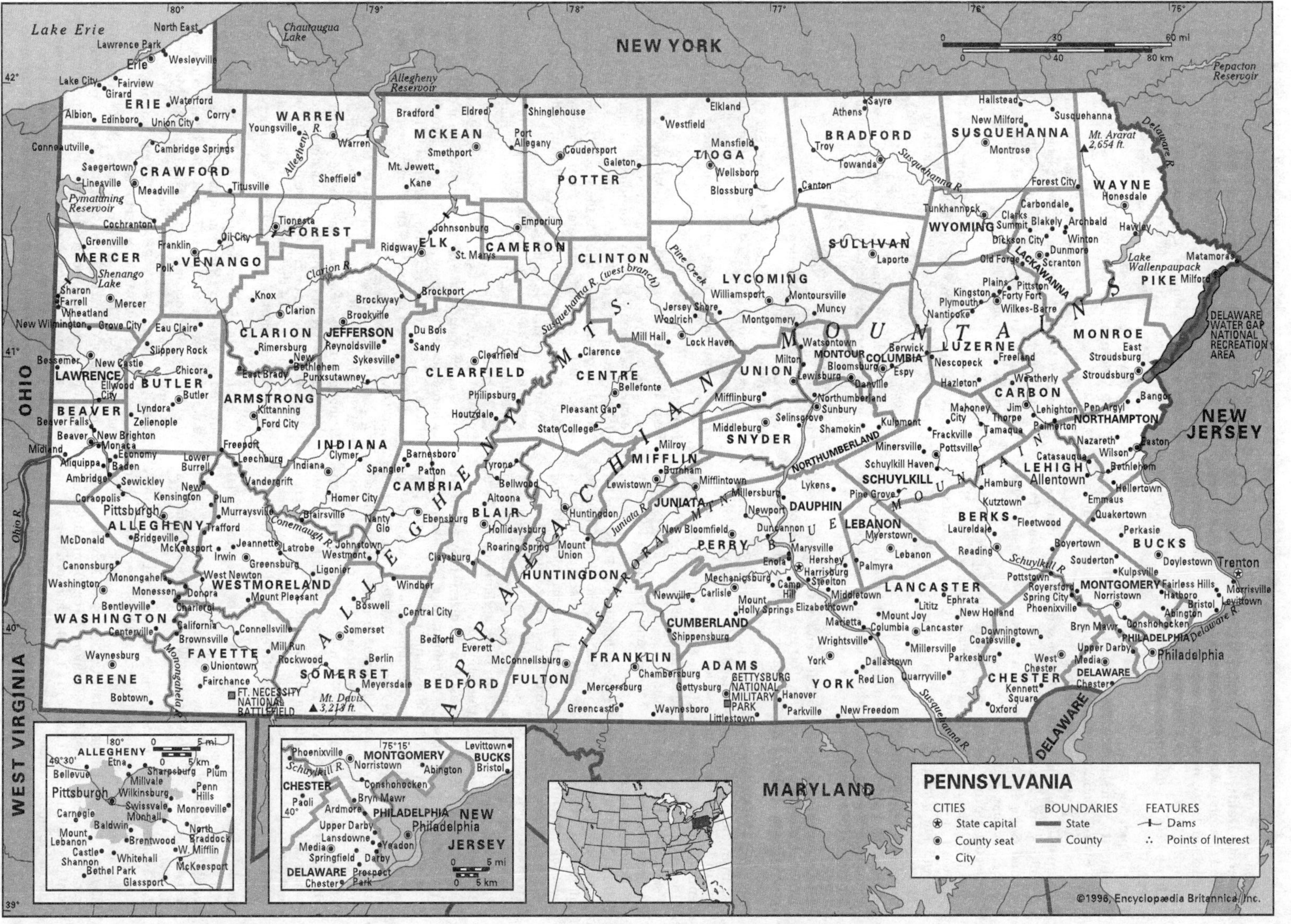

PENNSYLVANIA
CITIES
State capital
County seat
City
BOUNDARIES
State
County
FEATURES
Dams
Points of Interest
©1996, Encyclopædia Britannica, Inc.
NEW YORK
NEW JERSEY
MARYLAND
DELAWARE
WEST VIRGINIA
OHIO
Lake Erie
APPALACHIAN MTS.
ALLEGHENY MOUNTAINS
BLUE MOUNTAIN
TUSCARORA MTN.
DELAWARE WATER GAP NATIONAL RECREATION AREA
GETTYSBURG NATIONAL MILITARY PARK
FT. NECESSITY NATIONAL BATTLEFIELD
Mt. Davis 3,213 ft.
Mt. Ararat 2,654 ft.
ERIE
CRAWFORD
MERCER
LAWRENCE
BEAVER
BUTLER
VENANGO
WARREN
FOREST
CLARION
ARMSTRONG
ALLEGHENY
WASHINGTON
GREENE
FAYETTE
WESTMORELAND
INDIANA
JEFFERSON
ELK
MCKEAN
POTTER
CAMERON
CLEARFIELD
CAMBRIA
SOMERSET
BEDFORD
BLAIR
HUNTINGDON
FULTON
FRANKLIN
CENTRE
CLINTON
TIOGA
LYCOMING
UNION
SNYDER
MIFFLIN
JUNIATA
PERRY
CUMBERLAND
ADAMS
YORK
DAUPHIN
LEBANON
LANCASTER
CHESTER
DELAWARE
MONTGOMERY
PHILADELPHIA
BUCKS
BERKS
SCHUYLKILL
NORTHUMBERLAND
MONTOUR
COLUMBIA
SULLIVAN
BRADFORD
SUSQUEHANNA
WYOMING
LUZERNE
LACKAWANNA
WAYNE
PIKE
MONROE
CARBON
LEHIGH
NORTHAMPTON
Harrisburg
Pittsburgh
Philadelphia
Erie
Allentown
Scranton
Wilkes-Barre
Reading
Lancaster
York
Altoona
Johnstown
Trenton
Susquehanna R.
Delaware R.
Allegheny R.
Monongahela R.
Ohio R.
Juniata R.
Schuylkill R.
Clarion R.
Conemaugh R.
Pine Creek
Lake Wallenpaupack
Allegheny Reservoir
Chautauqua Lake
Pymatuning Reservoir
Shenango Lake
Pepacton Reservoir

River on the NW and the Yellow River on the NE; the city of Pensacola is on its W shore.

Pensacola Dam; *formerly* **Grand River Dam.** Dam across Grand (Neosho) River, NE Oklahoma; height 145 ft. (44 m.); completed 1940; impounds water for power; forms lake 64 sq. mi. (166 sq. km.) known as **Grand Lake O' The Cher·o·kees** \ə-thə-'cher-ə-,kēz\ *or* **Lake O' The Cherokees**.

Penselwood. See PEN.

Pens·hurst \'penz-,hərst\. Town, Kent, SE England, 4.5 mi. (7 km.) SW of Tonbridge; mansion of Sidney family, birthplace of poet and politician Sir Philip Sidney 1554.

Pen·tap·o·lis \pen-'ta-pə-lis\. One of some ancient groups of five cities, specifically: in Italy: Rimini, Ancona, Fano, Pesaro, and Senigallia; in Cyrenaica: Apollonia, Arsinoë, Berenice, Cyrene, and Barka.

Pen·te·cost \'pen-ti-,kȯst\ *or Fr.* **Pen·te·côte** \,pä^{n}t-'kōt\. Island, NE Vanuatu, SW Pacific Ocean, 5 mi. (8 km.) S of Maéwo I. and ab. 60 mi. (95 km.) SE of Espíritu Santo; 28 mi. (45 km.) long by 7 mi. (11 km.) wide; pop. (1991e) 11,336; copra, coffee.

Pentelikon *also* **Pentelicus.** See PENDELIKÓN.

Pen·thièvre \pe^n-'tyevr^ə\. Ancient countship, Brittany, NW France, within region of present Cotes-du-Nord dept.; ✻ (beginning 1134) Lamballe, later ✻ Guingamp; became duchy 1569.

Pen·tic·ton \pen-'tik-tən\. City, at S end of Okanagan Lake, S British Columbia, Canada, ab. 160 mi. (255 km.) E of Vancouver; pop. (1991c) 27,258; lumber; ships fruit; incorp. 1948.

Pent·land Firth \'pent-lənd\. Channel separating the Orkney Is. from the mainland of Scotland; 14 mi. (23 km.) long by 6.5 to 8 mi. (10 to 13 km.) wide.

Pentland Hills. Range of hills in Strathclyde, Lothian, and Borders regions, SE Scotland; highest peak **Scald Law** \'skȯld-'lȯ\ 1898 ft. (579 m.).

Pe·ñue·les \,pā-nyü-'ā-lās\. Municipality, S Puerto Rico; NW of Ponce; pop. (1990c) 22,515.

Pen·za \'pen-zə\. City, ✻ of Penza Oblast, cen. Russia in Europe; on left bank of Sura River 225 mi. (362 km.) W of Samara; pop. (1992e) 552,000; industrial center, producing industrial machinery, diesel engines, bicycles, lumber, watches, paper; ships grain and livestock; founded 1666.

Pen·zance \pen-'zans, pən-\. Seaside resort, Cornwall, SW England, on English Channel 65 mi. (105 km.) WSW of Plymouth; pop. (1981c) 19,210; ships agricultural products. Birthplace of chemist Sir Humphry Davy 1778.

Penza Oblast \'ō-bləst, -,blast\ *or* **Pen·zen·ska·ya Oblast'** \pən-'zen-skə-yə-'ō-bləst^y\. Administrative subdivision of cen. Russia in Europe; 16,680 sq. mi. (43,201 sq. km.); pop. (1992e) 1,514,000; ✻ Penza. Occupies part of cen. Russian plateau (highest point 1089 ft. or 332 m.) cut by three streams: Moksha, Sura, and Khoper. Principal economic activities grain farming, engineering, and food processing.

Pen·zhin·ska·ya Gu·ba \,pen-'zhin-skə-yə-'gü-bə\ *or* **Pen·zhi·na Bay** \'pen-zhə-nə\. Bay on the coast of Koryak Autonomous Okrug, NE Russia in Asia, bet. Kamchatka Penin. and the mainland, a NE extension of Zaliv Shelikhova, Sea of Okhotsk; receives the **Penzhina River,** ab. 400 mi. (645 km.) long.

People's Democratic Republic of Yemen. See YEMEN, PEOPLE'S DEMOCRATIC REPUBLIC OF.

People's Republic of China. See CHINA.

Pe·o·ria \pē-'ōr-ē-ə\. **1.** County, NW cen. Illinois. See table at ILLINOIS.

2. Town, Maricopa co., SW cen. Arizona, 3 mi. (4.8 km.) W and NW of Phoenix; pop. (1990c) 50,618; pop. more than quadrupled bet. 1980 and 1990.

3. *1814–25* **Fort Clark** \'klärk\. City, ⊗ of Peoria co., NW cen. Illinois, on expansions of Illinois River 67 mi. (108 km.) N of Springfield; pop. (1990c) 113,504; transportation and industrial center, producing earth-moving machinery, chemicals, food products; large distilleries and breweries; in an agricultural region; Bradley Univ. (1897). First settlement on site was French fort estab. by explorer René-Robert Cavelier, Sieur de La Salle 1680; incorp. as town 1835, as city 1845.

Peoria Heights. Village, Peoria co., NW cen. Illinois, on Upper Peoria Lake; surrounded by Peoria on three sides; pop. (1990c) 6930.

Peoria Lake. Expansion of Illinois River at Peoria, Illinois; created along with its N extension (called **Upper Peoria Lake**) by **Peoria Dam,** just S of the city.

Peper Bay. See LADY, TELUK.

Pep·in \'pe-pən\. County in W Wisconsin. See table at WISCONSIN.

Pepin, Lake. Lake, along Minnesota-Wisconsin boundary from Red Wing, Minnesota, to Wabasha, Minnesota; ab. 34 mi. (55 km.) long by as much as 2 to 4 mi. (3 to 6 km.) wide; an expansion of Mississippi River as it passes bet. limestone bluffs as much as 400 ft. (120 m.) high, weathered into unusual shapes.

Pep·per·ell \'pe-pə-rəl\. Town, Middlesex co., NE Massachusetts, 11 mi. (18 km.) NE of Fitchburg; pop. (1990c) 10,098.

Pep·per Pike \'pe-pər\. Village, Cuyahoga co., N Ohio, 12 mi. (19 km.) E of Cleveland; pop. (1990c) 6185; Ursuline Coll. (1871).

Pe·quan·nock \pi-'kwä-nək\. River, N New Jersey; flows from E Sussex co. SE and unites at Pompton with Ramapo and Ringwood rivers to form Pompton River.

Pequawket. See KEARSARGE NORTH.

Pe·que·ní \,pā-kā-'nē\. River in Panama E of the Panama Canal; flows SW into Madden Lake.

Pequeri. See PIQUIRI.

Pe·quon·nock \pi-'kwȯ-nək\. **1.** River, SW Connecticut; rises in cen. Fairfield co., flows S into Long Island Sound at Bridgeport.

2. Former name of Bridgeport, Connecticut. See BRIDGEPORT 3.

Pera. See BEYOĞLU.

Pe·ra·de·ni·ya \,pā-rə-'dā-nē-yə\. Village, cen. Sri Lanka, 3 mi. (5 km.) SW of Kandy (*q.v.*); botanic gardens.

Pe·raea *or* **Pe·rea** \pə-'rē-ə\. Region in ancient Palestine, E of Jordan River ("beyond Jordan," from Greek, literally, "[the country] on the other side [of the river]"); part of the earlier region of Gilead and extending from Jabesh-gilead on the N to the Arnon River on the S; formed with Galilee part of the Tetrarchy of Herod Antipas.

Pe·ra·hu \pə-'rä-hü\ *or* **Pra·hoe** \'prä-hü\ *or* **Prau** \'prä-ü\. Mountain, cen. Java, Indonesia, SW of Semarang; 10,285 ft. (3135 m.).

Pe·rak \'per-ə, 'pir-ə—*sic*\. **1.** River, Perak state, Malaysia; rises in NE part of the state, flows WSW and S to ab. 4°N where it turns sharply W at Telok Anson into the Strait of Malacca; 252 mi. (405 km.) long; navigable for small craft for nearly its entire course. Its chief tributary is the Kinta (see KINTA VALLEY).

2. A state of Malaysia, on W coast of Malay Penin., bounded on N by Penang, Kedah, and Thailand, on E by Kelantan and Pahang, on S by Selangor, and on W by Strait of Malacca; ✻ Ipoh; has two N and S parallel mountain ranges with the Perak River bet. them; on E border are peaks (6000 to 7000 ft. or 1830 to 2135 m.) of the main range of the Malay Penin.; rubber, rice, coconuts, tin; fishing; good road network. See table at MALAYSIA.

History: In early times region settled by Malays; conquered by Siamese 1818 but an independent state 1824–74; taken over by the British 1874 and joined the Federated Malay States 1895; became part of Federation of Malaya 1948; became a state of Malaysia 1963.

Pe·ra·via \,pā-rä-'vē-ä\. Province, S cen. Dominican Republic. See table at DOMINICAN REPUBLIC.

Per·cé \per-'sā\. Town, E Gaspé Penin., SE Quebec, Canada, on coast S of Gaspé Bay; pop. (1991c) 4028; a popular resort, noted for its scenery; nearby is small island, the **Percé Rock,** a bird sanctuary. Settled by missionaries in 17th cent.

Perche \'persh\. Historical division in N France, now included in depts. of Orne, Eure-et-Loir, and Eure; Mortagne and Nogent-le-Rotrou were its ✻s at various times; dairy-farming, stock-raising region, noted esp. for its breed of heavy draft horses (Percherons).

Per·di·do \pər-'dē-dō\. River, S Alabama; rises in Escambia co., flows S and forms boundary bet. SE Alabama and NW Florida; empties into **Perdido Bay,** an inlet of the Gulf of Mexico; ab. 60 mi. (95 km.) long.

Per·di·do, Mount \per-'thē-thō\ *or Fr.* **Mont Per·du** \,mōn-per-'dœ\. Peak in the cen. Pyrenees, NE Spain, on French border S of Luz-St.-Sauveur; 11,004 ft. (3354 m.).

Pe·rei·ra \pe-'rā-rä\. City, ✻ of Risaralda dept., W cen. Colombia, just S of Manizales; pop. (1992e) 336,000; ships livestock; technical university (1958).

Pe·re·kop \,per-ə-'käp\. **1.** Isthmus connecting Crimea with mainland Ukraine; bet. 4 and 14 mi. (6 and 23 km.) wide. Here Bolsheviks defeated Gen. Baron Pyotr Wrangel's White Army in Russian Civil War 1920; in WWII occupied by Germans 1941–43.

2. Village at N end of isthmus; ruins of ancient Greek and Tatar fortifications.

Père–La·chaise \,per-lȧ-'shez\. Cemetery in E section of Paris, France; burial place of many well-known people.

Peremyshl. See PRZEMYŚL.

Pereslavl'. See PLESHCHEYEVO.

Pe·re·slavl'–Za·les·skiy *or* **Pe·re·slavl–Za·les·ski** \,pir-i-'slȧv-ᵊl-zȧ-'lyes-kē\. Town on Pleshcheyevo Lake, S Yaroslavl' Oblast, cen. Russia in Europe; an old town, in early times in the Rostov-Suzdal' principality; from c. 1300 in the Moscow principality.

Pe·re·ya·slav \,pir-i-yə-'slȧf\. Medieval principality on the N bank of the Dnieper in E cen. Europe E of Kiev 11th–13th cents.; chief town Pereyaslav (now Pereyaslav-Khmel'nits'kiy).

Pereyaslav–Khmel'·nyt·s'kyy *or* **Pereyaslav–Khmel·nyt·sky** *or Russ.* **Pereyaslav–Khmel'·nit·skiy** \-kmelʸ-'nit-skē\; *formerly* **Pereyaslav.** Town, E Kiev subdivision, Ukraine, on a small tributary near the left bank of the Dnieper, 50 mi. (80 km.) SE of Kiev; an agricultural town that has been historically important; known since 10th cent.; chief town of principality from 1054; plundered by Tatars 1239; site of decisive battle in which Polish forces were defeated by Kievan Cossacks 1630; a key town during revolution against Poland led by Bohdan Khmelnytsky; treaty signed here 1654 allying Ukraine with Russia; occupied by Germans in both World Wars.

Pereyaslav–Ryazanskiy. See RYAZAN' 2.

Per·ga \'pər-gə\ *or* **Per·ge** \-gē\. City of ancient Pamphylia, Asia Minor; its ruins are NE of modern Antalya, Turkey; here Sts. Paul and Barnabas began their first mission in Asia Minor (*Acts* xiii. 13).

Per·ga·mi·no \,per-gä-'mē-nō\. City, N Buenos Aires prov., E Argentina, 141 mi. (227 km.) WNW of the city of Buenos Aires; pop. (1980p) 68,989.

Per·ga·mum \'pər-gə-məm\ *or* **Per·ga·mus** \-məs\; *Gk.* **Per·ga·mon** \-,män\ *or* **Per·ga·mos** \-məs, -,mäs\. Ancient Greek kingdom, W Asia Minor; at its height under Eumenes I and his successors the Attalids, 263–133 B.C.; became ally of Rome and on death of Attalus III kingdom bequeathed to Romans; divided bet. new prov. of Asia and neighboring kingdoms; its ✻ Pergamum (now Bergama, *q.v.*).

Perge. See PERGA.

Per·gi·ne Val·su·ga·na \'per-jē-nā-,väl-sü-'gä-nä\. Commune, Trento prov., Trentino-Alto Adige, NE Italy, 5 mi. (8 km.) E of the commune of Trento; pop. (1981p) 13,613; restored 13th cent. castle.

Per·go·la \'per-gō-lä\. Commune, Pesaro e Urbino prov., Marche, cen. Italy, 25 mi. (40 km.) SSW of Pesaro; pop. (1981p) 7810; cathedral.

Per·gu·sa, Lake of \per-'gü-sä\. See ENNA 2.

Per·i·bon·ca \,per-ə-'bäŋ-kə\. River, S cen. Quebec, Canada; rises in cen. Quebec, flows S into Lac St.-Jean; 280 mi. (451 km.) long.

Pe·ri·co \pā-'rē-kō\. **1.** Town and municipality, Matanzas prov., W cen. Cuba; town is on railroad line 20 mi. (32 km.) SE of Cárdenas; munic. pop. (1981p) 28,923.

2. Small fortified island, Panama, in Bay of Panama, just off SE end of Panama Canal.

Pé·riers \pā-'ryā\. Town, Manche dept., NW France, 14 mi. (23 km.) NW of St.-Lô; taken in battle for St.-Lô July 1944.

Pé·ri·gord \,pā-rē-'gȯr\. Old division of N Guienne prov., SW France; ✻ Périgueux.

Pé·ri·gueux \,pā-rē-'gœ\; *anc.* **Ve·su·na** \vi-'sü-nə\. Commune, ✻ of Dordogne dept., SW cen. France, 66 mi. (106 km.) ENE of Bordeaux; pop. (1990c) 34,848; road and rail junction; hardware, chemicals, truffles; printing of postage stamps; 12th cent. cathedral; Roman remains (amphitheater, baths, tower of temple to the deity Vésone). A settlement of the Petrocorii, a Gallic tribe; beginning 5th cent. medieval town developed around an abbey; suffered heavily in Wars of Religion 16th cent.

Pe·rim \pə-'rim\ *or Arab.* **Ba·rīm** \bə-'rēm\. Island in Bab el-Mandeb Strait at the entrance to the Red Sea, part of Yemen; 96 mi. (154 km.) W of Aden; 5 sq. mi. (13 sq. km.); came under British control as part of Aden Protectorate 1857; included in British colony of Aden 1937; became part of independent People's Democratic Republic of Yemen 1967; formerly site of coaling station.

Pe·ri·sté·ri·on \,per-ē-'ster-ē-,ȯn\ *or* **Pe·ri·sté·ri** \-'ster-ē\. Town, just NW of Athens, E Greece.

Pe·ri·to Mo·re·no National Park \pā-'rē-tō-mō-'rā-nō\. National park, S Argentina on Chilean border; ab. 330 sq. mi. (855 sq. km.); remote Andean peaks and glacial features.

Pe·ri·yar \,per-i-'yär\. River, cen. Kerala, S India; flows N and W to Arabian Sea N of Cochin; ab. 140 mi. (225 km.) long; navigable for 60 mi. (97 km.); in hills in Travancore has dam (completed 1895) impounding water for irrigation.

Per·kam, Cape \pər-'käm\; *formerly* **Cape d'Ur·ville** \'dər-,vil\. Cape on N coast of Irian Jaya, Indonesia, just E of Teluk Cenderawasih near mouth of the Mamberamo River.

Per·ka·sie \'pər-kə-sē\. Borough, Bucks co., SE Pennsylvania, 18 mi. (29 km.) SSE of Allentown; pop. (1990c) 7878.

Per·kins \'pər-kinz\. Name of counties in two states of the U.S. See tables at NEBRASKA and SOUTH DAKOTA.

Perkins, Mount. Peak in the Sierra Nevada, E Fresno co., S cen. California; 12,557 ft. (3827 m.).

Perlas, Archipiélago de las. See PEARL ISLANDS.

Perlas, Cayos de. See PEARL CAYS.

Per·las, Pun·ta de \,pün-tä-thā-'per-läs\ *or Eng.* **Pearl Point** \'pərl\. Cape projecting S on E cen. coast of Nicaragua, enclosing Perlas Lagoon.

Perlas Lagoon *also* **Pearl Lagoon.** Inlet of the Caribbean Sea on E cen. coast of Nicaragua.

Per·lis \'per-lis\. A state of Malaysia, Malay Penin., bounded on NW, N, and NE by Thailand, on SE by Kedah, and on SW by Andaman Sea; ✻ Kangar; smallest state of Malaysia. See table at MALAYSIA.

History: Until 1821 subject to Kedah; made separate state by the Siamese 1841; came under British protection by treaty of 1909, in which Siam (Thailand) ceded to Great Britain its rights over the state; became one of the five Unfederated Malay States of British Malaya; part of Federation of Malaya 1948; became a state of Malaysia 1963.

Perm' *or* **Perm** \'pərm, 'permʸ\; *formerly* **Mo·lo·tov** \'mä-lə-,tȯf, 'mȯ-, 'mō-, -,tȯv\. City, ✻ of Perm' Oblast, W Russia in Europe, W of Ural Mts. on Kama River; pop. (1992e) 1,099,000; manufactures lumber products, leather, chemicals; oil refining. On site of village founded 16th cent.; copper-smelting plant estab. here in early 18th cent.; received name of Perm' 1780; officially called Molotov 1940–57.

Për·met \pər-'met\ *or* **Pre·met** \prə-'met\. **1.** District of S Albania. See table at ALBANIA.

2. Town, its ✻, on the Vijosë River.

Perm' Oblast \'ō-bləst, -,blast\; *or* **Perm·ska·ya Oblast'** \'permʸ-skə-yə-'ō-bləstʸ\; *from 1940–57* **Molotov Oblast.**

\ə\ abut \ᵊ\ kitten, Fr table \ər\ further \a\ ash \ā\ ace \ä\ cot, cart \ȧ\ Fr bac \au̇\ out \b\ Span Avila \ch\ chin \e\ bet \ē\ easy \g\ go \i\ hit \ī\ ice \j\ job \k\ Ger ich, Buch \ⁿ\ Fr vin \ŋ\ sing \ō\ go \ȯ\ all \ȯ\ law \œ\ Fr bœuf \œ̄\ Fr feu \ȯi\ boy \th\ thin \th\ this \ü\ loot \u̇\ foot \ue\ Ger füllen \üe\ Fr rue \y\ yet \ʸ\ Fr digne \'dēnʸ\, nuit \'nwʸē\ \yü\ few \yu̇\ fury \zh\ vision

Administrative subdivision of Russia in Europe; 62,008 sq. mi. (160,601 sq. km.); pop. (1992e) 3,109,000; ✻ Perm; traversed by the Kama and its tributary the Chusovaya, and along its E border by the W foothills of the Ural Mts. Important mineral reserves, esp. potassium, salt. In early times occupied by a Finnic people, the Permiaks, whence the name of the autonomous okrug (Komi-Permyak, estab. 1925) in NW part; came under Moscow 15th cent.; organized as a subdivision of the Russian S.F.S.R. in 1938.

Per·nam·bu·co \ˌpər-nəm-ˈbü-kü\. **1.** State, E Brazil; ✻ Recife; sugarcane, coffee, cotton, corn; scene of several insurrections in 19th cent. See table at BRAZIL.
2. City, its ✻. See RECIFE.

Per·nik \ˈper-nik\. Town, W Bulgaria, ab. 15 mi. (24 km.) SW of Sofia; pop. (1991e) 99,643; steelworks.

Pernov *or* **Pernau.** See PÄRNU.

Pé·ronne \pā-ˈrȯn\. Town, Somme dept., N France, ab. 35 mi. (56 km.) N of Amiens on Somme River; site of meeting bet. Charles the Bold, duke of Burgundy, and Louis XI of France in which Louis was forced into a humiliating treaty 1468; taken by British under Arthur Wellesley, duke of Wellington, 1815; occupied by Germans 1870–71 and in WWI; suffered damage in WWII.

Perouse Bay, La. See LA PEROUSE BAY.

Pérouse Strait, La. See SŌYA STRAIT.

Perovsk. See QYZYLORDA 2.

Per·pet·ua, Cape \pər-ˈpe-chə-wə\. Cape on SW extremity of Lincoln co., W Oregon.

Per·pi·gnan \ˌper-pē-ˈnyäⁿ\. City, ✻ of Pyrénées-Orientales dept., S France, near Mediterranean Sea 96 mi. (154 km.) S of Toulouse; pop. (1990c) 108,049; major tourist resort; trades in wine, fruit, and vegetables; 14th–15th cent. cathedral; 14th cent. exchange; 13th–14th cent. castle; 17th–18th cent. citadel. Said to have been founded in 10th cent.; ✻ of Roussillon 12th cent. and of kingdom of Majorca 1276–1344; chartered 1197; united to France 1659.

Per·quim·ans \pər-ˈkwi-mənz\. County of NE North Carolina. See table at NORTH CAROLINA.

Perrégaux. See MOHAMMADIA.

Perreux–sur–Marne, Le. See LE PERREUX-SUR-MARNE.

Per·rine \ˈpər-ˌīn\. Unincorporated settlement, Miami-Dade co., SE Florida, SW of Miami; pop. (1990c) 15,576.

Per·ris \ˈper-əs\. City, Riverside co., SE California, 37 mi. (60 km.) W of Palm Springs; pop. (1990c) 21,460; pop. more than tripled bet. 1980 and 1990.

Per·ro, La·gu·na del \lə-ˈgü-nə-del-ˈper-ō\. Lake in cen. Torrance co., cen. New Mexico.

Per·rot, Ile \ˌēl-pə-ˈrō\. Island in St. Lawrence River, Quebec, E Canada, SW of Montreal I.; lies bet. Lac des Deux-Montagnes and Lake St. Louis; administratively a part of Vaudreuil-Soulanges co., Quebec; in SE part is town of Ile Perrot; connected by bridges with Montreal I. and with mainland at Vaudreuil.

Per·ry \ˈper-ē\. **1.** Name of counties in 10 states of the U.S. See tables at ALABAMA, ARKANSAS, ILLINOIS, INDIANA, KENTUCKY, MISSISSIPPI, MISSOURI, OHIO, PENNSYLVANIA, TENNESSEE.
2. City, ⊗ of Taylor co., N Florida, 48 mi. (77 km.) ESE of Tallahassee; pop. (1990c) 7151; wood products.
3. City, ⊗ of Houston co., cen. Georgia; pop. (1990c) 9452.
4. City, Dallas co., S cen. Iowa, 32 mi. (51 km.) WNW of Des Moines; pop. (1990c) 6652.
5. Village, Wyoming co., W New York, 37 mi. (60 km.) SSW of Rochester; pop. (1990c) 4219.
6. City, ⊗ of Noble co., N Oklahoma, 36 mi. (58 km.) E of Enid; pop. (1990c) 4978.

Per·rys·burg \ˈper-ēz-ˌbərg\. Village, Wood co., NW Ohio, on Maumee River 8 mi. (13 km.) SSW of Toledo; pop. (1990c) 12,551; site of one of North America's largest Islamic mosques.

Per·ry's Victory and International Peace Memorial \ˈper-ēz\. Site, at Put-in-Bay on South Bass I., Ohio, in Lake Erie, dedicated 1913, commemorating 100 years of peace bet. Great Britain and the U.S. following American naval commander Oliver Hazard Perry's victory over British fleet in battle of Lake Erie Sept. 10, 1813.

Per·ry·ton \ˈper-ē-tən\. City, ⊗ of Ochiltree co., NW Texas, in the Panhandle near the Oklahoma boundary, 58 mi. (93 km.) N of Pampa; pop. (1990c) 7607.

Per·ry·ville \ˈper-ē-ˌvil\. **1.** City, ⊗ of Perry co., cen. Arkansas; pop. (1990c) 1141.
2. City, Boyle co., E cen. Kentucky, 40 mi. (64 km.) SW of Lexington; pop. (1990c) 815; scene of battle Oct. 8, 1862 bet. Confederates under Gen. Braxton Bragg and Union forces under Gen. Don Carlos Buell which resulted in withdrawal of Confederates from Kentucky.
3. City, ⊗ of Perry co., E Missouri, 35 mi. (56 km.) NNW of Cape Girardeau; pop. (1990c) 6933.

Per·sep·o·lis \pər-ˈse-pə-lis\. Ancient city, a ✻ of Persia; its ruins lie ab. 30 mi. (48 km.) NE of Shīrāz, SW cen. Iran, covering extensive area and comprising palaces of early Persian kings, great staircase, halls, and treasury. Succeeded Pasargadae as ✻; partially destroyed by Macedonian King Alexander the Great c. 330 B.C.; place remained of some importance until Arab period. Nearby at Naksh-i-Rustam are notable rock tombs of Persian King Darius and others. Excavations in vicinity have disclosed remains of villages much older, perhaps of c. 4000 B.C.

Per·se·ver·ance Bay \ˌpər-sə-ˈvir-əns\. Bay in SW coast of St. Thomas I., Virgin Is. of the U.S.

Per·shing \ˈpər-shiŋ\. County in NW Nevada. See table at NEVADA.

Persia. See IRAN.

Persian Baluchistan. See BALUCHISTAN 1.

Persian Empire. See *History* at IRAN.

Per·sian Gulf \ˈpər-zhən\. **1.** *or* **Ara·bi·an Gulf** \ə-ˈrā-bē-ən\; *anc.* **Si·nus Per·si·cus** \ˈsī-nəs-ˈpər-si-kəs\. Arm of the Arabian Sea; 550 mi. (885 km.) long by 200 mi. (322 km.) max. width; 88,800 sq. mi. (229,992 sq. km.); av. depth 328 ft. (100 m.); connected with Gulf of Oman and Arabian Sea through Strait of Hormuz; Bahrain and Qeshm only islands of importance. The gulf was scene of a war Jan. 1991 prompted by Iraq's invasion of Kuwait Aug. 1990.
2. Former province of S Iran bordering on Persian Gulf.

Persian Gulf States. Term commonly applied to a number of states on E coast of Arabian Penin.: Bahrain (island group in Persian Gulf), Qatar, and the United Arab Emirates (*qq.v.*); sometimes thought to include also Kuwait and Oman.

Persis. See FĀRS.

Per·son \ˈpərs-ᵊn\. County in N North Carolina. See table at NORTH CAROLINA.

Perth \ˈpərth\. **1.** City, ✻ of Western Australia, Australia, on Swan River 10 mi. (16 km.) from its mouth; pop. (1991c) 80,517; commercial, financial, and transportation center of Western Australia; ships agricultural products and minerals; Univ. of Western Australia (1911), Murdoch Univ. (1975). Founded 1829; made city 1856; developed rapidly after discovery of goldfields at Coolgardie 1890 and opening of Fremantle Harbor 1897.
2. County, in SE Ontario, Canada. See table at ONTARIO.
3. Town, ⊗ of Lanark co., SE Ontario, Canada, 45 mi. (72 km.) SW of Ottawa; pop. (1991c) 5574.
4. *also* **Perth·shire** \-ˌshir, -shər\. Former county, cen. Scotland; ⊗ Perth; rivers Forth, Tay; region has some of the finest scenery in Scotland, in the Grampian Mts. and on the shores of its many lochs.
5. Burgh, Tayside region, cen. Scotland, on the Tay River 32 mi. (51 km.) NW of Edinburgh; pop. (1981c) 43,009; market center; distilleries, dyeworks, glass factories, jute mills; a Roman settlement; made a royal burgh 1210; ✻ of Scotland until 1437 when James I of Scotland was murdered here; at St. John's church (15th cent.) religious reformer John Knox preached in 1559 his denunciation of idolatry, resulting in plundering of town's monasteries and altars.

Perth Am·boy \ˌpərth-ˈam-ˌbȯi\. City and port of entry, Middlesex co., cen. New Jersey, on Raritan Bay at mouth of Raritan River 17 mi. (27 km.) SSW of Newark; pop. (1990c) 41,967; steel, electrical equipment, chemicals, paints, clothing; food processing, oil refining. Settled late 17th cent.; ✻ of East Jersey 1686–1702 and, with Burlington, alternate ✻ of

New Jersey until 1790; incorp. as city 1718; a summer resort in first half of 19th cent.

Per·tuis \per-ˈtwē\. Town, Vaucluse dept., SE France, 38 mi. (61 km.) SE of Avignon; ancient clock tower and 14th cent. church.

Pe·ru \pə-ˈrü, *Span.* pā-\. **1.** Republic, W South America, bounded on N by Ecuador and Colombia, on E by Brazil and Bolivia, on S tip by Chile, and on W by the Pacific Ocean; 496,222 sq. mi. or 1,285,215 sq. km. (incl. 1914 sq. mi. or 4957 sq. km. of Lake Titicaca and 14 sq. mi. or 36 sq. km. of insular possessions); pop. (1993e) 22,916,000; ✻ Lima.

Physical features: Greater part covered by Andes: main range, Cordillera Occidental, parallel to coast; Cordillera de Carabaya and Cordillera Oriental in SE, and Cordillera Huayhuash in cen. part; has many subsidiary ranges, esp. in S. Highest peak Huascarán 22,205 ft. (6768 m.) in W; others Nevado Coropuna 21,079 ft. (6425 m.), Solimana, Salcantay, Nevado Ausangate, and the volcanoes Misti and Yucamani in S; many peaks bet. 17,000 and 20,000 ft. (5182 and 6096 m.). Coastline ab. 1400 mi. (2255 km.) long; coastal belt, 40 to 100 mi. (64 to 161 km.) wide, bet. Pacific Ocean and coastal ranges; to the E are many valleys and plateaus shut in by the mountains and watered by streams of the Amazon system; in NE is extensive plain.

Rivers, lakes: Marañón in N, its many tributaries, esp. Napo, Tigre, Pastaza, and Huallaga; Ucayali in E and its great headstreams Urubamba and Apurímac; sources of Purús and Madre de Dios in SE; in extreme N the Putumayo forms boundary with Colombia; many short streams in coastal belt. Includes NW half of large Lake Titicaca (*q.v.*).

Chief products: Cotton, sugar, potatoes, corn, coffee; wool; fishing; copper, lead, zinc, silver, oil; a major source of coca.

Chief cities: Lima, Arequipa, Callao, Trujillo.

History: Seat of Inca empire, estab. c. 1230 with its ✻ at Cuzco, which by mid-15th cent. ruled parts of modern Colombia, Ecuador, Peru, Bolivia, Chile, and Argentina; visited by Spanish explorer Francisco Pizarro c. 1527; finally conquered by Pizarro and fellow Spanish soldier Diego de Almagro 1533; Lima (*q.v.*) founded 1535; scene of strife bet. rival conquistadores 1537–55; in 1542 Spanish established viceroyalty of Peru which, up to 18th cent., included Panama and all of Spanish South America except Venezuela (see also UPPER PERU); New Granada (*q.v.*) 1717 and Buenos Aires (La Plata) 1776 were made separate viceroyalties; Indians led by Tupac Amarú revolted 1780; Peru declared its independence of Spain under Argentinian leader José Francisco de San Martín 1821, but did not achieve final freedom until 1824; fought Spain 1866; defeated in War of the Pacific with Chile 1879–83, and lost Tarapacá and occupation of the settlements of Tacna and Arica; received Tacna (*q.v.*) 1929 after long dispute with Chile; in dispute with Colombia over Leticia (*q.v.*) 1932–33; boundary with Ecuador under dispute for many years, but not settled until 1942 when greater part of Amazon Basin was assigned to Peru. In WWII broke off relations with Axis powers 1942; government overthrown by military junta 1968; civilian rule returned 1980; President Alberto Fujimari suspended constitution 1992.

2. City, La Salle co., N Illinois, on Illinois River 15 mi. (24 km.) W of Ottawa; pop. (1990c) 9302.

3. City, ⊗ of Miami co., N cen. Indiana, 18 mi. (29 km.) N of Kokomo; pop. (1990c) 12,843. Birthplace of American composer and lyricist Cole Porter 1891.

4. Village, Nemaha co., SE Nebraska, on Missouri River 58 mi. (93 km.) ESE of Lincoln; pop. (1990c) 1110; Peru State Coll. (1867).

Peru–Chile Trench. Ocean trench, SE Pacific Ocean, extending approx. length of and parallel to W coast of South America in general N to S direction; subduction zone according to theory of plate tectonics.

Peru Current *or* **Hum·boldt Current** \ˈhəm-ˌbōlt\ *also* **Peru Coastal Current.** A cold ocean current formed as a division of the west-wind drift of the South Pacific Ocean and directed N along the coast of Chile and Peru.

Pe·ru·gia \pā-ˈrü-jä\. **1.** Lake, Italy. See TRASIMENO.

2. Province of Umbria, Italy. See table at ITALY.

3. *anc.* **Pe·ru·sia** \pə-ˈrü-zhə\. Commune, ✻ of Umbria region and ✻ of Perugia prov., cen. Italy, bet. Tiber River and Lake Trasimeno 85 mi. (137 km.) N of Rome; pop. (1991p) 143,698; textiles, confectionery; tourism; remains of Etruscan arch; Maggiore Fountain (1278); Palazzo dei Priori (13th–15th cents.); 14th–15th cent. cathedral; 14th cent. church of San Domenico and several other notable churches; university (founded 1200, received university status 1308).

History: One of the 12 major cities of the Etruscans; came under Rome 310 B.C.; burned during Roman civil wars first cent. B.C.; became Lombard duchy 592 A.D.; in c. 1540 became a possession of the church; to kingdom of Italy 1860; in WWII taken by British June 1944.

Perur. See COIMBATORE.

Perusia. See PERUGIA 3.

Per·vo·mays'k *also* **Per·vo·maisk** *or Russ.* **Per·vo·maysk** \ˌpir-və-ˈmīsk\. **1.** *formerly* **Ol·vi·o·pol** \ˌəl-vē-ˈō-ˌpȯl\. Town, S cen. Ukraine, on Bug River 112 mi. (180 km.) N of Odessa; pop. (1991e) 84,000.

2. Town, E Ukraine, ab. 33 mi. (55 km.) W of Luhans'k; pop. (1991e) 52,000.

Per·vo·ural'sk *or* **Per·vo·uralsk** \ˌpir-və-ˈrälʸsk\. Town, Sverdlovsk Oblast, W Russia in Asia, ab. 25 mi. (40 km.) WNW of Yekaterinburg; pop. (1992e) 144,000.

Per·vyy Ku·ril'·skiy Pro·liv \ˈper-vē-ku̇-ˈrilʸ-skē-ˌprə-ˈlyēf\ *or Eng.* **First Ku·rile Strait** *or* **First Ku·ril Strait** \ˈkyu̇r-ˌēl, kyu̇-ˈrēl\. Channel, separating Kuril Is. from S end of Kamchatka Penin. and connecting the Sea of Okhotsk with Bering Sea; ab. 7 mi (11 km.) wide.

Pe·sa·ro \ˈpā-zä-ˌrō\; *anc.* **Pi·sau·rum** \pə-ˈsȯr-əm, pī-\. Seaport, ✻ of Pesaro e Urbino prov., Marche, cen. Italy, on the Adriatic 85 mi. (137 km.) NE of Florence; pop. (1991p) 88,500; seaside resort; in agricultural region; cathedral with c. 14th cent. facade; 15th cent. ducal palace; 15th cent. fortress; 15th cent. Villa Imperiale.

History: Ruled successively by Umbrians, Etruscans, and Senonian Gauls; one of the five cities of the Pentapolis; became Roman colony c. 184 B.C.; destroyed by Ostrogoths 536 A.D.; to Malatesta family 1285, Sforzas 1445, and Rovveres 1512; part of Papal States 1631 ff. Birthplace of composer Gioacchino Rossini 1792.

Pesaro e Ur·bi·no \ā-ür-ˈbē-nō\. Province of Marche, Italy. See table at ITALY.

Pescadores. See P'ENG-HU 1.

Pes·ca·do·res, Point \ˌpā-skä-ˈt͟hō-rās\. Cape extending into Pacific Ocean on the coast of S Peru.

Pe·sca·ra \pe-ˈskä-rä\. **1.** Lower course of the Aterno River, SE cen. Italy. See ATERNO.

2. Province of Abruzzi, Italy. See table at ITALY.

3. *anc.* **Ater·num** \ə-ˈtər-nəm\. Seaport, ✻ of Pescara prov., Abruzzi, cen. Italy, on the Adriatic at mouth of Pescara River 98 mi. (158 km.) ENE of Rome; pop. (1991p) 121,367; textiles; tourism, fishing, shipbuilding. Made provincial ✻ 1927; badly damaged in WWII.

Pescara. Apennine pass. See table at APENNINES.

Pe·schie·ra del Gar·da \pes-ˈkyā-rä-del-ˈgär-dä\ *or* **Peschiera.** Commune, Verona prov., Veneto, NE Italy, on SE shore of Lake Garda at source of Mincio River 16 mi. (26 km.) W of the commune of Verona; pop. (1981p) 8738; a former frontier fortress, one of Quadrilateral cities (Peschiera, Mantua, Verona, Legnago) important to Austria's control of N Italy.

Pe·schio, Mount \ˈpes-kyō\. Mountain in S range of Alban Hills, W Italy, just N of Velletri; 3080 ft. (939 m.); in WWII taken by Americans June 1944.

Pe·scia \ˈpā-shä\. Commune, Pistoia prov., Tuscany, cen. Italy, 14 mi. (23 km.) W of the commune of Pistoia; pop. (1991p) 18,116; paper; 14th cent. church.

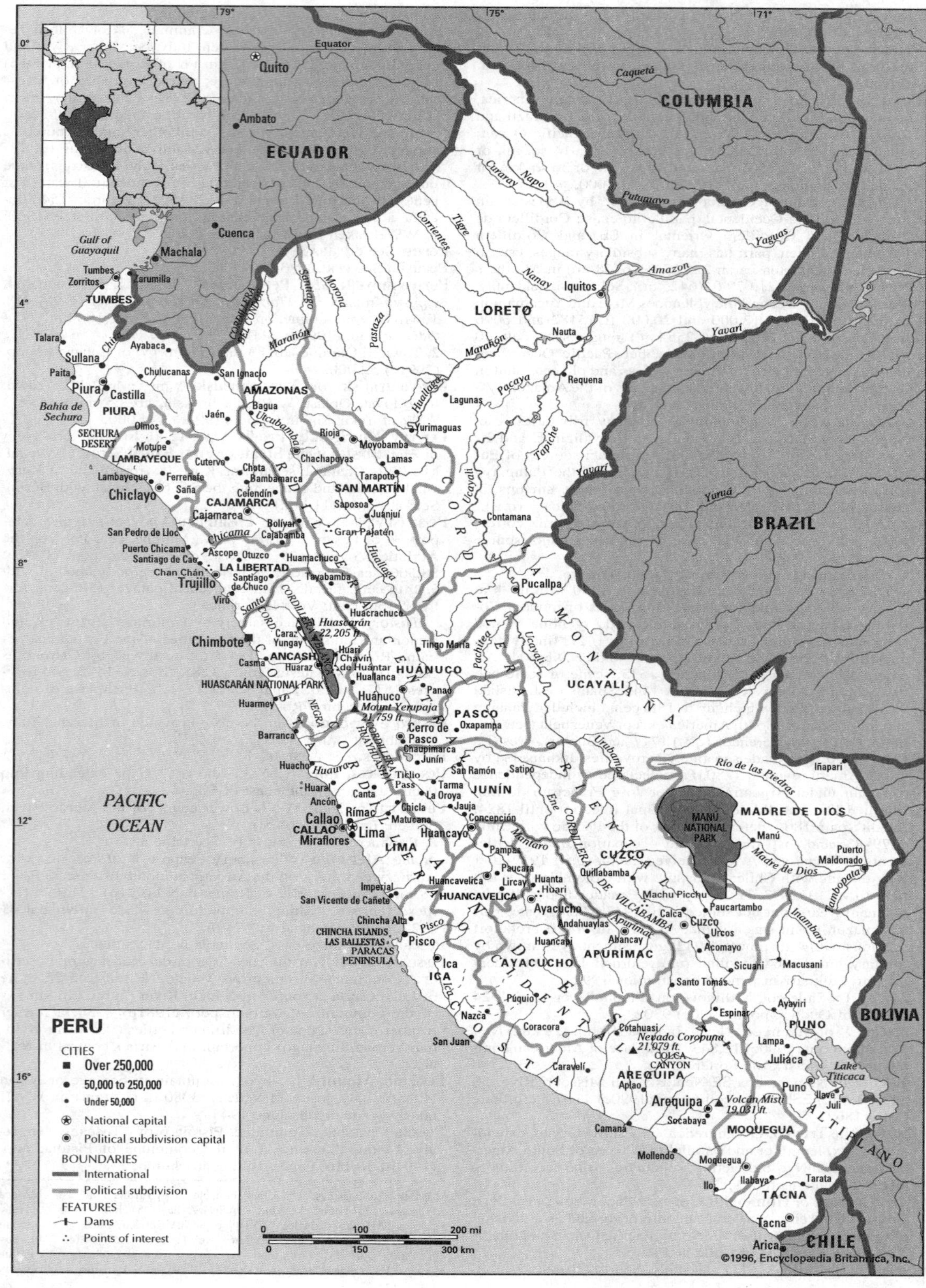
PERU
CITIES
Over 250,000
50,000 to 250,000
Under 50,000
National capital
Political subdivision capital
BOUNDARIES
International
Political subdivision
FEATURES
Dams
Points of interest
0 100 200 mi
0 150 300 km
©1996, Encyclopædia Britannica, Inc.
ECUADOR
COLUMBIA
BRAZIL
BOLIVIA
CHILE
PACIFIC OCEAN
Equator
Quito
Ambato
Cuenca
Machala
Gulf of Guayaquil
TUMBES
LORETO
AMAZONAS
PIURA
LAMBAYEQUE
CAJAMARCA
SAN MARTÍN
LA LIBERTAD
ANCASH
HUÁNUCO
UCAYALI
PASCO
JUNÍN
LIMA
CALLAO
HUANCAVELICA
ICA
AYACUCHO
APURÍMAC
CUZCO
MADRE DE DIOS
PUNO
AREQUIPA
MOQUEGUA
TACNA
Iquitos
Nauta
Requena
Pucallpa
Chiclayo
Trujillo
Chimbote
Callao
Lima
Miraflores
Huancayo
Ayacucho
Cuzco
Arequipa
Puno
Juliaca
Tacna
Arica
Huascarán 22,205 ft.
Mount Yerupaja 21,759 ft.
Nevado Coropuna 21,079 ft.
Volcán Misti 19,031 ft.
HUASCARÁN NATIONAL PARK
MANÚ NATIONAL PARK
SECHURA DESERT
COLCA CANYON
ALTIPLANO
Lake Titicaca
Amazon
Marañón
Ucayali
Huallaga
Napo
Putumayo
Caquetá
Yavarí
Madre de Dios
Urubamba
Apurímac
Mantaro
CORDILLERA DEL CÓNDOR
CORDILLERA BLANCA
CORDILLERA DE VILCABAMBA
Machu Picchu
Chan Chán

Pe·sha·war \pə-'shä-wər, -'shau̇-ər\. City, ✻ of North-West Frontier prov., Pakistan, on Bara River, tributary of the Kabul, 240 mi. (386 km.) NW of Lahore; met. area pop. (1981p) 555,000; strategically important because of its location 9 mi. (14 km.) from S entrance to Khyber Pass and has an important military cantonment; has cottage industries producing copperware, leather goods, pottery, and knives; notable bazaars trading in hides, wool, carpets, and fruit; university (1950).

History: Was ✻ of Indo-Scythian Kushan dynasty c. first cent. A.D.; annexed by Sikhs under Ranjit Singh 1823; to British 1849; under British rule an important military base against the Afghans and border tribes.

Pesh·ko·pi \pesh-'kȯ-pē\. Town, ✻ of Dibër dist., Albania, near border with Republic of Macedonia, ab. 44 mi. (71 km.) NE of Tiranë.

Pesh·ti·go \'pesh-ti-ˌgō\. **1.** River, NE Wisconsin; rises in Forest co., flows SE into Green Bay S of Marinette; ab. 150 mi. (240 km.) long.

2. City, Marinette co., NE Wisconsin, on Peshtigo River 6 mi. (10 km.) WSW of Marinette; pop. (1990c) 3154. Destroyed by fire Oct. 8, 1871, same day as great fire in Chicago.

Pes·quei·ra \pis-'kā-rə\. City, E cen. Pernambuco state, E Brazil, on railroad line 115 mi. (185 km.) W of Recife; munic. pop. (1991p) 57,448.

Pes·sac \pe-'sák\. Commune, Gironde dept., SW France, 4 mi. (6 km.) SSW of Bordeaux; produces wines.

Pes·si·nus \'pe-sə-nəs\. Ancient city, Galatia, Asia Minor (its site now in Turkey in Asia); site of principal shrine of Cybele, the great nature goddess of Phrygia, who was known here as Agdistis or Dindymene, from Mt. Dindymus nearby, also called Mt. Agdistis.

Pest \'pest, 'pesht\. **1.** County of N cen. Hungary. See table at HUNGARY.

2. Former town, Hungary. See BUDAPEST.

Pe·ta·cal·co Bay \ˌpe-tä-'käl-kō\. Inlet of the Pacific Ocean on SW coast of Mexico, chiefly in NW Guerrero state.

Pe·tach Tik·va *or* **Pe·tah Tiq·wa** \'pe-tək-'tik-və\. Town, Israel, 7 mi. (11 km.) NE of Tel Aviv-Jaffa; pop. (1992e) 148,900; chemicals, textiles, agricultural machinery; founded c. 1883 as one of first Jewish agricultural settlements of Zionist movement; incorp. as a city 1937.

Pet·al \'pet-^{ə}l\. City, Forrest co., SE Mississippi, NE of Hattiesburg; pop. (1990c) 7883.

Pe·ta·ling Ja·ya \pə-'tä-liŋ-'jī-ə\. City, West Malaysia, Malaysia, ab. 7 mi. (11 km.) SW of Kuala Lumpur.

Pet·a·lu·ma \ˌpet-^{ə}l-'ü-mə\. City, Sonoma co., W California, on Petaluma River 16 mi. (26 km.) S of Santa Rosa; pop. (1990c) 43,184; dairy products; poultry farms; first settled by Mexicans 1833; World Coll. West (1971).

Pé·tange \pā-'tä^{n}zh\. Commune, Grand Duchy of Luxembourg, in SW part N of Differdange; pop. (1991c) 12,345.

Pe·ta·re \pā-'tä-rā\. City, N Venezuela, ESE of Caracas; pop. (1990e) 531,866.

Pet·a·wa·wa \ˌpe-tə-'wä-wə\. Village, Renfrew co., SE Ontario, Canada; pop. (1991c) 5793.

Petch. See PEĆ.

Petchabun. See PHETCHABUN.

Petchaburi. See PHETCHABURI.

Pe·tén \pe-'ten\. Department of N Guatemala. See table at GUATEMALA.

Petén It·zá, La·go \'lä-gō-pe-ˌten-ēt-'sä\ *also* **Lago de Flo·res** \t͟hā-'flō-rās\. Lake, cen. Petén dept., Guatemala; ab. 27 mi. (43 km.) long; 38 sq. mi. (98 sq. km.).

Pe·ter·bor·ough \'pēt-ər-ˌbər-ō\. **1.** *or* **Pe·ter·boro.** Town, Hillsborough co., S New Hampshire, 16 mi. (26 km.) E of Keene; pop. (1990c) 5239; summer resort; apple orchards; ball bearings, basketry, electrical and electronic equipment, technical magazines, software, injection molds, woodenware; settled 1749; first tax-supported free public library in U.S. estab. here 1833; site of the MacDowell colony organized 1907 as a summer residence for composers and writers.

2. County in SE Ontario, Canada. See table at ONTARIO.

3. City, ⊗ of Peterborough co., SE Ontario, Canada, on Otonabee River and Trent Canal 13 mi. (21 km.) N of W end of Rice Lake; pop. (1991c) 68,371; machinery, boats, marine hardware, lumber, watches; Trent Univ. (1963); sawmills estab. on site 1821; town founded 1825; incorp. as city 1905.

4. City, Cambridgeshire, cen. England, on the Nene 75 mi. (121 km.) N of London; pop. (1981p) 88,346; railroad junction; produces diesel engines; sugar refining, brickmaking; cathedral (begun 12th cent.), burial place of Catherine of Aragon, first wife of Henry VIII.

Peterborough, Soke of. See HUNTINGDON AND PETERBOROUGH.

Petergof *or* **Peterhof.** See PETRODVORETS.

Pe·ter·head \'pē-tər-'hed\. Seaport burgh, Grampian region, NE Scotland, on a peninsula 30 mi. (48 km.) NE of Aberdeen; pop. (1981c) 17,085; woolens, canned goods; one of Great Britain's most important fishing ports; founded 1593; James Francis Edward Stuart (the Old Pretender), claimant to the English throne, landed here 1715.

Peter Island. One of the British Virgin Is., West Indies, S of Tortola.

Peterlingen. See PAYERNE.

Pe·ter·mann Glacier \'pē-tər-mən\. Glacier, N Greenland; 78 mi. (126 km.) long, 9 mi. (14 km.) wide near its terminus.

Pe·te·roa \ˌpā-tā-'rō-ä\. Volcanic peak, E cen. Chile, near border of W Mendoza prov., W Argentina; 13,419 ft. (4090 m.).

Pe·ters·burg \'pē-tərz-ˌbərg\. **1.** Fishing town, SE Alaska, ab. 35 mi. (55 km.) NNW of Wrangell; pop. (1990c) 3207.

2. City, ⊗ of Menard co., cen. Illinois, 20 mi. (32 km.) NW of Springfield; pop. (1990c) 2261; nearby is restored pioneer village of New Salem, home of Abraham Lincoln 1831–37.

3. City, ⊗ of Pike co., SW Indiana, 18 mi. (29 km.) SE of Vincennes; pop. (1990c) 2449.

4. City, SE Virginia, at head of navigation of Appomattox River 23 mi. (37 km.) S of Richmond; area 8 sq. mi. (21 sq. km.); pop. (1990c) 38,386; an independent city; manufactures tobacco products, luggage, clothing, optical equipment; Virginia State Univ. (1882), Richard Bland Coll. (1961). Fort built on site 1645; town estab. 1748; incorp. as town 1784 and as city 1850; in Civil War besieged by Union forces under Gens. Ulysses S. Grant and George Meade June 1864–Apr. 1865 when Confederate forces were forced to withdraw to W, abandoning Petersburg and Richmond, and to surrender at Appomattox (*q.v.*); nearby is **Petersburg National Battlefield** (see UNITED STATES, *National Historical Parks*).

5. Town, ⊗ of Grant co., NE West Virginia, 32 mi. (51 km.) S of Keyser; pop. (1990c) 2360.

Pe·ters·ham \'pē-tərz-ˌham\. Town, Worcester co., cen. Massachusetts, ab. 25 mi. (40 km.) NW of the city of Worcester; pop. (1990c) 1131; site of Harvard Forest, 2100 acres (851 hectares), bird sanctuary (1000 acres or 405 hectares) and experiment station for Harvard University's School of Forestry.

Pe·ter I Island \'pē-tər-t͟hə-'fərst\. Island off Antarctica in Bellingshausen Sea NE of Thurston I.; 68°47′S, 90°35′W; 14 mi. (23 km.) long; discovered and named by Russian explorer Fabian von Bellingshausen 1821; claimed by Norway 1931.

Pe·ter the Great Bay \'pē-tər\ *or Russ.* **Za·liv Pet·ra Ve·li·ko·go** \ˌzä-'lēf-pə-'trä-və-'lē-kə-və\. Inlet of Sea of Japan at S end of Primorskiy Kray, SE Russia in Asia; its two arms, Amur Bay and Ussuri Bay, are on either side of the peninsula on which Vladivostok is situated.

Pétervárad *or* **Peterwardein.** See PETROVARADIN.

Pé·tion·ville \ˌpā-tyō^{n}-'vēl\. Town, Haiti; an E suburb of Port-au-Prince; pop. (1982p) 35,333.

Petit Andely, Le. See LES ANDELYS.

Pet·it Bois Island \'pe-tē-ˌbwä\. Island off coast of SE Mississippi, on Alabama-Mississippi boundary, bet. Mississippi Sound and the Gulf of Mexico.

\ə\ abut \ᵊ\ kitten, Fr table \ər\ further \a\ ash \ā\ ace \ä\ cot, cart \á\ Fr bac \au̇\ out \b\ Span Avila \ch\ chin \e\ bet \ē\ easy \g\ go \i\ hit \ī\ ice \j\ job \k\ Ger ich, Buch \$^{n}$\ Fr vin \ŋ\ sing \ō\ go \ȯ\ all \ȯ\ law \œ\ Fr bœuf \œ̄\ Fr feu \ȯi\ boy \th\ thin \t͟h\ this \ü\ loot \u̇\ foot \ue\ Ger füllen \ue̅\ Fr rue \y\ yet \$^{y}$\ Fr digne \'dēn^{y}\, nuit \'nw^{y}ē\ \yü\ few \yu̇\ fury \zh\ vision

Pe·tit–Bourg \pə-'tē-'bür\. Town on E coast of Basse-Terre I., French overseas dept. of Guadeloupe, West Indies.

Petit–Ca·nal \pə-,tē-kə-'nal\. Commune, W coast of Grande-Terre I., French overseas dept. of Guadeloupe, West Indies.

Petit–Charenton. See SAINT-MAURICE.

Pet·it·co·di·ac \,pe-tē-'kō-dē-,ak\. River, SE New Brunswick, Canada; flows NE, E, and then S through wide estuary (20 mi. or 32 km. long) to inlet of Chignecto Bay; ab. 60 mi. (97 km.) long. Moncton is on it.

Petitjean. See SIDI KACEM.

Pe·tit Ma·nan Point \pə-,tēt-mə-'nan\. SW point of Washington co., SE Maine, on a peninsula jutting into the Atlantic.

Petit–Quevilly, Le. See LE PETIT-QUEVILLY.

Petit–Saint–Bernard. Pass in the Alps. See table at ALPS.

Pet·it·sik·a·pau Lake \,pe-tē-'si-kə-,paù\. Lake, W Labrador, Canada, on border of Quebec, in the NW part of the chain of lakes out of which the Churchill River flows.

Pe·to \'pā-tō\. Town, Yucatán state, on Yucatán Penin., SE Mexico; railroad terminus 70 mi. (113 km.) SE of Mérida.

Pe·to·ne \pə-'tō-nē\. Borough, S North I., New Zealand, NE suburb of Wellington on Port Nicholson; pop. (1981c) 8113.

Pe·tos·key \pə-'täs-kē\. City, ⊗ of Emmet co., N Michigan, on Lake Michigan 31 mi. (50 km.) SW of Cheboygan; pop. (1990c) 6056; summer resort; North Central Michigan Coll. (1958).

Pe·tra \'pē-trə, 'pe-\. Ruined city, SW Jordan, just W of modern **Wā·dī Mū·sá** \'wä-dē-'mü-sə\; usu. identified with **Se·la** \'sē-lə\, ancient ✻ of Edom, from which the Edomites were driven by 4th cent. B.C. by the Nabataeans whose ✻ it became; rock city in narrow valley; has notable temples and tombs carved in rose, crimson, and purple sandstone of surrounding hills; was a wealthy commercial city for several centuries with important caravan trade; became part of Roman prov. of Arabia c. 106 A.D. Captured by Muslims in 7th cent. and by Crusaders in 12th cent. Its ruins discovered by Swiss traveler Johann Ludwig Burckhardt in 1812.

Petra Velikogo, Zaliv. See PETER THE GREAT BAY.

Pe·trich \'pe-trich\. Town, SW Bulgaria, ab. 44 mi. (71 km.) SSE of Blagoevgrad.

Pet·ri·fied Forest National Park \'pe-trə-,fīd\. See UNITED STATES, *National Parks.*

Petrikau. See PIOTRKÓW TRYBUNALSKI.

Pet·ri·la \,pe-'trē-lə\. Town, Hunedoara co., W cen. Romania, ab. 35 mi. (56 km.) SE of Deva; pop. (1989c) 28,536.

Petroaleksandrovsk. See TURTKUL'.

Pet·ro·dvo·rets \,pi-trə-dvär-'yets\; *formerly* **Len·insk** \'lye-nēnsk\; *later* **Pe·ter·hof** \'pē-tər-,hòf, -,häf\ *or* **Pe·ter·gof** \-,gòf, -,gäf\. Coastal town, NW St. Petersburg Oblast, W Russia in Europe, 12 mi. (19 km.) W of the city of St. Petersburg; founded by Czar Peter the Great as a country estate; contains grand palace and smaller palaces (begun 1714) surrounded by vast park containing over 120 fountains; present name adopted 1944.

Petrograd. See SAINT PETERSBURG.

Petrokov. See PIOTRKÓW TRYBUNALSKI.

Pe·tro·kre·post' \,pi-trə-'kre-pəst[y]\; *formerly* **Shlis·sel'burg** \'shlis-[ə]l-,bùrk\ *or Ger.* **Schlüs·sel·burg** \'shlœs-[ə]l-,bùrk\. Town, NW St. Petersburg Oblast, W Russia in Europe, on S bank of Neva River at SW corner of Lake Ladoga. A Novgorodian town founded 1323; captured by Russian Czar Peter the Great from Sweden 1702; fortress on island in Neva River became imperial prison in which for nearly 200 years many noted prisoners were kept; prison abolished 1917 and later made a state museum. In WWII fortress used in defense against Germans.

Pe·tro·le·um \pə-'trō-lē-əm\. County in cen. Montana. See table at MONTANA.

Pe·tro·lia \pə-'trō-lē-ə\. Town, Lambton co., SE Ontario, Canada, 14 mi. (23 km.) ESE of Sarnia-Clearwater; pop. (1991c) 4594; production center of historically important oil field.

Pe·tro·li·na \,pe-trü-'lē-nə\. City, SW Pernambuco state, E Brazil, near Bahia border; pop. (1991p) 123,857.

Pe·tro·na Point \pe-'trō-nä\. Cape on S coast of Puerto Rico, E of Ponce.

Pet·ro·pav·lovsk \,pi-trə-'páv-ləfsk\. City, ✻ of North Kazakhstan subdivision, N Kazakhstan, on the Trans-Siberian R.R. 170 mi. (274 km.) W of Omsk and on the right bank of the Ishim River; pop. (1991e) 248,300; industrial center; city founded 1752.

Petropavlovsk–Kam·chat·skiy *also* **Petropavlovsk–Kam·chat·ski** \-kám-'chát-skē\; *formerly* **Petropavlovsk.** Seaport town on E coast of S end of Kamchatka Penin., Kamchatka Oblast, E Russia in Asia; pop. (1992e) 273,000; shipbuilding; fishing fleets; sawmills; naval base; town founded 1740.

Pe·tró·po·lis \pe-'trò-pü-lēs\. City, Rio de Janeiro state, SE Brazil, 27 mi. (43 km.) N of the city of Rio de Janeiro; munic. pop. (1991p) 255,211; residential and light industrial center; former imperial palace (now a museum), university (1961). Founded 1845; site of signing of Inter-American Treaty of Reciprocal Assistance 1947.

Pe·tro·şa·ni \,pe-trō-'shän\ *also* **Pe·tro·şe·ni** \-'shān\ *or Hung.* **Pe·tro·zsény** \'pe-trō-,zhān-yə\ *or Ger.* **Pe·tro·schen** \'pā-trə-,shān\. Town, Hunedoara co., W Romania, ab. 40 mi. (65 km.) SE of Deva; munic. pop. (1989c) 53,324; coal.

Pet·ro·va·ra·din \,pe-trə-və-'räd-,ēn\ *or Ger.* **Pe·ter·war·dein** \,pā-tər-vär-'dīn\ *or Hung.* **Pé·ter·vá·rad** \'pā-ter-,vär-,öd\. Commune, N Serbia, Yugoslavia, on S bank of the Danube opp. Novi Sad; scene of battle 1716 in which Austrian Gen. Prince Eugene of Savoy defeated the Turks.

Petrovgrad. See ZRENJANIN.

Petrovsk. See MAKHACHKALA.

Pet·ro·za·vodsk \,pi-trə-zə-'vòtsk\ *or* **Ka·li·ninsk** \kə-'lē-nənsk\. City, ✻ of Karelia Rep., NW Russia in Europe, in S part on NW shore of Lake Onega 185 mi. (298 km.) NE of St. Petersburg; pop. (1992e) 280,000; lumber, furniture; founded by Czar Peter the Great as ironworks 1703.

Petrozsény. See PETROŞANI.

Petsamo. See PECHENGA.

Pet·tis \'pe-təs\. County in W cen. Missouri. See table at MISSOURI.

Petuna. See FUYU.

Pet·worth \'pet-,wərth\. Village, West Sussex, England, ab. 42 mi. (68 km.) SSW of London; Petworth House, formerly owned by Percy family, longtime members of English nobility.

Peu·ce Island \'pyü-sē\. Ancient name of marshy region at mouth of Danube on the Black Sea where two islands are formed by the arms of the river; area now on NE coast of Romania on Moldova border.

Pev·en·sey \'pe-vən-zē, -sē\. Village, East Sussex co., S England, on coast W of Hastings; pop. (1981c) 2668; remains of walls of Roman fort; ruins of Norman castle; site of landing of William the Conqueror, duke of Normandy, 1066.

Pe·wau·kee \pi-'wò-kē\. Village, Waukesha co., SE Wisconsin, 18 mi. (29 km.) W of Milwaukee; pop. (1990c) 4941.

Pé·ze·nas \pāz-'näs\. Town, Hérault dept., S France, 25 mi. (40 km.) SW of Montpellier; residence 1655–56 of dramatist Molière.

Pfäf·fi·kon \'pfe-fi-,kòn\. Village, Zürich canton, Switzerland, ab. 12 mi. (19 km.) E of the city of Zürich; pop. (1980c) 8306; located at N end of **Lake of Pfäffikon** (*Ger.* **Pfäf·fi·ker See** \'pfe-fi-kər-,zā\), a marshy lake noted for many evidences of ancient lake dwellers found on its shores.

Pfalz. See PALATINATE.

Pforta. See SCHULPFORTE.

Pforz·heim \'pfòrts-,hīm\. City, Baden-Württemberg, Germany, on border of the Black Forest 16 mi. (26 km.) SE of Karlsruhe; pop. (1992e) 115,547; center of jewelry and watch industry; also produces paper and machinery; 11th–15th cent. castle church; humanist Johannes Reuchlin born here 1455.

Phaes·tus \'fes-təs, 'fēs-\ *also* **Phais·tos** \'fīs-təs\. Ancient city in S Crete, SW of Knossos, near the shore of the Bay of Messara; site of a Minoan palace.

Pha·le·ron \fə-'lir-ən\ *or* **Pha·le·rum** \-'lir-əm\. Town, an early port of Athens, in Attica, E part of ancient Greece, on **Phaleron Bay;** E of Piraeus, by which it was superseded in 5th cent. B.C.

Phal·tan \ˈpəl-tən\. **1.** Former Indian state, now part of Maharashtra state, W India; 391 sq. mi. (1013 sq. km.); merged with Bombay state 1948.

2. Town, its ✻, ab. 50 mi. (81 km.) SE of Pune.

Phan·a·go·ria \ˌfa-nə-ˈgōr-ē-ə\. Ancient city, Greece, on N shore of Pontus Euxinus at entrance to Palus Maeotis (Sea of Azov).

Phang·nga \ˈpäŋ-ˌgä\. **1.** *or* **Ko Phangnga** \ˈkȯ\. Island (Thai *ko*) in SW Gulf of Thailand, 8 mi. (13 km.) N of Ko Samui.

2. *or* **Pang–nga.** Town, SW Thailand, near W coast of Malay Penin. 40 mi. (64 km.) N of Phuket; pop. (1991e) 8540.

Phanom Dang Raek. See DANGREK MOUNTAINS.

Phanos. See FANO.

Phan Rang *or* **Phan·rang** \ˈpän-räŋ\. Coastal town, S Vietnam, 165 mi. (266 km.) ENE of Ho Chi Minh City on river 7 mi. (11 km.) from **Phan Rang Bay,** an inlet of South China Sea.

Phan Thiet \ˈpän-ˈtyet\. Seaport, S Vietnam, ENE of Ho Chi Minh City; pop. (1989c) 114,236.

Pha·rae \ˈfar-ē\. Ancient town of E Messenia, SW Peloponnese, S Greece, near modern city of Kalamata.

Pharnacia. See GİRESUN 2.

Pha·ros \ˈfar-ˌäs\. Peninsula in Lower Egypt; in ancient times an island on which was located a notable lighthouse, one of the Seven Wonders of the Ancient World; now part of the site of the city of Alexandria.

Phar·par \ˈfär-pər\. A river of Damascus (*2 Kings* v. 12); identified by some with the Awaj, a river some distance to the S of the present city of Damascus.

Pharr \ˈfär\. City, Hidalgo co., S Texas, 2 mi. (3 km.) E of McAllen; pop. (1990c) 32,921.

Phar·sa·lus \fär-ˈsā-ləs\; *Gk.* **Phár·sa·los** \ˈfär-sä-ˌlös\ *or* **Phar·sa·la** \ˈfär-sə-lə\; *mod.* **Fár·sa·la** \ˈfär-sä-lä\. Town, S Larissa dept., E Thessaly, E cen. Greece, near the Enipeus River; nearby, on the **Pharsalian Plain,** was scene of Roman Gen. Julius Caesar's decisive defeat of rival Gen. Pompey the Great 48 B.C.

Pharus. See HVAR.

Pha·se·lis \fə-ˈsē-ləs\. Coastal town in ancient Lycia, Asia Minor, near border of Pamphylia.

Pha·sis \ˈfā-sis\. **1.** Ancient Greek colony. See POTI.

2. River, W Republic of Georgia. See RIONI.

Phatnitic. See DAMIETTA 1.

Phat·tha·lung *or* **Pa·ta·lung** *also* **Pa·da·lung** \ˈpät-ᵊl-ˌu̇ŋ\. Town, SW Thailand, on W shore of Lake Thale Luang in Malay Penin. 50 mi. (81 km.) NW of Songkhla; pop. (1991e) 33,177.

Pha·yao \pä-ˈyau̇\. Town, N Thailand, NE of Chiang Mai; pop. (1992e) 23,148.

Phazania. See FEZZAN.

Phelps \ˈfelps\. Name of counties in two states of the U.S. See tables at MISSOURI and NEBRASKA.

Phelps Lake. Lake in SE Washington co., E North Carolina, in swampland bet. Albemarle Sound and Pamlico Sound.

Phenice. See PHOENIX 3.

Phenicia. See PHOENICIA.

Phe·nix City \ˈfē-niks\. City, a ⊗ of Russell co., E Alabama, on Chattahoochee River across from Columbus, Georgia; pop. (1990c) 25,312; lumber, wood products; dairy farms.

Phe·rae \ˈfir-ē\. Ancient town in SE Thessaly, E cen. Greece, ab. 27 mi. (43 km.) SE of Larissa. In mythology the home of King Admetus; historically, in first half of the 4th cent. B.C., its tyrants controlled Thessaly.

Phet Buri. See PHETCHABURI.

Phet·cha·bun \ˌpet-chä-ˈbün\ *also* **Pet·cha·bun** \ˌpet-chä-ˈbün\ *or* **Bej·ra·bu·ra·na** \ˌpet-chä-ˈbün—*sic*\. Town, N Thailand, on Sak River 70 mi. (113 km.) SE of Phitsanulok; pop. (1991e) 28,484.

Phet·cha·bu·ri \ˈpet-bu̇-ˌrē—*sic*\ *or* **Phet Bu·ri** \ˈpet-bu̇-ˌrē\ *also* **Pet·cha·bu·ri** \ˈpet-bu̇-ˌrē—*sic*\. Seaport town, cen. Thailand, on NW shore of Gulf of Thailand and on railroad line 60 mi. (97 km.) SW of Bangkok; pop. (1992e) 33,968.

Phi·chit \ˈpi-ˈchit\ *also* **Pi·chit** *or* **Bi·chit·ra** \ˈpi-ˈchit—*sic*\. Town, N Thailand, on Nan River 55 mi. (89 km.) N of Nakhon Sawan; pop. (1991e) 24,506.

Phi·ga·lia \fi-ˈgāl-yə\. Ancient city in SW Arcadia, cen. Peloponnese, S Greece, near N border of Messenia; ab. 4 mi. (6 km.) to the E is **Bas·sae** \ˈba-sē\, site of a temple of Apollo, still preserved, in which were the Phigalian marbles or sculptures (since 1814 in the British Museum); these form a frieze ab. 101 ft. (31 m.) long and 2 ft. (0.6 m.) high, representing in marble in high relief battles bet. Greeks and Amazons and bet. Lapithae, a legendary people from Thessaly, and centaurs.

Phil·a·del·phia \ˌfi-lə-ˈdel-fyə, -fē-ə\. **1.** County in SE Pennsylvania. See table at PENNSYLVANIA.

2. City, ⊗ of Neshoba co., E cen. Mississippi, 38 mi. (61 km.) NNW of Meridian; pop. (1990c) 6758; lumber; diversified agriculture.

3. City, ⊗ of and coextensive with Philadelphia co., SE Pennsylvania, at confluence of Delaware and Schuylkill rivers; pop. (1990c) 1,585,577; largest city in the state; a commercial, financial, industrial, cultural, and transportation center; major deepwater port; petroleum refineries; electrical machinery, chemical, and food industries; Independence National Historical Park incl. the Liberty Bell. Numerous educational institutions: Univ. of Pennsylvania (1740), Philadelphia Coll. of Pharmacy and Science (1821), Thomas Jefferson Univ. (1824), St. Charles Borromeo Seminary (1832), Moore Coll. of Art and Design (1844), Hahnemann Univ. (1848), Spring Garden Coll. (1850), St. Joseph's Univ. (1851), La Salle Univ. (1863), Philadelphia Univ. of the Arts (1870), Chestnut Hill Coll. (1871), Philadelphia Coll. of Textiles and Science (1884), Temple Univ. (1884), Drexel Univ. (1891), Pennsylvania Coll. of Optometry (1919), Curtis Institute of Music (1924), Holy Family Coll. (1954), Community Coll. of Philadelphia (1965); had first daily newspaper in the U.S. (*Pennsylvania Packet,* 1784); has oldest art museum in U.S., (1805, renovated 1994), and first hospital estab. in U.S., Pennsylvania Hospital (1751).

History: Delaware Indians original occupants of site; first European settlement on site made by colony of Swedes in 1640s; William Penn granted land from British crown 1681 and city laid out 1682; chartered 1701; received many immigrants from Scotland, Ireland, and Germany in early 18th cent.; dominant in shaping policies of nearby colonies in 18th cent.; statesman, scientist, and philosopher Benjamin Franklin moved to the city 1723. Prominent in opposing British policies; First Continental Congress met in Carpenters' Hall Sept. 1774; Second Continental Congress in the State House (Independence Hall) May 1775; Declaration of Independence signed in Independence Hall 1776; city held by British 1777–78; Constitutional Convention met in Independence Hall 1787 and adopted Sept. 17, 1787 the Constitution of the United States. Largest and most important city in U.S. in early 19th cent.; ✻ of Pennsylvania 1683–1799, and ✻ of U.S. 1790–1800; financial center of U.S. until mid-19th cent.; leader in antislavery movement; held Centennial Exposition 1876.

4. Town, Jordan. See AMMAN.

5. City, Turkey in Asia. See ALAŞEHİR.

Phi·lae \ˈfī-lē\. Former island in the Nile River, in Upper Egypt; site of ancient temples and monuments which were moved before the island was submerged by waters behind Aswān High Dam.

Phi·lia·tra \ˌfēl-yä-ˈträ\ *or Gk.* **Fi·li·trá** \ˌfē-lē-ˈträ\. Commune, Messenia dept., SW Peloponnese, S Greece, on Ionian Sea.

Phil·ip \ˈfi-ləp\. City, ⊗ of Haakon co., W cen. South Dakota, on Bad River 70 mi. (113 km.) WSW of Pierre; pop. (1990c) 1077.

\ə\ abut \ᵊ\ matches \ᵊ\ kitten, Fr table \ər\ further \a\ ash \ā\ ace \ä\ cot, cart \á\ Fr bac \au̇\ out \b̲\ Span Avila \ch\ chin \e\ bet \ē\ easy \g\ go \i\ hit \ī\ ice \j\ job \k̲\ Ger ich, Buch \ⁿ\ Fr vin \ŋ\ sing \ō\ go \ȯ\ all \ó\ law \œ\ Fr bœuf \œ̄\ Fr feu \ȯi\ boy \th\ thin \th̲\ this \ü\ loot \u̇\ foot \ue\ Ger füllen \ue̅\ Fr rue \y\ yet \ʸ\ Fr digne \ˈdēnʸ\, nuit \ˈnwʸē\ \yü\ few \yu̇\ fury \zh\ vision

Phil·ip·haugh \ˈfi-ləp-ˌhȯ\. Village, S Scotland, 2 mi. (3 km.) W of Selkirk; scene of battle in English Civil War 1645 in which James Graham, the Royalist earl of Montrose was surprised and defeated by pro-Parliamentarian forces of Gen. David Leslie.

Philippeville. See SKIKDA.

Phil·ip·pi \ˈfi-lə-pē\. City, ⊗ of Barbour co., N West Virginia, 19 mi. (31 km.) ESE of Clarksburg; pop. (1990c) 3132; scene of early battle in Civil War 1861 in which Union forces routed the Confederates; Alderson-Broaddus Coll. (1871).

Phi·lip·pi \ˈfi-lə-ˌpī, fə-ˈli-ˌpī\ *or* **Fí·lip·poi** \ˈfē-lē-ˌpē\. Ruined town in Drama dept., N cen. Macedonia, Greece, ab. 10 mi. (16 km.) from the Aegean Sea; fortified by King Philip II of Macedon c. 357 B.C.; scene of battle 42 B.C. in which Octavian (later Emperor Augustus) and Mark Antony defeated Julius Caesar's assassins Brutus and Cassius; place where St. Paul first preached the gospel in Europe.

Phil·ip·pines \ˈfi-lə-ˌpēnz, ˌfi-lə-ˈ\; *officially* **Republic of the Philippines** *or Pilipino* **Re·pu·bli·ka ng Pi·li·pi·nas** \re-ˈpüv-lē-kä-näŋ-pē-lē-ˈpē-näs\ *or Span.* **Re·pú·bli·ca de Fi·li·pi·nas** \re-ˈpü-blē-kä-thä-ˌfē-lē-ˈpē-näs\; *frequently* **Philippine Islands** *or Span.* **Is·las Fi·li·pi·nas** \ˈēz-läs-ˌfē-lē-ˈpē-näs\. Republic, an archipelago of ab. 7100 islands lying approx. 500 mi. (805 km.) off the SE coast of Asia; 115,651 sq. mi. (299,536 sq. km.); pop. (1993e) 64,954,000; ✻ Manila.

Physical features: N to S extent of the archipelago is ab. 1152 mi. (1854 km.), E to W extent ab. 688 mi. (1107 km.); has several sizable interisland seas—Sulu, Mindanao, Visayan, Sibuyan, Samar—and the irregular coastlines of many of the islands form many bays and fine harbors, such as Manila Bay, Lingayen Gulf, Leyte Gulf, Iligan Bay, and Davao Gulf. The San Bernardino Strait and Verde Island Passage together form the main ship lane across the archipelago from the Pacific to Manila and farther S Surigao Strait and Mindanao Sea provide a similar route across S part. Archipelago forms part of W Pacific volcanic chain, hence all islands are mountainous with chief ranges in N Luzon; highest peak Apo 9690 ft. (2954 m.) in SE Mindanao; ab. 20 mountains are volcanic peaks, esp. Taal and Mayon. Practically all islands are well watered but only Luzon and Mindanao have large streams (Cagayan, Pampanga, Agno, Agusan, Mindanao); Laguna de Bay and Taal on Luzon and Lanao on Mindanao are the chief lakes. Fertile volcanic soil is source of great variety of tropical products; major islands include: Bohol, Catanduanes, Cebu, Leyte, Luzon, Masbate, Mindanao, Mindoro, Negros, Palawan, Panay, Samar (for further information, see their individual entries).

Chief products: Rice, corn, copra, fruit, sugar, timber; iron ore, gold, nickel, copper, manganese; manufacturing: textiles, footwear, clothing; electronics assembly; food processing.

Chief cities: Quezon City, Manila, Davao, Caloocan, Cebu, Zamboanga, Pasay, Bacolod, Cagayan de Oro, Iloilo.

Political divisions: Divided into the following 14 regions and 75 provinces (for pronunciation of their names, see their individual entries):

NAME	AREA (sq. mi.)	AREA (sq. km.)	POP. (1990c)	CAPITAL
Bicol	6,810	17,638	3,909,799	
Albay	986	2,554	903,023	Legazpi
Camarines Norte	816	2,113	390,982	Daet
Camarines Sur	2,034	5,268	1,305,919	Pili
Catanduanes[1]	584	1,513	187,000	Virac
Masbate	1,563	4,048	599,915	Masbate
Sorsogon	827	2,142	522,960	Sorsogon
Cagayan Valley	14,865	38,502	2,816,243	
Batanes	81	210	15,026	Basco
Cagayan	3,476	9,003	829,974	Tuguegarao
Ifugao	972	2,517	147,281	Lagawe
Isabela	4,118	10,666	1,080,341	Ilagan
Kalinga-Apayao	2,721	7,047	211,775	Tabuk
Mountain Province	810	2,098	116,535	Bontoc
Nueva Vizcaya	1,507	3,904	301,179	Bayombong
Quirino	1,180	3,057	114,132	Cabarroquis
Central Luzon	7,039	18,231	6,198,957	
Bataan	530	1,373	425,803	Balanga
Bulacan	1,014	2,625	1,505,219	Malolos
Nueva Ecija	2,040	5,284	1,312,610	Palayan
Pampanga	842	2,181	1,532,682	San Fernando
Tarlac	1,179	3,054	859,651	Tarlac
Zambales	1,434	3,714	562,992	Iba
Central Mindanao	8,994	23,293	3,171,368	
Cotabato	2,603	6,742	763,995	Kidapawan
Lanao del Norte	1,203	3,115	614,092	Iligan
Lanao del Sur	1,486	3,850	599,637	Marawi
Maguindanao	2,046	5,298	757,739	Maganoy
Sultan Kudarat	1,656	4,288	435,905	Isulan
Central Visayas	5,774	14,953	4,593,151	
Bohol	1,590	4,118	948,315	Tagbilaran
Cebu	1,965	5,089	2,645,735	Cebu
Negros Oriental[2]	2,086	5,402	925,311	Dumaguete
Siquijor	133	344	73,790	Siquijor
Eastern Visayas	8,275	21,433	3,055,184	
Eastern Samar[3]	1,676	4,341	329,335	Borongan
Leyte[4,5]	2,420	6,268	1,486,522	Tacloban
Northern Samar[3]	1,350	3,498	383,654	Catarman
Southern Leyte[5]	670	1,735	321,940	Maasin
Western Samar[3]	2,159	5,591	533,733	Catbalogan
Ilocos	7,517	19,470	4,220,895	
Abra	1,535	3,976	184,743	Bangued
Benguet	1,025	2,655	485,546	La Trinidad
Ilocos Norte	1,312	3,398	461,661	Laoag
Ilocos Sur	996	2,580	519,930	Vigan
La Union	576	1,492	548,742	San Fernando
Pangasinan	2,073	5,369	2,020,273	Lingayen
National Capital[6]	146	378	9,201,000	
Northern Mindanao	10,938	28,328	3,509,000	
Agusan del Norte[1]	1,000	2,590	465,000	Butuan
Agusan del Sur[1]	3,462	8,966	421,000	Prosperidad
Bukidnon[1]	3,202	8,293	844,000	Malaybalay
Camiguin[1]	89	230	64,000	Mambajao
Misamis Occidental[1]	749	1,940	424,000	Oroquieta
Misamis Oriental[1]	1,378	3,569	865,000	Cagayan de Oro
Surigao del Norte[1]	1,058	2,740	426,000	Surigao
Southern Mindanao	12,304	31,866	4,457,076	
Davao	3,138	8,127	1,055,016	Tagum
Davao del Sur	2,462	6,377	1,482,648	Digos
Davao Oriental	1,994	5,164	394,697	Mati
South Cotabato	2,952	7,645	1,072,617	Koronadal
Surigao del Sur	1,758	4,553	452,098	Tandag
Southern Tagalog	18,116	46,921	8,256,784	
Aurora	1,251	3,240	139,586	Baler
Batangas	1,222	3,165	1,467,783	Batangas
Cavite	497	1,287	1,152,534	Trece Martires
Laguna	679	1,759	1,370,232	Santa Cruz
Marinduque	370	958	185,524	Boac
Mindoro Occidental	2,270	5,879	282,593	Mamburao
Mindoro Oriental	1,685	4,364	550,049	Calapan
Palawan	5,751	14,896	528,287	Puerto Princesa
Quezon	3,362	8,707	1,372,381	Lucena
Rizal	505	1,309	980,194	Pasig
Romblon	524	1,357	227,621	Romblon
Western Mindanao	7,214	18,684	3,159,197	
Basilan	512	1,327	243,091	Isabela
Sulu	618	1,600	469,971	Jolo
Tawi-tawi	420	1,087	228,204	Bato-Bato
Zamboanga del Norte	2,555	6,618	673,774	Dipolog
Zamboanga del Sur	3,109	8,052	1,544,157	Pagadian
Western Visayas	7,809	20,225	5,393,333	
Aklan[7]	702	1,818	380,497	Kalibo
Antique[7]	974	2,523	406,361	San Jose de Buenavista
Capiz[7]	1,017	2,634	584,091	Roxas
Iloilo[7,8]	2,056	5,325	1,765,476	Iloilo
Negros Occidental[2]	3,060	7,925	2,256,908	Bacolod
Autonomous Regions				
Cordillera[6]	7,063	18,293	1,304,000	
Muslim Mindanao[6]	4,570	11,836	2,103,000	

[1] Pop. (1993e).
[2] Comprise the island of Negros.
[3] Comprise the island of Samar.
[4] Includes the subprovince of Biliran.
[5] Comprise the island of Leyte.
[6] Pop. (1995e).
[7] Comprise the island of Panay.
[8] Includes the subprovince of Guimaras.

History: Earliest inhabitants probably Negritos coming from mainland of Asia, followed by, among others, Malays; Muslims settled in S in 15th cent. Discovered by Portuguese navigator Ferdinand Magellan 1521 and first successful settlement made by Spanish under the explorer Miquel López de Legazpi 1565; Manila founded 1571. In first two centuries many conflicts with Moros in S. In 1762–63 Manila captured and held by British; generally in 18th and 19th cents. Spanish control strengthened; many revolts of Filipino peoples occurred, the most serious being the Revolt of 1896; in Spanish-American War battle of Manila Bay May 1898 and

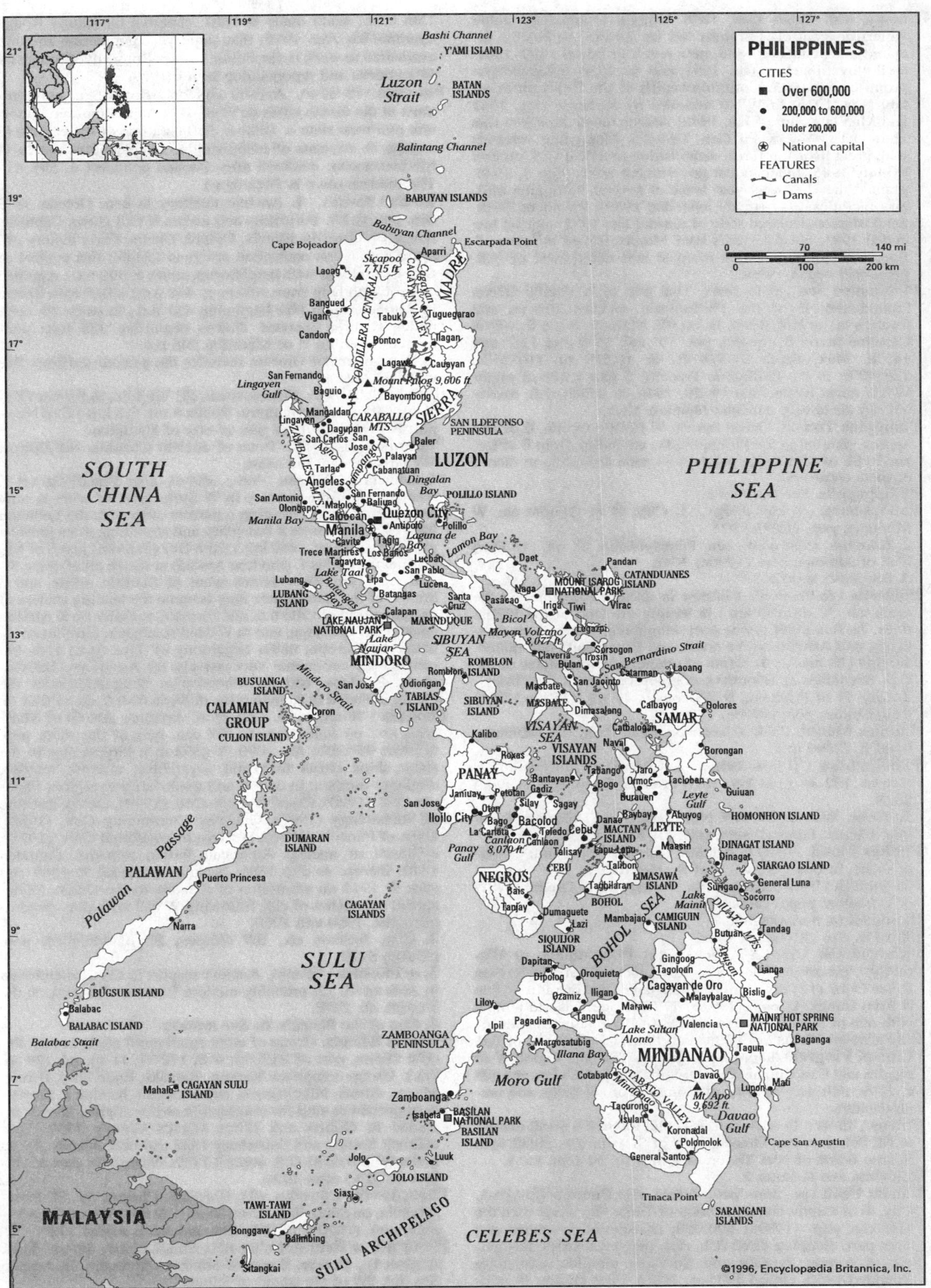
PHILIPPINES
CITIES
Over 600,000
200,000 to 600,000
Under 200,000
National capital
FEATURES
Canals
Dams
0 70 140 mi
0 100 200 km
117°
119°
121°
123°
125°
127°
21°
19°
17°
15°
13°
11°
9°
7°
5°
Bashi Channel
Y'AMI ISLAND
Luzon Strait
BATAN ISLANDS
Balintang Channel
BABUYAN ISLANDS
Babuyan Channel
Cape Bojeador
Escarpada Point
Aparri
Sicapoo 7,715 ft
Laoag
Cagayan
CAGAYAN VALLEY
MADRE
SIERRA
Bangued
Vigan
Tabuk
Tuguegarao
CORDILLERA CENTRAL
Candon
Bontoc
Ilagan
Lagawe
Cauayan
San Fernando
Lingayen Gulf
Mount Pulog 9,606 ft.
Baguio
Bayombong
Mangaldan
Lingayen
Dagupan
CARABALLO MTS.
San Carlos
San Jose
SAN ILDEFONSO PENINSULA
Baler
ZAMBALES MTS.
Agno
Pampanga
Palayan
LUZON
Tarlac
Cabanatuan
SOUTH CHINA SEA
PHILIPPINE SEA
Angeles
Dingalan Bay
San Fernando
Baliuag
POLILLO ISLAND
San Antonio
Olongapo
Malolos
Caloocan
Quezon City
Manila Bay
Manila
Antipolo
Polillo
Taguig
Laguna de Bay
Lamon Bay
Cavite
Trece Martires
Los Baños
Tagaytay
Lucban
Daet
Pandan
Lake Taal
San Pablo
CATANDUANES ISLAND
Lubang
Batangas Bay
Lipa
Lucena
MOUNT ISAROG NATIONAL PARK
Naga
LUBANG ISLAND
Batangas
Santa Cruz
Pasacao
Iriga
Tiwi
Virac
Calapan
MARINDUQUE
LAKE NAUJAN NATIONAL PARK
Bicol
Lake Naujan
Mayon Volcano 8,077 ft.
Legazpi
SIBUYAN SEA
Sorsogon
MINDORO
ROMBLON ISLAND
Claveria
Irosin
San Bernardino Strait
Romblon
Bulan
BUSUANGA ISLAND
Mindoro Strait
Laoang
Catarman
San José
Odiongan
Masbate
San Jacinto
TABLAS ISLAND
CALAMIAN GROUP
Coron
SIBUYAN ISLAND
MASBATE
Calbayog
Dolores
Dimasalang
SAMAR
CULION ISLAND
Catbalogan
VISAYAN SEA
Kalibo
Naval
Borongan
Roxas
VISAYAN ISLANDS
PANAY
Bantayan
Tabango
Jaro
Ormoc
Tacloban
Bogo
Gadiz
San Jose
Januay
Pototan
Silay
Sagay
Burauen
Leyte Gulf
Guiuan
Iloilo City
Oton
Bago
Bacolod
Baybay
Abuyog
HOMONHON ISLAND
San Fernando
La Carlota
Toledo
Cebu
Danao
Palawan Passage
DUMARAN ISLAND
Canlaon 8,070 ft.
Canlaon
MACTAN ISLAND
LEYTE
Panay Gulf
Talisay
Lapu-Lapu
Maasin
DINAGAT ISLAND
CEBU
Dinagat
PALAWAN
NEGROS
Talibon
LIMASAWA ISLAND
SIARGAO ISLAND
Puerto Princesa
General Luna
Bais
Tagbilaran
Lake Mainit
Surigao
Socorro
Palawan
Tanjay
BOHOL
Dumaguete
DIUATA MTS.
CAGAYAN ISLANDS
BOHOL SEA
Mambajao
CAMIGUIN ISLAND
Narra
Lazi
Butuan
Tandag
SIQUIJOR ISLAND
Agusan
SULU SEA
Gingoog
Dapitan
Tagoloan
Dipolog
Oroquieta
Lianga
Cagayan de Oro
BUGSUK ISLAND
Iligan
Malaybalay
Bislig
Balabac
Ozamiz
Marawi
Liloy
Tangub
Valencia
BALABAC ISLAND
Ipil
Pagadian
MAINIT HOT SPRING NATIONAL PARK
Balabac Strait
Lake Sultan Alonto
ZAMBOANGA PENINSULA
Margosatubig
Baganga
Illana Bay
MINDANAO
Tagum
Moro Gulf
Cotabato
COTABATO VALLEY
Davao
Mati
Mahalu
CAGAYAN SULU ISLAND
Mindanao
Mt. Apo 9,692 ft.
Lupon
Zamboanga
Tacurong
Davao Gulf
Isabela
BASILAN NATIONAL PARK
Isulan
Koronadal
BASILAN ISLAND
Polomolok
Cape San Agustin
General Santos
Jolo
Luuk
JOLO ISLAND
Siasi
Tinaca Point
TAWI-TAWI ISLAND
SARANGANI ISLANDS
MALAYSIA
Bonggaw
Balimbing
SULU ARCHIPELAGO
CELEBES SEA
Sitangkai

treaty with Spain Dec. 1898 brought archipelago under American control; Filipinos led by Emilio Aguinaldo declared independence 1898; new revolt followed 1899–1901; civil government estab. 1901 and in 1934 independence promised for 1945. **Commonwealth of the Philippines** estab. Nov. 1935. In WWII attacked by Japanese Dec. 1941 and Manila captured Jan. 1942; islands under Japanese rule until Oct. 1944, when Gen. Douglas MacArthur returned with great invasion force, establishing practical U.S. control by July 1945. Independent government estab. July 4, 1946; granted the U.S. a 99-year lease of several Philippine military facilities 1947 (treaty amended 1959); President Ferdinand Marcos declared state of martial law 1972; martial law ended 1981, but five years later Marcos forced to leave office; U.S. military leases revoked and withdrawal of U.S. personnel began 1990s.

Phil·ip·pine Sea \ˈfi-lə-ˌpēn\. That part of W Pacific Ocean immediately E of the Philippines; touches Taiwan and Ryukyu Is. on NW, Bonin Is. on NE, Mariana Is. on E, and W Caroline Is. on S; roughly bet. 10° and 25°N and 125° and 145°E. Max. depth 34,578 ft. or 10,539 m. (10°24′N, 126°40′E; in the Philippine Trench); S part scene of major WWII naval battle June 19–20, 1944, in which U.S. carrier aircraft decisively defeated Japanese fleet.

Philippine Trench. Ocean trench, W Pacific Ocean, E of and approx. parallel to the Philippine Is., extending from E of Luzon to SE of Mindanao; subduction zone according to theory of plate tectonics.

Philippopolis. See PLOVDIV 2.

Phil·ips·burg \ˈfi-ləps-ˌbərg\. **1.** City, ⊗ of Granite co., W Montana; pop. (1990c) 925.
2. Borough, Centre co., cen. Pennsylvania, 28 mi. (45 km.) NNE of Altoona; pop. (1990c) 3048.
3. See SAINT MARTIN.

Phi·lis·tia \fə-ˈlis-tē-ə\. Country in ancient Palestine, on the coast, ab. 50 mi. (80 km.) in length; the land of the Philistines. Its five chief towns (city-kingdoms) were Gaza, Ashkelon, and Ashdod on the coast, and Ekron and Gath inland.

Phil·lips \ˈfi-ləps\. **1.** Name of counties in four states of the U.S. See tables at ARKANSAS, COLORADO, KANSAS, MONTANA.
2. City, ⊗ of Price co., N Wisconsin, 47 mi. (76 km.) W of Rhinelander; pop. (1990c) 1592.

Phillips, Mount. Peak, Glacier National Park, NW Montana; 9480 ft. (2890 m.).

Phil·lips·burg \ˈfi-ləps-ˌbərg\. **1.** City, ⊗ of Phillips co., N Kansas, 102 mi. (164 km.) NNW of Great Bend; pop. (1990c) 2828.
2. Town, Warren co., NW New Jersey, on Delaware River opp. Easton, Pennsylvania; pop. (1990c) 15,757.

Phillips Island. Island in Atlantic Ocean off SE South Carolina coast, in Beaufort co., S of St. Helena I.

Phi·lo·math \ˈfi-lə-ˌmath\. City, Benton co., W Oregon, WSW of Corvallis; pop. (1990c) 2983.

Philomelion. See AKŞEHİR.

Phintias. See LICATA.

Phit·sa·nu·lok \ˈpit-ˌsä-nu̇-ˈlōk\ *also* **Pit·sa·nu·lok** *or* **Bis·nu·lok** \ˈpit-ˌsä-nu̇-ˈlōk—*sic*\. Town, N cen. Thailand, on Nan River 75 mi. (121 km.) N of Nakhon Sawan and on railroad line N from Bangkok; pop. (1991e) 77,672; rice; has old temple with one of most venerated images of Buddha in Thailand.

Phle·grae·an Fields *or* **Phlegraean Plain** \flə-ˈgrē-ən\ *or Ital.* **Cam·pi Fle·grei** \ˈkäm-pē-flā-ˈgrā-ē\. Volcanic region W of Naples and E of Cumae, S Italy; Solfatara, which last erupted c. 1199, still active; ruins of Roman thermal baths and amphitheaters.

Phli·us \ˈflī-əs\. In ancient times chief town of a small district of NE Peloponnese, Greece, SSW of Sicyon; usu. allied with Sparta; home of poet Timon of Phlius (c. 3d cent. B.C.).

Phlórina. See FLORINA 2.

Phnom Penh \pə-ˈnòm-ˈpen, -ˈnäm\ *also* **Pnom·penh** \pə-\. City, ✻ of Cambodia, at junction of Tonle Sap River with the Mekong; pop. (1989e) 800,000; transportation center and river port, shipping dried fish, rice, pepper; textiles; has palace of former dynasty and Buddhist temples; university (founded 1956, closed 1975–c. 1988). First chosen ✻ mid-15th cent.; again made ✻ 1867; captured by Khmer Rouge Communists Apr. 1975; that same year population forcibly evacuated to work in the fields; Khmer Rouge overthrown by Vietnamese and repopulation begun 1979.

Pho·caea \fō-ˈsē-ə\. Ancient city on Aegean Sea, northernmost of the Ionian cities on W coast of Asia Minor; an important maritime state c. 1000–c. 550 B.C., one of the earliest to engage in voyages of colonization; founded Massilia in W Mediterranean; declined after Persian conquest c. 545 B.C. The modern town is Foça (*q.v.*).

Pho·cis \ˈfō-sis\. **1.** Ancient territory in cen. Greece. In S cen. part is Mt. Parnassus and across N half flows Cephisus River. Chief towns Elateia, Delphi, Daulis. Early history obscure but at first controlled oracle at Delphi; lost control of Delphi after war with neighboring states c. 590 B.C.; regained control with help from Athens c. 448 B.C.; allied with Sparta in Peloponnesian War beginning 431 B.C.; in early 4th cent. under Thebes; opposed Thebes beginning 355 B.C.; conquered by Philip II of Macedon 346 B.C.
2. Department of Greece; includes the ancient territory. See table at GREECE.

Phoe·bus \ˈfē-bəs\. Former town, SE Virginia, in former Elizabeth City co., on Hampton Roads 8 mi. (13 km.) E of Newport News; since 1952 part of city of Hampton.

Phoe·ni·ce \fi-ˈnī-sē\. Town of ancient Chaonia, NW Epirus, NW Greece, near the coast.

Phoe·ni·cia \fi-ˈni-shə, -ˈnē-, -shē-ə\ *also* **Phe·ni·cia** \fi-\. Ancient maritime country in W Syria (part of what is now modern Lebanon), forming a narrow strip with the Lebanon Mts. as an indefinite E boundary and stretching at its greatest extent ab. 160 mi. (260 km.) from Dor (Tantura) just S of Mt. Carmel to Aradus I. (modern Arwad) at the N; chief cities Sidon and Tyre. Phoenicians were of Semitic origin and a branch of the Canaanites; they became the leading traders of ancient world c. 1200 B.C. and founded colonies on N African coast, incl. Carthage, and in W Mediterranean; introduced alphabet to Europe; under hegemony of Tyre (*q.v.*) 11th–8th cents. B.C.; conquered successively by Assyrians, Babylonians, Persians, and by Macedonian King Alexander the Great; included in Roman prov. of Syria 64 B.C. (see SYRIA 1).

Phoe·nix \ˈfē-niks\. **1.** City, ✻ of Arizona, also ⊗ of Maricopa co., on Salt River in SW cen. part of the state; pop. (1990c) 983,403; alt. 1090 ft. (332 m.); largest city in the state; ships citrus fruit and vegetables; aircraft, textiles, clothing; tourism; in cotton and truck-farming region; Phoenix Coll. (1920), Grand Canyon Coll. (1949), DeVry Institute of Technology (1967), Gateway Community Coll. (1968), Univ. of Phoenix (1976), Western International Univ. (1978); evidence of ancient American Indian remains. Founded 1870; incorp. as city 1881; became territorial ✻ 1889 and state ✻ 1912 on admission of Arizona to the Union. Widespread expansion of city following WWII with pop. quadrupling bet. 1950 and 1960.
2. City, Jackson co., SW Oregon, SE of Medford; pop. (1990c) 3239.
3. *or* **Phe·nice** \ˈfē-nis\. Ancient seaport in Crete, mentioned in *Acts* xxvii. 12; probably modern **Lou·tro** \ˈlü-ˌtrò\ on the S coast, ab. 24°E.
4. One of the Phoenix Is. See RAWAKI.

Phoenix Islands. Group of eight small coral atolls in cen. Pacific Ocean, part of Kiribati; 4°S, 172°W; 11 sq. mi. (29 sq. km.). Group comprises Kanton, Rawaki, Enderbury, Birnie, Manra, Orona, Nikumaroro, and McKean. Kanton I. formerly important as stop for transpacific airline flights; islands included in Gilbert and Ellice Islands Colony 1937; U.S. claimed Kanton and Enderbury 1938 and both islands placed under joint British-U.S. control 1939; Phoenix Is. part of Gilbert Is. (*q.v.*) after 1976.

Phoe·nix·ville \ˈfē-niks-ˌvil\. Borough, Chester co., SE Pennsylvania, on Schuylkill River 24 mi. (39 km.) NW of Philadelphia; pop. (1990c) 15,066; iron and steel; settled 1720.

Phour·noi *or* **Foúr·noi** \ˈfu̇r-nē\. Small island, Sámos dept., Aegean Is., Greece, N part of Southern Sporades, in Aegean Sea just SW of the island of Sámos.

Phrae *or* **Prae** \ˈprä\. Town, N Thailand, on Yom River 90 mi. (145 km.) N of Phitsanulok; pop. (1991e) 17,681.

Phra Na·khon Si Ayut·tha·ya \ˌprä-nä-ˈkȯn-sē-ˌä-yü-ˈtī-ə\; *usu. shortened to* **Ayutthaya** *also* **Ayu·tha·ya** *or* **Ayu·thia** \ˌä-yü-ˈtī-ə\. City, S Thailand, 40 mi. (64 km.) N of Bangkok, on an island in the lower Chao Phraya; pop. (1991e) 60,561; intersected by many canals and many of its inhabitants live on boats; chief town of a rich agricultural section; numerous remains of Buddhist shrines and temples. Founded 1350 and was Siamese ✻ until 1767 when it was destroyed by the Burmese.

Phryg·ia \ˈfri-jē-ə\. Ancient country, W cen. Asia Minor. Settled as early as 13th cent. B.C. by people perhaps of Thracian origin who occupied extensive lands along Black Sea and Aegean coasts; gradually driven E and S, Phrygians made their home in the plateau region bounded on N by Bithynia, on E by Cappadocia and Lycaonia, on S by Pisidia and Lycia, and on W by Caria, Lydia, and Mysia. Reached height of power 8th cent. B.C.; conquered by Lydia 7th cent. B.C.; afterwards was source of slaves for Greece but not without influence in arts and religion. Conquered by Persia 546 B.C.; passed into power of Macedonian King Alexander the Great 333 B.C. and soon after 301 became a part of the new kingdom founded by one of his generals, Seleucus Nicator, first ruler of the Seleucid dynasty; fell into Roman hands 133 B.C. and most of it became part of prov. of Asia; under Byzantine Empire name disappeared from record.

Phthia \ˈthī-ə\; *later* **Phthi·o·tis** \thī-ˈō-tis\. Ancient name of district in S Thessaly, NE Greece, now in Central Greece region. In Homer's *Iliad*, Phthia was the residence of Achilles.

Phthi·o·tis \fthē-ˈō-tēs, thī-ˈō-tis\. Department of Greece. See table at GREECE.

Phthiotis and Phocis. Former department of Greece, now subdivided into Phthiotis and Phocis depts.

Phu Ka·dueng National Park \ˈpü-kä-ˈdu̇ŋ\. National park, Thailand; 134 sq. mi. (347 sq. km.); waterfalls.

Phu·ket *also* **Pu·ket** *or* **Bhu·ket** \ˈpü-ˈket\. **1.** *formerly* **Sa·lang** \sä-ˈläŋ\ *or* **Junk·sey·lon** \ˌjəŋk-si-ˈlän\. Island, SW Thailand, off W coast of Malay Penin. in Andaman Sea; 309 sq. mi. (800 sq. km.); pop. (1991e) 174,744; large tin mines. **2.** Seaport town, at S end of island; pop. (1991e) 42,913; one of the chief Thai ports on Indian Ocean; ships tin, rubber, charcoal, and fish.

Phul·kian States \ˈpül-kyän\. Patiala, Nabha, and Jind, former states of E and SE Punjab, now part of Punjab and Haryana states, India; 8188 sq. mi. (21,207 sq. km.); the name is derived from their common ancestral ruler.

Phumi Banam. See BANAM.

Phu·quoc \ˈpü-ˈkwu̇k\. Island in SE part of Gulf of Thailand, off S shore of Cambodia S of Kampot.

Phu·tha·di·tjha·ba \ˌpü-tä-dē-ˈchä-bä\. Town, Free State, Rep. of South Africa, near northernmost point of Lesotho; urban area pop. (1985c) 21,453; formerly ✻ of Qwa Qwa enclave.

Phy·le \ˈfī-lē\. Site of an ancient fortress, now in ruins, 11 mi. (18 km.) NNW of Athens, Attica dept., Greece. Base used by Athenian Gen. Thrasybulus and his followers in their operations against the Thirty Tyrants 404–403 B.C.

Pia·cen·za \pyä-ˈchen-sä\. **1.** Province of Emilia-Romagna, Italy. See table at ITALY.
2. *anc.* **Pla·cen·tia** \plə-ˈsen-ch(ē-)ə\. Commune, its ✻, on Po River 40 mi. (64 km.) SE of Milan; pop. (1991p) 102,252; chemicals, office furniture; in cereal-farming and wine-producing region; 12th–13th cent. cathedral with 14th cent. campanile; 13th cent. town hall; 16th cent. Farnese palace (uncompleted).
History: Founded by Romans 218 B.C.; destroyed by Gauls 200 B.C. and later rebuilt; made W terminus of ancient Roman Aemilian Way; became part of Lombard League 12th cent.; under Visconti family 14th cent., Sforza family, and popes 1512; given together with Parma to Farnese family by Pope Paul III 1545; part of duchy of Parma and Piacenza 1545–1860; became part of kingdom of Italy 1860.

Pi·ai, Cape \pē-ˈī\. Cape, Malaysia, S Malay Penin., 1°15′N; most southerly point on Asian mainland.

Pia·no·sa \ˌpē-ä-ˈnō-sä\. **1.** *anc.* **Pla·na·sia** \plə-ˈnā-zhə\. Small island, Italy, in the Mediterranean Sea SW of the island of Elba; 4 sq. mi. (10 sq. km.); highest point 95 ft. (29 m.); attached to Livorno prov.
2. Islet, Italy, in cen. Adriatic Sea N of Gargano Promontory and 14 mi. (23 km.) NE of Tremiti Is.

Pia·pa·yung·an, Mount \pē-ˌä-pə-ˈyu̇ŋ-ən\. Mountain, SE Lanao del Sur prov., Mindanao, Philippines, on Cotabato boundary E of Mt. Ragang; 8725 ft. (2659 m.).

Pia·secz·no \pyä-ˈsech-nō\. Town, Warszawa prov., Poland, ab. 15 mi. (24 km.) S of Warsaw; pop. (1989e) 24,348.

Pia·stow \ˈpyä-stüf\. Commune, Warszawa prov., NE cen. Poland; pop. (1989e) 23,836.

Piatigorsk. See PYATIGORSK.

Pia·tra–Ne·amţ \ˈpyä-trä-ˈnyäms\. City, ⊗ of Neamţ co., NE Romania, in foothills of the Carpathians and on Bistriţa River ab. 25 mi. (40 km.) W of Roman; pop. (1989c) 115,782; food products, furniture, fertilizer, paper; 15th cent. church.

Pi·att \ˈpī-ət\. County in cen. Illinois. See table at ILLINOIS.

Piauí; *formerly* **Piau·hy** \pyau̇-ˈē\. State, NE Brazil; ✻ Teresina; cotton; first European settlements in region 17th cent. See table at BRAZIL.

Piauí, Serra do. See SERRA DO PIAUÍ.

Pia·ve \ˈpyä-vā\. River, NE Italy; rises in the Carnic Alps S of Lienz, flows S and SE into the Adriatic Sea 22 mi. (35 km.) ENE of Venice; 137 mi. (220 km.) long; scene of battles 1917–18, when it became the line of defense of the Italians after their retreat from Caporetto; the Austrians made several unsuccessful attempts to cross the river.

Piaz·za Ar·me·ri·na \ˈpyät-sä-ˌär-mā-ˈrē-nä\; *Sicilian* **Chiaz·za** \ˈkyät-sä\. Commune, Enna prov., cen. Sicily, Italy, 13 mi. (21 km.) SSE of the commune of Enna; pop. (1991p) 22,384; cathedral.

Pi·bor \ˈpē-ˌbȯr\. River, SE Sudan; flows N and unites with Baro River on border of W Ethiopia to form Sobat River; ab. 200 mi. (320 km.) long.

Pic \ˈpēk\. French term meaning "peak" or "mountain"; for some entries beginning with *Pic*, see the distinguishing element.

Pi·ca·ra Point \pi-ˈkär-ə\. Tip of long narrow peninsula on N coast of St. Thomas I., Virgin Is. of the U.S., West Indies, which forms E side of Magens Bay.

Pi·car·die \ˌpē-kȧr-ˈdē\. Region of N France, lying mostly S of historical Picardy. See table at FRANCE.

Pic·ar·dy \ˈpi-kər-dē\ *or Fr.* **Pi·car·die** \ˌpē-kȧr-ˈdē\. Historical region of N France; bounded before 1790 on N by Strait of Dover, Artois, and Flanders, E by Champagne, S by Île-de-France, SW by Normandy, W by English Channel; watered by Somme River.
History: In 13th cent. area included countships of Amienois and Vermandois under French king; military government organized c. 1350 by Valois family; joined to Burgundy 1435; province of France 1482 until Revolution; region scene of heavy fighting in WWI and WWII.

Pic·a·yune \ˌpi-kē-ˈyün, -kə-ˈyün\. City, Pearl River co., S Mississippi, 35 mi. (56 km.) WNW of Gulfport; pop. (1990c) 10,633.

Pi·ce·num \pī-ˈsē-nəm\. Ancient district in E Italy, on the Adriatic Sea; became Roman province 3d cent. B.C.; chief towns Ancona and Asculum.

Pi·chin·cha \pē-ˈchēn-chä\. **1.** Volcano, Ecuador, NW of the city of Quito; 15,173 ft. (4625 m.); scene of battle 1822 in which rebels under Antonio José de Sucre defeated Spanish royalists. See ECUADOR.
2. Province of N cen. Ecuador. See table at ECUADOR.

Pichit. See PHICHIT.

Pichones, Cayos. See PIGEON CAYS.

Pick·a·way \ˈpi-kə-ˌwā\. County in S cen. Ohio. See table at OHIO.

Pick·ens \'pi-kənz\. **1.** Name of counties in three states of the U.S. See tables at ALABAMA, GEORGIA, SOUTH CAROLINA.
2. Town, ⊗ of Pickens co., NW South Carolina, 19 mi. (31 km.) W of Greenville; pop. (1990c) 3042.

Pick·er·ing \'pi-kə-riŋ\. Town, SE Ontario, Canada, NE of Toronto; pop. (1991c) 68,631.

Pick·ett \'pi-kət\. County in N Tennessee. See table at TENNESSEE.

Pick·wick Landing Dam \'pik-wik\. Dam in Tennessee River, Hardin co., SW Tennessee, at village of **Pickwick Dam,** forming **Pickwick Lake** extending along the Alabama-Mississippi boundary and into Lauderdale co., NW Alabama. See table at TENNESSEE VALLEY AUTHORITY.

Pi·co. **1.** *Span.* \'pē-kō, *Port.* -kü\. Spanish and Portuguese name for "mountain" or "peak"; for names beginning with *Pico,* see the distinguishing element.
2. \'pē-kō\. Town, Argentina. See GENERAL PICO.
3. \'pē-kü\. Island, cen. Azores; 167 sq. mi. (433 sq. km.); pop. (1991p) 15,129; chief town Lajes do Pico; highest point 7711 ft. or 2350 m. (see ALTO, PICO).

Pico Ri·ve·ra \'pē-kō-rə-'vir-ə\. City, Los Angeles co., SW California, SE of the city of Los Angeles; pop. (1990c) 59,177.

Pic·qui·gny \,pē-kē-'nyē\. Commune, Somme dept., N France, 8 mi. (13 km.) NW of Amiens; treaty signed here 1475 bet. Edward IV of England and Louis XI of France.

Pic·ton \'pik-tən\. **1.** Town, ⊗ of Prince Edward co., SE Ontario, Canada, on inlet of Lake Ontario 16 mi. (26 km.) SE of Belleville; pop. (1991c) 4373.
2. Borough and port on inlet of Cook Strait, NE South I., New Zealand; pop. (1987e) 4160.

Picton Channel. Strait, W of Wellington I., off SW coast of Chile, connecting Trinidad Gulf with the Pacific.

Pic·tou \'pik-tü\. **1.** County, N Nova Scotia, Canada. See table at NOVA SCOTIA.
2. Town, its ⊗, on **Pictou Harbor,** an inlet of Northumberland Strait; pop. (1991c) 4134; coastal port and trawler-fleet base; lobster fisheries; Pictou Academy (1818); town founded 1763 by colonists from Pennsylvania.

Pic·tured Rocks \'pik-chərd\. Cliffs on S shore of Lake Superior, in Alger co., N Upper Penin. of Michigan; erosion features.

Pi·du·ru·ta·la·ga·la \,pi-də-,rüt-ᵊl-'ä-gə-lə\. Mountain, highest peak in Sri Lanka, ab. 60 mi. (95 km.) E of Colombo; 8281 ft. (2524 m.).

Piedad, La. See LA PIEDAD.

Pied·mont \'pēd-,mänt\. **1.** An upland belt, that part of the Atlantic plain of E U.S. lying E of the Blue Ridge and Appalachian Mts., extending from the Hudson River to cen. Alabama.
2. City, Calhoun co., NE Alabama, 20 mi. (32 km.) E of Gadsden; pop. (1990c) 5288.
3. Residential city, Alameda co., W California, suburb of Oakland, 5 mi. (8 km.) E of San Francisco Bay; pop. (1990c) 10,602.
4. *or Ital.* **Pie·mon·te** \pyā-'mȯn-tā\. Autonomous region, NW Italy; borders on France and Switzerland; ✻ Turin; almost entirely surrounded by mountains; slopes to fertile plain producing grains, wine, dairy products; industries include automobiles, textiles, glass. In ancient times part of Transpadane Gaul; held from 11th cent. by house of Savoy (*q.v.*); leader in move to unite Italy 19th cent.; ruler Victor Emmanuel II became king of unified Italy 1861; administrative region estab. 1948; received limited autonomy 1970. See table at ITALY.

Piedras, Las. See LAS PIEDRAS.

Pi·e·dras Blan·cas Point \pē-'ā-drəs-'blaŋ-kəs\. Point on NW coast of San Luis Obispo co., SW California.

Pie·dras Ne·gras \'pyā-t͟hräs-'nā-gräs\. **1.** Archaeological site on right bank of the Usumacinta River, NW Guatemala; original location of Mayan sculptural art now in national museum.
2. *formerly* **Ciu·dad Por·fi·rio Dí·az** \syü-'t͟hät͟h-pȯr-'fē-rē-ō-'t͟hē-äs\. City, Coahuila state, NE Mexico, on the Rio Grande opp. Eagle Pass, Texas, with which it is connected by an international bridge; munic. pop. (1990p) 98,177; N terminus of Mexican National Railways.

Pie·dras Point \'pyā-t͟hräs\. Cape on E cen. coast of Argentina, SE of Buenos Aires, extending into the Río de la Plata opp. Brava Point in Uruguay. See BRAVA POINT.

Pie·gan, Mount \pē-'gan\. Peak, Glacier National Park, NW Montana; 9230 ft. (2813 m.).

Pie·ka·ry Śląs·kie \,pye-'kä-rē-'shləs-kē\. Town, Katowice prov., S Poland, ab. 12 mi. (19 km.) NNW of the city of Katowice; pop. (1989e) 68,277.

Piek·sä·mä·ki \'pē-ek-sa-ma-kē\. Town, Mikkeli prov., S Finland, ab. 45 mi. (70 km.) N of the city of Mikkeli; pop. (1980c) 13,844.

Pie·li·nen, Lake \'pē-e-,lē-nen\ *also* **Pie·lis·jär·vi** \'pē-e-lēs-,yar-vē\. Lake, Kuopio prov., SE Finland; 56 mi. (90 km.) long, 422 sq. mi. (1093 sq. km.).

Pie·man \'pī-mən\. River, NW Tasmania, Australia; rises on W edge of cen. highlands and flows W to Indian Ocean; ab. 70 mi. (115 km.) long.

Piemonte. See PIEDMONT 4.

Pien–ching. See KAIFENG.

Pierce \'pirs\. **1.** Name of counties in five states of the U.S. See tables at GEORGIA, NEBRASKA, NORTH DAKOTA, WASHINGTON, WISCONSIN.
2. City, ⊗ of Pierce co., NE Nebraska; pop. (1990c) 1615.

Pi·e·ria \pī-'ir-ē-ə\. **1.** Department of Central Macedonia, Greece. See table at GREECE.
2. A region of ancient Macedonia, W of the Gulf of Salonika; seat of worship of the Muses; location of Mt. Olympus.

Pierre \'pir\. City, ✻ of South Dakota, also ⊗ of Hughes co., cen. South Dakota, on Missouri River; pop. (1990c) 12,906; in farming region; recreation, tourism. Area orig. inhabited by Arikara Indians; European settlement founded as railroad terminus 1880; named state ✻ 1889.

Pierre·fitte–sur–Seine \pyer-'fēt-sūr-'sān, -'sen\. Commune, Seine-St.-Denis dept., N France, N suburb of Paris.

Pierre·fonds \pyer-'fōⁿ\. **1.** City, Montreal co., S Quebec, Canada; pop. (1991c) 48,735.
2. Town, E Oise dept., N France, SE of Compiègne; château, built c. 1400, torn down by Louis XIII early 17th cent., restored by French architect Eugène-Emmanuel Viollet-le-Duc 1857 ff.

Pier·son \'pirs-ᵊn\. Town, Volusia co., E Florida; pop. (1990c) 2988.

Pi·e·rus \'pī-ə-rəs\. Mountain in ancient Pieria, Macedonia, Greece, N of Mt. Olympus.

Pieš·t'a·ny \'pyesh-tyä-nē\ *or Hung.* **Pös·tyén** \'pœsh-,tyān\ *or Ger.* **Pis·tyan** \'pis-,tyän\. Town, W Slovakia, on Váh River ab. 45 mi. (70 km.) NE of Bratislava; pop. (1991p) 32,999.

Pie·tar·saa·ri \'pē-e-tär-,sä-rē\ *or Swed.* **Ja·kob·stad** \'yä-ku̇p-,städ\. Seaport, Vaasa prov., W Finland, on the Baltic Sea; pop. (1992e) 19,988; trade center; exports lumber; formed 1652; birthplace of the national poet Johan Ludvig Runeberg 1804.

Pietas Julia. See PULA.

Pie·ter·mar·itz·burg \,pē-tər-'mar-əts-,bərg\. City, S cen. KwaZulu-Natal prov., E Rep. of South Africa, 40 mi. (64 km.) W of Durban; pop. (1985c) 133,809; footwear, aluminum and rubber products, furniture; rice mill; in area growing wattle trees. Founded c. 1838 and named after two Boer leaders, Pieter Retief and Gerrit Maritz; made ✻ of Natal 1856.

Pie·ters·burg \'pē-tərz-,bərg\. Town, Northern prov., NE Rep. of South Africa, 150 mi. (241 km.) NNE of Pretoria; pop. (1985c) 29,909; in rich agricultural region; gold, asbestos, and corundum are found in area. For a time headquarters of Dutch forces during Boer War.

Pietola. See VIRGILIO.

Pie·tra·per·zia \,pye-trä-'pert-syä\. Commune, Enna prov., cen. Sicily, Italy, 13 mi. (21 km.) SW of the commune of Enna; pop. (1981p) 10,995.

Pie·tra·san·ta \,pye-trä-'sän-tä\. Commune, Lucca prov., Tuscany, cen. Italy, 16 mi. (26 km.) NW of the commune of Lucca; pop. (1991p) 24,723; 14th cent. cathedral; marbleworks.

Piet Re·tief \ˈpēt-rə-ˈtēf\. Town, Mpumalanga prov., NE Rep. of South Africa, near Swaziland border.

Pi·geon \ˈpi-jən\. **1.** River, extreme NE Minnesota; flows into N Lake Superior, forms section of U.S.-Canada boundary; 40 mi. (64 km.) long.

2. River, E Tennessee; rises in W North Carolina, flows NW across Tennessee border and into French Broad River in W Cocke co.; 75 mi. (121 km.) long.

Pigeon Cays *or Span.* **Ca·yos Pi·cho·nes** \ˈkī-ōs-pē-ˈchō-nās\. Group of small islands in Caribbean Sea off E coast of Honduras.

Pigeon Forge \ˈfȯrj\. City, Sevier co., E Tenessee, N of Great Smoky Mountains National Park; pop. (1990c) 3027.

Pigeon Peak. Mountain, La Plata co., SW Colorado; 13,961 ft. (4255 m.).

Pig·gott \ˈpi-gət\. City, a ⊗ of Clay co., NE corner of Arkansas, 49 mi. (79 km.) NE of Jonesboro; pop. (1990c) 3777.

Pignerol. See PINEROLO.

Pigs, Bay of \ˈpigz\ *or* **Ba·hía de Co·chi·nos** \bä-ˈhē-ä-ˌt͟hä-kō-ˈchē-nōs\. Bay on SW coast of Las Villas prov., W cen. Cuba; scene of attempted invasion of Cuba by forces opposed to the rule of Fidel Castro April 1961.

Pihkva–Järv. See PSKOV and PSKOV, LAKE.

Pike \ˈpīk\. Name of counties in 10 states of the U.S. See tables at ALABAMA, ARKANSAS, GEORGIA, ILLINOIS, INDIANA, KENTUCKY, MISSISSIPPI, MISSOURI, OHIO, PENNSYLVANIA.

Pike o' Stickle. See LANGDALE PIKES.

Pikes Peak \ˈpīks\. Mountain, El Paso co., E cen. Colorado, near Colorado Springs; 14,110 ft. (4301 m.); tourist destination noted for view from its summit; has mountain railroad and road to summit. Discovered 1806 by American explorer Lieut. Zebulon M. Pike.

Pikes·ville \ˈpīks-ˈvil\. Unincorporated settlement, Baltimore co., cen. Maryland, NW of the city of Baltimore; pop. (1990c) 24,815.

Pike·ville \ˈpīk-ˌvil\. **1.** City, ⊗ of Pike co., E Kentucky, 42 mi. (68 km.) ENE of Hazard; pop. (1990c) 6324; Pikeville Coll. (1889).

2. Town, ⊗ of Bledsoe co., SE cen. Tennessee; pop. (1990c) 1771.

Pik Pobedy. See POBEDA PEAK.

Pi·ła \ˈpē-wä\ *or Ger.* **Schnei·de·mühl** \ˈshnī-də-ˌmu̇̄l\. **1.** Province, W cen. Poland. See table at POLAND.

2. City, its ✻, ab. 55 mi. (90 km.) N of Poznań; pop. (1989e) 71,509; railroad junction; ships potatoes; sawmills, railroad shops. Chartered c. 14th cent.; made city 1513; to Prussia 1772; largely destroyed in WWII; assigned to Poland by Potsdam Conference 1945.

Pi·lar \pē-ˈlär\. **1.** Town, Buenos Aires prov., E cen. Argentina, ab. 28 mi. (45 km.) NW of the city of Buenos Aires; pop. (1980p) 74,629.

2. *or* **Vil·la del Pilar** \ˈvē-yä-ˌt͟hel-\. Town and river port, ✻ of Ñeembucú dept., SW cen. Paraguay, on Paraguay River opp. the mouth of the Bermejo 120 mi. (193 km.) SW of Asunción; pop. (1992p) 19,151; ships agricultural produce; sawmills, distilleries; founded 1779.

3. Municipality, Sorsogon prov., Luzon, Philippines, on inlet W of Sorsogon Bay 22 mi. (35 km.) W of Sorsogon; pop. (1980c) 45,579.

4. Municipality, Capiz prov., Panay, Philippines, on S shore of Pilar Bay 18 mi. (29 km.) ESE of Roxas; pop. (1980c) 30,104.

5. Municipality, Cebu prov., Philippines. See PONSON.

Pilar, Cape *or* **Cape Pil·lar** \ˈpi-lər\. Cape on Desolación I. at W entrance into Strait of Magellan, off S coast of South America.

Pilar Bay. Inlet of SE Sibuyan Sea in NE Capiz prov., Panay, Philippines.

Pi·lat \pē-ˈlä\. Peak in the Cévennes Range, Loire dept., SE cen. France; 4704 ft. (1434 m.).

Pi·la·tus \pē-ˈlä-tu̇s\. Peak, Obwalden demicanton, cen. Switzerland, near border of Lucerne canton; 6983 ft. (2128 m.); railway.

Pil·co·ma·yo \ˌpēl-kō-ˈmä-yō\. River, S cen. South America; rises in E Andes Mts., W cen. Bolivia, flows SE and forms boundary bet. Argentina and the Chaco region of Paraguay; empties into Paraguay River at Asunción; ab. 1000 mi. (1610 km.) long. See CONFUSO.

Pi·li \ˈpē-lē\. **1.** Peak in the Andes, N Chile; 19,849 ft. (6050 m.).

2. Municipality, Camarines Sur prov., Luzon, Philippines, on railroad line 8 mi. (13 km.) SE of Naga; pop. (1980c) 43,181.

Pi·li·bhit \ˌpē-li-ˈbēt\. Town, N Uttar Pradesh, N India, ab. 50 mi. (80 km.) N of Shahjahanpur; pop. (1991p) 106,329; 18th cent. mosque.

Pi·li·ca \pē-ˈlēt-sä\ *or* **Pi·li·tsa** \pē-ˈlēt-sä\. River, Poland; rises in SW Poland, flows N and NE into Vistula River above Warsaw; 195 mi. (314 km.) long.

Pi·lim·sit \ˌpi-lim-ˈsit\; *formerly* **Iden·burg** \ˈī-dən-ˌbərg\. Peaks in Sudirman Range, W Irian Jaya, Indonesia; highest point 15,784 ft. (4811 m.).

Pílion Óros. See PELION, MOUNT.

Pilipinas, Republika ng. See PHILIPPINES.

Pilitsa. See PILICA.

Pil·lar, Cape \ˈpi-lər\. **1.** SE point of Tasmania, Australia, at S end of Tasman Penin., extending into Tasman Sea.

2. Cape, Strait of Magellan. See PILAR, CAPE.

Pillar Mountain. Peak, Cumbria co., NW England, in the Lake District; 2927 ft. (892 m.).

Pillars of Her·cu·les \ˈhər-kyə-ˌlēz\. The two promontories at E end of Strait of Gibraltar: Rock of Gibraltar in Europe, and Jebel Musa at Ceuta in Africa. Fabled to have been set there by Hercules as a memorial in his travels to seize the cattle of the three-bodied giant Geryon.

Pillau. See BALTIYSK.

Pill·nitz \ˈpil-nits\. Village on the Elbe just SE of Dresden, Germany; site of 18th cent. castle, former residence of Saxon kings; scene of conference Aug. 1791 at which Holy Roman Emperor Leopold II and Frederick William II, king of Prussia, reached agreement regarding policy toward France.

Pills·bury Sound \ˈpilz-ber-ē, -bə-rē\. Body of water off N coast of E end of St. Thomas I., Virgin Is. of the U.S., West Indies.

Pi·lo·ña \pē-ˈlō-nyä\. Commune, Asturias prov., NW Spain, 24 mi. (39 km.) E of Oviedo; pop. (1991c) 9672.

Pílos. See PYLOS.

Pi·lot Knob \ˈpī-lət\. **1.** Peak, San Juan and San Miguel cos., SW Colorado; 13,750 ft. (4191 m.).

2. Peak, cen. Idaho co., N cen. Idaho; ab. 7135 ft. (2175 m.).

Pilot Peak. **1.** Mountain on S boundary of Plumas co., NE California, in the Sierra Nevada; 7508 ft. (2288 m.).

2. Mountain, cen. Boise co., W cen. Idaho; 8560 ft. (2609 m.).

3. Mountain, N Valley co., W cen. Idaho; 8061 ft. (2457 m.).

4. Mountain, S Mineral co., SW Nevada; ab. 9187 ft. (2800 m.); highest in Excelsior Mts.

5. Mountain, NW Park co., in the Absaroka Range, NW Wyoming; 11,708 ft. (3568 m.).

Pilsen. See PLZEŇ.

Pilt·down *or* **Pilt Down** \ˈpilt-ˌdau̇n\. Locality in East Sussex, S England, ab. 7 mi. (11 km.) N of Lewes; site of discovery 1909–15 of skull and jawbone fragments orig. thought to derive from a distinctive early Pleistocene hominoid but in the 1950s shown to be the product of a deliberate hoax.

Pi·ma \ˈpē-mə\. County in S Arizona. See table at ARIZONA.

Pi·men·tel \ˌpē-men-ˈtel\. Seaport, NW Peru, 8 mi. (13 km.) from Chiclayo; pop. (1981p) 11,456.

Pim·li·co \ˈpim-li-ˌkō\. SW neighborhood of London, England, bet. Westminster and Chelsea; includes Belgravia.

Pi·ná·cu·lo \pē-ˈnä-kü-ˌlō\. Peak, SW Santa Cruz prov., S Argentina, near Chilean border; 7090 ft. (2161 m.).

Pi·nal \pə-ˈnal\. County in S Arizona. See table at ARIZONA.

Pin·a·le·no Mountains \ˌpin-ᵊl-ˈā-nō\. Mountain range, incl. Mt. Graham (*q.v.*), in Graham co., SE Arizona.

Pinal Peak. Mountain in SW Gila co., SE cen. Arizona; ab. 7850 ft. (2395 m.).

Pi·na·ma·la·yan \ˌpē-nä-mä-ˈlä-ˌyän\. Municipality, Mindoro Oriental prov., in center of E coast of Mindoro I., Philippines, on coastal highway 33 mi. (53 km.) SE of Calapan; pop. (1980c) 48,431.

Pi·na·mung·a·jan \ˌpē-nä-ˌmůŋ-ˈä-ˌhän\. Municipality, Cebu prov., on W coast of Cebu I., Philippines, in cen. part on Tanon Strait 22 mi. (35 km.) WSW of City of Cebu; pop. (1980c) 31,394.

Pinang. See PENANG 1.

Pinang, Pulau. See PENANG 2.

Pi·nar del Río \pē-ˈnär-t͟hel-ˈrē-ō\. **1.** Province of W Cuba. See table at CUBA.
2. City, its ❋; pop. (1990e) 121,774.

Pi·na·tu·bo, Mount \ˌpē-nä-ˈtü-bō\. Mountain on boundary bet. E Zambales and W Pampanga provs., Luzon, Philippines; 5770 ft. (1759 m.); erupted June 1991.

Pin·cher Creek \ˈpin-chər\. Town, SW Alberta, Canada, N of Waterton-Glacier International Peace Park; pop. (1991c) 3660.

Pin·chot, Mount \ˈpin-ˌshō\. **1.** Peak in the Sierra Nevada, in E Fresno co., S cen. California; 13,495 ft. (4113 m.).
2. Peak in Glacier National Park, NW Montana; 9375 ft. (2858 m.).

Pinciacum. See POISSY.

Pinck·ney·ville \ˈpiŋk-nē-ˌvil\. City, ⊗ of Perry co., SW Illinois, 34 mi. (55 km.) SW of Mount Vernon; pop. (1990c) 3372.

Pin·court \ˈpin-ˌkōrt\. Town, S Quebec, Canada; pop. (1991c) 9639.

Pin·da·ré \ˌpēn-dä-ˈrā\. River, Maranhão state, NE Brazil; flows NE into Mearim River just before it enters São Marcos Bay; ab. 200 mi. (320 km.) long.

Pin·dus Mountains \ˈpin-dəs\ *or Gk.* **Pín·dhos Óros** \ˈpēn-thös-ˈö-rös\. **1.** In modern times, range of mountains in NW Greece, extending into Albania; ab. 68 mi. (109 km.) long; av. width 20 mi. (32 km.); highest point 8136 ft. (2480 m.).
2. In classical times, the mountains forming the boundary bet. Epirus and Thessaly.

Pine \ˈpīn\. **1.** County in E Minnesota. See table at MINNESOTA.
2. River, E British Columbia, Canada; flows E and N into Peace River near Fort St. John; ab. 125 mi. (200 km.) long.

Pine, Cape. Cape, SE Newfoundland, Canada, W of Cape Race.

Pine Bluff *before 1832* **Mount Marie** \mə-ˈrē\. Commercial city, ⊗ of Jefferson co., SE cen. Arkansas, on Arkansas River 43 mi. (69 km.) SE of Little Rock; pop. (1990c) 57,140; cotton market; lumber and wood products, chemicals; Univ. of Arkansas at Pine Bluff (1873). Settled 1819; incorp. 1839; successfully defended by Union forces against Confederate attack Oct. 25, 1863.

Pine City. City, ⊗ of Pine co., E Minnesota, 60 mi. (97 km.) N of Minneapolis; pop. (1990c) 2613.

Pine Creek. River, N cen. Pennsylvania; rises in Potter co., N Pennsylvania, flows E and S into W branch of Susquehanna River in S Lycoming co.; ab. 100 mi. (160 km.) long.

Pine·dale \ˈpīn-ˌdāl\. Town, ⊗ of Sublette co., W Wyoming; pop. (1990c) 1181.

Pine Flat Dam. See UNITED STATES, *Dams and Reservoirs.*

Pine Forest Range. Range in Humboldt co., NW Nevada; includes Duffer Peak 9458 ft. (2883 m.).

Pi·neg·ska·ya Yen·ta·la \ˌpē-ˈneg-skə-yə-ˈyen-ˌtä-lə\. River, Arkhangel'sk Oblast, N Russia in Europe; flows into the Northern Dvina near its mouth; 407 mi. (655 km.) long.

Pine Hill. Borough, Camden co., SW New Jersey, 13 mi. (21 km.) SSE of the city of Camden; pop. (1990c) 9854.

Pine·hurst \ˈpīn-ˌhərst\. **1.** Town and winter resort, Moore co., cen. North Carolina, ab. 65 mi. (105 km.) SW of Raleigh; pop. (1990c) 5103; PGA World Golf Hall of Fame; town estab. 1895.
2. City, Orange co., E Texas; pop. (1990c) 2682.

Pine Island. Island off W coast of Lee co., SW Florida, S of Charlotte Harbor; 31 sq. mi. (80 sq. km.).

Pine Island Sound. Sound W of Pine I. and E of outer island chain off coast of Lee co., SW Florida.

Pine Lawn. City, St. Louis co., E Missouri, NW suburb of the city of St. Louis; pop. (1990c) 5092.

Pi·nel·las \pī-ˈne-ləs\. Coastal county in cen. W Florida Penin., Florida. See table at FLORIDA.

Pinellas Park. City, Pinellas co., W cen. Florida, N of St. Petersburg; pop. (1990c) 43,426.

Pinellas Peninsula. Peninsula, Pinellas co., cen. W Florida Penin., Florida, W of Tampa Bay; St. Petersburg is situated at its S end.

Pine Mountain. Range extending along N section of Kentucky-Virginia boundary.

Pine Point. **1.** Cape on W shore of Dixie co., NW Florida Penin., extending into the Gulf of Mexico.
2. Extreme S point, Cumberland co., SW Maine.

Pi·ne·ro·lo \ˌpē-nā-ˈrō-lō\ *or Fr.* **Pi·gne·rol** \pē-nyə-ˈrōl\. Commune, Torino prov., Piedmont, NW Italy, at foot of Alps 22 mi. (35 km.) SW of Turin; pop. (1989c) 35,900; textile mills, printing plants; 15th–16th cent. cathedral; 14th cent. palace. First mentioned 10th cent.; successively under Savoy and France.

Pines, Isle of \ˈpīnz\. **1.** Island in Caribbean Sea. See ISLA DE LA JUVENTUD.
2. Island, Pacific Ocean. See PINS, ÎLE DES.

Pine·town \ˈpīn-ˌtau̇n\. Town, KwaZulu-Natal prov., Rep. of South Africa, ab. 10 mi. (16 km.) WNW of Durban; pop. (1985c) 55,770.

Pine·view Dam \ˈpīn-ˌvyü\. Dam across Ogden River E of Ogden, Utah; height 132 ft. (40 m.); completed 1937; impounds water, **Pineview Reservoir,** for irrigation.

Pine·ville \ˈpīn-ˌvil, -vəl\. **1.** City, ⊗ of Bell co., SE Kentucky; pop. (1990c) 2198.
2. City, Rapides parish, cen. Louisiana, 5 mi. (8 km.) NE of Alexandria; pop. (1990c) 12,251; Louisiana Coll. (1906).
3. Town, ⊗ of McDonald co., SW Missouri; pop. (1990c) 580.
4. Town, Mecklenburg co., S North Carolina, on South Carolina border; pop. (1990c) 2970; birthplace 1795 of James Knox Polk, 11th president of the U.S., nearby.
5. Town, ⊗ of Wyoming co., S West Virginia; pop. (1990c) 865.

Pin·ey Point Village \ˈpī-nē-ˌpȯint\. City, Harris co., SE Texas, in an enclave surrounded by Houston; pop. (1990c) 3197.

Ping \ˈpiŋ\ *or* **Me·ping** \ˈmā-\. River, W Thailand; rises N of Chiang Mai, flows SSE to join with the Nan at Nakhon Sawan to form Chao Phraya; ab. 300 mi. (485 km.) long.

Ping·e·lap \ˈpiŋ-ə-ˌlap\. Group of three small islands halfway bet. Pohnpei and Kosrae, E Caroline Is., W Pacific Ocean; part of Federated States of Micronesia.

Pingkiang. See HARBIN.

Ping·liang *or W.-G.* **P'ing–liang** \ˈpiŋ-ˈlyäŋ\. Town, E Gansu prov., N cen. China, 170 mi. (274 km.) E of Lanzhou near Ningxia Huizu border.

P'ing–tung \ˈpiŋ-ˈdu̇ŋ\. Municipality, SW Taiwan, ENE of Kao-hsiung; pop. (1993e) 213,309.

Ping·xiang *or W.-G.* **P'ing–hsiang** \ˈpiŋ-ˈshyäŋ\; *formerly* **Ping·siang** \ˈpiŋ-ˈshyäŋ\. **1.** Town, W Jiangxi prov., SE China, SE of Changsha, Hunan.
2. Town, SW Guangxi Zhuangzu, S China, on Vietnam border.

Pi·nhei·ro \pē-ˈnyer-ü\. City, Maranhão state, NE Brazil, ab. 50 mi. (80 km.) W of São Luís; munic. pop. (1991p) 82,439.

Pi·ni \ˈpē-nē\. See BATU.

Pi·ni·ós \ˌpē-nē-ˈös\ *or* **Pe·ne·us** \pi-ˈnē-əs\ *also* **Pe·nei·us** \-ˈnē-\; *formerly* **Sa·lam·bria** \sə-ˈlam-brē-ə\. River, Thessaly, N cen. Greece; rises in Pindus Mts., flows SE and ENE through plain of Thessaly and Vale of Tempe into the Gulf of Salonika; ab. 125 mi. (200 km.) long.

Pin·kiang \ˈbin-ˈjyäŋ, ˈbiŋ-\. **1.** Former province (1934–45), E cen. Manchukuo; 24,651 sq. mi. (63,846 sq. km.); ❋ Harbin.
2. *or* **Pingkiang.** City, China. See HARBIN.

Pink·ie \ˈpiŋ-kē\. Battlefield near Edinburgh, Scotland; scene of victory of English duke of Somerset over the Scots 1547.

Pinna. See PENNE.

Pin·na·cles National Monument \ˈpi-nə-kəlz\. See UNITED STATES, *National Monuments.*

Pin·ne·berg \ˈpi-nə-ˌberk\. Town, Schleswig-Holstein, Germany, on Pinnau River 12 mi. (19 km.) NW of Hamburg; pop. (1980c) 36,683.

Pi·nole \pi-ˈnōl\. City, Contra Costa co., W California, N of Oakland; pop. (1990c) 17,460; pop. more than doubled bet. 1960 and 1970.

Pin·op·o·lis Dam \ˈpī-ˈnä-pə-lis\. Dam across Cooper River, cen. Berkeley co., SE South Carolina; height 140 ft. (43 m.); completed 1941; impounds water, Lake Moultrie, for waterpower.

Pinopolis Reservoir. See MOULTRIE, LAKE.

Pi·nos \ˈpē-nōs\. Municipality, Zacatecas state, Mexico, 70 mi. (113 km.) SE of the city of Zacatecas; pop. (1990p) 59,386.

Pi·nos, Mount \ˈpē-nōs\. Peak, N Ventura co., SW California, in the Coast Ranges (*q.v.*); 8831 ft. (2692 m.).

Pi·nos–Puen·te \ˈpē-nōs-ˈpwen-tā\. Commune, Granada prov., S Spain, 11 mi. (18 km.) NW of the city of Granada; pop. (1991c) 13,132.

Pins, Île des \ˌēl-dā-ˈpen\ *or Eng.* **Isle of Pines** \ˈpīnz\ *also* **Ku·nie** \kü-ˈnē-ā\. Island in SW Pacific Ocean 31 mi. (50 km.) SE of S end of New Caledonia I.; 58 sq. mi. (150 sq. km.); formerly used as French convict station; administratively part of New Caledonia.

Pinsk *or Pol.* **Pińsk** \ˈpinsk\. Town, Brest subdivision, Belarus, 103 mi. (166 km.) E of the city of Brest at confluence of the Pina and Pripet rivers; pop. (1991e) 123,800; furniture; shipbuilding and repairing. First mentioned 1097; ✽ of an early Russian principality of the same name; to Lithuania in 14th cent. and then to Poland; to Russia under Second Partition 1793; returned to Poland 1921 but to U.S.S.R. in agreement with Poland following WWII.

Pinsk Marshes. See POLESYE.

Pinsk Oblast \ˈȯ-bləst, -ˌblast\. Former subdivision of the Belorussian S.S.R., U.S.S.R.; ✽ Pinsk; abolished 1954.

Pin·ta Island \ˈpēn-tä\ *also* **Ab·ing·don Island** \ˈa-biŋ-dən\. One of the Galápagos Is. (*q.v.*), Ecuador.

Pintuaria. See TENERIFE.

Pint·wa·ter Range \ˈpīnt-ˌwȯ-tər, -ˌwä-\. Small range in N Clark co., SE Nevada, extending N into Lincoln co.; highest peak 6370 ft. (1942 m.).

Pin·yon Peak \ˈpin-yən\. Mountain, NW Custer co., cen. Idaho; 9945 ft. (3031 m.).

Pi·oche \pē-ˈōch\. Village, ⊗ of Lincoln co., E Nevada.

Piol·tel·lo \pyȯl-ˈtel-lō\. Commune, Milano prov., Lombardy, N Italy; pop. (1989c) 33,414.

Piom·bi·no \pyōm-ˈbē-nō\. Commune, Livorno prov., Tuscany, cen. Italy, on Ligurian Sea 43 mi. (69 km.) S of commune of Livorno; pop. (1989c) 37,613; seaport with iron and steel works; under Pisan rule in the Middle Ages; ceded to the Viscontis 1399; became principality 1594; passed to Ludovisi family 1634 and to Buoncompagni family 1706; to French 1801; to Tuscany 1815.

Pi·o·neer Valley \ˌpī-ə-ˈnir\. The valley through which the Connecticut River flows in Massachusetts—often used of all of Hampden, Hampshire, and Franklin cos.

Pio·tr·ków \ˈpyȯ-tər-ˌküf\. Province, cen. Poland. See table at POLAND.

Pio·tr·ków Try·bu·nal·ski \ˈpyȯ-tər-ˌküf-ˌtri-bü-ˈnäl-skē\ *or Russ.* **Pe·tro·kov** \ˈpet-rə-ˌkȯf, -ˌkȯv\ *or Ger.* **Pe·tri·kau** \ˈpā-tri-ˌkau̇\. Commune, ✽ of Piotrków prov., cen. Poland, 28 mi. (45 km.) SSE of Łódź; pop. (1989e) 80,529; textiles. Seat of Polish tribunal 1578 ff.—hence its name.

Pio XII \ˈpē-ü-ˌdü-ō-ˈdā-sē-ˌmü\. Municipality, Maranhão state, NE Brazil, ab. 100 mi. (160 km.) WSW of São Luís.

Pi·per Peak \ˈpī-pər\. Mountain, W Esmeralda co., SW Nevada; ab. 9447 ft. (2879 m.).

Pipe Spring National Monument \ˈpīp\. See UNITED STATES, *National Monuments.*

Pipe·stone \ˈpīp-ˌstōn\. **1.** County in SW Minnesota. See table at MINNESOTA. **2.** City, its ⊗, 40 mi. (64 km.) SW of Marshall; pop. (1990c) 4554; agriculture; just to the N is **Pipestone National Monument** (see UNITED STATES, *National Monuments*).

Piq·ua \ˈpi-kwä, -kwə\. City, Miami co., W Ohio, 27 mi. (43 km.) N of Dayton; pop. (1990c) 20,612; clothing, automobiles; Edison State Community Coll. (1973); settled 1797 on site of former Shawnee Indian village; at first called Washington; renamed Piqua 1816; important canal port in early 19th cent.

Pi·qui·ri \ˌpē-kē-ˈrē\ *or* **Pe·que·ri** \ˌpā-\. River, Paraná state, S Brazil; flows NW into the Paraná; ab. 200 mi. (320 km.) long.

Pi·ra·ci·ca·ba \ˌpē-rä-sē-ˈkä-bə\. City, SE cen. São Paulo state, SE Brazil, 42 mi. (68 km.) WNW of Campinas; pop. (1991p) 223,170; ships sugar, coffee; sugar mills, distillery.

Pi·rae·us \pī-ˈrē-əs\ *or* **Pi·rai·evs** *also* **Pei·rae·us** \pī-ˈrē-əs\ *or Gk.* **Pi·rai·éus** \ˌpē-re-ˈefs\. Seaport city, Greece, on the Saronic Gulf 5 mi. (8 km.) SW of Athens; pop. (1991p) 169,622; principal railroad terminus and seaport of Greece; chemical, shipbuilding, and engineering industries.

History: Fortification of Piraeus planned and begun by the statesman-general Themistocles 493 B.C.; "long walls," a fortified barrier connecting Athens and the port, built c. 460–c. 454 B.C.; city laid out in grid pattern according to plan by the architect Hippodamus 450 B.C.; long walls destroyed by Sparta 404 B.C. but rebuilt 393 B.C.; city burned by Romans under Sulla 86 B.C. Began modern development mid-19th cent.; heavily damaged by bombing in WWII.

Piragua. See PARAGUA 1.

Piraiéus *or* **Piraievs.** See PIRAEUS.

Pi·rá·mi·de \pē-ˈrä-mē-ˌthā\. Peak, S Chile, W of Lake San Martín; 11,090 ft. (3380 m.).

Pi·ran \pē-ˈrän\ *or Ital.* **Pi·ra·no** \pē-ˈrä-nō\. Seaport, Slovenia, ab. 45 mi. (70 km.) WNW of Rijeka; 14th cent. church.

Pi·ra·nhas \pē-ˈrȧ-nyəs\. River, NE Brazil; flows N through Rio Grande do Norte state into Atlantic Ocean; ab. 250 mi. (400 km.) long.

Pi·ra·po·ra \ˌpē-rȧ-ˈpōr-ə\. City, Minas Gerais state, E Brazil, on the São Francisco 190 mi. (306 km.) NNW of Belo Horizonte; munic. pop. (1980c) 32,709.

Pi·ras·su·nun·ga \ˌpē-rȧ-sü-ˈnu̇ŋ-gə\. City, São Paulo state, SE Brazil, 60 mi. (97 km.) NNW of Campinas; munic. pop. (1991p) 56,737.

Pi·ray \pē-ˈrī\. River, cen. Bolivia; flows N into the Río Grande; 150 mi. (241 km.) long.

Pírgos. See PYRGOS.

Pi·riá·po·lis \ˌpēr-ˈyä-pō-ˌlēs\. Town, Maldonado dept., S Uruguay, on coast 50 mi. (80 km.) E of Montevideo.

Pirineos. See PYRENEES.

Pir·ma·sens \ˈpir-mə-ˌzens\. City, North Rhineland-Palatinate, Germany, 40 mi. (64 km.) WNW of Karlsruhe; pop. (1992e) 47,801; manufactures leather goods, esp. footwear. Came under French control 1794; passed to Bavaria 1816; severely damaged in WWII.

Pir·na \ˈpir-nə\. City, Saxony, E Germany, on Elbe River 11 mi. (18 km.) SE of Dresden; pop. (1981c) 48,001; glass, paper, artificial silk; 16th cent. castle; first mentioned 13th cent.; site of Saxon surrender to king of Prussia 1756.

Piroe. See PIRU.

Pi·rot \ˈpē-rōt\. Town, Serbia, E Yugoslavia, on the Nišava River ab. 33 mi. (53 km.) ESE of Niš; handwoven carpets. Became part of Serbia 1878.

Pir Pan·jal \ˈpēr-ˌpən-ˈjäl\. Mountain range, SW Jammu and Kashmir, N India; highest point over 19,000 ft. (5790 m.).

Pi·ru *or Du.* **Pi·roe** \ˈpir-ü\. Village at W end of Ceram I., Indonesia, at head of **Piru Bay,** an inlet of Ceram Sea nearly closed by Ambon I.

Pi·sa \ˈpē-zə; *Ital.* -sä\. **1.** Province of Tuscany, W Italy. See table at ITALY.

2. *anc.* **Pi·sae** \ˈpī-sē\. Commune, its ✻, on Arno River 43 mi. (69 km.) SW of Florence; pop. (1991p) 98,006; glass; tourism; notable buildings include cathedral (begun 11th cent.), 12th–14th cent. baptistery, leaning tower (campanile of cathedral, built 1174–c. 1350, deviating 16.5 ft. or 5 m. from the perpendicular), 14th cent. Palazzo Gambacorti, Palazzo de Medici (prefecture), 14th cent. church of Santa Maria della Spina, and numerous other churches; university (1343).

History: Orig. probably an Etruscan town; became Roman colony c. 180 B.C.; rose to prominence in Italy in Middle Ages; conquered Sardinia and Corsica 11th cent.; defeated Arabs near Palermo 1063; sided with Ghibellines in support of the Holy Roman emperor 13th–14th cents.; defeated in long struggle with Genoa at battle of Meloria 1284; fell to Florence 1406; Council of Pisa held 1409 (rival popes Gregory XII and Benedict XIII deposed and Pope Alexander V elected, but decision not recognized); as part of grand duchy of Tuscany, became part of kingdom of Italy 1860; scene of heavy fighting in WWII 1944. Birthplace of astronomer and physicist Galileo 1564.

Pi·sa·gua \pē-ˈsä-gwä\. Seaport, Tarapacá region, N Chile, ab. 40 mi. (64 km.) N of Iquique; formerly belonged to Peru; taken by Chilean Army 1879 in War of the Pacific; ceded to Chile 1883.

Pisaurum. See PESARO.

Pis·cat·a·qua \pi-ˈska-tə-ˌkwȯ\. River, Maine and New Hampshire; 12 mi. (19 km.) long; forms part of Maine-New Hampshire boundary; tidal harbor from Portsmouth to the sea (3 mi. or 4.8 km.) one of the best in U.S.

Pis·cat·a·quis \pi-ˈska-tə-kwis\. County in N cen. Maine. See table at MAINE.

Pis·cat·a·way \pi-ˈska-tə-ˌwā\. Village, part of Piscataway township, Middlesex co., cen. New Jersey, N of Raritan River and E of New Brunswick; township pop. (1990c) 47,089.

Pis·co \ˈpē-skō\. Seaport on Pisco Bay, SW Peru, 130 mi. (209 km.) S of Callao; pop. (1981p) 55,749.

Pi·se·co Lake \pə-ˈsē-kō\. Lake, S Hamilton co., NE cen. New York; ab. 5 mi. (8 km.) long; drains S through Sacandaga River into Great Sacandaga Lake.

Pí·sek \ˈpē-ˌsek\. Town, SW Czech Republic, 55 mi. (88 km.) SW of Prague on Otava River; pop. (1989c) 29,617.

Pis·gah, Mount \ˈpiz-gə\. **1.** Peak in the Catskill Mts., Delaware co., S New York; 3345 ft. (1020 m.).

2. Ridge of Abarim Mts. in ancient Palestine, E of N end of the Dead Sea; highest point 2644 ft. (806 m.); now in Jordan; **Ne·bo** \ˈnē-bō\ was an alternative name for it or the name of its peak.

Pi·shin \pi-ˈshēn\. Area, N Baluchistan, Pakistan, N of Quetta; ceded to British by Afghanistan 1879.

Pishin Lo·ra \ˈlōr-ə\. River, W Pakistan; flows SW into Hamun-i-Lora; ab. 300 mi. (485 km.) long; part of its course is in SE Afghanistan.

Pishpek. See BISHKEK.

Pi·sid·ia \pə-ˈsi-dē-ə, pī-\. Ancient country, S Asia Minor, cut off from the Mediterranean by Pamphylia; bounded on NW by Phrygia, on NE by Lycaonia, on SE by Cilicia, and on SW by Lycia. A mountainous region; its inhabitants never entirely subdued until country was incorp. into Roman prov. of Galatia early first cent. A.D.; later, part of Pisidia included in Lycia and Pamphylia; under Roman Emperor Diocletian became part of diocese of Asia.

Pisino. See PAZIN.

Pis·ki \ˈpish-kē\. Village on Mureşul River, S Transylvania, Romania, SW of Alba Iulia; scene of victory of Hungarians under Polish Gen. Józef Bem over Austrians Feb. 1849.

Pis·mo Beach \ˈpiz-mō\. City, San Luis Obispo co., SW California, on Pacific Ocean 65 mi. (105 km.) NW of Santa Barbara; pop. (1990c) 7669; beach resort.

Pisse·vache \pēs-ˈväsh\. Waterfall in Valais canton, SW cen. Switzerland; 215 ft. (66 m.) high.

Pi·sto·ia \pē-ˈstȯi-ä\. **1.** Province of Tuscany, W Italy. See table at ITALY.

2. *anc.* **Pis·to·ria** \pis-ˈtōr-ē-ə\ *or* **Pis·to·ri·ae** \pis-ˈtōr-ē-ˌē, -ˈtȯr-\. Commune, its ✻, 17 mi. (27 km.) NW of Florence; pop. (1991p) 87,275; railroad junction; shoes, glass; tanneries, flower nurseries; 12th–13th cent. cathedral with 14th cent. baptistery; Ospedale del Ceppo, founded 13th cent.; 12th cent. church of Sant'Andrea; 12th–14th cent. church of San Giovanni Fuorcivitas.

History: Scene of final defeat and death of Roman politician Catiline 62 B.C.; became free commune 11th cent.; important banking center 12th–13th cents.; under Florence in early 14th cent.; to Tuscany 1530 and to kingdom of Italy 1860.

Pistyan. See PIEŠT'ANY.

Pis·tyll Cain Falls \ˈpis-təl-ˈkīn, -tihl-\. Falls in Prysor River, Gwynedd co., Wales; 150 ft. (46 m.) high.

Pistyll Rhai·adr \ˈpis-təl-ˈrī-ə-dər, -tihl-\. Falls in **Rhaiadr River,** Wales in Clwyd co. on border with Powys co.; 230 ft. (70 m.) high.

Pi·suer·ga \pē-ˈswer-gä\. River, N Spain; rises in the Cantabrian Mts., flows SSW into Duero River 9 mi. (14 km.) below Valladolid; 171 mi. (275 km.) long.

Pit \ˈpit\. River, N California; has source in N Modoc co., NE California, and flows S and W into the Sacramento in W cen. Shasta co.; ab. 200 mi. (320 km.) long.

Pi·tan·ga \pē-ˈtäŋ-gə\. Municipality, Paraná state, S Brazil, 150 mi. (241 km.) WNW of Curitiba; pop. (1991p) 64,519.

Pit·cairn \ˈpit-ˌkarn\. Borough, Allegheny co., SW Pennsylvania, 13 mi. (21 km.) E of Pittsburgh; pop. (1990c) 4087.

Pitcairn Island. **1.** British colony, S Pacific Ocean, annexed 1839, consisting of Pitcairn I. (see PITCAIRN ISLAND 2), with the uninhabited islands of Henderson (12 sq. mi. or 31 sq. km.), Ducie (2.5 sq. mi. or 6 sq. km.), and Oeno (2 sq. mi. or 5 sq. km.), annexed 1902.

2. Island in S Pacific Ocean, 25°04′S, 130°05′W, ab. 100 mi. (160 km.) SSE of nearest island of the Tuamotus and equidistant bet. Tahiti and Easter I.; 2.5 mi. (4 km.) long; area 1.75 sq. mi. (5 sq. km.); pop. (1991c) 62; only village Adamstown. Of volcanic origin; highest point ab. 1000 ft. (305 m.); has fertile soil.

History: Discovered by British naval officer Philip Carteret 1767; uninhabited until 1790 when settled by the mutineers from the English ship *Bounty* and their Tahitian companions; their settlement discovered 1808; due to overpopulation inhabitants removed to Norfolk I. 1856; some later returned to Pitcairn and their descendants constitute present population of island.

Pitch Lake \ˈpich\. Deposit of natural asphalt in SW Trinidad, West Indies; extends over 114 acres (46 hectares).

Pi·te \ˈpē-tə\. River, N Sweden; rises in Pieska Lake near Norwegian border, flows SE into the head of the Gulf of Bothnia; 230 mi. (370 km.) long.

Pi·teå \ˈpē-tə-ˌō\. Seaport town, S Norrbotten prov., N Sweden, at mouth of the Pite River on the Gulf of Bothnia; pop. (1989c) 39,516.

Pi·teş·ti \pē-ˈtesht\. City, ⊗ of Argeş co., S cen. Romania, on Argeş River 70 mi. (113 km.) NW of Bucharest; pop. (1989c) 162,395; produces petrochemicals, footwear, food products, wine.

Pi·thom \ˈpī-thəm\. City of ancient Egypt, near Ismailia in E Goshen; probably identical with ancient Heroopolis; one of the treasure cities built for Pharaoh by the Hebrews (*Exod.* i. 11).

Pi·ti \ˈpē-tē\. Town and port of entry on Apra Harbor, W Guam, W Pacific Ocean.

Pit·kin \ˈpit-kən\. County in W cen. Colorado. See table at COLORADO.

Pit·man \ˈpit-mən\. Residential borough, Gloucester co., SW New Jersey, 15 mi. (24 km.) S of Camden; pop. (1990c) 9365.

Pi·ton \pē-ˈtōⁿ\. French word for "mountain peak," used esp. in the French West Indies and the Mascarene Is.; for names beginning with *Piton,* see the distinguishing element. **The Pi·tons** \pē-ˈtōⁿ\ of St. Lucia I. are two conical mountains (2619 ft. or 798 m. and 2461 ft. or 750 m.) forming prominent landmarks.

Pit·rea·vie \pit-ˈrē-vē\. Village on Firth of Forth, Scotland, 2.75 mi. (4.4 km.) SE of Dunfermline; site of NATO naval facilities.

Pitsanulok. See PHITSANULOK.
Pitt \ˈpit\. County in E North Carolina. See table at NORTH CAROLINA.
Pitt, Mount. See MCLOUGHLIN, MOUNT.
Pitt Island. **1.** Island off W coast of British Columbia, Canada, bet. Banks I. and the mainland S of mouth of Skeena River; 537 sq. mi. (1391 sq. km.).
2. Island, Pacific Ocean. See CHATHAM ISLANDS.
Pitt Lake. Lake, SW British Columbia, Canada; 21 sq. mi. (54 sq. km.); formed by a widening of the **Pitt River** near its junction with the Fraser River E of Vancouver.
Pitts·boro \ˈpits-ˌbər-ō\. **1.** Village, ⊗ of Calhoun co., N cen. Mississippi; pop. (1990c) 277.
2. Town, ⊗ of Chatham co., cen. North Carolina; pop. (1990c) 1436.
Pitts·burg \ˈpits-ˌbərg\. **1.** County in SE Oklahoma. See table at OKLAHOMA.
2. City, Contra Costa co., W California, near mouth of Sacramento River at its confluence with the San Joaquin; pop. (1990c) 47,564.
3. City, Crawford co., SE Kansas, 30 mi. (48 km.) S of Fort Scott; pop. (1990c) 17,775; coal mines; Pittsburg State Univ. (1903).
4. City, ⊗ of Camp co., NE Texas, 42 mi. (68 km.) NW of Marshall; pop. (1990c) 4007.
Pitts·burgh \ˈpits-ˌbərg\. City, ⊗ of Allegheny co., SW Pennsylvania, at confluence of Allegheny and Monongahela rivers where they form the Ohio; pop. (1990c) 369,879; 2d largest city in Pennsylvania; major inland river port and transportation and service center; formerly a major steel-production center; electrical equipment, glass; oil refining; Univ. of Pittsburgh (1787), Pittsburgh Theological Seminary (1794), Chatham Coll. (1869), Duquesne Univ. (1878), Carnegie Mellon Univ. (1900), Carlow Coll. (1929), Point Park Coll. (1960), La Roche Coll. (1963), Community Coll. of Allegheny County, Allegheny Campus (1965); Carnegie museums; Hartwood re-created English country estate; zoo; Phipps Conservatory; Three Rivers Stadium (1970). French built Fort Duquesne on site 1754; fort captured by British 1758 and site renamed Pitt; settlement begun 1760; incorp. as borough 1794 and as city 1816; in 19th cent. developed rapidly as steel-manufacturing center; American Federation of Labor estab. in Pittsburgh 1881; since WWII scene of notable urban renewal projects. Birthplace of songwriter Stephen Collins Foster 1826.
Pittsburg Landing. Hamlet, Hardin co., SW Tennessee, on W bank of Tennessee River; scene of battle, usu. called battle of Shiloh from the name of the nearby church, Apr. 6–7, 1862 in which Confederates under Gen. Albert Sidney Johnston made successful surprise attack on Gen. Ulysses S. Grant's Union forces who, however, with fresh reinforcements finally compelled Confederate withdrawal. See *Shiloh National Military Park* at UNITED STATES, *National Historical Parks.*
Pitts·field \ˈpits-ˌfēld\. **1.** City, ⊗ of Pike co., W Illinois, 40 mi. (64 km.) ESE of Quincy; pop. (1990c) 4231.
2. Town, Somerset co., W Maine, 20 mi. (32 km.) NNE of Waterville; pop. (1990c) 4190.
3. City, ⊗ of Berkshire co., W Massachusetts, on Housatonic River 40 mi. (64 km.) WNW of Springfield; pop. (1990c) 48,622; alt. 1015 ft. (309 m.); summer resort, ski slopes nearby, in area noted for music and drama; produces paper, chemicals, electrical equipment; Berkshire Community Coll. (1960); incorp. as town 1761, as city 1889.
4. Town, Merrimack co., S cen. New Hampshire, on Suncook River 12 mi. (19 km.) NE of Concord; pop. (1990c) 3701.
Pitts·ford \ˈpits-fərd\. Town, Rutland co., Vermont; pop. (1990c) 2919.
Pitts·ton \ˈpit-stən\. City, Luzerne co., E Pennsylvania, on Susquehanna River 8 mi. (13 km.) NE of Wilkes-Barre; pop. (1990c) 9389; settled 1762; incorp. as city 1894.
Pitt·syl·va·nia \ˌpit-səl-ˈvān-yə, -ˈvā-nē-ə\. County in S Virginia. See table at VIRGINIA.
Pit·y·u·sae \ˌpi-tē-ˈyü-sē\. Ancient name (*Eng.* Pine Islands) of W group of Balearic Is., W Mediterranean Sea, comprising the two islands Ebusus (Ibiza) and Ophiusa (Formentera).
Piu·ra \ˈpyü-rä\. **1.** River, N Peru; flows W into Pacific Ocean; ab. 150 mi. (240 km.) long.
2. City, NW Peru, on Piura River ab. 35 mi. (56 km.) SE of its port Paita; pop. (1990e) 315,800; cotton market with cotton gins and cottonseed-oil mills; two universities; oldest Spanish city in Peru, founded by Francisco Pizarro 1532.
Pi·ute \pī-ˈyüt\. County in S cen. Utah. See table at UTAH.
Piute Dam. Dam on Sevier River, cen. Piute co., S cen. Utah; 98 ft. (30 m.) high; completed 1914; forms **Piute Reservoir** used for irrigation.
Piz Bernina. See BERNINA.
Piz·zo \ˈpēt-sō\ *or in full* **Pizzo di Ca·la·bria** \dē-kä-ˈlä-brē-ä\. Seaport, Catanzaro prov., cen. Calabria, S Italy, on Tyrrhenian Sea; pop. (1981p) 9013; scene of trial and execution 1815 of French cavalry leader and former king of Naples Joachim Murat.
Pizzo Bernina. see BERNINA.
Pla·cen·tia \plə-ˈsen-chə\. **1.** City, Orange co., SW California, 20 mi. (32 km.) ENE of Long Beach; pop. (1990c) 41,259; incorp. 1926; grew rapidly in 1960s.
2. Commune, Italy. See PIACENZA 2.
3. Town, SE Newfoundland, Canada, on E shore of Placentia Bay 62 mi. (100 km.) WSW of St. John's; pop. (1991c) 1954. Founded 1662 by the French, who fortified it and held it until Treaty of Utrecht 1713.
Placentia Bay. Wide inlet of Atlantic Ocean, SE Newfoundland, Canada, W of St. John's; ab. 75 mi. (120 km.) long; Argentia and Placentia are on its E shore. Here meetings bet. U.S. President Franklin D. Roosevelt and British Prime Minister Winston Churchill on board their respective battleships *Augusta* and *Prince of Wales* Aug. 1941 culminated in signing of Atlantic Charter.
Plac·er \ˈpla-sər\. County in E California. See table at CALIFORNIA.
Plac·er Mountain \ˈpla-sər, ˈplā-\. Peak, cen. Santa Fe co., N cen. New Mexico; 8928 ft. (2721 m.).
Plac·er·ville \ˈpla-sər-ˌvil\. City, ⊗ of El Dorado co., E California, 36 mi. (58 km.) ENE of Sacramento; pop. (1990c) 8355.
Pla·ce·tas \plä-ˈsā-täs\. Town and municipality, Las Villas prov., W cen. Cuba; town pop. (1990e) 49,917; town is railroad junction point 20 mi. (32 km.) SE of Santa Clara.
Plac·id, Lake \ˈpla-səd\. **1.** Lake, N Essex co., NE New York; ab. 5 mi. (8 km.) long and 1.5 mi. (2 km.) max. width; elev. 1860 ft. (567 m.).
2. Village, New York. See LAKE PLACID.
Plad·da \ˈpla-də\. Low rocky island in Firth of Clyde, S of Arran I., off SW coast of Scotland; lighthouse.
Plain·edge \ˈplā-ˌnej\. Unincorporated settlement, Nassau co., SE New York, in cen. Long Island; pop. (1990c) 8739.
Plaines d'Abraham. See ABRAHAM, PLAINS OF.
Plain·field \ˈplān-ˌfēld\. **1.** Town, SE Windham co., NE Connecticut, on Quinebaug River; pop. (1990c) 14,363; incorp. 1699.
2. Village, Will co., NE Illinois, 8 mi. (13 km.) NW of Joliet; pop. (1990c) 4557.
3. Town, Hendricks co., cen. Indiana, 14 mi. (23 km.) W of Indianapolis; pop. (1990c) 10,433.
4. City, Union co., NE New Jersey, 11 mi. (18 km.) WSW of Elizabeth; pop. (1990c) 46,567; residential; produces electronic components, printing supplies, clothing; became township 1847; incorp. as city 1869.
Plains \ˈplānz\. **1.** City, Sumter co., SW cen. Georgia; pop. (1990c) 716; birthplace 1924 of Jimmy Carter, 39th president of the U.S.
2. Town, ⊗ of Yoakum co., NW Texas; pop. (1990c) 1422.
Plains of Abraham. See ABRAHAM, PLAINS OF.

Plain·view \ˈplān-ˌvyü\. **1.** City, Wabasha co., SE Minnesota, 18 mi. (29 km.) NE of Rochester; pop. (1990c) 2768.
2. Unincorporated settlement, Nassau co., SE New York, on Long Island E of New York City; pop. (1990c) 26,207.
3. City, ⊗ of Hale co., NW Texas, 42 mi. (68 km.) N of Lubbock; pop. (1990c) 21,700; agricultural implements; diversified agriculture; Wayland Baptist Univ. (1908).

Plain·ville \ˈplān-ˌvil\. **1.** Town, SW Hartford co., N Connecticut, W of New Britain; pop. (1990c) 17,392.
2. Town, Norfolk co., E Massachusetts, 27 mi. (43 km.) SW of Boston; pop. (1990c) 6871.

Plain·well \ˈplān-ˌwel, -wəl\. City, Allegan co., SW Michigan, 11 mi. (18 km.) N of Kalamazoo; pop. (1990c) 4057.

Plais·tow \ˈpla-ˌstō\. Town, Rockingham co., SE New Hampshire; pop. (1990c) 7316.

Plaka. See MELOS 3.

Plá·ka, Cape \ˈplä-kä\; *formerly* **Cape Sal·mo·ne** \sal-ˈmō-nē\. Cape at E end of island of Crete, Greece, S of Cape Sidero; mentioned in St. Paul's account of his 4th journey (*Acts.* xxvii. 7).

Planalto Central. See BRAZILIAN HIGHLANDS.

Planalto do Mato Grosso. See MATO GROSSO, PLANALTO DO.

Planasia. See PIANOSA 1.

Planches, Les. See LES PLANCHES.

Planka, Cape. See PLOČA, CAPE.

Plan·kin·ton \ˈplaŋ-kən-tən\. City, ⊗ of Aurora co., SE cen. South Dakota; pop. (1990c) 604.

Pla·no \ˈplā-nō\. **1.** City, Kendall co., NE Illinois, 26 mi. (42 km.) WNW of Joliet; pop. (1990c) 5104.
2. City, Collin co., NE Texas, 15 mi. (24 km.) N of Dallas; pop. (1990c) 128,713; grain farms; electronics; grew rapidly in 1970s and 1980s.

Plan·ta·tion \plan-ˈtā-shən\. City, Broward co., SE Florida; W of Fort Lauderdale; pop. (1990c) 66,692; pop. more than doubled bet. 1970 and 1980.

Plant City \ˈplant\. City, Hillsborough co., W cen. Florida Penin., 20 mi. (32 km.) E of Tampa; pop. (1990c) 22,754.

Plaque·mine \ˈplak-mən\. Town, ⊗ of Iberville parish, S Louisiana, on Mississippi River 13 mi. (21 km.) SSW of Baton Rouge; pop. (1990c) 7186; site of Plaquemine Locks, with a lift of 55 ft. (17 m.), built 1909 to connect **Bayou Plaquemine** and the Intracoastal Canal with the Mississippi River; incorp. 1838.

Plaque·mines \ˈplak-mənz\. Parish in SE Louisiana. See table at LOUISIANA.

Pla·ri·del \ˌplä-rē-ˈdel\. Municipality, Misamis Occidental prov., Mindanao, Philippines, on S shore of Mindanao Sea NW of Iligan Bay; pop. (1980c) 26,060.

Pla·sen·cia \plä-ˈsen-syä\. Commune, Cáceres prov., W Spain, 43 mi. (69 km.) NNE of the commune of Cáceres; pop. (1991c) 36,060; agricultural products; old cathedral (13th–14th cent.) and newer cathedral (begun 15th cent.); founded by Castilian King Alfonso VIII 12th cent.

Plas·sey \ˈpla-sē\ *also* **Pa·lā·shi** \pə-ˈlä-shē\. Village, West Bengal, NE India, on E bank of Bhagirathi River ab. 80 mi. (130 km.) N of Calcutta; site of decisive victory of British forces under Robert Clive over the nabob of Bengal 1757, opening way for British domination of India.

Plata *or* **Plata, La.** See LA PLATA.

Plata, Río de la \ˈrē-ō-ˌthā-lä-ˈplä-tä\ *or Eng.* **River Plate** \ˈplāt\. Estuary of Paraná and Uruguay rivers, bet. Uruguay and Argentina; ab. 170 mi. (275 km.) long; at mouth max. width is ab. 140 mi. (220 km.), at Montevideo ab. 60 mi. (97 km.), opp. Buenos Aires and above, 25 to 28 mi. (40 to 45 km.). Discovered by Spanish navigator Juan Díaz de Solís 1516; explored by Ferdinand Magellan of Portugal 1520 and by the English navigator Sebastian Cabot, commanding a Spanish expedition 1527–29; first permanent settlement in La Plata region was at Asunción 1537.

Pla·taea \plə-ˈtē-ə\ *or* **Pla·tae·ae** \-ˈtē-ˌē\. Ancient city in S Boeotia, E cen. Greece, 8 mi. (13 km.) S of Thebes and near Attica border. Allied with Athens from 519 B.C.; sent 1000 men to aid Athenians at Marathon 490 B.C.; scene 479 B.C. of the defeat of Mardonius and the Persians by Pausanias and the Greeks that assured the independence of Greece; repulsed attack by Thebes 431 B.C.; besieged by Sparta for two years 429–427 and destroyed; rebuilt but destroyed again by Thebans 373 B.C.; came under Philip II of Macedon c. 338 B.C.

Plate, River. See PLATA, RÍO DE LA.

Pla·teau \pla-ˈtō\. State of cen. Nigeria. See table at NIGERIA.

Plateau Mountain. Peak in the Catskill Mts., Greene co., SE New York; 3840 ft. (1170 m.).

Pla·to \ˈplä-tō\. Town, Magdalena dept., N Colombia, on the Magdalena River ab. 65 mi. (105 km.) SE of Cartagena.

Platte \ˈplat\. **1.** River, S Iowa and NW Missouri; rises in Union co., S Iowa, enters Missouri River in Platte co., NW Missouri, ab. 15 mi. (24 km.) NW of Kansas City, Kansas; ab. 300 mi. (485 km.) long.
2. River, cen. Nebraska; formed by confluence of North Platte and South Platte in Lincoln co., SW cen. Nebraska, flows E into Missouri River below Omaha; 310 mi. (499 km.) long (with North Platte ab. 930 mi. or 1495 km.).
3. Name of counties in three states of the U.S. See tables at MISSOURI, NEBRASKA, WYOMING.

Platte City. City, ⊗ of Platte co., NW Missouri; pop. (1990c) 2947.

Plattensee. See BALATON, LAKE.

Platte·ville \ˈplat-ˌvil\. City, Grant co., SW corner of Wisconsin, 60 mi. (97 km.) WSW of Madison; pop. (1990c) 9708; dairy products; zinc mines in vicinity; Univ. of Wisconsin–Platteville (1866).

Platts·burg \ˈplats-ˌbərg\. **1.** City, ⊗ of Clinton co., NW Missouri, 33 mi. (53 km.) N of Kansas City; pop. (1990c) 2248.
2. City, New York. See PLATTSBURGH.

Platts·burgh *also* **Platts·burg** \ˈplats-ˌbərg\. City, ⊗ of Clinton co., NE corner of New York, on W shore of Lake Champlain 20 mi. (32 km.) S of Canadian border; pop. (1990c) 21,255; summer resort; pulp and paper products; State Univ. of New York Coll. at Plattsburgh (1889), Clinton Community Coll. (1966). Settled c. 1785; incorp. as city 1902; at battle of Plattsburgh, American naval victory over British fleet nearby on Lake Champlain caused invading British land forces to retreat Sept. 1814.

Platts·mouth \ˈplat-sməth, -ˌsmau̇th\. City, ⊗ of Cass co., E Nebraska, on Missouri River 17 mi. (27 km.) S of Omaha; pop. (1990c) 6412; diversified agriculture.

Plau·en \ˈplau̇-ən\; *formerly* **Plauen im Vogt·land** \im-ˈfōk-ˌtlänt\. City, Saxony, E Germany, on Weisse Elster 29 mi. (47 km.) SW of Zwickau; pop. (1992e) 70,856; manufactures lace, textiles, machinery; 12th cent. church; 13th cent. castle. To Saxony 1466. A former ✻ of Vogtland.

Pla·ya, Point \ˈplī-ä\. Cape extending into Atlantic Ocean from E Venezuela coast, near Guyana boundary.

Pleas·ant, Lake \ˈple-zənt\. **1.** Reservoir, W cen. Arizona, on boundary of Yavapai and Maricopa cos.; formed by dam across Agua Fria River completed 1927 to impound water for irrigation and waterpower.
2. Lake, S cen. Hamilton co., NE cen. New York.

Pleasant, Mount. See EISENHOWER, MOUNT.

Pleasant Bay. **1.** Inlet of Atlantic Ocean, S coast of Washington co., SE Maine.
2. Inlet of Atlantic Ocean, SE coast of Cape Cod, SE Massachusetts.

Pleasant Grove. **1.** City, Jefferson co., cen. Alabama, 6 mi. (10 km.) W of Birmingham; pop. (1990c) 8458.
2. City, Utah co., N cen. Utah, 10 mi. (16 km.) NNW of Provo; pop. (1990c) 13,476.

Pleasant Hill. **1.** City, Contra Costa co., W California, NE of Oakland; pop. (1990c) 31,585; Diablo Valley Coll. (1949).
2. City, Polk co., Iowa; pop. (1990c) 3671.
3. Village, Sabine parish, W Louisiana, 60 mi. (97 km.) S of Shreveport; pop. (1990c) 824; scene of battle Apr. 1864 in which Confederates closing in on Union forces were routed by Union reinforcements under Gen. Andrew Jackson Smith.
4. City, Cass co., W Missouri; pop. (1990c) 3827.

Pleasant Hills. Borough, Allegheny co., SW Pennsylvania, S suburb of Pittsburgh; pop. (1990c) 8884.

Pleasant Island. See NAURU.

Pleas·an·ton \ˈplez-ᵊn-tən\. **1.** City, Alameda co., W California, 15 mi. (24 km.) E of San Francisco Bay; pop. (1990c)

50,553; pop. has increased twelvefold since 1960.
2. City, Atascosa co., S Texas, 33 mi. (53 km.) S of San Antonio; pop. (1990c) 7678.

Pleas·ant Prairie \ˈple-zənt\. Village, Kenosha co., SE Wisconsin; 3 mi. (5 km.) W of the city of Kenosha; pop. (1990c) 11,961.

Pleasant Ridge. City, Oakland co., SE Michigan; residential suburb of Detroit; pop. (1990c) 2775.

Pleas·ants \ˈplez-^{ə}nts\. County in NW West Virginia. See table at WEST VIRGINIA.

Pleasant View. City, Weber co., Utah, N of Ogden; pop. (1990c) 3603.

Pleas·ant·ville \ˈplez-^{ə}nt-ˌvil\. **1.** City, Atlantic co., SE New Jersey, 5 mi. (8 km.) WNW of Atlantic City; pop. (1990c) 16,027.
2. Residential village, Westchester co., SE New York, 30 mi. (48 km.) NNE of New York City; pop. (1990c) 6592.

Plea·sure Ridge Park \ˈple-zhər\. Unincorporated settlement, Jefferson co., N cen. Kentucky; pop. (1990c) 25,131.

Pleis·se \ˈplī-sə\. River, Saxony, Germany; flows N to the Weisse Elster at Leipzig; ab. 60 mi. (97 km.) long.

Plen·ty, Bay of \ˈplen-tē\. Large inlet of Pacific Ocean, NE coast of North I., New Zealand.

Plenty Coups Peak \ˈplent-ē-ˈküs\. Mountain, W Park co., NW Wyoming, on boundary of Yellowstone National Park; 10,937 ft. (3334 m.).

Plen·ty·wood \ˈplen-tē-ˌwu̇d\. City, ⊗ of Sheridan co., NE corner of Montana; pop. (1990c) 2136.

Plesh·che·ye·vo \plesh-ˈchā-ə-və\; *formerly* **Pe·re·slavl'** \ˌper-ə-ˈslȧ-vəl^{y}\. Small lake, S Yaroslavl' Oblast, cen. Russia in Europe; on it the first vessels of the Russian Navy were built late 17th cent. by Peter the Great.

Pless. See PSZCZYNA.

Ples·sis·ville \ˈple-sē-ˌvil\. Town, S Quebec, Canada, 24 mi. (39 km.) WNW of Thetford Mines; pop. (1991c) 7042.

Plét·i·pi, Lac \ˌlȧk-ˌplā-tē-ˈpē\. Lake, S cen. Quebec, Canada; 138 sq. mi. (357 sq. km.); outlets S through Outardes River.

Plet·ten·berg \ˈplet-^{ə}n-ˌberk\. City, North Rhine-Westphalia, Germany, 45 mi. (72 km.) NE of Cologne; pop. (1980c) 29,046.

Ple·ven \ˈple-ven\ *or* **Plev·na** \ˈplev-nä\. City, N Bulgaria, 85 mi. (137 km.) NE of Sofia; pop. (1991e) 138,323; market center in agricultural region; produces textiles, cement, tobacco products; food processing; in 1877 taken from the Turks by the Russians after a 143-day siege.

Pley·ben \plā-ˈbe^{n}\. Town, Finistère dept., NW France, ab. 16 mi. (26 km.) N of Quimper; 16th cent. church with interesting wood carvings.

Plo·ča, Cape \ˈplō-chä\; *formerly* **Cape Plan·ka** \ˈpläŋ-kä\. Cape, Croatia, on the coast W of Split at 43°30′N, 15°58′E.

Płock \ˈpwȯtsk\ *or Ger.* **Plozk** \ˈplȯtsk\. **1.** Province, NE cen. Poland. See table at POLAND.
2. Commune, its ✻, on Vistula River 55 mi. (89 km.) WNW of Warsaw; pop. (1989e) 121,996; market town; 12th cent. cathedral (containing tombs of Polish kings). Under Prussia 1793–1806; included in Grand Duchy of Warsaw under French Emperor Napoléon 1807; under Russia 1815–1918.

Plöck·en \ˈplœ-kən\ *or Ital.* **Mon·te Cro·ce** \ˈmȯn-tā-ˈkrō-chā\. Pass over the Carnic Alps bet. S Carinthia, Austria, and Friuli-Venezia Giulia, Italy; alt. 4298 ft. (1310 m.); connects upper valley of the Drava with N Italy.

Ploen. See PLÖN.

Plo·ër·mel \ˌplō-er-ˈmel\. Town, Morbihan dept., NW France, ab. 25 mi. (40 km.) NNE of Vannes; 16th cent. church of St. Armel, named for the hermit who lived in the district in 6th cent. and after whom the town is named.

Plo·ieş·ti *or* **Plo·eş·ti** \plȯ-ˈyesht\. City, ⊗ of Prahova co., SE cen. Romania, 35 mi. (56 km.) N of Bucharest; pop. (1989c) 247,502; center of important oil fields; furniture, textiles, leather goods; oil refineries, petrochemical plants; heavily bombed by Allies in WWII.

Plomb du Can·tal \ˌplō^{n}-dūe-kä^{n}-ˈtȧl\. Peak in the Auvergne Mts., cen. France; 6094 ft. (1858 m.).

Plön *or* **Ploen** \ˈplœn\. Commune, E Schleswig-Holstein, Germany, SE of Kiel on Grosser Plöner See (lake).

Plott Bal·sam Mountain \ˌplät-ˈbȯl-səm\. Peak, Haywood co., W North Carolina; 6200 ft. (1890 m.).

Plou·gas·tel–Da·ou·las \ˌplü-gäs-ˈtel-dä-ü-ˈläs\. Commune, W Finistère dept., NW France, on a bay which separates it from Brest to the W.

Plov·div \ˈplȯv-ˌdif, -ˌdiv\. **1.** Region of cen. Bulgaria. See table at BULGARIA.
2. *or Gk.* **Phil·ip·pop·o·lis** \ˌfē-lē-ˈpō-pō-ˌlēs\; *anc.* **Eu·mol·pi·as** \yu̇-ˈmäl-pē-əs\. City, its ✻, on the Maritsa N of the Rhodope Mts.; pop. (1991e) 379,083; railroad junction; market town in region producing rice, fruit, and tobacco; produces textiles, metal products; food processing; ruins of 13th cent. fortress. Fell to Macedonians under Philip II 341 B.C.; annexed to Rome 46 A.D. and made ✻ of Thrace under name of Trimontium; frequently sacked, often changing hands, during the Middle Ages; taken by Turks 1364; to Bulgaria 1885.

Plozk. See PŁOCK.

Plum \ˈpləm\. Borough, Allegheny co., SW Pennsylvania, E suburb of Pittsburgh; pop. (1990c) 25,609.

Plu·ma·jes Point \plü-ˈmä-hās\. Cape, W coast of Cuba, S of Guadiana Bay.

Plu·mas \ˈplü-məs\. County in NE California. See table at CALIFORNIA.

Plum Island. **1.** Island in Atlantic Ocean off NE coast of Essex co., NE Massachusetts, just S of mouth of the Merrimack River; 8.5 mi. (14 km.) long.
2. Island, E end of Long Island Sound, off NE extremity of Long Island, New York; 3 mi. (5 km.) long.

Plym·outh \ˈpli-məth\. **1.** Name of counties in two states of the U.S. See tables at IOWA and MASSACHUSETTS.
2. Town, Litchfield co., NW Connecticut, N of Waterbury; pop. (1990c) 11,822; settled 1728; incorp. 1795.
3. City, ⊗ of Marshall co., N Indiana, 23 mi. (37 km.) S of South Bend; pop. (1990c) 8303; dairy products, fertilizer.
4. Town, ⊗ of Plymouth co., SE Massachusetts, on Plymouth Bay 18 mi. (29 km.) SE of Brockton; pop. (1990c) 45,608; cordage works, boatyards, fisheries; cranberries; tourist attractions include Plymouth Rock, re-created Plimoth Plantation, re-created Mayflower II, Pilgrim Hall Museum, a wax museum, and a cranberry farm open to visitors; site of first permanent European settlement in New England, the **Colony of New Plymouth,** founded by the Pilgrims 1620; governed under Mayflower Compact until 1691 when it became part of Massachusetts Bay Colony.
5. City, Wayne co., SE Michigan, ab. 11 mi. (18 km.) W of Detroit; pop. (1990c) 9560.
6. City, Hennepin co., SE Minnesota, NW suburb of Minneapolis; pop. (1990c) 50,889; pop. has quintupled since 1960.
7. Town, Grafton co., W New Hampshire, on Pemigewasset River 20 mi. (32 km.) NW of Laconia; pop. (1990c) 5811; summer resort; Plymouth State Coll. (1871).
8. Town, ⊗ of Washington co., E North Carolina, 10 mi. (16 km.) S of W end of Albemarle Sound; pop. (1990c) 4328.
9. Borough, Luzerne co., E Pennsylvania, on Susquehanna River 4 mi. (6 km.) W of Wilkes-Barre; pop. (1990c) 7134.
10. Town, Windsor co., E Vermont, ab. 14 mi. (23 km.) SE of Rutland; pop. (1990c) 440; birthplace (1872) and grave of Calvin Coolidge, 30th president of the U.S.
11. City, Sheboygan co., E Wisconsin, 13 mi. (21 km.) W of the city of Sheboygan; pop. (1990c) 6769.
12. City, Devon, SW England, on Plymouth Sound bet. Plym and Tamar estuaries 190 mi. (306 km.) WSW of London; pop. (1991p) 238,800; manufactures machine tools, precision instruments, chemicals; Devonport naval dockyard, a major facility of the British Navy. Chartered 1439; port from which English fleet sailed against the Spanish Armada 1588; last port touched by *Mayflower* before voyage to America 1620;

\ə\ abut \ə\ matches \$^{ə}$\ kitten, Fr table \ər\ further \a\ ash \ā\ ace
\ä\ cot, cart \ȧ\ Fr bac \au̇\ out \b\ Span Avila \ch\ chin \e\ bet \ē\ easy
\g\ go \i\ hit \ī\ ice \j\ job \k\ Ger ich, Buch \$^{n}$\ Fr vin
\ŋ\ sing \ō\ go \ȯ\ all \ȯ\ law \œ\ Fr bœuf \œ̄\ Fr feu \ȯi\ boy
\th\ thin \t͟h\ this \ü\ loot \u̇\ foot \ue\ Ger füllen \ūe\ Fr rue
\y\ yet \$^{y}$\ Fr digne \ˈdēn^{y}\, nuit \ˈnw^{y}ē\ \yü\ few \yu̇\ fury \zh\ vision

dockyard estab. 1690; heavily damaged by German air raids in WWII but now rebuilt.

13. Seaport, ✻ of Montserrat, Leeward Is., West Indies, on SW coast; pop. (1980p) 1623; destroyed during volcanic eruption 1997.

Plymouth Bay. Inlet of Atlantic Ocean on E coast of Plymouth co., SE Massachusetts.

Plymouth Colony. See PLYMOUTH 4.

Plymouth Sound. Inlet of the English Channel, SW coast of England, on the boundary bet. Devon and Cornwall; site of the city of Plymouth.

Pl·zeň \ˈpəl-zen\ *or Ger.* **Pil·sen** \ˈpil-zən\. City, W Czech Republic, 52 mi. (84 km.) WSW of Prague; pop. (1991p) 173,129; produces railway rolling stock, munitions, heavy industrial machinery; paper, pottery; breweries; university (1991); Gothic church and 16th cent. town hall. First mentioned 10th cent.; chartered c. 1290; developed as industrial center from mid-19th cent.

Pnompenh. See PHNOM PENH.

Po \ˈpȯ, ˈpō\; *anc.* **Pa·dus** \ˈpā-dəs\ *also, in mythology,* **Erid·a·nus** \i-ˈrid-ᵊn-əs\. River, N Italy; rises on the slopes of Mt. Viso, flows NE to Turin and then E across Piedmont and Lombardy into the Adriatic Sea through several mouths; 405 mi. (652 km.) long; navigable to beyond Turin. Its chief tributaries in the W are the Dora Baltea, Dora Riparia, and Tanaro; others, from the N, serving as outlets of the Alpine lakes, are the Ticino, Adda, Oglio, and Mincio. Important industrial cities in its valley (Milan, Turin, Padua, Verona, Brescia).

Po·ás \ˈpwäs\. Volcano, Costa Rica, ab. 19 mi. (31 km.) NW of the city of San José; 8872 ft. (2704 m.).

Po·be·da Peak \pȧ-ˈbye-də\ *or Russ.* **Pik Po·be·dy** \ˈpēk-pȧ-ˈbye-dē\. Mountain, Kyrgyzstan, on border with Xinjiang Uygur, China; 24,406 ft. (7439 m.); highest in Tian Shan Range.

Po·ca·hon·tas \ˌpō-kə-ˈhän-təs\. **1.** Name of counties in two states of the U.S. See tables at IOWA and WEST VIRGINIA.

2. City, ⊗ of Randolph co., NE Arkansas, on Black River 33 mi. (53 km.) NNW of Jonesboro; pop. (1990c) 6151.

3. City, ⊗ of Pocahontas co., NW cen. Iowa, 30 mi. (48 km.) NW of Fort Dodge; pop. (1990c) 2085.

Po·ca·tel·lo \ˌpō-kə-ˈte-lō, -lə\. City, ⊗ of Bannock co., SE Idaho, at the junction of two interstates, 60 mi. (97 km.) N of Utah border and 70 mi. (113 km.) W of Wyoming border; pop. (1990c) 46,080; produces dairy products; railroad shops; Idaho State Univ. (1901); settled 1882; incorp. as city 1893.

Pochow. See BO XIAN.

Po·chu·tla \ˌpō-ˈchüt-lä\. Municipality, Oaxaca state, Mexico, 95 mi. (153 km.) S of the city of Oaxaca.

Pock·ling·ton Reef \ˈpä-kliŋ-tən\. Reef in S Solomon Sea, off SW Solomon Is., W Pacific Ocean.

Po·co·la \pə-ˈkō-lə\. Town, Le Flore co., E Oklahoma, near Arkansas border; pop. (1990c) 3664.

Po·co·moke \ˈpō-kə-ˌmōk\. River, SE Maryland; rises in S Delaware, flows S across Maryland border and into Pocomoke Sound in SE Somerset co.; ab. 55 mi. (90 km.) long.

Pocomoke City. City, Worcester co., SE Maryland, 22 mi. (35 km.) S of Salisbury; pop. (1990c) 3922.

Pocomoke Sound. Inlet of Chesapeake Bay, S coast of Somerset co., Maryland, and NW coast of Accomac co., Virginia, receiving Pocomoke River on NE.

Po·co·no Mountains \ˈpō-kə-ˌnō\. Ridge, E Pennsylvania, chiefly in Pike, Monroe, and Carbon cos.; extends parallel with and ab. 15 mi. (24 km.) NW of Kittatinny Mt.; ab. 1600 ft. (490 m.) high.

Po·ços de Cal·das \ˈpȯ-ˌsüs-dē-ˈkäl-des\. Health and tourist resort, Minas Gerais state, E Brazil; munic. pop. (1991p) 110,152; alt. ab. 4000 ft. (1220 m.); sulfur baths.

Po·co·to·paug Lake \ˈpō-kə-tə-ˌpȯg\. Lake, NE Middlesex co., S Connecticut; outlet is stream flowing S into Salmon River.

Pod·go·ri·ca *also* **Pod·go·ri·tsa** \ˈpȯd-ˌgȯr-ēt-sä\; *1946–92* **Ti·to·grad** \ˈtē-tȯ-ˌgräd\. City, ✻ of Montenegro, S Yugoslavia; pop. (1991p) 152,242; aluminum; under Turks mid-15th cent. to late 19th cent. when returned to Montenegro.

Po di Pri·ma·ro \ˈpȯ-dē-prē-ˈmä-rō\. Name applied to the lower course of the Reno River, Italy.

Podium Anicensis. See LE PUY.

Podkamennaya Tunguska. See TUNGUSKA.

Podkarpatská Rus. See ZAKARPATS'KA.

Po·do·lia \pə-ˈdō-lē-ə, -ˈdōl-yə\ *or Russ.* **Po·dol'sk** \pə-ˈdȯlʸsk\. Former region bet. Southern Bug and Dniester rivers, SE Europe; now in W Ukraine, nearly coextensive with Khmel'nyts'kyy subdivision; seized from the Tatars by grand duke of Lithuania c. 1360; W part incorp. in medieval kingdom of Poland 1431; held by Turks 1672–99; small area in W to Austria 1772 and remainder to Russia 1793.

Po·dol'sk \pə-ˈdȯlʸsk\. **1.** Former region, S Europe. See PODOLIA.

2. *or* **Po·dolsk** \-ˈdȯlsk\. Town, Moscow Oblast, W cen. Russia in Europe, on railroad line 25 mi. (40 km.) S of the city of Moscow; pop. (1992e) 208,000; manufactures sewing machines, cables, cement; chartered 1781.

Po·dor \ˈpō-ˌdȯr\. Town, N Senegal, across Senegal River from Mauritania.

Poelau. See PULAU.

Poel·ka·pel·le *or* **Poel·ca·pel·le** \ˌpül-kə-ˈpe-lə\. Small commune, West Flanders prov., NW Belgium, NNE of Ieper (Ypres); many cemeteries and memorials from WWI in area.

Poerwakarta. See PURWAKARTA.

Poerwodadi. See PURWODADI.

Poerwokerto. See PURWOKERTO.

Poeting. See PUTING, TANJUNG.

Poge, Cape \ˈpōj\. NE point of Chappaquiddick I., Massachusetts, E of Martha's Vineyard.

Pog·gi·bon·si \ˌpōj-jē-ˈbōn-sē\. Commune, Siena prov., Tuscany, cen. Italy, 16 mi. (26 km.) NW of the commune of Siena; pop. (1991c) 26,318; 13th cent. church and convent.

Pog·ra·dec \ˌpȯ-grä-ˈdets\. **1.** District of E Albania. See table at ALBANIA.

2. Town, its ✻, ab. 55 mi. (90 km.) SE of Tiranë.

Po Hai. See BO HAI.

P'o·hang \ˈpō-ˈhäŋ\. Town, North Kyŏngsang prov., South Korea, ab. 66 mi. (106 km.) NNE of Pusan; pop. (1985c) 260,691; steel.

Poh·jois–Kar·ja·la \ˈpȯ-yȯis-ˈkär-yä-lä\. Province of E Finland. See table at FINLAND.

Pohn·pei \ˈpōn-ˌpā\; *mostly formerly* **Po·na·pe** \ˈpō-nä-ˌpā\. Island of the Senyavin I. group in the Federated States of Micronesia, 410 mi. (660 km.) E of Chuuk; 6°58′N, 158°31′E; area 129 sq. mi. (334 sq. km.); with eight nearby coral atolls constitutes a state, 133 sq. mi. (344 sq. km.); pop. (1980c) 22,081; ✻ Kolonia. The island is one of the largest in the cen. Pacific, very fertile and hilly; surrounded by a barrier reef enclosing many small islands. Settled all around the coast, but practically uninhabited in the interior. Notable for its many ruins of an earlier population; houses seat of government for Federated States of Micronesia.

Pohsien. See BO XIAN.

Poictiers. See POITIERS.

Poin·sett \ˈpȯin-ˌset, -sit\. County in NE Arkansas. See table at ARKANSAS.

Poinsett, Lake. Lake, S Hamlin co. extending into NW Brookings co., E South Dakota.

Point Barrow. See BARROW, POINT.

Point Buenos Aires. See BUENOS AIRES, POINT.

Point de Galle. See GALLE.

Pointe a la Hache \ˈpȯint-ˌa-lə-ˈhash\. Village, ⊗ of Plaquemines parish, SE Louisiana.

Pointe-à-Pi·tre \ˌpweⁿt-ə-ˈpētrᵊ\. Seaport, SW Grande-Terre I., E Guadeloupe, West Indies; largest town in Guadeloupe; pop. (1990c) 26,083; founded mid-17th cent.

Pointe Aux Barques. See AUX BARQUES, POINTE.

Pointe Claire \ˌpȯint-ˈklar\. City, Montreal I., S Quebec, Canada, on St. Lawrence River 15 mi. (24 km.) WSW of the city of Montreal; pop. (1991c) 27,647.

Pointe Cou·pee \ˈpoint-kü-ˈpē\. Parish in SE cen. Louisiana. See table at LOUISIANA.

Point Edward \ˈed-wərd\. Village, Lambton co., SE Ontario, Canada, on Lake Huron 3 mi. (5 km.) N of Sarnia-Clearwater; pop. (1991c) 2336.

Pointe–Noire \ˌpwe^{n}t-ˈnwär\. City and port, SW Rep. of the Congo, on the Atlantic Ocean 230 mi. (370 km.) SW of Brazzaville; met. area pop. (1992e) 576,206; commercial center; oil industry; port facilities constructed 1934–39; was ✻ of Middle Congo 1950–58.

Point For·tin \ˈfȯr-tin\. Borough, SW Trinidad, Trinidad and Tobago, West Indies; pop. (1990c) 20,025.

Point Hueneme. See PORT HUENEME.

Point Judith. See NARRAGANSETT.

Point Mountain. Peak in Glacier National Park, NW Montana; 8300 ft. (2530 m.).

Point Pe·lee National Park \ˈpē-lē\. See CANADA, *National Parks.*

Point Pleas·ant \ˈplez-ᵊnt\. **1.** Borough and seaside resort, Ocean co., E New Jersey, on Atlantic Ocean 10 mi. (16 km.) S of Asbury Park; pop. (1990c) 18,177.

2. Village, S Clermont co., SW Ohio, on the Ohio River; birthplace (1822) of Ulysses S. Grant, 18th president of the U.S.

3. City, ⊗ of Mason co., W West Virginia, on Ohio River 35 mi. (56 km.) NNE of Huntington; pop. (1990c) 4996; iron foundries; incorp. 1833.

Point Pleasant Beach. Borough and seaside resort, Ocean co., E New Jersey, near Point Pleasant; pop. (1990c) 5112.

Point Pudjut. See PUJUT, TANJUNG.

Point Rob·erts \ˈrä-bərts\. **1.** The tip of a peninsula, NW Washington, extending S into Strait of Georgia from British Columbia, Canada; separated from mainland of Whatcom co. by Boundary Bay.

2. Village on point.

Point San Blas. See EL PORVENIR.

Point Suc·cess \sək-ˈses\. Mountain in Mt. Rainier National Park, W cen. Washington; ab. 14,150 ft. (4315 m.).

Pois·sy \pwȧ-ˈsē\; *anc.* **Pin·ci·a·cum** \pin-ˈsī-ə-kəm\. Commune, Yvelines dept., N France, on Seine River 11 mi. (18 km.) WNW of Paris; pop. (1990c) 36,864; 12th cent. church. Scene of unsuccessful conference bet. Catholic and Protestant leaders 1561; birthplace of Louis IX, known as St. Louis, 1214.

Poi·tiers \pwä-ˈtyā\; *formerly* **Poic·tiers** \pwä-ˈtyā\; *anc.* **Li·mo·num** \lə-ˈmō-nəm\. City, ✻ of Vienne dept., W cen. France, 100 mi. (161 km.) ESE of Nantes; pop. (1990c) 82,507; railroad junction; market town; wine, chemicals, rubber products; cathedral (begun 12th cent.); palace of former counts of Poitiers; several notable Romanesque churches; university (1431).

Poi·tou \pwä-ˈtü\. Historical region of W cen. France; bounded on NW by Brittany, on N by Anjou, on NE by Touraine, on E by Marche, on SE by Limousin, on S by Angoumois, Saintonge, and Aunis, and on W by Atlantic Ocean; ✻ Poitiers; watered by Sèvre Nantaise and Sèvre Niortaise rivers.

History: Inhabited by ancient Pictones; conquered by Romans and made part of Aquitania; conquered by Visigoths 5th cent. A.D.; Visigoths under Alaric II defeated near Poitiers by Franks under Clovis 507; Arabs defeated by Frankish ruler Charles Martel 732 on a site bet. Poitiers and Tours; came under counts of Poitiers 9th cent.; important center of Romanesque art 11th–12th cent.; as part of Aquitaine came under English crown on marriage of Eleanor of Aquitaine to Henry II of England 1152; confiscated by Philip Augustus of France 1204; occupied 1356–72 by English after major defeat of French King John the Good by Edward, the Black Prince, 1356 at Maupertuis, near Poitiers; afterwards appanage of Jean de France, duc de Berry, until reunited with French crown 1417; province of France until Revolution, when territory was divided into three departments, Vendée, Deux-Sèvres, and Vienne.

Poitou–Cha·rentes \-shȧ-ˈrä^{n}t\. Region of W France. See table at FRANCE.

Pojezierze Mazurskie. See MASURIA.

Po·kha·ra \ˈpō-kə-rə\. City, cen. Nepal; pop. (1991c) 95,286; airport.

Pok Liu Chau. See LAMMA.

Po–ko–to Shan. See BOGDA SHAN.

Pokrovsk. See ENGEL'S.

Pola. See PULA.

Po·land \ˈpō-lənd\. **1.** *or Pol.* **Pols·ka** \ˈpȯl-skä\; *officially* **Republic of Poland** *or Pol.* **Rze·czy·pos·po·li·ta Polska** \ˌzhech-pȯ-ˈspȯ-lē-tä-ˈpȯl-skä\. Republic, cen. Europe, bounded on N by the Baltic Sea and Kaliningrad Oblast of Russia, on NE by Lithuania, on E by Belarus and Ukraine, on S by Slovakia and the Czech Republic, and on W by Germany; 120,756 sq. mi. (312,758 sq. km.); pop. (1989e) 38,038,400; ✻ Warsaw.

Physical features: N and cen. regions are essentially flat and characterized by morainic topography; area along S boundary is mountainous, with highest peak Rysy, 8197 ft. (2499 m.).

Chief products: Wheat, potatoes, rye, sugar beets; livestock; coal, sulfur, copper, zinc, lead; manufacturing: chemicals, iron and steel, machinery, motor vehicles, textiles; shipbuilding, food processing.

Chief cities: Warsaw, Łódź, Kraków, Wrocław, Poznań, Gdańsk, Szczecin, Katowice.

Political divisions: Divided into the following 49 provinces (for pronunciation of their names, see their individual entries):

NAME	AREA (sq. mi.)	AREA (sq. km.)	POP. (1989c)	CAPITAL
Biała Podlaska	2,065	5,348	304,500	Biała Podlaska
Białystok	3,882	10,055	690,300	Białystok
Bielsko-Biała	1,430	3,704	895,300	Bielsko-Biała
Bydgoszcz	3,996	10,349	1,106,600	Bydgoszcz
Chełm	1,493	3,866	246,200	Chełm
Ciechanów	2,456	6,362	427,000	Ciechanów
Częstochowa	2,387	6,182	776,100	Częstochowa
Elbląg	2,356	6,103	476,600	Elbląg
Gdańsk	2,855	7,394	1,423,300	Gdańsk
Gorzów	3,276	8,484	498,300	Gorzów Wielkopolski
Jelenia Góra	1,690	4,378	517,000	Jelenia Góra
Kalisz	2,514	6,512	708,300	Kalisz
Katowice	2,568	6,650	3,968,300	Katowice
Kielce	3,556	9,211	1,126,000	Kielce
Konin	1,984	5,139	467,600	Konin
Koszalin	3,270	8,470	504,200	Koszalin
Kraków	1,256	3,254	1,227,800	Kraków
Krosno	2,202	5,702	491,800	Krosno
Legnica	1,559	4,037	512,000	Legnica
Leszno	1,604	4,154	384,500	Leszno
Łódź	588	1,523	1,142,700	Łódź
Łomża	2,581	6,684	345,600	Łomża
Lublin	2,622	6,792	1,013,400	Lublin
Nowy Sącz	2,153	5,576	692,200	Nowy Sącz
Olsztyn	4,756	12,327	748,500	Olsztyn
Opole	3,295	8,535	1,014,900	Opole
Ostrołęka	2,509	6,498	395,000	Ostrołęka
Piła	3,168	8,205	478,000	Piła
Piotrków	2,419	6,266	642,000	Piotrków Trybunalski
Płock	1,976	5,117	515,400	Płock
Poznań	3,147	8,151	1,327,900	Poznań
Przemyśl	1,713	4,437	405,100	Przemyśl
Radom	2,816	7,294	748,300	Radom
Rzeszów	1,698	4,397	717,400	Rzeszów
Siedlce	3,281	8,499	649,300	Siedlce
Sieradz	1,880	4,869	408,000	Sieradz
Skierniewice	1,529	3,960	418,200	Skierniewice
Słupsk	2,878	7,453	410,400	Słupsk
Suwałki	4,050	10,490	466,300	Suwałki
Szczecin	3,854	9,981	967,300	Szczecin
Tarnobrzeg	2,426	6,283	596,400	Tarnobrzeg
Tarnów	1,603	4,151	666,000	Tarnów
Toruń	2,065	5,348	655,700	Toruń
Wałbrzych	1,609	4,168	741,200	Wałbrzych
Warszawa	1,462	3,788	2,419,100	Warsaw
Włocławek	1,700	4,402	428,900	Włocławek
Wrocław	2,427	6,287	1,126,300	Wrocław
Zamość	2,695	6,980	489,800	Zamość
Zielona Góra	3,424	8,868	657,400	Zielona Góra

History: Slavic tribes in region around Poznań united under Piast dynasty 10th cent.; history of Polish state dates from 966, when Piast ruler Mieszko I adopted Christianity; kingdom of Poland estab. 1025; kingdom divided 1138 after death of Bolesław III; invaded by Mongols 1241; reunification begun 14th cent.; marriage of Piast Princess Jadwiga to grand duke of Lithuania 1386 established Jagellon dynasty ruling Poland and Lithuania; after long struggle with Teutonic Knights, obtained West Prussia and East Prussia (*q.v.*) 1466; 15th and 16th cents. considered Poland's golden age; after 1572, Polish crown became elective, and the nobility stronger than the monarch; in 17th cent. wars with Sweden and Russia led to loss of much territory. New wars and political weakness led to three partitions: 1772, 1793, and 1795, in which Poland was completely dismembered and divided among Russia, Prussia, and Austria. Grand Duchy of Warsaw established by the French Emperor Napoléon 1807 from lands formerly partitioned to Prussia and Austria; following the Congress of Vienna 1815, Poland again divided among Prussia, Austria, and Russia; organized as autonomous kingdom (frequently called **Congress Poland**) in personal union with Russia; lost autonomy after Polish Revolt 1830–31; after unsuccessful rising of Jan. 1863, became merely a Russian province and intensive policy of Russification put into effect; occupied by Germans and Austrians in WWI; proclaimed independent republic 1918. West Prussia, except Danzig (see GDAŃSK 2), ceded by Germany 1919 (see also POLISH CORRIDOR); Soviet-Polish boundaries determined 1921; governed by 1921 constitution, amended after Józef Piłsudski's coup d'état 1926; 1935 constitution formally ended democratic parliamentary rule; invasion by Germany and U.S.S.R. 1939 precipitated WWII; as result of treaty bet. Germany and U.S.S.R., W part annexed to Germany, cen. sector constituted into German-controlled Government Gen-

eral of Poland, and E part incorp. in U.S.S.R. After German invasion of U.S.S.R. 1941, all of Poland under Nazis who undertook to purge Polish culture and large Jewish population; reoccupied by Soviet armies in 1944 and 1945. After WWII part E of Curzon Line (*q.v.*) taken by U.S.S.R. and added to Belorussian and Ukrainian S.S.R.'s; received Danzig, S two thirds of East Prussia, and regions of Germany E of the Oder and Neisse rivers; establishment of Soviet-dominated government following controlled elections 1947; adopted new constitution 1952; became a member of the Warsaw Treaty Organization 1955; participated with U.S.S.R. in invasion of Czechoslovakia 1968; its W boundary recognized as permanent by West Germany 1970. Workers' strikes incited by shipyard worker Lech Wałesa 1980 followed by imposition of martial law Dec. 1981–July 1983; negotiations with labor leaders reopened 1989, resulting in major political reforms and victory of labor party in free elections; Germany reaffirmed W boundary 1991.

2. Village, Mahoning co., NE Ohio, 7 mi. (11 km.) SW of Youngstown; pop. (1990c) 2992.

Polangen. See PALANGA.

Po·lan·gui \pȯ-'läŋ-gē\. Municipality, Albay prov., Luzon, Philippines, on railroad line ab. 19 mi. (31 km.) NW of Legazpi; pop. (1990c) 61,556.

Po·lar Plateau \'pō-lər\. High region covered by ice cap surrounding the South Pole; av. height 6000 ft. (1830 m.).

Polar Regions. Regions around the North Pole (**North Polar Regions**) and the South Pole (**South Polar Regions**); North Pole first reached by American explorer Robert E. Peary 1909; first flown over by American aviator Richard Byrd 1926; first reached by submarine (the U.S. submarine *Nautilus*) 1958; Soviet nuclear icebreaker *Arktika* first surface ship to arrive 1978. South Pole first reached by Norwegian explorer Roald Amundsen 1911; Byrd first to fly over 1929; both regions extensively explored before and after WWII; conditions of extreme cold and fields of ice are of much wider extent around the South Pole. See ARCTIC, THE; ANTARCTIC REGIONS; MAGNETIC POLE; SOUTH POLE; NORTH POLE.

Po·latsk \'pȯ-lətsk\; *mostly formerly* **Po·lotsk** \'pȯ-lətsk\. City, Vitsyebsk administrative subdivision, Belarus, on right bank of the Western Dvina River 60 mi. (97 km.) NW of the city of Vitsyebsk; pop. (1991e) 78,700; market town; lumber; oil refinery; ✻ of former Polotsk Oblast.

History: First mentioned 862; as a ✻ of the principality of Polotsk a major trade center; in 14th cent. came under Lithuania; became free city 1498; held by Russians 1563–79 and permanently acquired by Russians 1772; occupied by Germany 1941–43.

Pole Mountain \'pōl\. Peak, Hinsdale co., SW Colorado; 13,737 ft. (4187 m.).

Po·le·sie \pȯ-'le-sye\. Former department of Poland; ab. 14,160 sq. mi. (36,675 sq. km.); ✻ Brest Litovsk; now divided bet. Belarus and Ukraine.

Po·le·si·ne \pə-'lā-zē-nā\. Region, NE Italy, the lowland bet. lower Po and lower Adige rivers, ab. equivalent to Rovigo prov., S Veneto.

Po·les·ye *or* **Po·les'·ye** \pȯ-'lye-sye\ *or* **Pri·pet Marshes** \'pri-ˌpet, -pət\ *or* **Pri·pyat Marshes** \'pri-pyət\ *also* **Pinsk Marshes** \'pinsk\. Extensive marshlands, S Belarus and NW Ukraine, chiefly on both sides of the Pripyat' River (*q.v.*); ab. 300 mi. (485 km.) E and W and 140 mi. (225 km.) N and S; largest tract of swamp in Europe; formerly in E Poland. Densely wooded and largely uninhabited; draining projects since 1870s have reclaimed some sections for agriculture. Formerly marked a natural boundary bet. Poland and U.S.S.R. and for centuries have greatly affected the strategy of military invasions or mass movements of peoples.

Po·lev·skoi *or* **Po·lev·skoy** \pə-ləf-'skȯi\. Town, Sverdlovsk Oblast, W Russia in Asia, ab. 30 mi. (48 km.) SW of Yekaterinburg; pop. (1991e) 71,900.

Pol·gár \'pȯl-gär\ *or* **Ti·sza·pol·gár** \'tē-sö-ˌpȯl-gär\. Commune, Hajdú-Bihar co., E Hungary, 35 mi. (56 km.) NW of Debrecen, E of Tisza River; pop. (1980p) 9429.

Po·li·ca·stro, Gulf of \ˌpō-lē-'käs-trō\. Inlet of Tyrrhenian Sea, SW coast of Italy, S of the Gulf of Salerno.

Po·li·ce \pȯ-'lēt-se\. Commune, Szczecin prov., NW Poland; pop. (1989e) 33,597.

Po·li·gna·no a Ma·re \ˌpȯ-lē-'nyä-nō-ä-'mä-rā\. Commune, Bari prov., Puglia, SE Italy, on the Adriatic 21 mi. (34 km.) ESE of the seaport of Bari; pop. (1981p) 14,634.

Po·lil·lo \pȯ-'lē-yō\. **1.** Group of islands in Pacific Ocean off E coast of Luzon, Philippines, on N side of Lamon Bay; total area ab. 297 sq. mi. (769 sq. km.); comprises Polillo, Jomalig, Patnanongan, Palasan, and ab. 17 islets; part of Quezon prov.

2. Largest island of the Polillo group, 14°50′N, 121°50′E; 234 sq. mi. (606 sq. km.); separated from Luzon mainland by **Polillo Strait** (36 mi. or 58 km. long, 12 to 18 mi. or 19 to 29 km. wide).

Po·lish Corridor \'pōl-ish\. A strip of land in N part of Poland, in former West Prussia extending to Gdańsk and the Baltic Sea; ab. 90 mi. (145 km.) long; 25 to 55 mi. (40 to 89 km.) wide. By Treaty of Versailles 1919 taken from Germany and assigned to Poland but with the provisions of the establishment of the Free City of Danzig (see GDAŃSK 2) and of the development of Gdynia as Polish port. After WWI caused much friction bet. Germany and Poland and in 1939 was an immediate cause of WWII; occupied by Germany 1939 but after 1945 returned with Danzig to Poland.

Polish Silesia. See SILESIA.

Polk \'pōk\. **1.** Name of counties in 12 states of the U.S. See tables at ARKANSAS, FLORIDA, GEORGIA, IOWA, MINNESOTA, MISSOURI, NEBRASKA, NORTH CAROLINA, OREGON, TENNESSEE, TEXAS, WISCONSIN.

2. Residential borough and resort, Venango co., NW Pennsylvania, 13 mi. (21 km.) WSW of Oil City; pop. (1990c) 1267.

Pol·la·chi \pō-'lä-chē\. Town, W Tamil Nadu, S India, 90 mi. (145 km.) SE of Calicut; pop. (1991p) 87,012.

Pol·len·sa, Bay of \pōl-'yen-sä\. Bay on N coast of the island of Majorca, W Mediterranean Sea.

Pol·len·za \pō-'len-sä\; *anc.* **Pol·len·tia** \pə-'len-shē-ə\. Commune, Macerata prov., S cen. Marche, cen. Italy; pop. (1981p) 5581; scene of battle 402 A.D. bet. Roman Gen. Stilicho and Goths under Alaric who subsequently retired from Italy.

Pol·li·no, Mon·te \'mȯn-tā-pō-'lē-nō\. Mountain, highest in Lucanian Apennines. See table at APENNINES.

Pol·lock, Mount \'pä-lək\. Peak on Continental Divide in Glacier National Park, NW Montana; 9211 ft. (2808 m.).

Pol·lux \'pä-ləks\. Peak in the Pennine Alps. See ZWILLINGE.

Pollux Peak. Mountain in Yellowstone National Park, NW Wyoming; 11,067 ft. (3373 m.).

Po·lo \'pō-lō\. City, Ogle co., N Illinois, 34 mi. (55 km.) SW of Rockford; pop. (1990c) 2514.

Po·lo·chic \ˌpō-lō-'chēk\. River, S cen. Guatemala; flows ESE into Lake Izabal; ab. 180 mi. (290 km.) long.

Po·lotsk \'pȯ-lətsk\. **1.** Medieval principality in the region S of Lake Peipus, N Europe; retained autonomy from Kiev 11th–12th cents.

2. City, Belarus. See POLATSK.

Polotsk Oblast \'ȯ-bləst, -ˌblast\. Former subdivision of N Belorussian S.S.R., U.S.S.R.; ✻ Polotsk; abolished 1954.

Polska. See POLAND.

Pol·son \'pōl-sən\. City, ⊗ of Lake co., NW Montana, on S end of Flathead Lake; pop. (1990c) 3283; lake resort.

Pol·ta·va \pəl-'tä-və\ *also* **Pul·to·va** *or* **Pul·to·wa** \pəl-'tō-və\. **1.** Administrative subdivision, cen. Ukraine; 11,120 sq. mi. (28,801 sq. km.); pop. (1991e) 1,756,900; ✻ Poltava; crossed by the Psel and Vorskla, tributaries of the Dnieper.

2. City, its ✻, on right bank of Vorskla River 85 mi. (137 km.) WSW of Kharkiv; pop. (1991e) 320,000; textiles, leather goods, flour, clothing, machinery.

History: Town first mentioned 1174 but believed to date from c. 9th cent.; taken from Tatars by Lithuania 14th cent.; in 17th cent. a Cossack stronghold; scene of decisive battle July 8, 1709, in which Russians under Czar Peter the Great defeated the Swedes under Charles XII, a battle which marked the emergence of Russia as a major European power.

Poltoratsk. See ASHKHABAD.

Po·lu·os·trov \ˌpə-lü-ˈȯ-strəf\. Russian word meaning "peninsula". For names of peninsulas containing this word, see the 2d element.

Po·lyar·ny *or* **Po·lyar·nyy** \ˌpəl-ˈyär-nē\. Small ice-free port at mouth of Tuloma River, NW Murmansk Oblast, NW Russia in Europe; now largely replaced as a port by Murmansk.

Po·lyg·y·ros \pō-ˈli-jə-ˌräs\ *or Gk.* **Po·lý·gy·ros** \pō-ˈlē-yē-ˌrōs\. Town, ✻ of Chalcidice dept., S Macedonia, NE Greece, in center of peninsula ab. 30 mi. (48 km.) SE of Thessaloníki; pop. (1981p) 5228.

Pol·y·ne·sia \ˌpä-lə-ˈnē-zhə, -shə\. Islands of the cen. Pacific Ocean, bet. 30°N and 47°S; a subdivision of Oceania. They include the large islands of New Zealand and the groups of the Hawaiian Is., Samoa, Line Is., French Polynesia, Cook Is., Phoenix Is., Tuvalu, Tonga, and Easter I. The islands are mostly small; many are coral atolls, others are of volcanic origin. The greater part of the inhabitants are Polynesians, perhaps related to the Malay, but many are of mixed origin. Their languages belong to a subfamily of the Austronesian languages. Foremost representatives are the Hawaiians, Maoris, Marquesans, Samoans, Tongans, and Tahitians.

Polynésie française. See FRENCH POLYNESIA.

Pom·er·a·nia \ˌpä-mə-ˈrā-nē-ə, -nyə\ *or Ger.* **Pom·mern** \ˈpȯ-mərn\. Historical region NW cen. Europe, on Baltic Sea; at its greatest extent comprising the territory bet. Stralsund and the Vistula and incl. Rügen I. Occupied by Slavic and other peoples, entire area bet. Oder and Vistula rivers conquered by Bolesław III of Poland 1113–35; in 12th cent. W part penetrated by Germans who erected duchy of Pomerania (included territory on both sides of the lower Oder); E part (see POMERELIA) came under Teutonic Knights and was returned to Poland 1466 as part of West Prussia. Duchy came under Brandenburg which divided it with Sweden 1648, keeping the part E of the Oder, **Farther Pomerania** (*Ger.* **Hin·ter·pom·mern** \ˈhin-tər-ˌpȯ-mərn\), and giving to Sweden **Hither Pomerania** (*Ger.* **Vor·pom·mern** \ˈfōr-\), incl. both banks of the Oder as well as territory to the W, with Rügen I. and Usedom I.; Sweden ceded S part of Hither Pomerania to Prussia 1720, keeping N part, **Swedish Pomerania** (the island of Rügen and the adjoining territory on the mainland N of the Peene River), until 1815 when it also was ceded to Prussia. The section E of the Oder (but incl. Szczecin, mainly on left bank) assigned to Poland by the Potsdam Conference 1945.

Pom·er·an·i·an Bay \ˌpä-mə-ˈrā-nē-ən, -nyən\ *or* **Bay of Pomerania** *or Ger.* **Pom·mer·sche Bucht** \ˈpȯ-mər-shə-ˈbu̇kt\. Widemouthed inlet of Baltic Sea bet. NE Germany and NW Poland.

Pom·er·e·lia \ˌpä-mə-ˈrē-lē-ə, -ˈrēl-yə\ *or Ger.* **Pom·me·rel·len** \ˌpȯ-mə-ˈre-lən\. Historical region N Europe, on the Baltic Sea W of the Vistula; orig. part of Pomerania (*q.v.*) but gradually separated from it and was distinct from it when the duchy of Pomerania was created in 12th cent.; came under Teutonic Knights c. 1308; returned to Poland 1466; in First Partition of Poland 1772 came under Prussia; to Poland again 1919; occupied by Germany 1939 but after 1945 returned to Poland.

Pom·er·oy \ˈpä-mə-ˌrȯi\. **1.** Village, ⊗ of Meigs co., SE Ohio, on Ohio River 38 mi. (61 km.) SW of Marietta; pop. (1990c) 2259.

2. City, ⊗ of Garfield co., SE Washington, 27 mi. (43 km.) SW of Pullman; pop. (1990c) 1393.

Po·me·zia \pȯ-ˈmād-zyä\. Commune, Roma prov., Lazio, Italy; pop. (1989c) 37,713.

Pom·fret \ˈpəm-fret, -frit\. Residential town, N cen. Windham co., NE Connecticut, WSW of Putnam; pop. (1990c) 3102.

Po·mi·glia·no d'Ar·co \ˌpō-mēl-ˈyä-nō-ˈdär-kō\. Commune, Napoli prov., Campania, S Italy, at N foot of Vesuvius 8 mi. (13 km.) NE of Naples; pop. (1991p) 42,685.

Pommerellen. See POMERELIA.

Pommern. See POMERANIA.

Pommersche Bucht. See POMERANIAN BAY.

Po·mo·na \pə-ˈmō-nə\. **1.** City, Los Angeles co., SW California, 25 mi. (40 km.) E of the city of Los Angeles; pop. (1990c) 131,723; residential and commercial suburb of Los Angeles; California State Polytechnic Univ., Pomona (1938), Coll. of Osteopathic Medicine of the Pacific (1977); city founded 1875; incorp. 1888.

2. Village, Rockland co., SE New York; pop. (1990c) 2611.

3. *or* **Main·land** \ˈmān-ˌland, -lənd\. Largest of the Orkney Is. (*q.v.*), off N coast of Scotland; 190 sq. mi. (492 sq. km.); chief towns Kirkwall and Stromness.

Po·mo·rze \pȯ-ˈmȯ-zhā\. Former department of Poland; ✻ Toruń; formed 1921 from part of West Prussia.

Pomorze Zachodnie. See SZCZECIN 1.

Pompaelo. See PAMPLONA 2.

Pom·pa·no Beach \ˈpäm-pə-nō, ˈpəm-\. City, Broward co., SE Florida, near Atlantic Ocean 32 mi. (52 km.) N of Miami; pop. (1990c) 72,411; resort; truck farms, citrus fruit; moved inland to present site after hurricane 1928.

Pom·pei \päm-ˈpā\; *before 1928* **Val·le di Pompei** \ˈvä-lā-dē-\. Commune, Napoli prov., Campania, S Italy, 14 mi. (23 km.) ESE of Naples; pop. (1991p) 25,080; much-visited pilgrimage church; geophysical observatory; near ancient Pompeii (*q.v.*).

Pom·pe·ii \päm-ˈpā, -ˈpā-ˌē\. Ancient city, Campania, S Italy, 15 mi. (24 km.) SE of Naples near the foot of Vesuvius and near Herculaneum (*q.v.*); founded 6th cent. B.C. or earlier by Oscans; came under Greek and Etruscan influence; occupied by Samnites late 5th cent. B.C.; allied with Rome 290 B.C. and became a Roman colony by 80 B.C.; devasted by earthquake 63 A.D.; partly rebuilt when it was completely destroyed by the eruption of Vesuvius 79 A.D. and buried under 20 ft. (6 m.) of volcanic debris and ashes; 2,000 of the 20,000 inhabitants perished, as well as the Roman scholar Pliny the Elder. Excavations begun 1748 and now three fourths of the city uncovered, revealing its regular plan, the forum, temples, baths, theaters, and many dwellings, incl. villas of Roman nobles.

Pomp·ton \ˈpämp-tən\. Short river, N New Jersey; formed just S of Pompton Lakes by confluence of Pequannock, Ramapo, and Ringwood rivers; flows S into Passaic River.

Pompton Lakes. Borough, Passaic co., N New Jersey, 9 mi. (15 km.) NW of Paterson; pop. (1990c) 10,539; settled 1682.

Ponape. See POHNPEI.

Pon·ca \ˈpäŋ-kə\. City, ⊗ of Dixon co., NE Nebraska; pop. (1990c) 877.

Ponca City. City, Kay co., N Oklahoma, on Arkansas River 52 mi. (84 km.) ENE of Enid; pop. (1990c) 26,359; oil-drilling equipment; oil refining, food processing; oil wells; city founded 1893.

Pon·ce \ˈpȯn-sā\. Seaport city, S Puerto Rico, 140 mi. (225 km.) SW of San Juan; munic. pop. (1990c) 187,749; principal city of S Puerto Rico; exports sugar; produces cement, textiles, footwear, rum, and paper; Pontifical Catholic Univ. of Puerto Rico (1948); made city 1877.

Ponce de Le·on Bay \ˈpäns-də-ˈlē-ən\. Inlet of Gulf of Mexico on SW coast of Florida, from Cape Sable to Cape Romano.

Pon·cha·tou·la \ˌpän-chə-ˈtü-lə\. City, Tangipahoa parish, SE Louisiana, 41 mi. (66 km.) NNW of New Orleans; pop. (1990c) 5425.

Pon·dera \ˌpän-də-ˈrā\. County in NW Montana. See table at MONTANA.

Pon·di·cher·ry \ˌpän-də-ˈcher-ē, -ˈsher-\ *or Fr.* **Pon·di·ché·ry** \ˌpōⁿ-dē-shā-ˈrē\. **1.** Union territory of India; ✻ Pondicherry; composed of four widely-separated former French coastal settlements: Mahe (in Kerala state), Yanam (in Andhra Pradesh), and Karikal and Pondicherry (both in Tamil Nadu); formed 1963. See table at INDIA.

2. Seaport, its ✻; pop. (1991p) 202,648; an open roadstead but with good trade; has textile industry; ✻ of former French India. Founded by French 1674; held by Dutch 1693–97; several times taken by British 1761, 1778, 1793, 1803 but each time restored; French possession 1816–1954.

Pon·do·land \ˈpän-dō-ˌland\. Region, Eastern Cape prov., S Rep. of South Africa, on coast of Indian Ocean bet. Mtata River and KwaZulu-Natal border (Mtamvuna River); 3906 sq. mi. (10,117 sq. km.); ✻ Port St. Johns. Settled by Pondos (Mpondos), a Bantu-speaking people. Annexed to Cape Colony 1894.

Ponente, Riviera di. See RIVIERA.

Pon·fer·ra·da \ˌpȯn-fer-ˈrä-t͟hä\. Commune, León prov., NW Spain, 50 mi. (81 km.) WSW of the city of León; pop. (1991p) 59,690.

Pon·go de Man·se·ri·che \ˈpȯŋ-gō-t͟hā-ˌmän-sā-ˈrē-chā\. Narrows (*pongo*), Peru, through which the Marañón River flows after its major curve around to the E in N Peru; ab. 2000 ft. (610 m.) deep; flow is very rapid and the gorge narrows to as little as 100 ft. (30 m.) width in places.

Pon·go·lo \pȯŋ-ˈgō-lō\. River, Rep. of South Africa, flowing bet. SE Mpumalanga and N KwaZulu-Natal provs.; ab. 120 mi. (195 km.) long; unites with Usutu River to form Maputo River in Mozambique.

Po·nien·te, Is·las de \ˈēs-läs-t͟hā-pō-ˈnyen-tā\. Early Spanish name of the Philippines—literally "Western Islands," because lying to the W (beyond Mexico) within the lands of the Far East claimed by Spain.

Pon·na·ni \pə-ˈnä-nē\. **1.** River, W Tamil Nadu and cen. Kerala, S India; flows W to Arabian Sea at Ponnani; 120 mi. (193 km.) long; part of its course forms N boundary of Cochin.

2. Seaport town, Kerala, SW India, at mouth of Ponnani River, 38 mi. (61 km.) S of Calicut; pop. (1991p) 51,754.

Po·no·ro·go \ˌpō-nō-ˈrō-gō\. Market town, East Java prov., Indonesia, 20 mi. (32 km.) S of Madiun; pop. (1980c) 73,991.

Pons Aelii. See NEWCASTLE 5.

Pon·son \pȯn-ˈsȯn\. Island, easternmost of Camotes Is., Cebu prov., Philippines; 13 sq. mi. (34 sq. km.); coextensive with municipality of Pilar.

Pons Vetus. See PONTEVEDRA 4.

Pon·ta Del·ga·da \ˌpȯn-tə-del-ˈgä-də\. **1.** Former district of Portugal, comprised of São Miguel and Santa Maria islands, Azores.

2. Seaport commune, ✻ of Azores, Portugal, on SW coast of São Miguel I.; munic. pop. (1991p) 21,091; commercial and tourist center; exports pottery, hats, distilled liquors, and citrus fruit.

Ponta Gros·sa \ˌpōn-tə-ˈgrȯ-sə\. City, Paraná state, S Brazil, 60 mi. (97 km.) WNW of Curitiba; munic. pop. (1991p) 233,517; lumber, tea, cereals, livestock.

Pont–à–Mous·son \ˌpȯⁿt-ä-mü-ˈsōⁿ\. Commune, Meurthe-et-Moselle dept., NE France, on Moselle River 12 mi. (19 km.) NNW of Nancy. University founded here 1572 (transferred to Nancy 1768); commune taken by Louis XIII of France 1633; a frontline position in WWI; badly damaged in WWII.

Pontarfynach. See DEVIL'S BRIDGE.

Pon·tar·lier \ˌpȯⁿ-tär-ˈlyā\. Commune, Doubs dept., E France, on Doubs River near Swiss border 29 mi. (47 km.) SSE of Besançon.

Pon·ta São Se·bas·tião \ˈpȯn-tə-ˌsau̇ⁿ-se-ˌbäs-ˈtyau̇ⁿ\. Cape, extending into Mozambique Channel on SE coast of Mozambique, N of Inhambane.

Pon·tas·sie·ve \ˌpōn-tä-ˈsyā-vā\. Commune, Firenze prov., Tuscany, cen. Italy, on the Arno 10 mi. (16 km.) E of Florence; pop. (1981p) 20,057.

Pont–Au·de·mer \ˌpȯⁿ-tōd-ˈmer\. Commune, Eure dept., N France, ab. 39 mi. (63 km.) NW of Évreux; a river port on the Risle, a tributary of the Seine.

Pont–Aven \ˌpȯⁿ-tə-ˈven\. Village at head of estuary on coast of Bay of Biscay, Finistère dept., Brittany, NW France, ab. 18 mi. (29 km.) WNW of Lorient. Artist colony; in late 19th cent. home of Paul Gauguin, among others.

Pont·char·train, Lake \ˈpän-chər-ˌtrān, ˌpän-chər-ˈ\. Lake, SE Louisiana; ab. 40 mi. (64 km.) long; 630 sq. mi. (1632 sq. km.); connected through Lake Borgne with Gulf of Mexico, and by canal with Mississippi River; spanned by world's longest causeway (total length 23.8 mi. or 38.4 km.). The city of New Orleans lies bet. it and the Mississippi River.

Pont du Fahs. See QANṬARAT AL-FAḤṢ.

Pon·te·ca·gna·no Fai·a·no \ˌpȯn-te-kä-ˈnyä-nō-fī-ˈä-nō\. Commune, Salerno prov., Campania, S Italy; pop. (1989c) 22,622.

Pon·te·cor·vo \ˌpōn-te-ˈkȯr-vō\. Commune, Frosinone prov., Lazio, cen. Italy, 21 mi. (34 km.) SE of the commune of Frosinone; pop. (1981p) 12,216; a former principality; largely destroyed in WWII.

Pon·te·de·ra \ˌpōn-tā-ˈder-ä\. Commune, Pisa prov., Tuscany, cen. Italy, on the Arno 13 mi. (21 km.) ESE of the commune of Pisa; pop. (1991c) 27,107.

Pon·te·fract \ˈpän-ti-ˌfrakt, ˈpəm-frət\. Town, West Yorkshire, N England, near confluence of Aire and Calder rivers 13 mi. (21 km.) S of Leeds; pop. (1981c) 29,047; licorice confectionary ("Pomfret cakes"), leather goods. Town grew around Norman castle, scene of the death of King Richard II 1400 and of imprisonment of Charles, duke of Orleans, after defeat at Agincourt 1415; castle dismantled 1649 after English Civil War and now only ruins remain.

Pon·te No·va \ˌpōn-tə-ˈnȯ-və\. City, SE Minas Gerais state, E Brazil, 75 mi. (121 km.) SE of Belo Horizonte; munic. pop. (1991p) 56,689.

Pon·te·ve·dra \ˌpȯn-tā-ˈvā-drä\. **1.** Municipality, Negros Occidental, Negros, Philippines, on Guimaras Strait 20 mi. (32 km.) S of City of Bacolod; pop. (1980c) 33,258.

2. Municipality, NE Capiz prov., Panay, Philippines, just W of head of Pilar Bay 13 mi. (21 km.) SE of Roxas; pop. (1980c) 30,489.

3. Province of NW Spain. See table at SPAIN.

4. *anc.* **Pons Ve·tus** \pänz-ˈvē-təs, -ˈve-\. Commune, ✻ of Pontevedra prov., NW Spain, on inlet of Atlantic Ocean 65 mi. (105 km.) SW of Lugo; pop. (1991p) 71,182; trades in grain and fruit; produces textiles, pottery, leather, hats, fertilizers; 16th cent. church; Roman bridge; in Middle Ages an important shipbuilding center and port.

Ponthierville. See UBUNDU.

Pon·thieu \pōⁿ-ˈtyœ̄\. Ancient region in N France, in Picardy; ✻ Abbeville; annexed to Aquitaine 831; passed to Castile 13th cent.; held by England (acquired through marriage of Eleanor of Castile to Edward I) almost continuously 1272–1369; to French crown 1477.

Pon·ti·ac \ˈpän-tē-ˌak\. **1.** City, ⊗ of Livingston co., NE cen. Illinois, 35 mi. (56 km.) NNE of Bloomington; pop. (1990c) 11,428; gloves; grain farms.

2. City, ⊗ of Oakland co., SE Michigan, 25 mi. (40 km.) NNW of Detroit; pop. (1990c) 71,166; motor-vehicle manufacturing; rubber, paint; settled 1818; chartered as city 1861.

3. County, in SW Quebec, Canada. See table at QUEBEC.

Pontiae. See PONZA ISLANDS.

Pon·ti·a·nak \ˌpän-tē-ˈä-nək\. City, ✻ of West Kalimantan prov., W Borneo, Indonesia, at mouth of small stream on N edge of Kapuas Delta; pop. (1990c) 398,357; exports rubber, sugar, and palm oil; shipbuilding; in region producing coconuts, pepper, rice, tobacco, and sugar. Founded 1772 as ✻ of a sultanate supported by the Dutch East India Co.; later became chief gold-exporting port of Borneo.

Pontine Islands. See PONZA ISLANDS.

Pon·ti·no, Agro \ˈä-grō-pōn-ˈtē-nō\ *or* **Pon·tine Marshes** \ˈpän-ˌtīn, -ˌtēn\. Area in SW Lazio, cen. Italy; ab. 290 sq. mi. (751 sq. km.); bounded on N by the Lepini Mts., separated from sea by low sand hills which prevent natural drainage. Traversed by the Appian Way, built c. 312 B.C. but in later Roman times became an unhealthful region of malarial swamps; most recent reclamation projects begun 1920s under dictator Benito Mussolini; has several settlements built in the 1930s, incl. Latina (*q.v.*) and **Pon·ti·nia** \pōn-ˈtē-nyə\. In SE part on a promontory is Monte Circeo (*q.v.*).

\ə\ abut \ə\ matches \ᵊ\ kitten, Fr table \ər\ further \a\ ash \ā\ ace
\ä\ cot, cart \ȧ\ Fr bac \au̇\ out \b̲\ Span Avila \ch\ chin \e\ bet \ē\ easy
\g\ go \i\ hit \ī\ ice \j\ job \k̲\ Ger ich, Buch \ⁿ\ Fr vin
\ŋ\ sing \ō\ go \ȯ\ all \ȯ\ law \œ\ Fr bœuf \œ̄\ Fr feu \ȯi\ boy
\th\ thin \t͟h\ this \ü\ loot \u̇\ foot \ue\ Ger füllen \ue̅\ Fr rue
\y\ yet \ʸ\ Fr digne \ˈdēnʸ\, nuit \ˈnwʸē\ \yü\ few \yu̇\ fury \zh\ vision

Pontisarae. See PONTOISE.

Pon·ti·vy \ˌpōⁿ-tē-ˈvē\. Town, Morbihan dept., NW France, ab. 30 mi. (48 km.) NNW of Vannes; made military headquarters of Brittany by Emperor Napoléon; known as Napoléonville until 1871.

Pon·toise \pōⁿ-ˈtwäz\; *anc.* **Bri·va Is·a·rae** \ˈbrī-və-ˈi-sə-rē\ *also* **Pon·tis·a·rae** \pän-ˈti-sə-rē\. Commune, ✻ of Val-d'Oise dept., N France, on Oise River 18 mi. (29 km.) NNW of Paris; pop. (1990c) 28,463; market center and residential suburb of Paris; 12th–16th cent. cathedral; 16th cent. church. Came under French crown 1064 and made ✻ of French Vexin; occupied by English twice in first half of 15th cent.; Parliament of Paris exiled here 1753.

Pon·to·toc \ˈpän-tə-ˌtäk\. **1.** Name of counties in two states of the U.S. See tables at MISSISSIPPI and OKLAHOMA.
2. City, ⊗ of Pontotoc co., N Mississippi, 17 mi. (27 km.) W of Tupelo; pop. (1990c) 4570.

Pon·tre·mo·li \ˌpōn-tre-ˈmō-lē\. Commune, Massa-Carrara prov., Tuscany, W Italy, 28 mi. (45 km.) NNW of Carrara; pop. (1981p) 10,135.

Pont Rouge \ˈpōⁿ-ˈrüzh\. Village, Portneuf co., S Quebec, Canada, on Jacques Cartier River and on railroad line 25 mi. (40 km.) W of Quebec City; pop. (1991c) 4133.

Pont–Saint–Es·prit \ˈpōⁿ-ˌseⁿ-tes-ˈprē\. Town, Gard dept., S France; on the Rhone which is here crossed by a 13th–14th cent. bridge built by friars, widened in 1860.

Pon·tus \ˈpän-təs\. **1.** Ancient country in NE Asia Minor, orig. that part of Cappadocia along the shore of Pontus Euxinus (Black Sea) E of Halys River; ancient ✻ Amasia. As kingdom, bounded on E by Armenia, on S by Cappadocia and Galatia, and on W by Bithynia. Mountainous, watered by Iris River. Kingdom estab. 4th cent. B.C. and continued with expanding borders until 66 B.C. when its last king, Mithradates the Great, was overcome by Roman Gen. Pompey the Great; incorp. into Roman Empire 63 B.C. Chief cities Trapezus (see TRABZON), Amasia, Cerasus, Neocaesarea, and Cotyora.
2. *or* **Pontus Euxinus.** See BLACK SEA.

Pon·ty·pool \ˌpän-ti-ˈpül\. Town, Gwent co., SE Wales, on the Afon Llwydd 25 mi. (40 km.) NW of Bristol, England; pop. (1981c) 36,301; steel, glass, rubber, nylon products; coal mines in vicinity; iron mining began late 16th cent.

Pon·ty·pridd \ˌpän-ti-ˈprēth\. Town, Mid Glamorgan co., S Wales; pop. (1981c) 29,796; electrical equipment, cables; coal mining formerly significant; notable 18th cent. bridge from which community takes its name.

Pon·za Islands \ˈpōnt-sä\ *also* **Pon·tine Islands** \ˈpän-ˌtīn, -ˌtēn\ *or* **Pon·zia·ne Islands** \pōn-ˈtsyä-nā\; *anc.* **Pon·ti·ae** \ˈpän-shē-ˌē\. Island group in Tyrrhenian Sea W of Naples, SW Italy; administratively a part of Napoli prov., Campania; chief island **Ponza** \ˈpōnt-sə\; used as a place of banishment in ancient times and again under dictator Benito Mussolini.

Poole \ˈpül\. Port town, Dorset, S England, on **Poole Harbour,** large nearly landlocked bay of English Channel 40 mi. (64 km.) W of Portsmouth; pop. (1991p) 130,900; yachting center; manufactures chemicals, boats; chartered 1248.

Pool·er \ˈpü-lər\. City, Chatham co., E Georgia, 10 mi. (16 km.) W of Savannah; pop. (1990c) 4453.

Pool Malebo. See MALEBO, POOL.

Poona. See PUNE.

Po·o·pó, Lake \ˌpō-ō-ˈpō\ *also* **Lake Aul·la·gas** \aú-ˈyä-gäs\. Lake in W cen. Bolivia at alt. of 12,000 ft. (3658 m.); 977 sq. mi. (2530 sq. km.); max. depth 15 ft. (6 m.); receives Desaguadero River from Lake Titicaca to the N.

Po·pa, Mount \ˈpō-pə\. Extinct volcano, cen. Myanmar, highest peak in Pegu Yoma range; 4981 ft. (1518 m.).

Po·pa·yán \ˌpō-pä-ˈyän\. City, ✻ of Cauca dept., SW Colombia, S of Cali at foot of Mt. Puracé; pop. (1992e) 203,800; alt. 5700 ft. (1737 m.); primarily a cultural center with some local industry; university (1827). Founded 1537; during the colonial era center of a mining region and an important residential, administrative, and religious center; struck by severe earthquake March 1983.

Pope \ˈpōp\. Name of counties in three states of the U.S. See tables at ARKANSAS, ILLINOIS, MINNESOTA.

Popes Creek \ˈpōps\. Small stream in Westmoreland co., Virginia, flowing into the Potomac; Wakefield, George Washington's birthplace, is on its left bank.

Pop·lar Bluff \ˈpä-plər\. City, ⊗ of Butler co., SE Missouri, 63 mi. (101 km.) WSW of Cape Girardeau; pop. (1990c) 16,996; market town; ships farm products; Three Rivers Community Coll. (1966); city founded 1850.

Pop·lar·ville \ˈpä-plər-ˌvil\. Town, ⊗ of Pearl River co., S Mississippi, 37 mi. (60 km.) SSW of Hattiesburg; pop. (1990c) 2561; Pearl River Community Coll. (1909).

Popo, Grand. See GRAND POPO.

Po·po Agie \pə-ˈpō-zhə, -zē-ə\. River, W cen. Wyoming; rises in Wind River Range, SW Fremont co., flows NE and unites with Wind River to form Bighorn River.

Po·po·ca·té·petl \ˌpō-pə-ˈkat-ə-ˌpet-ᵊl, -ˌkat-ə-ˈ, *Span.* ˌpō-pō-kä-ˈtā-pe-təl\. Volcano, Puebla state, SE cen. Mexico, 30 mi. (48 km.) W of the city of Puebla; ab. 17,887 ft. (5450 m.); contains crater over 0.5 mi. (0.8 km.) in circumference and 250 ft. (76 m.) deep.

Po·po·ma·na·siu, Mount \ˌpō-pō-mä-ˈnä-sē-ˌü\. Peak in Kavo Mts. near S coast, Guadalcanal I., SE Solomon Is., W Pacific Ocean; 7648 ft. (2331 m.).

Pop·pi \ˈpō-pē\. Commune, Arezzo prov., E Tuscany, cen. Italy, on Arno River; pop. (1981p) 5725; 13th cent. castle.

Pop·rad \ˈpōp-rät\. Town, N Slovakia; pop. (1989c) 52,362.

Pop·u·lo·ni·um \ˌpä-pyə-ˈlō-nē-əm\ *or* **Pu·plu·na** \pü-ˈplü-nə\. Ancient town of Etruria, Italy, on coast of Ligurian Sea N of Piombino; iron from nearby island of Elba supplied metal manufactures; has remains of Etruscan walls and tombs and ruins of a medieval castle; besieged by Roman Gen. Sulla 82 B.C.

Po·quis \ˈpō-kēs\. Peak, E Antofagasta region, N Chile, near Argentine boundary; 18,832 ft. (5740 m.).

Po·quos·on \pə-ˈkwō-sən\. Independent city, York co., SE Virginia, 9 mi. (14 km.) N of Newport News; pop. (1990c) 11,005.

Po·ra·li \pō-ˈrä-lē\ *or* **Pu·ra·li** \pü-ˈrä-lē\. River, SE Baluchistan, Pakistan; flows S into Sonmiani Bay.

Por·ban·dar \pōr-ˈbən-dər\. **1.** Former Indian state, now part of Gujarat state, W India, on Arabian Sea; 642 sq. mi. (1663 sq. km.).
2. Town, its ✻, on Arabian Sea 275 mi. (442 km.) NW of Bombay; pop. (1991p) 160,043; port with extensive coastal trade. Birthplace of nationalist and spiritual leader Mahatma Gandhi 1869.

Por·cher Island \ˈpōr-chər\. Island off W British Columbia, Canada, N of Pitt I. and near mouth of Skeena River; 205 sq. mi. (531 sq. km.).

Por·cu·pine \ˈpōr-kyə-ˌpīn\. River, N Yukon Terr., Canada, and NE Alaska; flows N then W to Yukon River at Fort Yukon, Alaska; 448 mi. (721 km.) long.

Porcupine Mountains. Range in Gogebic and Ontonagon cos., NW extremity of Michigan's Upper Penin.; highest point **Porcupine Mountain** 1958 ft. (597 m.), in Ontonagon co.

Por·de·no·ne \ˌpōr-de-ˈnō-nā\ *or Ger.* **Por·te·nau** \ˈpōrt-ᵊn-ˌaú\. **1.** Province of Friuli-Venezia Giulia, Italy. See table at ITALY.
2. Commune, ✻ of Pordenone prov., Friuli-Venezia Giulia, NE Italy, 37 mi. (60 km.) SW of Udine; pop. (1991p) 49,746; notable 13th–14th cent. campanile. Destroyed in local war 1233; passed to Venice 1508; became part of Italy 1866.

Po·reč \ˈpō-ˌrech\ *or Ital.* **Pa·ren·zo** \pä-ˈrent-sō, -ˈren-zō\. Commune in W Croatia, on coast of Istria Penin. 30 mi. (48 km.) NNW of Pula; 6th cent. basilica; before 1947 belonged to Italy.

Porfirio Díaz, Ciudad. See PIEDRAS NEGRAS 2.

Po·ri \ˈpōr-ē\ *or Swed.* **Björ·ne·borg** \ˈbyœr-nə-ˌbōr, -ˌbōr-ē\. Seaport, Turku ja Pori prov., SW Finland; pop. (1989c) 76,456; shipping center; manufactures paper; copper refineries. See TURKU.

Po·ri·rua \ˌpo-rə-ˈrü-ə\. City, New Zealand, near SW tip of North I., NNE of Wellington; pop. (1991c) 46,601.

Pork·ka·la Peninsula \ˈpōr-kä-lä\. Small tongue of land, S Finland, projecting into the Gulf of Finland ab. 19 mi. (31 km.) W of Helsinki; ceded by Finland to U.S.S.R. in exchange for Hangö 1944; returned to Finland 1956.

Por·la·mar \ˌpȯr-lä-ˈmär\. Port, Nueva Esparta state, Venezuela, chief town of Margarita I., in Caribbean Sea off N coast of Venezuela.

Po·ro \ˈpō-rō\. Island, Cebu prov., Philippines; 39 sq. mi. (101 sq. km.); pop. (1980c) 17,717; coextensive with municipalities of Poro and Tudela; cen. island of Camotes group.

Po·ron·gos, La·gu·na de \lä-ˈgü-nä-ˌt͟hā-pō-ˈrȯŋ-gōs\. Swamp region in NE Córdoba prov., N cen. Argentina, N of Mar Chiquita; no outlet. Includes **La·go de los Pa·tos** \ˈlä-gō-ˌt͟hā-lȯs-ˈpä-tōs\.

Por·que·rolles \ˌpȯr-kə-ˈrȯl\. One of the Hyères Is. (*q.v.*), of France.

Pors·ang·en Fjord \ˈpȯr-ˌsäŋ-ən\ *also* **Pors·ang·er Fjord** \-ˌsäŋ-ər\. Inlet of Arctic Ocean on N coast of Norway; extends S inland 249 mi. (401 km.).

Pors·grunn \ˈpȯrs-ˌgrün\. Seaport, Telemark co., S Norway, near coast NW of Larvik; pop. (1990c) 31,209; noted for its manufacture of porcelain.

Por·suk \pȯr-ˈsük\ *or* **Pur·sak** \pu̇r-ˈsäk\. River, W Turkey in Asia; rises near Murat Dağı and flows N and E into Sakarya River; ab. 200 mi. (320 km.) long.

Port Ad·e·laide \ˈad-ᵊl-ˌād\. City, SE South Australia, Australia, on Gulf St. Vincent at mouth of Torrens River; pop. (1991c) 38,205; seaport of Adelaide.

Port·a·down \ˌpōr-tə-ˈdau̇n\. City, Armagh dist., S Northern Ireland; pop. (1981c) 21,333; linen.

Por·tage \ˈpōr-tij\. **1.** Name of counties in two states of the U.S. See tables at OHIO and WISCONSIN.
2. Town, Porter co., NW Indiana, NW of Valparaiso; pop. (1990c) 29,060.
3. City, Kalamazoo co., SW Michigan, 8 mi. (13 km.) S of the city of Kalamazoo; pop. (1990c) 41,042.
4. Borough, Cambria co., SW cen. Pennsylvania, 15 mi. (24 km.) ENE of Johnstown; pop. (1990c) 3105.
5. City, ⊗ of Columbia co., S cen. Wisconsin, on Wisconsin River 34 mi. (55 km.) N of Madison; pop. (1990c) 8640; plastics; diversified agriculture; fort built on site 1828; previously site of a 1.5-mile (2.4-kilometer) portage bet. Fox and Wisconsin rivers, now connected by a canal.

Portage Falls. Waterfall in the Genesee River, W New York, 45 mi. (72 km.) SSW of Rochester; 110 ft. (34 m.) high.

Portage Lake. **1.** Lake, N cen. Aroostook co., N Maine.
2. Lake, Houghton co., in Michigan's Upper Penin., an inlet of Keweenaw Bay; Keweenaw Waterway (see KEWEENAW PENINSULA) passes through it.

Portage la Prai·rie \lə-ˈprer-ē\. City, S Manitoba, Canada, on Assiniboine River 54 mi. (87 km.) W of Winnipeg; pop. (1991c) 13,186; railroad center; dairy products, bricks; ships grain; fort built on site 1738; settlement begun c. 1851.

Por·tage·ville \ˈpōr-tij-ˌvil\. City, New Madrid co., SE Missouri, 18 mi. (29 km.) N of Caruthersville; pop. (1990c) 3401.

Port Al·ber·ni \al-ˈbər-nē\. Resort city, E cen. Vancouver I., British Columbia, Canada, at head of Alberni Canal 75 mi. (121 km.) W of Vancouver; pop. (1991c) 18,403; fisheries, pulp mills.

Por·ta·le·gre \ˌpu̇r-tá-ˈle-grē\. **1.** District of E cen. Portugal. See table at PORTUGAL.
2. Once-fortified commune, its ✻, near Spanish frontier 100 mi. (161 km.) ENE of Lisbon; pop. (1991p) 25,623; woolens, cork; 16th cent. cathedral.

Por·tal·es \pȯr-ˈta-ləs\. City, ⊗ of Roosevelt co., E New Mexico, 18 mi. (29 km.) SW of Clovis; pop. (1990c) 10,690; truck farms; Eastern New Mexico Univ. (1934).

Port Al·fred \ˈal-frəd, -fərd\. Resort town, Eastern Cape prov., S Rep. of South Africa, at mouth of Kowie River 80 mi. (129 km.) ENE of Port Elizabeth; founded 1825.

Port Al·le·ga·ny \ˌa-lə-ˈgā-nē\. Borough, McKean co., N Pennsylvania, on Allegheny River 22 mi. (35 km.) ESE of Bradford; pop. (1990c) 2391.

Port Al·len \ˈa-lən\. City, ⊗ of West Baton Rouge parish, SE cen. Louisiana, on Mississippi River opp. Baton Rouge; pop. (1990c) 6277.

Port Amelia. See PEMBA 2.

Port An·ge·les \ˈan-jə-ləs\. City and port of entry, ⊗ of Clallam co., NW Washington, on Strait of Juan de Fuca opp. Victoria, Canada, and 65 mi. (105 km.) WNW of Seattle; pop. (1990c) 17,710; resort; wood and paper products; commercial fisheries; dairy farms; Peninsula Coll. (1961).

Port An·to·nio \an-ˈtō-nē-ˌō\. Seaport, NE Jamaica, West Indies, 26 mi. (42 km.) NE of Kingston (75 mi. or 121 km. by coastal railroad) on a bay divided in two parts by a promontory; pop. (1991p) 13,246; ships bananas.

Port Apra. See APRA HARBOR.

Port Aransas. See ARANSAS PASS 2.

Port Ar·thur \ˈär-thər\. **1.** City and port of entry, Jefferson co., SE Texas, on Sabine Lake 18 mi. (29 km.) S of Beaumont; pop. (1990c) 58,724; oil refineries and petrochemical plants; deepwater channels connect it with Gulf of Mexico and make it a major petroleum-shipping port; Lamar Univ.–Port Arthur campus (1909). Founded in 1895 as S terminus of Kansas City Southern R.R.
2. Settlement, Tasmania, Australia. See TASMAN PENINSULA.
3. City, Ontario, Canada. See THUNDER BAY 5.
4. Seaport, Liaodong prov., China. See LÜSHUN.

Port Au·gus·ta \ȯ-ˈgəs-tə, ə-ˈgəs-\. Seaport, S South Australia, Australia, at head of Spencer Gulf 175 mi. (282 km.) NNW of Adelaide; pop. (1991c) 14,965; trading center and shipping point for wheat-growing and sheep-raising region.

Port–au–Prince \ˌpōr-tō-ˈprins, -ˈprans\. Seaport, ✻ of Haiti, Hispaniola I., West Indies, on SE shore of Golfe de la Gonâve; pop. (1992e) 752,600, met. area pop. 1,255,078; principal port and commercial center of the republic; produces sugar, flour, cottonseed oil, and textiles; Univ. of Haiti (1920). Founded by French 1749; destroyed by earthquakes 1751 and 1770.

Port·bail \pȯr-ˈbā\. Town, Manche dept., NW France, near W coast of Cotentin Penin., Normandy, ab. 20 mi. (30 km.) W of Carentan; its capture by Allies June 1944 opened up corridor across the peninsula.

Port Blair \ˈblar\. Seaport town, ✻ of Andaman and Nicobar Is. union territory, India, on SE coast of South Andaman I.; 11°39′N, 92°45′E; pop. (1991p) 74,810; good harbor. First occupied by British 1789, but soon abandoned; made a penal colony 1858; occupied by Japanese 1942–45; penal colony abolished 1945.

Port Bou \pōrt-ˈbō\. Town, Gerona prov., NE Spain, on coast and on French border; pop. (1991c) 1913.

Port–Bouët \pȯr-ˈbwā\. Seaport, Ivory Coast, port of Abidjan on S side of lagoon opp. the ✻.

Port Bur·well \ˈbər-ˌwel, -wəl\. Harbor on SW coast of Killinek I., NE Quebec, Canada, just off N tip of Labrador.

Port–Car·tier \ˌpȯr-kär-ˈtyā\. Town, Quebec, Canada; pop. (1991c) 7383.

Port Chal·mers \ˈchal-mərz, ˈchä-mərz\. Borough, SE South I., New Zealand, on Otago Harbour 10 mi. (16 km.) NE of Dunedin; pop. (1981c) 2917.

Port Ches·ter \ˈpōrt-ˌches-tər\. Village, Westchester co., in Rye township (*q.v.*), SE New York, on Long Island Sound 25 mi. (40 km.) NE of New York City, near Connecticut boundary; pop. (1990c) 24,728; residential suburb of New York.

Port Clar·ence \ˈklar-əns\. Inlet at W end of Seward Penin., NW of Nome, W Alaska.

Port Clin·ton \ˈklint-ᵊn\. City, ⊗ of Ottawa co., N Ohio, on Lake Erie 30 mi. (48 km.) ESE of Toledo; pop. (1990c) 7106.

Port Col·borne \ˈkōl-bərn\. City, Niagara munic. region, SE Ontario, Canada, on NE shore of Lake Erie at S end of Welland Canal; pop. (1991c) 18,766; steel mill, nickel refinery.

Port Con·way \ˈkän-wā\. Hamlet, S King George co., NE Virginia, on the Rappahannock; birthplace 1751 of James Madison, 4th president of the U.S.

Port Cooper. See LYTTELTON.

\ə\ **abut** \ᵊ\ **matches** \ᵊ\ kitten, Fr table \ər\ **further** \a\ **ash** \ā\ **ace** \ä\ cot, cart \á\ Fr bac \au̇\ **out** \b̲\ Span Avila \ch\ **chin** \e\ **bet** \ē\ **easy** \g\ **go** \i\ **hit** \ī\ **ice** \j\ **job** \k̲\ Ger **ich**, **Buch** \ⁿ\ Fr vin \ŋ\ **sing** \ō\ **go** \ȯ\ **all** \ȯ\ **law** \œ\ Fr **bœuf** \œ̄\ Fr **feu** \ȯi\ **boy** \th\ **thin** \t͟h\ **this** \ü\ **loot** \u̇\ **foot** \ue\ Ger **füllen** \ue̅\ Fr **rue** \y\ **yet** \ʸ\ Fr digne \ˈdēnʸ\, nuit \ˈnwʸē\ \yü\ **few** \yu̇\ **fury** \zh\ **vision**

Port Co·quit·lam \kō-ˈkwit-ləm\. City, SW British Columbia, Canada, just N of the Fraser River 15 mi. (24 km.) E of Vancouver; pop. (1991c) 36,773.

Port Cred·it \ˈkre-dət\. Community, Peel munic. region, SE Ontario, Canada, on Lake Ontario 13 mi. (21 km.) WSW of Toronto.

Port Cros \pȯr-ˈkrō\. One of the Hyères Is. (*q.v.*).

Port–Cros National Park. National park, S France; 58 sq. mi. (150 sq. km.); estab. 1963.

Port Cyg·net \ˈsig-nət\. Town, S Tasmania, Australia, on coast near mouth of Huon River 25 mi. (40 km.) S of Hobart; pop. (1991c) 3114.

Port Darwin. See DARWIN.

Port–de–France. See NOUMÉA.

Port–de–Paix \ˌpȯr-də-ˈpā\. Seaport, NW Haiti, 35 mi. (56 km.) N of Gonaïves and opp. Tortuga I.; pop. (1982p) 17,633.

Port De·pos·it \di-ˈpä-zət\. Town, Cecil co., NE corner of Maryland, on the Susquehanna at a place where the riverbanks are 200-foot (61-meter) cliffs; pop. (1990c) 685.

Port–des–Galets. See LE PORT.

Port Dick·son \ˈdik-sən\. Seaport, SW coast of Negeri Sembilan state, Malaysia; pop. (1980c) 85,552; terminus of railroad branch line from Seremban; shipping point; health resort.

Port Durnford. See BUR GAVO.

Port Eads \ˈēdz\. Locality, Plaquemines parish, extreme SE Louisiana, at mouth of middle course of Mississippi River in the delta.

Port Eliz·a·beth \i-ˈli-zə-bəth\. Town, Eastern Cape prov., S Rep. of South Africa, on W side of Algoa Bay ab. 410 mi. (660 km.) E of Cape Town; pop. (1985c) 272,844; one of the republic's major seaports, shipping citrus fruit and mineral ores; center of automobile industry; notable seaside resort; Univ. of Port Elizabeth (1964). British fort built nearby 1799; founded 1820; developed after completion of Kimberley railroad 1873.

Port El·len \ˈe-lən\. Seaport village, S coast of Islay I., Inner Hebrides, Strathclyde region, W Scotland; pop. (1981p) 1021.

Portenau. See PORDENONE.

Port–en–Bes·sin \ˌpȯr-äⁿ-be-ˈseⁿ\. Village, Calvados dept., Normandy, NW France, ab. 5 mi. (8 km.) N of Bayeux on shore of Bay of the Seine.

Por·ter \ˈpōr-tər\. **1.** County in NW Indiana. See table at INDIANA.
2. Town, Porter co., NW Indiana, NNW of Valparaiso; pop. (1990c) 3118.

Porter Mountain. Peak in the Adirondack Mts., Essex co., NE New York; 4070 ft. (1241 m.).

Por·ter·ville \ˈpōr-tər-ˌvil\. City, Tulare co., S cen. California, 45 mi. (72 km.) N of Bakersfield; pop. (1990c) 29,563; Porterville Coll. (1927).

Port Es·sing·ton \ˈe-siŋ-tən\. Inlet of Arafura Sea, N coast of Coburg Penin., Northern Terr., Australia; lies within area set aside as a park.

Port–Étienne. See NOUADHIBOU.

Port Florence. See KISUMU.

Port Fos·ter \ˈfȯs-tər, ˈfäs-\. See SOUTH SHETLAND ISLANDS.

Port Francqui. See ILEBO.

Port Fu·ad \ˈfü-ˌäd\ *or Arab.* **Būr Fu'ād** \ˌbu̇r-fü-ˈäd\. Seaport, NE Egypt, at N end of Suez Canal opp. Port Said.

Port–Gen·til \ˌpȯr-zhäⁿ-ˈtē\. Town, W Gabon, 100 mi. (161 km.) SW of Libreville, at mouth of Ogooué River; pop. (1987e) 164,000; the nation's chief seaport; plywood; oil refining and shipment.

Port Gib·son \ˈgib-sən\. Town, ⊗ of Claiborne co., SW Mississippi, 28 mi. (45 km.) S of Vicksburg; pop. (1990c) 1810; scene of victory May 1, 1863 by Gen. Ulysses S. Grant over Confederates on his march to Vicksburg.

Port Glas·gow \ˈglas-kō, ˈglaz-, -gō\. Burgh, Strathclyde region, SW Scotland, on the Clyde; pop. (1981p) 21,554; a seaport with shipbuilding yards; adjoins Greenock.

Port Hack·ing \ˈha-kiŋ\. Inlet of South Pacific Ocean, New South Wales, SE Australia, just S of Botany Bay.

Port Hamilton. See KŎMUN-DO.

Port Har·court \ˈhär-kərt\. Seaport, ✱ of Rivers State, S Nigeria, on the Bonny River ab. 40 mi. (64 km.) from the sea; pop. (1991e) 361,800; railroad terminus; oil refining; ships palm products, coal, tin, and peanuts; produces cement and cigarettes; Univ. of Port Harcourt (1975; present status 1977), Rivers State Univ. of Science and Technology (1980); town laid out 1912; connected by rail 1916 to Enugu coalfields.

Porth·cawl \pōrth-ˈkȯl, pȯrth-\. Town, Mid Glamorgan co., S Wales; pop. (1981c) 15,625; seaside resort.

Port Hed·land \ˈhed-lənd\. Port, Western Australia, Australia, ab. 820 mi. (1320 km.) NNE of Perth; pop. (1991c) 12,599; mineral port, exporting esp. iron ore.

Porthmadog. See PORTMADOC.

Port Hood \ˈhu̇d\. Town, ⊗ of Inverness co., NE Nova Scotia, Canada, port on W coast of Cape Breton I.

Port Hope \ˈhōp\. Town, Northumberland co., SE Ontario, Canada, port on Lake Ontario 62 mi. (100 km.) ENE of Toronto; pop. (1991c) 11,505.

Port Hud·son \ˈhəd-sən\. Village, East Baton Rouge parish, Louisiana, on Mississippi River; besieged by Union forces under Gen. Nathaniel P. Banks for six weeks 1863; surrendered July 9, after fall of Vicksburg.

Port Hue·ne·me \wī-ˈnē-mē\ *also* **Hueneme.** City, Ventura co., S California, on Santa Barbara Channel ab. 40 mi. (64 km.) W of Los Angeles, near **Point Hueneme;** pop. (1990c) 20,319; naval facility since WWII.

Port Hu·ron \ˈhyu̇r-ən, -ˌän\. City, ⊗ of St. Clair co., SE Michigan, at Lake Huron end of St. Clair River; pop. (1990c) 33,694; paper, automobile parts, salt; summer resort; St. Clair Co. Community Coll. (1923). French fort built on site 1686; U.S. fort built 1814; incorp. as village 1849 and as city 1857; early home of inventor Thomas A. Edison.

Por·ti·ci \ˈpōr-tē-ˌchē\. Commune, Napoli prov., Campania, S Italy, on Bay of Naples 4 mi. (6 km.) ESE of Naples; pop. (1991p) 67,824; residential and resort suburb of Naples.

Porţile de Fier. See IRON GATE.

Portillo de los Patos. See LOS PATOS.

Por·ti·mão \ˌpōr-tē-ˈmau̇ⁿ\ *or* **Vi·la No·va de Portimão** \ˈvē-lə-ˈnō-və-dē-\. Commune, Faro dist., S Portugal, near Atlantic Ocean 24 mi. (39 km.) WNW of the commune of Faro; pop. (1991p) 16,967; fisheries; fish canneries, esp. for tuna, sardines.

Port Is·a·bel \ˈi-zə-ˌbel\. City, Cameron co., S Texas, on Gulf of Mexico 20 mi. (32 km.) ENE of Brownsville; pop. (1990c) 4467.

Port Jack·son \ˈjak-sən\. Inlet of South Pacific Ocean, New South Wales, SE Australia, forming an exceptionally good natural harbor; city of Sydney is on its S shore and N suburbs of Sydney on its N shore; has width of about 1.5 mi. (2.4 km.) at its mouth; ab. 8 mi. (13 km.) long to the point where it merges with the mouth of the Parramatta River. Its shores are irregular, broken by steep points that enclose bays that form smaller harbors. Great bridge across the harbor opened 1932.

Port Jef·fer·son \ˈje-fər-sən\. Village, Suffolk co., SE New York, on Long Island, on Long Island Sound ab. 13 mi. (21 km.) N of Patchogue; pop. (1990c) 7455.

Port Jer·vis \ˈjər-vəs\. City and summer resort, Orange co., SE New York, on Delaware River 38 mi. (61 km.) W of Newburgh; pop. (1990c) 9060; settled c. 1698; incorp. 1907.

Port Judith. See NARRAGANSETT.

Port Ke·lang \kə-ˈläŋ\; *formerly* **Port Swet·ten·ham** \ˈswet-nəm, -əⁿ-əm\. Seaport town, W Selangor state, Malaysia, 27 mi. (43 km.) SW of Kuala Lumpur; pop. (1980c) 192,080; terminus of railroad line from Kuala Lumpur.

Port Ken·ne·dy \ˈke-nə-dē\. See THURSDAY ISLAND.

Port·land \ˈpōrt-lənd\. **1.** Town, N Middlesex co., S Connecticut, on Connecticut River NE of Middletown; pop. (1990c) 8418; boat repair and services; petroleum distribution; settled c. 1690; incorp. 1841.
2. City, ⊗ of Jay co., E Indiana, 26 mi. (42 km.) NE of Muncie; pop. (1990c) 6483; birthplace of inventor Elwood Haynes 1857.
3. Seaport city, ⊗ of Cumberland co., SW Maine, on Casco Bay; pop. (1990c) 64,358; commercial center of SW Maine; good harbor and major oil port; produces pulp and paper,

lumber, chemicals, machinery; fishing, shipbuilding, printing; Westbrook Coll. (1831), Univ. of Southern Maine (1878), Portland School of Art (1882); settled 1632; destroyed by Indians 1676 and 1690; bombarded by the British 1775; incorp. as town 1786; state ✻ 1820–32; incorp. as city 1832; destructive fire 1866. Birthplace of poet Henry Wadsworth Longfellow 1807.

4. Village, Ionia co., S cen. Michigan, 21 mi. (34 km.) NW of Lansing; pop. (1990c) 3889.

5. City and port, ⊗ of Multnomah co., NW Oregon, on Willamette River 10 mi. (16 km.) SE of its confluence with Columbia River; pop. (1990c) 437,319; largest city and principal port in the state; site of Fremont Bridge (steel arch; main span 1255 ft. or 366 m.; completed 1973) spanning Willamette River; exports lumber, aluminum, and wheat; produces chemicals, electronic components; shipyards, meatpacking plants. Lewis and Clark Coll. (1867), Univ. of Portland (1901), Reed Coll. (1909), Concordia Coll. (1905), Pacific Northwest Coll. of Art (1909), Multnomah School of the Bible (1936), Warner Pacific Coll. (1937), Portland State Univ. (1946), Judson Baptist Coll. (1956), Columbia Christian Coll. (1956), Portland Community Coll. (1961), Bassist Coll. (1963), Oregon Health Sciences Univ. (1974). Laid out 1844; incorp. 1851; developed as supply center for NW gold rushes in 2d half of 19th cent.

6. Town, Sumner co., N Tennessee, 33 mi. (53 km.) NE of Nashville; pop. (1990c) 5165.

7. City, Nueces and San Patricio cos., S Texas, on Corpus Christi Bay 12 mi. (19 km.) NE of Corpus Christi; pop. (1990c) 12,224.

8. Town, SW Victoria, SE Australia, on **Portland Bay** 185 mi. (298 km.) WSW of Melbourne; pop. (1991p) 10,136.

Portland, Cape. Cape on NE coast of Tasmania, Australia, on Banks Strait, 40°45′S, 147°57′E.

Portland, Isle of. See ISLE OF PORTLAND.

Portland Bay. See PORTLAND 8.

Portland Bight; *formerly* **Old Harbour Bay.** Gulf, SE coast of Jamaica, West Indies; several areas around the bight leased 1940 by Great Britain to the U.S. as naval and air bases.

Portland Bill. See ISLE OF PORTLAND.

Portland Canal. Narrow inlet bet. SE Alaska and W British Columbia, Canada, 55°N, 130°W; ab. 80 mi. (130 km.) long; inlet is very deep with steep sides and in some places mountains 5000 to 6000 ft. (1525 to 1830 m.) on both sides.

Portland Point. Cape projecting into the Caribbean Sea from S coast of Jamaica, on SW side of Portland Bight.

Port·laoigh·i·se \ˌpōrt-ˈlē-shə\ *or* **Port Laoi·se** \ˌpōrt-ˈlē-shə\ *or* **Mary·bor·ough** \ˈmar-ē-ˌbər-ə\. Town, ⊗ of co. Laoighis, cen. Ireland; pop. (1986c) 3773; remains of old castle.

Port La·vaca \lə-ˈva-kə\. City, ⊗ of Calhoun co., S Texas, 25 mi. (40 km.) SE of Victoria; pop. (1990c) 10,886; aluminum products; oil and gas wells.

Port Li·món. See PUERTO LIMÓN.

Port Lin·coln \ˈliŋ-kən\. Town, S South Australia, Australia, near mouth of Spencer Gulf on W side, 175 mi. (282 km.) W of Adelaide; pop. (1991c) 11,809; harbor.

Port Lo·ko \ˈlō-kō\. Town, NW Sierra Leone, 35 mi. (56 km.) NE of Freetown.

Port–Lou·is \pȯr-ˈlwē\. Seaport town, NW Grande-Terre I., French overseas dept. of Guadeloupe, West Indies.

Port Lou·is \ˈlü-əs, ˈlü-ē, lu̇-ˈē\. Seaport city, ✻ of Mauritius, in Indian Ocean E of Madagascar; pop. (1991e) 142,645; principal commercial center of the island, exports sugar; Univ. of Mauritius (1965); city founded by the French c. 1736.

Port Lyautey. See KENITRA.

Port Lyt·tel·ton \ˈlit-ᵊl-tən\. Inlet of South Pacific, E coast of South I., New Zealand; ab. 9 mi. (14 km.) long; forms harbor of Lyttelton, the shipping port of Christchurch to the N.

Port Mac·quar·ie \mə-ˈkwär-ē\. Town, E New South Wales, SE Australia, on Pacific Ocean at mouth of Hastings River 200 mi. (322 km.) NNW of Sydney; pop. (1991c) 26,798; port for dairying and agricultural region.

Port·mad·oc \pōrt-ˈma-dək\ *or* **Porth·mad·og** \pȯrth-ˈma-dȯg\. Town, Gwynedd co., NW Wales, on NE coast of Cardigan Bay; pop. (1981p) 3927; ships slate.

Port Madryn. See PUERTO MADRYN.

Port Mahon. See MAHÓN.

Port Ma·ria \mə-ˈrē-ə\. Seaport, N Jamaica, West Indies, 28 mi. (45 km.) NNW of Kingston; pop. (1991p) 7651.

Port Math·ur·in \ˈma-thə-rin\. Chief settlement of Rodriquez I. in the Indian Ocean.

Port Mel·bourne \ˈmel-bərn\. Town, S Victoria, SE Australia, SW suburb of Melbourne on Port Phillip Bay; pop. (1991c) 7496.

Port Mol·ler \ˈmä-lər\. Inlet and harbor, N coast of Alaska Penin., SW Alaska; an inlet of Bering Sea.

Port Moo·dy \ˈmü-dē\. City, SW British Columbia, Canada, at head of Burrard Inlet 12 mi. (19 km.) E of Vancouver; pop. (1991c) 17,712; resort.

Port Mores·by \ˈmōrz-bē\. Seaport, ✻ of Papua New Guinea, on SE coast of the Gulf of Papua; pop. (1990c) 193,242; large sheltered harbor; commercial center; university (1965). Harbor explored by British Capt. John Moresby 1873 and mission soon established; in WWII an Allied base.

Port Nech·es \ˈnā-chəz\. City, Jefferson co., SE Texas, near mouth of Neches River 13 mi. (21 km.) ESE of Beaumont; pop. (1990c) 12,974.

Port Nel·son \ˈnel-sən\. The mouth of the Nelson River, NE Manitoba, Canada; site of first post in Manitoba, estab. 1682 by Hudson's Bay Company.

Port·neuf \pȯr-ˈnœf\. County, S Quebec, Canada. See table at QUEBEC.

Port Nich·ol·son \ˈni-kəl-sən\ *also* **Wel·ling·ton Harbour** \ˈwe-liŋ-tən\. Harbor, SW extremity of North I., New Zealand, an inlet of Cook Strait; the city of Wellington is located on it.

Port Nol·loth \ˈnä-ləth\. Seaport town, Northern Cape prov., W Rep. of South Africa, on Atlantic Ocean 50 mi. (80 km.) SSE of mouth of Orange River; in barren country; diamonds found in vicinity.

Porto \ˈpōr-tü\. **1.** District of NW Portugal. See table at PORTUGAL.

2. *also* **Opor·to** \ō-ˈpȯr-tü\. Seaport city, its ✻, on right bank of Douro River 2 mi. (3.2 km.) from its mouth and 170 mi. (274 km.) NE of Lisbon; pop. (1991p) 310,600; its harbor is at Leixões; exports wine (port wine named after the city), cork, olives; fishing, manufacturing; restored 12th–14th cent. cathedral; medieval church; 18th cent. Torre dos Clérigos; several museums and other notable buildings; university (1911).

History: Roman town; held by Visigoths 540–716 and by Moors 716–997; an important city in its area to 12th cent.; established port-wine trade 1678; scene of British victory over French during Peninsular War 1809; besieged in civil conflict 1832–33. Birthplace of Henry the Navigator 1394.

Pôrto Ale·gre \ä-ˈlā-grē\. Seaport city, ✻ of Rio Grande do Sul state, S Brazil, on inlet at N end of Lagoa dos Patos; munic. pop. (1989e) 1,300,000; most important Brazilian commercial center S of São Paulo; exports rice, tobacco, grapes, meat, and hides; produces leather, lard, textiles, chemicals, beer, metal goods; shipyards, meatpacking plants; Federal Univ. (1934), Catholic Univ. (1948). Founded c. 1742 by immigrants from the Azores; became ✻ of state 1807; in 19th cent. received considerable German and Italian immigrant populations.

Porto Amélia. See PEMBA 2.

Porto Bardia. See BARDĪYAH.

Por·to·be·lo *also* **Por·to Bel·lo** \ˌpōr-tō-ˈbe-lō\ *or* **Puer·to Bel·lo** \ˌpwer-tō\. Seaport village on the Caribbean coast of Panama, 20 mi. (32 km.) NE of Colón; pop. (1990p) 3026; in banana-growing area; ruins of early Spanish settlement and fortifications. Harbor visited and named by Christopher Columbus 1502; town founded 1597; became thriving port for Spanish colonial trade; terminus at N end of Spanish causeway across isthmus. English mariner Sir Francis Drake died aboard ship off the town and was buried at sea 1596.

Porto d'Anzio. See ANZIO.

Porto Edda. See SARANDË 2.

Porto Em·pe·do·cle \ˈpōr-tō-em-ˈpe-dō-ˌklā\. Seaport commune, Agrigento prov., SW Sicily, Italy, on Mediterranean 4 mi. (6 km.) SW of the commune of Agrigento; pop. (1981p) 16,079.

Porto Farina. See GHĀR AL-MILḤ.

Por·to·fer·ra·io \ˌpōr-tō-fe-ˈrä-yō\. Seaport commune, Livorno prov., Tuscany, Italy, on N coast of Elba I. 48 mi. (77 km.) S of commune of Livorno; pop. (1981p) 10,755; chief port of Elba I. French Emperor Napoléon lived here while in exile 1814–15.

Por·to·fi·no \ˌpōr-tō-ˈfē-nō\. Commune, Genova prov., Liguria, NW Italy, on coast SSW of Rapallo; pop. (1991p) 605; tourist resort; fishing.

Port–of–Spain *or* **Port of Spain.** Seaport, ✻ of Trinidad and Tobago, and formerly ✻ of West Indies (Federation), in NW part of island of Trinidad on Gulf of Paria; pop. (1990c) 50,878; commercial center and a principal port and air transport center for the Caribbean; produces rum, beer, lumber, textiles; exports oil, sugar, citrus fruit, and asphalt.

Porto Grande. See MINDELO.

Por·to·gru·a·ro \ˌpōrt-ō-grü-ˈär-ō\. Commune, Venezia prov., Veneto, NE Italy, 34 mi. (55 km.) NE of Venice; pop. (1991p) 24,983; 14th cent. Gothic palace.

Por·to·la Valley \pòr-ˈtō-lə\. City, San Mateo co., W California, 19 mi. (31 km.) WNW of San Jose; pop. (1990c) 4194.

Porto–No·vo \ˌpōr-tō-ˈnō-vō\. **1.** Seaport town, ✻ of Benin, in SE part on coastal lagoon; pop. (1982e) 208,258; commercial center; probably founded 16th cent.; seat of small native kingdom; Portuguese established trading post 17th cent.; became center of slave trade; became French protectorate 1863 and ✻ of French West African colony of Dahomey 1904.

2. Seaport town, Tamil Nadu, SE India, 35 mi. (56 km.) S of Pondicherry. Site of British soldier Sir Eyre Coote's victory July 1781 over Indian ruler Hyder Ali, important to British expansion in S India.

Port Or·ange \ˈòr-inj, ˈär-, -ənj\. City, Volusia co., E Florida, on Atlantic coast 5 mi. (8 km.) SE of Daytona Beach; pop. (1990c) 35,317; grew rapidly in 1970s and 1980s.

Port Or·chard \ˈòr-chərd\. Town, ⊗ of Kitsap co., W Washington, on Puget Sound 15 mi. (24 km.) WSW of Seattle; pop. (1990c) 4984; resort; naval facility.

Porto Rico. See PUERTO RICO.

Porto San·to \ˌpōr-tō-ˈsän-tō\. One of the Madeira Is., 26 mi. (42 km.) NE of the island of Madeira; 7 mi. (11 km.) long; 17 sq. mi. (44 sq. km.); first island of the group to be sighted by Portuguese navigator João Gonçalves Zarco 1418.

Porto Tor·res \ˈpōr-tō-ˈtōr-res\; *anc.* **Tur·ris Lib·i·so·nis** \ˈtər-is-ˌli-bi-ˈsō-nis\. Seaport, Sassari prov., NW Sardinia, Italy; pop. (1991p) 21,173; Roman ruins, 12th cent. basilica.

Porto–Vec·chio \ˈpōr-tō-ˈvek-kyō\. Seaport, SE Corsica, France, on a very shallow inlet of the Tyrrhenian Sea; cork-oak forests and salt deposits nearby.

Pôr·to Vel·ho \ˈpōr-tü-ˈvel-yü\ *also* **Velho.** Town, ✻ of Rondônia, W Brazil, on the Madeira River; munic. pop. (1991p) 286,400; commercial center; rubber, lumber, and medicinal plants.

Por·to·vie·jo \ˌpōr-tō-ˈvyā-hō\ *also* **Puer·to·vie·jo** \ˌpwer-tō-ˈvyā-hō\. Town, ✻ of Manabí prov., W Ecuador, on E bank of **Portoviejo River** 90 mi. (145 km.) NW of Guayaquil; pop. (1990c) 132,937; technical university (1952); founded 1535 near coast; moved to present location 1628.

Port·pat·rick \pōrt-ˈpa-trik\. Village, Dumfries and Galloway region, SW Scotland; nearest port of Great Britain to Ireland.

Port Pat·te·son \ˈpa-tə-sən\. See VANUA LAVA.

Port Phil·lip Bay \ˈfī-ləp\ *also* **Port Phillip.** Harbor of Melbourne, S Victoria, SE Australia; 31 mi. (50 km.) long by 20 mi. (32 km.) wide; 800 sq. mi. (2072 sq. km.). First attempt at settlement by English on bay made in 1803.

Port Pir·ie \ˈpir-ē\. Seaport, S South Australia, Australia, on E side of Spencer Gulf at its N end, 125 mi. (201 km.) NNW of Adelaide; pop. (1991c) 14,398; ships lead, wheat; ore smelters; the principal outlet for the Broken Hill mines.

Port Ra·da·ma Bay \ˈra-də-ˌmä\. Inlet of Mozambique Channel, NW coast of Madagascar.

Port Ra·di·um \ˈrā-dē-əm\. Settlement on E shore of Great Bear Lake, NW cen. mainland part of Northwest Territories, Canada, just S of Arctic Circle; site of formerly important pitchblende mine.

Port Re·pub·lic \ri-ˈpə-blik\. Village, Rockingham co., NW Virginia, in Shenandoah Valley; site of Confederate victory June 9, 1862, bringing to a successful close Gen. Thomas "Stonewall" Jackson's Shenandoah Valley campaign.

Port Rex. See EAST LONDON.

Port Rich·mond \ˈrich-mənd\. Neighborhood on N shore of Staten I. (Richmond co.), New York City, across Kill Van Kull from Bayonne, New Jersey; a business center for the island.

Port Roy·al \ˈròi-əl\. **1.** Town on **Port Royal Island,** one of the Sea Is., in Beaufort co., S South Carolina; pop. (1990c) 2985; tourist resort; fisheries; colony of French Huguenots founded here by Jean Ribault 1562, but soon abandoned; area occupied by Spanish 16th–17th cents.; in early 19th cent. a prosperous cotton-growing center.

2. Town, Canada. See ANNAPOLIS ROYAL.

3. Fortified town at entrance to Kingston harbor, SE Jamaica, West Indies; notorious as base of buccaneering operations 17th cent.; destroyed by earthquakes 1692 and 1907; formerly a British naval station; use of dockyard leased to U.S. 1940.

Port Royal National Historic Park. Reservation, W Nova Scotia, Canada.

Port Royal Sound. Inlet of Atlantic Ocean bet. islands of St. Helena and Hilton Head off SE coast of South Carolina at entrance to Broad River.

Port·rush \pōrt-ˈrəsh\. Town, N coast of Coleraine dist., NE Northern Ireland; pop. (1981c) 5114; seaside resort and seaport; nearby is Giant's Causeway (*q.v.*).

Port Said \ˈsīd, sä-ˈēd\ *or Arab.* **Būr Saʻīd** \ˈbür-sä-ˈēd\. Seaport city, constituting the Port Said governorate, NE Egypt, on the Mediterranean Sea at N end of the Suez Canal, on a narrow sand strip bet. Mediterranean Sea and Lake Manzala; exports rice, cotton, salt. Founded 1859 and formerly the most important coaling station in the world; landing point of French and British troops Nov. 1956 in intervention caused by Egyptian nationalization of Suez Canal; harbor closed 1967–75 after six-day Arab-Israeli War; city revitalized after 1975. See table at EGYPT.

Port Saint Joe \ˈjō\. City, Gulf co., NW Florida, 75 mi. (121 km.) SW of Tallahassee on St. Joseph Bay; pop. (1990c) 4044.

Port Saint Johns \ˈjänz\ *or* **Umzi·mvu·bu** \ˌùm-zēm-ˈvü-bü\. Seaport town, Eastern Cape prov., Rep. of South Africa, at mouth of Mzimbuvu River.

Port Saint Lu·cie \ˈlü-sē\. City, St. Lucie co., E Florida, S of Fort Pierce; pop. (1990c) 55,866; pop. more than tripled in 1980s.

Port Sand·wich \ˈsand-wich\. Port, Vanuatu. See MALEKULA.

Port·sea \ˈpōrt-sē\. **1.** Island off S coast of Hampshire, S England; 4 mi. (6 km.) long and 2.5 to 3 mi. (4 to 5 km.) wide; site of the city of Portsmouth.

2. Ward of Portsmouth, Hampshire, S England; Portsmouth dockyards and naval station.

Port Shep·stone \ˈshep-stən\. Town at mouth of Mzimkulu River, S KwaZulu-Natal prov., E Rep. of South Africa, 72 mi. (116 km.) SSW of Durban.

Port Simp·son \ˈsimp-sən\. Indian reserve, W British Columbia, Canada, on coast 25 mi. (40 km.) N of Prince Rupert and on S side of entrance to Portland Canal; pop. (1991c) 785.

Ports·lade by Sea \ˈpōrt-ˌslād\. Town, East Sussex, S England, near Brighton; pop. (1981p) 18,128; manufacturing center; Roman and Anglo-Saxon remains nearby.

Ports·mouth \ˈpōrt-sməth\. **1.** Seaport city and port of entry, Rockingham co., SE New Hampshire, on Atlantic Ocean at mouth of Piscataqua River; pop. (1990c) 25,925; tourism; financial services; Portsmouth Naval Shipyard estab. 1800 on Seavy's I. (part of Kittery, Maine) principally noted for construction and repair of submarines. Settled 1623; ❋ of provincial government 1679–1775 and ❋ of state until 1808; incorp. as city 1849; shipyard was site of the signing of the peace treaty ending the Russo-Japanese War 1905.

2. City, ⊗ of Scioto co., S Ohio, on Ohio River at mouth of Scioto River; pop. (1990c) 22,676; chemicals, plastics, footwear; prehistoric Indian mounds and earthworks nearby; Shawnee State Univ. (1975); city founded 1803.

3. Town, Newport co., SE Rhode Island, on N end of Rhode Island (island) and on the Sakonnet River 8 mi. (13 km.) NNE of Newport; pop. (1990c) 16,857; settled 1638; scene of battle of Rhode Island 1778 in American Revolution.

4. Seaport city, SE Virginia, on Elizabeth River opp. Norfolk; 18 sq. mi. (47 sq. km.); pop. (1990c) 103,907; politically independent; with Norfolk and Newport News comprises Port of Hampton Roads; transportation center; manufactures chemicals, fertilizer; shipyards, railroad shops; Tidewater Community Coll. (1968). City laid out 1750; suffered from yellow-fever epidemic 1855; incorp. as city 1858; U.S. Navy Yard evacuated and burned by Union troops in Civil War 1861 but recaptured 1862.

5. Seaport, Hampshire, S England, on island of Portsea in English Channel 65 mi. (105 km.) SW of London; pop. (1991p) 174,700; major naval base; shipyards; cathedral (dates from 12th cent.); is noted seaside resort. Founded and received first charter 1194; naval dockyard estab. 1496; became city 1926; suffered extensive damage from German bombing in WWII. Birthplace of author Charles Dickens 1812.

6. Seaport on NW coast of Dominica, Windward Is., West Indies.

Portsmouth Island. Island off cen. North Carolina coast, bet. S Pamlico Sound and Atlantic Ocean; 7 sq. mi. (18 sq. km.).

Port Stan·ley \ˈstan-lē\. **1.** Village, Elgin co., SE Ontario, Canada, on Lake Erie 8 mi. (13 km.) S of St. Thomas; pop. (1991c) 2223; serves as port for St. Thomas and London (Ontario).

2. Town, Falkland Is. See STANLEY 6.

3. Port, Vanuatu. See MALEKULA.

Port Ste·phens \ˈstē-vənz\. Good harbor on E coast of New South Wales, SE Australia, ab. 90 mi. (145 km.) NE of Sydney; pop. (1991c) 43,735.

Port Sual. See SUAL.

Port Su·dan \sü-ˈdan, -ˈdän\. City, NE Sudan, ab. 400 mi. (645 km.) NE of Khartoum; pop. (1983c) 206,727; principal port of Sudan, exporting hides and skins, gum, cotton, and oilseeds; terminus of railroad line from the Nile Valley; founded 1906.

Port Sul·phur \ˈsəl-fər\. Unincorporated settlement, Palquemines parish, SE Louisiana, on Mississippi River 20 mi. (32 km.) SE of New Orleans; pop. (1990c) 3523.

Port Sun·light \ˈsən-ˌlīt\. Town, Merseyside co., NW England, on S bank of the Mersey near Liverpool; founded as a model industrial town 1888 by William Hesketh Lever, viscount Leverhulme, chairman of Lever Bros. Ltd., soap manufacturers.

Port Su·san \ˈsüz-ᵊn\. Inlet in upper Puget Sound, NW Washington, bet. Camano I. and Snohomish co.

Port Swettenham. See PORT KELANG.

Port Tal·bot \ˈtȯl-bət, ˈtal-\. Port, West Glamorgan co., SE Wales; pop. (1991p) 49,900; ships metal goods; large ironworks.

Port Tau·fiq \tau̇-ˈfēk\ *or Arab.* **Būr Taw·fīq** \ˈbür-tau̇-ˈfēk\. Town, port of Suez, Egypt, at S end of Suez Canal at head of Gulf of Suez; railroad terminus.

Port Town·send \ˈtau̇n-zənd\. City and port of entry, ⊗ of Jefferson co., W Washington, on W side of entrance to Puget Sound 30 mi. (48 km.) WNW of Everett; pop. (1990c) 7001; settled 1851; incorp. as city 1860; in late 19th cent. a major lumber port.

Por·tu·gal \ˈpōr-chi-gəl, ˌpür-tü-ˈgäl\; *anc.* **Lu·si·ta·nia** \ˌlü-sə-ˈtā-nē-ə, -nyə\. Republic, occupying W section of the Iberian Penin., bounded on N and E by Spain, and on S and W by the Atlantic Ocean; 35,383 sq. mi. (91,642 sq. km.); pop.

(1992e) 10,429,000; ✻ Lisbon; includes the Azores and Madeira Is.

Physical features: Its 500-mile (805-kilometer) coastline affords good harbors only at the mouths of the principal rivers: the Tagus in cen. part, the Guadiana in S flowing into Gulf of Cádiz, the Douro and the Minho in the N; each of these rises in Spain, forms in part of its course a portion of the Portugal-Spain boundary, and flows through narrow gorges and restricted valleys; there are no inland lakes but there are lagoons at Aveiro and at Lisbon at the mouth of the Tagus. Mountains are parts of the E to W ranges of the Iberian Penin.: the highest, the Serra da Estrela 6532 ft. (1991 m.), the W extension of the Sierra de Guadarrama; the mountains in the N, a SW extension of the Cantabrian Mts.; and those in the S, a SW extension of the Guadalupe Mts.

Chief products: Wheat, corn, olives, potatoes, wines; fishing; cork; iron ore, tungsten; manufacturing: textiles, iron and steel, chemicals; tourism.

Chief cities: Lisbon, Porto, Amadora.

Political divisions: Divided into the following 18 districts and 2 autonomous regions (for pronunciation of their names, see their individual entries):

NAME	AREA (sq. mi.)	AREA (sq. km.)	POP. (1992e)	CAPITAL
Districts				
Aveiro	1,046	2,709	657,600	Aveiro
Beja	3,954	10,241	166,300	Beja
Braga	1,054	2,730	748,300	Braga
Bragança	2,527	6,545	156,500	Bragança
Castelo Branco	2,588	6,703	213,300	Castelo Branco
Coimbra	1,527	3,955	426,400	Coimbra
Évora	2,855	7,394	172,900	Évora
Faro	1,958	5,071	340,600	Faro
Guarda	2,122	5,496	186,400	Guarda
Leiria	1,357	3,515	427,700	Leiria
Lisboa	1,066	2,761	2,062,300	Lisbon
Portalegre	2,274	5,890	133,400	Portalegre
Porto	881	2,282	1,626,200	Porto
Santarém	2,583	6,690	441,100	Santarém
Setúbal	1,989	5,152	715,300	Setúbal
Viana do Castelo	814	2,108	247,800	Viana do Castelo
Vila Real	1,637	4,240	235,300	Vila Real
Viseu	1,938	5,019	399,100	Viseu
Autonomous Regions				
Azores	905	2,344	236,500	Ponta Delgada
Madeira	308	798	253,000	Funchal

History: Inhabited in ancient times by Lusitanians who were subjugated by Rome from 2d cent. B.C.; conquered by Visigoths in 5th cent. A.D. and invaded by Moors 711; N portion of country restored to Christianity by 11th cent.; county of Portugal granted to Henry of Burgundy by king of Leon and Castile c. 1095; became independent kingdom under Afonso I (1140–85); expanded its territory southward, expelling Moors from Algarve in S in mid-13th cent.; after 1385, ruled by Aviz dynasty under whom it came to flourish as maritime and colonial power; in 15th and 16th cents., Portuguese opened African coast, found Cape route to Indies, colonized Brazil, and secured trade monopoly in India and East Indies; Lisbon (*q.v.*) became European trading center; Spanish dependency 1580–1640; lost much of empire to the Dutch and English in 17th and 18th cents.; made trade agreement with Great Britain 1703; occupied by French 1807–11; its revolt 1820 inaugurated unsettled period during which it lost Brazil; proclaimed republic 1910; in war against Germany 1916–18; dictatorship set up following military coup 1926; new corporative constitution adopted 1933; neutral in WWII but friendly to Allies; became a member of NATO 1949, of the UN 1955; Portuguese possessions in India annexed by India 1961; 1960s marked by anti-Portuguese guerrilla activity in its African possessions; dictatorship overturned by anticolonialist military 1974; Cape Verde Is., East Timor (formerly Portuguese Timor) and African possessions (Angola, Guinea-Bissau, and Mozambique) granted independence 1974–75; new constitutions adopted 1976 and 1982; joined European Economic Community Jan. 1, 1986.

Por·tu·ga·le·te \ˌpōr-tü-gä-ˈlā-tā\. Commune, Vizcaya prov., N Spain, on Bay of Biscay 5 mi. (8 km.) NW of Bilbao; pop. (1991c) 55,823.

Por·tu·gue·sa \ˌpōr-tü-ˈgā-sä\. **1.** River, W Venezuela; flows SE to join the Apure River 5 mi. (8 km.) above San Fernando; ab. 240 mi. (385 km.) long.

2. State of W cen. Venezuela. See table at VENEZUELA.

Por·tu·guese Con·go \ˈpōr-chi-gēz-ˈkäŋ-gō\. A former name of Cabinda (*q.v.*) exclave of Angola, N of the mouth of the Congo.

Portuguese East Africa. Region formerly incl. most of the E coast of Africa. See MOZAMBIQUE 1.

Portuguese Guinea. See GUINEA–BISSAU.

Portuguese India. Name formerly applied to the possessions of Portugal on the W coast of India; 3814 sq. mi. (9878 sq. km.); ✻ Pangim (Panaji), in Goa; annexed 1961 by India and now the union terr. of Daman and Diu and the state of Goa.

Portuguese Ny·as·a·land \nī-ˈa-sə-ˌland, nē-\. Former name of N part of Mozambique.

Portuguese Timor. See EAST TIMOR.

Portuguese West Africa. See ANGOLA 1.

Portus Gaditanus. See PUERTO REAL.

Portus Iulius. See AVERNUS, LAKE.

Portus Lemanis. See LYMPNE.

Portus Magnus. See ALMERÍA 2.

Portus Magonis. See MAHÓN.

Port–Vi·la \ˌpȯr-vē-ˈlä, ˈvē-lä\ *or* **Vila** \vē-ˈlä, ˈvē-lä\. Seaport, ✻ of Vanuatu, SW Efate I., SW Pacific Ocean; pop. (1991e) 18,905.

Port Vue \ˈvyü\. Borough, Allegheny co., SW Pennsylvania, 10 mi. (16 km.) SE of Pittsburgh; pop. (1990c) 4641.

Port Wash·ing·ton \ˈwȯ-shiŋ-tən, ˈwä-\. **1.** Unincorporated settlement, Nassau co., SE New York, on Long Island, on hill overlooking Manhasset Bay, Long Island Sound ab. 6 mi. (10 km.) NW of Mineola; pop. (1990c) 15,387; resort and yachting center.

2. City, ⊗ of Ozaukee co., E Wisconsin, on Lake Michigan 25 mi. (40 km.) N of Milwaukee; pop. (1990c) 9338.

Port Washington North. Village, Nassau co., SE New York; pop. (1990c) 2736.

Port Weld \ˈweld\. Seaport, NW Perak state, Malaysia.

Port Went·worth \ˈwent-ˌwərth\. City, Chatham co., SE Georgia, 5 mi. (8 km.) N of Savannah; pop. (1990c) 4012.

Porvenir, El. See EL PORVENIR.

Por·voo \ˈpȯr-ˌvȯ\ *or Swed.* **Bor·gå** \ˈbȯr-ˌgō\. Seaport, Uusimaa prov., S Finland, E of Helsinki on the Gulf of Finland; pop. (1989c) 20,287; exports lumber; publishing; 15th cent. cathedral. Founded 1346; place where Finnish diet took oath of allegiance 1809 to Alexander I of Russia; home of the national poet Johan Ludvig Runeberg.

Porz am Rhein \ˈpȯrts-äm-ˈrīn\; *formerly* **Heu·mar** \ˈhȯi-ˌmär\. Commune, North Rhine-Westphalia, Germany, ESE suburb of Cologne on the Rhine.

Po·sa·das \pō-ˈsä-t͟häs\. Town, ✻ of Misiones prov., NE Argentina, on the Paraná River opp. the Paraguayan town of Encarnación; pop. (1991p) 219,824.

Poseidonia. See PAESTUM.

Po·sen \ *U.S.* ˈpō-zən, -sən; *Pol.* ˈpō-zən\. **1.** Village, Cook co., NE Illinois, 3 mi. (4.8 km.) S of Chicago; pop. (1990c) 4226.

2. Former province of Prussia (from 1793 to 1919); now part of W Poland.

3. City, Poland. See POZNAŃ.

Poset Bay *or* **Poseta Bay.** See POSYETA BAY.

Po·sey \ˈpō-zē\. County in SW corner of Indiana. See table at INDIANA.

Po–shan. See BOSHAN.

Posht·kūh \ˌpōsht-ˈkü\ *or* **Posht–e–Kūh** \ˌpōsh-tē-ˈkü\. Mountain range, W Iran, extending NW to SE along the boundary with Iraq; highest point 5092 ft. (1552 m.); source of a headstream of the Karkheh River.

Po·si·li·po \pō-ˈzē-lē-ˌpō\. Promontory, SW of Naples, Italy; pierced by the "Grotto," a tunnel 2264 ft. (690 m.) long, from 20 to 32 ft. (6 to 10 m.) wide, and from 23 to 71 ft. (7 to 22 m.) high.

Po·si·ta·no \ˌpō-zē-ˈtä-nō\. Town, Salerno prov., Campania, Italy, on N coast of Gulf of Salerno 6 mi. (10 km.) E of Sorrento; pop. (1981p) 3489; resort.

Posnania. See POZNAŃ.

Po·so \ˈpō-sō\. Town, N Sulawesi, Indonesia, on S coast of Gulf of Tomini and N of Lake Poso.

Poso, Lake. Lake, cen. Sulawesi, Indonesia; has been sounded to depth of 1000 ft. (305 m.).

Püss·neck \ˈpœs-ˌnek\. City, Thuringia, E cen. Germany, 33 mi. (53 km.) SE of Erfurt.

Possum Kingdom Dam. See MORRIS SHEPPARD DAM.

Post \ˈpōst\. City, ⊗ of Garza co., NW Texas, 40 mi. (64 km.) SSE of Lubbock; pop. (1990c) 3768.

Pos·toj·na \ˈpō-stȯi-nä\ *or Ital.* **Pos·tu·mia** \pō-ˈstü-myä\ *or Ger.* **Adels·berg** \ˈäd-ᵊls-ˌberk\. Commune, SW Slovenia, ENE of Trieste, Italy; in NE Italy 1919–47; stalactite caves nearby.

Pöstyén. See PIEŠŤANY.

Po·sye·ta Bay *or* **Po·se·ta Bay** \pə-ˈsye-tə\ *or* **Po·set Bay** \pə-ˈsyet\. Inlet of Sea of Japan, S tip of Primorskiy Kray, SE Russia in Asia, just SW of Peter the Great Bay.

Po·ta·ro \pō-ˈtär-ō\. River, cen. Guyana; flows E into Essequibo River; ab. 100 mi. (160 km.) long.

Po·ta·to Knob \pə-ˈtā-tō\. Peak, Yancey and Buncombe cos., W North Carolina; 6420 ft. (1957 m.).

Potch·ef·stroom \ˈpä-chəf-ˌstrüm\. Town, SE North West prov., NE Rep. of South Africa, 75 mi. (121 km.) SW of Johannesburg; pop. (1985c) 43,766; center of cattle-raising area. Founded 1838; first Boer settlement in Transvaal; ✻ until 1860; scene of capture of British forces by Boers 1880–81; occupied by British during Boer War 1900.

Po·teau \ˈpō-ˌtō\. **1.** River, E Oklahoma; flows N in Le Flore co. and empties into Arkansas River on the Arkansas border; ab. 90 mi. (145 km.) long.

2. City on Poteau River, ⊗ of Le Flore co., E Oklahoma, 9 mi. (14 km.) W of Arkansas border; pop. (1990c) 7210; Carl Albert State Coll. (1934).

Po·teet \pō-ˈtēt\. City, Atascosa co., S Texas, 29 mi. (47 km.) S of San Antonio; pop. (1990c) 3206.

Po·ten·za \pō-ˈtent-sä\. **1.** River, NE cen. Italy; flows ENE into Adriatic Sea 2.5 mi. (4 km.) ESE of Loreto; ab. 60 mi. (95 km.) long.

2. Province of Basilicata, Italy. See table at ITALY.

3. *anc.* **Po·ten·tia** \pə-ˈten-chē-ə\. Commune, ✻ of Basilicata, also ✻ of Potenza prov., S Italy, 84 mi. (135 km.) SE of Naples; pop. (1989c) 68,046; railroad junction in an agricultural area; ships fruit and vegetables; cathedral and three medieval churches. Roman city founded 2d cent. B.C.; in Middle Ages under a succession of feudal overlords; in 1860 was first town in S Italy to expel Bourbons.

Po·ter·la, Col·lado de la \kō-ˈlyä-t͟hō-ˌt͟hā-lä-pō-ˈter-lä\ *or Fr.* **Pas·sage de Ta·ra·die** \pä-ˈsäzh-də-tär-ə-ˈdē\; *formerly* **Col de Pour·ta·let** \ˈkȯl-də-ˌpür-tȧ-ˈlā\. Mountain pass in W Pyrenees on boundary bet. Spain and SW France, E of Col de Somport (*q.v.*); 5468 ft. (1667 m.).

Pot·gie·ters·rust \ˈpȯt-ˌk͟ē-tərz-ˌrəst\. Town, Northern prov., NE Rep. of South Africa, on branch of Limpopo River 125 mi. (201 km.) NNE of Pretoria.

Pothea. See KALYMNOS 2.

Potholes Reservoir. See MOSES LAKE 1.

Po·ti \ˈpȯ-tē\. Seaport town, W Republic of Georgia, on Black Sea at mouth of Rioni River, 40 mi. (64 km.) N of Rioni; pop. (1991e) 51,100; ships manganese; fishing fleet; on site of ancient **Phasis,** Greek colony estab. 6th cent. B.C.; modern town developed in 1880s with construction of artificial harbor and rail link to Trans-Caucasus R.R.

Pot·i·daea \ˌpä-tə-ˈdē-ə\. Ancient city of Macedonia, on the narrow isthmus joining Pallene Penin. to the Chalcidice mainland; its site is ab. 40 mi. (64 km.) SE of Thessoloníki. A Corinthian colony, founded c. 600 B.C.; resisted siege by Persian invaders 5th cent. B.C.; its revolt from Athens 432 B.C. was one of the causes of Peloponnesian War; taken by Athenians c. 430 B.C. after siege of two years; taken again by Philip II of Macedon 356 B.C. and destroyed; rebuilt early 4th cent. B.C. by Macedonian King Cassander as **Cas·san·dreia** \ˌka-ˌsan-ˈdrī-ə\, which became a prosperous city; finally destroyed by Huns in Middle Ages.

Pot Mountain \ˈpät\. Peak, E Clearwater co., NE Idaho; 7175 ft. (2187 m.).

Po·to·mac \pə-ˈtō-mək, -mik\. River, E U.S. in West Virginia, Virginia, and Maryland; formed by confluence of N branch (ab. 110 mi. or 175 km. long, flows NE from Tucker co., West Virginia, forms West Virginia-Maryland boundary) and S branch (ab. 140 mi. or 225 km. long, rises in Pendleton co., West Virginia) on N boundary of Hampshire co., NE West Virginia; flows E and SE to form West Virginia-Maryland and Virginia-Maryland boundaries and empties into Chesapeake Bay; 287 mi. (462 km.) long; navigable for large vessels to Washington, D.C.; above Washington are the Great Falls (*q.v.*).

Po·to·si \pə-ˈtō-sē\. City, ⊗ of Washington co., E Missouri, 58 mi. (93 km.) SW of St. Louis; pop. (1990c) 2683.

Po·to·sí \ˌpō-tō-ˈsē\. **1.** Department of SW Bolivia. See table at BOLIVIA.

2. City, its ✻, situated at base of the noted silver-producing Cerro Potosí ab. 50 mi. (80 km.) S of Sucre; pop. (1992p) 112,291; one of the highest cities in the world, at an alt. of over 13,700 ft. (4176 m.); a major industrial center, producing footwear, furniture, electrical equipment, and beverages; tin, lead, copper mines and refineries; university (1892). Founded 1545 after discovery of silver in neighboring mountain; at one time most populous city in Latin America; pop. declined drastically with slackening of silver production, but expanded 19th–20th cents. with the introduction of tin mining and other industries.

Potosi Mountain \pə-ˈtō-sē\. Peak in SW Clark co., SE Nevada; 8504 ft. (2592 m.).

Potosi Peak. Mountain, in Ouray co., SW Colorado; 13,790 ft. (4203 m.).

Po·to·tan \pō-ˈtō-tän\. Municipality, Iloilo prov., Panay, Philippines, near right bank of Jalaud River and on railroad line 17 mi. (27 km.) N of City of Iloilo; pop. (1980c) 44,624.

Pots·dam \ˈpäts-ˌdam\. **1.** Village, St. Lawrence co., N New York, 27 mi. (43 km.) E of Ogdensburg; pop. (1990c) 10,251; paper, dairy products; State Univ. of New York Coll. at Potsdam (1816), Clarkson Univ. (1896).

2. District, of former East Germany; now split bet. Brandenburg and Saxony-Anhalt.

3. City, ✻ of Brandenburg state, Germany and formerly of Potsdam dist., East Germany, on Havel River 17 mi. (27 km.) SW of Berlin; pop. (1992e) 139,025; railroad locomotives, textiles; several scientific and technical institutes; town hall (18th cent.); three large parks; museum.

History: First mentioned as Slav settlement 10th cent.; received munic. charter 14th cent.; became electoral residence of margrave of Brandenburg mid-17th cent. and chief residence of Hohenzollern kings of Prussia; town grew under Frederick the Great, who built the rococo Sans Souci Palace (1745–47); at the end of WWII site of conference of American, British, and Soviet leaders July 17–Aug. 2, 1945, at which the details of the intended administration of Germany were determined and at which lands of E Germany (E of Oder and Neisse rivers) were assigned to Poland.

Pot·ta·wat·o·mie \ˌpä-tə-ˈwä-tə-mē\. Name of counties in two states of the U.S. See tables at KANSAS and OKLAHOMA.

Pot·ta·wat·ta·mie \ˌpä-tə-ˈwä-tə-mē\. County in SW Iowa. See table at IOWA.

Pot·ter \ˈpä-tər\. Name of counties in three states of the U.S. See tables at PENNSYLVANIA, SOUTH DAKOTA, TEXAS.

Pot·ter·ies, The \ˈpä-tə-rēz\. District in Staffordshire, W cen. England, noted for its production of china and earthenware; comprises what is sometimes called the Five Towns (actually six): Stoke-on-Trent and the surrounding formerly separate towns of Burslem, Fenton, Hanley, Longton, and Tunstall;

setting of Arnold Bennett's trilogy of novels *Clayhanger* (1910), *Hilda Lessways* (1911), and *These Twain* (1916).

Pot·ters Bar \ˈpä-tərz\. Town, Hertfordshire, S England, 14 mi. (23 km.) NNW of London; pop. (1981p) 23,159.

Potts·town \ˈpäts-ˌtau̇n\. Borough, Montgomery co., SE Pennsylvania, on Schuylkill River 17 mi. (27 km.) ESE of Reading; pop. (1990c) 21,831; became important in metallurgical industry early 18th cent.; town laid out c. 1752; incorp. as borough 1815.

Potts·ville \ˈpäts-ˌvil\. City, ⊗ of Schuylkill co., E cen. Pennsylvania, on Schuylkill River 28 mi. (45 km.) NNW of Reading; pop. (1990c) 16,603; aluminum products, clothing, footwear; formerly significant anthracite coal mines. Permanently settled c. 1800; incorp. as borough 1828; in 1860s and 1870s a center of the activities of the Molly Maguires, a secret miners' society.

Pough·keep·sie \pə-ˈkip-sē, pō-\. City and river port, ⊗ of Dutchess co., SE New York, on E bank of Hudson River 65 mi. (105 km.) N of New York City; pop. (1990c) 28,844; railroad and highway bridges across the Hudson; computers, ball bearings, chemicals, medical equipment, fabricated rubber products; Vassar Coll. (1861), Marist Coll. (1929), Dutchess Community Coll. (1957). Settled by Dutch 1683; made temporary state ✻ 1777; incorp. as city 1854.

Pouls·bo \ˈpȯlz-bō\. City, Kitsap co., W cen. Washington, NW of Seattle; pop. (1990c) 4848.

Poult·ney \ˈpōlt-nē\. **1.** River, W Vermont; rises in N Rutland co., flows NW, W, and SW into S end of Lake Champlain, forming for a short distance the New York-Vermont state boundary; ab. 35 mi. (55 km.) long.

2. Village on Poultney River in the town of Poultney, Rutland co., W Vermont, 15 mi. (24 km.) WSW of the city of Rutland; pop. (1990c) 1731 (village), 3498 (town); Green Mountain Coll. (1834).

Poul·ton–le–Fylde \ˈpül-tən-lə-ˈfīld\. Town, Lancashire, NW England, 15 mi. (24 km.) NW of Preston; pop. (1981p) 17,608.

Pour·ri, Mont \ˌmōⁿ-pü-ˈrē\. Peak in the Graian Alps, E France; 12,405 ft. (3781 m.).

Pourtalet, Col de. See POTERLA, COLLADO DE LA.

Pou·so Ale·gre \ˈpō-zü-ə-ˈle-grē\. City, S Minas Gerais state, E Brazil, 180 mi. (290 km.) WNW of Rio de Janeiro; munic. pop. (1991p) 81,768.

Poŭthĭsăt. See PURSAT.

Po·vazs·ka By·stri·ca \ˈpȯ-väsh-kä-ˈbi-strēt-sä\. Town, W Slovakia, on the Váh River; pop. (1989c) 40,380.

Pov·er·ty Bay \ˈpä-vər-tē\. Inlet of Pacific Ocean, E coast of North I., New Zealand; the city of Gisborne is on it.

Poverty Point National Monument. See UNITED STATES, *National Monuments.*

Pó·voa de Var·zim \ˈpȯ-vwə-dē-vər-ˈzēm\. Commune, Porto dist., NW Portugal, on Atlantic Ocean 20 mi. (32 km.) NNW of the city of Porto; pop. (1990c) 23,729; seaside resort; birthplace of novelist José Maria Eça de Queirós 1845.

Po·way \ˈpō-wā\. City, San Diego co., SW California, bordering on the NE part of the city of San Diego; pop. (1990c) 43,516.

Pow·der \ˈpau̇-dər\. **1.** River, E Oregon; rises in S Baker co., flows N and then curves SE into Snake River on E cen. boundary of Baker co.; 150 mi. (241 km.) long.

2. River, N Wyoming and SE Montana; formed by confluence of forks in Johnson co., N Wyoming, flows N across Montana border into Yellowstone River in Prairie co., E Montana; 375 mi. (603 km.) long.

Powder River. **1.** Name of two rivers, United States. See POWDER.

2. County in SE Montana. See table at MONTANA.

Powder Springs. City, Cobb co., NW Georgia, 18 mi. (29 km.) WNW of Atlanta; pop. (1990c) 6893.

Pow·ell \ˈpau̇-əl\. **1.** River, NE Tennessee; rises in Wise co., SW Virginia, flows SW across Tennessee border and into Clinch River at Norris Dam; ab. 150 mi. (240 km.) long.

2. Name of counties in two states of the U.S. See tables at KENTUCKY and MONTANA.

3. City, Park co., NW Wyoming, 22 mi. (35 km.) NNE of Cody; pop. (1990c) 5292; Northwest Coll. (1946).

Powell, Lake. Artificial lake in Colorado River, S Utah and across border into N Arizona; 252 sq. mi. (653 sq. km.); alt. 3700 ft (1128 m.); created by Glen Canyon Dam.

Powell, Mount. Peak on border bet. Eagle and Summit cos., cen. Colorado; 13,534 ft. (4125 m.).

Powell River. **1.** River in Tennessee. See POWELL 1.

2. Town, S British Columbia, Canada, on Strait of Georgia 80 mi. (129 km.) NW of Vancouver; produces pulp and newsprint.

Pow·er \ˈpau̇-ər\. County in SE Idaho. See table at IDAHO.

Pow·e·shiek \ˈpau̇-ə-ˌshēk\. County in SE cen. Iowa. See table at IOWA.

Pow·ha·tan \ˌpau̇-ə-ˈtan\. **1.** County in E cen. Virginia. See table at VIRGINIA.

2. Village, its ⊗.

Pow·nal \ˈpau̇-nəl\. Town, Bennington co., SW Vermont, near Massachusetts and New York borders; pop. (1990c) 3485.

Pow·ys \ˈpō-əs\. **1.** Ancient Welsh kingdom, E Wales, roughly corresponding to former Montgomery co.

2. County, E Wales; includes former Brecknock, Montgomery, and Radnor cos. See table at WALES.

Po·yang Hu *or* **P'o–yang Hu** \ˈpō-ˈyäŋ-ˈhü\. Lake, N Jiangxi prov., SE China; 90 mi. (145 km.) long and 20 mi. (32 km.) wide; 1073 sq. mi. (2779 sq. km.); 2d largest lake in China; receives the Gan (the largest) and practically all other rivers of Jiangxi; its outlet is the Gan.

Poy·gan, Lake \ˈpȯi-gən\. Lake, W Winnebago co., E Wisconsin; extends W into Waushara co.; ab. 10 mi. (16 km.) long by 3 mi. (5 km.) wide; an expansion of Wolf River.

Po·ža·re·vac \pō-ˈzhär-ə-ˌväts\ *or Ger.* **Pas·sa·ro·witz** \pä-ˈsär-ə-ˌvits\. Town, Serbia, Yugoslavia, 35 mi. (56 km.) ESE of Belgrade, near the Morava River; scene of signing of treaty 1718 bet. Turkey, Austria, and Venice.

Po·za Ri·ca \ˌpō-sä-ˈrē-kä\ *or in full* **Poza Rica de Hi·dal·go** \-ˌt͟hā-ē-ˈt͟häl-gō\. Municipality, Veracruz state, Mexico, 120 mi. (193 km.) S of Tampico; munic. pop. (1990p) 151,201.

Požega. See SLAVONSKA POŽEGA.

Po·zières \ˌpȯ-ˈzyer\. Village, Somme dept., N France, NE of Albert near Bapaume; during WWI captured by Australians July 1916.

Poz·nań \ˈpȯz-ˌnän, -ˌnan\ *or Ger.* **Po·sen** \ˈpōz-ᵊn\ *also* **Pos·na·nia** \päz-ˈnā-nē-ə\. **1.** Province of W cen. Poland. See table at POLAND.

2. City, its ✻, on both banks of the Warta River 167 mi. (269 km.) W of Warsaw; pop. (1989e) 588,715; archiepiscopal see (primacy of Poland); center of metallurgical, chemical, textile, and food processing industries; Gothic-style cathedral; Renaissance town hall; numerous educational institutions.

History: One of the oldest cities in Poland, dating from 9th cent. A.D.; reached height of prosperity as important European trading center 15th–17th cents. but declined due to Great Northern War (1700–1721); to Prussia 1793; part of Grand Duchy of Warsaw 1807–15 and then reverted to Prussia; to Poland 1918; in WWII occupied by Germans 1939–45; suffered extensive damage but has been largely rebuilt; scene of riots June 1956 which led to changes in leadership of Communist party.

Po·zo·blan·co \pō-sō-ˈblaŋ-kō\. Commune, Córdoba prov., S Spain, 34 mi. (55 km.) N of the city of Córdoba; pop. (1991c) 15,363.

Po·zo Co·lo·ra·do \ˈpō-sō-ˌkō-lō-ˈrä-t͟hō\. Town, ✻ of Presidente Hayes dept., cen. Paraguay.

Pozsega. See SLAVONSKA POŽEGA.

Pozsony. See BRATISLAVA.

Poz·zal·lo \pȯt-ˈzä-lō\. Commune, Ragusa prov., SE Sicily, Italy, 15 mi. (24 km.) SSE of the commune of Ragusa; pop. (1981p) 14,755.

Poz·zuo·li \pȯt-ˈswȯ-lē\; *anc.* **Pu·te·o·li** \pyu̇-ˈtē-ə-ˌlī, pə-ˈtē-\ *or* **Di·cae·ar·chia** \ˌdī-kē-är-ˈkī-ə, -ˈkē-\. Commune, Napoli prov., Campania, S Italy, on **Bay of Pozzuoli** 6 mi. (10 km.) W of Naples; pop. (1989c) 76,121; machinery, cement; fishing, food processing; cathedral (incorporating parts of ancient Roman temple) and extensive Roman remains, incl. a semi-submerged market, baths, amphitheater, and necropolis with painted underground chambers. Founded 6th cent. B.C. by Greeks; became Roman colony 194 B.C.; important commercial center under Roman Empire; declined during Middle Ages due to local volcanic activity and barbarian invasions. Nearby is Lake Avernus, the legendary mouth of Hades.

Pra·chin Bu·ri *or* **Pra·chin·bu·ri** \ˈprä-ˌchin-bu̇-ˌrē\. Town, cen. Thailand, on railroad line 65 mi. (105 km.) ENE of Bangkok; pop. (1991e) 21,806.

Pra·chu·ap Khi·ri Khan *or* **Pra·chu·ab Gi·ri·khand** \ˈprä-chü-ˌäp-ˌkir-ē-ˈkän\. Town and seaport, S cen. Thailand, on W coast of Gulf of Thailand, E upper Malay Penin., 140 mi. (225 km.) SSW of Bangkok; pop. (1991e) 14,252.

Prác·ti·cos, Point \ˈpräk-tē-ˌkōs\. Cape on NE coast of Camagüey prov., E cen. Cuba.

Prades \ˈpräd\. Commune, Pyrénées-Orientales dept., S France, 25 mi. (40 km.) SW of Perpignan; 9th cent. abbey where annual music festivals founded 1950 by Spanish musician Pablo Casals are held.

Prae. See PHRAE.

Praeneste. See PALESTRINA.

Prae·nes·ti·na, Via \ˈvī-ə-ˌprē-nes-ˈtī-nə\. Ancient road, Italy, from Rome to Praeneste; ab. 23 mi. (37 km.) long.

Præstø \ˈpres-ˌtœ\. Town, Storstrøm co., S Sjælland I., Denmark, on **Præstø Fjord;** pop. (1981c) 6818.

Prague \ˈpräg\ *or Czech* **Pra·ha** \ˈprä-hä\ *or Ger.* **Prag** \ˈpräk\. City, ✱ of Czech Republic and formerly ✱ of Czechoslovakia, on both sides of the Vltava (Moldau) River; pop. (1989c) 1,214,772; major commercial and industrial center, producing aircraft, motor vehicles, machine tools, chemicals; food processing, printing, brewing; cathedral (begun 14th cent.); Romanesque basilica; Prague Castle (founded 9th cent., now presidential palace); neo-Renaissance national museum; several notable churches; Charles Univ. (1348) and several other educational institutions.

History: First historically recorded settlement on site in 9th cent. A.D.; by 14th cent. one of the leading cultural and trade centers of Central Europe; center of Hussite movement early 15th cent.; center of opposition to Hapsburgs early 17th cent. which led to Defenestration of Prague 1618, in which Hapsburg officials were thrown from windows of palace (one of the precipitating events of the Thirty Years' War); scene of victory of Prussians under Frederick the Great over the Austrians 1757; site of Congress of Prague 1813, in which allied powers failed to come to agreement with French Emperor Napoléon; scene of signing of peace treaty bet. Prussia and Austria 1866 ending Austro-Prussian (Seven Weeks') War. Became ✱ of independent Czechoslovakia 1918; under German occupation 1939–45; occupied by U.S.S.R. and other Warsaw Pact military forces Aug. 1968 in order to prevent Czech political liberalization; center of movement that led to peaceful overthrow of Czechoslovakia's Communist government 1989.

Prahoe. See PERAHU.

Pra·ho·va \ˈprä-hō-vä\. County of S cen. Romania. See table at ROMANIA.

Prah·ran \prə-ˈran\. City, S Victoria, SE Australia, SE suburb of Melbourne; pop. (1991c) 42,193.

Praia \ˈprī-ə\. Town, ✱ of Cape Verde Is., on São Tiago I.; pop. (1990p) 61,797.

Praia de Copacabana. See COPACABANA BEACH.

Prai·rie \ˈprer-ē\. Name of counties in two states of the U.S. See tables at ARKANSAS and MONTANA.

Prairie du Chien \ˌprer-ē-də-ˈshēn\. City, ⊗ of Crawford co., SW Wisconsin, on Mississippi River near its confluence with the Wisconsin River 53 mi. (85 km.) S of La Crosse; pop. (1990c) 5659. French trading post estab. 1673 and fort built 1685; settlement 1781 by French Canadians; site of American Fur Company post c. 1820; incorp. as city 1872.

Prairie Grove. City, Washington co., NW Arkansas, 10 mi. (16 km.) S of Fayetteville; pop. (1990c) 1761; scene of battle Dec. 7, 1862 in which Union troops under Gen. Francis J. Herron defeated Confederate forces of Gen. Thomas C. Hindman.

Prairie Provinces. Unofficial name for the Canadian provinces of Manitoba, Saskatchewan, and Alberta.

Prai·ries, Ri·vière des \rē-ˈvyer-dā-pre-ˈrē\. River, Canada, part of the course of the St. Lawrence River N of Montreal I., separating it from Jesus I., S Quebec; flows NE; ab. 28 mi. (45 km.) long.

Prairie View. City, Waller co., SE Texas, NW of Houston; pop. (1990c) 4004; Prairie View A&M Univ. (1876).

Prairie Village. City, Johnson co., NE Kansas, S of Kansas City; pop. (1990c) 23,186.

Pralls Island \prȯlz\. Uninhabited island in Arthur Kill off W shore of Staten I., New York City, New York; part of Richmond co.

Pram·ba·nan \präm-ˈbä-ˌnän\ *also* **Bram·ba·nan** \bräm-\. Town, S cen. Java, Indonesia, on Yogyakarta border and on railroad line ab. 12 mi. (19 km.) ENE of Yogyakarta; nearby are ruins of many Hindu temples (some restored), built 8th–10th cents.

Pran·hi·ta \ˈprä-ni-ˌtä\. River, E Maharashtra, cen. India; formed by confluence of Wainganga and Wardha rivers, flows S, forming part of boundary bet. Maharashtra and Andhra Pradesh, to Godavari River; ab. 80 mi. (130 km.) long.

Pras·lin \prä-ˈle^{n}\. See SEYCHELLES.

Pra·so·ne·si, Cape \ˌprä-sə-ˈnē-sē\ *or Gk.* **Cape Pra·so·ní·si** \ˌprä-sō-ˈnē-sē\ *or* **Cape Pras·so** \ˈprä-sō\. Cape at S extremity of the island of Rhodes, Greece.

Pra·tap·garh \prə-ˈtəp-ˌgär\. Town, S Rajasthan, India, ab. 78 mi. (126 km.) SE of Udaipur; pop. (1991p) 29,415; served as ✱ of former state of Partabgarh.

Pra·tas \ˈprä-təs\. Cluster of reefs and islets in South China Sea bet. Hong Kong and Luzon, Philippines, ab. 200 mi. (320 km.) SE of Hong Kong.

Pra·ter, Mount \ˈprā-tər\. Peak in the Sierra Nevada, E Fresno co., S cen. California; 13,501 ft. (4115 m.).

Prätigau. See PRÄTTIGAU.

Pra·to \ˈprä-tō\. Commune, Firenze prov., Tuscany, W Italy, 11 mi. (18 km.) NW of Florence; pop. (1989c) 165,888; woolens, weaving machinery, cement; 12th–15th cent. cathedral; 15th cent. church; 13th cent. castle; 14th cent. city walls. Became important wool-manufacturing center in Middle Ages; came under Florence c. 1350; sacked by Spanish 1512.

Pratt \ˈprat\. **1.** County in S cen. Kansas. See table at KANSAS.
2. City, its ⊗, 54 mi. (87 km.) WSW of Hutchinson; pop. (1990c) 6687; grain farms; Pratt Community Coll. (1938).

Prät·ti·gau *or* **Prä·ti·gau** \ˈprā-ti-ˌgau̇, ˈpre-\. Highland valley in N Graubünden canton, E Switzerland, NE of Chur.

Pratt·ville \ˈprat-ˌvil, -vəl\. City, ⊗ of Autauga co., cen. Alabama, 12 mi. (19 km.) NW of Montgomery; pop. (1990c) 19,587; settled 1816.

Prau. See PERAHU.

Prav·dinsk \ˈpräv-dēnsk\ *or Ger.* **Fried·land** \ˈfrēt-ˌlänt\. Town, Kaliningrad Oblast, W Russia in Europe, ab. 27 mi. (43 km.) SE of the city of Kaliningrad; formerly in East Prussia, Germany; battle June 14, 1807 in which the Russians under Gen. Leonty Bennigsen were defeated by French under Emperor Napoléon, who proceeded to occupy Königsberg (now Kaliningrad).

Pra·via \ˈprä-vē-ə\. Commune, Asturias prov., NW Spain, 19 mi. (31 km.) NW of Oviedo; pop. (1991c) 10,016.

Prebeza. See PREVEZA.

Pre·ble \ˈpre-bəl\. County in SW Ohio. See table at OHIO.

Prêcheur, Le. See LE PRÊCHEUR.

Pre·dap·pio \prē-ˈdä-pyō\. Village, Forlì prov., SE Emilia-Romagna, N Italy, ab. 10 mi. (16 km.) SSW of the commune of Forlì; pop. (1981p) 6205; birthplace of dictator Benito Mussolini 1883.

\ə\ abut \ˈə\ matches \$^{ə}$\ kitten, Fr table \ər\ further \a\ ash \ā\ ace \ä\ cot, cart \ȧ\ Fr bac \au̇\ out \b\ Span Avila \ch\ chin \e\ bet \ē\ easy \g\ go \i\ hit \ī\ ice \j\ job \k\ Ger ich, Buch \$^{n}$\ Fr vin \ŋ\ sing \ō\ go \ȯ\ all \ȯ\ law \œ\ Fr bœuf \œ̄\ Fr feu \ȯi\ boy \th\ thin \th\ this \ü\ loot \u̇\ foot \ue\ Ger füllen \ue̅\ Fr rue \y\ yet \$^{y}$\ Fr digne \ˈdēn^{y}\, nuit \ˈnw^{y}ē\ \yü\ few \yu̇\ fury \zh\ vision

Pre·daz·zo \ˌpre-ˈdät-sō\. Commune, Trento prov., S Trentino-Alto Adige, N Italy; in Dolomites on a tributary of the Adige SE of Bolzano; pop. (1981p) 4058.

Pre·deal Pass \ˌpre-dē-ˈäl\ *or Hung.* **Tö·mös Pass** \ˈtœ-ˌmœsh\. Chief pass in the Transylvanian Alps, Romania, 10 mi. (16 km.) S of Braşov; 45°28′N, 25°36′E; alt. 3445 ft. (1050 m.).

Predkavkaz'ye. See CISCAUCASIA.

Před·most \pər-ˈzhed-ˌmȯst\. Village, cen. E Czech Republic, near Přerov; site of extensive Paleolithic remains; excavations since 1880 have uncovered human burials, flint implements, ivory and bone carvings, mammoth remains.

Pre·gol·ya \ˌpre-ˈgōl-yə\ *or Ger.* **Pre·gel** \ˈprā-gəl\. Navigable river, W Russia in Europe; flows W through Kaliningrad Oblast into Vislinski Zaliv; ab. 80 mi. (130 km.) long; its main course assigned to U.S.S.R. by the Potsdam Conference 1945.

Prei·gnac \ˌpre-ˈnyäk\. Commune, Gironde dept., SW France; produces white wine (see SAUTERNES).

Premet. See PËRMET.

Pre·mont \ˈprē-ˌmänt\. City, Jim Wells co., S Texas, 20 mi. (32 km.) SW of Kingsville; pop. (1990c) 2914.

Pren·tiss \ˈpren-təs\. **1.** County in NE Mississippi. See table at MISSISSIPPI.

2. Town, ⊗ of Jefferson Davis co., S Mississippi; pop. (1990c) 1487.

Prenz·lau \ˈprents-ˌlau̇\. City, Brandenburg, NE Germany, 30 mi. (48 km.) SE of Neubrandenburg; pop. (1981c) 22,811; town walls (c. 13th cent.); several churches. Became city 1234; to Brandenburg 1250; scene of Prussian surrender to French 1806.

Prep·a·ris Channels \ˈpre-pə-rəs\. Passage in E Bay of Bengal, bet. Cape Negrais, Myanmar and the mouths of the Irrawaddy on the N and Great and Little Coco islands of the Andamans on the S; 140 mi. (225 km.) wide; the channel is divided in the center by the **Preparis Isles** into **Preparis North Channel** and **Preparis South Channel.**

Pře·rov \pər-ˈzher-ˌȯf\ *or Ger.* **Pre·rau** \ˈprā-ˌrau̇\. Town, cen. E Czech Republic, ab. 40 mi. (64 km.) NE of Brno; pop. (1989c) 51,922.

Pré–Saint–Gervais, Le. See LE PRÉ-SAINT-GERVAIS.

Pres·cot \ˈpres-kət\. Town, Merseyside, NW England, 7 mi. (11 km.) E of Liverpool; pop. (1981p) 10,992.

Pres·cott \ˈpres-kət, -ˌkät\. **1.** City, ⊗ of Yavapai co., cen. Arizona, 78 mi. (126 km.) NNW of Phoenix; pop. (1990c) 26,455; alt. 5347 ft. (1630 m.); health resort; trade center in agricultural and mining region; Prescott Coll. (1966); territorial ✱ 1864–67, and again 1877–89; annual "Frontier Days" rodeo 1888 ff.

2. Commercial city, ⊗ of Nevada co., SW Arkansas, 48 mi. (77 km.) NE of Texarkana; pop. (1990c) 3673.

3. City, Pierce co., W Wisconsin, at the point where the St. Croix River flows into the Mississippi; pop. (1990c) 3243.

4. Town, ⊗ of Grenville co., SE Ontario, Canada, on St. Lawrence River 50 mi. (80 km.) S of Ottawa; pop. (1991c) 4512; founded 1810.

Prescott and Rus·sell \ˈrə-səl\. County, Ontario, Canada. See table at ONTARIO.

Prescott Valley. Town, Yavapai co., cen. Arizona, NE of Prescott; pop. (1990c) 8858.

Pres·i·den·cy \ˈpre-zə-dən-sē, -ˌden-\. Former division in S Bengal prov., NE British India; 16,402 sq. mi. (42,481 sq. km.); ✱ Calcutta; in 1947 divided bet. newly established West Bengal state, India, and East Pakistan (now Bangladesh).

Pre·si·den·te Hayes \ˌprā-sē-ˈden-tā-ˈīs, -ˈhāz\. Department of W cen. Paraguay. See table at PARAGUAY.

Pre·si·den·te Pru·den·te \ˌprā-sē-ˈden-tā-prü-ˈden-tā\. City, SW São Paulo state, SE Brazil, on railroad line near Paraná River; munic. pop. (1991p) 165,447.

Presidente Vargas. See ITABIRA.

Pres·i·den·tial Range \ˌpre-zə-ˈden-chəl\. Range of the White Mts., chiefly in S Coos co., N New Hampshire, bet. Pinkham Notch on E and Crawford Notch on W; highest peak Mt. Washington 6288 ft. (1917 m.).

Pre·sid·io \prə-ˈsi-dē-ˌō\. County in W Texas. See table at TEXAS.

Pre·šov \ˈpre-ˌshau̇\. Town, cen. E Slovakia, 20 mi. (32 km.) N of Kosiče; pop. (1989c) 89,081; rail and road junction; textiles; distilling; first mentioned 13th cent.; partly destroyed by fire 1887.

Pres·pa, Lake \ˈpres-pə\ *or Serbo-Croat.* **Pres·pan·sko Je·ze·ro** \ˈpres-pən-ˌskō-ˈyez-ə-ˌrō\. Lake on the boundary bet. Republic of Macedonia, Albania, and Greece; 14 mi. (23 km.) long by 8 mi. (13 km.) wide; drains NW into Lake Ohrid through a subterranean channel. Near it is the smaller lake, **Mi·krí Prés·pa** \mē-ˈkrē-ˈpres-pä\.

Presque Isle. 1. \presk-ˈīl\. Peninsula, NW Pennsylvania, in Lake Erie, forming **Presque Isle Bay,** harbor of Erie; state park.

2. \presk-ˈēl\. County in NE Michigan. See table at MICHIGAN.

3. \presk-ˈīl\. City, Aroostook co., N Maine, 40 mi. (64 km.) N of Houlton; pop. (1990c) 10,550; potatoes; Univ. of Maine at Presque Isle (1903).

Press, Mount \ˈpres\. Mountain, Antarctica, 78°05′S, 85°58′W; 12,566 ft. (3830 m.).

Pressburg. See BRATISLAVA.

Pres·tat·yn \pres-ˈtat-ᵊn\. Resort town, Clwyd co., NE Wales; pop. (1981p) 16,439.

Pres·teigne \pres-ˈtēn\. Town, E Powys co., E Wales; pop. (1981p) 1517.

Pres·ton \ˈpres-tən\. **1.** County in N West Virginia. See table at WEST VIRGINIA.

2. Town, N cen. New London co., SE Connecticut, SE of Norwich; pop. (1990c) 5006.

3. City, ⊗ of Webster co., W Georgia; pop. (1990c) 388.

4. City, ⊗ of Franklin co., SE Idaho, 65 mi. (105 km.) SSE of Pocatello; pop. (1990c) 3710.

5. City, ⊗ of Fillmore co., SE Minnesota, 30 mi. (48 km.) SE of Rochester; pop. (1990c) 1530.

6. City, Victoria, Australia, a NNE suburb of Melbourne; pop. (1991c) 76,996.

7. Former town, Waterloo co., SE Ontario, Canada, on Grand River 8 mi. (13 km.) ESE of Kitchener; now merged with Galt and Hespeler to form Cambridge (*q.v.*).

8. Town, ⊗ of Lancashire, England, on the Ribble 30 mi. (48 km.) NNE of Liverpool; pop. (1991p) 126,200; port, market town, and industrial center, producing aircraft, motor vehicles, chemicals, plastics, textiles; received first charter 1179; important Royalist center during the English Civil War; made county borough (administrative county) 1889.

Pres·ton·pans \ˈpres-tən-ˌpanz\. Burgh, Lothian region, SE Scotland, 8 mi. (13 km.) E of Edinburgh; pop. (1981p) 7620; scene of a rout of troops under Sir John Cope by Prince Charles Edward Stuart (the Young Pretender) and his Highlanders Sept. 1745.

Pres·tons·burg \ˈpres-tənz-ˌbərg\. City, ⊗ of Floyd co., E Kentucky, 20 mi. (32 km.) NW of Pikeville; pop. (1990c) 3558.

Prest·wich \ˈprest-ˌwich\. Borough, Greater Manchester, NW England, 5 mi. (8 km.) NNW of Manchester; pop. (1981p) 31,198; residential; textile mills.

Prest·wick \ˈprest-ˌwik\. Burgh, Strathclyde region, SW Scotland, ab. 3 mi. (5 km.) N of Ayr; pop. (1981c) 13,600; tourist resort; noted golf course; international airport.

Pre·to·ria \pri-ˈtōr-ē-ə, -ˈtȯr-\. City, administrative ✱ of the Rep. of South Africa; in Gauteng prov., on small tributary of Limpopo River ab. 34 mi. (55 km.) N of Johannesburg; pop. (1985c) 443,059; formerly ✱ of Transvaal; iron and steel industry; Univ. of South Africa (1873), Univ. of Pretoria (1930).

History: Founded 1855 by Marthinus W. Pretorius, first president of South African Republic, and named after his father, the Boer Voortrekker leader Andries Pretorius. Chosen ✱ of South African Republic (Transvaal) 1860; in Boer War surrendered to British commander Lord (Frederick) Roberts June 1900; articles of peace ending war signed here May 31, 1902; made administrative seat of Union (now Republic) government 1910. Home and burial place of S. J. Paulus Kruger, president of South African Republic 1883–1900.

Pretoria–Wit·wa·ters·rand–Ver·een·ig·ing \-'wit-ˌwä-tərs-ˌränd-fər-'ā-nə-giŋ\. See *Gauteng* in table at SOUTH AFRICA, REPUBLIC OF.

Pret·ty·boy Dam \'prit-ē-ˌbȯi\. Dam across Gunpowder River, N Baltimore co., NE Maryland; height 153 ft. (47 m.); completed 1934; forms **Prettyboy Reservoir,** chief reserve for water supply of Baltimore.

Preussen. See PRUSSIA.

Preussisch Eylau. See BAGRATIONOVSK.

Preussisch–Stargard. See STAROGARD GDAŃSKI.

Pré·ve·za *also* **Pre·be·za** \'pre-ve-ˌzä\. **1.** Department of Epirus region, W Greece. See table at GREECE.
2. Seaport town, its ✻, at entrance to Amvrakikós Kólpos; pop. (1991p) 15,512; ships dairy products, olives, hides; founded 290 B.C.; for a while superseded by Nicopolis, the Roman town just to N of it; developed in Middle Ages; occupied by Venetians 1499; taken by French 1797; the following year taken by Ali Paşha for Turkey; recovered from Turks by Greeks 1912.

Prib·i·lof Islands \'pri-bə-ˌlȯf\ *also* **Fur Seal Islands** \'fər-'sēl\. Group of islands in SE Bering Sea, Alaska, ab. 180 mi. (290 km.) N of Unalaska; comprise St. Paul and St. George, and three islets. Islands are hilly with no harbors; noted as fur-seal grounds and habitat of blue and white foxes and breeding place of enormous numbers of birds. Visited annually by a high percentage of the fur seals of the world; commercial killing operations governed by convention signed by U.S., U.S.S.R., Japan, and Canada 1957. First visited 1786 by Russian explorer Gavril Pribylov; leased to commercial companies 1870 to 1910 whose methods nearly exterminated the seals; taken over by U.S. 1910.

Pří·bram \pər-'shē-bräm\. Town, W cen. Czech Republic, in mountainous region 33 mi. (53 km.) SW of Prague; pop. (1989c) 40,370; silver and gold mines several centuries old.

Price \'prīs\. **1.** River, E cen. Utah; flows through cen. Carbon and NE Emery cos. into Green River; in Carbon co., flows through a steep-walled canyon.
2. County in N Wisconsin. See table at WISCONSIN.
3. City, ⊗ of Carbon co., E cen. Utah, on Price River 62 mi. (100 km.) SE of Provo; pop. (1990c) 8712; coal mines; Coll. of Eastern Utah (1937).

Price Peak. Mountain in the Sierra Nevada, E Tuolumne co., cen. California; 10,716 ft. (3266 m.).

Prich·ard \'pri-chərd\. City, Mobile co., SW corner of Alabama, 3 mi. (5 km.) W of the city of Mobile; pop. (1990c) 34,311; cotton-processing and chemical industries; incorp. 1925.

Pri·e·go de Cór·do·ba \prē-'ā-gō-t͟hä-'kȯr-t͟hō-vä\. Commune, Córdoba prov., S Spain, 48 mi. (77 km.) SE of the city of Córdoba; pop. (1991c) 21,177; several baroque churches; Moorish castle.

Pri·e·ne \prī-'ē-nē\. Ancient Greek city in W Asia Minor, near the mouth of the Maeander River (*mod.* Menderes); site of archaeological excavations SW of present-day Söke, W Turkey in Asia. One of the 12 Ionian Cities, active in Ionian revolt; prosperous under Roman and Byzantine dominion; seized by Ottomans late in 13th cent.

Pries·ka \'prē-skə\. Town, cen. Northern Cape prov., S Rep. of South Africa, on Orange River 150 mi. (241 km.) WSW of Kimberley.

Priest Lake \'prēst\. Lake, N Bonner co., N Idaho; 24 mi. (39 km.) long by 14 mi. (23 km.) wide.

Prie·vid·za \'pre-vid-zä\. Town, W cen. Slovakia, ab. 80 mi. (130 km.) NE of Bratislava; pop. (1989c) 52,389.

Pri·lep \'prē-ˌlep\. City, S Republic of Macedonia, ab. 47 mi. (76 km.) S of Skopje; pop. (1991p) 98,327; 14th cent. monastery; important in Middle Ages; occupied by Bulgaria 1916–18; birthplace of Serbian hero Marko Kraljević c. 1335.

Pri·lu·ki \pri-'lü-kē\. Town, S Chernihiv subdivision, Ukraine, ab. 85 mi. (135 km.) E of Kiev; pop. (1991e) 73,000; dates from 11th cent.

Prime Me·rid·i·an \'prīm-mə-'ri-dē-ən\. The meridian of 0° long. which runs through the original site of the Royal Greenwich Observatory at Greenwich, England, and from which other longitudes are reckoned.

Pri·me·ro \prē-'mā-rō\. River, Córdoba prov., N cen. Argentina; flows NE into Mar Chiquita; ab. 130 mi. (210 km.) long.

Prim·ghar \'prim-ˌgär\. City, ⊗ of O'Brien co., NW Iowa; pop. (1990c) 950.

Pri·mor·je \'prē-mȯr-ˌyā\ *or* **Pri·mor·ska** \'prē-mȯr-ˌskä\. Former county, W Yugoslavia; 7476 sq. mi. (19,363 sq. km.); ⊗ Split; now chiefly in Croatia and Bosnia and Herzegovina.

Pri·morsk \prē-'mȯrsk\; *formerly* **Koi·vis·to** \'kȯi-vis-ˌtȯ\; *or earlier* **Björ·kö** \'byœr-ˌkœ\. Town, St. Petersburg Oblast, W Russia in Europe, formerly in SE Finland, opp. the island **Os·trov Bol'·shoy Be·re·zo·vyy** \'ȯs-trəf-bȯl-'shȯi-ˌbir-'yō-zə-vē\ (*formerly* **Koivisto Island**) at E end of Gulf of Finland; port of Vyborg (formerly Viipuri) ab. 20 mi. (32 km.) S of it on Karelian Isthmus. Scene of treaty signing July 1905 bet. William II of Germany and Nicholas II of Russia, in an unsuccessful attempt to form a coalition against Great Britain; in war bet. U.S.S.R. and Finland 1939–40 forts on island marked W end of Mannerheim Line; scene of severe fighting; captured by U.S.S.R. Mar. 1940.

Pri·mor·skiy Kray *or* **Pri·mor·ski Krai** \prē-'mȯr-skē-'krī\ *or* **Pri·mo·rye Territory** \prē-'mȯr-yə\ *or* **Mar·i·time Territory** \'mar-ə-ˌtīm\. Territory of SE Russia in Asia, 64,054 sq. mi. (165,900 sq. km.); pop. (1992e) 2,309,000; ✻ Vladivostok; at the extreme S along the Tumen River it touches North Korea, and along its entire coast stretch the Sikhote-Alin' Mts. At its S end on Peter the Great Bay is Vladivostok, the finest Russian seaport on the Pacific littoral; to the N along the valley of the Ussuri is rich agricultural country and timberland; coal, lead, zinc; fishing. Ussuriysk is an important industrial center. Formerly included in Maritime Prov. and in Far Eastern Region (*qq.v.*); made a territory 1938.

Prince \'prins\. County in W Prince Edward I., Canada. See table at PRINCE EDWARD ISLAND.

Prince Albert \'al-bərt\. City, S cen. Saskatchewan, Canada, on North Saskatchewan River 83 mi. (134 km.) NNE of Saskatoon; pop. (1991c) 34,181; resort; packing plants, oil refineries; founded 1866 as Presbyterian mission.

Prince Albert National Park. See CANADA, *National Parks.*

Prince Albert Peninsula. NW section of Victoria I., W Arctic Archipelago, Northwest Territories, Canada.

Prince Albert Sound. Inlet, W Victoria I., W Arctic Archipelago, Northwest Territories, Canada.

Prince Charles Foreland \'chärlz\. Island, Norway, W of Spitsbergen I., from which it is separated by **Foreland Sound;** 60 mi. (97 km.) long; area 241 sq. mi. (624 sq. km.); has high mountain peaks.

Prince Charles Island. Island of Arctic Archipelago, SE Nunavut, Canada, in Foxe Basin; 3639 sq. mi. (9425 sq. km.).

Prince Ed·ward \'ed-wərd\. **1.** County in S cen. Virginia. See table at VIRGINIA.
2. County in SE Ontario, Canada. See table at ONTARIO.

Prince Edward Island. Island in the Gulf of St. Lawrence, constituting a province of Canada; 2184 sq. mi. (5657 sq. km.); pop. (1991c) 129,765; ✻ Charlottetown. Separated from New Brunswick and Nova Scotia by Northumberland Strait, but connected to New Brunswick by Confederation Bridge (8 mi. or 13 km. long), opened 1997; very irregular in shape with many deep inlets. Highest point ab. 465 ft. (142 m.); livestock raising, fishing; vegetables; tourism.

Political divisions: Divided into the following three counties:

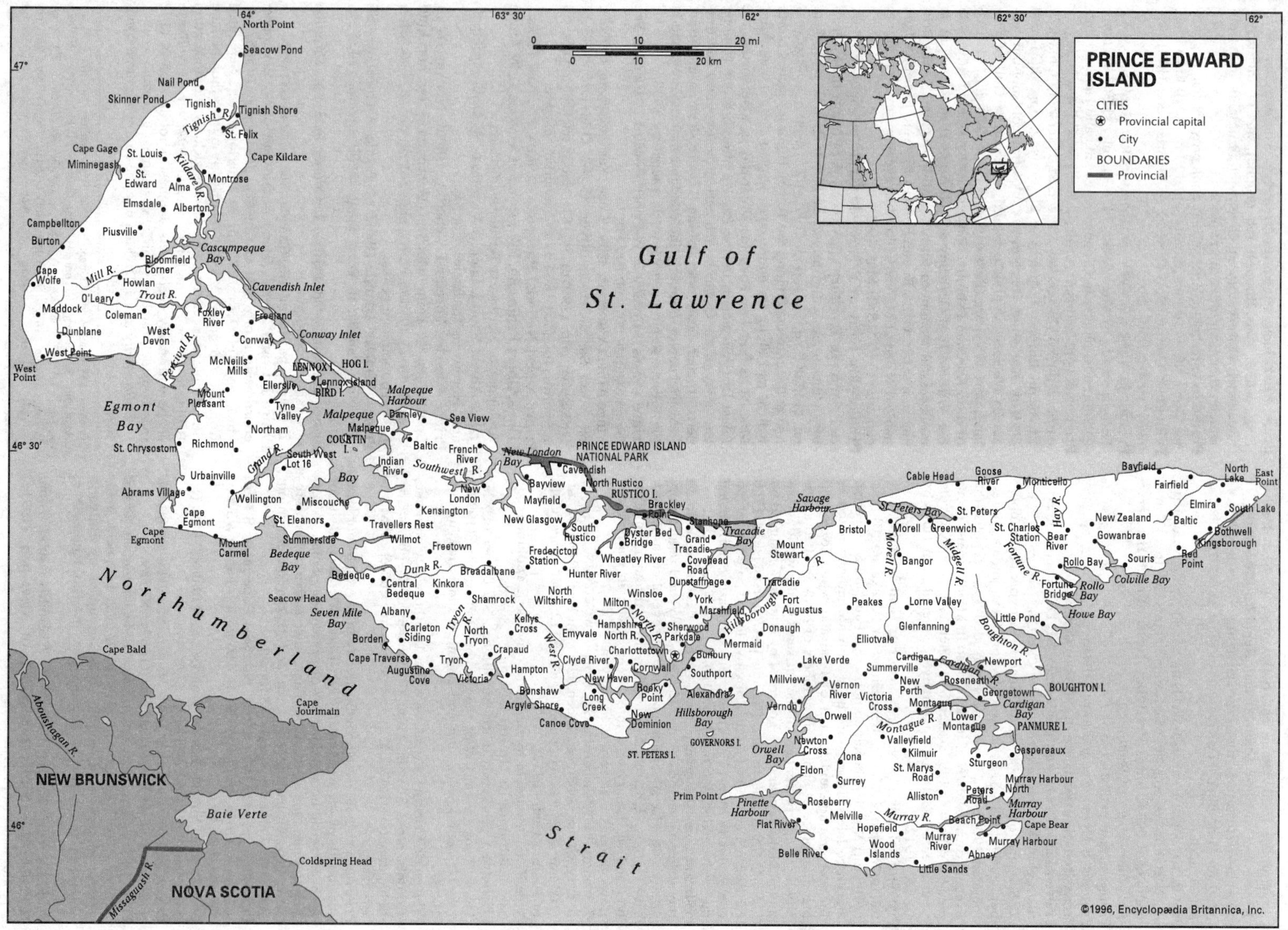
PRINCE EDWARD ISLAND
CITIES
Provincial capital
City
BOUNDARIES
Provincial
Gulf of St. Lawrence
Northumberland Strait
PRINCE EDWARD ISLAND NATIONAL PARK
NEW BRUNSWICK
NOVA SCOTIA
Egmont Bay
Malpeque Bay
Bedeque Bay
Seven Mile Bay
Hillsborough Bay
Orwell Bay
Pinette Harbour
Cardigan Bay
Murray Harbour
Rollo Bay
Colville Bay
Howe Bay
Savage Harbour
Tracadie Bay
St. Peters Bay
Cascumpeque Bay
Malpeque Harbour
New London Bay
Baie Verte
Conway Inlet
Cavendish Inlet
Charlottetown
Summerside
Souris
Georgetown
Montague
Kensington
Tignish
Alberton
O'Leary
North Point
West Point
East Point
Cape Egmont
Cape Traverse
Borden
Cavendish
North Rustico
Stanhope
Cornwall
Murray River
Wood Islands
Belle River
Flat River
Hillsborough R.
West R.
North R.
Dunk R.
Morell R.
Midgell R.
Fortune R.
Montague R.
Murray R.
Boughton R.
Kildare R.
Trout R.
Mill R.
Percival R.
Tryon R.
Hay R.
Southwest R.
Grand R.
Missaguash R.
Aboushagan R.
LENNOX I.
HOG I.
BIRD I.
COURTIN I.
RUSTICO I.
GOVERNORS I.
ST. PETERS I.
BOUGHTON I.
PANMURE I.
Cape Bald
Cape Jourimain
Coldspring Head
Prim Point
Seacow Head
0 10 20 mi
0 10 20 km
64°
63° 30'
62°
62° 30'
47°
46° 30'
46°
©1996, Encyclopædia Britannica, Inc.

NAME	AREA[1] (sq. mi.)	AREA[1] (sq. km.)	POP. (1991c)	CO. SEAT
Kings	641	1,660	19,328	Georgetown
Prince	778	2,015	43,241	Summerside
Queens	765	1,981	67,196	Charlottetown

[1]Area = land area.

History: Discovered by French explorer Jacques Cartier 1534; French explorer Samuel de Champlain called it **Île-St.-Jean** \\,ēl-sa^n-'zhä^n\\ *or Eng.* **Isle St. John** \\,īl-sānt-'jän, -sənt-\\; renamed 1799 after Edward, duke of Kent; colonized by French c. 1720; occupied by Great Britain 1758; annexed to Nova Scotia 1763 and became separate colony 1769; site of conference 1864 which prepared the way for formation of Canadian Confederation; settled by Scottish immigrants at beginning of 19th cent.; entered Confederation 1873.

Prince Edward Island National Park. See CANADA, *National Parks.*

Prince Edward Islands. Two uninhabited islands, S Indian Ocean, 46°35′S, 37°56′E; 1200 mi. (1931 km.) SE of Cape Town; belong to Rep. of South Africa.

Prince Fred·er·ick \\'fre-də-rik\\. Unincorporated settlement, ⊗ of Calvert co., S Maryland; pop. (1990c) 1885.

Prince George \\'jȯrj\\. **1.** County in SE Virginia. See table at VIRGINIA.
2. Village, its ⊗.
3. City, cen. British Columbia, Canada, at confluence of Fraser and Nechako rivers; pop. (1991c) 69,653; summer resort; lumber; diversified agriculture.

Prince Georg·es *or* **Prince Georg·e's** \\'jȯr-jəz\\. County in S cen. Maryland. See table at MARYLAND.

Prince Har·ald Coast \\'har-əld\\. Section of coast, East Antarctica, on Indian Ocean, ab. 69°31′S, 36°E; part of Queen Maud Land.

Prince Island. See PRÍNCIPE ISLAND.

Prince of Wales, Cape \\'wālz\\. Cape on Bering Strait at W tip of Seward Penin., Alaska; most westerly point of mainland of North America, 65°40′N, 168°05′W.

Prince of Wales Island. **1.** Largest island of Alexander Archipelago, in S part, SE Alaska; ab. 135 mi. (215 km.) long by 40 mi. (65 km.) wide; 2587 sq. mi. (6700 sq. km.). Largest settlement Craig.
2. Island in Torres Strait W of Cape York, Queensland, Australia, just S of Thursday I.
3. Island, cen. Arctic Archipelago, Nunavut, Canada, bet. Victoria I. and Somerset I.; 12,830 sq. mi. (33,230 sq. km.).
4. Island, Malaysia. See PENANG 1.

Prince of Wales–Out·er Ketch·i·kan \\-'au̇-tər-'ke-chi-,kan\\. Division in Alaska. See table at ALASKA.

Prince of Wales Strait. Narrow channel bet. Banks I. and NW Victoria I., in SW Arctic Archipelago, Northwest Territories, Canada; ab. 170 mi. (274 km.) long.

Prince Olav Coast \\'ō-ləf, -ləv\\. Section of coast of Antarctica, on Indian Ocean, 68°30′S, bet. 39° and 49°30′E; a part of Queen Maud Land; discovered 1930.

Prince Pat·rick Island \\'pa-trik\\. Island, one of the Parry Is., W Arctic Archipelago, Northwest Territories, Canada; 6081 sq. mi. (15,750 sq. km.).

Prince Re·gent Inlet \\'rē-jənt\\. Channel bet. E Somerset I. and NW Baffin I., off N Canada mainland; connects with Gulf of Boothia on the S and Lancaster Sound on the N; ab. 60 mi. (95 km.) wide.

Prince Ru·pert \\'rü-pərt\\. City, W British Columbia, Canada, on Pacific Ocean at head of Dixon Entrance 10 mi. (16 km.) N of mouth of Skeena River; pop. (1991c) 16,620; important port and W terminus of Canadian National R.R.; service center for lumbering, fishing, and mining area.

Prince Rupert's Land. See RUPERT'S LAND.

Princes Islands. See KIZIL ISLANDS.

Prin·cess Anne \\'prin-səs-'an\\. Town, ⊗ of Somerset co., SE Maryland; pop. (1990c) 1666; Univ. of Maryland Eastern Shore (1886).

Princess As·trid Coast \\'as-trid\\. Section of coast of East Antarctica, on South Atlantic Ocean, ab. 74°45′S, bet. 5° and 20°30′E; part of Queen Maud Land.

Princess Char·lotte Bay \\'shär-lət\\. Inlet of Coral Sea on NE coast of Queensland, Australia, W of Cape Melville.

Princess Mar·tha Coast \\'mär-thə\\; *formerly* **Crown Princess Martha Land.** Section of coast of Antarctica E of Coats Land and of Weddell Sea; ab. 72°S, 7°30′W; largely ice-covered; a part of Queen Maud Land.

Princess Ragn·hild Coast \\'räŋ-ən-,hil\\. Section of coast of Antarctica, ab. 70°15′S, bet. 20°30′ and 34°E; part of Queen Maud Land.

Princess Royal Island. Island off the coast of British Columbia, Canada, 52°57′N, 128°49′W; borders on Caamaño Sound on the W; 870 sq. mi. (2253 sq. km.).

Prince·ton \\'prin-stən\\. **1.** City, ⊗ of Bureau co., N Illinois, 33 mi. (53 km.) W of Ottawa; pop. (1990c) 7197.
2. Residential city, ⊗ of Gibson co., SW Indiana, 27 mi. (43 km.) N of Evansville; pop. (1990c) 8127.
3. City, ⊗ of Caldwell co., W Kentucky, 42 mi. (68 km.) E of Paducah; pop. (1990c) 6940.
4. Village, Mille Lacs co., E cen. Minnesota, 28 mi. (45 km.) E of St. Cloud; pop. (1990c) 3719.
5. City, ⊗ of Mercer co., N Missouri, 42 mi. (68 km.) N of Chillicothe; pop. (1990c) 1021.
6. Borough, Mercer co., W cen. New Jersey, 11 mi. (18 km.) NNE of Trenton; pop. (1990c) 12,016; residential and educational center; research facilities; Princeton Univ. (1746), Princeton Theological Seminary (1812), Westminster Choir Coll. (1926). Founded by Quakers 1696; scene of defeat of British detachment by American troops under Gen. George Washington 1777; seat of Continental Congress June–Nov. 1783.
7. City, ⊗ of Mercer co., S West Virginia, 11 mi. (18 km.) NE of Bluefield; pop. (1990c) 7043. Settled 1826; scene of engagements in Civil War May 16, 1862.

Princeton, Mount. Peak in Sawatch Range, Chaffee co., cen. Colorado; 14,197 ft. (4327 m.).

Prince·ville \\'prins-,vil\\. Town, Arthabaska co., S Quebec, Canada, 54 mi. (87 km.) SW of Quebec City; pop. (1991c) 3914.

Prince Wil·liam \\'wil-yəm\\. County in NE Virginia. See table at VIRGINIA.

Prince William Sound. Inlet of Gulf of Alaska, S Alaska, E of Kenai Penin.; 90 to 100 mi. (145 to 160 km.) across; Montaque I. and Hinchinbrook I. lie across its entrance; site of largest oil-tanker spill up to then in U.S. history March 24, 1989.

Prín·ci·pe Island \\'prin-si-pē\\ *also* **Prince Island** \\'prins\\. Island, São Tomé and Príncipe, in the Gulf of Guinea, N of São Tomé; 42 sq. mi. (109 sq. km.); site of English astronomer Arthur Eddington's solar-eclipse observations May 29, 1919, which provided confirmation of physicist Albert Einstein's general relativity theory; with São Tomé (*q.v.*) received independence from Portugal July 1975, becoming republic of São Tomé and Príncipe (*q.v.*).

Prine·ville \\'prīn-,vil\\. City, ⊗ of Crook co., cen. Oregon, 30 mi. (48 km.) NE of Bend; pop. (1990c) 5355.

Prinkipo. See BÜYÜKADA.

Prinsen. See PANAITAN.

Prin·za·pol·ka *or* **Prin·za·pol·ca** \\,prēn-sä-'pōl-kä\\. **1.** River, E cen. Nicaragua; flows E into the Caribbean Sea at the seaport of Prinzapolka; ab. 120 mi. (195 km.) long.
2. Seaport on E coast of Nicaragua, at mouth of Prinzapolka River.

Pri·or Lake \\'prī-ər\\. City, Scott co., SE Minnesota, SW of Minneapolis; pop. (1990c) 11,482.

Pri·o·zersk \\,prē-ə-'zyȯrsk\\; *formerly* **Keks·golm** \\'keks-,gōm\\ *or Finnish* **Kä·ki·sal·mi** \\'ka-kē-,säl-mē\\ *or Swed.* **Kex·holm** \\'keks-,hȯlm\\. Town, St. Petersburg Oblast, W

Russia in Europe, on W shore of Lake Ladoga 75 mi. (121 km.) N of the city of St. Petersburg; has rail connection with St. Petersburg. Developed in Middle Ages; changed hands several times bet. Russians and Swedes; ceded to Russia by Sweden 1721; fell to Finland 1917; ceded to U.S.S.R. by treaty 1940; retaken by Germans and Finns 1941 but returned by treaty 1944.

Pripet Marshes *or* **Pripyat Marshes.** See POLESYE.

Pri·pyat' \ˈpri-pyət\ *or Pol.* **Pry·peć** \ˈpri-ˌpech\ *or* **Pri·pet** \ˈpri-ˌpet, -pət\. River, NW Ukraine and S Belarus; rises W of Kovel' (formerly in Poland) and flows E through the Polesye (*q.v.*) to the Dnieper in NW Ukraine, joining it near Belarus border 50 mi. (81 km.) N of Kiev; 500 mi. (805 km.) long. Navigable for 300 mi. (483 km.) and connected by canals with the Bug (tributary of the Vistula) and Neman rivers. Has many tributaries flowing through the marshes.

Prishib. See LENINSK 2.

Priš·ti·na \ˈprēsh-tē-ˌnä\. Town, ✻ of Kosovo autonomous area, Serbia, S Yugoslavia, ab. 48 mi. (77 km.) NNW of Skopje, Republic of Macedonia; pop. (1981c) 148,656; in medieval period a ✻ of Serbian empire; 14th cent. monastery nearby.

Pri·vas \prē-ˈvä\. Commune, ✻ of Ardèche dept., SE France, W of Rhone River 107 mi. (172 km.) NNW of Marseille; a Protestant stronghold in 16th cent.

Priz·ren \ˈpriz-ˌren, ˈprēz-\. Town, Serbia, S Yugoslavia, ab. 40 mi. (65 km.) WNW of Skopje, Republic of Macedonia; pop. (1981c) 134,525; burial place of Serbian King Stephen Dušan (d. 1355); many mosques; a ✻ of Serbian empire in medieval period.

Pro·bo·ling·go \ˌprō-bō-ˈliŋ-gō\. Seaport city, N coast of East Java prov., Indonesia, on Madura Strait 45 mi. (72 km.) SE of Surabaya; pop. (1990c) 177,120; fisheries.

Pro·ci·da \ˈprō-chē-dä\; *anc.* **Proch·y·ta** \ˈprä-ki-tə\. **1.** Island in the Bay of Naples, Campania, Italy; ab. 2 mi. (3 km.) long; pop. (1991p) 10,440; highest point 250 ft. (76 m.); consists of volcanic craters.

2. Town on NE coast of Procida Island, Italy; has castle used as a prison.

Proconnesus. See MARMARA.

Proc·tor \ˈpräk-tər\. **1.** City, St. Louis co., NE Minnesota, 7 mi. (11 km.) SW of Duluth; pop. (1990c) 2974; before 1939 called **Proc·tor·knott** \-ˌnät\.

2. Town, Rutland co., W Vermont, 5 mi. (8 km.) NNW of the city of Rutland; pop. (1990c) 1979; center of marble industry.

Prod·da·tur \ˈprä-də-ˌtu̇r\. Town, S Andhra Pradesh, S India, on Penner River 160 mi. (257 km.) NW of Madras; pop. (1981c) 107,068.

Profile Mountain. See CANNON MOUNTAIN 2.

Pro·gre·so \prō-ˈgre-sō\. Seaport, Yucatán state, SE Mexico; munic. pop. (1990p) 37,806; port for Mérida; formerly known for hemp production.

Progreso, El. See EL PROGRESO.

Prokletije. See NORTH ALBANIAN ALPS.

Pro·ko·pyevsk \prə-ˈkȯp-yifsk\. City, Kemerovo Oblast, S Russia in Asia, in S end of Kuznetsk Basin 17 mi. (27 km.) NW of Novokuznetsk; pop. (1992e) 272,000; coal mining; flour mills, grain elevators; modern development dates from 1920s.

Proliv Dmitriya Lapteva. See DMITRIYA LAPTEVA PROLIV.

Proliv Karskiye Vorota. See KARA STRAIT.

Proliv Vil'kitskogo. See VILKITSKI STRAIT.

Prome \ˈprōm\ *or* **Pyè** \ˈpyā\. Town, Myanmar, on left bank of the Irrawaddy 150 mi. (241 km.) NNW of Yangon; ab. 5 mi. (8 km.) SE is site of ✻ of Pyu state overcome by Burmese in 9th cent. A.D.

Promontore, Cape. See KAMENJAK, CAPE.

Promontorio del Gargano. See GARGANO PROMONTORY.

Promontorium Sacrum. See SAINT VINCENT, CAPE 2.

Prom·on·to·ry Point \ˈprä-mən-ˌtōr-ē\. Point forming S end of elevated peninsula extending into N part of Great Salt Lake, Box Elder co., NW corner of Utah; its coastline traversed by Lucin Cutoff of Southern Pacific R.R. To the N ab. 30 mi. (48 km.) is **Promontory,** locality 30 mi. (48 km.) W of Brigham City where on May 10, 1869 last spike was driven completing first transcontinental railroad in U.S., commemorated by a monument.

Prophetstown. See BATTLE GROUND.

Propontis. See MARMARA, SEA OF.

Pro·priá \ˌprō-prē-ˈä\. City, Sergipe state, E Brazil, on the São Francisco 55 mi. (89 km.) NNE of Aracaju; munic. pop. (1980c) 21,342.

Proskurov. See KHMEL'NYTS'KYY 2.

Pros·pect \ˈprä-ˌspekt\. Town, New Haven co., S Connecticut, 4 mi. (6 km.) SE of Waterbury; pop. (1990c) 7775.

Prospect Heights. City, Cook co., NE Illinois, 10 mi. (16 km.) NW of Chicago and just N of Mount Prospect; pop. (1990c) 15,239.

Pros·pec·tors Mountain \ˈprä-ˌspek-tərz\. Peak in S Grand Teton National Park, NW Wyoming; ab. 11,235 ft. (3425 m.).

Prospect Park. 1. Residential borough, Passaic co., N New Jersey, 2 mi. (3 km.) N of Paterson; pop. (1990c) 5053.

2. Borough, Delaware co., SE Pennsylvania, 10 mi. (16 km.) SW of Philadelphia; pop. (1990c) 6764.

Prospect Point. See NIAGARA FALLS 1.

Prospect Reservoir. Reservoir, New South Wales, SE Australia, ab. 12 mi. (19 km.) W of Sydney.

Pros·pe·ri·dad \prȯ-ˌsper-ē-ˈdäd, -ˈthäth\. Municipality, ✻ of Agusan del Sur prov., Mindanao, Philippines; pop. (1980c) 33,824.

Pros·ser \ˈprä-sər\. City, ⊗ of Benton co., S Washington, on Yakima River 48 mi. (77 km.) SE of the city of Yakima; pop. (1990c) 4476; fruit, livestock farms.

Pro·stě·jov \ˈprȯs-tye-ˌyȯf\ *or Ger.* **Pross·nitz** \ˈprȯ-snits\. City, E cen. Czech Republic, ab. 30 mi. (48 km.) NE of Brno; pop. (1991p) 50,102; textile mills.

Pro·vence \prȯ-ˈvän^n^s\ *or Lat.* **Pro·vin·cia** \prə-ˈvin-chē-ə\. Historical region of SE France; bounded anciently on N by Dauphiné, on E by countship of Nice, on S by Mediterranean, on W by Languedoc, and on NW by Comtat Venaissin; ✻ Aix; watered by Durance and Rhone rivers; diverse topography, incl. plateaus in W, Alpine chains in E, ancient massifs along sea, and extensive plains; one of the major provincial governments of ancien régime; its language, Provençal, important in medieval literature and, since 19th cent. revival, significant in modern literature.

History: Part of Roman Gallia Narbonensis (see GAUL); invaded by Visigoths, Burgundians, and Ostrogoths; came under Franks 6th cent. A.D.; became part of realm of Holy Roman Emperor Lothair I by Treaty of Verdun 843; became separate kingdom 855; united with Burgundy c. 934 and again with Holy Roman Empire 1032; as countship came under Barcelona c. 1113; passed as dowry to Charles of Anjou, king of Naples and Sicily, 1246; came under French crown 1481; suffered in Wars of Religion (1562–98); province of France until Revolution.

Provence–Alpes–Côte d'A·zur \-ˌalp-ˌkōt-da-ˈzu̇r\. Region of SE France. See table at FRANCE.

Prov·i·dence \ˈprä-və-dəns, -ˌdens\. **1.** Navigable river, a N arm of Narragansett Bay, formed by the confluence of two small rivers in the city of Providence, Rhode Island.

2. County in N Rhode Island. See table at RHODE ISLAND.

3. City, Webster co., W Kentucky, 33 mi. (53 km.) WSW of Henderson; pop. (1990c) 4123.

4. Town, Maryland. See ANNAPOLIS 1.

5. City and port of entry, ✻ of Rhode Island and ⊗ of Providence co., N Rhode Island, at head of Providence River; pop. (1990c) 160,728; excellent harbor; jewelry, rubber goods, electronic equipment, machinery, machine tools. Brown Univ. (1764), Rhode Island Coll. (1854), Rhode Island School of Design (1877), Johnson and Wales Coll. (1914), Providence Coll. (1917).

History: Founded by clergyman Roger Williams 1636 as refuge for religious dissenters; partly destroyed 1676 in King Philip's War; Rhode Island Independence Act signed in Old State House May 4, 1776; in 18th cent. a major port in West Indies trade and in 19th cent. important center of textile industry; incorp. as city 1831.

6. City, Cache co., N Utah; pop. (1990c) 3344.

7. Hamlet, Canada. See FORT PROVIDENCE.
8. Island, Seychelles, in the Indian Ocean; NNE of Madagascar, at 9°14′S, 51°02′E; ab. 0.5 sq. mi. (0.8 sq. km.).

Providence Bay *or Russ.* **Pro·vi·de·ni·ya Bukh·ta** \ˌprə-vi-ˈde-nē-ə-ˈbük-tə\. Inlet of Bering Sea, SE of Chukchi Penin., Magadan Oblast, NE Russia in Asia.

Providence Channel, North West *and* **North East Providence Channel.** Channels in Bahamas, bet. Atlantic Ocean and the Straits of Florida, S of Grand Bahama I. and Abaco I. and N of Bimini, Berry Is., and Eleuthera.

Providence Plantations. See RHODE ISLAND 2.

Pro·vi·den·cia, Is·la de \ˈēs-lä-thā-prō-bē-ˈthen-syä\. Small island, Colombia, in W Caribbean Sea off E coast of Nicaragua; with San Andrés I. constitutes the dept. of San Andrés y Providencia. Claimed by Nicaragua 1986.

Prov·i·den·ci·a·les \ˌpräv-ə-ˌden-sē-ˈä-lis\. One of the Caicos Is. See TURKS AND CAICOS ISLANDS.

Provideniya Bukhta. See PROVIDENCE BAY.

Prov·ince·town \ˈpräv-ins-ˌtaùn\. Town, Barnstable co., SE Massachusetts, on N tip of Cape Cod; pop. (1990c) 3561; commercial fisheries; popular resort; Pilgrim Monument; art galleries. First landing place of Pilgrims Nov. 20 (Nov. 11 Old Style), 1620; Mayflower Compact drawn up in harbor same day; incorp. 1727; Provincetown Players theater group originated here 1915.

Province Welles·ley \ˈwelz-lē\. Formerly used name for mainland section of Penang state, Malaysia. Ceded to Great Britain by Kedah 1800 and became part of Penang settlement; included in Penang state 1957.

Provincia. See PROVENCE.

Pro·vins \prō-ˈveⁿ\. Town, E Seine-et-Marne dept., N France, ab. 25 mi. (40 km.) E of Melun; pop. (1990c) 12,171; clay pits; three medieval churches; 12th cent. ramparts and keep; fl. 12th–13th cents.; suffered in the Wars of Religion during which it was besieged and taken by French King Henry IV 1592.

Pro·vo \ˈprō-vō\. **1.** River, N cen. Utah; rises in W end of Uinta Mts., flows SW into Utah Lake; ab. 40 mi. (64 km.) long; dammed for irrigation and for Provo and Salt Lake City water supply.
2. City, ⊗ of Utah co., N cen. Utah, on Provo River 3 mi. (5 km.) from Utah Lake 45 mi. (72 km.) SSE of Salt Lake City; pop. (1990c) 86,835; manufactures steel and steel products, electronic components; tourist center; Brigham Young Univ. (1875); city founded 1849 by Mormons.

Provo Peak. Mountain, Utah co., N cen. Utah, E of the city of Provo in the Wasatch Range; 11,068 ft. (3374 m.).

Prow·ers \ˈprō-ərz\. County in SE Colorado. See table at COLORADO.

Proy·art \prwä-ˈyär\. Village, Somme dept., N France, 12 mi. (19 km.) SW of Péronne; site of WWI battle 1918.

Pru·dence Island \ˈprüd-ᵊns\. Island in Narragansett Bay, a part of Newport co., Rhode Island.

Pru·den·tó·po·lis \ˌprü-den-ˈtò-pù-lēs\. Municipality, Paraná state, S Brazil, 110 mi. (177 km.) WNW of Curitiba; pop. (1980c) 40,088.

Prud·hoe \ˈprə-ˌdō, ˈprəd-hō\. Town, Northumberland, N England, on the Tyne 11 mi. (18 km.) W of Newcastle upon Tyne; pop. (1981p) 11,820.

Prud·hoe Bay \ˈprü-dō\. Inlet, Beaufort Sea, N Alaska, 200 mi. (322 km.) ESE of Point Barrow; center of oil-drilling activities since 1968; pop. of unincorporated settlement (1990c) 47.

Prud·nik \ˈprüd-nik\; *Ger.* **Neu·stadt** \ˈnòi-ˌshtät\ *or* **Neustadt in Ober·schle·si·en** \in-ˌō-bər-ˈshlā-zyən\. City, S Opole prov., S Poland, W of Zabrze near Czech Republic border; pop. (1989e) 24,626; formerly in Germany. Assigned to Poland by Potsdam Conference 1945.

Prusa. See BURSA 2.

Prus·sia \ˈprə-shə\ *or Ger.* **Preus·sen** \ˈpròis-ᵊn\. Former German state, N cen. Germany; ✻ Berlin.
History: Early Prussians a people of Baltic stock dwelling along shore E of the Vistula; finally conquered, Christianized, and colonized by Teutonic Knights 13th cent. (see EAST PRUSSIA); in 1466, W Prussia ceded by Teutonic Knights to Poland, while E Prussia became Polish fief; E Prussia secularized and erected into duchy under Polish suzerainty 1525; in 1618 it passed by inheritance to the Hohenzollern elector of Brandenburg; became independent from Poland 1660; kingdom of Prussia erected from all holdings of Brandenburg (*q.v.*) 1701; became strong military state, esp. under Frederick the Great 1740–86; by 1815 expanded to include W Pomerania, Silesia, W part of Poland incl. West Prussia, Rhine Prov., and part of Saxony; strong German customs union (Ger. *Zollverein*) estab. under Prussian leadership 1834; until 1918 ruled according to 1850 constitution; after war against Austria 1866, Prussian land stretched continuously across N two thirds of Germany; held leading position in North German Confederation 1867–71; German Empire (see GERMANY), of which Prussian king became Emperor William I, founded under Prussian leadership 1871; after WWI lost much territory by Treaty of Versailles and became subsidiary to German Weimar Republic; after WWII by decision of Potsdam Conference 1945 lost the entire E part to Poland and the U.S.S.R.; formally abolished by the Allied Control Council Mar. 1, 1947.

Prussia, East *and* **Prussia, West.** See EAST PRUSSIA and WEST PRUSSIA.

Prusz·ków \ˈprüsh-ˌküf\. Commune, Warszawa prov., NE cen. Poland, 7 mi. (11 km.) WSW of Warsaw; pop. (1989e) 52,908.

Prut \ˈprüt\ *or Ger.* **Pruth** \ˈprüt\. River, E boundary of Romania; rises in SW Ukraine, in the Carpathian Mts. and flows SSE into the Danube at Reni, below Galaţi, 75 mi. (121 km.) from the Black Sea; 565 mi. (909 km.) long; formerly almost entirely within Romania, separating Moldavia from Bessarabia (now part of Moldova). Treaty of the Pruth, by which Russian Czar Peter the Great was compelled by the Turks to return Azov, signed on its banks 1711.

Pry·or *or* **Pryor Creek** \ˈprī-ər\. City, ⊗ of Mayes co., NE Oklahoma, 41 mi. (66 km.) ENE of Tulsa; pop. (1990c) 8327.

Prypeć. See PRIPYAT′.

Pry·sor \ˈprī-zər\. River, Gwynedd co., Wales. See PISTYLL CAIN FALLS.

Przas·nysz \ˈpshäs-nish\. Commune, W Ostrołęka prov., NE cen. Poland, 53 mi. (85 km.) N of Warsaw; pop. (1981p) 14,483; in WWI scene of battles bet. Germans and Russians Feb. 1915.

Prze·myśl \ˈpshe-mish-ᵊl\ *or Russ.* **Pe·re·myshl** \ˌper-ə-ˈmi-shəl\. **1.** Province, SE Poland. See table at POLAND.
2. City, its ✻, on San River near border of Ukraine, and ab. 30 mi. (48 km.) SE of Rzeszów; pop. (1989e) 68,061; metal- and timber-working. Founded before 10th cent.; to Poland c. 1340; to Austria 1772; in WWI a major Austrian fortress, besieged by Russians 1914–15; to Poland 1918; during WWII divided by German-Soviet frontier.

Przhe·val′sk \ˌpər-zhə-ˈvälsk\; *1869–89 and 1921–39* **Ka·ra·kol** \ˌkär-ə-ˈkəl\. Town, NE Kyrgyzstan, at E end of Issyk-Kul; pop. (1991e) 64,300; center of agricultural region and of trade routes E and N. Founded 1869; name changed 1889 in honor of the Russian explorer Nikolay M. Przhevalsky, who died here 1888.

Psa·rá \psä-ˈrä\ *also* **Ipsa·ra** \ˌēp-sə-ˈrä\; *anc.* **Psy·ra** \ˈsī-rə\. One of the Aegean Is., Greece, W of Chios; 35 sq. mi. (91 sq. km.); captured by Turkey 1824; after Balkan War annexed to Greece 1914.

Psel *or* **Psiol** \ˈpsy-òl\. River, E cen. Europe, mostly in Ukraine; rises in Kursk Oblast, Russia, and flows S to the Dnieper near Kremenchug, Ukraine; 445 mi. (716 km.) long; has winding course through fertile region.

Psiloritis, Mount. See IDA, MOUNT.

Pskov \ˈpskòf\ *or Estonian* **Pih·kva** \ˈpēk-ˌvä\. City, ✻ of Pskov Oblast, W Russia in Europe, on Velikaya River near SE shore of Lake Pskov, 155 mi. (249 km.) SW of St. Petersburg;

pop. (1992e) 209,000; important railroad junction; produces linen, machinery; 17th cent. cathedral.

History: One of the oldest and historically most important Russian cities; dates from at least 9th cent. A.D.; growth and history paralleled that of Novgorod; occupied by Teutonic Knights 1241–42; subject to Novgorod until 1348, when it gained independence; came under rule of Moscow 1510; sacked by Czar Ivan the Terrible 1570; besieged 1581 by King Stephen Báthory of Poland; in WWII occupied by the Germans 1941–44 and suffered considerable damage.

Pskov, Lake *or Estonian* **Pih·kva Järv** \ˈpēk-ˌvä-ˈyarv\. S arm of Lake Peipus, N cen. Europe; bet. Estonia and W Pskov Oblast, Russia; 274 sq. mi. (710 sq. km.).

Pskov Oblast \ˈo-bləst, -ˌblast\. Subdivision of NW Russia in Europe; 21,351 sq. mi. (55,299 sq. km.); pop. (1992e) 841,000; ✱ Pskov. Occupies basins of Lovat', Shelon, and Velikaya rivers and includes part of Lake Peipus with many minor lakes and swamps; principal economic activity agriculture, esp. flax growing and dairying.

Psyra. See PSARÁ.

Pszczy·na \ˈpshchi-nä\ *or Ger.* **Pless** \ˈples\. Town, SE Katowice prov., SW Poland, ab. 20 mi. (32 km.) S of the city of Katowice; pop. (1989e) 39,378. Grew up around castle of Piast dynasty (12th cent.); to Silesia 19th cent.; to Poland after WWI.

Ptar·mi·gan Peak \ˈtär-mi-gən\. Mountain, Park and Lake cos., cen. Colorado; 13,736 ft. (4187 m.).

Pteria. See BOGAZKÖY.

Ptol·e·ma·ïs \ˌtä-lə-ˈmā-əs\. **1.** Ancient town, Egypt, on left bank of the Nile, ab. 225 mi. (360 km.) S of Memphis.
2. Seaport city, Israel. See ACRE.
3. Town, Libya. See TOLMETA.

Pu·call·pa \pü-ˈkī-pä\. Town, E Peru, on the lower Ucayali River; pop. (1990e) 153,000.

Pucelancyrcan. See PUCKLECHURCH.

Pu·ch'ŏn \ˈpü-ˈchon\. City, NW South Korea; pop. (1985c) 456,292.

Pu·cio Point \ˈpü-sē-ˌō\. NW point of Panay I. and of Antique prov., Philippines; marks boundary with Capiz.

Puck·a·way, Lake \ˈpə-kə-ˌwā\. Lake in W Green Lake co., cen. Wisconsin.

Puck·le·church \ˈpə-kəl-ˌchərch\; *Old English* **Pu·clan·cyr·can** *also* **Pu·ce·lan·cyr·can** \ˌpü-klə-ˈchuer-chən\. Village, SW England, ab. 10 mi. (16 km.) NE of Bristol; Edmund I, king of the English, killed here 946; site now in Avon co.

Pudjut, Point. See PUJUT, TANJUNG.

Pud·sey \ˈpəd-zē\. Town, West Yorkshire, N England, 6 mi. (10 km.) W of Leeds; pop. (1981p) 38,977; textiles; tanneries.

Pu·duk·kot·tai \ˌpu-dək-ˈkō-ˌtī\. **1.** Former Indian state, now part of Tamil Nadu state, S India, bet. Thanjavur and Madura; 1185 sq. mi. (3069 sq. km.).
2. Town, its ✱, 38 mi. (61 km.) SSW of Thanjavur.

Pue·bla \ˈpwe-blä\. **1.** State of SE cen. Mexico. See table at MEXICO.
2. *or in full* **Puebla de Za·ra·go·za** \t͟hā-ˌsä-rä-ˈgō-sä\. City, its ✱, ab. 75 mi. (120 km.) SE of Mexico City; pop. (1990p) 1,054,921; alt. 7093 ft. (2162 m.); diversified light industry, incl. onyx, tiles, cotton, glass, pottery; two universities; notable for Spanish colonial architecture; 16th cent. cathedral; several churches; 18th cent. theater; many museums.

History: Founded as **Puebla de los An·gel·es** \t͟hā-lōs-ˈäŋ-he-lās\ by Spanish 1532; in Mexican War occupied by U.S. forces under Gen. Winfield Scott 1847; scene of victory of Mexicans under Gen. Ignacio Zaragoza over French May 5, 1862; occupied by French 1863 and recaptured by Gen. Porfirio Díaz 1867.

Pueb·lo \ˈpwe-blō, pyü-ˈe-\. **1.** County in SE cen. Colorado. See table at COLORADO.
2. City, its ⊗, on Arkansas River 42 mi. (68 km.) SSE of Colorado Springs; pop. (1990c) 98,640; alt. 4690 ft. (1430 m.); manufactures steel; center of an irrigated agricultural region and near the major Colorado coalfields; high-tech industry; Univ. of Southern Colorado (1933); U.S. Army ordnance depot. Estab. as trading post 1842; incorp. as city 1885; severely damaged by floods 1921.

Pueblo Bo·ni·to \ˈpwe-blō-bə-ˈnē-tō\. Largest of prehistoric pueblo ruins, Chaco Culture National Historical Park, New Mexico; town fl. 10th–12th cents.

Pueblo Gran·de \ˈpwe-blō-ˈgran-dē\. Prehistoric ruin, E Phoenix, Arizona; surrounded on three sides by a wall containing a remarkable amount of stone for a pueblo ruin; museum.

Pue·blo Li·bre \ˈpwe-blō-ˈlē-brā\. Community, W Peru, in Lima-Callao met. area; pop. (1990e) 94,647.

Pueblonuevo. See PEÑARROYA-PUEBLONUEVO.

Pue·blo Vie·jo, La·gu·na del \lä-ˈgü-nä-t͟hel-ˈpwe-blō-ˈvyā-hō\. Inlet of Gulf of Mexico in E cen. Mexican coast, S of the mouth of the Pánuco River.

Puen·te Al·to \ˈpwen-tā-ˈäl-tō\. City, Santiago region, cen. Chile, just S of the city of Santiago; pop. (1992c) 254,534.

Puen·te del In·ca \ˈpwen-tā-t͟hel-ˈēŋ-kä\. Natural bridge in the Andes, W Argentina, W of city of Mendoza; height 65 ft. (20 m.) over the Cuevas River; length of span 70 ft. (21 m.); width 90 ft. (27 m.).

Puente–Ge·nil \-hā-ˈnēl\. Commune, Córdoba prov., S Spain, 35 mi. (56 km.) S of the city of Córdoba; pop. (1991p) 26,387; agricultural products; stone quarries.

Pu·eo Point \pü-ˈā-ō\. Cape on E cen. coast of Niihau I., Hawaii.

Puer·co \ˈpwer-kō\. River, NW New Mexico and E Arizona; rises in McKinley co., NW New Mexico, flows SW across Arizona border and joins the Little Colorado River in E cen. Arizona, in Navajo co.; ab. 120 mi. (195 km.) long.

Puer·ta, Point \ˈpwer-tä\. Cape on E coast of Puerto Rico.

Puerto, El. See PUERTO DE SANTA MARÍA.

Puer·to Ai·sén \ˈpwer-tō-ī-ˈsān\. Commune, Aisén del General Carlos Ibáñez del Campo region, S Chile; pop. (1992c) 19,488.

Puer·to Ar·muel·les \ˈpwer-tō-är-ˈmwā-yās\. Pacific coast port, Chiriquí prov., extreme W Panama, on Charco Azul Bay; pop. (1980p) 12,488.

Puerto Arrecife. See ARRECIFE.

Puer·to Aya·cu·cho \ˈpwer-tō-ˌī-ä-ˈkü-chō\. Town, ✱ of Amazonas terr., S Venezuela, on the Orinoco River and on Colombian border; pop. (1990p) 35,865.

Puerto Bar·rios \ˈpwer-tō-ˈbär-rē-ˌōs\. Seaport, ✱ of Izabal dept., E Guatemala, on Gulf of Honduras ab. 150 mi. (240 km.) NE of Guatemala City; pop. (1993e) 39,088; ships bananas.

Puerto Bello. See PORTOBELO.

Puer·to Ber·río \ˈpwer-tō-ˈber-rē-ˌō\. River port, Antioquia dept., NW Colombia, on Magdalena River ab. 320 mi. (515 km.) S of Barranquilla; pop. (1985c) 22,084.

Puer·to Bo·lí·var \ˈpwer-tō-bō-ˈlē-ˌvär\. Port on SW coast of Ecuador, 75 mi. (121 km.) S of Guayaquil; the port of Machala (*q.v.*).

Puer·to Ca·bel·lo \ˈpwer-tō-kä-ˈbā-yō\. Seaport, Carabobo state, N Venezuela, 70 mi. (113 km.) W of Caracas; pop. (1990p) 145,759; the port of Valencia, exporting agricultural produce. During colonial period frequently sacked by pirates; in War of Independence held by royalist forces 1812–23.

Puer·to Car·re·ño \ˈpwer-tō-kär-ˈrā-nyō\. Town, ✱ of Vichada dept., E Colombia, at the junction of Meta and Orinoco rivers; pop. (1985c) 3987.

Puer·to Cas·til·la \ˈpwer-tō-kä-ˈstē-yä\. Seaport on N coast of Honduras, across a bay just N of Trujillo.

Puer·to Co·lom·bia \ˈpwer-tō-kō-ˈlōm-bē-ä\. Coastal commune, Atlántico dept., N Colombia, 12 mi. (19 km.) NW of Barranquilla, and formerly its port; now a seaside resort.

Puer·to Cor·tes \ˈpwer-tō-kor-ˈtes\. Seaport, Cortés dept., NW Honduras, on the Gulf of Honduras; pop. (1989e) 31,900; largest Atlantic port in Honduras; oil refinery; has a free-trade zone; founded c. 1525.

Puer·to del Ro·sa·rio \ˈpwer-tō-t͟hel-rō-ˈsä-rē-ō\; *formerly* **Puerto de Ca·bras** \də-ˈkäb-rəs\. Chief port of Fuerteventura I., Canary Is., Spain; pop. (1991c) 16,485.

Puerto de San José. See SAN JOSÉ 3.

Puer·to de San·ta Ma·ría \ˈpwer-tō-t͟hā-ˈsän-tä-mä-ˈrē-ä\ *or* **El Puerto de Santa María** \el-\. Commune, Cádiz prov., SW Spain, on Bay of Cádiz at mouth of Guadalete River 8 mi.

(13 km.) NE of the city of Cádiz; pop. (1991c) 65,517; produces and exports sherry; manufactures soap; Gothic church.

Puer·to De·se·a·do \ˈpwer-tō-ˌthā-sä-ˈä-thō\. Town and bay on E coast of Santa Cruz prov., S Argentina, at the mouth of Deseado River; pop. (1980p) 4017.

Puerto de Ibañeta. See RONCESVALLES.

Puer·to La Cruz \ˈpwer-tō-lä-ˈkrüz, -ˈkrüs\. City and port, Anzoátegui state, N Venezuela, NE of Barcelona; pop. (1990e) 60,546.

Puer·to Lem·pi·ra \ˈpwer-tō-lem-ˈpē-rä\. Town, ✻ of Gracias a Dios dept., E Honduras; pop. (1988p) 1910.

Puer·to Li·món \ˈpwer-tō-lē-ˈmōn\ *or* **Limón** *also* **Port Limón.** Seaport, ✻ of Limón prov., E cen. Costa Rica; pop. (1991e) 50,939; chief port of Costa Rica; center of the banana trade; exporting port for coffee shipments.

Puer·tol·la·no \ˌpwer-tō-ˈlyä-nō\. Commune, Ciudad Real prov., S cen. Spain, 24 mi. (39 km.) SSW of the commune of Ciudad Real; pop. (1991p) 50,910; mineral baths; coal, iron, lead, manganese mines.

Puer·to Ma·dryn \ˈpwer-tō-ˈmä-thrēn\ *also* **Port Madryn.** Seaport, on NE coast of Chubut prov., S Argentina, on New Gulf; pop. (1980p) 20,709.

Puer·to Mal·do·na·do \ˈpwer-tō-ˌmäl-dō-ˈnä-thō\. Town, SE Peru, at junction of the Tambopata and Madre de Dios rivers ab. 525 mi. (845 km.) E of Lima; pop. (1990e) 21,200.

Puerto México. See COATZACOALCOS 2.

Puer·to Montt \ˈpwer-tō-ˈmȯnt\. Seaport, ✻ of Los Lagos region, S cen. Chile, 12 mi. (19 km.) S of Lake Llanquihue; pop. (1982c) 84,410; terminus of the S railroad.

Puer·to Mu·tis \ˈpwer-tō-ˈmü-tē\. Pacific coast port, SW cen. Panama, at the head of the Gulf of Montijo.

Puer·to Na·ta·les \ˈpwer-tō-nä-ˈtä-lās\. Town, Magallanes y Antártica Chilena region, S Chile, N of the Strait of Magellan near Argentine border.

Puerto Orotava. See LA OROTAVA.

Puer·to Pa·dre \ˈpwer-tō-ˈpä-drā\. Town, E Cuba, on inlet on N coast NW of Holguín; munic. pop. (1990e) 57,343.

Puer·to Pi·nas·co \ˈpwer-tō-pē-ˈnäs-kō\. Town, Boquerón dept., NW Paraguay, on W bank of Paraguay River ab. 178 mi. (286 km.) N of Asunción.

Puer·to Pla·ta \ˈpwer-tō-ˈplä-tä\. **1.** Province, N Dominican Republic. See table at DOMINICAN REPUBLIC.
2. *formerly* **San Fe·li·pe de Puerto Plata** \ˌsän-fā-ˈlē-pā-thā-\. Commune and seaport city, its ✻; munic. pop. (1983e) 47,000; exports tobacco, sugar, hides, coffee, cacao, hardwoods.

Puerto Presidente Stroessner. See CIUDAD DEL ESTE.

Puer·to Prin·ce·sa \ˈpwer-tō-prin-ˈsā-sä\. Municipality, ✻ of Palawan I., Philippines, on sheltered harbor in cen. part of E coast; pop. (1990p) 92,000; handles most of the trade of the island. In Spanish times a penal colony; in WWII occupied by American forces Mar. 1945.

Puerto Príncipe. See CAMAGÜEY.

Puer·to Re·al \ˈpwer-tō-rā-ˈäl\; *anc.* **Por·tus Gad·i·ta·nus** \ˈpōr-təs-ˌga-də-ˈtā-nəs, -ˈta-\. Seaport, Cádiz prov., SW Spain, on Bay of Cádiz 7 mi. (11 km.) E of the city of Cádiz; pop. (1991c) 29,638; rebuilt 1488 by Spanish monarchs Ferdinand of Aragon and Isabella of Castile.

Puer·to Ri·co \ˈpwer-tō-ˈrē-kō, ˈpōr-tə-\; *officially* **Commonwealth of Puerto Rico** *or Span.* **Esta·do Li·bre Aso·ci·a·do Puerto Rico** \e-ˈstä-thō-ˈlē-brā-ä-ˌsō-ˈsyä-thō\; *formerly* **Por·to Rico** \ˈpōr-tō-ˈrē-kō\. A self-governing commonwealth in union with the U.S., an island of the West Indies, 70 mi. (113 km.) E of Hispaniola; 3435 sq. mi. (8897 sq. km.); pop. (1993e) 3,612,000; ✻ San Juan.

Physical features: Has coastal plain, narrow in S, mountain ranges in interior, highest point Cerro de Punta 4389 ft. (1338 m.); rivers not useful for navigation; the few lakes are very small and are located in the coastal plain.

Chief products: Sugar, tobacco, fruits; livestock raising; textiles, pharmaceuticals, metal products, petrochemicals, rum; tourism.

Chief municipalities: San Juan, Bayamon, Ponce, Carolina Caguas, Mayagüez.

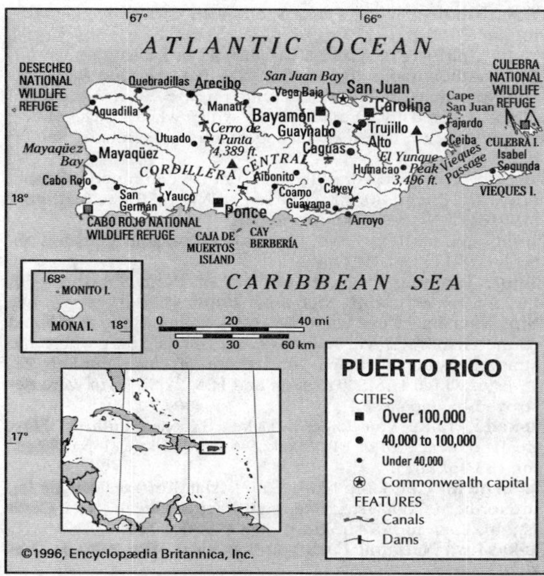

History: Inhabited by Arawak Indians when Christopher Columbus arrived 1493; colonization begun when Spanish explorer Juan Ponce de León founded Caparra 1508; Caparra abandoned but San Juan founded nearby 1521; gold supply depleted by mid-15th cent. and economic development of island declined; attacks by French, English, and Dutch prompted fortification of San Juan 16th cent.; occupied by American troops during Spanish-American War 1898 and ceded to U.S. by Treaty of Paris later in year; Puerto Ricans granted U.S. citizenship 1917; on adoption of constitution 1952 became a commonwealth with autonomy in internal affairs; commonwealth status reapproved by electorate in 1967 and 1993 plebiscites.

Puerto Rico Trench. Ocean trench, W Atlantic Ocean, extending approx. from NE of Hispaniola to NE of St. Martin in a general E to W direction; subduction zone according to theory of plate tectonics; contains deepest known part of Atlantic Ocean, at 19°35′N, 68°17′W, 28,374 ft. (8648 m.).

Puer·to Val·lar·ta \ˈpwer-tō-bä-ˈyär-tä\. Coastal town and resort, Jalisco state, W cen. Mexico; munic. pop. (1990p) 111,175.

Puer·to Va·ras \ˈpwer-tō-ˈvä-räs\. City on Lake Llanquihue, Los Lagos region, S cen. Chile, ab. 12 mi. (19 km.) N of Puerto Montt.

Puertoviejo. See PORTOVIEJO.

Puer·to Wil·ches \ˈpwer-tō-ˈwēl-chās\. River port, Santander dept., N cen. Colombia, on Magdalena River N of Barrancabermeja.

Pu·ga·chev \ˌpü-gə-ˈchȯf\ *also* **Pu·ga·chevsk** \ˌpü-gə-ˈchȯfsk\; *formerly* **Ni·ko·la·evsk** *or* **Ni·ko·la·yevsk** \ˌni-kə-ˈlī-əfsk\. Town, E Saratov Oblast, Russia in Europe, 120 mi. (193 km.) ENE of the city of Saratov on the navigable Irgiz River; terminus of a branch of the Saratov-Oral railroad.

Puget Sound \ˈpyü-jət\. Arm of Pacific Ocean extending S in W Washington from E end of Strait of Juan de Fuca through Admiralty Inlet; ab. 80 mi. (130 km.) long at its greatest extent; 561 sq. mi. (1453 sq. km.); important U.S. naval shipyard at Bremerton is on its W shore opp. Seattle. Explored by British navigator George Vancouver 1792.

Pugh, Mount \'pyü\. Peak, Snohomish co., NW cen. Washington; 7150 ft. (2179 m.).

Puglia \'pü-lyä\ *or* **Apu·lia** \ä-'pü-lyä\ *or* **Le Pu·glie** \lə-pü-'lyā\. Autonomous region, SE Italy, bet. Adriatic Sea on N and Apennines and Gulf of Taranto on S; ✻ Bari; vast coastal plain; watered by Ofanto River; wine, wheat, oats, olives, fruits, tobacco; livestock raising, fishing; chemicals. See table at ITALY.

Puig·cer·dá \,pwēg-ther-'thä\. Frontier commune, Gerona prov., NE Spain, 80 mi. (129 km.) NNW of Barcelona; pop. (1991c) 6329. See BOURG-MADAME.

Pu·ji·lí \,pü-hē-'lē\. Town, Cotopaxi prov., cen. Ecuador, ab. 50 mi. (80 km.) S of Quito.

Pu·jut, Tan·jung \'tän-,jüŋ-pü-'jůt\ *or* **Point Pu·djut** \pü-'jůt\; *formerly* **Saint Nich·o·las Point** \'ni-kə-ləs\ *or Du.* **Sint Ni·co·laas Punt** \sint-'nē-kə-läs-'pənt\. Cape at NW end of the island of Java, Indonesia, on Sunda Strait where the strait opens into Java Sea. Naval battle off this point Feb. 28, 1942 in which U.S.S. *Houston* and H.M.A.S. *Perth* were destroyed by Japanese.

Pu·ka·ki, Lake \pů-'kä-kē\. Lake, S cen. South I., New Zealand, near foot of Mt. Cook; 9.5 mi. (15 km.) long; 32 sq. mi. (83 sq. km.).

Pu·ka·pu·ka \,pü-kä-'pü-kä\. Chief island of the Danger Is., in Northern Cook Is. group, cen. Pacific Ocean, N of Cook Is.; ab. 2 sq. mi. (5 sq. km.); pop. (1986c) 761.

Pu·kas·kwa National Park \pü-'kas-kwə\. See CANADA, *National Parks.*

Pu·kë \'pü-kə\. **1.** District of N Albania. See table at ALBANIA.

2. Town, its ✻, ab. 50 mi. (80 km.) N of Tiranë.

Puket. See PHUKET.

Pu·kou *or* **P'u–k'ou** *also* **Pu·kow** \'pü-'kō\. Port on N bank of the Chang, W Jiangsu prov., E China, opp. Nanjing; on railroad line 628 mi. (1011 km.) from Tianjin.

Pu·la \'pü-lä\ *also* **Pulj** \'pül-yə\ *or Ital.* **Po·la** \'pō-lä\; *anc.* **Pi·e·tas Ju·lia** \'pī-ə-,tas-'jül-yə\. City, Croatia, on the Adriatic Sea ab. 45 mi. (70 km.) SW of Rijeka; pop. (1991c) 62,690; naval base and shipbuilding center; seaside resort; considerable Roman remains (incl. temple, amphitheater, and triumphal arch); Byzantine basilica.

History: Came under Rome 2d cent. B.C.; declined during Middle Ages; taken by Venetians 12th cent.; scene of Genoese victory over Venetians 1379; to Austria 1797; became chief Austro-Hungarian naval station; to Italy by treaty 1920; assigned to Yugoslavia by treaty of 1947.

Pu·lan·gi \pü-'läŋ-gē\. See MINDANAO 2.

Pu·lar \pü-'lär\. Peak, E Antofagasta region, N Chile, near Argentine border; 20,423 ft. (6225 m.).

Pu·las·ki \pə-'las-kē, pyů-\. **1.** Name of counties in seven states of the U.S. See tables at ARKANSAS, GEORGIA, ILLINOIS, INDIANA, KENTUCKY, MISSOURI, VIRGINIA.

2. Village, a ⊗ of Oswego co., cen. New York, near Lake Ontario 30 mi. (48 km.) SSW of Watertown; pop. (1990c) 2525.

3. City, ⊗ of Giles co., S Tennessee, 28 mi. (45 km.) S of Columbia; pop. (1990c) 7895; Martin Methodist Coll. (1870).

4. Town, ⊗ of Pulaski co., SW Virginia, in Allegheny Mts. 52 mi. (84 km.) WSW of Roanoke; pop. (1990c) 9985.

Pu·lau \'pü-,laů\ *also* **Poe·lau** \'pü-\ *or* **Pu·lo** \-,lō\. Malay term meaning "island," often used with names of islands in the Malay Archipelago, as **Pulau Langkawi** (see LANGKAWI, PULAU).

Pulau Pinang. See PENANG 2.

Pu·ła·wy \pü-'wä-və\. Commune, Lublin prov., E Poland, on E bank of Vistula River ab. 30 mi. (48 km.) WNW of the city of Lublin; pop. (1989e) 52,207; formerly seat of Czartoryski family (influential in Polish government esp. 18th–19th cents.).

Pul·i·cat \'pə-li-kət\. **1.** Town, Tamil Nadu, S India, at S end of Pulicat Lake; became Dutch post 1610; long chief Dutch settlement on Coromandel Coast; became British 1825.

2. Town, India. See PALGHAT.

Pulicat Lake. Shallow lagoon in Andhra Pradesh and Tamil Nadu, India, ab. 37 mi. (60 km.) along coast W of Sriharikota I.

Pulj. See PULA.

Pul·ko·vo \'pül-kə-və\. Village, cen. St. Petersburg Oblast, W Russia in Europe, 11 mi. (17 km.) S of the city of St. Petersburg; seat of national observatory 30°19′40″E, 59°46′19″N, founded 1839. Badly damaged in WWII, reopened 1954.

Pul·liam Bluff \'pül-yəm\. Peak, S Brewster co., W Texas; 6921 ft. (2110 m.).

Pull·man \'půl-mən\. **1.** Former industrial suburb of Chicago, Illinois; founded 1880; since 1889 a SE section of Chicago.

2. City, Whitman co., SE Washington, 65 mi. (105 km.) S of Spokane; pop. (1990c) 23,478; diversified agriculture; Washington State Univ. (1890).

Pulo. See PULAU.

Pu·log, Mount \'pü-,lȯg\. Highest peak in N Luzon, Philippines, at S end of Cordillera Central; 9606 ft. (2928 m.).

Pultova *or* **Pultowa.** See POLTAVA.

Puł·tusk \'pü-,tüsk\. Commune, SE Ciechanów prov., NE cen. Poland, on Narew River 32 mi. (52 km.) N of Warsaw; pop. (1981p) 15,218. Scene of Saxon defeat by Charles XII of Sweden 1703; Russians defeated by French under Emperor Napoléon 1806.

Pu·lu·wat \,pü-lü-'wät\. Atoll, cen. Caroline Is., Kiribati, W Pacific Ocean, 180 mi. (290 km.) W of Chuuk.

Pum·mel Peak \'pə-məl\. Mountain, S Brewster co., W Texas; 6630 ft. (2021 m.).

Pu·ná \pü-'nä\. Island in the Gulf of Guayaquil, SW Ecuador; 29 mi. (47 km.) long.

Puna de Atacama. See ATACAMA, PUNA DE.

Pu·na·kha \'pü-nə-kə\. Town, a former ✻ of Bhutan; pop. (1982e) 1100.

Puncak Jaya. See JAYA, PUNCAK.

Punchbowl. See HONOLULU 2.

Pu·ne \'pü-nə\; *mostly formerly* **Poo·na** \'pü-nə\. City, Maharashtra, W India, on tributary of the Bhima River 80 mi. (129 km.) ESE of Bombay; pop. (1991c) 1,566,651; rail and road junction; textiles, paper, chemicals, soap; several notable palaces and temples; extensive public gardens; numerous educational and scientific institutions; headquarters of southern command of Indian Army; university (1948). Former ✻ of Maratha empire; came under British rule 1817.

Pún·goè *or* **Pun·gwe** \'půŋ-gwə\ *or Port.* **Pun·gue** \'půŋ-gwə\. River, S cen. Mozambique; flows SE into Indian Ocean at Beira; ab. 200 mi. (320 km.) long.

Pun·jab \,pən-'jäb, -'jab, 'pən-,\ *or Hind.* **Pan·jāb** \,pən-'jäb\. **1.** Former province of British India; 99,089 sq. mi. (256,641 sq. km.); included a number of Indian states under Punjab government; ✻ Lahore, summer ✻ Simla. Divided Aug. 1947 into East Punjab (*q.v.*), India, and West Punjab (see PUNJAB 4), Pakistan. Greater part occupied the valleys of the Indus and the five great tributaries (hence its name, Persian *panj* five and *āb* waters) of the Indus: Jhelum, Chenab, Ravi, Beas, and Sutlej; these rivers now chiefly in West Punjab, the Sutlej forming part of the boundary. NE part (in East Punjab) is wholly in the Himalayas. Location of advanced Indus Valley civilization, brought to end by arrival of Aryans c. 1500 B.C.; became part of Persian Empire c. 500 B.C.; invaded by Macedonian King Alexander the Great 326 B.C.; under Maurya dynasty 322–185 B.C.; in succeeding centuries tributary to various rulers; conquered by Muslims under Afghan Sultan Maḥmūd of Ghaznī early 11th cent.; prospered under Moguls 16th–18th cents.; after Sikh Wars annexed to British India 1849; North-West Frontier prov. set apart 1901; constituted autonomous province 1937. See PAKISTAN.

2. Former state, India. See EAST PUNJAB.

3. *or* **Pun·jabi Su·ba** \pən-'jä-bē-'sü-bə, -'ja-\. State, N India, formed from former Punjab state; ✻ Chandigarh; wheat, cotton, millets; important irrigation projects; largest cities: Ludhiana, Amritsar, Chandigarh, Jullundur; formed 1966; came under direct Federal rule 1987–1992. See table at INDIA.

4. *formerly* **West Punjab** *or* **Western Punjab.** Province, Pakistan; ✻ Lahore; chief cities: Lahore, Faisalabad, Rawalpindi, Multan, Gujranwala; formed 1947 from former Punjab prov.; provincial status abolished 1955, reestablished 1970. See table at PAKISTAN.

Punjab States. Former grouping of Indian states under Punjab government; ✻ Lahore.

Punjab States Agency. Former group of 45 Indian states and estates in the Punjab (see PUNJAB 1), India; in political relations with the crown representative through the resident at Lahore. The 14 most important of these (incl. Patiala, Bahawalpur, Khairpur, Chamba, Jind) had an area of 38,146 sq. mi. (98,798 sq. km.); a 2d group, known as **Punjab Hill States** (most important Tehri Garhwal and Sirmur), had an area of 11,375 sq. mi. (29,461 sq. km.).

Pu·no \ˈpü-nō\. Town, SE Peru, on W shore of Lake Titicaca 218 mi. (351 km.) by rail E of Arequipa; pop. (1990e) 99,600; alt. 12,641 ft. (3853 m.); technical university (19th cent.), university (1961).

Pun Run, Lake \pün-ˈrün\. Lake, cen. Peru; alt. ab. 14,200 ft. (4330 m.).

Punt \ˈpu̇nt\. Ancient Egyptian name for a part of Africa probably along S coast of Red Sea to Gulf of Aden (modern coastal Eritrea and Djibouti). Visited by Egyptian expeditions as early as 23d cent. B.C.; voyage there of Egyptian Queen Hatshepsut 15th cent. B.C. depicted in reliefs in the Deir el-Bahri temple near Thebes; was source of incense, ivory, and ostrich feathers for Egypt.

Punta, Cerro de. See CERRO DE PUNTA.

Pun·ta Al·ta \ˈpün-tä-ˈäl-tä\. Town, Buenos Aires prov., E cen. Argentina, ab. 20 mi. (30 km.) SE of Bahia Blanca.

Pun·ta Are·nas \ˈpün-tä-ä-ˈrā-näs\ *or 1927–37* **Ma·gal·la·nes** \ˌmä-gä-ˈyä-näs\. Seaport city, ✻ of Magallanes y Antártica Chilena region, S Chile, on Brunswick Penin; pop. (1982c) 95,332; formerly ✻ of Magallanes prov.; ships meat, wool; military and naval facilities; southernmost city in Chile (53°10′S); founded 1849.

Punta Argentera. See ARGENTERA, PUNTA.

Punta de Aguja. See AGUJA, POINT.

Pun·ta del Es·te \ˈpün-tä-t͟hel-ˈes-tā\. Town, Maldonado dept., S Uruguay, 70 mi. (113 km.) E of Montevideo; seaside resort. In 1962 site of Inter-American Foreign Ministers Conference at which suspension of Cuba from active membership in the Organization of American States (*q.v.*) was agreed upon.

Punta del Faro. See FARO, CAPE.

Pun·ta Gor·da \ˌpən-tə-ˈgȯr-də\. **1.** City, ⊗ of Charlotte co., SW Florida, on Charlotte Harbor 20 mi. (32 km.) in from Gulf of Mexico; pop. (1990c) 10,747; fishing resort.
2. Seaport, ✻ of Toledo dist., S Belize; pop. (1990p) 2585.

Punta Mico. See MONKEY POINT.

Punta Mita. See MITA POINT.

Pun·ta·re·nas \ˌpün-tä-ˈrā-näs\. **1.** Province of W cen. Costa Rica. See table at COSTA RICA.
2. Seaport, its ✻, on Gulf of Nicoya; exports bananas and coffee; processes fish.

Puntilla, La. See LA PUNTILLA.

Pun·to Fi·jo \ˈpün-to-ˈfē-hō\. Town, Falcón state, NW Venezuela, on SW coast of Paraguaná Penin.; pop. (1990e) 91,345.

Punx·su·taw·ney \ˌpəŋk-sə-ˈtȯ-nē\. Borough, Jefferson co., W cen. Pennsylvania, 17 mi. (27 km.) SW of Du Bois; pop. (1990c) 6782; focus of U.S. Groundhog Day observance.

Pu·pa·yax \ˌpü-pä-ˈyäsh\. Peak, W Bolivia, NE of Lake Titicaca; 19,080 ft. (5816 m.).

Pupluna. See POPULONIUM.

Pu·ra·cé \ˌpü-rä-ˈsā\. Active volcano, SW cen. Colombia, just SE of Popayán; 15,604 ft. (4756 m.); main feature in **Puracé National Park,** estab. 1961.

Purali. See PORALI.

Pu·ra·ri \pu̇-ˈrär-ē\. River, E cen. New Guinea I., Papua New Guinea; flows generally SSE to Gulf of Papua; ab. 170 mi. (275 km.) long.

Pur·beck, Isle of \ˈpər-ˌbek\. Peninsula in Dorset, S England; extends E into English Channel; 12 mi. (19 km.) long; harbor of Poole is on N; source of Purbeck marble, onshore oil.

Pur·cell \pər-ˈsel\. City, ⊗ of McClain co., cen. Oklahoma, on Canadian River 34 mi. (55 km.) S of Oklahoma City; pop. (1990c) 4784.

Pur·cell Mountains \ˈpər-səl, pər-ˈsel\. Subsidiary mountain range in SE British Columbia, Canada, bet. the Selkirk Mts. and the main range of the Rocky Mts.; highest Mt. Farnham 11,343 ft. (3457 m.).

Pur·ga·toire \ˈpər-gə-ˌtwär, ˈpi-kət-ˌwīr\. River, S and SE Colorado; rises in W Las Animas co., flows NE into Arkansas River in Bent co.; 186 mi. (299 km.) long.

Pur·ga·to·ry Peak \ˈpər-gə-ˌtōr-ē\. Mountain, Costilla and Las Animas cos., S Colorado, in the Sangre de Cristo Mts.; 13,719 ft. (4182 m.).

Pu·ri \ˈpu̇r-ē\ *also* **Ja·gan·nath** \ˈjə-gə-ˌnät\ *or* **Jug·ger·naut** \ˈjə-gər-ˌnȯt, -ˌnät\. Seaport town, E Orissa, E India, on Bay of Bengal 260 mi. (418 km.) SSW of Calcutta; pop. (1991p) 124,835. One of the major centers of Hindu pilgrimage. Main temple (12th cent.) sacred to Krishna under the name Jagannath; scene of many festivals, incl. the Rathayātrā, at which the image of Jagannath is pulled through the streets on a huge cart with 16 enormous wheels.

Puriramya. See BURIRAM.

Pur·me·rend \ˌpər-mə-ˈrent\. Commune, North Holland prov., W Netherlands, 8 mi. (13 km.) NNE of Amsterdam; pop. (1992c) 62,504.

Pur·na \ˈpu̇r-nə\. River, cen. India; flows SE in NW Hyderabad to the upper Godavari River;ab. 220 mi. (355 km.) long.

Pūr·nia *also* **Pur·nea** \ˈpər-nē-ə\. Town, NE Bihar, NE India, N of the Ganges ab. 50 mi. (80 km.) NE of Bhagalpur; pop. (1991p) 135,995; trades in rice and jute.

Pursak. See PORSUK.

Pur·sat \ˈpu̇r-ˈsät\ *also* **Poŭ·thĭ·săt** \ˈpu̇r-ˈsät—*sic*\. Town, cen. Cambodia, S of the Tonle Sap and on railroad line 100 mi. (161 km.) NW of Phnom Penh; pop. (1987e) 16,000.

Pu·ruán·di·ro \pür-ˈwän-dē-rō\. Town, Michoacán state, SW Mexico, just W of Lake Cuitzeo; munic. pop. (1990p) 70,964.

Pu·ru·lia \pə-ˈrü-lē-ə\. Town, West Bengal, NE India, 140 mi. (225 km.) WNW of Calcutta; pop. (1991p) 92,574; road junction.

Pu·rus \pü-ˈrüs\. Navigable river, NW cen. South America; rises in Andes in SE Peru, flows NE across Amazonas state, Brazil, and into Amazon River above Manaus; ab. 2100 mi. (3380 km.) long.

Pur·wa·kar·ta *or Du.* **Poer·wa·kar·ta** \ˌpu̇r-wə-ˈkär-tə\. Town, West Java prov., Indonesia, ab. 60 mi. (95 km.) SE of Jakarta.

Pur·wo·da·di *or Du.* **Poer·wo·da·di** \ˌpu̇r-wə-ˈdä-dē\. Town, Central Java prov., Indonesia; railroad junction point 35 mi. (56 km.) ESE of Semarang.

Pur·wo·ker·to *or Du.* **Poer·wo·ker·to** \ˌpu̇r-wə-ˈker-tō\. Town, Central Java prov., Indonesia, just NW of Banjumas.

Pu·san \ˈpü-ˌsän\ *or Jp.* **Fu·san** \ˈfü-ˌsän\. City, SE South Korea, ab. 200 mi. (320 km.) SSE of Seoul; pop. (1990e) 3,825,000; has special city (provincial) status; major seaport and industrial center, with shipbuilding, textile, and metallurgical industries; rice mills, salt refineries; opened to Japanese trade 1876 and to general foreign trade 1883; developed into major port under Japanese rule 1910–45; during Korean War, center of a beachhead held by UN forces 1950 and later provisional ✻. See table at KOREA, SOUTH.

Push·kar Lake \ˈpu̇sh-kər\. Lake in E cen. Rajasthan, NW cen. India, 7 mi. (11 km.) W of Ajmer; one of India's most sacred waters, it is scene of annual pilgrim fair and site of only temple in India dedicated to Brahma.

Push·kin \ˈpu̇sh-kən\; *or 1918–37* **Det·sko·ye Se·lo** \ˈdet-skə-yə-sə-ˈlō\; *earlier* **Tsar·sko·ye Se·lo** \ˈtsär-skə-yə-sə-ˈlō\. Town, NW St. Petersburg Oblast, W Russia in Europe; pop. (1991e) 95,300; a residential and resort suburb of St. Petersburg.

History: Site presented by Russian Czar Peter the Great to his wife Catherine c. 1710 as summer residence, Tsarskoye Selo ("The Czar's [Tsar's] Village"). Present palace begun 1752; was an important imperial residence until 1917 Bolshevik Revolution, when town was subsequently renamed

Detskoye Selo ("Children's Village") and converted into a health resort; name changed 1937 to Pushkin in honor of the Russian poet who studied in the lyceum there; palace buildings severely damaged in WWII but extensive restoration work has been undertaken since 1945.

Push·ki·no \ˈpu̇sh-kə-nə\. Town, Moscow Oblast, W cen. Russia in Europe, 20 mi. (32 km.) NE of the city of Moscow; pop. (1991e) 75,800.

Push·ma·ta·ha \ˌpu̇sh-mə-ˈtä-hä, -hȯ\. County in SE Oklahoma. See table at OKLAHOMA.

Pu·ster·tal \ˈpu̇s-tər-ˌtäl\ *or* **Val Pu·ste·ria** \ˈväl-ˌpü-stə-ˈrē-ə\. Valley, N of the Carnic Alps, NE Italy and W Carinthia, Austria.

Pu·tao \pü-ˈtau̇\; *formerly* **Fort Hertz** \ˈərts\. Town in extreme N of Myanmar, S of Namni Pass.

Pu·teaux \pǖ-ˈtō\. Commune, Hauts-de-Seine dept., N France, NW suburb of Paris on Seine River; pop. (1990c) 42,917.

Puteoli. See POZZUOLI.

Pu·ti·gna·no \ˌpü-tē-ˈnyä-nō\. Commune, Bari prov., Puglia, SE Italy, 23 mi. (37 km.) SE of the seaport of Bari; pop. (1989c) 27,254.

Put–in–Bay \ˌpu̇t-ˌin-ˈbā\. Bay in South Bass I., Lake Erie, in Ottawa co., Ohio; scene of Commodore Oliver Perry's victory over the British fleet 1813.

Pu·ting, Tan·jung *or Du.* **Tand·joeng Poe·ting** \ˈtän-ˌjüŋ-ˈpü-ˌtiŋ\. Cape on SW coast of Borneo, Indonesia, projecting into Java Sea, 3°31′S, 111°46′E.

Put·na \ˈpüt-nä\. River, NE Romania; flows N, E, and SE into Siret River; 81 mi. (130 km.) long.

Put·nam \ˈpət-nəm\. **1.** Name of counties in nine states of the U.S. See tables at FLORIDA, GEORGIA, ILLINOIS, INDIANA, MISSOURI, NEW YORK, OHIO, TENNESSEE, WEST VIRGINIA.
2. City, Windham co., NE Connecticut, on Quinebaug River at mouth of Mill River 21 mi. (34 km.) NE of Willimantic; pop. (1990c) 9031; waterfall near center of city; incorp. 1895.

Put·ney \ˈpət-nē\. Ward of Wandsworth met. borough, London, England.

P'u–t'o Shan. See PUTUO SHAN.

Putrid Sea. See SIVASH SEA.

Put·ta·lam \ˈpət-ᵊl-əm\. Seaport town, NW Sri Lanka, 80 mi. (129 km.) N of Colombo; pop. (1981p) 21,463.

Puttiala. See PATIALA.

Pu·tu·ma·yo \ˌpü-tü-ˈmä-yō\. **1.** River, NW South America; rises in SW Colombia, flows SE, forming large section of Peru-Colombia boundary, crosses border into Brazil, where it is known as the **Içá** \ē-ˈsä\, and empties into Amazon River; ab. 980 mi. (1575 km.) long; flows through rubber-producing region.
2. Department of S Colombia. See table at COLOMBIA.

Pu·tuo Shan \ˈpü-ˈtwȯ-ˈshän\ *or W.-G.* **P'u–t'o Shan** \ˈpü-ˈtō-ˈshän\. Small island in Zhoushan Archipelago, Zhejiang prov., E China, just SE of Zhoushan I.; a sacred area of Chinese Buddhism; numerous temples and monasteries; noted as scenic area.

Pu'·u·ho·nua o Ho·nau·nau National Historical Park \ˌpü-ü-hō-ˈnü-ä-ō-hō-ˈnau̇-ˌnau̇\. See UNITED STATES, *National Historical Parks.*

Puu Ku·kui \ˌpü-kü-ˈkü-ē\. Mountain, Maui I., at W end, Hawaii; 5787 ft. (1764 m.).

Puu·la·ve·si \ˈpü-lä-ˌvā-sē\. Lake, Mikkeli prov., S Finland; 154 sq. mi. (399 sq. km.).

Puu Poa Point \ˈpü-ˈpō-ä\. Cape on N coast of Kauai I., Hawaii.

Puy, Le. See LE PUY.

Puy·al·lup \pyü-ˈa-ləp\. **1.** River, W cen. Washington; flows NW into Puget Sound at Tacoma; ab. 50 mi. (80 km.) long.
2. City, Pierce co., W cen. Washington, on Puyallup River 8 mi. (13 km.) ESE of Tacoma; pop. (1990c) 23,875.

Puy–de–Dôme \ˌpwē-də-ˈdōm\. Department of S cen. France. See table at FRANCE.

Puy de Dôme. See DÔME, PUY DE.

Puy de Sancy. See SANCY, PUY DE.

Pu·ye·hue, La·go \ˈlä-gō-pü-ˈyā-wā\. Lake in Los Lagos region, S cen. Chile, N of Puerto Montt.

Puyehue National Park. National park, S cen. Chile E of Osorno, on Argentina border; 290 sq. mi. (751 sq. km.); volcanic activity; park estab. 1941.

Puy–en–Velay, Le. See LE PUY.

Puy·mo·rens, Col de \ˈkȯl-də-ˌpwē-mȯ-ˈräⁿs\. Mountain pass, Pyrénées-Orientales dept., S France, in the Pyrenees just NE of Andorra; 6335 ft. (1931 m.).

Pu·yo \ˈpü-yō\. Town, ✻ of Pastaza prov., cen. Ecuador; pop. (1990c) 14,438.

Pwa·ni \ˈpwä-nē\ *or Eng.* **Coast.** Administrative region of E Tanzania. See table at TANZANIA.

Pwll·he·li \pül-ˈhe-lē\. Town, Gwynedd co., NW Wales, on S coast of Lleyn Penin. on Cardigan Bay; pop. (1981p) 3989; seaside resort.

Pyandzh. See PANJ.

Pya·pon \pyä-ˈpōn\. Town, Myanmar, in delta of the Irrawaddy 45 mi. (72 km.) SW of Yangon; pop. (1983c) 39,862.

Pyarnu. See PÄRNU.

Pya·si·na \ˈpyä-sə-nə\. River, Krasnoyarsk Kray, N Russia in Asia; in W part of Taymyr Penin., flows N into the Arctic Ocean; 506 mi. (814 km.) long.

Pya·ti·gorsk *also* **Pia·ti·gorsk** \pi-tē-ˈgȯrsk\. Town, S Stavropol' Kray, S Russia in Europe, on a tributary of the Kuma River 140 mi. (225 km.) WNW of Grozny, Chechnya; pop. (1992e) 132,000; health resort, with mineral springs; on a plateau on the N slopes of the Caucasus.

Pyd·na \ˈpid-nə\. Ancient town in Macedonia, N Greece; ruins on W shore of Gulf of Salonika. Scene of battle nearby 168 B.C. in which the Romans under Lucius Aemilius Paulus defeated the Macedonians under their last king, Perseus, thus bringing to an end the independent Macedonian kingdom.

Pyè. See PROME.

Pyeitawinzu Myanma Naingngandaw. See MYANMAR.

Py·hä·kos·ki \ˈpyü-he-ˌkȯ-skē\. Rapids in Oulu River near its mouth SE of Oulu, W Finland; name means "Holy Rapids."

Pyin·ma·na \ˈpyin-mä-ˌnä\. Town on the Sittang River, Mandalay division, Myanmar; on railroad line 150 mi. (241 km.) S of Mandalay.

Py·los \ˈpī-ˌläs\ *or Gk.* **Pí·los** \ˈpē-ˌlȯs\. **1.** Seaport, Greece. See NAVARINO 2.
2. Town, NW Peloponnese, Greece, on the Peneus River.

P'yŏng·yang \ˌpyəŋ-ˈyaŋ, ˌpyȯŋ-, -ˈyäŋ\ *or Jp.* **Hei·jo** \ˈhā-ˌjō\. City, ✻ of North Korea, on the Taedong River 30 mi. (48 km.) from its mouth; 77 sq. mi. (199 sq. km.); pop. (1987e) 2,355,000; a center of heavy industry, with iron and steel, chemical, rubber, and textile plants, an arsenal, and railroad workshops; university (1946).
History: Founded more than 3,000 years ago; invaded by Chinese, who established colony, c. 108 B.C.; ✻ of Koguryŏ kingdom 427 A.D. until 668 A.D. when it was subjugated by Chinese invaders; devastated by Japanese c. 1592; made an industrial center under Japanese rule 1910–45; captured by UN forces during Korean War 1950 but retaken by Chinese Communist troops; suffered extensive damage from UN air raids but has been largely rebuilt since 1953.

Pyr·a·mid Lake \ˈpir-ə-ˌmid\. Lake, S Washoe co., NW Nevada; ab. 30 mi. (50 km.) long by 4 to 13 mi. (6 to 20 km.) wide; 188 sq. mi. (487 sq. km.); remnant of Lake Lahontan.

Pyramid Mountain. **1.** Peak in Glacier National Park, NW Montana; 8100 ft. (2470 m.).
2. Peak, Chelan co., cen. Washington; 8245 ft. (2513 m.).

Pyramid Peak. **1.** Mountain in the Sierra Nevada, E cen. Eldorado co., E California; 9983 ft. (3043 m.).
2. Mountain, Pitkin co., W cen. Colorado; 14,018 ft. (4273 m.).
3. Mountain, NE Lemhi co., E cen. Idaho; 9594 ft. (2924 m.).
4. Mountain, N Cascade Range, NW Washington; 7800 ft. (2400 m.).
5. Mountain on E boundary of Yellowstone National Park, NW Wyoming; 10,497 ft. (3199 m.).

Pyramus. See CEYHAN 1.

Pyr·e·nees \ˈpir-ə-ˌnēz\ *or Fr.* **Py·ré·nées** \pē-rā-ˈnā\ *or Span.* **Pi·ri·ne·os** \ˌpē-rē-ˈnā-ōs\; *anc.* **Pyr·e·naei Mon·tes** \ˌpir-ə-

ˈnē-ī-ˈmän-tēz\. Mountain range extending along the France-Spain border from the Bay of Biscay to the SW coast of the Gulf of Lion; ab. 270 mi. (435 km.) long; highest peak Pico de Aneto 11,168 ft. (3404 m.) in the Maladetas in cen. part; an historically effective barrier bet. the two countries, has principal highways only at ends near coasts; traversed by few passes, notably Somport, Poterla, and Puymorens, all over 5000 ft. (1500 m.), and the pass at Roncesvalles 3576 ft. (1090 m.), made famous by the 12th cent. epic poem *Chanson de Roland*, based on a battle there 778; pass often used by invading armies; mountains noted for many streams (*gaves*), waterfalls, and cirques.

Pyrénées–At·lan·tiques \-ˌȧt-län-ˈtēk\. Department of France. See table at FRANCE.

Pyrénées–Or·ien·tales \-ˌȯr-yäⁿ-ˈtȧl\. Department of France. See table at FRANCE.

Pyr·gos \ˈpir-gȯs\ *or Gk.* **Pír·gos** \ˈpir-gös\. Town, ✱ of Elis dept., Peloponnese, Greece, 120 mi. (193 km.) W of Athens; pop. (1991p) 27,248.

Py·rox·ene Peak \pə-ˈräk-sēn\. Peak, Madison co., SW Montana; 9000 ft. (2750 m.).

Py·sko·wi·ce \ˌpə-skȯ-ˈvēt-se\. Town, Katowice prov., S Poland, ab. 20 mi. (30 km.) WNW of the city of Katowice; pop. (1989e) 21,291.

Pytho. See DELPHI 2.

Pyu \ˈpyü\. Town, Myanmar, on railroad line and highway W of the Sittang 30 mi. (48 km.) S of Toungoo.

Q

Qaa·naaq \kä-ˈnäk\ *or* **Thule** \ˈtü-lē, ˈthü-\. Settlement, NW Greenland, on coast of Hayes Penin. N of Cape York; pop. (1980c) 771; Danish trading post founded 1910 by explorer Knud Rasmussen; site of U.S. air base since WWII.

Qabes *or* **Qābis.** See GABÈS.

Qaḍārif, Al–. See GEDAREF.

Qādisīyah, al–. See KADISIYA.

Qafsah. See GAFSA.

Qāhirah, Al–. See CAIRO 2 (Egypt).

Qai·dam \ˈchī-ˈdäm\ *or W.-G.* **Ch'ai–ta–mu** \ˈchī-ˈdä-ˈmə̇\; *also* **Tsai·dam** \ˈchī-ˈdäm\. Intermontane basin, Qinghai prov., W cen. China; a sandy swamp region with salt lakes; alt. 9000 ft. (2743 m.).

Qain. See QĀYEN.

Qais. See QEYS.

Qal·lā·bāt \ˌkȧ-lä-ˈbät\ *or* **Gal·la·bat** \gä-ˈla-bat\. Town, E Sudan, on Ethiopian border NW of Lake Tana.

Qalunya. See EMMAUS 2.

Qal·yûb *also* **Kal·yub** \käl-ˈyüb\. Town, Qalyubīya gov., Egypt, 10 mi. (16 km.) N of Cairo, at head of Nile Delta; pop. (1986p) 86,684.

Qal·yu·bī·ya *also* **Kal·yu·bi·ya** \ˌkäl-yu̇-ˈbē-yə\. Governorate of N Egypt. See table at EGYPT.

Qa·mar, Ghub·bat al \ˈgu̇-bət-ˌȧl-ˈkä-mər\ *or* **Qamr Bay** \ˈkä-mər\; *mostly formerly* **Ka·mar Bay** \ˈkä-mər\. Inlet of the Arabian Sea, E Yemen, S coast of Arabian Penin., E of Cape Fartak.

Qamaran. See KAMARAN.

Qāmishlī, Al. See AL QĀMISHLĪ.

Qamr Bay. See QAMAR, GHUBBAT AL.

Qan·da·hār *or* **Kan·da·hār** \ˌkən-də-ˈhär, ˈkən-də-ˌ\; *anc.* **Al·ex·an·dria Ar·a·cho·si·o·rum** \ˌa-lig-ˈzan-drē-ə-ˌar-ə-ˌkō-zē-ˈōr-əm\. Commercial city, S Afghanistan, 300 mi. (483 km.) SW of Kabul; 2d city in size in the country; at elev. of 3300 ft. (1006 m.); connected with Quetta over the Chaman Pass; has long been a trading center both for imports and exports.

History: Held by Mogul Empire of India (*q.v.*) after its capture by Bābur (Emperor Ẓahīr-ud-Dīn Mūḥammad); captured c. 1625 by Shāh ʻAbbās I of Persia; center of successful Afghan uprising against Persia 1706–08; independent until 1737; under Aḥmad Shāh Durrānī early 18th cent., one of the capitals of Afghanistan (*q.v.*); held by British 1839–42 and 1879–81, during the latter period its garrison relieved 1880 by memorable march of British Gen. Frederick Roberts.

Qanṭarah, Al *or* **Qantara, El** *or* **Qantara.** See AL QANṬARAH.

Qan·ṭa·rat al–Faḥṣ \ˈkän-tə-rət-ȧl-ˈfäks, -ˈfäs\; *formerly* **Pont du Fahs** \ˌpōⁿ-dᵫ-ˈfäs\. Town, N Tunisia, ab. 12 mi. (19 km.) W of Zaghwān; scene of battles in WWII 1943.

Qaqortoq. See JULIANEHÅB.

Qa·ra Dagh \ˈkär-ə-ˈdä\. **1.** Mountain range, NW Iran, S of Araks River; highest point 9545 ft. (2909 m.).

2. Mountain range, NE Iraq, on Iranian border, SE end of mountains of Kurdistan; highest point 5923 ft. (1805 m.).

Qa·ra·ghan·dy \ˌkä-rä-ˈgän-də\ *or* **Ka·ra·gan·da** \ˌkär-ə-ˈgän-də\. **1.** Administrative subdivision of Kazakhstan, NW of Lake Balkhash; 153,977 sq. mi. (398,800 sq. km.); pop. (1991e) 1,339,900; ✻ Qaraghandy; extensive steppe region; coal deposits; an oblast of U.S.S.R. until 1991.

2. City, its ✻, NE cen. Kazakhstan; on railroad line 135 mi. (217 km.) SSE of Astana; pop. (1991e) 608,600; iron and steel foundries.

Qara Kul. See KARAKUL.

Qaraqorum. See KARAKORUM.

Qa·reh \ˈkär-ə\ *also* **Ka·ra** \ˈkär-ə\. River, NW Iran; flows N into Araks River on Azerbaijan border; ab. 160 mi. (255 km.) long.

Qarkilik. See RUOQIANG.

Qar·qan \ˈchär-ˌchän\. **1.** *or W.-G.* **Ch'e–erh–ch'en** \ˈchə-ˈər-ˈchən\. River, W China; flows from N slopes of cen. Kunlun Shan N and NE along SE border of Taklimakan Desert to Lop Nur; ab. 420 mi. (675 km.) long.

2. Town and oasis, Xinjiang Uygur, China. See QIEMO.

Qarqannah, Juzur. See KERKENNAH ISLANDS.

Qarqar. See KARKAR 2.

Qars. See KARS.

Qārūn, Birket *or* **Qarun, Lake.** See BIRKET QĀRŪN.

Qar·yat az Zu·way·tī·nah \ˈkär-yət-ˌaz-ˌzü-wā-ˈtē-nə\; *frequently shortened to* **Az Zuwaytīnah;** *also* **Ez Zue·ti·na** \ˌez-ˌzü-e-ˈtē-nə\. Town, on coastal road, N Libya, on E shore of Gulf of Sidra ab. 40 mi. (65 km.) S of Benghazi.

Qāsh, Al–. See MAREB.

Qasr, Al– *or* **Qasr, El.** See AL-QASR.

Qasr al–Az·raq \ˈkäs-rȧl-ˈȧz-rək\. Town and oasis, N Jordan, 55 mi. (88 km.) E of Amman.

Qaṣrayn, Al–. See AL-QAṢRAYN.

Qa·tar *also* **Ka·tar** \ˈkä-tər, ˈgə-\. Independent emirate, SW Asia, occupying a peninsula on Arabian Penin. projecting into SW Persian Gulf; area ab. 4400 sq. mi. (11,395 sq. km.); ab. 160 mi. (255 km.) long; pop. (1993e) 539,000; ✻ Doha; consists chiefly of low hills and sandy areas; produces oil, natural gas; fish; early inhabitants were nomads and fishermen; partly controlled from Bahrain by Khalīfah family during 18th and 19th cents.; entered into treaty relations with Great Britain 1868; became British protectorate 1916; oil discovered 1940 but not commercially exploited until 1949; became independent state and a member of the UN 1971; joined other Arab nations in establishing Gulf Cooperation Council (GCC) 1981; served as base for air strikes against Iraq in Persian Gulf War 1991.

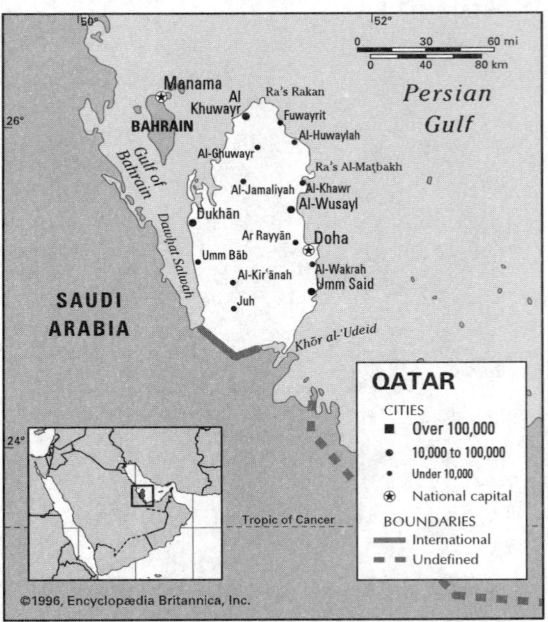

Qatif *or* **Qaṭīf, Al.** See AL QAṬĪF.

Qatrānah, Al– *or* **Qatrana, El** *or* **Qatrana.** See AL-QATRĀNAH.

Qat·ta·ra Depression \kə-'tär-ə\. Low area in N Egypt, 130 mi. (209 km.) W of Cairo and 40 mi. (64 km.) S of the seacoast; ab. 7000 sq. mi. (18,130 sq. km.); deepest point 440 ft. (134 m.) below sea level; because it was impassable to armies and vehicles, it formed the anchor at S end of British defense line at El-Alamein in NW Egypt July 1942, stopping German Field Marshal Erwin Rommel's invasion; followed by Allied success, Oct.–Nov. 1942, at El-Alamein (*q.v.*).

Qā·yen *or* **Qa·in** \kä-'ēn\. Town, Khorāsān prov., E Iran, 175 mi. (282 km.) S of Mashhad; pop. (1986c) 15,955; situated in a broad valley at 4500 ft. (1372 m.) alt.; raises saffron and manufactures carpets and felts. A very old town near the Afghanistan border; has often changed overlords.

Qayrawān, al–. See KAIROUAN.

Qaz·vīn *or* **Kaz·vin** \kaz-'vēn\. **1.** Former province of NW Iran; 9826 sq. mi. (25,449 sq. km.).

2. City, Zanjan prov., NW Iran, ab. 90 mi. (145 km.) NW of Tehran; pop. (1986c) 248,591; important communications center; textile and flour mills. Founded under Sassanid dynasty 3d or 4th cent. A.D.; flourished under Muslims 7th cent.; fortified by Caliph Hārūn al-Rashīd 8th cent.; ✻ of Persia 1548–98; has suffered much from earthquakes.

Qe·na *also* **Ke·na** \'kē-nə, 'kā-\ *or* **Qi·na** \'kē-\. **1.** Governorate of Egypt. See table at EGYPT.

2. *anc.* **Cae·ne** \'sē-nē\ *or* **Cae·nep·o·lis** \si-'ne-pə-lis\. City, its ✻, Upper Egypt, on right bank of the Nile at the bend below Luxor and 280 mi. (451 km.) SSE of Cairo; pop. (1991e) 137,000; a trade center, noted for its manufacture of water jars and bottles.

Qena, Wa·di \'wä-dē\. Watercourse in E cen. Egypt, extending S to the Nile River at Qena.

Qe·qer·tar·su·aq \ˌke-ker-ˌtär-'sü-äk\. **1.** *or* **Dis·ko** \'dis-kō\. Island in Davis Strait, on W coast of Greenland, 70°N; 3200 sq. mi. (8288 sq. km.); coal; the town of Qeqertarsuaq is on S shore.

2. *or* **God·havn** \'gōt͟h-ˌhau̇n\. Town, W Greenland, on Davis Strait on S coast of Qeqertarsuaq I., 69°15′N, 53°33′W; pop. (1980c) 1012; an administrative center; formerly important in whaling industry; has radio and other scientific stations.

Qe·qer·tar·suup Tu·nua Bay \ˌke-ker-ˌtär-'süp-tü-'nü-ä\ *or* **Dis·ko Bay** \'dis-kō\. Bay, Greenland, on W coast, S of Qeqertarsuaq I.

Qesari, Ḥorbat. See CAESAREA 2.

Qeshm \'kesh-ᵊm\ *or* **Qishm** *also* **Kishm** \'kish-ᵊm\. **1.** *anc.* **Oa·rac·ta** \ˌō-ə-'rak-tə\. Island, Iran, at SE end of Persian Gulf, off S coast in Strait of Hormuz; 516 sq. mi. (1336 sq. km.); pop. (1986c) 9682; administratively part of Lorestān prov.; separated from mainland by Clarence Strait. Island is generally rocky and barren but has some fertile areas, producing dates and melons.

2. Chief town of Qeshm I., Iran; at E tip of island.

Qeys \'kīs\ *also* **Qais** *or* **Kais** \'kīs\. Island in SE Persian Gulf, ab. 10 mi. (16 km.) off S coast of Iran; under Arabs in Middle Ages an important trade center, providing a market where goods of the Middle East were exchanged; declined after 14th cent.

Qe·zel Ow·zan \'ke-zəl-au̇-'zan\ *also* **Qi·zil Uzun** \'ki-zəl-yu̇-'zün\ *or* **Ki·zil Uzen** \'ki-zəl-ü-'zen\. River, NW Iran; rises in mountains SE of Daryācheh-ye Orūmīyeh and flows N then SE, then turns NE through the Elburz Mts. to Caspian Sea E of Rasht; ab. 450 mi. (725 km.) long; called Safīd in its lower course.

Qiang·tang *or* *W.-G.* **Ch'iang–t'ang** \'chyäŋ-'täŋ\. N region of Tibet, China; a desert plateau at av. alt. of 17,000 ft. (5182 m.); has many lakes.

Qie·mo \'chye-'mō\ *or* **Qar·qan** \'char-'chan\ *or* *W.-G.* **Ch'ieh–mo** \'chye-'mō\ *or* **Cher·chen**\'cher-'chen\. Town and oasis, S Xinjiang Uygur, W China, on Qarqan River; on major routes of transportation.

Qifṭ \'kift\; *anc.* **Cop·tos** \'käp-təs\. Village in Qena governorate, Egypt, on right bank of the Nile, an ancient city N of Thebes; Coptos was starting point of caravan route from the Nile to Berenice on the Red Sea.

Qi·lian Shan *or* *W.-G.* **Ch'i–lien Shan** \'chē-'lyan-'shän\ *or* **Nan Shan** \'nän-'shän\. Mountain range on border bet. Qinghai and Gansu provs., cen. China, running NW to SE; forms NE rampart of Plateau of Tibet; peaks 18,000 to more than 20,000 ft. (5400 to more than 6000 m. high); traversed by passes 12,000 to 14,000 ft. (3650 to 4260 m.); long valleys; Qinghai Hu (lake) at E end.

Qina. See QENA.

Qing·dao \'chiŋ-'dau̇\ *or* *W.-G.* **Ch'ing–tao** \'chiŋ-'dau̇\ *or* **Tsing·tao** \'chiŋ-'dau̇\ *or* *Ger.* **Tsing·tau** \'tsiŋ-'tau̇\. City, Shandong prov., NE China, on S coast; roughly equidistant (ab. 345 mi. or 555 km.) from Beijing and Shanghai; pop. (1990c) 1,459,195.

History: A fishing village until late 19th cent.; naval base estab. 1891; part of Kiaochow territory occupied by Germany 1897 and leased to Germany for 99 years in 1898; modern city constructed 1898–1914; occupied by Japanese 1914–22, when it was returned to China; again occupied by Japanese 1938–45, during Sino-Japanese War; developed industrially under Communist rule after 1949.

Qing·hai \'chiŋ-'hī\. **1.** *or* *W.-G.* **Ch'ing–hai** \'chiŋ-'hī\; *mostly formerly* **Ko·ko Nor** \'kō-ˌkō-'nōr\ *or* **Ku·ku Nor** \'kü-ˌkü-'nōr\. Lake, NE Qinghai prov., China; 1625 sq. mi. (4209 sq. km.); 68 mi. (109 km.) long; max. depth 125 ft. (38 m.); lies at alt. 10,515 ft. (3205 m.).

2. *or* *W.-G.* **Tsing·hai** *or* **Ch'ing Hai** \'chiŋ-'hī\ *also* **Ko·ko Nor** \'kō-kō-'nu̇r\. Province, W cen. China, bounded on NW by Xinjiang Uygur, on N, NE, and E by Gansu, on SE by Sichuan, on S and SW by Tibet, and on W by Tibet and Xinjiang Uygur; ✻ Xining.

Physical features: Forms NE part of Plateau of Tibet with the greater part above 10,000 ft. (3048 m.); at the NW and in the center is Qaidam swamp at an elev. of ab. 9000 ft. (2745 m.). On the N border, partly in Gansu prov., is the Qilian Shan; in the W cen. part is the E end of the Kunlun Shan, the E extension of which is the A'nyêmaqên Shan reaching heights from 18,000 to 23,490 ft. (5486 to 7160 m.); in this range the Huang has its source, winding in its upper course through E end of the province in tremendous gorges. See table at CHINA.

Qing·jiang *or* *W.-G.* **Ch'ing–chiang** \'chiŋ-'jyäŋ\; *formerly* **Hwai·yin** \'hwī-'yin\. City, cen. Jiangsu prov., E China; pop. (1990c) 239,675.

Qin·huang·dao *or* *W.-G.* **Ch'in–huang–tao** \'chin-'hwäŋ-'dau̇\ *or* **Chin·wang·tao** \'chin-'wäŋ-'dau̇\. Seaport town on Bo Hai, NE Hebei prov., NE China; glass manufacture; former treaty port.

Qin·ling Shan·di \'chin-'liŋ-'shän-ˌdē\ *or* *W.-G.* **Ch'in Ling Shan** \'chin-'liŋ-'shän\; *formerly* **Tsin·ling Shan** \'chin-\. Mountain range in N China, running E to W from SE Gansu across cen. Shaanxi into W Henan; watershed bet. Wei and Han rivers; highest peak 13,474 ft. (4107 m.).

Qiong·shan \'chyu̇ŋ-'shän\ *or* **Qiong·zhou** \-'jō\ *or* *W.-G.* **Ch'iung–shan** \'chyu̇ŋ-'shän\ *or* **Ch'iung–chou** \-'jō\. City, ✻ of Hainan I., on NE coast, SW Guangdong prov., SE China; its outport is Haikou; opened to foreign trade 1858 by Treaty of Tientsin but not actually used until 1876.

Qi·qi·har \'chē-'chē-'här\ *or* *W.-G.* **Ch'i–ch'i–ha–erh** \'chē-'chē-ˌhä-'ər\; *formerly* **Lung·kiang** \'lu̇ŋ-'chyäŋ\ *or* *Jp.* **Tsi·tsi·har** \'tsē-ˌtsē-ˌhär\. City and port, Heilongjiang prov., China, on left bank of Nen River 170 mi. (274 km.) NW of Harbin.

Qirghiz. See KIRGHIZ.

Qishm. See QESHM.

Qishn \'kish-ᵊn\. Coastal town, Yemen, ab. 190 mi. (305 km.) NE of Al Mukallā; ✻ of former Mahra sultanate.

Qi·shon *or* **Ki·shon** \'kī-ˌshän, 'ki-\. River, N Israel; rises near Mt. Gilboa and flows NW through the Plain of Esdraelon to the Mediterranean just N of Haifa; 45 mi. (72 km.) long. On its banks the Canaanite Gen. Sisera was defeated by the Israelites (*Judges* v. 21) and the prophets of Baal slain by the prophet Elijah (*1 Kings* xviii. 40).

Qi·tai *or W.-G.* **Ch'i–t'ai** \ˈchē-ˈtī\ *or* **Ku·cheng·tze** \ˈkü-ˈchəŋ-ˈdzə\. Town, cen. Xinjiang Uygur, W China, ab. 85 mi. (135 km.) E of Ürümqi, on N highway from Hami to Ürümqi.

Qi·yang *or W.-G.* **Ch'i–yang** *also* **Ki·yang** \ˈchē-ˈyäŋ\. Town, Hunan prov., SE cen. China; in WWII an American outpost captured by Japanese Sept. 1944.

Qizilkum. See KYZYL KUM.

Qizil Orda. See QYZYLORDA 2.

Qizil Qum. See KYZYL KUM.

Qizil Uzun. See QEZEL OWZAN.

Qom \ˈkōm\ *also* **Qum** \ˈku̇m\. Town, Markazi prov., NW cen. Iran, 75 mi. (121 km.) SSW of Tehran; pop. (1986c) 543,139; textiles; center of grain and cotton region and important junction for several highways; has numerous Muslim shrines and as site of shrine of Fāṭima, sister of Imam ʻAlī ar-Riḍā, is a place for Shiite pilgrimages.

Qomul. See HAMI.

Qor·mi \ˈkȯr-mē\. Town, Malta, 3 mi. (5 km.) SW of Valletta; pop. (1988c) 18,841.

Qos·ta·nay *or* **Kus·ta·nay** *also* **Kus·ta·nai** \ˌku̇s-tə-ˈnī\. **1.** Administrative subdivision of Kazakhstan; 75,367 sq. mi. (195,201 sq. km.); pop. (1991e) 1,074,400; ✻ Qostanay; wheat, cattle, sheep.

2. Town, its ✻, N Kazakhstan, on left bank of Tobol River 170 mi. (274 km.) E of Magnitogorsk, Russia; pop. (1991e) 233,900; market for grains of surrounding fertile black-earth area; founded 1879.

Quab·bin Reservoir \ˈkwä-bin\. Reservoir, W cen. Massachusetts; created 1939 by damming of Swift River.

Qua·boag \ˈkwä-ˌbäg\. River, cen. Massachusetts; rises in **Quaboag Pond** in S cen. Worcester co., flows W and joins Swift River in N Hampden co., to form Chicopee River.

Quad Cities \ˈkwäd\. Grouping of nearby cities, NW Illinois and SE Iowa—East Moline, Moline, and Rock Island, Illinois and Davenport, Iowa—an unofficial designation.

Quad·rant Mountain \ˈkwä-drənt\. Peak in Yellowstone National Park, NW Wyoming; 10,200 ft. (3109 m.).

Quake Lake \ˈkwāk\ *or* **Earth·quake Lake** \ˈərth-ˌkwāk\. Lake, S Montana, below Hebgen Dam on Madison River; formed 1959 by an earthquake.

Quak·er·town \ˈkwā-kər-ˌtau̇n\. Borough, Bucks co., SE Pennsylvania, 13 mi. (21 km.) S of Allentown; pop. (1990c) 8982; founded by Quakers 1715.

Qua·nah \ˈkwä-nə\. City, ⊗ of Hardeman co., N Texas, 24 mi. (39 km.) WNW of Vernon; pop. (1990c) 3413.

Quan Dao Hoang Sa. See PARACEL ISLANDS.

Quan·da·ry Peak \ˈkwän-drē\. Mountain, Summit co., cen. Colorado; 14,265 ft. (4348 m.).

Quang Ngai *or* **Quang·ngai** \ˈkwäŋ-ˈgī\. Coastal town, cen. Vietnam, ab. 130 mi. (210 km.) SE of Hue; pop. (1989c) 34,402.

Quang Tri *or* **Quang·tri** \ˈkwäŋ-ˈtrē\. Town, cen. Vietnam, on coastal railroad line 30 mi. (48 km.) NW of Hue.

Quan Long *or* **Ca·mau** \kə-ˈmau̇\. Town, near S tip of Vietnam, near Mui Bai Bung.

Quan·ti·co \ˈkwän-tə-ˌkō\. Town, Prince William co., NE Virginia, on Potomac River 18 mi. (29 km.) NNE of Fredericksburg; pop. (1990c) 670; U.S. Marine Corps facility, first estab. as a naval base in Revolutionary War; made a permanent Marine Corps base 1918.

Quan·tock Hills \ˈkwän-tək\. Range of hills, NW Somersetshire, SW England; highest point 1262 ft. (385 m.).

Quan·zhou *or W.-G.* **Ch'üan–chou** \ˈchwän-ˈjō\ *or* **Chuan–chow** \ˈchwän-ˈchau̇\; *formerly* **Tsin·kiang** \ˈchin-ˈjyäŋ\. Town, Fujian prov., SE China, ab. 90 mi. (145 km.) SW of Fuzhou; 11th cent. mosque; ancient pagodas; 7th cent. temple; museum; university; has been identified with Zaytūn (or Zaiton) described by Venetian traveler Marco Polo and by Muslim traveler Ibn Baṭṭūṭah as one of the great ports in the East during the Middle Ages; probably (as Zaiton) the origin for the English word *satin*, cloth being an important export; declined after 15th cent.

Qu'Ap·pelle \kwä-ˈpel\. River, S Saskatchewan, Canada; flows E across Manitoba border and into the Assiniboine River; ab. 270 mi. (435 km.) long; Moose Jaw is near its source.

Qua·raí \ˌkwär-ä-ˈē\. River, forming W section of Uruguay-Brazil boundary; flows W into Uruguay River; ab. 160 mi. (255 km.) long.

Quare·gnon \ˌkȧr-ˈnyō^{n}\. Commune, Hainaut prov., SW Belgium, just W of Mons; pop. (1991c) 19,572.

Quarnero. See KVARNER.

Quarnerolo. See KVARNERIĆ.

Quar·to \ˈkwär-tō\. Commune, Napoli prov., Campania, S Italy; pop. (1989c) 28,258.

Quar·tu Sant'·Ele·na \ˈkwär-tü-sän-ˈte-le-ˌnä\. Commune, Cagliari prov., S Sardinia, Italy, 4 mi. (6 km.) E of the seaport of Cagliari; pop. (1991p) 61,460.

Quatre Bornes \ˌkȧ-trə-ˈbȯrn\. Residential town, Mauritius, bet. Port Louis and Curepipe; pop. (1991e) 66,572.

Quatre Bras \-ˈbrä\. Village, Brabant prov., cen. Belgium, ab. 20 mi. (32 km.) SSE of Brussels; battlefield where forces under Arthur Wellesley, duke of Wellington, defeated the French under Marshal Michel Ney June 1815, just before the battle of Waterloo.

Quay \ˈkwā\. County in E New Mexico. See table at NEW MEXICO.

Qu·ba *or* **Ku·ba** \ˈkü-bə\. Town, NE Azerbaijan, on E slopes of Caucasus Mts. 95 mi. (153 km.) NW of Baku.

Qu·chan *also* **Ku·chan** \kü-ˈchän\. Town, N Khorāsān prov., NE Iran, on highway 80 mi. (129 km.) NW of Mashhad; pop. (1986c) 66,531; chief product grain. In 1893 destroyed by earthquake with great loss of life, but rebuilt.

Quds, Al–. See JERUSALEM 3.

Quean·bey·an \ˈkwēn-bē-ən, kwēn-ˈ\. Town, SE New South Wales, SE Australia; pop. (1991c) 24,942; SE suburb of Canberra, outside Australian Capital Terr.

Qué·ant \kā-ˈä^{n}\. Village, Pas-de-Calais dept., N France, 11 mi. (18 km.) W of Cambrai; fortress on the Hindenburg Line during WWI. See DROCOURT.

Que·bec \kwi-ˈbek\ *or Fr.* **Qué·bec** \kā-ˈbek\. **1.** Province, E Canada, bounded on N by Hudson Strait, on E by Labrador and Gulf of St. Lawrence, on SE by New Brunswick, on S by U.S. and Ottawa River, and on W by Ontario prov., James Bay, and Hudson Bay; ✻ Quebec. See table at CANADA.

Physical features: Its general elevation is low but the Canadian Shield N of Quebec (city) averages ab. 2000 ft. (610 m.); the mountains of the Gaspé Penin. are the highest in the province (Mt. Jacques Cartier 4160 ft. or 1268 m.). Has many large lakes, incl. Lac St.-Jean, Mistassini, Minto, Bienville; in the S in the populous part is the great artery of the St. Lawrence with its many tributaries. Relief running generally NE and SW forms the watershed for many rivers flowing W and NW into Hudson Bay and NE into Ungava Bay.

Chief products and economic activities: Agriculture; copper, iron ore, asbestos, gold, zinc; manufacturing; mineral processing; pulp and paper; hydroelectric power production.

Chief cities: Montreal, Laval, Quebec, Longueuil.

Political divisions: Divided into the following 99 counties (for pronunciation of their names, see their individual entries):

NAME	AREA (sq. mi.)	AREA (sq. km.)	POP. (1991c)
Abitibi	3,090	8,003	25,334
Abitibi-Ouest	1,300	3,367	24,109
Acton	223	578	14,613
Antoine-Labelle	5,755	14,906	32,019
Argenteuil	485	1,255	27,232
Arthabaska	732	1,896	60,257
Asbestos	298	772	15,381
Avignon	1,407	3,645	15,494
Beauce-Sartigan	749	1,939	44,218
Beauharnois-Salaberry	179	462	59,785
Bécancour	439	1,136	19,175
Bellechasse	629	1,629	29,475
Bonaventure	1,696	4,393	19,848
Brome-Missisquoi	598	1,548	45,257
Champlain	63	163	312,734
Charlevoix	1,451	3,757	13,547
Charlevoix-Est	917	2,375	17,413
Coaticook	449	1,162	15,758

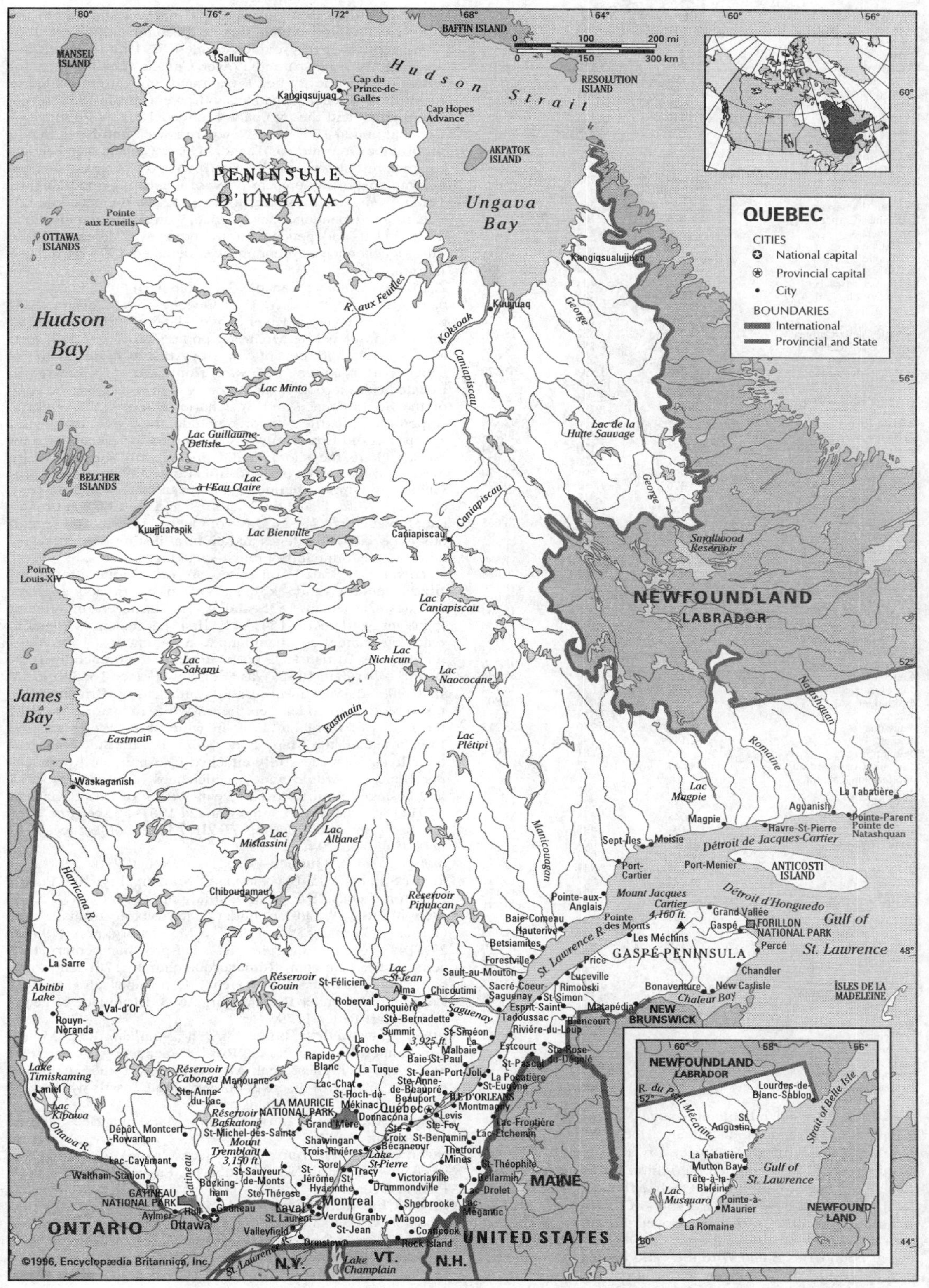
QUEBEC
CITIES
National capital
Provincial capital
City
BOUNDARIES
International
Provincial and State
Hudson Bay
James Bay
Hudson Strait
Ungava Bay
PENINSULE D'UNGAVA
NEWFOUNDLAND
LABRADOR
GASPÉ PENINSULA
Gulf of St. Lawrence
ANTICOSTI ISLAND
ONTARIO
UNITED STATES
MAINE
NEW BRUNSWICK
N.Y.
VT.
N.H.
Montreal
Québec
Ottawa
Laval
Salluit
Kangiqsujuaq
Kuujjuaq
Kangiqsualujjuaq
Kuujjuarapik
Waskaganish
Chibougamau
Caniapiscau
Sept-Îles
Port-Cartier
Baie-Comeau
Rimouski
Chicoutimi
Jonquière
Trois-Rivières
Sherbrooke
Gaspé
Val-d'Or
Rouyn-Noranda
La Sarre
Mount Jacques Cartier 4,160 ft.
Mount Tremblant 3,150 ft.
Smallwood Reservoir
Lac Mistassini
Lac Minto
Lac Bienville
Lac Caniapiscau
Lac Sakami
Réservoir Gouin
Réservoir Pipmuacan
Lac St-Jean
Détroit de Jacques-Cartier
Détroit d'Honguedo
St. Lawrence R.
Ottawa R.
Saguenay
Eastmain
Koksoak
George
Manicouagan
Romaine
Natashquan
FORILLON NATIONAL PARK
LA MAURICIE NATIONAL PARK
GATINEAU NATIONAL PARK
ÎLES DE LA MADELEINE
BAFFIN ISLAND
RESOLUTION ISLAND
AKPATOK ISLAND
MANSEL ISLAND
OTTAWA ISLANDS
BELCHER ISLANDS
Lourdes-de-Blanc-Sablon
Strait of Belle Isle
©1996, Encyclopædia Britannica, Inc.

NAME	AREA (sq. mi.)	AREA (sq. km.)	POP. (1991c)
D'Autray	459	1,188	35,727
Denis-Riverin	1,991	5,156	14,019
Desjardins	98	254	49,076
Deux-Montagnes	93	241	71,218
Drummond	628	1,627	79,654
Francheville	436	1,128	137,458
Joliette	124	321	48,303
Kamouraska	745	1,929	23,268
La Côte-de-Beaupré	1,925	4,985	21,214
La Côte-de-Gaspé	1,600	4,143	20,903
Lac-Saint-Jean-Est	1,055	2,733	51,963
La Haute-Côte-Nord	5,141	13,316	13,541
La Haute-Yamaska	292	755	73,351
La Jacques-Cartier	1,228	3,180	23,282
Lajemmerais	160	414	85,720
La Matapédia	2,080	5,388	20,930
L'Amiante	736	1,905	45,851
La Mitis	886	2,294	20,157
La Nouvelle-Beauce	306	793	24,362
La Rivière-du-Nord	176	455	73,896
L'Assomption	98	253	91,537
Laval	95	245	314,398
La Vallée-de-la-Gatineau	4,873	12,622	18,706
La Vallée-du-Richelieu	214	555	105,032
Le Bas-Richelieu	229	593	53,909
Le Centre-de-la-Mauricie	498	1,291	67,379
Le Domaine-du-Roy	7,202	18,653	33,239
Le Fjord-du-Saguenay	17,569	45,503	172,793
Le Granit	1,055	2,733	20,993
Le Haut-Richelieu	359	930	92,889
Le Haut-Saint-François	911	2,359	20,769
Le Haut-Saint-Laurent	452	1,170	21,864
Le Haut-Saint-Maurice	10,821	28,026	16,272
L'Érable	498	1,291	24,680
Les Basques	476	1,232	10,325
Les Chutes-de-la-Chaudière	162	419	67,479
Les Collines-de-l'Outaouais	748	1,938	28,894
Les Etchemins	697	1,806	18,668
Les Îles-de-la-Madeleine	78	202	13,991
Les Jardins-de-Napierville	308	797	21,977
Les Laurentides	948	2,455	31,580
Les Maskoutains	499	1,292	76,828
Les Moulins	102	264	91,156
Les Pays-d'en-Haut	285	739	23,088
Le Val-Saint-François	539	1,397	32,304
L'Île-d'Orléans	75	195	6,938
L'Islet	808	2,092	19,938
Lotbinière	636	1,647	26,633
l'Outaouais	181	470	201,536
Manicouagan	12,270	31,780	36,108
Maria-Chapdelaine	14,932	38,674	28,164
Maskinongé	773	2,002	23,802
Matane	1,279	3,312	24,334
Matawinie	4,147	10,740	35,253
Mékinac	2,141	5,544	13,629
Memphrémagog	495	1,281	35,984
Minganie-Côte-Nord-du-Golfe-Saint-Laurent	38,661	100,132	12,845
Mirabel	190	492	17,971
Montcalm	278	720	32,872
Montmagny	648	1,678	23,667
Montréal	191	494	1,775,871
Nicolet-Yamaska	386	1,001	23,897
Pabok	1,187	3,075	21,713
Papineau	1,138	2,947	19,526
Pontiac	6,022	15,597	15,111
Portneuf	1,515	3,924	43,179
Quebec	210	543	490,271
Rimouski-Neigette	994	2,575	51,290
Rivière-du-Loup	490	1,269	31,485
Robert-Cliche	316	819	18,586
Roussillon	163	422	118,355
Rouville	208	540	31,370
Rouyn-Noranda	2,316	5,999	42,033
Sept-Rivières-Caniapiscau	34,947	90,514	40,730
Sherbrooke	163	422	127,224
Témiscamingue	7,316	18,949	17,381
Témiscouata	1,496	3,874	23,348
Territoire nordique	286,451	741,907	36,310
Thérèse-De Blainville	79	204	104,693
Vallée-de-l'Or	10,488	27,165	43,121
Vaudreuil-Soulanges	329	852	84,503

History: Original inhabitants Inuits and members of Algonquin, Cree, and other Indian tribes; 1534–42 Gaspé Penin. and valley of St. Lawrence River visited by explorer Jacques Cartier who claimed the region for France, but settlement not begun until city of Quebec founded; lost to British in French and Indian War 1754–63 (see QUEBEC 3). As first set up under the British, comprised the valleys of the Ottawa and lower St. Lawrence rivers; Quebec Act 1774 extended boundaries S and W to the Ohio and Mississippi rivers; as result of American Revolution, received many Loyalist settlers in region W of the Ottawa and lost to the U.S. 1783 region which was to become Northwest Terr. (*q.v.*); remainder of province divided 1791 into Upper Canada (chiefly English) and Lower Canada (chiefly French); struggle for authority bet. French and English groups led to rebellion by French Canadians in Lower Canada 1837; rebellion quelled and the two parts reunited 1841 as Province of Canada; united 1867 with New Brunswick and Nova Scotia to form the Dominion of Canada, Upper Canada then becoming the present prov. of Ontario (*q.v.*) and Lower Canada becoming part of the present prov. of Quebec; gained Ungava Penin. from Northwest Territories 1912. Parti Québecois, advocating independence for Quebec, won provincial elections 1976, but its independence referendum was defeated 1980; 2d independence referendum was defeated 1995 by a close margin.

2. County, Quebec, Canada. See table at QUEBEC 1.

3. *or* **Quebec City.** City, ✱ of Quebec prov., Canada, on N bank of St. Lawrence River above Island of Orleans and 180 mi. (290 km.) below Montreal; pop. (1991c) 167,517; met. area pop. 645,550; port of entry for Atlantic vessels with excellent harbor 300 mi. (483 km.) from Gulf of St. Lawrence. Located upon a rocky promontory which rises from the edge of the St. Lawrence and St. Charles rivers in sheer cliffs; shipbuilding; textiles; exports include grain, pulp and paper; consists of old Lower Town, with narrow streets and ancient houses along the shore, and Upper Town, surrounded by massive wall, part of early fortifications. Notable for its provincial government buildings, Anglican cathedral, 17th cent. church of Notre Dame des Victoires, and the Château Frontenac; Laval Univ. (1852), Univ. of Quebec (1969), and several other specialized colleges and cultural institutions. Its population is predominantly French-speaking.

History: Located on site of old Indian town of **Stad·a·co·na** \ˌsta-də-ˈkō-nə\, visited by French explorer Jacques Cartier in 1535 and 1541; unsuccessful attempt made at settlement 1541–42; first permanent settlement made by Samuel de Champlain as a trading post 1608. Captured by the British 1629 but returned to the French by Treaty of St.-Germain 1632. Was ✱ of New France 1663 to 1763. In 1690 and 1711 unsuccessfully attacked by British fleets; taken by British under Gen. James Wolfe in historic battle of the Plains of Abraham 1759 in which both Wolfe and the French leader, the Marquis de Montcalm de St.-Véran, lost their lives; unsuccessfully attacked by American troops under Benedict Arnold and Gen. Richard Montgomery 1775 and besieged until following year. Was ✱ of Lower Canada 1791–1841 and ✱ of United Canada 1851–55; became ✱ of Quebec prov. 1867. During WWII, Allied Conferences held here 1943 and 1944.

Quebec West *or* **Québec–Ouest.** See VANIER 2.

Que·bra·dil·las \ˌkā-brä-ˈt͟hē-yäs\. Municipality, NW Puerto Rico; on N coast ENE of Aguadilla; pop. (1990c) 21,425.

Qued·lin·burg \ˈkfād-lən-ˌbu̇rk\. City, Saxony-Anhalt, cen. Germany, 33 mi. (53 km.) SSW of Magdeburg; pop. (1992e) 27,514; precision instruments; seed-growing center; 16th cent. castle; 12th cent. Romanesque church; 17th cent. town hall; city fortified 922 by Henry I; member of Hanseatic League; came under Brandenburg 1698. Birthplace of geographer Carl Ritter 1779.

Queen Al·ex·an·dra Range \ˈkwēn-ˌa-lig-ˈzan-drə\. Mountain range, Victoria Land, Ross Dependency, Antarctica; 84°S, 168°E; highest peak Mt. Kirpatrick 14,855 ft. (4528 m.); in 1969 site of discovery of vertebrate fossils which supported theory of continental drift.

Queen Annes \ˈanz\. County in E Maryland. See table at MARYLAND.

Queen Car·o·la Harbour \ˈkar-ə-lə, kə-ˈrō-lə\. Anchorage on W coast of Buka I., NW Solomon Is., Papua New Guinea, W Pacific Ocean.

Queen Char·lotte Islands \ˈshär-lət\. Group of ab. 150 islands off W British Columbia, Canada, separated from mainland by Hecate Strait and from islands of S Alaska on the N by Dixon Entrance; 3705 sq. mi. (9596 sq. km.); pop. (1986c) 3368; lumber, fish. Main islands are Graham (2491 sq. mi. or 6452 sq. km.), Moresby (991 sq. mi. or 2567 sq. km.), Louise, Lyell, Kunghit, and several smaller islands. Chief village, Masset. Inhabitants once mainly Haida Indians but population suffered drastically after contact with outsiders.

Queen Charlotte Sound. Body of water off W British Columbia coast, W Canada, bet. N end of Vancouver I. and S Queen Charlotte Is.

Queen Charlotte Strait. Channel bet. N Vancouver I. and the mainland of Canada, connecting Queen Charlotte Sound with Johnstone Strait.

Queen Eliz·a·beth Islands \i-'li-zə-bəth\. Islands of N Canada, N of the water passage extending from M'Clure Strait to Lancaster Sound; includes the Parry Is., Sverdrup Is., Devon, and Ellesmere.

Queen Elizabeth National Park *or* **Ru·wen·zo·ri National Park** \ˌrü-wen-'zōr-ē\. National park, SW Uganda; 764 sq. mi. (1979 sq. km.); varied scenery, incl. tropical forests, grassland, and volcanic craters; noted for its wildlife; estab. 1952.

Queen Mary Coast \'mer-ē, 'mā-rē\. Region of Antarctica extending E from Cape Filchner, 91°53′E, to ab. 102°E at the Antarctic Circle W of Wilkes Land.

Queen Maud Gulf \'mȯd\. Gulf, Arctic Ocean, Nunavut, Canada, bet. SE Victoria I. and the mainland.

Queen Maud Land. Section of Antarctica W of Enderby Land at 20°W to 45°E and extending S to Polar Plateau and to Coats Land on the W; claimed by Norway 1939 and later declared a dependency; Prince Olav Coast forms a part of its coast.

Queen Maud Mountains. Mountain range, S Ross Dependency, Antarctica, S of Ross Ice Shelf; extends 500 mi. (805 km.) SE from 84°S and from 175°E to 145°W, on edge of Polar Plateau.

Queen's. See LAOIGHIS.

Queens \'kwēnz\. **1.** County in SE New York. See table at NEW YORK.

2. Borough of New York City, New York, on W end of Long Island, coextensive with Queens co.; 108 sq. mi. (280 sq. km.); pop. (1990c) 1,951,598; largest in area of five boroughs of New York City; extends from Brooklyn to Long Island Sound, Newtown Creek, and East River; connected with the Bronx by Hell Gate, Whitestone, and Throggs Neck bridges and with Manhattan by Queensboro Bridge, Queens-Midtown Tunnel, and railroad tunnels beneath East River; has ab. 200 mi. (320 km.) of waterfront; governed as part of New York City (see NEW YORK 3); has a borough president, with local and county functions conducted independently of central munic. government; La Guardia Airport, Kennedy (formerly Idlewild) International Airport; Shea Stadium; St. John's Univ. (1870) in Jamaica. Settled by Dutch c. 1635; chartered as borough 1898; includes former Long Island City (*q.v.*) and former towns of Newtown, Flushing, and Jamaica (*qq.v.*).

3. County, in S New Brunswick, Canada. See table at NEW BRUNSWICK.

4. County in SW Nova Scotia, Canada. See table at NOVA SCOTIA.

5. County in cen. Prince Edward I., Canada. See table at PRINCE EDWARD ISLAND.

Queens Channel. Inlet of Joseph Bonaparte Gulf, NW Northern Terr., Australia; receives Victoria River.

Queens·cliffe \'kwēnz-ˌklif\. Seaport, S Victoria, SE Australia, at mouth of Port Phillip Bay 40 mi. (64 km.) SSW of Melbourne; pop. (1991p) 3121.

Queens·land \'kwēnz-ˌland, -lənd\. State, NE Australia; ✻ Brisbane. See table at AUSTRALIA.

Physical features: E half contains parallel N and S ranges of Great Dividing Range (Eastern Highlands) with highest part in the Atherton Plateau in the N; highest peak in the state, Mt. Bartle Frere, 5289 ft. (1612 m.). Low coastlands along W side of Cape York Penin.; cen. and S parts slope gradually to W (Artesian Basin) where upper tributaries of the Darling and Cooper Creek rise. Several streams (incl. Mitchell, Gilbert, Flinders) flow W or NW to Gulf of Carpentaria; others (Burdekin, Brisbane, Fitzroy) enter S Pacific. Along NE coast for ab. 1250 mi. (2010 km.) extends Great Barrier Reef (*q.v.*). N point is Cape York, separated by Torres Strait from S New Guinea. Largest island is Fraser, off SE coast.

Chief products: Wheat, fruit, sugarcane, dairy products; bauxite, copper, lead, zinc; livestock; oil field.

Chief towns: Brisbane, Gold Coast, Toowoomba, Townsville, and Ipswich.

History: Inhabited by Australian aborigines when coast explored by English Capt. James Cook 1770; first settlement (penal) on Moreton Bay 1824; officially opened to free settlers 1842. Part of New South Wales until 1859; became one of states of Commonwealth of Australia 1901.

Queens·ton \'kwēn-ˌstən\. Village, Lincoln co., Ontario, Canada, on Niagara River; scene of unsuccessful attempt Oct. 1812 by U.S. forces under Maj. Gen. Stephen Van Rensselaer to invade Canada; U.S. force that had gained the heights above the village was captured by the British; often referred to as battle of Queenston Heights.

Queens·town \'kwēn-ˌstau̇n\. **1.** Town and seaport, SW Ireland. See COBH.

2. Town, W Tasmania, Australia, 12 mi. (19 km.) NW of N end of Macquarie Harbour; pop. (1991c) 3368; formerly center of mining region; produced gold, silver, and copper.

3. Town, cen. Eastern Cape prov., S Rep. of South Africa, in upper valley of Great Kei River 160 mi. (257 km.) NE of Port Elizabeth; pop. (1985c) 17,996; in district producing wool and wheat; founded 1853.

Queen Victoria Park. See NIAGARA FALLS 1.

Quel·i·ma·ne *or* **Quil·i·ma·ne** *also* **Ki·li·ma·ne** \kə-lē-'mä-nə\ *or* **Kil·main** \kil-'mān\. **1.** River, Mozambique, N of the Zambezi.

2. Seaport town, ✻ of Zambézia prov., Mozambique, on Quelimane River ab. 14 mi. (23 km.) inland from its mouth; pop. (1991e) 146,206.

Quelpart. See CHEJU 1.

Que·luz \ke-'lüsh\. Town, SW Portugal, just NW of Lisbon; pop. (1991p) 61,300; 18th cent. palace.

Que·ma·do de Güi·nes \kā-'mä-thō-thā-'gwē-nās\. Town and municipality, Las Villas prov., W cen. Cuba; town 32 mi. (51 km.) NW of Santa Clara; munic. pop. (1981p) 22,458.

Que·moy \ki-'mȯi\ *or Chin.* **Jin·men** \'jin-'mən\. Island, off SE coast of China, in Taiwan Strait E of Xiamen; with **Little Quemoy (Xiaojinmen)**, island to the W, and several islets, comprises the Quemoy Is. group; garrisoned by Taiwan government since 1950.

Que·na·ma·ri Knot \ˌkā-nä-'mä-rē-'nät\. Mountain, SE Peru, NW of Lake Titicaca; 19,193 ft. (5850 m.).

Que·pos, Point \'kā-pȯs\. Cape on W cen. coast of Costa Rica, projecting into the Pacific Ocean.

Que Que. See KWEKWE.

Quer·cy \ker-'sē\. Ancient county, S France; in region now occupied by depts. of Lot and Tarn-et-Garonne; occupied by Franks 6th cent.; contested by England and France throughout Middle Ages; united with French crown 1472; suffered severely during religious wars of 16th cent.

Que·ré·ta·ro \kā-'rā-tä-ˌrō\. **1.** State of cen. Mexico. See table at MEXICO.

2. City, its ✻, 160 mi. (257 km.) NW of Mexico City; munic. pop. (1990p) 454,049; alt. 5900 ft. (1798 m.); opal mines; 18th cent. aqueduct; university (1951); city founded by Spanish 1531 on site of a pre-Aztec settlement; scene of execution of Emperor Maximilian 1867.

Quer·furt \'kfer-ˌfürt\. Commune, Saxony-Anhalt, E cen. Germany; 12th cent. church; came under Magdeburg archbishopric 1496; to Saxony 1635; to Prussia 1815.

Ques·nel \kə-'nel\. **1.** River, S cen. British Columbia, Canada; flows NW out of **Quesnel Lake** (100 sq. mi. or 259 sq. km.) into Fraser River; 64 mi. (103 km.) long.

2. Town, British Columbia, Canada, 60 mi. (97 km.) S of Prince George; pop. (1991c) 8179; timber, gold mining; agriculture.

Quesnoy, Le. See LE QUESNOY.

Quet·ta \'kwe-tə\. Town, ✻ of Baluchistan, Pakistan, 450 mi. (724 km.) WSW of Lahore; pop. (1981c) 285,719; important rail junction; regional trade center; university (1970); town located on a plain enclosed by high mountains; controls Bolan and Khojak passes and routes heading into S Afghanistan. Occupied by British 1876; developed into a strong fortress; practically destroyed in severe earthquake June 1935, but rebuilt.

Quetzalcoalco. See COATZACOALCOS.

Quet·zal·te·nan·go *or* **Que·zal·te·nan·go** \ket-,säl-tā-'näŋ-gō\. **1.** Department of SW Guatemala. See table at GUATEMALA.
2. City, its ✻; munic. pop. (1981p) 72,745; alt. 7800 ft. (2377 m.).

Que·ve·do \kā-'bā-thō\. Town, Los Rios prov., W cen. Ecuador, ab. 55 mi. (90 km.) N of Babahoyo; pop. (1990c) 86,910.

Quezaltenango. See QUETZALTENANGO.

Que·zon \'kā-,sōn\; *formerly* **Ta·ya·bas** \tī-'yä-bäs\. Province, E and S cen. Luzon, Philippines; ✻ Lucena. Forms a long strip of territory of very irregular shape along the Pacific or E coast of Luzon; mountainous, with S end of the Sierra Madre in the N and continuation of range, sometimes known as the Caraballo Sur, to the S; coastline includes many indentations, esp.: Baler Bay, Lamon Bay, and on S coast Ragay Gulf, Tayabas Bay, and Mompog Pass separating it from the island of Marinduque. Includes islands of Polillo group and Alabat on Pacific coast. See table at PHILIPPINES.

History: Explored by Spaniards soon after settlement of Manila; original province created 1591; suffered from depredations of Moro pirates until late 19th cent.; center of unsuccessful Filipino revolt 1841.

Quezon City. City, Luzon I., Philippines, adjoining Manila on the NE; pop. (1990p) 1,632,000; was official ✻ of the Philippines 1948–76; university (1908).

Qu·fu *or W.-G.* **Ch'ü–fu** \'chü-'fü\ *or* **Ch'ü–fou** \-'fō\ *or* **Ku·fow** \'chü-'faü\. Town, W Shandong prov., NE China, ab. 65 mi. (105 km.) S of Jinan. Residence of philosopher Confucius during most of his life and of his descendants (K'ung family) to the present day; 1 mi. (1.6 km.) N is cemetery containing tomb of Confucius and graves of thousands of his descendants. Town has great Confucian temple; original small structure built 478 B.C., but was rebuilt or renovated by successive emperors.

Quiaca, La. See LA QUIACA.

Quiangan. See KIANGAN.

Quib·dó \kēb-'dō\. City, ✻ of Chocó dept., W Colombia, on the Atrato River 80 mi. (129 km.) WNW of Manizales; pop. (1992e) 119,000.

Qui·be·ron \,kēb-'rōn\. Town, Morbihan dept., NW France; at tip of **Quiberon Peninsula,** a narrow, sandy peninsula 6 mi. (10 km.) long forming W side of **Quiberon Bay,** site of naval battle 1759 during Seven Years' War, in which English fleets under Adm. Edward Hawke defeated the French. Scene 1795 of defeat of French royalists who landed at base of peninsula but were driven back by forces of Gen. Louis-Lazare Hoche.

Qui·ça·ma National Park \kē-'sä-mə\. National park, Angola; 3846 sq. mi. (9961 sq. km.); varied wildlife; estab. 1957.

Qui·ché \kē-'chā\. Department of W cen. Guatemala. See table at GUATEMALA.

Quie·pe \kē-'ā-pē\. Island in Atlantic Ocean off SE coast of Bahia state, Brazil, 70 mi. (113 km.) SSW of Salvador.

Quié·vrain \kyā-'vren\. Commune, Hainaut prov., Belgium, on the French frontier bet. Mons and Valenciennes; pop. (1991c) 6928.

Quilimane. See QUELIMANE.

Quill Lakes \'kwil\. Two connected lakes, SE cen. Saskatchewan, Canada; 236 sq. mi. (611 sq. km.).

Quil·lo·ta \kē-'yō-tä\. Town, Valparaíso region, cen. Chile, 30 mi. (48 km.) NE of the seaport of Valparaíso; pop. (1992c) 68,284.

Quil·mes \'kēl-,mās\. City, Buenos Aires prov., E Argentina, suburb of the city of Buenos Aires; pop. (1991p) 509,445; industrial center; founded 1666.

Qui·lon \'kwē-,lön\ *also* **Kol·lam** \'kä-ləm\. Town, SE Kerala, S India, on Malabar Coast 130 mi. (209 km.) SW of Madurai; pop. (1981e) 167,583; seaport with extensive trade.

Quil·pué \kēl-'pwā\. City, Valparaíso region, cen. Chile, ab. 10 mi. (16 km.) E of the seaport of Valparaíso; pop. (1992c) 102,824.

Quim·per \ken-'per\. Commune, ✻ of Finistère dept., NW France, near Bay of Biscay 112 mi. (180 km.) W of Rennes; pop. (1990c) 62,541; 13th–16th cent. Gothic cathedral; manufactures pottery (called Quimper or Brittany ware); tourism; ✻ of old countship of Cornouaille.

Quim·per·lé \,ken-per-'lā\. Commercial town, Finistère dept., NW France, ab. 13 mi. (21 km.) NW of Lorient; restoration of an 11th cent. Romanesque abbey church of Ste.-Croix.

Quim·sa·cha·ta \,kēm-sä-'chä-tä\. Peak, N Chile, W of Lake Poopó; 19,882 ft. (6060 m.).

Quim·sa·cruz \,kēm-sä-'krüs\. Peak, W Bolivia, SE of Lake Titicaca; 19,357 ft. (5900 m.).

Qui·na·la·sag \,kē-nä-lä-'säg\. Island, NE Camarines Sur prov., Luzon, Philippines, in Pacific off N coast of Caramoan Penin.; 13 sq. mi. (34 sq. km.).

Qui·na·ta \kē-'nä-tä\. Peak, S Venezuela, N of the Orinoco; 7415 ft. (2260 m.).

Qui·na·uan Point \kē-'nä-wän\. Point, SW coast of Bataan Penin., Luzon, Philippines; extends into South China Sea WNW of Mariveles, 14°29′N, 120°23′E.

Qui·nault Lake \kwi-'nölt\. Lake, N Grays Harbor co., W Washington, on W slope of Coast Range; traversed by **Quinault River** which rises to the NE in Jefferson co. and flows SW to the Pacific Ocean.

Quin·cy \'kwin-sē; *in Mass.* 'kwin-zē\. **1.** Unincorporated village, ⊗ of Plumas co., NE California; area pop. (1990c) 4271.
2. City, ⊗ of Gadsden co., N Florida, 20 mi. (32 km.) WNW of Tallahassee; pop. (1990c) 7444.
3. City, ⊗ of Adams co., W Illinois, on Mississippi River across from NE Missouri; pop. (1990c) 39,681; commercial, industrial, and distribution center in agricultural area; Quincy Coll. (1860), John Wood Community Coll. (1974); city settled 1822.
4. City, Norfolk co., E Massachusetts, 8 mi. (13 km.) S of Boston; pop. (1990c) 84,985; previously famous for its granite quarries; Eastern Nazarene Coll. (1918), Quincy Junior Coll. (1958); birthplace of John Adams (1735), 2d president of the U.S. and of John Quincy Adams (1767), 6th president of the U.S.; began as trading post estab. 1625; until 1792 a part of Braintree.
5. City, Grant co., cen. Washington, 120 mi. (193 km.) WSW of Spokane; pop. (1990c) 3738.

Quin·dío \kēn-'dē-ō\. Department of W Colombia. See table at COLOMBIA.

Quindío Pass. Mountain pass in the Cordillera Central, in Colombia, 4°38′N, 75°32′W; alt. 11,435 ft. (3485 m.).

Quin·e·baug \'kwi-nə-,bög\. River, S Massachusetts and E Connecticut; rises in E Hampden co., SW Massachusetts, flows SE across Connecticut border, then S across E Connecticut into the Shetucket N of Norwich; ab. 100 mi. (160 km.) long.

Qui·né·ville \,kē-,nā-'vēl\. Commune, Manche dept., NW France, on E coast of Cotentin Penin. ab. 17 mi. (27 km.) SE of Cherbourg.

Qui Nhon *or* **Qui·nhon** \kwē-'nyön\. Town on coast of S Vietnam; pop. (1989c) 159,852; near site of ancient Cham ✻; port upgraded for military use by U.S. 1965.

Quinn Canyon Mountains \'kwin\. Small range in W Lincoln co. and E cen. Nye co., SE cen. Nevada.

Quin·ni·pi·ac \,kwi-nə-pē-'ak\. **1.** River, cen. Connecticut; rises in SW Hartford co., flows S through cen. New Haven co. and empties into New Haven Harbor.
2. City, Connecticut. See *History* at NEW HAVEN.

Quin·sig·a·mond, Lake \kwin-ˈsi-gə-mənd\. Lake in cen. Worcester co., cen. Massachusetts, on E border of city of Worcester.

Quin·ta·na Roo \kēn-ˈtä-nä-ˈrō\. State, E Yucatán Penin., SE Mexico; ✻ Chetumal; territory created from parts of Yucatán and Campeche states 1902; became a state 1974; has many Mayan ruins. See table at MEXICO.

Quin·te, Bay of \ˈkwin-tē\. Inlet of Lake Ontario, SE Ontario, Canada, extending N of Prince Edward co. and from Trenton E to Napanee; connected with Georgian Bay by Trent Canal (see TRENT 2); resort area; has many inlets and islands.

Quin·to \ˈkēn-tō\. River, Córdoba prov., N cen. Argentina; rises in San Luis prov.; flows ESE into a marsh; ab. 250 mi. (400 km.) long.

Quion·ga \ˈkyȯŋ-gä\. Village, NE Mozambique. See KIONGA TRIANGLE.

Qui·raing \kwi-ˈraŋ\. Mountain in N Skye I., off NW coast of Scotland; 1779 ft. (542 m.); remarkable rock formations.

Qui·ri·guá \ˌkē-rē-ˈgwä\. Ancient Mayan city in E Guatemala, in valley of the Motagua; known for its stelae and zoomorphs.

Quir·i·nal \ˈkwir-ən-ᵊl\. One of the Seven Hills of Rome, Italy. See SEVEN HILLS.

Qui·ri·no \kē-ˈrē-nō\. Province, N cen. Luzon, Philippines; ✻ Cabarroquis. See table at PHILIPPINES.

Qui·ro·ga, Point \kē-ˈrō-gä\. Cape, NE Chubut prov., S Argentina, W of entrance to Gulf of San José opp. Point Buenos Aires (*q.v.*).

Quiros. See SWAINS.

Quis·ling Cove \ˈkwiz-liŋ\. Inlet on NW coast of Kiska I. in the Aleutians, Alaska.

Qui·ta Sue·ño Bank \ˈkē-tä-ˈswā-nyō\. Shoal in W Caribbean Sea off NE coast of Nicaragua.

Quit·man \ˈkwit-mən\. **1.** Name of counties in two states of the U.S. See tables at GEORGIA and MISSISSIPPI.
2. City, ⊗ of Brooks co., S Georgia, 17 mi. (27 km.) W of Valdosta; pop. (1990c) 5292.
3. City, ⊗ of Clarke co., E Mississippi; pop. (1990c) 2736.
4. City, ⊗ of Wood co., NE Texas; pop. (1990c) 1684.

Qui·to \ˈkē-tō\. **1.** Former Spanish presidency, now Ecuador (*q.v.*); won independence and incorp. with Gran Colombia (*q.v.*) under presidency of South American liberator Simón Bolívar 1822.
2. City, ✻ of Ecuador, also ✻ of Pichincha prov., on fertile plateau ab. 114 mi. (183 km.) from the Pacific coast and 170 mi. (274 km.) NE of Guayaquil; lies almost on the Equator just SE of the volcano Pichincha; pop. (1990c) 1,100,847; ab. 9300 ft. (2835 m.); textiles, pharmaceuticals; Spanish colonial architecture; 16th cent. monastery church of San Francisco; has a technical institute and two universities; observatory.
History: A pre-Columbian town, captured by the Incas 1487; taken by the Spanish under Sebastián de Belalcázar 1534; became seat of audiencia 1563; during Spanish rule, ✻ of presidency of Quito; scene of independence revolt 1809; nearby Pichincha scene of victory over the Spanish by rebels under Gen. Antonio José de Sucre May 24, 1822 resulting in Ecuadorean independence; has suffered repeatedly from earthquakes.

Qui·vi·ra \ki-ˈvir-ə\. Mythical town of fabulous wealth, generally located near Great Bend, Barton co., cen. Kansas; sought 1541 by Spanish explorer Francisco Coronado; the pueblo at Gran Quivira (now part of Salinas Pueblo Missions National Monument) was at one time mistakenly identified with it (see UNITED STATES, *National Monuments*).

Qui·xa·dá \ˌkē-shə-ˈdä\. Municipality, Ceará state, NE Brazil, ab. 100 mi. (160 km.) S of Fortaleza; pop. (1991p) 72,291.

Qui·xe·ra·mo·bim \ki-ˌsher-ə-mō-ˈbēm\. Municipality, Ceará state, NE Brazil, 30 mi. (48 km.) SW of Quixadá; pop. (1991p) 59,115.

Qum. See QOM.

Qumran *or* **Qumran, Khirbat** *or* **Qumran, Khirbet.** See KHIRBAT QUMRAN.

Qunaytirah, Al *or* **Qunaytirah, El.** See AL QUNAYTIRAH.

Quoich, Loch \ˈkȯik̲, ˈkȯik\. Lake in W Highland region, NW Scotland.

Qŭ·qon \kə-ˈkȯn\ *or* **Ko·kand** \kə-ˈkänt\. **1.** Region, E Uzbekistan, around towns of Qŭqon and Fergana; became powerful khanate in 18th cent.; ab. 1760 recognized Chinese sovereignty; after 1800 came into conflict with other Turkic peoples of Turkistan and finally with the Russians; conquered by Russia 1876; made a province of Turkistan under ancient name of Fergana (Farghona); became part of newly formed Uzbek S.S.R., U.S.S.R., 1924, and of independent Uzbekistan 1991.
2. City, Fergana subdivision, E Uzbekistan, ab. 100 mi. (160 km.) SE of Tashkent; pop. (1991e) 175,000; important rail and trade center in a fertile oasis region; center for textile industry. Settlement dates back to at least 10th cent.; town founded c. 1732; chief town of Qŭqon khanate.

Qŭr·ghon·tep·pa \ku̇r-ˌgän-te-ˈpä\ *or* **Kur·gan–Tyu·be** \ku̇r-ˈgän-tyü-ˈbā\. Town, SW Tajikistan; 40 mi. (64 km.) S of Dushanbe; pop. (1991e) 58,400.

Qurna, Al–. See AL QURNAH.

Qur·nat as Saw·dā' *or* **Qur·net es Sa·ou·da** *or* **Qurnet es Sau·da** \ˈku̇r-nit-ˌes-ˈsau̇-dä\ *also* **Qor·net es Saouda** \ˈkȯr-\. Mountain in the Lebanon Mts., N Lebanon; 10,131 ft. (3088 m.); highest peak in Lebanon.

Qurqās, Abu. See ABU QURQĀS.

Qu·seir \ku̇-ˈsār\ *or* **Al Qu·ṣayr** \ˌal-ku̇-ˈsār\ *also* **El Qu·seir** \ˌel-\; *mostly formerly* **Kos·seir** \kȯ-ˈser\. Seaport, E Egypt, on the Red Sea E of Qena; on ancient caravan route to the Nile.

Qusur, Al–. See LUXOR.

Qu Xian *or* **Qu·xian** *or W.-G.* **Ch'ü-hsien** \ˈchü-ˈshyen\. City, W Zhejiang prov., E China, on railroad line 120 mi. (193 km.) SW of Hangzhou.

Qwa Qwa \ˈkwä-ˌkwä\. Former black enclave, Orange Free State, Rep. of South Africa, on the border with Lesotho; estab. 1974.

Qy·zyl·or·da \kə̇-ˌsil-ər-ˈdä\ *or* **Kzyl–Or·da** \ˈksil-ər-ˈdä\. **1.** Administrative subdivision of Kazakhstan, in S part E of Aral Sea; traversed by lower course of the Syr Dar'ya; 85,135 sq. mi. (220,500 sq. km.); pop. (1991e) 664,900; ✻ Qyzylorda; grain.
2. *also* **Qi·zil Orda** \kə-ˌzil-\; *formerly* **Pe·rovsk** \pi-ˈrȯfsk\. Town, its ✻, S cen. Kazakhstan; 315 mi. (507 km.) NW of Tashkent, Uzbekistan, on N bank of the Syr Dar'ya; pop. (1991e) 158,200.

\ə\ **abut** \ə̇\ **matches** \ᵊ\ **kitten**, Fr **table** \ər\ **further** \a\ **ash** \ā\ **ace** \ä\ **cot, cart** \ȧ\ Fr **bac** \au̇\ **out** \b̲\ Span **Avila** \ch\ **chin** \e\ **bet** \ē\ **easy** \g\ **go** \i\ **hit** \ī\ **ice** \j\ **job** \k̲\ Ger **ich, Buch** \ⁿ\ Fr **vin** \ŋ\ **sing** \ō\ **go** \ȯ\ **all** \ȯ\ **law** \œ\ Fr **bœuf** \œ̄\ Fr **feu** \ȯi\ **boy** \th\ **thin** \t͟h\ **this** \ü\ **loot** \u̇\ **foot** \u̇e\ Ger **füllen** \üe\ Fr **rue** \y\ **yet** \ʸ\ Fr **digne** \ˈdēnʸ\, **nuit** \ˈnwʸē\ \yü\ **few** \yu̇\ **fury** \zh\ **vision**

R

Raab. **1.** River, Austria and Hungary. See RÁBA.
2. City, Hungary. See GYOR.

Raa·he \ˈrä-hā\. Town, Oulu prov., W Finland, on Gulf of Bothnia 35 mi. (56 km.) SW of the seaport of Oulu; founded 1649.

Raal·te \ˈräl-tə\. Commune, Overijssel prov., E Netherlands, 12 mi. (19 km.) SE of Zwolle; pop. (1981e) 25,311.

Raamses. See RAMSES.

Raa·say, Sound of \ˈrä-zā\. Channel bet. E Skye I. and Raasay I. in the Inner Hebrides, off NW coast of Scotland.

Raasay Island. One of the Inner Hebrides, NE of Skye I., off NW coast of Scotland; 13 mi. (21 km.) long; administratively a part of Highland region.

Raas Xaafuun. See HAFUN, RAS.

Rab \ˈräb\ *or Ital.* **Ar·be** \ˈär-bā\. **1.** Island, Croatia, E of the Kvarnerić at the head of the Adriatic Sea; 36 sq. mi. (93 sq. km.); pop. (1991p) 9495; resort.
2. Town on W coast of the island.

Ra·ba \ˈrä-bə\. Town on Bima Bay, NE coast of Sumbawa I., Lesser Sunda Is., Indonesia.

Rá·ba \ˈrä-bö\ *or Ger.* **Raab** \ˈräp\. Navigable river, SE Austria and W Hungary; rises in Styria, Austria, flows E and NE across Hungarian border and into the Danube; 159 mi. (256 km.) long.

Ra·bat \rä-ˈbät\ *or* **Vic·to·ria** \vik-ˈtōr-ē-ə\. Chief town, Gozo I., Malta; pop. (1992e) 13,235.

Ra·bat \rə-ˈbät\. City, ✻ of Morocco, on Atlantic coast 57 mi. (92 km.) NE of Casablanca, situated at the mouth of the Bou Regreg opp. Salé (*q.v.*); pop. (1982c) 518,616; textiles, carpets, asbestos; 12th cent. tower and ramparts; estab. 12th cent. as a fortress by ʻAbd al-Muʼmin, founder of Almohad dynasty; declined 13th cent.; with neighboring town of Salé, center of piracy 17th cent.; ✻ of French protectorate after 1912.

Ra·baul \rə-ˈbau̇l\. Town and port on NE New Britain I., Papua New Guinea, in Bismarck Archipelago, W Pacific Ocean; pop. (1990c) 17,022; ships copra and coconut oil. On Simpson Harbour, the inner, landlocked part of Blanche Bay, and almost surrounded by active and extinct volcanoes.
History: Estab. as ✻ of German New Guinea 1910; became ✻ of Terr. of New Guinea 1921; after destructive eruptions of Mts. Tavurvur and Vulcan 1937, ✻ finally moved to Lae 1941. In WWII occupied by Japanese from 1942; destroyed by Allied bombing but rebuilt; again damaged by volcanic eruptions 1994.

Rabbah Ammon *or* **Rabbath Ammon.** See AMMAN.

Rab·bit Ears Pass \ˈra-bət-ˌirz\. Mountain highway pass, Jackson, Routt, and Grand cos., N Colorado, in Park Range of Rocky Mts.; 9462 ft. (2884 m.); in a small range called the **Rabbit Ears Range** named for peculiar formation on summit of **Rabbit Ears Peak** 10,719 ft. (3267 m.).

Ra·bun \ˈrā-bən\. County in Georgia. See table at GEORGIA.

Ra·cal·mu·to \ˌrä-käl-ˈmü-tō\. Commercial commune, Agrigento prov., SW Sicily, Italy, 11 mi. (18 km.) NE of the commune of Agrigento; pop. (1981p) 10,265.

Rac·co·ni·gi \ˌrä-kō-ˈnē-jē\. Town, Cuneo prov., SW Piedmont, NW Italy, 24 mi. (39 km.) S of Turin; pop. (1981p) 9759; royal palace and park of the ruling house of Savoy.

Rac·coon \ra-ˈkün, rə-\. River, Iowa; rises in Buena Vista co., in the NW part of the state, flows SE into Des Moines River at Des Moines; 200 mi. (322 km.) long.

Raccoon Mountains. Ridge, NE Alabama, chiefly in De Kalb and Jackson cos.; ab. 2000 ft. (610 m.) high; runs from NE to SW parallel with course of Tennessee River in that area.

Raccoon Point. Point at W tip of Isles Dernieres, off S coast of Terrebonne parish, SE Louisiana.

Race, Cape \ˈrās\. SE point of Newfoundland, Canada, extending into the Atlantic Ocean 46°40′N, 53°10′W.

Race, The. Strait S of SE Connecticut, bet. Fishers I. and islands off NE Long Island, connecting Long Island Sound with Block Island Sound and the Atlantic Ocean.

Race of Al·der·ney \ˈól-dər-nē\. Dangerous channel, English Channel, bet. the island of Alderney and the coast of France.

Race Point. Small peninsula at tip of Cape Cod, SE Massachusetts, N of Provincetown; lighthouse.

Rach Gia \ˈrät-ˈzhä\. Port city, S Vietnam, on a bay of the Gulf of Thailand; pop. (1989c) 137,784.

Ra·ci·bórz \rä-ˈchē-ˌbu̇sh\ *or Ger.* **Ra·ti·bor** \ˈrä-tə-ˌbȯr\. City, SW Katowice prov., S Poland, 42 mi. (68 km.) SSE of Opole on Odra (Oder) River near Czech Republic border; pop. (1989e) 62,833; 15th cent. Gothic church. Chartered 13th cent. and later ✻ of an independent principality which came under Bohemia 1327; to Prussia 1742; returned to Poland 1945.

Ra·cine \rə-ˈsēn, rā-\. **1.** County in SE Wisconsin. See table at WISCONSIN.
2. City, its ⊗, on Lake Michigan 23 mi. (37 km.) S of Milwaukee; pop. (1990c) 84,298; lake port; produces agricultural machinery, automobile parts, electrical equipment, wax; founded 1834; incorp. as city 1848.

Radak. See RATAK.

Ră·dă·u·ţi *or* **Ra·da·u·tsi** \ˌrə-də-ˈüt-sē\ *or Ger.* **Ra·dautz** \ˈrä-ˌdau̇ts\. Town, Suceava co., N Romania, ab. 20 mi. (32 km.) NW of the town of Suceava; pop. (1989c) 30,479; 14th cent. church.

Rad·cliff \ˈrad-ˌklif\. City, Hardin co., cen. Kentucky; pop. (1990c) 19,772; grew rapidly in 1970s.

Rad·cliffe \ˈrad-ˌklif\. Town, Greater Manchester, NW England, on the Irwell 8 mi. (13 km.) NNW of Manchester; pop. (1981p) 30,501; chemicals.

Ra·de·berg \ˈrä-də-ˌberk\. City, Saxony, E Germany, 8 mi. (13 km.) NE of Dresden; pop. (1981c) 16,906; 16th cent. castle.

Ra·de·beul \ˈrä-də-ˌbȯil\. City, Saxony, E Germany, NW suburb of Dresden on Elbe River; pop. (1981c) 33,990.

Ra·de·vorm·wald \ˈrä-də-ˌfȯrm-ˌvält\. City, North Rhine-Westphalia, Germany, 25 mi. (40 km.) E of Düsseldorf; pop. (1980c) 23,607.

Rad·ford \ˈrad-fərd\. Independent city, Montgomery co., W Virginia, 14 mi. (23 km.) ENE of Pulaski; 5 sq. mi. (13 sq. km.); pop. (1990c) 15,940; Radford Univ. (1910).

Ra·dhan·pur \ˈräd-ᵊn-ˌpu̇r\. **1.** Former Indian state, now part of Gujarat state, India.
2. Town, its ✻, ab. 85 mi. (135 km.) NW of Ahmadabad.

Rad·nor \ˈrad-nər\. Urban township, Delaware co., SE Pennsylvania, W of Philadelphia; pop. (1990c) 28,703; Cabrini Coll. (1957).

Rad·nor·shire \ˈrad-nər-ˌshir, -shər\ *or* **Rad·nor** \ˈrad-nər\. Former county, E Wales; ⊗ Presteigne. See POWYS.

Ra·dom \ˈrä-ˌdȯm\. **1.** Province, E cen. Poland. See table at POLAND.
2. Commune, its ✻, 37 mi. (60 km.) NE of Kielce; pop. (1989e) 226,317; railroad junction; produces leather goods, glass, tobacco products, chemicals; first mentioned 12th cent.; received town rights 14th cent.; to Austria 1795; under Grand Duchy of Warsaw 1807–15; returned to Poland 1918.

Ra·dom·sko \rə-ˈdȯm-skō\ *or Russ.* **No·vo·ra·domsk** \ˌnə-və-rə-ˈdȯmsk\. Commune, SW Piotrków prov., cen. Poland, 48 mi. (77 km.) S of Łódź; pop. (1989e) 50,340.

Ra·do·myshl *or* **Ra·do·mysl** \ˌrä-də-ˈmish-ᵊl\. Town, E Zhytomyr subdivision, Ukraine, on left bank of Teterev River 55 mi. (88 km.) W of Kiev.

Rae Ba·re·li \ˌrī-bə-ˈrā-lē\. Town, S cen. Uttar Pradesh, N India, 45 mi. (72 km.) SSE of Lucknow; pop. (1991p) 130,101; trade center; has 15th cent. fort and several fine mosques.

Rae·ford \ˈrā-fərd\. City, ⊗ of Hoke co., S North Carolina, 20 mi. (32 km.) WSW of Fayetteville; pop. (1990c) 3469.

Rae Strait \ˈrā\. Channel, Nunavut, Canada, bet. E King William I. and mainland.

Rae·tia *or* **Rhae·tia** \ˈrē-shē-ə\. Ancient province of Rome S of the Danube River; included most of what are now Tirol and Vorarlberg in Austria and Graubünden in E Switzerland. Bounded on N by Vindelicia, on E by Noricum, on S by Italy, and on W by Gaul. Original inhabitants an Ilyrian and Celtic people; added to Roman Empire 15 B.C.; Roman province at first included Vindelicia.

Raetia Secunda. See VINDELICIA.

Raeticae, Alpes. See *Rhaetian Alps* in table at ALPS.

Rae·va·vae \ˌrī-vä-ˈvī\. See TUBUAI ISLANDS.

Ra·fah *also* **Ra·fa** \ˈrä-fə\; *anc.* **Ra·phia** \rə-ˈfī-ə\. Town divided by border bet. Gaza Strip and Sinai Penin., Egypt, ab. 2 mi. (3 km.) S of the Mediterranean coast; scene of battle 720 B.C. when Sargon II of Assyria defeated the Egyptians, and in 217 B.C. scene of the defeat of Syrian King Antiochus the Great by Ptolemy IV Philopator of Egypt. From 1967–82 entirely within Israeli-occupied territory; international border estab. 1982 bet. Egypt and Israel divided city.

Ra·fa·e·la \ˌrä-fä-ˈā-lä\. City, Santa Fe prov., E cen. Argentina, 50 mi. (80 km.) NW of the city of Santa Fe; pop. (1980p) 53,152.

Ragae. See RHAGAE.

Ra·gang, Mount \rä-ˈgäŋ\. Active volcano, SE Lanao del Sur prov., Mindanao, Philippines, on Cotabato boundary; 9235 ft. (2815 m.).

Ra·gay Gulf \rä-ˈgī\. An inland body of water of cen. Philippines, a N arm of the Sibuyan Sea in SE Luzon; ab. 60 mi. (95 km.) long and 32 mi. (50 km.) wide at its mouth or S end; Burias I. is S of its mouth.

Rages. See RHAGAE.

Rag·ged Island \ˈra-gəd\. One of the Bahamas, in Atlantic Ocean N of E end of Cuba and W of Acklins I.; with adjacent cays, 5 sq. mi. (13 sq. km.).

Ragged Top, Mount. Peak, Lawrence co., W South Dakota; 6207 ft. (1892 m.).

Rag·lan \ˈra-glən\. Town, Gwent co., SE Wales, 6.5 mi. (10 km.) SW of Monmouth; site of castle begun 15th cent.; gave title to Field Marshal Fitzroy Somerset, baron Raglan (d. 1855).

Ra·gu·sa \rä-ˈgü-sä\. **1.** Province of SE Sicily, Italy. See table at ITALY.

2. *anc.* **Hy·bla He·raea** \ˌhī-blə-hə-ˈrē-ə\. Commune, its ✻, 113 mi. (182 km.) SE of Palermo; pop. (1989c) 68,850; cement; oil wells, asphalt pits; 18th cent. cathedral.

3. Seaport, Croatia. See DUBROVNIK.

Ra·had, Ar \ˌär-ˈrä-ˌhad\ *or* **Rahad.** River, E Africa; rises in NW Ethiopia near Lake Tana, flows NW across border into Sudan and empties into the Blue Nile (Bahr al-Azraq); over 300 mi. (480 km.) long.

Rahaeng. See TAK.

Rahiroa. See RANGIROA.

Rah·way \ˈrȯ-ˌwā\. **1.** Short river, NE New Jersey; rises in Essex co., flows S through Union co., enters Arthur Kill 5 mi. (8 km.) S of Elizabeth.

2. City, Union co., NE New Jersey, on Rahway River 5 mi. (8 km.) SSW of Elizabeth; pop. (1990c) 25,325; chemicals, automobile parts, pharmaceuticals.

Ra·ia·tea \ˌrī-ə-ˈtā-ə\. One of the Leeward Is. group of the Society Is., French Polynesia, S Pacific Ocean, 130 mi. (209 km.) WNW of Tahiti and just S of Tahaa; 75 sq. mi. (194 sq. km.); highest point 3389 ft. (1033 m.).

Rai·chur \ˈrī-chər\. Town, W Karnataka, S cen. India, 110 mi. (177 km.) SW of Hyderabad, bet. the Krishna and Tungabhadra rivers; pop. (1991p) 157,477; contains a citadel and fort built c. 1300.

Rai·dak \ˈrī-ˌdäk\ *or* **Rai·dhak** \-ˌdäk\. River, W Bhutan; flows S across Indian border to the Brahmaputra.

Raidestos. See TEKİRDAĞ 2.

Rai·ganj \ˈrī-gənj\. Town, West Bengal, NE India, W of the Bangladesh border; pop. (1991p) 151,454.

Rai·garh \ˈrī-ˌgär\. **1.** Former Indian state, now part of Madhya Pradesh, NE India; 1444 sq. mi. (3740 sq. km.).

2. Town, its ✻, 185 mi. (298 km.) NW of Cuttack; pop. (1991p) 92,569.

Rain \ˈrīn\. Village, Bavaria, Germany, on the Lech River near its confluence with the Danube 22 mi. (35 km.) N of Augsburg. In battle here 1632 Flemish Gen. Johann Tserclaes, Graf von Tilly was defeated by King Gustavus II Adolph of Sweden and mortally wounded.

Rain·bow Bridge National Monument \ˈrān-bō\. See UNITED STATES, *National Monuments.*

Rainbow City. **1.** City, Etowah and St. Clair cos., NE Alabama; pop. (1990c) 7673.

2. *formerly* **Sil·ver City** \ˈsil-vər\. Town, cen. Panama, adjoining Cristobal.

Rainbow Peak. **1.** Mountain, N Valley co., W cen. Idaho; 9329 ft. (2843 m.).

2. Mountain, Glacier National Park, NW Montana; ab. 9890 ft. (3015 m.).

Raincy, Le. See LE RAINCY.

Rai·nier, Mount \rə-ˈnir, rā-\. Peak, Pierce co., W cen. Washington; 14,410 ft. (4392 m.); highest point in Cascade Range and in the state; sometimes called **Mount Ta·co·ma** \tə-ˈkō-mə\, from the Indian name; in Mount Rainier National Park (see UNITED STATES, *National Parks*).

Rains \ˈrānz\. County in NE Texas. See table at TEXAS.

Rainy \ˈrā-nē\. River, forming part of the Canada-U.S. boundary, bet. SW Ontario and N Minnesota; flows from Rainy Lake to Lake of the Woods, leaving Rainy Lake at Koochiching Falls; ab. 80 mi. (130 km.) long.

Rainy Lake. Lake on N boundary of Minnesota, bet. Minnesota and Canadian prov. of Ontario; area 360 sq. mi. (932 sq. km.); outlet of Rainy River.

Rainy River. District in SW corner of Ontario, Canada. See table at ONTARIO.

Rai·pur \ˈrī-ˌpu̇r\. Town, SE Madhya Pradesh, India, 162 mi. (261 km.) E of Nagpur; pop. (1991c) 438,639; university (1963).

Rai·ra·khol \ˈrī-rə-ˌkōl\. Former Indian state, NE India, N of the Mahanadi River; now part of NE Orissa state; 857 sq. mi. (2220 sq. km.).

Rai·sin \ˈrāz-ᵊn\. River, SE Michigan; rises in Hillsdale co., flows NE, curves SE, and turns E into Lake Erie at Monroe, in Monroe co.; ab. 115 mi. (185 km.) long. See MONROE 5.

Raja Peak. See RAYA, MOUNT.

Ra·ja·gri·ha \ˌrä-jə-ˈgrē-ə\. Ancient city, S Bihar, NE India, in the hills SSW of Bihar; ruins of stone walls; as ✻ of kingdom of Magadha under Bimbisara (reigned c. 520–490 B.C.), home for many years of Siddhārtha Gautama, founder of Buddhism. Now site of modern village of **Raj·gir** \ˈräj-ˌgir\, a place of pilgrimage.

Ra·jah·mun·dry \ˌrä-jə-ˈmu̇n-drē\. City, NE Andhra Pradesh, E India, on left bank of Godavari River 295 mi. (475 km.) NNE of Madras; pop. (1991c) 324,881; market town; paper mill; center of timber trade. A ✻ of the E Cālukya dynasty; taken by French 1753 from nizam of Hyderabad and by British 1757.

Ra·jang \ˈrä-ˌjäŋ\ *or* **Re·jang** \ˈrā-\. Chief river of cen. Sarawak, on island of Borneo, Malaysia; flows SW and W into South China Sea; ab. 350 mi. (565 km.) long; chief town on its course Sibu; navigable for ab. 80 mi. (130 km.); has wide delta.

Ra·ja·pa·lai·yam \ˌrä-jə-ˈpä-lī-yəm\. Town, Tamil Nadu, India, ab. 50 mi. (80 km.) SW of Madurai; pop. (1991p) 114,042.

Ra·ja·sthan \ˈrä-jə-ˌstän\. **1.** Region, India. See RAJPUTANA.

2. State, NW India; ✻ Jaipur; wheat, barley, sugarcane; silver, copper, gypsum, salt; largest cities: Jaipur, Jodhpur, Kota; organized 1948 as **Union of Rajasthan;** reorganized 1956 with addition of Ajmer and other areas. See table at INDIA.

Raj·garh \ˈräj-ˌgär\. **1.** Former state, Bhopal Agency, cen. India; now part of Madhya Pradesh state.
2. Town, its ✻, 80 mi. (129 km.) NE of Ujjain; pop. (1991p) 18,689; founded c. 1640.

Rajgir. See RAJAGRIHA.

Raj·kot \ˈräj-ˌkōt\. **1.** Former state, N cen. Kathiawar, W India; now part of Gujarat state.
2. Town, its ✻, 125 mi. (201 km.) WSW of Ahmadabad; pop. (1991c) 612,458; major railroad junction; college (1870), university (1967); a boyhood home of Indian nationalist and spiritual leader Mohandas Gandhi.

Raj·ma·hal Hills \ˈräj-mə-ˌhäl\. Low range of hills, E Bihar, NE India, S and W of the Ganges River; highest ab. 2000 ft. (610 m.).

Raj Nand·gaon *or* **Raj·nand·gaon** \räj-ˈnänd-ˌgaun\. Town, S Madhya Pradesh, E cen. India, 125 mi. (201 km.) E of Nagpur; pop. (1991p) 125,394; ✻ of former Nandgaon state.

Raj·pi·pla *mostly formerly* **Raj·pee·pla** \räj-ˈpē-plə\. **1.** Former Indian state, in Rewa Kantha Agency, W India; now part of Gujarat state.
2. Town, its ✻, NE of Surat.

Raj·pu·ta·na \ˌräj-pə-ˈtä-nə\ *or* **Ra·ja·sthan** \ˈrä-jə-ˌstän\. Region of NW India, formerly incl. the Rajputana Agency (*q.v.*) and Ajmer-Merwara prov. Region now comprises Rajasthan state and small sections of Madhya Pradesh and Gujarat. The Aravalli Range crosses the S part of the region from NE to SW; the NW part is largely desert (Thar Desert) but to the SE the country is generally quite fertile. Chief rivers Luni, Chambal, and Banas. Most of the population is Hindu. Before the coming of the Muslims 11th cent., several powerful dynasties ruled the region; Rajput dynasties maintained some independence under Muslims; under the Moguls 16th–17th cents. and the Marathas 18th cent. there was much disorder; the Rajput states came under British protection by treaties 1818; in 1948 most of area formed into Rajasthan state.

Rajputana Agency. Formerly the official name of a group of 21 states in the Rajputana region of India; 132,559 sq. mi. (343,328 sq. km.). The resident for the crown resided at Mount Abu and under him were four agencies: Jaipur Residency, Western Rajputana States, Eastern Rajputana States, and the Mewar and Southern Rajputana States (*qq.v.*).

Raj·sha·hi \räj-ˈshä-hē\. **1.** Former division, N Bengal, NE British India; 19,642 sq. mi. (50,873 sq. km.); divided 1947 bet. East Pakistan (now Bangladesh) and West Bengal, India. See EAST BENGAL and WEST BENGAL.
2. *formerly* **Ram·pur Bo·a·lia** \ˈräm-ˌpu̇r-bō-ˈä-lē-ə\. City, W Bangladesh, on Ganges River 125 mi. (201 km.) N of Calcutta; pop. (1991p) 324,532; university (1953).

Ra·ka·hanga \ˌrä-kə-ˈhäŋ-ə\. Atoll in the Northern Cook Is., cen. Pacific Ocean, N of the Cook Is. ab. 25 mi. (40 km.) NW of Manihiki; ab. 1.5 sq. mi. (4 sq. km.); pop. (1986c) 282; administratively part of Cook Is.; U.S. claim dropped 1983.

Ra·ka·ia \rə-ˈkī-ə\. River, E cen. South I., New Zealand; flows SE into Pacific Ocean; 90 mi. (145 km.) long.

Ra·ka·po·shi \ˌrə-kə-ˈpō-shē\ *or* **Ra·ka·pu·shi** \-ˈpü-\. Peak in the Karakoram Range, in region of Jammu and Kashmir under Pakistani control; 25,550 ft. (7788 m.).

Rakata. See KRAKATAU.

Ra·khine \rä-ˈkēn\; *formerly* **Ara·kan** \ˌär-ə-ˈkän, ˌar-ə-ˈkan\. State of Myanmar along the coast of NE Bay of Bengal; ✻ Sittwe; E border formed by Arakan Yoma Range; rice, tobacco. Conquered by Burmese 1784; ceded to British 1826 by treaty signed at Yandabu (*q.v.*); scene of heavy fighting bet. Japanese and Allied forces during WWII; long a scene of unrest bet. minority Muslim members of population and Burmese Army. See table at MYANMAR.

Rakka. See AR RAQQAH.

Ra·kov·nik \ˈrä-ko̊v-ˌnyēk\ *or Ger.* **Ra·ko·nitz** \ˈrä-kə-ˌnits\. Town, W Czech Republic, 33 mi. (53 km.) W of Prague; pop. (1980p) 16,233.

Ra·ku·to \ˈrä-kə-ˌtō\. River, South Korea; flows S into Korea Strait at Pusan; ab. 270 mi. (435 km.) long; navigable for ab. 125 mi. (200 km.).

Ra·leigh \ˈro̊-lē, ˈrä-\. **1.** County in S West Virginia. See table at WEST VIRGINIA.
2. Town, ⊗ of Smith co., S cen. Mississippi, ab. 45 mi. (70 km.) SE of Jackson; pop. (1990c) 1291.
3. City, ✻ of North Carolina, also ⊗ of Wake co., E cen. North Carolina, 50 mi. (80 km.) S of Virginia border; pop. (1990c) 207,951; retail and wholesale trade center, tobacco market; produces textiles, chemicals, electronic components. St. Mary's Coll. (1842), Peace Coll. (1857), Shaw Univ. (1865), St. Augustine's Coll. (1867), North Carolina State Univ. (1887), Meredith Coll. (1891). Site selected as ✻ 1788 and laid out 1792; in Civil War occupied by Union forces under Gen. William T. Sherman Apr. 1865. Birthplace 1808 of Andrew Johnson, 17th president of the U.S.

Raleigh Bay. Bay off E coast of North Carolina bet. Cape Hatteras and Cape Lookout.

Ra·lik \ˈrä-lik\. W chain of islands in the Marshall Is., W Pacific Ocean; includes 15 atolls and 3 coral islands in long chain of ab. 750 mi. (1205 km.). More important atolls Jaluit, Kwajalein, Wotho, and Enewetak.

Ralls \ˈro̊lz\. County in NE Missouri. See table at MISSOURI.

Ral·ston \ˈro̊l-stən\. City, Douglas co., E Nebraska, 5 mi. (8 km.) SW of Omaha; pop. (1990c) 6236.

Ramadi *or* **Ramādī, Ar.** See AR RAMĀDĪ.

Ra·mah \ˈrā-mə\. See ARIMATHEA.

Ramal, Ar. See RAMLEH.

Rām Al·lāh \ˈräm-ȧl-ˈlä\. Town in West Bank, N of Jerusalem and adjacent to Al Bīrah; pop. (1987e) 24,772. In area occupied by Israel 1967; Israeli troops withdrawn late 1995.

Ram·a·po \ˈra-mə-ˌpō\. River, S New York and N New Jersey; rises in New York N of the Ramapo Mts., flows SE traversing the range, then S and SW just S of the range to unite at Pompton (just S of Pompton Lakes) with the Pequannock and Ringwood rivers to form the Pompton River.

Ramapo Mountains. Range of the Appalachian Mts. extending NE to SW in S New York (Rockland and Orange cos.) and N New Jersey (Bergen co.); highest point 1164 ft. (355 m.).

Ra·mat Gan \rə-ˈmät-ˌgän\. Town, Israel, 2 mi. (3 km.) E of Tel Aviv-Jaffa; pop. (1992e) 122,700; university (1955); town founded 1921.

Ram·bouil·let \ˌrä^{n}-bü-ˈyā\. Town, Yvelines dept., N France, 28 mi. (45 km.) SW of Paris; pop. (1990c) 25,293; 14th–18th cent. chateau, now summer residence of the presidents of France; Forest of Rambouillet nearby.

Ram·bu·tyo \räm-ˈbü-tē-ˌō\. Island in Admiralty Is., Bismarck Archipelago, Papua New Guinea, W Pacific Ocean; 35 mi. (56 km.) ESE of Manus I.; 10 mi. (16 km.) long by 8 mi. (13 km.) wide; highest point 700 ft. (213 m.).

Ram·durg \ˈräm-ˌdu̇rg\. Former Indian state in Deccan and Kolhapur States, SW India; now part of Karnataka state; 166 sq. mi. (430 sq. km.); ✻ Ramdurg.

Rame Head \ˈrām\. Headland on the coast of Cornwall, SW England, on the W side of Plymouth Sound.

Ra·men·sko·ye \ˈrä-mən-skə-yə\. Town, Moscow Oblast, W cen. Russia in Europe, 27 mi. (43 km.) SE of the city of Moscow; pop. (1991e) 88,800.

Ra·mes·wa·ram \rä-ˈmes-wə-rəm\. **1.** Island, S Tamil Nadu, S India, bet. Palk Strait and the Gulf of Mannar, at the W end of Adam's Bridge.
2. Village on the island; has notable temple of Dravidian architecture, one of the most sacred of Hindu shrines; visited annually by thousands of pilgrims.

Ram·gan·ga \räm-ˈgəŋ-gə\. River, Uttar Pradesh, N India; rises in the Himalayas, flows S into the Ganges near Kannauj; ab. 350 mi. (565 km.) long; navigable for short distance only.

Ra·mil·lies–Of·fus \ˌrä-mē-yē-ō-ˈfue̅\ *also* **Ramillies.** Village, Brabant prov., cen. Belgium, 13 mi. (21 km.) NE of Namur; pop. (1991c) 4610; scene of battle in which troops under John Churchill, duke of Marlborough defeated the French under François de Neufville, duc de Villeroi 1706 in the War of the Spanish Succession.

Ram·la \ˈräm-lə\ *also* **Er Ram·le** \er-ˈräm-lə\. Town, ✻ of Central District, Israel, 12 mi. (19 km.) SE of Tel Aviv-Jaffa; pop. (1992e) 49,300; founded 716 by Arabs; captured by

Crusaders 1099 on march to Jerusalem; retaken by the Muslim Sultan Saladin 1187; after fighting bet. Arabs and Jews 1948, Arab population withdrew and Jewish settlers moved in.

Ramlat āl Wahībah. See WAHIBA SANDS.

Ram·leh \'räm-lə\ *or* **Ar Ra·mal** \är-'rä-ˌməl\. City, NE suburb and seaside resort of Alexandria, Egypt.

Ram·na·gar \'räm-nə-gər\. Village, Punjab, Pakistan, 55 mi. (88 km.) NNW of Lahore; site of battle 1848 in Second Sikh War in which Sikh forces retreated from the British.

Râmnicul–Sărat. See RÎMNICU-SĂRAT.

Râmnicul–Vâlcea. See RÎMNICU-VÎLCEA.

Ra·moth Gil·e·ad \'rā-ˌmäth-'gi-lē-əd\. Ancient town of Gilead, in present-day Jordan; its exact location not certainly identified; in the Bible, a city of refuge (*Deut.* iv. 43).

Ram·page Mountain \'ram-ˌpāj\. Peak in Glacier National Park, NW Montana; 6840 ft. (2085 m.).

Ram·pur \'räm-ˌpu̇r\. **1.** Former Indian state, N Uttar Pradesh, N India; 894 sq. mi. (2315 sq. km.); level and fertile country E of the Ganges, watered by the Kosi and Ramganga rivers. State founded 18th cent.; was last remnant of the Rohilla kingdom.

2. City, its ✻, on Kosi River 115 mi. (185 km.) E of Delhi; pop. (1991p) 242,752; produces sugar, pottery.

Rampur Boalia. See RAJSHAHI 2.

Ram·ree \'räm-rē\. **1.** Island in Bay of Bengal off W coast of Myanmar; ab. 50 mi. (80 km.) long; the town of Kyaukpyu is at its N end.

2. Village on E coast of island.

Rams·bot·tom \'ramz-ˌbä-təm\. Town, Greater Manchester, NW England, on the Irwell 12 mi. (19 km.) N of Manchester; pop. (1981p) 17,799; textiles.

Ram·ses \'ram-ˌsēz\ *also* **Ra·am·ses** \rā-'am-ˌsēz\. City of ancient Egypt, in Goshen probably near Tanis; one of the treasure cities built for Ramses II by the Hebrews (*Exod.* i. 11).

Ram·sey \'ram-zē\. **1.** Name of counties in two states of the U.S. See tables at MINNESOTA and NORTH DAKOTA.

2. City, Anoka co., E Minnesota, on the Mississippi, NW of Minneapolis; pop. (1990c) 12,408.

3. Residential borough, Bergen co., NE corner of New Jersey, 9 mi. (14 km.) N of Paterson; pop. (1990c) 13,228.

4. Town, Cambridgeshire, E cen. England, 65 mi. (105 km.) N of London; pop. (1981p) 5828; market town.

5. Town on NE coast of Isle of Man, England; seaside resort.

6. Island in St. George's Channel off SW coast of Wales, ab. 3 mi. (5 km.) W of St. David's Head, N of entrance to St. Brides Bay; ab. 2 mi. (3 km.) long.

Rams·gate \'ramz-ˌgāt, -gət\. Town, Kent, SE England, on North Sea 17 mi. (27 km.) N of Dover; pop. (1981c) 37,398; popular seaside resort; the Anglo-Saxon warriors Hengist and Horsa purportedly landed in vicinity with a band of followers from Jutland 449 A.D.; the missionary St. Augustine, who later became first archbishop of Canterbury, believed to have landed here 597.

Ram·tek \'räm-ˌtek\. Town, NE Maharashtra, India, 24 mi. (39 km.) NNE of Nagpur; long a sacred place for Hindus; has many old temples.

Ra·mu \'rä-mü\. River, New Guinea I., Papua New Guinea; flows NW and N; ab. 400 mi. (645 km.) long. In WWII its valley taken from Japanese by Allied forces 1943; scene of earthquake 1993.

Ra·na \'rä-nə\. **1.** River in cen. Norway; flows SW into Ranen Fjord.

2. Commune, Nordland co., N Norway; pop. (1990c) 24,646.

Ranan. See NANAM.

Ra·nau \'rä-ˌnau̇\. Lake in S end of Barisan Mts., S Sumatra, Indonesia.

Ran·ca·gua \rän-'kä-gwä, räŋ-\. City, ✻ of Libertador General Bernardo O'Higgins region, cen. Chile, 48 mi. (77 km.) S of Santiago; pop. (1982c) 139,925; copper mines in the vicinity; scene of a battle 1814 in which Chilean revolutionaries under Bernardo O'Higgins were overcome by Spanish royalists.

Rance \'räⁿs\. River, Brittany, NW France; flows N into the English Channel at St.-Malo; ab. 60 mi. (95 km.) long.

Ran·chi \'rän-chē\. Town, S Bihar, India; 210 mi. (338 km.) WNW of Calcutta; pop. (1991c) 599,306; summer ✻ of Bihar; steel, machine tools; university (1960).

Ran·cho Cor·do·va \'ran-chō-'kȯr-də-və\. Unincorporated settlement, Sacramento co., N cen. California; pop. (1990c) 48,731.

Ran·cho Cu·ca·mon·ga \'ran-chō-ˌkü-kə-'mäŋ-gə\. City, San Bernardino co., SE California, E of Los Angeles; pop. (1990c) 101,409.

Ran·cho Mi·rage \'ran-chō-mə-'räj\. City, Riverside co., SE California, SE of Palm Springs; pop. (1990c) 9778.

Ran·cho Pal·os Ver·des \'ran-chō-'pa-ləs-'vər-dēz\. City, Los Angeles co., SW California, on the coast, S of Torrance; pop. (1990c) 41,659.

Ran·chue·lo \ˌrän-'chwā-lō\. Municipality, Las Villas prov., W cen. Cuba, 14 mi. (23 km.) WSW of Santa Clara; pop. (1981p) 60,828.

Ran·co \'räŋ-kō\. Lake, S cen. Chile, ab. 40 mi. (64 km.) SE of Valdivia; resort.

Rand, The. See WITWATERSRAND.

Ran·dall \'rand-ᵊl\. County in NW Texas. See table at TEXAS.

Ran·dalls Island \'rand-ᵊlz\. Island in East River, New York, part of Manhattan borough; 194 acres (79 hectares); site of parks, playgrounds, a municipal stadium; meeting place of three arms of the Triborough Bridge.

Ran·daz·zo \ˌrän-'dät-sō\. Commune, Catania prov., E Sicily, Italy, on N slope of Mt. Etna 23 mi. (37 km.) NNW of the commune of Catania; pop. (1981p) 11,064; archaeological museum; 13th cent. church. In WWII captured by U.S. troops Aug. 1943.

Rand·burg \'ränd-ˌbu̇rg\. Town, Gauteng prov., Rep. of South Africa, just N of Johannesburg; urban area pop. (1985c) 74,347.

Ran·ders \'rä-nərs\. Seaport, Århus co., E Jutland Penin., Denmark, on the Gudenå River where it enters Randers Fjord 15 mi. (24 km.) from the Kattegat; pop. (1989e) 61,137; center of agricultural region; produces dairy products, beer, gloves; 15th cent. church; 18th cent. town hall.

Randers Fjord. Inlet of the Kattegat on NE cen. coast of Jutland Penin., Denmark; receives the Gudenå River.

Rand·fon·tein \'ränt-ˌfän-ˌtān\. City, Gauteng prov., NE Rep. of South Africa, 28 mi. (45 km.) W of Johannesburg; pop. (1985c) 43,763; produces textiles; at W end of Witwatersrand goldfields; the Randfontein gold mine is one of largest in the world.

Ran·dle·man \'rand-ᵊl-mən\. City, Randolph co., cen. North Carolina, S of Greensboro; pop. (1990c) 2612.

Ran·dolph \'ran-ˌdälf\. **1.** Name of counties in eight states of the U.S. See tables at ALABAMA, ARKANSAS, GEORGIA, ILLINOIS, INDIANA, MISSOURI, NORTH CAROLINA, WEST VIRGINIA.

2. Town, Norfolk co., E Massachusetts, 6 mi. (10 km.) N of Brockton; pop. (1990c) 30,093; residential.

3. City, ⊗ of Rich co., N Utah; pop. (1990c) 488.

4. Town, Orange co., E Vermont, SSW of Barre; pop. (1990c) 4764; manufactures wood-burning stoves and clothing; tourism. At **Randolph Center,** to E, is Vermont Technical Coll. (1957).

Randolph, Fort. See FORT RANDOLPH.

Rand·wick \'ran-dwik\. Municipality, E New South Wales, SE Australia, SE suburb of Sydney on Pacific Ocean and Botany Bay; pop. (1991c) 115,349.

Ra·nen Fjord \'rä-nən\ *or* **Ran·fjord** \'rän-ˌfyu̇r\. Inlet of Norwegian Sea on W coast of Norway opp. Dønna I.; receives Rana River from the E.

Rān·gā·mā·ti \ˌrəŋ-'gäm-ət-ē\. Town, SE Bangladesh, in Chittagong Hill Tracts; pop. (1991p) 56,216.

Rangasa, Tandjung. See MANDAR, GULF OF.

Rang·au·nu Bay \'räŋ-au̇-ˌnü\. Inlet of Pacific Ocean, NE coast of N extension of North I., New Zealand.

\ə\ abut \ᵊ\ kitten, Fr table \ər\ further \a\ ash \ā\ ace \ä\ cot, cart \å\ Fr bac \au̇\ out \b̲\ Span Avila \ch\ chin \e\ bet \ē\ easy \g\ go \i\ hit \ī\ ice \j\ job \k̲\ Ger ich, Buch \ⁿ\ Fr vin \ŋ\ sing \ō\ go \ȯ\ all \ȯ\ law \œ\ Fr bœuf \œ̄\ Fr feu \ȯi\ boy \th\ thin \th̲\ this \ü\ loot \u̇\ foot \ue\ Ger füllen \ue̅\ Fr rue \y\ yet \ʸ\ Fr digne \'dēnʸ\, nuit \'nwʸē\ \yü\ few \yu̇\ fury \zh\ vision

Range·ley Lakes \ˈrānj-lē\. Chain of lakes in Franklin and Oxford cos., in W Maine, incl. Rangeley, Mooselookmeguntic, Richardson (Upper Richardson, Lower Richardson), and Umbagog lakes, extending over 50 mi. (80 km.) in length and covering an area of 80 sq. mi. (207 sq. km.); elev. bet. 1200 and 1500 ft. (365 and 460 m.).

Rang·er \ˈrān-jər\. City, Eastland co., N cen. Texas, 40 mi. (64 km.) E of Abilene; pop. (1990c) 2803; Ranger Junior Coll. (1926).

Ranger Peak. Mountain, NE Idaho co., N cen. Idaho; 8810 ft. (2685 m.).

Rang·i·o·ra \ˌräŋ-ē-ˈōr-ə\. Borough, E South I., New Zealand, on inlet of Pegasus Bay 17 mi. (27 km.) N of Christchurch.

Rang·i·roa \ˌräŋ-i-ˈrō-ə\ *or* **Ra·hi·roa** \ˌrä-hi-\. Atoll, largest in the Tuamotu Archipelago, French Polynesia, in S Pacific Ocean, 200 mi. (322 km.) NNE of Tahiti; 29 sq. mi. (75 sq. km.); has good harbor within the lagoon.

Rang·i·tai·ki \ˌräŋ-i-ˈtī-kē\. River, cen. and N cen. North I., New Zealand; flows NE and N into Bay of Plenty; 120 mi. (193 km.) long.

Rang·i·ta·ta \ˌräŋ-i-ˈtä-tə\. River, E cen. South I., New Zealand; flows SE into Canterbury Bight; 75 mi. (121 km.) long.

Rang·i·tik·ei \ˌräŋ-i-ˈti-kē\. River, SW North I., New Zealand; flows S and SW into Cook Strait; 150 mi. (241 km.) long.

Rang·i·to·to \ˌräŋ-i-ˈtō-tō\. Island on E coast of North I., New Zealand, in outer harbor of Auckland; a lava cone 854 ft. (260 m.) high.

Rangoon. See YANGON.

Rang·pur \ˈrəŋ-ˌpu̇r\. Town, N Bangladesh, on tributary of Jamuna River; pop. (1991p) 220,849; carpets, tobacco products.

Ra·ni·ganj \ˈrä-ni-ˌgənj\. Town, West Bengal, NE India, on N bank of Damodar River ab. 105 mi. (170 km.) NW of Calcutta; pop. (1991p) 62,014.

Ra·ni·khet \ˈrä-ni-ˌket\. Hill station, NE Uttar Pradesh, N India, 75 mi. (121 km.) NE of Moradabad; alt. 6000 ft. (1829 m.).

Ran·kin \ˈraŋ-kən\. **1.** County in S cen. Mississippi. See table at MISSISSIPPI.
2. Borough, Allegheny co., SW Pennsylvania, on Monongahela River 7 mi. (11 km.) E of Pittsburgh; pop. (1990c) 2503.
3. City, ⊗ of Upton co., W Texas; pop. (1990c) 1011.

Ran·noch, Loch \ˈra-nək, -nək\. Lake, Tayside region, cen. Scotland; 9 mi. (14 km.) long.

Rann of Kutch. See KACHCHH, RANN OF.

Ra·nong \ˈrä-ˈnȯŋ\. Port, SW Thailand, on W coast of Malay Penin. at mouth of the Pakchan River ab. 8 mi. (13 km.) E of Victoria Point, Myanmar; pop. (1991e) 17,685.

Ran·pur \ˈrän-ˌpu̇r\. Former Indian state, NE India, now in Orissa state; 204 sq. mi. (528 sq. km.).

Ran·som \ˈran-səm\. County in SE North Dakota. See table at NORTH DAKOTA.

Ran·te·kom·bo·la \ˌrän-tə-ˈkȯm-bə-lə\. Mountain in N cen. part of the SW peninsula of Sulawesi, Indonesia, near Palopo; 11,335 ft. (3455 m.); highest point of Sulawesi.

Ran·te·ma·rio \ˌrän-tə-ˈmär-ē-ˌō\. Mountain in N cen. part of the SW peninsula of Sulawesi, Indonesia, near Palopo; 11,286 ft. (3440 m.).

Ran·toul \ran-ˈtül\. Village, Champaign co., E cen. Illinois, 15 mi. (24 km.) N of the city of Champaign; pop. (1990c) 17,212.

Raoeng. See RAUNG.

Ra·oul, Cape \ˈrau̇l\. S point of Tasman Penin., Tasmania, Australia, W of Cape Pillar and at E entrance to Storm Bay; extends into Tasman Sea.

Raoul Island \ˈrau̇l\ *or* **Sun·day Island** \ˈsən-dē\. Largest island of the Kermadec Is. (*q.v.*), New Zealand.

Ra·pa \ˈrä-pə\. Island at SE end of chain of Austral Is., French Polynesia, S Pacific Ocean, 27°36′S, 144°20′W; ab. 20 mi. (32 km.) in circumference; pop. (1988c) 516; mountainous (highest 2077 ft. or 633 m.); has harbor. Formerly had a large population of Polynesian origin. In early 19th cent. much visited by whalers and first missionaries arrived; diseases introduced by outsiders almost decimated indigenous population leading to stricter immigration rules.

Ra·pal·lo \rä-ˈpäl-lō\. Commercial seaport commune, Genova prov., Liguria, NW Italy, on **Gulf of Rapallo,** an inlet of Ligurian Sea, 16 mi. (26 km.) ESE of Genoa; pop. (1989c) 29,790; tourist resort; two treaties signed here after WWI: 1920 bet. Italy and Yugoslavia which made Fiume an independent city, and 1922 bet. U.S.S.R. and Germany in which both renounced claims to war indemnities.

Rapa Nui. See EASTER ISLAND.

Ra·pa Nui National Park \ˈrä-pä-ˈnü-ē\. National Park, Chile, on Easter I. (Rapa Nui); estab. 1935; contains giant stone figures.

Ra·pel \rä-ˈpel\. River, Chile; flows NW, enters Pacific Ocean SW of Santiago.

Ra·pha·na \rə-ˈfā-nə\. Town of the Decapolis (*q.v.*) in Greece.

Raphia. See RAFA.

Rap·i·dan \ˌra-pə-ˈdan\. River, N Virginia; rises in the Blue Ridge, flows E into Rappahannock River on boundary bet. Culpeper and Spotsylvania cos; ab. 70 mi. (115 km.) long.

Rap·id City \ˈra-pəd\. City, ⊗ of Pennington co., SW South Dakota, in E part of Black Hills 45 mi. (72 km.) E of Wyoming border; pop. (1990c) 54,523; tourism; produces building materials, flour, electronic equipment; gold, uranium, mica, silver mines; South Dakota School of Mines and Technology (1885), National Coll. (1941); settled 1876; incorp. 1882; suffered heavy losses in flood June 1972.

Ra·pides \ˌrä-ˈpēd\. Parish in cen. Louisiana. See table at LOUISIANA.

Ra·pi·do \ˈrä-pē-ˌdō\. Short river, SE Lazio, cen. Italy, flows SW past Cassino to the Liri; in WWII in campaign in Italy formed a German defense line, finally crossed by Allied troops May 1944.

Rap·pa·han·nock \ˌra-pə-ˈha-nək\. **1.** River, NE Virginia; rises in the Blue Ridge, Rappahannock co., flows SE forming a long estuary emptying into Chesapeake Bay; 212 mi. (341 km.) long; navigable to Fredericksburg; scene of several battles during Civil War.
2. County in N Virginia. See table at VIRGINIA.

Rappoltsweiler. See RIBEAUVILLÉ.

Rap·ti \ˈräp-tē\. River, Nepal and N India; flows NW in Nepal and then SE in Uttar Pradesh, India, to the Ghāghara River; ab. 400 mi. (645 km.) long; navigable in its lower course.

Ra·pu–Ra·pu \ˌrä-pü-ˈrä-pü\. **1.** Island, Albay prov., S Luzon, Philippines; 25 sq. mi. (65 sq. km.); chief town Rapu-Rapu.
2. Chief town on Rapu-Rapu I., Luzon, Philippines; munic. pop. (1980c) 25,176.

Raqqah, Ar. See AR RAQQAH.

Raq·uette \ˈra-kət\. River, N New York; rises in Hamilton co., flows N through St. Lawrence co. into St. Lawrence River near Massena; ab. 140 mi. (225 km.) long.

Raquette Lake. Lake, N Hamilton co., NE cen. New York; drains through stream flowing NE into Long Lake; ab. 10 mi. (16 km.) long; elev. 1775 ft. (541 m.); summer resort.

Rar·i·tan \ˈrar-ə-tən\. **1.** River, N cen. New Jersey; formed by confluence of branches in W Somerset co., flows E into Raritan Bay; ab. 75 mi. (120 km.) long.
2. Borough, Somerset co., N cen. New Jersey, 11 mi. (18 km.) WNW of New Brunswick; pop. (1990c) 5798.

Raritan Bay. Inlet of Atlantic Ocean in Middlesex co., cen. New Jersey; receives the Raritan River and Arthur Kill on the NW; city of Perth Amboy is on NW shore.

Rar·o·ton·ga \ˌrar-ə-ˈtäŋ-gə\. Chief island of the Cook Is., in SW part of group, S Pacific Ocean; 21°14′S, 159°46′W; 26 sq. mi. (67 sq. km.); pop. (1986c) 9826; chief village Avarua on N coast, ✻ of Cook Is.; exports copra, bananas. Highest point 2140 ft. (3443 m.). One of the most habitable of all Polynesian islands. First European visitors may have been mutineers from the British ship *Bounty* 1789; became British protectorate 1888; transferred to New Zealand 1901.

Ras \räs, ˈräs\. Arabic word meaning "cape"; for many names beginning with it, see the distinguishing element.

Ras al–Ge·nei·na \ˌräs-ˌál-gə-ˈnā-nə\. Mountain, S cen. Sinai Penin., NE Egypt; 5334 ft. (1626 m.); highest point of Egma Plateau.

Ra's al Khay·mah *or* **Ras al–Khai·mah** \ˌräs-ál-ˈk̲ī-mə\. **1.** Emirate. See table at UNITED ARAB EMIRATES.
2. Town, its ✻.

Ras ash–Sharbatāt. See SHARBATAT, CAPE.

Ras Asir. See CASEYR, RAAS.

Ra's at Tan·nū·rah \ˌräs-át-tá-ˈnü-rə\ *or* **Ras Ta·nu·ra** \ˌräs-tə-ˈnu̇r-ə\. Peninsula, cape (*ras*), and seaport on W coast of Persian Gulf, al-Hasa, Saudi Arabia, just E of Al Qaṭīf ab. 35 mi. (56 km.) NW of Bahrain; oil pipelines and refineries.

Ra's aṭ Ṭīb. See BON, CAPE.

Ras Banâs *also* **Ras Benas.** See BANÂS, RAS.

Ras Dashen *also* **Ras Da·shan** \ˌräs-də-ˈshän\. Peak in the Simyen Mts., N Ethiopia, NE of Gonder and Lake Tana; 15,158 ft. (4620 m.); highest peak in Ethiopia.

Rashīd. See ROSETTA.

Rashowa. See RASSHUA.

Rasht \ˈrasht\ *also* **Resht** \ˈresht\. City, ✻ of Gīlān prov., NW Iran, near the shore of the Caspian Sea; pop. (1986c) 2,900,897; silk-manufacturing center; has large trade, partly through its port of Bandor-e Anzali; connected by motor transport road with Qazvīn and Tehran to the SE. Occupied by Russia 1723–32; came under Russian sphere of influence by agreement with Great Britain 1907; suffered from Russian occupation in WWI and WWII.

Ras Muari. See MUARI, RAS.

Ra's Naṣrānī. See SHARM AL-SHEIKH.

Raso, Cabo. See NORTE, CABO.

Ras Sham·ra *or* **Ra's Sham·rah** \ˌräs-ˈsham-rä, -ˈshäm-\. Site of ancient city of Ugarit (*q.v.*), W Syria, near coast just N of Latakia; its archaeological objects, excavated since 1929, have been of very great value; they include clay tablets of 2d millennium B.C. bearing texts in a cuneiform alphabet (Ugaritic) and objects of art and daily use of the Middle Bronze Age.

Ras·shua \rə-ˈshü-ə\ *or Jp.* **Ra·sho·wa** \rä-ˈshō-wä\. Small island in cen. part of Kuril Is. chain, E Russia in Asia, NE of Shimushir.

Ras Tanura. See RA'S AT TANNŪRAH.

Ra·statt *also* **Ra·stadt** \ˈrä-ˌshtät\. City, Baden-Württemberg, Germany, 13 mi. (21 km.) SW of Karlsruhe; pop. (1980c) 37,297. Became residence of margrave of Baden 1705; Treaty of Rastatt signed here 1714 bet. Austria and France supplementing Treaty of Utrecht (ending War of the Spanish Succession); scene of insurrection against German government 1849.

Rastenburg. See KĘTRZYN.

Ra·tak \ˈrä-ˌtäk\ *or* **Ra·dak** \-ˌdäk\. E chain of islands in the Marshall Is., in W Pacific Ocean; includes 14 atolls and 2 coral islands in long chain of ab. 700 mi. (1130 km.). More important atolls are Mili, Majuro, Maloelap, Wotje, Likiep, and at extreme NW, Bikini.

Ratch·a·bu·ri *or* **Rat Bu·ri** \rät-ˈbu̇-ˌrē\. Town, SW Thailand, on Mae Klong River 50 mi. (80 km.) WSW of Bangkok; center of agricultural area.

Ra·the·now \ˈrä-tə-ˌnō\. City, Brandenburg, NE cen. Germany, on Havel River 33 mi. (53 km.) NW of Potsdam; pop. (1981c) 31,999; 16th cent. town hall. Suffered during Thirty Years' War 1618–48; occupied by the Swedes for a short time in 1675.

Rath·lin \ˈrath-lin\. Island in the North Channel off the NE coast of Northern Ireland; administratively in Moyle dist.; has ruins of castle where Scottish King Robert the Bruce took refuge 1306 after his defeat by the English.

Ra·thong \rä-ˈtȯŋ\. Mountain in the Himalayas, on the Nepal-Sikkim boundary; 24,913 ft. (7593 m.).

Ratibor. See RACIBÓRZ.

Ra·ting·en \ˈrä-tiŋ-ən\. City, North Rhine-Westphalia, Germany, 6 mi. (10 km.) N of Düsseldorf; pop. (1992e) 90,879; textiles, boilers; made city 1276.

Ratisbon *or* **Ratisbona.** See REGENSBURG.

Rätische Alpen. See *Rhaetian Alps* in table at ALPS.

Rat Island \ˈrat\. Small island in center of Rat Is., Alaska; 51°55′N, 178°20′E; E of Kiska and NW of Amchitka.

Rat Islands. Group of islands, W Aleutian Is., SW Alaska, extending from 175°45′E to 179°40′E; comprises Kiska (*q.v.*), Amchitka, Semisopochnoi, Rat, and a number of islets.

Rat·lam *or* **Rut·lam** \rət-ˈläm\. **1.** Former Indian state, now part of Madhya Pradesh state, India; 687 sq. mi. (1779 sq. km.).
2. Town, its ✻, 60 mi. (97 km.) NW of Indore; pop. (1991p) 183,370; textiles, pottery.

Ratmanov. See DIOMEDE ISLANDS.

Rat·na·gi·ri \rət-ˈnä-gə-rē\. Town, SW Maharashtra, W India, on Arabian Sea 136 mi. (219 km.) S of Bombay; pop. (1991p) 56,512; port of call for coastal vessels. Place where Thibau, the last king of Burma, was exiled by British after his defeat 1885 in the Third Anglo-Burmese War.

Rat·na·pu·ra \ˈrət-nə-ˌpu̇r-ə\. Town, SW cen. Sri Lanka, 42 mi. (68 km.) ESE of Colombo; pop. (1990e) 46,000; center of precious-stone industry. Nearby is Maha Saman Dewale, Buddhist temple.

Ra·ton \rə-ˈtōn, ra-, -ˈtün\. City, ⊗ of Colfax co., N New Mexico, 115 mi. (185 km.) NE of Santa Fe near Colorado border; pop. (1990c) 7372; alt. 6400 ft. (1950 m.).

Raton Pass. Mountain pass, Las Animas co., SE Colorado, on Colorado-New Mexico boundary just N of Raton, New Mexico; 7834 ft. (2388 m.); highway and railroad; formerly traversed by a branch of the Santa Fe Trail; used by Spanish of New Mexico in military expeditions in 18th and 19th cents. and by U.S. frontier army in 19th cent.

Raton Range. Range in SE Colorado, extending S across border into Colfax co., N New Mexico.

Rat Portage. See KENORA 2.

Rat·tray Head \ˈra-ˌtrā\. Cape on NE cen. coast of Scotland, S of Kinnairds Head; lighthouse.

Raub \ˈrau̇b\. Town, Pahang state, cen. peninsular Malaysia; pop. (1980c) 22,907.

Rau·far·höfn \ˈrȯi-ˌvär-ˌhœb-ᵊn\. Village and port on NE coast of Iceland near Cape Rifstangi.

Raukawa. See COOK STRAIT.

Rau·ku·ma·ra Range \rau̇-ˈkü-mə-rə\. Mountain range in NE North I., New Zealand.

Rau·ma \ˈrau̇-mä\. **1.** Seaport, Turku ja Pori prov., SW Finland, on the Gulf of Bothnia 25 mi. (40 km.) S of Pori; pop. (1989c) 29,937; exports lumber and cellulose; paper mills; chartered 15th cent.
2. River, cen. Norway; flows NW into Romsdalsfjord SE of Molde; has several waterfalls; its valley is called Romsdal (*q.v.*).

Ra·ung, Gu·nung \gu̇-ˈnu̇ŋ-rä-ˈu̇ŋ\ *or Du.* **Ra·oeng** \rä-ˈüŋ\. Mountain, E Java, Indonesia, the highest point of the Idjen volcanic plateau; 10,932 ft. (3332 m.).

Raurkela. See ROURKELA.

Ra·val·li \rə-ˈva-lē\. County in W Montana. See table at MONTANA.

Ra·va·nu·sa \ˌrä-vä-ˈnü-zä\. Commune, Agrigento prov., SW Sicily, Italy, 23 mi. (37 km.) ESE of the commune of Agrigento; pop. (1981p) 15,472.

Ra·vel·lo \rä-ˈve-lō\. Village, Salerno prov., S Campania, S Italy, 19 mi. (31 km.) W of the seaport of Salerno; pop. (1981p) 2314; 1227 ft. (374 m.) above the sea; 12th cent. church.

Ra·ve·na \rə-ˈvē-nə\. Village, Albany co., E New York, on Hudson River 11 mi. (18 km.) S of the city of Albany; pop. (1990c) 3547.

Ra·ven·na \rə-ˈve-nə, *It.* rä-ˈven-nä\. **1.** City, ⊗ of Portage co., NE Ohio, 15 mi. (24 km.) ENE of Akron; pop. (1990c) 12,069; settled 1799.
2. Province of Emilia-Romagna, Italy. See table at ITALY.

3. Commune, ✻ of Ravenna prov., Emilia-Romagna, N Italy, 61 mi. (98 km.) NE of Florence; pop. (1991p) 135,435; connected with the Adriatic Sea by a canal; produces wine, fertilizer; oil refining; exceptionally rich collection of Roman and Byzantine architectural remains, principally churches of the 5th–8th cents., incl. 6th cent. San Vitale with notable mosaics, 6th cent. mausoleum of Ostrogoth King Theodoric, 6th cent. basilica of San Apollinaire Nuovo.

History: Came under Rome 2d cent. B.C.; important naval station under Roman Emperor Augustus; became ✻ of the Western Roman Empire c. 402 A.D., of the barbarian kingdom of Odoacer c. 476, and of the Ostrogoth kingdom of Theodoric 493; flourished as ✻ of Byzantine Empire in Italy under Emperor Justinian and his successors 6th–8th cents.; passed to Lombards c. 751 but given to pope by conquering Franks 757; became independent republic in 12th cent.; subsequently ruled by Polenta family, by Venetians, and again by popes; became part of kingdom of Italy 1860. In WWII taken by Allies Dec. 1944.

Ra·vens·brück \ˌräv-ᵊns-ˈbrœk, ˈrāv-ᵊnz-ˌbru̇k\. Village, Brandenburg, NE Germany, N of Berlin; site of a Nazi concentration camp in WWII.

Ra·vens·burg \ˈräv-ᵊns-ˌbu̇rk, ˈrā-vənz-ˌbərg\. City, Baden-Württemberg, Germany, 47 mi. (76 km.) SSW of Ulm; pop. (1992e) 46,329; textiles, lumber, paper; several Gothic churches. Founded in 11th cent.; free imperial city 1276–1802; to Bavaria 1802.

Ra·ven·spur \ˈrā-vən-ˌspər\. Former seaport town, East Riding, Yorkshire, NE England, at mouth of the Humber near Spurn Head; landing place of exiled English King Edward IV 1471 in Wars of the Roses; town later swept away by sea.

Ra·vens·wood \ˈrā-vənz-ˌwu̇d\. Town, Jackson co., W West Virginia, on Ohio River 25 mi. (40 km.) SW of Parkersburg; pop. (1990c) 4189.

Ra·vi \ˈrä-vē\; *anc.* **Hy·dra·o·tes** \ˌhī-drə-ˈō-tēz\. River, N Pakistan; rises in the Himalayas, flows SW diagonally across Pakistan to the Chenab; NE of Lahore forms part of boundary bet. Pakistan and India; about 475 mi. (765 km.) long; one of the "Five Rivers" of the Punjab.

Rawa Harbour. See ARAWA HARBOUR.

Ra·wa·ki \rä-ˈwä-kē\; *formerly* **Phoe·nix** \ˈfē-niks\. One of the Phoenix Is. in cen. Pacific Ocean, SE of Enderbury I., 3°40′S, 170°43′W; ab. 3 sq. mi. (8 sq. km.); most fertile of the group.

Ra·wal·pin·di \ˌrä-wəl-ˈpin-dē, rau̇l-ˈ\. City, Punjab, Pakistan, 90 mi. (145 km.) ESE of Peshawar; met. area pop. (1981c) 966,000; locomotive works, iron foundry, oil refinery; textiles. Strategically located, controlling routes to Kashmir; before 1947 site of important British military station and now headquarters of Pakistan's army. Treaty signed here 1919 by which Great Britain recognized complete independence of Afghanistan; was temporary ✻ of Pakistan 1959–69.

Ra·wān·dūz \rä-ˈwän-ˌdu̇z\ *also* **Ru·wan·diz** \rə-ˈwän-ˌdiz\. Town in mountains of Kurdistan, NE Iraq, 80 mi. (129 km.) ENE of Mosul.

Rawḍah. See RODA.

Raw·don \ˈrȯ-dən\. Village, Montcalm co., S Quebec, Canada, 55 mi. (88 km.) N of Montreal; pop. (1991c) 3297.

Ra·wicz \ˈrä-vich\ *or Ger.* **Ra·witsch** \ˈrä-vich\. Commune, S Leszno prov., W cen. Poland, 50 mi. (80 km.) S of Poznań; pop. (1989e) 20,615.

Raw·ka \ˈräf-kä\. River, W Poland, a tributary of the Bzura; ab. 50 mi. (80 km.) long.

Raw·lins \ˈrȯ-lənz\. **1.** County in NW Kansas. See table at KANSAS.

2. City, ⊗ of Carbon co., S Wyoming, 28 mi. (45 km.) SW of confluence of Medicine Bow and North Platte rivers; pop. (1990c) 9380; state penitentiary; city founded 1868; incorp. 1886.

Raw·marsh \ˈrȯ-ˌmärsh\. Town, South Yorkshire, N England, near Rotherham; pop. (1981p) 18,985; coal mines in vicinity.

Raw·son \ˈrȯs-ᵊn, ˈrau̇-ˌsȯn\. Seaport, ✻ of Chubut prov., S cen. Argentina, near the mouth of Chubut River; munic. pop. (1991p) 100,132.

Raw·ten·stall \ˈrȯt-ᵊn-ˌstȯl\. Town, Lancashire, NW England, on the upper Irwell 17 mi. (27 km.) N of Manchester; pop. (1981p) 22,231; footwear, textiles.

Ray \ˈrā\. County in NW Missouri. See table at MISSOURI.

Ray, Cape. SW point of Newfoundland, Canada, on Cabot Strait opp. N tip of Cape Breton I.

Ray, Mount. Mountain, Antarctica, 85°07′S, 170°48′W; 12,808 ft. (3904 m.).

Ra·ya, Mount \ˈrä-yä, ˈrī-ə\ *or* **Ra·ja Peak** \ˈrä-jä\. Peak, Schwaner Mts., W cen. Borneo, Indonesia; 7474 ft. (2278 m.).

Rayak. See RIYAQ.

Ray·leigh \ˈrā-lē\. Town, Essex, SE England, 32 mi. (51 km.) ENE of London; pop. (1981p) 29,146.

Ray·mond \ˈrā-mənd\. **1.** Town, a ⊗ of Hinds co., SW cen. Mississippi, ab. 28 mi. (45 km.) ESE of Vicksburg; pop. (1990c) 2275; Hinds Community Coll. (1917); in Civil War scene of battle May 12, 1863, a victory for Union forces.

2. Town, Rockingham co., SE New Hampshire; pop. (1990c) 8713.

3. City, Pacific co., SW corner of Washington, on Willapa Bay 21 mi. (34 km.) S of Aberdeen; pop. (1990c) 2901.

Raymond Peak. Mountain in the Sierra Nevada in E Alpine co., E California; 10,075 ft. (3071 m.).

Ray·mond·ville \ˈrā-mənd-ˌvil\. City, ⊗ of Willacy co., S Texas, 42 mi. (68 km.) N of Brownsville; pop. (1990c) 8880.

Ray·more \ˈrā-ˌmōr\. City, Cass co., W Missouri, S of Kansas City; pop. (1990c) 5592.

Rayne \ˈrān\. City, Acadia parish, S Louisiana, 16 mi. (26 km.) W of Lafayette; pop. (1990c) 8502.

Rayn·ham \ˈrān-əm, -ˌham\. Town, Bristol co., SE Massachusetts, 10 mi. (16 km.) SSW of Brockton; pop. (1990c) 9867.

Ra·yong \rä-ˈyȯŋ\. Town, S Thailand, port on NE coast of Gulf of Thailand 80 mi. (129 km.) SE of Bangkok; pop. (1991e) 46,689.

Ray·side–Bal·four \ˈrā-ˌsīd-ˈbal-fər\. Town, Sudbury munic. region, SE Ontario, Canada; pop. (1991c) 15,039.

Raystown. See BEDFORD 8.

Ray·town \ˈrā-ˌtau̇n\. City, Jackson co., W Missouri, SE suburb of Kansas City; pop. (1990c) 30,601.

Ray·ville \ˈrā-ˌvil\. Town, ⊗ of Richland parish, NE Louisiana, 22 mi. (35 km.) E of Monroe; pop. (1990c) 4411.

Rayyān, Ar. See AR RAYYĀN.

Raz, Pointe du \ˌpweⁿt-dǖ-ˈrä\. Headland, W Finistère dept., NW France, S of Brest; 240 ft. (386 m.) high.

Razdan. See HRAZDAN.

Ra·zelm, Lake \rä-ˈzelm\. Coastal lake or lagoon, Tulcea co., SE Romania, just S of mouth of the Danube.

Raz·grad \ˈräz-ˌgrät\. Town, N Bulgaria, ab. 25 mi. (40 km.) N of Shumen; pop. (1991e) 57,305.

Ré, Île de \ˌēl-də-ˈrā\. Island in E Bay of Biscay, Charente-Maritime dept., W France; linked by bridge with La Rochelle; 16 mi. (26 km.) long; 33 sq. mi. (85 sq. km.); pop. (1982c) 11,396; chief town St.-Martin on NE coast.

Rea, Lough. See LOUGHREA.

Read·ing \ˈre-diŋ\. **1.** Residential town, Middlesex co., NE Massachusetts, 11 mi. (18 km.) N of Boston; pop. (1990c) 22,539.

2. City, Hamilton co., SW corner of Ohio, 9 mi. (14 km.) N of Cincinnati; pop. (1990c) 12,038.

3. City, ⊗ of Berks co., SE Pennsylvania, on Schuylkill River 50 mi. (80 km.) WNW of Philadelphia; pop. (1990c) 78,380; brick, motor-vehicle parts; foundries; Albright Coll. (1856), Alvernia Coll. (1958). Town laid out 1748; incorp. as borough 1783 and as city 1847.

4. Town, ⊗ of Berkshire, S England, on the Kennet at its confluence with the Thames 39 mi. (63 km.) W of London; pop. (1991p) 122,600; produces baked goods, computers, iron products; brewing and malting, printing, boatbuilding; Univ. of Reading (1926); Danish encamped on site 871; town received first charter 1253; Irish poet and playwright Oscar Wilde imprisoned here 1897.

Rea·gan \ˈrā-gən\. County in W Texas. See table at TEXAS.

Re·al \ˈrē-ˌȯl\. County in SW cen. Texas. See table at TEXAS.

Real, Cordillero. See ANDES.

Re·ao \rā-ˈau̇\ *also* **Cler·mont–Ton·nerre** \ˌkler-ˌmȯ^{n}-tō-ˈner\. Island in E part of the Tuamotu Archipelago, French Polynesia, S Pacific Ocean; 18°31′S, 136°23′W; 10 mi. (16 km.) long by 1.5 mi. (2.4 km.) wide; pop. (1988c) 452.

Rear·guard, Mount \ˈrir-ˌgärd\. Peak, S Carbon co., S Montana; 12,350 ft. (3764 m.).

Reate. See RIETI 2.

Re·bun \ˈrā-ˈbün\. Small Japanese island in N Sea of Japan, off NW coast of Hokkaidō.

Re·ca·na·ti \ˌrā-kä-ˈnä-tē\. Commune, Macerata prov., Marche, cen. Italy, 9 mi. (14 km.) NNE of the commune of Macerata; pop. (1981p) 18,485. Poet Giacomo Leopardi born here 1798.

Re·cherche, Archipelago of the \rə-ˈshersh\. Group of small islands in Indian Ocean off S coast of Western Australia, Australia, at W end of Great Australian Bight.

Re·chy·tsa *or* **Re·chi·tsa** \rə-ˈchit-sə\. Town, Homyel’ subdivision, Belarus, W of city of Homyel’; pop. (1991e) 69,400. Dates from before 12th cent.

Re·ci·fe \ri-ˈsē-fē\; *formerly* **Per·nam·bu·co** \ˌper-nəm-ˈbü-kü\. Seaport, ✻ of Pernambuco state, E Brazil, at mouth of Capibaribe River near Point Plata, easternmost point of South America; munic. pop. (1989e) 1,300,000; one of the leading ports of Brazil, with extensive modern facilities; naval base; federal university (1946) and other educational institutions. City is built partly on the mainland, partly on a peninsula and on an island in a lagoon formed by two rivers. Founded by Portuguese in first half of 16th cent.; raided and sacked by English privateers 1595; occupied by Dutch 1630–54; became ✻ of province 1823.

Recife, Cape. Cape on E coast of Eastern Cape prov., Rep. of South Africa, on W side of Algoa Bay 6 mi. (10 km.) SW of Port Elizabeth.

Reciţa. See REŞIŢA.

Reck·ling·hau·sen \ˌre-kliŋ-ˈhau̇z-^{ə}n\. City, North Rhine-Westphalia, Germany, 30 mi. (48 km.) SW of Münster; pop. (1992e) 125,966; textiles, machinery; coal mines, iron foundries, chemical plant; 13th–16th cent. church. Orig. a Saxon settlement; came under archbishop of Cologne 12th cent.; received city charter c. 1230; to Prussia 1815.

Re·co·a·ro Ter·me \ˌrā-kō-ˈä-rō-ˈter-mē\. Commune, NW Vicenza prov., SW cen. Veneto, NE Italy; pop. (1981p) 7819; mineral springs.

Re·cu·let \rə-kǖ-ˈlā\. Peak in Ain dept., E France, in the Jura Mts.; 5633 ft. (1717 m.).

Red \ˈred\. **1.** Navigable river, S cen. U.S.; rises in high plains in E New Mexico; flows E, crossing Texas Panhandle and then becoming boundary bet. Texas and Oklahoma and for a short distance boundary bet. Texas and Arkansas; turns S in SW Arkansas and crosses border into Louisiana, flows SE across Louisiana and into the Mississippi River; 1018 mi. (1638 km.) long.

2. River, N Tennessee; rises in Sumner co., flows NW across border of Kentucky, reenters Tennessee and flows SW into Cumberland River at Clarksville.

3. *or* **Red River of the North.** River, N cen. U.S. and S cen. Canada; formed by junction at Breckenridge, W Minnesota, of the Otter Tail River from the E and Bois de Sioux River from Lake Traverse to the S; flows N forming Minnesota-North Dakota boundary, crosses Canadian border and continues N to S Lake Winnipeg, S Manitoba, Canada; 355 mi. (571 km.) long. (ab. 700 mi. or 1125 km. with longest tributary). Chief tributaries the Sheyenne and Red Lake rivers in U.S. and the Assiniboine in Canada; drains rich wheat lands. In Canada first settled as Scottish colony known as Red River Settlement (*q.v.*).

4. *or in China* **Yuan** (*W.-G.* **Yüan**) \ˈywän\ *or in Vietnam* **Hong** \ˈhȯŋ\; *formerly* **Coi** \ˈkȯi\. River, SE Asia; rises in cen. Yunnan prov., S China, flows SE across N Vietnam, past Hanoi, into Gulf of Tonkin; ab. 500 mi. (805 km.) long; has wide fertile delta E of Hanoi.

Re·dan \ri-ˈdan\. Fortification, S part of Sevastopol’, Crimea, Ukraine; evacuated Sept. 1855 by Russians during Crimean War.

Redang. See GREAT REDANG.

Red Bank \ˈred-ˌbaŋk\. **1.** Residential and resort borough, Monmouth co., E cen. New Jersey, on Navesink River ab. 6 mi. (10 km.) inland from Atlantic Ocean, 15 mi. (24 km.) SE of Perth Amboy; pop. (1990c) 10,636.

2. Town, Hamilton co., SE Tennessee, near Chattanooga; pop. (1990c) 12,322.

Red Basin. See SICHUAN.

Red Bluff. City, ⊗ of Tehama co., N California, on Sacramento River 38 mi. (61 km.) NW of Chico; pop. (1990c) 12,363; diversified agriculture.

Red·boy \ˈred-ˌbȯi\. Mountain, Grant co., E cen. Oregon; 6021 ft. (1835 m.).

Red·bridge \ˈred-ˌbrij\. A borough of Greater London, SE England. See table at LONDON 4.

Red Bud \ˈred-ˌbəd\. City, Randolph co., SW Illinois, 28 mi. (45 km.) SSE of East St. Louis; pop. (1990c) 2918.

Red Cedar. River, W Wisconsin; flows from Barron co. S into Chippewa River in S Dunn co.; ab. 85 mi. (135 km.) long.

Red Cen·tre \ˈsen-tər\. The vast, remote, interior part of Australia; noted for its aridity and brightly colored landscape features.

Red·cliff \ˈred-ˌklif\. Town, cen. Zimbabwe, SSW of Kwekwe; pop. (1982c) 22,109.

Red Cloud \ˈred-ˌklau̇d\. City, ⊗ of Webster co., S Nebraska, on Republican River 35 mi. (56 km.) S of Hastings; pop. (1990c) 1204. Childhood home of author Willa Cather.

Red·cloud Peak \ˈred-ˌklau̇d\. Mountain, Hinsdale co., SW Colorado; 14,034 ft. (4278 m.).

Red Cone. Mountain, W Klamath co., S Oregon, N of Crater Lake; 7372 ft. (2247 m.).

Red Deer \ˈred-ˌdir\. **1.** River, S Alberta, Canada; rises in Banff National Park, SW Alberta, flows SE and E into the South Saskatchewan River near the Alberta boundary; 385 mi. (619 km.) long.

2. River, S cen. Canada; rises in E cen. Saskatchewan, flows E across border of Manitoba prov., through **Red Deer Lake** (100 sq. mi. or 259 sq. km.), into Lake Winnipegosis; ab. 140 mi. (225 km.) long.

3. City, S Alberta, Canada, on Red Deer River 85 mi. (137 km.) N of Calgary; pop. (1991c) 58,134; dairy products; petroleum; Red Deer Coll. (1964).

Red·ding \ˈre-diŋ\. **1.** City, ⊗ of Shasta co., N California, on Sacramento River 67 mi. (108 km.) NNW of Chico; pop. (1990c) 66,462; summer resort; Simpson Coll. (1921), Shasta Coll. (1949); pop. more than doubled bet. 1970 and 1980.

2. Town, cen. Fairfield co., SW Connecticut; pop. (1990c) 7927.

Red·ditch \ˈre-dich\. Town, Hereford and Worcester co., W cen. England, near Birmingham; pop. (1991p) 76,900; needles, fishing tackle, bicycles.

Red Eagle Mountain. Peak in Glacier National Park, NW Montana; 8800 ft. (2682 m.).

Red·field \ˈred-ˌfēld\. City, ⊗ of Spink co., NE cen. South Dakota, 41 mi. (66 km.) S of Aberdeen; pop. (1990c) 2770.

Redfield Mountain. Peak in the Adirondack Mts., Essex co., NE New York; 4606 ft. (1404 m.).

Red·fish Lake \ˈred-ˌfish\. Lake in W Custer co., cen. Idaho.

Red Hill. See MAUI 1.

Red Indian Lake. Lake, cen. Newfoundland, Canada; 37 mi. (60 km.) long, 64 sq. mi. (166 sq. km.); Exploits River flows into the lake.

Red Kaweah. See KAWEAH PEAKS.

Red Lake. **1.** Lake, Beltrami co., N Minnesota, divided into **Upper Red Lake** and **Lower Red Lake;** 38 mi. (61 km.) long; 451 sq. mi. (1168 sq. km.).

2. River, NW Minnesota; flows W out of Lower Red Lake, turns SW to empty into Red River of the North opp. Grand Forks, North Dakota; 196 mi. (315 km.) long.

3. County in NW Minnesota. See table at MINNESOTA.

\ə\ **abut** \ə\ matches \$^{ə}$\ kitten, Fr table \ər\ **further** \a\ **ash** \ā\ **ace**
\ä\ cot, cart \à\ Fr bac \au̇\ **out** \b̲\ Span Avila \ch\ **chin** \e\ **bet** \ē\ **easy**
\g\ **go** \i\ **hit** \ī\ **ice** \j\ **job** \k̲\ Ger **ich**, **Buch** \$^{n}$\ Fr vin
\ŋ\ **sing** \ō\ **go** \ȯ\ **all** \ȯ\ **law** \œ\ Fr **bœuf** \œ̄\ Fr **feu** \ȯi\ **boy**
\th\ **thin** \th̲\ **this** \ü\ **loot** \u̇\ **foot** \ue\ Ger **füllen** \ǖ\ Fr **rue**
\y\ **yet** \$^{y}$\ Fr digne \ˈdēn^{y}\, nuit \ˈnw^{y}ē\ \yü\ **few** \yu̇\ **fury** \zh\ **vision**

Red Lake Falls. City, ⊗ of Red Lake co., NW Minnesota, 17 mi. (27 km.) S of Thief River Falls; pop. (1990c) 1481.

Red·lands \ˈred-ləndz\. Residential city, San Bernardino co., SE California, 8 mi. (13 km.) ESE of the city of San Bernardino; pop. (1990c) 60,394; Univ. of Redlands (1907); city incorp. 1888.

Red Lick Mountain. Peak, Pocahontas co., E cen. West Virginia; 3533 ft. (1077 m.).

Red Li·on \ˈlī-ən\. Borough, York co., S Pennsylvania, 8 mi. (13 km.) SE of the city of York; pop. (1990c) 6130.

Red Lodge \ˈred-ˌläj\. City, ⊗ of Carbon co., S Montana, 57 mi. (92 km.) SW of Billings; pop. (1990c) 1958; resort.

Red·mond \ˈred-mənd\. **1.** City and resort, Deschutes co., cen. Oregon, 18 mi. (29 km.) NNE of Bend; pop. (1990c) 7163.

2. City, King co., W cen. Washington, 10 mi. (16 km.) NE of Seattle; pop. (1990c) 35,800; has grown rapidly since 1970.

Red Mountain. **1.** Peak in the Sierra Nevada, E Fresno co., S cen. California; 11,933 ft. (3637 m.).

2. Peak, Chaffee and Pitkin cos., W cen. Colorado; 13,500 ft. (4115 m.).

3. Peak, Glacier National Park, NW Montana; 9300 ft. (2835 m.).

4. Peak, S Lewis and Clark co., W cen. Montana; 8802 ft. (2683 m.).

5. Peak, Baker co., E Oregon; ab. 8925 ft. (2720 m.).

6. Peak, N Whatcom co., NW Washington; 7784 ft. (2373 m.).

Red·nitz \ˈrād-nits\. River, Bavaria, Germany; flows N to unite with the Pegnitz River at Fürth and form the Regnitz River; ab. 50 mi. (80 km.) long.

Red Oak \ˈred-ˌōk\. City, ⊗ of Montgomery co., SW Iowa, 37 mi. (60 km.) SE of Council Bluffs; pop. (1990c) 6264.

Re·don \rə-ˈdōⁿ\. Town, SW Ille-et-Vilaine dept., NW France, on the Vilaine ab. 38 mi. (61 km.) SSW of Rennes; on site of monastery founded 9th cent.

Re·don·da \ri-ˈdän-də\. Uninhabited island in the Leeward Is., West Indies; part of Antigua and Barbuda; ab. 1 sq. mi. (3 sq. km.); rocky, highest point 1000 ft. (305 m.).

Re·don·de·la \ˌrā-t͟hōn-ˈdā-lä\. Commune, Pontevedra prov., NW Spain, 15 mi. (24 km.) S of the commune of Pontevedra; pop. (1991c) 28,014; manufactures linen, china.

Re·don·do Beach \ri-ˈdän-dō\. Residential and resort city, Los Angeles co., SW California, on Pacific Ocean 17 mi. (27 km.) SE of center of Los Angeles; pop. (1990c) 60,167; incorp. 1892.

Re·doubt Volcano \ri-ˈdau̇t\. Volcano, S Alaska, ab. 18 mi. (29 km.) W of Cook Inlet; 10,197 ft. (3108 m.); erupted 1966, 1989.

Red Peak. **1.** Mountain in the Sierra Nevada, in E Yosemite National Park, cen. California; 11,699 ft. (3566 m.).

2. Mountain, Costilla and Las Animas cos., S Colorado; 13,600 ft. (4145 m.).

Red Point. Cape on SW coast of St. Thomas I., Virgin Is. of the U.S., West Indies.

Redriff. See ROTHERHITHE.

Red River. **1.** Name of a parish in NW Louisiana and a county in NE Texas. See tables at LOUISIANA and TEXAS.

2. Rivers. See RED.

Red River of the North. See RED 3.

Red River Settlement. Colony in valley of Red River of the North, now in Manitoba, Canada. Founded 1811 by Scottish leader Thomas Douglas, 5th earl of Selkirk; destroyed 1816 in conflict with North-West Fur Company, but restored 1817; united with Canada 1869 and absorbed into prov. of Manitoba 1870.

Red Rock River \ˈred-ˈräk\ *or* **Red Rock Creek.** River in Rocky Mts., Beaverhead co., SW Montana.

Red Russia. In 18th cent. a region of S Poland bet. Volhynia and the Carpathian Mts. in the area around the upper Dniester; now a part of W Ukraine and SE Poland.

Red·scar Bay \ˈred-ˌskär\. Small bay on S coast of New Guinea I., Papua New Guinea, N of Port Moresby.

Red Sea **1.** *anc.* **Si·nus Arab·i·cus** \ˈsī-nəs-ə-ˈra-bi-kəs\. Inland sea bet. Arabian Penin. and NE Africa; ab. 1200 mi. (1930 km.) long; 169,100 sq. mi. (437,969 sq. km.); on the N connects with Mediterranean Sea through the Gulf of Suez and the Suez Canal; on the S connects with Arabian Sea through the strait of Bab el Mandeb; in the Great Rift Valley (*q.v.*).

2. Part of Indian Ocean. See ERYTHRAEAN SEA.

3. Coastal governorate, E Egypt, on the Red Sea. See table at EGYPT.

Red Springs. Town, Robeson co., S North Carolina, 25 mi. (40 km.) SW of Fayetteville; pop. (1990c) 3799.

Red Tank. Town, cen. Panama, on the Panama Canal near the Pedro Miguel Locks.

Red Volta. See VOLTA, RED.

Red Willow. County in S Nebraska. See table at NEBRASKA.

Red Wing \ˈred-ˌwiŋ\. City, ⊗ of Goodhue co., SE Minnesota, on Mississippi River 40 mi. (64 km.) SE of St. Paul; pop. (1990c) 15,134; footwear.

Red·wood \ˈred-ˌwu̇d\. **1.** River, SW Minnesota; flows NE and E in Lyon and Redwood cos. into Minnesota River; ab. 90 mi. (145 km.) long.

2. County in SW Minnesota. See table at MINNESOTA.

Redwood City. City, ⊗ of San Mateo co., W California, 5 mi. (8 km.) W of San Francisco Bay and ab. 18 mi. (29 km.) SE of San Francisco; pop. (1990c) 66,072; center of electronics industry; rubber products, cement; residential; Cañada Coll. (1968); town laid out 1854.

Redwood Falls. City, ⊗ of Redwood co., SW Minnesota, on the Redwood River 33 mi. (53 km.) ENE of Marshall; pop. (1990c) 4859.

Redwood National Park. See UNITED STATES, *National Parks.*

Ree, Lough \ˈrē\. Lake, cen. Ireland, E of Roscommon; 16 mi. (26 km.) long and 1 to 7 mi. (2 to 11 km.) wide; 39 sq. mi. (101 sq. km.); the Shannon River flows S through the lake.

Reed City \ˈrēd\. City, ⊗ of Osceola co., cen. Michigan, 26 mi. (42 km.) SSW of Cadillac; pop. (1990c) 2379.

Reed·ley \ˈrēd-lē\. City, Fresno co., S cen. California, 20 mi. (32 km.) ESE of the city of Fresno; pop. (1990c) 15,791; Kings River Community Coll. (1926).

Reeds, Plain of \ˈrēdz\ *or Vietnamese* **Dong Thap Muoi** \ˈdȯŋ-ˈtäp-ˈmwȯi\. Swampy region, S Vietnam; a N extension of the Mekong Delta.

Reeds·burg \ˈrēdz-ˌbərg\. City, Sauk co., S cen. Wisconsin, 26 mi. (42 km.) W of Portage; pop. (1990c) 5834.

Reeds·port \ˈrēdz-ˌpōrt\. City, Douglas co., SW Oregon, on Pacific coast 66 mi. (106 km.) SW of Eugene; pop. (1990c) 4796.

Reef Point \ˈrēf\. Cape on NW coast of N extension of North I., New Zealand, forming S side of Ahipara Bay.

Reel·foot Lake \ˈrēl-ˌfu̇t\. Shallow lake, on boundary bet. Lake and Obion cos., NW Tennessee; ab. 18 mi. (29 km.) long; formed as result of the earthquake at New Madrid (*q.v.*) 1811–12.

Reeves \ˈrēvz\. County in W Texas. See table at TEXAS.

Re·fu·gio \rə-ˈfyu̇r-ē-ō—*sic*\. **1.** County in S Texas. See table at TEXAS.

2. Town, its ⊗, 38 mi. (61 km.) N of Corpus Christi; pop. (1990c) 3158; captured by Mexican forces in Texas Revolution 1836.

Re·gen \ˈrā-gən\. River, Bavaria, Germany; flows W out of Bohemian Forest, then S into the Danube River at Regensburg; 114 mi. (183 km.) long.

Re·gens·burg \ˈrā-gənz-ˌbu̇rk, -ˌbərg\; *formerly (Eng.)* **Rat·is·bon** \ˈra-təs-ˌbän, -təz-\; *medieval* **Rat·is·bo·na** \ˌra-təs-ˈbō-nə, -təz-\; *anc.* **Re·gi·num** \ri-ˈjī-nəm\ *or* **Cas·tra Re·gi·na** \ˈkas-trə-ri-ˈjī-nə\. Commercial city, Bavaria, Germany, on Danube River 65 mi. (105 km.) NNE of Munich; pop. (1992e) 123,002; road and rail junction and river port; produces electronics, chemicals; notable 13th–16th cent. Gothic cathedral, 14th–18th cent. town hall, 12th cent. bridge, and numerous other notable medieval buildings; university (1962).

History: Orig. a Celtic settlement; Roman town founded 179 A.D.; made episcopal see 739; made free imperial city 1245; in Thirty Years' War fell to Protestants 1633 but regained by imperial forces the following year; seat of imperial diet 1663–1803; stormed by French under Emperor Napoléon 1809; to Bavaria 1810; frequently bombed by Allies in WWII.

Reg·gio di Ca·la·bria \ˈred-jō-dē-kä-ˈlä-brē-ä\; *often shortened to* **Reggio** *or* **Reggio Calabria. 1.** Province of Calabria, S Italy. See table at ITALY.

2. *anc. Gk.* **Rhe·gi·on** \ˈrē-jē-ˌän\; *Lat.* **Rhe·gi·um** \ˈrē-jē-əm\. Seaport and industrial commune, its ✻, on Strait of Messina 202 mi. (325 km.) SSE of Naples; pop. (1991p) 169,709; tourist resort; exports dried herbs and essential oils for perfume and pharmaceutical industries; cathedral (rebuilt after earthquake 1908).

History: Founded by Greek colonists at end of 8th cent. B.C. as sister city to Zancle; allied with Athens 5th cent. B.C.; captured by tyrant Dionysius (the Elder) of Siracusae 387 B.C.; allied with Rome c. 280 B.C.; came successively under Visigoth and Ostrogoth kingdoms and under Byzantine Empire; conquered by Arabs 10th cent.; conquered by Normans under Robert Guiscard c. 1060 and became part of Kingdom of The Two Sicilies; devastated by earthquakes 1783 and 1908. Damaged by bombing in WWII.

Reggio nel·l'E·mi·lia \ˈred-jō-ˌnel-e-ˈmēl-yä\; *often shortened to* **Reggio** *or* **Reggio Emilia. 1.** Province of Emilia-Romagna, N Italy. See table at ITALY.

2. *anc.* **Re·gi·um Lep·i·di** \ˈrē-jē-əm-ˈle-pə-ˌdī\ *or* **Regium Lep·i·dum** \-dəm\. Commercial and industrial commune, its ✻, 71 mi. (114 km.) NNW of Florence; pop. (1991p) 131,419; produces wine, cheese, cement, electrical equipment, and pharmaceuticals; 9th–13th cent. cathedral. Founded by Romans 2d cent. B.C.; ruled largely by the Este family 1289–1859; became part of Italy 1860.

Re·ghin \ˈrā-gin\. Town, Mureş co., N cen. Romania, ab. 15 mi. (24 km.) NNE of Tîrgu Mureş; pop. (1989c) 39,045.

Re·gil·lus, Lake \ri-ˈji-ləs\. Ancient name of a small unidentified lake near Rome, Italy, possibly near Tusculum; scene of battle c. 496 B.C. in which Latins were defeated by the Romans.

Re·gi·na \ri-ˈjī-nə\. City, ✻ of Saskatchewan, Canada, in S part of province, 357 mi. (574 km.) W of Winnipeg; pop. (1991c) 179,178; transportation and commercial center in livestock and grain-farming region; produces steel, paint; oil refineries; Campion Coll. (1918), Luther Coll. (1926), Canadian Bible Coll. (1941), Univ. of Regina (1974). Founded 1882; ✻ of Northwest Territories of Canada 1882–1905; made ✻ of Saskatchewan on its formation as province 1905; headquarters of Royal Canadian Mounted Police until 1920.

Reginum. See REGENSBURG.

Región Metropolitana de Santiago. See *Santiago* in table at CHILE.

Registan. See RĪGESTĀN.

Regium Lepidi *or* **Regium Lepidum.** See REGGIO NELL'EMILIA 2.

Re·gla \ˈrā-g̅lä\. Former municipality, La Habana prov., W Cuba; pop. (1990e) 41,449; now part of Havana.

Reg·nitz \ˈräg-nits\. River, Bavaria, Germany; formed by confluence of Pegnitz and Rednitz rivers at Fürth, flows N into the Main River 3 mi. (5 km.) NW of Bamberg.

Regnum Parthorum. See PARTHIA.

Reg·u·la·tion Peak \ˌre-gyə-ˈlā-shən\. **1.** Mountain in the Sierra Nevada, in E Tuolumne co., cen. California; 10,500 ft. (3200 m.).

2. Mountain, E Yellowstone National Park, NW Wyoming; 10,000 ft. (3050 m.).

Re·ho·both \ri-ˈhō-bəth\. **1.** City, Sussex co., S Delaware. See REHOBOTH BEACH.

2. Town, Bristol co., SE Massachusetts, 10 mi. (16 km.) NNW of Fall River; pop. (1990c) 8656.

3. Town, cen. Namibia, on railroad line 50 mi. (80 km.) S of Windhoek; pop. (1991c) 21,654.

Rehoboth Bay. Inlet of Atlantic Ocean, on E coast of Sussex co., Delaware.

Rehoboth Beach *also* **Rehoboth.** City, Sussex co., S Delaware, on Atlantic Ocean just S of Delaware Bay; pop. (1990c) 1234; summer beach resort.

Re·ho·vot *or* **Re·ho·voth** \rə-ˈhō-ˌvōt, ˈrā-hȯ-ˌvȯt\. Town, Israel, ab. 4 mi. (6 km.) SW of Ramla; pop. (1992e) 83,000; pharmaceuticals, plastics; citrus orchards; Weizmann Institute of Science; town founded 1890 by Jewish immigrants from E Europe. Burial place of Chaim Weizmann, Israel's first president.

Rei. See REY.

Reich \ˈrīk, ˈrīk̲\. Literally "empire"; (1) orig., the Holy Roman Empire (the **First Reich**) from its founding in the 9th cent. to 1806; (2) the empire estab. by Prussian statesman Otto von Bismarck (the **Second Reich**) 1871–1918; (3) following the dissolution of the Second Reich and the succeeding German Republic (1918–33), the National Socialist (Nazi) state (the **Third Reich**) created by dictator Adolf Hitler and lasting from 1933 to 1945.

Rei·che·nau \ˈrī-k̲ə-ˌnau̇\. Island in W arm of Lake Constance, Baden-Württemberg, Germany, just W of Konstanz; ab. 2 sq. mi. (5 sq. km.); pop. (1991e) 4562. Site of Benedictine abbey founded 724.

Rei·chen·bach \ˈrīk̲-ᵊn-ˌbäk\. **1.** *or in full* **Reichenbach im Vogt·land** \im-ˈfōkt-ˌlänt\. City, Saxony, E Germany, 10 mi. (16 km.) SW of Zwickau; manufactures textiles, machinery. Chartered late 13th cent.

2. Town, Poland. See DZIERŻONIÓW.

3. Waterfall in Bern canton, Switzerland; comprises five cascades, with a drop of over 200 ft. (61 m.). Scene of final confrontation bet. Sir Arthur Conan Doyle's fictional detective Sherlock Holmes and his archenemy Prof. Moriarty.

Reichenberg. See LIBEREC.

Reichenhall. See BAD REICHENHALL.

Reich·stadt \ˈrīk-ˌshtät\. Village, N Czech Republic, just E of Česká Lípa; ducal castle; dukedom given to Napoléon II 1818; scene of signing of agreement bet. Austria-Hungary and Russia July 1876.

Reids·ville \ˈrēdz-ˌvil, -vəl\. **1.** City, ⊗ of Tattnall co., SE cen. Georgia; pop. (1990c) 2469.

2. City, Rockingham co., N North Carolina, 20 mi. (32 km.) NNE of Greensboro; pop. (1990c) 12,183; tobacco market.

Rei·gate \ˈrī-gət\. Town, Surrey, S England, 18 mi. (29 km.) S of London; pop. (1981p) 52,554; residential suburb of London; remnants of Norman castle; Norman church, burial place of Charles Howard, first earl of Nottingham, commander of English fleet that defeated Spanish Armada 1588.

Reikjavik. See REYKJAVÍK.

Reims *or* **Rheims** \ˈrēmz; *Fr.* ˈreⁿs\; *anc.* **Du·ro·cor·to·rum** \ˌdu̇r-ə-ko̊r-ˈtōr-əm, ˌdyu̇r-\; *later* **Re·mi** \ˈrē-ˌmī\. City, Marne dept., NE France, on Vesle River 83 mi. (134 km.) ENE of Paris; pop. (1990c) 185,164; rail and road junction and port on Aisne-Marne Canal; a major wine-producing center (esp. champagne) with an extensive network of caves for storage of wine beneath city and in vicinity; 13th cent. Gothic cathedral, one of the most notable cathedrals of France; university (1967).

History: Ancient ✻ of the Remi; said to be site of baptism of Frankish King Clovis and his officers 496; in Middle Ages a center of the textile trade; Philip Augustus crowned in cathedral 1179, and Reims cathedral thereafter (until 1830) the traditional coronation place of French kings, incl. Charles VII, who was crowned in presence of Joan of Arc 1429. Early medieval cathedral destroyed by fire early 13th cent.; present building begun 1211 and completed in 14th cent.; city shelled by Germans in WWI and suffered extensive damage, incl. partial destruction of cathedral; restoration of cathedral took place 1927–38 with aid of grant from American philanthropist John D. Rockefeller; scene in WWII of signature of unconditional German surrender May 7, 1945.

Rei·na Ade·lai·da Archipelago \ˈrā-nə-ˌäd-ᵊl-ˈī-də\. Group of islands in S Pacific Ocean, off SW coast of Chile, N of W end of the Strait of Magellan.

\ə\ abut \ə\ matches \ᵊ\ kitten, Fr table \ər\ further \a\ ash \ā\ ace \ä\ cot, cart \à\ Fr bac \au̇\ out \b̲\ Span Avila \ch\ chin \e\ bet \ē\ easy \g\ go \i\ hit \ī\ ice \j\ job \k̲\ Ger ich, Buch \ⁿ\ Fr vin \ŋ\ sing \ō\ go \ö\ all \ȯ\ law \œ\ Fr bœuf \œ̄\ Fr feu \ȯi\ boy \th\ thin \t̲h̲\ this \ü\ loot \u̇\ foot \ue\ Ger füllen \ue̅\ Fr rue \y\ yet \ʸ\ Fr digne \ˈdēnʸ\, nuit \ˈnwʸē\ \yü\ few \yu̇\ fury \zh\ vision

Rein·deer Island \ˈrān-ˌdir\. Island in cen. Lake Winnipeg, SE Manitoba, Canada.

Reindeer Lake. Lake, cen. Canada, lying on the N section of the Saskatchewan-Manitoba boundary; 2467 sq. mi. (6390 sq. km.); its outlet is the **Reindeer River,** 143 mi. (230 km.) long, flowing S to the Churchill.

Rei·no·sa \rā-ˈnō-sä\. Town, Cantabria prov., N Spain, on the Ebro ab. 4 mi. (6 km.) from its source; pop. (1991c) 12,593; in the Cantabrian Mts. at 2790 ft. (850 m.); resort.

Rein·stein, Mount \ˈrīn-ˌstīn\. Peak in the Sierra Nevada, in E Fresno co., S cen. California; 12,595 ft. (3839 m.).

Re·jaf \rə-ˈjaf\. River town, S Sudan, on the Bahr el Jebel just S of Juba.

Rejang. See RAJANG.

Re·ka·ta Bay \rə-ˈkä-tə\. Bay on NW coast of Santa Isabel I. in the NE Solomon Is., W Pacific Ocean; used as a base by the Japanese in WWII.

Re·li·zane \ˌre-lē-ˈzän\. Town, N Algeria, ENE of Oran; pop. (1987p) 80,091.

Re·ma·gen \ˈrā-ˌmäg-ᵊn\. Town, N Rhineland-Palatinate, Germany, on left bank of the Rhine 20 mi. (32 km.) NW of Koblenz; pop. (1992e) 15,460. Site of ancient Roman fortress. In Mar. 1945 town's Ludendorff Bridge (built 1916–18) was place where Allied troops crossed the Rhine River for the first time in WWII.

Rem·bang \ˈrem-ˌbäŋ\. Seaport town, Central Java prov., Indonesia, on coast 45 mi. (72 km.) ENE of Semarang.

Re·me·dios \rā-ˈmā-dyōs\ *or in full* **San Juan de los Remedios** \sän-ˈhwän-t͟hā-lōs-\. Town and municipality, Las Villas prov., W cen. Cuba; munic. pop. (1981p) 47,306; town near coast, 23 mi. (37 km.) E of Santa Clara.

Remi. See REIMS.

Re·mi·re·mont \rə-ˌmēr-ˈmōⁿ\. Commune, Vosges dept., NE France, on Moselle River 12 mi. (19 km.) SSE of Épinal; pop. (1990c) 9931; textiles, beer, iron castings; 14th–15th cent. church of abbey (founded 10th cent.).

Rem·pang \ˈrem-ˌpäŋ\. Island, Kepulauan Riau, Indonesia, SSE of Batam.

Rems \ˈrems\. River, Baden-Württemberg, Germany; flows into the Neckar River just N of Stuttgart; ab. 50 mi. (80 km.) long.

Rem·scheid \ˈrem-ˌshīt\. Manufacturing city, North Rhine-Westphalia, Germany, near the Wupper River 25 mi. (40 km.) ESE of Düsseldorf; pop. (1992e) 123,618; a center of German tool industry; iron products, cutlery.

Renaix. See RONSE.

Ren·de \ˈren-dā\. Commune, Cosenza prov., Calabria, S Italy; pop. (1989c) 30,044.

Ren·dez·vous Peak \ˈrän-di-ˌvü, -dā-\. Mountain, S of Grand Teton National Park, NW Wyoming; 10,924 ft. (3330 m.).

Rendina, Gulf of. See STRYMONIC GULF.

Ren·do·va \ren-ˈdō-və\. Island off SW cen. coast of New Georgia I., cen. Solomon Is., W Pacific Ocean; separated from New Georgia by Blanche Channel. In WWII seized by U.S. troops 1943.

Rends·burg \ˈrents-ˌbu̇rk\. City, Schleswig-Holstein, Germany, on Eider River and the Kiel Canal 13 mi. (21 km.) S of Schleswig; old section situated on an island in the Eider; pop. (1992e) 31,123; fertilizer, textiles; iron foundries; 13th cent. church; 16th cent. town hall. First mentioned 1199; chartered 1253; fortified late 17th cent.; stronghold of Schleswig-Holstein army during uprising against Denmark 1848; annexed by Prussia 1866.

Ren·frew \ˈren-ˌfrü\. **1.** County in SE Ontario, Canada. See table at ONTARIO.

2. Town, Renfrew co., SE Ontario, Canada, on Bonnechère River 32 mi. (51 km.) SE of Pembroke; pop. (1991c) 8134.

3. *or* **Ren·frew·shire** \-ˌshir, -shər\. Former county, SW Scotland; rivers Clyde, Gryfe; towns include Paisley, Greenock, Port Glasgow, Johnstone.

4. Burgh, Strathclyde region, SW Scotland, near S bank of the Clyde ab. 7 mi. (11 km.) W of Glasgow; pop. (1981p) 21,396; paint, rubber; shipbuilding.

Ren·kum \ˈreŋ-kəm\. Municipality, Gelderland prov., E Netherlands, on the Neder Rijn just W of Arnhem; pop. (1992e) 33,039.

Ren·nell \ˈren-ᵊl, rə-ˈnel\. Uplifted atoll of coral limestone, an island of the Solomon Is., in NE Coral Sea 120 mi. (193 km.) SW of San Cristóbal I., W Pacific Ocean, 11°40′S, 160°10′W; ab. 50 mi. (80 km.) long and 12 mi. (19 km.) wide. At its E end is largest expanse of enclosed freshwater in Pacific Ocean; 50 sq. mi. (130 sq. km.).

Rennes \ˈren\; *anc.* **Con·da·te** \kän-ˈdā-tē, -ˈdä-\ *or Breton* **Roa·zon** \ˈrō-ə-zən\. Industrial and commercial city, ✱ of Ille-et-Vilaine dept., NW France, at junction of Ille and Vilaine rivers 193 mi. (311 km.) WSW of Paris; pop. (1990c) 203,533; archiepiscopal see; railroad junction; agricultural and business center; produces automobiles, agricultural machinery, chemicals, electronics; printing; university (founded at Nantes 1461, transferred to Rennes 1735); cathedral. Became ✱ of Brittany in the Middle Ages; seat of parliament of Brittany 1561–1675; suffered widespread destruction from fire 1720 and in WWII 1944.

Re·no \ˈrē-nō\. **1.** County in cen. Kansas. See table at KANSAS.

2. City, ⊗ of Washoe co., NW Nevada, on Truckee River 20 mi. (32 km.) N of Lake Tahoe; pop. (1990c) 133,850; 2d largest city in the state; alt. 4490 ft. (1369 m.); distribution center; produces electronic components; tourist center with numerous gambling casinos, entertainment facilities, and outdoor recreation opportunities; planetarium; Univ. of Nevada, Reno (1864); site first settled 1859; town estab. 1868 with arrival of Central Pacific R.R.; incorp. 1879.

Re·no \ˈre-nō\; *anc.* **Re·nus** \ˈrē-nəs\. River, N Italy; rises in the Apennines, flows N and E into the Adriatic Sea N of Ravenna; 131 mi. (211 km.) long.

Rens·se·laer \ˌren-sə-ˈlir, ˈren-sə-lər\. **1.** County in E New York. See table at NEW YORK.

2. City, ⊗ of Jasper co., NW Indiana, 40 mi. (64 km.) NNW of Lafayette; pop. (1990c) 5045; St. Joseph's Coll. (1889) in a S suburb.

3. City, Rensselaer co., E New York, across Hudson River from Albany; pop. (1990c) 8255; suburb of Albany; chemicals.

Ren·ton \ˈrent-ᵊn\. City, King co., W cen. Washington, 12 mi. (19 km.) SSE of Seattle; pop. (1990c) 41,688; aircraft, steel products; clay pits; incorp. 1901.

Renus. See RENO.

Ren·ville \ˈren-vil\. Name of counties in two states of the U.S. See tables at MINNESOTA and NORTH DAKOTA.

Repelen–Baerl *or* **Repeln–Baerl.** See RHEINKAMP.

Re·pen·ti·gny \rə-ˌpäⁿ-tē-ˈnyē\. Town, L'Assomption co., S Quebec, Canada; pop. (1991c) 49,630; residential suburb of Montreal.

Re·pub·lic \ri-ˈpə-blik\. **1.** County in N Kansas. See table at KANSAS.

2. City, Greene co., SW Missouri; pop. (1990c) 6292.

3. Town, ⊗ of Ferry co., NE Washington; pop. (1990c) 940.

República de Panamá. See PANAMA.

República Dominicana. See DOMINICAN REPUBLIC.

República Federativa do Brasil. See BRAZIL.

Re·pub·li·can \ri-ˈpə-bli-kən\. River, cen. United States; rises in E Colorado, flows NE and E through S Nebraska, then SE through NE cen. Kansas to unite with the Smoky Hill River at Junction City in Geary co., Kansas, and form the Kansas River; 422 mi. (679 km.) long.

República Oriental del Uruguay. See URUGUAY.

Republic of Korea. See KOREA, SOUTH.

Republic of Vietnam. See VIETNAM, SOUTH.

République Centrafricaine. See CENTRAL AFRICAN REPUBLIC.

Re·pulse Bay \ri-ˈpəls, ˈrē-pəls\. **1.** Inlet of Pacific Ocean, E Queensland, Australia, bet. Mackay and Bowen, 20°36′S, 148°43′E.

2. Small inlet, Nunavut, Canada, at N end of Roes Welcome Sound, N Hudson Bay, in S part of isthmus connecting Melville Penin. with mainland.

Re·que·na \rā-ˈkā-nä\. Commune, Valencia prov., E Spain, 36 mi. (58 km.) W of the commune of Valencia; pop. (1991c)

17,484; produces wine; taken from Arabs by James I of Aragon c. 1238 and ceded to Castile 1244.

Re·sa·ca \ri-ˈsak-ə\. City, N Gordon co., NW Georgia; pop. (1990c) 410; scene of Civil War battle May 1864.

Re·sa·ca de la Pal·ma \ri-ˈsa-kə-ˌdā-lə-ˈpäl-mə\. Battlefield in Cameron co., S Texas, ab. 4 mi. (6 km.) N of Brownsville; scene of victory May 9, 1846 of Americans under Gen. Zachary Taylor over Mexicans under Gen. Mariano Arista; 2d encounter of the Mexican War; Mexicans driven across the Rio Grande.

Re·sen·de \ri-ˈzen-dē\. Municipality, Rio de Janeiro state, SE Brazil, 85 mi. (137 km.) WNW of the city of Rio de Janeiro; munic. pop. (1991p) 91,574.

Res·er·va·tion Peak \ˌre-zər-ˈvā-shən\. Mountain on E boundary of Yellowstone National Park, NW Wyoming; 10,629 ft. (3240 m.).

Re·serve \ri-ˈzərv\. Village, ⊗ of Catron co., W New Mexico, 70 mi. (113 km.) NNW of Silver City; pop. (1990c) 319.

Resht. See RASHT.

Resiczabánya. See REŞIŢA.

Resina. See ERCOLANO.

Re·sis·ten·cia \ˌrā-sēs-ˈten-syä\. City, ✱ of Chaco prov., N Argentina, on the bank of the Paraná River facing Corrientes; ships cattle, quebracho wood, hides.

Re·şi·ţa \ˈre-shēt-ˌsä\ *or* **Re·ci·ţa** \ˈre-chēt-ˌsä\ *or Hung.* **Re·si·cza·bá·nya** \ˈre-shēt-ˌsö-ˈbän-ˌyö\. Commune, ⊗ of Caraş-Severin co., SW Romania, 65 mi. (105 km.) SE of Arad; pop. (1989c) 110,260; center of iron and steel industry; heavy machinery, diesel engines, food products.

Resolution. See FORT RESOLUTION.

Res·o·lu·tion Island \ˌre-zə-ˈlü-shən\. **1.** Island, E Nunavut, Canada, off SE tip of Baffin I. and on N side of entrance to Hudson Strait; 387 sq. mi. (1002 sq. km.).

2. Island, New Zealand, off SW coast of South I.

Res·ti·gouche \ˈres-ti-ˌgüsh\. **1.** River, N New Brunswick, Canada; rises in NW New Brunswick, flows NW, then E in a wide estuary into Chaleur Bay; 130 mi. (209 km.) long; notable for its salmon.

2. County in N New Brunswick, Canada. See table at NEW BRUNSWICK.

Res·ton \ˈres-tən\. Unincorporated settlement, Fairfax co., NE Virginia, ab 15 mi. (24 km.) W of Washington, D.C.; pop. (1990c) 48,556; a planned community developed in the 1960s.

Res·ur·rec·tion Bay \ˌre-zə-ˈrek-shən\. Inlet of Gulf of Alaska, SE Kenai Penin., S Alaska; Seward at its head.

Re·tal·hu·leu \ˌrā-tä-lü-ˈlā-ü\. **1.** Department of SW Guatemala. See table at GUATEMALA.

2. Town, its ✱; munic. pop. (1993e) 37,559; in sugar- and coffee-growing region near the coast ab. 22 mi. (35 km.) SSW of Quetzaltenango.

Re·te·zat National Park \ˌre-te-ˈzät\. National park, Romania; 50 sq. mi. (130 sq. km.); conifer forest; chamois, lynx.

Re·thel \rə-ˈtel\. Commune, Ardennes dept., NE France, on the Aisne 20 mi. (32 km.) SW of Charleville-Mézières; seat of countship in Middle Ages; made a duchy 1581; acquired by Cardinal Jules Mazarin, the French prime minister, in 17th cent.; extensively damaged in both World Wars.

Re·thondes \rə-ˈtō^{n}d\. Village, Oise dept., N France, near Compiègne in the Forêt de Laigue; place where armistice of WWI was signed Nov. 11, 1918.

Re·thým·nē \re-ˈthēm-nē\. **1.** Department of Crete, Greece. See table at GREECE.

2. Seaport, its ✱. See RETHYMNON.

Re·thym·non \ˈre-thēm-ˌnōn\ *also* **Re·thým·nē** \re-ˈthēm-nē\ *or* **Re·ti·mo** \ˈre-tē-ˌmō, ˈrā-\. Seaport town, ✱ of Rethýmnē dept., on N coast of island of Crete, Greece, ab. 38 mi. (61 km.) W of Iráklion; pop. (1981p) 17,940.

Reti, Alpi. See *Rhaetian Alps* in table at ALPS.

Ré·u·nion \rē-ˈyün-yən\; *formerly* **Bour·bon** \ˈbu̇r-bən, bür-ˈbō^{n}\ *also* **Bo·na·parte** \ˈbō-nə-ˌpärt\. Island of the Mascarene Is., in the Indian Ocean 425 mi. (684 km.) E of Madagascar; of oval shape, ab. 39 mi. (63 km.) long by 28 mi. (45 km.) wide; 969 sq. mi. (2510 sq. km.); pop. (1993e) 634,000; ✱ St.-Denis, on N coast; constitutes an overseas department of France; exports sugar, vanilla. Mountainous, highest point Piton des Neiges 10,069 ft. (3069 m.) in cen. part; coast has few harbors; principal harbor at Le Port at NW corner; other towns St.-Paul, St.-Louis, and St.-Pierre. Uninhabited island discovered by Portuguese 1513, though previously known to Arabs; claimed by France 1638 and settled in mid-17th cent., first as penal colony, then by French East India Company, as Bourbon; first named Réunion 1793; occupied by British 1810–15; made overseas department of France 1946.

Reus \ˈre-üs\. Commune, Tarragona prov., NE Spain, 6 mi. (10 km.) WNW of the commune of Tarragona; pop. (1991p) 86,864; trades in fruit and wine; manufactures textiles, leather goods; flower nurseries; Gothic church. First mentioned late 12th cent.; began commercial development after establishment of English colony 1750; made city in 1840s.

Reuss \ˈrȯis\. **1.** River, cen. Switzerland; rises in S Uri canton, flows N through Urner See and Lake of Lucerne into Aare River near its junction with the Rhine River; 98 mi. (158 km.) long.

2. Name of two former principalities in Thuringia: one with ✱ Greiz, and the other with ✱ Gera. Both became part of Thuringia 1920.

Reu·ter Peak \ˈrü-tər\. Peak, Glacier National Park, NW Montana; 8700 ft. (2652 m.).

Reut·ling·en \ˈrȯit-liŋ-ən\. City, Baden-Württemberg, Germany, 19 mi. (31 km.) S of Stuttgart; pop. (1992e) 105,835; a major center of the textile industry; leather, paper, machinery; 13th cent. Gothic church. Founded before 1090; free imperial city 1240–1802; scene of victory of Swabian League over Count Ulrich von Württemberg 1377; to Württemberg 1802. Birthplace of American economist Georg Friedrich List 1789.

Revakantha. See REWA KANTHA.

Reval. See TALLINN.

Rev·da \ˈryev-də\. Town, Sverdlov'sk Oblast, W Russia in Asia, ab. 10 mi. (16 km.) WSW of Yekaterinburg; pop. (1991e) 66,000.

Rev·eil·le Range \ˈre-və-lē\. Range in cen. Nye co., S Nevada; highest point **Reveille Peak** 8910 ft. (2716 m.).

Revel. See TALLINN.

Rev·el·stoke \ˈrev-^{ə}l-ˌstōk\. City, SE British Columbia, Canada, on left bank of Columbia River just S of Mount Revelstoke National Park, ab. 100 mi. (160 km.) ENE of Kamloops; pop. (1991c) 7729; trade center in mining and resort region; lumber, beer.

Revelstoke, Mount. Mountain, SE British Columbia, Canada, just W of Selkirk Mts.; over 7000 ft. (2130 m.); comprises Mount Revelstoke National Park (see CANADA, *National Parks*).

Re·vere \ri-ˈvir\. City, Suffolk co., E Massachusetts, just N of the NE part of Boston; pop. (1990c) 42,786; residential; made city 1914.

Re·ver·mont \rə-ˌver-ˈmȯ^{n}\. W ridge of the Jura Mts., E Ain and E Jura depts., E France; highest point 2529 ft. (771 m.).

Re·vil·la·gi·ge·do *or* **Re·vil·la Gi·ge·do** \rā-ˈvē-yä-hē-ˈhā-t͟hō\. Group of islands, Mexico, in the Pacific Ocean ab. 450 mi. (725 km.) W of and under administrative control of the state of Colima, 19°N, 111°30′W; total area 320 sq. mi. (829 sq. km.). The largest of the group is Socorro, a rocky mountainous island 24 mi. (39 km.) long and 9 mi. (14 km.) wide. The westernmost island of the group is Roca Partida.

Re·vil·la·gi·ge·do Island \ri-ˌvi-lə-gə-ˈgē-dō, -ˈge-\. Island, SE Alaska, off mainland E of Prince of Wales I.; in SE Alexander Archipelago; 50 mi. (80 km.) long by 25 mi. (40 km.) wide; 1145 sq. mi. (2966 sq. km.). Ketchikan is on its SW coast.

Re·wa \ˈrā-wä\. Largest river on Viti Levu I., Fiji, SW Pacific Ocean; flows SE across E side of the island and empties into the Pacific Ocean; 90 mi. (145 km.) long; navigable for ab. 40 mi. (65 km.).

Re·wa \ˈrā-wə\. **1.** Former Indian state, now part of Madhya Pradesh state, cen. India; 12,830 sq. mi. (33,230 sq. km.); founded c. 1400 by Rajputs.
2. Town, Madhya Pradesh state, India, 110 mi. (177 km.) SSW of Allahabad; pop. (1991p) 128,918; former ✻ of Rewa state.

Re·wa Kan·tha *or* **Re·va·kan·tha** \ˌrā-wä-ˈkän-tə\. Former British agency, now mostly in Gujarat state, W India, chiefly on banks of lower Narmada River; 978 sq. mi. (2533 sq. km.).

Re·wa·ri \rā-ˈwär-ē\. Town, Haryana, N India, 50 mi. (80 km.) SW of Delhi; pop. (1991p) 75,294.

Rex·burg \ˈreks-ˌbərg\. City, ⊗ of Madison co., E Idaho, 25 mi. (40 km.) NE of Idaho Falls; pop. (1990c) 14,302; Ricks Coll. (1888); city founded 1883 by Mormons.

Rey. See RHAGAE.

Rey Island \ˈrā\ *or Span.* **Is·la del Rey** \ˈēs-lä-thel-ˈrā\. Island, largest of the Pearl Is., Panama, in Gulf of Panama; 15 mi. (24 km.) long; chief town San Miguel.

Reyes, Los. See LOS REYES.

Reyes, Point \ˈrāz\. Point at S extremity of peninsula jutting out on W coast of Marin co., California, ab. 30 mi. (48 km.) NW of Golden Gate; one of the windiest and foggiest places on W coast of United States S of Bering Sea.

Rey·kja·nes, Cape \ˈrā-kyä-ˌnes\. Cape on SW extremity of Iceland.

Reyk·ja·vík *also* **Reik·ja·vik** \ˈrā-kyä-ˌvēk, -ˌvik\. Seaport, ✻ of Iceland, on SW coast, 64°10′N, 21°58′W; pop. (1990c) 97,648; principal commercial and industrial center of the country, with food processing and textile industries; major fishing port; university (1911). Founded 874 by Norsemen; received munic. rights 1786; made seat of the parliament (*Althing*) 1843; became ✻ of newly independent Iceland 1918; in WWII, an American naval and air base; site of arms-control talks bet. U.S. and U.S.S.R. 1986.

Reyn·olds \ˈren-ᵊldz\. County in SE Missouri. See table at MISSOURI.

Reynolds, Mount. Peak in Glacier National Park, NW Montana; 9147 ft. (2788 m.).

Reyn·olds·burg \ˈren-ᵊldz-ˌbərg\. Village, Franklin and Licking cos., cen. Ohio, W of Columbus; pop. (1990c) 25,748; pop. size has more than tripled since 1960.

Reyn·olds·ville \ˈren-ᵊldz-ˌvil\. Borough, Jefferson co., W cen. Pennsylvania, 8 mi. (13 km.) WSW of Du Bois; pop. (1990c) 2818.

Rey·no·sa \rā-ˈnō-sä\. Municipality, Tamaulipas state, E Mexico, on the Rio Grande; munic. pop. (1990p) 281,618.

Rezā'īyeh, Daryācheh-ye. See ORŪMĪYEH, DARYĀCHEH-YE.

Re·zé \rə-ˈzā\. Commune, Loire-Atlantique dept., NW France, on Loire River opp. Nantes.

Rē·zek·ne \ˈrā-zek-ˌnā\; *formerly* **Rye·zhi·tsa** *or* **Re·zhi·tsa** \ˈre-zhit-sä\ *or Ger.* **Ro·sit·ten** \rō-ˈzit-ᵊn\. Town, E Latvia, 55 mi. (88 km.) NE of Daugavpils. Founded 1285 by Teutonic Knights; under Lithuanian and Polish rule most of period 1561–1772; came under Russian rule in First Partition of Poland 1772; as part of independent Latvia, occupied 1919–20 by Bolshevik forces; occupied by Germans in WWII.

Re·zon·ville \rə-zōⁿ-ˈvēl\. Commune, Moselle dept., NE France, just W of Metz; scene of battle in Franco-Prussian War Aug. 1870 in which Prussian attempts to push back retreating French troops were temporarily checked; an early engagement in the decisive battle of Mars-la-Tour (*q.v.*).

Rha. See VOLGA.

Rhaedestus. See TEKİRDAĞ 2.

Rhaetia. See RAETIA.

Rhaetian Alps. See table at ALPS.

Rha·gae *or* **Ra·gae** \ˈrā-ˌjē, -ˌjī\ *also* **Rha·ges** \ˈrā-jəz\; *bib.* **Ra·ges** \ˈrā-jəz\; *Gk.* **Eu·ro·pus** \yu̇-ˈrō-pəs\. City of ancient Media; its ruins are at modern **Rey** \ˈrā\ ab. 5 mi. (8 km.) S of Tehran, N Iran. Founded 3d millennium B.C.; under Sassanids (3d–7th cents. A.D.) was seat of Zoroastrianism; flourished under Arab rule in the Middle Ages; weakened by religious conflicts and finally destroyed by Mongols 13th cent. Birthplace c. 765 of Hārūn ar-Rashīd, caliph immortalized in *The Thousand and One Nights.*

Rhaiadr River. See PISTYLL RHAIADR.

Rham·nus \ˈram-nəs\. City of ancient Greece on coast of Attica, NE of Marathon; site of temple of goddess Nemesis, now in ruins.

Rhea \ˈrā\. County in E cen. Tennessee. See table at TENNESSEE.

Rhe·den \ˈrād-ᵊn\. Commune, Gelderland prov., E Netherlands, on IJssel River just E of Arnhem; pop. (1992e) 45,323; tourism.

Rhegion *or* **Rhegium.** See REGGIO DI CALABRIA 2.

Rhei·dol \ˈrī-ˌdōl, -ˌdäl\. River, cen. Wales; rises NW of Plynlimmon, flows SW and S, makes sharp turn W (site of Devil's Bridge, *q.v.*) and enters Cardigan Bay at Aberystwyth; 22 mi. (35 km.) long.

Rheims. See REIMS.

Rhein. See RHINE.

Rhei·ne \ˈrī-nə\ *also* **Rheine in West·fa·len** \in-vest-ˈfä-lən\. City, North Rhine-Westphalia, Germany, on Ems River 25 mi. (40 km.) NNW of Münster; pop. (1992e) 71,808; textiles, machinery; 15th cent. church; 15th cent. castle.

Rheinfall. See SCHAFFHAUSEN FALLS.

Rhein·fel·den \ˈrīn-ˌfel-dən\ *or* **Rhein·feld** \-ˌfelt\. Commune, NW Aargau canton, N Switzerland, on the Rhine; scene of battle 1638 during Thirty Years' War in which the Huguenot leader Henri, duc de Rohan, was mortally wounded.

Rhein·gau \ˈrīn-ˌgau̇\. Wine-producing region, Hesse, Germany, along the right bank of the Rhine below Wiesbaden.

Rhein·kamp \ˈrīn-ˌkamp\; *formerly* **Re·pe·len–Baerl** \ˈrā-pə-lən-ˈbärl\ *also* **Re·peln–Baerl** \ˈrā-pəln-\. City, North Rhine-Westphalia, Germany, 22 mi. (35 km.) NNW of Düsseldorf.

Rheinland. See RHINELAND.

Rheinland–Pfalz. See RHINELAND-PALATINATE.

Rhein·pfalz \ˈrīn-ˌpfälts\. German form of Rhine Palatinate. See PALATINATE.

Rhein·wald·horn \ˈrīn-ˌvält-ˌhȯrn\. Highest peak in the Adula Range, Lepontine Alps, SE Switzerland; 11,158 ft. (3401 m.).

Rhe·nea \ri-ˈnē-ə\ *or Gk.* **Ri·nía** \rē-ˈnē-ä\. Small island, N Cyclades, Greece, in S Aegean Sea W of Mykonos; bet. it and Mykonos is the island of Delos.

Rhe·nen \ˈrā-nən\. Commune, Utrecht prov., cen. Netherlands, on the Neder Rijn SE of the city of Utrecht; pop. (1981e) 17,041.

Rhenus. See RHINE.

Rhétiques, Alpes. See *Rhaetian Alps* in table at ALPS.

Rheydt \ˈrīt\. City, North Rhine-Westphalia, Germany, S of Mönchengladbach; 16th cent. castle.

Rhin \ˈreⁿ\. **1.** River. See RHINE.
2. Departments of France: **Bas–Rhin** \ˌbä-\ and **Haut–Rhin** \ˌō-\. See table at FRANCE.

Rhine \ˈrīn\ *or Ger.* **Rhein** \ˈrīn\ *or Fr.* **Rhin** \reⁿ\ *or Du.* **Rijn** \ˈrīn, ˈrān\; *anc.* **Rhe·nus** \ˈrē-nəs\. River, W Europe; formed by confluence of Hinterrhein and Vorderrhein rivers in SE Switzerland; flows through Lake Constance W, N, and NW to the North Sea, forming in its course W boundary of Liechtenstein and Austria, and SW boundary of Germany; 820 mi. (1319 km.) long; navigable to Basel, Switzerland. The Upper Rhine (*Ger.* Oberrhein) extends from Basel to Mainz; the Lower Rhine (*Ger.* Niederrhein) begins at Bonn and leaves Germany near Kleve; in its natural course through Netherlands it curves W and divides into two branches, the Neder Rijn to the N and the Waal to the S. One branch (IJssel) of the Neder Rijn flows N into IJsselmeer; the main course of the Neder Rijn is W, where it becomes known as the Lek, which in its natural course unites with the Merwede and continues to the North Sea as the Nieuwe Maas. The Waal in its natural course unites with the Maas (Meuse) and in its S arm flows into the Hollandsch Diep; its N arm, known as the Merwede, divides into the Oude Maas and Nieuwe Maas (see MEUSE), both entering the North Sea close together just S of the Hoek van Holland. In this wide delta are various islands of South Holland and Zeeland provs. of Netherlands. In all its course are many canals connecting with other streams in Netherlands and with the Rhone, Marne, and Danube systems in Germany and France. Its river trade is very extensive and both in German legend and history it has played a prominent part. Its main tributaries on the right the Neckar, Main, Lahn, Sieg, Ruhr, and Lippe; on the left the Aare, Ill, Nahe, Moselle, and Erft. Chief cities on its banks: Konstanz, Schaffhausen, Basel, Mannheim, Ludwigshafen, Mainz, Wiesbaden, Koblenz, Bonn, Cologne, Düsseldorf, Duisburg, and Rotterdam. In WWII its course was a major line of defense; first crossed by Allies Mar. 1945 by bridge at Remagen (*q.v.*).

Rhine, Falls of the. See SCHAFFHAUSEN FALLS.

Rhine·beck \ˈrīn-ˌbek\. Residential village, Dutchess co., SE New York, near E bank of the Hudson River 16 mi. (26 km.) N of Poughkeepsie and 5 mi. (8 km.) E of Kingston; pop. (1990c) 2725; Old Rhinebeck Aerodrome antique airplane museum.

Rhine·land \ˈrīn-ˌland, -lənd\ *or Ger.* **Rhein·land** \ˈrīn-ˌlänt\. Region, Germany, W of the Rhine River (left bank of the Rhine); ab. 9000 sq. mi. (23,300 sq. km.); chief city Cologne.

Rhine·land·er \ˈrīn-ˌlan-dər, -lən-\. City, ⊗ of Oneida co., N Wisconsin, 37 mi. (60 km.) NNW of Antigo; pop. (1990c) 7427; lumber, paper products; center of summer and winter resort region.

Rhineland–Pa·lat·i·nate \-pə-ˈlat-ᵊn-ət\ *or Ger.* **Rhein·land–Pfalz** \ˈrīn-ˌlänt-ˈpfälts\. A state of Germany, chiefly W of the Rhine; ✻ Mainz; grain crops, potatoes, sugar beets; vineyards; chemicals, footwear. See table at GERMANY.

Rhine Palatinate. See PALATINATE.

Rhine Province. Former province of Prussia; ✻ Koblenz; formed 1824 from Prussian territories on right and left banks of Rhine; after WWII absorbed by West German states of North Rhine-Westphalia and Rhineland-Palatinate (*qq.v.*).

Rhin–et–Mo·selle \ˌreⁿ-nā-mō-ˈzel\. Department of France 1801–15; ✻ Koblenz; comprised region on W bank of the Rhine which was given to France by Treaty of Lunéville 1801; to Prussia by Congress of Vienna 1815.

Rhinns of Galloway, The *or* **Rhinns, The.** See RINNS OF GALLOWAY, THE.

Rhinns of Islay *also* **Rhinns, The.** See RINNS OF ISLAY.

Rhinns Point. See RINNS OF ISLAY.

Rhinocolura. See AL ʻARĪSH.

Rhio. See BINTAN.

Rhio Archipelago. See RIAU, KEPULAUAN.

Rhir, Cape \ˈrir\; *formerly* **Cape Guir** \ˈgir\. Cape, SW coast of Morocco.

Rho \ˈrō\. Commune, Milano prov., Lombardy, N Italy, 8 mi. (13 km.) NW of Milan; pop. (1991p) 51,646.

Rhoda. See RODA.

Rhodanus. See RHONE.

Rhode Is·land \rō-ˈdī-lənd\. **1.** *also* **Aquid·neck Island** \ə-ˈkwid-ˌnek\. Island in Narragansett Bay, SE Rhode Island; 15 mi. (24 km.) long, 39 sq. mi. (101 sq. km.); the city of Newport is on its SW coast. Purchased from the Narragansett Indians by Anne Hutchinson, William Coddington, and other religious exiles from Massachusetts and settled at Portsmouth 1638; name officially changed to Rhode Island 1644.

2. *officially* **Rhode Island and Providence Plantations.** Northeastern seaboard state of U.S.A., bounded on N and E by Massachusetts, on S by the Atlantic Ocean, and on W by Connecticut; 50th state in area, 1212 sq. mi. (3139 sq. km.); 43d state in population, (1990c) 1,003,464; ✻ Providence; an original state of the Union, the 13th to ratify the U.S. Constitution, May 29, 1790. See table of states at UNITED STATES.

Nicknames: Ocean State, Little Rhody.

State flower: Violet.

Motto: Hope.

Rivers: Pawtuxet, Blackstone, and the Pawcatuck, forming lower SW boundary.

Highest point: Jerimoth Hill, 812 ft. (247 m.), in Providence co.

Chief industries: Jewelry making; electronics; historically important textile industry; tourism.

Chief cities: Providence, Warwick, Cranston, Pawtucket.

Political divisions: Divided into the following five counties (for pronunciation of their names, see their individual entries):

NAME	AREA[1] (sq. mi.)	AREA[1] (sq. km.)	POP. (1990c)	CO. SEAT
Bristol	25	65	48,859	Bristol
Kent	173	448	161,135	East Greenwich
Newport	108	280	87,194	Newport
Providence	416	1,077	596,270	Providence
Washington	331	857	110,006	West Kingston

[1] Area = land area.

History: Orig. settled by Narragansett Indians; Narragansett Bay explored by Florentine navigator Giovanni da Verrazano 1524; first permanent nonnative settlement founded by Roger Williams for religious dissenters at Providence 1636; scattered settlements united when charter granted by British King Charles II to Roger Williams 1663; charter provisions continued in effect until Dorr's Rebellion 1842, led by political activist Thomas Dorr, whose attempts to form an alternate government providing for extension of suffrage resulted in new state constitution 1843.

Rhoden, Appenzell Ausser *and* **Rhoden, Appenzell Inner.** See APPENZELL 1.

Rhodes \ˈrōdz\ *or* **Ró·dhos** *also* **Rho·dos** \ˈrö-ˌt͟hös\. **1.** *also* **Rho·dus** \ˈrō-dəs\ *or* **Ro·dos** \ˈrö-ˌt͟hös\. Greek island in the Southern Sporades (see SPORADES), SE Aegean Sea, off SW coast of Turkey in Asia, in the Dodecanese group; 45 mi. (72 km.) long by 22 mi. (35 km.) at greatest width; 540 sq. mi. (1399 sq. km.); pop. (1981c) 87,831. Has mountain range extending length of island, highest point Mt. Attairo 3986 ft. (1215 m.); mild climate and fertile soil; exports wine; tourism.

History: Settled by Dorians c. 1000 B.C. who established the city-states of Lindos, Camirus, and Ialysus; Rhodians in turn established numerous colonies in Mediterranean 7th–6th cents. B.C.; independent until conquered by Persia late 6th cent. B.C.; allied alternately with Athens and Sparta 5th–4th cents. B.C.; city of Rhodes founded c. 408 B.C.; occupied by Macedon 332 B.C.; entered period of greatest prosperity after death of Macedonian King Alexander the Great (323 B.C.) but declined during alliance with Rome 2d cent. B.C.; flourished again under Knights of St. John of Jerusalem from early 14th cent. A.D. until capitulation to Turks 1522; taken by Italy from Turkey 1912; to Greece 1947.

2. City, its ✻ and ✻ of the Dodecanese dept., Greece, at NE point of island; pop. (1981c) 40,392; commercial center and only large town of the island; two harbors; 14th cent. walls; 14th cent. Palace of the Grand Masters (restored 20th cent.); 15th cent. Hospital of the Knights.

History: Founded c. 408 B.C. as ✻ of Rhodian city-states; unsuccessfully besieged 305–304 B.C. by king of Macedon in retaliation for refusal to become his ally after death of his predecessor Alexander the Great (323 B.C.); Colossus of Rhodes, 100-foot (30-meter) high bronze statue of the sun-god Helios, one of the Seven Wonders of the Ancient World, erected c. 292–280 B.C. in commemoration of siege; statue destroyed in earthquake c. 225 B.C.

Rhodes, Inner *and* **Rhodes, Outer.** See APPENZELL 1.

Rho·de·sia \rō-ˈdē-zhə, -zhē-ə\. **1.** Region, cen. S Africa, S of Democratic Rep. of the Congo, now divided into Zimbabwe and Zambia; formerly administered by British South Africa Company; named after British colonial administrator Cecil J. Rhodes. Remains of Stone Age cultures 500,000 years old have been found in region.

2. Landlocked country, S Africa; since 1980 called Zimbabwe (*q.v.*).

Rhodesia and Ny·as·a·land, Federation of \nī-ˈa-sə-ˌland\. Former federation, S cen. Africa, consisting of Nyasaland, Southern Rhodesia, and Northern Rhodesia; formed 1953, dissolved 1963.

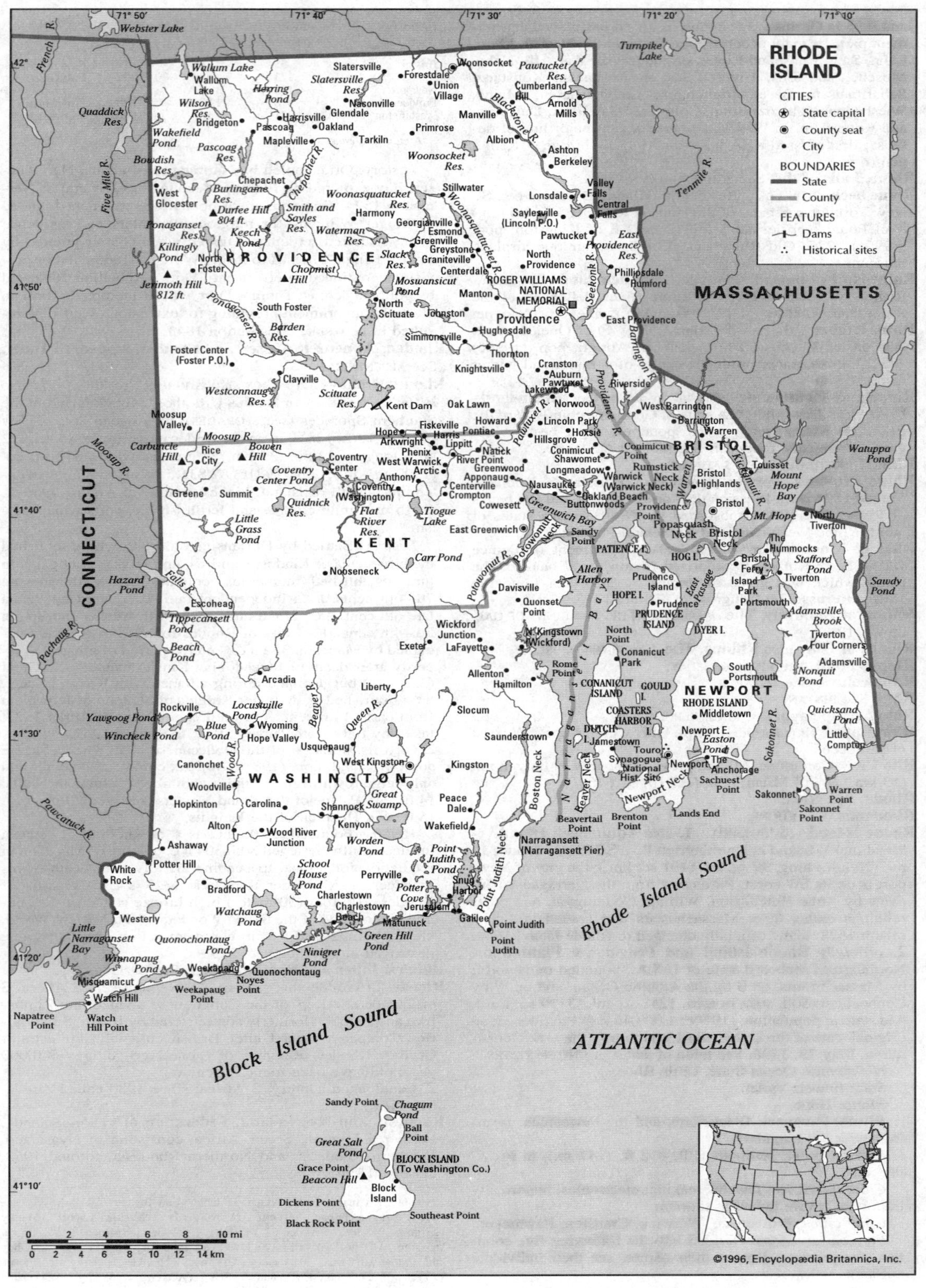
RHODE ISLAND
CITIES
State capital
County seat
City
BOUNDARIES
State
County
FEATURES
Dams
Historical sites
MASSACHUSETTS
CONNECTICUT
PROVIDENCE
KENT
WASHINGTON
BRISTOL
NEWPORT
71° 50′
71° 40′
71° 30′
71° 20′
71° 10′
42°
41°50′
41°40′
41°30′
41°20′
41°10′
Webster Lake
French R.
Quaddick Res.
Five Mile R.
Moosup R.
Hazard Pond
Pachaug R.
Pawcatuck R.
Wallum Lake
Wallum Lake
Wilson Res.
Herring Pond
Bridgeton
Harrisville
Pascoag
Glendale
Oakland
Wakefield Pond
Pascoag Res.
Mapleville
Tarkiln
Slatersville
Slatersville Res.
Nasonville
Forestdale
Woonsocket
Union Village
Primrose
Manville
Pawtucket Res.
Cumberland Hill
Arnold Mills
Blackstone R.
Albion
Ashton
Berkeley
Turnpike Lake
Bowdish Res.
Chepachet
Chepachet R.
Burlingame Res.
West Glocester
Durfee Hill 804 ft.
Smith and Sayles Res.
Woonsocket Res.
Woonasquatucket Res.
Stillwater
Harmony
Georgiaville
Esmond
Waterman Res.
Greenville
Greystone
Graniteville
Centerdale
Woonasquatucket R.
Lonsdale
Valley Falls
Central Falls
Saylesville (Lincoln P.O.)
Pawtucket
East Providence Res.
Tenmile R.
Ponaganset Res.
Keech Pond
Killingly Pond
North Foster
Chopmist Hill
Slack Res.
Jerimoth Hill 812 ft.
Moswansicut Pond
North Providence
Seekonk R.
Phillipsdale
Rumford
Ponaganset R.
North Scituate
Manton
ROGER WILLIAMS NATIONAL MEMORIAL
Providence
South Foster
Johnston
East Providence
Barden Res.
Simmonsville
Hughesdale
Barrington R.
Foster Center (Foster P.O.)
Thornton
Knightsville
Cranston
Auburn
Pawtuxet
Providence R.
Riverside
Clayville
Westconnaug Res.
Scituate Res.
Kent Dam
Oak Lawn
Lakewood
Norwood
West Barrington
Barrington
Warren
Moosup Valley
Hope
Fiskeville
Harris
Howard
Pawtuxet R.
Lincoln Park
Hoxsie
Carbuncle Hill
Rice City
Bowen Hill
Arkwright
Phenix
Pontiac
Lippitt
Hillsgrove
Conimicut Point
Conimicut
Shawomet
Natick
River Point
Coventry Center
Coventry Center Pond
West Warwick
Arctic
Greenwood
Apponaug
Anthony
Centerville
Crompton
Longmeadow
Warwick (Warwick Neck)
Rumstick Neck
Warren R.
Kickemuit R.
Bristol Highlands
Touisset
Mount Hope Bay
Watuppa Pond
Greene
Summit
Coventry (Washington)
Nausauket
Oakland Beach
Buttonwoods
Quidnick Res.
Flat River Res.
Tiogue Lake
Cowesett
Greenwich Bay
Providence Point
Bristol
Mt. Hope
North Tiverton
Little Grass Pond
East Greenwich
Potowomut Neck
Sandy Point
Popasquash Neck
Bristol Neck
The Hummocks
Stafford Pond
Carr Pond
Potowomut R.
PATIENCE I.
HOG I.
Bristol Ferry
Island Park
Tiverton
Sawdy Pond
Nooseneck
Allen Harbor
Falls R.
Escoheag
Davisville
Prudence Island
HOPE I.
Prudence
East Passage
Portsmouth
Quonset Point
PRUDENCE ISLAND
DYER I.
Adamsville Brook
Tippecansett Pond
Wickford Junction
North Point
Tiverton Four Corners
Beach Pond
Exeter
LaFayette
N. Kingstown (Wickford)
Conanicut Park
Adamsville
Narragansett Bay
Allenton
Rome Point
South Portsmouth
Nonquit Pond
Arcadia
Hamilton
CONANICUT ISLAND
GOULD I.
Liberty
RHODE ISLAND
Middletown
Locustville Pond
Beaver R.
Queen R.
Slocum
COASTERS HARBOR I.
Quicksand Pond
Rockville
Yawgoog Pond
Blue Pond
Wyoming
Hope Valley
DUTCH I.
Jamestown
Newport E.
Easton Pond
Sakonnet R.
Little Compton
Wincheck Pond
Usquepaug
Saunderstown
Touro Synagogue National Hist. Site
Newport
The Anchorage
Canonchet
West Kingston
Kingston
Beaver Neck
Sachuest Point
Wood R.
Boston Neck
Newport Neck
Sakonnet
Warren Point
Woodville
Great Swamp
Peace Dale
Sakonnet Point
Hopkinton
Carolina
Shannock
Beavertail Point
Brenton Point
Lands End
Alton
Kenyon
Wood River Junction
Wakefield
Worden Pond
Point Judith Neck
Narragansett (Narragansett Pier)
Ashaway
Point Judith Pond
Potter Hill
School House Pond
Perryville
White Rock
Snug Harbor
Bradford
Potter Cove
Charlestown
Rhode Island Sound
Watchaug Pond
Charlestown Beach
Jerusalem
Galilee
Westerly
Matunuck
Point Judith
Green Hill Pond
Little Narragansett Bay
Quonochontaug Pond
Point Judith
Ninigret Pond
Winnapaug Pond
Weekapaug
Quonochontaug
Misquamicut
Noyes Point
Watch Hill
Weekapaug Point
Napatree Point
Watch Hill Point
Block Island Sound
ATLANTIC OCEAN
Sandy Point
Chagum Pond
Ball Point
Great Salt Pond
BLOCK ISLAND (To Washington Co.)
Grace Point
Beacon Hill
Block Island
Dickens Point
Southeast Point
Black Rock Point
0 2 4 6 8 10 mi
0 2 4 6 8 10 12 14 km
©1996, Encyclopædia Britannica, Inc.

Rhodes Peak. Mountain, E Clearwater co., Idaho; 7950 ft. (2423 m.).

Rhod·o·pe \'rä-də-pē\ *also* **Ro·do·pi** \rō-'thō-pē\ *or Turk.* **Dos·pad Dagh** \dəs-ˌpät-'dä\ *or Bulg.* **Des·po·to Pla·ni·na** \'des-pō-ˌtō-ˌplä-nē-'nä\. **1.** Mountain range in Balkan Penin., SE Europe; runs SE from SW Bulgaria along border bet. Bulgaria and Macedonia, Greece; ab. 180 mi. (290 km.) long; highest point Musala 9596 ft. (2925 m.); lies bet. Balkan Mts. and Aegean Sea; in Roman Empire marked boundary bet. Thrace and Macedonia.

2. Department of Greece. See table at GREECE.

Rhodos. See RHODES.

Rhodus. See RHODES 1.

Rhön \'rœn\. Mountain range, NW Bavaria, E Hesse, and SW Thuringia, cen. Germany; highest peak Wasserkuppe 3116 ft. (950 m.); formerly on both sides of the East Germany-West Germany border.

Rhond·da \'rän-də, 'hrȯn-thä\; *formerly* **Ys·trad·y·fod·wg** \ˌəs-ˌtra-di-'vȯ-du̇g\. Town, Mid Glamorgan co., S Wales; pop. (1991p) 76,300; coal mining; in a valley region ab. 12 mi. (19 km.) long, 4 mi. (6 km.) wide, formed mainly by two rivers, the **Rhondda Fawr** \'vau̇r\ and the **Rhondda Fach** \'vak\ separated by ridge 600 to 1690 ft. (183 to 515 m.) high.

Rhone *or Fr.* **Rhône** \'rōn\; *anc.* **Rhod·a·nus** \'räd-ᵊn-əs\. River, Switzerland and France; rises in the Swiss Alps and flows SW to Martigny where it turns NW and flows into E end of Lake Geneva; issues from SW end of Lake Geneva, crosses French border through an opening in the Jura Mts., and continues S through Lyon, Avignon, and Tarascon to Arles; empties into the Gulf of Lion, S France, through several branches; 505 mi. (813 km.) long; navigable for ab. 300 mi. (485 km.); source of hydroelectric power esp. in its upper course.

Rhône \'rōn\. Department of E cen. France. See table at FRANCE.

Rhône–Alpes. Region of E France. See table at FRANCE.

Rhudd·lan \'rith-lən\. Civil parish of St. Asaph, Clwyd co., N Wales; pop. (1991p) 54,000; ruins of 13th cent. castle at which English King Edward I enacted 1284 the statute for the government of Wales.

Rhum, Isle of. See RUM, ISLE OF.

Rhyl \'ril\. Seaport at mouth of the Clwyd, N Clwyd co., NE Wales; pop. (1981c) 23,124; seaside resort.

Rhym·ney \'rəm-nē\. **1.** *or* **Rum·ney** \'rəm-nē\. River, S Wales; flows from S Powys co. SE along Gwent-Mid Glamorgan border and into South Glamorgan co. where it empties into the Bristol Channel E of Cardiff; ab. 30 mi. (48 km.) long.

2. Town, Mid Glamorgan co., SE Wales, on the Rhymney 38 mi. (61 km.) NW of Bristol; pop. (1981p) 7360.

Rhyndacus. See ATRANOS.

Rhy·o·lite \'rī-ə-ˌlīt\. Former town, S Nye co., S Nevada near Death Valley; boom mining city 1905–08 following Goldfield stampede.

Ria·chos \rē-'ä-chōs\. Small island in Atlantic Ocean off SE coast of Buenos Aires prov., Argentina.

Riad. See RIYADH.

Ri·al·to \rē-'al-tō\. **1.** Residential city, San Bernardino co., SE California, 4 mi. (6 km.) W of the city of San Bernardino; pop. (1990c) 72,388; pop. nearly doubled bet. 1980 and 1990.

2. Island and district on the Grand Canal, Venice, Italy; connected with San Marco I. by the **Rialto Bridge,** built ab. 1590, which has a double row of shops with a broad footway between.

Ri·au \'rē-ˌau̇\. Province of Sumatra, Indonesia. See table at INDONESIA.

Riau, Ke·pu·lau·an \ˌke-pu̇-'lau̇-ˌän\ *or Du.* **Ri·ouw Archipelago** \'rē-ˌau̇\ *or mostly formerly* **Rhio Archipelago** \'rē-ō\. Group of islands in Indonesia, off SE end of the Malay Penin., separated from Singapore by Singapore Strait; 2279 sq. mi. (5903 sq. km.). Comprises the islands of Bintan, Batam, Rempang, the Karimun group, and smaller islands; all, as well as Singapore I. (*q.v.*), were once part of Johor sultanate. Occupied by Japanese in WWII.

Riazan. See RYAZAN.

Ribachi Peninsula. See RYBACHIY, POLUOSTROV.

Rib·ble \'rib-ᵊl\. River, NW England; rises in North Yorkshire, flows S and W through Lancashire into the Irish Sea through an estuary extending from Preston.

Ribbon Fall *or* **Rib·bon Falls** \'rib-ᵊn\. Waterfall in Yosemite National Park, E cen. California; 1612 ft. (491 m.).

Ri·be \'rē-bə\. **1.** County of SW Jutland, Denmark. See table at DENMARK.

2. Town, its ⊗, on Ribe River; pop. (1989e) 17,864; iron, dairy products; 12th cent. cathedral; first mentioned 9th cent.

Ri·beau·vil·lé \rē-ˌbō-vē-'lā\ *or Ger.* **Rap·polts·wei·ler** \ˌrä-pȯlts-'vī-lər\. Commune, N Haut-Rhin dept., NE France; saline springs; two Gothic churches; ruins of three castles.

Ri·bei·ra. **1.** \ri-'bā-rə\. River, Paraná and São Paulo states, S Brazil; flows SW and SE into the Atlantic Ocean; ab. 200 mi. (320 km.) long.

2. \rē-'bā-rä\. Commune, La Coruña prov., NW Spain, 38 mi. (61 km.) SW of the commune of La Coruña and across the bay from Villagarcía de Arosa; pop. (1991c) 25,285.

Ribeira Gran·de \ri-'bā-rə-'grän-dē\. See SANTO ANTÃO.

Ri·bei·rão Prê·to \ˌrē-bī-'rau̇ⁿ-'prā-tü\. City, N cen. São Paulo state, SE Brazil, on railroad line 180 mi. (290 km.) NNW of the city of São Paulo; munic. pop. (1991p) 430,805; commercial city in center of rich coffee-growing region; also produces cereals, cotton, and sugar.

Ri·be·ra \rē-'bā-rä\. Commune, Agrigento prov., SW Sicily, Italy, 20 mi. (32 km.) NW of the commune of Agrigento; pop. (1989c) 20,945.

Ri·be·ral·ta \ˌrē-be-'räl-tä\. Town, El Beni dept., N Bolivia, on Beni River at its confluence with the Madre de Dios; rubber and nuts.

Ric·car·ton \'rik-ərt-ᵊn\. Borough, E South I., New Zealand, suburb of Christchurch; pop. (1981c) 6709.

Ric·cio·ne \rē-'chō-nā\. Commune, Forlì prov., SE Emilia-Romagna, N Italy, SE of Rimini on the Adriatic coast; pop. (1989c) 32,463; resort.

Rice \'rīs\. Name of counties in two states of the U.S. See tables at KANSAS and MINNESOTA.

Rice Lake. **1.** City, Barron co., NW Wisconsin, 45 mi. (72 km.) NNW of Chippewa Falls; pop. (1990c) 7998.

2. Lake, N Northumberland co., SE Ontario, Canada; 27 sq. mi. (70 sq. km.); forms part of Trent Canal system; fishing.

Rich \'rich\. County in N Utah. See table at UTAH.

Rich, Cape. Cape, SE Ontario, Canada, extending from N Grey co. into Georgian Bay.

Rich, Mount. Peak, Gilmer co., N Georgia; 4081 ft. (1244 m.).

Rich·ards Island \'ri-chərdz\. Large island in Beaufort Sea at mouth of Mackenzie River, NW Northwest Territories, Canada.

Rich·ard·son \'ri-chərd-sən\. **1.** County in SE corner of Nebraska. See table at NEBRASKA.

2. Village, E Alaska, on Tanana River and Alaska Highway, 45 mi. (72 km.) SE of Fairbanks.

3. City, Collin and Dallas cos., NE Texas, N of Dallas; pop. (1990c) 74,840; residential; electronics; Univ. of Texas at Dallas (1969).

Richardson Highway. Highway N from Valdez, S Alaska, to Fairbanks; 371 mi. (597 km.) long; completed 1923; now merges with Alaska Highway SE of Big Delta; from it a cutoff runs from Gulkana NE to Alaska Highway ESE of Tanacross; joined NNW of Copper Center by Glenn Highway from Anchorage on the W.

Richardson Lakes. Two connected lakes, **Upper Richardson Lake** and **Lower Richardson Lake,** N Oxford co., W Maine; part of the Rangeley Lakes (*q.v.*).

Richardson Mountains. Range in N Yukon Terr., Canada; av. height ab. 4000 ft. (1220 m.); highest point 6500 ft. (1980 m.); separates Porcupine River from lower Mackenzie River; forms an E extension of the Brooks Range of Alaska.

Rich·bor·ough \ˈrich-bə-rə\. Settlement, Kent, SE England, on the estuary of the Great Stour River SW of Ramsgate; on the site of ancient **Ru·tu·pi·ae** \rü-ˈtü-pē-ˌē, -ˈtyü-\, an important Roman port; ruins of castle where Watling Street (*q.v.*) begins; power station.

Rich·e·lieu \ˈri-shə-ˌlü\. River, S Quebec, Canada; flows N from Lake Champlain to the head of Lake St. Peter in the St. Lawrence River at Sorel; 210 mi. (338 km.) long. Noted for its scenery; in early times an important travel route. Visited by French explorer Samuel de Champlain 1609.

Rich·field \ˈrich-ˌfēld\. **1.** Village, Hennepin co., SE cen. Minnesota, just S of Minneapolis; pop. (1990c) 35,710.
2. Village, Summit co., NE Ohio, 16 mi. (26 km.) NW of Akron; pop. (1990c) 3117.
3. City, ⊗ of Sevier co., cen. Utah, on Sevier River; pop. (1990c) 5593; settled 1863.

Rich·i·buc·to \ˌri-shə-ˈbək-tō\. Town, ⊗ of Kent co., E New Brunswick, Canada, on inlet of Northumberland Strait; pop. (1991c) 1469; founded 1787.

Rich·land \ˈrich-lənd\. **1.** *or* **Richland Creek.** River, S Tennessee; rises in SW Marshall co., flows S into Elk River near Alabama border; 40 mi. (64 km.) long.
2. Name of a parish in NE Louisiana and of counties in six states of the U.S. See tables at ILLINOIS, LOUISIANA, MONTANA, NORTH DAKOTA, OHIO, SOUTH CAROLINA, WISCONSIN.
3. City, California. See ORANGE 2.
4. City, Rankin co., S cen. Mississippi; pop. (1990c) 4014.
5. City, Benton co., SE Washington, on the Columbia River WNW of Pasco; pop. (1990c) 32,315. Orig. a farming community; taken over 1942 by U.S. government for development as a residential community for employees of Hanford Engineer Works to NW. See HANFORD 2.

Richland Bal·sam \ˈbȯl-səm\. Peak, Haywood co., W North Carolina; 6540 ft. (1993 m.).

Richland Center. City, ⊗ of Richland co., SW Wisconsin, 53 mi. (85 km.) WNW of Madison; pop. (1990c) 5018.

Richland Hills. Town, Tarrant co., NE Texas, NE of Fort Worth; pop. (1990c) 7978.

Rich·lands \ˈrich-ləndz\. Town, Tazewell co., SW Virginia, 42 mi. (68 km.) NNE of Bristol; pop. (1990c) 4456.

Rich·mond \ˈrich-mənd\. **1.** Name of counties in four states of the U.S. See tables at GEORGIA, NEW YORK, NORTH CAROLINA, VIRGINIA.
2. Seaport city, Contra Costa co., W California, on E shore of San Francisco Bay 9 mi. (14 km.) NNW of Oakland; pop. (1990c) 87,425; chemicals, aircraft parts, electronic components; oil refineries; founded 1899.
3. City, ⊗ of Wayne co., E Indiana, 35 mi. (56 km.) SE of Muncie; pop. (1990c) 38,705; automobile parts, machine tools, machinery, fabricated metals; ships cut flowers; Earlham Coll. (1847), Indiana Univ. East (1971); settled 1806 by Quakers from North Carolina; incorp. as a city 1840.
4. City, ⊗ of Madison co., E cen. Kentucky, 24 mi. (39 km.) SSE of Lexington; pop. (1990c) 21,155; tobacco and livestock market; corn; Eastern Kentucky Univ. (1906); scene of battle Aug. 1862, the first Confederate victory in Kentucky.
5. Town, Sagadahoc co., S Maine, on Kennebec River 16 mi. (26 km.) S of Augusta; pop. (1990c) 3072.
6. City, Macomb co., SE Michigan, 19 mi. (31 km.) WSW of Port Huron; pop. (1990c) 4141.
7. City, ⊗ of Ray co., NW Missouri, 38 mi. (61 km.) ENE of Kansas City; pop. (1990c) 5738.
8. Borough, Richmond co., SE New York. See STATEN ISLAND 2.
9. Town, Washington co., S Rhode Island; pop. (1990c) 5351.
10. Town, ⊗ of Fort Bend co., SE Texas, ab. 20 mi. (32 km.) WSW of Houston; pop. (1990c) 9801.
11. City and port of entry, ✳ of Virginia and ⊗ of Henrico co., E cen. Virginia, on James River; 37 sq. mi. (96 sq. km.); pop. (1990c) 203,056; politically independent of the county; major tobacco market and commercial center; manufactures textiles, paper, food products; Union Theological Seminary (1812), Univ. of Richmond (1830), Virginia Commonwealth Univ. (1838), Virginia Union Univ. (1865), Presbyterian School of Christian Education (1914), J. Sargeant Reynolds Community Coll. (1972).
History: Developed around trading post estab. 1637; town laid out 1737; incorp. 1742; scene of 2d Virginia Convention 1775 at which Revolutionary leader Patrick Henry gave speech containing famous words "Give me liberty, or give me death"; made ✳ of Virginia 1779; figured prominently in Revolution; plundered and burned by British under former American general turned traitor Benedict Arnold 1781; incorp. as city 1782; scene of political leader Aaron Burr's trial for treason, at which he was acquitted, 1807; became the Confederate ✳ 1861 at beginning of Civil War and remained the major objective of the Union army until its capture 1865; evacuated and burned by residents 1865; rebuilt after war.
12. City, S Victoria, SE Australia, E suburb of Melbourne; pop. (1991c) 22,789.
13. County in E Nova Scotia, Canada. See table at NOVA SCOTIA.
14. City, S British Columbia, Canada, on an island S of Vancouver; pop. (1996c) 148,867.
15. Town, S Quebec, Canada, on St. Francis River 20 mi. (32 km.) NNW of Sherbrooke; pop. (1991c) 3123.
16. Borough, London. See RICHMOND UPON THAMES.

Richmond Bay. See MALPEQUE BAY.

Richmond Gulf. See GUILLAUME-DELISLE, LAC.

Richmond Heights. **1.** City, St. Louis co., E Missouri, 7 mi. (11 km.) W of the city of St. Louis; pop. (1990c) 10,448.
2. Village, Cuyahoga co., N Ohio, NE of Cleveland; pop. (1990c) 9611.

Richmond Hill. **1.** Peak in Lawrence co., W South Dakota; 6057 ft. (1846 m.).
2. Town, York munic. region, SE Ontario, Canada, 10 mi. (16 km.) N of Toronto; pop. (1991c) 80,142; residential; pop. more than doubled bet. 1981 and 1991.

Richmond upon Thames *or frequently* **Richmond.** A borough of London, SE England. See table at LONDON 4.

Rich Mountain. **1.** Mountain, Arkansas. See BLUE MOUNTAIN 1.
2. Locality, Randolph co., West Virginia; scene of battle July 1861 in which Gen. George McClellan's Union troops defeated the Confederates.

Rich·ton Park \ˈrich-tən\. Village, Cook co., NE Illinois, ab. 15 mi. (24 km.) SSW of Chicago; pop. (1990c) 10,523.

Rich·wood \ˈrich-ˌwu̇d\. City, Nicholas co., cen. West Virginia, 63 mi. (101 km.) E of Charleston; pop. (1990c) 2808.

Rick·en Tunnel \ˈrik-ᵊn\. Railroad tunnel, W St. Gall canton, NE Switzerland, E of Zürichsee; 5.34 mi. (8.59 km.) long.

Rick·mans·worth \ˈrik-mənz-ˌwərth\. Town, Hertfordshire, SE England, at confluence of Chess and Colne rivers 20 mi. (32 km.) WNW of London; pop. (1981p) 29,408.

Ricomagus. See RIOM.

Ridder. See LENINOGOR.

Rid·der·kerk \ˈri-dər-ˌkerk\. Commune, South Holland prov., SW Netherlands, on a delta island of the Rhine just E of Rotterdam; pop. (1992e) 45,834.

Ri·deau \ri-ˈdō\. Lake on S border of Lanark co., SE Ontario, Canada; its outlet is **Rideau River** which flows NE through Rideau Lake to the Ottawa River at Ottawa. The lake and river, with constructed section from Rideau Lake to Lake Ontario, form the **Rideau Canal,** 123.5 mi. (198.7 km.) long, connecting Kingston on Lake Ontario with the Ottawa River below Chaudière Falls. The canal divides the city of Ottawa; it was built 1826–32 by British government for military transport. Now used for pleasure craft; has branch 6.5 mi. (10.5 km.) long from Rideau Lake to Perth.

Ridge·crest \ˈrij-ˌkrest\. City, Kern co., S California, NE of Bakersfield; pop. (1990c) 27,725; U.S. Naval Weapons Center nearby to the N.

Ridge·field \ˈrij-ˌfēld\. **1.** Suburban residential town, W Fairfield co., SW Connecticut, on New York border; pop. (1990c) 20,919; incorp. 1709; site of Revolutionary War battle 1777.

2. Borough, Bergen co., NE corner of New Jersey, 8 mi. (13 km.) N of Jersey City; pop. (1990c) 9996.

Ridgefield Park. Village, Bergen co., NE New Jersey, 8 mi. (13 km.) ESE of Paterson; pop. (1990c) 12,454; residential.

Ridge·land \ˈrij-lənd\. **1.** City, Madison co., cen. Mississippi, just N of Jackson; pop. (1990c) 11,714.

2. Town, ⊗ of Jasper co., S South Carolina; pop. (1990c) 1071.

Ridge·wood \ˈrij-ˌwu̇d\. Village, Bergen co., NE New Jersey, 5 mi. (8 km.) NNE of Paterson; pop. (1990c) 24,152; scene of American and British encampments in Revolution.

Ridg·way \ˈrij-ˌwā\. Borough, ⊗ of Elk co., NW cen. Pennsylvania, 20 mi. (32 km.) N of Du Bois; pop. (1990c) 4793.

Riding, East *and* **Riding, North** *and* **Riding, West.** See YORKSHIRE.

Rid·ing Mountain \ˈrī-diŋ\. Plateau, SW cen. Manitoba, Canada, W of Lake Manitoba; highest point 2411 ft. (735 m.); forms main part of Riding Mountain National Park.

Riding Mountain National Park. See CANADA, *National Parks.*

Rid·ley \ˈrid-lē\. Township, Delaware co., SE Pennsylvania, SW of Philadelphia; pop. (1990c) 31,169.

Ridley Park. Residential borough, Delaware co., SE Pennsylvania, 10 mi. (16 km.) WSW of Philadelphia; pop. (1990c) 7592.

Riduna. See ALDERNEY.

Ried \ˈrēt\ *or* **Ried im Inn·kreis** \im-ˈin-ˌkrīs\. Town, Upper Austria, Austria, ab. 40 mi. (64 km.) W of Linz; pop. (1991c) 11,260; treaty of alliance bet. Austria and Bavaria signed here 1813.

Rieka. See RIJEKA.

Rie·sa \ˈrē-zä, -zə\. City, Saxony, E Germany, on Elbe River 39 mi. (63 km.) E of Leipzig; pop. (1992e) 44,393; developed around monastery 12th cent.; received first charter 1623.

Ries·co \rē-ˈes-kō\. Island, S Chile, N of the W end of Strait of Magellan; separated from Brunswick Penin. by Otway Water.

Rie·sen·ge·bir·ge *or* **Rie·sen Ge·bir·ge** \ˈrēz-ᵊn-gə-ˌbir-gə\ *or Eng.* **Gi·ant Mountains** \ˈjī-ənt\ *or Czech* **Krko·no·še** \ˈkər-kȯ-ˌnō-she\. Mountain range extending along boundary bet. SW Poland (in region formerly included in Silesia prov., Prussia, Germany) and N Czech Republic; part of Sudety Mts.; highest Sněžka 5256 ft. (1602 m.).

Rie·si \rē-ˈā-zē, -ˈe-\. Commune, Caltanissetta prov., cen. Sicily, Italy, 19 mi. (31 km.) SSE of the commune of Caltanissetta; pop. (1981p) 13,665.

Riet \ˈrēt\. River, SW Free State and E Northern Cape prov., cen. Rep. of South Africa; flows W into the Vaal; ab. 250 mi. (400 km.) long.

Rie·ti \rē-ˈā-tē, -ˈe-\. **1.** Province of Lazio, cen. Italy. See table at ITALY.

2. *anc.* **Re·a·te** \rē-ˈā-tē\. Commune, its ✻, 42 mi. (68 km.) NNW of Rome; pop. (1991p) 42,859; synthetic textiles, olive oil; 12th cent. cathedral; 13th cent. palace and city walls. In ancient times a ✻ of the Sabines; passed to Romans; passed to Papal States 14th cent. Believed to be birthplace of scholar Marcus Terentius Varro 116 B.C.

Rif *or* **Riff.** See ER RIF.

Rifāʻ, ar–. See AR-RIFĀʻ.

Riffe Lake \ˈrif\. Reservoir in Cowlitz River, Lewis co., SW Washington, formed by Mossyrock Dam (see UNITED STATES, *Dams and Reservoirs*).

Ri·fle \ˈrī-fəl\. City, Garfield co., W Colorado, NE of Grand Junction; pop. (1990c) 4636.

Rifs·tan·gi, Cape \ˈrifs-ˌtau̇ŋ-gē\. Cape, NE Iceland, W of Raufarhöfn.

Rift Valley \ˈrift\. **1.** Geological depression, Asia and Africa. See GREAT RIFT VALLEY.

2. Province of W Kenya. See table at KENYA.

Ri·ga \ˈrē-gə\ *or Lettish* **Rī·ga** \ˈrē-gə\. City and seaport, ✻ of Latvia, at S extremity of the Gulf of Riga on the Western Dvina River 9 mi. (15 km.) above its mouth; pop. (1989p) 915,000, incl. a sizable Russian minority; a principal Baltic port; produces diesel engines, electrical equipment, glass, chemicals, cement; shipyards; retains some medieval remains, incl. 13th cent. church, 14th cent. castle of the Livonian Order; university (1919).

History: Settled before 13th cent.; estab. as a trading settlement 1201 by bishop of Livonia and joined Hanseatic League 1282; dominated in Middle Ages by Teutonic Knights; fought over by Poles and Russians in 16th cent., and fell under Polish domination 1581; captured by Sweden 1621 and granted self-government; occupied by Russia 1710, and ceded to Russia by Sweden 1721; in WWI, civilians evacuated 1915; after much fighting, occupied by Germans 1917; independence of Latvia proclaimed at Riga 1918; ✻ of independent Latvia 1918–40; incorp. into U.S.S.R. 1940; in WWII taken by Germans 1941 and retaken by U.S.S.R. 1944; again ✻ of independent Latvia 1991 ff.

Riga, Gulf of. Inlet of NE Baltic Sea extending S into N coast of Latvia; ab. 100 mi. (160 km.) long by 60 mi. (97 km.) wide; receives the Western Dvina River.

Rig·by \ˈrig-bē\. City, ⊗ of Jefferson co., E Idaho, 15 mi. (24 km.) NE of Idaho Falls; pop. (1990c) 2681; settled by Mormons 1884.

Rī·ge·stān \ˌrē-gə-ˈstän\ *or* **Re·gi·stan** \ˈrā-gə-ˌstän, -ˌstan\. Extensive desert region, S Afghanistan.

Ri·gi *or* **Ri·ghi** \ˈrē-gē\. Mountain mass in cen. Switzerland, bet. Lake of Lucerne and Lake of Zug; highest peaks the **Rigi–Kulm** \-ˈku̇lm\ 5905 ft. (1800 m.) in NW, and **Rigi–Schei·degg** \-ˈshī-ˌdek\ 5462 ft. (1665 m.) in SE; ascended by Switzerland's oldest rack railway (completed 1871).

Rig·o·let \ˌri-gə-ˈlet\. Community, SE Labrador, Newfoundland, Canada, at head of Hamilton Inlet on narrows leading to Lake Melville; pop. (1991c) 334.

Ri·i·shi·ri \ˈrē-shē-ˌrē\. Island in N Sea of Japan, off NW coast of island of Hokkaidō, Japan.

Ri·je·ka \rē-ˈye-kə\ *or* **Ri·eka** \rē-ˈe-kə\ *or Ital.* **Fiu·me** \ˈfyü-mā\ *or Ger.* **Sankt Veit am Flaum** \ˌzäŋkt-ˌfīt-äm-ˈflau̇m\. Seaport, W Croatia, ab. 80 mi. (130 km.) WSW of Zagreb; pop. (1991c) 167,964; ships tobacco products; shipbuilding, oil refining; naval base, episcopal see; Roman triumphal arch; 13th cent. castle.

History: Orig. a Roman settlement; later in Byzantine Empire; independent duchy from 9th cent.; to Austria 15th cent.; in 18th cent. became free port, was united to Croatia, and gained autonomy under Hungarian crown; held by French in Napoleonic era; after WWI contended for by Italy and Yugoslavia; occupied by Italy in 1919; set up as independent free city 1920; occupied by Italy (Fascists) 1922, ceded by Yugoslavia 1924; in WWII held by Germans 1943–45, liberated by Yugoslavs; transferred to Yugoslavia by Italian peace treaty 1947; to independent Croatia 1991.

Rijn. See RHINE.

Rijs·wijk \ˈrīs-ˌvīk\ *or Eng.* **Rys·wick** \ˈriz-ˌwik\. Commune, South Holland prov., NW Netherlands, suburb of The Hague; pop. (1992e) 47,456; residential; 14th cent. church. The Treaty of Ryswick was signed here Sept. 20, 1697 by France with Netherlands, England, and Spain, ending War of the Grand Alliance; by this treaty, most prewar boundaries were restored, France acknowledged William III as king of England, conquests in America (King William's War) were mutually restored, and France was allowed to retain Alsace; separate treaty signed here Oct. 30, 1697 by France and the Holy Roman Empire.

Ri·kers Island \ˈrī-kərz\. Island in the East River off S coast of the Bronx, New York City, New York; attached to Bronx borough; large penitentiary.

Ri·ku·chu \ˈrē-kü-ˌchü\. Former province, N Honshū, Japan, now Iwate prefecture.

Ri·ku·zen \ˈrē-kü-ˌzen\. Former province, N Honshū, Japan, now part of Miyagi prefecture.

Ri·la Mountains \'rē-lä\. Range of mountains in SW Bulgaria, at W end of the Rhodope Mts.; highest point Musala Peak 9596 ft. (2925 m.); contains sources of Iskŭr, Maritsa, and Mesta rivers.

Ri·ley \'rī-lē\. County in NE cen. Kansas. See table at KANSAS.

Rí·mac \'rē-ˌmäk\. River, Peru; flows through the city of Lima into the Pacific Ocean; ab. 80 mi. (130 km.) long.

Ri·ma·ta·ra \ˌrē-mä-'tar-ə\. See AUSTRAL ISLANDS.

Ri·mav·ská So·bo·ta \'rē-ˌmaù-skä-'sò-bō-ˌtä\ *or Hung.* **Ri·ma·szom·bat** \'rē-mö-ˌsōm-ˌböt\. Town, S cen. Slovakia, ab. 60 mi. (95 km.) WSW of Kosĭce near the Hungarian border; pop. (1980p) 19,699; part of Hungary 1938–45.

Ri·mi·ni \'rē-mi-nē\; *anc.* **Arim·i·num** \ə-'ri-mə-nəm\. Seaport, Forlí prov., Emilia-Romagna, N Italy, on the Adriatic 27 mi. (43 km.) ESE of the commune of Forlí; pop. (1991p) 128,119; railroad junction; has flour mills and railroad shops, but is primarily a tourist center; has Roman remains incl. Arch of Augustus (first cent. B.C.) and Bridge of Tiberius (first cent. A.D.); ruins of 15th cent. Malatesta castle; 15th cent. Malatesta temple; several medieval churches.

History: Ancient Umbrian and Etruscan settlement; came under Rome 268 B.C.; was N terminus of Flaminian Way; scene of Council of Rimini 359 A.D.; under the Malatesta family 1239–1508; passed to Papal States until 1860 when it joined kingdom of Italy.

Rîm·ni·cu Să·rat \'rəm-nē-ˌkü-sə-'rät\ *or* **Râm·ni·cul–Sărat** \'rəm-nə-ˌkül-sə-'rät\. Town, Buzău co., SE cen. Romania, ab. 20 mi. (32 km.) NE of the city of Buzău; pop. (1989c) 39,307; commercial center; oil refining, textiles; has often been a battlefield; destructive fire 1854.

Rîmnicu Vîl·cea \-'vəl-chə\ *or* **Râmnicul–Vâl·cea** \-'vəl-chə\. City, ⊗ of Vîlcea co., S cen. Romania, ab. 100 mi. (160 km.) NW of Bucharest; pop. (1989c) 107,996; chemicals, woodworking products, leather; has cathedral and episcopal palace.

Ri·mou·ski \ri-'mü-skē\. City, S Quebec, Canada, on S bank of St. Lawrence River ab. 180 mi. (290 km.) NE of Quebec City; pop. (1991c) 30,873; lumber; tourist center; university (1969).

Rimouski–Nei·gette \-nā-'get\. County, Quebec, Canada. See table at QUEBEC.

Rimp·fisch·horn \'rimp-ˌfish-ˌhòrn\. Peak in the Pennine Alps, in Switzerland, N of Monte Rosa; 13,776 ft. (4199 m.).

Rimrock Lake. See TIETON DAM.

Rin·con \'riŋ-ˌkän\. Town, Effingham co., E Georgia, NW of Savannah; pop. (1990c) 2697.

Rin·cón \riŋ-'kòn\. Municipality, W Puerto Rico; pop. (1990c) 12,213; on coast SW of Aguadilla.

Rincón, Cer·ro \'ser-rō\. Peak, E Antofagasta region, N Chile, on Argentine boundary; 18,353 ft. (5594 m.).

Rincón Bay. Bay in S coast of Puerto Rico.

Rincon Peak. Mountain, E Pima co., S Arizona; 8465 ft. (2577 m.).

Rindge \'rinj\. Town, Cheshire co., SW corner of New Hampshire; pop. (1990c) 4941; Franklin Pierce Coll. (1962).

Rin·dja·ni, Gu·nung \'gü-nùŋ-rin-'jä-nē\. Volcanic peak, N part of Lombok I., Indonesia; 12,224 ft. (3726 m.); one of highest peaks of Malay Archipelago.

Rin·ge·ri·ke \'riŋ-ə-ˌrē-kə\. Commune, Buskerud co., S Norway; pop. (1990c) 27,275.

Ring·gold \'riŋ-ˌgōld\. **1.** County in S Iowa. See table at IOWA.

2. City, ⊗ of Catoosa co., NW Georgia; pop. (1990c) 1675.

Ring·kø·bing \'riŋ-ˌkœ-beŋ\. **1.** County of W Jutland, Denmark. See table at DENMARK.

2. Town, its ⊗, at N end of Ringkøbing Fjord; pop. (1989e) 16,944.

Ringkøbing Fjord. Lagoon, W cen. coast of Jutland, Denmark; receives Omme and Skjern rivers.

Ring·nes Islands \'riŋ-nes\. The Ellef Ringnes and Amund Ringnes islands of the Sverdrup Is., N Arctic Archipelago, Nunavut, Canada, W of Axel Heiberg I.

Ring of Fire. Belt of seismic and esp. volcanic activity roughly surrounding the Pacific Ocean; composed of the Andes, Pacific coastal regions of Central and North America, the Aleutians, Kamchatka Penin., the Kuril Is., the islands comprising Japan, Taiwan, the islands comprising the Philippines, E Indonesia, island arcs of the W Pacific Ocean, and New Zealand. Majority (approx. 70 percent) of historically recorded active volcanoes have occurred in this belt; these areas of geological activity coincide with locations at which crustal-plate subduction is occurring according to the theory of plate tectonics, and are believed to be a result of this subduction.

Ring·sa·ker \'riŋ-sä-kər\. Commune, Hedmark co., E Norway; pop. (1990c) 31,180.

Ring·vass·øy \'riŋ-vä-ˌsòi\. Island in Arctic Ocean off NW coast of Norway, SW of Vannøy I., in Troms co.; 253 sq. mi. (655 sq. km.).

Ring·wood \'riŋ-ˌwùd\. **1.** River, New York and N New Jersey; rises in Orange co., SE New York, flows S through Passaic co., New Jersey, and unites with Pequannock and Ramapo rivers to form Pompton River.

2. Borough, Passaic co., N New Jersey, 17 mi. (27 km.) NNW of Paterson; pop. (1990c) 12,623.

3. City, Victoria, Australia, an E suburb of Melbourne; pop. (1991c) 40,308.

Rinía. See RHENEA.

Rinns of Gal·lo·way, The \'rinz-əv-'ga-lə-ˌwā\ *or* **The Rinns** *also* **The Rhinns of Galloway** \'rinz\ *or* **The Rhinns.** Peninsula in Dumfries and Galloway region, on extreme SW coast of Scotland, W of Loch Ryan and Luce Bay and terminating on the N in Corsewall Point and on the S in the Mull of Galloway.

Rinns of Is·lay \'rinz-əv-'ī-lə, -ˌlā\ *or* **Rhinns of Islay** \'rinz\ *also* **The Rinns** *or* **The Rhinns.** Peninsula extending into the Atlantic Ocean on W coast of island of Islay, Inner Hebrides, off W coast of Scotland; terminates in **Rinns Point** *or* **Rhinns Point;** lighthouse.

Rin·tja \'rin-chä\. Small island off W end of Flores I., Indonesia, ESE of Komodo I.

Rio *Span.* 'rē-ō, *Port.* -ü\. **1.** For most names of rivers beginning with Rio (Span. *Río,* Port. *Rio,* "river"), see the distinguishing element.

2. City, Brazil. See RIO DE JANEIRO 2.

Rio Ar·ri·ba \'rē-ō-ə-'rē-bə\. County in N New Mexico. See table at NEW MEXICO.

Ri·o·bam·ba \ˌrē-ō-'bäm-bä\. City, ✻ of Chimborazo prov., cen. Ecuador, 110 mi. (177 km.) S of Quito and ab. 20 mi. (32 km.) SE of the volcano Chimborazo; pop. (1990c) 95,505; market town; produces textiles, carpets, footwear; original town a few miles distant settled by Spaniards 16th cent., destroyed by earthquake 1797; first constitution of republic of Ecuador proclaimed here 1830.

Rio Blan·co \'rē-ō-'blaŋ-kō\. County in NW Colorado. See table at COLORADO.

Río Blanco \'rē-ō-'bläŋ-kō\. Municipality, Veracruz state, Mexico, 4 mi. (6 km.) W of Orizaba.

Rio Bran·co \'rē-ü-'bräŋ-kü\. **1.** River in Brazil. See BRANCO, RIO.

2. City, ✻ of Acre state, W Brazil, on Acre River; munic. pop. (1991p) 196,923; rubber, timber, nuts.

Río Bra·vo \'rē-ō-'brä-vō\. **1.** *or* **Río Bravo del Nor·te** \t͟hel-'nòr-tā\. Mexican name of the Rio Grande, bet. U.S. and Mexico. See RIO GRANDE 1.

2. Municipality, Tamaulipas state, Mexico, 40 mi. (64 km.) W of Matamoros; pop. (1990p) 93,931.

Rio Cha·ma \'rē-ō-'chä-mä\. River, Colorado and N New Mexico; rises in Conejos co., S Colorado, flows S across state border and empties into the Rio Grande in SE Rio Arriba co., N New Mexico; ab. 100 mi. (160 km.) long.

Rio Cla·ro \'rē-ü-'klä-rü\. City, São Paulo state, SE Brazil, 90 mi. (145 km.) NW of the city of São Paulo; munic. pop. (1991p) 137,509.

Río Cuar·to \'rē-ō-'kwär-tō\. Town, Córdoba prov., cen. Argentina, ab. 125 mi. (200 km.) S of the city of Córdoba; pop. (1991p) 217,717; commercial center.

Rio de Ja·nei·ro \'rē-ü-dē-zhá-'nā-rü; 'rē-ō-ˌdā-zhə-'ner-ō, -ˌdē-, -'nir-\. **1.** State of SE Brazil; ✻ Rio de Janeiro. See table at BRAZIL.

2. *abbr.* **Rio** \ˈrē-ō\. Commercial seaport, ✱ of Rio de Janeiro state, SE Brazil, on SW shore of Guanabara Bay; pop. (1989e) 6,100,000; former ✱ of Brazil; principal port of Brazil and major transportation center; produces foodstuffs, tobacco products, clothing, chemicals, textiles; publishing, metalworking; federal university (1920) and several other educational institutions. Located on one of the largest harbors in the world, noted for its scenery; built on an alluvial plain. The mountains come down to the shore of the bay in places, notably in Pão de Açúcar (1296 ft. or 395 m.) at the entrance to the bay and just W of it the Corcovado (*q.v.*) 2310 ft. (704 m.). Noted for its numerous wide streets, public buildings, museums, and public parks and gardens; one of the leading tourist and resort centers of South America.

History: Guanabara Bay discovered by Portuguese early 16th cent.; first settled by French, but settlement expelled by Portuguese 1567; became important in 18th cent. after discovery of gold and diamonds in Minas Gerais as outlet for mineral exports; made ✱ of colony of Brazil 1763, of empire 1822, and of republic 1889; in 1960 was replaced as ✱ of Brazil by Brasilia (*q.v.*) and became ✱ of newly created Guanabara state (1960–75), and of Rio de Janeiro state 1975 ff.

Rio de Janeiro Bay. See GUANABARA BAY.

Río de la Plata. **1.** Estuary, South America. See PLATA, RÍO DE LA.

2. Viceroyalty, South America. See LA PLATA 3.

Rio Dell \ˌrē-ō-ˈdel\. City, Humboldt co., NW California, SE of Eureka; pop. (1990c) 3012.

Rio del Rey \ˈrē-ō-del-ˈrā\. Seaport and estuary on the coast of Cameroon, E of Cross River.

Río de Oro \ˈrē-ō-dā-ˈōr-ō\. **1.** Narrow bay on the coast of Río de Oro region, Western Sahara; harbor of Dakhla.

2. Historical region comprising the S two thirds of Western Sahara bet. Cape Blanc and 26°N.

Río Gal·le·gos \ˈrē-ō-gä-ˈyā-gōs\. River port, ✱ of Santa Cruz prov., S Argentina, near mouth of Gallegos River.

Rio Grande \ˈrē-ō-ˈgrand, ˈgrän-dā\. **1.** *in Mex.* **Río Bra·vo** \ˌrē-ō-ˈbrä-vō\ *or* **Río Bravo del Nor·te** \t͟hel-ˈnȯr-tā\. River, SW U.S. and N Mexico; rises in San Juan Mts. near E boundary of San Juan co., SW Colorado, flows SE, then S through San Luis Park and across cen. New Mexico, forms W and SW boundary of Texas and the Texas-Mexico boundary, and empties into the Gulf of Mexico; 1885 mi. (3033 km.) long; the section in S part of Brewster co., Texas, includes canyons of the Big Bend National Park.

2. County in S Colorado. See table at COLORADO.

3. Village, Gallia co., S Ohio; pop. (1990c) 995; Univ. of Rio Grande (1876).

Rio Gran·de \ˈrē-ü-ˈgrȧn-dē\. **1.** Name of a river in Africa and two rivers in Brazil. See GRANDE, RIO.

2. *or* **São Pe·dro do Rio Grande do Sul** \sau̇m-ˈpā-drü-dü … dü-ˈsül\. City, SE Rio Grande do Sul state, S Brazil, 150 mi. (241 km.) SSW of Pôrto Alegre; munic. pop. (1991p) 172,435; ships meat products, wool, hides, rice; textiles, canned meat and fish, footwear; oil refining; founded 1737 as fort on site nearby; moved to present site 1745.

Río Gran·de \ˈrē-ō-ˈgrän-dā\. **1.** Name of four rivers in Spanish America. See GRANDE, RÍO.

2. Town, Zacatecas state, cen. Mexico, on branch railroad line 80 mi. (129 km.) NNW of the city of Zacatecas; munic. pop. (1990p) 57,879.

3. Municipality, NE Puerto Rico, ESE of San Juan; pop. (1990c) 45,648.

Rio Grande City. Unincorporated settlement, ⊗ of Starr co., S Texas, on the Rio Grande; pop. (1990c) 9891.

Rio Grande de Cagayan. See CAGAYAN 1.

Rio Grande de Mindanao. See MINDANAO 2.

Rio Grande de Pampanga. See PAMPANGA 1.

Río Grande de Santiago. See SANTIAGO, RÍO.

Rio Gran·de do Nor·te \ˈrē-ü-ˈgrȧn-dē-dü-ˈnȯr-tē\. State, NE Brazil; ✱ Natal; interior is semiarid; agriculture; salt. See table at BRAZIL.

Rio Gran·de do Sul \ˈrē-ü-ˈgrȧn-dē-dü-ˈsül\. State, S Brazil; ✱ Pôrto Alegre. See table at BRAZIL.

Rio Grande Pyramid \ˈrē-ō-ˈgrand\. Peak, Hinsdale co., SW Colorado; 13,827 ft. (4215 m.).

Rio Grande Reservoir. Reservoir in upper course of Rio Grande River, cen. Hinsdale co., SW Colorado.

Rí·o·ha·cha *also* **Río Ha·cha** \ˌrē-ō-ˈä-chä\. Seaport, ✱ of La Guajira dept., N Colombia, on W side of base of La Guajira Penin. ab. 90 mi. (145 km.) E of Santa Marta; munic. pop. (1992e) 126,300; one of the oldest Spanish towns in Colombia, founded 1545; had major pearl industry until 18th cent.

Rioja, La. See LA RIOJA.

Riom \rē-ˈōⁿ\; *anc.* **Ri·com·a·gus** \rī-ˈkä-mə-gəs\. Commune, Puy-de-Dôme dept., S cen. France, 8 mi. (13 km.) N of Clermont-Ferrand; pop. (1990c) 19,302; ✱ of medieval duchy of Auvergne; scene of trial 1942 of such leaders of the Third Republic as Édouard Daladier, Léon Blum, Maurice G. Gamelin, and Paul Reynaud by a kangaroo court of the Vichy government on charges of unpreparedness for war; trial suspended amid challenges to the court's authority.

Río Muni. See MBINI.

Rion. See RIONI.

Río Ne·gro \ˈrē-ō-ˈnā-grō\. **1.** River, South America. See NEGRO, RÍO 3.

2. Province of cen. Argentina, ✱ Viedma. See table at ARGENTINA.

3. Department of W Uruguay. See table at URUGUAY.

Ri·o·ne·ro in Vul·tu·re \ˌrē-ō-ˈnā-rō-in-ˈvül-tü-rā\. Commune, Potenza prov., Basilicata, S Italy, 21 mi. (34 km.) NNW of the commune of Potenza; pop. (1981p) 12,225.

Ri·oni \rē-ˈȯ-nē, -nyē\ *or* **Ri·on** \rē-ˈȯn\; *anc.* **Pha·sis** \ˈfā-səs\. River, W Republic of Georgia; rises in the Caucasus Mts., flows SW and W to the Black Sea at Poti; 179 mi. (288 km.) long. Navigable for nearly half its course; has hydroelectric station at Kutaisi. The ancient Phasis famous in Greek legends concerning Colchis (*q.v.*), the Golden Fleece, and the Argonauts; for a time held to be boundary bet. Europe and Asia.

Rio Par·do \ˈre-ü-ˈpär-dü\. Municipality, Rio Grande do Sul state, S Brazil, 70 mi. (113 km.) W of Pôrto Alegre; pop. (1980c) 50,080.

Río Pie·dras \ˈrē-ō-ˈpyā-t͟hräs\. Section of San Juan, Puerto Rico; formerly comprised a separate city; annexed to San Juan 1951; Univ. of Puerto Rico, Río Piedras Campus (1903); botanical garden.

Rio Ran·cho \ˈrē-ō-ˈran-chō\. City, Sandoval co., NW cen. New Mexico, N of Albuquerque; pop. (1990c) 32,505.

Ríos, Los. See LOS RÍOS.

Río San Juan \ˈrē-ō-sän-ˈwän\. Department of S Nicaragua. See table at NICARAGUA.

Rio Tin·to \ˈrē-ü-ˈtēn-tü\. City, Paraíba state, E Brazil; munic. pop. (1980c) 13,432.

Ríotinto, Minas de. See MINAS DE RÍOTINTO.

Riou *or* **Riouw.** See BINTAN.

Riouw Archipelago. See RIAU, KEPULAUAN.

Río·ver·de *or* **Río Ver·de** \ˌrē-ō-ˈver-dē\. Town, San Luis Potosí state, cen. Mexico, 65 mi. (105 km.) ESE of the city of San Luis Potosí; munic. pop. (1990p) 86,196.

Rio Vis·ta \ˈrē-ō-ˈvis-tə\. City, Solano co., cen. California, on Sacramento River 32 mi. (52 km.) SSW of Sacramento; pop. (1990c) 3316.

Rip·ley \ˈri-plē\. **1.** Name of counties in two states of the U.S. See tables at INDIANA and MISSOURI.

2. City, ⊗ of Tippah co., N Mississippi, 28 mi. (45 km.) SW of Corinth; pop. (1990c) 5371.

3. City, ⊗ of Lauderdale co., W Tennessee, 23 mi. (37 km.) S of Dyersburg; pop. (1990c) 6188.

4. City, ⊗ of Jackson co., W West Virginia; pop. (1990c) 3023.

5. Town, Derbyshire, N cen. England, 10 mi. (16 km.) NNE of Derby; pop. (1981p) 18,691.

Rip·on \'ri-ˌpän\. **1.** City, San Joaquin co., cen. California, 11 mi. (18 km.) NW of Modesto; pop. (1990c) 7455.
2. City, Fond du Lac co., E Wisconsin, 20 mi. (32 km.) W of the city of Fond du Lac; pop. (1990c) 7241; home appliances; Ripon Coll. (1851); site of a Fourieristic communal settlement 1844–50; reputed birthplace of the Republican party, in a meeting Mar. 20, 1854, of Whigs, anti-Nebraska Democrats, and Free Soilers on the campus of Ripon Coll.
3. Town, North Yorkshire, N England, on the Ure 23 mi. (37 km.) N of Leeds; pop. (1981c) 13,232; trade center in agricultural section; 12th cent. Norman cathedral with 7th cent. Saxon remnants; Fountains Abbey ruins are at Studley Royal nearby.

Ripon Falls. Former waterfall in the Victoria Nile near where it issues from Lake Victoria, Uganda; now submerged by Owen Falls Dam.

Rip·shin Ridge \'rip-ˌshin\. Elevation, Carter co., NE Tennessee; 4500 ft. (1370 m.).

Ri·sa·ral·da \ˌrē-sä-'räl-dä\. Department of W Colombia. See table at COLOMBIA.

Ris·ca \'ris-kə\. Town, Gwent co., SE Wales, on the Ebbw River 26 mi. (42 km.) WNW of Bristol; pop. (1981p) 14,860.

Ris·don \'riz-dən\. Town, Tasmania, Australia, suburb of Hobart, ab. 4 mi. (6 km.) above it on the left bank of the Derwent; settled 1803.

Ri·shon le–Ziy·yon *or* **Rishon Le–Zi·on** \rē-'shȯn-lə-tsē-'yōn\. Town, Israel, ab. 8 mi. (13 km.) SE of Tel Aviv-Jaffa; pop. (1992e) 145,600.

Rish·ra \'rish-rə\. Town, West Bengal, NE India, on right bank of Hugli River 12 mi. (19 km.) N of Calcutta; pop. (1991p) 102,649; site of first power mill for spinning jute yarns set up in India 1855.

Rish·ton \'rish-tən\. Town, Lancashire, NW England, 22 mi. (35 km.) NNW of Manchester; pop. (1981p) 6212.

Ris·ing Sun \'rīz-iŋ-'sən\. City, ⊗ of Ohio co., SE Indiana, on Ohio River 60 mi. (97 km.) SE of Shelbyville; pop. (1990c) 2311.

Rising Wolf Mountain. Peak, Glacier National Park, NW Montana; 9505 ft. (2897 m.).

Ri·son \'rī-zən\. Commercial city, ⊗ of Cleveland co., S Arkansas; pop. (1990c) 1258.

Ris–Oran·gis \'rēz-ȯ-rän-'zhē\. Commune, Essonne dept., N France, ab. 15 mi. (24 km.) S of Paris.

Rist·na, Cape \'rist-nə\. W point of Hiiumaa I., Estonia, W of the mainland.

Ritch·ie \'ri-chē\. County in NW West Virginia. See table at WEST VIRGINIA.

Ritch·ie's Archipelago \'ri-chēz\. Island group in Andaman Is., India, E of South Andaman I.; largest islands Havelock, Henry Lawrence, and Neill.

Ri·to Al·to Peak \'rē-tō-'al-tō\. Mountain, Saguache and Custer cos., Colorado, in the Sangre de Cristo Mts.; 13,573 ft. (4137 m.).

Rit·ter, Mount \'ri-tər\. Peak in the Sierra Nevada, in NE Madera co., cen. California; 13,157 ft. (4010 m.).

Ritt·man \'rit-mən\. Village, Medina and Wayne cos., NE cen. Ohio, 15 mi. (24 km.) SW of Akron; pop. (1990c) 6147.

Ritz·ville \'rits-ˌvil\. City, ⊗ of Adams co., E Washington, 60 mi. (97 km.) SW of Spokane; pop. (1990c) 1725.

Riukiu Islands. See RYUKYU ISLANDS 1.

Ri·va \'rē-vä\. Commune, Trento prov., Trentino-Alto Adige, NE Italy, at N end of Lake Garda 19 mi. (31 km.) SW of the commune of Trento; pop. (1981p) 13,011; medieval castle; palaces of 14th and 15th cents.; held by Austria until c. 1919.

Ri·va·da·via \ˌrē-vä-'dä-vyä\. Town, Mendoza prov., W Argentina, 30 mi. (48 km.) SE of the city of Mendoza; pop. (1980p) 10,953.

Ri·van·na \rə-'va-nə\. River, cen. Virginia; rises in the Blue Ridge, flows E and SE into James River on SE boundary of Fluvanna co.; ab. 65 mi. (105 km.) long.

Ri·vas \'rē-ˌväs\. **1.** Department of SW Nicaragua. See table at NICARAGUA.
2. Town, its ✱, on W shore of Lake Nicaragua; pop. (1985e) 19,564.

Ri·ve·ra \rē-'b̲ā-rä\. **1.** Department of N Uruguay. See table at URUGUAY.
2. Town, its ✱, on Brazil border opp. Santana do Livramento, ab. 270 mi. (430 km.) N of Montevideo; pop. (1985c) 57,316; in livestock-farming region.

River·bank \'ri-vər-ˌbaŋk\. City, Stanislaus co., cen. California, 11 mi. (18 km.) NW of Modesto; pop. (1990c) 8547.

River Cess \'ses\. Coastal town, SW Liberia, in cen. part of coast ab. 40 mi. (64 km.) SE of Buchanan.

Riv·er·dale \'ri-vər-ˌdāl\. **1.** City, Clayton co., NW cen. Georgia, 14 mi. (23 km.) S of Atlanta; pop. (1990c) 9359.
2. Village, Cook co., NE Illinois, just S of Chicago; pop. (1990c) 13,671.
3. Town, Prince Georges co., S cen. Maryland, 8 mi. (13 km.) NE of Washington, D.C.; pop. (1990c) 5185.
4. City, Weber co., N Utah, 4 mi. (6 km.) S of Ogden; pop. (1990c) 6419.

River Edge. Borough, Bergen co., NE corner of New Jersey, 4 mi. (6 km.) N of Hackensack; pop. (1990c) 10,603.

River Falls. City, Pierce and St. Croix cos., W Wisconsin, 12 mi. (19 km.) NE of confluence of Mississippi and St. Croix rivers; pop. (1990c) 10,610; Univ. of Wisconsin–River Falls (1874).

River Forest. Residential village, Cook co., NE Illinois, 2 mi. (3.2 km.) W of Chicago; pop. (1990c) 11,669; Rosary Coll. (1901), Concordia Univ. (1864).

River Grove. Village, Cook co., NE Illinois, 3 mi. (4.8 km.) SE of Chicago's O'Hare International Airport; pop. (1990c) 9961; Triton Coll. (1964).

Riv·er·head \'ri-vər-ˌhed\. Town, ⊗ of Suffolk co., SE New York, at E end of Long Island, on the Peconic River; pop. (1990c) 8814; Suffolk County Community Coll.–Eastern Campus (1977).

Riv·er·i·na \ˌri-və-'rī-nə\. Area of S New South Wales, SE Australia, bounded on N by Murrumbidgee River and on S by Murray River; 26,533 sq. mi. (68,721 sq. km.); chief towns Albury and Wagga Wagga; flat fertile land, important for irrigated agriculture; sheep and wheat in W portion; in SE grows rice, truck crops; fruit (incl. wine grapes).

River Junction. See CHATTAHOOCHEE 3.

River Oaks. City, Tarrant co., NE Texas, NW suburb of Fort Worth; pop. (1990c) 6580.

River Point. Village, Kent co., cen. Rhode Island, ab. 7 mi. (11 km.) SW of Cranston; governmental center of the town of West Warwick.

River Rouge \'rüzh, 'rüj\. City, Wayne co., SE Michigan, on Detroit River just S of Detroit; pop. (1990c) 11,314; steel.

Riv·ers \'ri-vərz\. State of S Nigeria. See table at NIGERIA.

Riv·er·side \'ri-vər-ˌsīd\. **1.** County in SE California. See table at CALIFORNIA.
2. City, its ⊗, 10 mi. (16 km.) SSW of San Bernardino; pop. (1990c) 226,505; packs and ships oranges; electronics; Univ. of California, Riverside (1954), Riverside Community Coll. (1916), La Sierra Univ. (1922), California Baptist Coll. (1950); March Air Force Base nearby; settled in 1870s; incorp. 1883.
3. Subdivision of town of Greenwich, Connecticut. See GREENWICH 1.
4. Residential village, Cook co., NE Illinois, 4 mi. (6.4 km.) W of Chicago; pop. (1990c) 8774.
5. City, Platte co., Missouri; across the Missouri from Kansas City, Kansas; pop. (1990c) 3010.
6. Township, Burlington co., S cen. New Jersey, on Delaware River 10 mi. (16 km.) NE of Camden; pop. (1990c) 7974.

Riv·ers·leigh \'ri-vərz-ˌlē\. Site, W Queensland, Australia, ab. 115 mi. (185 km.) NW of Mount Isa; many fossils here of Miocene and Pliocene epochs reveal much about Australia's prehistoric life.

Riv·er·ton \'ri-vər-tən\. **1.** Village, Sangamon co., cen. Illinois, on Sangamon River; pop. (1990c) 2638.
2. Borough, Burlington co., S cen. New Jersey, on Delaware River 8 mi. (13 km.) NE of Camden; pop. (1990c) 2775.
3. City, Salt Lake co., Utah, 15 mi. (24 km.) S of Salt Lake City; pop. (1990c) 11,261.

4. City, Fremont co., cen. Wyoming, 25 mi. (40 km.) NE of Lander; pop. (1990c) 9202; livestock; oil wells, uranium mines; Central Wyoming Coll. (1966).

Riv·er·view \ˈri-vər-ˌvyü\. **1.** City, Wayne co., SE Michigan, S suburb of Detroit; pop. (1990c) 13,894.

2. Village, St. Louis co., E Missouri; pop. (1990c) 3242.

Riv·er·woods \ˈri-vər-ˌwu̇dz\. Village, Lake co., Illinois, NNW of Chicago; pop. (1990c) 2868.

Rives·altes \rēv-ˈzält\. Town, Pyrénées-Orientales dept., S France, 5 mi. (8 km.) N of Perpignan; wine.

Ri·vi·era \ˌri-vē-ˈer-ə\. Region bordering on Mediterranean Sea in SE France and NW Italy, esp. the coast extending from Cannes to La Spezia; noted for scenery and pleasant climate; one of the major tourist centers of W Europe. The Italian Riviera is divided into **Riviera di Po·nen·te** \ˌdē-pə-ˈnen-tā\ W of Genoa, and **Riviera di Le·van·te** \ˌdē-lə-ˈvän-tā\ E of Genoa; the French Riviera is also called **Côte d'Azur** \ˈkōt-də-ˈzu̇(ə)r\. See CORNICHE.

Ri·viera Beach \ri-ˈvir-ə\. City, Palm Beach co., SE Florida, just N of West Palm Beach; pop. (1990c) 27,639.

Ri·vière–du–Loup \rē-ˈvyer-dʊ̄-ˈlü\. **1.** County in S Quebec, Canada. See table at QUEBEC.

2. City, its ⊗, near St. Lawrence River; pop. (1991c) 14,017.

Ri·vière Noire, Pi·ton de la \pē-ˈtō^{n}-də-lä-ˌrē-ˌvyer-ˈnwär\. Highest mountain in Mauritius, in SW part; 2711 ft. (826 m.).

Ri·vière Sa·lée \rē-ˌvyer-sȧ-ˈlā\. Strait, extending bet. Basse-Terre and Grande-Terre, French overseas dept. of Guadeloupe, West Indies; 4 mi. (6 km.) long.

Rivières du Sud. See GUINEA 2.

Riv·ne \ˈriv-nə\ *or mostly formerly* **Rov·no** \ˈrȯv-nə\. **1.** Administrative subdivision of Ukraine; 7761 sq. mi. (20,101 sq. km.); pop. (1991e) 1,176,000; ✻ Rivne; sugar beets, timber.

2. *or Pol.* **Rów·ne** \ˈrȯv-ne\ *or Ger.* **Row·no** \ˈrȯv-nō\. Town, its ✻, ab. 110 mi. (180 km.) NE of L'viv; pop. (1991e) 239,000; railroad junction; produces machinery, chemicals, food products. Formerly in Poland; occupied by Soviet troops in 1939 and by Germans 1941–44.

Ri·vo·li \ˈrē-vō-lē\. Commune, Torino prov., Piedmont, NW Italy, 8 mi. (13 km.) W of Turin; pop. (1991p) 51,884.

Rivoli Ve·ro·ne·se \ˌver-ō-ˈnā-sā, -ˈnā-zā\. Commune, Verona prov., Veneto, NE Italy, on Adige River 14 mi. (23 km.) NW of the commune of Verona; pop. (1981p) 1623; scene of victory of French Emperor Napoléon over Austrians Jan. 15, 1797.

Rixhöft, Kap. See ROZEWIE, CAPE.

Ri·yadh \rē-ˈyäd\ *also* **Er Ri·ad** \ˌer-rē-ˈäd\ *or* **Riad.** City, ✻ of Saudi Arabia, in E cen. part ab. 235 mi. (380 km.) from Persian Gulf; pop. (1981e) 1,308,000; oil refining; formerly a walled city, but walls demolished in 1950s to make room for rapid expansion of modern quarters of the city; has royal palace and numerous mosques; university (1957); became ✻ 1932.

Ri·yaq \ri-ˈyäk\; *formerly* **Ra·yak** \rä-\. Town, E Lebanon, on railroad line just E of Zahle.

Rizaiyeh. See ORŪMĪYEH.

Ri·zal \ri-ˈzäl, -ˈsäl\. **1.** Province, cen. Luzon, Philippines; ✻ Pasig; along Manila Bay and the Pasig land is low and flat; in the N part are hills and low mountain ranges. The main stream of the province is the Pasig, flowing NNW from the Laguna de Bay and through the city of Manila to Manila Bay. On the S marked by two large arms of Laguna de Bay separated by peninsula ending in Tapao Point and by Talim I. See table at PHILIPPINES.

2. Municipality, Nueva Ecija prov., Luzon, Philippines, on upper Pampanga River 18 mi. (29 km.) NE of Cabanatuan; pop. (1980c) 31,407; university (1958).

Ri·ze \ˈrē-ze\; *formerly* **Ço·ruh** \ˈchō-rük\. **1.** Province of Turkey in Asia. See table at TURKEY.

2. Seaport, its ✻, on the Black Sea ab. 40 mi. (64 km.) E of Trabazon; pop. (1990p) 51,586.

Riz·zu·to, Cape \rēt-ˈsü-tō\. Cape on E coast of Calabria, S Italy, projecting into Ionian Sea N of Gulf of Squillace.

Rju·kan \rē-ˈü-ˌkän\. **1.** Waterfall in Telemark co., S Norway; 780 ft. (238 m.) high.

2. Town, Telemark co., S Norway, 75 mi. (121 km.) W of Oslo; in WWII German-run heavy-water plant sabotaged by Norwegians.

Road Town. Town, ✻ of British Virgin Is., on Tortola I., West Indies; pop. (1987e) 2500.

Roag, Loch \ˈrōg\. Inlet of Atlantic Ocean on W coast of island of Lewis with Harris, in the Outer Hebrides, off NW coast of Scotland.

Roane \ˈrōn\. Name of counties in two states of the U.S. See tables at TENNESSEE and WEST VIRGINIA.

Roan High Knob \ˈrōn\. Peak, Mitchell co., W North Carolina, on the Tennessee border; 6285 ft. (1916 m.).

Ro·anne \rō-ˈän\; *anc.* **Ro·dum·na** \rō-ˈdəm-nə\. Commune, Loire dept., SE cen. France, on Loire River 45 mi. (72 km.) NNW of St.-Étienne; pop. (1990c) 42,848; textiles, leather goods.

Ro·a·noke \ˈrō-ə-ˌnōk\. **1.** River, S Virginia and NE North Carolina; formed by confluence of forks in Montgomery co., W Virginia, flows E and SE across North Carolina border in NE Warren co., and continues SE into Albemarle Sound; 410 mi. (660 km.) long; navigable for 112 mi. (180 km.).

2. County in W cen. Virginia. See table at VIRGINIA.

3. City, Randolph co., E Alabama, 5 mi. (8 km.) W of Georgia border and 35 mi. (56 km.) NE of Martin Lake; pop. (1990c) 6362.

4. City, Roanoke co., W Virginia, 148 mi. (238 km.) W of Richmond; 26 sq. mi. (67 sq. km.); pop. (1990c) 96,397; politically independent of the county; railroad center; electrical equipment, clothing, furniture, textiles; Hollins Coll. (1842), Virginia Western Community Coll. (1966). Settled 1740; developed after growth of railroads; incorp. as city 1884.

Roanoke Island. Island near S entrance to Albemarle Sound, Dare co., North Carolina; 12 mi. (19 km.) long and ab. 3 mi. (5 km.) wide; Manteo, ⊗ of Dare co., is on it; at N end is Fort Raleigh, site of first English settlement in North America 1585, sent by navigator and historian Sir Walter Raleigh, remained only 10 months; site of a 2d colony 1587 with John White appointed governor by Raleigh; by 1590 all the colonists had vanished; during the Civil War island captured 1862 by Union forces under Gen. Ambrose Burnside. Birthplace of Virginia Dare 1587, first child born in America to English parents.

Roanoke Rapids. City, Halifax co., NE North Carolina, 35 mi. (56 km.) NNE of Rocky Mount; pop. (1990c) 15,722.

Roanoke Sound. Inlet of Atlantic Ocean bet. Roanoke I. and Bodie I. off NE coast of North Carolina.

Roar·ing Spring \ˈrōr-iŋ\. Borough, Blair co., S cen. Pennsylvania, 13 mi. (21 km.) S of Altoona; pop. (1990c) 2615.

Ro·a·tán \ˌrō-ä-ˈtän\. **1.** Island, largest of the Islas de la Bahía, Honduras, in the Caribbean Sea N of the mainland; 30 mi. (48 km.) long.

2. *also* **Cox·en Hole** \ˈkäk-sən\. Town on Roatán I., ✻ of Islas de la Bahía dept., Honduras; pop. (1988p) 3744; exports coconuts.

Roazon. See RENNES.

Rob·bins \ˈrä-bənz\. Village, Cook co., NE Illinois, S suburb of Chicago; pop. (1990c) 7498.

Rob·bins·dale \ˈrä-bənz-ˌdāl\. City, Hennepin co., SE cen. Minnesota, 5 mi. (8 km.) NW of Minneapolis; pop. (1990c) 14,396.

Rob·bins·ville \ˈrä-bənz-ˌvil\. Town and mountain resort, ⊗ of Graham co., W North Carolina; pop. (1990c) 709.

Ro·bert–Cliche \rō-ˈber-ˈklēsh\. County, Quebec, Canada. See table at QUEBEC.

Rob·ert Lee \ˌrä-bərt-ˈlē\. City, ⊗ of Coke co., W cen. Texas; pop. (1990c) 1276.

Robert Moses Dam. See UNITED STATES, *Dams and Reservoirs.*

Rob·erts \ˈrä-bərts\. Name of counties in two states of the U.S. See tables at SOUTH DAKOTA and TEXAS.

Roberts, Point. See POINT ROBERTS.

Rob·ert·son \ˈrä-bərt-sən\. **1.** Name of counties in three states of the U.S. See tables at KENTUCKY, TENNESSEE, TEXAS.
2. Town, SW cen. Western Cape prov., S Rep. of South Africa, in valley of the Bree River 85 mi. (137 km.) E of Cape Town.

Rob·erts·port \ˈrä-bərts-ˌpōrt\. Seaport, NW Liberia, NW of Monrovia and SE of mouth of Mano River.

Ro·ber·val \ˌrō-bər-ˈval\. City, S Quebec, Canada, on W shore of Lac St.-Jean; pop. (1991c) 11,628; summer resort.

Rob·e·son \ˈrä-bə-sən\. County in S North Carolina. See table at NORTH CAROLINA.

Robe·son Channel \ˈrōb-sən\. N section of passage in Artic Ocean bet. Ellesmere I. and Greenland, extending NE to Lincoln Sea.

Rob·in·son \ˈrä-bən-sən\. **1.** City, ⊗ of Crawford co., E Illinois, 28 mi. (45 km.) NE of Olney; pop. (1990c) 6740.
2. City, McLennan co., cen. Texas, 7 mi. (11 km.) SSE of Waco; pop. (1990c) 7111.

Robinson Crusoe Island. See MÁS A TIERRA.

Rob·ins Point \ˈrä-bənz\. Point at S tip of Harford co., NE Maryland, extending into upper Chesapeake Bay.

Rob·son, Mount \ˈräb-sən\. Peak, E British Columbia, Canada; 12,972 ft. (3954 m.); highest of the Rocky Mts. in Canada.

Robs·town \ˈräbz-ˌtau̇n\. City, Nueces co., S Texas, 15 mi. (24 km.) W of Corpus Christi; pop. (1990c) 12,849.

Ro·by \ˈrō-bē\. City, ⊗ of Fisher co., NW cen. Texas; pop. (1990c) 616.

Ro·ca, Cape \ˈrō-kə\ *or Port.* **Ca·bo da Ro·ca** \ˈkä-vü-t͟hə-ˈrō-kə\. Cape on SW cen. coast of Portugal, 9°30′W, 38°47′N; westernmost point in continental Europe.

Roca El Yunque. See EL YUNQUE 1.

Roca Par·ti·da \ˈrō-kä-pär-ˈtē-t͟hä\. Westernmost island of the Revillagigedo group (*q.v.*) in the Pacific Ocean off cen. Mexico.

Ro·cas \ˈrō-kəs\. Island, Brazil, in the Atlantic Ocean 125 mi. (201 km.) NE of Cape São Roque, NE mainland Brazil, 33°59′W, 3°52′S; comprises a biological reserve (estab. 1979).

Roccabruna. See ROQUEBRUNE.

Roc·ca·stra·da \ˌrō-kä-ˈsträ-dä\. Commune, Grosseto prov., Tuscany, NW Italy, 17 mi. (27 km.) NE of the commune of Grosseto; pop. (1981p) 10,028.

Roch \ˈräch\. River, Greater Manchester co., NW England; rises near West Yorkshire border, flows SW into the Irwell S of Bury; 12 mi. (19 km.) long.

Ro·cha \ˈrō-chä\. **1.** Department of SE Uruguay. See table at URUGUAY.
2. City, its ✻, 100 mi. (161 km.) E of Montevideo; pop. (1985c) 24,015.

Roch·dale \ˈräch-ˌdāl\. Town, Greater Manchester, NW England, on Roch River 10 mi. (16 km.) NNE of Manchester; pop. (1981p) 92,704; cotton textiles; founding place of modern cooperative movement, with Rochdale Society of Equitable Pioneers (1844). Birthplace of politician John Bright (1811) and comedienne Gracie Fields (1898).

Roche·fort \rȯsh-ˈfȯr\. **1.** Town, Namur prov., SE Belgium, 15 mi. (24 km.) SE of Dinant; pop. (1991c) 11,226.
2. *or unofficially* **Rochefort–sur–Mer** \-sūr-ˈmer\. City, Charente-Maritime dept., W France, on Charente River 17 mi. (27 km.) SSE of La Rochelle; pop. (1990c) 26,949; ships timber and dairy products; air force base; an 11th cent. fortified settlement; in 17th–19th cents. a fortified town with a large naval arsenal and shipyards; bombed in WWII.

Ro·chelle \rō-ˈshel\. City, Ogle co., N Illinois, 25 mi. (40 km.) S of Rockford; pop. (1990c) 8769.

Rochelle, La. See LA ROCHELLE.

Rochers du Calvados. See CALVADOS REEF.

Roch·es·ter \ˈrä-chə-stər, -ˌches-tər\. **1.** City, ⊗ of Fulton co., N Indiana, 40 mi. (64 km.) S of South Bend; pop. (1990c) 5969.
2. Town, Plymouth co., SE Massachusetts, NE of New Bedford; pop. (1990c) 3921.
3. City, Oakland co., SE Michigan, 9 mi. (15 km.) E of Pontiac; pop. (1990c) 7130; Oakland Univ. (1957).
4. City, ⊗ of Olmsted co., SE Minnesota, 70 mi. (113 km.) SSE of St. Paul; pop. (1990c) 70,745; dairy products, hospital supplies; Minnesota Bible Coll. (1913), Rochester Community Coll. (1915); seat of the Mayo Clinic, estab. 1889 by Dr. William James Mayo and his brother Dr. Charles Horace Mayo, one of the most widely known medical centers in the world.
5. City, Strafford co., SE New Hampshire, 9 mi. (15 km.) NNW of Dover; pop. (1990c) 26,630; paper, textiles; dairy farms.
6. City and port of entry, ⊗ of Monroe co., W New York, 70 mi. (113 km.) ENE of Buffalo; pop. (1990c) 231,636; port on New York State Barge Canal; manufactures cameras and photographic equipment and supplies, optical goods, precision tools, dental equipment, office equipment, machine tools; in a fruit- and truck-farming region. Rochester Institute of Technology (1829), Univ. of Rochester (1850), Roberts Wesleyan Coll. (1866), Nazareth Coll. of Rochester (1924), St. John Fisher Coll. (1948), Monroe Community Coll. (1961). First permanent settlement 1811; incorp. as village 1817, as city 1834; home of abolitionist Frederick Douglass from 1840s, N terminus of Underground Railroad, and center of abolitionist activity before Civil War; scene of 1848 spirit rappings of the Fox sisters, Margaret and Kate, the origin of modern U.S. Spiritualism; in late 19th cent. a major center of horticulture.
7. Residential borough, Beaver co., W Pennsylvania, on Ohio River 23 mi. (37 km.) NW of Pittsburgh; pop. (1990c) 4156.
8. *anc.* **Du·ro·bri·vae** \ˌdu̇r-ə-ˈbrī-vē, ˌdyu̇r-\. City, Kent, SE England, on the Medway 28 mi. (45 km.) ESE of London; pop. (1981p) 52,505; seaport; cement; 12th cent. cathedral; remains of 11th cent. Norman castle. Nearby is Gadshill (*q.v.*), the home of novelist Charles Dickens. Site of pre-Roman settlement, Roman town, and Norman stronghold.

Rochester Hills. City, Oakland co., SE Michigan, N of Detroit; pop. (1990c) 61,766; Michigan Christian Coll. (1955).

Roche–sur–Yon, La. See LA ROCHE-SUR-YON.

Rock \ˈräk\. **1.** River, S Wisconsin and N Illinois; rises in Washington co., SE Wisconsin, flows S and SW across NW corner of Illinois, and empties into the Mississippi in W Rock Island co., NW Illinois; 285 mi. (459 km.) long.
2. Name of counties in three states of the U.S. See tables at MINNESOTA, NEBRASKA, WISCONSIN.

Rock·all \ˈrä-ˌkȯl\. Tiny rock island in North Atlantic Ocean, ab. 250 mi. (400 km.) NW of Ireland, at 57°35′N, 13°48′W; claimed by Denmark (May 7, 1985) and Iceland (1978 and reiterated May 10, 1985).

Rock·a·way \ˈrä-kə-ˌwā\. Borough, Morris co., N New Jersey, 8 mi. (13 km.) N of Morristown; pop. (1990c) 6243.

Rockaway Beach. Beach on S shore of Long Island, in the borough of Queens, New York City, New York; on narrow **Rockaway Peninsula** which shelters Jamaica Bay from the Atlantic.

Rockaway Inlet. Channel on S shore at W end of Long Island, New York, connecting Jamaica Bay with the Atlantic; crossed by bridge (540-foot or 164-meter lift span), joining Brooklyn with Rockaway Beach.

Rock·bridge \ˈräk-ˌbrij\. County in W cen. Virginia. See table at VIRGINIA.

Rock·cas·tle \ˈräk-ˌka-səl\. County in SE cen. Kentucky. See table at KENTUCKY.

Rock·chuck, Mount \ˈräk-ˌchək\. Peak in cen. Grand Teton National Park, NW Wyoming; 11,150 ft. (3399 m.).

Rock Creek Butte. Peak in Baker co., NE Oregon; 9105 ft. (2775 m.); highest in Blue Mts.

Rock·dale \ˈräk-ˌdāl\. **1.** County in N cen. Georgia. See table at GEORGIA.
2. City, Milam co., cen. Texas, 33 mi. (53 km.) W of Bryan; pop. (1990c) 5235.
3. City, E New South Wales, SE Australia, S suburb of Sydney on W shore of Botany Bay; pop. (1991c) 84,074.

Rock·e·fel·ler Plateau \ˈrä-ki-ˌfe-lər\. Elevated region in Marie Byrd Land, Antarctica, E of Ross Dependency; at

80°S, 135°W; averages 2500 ft. (760 m.) to 4500 ft. (1370 m.); discovered 1934 by American explorer Adm. Richard E. Byrd.

Rock Falls. City, Whiteside co., NW Illinois, 50 mi. (80 km.) SW of Rockford; pop. (1990c) 9654.

Rock·ford \ˈräk-fərd\. **1.** Town, ⊗ of Coosa co., E cen. Alabama; pop. (1990c) 461; American Indian artifacts in vicinity.
2. City, ⊗ of Winnebago co., N Illinois, 80 mi. (129 km.) NW of Chicago; pop. (1990c) 139,426; machine tools, agricultural implements, paint, furniture; in agricultural region; Rockford Coll. (1847), Rock Valley Coll. (1964); founded 1834; incorp. as village 1839, as city 1852.
3. City, Kent co., W Michigan, 13 mi. (21 km.) NNE of Grand Rapids; pop. (1990c) 3750.
4. Township, Wright co., S cen. Minnesota; pop. (1990c) 3380.

Rock·hamp·ton \räk-ˈhamp-tən\. City, E Queensland, Australia, on Fitzroy River 325 mi. (523 km.) NNW of Brisbane; pop. (1993e) 61,631; railroad center and river port; railroad shops, meatpacking and freezing plants; center of coal-mining, livestock-raising, and agricultural region; made a municipality 1860.

Rock Hill. **1.** City, St. Louis co., E Missouri, 9 mi. (14 km.) W of the city of St. Louis; pop. (1990c) 5217.
2. City, York co., N South Carolina, 64 mi. (103 km.) N of Columbia; pop. (1990c) 41,643; textiles, paper; Winthrop Univ. (1886).

Rockies. See ROCKY MOUNTAINS.

Rock·ing·ham \ˈrä-kiŋ-ˌham\. **1.** Name of counties in three states of the U.S. See tables at NEW HAMPSHIRE, NORTH CAROLINA, VIRGINIA.
2. City, ⊗ of Richmond co., S North Carolina, 52 mi. (84 km.) W of Fayetteville; pop. (1990c) 9399.
3. Town, Windham co., SE corner of Vermont; pop. (1990c) 5484.
4. City, SW Western Australia, Australia, on the coast, S of Perth; pop. (1993e) 51,391.

Rock Island \räk-ˈī-lənd\. **1.** County in NW Illinois. See table at ILLINOIS.
2. City, its ⊗, on the Mississippi River 78 mi. (126 km.) NW of Peoria; pop. (1990c) 40,552; clothing, agricultural and electrical equipment; railroad shops, large U.S. government arsenal (1862); Augustana Coll. (1860); inhabited by American Indians prior to European settlement c. 1830s.
3. Populated place, S Quebec, Canada, on Vermont border 34 mi. (55 km.) SSW of Sherbrooke; pop. (1991c) 1067; is closely associated with Stanstead, Quebec, and Derby Line, Vermont.

Rock·land \ˈrä-klənd\. **1.** County in SE New York. See table at NEW YORK.
2. City, ⊗ of Knox co., S Maine, on W shore of Penobscot Bay 37 mi. (60 km.) ESE of Augusta; pop. (1990c) 7972; center of Penobscot Bay resort area; shopping and commercial center; fishing. Birthplace of poet Edna St. Vincent Millay 1892.
3. Town, Plymouth co., SE Massachusetts, 6 mi. (10 km.) ENE of Brockton; pop. (1990c) 16,123.
4. Town, Prescott and Russell co., SE Ontario, Canada, on Ottawa River 20 mi. (32 km.) ENE of Ottawa; pop. (1991c) 6771.

Rock·ledge \ˈräk-lej\. **1.** City, Brevard co., E cen. Florida, just S of Cocoa; pop. (1990c) 16,023.
2. Borough, Montgomery co., SE Pennsylvania, 10 mi. (16 km.) NNE of Philadelphia; pop. (1990c) 2679.

Rock·lin \ˈrä-klin\. City, Placer co., E California, 17 mi. (27 km.) NE of Sacramento; pop. (1990c) 19,033; pop. more than doubled bet. 1980 and 1990.

Rock·mart \ˈräk-ˌmärt\. City, Polk co., NW Georgia, 18 mi. (29 km.) SSE of Rome; pop. (1990c) 3356.

Rock of Cashel. See CASHEL.

Rock·port \ˈräk-ˌpōrt\. **1.** City, ⊗ of Spencer co., SW Indiana, on Ohio River 28 mi. (45 km.) E of Evansville; pop. (1990c) 2315.
2. Town, Knox co., S Maine, on W shore of Penobscot Bay 37 mi. (60 km.) E of Augusta; pop. (1990c) 2854.
3. Town, Essex co., NE corner of Massachusetts, on Atlantic Ocean 30 mi. (48 km.) NE of Boston; pop. (1990c) 7482; summer resort.
4. City and resort, ⊗ of Aransas co., S Texas, on Aransas Bay 28 mi. (45 km.) NE of Corpus Christi; pop. (1990c) 4753; tourism.

Rock Port. City, ⊗ of Atchison co., NW corner of Missouri; pop. (1990c) 1438.

Rock Rapids. City, ⊗ of Lyon co., NW corner of Iowa, 63 mi. (101 km.) N of Sioux City; pop. (1990c) 2601.

Rock River. See ROCK 1.

Rocks Point \ˈräks\. Cape on NW coast of South I., New Zealand, at N end of Karamea Bight.

Rock·springs \räk-ˈspriŋz\. Town, ⊗ of Edwards co., SW cen. Texas; pop. (1990c) 1339.

Rock Springs. City, Sweetwater co., SW Wyoming, 40 mi. (64 km.) N of Utah border; pop. (1990c) 19,050; coal mines, oil wells.

Rock·stand Knob \ˈräk-stand\. Peak in W North Carolina; 6002 ft. (1829 m.).

Rock·stone \ˈräk-ˌstōn, -stən\. Town, N Guyana, on E bank of the Essequibo River 58 mi. (93 km.) S of Georgetown.

Rock Valley. City, Sioux co., NW Iowa, 48 mi. (77 km.) N of Sioux City; pop. (1990c) 2540.

Rock·ville \ˈräk-ˌvil, -vəl\. **1.** Former city, N Connecticut; now a section of town of Vernon (*q.v.*).
2. Town, ⊗ of Parke co., W Indiana, 23 mi. (37 km.) NNE of Terre Haute; pop. (1990c) 2706.
3. City, ⊗ of Montgomery co., cen. Maryland, 15 mi. (24 km.) NNW of Washington, D.C.; pop. (1990c) 44,835; dates to Revolutionary period.

Rockville Centre. Village, Nassau co., SE New York, on Long Island 19 mi. (31 km.) ESE of New York City; pop. (1990c) 24,727; Molloy Coll. (1955).

Rock·wall \ˈräk-ˌwȯl\. **1.** County in NE Texas. See table at TEXAS.
2. City, its ⊗; pop. (1990c) 10,486.

Rock·well, Mount \ˈräk-ˌwel\. Peak in Glacier National Park, NW Montana; 9250 ft. (2819 m.).

Rockwell City. City, ⊗ of Calhoun co., NW cen. Iowa, 25 mi. (40 km.) WSW of Fort Dodge; pop. (1990c) 1981.

Rock·wood \ˈräk-ˌwu̇d\. **1.** City, Wayne co., SE Michigan, 20 mi. (32 km.) S of Detroit; pop. (1990c) 3141.
2. City, Roane co., E Tennessee, 6 mi. (10 km.) SE of Harriman; pop. (1990c) 5348.

Rocky \ˈrä-kē\. River, N Ohio; rises in Medina co., flows N and NE into Lake Erie on W boundary of the city of Cleveland.

Rocky Face. Peak, W North Carolina; 6031 ft. (1838 m.).

Rocky Ford. City, Otero co., SE Colorado, on Arkansas River 12 mi. (19 km.) WNW of La Junta; pop. (1990c) 4162.

Rocky Hill. **1.** Town, S Hartford co., N Connecticut, on W bank of Connecticut River; pop. (1990c) 16,554; settled c. 1650.
2. Borough, Somerset co., N cen. New Jersey, ab. 4 mi. (6 km.) NNE of Princeton; pop. (1990c) 693; Gen. George Washington wrote his farewell address to the army here 1783.

Rocky Knob. Peak, Towns co., N Georgia; 4164 ft. (1269 m.).

Rocky Mount. **1.** City, Edgecombe and Nash cos., NE North Carolina, 52 mi. (84 km.) E of Raleigh; pop. (1990c) 48,997; tobacco market; produces textiles, electronic components, chemicals; North Carolina Wesleyan Coll. (1956); city founded c. 1818.
2. Town, ⊗ of Franklin co., SW cen. Virginia; pop. (1990c) 4098.

\ə\ **abut** \ə\ **matches** \ᵊ\ **kitten,** Fr **table** \ər\ **further** \a\ **ash** \ā\ **ace** \ä\ **cot, cart** \á\ Fr **bac** \au̇\ **out** \b̲\ Span **Avila** \ch\ **chin** \e\ **bet** \ē\ **easy** \g\ **go** \i\ **hit** \ī\ **ice** \j\ **job** \k̲\ Ger **ich, Buch** \ⁿ\ Fr **vin** \ŋ\ **sing** \ō\ **go** \ȯ\ **all** \ȯ\ **law** \œ\ Fr **bœuf** \œ̄\ Fr **feu** \ȯi\ **boy** \th\ **thin** \t͟h\ **this** \ü\ **loot** \u̇\ **foot** \ue\ Ger **füllen** \ue̅\ Fr **rue** \y\ **yet** \ʸ\ Fr **digne** \ˈdēnʸ\, **nuit** \ˈnwʸē\ \yü\ **few** \yu̇\ **fury** \zh\ **vision**

Rocky Mountain. Peak, Union and Towns cos., N Georgia; 4586 ft. (1398 m.).

Rocky Mountain National Park. See UNITED STATES, *National Parks.*

Rocky Mountains *or* **Rock·ies** \ˈrä-kēz\. Mountain system, W North America, extending from the Mexican frontier to the Arctic, through Arizona, New Mexico, Colorado, Utah, Nevada, Wyoming, Idaho, and Montana, the Canadian provs. of Alberta and British Columbia, Yukon Terr. and Alaska; highest peak in U.S. section of this range is Mt. Elbert 14,433 ft. (4399 m.) in Colorado; highest in Canadian section Mt. Robson 12,972 ft. (3954 m.) in British Columbia.

Rocky Point. Point on SW coast of Los Angeles co., SW California, W of Long Beach, extending into Pacific Ocean.

Rocky River. City, Cuyahoga co., N Ohio, on Lake Erie 8 mi. (13 km.) W of Cleveland; pop. (1990c) 20,410; residential suburb of Cleveland.

Rocky Trail Peak. Peak, W North Carolina; 6488 ft. (1978 m.).

Ro·court \rȯ-ˈkür\. Commune, Liège prov., E Belgium, just N of the city of Liège; scene of battle Oct. 11, 1746 during War of Austrian Succession in which Austrian forces under Prince Charles of Lorraine were defeated by the French under Maurice, comte de Saxe.

Ro·croi *or* **Ro·croy** \rȯ-ˈkrwä\. Town, Ardennes dept., NE France, near Belgian frontier; pop. (1990c) 2565; well-preserved 17th cent. fortifications; scene of battle May 19, 1643 during Thirty Years' War in which the French under Louis, duc d'Enghien (called "the Great Condé"), thoroughly defeated the Spanish.

Ro·da *or* **Rho·da** \ˈrō-də\ *or* **Raw·ḍah** \ˈrō-də\. Island in the Nile River, N Egypt, near Cairo; site of an ancient Nilometer.

Roda, La. See LA RODA.

Ro·das \ˈrȯ-ˌt͟häs\. Municipality, Las Villas prov., W cen. Cuba, 15 mi. (24 km.) NNW of Cienfuegos; pop. (1981p) 29,831.

Ro·den·kir·chen \ˈrō-dən-ˌkir-k̲ən\. City, North Rhine-Westphalia, Germany, on Rhine River just S of Cologne.

Ro·dez \rȯ-ˈdāz, -ˈdes\; *anc.* **Seg·o·du·num** \ˌse-gə-ˈdü-nəm, -ˈdyü-\. Industrial and commercial commune, ✻ of Aveyron dept., S France, on Aveyron River 78 mi. (126 km.) NE of Toulouse; pop. (1990c) 26,794; tourism; textiles; agricultural trade center; 13th–16th cent. cathedral. Ancient Gallic ✻; became colony of Rome; made seat of bishopric 401; ✻ of Rouergue until 1789; in Middle Ages politically and physically divided bet. bishops and counts; Catholic stronghold in Wars of Religion 16th cent.

Rodg·ers Peak \ˈrä-jərz\. Mountain in Yosemite National Park, California, on E border of the park SSE of Mt. Lyell; 12,978 ft. (3956 m.).

Ródhos. See RHODES.

Ro·ding \ˈrō-diŋ\. River, SE England; flows S and SW into the Thames in E Greater London; 30 mi. (48 km.) long.

Ro·do·ni, Cape \rō-ˈdō-nē\ *or Alb.* **Kep i Ro·do·nit** \ˈkep-i-rō-ˈdō-nit\. Cape extending into Adriatic Sea, NW coast of Albania, N of Durrës.

Rodopi. See RHODOPE.

Rodos. See RHODES 1.

Rodosto. See TEKİRDAĞ 2.

Ro·dov·re \ˈrœ-t͟hȯ-rə\. Town, Copenhagen co., Denmark; pop. (1989e) 35,561.

Ro·dri·gues *also* **Ro·dri·guez** \rō-ˈdrē-ges\. Island of the Mascarene Is., in the Indian Ocean ab. 500 mi. (800 km.) E of Madagascar; 40 sq. mi. (104 sq. km.); pop. (1991e) 37,782; a dependency of Mauritius; highest point 1300 ft. (395 m.); many limestone caves in W part. Discovered by Portuguese c. 16th cent.; colonized by French 17th–18th cents.; taken by English c. 1810.

Rodumna. See ROANNE.

Roeb·ling \ˈrō-bliŋ\. Town, Burlington co., S cen. New Jersey, on Delaware River ab. 7 mi. (11 km.) S of Trenton; estab. 19th cent. by J. A. Roebling, founder of steel-cable factory which built Brooklyn Bridge and supplied cables for other well-known bridges.

Roe·buck Bay \ˈrō-ˌbək\. Inlet of Indian Ocean, NW Western Australia, Australia, just SW of Dampier Land, 19°04′S, 122°17′E.

Roe·land Park \ˈrō-lənd\. City, Johnson co., E Kansas, S suburb of Kansas City; pop. (1990c) 7706.

Roepat. See RUPAT.

Roer. See RUR.

Roer·mond \rür-ˈmȯnt\. Commune, Limburg prov., SE Netherlands near German border at confluence of the Rur and the Meuse rivers; pop. (1992e) 42,782; chemicals, paper, cigars, electrical equipment; 13th cent. Romanesque church; 15th cent. cathedral. In medieval times the chief town of Upper Gelderland (see GELDERLAND); became bishopric 16th cent.; under Hapsburgs 16th–18th cents.; to Netherlands 1839; heavily damaged in WWII.

Roe·se·la·re \ˌrü-sə-ˈlär-ə\ *or Fr.* **Rou·lers** \rü-ˈlers\. Commune, West Flanders prov., NW Belgium; pop. (1991c) 52,872; 15th cent. church; 18th cent. town hall; scene of battle 1794 during French Revolutionary Wars in which French under Gen. Jean-Charles Pichegru and Jacques-Alexandre Macdonald defeated the Austrians; in WWI occupied by Germans 1914–18, and heavily damaged.

Roes Wel·come Sound \ˈrōz-ˈwel-kəm\. Strait, S Nunavut, Canada, bet. W Southampton I. and the mainland; 170 mi. (274 km.) long and 50 to 115 mi. (80 to 185 km.) wide; a part of N Hudson Bay.

Rofreit. See ROVERETO.

Ro·ga·land \ˈrō-gə-ˌlän\. County of SW Norway. See table at NORWAY.

Rog·er Mills \ˌrä-jər-ˈmilz\. County in W Oklahoma. See table at OKLAHOMA.

Rog·ers \ˈrä-jərz\. **1.** County in NE Oklahoma. See table at OKLAHOMA.
2. Commercial city, Benton co., NW corner of Arkansas, 20 mi. (32 km.) N of Fayetteville; pop. (1990c) 24,692; mountain resort; pop. has quadrupled since 1960.

Rogers, Mount. Peak, Grayson and Smyth cos., SW Virginia; 5729 ft. (1746 m.); highest point in Virginia.

Rogers City. City, ⊗ of Presque Isle co., NE Michigan, on Lake Huron 30 mi. (48 km.) NW of Alpena; pop. (1990c) 3642; limestone quarries.

Rogers Pass. Pass in Selkirk Mts., SE British Columbia, Canada, NE of Revelstoke, through which passes the Canadian Pacific Railway; 4302 ft. (1311 m.); explored 1881 for Canadian Pacific Railway whose tracks ran through the pass 1886–1916 until superseded by tunnel; section of Trans-Canada Highway through the pass opened 1962.

Rogers Peak. Mountain in Glacier National Park, NW Montana; 7300 ft. (2225 m.).

Rog·ers·ville \ˈrä-jərz-ˌvil\. Town, ⊗ of Hawkins co., NE Tennessee; pop. (1990c) 4149.

Rog·ge·veld \ˈrä-gə-ˌfelt\. Mountain range, SW Rep. of South Africa, in Northern Cape prov. extending into Western Cape prov. W of Nieuwveld; highest point ab. 5700 ft. (1735 m.).

Ro·go·a·gua·do, Lake \ˌrō-gō-ä-ˈgwä-t͟hō\. Lake, N Bolivia; drains S and E into Mamoré River.

Rogue \ˈrōg\. River, SW Oregon; rises in Crater Lake National Park, flows S and SW into Pacific Ocean in W Curry co.; ab. 200 mi. (320 km.) long.

Ro·hil·khand \ˈrō-ˌhil-ˌkənd\ *also* **Ba·reil·ly** \bə-ˈrā-lē\. Region of N India; occupied since early part of 18th cent. by the Rohilla tribe of Afghans. An early Rohilla ruler was made nabob by the Delhi emperor; invaded by Marathas 1772, who were overcome 1774 by united forces of British and nabob of Oudh; became fragmented until it passed to British India 1801; widespread rebellious activity in Indian mutiny 1857–58. See RAMPUR.

Rohn·ert Park \ˈrō-nərt\. City, Sonoma co., W California, 7 mi. (11 km.) S of Santa Rosa; pop. (1990c) 36,326; Sonoma State Univ. (1960). The city's pop. more than tripled bet. 1970 and 1980.

Roh·tak \ˈrō-tək\. Town, Haryana, NW India, 44 mi. (71 km.) WNW of Delhi; pop. (1991p) 215,844; grain market; many prehistoric artifacts found here; 12th cent. mosque; 18th cent. border town bet. Sikh and Maratha empires.

Roi \ˈrȯi\. Islet of Kwajalein Atoll, Marshall Is.; site of Japanese airfield in WWII, taken by U.S. troops 1944.

Roi Et \ˌrȯi-ˈet\ *or* **Roi Ed** \ˈet\. Town, E Thailand, near the Chi River and 70 mi. (113 km.) SE of Khon Kaen; pop. (1991e) 33,507.

Ro·jo, Cape \ˈrō-hō\. **1.** Cape on coast of N Veracruz state, Mexico, extending into Gulf of Mexico.
2. Cape at SW end of Puerto Rico, on SE side of Mona Passage.

Ro·kan \ˈrō-ˌkän\. River, N cen. Sumatra, Indonesia; flows NE into the Strait of Malacca; 175 mi. (282 km.) long.

Ro·kel *also* **Ro·kelle** \rō-ˈkel\ *or* **Se·li** \ˈsā-lē\. River, Sierra Leone; flows S and W into Atlantic Ocean at Freetown; ab. 250 mi. (400 km.) long; called the Sierra Leone at its estuary.

Ro·ku·gō, Cape \ˈrō-kü-ˌgō\. Cape on W coast of Honshū, Japan, NW of Toyama Bay at end of Noto Penin.

Roland, Brèche–de–. See BRÈCHE–DE–ROLAND.

Ro·lette \ˌrō-ˈlet\. County in N North Dakota. See table at NORTH DAKOTA.

Rol·la \ˈrä-lə, -lē\. **1.** City, ⊗ of Phelps co., S cen. Missouri; pop. (1990c) 14,090; diversified agriculture; Univ. of Missouri–Rolla (1870).
2. City, ⊗ of Rolette co., N North Dakota; pop. (1990c) 1286; farms.

Roll·ing Fork \ˈrō-liŋ-ˈfȯrk\. City, ⊗ of Sharkey co., W Mississippi; pop. (1990c) 2444.

Rolling Hills Estates. City, Los Angeles co., SW California, 10 mi. (16 km.) W of Long Beach; pop. (1990c) 7789.

Rolling Meadows. City, Cook co., NE Illinois, NW suburb of Chicago; pop. (1990c) 22,591.

Rolling Mountain. Peak, San Juan co., SW Colorado; 13,694 ft. (4174 m.).

Rolling Thunder. Peak, N Grand Teton National Park, NW Wyoming; 10,902 ft. (3323 m.).

Rol·lins Pass \ˈrä-linz\. Mountain pass in Front Range of Rocky Mts., Boulder and Grand cos., N Colorado; 11,680 ft. (3560 m.).

Røm. See RØMØ.

Ro·ma \ˈrō-mə\. **1.** City, Starr co., S Texas, on the Rio Grande; pop. (1990c) 8059.
2. Town, SE Queensland, Australia, 275 mi. (442 km.) WNW of Brisbane; pop. (1993e) 6862; service center for an agricultural area.
3. Province of Lazio, Italy. See table at ITALY.
4. City, Italy. See ROME 3.
5. Island, Indonesia. See ROMANG.

Romae, Ducatus. See ROME, DUCHY OF.

Ro·ma·gna \rō-ˈmä-nyä\; *anc.* **Ro·ma·nia** \rō-ˈmā-nyə, -nē-ə\. A former province of the Papal States; ✻ Ravenna; under nominal papal control throughout Middle Ages; brought fully under papal control 16th cent. until 1796; as part of Emilia incorp. 1796–1814 in Italian republic and French Emperor Napoléon's kingdom of Italy; restored to Papacy 1815; annexed to kingdom of Sardinia 1860. Now forms part of the region of Emilia-Romagna, N Italy.

Ro·magne–sous–Mont·fau·con \rō-ˈmänʸ-sü-ˌmȯⁿ-fō-ˈkōⁿ\. Village, Meuse dept., NE France, near Montfaucon; site of a large American military cemetery.

Ro·main, Cape \rō-ˈmān\. Cape on island off mainland in Charleston co., South Carolina, extending into Atlantic Ocean.

Ro·maine \rō-ˈmān\. River, SE Quebec, Canada; rises in SW Labrador, flows S across Quebec into the Gulf of St. Lawrence opp. W end of Anticosti I.; 270 mi. (434 km.) long.

Ro·main·ville \rȯ-meⁿ-ˈvēl\. Commune, Seine-St.-Denis dept., N France, a NE suburb of Paris.

Ro·man \ˈrȯ-ˌmän\. City, Neamţ co., NE Romania, on railroad line 28 mi. (45 km.) N of Bacău; pop. (1989c) 77,021; tube-rolling mill, sugar refineries; city first mentioned 14th cent.

Romana, La. See LA ROMANA.

Roman Africa. See AFRICA, ROMAN.

Roman Apennines. See table at APENNINES.

Roman Campagna. See CAMPAGNA DI ROMA.

Ro·man Empire \ˈrō-mən\. The empire of ancient Rome, beginning with the imperial rule of Augustus 27 B.C.; at its greatest extent (c. 117 A.D.) included all S Europe, Britannia, N Africa, Egypt, Asia Minor, N coast of Pontus Euxinus (Black Sea), Armenia and regions S of the Caucasus, Mesopotamia and adjoining regions, Syria, Palestine, and NW corner of Arabia.
History: Founded following civil wars by victorious Octavian who gained control of Italy and the West 43–35 B.C. and of the East 31 B.C.; as Emperor Augustus 27 B.C.–14 A.D., Octavian established the principate and expanded the empire with the conquest and annexation of Egypt, parts of Asia Minor, areas S of the Danube from the Alps to the Black Sea, and N Spain; briefly held Germania to the Elbe, but withdrew to the Rhine; later emperors' major territorial additions (by 2d cent. A.D.) included Dacia, Thrace, parts of W Asia Minor, Mesopotamia, Arabia Petraea, Agri Decumates, and Britannia; territories consisted of senatorial and imperial provinces and of client states subject to the foreign policies of Rome; from 3d cent. suffered decline caused partly by external factors, such as pressure of Persia and of barbarian tribes from across the Danube and Germany, and partly by internal breakdown of trade and administrative system; lost Daria, Agri Decumates, and Mesopotamia; intermittently divided for administration 3d–4th cents. by line running from the Danube to Adriatic Sea S of Dalmatia; final division 395; for Eastern Empire after 395, see BYZANTINE EMPIRE; invaded and overwhelmed during 5th cent. by successive waves of Visigoths, Huns, Vandals, Ostrogoths, and others, retaining only Italian and some adjacent lands; largely ruled from Ravenna in 5th cent.; end of Western Empire conventionally dated 476 when the last emperor of the West, Romulus Augustulus, was deposed by German tribal leader Odoacer who abolished the office of emperor; for medieval "revival" of Rome's imperial authority in West, see HOLY ROMAN EMPIRE.

Ro·mang \ˈrō-ˌmäŋ\ *or* **Ro·ma** \ˈrō-mə\. Island, S Moluccas, Indonesia, E of Wetar I. and NE of Timor; ab. 15 mi. (24 km.) long by 10 mi. (16 km.) wide.

Ro·ma·nia *or* **Ru·ma·nia** *also* **Rou·ma·nia** \rō-ˈmä-nyä; rü-ˈmā-nē-ə, rō-, -nyə\. Republic, SE Europe, bounded on N by Ukraine, on NE by Moldova and Ukraine, on E by the Black Sea, on S by Bulgaria, and on W by Yugoslavia and Hungary; 91,699 sq. mi. (237,500 sq. km.); pop. (1993e) 22,789,000; ✻ Bucharest.
Physical features: In the N penetrated by the SE end of the Carpathian Mts., uniting in the center of the country with the E end of the Transylvanian Alps (highest point Moldoveanu 8343 ft. or 2543 m.). For the greater part consists of rolling and well-watered plains with fertile soil. Besides the Prut, other important tributaries of the Danube are Siret, Ialomiţa, Argeş (with its tributary the Dîmboviţa), Olt, Jiu, and Timiş (which enters the Danube in Yugoslavia); plains in Transylvania are watered by the Mureşul and Someşul, tributaries of the Tisza. Marshlands occur along the lower Danube and in its delta; its shoreline from Sulina at the mouth of the Danube extends ab. 125 mi. (200 km.) to a point N of Nos Kaliakra.
Chief products: Wheat, corn, barley, sugar beets, potatoes; livestock; oil, natural gas, bauxite, manganese, coal; manufacturing: textiles, chemicals, iron and steel, agricultural machinery, motor vehicles.
Chief cities: Bucharest, Constanţa, Iaşi, Timişoara, Cluj-Napoca, Galaţi, Braşov, Craiova.
Political divisions: Divided into the following counties (for pronunciation of their names, see their individual entries):

NAME	AREA (sq. mi.)	AREA (sq. km.)	POP. (1992p)	CAPITAL
Alba	2,396	6,206	414,200	Alba Iulia
Arad	2,944	7,625	487,400	Arad

NAME	AREA (sq. mi.)	AREA (sq. km.)	POP. (1992p)	CAPITAL
Argeș	2,616	6,775	680,600	Pitești
Bacău	2,540	6,579	736,100	Bacău
Bihor	2,898	7,506	634,100	Oradea
Bistrița-Năsăud	2,040	5,284	327,200	Bistrița
Botoșani	1,910	4,947	458,900	Botoșani
Brăila	1,817	4,706	392,100	Brăila
Brașov	2,058	5,330	642,500	Brașov
Bucharest (municipality)	526	1,362	2,351,000	Bucharest
Buzău	2,335	6,048	516,300	Buzău
Călărași	1,828	4,734	338,800	Călărași
Caraș-Severin	3,275	8,482	375,800	Reșița
Cluj	2,558	6,625	735,100	Cluj-Napoca
Constanța	2,713	7,027	748,000	Constanța
Covasna	1,425	3,691	232,600	Sfîntu Gheorghe
Dîmbovița	1,548	4,009	559,900	Tîrgoviște
Dolj	2,851	7,384	761,100	Craiova
Galați	1,702	4,408	639,900	Galați
Giurgiu	1,465	3,794	313,100	Giurgiu
Gorj	2,170	5,620	400,100	Tîrgu Jiu
Harghita	2,542	6,584	347,700	Miercurea-Ciuc
Hunedoara	2,698	6,988	548,000	Deva
Ialomița	1,889	4,892	304,000	Slobozia
Iași	2,103	5,447	806,800	Iași
Maramureș	2,390	6,190	538,500	Baia-Mare
Mehedinți	1,885	4,882	332,100	Drobeta-Turnu-Severin
Mureș	2,575	6,669	607,300	Tîrgu Mureș
Neamț	2,265	5,866	577,600	Piatra-Neamț
Olt	1,695	4,390	521,000	Slatina
Prahova	1,805	4,675	873,200	Ploiești
Sălaj	1,481	3,836	266,300	Zalău
Satu Mare	1,694	4,387	400,100	Satu Mare
Sibiu	2,085	5,400	452,800	Sibiu
Suceava	3,290	8,521	700,800	Suceava
Teleorman	2,223	5,758	482,300	Alexandria
Timiș	3,338	8,645	700,300	Timișoara
Tulcea	3,242	8,397	270,200	Tulcea
Vaslui	2,038	5,278	457,800	Vaslui
Vîlcea	2,194	5,682	436,300	Rîmnicu-Vîlcea
Vrancea	1,870	4,843	392,600	Focșani

History: For earlier history, see DACIA, MOLDAVIA, WALACHIA, and DANUBIAN PRINCIPALITIES; autonomous Danubian Principalities united and took name of Romania 1861; assisted Russia in Russo-Turkish War 1877–78, yet lost Bessarabia to Russia at war's end, gaining in compensation N Dobruja; complete independence from Turkey recognized by powers 1878; became kingdom 1881; in Balkan Wars, occupied and forced Bulgaria to cede S Dobruja 1913; maintained neutrality in WWI until entering on side of Allies 1916; disastrously defeated and overrun, but upon Allied victory, territory enlarged by addition of Bessarabia, Transylvania, E Banat, and Bukovina (*qq.v.*) 1918–20; with aim of preserving territorial integrity, entered into several mutual protection treaties in the interwar period, incl. the Little Entente 1921, and the Balkan Pact 1934 (see BALKAN STATES); in 1940 forced to cede Bessarabia and N Bukovina to U.S.S.R., part of N Transylvania to Hungary, and S Dobruja to Bulgaria; in WWII under authoritarian regime of Ion Antonescu fought on side of Germany, assisting in invasion of U.S.S.R. 1941 ff.; overrun by U.S.S.R. in 1944 and after coup d'état switched sides and fought remainder of war against the Axis; N Transylvania returned by treaty 1947; proclaimed people's republic Dec. 1947, and adopted soviet-style constitution 1948; became a member of the Warsaw Treaty Organization 1955; during 1960s adopted a foreign policy frequently differing from that of the U.S.S.R.; suffered large-scale economic losses 1970 due to severest floods in its history; Communist regime overthrown 1989; first free elections since 1937 held 1990; new constitution 1991.

Romania. 1. Part of region of Emilia-Romagna, Italy. See ROMAGNA.

2. European division of the Ottoman Empire. See RUMELIA.

Romania, Cape. See BULAT, CAPE.

Ro·ma·no, Cape \rō-ˈmä-nō\. Cape on island in Gulf of Mexico off W coast of Collier co., SW Florida.

Romano Cay \rō-ˈmä-nō-ˈkē, -ˈkā\. Island off N coast of Camagüey prov., E cen. Cuba, in the Camagüey Archipelago.

Ro·mans·horn \ˈrō-mäns-ˌhȯrn\. Commune, Thurgau canton, NE Switzerland, on S shore of Lake Constance; pop. (1980c) 7893.

Ro·mans–sur–Isère \rō-ˌmäⁿ-ˌsu̅e̅r-ē-ˈzer\. Commune, Drôme dept., SE France, on Isère River 11 mi. (18 km.) NE of Valence; pop. (1990c) 33,546; leather goods; 12th cent. church. Settlement arose around abbey founded 9th cent.; important city in the Dauphiné during Middle Ages.

Ro·man·zof, Cape \rō-ˈman-zəf\. Cape on W coast of Alaska; extends into Bering Sea, 61°47′N, 166°W.

Rom·blon \rȯm-ˈblȯn\. **1.** Province, cen. Philippines; an island group of the Visayan Is. in Sibuyan Sea SE of Mindoro and S of Luzon; comprises three large islands—Tablas, Sibuyan, and Romblon—and ab. 30 small and dependent islands; 524 sq. mi. (1357 sq. km.); pop. (1980c) 193,174; ✻ Romblon. Islands generally low except Sibuyan, which has peak 6745 ft. (2056 m.) high. Soil is fertile; chief crops abacá and copra. See table at PHILIPPINES.

History: Islands visited by Spaniards 16th cent.; received first missionaries 17th cent.; in 17th and 18th cents. often ravaged by Moros; organized into a comandancia 1853; civil government estab. 1901.

2. Smallest of the three important islands of Romblon group, E of N Tablas I. and W of Sibuyan; 32 sq. mi. (83 sq. km.).

3. Town, ✻ of Romblon prov., NW Romblon I., Philippines; pop. (1980c) 24,251; has excellent harbor; active trading port on interisland passage from San Bernardino Strait to Verde Island Passage.

Rombo, Ilhéus do. See SECOS, ILHÉUS.

Rome \ˈrōm\. **1.** City, ⊗ of Floyd co., NW Georgia, 55 mi. (88 km.) NW of Atlanta; pop. (1990c) 30,326; textiles; in farming region; Shorter Coll. (1873), Floyd Coll. (1970); founded 1834; Confederate rail and manufacturing center in Civil War; occupied by Union troops 1864.

2. City, a ⊗ of Oneida co., cen. New York, on Mohawk River 15 mi. (24 km.) WNW of Utica; pop. (1990c) 44,350; household appliances, graders, radiators. Site of native portage long before arrival of Europeans; fortified by British 18th cent. (site of Fort Stanwix National Monument since 1935); fort played prominent role in the American Revolution; nearby battle of Oriskany (*q.v.*) 1777; township organized 1796; Erie Canal begun here 1817; incorp. as village 1819, as city 1870.

3. *or Ital.* **Ro·ma** \ˈrō-mä\; *anc.* **Roma** \ˈrō-mə\. City, ✻ of Italy, also ✻ of Lazio region and ✻ of Roma prov., cen. Italy, on both sides of Tiber River 16 mi. (26 km.) from its mouth and 117 mi. (188 km.) NW of Naples; pop. (1991p) 2,693,383; the cultural, financial, and transportation center of Italy; printing and publishing; chemicals; motion-picture production; tourism; in ancient times ✻ of the Roman Empire (*q.v.*) and later ✻ of the Papal States. Early city built on seven hills (see SEVEN HILLS) enclosed by Servian Wall; city now extends along both banks of Tiber River and includes Vatican City, autonomous administrative center of the Roman Catholic Church (for account of papal properties in Rome, see VATICAN CITY); imperial Rome divided into 14 Augustan Regions and enclosed by the Aurelian Wall; modern city has notable public squares (Piazza del Popolo, Venezia, San Pietro, Barberini, among others), and city gates (Porta Pinciana, Porta Pia, Porta Maggiore, among others); notable churches include San Giovanni in Laterno, Santa Pudenziana, and Il Gesù; Univ. of Rome (1303) and several other educational institutions; numerous libraries; noted for its palaces, as the Barberini, Colonna, Corsini, Rospigliosi, Pallavicini, and Farnese; remains of ancient city include the Colosseum, catacombs, temples, baths (esp. the Baths of Caracalla), aqueducts, arches and Forum.

History: During c. 8th cent. B.C., early settlements on hills united to form one city (traditional date of founding of Rome 753 B.C.); predominantly Latin in population, but ruled as Etruscan city-kingdom to 6th cent. B.C.; according to tradition, republic founded 509 B.C.; began to establish control over neighboring settlements 5th cent. B.C.; captured for a short time and sacked by Gauls 390 B.C.; by 275 B.C. Rome, having defeated Etruscan towns, Latin League, Samnites, and Greek cities in S, was supreme in Italy; began overseas expansion in Punic Wars 264–241, 218–201, 149–146 B.C. (see CARTHAGE); conquered Sicily, Sardinia, Corsica, Cisalpine Gaul, much of Spain, Carthage, and former Carthaginian islands in the Mediterranean; by defeat of Macedonia (*q.v.*) 197 B.C., attained hegemony in Greece; gradually acquired Balearic Is., S Gaul, additional parts of Asia Minor and Africa, Cyrenaica, and Crete; under Generals Pompey the Great and Julius Caesar (first cent. B.C.) conquered Syria, Jerusalem, Cyprus, Gaul, and attempted (55 B.C.) to invade Britain; after battle of Actium 31 B.C., all of Roman lands were controlled by Octavian (Augustus), the first Roman emperor, 27 B.C. (for later history of Roman rule, see ROMAN EMPIRE); city of Rome the ✻ of Roman Empire until Emperor Constantine the Great dedicated Constantinople 330 A.D. (see İSTANBUL); sacked by Alaric and the Visigoths 410; after Ravenna (*q.v.*) became political ✻ of Italy, bishop of Rome, the chief defender of city, gradually obtained temporal authority and began to claim primacy among Western bishops; Duchy of Rome, a Byzantine fief, 6th–8th cents.; for its theoretical position as ✻ of revived Roman Empire, see HOLY ROMAN EMPIRE; seat of Papacy and (except 1309–77) of temporal rule of Papal States (*q.v.*); city declined amid factional strife 13th–14th cents. until absolute papal rule estab. 1420 by Martin V; became a center of Renaissance culture 15th–16th cents.; sacked by imperial armies of Holy Roman Emperor Charles V 1527; occupied by French who erected Roman republic 1798; annexed to French First Empire 1809, but restored to pope 1814; scene of republican revolt 1848–49; made ✻ of kingdom of Italy 1870 (see VATICAN CITY for part belonging to Papacy); in WWII captured by Allies June 4, 1944; scene of signing of Treaty of Rome 1957, establishing European Economic Community; site of Summer Olympic Games 1960.

Rome, Duchy of; *anc.* **Du·catus Ro·mae** \du̇-ˈkā-təs-ˈrō-mē, dyu̇-; -ˈkä-təs-ˈrō-ˌmē\. A division of the Byzantine Empire, 6th cent. to 8th cent., comprising most of modern Lazio, cen. Italy; later a province of the Papal States called **Patrimony of Saint Peter** \sānt-ˈpē-tər\.

Ro·meo \ˈrō-mē-ˌō\. Village, Macomb co., SE Michigan, 19 mi. (31 km.) NE of Pontiac; pop. (1990c) 3520.

Ro·me·o·ville \ˈrō-mē-ō-ˌvil\. Village, Will co., NE Illinois, 10 mi. (16 km.) N of Joliet; pop. (1990c) 14,074; Lewis Univ. (1932).

Rom·ney \ˈräm-nē\. **1.** City, ⊗ of Hampshire co., NE West Virginia, in E Panhandle on S branch of Potomac River 15 mi. (24 km.) ESE of Keyser; pop. (1990c) 1966; lumber; ships fruit; poultry, livestock farms.

2. Town, England. See NEW ROMNEY.

Romney Marsh \ˈräm-nē, ˈrəm-\. Coastal pasture tract in Kent, SE England, NE of Rye; 68 sq. mi. (176 sq. km.); before end of 13th cent. the Rother River flowed through it to the sea.

Rom·ny \ˈrȯm-nē\. Town, W Sumy subdivision, NE Ukraine, on upper Sula River 58 mi. (93 km.) W of the town of Sumy; pop. (1991e) 57,000.

Rø·mø \ˈrœ-ˌmœ\ *or* **Røm** \ˈrœm\. One of the North Frisian Is. in the North Sea off W coast of S Jutland Penin.; 39 sq. mi. (101 sq. km.); pop. (1981c) 833; belongs to Denmark.

Ro·mo·ran·tin–Lanthe·nay \ˌrȯ-mȯ-räⁿ-ˈteⁿ-ˌläⁿt-ˈnā\ *or* **Romorantin.** Town, Loir-et-Cher dept., N cen. France, ab. 24 mi. (39 km.) SE of Blois; remains of 15th cent. castle where Francis II signed edict that prevented establishment of the Inquisition in France 1560.

Roms·dal \ˈrüms-ˌdäl\. Valley of the Rauma (*q.v.*), Norway; steep mountains on either side, esp. Vinjatindane (Vengetinder) 5960 ft. (1817 m.), **Roms·dals·horn** \-ˌdäls-ˌhórn\ 5105 ft. (1556 m.), and Trolltindane (Troldtinder) 5876 ft. (1791 m.).

Roms·dals·fjord \ˈrüms-ˌdäls-ˌfyōr\. Long fjord of Norwegian Sea, W cen. Norway, E of Ålesund; Åndalsnes is at head of it; receives Rauma River.

Rom·sey \ˈrəm-zē\. Town, Hampshire, S England, ab. 7 mi. (11 km.) NW of Southampton; pop. (1981p) 12,941; brewing; farms; site of a Norman abbey church of 12th cent. with remains of an earlier Saxon church beneath it; naval commander and statesman Earl Mountbatten of Burma is buried in the abbey.

Rom·u·lus \ˈrä-myə-ləs\. City, Wayne co., SE Michigan, SW of Detroit; pop. (1990c) 22,897.

Roncador, Serra do. See SERRA DO RONCADOR.

Ron·ca·dor Bank *or* **Roncador Cay** \ˈróŋ-kä-ˌthór-ˈkē, -ˈkā\. Small island in W Caribbean Sea, off E coast of Nicaragua.

Roncador Reef. Reef, Solomon Is., S of Ontong Java and N of Santa Isabel, 6°13′S, 159°22′E.

Ron·ca·glia \rōŋ-ˈkäl-yä\. Former village, Piacenza prov., Emilia-Romagna, N Italy; now part of commune of Piacenza (*q.v.*); several diets held here (12th cent.) by Holy Roman emperors, esp. Frederick I.

Ron·ces·va·lles \ˌrón-thās-ˈbäl-ˌyās\ *or Fr.* **Ron·ce·vaux** \rōⁿs-ˈvō\. Commune in Navarra prov., N Spain; pop. (1991p) 35; in the Pyrenees ab. 5 mi. (8 km.) from the French boundary; medieval abbey; mountains here crossed by the **Puer·to de Iba·ñe·ta** \ˈpwer-tō-ˌthā-ˌē-bä-ˈnyā-tä\, a celebrated mountain pass 3648 ft. (1112 m.) high traditionally held to be place where Breton nobleman Roland met his death defending Frankish King (later Holy Roman Emperor) Charlemagne's retreating army in the battle of Roncesvalles 778.

Ron·ce·verte \ˈrän-sə-ˌvərt\. City, Greenbrier co., SE West Virginia, on Greenbrier River 26 mi. (42 km.) E of Hinton; pop. (1990c) 1754.

Ron·co \ˈrōŋ-kō\ *or in full* **Ronco Scri·via** \ˈskrē-vyä\. Commune, Genova prov., E cen. Liguria, NW Italy, N of Genoa; pop. (1981p) 4799; railroad tunnel 5.16 mi. (8 km.) long.

Ron·co·le \ˈróŋ-kō-ˌlā\ *or* **Le Roncole** \lā-\. Village, Parma prov., NW cen. Emilia-Romagna, N Italy, near Busseto (*q.v.*) S of Cremona; birthplace of composer Giuseppe Verdi 1813.

Ron·da \ˈrón-dä\. Commune, Málaga prov., S Spain, 40 mi. (64 km.) W of the city of Málaga; pop. (1991c) 33,900; produces grain, wine; manufactures flour, leather, soap, chocolates; Roman and Moorish remains; reconquered by Ferdinand II of Aragon 1485.

Ron·da·ne National Park \ˈrón-dä-nə\. National park, Norway; 222 sq. mi. (575 sq. km.); alpine region.

Ron·de·bosch \ˈrón-də-ˌbós\. Town, Western Cape prov., S Rep. of South Africa, ab. 6 mi. (10 km.) SE of Cape Town; founded 1657 by freed burghers, once servants of Dutch East India Company; site of British administrator Cecil Rhodes's home Groote Schuur, now location of Univ. of Cape Town (1918).

Ron·dô·nia \rōⁿ-ˈdō-nyə\; *formerly* **Gua·po·ré** \ˌgwä-pó-ˈrā\. State, W Brazil; ✻ Pôrto Velho; rubber; Brazil nuts; formerly (1943–1981) a territory. See table at BRAZIL.

Ron·dout \ˈrän-ˌdau̇t\. Former village in Ulster co., New York, on the Hudson River; now part of Kingston.

Rondout Reservoir. Reservoir in **Rondout Creek** in Ulster and Sullivan cos., SE New York, formed by Merriman Dam (see UNITED STATES, *Dams and Reservoirs*).

Ronge, Lac la \ˌlak-lə-ˈrōⁿzh\. Lake, N Saskatchewan, Canada; 552 sq. mi. (1430 sq. km.); its outlet flows N into Churchill River.

Rong·e·lap \ˈroŋ-ə-ˌlap\. Atoll, Marshall Is., W cen. Pacific Ocean, at NW end of Ratak Chain ab. 80 mi. (130 km.) E of Bikini Atoll; evacuated 1985 because of continuing radioactive contamination from nuclear weapons tests carried out at Eniwetok in the 1950s.

Rong·e·rik \ˈróŋ-ə-ˌrik\. Atoll, Marshall Is., W cen. Pacific Ocean, near NW end of Ratak Chain E of Bikini and Rongelap; place to which population of Bikini was first removed at time of atomic-bomb tests 1946, later moved elsewhere.

Ro·niu *or* **Roo·niu** \ˈrō-nē-ˌü\. Peak, on the SE peninsula of the island of Tahiti, French Polynesia, S Pacific Ocean; 4370 ft. (1332 m.).

Røn·ne \ˈrœ-nə\. Seaport, ⊗ of Bornholm co., on the W coast of Bornholm I., Denmark; pop. (1989e) 15,278.

Ron·ne·by \ˈró-nə-bē\. Town, Blekinge prov., S Sweden, ab. 14 mi. (23 km.) W of Karlskrona; pop. (1989c) 28,902.

Ron·ne Ice Shelf \ˈrō-nə\. Large area of shelf ice at head of Weddell Sea, Antarctica, bet. Ellsworth Land on W and Berkner I. and Filchner Ice Shelf on E; extends inland ab. 400 mi. (640 km.).

Ron·se \ˈrón-sə\ *or Fr.* **Re·naix** \rə-ˈnā\. Commune, East Flanders prov., NW cen. Belgium; pop. (1991c) 11,564.

Roo·de·poort \ˈrō-də-ˌpōrt\. City, Gauteng prov., NE Rep. of South Africa, 12 mi. (19 km.) W of Johannesburg; pop. (1985c) 141,764; residential community in gold-mining region; has iron and steel and woodworking industries; founded 1886 as gold-mining camp; declared a municipality 1904; scene of surrender of physician and statesman Dr. Leander Starr Jameson to the Boers 1896.

Roof Butte \ˈrüf, ˈru̇f\. Butte, NE Apache co., NE Arizona; 9808 ft. (2989 m.).

Rooke. See UMBOI.

Rooks \ˈru̇ks\. County in N Kansas. See table at KANSAS.

Rooniu. See RONIU.

Roor·kee *or* **Rur·ki** \ˈru̇r-kē\. Town, N Uttar Pradesh, N India, 19 mi. (31 km.) E of Saharanpur; pop. with cantonment (1991p) 80,236; headquarters of workers and shops for Ganges Canals; university (1948).

Roo·se·be·ke \ˈrō-sə-ˌbā-kə\. Village, East Flanders, Belgium, just E of Roeselare; scene of battle 1382 in which French forces quashed Flemish revolt.

Roo·sen·daal en Nis·pen \ˈrōs-ᵊn-ˌdäl-ən-ˈnis-pən\. Commune, North Brabant prov., S Netherlands; pop. (1992e) 61,354; machinery, furniture; founded 1268.

Roo·se·velt \ˈrō-zə-ˌvelt, -vəlt *also* ˈrü-\. **1.** Name of counties in two states of the U.S. See tables at MONTANA and NEW MEXICO.

2. Unincorporated settlement, Nassau co., SE New York, on Long Island SW of Hempstead; pop. (1990c) 15,030.

3. City, Duchesne co., Utah; pop. (1990c) 3915.

Roosevelt, Mount. Peak, Lawrence co., W South Dakota; 5676 ft. (1730 m.).

Roosevelt, Rio \ˈrē-ü\; *formerly* **Rio da Dú·vi·da** \də-ˈdü-vi-də\ *or Eng.* **River of Doubt** \ˈdau̇t\. River, W cen. Brazil; rises in W Mato Grosso state, flows N into SE Amazonas state where it joins the Aripuanã River; ab. 400 mi. (640 km.) long; explored by Theodore Roosevelt, 26th president of the U.S., 1914; lower course of the Aripuanã sometimes called Rio Roosevelt also.

Roosevelt Island. **1.** Island, Potomac River, U.S. See THEODORE ROOSEVELT ISLAND.

2. *1921–73* **Wel·fare Island** \ˈwel-ˌfar\; *earlier* **Black·wells Island** \ˈblak-wəlz, -ˌwelz\. Island in East River, New York City, New York; 1.5 mi. (2.4 km.) long by 0.1 mi. (0.16 km.) wide; part of Manhattan borough; connected to Manhattan by tramway.

3. Ice-covered island, E Ross Ice Shelf, Ross Dependency, Antarctica, S of the Bay of Whales; ab. 90 mi. (145 km.) long.

Roosevelt Lake. See FRANKLIN D. ROOSEVELT LAKE.

Roosevelt Park. City, Muskegon co., W Michigan, 5 mi. (8 km.) S of the city of Muskegon; pop. (1990c) 3885.

Ro·per \ˈrō-pər\. River, NE Northern Terr., Australia; flows N and E to Limmen Bight on W side of Gulf of Carpentaria; ab. 325 mi. (525 km.) long, navigable for ab. 90 mi. (145 km.).

Ro·que·brune \ˌrók-ˈbrue̅n\ *or in full* **Roquebrune–Cap–Mar·tin** \-ˌkáp-mär-ˈteⁿ\ *or Ital.* **Roc·ca·bru·na** \ˌró-kä-ˈbrü-nä\. Commune, Alpes-Maritimes dept., SE France, near coast bet. Monaco and Menton; medieval village and fortress; formerly under princes of Monaco from whom it (with Menton) revolted 1848; independent 1848–60 when it became part of France.

Roque·fort–sur–Soul·zon \ˌrȯk-ˈfȯr-sᵫr-sül-ˈzō^{n}\. Town, SE Aveyron dept., S France; town built against limestone cliffs in which are caves where Roquefort cheeses are ripened.

Roques, Los. See LOS ROQUES.

Ro·rai·ma \rȯ-ˈrī-mä\. State, N Brazil; ✻ Boa Vista; cattle ranching; formed as a territory 1943; became a state 1990. See table at BRAZIL.

Roraima, Mount. Flat-topped mountain in Pacaraima Mts. at intersection of boundaries of Brazil, Venezuela, and Guyana; 9 mi. (14 km.) long by 3 mi. (5 km.) wide; highest point 9219 ft. (2810 m.); steep slopes, many waterfalls (one almost 2000 ft. or 610 m.), source of many rivers of Guyana, of the Amazon system to the S, and of Orinoco system to the W.

Rorke's Drift \ˈrȯrks\. Locality on a tributary of the Tugela River, N cen. KwaZulu-Natal prov., E Rep. of South Africa, 21 mi. (34 km.) SE of Dundee; scene of British defense against Zulus 1879.

Rør·os \ˈrœr-ˌōs\. Commune, SE Sør-Trøndelag co., cen. Norway 35 mi. (56 km.) by road from Swedish frontier; pop. (1980c) 5377; formerly a copper-mining center.

Ror·schach \ˈrȯr-ˌshäk\. Commune, St. Gall canton, NE Switzerland, on S shore of Lake Constance 6 mi. (10 km.) NE of the commune of St. Gall; pop. (1980c) 9878.

Ro·sa, Mon·te \ˈmȯn-tā-ˈrō-zä\. Mountain of the Pennine Alps, on the Switzerland-Italy border; a mountain mass, has 10 summits, the highest the Dufourspitze, highest point in the Pennine Alps. At alt. of 11,500 ft. (3505 m.) has Italian laboratory for nuclear research.

Ro·sa·les \rō-ˈsä-lās\. Municipality, Pangasinan prov., Luzon, Philippines, on left bank of the Agno 27 mi. (43 km.) ESE of Lingayen; pop. (1980c) 36,582.

Ro·sa·lie Peak \ˈrō-zə-lē\. Mountain, Park co., cen. Colorado; 13,575 ft. (4138 m.).

Ros·a·lind Bank \ˈrä-zə-lənd, ˈrō-\. Shoal in Caribbean Sea halfway bet. W Jamaica and E Honduras.

Ro·sa·rio \rō-ˈsär-ē-ˌō\. **1.** Commercial city, Santa Fe prov., E cen. Argentina, on the Paraná River 190 mi. (306 km.) NW of Buenos Aires; pop. (1980p) 875,623; ships grain, meat, hides, and sugar; flour mills; institutions of higher learning; several museums. Founded 1725; began development into major city late 19th cent.
2. Municipality, Batangas prov., Luzon, Philippines, 13 mi. (21 km.) NE of the municipality of Batangas; pop. (1980c) 54,252.
3. Municipality, La Union prov., Luzon, Philippines, 5 mi. (8 km.) from E shore of Lingayen Gulf; pop. (1980c) 29,331.

Rosario, Sierra del. See SIERRA DEL ROSARIO.

Rosario Cay. Cuban island in N Caribbean Sea, E of Isle of Pines.

Rosario de la Fron·te·ra \-del-ə-ˌfrən-ˈter-ə\. Town, Salta prov., N Argentina; pop. (1980p) 13,531; alt. 3200 ft. (975 m.).

Ro·sar·io Strait \rō-ˈzar-ē-ˌō\. Strait, NW Washington, lying bet. San Juan Is. on the W and Skagit co. on the E.

Ro·sas, Gulf of \ˈrō-ˌsäs\. Inlet of Mediterranean Sea on NE coast of Spain, S of Cape Creus.

Roscianum. See ROSSANO.

Ros·com·mon \rä-ˈskä-mən\. **1.** County in N cen. Michigan. See table at MICHIGAN.
2. Village, ⊗ of Roscommon co., N cen. Michigan; pop. (1990c) 858; Kirtland Community Coll. (1966).
3. County, N cen. Ireland, in Connacht prov.; ⊗ Roscommon; agriculture, coal mining. See table at IRELAND.
4. Town, ⊗ of co. Roscommon, N cen. Ireland; pop. (1986c) 1363; ruins of 13th cent. castle and of 13th cent. Dominican priory.

Ros·crea \räs-ˈkrā\. Town, NE co. Tipperary, S Ireland; pop. (1986c) 4378; ruins of priory founded in 7th cent.; remnants of 13th cent. castle.

Rose \ˈrōz\. Small uninhabited island in American Samoa, in SW cen. Pacific Ocean, ab. 70 mi. (113 km.) E of Tau.

Rose, Mount. Peak, S Washoe co., NW Nevada, in Carson Range; 10,778 ft. (3285 m.).

Ro·seau \rō-ˈzō\. **1.** County in NW Minnesota. See table at MINNESOTA.
2. Village, its ⊗, 20 mi. (32 km.) WSW of Lake of the Woods; pop. (1990c) 2396.
3. Seaport, ✻ of Dominica, Windward Is., West Indies; pop. (1991p) 15,853.

Rose·bud \ˈrōz-ˌbəd\. **1.** Creek, SE Montana; rises in E Big Horn co., flows NE into Yellowstone River in Rosebud co.; ab. 100 mi. (160 km.) long.
2. County in SE Montana. See table at MONTANA.

Rose·burg \ˈrōz-ˌbərg\. City, ⊗ of Douglas co., SW Oregon, 45 mi. (72 km.) E of Coos Bay; pop. (1990c) 17,032; sawmills, nickel mine; diversified agriculture; Umpqua Community Coll. (1964).

Rose·dale \ˈrōz-ˌdāl\. **1.** Former city, Wyandotte co., Kansas; annexed to Kansas City 1922.
2. City, a ⊗ of Bolivar co., NW Mississippi, on Mississippi River 31 mi. (50 km.) N of Greenville; pop. (1990c) 2595.

Ro·seg, Piz \ˌpēts-rō-ˈzej\. Mountain in the Rhaetian Alps, Switzerland, W of Piz Bernina; 12,936 ft. (3943 m.).

Rose Hill. See BEAU BASSIN.

Rose·land \ˈrōz-ˌland, -lənd\. Borough, Essex co., NE New Jersey, 10 mi. (16 km.) NW of Newark; pop. (1990c) 4847.

Ro·selle \rō-ˈzel\. **1.** City, Cook and Du Page cos., NE Illinois, W of Chicago; pop. (1990c) 20,819.
2. Residential borough, Union co., NE New Jersey, 2 mi. (3.2 km.) W of Elizabeth and adjoining Roselle Park; pop. (1990c) 20,314; first community in world to have streets lighted by incandescent bulbs; site of laboratory of inventor Thomas A. Edison in which he installed first electric lighting plant in world. Birthplace 1726 of Abraham Clark, signer of the Declaration of Independence.

Roselle Park. Residential borough, Union co., NE New Jersey, 3 mi. (5 km.) W of Elizabeth and adjoining Roselle; pop. (1990c) 12,805.

Rose·mead \ˈrōz-ˌmēd\. City, Los Angeles co., SW California, E of Alhambra; pop. (1990c) 51,638.

Rose·mère \ˌrōz-ˈmer, -ˈmi(ə)r\. Town, S Quebec, Canada, 15 mi. (24 km.) NW of Montreal; pop. (1991c) 11,198.

Rose·mont \ˈrōz-ˌmänt\. **1.** Village, Cook co., NE Illinois, site of highway interchanges bet. Chicago to the E and O'Hare International Airport to the W; pop. (1990c) 3995.
2. Locality, Montgomery co., SE Pennsylvania, ab. 6 mi. (10 km.) S of Norristown; Rosemont Coll. (1921).

Rose·mount \ˈrōz-ˌmau̇nt\. City, Dakota co., SE Minnesota; pop. (1990c) 8622.

Ro·sen·berg \ˈrōz-^{ə}n-ˌbərg\. **1.** City, Fort Bend co., SE Texas, ab. 19 mi. (30 km.) WSW of Houston; pop. (1990c) 20,183.
2. Town, Slovakia. See RUŽOMBEROK.

Rose·neath \ˈrōz-ˌnēth\. Parish, Strathclyde region, W cen. Scotland, on Gare Loch ab. 23 mi. (35 km.) NW of Glasgow; site of U.S. naval base in WWII.

Ro·sen·heim \ˈrōz-^{ə}n-ˌhīm\. City, Bavaria, Germany, at foot of Alps on Inn River 34 mi. (55 km.) SE of Munich; pop. (1992e) 56,704; lumber.

Rose Peak \ˈrōz\. Mountain, N Greenlee co., E Arizona; 8786 ft. (2678 m.).

Rose Point. Cape, NE Graham I., N Queen Charlotte Is., off W British Columbia, Canada.

Ro·se·to de·gli Abruz·zi \rō-ˈzā-tō-ˌdel-yē-ä-ˈbrüt-sē\. Commune, Teramo prov., Abruzzi, cen. Italy, on Adriatic Sea 17 mi. (27 km.) E of the commune of Teramo; pop. (1989c) 22,131.

Rose·town \ˈrōz-ˌtau̇n\. Town, Saskatchewan, Canada, 72 mi. (116 km.) SW of Saskatoon; pop. (1991c) 2519.

Ro·set·ta \rō-ˈze-tə\ *or Arab.* **Ra·shīd** \rä-ˈshēd\; *anc.* **Bol·bi·ti·ne** \ˌbäl-bə-ˈtī-nē\. **1.** Name given to W branch of Nile River in the Nile Delta, Egypt; ab. 146 mi. (235 km.) long; its mouth is the **Rosetta Mouth** (*anc.* **Bol·bi·tin·ic Mouth** \ˌbäl-bə-ˈti-nik\).

\ə\ abut \ə\ matches \$^{ə}$\ kitten, Fr table \ər\ further \a\ ash \ā\ ace \ä\ cot, cart \ȧ\ Fr bac \au̇\ out \b\ Span Avila \ch\ chin \e\ bet \ē\ easy \g\ go \i\ hit \ī\ ice \j\ job \k\ Ger ich, Buch \$^{n}$\ Fr vin \ŋ\ sing \ō\ go \ȯ\ all \ȯ\ law \œ\ Fr bœuf \œ̄\ Fr feu \ȯi\ boy \th\ thin \th\ this \ü\ loot \u̇\ foot \ue\ Ger füllen \ᵫ\ Fr rue \y\ yet \$^{y}$\ Fr digne \ˈdēn^{y}\, nuit \ˈnw^{y}ē\ \yü\ few \yu̇\ fury \zh\ vision

2. City, Beheira governorate, Egypt, on left bank of the Rosetta, ab. 9 mi. (14 km.) SSE of its mouth; pop. (1986p) 52,014. The Rosetta stone, a piece of black basalt, was found near here 1799; it bears a trilingual inscription (in hieroglyphics, demotic characters, and Greek) and furnished the clue to Jean-François Champollion, French Egyptologist, and others toward deciphering Egyptian hieroglyphics.

Rose·ville \ˈrōz-ˌvil\. **1.** City, Placer co., E California, 18 mi. (29 km.) NE of Sacramento; pop. (1990c) 44,685; pop. grew rapidly in 1980s.

2. Residential city, Macomb co., SE Michigan, 3 mi. (4.8 km.) NNE of Detroit; pop. (1990c) 51,412.

3. Village, Ramsey co., E Minnesota, N suburb of St. Paul; pop. (1990c) 33,485.

Ro·si·gna·no Ma·rit·ti·mo \ˌrō-zē-ˈnyä-nō-mä-ˈrē-tē-ˌmō\. Commune, Livorno prov., Tuscany, W Italy, near Ligurian Sea 10 mi. (16 km.) ESE of the commune of Livorno; pop. (1989c) 30,087.

Ro·sil·los Mountains \rō-ˈsē-yəs\. Range, S Brewster co., W Texas; highest ab. 5420 ft. (1650 m.).

Ro·şio·ri de Ve·de \rō-ˈshyōr-dā-ˈvā-dā\. Commune, Teleorman co., S Romania, ab. 58 mi. (93 km.) SW of Bucharest; pop. (1989c) 37,386; textiles, food products.

Rositten. See RĒZEKNE.

Ros·kil·de \ˈrȯs-ˌki-lə\. **1.** County, E Sjælland I., Denmark. See table at DENMARK.

2. City, ⊗ of Roskilde co., Denmark, at head of Roskilde Fjord, W of Copenhagen; pop. (1991e) 49,593; residential suburb of Copenhagen; ✻ of Denmark from 10th cent. to 1443; cathedral, dating from 12th cent. and containing Danish royal mausoleum; scene of the signing of the Peace of Roskilde 1658 bet. Denmark and Sweden.

Roskilde Fjord. E extension of Ise Fjord on N coast of Sjælland, Denmark; extends S inland for ab. 25 mi. (40 km.).

Ro·slavl' *or* **Roslavl** \ˈrȯ-ˌsläv-ᵊlʸ\. Town, S Smolensk Oblast, W Russia in Europe, ab. 65 mi. (105 km.) SE of the city of Smolensk; pop. (1991e) 60,700; in WWII occupied by Germans 1941–43.

Ros·lyn \ˈräz-lən\. Residential village, Nassau co., SE New York, on Long Island ab. 4 mi. (6 km.) N of Mineola; pop. (1990c) 1965; home and burial place of poet and editor William Cullen Bryant. Adjacent villages are **Roslyn Harbor** and **Roslyn Estates,** of which **Roslyn Heights** is the post office.

Ros·ny–sous–Bois \rō-ˌnē-sü-ˈbwä\. Commune, Seine-St.-Denis dept., N France, an E suburb of Paris.

Ro·so·li·ni \ˌrō-zō-ˈlē-nē\. Commune, Siracusa prov., SE Sicily, Italy, 25 mi. (40 km.) SW of seaport of Siracusa; pop. (1989c) 21,128.

Ross \ˈrȯs\. **1.** County in S Ohio. See table at OHIO.

2. Urban township, Allegheny co., SW Pennsylvania, N of Pittsburgh; pop. (1990c) 33,482.

Ross, Mount. Peak, Kerguelen I., in the Indian Ocean; 6430 ft. (1960 m.); highest point on the island.

Ross and Crom·ar·ty \ˈkrä-mər-tē\. Former county, N Scotland, incl. Lewis I. in the Outer Hebrides; ⊗ Dingwall; a mountainous region with many lochs.

Ros·sa·no \rȯ-ˈsä-nō\; *anc.* **Ros·ci·a·num** \ˌrä-sē-ˈā-nəm, -ˈa-\. Commune, Cosenza prov., Calabria, S Italy, near Gulf of Taranto 29 mi. (47 km.) NE of the commune of Cosenza; pop. (1989c) 35,213; archiepiscopal see; 10th cent. church; religious museum has valuable 6th cent. Byzantine manuscript of the Gospels.

Ross·bach \ˈrȯs-ˌbäk\. Village, Saxony-Anhalt, E cen. Germany, 8 mi. (13 km.) SW of Merseburg; scene of battle 1757, during Seven Years' War, in which Prussians under Frederick the Great defeated the French and Austrians.

Ross Barrier. See ROSS ICE SHELF.

Ross Dam. See UNITED STATES, *Dams and Reservoirs.*

Ross Dependency. Section of Antarctica lying S of 60°S and bet. 160°E and 150°W; includes Balleny Is., Coulman I., Ross I., Scott I., and the shores of Ross Sea (Edward VII Penin. and part of Victoria Land), also Little America and Roosevelt I. in the Ross Ice Shelf area; ab. 165,000 sq. mi. (427,350 sq. km.) land and 130,000 sq. mi. (336,700 sq. km.) permanent ice shelf; by act of British parliament placed under jurisdiction of New Zealand 1923.

Ros·seau, Lake \ˈrȯ-sō\. Lake in Muskoka Lake Region, Muskoka dist., SE Ontario, Canada; connected with Lake Joseph and Lake Muskoka (see MUSKOKA, LAKE).

Ros·sel \ˈrȯ-səl\. Island, easternmost of the Louisiade Archipelago, Papua New Guinea, in Solomon Sea 22 mi. (35 km.) NE of Tagula I.; ab. 21 mi. (34 km.) long by 7 mi. (11 km.) wide.

Ross·ford \ˈrȯs-fərd\. Village, Wood co., NW Ohio, 3 mi. (5 km.) S of Toledo; pop. (1990c) 5861.

Ross Ice Shelf. Ice shelf, Antarctica, bordering on S part of Ross Sea and extending inland over 500 mi. (800 km.); bordered on S and W by Transantarctic Mts. (see ANTARCTICA) and on E by Marie Byrd Land; its N edge, formerly known as **Ross Barrier,** extends ab. 500 mi. (800 km.) from Ross I. to Edward VII Penin. and rises 50 to 200 ft. (15 to 60 m.) high; discovered 1841 by Scottish explorer Capt. James Ross; in 20th cent. crossed by several expeditions to the interior, incl. those of Norwegian explorer Roald Amundsen and of English explorer Robert Scott 1911; region intensively explored and made site of several permanent research stations.

Ros·sig·nol, Lake \ˈrä-sig-ˌnäl\. Lake, SW Nova Scotia, Canada.

Ross Island. 1. Island, Weddell Sea, Antarctica. See JAMES ROSS ISLAND.

2. Island in Ross Sea, W Ross Dependency, Antarctica, at W end of Ross Ice Shelf; separated from Victoria Land by McMurdo Sound; highest point Mt. Erebus 12,450 ft. (3795 m.); has also Mt. Terror 10,750 ft. (3277 m.).

3. Island, Myanmar. See DAUNG ISLAND.

4. Island, Kerry, Ireland. See KILLARNEY, LAKES OF.

Rossiya. See RUSSIA.

Ross·land \ˈrȯs-ˌland, -lənd\. Residential city, SE British Columbia, Canada, near U.S. border 5 mi. (8 km.) W of Trail; pop. (1991c) 3557; winter resort.

Ross·lau \ˈrȯs-ˌlau̇\. City, Saxony-Anhalt, E Germany, on Elbe River N of Dessau.

Ros·so \ˈrȯ-sō\. Town, SW Mauritania, across Senegal River from Senegal; pop. (1988c) 27,783.

Ross of Mull. See MULL, ROSS OF.

Ross Quadrant. Former quarter section of Antarctica (*q.v.*) bet. 90°W and 180°W; now chiefly E part of Ross Dependency, Marie Byrd Land, and W part of Ellsworth Land.

Ross Sea. Arm of S Pacific Ocean bet. Victoria Land and Edward VII Penin., extending into Antarctica to ab. 85°S; on S borders an extensive area of Ross Ice Shelf. Discovered 1841 by Scottish explorer Capt. James Ross.

Ross·ville \ˈrȯs-ˌvil\. City, Walker co., NW Georgia, on Tennessee border 23 mi. (37 km.) WNW of Dalton; pop. (1990c) 3601; suburb of Chattanooga, Tenn.

Ros·tock \ˈrȯ-ˌstȯk, ˈräs-ˌtäk\. **1.** District of former East Germany.

2. *also* **Rostock–War·ne·mün·de** \-ˌvär-nə-ˈmue̅n-də\. City and seaport, Mecklenburg-West Pomerania, NE Germany, on the Warnow River 8 mi. (13 km.) from the Baltic and 41 mi. (66 km.) WSW of Stralsund; pop. (1981c) 234,475; produces diesel engines, chemicals; fishing center; a major shipbuilding center before German reunification; 15th cent. brick church; 15th cent. town hall; university (1419). Founded during 12th cent.; chartered 1218; member of Hanseatic League in 14th cent.; in WWII heavily damaged by Allied bombing. Birthplace of Prussian Field Marshal Gebhard Leberecht von Blücher 1742.

Ros·tov \rə-ˈstȯf, -ˈstȯv\. **1.** Medieval Russian principality, cen. Russia; united with Suzdal' (*q.v.*) as Rostov-Suzdal' (*q.v.*) principality; superseded by Vladimir and Moscow.

2. *formerly* **Rostov–Ya·ro·slav·ski** *or* **Rostov–Ya·ro·slav·skiy** \-ˌyir-ə-ˈsläf-skē\ *or* **Rostov–Ve·li·ki** *or* **Rostov–Ve·li·kiy** \-vi-ˈlē-kē\. Town, S Yaroslavl' Oblast, W cen. Russia in Europe, on small lake 35 mi. (56 km.) SW of Yaroslavl'; pop. (1991e) 36,400; handmade enamelware; 13th cent. cathedral; several 17th cent. churches. A very early Slavic town; ✻ of medieval Rostov-Suzdal' principality; came under Moscow 1474.

Rostov–na–Do·nu \-nä-ˈdȯ-nü\ *or Eng.* **Rostov–on–Don** \-ˈdän\. City, ✻ of Rostov Oblast, S Russia in Europe, on N bank of the Don ab. 28 mi. (45 km.) from its mouth on the Gulf of Taganrog (Sea of Azov); pop. (1992e) 1,027,000; an important industrial center, producing agricultural machinery, barges, electrical equipment, wire, road-making machinery, footwear, chemicals, tobacco products, wine; university (1917). Founded as customs post 1749; fortified 1761 and made town 1797; in WWII occupied by Germans and suffered extensive damage.

Rostov Oblast \ˈō-bləst, -ˌblast\ *or* **Ros·tov·ska·ya Oblast'** \rə-ˈstȯf-skə-yə\. Administrative subdivision of S Russia in Europe, on the lower Don; 38,919 sq. mi. (100,800 sq. km.); pop. (1992e) 4,363,000; ✻ Rostov-na-Donu. Consists largely of low fertile plains along the Don and its tributaries; wheat, corn, melons, barley; vineyards; coal mining; some heavy industry. Chief towns Rostov-na-Donu, Taganrog, Shakhty, Novocherkassk, Novoshakhtinsk. Region of the lower Don held by Tatars c. 13th–15th cents.; largely under Russian rule from mid-16th cent. except for S part which remained Turkish as part of Khanate of the Crimea until 18th cent.; long inhabited by the Don Cossacks, and approx. coextensive with former Terr. of the Don Cossacks (see DON COSSACKS, TERRITORY OF THE); in WWII, parts occupied by Germans 1941–43.

Ro·stov–Suz·dal' *or* **Ros·tov–Suz·dal** \-ˈsüz-dəl^{y}\. Medieval Russian principality, in cen. part of Russia, NE of modern Moscow; ✻ Rostov; chief towns Rostov, Suzdal', Vladimir (*q.v.*), Tver', and Moscow; absorbed 14th–15th cents. by rapidly growing Moscow principality.

Rostov–Veliki *or* **Rostov–Velikiy** *or* **Rostov–Yaroslavski** *or* **Rostov–Yaroslavskiy.** See ROSTOV 2.

Roşu. See TURNU ROŞU.

Røs·vatn \ˈrœs-ˌvät-^{ə}n\. Lake, S Nordland co., N Norway.

Ros·well \ˈräz-ˌwel, -wəl\. **1.** Residential city, Fulton co., NW cen. Georgia, 18 mi. (29 km.) N of Atlanta; pop. (1990c) 47,923; pop. more than doubled bet. 1980 and 1990.

2. City, ⊗ of Chavez co., SE New Mexico, 95 mi. (153 km.) N of Texas border; pop. (1990c) 44,654; ships livestock, cotton, fruit; oil wells; New Mexico Military Institute (1891); Eastern New Mexico Univ.–Roswell (1958). Founded 1871; incorp. 1891.

Ro·syth \rō-ˈsīth\. Village, Fife, E Scotland, on N shore of Firth of Forth; pop. (1981c) 10,061; site of naval base, a major base in WWI and WWII, now a base for nuclear-powered submarines.

Ro·ta \ˈrō-tə\. Island, S end of Mariana Is., W Pacific, midway bet. Guam and Tinian; ab. 35 sq. mi. (91 sq. km.); pop. (1990c) 2295; highest point 1612 ft. (491 m.); site of Japanese base used for invasion of Guam 1941, severely bombed by U.S. 1944 prior to retaking Guam.

Rotenturm. See TURNU ROŞU.

Ro·then·burg ob der Tau·ber \ˈrōt-^{ə}n-ˌbu̇rk-ˌȯp-dər-ˈtau̇-bər\. Commune, Bavaria, Germany, on Tauber River 31 mi. (50 km.) SSE of Würzburg; pop. (1992e) 11,771; textiles; medieval walls and town hall; became free imperial city 1274; at height of its prosperity at end of 14th cent.; to Bavaria 1803.

Roth·er \ˈrä-t͟hər\. **1.** River, Derbyshire and South Yorkshire, N England; flows into the Don at Rotherham; 21 mi. (34 km.) long.

2. Either of two small streams in S England: (1) in Hampshire and West Sussex; (2) in East Sussex (see ROMNEY MARSH).

Roth·er·ham \ˈrä-t͟hə-rəm\. Town, South Yorkshire, N England, at confluence of Rother and Don rivers 6 mi. (10 km.) NE of Sheffield; area pop. (1991p) 247,100; steel, iron, and brass products, machinery.

Roth·er·hithe \ˈrä-t͟hər-ˌhīt͟h\ *also* **Red·riff** \ˈred-ˌrif\. Parish in Southwark met. borough, London, England; terminus of Grand Surrey Canal.

Rothe·say \ˈräth-sē, -sā\. Burgh, Strathclyde region, Scotland on the island of Bute; pop. (1981p) 5408; naval base; resort; ruins of 11th cent. castle. "Duke of Rothesay" is highest Scottish title taken by the Prince of Wales.

Roth·schild \ˈräths-ˌchīld\. Village, Marathon co., cen. Wisconsin, 6 mi. (10 km.) S of Wausau; pop. (1990c) 3310.

Roth·well \ˈräth-ˌwel, -wəl\. Town, West Yorkshire, N England; pop. (1981p) 29,142.

Ro·ti \ˈrō-tē\ *or* **Rot·ti** \ˈrȯ-tē\. Island, Indonesia, SW of Timor; 50 mi. (80 km.) long by 14 mi. (23 km.) wide; 467 sq. mi. (1209 sq. km.); chief village Baa.

Roti Strait. Channel bet. SW end of Timor I. and the island of Roti, Indonesia; connects Savu Sea with Timor Sea.

Ro·to·a·va \ˌrō-tō-ˈä-və\. Locality on Fakarava Atoll, Tuamotu Archipelago, S Pacific Ocean; 16°03′S, 145°37′W; former headquarters of French administrator.

Rotomagus. See ROUEN.

Ro·to·ma·ha·na \ˌrō-tō-mə-ˈhä-nə\. Lake, N cen. North I., New Zealand, S of Lake Tarawera; 3.5 sq. mi. (9 sq. km.); 4 mi. (6 km.) long; famous for its sinter terraces which were destroyed by an eruption of Mt. Tarawera 1886.

Ro·ton·do, Mon·te \ˈmȯn-tā-rō-ˈtōn-dō\. Peak, in cen. part of the island of Corsica, France; 8612 ft. (2625 m.).

Rotondo, Piz·zo \ˈpēt-sō-rō-ˈtōn-dō\. Peak, Lepontine Alps, S cen. Switzerland; 10,472 ft. (3192 m.); highest in the St. Gotthard Range.

Ro·to·rua \ˌrō-tō-ˈrü-ə\. City, N cen. North I., New Zealand, at SW end of **Rotorua Lake** (31 sq. mi. or 80 sq. km.) 120 mi. (193 km.) SE of Auckland; pop. (1992e) 53,700; noted health resort with thermal springs. Area long populated by Maori before coming of Europeans.

Rot·ter·dam \ˈrȯ-tər-ˌdäm, ˈrä-tər-ˌdam\. **1.** Industrial and commercial city and seaport, South Holland prov., W Netherlands, on both sides of the Nieuwe Maas ab. 15 mi. (24 km.) from the North Sea; pop. (1992e) 589,707; one of the world's busiest cargo-handling ports; center of an extensive system of canals connecting it with the Rhine and all parts of the Netherlands; site of the Europoort, a complex of industrial sites and harbor basins opp. the Hoek van Holland, begun 1958; produces chemicals, paper, clothing; brewing, distilling, oil refining, shipbuilding; engineering; 15th cent. church; 17th cent. Schielandhaus; museum; public gardens.

History: Founded 13th cent. and a major commercial city from c. 1340; experienced great prosperity during late 16th and 17th cent.; occupied by French 1795–1813; in WWII center of city destroyed by German bombing 1940, largely reconstructed to new plan.

2. Town, Schenectady co., E New York, NW of the city of Schenectady; pop. (1990c) 28,395.

Rotti. See ROTI.

Rot·tum·er·oog \ˈrȯ-tə-mə-ˌrōg\. Island of Netherlands in the North Sea 4 mi. (6 km.) SW of Borkum; easternmost of the Dutch West Frisian Is.

Rott·weil \ˈrȯt-ˌvīl\. City, Baden-Württemberg, Germany, on Neckar River 49 mi. (79 km.) SSW of Stuttgart; pop. (1980c) 23,673. The rottweiler breed of dog originated here.

Ro·tu·ma \rō-ˈtü-mə\. Chief island of small group of eight islands, Fiji in SW Pacific Ocean, 12°30′S and 177°5′E, 220 mi. (354 km.) NNW of Fiji I.; ab. 8 mi. (13 km.) long, area 14 sq. mi. (36 sq. km.); pop. (1986c) 2688; administratively part of Fiji since 1881. Original Rotumans were pure Polynesians. Explored 1791 by British.

Rouad, Île. See ARWAD.

Rou·baix \rü-ˈbā\. City, Nord dept., N France, 7 mi. (11 km.) NE of Lille; pop. (1990c) 98,179; center of French textile industry; rubber and plastics factories; chartered 15th cent.; textile industry developed in 19th cent.; occupied by Germany in WWI and WWII.

Rou·en \ru̇-ˈä^{n}, -ˈän\; *anc.* **Ro·tom·a·gus** \rō-ˈtä-mə-gəs\. Commercial city and river port, ✻ of Seine-Maritime dept., N France, on right bank of Seine River 71 mi. (114 km.) NW of Paris; pop. (1990c) 105,470; ships wine; produces textiles, chemicals, paper, brandy. Has an exceptional number of notable buildings, incl. the 13th cent. Gothic cathedral (restored after heavy damage in WWII), 14th cent. abbey of St. Ouen (where national heroine Joan of Arc was sentenced to death 1431), 15th cent. church, late Gothic palace of justice (housing the law courts), museum, and several medieval houses; university (1964).

History: Founded in pre-Roman times; sacked by Normans 9th cent. A.D.; became medieval ✻ of Normandy; held by English 1066–1203 and 1419–49; Joan of Arc burned at the stake here 1431; taken by Huguenots 1562; produced famous soft-paste ceramic wares 17th–18th cents.; occupied by Germans 1870 in Franco-Prussian War; in WWII suffered heavy bombing damage. Birthplace of writers Pierre Corneille (1606), Bernard Fontenelle (1657), and Gustave Flaubert (1821).

Rou·ergue \rü-'erg\. Ancient province (until 1789) of S France, in region now comprising Aveyron dept. and a small part of Tarn-et-Garonne dept.; ✻ Rodez; medieval countship eventually attached to the crown by Henry IV.

Rouffaer. See TARIKU.

Roufiás. See ALPHEUS.

Rouge \'rüzh\. River, SW Quebec, Canada; flows S and empties into the Ottawa River in SW Argenteuil co.; ab. 120 mi. (190 km.) long.

Roulers. See ROESELARE.

Roum. See RUM.

Roumania. See ROMANIA.

Roumelia. See RUMELIA.

Round Butte Dam. See UNITED STATES, *Dams and Reservoirs.*

Round·house Rock \'raůnd-,haůs\. Peak, Cheyenne co., W Nebraska; 4255 ft. (1297 m.).

Round Lake. **1.** Small lake, W cen. Lake co., NE Illinois; surrounded by the villages of Round Lake, Round Lake Beach, and Round Lake Park.

2. Village, W cen. Lake co., NE Illinois, SW of Round Lake (sense 1); pop. (1990c) 3550.

Round Lake Beach. Village, W cen. Lake co., NE Illinois, N of Round Lake; pop. (1990c) 16,434.

Round Lake Park. Village, W cen. Lake co., NE Illinois, S of Round Lake; pop. (1990c) 4045.

Round Rock. Town, Williamson co., cen. Texas, 18 mi. (29 km.) N of Austin; pop. (1990c) 30,923; pop. more than doubled bet. 1980 and 1990.

Round·top \'raůnd-,täp\. **1.** Mountain, Scotts Bluff co., W Nebraska; 4419 ft. (1347 m.).

2. Elevation, Tioga co., N Pennsylvania; 2030 ft. (619 m.).

Round Top. Elevation forming a granite spur at S end of Cemetery Ridge (*q.v.*), Gettysburg, Pennsylvania; vantage point held by far left flank of Union forces on 2d and 3d days of battle of Gettysburg.

Round·up \'raůnd-,əp\. City, ⊗ of Musselshell co., cen. Montana, 45 mi. (72 km.) N of Billings; pop. (1990c) 1808.

Round·way Down \'raůn-dwā\. Hill near Devizes, Wiltshire, SW England; 796 ft. (243 m.); Parliamentarian forces defeated here by Royalists 1643.

Rour·ke·la *or* **Raur·ke·la** \rȯr-'kā-lə\. Town, Orissa, India, ab. 140 mi. (225 km.) NW of Cuttack; pop. (1981e) 321,326; iron and steel plant.

Rou·say \'raů-zē\. One of the Orkney Is. (*q.v.*), off N coast of Scotland; 5.25 mi. (8.4 km.) long by 4.5 mi. (7.2 km.) wide.

Rous·es Point \'raů-səz\. Village and port of entry, Clinton co., NE corner of New York, at the upper end of Lake Champlain at Canadian border 21 mi. (34 km.) N of Plattsburg; pop. (1990c) 2377.

Rous·sil·lon \,rü-sē-'yōn\. **1.** Historical region of S France, bounded anciently on N by Languedoc, on S by the Pyrenees, on W by Andorra, and on NW by Countship of Foix; ✻ Perpignan (12th cent. ff.). Inhabited orig. by Iberians; made part of Roman Gallia Narbonensis (see GAUL); subsequently came under Visigoths, Arabs, and Carolingian Franks; became separate county c. 10th cent.; united to Aragon 1172; included in kingdom of Majorca 13th–14th cents., then reunited to Aragon; acquired from Spain by Louis XIV of France 1659 (Treaty of the Pyrenees); province of France under ancien régime; approx. coextensive with dept. of Pyrénées-Orientales created after the French Revolution.

2. County, Quebec, Canada. See table at QUEBEC.

Routt \'raůt\. County in NW Colorado. See table at COLORADO.

Rou·ville \'rü-,vil\. County, S Quebec, Canada. See table at QUEBEC.

Rou·vroy \rü-'vrwä\. Commune, Pas-de-Calais dept., N France, 9 mi. (14 km.) NE of Arras.

Rouyn–No·ran·da \'rü-ən-nȯ-'ran-də, rü-'ēn-,nȯ-rän-'dä\. **1.** County, Quebec, Canada. See table at QUEBEC.

2. City, Rouyn-Noranda co., SW Quebec, Canada, 240 mi. (386 km.) NW of Ottawa and on railroad line N of Lake Timiskaming; pop. (1991c) 26,448; center of copper-mining and gold-mining district; settled 1920s; incorp. as a city 1948; has developed in close association with the city of Noranda.

Ro·va·nie·mi \'rȯ-vä-,nye-mē\. City, ✻ of Lappi prov., Finland, ab. 100 mi. (160 km.) N of Oulu; pop. (1992e) 33,954; destroyed by Germans in WWII, completely rebuilt, largely on designs of architect Alvar Aalto.

Ro·ven'·ki *or* **Rovenki** \'rȯ-vən-kē\. Town, Luhans'k subdivision, Ukraine, ab. 34 mi. (55 km.) S of city of Luhans'k; pop. (1991e) 59,000.

Ro·ve·re·to \,rō-vā-'rā-tō\ *or Ger.* **Ro·freit** \'rō-,frīt\. Commune, Trento prov., Trentino-Alto Adige, N Italy, on Adige River 13 mi. (21 km.) SSW of the commune of Trento; pop. (1991p) 31,617; tourism; chemicals, textiles, paper; medieval fortifications; art and historical collections; WWI museum. Scene of battle in which French Emperor Napoléon defeated the Austrians 1796; taken from Austrians by Italians in WWI. Birthplace of archaeologist Paulo Orsi (1859) and philosopher Antonio Rosmini-Serbati (1797).

Rove Tunnel \'rōv, 'rȯv\ *or Fr.* **Sou·ter·rain du Rove** \sü-ter-,en-dūē-'rȯv\. Tunnel, Bouches-du-Rhône dept., SE France, in the hills NW of Marseille; 4.5 mi. (7.2 km.) long, 59 ft. (18 m.) wide, and 50 ft. (15 m.) high; provides a sea-level passageway for the Marseille-Rhone Canal.

Ro·vi·a·na \,rō-vē-'ä-nə\. See NEW GEORGIA 2.

Ro·vi·go \rō-'vē-gō\. **1.** Province of Veneto, NE Italy. See table at ITALY.

2. Commune, its ✻, 36 mi. (58 km.) SW of Venice; pop. (1991p) 52,058; center of agricultural region; 16th cent. octagonal church; museum; cathedral; palaces; commune first mentioned 838; ruled by Este family until it came under Venice 1482; to Austria 1797; became part of Italy 1866.

Ro·vinj \'rō-,vēn-yə\; *Ital.* **Ro·vi·gno** \rō-'vē-nyō\ *or* **Rovigno d'I·stria** \-'dēs-trē-ä\. Seaport commune, Istria Penin., W Croatia, on Adriatic Sea 17 mi. (27 km.) NNW of Pula; pop. (1991c) 13,821; formerly in Italy.

Rovno. See RIVNE.

Rovuma. See RUVUMA 1.

Row·an *Ky.* 'raů-ən, *N.C.* 'rō-,an\. Name of counties in two states of the U.S. See tables at KENTUCKY and NORTH CAROLINA.

Row·lett \'raů-lət\. City, Dallas co., NE Texas; pop. (1990c) 23,260; pop. more than tripled bet. 1980 and 1990.

Row·ley \'raů-lē\. Town, Essex co., NE corner of Massachusetts, 22 mi. (35 km.) ENE of Lowell; pop. (1990c) 4452; settled 1638.

Równe *or* **Rowno.** See RIVNE 2.

Row·ter, Mount \'raů-tər\. Peak, Gunnison co., W cen. Colorado; 13,750 ft. (4191 m.).

Ro·xas \'rō-,häs\; *formerly* **Ca·piz** \'kä-,pēs\. Chartered city, ✻ of Capiz prov., Panay I., Philippines; pop. (1990p) 103,000; trades in rice.

Rox·boro \'räks-,bər-ō\. **1.** City, ⊗ of Person co., N North Carolina, 27 mi. (43 km.) N of Durham; pop. (1990c) 7332.

2. Town, Montreal co., S Quebec, Canada, 8 mi. (13 km.) W of the city of Montreal; pop. (1991c) 5879.

Rox·burgh \'räks-,bər-ə, -bə-rə\ *or* **Rox·burgh·shire** \-,shir, -shər\. Former county, SE Scotland; ⊗ Jedburgh; rivers Teviot, Tweed; mountainous region.

Rox·bury \'räks-,ber-ē, -bə-rē\. **1.** Residential district, S Boston, Massachusetts; formerly a city, founded 1630; became part of Boston 1868.

2. Town, Delaware co., S New York, 18 mi. (29 km.) E of Delhi; pop. (1990c) 2388; birthplace of railroad executive and financier Jay Gould 1836.

Rox·en, Lake \ˈrök-sən\. Lake, SE Sweden, bet. Lake Vättern and the Baltic Sea; ab. 16 mi. (26 km.) long; Linköping is near its S shore.

Ro·xo, Cape \ˈrō-shü\. Point on W coast of Africa, at S end of coast of Senegal, 12°20′N, 16°43′W.

Roy \ˈrȯi\. City, Weber co., NE Utah, SW of Ogden; pop. (1990c) 24,603.

Roy·al, Mount \ˈrȯi-əl\ *or Fr.* **Mont Roy·al** \ˌmōⁿ-rwä-ˈyäl\. A height in center of the city of Montreal, Quebec, Canada; 769 ft. (234 m.).

Roy·ale \rwä-ˈyal\. One of the Safety Is. (*q.v.*), French Guiana, off the N coast.

Royale, Isle. See ISLE ROYALE.

Royal Gorge. Scenic gorge of the Arkansas River just W of Canon City, S cen. Colorado; 4.5 mi. (7.2 km.) long; its red granite walls rise sheerly more than 1000 ft. (300 m.). Railroad runs through bottom of gorge; gorge crossed by Royal Gorge Suspension Bridge 1053 ft. (321 m.) above the Arkansas River.

Royal Leamington Spa. Town, England. See LEAMINGTON.

Royal Oak. City, Oakland co., SE Michigan, 3 mi. (4.8 km.) N of Detroit; pop. (1990c) 65,410; residential suburb of Detroit.

Royal Palm Beach. Village, Palm Beach co., Florida; pop. (1990c) 14,589; pop. more than quadrupled bet. 1980 and 1990.

Royal Society Range. Mountain range, Antarctica, ab. 77°55′S, N Victoria Land.

Royal Tsavo National Park. See TSAVO NATIONAL PARK.

Royal Tunbridge Wells. See TUNBRIDGE WELLS.

Roy·an \rwä-ˈyäⁿ\. Commune, Charente-Maritime dept., W France, on Atlantic Ocean at mouth of the Gironde; largely destroyed in WWII bombing, but since rebuilt.

Roye \ˈrwä\. Town, Somme dept., N France, 18 mi. (29 km.) N of Compiègne; scene of fighting in WWI.

Roy·ers·ford \ˈrȯi-ərz-fərd\. Borough, Montgomery co., SE Pennsylvania, on Schuylkill River 27 mi. (43 km.) NW of Philadelphia; pop. (1990c) 4458.

Roys·ton \ˈrȯi-stən\. **1.** City, Franklin, Hart, and Madison cos., NE Georgia, NE of Athens; pop. (1990c) 2758.

2. Town, South Yorkshire, N England; pop. (1981p) 8901.

Roy·ton \ˈrȯit-ᵊn\. Town, Greater Manchester co., NW England; pop. (1981p) 21,233.

Ro·ze·wie, Cape \rō-ˈzē-vyə\ *or Ger.* **Kap Rix·höft** \ˈkäp-ˈriks-ˌhœft\. Cape on coast of Poland projecting into the Baltic Sea just W of base of Hel Penin.

Rózsahegy. See RUŽOMBEROK.

Roz·za·no \rōd-ˈzä-nō\. Commune, Milano prov., Lombardy, N Italy; pop. (1989c) 39,100.

Rrëshen \ˈrə-shən\. Town, ✻ of Mirditë dist., N cen. Albania.

Ruacana Falls. See CUNENE.

Ruaha, Great. See GREAT RUAHA.

Ru·a·ha National Park \rü-ˈä-hä\. National park, Tanzania; 5000 sq. mi. (12,950 sq. km.); habitat for wildlife, incl. elephant, lion, ostrich, zebra; estab. 1964.

Ruanda. See RWANDA.

Ru·an·da–Urun·di \rü-ˈän-dä-ü-ˈrün-dē\ *also* **Belgian East Africa.** Former Belgian trust territory, cen. Africa; 20,916 sq. mi. (54,172 sq. km.); ✻ Usumbura; comprised two districts, Ruanda (now Rwanda) in N and Urundi (now Burundi) in S; formerly part of German East Africa, was ceded to Belgium after WWI; administered as mandate of the League of Nations, and later (1946) as trust territory of UN; united administratively with Belgian Congo 1925–60; divided 1962 into two independent countries, Rwanda and Burundi. See RWANDA and BURUNDI.

Ru·a·pe·hu, Mount \ˌrü-ə-ˈpā-hü\. Volcano, S cen. North I., New Zealand, in Tongariro National Park; 9175 ft. (2796 m.).

Ru·a·pu·ke \ˌrü-ə-ˈpü-kē\. Small island, New Zealand, at E end of Foveaux Strait off S coast of South I.

Rub‘ al–Kha·li \ˈrüb-al-ˈkȧ-lē\ *or* **Ar Ri·mal** \ˌär-rē-ˈmal\ *or Eng.* **Great Sandy Desert.** Desert region, S Arabian Penin., extending S from Nejd, Saudi Arabia to Ḥaḍramawt, Yemen and E into United Arab Emirates and Oman; ab. 250,000 sq. mi. (647,500 sq. km.); comprises a vast area of continuous sand that has been little explored.

Ru·bezh·no·ye \rü-ˈbyezh-nə-yə\. Town, Luhans'k subdivision, Ukraine, ab. 50 mi. (80 km.) NW of city of Luhans'k; pop. (1991e) 75,000.

Rubi. See RUVO DI PUGLIA.

Ru·bi·con \ˈrü-bi-ˌkän\ *or* **Ru·bi·co·ne** \ˌrü-bē-ˈkō-nā\. Small river, N cen. Italy; flows E into Adriatic Sea at 44°10′N just N of Rimini; with the Apennines, formed boundary bet. Italy and Cisalpine Gaul in the time of the ancient Roman republic. Its crossing in 49 B.C. by Julius Caesar with his army began a Roman civil war against Pompey the Great and the senate.

Ru·bi·doux, Mount \ˌrü-bi-ˈdü\. Rocky height in the city of Riverside, Riverside co., SE California; has on its top a cross dedicated to memory of Junípero Serra, Spanish missionary to the Indians inhabiting W North America.

Rubrum, Mare. See ERYTHRAEAN SEA.

Rub·tsovsk \ˈrüpt-ˌsȯfsk\. Town, Altay Kray, S Russia in Asia, ab. 80 mi. (130 km.) NE of Semey; pop. (1992e) 172,000.

Ru·by \ˈrü-bē\. Village, W cen. Alaska, on S bank of the Yukon ab. 240 mi. (390 km.) W of Fairbanks; pop. (1990c) 170.

Ruby Dome. See RUBY MOUNTAINS.

Ruby Lake. Lake in S Elko co. and N White Pine co., NE Nevada.

Ruby Mountains. Range chiefly in S Elko co., NE Nevada, extending S into White Pine co.; highest peak **Ruby Dome,** Elko co., 11,387 ft. (3471 m.).

Rück·er, Mount \ˈrü-kər\. Mountain, Antarctica, 78°11′S, 162°32′E; 12,520 ft. (3816 m.).

Ru·dall River National Park \ˈrü-ˌdȯl\. National park, N cen. Western Australia, Australia, one of the country's largest; an arid landscape with water holes.

Ru·da Śląs·ka \ˌrü-də-ˈshlōⁿ-skə\. Commune, Katowice prov., S Poland, just E of Zabrze; pop. (1989e) 169,789.

Rūd–e Māshkid. See MASHKEL.

Rud·kø·bing \ˈrü-ˌkœ-biŋ\. Town, Fyn co., Denmark, on W coast of Langeland I.; pop. (1981c) 6998.

Rud·nik Mountains \ˈrüd-nik\. Low mountain range in N Serbia, Yugoslavia; highest peak 3714 ft. (1132 m.).

Rud·ny \ˈrüd-nē\. Town, Kustanai subdivision, Kazakhstan, ab. 25 mi. (40 km.) SW of the town of Qostanay; pop. (1991e) 128,800.

Rudolf, Lake. See TURKANA, LAKE.

Ru·dolph \ˈrü-ˌdälf\. Island, northernmost of Franz Josef Land, Russia, in Arctic Ocean; meteorological station.

Ru·dol·stadt \ˈrüd-ᵊl-ˌshtät\. City, Thuringia, E cen. Germany, on Saale River 18 mi. (29 km.) S of Weimar; pop. (1981c) 31,287; chemicals, porcelain.

Rueil–Mal·mai·son \ˌrwā-ˌmal-mā-ˈzōⁿ\. Industrial commune, Hauts-de-Seine dept., N France, on Seine River 8 mi. (13 km.) W of Paris; pop. (1990c) 67,323; manufactures photographic supplies, pharmaceuticals, automobile parts; tombs of Empress Josephine and her daughter Queen Hortense.

Ru·fi·ji \rü-ˈfē-jē\. Navigable river, E Africa; rises in S cen. Tanzania; flows NE and E into Indian Ocean opp. island of Mafia; ab. 175 mi. (280 km.) long.

Ru·fisque \rü-ˈfēsk\. Commune, W Senegal, near Dakar and 10 mi. (16 km.) E of Cap Vert; pop. (1988c) 137,150; leather goods, cement, vegetable oils.

Rug·by \ˈrəg-bē\. **1.** City, ⊗ of Pierce co., N cen. North Dakota, 65 mi. (105 km.) E of Minot; pop. (1990c) 2909. Nearby is the point determined by the U.S. Geological Survey to be the geographic center of North America.

2. Town, Warwickshire, cen. England, on the Avon 28 mi. (45 km.) ESE of Birmingham; pop. (1991p) 83,400; railroad junction; electrical equipment; site of Rugby School (founded 1567), where the game of rugby was invented.

Ruge·ley \ˈrüj-lē\. Town, Staffordshire, W cen. England, 9 mi. (14 km.) SE of Stafford; pop. (1981p) 24,340.

Rü·gen \ˈrǖ-gən\. Island in the Baltic Sea, administratively part of Mecklenburg-West Pomerania, Germany, opp. Stralsund; largest island of Germany; 358 sq. mi. (927 sq. km.); pop. (1990e) 87,248; chief town Bergen. Separated by the narrow Strelasund from the mainland. Chief economic activity fishing. Has many prehistoric sites; seized by the Danes 1168; united with Pomerania 1325 and with Sweden 1648; became part of Prussia 1815.

Ruhr \ˈrür\. River, Germany; flows NW and W and joins the Rhine at **Ruhr·ort** \-ˌȯrt\ (a part of Duisburg); 146 mi. (235 km.) long; navigable to Witten, ab. 30 mi. (48 km.). The **Ruhr·ge·biet** \ˈrür-gə-ˌbēt\ *or* **Ruhr Valley** is a mining region with many industrial cities, incl. Essen, Bochum, Duisburg, Gelsenkirchen, and Dortmund. In WWI the district was of great military importance; occupied 1923–25 by France and Belgium because of Germany's default in war reparations; in WWII bombed severely and continuously 1942–45; occupied by Allies 1945.

Ru·i·do·so \ˌrü-ē-ˈdō-sō\. Village, Lincoln co., S cen. New Mexico, pop. (1990c) 4600.

Rui·vo, Pi·co \ˈpē-kü-rü-ˈē-vü\. Volcanic peak on the island of Madeira; 6106 ft. (1861 m.); highest point in the Madeira Is.

Ruiz, Ne·va·do del \ne-ˈbä-thō-ˌthel-rü-ˈēs, -ˈēz\. Volcanic peak in the Andes, in Tolima dept., W cen. Colombia; 17,716 ft. (5400 m.); destructive eruption Nov. 1985 resulted in more than 20,000 deaths.

Ru·ki \ˈrü-kē\. River, NW Democratic Rep. of the Congo; flows W into Congo River at Mbandaka at the Equator; ab. 250 mi. (400 km.) long; has several long tributaries, esp. the Busira.

Ru·kwa \ˈrü-kwä\. Region of W Tanzania; formerly part of Tabora region. See table at TANZANIA.

Rukwa, Lake. Shallow lake, SW Tanzania; ab. 20 mi. (32 km.) long.

Rule·ville \ˈrül-ˌvil, -vəl\. City, Sunflower co., W Mississippi; pop. (1990c) 3245.

Rum *or* **Rhum** \ˈrəm\. Island of the Inner Hebrides, off W coast of Scotland; 8 sq. mi. (21 sq. km.); administratively a part of Highland region.

Rum \ˈrüm\ *or* **Roum** \ˈrüm\ *also* **Ico·ni·um** \ī-ˈkō-nē-əm\. The Seljuq sultanate c. 12th–13th cents. occupying much of cen. and E Asia Minor; ✻ Iconium; declined 13th cent.; subsequently to Mongols.

Rum, Sound of. Channel bet. Isle of Rum and Eigg I. in the Inner Hebrides, off W coast of Scotland.

Ru·ma \ˈrü-mə\. Commune, Serbia, N Yugoslavia, 35 mi. (56 km.) NW of Belgrade.

Ru·mai·la \rü-ˈmī-lə, -ˈmā-\. Oil field, SE Iraq and extending across border into Kuwait; believed to be one of the world's largest oil reserves.

Rumania. See ROMANIA.

Rum Cay \ˈrəm\. One of the Bahamas, in the Atlantic Ocean SSW of San Salvador (Watling); 30 sq. mi. (78 sq. km.); pop. (with San Salvador [1980c]) 804.

Ru·me·lia *also* **Rou·me·lia** \rü-ˈmēl-yə, -ˈmē-lē-ə\. European (Balkan) division (*Turk.* "Rumeli," the land of the Romans or Byzantines, sometimes called **Ro·ma·nia** \rō-ˈmā-nē-ə, -nyə\) of the Ottoman Empire; of indefinite limits, but usu. included Albania, Macedonia, and Thrace. See EASTERN RUMELIA.

Ru·me·li Hi·sa·ri *or* **Ru·me·li·hi·sa·rı** \ˌrü-me-ˈlē-ˌhē-sä-ˈrə\. Village, Turkey in Europe, on the Bosporus NE of İstanbul of which it is a suburb; has fortifications built by Mehmed II c. 1452 in preparation for conquering Constantinople.

Rum·ford \ˈrəm-fərd\. Town, Oxford co., W Maine, 35 mi. (56 km.) NNW of Lewiston; pop. (1990c) 7078; paper.

Ru·mia \ˈrü-myä\. Town, Gdańsk prov., N Poland, ab. 20 mi. (32 km.) NNW of the city of Gdańsk; pop. (1989e) 37,064.

Rummel. See KÉBIR, OUED AL-.

Rumney. See RHYMNEY 1.

Ru·moi \rü-ˈmȯi\. Seaport, Hokkaidō prefecture, W coast of Hokkaidō, Japan, 65 mi. (105 km.) N of Sapporo; pop. (1990c) 32,428.

Rum·son \ˈrəm-sən\. Borough and summer resort, Monmouth co., E cen. New Jersey, 16 mi. (26 km.) SE of Perth Amboy; pop. (1990c) 6701.

Run·a·way, Cape \ˈrə-nə-ˌwā\. Cape on NE coast of North I., New Zealand, at E side of entrance to the Bay of Plenty.

Run·corn \ˈrəŋ-kərn\. New town, Cheshire, NW England, on the Mersey 10 mi. (16 km.) ESE of Liverpool; pop. (1981c) 64,412; terminus of the Bridgewater Canal; chemical manufacture; town estab. 1964.

Rung·we Mountain \ˈrüŋ-ˌwā\. Volcanic peak, SW Tanzania, N of Lake Malawi; 9713 ft. (2960 m.).

Run·nels \ˈrə-nəlz\. County in W cen. Texas. See table at TEXAS.

Run·ne·mede \ˈrə-nē-ˌmēd\. Residential borough, Camden co., SW New Jersey, 7 mi. (11 km.) S of the city of Camden; pop. (1990c) 9042; settled by Quakers 1683.

Run·ny·mede \ˈrə-nē-ˌmēd\. Meadow on S bank of the Thames in Surrey, S England, near Egham, W of Staines; Magna Carta signed by King John on June 15, 1215 probably either here or on an island in the river off the meadow.

Ruo \ˈrwȯ\ *or W.-G.* **Jo** \ˈjō\ *or* **Ho** \ˈhō\. River, N China, in Gansu and Nei Monggol; ab. 200 mi. (320 km.) long.

Ruo·qiang \ˈrwȯ-ˈchyäŋ\ *or W.-G.* **Jo–ch'iang** \ˈjō-ˈchyäŋ\ *or* **Qar·ki·lik** \ˈchär-kə-ˌlik\ *or* **Char·khlik** \ˈchär-ˌklik\. Town, S cen. Xinjiang Uygur, W China, on highway S of Taklimakan Desert 155 mi. (249 km.) NE of Qiemo.

Ru·pan·co, La·go \ˈlä-gō-rü-ˈpäŋ-kō\. Lake, S cen. Chile, N of Puerto Montt; 25 mi. (40 km.) long by 4 mi. (6 km.) wide.

Ru·pat *or Du.* **Roe·pat** \ˈrü-ˌpät\. Island of Indonesia, in the Strait of Malacca off E coast of Sumatra.

Ru·pel \rü-ˈpel\. Stream, N cen. Belgium; formed by confluence of the Dijle and Nethe rivers; flows NW into the Schelde 8 mi. (13 km.) SW of Antwerp; ab. 7 mi. (11 km.) long.

Rupella. See LA ROCHELLE.

Rupel Pass \ˈrü-pel\. Mountain pass, valley of Struma River, Macedonia, NE Greece; used by Germans in invasion of Greece 1941.

Ru·pert \ˈrü-pərt\. **1.** City, ⊗ of Minidoka co., S Idaho, on Snake River; pop. (1990c) 5455.
2. River, W Quebec, Canada; flows out of Lac Mistassini W into James Bay; 380 mi. (611 km.) long.

Ru·pert's Land \ˈrü-pərts\ *or in full* **Prince Rupert's Land** \ˈprins\. Historical region, mainland part of Canada, comprising drainage basin of Hudson Bay; granted 1670 by King Charles II to Hudson's Bay Company; purchased 1869 by Canada.

Rup·pert Coast \ˈrü-pərt, ˈrü-\. Section of Antarctica on coast of Marie Byrd Land E of Edward VII Penin. ab. 75°45′S, extending 140°30′W to 147°W.

Ru·pu·nu·ni \ˌrü-pü-ˈnü-nē\. River, Guyana; rises in SW and flows ab. 250 mi. (400 km.) N and E into Essequibo River.

Rur *or Du.* **Roer** \ˈrür\. River, W Europe; rises in the Hohe Venn Mts., Belgium, and flows through North Rhine-Westphalia, Germany to the Meuse at Roermund in Netherlands; 129 mi. (208 km.) long; fighting along its banks in WWII, esp. near Düren and Jülich; dam near source blown up 1945, delaying Allied advance.

Rurki. See ROORKEE.

Ru·ru·tu \rü-ˈrü-tü\. See AUSTRAL ISLANDS.

Rusaddir. See MELILLA.

Ru·se \ˈrü-sā\; *Turk.* **Rus·chuk** *also* **Rus·tchuk** \ˈrüs-ˈchük\. **1.** Region of N Bulgaria. See table at BULGARIA.
2. City, its ✻, on Danube River, ab. 155 mi. (250 km.) NE of Sofia; pop. (1991e) 192,365; textiles, agricultural machinery; tanning, oil refining; founded as Roman fortress; destroyed in 7th cent.; ceded by Ottomans to Bulgaria 1877.

Rusein, Piz. See TÖDI.

Rusellae. See GROSSETO 2.

Rush \ˈrəsh\. Name of counties in two states of the U.S. See tables at INDIANA and KANSAS.

Rush·den \ˈrəsh-dən\. Town, Northamptonshire, cen. England, 14 mi. (23 km.) ENE of Northampton; pop. (1981p) 22,253.

Rush·more, Mount \ˈrəsh-ˌmōr\. Peak in Black Hills, W South Dakota, NE of Harney Peak; 5600 ft. (1707 m.); faces of presidents George Washington, Thomas Jefferson, Theodore Roosevelt, and Abraham Lincoln, carved 1927–41 under direction of Gutzon Borglum, constitute **Mount Rushmore National Memorial.**

Rush·ville \ˈrəsh-ˌvil\. **1.** City, ⊗ of Schuyler co., W Illinois, 45 mi. (72 km.) ENE of Quincy; pop. (1990c) 3229.
2. City, ⊗ of Rush co., E cen. Indiana, 40 mi. (64 km.) ESE of Indianapolis; pop. (1990c) 5533.
3. City, ⊗ of Sheridan co., NW Nebraska; pop. (1990c) 1127.

Rusk \ˈrəsk\. **1.** Name of counties in two states of the U.S. See tables at TEXAS and WISCONSIN.
2. Town, ⊗ of Cherokee co., E Texas, 28 mi. (45 km.) E of Palestine; pop. (1990c) 4366.

Rusk, Mount. Peak in the Catskill Mts., Greene co., SE New York; 3680 ft. (1122 m.).

Ruspina. See MONASTIR 1.

Russ. See NEMAN.

Rus·sell \ˈrə-səl\. **1.** Name of counties in four states of the U.S. See tables at ALABAMA, KANSAS, KENTUCKY, VIRGINIA.
2. City, ⊗ of Russell co., cen. Kansas, 37 mi. (60 km.) N of Great Bend; pop. (1990c) 4781.
3. City, Greenup co., NE Kentucky, on Ohio River 5 mi. (8 km.) NNW of Ashland; pop. (1990c) 4014.
4. Borough and port, N North I., New Zealand, on Bay of Islands 115 mi. (185 km.) NNW of Auckland; has oldest buildings in New Zealand; site first chosen 1840 as ✻ of colony but soon transferred to Auckland.

Russell, Mount. Peak in the Sierra Nevada in W Inyo co., E California; 14,086 ft. (4293 m.).

Russell Cave National Monument. See UNITED STATES, *National Monuments.*

Russell Islands. Group comprising two islands and several islets, SE cen. Solomon Is., W Pacific Ocean, 30 mi. (48 km.) NW of Guadalcanal I.; of volcanic origin; in WWII, occupied by U.S. troops 1943.

Rus·sell·ville \ˈrə-səl-ˌvil\. **1.** City, ⊗ of Franklin co., NW Alabama, 20 mi. (32 km.) S of Wilson Dam and Tennessee River; pop. (1990c) 7812.
2. City, ⊗ of Pope co., NW cen. Arkansas, near Arkansas River 64 mi. (103 km.) NW of Little Rock; pop. (1990c) 21,260; Arkansas Tech Univ. (1909).
3. City, ⊗ of Logan co., S Kentucky, 35 mi. (56 km.) E of Hopkinsville; pop. (1990c) 7454.

Rüs·sels·heim \ˈrue-səls-ˌhīm\. City, Hesse, Germany, on the Main River 7 mi. (11 km.) E of Mainz; pop. (1992e) 59,996.

Rus·sia \ˈrə-shə\ *or Russ.* **Ros·si·ya** \rə-ˈsē-yə\. **1.** Former empire, E Europe and N and W Asia; ✻ St. Petersburg; its territories (except for Finland and Kars) later comprised the Union of Soviet Socialist Republics (U.S.S.R.). For geographical description, see UNION OF SOVIET SOCIALIST REPUBLICS. For history, see RUSSIA 3.
2. Popularly the name for the former Union of Soviet Socialist Republics.
3. *officially* **Rus·sian Federation** \ˈrə-shən\. Republic, E Europe and N Asia; main body of the country bounded on W by Black Sea, Ukraine, Belarus, Latvia, Estonia, and Finland, touches Norway on NW, bounded by Arctic Ocean on N, and by North Pacific Ocean on E, touches North Korea on SE, and on S borders China, Mongolia, Kazakhstan, Azerbaijan, and Republic of Georgia; 6,592,812 sq. mi. (17,075,383 sq. km.); pop. (1993e) 148,000,000; ✻ Moscow.

Physical features: Its mountains include the entire Ural Range and the various ranges of E Siberia, and its highest peaks are in Kamchatka; in Europe it contains the great plain of the Volga and Northern Dvina, in Asia the valleys of the Ob', Yenisey, Lena, and Amur; in the N in both continents is the belt of tundra, farther S extensive forests, steppes, and fertile areas.

Chief products: Wheat, flax, sugar beets, sunflower seeds, potatoes; timber, oil, natural gas; chemicals, motor vehicles.

Chief cities: Moscow, St. Petersburg, Nizhniy Novgorod, Novosibirsk, Yekaterinburg, Samara, Omsk, Chelyabinsk, Kazan', Ufa.

History: Region bet. the Dniester and Volga rivers inhabited from ancient times by various peoples, notably Slavs; overrun 8th cent. B.C.–6th cent. A.D. by successive nomadic peoples, incl. Scythians, Sarmatians, Goths, Huns, and Avars; entered from N c. 9th cent. by Varangians (Scandinavians) who established hegemony over Slavic settlements; Kievan Russia, a confederation of principalities ruled from Kiev emerged c. 10th cent. and subsequently maintained a network of largely river-borne trade from the Baltic to the Black Sea; Kiev lost supremacy 11th–12th cents. to independent principalities, such as Novgorod and Vladimir; Novgorod (*q.v.*) ascended in the N and was the only Russian principality to escape the domination of the Mongols (Tatars), who invaded and conquered the others in 13th cent.; Tatar Khanate of the Golden Horde, ✻ at Sarai, levied tribute on all Russia; lands in S and W came under Lithuanian control 13th–15th cents.; in 14th–15th cents. princes of Moscow (*q.v.*) rose to lead and began overthrow of Tatars and subjugation of rival principalities; under Ivan IV, first czar (crowned 1547), Russia conquered Astrakhan and Kazan' to SE and pushed E of the Urals into Siberia; end of the Rurik dynasty 1598 introduced period of political chaos in Russia ("Time of Troubles") which lasted until Michael Romanov was elected czar 1613; under Romanov dynasty 1613–1917; lost access to the Baltic in war with Sweden early 17th cent.; gained E Ukraine in war with Poland mid-17th cent.; in Great Northern War with Sweden 1700–21, Czar Peter the Great secured access to the Baltic with annexation of the Baltic Provinces, Ingria, and Karelia (*qq.v.*); under Empress Catherine the Great, late 18th cent., gained territory on N shore of Black Sea, Crimea, and part of the Caucasus region in wars with Ottoman Empire; also acquired Lithuania, Belarus, and most of W Ukraine in the partitions of Poland 1772, 1792, and 1795; annexed Finland from Sweden 1809; acquired Bessarabia in treaty with Ottomans 1812; invaded by forces of French Emperor Napoléon I 1812; received most of Grand Duchy of Warsaw 1815 after defeat of Napoléon; annexed Georgia, Armenia, and remainder of Caucasus territories throughout 19th cent.; Russian southward advance against Ottoman Empire of key importance to Europe (see CRIMEA); defeated in Crimean War 1853–56 by British, French, and Turkish forces; Chinese cession of left bank of the Amur and of right bank of the Ussuri (coastline along Sea of Japan), 1858 and 1860, marked active policy in Far East; sold Alaska (*q.v.*) to U.S. 1867; instituted policies of Russification in non-Russian regions of the empire 1860s ff.; in cen. Asia advanced to borders of Persia, Afghanistan (*q.v.*), and China; secured Sakhalin (1875) and rights in Manchuria and Liaodong Penin. (1898); defeat in Russo-Japanese War 1904–05 resulted in destruction of Baltic fleet, loss of control over Manchuria, loss of S half of Sakhalin, and end of active policy in Far East; defeat contributed to outbreak of unsuccessful popular revolution of 1905; vital Russian interests in the Balkans and the Straits brought about entry into WWI in opposition to the Central Powers 1914–17; popular overthrow of czarist regime Mar. 1917 marked beginning of government of soviets; Bolshevik Revolution of Nov. 1917 brought the main part of the former empire under Communist control under whom it was organized as Russian S.F.S.R. (coextensive with present-day Russia); by Treaty of Brest Litovsk (signed with Germany Mar. 3, 1918) E front hostilities of WWI ceased, and the Russian government gave up Finland, Estonia, Latvia, Lithuania, Poland, Belarus, Ukraine, Moldavia, and Transcaucasian Federation, but treaty annulled upon Allied-German armistice Nov. 11, 1918; period of unrest and civil war (1918–20) followed by severe famine 1921; state

RUSSIA
CITIES
Over 2,000,000
800,000 to 2,000,000
150,000 to 800,000
Under 150,000
Other localities
National capital
Political subdivision capital
BOUNDARIES
International
Political subdivision
FEATURES
Canals
Dams
Points of Interest
NORWEGIAN SEA
ARCTIC
Arctic Circle
SVALBARD (NORWAY)
FRANZ JOSEF LAND
SEVERNAYA
NORWAY
Oslo
DENMARK
Copenhagen
SWEDEN
Stockholm
GERMANY
FINLAND
Helsinki
BALTIC SEA
POLUOSTROV RYBACHIY
Pechenga
Murmansk
Severomorsk
LAPLAND NATURE RESERVE
Apatity
Kirovsk
KOLA PENINSULA
BARENTS SEA
KARA SEA
NOVAYA ZEMLYA
KARELIA
KARELIAN ISTHMUS
White Sea-Baltic Canal
WHITE SEA
Tallinn
ESTONIA
LATVIA
Baltiysk
Kaliningrad
Sovetsk
LITHUANIA
Vilnius
Riga
POLAND
Warsaw
Vyborg
Lake Ladoga
Lake Vyg
Onega
Pushkin
Gatchina
St. Petersburg
Pskov
Novgorod
Lake Il'men'
Staraya Russa
Petrozavodsk
Lake Onega
Severodvinsk
Arkhangel'sk
Kholmogory
KOLGUYEV ISLAND
KANIN PENINSULA
PECHORSKOYE MORE
VAYGACH ISLAND
YAMAL PENINSULA
BELYY ISLAND
BYRRAN
NORTH
GYDAN PENINSULA
Dudinka
Talnakh
Noril'sk
Khantayskoye Reservoir
Igarka
Turukhansk
Western Dvina
Minsk
BELARUS
Velikiye Luki
VALDAY HILLS
Vyshniy Volochek
DARVINSKIY NATURE RESERVE
Beloye Ozero
Nyandoma
Vel'sk
Cherepovets
Rybinsk Reservoir
Vologda
Northern Dvina
TIMAN RIDGE
Pechora
Nar'yan-Mar
NENETS A. OKRUG
Vorkuta
KOMI
Inta
Pechora
Mount Narodnaya 6,214 ft.
Ukhta
URAL MOUNTAINS
Salekhard
Gulf of Ob
Pur
Taz
Smolensk
Roslavl'
Tver'
Rybinsk
Yaroslavl'
Kostroma
Ivanovo
Sukhona
Kotlas
Veliki Ustyug
Syktyvkar
PECHORO-ILYCHSKIY NATURE RESERVE
Nadym
Novyy Urengoy
YAMALO-NENETS AUTONOMOUS OKRUG
Bryansk
Kaliningrad
Moscow
Elektrostal'
Kaluga
Oka
Podol'sk
Vladimir
Kolomna
Kovrov
Ryazan'
Dzerzhinsk
Nizhniy Novgorod
RUSSIAN PLAIN
Kiev
UKRAINE
Orel
Kursk
Uzlovaya
Yefremov
Stary Oskol
Gubkin
Lipetsk
Kulebaki
Vyatka
Kama
Kirovo-Chepetsk
Kudymkar
Solikamsk
Berezniki
KHANTY-MANSI AUTONOMOUS OKRUG
Noyabr'sk
Vasyugan'ye
Yenisey
Voronezh
Belgorod
Tambov
Dnieper
Donets
Yoshkar-Ola
Saransk
Cheboksary
Zelenodol'sk
Kazan'
Glazov
Izhevsk
Kizel
Lys'va
Krasnotur'insk
Serov
Khanty-Mansiysk
WEST
Surgut
Nizhnevartovsk
Strezhevoy
Nefteyugansk
Megion
Liski
Borisoglebsk
DONETS BASIN
Don
Sura
Penza
Kuznetsk
Bolgar
Volga
Balashov
Nizhnekamsk
Neftekamsk
Naberezhnye Chelny
Perm'
Krasnoural'sk
Nizhniy Tagil
Kirovograd
SEA OF AZOV
Taganrog
Mikhaylovka
Syzran'
Tol'yatti
Almetyevsk
Pervoural'sk
Yekaterinburg
Saratov
Engel's
Samara
Oktyabr'skiy
Rostov-na-Donu
Shakhty
Novocherkassk
Azov
Bataysk
Volgodonsk
Balakovo
Novokuibyshevsk
Ufa
Revda
Kamensk Ural'skiy
Tobol'sk
SIBERIAN
Volgograd
Volzhskiy
Sterlitamak
Zlatoust
Karabash
Tyumen'
Tobol
Ishim
Irtysh
Swamp
Ob
Ket'
Yenisey
Krasnodar
Kuban
CAUCASUS NATURE RESERVE
Tsimlyansk Reservoir
Sal'sk
Lake Elton
Salavat
Samara
Chelyabinsk
Miass
Beloretsk
Korkino
Troitsk
Kurgan
Ishim
Tara
PLAIN
Kolpashevo
Chulym
Maykop
Stavropol'
Sochi
Armavir
Elista
Yermolayevo
Orenburg
Mednogorsk
Magnitogorsk
Iriklinskoe Reservoir
Orsk
Borisoglebsk
Ural
Novotroitsk
Omsk
Tomsk
Asino
Cherkessk
Mount Elbrus 18,510 ft.
BLACK SEA
Nal'chik
Kuma
CASPIAN DEPRESSION
Astrakhan
Lake Chany
Tatarsk
Anzhero-Sudzhensk
Achinsk
Novosibirsk
Yurga
Kemerovo
Uzhur
Novosibirsk Reservoir
Ob'
Akademgorodok
GEORGIA
Vladikavkaz
Grozny
Nazran
Khasavyurt
TURKEY
Tbilisi
Makhachkala
Karasuk
Kamen'-na-Obi
Iskitim
Chernogorsk
Novokuznetsk
Abakan
Prokopyevsk
ARMENIA
Yerevan
Derbent
CAUCASUS MOUNTAINS
KULUNDA STEPPE
Barnaul
Biysk
Gorno-Altaysk
Rubtsovsk
ALTAY NATURE RESERVE
WESTERN
TANNU
KAZAKHSTAN
AZERBAIJAN
Baku
CASPIAN SEA
Kara-Bogaz Gol
ARAL SEA
Karaganda
Belukha 15,157 ft.
ALTAY SHAN
Lake Balkhash
IRAN
TURKMENISTAN
UZBEKISTAN
Tashkent
Bishkek
Almaty
KYRGYZSTAN
Ürümqi
Dushanbe
TAJIKISTAN
CHINA
AFGHANISTAN
PAKISTAN
1
2
3
4
5
6
7
8
9
10
11
12
13
14
15
16
17

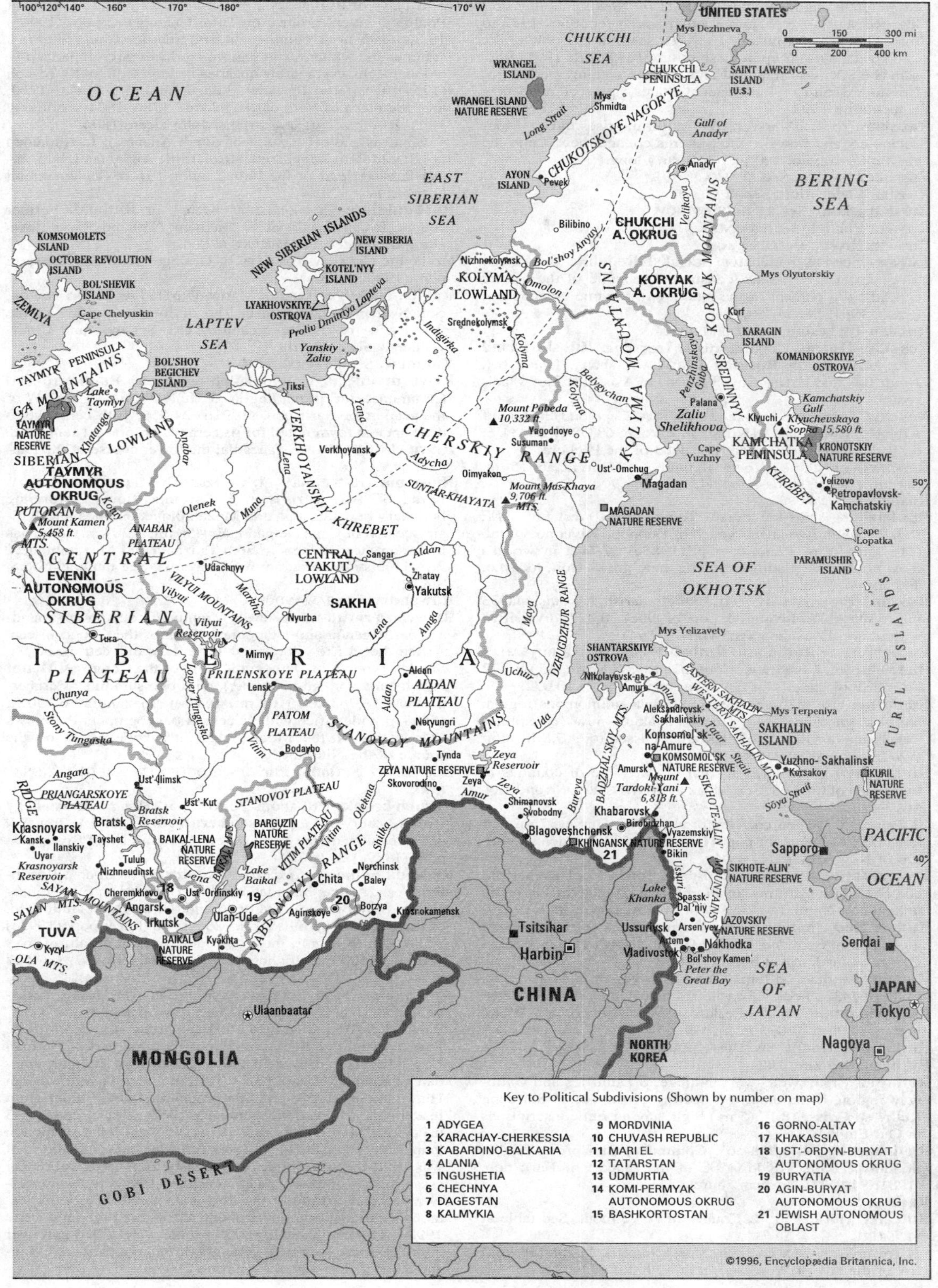

OCEAN
CHUKCHI SEA
EAST SIBERIAN SEA
LAPTEV SEA
BERING SEA
SEA OF OKHOTSK
SEA OF JAPAN
PACIFIC OCEAN
UNITED STATES
Mys Dezhneva
0 150 300 mi
0 200 400 km
WRANGEL ISLAND
WRANGEL ISLAND NATURE RESERVE
CHUKCHI PENINSULA
SAINT LAWRENCE ISLAND (U.S.)
Mys Shmidta
Long Strait
CHUKOTSKOYE NAGOR'YE
Gulf of Anadyr
Anadyr
AYON ISLAND
Pevek
Bilibino
CHUKCHI A. OKRUG
KORYAK A. OKRUG
KORYAK MOUNTAINS
KOLYMA MOUNTAINS
Mys Olyutorskiy
Korf
KARAGIN ISLAND
KOMANDORSKIYE OSTROVA
KOMSOMOLETS ISLAND
OCTOBER REVOLUTION ISLAND
BOL'SHEVIK ISLAND
NEW SIBERIAN ISLANDS
NEW SIBERIA ISLAND
KOTEL'NYY ISLAND
LYAKHOVSKIYE OSTROVA
Proliv Dmitriya Lapteva
Cape Chelyuskin
ZEMLYA
TAYMYR PENINSULA
BOL'SHOY BEGICHEV ISLAND
Nizhnekolymsk
Bol'shoy Anyuy
KOLYMA LOWLAND
Omolon
Srednekolymsk
Indigirka
Kolyma
Yanskiy Zaliv
Tiksi
Lake Taymyr
TAYMYR NATURE RESERVE
LOWLAND
SIBERIAN
Khatanga
Anabar
TAYMYR AUTONOMOUS OKRUG
PUTORAN
Mount Kamen 5,458 ft.
MTS.
ANABAR PLATEAU
Olenek
Muna
CENTRAL
EVENKI AUTONOMOUS OKRUG
SIBERIAN
PLATEAU
SIBERIA
VERKHOYANSKIY KHREBET
Yana
Verkhoyansk
Lena
Adycha
CHERSKIY RANGE
Mount Pobeda 10,332 ft.
Yagodnoye
Susuman
Balygychan
Ust'-Omchug
Oimyakon
Magadan
MAGADAN NATURE RESERVE
Mount Mas-Khaya 9,706 ft.
SUNTAR-KHAYATA MTS.
Penzhinskaya Guba
Palana
Zaliv Shelikhova
SREDINNYY
Kamchatskiy Gulf
Klyuchi
Klyuchevskaya Sopka 15,580 ft.
Cape Yuzhny
KAMCHATKA PENINSULA
KRONOTSKIY NATURE RESERVE
KHREBET
Yelizovo
Petropavlovsk-Kamchatskiy
Cape Lopatka
PARAMUSHIR ISLAND
KURIL ISLANDS
Udachnyy
CENTRAL YAKUT LOWLAND
Sangar
Aldan
Zhatay
Yakutsk
SAKHA
VILYUI MOUNTAINS
Markha
Vilyui
Nyurba
Vilyui Reservoir
Tura
Mirnyy
Amga
Maya
DZHUGDZHUR RANGE
Mys Yelizavety
SHANTARSKIYE OSTROVA
Nikolayevsk-na-Amure
Amur
EASTERN SAKHALIN MTS.
WESTERN SAKHALIN MTS.
Mys Terpeniya
SAKHALIN ISLAND
Aleksandrovsk-Sakhalinskiy
Tatar Strait
Komsomol'sk na-Amure
KOMSOMOL'SK NATURE RESERVE
Amursk
Mount Tardoki-Yani 6,818 ft.
Yuzhno-Sakhalinsk
Korsakov
KURIL NATURE RESERVE
Soya Strait
PRILENSKOYE PLATEAU
Lensk
Aldan
ALDAN PLATEAU
Uchur
Chunya
Stony Tunguska
Lower Tunguska
PATOM PLATEAU
STANOVOY MOUNTAINS
Neryungri
Uda
Vitim
Bodaybo
Tynda
Zeya Reservoir
ZEYA NATURE RESERVE
Zeya
Skovorodino
BADZHAL'SKIY MTS.
SIKHOTE-ALIN'
Bureya
Angara
Ust'-Ilimsk
RIDGE
PRIANGARSKOYE PLATEAU
Ust'-Kut
STANOVOY PLATEAU
Bratsk Reservoir
Bratsk
Krasnoyarsk
Kansk
Uyar
Ilanskiy
Tayshet
BAIKAL-LENA NATURE RESERVE
BARGUZIN NATURE RESERVE
Tulun
Nizhneudinsk
Krasnoyarsk Reservoir
VITIM PLATEAU
Olekma
Shilka
Amur
Shimanovsk
Svobodny
Blagoveshchensk
Khabarovsk
Birobidzhan
KHINGANSK NATURE RESERVE
Vyazemskiy
Bikin
Sapporo
SAYAN
BAIKAL MTS.
Lake Baikal
YABLONOVYY RANGE
Nerchinsk
Baley
Chita
Cheremkhovo
18
Ust'-Ordinskiy
19
20
Angarsk
Irkutsk
Ulan-Ude
Aginskoye
Borzya
Krasnokamensk
SAYAN MTS. MOUNTAINS
TUVA
Kyzyl
OLA MTS.
BAIKAL NATURE RESERVE
Kyakhta
Tsitsihar
Harbin
21
Ussuri
Lake Khanka
Spassk-Dal'niy
MOUNTAINS
SIKHOTE-ALIN' NATURE RESERVE
Ussuriysk
Arsen'yev
LAZOVSKIY NATURE RESERVE
Artem
Nakhodka
Vladivostok
Bol'shoy Kamen'
Peter the Great Bay
Sendai
JAPAN
Tokyo
Nagoya
CHINA
NORTH KOREA
Ulaanbaatar
MONGOLIA
GOBI DESERT
100° 120° 140° 160° 170° 180° 170° W
50°
40°
Key to Political Subdivisions (Shown by number on map)
1 ADYGEA
2 KARACHAY-CHERKESSIA
3 KABARDINO-BALKARIA
4 ALANIA
5 INGUSHETIA
6 CHECHNYA
7 DAGESTAN
8 KALMYKIA
9 MORDVINIA
10 CHUVASH REPUBLIC
11 MARI EL
12 TATARSTAN
13 UDMURTIA
14 KOMI-PERMYAK AUTONOMOUS OKRUG
15 BASHKORTOSTAN
16 GORNO-ALTAY
17 KHAKASSIA
18 UST'-ORDYN-BURYAT AUTONOMOUS OKRUG
19 BURYATIA
20 AGIN-BURYAT AUTONOMOUS OKRUG
21 JEWISH AUTONOMOUS OBLAST

Communist methods modified 1921 by New Economic Policy; Russian S.F.S.R. joined other soviet republics 1922 to form U.S.S.R.; for history 1922–91, see UNION OF SOVIET SOCIALIST REPUBLICS; upon dissolution of U.S.S.R. 1991, Russian S.F.S.R. was renamed and became leading member of Commonwealth of Independent States (*q.v.*); adopted new constitution 1993.

Rus·sian \ˈrə-shən\. River, NW California; rises in cen. Mendocino co. and flows S into Sonoma co. and then W into the Pacific Ocean; ab. 100 mi. (160 km.) long.

Russian America. See ALASKA.

Russian Federation. See RUSSIA 3.

Russian Island. See RUSSKIY, OSTROV.

Russian Poland. See POLAND 1.

Russian River. See RUSSIAN.

Russian So·vi·et Federated Socialist Republic \ˈsō-vē-ˌet, ˈsä-, -vē-ət\. The largest constituent republic of the former U.S.S.R. (76 percent of the total area); became independent Russia 1991. See RUSSIA 3.

Russian Turkestan. See TURKISTAN.

Rus·skiy, Os·trov \ˈó-strəf-ˈrüs-kē\ *or Eng.* **Rus·ski Island** \ˈrůs-kē, ˈrəs-\ *or* **Rus·sian Island** \ˈrə-shən\. Island bet. Amur Bay and Ussuri Bay, E Russia in Asia, just S of Vladivostok.

Rus·skiy Za·vo·rot \ˈrüs-kē-ˌzä-və-ˈrōt\. Cape on NE coast of Arkhangel'sk Oblast, N Russia in Europe; 68°58′N, 54°34′E; on E shore of Barents Sea N of delta of the Pechora.

Rus·ta·vi \rů-ˈstä-vē\. Town, Republic of Georgia, ab. 15 mi. (24 km.) SE of Tbilisi; pop. (1991e) 161,900.

Rustchuk. See RUSE.

Rus·ten·burg \ˈrůs-tən-ˌbůrk\. Town, North West prov., NE Rep. of South Africa, on branch of Limpopo River ab. 70 mi. (115 km.) W of Pretoria; pop. (1985c) 37,712; in world's most productive platinum-mining area; grows fruit, tobacco, and cotton.

Rus·ton \ˈrəs-tən\. City, ⊗ of Lincoln parish, N Louisiana, 33 mi. (53 km.) W of Monroe; pop. (1990c) 20,027; diversified agriculture; Louisiana Tech Univ. (1894).

Ruṭbah, Ar *or* **Rutba** *also* **Rutbah Wells.** See AR RUṬBAH.

Ru·te \ˈrü-te\. Commune, Córdoba prov., S Spain, 45 mi. (72 km.) SSE of the city of Córdoba; pop. (1991c) 10,072.

Ru·the·nia \rü-ˈthē-nyə, -nē-ə\. Former autonomous region, later a province of Czechoslovakia, now constitutes Zakarpats'ka subdivision, Ukraine. Passed to U.S.S.R. after WWII. See ZAKARPATS'KA.

Ruth·er·ford \ˈrə-t͟hər-fərd, -thər-\. **1.** Name of counties in two states of the U.S. See tables at NORTH CAROLINA and TENNESSEE.

2. Borough, Bergen co., NE corner of New Jersey, 7 mi. (11 km.) SSE of Paterson; pop. (1990c) 17,790; residential suburb of New York City.

Ruth·er·ford·ton \ˈrə-t͟hər-fərd-tən\. Town, ⊗ of Rutherford co., SW North Carolina, in Blue Ridge on edge of Piedmont upland belt 25 mi. (40 km.) W of Shelby; pop. (1990c) 3617.

Ruth·er·glen \ˈrə-t͟hər-ˌglen\. Former burgh, Strathclyde region, S cen. Scotland, on the Clyde 3 mi. (4.8 km.) SE of Glasgow; made royal burgh 1126.

Ruth·in \ˈrü-t͟hən, ˈri-thin\. Town, Clwyd co., N Wales; pop. (1981p) 4430; medieval castle; 14th cent. church of St. Peter.

Ruth Mountain \ˈrüth\. Peak, cen. Whatcom co., NW Washington; 6800 ft. (2073 m.).

Ruth Siple, Mount. See SIPLE, MOUNT.

Ruthven. See KINGUSSIE.

Ruth·well \ˈrət͟h-ˌwel, -wəl\. Village, S Dumfries and Galloway region, S Scotland, on Solway Firth; site of 8th cent. Ruthwell Cross, 18 ft. (5 m.) high, having runic inscriptions in Old English.

Ru·ti·glia·no \ˌrü-tē-ˈlyä-nō\. Commune, Bari prov., Puglia, SE Italy, 11 mi. (18 km.) SE of the seaport of Bari; pop. (1981p) 14,611; Norman church.

Rutlam. See RATLAM.

Rut·land \ˈrət-lənd\. **1.** County in W Vermont. See table at VERMONT.

2. Town, Worcester co., cen. Massachusetts, 12 mi. (19 km.) NW of the city of Worcester; pop. (1990c) 4936.

3. City, ⊗ of Rutland co., W Vermont, 22 mi. (35 km.) E of Poultney River entrance on Lake Champlain; pop. (1990c) 18,230; industrial, commercial, and transportation center in a summer and winter resort region; produces aircraft parts, plywood, machinery; marble quarries nearby; Coll. of St. Joseph (1954). Chartered by New Hampshire 1761; settled 1770; meeting place of Vermont legislature 1784–1804; made city 1892. Birthplace of industrialist John Deere 1804.

4. Small island off S point of South Andaman I., Andaman Is., Bay of Bengal; separated from Little Andaman I. by Duncan Passage; part of the Indian union terr. of Andaman and Nicobar Is.

Rut·land·shire \ˈrət-lənd-ˌshir, -shər\ *or* **Rutland.** Former county, E cen. England; ⊗ Oakham; Welland River flows along SE border. See LEICESTERSHIRE.

Rut·ledge \ˈrət-lij\. Town, ⊗ of Grainger co., NE Tennessee; pop. (1990c) 903.

Rüt·li \ˈrœt-lē\ *or* **Grüt·li** \ˈgrœt-\. Meadow in Uri canton, cen. Switzerland; legendary site of formation 1307 of the first league of the three cantons Uri, Schwyz, and Unterwalden against Austria.

Rutupiae. See RICHBOROUGH.

Ru·vo di Pu·glia \ˌrü-vō-dē-ˈpü-lyä\; *anc.* **Ru·bi** \ˈrü-ˌbī\. Commune, Bari prov., Puglia, SE Italy, 9 mi. (14 km.) W of the seaport of Bari; pop. (1991p) 24,556; 13th cent. cathedral; ancient town noted for its ceramic art 5th–3d cents. B.C.

Ru·vu \ˈrü-vü\. River, Tanzania; the lower course of the Pangani (*q.v.*).

Ru·vu·ma \rü-ˈvü-mä\. **1.** *or Port.* **Ro·vu·ma** \rů-ˈvü-mə\. River, SE Africa; rises in S Tanzania, flows E, forming boundary bet. Tanzania and Mozambique, empties into Indian Ocean N of Cape Delgado; ab. 450 mi. (720 km.) long; has important headstreams in both Tanzania and Mozambique.

2. Administrative region of S Tanzania. See table at TANZANIA.

Ruwandiz. See RAWĀNDŪZ.

Ru·wen·zo·ri \ˌrü-wən-ˈzōr-ē\. Mountain group on the boundary bet. Uganda and Democratic Rep. of the Congo in cen. Africa, bet. Lake Albert and Lake Edward; cen. peak Mt. Stanley (known in Democratic Rep. of the Congo as **Mount Nga·li·e·ma** \əŋ-ˌgä-lē-ˈā-mä\), with two summits, Margherita Peak 16,763 ft. (5109 m.) and Mt. Alexandra 16,750 ft. (5105 m.); identified with 2d cent. A.D. geographer Ptolemy's "Mountains of the Moon," anciently believed to be the source of the Nile.

Ruwenzori National Park. See QUEEN ELIZABETH NATIONAL PARK.

Ru·žom·be·rok \ˈrü-zhȯm-ˌbe-rȯk\ *or Hung.* **Ró·zsa·hegy** \ˈrō-zhö-ˌhej\ *or Ger.* **Ro·sen·berg** \ˈrōz-ᵊn-ˌberk\. Town, N cen. Slovakia, on the Váh 118 mi. (190 km.) NE of Bratislava; pop. (1989c) 29,937.

Rwan·da *or mostly formerly* **Ru·an·da** \rə-ˈwän-də\. Republic, E cen. Africa, bounded on N by Uganda, on E by Tanzania, on S by Burundi, and on W and NW by Democratic Rep. of the Congo; 10,169 sq. mi. (26,338 sq. km.); pop. (1993e) 7,584,000; ✱ Kigali; most of country lies at an alt. of over 5000 ft. (1500 m.); highest peak Karisimbi 14,787 ft. (4507 m.).

Chief products: Sorghum, pyrethrum, corn, beans, cassava, coffee, tea; livestock; cassiterite, wolframite.

History: Area ruled by a Tutsi monarchy 16th cent.–1959; governed through native monarchy, became part of German East Africa protectorate 1890–1916, then of Belgian mandate of Ruanda-Urundi (*q.v.*); Tutsi monarchy overthrown in Hutu uprising 1959; republic proclaimed 1961 under Hutu leadership; achieved independence 1962; military coup 1973 ushered in single-party rule 1973–91; Tutsi-led insurrection launched by Rwandan refugees from Uganda initiated civil war 1990–93; new multi-party constitution 1991; following assassination of the Rwandan president 1994, civil war briefly recommenced until Tutsi forces declared victory and established a coalition government; throughout the civil strife 1990–94 an estimated 200,000 people were killed and over 2,000,000 refugees fled to neighboring countries, esp. Tanzania and Zaire; new constitution 1995.

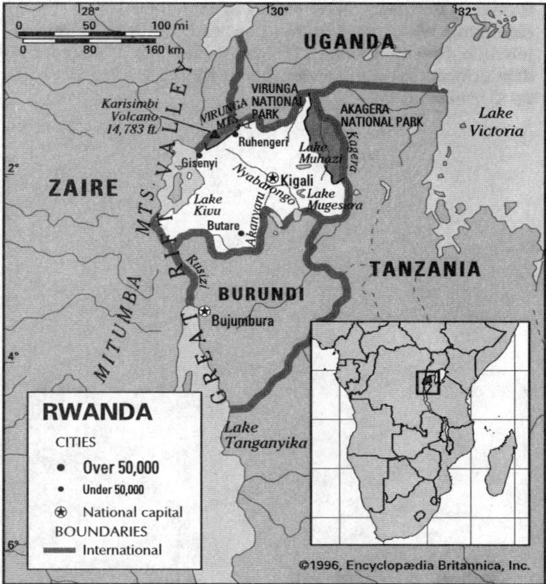

Ry·an, Loch \ˈrī-ən\. Inlet, Dumfries and Galloway region, on SW coast of Scotland; extends S inland ab. 9 mi. (14 km.) with the town of Stranraer at its head; land to its W forms N part of The Rinns of Galloway (*q.v.*); fine harbor.

Ryan Peak. Mountain, S Custer co., cen. Idaho; 11,794 ft. (3595 m.).

Rya·zan' or **Rya·zan** *also* **Ria·zan** \ri-ˈzän, -ˈzänʸ\. **1.** Medieval principality, cen. Russia, SE of Moscow; ✻ Old Ryazan'; included Murom to the NE and Kolomna on the Moskva. A border state of the Russian lands, was frequently in conflict; became independent of Kiev (*q.v.*) c. 12th cent.; overrun by Mongols 13th cent.; annexed by Moscow in 16th cent.

2. City, ✻ of Ryazan' Oblast, W cen. Russia in Europe, on right bank of Oka River 120 mi. (193 km.) SE of Moscow; pop. (1992e) 529,000; chemicals; oil refinery.

History: Town of **Old Ryazan'**, ✻ of the principality, founded (11th cent.) on site ab. 30 mi. (48 km.) SE; lost importance after destruction by Tatars 1237; ✻ later moved to **Pe·re·ya·slav–Rya·zan·skiy** \ˌpi-ri-ˈyä-sləf-ri-ˈzän-skē\, which passed to Moscow 1521 and took present name 1778.

Ryazan' Oblast *or* **Ryazan Oblast** \ˈȯ-bləst, -ˌblast\ *or* **Rya·zan·ska·ya Oblast'** \ri-ˈzän-skə-yə-ȯ-bləstʸ\. Administrative subdivision of W cen. Russia in Europe, crossed by Oka River; 15,290 sq. mi. (39,601 sq. km.); pop. (1992e) 1,344,000; ✻ Ryazan'. Level, well-watered area, with many lakes and some forest areas, chiefly agricultural, growing grain, sugar beets, vegetables, flax, and tobacco; only large town is Ryazan'; estab. as oblast 1937.

Ry·ba·chiy, Po·lu·os·trov \ˌpə-lə-ˈȯs-trəf-ri-ˈbä-chē\ *or* **Ry·ba·chi Peninsula** \ri-ˈbä-chē\ *or* **Rybachiy Peninsula** *also* **Ri·ba·chi Peninsula** \ri-\. Irregular land projection, extending into Barents Sea on NW coast of Murmansk Oblast, NW Russia in Europe, N of Kola Bay and Murmansk and NE of Pechenga; ab. 17 mi. (27 km.) wide; its base touches the former Finnish boundary line.

Ry·binsk \ˈri-bənsk\; *1946–57* **Shcher·ba·kov** \ˌshcher-bə-ˈkȯf\; *1984–89* **An·dro·pov** \än-ˈdrō-ˌpȯf\. City, Yaroslavl' Oblast, W cen. Russia in Europe, on right bank of the Volga; pop. (1992e) 252,000; engineering industries.

Rybinsk Reservoir *also* **Sea of Rybinsk.** Large lake, W cen. Russia in Europe, for the greater part in NW Yaroslavl' Oblast; 1757 sq. mi. (4551 sq. km.); formed 1940s by damming waters of upper Volga; on N receives the Suda and Sheksna rivers; formerly the world's largest man-made lake; comprises part of Volga-Baltic Waterway (*q.v.*).

Ryb·nik \ˈrib-nik\. Commune, Katowice prov., S Poland, 20 mi. (32 km.) SW of the city of Katowice; pop. (1989e) 142,588; coal mines.

Ry·dal \ˈrīd-ᵊl\. Village, Cumbria co., NW England, on **Rydal Water,** a small lake just E of Grasmere Lake; site of Rydal Mount, home of English poet William Wordsworth from 1813 to 1850; 2 mi. (3 km.) NW of the village are the **Rydal Falls.**

Ryde \ˈrīd\. **1.** Town on Isle of Wight, S England, in English Channel 6 mi. (10 km.) SW of Portsmouth; pop. (1981p) 24,346; seaside resort.

2. Municipality, E New South Wales, Australia, a NW suburb of Sydney; pop. (1991c) 90,197.

Rye \ˈrī\. **1.** Town, Rockingham co., SE New Hampshire, on Atlantic Ocean 4 mi. (6 km.) S of Portsmouth; pop. (1990c) 4612.

2. Residential city in town of Rye, Westchester co., SE New York, on Long Island Sound 24 mi. (39 km.) NE of New York City; pop. (1990c) 14,936 (city), 39,524 (town); settled 1660.

3. Town, East Sussex, S England; pop. (1981p) 4293; tourism; medieval gate and tower; incorp. 1289; one of the Cinque Ports (*q.v.*).

Rye·gate \ˈrī-ˌgāt\. Town, ⊗ of Golden Valley co., cen. Montana; pop. (1990c) 260.

Rye House. Village, Hertfordshire, SE England, 2 mi. (3 km.) from Ware; remains of manor house (Rye House), intended site of murder of Charles II and James, duke of York, in alleged assassination plot 1683. Whig parliamentary leader Lord William Russell and republican leader Algernon Sidney were implicated in the conspiracy and executed.

Ryezhitsa. See RĒZEKNE.

Ry·ma·nów \rə̇-ˈmä-ˌnüf\. Commune, Rzeszów prov., SE Poland, ab. 35 mi. (55 km.) SW of the commune of Rzeszów; pop. (1981p) 3242; Greek Catholic episcopal see; in foothills of Carpathian Mts.

Ryojun. See LÜSHUN.

Ryssel. See LILLE.

Ryswick. See RIJSWIJK.

Ry·sy \ˈri-sē\. Peak in Carpathian Mts., S Poland; 8197 ft. (2498 m.); highest mountain in Poland.

Ry·ton \ˈrīt-ᵊn\. Town, Tyne and Wear co., N England, on the Tyne 6 mi. (10 km.) W of Newcastle upon Tyne; pop. (1981p) 15,023.

Ryu·kyu Islands \rē-ˈyü-ˌkyü\. **1.** *also* **Riu·kiu Islands** \rē-ˈyü-ˌkyü\ *or* **Nan·sei Islands** \ˌnän-ˈsā\; *Jp.* **Ryukyu Ret·tō** \ˈre-tō\; *also* **Lu·chu Islands** *or* **Loo·choo Islands** \ˈlü-ˌchü\. Island chain, Japan, in W Pacific Ocean, extending in a 600-mile-long (970-kilometer-long) arc bet. Taiwan and Kyūshū, Japan; includes Sakishima, Okinawa, and Amami island groups; 848 sq. mi. (2196 sq. km.); pop. (1990c) 1,222,458; chief town Naha on Okinawa I.; highest point in N, a volcano 3215 ft. (980 m.) on Nakano Shima in Tokara Is. (part of Amami group).

History: Site of ancient independent kingdoms; became tributary to China 14th cent., and to Japan as well 15th cent.; became integral part of Japan by 1879; scene of heavy fighting toward end of WWII, and after WWII placed under U.S. administration 1945; Amami group returned to Japan 1953; remainder returned to Japan 1972.

2. Administrative region of Japan consisting of the Ryukyu Is.

Ryukyu Trench. Ocean trench, W Pacific Ocean, E of and approx. parallel to the Ryukyu Is., extending from E of Kyūshū to E of Taiwan; subduction zone according to theory of plate tectonics.

Rzeczypospolita Polska. See POLAND.

Rze·szów \ˈzhe-ˌshüf\. **1.** Province of SE Poland. See table at POLAND.

2. Industrial commune, its ❋, ab. 95 mi. (155 km.) E of Kraków; pop. (1989e) 150,754; textiles, metal goods; c. 17th cent. castle; made town mid-14th cent.; under Austrian rule 1772–1918.

Rzhev \ər-ˈzhef, rə-ˈzhef, -ˈzhev\. City, S Tver' Oblast, W cen. Russia in Europe, on both banks of the upper Volga 125 mi. (201 km.) WNW of Moscow; pop. (1991e) 70,900; railroad junction; first mentioned 1216 and formerly ❋ of an independent princedom; came under rule of Moscow 1390; occupied by Germans in WWII.

S

Saadani. See SADANI.

Saa·le \ˈzä-lə, ˈsä-\. River, E cen. Germany; rises in the Fichtelgebirge, NE Bavaria, and flows N into the Elbe River 18 mi. (29 km.) SE of Magdeburg; 265 mi. (426 km.) long.

Saale, Frän·ki·sche \ˈfreŋ-ki-shə-ˈzä-lə\. River, Bavaria, Germany; rises in the Rhön Mts., flows SW into Main River NW of Würzburg; ab. 70 mi. (115 km.) long.

Saal·feld \ˈzäl-ˌfelt\ *also* **Saalfeld an der Saa·le** \än-dər-ˈzä-lə\. City, Thuringia, E cen. Germany, on Saale River 29 mi. (47 km.) SSE of Erfurt; pop. (1992e) 32,641; iron and steel, electrical equipment; 13th cent. monastery, now a museum; 16th cent. town hall; present town dates to 13th cent.

Saa·ne \ˈzä-nə\ *or Fr.* **Sa·rine** \sȧ-rēn\. River, SW Switzerland; rises in Bernese Alps, flows N through Fribourg canton and into Aare River 10 mi. (16 km.) WNW of Bern; 80 mi. (129 km.) long.

Saar \ˈsär, ˈzär\ *or Fr.* **Sarre** \ˈsȧr\. **1.** River, Moselle dept., France, and Saarland and Rhineland-Palatinate, Germany; flows N and NNW across German border to the Mosel (Moselle) just above Trier; 75 mi. (121 km.) long. **2.** State, Germany. See SAARLAND.

Saar·brück·en \zär-ˈbrue-kən, sär-ˈbru̇-kən\ *or Fr.* **Sar·re·bruck** \sȧr-ˈbrūek\. Industrial city, ✻ of Saarland, Germany, on Saar River on France-Germany frontier ab. 39 mi. (63 km.) SE of Trier; pop. (1992e) 192,030; major center of iron and steel industry; also produces optical instruments, cement, beer; printing, coal mining; 18th cent. castle; 18th cent. town hall; 13th cent. Gothic church; university (1948).

History: Site of Roman settlement, and later of Frankish castle; received charter 1321; under counts of Nassau-Saarbrücken 14th cent.–1793; to France 1793–1815; to Prussia 1815; after WWI made ✻ of government of the Saar (see SAARLAND); to Germany 1935 and made ✻ of Saarland state; heavily bombed in WWII.

Saa·re·maa *or* **Sa·re·ma** \ˈsär-ə-ˌmä\; *Ger.* **Oe·sel** \ˈœ-zəl\. Island, Estonia, in E Baltic Sea NW of Gulf of Riga; 1050 sq. mi. (2720 sq. km.); livestock raising, fishing. Conquered by Brothers of the Sword (Livonian Knights) 13th cent.; passed to Denmark 16th cent., then to Sweden 1645; as part of Livonia was united to Russia 1721; became part of Estonia 1918; occupied by Germans in WWII.

Saargemünd. See SARREGUEMINES.

Saar·land \ˈzär-ˌlänt, ˈsär-ˌland\ *or* **Saar·ge·biet** \-gə-ˌbēt\ *also* **Saar** \ˈzär, ˈsär\ *or Fr.* **Sarre** \ˈsȧr\. A state of Germany; ✻ Saarbrücken; iron and steel; coal mining.

History: Ceded to France 1790s, but by Treaty of Paris 1815 divided bet. Prussia and Bavaria; after WWI, by Treaty of Versailles 1919, coal mines assigned to France and territory placed under administration of the League of Nations; returned to Germany by plebiscite 1935; after WWII occupied by French; rejected French-German arrangement for autonomy 1955, and became a state of West Germany 1957. See table at GERMANY.

Saar·lou·is \zär-ˈlü-ē, sär-; ˌsär-ˈlwē\; *1936–45* **Saar·lau·tern** \zär-ˈlau̇-tərn, sär-\. Manufacturing commune, Saarland, Germany, on left bank of the Saar 11 mi. (18 km.) WNW of Saarbrücken; pop. (1992e) 38,265; founded 1680 by Louis XIV; birthplace of Marshal Michel Ney 1769; heavily damaged during WWII.

Sa·ba \ˈsä-bə, ˈsä-\. Island, NE West Indies, in Leeward Is. 16 mi. (26 km.) NW of St. Eustatius; 5 sq. mi. (13 sq. km.); pop. (1990c) 1119; chief settlement The Bottom; part of Netherlands Antilles; an extinct volcano, its coasts are sheer cliffs ab. 2800 ft. (850 m.) high; settled by Dutch 1632.

Saba *or* **Saba'.** see SHEBA.

Ša·bac \ˈshä-ˌbäts\. Town, Serbia, Yugoslavia, 40 mi. (64 km.) W of Belgrade on Sava River; trade center and river port.

Sa·ba·dell \ˌsä-bä-ˈthel\. Commune, Barcelona prov., NE Spain, 8 mi. (13 km.) NNW of the city of Barcelona; pop. (1991p) 184,460; ships agricultural products, wine; manufactures textiles, leather.

Sa·bae \sä-ˈbä-ā\. City, Fukui prefecture, Honshū, Japan, 13 mi. (21 km.) S of the city of Fukui; pop. (1990p) 62,284.

Sa·bah \ˈsä-bä\; *formerly* **British North Bor·neo** \ˈbȯr-nē-ˌō\ *also* **North Borneo.** A state of Malaysia, NE island of Borneo; ✻ Kota Kinabalu. Almost all mountainous with highest ranges parallel with W coast (highest mountain Kinabalu, 13,455 ft. or 4101 m., highest on island of Borneo); cut by open river valleys, esp. the Kinabatangan and Labuk in the E; has coastline of 900 mi. (1450 km.) bordering on South China Sea, Sulu Sea, and Celebes Sea; much indented by bays, esp. on E coast; coconuts, rice, rubber, timber. See table at MALAYSIA.

History: English attempts at settlement in 17th and 18th cents. unsuccessful; granted by sultans of Brunei and Sulu to British North Borneo Company, chartered in 1881; territory proclaimed British protectorate 1888 but continued to be administered by company until WWII; occupied by Japanese 1941; recovered in part by Allies in last months of war; became a British colony 1946 and a state of Malaysia 1963.

Sa·ba·ki \sä-ˈbä-kē\. River, SE Kenya, formed by confluence of Athi and Tsavo rivers, flows E into Indian Ocean; ab. 120 mi. (190 km.) long.

Sa·ba·lān \ˌsä-bə-ˈlän\ *or* **Sa·va·lan** \-və-\. Peak, East Azerbaijan prov., NW Iran, ab. 85 mi. (135 km.) E of Tabrīz; 15,784 ft. (4811 m.).

Sa·ba·na, Ar·chi·pié·la·go de \ˌär-chē-ˈpyā-lä-ˌgō-thā-sä-ˈbä-nä\. Group of islands off N coast of Las Villas prov., W cen. Cuba.

Sabana Gran·de \ˈgrän-dā\. Municipality, SW Puerto Rico, WNW of Ponce; pop. (1990c) 22,843.

Sa·ba·na·lar·ga \sä-ˌbä-nä-ˈlär-gä\. Town, Atlántico dept., N Colombia, 30 mi. (48 km.) S of Barranquilla.

Sa·ba·ne·ta \ˌsä-bä-ˈnā-tä\ *or* **San·tia·go Ro·drí·guez** \sän-ˈtyä-ˌgō-rȯ-ˈthrē-ges\. Town, ✻ of Santiago Rodríguez prov., Dominican Republic; pop. (1981c) 9170.

Sa·bang \ˈsä-ˌbäŋ\. Seaport on the island of We off N Sumatra, Indonesia; pop. (1990c) 24,416; good harbor; held by Japanese in WWII and used as a fueling center.

Sa·ba·ri \ˈsə-bə-rē\. River, E cen. India; rises in S Orissa and flows SW along SE boundary of Madhya Pradesh into Godavari River in N Andhra Pradesh; ab. 130 mi. (210 km.) long.

Sabaria. See SZOMBATHELY.

Sa·bar Kan·tha \ˌsə-bər-ˈkən-tə\. Former subdivision of Western India States, India; 5408 sq. mi. (14,007 sq. km.); was in N Gujarat.

Sa·bar·ma·ti \ˌsä-bər-ˈmə-tē\. River, W India; rises in the Aravalli Range in Rajasthan, flows S into the head of Gulf of Khambhat, W of the mouth of Mahi River; ab. 250 mi. (400 km.) long.

Sabastīyah. See SAMARIA 2.

Sabatinus. See BRACCIANO, LAKE.

Sa·bau·dia \sä-ˈbau̇-dyə\. Town, Latina prov., SW Lazio; cen. Italy, on the coast N of Monte Circeo; pop. (1981p) 12,430; built on reclaimed land in Agro Pontino.

Sabbioncello. See PELJEŠAC.

Sa·be·ta Peak \sə-ˈbā-tə\. Mountain, Chaffee co., cen. Colorado; 13,600 ft. (4145 m.).

Sab·hā *or* **Sab·hah** \ˈsab-ˌhä\ *or* **Seb·ha** \ˈseb-ˌhä\. Town, SW Libya.

Sabi. See SAVE.

Sa·bi·nal Cay \ˌsä-b̄ē-ˈnäl\. Island off NE coast of Camagüey prov., E cen. Cuba, in the Camagüey Archipelago.

Sa·bi·nas \sä-ˈb̄ē-näs\. **1.** River, Mexico. See SALADO 2. **2.** Town, Coahuila state, NE Mexico, on Sabinas River 70 mi. (113 km.) SW of Piedras Negras.

Sa·bine \sə-ˈbēn\. **1.** Navigable river, E Texas and W Louisiana; formed by confluence of forks in Hunt co., NE Texas, flows SE to Louisiana border, forming S section of Texas-Louisiana boundary, and empties through Sabine Lake and Sabine Pass into the Gulf of Mexico; 360 mi. (579 km.) long; drains an area of 9733 sq. mi. (25,208 sq. km.); has two large reservoirs and forms a link in the Gulf Intracoastal Waterway. **2.** Name of a parish in W Louisiana and a county in E Texas. See tables at LOUISIANA and TEXAS.

Sabine, Cape. Point on E coast of Ellesmere I., N Canada, extending into Smith Sound; here part of U.S. Army officer Adolphus Greely's Arctic expedition perished 1883–84.

Sabine, Mount. Peak in Admiralty Mts., Victoria Land, Antarctica, 71°55′S, 169°33′E; 12,198 ft. (3718 m.).

Sabine Crossroads. Hamlet, DeSoto parish, Louisiana, ab. 40 mi. (64 km.) S of Shreveport; site of battle Apr. 8, 1864 in which Union forces under Gen. Nathaniel Banks were defeated by Confederates under Gen. Richard Taylor.

Sabine Lake. Lake bet. Louisiana and Texas, 5 mi. (8 km.) from the Gulf of Mexico, formed by expansion of Sabine River, which flows through it and Sabine Pass to the Gulf of Mexico.

Sabine–Nech·es Waterway \-ˈnā-chəz\. System of waterways at Port Arthur, Texas; includes the ship canal at Port Arthur, Sabine Pass, and the **Sabine–Neches Canal** which comprises the Neches River as far as Beaumont and the Sabine River as far as Orange; part of the Gulf Intracoastal Waterway.

Sabine Pass. Outlet for Sabine River extending from Sabine Lake to Gulf of Mexico on boundary bet. Louisiana and Texas.

Sab·khat al–Kur·zī·yah \ˈsäb-ˌk̲ät-äl-ku̇r-ˈzē-yə\ *or* **Seb·khet el Kour·zia** \ˈseb-ˌk̲et-el-ˈku̇r-zē-ə\. Saline lake, N cen. Tunisia, W of Zaghwān.

Sabkhat Tāwurghā'. See SEBCHA DI TAUORGA.

Sa·ble, Cape \ˈsā-bəl\. **1.** Cape at SW tip of Florida Penin. in Monroe co., enclosing Whitewater Bay, 25°12′N, 81°05′W; lies within Everglades National Park. **2.** Headland, SW Nova Scotia, Canada, on an islet S of Cape Sable I.

Sable Island. Low, sandy island, Nova Scotia, Canada, in North Atlantic Ocean 115 mi. (185 km.) SE of Cape Canso, 43°55′N, 59°50′W; ab. 20 mi. (32 km.) long and 1 mi. (2 km.) wide, the exposed part of a sandbar along W edge of Gulf Stream. Dangerous to navigation and the scene of numerous shipwrecks; site of unsuccessful French colony 1598–1603; two lighthouses built 1873.

Sables–d'Olonne, Les. See LES SABLES-D'OLONNE.

Sa·blé–sur–Sarthe \sȧ-ˈblā-sūr-ˈsärt\. Commune, SW Sarthe dept., NW France, on the Sarthe; restored medieval castle.

Sab·ra·ta \ˈsa-brə-tə\ *or* **Sabrātah** *or* **Abrot·o·num** \ə-ˈbrät-ᵊn-əm\. Ancient town, Roman Africa, on coast 48 mi. (77 km.) W of Tripoli; founded 4th cent. B.C. by Carthaginians; one of three chief cities of Tripolis (see TRIPOLI 1); remains include Roman and Byzantine fortifications, temples, forum, theater, basilica, and churches.

Sa·bra·ton \ˈsā-brə-tən\. Former industrial town, Monongalia co., West Virginia; annexed to Morgantown 1949; site of settlement (founded 1758) destroyed by Mingo Indians 1759.

Sabrina. See SEVERN 4.

Sa·bri·na Coast \sə-ˈbrī-nə, -ˈbrē-\. Section of coast of Wilkes Land, Antarctica, on Indian Ocean at ab. 67°S, bet. 117° and 119°30′E; probably first sighted 1839 by British.

Sab·tang \säb-ˈtäŋ\. Island, most southerly of Batan Is., N Philippines; 13 sq. mi. (34 sq. km.).

Şa·byā \ˈsä-ˌbyä\. City, Saudi Arabia, near Yemen border, at foot of mountain range ab. 40 mi. (65 km.) inland from Red Sea.

Sab·za·war. See SHĪNDAND.

Sab·ze·vār \ˌsab-zə-ˈvär\. Town, Khorāsān prov., NE Iran, 110 mi. (177 km.) W of Mashhad; pop. (1986c) 129,103; on the highway to Tehran.

Sac \ˈsȯk\. County in W Iowa. See table at IOWA.

Sac·an·da·ga \ˌsa-kən-ˈdȯ-gə\. River, E New York; rises in Piseco Lake and flows SE through Great Sacandaga Lake into the Hudson River in N Saratoga co; ab. 50 mi. (80 km.) long.

Sacandaga Reservoir. See GREAT SACANDAGA LAKE.

Sa·ca·te·pé·quez \ˌsä-kä-tā-ˈpā-kās\. Department of S cen. Guatemala. See table at GUATEMALA.

Sac·ca·rel·lo \ˌsä-kä-ˈrel-lō\. Mountain, NW Italy, on boundary bet. Liguria and Piedmont; highest point in the Ligurian Alps. See table at ALPS.

Sac City \ˈsȯk\. City, ⊗ of Sac co., W Iowa, 43 mi. (69 km.) W of Fort Dodge; pop. (1990c) 2492.

Sac·co \ˈsäk-kō\. River, cen. Italy; flows SE, joins the Liri S of Frosinone.

Să·ce·le \sə-ˈche-lā\. Town, Braşov co., cen. Romania, ab. 5 mi. (8 km.) ESE of the city of Braşov; pop. (1989c) 34,661.

Sach·seln \ˈzäks-ᵊln\. Commune, Obwalden demicanton, cen. Switzerland, near Sarnen; nearby is birthplace of Swiss religious Nicholas of Flüe 1417.

Sachsen. See SAXONY.

Sächsische Schweiz. See SAXON SWITZERLAND.

Sa·ci·le \sä-ˈchē-lā\. Commune, Pordenone prov., Friuli-Venezia Giulia, NE Italy, 23 mi. (37 km.) NE of Udine; pop. (1981p) 16,428; 15th cent. cathedral.

Sack·ets Harbor \ˈsa-kəts\. Village, Jefferson co., N New York, on Lake Ontario 11 mi. (18 km.) WSW of Watertown; pop. (1990c) 1313; settled 1801; during War of 1812, when it served as U.S. naval station, scene of several engagements.

Säck·ing·en \ˈze-kiŋ-ən\. Town, SW Baden-Württemberg, Germany, on the Rhine E of Basel; scene of writer Josef Victor von Scheffel's epic poem *Der Trompeter von Säckingen.*

Sack·ville \ˈsak-ˌvil\. Town, Westmorland co., SE New Brunswick, Canada, 25 mi. (40 km.) SE of Moncton and near the Nova Scotia boundary; pop. (1991c) 5494; paper products; diversified agriculture; Mount Allison Univ. (1839).

Sa·co \ˈsȯ-kō\. **1.** River, E cen. New Hampshire and SW Maine; rises in White Mts. W of Mt. Washington, NE cen. New Hampshire, flows S and SE across Maine border and SE into Atlantic Ocean 6 mi. (10 km.) below the city of Saco, York co., SW Maine; 104 mi. (167 km.) long. **2.** Residential city, York co., SW Maine, on Saco River just N of Biddeford; pop. (1990c) 15,181.

Sacralias. See ZALLAKA.

Sac·ra·men·to \ˌsa-krə-ˈmen-tō\. **1.** River, NW California; rises near Mt. Shasta in Siskiyou co., and flows S into Suisun Bay, E extension of San Francisco Bay; ab. 320 mi. (515 km.) long; navigable for 180 mi. (290 km.). **2.** County in N cen. California. See table at CALIFORNIA. **3.** City, ✻ of California and ⊗ of Sacramento co., N cen. California, on Sacramento River at the head of navigation 72 mi. (116 km.) NE of San Francisco; pop. (1990c) 369,365; became a deepwater seaport with completion of a ship channel 1963; transportation center; market and commercial center for farming region; food proccessing; aerospace industries; California State Railroad Museum; Sacramento City Coll. (1916), California State Univ., Sacramento (1947), American River Coll. (1955). Site first settled 1839 by John Sutter; an important trading center in California gold rush (1840s–50s); made state ✻ 1854; terminus of California's first railroad 1856, of Pony Express 1860, and of first transcontinental railroad 1869.

Sacramento Mountains. Range in S New Mexico, in Otero co. and extending N into Lincoln co. and E into Chaves and Eddy cos.; in center of region bet. the Pecos River and the Rio Grande; name sometimes includes range to the S known as Guadalupe Mts.

Sa·cri·fi·cios \ˌsä-krē-ˈfē-syōs\. Small island in the Gulf of Mexico, 3 mi. (5 km.) S of the city of Veracruz, Mexico; a place of sacrifice under the Aztecs.

Sacrum Promontorium. See CORSE, CAPE.

Sada, Cape. See ASHIZURI, CAPE.

Sá da Bandeira. See LUBANGO.

Sa·da·ni *or* **Saa·da·ni** \sä-ˈdä-nē\. Seaport, Tanzania, opp. Zanzibar I.

Saddle. See MOTA LAVA.

Sad·dle·back \ˈsad-ᵊl-ˌbak\ *or* **Blen·cath·a·ra** \blen-ˈka-thə-rə\. Mountain, Cumbria, NW England, in the Lake District 4.25 mi. (6.8 km.) NE of Keswick; 2847 ft. (868 m.).

Saddleback Mountain. **1.** Peak in Santa Ana Mts., S California.
2. Peak, Franklin co., W Maine, near Rangeley Lakes; 4116 ft. (1255 m.); ski slopes.
3. Peak in the Adirondack Mts., Essex co., NE New York; 4530 ft. (1381 m.).

Saddle Brook. Urban township, Bergen co., NE New Jersey, E of Paterson; pop. (1990c) 13,296.

Saddle Mountain. **1.** Peak on E boundary of Idaho co., N cen. Idaho; 8225 ft. (2507 m.).
2. Peak, Clatsop co., NW corner of Oregon; 3283 ft. (1001 m.).
3. Peak, S cen. Klamath co., S Oregon; 6841 ft. (2085 m.).
4. Peak, E Yellowstone National Park, NW Wyoming; 10,670 ft. (3252 m.).

Saddle Mountains. Range in S Kittitas and S Grant cos., cen. Washington.

Sa·di·ya \ˈsə-dē-ə\. Town, Assam, NE India, ab. 575 mi. (925 km.) NE of Calcutta; supply base and starting point for routes to China in WWII.

Sa·do \ˈsä-dō\. Mountainous island in E Sea of Japan, off NW coast of island of Honshū, Japan; 331 sq. mi. (857 sq. km.); rice growing, fishing; tourism; in early times, a place of exile.

Sa·do \ˈsȧ-dü\. River, S Portugal; flows NW into Atlantic Ocean at Setúbal; 110 mi. (177 km.) long; wide estuary.

Saena Julia. See SIENA 2.

Safad. See Z̲EFAT.

Safāqis. See SFAX.

Safed. See Z̲EFAT.

Sa·fed Koh \sə-ˌfed-ˈkō\. Mountain range, E Afghanistan, SE of Kabul on Pakistani border, an offshoot of the Hindu Kush; its remarkable evenness of height presents appearance of towering wall; highest peak Mt. Sikaram 15,619 ft. (4761 m.). Peiwar Pass is at W end.

Safe·ty Harbor \ˈsāf-tē-\. City, Pinellas co., W cen. Florida Penin., N of St. Petersburg; pop. (1990c) 15,124; pop. more than doubled bet. 1980 and 1990.

Safety Islands *or Fr.* **Îles du Sa·lut** \ˌēl-dūē-sȧ-ˈlūē\. French group of three islands, in the Atlantic Ocean 7 mi. (11 km.) off the N coast of French Guiana; Royale, Joseph, and Devil's I., used by France for a penal settlement until 1938.

Saffi. See SAFI.

Saf·ford \ˈsa-fərd\. City, ⊗ of Graham co., SE Arizona, on Gila River; pop. (1990c) 7359.

Saf·fron Wal·den \ˈsa-frən-ˈwȯl-dən\. Town, Essex, SE England, 40 mi. (64 km.) NNE of London; pop. (1981c) 12,592; saffron cultivation was an important occupation from 14th to 18th cents.

Saffuriyah. See ZIPPORI.

Sa·fi *or* **Saf·fi** \ˈsa-fē\. Seaport, W cen. Morocco, SW of Casablanca; pop. (1982c) 197,309; sardine canneries; chemicals, fertilizer; 16th cent. Portuguese fortress; mosque; during WWII Allies landed here 1942.

Sa·fīd Rud \sa-ˈfēd-ˈrüd\ *or* **Se·fid Rud** \se-ˈfēd\. The lower course of the Qezel Owzan River (*q.v.*), Iran.

Sa·fo·no·vo \sə-ˈfȯ-nə-vȯ\. Town, Smolensk Oblast, W Russia in Europe, ab. 50 mi. (80 km.) ENE of the city of Smolensk; pop. (1991e) 56,300.

Sa·ga \ˈsä-gä\. **1.** Prefecture, NW Kyūshū, Japan; ✻ Saga. See table at JAPAN.
2. City, its ✻, near coast of Shimabara Bay 43 mi. (69 km.) NE of Nagasaki; pop. (1992e) 170,145; textiles, ceramics.

Sag·a·da·hoc \ˌsa-gə-də-ˈhäk, ˈsa-gə-də-ˌhäk\. **1.** Early name for the Kennebec River, Maine. See KENNEBEC 1.
2. Coastal county in S Maine. See table at MAINE.

Sa·gaing \sə-ˈgīŋ\. **1.** Division, of Myanmar. See table at MYANMAR.
2. Town, its ✻, on right bank of the Irrawaddy opp. Ava 10 mi. (16 km.) W of Mandalay; river port; linked by rail to Myitkyina; numerous pagodas; bridge over the Irrawaddy; founded 14th cent. as ✻ of a Shan kingdom; formerly a ✻ of Burma (18th cent.).

Sa·ga·mi·ha·ra \ˌsä-gä-mē-ˈhä-rä\. City, Kanagawa prefecture, Honshū, Japan; pop. (1990p) 531,562.

Sa·ga·mi Sea \sä-ˈgä-mē\; *Jp.* **Sagami–na·da** \-ˈnä-dä\. Widemouthed bay on SE coast of Honshū, Japan, in Kanagawa prefecture SSW of Tokyo.

Sagan. See ŻAGAŃ.

Sa·gan·thit Island \ˌsä-gən-ˈtēt\; *formerly* **Sel·lore Island** \sə-ˈlōr\. Island in Mergui Archipelago (*q.v.*), Myanmar.

Sa·gar \ˈsä-gər\. **1.** *also* **Sa·gar·dwip** \-ˌdwip\. Island at the mouth of the Hugli River, S West Bengal, NE India; pilgrimage site.
2. *or* **Sau·gor** \ˈsȯ-gər, ˈsä-\. Town, N Madhya Pradesh, India, 180 mi. (290 km.) N of Nagpur; pop. (1991p) 195,106; university (1946); Maratha fort.

Sa·gay \sä-ˈgī\. Municipality, N Negros, Philippines, on Visayan Sea 37 mi. (60 km.) NE of City of Bacolod; pop. (1980c) 99,118.

Saghalien. See SAKHALIN.

Sag Harbor \ˈsag\. Village, Suffolk co., SE New York, at E end of Long Island, S of Shelter I., on Gardiners Bay 25 mi. (40 km.) W of Montauk Point; pop. (1990c) 2134; tourism; in mid-19th cent. an important whaling port.

Sag·i·naw \ˈsa-gə-ˌnȯ\. **1.** Navigable river, cen. Michigan; formed by confluence of the Flint and Shiawassee rivers, flows N into Saginaw Bay; 20 mi. (32 km.) long.
2. County in cen. Michigan. See table at MICHIGAN.
3. City, its ⊗, on Saginaw River 36 mi. (58 km.) NNW of Flint; pop. (1990c) 69,512; port of entry, commercial and transportation center; in sugar-beet and bean-farming region. Settlement developed around fur trading post founded 1816; incorp. 1857; combined with East Saginaw to form Saginaw 1889.
4. City, Tarrant co., Texas; pop. (1990c) 8551.

Saginaw Bay. Inlet of Lake Huron on coast of E cen. Michigan, SE of Arenac co., E of Bay co., NW of Tuscola co., and W of Huron co.

Sa·go·ne, Bay of \sä-gō-ˈnā, sä-ˈgō-nā\ *or Fr.* **Anse de Sa·gone** \ˌäⁿs-də-sȧ-ˈgȯn\. Inlet on W coast of Corsica, France, N of Ajaccio.

Sagra, La. See LA SAGRA.

Sagres. See SAINT VINCENT, CAPE 2.

Sagrus. See SANGRO.

Sa·guache \sə-ˈwäch\. **1.** County in S Colorado. See table at COLORADO.
2. Town, its ⊗; pop. (1990c) 584.

Sa·gua de Tá·na·mo \ˈsä-gwä-t͟hā-ˈtä-nä-ˌmō\. Municipality, E Cuba, near N coast 33 mi. (53 km.) N of Guantánamo; pop. (1981p) 57,525.

Sa·gua la Gran·de \ˈsä-gwā-lä-ˈgrän-dā\. **1.** River, N Las Villas prov., W cen. Cuba; flows N.
2. City, W cen. Cuba; munic. pop. (1990e) 56,263; railroad center 30 mi. (48 km.) NNW of Santa Clara.

Sa·gua·ro Lake \sə-ˈgwär-ō, -ˈwär-\. See STEWART MOUNTAIN DAM.

Saguaro National Monument. See UNITED STATES, *National Monuments.*

Sag·ue·nay \ˌsa-gə-ˈnā\. River, S Quebec, Canada; flows from Lac St.-Jean E into St. Lawrence River at Tadoussac; 105 mi. (169 km.) long; incl. the Peribonca River, ab. 475 mi. (765 km.) long. Leaves Lac St.-Jean by two channels, Big Discharge and Little Discharge, which enclose the island of Alma (see ALMA 7). Its fall 314 ft. (96 m.) is a source of hydroelectric power and its shores are in many places high cliffs 1000 to 1800 ft. (300 to 550 m.). Noted for its scenery, recreation, and as a resort.

Sa·guia el Ham·ra \ˈsä-gyä-ˌel-ˈäm-rə, -ˈhäm-\. Historical region comprising the N third of Western Sahara bet. the Moroccan border and 26°N lat.

Sa·gui·et el Ham·ra \sȧ-ˈgē-ət-ˌel-ˈhȧm-rə\ *or* **Sa·guia El Hamra** *also* **Se·kia el Hamra** \sə-ˈgē-ə-ˌel-\. River, Western Sahara.

Sa·gun·to \sä-ˈgün-tō\; *formerly* **Mur·vie·dro** \mür-ˈvyā-thrō\; *anc.* **Sa·gun·tum** \sə-ˈgən-təm\. Commune, Valencia prov., E Spain, near Mediterranean 15 mi. (24 km.) NNE of the commune of Valencia; pop. (1991c) 55,457; agricultural products; garrisoned castle; ancient Roman theater and other Roman and Greek remains.

History: Perhaps settled by Greeks c. 3d cent. B.C.; allied with Rome when taken by Carthaginian Gen. Hannibal 219 B.C., event which started Second Punic War; captured by Moors early 8th cent. A.D.; conquered by James I of Aragon c. 1238; in Peninsular War captured by French under Adm. Louis-Gabriel Suchet 1808; end of first Spanish Republic proclaimed here 1874 and Bourbons, in person of Alfonso XII, restored to throne; medieval name (Murviedro) discarded in favor of earlier name (Sagunto) 1877.

Sa·ha·gún \ˌsä-ä-ˈgün\. Commune, León prov., Spain; pop. (1991c) 3413; ruins of Benedictine monastery.

Sahama. See SAJAMA, NEVADO.

Sa·hand, Kūh–e \ˈkü-he-sä-ˈhänd\. Mountain, NW Iran, E of Daryācheh-ye Orūmīyeh and just S of Tabrīz; 12,105 ft. (3690 m.).

Sa·hara \sə-ˈhar-ə, -ˈhär-\ *or Arab.* **Sah·ra** \ˈsä-ˌhrä\. Vast region of deserts and oases, N Africa; extends from Atlas Mts. and Atlantic coast of Western Sahara E to Red Sea; ab. 3,500,000 sq. mi. (9,065,000 sq. km.); of varied surface and irregular relief, ranging from 100 ft. (30 m.) below sea level to more than 11,000 ft. (3350 m.) above. See LIBYAN DESERT.

Saharan Atlas. See ATLAS MOUNTAINS.

Sa·ha·ran·pur \sə-ˈhär-ən-ˌpu̇r\. City, NW Uttar Pradesh, N India, 100 mi. (161 km.) NNE of Delhi; pop. (1991c) 374,945; paper, sugar, railroad workshops; founded c. 1340.

Sa·hel \sä-ˈhel\. Semidesert S fringe of the Sahara, N Africa, stretching from Mauritania and Senegal to Chad.

Sa·hi·wal \ˈsä-hē-ˌwäl, -ˌväl\; *formerly* **Mont·gom·ery** \mənt-ˈgəm-rē, mänt-, -ˈgäm-\. Town, Punjab, Pakistan, on Bari Doab Canal 92 mi. (148 km.) SW of Lahore; pop. (1981c) 152,000; founded c. 1865.

Sahra. See SAHARA.

Sa·hua·yo \sä-ˈwä-yō\ *or in full* **Sahuayo de Por·fi·rio Dí·az** \thā-pōr-ˈfē-rē-ō-ˈthē-äs\. Municipality, Michoacán state, Mexico, 62 mi. (100 km.) NW of Uruapan; pop. (1990p) 48,426; livestock raising; diversified agriculture.

Sai·bai \ˈsī-ˌbī\. Island, Australia, off S coast of New Guinea I., WSW of Daru and on N side of Torres Strait.

Sa·i·da \sī-ˈdä\. **1.** Town, N Algeria, on S slopes of Little Atlas Mts; pop. (1987p) 80,825.

2. Seaport, Lebanon. See SIDON.

Saida Mountains. Range of the Atlas Mts., in Maritime Atlas, NW Algeria; highest peak ab. 3870 ft. (1180 m.).

Sai·dor \ˈsī-ˌdȯr\. Coastal town, E coast of New Guinea I., Papua New Guinea, on Vitiaz Strait ab. 55 mi. (88 km.) ESE of Madang; has good harbor.

Said·pur \ˈsīd-ˌpu̇r\. Town, N Bangladesh, ab. 165 mi. (265 km.) NNW of Dhaka; pop. (1991p) 110,494.

Sai·gō \ˈsī-gō\. See OKI ARCHIPELAGO.

Saigon. See HO CHI MINH CITY.

Sai·la·na \sī-ˈlä-nə\. Former Indian state, W cen. India; 300 sq. mi. (777 sq. km.); joined Union of Rajasthan June 26, 1947.

Sai–li–mu Hu. See SAYRAM HU.

Sail·ly–Sail·li·sel \sȧ-ˌyē-sȧ-yē-ˈzel\. Village, Somme dept., N France, 6 mi. (10 km.) N of Péronne; severe fighting 1916 to 1918, esp. during battle of the Somme July to Nov. 1916.

Sai·maa, Lake \ˈsī-ˌmä\. Lake, SE Finland; 680 sq. mi. (1761 sq. km.); drains E through Vuoksi River into Lake Ladoga.

Sain–ni \ˈsīn-ˈnē\. Town, ✻ of South P'yŏngan prov., North Korea.

Saint *Eng.* ˈsānt, sənt; *Fr.* ˌsaⁿ\. The following are foreign equivalents for the word "saint" often occurring in placenames: *Fr.*, Saint or Sainte; *Ital. and Span.*, San, Santa, Santo; *Port.*, São; *Ger. and Scandinavian*, Sankt; *Rom.*, Sfânta, Sfântul; *Du.*, Sint; *Slovak*, Svätý; *Serb.*, Sveti; *Bulg.*, Svetiya; *Russ.*, Svyatoy; *Hung.*, Szent; *Gk.*, Hagion, Hagios.

Saint Abb's Head \ˈabz\. Cape, SE coast of Scotland, near English border, projecting into North Sea; lighthouse.

Saint–Acheul \ˌsaⁿt-ə-ˈshœl\. Hamlet, Somme dept., N France, near Amiens. Lower Paleolithic axes found here c. 1835 furnishing typical artifacts of Acheulean technology.

Saint Ag·nes Head \ˈag-nəs\. Promontory, W coast of Cornwall, SW England, WNW of Truro.

Saint Aignan. See MISIMA.

Saint Al·bans \ˈȯl-bənz\. **1.** City, ⊗ of Franklin co., NW Vermont, near Lake Champlain 29 mi. (47 km.) N of Burlington; pop. (1990c) 7339; dairy products, maple syrup; baby food; settled 1763; town attacked and bank looted in 1864 by Confederate soldiers crossing from Canada in attempt to shake Northerners.

2. City, Kanawha co., W cen. West Virginia, on Kanawha River 12 mi. (19 km.) W of Charleston; pop. (1990c) 11,194; machine shops; truck farms.

3. *anc.* **Ver·u·la·mi·um** \ˌver-u̇-ˈlā-mē-əm, ˌver-yu̇-\. City, Hertfordshire, SE England, 20 mi. (32 km.) NNW of London; pop. (1991p) 122,400; electrical equipment, musical instruments; printing; 11th–14th cent. cathedral (former abbey church) with one of the longest Gothic naves in the world; abbey founded 793 and prominent in the Middle Ages, being the home of notable chroniclers incl. Roger of Wendover, Matthew Paris, and Thomas Walsingham; site of two royal battles during Wars of the Roses 1455 and 1461; after dissolution of abbey, city received first charter 1553.

Saint Al·ban's Head \ˈȯl-bənz\. Headland on the coast of Dorset, S England.

Saint Al·bert \ˈal-bərt\. Town, Alberta, Canada, 5 mi. (8 km.) NW of Edmonton; pop. (1991c) 42,146; agriculture.

Saint–Amand–les–Eaux \ˌsaⁿt-ə-ˈmäⁿ-lā-ˈzō\; *sometimes shortened to* **Saint–Amand.** City, Nord dept., N France, 22 mi. (35 km.) SE of Lille; textiles, foundry products; thermal springs; built around abbey founded 647 by St. Amand; center for production of faïence in 18th cent.

Saint An·dré, Cape \ˌsaⁿt-äⁿ-ˈdrā\. Cape extending into Mozambique Channel on NW cen. coast of Madagascar.

Saint An·drews \ˈan-ˌdrüz\. **1.** Unincorporated settlement, Richland co., cen. South Carolina; pop. (1990c) 25,692.

2. Town, ⊗ of Charlotte co., SW New Brunswick, Canada, on Passamaquoddy Bay at mouth of St. Croix River; pop. (1991c) 1652; summer resort.

3. Seaport burgh, Fife region, E Scotland, on **Saint Andrews Bay** 13 mi. (21 km.) SE of Dundee; pop. (1981p) 11,302; noted seaside and golfing resort; St. Andrews Univ. (c. 1411, oldest university in Scotland); ruins of 12th–13th cent. cathedral, former seat of the primate of Scotland; 13th cent. castle; received charter 1160 and was one of the principal towns in Scotland during the Middle Ages.

Saint An·drew Sound \ˈan-ˌdrü\. Inlet of Atlantic Ocean on NE coast of Camden co., SE Georgia, receiving the Satilla River on the W.

Saint Ann \ˈan\. City, St. Louis co., E Missouri, NW suburb of the city of St. Louis; pop. (1990c) 14,489.

Saint Ann Bay. See SAINT ANN'S BAY 1.

Saint Anne \ˈan\. Town, ✻ of Alderney I., Channel Is., United Kingdom.

Saint Ann's Bay **1.** *also* **Saint Ann Bay.** Inlet of Atlantic Ocean in NE Cape Breton I., Nova Scotia, Canada.

2. Town on N coast of island of Jamaica, West Indies; pop. (1991p) 10,518.

Saint Ann's Head. Cape on SW extremity of Wales, N of entrance to Milford Haven; lighthouse.

Saint An·tho·ny \ˈant-thə-nē\. **1.** City, ⊗ of Fremont co., E Idaho, 40 mi. (64 km.) NE of Idaho Falls; pop. (1990c) 3010.
2. City, Hennepin and Ramsey cos., Minnesota, N suburb of Minneapolis; pop. (1990c) 7727.
3. Seaport, NE Newfoundland, Canada, on Atlantic Ocean 20 mi. (32 km.) S of Cape Bauld; pop. (1991c) 3164.

Saint Anthony, Falls of *or* **Saint Anthony's Falls.** Waterfall in the Mississippi River in the center of the city of Minneapolis, Minnesota; ab. 50 ft. (15 m.) high; total fall incl. rapids above and below is ab. 85 ft. (26 m.); furnishes industrial power. Visited c. 1680 by French missionary Louis Hennepin; center of first village in area in mid-19th cent.

Saint As·aph \ˈā-səf\. City, Clwyd co., NE Wales; parish pop. (1981c) 3401; cathedral, one of smallest in Great Britain.

Saint Au·gus·tine \ˈȯ-gə-ˌstēn\. City, ⊗ of St. Johns co., NE Florida, on Atlantic Ocean 35 mi. (56 km.) SE of Jacksonville; pop. (1990c) 11,692; port of entry; winter and summer resort; Flagler Coll. (1968). Oldest permanent existing European settlement on continent of North America; founded by Pedro Menéndez de Avilés 1565; burned by English navigator Sir Francis Drake 1586; great stone fort of Castillo de San Marcos begun by Spanish 1672; attacked by South Carolina troops and British soldier James Oglethorpe, founder of Georgia, in 18th cent.; a refuge of Loyalists during American Revolution; held by Union troops in Civil War from 1862 (see FLORIDA).

Saint Augustine Beach. City, St. Johns co., NE Florida, on Anastasia I., SE of St. Augustine; pop. (1990c) 3657.

Saint Augustine Inlet. Narrow strait leading from Atlantic Ocean through barrier reef opp. cen. St. Johns co., NE Florida.

Saint Aus·tell \ˈȯst-ᵊl\. Town, Cornwall, SW England, on **Saint Austell Bay** 28 mi. (45 km.) W of Plymouth; pop. (1981c) 20,585; center of kaolin production in England.

Saint-Avold \ˌseⁿt-ä-ˈvȯl\. Town, Moselle dept., NE France, 23 mi. (37 km.) E of Metz; U.S. military cemetery.

Saint-Bar·thé·le·my *or* **Saint-Barthélemy** \seⁿ-ˌbär-ˌtāl-ˈmē\; *informally* **Saint Bart's** \ˌsānt-ˈbärts\. Island in French overseas dept. of Guadeloupe, West Indies, in Leeward Is.

Saint-Ba·sile-le-Grand \ˌseⁿ-bä-ˈzēl-lə-ˈgräⁿ\. Town, S Quebec, Canada, E of Longueil; pop. (1991c) 10,127.

Saint Bath·ans, Mount \ˈba-thənz\. Peak, S cen. South I., New Zealand; 6842 ft. (2085 m.).

Saint Bees Head \ˈbēz\. Cape on NW coast of England, projecting into Irish Sea S of entrance to Solway Firth; lighthouse.

Saint Ber·nard \ˌsānt-bər-ˈnärd\. **1.** Parish in SE Louisiana. See table at LOUISIANA.
2. City, Hamilton co., SW corner of Ohio, 5 mi. (8 km.) N of Cincinnati; pop. (1990c) 5344; suburb of Cincinnati.
3. Two passes, Great St. Bernard and Little St. Bernard, in Alps. See table at ALPS.

Saint Bonaventure. See ALLEGANY 2.

Saint Bon·i·face \ˈbä-nə-ˌfās\. Community, Winnipeg area, S Manitoba, Canada, on Red River; stockyards, oil refineries, packing plants, flour mills; founded 1818, incorp. as city 1908. Birthplace of 19th cent. Métis rebel Louis Riel 1844; important French-Canadian and Roman Catholic community for W Canada.

Saint Boniface de Sha·win·i·gan \də-shə-ˈwi-ni-gən\. Village, S Quebec, Canada, 18 mi. (29 km.) NW of Trois-Rivières; pop. (1991c) 3813.

Saint Bon·i·fa·cius \ˌbä-nə-ˈfā-shəs\. City, Hennepin co., SE cen. Minnesota; pop. (1990c) 1180; St. Paul Bible Coll. (1916).

Saint Botolph's Town. See BOSTON 3.

Saint Brandon Shoals. See CARGADOS CARAJOS SHOALS.

Saint Bride's Bay \ˈbrīdz\. Inlet of St. George's Channel on the SW extremity of Wales.

Saint-Bri·euc \ˌseⁿ-brē-ˈœ\. City, ✻ of Côtes-du-Nord dept., NW France, on English Channel 70 mi. (113 km.) NE of Quimper; pop. (1990c) 47,370; railroad junction, commercial center, coastal and fishing port; 13th cent. fortress-cathedral; founded c. 5th cent. A.D. by St. Brieuc, a Welsh monk; sacked by Spanish 1592.

Saint Bru·no de Mon·tar·ville \ˌseⁿ-brü-ˈnō-də-ˌmōⁿ-tär-ˈvēl\. Town, S Quebec, Canada, 10 mi. (16 km.) E of Montreal; pop. (1991c) 23,849.

Saint Cath·a·rine, Lake *also* **Lake Cath·er·ine** \ˈka-thrin, -thə-rin\. Lake in SW Rutland co., W Vermont.

Saint Cath·a·rines \ˈka-thrinz, -thə-rinz\. City, ⊗ of Niagara munic. region, SE Ontario, Canada, on Welland Canal just S of Lake Ontario; pop. (1991c) 129,300; automobile parts, machinery, electrical equipment, hosiery; packs and ships fruit; Brock Univ. (1962); settled 1790; incorp. as town 1845, as city 1876.

Saint Cath·er·ine, Mount. Mountain, N Grenada I., Grenada, West Indies; 2757 ft. (840 m.); highest point on the island.

Saint Catherine Point. Cape on N extremity of Bermuda I., Bermuda, W North Atlantic Ocean.

Saint Cath·er·ines Island. Island in Atlantic Ocean, off E mainland of Liberty co., SE Georgia; 21 sq. mi. (54 sq. km.).

Saint Catherine's Point. Cape on S tip of Isle of Wight, off S coast of England; lighthouse.

Saint Catherines Sound. Inlet of Atlantic Ocean on E coast of Liberty co., SE Georgia.

Saint-Cha·mond \ˌseⁿ-shə-ˈmōⁿ\. Commune, Loire dept., SE cen. France, 7 mi. (11 km.) NE of St.-Étienne.

Saint Charles \ˈchärlz\. **1.** Name of a parish in SE Louisiana and of a county in E Missouri. See tables at LOUISIANA and MISSOURI.
2. City, Kane co., NE Illinois, 37 mi. (60 km.) W of Chicago; pop. (1990c) 22,501.
3. City, Winona co., SE Minnesota, ESE of Rochester; pop. (1990c) 2642.
4. City, ⊗ of St. Charles co., E Missouri, on Missouri River; pop. (1990c) 54,555; Lindenwood Coll. (1827); settled 1769; incorp. as city 1849; ✻ of Missouri Terr., and first ✻ of state 1821–26.

Saint Christopher. See SAINT KITTS.

Saint Christopher-Nevis *or* **Saint Christopher and Nevis.** See SAINT KITTS-NEVIS.

Saint Christopher-Nevis-Anguilla. See SAINT KITTS-NEVIS.

Saint Clair \ˈklar\. **1.** Navigable river, SE Michigan; connects Lake Huron with Lake St. Clair; forms part of U.S.-Canada boundary; ab. 40 mi. (65 km.) long.
2. Name of counties in four states of the U.S. See tables at ALABAMA, ILLINOIS, MICHIGAN, MISSOURI.
3. City, St. Clair co., SE Michigan, on St. Clair River 10 mi. (16 km.) S of Port Huron; pop. (1990c) 5116.
4. City, Franklin co., E Missouri, 50 mi. (80 km.) SW of St. Louis; pop. (1990c) 3917.
5. Borough, Schuylkill co., E cen. Pennsylvania, 4 mi. (6 km.) WNW of Pottsville; pop. (1990c) 3524.

Saint Clair, Lake. **1.** Lake bet. state of Michigan and Canadian prov. of Ontario; the U.S.-Canada boundary passes through it; ab. 30 mi. (48 km.) long; area ab. 450 sq. mi. (1150 sq. km.), max. depth 26 ft. (8 m.); connects with Lake Huron by St. Clair River, and with Lake Erie by Detroit River.
2. Lake, E cen. Tasmania, Australia, source of Derwent River; 9 mi. (14 km.) long; ab. 16 sq. mi. (41 sq. km.); noted for its scenery and fishing; in Cradle Mountain–Lake St. Clair National Park.

Saint Clair Shores. City, Macomb co., SE Michigan, on Lake St. Clair 13 mi. (21 km.) NE of Detroit; pop. (1990c) 68,107; residential; boating center.

Saint Clairs·ville \ˈklarz-ˌvil\. City, ⊗ of Belmont co., E Ohio, 24 mi. (39 km.) SSW of Steubenville; pop. (1990c) 5162.

Saint-Claude \seⁿ-ˈklōd\; *anc.* **Con·da·te** \kän-ˈdā-tē\. Commune, Jura dept., E France; gem cutting; 15th cent. cathedral. Founded in pre-Roman times.

Saint Clem·ent Bay \ˈkle-mənt\. Inlet of Potomac River on SW shore of St. Marys co., S Maryland.

Saint–Cloud \seⁿ-ˈklü\. Commune, Hauts-de-Seine dept., N France, WSW suburb of Paris near Seine River; pop. (1990c) 28,673; national porcelain factory (formerly located at Sèvres); formerly residence of French monarchs; scene of murder of Henry III 1589; scene of Napoléon's coup of the 18th Brumaire 1799 and his declaration as emperor 1804.

Saint Cloud \ˌsānt-ˈklau̇d\. **1.** City, Osceola co., cen. Florida Penin., 23 mi. (37 km.) S of Orlando; pop. (1990c) 12,453. **2.** City, ⊗ of Stearns co., but also in Benton and Sherburne cos., cen. Minnesota, on Mississippi River 58 mi. (93 km.) NW of Minneapolis; pop. (1990c) 48,812; metalworking; railroad shops; St. Cloud State Univ. (1869); settled 1850s; incorp. as city 1868.

Saint–Cons·tant \ˌseⁿ-kōⁿ-ˈstäⁿ\. Town, S Quebec, Canada, ab. 10 mi. (16 km.) S of Montreal; pop. (1996c) 21,933.

Saint Croix \ˈkrȯi\. **1.** River forming S section of boundary bet. Maine and the Canadian prov. of New Brunswick; flows S from Chiputneticook Lakes into Passamaquoddy Bay; 129 mi. (208 km.) long.
2. River, NW Wisconsin and E Minnesota; rises in Douglas co., NW Wisconsin, flows SW and forms part of Wisconsin-Minnesota boundary until it empties into the Mississippi below St. Paul; 164 mi. (264 km.) long; navigable ab. 54 mi. (87 km.) to **The Dalles** \ˈdalz\, a deep gorge.
3. County in W Wisconsin. See table at WISCONSIN.
4. *also* **San·ta Cruz** \ˈsan-tə-ˈkrüz\. Largest island of the Virgin Is. of the U.S., West Indies, ab. 37 mi. (60 km.) S of St. Thomas; 84 sq. mi. (218 sq. km.); pop. (1990c) 50,139; most populous of the U.S. Virgin Is.; chief town Christiansted; only other town is Frederiksted, at W end; tourism; rum. Visited 1493 by explorer Christopher Columbus; in turn became possession of Dutch, English, Spanish, and French; purchased by Denmark 1753; sold to U.S. 1917.

Saint Croix Island International Historic Site. Reservation, E Maine, on border with Canada; 35.39 acres (14 hectares); commemorates French settlement of 1604; estab. as a national monument 1949; redesignated 1984.

Saint–Cyr–l'École \seⁿ-ˌsēr-lā-ˈkȯl\. Commune, Yvelines, N France, 3 mi. (5 km.) W of Versailles; site of military school estab. 1808 by Emperor Napoléon and destroyed 1944; school relocated at Coëtquidan after WWII.

Saint David. See MAPIA.

Saint David Island \ˈdā-vəd\. Island, NE Bermuda Is., Bermuda, W North Atlantic Ocean, N of Castle Harbour.

Saint Da·vids \ˈdā-vədz\. Locality, Delaware co., SE Pennsylvania, W of Philadelphia; Eastern Coll. (1932).

Saint Da·vid's \ˈdā-vədz\ *or Welsh* **My·nyw** \ˈmə-nyü\; *anc.* **Me·ne·via** \mə-ˈnē-vē-ə\. Parish, Dyfed co., SW Wales; pop. (1981c) 1930; 12th–14th cent. cathedral; see of Menevia perhaps founded in 6th cent. by St. David, patron saint of Wales; shrine of St. David was pilgrimage site in Middle Ages.

Saint Davids Head. Cape at E end of St. David I., NE Bermuda Is.; Bermuda, W North Atlantic Ocean, easternmost point of the islands, 32°22′N, 64°38′W.

Saint David's Head. Cape, Dyfed co., SW coast of Wales, extending into St. George's Channel; cliffs ab. 100 ft. (30 m.) high; westernmost point of Wales, 51°55′N, 5°19′W.

Saint–De·nis \ˌseⁿ-də-ˈnē\. **1.** Commune, Seine-St.-Denis dept., N France, 7 mi. (11 km.) NNE of Paris; pop. (1990c) 90,806; chemicals, diesel engines, pharmaceuticals; 12th cent. Gothic abbey church containing tombs of French monarchs, among them Louis XII, Anne of Brittany, Henry II, Catherine de Médicis, Francis I, Claude of France, Louis XVI, Marie Antoinette, Louis XIII; abbey of St.-Denis founded here c. 626 by the Merovingian King Dagobert I; philosopher and theologian Peter Abelard resided here as monk in 12th cent.; the banner of St. Denis, the oriflamme, served as royal standard from reign of Louis VI (early 12th cent.) until reign of Charles VI (late 14th–early 15th cent.); called **Fran·ciade** \fräⁿ-ˈsyäd\ during the Revolution.
2. City, ✱ of French island of Réunion in the Indian Ocean, on N coast; pop. (1990c) 100,926.

Saint–Denis–du–Sig. See SIG.

Saint–Denis–le–Gast \-lə-ˈgäst\. Commune, Manche dept., NW France, 12 mi. (19 km.) N of Avranches; scene of breakthrough of U.S. armored forces July 30, 1944 in WWII.

Saint–Dié \ˌseⁿ-ˈdyā\. Commune, Vosges dept., NE France, on Meurthe River 25 mi. (40 km.) ENE of Épinal; pop. (1990c) 23,670; 12th cent. cathedral; built around a monastery founded by St. Deodatus in 7th cent.

Saint–Di·zier \ˌseⁿ-dē-ˈzyā\; *anc.* **Des·i·de·rii Fa·num** \ˌde-sə-ˈdir-ē-ˌī-ˈfā-nəm\. Commune, Haute-Marne dept., NE France, on Marne River 39 mi. (63 km.) N of Chaumont; pop. (1990c) 35,558; iron and bronze foundries. Besieged by forces of Holy Roman Emperor Charles V in 1544.

Saint Do·mingue \ˌseⁿ-dȯ-ˈmeⁿg\. French form of Santo Domingo, early name of Haiti, sometimes applied to entire island (see HISPANIOLA).

Sainte–Adresse \ˌseⁿt-ȧ-ˈdres\. Commune, Seine-Maritime dept., N France, near Le Havre; seat of Belgian government Oct. 1914 to Dec. 1918 during WWI.

Sainte Agathe des Monts \ˌseⁿt-ȧ-ˌgät-dā-ˈmōⁿ\. Resort town, S Quebec, Canada, 52 mi. (84 km.) NW of Montreal; pop. (1991c) 5452.

Sainte–Anne \seⁿt-ˈȧn\. Commune and village, S coast of Grande-Terre I., Guadeloupe, West Indies.

Sainte Anne **1.** \sānt-ˈan, sənt-\. Fort, Vermont. See FORT SAINTE ANNE.
2. *Fr.* seⁿt-ȧn\. River, S Quebec, Canada; flows S into the St. Lawrence at Ste. Anne de Beaupré; ab. 50 mi. (80 km.) long.

Sainte Anne de Beau·pré \seⁿt-ˈȧn-də-bō-ˈprā\. Village, S Quebec, Canada, on St. Lawrence River 21 mi. (34 km.) NE of Quebec City; pop. (1991c) 3146; site of shrine to St. Anne since 1658; 20th cent. basilica.

Sainte Anne de Belle·vue \-də-bel-ˈvü\. Town at SW end of Montreal I., S Quebec, Canada, on Lake St. Louis 21 mi. (34 km.) WSW of Montreal; pop. (1991c) 4030; Macdonald Coll. of Agriculture.

Sainte Anne des Monts \-dā-ˈmōⁿ\. Town, on Gaspé Penin., SE Quebec, Canada, on St. Lawrence River at its mouth; pop. (1991c) 5652.

Sainte Anne's Point. See FREDERICTON.

Sainte–Baume \seⁿt-ˈbōm\. Mountain chain in Bouches-du-Rhône and Var depts., SE France; highest point 3260 ft. (994 m.); site of grotto where St. Mary Magdalene is thought to have been sheltered; popular place of pilgrimage.

Sainte Croix \seⁿ-tə-ˈkrwä, sānt-ˈkrȯi\. Village, ⊗ of Lotbinière co., S Quebec, Canada, on S bank of the St. Lawrence River 28 mi. (45 km.) SW of Quebec City; pop. (1991c) 1650.

Sainte Fa·mille \ˌseⁿt-fȧ-ˈmēʸ\. Parish village, S Quebec, Canada, on N shore of Orleans I., 28 mi. (45 km.) NE of Quebec City; pop. (1991c) 942.

Sainte–Foy \seⁿt-ˈfwä\. City, Quebec co., S Quebec, Canada, 4 mi. (6 km.) SW of Quebec City; pop. (1991c) 71,133.

Sainte Gen·e·vieve \sānt-ˈje-nə-ˌvēv, sənt-\. **1.** County in E Missouri. See table at MISSOURI.
2. City, its ⊗, on Mississippi River 46 mi. (74 km.) S of St. Louis; pop. (1990c) 4411; diversified agriculture; site of first permanent settlement in Missouri c. 1735.

Sainte Ge·ne·viève \ˌseⁿt-ˌzhə-nə-ˈvyev\. Town, ⊗ of Champlain co., S Quebec, Canada, on Batiscan River near its mouth; pop. (1991c) 3197.

Sainte–Geneviève–des–Bois \-dā-ˈbwä\. Commune, Essonne dept., N France, ab. 15 mi. (24 km.) S of Paris.

Sainte–Ju·lie \ˌseⁿt-zhü-ˈlē\. Town, S Quebec, Canada, ab. 15 mi. (24 km.) E of Montreal; pop. (1996c) 24,030.

Sainte Ju·lienne \ˌseⁿt-zhü-ˈlyen\. Parish village, ⊗ of Montcalm co., S Quebec, Canada, 32 mi. (51 km.) N of Montreal; pop. (1991c) 6092.

Saint Eli·as, Cape \ˌsānt-ə-ˈlī-əs\. Point, S end of Kayak I., off SE coast of Alaska.

Saint Elias, Mount. **1.** Peak in the St. Elias Mts., on the boundary bet. SW Yukon Terr., Canada, and E Alaska; 18,008 ft. (5489 m.)
2. Mountain peaks, Greece. See HAGIOS ELIAS, MOUNT.

Saint Elias Mountains *also* **Saint Elias Range.** Mountain range, SW Yukon Terr., Canada, and E Alaska, near the Pacific Ocean; ab. 250 mi. (400 km.) long; highest peak Mt. Logan 19,850 ft. (6050 m.). On its S slopes are the Malaspina and Guyot glaciers in Alaska.

Sainte–Marguerite. See LÉRINS, ÎLES DE.

Sainte Ma·rie \ˈseⁿt-ˈmȧ-rē, ˌsānt-mə-ˈrē\. Town, Beauce-Sartigan co., S Quebec, Canada, on Chaudière River 28 mi. (45 km.) SSE of Quebec City; pop. (1991c) 10,542.

Sainte–Marie, Cape. Extreme S tip of Madagascar.

Sainte–Marie–aux–Mines \ˌseⁿt-mȧ-ˌrē-ō-ˈmēn\ *or Ger.* **Mar·kirch** \ˈmär-ˌkirk\. Commune, Haut-Rhin dept., NE France; silver, copper, and lead mines in the vicinity, worked 9th–18th cents.

Sainte–Marie, Île. See NOSY BORAHA.

Sainte–Me·ne·hould \ˌseⁿt-mə-ˈnü\. Commune, NE Marne dept., NE France, on the Aisne; on W border of the Argonne Forest.

Sainte–Mère–Église \ˌseⁿt-ˌmer-ā-ˈglēz\. Commune, Manche dept., NW France, ab. 20 mi. (32 km.) SE of Cherbourg; taken June 1944 by U.S. paratroops early in invasion of Normandy.

Saintes \ˈseⁿt\; *anc.* **Me·di·o·la·num San·to·num** \ˌmē-dē-ō-ˈlā-nəm-san-ˈtō-nəm, -ˈla-\ *or* **Mediolanum.** City, Charente-Maritime dept., W France, on Charente River 40 mi. (64 km.) SE of La Rochelle; pop. (1990c) 27,546; market town; produces brandy; 15th cent. cathedral; Roman amphitheater. Ancient center of the Santones, a Gallic tribe; ✻ of old prov. of Saintonge; scene of defeat of Henry III of England by Louis IX 1242.

Saintes, Îles des *or* **Saintes, Les.** See ÎLES DES SAINTES.

Sainte Scholastique. See MIRABEL 2.

Saint–Es·tèphe \seⁿt-es-ˈtef\. Commune, Gironde dept., SW France, on the Gironde ab. 25 mi. (40 km.) NNW of Bordeaux; in the Médoc; red wines from the Châteaux Cos d'Estournel and Montrose.

Sainte Thé·rèse \ˌseⁿt-tā-ˈrez, ˌsānt-tə-ˈrēs\. **1.** Island, in the St. Lawrence at the foot of Montreal I., S Quebec, Canada; ab. 3 mi. (5 km.) long.
2. Town, S Quebec, Canada, 18 mi. (29 km.) NW of Montreal; pop. (1991c) 24,158.

Saint–Étienne \ˌseⁿt-ā-ˈtyen\. City, ✻ of Loire dept., SE cen. France, 32 mi. (51 km.) SW of Lyon; pop. (1990c) 201,569; important center of textile and dyeing industry; also produces alloy steels, small arms and ammunition; government armaments factory, coal mines historically important. A primary city in French industrial revolution; first steel mill in France and terminus of first French railway.

Saint–Étienne–du–Rou·vray \-dœ̄-ˌrü-ˈvrā\. Commune, Seine-Maritime dept., N France, 3 mi. (5 km.) S of Rouen; textiles.

Saint Eus·tache \ˌseⁿt-œ̄-ˈstȧsh\. Town, Deux Montagnes co., S Quebec, Canada, on Rivière des Mille Îles across from Jesus I.; pop. (1991c) 37,278.

Saint Eu·sta·ti·us \ˌsānt-yu̇-ˈstā-shəs\. Small island of the Leeward Is., West Indies, NW of St. Kitts; 8 sq. mi. (21 sq. km.); pop. (1990c) 1715; part of the Netherlands Antilles; settled by French 1625; became Dutch 1632; sacked by English 1781.

Saint Fé·li·cien \seⁿ-ˌfā-lēs-ˈyeⁿ, ˌsānt-fə-ˈli-shən\. Town, Le Domaine-du-Roy co., S Quebec, Canada, on Chamouchouane River near its mouth, W of Lac St.-Jean; pop. (1991c) 9340; lumber; potatoes, vegetables.

Saint–Flo·rent, Gulf of \ˌseⁿ-flō-ˈräⁿ\. Inlet, NW coast of Corsica, France; the town of **Saint–Florent** is on it.

Saint–Flour \seⁿ-ˈflür\. Commune, E Cantal dept., S cen. France; built on a steep rock; 14th–15th cent. cathedral.

Saint Fran·cis \sānt-ˈfran-səs\. **1.** River, N Maine; with **Lake Saint Francis** (actually an expansion of the river) forms a section of the extreme N boundary of Maine and flows into St. John River.
2. River, SE Missouri and E Arkansas; rises in Iron co., SE Missouri, flows S and forms section of boundary bet. SE Missouri and NE Arkansas, continues S through E Arkansas into Mississippi River; 425 mi. (684 km.) long; navigable 125 mi. (201 km.).
3. County in E Arkansas. See table at ARKANSAS.
4. City, ⊗ of Cheyenne co., NW corner of Kansas; pop. (1990c) 1495.
5. City, Anoka co., E Minnesota; pop. (1990c) 2538.
6. City, Milwaukee co., SE Wisconsin, SW of the city of Milwaukee; pop. (1990c) 9245.
7. *or Fr.* **Saint–Fran·çois** \seⁿ-fräⁿ-ˈswȧ\. River, S Quebec, Canada; flows SW out of Lake St. Francis, then NW into Lake St. Peter in the St. Lawrence River below Sorel; 165 mi. (265 km.) long.

Saint Francis, Cape. **1.** Cape, Canada. See FRANCIS, CAPE.
2. Cape on SE coast of Eastern Cape prov., S Rep. of South Africa, W of St. Francis Bay.

Saint Francis, Lake. **1.** Lake in N Maine. See SAINT FRANCIS 1.
2. Lake, S Quebec and SE Ontario, Canada, 35 mi. (56 km.) SW of the city of Montreal, formed by a widening of the St. Lawrence River; 88 sq. mi. (228 sq. km.).
3. Lake, S Quebec, Canada. See SAINT FRANCIS 7.

Saint Francis Bay. Bay, Eastern Cape prov., S Rep. of South Africa, E of Cape St. Francis.

Saint Fran·cis·ville \ˌsānt-ˈfran-səs-ˌvil\. Town, ⊗ of West Feliciana parish, E cen. Louisiana; pop. (1990c) 1700.

Saint–Fran·çois \ˌseⁿ-fräⁿ-ˈswȧ; sānt-ˈfran-səs, sənt-\. **1.** River, Canada. See SAINT FRANCIS 7.
2. Commune, SE coast of Grande-Terre I., French overseas dept. of Guadeloupe, West Indies.

Saint Fran·cois \ˌsānt-ˈfran-səs\. County in E Missouri. See table at MISSOURI.

Saint Fran·çois du Lac \ˌseⁿ-fräⁿ-ˌswȧ-dœ̄-ˈlȧk\. Village, S Quebec, Canada, S of Lake St. Peter and ab. 25 mi. (40 km.) SE of Trois-Rivières; pop. (1991c) 912.

Saint Fran·cois Mountains \ˌsānt-ˈfran-səs\. Mountains, SE Missouri, in Ozark Plateau, S of Flat River; highest peak Taum Sauk Mt. 1772 ft. (540 m.).

Saint Ga·bri·el \seⁿ-ˌgȧ-brē-ˈel\. Village, S Quebec, Canada, 42 mi. (68 km.) W of Trois-Rivières on S shore of Lake Maskinongé; pop. (1991c) 2716.

Saint Gall \sānt-ˈgȯl, sənt-, -ˈgäl\ *or Ger.* **Sankt Gal·len** \zäŋkt-ˈgä-lən\ *or Fr.* **Saint–Gall** \seⁿ-ˈgȧl\. **1.** Canton, Switzerland, in Alps; includes Lake Wallen and part of Lake Constance; pastures; textile manufacturing. See table at SWITZERLAND.
2. Commune, its ✻, NE Switzerland, 39 mi. (63 km.) E of Zürich; pop. (1989c) 73,889; embroidery work, linen and cotton textiles, glass, metal goods; 18th cent. baroque cathedral (formerly abbey church); notable library containing numerous manuscripts; public parks. Developed around Benedictine abbey founded c. 747 on site of hermitage of Irish missionary St. Gall (c. 612); from 1206 abbots ruled town as princes of Holy Roman Empire; joined Swiss Confederation 1454 and became independent of abbey; ✻ of canton 1803; abbey a notable center of learning in early Middle Ages.

Saint–Gau·dens \ˌseⁿ-gō-ˈdeⁿs\. Town, Haute-Garonne dept., S France, ab. 50 mi. (80 km.) SSW of Toulouse; 11th–12th cent. church; important in medieval times.

Saint George \ˈjȯrj\. **1.** Town, Knox co., S Maine, on Atlantic Ocean inlet 36 mi. (58 km.) ESE of Augusta; pop. (1990c) 2261; on the site of Fort St. George, built 1809 and captured by British 1814.
2. Post office station, ⊗ of Richmond co., SE New York, N Staten I. on Upper New York Bay. See STATEN ISLAND 2.
3. Town, ⊗ of Dorchester co., SE South Carolina, 28 mi. (45 km.) SSE of Orangeburg; pop. (1990c) 2077.
4. City, ⊗ of Washington co., SW corner of Utah, 50 mi. (80 km.) SSW of Cedar City; pop. (1990c) 28,502; resort; diversified agriculture; tourism; Dixie Coll. (1911); pop. more than doubled bet. 1980 and 1990.

5. Town, S coast of St. George's I., N Bermuda Is., Bermuda, W North Atlantic Ocean; pop. (1991c) 1648; founded 1612, first settlement in Bermuda; was ✻ until 1815.

Saint George, Cape. **1.** Cape, S extremity of St. George I., in Gulf of Mexico, off S coast of Franklin co., NW Florida.
2. Peninsula, SE New South Wales, SE Australia, S of Beecroft Head and with it enclosing Jervis Bay.
3. Cape and peninsula, N of St. Georges Bay, SW Newfoundland, Canada.
4. Cape, S point of New Ireland, Bismarck Archipelago, Papua New Guinea, 4°52′N, 152°52′E, at N end of Solomon Sea.

Saint George, Point. Point on W coast of Del Norte co., NW California.

Saint George Channel. See SAINT GEORGE'S CHANNEL 1.

Saint George Island. **1.** Island off coast of Franklin co., NW Florida, bet. Gulf of Mexico on the S and St. George Sound and Apalachicola Bay on the N; 13 sq. mi. (34 sq. km.).
2. Island in Potomac River near its mouth, in St. Marys co., S Maryland.
3. Island, most southerly of Pribilof Is. (*q.v.*) in Bering Sea, Alaska; 10 mi. (16 km.) long by ab. 4 mi. (6 km.) wide; 27 sq. mi. (70 sq. km.).
4. Island, Azores, N Atlantic Ocean. See SÃO JORGE.
5. Island in the delta of the Danube, Romania. See SFÎNTU GHEORGHE.

Saint Georges \se^{n}-'zhȯrzh\. Town, E French Guiana, NE South America, ab. 90 mi. (145 km.) SE of Cayenne on Oyapock River; pop. (1982c) 1199.

Saint–Georges \se^{n}-'zhȯrzh\. Town, Beauce-Sartigan co., S Quebec, Canada, on E bank of Chaudière River 30 mi. (48 km.) E of Thetford Mines; pop. (1991c) 19,583; pop. grew rapidly in 1980s.

Saint George's *or* **Saint Georges** \ˌsānt-'jȯr-jəz\. **1.** Seaport town, SW Newfoundland, Canada, at E end of St. Georges Bay; pop. (1991c) 1678.
2. Town on Grenada I., Grenada, West Indies; ✻ of Grenada; pop. (1981e) 29,400. Scene of fighting during U.S. and Caribbean forces intervention 1983.

Saint Georges Bay. Inlet of S Gulf of St. Lawrence bet. Nova Scotia and SW Cape Breton I., Canada.

Saint George's Bay. Inlet of E Gulf of St. Lawrence in SW Newfoundland, Canada.

Saint Georges Cay. Small island in Caribbean Sea off NE coast of Belize; resort; scene of British defeat of Spanish Sept. 1798 that assured British possession of Belize (then British Honduras).

Saint George's Channel. **1.** *or* **Saint George Channel.** Passage bet. S end of New Ireland on E and NE New Britain on W, Bismarck Archipelago, Papua New Guinea; ab. 20 mi. (32 km.) wide; connects Bismarck Sea with Solomon Sea.
2. Strait bet. Wales on the E and Ireland on the W; joins Atlantic Ocean and Irish Sea, ab. 100 mi. (160 km.) N to S and bet. 50 and 95 mi. (80 and 153 km.) E to W.

Saint George's Island. An island in N Bermuda Is., Bermuda, W North Atlantic Ocean, on W side of Castle Harbour; pop. (1980c) 2940; first of the islands to be colonized by English 1612, settlement at St. George on S coast.

Saint George Sound. Inlet of Gulf of Mexico in S coast of Franklin co., NW Florida.

Saint–Ger·main \ˌse^{n}-zhər-'me^{n}\ *or in full* **Saint–Germain–en–Laye** \-ä^{n}-'lā\. Commune, Yvelines dept., N France, on Seine River 11 mi. (18 km.) WNW of Paris; pop. (1990c) 41,710; summer resort; Parisian residential suburb; noted for extensive forest and park; terrace of St.-Germain one of the most notable promenades in Europe; Renaissance castle birthplace of Henry II (1519), Charles IX (1550), Louis XIV (1638); residence of James II of England after 1688 revolution; site of court of Louis XIV until 1682; notable treaties signed here 1632, 1679, and esp. 1919 bet. Allied Powers and Austria.

Saint–Gilles \se^{n}-'zhēl\. **1.** *or Flemish* **Sint–Gil·lis** \sint-'gi-ləs\. Commune, Brabant prov., cen. Belgium, a suburb of Brussels; pop. (1991c) 42,684.
2. Town, Gard dept., S France, ab. 12 mi. (19 km.) SSE of Nîmes; medieval countship held by counts of Toulouse; former site of Benedictine abbey founded 9th cent. and popular pilgrimage center in Middle Ages; extant abbey church has noted 12th cent. facade and crypt.

Saint–Go·bain \ˌse^{n}-gō-'be^{n}\. Town, Aisne dept., N France, ab. 7 mi. (11 km.) NW of Laon; in the **Fo·rêt de Saint–Gobain** \fō-ˌre-də-\; site of glass factories estab. 1685 and subsequently linked with other manufactures as part of mammoth chemical enterprise.

Saint Gott·hard *or* **Saint Got·hard** \sānt-'gä-tərd, sənt-; ˌse^{n}-gə-'tär\ *also Ger.* **Sankt Gotthard** \zäŋkt-'gȯt-ˌhärt\. **1.** Mountain range of the Lepontine Alps, mostly bet. Uri and Ticino cantons, SE cen. Switzerland; highest peak Pizzo Rotondo 10,472 ft. (3192 m.).
2. Alpine pass and tunnel. See table at ALPS.

Saint Gotthard. See SZENTGOTTHÁRD.

Saint Gow·an's Head \'gau̇-ənz\. Cape, SW corner of Wales, S of Pembroke.

Saint He·le·na \ˌsānt-hə-'lē-nə\. **1.** Parish in E Louisiana. See table at LOUISIANA.
2. City, Napa co., W cen. California, 22 mi. (35 km.) N of San Pablo Bay; pop. (1990c) 4990; wine; tourism.
3. British island in South Atlantic Ocean, ab. 1200 mi. (1950 km.) from W coast of Africa, 15°57′S, 5°42′W; 47 sq. mi. (122 sq. km.); pop. (1991e) 5644; ✻ Jamestown; exports flax and cordage; with Ascension I. (since 1922) and the Tristan da Cunha Is. (since 1938) constitutes a British crown colony (119 sq. mi. or 308 sq. km.; pop. [1993e] 7400). The crater rim of a volcano long extinct; highest point 2704 ft. (824 m.); marked by gorges and valleys, many springs, and plains in the NE. Discovered May 1502 by a Portuguese navigator; first visited by English 1588; granted to British East India Company 1659; French Emperor Napoléon's place of exile 1815–21; declined in importance as port of call after opening of Suez Canal 1869.

Saint Hel·e·na Bay \'he-lə-nə\. Bay, W coast of Western Cape prov., Rep. of South Africa.

Saint Hel·e·na Island \'he-lə-nə\. Island, Beaufort co., S South Carolina; ab. 13 mi. (21 km.) long.

Saint Helena Sound. Inlet on N coast of St. Helena I., South Carolina.

Saint Hel·ens \'he-lənz\. **1.** City and river port, ⊗ of Columbia co., NW Oregon, on Columbia River 25 mi. (40 km.) N of Portland; pop. (1990c) 7535.
2. Town, Merseyside, NW England, 10 mi. (16 km.) ENE of Liverpool; pop. (1981p) 98,769; important glassmaking center.

Saint Helens, Mount. Volcanic peak, NW Skamania co., S Washington; 8366 ft. (2550 m.); over 9600 ft. (2925 m.) before 1980 eruption; **Mount Saint Helens National Volcanic Monument** estab. 1982 (see UNITED STATES, *National Monuments*).

Saint Hel·ier \'hel-yər\. Commercial town and civil parish on the island of Jersey, Channel Is., United Kingdom, in the English Channel 122 mi. (196 km.) SSW of Southampton; ✻ of Jersey bailiwick; pop. (1991c) 28,123; residential community and seaside resort; residence of French writer Victor Hugo 1852–55; Victoria Coll. (1852).

Saint–Honorat. See LÉRINS, ÎLES DE.

Saint Hu·bert \ˌse^{n}-ᵫ-'ber\. Town, Quebec, E Canada, just E of Montreal; pop. (1991c) 74,027.

Saint Hy·a·cinthe \sānt-'hī-ə-ˌsinth, sənt-, ˌsant-yə-'sant\. City, S Quebec, Canada, on Yamaska River 34 mi. (55 km.) ENE of Montreal; pop. (1991c) 39,292; clothing, silk; in agricultural area; Séminaire de St.-Hyacinthe (1811), L'École de Médicine Vétérinaire (1886), Coll. St.-Maurice (1935); settled 1760.

Saint Ig·nace \'ig-nəs\. City, ⊗ of Mackinac co., SE Upper Penin. of Michigan, on Straits of Mackinac; pop. (1990c) 2568; summer resort; diversified agriculture. Founded as mission 1671 by French explorer and missionary Père Jacques Marquette; fort built later; lost importance during 18th cent., as pop. settled elsewhere; supposed burial place of Père Marquette.

Saint Ignace Island. Island in N Lake Superior, W of Simpson I., SW Ontario, Canada.

Saint–Imier \ˌse^{n}t-ē-ˈmyā\. Commune, Bern canton, Switzerland, ab. 12 mi. (19 km.) W of Biel; pop. (1980c) 5430.

Saint Ives \ˈīvz\. **1.** Town, Cambridgeshire, England, on the Great Ouse River; pop. (1981c) 12,331.

2. Town, on NW coast of Cornwall, SW England, on **Saint Ives Bay** 60 mi. (97 km.) W of Plymouth; pop. (1981p) 10,985; seaside resort.

Saint Jacques, Cape. See VUNG TAU 1.

Saint James \ˈjāmz\. **1.** Parish in SE Louisiana. See table at LOUISIANA.

2. City, ⊗ of Watonwan co., S Minnesota, 33 mi. (53 km.) WSW of Mankato; pop. (1990c) 4364.

3. City, Phelps co., S cen. Missouri, 10 mi. (16 km.) E of Rolla; pop. (1990c) 3256.

Saint James, Cape. Cape, S tip of Kunghit I., S Queen Charlotte Is., off W British Columbia, Canada; 51°56′N, 131°01′W.

Saint–Jean. See SAINT-JEAN-SUR-RICHELIEU.

Saint–Jean, Île–. See PRINCE EDWARD ISLAND.

Saint–Jean, Lac \ˌlák-se^{n}-ˈzhä^{n}\ *or Eng.* **Lake Saint–Jean** \ˌsānt-ˈzhän, sint-\. Lake, S Quebec, Canada; 414 sq. mi. (1072 sq. km.); receives the Chamouchouane, Mistassini, and Peribonca rivers on the N; its outlet is the Saguenay River (*q.v.*) to the E, leaving by two channels. Popular with tourists and fishermen.

Saint–Jean–d'Acre. See ACRE.

Saint–Jean–d'An·gé·ly \-ˌdä^{n}-zhā-ˈlē\. Town, Charente-Maritime dept., W France, ab. 35 mi. (56 km.) SE of La Rochelle; in 16th cent. a strong Protestant center; Benedictine abbey attacked by Huguenots 1569; town taken by Louis XIII 1621.

Saint–Jean–de–Luz \-də-ˈlu̅e̅z\. Coast town, Pyrénées-Atlantiques dept., SW France, on the Bay of Biscay SW of Biarritz near Spanish border; pop. (1990c) 13,181; a Basque town; old fishing center, first to send boats to Newfoundland cod grounds 1520; still important fishing port; popular resort.

Saint–Jean–de–Mau·rienne \də-mȯr-ˈyen\. Town, Savoie dept., E France, SE of Chambéry; bishopric founded 6th cent.; cathedral from 11th cent.; Allied conference Apr. 1917 during WWI.

Saint–Jean–Port–Jo·li \-pȯr-zhȯ-ˈlē\. Municipality, ⊗ of L'Islet co., S Quebec, Canada, on S bank of St. Lawrence River 55 mi. (89 km.) NE of Quebec City; pop. (1991c) 3369.

Saint–Jean–sur–Rich·e·lieu \-su̅e̅r-ˌrē-shə-ˈlyœ\ *or* **Saint–Jean.** City, S Quebec, Canada, on Richelieu River 21 mi. (34 km.) SE of Montreal; pop. (1991c) 37,607; paper products, textiles, metal goods, sewing machines. First fortified by French 17th cent.; site of prolonged conflict bet. British holding fort and Americans en route to Montreal 1775; British base in American Revolution.

Saint–Jé·rôme \ˌse^{n}-zhā-ˈrōm\. City, SW Quebec, Canada, 28 mi. (45 km.) NW of Montreal; pop. (1991c) 23,384; textiles; tourist center; settled 1834.

Saint John \ˌsānt-ˈjän\. **1.** Town, Lake co., NW Indiana, SSW of Gary; pop. (1990c) 4921.

2. City, ⊗ of Stafford co., cen. Kansas, 47 mi. (76 km.) W of Hutchinson; pop. (1990c) 1357.

3. City, St. Louis co., E Missouri, W suburb of the city of St. Louis; pop. (1990c) 7466.

4. River, NE United States and SE Canada; rises in NW Maine (Somerset co.), flows NE and for 80 mi. (129 km.) forms a part of the boundary bet. Maine and New Brunswick, turns SE through W New Brunswick, then E and S to Bay of Fundy at St. John; 418 mi. (673 km.) long. Navigable to Fredericton (81 mi. or 130 km.) for large vessels, Fredericton to Grand Falls and for ab. 65 mi. (120 km.) above Grand Falls for smaller boats. At Grand Falls, ab. 220 mi. (355 km.) from its mouth, is great cataract ab. 75 ft. (25 m.) high; at its mouth in St. John Harbor narrowed to gorge 450 ft. (137 m.) wide with sides ab. 100 ft. (30 m.) high; strong tides result in the Reversing Falls phenomenon. Chief tributaries Allagash and Aroostook in Maine, Madawaska in Quebec, and Tobique and Nashwaak in New Brunswick.

5. County in S New Brunswick, Canada. See table at NEW BRUNSWICK.

6. Seaport city, ⊗ of St. John co., S New Brunswick, Canada, on Bay of Fundy at mouth of St. John River; pop. (1991c) 74,969; largest city in the province and its principal port, with a large ice-free harbor; commercial center; pulp and paper products; shipyards; tourism.

History: Area visited by French explorer Samuel de Champlain 1604; settled and fortified by French 1630s; scene of 18th cent. struggles involving Acadians, Americans, and British; settled by Loyalists 1783 and chartered as first city in Canada 1785; from late 18th cent. a major lumber and shipbuilding center; suffered destructive fire 1877.

7. River, cen. Liberia; rises on NE boundary, flows SW to Atlantic Ocean near Buchanan; 120 mi. (193 km.) long.

Saint John, Cape. Cape, N coast of Newfoundland, Canada, NW point of entrance to Notre Dame Bay.

Saint John, Isle. See PRINCE EDWARD ISLAND.

Saint John, Mount. Peak, cen. Grand Teton National Park, NW Wyoming; 11,412 ft. (3478 m.).

Saint John Island. **1.** One of the Virgin Is. of the U.S., West Indies, 4 mi. (6 km.) E of St. Thomas; 20 sq. mi. (52 sq. km.); pop. (1990c) 3504; highest point 1286 ft. (392 m.); produces bay leaves for bay rum industry of St. Thomas. See VIRGIN ISLANDS.

2. Island off Guangdong prov., SE China. See SHANGCHUAN.

Saint John River. See SAINT JOHN 4.

Saint Johns \ˌsānt-ˈjänz\. **1.** Navigable river, E Florida; rises in Brevard co., E cen. Florida, flows N into Atlantic Ocean NE of Jacksonville; 285 mi. (459 km.) long.

2. County on NE coast of Florida. See table at FLORIDA.

3. City, ⊗ of Apache co., E Arizona; pop. (1990c) 3294.

4. City, ⊗ of Clinton co., S cen. Michigan, 20 mi. (32 km.) N of Lansing; pop. (1990c) 7284.

Saint John's \ˌsānt-ˈjänz\. **1.** City, ✳ of Antigua and Barbuda, Leeward Is., West Indies; pop. (1986e) 36,000; tourism.

2. City, ✳ of Newfoundland, Canada, on Atlantic Ocean on the SE coast; pop. (1991c) 95,770; commercial center and principal port of Newfoundland; good natural harbor; terminus of the railroad across the island; fishing and fish processing; shipbuilding; textiles; Queen's Coll. (1841), Memorial Univ. of Newfoundland (1925). Probably visited by explorer for England John Cabot 1497; small fishing base from early 16th cent.; colonized by British under navigator Sir Humphrey Gilbert 1583; attacked several times by French but securely British from 1762; British naval base during Revolutionary War and War of 1812.

Saint Johns·bury \ˌsānt-ˈjänz-ˌber-ē, -bə-rē\. Town, ⊗ of Caledonia co., NE Vermont, 39 mi. (63 km.) ENE of Montpelier; pop. (1990c) 7608; dairy and maple-sugar products; dairy farms; settled 1786.

Saint John's Point. Cape, NE coast of Northern Ireland, S of Strangford Lough and at N side of entrance to Dundrum Bay; lighthouse.

Saint Johns·ville \ˌsānt-ˈjänz-ˌvil\. Town, Montgomery co., E New York, on Mohawk River 30 mi. (48 km.) E of Utica; pop. (1990c) 2773.

Saint John the Bap·tist \ˈbap-tist\. Parish in SE Louisiana. See table at LOUISIANA.

Saint Jo·seph \ˈjō-zəf, -səf\. **1.** River, S Michigan and NW Indiana; rises in Hillsdale co., S Michigan, flows W along S Michigan, curves S and W in NW Indiana, then NW into Lake Michigan at St. Joseph, W Berrien co., SW Michigan; 210 mi. (338 km.) long; navigable for a short distance.

2. River, S Michigan, NW Ohio, and NE Indiana; rises in S Michigan, flows SW across NW corner of Ohio and unites with St. Marys River at Fort Wayne in Allen co., NE Indiana, to form the Maumee River; over 100 mi. (160 km.) long.

3. Name of counties in two states of the U.S. See tables at INDIANA and MICHIGAN.

\ə\ **abut** \ə\ matches \$^{ə}$\ kitten, Fr table \ər\ **further** \a\ **ash** \ā\ **ace** \ä\ cot, cart \á\ Fr bac \au̇\ **out** \b\ Span Avila \ch\ **chin** \e\ **bet** \ē\ **easy** \g\ **go** \i\ **hit** \ī\ **ice** \j\ **job** \k\ Ger **ich**, Buch \$^{n}$\ Fr vin \ŋ\ **sing** \ō\ **go** \ȯ\ **all** \ȯ\ **law** \œ\ Fr **bœuf** \œ̄\ Fr **feu** \ȯi\ **boy** \th\ **thin** \t͟h\ **this** \ü\ **loot** \u̇\ **foot** \ue\ Ger **füllen** \u̅e̅\ Fr **rue** \y\ **yet** \$^{y}$\ Fr digne \ˈdēn^{y}\, nuit \ˈnw^{y}ē\ \yü\ **few** \yu̇\ **fury** \zh\ **vision**

4. Town, ⊗ of Tensas parish, NE Louisiana; pop. (1990c) 1517.
5. City, ⊗ of Berrien co., SW corner of Michigan, on Lake Michigan at mouth of St. Joseph River 49 mi. (79 km.) WSW of Kalamazoo; pop. (1990c) 9214; automobile parts; processes fruit; summer resort.
6. City, Stearns co., cen. Minnesota, 7 mi. (11 km.) W of St. Cloud; pop. (1990c) 3294; Coll. of St. Benedict (1887).
7. City, ⊗ of Buchanan co., NW Missouri, on Missouri River 55 mi. (88 km.) NNW of Kansas City; pop. (1990c) 71,852; grain and livestock market; meatpacking, flour milling; Missouri Western State Coll. (1915). Settled 1826 as trading post; town laid out 1843; chartered as city 1851; E terminus of the Pony Express 1860–61.
8. Town, St. Croix co., W Wisconsin; pop. (1990c) 2657.

Saint Joseph, Lake. Lake, SW Ontario, Canada; 187 sq. mi. (484 sq. km.); a source of the Albany River flowing into James Bay.

Saint Joseph Bay *or* **Saint Josephs Bay.** Inlet of Gulf of Mexico on SW coast of Gulf co., NW Florida.

Saint–Joseph–d'Al·ma \ˌse^{n}-zhō-'zef-dȧl-'mä\ *or since 1954* **Alma** \ȧl-'mä, 'al-mə\. City, S Quebec, Canada, on S bank of Saguenay River 5 mi. (8 km.) E of Lac St.-Jean; pop. (1991c) 25,910; paper mills, aluminum plant; nearby **Isle Ma·ligne** \ˌēl-mȧ-'lēn^{y}\ is a major hydroelectric station on the Saguenay.

Saint–Joseph–de–Beauce \ˌse^{n}-zhō-'zef-də-'bōs\. Town, Beauce-Sartigan co., S Quebec, Canada, 38 mi. (61 km.) SSE of Quebec City; pop. (1991c) 3111.

Saint Joseph Island. **1.** See SAN JOSE 1.
2. Island belonging to Ontario, Canada, at N end of Lake Huron, just E of Chippewa co., Michigan; ab. 19 mi. (31 km.) long.

Saint Joseph Point *or* **Saint Josephs Point.** Point at N end of narrow **Saint Joseph Peninsula** extending from SW coast of Gulf co., NW Florida, into Gulf of Mexico and enclosing St. Joseph Bay.

Saint Joseph River. See SAINT JOSEPH 1.

Saint Josephs Bay. See SAINT JOSEPH BAY.

Saint Josephs Point. See SAINT JOSEPH POINT.

Saint–Josse–ten–Noo·de \se^{n}-ˌzhȯs-tä^{n}-'nōd\ *or Flemish* **Sint–Joost–ten–Noode** \sint-ˌyōst-tə-'nō-də\. Commune, Brabant prov., cen. Belgium, a suburb of Brussels; pop. (1991c) 21,317.

Saint–Jo·vite \ˌse^{n}-zhō-'vēt\. Village, S Quebec, Canada, 65 mi. (105 km.) NW of Montreal; pop. (1991c) 4118.

Saint–Ju·lien–Beyche·velle \ˌse^{n}-zhül-'ye^{n}-bāsh-'vel\ *or* **Saint–Julien.** Commune, Gironde dept., SW France, on the Gironde estuary near Pauillac; wine.

Saint–Ju·nien \ˌse^{n}-zhū̅-'nye^{n}\. Commune, Haute-Vienne dept., W cen. France, 18 mi. (29 km.) WNW of Limoges; hydroelectric power plant; produces leather.

Saint Just \'jəst\ *or* **Saint Just in Pen·with** \pen-'with\. Town, Cornwall, SW England, ab. 4 mi. (6 km.) N of Land's End; pop. (1981p) 4047; amphitheater where miracle plays were produced in medieval times.

Saint Kil·da \'kil-də\. **1.** Municipality, S Victoria, SE Australia, SE suburb of Melbourne on Port Phillip Bay; pop. (1991c) 45,481; residential community and seaside resort.
2. Borough, SE South I., New Zealand, S suburb of Dunedin on Pacific coast; pop. (1981c) 6147.
3. Island, westernmost of the Outer Hebrides, Scotland, in the Atlantic Ocean W of the Sound of Harris, at 57°49′N, 8°36′W; nonpermanent pop. (1981c) 46; max. elev. 1220 ft. (372 m.); important breeding place and reserve for gannets.

Saint Kitts \'kits\ *or* **Saint Chris·to·pher** \'kris-tə-fər\. Island, Leeward Is., West Indies; 68 sq. mi. (176 sq. km.); ✻ Basseterre; administratively united with Nevis (see SAINT KITTS-NEVIS). Has long narrow point of land extending to SE, its tip separated by strait 2 mi. (3.2 km.) wide from island of Nevis. Mountainous, of volcanic origin; fertile and well watered; highest point at NW end 4314 ft. (1315 m.); Mt. Misery 3792 ft. (1156 m.) in center; only towns are Basseterre and Old Road.
History: Carib island when visited by explorer Christopher Columbus 1493; settled by British 1623, the first of Leeward Is. to be colonized by British; French settlers arrived c. 1625; slaves imported from Africa to harvest sugar 17th–18th cents.; repeated clashes bet. French and British until British control validated in 1783; united with Nevis 1882; gained independence with Nevis Sept. 19, 1983.

Saint Kitts–Nevis \'kits-'ne-vəs\ *or* **Saint Kitts and Nevis** *or* **Saint Chris·to·pher–Nevis** \'kris-tə-fər-\ *or* **Saint Christopher and Nevis.** Independent state, Leeward Is., West Indies, consisting of St. Kitts, Nevis, and Sombrero; 104 sq. mi. (269 sq. km.); pop. (1994e) 41,800; ✻ Basseterre; tourism.
Chief products: Sugar, electronic components, garments.
History: Became a self-governing state (in association with Great Britain) 1967; was constitutionally united with Anguilla (forming **Saint Christopher–Nevis–Anguilla**) 1967–71; gained independence 1983.

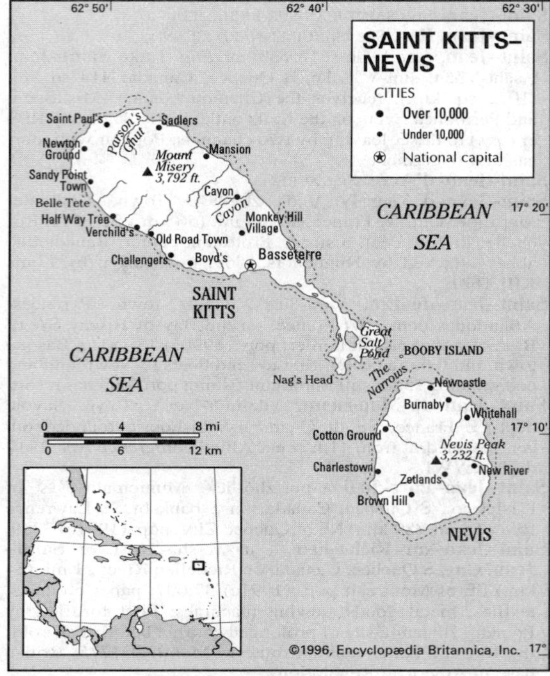

Saint–Lam·bert \ˌse^{n}-lä^{n}-'ber; sānt-'lam-bərt, sənt-\. Residential city, S Quebec, Canada, on St. Lawrence River opp. Montreal; pop. (1991c) 20,976.

Saint Lan·dry \'lan-drē\. Parish in S cen. Louisiana. See table at LOUISIANA.

Saint–Lau·rent \ˌse^{n}-lō-'rä^{n}, ˌsant-lō-'rent\. **1.** City, Montreal I., S Quebec, Canada, 6 mi. (10 km.) W of the city of Montreal; pop. (1991c) 72,402; chemicals, aircraft; Coll. de St.-Laurent (1847), Seminaire Ste.-Croix (1899), Coll. Basile-Moreau (1929).
2. *or* **Saint Laurent du Ma·ro·ni** \dū̅-ˌmȧ-rō-'nē\. Seaport, N French Guiana, on the Maroni near its mouth; pop. (1982c) 6971.

Saint–Laurent–sur–Mer \-sū̅r-'mer\. Commune, Calvados dept., NW France, on the coast of the Bay of the Seine 8 mi. (13 km.) NW of Bayeux. An American beachhead in Allied invasion of Normandy June 6, 1944; large artificial harbor destroyed in gale June 19–22, forcing Allies to rely on one at Arromanches-les-Bains.

Saint Law·rence \'lȯr-əns, -'lär-\. **1.** County in N New York. See table at NEW YORK.
2. Navigable river, S Quebec and SE Ontario provs., Canada; flows NE out of Lake Ontario into the Gulf of St. Lawrence; ab. 760 mi. (1225 km.) long; incl. the waterway provided by

the Great Lakes, ab. 2000 mi. (3220 km.) long. Leaving Lake Ontario the St. Lawrence proper passes through the Thousand Is. (*q.v.*) and for ab. 120 mi. (195 km.) forms the boundary bet. New York state and Ontario; on entering Quebec prov. it widens into Lake St. Francis, then passes through Lake St. Louis and the Lachine Rapids past Montreal I.; at Sorel passes through another expansion, Lake St. Peter, and below Quebec around Orleans I. into a wide stream fully 90 mi. (145 km.) wide at its mouth in the Gulf of St. Lawrence. Its chief tributaries are the Ottawa, St. Maurice, and Saguenay on the N, and the Richelieu, Yamaska, St. Francis, and Chaudière on the S. Chief cities on it are Ogdensburg (New York), Kingston and Cornwall (Ontario), and Montreal, Sorel, Trois-Rivières, and Quebec (Quebec). The headstream of the greater St. Lawrence is the St. Louis River in Minnesota; then the waterway passes through Lake Superior, the St. Marys River (by the Sault Ste. Marie Canals, *q.v.*), Lake Huron, St. Clair River, Lake St. Clair, Detroit River, Lake Erie, Niagara River (by the Welland Canal, *q.v.*), and Lake Ontario into the St. Lawrence proper. See SAINT LAWRENCE SEAWAY.

Saint Lawrence, Cape. Point, N coast of Cape Breton I., Canada, on Gulf of St. Lawrence, W of Cape North.

Saint Lawrence, Gulf of. Deep gulf of the Atlantic Ocean off E coast of Canada, bet. Newfoundland and the Canadian mainland (Quebec, New Brunswick, and Nova Scotia provs.); receives the St. Lawrence River in the NW; connected with the Atlantic Ocean through the Strait of Belle Isle on the NE (N of Newfoundland), Cabot Strait on the E (bet. Newfoundland and Cape Breton I.), and Strait of Canso on SE (bet. Nova Scotia mainland and Cape Breton I.). Has many islands, Anticosti, Prince Edward (province), Magdalen Is., and islands along the shores.

Saint Lawrence Island. Island, W Alaska, in the Bering Sea 150 mi. (241 km.) S of Bering Strait and 118 mi. (190 km.) from nearest Alaskan mainland; 95 mi. (153 km.) long by ab. 10 to 35 mi. (16 to 56 km.) wide; 1712 sq. mi. (4434 sq. km.); highest point 2204 ft. (672 m.). Chief settlement Savoonga on N cen. coast; Inuit island visited by Dutch explorer Vitus Bering 1728; site of extensive archaeological work.

Saint Lawrence Islands National Park. See CANADA, *National Parks.*

Saint Lawrence Seaway. Waterway, Canada and U.S., along upper St. Lawrence River bet. Montreal and Lake Ontario, in Ontario, Quebec, and New York; permits passage of deep-draft vessels bet. Atlantic Ocean and Great Lakes; includes a system of canals, locks, and dams; important route for shipment of bulk cargoes such as grain and iron ore; hydroelectric power project; constructed 1954–59.

Saint Laz·a·rus, Islands of \ˈla-zə-rəs\. Portuguese explorer Ferdinand Magellan's name for Philippine Is.

Saint Leo \ˈlē-ō\. Town, Pasco co., Florida, NE of Tampa; pop. (1990c) 1009; St. Leo Coll. (1889).

Saint–Lé·o·nard \ˌseⁿ-ˌlā-ȯ-ˈnär; sānt-ˈle-nərd, sənt-\. City, Montreal co., S Quebec, Canada, 4 mi. (6 km.) N of city of Montreal; pop. (1991c) 73,120; residential suburb of Montreal.

Saint–Léonard–de–No·blat \-də-nȯ-ˈblä\. Town, Haute-Vienne dept., W cen. France, ab. 12 mi. (19 km.) E of Limoges; 11th–13th cent. Romanesque church.

Saint–Lô \seⁿ-ˈlō; sānt-ˈlō, sənt-\; *anc.* **Bri·o·ve·ra** \ˌbrī-ə-ˈvir-ə\; *later* **Lau·dus** \ˈlȯ-dəs\. Commune, ✻ of Manche dept., NW France, 34 mi. (55 km.) W of Caen; pop. (1990c) 22,819; market town; food processing.

History: Fortified by Frankish King (later Holy Roman Emperor) Charlemagne; attacked by Norsemen c. 889, Geoffrey Plantagenet, count of Anjou, c. 1141, and Edward III of England c. 1346. German defense base attacked by Allies July 7, 1944 in invasion of Normandy; its capture July 18 after severe fighting resulted in unhinging entire W end of German line and was followed by Allied breakthrough; town almost entirely destroyed in the fighting.

Saint–Lou·is \ˌseⁿ-ˈlwē\. **1.** Commune, Haut-Rhin dept., NE France, on the Swiss border.

2. Town on SW coast of the island of Réunion in the Indian Ocean; pop. (1982c) 32,045.

3. City, Senegal, on **Saint–Louis Island** at mouth of the Senegal River; pop. (1992e) 125,717; first settled by French c. 1638; ✻ of French West Africa 1895–1902 and ✻ of Senegal 1902–58.

Saint Louis \ˌsānt-ˈlü-əs\. **1.** River, NE Minnesota; rises near E border of St. Louis co., flows SW, then turns SE to empty into Lake Superior at Duluth; 160 mi. (257 km.) long; sometimes considered the ultimate source of the St. Lawrence River.

2. Name of counties in two states of the U.S. See tables at MINNESOTA and MISSOURI.

3. City, Gratiot co., cen. Michigan, 17 mi. (27 km.) SSE of Mount Pleasant; pop. (1990c) 3828.

4. City, Missouri, on Mississippi River ab. 10 mi. (16 km.) below its confluence with the Missouri; pop. (1990c) 396,685; independent of St. Louis co.; 2d largest city in the state; major river port; manufactures aircraft, chemicals, electrical equipment, iron and steel products, beer; automobile-assembly plants. St. Louis Univ. (1818), Concordia Seminary (1839), Eden Theological Seminary (1850), Washington Univ. (1853), Harris-Stowe State Coll. (1857), St. Louis Coll. of Pharmacy (1864), Maryville Univ. of St. Louis (1872), Kenrick-Glennon Seminary (1900), Webster Univ. (1915), Fontbonne Coll. (1917), St. Louis Conservatory of Music (1924), Aquinas Institute of Theology (1939), Covenant Theological Seminary (1956), St. Louis Community Coll. (four campuses, 1962), Univ. of Missouri–St. Louis (1963). See table at MISSOURI.

History: Settled 1764 by French fur trader and pioneer Pierre Laclède of New Orleans unaware that land was ceded to Spain by France 1762; under Spanish rule 1770–1800; formally American 1804 and territorial ✻ until 1821; made city 1822; large influx of American and foreign immigrants and rise as vital transportation and manufacturing center 19th cent.; Union base in Civil War; site 1904 of Louisiana Purchase Exposition and Olympic Games; efforts at urban renewal mid–late 20th cent.; lost nearly half its 1960 pop. in the following 30 years.

Saint Louis, Lake \seⁿ-ˈlwē\. Lake, S Quebec, Canada, SW of Montreal and below Ile Perrot, 57 sq. mi. (148 sq. km.); formed by a widening of St. Lawrence River.

Saint–Louis Island. See SAINT-LOUIS 3.

Saint Louis Park \ˈlü-əs\. City, Hennepin co., SE cen. Minnesota, just W of Minneapolis; pop. (1990c) 43,787; suburb of Minneapolis.

Saint Louis River. See SAINT LOUIS 1.

Saint–Luc \seⁿ-ˈlūek, sānt-ˈlük\. Town, Quebec, Canada; pop. (1991c) 15,008.

Saint Lu·cia \sānt-ˈlü-shə, sənt-; ˌsānt-lü-ˈsē-ə\. Island, an independent state of the Windward Is., E West Indies, S of Martinique and N of St. Vincent; 238 sq. mi. (616 sq. km.); pop. (1989e) 148,183; ✻ Castries; high mountainous volcanic mass; Mt. Gimie 3117 ft. (950 m.) is in S cen. part and The Pitons (2619 ft. or 798 m. and 2461 ft. or 750 m.) are on SW coast; has rich soil; exports cocoa, spices, coconuts, bananas, citrus fruit, livestock; electronic components, beverages, cardboard boxes, clothing; tourism.

History: Caribs replaced early Arawak inhabitants c. 800–1300 A.D.; violently resisted French and English colonists mid-17th cent.; treaty with French 1660; island disputed by French and English until 1814 Treaty of Paris gave Great Britain control; African slaves used in sugar harvest freed c. 1838; bay leased by Great Britain to U.S. for naval base 1940; internal self-government under Great Britain began 1967; independence achieved Feb. 22, 1979.

Saint Lucia, Cape. Cape extending into Indian Ocean on E cen. coast of KwaZulu-Natal prov., Rep. of South Africa.

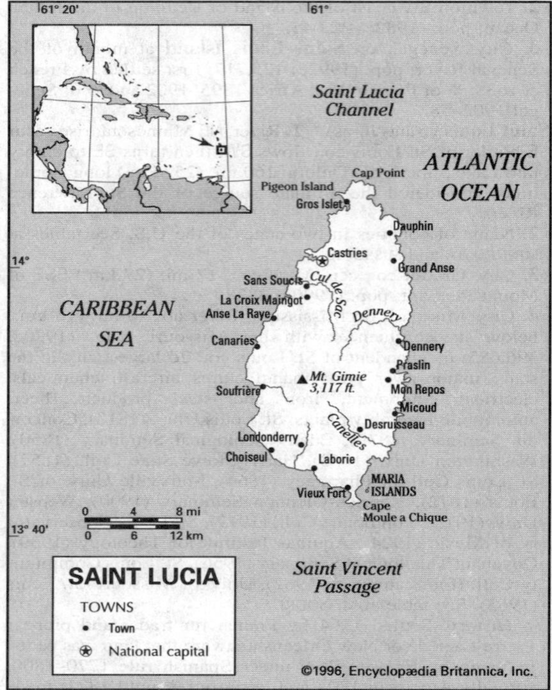

Saint Lucia, Lake. Inlet of Indian Ocean, on E coast of KwaZulu-Natal prov., Rep. of South Africa, N of Cape St. Lucia.

Saint Lucia Channel. Channel bet. the islands of Martinique and St. Lucia in the West Indies.

Saint Lu·cie \ˈlü-sē\. County on cen. E coast of Florida. See table at FLORIDA.

Saint Lucie Canal. Canal, S Florida, linking the Atlantic coast at Stuart with Lake Okeechobee; part of the Okeechobee Waterway (*q.v.*).

Saint Lucie Inlet. Narrow strait leading from Atlantic Ocean through barrier reef off NE coast of Martin co., SE Florida; E terminus of St. Lucie Canal.

Saint–Maix·ent–l'École \ˌsen-ˌmek-ˈsän-lā-ˈkȯl\. Town, Deux-Sèvres dept., W France, 15 mi. (24 km.) NE of Niort by rail; rebuilt abbey church on site of 5th cent. Benedictine monastery; military school and museum.

Saint–Ma·lo \ˌsen-mȧ-ˈlō\. Commercial seaport, Ille-et-Vilaine dept., NW France, on rocky island in Atlantic Ocean at mouth of Rance River 40 mi. (64 km.) NNW of Rennes; pop. (1990c) 49,274; fishing port, tourist resort, yachting center; ships fruit and vegetables; Renaissance church; 15th cent. castle; town hall; customhouse. Site of a monastery in 6th cent.; became episcopal see in 12th cent.; headquarters of many privateers esp. 17th and 18th cents.; episcopal see ended 1790. German forces burned most of city Aug. 1944 while losing it to Allies. Birthplace of explorer Jacques Cartier 1491.

Saint–Malo, Gulf of. Inlet of English Channel, NW coast of France, bet. peninsulas of Normandy and Brittany.

Saint–Man·dé \ˌsen-män-ˈdā\. Commune, Val-de-Marne dept., N France, ESE suburb of Paris near the Bois de Vincennes.

Saint Marc \sānt-ˈmärk, sənt-; sen-ˈmȧrk\. Town, W Haiti, 44 mi. (71 km.) NW of Port-au-Prince; pop. (1982c) 24,165.

Saint–Marc–des–Car·rières \sen-ˈmȧrk-dā-kär-ˈyer\. Village, Portneuf co., S Quebec, Canada, 40 mi. (64 km.) W of Quebec City; pop. (1991c) 2844.

Saint Mar·ga·rets Bay \ˈmär-grəts, -gə-rəts\. Inlet of Atlantic Ocean, S Nova Scotia, Canada, SW of Halifax.

Saint Mar·ies \mə-ˈrēz\. City, ⊗ of Benewah co., NW Idaho, 30 mi. (48 km.) SSE of Coeur d'Alene; pop. (1990c) 2442.

Saint Mark \ˈmärk\. The island of San Marco, E part of Venice, Italy. See *History* at VENICE 4.

Saint Mar·tin \ˈmärt-ən\. Parish in S Louisiana. See table at LOUISIANA.

Saint Martin *or Du.* **Sint Maar·ten** \sint-ˈmärt-ən\. Island in Leeward Is. group E of British Virgin Is., E West Indies, ab. 43 mi. (69 km.) NNW of St. Kitts; 33 sq. mi. (85 sq. km.); N section is a dependency of the French overseas dept. of Guadeloupe and has area of 20 sq. mi. (52 sq. km.) and pop. (1990c) 25,518; chief town Marigot; S section is administratively a part of Netherlands Antilles, and has area of 13 sq. mi. (34 sq. km.) and pop. (1990c) 31,722; ✱ Philipsburg. Produces salt; tourism. Divided 1648 bet. French and Dutch.

Saint Martin, Lake. Lake, S cen. Manitoba, Canada, E of N Lake Manitoba; 125 sq. mi. (324 sq. km.); Dauphin River, connecting Lake Manitoba and Lake Winnipeg, passes through it.

Saint–Martin–Bou·logne \ˌsen-mär-ˈten-bü-ˈlȯnʸ\. Commune, Pas-de-Calais dept., N France, suburb of Boulogne.

Saint–Martin–d'Hères \-ˈder\. Town, Isère dept., SE France, just E of Grenoble.

Saint Mar·tin·ville \ˈmärt-ən-ˌvil\. City, ⊗ of St. Martin parish, S Louisiana, 13 mi. (21 km.) ESE of Lafayette; pop. (1990c) 7137; settled 1760; influx of Acadians expelled from Nova Scotia 1765, incl. the lovers immortalized in poet Henry Wadsworth Longfellow's *Evangeline;* a refuge for royalists fleeing French Revolution.

Saint Mary \ˈmar-ē, ˈmer-\. **1.** Parish in S Louisiana. See table at LOUISIANA.
2. River, SW Alberta, Canada, and NW Montana; rises in **Saint Mary Lake,** Glacier National Park, NW Montana, and flows NNE to the Oldman River near Lethbridge, Alberta; ab. 75 mi. (120 km.) long.

Saint Mary, Cape. Point of land, SE Canada, projecting W along W coast of Nova Scotia on S side of entrance to **Saint Mary Bay,** a narrow inlet of the Atlantic ab. 40 mi. (64 km.) long, in Digby co.

Saint Mary, Island of *or* **Saint Mary's Island.** Island, Gambia, in the Gambia River near its mouth; site of the town of Banjul, ✱ of Gambia.

Saint Mary Lake. See SAINT MARY 2.

Saint Mary Peak. Highest peak in North Flinders Range, E South Australia, Australia, NNE of Port Augusta; 3838 ft. (1170 m.).

Saint Mary River. See SAINT MARY 2.

Saint Marys \ˈmar-ēz, ˈmer-\. **1.** River, SE Georgia and NE Florida; rises in Okefenokee Swamp, SE Georgia, forms a section of E Georgia-Florida boundary, and empties into Cumberland Sound N of Amelia I. and NNE of Jacksonville; 175 mi. (282 km.) long.
2. River, E Michigan on Upper Penin.; flows from Whitefish Bay on Lake Superior; ab. 70 mi. (115 km.) long; forms boundary bet. U.S. and Canada; descends ab. 20 ft. in a mile (4 m. in a kilometer) at **Saint Marys Falls** where canals have been built (see SAULT SAINTE MARIE CANALS), then flows around Sugar I. and Neebish I., W of St. Joseph I. (Canada), and through Detour Passage into N end of Lake Huron.
3. River, NW Ohio and NE Indiana; rises in Auglaize co., Ohio, flows N and NW to unite with St. Joseph River at Fort Wayne, Allen co., NE Indiana, and form the Maumee River; ab. 110 mi. (175 km.) long.
4. County in S Maryland. See table at MARYLAND.
5. City, Camden co., SE Georgia, 29 mi. (47 km.) S of Brunswick; pop. (1990c) 8187.
6. Village, Maryland. See SAINT MARYS CITY.
7. City, Auglaize co., W Ohio, on Lake St. Marys 20 mi. (32 km.) SW of Lima; pop. (1990c) 8441; settled late 18th cent.
8. Borough, Elk co., NW cen. Pennsylvania, 24 mi. (39 km.) NNE of Du Bois; pop. (1990c) 5511; agriculture.
9. City, ⊗ of Pleasants co., NW West Virginia, on Ohio River; pop. (1990c) 2148.

Saint Mary's. Town, Perth co., SE Ontario, Canada, on Thames River 20 mi. (32 km.) N of London; pop. (1991c) 5496.

Saint Marys, Lake *also* **Grand Lake** *or* **Grand Reservoir.** Lake, Auglaize and Mercer cos., W Ohio, 9 mi. (15 km.) long and 3 mi. (5 km.) wide; formed by damming Wabash River.

Saint Mary's Bay. Inlet of Atlantic Ocean, SE Newfoundland, Canada; ab. 40 mi. (64 km.) long.

Saint Marys City; *formerly* **Saint Marys.** Village, St. Marys co., S Maryland; St. Mary's Coll. of Maryland (1840); first European settlement in Maryland 1634 by Leonard Calvert, who purchased small village from Piscataways; ✻ of Maryland until 1694, followed by decline; revived 1934 during tercentenary celebration and now an historical village.

Saint Marys Falls. See SAINT MARYS 2.

Saint Mary's Island. See SAINT MARY, ISLAND OF.

Saint Mary's Loch. Lake, Borders region, SE Scotland; 3 mi. (5 km.) long; max. depth 153 ft. (47 m.).

Saint Marys River. Name of three rivers in the U.S. See SAINT MARYS.

Saint–Ma·thieu, Pointe de \ˌpweⁿt-də-ˌseⁿ-mȧ-ˈtyœ̄\. Cape on the NW coast of France, near Brest.

Saint Mat·thew Island \ˈmath-yü\. **1.** Island, cen. Bering Sea, Alaska, 63°30′N, 170°30′W, 135 mi. (217 km.) W of Nunivak I.; 123 sq. mi. (319 sq. km.); includes Hall I. off NW; uninhabited.

2. Island, Mergui Archipelago. See ZADETSKYI ISLAND.

Saint Mat·thews \ˈmath-ˌyüz\. **1.** City, Jefferson co., N cen. Kentucky, E suburb of Louisville; pop. (1990c) 15,800.

2. Town, ⊗ of Calhoun co., cen. South Carolina, 13 mi. (21 km.) NNE of Orangeburg; pop. (1990c) 2345.

Saint Mat·thi·as Group \mə-ˈthī-əs\ *or* **Mus·sau Islands** \mü-ˈsau̇\. Group of small islands in N Bismarck Archipelago, W Pacific Ocean, NNW of island of New Hanover; largest is Mussau; Emira I. in S part of group occupied by U.S. marines 1944 in WWII.

Saint–Maur–des–Fos·sés \seⁿ-ˌmȯr-dā-fȯ-ˈsā\. Commune, Val-de-Marne dept., N France, SE suburb of Paris on Marne River; pop. (1990c) 77,492; residential.

Saint–Mau·rice \ˌseⁿ-mȯ-ˈrēs\; *formerly* **Pe·tit–Cha·ren·ton** \pə-ˈtē-ˌshȧ-räⁿ-ˈtōⁿ\. Commune, Val-de-Marne dept., N France, SE suburb of Paris.

Saint–Maurice \ˌseⁿ-mȯ-ˈrēs, ˌsānt-; sānt-ˈmȯr-əs, sənt-, -ˈmär-\. River, S Quebec, Canada; flows S from Gouin Reservoir into the St. Lawrence River at Trois-Rivières; 325 mi. (523 km.) long; chief tributary the Mattawin from the W. See SHAWINIGAN.

Saint Mi·chael \ˌsānt-ˈmī-kəl\. **1.** Village, W Alaska, on S coast of Norton Sound and SW of Unalakleet; pop. (1990c) 295.

2. City, Wright co., S cen. Minnesota, NW of Minneapolis; pop. (1990c) 2506.

3. Island, Azores. See SÃO MIGUEL.

Saint Mi·chaels Bay \ˈmī-kəlz\. Bay, E coast of Labrador, Canada, 52°44′N.

Saint Michael's Mount. Lofty rock in Mounts Bay, Cornwall, SW England; seat of an ancient castle.

Saint–Mi·hiel \ˌseⁿ-mē-ˈyel\. Commune, Meuse dept., NE France; pop. (1990c) 5435; battle Sept. 1918, one of the principal battles at the close of WWI; Germans driven from salient (held since 1914) in first major American offensive under Gen. John Pershing.

Saint–Mo·ritz \ˌsānt-ˈmȯ-rits\ *or Ger.* **Sankt Moritz** \ˌzäŋkt\ *or Romansh* **San Mu·rez·zan** \ˌsän-mü-ˈret-ˌsän\. Commune, Graubünden canton, E Switzerland, on Inn River in upper Engadine 28 mi. (45 km.) SSE of Chur; pop. (1980c) 5900; major winter resort; thermal springs; site of Winter Olympic Games 1928 and 1948.

Saint–Na·zaire \ˌseⁿ-nȧ-ˈzer\. Seaport, Loire-Atlantique dept., NW France, at mouth of Loire River 33 mi. (53 km.) WNW of Nantes; pop. (1990c) 66,087; major shipbuilding center and fishing port; produces aircraft, chemicals, steel, fertilizers; food canning.

History: Believed to occupy site of ancient **Car·bi·lo** \ˈkär-bə-ˌlō\ where Romans built a fleet 56 B.C.; developed as a port from mid-19th cent.; in WWI a major port of debarkation for American Expeditionary Force 1917–18; in WWII a German submarine base 1940–44; in 1942 scene of British commando raid which destroyed principal dock; surrounded by Allied forces Aug. 1944 and surrendered May 1945; town almost entirely destroyed in war but since rebuilt.

Saint Neots \ˈnēts\. Town, Cambridgeshire, England, ab. 50 mi. (80 km.) N of London; pop. (1981p) 21,185; 15th cent. church and old stone bridge.

Saint Nicholas. See SÃO NICOLAU.

Saint Nich·o·las, Mount \ˈni-kləs, -kə-ləs\. Peak in Glacier National Park, NW Montana; 9380 ft. (2859 m.).

Saint Nicholas–les–Cîteaux. See CÎTEAUX.

Saint Nicholas Point. See PUJUT, TANJUNG.

Saint–Ni·co·las \ˌseⁿ-ˌnē-kȯ-ˈlä\. **1.** Commune, Belgium. See SINT-NIKLAAS.

2. Commune, Liège prov., E Belgium, W suburb of the city of Liège; pop. (1991c) 23,817.

3. *or* **Saint Nicolas de Port** \də-ˈpȯr\. Commune, Meurthe-et-Moselle dept., NE France, ab. 8 mi. (15 km.) SE of Nancy; 15th–16th cent. Flamboyant church; noted for fairs which have been held since 12th cent.

Saint–Omer \ˌseⁿt-ȯ-ˈmer\. Commune, Pas-de-Calais dept., N France, 40 mi. (64 km.) NW of Arras; pop. (1990c) 15,304; ships fruit and vegetables; produces paper, textiles; 13th–15th cent. church; museums; library. Monastery founded on site by St. Omer 7th cent.; taken for France by Louis XIV 1677; British headquarters in WWI 1914–16; heavily damaged in both World Wars.

Sain·tonge \seⁿ-ˈtōⁿzh\. Ancient province of France, on the Bay of Biscay N of the Gironde; comprised most of present dept. of Charente-Maritime and small part of Charente; ✻ Saintes; country of an ancient Gallic people; part of Aquitaine from 9th cent.; passed to England 1152; regained for France by soldier Bertrand du Guesclin 1371; a crown possession 1375.

Saint–Ou·en \seⁿ-ˈtweⁿ\. Commune, Seine-St.-Denis dept., N France, N suburb of Paris on Seine River; pop. (1990c) 42,611.

Saint–Pas·cal \ˌseⁿ-pȧs-ˈkȧl\. Town, ⊗ of Kamouraska co., S Quebec, Canada, 85 mi. (137 km.) ENE of Quebec City, near right bank of St. Lawrence River and on highway to Gaspé Penin.; pop. (1991c) 2578.

Saint–Paul \seⁿ-ˈpȯl\. City on NW coast of Réunion I.; pop. (1990c) 11,006.

Saint Paul \ˌsānt-ˈpȯl\. **1.** City, ✻ of Minnesota and ⊗ of Ramsey co., E Minnesota, on Mississippi River just E of Minneapolis; pop. (1990c) 272,235; transportation and commercial center; livestock market; produces automobiles, chemicals, electronic equipment, abrasives, construction equipment; breweries, oil refineries, printing plants. Hamline Univ. (1854), Bethel Coll. (1871), Bethel Theological Seminary (1871), Macalester Coll. (1874), Univ. of St. Thomas (1885), Concordia Coll. (1893), William Mitchell Coll. of Law (1900), Northwestern Coll. (1902), Coll. of St. Catherine (1905), St. Paul Technical Coll. (1922), Coll. of Associated Arts (1924), Metropolitan State Univ. (1971). First settled 1838–40 by civilians expelled from military property of nearby Fort Snelling; ✻ of Minnesota Terr. 1849 and ✻ of state 1858; incorp. as city 1854. St. Paul and adjacent Minneapolis are often referred to as the Twin Cities.

2. City, ⊗ of Howard co., E cen. Nebraska, 21 mi. (34 km.) N of Grand Island; pop. (1990c) 2009.

3. Town, Alberta, Canada, 90 mi. (145 km.) ENE of Edmonton; pop. (1991c) 4881.

4. River, W Africa; flows from Guinea, forms part of Guinea-Liberia boundary, and flows through Liberia into the Atlantic Ocean near Monrovia; ab. 125 mi. (200 km.) long.

5. *Fr.* \seⁿ-'pȯl\. Uninhabited island, S Indian Ocean, 38°43′S, 77°32′E, just S of Amsterdam I.; part of French Southern and Antarctic Territories.

Saint Paul, Cape. Cape extending into the Bight of Benin on SE coast of Ghana, E of the mouth of the Volta River.

Saint Paul Island. **1.** Island, most northerly of Pribilof Is. (*q.v.*) in Bering Sea, Alaska; 35 sq. mi. (91 sq. km.); 13 mi. (21 km.) long by ab. 6 mi. (10 km.) wide.

2. Island, Cabot Strait, E Canada, ab. 14 mi. (23 km.) off Cape North, N Cape Breton I., at entrance to Gulf of St. Lawrence; lighthouse.

3. Uninhabited French island in S Indian Ocean, just S of Amsterdam I., at 38°43′S, 77°32′E; 3 sq. mi. (8 sq. km.).

Saint Paul Park. City, Washington co., E Minnesota, on Mississippi River 9 mi. (15 km.) SSE of St. Paul; pop. (1990c) 4965.

Saint Paul's Bay. See BAIE SAINT PAUL.

Saint Pe·ter \'pē-tər\. City, ⊗ of Nicollet co., S Minnesota, on Minnesota River 12 mi. (19 km.) N of Mankato; pop. (1990c) 9421; Gustavus Adolphus Coll. (1862).

Saint Peter, Lake. Lake, S Quebec, Canada, 60 mi. (97 km.) NE of the city of Montreal; 142 sq. mi. (368 sq. km.); formed by a widening of St. Lawrence River.

Saint Peter and Saint Paul Rocks *or Port.* **Pe·ne·dos de São Pe·dro e São Pau·lo** \pə-ˌnā-düs-dē-säⁿ-'pā-drü-ē-säⁿ-'pau̇-ˌlü\. Group of volcanic rocks in the Atlantic Ocean, 0°56′N, 29°22′W, ab. 600 mi. (965 km.) NE of Natal, Brazil.

Saint Peter Port. Town and civil parish, Guernsey, Channel Is.; United Kingdom; pop. (1991c) 16,648; ✱ of Guernsey bailiwick; site of Hauteville House, residence of French writer Victor Hugo 1856–70.

Saint Pe·ters \'pē-tərz\. **1.** City, St. Charles co., E Missouri, WNW of St. Louis; pop. (1990c) 45,779.

2. Town, NE suburb of Adelaide, SE South Australia, Australia; pop. (1981c) 8458.

Saint Peter's. See BROADSTAIRS.

Saint Pe·ters·burg \'pē-tərz-ˌbərg\. **1.** City, Pinellas co., W cen. Florida Penin., on W shore of Tampa Bay; pop. (1990c) 238,629; ships fruit and vegetables; winter resort, yachting and sportfishing center; St. Petersburg Junior Coll. (1927), Eckerd Coll. (1958); railway arrived 1888; incorp. as town 1892.

2. *or to Russians* **Sankt–Pe·ter·burg** \'sȧnkt-ˌpʸə-tʸər-'bu̇rk\; *1914–24* **Pet·ro·grad** \'pe-trə-ˌgrät, -ˌgrad\; *1924–91* **Len·in·grad** \ˌli-nən-'grät, 'le-nən-ˌgrad\. City, ✱ of St. Petersburg Oblast, W Russia in Europe; at E end of Gulf of Finland; pop. (1993e) 4,952,000; ✱ of Russian empire 1712–1917; 2d largest city in Russia, and an important port built on the Neva delta; an industrial center with shipbuilding, heavy engineering, electrical equipment, chemical, printing, and food-processing industries; A.A. Zhdanov State Univ. (1819) and numerous other educational institutions; libraries incl. the Saltykov-Shchedrin public library (1795; contains ab. 12 million volumes); major cultural center, incl. publishing, theater, and music; intersected by many canals, crossed by more than 600 bridges; many fine buildings (Academy of Sciences, Winter Palace [1754–62], Palace of Art, St. Isaac's Cathedral [1818–58], Peter and Paul Fortress, and museums), making it a major center for Western tourism.

History: Founded 1703 by Czar Peter the Great as his "window on Europe" and in 1712 made ✱ of Russia (though area was nominally Swedish until 1821); scene of liberal Decembrist revolt 1825 and "Bloody Sunday" attack on workers marching on Winter Palace to petition czar 1905; renamed Petrograd 1914; original center of Bolshevik Revolution in 1917 but ✱ of Soviet Russia moved to Moscow March 1918; renamed Leningrad 1924; in WWII underwent siege by Germans Sept. 1941–Jan. 1944 during which perhaps one million persons died; from 1990 reformist city council and mayor helped swing country from Communist control; regained original city name 1991.

Saint Petersburg Beach. City, Pinellas co., W cen. Florida; pop. (1990c) 9200.

Saint Petersburg Oblast; *formerly* **Leningrad Oblast.** Administrative subdivision of W Russia in Europe, bounded on N by Karelia Rep. and on W by Estonia; 33,166 sq. mi. (85,900 sq. km.); pop. (1991e) 6,705,000; ✱ St. Petersburg; approx. two thirds of Lake Ladoga lies within its borders. Its principal streams are the Neva (outlet of Lake Ladoga), Svir (outlet of Lake Onega), and Volkhov (outlet of Lake Ilmen). Level country with forests and some marshlands; has considerable agricultural development; mining; timberworking in E. Its manufacturing industries highly developed and varied, esp. in St. Petersburg, which is by far the oblast's largest city. Region early settled by Finnish peoples; for several centuries nominally subject to Novgorod but contended for by Swedes; part included in Ingria (*q.v.*) 1617–1703 but with capture of Swedish fort on the Neva by Czar Peter the Great 1703, history of region centers on St. Petersburg (*q.v.*). After WWII extended to include all of Karelian Isthmus, N part of which was formerly in Finland.

Saint Phil·ip and Saint James Bay \'fi-ləp ... 'jāmz\. Large inlet on N coast of Espíritu Santo I., Vanuatu, SW Pacific, bet. two peninsulas.

Saint–Pierre \sānt-'pir, sənt-; *Fr.* seⁿ-'pyer\. **1.** Town, Montreal I., S Quebec, Canada, on N bank of Lachine Canal bet. Montreal and Lachine; pop. (1991c) 4967.

2. Small island off S coast of Newfoundland, Canada, in Atlantic Ocean; part of French terr. of St.-Pierre and Miquelon; 10 sq. mi. (26 sq. km.); pop. (1982c) 5415; chief town St.-Pierre; rocky and of very irregular shape.

3. Town on St.-Pierre I. off Newfoundland, Canada; pop. (1990p) 5007; seat of government of terr. of St.-Pierre and Miquelon; its harbor is port for fishing fleet.

4. Small island in the Indian Ocean 240 mi. (386 km.) NNE of Madagascar; ab. 0.5 sq. mi. (1.3 sq. km.); belongs to Seychelles.

5. Town, French overseas dept. of Martinique, West Indies; pop. (1990c) 5045; had pop. of 30,000 before its destruction by volcanic eruption of Mt. Pelée 1902; only survivor was a prisoner in an underground cell.

6. Town, SW coast of the island of Réunion, Indian Ocean; pop. (1982c) 50,419.

Saint–Pierre and Miq·ue·lon \'mi-kə-ˌlän\ *or Fr.* **Saint–Pierre et Mi·que·lon** \seⁿ-'pyer-ā-mē-'klōⁿ\. French overseas territorial collectivity consisting of two small islands, St.-Pierre and Miquelon, in the Atlantic Ocean just S of Newfoundland, Canada; 93 sq. mi. (241 sq. km.); pop. (1993e) 6400; ✱ St.-Pierre; exports dried and frozen cod; tourism.

History: Settled 1604 by Basque and Breton fishermen; changed hands several times bet. France and Britain until 1814 treaty made French possession final; long dispute over French rights to the French Shore (*q.v.*) ended 1904. Classified as a French territory 1946, department 1976, territorial collectivity 1985.

Saint–Pierre–de–Chartreuse. See CHARTREUSE, LA GRANDE.

Saint–Pol–de–Lé·on \seⁿ-ˌpȯl-də-lā-'ōⁿ\. Town, Finistère dept., NW France, ab. 30 mi. (48 km.) NE of Brest and ab. 1 mi. (2 km.) from the coast; 13th–14th cent. cathedral.

Saint–Pol–sur–Mer \sūr-'mer\; *sometimes shortened to* **Saint–Pol.** Commune, Nord dept., N France, WSW suburb of Dunkerque.

Saint–Priest \seⁿ-'prēst\. Commune, NW Isère dept., SE France.

Saint–Pri·vat–la–Mon·tagne \ˌseⁿ-prē-'vä-lä-mōⁿ-'tänʸ\ *or* **Saint–Privat.** Village, Moselle dept., NE France, 7 mi. (11 km.) NW of Metz and near Gravelotte (*q.v.*).

Saint–Quen·tin \ˌseⁿ-käⁿ-'teⁿ; sānt-'kwent-ᵊn, sənt-\. Commune, Aisne dept., N France, on Somme River 25 mi. (40 km.) NW of Laon; pop. (1990c) 62,085; textiles, iron goods, chemicals, machinery; 13th–15th cent. church; 14th–16th cent. city hall; important center of cloth industry during Middle Ages; chief city of old prov. of Vermandois, came under French crown 1191; scene of Spanish victory over the French 1557; center of major battle won by the Germans in Franco-Prussian War Jan. 1871; in WWI scene of decisive British breakthrough, Sept.–Oct. 1918.

Saint–Ra·pha·ël \ˌseⁿ-ˌrȧ-fā-'el\. **1.** Village, ⊗ of Bellechasse co., S Quebec, Canada, 24 mi. (39 km.) E of Quebec City; pop. (1991c) 1285; agriculture.

2. Town, Var dept., SE France, on the Riviera ab. 18 mi. (29 km.) SW of Cannes; in WWII scene of severe fighting Aug. 1944 during Allied invasion of S France.

Saint–Ray·mond \ˌse^{n}-rā-ˈmȯ^{n}; sānt-ˈrā-mənd, sənt-\. Town, Portneuf co., S Quebec, Canada, on Ste. Anne River 28 mi. (45 km.) W of Quebec City; pop. (1991c) 3373.

Saint–Ré·mi \ˌse^{n}-rā-ˈmē\. Town, S Quebec, Canada, 17 mi. (27 km.) S of Montreal; pop. (1991c) 5768.

Saint–Ré·my–de–Pro·vence \ˌse^{n}-rā-ˌmē-də-prȯ-ˈvä^{n}s\ *or* **Saint–Rémy.** Town, Bouches-du-Rhône dept., SE France, ab. 15 mi. (24 km.) NE of Arles.

Saint–Ri·quier \ˌse^{n}-rē-ˈkyā\. Town, Somme dept., N France, ab. 8 mi. (13 km.) NE of Abbeville; 13th–15th cent. church remaining from abbey founded 7th cent.

Saint–Ro·mu·ald \se^{n}-rȯm-ˈwäld\ *or* **Saint Romuald–d'Etch·e·min** \-dech-ˈme^{n}\. City, S Quebec, Canada, ab. 6 mi. (10 km.) SW of Levis; pop. (1991c) 9830.

Saint–Sau·veur–le–Vi·comte \ˌse^{n}-sō-ˈvœr-lə-vē-ˈkō^{n}t\. Commune, Manche dept., NW France, 18 mi. (29 km.) S of Cherbourg. Contested by French and English in Hundred Years' War; belonged to English soldier Sir John Chandos 1360–70; in WWII taken by Allies June 1944.

Saint Sé·bas·tien, Cape \ˌsānt-sə-ˈbas-chən, ˌse^{n}-ˌsā-bȧs-ˈtye^{n}\. Cape extreme NW coast of Madagascar, projecting into N Mozambique Channel.

Saint Si·mons Island \ˈsī-mənz\. Island, E coast of Glynn co., SE Georgia, in Atlantic Ocean S of entrance to Altamaha Sound; 36 sq. mi. (93 sq. km.).

Saint So·phia Ridge \sə-ˌfī-ə\. Peak, Ouray and San Miguel cos., SW Colorado; 13,100 ft. (3993 m.).

Saint Ste·phen \ˈstē-vən\. Town, Charlotte co., SW New Brunswick, Canada, on St. Croix River 15 mi. (24 km.) NW of its mouth and at head of navigation; pop. (1991c) 4931; lumber; diversified agriculture.

Saint Tam·ma·ny \ˈta-mə-nē\. Parish in SE Louisiana. See table at LOUISIANA.

Saint Thom·as \ˈtä-məs\. **1.** City, ⊗ of Elgin co., SE Ontario, Canada, near Lake Erie 15 mi. (24 km.) S of London; pop. (1991c) 29,990; electric motors, aircraft parts, bearings, tile; automobile assembly; Alma Coll. (1878); settled c. 1810.

2. Island, Gulf of Guinea, E Atlantic Ocean. See SÃO TOMÉ 1.

3. Island, Virgin Is. of the U.S., West Indies, ab. 40 mi. (64 km.) E of Puerto Rico; separated from Culebra I. on W by Virgin Passage; 28 sq. mi. (73 sq. km.); pop. (1990c) 48,166; ✻ Charlotte Amalie (also ✻ of U.S. Virgin Is.) on S coast; 2d in size and commercially the most important of the group; of volcanic origin, with range of hills traversing island E to W (highest point 1556 ft. or 474 m.). Coastline much indented, with **Saint Thomas Harbor,** the harbor of Charlotte Amalie, a good anchorage; has fueling and repair facilities. Produces rum and bay rum; tourism; Univ. of the Virgin Islands (1962). Visited by explorer Christopher Columbus 1493; unsuccessful settlements by Dutch 1657 and by Danes 1666 followed by permanent Danish one 1672; a major center of slavery 17th–19th cents.; in 19th cent. twice held temporarily by English. See VIRGIN ISLANDS and WEST INDIES.

4. Town, St. Thomas I., Virgin Is. of the U.S. See CHARLOTTE AMALIE.

Saint Tho·mé \ˌsānt-tō-ˈmā\ *or Port.* **São To·mé** \ˌsau̇^{n}-tu̇-ˈmā\. Orig. Portuguese fort (1615–69) on Coromandel Coast, India; now part of the city of Madras (*q.v.*). Occupied by English 1749; battle bet. French and English 1759.

Saint–Tite \se^{n}-ˈtēt\. Town, Champlain co., S Quebec, Canada, 27 mi. (43 km.) N of Trois-Rivières; pop. (1991c) 2654.

Saint–Trond. See SINT-TRUIDEN.

Saint–Tro·pez \ˌse^{n}-trō-ˈpā\. Commune, Var dept., SE France, on Bay of St. Tropez, SSW of Fréjus; noted seaside resort.

Saint Ubes. See SETÚBAL 2.

Saint–Va·lé·ry–sur–Somme \ˌse^{n}-ˌvȧ-lā-ˌrē-sūr-ˈsȯm\. Town, Somme dept., NE France, on S side of mouth of the Somme; point of departure of William the Conqueror, duke of Normandy, in 1066 for invasion of England. See DIVES.

Saint–Ve·nant \se^{n}v-ˈnä^{n}\. Commune, Pas-de-Calais dept., N France, on the Leie River N of Béthune.

Saint Vin·cent \ˈvint-sənt\. **1.** Island off SW coast of Franklin co., NW Florida, bet. Apalachicola Bay on E and Gulf of Mexico on W; 19 sq. mi. (49 sq. km.); a wildlife refuge.

2. Island, Cape Verde Is. See SÃO VICENTE 2.

3. Principal island of St. Vincent and the Grenadines (*q.v.*), S of St. Lucia and W of Barbados; ab. 18 mi. (29 km.) long by 11 mi. (18 km.) wide; area 133 sq. mi. (344 sq. km.); ✻ Kingstown; volcanic, with many hills and valleys; highest point Soufrière volcano 4048 ft. (1234 m.); has botanical garden estab. 1768.

History: Caribs, who arrived c. 1300, strongly resisted colonial settlement until 18th cent.; perhaps sighted by explorer Christopher Columbus 1498; British possession confirmed 1763 but under French 1779–83 when British again gained control; failed Carib uprising 1795–96 resulted in deportation of Caribs 1797; slavery begun by French and British ended 1834. Has suffered much from hurricanes and volcanic eruptions (esp. Soufrière 1902); became with the N Grenadines self-governing 1969; independent 1979.

4. City, Brazil. See SÃO VICENTE 1.

Saint Vincent, Cape. **1.** Cape on W coast of Madagascar, 21°57′S, 43°16′E.

2. *or Port.* **Ca·bo de São Vi·cen·te** \ˈkä-bü-dē-ˌsau̇^{n}-vē-ˈsān-tē\; *Roman name* **Pro·mon·to·ri·um Sa·crum** \ˌprä-mən-ˈtōr-ē-əm-ˈsā-krəm\. Cape, SW point of Portugal, ab. 118 mi. (190 km.) S of Lisbon. Regarded by some ancient geographers as westernmost point of Europe or the world. Near **Sa·gres** \ˈsä-grēsh\ 3 mi. (5 km.) E, Prince Henry the Navigator estab. c. 1420 his school of navigation and observatory; lighthouse now on site of ruins. In naval battle off cape, English Adm. Sir John Jervis defeated Spanish fleet 1797; other naval battles off the cape were: defeat of English and Dutch 1693 by French Adm. Anne-Hilarion de Tourville; defeat of Spanish 1780 by English Adm. George Rodney; and defeat 1833 of fleet of Portuguese usurper Dom Miguel by fleet of his brother Dom Pedro I under Sir Charles Napier, British naval commander.

Saint Vincent, Gulf. Gulf, South Australia, Australia, E of Yorke Penin.; ab. 100 mi. (160 km.) long; connected with Indian Ocean by Investigator Strait on SW and Backstairs Passage on S; Kangaroo I. across its entrance; Adelaide and Port Adelaide, its seaport, are on its E shore.

Saint Vincent and the Grenadines. Self-governing state of the Windward Is., West Indies; comprises St. Vincent I. and the N Grenadines (incl. Union and Bequia); 150 sq. mi. (389 sq. km.); pop. (1993e) 109,000; ✻ Kingstown, on SW coast of St. Vincent I.; chief product bananas; tourism; became independent 1979.

Saint Vital, Point \ˈvī-təl\. Point in SE Chippewa co., E Michigan on Upper Penin., extending into Lake Huron.

Saint–Vith \se^{n}-ˈvēt\ *or* **Sankt–Vith** \zäŋkt-ˈvēt\. Town, Liège prov., E Belgium, near border of Grand Duchy of Luxembourg 35 mi. (56 km.) SE of Liège; pop. (1991c) 8623; formerly German. In WWII in the Battle of the Bulge (E Belgium), taken by Germans Dec. 1944 and retaken by U.S. troops after severe fighting Jan. 23, 1945.

Saint Yves. See SETÚBAL 2.

Sai·pan \sī-ˈpän, -ˈpan, ˈsī-ˌ\. **1.** Island, S cen. Northern Mariana Is., W Pacific Ocean; 14 mi. (23 km.) long and 2 to 5 mi. (3 to 8 km.) wide; area 70 sq. mi. (181 sq. km.); pop. (1990c) 38,896. Hilly with highest point 1551 ft. (473 m.); at N end, Marpi Point, are high cliffs. On SE coast is wide inlet, Magicienne Bay; best anchorage is Tanapag Harbor on W coast just N of Garapan. Spanish possession 1565–1899; German 1899–1914; included in Japanese mandate under League of Nations 1920, and developed as naval base with several airfields; in WWII captured by U.S. troops after severe fighting June 15–July 9, 1944; developed into major American air base, used Nov. 1944 to end of war.

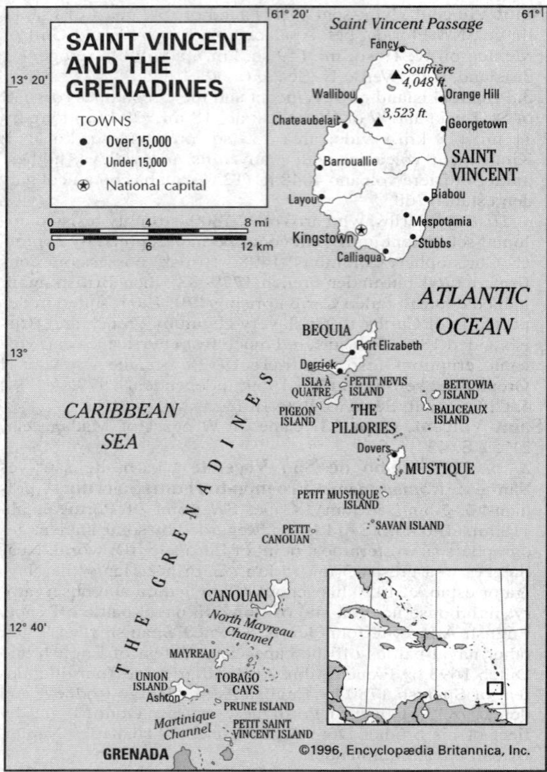

2. Village, W coast of Angaur I., S Palau, W Pacific Ocean.

Sairam Nor. See SAYRAM HU.

Sairussu. See SAYR USA.

Sa·ïs \ˈsā-is\. Important city in ancient Egypt, in the Nile Delta on the Canopic branch of the river; 30°57′N, 30°48′E; ancient ❋ of Lower Egypt.

Saishu. See CHEJU 2.

Saishu To. See CHEJU 1.

Sai·ta·ma \ˈsī-tä-mä, sī-ˈtä-mä\. Prefecture, Honshū, Japan; ❋ Urawa; sericulture; textiles. See table at JAPAN.

Sa·ja·ma, Ne·va·do \nā-ˈbä-thō-sä-ˈhä-mä\ *also* **Sa·ha·ma** \sä-ˈhä-mä\. Peak, W Bolivia, near Chilean boundary; 21,391 ft. (6520 m.); area set aside as **Sajama National Park** 1945.

Sa·jó \ˈsö-yō\. River, cen. Europe; rises in S Slovakia, flows S and SE to the Tisza in NE Hungary; 125 mi. (201 km.) long.

Sa·ka·do \sä-ˈkä-dō\. City, Saitama prefecture, Honshū, Japan; pop. (1990p) 95,736.

Sa·kai \ˈsä-ˌkī\. City, Ōsaka prefecture, W cen. Honshū, Japan, 6 mi. (10 km.) S of the city of Ōsaka on Ōsaka Bay; pop. (1990p) 807,859; machinery, chemicals, fertilizer, automobile parts; numerous earthen tombs, incl. that of Emperor Nintoku (d. 399 A.D.); in 16th cent. a leading seaport but declined after silting up of harbor.

Sa·kai·de \sä-ˈkī-dā\. Port city, Kagawa prefecture, Shikoku, Japan, 12 mi. (19 km.) W of Takamatsu; pop. (1990p) 63,878.

Sa·kā·kah *also* **Sa·ka·ka** \sə-ˈkäk-ə\. Town, N Nejd, Saudi Arabia, ab. 35 mi. (55 km.) ENE of Al Jawf.

Sak·a·ka·wea, Lake \ˌsa-kə-kə-ˈwē-ə\; *formerly* **Garrison Reservoir** \ˈgar-ə-sən\. Reservoir, W cen. North Dakota; ab. 200 mi. (320 km.) long on Missouri River; easternmost part called Lake Audubon; formed behind Garrison Dam (see UNITED STATES, *Dams and Reservoirs*).

Sakartvelos. See GEORGIA, REPUBLIC OF.

Sa·kar·ya \sə-ˈkär-yə\; *anc.* **San·gar·i·us** \saŋ-ˈgar-ē-əs\. **1.** River, NW Turkey in Asia; rises in mountains N of Afyon and flows in double curve E, W, and N into the Black Sea 80 mi. (129 km.) E of the Bosporus; 510 mi. (821 km.) long. The Porsuk and Ankara are its chief tributaries; Adapazarı is chief town on its banks. **2.** Province of Turkey in Asia; ❋ Adapazarı. See table at TURKEY.

Sa·ka·ta \sä-ˈkä-tä, ˈsä-kä-ˌtä\. Seaport city, Yamagata prefecture, N Honshū, Japan, 85 mi. (137 km.) N of Niigata; pop. (1990p) 100,808; Shinto shrine.

Sa·kha \ˈsä-kə\ *or* **Ya·ku·tia** \yə-ˈkü-shē-ə\. Republic, E cen. Siberia, E Russia in Asia; 1,198,146 sq. mi. (3,103,198 sq. km.); pop. (1992e) 1,093,000; ❋ Yakutsk.

Physical features: Bounded on the N by the Arctic Ocean (Laptev and East Siberian seas), on the E by Khabarovsk Kray, on S by Chita and Irkutsk oblasts, and on W by Krasnoyarsk Kray (Evenki and Taymyr autonomous okrugs). Includes nearly the whole great basin of the Lena (*q.v.*), as well as the valleys of the Olenek, Yana, Indigirka, and Kolyma; largely plain, with tundra in the N and mountain ranges (Verkhoyansk and Cherski) in the E; highest peaks 8000 to 10,200 ft. (2450 to 3100 m.). Includes New Siberian Is. and Lyakhovskiye Ostrova in the Arctic. Extremely severe climate, the towns of Verkhoyansk and Oimyakon being two of the coldest places on Earth.

Chief products: Economic activity includes reindeer herding and fishing; substantial timber resources; cattle; gold and diamonds, also tin, salt and coal; food products.

History: Highway system has expanded since WWII. Fort at Yakutsk founded 1632 and first gold mines worked mid-19th cent.; organized as autonomous republic 1922, an A.S.S.R. (**Ya·kutsk A.S.S.R.** \yə-ˈkütsk\ *or* **Ya·kut A.S.S.R.** \yə-ˈküt\ *also* **Yakutia**) of the U.S.S.R. before 1991.

Sa·kha·lin \ˌsä-kä-ˈlēn; ˈsak-ə-ˌlēn, -lən\; *formerly* **Sa·ghal·ien** \ˌsä-gəl-ˈyen\ *or Jp.* **Ka·ra·fu·to** \ˌkä-rä-ˈfü-tō\. Island, Sakhalin Oblast, E Russia in Asia, N of Japan in W part of Sea of Okhotsk; 28,597 sq. mi. (74,066 sq. km.); 589 mi. (948 km.) long, 16 to 100 mi. (26 to 161 km.) wide, av. width 62 mi. (100 km.); separated from Russian mainland on W by Tatar Strait and from Hokkaidō, Japan, on S by Sōya Strait; in SE are two large inlets Terpeniya Bay and Aniva Bay; covered with forests; in S mountainous, highest point 5277 ft. (1608 m.); fishing, lumbering, coal mining; oil wells.

History: Explored by Russians and Japanese 18th–19th cents.; first settled by Russians 1853, came entirely under Russian control 1875 when Japan ceded it in exchange for Kuril Is.; used as a penal colony in czarist Russia; occupied by Japanese 1905; S part below 50°N granted to Japan by Treaty of Portsmouth 1905, returned to U.S.S.R. 1945 after defeat of Japan by Allies in WWII.

Sakhalin, Gulf of. Inlet of Sea of Okhotsk bet. N end of Sakhalin I. and mainland of Khabarovsk Kray, E Russia in Asia; on S connects with Tatar Strait.

Sakhalin Oblast \ˈȯ-bləst, -ˌblast\ *or* **Sa·kha·lin·ska·ya Oblast′** \sə-ˌkə-ˈlēn-skə-yə-ˈȯ-bləstʸ\. Subdivision of Russia in Asia, consisting of Sakhalin I. and the Kuril Is.; 33,629 sq. mi. (87,099 sq. km.); pop. (1992e) 719,000. See KURIL ISLANDS and SAKHALIN.

Sakhar. See SUKKUR.

Sakhara. See SAQQARA.

Şäki. See SHEKI.

Sakız. See CHIOS.

Sa·ki·shi·ma Islands \ˌsä-kē-ˈshē-mä\. Group of ab. 20 small islands in S section of Ryukyu Is. (*q.v.*), in W Pacific Ocean off E coast of N Taiwan; 343 sq. mi. (888 sq. km.); all formed of coral reefs. Largest are Miyako, Ishigaki, and Iriomote.

Sak·ma·ra \sək-ˈmär-ə\. River, E Russia in Europe; rises in S Ural Mts. in Bashkortostan Rep. and flows S and W to the Ural River at Orenburg; 440 mi. (708 km.) long.

Sa·kon Na·khon \sə-ˈkȯn-nə-ˈkȯn\ *or* **Sa·kol Na·korn** \sə-ˈkȯn-nə-ˈkȯn—*sic*\. Town, NE Thailand, on a small lake with outlet to the Mekong, 50 mi. (80 km.) W of Nakhon Phanom; pop. (1991e) 47,869.

Sa·kon·net River \sə-ˈkä-nət, -ˈkə-\. Inlet of Atlantic Ocean extending into Newport co., SE Rhode Island, E of Rhode I. (island).

Sakota. See SEKOTA.

Sak·ti \ˈsək-tē\. Former Indian state, now part of Madhya Pradesh, India, 45 mi. (72 km.) E of Bilaspur; 137 sq. mi. (355 sq. km.); ✱ Sakti.

Sa·ku·ra \sä-ˈkü-rä\. City, Chiba prefecture, SE Honshū, Japan; pop. (1990p) 144,688.

Sakurajima. See ON-TAKE.

Sal \ˈsäl\. One of the Cape Verde Is., N of Boa Vista; 83 sq. mi. (215 sq. km.); salt.

Sal, Cay \ˈsal\. Islet in W Bahamas. See CAY SAL BANK.

Sala. See IJSSEL.

Šal·'a \ˈshäl-yä\. Town, W Slovakia; pop. (1989c) 24,717.

Sa·la·ber·ry de Val·ley·field \ˌsà-là-be-ˈrē-də-ˌvà-lā-ˈfēld, ˈsa-lə-ˌber-ē-də-ˈva-lē-ˌfēld\; *often shortened to* **Valleyfield.** City, Beauharnois co., S Quebec, Canada, on S shore of Lake St. Francis on an island formed by St. Lawrence Seaway Canal, 35 mi. (56 km.) SW of Montreal; pop. (1991c) 27,598; produces chemicals, food products; founded c. 1870.

Sa·la·dil·lo \ˌsä-lä-ˈdē-yō\. Name of several rivers in Argentina, esp.: (1) the upper course of the Dulce (*q.v.*); (2) river in N cen. part, in Córdoba prov., flowing E, joining Tercero River to form the Carcaraña, a tributary of the Paraná.

Sa·la·do \sä-ˈlä-t͟hō\. **1.** River, E Cuba; flows W into Cauto River; 60 mi. (97 km.) long.

2. River, Coahuila and Nuevo León states, NE Mexico; flows SE into the Rio Grande River; ab. 250 mi. (400 km.) long; in upper course known as the **Sa·bi·nas** \sä-ˈbē-näs\.

Salado, Río \ˈrē-ō-sä-ˈlä-t͟hō\. **1.** Name of three rivers in Argentina: (1) river in N part; more than 1100 mi. (1770 km.) long; rises in Andes and flows SE into the Paraná River at Santa Fe; (2) river in W part; ab. 850 mi. (1370 km.) long; flows S forming boundary bet. Mendoza and San Luis provs., turns SE and empties into Colorado River; known as **Des·a·gua·de·ro** \ˌthā-ˌsä-gwä-ˈt͟hā-rō\ in its upper course, and as **Cha·di·leo** \ˌchä-t͟hē-ˈlā-ō\ in its course through La Pampa prov.; (3) river in E part, in Buenos Aires prov.; ab. 400 mi. (650 km.) long; flows W into Samborombón Bay.

2. Small river, Cádiz prov., S Spain near Tarifa; battle on its bank 1340 in which Alfonso XI of Castile as ally of Alfonso IV of Portugal defeated the Moors.

Salado Bay. Inlet of Pacific Ocean on W coast of Atacama prov., N cen. Chile.

Salahiyeh. See DURA-EUROPOS.

Sălaj \sə-ˈläzh\. County of NW Romania. See table at ROMANIA.

Sa·lak, Gu·nung \ˈgü-nu̇ŋ-ˈsä-läk\. Volcano, W Java, Indonesia, SW of Bogor; 7252 ft. (2210 m.). Severe eruptions 1669 and 1699.

Sa·lā·lah \sà-ˈlà-lə\. Coastal town, Oman, ab. 80 mi. (130 km.) E of Yemen border; formerly known for frankincense trade.

Sa·la·má \ˌsä-lä-ˈmä\. Town, ✱ of Baja Verapaz dept., cen. Guatemala; munic. pop. (1993e) 12,794.

Sal·a·man·ca \ˌsa-lə-ˈmaŋ-kə\. City, Cattaraugus co., SW New York, on Allegheny River 13 mi. (21 km.) WNW of Olean; pop. (1990c) 6566; within Allegany Indian Reservation, from whom ground is leased.

Sa·la·man·ca \ˌsä-lä-ˈmäŋ-kä\. **1.** Town, Guanajuato state, cen. Mexico, 17 mi. (27 km.) S of the city of Guanajuato; munic. pop. (1990p) 206,275; oil refining; in agricultural region.

2. Province of W Spain. See table at SPAIN.

3. *anc.* **Sal·man·ti·ca** \sal-ˈman-ti-kə\ *or* **Hel·man·ti·ca** \hel-\. Commune, ✱ of Salamanca prov., W Spain, on Tormes River 107 mi. (172 km.) WNW of Madrid; pop. (1991c) 162,888; center of an agricultural region; two cathedrals (12th cent. Romanesque and 16th–18th cent. Gothic); Roman bridge; notable colonnaded square, the Plaza Mayor, lined with Renaissance buildings; Univ. of Salamanca (c. 1200; one of the major universities of medieval Europe), Pontifical Univ. of Salamanca (1940).

History: Important city of ancient Spain, conquered by Carthaginian commander Hannibal c. 220 B.C.; became Roman station on the "Silver Road" from Emerita Augusta (Mérida) to Asturica Augusta (Astorga); captured by Moors 8th cent.; reconquered by Christians late 11th cent. and gradually repopulated; in Peninsular War occupied by the French, and scene of a victory of the British under Gen. Arthur Wellesley (later duke of Wellington), over the French 1812.

Sal·a·maua \ˌsä-lä-ˈmau̇-ä\. Coastal town, New Guinea I., Papua New Guinea, on W shore of Huon Gulf ab. 19 mi. (31 km.) S of Lae; has good harbor. Seized by Japanese during WWII 1942; made a military base; captured by Allied forces 1943.

Salambria. See PINIÓS.

Sal·a·mis \ˈsa-lə-məs\ *or* **Sal·a·mís** \ˌsä-lä-ˈmēs\. **1.** Chief city of Cyprus in ancient times, on E coast; its site 3 mi. (5 km.) N of Famagusta. Had active trade with Phoenicia, Egypt, and Cilicia. According to tradition founded by Teucer, a hero of the Trojan War; was a major Hellenic center during struggle bet. Greece and Persia; scene of naval victory 449 B.C. for Greeks and again 306 B.C. when Demetrius I defeated Ptolemy I of Egypt. Visited by Sts. Paul and Barnabas (*Acts* xiii. 4, 5). Under the Byzantine Empire known as **Con·stan·tia** \kən-ˈstan-chē-ə\, after Constantius II who rebuilt it 337–361; abandoned after destruction by Arabs 647–48.

2. *also* **Kou·lou·ri** \kü-ˈlü-rē\. Island in the Saronic Gulf, Attica dept., Greece, near Piraeus; 37 sq. mi. (96 sq. km.); pop. (1981c) 28,574; naval base; forms an irregular semicircle with large inlet on the W and is S boundary of Bay of Eleusis. Important naval battle fought 480 B.C. in narrow strait off NE coast, in which allied Greeks under Athenian Themistocles defeated Persians under King Xerxes. See CYNOSURA.

3. *also* **Koulouri.** Commune on NE Salamis I., Greece, W of Piraeus.

Sal·a·mon·ie \ˈsa-lə-ˌmō-nē\. River, Indiana; flows NW from SE Jay co. to Wabash River in E Wabash co.; ab. 100 mi. (160 km.) long.

Salang. See PHUKET 1.

Sa·lar de Uyu·ni. See UYUNI.

Sa·lar·i·an Way \sə-ˈlar-ē-ən\ *or Lat.* **Via Sa·lar·ia** \ˈvē-ə-sə-ˈlar-ē-ə\. Road in ancient Roman Empire from Rome NE through Reate (Rieti) and Asculum Picenum (Ascoli Piceno) to Adriatic coast; ab. 150 mi. (240 km.) long; route by which the Sabines got their salt from the sea.

Sa·las \ˈsä-läs\. Commune, Asturias prov., NW Spain, 24 mi. (39 km.) WNW of Oviedo; pop. (1991c) 8157.

Sa·la·sun·go Dan·da \ˌsä-lə-ˌsüŋ-gō-ˈdən-də\. Mountain in the Himalayas, on the China-Nepal boundary; 24,299 ft. (7406 m.).

Salatan, Cape. See SELATAN, TANJUNG.

Sa·la·ti·ga \ˌsä-lə-ˈtē-gə\. Town, Central Java prov., Indonesia, ab. 25 mi. (40 km.) S of Semarang; pop. (1990c) 98,072.

Sa·la·vat \sə-ˈlä-vät\. Town, Bashkortostan Rep., E Russia in Europe, ab. 100 mi. (160 km.) S of Ufa; pop. (1992e) 152,000.

Sa·la·wa·ti \ˌsä-lə-ˈwä-tē\. Island off W Doberai Penin., NW Irian Jaya, Indonesia; separated by narrow channel from New Guinea mainland; greatest diameter ab. 30 mi. (48 km.).

Salayar *or* **Salayer.** See SELAYAR.

Salayar Strait *or* **Salayer Strait.** See SELAYAR STRAIT.

Sa·la y Gó·mez \ˈsä-lä-ē-ˈg̅ō-mās\. Uninhabitable rocky island in S Pacific Ocean, 210 mi. (338 km.) ENE of Easter I., 26°28′S, 105°28′W; belongs to Chile.

Sal·can·tay \ˌsäl-kän-ˈtī\. Peak in Cordillera Oriental, Peru, NW of Cuzco; 20,574 ft. (6271 m.).

Sal·ce·do \säl-ˈsā-t͟hō\. **1.** Province, N cen. Dominican Republic. See table at DOMINICAN REPUBLIC.

2. Town, its ✱; pop. (1981c) 10,651.

Sal·chak·et \sal-ˈcha-kət\. Village on Tanana River and on Alaska Highway, E Alaska, 36 mi. (58 km.) SE of Fairbanks.

Sal·combe \ˈsȯl-kəm\. Town, Devon, SW England, on English Channel; pop. (1981p) 2374; resort.

Saldae. See BEJAÏA.

Sal·da·nha Bay \sal-ˈda-nyə\. Bay on W coast of Western Cape prov., Rep. of South Africa, at 33°04′S, 18°E.

Salduba. See SARAGOSSA.

Sale \ˈsāl\. **1.** Town, SE Victoria, SE Australia, 120 mi. (193 km.) ESE of Melbourne; pop. (1991c) 13,858; chief town of Gippsland in a fertile agricultural district.

2. Town, Greater Manchester, NW England, on the Mersey 5 mi. (8 km.) SW of Manchester; pop. (1981p) 57,824; residential suburb of Manchester.

Sa·lé \sa-ˈlā\ *or Arab.* **Sla** \ˈslä\ *also* **Sal·lee** *or* **Sa·li** \ˈsal-ē\. City, NW Morocco, at the mouth of the Bou Regreg opp. Rabat of which it is a suburb; pop. (1982c) 289,391; founded 11th cent.; important port in Middle Ages; in 17th cent. an independent republic and a center of the Barbary pirates (sometimes called *Sallee rovers*).

Sa·le·ba·bu *or* **Sa·le·ba·boe** \ˌsä-lə-ˈbä-bü\. One of the Talaud Is. (*q.v.*), Indonesia.

Sa·leh Bay \ˈsä-lē\. Large inlet of Flores Sea on N coast of Sumbawa I., Lesser Sunda Is., Indonesia, ab. 45 mi. (72 km.) long by 22 mi. (35 km.) wide. Nearly cuts the island into two parts; its entrance nearly closed by Mojo I.

Sa·le·khard \ˌsə-le-ˈkärt\. Town, ✻ of Yamalo-Nenets Autonomous Okrug, NW Russia in Asia.

Sa·lem \ˈsā-ləm\. **1.** County in SW New Jersey. See table at NEW JERSEY.

2. City, ⊗ of Fulton co., N Arkansas; pop. (1990c) 1474.

3. City, ⊗ of Marion co., S cen. Illinois, 13 mi. (21 km.) ENE of Centralia; pop. (1990c) 7470; apple orchards; birthplace of lawyer and politician William Jennings Bryan 1860.

4. City, ⊗ of Washington co., S Indiana, 28 mi. (45 km.) NW of New Albany; pop. (1990c) 5619; birthplace of statesman John Hay 1838.

5. City, a ⊗ of Essex co., NE Massachusetts, on Atlantic Ocean 14 mi. (23 km.) NE of Boston; pop. (1990c) 38,091; residential suburb of Boston; produces leather goods; tourism; Salem State Coll. (1854). Peabody and Essex historical and art museum; Salem Maritime National Historic Site, incorporating part of 18th cent. waterfront and several merchants' houses. Founded 1626; scene of witchcraft hysteria 1692, in which 20 persons were executed; a leading American port in the East Indies and China trade late 18th–early 19th cents.; birthplace of author Nathaniel Hawthorne 1804.

6. City, ⊗ of Dent co., SE cen. Missouri, 26 mi. (42 km.) SSE of Rolla; pop. (1990c) 4486; footwear; agriculture.

7. Town, Rockingham co., SE New Hampshire, 12 mi. (19 km.) E of Nashua; pop. (1990c) 25,746. Part of Haverhill, Massachusetts until 1741; incorp. 1750.

8. City, ⊗ of Salem co., SW New Jersey, on Salem Creek near its confluence with Delaware River 16 mi. (26 km.) WNW of Bridgeton; pop. (1990c) 6883; manufactures glass containers, linoleum; English Quaker settlement founded 1675; made port of entry 1682; scene of fighting in American Revolution; incorp. as city 1858.

9. Former city, Forsyth co., North Carolina; now part of Winston-Salem (*q.v.*).

10. City, Columbiana co., E Ohio, 17 mi. (27 km.) SW of Youngstown; pop. (1990c) 12,233; machinery, tools and dies; founded 1801; a stop on the Underground Railroad.

11. City, ✻ of Oregon and ⊗ of Marion co., NW Oregon, on Willamette River 44 mi. (71 km.) SSW of Portland; pop. (1990c) 107,786; marketing and distributing center of agricultural area (esp. fruit and vegetables, livestock); food processing; Willamette Univ. (1842), Chemeketa Community Coll. (1954). Founded 1840; territorial ✻ 1851, continued as ✻ of state of Oregon 1859.

12. City, ⊗ of McCook co., SE South Dakota; pop. (1990c) 1289.

13. City, ⊗ of Roanoke co., W cen. Virginia, 8 mi. (13 km.) W of Roanoke; 8 sq. mi. (21 sq. km.); pop. (1990c) 23,756; politically independent; Roanoke Coll. (1842).

14. City, Harrison co., N West Virginia, 13 mi. (21 km.) W of Clarksburg; pop. (1990c) 2063; Salem-Teikyo Univ. (1888).

15. City, cen. Tamil Nadu, S India, 175 mi. (282 km.) SW of Madras; pop. (1991c) 366,712; trade center; handwoven cotton textiles.

Sa·le·mi \sä-ˈle-mē\. Commune, Trapani prov., NW Sicily, Italy, 22 mi. (35 km.) SE of the seaport of Trapani; pop. (1981p) 12,289; patriot Giuseppe Garibaldi declared himself dictator of Sicily here May 1860 in the name of Victor Emmanuel II.

Sa·len·ti·na \ˌsä-len-ˈtē-nä\ *also* **Sal·en·tine** \ˈsa-lən-ˌtēn, -ˌtīn\. Peninsula, Puglia, S Italy; from the ancient name, Sallentinum Promontorium, of Cape Santa Maria di Leuca at its tip.

Saleph. See GÖKSU 1.

Sa·ler·no \sə-ˈler-nō\. **1.** Province of Campania, S Italy. See table at ITALY.

2. *anc.* **Sa·ler·num** \sə-ˈlər-nəm\. Seaport, its ✻, S Italy, on Gulf of Salerno 29 mi. (47 km.) ESE of Naples; pop. (1989c) 152,159; manufactures textiles, machinery, ceramics, building materials, ironwork; 11th cent. cathedral said to contain tomb of St. Matthew and containing tomb of Pope Gregory VII; Lombard and Roman remains.

History: Founded by Romans c. 197 B.C.; taken by Lombards 646 and became independent Lombard ✻ 839; seized by Norman leader Robert Guiscard c. 1076; site of the first medical school of medieval Europe, founded c. 9th cent.; in WWII scene of major U.S. troop landing Sept. 9, 1943, and occupied by U.S. troops Sept. 18 after severe fighting.

Salerno, Gulf of; *anc.* **Bay of Paes·tum** \ˈpes-təm, ˈpē-\. Inlet of Tyrrhenian Sea on SW coast of Italy, S of the Bay of Naples.

Sal·ford \ˈsȯl-fərd\. City, Greater Manchester, NW England, on the Irwell adjacent to Manchester; pop. (1981c) 98,343; major port on Manchester Ship Canal; textiles, machinery, electronic products, rubber goods; Univ. of Salford (1967); received first charter 1230; incorp. as munic. borough 1844, as city 1926.

Sal·gó·tar·ján \ˈshöl-gō-ˌtör-ˌyän\. City, ⊗ of Nógrád co., N Hungary, 52 mi. (84 km.) NE of Budapest; pop. (1991e) 49,700.

Sal·hu·tu, Mount *or* **Mount Sal·hoe·toe** \säl-ˈhü-tü\. Peak, Moluccas, Indonesia; 3360 ft. (1024 m.); highest point on Ambon I.

Sali. See SALÉ.

Sa·li·da \sə-ˈlī-də\. City, ⊗ of Chaffee co., cen. Colorado, on Arkansas River 65 mi. (105 km.) WSW of Colorado Springs; pop. (1990c) 4737.

Salihorsk. See SOLIGORSK.

Sa·li·na \sə-ˈlī-nə\. City, ⊗ of Saline co., Kansas, on Smoky Hill River 58 mi. (93 km.) NNE of Hutchinson; pop. (1990c) 42,303; trade center in wheat-farming area; grain milling; Kansas Wesleyan Univ. (1886); founded 1858; incorp. 1870.

Sa·li·na \sä-ˈlē-nä\; *anc.* **Did·y·me** \ˈdi-di-mē\. One of the Lipari Is. (*q.v.*), S Italy; 5 mi. (8 km.) long; chief town Malfa.

Sa·li·na Cruz \sä-ˈlē-nä-ˈkrüs\. Seaport, Oaxaca state, Mexico, on the Gulf of Tehuantepec; pop. (1990p) 66,147.

Sa·li·nas \sə-ˈlē-nəs\. **1.** River, W California; rises in S cen. San Luis Obispo co. and flows NW into Monterey Bay on NW coast of Monterey co.; 150 mi. (241 km.) long.

2. City, ⊗ of Monterey co., W California, 10 mi. (16 km.) E of Monterey Bay and 47 mi. (76 km.) SSE of San Jose; pop. (1990c) 108,777; center of a major truck-farming region; Hartnell Coll. (1920); settled 1856; incorp. 1874. Birthplace of author John Steinbeck 1902.

3. Seaport town and resort on Santa Elena Penin., W Guayas prov., W Ecuador, ab. 70 mi. (113 km.) W of Guayaquil.

4. Municipality, S Puerto Rico, E of Ponce; pop. (1990c) 28,335.

5. See USUMACINTA.

Salinas, Cape. Cape, S tip of the island of Majorca, W Mediterranean Sea.

Salinas, Point. Cape, NE coast of Puerto Rico, W of entrance to San Juan harbor.

Salinas Bay. Inlet of Pacific Ocean, extreme NW coast of Costa Rica.

Salinas Pueblo Missions National Monument; *formerly* **Salinas National Monument;** *earlier* **Gran Quivira National Monument.** See UNITED STATES, *National Monuments.*

Sa·line \sə-ˈlēn\. **1.** River, S cen. Arkansas; rises in Saline co., flows S into the Ouachita near the Louisiana boundary; ab. 175 mi. (282 km.) long; navigable for 100 mi. (161 km.).
2. River, Kansas; rises in W Thomas co., NW Kansas, flows E into Smoky Hill River near Salina, Saline co., cen. Kansas; ab. 200 mi. (320 km.) long.
3. Name of counties in five states of the U.S. See tables at ARKANSAS, ILLINOIS, KANSAS, MISSOURI, NEBRASKA.
4. City, Washtenaw co., SE Michigan, 9 mi. (14 km.) S of Ann Arbor; pop. (1990c) 6660.

Saline di Barletta. See MARGHERITA DI SAVOIA.

Saline Lake. Lake, N cen. Louisiana, on boundary bet. Winn and Natchitoches parishes.

Salis·bury \ˈsȯlz-ˌber-ē, ˈsalz-, -bə-rē\. **1.** Town, NW Litchfield co., NW Connecticut, on New York and Massachusetts borders; pop. (1990c) 4090; settled 1719, incorp. 1741; source of iron mid-18th cent.
2. City, ⊗ of Wicomico co., SE Maryland, 50 mi. (80 km.) ENE of mouth of Potomac River; pop. (1990c) 20,592; port; farms; Salisbury State Univ. (1925).
3. Town, Essex co., NE corner of Massachusetts, 27 mi. (43 km.) ENE of Lowell; pop. (1990c) 6882.
4. City, ⊗ of Rowan co., cen. North Carolina, in Piedmont section 37 mi. (60 km.) NNE of Charlotte; pop. (1990c) 23,087; Catawba Coll. (1851), Livingstone Coll. (1879); settled 1753; incorp. 1755; on Civil War site of camp for Union prisoners where thousands died.
5. City, Rhodesia (now Zimbabwe). See HARARE.
6. *also* **New Sar·um** \ˈsar-əm\. City, Wiltshire, S England, on the Avon 22 mi. (35 km.) NW of Southampton; pop. (1981c) 37,831; ⊗ of former Wiltshire co.; 13th cent. cathedral with the tallest spire (404 ft. or 123 m.) in England; tourist center; brewing, tanning, printing; livestock market. City developed around cathedral begun 1220; near site of Old Sarum (*q.v.*).

Salisbury Island. Island, W end of Hudson Strait, SE Nunavut, Canada, S of Foxe Penin.; 312 sq. mi. (808 sq. km.).

Salisbury Plain. Undulating tract of land, Wiltshire, S England, near the city of Salisbury; av. elev. 400 ft. (122 m.); highest point **West·bury Down** \ˈwest-ˌber-ē, -bə-rē\ 775 ft. (236 m.); contains Stonehenge (*q.v.*).

Salisbury Sound. Channel, SE Alaska, bet. S Chichagof I. and N Baranof I.

Sal·ke·hatch·ie \ˌsȯl-kə-ˈha-chē\. River, S South Carolina; rises in W Barnwell co., flows SE to unite with Little Salkehatchie River and form Combahee River; 60 mi. (97 km.) long.

Sallee. See SALÉ.

Sallentinum Promontorium. See SANTA MARIA DI LEUCA, CAPE.

Sal·li·saw \ˈsa-lə-ˌsȯ\. City, ⊗ of Sequoyah co., E Oklahoma, 39 mi. (63 km.) SE of Muskogee; pop. (1990c) 7122; service center for outdoor recreational activities; agriculture; home of American Indian scholar Sequoya nearby.

Sallūm, As–. See SALŪM.

Salmantica. See SALAMANCA 3.

Salm·on \ˈsa-mən\. **1.** River, cen. Connecticut; rises in S Tolland co., flows SW into Connecticut River.
2. River, cen. Idaho; rises in S Custer co., cen. Idaho, flows N, then W across Idaho, and again N to empty into Snake River at S extremity of Nez Perce co., W Idaho; 420 mi. (676 km.) long.
3. City, ⊗ of Lemhi co., E cen. Idaho, at confluence of Salmon and Lemhi rivers; pop. (1990c) 2941.

Salmon Dam. Dam across **Salmon Falls Creek**, a S tributary of Snake River, Twin Falls co., SW Idaho; height 220 ft. (67 m.); completed 1912; impounds water for irrigation. Reservoir known as **Salmon Falls Creek Reservoir** *or* **Salmon Creek Reservoir**. See CEDAR CREEK DAM.

Salmone, Cape. See PLÁKA, CAPE.

Salmon River Mountains. Group of mountain ranges, chiefly in Valley, Custer, and Lemhi cos., cen. Idaho; highest peak 10,328 ft. (3148 m.). See SAWTOOTH RANGE.

Sa·lo·ma·gue Harbor \ˌsä-lō-ˈmä-gā\. Inlet and sheltered anchorage on N coast of Ilocos Sur prov., Luzon, Philippines, 15 mi. (24 km.) N of Vigan; 17°46′N, 120°24′E.

Sa·lo·nae \sə-ˈlō-nē\ *or* **Sa·lo·na** \-nə\. Military base 119–18 B.C., in ancient Roman Empire; attacked several times first cent. B.C.; ✻ of Illyricum; residence (after his abdication) 305–313 A.D. of Roman Emperor Diocletian (born nearby c. 245) who built palace on site of Spalatum (see SPLIT) 3 mi. (5 km.) S; destroyed by Avars early 7th cent.

Sa·lon·ga National Park \sä-ˈlȯŋ-gä\. National park, W cen. Democratic Rep. of the Congo, in two sections.

Salonika. See THESSALONÍKI.

Sa·lon·i·ka, Gulf of \sə-ˈlä-ni-kə\ *or Gk.* **Ther·ma·ï·kós Kól·pos** \ther-ˌmä-ē-ˈkös-ˈkȯl-pös\; *anc.* **Ther·ma·i·cus Si·nus** \thər-ˈmā-ə-kəs-ˈsī-nəs\. Arm of the NW Aegean Sea, extending into NE coast of Greece, E of Thessaly and W of Chalcidice and Kassándra penins.

Saloniki. See THESSALONÍKI.

Sa·lon·ta \ˈsä-lȯn-tä\ *or Hung.* **Nagy·sza·lon·ta** \ˈnöt-ˌsö-lȯn-ˌtö\. City, W Romania, near Hungarian border, 25 mi. (40 km.) SSE of Oradea; transferred to Hungary 1940–45.

Salop. See SHROPSHIRE 2.

Sa·loum *or* **Sa·lum** \sä-ˈlüm\. River, Senegal; flows into Atlantic Ocean just N of Gambia; 100 mi. (161 km.) long; navigable for 60 mi. (97 km.); has wide mouth containing many islands; town of Kaolack is on it.

Sal·sette \sal-ˈset\. Island, N of Bombay I., India; 18 mi. (29 km.) long; 246 sq. mi. (637 sq. km.); taken by Marathas from Portuguese 1739 and by British 1774; has numerous Buddhist cave shrines.

Sal'sk *or* **Salsk** \ˈsälsk\. Town, S Rostov Oblast, S Russia in Europe; pop. (1991e) 62,200; railroad junction point S of the Manych; taken by Germans in Caucasus drive 1942; retaken by U.S.S.R. 1943.

Sal·so \ˈsäl-sō\. River, Sicily, Italy; flows from La Madonie into the Mediterranean Sea; 89 mi. (143 km.) long.

Sal·so·mag·gio·re Ter·me \ˌsäl-sō-mä-ˈjōr-ā-ˈter-mā\. Commune, Parma prov., Emilia-Romagna, N Italy, 18 mi. (29 km.) W of Parma; pop. (1981p) 17,750; mineral baths.

Salt \ˈsȯlt\. **1.** River, Arizona; rises in Apache co., E Arizona, flows W into Gila River in Maricopa co. W of Phoenix; 200 mi. (322 km.) long; in Phoenix the channel is usu. dry as result of upstream dams; water used for irrigation and waterpower through a system of dams forming a 60-mile (97-kilometer) chain of lakes that include Theodore Roosevelt Dam and Theodore Roosevelt Lake, Horse Mesa Dam and Apache Lake, Stewart Mountain Dam and Saguaro Lake.
2. River, N cen. Kentucky; rises in Boyle co., cen. Kentucky, flows N, then W into Ohio River below Louisville; ab. 100 mi. (160 km.) long.
3. River, NE Missouri; rises in Schuyler co., N Missouri, flows SE into Mississippi River in E Pike co., E Missouri; 200 mi. (322 km.) long.

Sal·ta \ˈsäl-tä\. **1.** Province of NNW Argentina. See table at ARGENTINA.
2. City, its ✻, 140 mi. (225 km.) NW of San Miguel de Tucumán; pop. (1991p) 373,857; produces tobacco products, leather, livestock; timber; flour; cathedral; university (1967); city founded 1582; scene of defeat of Spanish royalist forces by Gen. Manuel Belgrano 1813.

Salt Block Mountain. Peak, Garrett co., NW corner of Maryland; 2768 ft. (844 m.).

Salt·burn–by–the–Sea \ˈsȯlt-bərn\. Resort town, Cleveland, NE England.

Salt Cay. One of Turks Is., Turks and Caicos Is.; pop. (1990c) 211. See TURKS AND CAICOS ISLANDS.

Salt·coats \ˈsȯlt-ˌkōts\. Seaport burgh, Strathclyde region, SW Scotland, on the Firth of Clyde 30 mi. (48 km.) SW of Glasgow; pop. (1981p) 12,807; formerly known for its salt mines and for shipbuilding.

Sal·tee Islands \ˈsȯl-tē\. Two small islands, St. George's Channel, off SE coast of Ireland, E of Waterford.

\ə\ **abut** \ˈə\ matches \ᵊ\ kitten, Fr table \ər\ **further** \a\ **ash** \ā\ **ace** \ä\ **cot, cart** \à\ Fr bac \au̇\ **out** \b\ Span Avila \ch\ **chin** \e\ **bet** \ē\ **easy** \g\ **go** \i\ **hit** \ī\ **ice** \j\ **job** \k\ Ger **ich, Buch** \ⁿ\ Fr vin \ŋ\ **sing** \ō\ **go** \ȯ\ **all** \ȯi\ **law** \œ\ Fr **bœuf** \œ̄\ Fr **feu** \ȯi\ **boy** \th\ **thin** \th\ **this** \ü\ **loot** \u̇\ **foot** \ue\ Ger **füllen** \ue̅\ Fr **rue** \y\ **yet** \ʸ\ Fr digne \ˈdēnʸ\, nuit \ˈnwʸē\ \yü\ **few** \yu̇\ **fury** \zh\ **vision**

Salt Fjord \ˈsȯlt\. Inlet of Norwegian Sea, NW coast of Norway, extending E from SE entrance to Vestfjorden, in Nordland co.

Salt Fork. River, NW Texas; unites with Double Mountain Fork in Stonewall co. to form the Brazos River.

Salt·holm \ˈsält-ˌhȯlm, ˈsȯlt-\. Island in the Sjælland group, Denmark, in the Øresund, opp. Copenhagen; 4.5 mi. (7 km.) long; 6 sq. mi. (16 sq. km.).

Sal·til·lo \säl-ˈtē-yō\. City, ✻ of Coahuila state, NE Mexico, ab. 660 mi. (1060 km.) N of Mexico City; munic. pop. (1990p) 440,845; alt. 5244 ft. (1598 m.); commercial center; produces textiles and flour; noted for serapes; gold, lead, silver, coal mines; summer resort; cathedral; university (1957); city founded 1575.

Salt Island. One of the British Virgin Is., West Indies.

Salt Lake. County in N Utah. See table at UTAH.

Salt Lake City. City, ✻ of Utah and ⊗ of Salt Lake co., N Utah, on Jordan River 13 mi. (21 km.) E of Great Salt Lake; pop. (1990c) 159,936; alt. 4390 ft. (1338 m.); largest city in the state; produces steel and iron products, electronic components; copper, silver, lead smelting, oil refining; Univ. of Utah (1850), Westminster Coll. of Salt Lake City (1875), Latter-day Saints Business Coll. (1886), Salt Lake Community Coll. (1947); notable buildings include Mormon Temple and Tabernacle, state capitol, and two cathedrals. Headquarters of the Mormon Church since 1847.

History: Settled by Mormons under leadership of Brigham Young 1847; developed as station on route to California during gold rush 1849 ff.; served successively as ✻ of provisional state of Deseret (*q.v.*), of Utah Terr. (1856–96), and of state of Utah (from 1896); prominent in "Utah War" of 1857–58 and further disputes bet. U.S. government and Mormon Church to ab. 1890.

Salt Lake Region. Extensive region, SW cen. Western Australia, Australia; contains many salt lakes; rich mining region, esp. in gold.

Sal·to \ˈsäl-tō\. **1.** Town, Buenos Aires prov., E Argentina, 107 mi. (172 km.) WNW of the city of Buenos Aires; pop. (1980p) 18,462.

2. Department of NW Uruguay. See table at URUGUAY.

3. City and port, ✻ of Salto dept., NW Uruguay, at head of navigation on E bank of Uruguay River opp. Concordia, Argentina, 260 mi. (418 km.) NW of Montevideo; pop. (1985c) 80,823; produces wines and nonalcoholic fruit drinks; shipyards.

Sal·to del Gui·a·rá \ˈsäl-tō-t͟hel-ˌgē-ä-ˈrä\. Town, ✻ of Canendiyú dept., E Paraguay.

Sal·ton Sea \ˈsȯlt-ᵊn\. Saline lake, Riverside and Imperial cos., SE California; 360 sq. mi. (932 sq. km.); ab. 235 ft. (70 m.) below sea level; formerly a depression 280 ft. (85 m.) below sea level; became a lake 1891 but later dried up; lake began to form again 1893; flooded 1905 by water from the Colorado River that broke through levees weakened by a gap made for irrigation; break in levees closed July 1907; level now sustained by irrigation runoff.

Salt·pond \ˈsȯlt-ˌpänd\. Seaport town, S Ghana, just E of Cape Coast.

Salt Range. Mountain range, Punjab, Pakistan, bet. the Indus and Jhelum rivers; highest peak 4074 ft. (1242 m.); salt beds.

Salt River. Name of three rivers in the U.S. See SALT.

Salt River Bay National Historical Park. See UNITED STATES, *National Historical Parks.*

Salt River Indian Reservation. Reservation, S cen. Arizona, on N side of Salt River, E and S of Scottsdale; pop. (1990c) 4852.

Salt Sea. An occasional biblical name for the Dead Sea (*Num.* xxxiv. 3; *Josh.* xv. 2).

Salt·sjö·bad·en \ˈsält-ˌshœ-ˌbäd-ᵊn\. Town, SE Sweden; a Baltic resort and SE suburb of Stockholm.

Salt·ville \ˈsȯlt-ˌvil\. Town, Smyth and Washington cos., SW Virginia, 32 mi. (51 km.) NE of Bristol; pop. (1990c) 2300; scene of engagement during Civil War 1864.

Sa·lu·a·fa·ta \ˌsä-lü-ä-ˈfä-tä\. Harbor, N coast of Upolu I., Samoa, SW cen. Pacific Ocean; formerly (1879–99) a German coaling station.

Saluces *or* **Saluciae.** See SALUZZO.

Sa·lu·da \sə-ˈlü-də\. **1.** River, W cen. South Carolina; rises in Blue Ridge, NW South Carolina, flows SE through Lake Murray and unites near Columbia with Broad River to form Congaree River.

2. County in W South Carolina. See table at SOUTH CAROLINA.

3. Town, ⊗ of Saluda co., W South Carolina, 27 mi. (43 km.) ESE of Greenwood; pop. (1990c) 2798.

4. Village, ⊗ of Middlesex co., E Virginia.

Saluda Dam. Dam across Saluda River in W cen. South Carolina, W of Columbia; completed 1930.

Salum. See SALOUM.

Sa·lûm \sə-ˈlüm\ *or* **Sol·lum** \sə-ˈlüm\ *also* **As–Sal·lüm** \ˌas-\; *anc.* **Cat·a·bath·mus Mag·na** \ˌka-tə-ˈbath-məs-ˈmag-nə\. Village, extreme NW Egypt, on the **Gulf of Salûm,** an inlet of the Mediterranean Sea, ab. 275 mi. (440 km.) W of Alexandria. Successively taken in North African campaigns of WWII by Italians, British, Germans, and finally by British.

Salut, Îles du. See SAFETY ISLANDS.

Sa·luz·zo \sä-ˈlüt-sō\ *or Fr.* **Sa·luces** \sa-ˈlüs\; *anc.* **Sa·lu·ci·ae** \sə-ˈlü-sē-ˌē\. Commune, Cuneo prov., Piedmont, NW Italy, 18 mi. (29 km.) NW of the commune of Cuneo; pop. (1991p) 15,829; early 16th cent. cathedral; castle. Center of medieval marquisate from 12th cent.; to France 1548, Savoy 1601.

Sal·va·dor \ˌsal-vȧ-ˈdōr\ *or* **Ba·hia** \bä-ˈē-ə\ *also* **São Salvador** \ˌsaùⁿ-ˌsal-vȧ-ˈdōr\. Seaport city, ✻ of Bahia state, E Brazil, on All Saints Bay ab. 225 mi. (360 km.) SSW of Recife; pop. (1989e) 2,000,000; on a peninsula with the modern part of the city on heights back of the harbor; modern port, shipping tobacco, sugar, hides, hardwoods, diamonds, oil; produces textiles, tobacco products, leather, metal goods; tourism; university (1946), Catholic university (1961); naval base and dockyard; 16th cent. chapel, 17th cent. cathedral, and many other buildings dating from 17th and 18th cents.

History: Town (in early times usually called Bahia) founded by Tomé de Sousa of Portugal 1549; African slaves imported to work on sugar plantations from 16th cent.; under Dutch 1624–25; ✻ of viceroyalty of Brazil; ✻ moved to Rio de Janeiro 1763.

Salvador, El. See EL SALVADOR.

Salvador, Lake \ˈsal-və-ˌdȯr\. Lake, St. Charles, Jefferson, and Lafourche parishes, SE Louisiana; joined to Gulf Intracoastal Waterway system.

Sal·va·ges \säl-ˈvȧ-zhēsh\ *or* **Sel·va·gens** \sel-ˈva-zhāⁿsh\. Group of small uninhabited islands of the Madeira Is., Portugal, ab. 180 mi. (290 km.) SSE of Madeira I.

Sal·va·tier·ra \ˌsäl-b̲ä-ˈtyär-rä\. Town, Guanajuato state, cen. Mexico, on railroad line near Lake Cuitzeo ab. 125 mi. (200 km.) NW of Mexico City; munic. pop. (1990p) 96,950.

Sal·ween \ˈsal-ˌwēn\; *Chin.* **Nu** \ˈnü\. River, SE Asia; rises in Plateau of Tibet, E Tibet, China, flows E through S Sichuan, then S through W Yunnan prov. of SW China; continues S through Myanmar, its lower course forming a section of Thailand-Myanmar boundary; empties into Gulf of Martaban at Moulmein; ab. 1500 mi. (2415 km.) long; has few tributaries; its lower course scene of fighting in WWII early 1942; its middle course in N Myanmar scene of fighting in 1944, esp. in May.

Sal·yan \səl-ˈyän\ *or* **Sal'·ya·ny** \-ˈyä-nē\. Town, SE Azerbaijan, on the Kura in its delta 72 mi. (116 km.) SW of Baku.

Sal·yers·ville \ˈsal-yərz-ˌvil\. City, ⊗ of Magoffin co., E Kentucky; pop. (1990c) 1917.

Sal·zach \ˈzäl-ˌtsäk̲\. River, W Austria; rises in N slopes of Hohe Tauern, flows E and N through Salzburg state past Salzburg to the German border; continues N, forming part of the boundary bet. Bavaria, Germany, and Upper Austria; empties into Inn River ab. 30 mi. (48 km.) N of Salzburg; 139 mi. (224 km.) long. See GOLLINGER.

Salz·burg \ˈsȯlz-ˌbərg, ˈsälz-, ˈsalz-, -ˌbùrg; *Ger.* ˈzälts-ˌbùrk\. **1.** State of cen. Austria. See table at AUSTRIA.

2. *anc.* **Ju·va·vum** \jü-ˈvā-vəm\. City, its ✻, on Salzach River 71 mi. (114 km.) ESE of Munich, Germany; pop. (1991c) 143,971; one of Austria's principal tourist centers and one of the major music centers of W Europe; two archiepiscopal palaces; notable 17th cent. cathedral; numerous notable churches and houses; university (founded 1622, reestablished 1964). Founded c. 696 on Celtic and Roman site; ruled by prince-archbishops for over 1000 years from 798; secularized 1802; birthplace of composer Wolfgang Amadeus Mozart 1756.

Salz·git·ter \ˈzälts-ˌgi-tər\; *until 1951* **Wa·ten·stedt–Salzgitter** \ˈvät-ᵊn-ˌshtet-\. City, SE Lower Saxony, Germany, SW of Brunswick; pop. (1992e) 115,381; major center of metallurgical industry; also produces motor vehicles, railroad cars, television sets, textiles, and pharmaceuticals; created 1942 out of several towns (incl. original Salzgitter).

Salz·kam·mer·gut \ˈzälts-ˌkä-mər-ˌgüt\. Region, Styria, Salzburg, and Upper Austria states of Austria; contains great salt deposits, used from prehistoric times. Now a resort area with lakes, mountains (Dachstein) in S part, and several small towns, incl. Hallstatt (*q.v.*), noted for its early cultural remains.

Salzuflen, Bad. See BAD SALZUFLEN.

Salz·we·del \ˈzälts-ˌvād-ᵊl\. City, Saxony-Anhalt, Germany, 55 mi. (88 km.) NNW of Magdeburg; pop. (1981c) 22,882; received charter 1233; a member of Hanseatic League 13th–16th cents.

Sa·ma \ˈsä-mä\. River, S Peru; flows into Pacific Ocean; ab. 250 mi. (400 km.) long.

Sa·ma de Lan·greo \ˈsä-mä-t͟hä-läŋ-ˈgrā-ō\; *sometimes shortened to* **Sama** *or* **Langreo.** Commune, Asturias prov., NW Spain, 14 mi. (23 km.) SE of Oviedo; pop. (1991c) 51,710.

Samakov. See SAMOKOV.

Sa·mal \ˈsä-ˌmäl\. Island, N end of Davao Gulf, Davao del Norte prov., Mindanao, Philippines; 96 sq. mi. (249 sq. km.); coextensive with municipality of Samal. Forms shelter for Davao harbor to the W.

Sa·ma·les \sä-ˈmä-lās\. Group of islands, E Sulu Archipelago, Philippines, E of Jolo and SW of Basilan; ab. 45 sq. mi. (115 sq. km.); comprises ab. 20 small islands: largest, Tongquil I. (19 sq. mi. or 49 sq. km.) and most important, Balanguingui I.

Sa·ma·ná \ˌsä-mä-ˈnä\. **1.** Province of NE Dominican Republic. See table at DOMINICAN REPUBLIC.

2. *formerly* **San·ta Bár·ba·ra de Samaná** \ˈsän-tä-ˈbär-bä-rä-t͟hā-\. Commune, its ✻; pop. (1981c) 5023; cacao, coconuts, rice; tropical woods.

Samaná, Bay of. Inlet on NE coast of Dominican Republic; extends E and W, protected on N by **Cape Samaná** which extends E from coast; ab. 40 mi. (65 km.) long.

Samana Cay *or* **At·wood Cay** \ˈat-wu̇d\. Small island, cen. Bahamas, 23°9′N, 73°54′W; thought by some to be explorer Christopher Columbus' San Salvador instead of modern San Salvador (*q.v.*).

Samanala. See ADAM'S PEAK.

Samannûd. See SEBENNYTOS.

Samanti. See YENICE.

Sa·mar \ˈsä-ˌmär\. Island, one of the Visayan Is., E Philippines; touches San Bernardino Strait on NW, Pacific Ocean on N and E, Leyte Gulf on S, and Samar Sea on W; on SW separated from Leyte by very narrow San Juanico Strait; 150 mi. (241 km.) long from NW to SE and ab. 75 mi. (120 km.) at widest point; 3d in size of the Philippines group. Constitutes with several small adjacent islands three provinces: **Eastern Samar** (✻ Catbalogan), **Northern Samar** (✻ Catarman), **Western Samar** (✻ Borongan). Irregular shape, having many inlets and offshore islands; has very rugged surface so that density of population is not large; mountains low, highest point 2789 ft. (850 m.) in N cen. part. Well watered, with many short navigable rivers on both coasts; experiences violent typhoons. Though agriculture not extensively pursued, rice, coconuts, and abacá are raised.

History: Visited 1521 by Spaniards on explorer Magellan's world trip; scene of extremely violent conflict bet. natives and U.S. forces 1901; granted civil government June 1902; in WWII came under Japanese control 1942; retaken by U.S. 1944.

Samar, Eastern. See EASTERN SAMAR.

Samar, Northern. See NORTHERN SAMAR.

Samar, Western. See WESTERN SAMAR.

Sa·ma·ra \sə-ˈmär-ə\. **1.** River, Orenburg and Samara oblasts, E Russia in Europe; flows W into the Volga River at Samara; ab. 360 mi. (580 km.) long. Buzuluk is on it.

2. *1935–91* **Kuy·by·shev** *also* **Kui·by·shev** \ˈkü-ē-bə̇-shəf\. City and river port, ✻ of Samara Oblast, E Russia in Europe, on left bank of the Volga at loop where it reaches farthest point E and where Samara River joins it, 550 mi. (885 km.) SE of Moscow; pop. (1992e) 1,239,000; machinery and machine tools, cables, bearings, railway equipment, chemicals; flour milling, shipbuilding, oil refining, food processing, brewing; university (1919). A trading center since end of 18th cent. with the Kirgiz Steppe region and cities of Turkistan. Estab. 1586; scene of Russian Cossack Yemelyan Ivanovich Pugachov's rebellion against Catherine the Great 1773–74; in WWII became temporary ✻ of U.S.S.R. Oct. 1941 when Moscow was threatened by German advance.

Sa·ma·rai \ˌsä-mä-ˈrī\. **1.** Island, Papua New Guinea, ab. 3 mi. (5 km.) off SE tip of New Guinea I., just SE of Milne Bay; ab. 60 acres (24 hectares).

2. Township on Samarai island; commercial center; copra. Destroyed by Japanese Jan. 1942; since rebuilt.

Samarang. See SEMARANG.

Samara Oblast \-ˈō-ˌblast, -bləst\ *or* **Sa·mar·ska·ya Oblast'** \sə-ˈmȧr-skə-yə-ˈȯ-bləstʸ\; *formerly* **Kuy·by·shev Oblast** *also* **Kui·by·shev Oblast** \ˈkü-ē-bə̇-shəf\. Subdivision of E Russia in Europe; 20,695 sq. mi. (53,600 sq. km.); pop. (1992e) 3,296,000; ✻ Samara; traversed by the Volga which here makes a great bend to the E; tableland region W of river, flat steppes to the E; wheat, corn, sunflowers; oil, natural gas; petrochemicals; engineering.

Sa·mar·ia \sə-ˈmar-ē-ə\. **1.** Region, ancient Palestine, in cen. part, extending from the Mediterranean to the Jordan River and lying S of Galilee and N of Judaea; name of territory originated from town of Samaria; in first millennium B.C. also a province of Assyria, Babylonia, and Persia; in 6 A.D. made by Roman Emperor Augustus a division of the Roman prov. of Judaea.

2. Ancient city, ✻ of Samaria; its ruins at **Sa·bas·tī·yah** \sə-ˈbȯs-tē-ə\ now in region of Jordan occupied by Israel 1967; the holy city of the Samaritans; built on a hill c. 880 B.C. by King Omri as new ✻ of Northern Kingdom of Israel; strengthened by his son King Ahab; taken by Assyrians Shalmaneser V and Sargon II c. 724–721 B.C. (*2 Kings* xvii. 3–6); inhabitants transported into captivity; taken by Macedonian King Alexander the Great c. 332 B.C. and by Judaean John Hyrcanus I c. 110 B.C., who destroyed it; rebuilt by later Judaean King Herod the Great.

Sam·a·rin·da \ˌsa-mə-ˈrin-də\. Coastal town, ✻ of East Kalimantan prov., E Borneo, Indonesia, on lower course of Mahakam River ab. 30 mi. (50 km.) from its mouth; pop. (1990c) 407,339; important trading town for products of the river region, also for nearby coal and oil fields; university (1962).

Samarkand. See SAMARQAND.

Samarobriva. See AMIENS.

Sam·ar·qand \ˌsä-mər-ˈkänd\ *or* **Sa·mar·kand** \ˈsa-mər-ˌkand\. **1.** Former province, Russian Turkestan, now part of Uzbekistan; ab. 26,620 sq. mi. (68,946 sq. km.).

2. Administrative subdivision of Uzbekistan; 11,274 sq. mi. (29,200 sq. km.); pop. (1991e) 2,386,200; ✻ Samarqand; wheat, cotton, fruit; sheep, goats; sericulture; formed 1938; before 1991 comprised an oblast of Uzbek S.S.R., U.S.S.R.

3. City, its ✻, in the fertile valley of the Zerayshan 180 mi. (290 km.) SW of Tashkent, on W spur of Altay Shan; pop. (1991e) 370,500; alt. 2330 ft. (710 m.); has railroad connections with Orenburg, Russia and the S Caspian; produces motor-vehicle parts, silk, canned fruit, textiles, wine, leather, footwear; tobacco; has many medieval structures; has several Muslim educational institutions, tomb of Turkic ruler Timur (Tamerlane), numerous monuments, several mosques.

History: One of the oldest cities in cen. Asia; as **Ma·ra·can·da** \ˌmar-ə-ˈkan-də\, ✻ of Sogdiana, destroyed by Macedonian King Alexander the Great 329 B.C.; important point on Silk Road from China to Europe first millennium A.D.; taken by Arabs 712; under Samanids (9th–10th cents.) and successors a notable center of Arab culture; destroyed by Mongol conqueror Genghis Khan 1220 but made ✻ of Timur's (Tamerlane's) empire c. 1370; fell c. 1500 to Uzbeks; also came under emir of Bukhara and the Russians, who took it 1868; in 1924 incorp. in Uzbek S.S.R. and its ✻ until 1930.

Sāmarrā' \sə-ˈmär-ə\. Town, N cen. Iraq, 65 mi. (105 km.) NNW of Baghdad, on the E bank of the Tigris River; head of navigation for small vessels. In 9th cent. residence of Abbassid rulers; sacred to Shiite Muslims.

Samar Sea \ˈsä-mär\. Interisland body of water, E Philippines, bounded by Luzon on N, Samar on E, Leyte on S, and Masbate on W; connects by San Bernardino Strait with the Pacific on N and joins Visayan Sea on SW.

Samāwah, As *also* **Samawa.** See AS SAMĀWAH.

Şamaxı. See SHEMAKHA.

Sam·bal·pur \ˈsəm-bəl-ˌpu̇r\. Town, N Orissa, E India, on N bank of Mahanadi River 140 mi. (225 km.) NW of Cuttack; pop. (1991p) 192,917.

Sam·bas \ˈsäm-bäs\. River, NW West Kalimantan prov., Borneo, Indonesia; flows W and SW into South China Sea; ab. 90 mi. (145 km.) long.

Sam·bhal \ˈsəm-bəl\. Town, NW cen. Uttar Pradesh, N India, 80 mi. (129 km.) E of Delhi; pop. (1991p) 150,012; sugar, calico; important Muslim ✻ in late 15th–16th cents.

Sam·bhar Lake \ˈsäm-bər\. Salt lake, E cen. Rajasthan, India, W of Jaipur.

Sam·bir \ˈsäm-bir\ *or* **Sam·bor** \-bər\. Town, L'viv subdivision, W Ukraine, on Dniester River 50 mi. (81 km.) WSW of the city of L'viv; pop. (1991c) 34,632; formerly in Poland; a railroad-junction town.

Sam·bo·rom·bón Bay \ˌsäm-bō-ˌrōm-ˈbōn\. Inlet of Atlantic Ocean, on E coast of Buenos Aires prov., E Argentina, S of the mouth of Río de la Plata.

Sambre \ˈsäⁿbrᵊ\. River, N France and S cen. Belgium; rises in Aisne dept., N France, flows ENE across the Belgian border and into the Meuse River at Namur; ab. 120 mi. (195 km.) long; during WWI scene of British victory Nov. 1918.

Sam·mam·ish Lake \sə-ˈma-mish\. Lake, King co., W cen. Washington; 9 mi. (15 km.) long.

Samnan. See SEMNĀN.

Sam·ni·um \ˈsam-nē-əm\. Country in ancient cen. Italy, the modern Abruzzi region and part of Campania region. Its inhabitants, the Samnites, spoke Oscan; conquered by Romans 290 B.C.

Sa·moa \sə-ˈmō-ə\ *also* **Samoa Islands;** *formerly* **Navigators Islands.** Group of islands, SW cen. Pacific Ocean, N of Tonga and NE of Fiji, bet. 13°26′ and 14°22′S lat. and 168° and 172°48′W long.; 1209 sq. mi. (3131 sq. km.); divided into **American Samoa,** islands E of 171°W long., 76 sq. mi. (197 sq. km.), and **Samoa** (*formerly* **Western Samoa**), islands W of 171°W long., 1133 sq. mi. (2935 sq. km.). Islands are volcanic, with soil generally fertile; the island group was probably for centuries a cradle of Polynesian settlement.

History: First settled c. 1100 B.C. by early Polynesians; visited 1722 by Dutchman Jacob Roggeveen; visited 1768 and named Navigators Islands by French navigator Louis de Bougainville; Christian mission from London arrived 1830 and Germans c. 1855; visited by U.S. naval officers Charles Wilkes 1839 and Richard Meade 1872, the latter visit resulting in use of Pago Pago (*q.v.*) as U.S. naval base; U.S., British, and German interest in islands produced period of international friction and internal dissension culminating in civil war and German intervention 1887; neutrality and independence of islands under three-power supervision estab. by tripartite agreement 1889; islands divided bet. U.S. and Germany 1899, Britain having ceded its interests to Germany in exchange for territory elsewhere; German Samoa mandated to New Zealand 1919, achieved independence 1962. See AMERICAN SAMOA and WESTERN SAMOA.

Sam·o·gi·tia \ˌsa-mə-ˈji-shə\ *or Lith.* **Že·mai·ti·ja** \ˌzhe-mī-ˈtē-yə\. Baltic region, coextensive with most of modern Lithuania, a lowland country N of the Neman; in 14th cent. held by Teutonic Knights; surrendered to Poland and Lithuania by Treaty of Thorn (Toruń) 1411; to Lithuania 1422.

Sa·mo·kov *also* **Sa·ma·kov** \ˈsä-mə-ˌko̊f, -ˌko̊v\. Town, Sofia prov., W Bulgaria, 30 mi. (48 km.) SSE of the city of Sofia.

Sá·mos \ˈsä-mös, ˈsā-ˌmäs\. **1.** *or Turk.* **Su·sam** \sü-ˈsäm\. Island in the Aegean Sea off W coast of Turkey; 184 sq. mi. (477 sq. km.); pop. (1991p) 41,850; with Ikaria I. and several other islets forms a department of Greece (see table at GREECE); by some considered an island of the Southern Sporades (see SPORADES). Produces olives, wine, tobacco, cotton; mountainous, with highest point 4725 ft. (1440 m.) at W end.

History: Settled by Ionians 11th cent. B.C. and by 7th cent. B.C. one of the principal commercial centers of Greece; under the tyrant Polycrates (late 6th cent. B.C.) a major cultural center, esp. in sculpture; notable temple of Hera built. Under Persia 522–479 B.C.; a member of Delian League and then subject variously to Athens, Sparta, Rome, and Byzantium; under the Ottoman Empire 1475–1912; restored to Greece 1912–13. Birthplace of mathematician Pythagoras c. 580 B.C.

2. Ancient town on SE coast of Sámos I., one of the 12 Ionian Cities; now in ruins.

Sa·mos·a·ta \sə-ˈmä-sə-tə\ *or* **Sam·sat** \säm-ˈsät\. Ancient city, Syria, on right bank of Euphrates River ab. 30 mi. (48 km.) NNW of Edessa (*mod.* Urfa); Kurdish village of Samsat, SE Turkey in Asia, on its site. In ancient times an important river crossing and caravan station. Was ✻ of Hellenistic kingdom of Commagene (*q.v.*) under Seleucids and of a division of Roman prov. of Syria 72 A.D.

Sa·mo·sir \ˌsä-mō-ˈsir\. Island in Lake Toba, N cen. Sumatra I., Indonesia; 30 mi. (48 km.) long, ab. 10 mi. (16 km.) wide.

Sam·o·thrace \ˈsa-mə-ˌthrās\ *or Gk.* **Sa·mo·thrá·ki** \ˌsä-mö-ˈthrä-kē\; *anc.* **Sam·o·thra·ce** \ˌsa-mə-ˈthrā-sē\ *or* **Sam·o·thra·cia** \ˌsa-mə-ˈthrā-shə\. **1.** Greek island, NE Aegean Sea, part of Evros dept., Thrace, Greece; 14 mi. (23 km.) NNW of Turkish island of Gökceada; 69 sq. mi. (179 sq. km.); pop. (1981c) 2871; sponge fisheries. Has prominent peak 5577 ft. (1700 m.), the highest point on any of the Aegean Is.; visited by St. Paul (*Acts* xvi. 11); famous sculpture known as Nike of Samothrace (now in the Louvre, Paris) found here 1863. See AEGEAN ISLANDS.

2. Town on Samothrace I. near N coast.

Sam·pa·loc Point \säm-ˈpä-lo̊k\. Point at SW side of entrance to Subic Bay, S Zambales prov., Luzon, Philippines.

Sampanmangio, Cape. See SEMPANG MANGAYAU, TANJONG.

Samp·son \ˈsamp-sən\. County in SE North Carolina. See table at NORTH CAROLINA.

Sam Ray·burn Reservoir \ˈsam-ˈrā-bərn\. Reservoir, E Texas, SE of Nacodoches; formed by dam on Angelina River.

Samsat. See SAMOSATA.

Samshui. See HEKOU 1.

Samsø \ˈsäm-ˌsœ\. Island in Sjælland group, forming a part of Denmark, lying bet. W tip of the island of Sjælland and the E coast of Jutland Penin.; 15 mi. (24 km.) long; 44 sq. mi. (114 sq. km.).

Sam·son \ˈsamp-sən\. City, Geneva co., SE Alabama, 8 mi. (13 km.) N of Florida border and 40 mi. (64 km.) WSW of Dothan; pop. (1990c) 2190.

Sam's Point \ˈsamz\. Peak, Ulster co., SE New York; 2289 ft. (698 m.); highest peak in the Shawangunk Mts.

Sam·sun \säm-ˈsün\. **1.** Province of Turkey in Asia. See table at TURKEY.

2. *anc.* **Ami·sus** \ə-ˈmī-səs\. Seaport city, its ✻, on **Samsun Bay,** an inlet of the Black Sea, ab. 200 mi. (320 km.) NE of Ankara; pop. (1990c) 303,979; located bet. the deltas of the Kızıl Irmak and the Yeşil Irmak; ships tobacco and wool; produces cigarettes and textiles. Ancient Amisus one of the principal Greek cities on the Black Sea (Euxine); prominent on the trade route from Central Asia in Middle Ages.

Sam·thar \ˈsəm-tər\. **1.** Former Indian state, now part of Uttar Pradesh, N India; 189 sq. mi. (490 sq. km.).
2. Town, its ✻, 55 mi. (89 km.) SE of Gwalior.

Sa·mui, Ko \ˈkō-sä-ˈmü-ē\. Island (Thai *ko*), Thailand, in SW Gulf of Thailand off E coast of Isthmus of Kra 65 mi. (105 km.) N of Nakhon Si Thammarat.

Sa·mut Pra·kan \sä-ˈmu̇t-prä-ˈkän\ *or locally* **Pak·nam** \päk-ˈnäm\. Town, S cen. Thailand, lower port of Bangkok where the Chao Phraya empties into Gulf of Thailand, 12 mi. (19 km.) SSE of the ✻; pop. (1991e) 71,538.

Samut Song·khram \ˌsəŋ-ˈkräm\; *formerly* **Me·klong** \mə-ˈklȯŋ\. Seaport, W Thailand, at mouth of Mae Klong River 40 mi. (64 km.) SW of Bangkok; pop. (1991e) 34,047.

San. See SAINT.

San \ˈsän\. River, SE Poland; flows out of the Carpathian Mts. NNW into Vistula River 4 mi. (6 km.) NE of Sandomierz; 247 mi. (397 km.) long; at one time formed part of boundary bet. W Ukraine and Poland; battle line May 1915 bet. German and Russian forces.

San·aa *or* **San·a·'a** *or* **Sana** *or* **San·'a** \sän-ˈä\. City, ✻ of Yemen, SW Arabian Penin., ab. 40 mi. (64 km.) from its port of Al Ḩudaydah with which it is connected by road; pop. (1986c) 427,185; alt. 7250 ft. (2210 m.); commercial center; jewelry; textiles; walled city with eight gates and numerous mosques. Founded c. first cent. A.D.; a Zaidi imamate from c. 860; under Turks 1872–1918; became ✻ of imam of Yemen 1918 and of Yemen Arab Republic 1962; ✻ after unification with People's Democratic Republic of Yemen 1990.

Sa·na·fi·ri \ˌsȧ-nȧ-ˈfē-rē\. Island in Red Sea. See TĪRĀN.

Sa·na·ga \ˌsä-nä-ˈgä\. River, Cameroon; flows WSW into the Bight of Biafra opp. the island of Bioko; ab. 325 mi. (525 km.) long.

San Agus·tin, Cape \ˌsän-ˌä-gü-ˈstēn\. S extremity of long peninsula marking E side of Davao Gulf, Mindanao, Philippines, 6°16′N, 126°11′E.

San Am·bro·sio \ˌsän-äm-ˈbrō-syō\. Island in Pacific Ocean, ab. 550 mi. (885 km.) off W cen. coast of Chile, close to San Félix I.; belongs to Chile.

Sa·na·na \sə-ˈnä-nə\. **1.** *formerly* **Su·la Be·si** \ˈsü-lə-bə-ˈsē\ *or* **Besi.** Island, smallest but most important of the three islands of the Sula Is., Indonesia; E of Sulawesi.
2. Village, N end of Sanana I.

Sa·nan·daj \ˌsä-nən-ˈdäj\ *or* **Sin·neh** \si-ˈnā\. Town, ✻ of Kordestān prov., NW Iran, on highway to Mosul 100 mi. (161 km.) NNW of Hamadān; pop. (1986c) 204,537.

Sa·nan·di·ta \ˌsä-nən-ˈdē-tə\. Town, S Bolivia, near the Argentine border.

San An·dre·as \ˌsan-an-ˈdrā-əs\. Village, ⊗ of Calaveras co., cen. California; pop. (1990c) 2115.

San Andreas Fault. Zone of transform faults at the boundary bet. two tectonic plates, extending along the coast of N California, through the San Francisco Penin., and SE toward the head of the Gulf of California; movement along part of this zone is frequently the cause of earthquakes in the region, and caused the San Francisco earthquake of 1906.

San An·drés \ˌsän-än-ˈdrās\. **1.** Small island in Caribbean Sea, off E coast of Nicaragua; belongs to Colombia; claimed by Nicaragua 1986.
2. Town on island, ✻ of San Andrés y Providencia dept., Colombia; munic. pop. (1992e) 37,700; ships oranges and copra.

San Andrés It·za·pa \ēt-ˈsä-pä\. Town, Chimaltenango dept., S cen. Guatemala; pop. (1981c) 11,809.

San An·dres Mountains \ˌsän-än-ˈdrās\. Range, chiefly in S Socorro and N Dona Ana cos., S cen. New Mexico, E of the Rio Grande.

San Andrés Tux·tla \ˈtüs-ˌtlä\ *also* **Tuxtla.** Town, Veracruz state, E Mexico, 80 mi. (129 km.) SE of the seaport of Veracruz; pop. (1990c) 49,658.

San Andrés y Pro·vi·den·cia \ē-ˌprō-b̲e-ˈdān-syä\. Islands, Caribbean Sea, E of Nicaragua; constitute a department of Colombia. See table at COLOMBIA.

San An·ge·lo \san-ˈan-jə-lō\. City, ⊗ of Tom Green co., W cen. Texas, 77 mi. (125 km.) SSW of Abilene; pop. (1990c) 84,474; alt. 1845 ft. (562 m.); wool market; Angelo State Univ. (1928); Goodfellow Air Force Base; city founded 1869.

San An·sel·mo \ˌsan-an-ˈsel-mō\. Town, Marin co., W California, 14 mi. (23 km.) NW of San Francisco; pop. (1990c) 11,743; San Francisco Theological Seminary (1871).

San An·to·nio \ˌsan-an-ˈtō-nē-ˌō, *Span.* ˌsän-än-ˈtō-nyō\. **1.** River, S Texas; rises in city of San Antonio, receives waters of Medina River in Bexar co., flows SE through Wilson, Karnes, and Goliad cos., forms boundary line bet. Refugio and Victoria cos., and empties into San Antonio Bay; 180 mi. (290 km.) long.
2. City and port of entry, ⊗ of Bexar co., S cen. Texas, on San Antonio River ab. 80 mi. (130 km.) SW of Austin; pop. (1990c) 935,933; clothing; tourist center; attractions include the River Walk (Paseo del Rio), Tower of the Americas, McNay Art Institute, a zoo, and the Alamo in **San Antonio Missions National Historical Park** (estab. 1978; see UNITED STATES, *National Historical Parks*); St. Mary's Univ. (1852), Trinity Univ. (1869), Incarnate Word Coll. (1881), St. Philip's Coll. (1898), Oblate School of Theology (1903), Our Lady of the Lake Univ. (1911), San Antonio Coll. (1925), Univ. of Texas at San Antonio (1969), Palo Alto. Coll. (1987). Military aviation center, with Kelly, Lackland, and Randolph Air Force bases; Fort Sam Houston (1865).
History: Franciscan mission San Antonio de Valero (later the Alamo) and presidio of San Antonio de Bexar founded 1718; first civil municipality, San Fernando, founded 1731; all three consolidated into San Antonio de Bexar c. 1794; became city 1837. Prominent in Mexican Revolution and Texas Revolution; in Texas Revolution a military base, captured by Mexicans in historic siege of the Alamo and recaptured by Texans after their victory at San Jacinto 1836.
3. Seaport and resort, Santiago prov., cen. Chile, 58 mi. (93 km.) W of Santiago; pop. (1992c) 77,719; extensive earthquake damage Mar. 3, 1985.
4. Town, Central dept., cen. Paraguay, on Paraguay River SE of Asunción; pop. (1982p) 5320.
5. Municipality, Nueva Ecija prov., Luzon, Philippines, near right bank of Pampanga River W of San Isidro and 14 mi. (23 km.) SSW of Cabanatuan; pop. (1980c) 42,969.
6. Municipality, SW Zambales prov., Luzon, Philippines, near coast ab. 65 mi. (105 km.) NW of Manila; pop. (1980c) 22,382; U.S. troops landed on coast bet. here and San Narciso 1945.

San Antonio, Cabo. \ˈkä-bō-ˌsän-än-ˈtō-nyō\. **1.** Cape extending into Atlantic Ocean on E coast of Buenos Aires prov., E Argentina, S of Samborombón Bay.
2. Cape, W extremity of Cuba, projecting into Yucatán Channel.
3. Cape, N coast of Alicante prov., SE Spain.

San Antonio Bay. Inlet of Gulf of Mexico, S Calhoun co., S Texas, receiving San Antonio River on N.

San Antonio de las Ve·gas \ˌt̲h̲ā-läs-ˈb̲ā-gäs\. Municipality, La Habana prov., W Cuba, just S of Havana.

San Antonio de las Vuel·tas \ˌt̲h̲ā-läs-b̲wāl-täs\. Municipality, Las Villas prov., W cen. Cuba, 16 mi. (26 km.) ENE of Santa Clara.

San Antonio de los Ba·ños \ˌt̲h̲ā-lōs-ˈbä-nyōs\. Municipality and town, La Habana prov., W Cuba; munic. pop. (1990e) 33,120; town 20 mi. (32 km.) SW of Havana.

San Antonio de los Co·bres \ˌt̲h̲ā-lōs-ˈkō-brās\. Town, Salta prov., NW Argentina, 75 mi. (121 km.) NW of the city of Salta; pop. (1980p) 2357.

San Antonio Peak. **1.** *formerly* **Mount Baldy** \ˈbȯl-dē\. Mountain, Los Angeles co., S California; 10,064 ft. (3068 m.); highest peak in San Gabriel Mts.

\ə\ abut \ᵊ\ matches \ᵊ\ kitten, Fr table \ər\ further \a\ ash \ā\ ace \ä\ cot, cart \ȧ\ Fr bac \au̇\ out \b\ Span Avila \ch\ chin \e\ bet \ē\ easy \g\ go \i\ hit \ī\ ice \j\ job \k̲\ Ger ich, Buch \ⁿ\ Fr vin \ŋ\ sing \ō\ go \ȯ\ all \ȯ\ law \œ\ Fr bœuf \œ̄\ Fr feu \ȯi\ boy \th\ thin \t̲h̲\ this \ü\ loot \u̇\ foot \ue\ Ger füllen \ue̅\ Fr rue \y\ yet \ʸ\ Fr digne \ˈdēnʸ\, nuit \ˈnwʸē\ \yü\ few \yu̇\ fury \zh\ vision

2. Mountain, NE Rio Arriba co., N New Mexico; 10,908 ft. (3325 m.).

San Au·gus·tine \san-'ò-gəs-ˌtēn\. **1.** County in E Texas. See table at TEXAS.

2. Town, its ⊗, 37 mi. (60 km.) ENE of Lufkin; pop. (1990c) 2337.

San Be·ne·det·to del Tron·to \ˌsän-ˌbā-nā-'dā-tō-del-'trón-tō\. Seaport, Ascoli Piceno prov., Marche, cen. Italy, on Adriatic Sea 16 mi. (26 km.) ENE of the commune of Ascoli Piceno; pop. (1989c) 45,241.

San Be·ni·to \ˌsan-bə-'nē-tō\. **1.** County in W California. See table at CALIFORNIA.

2. City, Cameron co., S Texas, 18 mi. (29 km.) N of Brownsville; pop. (1990c) 20,125.

San Ber·nar·di·no \ˌsan-ˌbər-nə-'dē-nō, *locally also* ˌsan-bər-'dü\. **1.** County in SE California. See table at CALIFORNIA.

2. City, its ⊗, ab. 62 mi. (100 km.) E of Los Angeles; pop. (1990c) 164,164; manufactures steel; foundries, railroad shops; San Bernardino Valley Coll. (1926), California State Univ., San Bernardino (1960); site named 1810; founded 1851 by Mormons.

3. Islet, Philippines. See SAN BERNARDINO STRAIT.

4. Mountain pass in Lepontine Alps, Graubünden canton, SE Switzerland; alt. 6773 ft. (2064 m.).

San Bernardino Mountain. Peak in San Bernardino Mts., S California; ab. 10,630 ft. (3240 m.).

San Bernardino Mountains. Mountain range, SW San Bernardino co., extending SE into cen. Riverside co., S California; one of the series of ranges bordering the Mojave Desert on the SW; bet. the San Gabriel Mts. and the San Jacinto Mts.; highest point San Gorgonio Mt., 11,502 ft. (3506 m.), located at SE end.

San Bernardino Strait. Strait bet. S Sorsogon prov., SE Luzon, and N end of Samar I., Philippines; ab. 27 mi. (43 km.) long by 5 mi. (8 km.) wide at narrowest point; by some extended to include Ticao Pass (*q.v.*). The main entrance to the Philippines from the E forming with the Sibuyan Sea and Verde Island Passage the main channel for ships from U.S. and the Pacific to Manila and the South China Sea. In Pacific at E end is the islet of **San Bernardino** 7 mi. (11 km.) off Bulusan, on which is one of the major lighthouses in the archipelago. Scene of naval battle Oct. 1944 in which part of Japanese fleet was defeated by U.S. during Leyte Gulf (*q.v.*) conflict.

San Bernardino Valley. Fertile valley, SW San Bernardino co., SE California; watered by small streams.

San Ber·nar·do \ˌsän-ber-'när-dō\. **1.** City, Santiago prov., cen. Chile, 10 mi. (16 km.) S of the city of Santiago; pop. (1992c) 188,580.

2. Group of small islands in the Caribbean Sea, off NW coast of Colombia, at entrance to Gulf of Morrosquillo.

San Blas \sän-'bläs\. Municipality, Nayarit state, Mexico, on Pacific Ocean 25 mi. (40 km.) W of Tepic.

San Blas, Cape. Low point of land projecting into Gulf of Mexico from SW coast of Gulf co., NW Florida.

San Blas, Gulf of *or Span.* **Gol·fo de San Blas** \'gōl-fō-ˌthā-\. Inlet of the Caribbean Sea on the N coast of Panama, E of the Panama Canal.

San Blas, Point. Cape, N coast of Panama, N of the Gulf of San Blas.

San Blas Range *or* **Cor·dil·le·ra de San Blas** \ˌkōr-thē-'yā-rä-thā-\. Range, NE Panama, S of the Gulf of San Blas.

San·born \'san-bərn\. County in SE cen. South Dakota. See table at SOUTH DAKOTA.

San Bru·no \san-'brü-nō\. City, San Mateo co., W California, S of San Francisco; pop. (1990c) 38,961; residential.

San Buenaventura. See VENTURA 2.

San Car·los \san-'kär-lōs, *Span.* sän-\. **1.** River, SE Arizona; forms part of NW boundary of Graham co.; flows in curve W to S and into **San Carlos Lake** (*or* **San Carlos Reservoir**), formed by the Coolidge Dam.

2. Residential city, San Mateo co., W California, 17 mi. (27 km.) SE of San Francisco; pop. (1990c) 26,167.

3. River, Costa Rica; flows NE into the San Juan River; 75 mi. (121 km.) long.

4. City, ✱ of Río San Juan dept., S Nicaragua, on SE shore of Lake Nicaragua; pop. (1985e) 5103.

5. Chartered city, Pangasinan prov., Luzon, Philippines, 10 mi. (16 km.) SE of Lingayen; pop. (1990p) 124,000; largest town in the province; on border of delta of Agno River.

6. Chartered city, NE Negros Occidental, Negros, Philippines, near N end of Tanon Strait 33 mi. (53 km.) ESE of City of Bacolod; pop. (1990p) 106,000; sugar.

7. Town, ✱ of Cojedes state, NW cen. Venezuela, ab. 130 mi. (210 km.) SW of Caracas; pop. (1990p) 50,339.

San Carlos de Ancud. See ANCUD.

San Carlos de Bariloche. See BARILOCHE.

San Carlos Lake *or* **San Carlos Reservoir.** See SAN CARLOS 1.

San Ca·scia·no in Val di Pe·sa \ˌsän-kä-'shä-nō-ēm-'väl-dē-'pā-sä\. Commune, Firenze prov., Tuscany, W Italy, 10 mi. (16 km.) SW of Florence; pop. (1981p) 15,275.

San Ca·tal·do \ˌsän-kä-'täl-dō\. Commune, Caltanissetta prov., cen. Sicily, Italy, 4 mi. (6 km.) W of the commune of Caltanissetta; pop. (1989c) 23,496.

Sán·chez \'sän-chās\. Seaport, Samaná prov., NE Dominican Republic, 24 mi. (39 km.) from the commune of Samaná; munic. pop. (1981p) 21,153.

Sánchez Ra·mí·rez \rä-'mē-rās\. Province, cen. Dominican Republic. See table at DOMINICAN REPUBLIC.

San·chi \'sän-chē\. Village, W Madhya Pradesh, N cen. India, ab. 23 mi. (37 km.) NE of Bhopal. Site of several Buddhist stupas, among the oldest buildings now standing in India; erected 3rd–1st cents. B.C. The Great Stupa is a memorial shrine in the shape of a solid dome of stone and brick, ab. 103 ft. (31 m.) in diameter and 42 ft. (13 m.) high; begun under King Aśoka c. 250 B.C.

San–ch'ung *or* **San·chung** \'sän-'chu̇ŋ\. Municipality, N Taiwan, W of Taipei; pop. (1993e) 382,003.

San Ci·pri·a·no Bay \san-ˌsi-prē-'ä-nō\. Bay, NW Africa, on SW coast of Western Sahara, 22°20′N, 16°35′W.

San Cle·men·te \ˌsan-klə-'men-tē\. City, Orange co., SW California, SE of Los Angeles; pop. (1990c) 41,100; vacation home of Richard M. Nixon, 37th president of the U.S.

San Clemente Island. Island, SW part of Channel Is. in Pacific Ocean, SW California; S of Santa Catalina I.; 57 sq. mi. (148 sq. km.); part of Los Angeles co.

San·co Point \säŋ-'kō\. Point, E coast of Mindanao, Philippines, at S end of Surigao del Sur prov., 8°14′N, 126°25′E.

San Cris·to·bal \ˌsän-krēs-'tō-bäl\. Mountain, SE border of Laguna prov., Luzon, Philippines; ab. 4900 ft. (1500 m.); an extinct volcano with freshwater lake in its crater.

San Cris·tó·bal \ˌsän-krēs-'tō-bäl\. **1.** Municipality, Pinar del Río prov., W Cuba, on railroad line 45 mi. (72 km.) ENE of city of Pinar del Río; pop. (1981c) 58,520.

2. Province, E cen. Dominican Republic. See table at DOMINICAN REPUBLIC.

3. Municipality, ✱ of San Cristóbal prov., S Dominican Republic, 25 mi. (40 km.) WSW of Santo Domingo; pop. (1981p) 123,740; in an area producing rice, sugar, coffee, fruits, and vegetables; founded 1575.

4. *also* **Chat·ham Island** \'cha-təm\. One of the Galápagos Is. (*q.v.*), off coast of Ecuador; ab. 24 mi. (39 km.) long, 8 mi. (13 km.) wide; produces sugarcane, coffee.

5. Lake in the Valley of Mexico, cen. Mexico, 12 mi. (19 km.) NNE of Mexico City.

6. *or in full* **San Cristóbal de las Ca·sas** \ˌthā-läs-'kä-säs\. City, Chiapas state, SE Mexico, ab. 40 mi. (64 km.) E of Tuxtla; pop. (1990p) 89,251.

7. *or* **Ma·ki·ra** \mä-'kē-rä\ *also* **San Cris·to·val** \ˌsän-krēs-'tō-väl\. Island in S Solomon Is., W Pacific Ocean, 38 mi. (61 km.) SE of Guadalcanal; 80 mi. (129 km.) long and 22 mi. (35 km.) wide at greatest width; 1270 sq. mi. (3289 sq. km.); pop. (1986c) 17,003; mountainous; most of its settlements, incl. Kirakira, location of the government station, and Star Harbour, are along the N shore.

8. City, ✱ of Táchira state, W Venezuela, in mountains at SW end of Cordillera de Mérida and S of Lake Maracaibo, near Colombian border; pop. (1990p) 220,697; elev. 2700 ft. (823 m.); textiles, leather products, footwear, cigarettes, cement;

ships coffee; founded 1561; heavily damaged by earthquake 1875.

Sanc·ti Spí·ri·tus \'säŋk-tē-'spē-rē-ˌtüs\. **1.** Province of W cen. Cuba. See table at CUBA.
2. City, its ✻, 45 mi. (72 km.) SE of Santa Clara; pop. (1990e) 85,499; trading center for sugar, tobacco, and cattle; founded c. 1516, oldest inland city of Cuba.

San Cui·cuil·co \ˌsän-kwē-'kwēl-kō\ *or* **Cuicuilco.** Hill, Mexico, comprising an archaeological site ab. 12 mi. (19 km.) S of Mexico City; artificial mound, ab. 410 ft. (125 m.) in diameter, orig. ab. 52 ft. (16 m.) high; probably an ancient temple.

San·cy, Puy de \ˌpwē-də-ˌsä^{n}-'sē\. Peak, Puy-de-Dôme dept., S cen. France; 6186 ft. (1886 m.); highest peak of the Monts Dore in the Auvergne Mts.

San·da·kan \ˌsän-dä-'kän\. Seaport town, Sabah, Malaysia, on island of Borneo, on **Sandakan Harbour,** an inlet of the Sulu Sea having a length of 15 mi. (24 km.) and an entrance 1.25 mi. (2 km.) wide; pop. (1980c) 70,420; ✻ of former British North Borneo, suffered much destruction during Japanese occupation in WWII; ✻ transferred to Jesselton (now Kota Kinabalu) 1947.

Sandalwood Island. See SUMBA.

San·day \'san-dā\. Island, NE part of the Orkney Is. (*q.v.*) off N coast of Scotland; 12 mi. (19 km.) long.

Sand·bach \'sand-ˌbach\. Town, Cheshire, NW England, 24 mi. (39 km.) S of Manchester.

San·de·fjord \'sä-nə-ˌfyür\. Seaport, Vestfold co., SE Norway, SSW of Oslo near the mouth of Oslo Fjord; pop. (1990c) 35,888; historically a base for whaling fleets operating in Arctic waters; shipping; chemical works.

San·ders \'san-dərz\. County in NW Montana. See table at MONTANA.

San·der·son \'san-dər-sən\. Unincorporated settlement, ⊗ of Terrell co., W Texas, 55 mi. (89 km.) SSE of Fort Stockton; pop. (1990c) 1128.

San·ders·ville \'san-dərz-ˌvil\. City, ⊗ of Washington co., cen. Georgia, 58 mi. (95 km.) SW of Augusta; pop. (1990c) 6290; kaolin.

Sand·gate \'sand-ˌgāt\. Seaport town, SE Queensland, Australia, suburb of Brisbane; pop. (1981c) 6776.

Sand·ham·mar, Cape \'sänd-ˌhä-mər\. Cape, S extremity of Sweden, projecting into Baltic Sea at S side of Hanö Bay.

Sand·hurst \'sand-ˌhərst\. **1.** City, Australia. See BENDIGO.
2. Town, Berkshire, S England. Nearby is Royal Military Coll., founded 1799 and merged 1947 with Royal Military Academy at Woolwich.

San·dia Mountains \san-'dē-ə\. Range, SE Sandoval co., NW cen. New Mexico, E of Albuquerque; highest point 10,678 ft. (3255 m.).

San Di·e·go \ˌsan-dē-'ā-gō\. **1.** Coastal county in SW corner of California. See table at CALIFORNIA.
2. Seaport city and port of entry, its ⊗, on San Diego Bay ab. 12 mi. (19 km.) N of the Mexican border; pop. (1990c) 1,110,549; a center of the electronics and aircraft industries; tuna fisheries; tourism; in a major truck- and fruit-farming area; numerous military and esp. naval installations. San Diego State Univ. (1897), Point Loma Nazarene Coll. (1902), San Diego City Coll. (1914), California Western School of Law (1927), Univ. of San Diego (1949), United States International Univ. (1952), San Diego Mesa Coll. (1962), San Diego Miramar Coll. (1969), California School of Professional Psychology–San Diego (1969); National Univ. (1971); notable zoological park. Bay discovered by explorer Juan Cabrillo 1542 and settled as Spanish presidio by Gaspar de Portolá 1769; mission (California's first) dedicated 1769; organized as pueblo 1834; captured from Mexico by Commodore Robert Field Stockton 1846; incorp. 1850.
3. City, ⊗ of Duval co., S Texas, 50 mi. (81 km.) W of Corpus Christi; pop. (1990c) 4983.

San Di·e·go, Cape \ˌsän-dē-'ā-gō\. Cape, E end of Tierra del Fuego I., S Argentina.

San Diego Bay. Inlet of Pacific Ocean, San Diego co., SW corner of California; 12 mi. (19 km.) long, 1 to 3 mi. (2 to 5 km.) wide; 22 sq. mi. (57 sq. km.); landlocked; forms harbor for the city of San Diego.

San Di·e·go de la Unión \ˌsän-dē-'ā-gō-ˌthā-lä-ü-'nyȯn\. Municipality, Guanajuato state, Mexico, 60 mi. (97 km.) NE of León.

San Diego del Val·le \del-'vī-yā\. Municipality, Las Villas prov., W cen. Cuba, 12 mi. (19 km.) NW of Santa Clara.

San Di·mas \san-'dē-məs\. City, Los Angeles co., SW California, 25 mi. (40 km.) E of the city of Los Angeles; pop. (1990c) 32,397; citrus fruit.

Sand Island \'sand\. **1.** Island, Lake Superior. See APOSTLE ISLANDS.
2. Island, Pacific Ocean. See MIDWAY.

Sandju. See SANJU.

Sand·nes \'sän-nəs\. Municipality, Rogaland co., SW Norway, ab. 9 mi. (15 km.) S of Stavanger; pop. (1990c) 44,340.

Sandø \'sä-ˌnœ\. Island in S part of the Faeroe Is. (*q.v.*), in North Atlantic Ocean, N of British Isles; 48 sq. mi. (124 sq. km.); pop. (1981c) 1706.

San·do·mierz \sän-'dȯ-myesh\ *or Russ.* **San·do·mir** \ˌsán-də-'myir\. Commune, cen. Tarnobrzeg prov., SE cen. Poland, on Vistula River 52 mi. (84 km.) ESE of Kielce; pop. (1989e) 23,869; sulfur, glass products; Romanesque church; Gothic cathedral. Founded by 11th cent. and ✻ of an independent principality c. 1139; gained town rights 1286; to Austria 1772 and to Russia 1815–1918.

San Domino. See TREMITI ISLANDS.

San Do·nà di Pia·ve \ˌsän-dō-'nä-dē-'pyä-vā\. Commune, Venezia prov., Veneto, NE Italy, on Piave River 19 mi. (31 km.) NE of Venice; pop. (1989c) 33,380.

San Do·na·to Mi·la·ne·se \ˌsän-dō-'nä-tō-ˌmē-lä-'nā-sā\. Commune, Milano prov., Lombardy, N Italy; pop. (1989c) 32,076.

San·do·val \san-'dō-vəl\. County in NW cen. New Mexico. See table at NEW MEXICO.

San·do·way \'san-də-ˌwā\. Town, Myanmar, near coast of Bay of Bengal 63 mi. (101 km.) WSW of Prome; pop. (1983c) 12,238; seaside resort.

San·down \'san-ˌdau̇n\. Seaside resort, SE Isle of Wight, S England.

Sandown Park. Fashionable racecourse near Esher, Surrey, S England.

Sand·point \ˌsand-'pȯint\. City, ⊗ of Bonner co., N Idaho, on Pend Oreille Lake, 45 mi. (72 km.) N of Coeur d'Alene; pop. (1990c) 5203; ski resort.

San·dray \'san-ˌdrā\. See BARRA.

San·dring·ham \'san-driŋ-əm\. **1.** City, Victoria, Australia, a SSE suburb of Melbourne; pop. (1991c) 30,319.
2. Village, Norfolk, E England, near E shore of the Wash; Sandringham House, royal residence.

Sand Springs. City, Tulsa co., NE Oklahoma, on Arkansas River 8 mi. (13 km.) W of the city of Tulsa; pop. (1990c) 15,346.

San·du \'sän-'dü\ *or W.-G.* **San–tu** \-'dü\ *or* **San·tuao** \-'dwau̇\. Seaport, on an island, NE Fujian prov., SE China, ab. 48 mi. (77 km.) NE of Fuzhou; formerly had large tea trade.

San·dus·ky \sən-'dəs-kē, san-\. **1.** River, N Ohio; rises in W Richland co., N cen. Ohio, flows W, then N into Sandusky Bay; ab. 150 mi. (240 km.) long.
2. County in N Ohio. See table at OHIO.
3. City, ⊗ of Sanilac co., E Michigan, 38 mi. (61 km.) NNW of Port Huron; pop. (1990c) 2403.
4. City and port of entry, ⊗ of Erie co., N Ohio, on Lake Erie 50 mi. (81 km.) W of Cleveland; pop. (1990c) 29,764; automobile parts, paper products; wineries; ships coal; tourism; settled 1816; incorp. 1824.

Sandusky Bay. Inlet of Lake Erie on N coasts of Sandusky and Erie cos., N Ohio; the city of Sandusky lies S of the entrance to the bay.

Sand·vi·ken \ˈsand-ˌvē-kən\. Town, Gävleborg prov., Sweden, WSW of Gävle; pop. (1993e) 39,515.

Sand·wich \ˈsand-wich\. **1.** City, De Kalb and Kendall cos., N Illinois, 30 mi. (48 km.) WNW of Joliet; pop. (1990c) 5567.
2. Town, Barnstable co., SE Massachusetts, just S of Cape Cod end of Cape Cod Canal; pop. (1990c) 15,489; noted for glass made here 1825–88. Cape's oldest European settlement, founded 1637.
3. Town, Kent, SE England; pop. (1981c) 4254; one of the Cinque Ports; noted golf links.

Sandwich Island. See EFATE.

Sandwich Islands. See HAWAII 2.

Sandwich Mountain. Mountain, Carroll and Grafton cos., New Hampshire, at W end of Sandwich Range; 3993 ft. (1217 m.).

Sandwich Range. S range of the White Mts., New Hampshire; highest point Mt. Passaconaway 4060 ft. (1238 m.); includes Mt. Chocorua 3475 ft. (1059 m.).

San·dwip \ˈsən-ˌdwēp\. Island, E mouth of the Ganges-Brahamaputra Delta, Bangladesh; 126 sq. mi. (326 sq. km.).

Sandy \ˈsan-dē\. **1.** River, W Maine; rises in W Franklin co., flows SE and E into Kennebec River in S Somerset co.; 55 mi. (89 km.) long.
2. River, Kentucky and West Virginia. See BIG SANDY 2.
3. City, Salt Lake co., N Utah, 13 mi. (21 km.) S of Salt Lake City; pop. (1990c) 75,058; pop. grew very rapidly in 1970s.

Sandy Cape. Cape, N point of Fraser I. off SE coast of Queensland, Australia, 24°42′S, 153°17′E.

Sandy Hook. **1.** Peninsula, NE Monmouth co., E cen. New Jersey, ab. 15 mi. (24 km.) S of S tip of Manhattan I.; 6 mi. (10 km.) long; encloses **Sandy Hook Bay** (inlet of Raritan Bay) on W; oldest working lighthouse in U.S.
2. Subdivision of town of Newtown, Connecticut. See NEWTOWN 1.
3. City, ⊗ of Elliott co., NE Kentucky; pop. (1990c) 548.

Sa·nem \sä-ˈnem\. Commune, Grand Duchy of Luxembourg, in SW part ESE of Pétange; pop. (1990e) 11,300.

San Es·ta·nis·lao \ˌsän-es-ˌtä-nē-ˈslau̇\. Town, San Pedro dept., cen. Paraguay, 90 mi. (145 km.) NE of Asunción; pop. (1982p) 5538.

San Eugenio *also* **San Eugenio del Cuareim.** See ARTIGAS 2.

San Fa·bian \ˌsän-fä-ˈbyän, san-ˈfā-bē-ən\. Municipality, Pangasinan prov., Luzon, Philippines, on SE shore of Lingayen Gulf 13 mi. (21 km.) ENE of Lingayen; pop. (1980c) 42,018; important coast town.

San Fe·li·ce sul Pa·na·ro \ˌsän-fā-ˈlē-chā-ˌsül-pä-ˈnä-rō\. Commune, Modena prov., Emilia-Romagna, N Italy, 17 mi. (27 km.) NE of the commune of Modena; pop. (1981p) 9423.

San Fe·li·pe \ˌsän-fā-ˈlē-pā\. **1.** Town, Austin co., SE cen. Texas, W of Houston; pop. (1990c) 618; settled by Steven F. Austin 1822.
2. City, Valparaíso region, cen. Chile, ab. 48 mi. (77 km.) N of Santiago.
3. Town, ✻ of Guainía dept., E Colombia.
4. Mountain, cen. Oaxaca state, SE Mexico, N of the city of Oaxaca; 10,207 ft. (3111 m.).
5. City, ✻ of Yaracuy state, NW Venezuela, 125 mi. (201 km.) W of Caracas; pop. (1990p) 65,793.

San Felipe de Puerto Plata. See PUERTO PLATA 2.

San Feliu de Guixols. See SANT FELIU DE GUIXOLS.

San Fé·lix \sän-ˈfā-lēks\. Island in Pacific Ocean, ab. 600 mi. (965 km.) off W cen. coast of Chile, close to San Ambrosio I.; belongs to Chile.

San Fer·di·nan·do di Pu·glia \ˌsän-fer-dē-ˈnän-dō-dē-ˈpül-yä\. Commune, Foggia prov., Puglia, SE Italy, 29 mi. (47 km.) SE of the commune of Foggia; pop. (1981p) 12,843.

San Fer·nan·do \ˌsan-fər-ˈnan-dō, *Span.* ˌsän-fer-ˈnän-dō\. **1.** City, Los Angeles co., SW California, enclave of the city of Los Angeles; pop. (1990c) 22,580; San Fernando Rey de España mission (founded 1797) nearby.
2. Seaport, Buenos Aires prov., E Argentina, on the Río de la Plata just N of the city of Buenos Aires; pop. (1980p) 128,939; part of Buenos Aires met. area.
3. City, Libertador General Bernardo O'Higgins region, cen. Chile, 80 mi. (129 km.) S of Santiago; pop. (1982c) 32,432; founded 1742.
4. River, N Tamaulipas state, Mexico; rises in mountains S of Monterrey and flows E into Laguna Madre; ab. 170 mi. (275 km.) long.
5. Municipality, E coast of Cebu I., Philippines, on Bohol Strait 17 mi. (27 km.) SW of City of Cebu; pop. (1980c) 28,324.
6. Municipality, ✻ of La Union prov., Luzon, Philippines, on the coast 45 mi. (72 km.) N of Dagupan; pop. (1989e) 82,797; has a harbor sheltered by San Fernando Point and coastal trade with Manila and other ports; on main W coast highway and terminus of railroad to Manila.
7. Municipality, ✻ of Pampanga prov., cen. Luzon, Philippines, 35 mi. (56 km.) NNW of Manila; pop. (1980c) 110,891.
8. *formerly* **Is·la de Le·ón** \ˈēs-lä-ˌthā-lā-ˈōn\. Seaport and naval base, Cádiz prov., SW Spain, 7 mi. (11 km.) SE of the city of Cádiz; pop. (1991p) 85,191; dockyard and arsenal; naval academy; observatory; produces salt.
9. Seaport, Trinidad and Tobago, West Indies, in SW Trinidad; pop. (1990c) 30,092; founded 1786.
10. *or in full* **San Fernando de Apu·re** \ˌthā-ä-ˈpü-rā\. Town, ✻ of Apure state, W Venezuela, on Apure River 185 mi. (289 km.) S of Caracas; pop. (1990p) 72,733; river port; livestock, hides.

San Fernando de Ata·ba·po \thā-ˌä-tä-ˈbä-pō\. Town, former ✻ of Amazonas terr., S Venezuela, on the Atabapo and Orinoco rivers.

San Fernando de Monte Cristi. See MONTE CRISTI 2.

San Fernando Point. Point on coast of NW Luzon, La Union prov., Philippines, 16°37′N, 120°16′E, just W of San Fernando and marking northeasternmost point of Lingayen Gulf.

San Fernando Valley. Valley, Los Angeles co., S California, NW of cen. Los Angeles; partly included in city of Los Angeles; orig. a farming area, but now many suburban residential communities.

San·ford \ˈsan-fərd\. **1.** City, ⊗ of Seminole co., cen. Florida Penin., 20 mi. (32 km.) NNE of Orlando; pop. (1990c) 32,387; citrus orchards; Seminole Community Coll. (1965).
2. Town, York co., SW Maine, 34 mi. (55 km.) SW of Portland; pop. (1990c) 20,463.
3. City, ⊗ of Lee co., cen. North Carolina, 31 mi. (50 km.) NNW of Fayetteville; pop. (1990c) 14,475.

Sanford, Mount. Mountain at W end of Wrangell Mts., S Alaska; 16,237 ft. (4949 m.).

San Fran·cis·co \ˌsan-frən-ˈsis-kō, -fran-; *Span.* ˌsän-frän-ˈsēs-kō\. **1.** River, W New Mexico and E Arizona; rises in Catron co., W New Mexico, flows W across Arizona border and into the Gila River in Greenlee co., SE Arizona; 105 mi. (169 km.) long.
2. County in W California. See table at CALIFORNIA.
3. Seaport city, its ⊗, on W side of San Francisco Bay and on Pacific Ocean and Golden Gate; pop. (1990c) 723,959; exceptionally good harbor; connected with Marin co. to the N by Golden Gate Bridge and with Oakland to the E by the San Francisco-Oakland Bay Bridge; commercial, financial, and industrial center; ships food products, fruit, cotton, mineral ores; produces aircraft and missile parts, canned goods, plastic and rubber products, textiles; printing and publishing; fishing; important tourist and cultural center; attractions include cable cars, the Old U.S. Mint, Coit Tower (firefighters memorial), and the Transamerica Pyramid Building. Univ. of San Francisco (1855), Heald Institute of Technology (1863), Univ. of California, San Francisco (1864), San Francisco Art Institute (1871), San Francisco State Univ. (1899), Golden Gate Univ. (1901), California Coll. of Podiatric Medicine (1914), San Francisco Conservatory of Music (1917), Academy of Art Coll. (1929), San Francisco Coll. of Mortuary Science (1930), City Coll. of San Francisco (1935), New Coll. of California (1971); Treasure Island Naval Station.

History: Bay sighted 1769 by Spanish explorers with Don Gaspar de Portolá; mission and presidio founded 1776; pueblo of Yerba Buena developed nearby; came under Mexican control after Mexican independence 1821; occupied by

U.S. naval forces 1846; name changed to San Francisco 1847; city grew rapidly after discovery of gold in nearby areas; incorp. as city 1850; terminus of first transcontinental railroad 1869; suffered extensive damage from earthquake and fire Apr. 18, 1906 (see SAN ANDREAS FAULT); scene of organization meeting of the UN 1945; U.S.-Japan peace treaty signed here 1951; prominent in cultural upheaval of 1960s; suffered heavy earthquake damage 1989.

4. Town, Córdoba prov., N cen. Argentina, midway bet. Córdoba and Santa Fe; pop. (1980c) 51,932.

5. Island, river, and municipality in Brazil. See SÃO FRANCISCO.

6. Town, ✻ of Morazán dept., NE El Salvador.

7. Municipality on SE coast of Pacijan I., Camotes Is., Cebu prov., Philippines, ab. 41 mi. (66 km.) NE of City of Cebu; pop. (1980c) 28,806; largest town of the Camotes.

San Francisco, Pa·so de \ˈpä-sō-t͟hā-\. Mountain pass in the Andes, on border, bet. NW Argentina and NE Chile; alt. 14,025 ft. (4275 m.).

San Francisco Bay. Inlet of Pacific Ocean, W cen. California, connecting with the Pacific through the Golden Gate (*q.v.*); ab. 60 mi. (97 km.) long (N to S, incl. San Pablo Bay) and 3 to 12 mi. (5 to 19 km.) wide; the city of San Francisco is S of its Pacific entrance and the city of Oakland is on its E shore. See SAN PABLO BAY and SUISUN BAY.

San Francisco de la Selva. See COPIAPÓ.

San Francisco del Rin·cón \ˌt͟hel-rēŋ-ˈkōn\. Town, Guanajuato state, cen. Mexico, 35 mi. (56 km.) W of the city of Guanajuato; munic. pop. (1990p) 83,617.

San Francisco de Ma·co·rís \t͟hā-ˌmä-kō-ˈrēs\. City, ✻ of Duarte prov., N cen. Dominican Republic, ab. 60 mi. (97 km.) NNW of Santo Domingo; pop. (1986e) 71,850; trade center for agricultural region.

San Francisco de Pau·la, Cape \t͟hā-ˈpau̇-lä\. Cape extending into Atlantic Ocean on E coast of Santa Cruz prov., S Argentina.

San Francisco Maritime National Historical Park. See UNITED STATES, *National Historical Parks.*

San Francisco Mountains. Mountain range, W Catron co., W New Mexico, extending across border into Arizona.

San Francisco Peaks *also* **San Francisco Mountain.** Three peaks in S cen. Coconino co., N Arizona: Humphreys (*also* **San Francisco Mountain**) 12,633 ft. (3851 m.), highest point in Arizona; Agassiz 12,340 ft. (3761 m.); and Fremont 11,940 ft. (3639 m.).

San Fra·tel·lo \ˌsän-frä-ˈte-lō\. Commune, Messina prov., NE Sicily, Italy, 54 mi. (87 km.) WSW of the seaport of Messina; pop. (1981p) 5199.

San Fructuoso. See TACUAREMBÓ 2.

Sanga. See SANGHA.

San Ga·bri·el \san-ˈgā-brē-əl, *Span.* sän-ˌgä-brē-ˈel\. **1.** River, SW California; rises in San Gabriel Mts., flows SW across Los Angeles co. into Pacific Ocean near Long Beach; ab. 75 mi. (120 km.) long.

2. Residential city, Los Angeles co., SW California, 8 mi. (13 km.) E of the city of Los Angeles; pop. (1990c) 37,120; San Gabriel Arcángel mission (founded 1771) was starting point for colonizers of Los Angeles 1781.

3. Town, Carchi prov., N Ecuador, ab. 80 mi. (130 km.) NNE of Quito, in Andes.

4. Cape, E cen. Baja California, NW Mexico, projecting into the Gulf of California.

San Gabriel Mountains. Mountain range, SW California, SW of Mojave Desert, and NNE of coastal plain in which Los Angeles is situated; chiefly in Los Angeles co.; highest point San Antonio Peak 10,080 ft. (3072 m.).

San Gabriel No. 1 Dam *and* **San Gabriel Reservoir.** See UNITED STATES, *Dams and Reservoirs.*

San·ga·mon \ˈsaŋ-gə-mən\. **1.** River, cen. Illinois; rises in S McLean co., flows SW and W into Illinois River at NW extremity of Cass co.; ab. 250 mi. (400 km.) long.

2. County in cen. Illinois. See table at ILLINOIS.

Sangarius. See SAKARYA.

Sanga Sanga \säŋ-ˈä-säŋ-ˈä\. Island, SW Sulu Archipelago, SW Philippines, separated by narrow strait from W Tawi-tawi I.; 18 sq. mi. (47 sq. km.); forms part of Banggaw municipality.

San·gatte \sän-ˈgåt\. Town, Pas-de-Calais dept., N France, on Strait of Dover; terminus of Channel Tunnel connecting with Folkestone, England.

San·gay \säŋ-ˈgī\. Volcano, cen. Ecuador; 17,159 ft. (5230 m.).

Sang–chu. See SANJU.

Sang·er \ˈsaŋ-ər\. **1.** City, Fresno co., S cen. California, 14 mi. (23 km.) ESE of the city of Fresno; pop. (1990c) 16,839.

2. City, Denton co., N Texas, N of city of Denton; pop. (1990c) 3508.

Sang·er·hau·sen \ˈzäŋ-ər-ˌhau̇z-ᵊn\. City, Saxony-Anhalt, cen. Germany, 37 mi. (60 km.) NNE of Erfurt; pop. (1981c) 33,831; first mentioned 991.

San Ger·mán \ˌsäŋ-her-ˈmän\. Town and municipality, SW Puerto Rico; pop. (1990c) 11,977 (town), 34,962 (munic.); in sugarcane and coffee-farming region; Inter American Univ. of Puerto Rico, San Germán Campus (1912); 16th cent. church; founded 1511, moved to present site c. 1570.

San Germano. See CASSINO.

Sang·er·ville \ˈsaŋ-ər-ˌvil\. Town, Piscataquis co., N cen. Maine, 8 mi. (13 km.) W of Dover-Foxcroft; pop. (1990c) 1398; birthplace of inventor Sir Hiram Maxim 1840.

San·gha *or* **San·ga** \ˈsäŋ-gä\. River, Rep. of the Congo; flows S into the Congo River; ab. 400 mi. (645 km.) long.

Sang·i·he Islands \säŋ-ˈgē-ə\ *or* **Sangi Islands** \ˈsäŋ-ē\. Group of volcanic islands, Indonesia, bet. NE end of Sulawesi and S end of Mindanao I. and SW of the Talaud group; 314 sq. mi. (813 sq. km.); main islands are Sangihe, Siau, Tahulandang, and Biaro. Largest of the group at N end, **Sangihe** *or formerly* **Great Sang·ir** \ˈsäŋ-ˌir\, ab. 30 mi. (48 km.) long by 8 to 17 mi. (13 to 27 km.) wide, suffered from eruptions of volcano Gunung Awu (6102 ft. or 1860 m.) in 1856 and 1892; has fertile soil; produces copra, hemp, and nutmegs.

San Gil \säŋ-ˈhēl\. Town, Santander dept., N cen. Colombia, S of Bucaramanga.

San Gi·mi·gna·no \ˌsän-ˌjē-mē-ˈnyä-nō\. Commune, Siena prov., Tuscany, cen. Italy, 19 mi. (31 km.) NW of the commune of Siena; pop. (1991p) 7043; wine; tourism; numerous medieval towers, walls, gates; 13th cent. palace, 12th cent. former cathedral, and 13th cent. church of St. Augustine.

San Gior·gio a Cre·ma·no \sän-ˈjōr-jō-ˌä-krä-ˈmä-nō\. Commune, Napoli prov., Campania, S Italy, on Bay of Naples 3 mi. (5 km.) SE of Naples; pop. (1991p) 62,168.

San Giorgio Mag·gio·re \mä-ˈjōr-ā\. Island in the Lagoon of Venice, NE Italy; has church designed by Andrea Palladio.

San Gio·van·ni in Fio·re \ˌsän-jō-ˈvä-nē-in-ˈfyō-rā\. Commune, Cosenza prov., Calabria, S Italy, 23 mi. (37 km.) SE of the commune of Cosenza; pop. (1981p) 20,154; 12th cent. convent.

San Giovanni in Per·si·ce·to \in-ˌper-sē-ˈchā-tō\. Commune, Bologna prov., Emilia-Romagna, N Italy, 13 mi. (21 km.) NNW of the commune of Bologna; pop. (1981p) 22,301.

San Giovanni Ro·ton·do \rō-ˈtōn-dō\. Commune, Foggia prov., Puglia, SE Italy, 19 mi. (21 km.) NNE of the commune of Foggia; pop. (1991p) 24,363.

San Giovanni Val·dar·no \väl-ˈdär-nō\. Commune, Arezzo prov., Tuscany, W Italy, 20 mi. (32 km.) WNW of the commune of Arezzo; pop. (1981p) 19,532.

Sangir, Great. See SANGIHE ISLANDS.

San Giu·lia·no Mi·la·ne·se \ˌsän-jü-ˈlyä-nō-ˌmē-lä-ˈnā-sā\. Commune, Milano prov., Lombardy, N Italy; pop. (1989c) 32,355.

San Giuliano Ter·me \ˈter-mā\; *formerly* **Ba·gni San Giuliano** \ˈbän-yē\. Commune, Pisa prov., Tuscany, cen. Italy, 6 mi. (10 km.) NNE of the commune of Pisa; pop. (1991p) 27,999; warm mineral springs.

San Giu·sep·pe Ve·su·via·no \ˌsän-jü-ˈsep-pā-ˌvā-sü-ˈvyä-nō\. Commune, Napoli prov., Campania, S Italy, 12 mi. (19 km.) E of Naples; pop. (1989c) 25,781.

San·gley Point \säŋ-ˈglā\. Point, NE tip of Cavite Penin., NE Cavite prov., Luzon, Philippines, on N side of entrance to Cañacao Bay; part of Cavite naval base.

San·gli \ˈsäŋ-glē\. **1.** Former Indian state, now part of Maharashtra state, India; 1146 sq. mi. (2968 sq. km.); a former Southern Maratha state.
2. Town, Maharashtra, India, on Krishna River 190 mi. (306 km.) SE of Bombay; pop. (1991p) 363,728; trades in peanuts; produces textiles, cigarettes, brass vessels.

San Gor·go·nio Mountain \ˌsan-gȯr-ˈgō-nē-ō\. Peak, San Bernardino co., S California; 11,502 ft. (3506 m.); highest of San Bernardino Mts. and of S California.

San Gorgonio Pass. Mountain pass, SE end of San Bernardino Mts., San Bernardino co., S California; 1500 ft. (457 m.); a gateway bet. San Gorgonio Mt. and San Jacinto Peak and connecting the San Bernardino Valley with the Coachella Valley.

San·gre de Cris·to Mountains \ˈsaŋ-grē-də-ˈkris-tō\. A range of the Rocky Mts., extending from Chaffee co., cen. Colorado, to Santa Fe co., N cen. New Mexico; highest peak Blanca Peak 14,345 ft. (4372 m.).

Sangre de Cristo Pass. Mountain pass, Costilla co., S Colorado, in the Sangre de Cristo Mts. of the Rocky Mts.; 9459 ft. (2883 m.); used before 1800; abandoned road.

San·gro \ˈsäŋ-grō\; *anc.* **Sa·grus** \ˈsā-grəs\. River, SE cen. Italy; flows out of the Apennines NE into the Adriatic Sea 12 mi. (19 km.) SE of Ortona; ab. 65 mi. (105 km.) long.

San·grur \ˈsəŋ-grůr\. Town, Punjab, NW India, in N part of state 58 mi. (93 km.) W of Ambala; pop. (1991p) 56,374.

Sanhsing. See YILAN.

San·i·bel Island \ˈsa-nə-bəl\. Island in Gulf of Mexico, off SW coast of Lee co., SW Florida; 16 sq. mi. (41 sq. km.).

San Ig·na·cio \ˌsän-ēg-ˈnä-syō\. **1.** *formerly* **El Ca·yo** \el-ˈkī-ō\ *or* **Cayo.** Town, ✻ of Cayo dist., W Belize; pop. (1992e) 9533.
2. Town, cen. Misiones dept., S Paraguay; pop. (1992p) 11,584.

San·i·lac \ˈsa-nə-ˌlak\. County in E Michigan. See table at MICHIGAN.

San Il·de·fon·so \ˌsän-ˌēl-dā-ˈfȯn-sō\. **1.** Municipality, Bulacan prov., Luzon, Philippines, on E side of Candaba Swamp near Pampanga border; pop. (1980c) 44,931.
2. *or* **La Gran·ja** \lä-ˈgrän-hä\. Commune, Segovia prov., cen. Spain, 7 mi. (11 km.) SE of the commune of Segovia; pop. (1991p) 4897; seat of former summer palace of kings of Spain; scene of two treaties bet. Spain and France: 1796, by which Spain joined France against England; and 1800, by which France (First Consul Napoléon Bonaparte, later Emperor Napoléon) secured Louisiana in exchange for lands to enlarge Parma, Italy (under Spanish Bourbons).

San Ildefonso, Cape. Point, E coast of Luzon, Quezon prov., Philippines, SE of entrance to Casiguran Sound, 16°01′N, 122°E.

San–in Kai·gan National Park \ˌsän-ˌēn-kī-ˈgän\. National park, Honshū, Japan; 35 sq. mi. (91 sq. km.); coastal region; estab. 1964.

San Isi·dro \ˌsän-ē-ˈsē-thrō\. **1.** Town, Buenos Aires prov., E cen. Argentina; pop. (1991p) 299,022; part of Buenos Aires met. area.
2. Municipality, Leyte prov., on **San Isidro Bay,** NW coast of Leyte I., Philippines, 45 mi. (72 km.) WNW of Tacloban; pop. (1980c) 22,285.
3. Municipality, Nueva Ecija prov., Luzon, Philippines, 13 mi. (21 km.) S of Cabanatuan; pop. (1980c) 28,550.

Sanitary and Ship Canal. See ILLINOIS WATERWAY.

San Ja·cin·to \ˌsan-jə-ˈsin-tō, ˌsän\. **1.** River, SE Texas; flows from Walker co. into Galveston Bay; ab. 85 mi. (140 km.) long; battle near its mouth Apr. 21, 1836 in which Americans under Gen. Sam Houston decisively defeated Mexicans under Gen. Antonio López de Santa Anna.
2. County in E Texas. See table at TEXAS.
3. City, Riverside co., SE California, 23 mi. (37 km.) W of Palm Springs; pop. (1990c) 16,210.
4. Municipality, E coast of Ticao I., Masbate prov., Philippines; port on Ticao Pass; pop. (1980c) 20,612.

San Jacinto Mountains. Range, chiefly in Riverside co., SW California, extending SE toward Salton Sea; highest peak **San Jacinto Peak** 10,804 ft. (3293 m.); generally considered as one of the Coast Ranges.

San·jō \ˈsän-ˈjō\. City, Niigata prefecture, Honshū, Japan, 24 mi. (39 km.) S of the city of Niigata; pop. (1990p) 85,824.

San Joa·quin \ˌsan-wä-ˈkēn, ˌsän\. **1.** River, cen. California; formed by junction of forks in SE Madera co., flows W then NW into Sacramento River near its mouth; 350 mi. (563 km.) long; navigable 88 mi. (142 km.) for oceangoing vessels. **Flor·ence Lake Dam** \ˈflȯr-əns\ (completed 1926; 166 ft. or 51 m. high) at upper end of its S fork in NE Fresno co. forms **Florence Lake,** from which water is diverted to **Hun·ting·ton Lake** \ˈhən-tiŋ-tən\ 14 mi. (23 km.) SW, where water from Big Creek tributary is impounded for hydroelectric power; ab. 8 mi. (13 km.) SSW of Huntington Lake is **Sha·ver Lake** \ˈshā-vər\, another reservoir for waterpower, formed by **Shaver Lake Dam** (completed 1927; 198 ft. or 60 m. high) across Stevenson Creek tributary; lower in course bet. Fresno and Madera cos. is **Fri·ant Dam** \ˈfrī-ənt\ (completed 1942, 319 ft. or 97 m. high).
2. County in cen. California. See table at CALIFORNIA.
3. Municipality, Iloilo prov., Panay, Philippines, at W end of Iloilo Strait on Panay Gulf 31 mi. (50 km.) WSW of City of Iloilo; pop. (1980c) 34,525.

San Joaquin Ridge. Mountain, San Miguel co., SW Colorado; 13,446 ft. (4098 m.).

San Jor·ge \ˌsäŋ-ˈhȯr-hā\. **1.** River, N Colombia; flows NE into Cauca River; ab. 250 mi. (400 km.) long; lower course through marshy region.
2. Lake port, W cen. shore of Lake Nicaragua, Rivas dept., SW Nicaragua; connected by rail with Rivas and the Pacific port of San Juan del Sur.
3. Small island, Solomon Is. in W Pacific Ocean, off SE coast of Santa Isabel I., with which it forms Thousand Ships Bay.

San Jorge, Gulf of. Inlet of Mediterranean Sea on E coast of Spain, S of Tarragona and N of Cape Tortosa.

San Jorge Bay. Inlet of NE Gulf of California, NW coast of the state of Sonora, Mexico.

San Jorge Gulf. Widemouthed inlet of Atlantic Ocean on E coast of Chubut and Santa Cruz provs., S Argentina.

San Jo·se \ˌsan-hō-ˈzā, *Span.* ˌsäŋ-hō-ˈsā\. **1.** *also* **Saint Joseph.** Island, Aransas co., S Texas, bet. Aransas Bay and Gulf of Mexico.
2. City, ⊗ of Santa Clara co., W California, on Coyote and Guadalupe rivers, SE of San Francisco Bay and ab. 40 mi. (64 km.) SE of San Francisco; pop. (1990c) 782,248; computers, aerospace and electronic components, wine, fruit, and vegetables; in truck- and fruit-farming region; San Jose State Univ. (1857), San Jose City Coll. (1921), San Jose Christian Coll. (1939). Founded 1777; first civil community in California; first state ✻ 1849–51; incorp. 1850.
3. Municipality, Nueva Ecija prov., cen. Luzon, Philippines, ab. 21 mi. (34 km.) N of Cabanatuan; pop. (1980c) 64,254.
4. Municipality, Mindoro Occidental prov., SW coast of Mindoro I., Philippines; pop. (1980c) 66,262.

San Jo·sé \ˌsäŋ-hō-ˈsā\. **1.** Province of cen. Costa Rica. See table at COSTA RICA.
2. City, ✻ of Costa Rica and of San José prov.; pop. (1991e) 289,456; commercial and industrial center of the country; food processing; coffee; tourism; cathedral; Univ. of Costa Rica (1940). Founded c. 1738; made ✻ 1823; developed during 19th cent. as center of coffee production.
3. *or in full* **Puerto de San José.** Seaport, Escuintla dept., S Guatemala; munic. pop. (1981c) 23,099; chief exports coffee, sugar, forest products.
4. Island off SE coast of Baja California, Mexico, in the Gulf of California; 20 mi. (32 km.) long.
5. Island, Pearl Is., Panama, in Gulf of Panama, of the country's Pacific coast; ab. 25 sq. mi. (65 sq. km.).
6. Department of S Uruguay. See table at URUGUAY.

7. City, ✻ of San José dept., S Uruguay, on San José River 55 mi. (88 km.) NW of Montevideo; livestock.

San José, Gulf of. Inlet of Gulf of San Matías, NE coast of Chubut prov., S Argentina; enclosed by Valdés Penin.

San Jose de Bue·na·vis·ta \dā-,bwā-nä-'vēs-tä\. Municipality, ✻ of Antique prov., in S part, Panay, Philippines; port on coast of Sulu Sea; pop. (1980c) 30,266.

San José de Cúcuta. See CÚCUTA.

San José de Gua·ni·pa \t͟hā-'gwä-nē-pä\. Town, Anzoategui, N Venezuela, just E of El Tigre; pop. (1990c) 42,438.

San José de las La·jas \,t͟hā-läs-'lä-,häs\. Municipality, La Habana prov., W Cuba; railroad junction point SE of Havana; pop. (1990e) 42,200.

San José del Gua·via·re \t͟hel-gwä-'vyä-rā\. Town, ✻ of Guaviare dept., cen. Colombia.

San·ju *or W.-G.* **Sang–chu** \'säŋ-'jü\ *also* **San·dju** \'sän-'jü\. Town, Xinjiang Uygur, W China, on N slope of Kunlun Shan; pop. (1990c) 51,868.

San Juan \san-'wän, 'hwän, *Span.* sän-'hwän\. **1.** River, Colorado, New Mexico, and Utah; rises in Archuleta co., S Colorado, flows SW across New Mexico border, bends W then NW across SW Colorado into Utah, and empties into Colorado River in SW San Juan co., SE Utah; 360 mi. (579 km.) long; important in projects for development of the upper Colorado.

2. Name of counties in four states of the U.S. See tables at COLORADO, NEW MEXICO, UTAH, WASHINGTON.

3. City, Hidalgo co., S Texas, 6 mi. (10 km.) E of McAllen; pop. (1990c) 10,815.

4. River, W Argentina; main course flows ESE in San Juan prov., forming a headstream of the Desaguadero (Río Salado); ab. 160 mi. (255 km.) long.

5. Province of W Argentina. See table at ARGENTINA.

6. City, ✻ of San Juan prov., W Argentina, 100 mi. (161 km.) N of Mendoza; commercial city with food-processing industries; founded 1562; largely destroyed by earthquake 1944; birthplace 1811 of Domingo Faustino Sarmiento, president of Argentina 1868–74.

7. River, W Colombia; flows S and W into the Pacific Ocean; ab. 200 mi. (320 km.) long; the Calima is a tributary.

8. Peak, S Las Villas prov., W cen. Cuba; 3722 ft. (1134 m.).

9. Province of W cen. Dominican Republic. See table at DOMINICAN REPUBLIC.

10. River, Nuevo León and Tamaulipas, NE Mexico; flows NE into Rio Grande; ab. 150 mi. (240 km.) long.

11. River, S Nicaragua; flows E out of Lake Nicaragua into the Caribbean Sea; forms E section of Nicaragua-Costa Rica boundary; 120 mi. (193 km.) long.

12. Municipality, Dominican Republic. See SAN JUAN DE LA MAGUANA.

13. *formerly* **Bol·bok** \bȯl-'bȯk\. Municipality, Batangas prov., Luzon, Philippines, ab. 4 mi. (6 km.) inland from Tayabas Bay; pop. (1980c) 59,345.

14. Seaport and municipality, ✻ of Puerto Rico, on NE coast; pop. (1990c) 437,745; oldest part built on an island in a large bay which has a narrow entrance, connected with mainland by a causeway and bridges; exports (chiefly to mainland U.S.) sugar, tobacco; clothing, cigars and cigarettes; tourism; cathedral (16th cent.); church (16th cent.); Univ. of Puerto Rico, Medical Sciences Campus (1912). Burial place of Spanish explorer Juan Ponce de León.

History: Site first visited by Spanish explorer Juan Ponce de León who made a settlement 1508 on the mainland (see CAPARRA); in 1521 Caparra abandoned and site on island settled; fortifications begun 1533, El Morro Castle begun 1539; attacked by English under naval commanders Sir Francis Drake and Sir John Hawkins 1595; held by the British under Lord George de Clifford for a short time 1598; sacked by the Dutch 1625; attacked again unsuccessfully by British 1797; occupied by Americans 1898.

15. *or in full* **San Juan de los Mor·ros** \,t͟hā-lōs-'mōr-rōs\. Town, ✻ of Guárico state, N cen. Venezuela, 50 mi. (80 km.) SW of Caracas; pop. (1990c) 67,791.

San Juan, Cape. **1.** Cape, extending into the Gulf of Guinea on the SW coast of Mbini, Equatorial Guinea, at N side of entrance to Corisco Bay.

2. Cape, NE tip of Puerto Rico; lighthouse.

3. Cape, E tip of Isla de los Estados, in South Atlantic Ocean off E point of Tierra del Fuego I.

San Juan, Point. Cape, S coast of Camagüey prov., E cen. Cuba, at N entrance to Golfo de Guacanayabo.

San Juan Bau·tis·ta \bau̇-'tēs-tä\. **1.** City, Mexico. See VILLAHERMOSA.

2. Town, ✻ of Misiones dept., S Paraguay, 240 mi. (386 km.) SE of Asunción; munic. pop. (1992p) 8164.

San Juan Bautista Tuxtepec. See TUXTEPEC.

San Juan Cap·is·tra·no \,ka-pə-'strä-nō\. City, Orange co., SW California, SE of Los Angeles; pop. (1990c) 26,183; site of Spanish mission founded 1776 by Father Junípero Serra. The mission is known for its swallows, which regularly fly off on Oct. 23 and return to their nests on Mar. 19.

San Juan·ci·to \,sän-hwän-'sē-tō\. Town, S cen. Honduras, 20 mi. (32 km.) NE of Tegucigalpa; historically significant silver and gold mines.

San Juan de la Ma·gua·na \,thā-lä-mä-'gwä-nä\ *or* **San Juan.** Municipality, ✻ of San Juan prov., Dominican Republic, 85 mi. (137 km.) NW of Santo Domingo.

San Juan del Mon·te \t͟hel-'mȯn-tā\. Municipality, W Rizal prov., Luzon, Philippines, N of the Pasig; borders on Manila to the W and on Quezon City to the N.

San Juan del Nor·te \t͟hel-'nȯr-tā\; *formerly* **Grey·town** \'grā-,tau̇n\. Seaport, extreme SE coast of Nicaragua, at mouth of San Juan River. Occupied by Great Britain 1848; used in gold rush 1849 as terminus of isthmian crossing.

San Juan de los Morros. See SAN JUAN 15.

San Juan de los Remedios. See REMEDIOS.

San Juan del Río \t͟hel-'rē-ō\. Town, Querétaro state, cen. Mexico, 25 mi. (40 km.) SE of the city of Querétaro; munic. pop. (1990p) 125,335.

San Juan del Sur \t͟hel-'sür\. Seaport on SW coast of Rivas dept., SW Nicaragua; outlet for products of S and SW Nicaragua, esp. coffee and sugar.

San Juan de Sal·va·men·to \t͟hā-,säl-vä-'men-tō\. See ESTADOS, ISLA DE LOS.

San Juan de Ulúa \t͟hā-ü-'lü-ä\ *also* **San Juan de Ul·loa** \,t͟hā-ü-'yō-ä\. Small island off Veracruz, Mexico, 19°12′N, 96°08′W; contains a fort built for defense of the harbor.

San Juan Hill. Elevation near Santiago de Cuba, E Cuba; captured by Cubans and American troops in Spanish-American War 1898. See EL CANEY.

San Jua·ni·co Strait \,sän-hwä-'nē-kō\. Narrow passage extending E and S bet. SW Samar and NE Leyte, Philippines, from Samar Sea to San Pedro Bay; 25 mi. (40 km.) long and from 0.2 to 3 mi. (0.3 to 5 km.) wide. Noted for its scenery and navigable to medium-sized ships, but dangerous because of swift current and numerous islands. Has many pueblos on its banks; Tacloban at its S end. In occupation of Leyte secured on both sides by U.S. forces Oct. 1944.

San Juan Islands. Group of islands, bet. Haro and Rosario straits, off NW Washington, incl. Orcas I. (59 sq. mi. or 153 sq. km.), San Juan I. (56 sq. mi. or 145 sq. km.; see *San Juan Island National Historical Park* at UNITED STATES, *National Historical Parks*), and Lopez I. (26 sq. mi. or 67 sq. km.), and constituting as a group San Juan co., Washington.

San Jua·ni·to \,sän-hwä-'nē-tō\. Small island of the Islas Marías group (*q.v.*) in the Pacific Ocean off W cen. Mexico.

San Juan Ji·qui·pil·co \,hē-kē-'pēl-kō\ *or* **Jiquipilco.** Town, México state, cen. Mexico.

San Juan Mountains. A range of the Rocky Mts., SW Colorado, extending NW and SE through several counties; several peaks above 14,000 ft. (4267 m.); highest are Uncompahgre Peak 14,309 ft. (4361 m.), Mt. Wilson 14,246 ft. (4342 m.), and Mt. Sneffels 14,150 ft. (4313 m.); terrain is rugged and well-forested.

San Juan Teotihuacán. See TEOTIHUACÁN.

San Juan y Mar·tí·nez \ˌē-mär-ˈtē-nās\. Municipality, Pinar del Río prov., W Cuba; on railroad line 15 mi. (24 km.) SW of the city of Pinar del Río.

San Ju·lián \ˌsän-hül-ˈyän\. Seaport, Santa Cruz prov., S Argentina, ab. 200 mi. (320 km.) N of E entrance to Strait of Magellan; Portuguese navigator Ferdinand Magellan wintered here 1520 on his circumnavigation voyage, put down mutiny.

San Jus·to \sän-ˈhüs-tō\. Town, Buenos Aires prov., E cen. Argentina, ab. 10 mi. (16 km.) WSW of the city of Buenos Aires; pop. (1980c) 14,135; part of Buenos Aires met. area.

Sankt. See SAINT.

Sankt Andrä. See SZENTENDRE.

Sankt An·ton am Arl·berg \zäŋkt-ˈän-ˌtōn-äm-ˈärl-ˌberk\. Village resort and winter sports center, Tirol, W Austria, at E end of Arlberg Tunnel; alt. 4221 ft. (1287 m.).

Sankt Beatenberg. See BEATENBERG.

Sankt Gallen. See SAINT GALL.

Sankt Go·ars·hau·sen \ˌzänkt-ˌgō-ärs-ˈhau̇-zən\ *or* **Sankt Go·ar** \gō-ˈär\. Town, Rhineland-Palatinate, Germany, on the Rhine River 24 mi. (39 km.) WNW of Wiesbaden; Lorelei (*q.v.*) nearby.

Sankt Gotthard. See SAINT GOTTHARD.

Sankt Ing·bert \zäŋkt-ˈiŋ-bert\. Town, Saarland, Germany, ab. 7 mi. (11 km.) NE of Saarbrücken; pop. (1980c) 41,844.

Sankt Joachimsthal. See JÁCHYMOV.

Sankt Michel. See MIKKELI 2.

Sankt Moritz. See SAINT-MORITZ.

Sankt–Peterburg. See SAINT PETERSBURG 2.

Sankt Pöl·ten \zäŋkt-ˈpœlt-ᵊn\. City, ❋ of Lower Austria, Austria, 35 mi. (56 km.) W of Vienna; pop. (1991c) 50,026; railroad junction; cathedral; chartered 1159.

Sankt Veit am Flaum. See RIJEKA.

Sankt–Vith. See SAINT-VITH.

San·ku·ru \säŋ-ˈkü-rü\. River, Democratic Rep. of the Congo; flows WNW and empties into Kasai River; 750 mi. (1207 km.) long; upper course called the Lubilash (*q.v.*).

San Lá·za·ro, Cape \ˌsän-ˈlä-zä-rō\. Point, SW coast of Baja California, Mexico, extending into the Pacific Ocean W of Magdalena Bay.

San Laz·za·ro di Sa·ve·na \sän-lät-ˈsä-rō-dē-sä-ˈvā-nä\. Commune, Bologna prov., Emilia-Romagna, N Italy; pop. (1989c) 30,225.

San Le·an·dro \ˌsan-lē-ˈan-drō\. City, Alameda co., W California, 15 mi. (24 km.) SE of Oakland; pop. (1990c) 68,223; residential; incorp. 1872.

Şanlıurfa. See URFA 2.

San Lo·ren·zo \ˌsan-lə-ˈren-zō, *Span.* ˌsän-lō-ˈren-zō\. **1.** Unincorporated settlement, Alameda co., W California, SE of Oakland; pop. (1990c) 19,987.

2. Peak, NW Santa Cruz prov., S Argentina, on border of Chile; 12,136 ft. (3699 km.).

3. Town, Santa Fe prov., N cen. Argentina, ab. 20 mi. (32 km.) NNW of Rosario; pop. (1980p) 78,983.

4. Town, Valle dept., S Honduras, on an inlet of the Gulf of Fonseca 80 mi. (129 km.) by road S of Tegucigalpa; pop. (1988p) 15,294.

5. City, Paraguay, ESE of Asunción; pop. (1992p) 133,311.

6. Municipality, E Puerto Rico; on railroad line SE of San Juan; pop. (1990c) 35,163.

San Lorenzo, Cape. Cape extending into Pacific Ocean on W cen. coast of Ecuador.

San Lorenzo Island. Island, Peru, in the Pacific Ocean off the city of Callao; ab. 5 mi. (8 km.) long.

San·lú·car de Bar·ra·me·da \sän-ˈlü-ˌkär-t͟hā-ˌbä-rä-ˈmā-t͟hä\. Seaport, Cádiz prov., SW Spain, at mouth of Guadalquivir River 18 mi. (29 km.) NW of the city of Cádiz; pop. (1991p) 55,934; produces wine, flour; tourism; 14th cent. church; palace of dukes of Medina Sidonia; starting place of explorer Christopher Columbus's 3d voyage 1498 and of Portuguese navigator Ferdinand Magellan's voyage of circumnavigation 1519.

San Lu·cas, Cape \sän-ˈlü-käs\. Cape, S extremity of Baja California, Mexico, extending into the Pacific Ocean.

San Lu·is \san-ˈlü-is\. **1.** City, Yuma co., Arizona, on Colorado River and Mexican border in southwestern corner of the state; pop. (1990c) 4212.

2. City, ⊗ of Costilla co., S Colorado; pop. (1990c) 800; one of Colorado's oldest towns.

San Lu·is \ˌsän-ˈlwēs\. **1.** Province of cen. Argentina. See table at ARGENTINA.

2. City, its ❋, 150 mi. (241 km.) ESE of Mendoza; pop. (1991p) 121,146; hydroelectric power production; city founded 1596.

3. Municipality, Santiago de Cuba prov., E Cuba; on railroad line just N of seaport of Santiago de Cuba; pop. (1990e) 33,230.

San Luis Creek *and* **San Luis Dam.** See UNITED STATES, *Dams and Reservoirs.*

San Luis d'Apra. See APRA HARBOR.

San Luis de la Paz \ˌsän-ˈlwēs-ˌthā-lä-ˈpäs\. Municipality, Guanajuato state, Mexico, 75 mi. (121 km.) ENE of León; pop. (1990p) 78,947.

San Luis Obis·po \san-ˌlü-is-ə-ˈbis-pō\. **1.** County in SW California. See table at CALIFORNIA.

2. City, its ⊗, 12 mi. (19 km.) from Pacific Ocean and ab. 80 mi. (130 km.) NW of Santa Barbara; pop. (1990c) 41,958; California Polytechnic State Univ., San Luis Obispo (1901), Cuesta Coll. (1963). Spanish mission founded 1772; incorp. as city 1856.

San Luis Park *or* **San Luis Valley** \san-ˈlü-is\. An area of irrigated land bet. mountain ranges in S Colorado; ab. 120 mi. (195 km.) long, 60 mi. (95 km.) wide; southernmost of a chain of high, grassy areas enclosed by snowcapped peaks (see NORTH PARK).

San Luis Peak. Mountain, Saguache co., S Colorado; 14,014 ft. (4271 m.).

San Luis Po·to·sí \sän-ˈlwēs-pō-tō-ˈsē\. **1.** State of cen. Mexico. See table at MEXICO.

2. City, its ❋, NE of León; munic. pop. (1990p) 525,819; major industrial center, producing rope, footwear, textiles, arsenic; large smelting and refining plants; silver mines; in agricultural region; cathedral; several notable churches; university (1923). Franciscan mission founded c. 1583; seat of revolutionary and statesman Benito Juárez's government 1863; place where Francisco Madero drew up basic social and political program of Mexican Revolution 1910.

San Luis Río Co·lo·ra·do \sän-ˈlwēs-ˈrē-ō-ˌkō-lō-ˈrä-t͟hō\. Municipality, Sonora state, Mexico, 45 mi. (72 km.) ESE of Mexicali; pop. (1990p) 111,508.

San Luis Valley. See SAN LUIS PARK.

San Mar·co \sän-ˈmär-kō\. One of the two large islands of Venice, Italy; in English often known as St. Mark (*q.v.*).

San Marco in La·mis \in-ˈlä-mis\. Commune, Foggia prov., Puglia, SE Italy, 17 mi. (27 km.) NE of the commune of Foggia; pop. (1981p) 15,383.

San Mar·cos \san-ˈmär-kəs, *Span.* sän-ˈmär-kōs\. **1.** City, San Diego co., SW California, 22 mi. (35 km.) NNW of the city of San Diego; pop. (1990c) 38,974; California State Univ., San Marcos (1990).

2. City and resort, ⊗ of Hays co., S cen. Texas, 30 mi. (48 km.) S of Austin; pop. (1990c) 28,743; Southwest Texas State Univ. (1899).

3. Department of W Guatemala. See table at GUATEMALA.

4. Town, ❋ of San Marcos dept., Guatemala; pop. (1994e) 11,379; coffee trade.

San Marcos de Arica. See ARICA.

San Ma·ri·no \ˌsan-mə-ˈrē-nō\. **1.** Suburban residential city, Los Angeles co., SW California, 2 mi. (3.2 km.) E of the city of Los Angeles and just S of Pasadena; pop. (1990c) 12,959.

2. \sän-mä-ˈrē-nō\. Republic, cen. Italian Penin., on Mt. Titano, S Europe, 11 mi. (18 km.) SSW of Rimini, Italy; 24 sq. mi. (62 sq. km.); pop. (1993e) 24,000; ❋ San Marino; one of the smallest republics in the world and claims to be oldest state in Europe; legislative powers vested in grand council of 60 members elected by popular vote; executive powers vested in two regents appointed by grand council every six months; judicial powers vested in magistrates of Italian citizenship. First treaty of friendship with Italy 1862; exports wine; agriculture; tourism.

History: Traditionally thought to have been founded in 4th cent. by St. Marinus of Dalmatia; except for a few short periods has preserved its independence; protected by Montefeltro family of Urbino in Middle Ages against Malatesta family; its independence recognized by Papacy 1631. Under Fascists in WWII; governed by Communist-Socialist coalition 1945–57.

3. City, its ✱; pop. (1992e) 2397; built around hermitage dating from c. 5th cent. A.D.; entered by one road; city walls, governor's palace, six churches, town hall, and other public buildings.

San Mar·tín \ˌsän-mär-ˈtēn\. **1.** Town, Buenos Aires prov., E Argentina. See GENERAL SAN MARTÍN.

2. Town, Mendoza prov., W Argentina, 30 mi. (48 km.) SE of the city of Mendoza; pop. (1980c) 29,746.

San Martín, Lake. Lake, S South America, on border bet. S Aysén prov. in Chile and SW Santa Cruz prov. in Argentina.

San Martín del Rey Au·re·lio \t̲hel-ˈrā-au̇-ˈrā-lē-ˌō\. Commune, Asturias prov., NW Spain, 7 mi. (11 km.) SE of Oviedo; pop. (1991c) 23,765; stock raising; coal mines.

San Martín Tex·me·lu·cán \ˌtās-mā-lü-ˈkän\. Town, Puebla state, SE cen. Mexico, NW of city of Puebla; munic. pop. (1990p) 94,532.

San Ma·teo \ˌsan-mə-ˈtā-ō\. **1.** Coastal county in W California. See table at CALIFORNIA.

2. Residential city, San Mateo co., W California, on SW shore of San Francisco Bay; pop. (1990c) 85,486; Coll. of San Mateo (1922); town site platted 1863.

San Ma·tías Gulf \ˌsän-mä-ˈtē-äs\. Inlet of Atlantic Ocean in SE Río Negro prov., S cen. Argentina, enclosed on S by Valdés Penin. in Chubut prov.

San·men Bay \ˈsän-ˈmən\. Bay on E coast of Zhejiang prov., E China, S of Ningbo.

San Mi·che·le, Mon·te \ˈmȯn-tē-ˌsän-mē-ˈke-lā\. Mountain, Friuli-Venezia Giulia, NE Italy, E of the Isonzo, dominating Gorizia to the NE and the Kras to the SE.

San Mi·guel \ˌsan-mə-ˈgil\. **1.** River, SW Colorado; rises in San Juan Mts. in SE San Miguel co. and flows NW into the Dolores River in W Montrose co.; ab. 85 mi. (135 km.) long.

2. Name of counties in two states of the U.S. See tables at COLORADO and NEW MEXICO.

San Mi·guel \ˌsän-mē-ˈgel\. **1.** River, E Bolivia; flows NNW into Guaporé River on the Brazil-Bolivia boundary; ab. 475 mi. (765 km.) long; sometimes known as the **Ito·na·mas** \ˌē-tō-ˈnä-mäs\ in its lower course.

2. Volcano, El Salvador. See EL SALVADOR.

3. Department of E El Salvador. See table at EL SALVADOR.

4. City, ✱ of San Miguel dept., E El Salvador, ab. 65 mi. (105 km.) E of San Salvador at foot of San Miguel volcano (6957 ft. or 2120 m.); pop. (1992c) 182,817; commercial center; produces leather goods, flour, textiles; founded 1530.

5. Municipality, Mexico. See SAN MIGUEL DE ALLENDE.

6. Seaport town, N Rey I., Pearl Is., Panama.

7. Island, Albay prov., Luzon, Philippines, smallest of group off E coast of Luzon bet. Lagonoy Gulf and Tabaco Bay NW of Cagraray I.; 8 sq. mi. (21 sq. km.); forms part of Tabaco municipality.

8. Municipality, Bulacan prov., Luzon, Philippines, 23 mi. (37 km.) NNE of Malolos; pop. (1980c) 73,113.

San Miguel, Gulf of *or Span.* **Gol·fo de San Miguel** \ˈgōl-fō-t̲hā-\. Inlet of the Gulf of Panama, extending E into SE Panama.

San Miguel Bay. Large inlet of Pacific Ocean, N coast of SE Luzon, Philippines, bet. Camarines Norte prov. on NW and Camarines Sur on S and E; ab. 25 mi. (40 km.) long by 12 to 17 mi. (19 to 27 km.) wide.

San Miguel de Al·len·de \ˌt̲hā-ä-ˈyen-dā\ *also* **Allende.** Municipality, Guanajuato state, cen. Mexico; pop. (1990p) 110,057; several churches; colonial buildings; cultural center.

San Miguel de la Palma. See LA PALMA 3.

San Miguel de Tu·cu·mán \t̲hā-ˌtü-kü-ˈmän\ *or* **Tucumán.** City, ✱ of Tucumán prov., N Argentina, at foot of E ranges of the Andes on a tributary of the Dulce River; pop. (1991p) 473,014; center of sugar industry; university (1914), private university (1965). Founded 1565, moved to present site 1580; in 1776 became part of viceroyalty of La Plata; independence of Argentina was first proclaimed here at the first congress of the republic 1816. See *History* at ARGENTINA.

San Miguel Island \ˌsan-mə-ˈgil\. Island, NW end of Channel Is. in Pacific Ocean; part of Santa Barbara co., SW California; separated from mainland by Santa Barbara Channel.

San Miguel Passage. Strait bet. Santa Rosa I. and San Miguel I., off S Santa Barbara co., SW California.

San Miguel Peak. Mountain, Dolores and San Miguel cos., SW Colorado; 13,700 ft. (4176 m.).

San Mi·nia·to \ˌsän-mē-ˈnyä-tō\. Commune, Pisa prov., Tuscany, cen. Italy, 23 mi. (37 km.) ESE of the commune of Pisa; pop. (1989c) 25,201; cathedral.

San Murezzan. See SAINT-MORITZ.

San Nar·ci·so \ˌsän-när-ˈsē-sō\. Municipality, Zambales prov., Luzon, Philippines, on coast road ab. 75 mi. (120 km.) NW of Manila; pop. (1980c) 19,119; U.S. troops landed near here Jan. 1945.

San·ni·can·dro Gar·ga·ni·co \ˌsä-nē-ˈkän-drō-gär-ˈgä-nē-ˌkō\. Commune, Foggia prov., Puglia, SE Italy, 25 mi. (40 km.) N of the commune of Foggia; pop. (1981p) 18,642.

San Ni·co·las \ˌsän-ˌnē-kō-ˈläs\. **1.** Village, Aruba. See SINT NICOLAAS.

2. Municipality, Pangasinan prov., Luzon, Philippines, on E tributary of the Agno 105 mi. (169 km.) NNW of Manila; pop. (1980c) 23,243.

San Ni·co·lás \ˌsän-ˌnē-kō-ˈläs\. **1.** *or in full* **San Nicolás de los Ar·ro·yos** \ˌthā-lōs-är-ˈrō-yōs\. Town, Buenos Aires prov., E cen. Argentina, on Paraná River; pop. (1980p) 96,313; river port, exporting grains and wool; steel mill, electric power plant; town founded 1748.

2. Municipality, La Habana prov., W Cuba, 35 mi. (56 km.) SE of Havana; pop. (1981p) 18,458.

San Nic·o·las Island \san-ˈni-kə-ləs\. Island, cen. Channel Is. in Pacific Ocean; part of Ventura co., SW California.

Sânnicolaul–Mare. See SÎNNICOLAU MARE.

San·nois \sä-ˈnwä\. Commune, Val-d'Oise, N France, NNW suburb of Paris.

Sa·no \ˈsä-ˌnō\. City, Tochigi prefecture, Honshū, Japan, 49 mi. (79 km.) N of Tokyo; pop. (1990p) 83,484.

Sa·nok \ˈsä-ˌnȯk\. Commune, Krosno prov., SE Poland, on San River 35 mi. (56 km.) S of Rzeszów; pop. (1989e) 39,419.

San Pab·lo \san-ˈpa-blō\. City, Contra Costa co., W California, N of Berkeley; pop. (1990c) 25,158; Contra Costa Coll. (1949).

San Pa·blo \sän-ˈpä-blō\. Chartered city, S Laguna prov., Luzon, Philippines, 17 mi. (27 km.) SW of Santa Cruz; pop. (1990p) 161,000; ships copra; an important rail and highway center in a valley near several small crater lakes; incorp. 1940.

San Pab·lo Bay \san-ˈpa-blō\. North extension of San Francisco Bay (*q.v.*), W cen. California.

San Pantaleo *or* **San Pantaleone.** See MOTYA.

San Pas·qual *or* **San Pas·cual** \ˌsan-pə-ˈskwȯl\. Locality, W cen. San Diego co., SW California; site of battle 1846 in which U.S. troops under Gen. Stephen W. Kearny suffered greater losses but were not prevented by Spanish-Californian troops from reaching San Diego; now a state historical park.

San Pa·tri·cio \ˌsan-pə-ˈtri-shē-ˌō\. Coastal county in S Texas. See table at TEXAS.

San Pe·dro \san-ˈpē-drō, -ˈpā-\. **1.** River, SE Arizona; flows NW into the Gila River in Pinal co.; ab. 100 mi. (160 km.) long.

2. Former city, Los Angeles co., SW California; annexed to the city of Los Angeles 1909; harbor; port of entry; U.S. military facilities.

San Pe·dro \sän-'pā-t͟hrō\. **1.** Town, Buenos Aires prov., E cen. Argentina, port on the Paraná River 90 mi. (145 km.) NW of the city of Buenos Aires; pop. (1980p) 27,058.

2. River, S cen. Camagüey prov., E cen. Cuba; flows SW and W into Caribbean Sea; ab. 60 mi. (95 km.) long; the city of Camagüey is situated on its upper course.

3. *or* **San–Pé·dro** \sän-'pā-drō\. Town, SW Ivory Coast; a port on Gulf of Guinea; pop. (1988c) 70,587.

4. River, Durango and Nayarit states, W Mexico; flows S and W past Tuxpan to the Pacific; ab. 250 mi. (400 km.) long.

5. *or in full* **San Pedro de las Co·lo·nias** \ˌthā-läs-kō-'lō-nyäs\. Municipality, Coahuila state, NE Mexico, 40 mi. (64 km.) NE of Torreón; wheat.

6. Department of cen. Paraguay. See table at PARAGUAY.

7. Town, ✱ of San Pedro dept., cen. Paraguay, on Jejui Guazú River ab. 90 mi. (145 km.) N of Asunción; pop. (1985e) 3569.

San Pe·dro, Point. **1.** \san-'pē-drō\. Point, NW coast of San Mateo co., W California.

2. \sän-'pā-t͟hrō\. Cape, SW Antofagasta region, N Chile, S of Nuestra Señora Bay.

San Pe·dro Bay. **1.** \san-'pē-drō\. Inlet of San Pedro Channel, S Los Angeles co., California; the city of Long Beach is on it; discovered 1542 by Portuguese explorer Juan Rodríguez Cabrillo in service to Spain.

2. \sän-'pā-t͟hrō\. Inlet of Pacific Ocean, SW cen. coast of Chile, NW of Puerto Montt.

3. Inlet of Leyte Gulf, E Philippines, bet. SW Samar and NE Leyte; connects by San Juanico Strait with Samar Sea. Tacloban is at its NW corner.

San Pe·dro Car·chá \sän-'pā-t͟hrō-kär-'chä\. Town, Alta Verapaz dept., cen. Guatemala; pop. (1981c) 54,421.

San Pe·dro Channel \san-'pē-drō\. Strait bet. S California mainland and Santa Catalina I., off W coast of Orange co., SW California.

San Pe·dro Cho·lu·la \sän-'pā-t͟hrō-chō-'lü-lä\. Municipality, Puebla state, Mexico, 10 mi. (16 km.) W of the city of Puebla; pop. (1990p) 77,923.

San Pedro de las Colonias. See SAN PEDRO 5.

San Pedro del Durazno. See DURAZNO 2.

San Pe·dro de Ma·co·rís \sän-'pā-t͟hrō-t͟hā-ˌmä-kō-'rēs\. **1.** Province of SE Dominican Republic. See table at DOMINICAN REPUBLIC.

2. Municipality, its ✱, 40 mi. (64 km.) E of Santo Domingo; pop. (1986e) 86,950; exports sugar, molasses, and livestock; manufactures clothing, soap, alcohol; notable for producing good baseball players.

San Pe·dro Már·tir, Sier·ra \'syer-rä-sän-'pā-t͟hrō-'mär-ˌtēr\. Mountain range, N Baja California, Mexico.

San Pe·dro Mountain \san-'pē-drō\. Peak, SW Rio Arriba co., NW cen. New Mexico; 10,624 ft. (3238 m.).

San Pe·dro Sa·ca·te·pé·quez \sän-'pā-t͟hrō-ˌsä-kä-tā-'pā-kās\. Town, San Marcos dept., W Guatemala, ab. 20 mi. (32 km.) NW of Quetzaltenango; munic. pop. (1981c) 37,523.

San Pe·dro Su·la \sän-'pā-t͟hrō-'sü-lä\. Town, ✱ of Cortés dept., NW Honduras, ab. 100 mi. (160 km.) NW of Tegucigalpa; pop. (1989e) 300,400; commercial center; ships bananas; produces foodstuffs, clothing, beverages, tobacco products, soap, furniture, building materials.

San Pe·dro y San Pab·lo Te·pos·co·lu·la \sän-'pā-t͟hrō-ē-sän-'pä-b͟lō-tā-ˌpō-skō-'lü-lä\. Municipality, Oaxaca state, Mexico, 60 mi. (97 km.) NW of the city of Oaxaca.

San·pete \'san-ˌpēt\. County in cen. Utah. See table at UTAH.

San Pie·tro \sän-'pyā-trō\. Island in Mediterranean Sea, off SW coast of the island of Sardinia; part of Cagliari prov., Italy; 20 sq. mi. (52 sq. km.); chief town Carloforte.

San Pitch \san-'pich\. River, cen. Utah; flows SW through Sanpete co. into Sevier River; ab. 60 mi. (95 km.) long.

Sanpo. See ZANGBO.

San·quhar \'saŋ-kər\. Burg, Dumfries and Galloway region, Scotland, 26 mi. (42 km.) NW of Dumfries by rail; pop. (1981p) 2169; scene of publication by Richard Cameron 1680 and James Renwick 1685 of the Covenanters' declarations renouncing allegiance to Charles II and James VII (who ruled England as James II); ruined castle.

San Quin·tín Glacier \sän-kēn-'tēn\. Glacier in Andes, Chile; 35 mi. (56 km.) long; ab. 4 mi. (6 km.) wide near its terminus.

San Ra·fael \ˌsan-rə-'fel\. **1.** River, E cen. Utah; flows SE through Emery co. into Green River; ab. 90 mi. (145 km.) long.

2. Residential city, ⊗ of Marin co., W California, 10 mi. (16 km.) N of San Francisco; pop. (1990c) 48,404; Dominican Coll. of San Rafael (1890).

San Ra·fa·el \ˌsän-ˌrä-fä-'el\. Town, Mendoza prov., W cen. Argentina, 120 mi. (193 km.) S of city of Mendoza; pop. (1980p) 70,477; agricultural district.

San Rafael National Park. National park, Chile; 2278 sq. mi. (5900 sq. km.); rare animals; estab. 1945.

San Ra·mon \ˌsan-rə-'mōn\. City, Contra Costa co., W California, 11 mi. (18 km.) E of the S part of Oakland; pop. (1990c) 35,303.

San Re·mi·gio \ˌsän-rā-'mē-hē-ˌō\. Municipality, Cebu prov., on NW coast of Cebu I., Philippines, at N end of Tanon Strait 56 mi. (90 km.) N of City of Cebu; pop. (1980c) 29,412.

San Re·mo *or* **San·re·mo** \sän-'rā-mō\. Seaport, Imperia prov., Liguria, NW Italy, on Ligurian Sea 12 mi. (19 km.) WSW of Imperia; pop. (1991p) 55,786; important year-round resort; flower market; 13th cent. Romanesque cathedral. Site of international conference 1920 of representatives of countries in WWI.

San Ro·mán, Cape \ˌsän-rō-'män\. Cape, N extremity of Paraguaná Penin., NW Venezuela.

San Sa·ba \san-'sa-bə\. **1.** River, Texas; flows ENE from Schleicher co. to Colorado River on E boundary of San Saba co.; 100 mi. (161 km.) long.

2. County in cen. Texas. See table at TEXAS.

3. Town, its ⊗, cen. Texas, on San Saba River; pop. (1990c) 2626.

San Sal·va·dor \san-'sal-və-ˌdȯr, *Span.* sän-ˌsäl-b͟ä-'t͟hȯr\. **1.** *formerly* **Wat·lings** \'wät-liŋz\. One of the Bahamas, ESE of Cat I. (*q.v.*) at 24°0′N, 74°30′W; 60 sq. mi. (155 sq. km.); pop. (1990c) 465; often identified with the first landfall of explorer Christopher Columbus in the New World 1492, an island which Columbus said was called **Gua·na·ha·ni** \ˌgwän-ə-'hän-ē\ before he renamed it San Salvador; has lighthouse near NE end. See SAMANA CAY.

2. Peak in SW El Salvador; 6187 ft. (1886 m.).

3. Department of SW cen. El Salvador. See table at EL SALVADOR.

4. City, ✱ of El Salvador, also ✱ of San Salvador dept., 23 mi. (37 km.) from the port of La Libertad; pop. (1987e) 481,397; the republic's financial, commercial, and industrial center; produces textiles and clothing, leather and wood products, liquors, soap, cigars; meatpacking; cathedral; national observatory; national library; has several universities incl. Univ. of El Salvador (1841). City founded 1525 and estab. on present site 1528; ✱ of El Salvador since 1839 except for 1854–59; destructive earthquakes 1854, 1873, and 1986, when over 900 died.

5. *also* **James Island** \'jāmz\ *or* **San·ti·a·go** \ˌsan-tē-'ä-gō, sän-'tyä-gō\. Island, one of the Galápagos Is. (*q.v.*), Ecuador; rises to 1700 ft. (518 m.); of volcanic origin.

San Salvador de Jujuy. See JUJUY 2.

San·sa·por \'san-sə-ˌpȯr\. Village, NW coast of Doberai Penin., NW Irian Jaya, Indonesia, opp. Waigeo I. and NE of Sorong. In WWII advance of Allies toward the Philippines, seized by U.S. forces July 1944; this led a little later to occupation of Morotai.

San Se·bas·tián \ˌsän-sā-ˌb͟äs-'tyän\. **1.** Municipality, NW Puerto Rico, SE of Aguadilla; pop. (1990c) 38,799.

2. Chief town and port, Gomera I., Canary Is., Spain.

San Sebastián, Cape. Cape, NE coast of Tierra del Fuego I., Argentina, off S South America.

San Sebastián Bay. Bay, NE coast of Tierra del Fuego I., Argentina.

Sansego. See SUŠAK.

San·se·pol·cro \ˌsän-se-'pōl-krō\. Commune, Arezzo prov., Tuscany, W Italy, on Tiber River 15 mi. (24 km.) ENE of the commune of Arezzo; pop. (1981p) 15,138; birthplace of artist Piero della Francesca c. 1420.

San Ser·vo·lo \sän-ˈser-vō-ˌlō\. Island in the Lagoon of Venice, NE Italy.

San Se·ve·ri·no Mar·che \ˌsän-ˌsā-vā-ˈrē-nō-ˈmär-kā\. Commune, Macerata prov., Marche, cen. Italy, near Potenza River 16 mi. (26 km.) WSW of the commune of Macerata; pop. (1981p) 13,009; archaeological museum.

San Se·ve·ro \ˌsän-sā-ˈvā-rō\. Commune, Foggia prov., Puglia, SE Italy, 20 mi. (32 km.) NNW of the commune of Foggia; pop. (1991p) 55,376; center of agricultural region; episcopal see.

Sansing. See YILAN.

San·som Park *or* **Sansom Park Village** \ˈsan-səm\. City, Tarrant co., N Texas, an enclave of Fort Worth; pop. (1990c) 3928.

San Stefano. See YEŞILKÖY.

Sant *or* **Santh** \ˈsənt\. Former Indian state, now part of Gujarat state, W India; 390 sq. mi. (1010 sq. km.).

Santa. See SAINT.

San·ta \ˈsän-tä\. River, N cen. Peru; empties into Pacific Ocean at Chimbote ab. 75 mi. (120 km.) SE of Trujillo; ab. 200 mi. (320 km.) long; large hydro plant on its banks.

San·ta Ana \ˌsan-tə-ˈa-nə, *Span.* ˌsän-tä-ˈä-nä\. **1.** Residential and commercial city, ⊗ of Orange co., SW California, 11 mi. (18 km.) E of Long Beach; pop. (1990c) 293,742; Rancho Santiago Community Coll. (1915); city founded 1869; incorp. 1886.
2. Department of NW El Salvador. See table at EL SALVADOR.
3. City, ✻ of Santa Ana dept., NW El Salvador, 50 mi. (80 km.) NW of San Salvador; pop. (1987e) 232,210; important commercial and industrial center; ships coffee; produces textiles, leather products, cigars; distilling; **Santa Ana Volcano** ab. 7755 ft. (2365 m.) is nearby.
4. Peak on Paraguaná Penin., NW Venezuela; 2625 ft. (800 m.).

Santa Ana Bay. Bay, NW Africa, on SW coast of Western Sahara.

Santa Ana de Coro. See CORO.

Santa Ana Mountains. Range of mountains along border bet. Orange and Riverside cos., S California; highest point 5685 ft. (1733 m.).

Santa Ana Volcano. See SANTA ANA 3.

San·ta Bar·ba·ra \ˌsan-tə-ˈbär-bə-rə\. **1.** County in SW California. See table at CALIFORNIA.
2. Residential city, its ⊗, on Santa Barbara Channel ab. 80 mi. (130 km.) NW of Los Angeles; pop. (1990c) 85,571; seaside resort; oil; livestock farms; Univ. of California, Santa Barbara (1891), Westmont Coll. (1940), Brooks Institute of Photography (1945), Santa Barbara City Coll. (1946), Center for the Study of Democratic Institutions; Vandenburg Air Force Base. Spanish presidio founded 1782, mission 1786; incorp. as city 1850.
3. Municipality, cen. Pangasinan prov., Luzon, Philippines, 12 mi. (19 km.) E of Lingayen; pop. (1980c) 37,001.
4. Municipality, Iloilo prov., Panay, Philippines, on Jaro River and on railroad line 12 mi. (19 km.) NNW of City of Iloilo; pop. (1980c) 32,693.

San·ta Bár·ba·ra \ˌsän-tä-ˈbär-bä-rä\. **1.** Department of W Honduras. See table at HONDURAS.
2. Town, its ✻; pop. (1988p) 9957.

Santa Barbara Channel. Strait bet. S California mainland and the island chain of Santa Barbara Is., off coast of Santa Barbara and Ventura cos., SW California.

Santa Bárbara de Samaná. See SAMANÁ 2.

Santa Barbara Island. Island, cen. Channel Is. in Pacific Ocean, part of Santa Barbara co., SW California; part of island included in Channel Islands National Monument (see UNITED STATES, *National Parks*).

Santa Barbara Islands. See CHANNEL ISLANDS 2.

San·ta Cat·a·li·na \ˌsan-tə-ˌkat-ᵊl-ˈē-nə\. **1.** *or* **Catalina.** Island, SW Channel Is. in Pacific Ocean, part of Los Angeles co., SW California; 70 sq. mi. (181 sq. km.); tourist resort.
2. Small island in lower Gulf of California, off SE coast of Baja California, Mexico.

Santa Catalina, Gulf of. Inlet of Pacific Ocean, W coast of Orange and San Diego cos., SW California.

Santa Catalina Mountains. Small range, NE Pima and SE Pinal cos., S Arizona; highest point Mt. Lemmon 9157 ft. (2791 m.).

San·ta Ca·ta·ri·na \ˌsän-tä-ˌkä-tä-ˈrē-nä\. **1.** Island in Atlantic Ocean, off E cen. coast of Santa Catarina state, S Brazil.
2. State, S Brazil; ✻ Florianópolis; corn, livestock, coal. See table at BRAZIL.
3. City, Nuevo León, Mexico, 5 mi. (8 km.) W of Monterrey.

San·ta Clara \ˌsan-tə-ˈklar-ə\. **1.** River, California; rises in Los Angeles co. and flows W through Ventura co. to Santa Barbara Channel near the city of Ventura; ab. 75 mi. (120 km.) long.
2. County in W California. See table at CALIFORNIA.
3. City, Santa Clara co., W California, 5 mi. (8 km.) NW of San Jose; pop. (1990c) 93,613; produces chemicals; in fruit- and truck-farming area; Santa Clara Univ. (1851), Santa Clara mission. City settled 1777 as Franciscan mission; incorp. 1852.

Santa Clara. **1.** Municipality, ✻ of Villa Clara prov., W cen. Cuba, ab. 165 mi. (265 km.) ESE of Havana; pop. (1990e) 194,354; railroad junction; sugar and tobacco; university (c. 1949); founded 1689.
2. Island, Pacific Ocean. See JUAN FERNÁNDEZ.

Santa Clara Bay. Bay, N coast of Matanzas prov., W cen. Cuba, E of Cárdenas Bay.

San·ta Cla·ri·ta \ˌsan-tə-klə-ˈrē-tə\. City, Los Angeles co., California, N of the city of Los Angeles; pop. (1990c) 110,642.

San·ta Co·lo·ma de Gra·ma·net \ˌsän-tä-kō-ˈlō-mä-t͟hā-ˌgrä-mä-ˈnet\. Commune, Barcelona prov., NE Spain, N suburb of the city of Barcelona; pop. (1991p) 132,173.

San·ta Cruz \ˌsan-tə-ˈkrüz\. **1.** Island, NW end of Channel Is. in Pacific Ocean; part of Santa Barbara co., SW California; separated from mainland by Santa Barbara Channel.
2. River, S Arizona; rises in E Pima co. S of Tucson, flows NW into Gila River in NW Pinal co.; ab. 150 mi. (240 km.) long.
3. Name of counties in two states of the U.S. See tables at ARIZONA and CALIFORNIA.
4. City, ⊗ of Santa Cruz co., W California, at N end of Monterey Bay; pop. (1990c) 49,040; tourist center; Univ. of California, Santa Cruz (1965); Spanish mission founded 1791; incorp. 1866.
5. Island, Virgin Islands of the U.S. See SAINT CROIX 4.

San·ta Cruz \ˌsan-tə-ˈkrüz, *Span.* ˌsän-tä-ˈkrüs\. **1.** River, S Argentina; flows E out of Lake Argentino in W Santa Cruz prov. and empties into Atlantic Ocean at the port of Santa Cruz; ab. 250 mi. (400 km.) long.
2. Province of S Argentina; ✻ Río Gallegos. See table at ARGENTINA.
3. Port, E Santa Cruz prov., S Argentina, at mouth of Santa Cruz River.
4. Department of E Bolivia. See table at BOLIVIA.
5. City, ✻ of Santa Cruz dept., E Bolivia, on the Piray River ab. 180 mi. (290 km.) NE of Sucre; pop. (1992p) 694,616; sugar, rum, rice, leather goods, lumber; oil refinery; university (1880); city estab. c. 1560 and moved to present site 1595.
6. *also* **In·de·fat·i·ga·ble Island** \ˌin-di-ˈfa-ti-gə-bəl\. One of the Galápagos Is. (*q.v.*), Ecuador.
7. Municipality, Ilocos Sur prov., Luzon, Philippines, on coast highway; pop. (1980c) 23,027.
8. Municipality, ✻ of Laguna prov., Luzon, Philippines, on SE shore of Laguna de Bay 34 mi. (55 km.) SE of Manila; pop. (1980c) 60,620; connected by highway, railroad, and boat with Manila.
9. Municipality, Zambales prov., W Luzon, Philippines, on coast 30 mi. (48 km.) N of Iba; pop. (1980c) 35,665.

10. Municipality, NE coast of Marinduque I., Philippines, 18 mi. (29 km.) E of Boac; pop. (1980c) 51,846.

11. Municipality, Davao del Sur prov., Mindanao, Philippines, on W shore of Davao Gulf 21 mi. (34 km.) SW of City of Davao; pop. (1980c) 48,276.

12. Chief island of Santa Cruz Is., SW Pacific Ocean. See NENDO.

Santa Cruz Bay. Inlet of Atlantic Ocean, E cen. coast of Santa Cruz prov., S Argentina; receives the Santa Cruz and Chico rivers from the W and NW.

Santa Cruz Channel. Strait bet. Santa Cruz I. and Santa Rosa I., off S coast of Santa Barbara co., SW California.

San·ta Cruz da Gra·ci·o·sa \ˌsä^n-tə-ˈkrüzh-də-grȧ-ˈsyȯ-zə\; *sometimes shortened to* **Santa Cruz.** Chief town of Graciosa I., cen. Azores, Portugal.

Santa Cruz de Bravo. See FELIPE CARRILLO PUERTO.

San·ta Cruz de Ju·ven·ti·no Ro·sas \ˈsän-tä-ˈkrüz-t͟hā-ˌhü-ven-ˈtē-nō-ˈrō-säs\. Municipality, Guanajuato state, cen. Mexico; pop. (1990p) 56,672.

Santa Cruz de la Pal·ma \ˌt͟hā-lä-ˈpäl-mä\. Chief town, La Palma I., Canary Is., Spain.

Santa Cruz del Nor·te \t͟hel-ˈnȯr-tā\. Town, La Habana prov., W Cuba; pop. (1981p) 25,852.

Santa Cruz del Qui·ché \t͟hel-kē-ˈchā\. Town, ✻ of Quiché dept., W cen. Guatemala, ab. 60 mi. (95 km.) NW of Guatemala City; pop. (1993e) 16,666.

Santa Cruz del Seibo *or* **Santa Cruz del Seybo.** See EL SEIBO 2.

Santa Cruz del Sur \t͟hel-ˈsür\. Municipality, Camagüey prov., E cen. Cuba, on S coast 50 mi. (80 km.) S of the city of Camagüey; pop. (1981p) 50,353.

Santa Cruz de Te·ne·ri·fe \t͟hā-ˌtā-nā-ˈrē-fā\. **1.** Province of Spain. See table at SPAIN.

2. Seaport, its ✻, W Canary Is., Spain, on N coast 57 mi. (92 km.) NW of Las Palmas; pop. (1991p) 189,317; principal city of Tenerife I.; ships tomatoes; manufactures wine, pottery; oil refinery; tourism; founded c. 1494; attacked by British 1657 and 1797; developed rapidly after c. 1887.

San·ta Cruz do Sul \ˌsä^{n}n-tə-ˈkrüzh-dü-ˈsül\. City, E cen. Rio Grande do Sul state, S Brazil, 80 mi. (129 km.) WNW of Pôrto Alegre; munic. pop. (1991p) 117,795.

San·ta Cruz Islands \ˈsan-tə-ˈkrüz\. Island group; part of the Solomon Is., in SW Pacific Ocean, N of Vanuatu; 362 sq. mi. (938 sq. km.); chief island Nendo. Other islands are Vanikoro, Utupua, and a number of islets, incl. Tinakula, an active volcano. Rarely visited; limited trade in copra. Visited 1595 by Spanish explorer Álvaro de Mendaña de Neira. In large WWII naval battle Oct. 1942 U.S. forces inflicted heavy damage on Japanese but lost carrier *Hornet.*

San·ta Ele·na \ˌsan-tä-ā-ˈlā-nä\. Peninsula, W Guayas prov., W Ecuador, on N side of the Gulf of Guayaquil; its tip is La Puntilla and on its N side is **Santa Elena Bay;** site of Ecuador's principal oil field; seaside resort region.

Santa Elena, Cape. Cape, NW coast of Costa Rica, extending into the Pacific Ocean.

Santa Elena Bay. See SANTA ELENA.

Santa Eugenia, Point. See EUGENIA, POINT.

San·ta Fe \ˌsan-tə-ˈfā, ˈsan-tə-ˌ\. **1.** River, N Florida Penin.; flows from E Alachua co. W into the Suwannee River; ab. 70 mi. (115 km.) long.

2. County in N cen. New Mexico. See table at NEW MEXICO.

3. City, ✻ of New Mexico and ⊗ of Santa Fe co., N cen. New Mexico, ab. 40 mi. (64 km.) W of Las Vegas, bet. the Pecos River and the Rio Grande; pop. (1990c) 55,859; alt. 6950 ft. (2118 m.); major tourist center; noted for Indian and Mexican handicrafts; Coll. of Santa Fe (1947), St. John's Coll. (1964). Notable buildings include Palace of the Governors (c. 1610, museum since 1914), San Miguel Mission (17th cent.), cathedral. Has large Mexican-American population; Indian pueblos and Bandelier National Monument in vicinity.

History: Oldest ✻ in U.S., founded by Spanish 1609–10; a mission and exploration center in colonial era; occupied by Pueblo Indians 1680–92; after Mexican independence 1821 became center of trade with U.S.; W terminus of Santa Fe Trail (*q.v.*); occupied by U.S. forces under Gen. Stephen W. Kearny 1846; made territorial ✻ 1851.

4. City, Galveston co., SE Texas, SE of Houston; pop. (1990c) 8429.

5. Province of N cen. Argentina. See table at ARGENTINA.

6. City, ✻ of Santa Fe prov., Argentina, on E bank of Salado River 90 mi. (145 km.) N of Rosario; pop. (1991p) 442,214; ships grain, flax, and cotton; National Univ. of the Litoral (1919), Catholic Univ. (1960); city founded 1573, moved to present site 1651; here Argentine constitution adopted by convention 1853.

7. *also* **Santa Fe de Bo·go·tá** \t͟hā-ˌb͟ō-gō-ˈtä\. City, Colombia. See BOGOTÁ 2.

8. Village, Nueva Vizcaya prov., Luzon, Philippines, N of Balete Pass and ab. 25 mi. (40 km.) SSW of Bayombong; in WWII scene of severe fighting in U.S. conquest of Luzon 1945.

Santa Fe Bal·dy \ˈbȯl-dē\; *formerly* **Baldy Peak.** Mountain, Santa Fe co., New Mexico; 12,622 ft. (3847 m.).

Santa Fe Peak. Mountain, Summit and Clear Creek cos., cen. Colorado; 13,146 ft. (4007 m.).

Santa Fe Springs. City, Los Angeles co., SW California, N of Long Beach; pop. (1990c) 15,520.

Santa Fe Trail. Former commercial route to the West, now a national historic trail, cen. U.S.; started in W Missouri (first at Franklin, now nonexistent, then at Independence, and later at Westport, now Kansas City); ab. 1200 mi. (1930 km.) long; used esp. 1821–80; proceeded along the prairie divide bet. the tributaries of the Kansas and Arkansas rivers to site of Great Bend, Kansas, followed the Arkansas almost to the mountains, then turned S to Santa Fe, here giving a choice of three routes: the westernmost branch, the Taos Trail, crossed the Sangre de Cristo Range at La Veta Pass, the middle branch went through Raton Pass (*q.v.*), and the shortest route, from present site of Cimarron, Kansas, went SW across Cimarron Valley; trail first traced by trader William Becknell 1821; wagons used on his 2d trip 1822 and thereafter by many traders until 1880 when completion of railroad to Santa Fe reduced importance of the wagon road.

Sant'·Aga·ta de' Go·ti \sänt-ˌä-gä-tä-dā-ˈgō-tä\. Commune, Benevento prov., Campania, S Italy, 15 mi. (24 km.) WSW of the commune of Benevento; pop. (1981p) 11,236.

Sant'Agata di Mi·li·tel·lo \dē-ˌmē-lē-ˈtel-lō\. Commune, Messina prov., NE Sicily, Italy, on Tyrrhenian Sea 52 mi. (84 km.) WSW of Messina; pop. (1981p) 12,110.

San·ta Ge·no·ve·va \ˈsän-tä-ˌhā-nō-ˈvā-vä\. Mountain, S Baja California, Mexico; 7894 ft. (2406 m.).

San·ta Inés \ˈsän-tä-ē-ˈnes\. Island in Tierra del Fuego Archipelago (*q.v.*), Chile; separated from Brunswick Penin. on E by Strait of Magellan.

San·ta Is·a·bel \ˈsan-tə-ˈi-zə-ˌbel\. **1.** Mountain on island of Bioko, Equatorial Guinea; 9865 ft. (3007 m.); highest peak in Equatorial Guinea.

2. See MALABO.

3. Municipality, S Puerto Rico, on coast E of Ponce; pop. (1990c) 19,318.

4. *or* **Isabel** *also Span.* **Ys·a·bel** \ˈē-sä-ˌb͟el\. Island in E cen. Solomon Is., W Pacific Ocean, ab. 40 mi. (64 km.) E of SE Choiseul I. and separated from it by Manning Strait; ab. 140 mi. (225 km.) long; 1460 sq. mi. (3781 sq. km.); pop. (1986c) 13,514. Has mountain chain the length of the island; highest peak Mt. Marescot ab. 3900 ft (1190 m.). Under German control 1886–99. Rekata Bay on NW coast was a Japanese base in 1942–43.

San·ta Lu·cía \ˈsän-tä-lü-ˈsē-ä\. River, Uruguay; flows into Río de la Plata 7 mi. (11 km.) NW of Montevideo; ab. 125 mi. (200 km.) long.

San·ta Lu·cia Range \ˈsan-tə-lü-ˈsē-ə\. Mountain range, Monterey and San Luis Obispo cos., SW California; one of the Coast Ranges.

San·ta Lu·zia \ˈsän-tə-lü-ˈzē-ə\. One of the Cape Verde Is.; 18 sq. mi. (47 sq. km.); highest point 1296 ft. (395 m.).

San·ta Mar·ga·ri·ta \ˈsän-tä-ˌmär-gä-ˈrē-tä\. Island in Pacific Ocean off SW coast of Baja California, Mexico, at the entrance to Magdalena Bay.

San·ta Mar·ghe·ri·ta Li·gu·re \ˈsän-tä-ˌmär-gā-ˈrē-tä-lē-ˈgü-rā\. Commune, Genova prov., Liguria, NW Italy, on Ligurian Sea 16 mi. (26 km.) ESE of Genoa; pop. (1981p) 12,321; lacemaking; resort.

San·ta Ma·ria \ˈsan-tə-mə-ˈrē-ə\. **1.** River, W Arizona; rises in Yavapai co., flows W to join Big Sandy River and form Williams River; ab. 45 mi. (70 km.) long.
2. City, Santa Barbara co., SW California, 52 mi. (84 km.) NW of the city of Santa Barbara; pop. (1990c) 61,284; experienced large pop. growth in 1960s and again in 1980s.
3. Cape, SW cen. coast of Angola, N of Cape Santa Marta.
4. \ˈsän-tä-mä-ˈrē-ä\. Island, SE Azores, Portugal; 42 sq. mi. (109 sq. km.); highest point 1936 ft. (590 m.). Allied air base built 1944.
5. \ˈsȧn-tə-mȧ-ˈrē-ə\. City, cen. Rio Grande do Sul state, S Brazil, ab. 150 mi. (240 km.) W of Porto Alegre and connected with it by rail; munic. pop. (1980c) 181,685; transportation center; ships livestock; railroad shops, meatpacking plants, tanneries; university (1960).
6. Municipality, Bulacan prov., Luzon, Philippines, 10 mi. (16 km.) E of Malolos; pop. (1980c) 58,743.

San·ta Ma·ría \ˈsän-tä-mä-ˈrē-ä\. **1.** Volcanic peak, SW Mendoza prov., W Argentina; 6200 ft. (1890 m.).
2. Island in Pacific Ocean off W cen. coast of Chile, at entrance to Gulf of Arauco.
3. *also* **Charles Island** \ˈchärlz\. One of the Galápagos Is. (*q.v.*), Ecuador.
4. Volcano in Sierra Madre Range near Quetzaltenango, Guatemala; 12,375 ft. (3772 m.); eruption killed 1000 people 1902.
5. *or* **Gaua** \ˈgau̇-ə\. One of the Banks Is., N Vanuatu, SW Pacific Ocean; ab. 12 mi. (19 km.) long by 10 mi. (16 km.) wide; has central peak 2300 ft. (701 m.).

Santa Maria, Cape. Cape on island off coast of Faro dist., S Portugal.

Santa María, Cape. Cape projecting from SE coast of Uruguay.

Santa Maria Bay. Bay, NW coast of St. Thomas I., Virgin Is. of the U.S., West Indies.

Santa Maria Ca·pua Ve·te·re \ˈkä-pwä-ˈvā-tā-rā\. Commune, Caserta prov., Campania, S Italy, 16 mi. (26 km.) N of Naples; pop. (1989c) 32,626; Roman ruins.

Santa María Cay. Island off NE coast of Las Villas prov., W cen. Cuba.

Santa María de Je·sús \t͟hā-hā-ˈsüs\. Town, Sacatepéquez dept., S cen. Guatemala; pop. (1981c) 8289.

Santa María del Buen Ai·re \ˌt͟hel-bwān-ˈī-rā\. See BUENOS AIRES 3.

Santa María del Ro·sa·rio \ˌt͟hel-rō-ˈsär-ē-ˌō\. Former municipality, La Habana prov., W Cuba; now part of Havana.

Santa Maria di Leu·ca, Cape \dē-ˈleu̇-kä\; *anc.* **Sal·len·ti·num Pro·mon·to·ri·um** \ˌsa-lən-ˈtī-nəm-ˌprä-mən-ˈtōr-ē-əm\. Cape, SE coast of Puglia, SE Italy, on SE side of entrance to the Gulf of Taranto. See SALENTINA PENINSULA.

Santa María la Antigua del Darién. See DARIÉN 1.

San·ta Mar·ta \ˈsän-tä-ˈmär-tä\. Seaport, ✻ of Magdalena dept., N Colombia, on coast 50 mi. (80 km.) E of Barranquilla; munic. pop. (1992e) 286,500; episcopal see; tourist resort; ships bananas; university (1966). Founded 1525, the oldest city in Colombia; became banana-shipping center late 19th cent.; connected with Bogotá by railroad 1961.

Santa Marta, Cape. Cape on SW cen. coast of Angola.

Santa Marta, Sierra Nevada de. See SIERRA NEVADA DE SANTA MARTA.

Santa Marta Gran·de, Cape \ˈgrȧn-dē\. Cape on E coast of Santa Catarina state, S Brazil.

Santa Maura. See LEVKÁS.

San·ta Mon·i·ca \ˈsan-tə-ˈmä-ni-kə\. City, Los Angeles co., SW California, on Santa Monica Bay 15 mi. (24 km.) W of center of Los Angeles; pop. (1990c) 86,905; orig. a seaside resort; aircraft; business center; Santa Monica Coll. (1929); city laid out 1875 as terminus of projected railroad; incorp. 1886.

San·ta·na do Li·vra·men·to \sȧn-ˈtä-nə-dü-ˌlē-vrə-ˈmen-tü\; *formerly* **Livramento.** City, Rio Grande do Sul state, S Brazil, on Uruguay border opp. Rivera; munic. pop. (1991p) 72,950.

Sant'·Ana·sta·sia \sän-ˌtä-nä-ˈstä-syä\. Commune, Napoli prov., Campania, S Italy, near Mt. Vesuvius 7 mi. (11 km.) E of Naples; pop. (1989c) 27,914.

San·tan·der \ˌsän-ˌtän-ˈder\. **1.** Department of N cen. Colombia. See table at COLOMBIA.
2. Province of N Spain. See *Cantabria* in table at SPAIN.
3. Seaport, ✻ of Cantabria autonomous community and ✻ of Cantabria prov., N Spain, on Bay of Biscay 212 mi. (341 km.) N of Madrid; pop. (1991c) 191,079; major seaport and summer resort; produces paper, glass, soap, textiles, chemicals; shipyards; fish processing; university (1972); caves of Altamira and Castillo nearby. Sacked by French under Marshal Nicolas-Jean Soult 1808; in 1941 center of town destroyed by fire.

Sant'·An·ge·lo Lo·di·gia·no \sän-ˈtän-je-lō-ˌlō-dē-ˈjä-nō\. Commune, Milano prov., Lombardy, N Italy, 20 mi. (32 km.) SE of Milan; pop. (1981p) 11,389.

San·ta·no·ni Peak \ˌsan-tə-ˈnō-nē\. Mountain in the Adirondack Mts., Essex co., NE New York; ab. 4620 ft. (1410 m.).

Sant'·An·ti·mo \sän-ˈtän-tē-ˌmō\. Commune, Napoli prov., Campania, S Italy, 6 mi. (10 km.) N of Naples; pop. (1989c) 31,619.

Sant'·An·ti·o·co \ˌsän-tän-ˈtē-ō-ˌkō\. **1.** Island in Mediterranean Sea off SW coast of the island of Sardinia, Italy; 41 sq. mi. (106 sq. km.); attached to Cagliari prov., Italy; connected with Sardinia by a causeway.
2. *anc.* **Sul·ci** \ˈsəl-ˌsī\. Town on the island; pop. (1991p) 12,272; founded by Phoenicians; antiquities include catacombs and Punic and Roman necropolis.

San·ta Pau·la \ˌsan-tə-ˈpȯ-lə\. City, Ventura co., SW California, 33 mi. (53 km.) E of Santa Barbara; pop. (1990c) 25,062; Thomas Aquinas Coll. (1971).

Sant'·Ar·can·ge·lo di Ro·ma·gna \ˌsän-tär-ˈkän-je-ˌlō-dē-rō-ˈmä-nyä\. Commune, Forlì prov., Emilia-Romagna, N Italy, 23 mi. (37 km.) ESE of the commune of Forlì; pop. (1981p) 15,948.

San·ta·rém \ˌsȧn-tə-ˈrem\. **1.** City, W Pará state, N Brazil, on right bank of Amazon River at its juncture with the Tapajós; munic. pop. (1991p) 265,105; important river port, shipping rosewood oil, lumber, and rubber; center of an agricultural area; founded 1661.
2. District of W cen. Portugal. See table at PORTUGAL.
3. Commune, ✻ of Santarém dist., W cen. Portugal, on right bank of Tagus River 43 mi. (69 km.) NE of Lisbon; pop. (1991p) 62,162; tourism; 17th cent. seminary; 13th cent. church; reconquered from Moors 1147.

San·ta·ren Channel \ˌsän-tä-ˈren\ *also* **San·ta·rem Channel** \-ˈrem\. Channel, W Bahamas, bet. Great Bahama Bank on E and Cay Sal Bank on W, and N of cen. part of Cuba.

San·ta Ri·ta \ˈsȧn-tə-ˈrē-tə\. City, Paraíba state, E Brazil; munic. pop. (1991p) 94,412; a SW suburb of João Pessóa.

San·ta Ro·sa \ˈsan-tə-ˈrō-zə, *Span.* ˈsän-tä-ˈrō-sä\. **1.** Coastal county in NW Florida. See table at FLORIDA.
2. City, ⊗ of Sonoma co., W California, 50 mi. (80 km.) NNW of San Francisco; pop. (1990c) 113,313; fruit; Santa Rosa Junior Coll. (1918); home and experimental gardens of horticulturist Luther Burbank; nearby are geysers, petrified forest, and redwood forest; incorp. 1868.
3. City, ⊗ of Guadalupe co., E cen. New Mexico, on Pecos River; pop. (1990c) 2263.
4. Town, ✻ of La Pampa prov., S cen. Argentina, ab. 180 mi. (290 km.) NW of Bahia Blanca; pop. (1991p) 78,057; university (1958).
5. Department of S Guatemala. See table at GUATEMALA.
6. *or in full* **Santa Rosa de Co·pán** \ˌt͟hā-kō-ˈpän\. Town, ✻ of Copán dept., W Honduras; pop. (1989e) 20,300; center of

a mining area; 35 mi. (56 km.) to the W is ruined city of Copán, important in the Classic period of the Mayas; ruins include courtyards, ball court, stone columns, and noted hieroglyphic stairs.

7. Municipality on W shore of Laguna de Bay, Laguna prov., Luzon, Philippines; pop. (1980c) 64,325.

Santa Rosa de Ca·bal \thā-kä-'bäl\. Town, Risaralda dept., W cen. Colombia, on E slope of Cordillera Occidental 30 mi. (48 km.) SW of Manizales; munic. pop. (1985c) 40,396.

Santa Rosa Island. 1. Island at NW end of Channel Is. in Pacific Ocean; part of Santa Barbara co., SW California; separated from mainland by Santa Barbara Channel.

2. Narrow island in Gulf of Mexico, lying along S coast of Santa Rosa and Okaloosa cos., NW Florida; part of Escambia co.

Santa Rosa Mountains. Small range, Humboldt co., N Nevada; highest peak 9731 ft. (2966 m.).

Santa Tecla. See NUEVA SAN SALVADOR.

San·tee \san-'tē, 'san-,\. **1.** River, SE cen. South Carolina; formed by confluence of Congaree and Wateree rivers, flows SE into Atlantic Ocean; 143 mi. (230 km.) long.

2. City, San Diego co., S California, E of city of San Diego; pop. (1990c) 52,902.

Santee Dam. Dam across Santee River, bet. Clarendon and Berkeley cos., SE cen. South Carolina; 60 ft. (18 m.) high; completed 1941; provides power from water impounded in **Lake Mar·i·on** \'mar-ē-ən\, a broad lake 40 mi. (64 km.) long extending back to junction of Congaree and Wateree rivers.

San·teet·lah, Lake \san-'tēt-lə\. Lake, Graham co., W North Carolina, in resort area of Great Smoky Mts. SW of the national park; ab. 5 sq. mi. (13 sq. km.).

Sant'·El·pi·dio a Ma·re \,sän-tāl-'pē-dyō-ä-'mär-ē\. Commune, Ascoli Piceno prov., Marche, cen. Italy, near Adriatic coast 22 mi. (35 km.) NNE of the commune of Ascoli Piceno; pop. (1981p) 15,042.

Sant·e·ra·mo in Col·le \,sän-tā-'rä-mō-in-'kòl-lā\. Commune, Bari prov., Puglia, SE Italy, 23 mi. (37 km.) SSW of the seaport of Bari; pop. (1989c) 24,212.

Sant'·Eu·fe·mia, Gulf of \,sän-,teù-'fām-yä\; *anc.* **Gulf of Hip·po·ni·a·tes** \hi-,pō-nē-'ā-,tēz\ *or* **Gulf of Vi·bo** \'vī-bō\. Inlet of Tyrrhenian Sea, W coast of Calabria, S Italy.

Sant Fe·liu de Gui·xols \'sänt-fāl-'yü-thā-gē-'shòls\ *or* **San Feliu de Guixols** \'sän\. Seaport, Gerona prov., Catalonia, NE Spain; pop. (1991c) 16,051.

Santh. See SANT.

San·tia·go \,san-tē-'ä-gō, *Span.* sän-'tyä-gō, *Port.* ,san-'tyä-gü\. **1.** City, W Rio Grande do Sul state, S Brazil, 70 mi. (113 km.) NW of Santa Maria; munic. pop. (1991p) 51,759.

2. One of the Cape Verde Is. See SÃO TIAGO.

3. Former province of cen. Chile.

4. *or in full* **Re·gión Met·ro·po·li·ta·na de Santiago** \rā-'gyōn-,mā-trō-,pò-lē-'tä-nə-də-\. Region of cen. Chile. See table at CHILE.

5. *or* **San·tia·go de Chi·le** \sän-'tyä-gō-thā-'chē-lā\. City, ✱ of Chile, also ✱ of Santiago region, in cen. Chile, ab. 70 mi. (115 km.) ESE of Valparaíso on the Mapocho River; formerly, ✱ of Santiago prov.; met. area pop. (1982c) 3,902,356; on a plain at an alt. of 1706 ft. (520 m.) within view of the Andes to the E; economic and cultural center of Chile, archiepiscopal see, and the principal industrial city, producing textiles, footwear, and foodstuffs; numerous public buildings, incl. 18th cent. cathedral, national legislature, presidential palace, museums, libraries, and an extensive system of parks; Univ. of Chile (1738), Catholic Univ. (1888), Technical Univ. (1947).

History: Founded by Spanish soldier Pedro de Valdivia 1541; has suffered frequently from earthquakes, floods, and civil disorders; occupied by forces under liberator José de San Martín 1817; made ✱ of independent Chile 1818.

6. Seaport, Cuba. See SANTIAGO DE CUBA 2.

7. Province, N cen. Dominican Republic. See table at DOMINICAN REPUBLIC.

8. *or* **San·tia·go de los Ca·bal·le·ros** \sän-'tyä-gō-thā-,lōs-,kä-bä-'yā-rōs\. Commune, ✱ of Santiago prov., N cen. Dominican Republic, on banks of the Río Yaque; pop. (1986e) 308,400; produces pharmaceuticals, tobacco products, coffee; university (1962); founded c. 1500; rebuilt after destruction by earthquake 1564.

9. River, SE Ecuador and NW Peru; formed by confluence of Paute and Zamora rivers in SE Ecuador, flows E across border of Peru, and S into Marañón River; ab. 130 mi. (210 km.) long.

10. One of the Galápagos Islands, Ecuador. See SAN SALVADOR 5.

11. Town, ✱ of Veraguas prov., SW cen. Panama; pop. (1990p) 43,678.

12. Island marking NW corner of Lingayen Gulf, Pangasinan prov., Luzon, Philippines, opp. Bolinao municipality; 8 sq. mi. (21 sq. km.).

13. Municipality, Isabela prov., Luzon, Philippines, junction point on main highway N from cen. Philippines to Cagayan Valley; pop. (1980c) 69,877.

14. *or* **Santiago de Com·pos·te·la** \thā-,kòm-pō-'stā-lä\. Commune, ✱ of Galicia autonomous community, La Coruña prov., NW Spain, 32 mi. (51 km.) SW of the commune of La Coruña; pop. (1991c) 87,807; brandy, linen, paper, soap, silverwork, engraved wood; 11th–13th cent. Romanesque cathedral said to be built on tomb of the apostle St. James; 16th cent. pilgrim hospice; university (c. 1501). Alleged tomb of St. James discovered 9th cent. A.D.; soon became one of the principal places of pilgrimage in Europe.

Santiago, Cape. Point, SW coast of Batangas prov., Luzon, Philippines, in Verde Island Passage on SW side of entrance to Balayan Bay.

Santiago, Mount *or Span.* **Cer·ro Santiago** \'ser-rō\. Mountain, W Panama; 9269 ft. (2825 m.); highest in Tabasará Mts.

San·tia·go, Río *or in full* **Río Gran·de de Santiago** \'rē-ō-'grän-dā-thā-sän-'tyä-gō\. River, SW Mexico; rises ab. 18 mi. (29 km.) W of Mexico City, flows through Lake Chapala W into the Pacific Ocean; length below Lake Chapala 340 mi. (547 km.); known as **Río Ler·ma** \'ler-mä\ above Lake Chapala; length incl. Río Lerma ab. 600 mi. (965 km.). See JUANACATLÁN.

Santiago Ati·tlán \,ä-tēt-'län\; *formerly* **Atitlán.** Town, Sololá dept., S Guatemala, on S shore of Lake Atitlán; munic. pop. (1981c) 19,447.

Santiago Bay. See SANTIAGO DE CUBA BAY.

Santiago de Chile. See SANTIAGO 5.

Santiago de Compostela. See SANTIAGO 14.

Santiago de Cu·ba \thā-'kü-bä\. **1.** Province of S Cuba. See table at CUBA.

2. *or sometimes shortened to* **Santiago.** Seaport, its ✱, on S coast of Cuba; munic. pop. (1990e) 405,354; 2d largest city in Cuba; on a landlocked bay 6 mi. (10 km.) long by 3 mi. (5 km.) wide, connected with the Caribbean by a narrow channel passing beneath El Morro Castle (alt. 200 ft. or 61 m.); ships iron, manganese and copper ore, sugar, rum, tobacco products; distilleries; university (1947).

History: Founded by Spanish 1514 and moved to present site 1522; ✱ of Cuba until 1589; point of departure for the expedition of conquistador Hernán Cortés to Mexico 1518. In the Spanish-American War center of military activity (see EL CANEY and SAN JUAN HILL) and scene of destruction of Spanish fleet July 1898, final major event of the war; scene of attack of band of revolutionaries under Fidel Castro on Moncada army barracks 1953, the date (26th of July) of which gave its name to Castro's revolutionary movement.

Santiago de Cuba Bay; *formerly* **Santiago Bay.** Bay, S coast of E Cuba.

Santiago de Guayaquil. See GUAYAQUIL.

Santiago de las Ve·gas \,thā-läs-'vā-gäs\. Former municipality, La Habana prov., W Cuba; now part of Havana.

Santiago de la Vega. See SPANISH TOWN.

Santiago del Es·te·ro \,thel-es-'tā-rō\. **1.** Province of N Argentina. See table at ARGENTINA.

2. City, its ✱, on the Dulce River 88 mi. (142 km.) SE of San Miguel de Tucumán; pop. (1991p) 201,709; in a semi-arid region producing grain, cotton, and flax; founded 1553; oldest continuous European settlement in Argentina.

Santiago de los Caballeros. See SANTIAGO 8.

Santiago Ix·cuin·tla \ē-'skwēnt-lä\. Town, Nayarit state, W Mexico, on the Río Santiago ab. 20 mi. (32 km.) from its mouth; munic. pop. (1990p) 98,308.

Santiago Mountains. Range, W cen. Brewster co., W Texas, extending S to the Rio Grande; across the river in Mexico the range is called Del Carmen Mts.

Santiago Peak. Mountain, W cen. Brewster co., W Texas; 6521 ft. (1988 m.).

Santiago Ro·drí·guez \rō-'drē-gās\. **1.** Province, NW Dominican Republic. See table at DOMINICAN REPUBLIC.
2. Town, Dominican Republic. See SABANETA.

Santiago Tux·tla \'tüst-lä\. Town, Veracruz state, E Mexico; munic. pop. (1990p) 51,289.

San·ti·am \ˌsan-tē-'am\. River, NW Oregon; formed by confluence of north and south branches on SW boundary of Marion co., flows W into Willamette River; length with longest branch ab. 75 mi. (120 km.).

San·ti·pur \'sän-ti-ˌpu̇r\. Town, West Bengal, NE India, on left bank of Hugli River 45 mi. (72 km.) N of Calcutta; pop. (1991p) 109,911.

Santi Quaranta. See SARANDË 2.

Sän·tis *or* **Sen·tis** \'zen-tis\. Peak in the Alps of NE Switzerland; 8205 ft. (2501 m.).

Santo. See SAINT.

Santo. **1.** Island, Vanuatu. See ESPÍRITU SANTO 1.
2. Town, Vanuatu. See LUGANVILLE.

San·to, Mount \'sän-tō\. Mountain, W coast of Espíritu Santo I., Vanuatu, SW Pacific; 5420 ft. (1652 m.).

San·to Agos·ti·nho, Cape \'sȧn-tü-ˌȧ-gu̇s-'tē-nyü\. Cape extending into Atlantic Ocean on E coast of Pernambuco state, E Brazil, S of Recife.

San·to Ama·ro \'sȧn-tü-ȧ-'mä-rü\. City, E Bahia state, E Brazil, ab. 30 mi. (48 km.) NW of Salvador; munic. pop. (1991p) 54,146.

San·to An·dré \'sȧn-tü-ȧn-'dre\. City, São Paulo state, SE Brazil; munic. pop. (1991p) 613,672.

San·to Ân·ge·lo \'sȧn-tü-'ȧ^{n}-zhā-lü\. Municipality, Rio Grande do Sul state, S Brazil, 220 mi. (354 km.) NW of Pôrto Alegre; pop. (1991p) 59,688.

San·to An·tão \'sȧn-tü-ȧn-'tau̇^{n}\. Island in extreme NW of the Cape Verde Is.; 30 sq. mi. (78 sq. km.); pop. (1990p) 43,272; chief settlement is Ribeira Grande; highest point 6493 ft. (1979 m.); produces coffee, sugar, and fruit.

San·to An·tô·nio \'sȧn-tü-ȧn-'tō-nyü\. Municipality, Rio Grande do Sul state, S Brazil, 40 mi. (64 km.) NE of Pôrto Alegre.

San·to An·to·nio de Je·sus \'sȧn-tü-än-'tō-nyō-ˌthā-hā-'süs\. City, Bahia state, E Brazil, W of Salvador; pop. (1991p) 52,770.

San·to Do·min·go \'san-tō-də-'miŋ-gō, *Span.* 'sän-tō-thō-'mēŋ-gō\. **1.** Municipality, Las Villas prov., W cen. Cuba, 20 mi. (32 km.) NW of Santa Clara; pop. (1990c) 114,422.
2. Spanish colony that preceded Dominican Republic. See HISPANIOLA and DOMINICAN REPUBLIC.
3. *formerly* **Ciu·dad Tru·jil·lo** \syü-'thäth-trü-'hē-yō\. City, ✻ of the Dominican Republic; pop. (1986e) 1,600,000; constitutes with surrounding region the National District (533 sq. mi. or 1380 sq. km.); commercial and cultural center of the republic and its principal seaport; exports sugar; tourism; three universities; cathedral (early 16th cent.); lighthouse containing reputed tomb of explorer Christopher Columbus.
History: Founded 1496 by Christopher Columbus' brother Bartolomé; the oldest continuous European settlement in the Americas; repelled British attack 1655; largely destroyed by hurricane 1930; from 1936 to 1961 named Ciudad Trujillo after President Rafael Leonidas Trujillo Molina; renamed after assassination of Trujillo 1961.
4. Early name of the island of Hispaniola. See HISPANIOLA.

Santo Domingo, Point. Cape on SW coast of Pinar del Río prov., W Cuba, on N side of Cortés Bay.

Santo Domingo de Basco. See BASCO.

Santo Domingo de los Co·lo·ra·dos \thā-ˌlōs-ˌkō-lō-'rä-thōs\. City, NW cen. Ecuador, W of Quito; pop. (1990c) 114,422.

Santo Domingo Tehuantepec. See TEHUANTEPEC.

San Tomé de Guayana. See CIUDAD GUAYANA.

Santorin *or* **Santorini.** See THÍRA.

San·tos \'sȧn-tüs\. Seaport, SE São Paulo state, SE Brazil, 45 mi. (72 km.) SSE of the city of São Paulo, of which it is the port, and ab. 200 mi. (320 km.) WSW of Rio de Janeiro; munic. pop. (1991p) 428,526; on an island in a tidal inlet (sometimes called **Santos River**); one of the principal ports of Brazil and the largest coffee-exporting port in the world, with extensive modern dock and warehouse facilities; also exports bananas, beef, oranges. Its suburb, Guarujá (pop. 98,918), is a seaside resort; seaport founded c. 1536; sacked by English privateer Thomas Cavendish 1591.

San·tos Du·mont \'sȧn-tüs-dü-'mȯ^{n}t\. City, Minas Gerais state, E Brazil; munic. pop. (1980c) 39,985.

Santos River. See SANTOS.

San·to Sti·no di Li·ven·za \'sän-tō-'stē-nō-dē-lē-'vent-sä\. Commune, Venezia prov., Veneto, NE Italy, 22 mi. (35 km.) NE of Venice; pop. (1981p) 11,130.

San·to To·mas \'sän-tō-tō-'mäs\. Municipality, Batangas prov., Luzon, Philippines, NE of Lake Taal; pop. (1980c) 43,010.

Santo Tomas, Mount. Mountain, Benguet prov., Luzon, Philippines, S of Baguio; 7406 ft. (2257 m.).

Santo Tomé de Guayana. See CIUDAD GUAYANA.

San–tu *or* **Santuao.** See SANDU.

San Va·len·tín, Cer·ro \'ser-rō-ˌsän-ˌvä-len-'tēn\. Peak, S Chile, W of Lake Buenos Aires; 13,314 ft. (4058 m.).

San Vi·cen·te \'sän-vē-'sen-tā\. **1.** Peak, El Salvador; ab. 7155 ft. (2180 m.).
2. Department of cen. El Salvador. See table at EL SALVADOR.
3. City, its ✻; pop. (1987e) 70,414; industrial and commercial center; trades in tobacco, coffee, sugarcane; textiles; founded 1635 on site of ancient Aztec settlement.

San Vicente de Al·cán·ta·ra \thā-äl-'kän-tä-rä\. Commune, Badajoz prov., SW Spain, 35 mi. (56 km.) NNW of the city of Badajoz; pop. (1991c) 6102.

San Vi·to \sän-'vē-tō\. Cape on NW coast of Sicily, Italy.

San Vito al Ta·glia·men·to \äl-ˌtä-lyä-'men-tō\. Commune, Pordenone prov., Friuli-Venezia Giulia, NE Italy, 22 mi. (35 km.) WSW of Udine; pop. (1981p) 11,873.

San Vito dei Nor·man·ni \ˌdā-nȯr-'mä-nē\. Commune, Brindisi prov., Puglia, SE Italy, 13 mi. (21 km.) WNW of the seaport of Brindisi; pop. (1989c) 20,727.

San·ya·ti \sän-'yä-tē\. River, N cen. Zimbabwe; flows NW into Zambezi River; ab. 260 mi. (420 km.) long.

São. See SAINT.

São Ber·nar·do do Cam·po \sau̇^{n}m-ber-'när-dü-dü-'käm-pü\. Municipality, São Paulo state, SE Brazil, 13 mi. (21 km.) SE of the city of São Paulo; pop. (1991p) 565,171.

São Bor·ja \sau̇^{n}m-'bōr-zhə\. City, W Rio Grande do Sul state, S Brazil, on W bank of Uruguay River on Argentine border; munic. pop. (1980c) 58,281.

São Brás de Al·por·tel \sau̇^{n}m-'brāzh-dē-ˌäl-pȯr-'tel\. Commune, Faro dist., S Portugal, 10 mi. (16 km.) N of the commune of Faro; pop. (1981p) 7227.

São Ca·e·ta·no do Sul \ˌsau̇^{n}ŋ-kī-'tä-nü-dü-'sül\. Municipality, São Paulo state, SE Brazil, 7 mi. (11 km.) SE of the city of São Paulo; pop. (1991p) 149,125.

São Car·los \sau̇^{n}ŋ-'kär-lüs\. City, E cen. São Paulo state, SE Brazil, on railroad line 130 mi. (209 km.) NW of the city of São Paulo; pop. (1980c) 119,630.

São Fi·de·lis \sau̇^{n}m-fē-'de-lēs\. Municipality, Rio de Janeiro state, SE Brazil; pop. (1980c) 34,928.

São Fran·cis·co \ˌsau̇^{n}m-frä^{n}-'sēs-kü\ *also* **San Francisco.** **1.** Island off NE coast of Santa Catarina state, Brazil; 20 mi. (32 km.) long.
2. River, E Brazil; rises in S cen. Minas Gerais state, flows N, NE, and E into Atlantic Ocean S of Maceió; 1988 mi. (3199 km.) long.

\ə\ **abut** \ˈə\ **matches** \ᵊ\ **kitten**, Fr **table** \ər\ **further** \a\ **ash** \ā\ **ace** \ä\ **cot, cart** \ȧ\ Fr **bac** \au̇\ **out** \b̲\ Span **Avila** \ch\ **chin** \e\ **bet** \ē\ **easy** \g\ **go** \i\ **hit** \ī\ **ice** \j\ **job** \k̲\ Ger **ich, Buch** \$^{n}$\ Fr **vin** \ŋ\ **sing** \ō\ **go** \ȯ\ **all** \ȯ\ **law** \œ\ Fr **bœuf** \œ̄\ Fr **feu** \ȯi\ **boy** \th\ **thin** \th̲\ **this** \ü\ **loot** \u̇\ **foot** \ue\ Ger **füllen** \ue̅\ Fr **rue** \y\ **yet** \$^{y}$\ Fr **digne** \'dēn^{y}\, **nuit** \'nw^{y}ē\ \yü\ **few** \yu̇\ **fury** \zh\ **vision**

3. Municipality, Minas Gerais state, E Brazil, 280 mi. (451 km.) NNW of Belo Horizonte; pop. (1991p) 70,081.

São Francisco do Sul \dü-'sül\; *formerly* **São Francisco.** Seaport town, Santa Catarina state, S Brazil, on São Francisco I. 90 mi. (145 km.) N of Florianópolis; munic. pop. (1980c) 20,606.

São Ga·bri·el \saúⁿŋ-gä-'bryel\. City, Rio Grande do Sul state, S Brazil, 60 mi. (97 km.) SW of Santa Maria; munic. pop. (1991p) 59,107.

São Gon·ça·lo \ˌsaúⁿŋ-gōⁿ-'sä-lü\. City, Rio de Janeiro state, SE Brazil, on E side of Guanabara Bay opp. the city of Rio de Janeiro; munic. pop. (1991p) 747,891.

São João \saúⁿ-'zhwaúⁿ\. Island off N coast of Maranhão state, NE Brazil, at entrance to Turiaçu Bay.

São João da Bar·ra \də-'bä-rə\. Municipality, Rio de Janeiro state, SE Brazil, 160 mi. (257 km.) NNE of the city of Rio de Janeiro; pop. (1991p) 59,194.

São João da Boa Vis·ta \də-ˌbō-ə-'vēsh-tə\. City, E São Paulo state, SE Brazil, 110 mi. (177 km.) N of the city of São Paulo; munic. pop. (1991p) 69,032.

São João del Rei \del-'rā\. City, S Minas Gerais state, E Brazil, 82 mi. (132 km.) S of Belo Horizonte; pop. (1991p) 63,680; museums include a rail museum at the train station.

São João de Me·ri·ti \dē-mi-rē-'tē\. Municipality, Rio de Janeiro state, SE Brazil; pop. (1991p) 425,038.

São Jor·ge \saúⁿ-'zhór-zhē\ *or Eng.* **Saint George** \sānt-'jórj\. Island, cen. Azores, Portugal, W of Terceira; 85 sq. mi. (220 sq. km.).

São Jo·sé Bay \ˌsaúⁿ-zhō-'ze\. Bay, in Maranhão state, on NE coast of Brazil, SE of Maranhão I.

São José do Rio Par·do \dü-'rē-ü-'pär-dü\. City, E São Paulo state, SE Brazil, 135 mi. (217 km.) N of the city of São Paulo; munic. pop. (1980c) 36,186.

São José do Rio Prêto \dü-'rē-ü-'pre-tü\. Municipality, São Paulo state, SE Brazil; pop. (1991p) 283,281.

São José dos Cam·pos \düsh-'kàm-püs\. City, São Paulo state, SE Brazil, ab. 50 mi. (80 km.) NNE of the city of São Paulo; munic. pop. (1991p) 442,728.

São Le·o·pol·do \saúⁿ-lyō-'pōl-dü\. City, Rio Grande do Sul state, S Brazil; N suburb of Pôrto Alegre; munic. pop. (1991p) 167,740; railroad center.

São Lou·ren·ço \ˌsaúⁿ-lō-'rāⁿ-sü\. **1.** River, SW Brazil; flows from Mato Grosso state SW through Pantanal into Paraguay River in Mato Grosso do Sul state near Bolivian border; ab. 300 mi. (485 km.) long; the Cuiabá is a tributary on the N.

2. Health resort, S Minas Gerais state, E Brazil, ab. equidistant from Rio de Janeiro and São Paulo; munic. pop. (1980c) 24,071; alt. ab. 2800 ft. (855 m.) on N slopes of Serra da Mantiqueira.

São Luís \ˌsaúⁿ-'lwēs\. **1.** *or* **São Luís do Ma·ra·nhão** \dü-ˌmä-rà-'nyaúⁿ\ *or* **Maranhão.** Island off N coast of Maranhão state, NE Brazil, bet. São Marcos Bay on the W and São José Bay on the E; 28 mi. (45 km.) long; site of the state ✱, São Luís.

2. Seaport city, ✱ of Maranhão state, NE Brazil, on the island of São Luís; munic. pop. (1991p) 695,780; exports agricultural products, lumber, balsam; produces sugar, chocolate; 17th cent. cathedral; several museums. Founded by French 1612; taken by Portuguese 1615; held by Dutch 1641–44; made bishopric 1677.

São Luís Gon·za·ga \ˌsaúⁿ-'lwēs-gón-'zä-gə\. City, NW Rio Grande do Sul state, S Brazil, 95 mi. (153 km.) NNW of Santa Maria; pop. (1980c) 47,627.

São Manuel. See TELES PIRES.

São Mar·cos Bay \saúⁿ-'mär-küs\. Inlet of Atlantic Ocean on NE coast of Brazil, in Maranhão state, W of São Luís I.

São Mi·guel \ˌsaúⁿ-me-'gel\ *or Eng.* **Saint Mi·chael** \sānt-'mī-kəl\. Island, E Azores, Portugal; 288 sq. mi. (746 sq. km.); chief town Ponta Delgada; largest island of the group.

Sa·o·na Island \sä-'ō-nə\. Small island, Dominican Republic, West Indies, in the N cen. Caribbean Sea off the country's SE coast; 13 mi. (21 km.) long.

Saône \'sōn\; *anc.* **Arar** \'ā-ˌrär\. River, E France; rises in Vosges dept., NE France, flows SSW into Rhone River at Lyon; 298 mi. (479 km.) long; receives the Doubs from the E; navigable for 233 mi. (375 km.).

Saône, Haute– \ōt-'sōn\. Department of E France. See table at FRANCE.

Saône–et–Loire \'sōn-ā-'lwär\. Department of E cen. France. See table at FRANCE.

São Ni·co·lau \ˌsaúⁿ-ˌnē-kü-'laú\ *or Eng.* **Saint Nich·o·las** \sānt-'ni-kə-ləs\. One of the Cape Verde Is.; 30 mi. (48 km.) long; 132 sq. mi. (342 sq. km.); pop. (1990p) 13,577; highest point 4278 ft. (1304 m.). One of first of the group to be colonized.

São Pau·lo \saúⁿm-'paú-lü, -lō\. **1.** State, SE Brazil; ✱ São Paulo; Brazil's most populous state; important industrial and agricultural region. See table at BRAZIL.

2. City, its ✱, on the Tietê River 45 mi. (72 km.) NNW of Santos, its port; munic. pop. (1989e) 10,900,000; largest city and principal industrial center of Brazil; transportation center; produces steel, motor vehicles, machine tools, and a wide range of consumer goods incl. textiles, household appliances, furniture, foodstuffs, pharmaceuticals; oil refineries, chemical plants; has an extensive complex of residential suburbs and a notable system of public parks, a large stadium, art museum, and libraries; important cultural and publishing center; three universities, incl. Univ. of São Paulo (1934).

History: Founded by Portuguese Jesuits 1554; base for exploration in 17th cent.; became seat of captaincy 1681 and city 1711; in 1822 scene of declaration of Brazilian independence by Emperor Pedro I; developed rapidly as industrial center from late 19th cent. and became one of the world's largest cities.

São Paulo de Loanda. See LUANDA 2.

São Pedro do Rio Grande do Sul. See RIO GRANDE 2.

São Ro·que, Cape \saúⁿ-'ró-kē\ *or* **Ca·bo de São Roque** \'kä-bō-dē-\. Cape, E coast of Rio Grande do Norte, NE Brazil, N of Natal.

São Sal·va·dor \saúⁿ-ˌsäl-và-'dōr\. Seaport, E Brazil. See SALVADOR.

São Salvador do Congo. See M'BANZA CONGO.

São Se·bas·tião \ˌsaúⁿ-ˌsā-bà-'styaúⁿ\. Island, Brazil, in Atlantic Ocean off NE coast of São Paulo state.

São Se·bas·tião, Ponta. See PONTA SÃO SEBASTIÃO.

São Tia·go \ˌsaúⁿ-'tyä-gü, -gō\ *also* **San·ti·a·go** \ˌsan-tē-'ä-gō\. Largest of the Cape Verde Is.; 383 sq. mi. (992 sq. km.); pop. (1990p) 171,433; chief town Praia, ✱ of the group; highest point 4562 ft. (1390 m.); mountainous, many ravines and streams; grows coffee, oranges, sugarcane.

São To·mé \ˌsaúⁿ-tü-'mā\. **1.** *or* **São Tho·mé** *or Eng.* **Saint Thom·as** \sānt-'tä-məs\. Island, São Tomé and Príncipe; on the Equator, W of African mainland; 330 sq. mi. (855 sq. km.); chief town São Tomé, ✱ of São Tomé and Príncipe (*q.v.*).

2. Town, ✱ of São Tomé and Príncipe, on NE São Tomé I.

3. Part of the city of Madras, India, orig. a Portuguese port. See SAINT THOMÉ.

São Tomé, Cape. Cape extending into Atlantic Ocean on NE coast of Rio de Janeiro state, SE Brazil.

São To·mé and Prín·ci·pe *or* **Sao Tome and Prin·ci·pe** \saúⁿ-tü-'mā ... 'prēn-sē-pē\. Independent state, W Africa, comprising the islands of São Tomé and Príncipe, in Gulf of Guinea; 372 sq. mi. (963 sq. km.); pop. (1994e) 128,000; ✱ São Tomé. Chief products: copra, cocoa, palm kernels, bananas, coffee, fish. Until 1975 a Portuguese overseas province (**São Tomé e Príncipe** \-ē-'prēn-sē-pē\).

São Vi·cen·te \ˌsaúⁿn-vē-'sāⁿn-tē\ *or Eng.* **Saint Vin·cent** \sānt-'vin-sənt\. **1.** City, São Paulo state, SE Brazil, on same island with Santos, SSE of the city of São Paulo; munic. pop. (1991p) 254,718. Settled early 16th cent. on São Paulo coast.

2. One of the Cape Verde Is.; 88 sq. mi. (228 sq. km.); pop. (1990p) 51,257; chief town Mindelo; highest point 2539 ft. (774 m.).

São Vicente, Cabo de. See SAINT VINCENT, CAPE 2.

Sa·pé \ˌsä-'pā\. Municipality, Paraíba state, E Brazil, just W of Joáo Pessoa; pop. (1991p) 58,540.

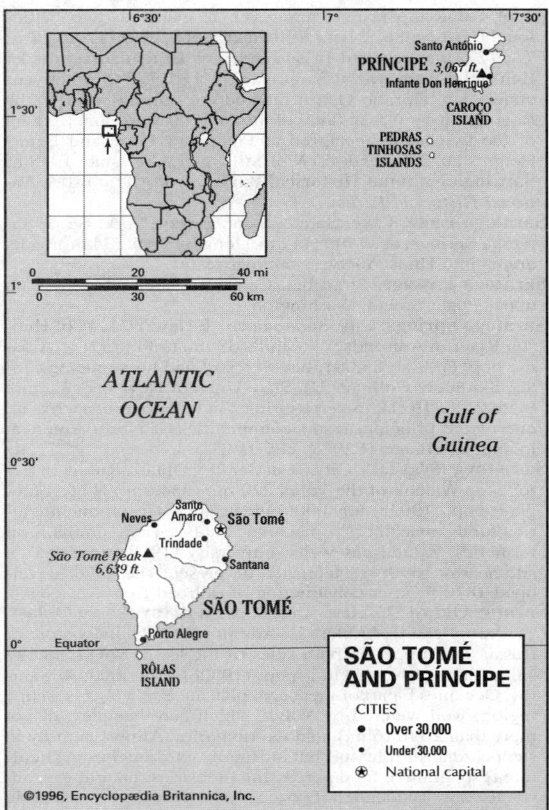

Sa·pe·le \sä-'pā-lā\. Port in Niger Delta, S Nigeria; pop. (1991e) 122,800; on the Benin River at the junction of its headstreams.

Sap·e·lo Island \'sa-pə-lō\. Island in Atlantic Ocean, off E mainland of McIntosh co., SE Georgia; largely a nature preserve; to the NW is **Sapelo Sound**.

Sa·pe Strait \'sä-pā\. Channel, bet. E end of Sumbawa I. and Komodo I. (part of Flores group), Lesser Sunda Is., Indonesia; ab. 13 mi. (21 km.) wide; connects Flores Sea with Indian Ocean.

Sapoedi. See SAPUDI.

Sap·pa \'sa-pə\. Creek, NW Kansas and SW Nebraska; rises in Sherman co., NW Kansas, flows NE into Nebraska and joins Beaver Creek 10 mi. (16 km.) before emptying into Republican River in Harlan co.; ab. 150 mi. (240 km.) long.

Sap·phire Mountains \'sa-,fīr\. A range of the Rocky Mts. in W Montana, extending along the boundary bet. Granite and Ravalli cos.; highest peak 8995 ft. (2742 m.).

Sap·po·ro \sä-'pō-rō\. City, ✱ of Hokkaidō prefecture, Hokkaidō I., Japan, in W part near head of Ishikari Bay; pop. (1990p) 1,671,765; commercial center of Hokkaidō; manufactures flour, lumber, beer; printing and publishing; winter-sports center; Hokkaidō Univ. (1876). City founded 1871 by Japanese government as center for the development of the island; site of Winter Olympic Games 1972.

Sa·pu·caia \,sä-pü-'kī-ə\. Small island in Guanabara Bay, Brazil, N of the city of Rio de Janeiro and S of Bom Jesús I.

Sa·pu·di *or Du.* **Sa·poe·di** \sə-'pü-dē\. Island, Malay Archipelago, in East Java prov., Indonesia, E of Madura I.; area with adjacent small islands, 94 sq. mi. (243 sq. km.).

Sa·pul·pa \sə-'pəl-pə\. City, ⊗ of Creek co., E cen. Oklahoma, 13 mi. (21 km.) SSW of Tulsa; pop. (1990c) 18,074; pottery, glassware.

Saq·qa·ra *or* **Saq·qā·rah** *or* **Sak·ka·ra** \sə-'kär-ə\. Site of ancient ruins, Lower Egypt, just NE of the present-day village of Saqqara; Step Pyramid, the oldest Egyptian pyramid, built by Djoser, 2d king of the IIId dynasty; also pyramids of the Vth and VIth dynasties and many mastabas.

Sa·ra \'sä-rä\. Municipality, Iloilo prov., Panay, Philippines, 48 mi. (77 km.) NE of City of Iloilo; pop. (1980c) 28,838.

Sarabat. See GEDİZ.

Sarābīt al–Khadím. See SERABIT EL KHADIM.

Sa·ra Bu·ri *or* **Sa·ra·bu·ri** \,sär-ə-'bu̇r-ē\. Town, S Thailand, on right bank of the Sak River and on the railroad line 20 mi. (32 km.) NE of Phra Nakhon Si Ayutthaya and ab. 65 mi. (105 km.) NE of Bangkok; pop. (1991e) 64,915.

Sar·a·gos·sa \,sar-ə-'gä-sə\ *or Span.* **Za·ra·go·za** \,zä-rä-'gō-sä\; *anc.* **Sal·du·ba** \sal-'dü-bə, -'dyü-\; *later* **Cae·sar·au·gus·ta** \,sē-zə-rȯ-'gəs-tə\. City, ✱ of Aragon autonomous community, and of Zaragoza prov., NE Spain, on Ebro river 170 mi. (274 km.) NE of Madrid; pop. (1991c) 594,394; manufactures agricultural machinery, cement, chemicals, textiles, soap, paper, glass; two cathedrals, La Seo (12th–16th cent. Gothic) and El Pilar (17th cent.); two 14th cent. Gothic churches, La Lonja (16th cent. Gothic); several palaces; university (1474).

History: Celtiberian settlement of Salduba taken by Romans late first cent. B.C. and made colony; made episcopal see 3d cent. A.D.; taken by Moors c. 714; reconquered by Alfonso I of Aragon 1118 and ✱ of Aragon until 15th cent.; in 1808–09 underwent two sieges by French, commemorated in "The Maid of Saragossa" in English poet Lord Byron's *Childe Harold.*

Sa·rai \sä-'rī\. City, ancient ✱ of the Khanate of the Golden Horde, near modern Leninsk (*q.v.*), Volgograd Oblast, S Russia in Europe, E of lower Volga. Founded by Batu Khan 1241 near Astrakhan (*q.v.*) and refounded at newer site 14th cent. by Berke (Baraka) Khan; for 200 years the Tatar (Kipchak) seat of government to which Russians paid tribute; seized by a vassal of Turkic ruler Timur 1382; declined after 1480 when Ivan III overcame the Tatars.

Sa·rai·ke·la \sə-'rī-kə-lə\. **1.** Former Indian state, now part of Bihar state, NE India; 446 sq. mi. (1155 sq. km.); ✱ Saraikela.
2. Town, S Bihar state, India; pop. (1991p) 11,180; served as ✱ of former Saraikela state.

Sa·ra·je·vo \'sä-rä-ye-,vȯ, *angl.* ,sar-ə-'yā-vō, ,sär-\. City, ✱ of Bosnia and Herzegovina, ab. 125 mi. (200 km.) SW of Belgrade, Yugoslavia; pop. (1991p [pre-civil war]) 525,980; in valley of upper Bosna River at alt. 1800 ft. (549 m.); formerly produced tobacco products, sugar, beer; university (1949); notable 15th cent. mosque.

History: Site of a Roman rest station nearby; citadel built by Hungarians c. 1262; occupied by Turks 15th cent.; sacked by Hungarians 1480; burned by Austrians 1697; came under Austrian rule 1878. In 1914 was scene of assassination of Archduke Francis Ferdinand by a Serbian nationalist, which precipitated WWI; joined to Yugoslavia 1918; in WWII occupied by Germans 1941–45; site of Winter Olympic Games 1984; attacked by Serbs following declaration of independence by Bosnia and Herzegovina (*q.v.*) 1992 and suffered extensive damage in ensuing war.

Sa·rakhs \sə-'raks\. Fortified town, Khorāsān prov., NE Iran; on Harī River at Turkmenistan border 90 mi. (145 km.) ENE of Mashhad.

Sa·ra·land \'sar-ə-,land\. City, Mobile co., SW Alabama, 10 mi. (16 km.) N of the city of Mobile; pop. (1990c) 11,751.

Sa·ra·mac·ca \,sä-rä-'mä-kə\. River, cen. and N cen. Suriname; flows N into Atlantic Ocean; ab. 250 mi. (400 km.) long.

Saramati. See ARAKAN YOMA.

\ə\ abut \ᵊ\ matches \ᵊ\ kitten, Fr table \ər\ further \a\ ash \ā\ ace
\ä\ cot, cart \å\ Fr bac \au̇\ out \b\ Span Avila \ch\ chin \e\ bet \ē\ easy
\g\ go \i\ hit \ī\ ice \j\ job \k\ Ger ich, Buch \ⁿ\ Fr vin
\ŋ\ sing \ō\ go \ȯ\ all \ȯ\ law \œ\ Fr bœuf \œ̄\ Fr feu \ȯi\ boy
\th\ thin \t͟h\ this \ü\ loot \u̇\ foot \ue\ Ger füllen \ue̅\ Fr rue
\y\ yet \ʸ\ Fr digne \'dēnʸ\, nuit \'nwʸē\ \yü\ few \yu̇\ fury \zh\ vision

Sa·ran \sä-'rän\. Town, Qaraghandy subdivision, Kazakhstan, ab 15 mi. (24 km.) WSW of city of Qaraghandy; pop. (1991e) 62,600.

Sa·ra·na \sə-'rä-nə\. Valley and pass in mountains of NE Attu I., W Aleutian Is., Alaska, leading from **Sarana Bay** on S to Chichagof Harbor to the N.

Sar·a·nac \'sar-ə-,nak\. River, NE New York; outlet of Saranac Lakes in Franklin co., flows NE into Lake Champlain at Plattsburg; ab. 100 mi. (160 km.) long.

Saranac Lake. Village, Essex and Franklin cos., NE New York, near Lower Saranac Lake 36 mi. (58 km.) S of Malone; pop. (1990c) 5377; in Adirondack region at alt. of 1600 ft. (488 m.); summer and winter sports resort; North Country Community Coll. (1967); settled 1819.

Saranac Lakes. Three lakes in S Franklin co., NE New York, **Upper Saranac Lake** ab. 8 mi. (13 km.) long, **Middle Saranac Lake** ab. 2.5 mi. (4 km.) wide, and **Lower Saranac Lake** ab. 5 mi. (8 km.) long; elev. 1540 ft. (469 m.).

Sa·ran·dë \sə-'rän-də\. **1.** District of S Albania. See table at ALBANIA.

2. *formerly* **San·ti Qua·ran·ta** \'sän-tē-kwə-'rän-tə\ *or* **Por·to Ed·da** \'pȯr-tō-'e-də\. Seaport, its ✻, on the Adriatic NE of the island of Corfu; developed as commercial port under Italian occupation in WWI.

Sa·ran·ga·ni Bay \,sär-ən-'gä-nē\. Inlet of Celebes Sea, S Mindanao, in S part of South Cotabato prov., Philippines; 19 mi. (31 km.) long by 9 mi. (14 km.) wide. Town of Buayan at its head.

Sarangani Islands. Island group, S Davao del Sur prov., Mindanao, Philippines, 8 mi. (13 km.) off Tinaca Point SW of entrance to Davao Gulf; 36 sq. mi. (93 sq. km.); comprises two islands, Balut and **Sarangani** (smaller and easternmost of the two, ab. 14 sq. mi. or 36 sq. km.), and an islet.

Sarangani Strait. Passage bet. Sarangani Is. and S tip of Mindanao, Philippines.

Sa·ran·garh \'sär-ən-,gär\. **1.** Former Indian state, now part of Madhya Pradesh state, India; 541 sq. mi. (1401 sq. km.). **2.** Town, its ✻, 60 mi. (97 km.) W of Sambalpur.

Sa·ransk \sə-'rȧsk\. Town, ✻ of Mordvinia Rep., cen. Russia in Europe, in cen. part, on a branch of the Moscow-Samara railroad, W of Simbirsk; pop. (1992e) 322,000; railroad junction; machinery, pharmaceuticals; university (1957); founded 1641.

Sa·ra·pi·quí \,sä-rä-pē-'kē\. River of Costa Rica; flows N into San Juan River; link in waterway from cen. Costa Rica to the Caribbean Sea.

Sa·ra·pul \sȧ-'rȧ-pül\. Town, SE Udmurtia Rep., E Russia in Europe, on Kama River 35 mi. (56 km.) SE of Izhevsk; pop. (1992e) 111,000; center of an agricultural area.

Sa·ra·sa·ra \,sä-rä-'sä-rä\. Peak in Cordillera Occidental, Peru; 17,923 ft. (5463 m.).

Sar·a·so·ta \,sar-ə-'sō-tə\. **1.** County in W cen. Florida. See table at FLORIDA.

2. City, its ⊗, on Gulf of Mexico 15 mi. (24 km.) S of mouth of Tampa Bay; pop. (1990c) 50,961; winter resort; truck and livestock farms; Ringling School of Art and Design (1931), New Coll. of the Univ. of South Florida (1960); John and Mable Ringling Museum of Art.

Sarasota Bay. Inlet of Gulf of Mexico on coast of NW Sarasota and SW Manatee cos., W Florida Penin.

Sa·ras·va·ti \'sär-əs-,və-tē\ *or* **Sa·ras·wa·ti** \-,wə-tē\. **1.** A sacred Hindu river of Punjab (region now divided bet. India and Pakistan); frequently mentioned in the Vedas and identified with the goddess Sarasvati. In early times held to be the Indus, later one of its tributaries; its modern equivalent, thought to be the **Sar·su·ti** \'sär-sət-ē\, loses itself in the sands of NW India.

2. River, W India; rises in S Rajasthan and flows SW to Little Rann of Kachchh, Gujarat; ab. 120 mi. (195 km.) long.

Sar·a·to·ga \,sar-ə-'tō-gə\. **1.** County in E New York. See table at NEW YORK.

2. City, Santa Clara co., W California, SW of San Jose; pop. (1990c) 28,061; residential; West Valley Coll. (1963).

3. Former village, now Schuylerville (*q.v.*), on W bank of Hudson River, Saratoga co., E New York, ab. 10 mi. (16 km.) E of Saratoga Springs; has given its name to two battles fought just to the S, near Stillwater, Sept. 19, 1777 and Oct. 7, 1777, that resulted in surrender of British forces under Gen. John Burgoyne at Saratoga Oct. 17, 1777 to Americans under Gen. Horatio Gates; marked the turning point of the Revolutionary War in favor of the Americans. Actual fighting of the two battles occurred at Freeman's Farm and Bemis Heights ab. 3 mi. (5 km.) N of Stillwater; site estab. 1948 as **Saratoga National Historical Park** (see UNITED STATES, *National Historical Parks*).

Saratoga Lake. Lake, Saratoga co., E New York, SE of Saratoga Springs; ab. 7 mi. (11 km.) long by 2 mi. (3 km.) wide; drains into Hudson River; summer resort.

Saratoga Passage. Strait bet. Camano I. and Whidbey I. in upper Puget Sound, Washington.

Saratoga Springs. City, Saratoga co., E New York, W of Hudson River in Adirondack foothills 33 mi. (53 km.) N of Albany; pop. (1990c) 25,001; health resort and horse-racing center; Skidmore Coll. (1903), State Univ. of New York Empire State Coll. (1971); mineral springs; in latter part of 19th cent. one of the principal resort communities of North America; incorp. as village 1826, as city 1915.

Sa·ra·tov \sə-'rä-təf\. City, ✻ of Saratov Oblast, Russia in Europe, on W bank of the Volga 220 mi. (354 km.) N of Volgograd; pop. (1992e) 909,000; industrial center, producing agricultural machinery, machine tools; flour mills, oil refineries, natural-gas wells; university (1919); founded on site nearby 1590; reestablished on present site 1674; developed 1870 ff. after construction of railroad from Moscow.

Saratov Oblast \'ȯ-bləst, -,blast\ *or* **Sa·ra·tov·ska·ya Oblast'** \sə-'rä-təf-skə-yə-'ȯ-bləstʸ\. Administrative subdivision of Russia in Europe, on both sides of the lower Volga; 38,687 sq. mi. (100,199 sq. km.); pop. (1992e) 2,711,000; ✻ Saratov. Occupies E part of great cen. plateau; E of Volga is steppe region; well watered by Volga, which here has elev. of not more than 20 ft. (6 m.), and its tributaries. Almost entirely in steppe zone; fertile soil but suffers from droughts. Agriculture (esp. grains), food processing industries; natural gas, oil.

History: Evidence of occupation dates to prehistoric times; came under the Khazars in 8th and 9th cents.; under Russian S.F.S.R. included in the Lower Volga Area 1928; reorganized as a separate region 1934; became oblast 1936.

Sa·ra·via \sə-'rā-vē-ə\. Municipality, Negros Occidental, Negros, Philippines, near coast 15 mi. (24 km.) N of City of Bacolod.

Sa·ra·wak \sə-'rä-wäk, -,wä\. **1.** A state of Malaysia, on NW island of Borneo, bordering on Sabah (with which it constitutes East Malaysia), Brunei, and Indonesian Borneo; ✻ Kuching; pepper, hardwood, rice, rubber, oil; coastline of 450 mi. (724 km.) extends along South China Sea on W and NW. Has several navigable rivers (Rajang, Baram, Limbang, and Batang Lupar); generally mountainous, esp. along E and S borders. See table at MALAYSIA.

History: Brunei (*q.v.*) visited in 1839 by Sir James Brooke who sought to quell piracy; S part of Brunei (orig. ab. 7000 sq. mi. or 18,130 sq. km.) ceded 1841 to Brooke by sultan and became independent state of Sarawak; became a British protectorate 1888 and governed for three generations by the Brooke family; during WWII occupied by Japanese 1941–45; became British crown colony 1946; joined Malaysia 1963.

2. Town, its ✻. See KUCHING.

Sar·bi·no·wo \,sär-bi-'nȯ-vȯ\ *or Ger.* **Zorn·dorf** \'tsȯrn-,dȯrf, 'zȯrn-\. Village, Zielona Góra prov., W Poland; formerly in Prussia; scene of battle 1758 during the Seven Years' War in which the Prussians under Frederick the Great defeated the Russians under Count William of Fermor.

Sar·celles \sȧr-'sel\. Commune, Val-d'Oise dept., N France, ab. 9 mi. (14 km.) N of Paris.

Sar·da \'sär-də\. River, N India; rises in N Uttar Pradesh, flows S (as Kali River) along border of W Nepal, then SE through Uttar Pradesh into Ghaghara River NE of Lucknow; ab. 220 mi. (355 km.) long.

Sar·din·ia \sär-'di-nē-ə, -nyə\ *or Ital.* **Sar·de·gna** \sär-'dān-yä\. Island, Italy, in the Mediterranean Sea, W of S Italian

Penin.; 9301 sq. mi. (24,090 sq. km.); pop. (1991p) 1,645,192; ✻ Cagliari; politically, together with some minor islands, constitutes an autonomous region of Italy (see table at ITALY); mountainous, highest point 6017 ft. (1834 m.) in E cen. part; chief rivers Tirso in center, Samassi in S, and Flumendosa in SE; separated on N from Corsica, France, by Strait of Bonifacio; more important inlets on its coast are Gulf of Asinara on NW, Oristano on W, and Cagliari on S. Chief towns Cagliari and Sassari.

History: Settled by Phoenicians c. 800 B.C. followed by Greeks; came under control of Carthage 6th cent. B.C.; taken by Romans 238 B.C.; in Vandal kingdom 5th cent. A.D.; part of Byzantine Empire 6th cent.; from 8th into 11th cent. frequently invaded by Arabs; Pisa and Genoa gained control 11th cent.; passed to house of Aragon early 14th cent.; held by Austria 1713–20; ceded to Savoy 1720 in exchange for Sicily, after which ruler of Savoy and Piedmont took title king of Sardinia (see SAVOY); became part of Italy 1861.

Sar·dis \ˈsär-dəs\. **1.** Town, a ⊗ of Panola co., NW Mississippi, 40 mi. (64 km.) ENE of Clarksdale; pop. (1990c) 2128; site of a dam and reservoir designed to control flood waters in the Tallahatchie River basin.

2. *or* **Sar·des** \ˈsär-dēz\. Ancient city in Asia Minor, in a strategic position in the Hermus Valley ab. 50 mi. (80 km.) E of Smyrna; chief city and ✻ of ancient kingdom of Lydia from 7th cent. B.C.; fell to Persians c. 546 B.C.; passed to Romans 133 B.C.; destroyed by earthquake 17 A.D.; rebuilt by Romans; one of the Seven Churches of Asia Minor addressed in the New Testament Book of Revelations; destroyed 1402 by Turkic ruler Timur. Site has many ruins, esp. of a major Ionic temple; earliest known coins (700 B.C.) found here.

Sardis Lake. Reservoir, N Mississippi; created 1940 by damming of Tallahatchie River for flood control.

Sa·reks National Park \ˈsär-ˌeks\. National park, N Sweden; 735 sq. mi. (1904 sq. km.); one of the largest wilderness regions in W Europe; glaciers; estab. 1909.

Sa·rek·tjåk·ko \ˌsär-ek-ˈchȯ-kō\. Peak in Kjølen Mts., N Sweden, near source of Luleålv River; 6854 ft. (2089 m.).

Sarema. See SAAREMAA.

Sar–e Pol *or* **Sar–i–pul** \ˈsär-ē-ˌpōl\ *or* **Sir–i–pul** \ˈsir-\. Town, N Afghanistan, 75 mi. (121 km.) SW of Mazār-e Sharīf; chief town of a former khanate of the same name.

Sa·rep·ta \sə-ˈrep-tə\ *or* **Zar·e·phath** \ˈzar-ə-ˌfath\. Ancient town of Phoenicia, subject to Sidon, on the coast ab. 8 mi. (13 km.) S of it; residence of the prophet Elijah (*1 Kings* xvii. 8–24).

Sa·re·ra Bay. See CENDERAWASIH, TELUK.

Sar·gas·so Sea \sär-ˈga-sō\. The large tract of comparatively still water in the North Atlantic Ocean; usu. considered as lying bet. the parallels 20° to 35°N and the meridians 30° to 70°W; so named from the floating seaweed there.

Sar·gent \ˈsär-jənt\. County in SE North Dakota. See table at NORTH DAKOTA.

Sar·go·dha \sər-ˈgō-də\. Town, Punjab, Pakistan, 106 mi. (171 km.) WNW of Lahore; met. area pop. (1981c) 291,362; railroad junction and industrial center, producing textiles, soap, chemicals, flour, and vegetable oils; grain market.

Sarh \ˈsär\; *formerly* **Fort–Ar·cham·bault** \ˌfȯr-ˌär-shäⁿ-ˈbō\. City, S Chad, on Chari River; pop. (1992e) 129,600.

Sā·rī \sä-ˈrē\. Town, ✻ of Māzanderān prov., N Iran, 17 mi. (27 km.) E of Bābol; pop. (1986c) 141,020.

Sa·ria·ya \ˌsär-ˈyä-yə\. Municipality, Quezon prov., Luzon, Philippines, 7 mi. (11 km.) WNW of Lucena; pop. (1980c) 74,148.

Sa·ri Ba·ir \ˌsär-ē-bä-ˈyir\ *or Turk.* **Sa·rı Ba·yır** \ˈsä-rə-bä-ˈyər\. Rugged hills in cen. Gallipoli Penin., Turkey in Europe; scene of WWI battle 1915.

Sa·ri·gan \ˌsär-i-ˈgän\ *or* **Sa·ri·guan** \-ˈgwän\. Small island, Northern Mariana Is., 100 mi. (161 km.) N of Saipan, 16°42′N, 145°47′E; highest point 1801 ft. (549 m.).

Sa·rı·ka·miş *or* **Sa·ri·ka·mish** \ˌsär-i-kä-ˈmish\. Town, SW Kars prov., NE Turkey in Asia, ab. 30 mi. (48 km.) SW of the city of Kars; formerly included in Russian Armenia. Scene of battle Dec. 1914 in WWI in which Turks were decisively defeated by Russians.

Sarine. See SAANE.

Sar–i–pul. See SAR-E POL.

Sarī Qūl. See ZORKUL, LAKE.

Sa·ri·ta \sə-ˈrē-tə\. Village, ⊗ of Kenedy co., S Texas.

Sa·ri·wŏn \ˈsä-ˈrē-ˈwən\. Town, SW North Korea, 36 mi. (58 km.) S of P'yŏngyang.

Sar·ju \ˈsär-jü\. River, W Nepal and Uttar Pradesh, N India; flows NW and S into the Ghāghara River; ab. 150 mi. (240 km.) long.

Sark \ˈsärk\. **1.** *or Fr.* **Sercq** \ˈserk\. One of the Channel Is., United Kingdom, in the English Channel; 2 sq. mi. (5 sq. km.); pop. (1986e) 500; comprises **Great Sark** and **Little Sark** connected by an isthmus; included in Guernsey bailiwick.

2. Small stream, S Scotland. See ESK 2.

Sar·kad \ˈshör-ˌköd\. Commune, Békés co., SE Hungary, 60 mi. (96 km.) S of Debrecen, near Romanian border; pop. (1980p) 11,937.

Sar·lat \sär-ˈlä\ *or* **Sarlat–la–Ca·né·da** \-lȧ-kȧ-ˈnā-də\. Town, Dordogne dept., SW cen. France, ab. 32 mi. (51 km.) SE of Périgueux; 16th cent. cathedral; numerous old houses (14th–17th cents.).

Sar·ma·tia \sär-ˈmā-shə\. Land of Sarmatians (fl. 6th cent. B.C.–4th cent. A.D.) without definite boundaries in S Russia in Europe and E Balkans.

Sar·mien·to \ˌsär-ˈmyen-tō\. See GENERAL SARMIENTO.

Sarmiento, Mount. Peak, in SW Tierra del Fuego I., Chile; 7218 ft. (2200 m.).

Sar·mi·zeg·e·tu·sa \ˈsär-mē-ˌze-jə-ˈtü-sə\. Ancient town, SW cen. Dacia, ESE of modern Lugoj in W Romania; ✻ of Dacia; captured by Roman Emperor Trajan early 2d cent. A.D.

Sar·nath \sär-ˈnät\. Archaeological site, Uttar Pradesh, N India, 3.5 mi. (6 km.) N of Varanasi; here was the Deer Park in which Buddha first taught. Ruins consist of building remains, the great stupa commemorating the site of Buddha's first sermon, and remains of 3d cent. B.C. Emperor Aśoka's memorial pillar.

Sar·nen \ˈzär-nən\. Commune, ✻ of Obwalden demicanton and of former Unterwalden canton, cen. Switzerland, 37 mi. (60 km.) E of Bern; pop. (1989c) 8328; resort.

Sarnen, Lake of *or Ger.* **Sar·ner See** \ˈzär-nər-ˌzā\. Lake, Obwalden demicanton, cen. Switzerland; ab. 4 mi. (6 km.) long and 1 mi. (2 km.) wide; 3 sq. mi. (8 sq. km.); max. depth 170 ft. (52 m.).

Sarner–Aa. See AA 2.

Sar·nia–Clear·wa·ter \ˈsär-nē-ə-ˈklir-ˌwȯ-tər, -ˌwä-\. City, ⊗ of Lambton co., SE Ontario, Canada, on St. Clair River at S end of Lake Huron; pop. (1991c) 74,167; opp. Port Huron, Michigan, and connected with it by railroad tunnel and highway bridge; important lake port; petrochemicals, plastics; oil refineries, saltworks. Settled 1807 by French and 1833 by English.

Sar·no \ˈsär-nō\. Commune, Salerno prov., Campania, S Italy, 12 mi. (19 km.) NW of the seaport of Salerno; pop. (1991p) 27,816; sulfur springs nearby.

Saron, Plain of. See SHARON, PLAIN OF.

Sa·ron·ic Gulf \sə-ˈrä-nik\ *also* **Gulf of Ae·gi·na** \ē-ˈjī-nə\ *or Gk.* **Sa·ro·ni·kós Kól·pos** \sä-ˈrō-nē-ˌkōs-ˈköl-ˌpōs\; *anc.* **Si·nus Sa·ron·i·cus** \ˈsī-nəs-sə-ˈrä-ni-kəs\. Inlet of Aegean Sea on SE coast of Greece, S of Attica dept.

Sa·ron·no \sä-ˈrȯn-nō\. Commune, Varese prov., Lombardy, N Italy, 18 mi. (29 km.) SE of the commune of Varese; pop. (1989c) 38,665; pilgrimage church begun late 15th cent.

Sa·ros Gulf \ˈsar-ˌäs\. Inlet of NE Aegean Sea extending E into SW coast of Turkey in Europe, at the base of Gallipoli Penin.

Sarps·borg \ˈsärps-ˌbȯr\. City, ⊗ of Østfold co., SE Norway, on W bank of Glåma River; pop. (1990c) 11,782; paper mills; founded early 11th cent.; destroyed c. 1567; rebuilt 1838.

Sarps·foss \ˈsärps-ˌfȯs\. Waterfall in Glåma River near its mouth, Østfold co., SE Norway; 60 ft. (18 m.) high and 164 ft. (50 m.) wide.

Sar·py \ˈsär-pē\. County in E Nebraska. See table at NEBRASKA.

Sarre. **1.** River, France. See SAAR 1.
2. State, Germany. See SAARLAND.

Sarre, La. See LA SARRE.

Sarrebruck. See SAARBRÜCKEN.

Sarre·gue·mines \ˌsär-gə-ˈmēn\; *formerly* **Saar·ge·münd** \ˌzär-gə-ˈmuent\. Town, Moselle dept., NE France, on Sarre River at German border 42 mi. (68 km.) E of Metz.

Sar·ria \ˈsär-yä\. Commune, Lugo prov., NW Spain, 19 mi. (31 km.) SSE of the commune of Lugo; pop. (1991c) 12,611.

Sars, Le. See LE SARS.

Sar·si·na \ˈsärs-ᵊn-ə\. Ancient town in mountains of N Umbria, cen. Italy; possibly birthplace of Roman playwright Plautus c. 254 B.C.

Sars·toon *or* **Sars·tún** \sär-ˈstün\. River, E cen. Guatemala; flows E into the Gulf of Amatique; forms S boundary of Belize; ab. 70 mi. (115 km.) long.

Sarsuti. See SARASVATI 1.

Sarthe \ˈsärt\. **1.** River, NW France; rises in Orne dept., flows S to unite with Mayenne River near Angers and form Maine River; 177 mi. (285 km.) long.
2. Department of NW France. See table at FRANCE.

Sar·trou·ville \ˌsär-trü-ˈvēl\. Commune, Yvelines dept., N France, NW suburb of Paris on Seine River.

Sarum, New. See SALISBURY 6.

Sarum, Old. See OLD SARUM.

Sarus. See SEYHAN 1.

Sa·ry·su \ˌsär-ē-ˈsü\. River, cen. Kazakhstan; flows S into the desert, not quite reaching the Syr Dar'ya; ab. 520 mi. (835 km.) long.

Sar·za·na \särd-ˈzä-nä\. Commune, La Spezia prov., Liguria, NW Italy, 7 mi. (11 km.) E of the seaport of La Spezia; pop. (1991p) 19,557; cathedral begun early 13th cent.

Sa·sa·la·guan, Mount \ˌsä-sä-lä-ˈgwän\. Mountain at S end of Guam, Mariana Is.; 1120 ft. (341 m.).

Sa·sa·ram \ˈsə-sə-ˌräm\. Town, W Bihar, NE India, 90 mi. (145 km.) WSW of Patna; pop. (1991p) 98,220; contains tomb of Emperor Shēr Shāh (reigned 1540–45), one of India's most notable examples of Pathan architecture, and tombs of Shēr Shāh's father and son.

Sasau. See SÁZAVA.

Sa·se·bo \ˈsä-sā-ˌbō\. Seaport city on large inlet of outer Ōmura Bay, Nagasaki prefecture, NW Kyūshū, Japan; pop. (1992c) 245,017; a commercial and fishing port; formerly site of a large naval base (estab. late 19th cent.); heavily bombed during WWII.

Saseno. See SAZAN.

Sa·ser Kan·gri \ˈsäs-ər-ˈkäŋ-grē\. Mountain in the Karakoram Range, in part of Jammu and Kashmir controlled by India; 25,172 ft. (7672 m.).

Sas·katch·e·wan \sə-ˈska-chə-wən, sa-, -ˌwän\. **1.** River, SW and S cen. Canada, flowing from the Rocky Mts. E into N Lake Winnipeg; upper part divided into two branches, **North Saskatchewan** (760 mi. or 1223 km.) and **South Saskatchewan** (865 mi. or 1392 km.); length of river after confluence of its branches, E of Prince Albert, 340 mi. (547 km.). The South Saskatchewan with its tributary the Bow along with the Nelson River have a total length of 1600 mi. (2574 km.). The main tributaries of the North Saskatchewan are the Battle, Brazeau, and Clearwater; of the South Saskatchewan the Red Deer, Bow, and Oldman.
2. Province, W Canada, cen. province of the Prairie Provinces, bounded on N by Northwest Territories, on E by Manitoba, on S by U.S. (North Dakota and Montana), and on W by Alberta; ✻ Regina. See table at CANADA.
Physical features: Entirely a plains region with prairie in S and wooded country containing many lakes and swamps in N. Highest point in SW corner 4546 ft. (1386 m.); av. elev. 1000 to 2000 ft. (305 to 610 m.). Watered in N by headstreams of the Mackenzie flowing into Lake Athabaska, in cen. part by the Churchill, in S cen. and SW by the Saskatchewan and branches, and in the SE by Assiniboine and tributaries. Lakes include Athabaska (E half), Reindeer, Wollaston, Churchill, Rouge.
Chief products: Wheat, oats, barley; livestock raising; potash, oil, natural gas, uranium, copper.
Chief cities: Saskatoon, Regina, Prince Albert, Moose Jaw.
History: For two centuries 1670–1869 region controlled by Hudson's Bay Company; explored by Englishman Henry Kelsey early 1690s; part of Northwest Terr. to 1869 with few settlements before that date; became part of Dominion of Canada 1870; estab. as a province 1905.
3. Former district, cen. Canada, bet. Athabaska on N and Assiniboia on S, bet. 52° and 55°N; 101,000 sq. mi. (261,590 sq. km.); ✻ Battleford; formed 1882 out of Northwest Territories; most of it included in Saskatchewan prov. 1905.

Sas·ka·toon \ˌsas-kə-ˈtün\. City, S cen. Saskatchewan, Canada, on South Saskatchewan River 150 mi. (241 km.) NW of Regina; pop. (1991c) 186,058; center of an important grain-farming region; creameries, meatpacking plants, flour mills, oil refineries, potash mines; museum; symphony; Univ. of Saskatchewan (1907), St. Andrew's Coll. (1912), Lutheran Theological Seminary (1913), St. Thomas More Coll. (1936); settled 1883.

Sas·ol·burg \ˈsä-səl-ˌbərg\. Town, near N border of Free State, Rep. of South Africa, S of Johannesburg; area pop. (1985c) 29,310.

Sason. See SAZAN.

Sas·sa·fras \ˈsa-sə-ˌfras\. River, NE Maryland; rises in NW Delaware, flows W into upper Chesapeake Bay; ab. 20 mi. (32 km.) long.

Sassafras Mountain. Peak, Pickens co., NW South Carolina; ab. 3560 ft. (1085 m.); highest point in the state.

Sas·san·dra \sə-ˈsan-drə\. **1.** River, W Ivory Coast, flows S into the Atlantic Ocean; ab. 350 mi. (565 km.) long.
2. Seaport at mouth of Sassandra River, SW Ivory Coast, 145 mi. (233 km.) W of Abidjan.

Sas·sa·ri \ˈsä-sä-rē\. **1.** Province of Sardinia, Italy. See table at ITALY.
2. Commune, its ✻, 110 mi. (177 km.) NNW of Cagliari; pop. (1991p) 116,989; trades in agricultural produce; cathedral; two Romanesque churches; university (estab. 1562, university status 1617). In Middle Ages came under Genoa 1284; to Aragon 1323; to house of Savoy with all of Sardinia 1720.

Sasseno. See SAZAN.

Sas·so·fer·ra·to \ˌsä-sō-fer-ˈrä-tō\. Commune, Ancona prov., Marche, cen. Italy, 37 mi. (60 km.) WSW of the seaport of Ancona; pop. (1981p) 7277; nearby at ancient town of **Sen·ti·num** \sen-ˈtī-nəm\ Romans defeated allied Etruscan, Samnite, and Gaulish forces 295 B.C., thereby establishing themselves in cen. Italy.

Sasstown. See SASTOWN.

Sas·suo·lo \sä-ˈswȯ-lō\. Commune, Modena prov., Emilia-Romagna, N Italy, 11 mi. (18 km.) SW of the commune of Modena; pop. (1981p) 39,931.

Sas·town *or* **Sass·town** \ˈsas-ˌtau̇n\. Coastal town, SE Liberia, 53 mi. (85 km.) WNW of Cape Palmas.

Sa·ta, Cape \ˈsä-tä\. Cape, S extremity of Kyūshū, Japan.

Sa·ta·ra \sə-ˈtär-ə\. Town, S Maharashtra, W India, near Krishna River 120 mi. (193 km.) SE of Bombay; pop. (1991p) 95,133; 12th cent. fort; came under Muslim rule 14th cent.; under Marathas was at one time ✻ of the Maratha kingdom; came under British rule mid-19th cent.

Sat·el·lite Beach \ˈsat-ᵊl-ˌīt\. Town, Brevard co., E Florida, on Atlantic coast 15 mi. (24 km.) SSE of Cocoa; pop. (1990c) 9889.

Sa·til·la \sə-ˈti-lə\. River, S and SE Georgia; rises in Irwin co., flows E, S, and again E into St. Andrew Sound; ab. 220 mi. (355 km.) long; navigable at its mouth.

Satit. See TEKEZE.

Sat·ka \ˈsät-kə\; *formerly* **Sat·kin·ski Za·vod** \sät-ˈkin-skē-zə-ˈvȯt, -ˈvȯd\. Town, Chelyabinsk Oblast, W Russia in Asia, ab. 100 mi. (160 km.) W of the city of Chelyabinsk; pop. (1991e) 51,100.

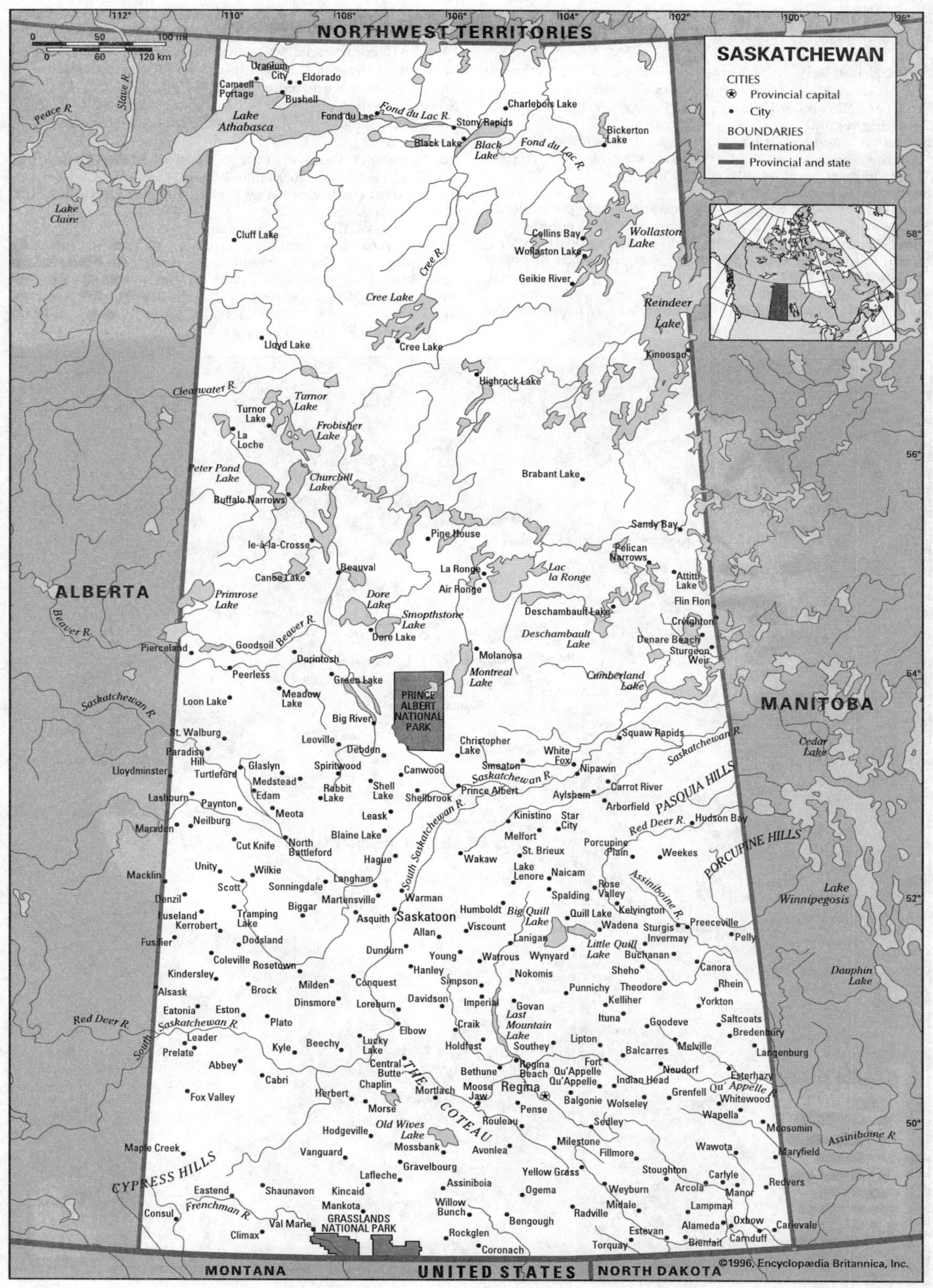
SASKATCHEWAN
CITIES
Provincial capital
City
BOUNDARIES
International
Provincial and state
0 50 100 mi
0 60 120 km
112°
110°
108°
106°
104°
102°
100°
98°
58°
56°
54°
52°
50°
NORTHWEST TERRITORIES
ALBERTA
MANITOBA
MONTANA
UNITED STATES
NORTH DAKOTA
Uranium City
Eldorado
Camsell Portage
Bushell
Lake Athabasca
Fond du Lac
Fond du Lac R.
Stony Rapids
Charlebois Lake
Black Lake
Black Lake
Fond du Lac R.
Bickerton Lake
Peace R.
Slave R.
Lake Claire
Cluff Lake
Cree R.
Collins Bay
Wollaston Lake
Wollaston Lake
Geikie River
Cree Lake
Cree Lake
Reindeer Lake
Kinoosao
Lloyd Lake
Highrock Lake
Clearwater R.
Turnor Lake
Turnor Lake
La Loche
Frobisher Lake
Peter Pond Lake
Churchill Lake
Brabant Lake
Buffalo Narrows
Pine House
Sandy Bay
Ile-à-la-Crosse
Pelican Narrows
La Ronge
Lac la Ronge
Air Ronge
Attitti Lake
Canoe Lake
Beauval
Primrose Lake
Dore Lake
Smoothstone Lake
Dore Lake
Deschambault Lake
Deschambault Lake
Flin Flon
Creighton
Beaver R.
Beaver R.
Pierceland
Goodsoil
Dorintosh
Molanosa
Denare Beach
Sturgeon Weir
Peerless
Green Lake
Montreal Lake
Cumberland Lake
PRINCE ALBERT NATIONAL PARK
Saskatchewan R.
Meadow Lake
Loon Lake
Big River
St. Walburg
Leoville
Christopher Lake
Squaw Rapids
Saskatchewan R.
Cedar Lake
Paradise Hill
Debden
White Fox
Lloydminster
Turtleford
Glaslyn
Spiritwood
Canwood
Smeaton
Nipawin
Medstead
Shell Lake
Saskatchewan R.
Lashburn
Edam
Rabbit Lake
Shellbrook
Prince Albert
Aylsham
Carrot River
PASQUIA HILLS
Paynton
Meota
Arborfield
Marsden
Neilburg
Leask
Kinistino
Star City
Hudson Bay
Blaine Lake
Red Deer R.
PORCUPINE HILLS
Cut Knife
North Battleford
South Saskatchewan R.
Melfort
Porcupine Plain
Weekes
Unity
Wilkie
Hague
Wakaw
St. Brieux
Macklin
Scott
Sonningdale
Langham
Lake Lenore
Naicam
Assiniboine R.
Lake Winnipegosis
Denzil
Martensville
Warman
Rose Valley
Spalding
Luseland
Tramping Lake
Biggar
Asquith
Saskatoon
Humboldt
Big Quill Lake
Quill Lake
Kelvington
Kerrobert
Allan
Viscount
Wadena
Sturgis
Preeceville
Fusilier
Dodsland
Lanigan
Little Quill Lake
Invermay
Pelly
Coleville
Dundurn
Young
Watrous
Wynyard
Buchanan
Kindersley
Rosetown
Hanley
Nokomis
Sheho
Canora
Alsask
Brock
Milden
Conquest
Simpson
Punnichy
Theodore
Dauphin Lake
Dinsmore
Davidson
Imperial
Rhein
Eatonia
Eston
Loreburn
Govan
Kelliher
Yorkton
Red Deer R.
South Saskatchewan R.
Plato
Last Mountain Lake
Ituna
Goodeve
Saltcoats
Leader
Elbow
Craik
Bredenbury
Prelate
Kyle
Beechy
Lucky Lake
Holdfast
Southey
Lipton
Balcarres
Melville
Langenburg
Abbey
Central Butte
Regina Beach
Fort Qu'Appelle
Neudorf
Esterhazy
Cabri
Chaplin
Bethune
Qu'Appelle
Indian Head
Qu'Appelle R.
THE COTEAU
Mortlach
Moose Jaw
Regina
Grenfell
Whitewood
Fox Valley
Herbert
Balgonie
Wolseley
Morse
Pense
Wapella
Old Wives Lake
Rouleau
Sedley
Hodgeville
Moosomin
Assiniboine R.
Maple Creek
Mossbank
Milestone
Vanguard
Avonlea
Fillmore
Wawota
Maryfield
CYPRESS HILLS
Gravelbourg
Lafleche
Yellow Grass
Stoughton
Carlyle
Redvers
Eastend
Shaunavon
Kincaid
Assiniboia
Ogema
Weyburn
Arcola
Manor
Frenchman R.
Mankota
Willow Bunch
Midale
Lampman
Consul
Val Marie
GRASSLANDS NATIONAL PARK
Bengough
Radville
Oxbow
Alameda
Carievale
Climax
Rockglen
Estevan
Carnduff
Coronach
Torquay
Bienfait
©1996, Encyclopædia Britannica, Inc.

Sat·na *or* **Sut·na** \ˈsət-nə\. Town, NE Madhya Pradesh, NE India, 90 mi. (145 km.) SW of Allahabad; pop. (1991p) 156,321.

Sá·tor·al·jaúj·hely \ˈshä-ˌtōr-ȯi-ˌjaůj-ˌhā\. City, Borsod-Abaúj-Zemplén co., NE Hungary, on a tributary of the Bodrog near Slovakian border; pop. (1980p) 19,252; in grape-growing region.

Sat·pu·ra Range \ˈsät-pə-rə\. Range of hills, W cen. India, bet. the Narmada and Tapti rivers; av. elev. ab. 3000 ft. (915 km.); highest point 4429 ft. (1350 m.).

Satrunjaya. See PALITANA 2.

Sa·tsu·ma \ˈsät-sü-ˌmä, sät-ˈsü-mä\. Former province, S Kyūshū, Japan, now in Kagoshima prefecture; noted for its pottery, dating from 16th cent. Held as fief by powerful Shimazu family clan 17th–19th cents.; reorganized as Kagoshima prefecture 1867.

Sattima. See LESATIMA.

Sa·tu Ma·re \ˈsä-tü-ˈmä-rā\. **1.** County of NW Romania. See table at ROMANIA.

2. *or Hung.* **Szat·már–Né·me·ti** \ˈsȯt-ˌmär-ˈnā-me-tē\. City, its ✻, near Hungarian border on Someşul River; pop. (1989c) 136,881; commercial and industrial center, producing machinery, rolling stock, electric motors, food products, furniture; palace; mentioned early 13th cent.

Sa·tun \sä-ˈtün\ *also* **Sa·tul** *or* **Se·tul** \sä-ˈtün—*sic*\. **1.** Area of SW Thailand; formerly one of the Malay States under Thai protection.

2. Town, SW Thailand, near W coast of Malay Penin., just NNW of Perlis state in Malaysia; pop. (1991e) 21,844.

Sa·tur·ni·an \sə-ˈtər-nē-ən\. Original name of Capitoline Hill. See SEVEN HILLS.

Sau. See SAVA 1.

Sa·u·di Ara·bia \ˈsaů-dē-ə-ˈrā-bē-ə, sä-ˈü-dē\; *officially* **Kingdom of Saudi Arabia** *or Arab.* **Al–Mam·la·kah al–ʻAra·bī·yah as–Sa·ʻūdī·yah** \ȧl-ˈmȧm-lə-kə-ȧl-ˌȧ-rə-ˈbē-yə-ˌȧs-ˌsä-ü-ˈdē-yə\. Kingdom, Arabian Penin., SW Asia; ab. 865,000 sq. mi. (2,240,350 sq. km.); pop. (1993e) 17,419,000; ✻ Riyadh.

Physical features: A plateau region, av. elev. 2500 ft. (762 m.), with band of highlands having elevations of 7000 to 10,000 ft. (2134 to 3048 m.) in W near Red Sea coast in Hejaz; includes great deserts of An Nafūd (in the N) and Rub' al Khali (in the S).

Chief export: Oil (one of the world's largest producers); other products include natural gas, gypsum; dates, wheat; desalinated water, petrochemicals; pastoralism.

Chief towns: Riyadh, Jidda, Mecca.

History: A dual kingdom formed 1927 by Ibn Sa'ūd as king of Nejd and Hejaz (*qq.v.*) and as a single kingdom named Saudi Arabia 1932; engaged in war with Yemen Arab Republic over boundary dispute 1934; oil discovered 1938; neutral in WWII until declaration of war on Germany 1945; joined UN and was founding member of Arab League 1945; supported Arab cause in Arab-Israeli conflicts; Saudi Arabia-Oman boundary dispute basis of friction with Great Britain during early 1950s; supported royalists in Yemen Arab Republic's civil war of 1960s; founding member of OPEC 1960; participated in oil embargo 1973; joined Gulf Cooperation Council 1981; participated in Persian Gulf War against Iraq 1991.

Sauer. See SÛRE.

Sau·ga·tuck \ˈsȯ-gə-ˌtək\. **1.** River, SW Connecticut; rises in cen. Fairfield co., flows S into Long Island Sound; ab. 20 mi. (32 km.) long.

2. City, Allegan co., SW Michigan, SW of Grand Rapids; pop. (1990c) 954; Lake Michigan resort and artists colony.

Saugeen Peninsula. See BRUCE PENINSULA.

Sau·ger·ties \ˈsȯ-gər-ˌtēz\. Village, Ulster co., SE New York, on W side of Hudson River 11 mi. (18 km.) N of Kingston; pop. (1990c) 3915; former river port.

Saugor. See SAGAR 2.

Sau·gus \ˈsȯ-gəs\. **1.** Town, Essex co., NE corner of Massachusetts, 8 mi. (13 km.) NNE of Boston; pop. (1990c) 25,549; site of the nation's first successful ironworks.

2. Former name of Lynn, Massachusetts. See LYNN 2.

Saujbulagh. See MAHĀBĀD.

Sauk \ˈsȯk\. **1.** River, cen. Minnesota; flows from Osakis Lake, SW Todd co., to Mississippi River above St. Cloud; 120 mi. (193 km.) long.

2. County in S cen. Wisconsin. See table at WISCONSIN.

Sauk Centre. City, Stearns co., cen. Minnesota, on the Sauk River; pop. (1990c) 3581; dairy farms; birthplace of Sinclair Lewis 1885 and setting for several of his novels.

Sauk Rapids. Village, Benton co., cen. Minnesota, on Mississippi River 3 mi. (5 km.) N of St. Cloud; pop. (1990c) 7825.

Sauk Village. Village, Cook co., NE Illinois, S of Chicago, near the Indiana border; pop. (1990c) 9926.

Saulk·ville \ˈsȯk-vil, ˈsäk-\. Village, Ozaukee co., SE Wisconsin, 10 mi. (16 km.) N of Milwaukee; pop. (1990c) 3695.

Sault Sainte Ma·rie \ˌsü-ˌsānt-mə-ˈrē\. **1.** City, ⊗ of Chippewa co., E Upper Penin. of Michigan, at the falls on St. Marys River (*q.v.*) bet. Lake Huron and Lake Superior; pop. (1990c) 14,689; opp. Canadian city of the same name; dairy products, lumber; center of a summer-resort region; Fort Brady (estab. 1822); Lake Superior State Univ. (1946). Site reached by French explorers Étienne Brulé c. 1618 and Jean Nicolet 1634; mission founded by Jacques Marquette 1668; taken by British 1762; ceded to U.S. 1783; first locks built 1855; incorp. as village 1879, as city 1887.

2. City, ⊗ of Algoma dist., S Ontario, Canada, at the falls on St. Marys River opp. Sault Sainte Marie, Michigan; pop. (1991c) 81,476; iron and steel, coke, lumber, chemicals, beer; in summer-resort region; site reached by French explorer Étienne Brulé 1622; mission estab. 1668; ceded to British 1763; first lock built 1797–98 and destroyed in War of 1812; incorp. as town 1887, as city 1912.

Sault Sainte Marie Canals *or* **Soo Canals** \ˈsü\. Two U.S. ship canals and a Canadian ship canal, St. Marys Falls on St. Marys River (*q.v.*) in E cen. North America; first U.S. canal completed 1855; since then replaced and enlarged; now divided: the N canal (U.S.), completed 1919, is 1.61 mi. (2.59 km.) long, 80 ft. (24 m.) wide and 24.5 ft. (7.5 m.) deep; the S canal (U.S.), completed 1896, is 1.56 mi. (2.5 km.) long, 100 ft. (31 m.) wide and 18 ft. (5.5 m.) deep; the Canadian canal, completed 1895, is 1.38 mi. (2.22 km.) long, 150 ft. (46 m.) wide and 22 ft. (7 m.) deep; there are five locks (one on the Canadian canal), one of the two largest, the Davis lock, being 1350 ft. (411 m.) long bet. the gates, 80 ft. (24 m.) wide and having a lift of 20.5 ft. (6.2 m.).

Sau·mur \sō-ˈmu̅e̅r\. Commune, Maine-et-Loire dept., W France, on Loire River 28 mi. (45 km.) SE of Angers; pop. (1990c) 31,894; mushrooms; 14th–16th cent. chateau; 16th cent. town hall; 12th cent. church; site of cavalry school (estab. 1768, now training center for French armored forces). Taken by count of Anjou Fulk III (Nerra) c. 1026 from counts of Blois; passed to French crown early 13th cent.; Protestant school estab. late 16th cent.; in 16th–17th cents. a major center of French Protestantism and declined after revocation of Edict of Nantes 1685; in WWII heavily damaged in fighting 1940.

Sau·mu·rois \ˌsō-mu̅e̅r-ˈwä\. Historical region of NW France; bounded on N by Anjou, on E by Touraine, on S and W by Poitou; now included in Maine-et-Loire and Vienne depts.; ✻ Saumur.

Saun·ders \ˈsȯn-dərz\. County in E Nebraska. See table at NEBRASKA.

Saunders, Cape. Cape, SE coast of South I., New Zealand, S of entrance to Otago Harbour.

Sau·rash·tra \sau̇-ˈräsh-trə\. Former state, W India; roughly coextensive with Kathiawar Penin.; estab. 1948; in 1956 became part of Bombay state; since 1960 in Gujarat state.

Sau·ri·mo \sau̇-ˈrē-mü, -mō\. Town, ✻ of Lunda Sul prov., NE Angola.

Sau·sa·li·to \ˌsȯ-sə-ˈlē-tō\. Suburban residential city, Marin co., W California, on San Francisco Bay 3 mi. (5 km.) NW of San Francisco; pop. (1990c) 7152.

Sau·ternes \sō-ˈtern, sȯ-, -ˈtərn\. Commune, Gironde dept., SW France, on tributary of the Garonne ab. 20 mi. (32 km.) SSE of Bordeaux; center of a district incl. Barsac, Bommes, Preignac, and Fargues, noted for production of white wine.

Sa·va \ˈsä-vä\. **1.** *or* **Sa·ve** \ˈsä-və\ *or Ger.* **Sau** \ˈzau̇\ *or Hung.* **Szá·va** \ˈsä-ˌvö\; *anc.* **Sa·vus** \ˈsā-vəs\. River, S Europe; rises in Slovenia near Italian border, flows E through Croatia, along border bet. Croatia and Bosnia and Herzegovina, and across half of N Yugoslavia into Danube River at Belgrade; 584 mi. (940 km.) long; navigable for 362 mi. (582 km.).

2. Former county, N Yugoslavia; ⊗ Zagreb; later Savska co.; now approx. coextensive with Croatia.

Sav·age \ˈsa-vij\. Village, Scott co., SE Minnesota, 9 mi. (14 km.) E of Minneapolis; pop. (1990c) 9906.

Savage Island. See NIUE.

Sav·age's Station \ˈsa-vi-jəz\. Battle site near Richmond, Virginia, where Confederates made unsuccessful attack on Union troops June 29, 1862, one of the "Seven Days' Battles" of the Civil War.

Sa·vai'i *or* **Sa·vaii** \sə-ˈvī-ē\. Island, Samoa, in SW Pacific Ocean; 700 sq. mi. (1813 sq. km.); largest island in Samoa group; has many rocky mountains, several of them semiactive volcanoes; highest point Mauga Silisili 6095 ft. (1856 m.).

Savalan. See SABALĀN.

Sa·van·na \sə-ˈva-nə\. City, Carroll co., NW Illinois, on Mississippi River 55 mi. (88 km.) WSW of Rockford; pop. (1990c) 3819.

Sa·van·nah \sə-ˈva-nə\. **1.** Navigable river, E Georgia; formed by confluence of Tugaloo and Seneca rivers in W Anderson co., NW South Carolina, flows SE forming Georgia-South Carolina boundary, and empties into Atlantic Ocean at Savannah; 314 mi. (505 km.) long.

2. City, ⊗ of Chatham co., SE Georgia, at mouth of Savannah River; pop. (1990c) 137,560; oldest city in Georgia and its principal seaport; cotton market; paper products, sugar, fertilizers, chemicals; shipyards; Savannah State Coll. (1890), Armstrong State Coll. (1935), Savannah Coll. of Art and Design (1978). First English settlement in Georgia, founded by James Oglethorpe 1733; ✻ of prov. and later state of Georgia 1754–86; in Civil War captured by Union forces under Gen. William T. Sherman Dec. 21, 1864.

3. City, ⊗ of Andrew co., NW Missouri, 14 mi. (23 km.) N of St. Joseph; pop. (1990c) 4352.

4. Town, ⊗ of Hardin co., SW Tennessee, on Tennessee River 45 mi. (72 km.) ESE of Jackson; pop. (1990c) 6547.

Sa·van·na·khet \sə-ˌvä-nə-ˈket\. Town, S Laos, on Mekong River ab. 130 mi. (210 km.) NW of Pakxē; pop. (1985c) 96,652.

Savanna–la–Mar \-lə-ˈmär\. Seaport on S coast at W end of Jamaica, West Indies; pop. (1991p) 16,553.

Sa·vant·va·di \ˌsä-vənt-ˈvä-dē\ *or* **Sa·want·wa·di** \ˌsä-wənt-ˈwä-dē\. **1.** Former state, India, now part of Maharashtra state; 937 sq. mi. (2427 sq. km.).

2. Town, Maharashtra state, W India, near coast 63 mi. (101 km.) SSW of Kolhapur; formerly ✻ of Savantvadi state.

Savaria. See SZOMBATHELY.

Sa·ve \ˈsä-vē\ *or Eng.* **Sa·bi** \ˈsä-bē\. River, SE Africa; rises in Zimbabwe, flows ESE across border into Mozambique, continues E across S Mozambique into Mozambique Channel; ab. 400 mi. (645 km.) long; its large tributary in Zimbabwe is the **Lun·di** \ˈlən-dē\ River.

Save 1. \ˈsȧv\. River, S France; rises on the slopes of the Pyrenees, flows NE into Garonne River 15 mi. (24 km.) NNW of Toulouse; ab. 90 mi. (145 km.) long.

2. River, S Europe. See SAVA 1.

Sa·verne \sə-ˈvern\ *or* **Za·bern** \ˈtsä-bərn\. Commune, Bas-Rhin dept., NE France, ab. 20 mi. (32 km.) NW of Strasbourg; important in Roman times when it was called **Tres Ta·ber·nae** \ˌtrēz-tə-ˈbər-nē\; held by bishops of Metz under the Carolingians and by the bishops of Strasbourg 13th–18th cents.; several ruined castles in vicinity; scene of incident ("Zabern affair") Nov. 1913 just before WWI when a German officer insulted Alsatian civilians leading to problems within Germany.

Savezna Republika Jugoslavija. See YUGOSLAVIA.

Sa·vi·glia·no \ˌsä-vēl-ˈyä-nō\. Commune, Cuneo prov., Piedmont, NW Italy, 18 mi. (29 km.) NE of the commune of Cuneo; pop. (1981p) 18,650; abbey; notable church.

Sa·vi·gny–sur–Orge \ˌsȧ-vē-ˈnyē-su̇r-ˈȯrzh\. Commune, Essonne dept., N France, 9 mi. (14 km.) S of Paris.

Sa·vo \ˈsä-vō\. Small island, SE Solomon Is., W Pacific Ocean, ab. 8 mi. (13 km.) N of W end of Guadalcanal I. (Cape Esperance) and 18 mi. (29 km.) W of Florida I.; highest point 1600 ft. (488 m.). Notable for naval and air battles in Guadalcanal campaign of WWII, 1942.

Savoia. See SAVOY.

Sa·voie \sȧ-ˈvwä\. **1.** Department of France. See table at FRANCE.

2. Region, France and Italy. See SAVOY.

Sa·vo·na \sä-ˈvō-nä\. **1.** Province of Liguria, NW Italy. See table at ITALY.

2. Seaport, its ✻, on Gulf of Genoa 23 mi. (37 km.) WSW of Genoa; pop. (1991p) 67,137; iron and steel, glass; tanning, shipbuilding, food processing; late 16th cent. cathedral. First mentioned c. 205 B.C.; destroyed by Lombards c. 640; under Genoese rule 1528 ff.; under French 1805–15; to Savoy 1815; heavily bombed in WWII.

Sa·von·lin·na \ˈsä-vȯn-ˌlēn-nä\. City, Mikkeli prov., S Finland; pop. (1989c) 28,524; built on a large island in the Lake Saimaa region; 15th cent. castle; summer resort; founded 1639; during 18th cent. strategically important in Russo-Swedish wars.

Sa·voon·ga \sə-ˈvüŋ-gə\. City on N coast of St. Lawrence I., Bering Sea, Alaska; pop. (1990c) 519.

Sa·voy \sə-ˈvȯi\ *or Fr.* **Sa·voie** \sȧ-ˈvwȧ\ *or Ital.* **Sa·vo·ia** \sä-ˈvȯ-yä\. Historical region of SE France and NW Italy, of varying limits, now chiefly in French depts. of Haute-Savoie and Savoie; chief city Chambéry.

History: From 11th cent., counts of Savoy ruled area in region of W Alps as part of kingdom of Arles (*q.v.*) under suzerainty of Holy Roman Empire; became virtually independent and expanded its territory to include plain of Piedmont in Italy; elevated to duchy 1416 by Emperor Sigismund; territory scene of fighting in many wars; at times allied with France, at times with Italy; involved in wars bet. France and Spain with alternating allegiances; by Treaty of Utrecht 1713 received island of Sicily and held it until 1720 when it was exchanged for the island of Sardinia and the kingdom of Sardinia was formed (included Piedmont, Savoy, and island of Sardinia), the dukes of Savoy becoming kings of Sardinia; Savoy and Piedmont ceded to France late 18th cent.; areas restored and Genoa acquired 1815; in 1860 Sardinia, Genoa, and Piedmont joined other states of Italy to form kingdom of Italy with house of Savoy ruling through 1946, while terr. of Savoy, with Nice (*q.v.*), was ceded to France.

Savoy Alps. See table at ALPS.

Sav·ska \ˈsäv-skə\. Former county, N and NW Yugoslavia; ⊗ Zagreb; formed 1929, dissolved after WWII; coextensive with a large part of Croatia.

Sa·vu *or* **Sa·wu** *or Du.* **Sa·woe** \ˈsä-vü\. Island of the Lesser Sunda Is., Indonesia, WSW of Timor and SE of Sumba; 23 mi. (37 km.) long by 10 mi. (16 km.) wide; with nearby islands 200 sq. mi. (518 sq. km.); only port Seba on NW coast.

Savus. See SAVA 1.

Sa·vu·sa·vu Bay \ˌsä-vü-ˈsä-vü\. Inlet, S coast of Vanua Levu I., Fiji, W Pacific Ocean.

Savu Sea *or* **Sawu Sea** *or Du.* **Sawoe–Zee** \ˌsä-vü-ˈzā\. Part of Indian Ocean bordering Indonesia, lying S of Flores, Lomblen, and Pantar islands, W of Timor, N of Savu I., and E of Sumba I.; connected with Timor Sea by Roti Strait.

Sa·wan·kha·lok \sä-ˌwän-kä-ˈlōk\ *or* **Swan·ka·lok** \ˌswän-kä-ˈlōk\. Village, W Thailand, on left bank of Yom River 40 mi. (64 km.) NW of Phitsanulok; pop. (1991e) 20,433.

Sawantwadi. See SAVANTVADI.

Sa·watch Range \sə-ˈwäch\. A range of the Rocky Mts., cen. Colorado; highest peak Mt. Elbert, 14,433 ft. (4399 m.).

Sawfajjīn. See SOFEGGIN.

Saw Grass Lake \ˈsȯ-ˌgras\. Lake in S Brevard co., E cen. Florida; outlet St. Johns River flowing N.

Sawhāj. See SOHÂG.

Sawoe. See SAVU.

Sawoe–Zee. See SAVU SEA.

Saw·teeth \ˈsȯ-ˌtēth\. Mountain in Adirondack Mts., Essex co., NE New York; 4138 ft. (1261 m.).

Saw·tooth Mountain \ˈsȯ-ˌtüth\. Peak, Jeff Davis co., W Texas; 7748 ft. (2362 m.).

Sawtooth Range. Large group of mountain ranges, Custer, Blaine, and Camas cos., S cen. Idaho, just S of Salmon River Mts.; 40 mi. (64 km.) long; contains a number of peaks above 10,000 ft. (3050 m.), many alpine lakes, and the sources of Boise and Big Wood rivers; resort area and game reserves.

Sawtooth Ridge. Ridge in N cen. Washington, extending along the NE shore of Lake Chelan and along boundary bet. Okanogan and Chelan cos.

Sawu. See SAVU.

Sawu Sea. See SAVU SEA.

Saw·yer \ˈsȯ-yər\. County in NW Wisconsin. See table at WISCONSIN.

Saxa Ru·bra \ˌsak-sə-ˈrü-brə\. Town of ancient Etruria, Italy, on Flaminian Way ab. 9 mi. (14 km.) N of Rome, just W of the Tiber; scene 312 A.D. of Roman Emperor Constantine the Great's victory over Maxentius, rival claimant to the throne, who was drowned in crossing the **Mil·vi·an Bridge** \ˈmil-vē-ən\; (*Lat.* **Pons Mul·vi·us** \ˈpänz-ˈməl-vē-əs, ˈpȯns-ˈmu̇l-vē-u̇s\; *mod.* **Pon·te Mol·le** \ˈpȯn-tā-ˈmȯ-lā\) just N of Rome; the battle, usually called the "battle of Milvian Bridge," is associated with the legend of the appearance of a cross and the words, *in hoc signo vinces* ("by this sign thou shalt conquer"), in the sky, which led Constantine to accept Christianity and to become emperor of Western Roman Empire as well as of Eastern Roman Empire.

Saxe \ˈsäks, ˈsaks\. French name of Saxony (*q.v.*) used in English chiefly in names of former duchies in Thuringia; these were **Saxe–Al·ten·burg** \-ˈält-ᵊn-ˌbu̇rk\ in the E, **Saxe–Wei·mar–Ei·se·nach** \-ˈvī-ˌmär-ˈīz-ᵊn-ˌäk, -ˌäk\ in the N and W and SE (grand duchy after 1815), **Saxe–Mei·ning·en** \-ˈmī-niŋ-ən\ in the SW, **Saxe–Go·tha** \-ˈgō-tə, -thə\ in the NW, and **Saxe–Co·burg** \-ˈkō-ˌbu̇rk\ in the S, which united in 1826 as **Saxe–Coburg–Gotha.** All made part of Thuringia 1920 except Saxe-Coburg which joined Bavaria.

Saxe–Lau·en·burg \-ˈlau̇-ən-ˌbu̇rk, -ˌbərg\. Former German duchy located in Saxony (*q.v.*).

Saxe–Wit·ten·berg \-ˈvit-ᵊn-ˌberk, -ˈwit-ᵊn-ˌbərg\. Former German duchy located in Saxony (*q.v.*).

Sax·on Switzerland \ˈsak-sən\ *or Ger.* **Säch·si·sche Schweiz** \ˈzek-si-shə-ˈshfīts\. Mountainous region, Saxony, E Germany, SE of Dresden.

Sax·o·ny \ˈsak-sə-nē\ *or Ger.* **Sach·sen** \ˈzäk-sən\. **1.** Historical region and former state of Germany.

History: Occupied by the Saxons who controlled much of N Germany W of the Elbe until finally subdued by Frankish King (later Holy Roman Emperor) Charlemagne late 8th cent. A.D.; as duchy of East Frankish kingdom, repulsed Wends and incorporated Thuringia; its duke elected German king as Henry I in 919 (first of Saxon line); extended E of the Elbe by Duke Henry the Lion from whom Holy Roman Emperor Frederick Barbarossa took duchy, splitting it up 1180; two widely-separated areas retained Saxon name as **Saxe–Lauenburg** (Lauenburg lands absorbed by Hanover 1689), and **Saxe–Wittenberg**, ruled jointly by Ascanian family to 1260 and thereafter by separate dynasties; Wittenberg line gained electoral status 1356; electorate passed to margrave of Meissen 1422; in 15th cent., electoral and ducal Saxony (which broke into separate small duchies) belonged to two lines of Wettin rulers and the name Saxony applied to Wettin holdings in cen. and E Germany; conquered by French Emperor Napoléon and made kingdom 1806; lost N part of territory to Prussia (became Prussian prov. of Saxony) 1815; rest of kingdom became member of German Confederation; part of German Empire 1871–1918; republic and free state in Weimar Republic 1919–33; state 1933–45; abolished 1952 when divided among the East German districts of Cottbus, Dresden, Karl-Marx-Stadt, and Leipzig.

2. State of reunified Germany, approx. equivalent to the pre-WWII state. See table at GERMANY.

Saxony–An·halt \-ˈän-ˌhält\. State of Germany. See table at GERMANY.

Say \ˈsī\. Town, W Niger, on Niger River ab. 30 mi. (48 km.) SE of Niamey.

Sa·ya·ma \sä-ˈyä-mä\. City, Saitama prefecture, Honshū, Japan; pop. (1990p) 157,307.

Sa·yan Mountains \sə-ˈyän\. Mountain range, S Russia in Asia, extending E and W bet. Tuva Rep. and Krasnoyarsk Kray and Irkutsk Oblast; av. height 7000 to 9000 ft. (2150 to 2750 m.); highest peak Munku-Sardyk 11,451 ft. (3490 m.); Siberian side is steep; at ab. 92°E pierced by the upper Yenisey.

Saybrook. See DEEP RIVER 2.

Saybrook Colony. An early settlement in Connecticut. See *History* at CONNECTICUT.

Saydā. See SIDON.

Say·ram Hu \sī-ˈräm-ˈhü\ *or W.-G.* **Sai–li–mu Hu** \ˈsī-ˈlē-ˈmü-ˈhü\ *or mostly formerly* **Sai·ram Nor** \sī-ˈräm-ˈnȯr\ *or* **Zai·ram Nor** \zī-\. Lake, NW Xinjiang Uygur, W China, S of the Alataw Shan.

Sayre \ˈsā-ər, ˈser\. **1.** City, ⊗ of Beckham co., W Oklahoma, 43 mi. (69 km.) WSW of Clinton; pop. (1990c) 2881.

2. Borough, Bradford co., N Pennsylvania, on Susquehanna River at New York border; pop. (1990c) 5791.

Sayre·ville \ˈsā-ər-ˌvil, ˈser-\. Borough, Middlesex co., cen. New Jersey, on Raritan Bay inlet 5 mi. (8 km.) ESE of New Brunswick; pop. (1990c) 34,986.

Sayr Usa \ˈsīr-ˈü-sə\ *or* **Sair·us·su** \ˈsīr-ˈü-sə\. Village, SE Mongolia, on N edge of the Gobi.

Sa·yu·la \sä-ˈyü-lä\. Town, Jalisco state, W cen. Mexico, on **Lake Sayula,** SW of Lake Chapala.

Say·ville \ˈsā-ˌvil\. Unincorporated settlement, Suffolk co., SE New York, on Long Island and Great South Bay, ab. 5 mi. (8 km.) SW of Patchogue; pop. (1990c) 16,550.

Sa·zan \ˈsä-ˌzän\ *or Ital.* **Sa·se·no** *also* **Sas·se·no** \ˈsä-se-nō\; *anc.* **Sa·son** \ˈsā-sən\. Small island in N Strait of Otranto at the entrance to the harbor of Vlorë, Albania, opp. the heel of Italy; ab. 4 mi. (6 km.) long; ab. 2 sq. mi. (5 sq. km.). Occupied by Italy 1914 and held as a naval base until its return by treaty 1947.

Sá·za·va \ˈsä-zä-vä\ *or Ger.* **Sa·sau** \ˈzä-ˌzau̇\. River, cen. Czech Republic; flows W into Vltava River 12 mi. (19 km.) S of Prague; 135 mi. (217 km.) long.

Sbeït·la \ˈzbāt-lə\; *anc.* **Su·fet·u·la** \sü-ˈfe-tə-lə\. Town, N cen. Tunisia, ab. 100 mi. (160 km.) WNW of the port of Sfax and on railroad line leading NE to Sousse; ancient Roman town estab. first cent. A.D.; ruins include the forum, temples, triumphal arch.

Sca·fa·ti \skä-ˈfä-tē\. Commune, Salerno prov., Campania, S Italy, 14 mi. (23 km.) WNW of the seaport of Salerno; pop. (1989c) 39,887.

Sca Fell *or* **Sca·fell** \ˈskȯ-ˌfel\. Mountain, Cumbria, NW England, in the Lake District 11 mi. (18 km.) SW of Keswick; 3162 ft. (964 m.); 2d highest peak in England.

Scafell Pike. Peak, Cumbria, NW England, in Cumbrian Mts. 1 mi. (2 km.) NE of Sca Fell; 3210 ft. (978 m.); highest peak in England.

Scaldis. See SCHELDE.

Scald Law. See PENTLAND HILLS.

Scale Force \ˈskāl-ˈfōrs\. Waterfall, Lake District, NW England, in Cumbria near Keswick; 125 ft. (38 m.) high.

Scamander. See MENDERES 2.

Scan·dia \ˈskan-dē-ə\. Ancient name of S Scandinavia.

Scan·dia·no \skän-ˈdyä-nō\. Commune, Reggio nell'Emilia prov., Emilia-Romagna, N Italy, 8 mi. (13 km.) SE of the commune of Reggio nell'Emilia; pop. (1989c) 22,099.

Scan·dic·ci \skän-ˈdē-chē\. Commune, Firenze prov., Tuscany, W Italy, ab. 3 mi. (5 km.) SW of Florence; pop. (1991p) 53,264.

Scan·di·na·via \ˌskan-də-ˈnā-vē-ə, -vyə\. **1.** *or* **Scan·di·na·vi·an Peninsula** \-ˈnā-vē-ən\. Peninsula N Europe, comprising Norway and Sweden; ab. 289,500 sq. mi. (749,800 sq. km.).

2. Ancient name of the country of the Norsemen.

3. Name of region of N Europe, encompassing Denmark, Norway, and Sweden; sometimes expanded to include Finland and Iceland.

Scania. See SKÅNE.

Scan·tic \ˈskan-tik\. River, N cen. Connecticut; rises in Hampden co., S Massachusetts, flows SW into Hartford co., N Connecticut, and into Connecticut River N of Windsor.

Scapa Flow \ˈska-pə-ˈflō\. Sea basin in Orkney Is., off N coast of Scotland; 15 mi. (24 km.) long and 8 mi. (13 km.) wide; chief British naval base in WWI; in it Germans scuttled their fleet after the war 1919; in WWII again a major naval base which was closed 1956.

Scap·poose \skə-ˈpüs\. City, Columbia co., NW Oregon, NW of Portland; pop. (1990c) 3529.

Scar·ba \ˈskär-bə\. Island in the Inner Hebrides, W coast of Scotland, N of Jura; 5 sq. mi. (13 sq. km.); highest point 1470 ft. (448 m.).

Scar·boro *or* **Scar·bor·ough** \ˈskär-ˌbər-ō\. Town, Cumberland co., SW Maine, 7 mi. (11 km.) S of Portland; pop. (1990c) 12,518.

Scar·bor·ough \ˈskär-ˌbər-ō\. **1.** Town, Maine. See SCARBORO.

2. City, SE Ontario, Canada; part of Toronto Metropolitan Municipality; pop. (1991c) 524,598.

3. Town, North Yorkshire, N England, on North Sea 37 mi. (60 km.) N of Hull; pop. (1991p) 107,800; site of ancient Roman signal station 4th cent. A.D.; a seaside resort since the late 17th cent.
4. Town, Tobago. See TOBAGO.
Scardona. See SKRADIN.
Scarp \ˈskärp\. Small island of the Outer Hebrides, off NW coast of Scotland, W of the island of Lewis with Harris; 3 mi. (5 km.) long; administratively a part of Western Isles region.
Scarpanto. See KARPATHOS.
Scarpanto Strait. See KARPATHOS STRAIT.
Scarpe \ˈskärp\. River, Pas-de-Calais dept., N France; flows into Schelde River; 62 mi. (100 km.) long.
Scars·dale \ˈskärz-ˌdāl\. Residential village, Westchester co., SE New York, 20 mi. (32 km.) NNE of New York City; pop. (1990c) 16,987.
Scat·tery Island \ˈska-tə-rē\. See KILRUSH.
Sceaux \ˈsō\. Town, Hauts-de-Seine dept., N France, S of Paris; site of castle, destroyed during the Revolution, which was scene during 17th cent. of literary court of the duchesse du Maine; present castle built 19th cent. Known for porcelain and earthenware production 18th cent.
Schaan \ˈshän\. Town, W Liechtenstein, ab. 2 mi. (3 km.) NNW of Vaduz; pop. (1980p) 4552.
Schaer·beek *or Flem.* **Schaar·beek** \ˈsk̲är-ˌbāk\. Commune, Brabant prov., cen. Belgium, a NE suburb of Brussels; pop. (1991c) 102,702.
Scha·fer \ˈshā-fər\. Village, former ⊗ of McKenzie co., W North Dakota, near **Schafer Springs**.
Schaff·hau·sen \shäf-ˈhau̇z-ᵊn\. **1.** Canton in Switzerland. See table at SWITZERLAND.
2. Commune, its ✻, N cen. Switzerland, on Rhine River 23 mi. (37 km.) N of Zürich; pop. (1989c) 34,101; textiles, watches; 11th cent. minster; 16th cent. castle; owes industrial development to power derived from Schaffhausen Falls (*q.v.*) in Rhine River.
Schaffhausen Falls *or* **Falls of the Rhine** *or Ger.* **Rhein·fall** \ˈrīn-ˌfäl\. Waterfall in Rhine River near Schaffhausen, Switzerland; 65 ft. (20 m.) high and 377 ft. (115 m.) wide.
Schar·hörn \ˈshär-ˌhœrn\. Small island in Heligoland Bight, Germany, at mouth of Elbe River.
Schässburg. See SIGHIŞOARA.
Schaulen. See ŠIAULIAI.
Schaum·burg \ˈshȯm-ˌbərg\. Village, Cook and Du Page cos., NE Illinois, ab. 15 mi. (23 km.) WNW of Chicago; pop. (1990c) 68,586; site of one of world's largest enclosed shopping malls.
Schaumburg–Lip·pe \ˈshau̇m-ˌbu̇rk-ˈli-pə\. Former German state, now part of Lower Saxony, Germany; 131 sq. mi. (339 sq. km.); ✻ Bückeburg; formed 1640; became principality 1807; joined German Confederation 1815; joined Weimar Republic 1918; in 1946 made part of Lower Saxony state.
Scheggia. Pass in the Apennines. See table at APENNINES.
Schei·degg \ˈshī-ˌdek\. Village, Bern canton, cen. Switzerland, E of Lauterbrunnen in the Bernese Alps; alt. 6762 ft. (2061 m.); resort and starting point of Jungfrau railway; lies on **Little Scheidegg** (*Ger.* **Klei·ne Scheidegg** \ˈklī-nə\), pass N of the Jungfrau and leading from Lauterbrunnen to Grindelwald; noted for view; to NE is **Great Scheidegg** (*Ger.* **Gros·se Scheidegg** \ˈgrō-sə\), pass at 6434 ft. (1961 m.) leading from Grindelwald to the valley of the Aare; just NW of the Wetterhorn.
Schel·de \ˈsk̲el-də\ *or* **Scheldt** \ˈskelt\ *or Fr.* **Es·caut** \es-ˈkō\; *anc.* **Scal·dis** \ˈskal-dəs\. Navigable river, W Europe; rises in Aisne dept., N France, flows N and NE through W Belgium to the city of Antwerp, turns NW and empties into the North Sea through two estuaries, Oosterschelde and Westerschelde, in Netherlands; 270 mi. (434 km.) long.
Schell Creek Range \ˈshel\. Mountain range, E White Pine co., E Nevada.
Sche·nec·ta·dy \skə-ˈnek-tə-dē\. **1.** County in E New York. See table at NEW YORK.
2. City, its ⊗, on Mohawk River 13 m. NW of Albany; pop. (1990c) 65,566; center of electrical industry; electronic equipment; also manufactures wire; locomotive works; atomic research facilities; Union Coll. (1795), Schenectady County Community Coll. (1968). Settled 1661; village destroyed by French and Indians 1690; chartered as borough 1765, as city 1798; became center of locomotive building c. 1850 and of electrical industry late 19th cent.
Scher·er·ville \ˈshir-ər-ˌvil\. Town, Lake co., NW Indiana, 10 mi. (16 km.) S of Hammond; pop. (1990c) 19,926.
Scheria. See CORFU.
Schertz \ˈshərts\. Town, Bexar and Guadalupe cos., S cen. Texas, 17 mi. (27 km.) NE of San Antonio; pop. (1990c) 10,555.
Sche·ve·ning·en \ˈsk̲ā-və-ˌniŋ-ə\. Seaside resort, part of The Hague, South Holland prov., SW Netherlands.
Schie·dam \sk̲ē-ˈdäm\. Commune, South Holland prov., SW Netherlands, 3 mi. (5 km.) W of Rotterdam near the Meuse; pop. (1992e) 71,117; machinery, glass; gin distilling, shipbuilding; chartered 1273.
Schie·hal·lion \shē-ˈhal-yən\. Peak, Tayside region, cen. Scotland; 3547 ft. (1081 m.).
Schier·mon·nik·oog \ˌsk̲ir-ˌmȯ-ni-ˈkōk̲\. Island, Netherlands, easternmost of the West Frisian Is., 10 mi. (16 km.) E of Ameland I.; 8 mi. (13 km.) long; 12 sq. mi. (31 sq. km.); lighthouse; administratively a part of Friesland prov.
Schif·fer·stadt \ˈshi-fər-ˌshtät\. Commune, SE Rhineland-Palatinate, Germany, in valley of the Rhine 7 mi. (11 km.) SSW of Ludwigshafen; pop. (1980c) 17,250.
Schil·ler Park \ˈshi-lər\. Village, Cook co., NE Illinois, suburb of Chicago located bet. the city to the E and O'Hare International Airport to the W; pop. (1990c) 11,189.
Schil·tig·heim \shēl-tē-ˈkem, ˈshil-tik̲-ˌhīm\. Commune, Bas-Rhin dept., NE France, NW suburb of Strasbourg.
Schio \ˈskē-ō\. Commune, Vicenza prov., Veneto, NE Italy, near Monti Lessini 16 mi. (26 km.) NW of the commune of Vicenza; pop. (1991p) 35,940; cathedral.
Schlei \ˈshlī\ *or Dan.* **Sli** \ˈslē\. Inlet of the Baltic Sea in E Schleswig-Holstein, Germany.
Schlei·cher \ˈshlī-kər, ˈslī-\. County in W cen. Texas. See table at TEXAS.
Schlesien. See SILESIA.
Schles·wig \ˈshlās-ˌvik̲; ˈshles-ˌwig, -ˌwik\ *or Dan.* **Sles·vig** \ˈslās-vē\. **1.** Historical region of NW Germany; a former duchy of the Danish crown, now largely in Schleswig-Holstein, Germany.
History: Danish duchy from early 12th cent.; entered personal union with Holstein (*q.v.*) 1460; with Holstein, object of conflict bet. Denmark and German Confederation 1848–50 and bet. Austria and Prussia in Austro-Prussian (Seven Weeks') War 1866; annexed to Prussia with Holstein, forming prov. of Schleswig-Holstein (*q.v.*) 1866.
2. Seaport city, Schleswig-Holstein, Germany, at W end of Schlei Inlet 70 mi. (113 km.) NNW of Hamburg; pop. (1992e) 26,938; 13th cent. cathedral; Gottorp Castle, ducal residence orig. built 13th cent., present structure 16th–18th cents. Site of church 850; chartered 1200; Danish administrative center for duchies of Holstein and Schleswig 1721–1848; ✻ of Prussian prov. of Schleswig-Holstein 1867–1917.
Schleswig–Hol·stein \-ˈhȯl-ˌshtīn, -ˈhōl-ˌstīn\. A state of Germany; ✻ Kiel; rye, potatoes, sugar beets, wheat; livestock; textiles; shipbuilding. For history prior to 1866, see HOLSTEIN and SCHLESWIG. Former duchies of Schleswig and Holstein annexed to Prussia as prov. of Schleswig-Holstein 1866; N part of Schleswig awarded to Denmark by plebiscite 1920 (see SOUTH JUTLAND), remainder became a state of West Germany 1946. See table at GERMANY.
Schlettstadt. See SÉLESTAT.
Schley \ˈslī\. County in SW cen. Georgia. See table at GEORGIA.
Schlüsselburg. See PETROKREPOST'.
Schmal·kal·den \ˈshmäl-ˌkäl-dən\; *Eng.* **Smal·kald** *or* **Smal·cald** \ˈsmȯl-ˌkȯld\. City, Thuringia, cen. Germany, 30 mi. (48 km.) SW of Erfurt; pop. (1981c) 17,348; 15th cent. town hall; Schmalkaldic League formed here 1531 to defend against Roman Catholic retribution on those churches which had adopted the Reformation.

Schnecks·ville \ˈshneks-ˌvil\. Unincorporated settlement, Lehigh co., E Pennsylvania; Lehigh Co. Community Coll. (1966).

Schnee·berg \ˈshnā-ˌberk\. **1.** City, Saxony, E Germany, 22 mi. (35 km.) SW of Chemnitz; pop. (1981c) 21,398; 16th cent. church.

2. Highest peak in the Fichtelgebirge, NE Bavaria, Germany, NE of Bayreuth; 3453 ft. (1053 m.).

Schneekoppe. See SNĚŽKA.

Schneidemühl. See PIŁA.

Scho·field Bar·racks \ˈskō-ˌfēld-ˈbar-əks\. City, Honolulu co., Hawaii, 18 mi. (29 km.) NW of the city of Honolulu; pop. (1990c) 19,597.

Scho·har·ie \skō-ˈhar-ē\. **1.** County in E New York. See table at NEW YORK.

2. Village, its ⊗; pop. (1990c) 1045.

Schö·ne·beck \ˈshœ-nə-ˌbek\. City, Saxony-Anhalt, E cen. Germany, on left bank of Elbe River 10 mi. (16 km.) SSE of Magdeburg; salt mines.

Schön·hau·sen \ˌshœn-ˈhau̇z-ᵊn\. Village, Saxony-Anhalt, NE cen. Germany, on the Elbe ab. 35 mi. (56 km.) NNE of Magdeburg; birthplace of Prussian statesman Otto von Bismarck 1815.

Schoo·dic Lake \ˈskü-dik\. Lake, in SE Piscataquis co., cen. Maine.

Schoodic Point. Point, SE Hancock co., SE Maine.

School·craft \ˈskül-ˌkraft\. County in Upper Penin. of Michigan. See table at MICHIGAN.

Schoo·ten *or* **Scho·ten** \ˈsk̲ōt-ᵊn\. Commune, Antwerp prov., N Belgium, just NE of the city of Antwerp; pop. (1991c) 31,094.

Schorn·dorf \ˈshȯrn-ˌdȯrf\. Town, Baden-Württemberg, Germany, ab. 15 mi. (24 km.) W of Stuttgart; pop. (1980c) 33,631.

Schou·ten Islands \ˈskau̇t-ᵊn, ˈskau̇-tə\. **1.** *also* **Mi·so·re Islands** \mi-ˈsȯ-rē\. Island group across the entrance to Teluk Cenderawasih, off N coast of Irian Jaya, Indonesia, in W Pacific Ocean; 1231 sq. mi. (3188 sq. km.); chief islands Biak, Supiori, and Numfoor.

2. Group of small islands, off NE coast of island of New Guinea; part of Papua New Guinea.

Schou·wen \ˈsk̲au̇-və\. Island in Zeeland prov., SW Netherlands, in estuary of Schelde River; 88 sq. mi. (228 sq. km.); chief town Zierikzee. See DUIVELAND.

Schram·berg \ˈshräm-ˌberk\. City, Baden-Württemberg, Germany, 30 mi. (48 km.) NE of Freiburg; pop. (1980c) 19,157.

Schreck·horn, Gross \ˌgrōs-ˈshrek-ˌhȯrn\. Peak in the Bernese Alps, SW cen. Switzerland, N of the Finsteraarhorn and S of the Wetterhorn; 13,379 ft. (4078 m.).

Schroon \ˈskrün\. River, NE New York; rises in cen. Essex co., flows S through Schroon Lake into Hudson River in cen. Warren co.; ab. 50 mi. (80 km.) long.

Schroon Lake. Lake, Essex co., NE New York; 10 mi. (16 km.) long by 1.5 mi. (2.4 km.) wide; the Schroon River flows through it.

Schroon Mountain. Peak in Adirondack Mts., Essex co., NE New York; 3200 ft. (975 m.).

Schul·pfor·te *or* **Schul·pfor·ta** \shülp-ˈfȯr-tə\ *or* **Pfor·ta** \ˈpfȯr-tə\. Village, N Hesse, Germany, 2 mi. (3 km.) SW of Naumburg on the Saale; site of school founded 1543 by Maurice, duke of Saxony, which occupies a former Cistercian monastery founded 12th cent.

Schurz, Mount \ˈshu̇rts\. Peak, W Park co., NW Wyoming; 11,139 ft. (3395 m.).

Schütt, Great. See GREAT SCHÜTT.

Schütt, Little. See SZIGETKÖZ.

Schuy·ler \ˈskī-lər\. **1.** Name of counties in three states of the U.S. See tables at ILLINOIS, MISSOURI, NEW YORK.

2. City, ⊗ of Colfax co., E Nebraska, on Platte River 30 mi. (48 km.) W of Fremont; pop. (1990c) 4052.

Schuy·ler·ville \ˈskī-lər-ˌvil\. Village, Saratoga co., E New York, on W bank of Hudson River 32 mi. (52 km.) N of Albany; pop. (1990c) 1364; settled 1689 and called Saratoga; incorp. as Schuylerville 1831; for history, see SARATOGA 3.

Schuyl·kill \ˈskü-kəl, ˈskül-ˌkil\. **1.** River, SE Pennsylvania; rises in Schuylkill co., E cen. Pennsylvania, flows SE into Delaware River at Philadelphia; 130 mi. (209 km.) long.

2. County in E cen. Pennsylvania. See table at PENNSYLVANIA.

Schuylkill Haven. Borough, Schuylkill co., E cen. Pennsylvania, on Schuylkill River 5 mi. (8 km.) S of Pottsville; pop. (1990c) 5610.

Schwa·bach \ˈshfä-ˌbäk̲\. City, N Bavaria, Germany, 8 mi. (13 km.) SSW of Nürnberg; pop. (1980c) 35,387; 15th cent. church; chartered 1371.

Schwaben. See SWABIA.

Schwä·bisch Gmünd \ˈshfe-bish-ˈgmu̅ent\ *also* **Gmünd.** City, Baden-Württemberg, Germany, 28 mi. (45 km.) E of Stuttgart; pop. (1992e) 61,358; chartered as city 1162; free city from 1268 until 1803 when it passed to Württemberg.

Schwäbisch Hall \ˈhäl\ *also* **Hall.** City, Baden-Württemberg, Germany, 34 mi. (55 km.) NE of Stuttgart; pop. (1992e) 33,006; historically a salt-mining center; 16th cent. church.

Schwa·ner Mountains \ˈskfä-nər\. Range in SW cen. Borneo, Indonesia, S of the Kapuas River; highest peak Mt. Rayo 7474 ft. (2278 m.).

Schwang·au \ˈshfäŋ-ˌgau̇\. Village, SW Bavaria, Germany, NE of Füssen; two 19th cent. castles.

Schwarze Elster. See ELSTER.

Schwarzwald. See BLACK FOREST.

Schwe·chat \ˈshfe-ˌkät\. Town, Lower Austria, Austria, on the Leitha, SE suburb of Vienna; pop. (1991c) 14,669; site of international airport serving Vienna.

Schwedt *or in full* **Schwedt an der Oder** \ˈshfāt-än-der-ˈō-dər\. City, Brandenburg, E Germany, 50 mi. (81 km.) NE of Berlin; pop. (1992e) 49,443; tobacco processing; chemicals, paper; passed from Pomerania to Brandenburg 15th cent.; largely destroyed in WWII.

Schweidnitz. See ŚWIDNICA.

Schwein·furt \ˈshfīn-ˌfu̇rt\. City, Bavaria, Germany, on Main River 66 mi. (106 km.) E of Frankfurt am Main; pop. (1992e) 54,520; machinery; ball-bearings (esp. important in WWII); river port; 16th cent. church; 16th cent. town hall; first mentioned 791; made free imperial city 1254; passed to Bavaria 1803. Birthplace of poet Friedrich Rückert 1788.

Schweiz. See SWITZERLAND.

Schwelm \ˈshfelm\. City, North Rhine-Westphalia, Germany, E of Wuppertal; pop. (1980c) 31,108.

Schwen·ning·en. See VILLINGEN-SCHWENNINGER.

Schwe·rin \shfā-ˈrēn\. **1.** District of former East Germany; now largely in Mecklenburg-West Pomerania state.

2. City, ✻ of Mecklenburg-West Pomerania state, Germany and formerly of Schwerin dist., East Germany, on SW shore of Lake Schwerin; pop. (1992e) 125,959; cigarettes, pharmaceuticals; food processing; 13th–15th cent. Gothic cathedral; mentioned 1018; chartered 1160.

Schwerin, Lake *or Ger.* **Schwe·ri·ner See** \ˈshfā-ri-nər-ˌzā\. Lake, Mecklenburg-West Pomerania, N Germany, 8 mi. (13 km.) S of Wismar; 14 mi. (23 km.) long; 24 sq. mi. (62 sq. km.); max. depth 177 ft. (54 m.); drains into the Elbe River.

Schwer·te \ˈshfer-tə\. City, North Rhine-Westphalia, Germany, on Ruhr River 7 mi. (11 km.) SSE of Dortmund; pop. (1992e) 50,673.

Schwiebus. See ŚWIEBODZIN.

Schwyz *also* **Schwiz** \ˈshfēts\. **1.** Canton, Switzerland. See *History* and table at SWITZERLAND.

2. Commune, its ✻, E cen. Switzerland, 22 mi. (35 km.) E of Lucerne; pop. (1989c) 12,596; tourism.

Sciac·ca \ˈshä-kä\. Seaport, Agrigento prov., SW Sicily, Italy, on Mediterranean Sea 30 mi. (48 km.) NW of the commune of Agrigento; pop. (1991p) 40,433; hot sulfur springs nearby.

Sci·cli \ˈshē-klē\. Commune, Ragusa prov., SE Sicily, Italy, 9 mi. (15 km.) S of the commune of Ragusa; pop. (1991p) 24,635.

Scil·la \ˈsi-lə, ˈshē-lə\; *anc.* **Scyl·la** \ˈsi-lə\. Legendary site of headland projecting into the Strait of Messina from the coast of Reggio di Calabria prov., S Italy; notable in Greek mythology. See CHARYBDIS.

Scilly. See MANUAE 2.

Scil·ly, Isles of *or* **Scilly Isles** *or* **Scilly Islands** \ˈsi-lē\. Group of 140 small islands off Land's End, SW England; 6 sq. mi. (16 sq. km.); pop. (1991p) 2900; main town Hugh Town; administratively a part of Cornwall; tourism, market gardening, and flower growing; formerly a haunt of pirates, and later of smugglers.

Scio. See CHIOS.

Sci·o·to \sī-ˈō-tə\. **1.** River, cen. and S Ohio; rises in Auglaize co., W Ohio, flows E, then S through Columbus and Chillicothe to empty into Ohio River at Portsmouth, S Scioto co., S Ohio; ab. 237 mi. (381 km.) long.
2. County in S Ohio. See table at OHIO.

Scit·u·ate \ˈsi-chə-wət\. **1.** Town, Plymouth co., SE Massachusetts, on Atlantic Ocean 16 mi. (26 km.) ENE of Brockton; pop. (1990c) 16,786; summer resort; settled c. 1630; incorp. 1636.
2. Town, Providence co., N Rhode Island, W of Cranston; pop. (1990c) 9796; settled 1710.

Scituate Dam *and* **Scituate Reservoir.** See GAINER MEMORIAL DAM.

Sco·bey \ˈskō-bē\. City, ⊗ of Daniels co., NE Montana; pop. (1990c) 1154.

Scodra. See SHKODËR 2.

Sco·field Reservoir \ˈskō-ˌfēld\. Reservoir in NW Carbon co., E cen. Utah.

Scone \ˈskün\. **1.** Shire, cen. E New South Wales, Australia, NNW of Sydney; pop. (1991c) 9379.
2. Parish, Tayside region, Scotland, just NE of Perth; **New Scone** is a modern village; **Old Scone,** site of abbey founded 1115, destroyed 1559; Scottish kings crowned at Scone until 1651; the *Stone of Scone* or *Stone of Destiny* upon which early Scottish kings sat at coronation is said to have been brought to Scone by Kenneth I MacAlpin, traditional founder of Scottish kingdom; it was taken to England by Edward I 1296 and is now in Westminster Abbey beneath the coronation chair.

Sconset. See SIASCONSET.

Sco·pus, Mount \ˈskō-pəs\ *or Heb.* **Har HaZofim** \ˈhär-ˌhä-zō-ˈfēm\. Mountain, N extension of the Mount of Olives, NE of Jerusalem, Israel; 2694 ft. (821 m.). Site of old campus of Hebrew Univ., dedicated 1925; an Israeli exclave surrounded by Jordanian-held territory 1949–67; reunited with Israel after the 1967 Arab-Israeli War.

Scores·by Sound \ˈskōrz-bē\. Large inlet of Norwegian Sea on E coast of Greenland, in cen. part just N of 70°N; has many fjords and two large islands; length of NW fjord 280 mi. (451 km.). On N side of entrance is the settlement of Ittoqqortoormiit.

Scoresbysund. See ITTOQQORTOORMIIT.

Scotch Plains \ˈskäch\. Urban township, Union co., NE New Jersey, 10 mi. (16 km.) W of Elizabeth; pop. (1990c) 21,160.

Sco·tia \ˈskō-shə\. **1.** Village, Schenectady co., E New York, on Mohawk River 15 mi. (24 km.) NW of Albany; pop. (1990c) 7359; residential suburb.
2. Medieval Latin name of Scotland, still sometimes used poetically and in the modern names Nova Scotia and Scotia Sea.

Scotia Sea. Part of South Atlantic SE of Falkland Is. and South America; bordered by South Sandwich Is., South Georgia I., and South Orkney Is.

Scot·land \ˈskät-lənd\. **1.** North part of the island of Great Britain, a part of the United Kingdom of Great Britain and Northern Ireland, bounded on N by the Atlantic Ocean, on E by the North Sea, on S by England and the Irish Sea, and on W by the Atlantic Ocean; 29,797 sq. mi. (77,174 sq. km.); pop. (1991e) 5,102,400; ✱ Edinburgh.

Physical features: Greatest length of mainland 274 mi. (441 km.), Mull of Galloway to Cape Wrath (see also DUNNET HEAD and JOHN O'GROAT'S HOUSE); greatest width 154 mi. (248 km.). Divided physically into three regions: (1) Highlands (see NORTHERN HIGHLANDS), nearly two thirds of N part of country, comprising the Grampians and many smaller ranges; highest Ben Nevis 4406 ft. (1343 m.); noted for scenery; (2) Central Lowlands, valleys of the Clyde, Tay, and Forth rivers; (3) Southern Uplands, in S, with ranges of hills in which highest points are 2600 to 2700 ft. (790 to 820 m.); Cheviot Hills and Tweed River on English border. Includes three large island groups: Shetland Is. in N, Orkney Is., separated from mainland by Pentland Firth, and Hebrides (*qq.v.*), and many islands off W coast (largest Mull, Islay, Jura, Arran, Bute, and Rum); has many deep inlets (firths): Forth, Clyde, Moray, Solway, Lorn.

Chief products: Barley; livestock raising, fishing; oil; coal; manufacturing: textiles, electronics, whisky; shipbuilding.

Chief cities: Glasgow and Edinburgh.

Political divisions: Divided (1975) into the following administrative regions:

NAME	AREA (sq. mi.)	AREA (sq. km.)	POP. (1993e)	ADMINISTRATIVE HEADQUARTERS
Regions				
Borders	1,814	4,698	105,300	Newtown St. Boswells
Central	1,017	2,635	272,900	Stirling
Dumfries and Galloway	2,481	6,425	147,900	Dumfries
Fife	509	1,319	351,200	Glenrothes
Grampian	3,358	8,698	528,100	Aberdeen
Highland	9,806	25,398	206,900	Inverness
Lothian	662	1,716	753,900	Edinburgh
Strathclyde	5,214	13,503	2,286,800	Glasgow
Tayside	2,893	7,492	395,200	Dundee
Island Administrative Areas				
Orkney	377	976	19,760	Kirkwall
Shetland	553	1,433	22,830	Lerwick
Western Isles	1,119	2,898	29,410	Stornoway

Prior to 1975 divided into the following counties: Aberdeen, Angus, Argyll, Ayr, Banff, Berwick, Bute, Caithness, Clackmannan, Dumfries, Dunbarton, East Lothian, Fife, Inverness, Kincardine, Kinross, Kirkcudbright, Lanark, Midlothian, Moray, Nairn, Orkney, Peebles, Perth, Renfrew, Ross and Cromarty, Roxburgh, Selkirk, Stirling, Sutherland, West Lothian, Wigtown, Zetland.

History: Occupied by Picts when invaded by Romans after 80 A.D.; area S of rampart from Firth of Forth to Clyde River held briefly by Romans (see UNITED KINGDOM); in 5th cent., included four kingdoms: of the Picts in highlands N of Forth, of Scots (of Irish extraction) in W highlands, of Britons in Strathclyde in S, and of Angles in Northumbria in SE; Picts Christianized by St. Columba c. 565; in 685 Picts broke Anglo-Saxon power on border; invaded by Norse from late 8th cent.; Scottish unification began under Kenneth I MacAlpin, king of Scots who became also king of Picts 843; Lothian and Strathclyde joined to kingdom 11th cent.; from 11th cent., came under anglicizing influence; its ruler was forced to do homage to English crown 1174, the source of frequent future disputes; defeated in war with England late 13th cent.; Robert the Bruce proclaimed himself king 1306 and won independence from England in battle at Bannockburn 1314; ruled by house of Stuart 1371–1688; acquired Orkneys and Shetlands 1472; in frequent intermittent conflict with England until accession of King James VI of Scotland as James I of England brought about personal union of two kingdoms 1603; united with England by parliamentary act 1707 (see UNITED KINGDOM).
2. Name of counties in two states of the U.S. See tables at MISSOURI and NORTH CAROLINA.

Scotland Neck. Town, Halifax co., NE North Carolina, 25 mi. (40 km.) ENE of Rocky Mount; pop. (1990c) 2575.

Scott \ˈskät\. **1.** Name of counties in 11 states of the U.S. See tables at ARKANSAS, ILLINOIS, INDIANA, IOWA, KANSAS, KENTUCKY, MINNESOTA, MISSISSIPPI, MISSOURI, TENNESSEE, VIRGINIA.
2. Urban township, Allegheny co., SW Pennsylvania, SW of Pittsburgh; pop. (1990c) 17,118.
3. Town, Lafayette parish, S Louisiana; a suburb W of the city of Lafayette; pop. (1990c) 4912.

Scott, Cape. Cape, NW tip of Vancouver I., off W British Columbia, Canada.

Scott, Mount. **1.** Peak, Wichita Mountains, SW Oklahoma; 2464 ft. (751 m.); highest point in range.
2. Peak, W Klamath co., near E shore of Crater Lake, S Oregon; 8926 ft. (2721 m.).

Scott Air Force Base; *formerly* **Scott Field.** United States military facility, 6 mi. (10 km.) E of Belleville, St. Clair co., Illinois.

Scott City. **1.** City, ⊗ of Scott co., W Kansas, 72 mi. (116 km.) NW of Dodge City; pop. (1990c) 3785.
2. City, Scott co., SE Missouri, near the Illinois border; pop. (1990c) 4292.

Scott·dale \ˈskät-ˌdāl\. Borough, Westmoreland co., SW Pennsylvania; pop. (1990c) 5184.

Scott Field. See SCOTT AIR FORCE BASE.

Scott Island. Small island N of Ross Sea, Ross Dependency, Antarctica, ab. 315 mi. (505 km.) NE of Cape Adare, 67°24′S, 179°55′W.

Scott Peak. Highest mountain in Bitterroot Range, E Idaho; 11,393 ft. (3473 m.).

Scotts·bluff \ˈskäts-ˌbləf\. City, Scotts Bluff co., W Nebraska, on North Platte River 20 mi. (32 km.) E of Wyoming border; pop. (1990c) 13,711; Western Nebraska Community Coll.–Scottsbluff Campus (1926).

Scotts Bluff. **1.** Butte, Scotts Bluff co., W Nebraska; 4662 ft. (1421 m.); site of **Scotts Bluff National Monument** (see UNITED STATES, *National Monuments*).
2. County in W Nebraska. See table at NEBRASKA.

Scotts·boro \ˈskäts-ˌbər-ō\. City, ⊗ of Jackson co., NE Alabama; pop. (1990c) 13,786; lumber; farming. Scene 1931 of the famous "Scottsboro Case" which produced landmark Supreme Court decisions in constitutional law and civil rights.

Scotts·burg \ˈskäts-ˌbərg\. City, ⊗ of Scott co., SE Indiana, 27 mi. (43 km.) N of New Albany; pop. (1990c) 5334.

Scotts·dale \ˈskäts-ˌdāl\. **1.** City, Maricopa co., SW cen. Arizona, E suburb of Phoenix; pop. (1990c) 130,069; grew rapidly in 1960s.
2. Town, NE Tasmania, Australia, 28 mi. (45 km.) NE of Launceston; pop. (1991c) 4694.

Scotts·ville \ˈskäts-ˌvil\. City, ⊗ of Allen co., S Kentucky, 23 mi. (37 km.) SE of Bowling Green; pop. (1990c) 4278.

Scran·ton \ˈskrant-ᵊn\. City, ⊗ of Lackawanna co., NE Pennsylvania, 20 mi. (32 km.) W of Lake Wallenpaupack; pop. (1990c) 81,805; textiles, clothing, electronic equipment, plastic, metal products; formerly important coal mines; Univ. of Scranton (1888), Lackawanna Junior Coll. (1894), Marywood Coll. (1915), International Correspondence Schools Center for Degree Studies (1975).

Screv·en \ˈskriv-ᵊn\. County in E Georgia. See table at GEORGIA.

Scroo·by \ˈskrü-bē\. Village, Nottinghamshire, cen. England, ab. 18 mi. (29 km.) E of Sheffield; home of William Brewster and other Pilgrims who later founded Plymouth Colony in New England.

Scru·ton Peak \ˈskrüt-ᵊn\. Mountain, Pennington co., SW South Dakota; 5950 ft. (1814 m.).

Scu·gog, Lake \ˈskyü-ˌgäg\. Lake at junction of Ontario, Durham, and Victoria cos., SE Ontario, Canada; 39 sq. mi. (101 sq. km.); connects with Trent Canal by Scugog River.

Scultenna. See PANARO.

Scun·thorpe \ˈskən-ˌthȯrp\. Town, Humberside, E England, 18 mi. (29 km.) WSW of Hull; pop. (1991p) 60,500; iron and steel, clothing; food processing.

Scupi. See SKOPJE.

Scur·die Ness \ˈskər-dē-ˈnes\. Headland on E coast of Scotland, S of Montrose; lighthouse.

Scur·ry \ˈskər-ē\. County in NW cen. Texas. See table at TEXAS.

Scu·ta·ri \ˈskü-tä-rē\ *or Serb.* **Ska·dar** \ˈskä-ˌdär\. **1.** District and town, Albania. See SHKODËR.
2. Town, Turkey in Asia. See ÜSKÜDAR.

Scutari, Lake *or Albanian* **Li·qen i Shkod·rës** \ˌlē-kə-nē-ˈshkō-drəs\; *anc.* **Pa·lus La·be·a·tis** \ˈpā-ləs-ˌlā-bē-ˈā-tis\. Lake on boundary bet. Montenegro, SW Yugoslavia, and NW Albania; 143 sq. mi. (371 sq. km.); receives Morača River on the N and drains into Buenë River in Albania; Shkodër, Albania is at its SE end.

Scylla. See SCILLA.

Scyros. See SKYROS.

Scyth·ia \ˈsi-thē-ə\. Ancient name of sections of Europe and Asia now included in Ukraine, Russia, and Kazakhstan; the country had undefined boundaries, but the Scythians, a nomadic people known for their horsemanship, dwelt chiefly in the steppes N and NE of the Black Sea and in the region E of Aral Sea. They are mentioned as early as the 7th cent. B.C. when they were driven out of Media; slowly conquered by the Sarmatians beginning 4th cent. B.C.

Scythopolis. See BET SHE'AN.

Sea Bright \ˈsē-ˌbrīt\. Borough, Monmouth co., New Jersey, on Atlantic Ocean; pop. (1990c) 1693.

Sea·brook \ˈsē-ˌbru̇k\. **1.** Town, Rockingham co., SE New Hampshire, on Atlantic Ocean 13 mi. (21 km.) S of Portsmouth; pop. (1990c) 6503.
2. City, Harris co., SE Texas, on Galveston Bay SE of Houston; pop. (1990c) 6685.

Sea Cliff. Residential village, Nassau co., SE New York, on Long Island, on Long Island Sound 21 mi. (34 km.) ENE of New York City; pop. (1990c) 5054.

Sea·ford \ˈse-fərd\. **1.** City, Sussex co., Delaware, on Nanticoke River 15 mi. (24 km.) W of Georgetown; pop. (1990c) 5689.
2. \ˈse-fərd\. Unincorporated settlement, Nassau co., SE New York, on Long Island E of New York City; pop. (1990c) 15,597.
3. \ˈsē-fərd, sē-ˌfȯrd\. Town, East Sussex, S England; pop. (1981p) 17,785; seaside resort.

Sea·forth, Loch \ˈsē-ˌfōrth\. Inlet of the Minch on E coast of island of Lewis with Harris off NW coast of Scotland, in the Outer Hebrides.

Sea Gardens. E part of harbor of Nassau, New Providence I., Bahamas.

Sea·go·ville \ˈsē-gō-ˌvil\. City, Dallas co., NE Texas, bordering the city of Dallas on the SE; pop. (1990c) 8969.

Sea·ham \ˈsē-əm\; *formerly* **Seaham Harbour.** Port town, Durham, N England, 16 mi. (26 km.) SE of Newcastle upon Tyne; pop. (1981p) 21,130.

Sea Islands. Chain of islands in Atlantic Ocean off coasts of South Carolina, Georgia, and a small stretch of N Florida; noted for the production of sea-island cotton.

Seal \ˈsēl\. River, N Manitoba, Canada; flows E through a chain of lakes into Hudson Bay; ab. 240 mi. (385 km.) long.

Seal, Cape. Cape, SE coast of Western Cape prov., S Rep. of South Africa.

Sea·lark Channel \ˈsē-lärk\. Channel, bet. Guadalcanal and Florida islands, SE Solomon Is., W Pacific Ocean; ab. 3 mi. (5 km.) wide. See FLORIDA ISLAND.

Seal Beach. City, Orange co., SW California, on Pacific Ocean just below Long Beach; pop. (1990c) 25,098.

Seale \ˈsēl\. Town, a ⊗ of Russell co., E Alabama.

Seal Islands. See LOBOS ISLANDS.

Seal Rock. Island in Pacific Ocean, in Lincoln co., W Oregon.

Sea·ly \ˈsē-lē\. City, Austin co., SE cen. Texas, ab. 30 mi. (48 km.) W of Houston; pop. (1990c) 4541; agriculture.

Sea of Rybinsk. See RYBINSK RESERVOIR.

Sea Point. Town, Western Cape prov., S Rep. of South Africa, suburb (incl. Green Point) 4 mi. (6 km.) W of Cape Town on Table Bay.

Sear·cy \ˈsər-sē\. **1.** County in N Arkansas. See table at ARKANSAS.
2. City, ⊗ of White co., NE cen. Arkansas, 48 mi. (77 km.) NE of Little Rock; pop. (1990c) 15,180; Harding Univ. (1924).

\ə\ abut \ᵊ\ kitten, Fr table \ər\ further \a\ ash \ā\ ace \ä\ cot, cart \ȧ\ Fr bac \au̇\ out \b̶\ Span Avila \ch\ chin \e\ bet \ē\ easy \g\ go \i\ hit \ī\ ice \j\ job \k\ Ger ich, Buch \ⁿ\ Fr vin \ŋ\ sing \ō\ go \ȯ\ all \ȯ\ law \œ\ Fr bœuf \œ̄\ Fr feu \ȯi\ boy \th\ thin \t͟h\ this \ü\ loot \u̇\ foot \ue\ Ger füllen \ue̅\ Fr rue \y\ yet \ʸ\ Fr digne \ˈdēnʸ\, nuit \ˈnwʸē\ \yü\ few \yu̇\ fury \zh\ vision

Searles Lake \ˈsərlz\. Dry lake bed, N San Bernardino co., SE California; extends a little way into Inyo co.; important source of minerals.

Sea·side \ˈsē-ˌsīd\. **1.** City, Monterey co., W California, N of the city of Monterey; pop. (1990c) 38,901; pop. grew rapidly in 1960s.
2. City and seaside resort, Clatsop co., NW corner of Oregon, on Pacific Ocean 15 mi. (24 km.) S of Astoria; pop. (1990c) 5359; summer resort.

Seat Pleas·ant \sēt-ˈplez-ᵊnt\. City, Prince Georges co., S cen. Maryland, just E of the easternmost point of Washington, D.C.; pop. (1990c) 5359.

Se·at·tle \sē-ˈat-ᵊl\. City, ⊗ of King co., W cen. Washington, bet. Elliott Bay of Puget Sound and Lake Washington (*q.v.*); pop. (1990c) 516,259; seaport important in trade with Asian countries; largest city in the state and the commercial, industrial, and financial center of the Pacific Northwest; ships grain; fish and timber market; supply center for fishing and lumbering industries; produces aircraft; shipyards, canneries; tourist center; Space Needle (landmark from 1962 world's fair); Seattle Art Museum housing notable collections of Asian, Northwest American Indian, and African art; Museum of Flight. Univ. of Washington (1861), Seattle Pacific Univ. (1891), Seattle Univ. (1891), Griffin Coll. (1909), Cornish Coll. of the Arts (1914), Shoreline Community Coll. (1964), Seattle Central Community Coll. (1966), North Seattle Community Coll. (1970), South Seattle Community Coll. (1970).
History: First settled 1851; platted and became ⊗ 1853; incorp. 1869; suffered from severe fire 1889; became important commercial center during Alaskan gold rush 1897 ff.; further expanded as seaport following opening of Panama Canal 1914 and during WWI; became a center of the aircraft industry during WWII. Site of Alaska-Yukon-Pacific Exposition 1909 and of Century 21 Exposition 1962.

Se·ba·go Lake \sə-ˈbā-gō\. Lake in cen. Cumberland co., SW Maine; ab. 13 mi. (21 km.) long by 10 mi. (16 km.) wide; resort.

Sebastea. See SIVAS 2.

Se·bas·tian \si-ˈbas-chən\. **1.** County in W Arkansas. See table at ARKANSAS.
2. City, Indian River co., cen. E coast of Florida; pop. (1990c) 10,205; outdoor recreation.

Sebastian, Cape. Cape on W coast of Curry co., SW corner of Oregon.

Se·bas·tián Viz·ca·í·no, Ba·hía \bä-ˈē-ä-ˌsā-bäs-ˈtyän-ˌbēs-kä-ˈē-nō\. Large inlet of Pacific Ocean on W coast of Baja California, Mexico.

Se·bas·ti·cook Lake \si-ˈbas-ti-ˌku̇k\. Lake, S cen. Maine, near SW boundary of Penobscot co.

Se·bas·to·pol \sə-ˈbas-tə-pəl, -ˌpōl\. City, Sonoma co., W California, 7 mi. (11 km.) SW of Santa Rosa; pop. (1990c) 7004.

Sebastopol. See SEVASTOPOL'.

Seb·cha di Tau·or·ga \ˈseb-kə-ˌdē-tau̇-ˈȯr-gə\ *or* **Sab·khat Tā·wur·ghā'** \ˈsäb-ˌkät-tä-ˈwu̇r-gə\. Salt marsh, N Libya, extending along W shore of the Gulf of Sidra.

Sebenico. See ŠIBENIK.

Se·ben·ny·tos *or* **Se·ben·ny·tus** \si-ˈbe-nə-təs\; *mod.* **Sa·man·nûd** *or* **Se·me·nud** \ˌsa-ma-ˈnüd\. City of ancient Egypt, in Nile Delta on W bank of Damietta Mouth; ruins are SW of El Mansûra.

Se·beş \ˈsā-besh\. Town, Alba co., Romania; pop. (1989c) 31,968.

Seb·ha. See SABHĀ.

Şe·bin·ka·ra·hi·sar \she-ˈbin-kä-rä-hi-ˈsär\; *anc.* **Ka·ra·his·sar** \kä-rä-hi-ˈsär\. Town, Giresun prov., N Turkey in Asia; alt. 4860 ft. (1481 m.).

Sebkhet el Kourzia. See SABKHAT AL-KURZĪYAH.

Se·boe·is Lake \si-ˈbō-əs\. Lake, SE Piscataquis co., cen. Maine.

Seboekoe. See SEBUKU.

Se·boo·mook Lake \si-ˈbü-mək\. Lake, cen. Somerset co., W Maine, an expansion of the W branch of the Penobscot River just E of junction of its headstreams; ab. 12 mi. (19 km.) long.

Se·bou *or* **Se·bu** \sə-ˈbü\. River, NW Morocco; flows N, then W into Atlantic Ocean N of Rabat; ab. 180 mi. (290 km.) long; navigable to Kenitra for oceangoing vessels and as far as Fès for smaller boats.

Seb·ra, Bay of \ˈse-brə\. See BIZERTE.

Se·bring \ˈsē-briŋ\. **1.** City, ⊗ of Highlands co., cen. Florida Penin., 50 mi. (81 km.) SE of Lakeland; pop. (1990c) 8900; citrus orchards.
2. City, Mahoning co., NE Ohio, 21 mi. (34 km.) SW of Youngstown; pop. (1990c) 4848.

Sebta. See CEUTA.

Sebu. See SEBOU.

Se·bu·ku *or Du.* **Se·boe·koe** \sə-ˈbü-kü\. Small island in SW Makassar Strait, E of Laut I., SE of Borneo, Indonesia.

Se·cau·cus \si-ˈkȯ-kəs\. Town, Hudson co., NE New Jersey, 5 mi. (8 km.) NNW of Jersey City; pop. (1990c) 14,061.

Sec·chia \ˈsāk-kyä\. River, N Italy; rises in the Apennines, flows N into Po River 12 mi. (19 km.) SE of Mantua; 97 mi. (156 km.) long.

Se·chu·ra, Ba·hía de \bä-ˈē-ä-ˌthā-sā-ˈchü-rä\ *or Eng.* **Bay of Sechura.** Inlet of Pacific Ocean on NW coast of Peru.

Sechura Desert. Desert, N coast of Peru; N to S extent ab. 65 mi. (105 km.) long, E to W extent ab. 40 mi. (65 km.) wide.

Se·cos, Ilhé·us \il-ˈyā-üs-ˈsā-küs\ *or* **Ilhéus do Rom·bo** \dü-ˈrȯm-bü\. Group of small uninhabited islands, Cape Verde Is., N of Brava I. and W of Fogo I.

Sec·re·tary Island \ˈse-krə-ˌter-ē\. Island off SW coast of South I., New Zealand.

Se·cun·der·a·bad *also* **Si·kan·dar·a·bad** \si-ˈkən-də-rə-ˌbad, -ˌbäd\. Town and cantonment, N Andhra Pradesh, S cen. India, part of Hyderabad; pop. (1991p) 167,461; railroad center. Formerly one of the largest of the British military stations in India.

Sé·cu·re \ˈsā-kü-ˌrā\. River, cen. Bolivia; flows E and NE into the Mamoré; ab. 150 mi. (240 km.) long.

Se·da·lia \si-ˈdāl-yə\. City, ⊗ of Pettis co., W cen. Missouri, 58 mi. (93 km.) W of Jefferson City; pop. (1990c) 19,800; packs and ships agricultural produce; site of annual Missouri State Fair; State Fair Community Coll. (1966); city founded c. 1860.

Se·dan 1. \si-ˈdan\. City, ⊗ of Chautauqua co., SE Kansas, 28 mi. (45 km.) WSW of Independence; pop. (1990c) 1306.
2. \sə-ˈdäⁿ, -ˈdan\. City, Ardennes dept., NE France, on Meuse River 11 mi. (18 km.) ESE of Mézières; pop. (1990c) 22,407; woolens, chemicals. Scene of decisive battle of Franco-Prussian War, resulting in French defeat and surrender of French Emperor Napoléon III 1870; occupied by Germany during WWI and WWII.

Sedd el Bahr \ˈsed-al-ˈbär\ *or Turk.* **Sedd·ül·ba·hir** \ˈsed-œl-bä-ˈhir\. Village on the S end of Gallipoli Penin., Turkey in Europe; just E of Cape İlyasbaba; one of the landing places of British forces 1915 during Gallipoli campaign in WWI.

Sedge·moor \ˈsej-ˌmōr, -ˌmu̇r\. Tract of moorland in Somerset, SW England; scene of James Scott, duke of Monmouth's defeat July 1685 by forces of James II.

Sedg·wick \ˈsej-ˌwik\. Name of counties in two states of the U.S. See tables at COLORADO and KANSAS.

Sed·li·ce \ˈsed-lit-ˌsā\ *or Ger.* **Sed·litz** \ˈzed-lits, ˈsed-\. Town, W Czech Republic, 11 mi. (18 km.) NW of Písek; gave name to Seidlitz powders.

Se·do·na \si-ˈdō-nə\. City, Coconino co., cen. Arizona, 28 mi. (45 km.) S of Flagstaff; pop. (1990c) 7720; retirement community, artist colony; tourism.

Se·dro–Wool·ley \ˈsē-drō-ˈwu̇-lē\. City, Skagit co., NW Washington, on Skagit River 20 mi. (32 km.) SSE of Bellingham; pop. (1990c) 6031; lumbering, agriculture.

Sedunum. See SION.

See·heim \ˈsē-ˌhām\. Town, S Namibia, on Fish River; elev. 2300 ft. (701 m.); railroad junction point.

See·konk \ˈsē-ˌkäŋk\. **1.** Navigable river, NE Rhode Island; formed by the widened Blackstone River at Pawtucket; the most northerly point of Narragansett Bay tidewater, flows S into Providence River at Providence; ab. 5 mi. (8 km.) long.
2. Town, Bristol co., SE Massachusetts, 10 mi. (16 km.) NW of Fall River; pop. (1990c) 13,046.

Seeland. See SJÆLLAND.
Seeonee. See SEONI.
Sefid Rud. See SAFĪD RUD.
Se·frou \sə-'frü\. Town, N cen. Morocco, ab. 20 mi. (32 km.) SE of Fès.
Sef·ton \'sef-tən\. Mountain range in the Southern Alps, W cen. South I., New Zealand; highest peak 10,359 ft. (3157 m.).
Sefurieh. See ZIPPORI.
Se·ga·mat \sə-gä-'mät\. Town, Johor state, West Malaysia (see MALAYSIA), roughly halfway bet. Kuala Lumpur and Johor Baharu; pop. (1980c) 34,008.
Se·ges·ta \sē-'jes-tä\ *or* **Se·ges·te** \-tā\. Ancient city in NW Sicily; its ruins, near modern Alcamo, include a well-preserved theater 3d cent. B.C. and the temple of Artemis, begun c. 425 B.C. Often in disputes with Selinus; allied with Carthage 409 B.C.; sacked by Agathocles, tyrant of Siracusae 307 B.C.; allied with Rome in First Punic War.
Segesvár. See SIGHIŞOARA.
Segodunum. See RODEZ.
Segontia. See SIGÜENZA.
Sé·gou \sā-'gü\ *also* **Se·gu** \sā-'gü\. Town, S Mali, on Niger River, 120 mi. (193 km.) ENE of Bamako; pop. (1987p) 88,877.
Se·go·via \sā-'gō-vyä\. **1.** River, Nicaragua. See COCO.
2. Province of cen. Spain. See table at SPAIN.
3. Commune, ✻ of Segovia prov., cen. Spain, 40 mi. (64 km.) NNW of Madrid; pop. (1991p) 54,142; rubber products, flour, pottery; a walled town with a restored 14th–15th cent. alcazar, 16th cent. Gothic cathedral, Roman aqueduct, and several Romanesque churches. Founded c. 700 B.C. and important under Romans; taken by Moors early 8th cent. A.D. and reconquered by Alfonso VI of Castile 1079; became royal residence 13th cent.; sacked by French 1808.
Seg Oze·ro \ˌsek-'ȯ-zir-ə\. Lake, Karelia Rep., NW Russia in Europe; 303 sq. mi. (785 sq. km.).
Se·gra·te \sā-'grä-tā\. Commune, Milano prov., Lombardy, N Italy; pop. (1989c) 33,255.
Se·gre \'sā-grā\. River, Catalonia, NE Spain; rises in the Pyrenees, flows SW past Lérida into Ebro River; 162 mi. (261 km.) long.
Segu. See SÉGOU.
Se·guam \sā-'gwäm\. Island of the Andreanof group in the Aleutians, SW Alaska, separated on the E from Amukta I. by Amukta Pass and on the W from Amlia I. by **Seguam Pass.**
Se·guin \sə-'gēn\. City, ⊗ of Guadalupe co., S cen. Texas, 33 mi. (53 km.) ENE of San Antonio; pop. (1990c) 18,853; cotton, corn produced in area; hydroelectric power generation nearby; Texas Lutheran Coll. (1891).
Se·gun·do \sā-'gün-dō\. River, Córdoba prov., N cen. Argentina; flows ENE into Mar Chiquita; ab. 200 mi. (320 km.) long.
Se·gu·ra \sā-'gü-rä\. River, SE Spain; rises in Sierra de Segura, flows E and SE into the Mediterranean Sea; 202 mi. (325 km.) long.
Segura, Sier·ra de \'syer-rä-ˌthā-\. Mountain range mostly in Jaén and Albacete provs., SE Spain; highest peak 5935 ft. (1809 m.).
Sehome. See BELLINGHAM 2.
Se·hore \sə-'hōr\. Town, W Madhya Pradesh, cen. India, 20 mi. (32 km.) WSW of Bhopal; pop. (1991p) 71,437.
Seibo, El. See EL SEIBO.
Seibus. See SEYBOUSE.
Seierø. See SEJERØ.
Seierø Bight. See SEJERØ BIGHT.
Seihun. See SEYHAN.
Sei·kan Tunnel \'sā-ˌkän\. Rail tunnel, Japan, under Tsugaru Strait from Aomori, Honshū to Hakodate, Hokkaidō; 33.4 mi. (53.7 km.) long; opened 1988.
Sei·land \'sā-ˌlän\. Island in Finnmark co., in Arctic Ocean off NW coast of Norway; 226 sq. mi. (585 sq. km.).
Seille \'sā\. River, Lorraine, NE France; flows W and NW to the Moselle at Metz; 80 mi. (129 km.) long; forms part of S boundary of Moselle dept.
Seim. See SEYM.
Sei·nä·jo·ki \'sā-na-ˌyȯ-kē\. Town, Vaasa prov., SW cen. Finland; pop. (1989c) 27,505; railroad junction point; founded 1931.
Seine \'sān, 'sen\; *anc.* **Seq·ua·na** \'se-kwə-nə\. River, N France; rises in Côte-d'Or dept., E France; flows NW through Paris and on into the English Channel near Le Havre; 482 mi. (776 km.) long; navigable for ab. 350 mi. (565 km.); spanned at its mouth by Pont de Normandie Bridge, longest cable-stayed bridge in world (main span 2808 ft. or 856 m.; completed 1994), connecting Le Havre and Honfleur.
Seine, Bay of the *or Fr.* **Baie de la Seine** \ˌbād-lä-'sen\. Inlet of the English Channel, N coast of Normandy, NW France; along its curving coastline, from Cotentin Penin. on W to mouth of the Seine on E, are many popular spas.
Seine–et–Marne \-ā-'märn\. Department of N France. See table at FRANCE.
Seine–Ma·ri·time \-ˌmä-rē-'tēm\; *formerly* **Seine–In·fé·ri·eure** \-ˌeⁿ-fer-'yœ̄r\. Department of N France. See table at FRANCE.
Seine–St.–Denis \ˌsān-seⁿ-də-'nē, ˌsen-\. Department of N France. See table at FRANCE.
Se·ir \'sē-ər, 'sir\. **1.** Country. See EDOM.
2. Mountain range of ancient Edom, along E side of Wadi al-'Arabah; now in Jordan; highest point Mt. Hor 4367 ft. (1331 m.).
Seis de Septiembre. See MORÓN 1.
Seishin. See CH'ŎNGJIN.
Seistan. See SISTĀN.
Se·je·rø \'sā-ər-ˌœ\; *mostly formerly* **Sei·erø** \'sā-ər-œ\. Small island off NW coast of Sjælland I., Denmark, in Sejerø Bight.
Sejerø Bight; *mostly formerly* **Seierø Bight.** Bay on NW coast of Sjælland I., Denmark.
Sekia el Hamra. See SAGUIET EL HAMRA.
Se·ki·ga·ha·ra \ˌse-kē-gä-'här-ä\. Town, SW Gifu prefecture, cen. Honshū, Japan, ab. 16 mi. (26 km.) WSW of the city of Gifu; pop. (1990p) 9545; site of battle in 1600 in which Tokugawa Ieyasu gained complete control of the government; resulting empire lasted to 1868.
Sek·ka, Ras ben \'räs-ben-sə-'kä\. Cape, N Tunisia; most northerly point of Africa, 37°21′N.
Se·kon·di–Ta·ko·ra·di \'se-kən-'dē-ˌtä-kə-'rä-dē\. Dual city and seaport, ✻ of Western Region, SW Ghana, 110 mi. (177 km.) WSW of Accra; pop. (1984c) 93,400; connected by rail with Kumasi; has modern port facilities and boatbuilding, cigarette-making, and railway-repair industries. Sekondi site of Dutch and British forts in 17th cent. and later became site of principal port of the Gold Coast; harbor constructed at Takoradi 1928; Sekondi and Takoradi united 1946; made city 1963.
Sela. City, ✻ of ancient Edom. See PETRA.
Se·lah \'sē-lə\. City, Yakima co., S Washington, 8 mi. (13 km.) NW of the city of Yakima; pop. (1990c) 5113.
Se·lang·or \sə-'läŋ-u̇r, sə-'laŋ-ˌgȯr\. A state of Malaysia, W coast of S Malay Penin., bounded on N by Perak, on E by Pahang and Negeri Sembilan, on S and W by Strait of Malacca; ✻ Shah Alam; generally level with mountain range along E boundary; rubber, rice, pineapples, tin. Crossed by the main railroad line along W coast of peninsula and by the branch from Kuala Lumpur to Port Kelang. See table at MALAYSIA. Became British protectorate 1874; became part of the Federated Malay States 1896 and of the Federation of Malaya 1948.
Selanik. See THESSALONÍKI.
Se·lar·gius \se-'lär-jüs\. Commune, Cagliari prov., Sardinia, Italy; pop. (1989c) 22,892.
Se·la·ru *or Du.* **Se·la·roe** \sā-'lä-rü\. Island of the Tanimbar group, in S Moluccas, Indonesia, E Malay Archipelago, off S

end of Jamdena I.; ab. 32 mi. (51 km.) long by 4 to 8 mi. (6 to 13 km.) wide.

Se·la·tan, Tan·jung *or Du.* **Tan·djoeng Selatan** \ˈtän-ˌjůŋ-sä-ˈlä-ˌtän\ *or Eng.* **Cape Se·la·tan** \sə-ˈlät-ᵊn\; *mostly formerly* **Cape Sa·la·tan** \sə-\. Cape, S coast of Borneo, Indonesia, projecting into Java Sea, 4°10′S, 114°38′E; southernmost point of the island of Borneo.

Selat Makasar. See MAKASSAR STRAIT.

Selat Surabaya. See SURABAYA STRAIT.

Selat Tebrau. See JOHORE STRAIT.

Se·la·yar *or* **Sa·la·yar** \sə-ˈlä-yər\; *mostly formerly* **Sa·la·yer** \-yər\. Long narrow island of Indonesia, in Flores Sea, 11 mi. (18 km.) off S coast of SW peninsula of Sulawesi, at entrance to Gulf of Bone; 51 mi. (82 km.) long; 259 sq. mi. (671 sq. km.).

Selayar Strait *or* **Salayar Strait;** *mostly formerly* **Salayer Strait.** Channel bet. Selayar I. and Sulawesi in the Malay Archipelago.

Selb \ˈzelp\. City, Bavaria, Germany, 40 mi. (64 km.) SSW of Zwickau; pop. (1980c) 21,207.

Sel·by \ˈsel-bē\. **1.** City, ⊗ of Walworth co., N South Dakota; pop. (1990c) 707.

2. Town, North Yorkshire, N England, on the Ouse River S of York; pop. (1991p) 88,200; thought to be birthplace of King Henry I 1068.

Sel·çuk \sel-ˈchük\; *formerly* **Aya So·luk** \ˌä-yä-sō-ˈlük\. Village, S İzmir prov., W Turkey in Asia, near site of ancient Ephesus (*q.v.*).

Sel·do·via \sel-ˈdō-vē-ə, -vyə\. City near S tip of Kenai Penin., S Alaska, on Cook Inlet; pop. (1990c) 316.

Se·le \ˈsā-le\. Short stream, Campania, S Italy; flows W to Gulf of Salerno ab. 8 mi. (13 km.) S of Salerno; ab. 20 mi. (32 km.) long.

Se·le·bi–Phi·kwe \se-ˈlā-bē-ˈpē-ˌkwā\ *or* **Selebi–Pi·kwe** \-ˈpē-\. Town, E Botswana; pop. (1991c) 39,772; developed as a result of nearby copper- and nickel-mining operations.

Se·lem·dzha \ˌsel-yim-ˈjä\. River, main tributary of the Zeya in S Khabarovsk Kray, E Russia in Asia; rises in SE spurs of Stanovoi Mts. and flows SW to the Zeya ab. 120 mi. (195 km.) NE of Blagoveshchensk; 376 mi. (605 km.) long.

Se·len·ga \ˌsi-liŋ-ˈgä\ *or in Mongolia* **Se·len·ge** \ˈse-leŋ-ˌgā\. River, N cen. Asia; rises near Uliastay in W Mongolia and flows E; joined by the Orhon near Russian border which it crosses, flows N through Buryatia Rep., turns W at Ulan-Ude to enter Lake Baikal on SE; 620 mi. (998 km.) long.

Sé·les·tat \sā-les-ˈtä\ *or Ger.* **Schlett·stadt** \ˈshlet-ˌshtät\. Commune, Bas-Rhin dept., NE France, near Ill River 34 mi. (55 km.) SW of Strasbourg. Became free city 13th cent.; taken by Swedes 1632; taken by French 1634; taken by Germans 1870; reverted to French rule 1918.

Se·leu·cia \sə-ˈlü-shə, -shē-ə\. Name of several cities in ancient Syria and Asia Minor, esp.: (1) *or* **Seleucia Tra·che·o·tis** \ˌtrā-kē-ˈō-təs\. Ancient city, Cilicia, SE Asia Minor, SW of Tarsus, on the Calycadnus (*mod.* Göksu) near its mouth; site of modern Silifke. (2) *or* **Seleucia on the Ti·gris** \ˈtī-grəs\. City, now in ruins, on W bank of the Tigris, cen. Iraq, opp. Ctesiphon and ab. 20 mi. (32 km.) SSE of Baghdad. Founded by Seleucus I Nicator late 4th cent. B.C. as eastern ✱; became chief city of E **Seleucid Empire;** developed extensive trade and at one time was said to have 600,000 inhabitants; sacked by Romans c. 162 A.D. See PARTHIA. (3) *or* **Seleucia Pi·e·ria** \pī-ˈir-ē-ə, -ˈer-\. Ancient port of Antioch, now in SW Hatay, S Turkey in Asia; founded by Seleucid King Seleucus I Nicator c. 300 B.C. as the port of Antioch; held by Egyptians 3d cent. B.C. but recovered c. 219 B.C. by Seleucid King Antiochus the Great; became independent c. 108 B.C. and its freedom confirmed by Roman Gen. Pompey the Great; port damaged in earthquake 526 A.D.; city declined thereafter.

Seli. See ROKEL.

Se·li·ger \si-lē-ˈgyer\. Lake, W Tver' Oblast, W Russia in Europe; 57 mi. (92 km.) long; 104 sq. mi. (269 sq. km.); discharges into headwaters of the Volga River.

Se·lins·grove \ˈsē-lənz-ˌgrōv\. Borough, Snyder co., cen. Pennsylvania, on Susquehanna River; pop. (1990c) 5384; Susquehanna Univ. (1858).

Se·li·nus \si-ˈlī-nəs\. Greek city, S coast of ancient Sicily; its ruins are SSE of Castelvetrano; founded 7th cent. B.C.; destroyed by Carthaginians 409 B.C.; partly rebuilt but razed by Carthage 250 B.C.

Sel·kirk \ˈsel-ˌkərk\. **1.** Resort town, SE Manitoba, Canada, on Red River 23 mi. (37 km.) NNE of Winnipeg, near S end of Lake Winnipeg; pop. (1991c) 9815; lake port, boatbuilding; steel foundries; truck farms in area; tourism. Founded near the Red River Settlement (estab. 1811) of Thomas Douglas, earl of Selkirk.

2. *or* **Sel·kirk·shire** \-ˌshir, -shər\. Former county, SE Scotland; ⊗ Selkirk; hilly region; writer Sir Walter Scott was appointed sheriff of Selkirk in 1799.

3. Burgh, cen. Borders region, SE Scotland, on Ettrick River; pop. (1981p) 5417; market town; woolens.

Selkirk Mountains *also* **the Sel·kirks** \ˈsel-ˌkərks\. Mountain range, SE British Columbia, Canada, within the Big Bend of the Columbia River, W of the Rocky Mts.; ab. 200 mi. (320 km.) long; highest peak Mt. Sir Sandford 11,555 ft. (3522 m.). Crossed by the Canadian Pacific Railways at Rogers Pass near the Illecillewaet Glacier (*q.v.*), contains part of Glacier National Park and Mount Revelstoke National Park (see CANADA, *National Parks*).

Sel·la·sia \sə-ˈlā-zhə\. Town in ancient Laconia, SE Peloponnese, S Greece, ab. 5 mi. (8 km.) N of Sparta; scene of battle 222 or 221 B.C. in which Antigonus Doson, king of Macedonia, defeated the Spartans under Cleomenes III.

Selle \ˈsel\. Small river in Nord dept., N France, flowing into Schelde River.

Sel·lers·burg \ˈse-lərz-ˌbərg\. Town, Clark co., SE Indiana; pop. (1990c) 5745.

Sel·lers·ville \ˈse-lərz-ˌvil\. Borough, Bucks co., SE Pennsylvania, 19 mi. (31 km.) SSE of Allentown; pop. (1990c) 4479; founded 1738.

Sel·lery, Mount \ˈse-lər-ē\. Peak, Antarctica, 84°58′S, 172°45′W; 12,779 ft. (3895 m.).

Selling Tso. See SILING CO.

Sellore Island. See SAGANTHIT ISLAND.

Selm \ˈzelm\. Commune, North Rhine-Westphalia, Germany, 20 mi. (32 km.) S of Münster; pop. (1980c) 23,762.

Sel·ma \ˈsel-mə\. **1.** City, ⊗ of Dallas co., SW cen. Alabama, on Alabama River 40 mi. (64 km.) W of Montgomery; pop. (1990c) 23,755; produces cigars, wood products, agricultural machinery, automobile locks; Selma Univ. (1878); settled c. 1815; incorp. 1820; Confederate arsenal and supply depot in Civil War, destroyed by Union troops 1865; in 1965 scene of major civil rights demonstrations.

2. City, Fresno co., S cen. California, 15 mi. (24 km.) SE of the city of Fresno; pop. (1990c) 14,757.

3. Town, Johnston co., E North Carolina, 27 mi. (43 km.) SE of Raleigh; pop. (1990c) 4600.

Sel·mer \ˈsel-mər\. Town, ⊗ of McNairy co., SW Tennessee; pop. (1990c) 3838.

Sel·sey Bill \ˌsel-sē-ˈbil\. Headland on S coast of England, E of Portsmouth.

Selukwe. See SHURUGWI.

Selvagens. See SALVAGES.

Sel·vas \ˈsel-vəz\. Extensive forested region of the upper Amazon River basin in N cen. South America.

Selzaete. See ZELZATE.

Se·man \ˈse-ˌmän\; *formerly* **Se·me·ni** \ˈse-mə-nē\. River, cen. Albania, formed by confluence of two headstreams N of Berat; flows W to Adriatic Sea; 157 mi. (253 km.) long.

Se·mang·ka Bay \sā-ˈmäŋ-kə\. Bay on S end of Sumatra, Indonesia, W of Lampung Bay; opens on Sunda Strait.

Se·ma·rang *or* **Sa·ma·rang** \sə-ˈmär-ˌäŋ\. **1.** Former residency, Central Java prov., Indonesia; 2088 sq. mi. (5408 sq. km.); ✱ Semarang.

2. Seaport city, ✱ of Central Java prov., Indonesia, and formerly ✱ of Semarang residency, on N coast railroad line ab.

255 mi. (410 km.) E of Jakarta; pop. (1990c) 1,250,971; unprotected against NW monsoon; manufactures textiles; shipbuilding, fishing; exports rubber, coffee, sugar; university (c. 1957).

Semendria. See SMEDEREVO.

Semeni. See SEMAN.

Se·me·nov \sə-ˈmyȯ-nəf\. Highest peak of Kyrgyz Range, N Kyrgyzstan; 15,994 ft. (4875 m.).

Semenovka. See ARSEN'YEV.

Semenud. See SEBENNYTOS.

Se·me·ru, Gu·nung \ˈgü-ˌnu̇ŋ-sə-ˈmer-ü\. Active volcano, E Java I., Indonesia, SE of Malang; 12,060 ft. (3676 m.); highest mountain in Java; joins with Tengger Mts. to the N.

Se·mey \ˈse-mā\ *or* **Se·mi·pa·la·tinsk** \ˌse-mē-pə-ˈlä-tinsk\. **1.** Administrative subdivision of Kazakhstan, bounded on N by Altay Kray, Russia in Asia, and on SE by Xinjiang Uygur, China; 69,344 sq. mi. (179,601 sq. km.); pop. (1991e) 841,900; ✻ Semey. Economy predominantly agricultural (esp. grain); has deposits of copper and gold.
2. City, its ✻, on right bank of Irtysh River 445 mi. (716 km.) SE of Omsk, Russia; pop. (1991e) 344,700; center of meatpacking industry; produces footwear, textiles; founded 1718 and transferred to present site 1778.

Se·mi·chi Islands \sə-ˈmē-chē\. Small island group at W end of Aleutian Is., SW Alaska, in the Near Is. ESE of Attu; includes Shemya (*q.v.*).

Se·mi·di Islands \sə-ˈmē-dē\. Group of eight islands off the S coast of Alaska, 56°07′N, 156°44′W.

Semien Mountains. See SIMYEN MOUNTAINS.

Se·mi·na·ra \ˌse-mē-ˈnä-rä\. Commune, Reggio di Calabria prov., Calabria, S Italy, on W coast N of commune of Reggio di Calabria; pop. (1981p) 4214; once most fortified place in Calabria.

Sem·i·noe Dam \ˈse-mə-nō\. Dam across North Platte River, N Carbon co., S cen. Wyoming; height 295 ft. (90 m.); impounds water, **Seminoe Reservoir,** for flood control, irrigation, and power.

Sem·i·nole \ˈse-mə-ˌnōl\. **1.** Name of counties in three states of the U.S. See tables at FLORIDA, GEORGIA, OKLAHOMA.
2. City, Pinellas co., Florida, in cen. W Florida Penin., W of St. Petersburg; pop. (1990c) 9251.
3. City, Seminole co., cen. Oklahoma, 13 mi. (21 km.) ESE of Shawnee; pop. (1990c) 7071; oil refineries; Seminole Junior Coll. (1931).
4. City, ⊗ of Gaines co., NW Texas, 62 mi. (100 km.) N of Odessa; pop. (1990c) 6342.

Seminole, Lake. Reservoir in NW Florida and SW corner of Georgia; created by damming of Apalachicola River.

Semipalatinsk. See SEMEY.

Se·mi·ra·ra Islands \ˌsä-mē-ˈrä-rä\. Island group bet. SE Mindoro I. and NW Panay I., cen. Philippines; ab. 50 sq. mi. (130 sq. km.); marks S end of Tablas Strait; comprises three large islands, Semirara, Sibay, and Caluya, and several smaller ones.

Sem·i·so·poch·noi \ˌse-mi-sə-ˈpäch-ˌnȯi\. Small island in N part of Rat Is. group, Aleutians, SW Alaska, E of Kiska; sea-lion rookery.

Sem·li·ki \ˈsem-lē-kē\. River, E cen. Africa; connects Lake Edward and Lake Albert; ab. 110 mi. (175 km.) long.

Semlin. See ZEMUN.

Sem·me·ring Pass \ˈze-mə-riŋ\. Mountain pass in E Alps, Austria, 23 mi. (37 km.) SW of Wiener Neustadt, bet. Lower Austria and Styria; alt. 3232 ft. (985 m.); two railroad tunnels.

Sem·nān \sem-ˈnän\ *or* **Sam·nan** \sam-\. **1.** Province (formerly a governorship) of N cen. Iran. See table at IRAN.
2. Town, its ✻, on highway 110 mi. (177 km.) E of Tehran, S of Elburz Mts.; pop. (1986c) 64,891.

Se·mois \sə-ˈmwä\. River, SE Belgium and NE France; flows NW in Luxembourg prov., crosses French border and empties into the Meuse 9 mi. (14 km.) N of Mézières; ab. 120 mi. (195 km.) long.

Sem·pach \ˈzem-ˌpäk\. Commune, Lucerne canton, cen. Switzerland, on Lake of Sempach 8 mi. (13 km.) NW of the commune of Lucerne; pop. (1980c) 2237; near scene of victory of Swiss Confederation over Austrian army July 9, 1386 contributing to ultimate Swiss independence.

Sempach, Lake of *or Ger.* **Sem·pach·er See** \ˈzem-ˌpä-kər-ˌzā\. Lake, N cen. Switzerland, NW of Lake of Lucerne; ab. 4 mi. (6 km.) long by 1 mi. (2 km.) wide; ab. 5.5 sq. mi. (14 sq. km.); max. depth 285 ft. (87 m.); outlet to the N into Aare River.

Sem·pang Man·ga·yau, Tan·jong \ˈtän-ˌjȯŋ-səm-ˈpäŋ-ˈmäŋ-yō\ *or* **Cape Sempang Mangayau;** *mostly formerly* **Cape Sam·pan·man·gio** \ˌsäm-pən-ˈmän-jō\. N point of island of Borneo, Sabah, Malaysia, 7°02′N, 116°45′E.

Sempione. Alpine pass and tunnel. See table at ALPS.

Se·na \ˈsā-nä\. Town, Mozambique, on right bank of Zambezi River, ab. 125 mi. (200 km.) SE of Tete; pop. (1992e) 4281; in 16th cent. a Portuguese fortified garrison.

Sena Gallica. See SENIGALLIA.

Sena Julia. See SIENA 2.

Sen·a·to·bia \ˌse-nə-ˈtō-bē-ə, -ˈtō-byə\. City, ⊗ of Tate co., NW Mississippi, 45 mi. (72 km.) NE of Clarksdale; pop. (1990c) 4772.

Sen·dai \sen-ˈdī\. City, ✻ of Miyagi prefecture, N Honshū, Japan, near E coast 180 mi. (290 km.) N of Tokyo; pop. (1990p) 918,378; local consumer-goods industry; an important cultural center with university (1907) and several technical schools. Ruins of early 17th cent. castle.

Sen·e·ca \ˈse-ni-kə\. **1.** River, W cen. New York; flows from Seneca Lake at N end to Cayuga Lake (canalized, part of New York State Barge Canal system) then N and E joining the Oneida River to form the Oswego River; ab. 65 mi. (105 km.) long.
2. River, NW South Carolina; rises in Blue Ridge in W North Carolina, flows S across South Carolina border and unites with Tugaloo River W of Anderson to form the Savannah River; in its upper course called the **Ke·o·wee** \ˈkē-ə-ˌwē\.
3. Name of counties in two states of the U.S. See tables at NEW YORK and OHIO.
4. City, ⊗ of Nemaha co., NE Kansas, 50 mi. (80 km.) NE of Manhattan; pop. (1990c) 2027.
5. Town, Oconee co., NW South Carolina, 22 mi. (35 km.) WNW of Anderson; pop. (1990c) 7726.

Seneca Falls. Village, Seneca co., W cen. New York, on Seneca River 11 mi. (18 km.) W of Auburn; pop. (1990c) 7370; tourism; Women's Rights National Historical Park estab. 1980 (see UNITED STATES, *National Historical Parks*); scene of first women's-rights convention in U.S. 1848; site of National Women's Hall of Fame.

Seneca Lake. Lake, chiefly in Yates and Seneca cos., W New York; one of the Finger Lakes (*q.v.*); ab. 35 mi. (56 km.) long; 67 sq. mi. (174 sq. km.); max. depth ab. 600 ft. (183 m.); connected at N end with Cayuga Lake by canalized Seneca River, part of the New York State Barge Canal system.

Sen·e·gal \ˌse-ni-ˈgȯl\ *or Fr.* **Sé·né·gal** \sā-nā-ˈgȧl\. **1.** Republic, W Africa, bounded on N and NE by Mauritania, on E by Mali, on S by Guinea and Guinea-Bissau, and on W by the Atlantic Ocean; in S part Republic of the Gambia extends as exclave ab. 200 mi. (320 km.) on both sides of the Gambia River; 76,124 sq. mi. (197,161 sq. km.); pop. (1993e) 7,899,000; ✻ Dakar.

Physical features: Mostly low on coast and only slightly elevated in cen. part, with mountain region in SE; lower Senegal River and its chief tributary the Falémé form N and E boundary; other streams are the upper Gambia, the Casamance, and the wide estuary of the Saloum. Coastline extends ab. 120 mi. (195 km.) S from mouth of Senegal River to Cap Vert (its W point) and Dakar, thence S for 190 mi. (306 km.) (not incl. Gambia coast) to a point just SE of Cape Roxo.

Chief products: Peanuts, cotton, rice, millet, sorghum; livestock raising, fishing; phosphates, titanium, zircon.

History: Coast explored by Portugal 1445; first French settlement at St.-Louis (founded 1658); control of coastal region passed bet. French and English from late 17th to early 19th cents.; French possession recognized 1814; Gov. Louis-Léon Faidherbe expanded territory inland 19th cent.; became a territory within French Union 1946 and an autonomous republic within French Community 1958; member of Mali Federation 1959–60; became independent state 1960; entered confederation with Gambia called Senegambia 1982 which was dissolved 1989; in late 1980s, thousands of Senegalese in Mauritania and Mauritanians in Senegal returned to their native countries amid racial violence.

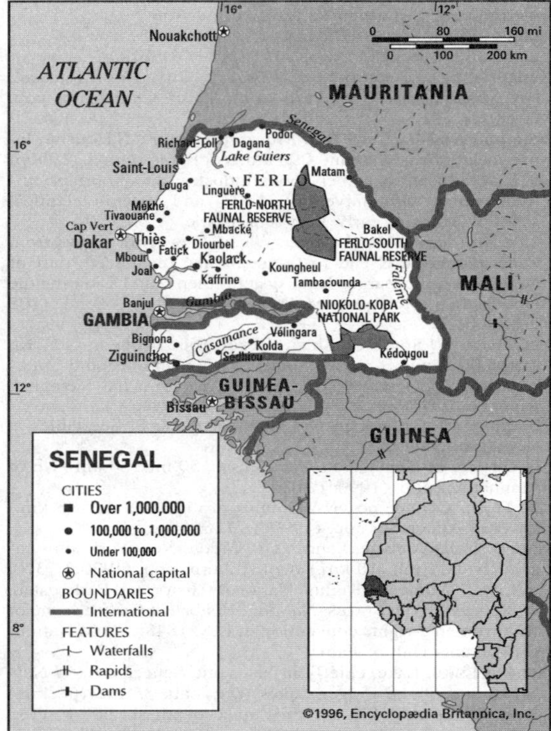

2. *or* **Sénégal.** River, W Africa; rises in the Fouta Djallon highlands of Guinea near the border of Sierra Leone, flows N and NW, forming the N boundary of the republic of Senegal, empties into Atlantic Ocean at St.-Louis; 1015 mi. (1633 km.) long; in its upper course, above its union at Bafoulabé with the Bakoye, known as Bafing River (*q.v.*); its chief tributary on the S is the Falémé, in E Senegal; navigable to the Bafing at high water.

Sen·e·gam·bia \ˌse-ni-ˈgam-bē-ə\. **1.** Region of the Senegal and Gambia rivers, W Africa, since 1904 mostly in Senegal and W Mali.
2. Former confederation, comprising Senegal and Gambia; formed 1982, dissolved 1989.

Senf·ten·berg \ˈzenf-tən-ˌberk\. City, Brandenburg, E Germany, on the Schwarze Elster 25 mi. (40 km.) NNW of Bautzen; pop. (1981c) 32,230.

Senglea. See BORMLA.

Seniavin Islands. See SENYAVIN ISLANDS.

Se·ni·gal·lia \ˌsā-ni-ˈgäl-yə\; *anc.* **Se·na Gal·li·ca** \ˈsē-nə-ˈga-li-kə\. Seaport, Ancona prov., Marche, cen. Italy, on Adriatic coast 18 mi. (29 km.) NW of the seaport of Ancona; pop. (1989c) 40,944; market town; 15th cent. castle; 18th cent. cathedral. Founded by Senonian Gauls; became Roman colony c. 289 B.C.; part of an ancient Pentapolis in Marche area of Italy.

Se·nio \ˈsān-yō, ˈsen-\. River, Emilia-Romagna, N Italy; rises in Apennines and flows NE to the Adriatic S of Comacchio; ab. 55 mi. (88 km.) long.

Senj \ˈsen-ye\ *or Hung.* **Zengg** \ˈzeŋ\. Seaport, Croatia.

Sen·ja \ˈsen-yə\. Island in Troms co., in Arctic Ocean off NW coast of Norway; 614 sq. mi. (1590 sq. km.).

Sen·lac \ˈsen-ˌlak\. Hill in East Sussex, S England, near Hastings; site of battle 1066 generally called "Battle of Hastings," the outcome of which allowed William the Conqueror to impose Norman rule over England.

Sen·lis \säⁿ-ˈlēs\. Town, Oise dept., N France, ab. 28 mi. (45 km.) NNE of Paris; pop. (1990c) 15,226; ancient town, has remains of Gallo-Roman walls; 12th cent. Gothic church.

Sen·nar *or* **Sen·naar** \sə-ˈnär\. **1.** Region and ancient kingdom, E Sudan, chiefly bet. the White Nile and Blue Nile.
2. Town, E Sudan, on the Blue Nile S of Wad Medani; ✱ of the ancient kingdom of Sennar; railroad terminus. Dam opened 1925 as Makwar Dam; name changed later to **Sennar Dam** (134 ft. or 41 m. high).

Senne \ˈsen\. River, W cen. Belgium; flows N out of Hainaut prov. through Brussels and into the Rupel River, a tributary of the Schelde; 64 mi. (103 km.) long.

Senne·terre \sen-ˈter\. Town, Abitibi co., SW Quebec, Canada, 300 mi. (483 km.) NW of Quebec City; pop. (1991c) 3563.

Sens \ˈsäⁿs\; *anc.* **Aged·in·cum** \ə-ˈje-diŋ-kəm\ *also later* **Sen·o·nes** \ˈse-nə-ˌnēz\. City, Yonne dept., NE cen. France, on Yonne River 32 mi. (51 km.) NNW of Auxerre; pop. (1990c) 27,755; electrical products, flour, dairy products; notable early Gothic cathedral (12th cent.) and remains of ancient fortifications. A Gallic ✱, later a large Roman settlement; important medieval bishopric; scene of 2d council condemning the teachings of theologian Peter Abelard 1140.

Sen·sun·te·pe·que \ˌsen-sün-te-ˈpā-kā\. Town, ✱ of Cabañas dept., N cen. El Salvador; pop. (1986e) 59,061; former center of indigo-growing region.

Sen·ta \ˈsen-tä\ *or Hung.* **Zen·ta** \ˈzen-tö\. City, Serbia, N Yugoslavia, on right bank of the Tisza River ab. 80 mi. (129 km.) NNW of Belgrade; trade center in agricultural region; scene of battle Sept. 1697 in which Austrian Gen. Prince Eugene of Savoy defeated the Turks.

Sen·ta·ni, Lake \sen-ˈtä-nē\. Small lake, NE Irian Jaya, Indonesia, ab. 10 mi. (16 km.) SW of Jayapura.

Sen·ti·nel, The \ˈsent-ᵊn-əl\. Mountain, Glacier National Park, NW Montana; 8100 ft. (2469 m.).

Sentinel Dome. Peak in the Sierra Nevada, E Fresno co., S cen. California; 9127 ft. (2782 m.).

Sentinel Peak. Mountain in the Adirondack Mts., Essex co., NE New York; 3858 ft. (1176 m.).

Sentinel Range *also* **Sentinel Mountains.** Group of high mountains, Ellsworth Land, Antarctica, bet. 77° and 78°S and bet. 86° and 92°30′W; highest peak Vinson Massif 16,860 ft. (5139 m.); discovered Nov. 1935 by American explorer Lincoln Ellsworth.

Sentinum. See SASSOFERRATO.

Sentis. See SÄNTIS.

Sen·to·sa \sen-ˈtō-sə\ *also* **Bla·kang Ma·ti** \ˈblä-ˌkäŋ-ˈmä-tē\. Island in Singapore Strait just S of Singapore; ab. 2 mi. (3.2 km.) long; strategically located for the defense of the harbor of Singapore.

Sen·ya·vin Islands *also* **Sen·ia·vin Islands** \ˈsen-yə-vin\. Island group, E part of the Caroline Is., W Pacific Ocean, 6°55′N, 158°E; chief island Pohnpei.

Seo de Urgel. See LA SEU D'URGELL.

Se·o·nath \ˌsā-ə-ˈnät\. River, E India; flows N and E in E Madhya Pradesh to Mahanadi River; ab. 200 mi. (320 km.) long.

Se·o·ni *also* **See·o·nee** \sā-ˈō-nē\. Town, S cen. Madhya Pradesh, E cen. India; pop. (1991p) 64,302.

Seoul \ˈsōl\ *also* **Kyong·song** \ˈkyȯŋ-ˈsȯŋ\ *or Jp.* **Kei·jo** \ˈkā-jō\. City, ✱ of South Korea, 40 mi. (64 km.) E of Inch'ŏn, its port; 237 sq. mi. (614 sq. km.); pop. (1985c) 9,639,110; has special city (provincial) status; commercial, cultural, and industrial center of South Korea, with textile and food-processing industries; several universities incl. Seoul National Univ. (1946); Ducksoo Palace, Changduk Palace.

History: ✻ of the Korean Yi dynasty 1392–1910; administrative center under Japanese rule 1910–45; made ✻ of U.S. military government 1945; made ✻ of South Korea 1948; suffered extensive damage in Korean War 1950–53; has been largely rebuilt since 1953; site of Summer Olympic Games 1988.

Sep·a·ra·tion Point *or* **Separation Head** \ˌse-pə-ˈrā-shən\. Cape, N coast of South I., New Zealand, forming SE side of Golden Bay and NW Point of Tasman Bay.

Se·pi \ˈsā-pē\. Village at SE tip of Santa Isabel I., Solomon Is.

Se·pik \ˈsā-pik\ *or Ger.* **Kai·se·rin Au·gus·ta** \ˈkī-zər-in-au̇-ˈgüs-tə\. River, NE New Guinea I., Papua New Guinea; ab. 600 mi. (965 km.) long; one of its headstreams is in Irian Jaya, Indonesia; navigable for ab. 300 mi. (485 km.).

Sepphoris. See ZIPPORI.

Sepsiszentgyörgy. See SFÎNTU-GHEORGHE.

Sept–Îles \se-ˈtēl\ *or Eng.* **Seven Isles.** City, SE Quebec, Canada, 250 mi. (402 km.) NE of Chicoutimi; pop. (1991c) 24,848; ships iron ore.

Sept–Îles, Les \lā-set-ˈēl\. Group of islands off the coast of Côtes-du-Nord dept., Brittany, NW France.

Sep·ti·ma·nia \ˌsep-tə-ˈmā-nē-ə\. Ancient territory, S France, from mouth of the Rhone to the Pyrenees on the S, and extending NW to the Cévennes Mts.

Sep·ti·mer Pass \ˈzep-tē-mər\. Mountain pass in the Rhaetian Alps, SE Switzerland, above Upper Engadine Valley; 7577 ft. (2309 m.).

Sept–Ri·vières–Ca·nia·pis·cau \ˌset-rē-ˈvyer-ˌka-nē-ə-ˌpis-ˈkau̇\. County, Quebec, Canada. See table at QUEBEC.

Sequana. See SEINE 1.

Se·quatch·ie \si-ˈkwä-chē\. **1.** River, SE cen. Tennessee; rises in S Cumberland co., flows SW into Tennessee River in S Marion co.

2. County in SE cen. Tennessee. See table at TENNESSEE.

Sequim \ˈskwim\. City, Clallam co., NW Washington, ESE of Port Angeles; pop. (1990c) 3616.

Se·quoia–Kings Canyon National Park \si-ˈkwȯi-ə\. Sequoia National Park and Kings Canyon National Park (see these names at UNITED STATES, *National Parks*); administered as a single unit.

Se·quoy·ah \si-ˈkwȯi-ə\. County in E Oklahoma. See table at OKLAHOMA.

Se·ra·bit el Kha·dim *or* **Sa·rā·bīt al–Kha·dím** \sə-rä-ˈbēt-al-k̲ä-ˈdēm\. Mountain, SW Sinai Penin., NE Egypt, in territory occupied by Israel 1967 to early 1980s; site of ancient Egyptian temple c. 2d millennium B.C.

Se·ra·fi·mo·vich \ˌser-ə-ˈfē-mə-vich\. Town, Volgograd Oblast, S Russia in Europe, on the Don NW of the city of Volgograd.

Se·raing \sə-ˈreⁿ\. Commune, Liège prov., E Belgium, on Meuse River SSW of the city of Liège; pop. (1991c) 60,838; a center of the Belgian metallurgical industry; machinery, glass.

Seram. See CERAM.

Ser·am·pore \ˈser-əm-ˌpōr\ *or* **Shrī·rām·pur** \ˈshrē-ˌräm-pu̇r\. Town, West Bengal, NE India, on right bank of Hugli River 13 mi. (21 km.) N of Calcutta; pop. (1991p) 137,087; jute and textile industry. Developed by Danes 18th cent. and known as **Fred·er·iks·na·gar** \ˈfre-də-riks-ˌnə-gər\; acquired by Great Britain 1845.

Seram Sea. See CERAM SEA.

Se·rang \ˈsā-ˌräŋ\. **1.** Island, Indonesia. See CERAM.

2. Town, West Java prov., Indonesia; pop. (1980c) 76,878; inland town on railroad line to Jakarta and 5 mi. (8 km.) S of old port of Banten.

Se·ra·vez·za \ˌse-rä-ˈvet-sä\. Commune, Lucca prov., Tuscany, cen. Italy, 17 mi. (27 km.) NW of the commune of Lucca; pop. (1981p) 13,026; cathedral.

Ser·bia \ˈsər-bē-ə\ *or Serb.* **Sr·bi·ja** \ˈsər-bē-ˌyä\; *mostly formerly* **Ser·via** \-vē-ə\. A constituent republic comprising 80 percent of the area of Yugoslavia; 34,115 sq. mi. (88,358 sq. km.); pop. (1992e) 9,823,000; ✻ Belgrade. Mountainous country with short ranges and spurs, running in various directions, highest on Bulgarian border; bordered on N by the Danube and traversed in E cen. part by the Morava and in cen. part by its tributaries the Western Morava and Ibar; textiles.

Chief cities: Belgrade, Novi Sad, Niš, Kragujevac, Podgorica, Subotica.

History: Settled by Serbs, 7th cent. A.D.; nominally under Byzantine suzerainty, by 9th cent. converted to Eastern Christianity; Nemanjic ruling dynasty founded by Stefan Nemanja c. 1169; territory expanded and became leading Slav kingdom under Stephen Dushan (1331–55) and controlled its greatest territory incl. areas comprising modern Serbia to the Danube, Albania, Macedonia, Montenegro, E Bosnia and Herzegovina, and N Greece; defeated by Turks at battle of Kosovo (*q.v.*) 1389; after period of resistance became part of Ottoman Empire 1459; revolted against Turkey under leadership of Karađorđe (Karageorge) 1804–13, and again in 1815–17, led by Miloš Obrenović; guaranteed autonomy 1829 and Miloš Obrenović recognized as hereditary prince 1830; secured withdrawal of Turkish garrisons 1867; made completely independent of Turkey 1878, but without control of Bosnia and Herzegovina (*q.v.*); defeated by Bulgaria (*q.v.*) 1885; threatened war after the annexation of Bosnia and Herzegovina by Austria 1908; with Bulgaria, Greece, and Montenegro founded Balkan League and defeated Turkey in First Balkan War 1912; received territory in Macedonia after Second Balkan War 1913; blamed by Austria for assassination of Archduke Francis Ferdinand and his wife (1914) leading to Austria's declaration of war on Serbia, ultimately precipitating WWI; after WWI became part of the Serb-dominated Kingdom of Serbs, Croats, and Slovenes 1918, renamed Yugoslavia (*q.v.*) 1929; made one of six federated republics of Yugoslavia in 1946; after the breakup of Yugoslavia, formed with Montenegro the Federal Republic of Yugoslavia 1992.

Ser·bi·an Republic of Bosnia and Herzegovina \ˈsər-bē-ən\. See BANJA LUKA.

Ser·bo·nis, Lake \sər-ˈbō-nəs\. Former lake and marsh, now dry, Lower Egypt, near coast E of Suez Canal.

Serbs, Croats, and Slovenes, Kingdom of the. See YUGOSLAVIA.

Ser·chio \ˈser-kyō, -kē-ō\. River, Tuscany, NW Italy; flows SE, SW, and W into the Ligurian Sea; ab. 60 mi. (95 km.) long.

Sercq. See SARK 1.

Serdica. See SOFIA 2.

Ser·do·bol'. See SORTAVALA.

Se·re·gno \se-ˈrān-yō\. Commune, Milano prov., Lombardy, N Italy, 13 mi. (21 km.) N of Milan; pop. (1989c) 38,440.

Se·re·kun·da \ˌse-re-ˈkün-dä\. City, W Gambia; pop. (1983c) 68,824.

Se·rem·ban \sə-ˈrem-bən\. Town, ✻ of Negeri Sembilan state, Malaysia, in W part of the state; pop. (1980c) 132,911; on coastal railroad line ab. 42 mi. (68 km.) NW of Melaka; connected with Port Dickson and Melaka by branch railroads.

Serena, La. See LA SERENA.

Serendib. See SRI LANKA.

Se·ren·ge·ti National Park \ˌser-ən-ˈge-tē\. National park, N Tanzania, in **Serengeti Plain**; park area 5700 sq. mi. (14,763 sq. km.); noted for its wildlife.

Seres. See SERRAI 2.

Se·ret \ˈser-ət\. River, W Ukraine; flows S and SE into Dniester River at Khotin; ab. 150 mi. (240 km.) long; formerly in SE Galicia, Poland.

Sereth. See SIRET.

Ser·geant Bluff \ˈsär-jənt\. City, Woodbury co., W Iowa, bordering the SE part of Sioux City; pop. (1990c) 2772.

Sergiopol. See AYAGUZ 2.

Ser·gi·pe \ser-ˈzhē-pē\. State, E Brazil; ✻ Aracaju; livestock raising; cotton, rice, tobacco, sugarcane. See table at BRAZIL.

Ser·gi·yev Po·sad \sir-ˈgyā-yif-pə-ˈsäd\; *1930–91* **Za·gorsk** \zə-ˈgȯrsk\; *before 1930* **Ser·giev·ski** \sir-ˈgyef-skē\ *or* **Sergiyev.** Town, Moscow Oblast, W cen. Russia in Europe, on railroad line 45 mi. (72 km.) NE of the city of Moscow; pop. (1991e) 115,600. Site of 14th cent. Trinity-St. Sergius monastery, architecturally significant and important as a place of pilgrimage; buildings include 15th cent. cathedral, 16th cent. cathedral, and 18th cent. bell tower.

Sergo. See STAKHANOV.

Ser·gy \ser-ˈzhē\. Village, Aisne dept., N France, 3 mi. (5 km.) SE of Fère-en-Tardenois; scene of heavy fighting 1918 during WWI.

Se·ria \sə-ˈrē-ə\. Town, W Brunei, ab. 45 mi. (70 km.) SW of Bandar Seri Begawan; pop. (1981c) 23,511; important oil fields nearby.

Ser·i·ca \ˈser-i-kə\. Name applied by ancient Greeks and Romans to a region of E Asia possibly equivalent to Manchuria; its people, the Seres, were said to have cultivated silkworms and made silken fabrics.

Sé·ri·fos *or* **Se·ri·phos** \sə-ˈrī-fəs, ˈse-rē-ˌfōs\. Island in W Cyclades, Aegean Sea, part of Cyclades dept., Greece, S of Kíthnos; ab. 25 sq. mi. (65 sq. km.).

Se·rin·ga·pa·tam \sə-ˌriŋ-gə-pə-ˈtam\. Town, Karnataka, S India, ab. 8 mi. (13 km.) N of Mysore. Former ✻ of Mysore (now Karnataka state) under Indian ruler Hyder Ali and his son and successor Tipu Sultan whose fort and palace were here on an island in Kāveri River; treaty signed here with the British 1792; in Fourth Mysore War 1799 besieged and captured by the British and Tipu killed; contains his mausoleum and that of his father.

Seringes–et–Nesles. See FÈRE-EN-TARDENOIS.

Seriphos. See SÉRIFOS.

Ser·ma·ta \ser-ˈmä-tə\. Island, Kepulauan Barat Daya, Indonesia, NE of Timor.

Ser·mi·de \ˈser-mē-dā\. Commune, Mantova prov., Lombardy, N Italy, on Po River 26 mi. (42 km.) ESE of Mantua; pop. (1981p) 7346.

Sermione. See SIRMIONE.

Ser·mo·ne·ta \ˌser-mȯ-ˈnā-tä\. Town, Latina prov., Lazio, cen. Italy, on edge of Agro Pontino NW of the commune of Latina; pop. (1981p) 6426.

Se·rov \ˈser-əf\; *formerly* **Na·dezh·dinsk** \nə-ˈdezh-ˌdinsk\. City, Sverdlovsk Oblast, W Russia in Asia, E of Ural Mts. on railroad line ab. 200 mi. (320 km.) N of Yekaterinburg; pop. (1992e) 106,000; steelmills; metallurgical center.

Se·ro·we \sə-ˈrō-wā\. Town, E Botswana, ab. 160 mi. (255 km.) NNE of Gaborone; pop. (1991c) 30,264.

Ser·pa \ˈser-pə\. Commune, Beja dist., S Portugal, near Guadiana River 17 mi. (27 km.) ESE of the commune of Beja; pop. (1981p) 19,750.

Ser·pent Mound \ˈsər-pənt-ˌmau̇nd\. Prehistoric serpent-shaped effigy earthwork, Adams co., S Ohio; ab. 1330 ft. (405 m.) long; 20 ft. (6 m.) wide at base, averages ab. 3 ft. (1 m.) high.

Ser·pent's Mouth \ˈsər-pənts-ˌmau̇th\. Strait bet. NE Venezuela and the S coast of the island of Trinidad; ab. 10 mi. (16 km.) wide; connects Gulf of Paria with the Atlantic Ocean.

Ser·pu·khov \ser-ˈpü-k̲əf\. City, Moscow Oblast, W cen. Russia in Europe, on railroad line and on navigable Oka River 56 mi. (90 km.) S of the city of Moscow; pop. (1992e) 141,000; textiles, synthetic silk; founded 1374 and orig. a fortified outpost of Moscow.

Ser·ra Aca·raí *also* **Serra Aca·ra·hy** \ˈser-rə-ˌȧ-kə-ˈrī\. Mountain range forming boundary bet. S Guyana and Brazil; highest peak ab. 2000 ft. (610 m.).

Ser·ra Cu·ru·pi·ra \ˈser-rə-ˌku̇r-u̇-pi-ˈrä\ *or Span.* **Sier·ra de Curupira** \ˈsyer-rä-ˌt̲h̲ā-ˌkü-rü-pē-ˈrä\. Mountain range, N South America, extending along a section of boundary bet. Venezuela and Brazil; highest peak 7675 ft. (2339 m.).

Ser·ra da Es·tre·la \ˈser-rə-dä-ish-ˈtre-lə\. Mountain range, Portugal; contains highest peak in Portugal, 6532 ft. (1991 m.).

Ser·ra da Man·ti·quei·ra \ˈser-rə-dä-ˌmȧn-tē-ˈkā-rə\. Mountain range, SE Brazil, on border of São Paulo, Minas Gerais, and Rio de Janeiro states; highest peak Pico das Agulhas Negras 9141 ft. (2786 m.).

Ser·ra das Di·vi·sões \ˈser-rə-däz-ˌdē-vē-ˈzōi^{n}s\. Mountain range, S cen. Brazil; highest point 2870 ft. (875 m.).

Ser·ra de Amam·baí \ˈser-rə-dē-ˌȧ-məm-ˈbī\ *or in Paraguay* **Cor·dil·le·ra de Amam·bay** \ˌkȯr-t̲h̲ē-ˈyā-rä-t̲h̲ā-ˌä-mäm-ˈbī\. Mountain range, S Mato Grosso state, SW Brazil, extending along a section of Brazil-Paraguay boundary; av. elev. ab. 1300 ft. (395 m.).

Ser·ra·di·fal·co \ˌser-rä-dē-ˈfäl-kō\. Commune, Caltanissetta prov., cen. Sicily, Italy, WSW of the commune of Caltanissetta; pop. (1981p) 6355.

Ser·ra do Es·tron·do \ˈser-rə-ˌdü-ēsh-ˈtrōn-dü\. Mountain range, N Goiás state, NE cen. Brazil, bet. the Araguaia and Tocantins rivers.

Ser·ra do Mar \ˈser-rə-dü-ˈmär\. Coastal mountain range, chiefly in Santa Catarina, Paraná, and São Paulo states, S Brazil; highest point 7423 ft. (2263 m.) in the Serra dos Órgãos.

Ser·ra do Mon·chi·que \ˈser-rə-ˌdü-mōn-ˈshē-kē\. Mountain range, S Portugal; highest point 2959 ft. (902 m.).

Ser·ra do Piauí \ˈser-rə-ˌdü-pyȧ-ˈwē\. Mountain range, NE Brazil, extending along boundary bet. Bahia and Piauí states.

Ser·ra do Ron·ca·dor \ˈser-rə-dü-ˌrōn-kə-ˈdȯr\. Mountain range, NE Mato Grosso state, cen. Brazil.

Ser·ra dos Ai·mo·rés \ˈser-rə-dü-ˌzī-mü-ˈres\. Mountain range, E Brazil, surrounding region formerly in dispute bet. Minas Gerais and Espírito Santo states; partitioned 1964 with 1515 sq. mi. (3924 sq. km.) to Minas Gerais and 2405 sq. mi. (6229 sq. km.) to Espírito Santo.

Ser·ra dos Or·gãos \ˈser-rə-dü-ˈzȯr-ˌgau̇^{n}s\ *or Eng.* **Or·gan Mountains** \ˈȯr-gən\. Mountain range, Rio de Janeiro state, SE Brazil, ab. 30 mi. (48 km.) from Rio de Janeiro; highest peak 7323 ft. (2232 m.).; part of the Serra do Mar; part of region estab. as **Serra dos Orgãos National Park** 1939 (39 sq. mi. or 101 sq. km.).

Ser·ra dos Pa·re·cis \ˈser-rə-düs-ˌpȧ-rē-ˈsēs\. Range of mountains, Mato Grosso state, SW Brazil, E of, and parallel with, the NE border of Bolivia; highest peak 2194 ft. (669 m.).

Ser·ra do Tom·ba·dor \ˈser-rə-dü-ˌtōm-bə-ˈdȯr\. Range of mountains, N cen. Mato Grosso state, SW Brazil.

Ser·ra Ge·ral \ˈser-rə-zhi-ˈräl\. Mountain range, E Santa Catarina state, S Brazil; highest peak 4133 ft. (1260 m.).

Sér·rai \ˈse-re\. **1.** Department of Central Macedonia region, Greece. See table at GREECE.
2. *also* **Ser·res** *or* **Ser·es** \ˈser-es\; *anc.* **Si·ris** \ˈsī-rəs\. City, its ✻, ab. 42 mi. (68 km.) NE of Thessaloníki; pop. (1981c) 46,317; ships cotton; occupied by Serbs 1345–71; taken by Turks late 14th cent.; taken by Bulgarians 1913 and occupied by them during WWI and WWII.

Ser·ra·nía de Cuen·ca \ˌser-rä-ˈnē-ä-t̲h̲ā-ˈkweŋ-kä\. Mountain range, Cuenca and Guadalajara provs., E cen. Spain; highest peak 6084 ft. (1854 m.).

Serranía de la Macarena. See MACARENA MOUNTAINS.

Serranía del Darién. See DARIÉN, SERRANÍA DEL.

Serranía de Tabasará. See TABASARÁ MOUNTAINS.

Ser·ra·nía Ima·ta·ca \ˌser-rä-ˈnē-ä-ˌē-mä-ˈtä-kä\. Mountain range, E Venezuela, S of delta of the Orinoco.

Ser·ra·no \ser-ˈrä-nō\. Island in Pacific Ocean off SW coast of Chile, N of Wellington I., 48°30′S, 74°43′W.

Serra Pacaraima. See PACARAIMA MOUNTAINS.

Serra Parima. See PARIMA, SERRA.

Ser·rat, Cape \sə-ˈrät\. Cape, N coast of Tunisia, W of Bizerte.

Serra Tumucumaque. See TUMUC-HUMAC MOUNTAINS.

Ser·ra Ua·ça·ri \ˈser-rə-wä-ˈsar-ē\ *or in Guyana* **Vas·sa·ri Mountains** \və-ˈsär-ē\. Mountain range forming part of boundary bet. S Guyana and Brazil, a W extension of Serra Acaraí; source of Essequibo River and of several rivers of Brazil.

Serres. See SERRAI 2.

Sert. See SIIRT.

Servia. See SERBIA.

Se·sa·jap \sə-'sä-ˌyäp\. River, NE part of island of Borneo; rises in NE Sarawak (Malaysia) and flows E in the Indonesian prov. of East Kalimantan to the Celebes Sea; ab. 200 mi. (320 km.) long; has large delta with many islands. See TARAKAN.

Se·sen·heim \'zā-zən-ˌhīm\. Village, N Alsace, France, ab. 18 mi. (29 km.) NNE of Strasbourg near the Rhine; noted as home of Friederike Brion, friend of German Romantic poet Johann Wolfgang von Goethe.

Se·she·go \se-'shā-gō\. Town, Northern prov., Rep. of South Africa, just NW of Pietersburg; area pop. (1985c) 32,895.

Se·sia \'sā-zē-ə, 'se-\. River, N Italy; rises on slopes of Monte Rosa, flows S into Po River 5 mi. (8 km.) E of Casale Monferrato; 86 mi. (138 km.) long.

Ses·sa Au·run·ca \'se-sä-au̇-'rüŋ-kä\; *anc.* **Sues·sa Aurunca** \'swe-sə-ȯ-'rəŋ-kə\. Commune, Caserta prov., Campania, S Italy, 33 mi. (53 km.) NNW of Naples; pop. (1989c) 24,247; 12th cent. cathedral; Roman ruins; sulfur springs.

Ses·tao \sā-'stau̇\. Commune, Vizcaya prov., N Spain, 5 mi. (8 km.) NW of Bilbao; pop. (1991c) 35,948.

Se·sto Fio·ren·ti·no \'ses-tō-ˌfyȯr-en-'tē-nō\. Commune, Firenze prov., Tuscany, cen. Italy, 5 mi. (8 km.) NW of Florence; pop. (1989c) 47,517.

Ses·tos \'ses-təs\. Ruined town on the Dardanelles (Hellespont), Turkey in Europe; at narrowest point of the strait opp. Abydos; N terminus of a bridge of boats built by Persian King Xerxes for the crossing of his armies for invasion of Greece c. 481 B.C. Scene of legend of Hero and Leander.

Sesto San Gio·van·ni \'ses-tō-ˌsän-jō-'vä-nē\. Commune, Milano prov., Lombardy, N Italy, NE suburb of Milan; pop. (1989c) 89,517.

Se·stri Le·van·te \'ses-trē-lā-'vän-tā\. Commune, Genova prov., Liguria, NW Italy, on Ligurian Sea 21 mi. (34 km.) ESE of Genoa; pop. (1989c) 20,790; winter and seaside resort.

Setabis. See JÁTIVA.

Sète; *formerly* **Cette** \'set\. Town, Hérault dept., S France, 18 mi. (29 km.) SSW of Montpellier on a strip of land which separates the Étang de Thau from the Mediterranean; pop. (1990c) 41,916; the principal seaport of S France after Marseille; large export trade in wine; produces chemicals, phosphates; distilleries, oil refineries, fisheries; seaside resort; port construction began 1666; birthplace of poet Paul Valéry 1871.

Se·te La·go·as \'se-tē-lə-'gō-əs\. City, Minas Gerais state, E Brazil, just N of Belo Horizonte; munic. pop. (1991p) 143,611.

Se·te Que·das \'se-tē-'kā-t͟həsh\; *formerly* **Guaí·ra** *or* **Guay·ra** \'gwī-rä\. Former cataract, in the Paraná River on boundary bet. Brazil and Paraguay; formed by a narrowing of the riverbed into a gorge ab. 200 ft. (60 m.) wide; now submerged by the lake formed by Itaipu Dam.

Se·ti \'sā-tē\. River, W Nepal; flows S into the Karnali River; ab. 120 mi. (195 km.) long.

Setia. See SEZZE.

Sé·tif \sā-'tēf\. Town, N Algeria, on railroad line 60 mi. (97 km.) NW of Constantine; pop. (1987p) 170,182; center of a grain-producing region; important town under Romans and Byzantines; scene of revolt against French rule and retaliatory massacre of Muslims 1945.

Setit. See TEKEZE.

Se·to \'se-tō\. City, Aichi prefecture, Honshū, Japan, 13 mi. (21 km.) ENE of Nagoya; pop. (1990p) 126,343.

Seto–naikai *also* **Seto no Uchi.** See INLAND SEA.

Set·tat \set-'tät\. City, Morocco, S of Casablanca; pop. (1982c) 65,203.

Set·ti·mo To·ri·ne·se \set-'tē-mō-ˌtō-rē-'nā-zā\. Commune, Torino prov., Piedmont, NW Italy, NE of Turin; pop. (1989c) 45,312.

Sett·su \'set-sü\. City, Ōsaka prefecture, Honshū, Japan; pop. (1990p) 87,465.

Se·tú·bal \sə-'tü-bəl\. **1.** District of SW Portugal. See table at PORTUGAL.

2. *formerly called in English* **Saint Ubes** \'yübz\ *or* **Saint Yves** \'īvz\. Seaport, its ✻, on **Bay of Setúbal** (receives the Sado River) 19 mi. (31 km.) SE of Lisbon; pop. (1990c) 77,285; good harbor; manufactures and trades in muscatel wine, corks, oranges, salt; shipbuilding; royal residence during the reign of King John II (1481–95).

Setul. See SATUN.

Seul, Lac \ˌlak-'sül\. Lake, W Ontario, Canada; 539 sq. mi. (1396 sq. km.); outlet is English River (a headstream of the Winnipeg).

Seul Choix Point \sə-'shwä\. Point on SE coast of Schoolcraft co., S Upper Penin. of Michigan, in Lake Michigan.

Se·van \sə-'vän\ *or* **Se·vang** \-'väŋ\ *or Turk.* **Gök·cha** \'gœk-chä\; *anc.* **Lych·ni·tis** \lik-'nī-təs\. Lake, N Armenia; 525 sq. mi. (1360 sq. km.); alt. 6279 ft. (1914 m.); surrounded by high mountains; largest lake in Armenia; its outlet is the Hrazdan, a tributary of the Araks; fisheries; water drawn from the Hrazdan River for hydroelectric plants 1940–78 caused a significant decrease in the lake's level.

Se·vas·to·pol' *or* **Se·vas·to·pol;** *mostly formerly* **Se·bas·to·pol** \sə-'vas-tə-ˌpōl, -ˌpȯl; ˌse-və-'stȯ-pəl, -'stō-\. Seaport city, SW Crimea, Ukraine, occupying a peninsula 40 mi. (64 km.) SW of Simferopol'; pop. (1991e) 366,000; on an inlet of the Black Sea (**Sevastopol' Bay**), which forms a good natural harbor. Principal base of the Russian Black Sea Fleet since early 19th cent., with extensive dockyard facilities and arsenals; has shipbuilding and food-processing industries; center of a region noted for health resorts.

History: Near site of Greek colony founded 5th cent. B.C. (for early history of area see CRIMEA); came under Russia 1783 and made site of naval base; commercial port opened 1808; besieged for 11 months 1854–55 by British, French, Turkish, and Sardinian forces during Crimean War; headquarters of White Army in Russian Civil War 1918–20; besieged for eight months by Germans in WWII; proclaimed a Russian city by Russian parliament 1993.

Seven Devils Mountains. Mountain range, W Idaho, E of Snake River in Adams and Idaho cos.; ab. 40 mi. (64 km.) long; highest point ab. 7900 ft. (2400 m.).

Seven Hills. City, Cuyahoga co., N Ohio, S of Cleveland; pop. (1990c) 12,339; residential.

Seven Hills. The seven hills in Rome (*q.v.*) on or about which the city was built: *Aventine, Caelian, Capitoline, Esquiline, Palatine* (according to tradition, the original city of Romulus built here 753 B.C.), *Quirinal,* and *Viminal.*

Seven Hunters. See FLANNAN ISLANDS.

Seven Isles. See SEPT-ÎLES.

Seven Mile Beach. Island off E cen. Cape May co., S New Jersey.

Sev·en·oaks \'se-vən-ˌōks\. Town, Kent, SE England, 20 mi. (32 km.) SSE of London; pop. (1991p) 106,100; residential; 15th cent. Knole House, a mansion formerly owned by royalty.

Seven Pines. See FAIR OAKS.

Seven Sisters *or* **Syv Sys·tre** \sue̅v-'sis-trə\. Waterfall in a small stream emptying into Stor Fjord on W coast of Norway.

Seven Troughs Peak. Mountain, W Pershing co., NW Nevada; 7480 ft. (2280 m.).

Sev·ern \'se-vərn\. **1.** Navigable inlet of Chesapeake Bay, E Anne Arundel co., cen. Maryland; ab. 10 mi. (16 km.) long; Annapolis is located 2 mi. (3 km.) from its mouth.

2. River, NW Ontario, Canada; has source in several large lakes in W Ontario, flows NE into Hudson Bay; 610 mi. (981 km.) long.

3. River, SE Ontario, Canada. See SIMCOE, LAKE.

4. *or Welsh* **Haf·ren** \'hä-vren\; *anc.* **Sa·bri·na** \sə-'brī-nə\. River, E Wales and W England; rises in E cen. Wales, flows in a curve NE, E, and S, crossing English border near Shrewsbury and continuing S into Bristol Channel; 180 mi. (290 km.) long; the "Shakespeare" Avon is one of its chief tributaries; bridge (across Severn) linking S Wales with Bristol opened 1960s.

Severnaya Dvina. See DVINA, NORTHERN.

Se·ver·na·ya Zem·lya \ˈsye-vir-nə-yə-zim-ˈlyä\; *Eng.* **Northern Land** *also* **North Land;** *formerly* **Nich·o·las II Land** \ˈni-kə-ləs-thə-ˈse-kənd\. Island group in Arctic Ocean, Krasnoyarsk Kray, N Russia in Asia, dividing Laptev Sea from Kara Sea, N of Taymyr Penin.; 14,286 sq. mi. (37,001 sq. km.); comprises three large islands, Bol'shevik, Komsomolets, and October Revolution, and a number of smaller ones; separated from mainland by Vilkitski Strait; discovered 1913.

Se·ve·ro·do·nets'k *or* **Se·ve·ro·do·netsk** \ˌsye-vir-ə-də-ˈnetsk\. Town, Luhans'k subdivision, Ukraine, ab. 45 mi. (70 km.) NW of the city of Luhans'k; pop. (1991e) 133,000.

Se·ve·rod·vinsk \ˌsye-vir-əd-ˈvin(t)sk\; *formerly* **Mo·lo·tovsk** \ˈmȯ-lə-təfsk\. Seaport town, NW Arkhangel'sk Oblast, N Russia in Europe, on Dvina Gulf across the delta of the Northern Dvina from the city of Arkhangel'sk; pop. (1992e) 250,000; exports timber.

Se·ve·ro–Ku·ril'sk\ˈsye-vir-ə-kə-ˈrilʸsk\. Town, E Russia in Asia; chief settlement on the island of Paramushir in the N Kuril Is.

Se·ve·ro·morsk \ˌsye-vir-ə-ˈmȯrsk\; *formerly* **Va·yen·ga** \və-ˈyen-gə, -ˈyeŋ-\. Town, Murmansk Oblast, N Russia in Europe, ab. 10 mi. (16 km.) NE of the city of Murmansk; pop. (1991e) 66,200.

Se·vier \sə-ˈvir\. **1.** River, SW cen. Utah; formed by confluence of forks in W Garfield co., S Utah, flows N, then turns SW in E Juab co., empties into Sevier Lake in cen. Millard co., W Utah; 279 mi. (449 km.) long.

2. Name of counties in three states of the U.S. See tables at ARKANSAS, TENNESSEE, UTAH.

Sevier Lake. Saline lake, Millard co., W Utah; ab. 25 mi. (40 km.) long; receives Sevier River from N; no outlet.

Se·vier·ville \sə-ˈvir-ˌvil\. Town, ⊗ of Sevier co., E Tennessee; pop. (1990c) 7178.

Se·vil·la \sā-ˈb̲ē-yä\. **1.** Town, Valle del Cauca dept., W Colombia; munic. pop. (1985c) 32,485.

2. Province of SW Spain. See table at SPAIN.

Se·ville \sə-ˈvil\ *or Span.* **Se·vil·la** \sā-ˈb̲ē-yä\; *anc.* **His·pa·lis** \ˈhis-pə-ləs\. City, ✻ of Andalucia autonomous community and ✻ of Sevilla prov., SW Spain, on Guadalquivir River 62 mi. (100 km.) NNE of Cádiz; pop. (1991p) 659,126; inland port with extensive facilities, exporting wine, citrus fruit, olives, and cork; agricultural implements, tobacco, pottery, porcelain ware; major shipyards. One of the principal tourist centers of Spain, with walks (*paseos*), the medieval pattern of Old Seville, and numerous notable buildings, incl. the cathedral (15th cent. Gothic), the Giralda (tower of the Almohads), one of the most notable Moorish structures in Spain (late 12th cent.), and the 12th cent. alcazar; university (1502). Birthplace of 17th cent. painters Diego Velázquez (1599) and Bartolomé Esteban Murillo (1617); noted for its processions and ceremonies during Holy Week.

History: Iberian settlement at early period; prosperous under Romans, chief city of Baetica; chief town of S Spain under Vandals and Visigoths 5th–8th cents.; captured 712 A.D. by Moors and became an important city in Western caliphate; captured 1248 by Ferdinand III of León and Castile; after 1492, center of Spanish colonial trade (Casa de Contratación, begun 1503); in 17th cent. declined in rivalry with Cádiz; occupied 1808–12 by French; site of Spanish-American Exhibition 1929; held by Nationalists during Civil War 1936–39; site of World Exposition 1992.

Se·vli·e·vo \sev-ˈlē-e-ˌvō\. Town, N cen. Bulgaria, ab. 15 mi. (24 km.) NW of Gabrovo.

Se·vran \sə-ˈvräⁿ\. Commune, Seine-St.-Denis dept., N France, ENE suburb of Paris.

Sè·vre Nan·taise \ˌse-vrə-näⁿ-ˈtez, -ˈtāz\. River, W France; rises in Deux-Sèvres dept., flows NW into Loire River opp. Nantes; ab. 80 mi. (130 km.) long.

Sè·vre Nior·taise \ˌse-vrə-nyȯr-ˈtez, -ˈtāz\. River, W France; rises in Deux-Sèvres dept., flows W into Bay of Biscay; ab. 95 mi. (155 km.) long.

Sè·vres \ˈsevrᵊ\. Commune, Hauts-de-Seine dept., N France, on Seine River 6 mi. (10 km.) SW of Paris; pop. (1990c) 22,057; site of national porcelain factory (transferred from Vincennes 1756) and ceramics museum; treaty signed here after WWI bet. Allies and Turkey 1920.

Sè·vres, Deux– \ˈdœ-ˈsevrᵊ\. Department of France. See table at FRANCE.

Se·wa·nee \sə-ˈwȯ-nē, -ˈwä-\. Unincorporated settlement, Franklin co., S Tennessee; pop. (1990c) 2128; Univ. of the South (1857).

Sew·ard \ˈsü-ərd\. **1.** Name of counties in two states of the U.S. See tables at KANSAS and NEBRASKA.

2. City, S Alaska, on Resurrection Bay, on SE shore of Kenai Penin.; pop. (1990c) 2699; important port, open all the year, and S terminal of government-owned Alaska railroad running N to Fairbanks; founded as a railroad terminus 1903; badly damaged by earthquake 1964.

3. City, ⊗ of Seward co., SE Nebraska, 22 mi. (35 km.) WNW of Lincoln; pop. (1990c) 5634; Concordia Coll. (1894).

Seward, Mount. **1.** Peak, Glacier National Park, NW Montana; 8879 ft. (2706 m.).

2. Peak in the Adirondack Mts., Franklin co., NE New York; 4404 ft. (1342 m.).

Seward–Ma·las·pi·na Glacier \-ma-ləs-ˈpē-nə\. Glacier in St. Elias Mts., SE Alaska and SW Yukon, Canada; 70 mi. (113 km.) long, ab. 43 mi. (69 km.) wide near its terminus.

Seward Peninsula. Peninsula, W Alaska, bet. Kotzebue Sound on N and Norton Sound on S; ab. 180 mi. (290 km.) long by 130 mi. (209 km.) wide; its W tip, Cape Prince of Wales on Bering Strait, is most westerly point of continent of North America; Nome is on its S coast.

Sew·ell \ˈsü-əl\. Town, Libertador General Bernardo O'Higgins region, cen. Chile; railroad terminus E of Rancagua at 8000 ft. (2440 m.); El Teniente copper mines at 10,000 ft. (3050 m.).

Se·wick·ley \si-ˈwi-klē\. Residential borough, Allegheny co., SW Pennsylvania, on Ohio River 12 mi. (19 km.) WNW of Pittsburgh; pop. (1990c) 4134.

Sexi. See ALMUÑÉCAR.

Seybo, El. See EL SEIBO.

Sey·bouse \sā-ˈbüz\ *or* **Sei·bus** \ˈsā-ˌbu̇s\. Unnavigable river, NE Algeria; flows N into the Mediterranean at Annaba; 145 mi. (233 km.) long.

Sey·chelles \sā-ˈshel, -ˈshelz\. Republic, consisting of a group of islands in the Indian Ocean, E of NE Tanzania, ab. 4°S and 56°E; 107 sq. mi. (277 sq. km.); pop. (1990e) 68,598; ✻ Victoria on Mahé; chief islands Mahé (58 sq. mi. or 150 sq. km.; pop. [1990e] 61,183), Praslin (7 sq. mi. or 18 sq. km.; pop. [1969e] 4867), and La Digue (6 sq. mi. or 15.5 sq. km.; pop. [1969e] 750); chief products coconuts and copra, cinnamon, fish; tourism. Known to Arab traders before claimed by French 1756; taken by English 1794 and later made a dependency of Mauritius; became a crown colony 1903 and a republic within the Commonwealth 1976; adopted new constitution 1993.

Sey·han \sā-ˈhän\ *or* **Sei·hun** \sā-ˈhün\ *also* **Si·hun** \si-ˈhün\. **1.** *anc.* **Sar·us** \ˈsar-əs\. River, S cen. Turkey in Asia; rises in NE Anti-Taurus Mts., flows SSW into the Mediterranean Sea E of Içel; 748 mi. (1204 km.) long; Adana is on left bank of its lower course; the Yenice is its chief tributary.

2. Province, Turkey in Asia. See *Adana* in table at TURKEY.

3. City, Turkey in Asia. See ADANA 2.

Seym *or* **Seim** \ˈsyām, ˈsām\. River, E cen. Europe; flows through Kursk Oblast of Russia and Sumy subdivision of Ukraine to the Desna River E of Chernihiv; 460 mi. (740 km.) long.

Sey·mour \ˈsē-ˌmōr\. **1.** Town, W New Haven co., S Connecticut, on Housatonic River N of Ansonia; pop. (1990c) 14,288; settled 1680; incorp. 1850; site of early successful woolen mill estab. early 19th cent.

2. City, Jackson co., S Indiana, 38 mi. (61 km.) ESE of Bloomington; pop. (1990c) 15,576.

3. City, ⊗ of Baylor co., N Texas, 48 mi. (77 km.) WSW of Wichita Falls; pop. (1990c) 3185.

4. City, Outagamie co., E Wisconsin; pop. (1990c) 2782.

Seymour, Mount. Peak, Franklin co., NE New York; 4120 ft. (1256 m.).

Seymour Island. Small island of Galápagos Is., E Pacific Ocean.

Seymour Lake. Lake, E Orleans co., N Vermont.

Seyne–sur–Mer, La. See LA SEYNE-SUR-MER.

Sé·zanne \ˌsā-ˈzän\. Town, SW Marne dept., NE France; in vicinity in WWI, battle of the Marne took place Sept. 1914.

Sez·ze \ˈsāt-sā, ˈset-\; *anc.* **Se·tia** \ˈsē-shē-ə\. Commune, Latina prov., Lazio, cen. Italy; pop. (1981p) 19,899; episcopal see; ancient Roman amphitheater and temple.

Sfânta *or* **Sfântul.** See SAINT.

Sfântu Gheorghe. See SFÎNTU GHEORGHE 1.

Sfântul–Gheorghe. See SFÎNTU GHEORGHE 2.

Sfax \ˈsfaks\ *or* **Sa·fā·qis** \sə-ˈfä-kis\. Seaport city, E Tunisia, on N shore of Gulf of Gabès; pop. (1989e) 221,770; exports phosphates, fruit, sponges, olive oil. Site of ancient settlements; occupied by Normans 12th cent. and Spanish 16th cent.; became stronghold for Barbary pirates; bombarded by French 1881; Axis base in WWII.

Sfîn·tu Gheor·ghe \ˈsfin-tü-ˈgyȯr-ge\ **1.** *or* **Sfân·tu Gheor·ghe** \ˈsfän-tü-\ *or Eng.* **Saint George.** Large island in cen. part of delta of the Danube, E Romania.
2. *or* **Sfân·tul–Gheorghe** \ˈsfän-tül-\ *or Hung.* **Sep·si·szent·györgy** \ˈshep-shi-ˌsent-ˈgyȯr-ge\. City, ⊗ of Covasna co., cen. Romania, in Transylvanian Alps on the upper Olt ab. 20 mi. (32 km.) NNE of Braşov; pop. (1989c) 72,092; textiles, furniture.

’s Gravenhage. See HAGUE, THE.

Sgurr nan Gil·lean \ˌskər-ˌnan-gə-ˈlēn\. Mountain, N Cuillin Hills, S Skye I., Inner Hebrides Is., off W coast of Scotland; 3167 ft. (965 m.).

Shaan·xi \ˈshän-ˈshē\ *or W.-G.* **Shen·si** \ˈshen-ˈsē\. Province, E cen. China, bounded on NW by Ningxia Huizu, on N by Nei Monggol, on E by Shanxi, Henan, and Hubei, on S by Sichuan, and on W by Gansu; ✻ Xi’an; separated from Shanxi by the Huang; crossed in cen. part by the Wei and Jing rivers and in the S by the Han; bordered on N by the Great Wall; divided climatically N and S by the Qinling Shandi (highest point 13,474 ft. or 4107 m.). Covered extensively by loess, which makes it agriculturally rich; chief crops include winter wheat, cotton, corn, tobacco, fruit; coal, manganese.
History: For several millennia a region in which Chinese civilization has developed; its ✻ Xi’an, under various names, was a chief city of the empire for long periods from 11th cent. B.C. to 9th cent. A.D.; suffered greatly during the Muslim rebellion 1860s and also from severe famine early 1920s; Chinese Communist leader Mao Tse Tung’s Long March ended here 1935 at Yan’an (*q.v.*) and area contributed greatly to rebuilding Communist forces in fight against Japanese and Nationalist forces. See table at CHINA.

Sha·ba \ˈshä-bə\; *formerly* **Ka·tan·ga** \kə-ˈtäŋ-gə, -ˈtaŋ-\; *earlier* **Elis·a·beth·ville** \i-ˈli-zə-bəth-ˌvil\. Administrative region, S Democratic Rep. of the Congo; ✻ Lubumbashi; noted esp. for its rich deposits of copper, uranium, cobalt, tin, iron, and gold; seceded 1960–63; subsequently reabsorbed, but political unrest persisted. See table at ZAIRE.

Shabani. See ZVISHAVANE.

Sha·beel·le \sha-ˈbe-lē\ *or in Ethiopia* **She·be·lē** \she-ˈbe-lē\. River, E Africa; rises in cen. Ethiopia, flows SE across border of Somalia, approaches the coast near Mogadishu, then turns SW and flows ab. 200 mi. (322 km.) parallel with the coast; becomes intermittent in its lower course, flowing through swamps and during wetter periods flowing into the Jubba River; 1250 mi. (2011 km.) long.

Sha·che \ˈshä-ˈchə\ *or* **Yar·kant** \yär-ˈkänt\; *W.-G.* **Sha–ch’e** \ˈshä-ˈchə\ *or* **Yar·kand** \yär-ˈkänd\ *also* **So–ch’e** \ˈsō-ˈchə\. Town and oasis, SW Xinjiang Uygur, W China, on Yarkant He at edge of Taklimakan Desert 100 mi. (161 km.) SE of Kashi; alt. 3900 ft. (1190 m.), at foot of N slope of Kunlun Shan; has for centuries been a trade center.

Shack·el·ford \ˈsha-kəl-fərd\. County in N cen. Texas. See table at TEXAS.

Shack·le·ton Ice Shelf \ˈsha-kəl-tən\. Large field of shelf ice, Queen Mary Coast, Antarctica; extends E at ab. 66°S, 100°E, and out into Indian Ocean for more than 130 mi. (209 km.); ab. 165 mi. (265 km.) long.

Shackleton Inlet. Inlet, W side of Ross Ice Shelf, Antarctica, 82°21′S, 163°15′E; ab. 10 mi. (16 km.) wide; occupied by glacier.

Shade’s Mills. See GALT 2.

Sha·drinsk \ˈshä-drinsk\. Town, NW Kurgan Oblast, W Russia in Asia, on a tributary of Tobol River; pop. (1991e) 88,500; on railroad line bet. Yekaterinburg and Kurgan.

Shad·well \ˈshad-ˌwel, -wəl\. Former estate, Albemarle co., Virginia, site ab. 5 mi. (8 km.) E of Charlottesville; birthplace 1743 of Thomas Jefferson, 3d president of the U.S.

Sha·dy·side \ˈshā-dē-ˌsīd\. Village, Belmont co., E Ohio, on Ohio River 27 mi. (43 km.) S of Steubenville; pop. (1990c) 3934.

Sha·fer Butte \ˈshā-fər\. Mountain, Boise co., W cen. Idaho; 7580 ft. (2310 m.).

Shafer Lake. Lake, NW Indiana, N of Freeman Lake (*q.v.*), formed in Tippecanoe River by Norway Dam.

Shaf·ter \ˈshaf-tər\. City, Kern co., S California, 17 mi. (27 km.) NW of Bakersfield; pop. (1990c) 8409.

Shafts·bury \ˈshafts-ˌber-ē, -bə-rē\. Town, Bennington co., SW Vermont; pop. (1990c) 3368.

Sha·ga·mu \shä-ˈgä-mü\. Town, SW Nigeria, 40 mi. (64 km.) SSW of Ibadan; pop. (1991e) 103,500.

Shag Rocks \ˈshag\. Group of rocks, South Atlantic Ocean, WNW of South Georgia I.; belongs to United Kingdom.

Shah·a·bad \ˈshä-hə-ˌbäd, ˈshȯ-\. Town, cen. Uttar Pradesh, N India, 80 mi. (129 km.) NW of Lucknow; pop. (1991p) 53,549.

Shah Alam \ˈshä-ˈä-ləm, ˈshȯ-\. Town, ✻ of Selangor state, Malaysia; located SE of Kuala Lumpur; pop. (1980c) 19,041.

Shah·da·ra \ˈshä-də-rə\. Suburb of Lahore, Punjab, Pakistan, ab. 5 mi. (8 km.) NW across the Ravi River; contains tomb of Mogul Emperor Jahāngīr.

Shāh Dhar \ˈshä-ˈdär\. Mountain in the Hindu Kush, Afghanistan; 23,082 ft. (7035 m.).

Sha He \ˈshä-ˈhə\ *or W.-G.* **Sha Ho** *also* **Sha–ho** \ˈshä-ˈhō\. Name of small river, NE China, a tributary of the Liao; its banks, site of battle Oct. 1904, in which the Russians were defeated by the Japanese during Russo-Japanese War.

Shāh Fu·lā·di \ˈshä-fü-ˈlä-dē, ˌshȯ-\. Highest peak in the Koh-i-Baba Range, E cen. Afghanistan; 16,872 ft. (5143 m.).

Shaḩ·ḩāt \shä-ˈkät\. Settlement, NE Libya, near the Mediterranean coast; site of the ancient city of Cyrene.

Shā·hī \shä-ˈhē\. **1.** Island, N cen. part of Daryācheh-ye Orūmīyeh, NW Iran; highest point 7161 ft. (2183 m.).
2. See GHAEM SHAHR.

Shahjahanabad. See DELHI 2.

Shah·ja·han·pur \ˌshä-jə-ˈhän-ˌpu̇r, ˌshȯ-\. City, cen. Uttar Pradesh, N India, on affluent of Ramganga River 100 mi. (161 km.) NW of Lucknow; pop. (1991p) 237,663; sugar, carpets. Founded 1647 and named for reigning emperor Shāh Jahān.

Sha Ho *also* **Sha–ho.** See SHA HE.

Shah·pu·ra \ˈshä-pu̇-rə, ˈshȯ-\. **1.** Former state, now part of Rajasthan state, NW India; 405 sq. mi. (1049 sq. km.).
2. Town, S cen. Rajasthan, NW India, 60 mi. (97 km.) SE of Ajmer; pop. (1991p) 23,646; former ✻ of Shahpura state.

Shahr–e Kord \ˈshär-ē-ˈkōrd\ *or* **Shahr Kord.** Town, ✻ of Chahār Mahāll va Bakhtīārī prov., W cen. Iran; pop. (1986c) 75,080.

Shahr–i–Zabul. See ZĀBOL.

Shāh·rūd *or* **Shah Rud** \ˌshä-ˈrüd, ˌshȯ-\. **1.** River, N Iran; flows W parallel with and S of the Elburz Mts. and empties into the Safīd Rūd 40 mi. (64 km.) S of Rasht; ab. 100 mi. (160 km.) long.
2. *or* **Emam·rud.** Town, Semnān prov., N Iran; ab. 210 mi. (340 km.) ENE of Tehran; pop. (1986c) 78,950.

Shaikh ‘Othman. See SHEIKH ‘OTHMAN.

Shak·er Heights \'shā-kər\. Residential city, Cuyahoga co., N Ohio, 8 mi. (13 km.) E of Cleveland; pop. (1990c) 30,831.

Sha·khri·sabz *or* **Sha·khri·syabz** \,shə-k̲ri-'syäps\. City, SE Uzbekistan, 40 mi. (64 km.) S of Samarqand; pop. (1991e) 53,200.

Shakh·ters'k *or* **Shakh·tersk** \shäk̲-'tyȯrsʸk, -'tersk\. Town, Donets'k subdivision, Ukraine, 31 mi. (50 km.) E of the city of Donets'k; pop. (1991e) 73,000.

Shakh·ty \'shäk-tē\; *formerly* **Ale·ksan·drovsk–Gru·shev·ski** \,ȧ-lik-'sȧn-drəfsk-grü-'shef-skē\. City, SW Rostov Oblast, S Russia in Europe, on railroad line ab. 35 mi. (55 km.) NE of Rostov-na-Donu; pop. (1992e) 228,000; mining town in E part of Donets coal region; iron foundries, breweries.

Sha·ki \'shä-kē\. Town, SW Nigeria, 95 mi. (153 km.) NNW of Ibadan; pop. (1991e) 153,700.

Shak·o·pee \'sha-kə-,pē\. City, ⊗ of Scott co., SE Minnesota, on Minnesota River 18 mi. (29 km.) SW of Minneapolis; pop. (1990c) 11,739.

Sha·la, Lake \'shä-lə\. Lake, cen. Ethiopia, ab. 110 mi. (177 km.) S of Addis Ababa.

Sha·ler \'shā-lər\. Urban township, Allegheny co., SW Pennsylvania, N of Pittsburgh; pop. (1990c) 30,533.

Sham, Jeb·el \'je-bəl-'shȧm\. Mountain in the Jebel Akdar, Oman, Arabian Penin.; 9927 ft. (3026 m.); highest peak in Oman.

Sha·māl Sī·nā' \shä-'mäl-sē-'nä\. Governorate of Egypt, on Sinai Penin. See table at EGYPT.

Sham·be \'shäm-be\. Town, SE Sudan, on Bahr el Jebel (Nile) NNW of Mongalla.

Sha·mian *or* **Sha–mien** \'shä-'myen\. Sandy island in Zhu River at Guangzhou, China, in SW part of city; ab. 0.11 sq. mi. (0.29 sq. km.). As result of Opium Wars set aside 1859 as foreign concession for British and French; returned to Chinese administration following WWII.

Shamo. See GOBI.

Sha·mo, Lake. See CHOMO LAKE.

Sha·mo·kin \shə-'mō-kən\. City, Northumberland co., E cen. Pennsylvania, 21 mi. (34 km.) WNW of Pottsville; pop. (1990c) 9184; formerly a coal-mining center.

Shan \'shän\; *formerly* **Federated Shan States** *also* **Shan States.** State, E Myanmar, part of which lies in Golden Triangle (*q.v.*); ✻ Taunggyi; original Shan States fl. 12th–16th cents.; in British expansion from India, came under British control 1887; states federated 1922; reconstituted as administrative unit within Burma on its independence 1948; lost some autonomy when Burma became socialist state 1974; experienced political unrest against central government late 20th cent. See table at MYANMAR.

Shandī. See SHENDI.

Shan·dong \'shän-'dủŋ\ *or W.-G.* **Shan·tung** \-'dủŋ\. Coastal province, NE China, bounded on NW by Hebei, on W by Hebei and Henan, and on S by Henan and Jiangsu; ✻ Jinan; its E part forms Shandong Penin. Bet. 1852 and 1938 and since 1947 traversed by lower course of the Huang; in the W crossed by the Grand Canal. Has two elevated regions: one in cen. part (highest point the sacred mountain of Tai Shan 5048 ft. or 1539 m.) and the other in E end of peninsula S of Yantai (highest point above 5000 ft. or 1525 m.). Has several good harbors, esp. Qingdao, Yantai, Weihai, and Penglai.

Chief products: Wheat, corn, millet; fishing; iron ore, gold.

History: Occupied by Chinese cultivators from very early times; became influential in Chinese history esp. because it was the birthplace of philosophers Confucius (K'ung Ch'iu) (c. 551 B.C.) and Mencius (Meng-tzu) (c. 371 B.C.), and because of Tai Shan (*q.v.*); early in first millennium A.D. established importance in maritime trading; when China was opened to foreign trade 19th cent., some areas leased to Great Britain and to Germany; in WWI Qingdao captured by Japanese army 1914 (returned 1922); occupied 1937 by Japanese; restored to China 1945; came under control of Communist forces 1948. See table at CHINA.

Shandong Peninsula *or Pinyin* **Shandong Ban·dao** \'bän-'daủ\ *or W.-G.* **Shan–tung Pan–tao** \'shän-'dủŋ-'bän-'daủ\. E section of Shandong prov., NE China, bet. Bo Hai (the Gulf of Chihli) and the Yellow Sea.

Shan·ga·ni \shäŋ-'gä-nē\. River, W cen. Zimbabwe; flows WNW into Zambezi River near Victoria Falls; 270 mi. (434 km.) long.

Shang–ch'iu. See SHANGQIU.

Shang·chuan *or W.-G.* **Shang–ch'uan** \'shäng-'chwen\ *also* **Chang·chuen** \'chäŋ-'chwen\ *or Eng.* **Saint John Island.** Island, Guangdong prov., S coast of China, SW of Macao.

Shang·hai \'shäŋ-'hī, 'shaŋ-\. City and seaport, E China, on Huangpu River 13 mi. (21 km.) from its mouth, 150 mi. (241 km.) SE of Nanjing; city pop. (1990c) 7,496,509; munic. pop. (1990c) 13,341,896; constitutes a special administrative unit; one of China's leading ports, with extensive harbor facilities; a major commercial and manufacturing center, producing textiles, steel, leather goods, chemicals, ships, motor vehicles; a major educational center, has several universities and colleges, incl. Shanghai Univ. (1895) and a medical university (1952); many museums, among them Shanghai museum; parks and gardens; Buddhist temple. See table at CHINA.

History: Settled c. 1000 A.D.; in an area of primarily agricultural importance until mid-19th cent.; opened to foreigners by Treaty of Nanking (1842) as one of first treaty ports; developed rapidly with increase of trade concession sections; Chinese Communist Party begun here 1921; scene of severe fighting in Sino-Japanese War 1930s; Japanese occupied city during WWII, after which it was restored to China; taken by Communists 1949; Shanghai Communique issued here 1972 marking diplomatic turning point easing relations bet. China and U.S.

Shangkiu. See SHANGQIU.

Shang·qiu \'shäŋ-'chyü\ *or W.-G.* **Shang–ch'iu** \-'chyü\ *also* **Shang·kiu** \-'chyü\. Town, E Henan prov., E cen. China, ab. 115 mi. (185 km.) ESE of Zhengzhou; pop. (1990c) 164,880.

Shang·rao *or W.-G.* **Shang–jao** \'shäŋ-'raủ\. Town, Jiangxi prov., SE China, ab. 130 mi. (210 km.) E of Nanchang; pop. (1990c) 132,455.

Shan·hai·guan *or W.-G.* **Shan–hai–kuan** \'shän-'hī-'gwen\; *formerly* **Lin·yü–kuan** \'lin-'yū̇-'kwen\. Town on Gulf of Liaodong, NE Hebei prov., NE China, at E end of Great Wall; ab. halfway bet. Beijing and Shenyang (260 mi. or 418 km. from either) and for centuries an important border town; first Chinese city occupied by the Manchus 1644 and scene of great activity in Boxer Rebellion 1900.

Shank·lin \'shaŋ-klin\. Seaside resort, SE Isle of Wight, S England.

Shan·non \'sha-nən\. **1.** Name of counties in two states of the U.S. See tables at MISSOURI and SOUTH DAKOTA. **2.** Navigable river, N, cen., and SW Ireland; rises in N co. Cavan, flows S through a number of lakes (incl. Lough Ree and Lough Derg) to Limerick, where it turns W and empties into Atlantic Ocean through a long, deep estuary; 230 mi. (370 km.) long; chief river in Ireland.

Shansi. See SHANXI.

Shan States. See SHAN.

Shan·tar·skiye Os·tro·va \shən-'tär-skyə-,əs-trə-'vȧ\ *or Eng.* **Shan·tar Islands** \shən-'tär\. Island group, W Sea of Okhotsk, Khabarovsk Kray, E Russia in Asia; crossed by 55°N.

Shan·tou \'shän-'tō\ *or W.-G.* **Shan–t'ou** \-'tō\ *or Eng.* **Swa·tow** \'swä-'taủ, -'tō\. Town, E Guangdong prov., SE China, at mouth of the Han on S side ab. 170 mi. (275 km.) NW of Hong Kong; pop. (1990c) 578,630; has excellent harbor; grew from small fishing village when opened to foreign trade mid-19th cent.; in WWII held by Japanese 1939–45; became c. 1980 one of China's "special economic zones" with privileges intended to encourage foreign trade and investment.

Shantung. See SHANDONG.

Shan–tung Pan–tao. See SHANDONG PENINSULA.

Shan·xi \'shän-'shē\ *or W.-G.* **Shan·si** \-'shē\. Province, NE China, bounded on N by Nei Monggol (Inner Mongolia), on E by Hebei, on S and SE by Henan, and on W by Shaanxi; ✻ Taiyuan; a plateau forming an intermediate region bet. arid Nei Monggol and the fertile plain of N China; its W and S boundaries are the Huang; a tributary, the Fen, traverses most of the province from NE to SW. Its N border is marked by a section of the Great Wall and farther S is crossed by another section. Covered by great loess deposits, it was the home of early Chinese agriculture; in its NE part is the sacred mountain Wutai Shan 9261 ft. (2823 m.), formerly visited by many pilgrims.

Chief products: Wheat, millet, cotton, tobacco; coal, iron ore.

Chief cities: Taiyuan and Datong.

History: For centuries has been an integral part of the various N kingdoms of China acting as buffer against invaders from N and serving as area for cen. trade routes; after the Revolution (1911) was ruled by warlord Yen Hsi-shan who instituted economic improvements; in Sino-Japanese War (1937–45) was in part occupied by Japanese forces and was the scene of much guerrilla warfare; came under Communist control 1949. See table at CHINA.

Shao·guan *or W.-G.* **Shao–kuan** \ˈshau̇-ˈgwen\ *also* **Ku·kong** \ˈkü-ˈkȯŋ\. City, N Guangdong, SE China, 125 mi. (201 km.) N of Guangzhou; pop. (1990c) 350,043; trading and coal-mining center.

Shao–hsing *also* **Shaohing.** See SHAOXING.

Shao–kuan. See SHAOGUAN.

Shao·xing *or W.-G.* **Shao–hsing** *also* **Shao·hing** \ˈshau̇-ˈshiŋ\. City, N Zhejiang prov., E China, ab. 40 mi. (64 km.) ESE of Hangzhou on rich delta plain; pop. (1990c) 179,818; center for trade in cotton and rice. An old town, seat of government of a powerful king of Yüeh in mid-first millennium B.C.

Shao·yang *or W.-G.* **Shao–yang** \ˈshau̇-ˈyäŋ\; *formerly* **Pao·king** \ˈbau̇-ˈchiŋ\. Town, cen. Hunan prov., SE cen. China, ab. 120 mi. (195 km.) SW of Changsha; pop. (1990c) 247,227.

Shap·in·say \ˈshap-ᵊn-ˌsā\. One of the Orkney Is. (*q.v.*) off N coast of Scotland; ab. 5 mi. (8 km.) long; ancestral home of American author Washington Irving.

Shaq·ra \ˈshȧ-krə\ *or* **Ash–Shaqrā** \ȧsh-\. Town, cen. Nejd, Saudi Arabia, ab. 100 mi. (160 km.) WNW of Riyadh.

Sha·raf·khā·neh \shə-ˌräf-kä-ˈne\ *or* **Sha·rif·kha·neh** \ˌshä-rəf-kə-ˈne\. Town, East Azerbaijan prov., NW Iran, on NE shore of Daryācheh-ye Orūmīyeh (*q.v.*).

Sha·ra·va·ti \shə-ˈrä-və-tē\. See JOG FALLS.

Shar·ba·tat, Cape \ˌshär-bə-ˈtȧt\ *or Arab.* **Ras ash–Sharba·tāt** \ˈräs-ȧsh-\. Cape, SE coast of Oman, SE Arabian Penin., extending into the Arabian Sea, NE of Cape Nus.

Shari. See CHARI.

Sharifkhaneh. See SHARAFKHĀNEH.

Shar·jah \ˈshär-jə\. **1.** Emirate. See *Ash Shāriqah* in table at UNITED ARAB EMIRATES.

2. Town, United Arab Emirates. See ASH SHĀRIQAH.

Shark Bay \ˈshärk\ *also* **Sharks Bay** \ˈshärks\. Large bay, inlet of Indian Ocean, W Western Australia, Australia, 25°30′S, 113°30′E; pearl fishing formerly important.

Shar·key \ˈshär-kē\. County in W Mississippi. See table at MISSISSIPPI.

Sharm al–Sheikh \ˈshärm-ȧl-ˈshēk, -ˈshāk\ *or Arab.* **Ra's Naṣ·rā·nī** \ˈrȧs-nȧs-ˈrä-nē\ *or Heb.* **Mif·raz Shlo·mo** \mi-ˌfräz-shlō-ˈmō\. Cape, S end of Sinai Penin. (*q.v.*), Egypt, opp. Tīrān I.; site of former Egyptian military base, captured by Israel 1956, restored to Egypt 1957; a UN emergency force was stationed there from 1957 until requested (1967) by Egypt to leave; captured by Israel during Arab-Israeli War 1967; returned to Egypt 1982.

Shar·on \ˈshar-ən\. **1.** Residential and resort town, W Litchfield co., NW Connecticut, S of Salisbury on New York border; pop. (1990c) 2928.

2. Residential town, Norfolk co., E Massachusetts, 9 mi. (14 km.) WNW of Brockton; pop. (1990c) 15,517.

3. City, Mercer co., W Pennsylvania, on Ohio border 18 mi. (29 km.) NNW of New Castle; pop. (1990c) 17,493; steel products; Shenango Valley campus of Pennsylvania State Univ. (1965).

Sharon, Plain of *also* **Plain of Sar·on** \ˈsär-ən\. Coastal plain, W Israel, extending from Mt. Carmel to Tel Aviv-Jaffa; ab. 50 mi. (80 km.) long by 10 mi. (16 km.) wide; very fertile.

Sharon Hill. Borough, Delaware co., SE Pennsylvania, 7 mi. (11 km.) WSW of Philadelphia; pop. (1990c) 5771.

Sharon Springs. City, ⊗ of Wallace co., W Kansas; pop. (1990c) 1148.

Shar·on·ville \ˈshar-ən-ˌvil\. City, Hamilton co., SW Ohio, 14 mi. (23 km.) NNE of Cincinnati; pop. (1990c) 13,153.

Sharp \ˈshärp\. County in N Arkansas. See table at ARKANSAS.

Sharp Mountain. Ridge, Schuylkill co., E cen. Pennsylvania, forming the S boundary of the Pottsville coal basin.

Sharps·burg \ˈshärps-ˌbərg\. **1.** Town, Washington co., N Maryland, on W side of Antietam Creek; pop. (1990c) 659; nearby is Antietam National Battlefield, commemorating battle (Sept. 1862) of Antietam (sometimes called battle of Sharpsburg) when Union forces under Gen. George McClellan met Gen. Robert E. Lee's first invasion of the North in the Civil War, causing Lee's withdrawal from Maryland into Virginia.

2. Borough, Allegheny co., SW Pennsylvania, on Allegheny River 6 mi. (10 km.) NE of Pittsburgh; pop. (1990c) 3781.

Sharps·ville \ˈshärps-ˌvil\. Borough, Mercer co., W Pennsylvania, 19 mi. (31 km.) NNW of New Castle; pop. (1990c) 4729.

Sharqāṭ, Ash. See ASH SHARQĀṬ.

Sharqī, Al–Jabal ash. See ANTI-LEBANON.

Shar·qī·ya \shȧr-ˈkē-yə\. Governorate of NE Egypt. See table at EGYPT.

Sha·shi *or W.-G.* **Sha–shih** \ˈshä-ˈshē, -ˈshir\ *also* **Sha·si** \ˈshä-ˈsē, -ˈshir\. Port, S Hubei prov., E cen. China, on N bank of the Chang, 83 mi. (134 km.) below Yichang; pop. (1990c) 281,352; an ancient city settled 2d millennium B.C.; has long functioned as commercial center; important port of region during Taiping Rebellion mid-19th cent.

Shas·ta \ˈshas-tə\. County in N California. See table at CALIFORNIA.

Shasta, Mount. Peak, cone of an extinct volcano, in Cascade Range, Siskiyou co., N California; 14,162 ft. (4317 m.); covered with glaciers; discovered 1827, first climbed 1854.

Shasta Dam *and* **Shasta Lake.** See UNITED STATES, *Dams and Reservoirs.*

Shasukotan. See SHIASHKOTAN.

Sha·to Plateau \ˈshä-tō\. Tableland, Coconino and Navajo cos., N Arizona.

Shatt al Ar·ab \ˈshat-ˌal-ˈar-əb\. Channel, SE Iraq, flowing SE into Persian Gulf; ab. 120 mi. (193 km.) long; formed by the confluence of the Tigris and Euphrates rivers, it is generally considered to begin at Al Qurnah, flowing past Iraqi port of Basra, past Khorramshahr and Ābādān in Iran, and entering the gulf near the port of Al Fāw in Iraq; forms in part the boundary bet. Iran and Iraq which has been long contested bet. the two countries; scene of Iraqi offensive 1980 to control wider territory, but which precipitated Iran-Iraq War; repeatedly fought over by Iran and Iraq during next several years; for ab. 60 mi. (97 km.) above Al Fāw, the waterway lies entirely within Iraq; navigation above Ābādān is difficult because of bar at Al Fāw and silt in the delta region. On E shore is Ābādān I. at N end of which it receives the Kārūn River. For the most part formed since ancient times because formerly Bassorah (Basra) was much nearer the sea.

Shatt al–Hodna. See HODNA, CHOTT EL.

Shaṭṭ al–Jarīd. See DJERID, CHOTT.

Shatt al–Melghir. See MELRHIR, CHOTT.

Shatt al–Shergui. See CHERGUI, CHOTT ECH.

Shatt Dijla. See TIGRIS.

Shaulyay. See ŠIAULIAI.

Sha·va·no Peak \ˈsha-və-ˌnō\. Mountain, Chaffee co., cen. Colorado; 14,229 ft. (4337 m.).

Shaver Lake *and* **Shaver Lake Dam.** See SAN JOAQUIN 1.

Sha·vers Mountain \ˈshā-vərz\. Ridge, E cen. West Virginia, extending along boundary bet. Randolph and Pocahontas cos.

Shaw·an·gunk Mountains \ˈshäŋ-gəm, -ˌgəŋk\. Range, part of Kittatinny Mt. (*q.v.*), SE New York; highest peak Sam's Point 2289 ft. (698 m.), in Ulster co.

Sha·wa·no \ˈshȯ-nō\. **1.** County in E cen. Wisconsin. See table at WISCONSIN.
2. City, its ⊗, 34 mi. (55 km.) WNW of Green Bay (city); pop. (1990c) 7598; diversified agriculture.

Shawano Lake. Lake, Shawano co., E cen. Wisconsin; ab. 6 mi. (10 km.) long and 3 mi. (5 km.) wide; drains into Wolf River.

Sha·win·i·gan \shə-ˈwi-ni-gən\; *formerly* **Shawinigan Falls.** City, St.-Maurice co., S Quebec, Canada, on St.-Maurice River 18 mi. (29 km.) NNW of Trois-Rivières; pop. (1991c) 19,931; aluminum, pulp and paper, chemicals, abrasives; founded c. 1900; ab. 2 mi. (3 km.) S is town of **Shawinigan–Sud** \-ˈsüd\. **Shawinigan Falls** (165 ft. or 50 m. high) furnishes power for local plants and light and power for Montreal 70 mi. (113 km.) distant.

Shaw·nee \shȯ-ˈnē, shä-\. **1.** County in NE Kansas. See table at KANSAS.
2. City, Johnson co., E Kansas, S suburb of Kansas City; pop. (1990c) 37,993.
3. City, ⊗ of Pottawatomie co., cen. Oklahoma, on North Canadian River 38 mi. (61 km.) ESE of Oklahoma City; pop. (1990c) 26,017; aircraft parts, clothing; oil wells; Oklahoma Baptist Univ. (1910), St. Gregory's Coll. (1915).

Shaw·nee·town \ˈshȯ-nē-ˌtau̇n, ˈshä-\. City, ⊗ of Gallatin co., SE Illinois, near Ohio River 10 mi. (16 km.) below its confluence with Wabash River; pop. (1990c) 1575.

Shaykh, Jabal ash–. See HERMON, MOUNT.

Shaykh Saʻīd. See CHEIK-SAÏD.

Shaykh ʻUthman. See SHEIKH ʻOTHMAN.

Shcha·ra \ˈshchä-rə\ *or Pol.* **Szcza·ra** \ˈshchä-rä\. River, W Belarus; flows NNW from Polesye to Neman River; ab. 100 mi. (160 km.) long.

Shche·ki·no \ˈshchȯ-ki-nə\. Town, Tula Oblast, W cen. Russia in Europe, ab. 15 mi. (24 km.) SSE of the city of Tula.

Shchel·ko·vo \ˈshchȯl-kə-ˌvə\. Town, Moscow Oblast, W cen. Russia in Europe, ab. 20 mi. (32 km.) NE of the city of Moscow.

Shcherbakov. See RYBINSK.

Shchu·chinsk \ˈshchü-ˌchinsk\; *formerly* **Shchuch'·ye** \ˈshchü-chʸē\. Town, Kokchetav subdivision, Kazakhstan, ab. 40 mi. (64 km.) NW of the town of Kokchetav; pop. (1991e) 56,000.

Shear, Mount \ˈshir\. Mountain, Antarctica, 78°21′S, 86°13′W; 13,100 ft. (3993 m.).

She·ba \ˈshē-bə\ *or* **Sa·ba** \ˈsā-bə\ *or Arab.* **Sa·ba'** \ˈsȧ-bə\. Ancient country, S Arabian Penin., SW Asia, probably included Yemen. Became important during first millennium B.C.; its inhabitants were Sabaeans, a Semitic people of very ancient culture; its language was closely related to Ethiopic and its people were early colonizers of Ethiopia. Wealthy and commercially strong because of its position on the India-Africa trade route (see story in Bible of Queen of Sheba's visit to Hebrew King Solomon, *1 Kings* x); declined c. 6th cent. A.D. A chief city was Mar'ib (*q.v.*).

Shebelē. See SHABEELLE.

She·ber·ghān *or* **Shi·bar·ghān** \ˌshi-bər-ˈgän\. Town, N Afghanistan.

She·boy·gan \shi-ˈbȯi-gən\. **1.** County in E Wisconsin. See table at WISCONSIN.
2. City, its ⊗, on Lake Michigan 51 mi. (82 km.) N of Milwaukee; pop. (1990c) 49,676; plastics, furniture, sausage, beer, cheese; Lakeland Coll. (1862).

Sheboygan Falls. City, Sheboygan co., E Wisconsin, 3 mi. (5 km.) W of the city of Sheboygan; pop. (1990c) 5823.

Shechem. See NĀBULUS.

Shed·i·ac \ˈshe-dē-ˌak\. Resort town, Westmorland co., SE New Brunswick, Canada, on Northumberland Strait 15 mi. (24 km.) ENE of Moncton; pop. (1991c) 4343.

Shee·lin, Lough \läk-ˈshē-lən\. Lake, S co. Cavan, N Ireland (republic), ENE of Longford; ab. 5 mi. (8 km.) long; drains SW through Inny River into Lough Ree.

Sheep Haven \ˈshēp\. Bay of Atlantic Ocean, N coast of co. Donegal, N Ireland (republic), W of Lough Swilly.

Sheep Mountain. **1.** Peak, Banner co., W Nebraska; 4507 ft. (1374 m.).
2. Peak, Snohomish co., NW cen. Washington; 6120 ft. (1865 m.).
3. Peak, Teton co., WSW Wyoming; 10,772 ft. (3283 m.).

Sheep Rock. Peak, Baker co., E Oregon; 6017 ft. (1834 m.).

Shef·field \ˈshe-ˌfēld\. **1.** Industrial city, Colbert co., NW Alabama, on Tennessee River near Wilson Dam; pop. (1990c) 10,380.
2. Town, Berkshire co., W Massachusetts, on Housatonic River 24 mi. (39 km.) S of Pittsfield; pop. (1990c) 2910.
3. City and county borough, South Yorkshire, N England, on the Don 68 mi. (109 km.) NNE of Birmingham; pop. (1991p) 499,700; center of the English cutlery industry; optical instruments, food products; formerly a major producer of steel, plated ware, and iron; Univ. of Sheffield (1905); former site of Norman castle (now ruins) where Mary, Queen of Scots, was held prisoner. Known as early as 14th cent. for its cutlery; developed as center of steel industry (incl. esp. armor plate and alloy steels) from mid-19th cent.

Sheffield Lake. City, Lorain co., N Ohio, on Lake Erie W of Cleveland; pop. (1990c) 9825.

She–hsien. See SHEXIAN.

Sheikh ʻOth·man *or* **Shaikh ʻOthman** \ˈshīk-ȯth-ˈmȧn, ˈshāk-\ *or* **Shaykh ʻUth·mān** \-ùth-\. Town, Yemen, on SW Arabian Penin., ab. 6 mi. (10 km.) N of Aden.

Shekh·u·pura \ˌshe-k̲ə-ˈpu̇r-ə\. Town, Punjab, Pakistan, NW of Lahore; pop. (1981c) 141,168.

She·ki *or* **Şä·ki** \ˈshe-kē\; *formerly* **Nu·kha** \nü-ˈk̲ä\. Town, N Azerbaijan, at foot of Caucasus Mts. 55 mi. (88 km.) NE of Gäncä. Once the center of a Tatar khanate, was taken over by Russians in 1819.

Shek·sna \shik-ˈsnä\. Navigable river, Vologda and Yaroslavl' oblasts, cen. Russia in Europe; flows S from Lake Beloye; near Cherepovets enters Rybinsk Reservoir (*q.v.*); ab. 280 mi. (450 km.) long; before 1940 entered the Volga River just W of Shcherbakov (now Rybinsk). Forms important part of the Volga-Baltic Waterway (*q.v.*).

She·lag·ski, Cape \shə-ˈläk-skē\ *or Russ.* **Mys She·lag·skiy** \ˈməs-shi-ˈläk-skē\. Point on N coast of Chukchi Autonomous Okrug, NE Russia in Asia, on East Siberian Sea, 70°06′N, 170°26′E.

Shel·burne \ˈshel-bərn\. **1.** Town, Chittenden co., NW Vermont, 6 mi. (10 km.) S of Burlington; pop. (1990c) 5871.
2. County in SW Nova Scotia, Canada. See table at NOVA SCOTIA.
3. Seaport town, ⊗ of Shelburne co., SW Nova Scotia, Canada, on inlet of Atlantic Ocean 43 mi. (69 km.) E of Yarmouth; pop. (1991c) 2245; received several thousand Loyalist settlers following American Revolution.

Shel·by \ˈshel-bē\. **1.** Name of counties in nine states of the U.S. See tables at ALABAMA, ILLINOIS, INDIANA, IOWA, KENTUCKY, MISSOURI, OHIO, TENNESSEE, TEXAS.
2. City, Bolivar co., NW Mississippi, 20 mi. (32 km.) SSW of Clarksdale; pop. (1990c) 2806.
3. City, ⊗ of Toole co., N Montana, 75 mi. (121 km.) NNW of Great Falls; pop. (1990c) 2763; oil wells.
4. City, ⊗ of Cleveland co., SW North Carolina, 21 mi. (34 km.) W of Gastonia; pop. (1990c) 14,669; textiles.
5. City, Richland co., N cen. Ohio, 11 mi. (18 km.) NW of Mansfield; pop. (1990c) 9564.

Shel·by·ville \ˈshel-bē-ˌvil\. **1.** City, ⊗ of Shelby co., cen. Illinois, 32 mi. (51 km.) SSE of Decatur; pop. (1990c) 4943.
2. City, ⊗ of Shelby co., cen. Indiana, 27 mi. (43 km.) SE of Indianapolis; pop. (1990c) 15,336; plastics, fiberglass, paper.
3. City, ⊗ of Shelby co., N cen. Kentucky, 20 mi. (32 km.) W of Frankfort; pop. (1990c) 6238.
4. City, ⊗ of Shelby co., NE Missouri; pop. (1990c) 582.
5. Town, ⊗ of Bedford co., S cen. Tennessee, 25 mi. (40 km.) S of Murfreesboro; pop. (1990c) 14,049; horsebreeding.

Shel·don \ˈshel-dən\. City, O'Brien co., NW Iowa, 32 mi. (51 km.) NW of Cherokee; pop. (1990c) 4937.

Shelia, Jebel. See CHÉLIA, DJEBEL.

Sheliff. See CHELIF.

She·li·kho·va, Za·liv \ˈshe-li-k̲ə-və-zə-ˈlʸif\. Gulf, Khabarovsk Kray, E Russia in Asia; ab. 200 mi. (320 km.) wide; Penzhinskaya Bay is an extension on the NE; its E shore is the NW part of Kamchatka Penin.

She·li·kof Strait \ˈshe-li-ko̊f\. Strait in N Pacific Ocean bet. mainland (Alaska Penin.) on W and Kodiak and Afognak islands on E; connects with Cook Inlet at N end; ab. 150 mi. (240 km.) long and 25 to 30 mi. (40 to 48 km.) wide.

Shel·ley \ˈshe-lē\. City, Bingham co., SE Idaho, 8 mi. (13 km.) SW of Idaho Falls; pop. (1990c) 3536.

Shell·har·bour \ˌshel-ˈhär-bər\. Coastal municipality, E New South Wales, Australia, S of Wollongong; pop. (1991c) 46,294.

Shell Lake. City, ⊗ of Washburn co., NW Wisconsin; pop. (1990c) 1161.

Shel·ter Island \ˈshel-tər\. Island, New York, bet. Little Peconic Bay and Gardiners Bay, E Long Island; 6 mi. (10 km.) long; site of a nature preserve.

Shel·ton \ˈshelt-ᵊn\. **1.** City, Fairfield co., SW Connecticut, on Housatonic River opp. Derby 8 mi. (13 km.) N of Long Island Sound; pop. (1990c) 35,418; settled 1697 as part of Stratford; separated from Stratford and later incorp. as town 1789; incorp. as city 1915.

2. City, ⊗ of Mason co., W Washington, on inlet of Puget Sound 17 mi. (27 km.) NW of Olympia; pop. (1990c) 7241.

She·ma·kha \ˌshe-mə-ˈkä\ *or* **Şa·ma·xı** \ˌsha-mə-ˈkē\. Town, E Azerbaijan, 65 mi. (105 km.) WNW of Baku on S slopes of E Caucasus Mts.; pop. (1991e) 25,300. An ancient trading town; former ✻ of Shirvan khanate, subject to Persia; taken and destroyed by Persian King Nāder Shāh 1742; rebuilt but annexed by Russians. Declined after earthquake 1902 and damage in Bolshevik Revolution 1917.

Shem·ya \ˈshem-yə\. Small island, one of the Semichi Is., at W end of Aleutian Is., SW Alaska, E of Attu; location of a U.S. Air Force station.

Shen·an·do·ah \ˌshe-nən-ˈdō-ə, ˌsha-nə-ˈdō-ə\. **1.** River, N Virginia; formed by junction of N and S forks in Warren co., flows NE across NE tip of West Virginia and empties into Potomac River at Harpers Ferry; 55 mi. (88 km.) long.

2. County in N Virginia. See table at VIRGINIA.

3. City, Page and Fremont cos., SW Iowa, 44 mi. (71 km.) SE of Council Bluffs; pop. (1990c) 5572.

4. Borough, Schuylkill co., E cen. Pennsylvania, 11 mi. (18 km.) N of Pottsville; pop. (1990c) 6221.

Shenandoah Mountain. Mountain ridge bet. Virginia and West Virginia; part of the Allegheny Mts.

Shenandoah National Park. See UNITED STATES, *National Parks.*

Shenandoah Valley. Valley, Virginia; ab. 110 mi. (175 km.) long, 25 mi. (40 km.) wide; drained by the Shenandoah River bet. the Allegheny and Blue Ridge mountains, and extending SW from Harpers Ferry; scene of important operations throughout Civil War, incl. Gen. Philip H. Sheridan's ride from Winchester to Cedar Creek where his arrival turned a Union defeat into victory (1865).

She·nan·go \shə-ˈnaŋ-gō\. River, W Pennsylvania; rises in Crawford co., flows S and joins Mahoning River 4 mi. (6 km.) SW of New Castle, Lawrence co., to form Beaver River; ab. 100 mi. (160 km.) long; dammed near Sharpsville to form **Shenango Lake**.

Shen–chen. See SHENZHEN.

Shen·di \ˈshen-dē\ *or* **Shan·dī** \ˈshän-\. Town, NE cen. Sudan, on right bank of Nile River 100 mi. (161 km.) NNE of Khartoum.

Shengking. See LIAONING.

Shensi. See SHAANXI.

Shen·yang *or* **Shen–yang** \ˈshən-ˈyäŋ\; *formerly* **Feng·tien** \ˈfəŋ-ˈtyen\; *traditionally* **Muk·den** \ˈmu̇k-dən, ˈmük-\ *also* **Mouk·den** \ˈmük-dən\. City, ✻ of Liaoning prov., NE China; pop. (1990c) 3,603,712; strategically located on the Hun River for control over N to S routes in S Manchurian plain; one of China's leading industrial cities, producing machinery, wires and cables, machine tools, flour, textiles, paper, and chemicals; trades in agricultural products. Divided into three major parts: old walled city, ab. 4 mi. (6 km.) in circumference; new town, orig. Japanese concession; the industrial area. Educational and cultural center; has notable palaces, mausoleums, and monuments.

History: City of ancient origins; ✻ of Manchu empire 1625–44, and base for Manchu conquest of China in 17th cent.; site of royal tombs and treasury during rule of Manchu dynasty 1644–1912; in Russo-Japanese War scene of major battle 1905 when it fell to Japanese; scene of "Mukden Incident" Sept. 1931 in which a nearby railway explosion was used as a pretext for Japanese military occupation of the city and then the rest of Manchuria (*q.v.*); occupied by Japanese 1931–45 and subsequently briefly by U.S.S.R.; scene of heavy fighting in Chinese Civil War 1947–48; occupied by Communist forces Nov. 1, 1948 and served as base for conquest of the rest of China.

Shen·zhen \ˈshən-ˈjen\; *W.-G.* **Shen–chen** \-ˈjen\ *or* **Bao·'an** \ˈbau̇-ˈan\; *W.-G.* **Pao–an** \ˈbau̇-ˈan\. City, S Guangdong prov., China, just N of Hong Kong; pop. (1990c) 350,727; developed rapidly after being designated a center for trade and foreign investment c. 1980.

She·paug \shə-ˈpo̊g\. River, W Connecticut; rises in N cen. Litchfield co., flows S into Housatonic River; ab. 35 mi. (55 km.) long.

She·pe·tiv·ka \shə-pi-ˈto̊f-kə\ *or* **She·pe·tov·ka** \-ˈto̊f-\. Town, N Khmel'nyts'kyy subdivision, Ukraine, 70 mi. (113 km.) W of Berdichev; pop. (1991e) 52,000; railroad junction on main line to Kovel'.

Shep·herd Islands \ˈshe-pərd\. Group of small islands, Vanuatu, SW Pacific Ocean; pop. (1991e) 3975.

Shep·herds·town \ˈshe-pərdz-ˌtau̇n\. Town, Jefferson co., NE West Virginia, in E Panhandle on Potomac River, ab. 15 mi. (24 km.) SW of Hagerstown, Maryland; pop. (1990c) 1287; Shepherd Coll. (1871).

Shep·herds·ville \ˈshe-pərdz-ˌvil\. City, ⊗ of Bullitt co., cen. Kentucky; pop. (1990c) 4805.

Shep·par·ton \ˈshe-pər-tən\. Town, N Victoria, SE Australia, on Goulburn River 102 mi. (164 km.) NNE of Melbourne; pop. (1991p) 25,251.

Shep·pey, Isle of \ˈshe-pē\. Island in mouth of the Thames, SE England; 9 mi. (14 km.) long; 35 sq. mi. (91 sq. km.); vegetables, sheep; bridge connections with Kentish mainland.

Shep·ton Mal·let \ˈshep-tən-ˈma-lət\. Town, Somerset, SW England, 22 mi. (35 km.) SW of Bath; pop. (1981p) 6306; 16th cent. market cross 50 ft. (15 m.) high.

She·qua·ga Falls \shə-ˈkwo̊-gə\. Waterfall in Montour Falls, New York; 156 ft. (48 m.) high.

Sher·born \ˈshər-bərn\. Town, Middlesex co., NE Massachusetts, 16 mi. (26 km.) SW of Boston; pop. (1990c) 3989.

Sher·borne \ˈshər-bərn\. Town, Dorset, S England, 50 mi. (80 km.) W of Southampton; pop. (1981p) 7572; trade center in agricultural area.

Sher·bro \ˈshər-ˌbrō\. Estuary, SW coast of Sierra Leone, opp. Sherbro I.

Sherbro Island. Island, SW coast of Sierra Leone; town of Bonthe is on its E coast.

Sher·brooke \ˈshər-ˌbru̇k\. **1.** County, S Quebec, Canada. See table at QUEBEC.

2. City, its ⊗, at confluence of Magog and St. Francis rivers 85 mi. (137 km.) E of Montreal; pop. (1991c) 76,429; produces machinery, leather and rubber products, footwear, paper, textiles; hydroelectric power plants; Séminaire de Sherbrooke, Univ. de Sherbrooke (1954). Founded by U.S. settlers 1802.

Sher·burne \ˈshər-bərn\. County in cen. Minnesota. See table at MINNESOTA.

Sherburne Peak. Mountain, Glacier National Park, NW Montana; 8500 ft. (2590 m.).

Shergui, Shatt al–. See CHERGUI, CHOTT ECH.

Sher·i·dan \ˈsher-əd-ᵊn\. **1.** Name of counties in five states of the U.S. See tables at KANSAS, MONTANA, NEBRASKA, NORTH DAKOTA, WYOMING.
2. City, ⊗ of Grant co., S cen. Arkansas; pop. (1990c) 3098.
3. City, Arapahoe co., NE cen. Colorado, just S of Denver; pop. (1990c) 4976.
4. City, ⊗ of Sheridan co., N Wyoming, 13 mi. (21 km.) S of Montana border; pop. (1990c) 13,900; tourist resort; Sheridan Coll. (1948).

Sheridan, Mount. **1.** Peak, Lake and Park cos., cen. Colorado; 13,700 ft. (4176 m.).
2. Peak, Yellowstone National Park, NW Wyoming; 10,308 ft. (3142 m.).

Sher·iff Knob \ˈsher-əf\. Peak, Union co., N Georgia; 3400 ft. (1036 m.).

Sher·iff·muir \ˈsher-əf-ˌmyu̇r, ˈsher-ē-ˌmyu̇r\. Battlefield, Central region, cen. Scotland, just W of the Ochil Hills; scene of battle 1715 in short-lived Jacobite rebellion in which the advance of the Jacobites under John Erskine, 6th earl of Mar, was checked by supporters of the house of Hanover under John Campbell, 2d duke of Argyll.

Sher·man \ˈshər-mən\. **1.** Name of counties in four states of the U.S. See tables at KANSAS, NEBRASKA, OREGON, TEXAS.
2. City, ⊗ of Grayson co., NE Texas, 60 mi. (97 km.) N of Dallas; pop. (1990c) 31,601; Austin Coll. (1849).

Sherman, Fort. See FORT SHERMAN.

Sherman, Mount. Peak, Park and Lake cos., cen. Colorado; 14,036 ft. (4278 m.).

Sher·rill \ˈsher-əl\. City, Oneida co., cen. New York, 19 mi. (21 km.) W of Utica; pop. (1990c) 2864.

Shershell. See CHERCHELL.

's Her·to·gen·bosch \ser-ˌtō-k̲ən-ˈbo̊s\ *or Fr.* **Bois–le–Duc** \ˌbwäl-ˈdu̅e̅k\. Commune, ✻ of North Brabant prov., S Netherlands, at the confluence of Aa and Dommel rivers; pop. (1981e) 81,471; railroad junction; Gothic cathedral of St. John; museum; received charter 1185; fortress until 1876. Birthplace of painter Hieronymus Bosch 1450.

Sher·wood \ˈshər-ˌwu̇d\. **1.** City, Pulaski co., cen. Arkansas, 5 mi. (8 km.) NE of Little Rock; pop. (1990c) 18,893; grew rapidly in 1970s and 1980s.
2. City, Washington co., NW Oregon, SW of Portland; pop. (1990c) 3093.

Sherwood Forest. Ancient royal forest, chiefly in Nottinghamshire, cen. England; remains of forest preserved in ducal estates around Worksop; associated with tales of legendary outlaw Robin Hood.

Shet·land \ˈshet-lənd\. **1.** *or* **Zet·land** \ˈzet-\ *or* **Shetland Islands.** Archipelago off N Scotland, 50 mi. (81 km.) NE of Orkney Is.; includes islands of Unst, Fetlar, Whalsay, Mainland, Foula, Papa Stour, Yell; 552 sq. mi. (1430 sq. km.); pop. (1991e) 22,270; ✻ Lerwick; constitutes Shetland administrative area; northernmost part of Great Britain. Long a Norse dependency; acquired by Scotland 1472.
2. Former county of Scotland. See ZETLAND.
3. *also* **Zetland.** Administrative area, N Scotland, comprising the Shetland Is.; fish processing, livestock raising (Shetland ponies); knitted goods, tweeds; terminal for North Sea oil. See table at SCOTLAND.

She·tuck·et \shē-ˈtə-kət\. River, E Connecticut; formed by confluence of Willimantic and Natchaug rivers at Willimantic, flows SE to unite with the Quinebaug and form the Thames; ab. 20 mi. (32 km.) long.

Shevchenko. See AQTAŪ.

She·wa \ˈshā-wə\ *or* **Shoa** \ˈshō-ə\. Historical region, cen. Ethiopia, in the area around Addis Ababa; location of several early kingdoms incl. that of Menelik II who became emperor of Ethiopia 1889.

She·xian *or* **She Xian** \ˈshə-ˈshyen\ *or W.-G.* **She–hsien** \-ˈshyen\; *formerly* **Hwei·chow** \ˈhwā-ˈchau̇\. City, SE Anhui prov., E China, S of Wuhu; pop. (1989e) 139,900.

Shey·enne \shī-ˈen, -ˈan\. River, cen. and SE North Dakota; rises in Sheridan co., cen. North Dakota, flows E, then S and again E into Red River of the North above Fargo; ab. 325 mi. (525 km.) long.

Shi·ash·ko·tan \shi-ˈäsh-kə-tən\; *formerly* **Sha·su·ko·tan** \ˈshä-ˈsu̇-ˈkō-ˈtän\. One of the Kuril Is. (*q.v.*), N part of chain, S of Onekotan; highest point 3097 ft. (944 m.).

Shi·a·was·see \ˌshī-ə-ˈwȯ-sē, -ˈwä-\. **1.** River, SE Michigan; flows from Oakland co. N to unite with Flint River to form Saginaw River in Saginaw co.; ab. 100 mi. (160 km.) long.
2. County in S cen. Michigan. See table at MICHIGAN.

Shibarghān. See SHEBERGHĀN.

Shi·bar Pass \ˈshē-bär\. Mountain pass, E Afghanistan, NW of Kabul, on highway to N Afghanistan; alt. 9800 ft. (2987 m.).

Shi·ba·ta \shē-ˈbä-tä\. City, Niigata prefecture, Honshū, Japan, 16 mi. (26 km.) E of the city of Niigata; pop. (1990p) 78,168.

Shibenik. See ŠIBENIK.

Shi·bīn al–Kawm *or* **Shi·bîn el Kôm** \shi-ˌbēn-al-ˈkōm\. Town, ✻ of Minūfīya governorate, Egypt, in Nile Delta 40 mi. (64 km.) NNW of Cairo; pop. (1991e) 153,000.

Shick·shock Mountains \ˈshik-ˌshäk\. Mountains, N Gaspé Penin., Quebec, Canada; highest point 4159 ft. (1268 m.).

Shiel, Loch \ˈshēl\. Lake, Highland region, W Scotland, 16 mi. (26 km.) W of Fort William; 16 mi. (26 km.) long and 1 mi. (1.6 km.) wide.

Shif·nal *or* **Shiff·nal** \ˈshif-nəl\. Parish, Shropshire, W England, 17 mi. (32 km.) E of Shrewsbury; market town; Tong (*q.v.*) is 3 mi. (5 km.) to the E.

Shi·ga \ˈshē-gä\. Prefecture, Honshū, Japan; ✻ Ōtsu. See table at JAPAN.

Shigatse. See XIGAZÊ.

Shih–an. See GUILIN.

Shi·he·zi \ˈshi-ˈhə-ˈdzə̇\ *or W.-G.* **Shih–ho–tzu** \ˈshi-ˈhə-ˈdzə̇\. City, N cen. Xinjiang Uygur, NW China, NW of Ürümqi; pop. (1990c) 299,676.

Shi·hor \ˈshī-ˌhȯr\ *or* **Si·hor** \ˈsī-\. Body of water, Egypt; referred to in the Bible and usu. thought to be the Nile River or one of its sections.

Shih–san–ling. See SHISANLING.

Shih–yen. See SHIYAN.

Shi·jia·zhuang *or W.-G.* **Shih–chia–chuang** *also* **Shih·kia·chwang** \ˈshi-ˈjyä-ˈjwäŋ\. City, ✻ of Hebei prov., NE China, ab. 75 mi. (120 km.) SW of Baoding; pop. (1990c) 1,068,439; industrial, cultural, and economic center.

Shi·kar·pur \shi-ˈkär-ˌpu̇r\. City, Sind, Pakistan, near right bank of Indus River 240 mi. (386 km.) NNE of Karachi; pop. (1981c) 88,138.

Shi·ko·ku \shē-ˈkō-kü\. **1.** The smallest of the four principal islands of Japan, S of Honshū and E of Kyūshū; 7245 sq. mi. (18,765 sq. km.); pop. (1990c) 4,195,106; separated from Honshū on E by Kii Channel and from Kyūshū on W by Bungo Strait; has no good harbors; crossed by range of high mountains with many branches; highest Ishizuchino 6500 ft. (1981 m.). From early times held in turn by feudal families until subjugated (c. 1590) by Shogun Hideyoshi Toyotomi; subdivided by him; daimiate of Tosa (old province in S part) powerful until Meiji Restoration 1868.
2. Administrative region of Japan consisting of the island of Shikoku. For subdivisions, see table at JAPAN.

Shi·ko·tan–tō \ˌshē-kō-ˈtän-tō\ *or* **Shikotan** \ˌshē-kō-ˈtän\. One of the Kuril Is. (*q.v.*), just E of Hokkaidō; claimed by Japan, but occupied by Russia (occupied by U.S.S.R. at end of WWII).

Shil·don \ˈshil-dən\. Town, Durham, N England, 25 mi. (40 km.) S of Newcastle upon Tyne; pop. (1981p) 17,443.

Shi·li·gu·ri \shi-ˈlē-ˌgu̇r-ē\ *or* **Si·li·gu·ri** \si-\. Town, West Bengal, India; pop. (1991p) 226,677; by direct line ab. 30 mi. (48 km.) SSE of Darjeeling and connected with it by narrow-gauge railroad 50 mi. (80 km.) long, ascending from 400 ft. (122 m.) to ab. 7000 ft. (2135 m.).

Shil·ka \ˈshil-kə\. **1.** River, SW cen. Chita Oblast, S Russia in Asia; formed by confluence of Ingoda and Onon rivers, flows NE to unite with the Argun to form the Amur River; 345 mi. (555 km.) long.
2. Town, N bank of the Shilka River, S Russia in Asia, ab. 110 mi. (177 km.) E of the city of Chita, on Trans-Siberian R.R.

Shilla. See SILLA.

Shil·le·lagh \shə-ˈlā-lē\. Village, SW co. Wicklow, Ireland; famous for its oaks; origin of the name for a cudgel, orig. applied only to cudgels made of oak or blackthorn.

Shil·ling·ton \ˈshi-liŋ-tən\. Borough, Berks co., SE Pennsylvania, 5 mi. (8 km.) SSW of Reading; pop. (1990c) 5062.

Shil·long \shi-ˈlȯŋ\. Town, ❋ of Meghalaya, NE India, in W cen. part 310 mi. (498 km.) NE of Calcutta; met. area pop. (1991p) 222,273; military cantonment; resort center. Became important as headquarters of a former district 1864 and as ❋ of Assam 1874; destroyed by earthquake 1897 but rebuilt.

Shi·loh \ˈshī-lō\. **1.** Village, St. Clair co., SW Illinois, SE of East St. Louis; pop. (1990c) 2655.
2. *or Arab.* **Khir·bat Say·lūn** \kir-ˈbät-sī-ˈlün, -sā-\. Site in West Bank, 15 mi. (24 km.) W of Jordan River on E slope of Mt. Ephraim; ruins of ancient village, meeting place and sanctuary of Israelites, where the Tabernacle was set up (*Josh.* xviii. 1) and where the Ark of the Covenant was kept until captured by the Philistines c. 1050 B.C.

Shiloh National Military Park. See UNITED STATES, *National Historical Parks.*

Shi·ma·ba·ra \shē-ˈmä-bä-rä\. Peninsula, W Kyūshū, Japan, E of Nagasaki; site of early establishment of Christianity; its persecuted inhabitants and those on nearby Amakusa Is. rebelled 1637–38; ab. 37,000 of them perished in siege and fall of castle stronghold ordered by Japanese Emperor Iemitsu, who was aided by a Dutch gunboat.

Shimabara Bay. Inlet of East China Sea, W coast of Kyūshū, Japan, NE of Nagasaki.

Shi·ma·ne \shē-ˈmä-nā\. Prefecture, Honshū, Japan; ❋ Matsue. See table at JAPAN.

Shi·ma·novsk \shi-ˈmä-nəfsk\. Town, S Amur Oblast, SE Russia in Asia, on Trans-Siberian R.R., 115 mi. (185 km.) N of Blagoveshchensk.

Shi·mi·zu \shē-ˈmē-zü\. Seaport, Shizuoka prefecture, on S coast of cen. Honshū, Japan, on Suruga Bay; pop. (1990p) 241,524; exports tea.

Shi·mo·da \shē-ˈmō-dä\. Seaport, Shizuoka prefecture, S Honshū, Japan, on SE coast of Izu Penin.; pop. (1990p) 30,081; visited by Commodore Matthew Perry and opened to U.S. commerce 1854; place where Townsend Harris, first U.S. consul general to Japan, established his office 1856.

Shi·mo·da·te \ˌshē-mō-ˈdä-tā\. City, Ibaraki prefecture, Honshū, Japan, 47 mi. (76 km.) NNE of Tokyo; pop. (1990p) 66,030.

Shi·mo·ga \shi-ˈmō-gə\. Town, cen. Karnataka, S India, on Tunga River (upper tributary of the Tungabhadra) 150 mi. (241 km.) WNW of Bangalore; pop. (1991p) 178,882; ships rice, pepper, and coffee; textiles, vegetable oils.

Shi·mo·no·se·ki \ˌshē-mō-nō-ˈse-kē\; *formerly* **Aka·ma·ga·se·ki** \ˌä-kä-ˌmä-gä-ˈse-kē\ *or* **Ba·kan** \ˈbä-ˌkän\. Seaport city, Yamaguchi prefecture, SW extremity of Honshū, Japan, on Shimonoseki Strait opp. Kitakyūshū and connected with it by tunnels under the straits; pop. (1990p) 262,643; modern port facilities, heavy industrial plants; controls W entrance of Inland Sea.
History: In 1185 scene of notable battle at Danno-ura (E end of town) in which Minamoto clan under Yoshitsune decisively defeated Taira clan. Bombarded 1864 by British, Dutch, French, and U.S. warships in retaliation against Choshu daimyo for firing on foreign ships; increased rapidly in prosperity after Meiji Restoration 1868; scene of signing of treaty of peace bet. Japan and China 1895.

Shimonoseki Strait. Narrow strait separating extreme SW Honshū and extreme N Kyūshū, Japan; only 0.25 mi. (0.4 km.) wide at its narrowest point; W outlet of Inland Sea, with strong tidal movements. Shimonoseki and Kitakyūshū are on opposite sides (1.5 mi. or 2.4 km. apart) but connected by tunnel under the strait.

Shi·mu·shir \shi-ˈmü-shir\; *formerly* **Shi·mu·shi·ru** \-shi-ˌrü\. One of the Kuril Is. (*q.v.*), in cen. part of chain.

Shin, Loch \ˈshin\. Lake, Highland region, N Scotland; 16.5 mi. (27 km.) long.

Shi·na·no \shē-ˈnä-nō\. River, W cen. Honshū, Japan; rises in Nagano prefecture, flows N into the Sea of Japan at Niigata; ab. 225 mi. (360 km.) long; longest river in Japan.

Shi·nar \ˈshī-nər, -ˌnär\. A country known to the early Hebrews, equivalent to all or part of Babylonia (*Gen.* xi. 2; xiv. 1).

Shin·bwi·yang \ˌshin-bwē-ˈyäŋ\. Town, N Myanmar, on the upper Chindwin at foot of Hukawng Valley.

Shin·chi·ku \ˈshēn-ˈchē-ˈkü\. Seaport city, NW coast of Taiwan, 37 mi. (60 km.) SW of Taipei.

Shīn·dand \ˈshin-ˌdənd\ *or* **Sab·za·war** \ˌsəb-zə-ˈwär\. Town, W Afghanistan, on highway 75 mi. (121 km.) S of Herāt.

Shingishu. See SINŬIJU.

Shinn, Mount \ˈshin\. Mountain, Antarctica, 78°27′S, 85°46′W; 15,750 ft. (4801 m.).

Shinn·ston \ˈshin-stən\. City, Harrison co., N West Virginia, 8 mi. (13 km.) N of Clarksburg; pop. (1990c) 2543.

Shinshu. See CHINJU.

Shi·nyan·ga \shē-ˈnyäŋ-gä\. **1.** Administrative region of N Tanzania. See table at TANZANIA.
2. Town, its ❋.

Shi·o·ga·ma \ˈshyō-gä-mä\. City, Miyagi prefecture, Honshū, Japan, 15 mi. (24 km.) NE of Sendai; pop. (1990p) 62,025.

Shi·o·no \shē-ˈō-nō\. Cape on S extremity of Honshū, Japan, in Wakayama prefecture.

Ship Island \ˈship\. Island, Gulf of Mexico, off SE coast of Harrison co., SE Mississippi; ab. 7 mi. (11 km.) long. In early part of 18th cent. harbor and base for French exploration of Gulf of Mexico coastal region; British naval base in War of 1812; point of contention in Civil War.

Ship·ka Pass *or* **Šip·ka Pass** \ˈship-kə\ *or Bulg.* **Ship·chen·ski Pro·khod** \shēp-ˈchen-skē-prə-ˈkȯd\. Mountain pass in the Balkan Mts., cen. Bulgaria, bet. Gabrovo on N and Kazanlŭk on S; alt. 4376 ft. (1334 m.); scene of major battles 1877 and 1878 during the Russo-Turkish War.

Ship·ley \ˈshi-plē\. Town, West Yorkshire, N England, on the Aire 10 mi. (16 km.) WNW of Leeds; pop. (1981p) 27,894; engineering, textile manufacture.

Ship·pan Point \ˈship-ᵊn\. Point on SW coast, Fairfield co., Connecticut, S of Stamford.

Shippegan Island. See LAMÈQUE, ÎLE.

Ship·pens·burg \ˈship-ᵊnz-ˌbərg\. Borough, Cumberland and Franklin cos., S Pennsylvania, 10 mi. (16 km.) NE of Chambersburg; pop. (1990c) 5331; Shippensburg Univ. of Pennsylvania (1871).

Ship Rock *or* **Ship·rock Peak** \ˈship-ˌräk\. Volcanic rock mass, San Juan co., NW New Mexico, W of Farmington; 7178 ft. (2188 m.); the object of Navajo legends.

Ship·shaw \ˈship-ˌshȯ\. River, S Quebec, Canada; a N tributary of the Saguenay flowing into it below Lac St.-Jean; ab. 90 mi. (145 km.) long; hydroelectric power.

Shi·ra \ˈshē-rä\ *also* **Shi·ra·ka·wa** \ˌshē-rä-ˈkä-wä\. River, W cen. Kyūshū, Japan; flows W through Kumamoto into Shimabara Bay.

Shiragami. See SHIRAKAMI.

Shi·rai·to–no–ta·ki \shē-ˈrī-tō-nō-ˈtä-kē\. Waterfall, S Honshū, Japan, near Fuji; 87 ft. (27 m.) high and 420 ft. (128 m.) wide.

Shi·ra·ka·mi \ˌshē-rä-ˈkä-mē, shē-ˈrä-kä-mē\ *or* **Shi·ra·ga·mi** \ˌshē-rä-ˈgä-mē, shē-ˈrä-gä-mē\. Cape at S extremity of Hokkaidō, Japan.

Shirakawa. See SHIRA.

Shi·rak, Steppe \ˈshir-ək\. Semidesert plain in E Republic of Georgia, bet. two N tributaries of the Kura SE of Tbilisi; oil fields.

Shi·ra·ku·mo–no–ta·ki \shē-ˈrä-ku̇-ˌmō-nō-ˈtä-kē\. Waterfall, cen. Honshū, Japan, W of Nikkō, E of Lake Chuzenji, and near the waterfall Kegon-no-taki; ab. 300 ft. (90 m.) high.

Shi·ra·ne \shē-ˈrä-nä\. Name of three mountains in Japan: (1) mountain, S cen. Honshū, W of Kōfu; several summits, highest 10,470 ft. (3191 m.); (2) mountain, Nagano prefecture, on border E of Nagano; 6908 ft. (2106 m.); and (3) mountain, Gumma prefecture, with two summits, in Nikkō Range W of Nikkō; 8456 ft. (2577 m.).

Shī·rāz \shē-ˈräz, -ˈraz\. Industrial and commercial city, ✻ of Fārs prov., SW cen. Iran, on highway from Tehran to Büshehr; pop. (1986c) 848,289; textiles, cement, sugar, fertilizers; university (1962); numerous notable mosques; birthplace of poets Saʻdī (13th cent.) and Ḥāfez (14th cent.), whose tombs are in city. Important in Middle Ages; reached peak 10th–11th cents.; often damaged by earthquakes. Ruins of ancient Persepolis (*q.v.*) lie ab. 35 mi. (55 km.) NE.

Shi·re *or* **Shi·ré** \ˈshir-ā, ˈshir-ē\ *or Port.* **Chi·re** \ˈshir-ə\. River, SE Africa, in S Malawi and cen. Mozambique; flows from Lake Malawi S into Zambezi River; ab. 250 mi. (400 km.) long; in Malawi has several cataracts, esp. Murchison Falls.

Shire Highlands *or* **Shiré Highlands.** Hill country, E bank of Shire River, S Malawi; alt. ab. 3000 ft. (915 m.).

Shi·re·to·ko–Mi·sa·ki \ˌshē-re-ˈtō-kō-mē-ˈsä-kē\ *or* **Cape Shiretoko.** Cape, NE extremity of Hokkaidō, Japan, in **Shiretoko National Park** (ab. 160 sq. mi. or 415 sq. km.; volcanic mountain ranges; estab. 1964).

Shi·ri·ya \shē-ˈrē-yä\. Cape, NE extremity of Honshū, Japan.

Shir·ley \ˈshər-lē\. Town, Middlesex co., NE Massachusetts, 7 mi. (11 km.) SE of Fitchburg; pop. (1990c) 6118.

Shirpurla. See LAGASH.

Shir·van \shir-ˈvän\. Medieval khanate, W shore of Caspian Sea S of the E end of the Caucasus Mts.; ✻ Shemakha. Subject to Persia 16th–19th cents.; conquered by Russian Czar Peter the Great 1722 but returned to Persia 1732; won again by Russia in Russo-Persian War (1804–13) and annexed 1813; now forms a part of NE Azerbaijan.

Shirwa, Lake. See CHILWA, LAKE.

Shi·san·ling *or W.-G.* **Shih–san–ling** \ˈshi-ˈsän-ˈliŋ\. Locality, Beijing municipality, NE China, NNW of the city of Beijing; site of Ming Tombs (or Thirteen Tombs), a semicircle of tombs of 13 of the 16 rulers of the Ming dynasty reached by an avenue (Sacred Way) under a great arch and bordered by large stone animals.

Shi·shal·din \shi-ˈshal-dən\. Volcano, S Unimak I., SW Alaska; 9372 ft. (2856 m.); has had several eruptions; locally known as "Smoking Moses."

Shish·ma·ref \ˈshish-mə-ˌref\. City on an island at entrance to **Shishmaref Inlet,** off NW coast of Seward Penin., W Alaska; pop. (1990c) 456.

Shit·tim \ˈshi-təm\. Valley in the West Bank, on W side of lower Jordan River N of Dead Sea; usually dry.

Shi·ve·luch, Sop·ka \ˈsȯp-kə-ˌshi-və-ˈlüch\. Volcano (*sopka*), Kamchatka Penin., Kamchatka Oblast, NE Russia in Asia; N end of Eastern Range; 15,580 ft. (4749 m.).

Shive·ly \ˈshīv-lē\. City, Jefferson co., N cen. Kentucky, S suburb of Louisville; pop. (1990c) 15,535.

Shi·yan \ˈshi-ˈyen\ *or W.-G.* **Shih–yen** \ˈshi-ˈyen\. City, NW Hubei prov., China; pop. (1990c) 273,786.

Shi·zu·o·ka \ˌshē-zu̇-ˈwō-kə, ˈshwō-ˌkä\. **1.** Prefecture, Honshū, Japan; ✻ Shizuoka. See table at JAPAN.
2. City, its ✻, 55 mi. (89 km.) SW of Tokyo, near W shore of Suruga Bay; pop. (1990p) 472,199; tea processing; center of higher education; its port is Shimizu. A residence of Ieyasu (d. 1616), founder of the Tokugawa shogunate.

Shkha·ra, Mount \sh̲kä-ˈrä\ *or Russ.* **Go·ra Shkha·ra** \gə-ˈrä-shk̲ə-ˈrä\. Mountain, N spur of Caucasus Mts. SE of Mt. Elbrus, in S Kabardino-Balkaria, S Russia in Europe, on Georgian border; 17,063 ft. (5201 m.).

Shko·dër \ˈshkō-dər\ *or* **Shko·dra** \-drə\ *or Ital.* **Scu·ta·ri** \ˈskü-tä-rē\. **1.** District of NW Albania. See table at ALBANIA.
2. *anc.* **Sco·dra** \ˈskō-drə\. Town, its ✻, bet. Drin River and Lake Scutari; pop. (1990e) 81,800; market town; produces textiles; 15th cent. citadel; cathedral. Ancient ✻ of Illyria; became Roman colony c. 168 B.C.; held by Venetians 1396–1479; stronghold of Albanian national hero George Kastrioti (Scanderbeg) in 15th cent.; under Turkish rule 1479–1913; in WWI occupied 1916 by Austria; became part of independent Albania 1921.

Shkodrës, Liqen i. See SCUTARI, LAKE.

Shkum·bin \ˈshküm-bēn\ *or* **Shkum·bi** \ˈshküm-bē\. River, cen. Albania, flowing into Adriatic Sea; ab. 50 mi. (81 km.) long; approx. the linguistic division line bet. the Ghegs of the N and the Tosks of the S.

Shlissel'burg. See PETROKREPOST'.

Shoa. See SHEWA.

Shoal·ha·ven \ˈshōl-ˌhā-vən\. City, SE New South Wales, Australia; pop. (1991c) 68,287.

Shoals \ˈshōlz\. Town, ⊗ of Martin co., SW Indiana, 40 mi. (64 km.) E of Vincennes; pop. (1990c) 853.

Shoal·wa·ter, Cape \ˈshōl-ˌwȯ-tər, -ˌwä-\. Cape, NW coast of Pacific co., SW Washington, at N entrance to Willapa Bay.

Shō·do \ˈshō-dō\ *or Jp.* **Shō·do·shi·ma** \ˌshō-dō-ˈshē-mä, shō-ˈdō-shē-mä\. Island on W side of Harima Sea, Japan, bet. the S coast of Honshū and the NE coast of Shikoku, W of Awaji I.

Shoe·bury Ness \ˈshü-bə-rē-ˈnes\. Cape on coast of Essex, SE England.

Shoe·bury·ness \ˈshü-bə-rē-ˌnes\. Village, a part of Southend-on-Sea, Essex, SE England, at mouth of Thames Estuary.

Sho·la·pur \ˈshō-lə-ˌpu̇r\ *or* **So·la·pur** \ˈsō-\. City, SE Maharashtra, W India, 170 mi. (274 km.) W of Hyderabad; pop. (1991c) 620,846; trade center; textiles; has old fort prominent in Deccan Wars (17th cent.); annexed by British 1818.

Shom·du \ˈshȯm-ˌdü\. Town, Lagos State, SW Nigeria.

Sho·mo·lu \shō-ˈmō-lü\. Town, SW Nigeria, a N suburb of Lagos; pop. (1993e) 137,100.

Shoot·ers Island \ˈshü-tərz\. Island, Newark Bay, close to N coast of Staten I., New York; part of Staten Island borough.

Shore·ham–by–Sea \ˈshōr-əm-bī-ˈsē\. Port, West Sussex, S England; pop. (1981c) 20,966.

Shore·view \ˈshōr-ˌvyü\. City, Ramsey co., E Minnesota, N suburb of St. Paul; pop. (1990c) 24,587.

Shore·wood \ˈshōr-ˌwu̇d\. **1.** Village, Will co., NE Illinois; pop. (1990c) 6264.
2. City, Hennepin co., SE cen. Minnesota; pop. (1990c) 5917.
3. Village, Milwaukee co., SE Wisconsin, 4 mi. (6 km.) N of the city of Milwaukee; pop. (1990c) 14,116.

Short·land Islands \ˈshȯrt-lənd\. Group of islands in NW Solomon Is., Papua New Guinea, W Pacific Ocean, in Bougainville Strait off S end of Bougainville; comprises **Shortland Island,** Fauro I., and other small islands. Japanese base in WWII.

Sho·sho·ne \shə-ˈshō-nē, -ˈshōn\. **1.** River, NW Wyoming; rises in Park co., flows NE into Bighorn River in N Big Horn co.; length with longest headstream ab. 120 mi. (195 km.); formed by uniting of two headstreams in Buffalo Bill Reservoir near Cody.
2. County in NE Idaho. See table at IDAHO.
3. City, ⊗ of Lincoln co., S Idaho; pop. (1990c) 1249.

Shoshone Dam. See BUFFALO BILL DAM.

Shoshone Falls. Waterfall in the Snake River, near Twin Falls, S Idaho; 210 ft. (64 m.) high.

Shoshone Lake. Lake, Yellowstone National Park, NW Wyoming, W of Yellowstone Lake; ab. 12 mi. (19 km.) long and 8 mi. (13 km.) wide; alt. 7800 ft. (2377 m.); a source of Snake River.

Shost·ka \shəst-ˈkä\. Town, Sumy subdivision, Ukraine, ab. 85 mi. (135 km.) NW of town of Sumy; pop. (1991e) 95,000.

Shott el Djerid. See DJERID, CHOTT.

Shot·tery \ˈshä-tə-rē\. Village, Warwickshire, cen. England, 1 mi. (1.6 km.) W of Stratford-upon-Avon; birthplace c. 1556 of Anne Hathaway, wife of William Shakespeare.

Shott Melghir. See MELRHIR, CHOTT.

Show Low \ˈshō-ˈlō\. City, Navajo co., E Arizona, 139 mi. (224 km.) SE of Flagstaff; pop. (1990c) 5019.

Shqipni *or* **Shqipri** *or* **Shqipëri.** See ALBANIA.

Shreve·port \ˈshrēv-ˌpōrt\. City, ⊗ of Caddo parish, NW Louisiana, on Red River 18 mi. (29 km.) E of Texas border; pop. (1990c) 198,525; commercial and industrial center; Centenary Coll. of Louisiana (1825), Louisiana State Univ. in Shreveport (1965); Barksdale Air Force Base; R.W. Norton

Art Gallery. Site acquired by white settlers from Caddo Indians 1835; Confederate state ⁕ at end of Civil War; developed notably after discovery of oil in region 1906.

Shrews·bury \ˈshrüz-ˌber-ē, -bə-rē\. **1.** Town, Worcester co., cen. Massachusetts, 5 mi. (8 km.) ENE of the city of Worcester; pop. (1990c) 24,146.

2. City, St. Louis co., E Missouri, W suburb of the city of St. Louis; pop. (1990c) 6416.

3. Borough, Monmouth co., E cen. New Jersey, 8 mi. (11 km.) NW of Asbury Park; pop. (1990c) 3096.

4. Borough, York co., SE Pennsylvania, 14 mi. (23 km.) SSE of the city of York; pop. (1990c) 2672.

5. *or* ˈshrōz-\. Town, ⊗ of Shropshire, W England, on the Severn (which surrounds it on three sides) 40 mi. (64 km.) NNW of Birmingham; pop. (1981c) 59,169; agricultural market; engineering.

History: Founded 5th cent. A.D.; as part of Welsh kingdom of Powys, called **Peng·wern** \ˈpeŋ-ˌwərn\; became part of Mercia at end of 8th cent. and named Scrobesbyrig (*mod.* Shrewsbury); became seat of one of oldest English earldoms, first granted c. 1074 to Roger de Montgomery who established an abbey; scene of much fighting with the Welsh 13th cent.; plain N of town scene of battle 1403 in which the rebellious Sir Henry Percy (Hotspur) was defeated and killed by forces of English King Henry IV.

Shrewsbury River. See NAVESINK RIVER.

Shrīrāmpur. See SERAMPORE.

Shrivijaya. See SRIVIJAYA.

Shrop·shire \ˈshräp-shər, -ˌshir\. **1.** *or* **Sal·op** \ˈsa-ləp, -ˌläp\. Former county, W England, on border of Wales.

2. *officially 1974–80* **Sal·op** \ˈsa-ləp, -ˌläp\. Administrative county, W England, comprising the former county; chief river Severn. See table at ENGLAND.

Shu \ˈshü\. Ancient kingdom, China; one of the Three Kingdoms (with Wu and Wei) formed at the breakup of the Chinese empire on the fall of the Eastern Han dynasty 220 A.D.; comprised Sichuan and most of Guizhou and Yunnan and lasted until 264 A.D.

Shuang·liao \ˈshwäŋ-ˈlyau̇\ *or* **Zheng·jia·tun** \ˈjəŋ-ˈjyä-ˈtün\ *or W.-G.* **Shuang–liao** \ˈshwäŋ-ˈlyau̇\ *or* **Cheng–chia–t'un** \ˈjəŋ-ˈjyä-ˈtün\; *formerly* **Liao·yuan** \ˈlyau̇-yue̅-ˈen\. Town, Jilin prov., NE China, on right bank of the Liao ab. 115 mi. (185 km.) N of Shenyang; formerly an important market city for E Mongolia; rapid growth in modern times began ab. 1876.

Shuang·ya·shan *or W.-G.* **Shuang–ya–shan** \ˈshwäŋ-ˈyä-ˈshän\. Town, Heilongjiang prov., NE China, ab. 240 mi. (385 km.) ENE of Harbin; pop. (1990c) 386,081.

Shu·brā al–Khay·mah \shu̇-ˈbrä-el-ˈkā-mə\. City, Egypt, N suburb of Cairo; pop. (1991e) 812,000.

Shuk·san, Mount \ˈshək-ˌsän\. Peak, cen. Whatcom co., NW Washington, in North Cascades National Park; ab. 9130 ft. (2783 m.).

Shu·ma·gin \ˈshü-mə-ˌgēn\. Island group off SE coast of Alaska Penin., SW Alaska, in Pacific Ocean; chief island is Unga.

Shu·men \ˈshü-ˌmen\. City, NE Bulgaria, ab. 50 mi. (80 km.) W of Varna; pop. (1991e) 110,754; important fort during Turkish rule (15th–19th cents.); played key role in Russo-Turkish Wars of 18th and 19th cents.; surrendered to Russians 1878.

Shum·shu \ˈshu̇m-ˌshü\; *formerly* **Shu·mu·shu** \ˈshü-mə-ˌshü\. Small island, one of the Kuril Is. (*q.v.*), off N point of Paramushir.

Shung·nak \ˈshəŋ-ˌnak\. City, NW Alaska, on N bank of upper Kobuk River; pop. (1990c) 223.

Shur, Wilderness of \ˈshər\. Desert region, N Sinai Penin., NE Egypt, near the Mediterranean Sea; traversed for three days by the Israelites (*Exod.* xv. 22).

Shu·ru·gwi \shü-ˈrü-gwē\; *formerly* **Se·lu·kwe** \se-ˈlü-kwā\. Town, cen. Zimbabwe; munic. pop. (1982c) 13,255; center of mining area; agricultural market.

Shu·rup·pak \shə-ˈrü-ˌpak\. Ancient city of Sumer, now the village of **Fa·ra** \ˈfär-ə\, SE Iraq, ab. 55 mi. (89 km.) NW of An Nāsirīyah; excavations have revealed dwellings dating back to late prehistoric period and cuneiform tablets from 4th millennium B.C.; most recent artifacts are from c. 2000 B.C.

Shūsh *or* **Shushan.** See SUSA 1.

Shūsh·tar \shüsh-ˈtär\. Town, Khūzestān prov., SW Iran, 50 mi. (81 km.) N of Ahvāz, on the Kārūn River at head of navigation; pop. (1986c) 65,840; has remains of an elaborate canal system dating from 5th cent. B.C. and of huge dams begun 3d cent. A.D.

Shu·swap Lake \ˈshü-swäp\. Lake, SE British Columbia, Canada, ab. 35 mi. (55 km.) W of Revelstoke; 120 sq. mi. (311 sq. km.), 42 mi. (68 km.) long; outlet is the Thompson River.

Shu·tar·gar·dan \ˈshü-ˌtär-gər-ˈdän\. Mountain pass at W end of Safed Koh, E Afghanistan; alt. 10,800 ft. (3292 m.); important in SE approach to Kabul.

Shu·ya \ˈshü-yə\. Town, cen. Ivanovo Oblast, cen. Russia in Europe, ab. 20 mi. (32 km.) SE of city of Ivanovo; pop. (1991e) 69,000.

Shwe·bo \ˈshwā-bō\. Town, Myanmar, 50 mi. (81 km.) NNW of Mandalay; pop. (1983c) 52,185. Birthplace 1714 of Alaungpaya, founder of last Burmese dynasty; later his ⁕.

Shwe·daung \ˈshwā-ˌdau̇ŋ\. Town, Myanmar, on Irrawaddy River just S of Prome.

Shwe·li \ˈshwā-lē\. River, SE Asia; flows SW out of Yunnan prov. in SW China where it is called the **Long·chuan** (*or W.-G.* **Lung–ch'uan** \ˈlu̇ŋ-ˈchwän\), crosses Myanmar-China boundary at Namhkam, continues SW, turns N and empties into Irrawaddy River below Katha, Myanmar; ab. 400 mi. (645 km.) long.

Shym·kent \shim-ˈkent\ *or* **Chim·kent** \chim-\. Town, ⁕ of South Kazakhstan subdivision, Kazakhstan, on Turkistan-Siberian R.R. 75 mi. (121 km.) N of Tashkent; pop. (1991e) 438,800; chemicals, food products; leadworks.

Si. 1. River, China. See XI.

2. River, Thailand. See CHI.

Sia·chen Glacier \ˈsyä-chən\. Glacier in Karakoram Range, in area controlled by Pakistan; 46 mi. (74 km.) long, ab. 2 mi. (3 km.) wide near its terminus.

Sia·han Range \ˈsyä-ˌhän\. Mountain range, W cen. Baluchistan, Pakistan; highest point 6775 ft. (2065 m.).

Si·al·kot \ˈsyäl-ˌkōt\. City, Punjab, Pakistan, near left bank of Chenab River 70 mi. (113 km.) N of Lahore; pop. (1981c) 302,009; fort and mausoleum of Nānak, founder of the Sikh religion (died c. 1539).

Siam. See THAILAND.

Siam, Gulf of. See THAILAND, GULF OF.

Sian *or* **Sianfu.** See XI'AN.

Siang. See XIANG.

Siangshan. See XIANGSHAN.

Siangtan. See XIANGTAN.

Siangyun. See XIANGYUN.

Sia·pa \ˈsyä-pä\. River, S Venezuela; flows W into Casiquiare River; ab. 200 mi. (320 km.) long.

Siar·gao \syär-ˈgau̇\. Island, part of Surigao del Norte prov., off NE coast of Mindanao, Philippines; 169 sq. mi. (438 sq. km.). Separated from Dinagat I. on the W by Dinagat Sound.

Si·a·scon·set \ˈskȯn-sət, -zət; ˌsī-əs-ˈkȯn-set\ *or locally* **Scon·set** \ˈskȯn-set, -zət\. Summer resort, Nantucket I., Massachusetts; orig. a fishing hamlet.

Sia·si \sē-ˈä-sē\. Chief island of Tapul group, cen. Sulu Archipelago, Sulu prov., Philippines; 30 sq. mi. (78 sq. km.).

Şiau \ˈshau̇\. See SANGIHE ISLANDS.

Šiau·liai \ˈshau̇-ˈlā\ *or Russ.* **Shau·lyay** \ˈshau̇-ˈlyī\ *or Ger.* **Schau·len** \ˈshau̇-lən\. City, N Lithuania, 75 mi. (121 km.) NNW of Kaunas; pop. (1992e) 149,000; leather and footwear industries; acquired by Russia in Third Partition of Poland 1795; suffered extensive damage in both World Wars.

Si·ba·lom \ˌsē-bä-ˈlȯm\. Municipality, Antique prov., Panay, Philippines, interior town 10 mi. (16 km.) NE of San Jose de Buenavista; pop. (1980c) 35,515.

Ši·be·nik \shē-ˈbe-nik\ *also* **Shi·be·nik** \shi-\ *or Ital.* **Se·be·ni·co** \ˌsā-bā-ˈnē-kō\. Seaport city, Croatia, 30 mi. (48 km.) NW of Split; pop. (1991c) 55,842; ships bauxite and wine; 15th–16th cent. cathedral; 16th cent. town hall.

Si·be·ria \sī-ˈbir-ē-ə\ *or Russ.* **Si·bir'** \si-ˈbirʸ\. Region, N cen. Asia, largely in Russia; extends from the Ural Mts. on the W to the Pacific Ocean on the E and from the Arctic Ocean on the N to cen. Kazakhstan and the boundaries of China and Mongolia on the S; ab. 5,000,000 sq. mi. (12,950,000 sq. km.); in an administrative sense, political subdivisions bordering on the Ural Mts. and the Pacific Ocean are not considered part of Siberia; constituent administrative units are: Altay Kray, Krasnoyarsk Kray, Chita, Irkutsk, Kemerovo, Novosibirsk, Omsk, and Tomsk oblasts, and Buryatia, Tuva, and Sakha republics.

Physical features: Bordered by Kara, Laptev, and East Siberian seas on N (parts of the Arctic Ocean) and by Bering Sea, Sea of Okhotsk, and Sea of Japan on E (parts of the Pacific). Has three large peninsulas, Taymyr, Chukchi, and Kamchatka; principal islands off its coasts are Severnaya Zemlya group, New Siberian Is., Wrangel, Komandorskiye Ostrova, and Sakhalin. The N belt along the Arctic Ocean consists of open, frozen tundra, rich in fur-bearing animals; in the W are low plains, some with extensive marshland; in the S and cen. parts are several plateaus; in the E and SE numerous mountain ranges: Eastern Range on Kamchatka, containing highest peak in Siberia (Klyuchevskaya Sopka 15,580 ft. or 4749 m.); Cherskiy Range, Chukotskoye Nagor'ye, Verkhoyansk Kolyma, Stanovoi, and Yablonovyy mountains, and the Sikhote-Alin' along the coast of the Sea of Japan; Sayan Mts. on the S border and Ural Mts. on the W. Its great rivers, the Ob', Yenisey, and Lena, flow N to the Arctic Ocean, and the Amur on its SE border flows E to Tatar Strait; other rivers are the Khatanga, Yana, Indigirka, Kolyma, and Anadyr. In the S is the large Lake Baikal.

Chief products: Coal, iron ore, gold, copper, lead, zinc; large oil fields in W brought into production 1966; spring wheat grown in S parts; lumbering, fishing along the coast.

Chief cities: Novosibirsk, Omsk, Krasnoyarsk, Irkutsk, Barnaul, Novokuznetsk, Kemerovo, Tomsk, Chita, Ulan-Ude.

History: Tatar Khanate of Sibir' conquered for Russia by Cossacks under Yermak Timofeyevich 1582; entire region gradually penetrated by Cossack explorers and fur traders in late 16th and 17th cents.; Sea of Okhotsk first reached c. 1640; Amur River basin in S abandoned to China by Treaty of Nerchinsk 1689; Siberia used as a place of exile and penal colony by Russian czars from 17th cent.; Chinese possessions N of Amur River and W of Ussuri River ceded to Russia 1858–60; connected with Russia in Europe by Trans-Siberian R.R., built 1891–1917. E Siberia the scene of anti-Bolshevik government of Adm. Aleksandr Kolchak 1918–1920; independent Far Eastern Republic formed under Bolsheviks 1920 but area made part of Russian S.F.S.R. 1922; during the 1930s extensive concentration and forced-labor camp network estab. by dictator Joseph Stalin. In WWII played an important role in the Soviet war effort due to relocation of many W Russian factories to the E; has undergone large-scale colonization and exploitation of its natural resources since WWII.

Si·be·rut *or Du.* **Si·be·roet** \ˌsē-bə-ˈrüt\. Island, Mentawai Is., off W coast of Sumatra opp. Padang, Indonesia.

Siberut Strait. Channel bet. Siberut I. on S and Buta Is. on N, Indonesia, off W coast of Sumatra; ab. 27 mi. (43 km.) wide.

Si·bi \ˈsē-bē\. Town, NE Baluchistan, Pakistan, on railroad line at S end of Bolan Pass, 73 mi. (118 km.) SE of Quetta; pop. (1981c) 23,043.

Si·bil·li·ni Mountains \ˌsē-bē-ˈlē-nē\. Range of the Roman Apennines, SW Marche, cen. Italy; includes Monte Vettare 8130 ft. (2478 m.), highest point in the Roman Apennines.

Si·bir' \si-ˈbirʸ\. **1.** Region, Asia. See SIBERIA.

2. *or* **Is·ker** \ˈis-kər\. Ancient town, ✻ of a Tatar khanate in W Siberia in 16th cent., near site of city of Tobol'sk, W Russia in Asia; captured 1581 by Yermak Timofeyevich, a hetman of the Don Cossacks, an event which marked beginning of Russian conquest of N Asia; town gave its name to the region, Siberia.

Si·biu \sē-ˈbē-ü\. **1.** County of cen. Romania. See table at ROMANIA.

2. City, its ⊗, N of the Transylvanian Alps; pop. (1989c) 184,036; commercial and industrial center producing machinery, textiles, footwear, trucks, clothing, food products, precision instruments, and leather goods; 15th cent. walls; Gothic Evangelical church; Brukenthal museum; present town founded by German settlers from Saxony 12th cent. on site of former Roman colony; destroyed by Tatars 1241; came under Austria 1699 and was for a time ✻ of Transylvania.

Sib·ley \ˈsi-blē\. **1.** County in S cen. Minnesota. See table at MINNESOTA.

2. City, ⊗ of Osceola co., NW Iowa, 46 mi. (74 km.) NNW of Cherokee; pop. (1990c) 2815.

Si·bol·ga \si-ˈbȯl-gə\. Coastal town, NW Sumatra, Indonesia, on Sibolga Bay; pop. (1990c) 71,895.

Sibolga Bay; *formerly* **Ta·pa·noe·li Bay** \ˌtä-pə-ˈnü-lē\. Inlet of the Indian Ocean, NW coast of Sumatra, Indonesia, opp. Nias I.; the town of Sibolga is on its NE shore.

Si·bo·ney \ˌsē-bō-ˈnā\. Town, S coast of Cuba, just E of Santiago de Cuba; with Daiquirí to the E was landing place of U.S. forces 1898 during Spanish-American War.

Si·bon·ga \sē-ˈbȯŋ-gä\. Municipality, Cebu prov., on E coast of Cebu I., Philippines, 28 mi. (45 km.) SW of City of Cebu; pop. (1980c) 27,513; has anchorage on Bohol Strait.

Sib·sa·gar \sib-ˈsä-gər\. Town, NE Assam, NE India, near left bank of the Brahmaputra River 85 mi. (137 km.) SW of Sadiya; pop. (1991p) 36,651; center of tea cultivation, oil production.

Si·bu \ˈsē-ˌbü\. Commercial town, W Sarawak, Malaysia, on island of Borneo, at head of delta of Rajang River 60 mi. (97 km.) upstream, and 115 mi. (185 km.) NE of Kuching; pop. (1980c) 85,231.

Si·bu·guey Bay \ˌsē-bü-ˈgā\. Large inlet of Moro Gulf, SE coast of Zamboanga prov., Mindanao, Philippines; its mouth is ab. 35 mi. (56 km.) wide from Olutanga I. on the E to SW peninsula on the W.

Si·bu·tu \ˌsē-bü-ˈtü\. Low, wooded island, westernmost of the Sulu Archipelago, Philippines; SW of Tawi-tawi and separated from it by Sibutu Passage; ab. 25 mi. (40 km.) SE of the NE point of Sabah, Malaysia; 39 sq. mi. (101 sq. km.). After conclusion of treaty with Spain 1898, by which Philippine possessions were ceded to U.S., it was discovered that this island was omitted; by a supplementary convention ceded to U.S. 1900.

Sibutu Passage. Channel, SW Sulu Archipelago, Philippines, separating Sibutu I. on the SW from Tawi-tawi I.; ab. 12 mi. (19 km.) wide; one of the main channels of navigation connecting Sulu Sea and Celebes Sea.

Si·bu·yan \ˌsē-bü-ˈyän\. Island, E part of Romblon prov., cen. Philippines, in Sibuyan Sea; 173 sq. mi. (448 sq. km.). Mountainous with **Mount Sibuyan** in center 6745 ft. (2056 m.), highest point in province.

Sibuyan Sea. Body of interisland water, cen. Philippines, NW of Visayan Sea; bordering it are Marinduque I. and S coast of Luzon on the N and enclosing it on other sides are the Visayan islands of Burias, Masbate, Panay, and Tablas. Sibuyan I. and Romblon I. are within it.

Si·ca·poo \ˌsē-kä-ˈpō\ *or* **Mount Pac·san** \päk-ˈsän\. Mountain in Cordillera Central, NW Luzon, Philippines; highest point 7715 ft. (2352 m.).

Sicca Veneria. See LE KEF.

Si·chuan \ˈsē-ˈchwän\ *or W.-G.* **Sze·chuan** *or* **Sze·chwan** \ˈse-ˈchwän, ˈsesh-ˈwän\. Province, S cen. China, bounded on N by Qinghai, Gansu, and Shaanxi provs., on E by Hubei and Hunan, on S by Guizhou and Yunnan, and on W by Tibet; ✻ Chengdu. Well-watered plateau province, heart of which is known as the Red Basin; crossed in S section by the Chang and in the cen. part by three of its tributaries, Min, Tuo, and Jialing, flowing N to S. On NE bordered by Daba Shan and on W by mountains rising steeply to border of Plateau of Tibet (edge of which is 10,000 to 20,000 ft. or 3048 to 6096 m.). In mountains in SE the Chang flows through the Chang Gorges (*q.v.*); rivers in the Red Basin are navigable and there is much river traffic. See table at CHINA.

Chief products: Rice, sweet potatoes, sugarcane, tobacco, cotton, wheat; coal, salt, gold, copper.

Chief cities: Chongqing and Chengdu.

History: Inhabited by Chinese first millennium B.C.; incorp. (c. 3d cent. B.C.) in empire under Chin dynasty; protected by its mountain barriers, not always in close association with ruling dynasties. After outbreak 1937 of war with Japan, government removed from coast to Chongqing establishing that city as ✻ of China; new status increased population and encouraged industrial and economic growth; headquarters of military forces during war with Japan and although area suffered from bombing, growth continued following end of war 1945.

Sic·i·lies, The Two \ˈsi-sə-lēz\. Former kingdom comprising the area of the island of Sicily and the S portion of mainland Italy (S of the former Papal States). Area of kingdom conquered by Normans in 11th cent. who then erected the Kingdom of Sicily; passed to Hohenstaufen control 12th cent. by marriage of its heiress to future Holy Roman Emperor Henry VI; under Emperor Frederick II (d. 1250), despite struggle with Papacy, the kingdom eclipsed other European states in cultural brilliance and administration; conquered by Charles of Anjou 1266–68; following revolt 1282, Sicily passed to house of Aragon, while Naples remained in Angevin hands; two kingdoms reunited under Alfonso of Aragon 1442, self-styled King of The Two Sicilies; crowns separated once again upon his death 1458 when his holdings were divided; following French intrigues in Naples (*q.v.*), the crowns were reunited by Spanish conquest 1503 and remained under Spanish control until the 18th cent.; kingdoms separated 1713 by Treaty of Utrecht with Naples passing to Austrian Hapsburgs and Sicily passing first to duke of Savoy and later to Austrians; Sicily and Naples conquered 1734 by Spanish Bourbons who reestablished the Kingdom of The Two Sicilies; Naples held by Napoleonic forces 1799 and 1806–15, Bourbon dynasty restored 1815; two crowns officially merged by Ferdinand 1816; Constitutionalists' revolt 1820–21 suppressed with assistance of Austrian forces; as result of Italian patriot Giuseppe Garibaldi's expedition 1860, joined Italian kingdom.

Sic·i·ly \ˈsi-sə-lē\; *Ital. and anc.* **Si·ci·lia** \si-ˈsil-yə, *Ital.* sē-ˈchēl-yä\; *anc. also* **Tri·nac·ria** \trə-ˈna-krē-ə, trī-\. Largest island in the Mediterranean Sea, W of extreme S point of the Italian Penin.; ✻ Palermo; politically, an autonomous region of Italy (see table at ITALY); separated from Italian mainland by narrow Strait of Messina and from Africa (NE Tunisia) by a narrow part of the Mediterranean (ab. 90 mi. or 145 km.). Volcano of Etna 10,902 ft. (3323 m.) dominates its E end; entire island is mountainous with most of it a plateau having highest range along N coast (highest point 6467 ft. or 1971 m.); rivers numerous but small, largest the Simeto. Coastline regular with several wide inlets, esp. Gulf of Castellammare on NW and Gulf of Catania on E; Cape Passero is SE point and chief islands are Lipari Is. off NE coast, Egadi Is. at W end, and Ustica I. farther out to NW in Tyrrhenian Sea.

Chief products: Wheat, citrus fruit, olives; sulfur; oil refining.

Chief cities: Palermo, Catania, Messina, Siracusa.

History: Colonized by Greeks 8th–6th cents. B.C.; Siracusa, island's leading city, successfully resisted Carthaginian invasion at Himera 480 B.C.; by 4th cent. B.C. W part of island under Carthaginian control; Carthaginian territory, conquered by Rome in 3d cent. B.C., became first Roman province; remainder of island fell to Rome in Second Punic War (218–201 B.C.); part of Vandal and Ostrogothic kingdoms and of Byzantine Empire 5th–6th cents. A.D.; overrun by Arabs 9th–10th cents.; Sicily and Naples conquered 11th cent. by Normans who founded a Kingdom of Sicily comprising these lands (see SICILIES, THE TWO); passed to Hohenstaufens 12th cent.; conquered 1266–68 by Charles of Anjou whose harsh rule caused uprising and massacre (Sicilian Vespers) 1282, his expulsion from Sicily, and the introduction of the rule of the house of Aragon (Naples remained in Angevin hands); Sicily remained under Spanish control until ceded to the duke of Savoy 1713 by the Treaty of Utrecht; passed to Austria 1720; conquered by Spanish Bourbons 1734 who also conquered Naples and reestablished the Kingdom of The Two Sicilies; see SICILIES, THE TWO for later history in connection with Italy. In WWII invaded by American and British troops 1943; received a degree of local autonomy 1947.

Si·cua·ni \sē-ˈkwä-nē\. Town, SE Peru; pop. (1981p) 41,602; alt. 11,650 ft. (3551 m.); highway and railroad junction point on the Urubama River 70 mi. (113 km.) SE of Cuzco.

Siculum Fretum. See MESSINA, STRAIT OF.

Si·cy·on \ˈsi-sē-ən\ *or Gk.* **Sik·y·on** \ˈsi-kē-ən\. Ancient city, NE Peloponnese, S Greece, ab. 10 mi. (16 km.) NW of Corinth and near the S shore of the Gulf of Corinth; chief town of the district of Sicyonia. Influential in Greek history, esp. under the tyrant Cleisthenes at beginning of 6th cent. B.C.; noted for its painting and pottery during this period. After 500 B.C. generally followed Sparta or Corinth; famous for school of art 4th cent. B.C. which produced the sculptor Lysippus; in 3d cent. B.C. was prominent under Aratus as a leader in the Achaean League; declined first cent. B.C.

Si·cy·o·nia \ˌsi-sē-ˈō-nē-ə\. Small district, NE Peloponnese, ancient Greece, comprising the territory immediately around the city of Sicyon; touched upon Corinth, Argolis, Arcadia, and Achaea.

Siddhpur. See SIDHPUR.

Si·de \ˈsē-də\. Ruins, S Turkey in Asia, on Gulf of Antalya; site of the chief port of ancient Pamphylia.

Side·ling Hill \ˈsīd-liŋ\. Ridge, extending SW in Huntingdon and Bedford cos. S Pennsylvania into Washington co., N Maryland; highest point 2195 ft. (669 m.).

Si·der·no \sē-ˈder-nō\. Commune, Reggio di Calabria prov., Calabria, S Italy, 33 mi. (53 km.) ENE of the commune of Reggio di Calabria; pop. (1981p) 15,642.

Si·de·ro, Cape \ˈsē-thē-ˌrō\ *or Gk.* **Sí·dhe·ros** \-ˌrōs\. Point, NE tip of Crete, Greece, projecting into Caso Strait.

Si·de·ro·kas·tron \ˌsē-thē-ˈrō-kä-ˌstrōn\ *or Gk.* **Ákra Si·dhi·ró·kas·tron** \ˈä-krä-ˌsē-thē-ˈrō-käs-ˌtrōn\; *Turk.* **De·mir His·sár** *or* **Demir Hi·sar** \ˈde-mir-hi-ˈsär\. Commune, Sérrai dept., cen. Macedonia, Greece, on Struma River near Bulgarian border NNW of city of Sérrai.

Sidh·pur *or* **Siddh·pur** \ˈsid-ˌpu̇r\. City, E Gujarat, W India, on Sarasvati River 63 mi. (101 km.) N of Ahmadabad; pop. (1991p) 50,858; very old town with ruins of ancient temple; a place of pilgrimage.

Si·di Abd·al·lah \ˈsē-dē-ab-ˈdu̇-lə\. See BIZERTE.

Sī·dī al–Ha·ni \ˈsē-dē-al-ˈhä-nē\. Salt depression, NE Tunisia, near coast.

Sī·dī Bar·rā·nī \ˈsē-dē-bə-ˈrä-nē\. Coastal village, NW Egypt, E of Buqbuq and W of Maṭrūḥ. In WWII scene of much fighting in North Africa campaign 1940–42.

Sidi Bel Ab·bès \ˈsē-dē-ˌbel-ə-ˈbes\. Commune, NW Algeria, 40 mi. (64 km.) S of Oran; pop. (1987p) 152,778; alt. 1552 ft. (473 m.); founded 1843; headquarters of the French Foreign Legion until Algerian independence (1962).

Si·di Ka·cem \ˈsē-dē-ˈkä-səm\; *formerly* **Pe·tit·jean** \pə-ˌtē-ˈzhä^{n}\. Town, N Morocco, W of Fès; pop. (1982c) 55,833.

Sid·law Hills \ˈsid-ˌlȯ\. Range of hills in Tayside region, cen. Scotland; highest point **Auch·ter·house Hill** \ˈȯk-tər-ˌhau̇s\ 1398 ft. (426 m.).

Sid·ley, Mount \ˈsid-lē\. Peak, Marie Byrd Land, Antarctica, 77°02′S, 126°05′W; 13,717 ft. (4181 m.); discovered 1934.

\ə\ **abut** \ə\ match**es** \$^{ə}$\ kitt**en**, Fr tab**le** \ər\ f**ur**th**er** \a\ **a**sh \ā\ **a**ce
\ä\ c**o**t, c**a**rt \ȧ\ Fr b**a**c \au̇\ **ou**t \b\ Span Avila \ch\ **ch**in \e\ b**e**t \ē\ **ea**sy
\g\ **g**o \i\ h**i**t \ī\ **i**ce \j\ **j**ob \k\ Ger i**ch**, Bu**ch** \$^{n}$\ Fr v**in**
\ŋ\ si**ng** \ō\ g**o** \ö\ **a**ll \ȯ\ l**aw** \œ\ Fr b**œu**f \œ̄\ Fr f**eu** \ȯi\ b**oy**
\th\ **th**in \th\ **th**is \ü\ l**oo**t \u̇\ f**oo**t \ue\ Ger f**ü**llen \ue̅\ Fr r**ue**
\y\ **y**et \$^{y}$\ Fr digne \ˈdēn^{y}\, nuit \ˈnw^{y}ē\ \yü\ **few** \yu̇\ **fu**ry \zh\ vi**si**on

Sid·mouth \ˈsid-məth\. Seaside resort, Devon, SW England, on English Channel at the mouth of the Sid 13 mi. (21 km.) ESE of Exeter; pop. (1981p) 12,446.

Sid·ney \ˈsid-nē\. **1.** City, ⊗ of Fremont co., SW corner of Iowa; pop. (1990c) 1253.

2. City, ⊗ of Richland co., E Montana, on Yellowstone River 50 mi. (80 km.) NE of Glendive; pop. (1990c) 5217.

3. City, ⊗ of Cheyenne co., W Nebraska, 61 mi. (98 km.) SE of Scottsbluff; pop. (1990c) 5959.

4. Village, Delaware co., S New York, on Susquehanna River 30 mi. (48 km.) ENE of Binghamton; pop. (1990c) 4720.

5. City, ⊗ of Shelby co., W Ohio, 30 mi. (48 km.) NW of Springfield; pop. (1990c) 18,710.

6. Village, British Columbia, Canada, on Vancouver I. 20 mi. (32 km.) N of Victoria; pop. (1991c) 10,082.

Si·do·ar·jo *or* **Si·do·ar·djo** \ˌsē-dō-ˈär-jō\. Town, East Java prov., Indonesia, near coast ab. 15 mi. (24 km.) S of Surabaya; pop. (1980c) 54,424.

Si·don \ˈsīd-ᵊn\ *or* **Sai·da** \sä-ē-ˈdä\ *or* **Say·dā** \ˈsī-də\ *also* **Zi·don** \ˈzīd-ᵊn\. Seaport, SW Lebanon, 22 mi. (35 km.) N of Tyre; pop. (1985e) 100,000; trade center in agricultural region; fishing port; Mediterranean terminus of oil pipeline from Saudi Arabian oil fields.

History: Ancient city founded 3d millennium B.C. and from 2d millennium a principal city of Phoenicia; parent-city to Tyre. Ruled successively by the major powers of ancient times, incl. Assyria (9th–7th cents. B.C.), Babylonia (6th cent. B.C.), and Persia (6th–4th cents. B.C.); conquered by Macedonian King Alexander the Great c. 330 B.C.; under Roman rule by first cent. B.C. but remained important; noted for its manufacture of glass and purple dyes; changed hands several times during the Crusades and finally fell to Muslims c. 1291; flourished under Turkish rule after 1517 but declined following expulsion of French traders 1791.

Sid·ra, Gulf of \ˈsi-drə\ *or* **Gulf of Sir·te** \ˈsir-ˌtā\ *or Arab.* **Kha·līj Surt** \kä-ˈlēj-ˈsu̇rt\; *anc.* **Syr·tis Ma·jor** \ˈsər-təs-ˈmā-jər\. Inlet of Mediterranean Sea, on N cen. coast of Libya.

Siebenbürgen. See TRANSYLVANIA 2.

Sie·ben·ge·bir·ge \ˈzē-bən-gə-ˌbir-gə\. Hills in the Westerwald, Germany, on right bank of the Rhine 6 mi. (10 km.) SSE of Bonn, incl. Drachenfels 1053 ft. (321 m.), Löwenburg 1506 ft. (459 m.), and Ölberg 1509 ft. (460 m.).

Siedl·ce \ˈshed-ᵊl-ˌtse\ *also* **Syed·lets** \ˈshed-ləts\. **1.** Province, NE cen. Poland. See table at POLAND.

2. Commune, its ✻, ab. 55 mi. (88 km.) ESE of Warsaw; pop. (1989e) 70,472; episcopal see; food processing; received town rights c. 1547; to Austria 1795 in Third Partition of Poland; part of Grand Duchy of Warsaw 1807–15 and then to Russia until 1918; site nearby of German concentration camps in WWII.

Sieg \ˈzēk\. River, Germany; flows W into the Rhine 2 mi. (3 km.) N of Bonn; ab. 80 mi. (130 km.) long.

Sieg·burg \ˈzēk-ˌbu̇rk, -ˌbərg\. City, North Rhine-Westphalia, Germany, on Sieg River 14 mi. (23 km.) SE of Cologne; pop. (1980c) 34,616; 12th cent. church.

Sie·gen \ˈzē-gən\. Industrial city, North Rhine-Westphalia, Germany, on Sieg River 49 mi. (79 km.) E of Cologne; pop. (1992e) 110,374; metal goods, machinery; iron mines nearby; 13th cent. church. Birthplace of Flemish painter Peter Paul Rubens 1577.

Sieg·fried Line \ˈsig-ˌfrēd, ˈzēk-ˌfrēt\ *or* **West·wall** \ˈwest-ˌwȯl\. In WWII the strong defense line in W Germany, extending from Swiss border, generally parallel with the Rhine and in the S opposite to the French Maginot Line. Penetrated by Allied forces 1944–45.

Sieg·lar \ˈzē-glər\. City, North Rhine-Westphalia, Germany, 6 mi. (10 km.) N of Bonn.

Sie·mia·no·wi·ce Śl¸a·skie \she-ˌmyä-nȯ-ˈvēt-se-ˈshlȯⁿ-skē-ə\; *formerly* **Siemianowice–Hu·ta Lau·ra** \-ˈhü-tə-ˈlau̇-rə\. Industrial city, Katowice prov., S Poland; pop. (1989e) 80,432; iron, hardware; coal mines nearby.

Si·em Re·ap \ˌsē-əm-ˈrē-əp\ *also* **Si·em·re·ab** \-əb\. Town, NW Cambodia, on highway just N of NW end of Tonle Sap; pop. (1987e) 13,000; official station for visitors to ruins of Angkor (*q.v.*).

Si·e·na \sē-ˈe-nä\. **1.** Province of Tuscany, W Italy. See table at ITALY.

2. *anc.* **Sae·na Ju·lia** \ˈsē-nə-ˈjül-yə\. Commune, its ✻, 33 mi. (53 km.) S of Florence; pop. (1989c) 58,278; produces Chianti wine; tourist center. Retains an essentially medieval appearance, with medieval walls and numerous notable churches and palaces, incl. the 12th–13th cent. Gothic-Romanesque cathedral with 14th cent. campanile, church of San Giovanni with 15th cent. baptismal font, Palazzo Pubblico (13th–14th cent.), Palazzo Piccolomini, Palazzo Buonsignori; Piazza del Campo, where horse races originating in medieval times are still run; university (1240).

History: Founded by Etruscans, passing later to Romans and Lombards; under Carolingian empire formed countship; became independent in 12th cent.; seat of pro-imperial Ghibellines and rival of Florence; conquered by Charles of Anjou, king of Naples and Sicily, 1270 and joined Guelph confederation; Sienese school of art reached peak early 14th cent., producing such painters as Duccio di Buoninsegna, Simone Martini, and Pietro and Ambrogio Lorenzetti; sculpture reached peak early 15th cent. under Jacopo della Quercia; came under the despot Pandolfo Petrucci 1487; conquered by Holy Roman Emperor Charles V 1555 and ceded to Florence 1557.

Sienyang. See XIANYANG.

Sie·radz \ˈsher-ˌäts\. **1.** Province, cen. Poland. See table at POLAND.

2. Commune, its ✻, on Warta River 35 mi. (56 km.) WSW of Łódź; pop. (1989e) 42,165; a very old city; fortified in Middle Ages.

Sie·ro \ˈsyā-rō\. Commune, Asturias prov., NW Spain, 9 mi. (14 km.) ENE of Oviedo; pop. (1991c) 44,033.

Si·er·ra \sē-ˈer-ə\. Name of counties in two states of the U.S. See tables at CALIFORNIA and NEW MEXICO.

Si·er·ra An·cha \sē-ˈer-ə-ˈan-chə\. Ridge, cen. Gila co., cen. Arizona, NE of Roosevelt Lake; highest point 7694 ft. (2345 m.).

Si·er·ra Blan·ca \sē-ˈer-ə-ˈblaŋ-kə\. **1.** Range, chiefly in N Otero and S Lincoln cos., S cen. New Mexico.

2. Village, ⊗ of Hudspeth co., W Texas.

Sierra Blanca Peak *or* **White Mountain.** Mountain, N Otero co., S New Mexico; 12,003 ft. (3659 m.).

Sier·ra de Al·ca·raz \ˈsyer-rä-ˌthā-ˌäl-kä-ˈräs\. Mountain range, mostly in Albacete prov., SW cen. Spain.

Sierra de Curupira. See SERRA CURUPIRA.

Sier·ra de Fa·ma·ti·na \ˈsyer-rä-ˌthā-ˌfä-mä-ˈtē-nä\. Mountain range in the Andes, in La Rioja prov., NW Argentina; highest peak **Ge·ne·ral Man·uel Bel·gra·no** \ˌhā-nā-ˈräl-män-ˈwel-bel-ˈgrä-nō\ 20,505 ft. (6250 m.).

Sier·ra de Ga·ta \ˈsyer-rä-thā-ˈgä-tä\. Mountain range, W Spain and E Portugal, separating the basins of the Tagus and Douro rivers; highest peak 5690 ft. (1734 m.).

Sier·ra de Gre·dos \ˈsyer-rä-thā-ˈgrä-thōs\. Mountain range, W cen. Spain, W of Madrid; highest peak Pico de Almanzor 8501 ft. (2591 m.).

Sierra de Guadalupe. See GUADALUPE MOUNTAINS 2.

Sier·ra de Gua·dar·ra·ma \ˈsyer-rä-thā-ˌgwä-thär-ˈrä-mä\. Mountain range, cen. Spain; highest peak Pico de Peñalara 7970 ft. (2429 m.).

Sier·ra de Juá·rez \ˈsyer-rä-thā-ˈhwä-räs\. Mountain range, N Baja California, Mexico; highest peak 6560 ft. (1999 m.).

Sier·ra de la Gi·gan·ta \ˈsyer-rä-ˌthā-lä-hē-ˈgän-tä\. Range, SE coast of Baja California, Mexico; highest peak 5760 ft. (1756 m.).

Sier·ra de la Ma·ca·re·na National Park \ˈsyer-rä-ˌthā-lä-ˌmä-kä-ˈrā-nä\. National park, Colombia; 4366 sq. mi. (11,308 sq. km.).

Sier·ra de la Ven·ta·na \ˈsyer-rä-ˌthā-lä-ben-ˈtä-nä\. Mountain range, S Buenos Aires prov., E cen. Argentina; highest peak 4077 ft. (1243 m.).

Sier·ra de los Ór·ga·nos \ˈsyer-rä-ˌthā-lōs-ˈōr-gä-ˌnōs\. Mountain range, W Pinar del Río prov., W Cuba; highest point 1938 ft. (591 m.).

Sier·ra del Ro·sa·rio \ˈsyer-rä-ˌthel-rō-ˈsär-yō\. Mountain range, N Pinar del Río prov., W Cuba.

Sierra de Luquillo. See LUQUILLO MOUNTAINS.

Sier·ra de Mi·sio·nes \ˈsyer-rä-ˌthā-mēs-ˈyō-nās\. Mountain range, NE Argentina, extending NE into S Brazil.

Si·er·ra Le·one \sē-ˌer-ə-lē-ˈōn, ˌsir-ə-\. **1.** Republic, W Africa, bounded on N and E by Guinea, on SE by Liberia, on S by Liberia and the Atlantic Ocean, and on W by the Atlantic Ocean; 27,699 sq. mi. (71,740 sq. km.); pop. (1993e) 4,491,000; ✱ Freetown, the country's only large city.

Physical features: Its coastal belt, ab. 350 mi. (565 km.) long and 30 to 50 mi. (48 to 80 km.) wide, characterized by mangrove swamps; N region consists of upland plateau, highest peak in Loma Mts. (Bintimane, 6390 ft. or 1948 m.).

Chief products: Palm kernels, coffee, cocoa, ginger, cassava, rice; bauxite, diamonds, iron ore, rutile; ab. 75 percent of labor force is engaged in agriculture.

History: Mende and Temne peoples settled in region beginning 15th cent.; Portuguese first visited coast c. 1460, soon followed by European slave traders; coastal settlement for freed slaves estab. under sponsorship of English philanthropists 1787 on land purchased from Temne chief, the future site of Freetown; settlement taken over by Sierra Leone Company 1792 and came under British crown 1808. Hinterland gradually penetrated and proclaimed a British protectorate 1896; achieved independence 1961; civilian government overthrown by armed forces 1967, restored 1968; became a republic 1971; new military government took over in 1992.

©1996, Encyclopædia Britannica, Inc.

2. River, Sierra Leone republic, the estuary of the Rokel River; flows into the Atlantic Ocean at Freetown.

Sierra Leone Peninsula. Peninsula extending into Atlantic Ocean on W coast of Sierra Leone; ab. 28 mi. (45 km.) long and 9 mi. (14 km.) wide.

Si·er·ra Mad·re \sē-ˈer-ə-ˈmä-drē\. **1.** Range, S Wyoming, extending S into N Colorado; part of the Continental Divide. **2.** City, Los Angeles co., SW California, just E of Pasadena; pop. (1990c) 10,762.

Sier·ra Ma·dre \ˈsyer-rä-ˈmä-thrā\. **1.** Range, chiefly in S Chiapas state, SE Mexico, extending SE into N Guatemala. **2.** Main mountain range of NE Luzon, Philippines, extending ab. 215 mi. (345 km.) along coast of Pacific Ocean, turning SW at its S end to join the Cordillera Central in N Nueva Vizcaya; averages 3500 to 5000 ft. (1070 to 1525 m.) with highest point 6068 ft. (1850 m.); name sometimes applied also to continuation of range S into Bicol Penin.

Sierra Madre del Sur \ˌthel-ˈsür\. Coastal range along SW and S coasts of Guerrero and Oaxaca states, S Mexico.

Sierra Madre Oc·ci·den·tal \ˌök-sē-ˌthen-ˈtäl\ *also* **Western Sierra Madre.** Range of mountains, Mexico, running parallel to Pacific Ocean coast and bordering cen. Mexican plateau on the W; ab. 700 mi. (1125 km.) long N to S; several peaks above 10,000 ft. (3048 m.).

Sierra Madre Orien·tal \ˌōr-ē-en-ˈtäl\ *also* **Eastern Sierra Madre.** Range of mountains, Mexico, running parallel to Gulf of Mexico coast and bordering Mexico's cen. plateau on the E; av. height ab. 7000 ft. (2135 m.), with some peaks above 10,000 ft. (3048 m.).

Sier·ra Ma·es·tra \ˈsyer-rä-mä-ˈes-trä\. Mountain range, E Cuba, extending W and E along the S coast; highest peak Pico Turquino 6540 ft. (1993 m.).

Sier·ra Mo·re·na \ˈsyer-rä-mō-ˈrā-nä\. Mountain range, SW Spain, bet. the Guadiana and Guadalquivir rivers; highest peak Estrella 4339 ft. (1323 m.).

Si·er·ra Ne·va·da \sē-ˈer-ə-nə-ˈva-də, -ˈvä-\. Mountain range, E California, extending into Nevada, parallel to the Coast Ranges; ab. 400 mi. (645 km.) long; highest peak Mt. Whitney 14,494 ft. (4418 m.). See CASCADE RANGE.

Sier·ra Ne·va·da \ˈsyer-rä-nā-ˈbä-thä\. Mountain range, mostly in Granada and Almería provs., S Spain; highest peak Mulhacén 11,408 ft. (3477 m.).

Sierra Nevada de Co·cuy \ˌthā-kō-ˈkwē\. Mountain ridge of the Cordillera Oriental, E Andes, in Colombia; highest point 18,021 ft. (5493 m.).

Sierra Nevada de Mérida. See CORDILLERA DE MÉRIDA.

Sierra Nevada de San·ta Mar·ta \thā-ˈsän-tä-ˈmär-tä\. Mountain range, N Colombia, on the Caribbean coast; highest peak 19,020 ft. (5797 m.).

Sier·ra Ne·va·da National Park \ˈsyer-rä-nā-ˈbä-thä\. National park, NW Venezuela; estab. 1952; contains snowcapped peaks of the Cordillera de Mérida incl. Pico Bolívar, Venezuela's highest mountain at 16,427 ft. (5007 m.).

Sierra Pacaraima. See PACARAIMA MOUNTAINS.

Sierra Parima. See PARIMA, SERRA.

Sierra San Pedro Mártir. See SAN PEDRO MÁRTIR, SIERRA.

Sier·ras de Cór·do·ba \ˈsyer-räs-thā-ˈkōr-thō-bä\. Mountain range, San Luis and W Córdoba provs., cen. Argentina; highest peak Champaquí 9459 ft. (2883 m.).

Si·er·ra Vis·ta \sē-ˈer-ə-ˈvis-tə\. City, Cochise co., SE Arizona, 50 mi. (80 km.) SE of Tucson; pop. (1990c) 32,983; Fort Huachuca army installation. The city's pop. more than tripled bet. 1970 and 1980.

Sierre \ˈsyār\. Commune, cen. Valais canton, Switzerland, on the Rhone; pop. (1980c) 13,050.

Sie·vers·hau·sen \ˈzē-vərs-ˌhau̇-zən\. Village, Lower Saxony, Germany, ab. 15 mi. (24 km.) E of Hannover; Duke Maurice of Saxony defeated Albert Alcibiades, margrave of Brandenburg, here 1553 but was mortally wounded.

Síf·nos *or* **Sif·nos** *or* **Siph·nos** \ˈsēf-ˌnōs\. **1.** Island, W Cyclades, Aegean Sea; part of Cyclades dept., Greece; 29 sq. mi. (75 sq. km.). **2.** Town on E coast of island.

Sig \ˈsēg\; *formerly* **Saint–De·nis–du–Sig** \ˌseⁿ-də-ˈnē-də-ˈsēg\. Commune, NW Algeria, just SE of Oran; pop. (1987p) 42,197.

Sigeum. See YENIŞEHIR.

Si·ghet Mar·ma·ţiei \ˈsē-get-ˌmär-mä-ˈtyā\ *or Hung.* **Má·ra·ma·ros·szi·get** \ˈmä-rö-ˌmö-rōsh-ˈsē-get\. City, Maramureş co., N Romania, 45 mi. (72 km.) E of Satu Mare near the Ukrainian border; pop. (1989c) 44,507; in Hungary 1940–47.

Si·ghi·şoa·ra \ˌsē-gē-ˈshwä-rä\ *or Hung.* **Se·ges·vár** \ˈshe-gesh-ˌvär\ *or Ger.* **Schäss·burg** \ˈshes-ˌbu̇rk\. City, Mureş

\ə\ abut \ə\ matches \ᵊ\ kitten, Fr table \ər\ further \a\ ash \ā\ ace \ä\ cot, cart \å\ Fr bac \au̇\ out \b\ Span Avila \ch\ chin \e\ bet \ē\ easy \g\ go \i\ hit \ī\ ice \j\ job \k\ Ger ich, Buch \ⁿ\ Fr vin \ŋ\ sing \ō\ go \ö\ all \ȯ\ law \œ\ Fr bœuf \œ̄\ Fr feu \ȯi\ boy \th\ thin \th\ this \ü\ loot \u̇\ foot \ue\ Ger füllen \ue̅\ Fr rue \y\ yet \ʸ\ Fr digne \ˈdēnʸ\, nuit \ˈnwʸē\ \yü\ few \yu̇\ fury \zh\ vision

co., cen. Romania, 45 mi. (72 km.) NE of Sibiu; pop. (1989c) 38,002; an old city built on a hill around a castle; founded c. 1200; battlefield 1849 where Russians defeated Hungarian revolutionaries.

Si·gir·i·ya \si-ˈgir-yə\ *or* **Si·giri** \si-ˈgir-ē\. Fortress rock, N cen. Sri Lanka, N of Kandy; ruined ancient ⁕ of Ceylon serving as refuge for King Kasyapa in 5th cent. A.D.

Sig·lu·fjör·dhur *or* **Sig·lu·fjör·dur** \ˈsig-lœ-ˌfyœr-thœr\. Town, N Iceland, in cen. part of N coast; pop. (1992e) 1744.

Sig·ma·ring·en \ˈzēk-mə-ˌriŋ-ən\. City, Baden-Württemberg, Germany, on Danube River 30 mi. (48 km.) S of Reutlingen; pop. (1980c) 15,079; site of a castle, the ancestral home of the Hohenzollerns; chartered in 13th cent.; became property of the Hohenzollerns 1535.

Sig·nal Hill \ˈsig-nᵊl\. **1.** Peak, Custer co., SW South Dakota; 6500 ft. (1981 m.).
2. City, Los Angeles co., SW California, surrounded by Long Beach; pop. (1990c) 8371.
3. Elevation, cen. St. Thomas I., Virgin Is. of the U.S., West Indies; 1504 ft. (458 m.).

Signal Hill National Historic Park. Reservation, St. John's, Newfoundland, Canada, overlooking the harbor of St. John's; site where first transatlantic wireless message was received 1901.

Signal Mountain. Town, Hamilton co., SE Tennessee, just N of Chattanooga; pop. (1990c) 7034.

Sig·our·ney \ˈsi-gər-nē\. City, ⊗ of Keokuk co., SE cen. Iowa, 25 mi. (40 km.) E of Oskaloosa; pop. (1990c) 2111.

Sigs·bee Deep \ˈsigz-bē\. Deepest point in Gulf of Mexico, in SW cen. part; 12,425 ft. (3787 m.).

Si·gua·nea Bay \ˌsē-gwä-ˈnā-ä\. Bay, W coast of Isla de la Juventud, Cuba, West Indies.

Si·gua·te·pe·que \ˌsē-gwä-tā-ˈpā-kā\. Town, Comayagua dept., W Honduras; pop. (1989e) 29,000.

Si·güen·za \sē-ˈgwān-sä\; *anc.* **Se·gon·tia** \si-ˈgän-shē-ə\. Municipality, Guadalajara prov., cen. Spain, ab. 70 mi. (113 km.) NE of Madrid; pop. (1991c) 4775.

Si·gui·ri \sē-ˈgē-rē\. Town, NE Guinea, on Niger River; pop. (1983p) 37,361.

Sihanoukville. See KOMPONG SOM.

Sihor. See SHIHOR.

Sihun. See SEYHAN.

Si·irt \si-ˈyirt\ *or* **Sert** \ˈsert\. **1.** Province of Turkey in Asia. See table at TURKEY.
2. Town, its ⁕, on a tributary of the Tigris 85 mi. (137 km.) E of Diyarbakır; pop. (1990p) 66,607; blankets.

Si·kai·a·na \ˌsē-kī-ˈä-nə\. Chief island of the Stewart Is., E Solomon Is., 110 mi. (177 km.) E of Malaita; has no entrance to its lagoon.

Si·kan·dar·a·bad \si-ˈkən-də-rə-ˌbäd\. **1.** Town, W Uttar Pradesh, N India; pop. (1991p) 61,035.
2. Town, N Andhra Pradesh, India. See SECUNDERABAD.

Si·kan·dra \si-ˈkən-drə\. Village, Uttar Pradesh, N India, 6 mi. (10 km.) NW of Agra; site of tomb of Mogul Emperor Akbar (d. 1605), a mausoleum of red sandstone.

Si·kang *also* **Hsi·kang** \ˈshē-ˈkäŋ\. Former province, S China, now part of Tibet and Sichuan; region forms E part of Plateau of Tibet with nearly all of it above 10,000 ft. (3048 m.); bordered on the S by the E end of the Himalayas with peaks as high as 25,000 ft. (7620 m.); E edge cut by the great gorges of three streams—Salween, Mekong, and Chang—all of which have their upper courses here; province dissolved 1955.

Si·kar \ˈsi-kər\. Town, NE Rajasthan, NW India, NW of Jaipur; pop. (1991p) 148,235.

Si·kas·so \si-ˈkä-sō\. Town, S Mali, ab. 190 mi. (305 km.) SE of Bamako near Ivory Coast boundary; pop. (1987p) 73,050.

Sikes·ton \ˈsīk-stən\. City, Scott and New Madrid cos., SE Missouri, 30 mi. (48 km.) S of Cape Girardeau; pop. (1990c) 17,641.

Si·kho·te–Alin' *or* **Si·kho·te–Alin** \ˌsē-k̲ə-ˈte-ə-ˈlēn\. Mountain range, E coast of Primorskiy Kray, SE Russia in Asia; ab. 650 mi. (1045 km.) long; av. height 4000 to 5000 ft. (1220 to 1525 m.); highest point 6083 ft. (1854 m.), at S end. Rich in lead and zinc.

Siking. See XI'AN.

Sik·i·nos \ˈsē-kē-ˌnōs\. Island, S Cyclades, Greece, in S Aegean Sea E of Melos and W of Ios; ab. 17 sq. mi. (44 sq. km.).

Sik·kim \ˈsi-kəm\. State, NE India; bounded on N and E by Tibet, China, on SE by Bhutan, on S by Bangladesh, and on W by Nepal; ⁕ Gangtok; located on S slope of the Himalayas, alt. of ranges from ab. 1000 ft. (305 m.) to Mt. Kanchenjunga 28,209 ft. (8598 m.), 3d highest mountain in the world, on W border; chief river the Tista. Major crops include corn, fruit, barley. Kingdom estab. 1642; invaded by Nepal 18th and 19th cents.; came under British influence 1817; ceded site of Darjeeling to Great Britain in 1835; in 1890 British protectorate recognized by China; became a protectorate of India 1950; became a state of India 1975. See table at INDIA.

Siktivkar. See SYKTYVKAR.

Sikyon. See SICYON.

Sil \ˈsēl\. River, NW Spain; rises in NW León prov., flows SSW into Miño River; ab. 100 mi. (160 km.) long.

Si·la·cay·oá·pan \ˌsē-lä-kī-ˈwä-pän\. Municipality, Oaxaca state, Mexico, 105 mi. (169 km.) WNW of the city of Oaxaca.

Silagian Mountains. See table at APENNINES.

Si·lang \sē-ˈläŋ\. Municipality, Cavite prov., Luzon, Philippines, ab. 30 mi. (48 km.) S of Manila; pop. (1980c) 52,321.

Si·lao \sē-ˈlau̇\. Town, Guanajuato state, cen. Mexico, just WSW of the city of Guanajuato; munic. pop. (1990p) 114,929.

Si·lay \sē-ˈlī\. Chartered city, Negros Occidental, Negros, Philippines, on Guimaras Strait 10 mi. (16 km.) N of City of Bacolod; pop. (1990p) 92,000; port.

Silay, Mount. Mountain, N Negros Occidental, Negros, Philippines; 5048 ft. (1539 m.).

Sil·char \sil-ˈchär\. Town, Assam, NE India, on highway to Manipur; pop. (1991p) 115,045; British supply base in Burma campaign in WWII.

Sil·ches·ter \ˈsil-ˌches-tər, -chəs-\. Village, N Hampshire, S England; site of ancient Roman town **Cal·le·va Atreb·a·tum** \kə-ˈlē-və-ə-ˈtre-bə-ˌtəm\, excavated beginning in the 1890s; walls, earth banks of a Roman amphitheater, and ruins of forum and baths were uncovered.

Si·ler City \ˈsī-lər\. Town, Chatham co., cen. North Carolina, 28 mi. (45 km.) SE of Greensboro; pop. (1990c) 4808.

Si·lers Bald \ˈsī-lərz\. Peak, Sevier co., E Tennessee, in Great Smoky Mountain National Park; 5607 ft. (1709 m.); a peak of the Great Smoky Mts. near the North Carolina border.

Si·le·sia \sī-ˈlē-zhə, sə-, -shē-ə\ *or Ger.* **Schle·si·en** \ˈshlā-zē-ən\. Historical region, E cen. Europe, lying mostly in SW Poland, with minor sections in adjoining areas of the Czech Republic and Germany.

History: For centuries a part of Poland and at one time divided into many principalities; passed to Bohemia 14th cent. and came under Holy Roman Empire; suffered in Hussite Wars (1425–35) and Thirty Years' War (1618–48); passed to Austrian Hapsburgs 1526; all of Silesia except extreme SSE ceded to Prussia by Austria 1742; Prussian Silesia subdivided into **Lower Silesia** (*Ger.* **Nie·der·schle·si·en** \ˈnē-dər-ˌ\) in the SE and **Upper Silesia** (*Ger.* **Ober·schle·si·en** \ˈō-bər-ˌ\) in the NW. Remaining Austrian Silesia made separate crown land 1849 and became part of newly formed Czechoslovakia 1918; contested area of Teschen divided bet. Czechoslovakia and Poland 1920; because of predominant Polish population, SE portion of Upper Silesia, which included many large mining and industrial communities, assigned to Poland 1921. Polish Silesia (**Śląsk** \ˈshlōⁿsk\) occupied by Nazi Germany 1939; after WWII by Treaty of Potsdam 1945 Polish Silesia was increased to include all of Silesia held by Germany before the war, except a small section included in the East German state of Saxony.

Si·lex, Mount \ˈsī-ˌleks\. Peak, San Juan co., SW Colorado; 13,650 ft. (4161 m.).

Sil·hou·ette \ˌsi-lə-ˈwet\. One of the Seychelles (*q.v.*); ab. 6 sq. mi. (16 sq. km.).

Sil·i·con Valley \ˈsi-lə-kən, -ˌkän\. Strip in Santa Clara co., W California bet. San Jose and Palo Alto; came into prominence in early 1980s as a center of high-technology industries, whence the name originates—an unofficial term.

Si·lif·ke \sē-lēf-'ke\. Town, S Turkey in Asia; pop. (1990p) 47,276. See SELEUCIA.

Siliguri. See SHILIGURI.

Si·ling Co \'sē-'liŋ-'gō\ *or W.-G.* **Ch'i–lin–ts'o** \'chē-'lin-'tsō\ *or* **Sel·ling Tso** \'se-liŋ-'tsō\ *or* **Zil·ling Tso** \'zi-liŋ-'tsō\. Lake, cen. Tibet, China; alt. 15,120 ft. (4609 m.).

Si·lis·tra \si-'lis-trə, -'lēs-\ *also* **Si·lis·tria** \si-'lis-trē-ə\; *anc.* **Du·ros·to·rum** \dů-'räs-tə-rəm, dyů-\. City, N Bulgaria, on Danube River 70 mi. (113 km.) ENE of Ruse; pop. (1991e) 56,229; ships grain. Founded as Roman camp; important fortress town under Byzantines and Bulgars; came under Ottoman Empire early 15th cent.; to Bulgaria 1878; belonged to Romania 1913–40.

Si·li·vri \si-li-'vrē\. Port on the Sea of Marmara, İstanbul prov., Turkey in Europe, ab. 35 mi. (56 km.) W of the city of İstanbul.

Sil·jan \'sil-ˌyän\. Lake, cen. Kopparberg prov., cen. Sweden; 137 sq. mi. (355 sq. km.); drains into Dal River.

Sil·ke·borg \'sil-kə-ˌbórg\. City, Århus co., E Jutland Penin., Denmark, 27 mi. (43 km.) W of the city of Århus; pop. (1989e) 47,889; health resort in **Silkeborg Lakes** region.

Silk Road *or* **Silk Route.** Former trade route, from c. 100 B.C., extending from E China up the valley of the Wei through Gansu prov. and Xinjiang Uygur autonomous region to the W; at Dunhuang, oasis town in extreme W Gansu, divided into two ancient caravan routes that led westward: (1) "South Road," along N Altun Shan and Kunlun Shan mountain ranges S of the Taklimakan to Hotan and Shache, thence W and S through high passes of Pamirs and Hindu Kush to the Oxus River (now Amu Dar'ya) and India; and (2) "North Road," along N edge of the Taklimakan through Kashi, thence by way of Fergana Valley to the Jaxartes River (now Syr Dar'ya) and towns of Turkistan; this "North Road" later became the "Middle Road" and was superseded by the true "North Road" from Anxi via Hami to its junction at Korla; routes were used for shipments of silk to Western markets and for travel by ambassadors, pilgrims, and early missionaries.

Sill, Mount \'sil\. Peak in the Sierra Nevada, Fresno co., S cen. California; 14,162 ft. (4317 m.).

Sil·la \'si-lə\ *also* **Shil·la** \'shi-lə\. Early Korean kingdom, in SE part of Korean Penin.; founded first cent. B.C. and emerged as important kingdom 4th–6th cents.; united Korea for the first time under the unified Silla dynasty (668–935).

Sil·laj·huay, Cor·dil·le·ra \ˌkór-t͟hē-'yā-rä-ˌsē-yä-'k̲wī\ *or* **Cordillera Sil·laj·guay** \-'gwī\. Range, W Bolivia, on the Chilean boundary NW of Uyuni; highest peak 19,669 ft. (5995 m.).

Sillein. See ŽILINA.

Sil·le·ry \'si-lə-rē, ˌsē-yə-'re\. **1.** City, Quebec co., S Quebec, Canada, 3 mi. (5 km.) SW of Quebec City; pop. (1991c) 12,519.

2. Village, Marne dept., NE France, just SE of Reims; noted for champagne.

Sil·li·man, Mount \'si-lə-mən\. Peak in the Sierra Nevada, N Tulare co., S cen. California, on border bet. Sequoia and Kings Canyon national parks; 11,188 ft. (3410 m.).

Si·loam Springs \'sī-lōm, -ləm\. City, Benton co., NW corner of Arkansas, in Ozarks 23 mi. (37 km.) NW of Fayetteville; pop. (1990c) 8151; John Brown Univ. (1919).

Sils, Lake of \'zils\ *or Ger.* **Sil·ser See** \'zil-zər-ˌzā\. Lake, Graubünden canton, E Switzerland, in SW part of Upper Engadine; 3 mi. (5 km.) long by ab. 1 mi. (2 km.) wide; 1.5 sq. mi. (4 sq. km.); max. depth 232 ft. (71 m.).

Sils·bee \'silz-bē\. City, Hardin co., E Texas, 19 mi. (31 km.) N of Beaumont; pop. (1990c) 6368.

Sil·vas·sa \ˌsil-vä-'sä\. Town, ✱ of Dadra and Nagar Haveli union terr., W India; pop. (1991p) 11,720.

Sil·ver Bank \'sil-vər\. Bank in Atlantic Ocean, off N coast of Hispaniola, West Indies.

Silver Bank Passage. Channel, N cen. West Indies, SE of Mouchoir Bank and NW of Silver Bank.

Silver Bay. City, Lake co., NE Minnesota, on Lake Superior 50 mi. (80 km.) NE of Duluth; pop. (1990c) 1894.

Silver Bow \'bō\. County in SW Montana. See table at MONTANA.

Silver City. 1. Former town, Owyhee co., SW Idaho, 37 mi. (60 km.) SW of Boise. Founded 1863 as gold- and silver-mining center; served as ⊗ 1866–1935; pop. peaked at 5,000 but gradually fell with end of mining activity. A number of buildings still remain.

2. Town, ⊗ of Grant co., SW New Mexico, in Rocky Mts., near the Continental Divide; pop. (1990c) 10,683; livestock; copper mining and processing. Western New Mexico Univ. (1893); Gila Cliff Dwellings National Monument to NE. Founded 1870 as Spanish settlement; incorp. 1876.

3. Town, cen. Panama. See RAINBOW CITY 2.

Silver Creek. 1. Small stream, El Dorado co., E California; dammed to form Union Valley Reservoir. See *Union Valley at* UNITED STATES, *Dams and Reservoirs.*

2. Village, Chautauqua co., SW corner of New York, on Lake Erie 28 mi. (45 km.) S of Buffalo; pop. (1990c) 2927.

Sil·ver·heels, Mount \'sil-vər-ˌhēlz\. Peak, Park co., cen. Colorado; 13,825 ft. (4214 m.).

Silver Lake. Village, Summit co., NE Ohio, NNE of Akron; pop. (1990c) 3052.

Silver Peak Mountains. Small range, W Esmeralda co., SW Nevada; highest peak ab. 9500 ft. (2900 m.).

Silver Plume Mountain \'plüm\. Peak, Clear Creek co., N cen. Colorado; 13,500 ft. (4115 m.).

Silver Run Peak. Mountain, Carbon co., S Montana; 12,610 ft. (3844 m.).

Silver Spring. Unincorporated settlement, Montgomery co., cen. Maryland, N suburb of Washington; pop. (1990c) 76,046.

Silver Springs. Locality, Marion co., N Florida, near Ocala; site of more than 100 springs which form a pond ab. 35 ft. (11 m.) deep, source of **Silver River,** navigable tributary of the Oklawaha to the E.

Sil·ver·tip Peak \'sil-vər-ˌtip\. Mountain, Park co., NW Wyoming; 10,400 ft. (3170 m.).

Sil·ver·ton \'sil-vər-tən\. **1.** Town, ⊗ of San Juan co., SW Colorado; pop. (1990c) 716.

2. Residential city, Hamilton co., SW corner of Ohio, 8 mi. (13 km.) NE of Cincinnati; pop. (1990c) 5859.

3. City, Marion co., Oregon, ENE of Salem; pop. (1990c) 5635.

4. City, ⊗ of Briscoe co., NW Texas; pop. (1990c) 779.

Sil·ves \'sēl-vish\. Town, S coast of Portugal, 18 mi. (29 km.) NNW of Faro; pop. (1981p) 31,352; Gothic cathedral; Moorish castle; town destroyed in earthquake 1755.

Sil·vies \'sil-vēz\. River, E cen. Oregon; rises in S Grant co., flows S into Malheur Lake, Harney co.; 75 mi. (121 km.) long.

Sil·vis \'sil-vəs\. City, Rock Island co., NW Illinois, 9 mi. (14 km.) E of the city of Rock Island; pop. (1990c) 6926.

Sil·vret·ta \sil-'vre-tə\. Mountain group along border bet. E Switzerland and SW Tirol, Austria; heights **Piz Li·nard** \'pēts-li-'närt\ 11,188 ft. (3410 m.), **Flucht·horn** \'flůk̲t-ˌhórn\ 11,162 ft. (3402 m.).

Sim, Cape \'sim\. Cape, SW coast of Morocco, 31°23′N, 9°51′W.

Simalur. See SIMEULUE.

Si·man·cas \sē-'mäŋ-käs\. Commune, Valladolid prov., N cen. Spain, 8 mi. (13 km.) SW of the commune of Valladolid; pop. (1991c) 1996; ancient city; national archives housed in the castle since mid-16th cent.; scene of victory of Ramiro II of León over Caliph 'Abd ar-Raḥmān III of Spain 939.

Si·mang·gang \sē-'mäŋ-ˌgäŋ\. Town, S Sarawak, Malaysia, NW Borneo, on Batang Lupar River 80 mi. (129 km.) ESE of Kuching; pop. (1980p) 68,405.

\ə\ abut \ᵊ\ kitten, Fr table \ər\ further \a\ ash \ā\ ace \ä\ cot, cart \å\ Fr bac \aů\ out \b̲\ Span Avila \ch\ chin \e\ bet \ē\ easy \g\ go \i\ hit \ī\ ice \j\ job \k̲\ Ger ich, Buch \ⁿ\ Fr vin \ŋ\ sing \ō\ go \ȯ\ all \ó\ law \œ\ Fr bœuf \œ̄\ Fr feu \ȯi\ boy \th\ thin \t͟h\ this \ü\ loot \ů\ foot \ue\ Ger füllen \ue̅\ Fr rue \y\ yet \ʸ\ Fr digne \'dēnʸ\, nuit \'nwʸē\ \yü\ few \yů\ fury \zh\ vision

Si·mang·ge·la \si-məŋ-ˈgē-lə\; *formerly* **Door·man** \ˈdōr-mən\ *or* **Doorman Top** \ˈtöp\. Peak, N cen. part of Maoke Mts., cen. Irian Jaya, Indonesia; 13,287 ft. (4050 m.) high.

Si·mao *or W.-G.* **Ssu–mao** *or* **Sze mao** \ˈsə-ˈmaů\. Town, S cen. Yunnan prov., S China, on Mekong (Lancang) River; former treaty port late 19th cent.

Si·ma·ra \sē-ˈmä-rä\. Island in Romblon group, Philippines, N of Tablas I.; 8 sq. mi. (21 sq. km.).

Si·mav \sē-ˈmäv\. **1.** River, NW Turkey in Asia; flows W and N; ab. 160 mi. (255 km.) long.

2. Town on upper Simav River, Kütahya prov., NW Turkey in Asia, 60 mi. (97 km.) E of Akhisar.

Sim·birsk \sim-ˈbirsk\; *1924–91* **Ul'·ya·novsk** *or* **Ul·ya·novsk** *also* **Ul·ia·novsk** \ül-ˈyä-nəfsk\. City, ✻ of Ul'yanovsk Oblast, SE cen. Russia in Europe, on right bank of the Volga 485 mi. (780 km.) ESE of Moscow; pop. (1992e) 656,000; river port and railroad junction; machinery, food products; built along the river on top of a hill, with a major railroad bridge across the Volga. Founded 1648; birthplace of Russian Communist leader V. I. Lenin (V. I. Ulyanov) 1870; renamed in his honor after his death in 1924.

Sim·coe \ˈsim-kō\. **1.** County in SE Ontario, Canada. See table at ONTARIO.

2. Town, ⊗ of Haldimand-Norfolk munic. region, SE Ontario, Canada, 20 mi. (32 km.) S of Brantford; pop. (1991c) 15,539; tobacco products.

Simcoe, Lake. Lake, SE Ontario, Canada, ab. 40 mi. (64 km.) N of Toronto; 271 sq. mi. (702 sq. km.), 30 mi. (48 km.) long by 20 mi. (32 km.) wide; outlet is Severn River flowing ab. 45 mi. (72 km.) N and W into Georgian Bay. Popular resort region; Barrie and Orillia are chief towns on it.

Si·me·to \sē-ˈmā-tō, -ˈme-\. River, E Sicily, Italy; rises W of Mt. Etna, flows E, S, and SE into Mediterranean S of Catania.

Si·meu·lue *or Du.* **Si·meu·loeë** \ˌsē-mə-ˈlü-ə\ *or* **Si·ma·lur** \sē-ˈmä-lůr\. Island, Indonesia, in the Indian Ocean off NW coast of Sumatra; 683 sq. mi. (1769 sq. km.), with adjacent islands 712 sq. mi. (1844 sq. km.); forest-covered with cen. ridge; highest point 1860 ft. (567 m.); surrounded by reefs.

Sim·fer·o·pol' *or* **Sim·fer·o·pol** \ˌsim-fə-ˈrö-pəlʸ, -ˈrō-\. City, Crimea, Ukraine, in S part, on Sevastopol'-Kharkiv railroad line; pop. (1991e) 353,000; machine tools, canned goods, wine.

History: Settled c. 16th cent. by Tatars as **Ak Me·chet** \ˌäk-mi-ˈchet\ on site of former ancient Scythian ✻; refounded under present name by Russians 1784; in WWII occupied by Germans 1941–44.

Sí·mi *or* **Si·mi** *or* **Sy·mē** *or* **Sy·mi** \ˈsē-ˌmē\. **1.** Island of the Dodecanese (*q.v.*), Greece, NW of Rhodes; 25 sq. mi. (65 sq. km.).

2. Town on the island.

Si·mi Valley \si-ˈmē\. City, Ventura co., SW California, NW of Los Angeles; pop. (1990c) 100,217; Ronald Reagan presidential library.

Sim·la \ˈsim-lə\. Town, ✻ of Himachal Pradesh, NW India, 53 mi. (85 km.) NE of Ambala; pop. (1991p) 81,463; hill resort, situated on a ridge of the Himalayas at elev. of 6600 to 8000 ft. or 2010 to 2440 m. (highest point Mt. Jakko). Passed to British 1816; formerly summer ✻ of British government of India.

Sim·me \ˈzi-mə\. River, SW cen. Switzerland; rises in S Bern canton, flows N and NE into Thunersee; ab. 35 mi. (55 km.) long.

Sim·o·ïs \ˈsi-mə-wəs\; *mod.* **Düm·rek** \ˈdœm-ˌrek\. Small river, Asia Minor, near ancient Troy; tributary of Scamander (*mod.* Menderes).

Si·mon's Town *or* **Si·mons·town** \ˈsī-mənz-ˌtaůn\. Town, SW Western Cape prov., S Rep. of South Africa, on W shore of False Bay 20 mi. (32 km.) S of Cape Town; pop. (1985c) 4373; fishing; naval base and dockyard facilities. Naval base estab. by Dutch 1741; made base of British South Atlantic Naval Squadron 1814; facilities transferred to Union (now Rep.) of South Africa 1957.

Simplon. Alpine pass and tunnel. See table at ALPS.

Simp·son \ˈsimp-sən\. **1.** Name of counties in two states of the U.S. See tables at KENTUCKY and MISSISSIPPI.

2. Trading post, Canada. See FORT SIMPSON.

3. Island, Chonos Archipelago, in Pacific Ocean off SW coast of Chile.

Simpson Desert. Desert, cen. Australia, largely in SE Northern Terr., extending S into South Australia and E into Queensland; ab. 50,000 sq. mi. (129,500 sq. km.); first land-crossing by a European 1939.

Simpson Harbour. Harbor, inner landlocked part of Blanche Bay, NE coast of New Britain I., Bismarck Archipelago, W Pacific Ocean, forming the harbor of Rabaul.

Simpson Peninsula. Peninsula, NE mainland part of Nunavut, Canada, bet. Pelly Bay on W and Committee Bay on E; ab. 40 mi. (64 km.) wide.

Simp·son·ville \ˈsimp-sən-ˌvil\. Town, Greenville co., NW South Carolina, 11 mi. (18 km.) SE of the city of Greenville; pop. (1990c) 11,708.

Sims·bury \ˈsimz-ˌber-ē, -bə-rē\. Town, NW cen. Hartford co., N Connecticut, S of Granby; pop. (1990c) 22,023; machine tools, safety fuses; dairy farms; incorp. 1670; first colonial copper coins (Higley coppers) minted here 1737.

Si·myen Mountains *or* **Se·mien Mountains** \si-ˈmyān\. Mountains, N Ethiopia; highest peak Ras Dashen 15,158 ft. (4620 m.).

Sin, Wilderness of \ˈsin\. Biblical region, Sinai Penin., NE Egypt; thought by some to be along SW coast, on E side of Gulf of Suez; traversed by the Israelites during the Exodus (*Exod.* xvi. 1; xvii. 1).

Si·na \ˈsē-nə\. River, SE Maharashtra, S cen. India; flows SE and empties into Bhima River; ab. 170 mi. (274 km.) long.

Si·nai \ˈsī-ˌnī, ˈsī-nē-ˌī, ˈsī-nā-ˌī\. Peninsula, NE Egypt, bet. Gulf of Suez on W and Gulf of Aqaba on E, at N end of Red Sea; 23,442 sq. mi. (60,715 sq. km.); very mountainous, contains plateaus of Al-Tih and Egma, and at S end Gebel Musa. Thinly populated esp. in interior; has oil fields and manganese deposits. Scene of the principal campaign of the Arab-Israeli War 1967; under Israeli occupation 1967–82.

Sinai, Mount. 1. *or* **Mount Ho·reb** \ˈhōr-ib, -ˌeb\. Biblical mountain often identified with Gebel Musa (see MUSA, GEBEL); site where God is thought to have given the Ten Commandments to Moses (*Exod.* iii. 1).

2. Mountain, S Sinai Penin., Egypt. See MUSA, GEBEL.

Si·na·ia \sē-ˈnī-ə\. Town, SE Prahova co., Romania, 21 mi. (34 km.) S of Braşov; pop. (1992p) 15,407; two palaces; town began around monastery founded 1695; developed in 1870s when chosen as royal summer residence.

Si·na·loa \ˌsē-nä-ˈlō-ä\. State of W Mexico. See table at MEXICO.

Si·na·lun·ga \ˌsē-nä-ˈlůŋ-gä\; *formerly* **Asi·na·lun·ga** \ä-ˌsē-\. Commune, Siena prov., Tuscany, W Italy, 23 mi. (37 km.) ESE of the commune of Siena; pop. (1981p) 11,517.

Sin·ce·le·jo \ˌsin-sā-ˈlā-hō\. Town, ✻ of Sucre dept., N Colombia, 80 mi. (129 km.) S of Cartagena; munic. pop. (1992e) 167,600.

Sin·clair's Bay \ˈsin-klarz, ˈsiŋ-\. Inlet of North Sea, extreme NE coast of Scotland, N of town of Wick.

Sind *or* **Sindh** \ˈsind\. **1.** River, cen. India; rises in Madhya Pradesh, flows NE through Gwalior into the Yamuna E of Gwalior; 240 mi. (386 km.) long.

2. Province, Pakistan, bounded on N by the provs. of Baluchistan and Punjab, on E and S by India, on SW by the Arabian Sea, and on W by Baluchistan; ✻ Karachi; region is generally flat, lying along both banks of the Indus; rice is chief crop; other exports are wheat, cotton, barley, oilseeds. A large area under cultivation is irrigated by Sukkur Barrage (*q.v.*). Chief cities Karachi, Hyderabad. See table at PAKISTAN.

History: Important evidence of prehistoric Indus Valley civilization in the region; came under Persian Empire late 6th cent. B.C.; invaded by Macedonian King Alexander the Great 325 B.C.; later part of the Mauryan empire of Candragupta Maurya (4th–3d cents. B.C.); conquered by Arabs c. 711 A.D.; annexed by Akbar as part of the Mogul Empire 1591 but later came under local Muslim dynasties; made treaties with British 1809 and 1820; invaded by British 1842 and annexed to British India as N part of Bombay presidency; constituted an autonomous province 1937; became part of Pakistan 1947; provincial status abolished 1955; province reestablished constituting larger territory 1970.

Sin·dan·gan \sin-ˈdäŋ-ˌgän\. Municipality, Zamboanga del Norte prov., Mindanao, Philippines, on E shore of **Sindangan Bay** (inlet of Sulu Sea ab. 100 mi. or 160 km. NNE of Zamboanga); pop. (1980c) 66,177.

Sin·dan·gla·ja \ˌsin-däŋ-ˈglī-ə\. Village and mountain health resort, W Java, Indonesia, on slope of Mt. Gede at 3500-foot (1067-meter) elev., SE of Bogor.

Sin·del·fing·en \ˈzin-dəl-ˌfiŋ-ən\. Town, Baden-Württemberg, Germany, ab. 9 mi. (14 km.) SW of Stuttgart; pop. (1992e) 59,514.

Sinder. See ZINDER.

Si·nes \ˈsē-nish\. Town, Setúbal dist., SW Portugal, on coast 35 mi. (56 km.) SSE of the seaport of Setúbal; pop. (1991p) 12,180; oil refinery. Birthplace of navigator Vasco da Gama c. 1460.

Si·ne·wit, Mount \ˈsi-nə-ˌwit\. Mountain, New Britain I., Bismarck Archipelago, W Pacific Ocean; 7999 ft. (2438 m.); highest peak on island.

Sinfeng. See XINFENG.

Si–ngan *or* **Singan–fu.** See XI'AN.

Sin·ga·pore \ˈsiŋ-ə-ˌpōr, ˈsiŋ-gə-\. **1.** Republic, SE Asia, S of the Malay Penin., comprising Singapore I. and several smaller adjacent islets; 225 sq. mi. (583 sq. km.); pop. (1989e) 2,685,400; ✻ Singapore. For economy, see SINGAPORE 2 and 3.

History: Included in the British colony of Straits Settlements 1826; in WWII occupied by Japanese 1942–45; made a separate British colony 1946 and became self-governing 1959; part of Federation of Malaysia 1963–65; became an independent republic 1965.

2. Island off S end of Malay Penin., SE Asia, comprising the main part of Singapore (see SINGAPORE 1); separated from the Malay Peninsula by Johore Strait (ab. 0.75 mi. or 1.2 km. wide) and from Batam and other islands of Kepulauan Riau on the S by Singapore Strait; 77 mi. (124 km.) N of the Equator; 209 sq. mi. (541 sq. km.). Hilly (highest point 581 ft. or 177 m.), well cultivated; vegetables, poultry; textiles; crossed by railroad connecting by causeway over Johore Strait with Johor Baharu and towns of Malaysia; Singapore (city) on S coast. Nominally under Dutch influence when city of Singapore founded by British East India Company; ceded to Great Britain 1824.

3. Seaport city, ✻ of Singapore (see SINGAPORE 1), on Singapore Strait; met. area pop. (1985e) 157,000; major entrepôt; banking center; shipbuilding, food processing; electrical equipment, apparel; chemical and petroleum products; two universities.

History: A Malay city of importance in 13th cent.; destroyed by Javanese 14th cent. and remained a ruin until refounded by British colonial administrator Sir Thomas Stamford Raffles 1819 for the East India Company; became ✻ of the Straits Settlements 1833. Developed as a great port and trade center and later as naval base; in WWII fell to Japanese Feb. 1942.

Singapore, Strait of. Channel bet. Singapore I. on the N and Batam, Bintan, and other islands of Kepulauan Riau on the S; ab. 50 mi. (80 km.) long by 10 mi. (16 km.) wide; connects South China Sea with Strait of Malacca.

Sin·ga·ra·ja *or* **Sin·ga·ra·dja** \ˌsiŋ-gə-ˈrä-jə\. Town, N Bali I., Indonesia; pop. (1980c) 63,794; important market facilities.

Sing Bu·ri *or* **Sin·gha·bu·ri** \ˌsiŋ-bə-ˈrē—*sic*\. Town, SW cen. Thailand, on the Chao Phraya and on railroad line 40 mi. (64 km.) N of Phra Nakhon Si Ayutthaya.

Sing·en \ˈziŋ-ən\. City, Baden-Württemberg, Germany, 15 mi. (24 km.) WNW of Konstanz; pop. (1992e) 44,274.

Singhasari. See SINGOSARI.

Sin·gi·da \siŋ-ˈgē-dä\. **1.** Administrative region, cen. Tanzania. See table at TANZANIA.

2. Town, its ✻.

Singidunum. See BELGRADE 2.

Sin·git·ic Gulf \sin-ˈji-tik\ *or Gk.* **Sin·gi·ti·kós Kól·pos** \sēŋ-ˌgē-tē-ˈkōs-ˈkōl-ˌpōs\. Inlet of Aegean Sea, NE coast of Greece, S of Chalcidice and bet. the peninsulas of Acte and Sithonia.

Sing·ka·rak \ˌsiŋ-kə-ˈräk\. Mountain lake, W Sumatra, Indonesia, NE of Padang; ab. 12 mi. (19 km.) long by 5 mi. (8 km.) wide.

Sing·ka·wang \siŋ-ˈkä-ˌwäŋ\. Town, West Kalimantan prov., Borneo, Indonesia, on South China Sea coast 70 mi. (113 km.) N of Pontianak; pop. (1980c) 82,416.

Sing·kep \ˈsiŋ-ˌkep\. Island, SW Lingga Archipelago, Indonesia, SW of Lingga I. and separated from E coast of Sumatra by Berhala Strait.

Sin·gle·shot Mountain \ˈsiŋ-gəl-ˌshät\. Peak, Glacier National Park, NW Montana; 7700 ft. (2347 m.).

Sin·gle·ton \ˈsiŋ-gəl-tən\. Town, E New South Wales, Australia, N of Sydney; pop. (1991c) 11,861.

Singora. See SONGKHLA.

Sin·go·sa·ri *or* **Sing·ha·sa·ri** \ˌsiŋ-ə-ˈsä-rē\ *also* **Tu·ma·pel** \tü-ˈmä-pəl\. A powerful Malay kingdom of E Java in the 13th cent. (1222–92) with ✻ at Singosari, now a village just N of Malang, Indonesia.

Sing Peak \ˈsiŋ\. Mountain in the Sierra Nevada, E Madera co., cen. California, on SE edge of Yosemite National Park; 10,552 ft. (3216 m.).

Sing Sing. See OSSINING.

Sining. See XINING.

Sinkiang. See *History* at XINJIANG UYGUR.

Sinkiang Uighur. See XINJIANG UYGUR.

Sinmin. See XINMIN.

Sin·na·ma·ry *or* **Sin·na·ma·rie** \ˌsē-nə-mə-ˈrē\. **1.** River, N French Guiana; flows N into Atlantic Ocean 70 mi. (113 km.) NW of Cayenne; ab. 100 mi. (160 km.) long.

2. Coastal town, N French Guiana; pop. (1982c) 1991.

Sinneh. See SANANDAJ.

Sin·ni \ˈsē-nē\ *or* **Sin·no** \ˈsē-nō\; *anc.* **Si·ris** \ˈsī-rəs\. River, S Italy; flows E into Gulf of Taranto 19 mi. (31 km.) SW of the mouth of Bradano River; ab. 60 mi. (95 km.) long.

Sîn·ni·co·lau Ma·re \sin-ˌnē-kə-ˈlau̇-ˈmä-rə\ *or* **Sân·ni·co·la·ul–Ma·re** \sən-ˌnē-kə-ˈlau̇l-ˈmä-rə\ *or Hung.* **Nagy·szent·mi·klós** \ˈnözh-sent-ˈmi-klōsh\. Commune, Timiş co., SW Romania, on the Mureş River 25 mi. (40 km.) SE of Szeged; an ancient Roman outpost; site of discovery in 1799 of remarkable gold ornamented utensils, probably of 10th cent. Turkish origin.

Sin·nū·ris \si-ˈnu̇r-əs\. Town, El Faiyûm governorate, Egypt, SE of Birket Qārūn; pop. (1986p) 55,323.

Sino. See GREENVILLE.

Si·nop \si-ˈnȯp\. **1.** Province of Turkey in Asia. See table at TURKEY.

2. *anc.* **Si·no·pe** \sə-ˈnō-pē\. Seaport, its ✻, on narrow part of a peninsula extending into the Black Sea; pop. (1990p) 25,631; good natural harbor; ruins of Byzantine castle.

History: Founded c. 7th cent. B.C. as a colony of Miletus; as seaport and terminus of caravan route became a major Greek trading city; ✻ of Pontic monarchy 183 B.C. ff.; taken by Rome 70 B.C.; came under Ottoman Empire c. 1451; scene of Russian naval victory over Turks 1853 at the outset of the Crimean War. Birthplace of Greek philosopher Diogenes (4th cent. B.C.) and of Pontic King Mithradates the Great (2d cent. B.C.).

Sin·o·pah Mountain \ˈsi-nə-ˌpä\. Peak, Glacier National Park, NW Montana; 8435 ft. (2571 m.).

Sinope. See SINOP 2.

Sin·qu \ˈsiŋ-kü\. River, Lesotho; a headstream of the Orange River.

Sinsiang. See XINXIANG.

Sint. See SAINT.

Sint Amands·berg \sint-ä-ˈmänts-ˌberk\; *formerly* **Mont–Saint–Amand** \ˌmōⁿ-ˌseⁿ-tä-ˈmäⁿ\. Commune, East Flanders prov., NW cen. Belgium; NE suburb of Ghent.

\ə\ abut \ᵊ\ kitten, Fr table \ər\ further \a\ ash \ā\ ace \ä\ cot, cart \à\ Fr bac \au̇\ out \b\ Span Avila \ch\ chin \e\ bet \ē\ easy \g\ go \i\ hit \ī\ ice \j\ job \k\ Ger ich, Buch \ⁿ\ Fr vin \ŋ\ sing \ō\ go \ȯ\ all \ȯ\ law \œ\ Fr bœuf \œ̄\ Fr feu \ȯi\ boy \th\ thin \t͟h\ this \ü\ loot \u̇\ foot \ue\ Ger füllen \ue̅\ Fr rue \y\ yet \ʸ\ Fr digne \ˈdēnʸ\, nuit \ˈnwʸē\ \yü\ few \yu̇\ fury \zh\ vision

Sint–Gillis. See SAINT-GILLES 1.
Sint–Joost–ten–Noode. See SAINT-JOSSE-TEN-NOODE.
Sint–Ka·te·lij·ne–Wa·ver \ˌsint-ˌkä-tə-ˈlā-nə-ˈvä-vər\ *or Fr.* **Wa·vre–Sainte–Ca·the·rine** \ˌvȧ-vrᵊ-seⁿt-kȧ-ˈtrēn\. Commune, Antwerp prov., Belgium; pop. (1991c) 18,266.
Sint–Lambrechts–Woluwe. See WOLUWE-SAINT-LAMBERT.
Sint Maarten. See SAINT MARTIN.
Sint Ni·co·laas \sint-ˈnē-kō-ˌläs\ *or* **San Ni·co·las** \sän-ˈnē-kō-ˌläs\. Village, SE coast of Aruba I., West Indies.
Sint Nicolaas Punt. See PUJUT, TANJUNG.
Sint–Ni·klaas \sint-ˈnē-kläs\ *or Fr.* **Saint–Ni·co·las** \ˌseⁿ-nē-kȯ-ˈlä\. Commune, East Flanders prov., NW cen. Belgium, 14 mi. (23 km.) ENE of Ghent; pop. (1992e) 68,300; railroad junction, market town; chartered 1513.
Sin·ton \ˈsint-ᵊn\. Town, ⊗ of San Patricio co., S Texas, 20 mi. (32 km.) N of Corpus Christi; pop. (1990c) 5549.
Sint–Pieters–Woluwe. See WOLUWE-SAINT-PIERRE.
Sin·tra; *mostly formerly* **Cin·tra** \ˈsēn-trə, ˈsin-\. Commune, Lisboa dist., W Portugal, 12 mi. (19 km.) NW of Lisbon; pop. (1991p) 262,447; marble quarries in the area; Moorish castle; 15th–16th cent. royal palace; convention signed here 1808 by French, English, and Portuguese military leaders at conclusion of Peninsular War. Notable for scenery celebrated by English poet Lord Byron in *Childe Harold's Pilgrimage.*
Sint–Trui·den \sint-ˈtrȯid-ᵊn\ *or Fr.* **Saint–Trond** \seⁿ-ˈtrōⁿ\. Commune, Limburg prov., NE Belgium, 20 mi. (32 km.) NW of Liège; pop. (1991c) 36,994; two medieval churches.
Sin·ŭi·ju \ˈsēn-ˈwē-ˈjü\ *or Jp.* **Shin·gi·shu** \ˈshiŋ-gē-ˌshü\. City, W North Korea, near mouth of Yalu River; pop. (1987e) 289,000.
Si·nus \ˈsī-nəs\. Latin for "gulf or bay"; in classical names, as Sinus Saronicus, see the 2d element or its anglicized form.
Sinus Aelaniticus. See AQABA, GULF OF.
Sinus Arabicus. See RED SEA 1.
Sinus Cantabricus. See BISCAY, BAY OF.
Sinus Corinthiacus. See CORINTH, GULF OF.
Sinus Gallicus. See LIONS, GULF OF.
Sinus Ligusticus. See LIGURIAN SEA.
Sinus Pagasaeus. See PAGASITIKÓS KÓLPOS.
Sinyang. See XINYANG.
Sio·fok \ˈshē-ō-ˌfōk\. Town, Somogy co., Hungary; pop. (1991e) 23,600.
Sion *or* **Mount Sion.** See ZION 2.
Sion \ˈsyōⁿ\ *or Ger.* **Sit·ten** \ˈzit-ᵊn\; *anc.* **Se·du·num** \si-ˈdü-nəm, -ˈdyü-\. Commune, ✱ of Valais canton, SW cen. Switzerland, 50 mi. (80 km.) S of Bern; pop. (1990c) 25,350; 13th cent. church; Gothic cathedral; 17th cent. town hall. Made episcopal see in 6th cent.; bishops of Sion were temporal rulers of Valais in Middle Ages.
Sioux \ˈsü\. Name of counties in three states of the U.S. See tables at IOWA, NEBRASKA, NORTH DAKOTA.
Sioux Center. City, Sioux co., NW Iowa, 40 mi. (64 km.) N of Sioux City; pop. (1990c) 5074; Dordt Coll. (1955).
Sioux City. City, ⊗ of Woodbury co., W Iowa, on Missouri River at confluence of Big Sioux and Floyd rivers; pop. (1990c) 80,505; alt. 1135 ft. (346 m.); meatpacking plants; grain market and trade center; Morningside Coll. (1894), Briar Cliff Coll. (1930), Western Iowa Tech Community Coll. (1966); city laid out 1848; incorp. 1857.
Sioux Falls. City, ⊗ of Minnehaha co., SE South Dakota, on Big Sioux River, ab. 75 mi. (120 km.) N of Sioux City, Iowa; pop. (1990c) 100,814; alt. 1395 ft. (425 m.); commercial and financial center in a livestock-farming region; agricultural machinery; North American Baptist Seminary (1850), Augustana Coll. (1860), Sioux Falls Coll. (1883). Founded 1857; abandoned during Sioux uprising 1862; military post estab. 1865; permanent settlement begun 1870; incorp. as city 1883.
Sioux Lookout. Town, Kenora dist., W Ontario, Canada, 120 mi. (193 km.) E of the town of Kenora; pop. (1991c) 3311.
Siphnos. See SÍFNOS.
Si·ping \ˈsə-ˈpiŋ\ *or W.-G.* **Ssu–p'ing** \ˈsə-ˈpiŋ\; *mostly formerly* **Sze·ping·kai** \ˈsə-ˈpiŋ-ˈgī\ *or* **Ssu·ping·chieh** \ˈsə-ˈpiŋ-ˈjye\. Town, Jilin prov., NE China, 70 mi. (113 km.) SSW of Changchun; pop. (1990c) 317,223.
Šipka Pass. See SHIPKA PASS.
Si·ple, Mount \ˈsī-pəl\; *formerly* **Mount Ruth Siple** \ˈrüth\. Mountain on coast of Marie Byrd Land, Antarctica, extending into the South Pacific at 73°15′S, 126°06′W bet. Wrigley Gulf and Amundsen Sea; 10,168 ft. (3099 m.).
Sipora. See SIPURA.
Sip·par \si-ˈpär\. City of ancient Babylonia on the right bank of the Euphrates River; ruins ab. 16 mi. (26 km.) SSW of Baghdad. From 3d millennium B.C. a center of worship of the Sumerian sun-god, Shamash. Excavations, begun in 1882, have uncovered remains of a large temple and many thousands of religious and historic clay tablets.
Sip·sey \ˈsip-sē\. Navigable river, NW Alabama; rises in NW Alabama, flows S into the Tombigbee River in S Pickens co., W cen. Alabama; ab. 85 mi. (140 km.) long.
Si·pu·ra *or Du.* **Si·po·ra** \sē-ˈpu̇r-ə\. Cen. island, Mentawai Is., Indonesia, off W coast of Sumatra; ab. 27 mi. (43 km.) long by 12 mi. (19 km.) wide.
Si·quia \ˈsē-kyä\. River, S cen. Nicaragua; flows E into the Escondido River; 95 mi. (153 km.) long.
Si·qui·jor \ˌsē-kē-ˈhȯr\. **1.** Island, one of the Visayan Is., S cen. Philippines, N of Mindanao; forms a province (see table at PHILIPPINES) and a part of Negros Oriental prov., Philippines; in NW part of Mindanao Sea, SE of Negros, S of Cebu, and SW of Bohol; 130 sq. mi. (337 sq. km.); ab. 12 mi. (19 km.) from N to S and 17 mi. (27 km.) E to W; chief municipality Siquijor. Hilly (highest point 1394 ft. or 425 m.), fertile, and most densely populated island of the archipelago; has several good harbors.
2. Municipality, ✱ of Siquijor prov., NW coast of Siquijor I., 16 mi. (26 km.) SE of Dumaguete; pop. (1980c) 17,533.
Si·ra·cu·sa \ˌsē-rä-ˈkü-zä\. **1.** Province of Sicily, Italy. See table at ITALY.
2. *or Eng.* **Syr·a·cuse** \ˈsir-ə-ˌkyüs, -ˌkyüz\; *anc.* **Syr·a·cu·sae** \ˌsir-ə-ˈkyü-sē, -zē\. Seaport, ✱ of Siracusa prov., SE Sicily, Italy, on Ionian Sea 130 mi. (209 km.) SE of Palermo; partly on Ortygia I. (separated from mainland by narrow canal); pop. (1989c) 124,606; salt processing, wine making; tourism; cathedral; castle; 14th cent. palaces; fountain (Fonte Aretusa); ruins include 5th cent. B.C. Greek temple and theater, parts of city walls and fortifications, altar of Hiero II (3d cent. B.C.), Roman amphitheater (2d cent. A.D.), and numerous catacombs.
History: Founded 734 B.C. by Corinthian colonists; became largest and most important city in Sicily, extending its influence throughout Sicily and S Italy; seized by tyrant of Gela 485 B.C.; ruled by despotic Hiero I 478–466; democratic government estab. c. 465; Athenians defeated by Syracusans in land and sea engagements 413; under Dionysius the Elder 405–367 and then Dionysius the Younger; under Agathocles the Tyrant 317–289; Carthaginians repulsed by Pyrrhus 278; Hiero II made king 270; fell to Romans 211 B.C. after three years of resistance; conquered by Byzantines 535 A.D. and made ✱ of Sicily; residence 663–668 of Emperor Constans II; conquered by Arabs 878 and later by Normans. Birthplace of Greek poet Theocritus (c. 310 B.C.) and of Greek mathematician Archimedes (c. 287 B.C.). Lost importance in medieval times. In WWII taken by British 1943.
Si·raj·ganj \si-ˈräj-ˌgənj\. Town, Bangladesh, on Jamuna River ab. 68 mi. (109 km.) NW of Dhaka; pop. (1991p) 100,003; river port, trading in jute cloth.
Sir Ed·ward Pel·lew Group \sər-ˈe-dwərd-pəl-ˈyü, -ˈpel-ˌyü\. Island group, Northern Terr., Australia; in SW part of Gulf of Carpentaria.
Si·ret \sē-ˈret\ *also* **Si·re·tul** \ˈsē-re-ˌtu̇l\ *or Ger.* **Se·reth** \ˈzā-ˌret\. River, cen. Europe; rises in the Carpathian Mts. in Ukraine, flows SSE into Romania to Danube River above Galati; ab. 280 mi. (450 km.) long; chief tributary the Bistrița.
Sirguja. See SURGUJA.
Si·rik, Cape \ˈsir-ik\ *or Malay* **Tan·jong Sirik** \ˈtän-ˌjȯŋ\. Cape, SW coast of Sarawak, E Malaysia, on an island in delta of Rajang River, projecting into South China Sea.
Sir–i–pul. See SAR-E POL.
Siris. **1.** City, Greece. See SÉRRAI 2.

2. River, Italy. See SINNI.

Sir·mio·ne \sēr-ˈmyō-nā\; *formerly* **Ser·mio·ne** \ser-\; *anc.* **Sir·mio** \ˈsir-mē-ˌō\. Port and village on **Sirmione Peninsula,** Brescia prov., Lombardy, N Italy, on S shore of Lake Garda.

Sir·mi·um \ˈsər-mē-əm\. Ancient city in Roman prov. of Pannonia; its site is on the Sava River near modern Sremska Mitrovica, Serbia, Yugoslavia.

Sir·mur *or* **Sir·moor** \sir-ˈmu̇r\ *also* **Na·han** \ˈnä-hən\. Former state, N India; 1091 sq. mi. (2826 sq. km.); now part of Himachal Pradesh state; ✱ Nahan.

Şir·nak \shir-ˈnäk\. Province of Turkey in Asia. See table at TURKEY.

Si·ro·hi \si-ˈrō-hē\. **1.** Former state, now part of Rajasthan state, NW India; 1988 sq. mi. (5149 sq. km.); region contains Mt. Abu (*q.v.*); hilly and covered with dense jungle.

2. Town, NW India; 53 mi. (85 km.) NW of Udaipur; pop. (1991p) 28,117; formerly ✱ of Sirohi state.

Síros. See SYROS.

Sir·sa \ˈsir-sə\. Town, W Haryana, NW India, on N edge of Thar Desert; pop. (1991p) 112,542.

Sir Sand·ford, Mount \sər-ˈsand-fərd\. Peak, in Selkirk Mts., SE British Columbia, Canada, ab. 50 mi. (80 km.) N of Revelstoke; 11,555 ft. (3522 m.); highest in range.

Sirt *or* **Sirte.** See SURT.

Sirte, Gulf of. See SIDRA, GULF OF.

Sir Wil·frid Lau·ri·er, Mount \sər-ˈwil-frəd-ˈlȯr-ē-ˌā, -ˈlär-\. Mountain, SE British Columbia, Canada; 10,843 ft. (3305 m.).

Si·sak \ˈsē-ˌsäk\ *or* **Si·sek** \-ˌsek\ *or Ger.* **Sis·sek** \ˈzi-sek\ *or Hung.* **Szi·szek** \ˈsi-sek\; *anc.* **Si·scia** \ˈsi-shē-ə\. Town, Croatia, on the Sava River 30 mi. (48 km.) SE of Zagreb; pop. (1991c) 60,564; ancient town in the Roman prov. of Pannonia; during 3d cent. had imperial mint; site of Turkish defeat by forces of the Holy Roman Empire 1593.

Si·sa·ket \ˌsē-sä-ˈkät\. Town, E Thailand; pop. (1992e) 39,480.

Sisapon. See ALMADÉN.

Sisimiut. See HOLSTEINSBORG.

Sis·ki·you \ˈsis-kē-ˌyü\. County in N California. See table at CALIFORNIA.

Siskiyou Mountains. Range, in SW Oregon and N California; highest 7533 ft. (2296 m.).

Sis·op·hon \ˈsi-sə-ˌpän\. Town, W Cambodia, ab. 40 mi. (64 km.) NNW of Battambang and near Thai border; ceded to French Indochina by Siam (Thailand) 1907.

Sissek. See SISAK.

Sis·se·ton \ˈsi-sə-tən\. City, ⊗ of Roberts co., NE corner of South Dakota, 53 mi. (85 km.) N of Watertown; pop. (1990c) 2181.

Si·stān \sē-ˈstän\ *or* **Sei·stan** \sā-\. Region, E Iran and SW Afghanistan. A depression with much marshland incl. Lake Helmand; corresponds nearly with ancient Drangiana. Under the Ṣafavids (1502–1736) played important part in Persian history; in 19th cent. was center of dispute bet. Persia and Afghanistan.

Sīstān, Daryācheh–ye. See HELMAND 1.

Sīs·tān va Ba·lū·che·stan \sē-ˈstän-ˌvä-bä-ˌlü-chi-ˈstän\ *or* **Balūchestān va Sīstān** \bä-ˌlü-chi-ˈstän-ˌvä-sē-ˈstän\. Province of SE Iran. See table at IRAN.

Sistova. See SVISHTOV.

Si·ta·mau \si-ˈtä-ˌmau̇\. Former state, cen. India; 191 sq. mi. (495 sq. km.); now part of Madhya Pradesh state.

Si·ta·pur \ˈsē-tə-ˌpu̇r\. Town, cen. Uttar Pradesh, N India, 50 mi. (80 km.) NNW of Lucknow; pop. (1991p) 120,595; grain market; manufactures plywood.

Si·tho·nia \si-ˈthō-nyə\ *or Gk.* **Si·tho·niá** \sē-t͟hō-ˈnyä\. Middle peninsula of Chalcidice, Macedonia, NE Greece, bet. Singitic Gulf on E and Gulf of Kassándra on W; ab. 31 mi. (50 km.) long; highest point 2470 ft. (753 m.).

Sit·ka \ˈsit-kə\. **1.** Division in Alaska. See table at ALASKA.

2. City, SE Alaska, on W coast of Baranof I. 932 mi. (1500 km.) N of Seattle, Washington; pop. (1990c) 8588; lumber; fisheries; tourism; Sheldon Jackson Coll. (1878); U.S. Coast Guard air station. Founded as **No·vo·ar·khan·gel'sk** \ˌnȯ-vō-ər-ˈkän-gilsk\ (**New Arch·an·gel** \nü-ˈär-ˌkān-jəl, nyü-\) by Russian fur trader Aleksandr Baranov 1804; became chief town of Russian America; site of formal transfer of Alaska from Russia to U.S. 1867; ✱ of Alaska under U.S. rule until 1900.

Sitka National Historical Park. See UNITED STATES, *National Historical Parks.*

Sitoebondo. See SITUBONDO.

Si·trah \ˈsi-trə\. Small island, Bahrain, Persian Gulf, off NW coast of Bahrain I.

Sit·tang \ˈsi-ˌtäŋ\. River, E cen. Myanmar; flows S into the head of the Gulf of Martaban; 260 mi. (418 km.) long; Toungoo and Pyinmana are on its banks. Scene of severe fighting in WWII.

Sit·tard \ˈsi-ˌtärt\. Commune, Limburg prov., SE Netherlands, 13 mi. (21 km.) NNE of Maastricht on German border; pop. (1992e) 46,314; railroad junction; chemicals, textiles, electronic components; chartered 1243.

Sit·taung \ˈsi-ˌtau̇ŋ\. Town, Sagaing div., W Myanmar, on right bank of Chindwin River near Manipur border.

Sitten. See SION.

Sit·ting·bourne \ˈsi-tiŋ-ˌbōrn\. Town, Kent, SE England, on Milton Creek 39 mi. (63 km.) ESE of London; paper; ships fruit; situated on the old route followed by pilgrims on their way to Canterbury (see WATLING STREET).

Sit·twe \ˈsit-ˌwē\; *formerly* **Ak·yab** \ak-ˈyab\. Port, ✱ of Rakhine state, Myanmar, on Bay of Bengal at mouth of Kaladan River; pop. (1983c) 107,621; rice mills.

Si·tu·bon·do *or Du.* **Si·toe·bon·do** \ˌsē-ˌtü-ˈbȯn-ˌdō\. Town, East Java prov., Indonesia, on railroad line near coast of SE Madura Strait.

Si·u·ri \sē-ˈyu̇r-ē\. Town, West Bengal, India, near Bihar border; pop. (1991p) 54,274.

Si·u·slaw \sī-ˈyü-ˌslȯ\. River, W Oregon; flows W into Pacific Ocean; ab. 60 mi. (96 km.) long; navigable 10 to 30 mi. (16 to 48 km.).

Siut. See ASYŪT.

Si·vas \sē-ˈväs\. **1.** Province of Turkey in Asia. See table at TURKEY.

2. *anc.* **Se·bas·tea** \sə-ˈbas-chē-ə\ *or* **Meg·a·lop·o·lis** \ˌme-gə-ˈlä-pə-lis\. City, its ✱, on right bank of upper Kızıl Irmak 225 mi. (362 km.) E of Ankara; pop. (1990c) 221,512; textiles, cement; notable 13th cent. Seljuq architecture. One of the principal cities of Asia Minor under Roman Emperor Diocletian and Byzantine Empire; came under Muslim rule 1080 and reached height of prosperity under Seljuq Turks late 12th cent.; sacked by Turkic ruler Timur c. 1400; restored under Ottoman rule mid-15th cent. ff.; site 1919 of national congress led by Mustafa Kemal (Atatürk), who later became first president of Turkey.

Si·va·sa·mu·dram \ˌsē-və-sə-ˈmü-drəm\. See CAUVERY.

Si·vash Sea \si-ˈvash\ *or* **Pu·trid Sea** \ˈpyü-trəd\. Area of salt lagoons and marshes, N and NE Crimea, Ukraine; enclosed by the Arabat Penin.; contains mineral salts.

Si·ve·rek \ˌsē-ve-ˈrek\. Town, Urfa prov., SE Turkey in Asia, ab. 50 mi. (80 km.) NE of the city of Urfa.

Si·wa \ˈsē-wə\; *anc.* **Am·mo·ni·um** \ə-ˈmō-nē-əm\. **1.** Oasis, Matrūh governorate, NW Egypt, N of Libyan Desert; ancient seat of oracle and temple of Zeus Ammon.

2. Town, in S part of the oasis; pop. (1986p) 7329.

Si·wa·lik Range *also* **Siwalik Hills** \si-ˈwä-lik\. Range of foothills, N India and Nepal, parallel with the main Himalayan system and extending more than 1000 mi. (1600 km.) SE from N Punjab, Pakistan, into Sikkim; notable for its geological formation, containing extensive paleontological remains.

Si·wan \si-ˈwän, -ˈvän\. Town, NW Bihar, India; pop. (1991p) 81,092.

\ə\ **abut** \ə\ **matches** \$^{ə}$\ **kitten, Fr table** \ər\ **further** \a\ **ash** \ā\ **ace**
\ä\ **cot, cart** \á\ **Fr bac** \au̇\ **out** \b̲\ **Span Avila** \ch\ **chin** \e\ **bet** \ē\ **easy**
\g\ **go** \i\ **hit** \ī\ **ice** \j\ **job** \k̲\ **Ger ich, Buch** \$^{n}$\ **Fr vin**
\ŋ\ **sing** \ō\ **go** \ö\ **all** \ȯ\ **law** \œ\ **Fr bœuf** \œ̄\ **Fr feu** \ȯi\ **boy**
\th\ **thin** \t͟h\ **this** \ü\ **loot** \u̇\ **foot** \ue\ **Ger füllen** \ue̅\ **Fr rue**
\y\ **yet** \$^{y}$\ **Fr digne** \ˈdēn^{y}\, **nuit** \ˈnw^{y}ē\ \yü\ **few** \yu̇\ **fury** \zh\ **vision**

Si·yeh, Mount \ˈsī-yə\. Peak, Glacier National Park, NW Montana; 10,014 ft. (3052 m.).

Sjæl·land \ˈshe-ˌlän\ *or Eng.* **Zea·land** \ˈzē-lənd\ *also* **See·land** \ˈzā-ˌlänt\. **1.** Group of islands, Denmark, in Danish territorial waters; 2901 sq. mi. (7114 sq. km.); pop. (1989e) 2,134,610; includes Sjælland, Møn, Samsø, Amager, Saltholm, and smaller islands.
2. Largest of the islands of Denmark; bounded on the N and NW by the Kattegat, on the W by Store Strait, on the S by narrow channels separating it from smaller islands, and on the E by the Baltic Sea and Øresund; 2709 sq. mi. (7016 sq. km.); pop. (1989e) 1,971,946.

Skadar. See SCUTARI.

Ska·ga Fjord \ˈskä-gə\. Inlet of the Arctic Ocean, N coast of Iceland.

Ska·gen \ˈskä-gən\. **1.** *or* **Skagen, Cape.** Cape, N Jutland, Denmark. See SKAW, THE.
2. Town, Nordjylland co., NE Jutland Penin., Denmark, at the N extremity of Jutland on The Skaw; pop. (1991e) 13,620; artists' colony.

Skagens Odde. See SKAW, THE.

Skag·er·rak *or* **Skag·e·rak** \ˈska-gə-ˌrak\. Broad arm of the E cen. North Sea, extending bet. Norway on the N and Denmark on the S, connecting with the Kattegat on the E; ab. 130 mi. (210 km.) long and more than 70 mi. (110 km.) wide.

Skag·it \ˈska-jət\. **1.** River, W North America; rises in British Columbia, flows S across Washington border and W into Skagit Bay, SW Skagit co.; 163 mi. (262 km.) long.
2. County in NW Washington. See table at WASHINGTON.

Skagit Bay. Inlet, NW Washington, on boundary bet. Skagit and Snohomish cos.

Skag·way \ˈskag-ˌwā\. City, SE Alaska, at head of Lynn Canal 80 mi. (129 km.) N of Juneau; pop. (1990c) 692; tourism; recreational railroad. Founded 1897 and a boom town in the Klondike gold rush 1897–1900 as starting point over Chilkoot and White passes to the Yukon goldfields.

Skag·way–Yak·u·tat–An·goon \ˈskag-ˌwā-ˈya-kə-ˌtat-aŋ-ˈgün\. Division in Alaska. See table at ALASKA.

Ska·ma·nia \skə-ˈmān-yə\. County in S Washington. See table at WASHINGTON.

Skå·ne \ˈskō-nə\ *or* **Sca·nia** \ˈskā-nyə\. Section of S Sweden, land area 4356 sq. mi. (11,282 sq. km.); pop. (1992e) 1,076,031; comprises provs. of Kristianstad and Malmöhus; fought over with Denmark prior to 1658.

Skan·e·at·e·les \ˌska-nē-ˈat-ləs, ˌski-\. Village and resort, Onondaga co., cen. New York, at N end of Skaneateles Lake 8 mi. (13 km.) E of Auburn; pop. (1990c) 2724; center of abolitionist activities before Civil War.

Skaneateles Lake. Lake, chiefly in Onondaga and Cayuga cos., cen. New York; 14 sq. mi. (36 sq. km.); ab. 16 mi. (26 km.) long and 1.5 mi. (2.4 km.) wide; one of the Finger Lakes (*q.v.*); outlet from N end flows into Seneca River.

Ska·ra·borg \ˈskär-ə-ˌbȯr, -ˌbȯr-ē\. Province of S Sweden. See table at SWEDEN.

Skar·du \ˈskär-dü\ *or* **Skar·do** \ˈskär-dō\. Town, S Asia, in region of Jammu and Kashmir under Pakistani control, ab. 95 mi. (155 km.) NNE of Srinagar; on left bank of the Indus above the great gorge, in the Himalayas at elev. of ab. 7500 ft. (2285 m.); chief town of Baltistan; scene of fighting 1948 bet. Indian and Pakistani forces.

Skar·ży·sko–Ka·mien·na \skär-ˈzhis-kō-kä-ˈmye-nä\. Commune, Kielce prov., Poland; pop. (1989e) 50,473.

Skaw, The \ˈskȯ\ *or Dan.* **Ska·gens Od·de** \ˈskä-gəns-ˈȯ-də\ *or* **Ska·gen** *or* **Cape Skagen** \ˈskä-gən\. Cape on N extremity of Jutland, Denmark; extends into the Skagerrak.

Ska·wi·na \skä-ˈvē-nä\. Commune, Kraków prov., S Poland; pop. (1989e) 23,607.

Sked·smo \ˈshedz-ˌmō\. Town, Akershus co., SE Norway; pop. (1990c) 33,679.

Skee·na \ˈskē-nə\. River, W British Columbia, Canada; rises in N cen. part of province, flows S and then W into Hecate Strait; 360 mi. (579 km.) long.

Skeg·ness \ˌskeg-ˈnes\. Town, Lincolnshire, E England, on North Sea 48 mi. (77 km.) SSE of Hull; pop. (1981p) 14,452; seaside resort.

Skei·dar·ar·jö·kull \ˈskā-thär-är-ˌyœ-küt-ᵊl\. Glacier, Iceland; ab. 35 mi. (55 km.) long, ab. 10 mi. (16 km.) wide near its terminus.

Skel·lef·te \she-ˈlef-tə\. River, Västerbotten and Norrbotten provs., N Sweden; flows SE into the Gulf of Bothnia; 255 mi. (410 km.) long.

Skel·lef·teå \she-ˈlef-tā-ˌō\. Coastal town, Västerbotten prov., N Sweden, at the mouth of Skellefte River; pop. (1993e) 75,734.

Skel·ligs \ˈske-ligz\. Three small islands, SW Ireland, off Bolus Head, co. Kerry: Great Skellig, Little Skellig, and Lemon Rock. Great Skellig has two lighthouses and the ruins of a monastery, said to be founded by the 7th cent. bishop St. Finan, once a place of pilgrimage.

Skel·mers·dale \ˈskel-mərz-ˌdāl\. New town, Lancashire, NW England, 13 mi. (21 km.) NE of Liverpool; pop. (1981p) 39,144; electronics; engineering.

Sker·ries \ˈsker-ēz\. Group of islets, S Irish Sea, off NW extremity of the island of Anglesey, Wales; lighthouse.

Sker·row, Loch \ˈsker-ō\. Lake, Dumfries and Galloway region, S Scotland; noted for scenery.

Ski·a·thos \ˈskī-ə-ˌthäs\ *or Gk.* **Skí·a·thos** \ˈskē-ä-ˌthȯs\. Island, Euboea dept., Northern Sporades (see SPORADES), Greece, in Aegean Sea in W end of the island group, nearest the mainland; 16 sq. mi. (41 sq. km.).

Ski·a·took \ˌskī-ˈtük, ˌskī-ə-, -ˈtu̇k\. Town, Tulsa and Osage cos., NE Oklahoma, N of Tulsa; pop. (1990c) 4910.

Skid·daw \ˈski-ˌdȯ\. Mountain, cen. Cumbria, NW England, in the Lake District E of Bassenthwaite Lake; 3053 ft. (930 m.).

Skid·e·gate Inlet \ˈski-di-gət\. Channel, Queen Charlotte Is., off W British Columbia, Canada, separating Graham I. from Moresby I.

Ski·en \ˈshā-ən, ˈshē-\. City, ⊗ of Telemark co., S Norway; pop. (1990c) 47,679; trade center; exports ores, lumber, and paper. Birthplace of playwright Henrik Ibsen 1828.

Ski·ens·elva \ˈshā-ən-ˌsel-və, ˈshē-\. River, S Norway; flows S into Skagerrak; 152 mi. (245 km.) long.

Skier·nie·wi·ce \ˌskyer-nye-ˈvēt-sä\. **1.** Province, cen. Poland. See table at POLAND.
2. Commune, its ✻, 42 mi. (68 km.) SW of Warsaw; pop. (1989e) 44,187; railroad junction point.

Ski·hist Mountain \ˈskē-ˌhist\. Peak, S British Columbia, Canada, W of Fraser River; 9659 ft. (2944 m.).

Skik·da \ˈskēk-də\; *formerly* **Phi·lippe·ville** \ˈfi-ləp-ˌvil, fə-ˈlēp-\. Seaport, NE Algeria; pop. (1987p) 128,747; exports oil, agricultural products; fishing; founded by French 1838.

Skip·ton \ˈskip-tən\. Town, North Yorkshire, N England; pop. (1981p) 13,246.

Skíros. See SKYROS.

Skjál·fan·da \ˈskyau̇l-ˌvän-dä\. River, NE cen. Iceland; flows N into Arctic Ocean W of Húsavík.

Skjeg·ge·dal \ˈshe-gə-ˌdäl\. Waterfall, in a small stream E of Hardanger Fjord, Hordaland co., SW Norway; 525 ft. (160 m.) high.

Skjern \ˈskyern\. River, W cen. Jutland, Denmark; flows W into Ringkøbing Fjord.

Skobelev. See FERGANA 2.

Sko·kie \ˈskō-kē\; *formerly* **Niles Center** \ˈnīlz\. Village, Cook co., NE Illinois, just N of Chicago; pop. (1990c) 59,432.

Sko·ko·mish \skō-ˈkō-mish\. River, W Washington; rises in Mason co., flows SW through Lake Cushman into Hood Canal; ab. 35 mi. (55 km.) long. See CUSHMAN, LAKE.

Sko·mer \ˈskō-mər\. Island, Wales, in St. George's Channel off SW coast, S of entrance to St. Bride's Bay.

Skop·e·los \ˈskä-pə-ˌläs\ *or Gk.* **Skó·pe·los** \ˈskō-pe-ˌlȯs\. **1.** Island, Northern Sporades (see SPORADES), Euboea dept., Greece; 37 sq. mi. (96 sq. km.); 2d largest island in the group.
2. Town on E coast of Skopelos I.

Skop·je \ˈskȯ-pye, -pyā\ *or* **Skop·lje** \ˈskȯp-lye, -lē-,ā\ *or Turk.* **Üs·küb** \ˈɶ-ˌskœb\ *also* **Üs·küp** \-ˌskœp\; *anc.* **Scu·pi** \ˈskyü-ˌpī\. City, ✻ of Republic of Macedonia, on Vardar River 200 mi. (322 km.) SSE of Belgrade; pop. (1991p) 563,301; educational center, road junction; steel, chemicals, beer, tobacco products, cement, glass. Important city in Roman prov. of Moesia Superior; a ✻ of medieval Serbia; under Turkish rule 1392–1913; incorp. in Yugoslavia 1918; occupied by Germans in WWII; made ✻ of Macedonia 1945; greatly destroyed by earthquake 1963; remained ✻ after Macedonia's independence 1992.

Skövde \ˈshœv-də\. Town, Skaraborg prov., S Sweden, bet. Lake Vättern and Lake Vänern; pop. (1993e) 48,460.

Skow·he·gan \skau̇-ˈhē-gən\. Town, ⊗ of Somerset co., W Maine, on Kennebec River; pop. (1990c) 8725.

Skra·din \ˈskrä-dēn\ *or Ital.* **Scar·do·na** \skär-ˈdō-nä\. Port on Krka River, Croatia, 35 mi. (56 km.) NW of Split.

Skra·par \skrä-ˈpär\. District of S cen. Albania. See table at ALBANIA.

Skunk \ˈskəŋk\. River, SE Iowa; rises in Hamilton co., N cen. part of the state, flows SE into the Mississippi below Burlington, in SE part of the state; 264 mi. (425 km.) long.

Skye \ˈskī\. Island of the Inner Hebrides off NW coast of Scotland; 48.5 mi. (78 km.) long, 670 sq. mi. (1735 sq. km.); pop. (1981c) 8139; administratively a part of Highland region; sheep and (West Highland) cattle raising; whisky distilling; noted for wild, mountainous scenery.

Sky·kje \ˈshü-hə, -kə\. Waterfall, Hordaland, SW Norway, near inner Hardanger Fjord; total drop 820 ft. (250 m.).

Sky·ko·mish \skī-ˈkō-mish\. River, NW cen. Washington; rises in Cascade Mts., flows W through S Snohomish co. and joins Snoqualmie River to form the Snohomish River.

Sky·light Mountain \ˈskī-ˌlīt\. Peak in the Adirondack Mts., Essex co., NE New York; 4926 ft. (1501 m.).

Sky·ring Water \ˈskī-ˌriŋ\. Large saltwater lake, Chile, extreme S mainland, NW of Otway Water.

Sky·ros \ˈskī-rəs, -ˌräs\; *Gk.* **Skí·ros** \ˈskē-ˌrȯs\ *also* **Scy·ros** \ˈsī-rəs\. **1.** Island, Northern Sporades (see SPORADES), Euboea dept., Greece, in N cen. Aegean Sea E of Euboea; 81 sq. mi. (210 sq. km.); largest island in the group. In Greek legend, place where the warrior Achilles sought refuge and where Athenian King Theseus was killed. Occupied by Athenians c. 475 B.C. Here the English poet, Rupert Brooke, died and was buried (1915).
2. Town on Skyros I., on NE coast; pop. (1981c) 2757.

Sla. See SALÉ.

Sla·gel·se \ˈslä-g̅əl-sə\. Town, Vestsjælland co., SW Sjælland, Denmark; pop. (1989e) 34,075. Remains of Viking fortress nearby.

Sla·ma·da·tang, Te·luk \te-ˈlu̇k-ˌslä-mä-ˈdä-ˌtäŋ\ *or Eng.* **Wel·come Bay** \ˈwel-kəm\ *or Du.* **Wel·komst Baai** \ˈvel-ˌkȯmst-ˈbī\. Inlet of Sunda Strait, W end of Java, Indonesia.

Sla·met, Gu·nung \ˈgü-ˌnu̇ŋ-ˈslä-ˌmet\. Peak, W cen. Java, Indonesia; 11,247 ft. (3428 m.).

Sla·ney \ˈslā-nē\. River, SE Ireland; rises in co. Wicklow, flows S through co. Wexford into Wexford Harbour; ab. 60 mi. (96 km.) long; navigable as far as Enniscorthy.

Slankamen. See NOVI SLANKAMEN.

Śląsk. See SILESIA.

Śląsk Dolny. See WROCŁAW 1.

Slate Mountain \ˈslāt\. Peak, cen. Coconino co., N cen. Arizona; 8209 ft. (2502 m.).

Sla·ters·ville \ˈslā-tərz-ˌvil\. Village, Providence co., N Rhode Island, ab. 4 mi. (6 km.) W of Woonsocket; seat of government for North Smithfield.

Sla·ti·na \ˈslä-tē-nä\. City, ⊗ of Olt co., S Romania, 30 mi. (48 km.) E of Craiova; pop. (1989c) 86,360; aluminum.

Slat·ing·ton \ˈslā-tiŋ-tən\. Borough, Lehigh co., E Pennsylvania, on Lehigh River 13 mi. (21 km.) NNW of Allentown; pop. (1990c) 4678.

Sla·ton \ˈslāt-ᵊn\. City, Lubbock co., NW Texas, 18 mi. (29 km.) SE of the city of Lubbock; pop. (1990c) 6078.

Slave \ˈslāv\ *also* **Great Slave.** River, W cen. Canada, bet. Lake Athabaska and Great Slave Lake; receives Peace River just below its outlet from Lake Athabaska and enters Great Slave Lake at Fort Resolution; 258 mi. (415 km.) long.

Slave Coast. Coastal region, W Africa, along the Bight of Benin and bet. the Benin and Volta rivers, approx. from 1° to 5°E long.; along coasts of Nigeria, Benin, and Togo; from c. 1500 to late 19th cent. a region of trade in slaves bet. European maritime countries and African rulers.

Slav·go·rod \ˈslȧv-gə-rət\. Agricultural town, W Altay Kray, SW Russia in Asia, on branch railroad line 210 mi. (338 km.) W of Barnaul.

Slav·kov u Brna \ˈsläf-ˌkȯf-ü-ˈbər-nä\; *often shortened to* **Slavkov;** *Ger.* **Aus·ter·litz** \ˈau̇s-tər-ˌlits\. Commune, E Czech Republic, 12 mi. (19 km.) ESE of Brno; has palace and church. Scene of battle 1805 in which French under Napoléon defeated combined forces of Russians and Austrians led by Russian commander Prince Mikhail Kutuzov, thus terminating Third Coalition against France.

Sla·vo·nia \slə-ˈvō-nē-ə, -nyə\ *or Serb.* **Sla·vo·ni·ja** \ˈslä-vȯ-ˌnē-yä\. Historical region, Croatia, bet. the Sava River on the S and the Drava and Danube rivers on N and E; 5152 sq. mi. (13,344 sq. km.); included in kingdom of Croatia formed 10th cent.; subsequent history follows closely that of Croatia (*q.v.*).

Sla·von·ska Po·že·ga \ˈslä-vȯn-skä-ˈpȯ-zhe-gä\ *also* **Požega** *or Hung.* **Po·zse·ga** \ˈpō-zhe-ˌgä\. Town, Croatia, N of the Sava ab. 90 mi. (145 km.) ESE of Zagreb.

Sla·von·ski Brod \ˈslä-vȯn-skē-ˈbrȯt\; *formerly* **Brod.** Town, Croatia, on Sava River 120 mi. (193 km.) WNW of Belgrade, Yugoslavia; pop. (1991c) 58,531.

Sla·vyans'k *or* **Sla·vyansk** *or* **Slo·vyansk** \slȧ-ˈvyȧnsʸk\. Town, N Donets'k subdivision, E Ukraine, on tributary of the Donets 55 mi. (88 km.) N of the city of Donets'k; pop. (1991e) 137,000; health resort; chemicals, pencils; founded 1676.

Slavyansk–na–Ku·ba·ni \-nä-kü-ˈbä-nē\. Town, Krasnodar Kray, S Russia in Europe, ab. 45 mi. (70 km.) NE of the city of Krasnodar; pop. (1991e) 58,500.

Slay·ton \ˈslāt-ᵊn\. City, ⊗ of Murray co., SW Minnesota, 27 mi. (43 km.) NNW of Worthington; pop. (1990c) 2147.

Slea·ford \ˈslē-fərd\. Town, Lincolnshire, E England, on the **Slea River** \ˈslē\ 32 mi. (51 km.) E of Nottingham; pop. (1981p) 8523.

Slea Head \ˈslā\. Cape, SW coast of Ireland, on N side of entrance to Dingle Bay.

Sleat, Point of \ˈslāt\. Cape, S tip of Skye I. in the Inner Hebrides, off NW coast of Scotland.

Sleat, Sound of. Body of water off W coast of Scotland, bet. SE coast of the island of Skye and the Scottish mainland.

Sleep·ing Bear Dunes \ˈslēp-iŋ-ˌber\. Area of sand dunes, W coast of Leelanau co., NW Michigan, along the shores of Lake Michigan.

Sleeping Deer Mountain \ˈdir\. Peak, W cen. Lemhi co., E cen. Idaho; 9885 ft. (3013 m.).

Sleepy Eye \ˈslē-pē-ˌī\. City, Brown co., S Minnesota, 37 mi. (60 km.) WNW of Mankato; pop. (1990c) 3694.

Sleepy Hol·low \ˌslē-pē-ˈhä-lō\. **1.** Valley, near Tarrytown, New York; made famous by author Washington Irving's *Legend of Sleepy Hollow.*
2. *formerly* **North Tarrytown.** Village, Westchester co., SE New York, on Hudson River, adjoining Tarrytown; pop. (1990c) 8152; burial place of author Washington Irving.

Slesvig. See SCHLESWIG.

Slezsko. See SILESIA.

Sli. See SCHLEI.

Sli·dell \slī-ˈdel\. Town, St. Tammany parish, SE Louisiana, 30 mi. (48 km.) NE of New Orleans; pop. (1990c) 24,124; Grantham Coll. of Engineering (1951).

Slide Mountain \ˈslīd\. **1.** Peak in the Sierra Nevada, E Tuolumne co., cen. California; 11,902 ft. (3628 m.).
2. Peak, N Clark co., E Idaho; on the Montana boundary; 10,200 ft. (3109 m.).
3. Highest peak in the Catskill Mts., Ulster co., SE New York; 4204 ft. (1281 m.).

Slie·drecht \ˈslē-ˌdrek̲t\. Commune, South Holland prov., SW Netherlands, on the lower Waal River SE of Rotterdam; pop. (1981e) 22,886.

Slie·ma \ˈslē-mä\. Town, E Malta, across bay NW of Valletta; pop. (1988c) 13,558.

Slieve Bin·gian \slēv-ˈbin-yən\. Mountain in Mourne Mts., SE Northern Ireland; 2449 ft. (746 m.).

Slieve Car \slēv-ˈkär\. Mountain, NW co. Mayo, NW Ireland; 2369 ft. (722 m.).

Slieve Com·me·dagh \slēv-ˈkä-mə-ˌdä\. Mountain in Mourne Mts., SE Down dist., SE Northern Ireland; 2512 ft. (766 m.).

Slieve Don·ard \slēv-ˈdän-ərd\. Highest peak in the Mourne Mts., SE Northern Ireland; 2796 ft. (852 m.).

Slieve Mish \slēv-ˈmish\. Mountain range, cen. co. Kerry, SW Ireland; 14 mi. (23 km.) long; highest peak 2796 ft. (852 m.).

Slieve Mis·kish \slēv-ˈmis-kish\. Mountain range, SW co. Cork, S Ireland, bet. Bantry Bay and Kenmare River; highest peak 2251 ft. (686 m.).

Slieve·more *or* **Slieve More** \slēv-ˈmōr\. Mountain, N coast of Achill I. off W coast of co. Mayo, W Ireland; 2204 ft. (672 m.).

Slieve·na·man *or* **Slieve–na–Man** \ˌslēv-nə-ˈmän\. Mountain, SE co. Tipperary, S Ireland, NE of Clonmel; 2364 ft. (720 m.).

Slieve Snaght \slēv-ˈsnäk̲t\. Mountain, co. Donegal, N Ireland (republic); 2014 ft. (614 m.).

Sli·go \ˈslī-gō\. **1.** County, Connacht prov., N Ireland (republic); ⊗ Sligo; livestock raising, dairy farming, fishing. See table at IRELAND.
2. Town and seaport, ⊗ of co. Sligo, N Ireland (republic), on **Sligo Bay** (inlet of Atlantic Ocean); pop. (1991p) 17,297. Ruins of 13th cent. Dominican abbey and 13th cent. castle. Nearby are megalithic remains and a cairn honoring Queen Maeve of Connacht.

Slip·pery Rock \ˈsli-pə-rē-ˈräk\. Borough, Butler co., W Pennsylvania, 17 mi. (27 km.) ENE of New Castle; pop. (1990c) 3008; Slippery Rock Univ. of Pennsylvania (1889).

Sli·ven \ˈslē-ven\ *or* **Sliv·no** \ˈslēv-nō\. City, E cen. Bulgaria, 60 mi. (96 km.) W of Burgas; pop. (1991e) 112,220; textiles; woodworking. Under Turkish rule 15th–19th cents.

Sliv·ni·tsa *or* **Sliv·ni·tza** *also* **Sliv·ni·ca** \ˈslēv-nēt-ˌsä\. Commune, Sofia prov., W Bulgaria, 19 mi. (31 km.) NW of city of Sofia; scene of battle 1885 in which the Bulgarians defeated the Serbs.

Sloan \ˈslōn\. Village, Erie co., W New York, adjoining Buffalo; pop. (1990c) 3830.

Sloan Peak. Mountain, Snohomish co., NW cen. Washington; 7835 ft. (2388 m.).

Sloats·burg \ˈslōts-ˌbərg\. Village, Rockland co., SE New York, near New Jersey state line 31 mi. (50 km.) NNW of New York City; pop. (1990c) 3035.

Slo·bo·zia \slō-ˈbȯ-zyə\. Town, ⊗ of Ialomiţa co., SE Romania, ab. 65 mi. (105 km.) ENE of Bucharest; pop. (1989c) 50,995.

Sloch·te·ren \ˈslȯk̲-tə-rə\. Commune, Groningen prov., NE Netherlands, 8 mi. (13 km.) E of city of Groningen; pop. (1981e) 14,004.

Slo·nim \ˈslȯ-nyim\ *or Pol.* **Sło·nim** \ˈswȯ-nēm\. Town, Hrodna subdivision, W Belarus, on Shchara River 43 mi. (69 km.) SSW of Novogrudok; pop. (1991e) 47,200; passed to Russia in Third Partition of Poland 1795; belonged to Poland 1921–45.

Slope \ˈslōp\. County in SW North Dakota. See table at NORTH DAKOTA.

Slot, The \ˈslät\ *or* **New Geor·gia Sound** \ˈjȯr-jə\. Long open-water passage, cen. Solomon Is., W Pacific Ocean, running NW to SE ab. 300 mi. (485 km.) from the Shortland Is. to Florida I. and Savo I. Named The Slot in WWII by Americans because it was the regular course followed by Japanese planes and vessels in their attempts to save Guadalcanal Aug. 1942–Jan. 1943.

Slough \ˈslau̇\. Town, Berkshire, SE cen. England, 20 mi. (32 km.) W of London; pop. (1991p) 98,600; paint, plastics, pharmaceuticals, electronic equipment, aircraft parts, automobile parts.

Slo·va·kia \slō-ˈvä-kē-ə, -ˈva-\ *or officially* **Slo·ven·ská Re·pu·bli·ka** \ˈslȯ-ven-ˌskä-rä-ˈpü-blē-ˌkä\ (**Slo·vak Republic** \ˈslō-ˌväk, -ˌvak\). Country, cen. Europe, bounded on W by Austria and Czech Republic, on N by Poland, on E by

Ukraine, and on S by Hungary; 18,923 sq. mi. (49,011 sq. km.); pop. (1993e) 5,329,000; ✱ Bratislava; rivers Váh and Hron; potatoes, sugar beets; livestock raising; iron ore; chief towns Bratislava and Košice.

History: Settled c. 6th cent. A.D. by Slovaks, a Slavic people; part of kingdom of Moravia in 9th cent.; conquered by Magyars c. 907, it remained in kingdom of Hungary (*q.v.*) until 1918; policy of enforced Magyarization from 1867 served to underline Slovak nationalism; Slovak National Council joined Czechs in forming Czechoslovakia (*q.v.*) 1918; Slovakian autonomy within a reorganized Czecho-Slovakia granted as a result of Munich Agreement 1938; Slovakia under leadership of President Josef Tiso became nominally independent under German protection 1939–45; Germans driven out by Allied forces 1945 and Slovakia joined reconstituted Czechoslovakia, maintaining theoretical equality with Czech lands; in 1969 a new equal partnership bet. Czechs and Slovaks established and **Slovak Socialist Republic** formed. Fall of Communist regime 1989 led to revival of interest in complete autonomy and on Jan. 1, 1993 independent country of Slovakia was created.

Slo·ve·nia \slō-ˈvē-nē-ə, -nyə\ *or Serb.* **Slo·ve·ni·ja** \slȯ-ˈvā-nē-yä\. Country, S Europe, bounded on E by Hungary and Croatia, on S by Croatia, on W by Italy, and on N by Austria; 7819 sq. mi. (20,251 sq. km.); pop. (1993e) 1,997,000; ✱ Ljubljana; textiles, steel; chief towns Ljubljana and Maribor.

History: Region settled by Slovenes in 6th cent. A.D.; came under Frankish empire of Charlemagne 8th cent., then under Germany as part of Holy Roman Empire; from late 13th cent. most of territory inhabited by Slovenes belonged to Austria except for period 1809–13 when it was part of Slavic Illyrian Provinces (*q.v.*) erected by French Emperor Napoléon; joined other S Slavs in proclaiming Kingdom of Serbs, Croats, and Slovenes 1918 (see YUGOSLAVIA); made a constituent republic of Yugoslavia in 1946 constitution; received section of former Italian Adriatic coastline 1947. Declared independence from Yugoslavia June 1991; independence internationally recognized 1992.

Slovyansk. See SLAVYANS'K.

Sło·wiń·ski National Park \swō-ˈvin-skē\. National park, Poland; 69 sq. mi. (179 sq. km.); migratory birds, dunes; estab. 1966.

Sloy, Loch \ˈslȯi\. Small lake, Strathclyde region, W Scotland, at NW end of Loch Lomond; ab. 1 mi. (1.6 km.) long; its outlet flows SE to Loch Lomond; site of huge hydroelectric project 1950.

Słu·bi·ce \swü-ˈbēt-sä\. City, SW Gorzów prov., W Poland, on E bank of the Oder River opp. Frankfurt an der Oder, Germany; pop. (1981p) 15,096; before boundary revisions of 1945 part of Frankfurt.

Sluis *or* **Sluys** \ˈslȯis\ *or Fr.* **Écluse** \ā-ˈklüez\. Commune, Zeeland prov., SW Netherlands; pop. (1981e) 3038; on the Belgian border and connected with sea by a canal; scene of naval battle 1340 in which Edward III of England almost completely destroyed the French fleet.

Sluis·kin \ˈslü-skən\. Waterfall, S side of Mt. Rainier, Pierce co., W cen. Washington; 300 ft. (91 m.) high.

Słu·pia \ˈswü-pē-ä\ *or Ger.* **Stol·pe** \ˈshtȯl-pə\. River, N Poland; flows NW into the Baltic Sea; 112 mi. (180 km.) long.

Słupsk \ˈswüpsk\ *or Ger.* **Stolp** \ˈshtȯlp\. **1.** Province, N Poland. See table at POLAND.

2. City, its ✱, 39 mi. (63 km.) ENE of Koszalin; pop. (1989e) 99,543. First mentioned 13th cent.; became city 1310; member of Hanseatic League; belonged to dukes of Pomerania until 1648, when it passed to Brandenburg; assigned to Poland by Potsdam Conference 1945.

Slutsk \ˈslütsk\. **1.** Town, Minsk subdivision, S cen. Belarus, 60 mi. (96 km.) S of the city of Minsk; pop. (1991e) 60,100; passed to Russia in Second Partition of Poland 1793.

2. Town, St. Petersburg Oblast, W Russia in Europe. See PAVLOVSK.

Sluys. See SLUIS.

Slyne Head \ˈslīn\. Cape, W co. Galway, W coast of Ireland, projecting into Atlantic Ocean; lighthouse.

Smaalenenes. See *Østfold* in table at NORWAY.

Små·land Highlands \ˈsmō-ˌländ\. Plateau region, S Sweden, S of Lake Vättern.

Smalcald *or* **Smalkald.** See SCHMALKALDEN.

Smal·ling·er·land \ˈsmä-liŋ-ər-ˌlänt\. Commune, Friesland prov., N Netherlands, on canal 12 mi. (19 km.) NE of Heerenveen; pop. (1992e) 50,289.

Small·wood Reservoir \ˈsmȯl-ˌwu̇d\; *formerly* **Mich·i·ka·mau Lake** \ˈmi-shi-kə-ˌmȯ\. Lake, W Labrador, Canada, largely in Newfoundland; 556 sq. mi. (1440 sq. km.).

Sme·de·re·vo \ˈsme-de-re-ˌvȯ\ *or Ger.* **Se·men·dria** \zā-ˈmen-drē-ə\. Town, Serbia, Yugoslavia, 25 mi. (40 km.) ESE of Belgrade on Danube River; trade center; 15th cent. fortress; ✱ of Serbia 1430–39 and 1444–59.

Sme·la \ˈsmye-lə\ *or* **Smi·la** \ˈsmyē-lə\. Town, Cherkassy subdivision, N cen. Ukraine, ab. 16 mi. (26 km.) SW of the city of Cherkassy.

Smeth·port \ˈsmeth-ˌpōrt\. Borough, ⊗ of McKean co., N Pennsylvania, 15 mi. (24 km.) SE of Bradford; pop. (1990c) 1734.

Smila. See SMELA.

Smi·ley Mountain \ˈsmī-lē\. Peak, S Custer co., cen. Idaho; 11,506 ft. (3507 m.).

Smith \ˈsmith\. Name of counties in four states of the U.S. See tables at KANSAS, MISSISSIPPI, TENNESSEE, TEXAS.

Smith Center. City, ⊗ of Smith co., N Kansas, 65 mi. (105 km.) WNW of Concordia; pop. (1990c) 2016.

Smith·ers \ˈsmi-thərz\. Village, British Columbia, Canada, 125 mi. (201 km.) ENE of Prince Rupert; pop. (1991c) 5029.

Smith·field \ˈsmith-ˌfēld\. **1.** Town, ⊗ of Johnston co., E North Carolina, 26 mi. (42 km.) SE of Raleigh; pop. (1990c) 7540.

2. Town, Providence co., N Rhode Island, 10 mi. (16 km.) NW of the city of Providence; pop. (1990c) 19,163; incorp. 1731;

\ə\ abut \ə\ matches \ᵊ\ kitten, Fr table \ər\ further \a\ ash \ā\ ace \ä\ cot, cart \á\ Fr bac \au̇\ out \b\ Span Avila \ch\ chin \e\ bet \ē\ easy \g\ go \i\ hit \ī\ ice \j\ job \k\ Ger ich, Buch \ⁿ\ Fr vin \ŋ\ sing \ō\ go \ȯ\ all \ȯ\ law \œ\ Fr bœuf \œ\ Fr feu \ȯi\ boy \th\ thin \th\ this \ü\ loot \u̇\ foot \ue\ Ger füllen \ue\ Fr rue \y\ yet \ʸ\ Fr digne \ˈdēnʸ\, nuit \ˈnwʸē\ \yü\ few \yu̇\ fury \zh\ vision

Bryant Coll. (1863).
3. City, Cache co., N Utah, 8 mi. (13 km.) N of Logan; pop. (1990c) 5566.
4. Town, Isle of Wight co., SE Virginia, on James River 13 mi. (21 km.) W of Newport News; pop. (1990c) 4686.
5. *or* **West Smithfield.** Site in London, England; formerly the location of tournaments, a trading center and place of executions; scene c. 1133–1840 of Bartholomew Fair, a great annual fair beginning on St. Bartholomew's Day; now location of a meat market.

Smith Island. **1.** Group of close islands, Lower Chesapeake Bay, SW Somerset co., SE Maryland, its S tip extending into Virginia; has ferry connections to both states.
2. Island in Atlantic Ocean at SE extremity of North Carolina; Cape Fear constitutes its S tip.
3. Island in Atlantic Ocean, S extremity of Northampton co., Virginia.

Smith·land \ˈsmith-lənd\. City, ⊗ of Livingston co., W Kentucky; pop. (1990c) 384.

Smith Peak. Mountain in Yosemite National Park, E Tuolumne co., cen. California; 7751 ft. (2362 m.).

Smiths Falls \ˈsmiths\. Town, Lanark co., SE Ontario, Canada, on Rideau River 41 mi. (66 km.) SSW of Ottawa; pop. (1991c) 9396.

Smith Sound. Channel, separating NW Greenland from coast of SE Ellesmere I.; ab. 50 mi. (80 km.) long by 35 mi. (56 km.) wide; connects Kane Basin with Baffin Bay.

Smith·ville \ˈsmith-ˌvil\. **1.** Town, ⊗ of De Kalb co., cen. Tennessee; pop. (1990c) 3791.
2. City, Bastrop co., S cen. Texas, on Colorado River 38 mi. (61 km.) ESE of Austin; pop. (1990c) 3196.

Smokies *or* **Smokies, Great.** See GREAT SMOKY MOUNTAINS.

Smoky \ˈsmō-kē\. River, W Alberta, Canada; rises in Rocky Mts. near British Columbia border and flows N into Peace River at the town of Peace River; 245 mi. (394 km.) long.

Smoky Cape. Cape, N New South Wales coast, SE Australia, 165 mi. (265 km.) NE of Newcastle.

Smoky Hill. River, cen. Kansas; rises in Cheyenne co., E Colorado, flows E through cen. Kansas to unite with the Republican River at Junction City in Geary co. and form the Kansas River; 540 mi. (869 km.) long.

Smoky Mountains. See GREAT SMOKY MOUNTAINS.

Smø·la \ˈsmœ-lə\. Island, Norway, in Norwegian Sea off W coast, WSW of Hitra I.

Smo·lensk \smō-ˈlensk, smə-ˈlyensk\. **1.** Medieval principality in W Russia in Europe S of Novgorod and W of Rostov-Suzdal'; ✻ Smolensk; created after breakup of Kievan state in 11th cent.; conquered by Mongols c. 1240; overcome c. 1400 by Lithuania.
2. City, ✻ of Smolensk Oblast, W Russia in Europe, on left bank of upper Dnieper River; pop. (1992e) 352,000; railroad junction and commercial center; cultural center with a cathedral, libraries and museums, and several educational institutions.
History: Important town in pre-Kievan Russia by 9th cent.; became major commercial center on trade route from Baltic Sea to Constantinople; ✻ of Smolensk principality; sacked by Mongols c. 1240; fell to Lithuania c. 1400; captured by Vasily III, grand prince of Moscow 1514; won by Poland 1611; returned to Russia by Treaty of Andrusovo 1667; burned during French invasion of Russia 1812; in WWII occupied by Germans 1941–43 and scene of heavy fighting.

Smolensk Oblast \ˈō-bləst, -ˌblast\ *or* **Smo·len·ska·ya Oblast'** \smə-ˈlyen-skə-yə-ˈō-bləstʸ\. Subdivision of W Russia in Europe; 19,228 sq. mi. (49,800 sq. km.); pop. (1992e) 1,163,000; ✻ Smolensk; occupies part of W plateau of Russia, containing source of the Dnieper River and of several headstreams of the Volga and Western Dvina; forest regions greatly reduced. Economy is largely agricultural: flax, potatoes; dairy farming; peat. Smolensk is by far the oblast's largest urban center. Territory contested 15th–17th cents. by Poland and Russia and ceded to Russia 1667.

Smo·lyan \smōl-ˈyän\. Town, S Bulgaria, ab. 40 mi. (64 km.) S of Plovdiv in Rhodope Mts. near Greek border; pop. (1988e) 51,172.

Smooth·face Mountain \ˈsmüt͟h-ˌfās\. Mountain, Yellowstone National Park, NW Wyoming; has two peaks, S 10,417 ft. (3175 m.) and N 10,500 ft. (3200 m.).

Smrčiny. See FICHTELGEBIRGE.

Smyr·na \ˈsmər-nə, ˈsmir-\. **1.** Short river, N cen. Delaware; forms section of boundary bet. New Castle and Kent cos.; empties into Delaware River.
2. Town, Kent co., cen. Delaware, 10 mi. (16 km.) N of Dover; pop. (1990c) 5231; state prison.
3. City, Cobb co., NW Georgia, 9 mi. (14 km.) NW of Atlanta; pop. (1990c) 30,981; residential suburb of Atlanta.
4. Town, Rutherford co., cen. Tennessee, 11 mi. (18 km.) NW of Murfreesboro; pop. (1990c) 13,647.
5. Province and seaport city, Turkey. See İZMİR.

Smyrna, Gulf of *and* **Smyrnaeus, Sinus.** See İZMİR, GULF OF.

Smyth \ˈsmīth\. County in SW Virginia. See table at VIRGINIA.

Snae·fell \ˈsnā-ˌfel\. Highest peak on the Isle of Man, off NW coast of England, in the Irish Sea; 2034 ft. (620 m.).

Snæ·fell \ˈsnī-ˌfel\. Mountain, W Iceland, NW of Reykjavík on peninsula on N side of Faxa Bay; 4744 ft. (1446 m.); contains the glacier **Snae·fells·jö·kull** \-ˌfels-ˌyœ-ˌkœd-ᵊl\.

Snaght, Slieve. See SLIEVE SNAGHT.

Snake \ˈsnāk\. **1.** River, NW United States; rises in Yellowstone National Park, NW Wyoming, flows S, then SW, W, and N across Idaho in a big arc; turns N and forms parts of Idaho-Oregon and Idaho-Washington boundaries; turns W at Lewiston, cuts across SE Washington and empties into the Columbia River in S Franklin co., SE Washington; 1038 mi. (1670 km.) long; on the Idaho-Oregon boundary has created a canyon more than 40 mi. (64 km.) long and more than 7000 ft. (2130 m.) deep at one point; has numerous notable springs; in section in S Idaho N of Twin Falls has several cascades, incl. Shoshone Falls (*q.v.*) and is used to irrigate the desert region to the S.
2. River, Minnesota; rises in S Aitkin co. E of Mille Lacs, flows S and E into St. Croix River in Pine co.; 135 mi. (217 km.) long.

Snake Creek. **1.** Creek, N Nebraska; rises in Sheridan co., flows E into Niobrara River in Cherry co.; 80 mi. (129 km.) long.
2. River, NE cen. South Dakota; rises in W Faulk co., flows E into James River in W Spink co.; ab. 60 mi. (100 km.) long.

Snake Mountain. Peak, Rabun co., NE Georgia; 3365 ft. (1026 m.).

Snake Range. Mountain range, E White Pine co., E Nevada; highest point Wheeler Peak 13,065 ft. (3982 m.); Great Basin National Park is in it.

Snares Islands \ˈsnarz\ *or* **The Snares.** Group of uninhabited islets, New Zealand, in S Pacific Ocean at 48°00′S, 166°30′E, SW of South I.; 15 sq. mi. (39 sq. km.).

Sneed·ville \ˈsnēd-ˌvil, -vəl\. Town, ⊗ of Hancock co., NE Tennessee; pop. (1990c) 1446.

Sneek \ˈsnāk\. Commune, Friesland prov., N Netherlands, 14 mi. (23 km.) SSW of Leeuwarden; pop. (1992e) 29,221; transportation center (canal and railroad) and market town.

Sneeu·berg \ˈsnā-ˌbərg\ *or* **Sneeuw·berg** \ˈsnā-u̇-ˌbərg\. Mountain range and peak, S cen. Rep. of South Africa; 8215 ft. (2504 m.).

Sneeuw Gebergte. See MAOKE MOUNTAINS.

Snef·fels, Mount \ˈsne-fəlz\. Peak in the San Juan Mts., Ouray co., SW Colorado; 14,150 ft. (4313 m.).

Snell·ville \ˈsnel-ˌvil\. City, Gwinnett co., N Georgia, ENE of Atlanta; pop. (1990c) 12,084; pop. quadrupled in 1960s and again in 1970s.

Snezh·no·ye \ˈsnyezh-nə-yə\. Town, Donets'k subdivision, Ukraine, ab. 45 mi. (72 km.) E of the city of Donets'k; pop. (1991e) 69,000.

Sněž·ka \ˈsnyesh-kə\ *or Ger.* **Schnee·kop·pe** \ˈshnā-ˌkȯ-pə\. Peak in Riesengebirge, on boundary bet. Czech Republic and Poland; 5256 ft. (1602 m.); highest peak in Riesengebirge.

Śniar·dwy \ˈshnyärd-vi\ *or Ger.* **Spir·ding** \ˈshpir-diŋ\. Lake, SW Suwałki prov., N Poland; 10 mi. (16 km.) long, 41 sq. mi. (106 sq. km.); max. depth 82 ft. (25 m.); largest lake in Poland; connected by canals with Lake Mamry and other smaller lakes. Formerly in Germany; to Poland after WWII.

Sni·zort, Loch \ˈsnē-ˌzȯrt\. Inlet of the Little Minch, N Skye I. in the Inner Hebrides, NW of Scotland.

Snø·het·ta \ˈsnœ̄-ˌhe-tə\. Snowcapped peak in cen. Norway, in the Dovrefjell Plateau; 7500 ft. (2286 m.).

Sno·ho·mish \snō-ˈhō-mish\. **1.** River, NW cen. Washington; formed by junction of Skykomish and Snoqualmie rivers in SW Snohomish co., flows NW into Puget Sound; 65 mi. (105 km.) long.
2. County in NW cen. Washington. See table at WASHINGTON.
3. City, Snohomish co., NW cen. Washington, 8 mi. (13 km.) SE of Everett; pop. (1990c) 6499.

Sno·qual·mie \snō-ˈkwäl-mē\. River, W cen. Washington; flows W and N in King co., crosses into Snohomish co. and joins Skykomish River to form Snohomish River; ab. 70 mi. (115 km.) long.

Snoqualmie Falls. Waterfall, Snoqualmie River, King co., W cen. Washington; ab. 270 ft. (80 m.).

Snow·don \ˈsnōd-ᵊn\ *or Welsh* **Yr Wydd·fa** \ˈər-ˈwid-fə\. Massif in Gwynedd co., NW Wales; has five peaks, the highest 3560 ft. (1085 m.) being the highest mountain in Wales; region often called **Snow·do·nia** \snō-ˈdō-nē-ə, -nyə\ and included in **Snowdonia National Park**.

Snow·flake \ˈsnō-ˌflāk\. Town, Navajo co., E Arizona; pop. (1990c) 3679.

Snow Hill \ˈsnō\. **1.** Town, ⊗ of Worcester co., SE Maryland, 18 mi. (29 km.) SSE of Salisbury; pop. (1990c) 2217.
2. Town, ⊗ of Greene co., E North Carolina; pop. (1990c) 1378.

Snow·mass Mountain \ˈsnō-ˌmas\. Peak, Pitkin and Gunnison cos., W cen. Colorado; 14,092 ft. (4295 m.).

Snow Mountains. See MAOKE MOUNTAINS.

Snow Peak. Mountain in the Sierra Nevada, in E Tuolumne co., cen. California; 10,933 ft. (3332 m.).

Snow·slip Mountain \ˈsnō-ˌslip\. Peak, Glacier National Park, NW Montana; 7290 ft. (2222 m.).

Snow Water Lake. Intermittent lake, E cen. Elko co., NE Nevada.

Snowy \ˈsnō-ē\. River, SE New South Wales and E Victoria, SE Australia; flows S from Australian Alps through **Snowy River National Park** and Gippsland to South Pacific Ocean; 278 mi. (447 km.) long; hydroelectric power project.

Snowy Mountain. Peak in the Adirondack Mts., Hamilton co., NE cen. New York; ab. 3900 ft. (1190 m.).

Snowy Mountains. Range of the Australian Alps (*q.v.*), E Victoria and SE New South Wales, Australia; site of recreational activities.

Sny·der \ˈsnī-dər\. **1.** County in cen. Pennsylvania. See table at PENNSYLVANIA.
2. City, ⊗ of Scurry co., NW cen. Texas, 33 mi. (53 km.) NW of Sweetwater; pop. (1990c) 12,195.

So·an \ˌsō-ˈän\ *or* **So·han** \ˌsō-ˈhän\. River, Punjab, Pakistan; flows from the Himalayas SW into the Indus River; ab. 130 mi. (210 km.) long.

Soap Lake \ˈsōp\. City, Grant co., cen. Washington, at S end of the Grand Coulee; pop. (1990c) 1149; on **Soap Lake,** containing minerals and salts.

Soar \ˈsōr\. River, Leicestershire, cen. England; flows N into the Trent 12 mi. (19 km.) ESE of Derby; 40 mi. (64 km.) long.

Soa Salt Pan. See MAKGADIKGADI PANS.

So·bat \ˈsō-ˌbat\. River, E cen. Africa; formed by confluence of Pibor and Baro rivers on extreme W border of Ethiopia; flows W into the White Nile River SW of Malakal, Sudan; length from source of the Baro 460 mi. (740 km.).

So·bo \ˈsō-bō\ *or* **So·bo·zan** \-ˈzän\. Peak, E cen. Kyūshū, Japan, E of Mt. Aso; 5766 ft. (1757 m.).

So·bral \sü-ˈbräl\. City, NW Ceará state, NE Brazil, 125 mi. (201 km.) W of Fortaleza; munic. pop. (1991p) 127,449.

So·braon \sō-ˈbrau̇n\. Village, Punjab, NW India, on right bank of the Sutlej; on opp. bank is site of 1846 battle in which British under Sir Hugh Gough were victors over the Sikhs, ending First Sikh War.

Soča. See ISONZO.

So·cha·czew \sȯ-ˈkä-ˌchef\. Commune, N Skierniewice prov., cen. Poland, 32 mi. (51 km.) W of Warsaw; pop. (1981p) 32,748.

So–ch'e. See SHACHE.

So·chi \ˈsō-chē\. Seaport town, S Krasnodar Kray, S Russia in Europe, on Black Sea near Republic of Georgia border 110 mi. (177 km.) SSE of the city of Krasnodar; pop. (1992e) 344,000; popular health resort with beaches, thermal and mineral springs; many sanatoriums.

So·cial Circle \ˈsō-shəl\. City, Walton co., N cen. Georgia, 38 mi. (61 km.) ESE of Atlanta; pop. (1990c) 2755.

Socialist People's Libyan Arab Jamahiriya. See LIBYA 2.

So·ci·ety Islands \sə-ˈsī-ə-tē\ *or Fr.* **Ar·chi·pel de la So·cié·té** \ˌär-kē-ˈpel-də-lä-ˌsȯ-syā-ˈtā\. Island group in W part of French Polynesia, S Pacific Ocean; 621 sq. mi. (1608 sq. km.); pop. (1988c) 162,573; ✻ Papeete. Comprises two groups: Windward Is. (Tahiti, Mooréa, and several islets); and the Leeward Is. (*q.v.*); chief island Tahiti. Volcanic in origin and mountainous; produces copra, pearls.

History: Claimed for Great Britain 1767 by Capt. Samuel Wallis; claimed for France 1768 by navigator Louis-Antoine de Bougainville but claim not immediately sustained; visited 1768 by mariner Capt. James Cook with a British Royal Society expedition (hence the name); made French protectorate 1843.

So·com·pa \sō-ˈkȯm-pä\. Volcanic peak, E Antofagasta region, N Chile, near Argentine border; 19,786 ft. (6031 m.).

So·cor·ro \sə-ˈkȯr-ō\. **1.** County in cen. New Mexico. See table at NEW MEXICO.
2. City, ⊗ of Socorro co., cen. New Mexico, on the Rio Grande 70 mi. (113 km.) S of Albuquerque; pop. (1990c) 8159; market for large area; New Mexico Institute of Mining and Technology (1889).
3. Town, El Paso co., W Texas, just SE of the city of El Paso; pop. (1990c) 22,995.
4. Island off coast of Chile. See GUAMBLIN.
5. Island, Revillagigedo group (*q.v.*), Pacific Ocean off cen. Mexico.

So·co·tra *or* **So·ko·tra** \sə-ˈkō-trə\ *or Arab.* **Su·qu·trā** \su̇-ˈkü-ˌträ\. Island, Yemen, in Indian Ocean, S of Arabian Penin., ab. 160 mi. (255 km.) ENE of Raas Caseyr, Somalia, E Africa; ab. 1200 sq. mi. (3110 sq. km.), 70 mi. (113 km.) long; ✻ Tamridah; mountainous interior, highest peak 4686 ft. (1428 m.); produces fish, ghee.

History: Known to the ancients; except for brief Portuguese occupation early 1500s was a possession of sultans of Mahra; came under British protection 1886; became part of People's Democratic Republic of Yemen 1967.

So·da Lake \ˈsō-də\. Large dry sink, at times a lake, in Mojave Desert, NE cen. San Bernardino co., California.

So·dan·ky·lä \ˈsȯ-dän-ˌkue̅-la\. Town, Lappi prov., N Finland, on tributary of Kemi River 55 mi. (88 km.) NNW of Kemijärvi; pop. (1980c) 10,103.

Soda Springs. City, ⊗ of Caribou co., SE Idaho, 45 mi. (72 km.) ESE of Pocatello; pop. (1990c) 3111.

Sod·dy–Dai·sy \ˌsä-dē-ˈdā-zē\. City, Hamilton co., SE Tennessee, 16 mi. (26 km.) NE of Chattanooga; pop. (1990c) 8240.

Sö·der·hamn \ˌsœ̄-dər-ˈhäm-ᵊn\. Seaport, Gävleborg prov., E Sweden, on an inlet of the Gulf of Bothnia; pop. (1989c) 29,538.

Sö·der·man·land \ˈsœ̄-dər-män-ˌländ\. Province of SE Sweden. See table at SWEDEN.

Sö·der·täl·je \ˌsœ̄-dər-ˈtel-yə\. Town, Stockholm prov., SE Sweden, a suburb of the city of Stockholm; pop. (1989c) 81,460; 12th cent. church.

Sod·om \ˈsä-dəm\. City in the plain of the Jordan, ancient Palestine; in the Old Testament notorious for its wickedness; destroyed, together with Gomorrah (*Gen.* x. 19; xviii. 20; xix. 24–28); sites of both cities unknown, possibly now beneath waters of Dead Sea.

So·dus \ˈsō-dəs\. Town, N Wayne co., W New York, on Lake Ontario ab. 25 mi. (40 km.) E of Rochester; pop. (1990c) 8877; includes the village of **Sodus Point** (pop. [1990c] 1190) on **Sodus Bay,** inlet of Lake Ontario.

Soebang. See SUBANG.

Soekaboemi. See SUKABUMI.

Soela Islands. See SULA ISLANDS.

Soemba. See SUMBA.

Soembawa. See SUMBAWA.

Soembing. See SUMBING.

Soenda Deep. See SUNDA DEEP.

Soenda Isles. See SUNDA ISLES.

Soenda Strait. See SUNDA STRAIT.

Soepiori. See SUPIORI.

Soerabaja. **1.** Former residency, Indonesia. See SURABAJA 1.

2. Seaport city, Indonesia. See SURABAYA.

Soerabaja Strait. See SURABAYA STRAIT.

Soerakarta. See SURAKARTA.

Soest **1.** \ˈsüst\. Commune, Utrecht prov., cen. Netherlands, 11 mi. (18 km.) NE of the city of Utrecht; pop. (1992e) 41,639; residential; founded 1029.

2. \ˈzōst\. City, North Rhine-Westphalia, Germany, 33 mi. (53 km.) N of Münster; pop. (1992e) 43,063; market town; 12th cent. cathedral; early 18th cent. town hall; first mentioned 836; chartered 12th cent.; important Hanseatic town.

So·fa·la \sō-ˈfä-lä\. **1.** Province of SE Mozambique. See table at MOZAMBIQUE.

2. Seaport village, Mozambique. See NOVA SOFALA.

So·feg·gin \sō-ˈfe-jin\ *or* **Saw·faj·jīn** \sȯ-ˈfa-ˌjēn\. Short river, N Libya, flows NE into W Gulf of Sidra, but dry at certain seasons.

So·fia *also* **So·phia** \ˈsō-fē-ə, ˈsȯ-, sō-ˈ\ *or Bulg.* **So·fi·ya** \ˈsȯ-fē-yä\. **1.** Region of W Bulgaria. See table at BULGARIA.

2. City, ✻ of Bulgaria, also ✻ of Sofia region; constitutes a separate administrative unit; pop. (1991e) 1,141,142; principal transportation center of Bulgaria; metallurgical, engineering, chemical, textile, and food-processing industries; cultural center of Bulgaria, with opera house, museums, 6th cent. church of St. Sofia, 19th cent. cathedral, university (estab. 1888, received university status 1904).

History: Originated as Thracian settlement c. 7th cent. B.C.; became important under Romans as **Ser·di·ca** \ˈsər-di-kə\; destroyed by Huns 447; rebuilt under Byzantine Empire; estab. as Bulgarian town 809 but again part of Byzantine Empire 1018–1185; ruled by Ottoman Turks 1382–1878; made ✻ of Bulgaria 1879; occupied by Germany in WWII.

So·ga·mo·so \ˌsō-gō-ˈmō-sō\. **1.** River, N cen. Colombia; flows N and NW into the Magdalena River; ab. 100 mi. (160 km.) long.

2. City, Boyacá dept., cen. Colombia, in the Cordillera Oriental 110 mi. (177 km.) NE of Bogotá; munic. pop. (1985c) 67,428.

Sog·di·a·na \ˌsäg-dē-ˈa-nə, -ˈä-, -ˈā-\. Province of NE Persian Empire; ✻ Maracanda (*mod.* Samarqand); became a satrapy under Persian ruler Darius I 6th cent. B.C.; conquered by Macedonian King Alexander the Great 329–327 B.C.; as part of Bactria, asserted its independence from Seleucid Empire c. 250 B.C.; fell to invading northern tribes 2d cent. B.C. For later history, see BUKHARA 1.

Sogne Fjord \ˈsȯŋ-nə-ˌfyȯrd\ *or* **Sog·ne·fjord·en** \-ˌfyȯr-dən\ *or* **So·gna·fjord·en** \ˈsȯŋ-nə-\. Inlet of Norwegian Sea, W coast of Norway, 61°10′N, 7°03′E; at 110 mi. (177 km.) Norway's longest fjord.

Sogn og Fjord·a·ne \ˌsȯŋ-ən-ȯ-ˈfyu̇r-ə-nə\. County of W Norway. See table at NORWAY.

So·god \ˈsō-ˌgōd\. Municipality, Philippines, at head of Sogod Bay, Southern Leyte prov., Leyte I.; pop. (1980c) 26,246.

Sogod Bay. Inlet of Mindanao Sea, S Leyte I., Philippines, ab. 35 mi. (55 km.) long and 4 to 8 mi. (6 to 13 km.) wide; Panaon I. forms part of its E shore and Limasawa I. is at its mouth.

So·hâg \ˈsō-ˌhäg, -ˌhaj\ *or* **Saw·hāj** \ˈsȯ-ˌhaj, ˈsau̇-\. **1.** Governorate of Upper Egypt. See table at EGYPT.

2. Town, its ✻, on W bank of the Nile 190 mi. (306 km.) NNW of Aswān; on main Cairo railroad line.

Sohan. See SOAN.

Sohar. See ṢUḤĀR.

So·ho \ˈsō-ˌhō, sō-ˈhō\. A district in London, England, S of Oxford Street; long a foreign quarter; noted for its restaurants and shops; esp. popular with tourists.

Soi·gnies \swä-ˈnyē\. Commune, Hainaut prov., SW Belgium, 23 mi. (37 km.) SSW of Brussels; pop. (1991c) 23,793.

Soi·roc·co·cha \ˌsȯi-rȯ-ˈkō-chä\. Peak in the Cordillera Oriental, Peru; 18,600 ft. (5669 m.).

Sois·sons \swä-ˈsōⁿ\; *anc.* **Au·gus·ta Sues·si·o·num** \ȯ-ˈgəs-tə-ˌswe-sē-ˈō-nəm\. Commune, Aisne dept., N France, on Aisne River 18 mi. (29 km.) SW of Laon; pop. (1990c) 32,144; 12th–13th cent. cathedral (heavily damaged in WWI); remains of abbey (founded 11th cent.).

History: In ancient times ✻ of Belgian Gaul; here Frankish King Clovis defeated the Roman governor Syagrius 486; became ✻ of Neustria in 6th cent.; Pépin the Short deposed Frankish King Childeric III, last of the Merovingians, here 751; scene of first council condemning the teachings of theologian Peter Abelard 1121; captured by Germans 1870, 1914, 1918; reduced to almost complete ruin by German bombardments in WWI.

Sō·ka \ˈsō-kä\. City, Saitama prefecture, Honshū, Japan, NNE of Tokyo; pop. (1990p) 206,129.

Sö·ke \sœ̄-ˈke\. Town, Aydın prov., SW Turkey in Asia, near coast at mouth of Menderes.

So·khon·do \sə-ˈk̲ȯn-də\. Highest peak in the Yablonovyy Mts., SW Chita Oblast, S Russia in Asia, near border with Mongolia; 7188 ft. (2191 m.).

So·ko·dé \sō-ˈkō-dā\. Town, cen. Togo; pop. (1981c) 48,098; one of Togo's most populous settlements.

So·kol \ˈsȯ-kəl\. Town, Vologda Oblast, cen. Russia in Europe, ab. 20 mi. (32 km.) NNE of the city of Vologda; pop. (1991e) 46,700.

So·ko·lov \ˈsȯ-kə-ləf\; *formerly* **Falk·nov** \ˈfälk-ˌnȯf\ *or Ger.* **Fal·ke·nau** \ˈfäl-kə-ˌnau̇\. Town, W Czech Republic, on Ohře River 11 mi. (18 km.) WSW of Karlovy Vary; pop. (1989c) 28,530.

So·ko·to \sō-ˈkō-tō\. **1.** Historical emirate, Sokoto state, Nigeria; ab. 25,000 sq. mi. (64,750 sq. km.). Once center of the Fulani Empire, estab. early 19th cent. after victory of Fulani leader Usman dan Fodio over Hausaland and incorporating most of present-day N and cen. Nigeria; made trade treaties with the British 1853 and 1885; became part of British protectorate of Nigeria 1903.

2. State of NW Nigeria. See table at NIGERIA.

3. Town, ✻ of Sokoto state, Nigeria, 250 mi. (402 km.) WNW of Kano; pop. (1991e) 180,900; commercial center; distribution of agricultural products; production of leather goods; sultan's palace; ✻ of former Fulani Empire.

Sokotra. See SOCOTRA.

Sol, Is·la del \ˈēs-lä-t̲h̲el-ˈsōl\. Island, W Bolivia, in Lake Titicaca; contains Incan ruins.

So·la de Vega \ˈsō-lä-t̲h̲ā-ˈb̲ā-gä\. Municipality, Oaxaca state, Mexico, 47 mi. (76 km.) SSW of the city of Oaxaca.

So·lai \sō-ˈlī\. Town, Rift Valley prov., W cen. Kenya, ab. 25 mi. (40 km.) N of Nakuru; terminus of railroad branch line.

Solana, La. See LA SOLANA.

So·la·na Beach \sə-ˈlä-nə, sō-\. City, San Diego co., S California, up the coast from the city of San Diego; pop. (1990c) 12,962; pop. more than doubled bet. 1970 and 1980, but declined slightly in 1980s.

So·la·no \sō-ˈlä-nō\. **1.** County in cen. California. See table at CALIFORNIA.

2. Municipality, Nueva Vizcaya prov., Luzon, Philippines, on Magat River ab. 5 mi. (8 km.) NE of Bayombong; pop. (1980c) 36,710.

Solapur. See SHOLAPUR.

Sol·dier Mountain \ˈsōl-jər\. Peak, Glacier National Park, NW Montana; 7460 ft. (2274 m.).

Sol·dot·na \säl-ˈdät-nə\. City, S Alaska, on Kenai Penin.; pop. (1990c) 3482.

Sole Bay. See SOUTHWOLD.

So·le·dad **1.** \ˈsä-lə-ˌdad\. City, Monterey co., W California, 35 mi. (56 km.) SE of the city of Monterey; pop. (1990c) 7146.

2. \ˌsō-lā-ˈthäth\. Town, Atlántico dept., N Colombia, S suburb of Barranquilla; munic. pop. (1985c) 169,681.

Solenhofen. See SOLNHOFEN.

So·lent, The \ˈsō-lənt\. Channel extending bet. the Isle of Wight and the mainland of S England; varies in width bet. 2 and 5 mi. (3 and 8 km.)

So·lesmes \sō-ˈlem\. **1.** Town, Nord dept., N France, E of Cambrai on Selle River.

2. Village, Sarthe dept., NW France, on Sarthe River ab. 23 mi. (37 km.) SW of Le Mans; Benedictine abbey noted for studies in Gregorian chant.

Sol·fa·ta·ra \ˌsȯl-fä-ˈtä-rä\. Crater, in volcanic region, Phlegraean Fields, W Naples, S Italy.

Sol·fe·ri·no \ˌsäl-fe-ˈrē-nō\. Village, Mantova prov., SE Lombardy, N Italy, 5 mi. (8 km.) W of the Mincio River; scene of indecisive battle 1859 bet. French and Piedmontese troops under Emperor Napoléon III and Austrians under Emperor Francis Joseph in which both sides suffered major losses.

So·li \ˈsō-ˌlī\ *or* **So·loi** \-ˌlȯi\. Ancient town, Cilicia, Asia Minor, on coast SW of Tarsus; founded by colonists from Rhodes; conquered by Macedonian King Alexander the Great 333 B.C.; in Mithradatic Wars first cent. B.C. destroyed by Armenian King Tigranes I; soon rebuilt by Roman statesman Pompey the Great. Source of the English word *solecism*, because of substandard form of Greek spoken there.

So·li·gny–la–Trappe \ˌsȯ-lē-ˈnyē-lȧ-ˈtrap\. Commune, Orne dept., NW France, NE of Alençon; site of La Trappe, monastery where the Trappist branch of the Cistercian monastic order was founded in the 17th cent.

So·li·gorsk \ˌsə-lē-ˈgȯrsk\ *or* **Sa·li·horsk** \ˌsə-lē-ˈhȯrsk\. City, S cen. Belarus; pop. (1991e) 96,000.

So·li·hull \ˌsō-lə-ˈhəl\. Town, West Midlands, England, 8 mi. (13 km.) SE of Birmingham; pop. (1991p) 194,100; light industries; motor vehicles.

So·li·kamsk \sə-li-ˈkämsk\. Town, Perm' Oblast, E Russia in Europe, on the Usolka River 125 mi. (201 km.) N of the city of Perm'; pop. (1992e) 110,000; chemical plants; town founded in 15th cent.

Sol'–Iletsk *or* **Sol–Iletsk** \ˌsȯl-yi-ˈlyetsk\; *formerly* **Iletska·ya Zash·chi·ta** \ē-ˈlyet-skī-yə-zäsh-ˈchē-tə\ *also* **Iletsk.** Town, Orenburg Oblast, E Russia in Europe; health resort.

So·li·ma·na \ˌsō-lē-ˈmä-nä\. Peak in the Cordillera Occidental, S Peru; 20,068 ft. (6117 m.).

So·li·mões \ˌsü-lē-ˈmōiⁿsh\. Brazilian name of upper Amazon River from Peruvian border to mouth of the Rio Negro.

So·ling·en \ˈzō-liŋ-ən, ˈsō-\. City, North Rhine-Westphalia, Germany, in the Ruhrgebiet (Ruhr Valley) 14 mi. (23 km.) ESE of Düsseldorf; pop. (1992e) 165,924; major center of cutlery industry; city chartered 1374; severely damaged by bombing in WWII but since rebuilt.

Sol·i·tar·io, El \el-ˌsä-lə-ˈtar-ē-ˌō\. Peak, Brewster and Presidio cos., W Texas; 5048 ft. (1539 m.).

Sol·len·tu·na \ˈsü-lən-ˌtᵫ-nə\. City, E Sweden, NNW of Stockholm; munic. pop. (1994e) 53,509.

Sól·ler \sōl-ˈyer\. Town, NW Majorca, Balearic Is., Spain; pop. (1991c) 10,238; tourist resort.

Sol·le·rod \ˈsœ-lə-ˌræth\. Town, Copenhagen co., Denmark; pop. (1989e) 30,865.

Sollum. See SALŪM.

Sol·na \ˈsōl-nä\. City, N suburb of Stockholm, Sweden; pop. (1989c) 51,427.

Soln·ho·fen \ˈzōln-ˌhōf-ᵊn\ *or* **So·len·ho·fen** \ˈzō-lən-\. Village, Bavaria, Germany. Many well-preserved fossilized remains (esp. of archaeopteryx of the Jurassic period) have been found in the area.

So·lo \ˈsō-lō\. **1.** River, cen. and NE cen. Java, Indonesia; rises in mountains near S coast, flows N then ENE into Java Sea opp. the W end of the island of Madura just N of Gresik; 335 mi. (539 km.) long; largest river in Java; navigable for small craft in much of its upper course.

2. City, Indonesia. See SURAKARTA 2.

So·logne \sȯ-ˈlȯn-yə, -ˈlōn\. Plateau region, cen. France; ab. 2000 sq. mi. (5180 sq. km.); a marshy district, now largely reclaimed and used for agriculture.

Soloi. See SOLI.

So·lo·lá \ˌsō-lō-ˈlä\. **1.** Department of SW cen. Guatemala. See table at GUATEMALA.

2. Town, its ✻; pop. (1993e) 14,408; alt. ab. 7000 ft. (2135 m.); market town; overlooks Lake Atitlán.

Sol·o·mon \ˈsä-lə-mən\. River, N cen. Kansas; formed by confluence of N and S forks in W Mitchell co., flows SE into Smoky Hill River in W Dickinson co.; 210 mi. (338 km.) long.

Solomon Islands. **1.** Island group, W Pacific Ocean, consisting of independent nation of the same name (see SOLOMON ISLANDS 2) and the N islands belonging to Papua New Guinea (Bougainville, Buka, and the Green Is.).

History: Islands first inhabited at least 4,000 years ago; first discovered by a European 1568 when Spanish navigator Álvaro de Mendaña de Neira landed at Santa Isabel I.; attempts at settlement failed and islands not visited again for nearly 200 years; Bougainville I. discovered by French navigator Louis-Antoine de Bougainville 1768; islands visited by missionaries and traders 18th and 19th cents.; by treaty of 1886 divided bet. Great Britain and Germany; islands in SW became British protectorate 1893; E islands and Santa Cruz group added to protectorate 1898–99; N islands S of Bougainville ceded to Great Britain by Germany 1900; Bougainville and Buka islands and Green Is. group remained under German control until WWI.

2. Independent island nation in Pacific Ocean, E of the island of New Guinea; 11,500 sq. mi. (29,785 sq. km.); pop. (1993e) 349,000; includes the islands of Guadalcanal, Malaita, San Cristóbal, Choiseul, Santa Isabel, Florida, and Rennell, the Russell, Shortland, Santa Cruz, and New Georgia Island groups, and small islands and reefs; ✻ Honiara, on Guadalcanal; copra, rice; fish; timber. Came under British protection in 1893–1900 and became **British Solomon Islands**; in WWII occupied by Japanese 1942, invaded by Americans who landed on Guadalcanal Aug. 1942; became internally self-governing 1976, independent 1978.

Solomon Sea. N part of Coral Sea; enclosed on the W by New Guinea, on NW by New Britain, and on E by the Solomon Is.

So·lon \ˈsō-lən\. City, Cuyahoga co., N Ohio, 13 mi. (21 km.) ESE of Cleveland; pop. (1990c) 18,548.

So·lor \sō-ˈlȯr\. Small mountainous island, Lesser Sunda Is., Indonesia, in Savu Sea, off E tip of Flores I. and W of Lomblen I.; 25 mi. (40 km.) long by 3 or 4 mi. (5 or 6 km.) wide; 114 sq. mi. (295 sq. km.). The islands of Solor, Adonara, and Lomblen are sometimes known as the **Solor Islands.**

So·lo·thurn \ˈzō-lə-ˌtu̇rn\. **1.** Canton, Switzerland. See table at SWITZERLAND.

2. Commune, ✻ of Solothurn canton, NW Switzerland, on Aare River 19 mi. (31 km.) N of Bern; pop. (1989c) 15,531; 18th cent. cathedral; 15th cent. town hall; 13th cent. clock tower; known in Roman times; free imperial city 1218.

So·lo·vets·kiye Ostro·va \ˌsə-lə-ˈvyet-skē-ə-ˈȯs-trə-və\ *or* *Eng.* **So·lo·vets·ki Islands** \ˌsä-lə-ˈvet-skē\. Island group, SW White Sea, Arkhangel'sk Oblast, Russia, 30 mi. (48 km.) E of Kem'; 134 sq. mi. (347 sq. km.); former place of exile; since 1970s a state historic and nature preserve. **Solovetski,** the largest, 100 sq. mi. (259 sq. km.), is site of a former monastery, built 15th cent.; in 16th and 17th cents. used as a fortress against Swedes; monastery held under siege 1668–76 when monks refused to accept reforms in Orthodox Church.

Solt \ˈshōlt\. Commune, Bács-Kiskun co., S Hungary, on the Danube ab. 50 mi. (80 km.) S of Budapest; pop. (1980p) 6911.

Šol·ta \ˈshōl-tä\ *or Ital.* **Sol·ta** \ˈsȯl-tä\. Island, Adriatic Sea, opp. Split, Croatia, 14 mi. (23 km.) long, 21 sq. mi. (54 sq. km.).

So·lu·tré \ˌsȯ-lüe-ˈtrā\ *or in full* **Solutré–Pouil·ly** \-pü-ˈyē\. Village, Saône-et-Loire dept., E cen. France, near Mâcon; site of rock shelter where prehistoric human remains have been found; type station of the Solutrean epoch of Paleolithic culture, distinguished by finely flaked stone implements.

Sol·vang \ˈsȯl-ˌvaŋ\. City, Santa Barbara co., SW California; pop. (1990c) 4741.

Sol·vay \ˈsäl-ˌvā\. Village, Onondaga co., cen. New York, just W of Syracuse; pop. (1990c) 6717.

Sol·way Firth \ˈsäl-ˌwā\. Inlet of Irish Sea, on the boundary bet. England and Scotland; extends inland 38 mi. (61 km.).

Solway Moss \ˈmȯs\. Swampy area, Cumbria, NW England, NW of Esk River near Scottish border; scene of battle 1542 in which the English defeated the Scots under King James V.

So·ma·lia \sō-ˈmä-lē-ə, sə-, -ˈmäl-yə\. Republic, E Africa, bounded on N by the Gulf of Aden, on E and S by the Indian Ocean, and on W by Kenya, Ethiopia, and Djibouti; 246,154 sq. mi. (637,539 sq. km.); pop. (1993e) 8,050,000; ✱ Mogadishu, which is by far the nation's largest city.

Physical features: Much of country semidesert; cen. and S regions flat, N hilly with highest peak Surud Ad 7894 ft. (2406 m.).

Chief products: Sorghum, corn, sugar, cotton, bananas; pastoralism is important.

History: For early history, see BRITISH SOMALILAND and ITALIAN SOMALILAND. Independent republic constituted 1960 by union of British Somaliland with Trust Territory of Somalia (formerly Italian Somaliland); military dictatorship estab. after 1969 coup; territorial war with Ethiopia 1977–78 followed by civil wars and internal strife bet. rival clans; area in N comprising former British Somaliland declared independence 1991; continuing civil strife prompted UN-sponsored U.S. peacekeeping forces to intervene 1992; U.S. forces withdrawn 1993 and all outside forces withdrawn 1995 but civil unrest continued.

So·ma·li·land \sō-ˈmä-lē-ˌland, sə-\. Historical name for the region of E Africa, bet. the Equator and the Gulf of Aden, incl. Somalia, Djibouti, and SE Ethiopia; ab. 300,000 sq. mi. (777,000 sq. km.).

Somaliland Protectorate. See BRITISH SOMALILAND.

Som·bor \ˈsōm-ˌbōr\ *or Hung.* **Zom·bor** \ˈzōm-ˌbōr\. City, Vojvodina autonomous prov., NW Yugoslavia, ab. 95 mi. (155 km.) NW of Belgrade; pop. (1991c) 48,789.

Som·bre·re·te \ˌsȯm-brā-ˈrā-tā\. Municipality, Zacatecas state, cen. Mexico, 83 mi. (134 km.) NW of the city of Zacatecas; pop. (1990p) 63,715.

Som·bre·ro \səm-ˈbrer-ō, säm-\. Small island associated with the British dependency of Anguilla, in Anegada Passage, West Indies, bet. Anegada and Anguilla Is.; former source of phosphate (reserves now exhausted).

Sombrero Channel. Strait bet. Katchall I. and Little Nicobar I. in the Nicobar Is., Bay of Bengal.

Som·er·dale \ˈsə-mər-ˌdāl\. Borough, Camden co., SW New Jersey, 10 mi. (16 km.) SE of the city of Camden; pop. (1990c) 5440.

Som·ers \ˈsəm-ərz\. **1.** Town, NW Tolland co., N Connecticut, E of Enfield; pop. (1990c) 9108; correctional institution; incorp. as town by Massachusetts 1734; annexed to Connecticut 1749.

2. Town, Kenosha co., SE Wisconsin; pop. (1990c) 7861.

Som·ers·by \ˈsə-mərz-bē\. Parish, Lincolnshire, E England, near Louth; birthplace of poet Alfred, Lord Tennyson 1809.

Som·er·set \ˈsə-mər-ˌset, -sət\. **1.** Name of counties in four states of the U.S. See tables at MAINE, MARYLAND, NEW JERSEY, PENNSYLVANIA.

2. City, ⊗ of Pulaski co., SE cen. Kentucky, 40 mi. (64 km.) S of Danville; pop. (1990c) 10,733.

3. Town, Bristol co., SE Massachusetts, 4 mi. (6 km.) N of Fall River; pop. (1990c) 17,655.

4. Borough, ⊗ of Somerset co., S Pennsylvania, 25 mi. (40 km.) SSW of Johnstown; pop. (1990c) 6454.

5. *or* **Somersetshire.** Former county, SW England. See SOMERSET 6.

6. Administrative county, SW England, incl. most of the former county except area in N in new county of Avon; ⊗ Taunton; dairy products, cider; tourism; chief towns: Taunton, Yeovil, Bridgwater. See table at ENGLAND.

Somerset Dam. Dam across branch of Deerfield River, W Windham co., S Vermont; height 106 ft. (32 m.); completed 1913; impounds water in **Somerset Reservoir.**

Somerset East. Town, Eastern Cape prov., S Rep. of South Africa, 83 mi. (134 km.) N of Port Elizabeth, at E end of Great Karoo. Founded 1825.

Somerset Island. Island, cen. Arctic Archipelago, Nunavut, Canada, E of Prince of Wales I. and N of Boothia Penin.; 9370 sq. mi. (24,268 sq. km.).

Somerset Nile. See NILE.

Som·er·set·shire \ˈsə-mər-set-ˌshir, -sət-, -shər\ *or* **Somerset.** Former county, SW England. See SOMERSET 6.

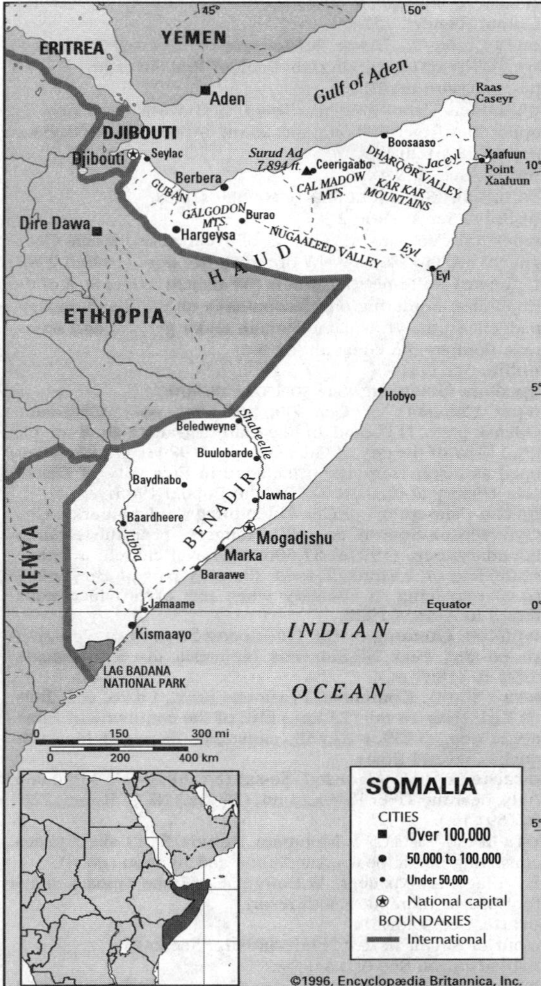

Somerset West. Town, Western Cape prov., S Rep. of South Africa, 30 mi. (48 km.) ESE of Cape Town near NE shore of False Bay; in agricultural district. See STRAND.

Somers Islands. See BERMUDA.

Som·ers Point \ˈsə-mərz\. City, Atlantic co., SE New Jersey, on Great Egg Harbor 10 mi. (16 km.) WSW of Atlantic City; pop. (1990c) 11,216; known as Egg Harbor in Revolutionary days.

Som·ers·worth \ˈsə-mərz-ˌwərth\. City, Strafford co., SE New Hampshire, on Salmon Falls River 5 mi. (8 km.) N of Dover; pop. (1990c) 11,249; incorp. as city 1893.

Som·er·ton \ˈsə-mərt-ᵊn\. City, Yuma co., SW corner of Arizona; pop. (1990c) 5282.

Som·er·vell \ˈsə-mər-ˌvel\. County in N cen. Texas. See table at TEXAS.

Som·er·ville \ˈsə-mər-ˌvil\. **1.** City, Middlesex co., NE Massachusetts, just W of the Charlestown section of Boston; pop. (1990c) 76,210. Settled 1630 as part of Charlestown; during Revolutionary War town's Old Powder House served as magazine of American army besieging the British in Boston; incorp. as town 1842 and as city 1871.

2. Borough, ⊗ of Somerset co., N cen. New Jersey, 10 mi. (16 km.) WNW of New Brunswick; pop. (1990c) 11,632; Raritan Valley Community Coll. (1968); during Revolutionary War, Gen. George Washington's headquarters 1778–79.

3. Town, ⊗ of Fayette co., SW Tennessee, 43 mi. (69 km.) E of Memphis; pop. (1990c) 2047.

So·meş \sō-ˈmesh\ *or* **So·me·şul** \sō-ˈme-shül\ *or Hung.* **Sza·mos** \ˈsö-ˌmōsh\. River, NE Hungary and NW Romania; formed by junction of **Someşul Mare** \ˈmä-rā\ (from Carpathians) and **Someşul Mic** \ˈmēk\ (rises in Bihor Mts.); flows NW into Tisza River; 145 mi. (233 km.) long.

Somma, Monte. See VESUVIUS.

Som·ma Ve·su·via·na \ˈsō-mä-vā-ˌzü-vē-ˈä-nə\. Commune, Napoli prov., Campania, S Italy, near Vesuvius 9 mi. (14 km.) NE of Naples; pop. (1989c) 28,216; damaged by volcanic eruption 1794.

Somme \ˈsȯm, ˈsäm, ˈsəm\. **1.** River, N France; rises near St.-Quentin in Aisne dept., flows W to Amiens and NW past Abbeville into the English Channel; 152 mi. (245 km.) long; scene 1916 of one of the major conflicts of WWI in which British and French launched an unsuccessful and costly attack on the German position. Area occupied by Germans during WWII.

2. Department of N France. See table at FRANCE.

Somme·py \sȯm-ˈpē\ *or* **Sommepy–Ta·hure** \-tä-ˈu̇r\. Village, Marne dept., NE France, 23 mi. (37 km.) E of Reims; American memorial to U.S. and French soldiers who fought in the region during WWI.

Sommerfeld. See LUBSKO.

Som·nath \sōm-ˈnät\ *or* **Pa·tan Somnath** \ˈpə-tən\. Port, S coast of Gujarat, W India, near Veraval; famous in Hindu legend as the spot where Krishna was mistakenly killed by a hunter's arrow. Site of temple of Siva, an important pilgrimage center; the original temple was sacked and destroyed c. 1024 by the Muslim invader Maḥmūd of Ghaznī, subsequently rebuilt and destroyed several times, and finally rebuilt again in 1950s.

So·mogy \ˈshō-ˌmōj\. County of SW Hungary. See table at HUNGARY.

So·mo·sier·ra Pass \ˌsō-mō-ˈsyer-rä\. Mountain pass in the Sierra de Guadarrama, cen. Spain; 4770 ft. (1454 m.).

So·mo·to \sō-ˈmō-tō\. Town, ✱ of Madriz dept., NW Nicaragua, near the Honduras border; pop. (1985e) 8561.

Som·port, Col de \ˌkȯl-də-sōⁿ-ˈpȯr\; *anc.* **Sum·mus Por·tus** \ˈsə-məs-ˈpōr-təs\. Mountain pass in W Pyrenees, N of Jaca, N Spain, on boundary bet. Huesca dept., Spain, and Pyrénées-Atlantiques dept., France; 5354 ft. (1632 m.); used by Muslim invaders from Spain in 8th cent.

Son \ˈsōn\ *or* **So·ne** \ˈsō-nā\. River, NE cen. India; rises in E Madhya Pradesh, flows NW, then E and NE to the Ganges River near Danapur; 475 mi. (764 km.) long; source of irrigation system for Bihar.

Sondags. See SUNDAYS.

Søn·der·borg \ˈsœn-dər-ˌbȯr\. **1.** Former county of Denmark, comprising Als I. and part of SE Jutland Penin.; now forms part of Sønderjylland co.; under German rule 1864–1920.

2. Town, Sønderjylland co., SW Als I. off SE coast of Jutland, Denmark, 17 mi. (27 km.) NE of Flensburg; pop. (1981c) 27,904; seaside resort; trade center of Als I.

Søn·der·jyl·land \ˈsœ-nər-ˌyu̅e̅-ˌlän\. County, S Jutland, Denmark. See table at DENMARK.

Son·ders·hau·sen \ˈzȯn-dərs-ˌhau̇z-ᵊn\. Commune, Thuringia, cen. Germany, N of Erfurt; pop. (1981c) 23,414; 16th–18th cent. palace.

Son·drio \ˈsȯn-drē-ˌō\. **1.** Province of Lombardy, Italy. See table at ITALY.

2. Commune, its ✱, on the Adda River 62 mi. (100 km.) NE of Milan; pop. (1989c) 22,708; transportation center near Bernina Pass; produces wines and textiles.

Sone. See SON.

So·ne·que·ra \ˌsō-nā-ˈkā-rä\. Peak, S Potosí dept., SW Bolivia; 18,652 ft. (5685 m.).

\ə\ **abut** \ᵊ\ matches \ᵊ\ kitten, Fr table \ər\ **further** \a\ **ash** \ā\ **ace**
\ä\ **cot, cart** \ȧ\ Fr bac \au̇\ **out** \b\ Span Avila \ch\ **chin** \e\ **bet** \ē\ **easy**
\g\ **go** \i\ **hit** \ī\ **ice** \j\ **job** \k\ Ger **ich, Buch** \ⁿ\ Fr vin
\ŋ\ **sing** \ō\ **go** \ö\ **all** \ȯ\ **law** \œ\ Fr **bœuf** \œ̄\ Fr **feu** \ȯi\ **boy**
\th\ **thin** \th\ **this** \ü\ **loot** \u̇\ **foot** \ue\ Ger **füllen** \u̅e̅\ Fr **rue**
\y\ **yet** \ʸ\ Fr digne \ˈdēnʸ\, nuit \ˈnwʸē\ \yü\ **few** \yu̇\ **fury** \zh\ **vision**

Song Da. See BLACK 9.
Son·gea \sȯŋ-ˈgā-ä\. Town, ✻ of Ruvuma region, S Tanzania, E of Lake Malawi; road junction and trade center.
Song·hai Empire *or* **Song·hay Empire** \ˈsȯŋ-ˌhī\. Muslim empire estab. c. 1000 in the region of the bend of the Niger in W cen. Sudan; chief town Gao; reached greatest extent early 16th cent.; fell to Moroccan forces 1591.
Song·hua \ˈsu̇ŋ-ˈhwä\ *or W.-G.* **Sung–hua** \ˈsu̇ŋ-ˈhwä\ *or angl.* **Sun·ga·ri** \ˌsu̇ŋ-gə-ˈrē\. River, NE China; rises in Changbai Shan on border of North Korea, flows NW past Jilin to join the Nen near Fuyu, then turns sharply E and NE through a fertile plain to join the Amur at Tongjiang; 1150 mi. (1850 km.) long; chief tributary of the Amur; navigable to Jilin.
Song·jiang \ˈsu̇ŋ-ˈjyäŋ\ *or W.-G.* **Sung–chiang** \ˈsu̇ŋ-ˈjyäŋ\ *also* **Sung·kiang** \ˈsu̇ŋ-ˈjyäŋ\. Town, Shanghai municipality, E China, on the Huangpu River; burial place of American military adventurer Frederick T. Ward, commander of "Ever-Victorious Army" during the Taiping Rebellion.
Songjin. See KIMCH'AEK.
Song·khla *or* **Song·kla** \ˌsȯŋ-ˈklä\ *or Malay* **Sin·go·ra** \siŋ-ˈgō(ə)r-ə\. Seaport, SW Thailand, on E coast of Malay Penin. 50 mi. (80 km.) NW of Pattani; pop. (1991e) 82,167; trade center and coastal port; tourism; fisheries.
Song·nam \ˈsȯŋ-ˈnäm\. City, NW South Korea; pop. (1985c) 447,692.
Song Shan *or W.-G.* **Sung Shan** \ˈsu̇ŋ-ˈshän\. Mountain, N Henan prov., E cen. China, ab. 35 mi. (56 km.) ESE of Luoyang; 4724 ft. (1440 m.); one of the Five Sacred Mountains of China.
Son·gwe \ˈsȯŋ-gwā\. River, E Africa; flows into N end of Lake Malawi; ab. 100 mi. (160 km.) long; forms N boundary of Malawi.
Song·zi Hu *or W.-G.* **Sung–tzu Ho** \ˈsu̇ŋ-ˈdzə-ˈhə\. River, S cen. China, in Hunan and Hubei provs.; flows N and NNW into the Chang.
Son·hat \ˈsōn-ˌhät\. Town, Madhya Pradesh, India. See KOREA.
So·ni·pat \ˈsō-nə-ˌpət\. Town, Haryana state, N India, N of New Delhi; pop. (1991p) 142,992.
Son La \ˈshən-ˈlä\. Town, NW Vietnam, in mountainous area.
Son·mi·a·ni Bay \ˌsōn-mē-ˈä-nē\. Inlet of Arabian Sea, S coast of Pakistan.
Son·ne·berg \ˈzȯ-nə-ˌberk\. City, Thuringia, SE cen. Germany, 44 mi. (71 km.) S of Erfurt; pop. (1992e) 26,366; a center of toy manufacturing; chartered 1349.
So·no·ma \sə-ˈnō-mə\. **1.** Coastal county in W California. See table at CALIFORNIA.
2. City, Sonoma co., W California, 13 mi. (21 km.) S of Santa Rosa; pop. (1990c) 8121; wineries; site of revolt by American settlers against Mexican garrison in which California Republic was proclaimed 1846.
So·no·ra \sə-ˈnōr-ə\. **1.** City, ⊗ of Tuolumne co., cen. California, 45 mi. (72 km.) E of Stockton; pop. (1990c) 4153.
2. City, ⊗ of Sutton co., SW cen. Texas, 65 mi. (105 km.) S of San Angelo; pop. (1990c) 2751.
3. River, Sonora state, NW Mexico; flows SW and W into upper Gulf of California near Tiburón I.; ab. 250 mi. (400 km.) long.
4. State of NW Mexico. See table at MEXICO.
So·no·ran Desert \sə-ˈnōr-ən\. Arid region, W North America, in SW Arizona, SE California, W Sonora state, Mexico, and N Baja California, Mexico; includes the Colorado Desert, Coachella Valley, and Imperial Valley (*qq.v.*).
Sonora Pass. Mountain pass, Mono, Alpine, and Tuolumne cos., E California; 9624 ft. (2933 m.); an important pass through the Sierra Nevada used by early emigrants and explorers.
Sonora Peak. Mountain on boundary bet. Mono and Alpine cos., E cen. California; 11,429 ft. (3484 m.).
Son·pur \ˈsōn-ˌpu̇r\. Former Indian state, now part of Orissa state, E India; 948 sq. mi. (2455 sq. km.).
Son·so·na·te \ˌsȯn-sō-ˈnä-tā\. **1.** Department of SW El Salvador. See table at EL SALVADOR.
2. City, its ✻; pop. (1986e) 78,790; center of rich agricultural region; founded 1524.
Son·tay \sōn-ˈtī\. Town, N Vietnam, on highway 25 mi. (40 km.) WNW of Hanoi; on right bank of Red River just S of its junction with the Black.
Sont·ho·fen \ˈzȯnt-ˌhōf-ᵊn\. Town, S Bavaria, Germany, on upper Iller River in mountains 25 mi. (40 km.) E of Bregenz; pop. (1980c) 20,149.
Sontius. See ISONZO.
Soo Canals. See SAULT SAINTE MARIE CANALS.
Soochow. See SUZHOU 2.
So·per·ton \ˈsō-pərt-ᵊn\. City, ⊗ of Treutlen co., E cen. Georgia, 90 mi. (145 km.) WNW of Savannah; pop. (1990c) 2797.
So·phe·ne \sō-ˈfē-nē\. District in SW ancient Armenia, E of the Euphrates, bordering on Mesopotamia on the S and on Cappadocia on the W; became Roman under general and statesman Pompey the Great ab. 63 B.C.
Sophia. See SOFIA.
Sopoetan, Goenoeng. See SOPUTAN, GUNUNG.
So·pot \ˈsȯ-ˌpȯt\ *or Ger.* **Zop·pot** \ˈtsȯ-ˌpȯt\. Commune, Gdańsk prov., N Poland, on the Gulf of Danzig ab. 8 mi. (13 km.) NNW of the city of Gdańsk; pop. (1989e) 47,195; developed as resort from 1823; included in Free City of Danzig (see *History* at GDAŃSK 2) 1919; to Poland 1945.
Sop·ron \ˈshō-ˌprōn\ *or Ger.* **Öden·burg** \ˈœd-ᵊn-ˌbu̇rk\. City, Győr-Moson-Sopron co., NW Hungary, near the Austrian boundary; pop. (1991e) 57,500; medieval church; a Roman settlement on a strategic road; the only part of Burgenland (*q.v.*) remaining in Hungary when rest of province transferred to Austria 1922.
So·pu·tan, Gu·nung *or Du.* **Goe·noeng So·poe·tan** \ˈgü-ˌnu̇ŋ-sō-ˈpü-tän\. Peak, NE Sulawesi, Indonesia, just S of Manado; 5994 ft. (1827 m.).
So·ra \ˈsō-rä\. Commune, Frosinone prov., Lazio, cen. Italy, on Liri River 14 mi. (23 km.) ENE of the commune of Frosinone; pop. (1989c) 27,158; cathedral; damaged by earthquakes several times.
So·rac·te \sə-ˈrak-te\ *or Ital.* **So·rat·te** \sō-ˈrät-tā\. Mountain, Italy, near the Tiber River 24 mi. (39 km.) NE of Rome; 2267 ft. (691 m.).
So·ra·ta \sō-ˈrä-tä\. **1.** Mountain, Bolivia, E of Lake Titicaca, consisting of the peaks Ancohuma and Illampu (*qq.v.*).
2. Village, La Paz dept., W Bolivia, E of Lake Titicaca and at foot of Mt. Illampu; health resort.
Soratte. See SORACTE.
Sorau *or* **Sorau in der Niederlausitz.** See ŻARY.
Sorbiodunum. See OLD SARUM.
So·rel \sȯ-ˈrel\. City, S Quebec, Canada, on S bank of St. Lawrence River at mouth of Richelieu River 35 mi. (56 km.) SW of Trois-Rivières; pop. (1991c) 18,786; clothing, textiles, plastics; founded 1672 around Fort Richelieu (erected 1642).
So·rell \sō-ˈrel\. Town, SE Tasmania, Australia, on Pitt Water 15 mi. (24 km.) ENE of Hobart; munic. pop. (1991c) 8468.
Sorell, Cape. Point, W coast of Tasmania, Australia, at entrance to Macquarie Harbour.
Sorell, Lake. Lake, E cen. Tasmania, Australia; 19 sq. mi. (49 sq. km.); source of Clyde River, a tributary of the Derwent.
So·ria \ˈsōr-ē-ä\. **1.** Province of N cen. Spain. See table at SPAIN.
2. Commune, its ✻, on Duero River 113 mi. (182 km.) NE of Madrid; pop. (1991c) 32,360.
So·ria·no \sōr-ˈyä-nō\. **1.** Department of SW Uruguay. See table at URUGUAY.
2. Town, Soriano dept., SW Uruguay, at mouth of the Río Negro 162 mi. (261 km.) NW of Montevideo; founded 1624, believed to be oldest settlement in Uruguay; transshipping point for Mercedes.
So·ro·ca \sə-ˈrō-kə\ *or* **So·ro·ki** \sə-ˈrō-kē\. Town, NE Moldova, on right bank of Dniester River 30 mi. (48 km.) SE of Mogilev Podol'skiy; raises fruit, corn, tobacco. Here in 15th cent. Prince Stephen the Great of Moldavia erected fortress and castle; to Russia 1812.
So·ro·ca·ba \ˌsȯr-ō-ˈkä-bə\. City, SE São Paulo state, SE Brazil, 68 mi. (109 km.) W of the city of São Paulo; munic. pop.

(1991p) 377,270; center of cotton-growing region; industrial and commercial center.

So·ro·ki. See SOROCA.

So·rol \sȯ-ˈrȯl\. Atoll, W Caroline Is., W Pacific Ocean, SE of Yap, 8°08′N, 140°23′E.

So·rong \ˈsȯ-ˌrȯŋ\. Port, Irian Jaya, Indonesia, on Dampier Strait, opp. N end of Salawati I.; was Japanese base in WWII.

Sør·øya \ˈsœ-ˌrȯi\. Island, off NW coast of Norway; 315 sq. mi. (816 sq. km.).

Sor·ren·to \sȯ-ren-tō\; *anc.* **Sur·ren·tum** \sə-ˈren-təm\. Seaport, Napoli prov., Campania, S Italy, on **Sorrento Peninsula** (*or* **Sur·ren·tine Peninsula** \ˈsər-en-ˌtēn\) on S side of Bay of Naples 17 mi. (27 km.) SE of Naples; pop. (1991p) 17,015; cathedral, Roman ruins. Seat of autonomous duchy in 7th cent.; birthplace of poet Torquato Tasso 1544; in WWII occupied by Allied forces during Salerno campaign Sept. 1943.

Sor·so·gon \ˌsȯr-sō-ˈgȯn\. **1.** Province, SE Luzon, Philippines; ✻ Sorsogon; comprises SE tip of Luzon; coastline irregular, its W coast being deeply indented by Sorsogon Bay. Mountainous, with Bulusan Volcano its most noted peak. Streams are short, but soil, of volcanic origin, is fertile. Hemp (abacá) is the main crop, but coconuts are also grown. See table at PHILIPPINES. Early in 17th cent. visited by Spaniards who established mission at Casiguran; many of the galleons used in the Manila-Acapulco trade built here; civil government estab. 1901.

2. Municipality, its ✻, at head of Sorsogon Bay; pop. (1980c) 60,574; port of call for vessels from Manila; has export trade in hemp.

Sorsogon Bay *or* **Sorsogon Gulf.** Landlocked body of water, cen. Sorsogon prov., Luzon, Philippines; opens onto Ticao Pass, NW of San Bernardino Strait; 19 mi. (31 km.) long and from 3 to 8 mi. (5 to 13 km.) wide.

Sor·ta·va·la \ˈsȯr-tä-ˌvä-lä\ *also* **Ser·do·bol'** \ˌsyir-də-ˈbȯlʸ\. Town, S Karelia Rep., NW Russia in Europe, on N shore of Lake Ladoga 120 mi. (193 km.) N of St. Petersburg; under Finnish administration 1917–40.

Sør–Trøn·de·lag \ˈsœr-ˈtrœn-də-ˌläg\. County of cen. Norway. See table at NORWAY.

Sõr·ve \ˈsər-və\ *or Ger.* **Swor·be** \ˈsvȯr-bə\. Peninsula, S Saaremaa I., Estonia.

Sos \ˈsōs\ *or in full* **Sos del Rey Ca·tó·li·co** \t͟hel-ˌrā-kä-ˈtō-lē-kō\. Commune, Zaragoza prov., N Spain, 60 mi. (97 km.) NNW of Saragossa; pop. (1991c) 940; birthplace of King Ferdinand II of Aragon 1452.

Sos·na \sə-ˈsnä\. River, Orel and Lipetsk oblasts, W Russia in Europe, flows E to join the Don E of Yelets; 188 mi. (302 km.) long.

Sos·no·wiec \sä-ˈsnō-ˌvyets\. Industrial city, Katowice prov., S Poland, 4 mi. (6 km.) E of the city of Katowice; pop. (1989e) 259,269; railroad junction; iron and steel, glass, textiles; coal mines nearby; developed as industrial center end of 19th cent.; received town rights 1902.

Sos·va \ˈsȯs-və\. River, chiefly in N Khanty-Mansi Autonomous Okrug, Tyumen' Oblast, W Russia in Asia; flows S and E to the Ob' in its lower course near the town of Berezovo; 556 mi. (895 km.) long.

So·ta·rá \ˌsō-tä-ˈrä\. Volcanic peak, SW Colombia, in the Cordillera Central S of Popayán; 14,550 ft. (4435 m.).

So·to la Ma·ri·na \ˈsō-tō-ˌlä-mä-ˈrē-nä\. River, cen. Tamaulipas state, Mexico; flows E into Gulf of Mexico; ab. 160 mi. (255 km.) long.

So·tra \ˈsō-trä\ *also* **Sto·re Sot·ra** \ˈstȯr-ə\. Island off SW coast of Norway, near Bergen; 67 sq. mi. (174 sq. km.).

Sot·te·ville–lès–Rou·en \sȯt-ˌvē-le-rü-ˈäⁿ\. Commune, Seine-Maritime dept., N France, S suburb of Rouen on left bank of Seine.

Sou·chez \sü-ˈshā\. Village, Pas-de-Calais dept., N France, 4 mi. (6 km.) SW of Lens; battle Sept. 1915 in which it was captured by the French.

Souda Bay. See SUDA BAY.

Soudan. See SUDAN.

Sou·der·ton \ˈsau̇-dərt-ᵊn\. Borough, Montgomery co., SE Pennsylvania, 26 mi. (42 km.) N of Philadelphia; pop. (1990c) 5957.

Soúdhas, Kólpos. See SUDA BAY.

Soueida. See AS SUWAYDĀ.

Soueidié. See SÜVEYDIYE.

Sou·flí·on \sü-ˈflē-ˌȯn\. Town, Évros dept., Eastern Macedonia and Thrace, NE Greece, ab. 32 mi. (50 km.) NE of Alexandroúpolis.

Sou·fri·ère \ˌsü-frē-ˈer\. **1.** *also* **Grande Soufrière** \ˈgräⁿd\. Volcano, S Basse-Terre I., French overseas dept. of Guadeloupe, West Indies; 4813 ft. (1467 m.).

2. Volcanic peak, S Montserrat, Leeward Is., West Indies; 3000 ft. (914 m.); highest point on island.

3. Town, W coast of St. Lucia I., West Indies; pop. (1988e) 9337.

4. *also* **La Soufrière** \lä-\. Volcano at N end of St. Vincent I., in the Windward Is., West Indies; 4048 ft. (1234 m.); violent eruption May 7, 1902, resulted in loss of more than 1500 lives; eruption 1979 for which one fifth of population was evacuated.

Souk–Ah·ras \sük-ˈar-ˌäs\ *also* **Suk–Ahras** \sük-ˈar-äs\; *anc.* **Ta·gas·te** \tə-ˈgas-tē\. Commune, NE Algeria, ab. 40 mi. (64 km.) S of Annaba; pop. (1987p) 83,015.

Sound, The. See ØRESUND.

Sou·ni·on, Cape \ˈsü-nē-ən\ *or* **Ákra Sou·ni·on** \ˈä-krä-ˈsü-nē-ˌȯn\; *formerly* **Cape Co·lon·na** \kə-ˈlō-nə\; *anc.* **Su·ni·um Prom·on·to·ri·um** \ˈsü-nē-əm-ˌprä-mən-ˈtōr-ē-əm\. Cape, E cen. Greece; summit contains ruins of ancient temple.

Sour. See TYRE.

Sou·ris \ˈsu̇r-əs\. River, S Canada; rises in S Saskatchewan, flows in curve SE, N, and NE through Saskatchewan, North Dakota, and Manitoba to the Assiniboine SE of Brandon; ab. 450 mi. (725 km.) long. In North Dakota also called the **Mouse** \ˈmau̇s\ River.

Sousse \ˈsüs\ *or* **Su·sa** \ˈsü-zə, -sə\; *anc.* **Had·ru·me·tum** \ˌha-drə-mē-təm\. Coastal town, NE Tunisia, on S shore of the Gulf of Hammamet; 9th cent. mosque and fortified monastery. An ancient city founded by the Phoenicians and important under the Carthaginians and Romans; important Arab city 9th–11th cents.; developed greatly under French protectorate 1881 ff.

Souterrain du Rove. See ROVE TUNNEL.

South \ˈsau̇th\. **1.** River, SE North Carolina; rises in E cen. North Carolina, flows S into Black River in E Bladen co.; ab. 70 mi. (115 km.) long.

2. Region of indefinite boundaries, SE United States; usu. thought to be bounded on the N by the Mason-Dixon Line.

South Africa, Republic of *or Afrikaans* **Re·pu·bliek van Suid–Afri·ka** \ˌrā-pü-ˈblēk-fän-ˌsȯit-ˈä-fri-kä\; *formerly* **Union of South Africa.** Republic, S Africa, bounded on E, S, and W by the Indian and Atlantic oceans (conventional boundary bet. the oceans at 20°E), on NW by Namibia, on N by Botswana and Zimbabwe, and on NE by Mozambique and Swaziland; the kingdom of Lesotho lies wholly within the republic; 471,445 sq. mi. (1,221,043 sq. km.); pop. (1989e) 30,193,000; administrative ✻ Pretoria, legislative ✻ Cape Town, judicial ✻ Bloemfontein.

Physical features: A plateau region with Drakensberg in E along boundary bet. Free State and KwaZulu-Natal; in the W half of the country an inner plateau is bordered on S by an escarpment roughly parallel with the coast which contains many short ranges 6000 to 8000 ft. (1830 to 2440 m.) in height; S of this escarpment is the Great Karoo, 2000 to 3000 ft. (610 to 915 m.) high, separated by the Groote Swartberg from the Little Karoo, 1000 to 2000 ft. (305 to 610 m.) high, along the S coast in Western Cape prov. (see KAROO); has much grassland (veld)—bush veld bet. the Great Karoo and the Orange River, and grass veld in the E and NE; desert or semidesert in much of the W and S part; bet. the Orange River and the Molopo is the S part of the Kalahari Desert. Chief

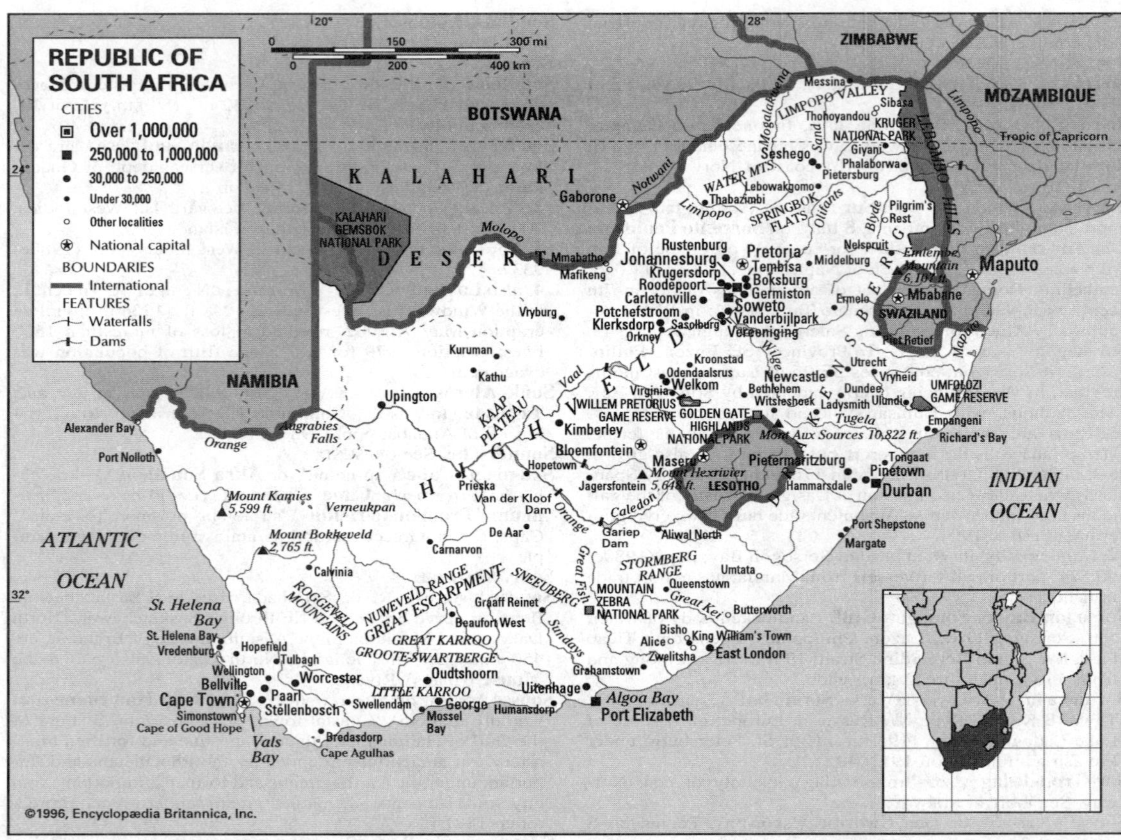

river the Orange, which with its tributary the Vaal traverses whole cen. part, flowing W to the Atlantic Ocean; many short streams along S and SE coast.

Chief products: Wheat, corn, fruit, sugarcane, sorghum, tobacco; livestock raising, fishing; gold, copper, coal, diamonds, asbestos, manganese, uranium, iron ore; chemicals, textiles, automobiles.

Chief cities: Cape Town, Durban, Johannesburg, Pretoria.

Political divisions: Prior to 1994 divided into the following provinces (for pronunciation of their names, see their individual entries): Cape Province, Natal, Orange Free State, and Transvaal. Now divided into the following nine provinces (for further details, see their individual entries):

NAME	AREA (sq. mi.)	AREA (sq. km.)	POP. (1994e)
Eastern Cape	65,483	169,600	6,504,000
Free State (formerly Orange Free State)	49,992	129,480	2,767,000
Gauteng (formerly Pretoria-Witwatersrand-Vereeniging)	7,262	18,810	6,864,000
KwaZulu-Natal	35,591	92,180	8,553,000
Mpumalanga (formerly Eastern Transvaal)	30,259	78,370	2,911,000
Northern (formerly Northern Transvaal)	47,598	123,280	5,013,000
Northern Cape	139,691	361,800	749,000
North West	44,861	116,190	3,349,000
Western Cape	49,950	129,370	3,635,000

History: Stone Age inhabitants were Bushmen and Hottentots; by 14th cent. A.D. had been settled by Bantu peoples; Cape of Good Hope settlement estab. by Dutch 1652, ceded to British 1814 (see CAPE PROVINCE); in 1836 Dutch settlers (Boers) left Cape in Great Trek N and E of Orange River; Orange Free State and Transvaal founded by Boers; Natal annexed to Cape Colony 1844, given separate government 1845; in 1877 British annexed South African Republic (Transvaal) which had been guaranteed its independence by Sand River Convention 1852; Kaffraria, Griqualand West, British Bechuanaland, Zululand, and Tongaland were annexed to provinces later in Union 1865–98; after Boers were defeated in South African (Boer) War 1899–1902, former Boer states met with Cape Colony and Natal in constitutional convention 1908; federal union went into effect 1910; received mandate to former German Southwest Africa 1919 after capturing it from German forces in WWI; declared war on Germany 1939; policy of apartheid formally instituted from 1948 ff.; became a republic and withdrew from the Commonwealth of Nations 1961; established the Transkei, a partly self-governing territory, 1963; granted independence to Bantustans ("homelands") of Transkei 1976, Bophuthatswana 1977, Venda 1979, Ciskei 1981 (that independence not recognized internationally); constitutional changes adopted 1983 allowing Asians and Coloreds limited government participation; under president Frederik Willem de Klerk began major reforms towards ending apartheid 1989; "homelands" reincorporated into South Africa subsequently; free and democratic elections 1994 brought Nelson Mandela to the presidency.

South African Republic. The Boer republic 1856–77 and 1881–1902 in S Africa, coextensive with Transvaal (*q.v.*).

South Am·boy \ˈam-ˌbȯi\. City, Middlesex co., cen. New Jersey, on Raritan Bay; pop. (1990c) 7863.

South America. Continent (4th in size), Western Hemisphere, comprising greater part of Latin America; 6,880,706 sq. mi. (17,821,029 sq. km.); ab. 4500 mi. (7240 km.) N to S and 3200 mi. (5150 km.) at max. width; pop. (1992e) 290,744,000.

Boundaries: On N, Caribbean Sea; chief inlets: Gulf of Darien, Gulf of Venezuela and Lake Maracaibo, Gulf of Paria; northernmost point, Point Gallinas in Colombia, 12°25′N; chief islands: Curaçao and Bonaire of Netherlands Antilles, Aruba, Margarita, and Trinidad and Tobago. On NE and E, Atlantic Ocean; chief inlets: mouth of Amazon, estuary of Río de la Plata, and in Argentina, Bahía Blanca, and San Matías Gulf and San Jorge Gulf; easternmost point, Point Coqueiros, just N of Recife, Brazil, 7°38′S, 34°47′W; off Brazil E of Cape São Roque is Fernando de Noronha I. and E of S extremity of Argentina lie the Falkland Is. On S, Drake Passage; Strait of Magellan borders on extreme S of mainland; to the S is large island of Tierra del Fuego and many adjacent smaller islands, incl. Horn I. on which is Cape Horn, generally considered the southernmost point of South America, 56°S; southernmost point of mainland is Cape Froward, S point of Brunswick Penin., Chile, 53°54′S. On W, Pacific Ocean; chief inlets: Corcovado Gulf and Gulf of Guayaquil; westernmost point, Point Pariñas, Peru, 81°20′W; islands: Galápagos Is., 600 mi. (965 km.) off Ecuador coast. On NW, Panama, republic and isthmus, connecting with Central America.

Mountains: On W side bordering the Pacific for entire length of continent are the Andes (*q.v.*); highest point Aconcagua 23,834 ft. (7265 m.). Other ranges: in N, chiefly in Venezuela and on border bet. Venezuela and the Guianas (on N) and Brazil (on S), the Serras Curupira, Parima, and Acaraí, and the Tumuc-Humac Mts.; in E, the highland of Brazil (Goiás, Minas Gerais, Bahia, São Paulo, and Paraná states) and the Planalto do Mato Grosso; and in S the mountains in Córdoba prov., Argentina. Lowland regions are known as the *llanos* in the N, the *selvas* of the Amazon, and the *pampas* of the Paraná basin; the Gran Chaco is the swamp region of the S cen. part.

Rivers: Amazon in N Brazil with headstreams in Colombia, Peru, and Bolivia and many large tributaries; Orinoco in the N (Venezuela and Colombia), connecting with Rio Negro of the Amazon system through the Casiquiare; Magdalena in Colombia, Essequibo in Guyana; in E, Paranaíba and São Francisco in E Brazil; in S, Uruguay (bet. Uruguay, Argentina, and Brazil), the Paraná system, with its two large headstreams the Alto Paraná and the Paraguay, and many tributaries, and in cen. and S Argentina the Salado, Negro, and Chubut; in W, in the Andes many short streams.

Lakes: Lake Titicaca (Peru and Bolivia), one of the highest large lakes in the world (alt. 12,500 ft. or 3810 m.); Poopó in Bolivia, Lagõa dos Patos in S Brazil, Lagoa Mirím in Uruguay and Brazil, Mar Chiquita in cen. Argentina; many resort lakes in S Andes, esp. Nahuel Huapí, Todos los Santos, Llanquihue.

Political divisions: Argentina, Aruba, Bolivia, Brazil, Chile, Colombia, Ecuador, Falkland Is., French Guiana, Guyana, Netherlands Antilles (Bonaire and Curaçao), Paraguay, Peru, Suriname, Trinidad and Tobago, Uruguay, and Venezuela.

South·amp·ton \saủth-'hamp-tən, saủ-'thamp-\. **1.** County in SE Virginia. See table at VIRGINIA.
2. Town, Hampshire co., W Massachusetts, 11 mi. (18 km.) NW of Springfield; pop. (1990c) 4478.
3. Village and seaside resort, Suffolk co., SE New York, on S shore of Long Island 33 mi. (53 km.) W of Montauk Point; pop. (1990c) 3980; Long Island Univ.–Southampton Campus (1963); near Shinnecock Indian Reservation; settled by Puritans from Massachusetts 1640.
4. City, Hampshire, S England, at head of Southampton Water 70 mi. (113 km.) WSW of London; pop. (1991p) 194,400; a major seaport, England's principal port for transatlantic passenger service, with extensive dock facilities; marine engineering; petrochemicals, electrical equipment, cables; Norman church; 12th cent. palace. Roman and Saxon settlements on the site; incorp. 1445; heavily damaged by German bombing in WWII, in which it was important U.S. naval base. Birthplace of hymn writer Isaac Watts (1674), composer Charles Dibdin (1745), painter Sir John Millais (1829), and naval commander John Jellicoe (1859).

Southampton Island. Island, N Hudson Bay, Nunavut, Canada; 15,700 sq. mi. (40,663 sq. km.).

Southampton Water. Estuary of the Test and Itchen rivers, Hampshire, S England.

South Andaman. One of the Andaman Is. (*q.v.*).

South An·na \'a-nə\. River, E cen. Virginia; flows SE to unite with North Anna River in E Hanover co. and form Pamunkey River; ab. 75 mi. (120 km.) long.

South Arabia, Federation of. Former federation, S Arabian Penin., consisting of territories controlled by native rulers in treaty relations with Great Britain; constituted 1959, dissolved and made part of South Yemen (see YEMEN, PEOPLE'S DEMOCRATIC REPUBLIC OF) 1967.

South Ar·gen·tine Peak \'är-jən-ˌtēn\. Mountain in Clear Creek and Summit cos., cen. Colorado; 13,600 ft. (4145 m.).

South Atlantic Ocean. See ATLANTIC OCEAN.

South Australia. State, S cen. Australia; ✻ Adelaide.

Physical features: Relatively little land above 2000 ft. (610 m.); in NW is extension of W plateau; in NE is large section (incl. Lake Eyre) with many mud and marsh depressions. In S part varied physiographic region: Nullarbor Plain in W, salt lakes and North Flinders Range in E, Eyre and Yorke penins. and Kangaroo I. in S. In SE an extension of Murray River lowland. Shoreline generally low but several good harbors on Spencer Gulf and Gulf St. Vincent, inlets of Indian Ocean. Chief river is lower course of Murray (ab. 500 mi. or 805 km. in South Australia).

Chief products: Wheat, barley, oats; wine; iron ore, opal, salt; livestock raising; motor vehicles. See table at AUSTRALIA.

History: Evidence of ancient human inhabitants; coast visited by Dutch 1627; British explorations by Matthew Flinders 1802 and Charles Sturt 1830 opened up S part; colonized as a British province 1836; first constitution 1856; included Northern Terr. (*q.v.*) 1863–1911; franchise extended to women 1894 who first voted in election of 1896; became a state of Commonwealth of Australia 1901.

South·aven \'saủ-ˌthā-vən\. City, DeSoto co., NW corner of Mississippi, just S of Memphis, Tennessee; pop. (1990c) 17,949.

South Bar·ring·ton \'bar-iŋ-tən\. Village, Cook co., NE Illinois, NW of Chicago; pop. (1990c) 2937.

South Bar·won \'bär-wən\. City, S Victoria, Australia; pop. (1991c) 40,772.

South Bass Island. See BASS ISLAND.

South Bay. City, Palm Beach co., SE Florida; pop. (1990c) 3558.

South Be·loit \bə-'lȯit\. City, Winnebago co., N Illinois, on Wisconsin border 16 mi. (26 km.) N of Rockford; pop. (1990c) 4072.

South Bend \'bend\. **1.** City, ⊗ of St. Joseph co., N Indiana, 68 mi. (109 km.) NW of Fort Wayne; pop. (1990c) 105,511; automobile parts, missiles; Indiana Univ. at South Bend (1922). Fur-trading post estab. 1820; incorp. as town 1835, as city 1865. See NOTRE DAME.
2. City, ⊗ of Pacific co., SW Washington, on Willapa Bay; pop. (1990c) 1551.

South Ber·wick \'bər-wik\. Town, York co., SW Maine, on New Hampshire border 24 mi. (39 km.) SW of Biddeford; pop. (1990c) 5877; birthplace of writer Sarah Orne Jewett 1849.

South Beveland. See BEVELAND.

South·bor·ough \'saủth-ˌbər-ə\. **1.** *also* **South·boro** \'saủth-ˌbər-ō\. Town, Worcester co., cen. Massachusetts, 14 mi. (23 km.) E of the city of Worcester; pop. (1990c) 6628.
2. Town, Kent, SE England, 27 mi. (43 km.) SSE of London; pop. (1981p) 9994.

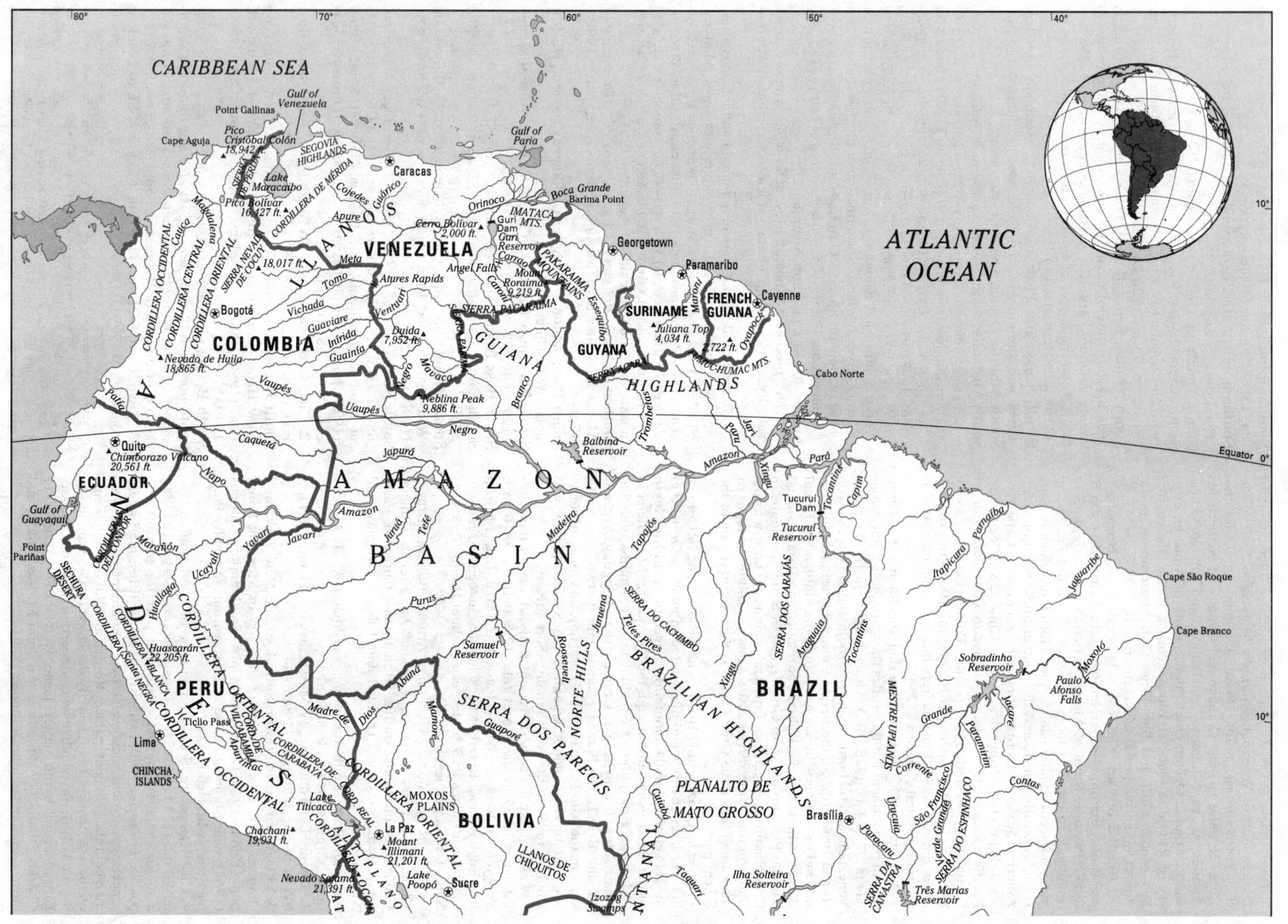

CARIBBEAN SEA
ATLANTIC OCEAN
Equator 0°
VENEZUELA
COLOMBIA
ECUADOR
PERU
BRAZIL
BOLIVIA
GUYANA
SURINAME
FRENCH GUIANA
Caracas
Bogotá
Quito
Lima
La Paz
Sucre
Brasília
Georgetown
Paramaribo
Cayenne
AMAZON BASIN
ANDES
LLANOS
GUIANA HIGHLANDS
BRAZILIAN HIGHLANDS
PLANALTO DE MATO GROSSO
SERRA DOS PARECIS
SERRA DO ESPINHAÇO
SERRA DA CANASTRA
SERRA DOS CARAJÁS
SERRA DO CACHIMBO
NORTE HILLS
MESTRE UPLANDS
PANTANAL
LLANOS DE CHIQUITOS
MOXOS PLAINS
SECHURA DESERT
CHINCHA ISLANDS
ALTIPLANO
CORDILLERA OCCIDENTAL
CORDILLERA CENTRAL
CORDILLERA ORIENTAL
CORDILLERA DE MÉRIDA
SIERRA NEVADA DE COCUY
CORDILLERA BLANCA
CORDILLERA NEGRA
CORDILLERA DEL CONDOR
CORD. DE VILCABAMBA
CORDILLERA DE CARABAYA
CORD. REAL
SERRA PACARAIMA
SERRA PARIMA
SERRA ACARAÍ
PAKARAIMA MOUNTAINS
IMATACA MTS.
TUMUC-HUMAC MTS.
SEGOVIA HIGHLANDS
Amazon
Orinoco
Negro
Madeira
Xingu
Tocantins
Araguaia
Tapajós
Purus
Juruá
Japurá
Caquetá
Napo
Marañón
Ucayali
Huallaga
Apurímac
Mamoré
Guaporé
Madre de Dios
Branco
Essequibo
Magdalena
Cauca
Meta
Apure
São Francisco
Parnaíba
Jaguaribe
Grande
Lake Maracaibo
Lake Titicaca
Lake Poopó
Gulf of Venezuela
Gulf of Paria
Gulf of Guayaquil
Point Gallinas
Cape Aguja
Point Pariñas
Cabo Norte
Cape São Roque
Cape Branco
Boca Grande
Barima Point
Pico Cristóbal Colón 18,942 ft.
Pico Bolívar 16,427 ft.
18,017 ft.
Nevado de Huila 18,865 ft.
Chimborazo Volcano 20,561 ft.
Huascarán 22,205 ft.
Chachani 19,931 ft.
Nevado Sajama 21,391 ft.
Mount Illimani 21,201 ft.
Neblina Peak 9,886 ft.
Duida 7,952 ft.
Mount Roraima 9,219 ft.
Cerro Bolívar 2,000 ft.
Juliana Top 4,034 ft.
2,722 ft.
Angel Falls
Atures Rapids
Paulo Afonso Falls
Guri Dam
Guri Reservoir
Tucuruí Dam
Tucuruí Reservoir
Balbina Reservoir
Samuel Reservoir
Sobradinho Reservoir
Três Marias Reservoir
Ilha Solteira Reservoir
Izozog Swamps
Ticlio Pass
80°
70°
60°
50°
40°
10°

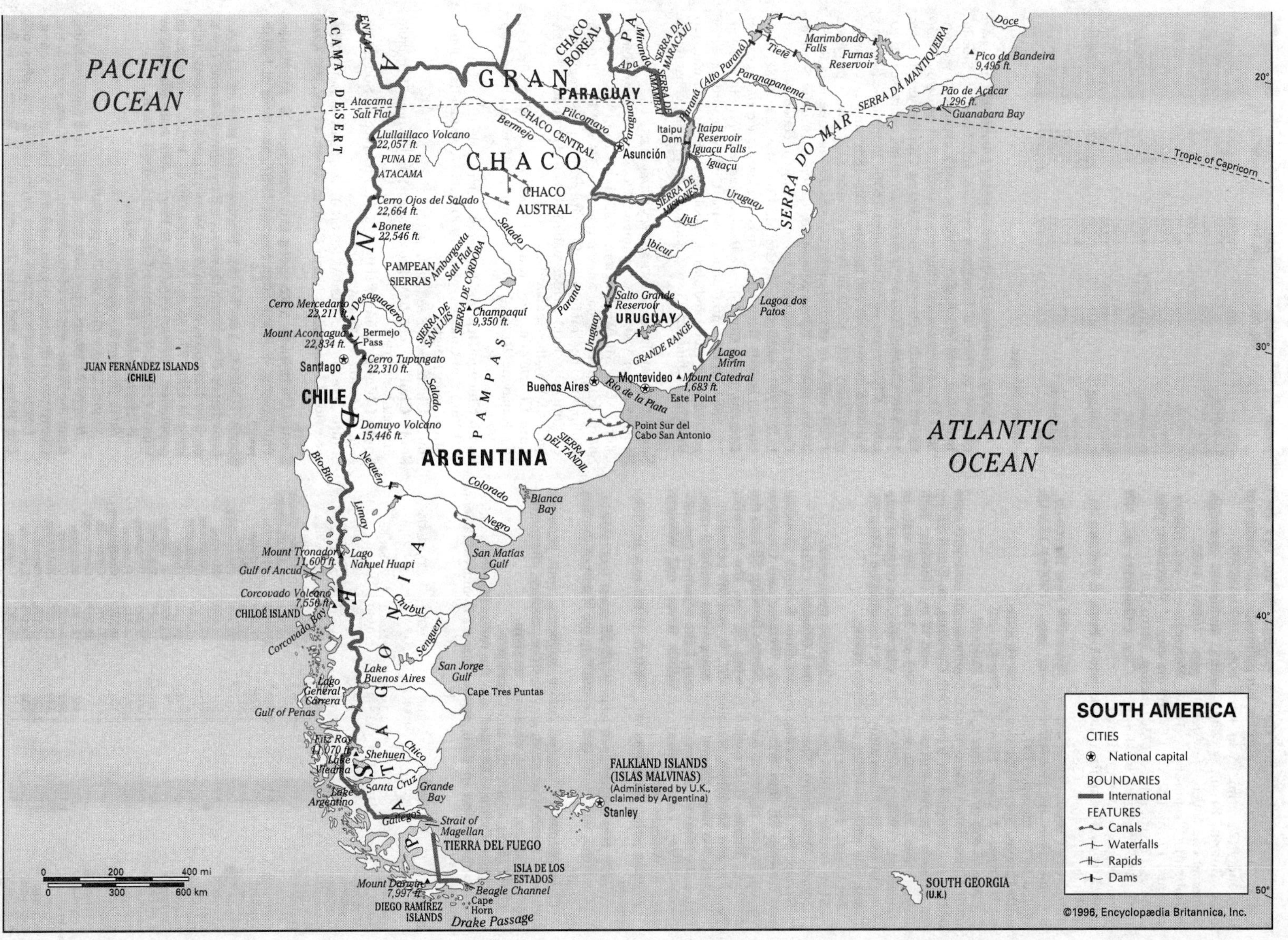
SOUTH AMERICA
CITIES
National capital
BOUNDARIES
International
FEATURES
Canals
Waterfalls
Rapids
Dams
©1996, Encyclopædia Britannica, Inc.
PACIFIC OCEAN
ATLANTIC OCEAN
Tropic of Capricorn
20°
30°
40°
50°
ACAMA DESERT
GRAN CHACO
CHACO BOREAL
CHACO CENTRAL
CHACO AUSTRAL
PARAGUAY
Asunción
URUGUAY
Montevideo
Buenos Aires
Río de la Plata
ARGENTINA
CHILE
Santiago
PAMPAS
SERRA DO MAR
SERRA DA MANTIQUEIRA
SERRA DA MARACAJU
SIERRA DE MISIONES
SIERRA DE CÓRDOBA
SIERRA DE SAN LUIS
SIERRA DEL TANDIL
GRANDE RANGE
PAMPEAN SIERRAS
Ambargasta Salt Flat
PUNA DE ATACAMA
Atacama Salt Flat
Llullaillaco Volcano 22,057 ft.
Cerro Ojos del Salado 22,664 ft.
Bonete 22,546 ft.
Cerro Mercedario 22,211 ft.
Mount Aconcagua 22,834 ft.
Cerro Tupungato 22,310 ft.
Bermejo Pass
Domuyo Volcano 15,446 ft.
Champaquí 9,350 ft.
Pico da Bandeira 9,495 ft.
Pão de Açúcar 1,296 ft.
Guanabara Bay
Mount Catedral 1,683 ft.
Este Point
Point Sur del Cabo San Antonio
Lagoa dos Patos
Lagoa Mirim
Itaipu Dam
Itaipu Reservoir
Iguaçu Falls
Marimbondo Falls
Furnas Reservoir
Salto Grande Reservoir
Paraná (Alto Paraná)
Paranapanema
Tietê
Iguaçu
Uruguay
Ibicuí
Ijuí
Apa
Miranda
Paraguay
Pilcomayo
Bermejo
Salado
Paraná
Desaguadero
Colorado
Negro
Neuquén
Limay
Chubut
Senguerr
Chico
Shehuen
Santa Cruz
Gallegos
Bío-Bío
Doce
Blanca Bay
San Matías Gulf
San Jorge Gulf
Cape Tres Puntas
Grande Bay
Lago Nahuel Huapi
Lake Buenos Aires
Lago General Carrera
Lake Viedma
Lake Argentino
Fitz Roy 11,070 ft.
Mount Tronador 11,600 ft.
Corcovado Volcano 7,559 ft.
Gulf of Ancud
Corcovado Bay
CHILOÉ ISLAND
Gulf of Penas
Strait of Magellan
TIERRA DEL FUEGO
ISLA DE LOS ESTADOS
Beagle Channel
Cape Horn
Mount Darwin 7,997 ft.
DIEGO RAMÍREZ ISLANDS
Drake Passage
FALKLAND ISLANDS (ISLAS MALVINAS) (Administered by U.K., claimed by Argentina)
Stanley
SOUTH GEORGIA (U.K.)
JUAN FERNÁNDEZ ISLANDS (CHILE)
0 200 400 mi
0 300 600 km

South Bos·ton \ˈbȯ-stən\. City, S Virginia, 28 mi. (45 km.) ENE of Danville; in Halifax co. but politically independent of the county; 2 sq. mi. (5 sq. km.); pop. (1990c) 6997.

South Bound Brook \ˈbau̇nd-ˌbru̇k\. Industrial borough, Somerset co., N cen. New Jersey; pop. (1990c) 4185.

South·bridge \ˈsau̇th-ˌbrij\. Town, Worcester co., cen. Massachusetts, 17 mi. (27 km.) SW of the city of Worcester; pop. (1990c) 17,816; settled 1730; incorp. 1816.

South Bur·ling·ton \ˈbər-liŋ-tən\. City, Chittenden co., NW Vermont; pop. (1990c) 12,809.

South Bur·ro Mountain \ˈbər-ō, ˈbu̇r-\. Peak, E Summit co., NE Utah; 12,746 ft. (3885 m.).

South·bury \ˈsau̇th-ˌber-ē, -bə-rē\. Town, NW New Haven co., S Connecticut, on Housatonic River; pop. (1990c) 15,818; settled 1673; incorp. 1787.

South Caicos. See TURKS AND CAICOS ISLANDS.

South Cape. 1. Cape, Hawaii I. See KA LAE. **2.** Cape, S end of Stewart I., New Zealand.

South Car·o·li·na \ˌkar-ə-ˈlī-nə\. Southeastern seaboard state of U.S.A., bounded on N by North Carolina, on E and SE by the Atlantic Ocean, and on S, SW, and W by Georgia; 40th state in area, 31,113 sq. mi. (80,583 sq. km.); 25th state in population, (1990c) 3,486,703; ✻ Columbia; an original state of the Union, the 8th to ratify the U.S. Constitution (May 23, 1788). See table of states at UNITED STATES.

Nickname: Palmetto State.

State flower: Yellow jasmine (Carolina jessamine).

Motto: Dum Spiro, Spero (While I Breathe, I Hope).

Rivers: Pee Dee, crossing border from S North Carolina and flowing SE into Winyah Bay; Wateree and Congaree uniting in cen. region to form the Santee flowing SE into the Atlantic; Edisto, in S region flowing SE into the Atlantic; Tugaloo and Savannah, forming NW, W, and SW boundary.

Lakes: No large natural lakes, but several artificial ones, incl. Lake Marion (see SANTEE DAM), Lake Moultrie (see PINOPOLIS DAM), Lake Murray in Saluda River, and Wateree Lake in Wateree River.

Highest point: Sassafras Mt., 3560 ft. (1085 m.), in Pickens co.

Islands: Has a number of islands off SE coast incl. Edisto, Hilton Head, and Parris and constituting the N part of the Sea Is. chain.

Chief products: Tobacco, cotton, soybeans, fruit, peanuts; livestock; lumbering; sand, gravel, stone; textiles, chemicals, paper products, cement, clothing; tourism.

Chief cities: Columbia and Charleston.

Political divisons: Divided into the following 46 counties (for pronunciation of their names, see their individual entries):

NAME	AREA[1] (sq. mi.)	AREA[1] (sq. km.)	POP. (1990c)	CO. SEAT
Abbeville	506	1,311	23,862	Abbeville
Aiken	1,100	2,849	120,940	Aiken
Allendale	418	1,083	11,722	Allendale
Anderson	775	2,007	145,196	Anderson
Bamberg	395	1,023	16,902	Bamberg
Barnwell	553	1,432	20,293	Barnwell
Beaufort	579	1,500	86,425	Beaufort
Berkeley	1,110	2,875	128,776	Moncks Corner
Calhoun	377	976	12,753	Saint Matthews
Charleston	939	2,432	295,039	Charleston
Cherokee	394	1,020	44,506	Gaffney
Chester	584	1,513	32,170	Chester
Chesterfield	792	2,051	38,577	Chesterfield
Clarendon	599	1,551	28,450	Manning
Colleton	1,049	2,717	34,377	Walterboro
Darlington	544	1,409	61,851	Darlington
Dillon	407	1,054	29,114	Dillon
Dorchester	569	1,474	83,060	St. George
Edgefield	481	1,246	18,375	Edgefield
Fairfield	696	1,803	22,295	Winnsboro
Florence	805	2,085	114,344	Florence
Georgetown	812	2,103	46,302	Georgetown
Greenville	793	2,054	320,167	Greenville
Greenwood	446	1,155	59,567	Greenwood
Hampton	562	1,456	18,191	Hampton
Horry	1,154	2,989	144,053	Conway
Jasper	652	1,689	15,487	Ridgeland
Kershaw	781	2,023	43,599	Camden
Lancaster	502	1,300	54,516	Lancaster
Laurens	711	1,841	58,092	Laurens
Lee	409	1,059	18,437	Bishopville
Lexington	717	1,857	167,611	Lexington
McCormick	306	793	8,868	McCormick
Marion	488	1,264	33,899	Marion
Marlboro	483	1,251	29,361	Bennettsville
Newberry	635	1,645	33,172	Newberry
Oconee	670	1,735	57,494	Walhalla
Orangeburg	1,106	2,865	84,803	Orangeburg
Pickens	501	1,298	93,894	Pickens
Richland	748	1,937	285,720	Columbia
Saluda	444	1,150	16,357	Saluda
Spartanburg	831	2,152	226,800	Spartanburg
Sumter	672	1,740	102,637	Sumter
Union	514	1,331	30,337	Union
Williamsburg	935	2,422	36,815	Kingstree
York	684	1,772	131,497	York

[1] Area = land area.

History: Evidence of Mound Builder inhabitants in W part of state; at time of European contact, inhabited by Siouan, Iroquoian, and Muskogean Indians; coast explored by Spanish 1521; unsuccessful attempts at settlement made by Spanish and French 16th cent.; included in Carolina grant given 1663 by Charles II to eight noblemen of his court (see CAROLINA); Charleston (*q.v.*) founded 1670; English settlements harassed by Spanish and Indians 17th–18th cents.; overthrew proprietary rule 1719 in favor of rule as a crown province 1729; scene of several engagements during American Revolution, notably Kings Mountain, Cowpens, Eutaw Springs, Camden, and Guilford Courthouse (*qq.v.*); ceded W lands to U.S. 1787; ratified U.S. Constitution May 23, 1788; first state to secede from Union, passing ordinance of secession Dec. 20, 1860; Confederate forces attacked Fort Sumter Apr. 12, 1861, in the initial action of the Civil War; ordinance of secession repealed and slavery abolished 1865; readmitted to the Union June 25, 1868; adopted its present constitution 1895.

South Carpathians. See TRANSYLVANIAN ALPS.

South Car·ter \ˈkär-tər\. Mountain, Coos co., N New Hampshire, NE of Mt. Washington; 4645 ft. (1416 m.).

South Channel. S part of entrance to Manila Bay, Luzon, Philippines, bet. mainland of Cavite prov. and Corregidor I.; 6.5 mi. (10 km.) wide; called **Bo·ca Gran·de** \ˈbō-kä-ˈgrän-dā\ by the Spaniards.

South Charleston. City, Kanawha co., W cen. West Virginia, on Kanawha River 4 mi. (6 km.) W of Charleston; pop. (1990c) 13,645.

South Chicago Heights. Village, Cook co., NE Illinois, 13 mi. (21 km.) S of Chicago; pop. (1990c) 3597; residential suburb of Chicago Heights.

South China Sea. See CHINA SEA.

South Chŏl·la \ˈchə-ˈlä\. Province of South Korea. See table at KOREA, SOUTH.

South Ch'ung·ch'ŏng \ˈchüŋ-ˈchȯŋ\. Province of South Korea. See table at KOREA, SOUTH.

South Con·cho \ˈkän-chō\. River, Texas; rises in Schleicher co., flows N and joins North Concho River; 41 mi. (66 km.) long.

South Co·ta·ba·to \ˌkō-tä-ˈbä-tō\. Province, S Mindanao, Philippines; ✻ Koronadal; formed 1967. See table at PHILIPPINES.

South Da·ko·ta \də-ˈkō-tə\. Northwestern state of U.S.A., bounded on N by North Dakota, on E by Minnesota and Iowa, on S by Nebraska, and on W by Wyoming and Montana; 16th state in area, 77,116 sq. mi. (199,730 sq. km.); 45th state in population, (1990c) 696,004; ✻ Pierre; 40th state admitted to Union (1889). See table of states at UNITED STATES.

Nickname: Mt. Rushmore State.

State flower: Pasqueflower.

Motto: Under God the People Rule.

Rivers: Missouri, bisecting state from N to S and receiving from the W the waters of the Moreau in the N cen. region, the Cheyenne in the cen. region, and the White in the S section.

Lakes: Numerous small lakes in E; on NE boundary are Big Stone Lake and Lake Traverse; in W in Butte co. is the

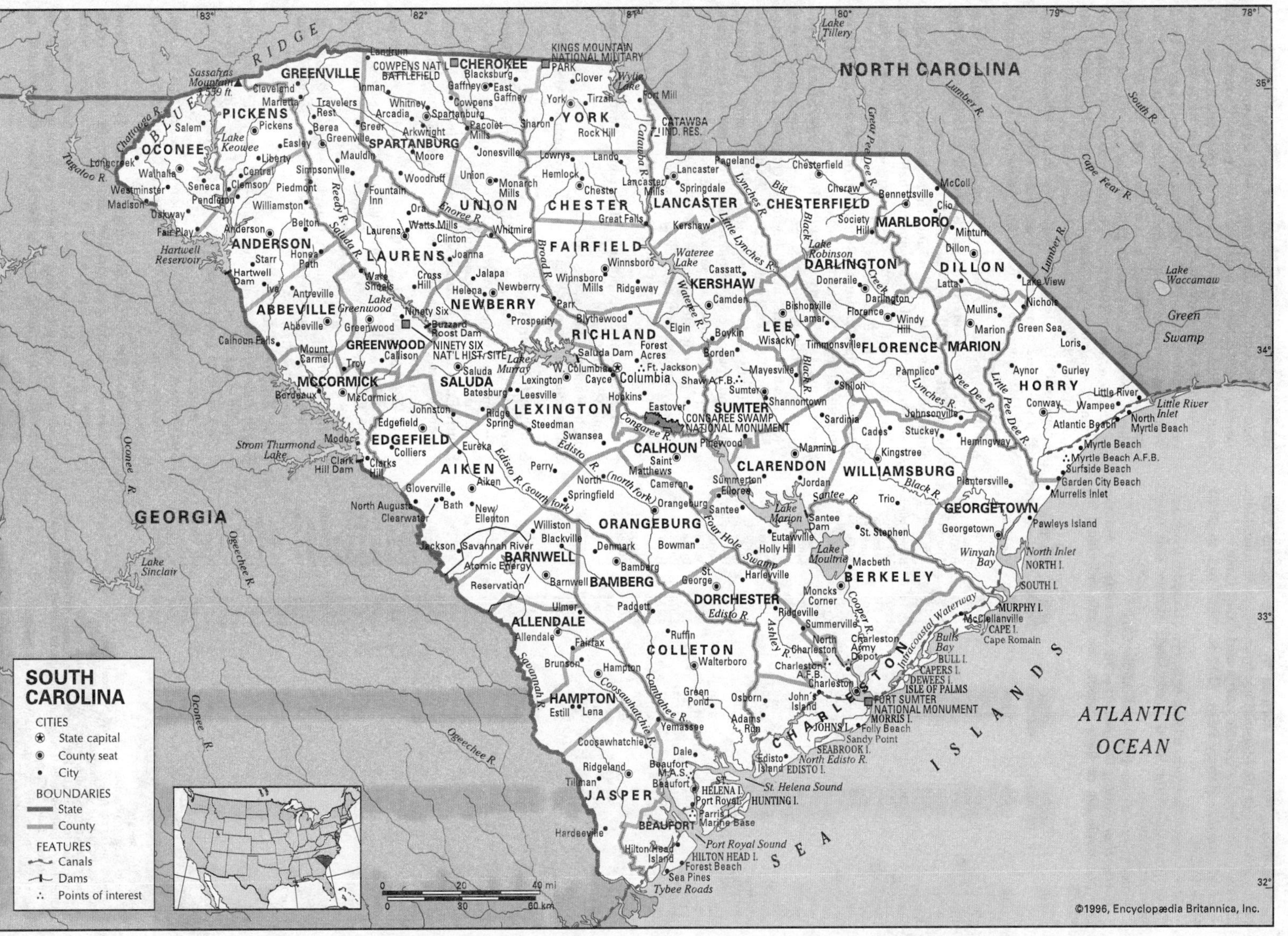
SOUTH CAROLINA
CITIES
State capital
County seat
City
BOUNDARIES
State
County
FEATURES
Canals
Dams
Points of interest
NORTH CAROLINA
GEORGIA
ATLANTIC OCEAN
SEA ISLANDS
BLUE RIDGE
Sassafras Mountain
OCONEE
PICKENS
GREENVILLE
SPARTANBURG
CHEROKEE
YORK
UNION
CHESTER
LANCASTER
CHESTERFIELD
MARLBORO
DILLON
HORRY
MARION
FLORENCE
DARLINGTON
LEE
KERSHAW
FAIRFIELD
NEWBERRY
LAURENS
ANDERSON
ABBEVILLE
GREENWOOD
McCORMICK
EDGEFIELD
SALUDA
RICHLAND
LEXINGTON
SUMTER
CLARENDON
WILLIAMSBURG
GEORGETOWN
BERKELEY
CHARLESTON
DORCHESTER
CALHOUN
ORANGEBURG
AIKEN
BARNWELL
BAMBERG
ALLENDALE
COLLETON
HAMPTON
JASPER
BEAUFORT
Columbia
KINGS MOUNTAIN NATIONAL MILITARY PARK
COWPENS NAT'L BATTLEFIELD
NINETY SIX NAT'L HIST. SITE
CONGAREE SWAMP NATIONAL MONUMENT
FORT SUMTER NATIONAL MONUMENT
Lake Murray
Lake Marion
Lake Moultrie
Strom Thurmond Lake
Hartwell Reservoir
Savannah R.
Santee R.
Intracoastal Waterway
0 20 40 mi
0 30 60 km
©1996, Encyclopædia Britannica, Inc.

Belle Fourche Reservoir formed by Belle Fourche Dam; large reservoirs in the Missouri are from NW to SE Lake Oahe and on the Nebraska border Lewis and Clark Lake.

Highest point: Harney Peak, 7242 ft. (2207 m.), in Black Hills in SW.

Chief products: Corn, wheat, oats, rye, flaxseed; livestock; gold; manufacturing: food processing; lumber and wood products; tourism.

Chief cities: Sioux Falls and Rapid City.

Political divisions: Divided into the following 67 counties (for pronunciation of their names, see their individual entries):

NAME	AREA[1] (sq. mi.)	AREA[1] (sq. km.)	POP. (1990c)	CO. SEAT
Aurora	709	1,836	3,135	Plankinton
Beadle	1,260	3,263	18,253	Huron
Bennett	1,181	3,059	3,206	Martin
Bon Homme	560	1,450	7,089	Tyndall
Brookings	800	2,072	25,207	Brookings
Brown	1,674	4,336	35,580	Aberdeen
Brule	818	2,119	5,485	Chamberlain
Buffalo	482	1,248	1,759	Gannvalley
Butte[2]	2,250	5,828	7,914	Belle Fourche
Campbell	732	1,896	1,965	Mound City
Charles Mix	1,097	2,841	9,131	Lake Andes
Clark	964	2,497	4,403	Clark
Clay	405	1,049	13,186	Vermillion
Codington	687	1,779	22,698	Watertown
Corson	2,470	6,397	4,195	McIntosh
Custer[3]	1,557	4,033	6,179	Custer
Davison	432	1,119	17,503	Mitchell
Day	1,030	2,668	6,978	Webster
Deuel	639	1,655	4,522	Clear Lake
Dewey[4]	2,351	6,089	5,523	Timber Lake
Douglas	435	1,127	3,746	Armour
Edmunds	1,154	2,989	4,356	Ipswich
Fall River	1,743	4,514	7,353	Hot Springs
Faulk	996	2,580	2,744	Faulkton
Grant	681	1,764	8,372	Milbank
Gregory	997	2,582	5,359	Burke
Haakon	1,816	4,703	2,624	Philip
Hamlin	511	1,323	4,974	Hayti
Hand	1,432	3,709	4,272	Miller
Hanson	430	1,114	2,994	Alexandria
Harding	2,682	6,946	1,669	Buffalo
Hughes	748	1,937	14,817	Pierre
Hutchinson	815	2,111	8,262	Olivet
Hyde	863	2,235	1,696	Highmore
Jackson[5]	1,872	4,848	2,811	Kadoka
Jerauld	527	1,365	2,425	Wessington Springs
Jones	973	2,520	1,324	Murdo
Kingsbury	818	2,119	5,925	De Smet
Lake	567	1,469	10,550	Madison
Lawrence	800	2,072	20,665	Deadwood
Lincoln	576	1,492	15,427	Canton
Lyman	1,683	4,359	3,638	Kennebec
McCook	575	1,489	5,688	Salem
McPherson	1,147	2,971	3,228	Leola
Marshall	848	2,196	4,844	Britton
Meade	3,465	8,974	21,878	Sturgis
Mellette	1,306	3,383	2,137	White River
Miner	570	1,476	3,272	Howard
Minnehaha	813	2,106	123,809	Sioux Falls
Moody	523	1,355	6,507	Flandreau
Pennington	2,779	7,198	81,343	Rapid City
Perkins	2,860	7,407	3,932	Bison
Potter	869	2,251	3,190	Gettysburg
Roberts	1,108	2,870	9,914	Sisseton
Sanborn	570	1,476	2,833	Woonsocket
Shannon[6,7]	2,100	5,439	9,902	
Spink	1,505	3,898	7,981	Redfield
Stanley	1,414	3,662	2,453	Fort Pierre
Sully	1,004	2,600	1,589	Onida
Todd[6]	1,388	3,595	8,352	
Tripp	1,620	4,196	6,924	Winner
Turner	612	1,585	8,576	Parker
Union	452	1,171	10,189	Elk Point
Walworth	718	1,860	6,087	Selby
Yankton	518	1,342	19,252	Yankton
Ziebach	1,981	5,131	2,220	Dupree

[1] Area = land area.
[2] Contains geographic center of the U.S.
[3] Contains (in S cen. part) Wind Cave National Park.
[4] Includes the previously unorganized Armstrong county.
[5] Includes the previously unorganized Washabaugh county.
[6] Two counties (occupied by Indian reservations) remain unorganized, being attached for judicial purposes to adjacent counties, as follows: Shannon (attached to Fall River), Todd (to Tripp).
[7] Includes the previously unorganized Washington county.

History: Evidence of prehistoric Mound Builders' settlements; at time of European contact, inhabited by several Indian tribes, incl. esp. the Arikara, who soon moved N, and several Dakota tribes; explored somewhat by French in 18th cent.; included in Louisiana Purchase 1803 and traversed by Lewis and Clark expedition 1804, 1806; fur trade with Indians conducted throughout 19th cent. until outbreak of Civil War; first permanent European settlement founded 1817, on future site of Fort Pierre, as a trading post; after several attempts, organized as part of Dakota Terr. (*q.v.*) 1861 with ✻ at Yankton; latter 19th cent. characterized by conflict with Indians, several insect plagues, and Black Hills gold rush (discovery 1874); admitted to Union Nov. 2, 1889 upon division of Dakota Terr. into two states; Pierre selected as state ✻ 1889; state constitution dates from 1889.

South Day·to·na \dā-'tō-nə\. City, Volusia co., E Florida; pop. (1990c) 12,482.

South Downs \'daùnz\. Range of low hills, extending W to E from SE Hampshire to S East Sussex in S England; highest point **But·ser Hill** \ˌbət-sər\ 889 ft. (271 m.).

Southeast Asia. Region of indefinite boundaries, SE Asia; usu. thought to include Myanmar, Thailand, Malaysia, Laos, Cambodia, and Vietnam, and often also Indonesia, Singapore, and the Philippines.

Southeast Asian Nations, Association of. See ASSOCIATION OF SOUTHEAST ASIAN NATIONS.

South–East Asia Treaty Organization *or abbr.* **SEATO** \'sē-tō\. Former military alliance, consisting of Australia, France, New Zealand, Pakistan, Philippines, Thailand, United Kingdom, United States; estab. by South-East Asia Collective Defense Treaty (Manila Pact) 1954; headquarters Bangkok, Thailand; purpose: to promote joint defense of the region against armed attack or subversive activities; U.S. restricted its own participation to cases of Communist agression, but agreed to consult on other matters as well; France and Pakistan became inactive from 1966–67; dissolved on June 30, 1977.

South East Cape SE point of Tasmania, Australia, on the South Pacific Ocean.

South–Eastern. See CROSS RIVER 2.

Southeast Fair·banks \'far-ˌbaŋks\. Division in Alaska. See table at ALASKA.

Southeast Indian Ridge. Ridge, S Indian Ocean floor, extending in an arc approx. from N of Amsterdam I. to SW of Tasmania in a general WNW to ESE direction; a center of oceanic crust formation according to theory of plate tectonics.

South East Islands. Group of islands, SE Indonesia, southeasternmost of the Moluccas; includes Tanimbar, Kai, and Aru islands.

South–East Su·la·we·si \ˌsü-lä-'wā-sē\. Province of Indonesia, on Sulawesi. See SULAWESI and table at INDONESIA.

South El·gin \'el-jən\. Village, Kane co., NE Illinois, 4 mi. (6 km.) S of Elgin; pop. (1990c) 7474.

South El Mon·te \el-'män-tē\. City, Los Angeles co., SW California, 10 mi. (16 km.) E of the city of Los Angeles; pop. (1990c) 20,850.

South Emporia. See EMPORIA 2.

South·end–on–Sea \'saù-ˌthend-ˌän-'sē\. Seaside resort, Essex, SE England, at mouth of estuary of the Thames 36 mi. (58 km.) E of London; pop. (1991p) 153,700; 12th cent. priory museum.

Southern Ae·ge·an \i-'jē-ən\. Region of Greece; 2041 sq. mi. (5286 sq. km.); pop. (1991c) 257,522. For subdivisions, see table at GREECE.

Southern Alps. Mountain range, W cen. South I., New Zealand, extending almost the entire length of the island; highest peak Mt. Cook 12,349 ft. (3764 m.); many peaks from 8000 to 11,000 ft. (2440 to 3350 m.); region noted for its scenery; only crossing place by railroad and highway is through Otira Gorge and Arthur's Pass, Christchurch to Greymouth.

Southern Bug. See BUG 2.

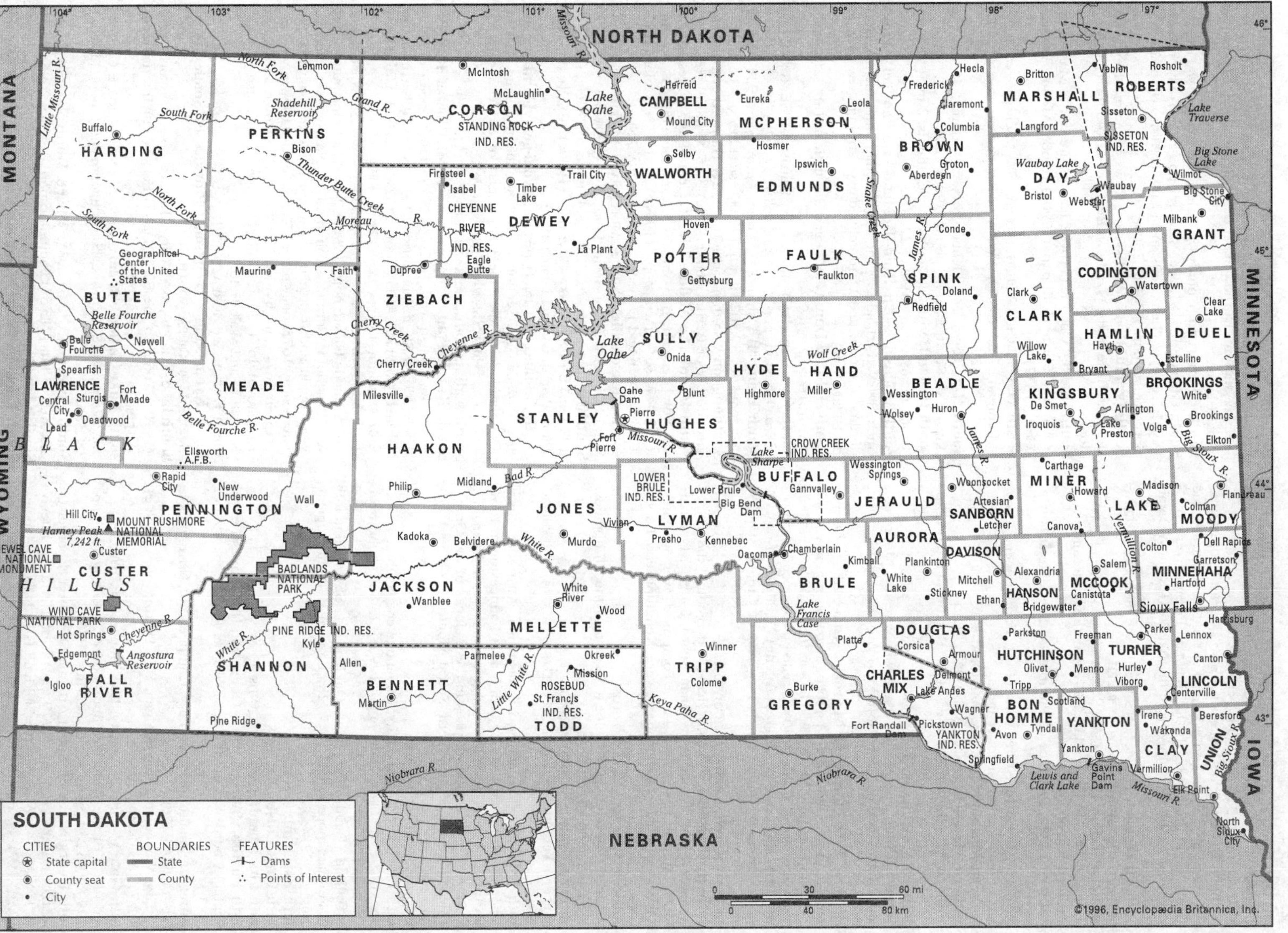
NORTH DAKOTA
MINNESOTA
IOWA
NEBRASKA
WYOMING
MONTANA
HARDING
PERKINS
CORSON
STANDING ROCK IND. RES.
CAMPBELL
McPHERSON
BROWN
MARSHALL
ROBERTS
SISSETON IND. RES.
WALWORTH
EDMUNDS
DAY
GRANT
DEWEY
CHEYENNE RIVER IND. RES.
POTTER
FAULK
SPINK
CODINGTON
BUTTE
ZIEBACH
SULLY
HYDE
HAND
CLARK
HAMLIN
DEUEL
LAWRENCE
MEADE
STANLEY
HUGHES
BEADLE
KINGSBURY
BROOKINGS
HAAKON
PENNINGTON
JONES
LOWER BRULE IND. RES.
CROW CREEK IND. RES.
BUFFALO
JERAULD
SANBORN
MINER
LAKE
MOODY
LYMAN
AURORA
DAVISON
HANSON
MCCOOK
MINNEHAHA
CUSTER
JACKSON
BRULE
FALL RIVER
SHANNON
PINE RIDGE IND. RES.
BENNETT
MELLETTE
ROSEBUD IND. RES.
TODD
TRIPP
GREGORY
DOUGLAS
CHARLES MIX
YANKTON IND. RES.
HUTCHINSON
TURNER
LINCOLN
BON HOMME
YANKTON
CLAY
UNION
BLACK HILLS
BADLANDS NATIONAL PARK
MOUNT RUSHMORE NATIONAL MEMORIAL
JEWEL CAVE NATIONAL MONUMENT
WIND CAVE NATIONAL PARK
Harney Peak 7,242 ft.
Geographical Center of the United States
Ellsworth A.F.B.
Lake Oahe
Oahe Dam
Lake Sharpe
Big Bend Dam
Lake Francis Case
Fort Randall Dam
Lewis and Clark Lake
Gavins Point Dam
Shadehill Reservoir
Belle Fourche Reservoir
Angostura Reservoir
Waubay Lake
Lake Traverse
Big Stone Lake
Missouri R.
Little Missouri R.
Grand R.
North Fork
South Fork
Thunder Butte Creek
Moreau R.
Cherry Creek
Cheyenne R.
Belle Fourche R.
Bad R.
White R.
Little White R.
Keya Paha R.
Niobrara R.
James R.
Snake Creek
Wolf Creek
Vermillion R.
Big Sioux R.
Pierre
Rapid City
Sioux Falls
Aberdeen
Watertown
Brookings
Huron
Mitchell
Yankton
Vermillion
Lemmon
Buffalo
Bison
McIntosh
McLaughlin
Herreid
Mound City
Eureka
Leola
Frederick
Hecla
Britton
Veblen
Rosholt
Sisseton
Wilmot
Big Stone City
Milbank
Webster
Waubay
Bristol
Langford
Claremont
Columbia
Groton
Selby
Hosmer
Ipswich
Trail City
Firesteel
Isabel
Timber Lake
La Plant
Eagle Butte
Dupree
Faith
Maurine
Hoven
Gettysburg
Faulkton
Conde
Doland
Redfield
Clark
Clear Lake
Willow Lake
Hayti
Bryant
Estelline
Onida
Blunt
Highmore
Miller
Wessington
Wolsey
De Smet
Iroquois
Arlington
Lake Preston
White
Volga
Elkton
Spearfish
Belle Fourche
Newell
Central City
Sturgis
Fort Meade
Deadwood
Lead
Cherry Creek
Milesville
Philip
Midland
Fort Pierre
Wall
New Underwood
Hill City
Custer
Hot Springs
Edgemont
Igloo
Kadoka
Belvidere
Murdo
Vivian
Presho
Kennebec
Lower Brule
Gannvalley
Wessington Springs
Woonsocket
Artesian
Letcher
Carthage
Howard
Madison
Canova
Flandreau
Colman
Dell Rapids
Garretson
Colton
Salem
Hartford
Chamberlain
Oacoma
Kimball
Plankinton
White Lake
Stickney
Mitchell
Ethan
Alexandria
Bridgewater
Canistota
Wanblee
White River
Wood
Kyle
Pine Ridge
Allen
Martin
Parmelee
Okreek
Mission
St. Francis
Winner
Colome
Burke
Platte
Corsica
Armour
Delmont
Lake Andes
Wagner
Pickstown
Springfield
Parkston
Olivet
Tripp
Menno
Scotland
Tyndall
Avon
Freeman
Hurley
Viborg
Parker
Lennox
Harrisburg
Canton
Centerville
Beresford
Irene
Wakonda
Elk Point
North Sioux City
104°
103°
102°
101°
100°
99°
98°
97°
46°
45°
44°
43°
SOUTH DAKOTA
CITIES
State capital
County seat
City
BOUNDARIES
State
County
FEATURES
Dams
Points of Interest
0 30 60 mi
0 40 80 km
©1996, Encyclopædia Britannica, Inc.

Southern Central India States. Former agency, group of Indian states, now part of Madhya Pradesh state, W cen. India; 5101 sq. mi. (13,212 sq. km.); chief state Dhar.

Southern Dec·can \ˈde-kən, -ˌkan\ *also* **Deccan Proper.** Plateau region, S India, in Karnataka, Andhra Pradesh, and Tamil Nadu; drained by the Krishna and Penner rivers; on S separated by a deep valley from the Nilgiri Hills in W Tamil Nadu. See DECCAN.

Southern District. District of S Israel. See table at ISRAEL.

Southern Flevoland. See ZUIDER ZEE.

Southern Indian Lake. Lake, NW Manitoba, Canada; 1060 sq. mi. (2745 sq. km.); Churchill River flows through it.

Southern Karoo. See KAROO.

Southern Leyte. Province of Philippines. See table at PHILIPPINES.

Southern Ma·ra·tha States \mə-ˈrä-tə\. Former agency, now part of Maharashtra state, W India.

Southern Mashonaland. See MASHONALAND.

Southern Matabeleland. See MATABELELAND.

Southern Min·da·nao \ˌmin-dä-ˈnau̇\ Region of the Philippines. See table at PHILIPPINES.

Southern Moytura. See MOYTURA.

Southern Pines \ˈpīnz\. Town and winter resort, Moore co., cen. North Carolina, 30 mi. (48 km.) W of Fayetteville; pop. (1990c) 9129.

Southern Protectorate of Mo·roc·co \mə-ˈrä-kō\. Former Spanish protectorate, SW Morocco; a coastal region extending from Cap Juby NE to Cape Dra at the mouth of the Drâa River and inland to ab. 8°40′W; ceded to Morocco 1958.

Southern Raj·pu·ta·na States Agency \ˌräj-pə-ˈtä-nə\. A former group of Indian states, now part of Gujarat state, W India.

Southern Rhodesia. See ZIMBABWE 2.

Southern Shan States \ˈshän, ˈshan\. S division of the former Federated Shan States (now Shan State), E cen. Myanmar; 36,416 sq. mi. (94,317 sq. km.); comprised over 30 states, some very small; among them were Kengtung and Lawksawk.

Southern Sporades. See SPORADES.

Southern Ta·ga·log \tä-ˈgä-ˌlȯg\. Region of the Philippines. See table at PHILIPPINES.

Southern Urals. See URAL MOUNTAINS.

Southern Yemen. See YEMEN, PEOPLE'S DEMOCRATIC REPUBLIC OF.

South Esk \ˈesk\. **1.** River, NE Tasmania, Australia; flows generally W then N to join North Esk at Launceston to form the Tamar; 120 mi. (193 km.) long; longest river in Tasmania.
2. River, E cen. Scotland; rises in the E slopes of the Grampian Mts., flows SE into North Sea at Montrose; 48.5 mi. (78 km.) long.
3. River, Scotland. See ESK 3.

South Eu·clid \ˈyü-kləd\. City, Cuyahoga co., N Ohio, 10 mi. (16 km.) E of Cleveland; pop. (1990c) 23,866; suburb of Cleveland.

South·field \ˈsau̇th-ˌfēld\. City, Oakland co., SE Michigan, S of Pontiac; pop. (1990c) 75,728; Lawrence Technological Univ. (1932).

South Foreland. See FORELAND.

South Fork Edisto. See EDISTO.

South Fox Island. See FOX ISLANDS 2.

South Ful·ton \ˈfu̇lt-ᵊn\. City, Obion co., NW Tennessee, on Kentucky border 35 mi. (56 km.) WNW of Paris; pop. (1990c) 2688.

South·gate \ˈsau̇th-ˌgāt\. **1.** City, Campbell co., N Kentucky; pop. (1990c) 3266.
2. City, Wayne co., SE Michigan, S of Detroit; pop. (1990c) 30,771; residential.

South Gate \ˈsau̇th-ˌgāt\. City, Los Angeles co., SW California, just E of the Watts neighborhood of Los Angeles; pop. (1990c) 86,284; grew rapidly during 1980s.

South Georgia. Island, South Atlantic Ocean on N border of Scotia Sea, ab. 1100 mi. (1770 km.) E of Tierra del Fuego, 54°15′S, 36°45′W; one of the Falkland Islands Dependencies (*q.v.*); 1450 sq. mi. (3756 sq. km.); chief town Grytviken Harbour; highest point 9625 ft. (2934 m.). Annexed to Great Britain by Capt. James Cook 1775; interior explored 1964–65; formerly a whaling base; now site of Antarctic research station. Burial place of Irish explorer Sir Ernest Shackleton.

South Glamorgan. County, S Wales. See table at WALES.

South Glens Falls. Village, Saratoga co., New York, on Hudson River opp. Glens Falls and 17 mi. (27 km.) NE of Saratoga Springs; pop. (1990c) 3506.

South Grand. River, W Missouri; flows SE across Henry co. into the Lake of the Ozarks in Benton co.; 140 mi. (225 km.) long.

South Had·ley \ˈhad-lē\. Town, Hampshire co., W Massachusetts, N of Springfield; pop. (1990c) 16,685; Mount Holyoke Coll. (1837).

South Haven. City, Van Buren co., SW Michigan, on Lake Michigan 37 mi. (60 km.) WNW of Kalamazoo; pop. (1990c) 5563.

South Hill. Town, Mecklenburg co., S Virginia, 45 mi. (72 km.) E of South Boston; pop. (1990c) 4217.

South Holland. Village, Cook co., NE Illinois, 3 mi. (4.8 km.) S of Chicago; pop. (1990c) 22,105.

South Holland *or Du.* **Zuid–Hol·land** \zȯit-ˈhȯ-länt\. Province, SW Netherlands; ✻ The Hague; other cities include Rotterdam, Leiden, and Dordrecht; dairy farming. See table at NETHERLANDS.

South Hol·ston Dam \ˈhōl-stən\. See table at TENNESSEE VALLEY AUTHORITY.

South Hous·ton \ˈhyü-stən\. City, Harris co., SE Texas, just SE of Houston; pop. (1990c) 14,207.

South Hsing·an \ˈshiŋ-ˈän\. Former province (1934–45), W Manchukuo; 30,502 sq. mi. (79,000 sq. km.).

South·ing·ton \ˈsə-t͟hiŋ-tən\. Town, SW Hartford co., N Connecticut, W of Berlin; pop. (1990c) 38,518; hardware.

South Island *also* **Middle Island.** Central and largest island of New Zealand; 525 mi. (845 km.) long; 59,439 sq. mi. (153,947 sq. km.); pop. (1991c) 881,537. Chief cities Christchurch and Dunedin. See NEW ZEALAND.

South Jacksonville. Village, Morgan co., W cen. Illinois, 30 mi. (48 km.) WSW of Springfield; pop. (1990c) 3187.

South Jor·dan \ˈjȯrd-ᵊn\. City, Salt Lake co., N Utah, 14 mi. (23 km.) S of Salt Lake City; pop. (1990c) 12,220; pop. has more than quadrupled since 1970.

South Jut·land \ˈjət-lənd\ *or Dan.* **Syd·li·ge Jyl·land** \ˈsu̅e̅t͟h-li-gə-ˈyu̅e̅-ˌlȧn\. S section of Jutland, the mainland part of Denmark; constitutes the Danish part of Schleswig (*q.v.*), known as **Nord Sle·svig** \ˈnȯr-ˈslis-vē\.

South Kalimantan. See KALIMANTAN, SOUTH.

South Kazakhstan. Administrative subdivision of Kazakhstan; 46,564 sq. mi. (120,601 sq. km.); pop. (1991e) 1,879,200; ✻ Shymkent; formed 1932 as **South Kazakhstan Oblast** \ˈȯ-bləst, -ˌblast\ of U.S.S.R.; called **Chim·kent Oblast** \chim-ˈkyent\ 1963–91.

South Kings·town \ˈkiŋ-stən, -ˌstau̇n\. Town, SE Washington co., S Rhode Island; pop. (1990c) 24,631; administrative center Wakefield. Former stronghold of Narraganset Indians, who fought and lost their last major battle of King Philip's War nearby 1675; once part of Kings Towne (Kingstown), incorp. in 1674 and divided into North Kingstown and South Kingstown in 1723; includes villages of Kingston, West Kingston, and Wakefield.

South Korea. See KOREA, SOUTH.

South Kyŏng·sang \ˈkyȯŋ-ˈsäŋ\. Province of South Korea. See table at KOREA, SOUTH.

South·lake \ˈsau̇th-ˌlāk\. City, Tarrant co., N Texas; pop. (1990c) 7065; to the SE is Dallas-Fort Worth International Airport.

South Lake Ta·hoe \ˈtä-ˌhō\. City, El Dorado co., E California, 75 mi. (121 km.) ENE of Sacramento; pop. (1990c) 21,586.

South Le·ba·non \ˈle-bə-nən\. Village, Warren co., SW Ohio, 28 mi. (45 km.) NE of Cincinnati; pop. (1990c) 2696.

South Llano. See LLANO 1.

South Lookout Peak. Mountain, San Juan and San Miguel cos., SW Colorado; 13,500 ft. (4115 m.).

South Loup \ˈlüp\. River, cen. Nebraska; rises in Logan co., flows E and SE to unite with North Loup and Middle Loup and form the Loup River; 152 mi. (245 km.) long.

South Ly·on \ˈlī-ən\. City, Oakland co., SE Michigan, 10 mi. (16 km.) NE of Ann Arbor; pop. (1990c) 5857.

South Magnetic Pole. See MAGNETIC POLE.

South Male. See MALE.

South Marsh Island. Island bet. Tangier Sound and Chesapeake Bay, NW Somerset co., SE Maryland.

South Melbourne. City, S Victoria, SE Australia, S suburb of Melbourne on Port Phillip Bay; pop. (1991c) 17,712.

South Miami. City, Miami-Dade co., SE Florida, 7 mi. (11 km.) SW of Miami; pop. (1990c) 10,404; incorp. 1926.

South Milwaukee. City, Milwaukee co., SE Wisconsin, on Lake Michigan 9 mi. (14 km.) S of the city of Milwaukee; pop. (1990c) 20,958.

South Moresby National Park. See CANADA, *National Parks.*

South Mountain. Ridge, S Pennsylvania and W Maryland; battle Sept. 14, 1862 (called Boonsboro by the Confederates) in which Union Gen. George McClellan defeated Confederate Gen. Robert E. Lee's army on its first invasion of the North, preliminary to the battle of Antietam.

South Na·han·ni \nə-ˈha-nē\. River, SW Northwest Territories, Canada; a N tributary of the Liard flowing SE from the Mackenzie Mts.; 350 mi. (563 km.) long.

South Na·varre Peak \nə-ˈvär\. Mountain, Chelan co., cen. Washington; 7800 ft. (2377 m.).

South Ne·gril Point \nə-ˈgril\. Cape, W end of Jamaica, West Indies, at S entrance to Long Bay.

South Norfolk. Former city, SE Virginia, on Elizabeth River 3 mi. (5 km.) S of Norfolk; merged 1963 with former county of Norfolk in new city of Chesapeake (*q.v.*).

South Norwalk. Former city, now a subdivision of town and city of Norwalk, Connecticut. See NORWALK 3.

South Ny·ack \ˈnī-ˌak\. Village, Rockland co., SE New York, on Hudson River near Nyack and 24 mi. (39 km.) N of New York City; pop. (1990c) 3352.

South Og·den \ˈȯg-dən, ˈäg-\. City, Weber co., N Utah; pop. (1990c) 12,105.

South·old \ˈsau̇th-ˌōld\. Unincorporated settlement in Southold town (pop. [1990] 19,836), Suffolk co., New York, on N extension of Long Island ab. 18 mi. (29 km.) NE of Riverhead; pop. (1990c) 5192.

South Orange. Village, Essex co., NE New Jersey, 5 mi. (8 km.) W of Newark; pop. (1990c) 16,390; together with Orange, East Orange, West Orange, and Maplewood, forms a suburban residential area outside New York City; Seton Hall Univ. (1856).

South Ork·ney Islands \ˈȯrk-nē\ *also* **South Ork·neys** \-nēz\. Group of islands, S Atlantic Ocean S of Scotia Sea, ab. 850 mi. (1370 km.) NE of Antarctic Penin., and SE of S extremity of South America, 61°S, 45°W; 240 sq. mi. (622 sq. km.); part of British Antarctic Terr. Largest island is Coronation I. Discovered 1821 by British and American sealers; part of Falkland Islands Dependencies until 1962; claimed by Argentina (*Span.* **Or·ca·das del Sur** \ȯr-ˈkä-t͟häs-ˌt͟hel-ˈsür\).

South Os·se·tia \ä-ˈsē-shē-ə\ *or* **South Os·se·ti·ya** \ä-ˈse-tē-yə\. Autonomous subdivision, N Republic of Georgia; 1506 sq. mi. (3901 sq. km.); pop. (1990e) 99,000; ✱ Ts'khinvali. High plateau region on S slopes of Caucasus; sheep farming. Formerly comprised **South Os·se·tian Autonomous Oblast** \ä-ˈsē-shən … ˈȯ-bləst, -ˌblast\ of Georgian S.S.R.; for early history, see ALANIA. Made an autonomous oblast of Georgia 1922; proclaimed independence from Republic of Georgia Sept. 20, 1990 and armed conflict followed.

South Pacific Ocean. See PACIFIC OCEAN.

South Pagai. See PAGAI.

South Paris. Unincorporated settlement, ⊗ of Oxford co., W Maine, 17 mi. (27 km.) WNW of Lewiston; pop. (1990c) 2320.

South Park. Tableland, Park co., cen. Colorado; contains source of the South Platte; with North Park, Middle Park, and San Luis Park (*qq.v.*) forms a N to S chain of grassy plateaus enclosed by snowcapped mountains.

South Pas·a·de·na \ˌpa-sə-ˈdē-nə\. **1.** Residential city, Los Angeles co., SW California, just E of the city of Los Angeles; pop. (1990c) 23,936; electronic components.
2. City, Pinellas co., cen. W coast of Florida; pop. (1990c) 5644.

South Pass. 1. One of the channels at the mouth of the Mississippi River (*q.v.*), at SW tip of Louisiana.
2. Pass, Fremont co., SW cen. Wyoming, at S end of Wind River Range; 7550 ft. (2301 m.); discovered 1812, first used for wagons 1832 by Capt. Benjamin Bonneville's exploring party. Nearby **South Pass City,** once-prosperous 19th cent. boomtown is now a tourist attraction. See OREGON TRAIL.

South Pitts·burg \ˈpits-ˌbərg\. City, Marion co., S Tennessee, on Tennessee River 24 mi. (39 km.) W of Chattanooga; pop. (1990c) 3295.

South Plain·field \ˈplān-ˌfēld\. Borough, Middlesex co., cen. New Jersey, 6 mi. (10 km.) NNE of New Brunswick; pop. (1990c) 20,489.

South Platte \ˈplat\. River, Colorado and W Nebraska; rises in NW Park co., cen. Colorado, flows SE then NE across Nebraska boundary to join the North Platte River in Lincoln co., SW cen. Nebraska, and form the Platte River; 424 mi. (682 km.) long.

South Point. 1. Cape, Hawaii I. See KA LAE.
2. Point, SE tip of Marsh I., off S coast of Louisiana.
3. Point, SE coast of Alpena co., NE Michigan, at S entrance to Thunder Bay.
4. Village, Lawrence co., S Ohio, on Ohio River 10 mi. (16 km.) SE of Ironton; pop. (1990c) 3823.

South Pole. The S extremity of Earth's axis, at 90°S lat.; S center from which start all meridians of longitude; the point from which the only direction is N. The area around it (**South Polar Regions:** see POLAR REGIONS) is a lofty plateau in W cen. part of Antarctica (*q.v.*). Pole first reached by Norwegian explorer Roald Amundsen 1911. See MAGNETIC POLE.

South·port \ˈsau̇th-ˌpōrt\. **1.** City, resort, and former ⊗ of Brunswick co., S North Carolina, at mouth of Cape Fear River 22 mi. (35 km.) S of Wilmington; pop. (1990c) 2369.
2. Town, SE Queensland, Australia, on Pacific Ocean 45 mi. (72 km.) SSE of Brisbane; seaside resort.
3. Town, Merseyside, NW England, on Irish Sea 17 mi. (27 km.) N of Liverpool; pop. (1981c) 90,962; seaside resort; golf courses.

South Portland. Residential city, Cumberland co., SW Maine, S suburb of Portland; pop. (1990c) 23,163.

South Riding. See TIPPERARY.

South River. 1. River, North Carolina. See SOUTH.
2. Borough, Middlesex co., cen. New Jersey, 6 mi. (10 km.) SE of New Brunswick; pop. (1990c) 13,692.

South Ron·ald·say \ˈrän-ᵊld-ˌsā\. One of the Orkney Is. (*q.v.*), off N coast of Scotland.

South Rus·sell \ˈrə-səl\. Village, Geauga co., NE Ohio, E of Cleveland; pop. (1990c) 3402.

South Saint Paul. City, Dakota co., SE Minnesota, on Mississippi River 4 mi. (6 km.) SSE of St. Paul; pop. (1990c) 20,197.

South Salt Lake. City, Salt Lake co., N Utah, ab. 4 mi. (6 km.) S of Salt Lake City; pop. (1990c) 10,129; incorp. 1938.

South Sand·wich Islands \ˈsan-dwich\. Group of small volcanic islands, South Atlantic Ocean at E end of Scotia Sea ab. 1350 mi. (2170 km.) ESE of Cape Horn, South America; 120 sq. mi. (311 sq. km.); part of the Falkland Islands Dependencies; discovered 1775.

South Sandwich Trench. Ocean trench, South Atlantic Ocean, extending in an arc from N to E to S of South Sandwich Is.; subduction zone according to theory of plate tectonics. See ATLANTIC OCEAN.

South San Francisco. City, San Mateo co., W California, 9 mi. (14 km.) S of San Francisco; pop. (1990c) 54,312; chemicals, steel; meatpacking; adjacent to San Francisco International Airport.

South Saskatchewan. See SASKATCHEWAN 1.

South·sea \ˈsau̇th-ˌsē\. Residential district and resort area in S part of Portsmouth, England, within the city limits on the Spithead; navy memorials.

South Sea *or Span.* **El Mar del Sur** \el-ˈmär-thel-ˈsür\. The Pacific Ocean—so named by Spanish explorer Vasco Núñez de Balboa on his discovery of it 1513. In the plural, **South Seas,** the waters of the Southern Hemisphere, esp. the South Pacific Ocean.

South Sea Islands. Islands of the South Pacific Ocean; equivalent in general usage to Oceania.

South Sea Mandated Territories. Collective name of the Caroline, Marshall, and Mariana (excluding Guam) Is. (*qq.v.*), in W Pacific Ocean N of the Equator; so called while they were under Japanese mandate 1920–45.

South Seas. See SOUTH SEA.

South Shet·land Islands \ˈshet-lənd\ *or* **South Shet·lands** \-ləndz\. Group of islands, British Antarctic Terr., N of the Antarctic Penin. and separated from its N tip by Bransfield Strait; S of Drake Passage and ab. 550 mi. (885 km.) SE of Cape Horn, bet. 61° and 63°S and bet. 54° and 63°W. Chief islands: Livingston, King George (the largest, with harbor at Admiralty Bay), Deception (with harbor at Port Foster and with a submerged volcano), Elephant, Clarence, and Greenwich. Rocky and mountainous, has several summer harbors with fishing activities. Discovered and claimed 1819 by British; whaling activities early 20th cent.; ownership a matter of dispute bet. Great Britain and the republics of Argentina and Chile.

South Shields \ˈshēldz\. Seaport, Tyne and Wear, N England, on North Sea at mouth of the Tyne 10 mi. (16 km.) E of Newcastle upon Tyne; pop. (1981c) 87,125; shipyards and marine engineering works; Roman fort excavated nearby; founded in 13th cent.; first lifeboat developed and launched here late 18th cent.

South·side \ˈsau̇th-ˌsīd, ˈsau̇s-\. City, Etowah co., NE Alabama; pop. (1990c) 5580.

South Sioux City \ˈsü\. City, Dakota co., NE Nebraska, across Missouri River from Sioux City, Iowa; pop. (1990c) 9677.

South Stradbroke. See STRADBROKE.

South Su·la·we·si \ˌsü-lä-ˈwā-sē\. Province of Indonesia, in Sulawesi. See SULAWESI and table at INDONESIA.

South Sumatra. Province of Indonesia, in Sumatra. See SUMATRA and table at INDONESIA.

South Sydney. City, E New South Wales, Australia; pop. (1991c) 77,818.

South Ta·ra·na·ki Bight \ˌtar-ə-ˈnä-kē\. Gulf, W coast of North I., New Zealand, ab. 75 mi. (120 km.) NW of Palmerston North.

South Te·ton \ˈtē-ˌtän\. Peak in cen. Grand Teton National Park, NW Wyoming; 12,514 ft. (3814 m.).

South Thompson. See THOMPSON 2.

South Tirol. See ALTO ADIGE.

South Toms River \ˈtämz\. Borough, Ocean co., E New Jersey, on inlet of Barnegat Bay; pop. (1990c) 3869.

South Tuc·son \ˈtü-ˌsän\. City, Pima co., S Arizona; pop. (1990c) 5093.

South Twin Mountain. See TWIN MOUNTAINS.

South Tyne. See TYNE 1.

South Uist \ˈyü-əst\. Island of the Outer Hebrides, off NW coast of Scotland, separated by Little Minch from Skye I.; administratively part of Western Isles region.

South Ump·qua \ˈəmp-kwȯ\. River, SW Oregon; rises in E Douglas co., flows E and then N uniting with North Umpqua River ab. 8 mi. (13 km.) NW of Roseburg to form the Umpqua River; 85 mi. (137 km.) long.

South Victoria Land. See VICTORIA LAND.

South Vietnam. See VIETNAM, SOUTH.

South·wark \ˈsə-thərk, ˈsau̇th-wərk\. A borough of Greater London, SE England. See table at LONDON 4.

South Waziristan. See WAZIRISTAN.

South We·ber \ˈwē-bər\. City, Davis co., N Utah, on the Weber River, S of Ogden; pop. (1990c) 2863.

South·well \ˈsau̇th-ˌwel, -wəl\. Parish, Nottinghamshire, N cen. England; cathedral; near place where Charles I surrendered himself to the Scots 1646.

South–West Africa. See NAMIBIA.

South West Cape. Cape, SW point of Tasmania, Australia.

Southwest Indian Ridge. Ridge, SW Indian Ocean floor, extending approx. from W of Prince Edward Is. to SE of Mascarene Is. in a general SW to NE direction; a center of oceanic crust formation according to theory of plate tectonics.

South West Islands. See BARAT DAYA, KEPULAUAN.

South West Miramichi. See MIRAMICHI BAY.

Southwest Pass. **1.** One of the channels at the mouth of the Mississippi River (*q.v.*).
2. Narrow strait, leading from Gulf of Mexico into Vermilion Bay, S Louisiana, bet. mainland of SE Vermilion parish and Marsh I.

Southwest Peak. See OTTER, PEAKS OF.

South·wick \ˈsau̇th-ˌwik\. **1.** Town, Hampden co., SW Massachusetts, WSW of Springfield; pop. (1990c) 7667.
2. Town, West Sussex, S England; pop. (1981p) 11,388.

South Williamsport. Borough, Lycoming co., N cen. Pennsylvania, S suburb of Williamsport; pop. (1990c) 6496.

South Windsor. Town, E Hartford co., N Connecticut, NE of Hartford; pop. (1990c) 22,090.

South·wold \ˈsau̇th-ˌwōld\. Town, Suffolk, E England; pop. (1981p) 1795; seaside resort; 15th cent. church; on **Southwold Bay** *or* **Sole Bay** \ˈsōl\, scene of naval battle bet. the Dutch under Adm. Michiel de Ruyter and the English and French under James, duke of York (later King James II), 1672.

South Yemen. See YEMEN, PEOPLE'S DEMOCRATIC REPUBLIC OF.

South Yorkshire. Metropolitan county, N England, incl. Barnsley, Doncaster, Rotherham, and Sheffield in former West Riding, Yorkshire; estab. 1974; lost its administrative function 1986. See table at ENGLAND.

Sout·pans·berg *or mostly formerly* **Zout·pans Berg** \ˈsau̇t-ˌpäns-ˌberg\. Mountain range, Northern prov., NE Rep. of South Africa; highest peak ab. 6700 ft. (2040 m.); a continuation of the Drakensberg.

So·vetsk \sə-ˈvyetsk\ *or Ger.* **Til·sit** \ˈtil-zit\. City, Kaliningrad Oblast, Russia in Europe, on left bank of Neman River 37 mi. (60 km.) NNW of Gusev; pop. (1991e) 42,300; trade center; 18th cent. town hall.
History: Founded in Middle Ages by Teutonic Knights; treaty bet. France, Russia, and Prussia signed here 1807; in section of East Prussia assigned to U.S.S.R. after WWII 1945.

So·vet·ska·ya Ga·van' *or* **So·vet·ska·ya Ga·van** \sə-ˈvyet-skī-yə-ˈgä-vənʸ\. Seaport town on Tatar Strait, N coast of Khabarovsk Kray, E Russia in Asia, 190 mi. (306 km.) SE of Komsomol'sk-na-Amure; pop. (1991e) 35,400.

Soviet Central Asia. See CENTRAL ASIA, SOVIET.

Soviet Union. See UNION OF SOVIET SOCIALIST REPUBLICS.

Sow·er·by Bridge \ˈsau̇-ər-bē\. Town, West Yorkshire, N England; pop. (1981p) 15,546.

So·we·to \sə-ˈwā-tō, -ˈwe-, -tü\. Township, NE Rep. of South Africa in Gauteng prov., adjoining SW Johannesburg; a black residential complex.

Sō·ya, Cape \ˈsō-ˌyä\ *or Jp.* **Sōya Misaki.** Cape on N extremity of Hokkaidō, Japan.

Sōya Strait *or* **La Pé·rouse Strait** \ˌlä-pā-ˈrüz\. Channel bet. NW Hokkaidō, Japan, and S tip of Sakhalin I., Russia; ab. 25 mi. (40 km.) wide.

Sozh \ˈsȯsh\. Navigable river, cen. Europe, an E tributary of the Dnieper; rises near Smolensk in W Russia in Europe and flows S in Smolensk Oblast into Belarus to join the Dnieper below Homyel'; 402 mi. (647 km.) long.

Sozopol. See APOLLONIA 2.

Spa \ˈspä, ˈspȯ\. Commune, Liège prov., E Belgium; pop. (1991c) 10,140; medicinal mineral springs. Origin of the word spa can be traced to here.

Spain \ˈspān\ *or Span.* **Es·pa·ña** \ā-ˈspä-nyä\; *anc.* **His·pa·nia** \hi-ˈspā-nē-ə, -ˈpa-, -nyə\. Kingdom, SW Europe,

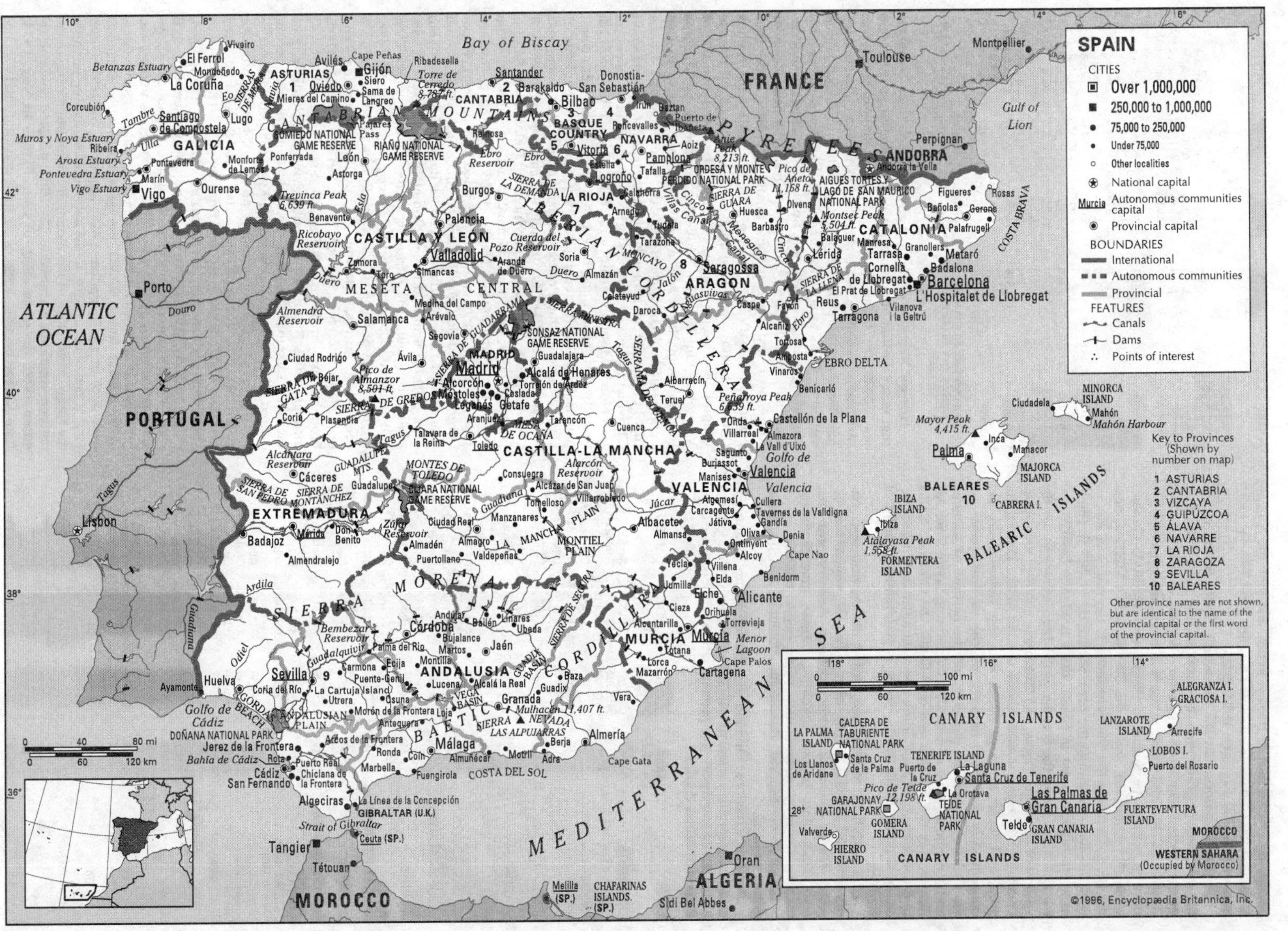
SPAIN
CITIES
Over 1,000,000
250,000 to 1,000,000
75,000 to 250,000
Under 75,000
Other localities
National capital
Murcia Autonomous communities capital
Provincial capital
BOUNDARIES
International
Autonomous communities
Provincial
FEATURES
Canals
Dams
Points of interest
Key to Provinces (Shown by number on map)
1 ASTURIAS
2 CANTABRIA
3 VIZCAYA
4 GUIPÚZCOA
5 ÁLAVA
6 NAVARRE
7 LA RIOJA
8 ZARAGOZA
9 SEVILLA
10 BALEARES
Other province names are not shown, but are identical to the name of the provincial capital or the first word of the provincial capital.
©1996, Encyclopædia Britannica, Inc.
Bay of Biscay
FRANCE
Gulf of Lion
ATLANTIC OCEAN
PORTUGAL
MEDITERRANEAN SEA
MOROCCO
ALGERIA
PYRENEES
ANDORRA
CANTABRIAN MOUNTAINS
IBERIAN CORDILLERA
MESETA CENTRAL
SIERRA MORENA
BAETIC CORDILLERA
BALEARIC ISLANDS
CANARY ISLANDS
GALICIA
ASTURIAS
CANTABRIA
BASQUE COUNTRY
NAVARRA
LA RIOJA
ARAGON
CATALONIA
CASTILLA Y LEÓN
MADRID
CASTILLA-LA MANCHA
VALENCIA
EXTREMADURA
ANDALUSIA
MURCIA
BALEARES
Madrid
Barcelona
Valencia
Sevilla
Saragossa
Málaga
Bilbao
Valladolid
Santiago de Compostela
Oviedo
Santander
Vitoria
Pamplona
Logroño
Mérida
Toledo
Murcia
Palma
Lisbon
Porto
Toulouse
Montpellier
Perpignan
Andorra la Vella
GIBRALTAR (U.K.)
Ceuta (SP.)
Melilla (SP.)
CHAFARINAS ISLANDS (SP.)
Tangier
Tétouan
Oran
Sidi Bel Abbes
Las Palmas de Gran Canaria
Santa Cruz de Tenerife
Pico de Teide 12,198 ft.
Mulhacén 11,407 ft.
WESTERN SAHARA (Occupied by Morocco)

occupying greater part of Iberian Penin. and incl. the Balearic Is. and the Canary Is.; 194,881 sq. mi. (504,742 sq. km.); pop. (1993e) 39,141,000; ✻ Madrid.

Physical features: On NE, separating Spain from France, the Pyrenees (highest Pico de Aneto 11,168 ft. or 3404 m.); greater part of peninsula is plateau (*meseta*), averaging 2000 ft. (610 m.) alt. and rising in the N in the Cantabrian Mts., in the cen. part in the Sierra de Gredos and Sierra de Guadarrama (N of Madrid), and in the SW the Sierra Morena; near the SE coast along the Mediterranean is the range of the Sierra Nevada, containing the peak Mulhacén 11,407 ft. (3477 m.), the highest point in Spain. Only lowlands besides the narrow strips along the E coast of the Mediterranean are the valleys of the Ebro, Tagus, and Guadiana, and esp. that of the Guadalquivir; other notable rivers are the Miño, Duero, Segura, and Jucár; no large lakes. Has few indentations and consequently few good harbors; on the Mediterranean are the Gulfs of Rosas and Almería and the harbors of Alicante and Málaga; at Strait of Gibraltar (separating Spain from Africa) is Bay of Gibraltar and on Atlantic the Golfo de Cádiz in S and harbors of La Coruña and Santander in N; its southernmost point, Point Tarifa, 36°N, is southernmost point of Europe.

Chief products: Wheat, rice, barley, olives, fruit (esp. citrus fruit and grapes), pulse, wine, olive oil, vegetables, esparto, hemp; livestock raising, fishing; mercury, iron ore, coal, lead, zinc, lignite, uranium, copper; manufacturing: textiles, footwear, automobiles, ships, paper; tourism.

Chief cities: Madrid, Barcelona, Valencia, Seville, Saragossa, Málaga.

Political divisions: Divided into the following 18 autonomous communities some of which in turn are subdivided into a number of provinces (for pronunciation of their names, see their individual entries):

NAME	AREA (sq. mi.)	AREA (sq. km.)	POP. (1991c)	CAPITAL
ANDALUSIA	33,694	87,267	6,940,522	Seville
Almería	3,388	8,775	455,496	Almería
Cádiz	2,851	7,384	1,078,404	Cádiz
Córdoba	5,297	13,179	754,452	Córdoba
Granada	4,838	12,530	790,515	Granada
Huelva	3,894	10,085	443,476	Huelva
Jaén	5,212	13,499	637,633	Jaén
Málaga	2,809	7,275	1,160,843	Málaga
Sevilla	5,406	14,002	1,619,703	Seville
ARAGON	18,398	47,651	1,188,817	Saragossa
Huesca	6,051	15,672	207,810	Huesca
Teruel	5,715	14,802	143,680	Teruel
Zaragoza	6,639	17,195	837,327	Saragossa
ASTURIAS	4,079	10,565	1,093,937	Oviedo
BALEARES[1]	1,936	5,014	709,138	Palma
BASQUE COUNTRY	2,803	7,260	2,104,041	Vitoria
Álava	1,176	3,046	272,447	Vitoria
Guipúzcoa	771	1,997	676,488	Donostia-San Sebastián
Vizcaya	853	2,209	1,155,106	Bilbao
CANARY ISLANDS	2,796	7,242	1,493,784	Santa Cruz de Tenerife
Las Palmas	1,569	4,064	767,969	Las Palmas de Gran Canaria
Santa Cruz de Tenerife	1,239	3,209	725,815	Santa Cruz de Tenerife
CANTABRIA[2]	2,042	5,289	527,326	Santander
CASTILLA-LA MANCHA	30,591	79,231	1,658,446	Toledo
Albacete	5,737	14,859	342,677	Albacete
Ciudad Real	7,625	17,749	475,435	Ciudad Real
Cuenca	6,587	17,060	205,198	Cuenca
Guadalajara	4,707	12,191	145,593	Guadalajara
Toledo	5,934	15,369	489,543	Toledo
CASTILLA Y LEÓN	36,368	94,193	2,545,926	Valladolid
Ávila	3,107	8,047	174,378	Ávila
Burgos	5,509	14,268	352,772	Burgos
León	5,972	15,467	525,896	León
Palencia	3,100	8,029	185,479	Palencia
Salamanca	4,763	12,336	357,801	Salamanca
Segovia	2,683	6,949	147,188	Segovia
Soria	3,972	10,287	94,537	Soria
Valladolid	3,166	8,200	494,207	Valladolid
Zamora	4,077	10,559	213,668	Zamora
CATALONIA	12,328	31,930	6,059,494	Barcelona
Barcelona	2,986	7,734	4,654,407	Barcelona
Gerona	2,273	5,887	509,628	Gerona
Lérida	4,644	12,028	353,455	Lérida
Tarragona	2,426	6,283	542,004	Tarragona
CEUTA AND MELILLA	13	33	124,215	
EXTREMADURA	16,063	41,603	1,061,852	Mérida
Badajoz	8,362	21,658	650,388	Badajoz
Cáceres	7,701	19,946	411,464	Cáceres
GALICIA	11,365	29,435	2,731,669	Santiago de Compostela
La Coruña	3,041	7,876	1,096,966	La Coruña
Lugo	3,785	9,803	384,365	Lugo
Orense	2,810	7,278	353,491	Orense
Pontevedra	1,729	4,478	896,847	Pontevedra
LA RIOJA[1]	1,944	5,035	263,434	Logroño
MADRID[1]	3,087	7,995	4,947,555	Madrid
MURCIA[1]	4,369	11,316	1,045,601	Murcia
NAVARRA[1]	4,024	10,422	519,277	Pamplona
VALENCIA	8,998	23,305	3,857,234	Valencia
Alicante	2,264	5,864	1,292,563	Alicante
Castellón	2,579	6,680	446,744	Castellón de la Plana
Valencia	4,156	10,764	2,117,927	Valencia

[1]Comprises both an autonomous community and a province.
[2]Comprises both an autonomous community and a province, the latter formerly called Santander.

History: Remains of Stone Age population (incl. Neanderthal man) throughout country, esp. cave paintings in N from ab. 25,000 B.C.; S and E coasts colonized 8th–6th cents. B.C. by Phoenicians and Greeks who had influence on the emerging Iberian culture of the native population; inland region settled by Celts at ab. the same time; Mediterranean coastal region conquered 3d cent. B.C. by Carthage which almost immediately ceded it to Rome; interior gradually brought under Rome over next two centuries, finally completed under Emperor Augustus 19 B.C.; Tarraconensis (Hither Spain), Bætica (Farther Spain), and Lusitania were provinces of Roman Empire; invaded by Vandals 5th cent. A.D.; Toledo the seat of Visigothic kingdom 6th–8th cents.; conquered by Muslims (Moors) from North Africa early 8th cent.; most of Iberian Penin. ruled by Umayyads 756–1031 (caliphate of Córdoba [*q.v.*] estab. 929), except in N where there arose various small Christian states, such as Asturias, León, Galicia, Navarre, Barcelona; Moorish territory ruled by Almoravids late 11th to early 12th cents., and by Almohads after mid-12th cent.; peninsula gradually reconquered by Christian kingdoms of Castile, Aragon, and Portugal; Spain united in 1479 as result of marriage (1469) of Ferdinand II of Aragon and Isabella of Castile (possessions of Aragon included Balearic Is., Sardinia, and Sicily); conquered Granada, last kingdom of Moors 1492; took kingdom of Naples 1503; annexed S Navarre 1515; in 1516 Spanish throne ascended by Charles I, Hapsburg ruler who brought Netherlands under rule of Spain and was elected Holy Roman Emperor Charles V 1519; in 16th cent. Spanish acquired huge colonial empire in New World, Philippines, and in N Africa; N Netherlands revolted 1568 and declared independence 1581 (recognized by Spain 1648, after 80 years of war); in wars with France in 2d half of 17th cent., lost Artois, Flanders, Roussillon, Cerdaña, and Franche-Comté; accession of Philip V 1700, first Bourbon, brought on war (War of Spanish Succession, 1701–14) through which Spain lost Gibraltar, Minorca, Sardinia, Two Sicilies, Luxembourg, and Spanish Netherlands; reconquered Kingdom of Two Sicilies 1734; regained Minorca in Treaty of Paris 1783; overrun by armies of French Emperor Napoléon 1809, scene of Peninsular War 1809–14; restored Bourbon ruler 1814; set up first republic 1873–74; in Spanish-American War lost Cuba, Puerto Rico, Philippines, Guam to U.S. 1898; set up 2d republic 1931; scene of civil war 1936–39 which resulted in collapse of republican (Loyalist) government and victory for the Insurgents under Gen. Francisco Franco who thereupon became chief of state; nominally neutral during WWII, but gave aid to Axis; excluded from UN at its inception 1945; approved by referendum 1947 a law of succession to the head of state making possible the future restoration of the monarchy; with improving international relations, admitted to UN 1955; adopted new constitution 1966; upon the death of Gen. Franco in Nov. 1975, Juan Carlos became king; with new constitution 1978 became parliamentary monarchy; became a member of NATO 1982, of EC 1986.

Spalato *or* **Spalatum.** See SPLIT.

Spal·ding \ˈspȯl-diŋ\. **1.** County in W cen. Georgia. See table at GEORGIA.

2. Town, Lincolnshire, E England, on the Welland; pop. (1981p) 18,223; flower bulbs.

Span·dau \ˈshpän-ˌdau̇\. District of Berlin, Germany, on the Spree River; first mentioned 12th cent.; received civic rights 1232; united with Berlin 1920; part of West Berlin, West Germany 1945–90.

Span·ish America \ˈspa-nish\. Those parts of America settled by Spaniards and now governed or occupied chiefly by their descendants; includes all of South America (except Brazil and the Guianas), Central America (except Belize), Mexico, Cuba, Puerto Rico, Dominican Republic, and some small islands in West Indies.

Spanish Fork. City, Utah co., N cen. Utah, 10 mi. (16 km.) S of Provo; pop. (1990c) 11,272; settled 1850.

Spanish Guinea. See EQUATORIAL GUINEA.

Spanish Main. The N coast of South America roughly bet. the Isthmus of Panama and the delta of the Orinoco River when it was under Spanish control.

Spanish March. Region, NE Spain, a boundary (*march*) region bet. the Pyrenees and the Ebro River, set up 795 A.D. by Frankish King (later Holy Roman Emperor) Charlemagne after his conquest of Catalonia 778. See *History* at CATALONIA.

Spanish Morocco. See MOROCCO 1.

Spanish Mountain. Peak in the Sierra Nevada, E Fresno co., S cen. California; 10,057 ft. (3065 m.).

Spanish Netherlands. S provinces of Netherlands; remained under Spain when seven N provinces formed Union of Utrecht 1579; parts ceded to France and Netherlands throughout 17th cent.; remainder held by Austria 1714–94, France 1794–1815, Netherlands 1815–30, and became independent kingdom of Belgium 1830. See BELGIUM and LUXEMBOURG.

Spanish Peaks. Two mountains in Huerfano and Las Animas cos., S Colorado; E peak 12,683 ft. (3866 m.) high, W peak 13,623 ft. (4152 m.) high; landmarks for early explorers and traders.

Spanish Point. Cape, W cen. coast of Bermuda I., Bermuda, extending W bet. Grassy Bay and Great Sound.

Spanish Sahara. See WESTERN SAHARA.

Spanish Town. Town, SE cen. Jamaica I., West Indies, ab. 20 mi. (32 km.) W of Kingston; pop. (1991p) 92,383; orig. called Santiago de la Vega; founded c. 1523; ✻ of Jamaica until 1872.

Spanish Wells. Island off N tip of Eleuthera I., Bahamas; 1 sq. mi. (2.6 sq. km.); pop. (1980c) 2274 (incl. Harbor Is.).

Sparks \ˈspärks\. City, Washoe co., NW corner of Nevada, on Truckee River 3 mi. (5 km.) E of Reno; pop. (1990c) 53,367; has grown rapidly since 1950.

Sparnacum. See ÉPERNAY.

Spar·ta \ˈspär-tə\. **1.** City, ⊗ of Hancock co., cen. Georgia; pop. (1990c) 1710.

2. City, Randolph co., SW Illinois, 45 mi. (72 km.) SE of East St. Louis; pop. (1990c) 4853.

3. Village, Kent co., W Michigan, 13 mi. (21 km.) N of Grand Rapids; pop. (1990c) 3968.

4. Town, ⊗ of Alleghany co., N North Carolina; pop. (1990c) 1957.

5. City, ⊗ of White co., cen. Tennessee, 17 mi. (27 km.) S of Cookeville; pop. (1990c) 4681.

6. City, ⊗ of Monroe co., W cen. Wisconsin, 23 mi. (37 km.) ENE of La Crosse; pop. (1990c) 7788.

7. *or* **Lac·e·dae·mon** \ˌla-sə-ˈdē-mən\. Ancient city of Greece, ✻ of ancient Laconia and chief city of the Peloponnese, on right bank of the Eurotas. A city-state of Dorian origin, founded c. 9th cent. B.C. as dual monarchy; developed as a strictly militaristic society; conquered Messenia 8th cent. B.C.; through military domination and coercion became leading state in Peloponnese and founder of Peloponnesian League 6th cent. B.C.; after long contest with Athens (see ATHENS 10), known as Peloponnesian Wars 460–404 B.C., Sparta attained hegemony in Greece; following numerous wars Spartan power broken by Thebes at battle of Leuctra 371 B.C.; lost independence when defeated by and forced to join Achaean League c. 192 B.C.; made part of Roman prov. of Achaea (*q.v.*) 146 B.C.; captured and destroyed by Visigoths 396 A.D.; later occupied by Byzantines and Franks. Ruins include remains of acropolis, agora, theater, temples.

8. *or Gk.* **Spár·ti** \ˈspär-tē\. Town, ✻ of Laconia dept., SE Peloponnese, S Greece, S of the remains of ancient city (see SPARTA 7); pop. (1991p) 15,496.

Spar·tan·burg \ˈspärt-ᵊn-ˌbərg\. **1.** County in NW South Carolina. See table at SOUTH CAROLINA.

2. City, ⊗ of Spartanburg co., NW South Carolina, at foot of Blue Ridge 30 mi. (48 km.) ENE of Greenville; pop. (1990c) 43,467; commercial, industrial, and distribution center; peaches; textiles, food products; catalog printing; Wofford Coll. (1854), Converse Coll. (1889), Spartanburg Methodist Coll. (1911), Spartanburg Technical Coll. (1961), Univ. of South Carolina–Spartanburg (1976); named for "Spartan" regiment of Revolutionary War militia raised in the area; several battles of the Revolution fought in vicinity, esp. at Cowpens and Kings Mountain battlefields; town founded as ⊗ 1785.

Spar·tel, Cape \spär-ˈtel\. Cape, NW coast of Morocco, at the Strait of Gibraltar.

Spárti. See SPARTA 8.

Spar·ti·ven·to \ˌspär-tē-ˈven-tō\. **1.** Cape, the SE point of Reggio di Calabria prov., S extremity of mainland of Italy.

2. Cape, S extremity of the island of Sardinia, Italy, in the Mediterranean Sea W of Italy.

Spassk–Dal'·niy *or* **Spassk–Dal·ni** \ˈspȧsk-ˈdäl-nyē\. City, SW Primorskiy Kray, SE Russia in Asia, on Trans-Siberian R.R. 120 mi. (193 km.) N of Vladivostok; pop. (1991e) 61,100.

Spa·tha, Cape \ˈspä-thä\ *or Gk.* **Ák·ra Spatha** \ˈä-krä\. Point at tip of peninsula on NW coast of Crete, Greece, NW of Canea.

Spav·i·naw Creek \ˈspa-və-ˌnȯ\. Stream, NE Oklahoma; dammed to form **Spavinaw Lakes,** impounding water used as supply for the city of Tulsa, located to the SW.

Spear·fish \ˈspir-ˌfish\. City, Lawrence co., W South Dakota, 12 mi. (19 km.) NNW of Lead; pop. (1990c) 6966; tourist resort, retirement community; lumbering; Black Hills State Univ. (1883).

Spearfish Peak. Mountain, Lawrence co., W South Dakota; 5976 ft. (1822 m.).

Spear·man \ˈspir-mən\. City, ⊗ of Hansford co., NW Texas, in the Texas Panhandle; pop. (1990c) 3197.

Spec·ta·cle Island \ˈspek-ti-kəl\. Island, Boston Harbor, Massachusetts.

Speed·way \ˈspēd-ˌwā\. Town, Marion co., cen. Indiana, completely surrounded by Indianapolis; pop. (1990c) 13,092; site of the Indianapolis Motor Speedway, where the annual 500-mile Indianapolis 500 race is held.

Speichern. See SPICHEREN.

Speights·town \ˈspīts-ˌtau̇n\. Town, NW Barbados I., Lesser Antilles, West Indies.

Spen·cer \ˈspen-sər\. **1.** Name of counties in two states of the U.S. See tables at INDIANA and KENTUCKY.

2. Town, ⊗ of Owen co., SW cen. Indiana, 14 mi. (23 km.) NW of Bloomington; pop. (1990c) 2609; birthplace of poet and playwright William Vaughn Moody 1869.

3. City, ⊗ of Clay co., NW Iowa; pop. (1990c) 11,066.

4. Town, Worcester co., cen. Massachusetts, 10 mi. (16 km.) W of the city of Worcester; pop. (1990c) 11,645.

5. Town, Rowan co., cen. North Carolina, NE suburb of Salisbury; pop. (1990c) 3219.

6. City, Oklahoma co., cen. Oklahoma, 7 mi. (11 km.) E of Oklahoma City; pop. (1990c) 3972.

\ə\ **abut** \ᵊ\ kitten, Fr table \ər\ **further** \a\ ash \ā\ ace \ä\ cot, cart \ȧ\ Fr bac \au̇\ **out** \b\ Span Avila \ch\ **chin** \e\ bet \ē\ **easy** \g\ go \i\ hit \ī\ ice \j\ job \k\ Ger ich, Buch \ⁿ\ Fr vin \ŋ\ sing \ō\ go \ö\ all \ȯ\ law \œ\ Fr bœuf \œ̄\ Fr feu \ȯi\ boy \th\ thin \t͟h\ this \ü\ loot \u̇\ foot \ue\ Ger füllen \ue̅\ Fr rue \y\ yet \ʸ\ Fr digne \ˈdēnʸ\, nuit \ˈnwʸē\ \yü\ **few** \yu̇\ fury \zh\ vision

7. Town, ⊗ of Van Buren co., cen. Tennessee; pop. (1990c) 1125.

8. City, ⊗ of Roane co., W cen. West Virginia, 35 mi. (56 km.) NNE of Charleston; pop. (1990c) 2279.

Spencer, Cape. **1.** Point, mainland of SE Alaska, on N side of entrance to Cross Sound.

2. Cape, S tip of Yorke Penin., SE South Australia, Australia, on E side of entrance to Spencer Gulf.

Spencer Gulf *also* **Spen·cer's Gulf** \ˈspen-sərz\. Large inlet, South Australia, Australia, bet. Yorke and Eyre penins.; 200 mi. (322 km.) long and ab. 90 mi. (145 km.) at its widest part; its entrance bet. Cape Catastrophe and Cape Spencer contains Thistle I.; explored by English mariner Matthew Flinders 1802.

Spen·cer·port \ˈspen-sər-ˌpōrt\. Village, Monroe co., W New York, 10 mi. (16 km.) NW of Rochester; pop. (1990c) 3606.

Spen·ny·moor \ˈspe-nē-ˌmu̇r\. Town, Durham, N England, 21 mi. (34 km.) S of Newcastle upon Tyne; pop. (1981p) 20,630; coal mines in area.

Spermunde Archipelago. See PABBIRING ARCHIPELAGO.

Sper·rin Mountains \ˈsper-ən\. Mountain range, W cen. Northern Ireland; highest peak 2240 ft. (683 m.).

Spe·su·tie Island \spə-ˈsü-shē-ə\. Island, upper Chesapeake Bay, easternmost point of Harford co., NE Maryland.

Spe·tsai *or Gk.* **Spé·tsai** \ˈspet-se\ *or Ital.* **Spez·zia** \ˈspet-sē-ä\. Island, Gulf of Argolis, Greece; 7 sq. mi. (18 sq. km.).

Spey \ˈspā\. River, Highland and Grampian regions, NE Scotland; flows NE into Moray Firth; 107 mi. (172 km.) long; noted for salmon fishing.

Spey·er \ˈshpī-ər\ *or angl.* **Spires** \ˈspīrz\; *anc.* **Civ·i·tas Ne·me·tum** \ˈsi-və-təs-ne-ˈmē-təm, -ˈne-mə-təm\; *later* **Spi·ra** \ˈspīr-ə\. City, Rhineland-Palatinate, W Germany, on the Rhine 22 mi. (35 km.) N of Karlsruhe; pop. (1992e) 47,456; port facilities; produces aircraft, wood products, textiles, chemicals, footwear, building materials, beer and wine; notable 11th cent. Romanesque cathedral (restored several times) containing remains of numerous German rulers; 18th cent. church. Birthplace of painter Anselm Feuerbach (1829) and of American businessman and financier Henry Villard (1835).

History: Orig. a Celtic settlement, town developed under Romans but was destroyed during barbarian invasions; bishopric from 7th cent.; became free imperial city 13th cent. and seat of numerous imperial diets, incl. famous Diet of Spires 1529 at which Lutherans protested the anti-Lutheran decree of the diet, giving rise to the term "Protestant"; destroyed by French 1689; part of French republic c. 1797–1815; passed to Bavaria 1815.

Spe·zia, Gulf of \ˈspet-sē-ä\. Small bay, inlet of Gulf of Genoa, on E coast of Genova prov., NW Italy; excellent harbor.

Spezia, La. See LA SPEZIA.

Spezzia. See SPETSAI.

Sphinx \ˈsfiŋks\. Peak, SE cen. Madison co., SW Montana; 10,860 ft. (3310 m.).

Spice Islands. See MOLUCCAS.

Spi·cer Islands \ˈspī-sər\. Two small islands, center of Foxe Basin, Nunavut, Canada.

Spi·che·ren *or* **Spick·e·ren** \spē-ˈkren\; *Ger.* **Spi·chern** \ˈshpi-k̲ərn\ *also* **Spei·chern** \ˈshpī-\. Village and heights, Moselle dept., France, E of Forbach; scene of early battle of Franco-Prussian War 1870 in which Germans defeated French.

Spie·ker·oog \ˈshpē-kə-ˌrōk\. Island, East Frisian Is., off NW coast of Germany bet. Langeoog and Wangerooge; ab. 5.5 sq. mi. (14.3 sq. km.).

Spij·ke·nis·se \ˈspī-kə-ˌni-sə\. Commune, South Holland prov., Netherlands; pop. (1992e) 69,655.

Spin·dale \ˈspin-ˌdāl\. Town, Rutherford co., SW North Carolina, 23 mi. (37 km.) W of Shelby; pop. (1990c) 4040; Isothermal Community Coll. (1966).

Spi·nea \spē-ˈnā-ä\. Commune, Venezia prov., Veneto, N Italy; pop. (1989c) 25,189.

Spink \ˈspink\. County in NE cen. South Dakota. See table at SOUTH DAKOTA.

Spi·on Kop \ˈspī-ən-ˌkäp, ˈspē-\. Hill, KwaZulu-Natal prov., Rep. of South Africa, 24 mi. (39 km.) WSW of Ladysmith; scene of battle Jan. 1900 during Boer War in which Boers defeated British.

Spira. See SPEYER.

Spirding. See ŚNIARDWY.

Spire Point \ˈspīr\. Peak, N cen. Washington, on boundary bet. Skagit and Chelan cos.; 8264 ft. (2519 m.).

Spires. See SPEYER.

Spirit Lake \ˈspir-ət\. **1.** Lake, Dickinson co., NW Iowa, on Minnesota border; ab. 10 mi. (16 km.) long; 9 sq. mi. (23 sq. km.).

2. City, ⊗ of Dickinson co., NW Iowa, on Spirit Lake; pop. (1990c) 3871.

Spiš·ská No·vá Ves \ˈspish-skä-ˈnō-vä-ˈves\ *or Hung.* **Igló** \ˈig-lō\ *or Ger.* **Zip·fer Neu·dorf** \ˈtsip-fər-ˈnȯi-ˌdȯrf\. Town, E Slovakia, ab. 35 mi. (56 km.) NW of Košice; pop. (1989c) 45,060.

Spit·head \ˌspit-ˈhed\. Roadstead, S coast of England, off Portsmouth's harbor bet. Portsea I. and the NE coast of the Isle of Wight; connects with the Solent on the W; formerly a frequent rendezvous of British fleet; scene 1797 of successful mutiny of the Channel fleet, whose crews demanded, and were granted, better pay and less severe working conditions.

Spits·ber·gen \ˈspits-ˌbər-gən\. Norwegian archipelago, Arctic Ocean, 360 mi. (579 km.) N of Norway; part of Svalbard; 23,641 sq. mi. (61,230 sq. km.); chief settlement Green Harbor; extensive coal deposits; chief islands Spitsbergen (formerly West Spitsbergen; 15,075 sq. mi. or 39,044 sq. km.), North East Land, Edge I., Barents I.; highest point Mt. Newton 5617 ft. (1712 m.), on Spitsbergen. Probably known to Vikings but discovered in modern times by Dutch navigator Willem Barents in 1596; possession disputed by several European nations in the interests of whaling rights (17th cent.) and later mining rights (20th cent.); granted by treaty to Norway 1920, possession formally taken 1925; towns and mines raided and damaged by both sides in WWII. See ARCTIC, THE.

Split \ˈsplit\ *or* **Spljet** \splē-ˈet\ *or Ital.* **Spa·la·to** \ˈspä-lä-ˌtō\; *anc.* **Spal·a·tum** \ˈspa-lə-təm\. Seaport on the Adriatic Sea, Croatia, ab. 105 mi. (170 km.) WSW of Sarajevo, Bosnia and Herzegovina; pop. (1991c) 200,459; good harbor; commercial center; tourism; cathedral (converted 7th cent. from mausoleum of Roman Emperor Diocletian); amphitheater; museum; art gallery.

History: Roman colony of Salonae (*q.v.*) founded nearby 78 B.C.; after its destruction by Avars 639 A.D. inhabitants estab. new town here within walls of former palace of Diocletian (early 4th cent.); came under Byzantine rule 9th cent., and after succession of rulers came under Venice 1420; to Austria 1797; held by French in Napoleonic era, then returned 1815 to Austria; to Yugoslavia 1918; to independent Croatia 1992.

Split Mountain. Peak in the Sierra Nevada, in Fresno and Inyo cos., SE cen. California; 14,058 ft. (4285 m.).

Splügen *or Ital.* **Spluga.** Alpine pass. See table at ALPS.

Spo·kane \spō-ˈkan\. **1.** River, E Washington; rises in Coeur d'Alene Lake, Kootenai co., N Idaho, flows W across Washington border and into Columbia River in N Lincoln co.; ab. 120 mi. (195 km.) long.

2. County in E Washington. See table at WASHINGTON.

3. City, ⊗ of Spokane co., E Washington, on falls of Spokane River 18 mi. (29 km.) W of Idaho border; pop. (1990c) 177,196; alt. ab. 1895 ft. (580 m.); lumber, aluminum; gateway to extensive recreational region and national parks; Gonzaga Univ. (1887), Whitworth Coll. (1890). Settled 1871; incorp. as village of **Spokane Falls** 1881; destroyed by fire 1889; reincorporated as city of Spokane 1890.

Spo·le·to \spō-ˈlā-tō\; *anc.* **Spo·le·ti·um** \spō-ˈlē-shē-əm\. Commune, Perugia prov., Umbria, cen. Italy, 30 mi. (48 km.) SE of the commune of Perugia; pop. (1991p) 37,057; center of olive-growing region; phosphorus, textiles; Roman ruins incl. walls, theater, bridge, arch; 12th cent. cathedral; numerous notable churches; annual arts festival.

History: Umbrian then Etruscan town; came under Rome 241 B.C.; episcopal see from 4th cent. A.D.; ✻ of Lombard duchy and one of principal cities of Italy 6th cent. ff.; declined after mid-8th cent. and came under papal rule 13th cent.; passed to kingdom of Italy 1860.

Spor·a·des \ˈspȯr-ə-ˌdēz\. Two groups of Greek islands, Aegean Sea: the **Northern Sporades** (*Gk.* **Vo·rí·ai Spo·rá·dhes** \vȯ-ˈrē-e-spȯ-ˈrä-thes\) and the **Do·dec·a·nese** \dō-ˈde-kə-ˌnēz, -ˌnēs\ *or* **Southern Sporades** (*Gk.* **Nó·ti·ai Sporádhes** \ˈnȯ-tē-e\). Chief islands of the Northern Sporades, off the mainland coast of Magnesia (Thessaly) and the island Euboea, are Skyros, Skopelos, Skiathos, and Iliodhrómia. For chief islands of the S group, see DODECANESE. Also included (in the Southern Sporades) by some geographers are the islands of Sámos, Ikaria, Chios, and Lesbos.

Spot Mountain \ˈspät\. Peak, Glacier National Park, NW Montana; 7800 ft. (2377 m.).

Spots·wood \ˈspäts-ˌwu̇d\. Borough, Middlesex co., cen. New Jersey, SE of New Brunswick; pop. (1990c) 7983.

Spot·syl·va·nia \ˌspät-səl-ˈvān-yə\. **1.** County in NE Virginia. See table at VIRGINIA.

2. Village, its ⊗, 11 mi. (18 km.) SW of Fredericksburg; scene of Civil War battles of Spotsylvania Court House May 8–21, 1864 (result indecisive) bet. Union troops under Gen. Ulysses S. Grant and Confederates under Gen. Robert E. Lee, included some of the bloodiest fighting of the war at the so-called "Bloody Angle" May 12.

Spot·ted Range \ˈspä-təd\. Small range, Clark, Lincoln, and S Nye cos., S Nevada.

Sprague \ˈsprāg\. **1.** River, S Oregon; rises in SW Lake co., flows W across Klamath co., into the Williamson River near Upper Klamath Lake.

2. Town, N New London co., SE Connecticut, N of Norwich; pop. (1990c) 3008.

Sprat·ly Islands \ˈsprat-lē\. Group of small islands, actually reefs, in cen. part of South China Sea, ab. 280 mi. (450 km.) SE of Camranh Bay and 775 mi. (1247 km.) NE of Singapore; seized by Japan in WWII and made submarine base; rights to islands renounced by Japan 1951; claims of all or part of group made by China, Vietnam, Philippines, Taiwan, Brunei, and Malaysia.

Spree \ˈshprā\. River, E Germany; rises in mountains near Czech border, flows N past Bautzen and Cottbus and through Berlin, where it joins the Havel River at Spandau; 247 mi. (75 km.) long; navigable for vessels of light draft.

Spree·wald \ˈshprā-ˌvält\. Woody and marshy area, E Germany, in valley of the Spree River, NW of Cottbus.

Sprem·berg \ˈshprem-ˌberk\. City, Brandenburg, E Germany, on Spree River 14 mi. (23 km.) S of Cottbus and 77 mi. (124 km.) SE of Berlin; pop. (1981c) 23,095.

Sprend·ling·en \ˈshprend-liŋ-ən\. City, Hesse, Germany, 7 mi. (11 km.) S of Frankfurt am Main.

Spring \ˈspriŋ\. River, NE Arkansas; rises in S Missouri, crosses Arkansas border in Fulton co., flows SE into Black River; ab. 60 mi. (97 km.) long.

Spring·bo·ro \ˈspriŋ-ˌbər-ō\. City, Warren co., SW Ohio, 15 mi. (24 km.) S of Dayton; pop. (1990c) 6590.

Spring City. Borough, Chester co., SE Pennsylvania, on Schuylkill River 28 mi. (45 km.) NW of Philadelphia; pop. (1990c) 3433.

Spring·dale \ˈspriŋ-ˌdāl\. **1.** City, Washington co., NW Arkansas, 12 mi. (19 km.) N of Fayetteville; pop. (1990c) 29,941.

2. City, Hamilton co., SW Ohio, N of Cincinnati; pop. (1990c) 10,621.

3. Borough, Allegheny co., SW Pennsylvania, on Allegheny River 14 mi. (23 km.) NE of Pittsburgh; pop. (1990c) 3992.

4. Town, Lexington co., cen. South Carolina; pop. (1990c) 3226.

5. Town, Newfoundland, Canada, 90 mi. (145 km.) E of Corner Brook; pop. (1991c) 3545.

Springer Mountain. Peak, Dawson co., N Georgia; 3782 ft. (1153 m.).

Spring·field \ˈspriŋ-ˌfēld\. **1.** Town, ⊗ of Baca co., SE corner of Colorado; pop. (1990c) 1475.

2. City, Bay co., NW Florida; 2 mi. (3 km.) E of Panama City; pop. (1990c) 8715.

3. City, ⊗ of Effingham co., E Georgia; pop. (1990c) 1415.

4. City, ✻ of Illinois and ⊗ of Sangamon co., cen. Illinois, on Sangamon River 185 mi. (298 km.) SW of Chicago; pop. (1990c) 105,227; electronic equipment, industrial tractors, electric meters, paints, flour. Home (became a National Historic Site 1971) and burial place of Abraham Lincoln, 16th president of the U.S.; Lincoln tomb and monument designed and executed by Larkin G. Meade, in Oak Ridge Cemetery; house in which Lincoln lived 1844–61; Dana-Thomas House designed by Frank Lloyd Wright; Springfield Coll. in Illinois (1929), Lincoln Land Community Coll. (1967), Sangamon State Univ. (1969). Settled 1818; incorp. as town 1832; made ✻ of Illinois 1837; incorp. as city 1840.

5. City, ⊗ of Washington co., cen. Kentucky, 25 mi. (40 km.) W of Danville; pop. (1990c) 2875; among records in the county courthouse is the certificate of marriage of Thomas Lincoln and Nancy Hanks, parents of Abraham Lincoln. See HARRODSBURG.

6. City, ⊗ of Hampden co., SW Massachusetts, on Connecticut River 5 mi. (8 km.) N of Connecticut border; pop. (1990c) 156,983; electrical equipment, chemicals, firearms, plastics; home of Merriam-Webster dictionary publishers. Springfield Coll. (1885), American International Coll. (1885), Western New England Coll. (1919), Springfield Technical Community Coll. (1965); site of Basketball Hall of Fame; city settled 1636; incorp. 1641; burned during King Philip's War 1675; scene of Shays' Rebellion 1786–87; site of United States Armory 1794–1968 (became a National Historic Site 1974). Birthplace of author Theodor Geisel (Dr. Seuss) 1904.

7. City, Calhoun co., S Michigan, 5 mi. (8 km.) W of Battle Creek; pop. (1990c) 5582.

8. City, ⊗ of Greene co., SW Missouri, ab. 150 mi. (240 km.) SSE of Kansas City; pop. (1990c) 140,494; alt. ab. 1300 ft. (395 m.); center of agricultural region, shipping poultry, livestock, dairy products; tourist center for Ozarks region; Drury Coll. (1873), Southwest Missouri State Univ. (1905), Central Bible Coll. (1922), Baptist Bible Coll. (1950), Evangel Coll. (1955); city settled 1820s; held briefly by Confederates 1861–62; home in 1860s of frontiersman James Butler "Wild Bill" Hickok.

9. Residential suburban township, Union co., NE New Jersey, ab. 6 mi. (10 km.) NW of Elizabeth; pop. (1990c) 13,420.

10. City, ⊗ of Clark co., W cen. Ohio, 23 mi. (37 km.) NE of Dayton; pop. (1990c) 70,487; produces engines; Wittenberg Univ. (1845), Clark State Community Coll. (1962); city settled 1799; made ⊗ 1818; incorp. as city 1850.

11. City, Lane co., W Oregon, on Willamette River just E of Eugene; pop. (1990c) 44,683.

12. Urban township, Delaware co., SE Pennsylvania, ab. 5 mi. (8 km.) NE of Chester; pop. (1990c) 24,160.

13. Urban township, Montgomery co., SE Pennsylvania, NW suburb of Philadelphia; pop. (1990c) 19,612.

14. City, ⊗ of Robertson co., N Tennessee, 23 mi. (37 km.) N of Nashville; pop. (1990c) 11,227.

15. Town, Windsor co., E Vermont, on Black River 33 mi. (53 km.) SE of Rutland; pop. (1990c) 9579.

16. Unincorporated settlement, Fairfax co., NE Virginia; pop. (1990c) 23,706.

Springfield, Lake. Artificial lake, Sangamon co., cen. Illinois; 15 mi. (24 km.) long; shoreline 45 mi. (72 km.); source of water supply for Springfield.

Spring Garden. Urban township, York co., S Pennsylvania, S of the city of York; pop. (1990c) 11,207.

Spring·hill \ˈspriŋ-ˌhil\. **1.** City, Webster parish, NW Louisiana, 38 mi. (61 km.) NNE of Shreveport; pop. (1990c) 5668.

2. Town, Cumberland co., N Nova Scotia, Canada, 15 mi. (24 km.) SE of Amherst; pop. (1991c) 4373; formerly an important coal-mining center.

Spring Lake. **1.** Village, Ottawa co., W Michigan, 14 mi. (23 km.) S of Muskegon; pop. (1990c) 2537.
2. Borough, Monmouth co., E cen. New Jersey, on Atlantic Ocean 6 mi. (10 km.) S of Asbury Park; pop. (1990c) 3499.
3. Town, Cumberland co., S cen. North Carolina; pop. (1990c) 7524.

Spring Lake Heights. Borough, Monmouth co., E cen. New Jersey, 6 mi. (10 km.) SSW of Asbury Park; pop. (1990c) 5341.

Spring Lake Park. Village, Anoka and Ramsey cos., E Minnesota, 11 mi. (18 km.) N of St. Paul; pop. (1990c) 6532.

Spring Mountains. Mountain range, W cen. Clark co., SE Nevada; highest Charleston Peak 11,919 ft. (3633 m.).

Springs \ˈspriŋz\. City, E Gauteng prov., NE Rep. of South Africa, 29 mi. (47 km.) E of Johannesburg; pop. (1985c) 68,235. Settled as coal-mining camp 1885; first gold mine opened 1908.

Spring·vale \ˈspriŋ-ˌvāl\. City, Victoria, Australia, a SE suburb of Melbourne; pop. (1991c) 89,478.

Spring Valley. **1.** City, Bureau co., N Illinois, on Illinois River 18 mi. (29 km.) W of Ottawa; pop. (1990c) 5246.
2. Village, Rockland co., SE New York; pop. (1990c) 21,802.
3. City, Harris co., SE Texas, surrounded by Houston; pop. (1990c) 3392.

Spring·view \ˈspriŋ-ˌvyü\. Village, ⊗ of Keya Paha co., N Nebraska; pop. (1990c) 304.

Spring·ville \ˈspriŋ-ˌvil\. **1.** Village, Erie co., W New York, 27 mi. (43 km.) SSE of Buffalo; pop. (1990c) 4310.
2. City, Utah co., N cen. Utah, just S of Provo; pop. (1990c) 13,950.

Sprottau. See SZPROTAWA.

Spruce Hill \ˈsprüs\. Peak, Berkshire co., W Massachusetts; 1974 ft. (602 m.). See HOOSAC MOUNTAINS.

Spruce Knob. Peak, Pendleton co., E West Virginia; 4861 ft. (1482 m.), highest point in the state.

Spruce Mountain. Peak, SE cen. Elko co., NE Nevada; 10,262 ft. (3128 m.).

Spruce·top \ˈsprüs-ˌtäp\. Peak in the Catskill Mts., Greene co., SE New York; 3620 ft. (1103 m.).

Spurn Head \ˈspərn\. Cape, E coast of England, in Humberside, at NE entrance to mouth of the Humber River; lighthouse.

Spurr, Mount \ˈspər\. Mountain peak, W of head of Cook Inlet, SW Alaska; ab. 11,100 ft. (3385 m.).

Spuy·ten Duy·vil Creek \ˈspīt-ᵊn-ˌdī-vəl\. Narrow channel, N of Manhattan I., New York, separating the island from the mainland and connecting Hudson and Harlem rivers.

Spy \ˈspē, ˈspī\. Commune, Namur prov., S Belgium, 6 mi. (10 km.) W of the commune of Namur; cave nearby in which two Neanderthal skeletons were found 1886 along with Mousterian remains.

Squam Lake \ˈskwäm\. Lake, cen. New Hampshire, on boundary bet. Grafton, Belknap, and Carroll cos.; ab. 6 mi. (10 km.) long and 4 mi. (6 km.) wide; resort.

Squa·pan *or* **Squa Pan** \ˈskwȯ-ˌpan\. Lake, E cen. Aroostook co., N Maine.

Squaw Peak \ˈskwȯ\. **1.** Mountain, E California, in the Sierra Nevada W of Lake Tahoe; 8884 ft. (2708 m.).
2. Mountain, SE Idaho co., N cen. Idaho; 8660 ft. (2640 m.).

Squaw Valley. Valley, E California, in the Sierra Nevada on E slopes of Squaw Peak; ski resort; site of Winter Olympic Games 1960.

Squil·la·ce, Gulf of \skwē-ˈlä-chā\. Inlet of Ionian Sea, S Italy.

Squin·za·no \skwēnt-ˈsä-nō\. Commune, Lecce prov., Puglia, SE Italy, 9 mi. (15 km.) NW of the commune of Lecce; pop. (1981p) 15,883.

Sra·gen \ˈsrä-gən\. Town, cen. Java, Indonesia, on railroad line ab. 17 mi. (27 km.) NE of Surakarta.

Śrā·vas·tī \shrä-ˈvəs-tē\. Ancient city, in NE Uttar Pradesh, N India; important religious center during Buddha's lifetime; ruins include those of a monastery.

Srbija. See SERBIA.

Sre·din·nyy Khre·bet \srə-ˈdē-nē-kri-ˈbyet\ *or Eng.* **Cen·tral Range** \ˈsen-trəl\. Mountain range extending the length of Kamchatka Penin., E Russia in Asia; av. height 3000 ft. (915 m.); highest Ichinskaya Sopka 11,800 ft. (3621 m.).

Srem. See SYRMIA.

Srem \ˈsrem\. Commune, Poznań prov., W cen. Poland, on Warta River; pop. (1989e) 27,768.

Srem·ska Mi·tro·vi·ca \ˈsrem-skä-ˈmē-trō-ˌvēt-sä\; *formerly* **Mitrovica** *or Ger.* **Mi·tro·witz** \ˈmē-trō-ˌvits\. Town, Serbia, NW Yugoslavia, on Sava River 42 mi. (68 km.) WNW of Belgrade; river port and commercial center; Roman ruins of Sirmium nearby.

Srem·ski Kar·lov·ci \ˈsrem-skē-ˈkär-lōv-tsē\ *or Ger.* **Karlo·witz** *also* **Car·lo·witz** \ˈkär-lō-ˌvits\ *or Hung.* **Kar·ló·cza** \ˈkär-lōt-sä\. Town, N Serbia, N Yugoslavia, on right bank of Danube River; pop. (1991p) 7398; trade center; cathedral; palace; scene of signing of Treaty of Karlowitz 1699 by Austria, Poland, Venice, and the Ottoman Empire in which the Ottomans formally ceded various lands in Europe which it had lost to conquest in the preceding war, thus marking the beginning of the disintegration of the Ottoman Empire.

Sri·ha·ri·ko·ta Island \ˌsrē-ˌhär-ə-ˈkō-tə\. Island off SE coast of India, N of Madras; 30 mi. (48 km.) long.

Sri·ka·ku·lam \ˌsrē-ˈkä-kə-ləm\. Town, NE Andhra Pradesh, S India; pop. (1991p) 88,464.

Sri Lanka \ˌsrē-ˈläŋ-kə\; *formerly* **Cey·lon** \sə-ˈlän, sē-, sā-\; *Arab.* **Ser·en·dib** \ˈser-ən-ˌdib, -ˌdip\ *or Lat. and Gk.* **Ta·prob·a·ne** \tə-ˈprä-bə-nē\. Independent state, consisting of an island in the Indian Ocean, S of India, with which it is connected by Adam's Bridge, a chain of shoals which divides Palk Strait on N from Gulf of Mannar on S; 25,332 sq. mi. (65,610 sq. km.); pop. (1994e) 17,829,500; ✻ Colombo; highest point Pidurutalagala 8281 ft. (2524 m.). Rich in tropical vegetation.

Chief products: Tea, rubber, coconuts; graphite, gemstones; textiles, clothing; fishing; tourism.

Chief cities: Colombo, Dehiwala-Mount Lavinia, Moratuwa.

History: Aboriginal inhabitants (Veddas) absorbed by immigrating Indo-Aryans from the Indian Subcontinent c. 5th cent. B.C., which then developed into Sinhalese population; Buddhism introduced 3d cent. and had spread island-wide by 2d cent.; Sinhalese kingdom centered at Anuradhapura grew along with Buddhist expansion to gain control of the island in 2d cent. B.C., kingdom survived largely intact until 10th cent. A.D.; reduced and threatened by invasions by S Indian peoples, esp. the Tamils, under whose pressure the center of the Sinhalese kingdom migrated to the SW; Sinhalese power rose and fell throughout 13th to 15th cents., while Tamil kingdom arose in the N in 14th cent., bringing large Hindu population to the island; throughout the period, island subjected to frequent foreign invasions from India, China, and Malaya; Portuguese first arrived 1505 and within a century had gained control over most coastal areas of the island; only remaining independent Sinhalese kingdom, centered at Kandy, enlisted Dutch assistance in expelling the Portuguese, but the Dutch merely replaced the Portuguese as an occupying power (by 1658); Dutch holdings surrendered to British 1796 who called it Ceylon and made it a crown colony 1802; cen. region (around Kandy) brought under control by 1815; nationalist activity in 20th cent. led to several constitutional reforms incl. representative government, universal adult suffrage, and finally independence 1948 with dominion status within the Commonwealth; parts bombed by Japanese airplanes 1942 in WWII; armed attempt to overthrow government suppressed 1971; new constitution 1972 established the Republic of Sri Lanka with presidential leadership; 1978 constitution strengthened presidency and renamed country Democratic Socialist Republic of Sri Lanka; armed Tamil insurgency arose in NE 1980s; Indian peace-keeping force occupied insurgent areas and fought with the rebels 1987–90; upon Indian withdrawal the insurgents resumed fighting with Sri Lankan forces and initiated terrorist activities, incl. assassinations and bombings; country's first woman president elected 1994; following failed peace talks 1995, hostilities resumed.

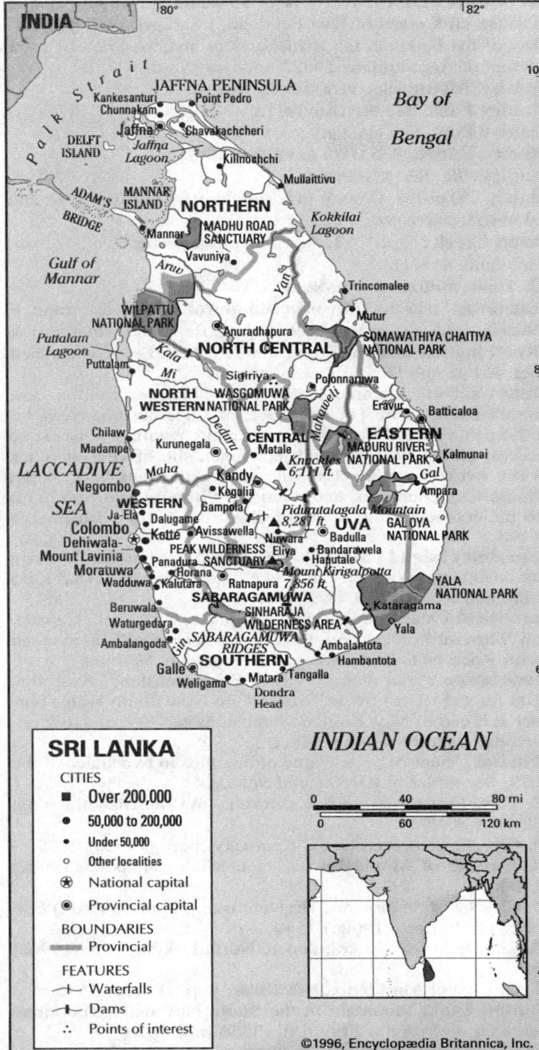

Sri·na·gar \srē-'nə-gər\ *also* **Kash·mir South** \'kash-mir, 'kazh-, kash-', kazh-'\. City, summer ✻ of Jammu and Kashmir, India, on Jhelum River 170 mi. (274 km.) N of Amritsar; pop. (1981c) 531,094; alt. 5250 ft. (1600 m.); carpets, silk, silver, leather, and copperware; woodcarving; tourism; numerous mosques and notable public gardens, palaces, museums, and fortress. Dal Lake with noted floating gardens lies to NE. Scene of Irish poet Thomas Moore's *Lalla Rookh.*

Sri·ran·gam \srē-'rəŋ-gəm\. Town, SE Tamil Nadu, S India, on island in Kāveri River 2 mi. (3 km.) N of Tiruchchirappalli and 30 mi. (48 km.) W of Thanjavur; pop. (1991p) 69,928; place of pilgrimage to notable large temple, consisting of seven concentric walled enclosures, and dedicated to the Hindu god Vishnu.

Sri·vi·ja·ya \ˌsrē-wi-'jō-yə\ *or* **Shri·vi·ja·ya** \ˌshrē-vi-\. Malayan empire of wide extent, SE Asia, 7th–14th cents. A.D. See MALAY ARCHIPELAGO.

Sri·vil·li·put·tur \ˌsrē-vi-li-pu̇-'tu̇r\. City, S Tamil Nadu, S India, 42 mi. (68 km.) SW of Madurai; pop. (1991p) 68,543.

Ssu–mao. See SIMAO.

Ssu–p'ing *or* **Ssupingchieh.** See SIPING.

Stabiae. See CASTELLAMMARE DI STABIA.

Stablo. See STAVELOT.

Stabroek. See GEORGETOWN 14.

Stadacona. See QUEBEC 3.

Sta·de \'shtä-də\. City, Lower Saxony, Germany, 22 mi. (35 km.) W of Hamburg; pop. (1992e) 43,116. First mentioned 10th cent.; member of Hanseatic League.

Städ·jan \'stād-ˌyän\. Peak, SW cen. Sweden, near the Norwegian border; 3710 ft. (1131 m.).

Stads·ka·naal \ˌstäts-kə-'näl\. Commune, Groningen prov., NE Netherlands; pop. (1992e) 32,924.

Stadt·lohn \'shtät-ˌlōn\. Town, North Rhine-Westphalia, Germany, W of Münster near Netherlands border; pop. (1980c) 16,723; scene of victory Aug. 6, 1623 of Catholic League under Gen. Johann Tserclaes, Graf von Tilly over Imperial forces.

Staf·fa \'sta-fə\. Small island, Inner Hebrides, Scotland, 7 mi. (11 km.) W of Mull; location of **Fin·gal's Cave** \ˌfiŋ-gəlz-\, 227 ft. (69 m.) long, 117 ft. (36 m.) high.

Staf·ford \'sta-fərd\. **1.** Name of counties in two states of the U.S. See tables at KANSAS and VIRGINIA.
2. Town, N Tolland co., N Connecticut, on Massachusetts border E of Somers; pop. (1990c) 11,091; includes borough of Stafford Springs; town founded 1719.
3. Town, Fort Bend and Harris cos., SE Texas, 2 mi. (3.2 km.) SW of Houston; pop. (1990c) 8397.
4. Village, ⊗ of Stafford co., NE Virginia.
5. County in England. See STAFFORDSHIRE.
6. Town, ⊗ of Staffordshire, W cen. England, 25 mi. (40 km.) NNW of Birmingham; pop. (1991p) 117,000; market town; electrical equipment, footwear. Birthplace of biographer, author, and fishing enthusiast Izaak Walton 1593.

Staf·ford·shire \'sta-fərd-ˌshir, -shər\ *or* **Staf·ford** \'sta-fərd\ *or* **Staffs** \'stafs\. **1.** Former county, W cen. England; chief towns Wolverhampton, Stoke-on-Trent, Dudley.
2. Administrative county, W cen. England, approx. equivalent to the former county; rivers the Trent and its tributaries; coal; pottery; brewing; contains much of the Black Country (*q.v.*). See table at ENGLAND.

Stafford Springs. Borough in town of Stafford, Connecticut; pop. (1990c) 4100; incorp. 1873.

Stag Dome \'stag\. Peak in the Sierra Nevada, in E Fresno co., S cen. California; 7707 ft. (2349 m.).

Sta·gi·ra \stə-'jī-rə\ *or* **Sta·gi·ros** \-rəs\. Town in ancient Macedonia, NE Greece, on E Chalcidice Penin., on Strymonic Gulf. Birthplace of philosopher Aristotle 384 B.C.

Staines \'stānz\. Town, Surrey, SE England, on the Thames 19 mi. (31 km.) WSW of London; pop. (1981c) 52,815.

Staked Plain. See LLANO ESTACADO.

Sta·kha·nov \stə-'kä-nəf\; *formerly* **Ka·di·yev·ka** *or* **Ka·di·ev·ka** \kə-'dē-yəf-kə\; *1937–43* **Ser·go** \'ser-gō\. Town, W Luhans'k subdivision, E Ukraine, pop. (1991e) 113,000.

Stakhanovo. See ZHUKOVSKIY.

Stalin. **1.** Seaport, Bulgaria. See VARNA 2.
2. City, Romania. See BRAŞOV 2.
3. City, Ukraine. See DONETS'K 2.

Stalinabad. See DUSHANBE.

Stalingrad. See VOLGOGRAD.

Stalingrad Oblast. See VOLGOGRAD OBLAST.

Stalinir. See TS'KHINVALI.

Stalino. See DONETS'K 2.

Stalinogorsk. See NOVOMOSKOVSK.

Stalino Oblast. See DONETS'K 1.

Stalin Peak. **1.** Peak, Slovakia. See GERLACHOVKA.
2. Peak, Tajikistan. See COMMUNISM PEAK.

Stalinsk. See NOVOKUZNETSK.

Sta·lo·wa Wo·la \stä-'lō-və-'vō-lə\. Town, Rzeszów prov., SE Poland, ab. 35 mi. (56 km.) NNE of Tarnobrzeg; pop. (1989e) 69,173.

Sta·ly·bridge \ˈstā-lē-ˌbrij\. Town, Greater Manchester; NW England, on the Tame River 10 mi. (16 km.) E of Manchester; pop. (1981p) 26,396; engineering; art gallery.

Stam·ford \ˈstäm-fərd\. **1.** City, Fairfield co., SW Connecticut, on Long Island Sound and New York border; pop. (1990c) 108,056; multiple corporate headquarters. Settled 1641; annexed to Connecticut 1662; city government formed within town 1893; town and city government consolidated 1949.

2. City, Jones and Haskell cos., NW cen. Texas, 35 mi. (56 km.) N of Abilene; pop. (1990c) 3817.

3. Market town, Lincolnshire, E England, on the Welland River 35 mi. (56 km.) SE of Nottingham; pop. (1981c) 16,393.

Stamford Bridge. Village, Humberside, N England, 8 mi. (13 km.) ENE of York; scene of battle 1066 in which English King Harold II defeated his brother Tostig and Harold Haardraade, king of Norway, Tostig's ally, just before battle of Hastings.

Stampalia. See ASTIPÁLIA.

Stam·pede Tunnel \ˈstam-ˌpēd\. Railroad tunnel, King and Kittitas cos., W cen. Washington, in Cascade Range; 9850 ft. (3002 m.) long.

Stan·ards·ville \ˈsta-nərdz-ˌvil\. Town, ⊗ of Greene co., N cen. Virginia; pop. (1990c) 257.

Stan·der·ton \ˈstan-dərt-ᵊn\. Town, S Mpumalanga prov., NE Rep. of South Africa, on Vaal River 90 mi. (145 km.) ESE of Johannesburg; in agricultural region.

Standing Indian. Mountain, Clay co., SW North Carolina; 5500 ft. (1680 m.).

Stan·dish \ˈstan-dish\. **1.** Town, Cumberland co., SW Maine, 15 mi. (24 km.) NW of Portland; pop. (1990c) 7678.

2. City, ⊗ of Arenac co., E Michigan; pop. (1990c) 1377.

Stand·ley Lake \ˈstand-lē\. Reservoir, Jefferson co., cen. Colorado, NW of Denver; formed c. 1909 by damming of a creek.

Stan·ford \ˈstan-fərd\. **1.** Unincorporated settlement, Santa Clara co., W California; pop. (1990c) 18,097; Stanford Univ. (1891).

2. Residential city, ⊗ of Lincoln co., E cen. Kentucky, 10 mi. (16 km.) SE of Danville; pop. (1990c) 2686.

3. Town, ⊗ of Judith Basin co., cen. Montana; pop. (1990c) 529.

Stang·er \ˈstaŋ-ər\. Town, E KwaZulu-Natal prov., E Rep. of South Africa, near coast 40 mi. (64 km.) NNE of Durban; burial place of Zulu warrior and chieftain Shaka.

Stan·hope \ˈstan-ˌhōp\. Borough, Sussex co., N New Jersey; pop. (1990c) 3393.

Stanimaka. See ASENOVGRAD.

Stanislau. See IVANO-FRANKIVS'K 2.

Stan·is·laus \ˈsta-nə-ˌslȯ, -ˌslȯs\. **1.** River, N cen. California; rises in Alpine co. near Nevada border, flows SW into San Joaquin River bet. San Joaquin and Stanislaus cos.; 95 mi. (153 km.) long. See MELONES DAM.

2. County in cen. California. See table at CALIFORNIA.

Stanislaus Peak. Mountain, S Alpine co., E cen. California, in the Sierra Nevada; 11,202 ft. (3414 m.).

Stanislav. See IVANO-FRANKIVS'K 2.

Stanislav Oblast. See IVANO-FRANKIVS'K 1.

Sta·ni·sła·wów \ˌstä-nē-ˈswä-ˌwüf\. **1.** Former department, SE Poland; now approx. coextensive with Ivano-Frankivs'k subdivision, Ukraine.

2. City, its ✱. See IVANO-FRANKIVS'K 2.

Stan·ke Di·mi·trov \ˌstän-ke-dē-ˈmē-trȯf\. Town, W Bulgaria, ab. 20 mi. (32 km.) W of Kyustendil.

Stan·ley \ˈstan-lē\. **1.** County in cen. South Dakota. See table at SOUTH DAKOTA.

2. City, ⊗ of Mountrail co., NW North Dakota; pop. (1990c) 1371.

3. *formerly* **Circular Head.** Town, NW Tasmania, Australia, on peninsula in Bass Strait 37 mi. (60 km.) WNW of Burnie; pop. (1981c) 603; Tasmanian port nearest to Melbourne; a seaside resort at the foot of the headland Circular Head (*q.v.*).

4. Town, Durham, N England, 18 mi. (29 km.) SSW of Newcastle upon Tyne; pop. (1981p) 41,210; coal mines.

5. Village, Durham, W England; pop. (1981p) 22,832.

6. *or* **Port Stanley.** Town, ✱ of Falkland Is., South Atlantic Ocean, on E coast of East Falkland; principal town and harbor of the Falkland Is.; British troops stationed nearby after defeat of Argentinians 1982.

Stanley, Mount. See RUWENZORI, MOUNT.

Stanley Falls. See BOYOMA FALLS.

Stanley Pool. See MALEBO, POOL.

Stanley Range. See MAIN BARRIER RANGE.

Stanleyville. See KISANGANI.

Stan·ly \ˈstan-lē\. County in S cen. North Carolina. See table at NORTH CAROLINA.

Stann Creek \ˈstan\. **1.** Administrative district, cen. Belize. See table at BELIZE.

2. Town, Belize. See DANGRIGA.

Stan·o·voy \ˌstȧ-nə-ˈvȯi\ *also* **Sta·no·voi.** Mountain range, E Russia in Asia, mostly bet. Sakha Rep. and Khabarovsk Kray; highest peak at E end 8268 ft. (2520 m.); watershed bet. Arctic and Pacific Ocean streams.

Stans \ˈshtäns\. Commune, ✱ of Nidwalden demicanton, cen. Switzerland, 7 mi. (11 km.) SSE of Lucerne; pop. (1989c) 6098; tourism; 17th cent. parish church with Romanesque tower; 18th cent. town hall; convents; site of Diet of Stans 1481 which averted civil war among the members of the Swiss Confederation, and admitted Fribourg and Solothurn to the confederation; scene of disastrous battle with French 1798.

Stans·bury Island \ˈstanz-ˌber-ē, -bə-rē\. Peninsula, formerly an island, in SW Great Salt Lake, Utah; 11.5 mi. (18.5 km.) long and 5.5 mi. (8.9 km.) wide.

Stan·stead \ˈstan-ˌsted\. Populated place, S Quebec, Canada, on Vermont border; pop. (1991c) 845; is closely associated with Rock Island, Quebec and Derby Line, Vermont.

Stan·thorpe \ˈstan-ˌthȯrp\. Town, SE Queensland, Australia, 100 mi. (161 km.) SW of Brisbane on New South Wales border at N end of New England Plateau; pop. (1991c) 4187; developed as a tin-mining center.

Stan·ton \ˈstant-ᵊn\. **1.** Name of counties in two states of the U.S. See tables at KANSAS and NEBRASKA.

2. City, Orange co., SW California, SW of Anaheim; pop. (1990c) 30,491.

3. City, ⊗ of Powell co., E Kentucky; pop. (1990c) 2795.

4. City, ⊗ of Montcalm co., cen. Michigan; pop. (1990c) 1504.

5. City, ⊗ of Stanton co., NE Nebraska, 12 mi. (19 km.) ESE of Norfolk; pop. (1990c) 1549.

6. City, ⊗ of Mercer co., W cen. North Dakota; pop. (1990c) 517.

7. City, ⊗ of Martin co., NW Texas; pop. (1990c) 2576.

Stanton Peak. Mountain in the Sierra Nevada, E Tuolumne co., cen. California; 11,666 ft. (3556 m.).

Sta·ples \ˈstā-pəlz\. City, Todd co., cen. Minnesota, 26 mi. (42 km.) W of Brainerd; pop. (1990c) 2754.

Staples, The. See FARNE ISLANDS.

Sta·ple·ton \ˈstā-pəl-tən\. **1.** Village, ⊗ of Logan co., cen. Nebraska, on an intermittent stream, NE of North Platte; pop. (1990c) 299.

2. Section of Staten Island, borough of New York City, New York. See STATEN ISLAND 2.

Sta·ra·cho·wi·ce \ˌstä-rä-ḵō-ˈvēt-se\. Town, Kielce prov., S Poland, ab. 25 mi. (40 km.) NE of the city of Kielce; pop. (1989e) 56,303.

Stara Planina. See BALKAN MOUNTAINS.

Starav, Ben. See BEN STARAV.

Sta·ra·ya Rus·sa \ˈstär-ə-yə-ˈrü-sə\. Town, cen. Novgorod Oblast, W Russia in Europe, 15 mi. (24 km.) S of Lake Il'men'; pop. (1991e) 41,700; resort, with mineral springs and parks. Town under Novgorod, dating at least to 12th cent.; later belonged to Moscow; in WWII occupied by Germans 1941–44 and scene of heavy fighting 1944.

Sta·ra Za·go·ra \ˈstär-ə-zə-ˈgȯr-ə\. City, cen. Bulgaria, on S slope of Balkan Mts. 50 mi. (81 km.) ENE of Plovdiv; pop. (1991e) 164,553; trade center; produces chemicals and fertilizers; site of ancient town; city destroyed during Russo-Turkish War 1877; rebuilt as planned town.

Star·buck \'stär-ˌbək\. Small island, Line Is., cen. Pacific Ocean, 5°37′S, 155°33′W; discovered 1823; once claimed by both Great Britain and U.S.; now part of Kiribati; U.S. claim dropped 1983.

Star City \'stär\. City, ⊗ of Lincoln co., SE Arkansas; pop. (1990c) 2138.

Star·gard Szcze·ciń·ski \'stär-gärt-shche-'chē^{n}-skē\; *formerly* **Stargard in Pom·mern** \in-'pō-mərn\. City, S cen. Szczecin prov., NW Poland, ab. 20 mi. (32 km.) ESE of the city of Szczecin; pop. (1989e) 69,953; medieval walls and gates; 13th cent. church; an early Hanse town; destroyed in Thirty Years' War; assigned to Poland following WWII by Potsdam Conference 1945.

Star Harbour. Inlet and trading station, N coast at extreme SE end of San Cristóbal I., SE Solomon Is., W Pacific Ocean.

Sta·ri Grad \'stä-rē-ˌgräd\ *or Ital.* **Cit·ta·vec·chia** \ˌchē-tä-'vek-kyä\. Seaport, NW coast of Hvar I., S Croatia.

Stark \'stärk\. Name of counties in three states of the U.S. See tables at ILLINOIS, NORTH DAKOTA, OHIO.

Starke \'stärk\. **1.** County in NW Indiana. See table at INDIANA.

2. City, ⊗ of Bradford co., NE Florida; pop. (1990c) 5226; strawberries; state prison.

Stark·ville \'stärk-ˌvil, -vəl\. City, ⊗ of Oktibbeha co., NE cen. Mississippi, 23 mi. (37 km.) W of Columbus; pop.(1990c) 18,458; dairy products; nearby is Mississippi State Univ. (1878).

Starn·berg \'shtärn-ˌberk\. Village, Bavaria, Germany, at N end of Starnberger See, ab. 10 mi. (16 km.) SSW of Munich.

Starn·ber·ger See \'shtärn-ˌber-gər-ˌzā\; *formerly* **Würm·see** \'vu̅e̅rm-ˌzā\ *or* **Wür·mer See** \'vu̅e̅r-mər-zā\. Lake, Bavaria, Germany, 15 mi. (24 km.) SSW of Munich; 12 mi. (19 km.) long, max. width 3 mi. (5 km.).

Sta·ro·dub \stə-ˌrə-'düp\. Town, W Bryansk Oblast, W Russia in Europe, 80 mi. (129 km.) SW of the city of Bryansk. An old town, important in Russian medieval history; destroyed by Mongols in 13th cent.; disputed among Russians, Lithuanians, and Poles down to late 17th cent. when it became permanently Russian; in WWII behind German lines 1941–43.

Sta·ro·gard Gdań·ski \stə-'rō-gärt-gə-'dän-skē\; *formerly* **Preus·sisch–Star·gard** \'prȯi-sish-'shtär-ˌgärt\. Commune, Gdańsk prov., N Poland, 64 mi. (103 km.) N of Toruń; pop. (1989e) 48,043.

Sta·ro·kon·stan·ti·nov \ˌstär-ə-ˌkən-stən-'tē-nəf\. Town, Khmel'nyts'kyy subdivision, W Ukraine, 160 mi. (257 km.) SSW of Kiev.

Star Peak. 1. Mountain, Gunnison and Pitkin cos., W cen. Colorado; 13,562 ft. (4137 m.).

2. Mountain, Chelan co., cen. Washington; 8400 ft. (2560 m.).

Starr \'stär\. County in S Texas. See table at TEXAS.

Start Point \'stärt\. **1.** Cape, S coast of Devon, SW England; at S end of **Start Bay,** wide inlet of English Channel on Devon coast S of Dartmouth; lighthouse.

2. Cape, NE tip of Sanday I., Orkney Is., off N coast of Scotland; lighthouse.

Starved Rock \'stärvd\. Locality, S bank of Illinois River, near Ottawa, La Salle co., N Illinois, 90 mi. (145 km.) SW of Chicago; narrow strip of high bluff above river, highest point 140 ft. (43 m.), steep on sides with flat top (0.5 acre or 0.2 hectare); now part of oldest (opened 1912) of Illinois' state parks. Of historical interest; visited by early European explorers, incl. René-Robert Cavelier, Sieur de La Salle and Henry de Tonti who erected Fort St. Louis here on summit 1682, abandoned 1702, burned by Indians 1721. Story of Illinois Indians starving on rock (c. 1770) while surrounded by enemy and having resources cut off gave rise to name.

Sta·ry Os·kol *or* **Sta·ryy Oskol** \'stä-rē-äs-'kōl\. Town, Belgorod Oblast, W Russia in Europe, ab. 70 mi. (115 km.) NE of the city of Belgorod; pop. (1992e) 184,000.

Stass·furt \'shtäs-ˌfu̇rt\. City, Saxony-Anhalt, E cen. Germany, 21 mi. (34 km.) S of Magdeburg.

State College. Borough, Centre co., cen. Pennsylvania, 22 mi. (35 km.) NW of Lewistown; pop. (1990c) 38,923; Pennsylvania State Univ.–University Park Campus (1855).

Stat·en Island \'stat-^{ə}n\. **1.** Island, New York Bay, New York, 5 mi. (8 km.) S of Manhattan; 64 sq. mi. (166 sq. km.); ab. 15.5 mi. (25 km.) long by 7 mi. (11 km.) wide; separated on E from Long Island by the Narrows and on W from New Jersey by narrow Arthur Kill connecting Newark Bay on N with Raritan Bay on S. Forms Staten Island (formerly Richmond) borough, New York City, and Richmond co., New York state; connected with Brooklyn by Verrazano-Narrows Bridge (suspension; main span 4260 ft. or 1298 m.; completed 1964) and with Bayonne, New Jersey, by Bayonne Bridge (steel arch; main span 1675 ft. or 511 m.; completed 1931). First permanent settlement made under Dutch 1661; passed to British 1664; scene 1776 of unsuccessful peace conference bet. British and Americans after battle of Long Island in American Revolution; as Richmond, became borough of New York City 1898. **Staten Island** was officially made the name of the borough in 1975.

2. *formerly* **Rich·mond** \'rich-mənd\. Borough, SW part of New York City, New York; coextensive with Richmond co.; 37 sq. mi. (96 sq. km.); pop. (1990c) 378,977; includes Staten I., Shooters I., Pralls I., Meadow I., part of Buckwheat I., a few small islands to W and N, and Hoffman I. and Swinburne I. in Lower New York Bay; separated from Long Island by the Narrows (spanned by Verrazano-Narrows Bridge) and from the mainland of New Jersey by Kill Van Kull on N (spanned by Bayonne Bridge) and Arthur Kill on W (crossed by Goethals Bridge to Elizabeth and by Outerbridge to Perth Amboy); munic. ferry connections with Manhattan. Has a 35-mile (56-kilometer) waterfront; residential sections and trade centers, incl. St. George (⊗ of Richmond co.), Port Richmond, West New Brighton, Tompkinsville, Stapleton, New Dorp, Tottenville; shipbuilding yards, printing plants, oil storage tanks and refineries. Wagner Coll. (1883, brought here from Rochester 1918); Sailors' Snug Harbor for retired sailors at New Brighton (*q.v.*). Governed as part of New York City; has a borough president, with local and county functions conducted independently of central munic. government. See also NEW YORK 3.

3. Island, Argentina. See ESTADOS, ISLA DE LOS.

Sta·ten·ville \'stāt-^{ə}n-ˌvil\. Town, ⊗ of Echols co., S Georgia, 20 mi. (32 km.) ESE of Valdosta.

State of Israel. See ISRAEL 2.

States, the. Colloquial name for United States of America (*q.v.*).

States·boro \'stāts-ˌbər-ō\. City, ⊗ of Bulloch co., E Georgia, 47 mi. (76 km.) WNW of Savannah; pop. (1990c) 15,854; Georgia Southern Univ. (1906).

States of the Church. See PAPAL STATES.

States·ville \'stāts-ˌvil, -vəl\. City, ⊗ of Iredell co., cen. North Carolina, 37 mi. (60 km.) N of Charlotte; pop. (1990c) 17,567; Mitchell Community Coll. (1852); city founded 1789.

Stato della Chiesa, Lo. See PAPAL STATES.

Statue of Liberty National Monument. See UNITED STATES, *National Monuments.*

Staub·bach Falls \'shtau̇p-ˌbäk\. Waterfall near Lauterbrunnen, Switzerland; 984 ft. (300 m.) high; slight flow.

Staun·ton 1. \'stȯnt-^{ə}n, 'stänt-\. City, Macoupin co., SW cen. Illinois, 32 mi. (51 km.) NE of East St. Louis; pop. (1990c) 4806.

2. \'stant-^{ə}n\. City, ⊗ of Augusta co., N cen. Virginia, 35 mi. (56 km.) WNW of Charlottesville; 9 sq. mi. (23 sq. km.); pop. (1990c) 24,461; politically independent; Mary Baldwin Coll. (1842). Birthplace (now a museum) of Woodrow Wilson, 28th president of the U.S., 1856. Founded 1736; during American Revolution Virginia Assembly briefly met here 1781; in Civil War twice occupied by Union forces, and served as supply base for both armies; was first city to adopt city manager form of government 1908.

\ə\ **abut** \ˈə\ **matches** \$^{ə}$\ **kitten, Fr table** \ər\ **further** \a\ **ash** \ā\ **ace**
\ä\ **cot, cart** \ȧ\ **Fr bac** \au̇\ **out** \b̲\ **Span Avila** \ch\ **chin** \e\ **bet** \ē\ **easy**
\g\ **go** \i\ **hit** \ī\ **ice** \j\ **job** \k\ **Ger ich, Buch** \$^{n}$\ **Fr vin**
\ŋ\ **sing** \ō\ **go** \ö\ **all** \ȯ\ **law** \œ\ **Fr bœuf** \œ̅\ **Fr feu** \ȯi\ **boy**
\th\ **thin** \t̲h̲\ **this** \ü\ **loot** \u̇\ **foot** \u̅e̅\ **Ger füllen** \u̅e̅\ **Fr rue**
\y\ **yet** \$^{y}$\ **Fr digne** \'dēn^{y}\, **nuit** \'nw^{y}ē\ \yü\ **few** \yu̇\ **fury** \zh\ **vision**

Sta·vang·er \stä-ˈväŋ-ər\. Seaport, ⊗ of Rogaland co., SW Norway, on **Stavanger Fjord,** a S branch of Bokn Fjord, 190 mi. (306 km.) WSW of Oslo; pop. (1990c) 97,570; fish canning, shipbuilding; center for coordination of offshore oil drilling; 12th cent. cathedral; two museums. Thought to have been founded in 8th cent.; made bishopric 12th cent. (see removed to Kristiansand 1682); made Lutheran bishopric c. 1925.

Stave·ley \ˈstāv-lē\. Town, Derbyshire, N cen. England; pop. (1981p) 17,828; chemicals.

Sta·ve·lot \stȧ-ˈvlō\ *or Flemish* **Sta·blo** \ˈstä-blō\. Commune, Liège prov., Belgium, on the Amblève River 21 mi. (34 km.) SE of the city of Liège; pop. (1991c) 6271; Benedictine abbey founded 651; in WWII in the Battle of the Bulge Dec. 1944–Jan. 1945, reached by Germans but held by Allies against further advance on Liège.

Stav·ro·pol' *or* **Stav·ro·pol** \ˈstä-vrə-pəlʸ\. **1.** *1935–43* **Vo·ro·shi·lovsk** \ˌvə-rə-ˈshi-ləfsk\. City, ✱ of Stavropol' Kray, S Russia in Europe, on tributary of upper Kalaus; pop. (1992e) 332,000; produces flour, wine, leather goods; founded 1777 as fortress.

2. Town, Samara Oblast, Russia. See TOL'YATTI.

Stavropol' Kray *or* **Stavropol Kray** \ˈkrī\; *formerly* **Or·dzho·ni·kid·ze Kray** \ȧr-jə-ni-ˈkid-zi-ˈkrī\. Territory, S Russia in Europe; 31,120 sq. mi. (80,600 sq. km.); pop. (1992e) 2,536,000; ✱ Stavropol'. Contains high land in W part and plain in the E, watered by Kuma and Terek rivers, the latter mostly on S border. Economy is principally agricultural (grain, sunflowers, flax, potatoes, livestock); natural gas fields. Chief settlements Stavropol', Pyatigorsk, Nevinnomyssk, Kislovodsk. Formed 1924, reorganized and renamed 1944.

Stav·ros *or* **Stav·rós** \stä-ˈvrōs\. Town, Chalcidice dept., S Macedonia, NE Greece, on NE coast of the Chalcidice Penin., on S shore of the Strymonic Gulf E of Thessaloníki.

Staw·ell \ˈstȯ-əl\. Town, W Victoria, SE Australia, 130 mi. (209 km.) WNW of Melbourne; pop. (1991p) 6340.

Stay·ton \ˈstāt-ᵊn\. City, Marion co., NW Oregon, 18 mi. (29 km.) SE of Salem; pop. (1990c) 5011.

Steam·boat Springs \ˈstēm-ˌbōt\. Town, ⊗ of Routt co., NW Colorado, on Yampa River 38 mi. (61 km.) E of Craig; pop. (1990c) 6695.

Stearns \ˈstərnz\. County in cen. Minnesota. See table at MINNESOTA.

Stę·bark \ˈstem-ˌbärk\ *or Ger.* **Tan·nen·berg** \ˈtän-ən-ˌberk\. Village, Olsztyn prov., N Poland, 15 mi. (24 km.) SE of Ostróda; site of two battles: (1) 1410, in which Teutonic Knights were defeated by the Lithuanians and Poles, and (2) Aug. 1914, in WWI, in which Germans severely defeated Russians. Before 1945 in East Prussia, Germany.

Steele \ˈstēl\. **1.** Name of counties in two states of the U.S. See tables at MINNESOTA and NORTH DAKOTA.

2. City, ⊗ of Kidder co., S cen. North Dakota; pop. (1990c) 762.

Steele, Mount. Peak in St. Elias Mts., SW Yukon Terr., Canada, near Alaskan border; 16,644 ft. (5073 m.).

Steel Mountain \ˈstēl\. Peak, N Elmore co., SW cen. Idaho; 9752 ft. (2972 m.).

Steel·ton \ˈstēl-tən\. Borough, Dauphin co., SE cen. Pennsylvania, on Susquehanna River just S of Harrisburg; pop. (1990c) 5152.

Steel·ville \ˈstēl-ˌvil\. City, ⊗ of Crawford co., SE cen. Missouri; pop. (1990c) 1465; nearby is the 1990 center of U.S. pop. as determined by the Bureau of the Census.

Steen·ker·ke \ˈstān-ˌker-kə\ *or* **Steen·kerque** \sten-ˈkerk, steⁿ-\ *also* **Stein·kirk** \ˈstīn-ˌkərk\. Village in Hainaut prov., SW Belgium; scene of battle July 23–Aug. 3, 1692 in which the French under Francois-Henri de Montmorency-Bouteville, duc de Luxembourg, defeated the English under William III.

Steens Mountain \ˈstēnz\. Mountain mass, SE Harney co., SE Oregon; highest point ab. 9700 ft. (2955 m.).

Steen·wijk \ˈstān-ˌvīk\. Commune, Overijssel prov., E Netherlands, ab. 7 mi. (11 km.) NNW of Meppel; pop. (1981e) 21,148.

Stee·ple \ˈstē-pəl\. Mountain, Cumbria, NW England, in the Lake District; two peaks, 2746 ft. (837 m.) and 2687 ft. (819 m.).

Steep Point \ˈstēp\. Westernmost point of mainland of Australia, 26°08′S, 113°08′E.

Stefanie, Lake. See CH'EW BAHIR.

Ste·fans·son Island \ˈste-fən-sən\. Island, cen. Arctic Archipelago, Canada, off NE coast of Victoria I.; 2890 sq. mi. (7485 sq. km.).

Stefansson Strait. Strait, bet. E Antarctic Penin. and Hearst I., Antarctica; 40 mi. (64 km.) long, 3 mi. (5 km.) wide at narrowest point; filled with shelf ice.

Stef·fen \ˈste-fen\. Peak, W Chubut prov., S Argentina, on Chilean border; 6916 ft. (2108 m.).

Ste·ger \ˈstā-gər\. Village, Cook and Will cos., NE Illinois, ab. 15 mi. (24 km.) S of Chicago; pop. (1990c) 8584.

Steier. See STEYR.

Steiermark. See STYRIA.

Stei·la·coom \ˈsti-lə-kəm\. Town, Pierce co., W cen. Washington, 10 mi. (16 km.) SW of Tacoma; pop. (1990c) 5728.

Steinamanger. See SZOMBATHELY.

Stein·bach \ˈstīn-ˌbak\. Town, Manitoba, Canada, 39 mi. (63 km.) SE of Winnipeg; pop. (1991c) 8213.

Steinkirk. See STEENKERKE.

Stein·kjer \ˈstān-ˌk̲ar\. Town, ⊗ of Nord-Trøndelag co., N cen. Norway, N of Levanger and at the head of Trondheim Fjord; pop. (1990e) 20,577; lumber port and railroad station; damaged in fighting 1940 in WWII.

Steins·øy \ˈstān-ˌsȯi\. Small island off Sogne Fjord, Norway, 58°59′N, 5°46′E; the most W point of Norway.

Stein·stück·en \ˈshtīn-ˌshtœ-kən\. Community, Brandenburg, NE cen. Germany; bet. Potsdam and Berlin; before reunification, comprised an exclave (31 acres or 13 hectares) of West Berlin in East Germany.

Stel·la·land \ˈste-lə-ˌland\. Former Boer republic, S Africa; ab. 5000 sq. mi. (12,950 sq. km.); ✱ Vryburg; estab. in W Transvaal 1882 as part of westward expansion of Boers (see GOSHEN 5); dissolved 1885 and became crown colony; region now part of North West prov., Rep. of South Africa.

Stel·lar·ton \ˈste-lərt-ᵊn\. Town, Pictou co., N Nova Scotia, Canada, 7mi. (11 km.) S of New Glasgow; pop. (1991c) 5237; coal mining formerly chief industry.

Stel·len·bosch \ˈste-lən-ˌbȯs, -ˌbu̇sh\. Residential town, SW Western Cape prov., S Rep. of South Africa, 25 mi. (40 km.) E of Cape Town; pop. (1985c) 38,602; produces wine and lumber; educational center, with Univ. of Stellenbosch (1918) and many schools; 2d oldest town in Rep. of South Africa (after Cape Town), founded 1679.

Stel·ler, Mount \ˈste-lər\. Mountain in Chugach Mts., S Alaska; 10,617 ft. (3236 m.); Bering Glacier is on it.

Stel·vio National Park \ˈstel-vē-ˌō\. National park, N Italy; alpine region; estab. 1935.

Stelvio Pass. Mountain pass, Ortler Mts., bet. Italy and Switzerland; 9045 ft. (2757 m.).

Ste·nay \stə-ˈnā\. Town, N Meuse dept., NE France, on Meuse River 26 mi. (42 km.) NNW of Verdun; an ancient frontier fortress, residence of the kings of Austrasia; last town taken by U.S. forces in WWI, on morning of Armistice Day Nov. 11, 1918.

Sten·dal \ˈshten-ˌdäl\. City, Saxony-Anhalt, NE Germany, 32 mi. (51 km.) NNE of Magdeburg; pop. (1992e) 48,360; chemicals, metal goods; sugar refining; numerous Gothic buildings; 12th cent. basilica; 15th cent. church; medieval town gates. Medieval origins, chartered 12th cent.; became member of the Hanseatic League 14th cent.

Stenón Karpathon. See KARPATHOS STRAIT.

Stepanakert. See XANKÄNDI.

Ste·phens \ˈstē-vənz\. Name of counties in three states of the U.S. See tables at GEORGIA, OKLAHOMA, TEXAS.

Ste·phen·son \ˈstē-vən-sən\. County in N Illinois. See table at ILLINOIS.

Ste·phen·ville \ˈstē-vən-ˌvil\. **1.** City, ⊗ of Erath co., N cen. Texas, 60 mi. (97 km.) SW of Fort Worth; pop. (1990c) 13,502; Tarleton State Univ. (1899).

2. Town on SW coast of Newfoundland, Canada, near head of St. Georges Bay; pop. (1991c) 7621.

Stepnoi. See ELISTA.

Steppes, the \ˈsteps\. Region, W cen. Asia. See KIRGIZ STEPPE.

Ster·ling \ˈstər-liŋ\. **1.** County in W cen. Texas. See table at TEXAS.

2. City, ⊗ of Logan co., NE Colorado, on South Platte River 40 mi. (64 km.) NE of Fort Morgan; pop. (1990c) 10,362; sugar refining; sugar beets; Northeastern Junior Coll. (1941).

3. City, Whiteside co., NW Illinois, 48 mi. (77 km.) SW of Rockford; pop. (1990c) 15,132; builders' hardware.

4. City, Rice co., cen. Kansas, on Arkansas River 20 mi. (32 km.) NW of Hutchinson; pop. (1990c) 2115; Sterling Coll. (1887).

5. Town, Worcester co., cen. Massachusetts, 10 mi. (16 km.) S of Fitchburg; pop. (1990c) 6481.

6. Unincorporated settlement, Loudon co., N Virginia, just NNE of Washington D.C.'s Dulles International Airport; pop. (1990c) 20,512.

Sterling, Mount. Peak, Haywood co., in E Great Smoky Mts., W North Carolina; 5835 ft. (1779 m.).

Sterling City. City, ⊗ of Sterling co., W cen. Texas; pop. (1990c) 1096.

Sterling Heights. City, Macomb co., SE Michigan, 7 mi. (11 km.) N of Detroit; pop. (1990c) 117,810; grew rapidly in 1970s.

Sterling Peak. Mountain, S Jackson co., SW Oregon; 7377 ft. (2249 m.).

Ster·li·ta·mak \ˌster-li-tə-ˈmák\. Town, S cen. Bashkortostan, E Russia in Europe, on left bank of Belaya River 75 mi. (121 km.) S of Ufa; pop. (1992e) 254,000; soda, cement, chemicals, synthetic rubber, oil refining; founded 1781; formerly ✻ of republic 1919–22.

Sterzing. See VIPITENO.

Stettin. See SZCZECIN 2.

Stet·tin·er Haff \shte-ˈtē-nər-ˈhäf\ *or Pol.* **Za·lew Szcze·ciń·ski** \ˈzä-ˌlev-shchet-ˈsēⁿ-skē\. Large lagoon on coast of Pomerania bet. NE Germany, and NW Poland, opening into Pomeranian Bay bet. the islands of Usedom (*Pol.* Uznam) and Wolin, which shut it off from the Baltic Sea; receives the Oder River.

Stett·ler \ˈstet-lər\. Town, Alberta, Canada, 90 mi. (145 km.) SSE of Edmonton; pop. (1991c) 4947.

Steu·ben \ˈstü-bən, ˈstyü-\. Name of counties in two states of the U.S. See tables at INDIANA and NEW YORK.

Steu·ben·ville \ˈstü-bən-ˌvil, ˈstyü-\. City, ⊗ of Jefferson co., E Ohio, on Ohio River 50 mi. (80 km.) S of Youngstown; pop. (1990c) 22,125; steel, chemicals, ferrous alloys; Franciscan Univ. of Steubenville (1946). Fort Steuben built on site 1786 but burned 1790; town laid out 1797; incorp. as city 1851.

Ste·ven·age \ˈstē-və-nij\. Town, Hertfordshire, SE England, 28 mi. (45 km.) N of London; pop. (1991p) 73,700; electronics industry.

Ste·vens \ˈstē-vənz\. Name of counties in three states of the U.S. See tables at KANSAS, MINNESOTA, WASHINGTON.

Ste·ven·son \ˈstē-vən-sən\. Town, ⊗ of Skamania co., S Washington; pop. (1990c) 1147.

Stevenson, Mount. Peak, Yellowstone National Park, NW Wyoming; 10,352 ft. (3155 m.).

Stevens Point. City, ⊗ of Portage co., cen. Wisconsin, 30 mi. (48 km.) S of Wausau; pop. (1990c) 23,006; paper, furniture, fishing tackle, beer; Univ. of Wisconsin–Stevens Point (1894).

Stew·art \ˈstü-ərt, ˈstyü-\. **1.** Name of counties in two states of the U.S. See tables at GEORGIA and TENNESSEE.

2. River, cen. Yukon Terr., Canada; flows W in S Klondike region to Yukon River; 331 mi. (533 km.).

Stewart Island. Island, Pacific Ocean, S of South I., New Zealand; 675 sq. mi. (1748 sq. km.); pop. (1987e) 540; mountainous.

Stewart Islands. Atoll group, 110 mi. (177 km.) E of N end of Malaita I., SE cen. Solomon Is., W Pacific Ocean; chief island Sikaiana.

Stewart Mountain Dam. Dam across Salt River, E Maricopa co., S cen. Arizona; height 207 ft. (63 m.); completed 1930; impounds water for power, forming **Sa·gua·ro Lake** \sə-ˈgwär-ō, -ˈwär-\ 10 mi. (16 km.) long.

Stewart Peak. Mountain, Saguache co., S Colorado; 13,980 ft. (4261 m.).

Stew·art·ville \ˈstü-ərt-ˌvil, ˈstyü-\. City, Olmsted co., SE Minnesota, 5 mi. (8 km.) S of Rochester; pop. (1990c) 4520.

Steyr \ˈshtīr\ *also* **Stei·er** \ˈshtī-ər\. City, Upper Austria, Austria, on **Steyr River** at its confluence with the Enns 16 mi. (26 km.) SSE of Linz; pop. (1991c) 39,337; motor vehicles, sporting firearms, tractors, iron goods; has a medieval center with 15th cent. church and 18th cent. town hall.

Stick·ney \ˈstik-nē\. Village, Cook co., NE Illinois, W suburb of Chicago; pop. (1990c) 5678.

Stig·ler \ˈsti-glər\. City, ⊗ of Haskell co., E Oklahoma, 38 mi. (61 km.) SSE of Muskogee; pop. (1990c) 2574.

Sti·kine \sti-ˈkēn\. River, NW British Columbia, Canada, and S Alaska; rises in Stikine Mts. and flows W and SW through the Coast Mts. and across S Alaska to the Pacific Ocean; 335 mi. (539 km.) long.

Stikine Mountains. Range, S Yukon and N British Columbia, Canada; ab. 400 mi. (645 km.) long; a range of the Rocky Mts.; highest peak Mt. Cushing 8676 ft. (2644 m.) in N British Columbia.

Sti·kle·stad \ˈsti-klə-ˌstä\. Village, Nord-Trøndelag co., N cen. Norway, on Trondheim Fjord NE of Trondheim; scene of battle in which King Olaf II of Norway was killed 1030.

Stil·fon·tein \ˈstil-ˌfän-ˌtān\. Town, North West prov., NE Rep. of South Africa, ab. 90 mi. (145 km.) SW of Johannesburg.

Still·wa·ter \ˈstil-ˌwò-tər, -ˌwä-\. **1.** County in S cen. Montana. See table at MONTANA.

2. City, ⊗ of Washington co., E Minnesota, on St. Croix River 15 mi. (24 km.) ENE of St. Paul; pop. (1990c) 13,882.

3. Village, Saratoga co., New York, on W bank of Hudson River ab. 21 mi. (34 km.) N of Albany; pop. (1990c) 7233; battle fought ab. 3 mi. (5 km.) N in Revolutionary War generally known as the battle of Saratoga. See SARATOGA 3.

4. City, ⊗ of Payne co., N cen. Oklahoma, 42 mi. (68 km.) S of Ponca City; pop. (1990c) 36,676; agriculture; gas wells; Oklahoma State Univ. (1890); city founded 1889.

Stillwater Range *or* **Stillwater Mountains.** Range, cen. Churchill co., W Nevada.

Stil·ton \ˈstilt-ᵊn\. Parish, Cambridgeshire, E cen. England; gives name to cheese now made chiefly in Leicestershire.

Stil·well \ˈstil-ˌwel, -wəl\. City, ⊗ of Adair co., E Oklahoma, 44 mi. (71 km.) E of Muskogee; pop. (1990c) 2663.

Stilwell Road. Former military highway, Asia, connecting NE India with Kunming, Yunnan prov., China; 1044 mi. (1680 km.) long; important esp. in WWII.

Stim·son, Mount \ˈstim-sən\. Peak, Glacier National Park, NW Montana; ab. 10,165 ft. (3098 m.).

Stin·nett \sti-ˈnet\. Town, ⊗ of Hutchinson co., NW Texas; pop. (1990c) 2166.

Štip \ˈshtēp\ *or Turk.* **Ish·tib** \ish-ˈtēp\. Town, Republic of Macedonia, 40 mi. (64 km.) SE of Skopje; an old town, in early times belonging to the Byzantines, later to the Serbs, and Turkish from 14th to 20th cents.

Stir·ling \ˈstər-liŋ\. **1.** *or* **Stir·ling·shire** \-shər, -ˌshir\. Former county, cen. Scotland; ⊗ Stirling; rivers Forth, Avon, Endrick, Carron; chief towns Stirling, Falkirk, Kilsyth, Grangemouth.

2. Burgh, ⊗ of Central region, S cen. Scotland, on the Forth River 36 mi. (58 km.) NW of Edinburgh; pop. (1981c) 38,842; Univ. of Stirling (1964). Early medieval castle, birthplace of James II of Scotland 1430; scene of the coronation of infant Mary, Queen of Scots, and James VI of Scotland; two battles nearby: (1) battle of Stirling Bridge 1297 in

which Scottish patriot Sir William Wallace defeated English, and (2) the battle of Bannockburn (*q.v.*) 1314.
3. Island, one of the Treasury Is. group off S end of Bougainville, Solomon Is., W Pacific Ocean.

Stirling Range. Mountain range, Papua New Guinea, SE New Guinea I., forming the SE extension of the Owen Stanley Range to the shores of Milne Bay.

Stirling Range National Park. National park, SW Western Australia, Australia; ab. 445 sq. mi. (1150 sq. km.); jagged mountains, sand plains.

Stjer·nø·ya \ˈstyer-nȯi-ə\. Island, Arctic Ocean off NW coast of Norway, in Finnmark co. S of Sørøya I.

Sto·bi \ˈstō-bē\. Ancient town of Paeonia (in Macedonia after 4th cent. B.C.) dating probably from the 6th cent. B.C.; esp. prominent in Roman times. Its ruins not far from Bitola in Republic of Macedonia.

Stochód. See STOKHOD.

Stock·ach \ˈshtȯ-ˌkäk\. Commune, Baden-Württemberg, Germany, NW of Konstanz; scene of two battles: (1) 1799 in which Charles Louis, archduke of Austria, defeated French under Gen. Jean-Baptiste Jourdan, and (2) 1800 in which French Gen. Victor Moreau defeated the Austrians under Gen. Paul Kray von Krajowa.

Stock·bridge \ˈstäk-ˌbrij\. Town, Berkshire co., W Massachusetts; pop. (1990c) 2408; summer resort in the Berkshire Hills.

Stock·e·rau \ˈshtȯ-kə-ˌraů\. City, Lower Austria, Austria, NNW of Vienna on arm of Danube River; pop. (1981c) 12,692; manufactures machinery, chemicals.

Stock·holm \ˈstäk-ˌhōlm, -ˌhōm, *Swedish* ˈstȯk-ˌhȯlm\. **1.** Province of SE Sweden. See table at SWEDEN.
2. Seaport city, ✻ of Sweden, also ⊗ of Stockholm prov., on the Baltic Sea; pop. (1993e) 684,576; largest city in Sweden and its cultural, commercial, and financial center; textiles, paper, chemicals, beer; printing, metalworking, food processing. Built on several islands and peninsulas. Has numerous notable buildings, incl. the city hall, Olympic stadium, Riddarkyrka (burial place of Swedish royalty and other notable figures), Nobel Institute, national museum, royal palace, 17th cent. cathedral; technical institute, university (1877).
History: According to tradition, founded by Swedish noble Birger Jarl c. 1250; became chief trade port of Sweden during Middle Ages, dominated by Hanseatic League; liberated from foreign domination c. 1523 by King Gustav I Vasa and became de facto ✻ of Sweden; developed rapidly during 17th cent. and was again extensively redeveloped during industrial growth of 19th cent.; site of Olympic Games 1912.

Stock·port \ˈstäk-ˌpōrt\. Town, Greater Manchester, NW England, on the Mersey 6 mi. (10 km.) S of Manchester; pop. (1991p) 276,800; textiles, hats, electronics; granted first charter 1220.

Stocks·bridge \ˈstäks-ˌbrij\. Town, South Yorkshire, N England; pop. (1981p) 14,015; steel.

Stock·ton \ˈstäk-tən\. **1.** City, ⊗ of San Joaquin co., cen. California, on San Joaquin River 53 mi. (85 km.) E of Oakland; pop. (1990c) 210,943; deepwater port and distribution center for agricultural produce of San Joaquin Valley; food processing; Univ. of the Pacific (1851), Humphreys Coll. (1896), San Joaquin Delta Coll. (1935). Founded 1847; supply and trade center during gold rush; made ⊗ 1850; the pop. has grown at an increasing rate since 1950.
2. City, ⊗ of Rooks co., N Kansas; pop. (1990c) 1507.
3. City, ⊗ of Cedar co., W Missouri; pop. (1990c) 1579.

Stockton Island. See APOSTLE ISLANDS.

Stock·ville \ˈstäk-ˌvil\. Village, ⊗ of Frontier co., S Nebraska; pop. (1990c) 32.

Stod·dard \ˈstä-dərd\. County in SE Missouri. See table at MISSOURI.

Sto·er, Point of \ˈstō-ər\. Cape, NW coast of Scotland, at S entrance to Eddrachillis Bay; lighthouse.

Stoke, East \ˈstōk\ *also* **Stoke.** Village, Nottinghamshire, N cen. England, near Newark-on-Trent; scene of battle 1487 in which Lambert Simnel, the pretender to a royal title, was defeated by Henry VII.

Stoke–on–Trent \-ˈtrent\. City, Staffordshire, W cen. England, 38 mi. (61 km.) N of Birmingham; pop. (1991p) 244,800; center of the Staffordshire pottery-making industry; coal mining; iron industry. Home of several of the pioneers in the pottery industry: Josiah Wedgwood (see BURSLEM), Josiah Spode, and Thomas and Herbert Minton. See POTTERIES, THE.

Stoke Po·ges \stōk-ˈpō-jəs, -jəz\. Parish, Buckinghamshire, SE cen. England; churchyard is burial site of poet Thomas Gray (d. 1771), and is generally considered the scene of his poem *An Elegy Written in a Country Church Yard.*

Stokes \ˈstōks\. **1.** County in N North Carolina. See table at NORTH CAROLINA.
2. Peak in Andes, S Chile, near Argentine border and E of Hanover I.; 7020 ft. (2140 m.).

Sto·khod \ˈstȯ-k̲ət\ *or Pol.* **Sto·chód** \-küt\. River, NW Ukraine; flows into Pripyat' River from the S; ab. 90 mi. (145 km.) long; formerly in Poland.

Stol·berg \ˈshtȯl-ˌberk\ *also* **Stolberg im Rhein·land** \im-ˈrīn-ˌlänt\. City, North Rhine-Westphalia, Germany, on Belgian border 7 mi. (11 km.) E of Aachen; pop. (1992e) 57,591; glass, textiles, chemicals.

Stol·bo·vo *or* **Stol·bo·va** \stəl-ˈbȯ-və\. Village, St. Petersburg Oblast, NW Russia in Europe, near S end of Lake Ladoga; treaty signed here 1617 ended war bet. Russia and Sweden and cut Russia off from Baltic Sea.

Stolp. See SŁUPSK.

Stolpe. See SŁUPIA.

Stone \ˈstōn\. **1.** Name of counties in three states of the U.S. See tables at ARKANSAS, MISSISSIPPI, MISSOURI.
2. Town, Staffordshire, W cen. England; pop. (1981p) 12,115.

Stone·ham \ˈstō-nəm\. Residential town, Middlesex co., NE Massachusetts, 9 mi. (14 km.) N of Boston; pop. (1990c) 22,203.

Stone·ha·ven \ˈstōn-ˌhā-vən\. Seaport burgh, SE Grampian region, E Scotland; pop. (1981p) 7885.

Stone·henge \ˈstōn-ˌhenj\. An assemblage of massive standing stones (megaliths), Salisbury Plain, 7 mi. (11 km.) N of Salisbury, England; construction and use occurred in several distinct periods from c. 3000 B.C. to c. 1000 B.C.; final site consisted of a circular ditch with interior circular mound surrounding the site except for an entrance gap to the NE from which radiates an ancient avenue; inside the earthworks were several rings of upright stones incl. a ring of large sandstone uprights formerly capped by a continuous series of lintel stones, a horseshoe arrangement of large sandstone trilithons, and a central stone (now lying flat, but formerly erect); several other stones adorn the site, as well as evidence of unused stone holes in the ground; the purpose of the site remains unknown, although many archaeologists agree that it was likely a site of religious ceremonies, and some attribute astronomical significance to the arrangement and orientation of the stones.

Stone Mountain. **1.** Massive monadnock of gray granite, De Kalb co., NW cen. Georgia, near Atlanta; at 1686 ft. (514 m.) high, largest in North America. Confederate memorial carved on the NE wall of the mountain; work began c. 1917 and continued periodically until 1967, incl. some work by Gutzon Borglum, sculptor of Mt. Rushmore.
2. Peak, Carter co., NE Tennessee; 3500 ft. (1067 m.).
3. City, De Kalb co., NW cen. Georgia; pop. (1990c) 6494.

Stone Park. Village, Cook co., NE Illinois ab. 3 mi. (5 km.) SSE of Chicago's O'Hare International Airport; pop. (1990c) 4383.

Stones River \ˈstōnz\. River, Tennessee; formed by confluence of E and W forks in N Rutherford co., flows N into Cumberland River E of Nashville; 60 mi. (97 km.) long; on W fork near Murfreesboro during Civil War occurred battle (also known as battle of Murfreesboro, *q.v.*) Dec. 31, 1862–Jan. 2, 1863, a drawn contest but strategic victory for Union forces; site of battle has been set aside as **Stones River National Battlefield** (see UNITED STATES, *National Historical Parks*).

Stone·wall \ˈstōn-ˌwäl\. **1.** County in NW Texas. See table at TEXAS.

2. Village, Gillespie co., cen. Texas, on Pedernales River; birthplace 1908 of Lyndon B. Johnson, 36th president of the U.S., nearby.

Ston·ey Creek \ˈstō-nē\. Town, Hamilton-Wentworth munic. region, SE Ontario, Canada, at W end of Lake Ontario; pop. (1991c) 49,968; scene of battle 1813 during War of 1812 in which the British defeated the Americans.

Ston·ing·ton \ˈstō-niŋ-tən\. Town, SE New London co., SE Connecticut, on Long Island Sound E of Groton; settled 1649. Includes (1) borough of Stonington; pop. (1990c) 16,919; incorp. 1801 (first such incorporation in Connecticut); formerly important fishing port; attacked by British during American Revolution (1775) and War of 1812 (1814), both attacks repulsed, and (2) Mystic (*q.v.*).

Stony Brook \ˈstō-nē-ˌbru̇k\. Unincorporated settlement, Suffolk co., E Long Island, SE New York; pop. (1990c) 13,726; State Univ. of New York at Stony Brook (1957).

Stony Creek \ˈstō-nē\. River, S Pennsylvania; flows N from Somerset co. to unite with the Little Conemaugh River at Johnstown and form the Conemaugh.

Stony Man Mountain. Peak, Shenandoah National Park, Page co., N Virginia; 4011 ft. (1223 m.).

Stony Mountain. Peak in the Catskill Mts., SE New York; 3844 ft. (1172 m.).

Stony Point. **1.** Point, W cen. coast of Jefferson co., N New York, extending into Lake Ontario SW of Sackets Harbor.

2. Village, Rockland co., SE New York; pop. (1990c) 12,814; named from a rocky promontory on the Hudson; in Revolutionary War an American blockhouse taken by British 1779 and fortified for commanding the Hudson; stormed and taken by Americans under Gen. Anthony Wayne July 15–16, 1779; immediately leveled and evacuated as untenable, refortified by British.

Stony Tunguska. See TUNGUSKA.

Sto·rå \ˈstō-rȯ\. River, NW cen. Jutland Penin., Denmark; flows W into North Sea; ab. 55 mi. (88 km.) long.

Sto·ra Sjö·fall·et \ˈstu̇r-ə-ˈshœ̄-ˌfä-lət\. Waterfall, upper Luleälv River, in **Stora Sjöfallet National Park,** N Sweden; 131 ft. (40 m.).

Stor·a·van \ˈstu̇r-ˌä-vən\. Lake, Västerbotten prov., N Sweden; 62 sq. mi. (161 sq. km.); drained by Skellefte River.

Stord \ˈstu̇rd\. Island in Hordaland co., off SW coast of Norway, ab. 30 mi. (48 km.) S of Bergen; 92 sq. mi. (238 sq. km.).

Store Bælt. See STORE STRAIT.

Store Sotra. See SOTRA.

Sto·re Strait \ˈstō-rə\ *or Dan.* **Sto·re Bælt** \ˈstō-rə-ˈbeld\ *or* **Great Belt** \ˈbelt\. Strait bet. Sjælland and Fyn islands, Denmark, connecting the Kattegat with the Baltic Sea; 40 mi. (64 km.) long, averages 10 mi. (16 km.) wide.

Sto·rey \ˈstōr-ē\. County in W Nevada. See table at NEVADA.

Stor Fjord \ˈstu̇r-ˌfyu̇r\. **1.** Fjord, Svalbard, Norway; separates the main island of Spitsbergen from Barents I. and Edge I.

2. Inlet of the Norwegian Sea, W coast of Norway; extends inland over 70 mi. (113 km.), E of Ålesund.

Stor·foss \ˈstu̇r-ˌfȯs\. Rapids in the Tana River, NE Norway, ab. 45 mi. (70 km.) from its mouth.

Storm Bay \ˈstȯrm\. Large inlet of South Pacific Ocean, SE Tasmania, Australia, bet. Tasman Penin. and Bruny I.; receives Derwent River.

Storm·berg \ˈstȯrm-ˌbərg\. Village, N Eastern Cape prov., Rep. of South Africa, S of Burgersdorp; scene of battle 1899 in Boer War in which the Boers defeated the English.

Storm·ber·ge \ˈstȯrm-ˌber-gə\. Mountain range, N Eastern Cape prov., Rep. of South Africa.

Storm King. Mountain in Highlands of the Hudson, SE New York, overlooking Hudson River on W bank N of West Point; 1355 ft. (413 m.).

Storm King Peak. Mountain, San Juan co., SW Colorado; 13,749 ft. (4191 m.).

Storm Lake. **1.** Lake, S Buena Vista co., NW Iowa.

2. City, ⊗ of Buena Vista co., NW Iowa, 20 mi. (32 km.) ESE of Cherokee; pop. (1990c) 8769; Buena Vista Coll. (1891).

Stor·mont \ˈstȯr-ˌmänt\. **1.** Former county of Ontario, Canada; now part of Stormont, Dundas and Glengarry co.

2. Seat of government of Northern Ireland, 4 mi. (6 km.) E of Belfast; parliament building (built 1928–32) situated in 300-acre (122-hectare) estate.

Stormont, Dundas and Glengarry. County, Ontario, Canada. See table at ONTARIO.

Storms, Cape of. See GOOD HOPE, CAPE OF 2.

Stormy Mountain \ˈstȯr-mē\. Peak, Chelan co., cen. Washington; 7219 ft. (2200 m.).

Stor·no·way \ˈstȯr-nə-ˌwā\. Seaport burgh, ⊗ of Western Isles administrative area, N Scotland, on Lewis with Harris I.; pop. (1981c) 13,409; chief town of Lewis with Harris; manufactures tweed.

Storrs \ˈstȯrz\. Unincorporated settlement, Tolland co., N Connecticut; pop. (1990c) 12,198; a subdivision of town of Mansfield; Univ. of Connecticut (1881). See MANSFIELD 1.

Stor·sjön \ˈstu̇r-ˌshœn\. Lake, Jämtland prov., W Sweden; 176 sq. mi. (456 sq. km.); Östersund is on its E shore.

Stor·strøm \ˈstȯr-strœm\. County, Denmark; includes S part of Sjælland I., Lolland I., Falster I., and Møn I. See table at DENMARK.

Stor·strøm·me Glacier \ˈstȯr-ˌstrœ-mə\. Glacier, Greenland; 81 mi. (130 km.) long, ab. 18 mi. (29 km.) wide near its terminus.

Stort \ˈstȯrt\. River, Essex and Hertfordshire, SE England; flows S and SW to the Lea at Hoddesdon; 22 mi. (35 km.) long.

Stor·u·man \ˈstü-rü-mən\. Lake, Västerbotten prov., N Sweden; 64 sq. mi. (166 sq. km.); drained by Ume River.

Sto·ry \ˈstōr-ē\. County in cen. Iowa. See table at IOWA.

Stough·ton \ˈstōt-ᵊn\. **1.** Town, Norfolk co., E Massachusetts, 5 mi. (8 km.) NW of Brockton; pop. (1990c) 26,777; plastics, machine tools.

2. City, Dane co., S Wisconsin, 14 mi. (23 km.) SSE of Madison; pop. (1990c) 8786.

Stour \ˈstau̇r, ˈstu̇r, ˈstōr\. **1.** \ *usu.* ˈstu̇r\. River, SE England; flows bet. Essex and Suffolk cos. and into North Sea at Harwich; 47 mi. (76 km.) long.

2. \ *usu.* ˈstau̇r\. River, S England; flows across Dorset from NW to SE, and empties into the Avon at Christchurch; 55 mi. (88 km.) long.

3. \ *usu.* ˈstu̇r\. River, Kent, SE England. See GREAT STOUR.

4. \ *usu.* ˈstau̇r *or* ˈstōr\. River, cen. England; rises in Oxfordshire and flows NW to the Avon 1.5 mi. (2 km.) SW of Stratford-upon-Avon, Warwickshire; 20 mi. (32 km.) long.

5. \ *usu.* ˈstau̇r\. River, W cen. England; rises in West Midlands co. and flows S into Hereford and Worcester co. past Kidderminster and into the Severn at Stourport; 20 mi. (32 km.) long.

Stour·bridge \ˈstau̇r-ˌbrij, ˈstōr-\. Town, West Midlands, W cen. England, on the Stour 11 mi. (18 km.) W of Birmingham; pop. (1981p) 54,661; glass.

Stour·port–on–Sev·ern \ˈstau̇r-ˌpōrt ... ˈse-vərn; ˈstu̇r-\. Town, Hereford and Worcester, W cen. England; pop. (1981p) 19,092.

Stow \ˈstō\. **1.** Town, Middlesex co., NE Massachusetts, 22 mi. (35 km.) NW of Boston; pop. (1990c) 5328.

2. City, Summit co., NE Ohio, NE of Akron; pop. (1990c) 27,702.

Stowey, Nether. See NETHER STOWEY.

Stra·bane \strə-ˈban\. **1.** Administrative district, W Northern Ireland. See table at IRELAND, NORTHERN.

2. Town, its ⊗, on Mourne and Finn rivers; pop. (1990e) 35,700; textiles.

Strad·broke \ˈstrad-ˌbrōk\. Former island off SE coast of Queensland, Australia, enclosing part of Moreton Bay; now split into **North Stradbroke** and **South Stradbroke** islands.

Straf·ford \ˈstra-fərd\. County in SE New Hampshire. See table at NEW HAMPSHIRE.

Stra·han \ˈstrȯ-ən\. Town, W Tasmania, Australia, at N end of Macquarie Harbour; pop. (1981c) 411.

Strahl·horn \ˈshträl-ˌhȯrn\. Peak in the Pennine Alps, Switzerland, N of Monte Rosa; 13,750 ft. (4191 m.).

Straits, The \ˈstrāts\. **1.** Name formerly used specifically to designate the Strait of Gibraltar (*q.v.*); later the Strait of Malacca.

2. The link bet. the Mediterranean and Black seas, incl. the Bosporus and Dardanelles (*qq.v.*); name came to be applied following Russian expansion to the Black Sea when the "Straits Question," the issue of fortification by Ottoman Empire and of terms of passage bet. Black Sea and Mediterranean, became a problem in European diplomacy; opened to passage of Russian vessels 1774; by Straits Convention (1841), the major European powers agreed to principle of closing Straits to non-Turkish war vessels whenever Ottoman Empire was at peace; crossed by British and French ships during Crimean War; after closure to merchant vessels in WWI, Allies attempted to reopen Straits in Dardanelles campaign 1915; occupied by Allies 1918 (see ZONE OF THE STRAITS); by terms of Treaty of Lausanne 1923, demilitarized and opened to ships of all nations; remilitarized by Turkey as provided by Convention of Montreux 1936, which also allows restriction of access against ships of non-Black Sea states.

Straits Settlements. Former British crown colony, on S and W coast of Malay Penin., incl. adjacent islands, comprising Singapore, Penang, and Melaka settlements.

History: United c. 1826 and administered by the government of India with ✻ at George Town; ✻ removed to Singapore 1836; taken from control of Indian government 1867 and made a crown colony under direct British control; in early 20th cent. Cocos Is., Christmas I., and Labuan incorp. into the colony; in WWII, under Japanese control 1941–45; Cocos Is. and Christmas I. ceded to Australia 1955 and 1958 respectively; Penang and Melaka made states of Federation of Malaya 1948, becoming states of Malaysia (*q.v.*) 1963; Singapore made a separate colony 1946, part of Malaysia 1963–65, independent republic 1965.

Stra·ko·ni·ce \ˈsträ-kȯ-ˌnyēt-se\. Town, SW Czech Republic; pop. (1989c) 24,963.

Stral·sund \ˈshträl-ˌzu̇nt, -ˌsu̇nt\. City, Mecklenburg-West Pomerania, NW Germany, on the Strelasund opp. Rügen I. in the Baltic; pop. (1992e) 71,618; shipbuilding, fish processing; 13th cent. church of St. Mary; 13th cent. town hall.

History: Chartered 1234; important member of Hanseatic League; besieged by Austrian Gen. Albrecht von Wallenstein 1628; repeatedly changed hands 17th–19th cents. until it passed to Prussia 1815; suffered considerable damage in WWII.

Strand \ˈstrand\. Town, SW Western Cape prov., S Rep. of South Africa, on NE shore of False Bay adjoining Somerset West.

Strang·ford Lough \ˈstraŋ-fərd-ˈläk, -ˈläk\. Inlet of Irish Sea, E coast of Northern Ireland; extends N inland ab. 19 mi. (31 km.) bet. the dists. of Ards and Down.

Stran·raer \stran-ˈrär\. Seaport burgh, Dumfries and Galloway region, SW Scotland, at head of Loch Ryan; pop. (1981p) 10,837; market town.

Stras·bourg \ˈsträs-ˌbu̇rg, ˈsträz-\ *or Ger.* **Strass·burg** \ˈshträs-ˌbu̇rk\; *anc.* **Ar·gen·to·ra·tum** \är-ˌjen-tə-ˈrā-təm\. Industrial and commercial city, ✻ of Bas-Rhin dept., NE France, on the Ill River ab. 2 mi. (3 km.) W of its confluence with the Rhine, 83 mi. (134 km.) SE of Metz; pop. (1990c) 255,937; important transportation center and major river port; produces pâté de foie gras, textiles, metal goods, beer, leather products, chemicals; printing, food processing, tourism; episcopal see; seat of Council of Europe. Numerous notable buildings, incl. medieval cathedral with noted 14th cent. astronomical clock, chamber of commerce, governor's palace, town hall, museums, former episcopal palace; university (founded 1537, university status 1621).

History: Important from ancient times because of strategic location; a Celtic settlement; passed to Romans; destroyed by Huns; in late 5th cent. restored by Franks; in 842 scene of Oath of Strasbourg which declared alliance bet. Charles the Bald and Louis the German, kings of the West and East Franks; attained status of free imperial city 1262; some work done here by German inventor Johannes Gutenberg on movable type 15th cent.; occupied by French 1681 and formally ceded 1697; under German rule 1871–1918; in WWII occupied by Germans 1940–44 and suffered considerable damage; monthly meeting place of European Union's European Parliament since 1979.

Strassburg. **1.** City, France. See STRASBOURG.

2. Town, Romania. See AIUD.

Strata Flor·i·da \ˈstra-tə-ˈflȯr-ə-də\ *or Welsh* **Ys·trad Fflur** \ˈəs-träd-ˈflir\. Site of former Cistercian abbey, Dyfed co., W Wales, SE of Aberystwyth near the Teifi River; flourished 12th cent., destroyed by fire at end of 13th cent.; few ruins.

Stratfield. See BRIDGEPORT 3.

Strat·ford \ˈstrat-fərd\. **1.** Town, SE Fairfield co., SW Connecticut, on Long Island Sound at mouth of Housatonic River E of Bridgeport; pop. (1990c) 49,389; aircraft and helicopters, chemicals, hardware, boats; historically important oystering center; settled 1639.

2. Borough, Camden co., SW New Jersey, 9 mi. (14 km.) SSE of the city of Camden; pop. (1990c) 7614.

3. City, ⊗ of Sherman co., NW Texas; pop. (1990c) 1781.

4. Estate, Westmoreland co., E Virginia, on Potomac River near George Washington Birthplace National Monument; birthplace of Confederate Gen. Robert E. Lee 1807.

5. City, ⊗ of Perth co., SE Ontario, Canada, 28 mi. (45 km.) W of Kitchener; pop. (1991c) 27,666; furniture; engineering industries; railroad shops; founded 1832; annual summer festival featuring performances esp. of William Shakespeare's plays.

6. Borough, W North I., New Zealand; pop. (1981c) 5518.

Stratford–upon–Avon *also* **Stratford–on–Avon** \-ˈā-vən\. Town, Warwickshire, cen. England, 21 mi. (34 km.) SSE of Birmingham; pop. (1981c) 20,911; tourism; birthplace (1564) and burial place of dramatist and poet William Shakespeare; his plays performed here at Royal Shakespeare Theatre during annual summer festival.

Strath·aird Point \ˈstrath-ˌard\. Cape, S coast of Skye I., Inner Hebrides, off NW coast of Scotland, projecting into Cuillin Sound.

Strath·clyde \strath-ˈklīd, strəth-\. **1.** Medieval Celtic kingdom of Scotland, S of the Clyde River; ✻ Dumbarton; estab. 6th cent.; threatened and ravaged by Picts and Vikings 8th and 9th cents.; suffered several defeats by English in 10th cent., and given to Scottish King Malcolm I by English King Edmund I mid-10th cent.; fully absorbed by Scotland 11th cent.; S part known as Cumbria.

2. Administrative region, W Scotland. See table at SCOTLAND.

Strathcona. See EDMONTON 2.

Strath·field \ˈstrath-ˌfēld\. Municipality, E New South Wales, Australia, a W suburb of Sydney; pop. (1991c) 25,833.

Strath·more \strath-ˈmōr, strəth-\. Valley of cen. Scotland, S of the Grampian Mts.

Strath·roy \strath-ˈrȯi\. Town, Middlesex co., SE Ontario, Canada, 22 mi. (35 km.) W of London; pop. (1991c) 10,566.

Strat·ton \ˈstrat-ᵊn\. Town, Cornwall, SW England; scene of battle May 1643 in which Royalists under Sir Ralph Hopton defeated Parliamentarians under the earl of Stamford.

Stratton Mountain. Peak, W Windham co., SE Vermont; 3936 ft. (1200 m.); recreation; the Appalachian National Scenic Trail traverses it.

Stra·tus \ˈstrā-təs, ˈstra-\. Chief town of ancient Acarnania, W Greece, on W bank of the Achelous River.

Strau·bing \ˈshtrau̇-biŋ\. City, Bavaria, Germany, on the Danube River 23 mi. (37 km.) ESE of Regensburg; pop. (1992e) 42,487; electrical equipment; 12th cent. church, two 15th cent. churches; earlier Roman settlement on site; present town dates to Middle Ages.

Straus·berg \ˈshtrau̇s-ˌberk\. City, Brandenburg, E Germany, 33 mi. (53 km.) NW of Frankfurt an der Oder; pop. (1981c) 24,439.

Straw·ber·ry \ˈstrȯ-ˌber-ē, -bə-rē\. River, N cen. Utah; rises in Wasatch co., flows E into Duchesne River in cen. Duchesne co.; ab. 60 mi. (95 km.) long.

Strawberry Mountain. Mountain, Grant co., E cen. Oregon; 9038 ft. (2755 m.).

Strawberry Point. NE point of Plymouth co., E Massachusetts, E of Hingham; marks the S limit of Massachusetts Bay.

Stream·wood \ˈstrēm-ˌwu̇d\. Village, Cook co., NE Illinois, 7 mi. (11 km.) ESE of Elgin; pop. (1990c) 30,987.

Strea·tor \ˈstrē-tər\. City, La Salle and Livingston cos., N Illinois, 50 mi. (80 km.) NE of Peoria; pop. (1990c) 14,121; building materials.

Street Mountain \ˈstrēt\. Peak in the Adirondack Mts., Essex co., NE New York; 4216 ft. (1285 m.).

Streets·boro \ˈstrēts-ˌbər-ō\. City, Portage co., NE Ohio, SE of Cleveland; pop. (1990c) 9932.

Strehlen. See STRZELIN.

Stre·la·sund \ˈshtrā-lə-ˌzu̇nt\. Strait bet. Rügen I. and the mainland, Mecklenburg and Pomerania, NE Germany; ab. 1.5 mi. (2 km.) wide and 15 to 20 mi. (24 to 32 km.) long; Stralsund is on its W shore.

Stre·sa \ˈstrā-zä\. Town, W shore of Lake Maggiore, Novara prov., NE Piedmont, NW Italy; pop. (1991p) 4636; scene of conference bet. representatives of France, Great Britain, and Italy Apr. 1935 in effort to show united opposition (Stresa front) to the rearmament of Germany (the coalition fell apart quickly, thus allowing German rearmament to proceed virtually unopposed).

Stret·ford \ˈstret-fərd\. Town, Greater Manchester, NW England, 4 mi. (6 km.) SW of Manchester; pop. (1981p) 47,600; chemicals, food products, textiles.

Strick·land \ˈstrik-lənd\. River, Papua New Guinea, New Guinea I.; main tributary of the Fly River; rises in mountains of cen. part of the island and flows S and SW through large swamp area to join the Fly on E ab. in the middle of its course; ab. 225 mi. (360 km.) long.

Striegau. See STRZEGOM.

Strimón, Gulf of *or* **Strimonikós Kolpos.** See STRYMONIC GULF.

Strip·ed Mountain \ˈstrī-pəd, ˈstrīpt\. Peak in the Sierra Nevada, E Fresno co., S cen. California; 13,160 ft. (4011 m.).

Strofádhes. See STROPHADES.

Strom·bo·li \ˈsträm-bō-ˌlē\. **1.** *anc.* **Stron·gy·le** \ˈsträn-jə-ˌlē\. Island, Lipari Is. (*q.v.*), Italy.

2. Active volcano, Stromboli I., Italy; 3038 ft. (926 m.); one of Europe's most active volcanoes, though major eruptions are rare.

Strom·lo, Mount \ˈsträm-lō\. Elevation, Australian Capital Terr., SE Australia, 7 mi. (11 km.) W of Canberra; astronomical observatory (74-inch or 2-meter telescope) of Australian National Univ.

Strømø \ˈstrœ-ˌmœ\. Largest island of Faeroe Is. (*q.v.*), Denmark; 28 mi. (45 km.) long; area 151 sq. mi. (391 sq. km.); chief town Tórshavn.

Strom Thurmond Lake. See CLARKS HILL LAKE.

Strongs·ville \ˈstrȯŋz-ˌvil\. City, Cuyahoga co., N Ohio, 14 mi. (23 km.) SSW of Cleveland; pop. (1990c) 35,308.

Strongyle. See STROMBOLI 1.

Stron·say \ˈsträn-ˌsā\. One of the Orkney Is. (*q.v.*) off N coast of Scotland; 7.25 mi. (12 km.) long.

Stroph·a·des \ˈstrō-fə-ˌdēz\ *or Gk.* **Stro·fá·dhes** \strō-ˈfä-thās\. Two small islands, Greece, in Ionian Sea, S of Zákinthos and ab. 30 mi. (48 km.) W of Peloponnese.

Stroud \ˈstrau̇d\. **1.** City, Lincoln co., cen. Oklahoma, 34 mi. (55 km.) NNE of Shawnee; pop. (1990c) 2666.

2. Town, Gloucestershire, SW cen. England, on Thames River and Severn Canal 8 mi. (13 km.) S of Gloucester; pop. (1991p) 108,300; diversified industry incl. wool cloth.

Strouds·burg \ˈstrau̇dz-ˌbərg\. Borough, ⊗ of Monroe co., E Pennsylvania, 30 mi. (48 km.) NNE of Allentown; pop. (1990c) 5312; in Blue Mts. region near the Delaware Water Gap and the Pocono foothills; site of Fort Penn (1776).

Stru·ma \ˈstrü-mə\ *or Gk.* **Stry·mon** \ˈstrī-mən, strē-ˈmōn\. River, SW Bulgaria and N Greece; rises SW of Sofia, flows S and SE into the Strymonic Gulf (Aegean Sea); 215 mi. (346 km.).

Strum·ble Head \ˈstrəm-bəl\. Cape, N side of SW projection of Wales, NE of St. David's Head.

Stru·mi·ca \ˈstrü-mēt-ˌsä\ *or* **Stru·mi·tsa** \-mēt-ˌsä\ *also* **Strum·ni·tza** \ˈstrüm-nēt-sä\. **1.** River, SE Republic of Macedonia and SW Bulgaria; flows E into the Struma River; ab. 50 mi. (80 km.) long.

2. Town, SE Republic of Macedonia, on Strumica River ab. 75 mi. (120 km.) SE of Skopje; passed from Turkish rule to Bulgarian 1913, and to Yugoslavia 1919; battlefield in the Balkan Wars and in both World Wars.

Struth·ers \ˈstrə-t͟hərz\. City, Mahoning co., NE Ohio, on Mahoning River 5 mi. (8 km.) SE of Youngstown; pop. (1990c) 12,284.

Stry *or* **Stryj.** See STRYY.

Strymon. See STRUMA.

Stry·mon·ic Gulf \strī-ˈmä-nik\ *or* **Gulf of Stri·món** \strē-ˈmōn, ˈstrī-mən\ *or Gr.* **Stri·mo·ni·kós Kol·pos** \strē-ˌmō-nē-ˈkōs-ˈkōl-ˌpōs\ *or* **Kol·pos Or·fa·nou** \ˈkōl-ˌpōs-ōr-ˈfä-nü\ *also* **Gulf of Or·fa·ni** \ōr-ˈfä-nē\ *or* **Gulf of Ren·di·na** \ren-ˈdē-nä\; *anc.* **Si·nus Stry·mon·i·cus** \ˈsī-nəs-strī-ˈmä-nə-kəs\. Inlet of Aegean Sea, NE coast of Greece, NE of Chalcidice Penin.; receives the Struma River.

Stry·pa \ˈstri-pə\. River, SW Ukraine; a tributary of the Dniester River bet. Ternopol' and Ivano-Frankivs'k; ab. 60 mi. (95 km.) long.12,284.

Stryy *or* **Stry** \ˈstrē\ *or Pol.* **Stryj** \ˈstrē\. **1.** River, W Ukraine; flows from the Carpathian Mts. NE to the Dniester River S of L'viv; 143 mi. (230 km.) long.

2. City, L'viv subdivision, SW Ukraine, on Stry River 44 mi. (71 km.) NW of Ivano-Frankivs'k; pop. (1991e) 68,000; annexed from Poland by Austria 1772; briefly held by Russians in WWI; to Poland 1919; to U.S.S.R. 1945.

Strze·gom \ˈsche-ˌgȯm\ *or Ger.* **Strie·gau** \ˈshtrē-ˌgau̇\. City, cen. Wałbrzych prov., SW Poland, 31 mi. (50 km.) WSW of Wrocław; pop. (1981p) 16,154; formerly in Germany; assigned to Poland by Potsdam Conference 1945.

Strzel·ce Opol·skie \ˈschelt-se-ȯ-ˈpȯl-skye\ *or Ger.* **Gross Streh·litz** \ˈgrōs-ˈshtrā-ˌlits\. Town, Opole prov., SW Poland, ab. 18 mi. (29 km.) SE of the city of Opole; pop. (1989e) 21,430.

Strze·lin \ˈsche-lēn\ *or Ger.* **Streh·len** \ˈshtrā-lən\. City, SE Wrocław prov., SW Poland, 22 mi. (35 km.) S of the city of Wrocław; pop. (1981p) 11,121; formerly in Germany; assigned to Poland by Potsdam Conference 1945.

Stu·art \ˈstü-ərt, ˈstyü-\. **1.** City, ⊗ of Martin co., SE Florida, on S end of Indian River 37 mi. (60 km.) N of West Palm Beach; pop. (1990c) 11,936; yachting and fishing resort.

2. Town, ⊗ of Patrick co., S Virginia; pop. (1990c) 965.

3. Town, Australia. See ALICE SPRINGS.

4. River, British Columbia, Canada; flows from Stuart Lake SE into Nechako River; 258 mi. (415 km.) long.

Stuart, Mount. Peak, SW Chelan co., cen. Washington; 9415 ft. (2870 m.).

Stuart Lake. Lake, cen. British Columbia, Canada; 139 sq. mi. (360 sq. km.); drains SE through Stuart River.

Stuart Range *also* **Stu·arts Range** \ˈstü-ərts, ˈstyü-\. Range of hills, N cen. South Australia, Australia, W of Lake Eyre and NW of Lake Torrens; mostly within a restricted weapons-testing area.

Stuhlweissenburg. See SZÉKESFEHÉRVÁR.

Stumpy Point \ˈstəm-pē\. Cape, NW St. Thomas I., Virgin Is. of the U.S., West Indies, at W entrance to Santa Maria Bay.

Stu·pi·no \ˈstü-pi-nə\; *formerly* **Elek·tro·voz** \e-ˌlyek-trə-ˈvȯz\. Town, Moscow Oblast, W cen. Russia in Europe, ab. 60 mi. (97 km.) SSE of the city of Moscow; pop. (1991e) 74,600.

Stu·ra di De·mon·te \'stü-rä-,dē-dā-'mōn-tā\. River, Piedmont, NW Italy; flows E and NE into Tanaro River; 44 mi. (71 km.) long.

Stur·bridge \'stər-,brij\. Town, Worcester co., cen. Massachusetts, 18 mi. (29 km.) SW of the city of Worcester; pop. (1990c) 7775; site of Old Sturbridge Village, a 19th cent. re-creation.

Stur·geon \'stər-jən\. River, SE Ontario, Canada; rises in E Ontario, flows SSE into Lake Nipissing; 110 mi. (177 km.) long.

Sturgeon Bay. City, ⊗ of Door co., NE Wisconsin, on Sturgeon Bay, an inlet of Green Bay, 38 mi. (61 km.) NE of Green Bay (city); pop. (1990c) 9176; canal connects Green Bay with Lake Michigan; vacation resort; shipyard, fruit-packing plant; grows cherries.

Sturgeon Falls. Town, Nipissing dist., SE Ontario, Canada, on N shore of Lake Nipissing 25 mi. (40 km.) W of North Bay; pop. (1991c) 5837.

Stur·gis \'stər-jəs\. **1.** City, St. Joseph co., S Michigan, 35 mi. (56 km.) S of Kalamazoo; pop. (1990c) 10,130.
2. City, ⊗ of Meade co., W South Dakota, in Black Hills 8 mi. (13 km.) ENE of Lead; pop. (1990c) 5330.

Stur·te·vant \'stər-tə-vənt\. Village, Racine co., SE Wisconsin, 7 mi. (11 km.) W of the city of Racine; pop. (1990c) 3803.

Stuts·man \'stəts-mən\. County in SE cen. North Dakota. See table at NORTH DAKOTA.

Stut·ter·heim \'stə-tər-,hīm\. Town, Eastern Cape prov., S Rep. of South Africa, ab. 40 mi. (64 km.) NW of East London.

Stutt·gart **1.** \'stət-,gärt, -gərt\. City, a ⊗ of Arkansas co., E Arkansas, 33 mi. (53 km.) NE of Pine Bluff; pop. (1990c) 10,420; rice.
2. \'shtüt-,gärt, 'stət-\. Industrial city, ❋ of Baden-Württemberg, Germany, on Neckar River 38 mi. (61 km.) ESE of Karlsruhe; pop. (1992e) 591,946; transportation center; produces electrical equipment, motor vehicles, machinery, textiles, chemicals, footwear, paper, musical instruments, beer; publishing center; several palaces; 12th–15th cent. church; university. Birthplace (1770) and early residence of philosopher Georg Wilhelm Friedrich Hegel; writer Johann Christoph Friedrich von Schiller studied medicine here 1770s. Founded c. 10th cent.; developed into town 13th cent.; became ❋ of counts of Württemberg 14th cent., of duchy 1495, and of kingdom of Württemberg 1806; in WWII heavily bombed; many historic buildings have since been rebuilt.

Stym·pha·lis \stim-'fā-ləs\; *Gk.* **Stym·fa·li·as** \,stēm-fä-'lē-äs\ *also* **Za·ra·ka** \,zä-rä-'kä\. Lake, NE Peloponnese, Greece; in ancient Arcadia; in Greek mythology the scene of the slaying by Hercules of the man-eating (Stymphalian) birds.

Styr \'stir\. River, NW Ukraine; flows N into Pripyat River in the Polesye Marshes, W of the Goryn; 271 mi. (436 km.) long; battles in area during both World Wars; formerly in E Poland.

Styr·ia \'stir-ē-ə\ *or Ger.* **Stei·er·mark** \'shtī-ər-,märk\. State, Austria; ❋ Graz; mountainous part of cen. and SE Austria watered by the Mur, Mürz, and Enns rivers; chief towns Graz, Leoben, and Bruck. Came under Romans as part of Noricum; became part of Carinthia under Frankish King (later Holy Roman Emperor) Charlemagne; became separate as a mark c. 11th cent.; became a duchy 1180; held by dukes of Austria 12th–13th cents.; came under the Hapsburgs 1276. See table at AUSTRIA.

Styx \'stiks\. River of the underworld in Greek mythology; its exact location is speculative.

Sua·kin \'swä-kin\ *or* **Sua·kim** \-kim\. Seaport on Red Sea, NE Sudan, S of Port Sudan.

Sual \'swäl\ *or* **Port Sual.** Municipality, NW Pangasinan prov., Luzon, Philippines, port on small harbor at SW corner of Lingayen Gulf ab. 11 mi. (18 km.) W of Lingayen; pop. (1980c) 15,796.

Su–ao *or* **Su·ao** \'sü-'aů\. Town, NE Taiwan; pop. (1992e) 51,376; important port.

Su·bang *or Du.* **Soe·bang** \'sü-,bäŋ\. Town, West Java prov., Indonesia, ab. 25 mi. (40 km.) NNE of Bandung; pop. (1980c) 52,117.

Su·bar·na·re·kha \sů-,bər-nə-'rā-kə\. River, Bihar and West Bengal, NE India; flows SE into Bay of Bengal SW of the mouth of the Hugli River and NE of Bāleshwar; ab. 290 mi. (465 km.) long.

Su·ba·sio, Mon·te \'mōn-tā-sü-'bä-zyō\. Mountain in cen. Apennines, Umbria, cen. Italy; 4232 ft. (1290 m.); town of Assisi is located on S slope of a W spur.

Sub·han Dağ·la·rı \sůp-'hän-,dä-lä-'rē\. Mountain range, E Turkey in Asia, N of Lake Van; highest point 14,547 ft. (4434 m.).

Su·bi·a·co \,sü-bē-'ä-kō\. Municipality, SW Western Australia, Australia, W suburb of Perth; pop. (1991c) 15,107.

Su·bia·co \sü-'byä-kō\. Commune, Roma prov., W Lazio, cen. Italy, 50 mi. (80 km.) E of Rome; pop. (1981p) 8890; site of monastery founded by St. Benedict c. 505; first printing press in Italy set up here 1464.

Su·bic \'sü-bik\ *or* **Su·big** \-big\. Municipality, S Zambales prov., Luzon, Philippines, at head of Subic Bay (*q.v.*) 35 mi. (56 km.) SSE of Iba; pop. (1980c) 30,340; one of the two harbors (see OLONGAPO) on Subic Bay.

Subic Bay *also* **Subig Bay.** Inlet of South China Sea, S Zambales prov., Luzon, Philippines; affords protected anchorage 35 mi. (56 km.) N of entrance to Manila Bay; ab. 7 mi. (11 km.) long. Its SE shore is part of Bataan prov.; mouth divided by small Grande I. U.S. naval base estab. here 1901; in WWII held by Japanese 1942–45; transferred to Philippines 1992.

Sub·lette \sə-'blet\. **1.** County in W Wyoming. See table at WYOMING.
2. City, ⊗ of Haskell co., SW Kansas; pop. (1990c) 1378.

Su·bo·ti·ca \'sü-bō-,tēt-sä\ *or* **Su·bo·ti·tsa** \-,tēt-sä\ *or Hung.* **Sza·bad·ka** \'sö-böt-,kö\ *or Ger.* **Ma·ria–The·re·si·o·pel** \mä-,rē-ə-te-,rā-zē-'ō-pəl\. City, Serbia, N Yugoslavia, near Hungarian border ab. 100 mi. (160 km.) NW of Belgrade; pop. (1991p) 150,666; iron goods, furniture, chemicals; first mentioned 1391; joined Yugoslavia 1918; occupied by Hungary during WWII.

Suc·coth \'sə-,käth, -,kōth\. **1.** Locality, ancient Egypt, E of the Nile Delta; first encampment of the Israelites in the Exodus (*Exod.* xii. 37; xiii. 20).
2. Town of ancient Palestine, E of the Jordan and near the N bank of the Jabbok (*Gen.* xxxiii. 17).

Su·cea·va *also* **Su·cza·wa** \sü-'chyä-vä\. **1.** River, N Romania; flows into the Siret River; ab. 110 mi. (175 km.) long.
2. County of N Romania. See table at ROMANIA.
3. Town, its ⊗, on the Suceava River; pop. (1989c) 105,921; wood products; food products; clothing; 14th cent. citadel; 16th cent. church; ❋ of Moldavia 14th cent.–1565.

Suchan. See PARTIZANSK.

Su·chia·te \sü-'chyä-tā\. River, W Guatemala; flows S and SW into Pacific Ocean; forms section of Guatemala-Mexico boundary.

Su·chi·te·pé·quez \sü-,chē-tā-'pā-kās\. Department of S Guatemala. See table at GUATEMALA.

Su·chi·to·to \,sü-chē-'tō-tō\. Town, Cuscatlán dept., cen. El Salvador; pop. (1986e) 44,852.

Suchou *or* **Suchow.** See XUZHOU.

Su–chou. See SUZHOU 2.

Suchow. **1.** Town, Gansu prov., China. See JIUQUAN.
2. City, Sichuan prov., China. See YIBIN.

Süchowfu. See XUZHOU.

Su·cia Bay \'sü-sē-ä\. Bay, S shore of Puerto Rico, enclosed by Cape Rojo on the W.

Suck \'sək\. River, W cen. Ireland; flows SSE in Connacht prov. into the Shannon River N of Lough Derg; 60 mi. (97 km.) long.

Su·cre \'sü-krā\. **1.** *formerly* **Chu·qui·sa·ca** \,chü-kē-'sä-kä\. City, constitutional ❋ of Bolivia, also ❋ of Chuquisaca dept., ab. 260 mi. (420 km.) SE of La Paz; pop. (1992p) 130,952; alt. 8530 ft. (2600 m.); oil refining; cement; seat of the national supreme court, and the archbishopric of La Plata; cathedral (1553); Univ. of San Francisco

Xavier (1624). Founded as Chuquisaca 1538; became ✻ of Charcas (see UPPER PERU) c. 1561; early scene of revolt against Spain 1809; site 1825 of signing of Bolivian declaration of independence; name changed 1840 to Sucre in honor of Antonio José de Sucre, first president of Bolivia; actual ✻ of Bolivia moved to La Paz 1898, but Sucre remains legal ✻.

2. Department of N Colombia. See table at COLOMBIA.

3. State of N Venezuela. See table at VENEZUELA.

Sucro. See ALCIRA.

Su·cum·bí·os \ˌsü-küm-ˈbē-ōs\. Province of Ecuador. See table at ECUADOR.

Suczawa. See SUCEAVA.

Sud, Massif du. See HOTTE, MASSIF DE LA.

Su·da \ˈsü-də\. River, W Vologda Oblast, N cen. Russia in Europe; flows SE and near Cherepovets enters the Rybinsk Reservoir (*q.v.*); 130 mi. (209 km.) long.

Suda Bay *also* **Sou·da Bay** \ˈsü-də\ *or Gk.* **Kól·pos Soú·dhas** \ˈköl-pös-ˈsü-t͟häs\. Inlet, N coast of Crete, Greece, near W end just E of Canea; shut in on NW by Akroteri Penin.; only good harbor on N coast.

Su·dan *or* **the Sudan** \sü-ˈdan, -ˈdän\ *or Fr.* **Sou·dan** \sü-ˈdä^n\ *or Arab.* **Bi·lād–es–Sūdān** \bi-ˌlad-as-sü-ˈdan\. **1.** Region, N cen. Africa, S of the Sahara and Libyan deserts—not a political unit; extends across the African continent from W coast 4000 mi. (6436 km.) to mountains of Ethiopia, with widest part nearly 1000 mi. (1610 km.); approx. area 2,000,000 sq. mi. (5,180,000 sq. km.). Includes major parts of republics of Senegal, Gambia, Guinea, Mali, Burkina Faso, Niger, Chad, Sudan, and the N sections of the countries bordering on the Atlantic from Guinea-Bissau to Cameroon; occupies the basin of the Senegal and cen. parts of the Niger and Nile basins and the Lake Chad region. Consists of desert, grassy steppes, and extensive plains; part of Africa N of the Equator under Muslim influence and in medieval times site of several indigenous empires incl. Bornu, Songhai, and Fulani.

2. *officially* **Republic of the Sudan** *or Arab.* **Jum·hūr·ī·yat as–Sū·dān** \ˌju̇m-hu̇r-ˈē-ət-as-sü-ˈdan\; *formerly* **An·glo–Egyp·tian Sudan** \ˌaŋ-glō-i-ˈjip-shən\. Republic, NE Africa, bounded on N by Egypt, on NE by the Red Sea, on E by Eritrea and Ethiopia, on S by Kenya, Uganda, and Democratic Rep. of the Congo, on W by Central African Rep. and Chad, and on NW by Libya; 967,500 sq. mi. or 2,505,825 sq. km. (largest country in Africa); pop. (1993e) 25,000,000; ✻ Khartoum.

Physical features: N region chiefly desert or semidesert; extreme S characterized by tropical rain forest; grassy plains in cen. region; W and NE parts of republic are hilly; the Nile flows the entire length of the country.

Chief products: Cotton, gum arabic, millet, sorghum, sesame, wheat, peanuts; livestock raising.

Chief cities: Khartoum and Khartoum North.

History: Evidence of prehistoric inhabitation dates back thousands of years; Nubia (*q.v.*) in the N came periodically under ancient Egypt's control; later, N was center of kingdom of Cush (*q.v.*); early medieval Christian kingdoms of the N collapsed upon influx of nomadic Arab (Muslim) settlers c. 14th cent.; conquered by Egypt 1820–21; under nominal Egyptian authority until 1882; ravaged by slave trade which Englishmen Sir Samuel Baker (1869–73) and Gen. Charles Gordon (1874–80) were appointed by the viceroy to suppress; after Sudanese revolt led by religious and nationalist leader Muḥammad Aḥmad ("al-Mahdī") 1883 in which Egyptian forces were defeated and expelled, Muslim theocracy erected 1885–98; conquered 1898 by Anglo-Egyptian forces sent to protect upper Nile from threat of French advance from W; jointly administered by Egypt and Great Britain as a condominium from 1899, Egypt excluded 1924–36, condominium reaffirmed 1936; granted internal autonomy 1953, independence 1956; government since 1956 characterized by often unstable military regimes punctuated by brief periods of ineffectual civilian parliamentary rule, successful military coups occurring in 1958, 1969, 1985, and 1989; protests, from 1950s forward, of the non-Muslim S population to the Muslim-dominated national government of the N led to armed rebellion 1963–72; rebellion halted upon granting of limited autonomy (1972–83) to the S as a unified region; hostilities resumed 1983 upon redivision of the region (further subdivision occurred 1994); rebellion punctuated by cease-fires 1988, 1993, 1995; S suffered from frequent famines 1980s–90s; refused to join coalition against Iraq during Persian Gulf War 1990–91.

Su·dan·ese Republic \ˌsü-də-ˈnēz, -ˈnēs\. The name of Mali (*q.v.*) for two years prior to its independence in 1960.

Sud·bury \ˈsəd-ˌber-ē, -bə-rē\. **1.** Town, Middlesex co., NE Massachusetts, 18 mi. (29 km.) W of Boston; pop. (1990c) 14,358; settled 1638; important town at time of Revolutionary War. Wayside Inn (first building 1686 known as Howe Tavern) subject of poet Henry Wadsworth Longfellow's *Tales of a Wayside Inn.*

2. District in SE Ontario, Canada. See table at ONTARIO.

3. Municipal region in SE Ontario, Canada. See table at ONTARIO.

4. Mining city, ⊗ of Sudbury dist. and Sudbury munic. region, SE Ontario, Canada, 38 mi. (61 km.) N of Georgian Bay and 165 mi. (265 km.) E of Sault Ste. Marie; pop. (1991c) 92,884; center of rich nickel-mining region; copper, platinum, and palladium mines also in area; lumbering and making of wood pulp; Laurentian Univ. (1960).

5. Town, Suffolk, E England, on the Stour 52 mi. (84 km.) NE of London; pop. (1981p) 9883; manufactures silk goods. Birthplace of painter Thomas Gainsborough 1727.

Sudd \ˈsu̇d\ *also* **as–Sudd** \as-ˈsu̇d\. Lowland swamp region, S Sudan; ab. 250 mi. (400 km.) long by 200 mi. (320 km.) wide; drained by Bahr al-Ghazal and Bahr el Jebel.

Su·derø \ˈsü-t͟hə-ˌrœ\. Island, Faeroe Is. (*q.v.*), Denmark, southernmost island of the group; 64 sq. mi. (166 sq. km.); pop. (1981c) 5803.

Sudest Island. See TAGULA ISLAND.

Sudeten. See SUDETY.

Su·de·ten·land \sü-ˈdāt-^{ə}n-ˌland, -ˌlänt\. Term orig. used for the mountainous region comprising the Sudety Mts. on N borders of Bohemia and Silesia, W cen. Europe; after the crisis of 1938 applied also to all the borderlands of Bohemia and Moravia inhabited by German-speaking people. These border regions inhabited largely by Germans when attached to the new state of Czechoslovakia 1919 following WWI; population relatively peaceful until roused by Nazi organizers from mid-1930s; the crisis which followed provided pretext for German dictator Adolf Hitler's demand of cession of Sudetenland to Germany 1938; ceded by Munich Agreement 1938 and occupied by German troops; restored to Czechoslovakia 1945 and most of German population expelled.

Su·de·ty *Czech* ˈsu̇-det-yē, *Polish* su̇-ˈde-tē\ *or Ger.* **Su·de·ten** \zü-ˈdāt-^{ə}n\ *or angl.* **Su·det·ic** \sü-ˈde-tik\ *also* **Su·de·tes** \sü-ˈdē-tēz\. Mountain ranges along part of boundary bet. N Czech Republic and S Poland, WNW of the Carpathians; highest peak Sněžka 5256 ft. (1602 m.); they consist of several smaller mountain groups or ranges, incl. the Riesengebirge and Eulengebirge.

Su·dir·man Range \su̇-ˈdir-mən\; *formerly* **Nas·sau Range** \ˈna-ˌsȯ\. Mountain range, cen. Irian Jaya, Indonesia, forming W end of Maoke Mts.; highest point Puncak Jaya 16,535 ft. (5040 m.); only 4°S of the Equator but covered with ice and glaciers; has great precipices.

Sud–Ki·vu \ˈsüd-ˈkē-vü\. Administrative region of Democratic Rep. of the Congo. See table at ZAIRE.

Sue·ca \su̇-ˈā-kä\. Commune, Valencia prov., E Spain, 22 mi. (35 km.) S of the commune of Valencia; pop. (1991c) 22,943; produces rice.

Sue Peaks \ˈsü\. Mountains, S Brewster co., W Texas; highest peak ab. 5855 ft. (1785 m.).

Suessa Aurunca. See SESSA AURUNCA.

Sues·su·la \'swes-yu̇-lə\. Ancient Samnite town, Campania, S Italy, N of modern Caserta, near the Caudine Forks; battle 343 B.C. in the First Samnite War.

Suez \sü-'ez, *chiefly Brit.* 'sü-iz\ *or Arab.* **As-Su·ways** \ˌas-su̇-'wās\. **1.** Governorate of NE Egypt. See SUEZ 2 and table at EGYPT.

2. City, constituting the governorate, at the N end of the Gulf of Suez and at the S terminus of the Suez Canal; pop. (1991e) 376,000; extensive port facilities; oil refineries and storage facilities, fertilizer plant; a port of departure for pilgrims to Mecca. In 7th cent. A.D. terminal point of canal connecting Red Sea with the Nile; under Ottoman Empire (16th cent.) became naval and commercial port; in 20th cent., repeatedly damaged in Egypt's conflicts with Israel; rebuilt since reopening of Suez Canal 1975.

Suez, Gulf of. NW arm of the Red Sea; joined to the Mediterranean Sea by the Suez Canal.

Suez, Isthmus of. Isthmus connecting NE Africa with Asia; 72 mi. (116 km.) wide; Gulf of Suez and the Red Sea on the S, and the E Mediterranean Sea on the N.

Suez Canal. Ship canal across Isthmus of Suez, NE Africa, connecting the Red Sea with the E Mediterranean; 101 mi. (163 km.) long from Suez to Port Said; nowhere less than 179 ft. (55 m.) wide; minimum depth of channel 40 ft. (12 m.). Passes along E edge of Lake Manzala and through Lake Timsah and the Bitter Lakes; Ismailia is principal town on its banks in cen. part.

History: Built 1859–69 under direction of French diplomat and canal promoter Ferdinand de Lesseps; opened Nov. 16, 1869; ownership orig. vested in French company in which British acquired controlling interest 1875; effectively under British control after establishment of British protectorate in Egypt 1882; nationalized by Egyptian government 1956, precipitating Anglo-French intervention Nov. 1956, in which canal closed until 1957; canal again closed 1967–1975 as result of Arab-Israeli War; its banks scene of considerable fighting bet. Egyptian and Israeli forces 1967–70, 1973.

Sufetula. See SBEÏTLA.

Suf·fern \ˈsə-fərn\. Village, Rockland co., SE New York, 28 mi. (45 km.) NNW of New York City; pop. (1990c) 11,055; Rockland Community Coll. (1959).

Suf·field \ˈsə-fēld\. Town, N Hartford co., N Connecticut, on Massachusetts border; pop. (1990c) 11,427; settled 1670; orig. incorp. by Massachusetts, later annexed to Connecticut 1749.

Suf·folk \ˈsə-fək, -ˌfȯk\. **1.** Name of counties in two states of the U.S. See tables at MASSACHUSETTS and NEW YORK.

2. Independent city, ⊗ of former Nansemond co., SE Virginia, on Nansemond River 18 mi. (29 km.) WSW of Portsmouth; pop. (1990c) 52,141; peanut market; building materials. Estab. 1742; burned by British in Revolution 1779; incorp. as town 1808; occupied by Union forces in Civil War 1862; incorp. as city 1910; merged with Nansemond co. 1974.

3. Former county, E England; divided into the administrative counties **East Suffolk** (871 sq. mi. or 2256 sq. km.; ⊗ Ipswich) and **West Suffolk** (611 sq. mi. or 1582 sq. km.; ⊗ Bury St. Edmunds).

4. County, E England, approx. equivalent to the former county; rivers include Waveney, Stour, Orwell, Alde; agriculture, fishing. See table at ENGLAND.

Suffolk Broads. See BROADS, THE.

Sug·ar·creek \ˈshu̇-gər-ˌkrēk\. Borough, Venango co., NW Pennsylvania, 10 mi. (16 km.) W of Oil City; pop. (1990c) 5532.

Sug·ar Creek \ˈshu̇-gər\. City, Jackson and Clay cos., W Missouri, 9 mi. (14 km.) E of Kansas City; pop. (1990c) 3982.

Sugar Hill. **1.** City, Gwinnett co., N Georgia, NE of Atlanta; pop. (1990c) 4557.

2. Settlement, W New Hampshire. See LISBON 3.

Sugar Land. City, Fort Bend co., SE Texas, 6 mi. (10 km.) SW of Houston; pop. (1990c) 24,529; pop. more than doubled bet. 1980 and 1990.

Sugar Loaf Hill \ˈshu̇-gər-ˌlōf\. Height, S Okinawa, Ryukyu Is., Japan, dominating approach to Shuri; scene of heavy fighting in 1945, recaptured by U.S. five times.

Sug·ar·loaf Key \ˈshu̇-gər-ˌlōf\. See FLORIDA KEYS.

Sugarloaf Mountain. **1.** Peak in Catskill Mts., Greene co., New York; 3647 ft. (1112 m.).

2. Peak in Le Flore co., E Oklahoma; 2630 ft. (802 m.).

3. Peak, Brazil. See PÃO DE AÇÚCAR.

Sugar Loaf Peak. Mountain, SE Elko co., NE Nevada; 8025 ft. (2446 m.).

Sugbu. See CEBU.

Suğ·la, Lake \ˈsü-lä\ *or Turk.* **Suğla Gö·lü** \gœ̄-ˈlue̅\. Lake (*gölü*), SW Turkey in Asia, N of the Gulf of Antalya and SE of Lake Beyşehir; 48 sq. mi. (124 sq. km.).

Şu·ḩār *or* **So·har** \su̇-ˈhär, -ˈkär\. Seaport town, Oman, SE Arabian Penin., on Gulf of Oman 140 mi. (225 km.) NW of Masqat.

Suhl \ˈzül\. **1.** District of former East Germany.

2. City, Thüringen, cen. Germany, 30 mi. (48 km.) SSW of Erfurt; pop. (1992e) 53,918; produces motorcycles, machinery, precision instruments, tools, sporting firearms; first mentioned 1239; famous for centuries for firearms manufacture; formerly ✻ of Suhl dist., East Germany.

Sui *or* **Sūi** \ˈsü-ē\. Village, Baluchistan, cen. Pakistan; pop. (1981p) 5000; airport; gas deposits nearby.

Sui·chuan *or W.-G.* **Sui–ch'uan** *or* **Sui·chwan** \ˈswē-ˈchwän\. Town, W Jiangxi prov., SE China, 50 mi. (80 km.) NW of Ganzhou; site of U.S. airfield during WWII, captured by Japanese late in the war.

Suid–Afrika, Republiek van. See SOUTH AFRICA, REPUBLIC OF.

Suifu. See YIBIN.

Suir \ˈshu̇r\. River, SE Ireland; rises in N co. Tipperary, flows S and E into Waterford Harbour; 114 mi. (183 km.) long.

Suisse. See SWITZERLAND.

Sui·sun Bay \sə-ˈsün\. Inlet of San Francisco Bay, W cen. California; lying on boundary bet. Contra Costa and Solano cos.; connected with San Pablo Bay by Carquinez Strait; crossed by Martinez Bridge, a vertical lift bridge with clearance of 291.5 ft. (89 m.).

Suisun City. City, Solano co., cen. California, 36 mi. (58 km.) SW of Sacramento; pop. (1990c) 22,686; pop. doubled bet. 1980 and 1990.

Su·i·ta \sü-ˈē-tä\. City, Ōsaka prefecture, Honshū, Japan; pop. (1990p) 345,187.

Suit·land–Silver Hill \ˈsüt-lənd-\. Unincorporated settlement, Prince Georges co., Maryland, E of Washington, D.C.; pop. (1990c) 35,111.

Sui·yuan \ˈswā-yü-ˈen\. Former province, N China; 112,493 sq. mi. (291,357 sq. km.); ✻ Hohhot.

Su·ka·bu·mi *or Du.* **Soe·ka·boe·mi** \ˌsü-kə-ˈbü-mē\. City, West Java prov., Indonesia, on railroad line 28 mi. (45 km.) SSE of Bogor; pop. (1990c) 119,981; health resort at S foot of Gunung Salak.

Suk–Ahras. See SOUK-AHRAS.

Sukarnapura. See JAYAPURA.

Sukarno, Mount. See JAYA, PUNCAK.

Su·ket \ˈsu̇-ˈkāt\. Former Indian state, now part of Himachal Pradesh state, N India; 392 sq. mi. (1015 sq. km.); ✻ Suket.

Sukhan–Darya Oblast. See SURKHANDARYA.

Su·kho·na \su̇-ˈk̲ō-nə\. River, chiefly in Vologda Oblast, N cen. Russia in Europe; rises in Lake Kubenskoe and flows E to unite with the Yug River near Veliki Ustyug in NE part of the region and form the Northern Dvina River; 358 mi. (576 km.) long.

Su·kho·thai *also* **Su·ko·tai** \ˈsu̇-kə-ˈtī\. Village, W Thailand, 30 mi. (48 km.) NW of Phitsanulok; nearby ruins of the old town contain several temples, Buddha statues, and other monuments; an early Thai settlement under Khmer rule; became ✻ of independent Thai state of the same name that fl. 13th–14th cents.

Su·khu·mi \ˈsu̇-k̲ə-mē\; *formerly* **Su·khum** \su̇-ˈküm\; *anc.* **Di·os·cu·ri·as** \ˌdī-əs-ˈkyu̇r-ē-əs\. Seaport town, ✻ of Abkhaz Rep., Republic of Georgia, on the Black Sea 100 mi. (161 km.) NW of Kutaisi; pop. (1991e) 120,000; formerly a popular resort; produces wine, canned fruit. Site of ancient Greek colony; later held by Romans, Byzantines, Turks, Russians; center of Abkhazian rebellion early 1990s, occupied by Georgian troops until it fell to rebel forces Sept. 1993.

Suk·ker·top·pen \ˈsu̇-kər-ˌtȯ-pən\ *or* **Ma·niit·soq** \mä-ˈnēt-ˌsȯk\. Headland and settlement, on an island on SW coast of Greenland, 65°25′N, 52°53′W, N of Nuuk; pop. (1980c) 3926.

Suk·kur \ˈsu̇-kər\ *or* **Sa·khar** \ˈsə-kər\. Town, Pakistan, on right bank of Indus River ab. 225 mi. (360 km.) NNE of Karachi; pop. (1981c) 193,000; textiles, vegetable oils, flour; center of major irrigation system, known as the Lloyd or Sukkur Barrage, completed 1932. Height of dam 190 ft. (58 m.).

Sukotai. See SUKHOTHAI.

Su·la \ˈsü-lə\. River, N cen. Ukraine; rises near Konotop and flows S to the Dnieper above Kremenchug; 250 mi. (402 km.) long.

Sula Besi. See SANANA 1.

Sulaimaniya. See SULAYMĀNĪYAH, AS-.

Su·lai·man Range \ˈsü-lī-ˌmän\. Mountain range, Pakistan, W of Indus River; highest, twin peaks at N end, Takht-i-Sulaiman ("throne of Solomon") 11,289 ft. (3441 m.).

Sula Islands *also* **Soe·la Islands** \ˈsü-lə\; *formerly* **Xul·la Islands** \ˈshü-lə\. Island group, Indonesia, part of the Moluccas, S of Molucca Sea and bet. Sulawesi on the W and the Ceram Sea on the E; 1873 sq. mi. (4851 sq. km.). Comprises islands of Taliabu, Mangole, and Sanana, and several small islands; grows sago, rice, sugarcane.

Su·la·we·si \ˌsü-lə-ˈwä-sē\ *also* **Cel·e·bes** \ˈse-lə-ˌbēz, sə-ˈlē-bēz\. Island, Indonesia, in Malay Archipelago E of Borneo, 1°45′N to 5°37′S, and 118°49′E to 125°05′E; 72,775 sq. mi. (188,487 sq. km.); pop. (1990c) 12,520,711; for administrative divisions, see table at INDONESIA.

History: Muslims arrived establishing ties with indigenous population c. 15th cent.; probably first visited by Portuguese 1512 while developing spice trade of the Moluccas; first foreign settlement on island was by Dutch 1607 at Makasar (now Ujung Pandang); scene in 17th cent. of various wars bet. Dutch and native sultans; direct Dutch rule gradually estab. by early 20th cent.; in WWII overrun by Japanese 1942; surrendered to Australians 1945; joined Republic of Indonesia 1950; Communist rebellion against central government suppressed 1965; unrest continued.

Su·lay·mā·nī·yah, as– \ås-ˌsü-lī-ˌmä-ˈnē-yə\ *also* **Su·lai·ma·ni·ya** \ˌsü-lī-ˌmä-ˈnē-yə\. Town, NE Iraq, in mountains 60 mi. (97 km.) E of Kirkuk near Iranian border; pop. (1985e) 279,424; market town; founded 1781.

Sulci. See SANT'ANTIOCO 2.

Sul·grave \ˈsəl-ˌgrāv\. Village, SW Northamptonshire, England, 7 mi. (11 km.) NE of Banbury; site of Sulgrave Manor, an ancestral home of George Washington, now a museum.

Sulimov. See CHERKESSK.

Su·li·na \sü-ˈlē-nä\. Port, Tulcea co., E Romania, on the Black Sea at the cen. mouth of the Danube.

Su·li·tjel·ma \ˌsü-li-ˈtyel-mə\ *or Swed.* **Su·li·tel·ma** \ˌsü-lē-ˈtel-mə\. Mountain mass in the Kjølen Mts., Norway, on the Swedish border, N of the Arctic Circle; 6280 ft. (1914 m.).

Sul·la·na \sü-ˈyä-nä\. City, NW Peru, 32 mi. (51 km.) NE of Paita; pop. (1990e) 154,800; cinchona bark.

Sul·li·van \ˈsə-lə-vən\. **1.** Name of counties in six states of the U.S. See tables at INDIANA, MISSOURI, NEW HAMPSHIRE, NEW YORK, PENNSYLVANIA, TENNESSEE.

2. City, ⊗ of Moultrie co., cen. Illinois, 25 mi. (40 km.) SE of Decatur; pop. (1990c) 4354.

3. City, ⊗ of Sullivan co., SW Indiana, 25 mi. (40 km.) S of Terre Haute; pop. (1990c) 4663.

4. City, Crawford and Franklin cos., SE cen. Missouri, 63 mi. (101 km.) SW of St. Louis; pop. (1990c) 5661.

Sullivan Island *or* **Sullivan's Island.** See LANBI KYUN.

Sul·lom Voe \ˈsü-ləm-ˈvō, ˈsə-\. Inlet, Mainland I., Shetland Is., Scotland; site of an important oil port of the same name.

Sul·ly \ˈsə-lē\. County in cen. South Dakota. See table at SOUTH DAKOTA.

Sul·lys Hill \ˈsə-lēz\. Former national park, Benson co., NE North Dakota, just S of Devils Lake; since c. 1932 a game preserve esp. for bison, elk, deer, geese.

Sul·mo·na \sül-ˈmō-nä\; *anc.* **Sul·mo** \ˈsəl-mō\. Commune, L'Aquila prov., Abruzzi, cen. Italy, 35 mi. (56 km.) SE of the commune of L'Aquila; pop. (1989c) 25,018; market town; cathedral; medieval churches; palace; aqueduct. Birthplace of poet Ovid (43 B.C.) and Pope Innocent VII (1336).

Sul·phur \ˈsəl-fər\. **1.** River, NE Texas; rises in Fannin co., flows E across Arkansas border and into Red River in SW Arkansas; 200 mi. (322 km.) long; formerly considered a fork (**Sulphur Fork**) of the Red River.

2. City, Calcasieu parish, SW Louisiana, 10 mi. (16 km.) W of Lake Charles; pop. (1990c) 20,125.

3. City, ⊗ of Murray co., S Oklahoma, 24 mi. (39 km.) NNE of Ardmore; pop. (1990c) 4824.

Sulphur Island. English language translation of Iwo Jima.

Sulphur Springs. City, ⊗ of Hopkins co., NE Texas, 27 mi. (43 km.) E of Greenville; pop. (1990c) 14,062.

Sultanabad. See ARĀK and ʿIRAQ-I-ʿAJAM.

Sul·tan Dağ·la·ri \sul-ˈtän-ˌdä-lä-ˈrē\. Mountain range, extending NW and SE in W cen. Turkey in Asia, N of Lake Beyşehir; highest point 8304 ft. (2531 m.).

Sul·tan Ku·da·rat \sul-ˈtän-ˌkü-dä-ˈrät\. Province, SW Mindanao, Philippines; ✻ Isulan. See table at PHILIPPINES.

Sul·tan·pur \sul-ˈtän-ˌpur\. **1.** Town, SE cen. Uttar Pradesh, N India, on right bank of Gomati River 60 mi. (97 km.) N of Allahabad; pop. (1991p) 76,567.

2. Town, India. See KULU.

Sultan sa Ba·ron·gis \sül-ˈtän-sä-bä-ˈroŋ-gēs\; *formerly* **Lam·bay·ong** \läm-ˈbī-oŋ\. Municipality, Cotabato prov., Mindanao, Philippines, ab. 45 mi. (72 km.) SE of Cotabato; pop. (1980c) 25,957.

Su·lu \ˈsü-lü\. **1.** Province, SW Philippines, in Sulu Archipelago; ✻ Jolo; fishing is most important industry. See table at PHILIPPINES.

2. Chief island and municipality, Sulu, Philippines. See JOLO.

Su·lu·an \sü-ˈlü-ˌän\. Small island, Philippines, 10 mi. (16 km.) E of Homonhon I. and ab. 13 mi. (21 km.) S of S point of Samar, Philippines; ab. 2 sq. mi. (5 sq. km.). Landmark for ships approaching cen. Philippines (Leyte Gulf or Surigao Strait) from the Pacific. Sighted by Portuguese navigator Ferdinand Magellan 1521.

Sulu Archipelago. Chain of islands, SW Philippines, bet. Mindanao and Borneo and incl. Basilan I., Jolo I., Sibutu I., and the following groups: Samales, Pangutaran, Tapul, and Tawi-tawi, all together ab. 400 named islands and more than 500 unnamed small islands in addition to many coral reefs; divided into Basilan, Sulu, and Tawi-tawi provs.

History: Visited by foreign traders (esp. from China) over 1000 years ago; inhabitants converted to Islam ab. the end of 14th cent.; struggled against Spanish from 16th cent. and did not come under Spanish control until 19th cent.; were ruled by Moro sultans; during these years, esp. in 17th and 18th cents., Moros conducted many destructive piratical raids against Spaniards and Filipinos of Visayan Is. and Luzon; archipelago finally became Spanish protectorate 19th cent.; came under U.S. 1899; sultan abdicated civil authority 1915; sultanate terminated by treaty of 1940, in which archipelago was ceded to Philippines.

Sulu Sea. Large interisland sea, SW Philippines, bordered on N by Cuyo Is., on E by islands of Panay, Negros, and W Mindanao, on SE by Sulu Archipelago, on SW by North Borneo, and on W and NW by Palawan I.; extends N and S ab. 350 mi. (565 km.) bet. 5° and 10°N and ab. 425 mi. (685 km.) E and W from Mindanao Sea entrance to Balabac Strait; open sea except for three small clusters of islands.

Sulz·bach \ˈzults-ˌbäk\. Town, Saarland, Germany, ab. 6 mi. (10 km.) NNW of Saarbrücken; pop. (1980c) 20,653.

Sulz·ber·ger Bay \ˈsəlz-ˌbər-gər\. Large inlet of Ross Sea, NW Marie Byrd Land, Antarctica, E of Edward VII Penin. and Little America, 77°S, 152°W; ab. 100 mi. (160 km.) wide; discovered 1929.

Sulzer Belchen. See GUEBWILLER, MOUNT.

Su·ma·tra \su-ˈmä-trə\. Island, W part of Indonesia, S of the Malay Penin.; 182,542 sq. mi. or 472,784 sq. km. (incl. small islands along its W and SE coasts); pop (1990c) 36,506,703; comprises three provinces **North Sumatra, South Sumatra,** and **West Sumatra** (see table at INDONESIA).

Physical features: Separated on NE from Malay Penin. by Strait of Malacca and at S end from Java by Sunda Strait. Divided into two almost equal parts by the Equator; 1060 mi. (1706 km.) long, max. width ab. 250 mi. (400 km.). Along its W coast extends for the length of the island the Barisan Mts. containing many peaks 6000 ft. (1830 m.) to 12,000 ft. (3660 m.); highest Kerintji 12,483 ft. (3805 m.); many peaks of volcanic origin, some active today. Its E and SE parts are jungle lowlands with numerous rivers having many tributaries—chief are Hari, Indragiri, Kampar, and Asahan; Lake Toba in the N is only large lake.

Chief products: Rice, corn, coffee, copra, tobacco, pepper, rubber, peanuts.

Chief cities: Medan and Palembang.

History: Coastal areas, on seaborne trade routes, had early contact with Hindu civilization; kingdom of Srivijaya (*q.v.*) arose 7th cent. and came to dominate much of the island; Islam introduced 13th cent.; visited by Venetian traveler Marco Polo c. 1292; fell under Madjapahit (*q.v.*) kingdom 14th–16th cents., followed by several independent Muslim principalities; trade with Europeans began early 16th cent.; slowly came under Dutch control, parts being acquired from native sultans by various treaties; was object of great rivalry with English, who held it for short periods during Napoleonic era; last remaining British possession (Bengkulu) given up

1824; Atjeh (*q.v.*) in N not overcome until early 20th cent.; occupied by Japanese during WWII; became part of independent Indonesia 1950.

Sum·ba *or Du.* **Soem·ba** \ˈsüm-bə\ *or Eng.* **San·dal·wood Island** \ˈsan-dᵊl-ˌwu̇d\. Island of the Lesser Sunda Is., Indonesia, S of Flores and SE of Sumbawa; 140 mi. (225 km.) long; max. width 50 mi. (80 km.); 4306 sq. mi. (11,153 sq. km.); pop. (1980c) 355,073; chief town Waingapu. Separated from Timor on the E by Savu Sea. Mainly a plateau of ab. 2000 ft. (610 m.) with highest point at 4019 ft. (1225 m.); has good harbors on N coast, esp. at Waingapu. Noted in 17th–19th cents. for its exported sandalwood trees, now found only in interior regions; produces rice, corn, tobacco, and exports copra; its chieftains brought by treaty under nominal control of Dutch 1756, renewed and revised several times in 19th cent.; became part of independent Indonesia 1950.

Sum·ba·wa *or Du.* **Soem·ba·wa** \süm-ˈbä-wə\. Island, Lesser Sunda Is., Indonesia, E of Lombok I. and W of Flores I.; 175 mi. (282 km.) long, max. width 55 mi. (88 km.); 5693 sq. mi. (14,745 sq. km.); pop. (1980c) 304,134. Separated on W from Lombok by Alas Strait and on E from Komodo I. (a dependency of Flores) by Sape Strait; has irregular coastline with deep indentation (Saleh Bay) in center of N coast; on NE coast is Bima Bay, one of best harbors in Indonesia. Mountainous throughout with highest point, the volcano Gunung Tambora, at tip of peninsula on N coast, 9350 ft. (2850 m.). Not highly developed but has fertile soil and tropical products of many kinds can be raised; horse and cattle raising important. Former tributary to Madjapahit kingdom, later fragmented into petty states; relations with Dutch first began 17th cent.; eruption of Gunung Tambora 1815 killed and displaced tens of thousands; repopulated from nearby islands; direct Dutch control estab. early 20th cent.; occupied by Japanese during WWII; became part of independent Indonesia 1950.

Sum·ba·wan·ga \ˌsüm-bä-ˈwäŋ-gä\. Town ✻ of Rukwa region, Tanzania.

Sum·be \ˈsu̇m-bā\; *formerly* **Ngun·za** \eŋ-ˈgu̇n-zə\; *earlier* **No·vo Re·don·do** \ˌnȯ-vō-re-ˈdän-dō\. Coastal town, W cen. Angola, ✻ of Cuanza Sul prov.

Sum·bing *or Du.* **Soem·bing** \ˈsüm-biŋ\. Volcanic peak, Central Java prov., Indonesia; 11,060 ft. (3371 m.); overlooks Magelang plain from the W.

Sum·burgh Head \ˈsəm-bə-rə\. Cape, S tip of Mainland I., Shetland Is., NNE of Scotland; lighthouse.

Su·me·dang \ˈsü-mə-ˌdäŋ\. Town, West Java prov., Indonesia, ab. 20 mi. (32 km.) E of Bandung.

Su·me·nep \ˈsü-mə-ˌnep\. Inland town, E end of Madura I., East Java prov., Indonesia.

Su·mer \ˈsü-mər\. The S division of ancient Babylonia in S Mesopotamia; region considered a cradle of civilization. Inhabited by a non-Semitic people from ab. the 4th millennium B.C., some influx of Semitic peoples from the N occurred; Sumerians were a non-Semitic people of uncertain origin, possibly immigrants from the E, under whom the world's first known true cities developed in this region c. 3000 B.C.; activities which flourished in these cities included irrigated agriculture, pottery, metalworking, and trade; these cities evolved into political entities (first-known city-states) which became loosely unified under the periodically shifting hegemony of one of the cities' kings, incl. esp. those of Kish, Erech, Ur, Nippur, and Lagash (*qq.v.*); gradually united with Akkadians to the N, esp. under Sargon of Akkad (ruled c. 2334–2279 B.C.), the first to rule the cities as a truly unified entity; upon collapse of the empire, the city-states again became largely independent until reunified under Ur (21st–20th cents. B.C.); this final Sumerian kingdom declined under both internal pressures and external invasions (esp. by Amorites); distinct Sumerian nation disappeared upon becoming part of empire of Babylonia under King Hammurabi 18th cent. B.C. Artifacts of Sumer provide evidence of earliest known system of writing (cuneiform), published codes of law, and potter's wheels, among other innovations.

Sumgait. See SUMQAYIT.

Su·mi·da \ˈsü-mē-dä, sü-ˈmē-\. River, SE Honshū, Japan; flows S through the city of Tokyo into Tokyo Bay; ab. 180 mi. (290 km.) long.

Sum·i·ton \ˈsə-mə-tən\. City, Walker co., NW cen. Alabama, NW of Birmingham; pop. (1990c) 2604.

Sum·mer Island \ˈsə-mər\. Island, Delta co., S Upper Penin. of Michigan, in N Lake Michigan at N entrance to Green Bay.

Summer Lake. Lake, cen. Lake co., S Oregon; ab. 15 mi. (24 km.) long.

Sum·mers \ˈsə-mərz\. County in S West Virginia. See table at WEST VIRGINIA.

Sum·mer·side \ˈsə-mər-ˌsīd\. Town, ⊗ of Prince co., W Prince Edward I., Canada, on Northumberland Strait 35 mi. (56 km.) W of Charlottetown; pop. (1991c) 7474; exports farm produce; summer resort; settled 1780 by Daniel Green, Quaker Loyalist from Pennsylvania.

Sum·mers·ville \ˈsə-mərz-ˌvil\. Town, ⊗ of Nicholas co., cen. West Virginia; pop. (1990c) 2906; ab. 6 mi. (10 km.) SSW is **Summersville Dam** (see UNITED STATES, *Dams and Reservoirs*).

Sum·mer·ville \ˈsə-mər-ˌvil\. **1.** City, ⊗ of Chattooga co., NW Georgia; pop. (1990c) 5025; incorp. 1839.
2. Town and resort, Dorchester co., SE South Carolina, 22 mi. (35 km.) NW of Charleston; pop. (1990c) 22,519; lumber; diversified industries; pop. more than tripled bet. 1980 and 1990.

Sum·mit \ˈsə-mət\. **1.** Elevation, McKean co., N Pennsylvania; 2252 ft. (686 m.).
2. Name of counties in three states of the U.S. See tables at COLORADO, OHIO, UTAH.
3. Village, Cook co., NE Illinois, just W of Chicago; pop. (1990c) 9971.
4. Town, Pike co., S Mississippi; pop. (1990c) 1566; Southwest Mississippi Community Coll. (1918).
5. Residential city, Union co., NE New Jersey, 10 mi. (16 km.) W of Newark; pop. (1990c) 19,757; site used as sentry point in Revolutionary War.

Summit Hill. Borough, Carbon co., E Pennsylvania, 28 mi. (45 km.) S of Wilkes-Barre; pop. (1990c) 3332.

Summit Mountain. Peak, Glacier National Park, NW Montana; 8770 ft. (2673 m.).

Summus Portus. See SOMPORT, COL DE.

Sum·ner \ˈsəm-nər\. **1.** Name of counties in two states of the U.S. See tables at KANSAS and TENNESSEE.
2. Town, a ⊗ of Tallahatchie co., NW Mississippi; pop. (1990c) 368.
3. City, Pierce co., W cen. Washington, 11 mi. (18 km.) E of Tacoma; pop. (1990c) 6281.

Sumner Lake *also* **Lake Sumner;** *formerly* **Al·a·mo·gor·do Reservoir** \ˌa-lə-mə-ˈgȯr-dō\. Reservoir, E cen. New Mexico, formed by Alamogordo Dam on Pecos River.

Su·mo·to \sü-ˈmō-tō\. Chief town of Awaji I. (*q.v.*), Hyōgo prefecture, Japan; pop. (1990p) 43,815.

Sum·pan·go \süm-ˈpäŋ-gō\. Town, Sacatepéquez dept., S cen. Guatemala; pop. (1981c) 13,046.

Šum·perk \ˈshu̇m-ˌperk\ *or Ger.* **Mäh·risch–Schön·berg** \ˈmer-ish-ˈshœn-ˌberk\. Town, NE Czech Republic, on Morava River 28 mi. (45 km.) NNW of Olomouc; pop. (1980p) 31,873.

Sum·pra·bum \ˌsu̇m-prä-ˈbu̇m, ˌsü-pə-yä-ˈbu̇n\. Town, N Myanmar, ab. 80 mi. (130 km.) N of Myitkyina and SE of Chaukan Pass.

Sum·qay·it \su̇m-ˈkī-it\ *or* **Sum·ga·it** \-ˈgī-it\. Town, Azerbaijan, ab. 15 mi. (24 km.) NE of Baku; pop. (1991e) 236,200; metallurgical and chemical industries.

Sum·ter \ˈsəmp-tər\. **1.** Name of counties in four states of the U.S. See tables at ALABAMA, FLORIDA, GEORGIA, SOUTH CAROLINA.

\ə\ **abut** \ᵊ\ **kitten, F table** \ər\ **further** \a\ **ash** \ā\ **ace** \ä\ **cot, cart** \a̱\ **Fr bac** \au̇\ **out** \ḇ\ **Span Avila** \ch\ **chin** \e\ **bet** \ē\ **easy** \g\ **go** \i\ **hit** \ī\ **ice** \j\ **job** \k̲\ **Ger ich, Buch** \ⁿ\ **Fr vin** \ŋ\ **sing** \ō\ **go** \ȯ\ **law** \ȯi\ **boy** \th\ **thin** \th̲\ **this** \ü\ **loot** \u̇\ **foot** \y\ **yet** \zh\ **vision**

\ə\ abut \ə̀\ matches \ᵊ\ kitten, Fr table \ər\ further \a\ ash \ā\ ace
\ä\ cot, cart \a̱\ Fr bac \au̇\ out \ḇ\ Span Avila \ch\ chin \e\ bet \ē\ easy
\g\ go \i\ hit \ī\ ice \j\ job \k̲\ Ger ich, Buch \ⁿ\ Fr vin
\ŋ\ sing \ō\ go \ȯ\ all \ȯ\ law \œ\ Fr bœuf \œ̄\ Fr feu \ȯi\ boy
\th\ thin \th̲\ this \ü\ loot \u̇\ foot \ue\ Ger füllen \u̅e\ Fr rue
\y\ yet \ʸ\ Fr digne \ˈdēnʸ\, nuit \ˈnwʸē\ \yü\ few \yu̇\ fury \zh\ vision

2. City, ⊗ of Sumter co., E cen. South Carolina, 42 mi. (68 km.) E of Columbia; pop. (1990c) 41,943; furniture, textiles, paints, chemicals; Shaw Air Force Base; Morris Coll. (1908), Univ. of South Carolina–Sumter (1966); founded late 18th cent.; grew rapidly in 1980s.

Su·my \ˈsü-mē\. **1.** Administrative subdivision of Ukraine, on N and E borders on Bryansk and Kursk oblasts of Russia; 9189 sq. mi. (23,800 sq. km.); pop. (1991e) 1,430,200; ✻ Sumy; fertile black-earth region, crossed by the Seym, Psel, and Vorskla rivers; sugar beets, hemp, tobacco; livestock.

2. Town, its ✻, near the Psel River 95 mi. (153 km.) NW of Kharkiv; pop. (1991e) 301,000; fertilizer, food products, machinery; founded as fortress 1652.

Sun \ˈsən\. River, NW cen. Montana; rises in W Teton co., flows S and E into Missouri River at Great Falls, Cascade co.; ab. 100 mi. (160 km.) long.

Sun·a·pee Lake \ˈsə-nə-ˌpē\. Lake, SW cen. New Hampshire, on boundary bet. Sullivan and Merrimack cos.; ab. 9 mi. (15 km.) long and from 1 to 3 mi. (2 to 5 km.) wide; summer resort.

Su·nart, Loch \ˈsü-nərt\. Inlet of the Atlantic Ocean, Highland region, W Scotland, S of Loch Shiel and N of Loch Linnhe.

Sun·belt \ˈsən-ˌbelt\. Region, S and SW United States; characterized by a warm climate, rapid pop. growth since 1970, and relatively conservative voting patterns.

Sun·bury \ˈsən-ˌber-ē, -bə-rē\. **1.** City, ⊗ of Northumberland co., E cen. Pennsylvania, on Susquehanna River 30 mi. (48 km.) SSE of Williamsport; pop. (1990c) 11,591. Site of native settlement prior to European arrival; Fort Augusta estab. 1756; laid out 1772; in 1883 inventor Thomas A. Edison set up and operated an early incandescent electric lighting plant here.

2. Town, S cen. Victoria, Australia, N of Melbourne; pop. (1991c) 18,533.

3. County in S cen. New Brunswick, Canada. See table at NEW BRUNSWICK.

4. *or in full* **Sunbury–on–Thames** \-ˈtemz\. Town, Surrey, SE England, 15 mi. (24 km.) WSW of London; pop. (1981p) 39,075; part of Greater London.

Sun·ch'ŏn \ˈsün-ˈchən\. Town, South Chŏlla prov., South Korea, ab. 19 mi. (30 km.) NW of Yŏsu; pop. (1985c) 135,612.

Sun City \ˈsən\. Unincorporated settlement, Maricopa co., SW cen. Arizona, W and NW of Phoenix; pop. (1990c) 38,126; has large retirement community.

Sun·cook \ˈsən-ˌku̇k\. River, S cen. New Hampshire; rises in **Suncook Lakes** (**Upper Suncook Lake** and **Lower Suncook Lake**), SE Belknap co., flows S into Merrimack River in SE Merrimack co.

Sun·da Deep *also* **Soen·da Deep** \ˈsən-də, ˈsün-\. One of the deepest parts of the Indian Ocean, off S coast of Java, Indonesia; 24,452 ft. (7453 m.).

Sunda Isles *or* **Soenda Isles.** Islands, Malay Archipelago, divided into two groups: (1) **Greater Sunda Islands,** comprising Java, Sumatra, Borneo, Sulawesi (*qq.v.*), and adjacent islands; 514,953 sq. mi. (1,333,728 sq. km.); and (2) **Lesser Sunda Islands,** comprising chain of islands E from Bali to and incl. Alor and Timor, but not Wetar; 29,441 sq. mi. (72,252 sq. km.).

Sun·dance \ˈsən-ˌdans\. Town, ⊗ of Crook co., NE corner of Wyoming; pop. (1990c) 1139; Devils Tower National Monument is 20 mi. (32 km.) to NW.

Sundarbans. See GANGES DELTA.

Sunda Strait *also* **Soenda Strait.** Channel bet. the islands of Sumatra and Java, Indonesia, connecting Java Sea with the Indian Ocean; 16 mi. (26 km.) wide at its narrowest part. In its center is volcanic island of Krakatau (*q.v.*); on S side of entrance is Panaitan I.; on N side two large bays of S Sumatra—Lampung and Semangka—open into it.

Sunday Island. See RAOUL ISLAND.

Sun·days \ˈsən-ˌdāz, -dēz\ *or* **Son·dags** \ˈsȯn-ˌdäks\ *also* **Sun·day** \-ˌdā, -dē\. River, Eastern Cape prov., Rep. of South Africa; flows into Algoa Bay; 250 mi. (402 km.) long.

Sunday Strait. Channel, the entrance to King Sound E of Cape Leveque, N Western Australia, Australia.

Sund·by·berg \ˌsu̇nd-bü̅-ˈbar\. City, Stockholm prov., SE Sweden, a NW suburb of the city of Stockholm; pop. (1993e) 30,719.

Sunderbunds. See GANGES DELTA.

Sun·der·land \ˈsən-dər-lənd\. **1.** Town, Franklin co., W Massachusetts, on Connecticut River, N of Northampton; pop. (1990c) 3399.

2. Seaport, Tyne and Wear, N England, on North Sea on S side of mouth of the Wear 12 mi. (19 km.) SE of Newcastle upon Tyne; pop. (1991p) 286,800; former shipbuilding center; shipping point, esp. for coal, glassware; coal mines; glass, automobile manufacturing. A very old town, frequently called **Wear·mouth** \ˈwir-məth\ in Saxon times; formerly included Monkwearmouth (*q.v.*) where St. Bede studied. **Bishop's Wearmouth,** an early settlement of the church on the S side of the river, is now within the town of Sunderland but was long used as the name of the port.

Sund·gau \ˈzu̇nt-ˌgau̇\. Historical region, S Alsace, chiefly in Haut-Rhin dept., NE France.

Sunds·vall \ˈsu̇nds-ˌväl\. Seaport, Västernorrland prov., E Sweden, on the Gulf of Bothnia; pop. (1993e) 94,329; trade center; exports lumber, wood pulp; chartered 1621.

Sun·flow·er \ˈsən-ˌflau̇-ər\. **1.** River, NW Mississippi; flows S from Coahoma co., to Yazoo River on border bet. Yazoo and Sharkey cos.; 240 mi. (386 km.) long.

2. County in W Mississippi. See table at MISSISSIPPI.

Sunflower, Mount. Hill, Wallace co., Kansas; 4039 ft. (1231 m.); highest elevation in Kansas.

Sungari. See SONGHUA.

Sungaria. See JUNGGAR.

Sung–chiang *or* **Sung·kiang** \ˈsu̇ŋ-ˈjyäŋ\. **1.** Former province, cen. Manchuria, China; 30,703 sq. mi. (79,521 sq. km.); ✻ Harbin.

2. Town, E China. See SONGJIANG.

Sun·gei Pa·ta·ni \ˈsüŋ-ˌgī-pə-ˈtä-nē\. Town, SW Kedah state, Malaysia, near coast ab. 15 mi. (24 km.) N of Butterworth.

Sun·gei Ujong \ˈsüŋ-ˌgī-ˈü-ˌjȯŋ\. Former state, W Malay Penin.; became a part of Negeri Sembilan state (*q.v.*) 1895.

Sung–hua. See SONGHUA.

Sungkiang. **1.** Former province, Manchuria, China. See SUNG-CHIANG 1.

2. Town, E China. See SONGJIANG.

Sung Shan. See SONG SHAN.

Sung–tzu Ho. See SONGZI HU.

Sunium Promontorium. See SOUNION, CAPE.

Su·ni·ya, Hor \hȯr-ˈsü-nē-yə\. Marshland region, SE Iraq, along W bank of lower Tigris; ab. 80 mi. (130 km.) long, 10 mi. (16 km.) wide.

Sunk Island \ˈsəŋk\. Parish in the estuary of the Humber, Humberside, England; 7334 acres (2970 hectares); formerly an islet.

Sun·land Park \ˈsən-ˌland\. City, Doña Ana co., S New Mexico, across the Rio Grande from El Paso, Texas; pop. (1990c) 8179.

Sun·light Peak \ˈsən-ˌlīt\. **1.** Mountain, La Plata co., SW Colorado; 14,059 ft. (4285 m.).

2. Mountain, W Park co., NW Wyoming; 11,977 ft. (3651 m.).

Sun·ny·side \ˈsə-nē-ˌsīd\. City, Yakima co., S Washington, 33 mi. (53 km.) SE of the city of Yakima; pop. (1990c) 11,238.

Sun·ny·vale \ˈsə-nē-ˌvāl\. City, Santa Clara co., W California, 8 mi. (11 km.) WNW of San Jose; pop. (1990c) 117,229; electronic equipment, cast-iron products; settled 1849; incorp. 1912; grew rapidly in 1960s.

Sun Prairie. City, Dane co., S Wisconsin, 11 mi. (18 km.) NE of Madison; pop. (1990c) 15,333.

Sun·rise \ˈsən-ˌrīz\. City, Broward co., SE Florida; pop. (1990c) 64,407; grew rapidly in 1980s.

Sun River. See SUN.

Sun·set \ˈsən-ˌset\. City, Davis co., N Utah, 7 mi. (11 km.) SW of Ogden; pop. (1990c) 5128.

Sunset Crater. Volcanic crater, cen. Coconino co., N cen. Arizona, E of San Francisco Peaks and ab. 15 mi. (24 km.) NE of Flagstaff; 5 sq. mi. (13 sq. km.); central feature of **Sunset Crater Volcano National Monument;** *formerly* **Sunset**

Crater National Monument (see UNITED STATES, *National Monuments*).

Sunset Hills. City, St. Louis co., E Missouri; pop. (1990c) 4915.

Sun·shine \ˈsən-ˌshīn\. City, Victoria, Australia, a NW suburb of Melbourne; pop. (1991c) 94,020.

Sunshine Peak. Mountain, Hinsdale co., SW Colorado; 14,001 ft. (4268 m.).

Sün·tel \ˈzᵫnt-ᵊl\ *or* **Sün·tel·berg** \-ˌberk\. Elevation, Lower Saxony, Germany, on N bank of Weser; 1433 ft. (437 m.); scene of defeat of Frankish army 8th cent. by Saxons, possibly under Saxon leader Wittekind.

Sun Valley. Resort center, Sawtooth Range, Blaine co., cen. Idaho, just N of Ketchum; originated with Sun Valley Lodge, built by Union Pacific R.R. 1936.

Sun·ya·ni \sün-ˈyä-nē\. Town, ✻ of Brong-Ahafo region, Ghana, on Kumasi-Pamu highway 80 mi. (129 km.) NW of Kumasi; pop. (1984c) 38,834.

Suo·men·lin·na \ˈsü-ȯ-men-ˌlin-nə\ *or Swed.* **Sve·a·borg** \ˌsfā-ə-ˈbȯrg, -ˈbȯr-ē\. Fortress on islands in the harbor of Helsinki, S Finland; built by the Swedes 1748; captured by Russians 1808; bombarded by French-British fleet 1855 in Crimean War.

Suomen Tasavalta *or* **Suomi.** See FINLAND.

Suo·mus·sal·mi \ˈsü-ȯ-mu̇s-ˌsäl-mē\. Town, Oulu prov., E Finland, near border with Karelia Rep., Russia 105 mi. (169 km.) E of the seaport of Oulu; pop. (1980c) 13,388.

Suō Sea *also* **Su·wo Sea** \ˈsü-wō\. The W part of the Inland Sea, Japan, bet. SW Honshū and NE Kyūshū.

Supanburi. See SUPHAN BURI.

Su·pe·ri·or \su̇-ˈpir-ē-ər\. **1.** Town, Pinal co., S Arizona; pop. (1990c) 3468; formerly silver mines, now copper.

2. Town, ⊗ of Mineral co., W Montana; pop. (1990c) 881.

3. City, Nuckolls co., S Nebraska, on Kansas border 43 mi. (69 km.) SSE of Hastings; pop. (1990c) 2397.

4. City, ⊗ of Douglas co., NW corner of Wisconsin, at extreme W end of Lake Superior opposite Duluth, Minnesota; pop. (1990c) 27,134; port of entry; railroad center and lake-transportation terminus; grain center and shipping point for iron and copper ore; manufactures flour, lumber products, marine equipment; oil refining; Univ. of Wisconsin–Superior (1893); growth began after discovery of iron ore in nearby Gogebic Range 1883.

Superior, Lake. Lake, U.S. and Canada, bounded on N and E by prov. of Ontario, Canada, on S by Michigan and Wisconsin, on W by Minnesota, the U.S.-Canada boundary passing through it; northernmost and westernmost of the five Great Lakes; at SE end connected by St. Marys River with Lake Huron; ab. 350 mi. (565 km.) long; area 31,800 sq. mi. (82,362 sq. km.); greatest depth 1333 ft. (406 m.); elev. 600 ft. (183 m.); area of drainage basin 80,100 sq. mi. (207,459 sq. km.); largest body of freshwater in the world.

Su·phan Bu·ri *or* **Su·pan·bu·ri** \ˌsü-ˌpän-bu̇-ˈrē\. Town, SW Thailand, on left bank of the Tha Chin 30 mi. (48 km.) WNW of Phra Nakhon Si Ayutthaya; pop. (1991e) 25,814.

Su·pi·o·ri *or* **Soe·pi·o·ri** \ˌsü-pē-ˈȯr-ē\. Island, N Irian Jaya, Indonesia, just W of Biak in the Schouten Is., N of Teluk Cenderawasih; ab. 17 mi. (27 km.) long by 6 mi. (10 km.) wide; very rugged surface with highest point 3392 ft. (1034 m.).

Suqutrā. See SOCOTRA.

Şūr *or* **Sur** \ˈsu̇r\. Seaport town, E Oman, SE Arabian Penin., on the Gulf of Oman 70 mi. (113 km.) SE of Masqat and near Ra's al Hadd.

Şūr. See TYRE.

Sur, Point \ˈsər\. Point, NW coast of Monterey co., W California.

Su·ra \ˈsu̇r-ə\. Ancient city of Babylonia, on a branch of the Euphrates SSW of Baghdad; site of famous Talmudic school 609 to 1038.

Su·ra \su̇-ˈrä\. River, cen. Russia in Europe; rises in E Penza Oblast and flows N through or on the border of Ul'yanovsk Oblast and Chuvash Rep. to the Volga below Nizhniy Novgorod; 537 mi. (864 km.) long; navigable to the city of Penza.

Su·ra·ba·ja *or Du.* **Soe·ra·ba·ja** \ˌsu̇r-ə-ˈbī-ə\. **1.** Former residency, now part of East Java prov., Indonesia; 1362 sq. mi. (3528 sq. km.); ✻ Surabaya. A small kingdom until overcome 17th cent. by Mataram; came under Dutch control mid-18th cent.; occupied by Japanese in WWII.

2. Seaport city, Indonesia. See SURABAYA.

Su·ra·ba·ya \ˌsu̇r-ə-ˈbī-ə\ *also* **Surabaja** *or Du.* **Soe·ra·ba·ja** \ˌsu̇r-ə-\. Seaport city, ✻ of East Java prov., Indonesia, at mouth of Kali Mas River on Surabaya Strait, near W end of Madura Strait; pop. (1990c) 2,483,871; major seaport, exporting sugar, rubber, coffee, and spices; produces textiles, glass, footwear, tobacco products; locomotive works, shipyards, oil refinery; principal Indonesian naval base, with dockyard facilities and naval college; Dutch colonial fort; zoo; large 19th cent. mosque; university (1954). Center of trade for centuries; came under Dutch control 18th cent. and became principal Dutch naval base in the East Indies; occupied by Japanese in WWII and suffered heavy bombing damage; a center of fighting in the postwar struggle for Indonesian independence 1945–49.

Surabaya Strait *or* **Selat Surabaya** *or* **Surabaja Strait;** *formerly* **Soerabaja Strait.** Narrow passage bet. NE Java and Madura I., Indonesia; connects Java Sea with W end of Madura Strait; ab. 24 mi. (39 km.) long.

Su·ra·kar·ta *or Du.* **Soe·ra·kar·ta** \ˌsu̇r-ə-ˈkärt-ə\. **1.** Former protected native principality, S cen. Java, Indonesia; 2331 sq. mi. (6037 sq. km.); ✻ Surakarta. Constituted a government of the former Netherlands East Indies. Founded 1755 at the breakup of Mataram sultanate; its prince (susuhunan) was under advice of Dutch resident from 19th cent.; occupied by Japanese in WWII; abolished upon recognition (1949) of Indonesian independence.

2. *also* **So·lo** \ˈsō-lō\. City, Central Java prov., Indonesia, 50 mi. (81 km.) SE of Semarang; pop. (1990c) 504,176; market for tobacco, sugar, rice, fruits; produces batik cloth, cigarettes, furniture, textiles; handicrafts; a cultural center; palaces of former native rulers; Dutch fort; university (1976); cultural museum. Was ✻ of Mataram sultanate in 18th cent.; became ✻ of Surakarta principality 18th–20th cents.

Su·ram Mountains \ˈsu̇r-ˌäm\. Mountain range, cen. Republic of Georgia, WNW of Tbilisi; ranges from 5000 to 6000 ft. (1525 to 1830 m.); separates the Rioni and Kura river basins and forms a connecting link bet. the Caucasus Mts. on N and highlands of Armenia on S; lowest point is **Suram Pass** (3500 ft. or 1067 m.); crossed by railroad (tunnel 2.5 mi. or 4 km. long) from Baku to Black Sea.

Su·rat \ˈsu̇r-ət, sə-ˈrat\. City, SE Gujarat, W India, on Tapti River near its mouth 150 mi. (241 km.) N of Bombay; pop. (1991c) 1,505,872; cotton, rice, paper, soap, silk, gold objects, silverware; several colleges.

History: Major seaport and commercial city from 16th cent.; destroyed by Portuguese early 16th cent.; conquered by Mogul Emperor Akbar 1573; British factory (trading station) founded c. 1608, the first in India and beginning of British Empire in India; seat of British Indian government until late 17th cent., when seat was moved to Bombay.

Surat Agency. Former agency, W India; comprised three small Indian states Bansda, Dharampur, and Sachin; later part of Gujarat States Agency; the states became part of India 1947.

Surat Tha·ni *or* **Su·rat·dha·ni** \ˌsü-ˌrät-ˈtä-nē\. Railroad town and port, SW Thailand, on Gulf of Thailand 70 mi. (113 km.) NW of Nakhon Si Thammarat; pop. (1991e) 41,103.

Sûre \ˈsu̅e̅r\ *or in Germany* **Sau·er** \ˈzau̇-ər\. River, W Europe; rises in Belgian prov. of Luxembourg, flows 107 mi. (172 km.) E across Grand Duchy of Luxembourg into Moselle River 7 mi. (11 km.) SW of Trier in Rhineland-Palatinate, Germany; navigable for ab. 40 mi. (64 km.).

Su·ren·dra·na·gar \su̇-ˌren-drə-ˈnə-gər\; *formerly* **Wadh·wan** \ˈwəd-ˌwän, ˈvəd-ˌvän\. Town, Gujaraat, India; a railroad junction 65 mi. (104 km.) WSW of Ahmadabad; area pop. (1991p) 166,309; served as ✻ of former Wadhwan state.

Su·resnes \sü-'rän, -'ren\. Commune, Hauts-de-Seine dept., N France, W suburb of Paris on Seine River; pop. (1990c) 36,950; automobiles, chemicals, perfumes; American military cemetery.

Surf·side \'sərf-ˌsīd\. Town, Miami-Dade co., SE Florida, on Atlantic coast 6 mi. (10 km.) N of Miami Beach; pop. (1990c) 4108.

Surfside Beach. Town, Horry co., E South Carolina, just down the coast from Myrtle Beach; pop. (1990c) 3845.

Sur·gu·ja \sůr-'gü-jə\ *or* **Sir·gu·ja** \sir-\. Former Indian state, now part of E Madhya Pradesh state, India; 6067 sq. mi. (15,714 sq. km.); ceded to British protection c. 1818; incorp. into Madhya Pradesh 1948.

Sur·gut \sůr-'güt\. Town, S Khanty-Mansi Autonomous Okrug, cen. W Russia in Asia, on right bank of Ob' River in swamp region 270 mi. (434 km.) NE of Tobol'sk; pop. (1992e) 260,000; incorp. 1965.

Su·ri·ba·chi, Mount \ˌsü-rē-'bä-chē\. Extinct volcano, S tip of Iwo Jima, in Volcano Is., Japan; 548 ft. (167 m.); in WWII taken by U.S. marines Feb. 1945 and flag raising on its summit provided one of the best known photographs relating to WWII.

Su·ri·gao \ˌsůr-ē-'gaů\. **1.** Former province, NE Mindanao, Philippines, now consisting of **Surigao del Nor·te** \del-'nȯr-tā\ and **Surigao del Sur** \del-'sůr\ (see table at PHILIPPINES).
2. Municipality, ✻ of Surigao del Norte prov., at N tip of mainland on narrow strait opp. Dinagat I.; pop. (1980c) 79,745; one of oldest Spanish towns in the Philippines.

Surigao Strait. Channel, SE Philippines, bet. Leyte I. on W and Dinagat I. on E and touching NE point of Mindanao on SE; connects Pacific Ocean with Mindanao Sea; 10 to 25 mi. (16 to 40 km.) wide; in WWII S division of Japanese fleet defeated here by U.S. fleet Oct. 1944.

Su·rin \sů-'rin\. Town, SE Thailand, on railroad line 95 mi. (153 km.) E of Nakhon Ratchasima; pop. (1991e) 39,984; annual elephant show.

Su·ri·na·me \ˌsůr-ə-'nä-mə\. **1.** River, N Suriname; flows N into Atlantic Ocean at Paramaribo; ab. 250 mi. (400 km.) long.
2. *also* **Su·ri·nam** \'sůr-ə-ˌnäm, -ˌnam\; *formerly also* **Netherlands Gui·a·na** \gē-'a-nə, gī-, -'ä-\ *or* **Dutch Guiana.** Republic, South America, bounded on N by the Atlantic Ocean, on E by French Guiana, on S by Brazil, and on W by Guyana; 63,251 sq. mi. (163,820 sq. km.); pop. (1990e) 403,000; ✻ Paramaribo; until 1975 an autonomous territory within the Netherlands realm.

Physical features: S and cen. parts consist of a forested plateau region and extensive savannas; mountain ranges in cen. part and S have peaks between 3300 and 4200 ft. or 1005 and 1280 m. and the Tumuc-Humac Mts. on Brazilian border reach 2700 to 3000 ft. (825 to 915 m.); S part never extensively explored. Has many rivers, esp. the Courantyne (or Corantijn) on Guyana border, the Maroni (or Marowijne) and its headstream, the Itany, on French Guiana border, and the Suriname, Saramacca, Coppename, and Commewijne flowing N through cen. part.

Chief products: Bauxite; rice, citrus fruit, bananas, sugarcane, shrimp; alumina, aluminum.

Chief city: Paramaribo is the only sizable city.

History: Inhabited by various native peoples prior to European settlement; coast sighted by explorer Christopher Columbus 1498; attempts at settlement 17th cent. by various European nations failed until first permanent settlement (British) sent by Lord Willoughby of Parham, governor of Barbados, 1651; seized by Dutch and was ceded to them by Treaty of Breda 1667; held by the English 1799–1802 and 1804–16; granted internal autonomy under the Dutch crown 1954; received independence Nov. 25, 1975; military coup 1980; new constitution 1987 returned government to civilian control; military control (1990–91) reestablished after a 2d coup 1990; peace made 1992 with rebel guerrilla groups.

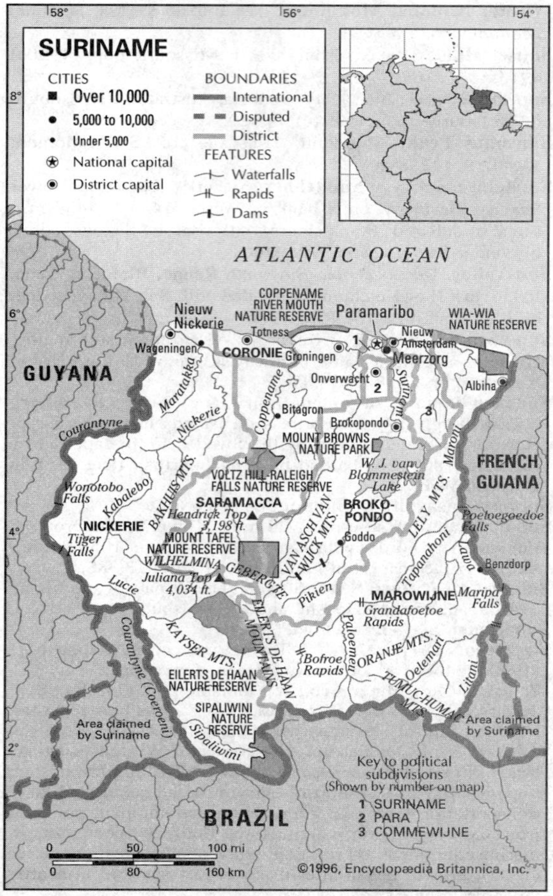

Sur·khan·dar·ya \ˌsür-k̲ən-dər-'yä\; *mostly formerly* **Su-khan–Dar·ya** \ˌsü-kən-dər-'yä\. Administrative subdivision of Uzbekistan, bet. Turkmenistan on W and Tajikistan on E and on the S bordering on Afghanistan; 8031 sq. mi. (20,800 sq. km.); pop. (1991e) 1,335,900; ✻ Termez; cotton, wheat.

Sur·khob *or* **Sur·khab** \sůr-'k̲äb\. River, Tajikistan; ab. 400 mi. (645 km.) long; a N tributary of the Amu Dar'ya.

Sur·ma \'sůr-mə\. River, NE India; rises in Manipur state, where it is called the Barak (*q.v.*), flows W into Bangladesh; ab. 560 mi. (900 km.) long.

Sur·prise \sər-'prīz\. Town, Maricopa co., Arizona, just NW of Phoenix; pop. (1990c) 7122.

Surrentine Peninsula *and* **Surrentum.** See SORRENTO.

Sur·rey \'sər-ē\. **1.** City, S British Columbia, Canada, SE of Vancouver; pop. (1991c) 245,173.
2. Former county, SE England.
3. Administrative county, SE England, approx. equivalent to the former county; rivers include the Wey, a tributary of the Thames; largely residential; market gardening. See table at ENGLAND.

Sur·ry \'sər-ē\. **1.** Name of counties in two states of the U.S. See tables at NORTH CAROLINA and VIRGINIA.
2. Town, ⊗ of Surry co., SE Virginia; pop. (1990c) 192.

Sur Sari. See GOGLAND.

Surt \'sərt, 'sůrt\ *or* **Sirt** \'sirt\ *or* **Sir·te** \'sir-tā\. Town, N Libya, SE of Miṣrātah on S shore of Gulf of Sidra; an historically important starting point for caravan routes.

Surt, Khalīj. See SIDRA, GULF OF.

Surt·sey \'sərt-sē\. Island off S Iceland; ab. 1 sq. mi. (3 sq. km.); formed by volcanic activity 1963; estab. as nature reserve 1965.

Su·rud Ad \'su̇r-əd-'äd\ *or* **Su·rud Cad** \-'käd\. Mountain, N Somalia, ab. 240 mi. (385 km.) NE of Hargeysa; 7894 ft. (2406 m.); highest peak in Somalia.

Su·ru·ga Bay \sü-'rü-gä\. Inlet of the Pacific Ocean, SE coast of Honshū, Japan, SW of Tokyo.

Su·sa \'sü-sə, -zə\. **1.** *bib.* **Shu·shan** \'shü-shən, -ˌshan\. Ancient city, ✻ of Elam (*q.v.*), now ruins at the village of **Shūsh** \'shüsh\ on the railroad line ab. 15 mi. (24 km.) S of Dezfūl, SW Iran. Settled in very early times, it came to be the winter residence of Achaemenian kings of Persia (6th cent. to 331 B.C.); its palace and treasure house were in a strong citadel; fell to Macedonian King Alexander the Great 331 B.C.; again Persian ✻ under Sāssānids; declined in Middle Ages; excavated c. 1850 ff. Scene of the biblical story of Esther, the Jewish queen of Persian King Ahasuerus (Xerxes I).
2. Town, Torino prov., W cen. Piedmont, NW Italy; E terminus of Mont Cenis Pass.
3. Town, Tunisia. See SOUSSE.

Su·šak \'sü-ˌshäk\ *or Ital.* **San·se·go** \'sän-sā-gō\. Island, SW of Lošinj I., Croatia, in group SE of Istria Penin.; 1.5 sq. mi. (4 sq. km.); formerly belonged to Italy; by treaty of 1947 assigned to Yugoslavia; became part of independent Croatia 1991.

Susam. See SÁMOS 1.

Su·san·ville \'süz-ᵊn-ˌvil\. City, ⊗ of Lassen co., NE California, at head of Honey Lake Valley 40 mi. (64 km.) E of Lassen Peak; pop. (1990c) 7279; Lassen Coll. (1925).

Susiana. 1. Ancient kingdom, Iran. See ELAM.
2. Province, Iran. See KHŪZESTĀN.

Su·sit·na \sü-'sit-nə\. River, S Alaska; flows W and S from E end of Alaska Range to Cook Inlet; 300 mi. (483 km.) long.

Sus·que·han·na \ˌsəs-kwə-'ha-nə\. **1.** River, cen. New York, Pennsylvania, and Maryland; rises in Otsego Lake, Otsego co., cen. New York, flows S across Pennsylvania border and across E Pennsylvania and NE corner of Maryland to empty into N Chesapeake Bay; 444 mi. (714 km.) long. By the use of canals it has been made navigable for a short distance from its mouth. The W branch, ab. 200 mi. (320 km.) long, rises in SW cen. Pennsylvania and flows NE and E across cen. Pennsylvania to unite with the Susquehanna near Sunbury, Northumberland co.
2. County in NE Pennsylvania. See table at PENNSYLVANIA.

Sus·sex \'sə-siks\. **1.** Name of counties in three states of the U.S. See tables at DELAWARE, NEW JERSEY, VIRGINIA.
2. Village, ⊗ of Sussex co., SE Virginia, S of Petersburg.
3. Village, Waukesha co., SE Wisconsin, 18 mi. (29 km.) NW of Milwaukee; pop. (1990c) 5039.
4. Town, Kings co., S New Brunswick, Canada, 43 mi. (69 km.) NE of St. John; pop. (1991c) 4132.
5. Anglo-Saxon kingdom, S England; traditionally thought to have been founded by Anglo-Saxon ruler Aelle after his defeat of the Britons c. 477, but little known about its early history; subject at times to neighboring kingdoms; part of Anglo-Saxon Heptarchy (*q.v.*); in conflict with Wessex in 8th cent. and in 825 became part of it.
6. Former county, S England, on the English Channel; divided into two administrative counties, **East Sussex** (⊗ Lewes) and **West Sussex** (⊗ Chichester); rivers Arun, Ouse, Rother, Adur. See table at ENGLAND.

Suth·er·land \'sə-t͟hər-lənd\ *or* **Suth·er·land·shire** \-ˌshir, -shər\. Former county, N Scotland; ⊗ Dornoch; mountainous region.

Sutherland Falls. Waterfall, South I., New Zealand, near W coast 16 mi. (26 km.) S of the head of Milford Sound; 1904 ft. (580 m.) high; one of the world's highest waterfalls, plunges down in three sections of 815, 751, and 338 ft. (248, 229, and 103 m.).

Suth·er·lin \'sə-t͟hər-lən\. City, Douglas co., SW Oregon, 15 mi. (24 km.) N of Roseburg; pop. (1990c) 5020.

Sut·lej \'sət-ˌlej\. River, Asia; rises in SW Tibet, China, flows W through the Himalayas across Himachal Pradesh and Punjab states, India, then SW across Punjab prov. of Pakistan, to join the Chenab and form the Panjnad (*q.v.*); 850 mi. (1368 km.) long; one of the "Five Rivers" of the Punjab; in its middle course important for irrigation projects.

Sutna. See SATNA.

Su·tro Tunnel \'sü-trō\. Drainage tunnel, near present site of Virginia City, Nevada; 4.5 mi. (7.2 km.) long; built (completed 1878) to drain the Comstock mine.

Sut·ter \'sə-tər\. County in N cen. California. See table at CALIFORNIA.

Sutter's Mill. See COLOMA.

Sut·ton \'sət-ᵊn\. **1.** County in SW cen. Texas. See table at TEXAS.
2. Town, Worcester co., cen. Massachusetts, 8 mi. (13 km.) SSE of the city of Worcester; pop. (1990c) 6824.
3. Town, ⊗ of Braxton co., cen. West Virginia; pop. (1990c) 939.
4. A borough of Greater London, SE England. See table at LONDON 4.

Sutton Cold·field \ˌsət-ᵊn-'kōld-ˌfēld\. Town, West Midlands, cen. England, 8 mi. (13 km.) NE of Birmingham; pop. (1981p) 86,494; residential suburb of Birmingham; pharmaceuticals.

Sutton in Ash·field *or* **Sutton–in–Ashfield** \-'ash-ˌfēld\. Town, Nottinghamshire, N cen. England, 13 mi. (21 km.) N of Nottingham; pop. (1981p) 41,270; textiles.

Sutton–on–the–Forest *also* **Sutton–in–the–Forest.** Village, North Yorkshire, England, 8 mi. (13 km.) N of York; residence (1738–59) of author Laurence Sterne.

Su·va \'sü-vä\. Seaport town, ✻ of Fiji, on SE coast of Viti Levu I., SW Pacific Ocean; pop. (1986c) 69,665; coconut processing; tourism; several institutions of higher learning, among them Univ. of the South Pacific (1968); has one of best harbors in South Pacific Ocean.

Suvalkai *or* **Suvalki.** See SUWAŁKI.

Sü·vey·di·ye \sue-'vā-dē-ye\ *or Fr.* **Souei·dié** \swā-'dyā\. Seaport town, S Turkey in Asia, just N of mouth of the Orontes River ab. 35 mi. (55 km.) S of İskenderun; nearby is site of ancient Seleucia (or Seleucia Pieria). See SELEUCIA (3).

Suvla Bay. See ANAFARTA BAY.

Suvorov. See SUWARROW.

Su·vo Ru·diš·te \ˌsü-vō-'rü-dish-ˌtā\. Highest peak in Kopaonik Range, Serbia, S cen. Yugoslavia; 7020 ft. (2140 m.).

Su·wa \'sü-wä, sü-'wä\. Lake, W cen. Honshū, Japan, within sight of Fuji; ab. 10 mi. (16 km.) in circumference; alt. 2600 ft. (793 m.).

Su·wał·ki \sü-'vau̇-kē\ *or Russ.* **Su·val·ki** \su̇-'väl-kē\ *or Lith.* **Su·val·kai** \su̇-'väl-kī\. **1.** Region, NE Poland, E of the Masurian Lakes; scene of several battles in WWI; after 1919 divided, N part to Lithuania, S part to Poland; assigned to Germany 1939 and after outbreak of war with U.S.S.R. held until retaken by U.S.S.R. 1944; part of Belorussian S.S.R. 1944–45 but ceded back to Poland Aug. 1945 (see BIAŁYSTOK).
2. Province, NE Poland. See table at POLAND.
3. City, its ✻, 68 mi. (109 km.) N of Białystok; pop. (1989e) 59,625; held by Germans in WWI and WWII.

Su·wan·nee \sə-'wä-nē\. **1.** River, SE Georgia and N Florida Penin.; rises in Ware co., SE Georgia, flows SW across Florida into Gulf of Mexico at Suwannee Sound; ab. 250 mi. (400 km.) long.
2. County in N Florida. See table at FLORIDA.

Suwannee Sound. Inlet of Gulf of Mexico, W coast of Levy co., NW Florida Penin., receiving Suwannee River on N.

Su·war·row \su̇-'wär-ō\ *or* **Su·vor·ov** \sü-'vȯr-əf\. Island, Pacific Ocean, in the Cook Is., 13°S and 163°W; pop. (1986c) 6; has good anchorage.

Suwaydā, As *or* **Suweida, Es** *or* **Suweidiya, Es.** See AS SUWAYDĀ.

Su·wŏn \'sü-'wən\. Town, ✻ of Kyŏnggi prov., South Korea, 18 mi. (29 km.) S of Seoul; pop. (1985c) 430,752; 18th cent. fortifications.

Suwo Sea. See SUŌ SEA.

Suz·dal' \'süz-dəl\. Principality, cen. Russia, during Middle Ages; united with Rostov (Rostov-Suzdal' principality), and later, c. 12th cent., with Vladimir (*q.v.*); ultimately absorbed by Moscow.

Su·zhou \'sü-'jō\. **1.** City, Gansu prov., China. See JIUQUAN. **2.** *or W.-G.* **Su–chou** \'sü-'jō\ *also* **Soo·chow** \'sü-'jō\; *formerly* **Wu·hsien** \'wü-'shyen\. City, S Jiangsu prov. E China, on the Grand Canal; pop. (1990c) 706,459; once surrounded by walls built c. 5th cent. B.C. Noted for its gardens, bridges, palaces, temples, and for its many pagodas, esp. one built 12th cent. A.D.

History: One of the oldest Chinese cities; founded c. 525 B.C.; ✻ of Wu, ancient feudal kingdom, 6th–5th cents. B.C.; received its present name under Sui dynasty 6th cent. A.D.; visited by Venetian traveler Marco Polo 13th cent.; destroyed mid-19th cent. in Taiping Rebellion but rebuilt; opened as treaty port 1896; occupied by Japanese 1937–45.

Su·zu·ka \sü-'zü-kä\. City, Mie prefecture, Honshū, Japan, ab. 28 mi. (45 km.) SW of Nagoya; pop. (1990p) 174,103.

Sval·bard \'sfäl-,bär\. Island group, Arctic Ocean, bet. 10° and 35°E and 74° and 81°N; 23,958 sq. mi. (62,052 sq. km.); includes Spitsbergen (*q.v.*) group and Bear I. (*q.v.*); coal deposits; Norwegian possession officially since 1925.

Svart \'sfärt\. **1.** Short river, S cen. Sweden; flows E into W end of Lake Hjälmaren at Örebro.

2. Short river, E Sweden; flows S into Lake Mälaren at Västerås.

Svart·i·sen *or* **Svart Isen** \'sfärt-,ēs-ᵊn\. Ice field, N Norway, on the Arctic Circle; ab. 230 sq. mi. (595 sq. km.); source of glaciers descending almost to sea level.

Svätý. See SAINT.

Sveaborg. See SUOMENLINNA.

Sve·a·land \'svā-ə-,länd\. Region, S cen. Sweden; 33,126 sq. mi. (85,796 sq. km.); pop. (1992e) 3,292,418; comprises an area of forest and lakes, farming and industry stretching the breadth of the country.

Svend·borg \'sfen-,bȯr\. Seaport, Fyn I., Denmark; pop. (1989e) 40,868; shipbuilding yards; textile mills, breweries; tobacco processing.

Sverd·lovsk \sfird-'lȯfsʸk\. See YEKATERINBURG.

Sverd·lovs'k *or* **Sverd·lovsk** \sfird-'lȯfsʸk\; *formerly* **Ime·ni Sverd·lo·va Rud·nik** \'ē-mā-nyē-'sverd-lə-və-'rüd-nik\. Town, Luhans'k subdivision, Ukraine, ab. 35 mi. (55 km.) SSE of the city of Luhans'k; pop. (1991e) 84,000.

Sverdlovsk Oblast \'ȯ-bləst, -,blast\ *or* **Sverd·lov·ska·ya Oblast'** \sfird-'lȯf-skə-yə\. Subdivision of W Russia in Asia; 75,212 sq. mi. (194,799 sq. km.); pop. (1992e) 4,719,000; ✻ Yekaterinburg. Crossed from N to S by Ural Mts. (*q.v.*) where tributaries of both the Tobol and Kama rise; for the most part lies on the E slopes of the mountains and has rich soil. Has extensive mineral resources (iron ore, manganese, cobalt, nickel, asbestos, bauxite, copper). Formed 1934.

Sver·drup Islands \'sfer-drəp\. Island group in Arctic Archipelago, N Nunavut, Canada, W of Ellesmere I.; chief islands Axel Heiberg, Ellef Ringnes, and Amund Ringnes.

Sverige. See SWEDEN.

Sveti *and* **Svetiya.** See SAINT.

Svet·lo·gorsk \,svit-lə-'gȯrsk\. City, SE cen. Belarus, on the Berezina River; pop. (1991e) 71,600.

Svetozarevo. See JAGODINA.

Svir' *or* **Svir** \'sfirʸ\. Navigable river, NE St. Petersburg Oblast, W Russia in Europe; flows from Lake Onega to Lake Ladoga; 139 mi. (224 km.) long; has large hydroelectric power station on its banks. Its course forms part of the Volga-Baltic Waterway (*q.v.*). Formed battle line in WWII bet. Finns and Soviets 1941.

Svi·shtov *or* **Svi·štov** \sfi-'shtȯf\ *or angl.* **Sis·to·va** \'sis-,tȯ-vä\. Town, N Bulgaria, on the Danube; pop. (1988e) 51,682. Treaty of Sistova signed here 1791 determining the boundary bet. Austria and Turkey; devastated in Russo-Turkish wars, esp. in 1878.

Svi·ya·ga \sfē-'yä-gə\. River, cen. Russia in Europe; rises in S Ul'yanovsk Oblast, flows N into Volga River just W of Kazan'; 245 mi. (394 km.) long; roughly parallels the Volga and approaches within 4 mi. (6 km.) of it near Simbirsk.

Svizzera. See SWITZERLAND.

Svo·bod·ny *or* **Svo·bod·nyy** \sfə-'bȯd-nē\. Town, Amur Oblast, SE Russia in Asia, on Zeya River and on Trans-Siberian R.R.; pop. (1991e) 81,400.

Svol·vær \'svül-,var\. Port, Austvågøy I., Norway; chief town of the Lofoten group.

Svyatoi. See SAINT.

Swa·bia \'swā-bē-ə\ *or Ger.* **Schwa·ben** \'shväb-ᵊn\. Duchy, medieval Germany, nearly coextensive with modern Baden-Württemberg, Hesse, and W Bavaria states, Germany. Original inhabitants were Suevi (whence its name) and Alamanni; conquered by Franks in 5th cent. A.D.; duchy from c. 10th cent.; ruled by Hohenstaufens c. 1077–1268; duchy ceased upon division in 1268. Several alliances of Swabian cities formed 14th–16th cents. (Swabian Leagues), esp. 1488–1534; region comprised a territorial division (circle) of the Holy Roman Empire 16th–19th cents. Chief cities of duchy Augsburg, Ulm, Freiburg, Konstanz.

Swad·lin·cote \'swäd-lin-,kōt\. Town, Derbyshire, N cen. England, 26 mi. (42 km.) NE of Birmingham; pop. (1981p) 23,388; coal mining; chinaware.

Swain \swān\. County in W North Carolina. See table at NORTH CAROLINA.

Swain Reefs. Coral reefs, S end of Great Barrier Reef, Queensland, Australia.

Swains \'swānz\ *also* **Qui·ros** \'kē-,rōs\; *formerly* **Gen·te Her·mo·sa** \'hān-tā-er-'mō-sä\. Island, American Samoa, SW cen. Pacific Ocean, 200 mi. (322 km.) NW of the island of Tutuila; 11°S, 171°W; 1 sq. mi. (3 sq. km.); pop. (1990c) 16; formerly a part of Tokelau under the jurisdiction of Gilbert and Ellice Islands Colony; transferred to U.S. 1925.

Swains·boro \'swānz-,bər-ō\. City, ⊗ of Emanuel co., E cen. Georgia, 33 mi. (53 km.) WNW of Statesboro; pop. (1990c) 7361; East Georgia Coll. (1970).

Swa·kop \'sfä-,kȯp\. River, Namibia; flows into Atlantic Ocean N of Walvis Bay; 250 mi. (402 km.) long.

Swa·kop·mund \'sfä-,kȯp-,mənt\. Town, W Namibia, on Atlantic Ocean 175 mi. (282 km.) W of Windhoek; pop. (1988e) 15,500; formerly chief port of German Southwest Africa but now silted up and closed to shipping; large uranium mine nearby; vacation resort.

Swale \'swāl\. River, Yorkshire, N England; flows S to unite with the Ure River and form the Ouse; 60 mi. (97 km.) long.

Swamp·scott \'swämp-skət\. Town, Essex co., NE corner of Massachusetts, on Massachusetts Bay 11 mi. (18 km.) NE of Boston; pop. (1990c) 13,650; summer resort.

Swan \'swän\. **1.** River, SW Western Australia, Australia; flows W to Indian Ocean; ab. 240 mi. (385 km.) long; called Avon in upper course. Perth situated on it near its mouth. Discovered and named 1697 by Dutch navigator Willem de Vlamingh.

2. River, E Saskatchewan and W Manitoba, Canada; flows NE into Swan Lake; ab. 110 mi. (175 km.) long.

Swan·age \'swä-nij\. Seaside resort, Dorset, S England, on English Channel 33 mi. (53 km.) SW of Southampton; pop. (1981p) 8647.

Swan Hill. City, N Victoria, Australia, across the Murray River from New South Wales; pop. (1991c) 9357.

Swan Islands *or* **Is·las San·ta·nil·la** \'ēs-läs-,sän-tä-'nē-lä\. Two small islands, W Caribbean Sea, N of Honduras; total area 1 sq. mi. (3 sq. km.); belong to Honduras.

Swankalok. See SAWANKHALOK.

Swan Lake. **1.** Lake, Nicollet co., S Minnesota.

2. Lake, W Manitoba, Canada; 118 sq. mi. (306 sq. km.); receives Swan River from SW and drains N into Lake Winnipegosis.

Swan·land \'swän-,land, -lənd\. Region, SW Western Australia, Australia—the plateau to the E of the Avon (upper Swan) River.

Swan Point. Point, SW shore of Kent co., NE Maryland, extending into upper Chesapeake Bay.

Swan Quarter. Town, ⊗ of Hyde co., E North Carolina.

Swan Range. A range of the Rocky Mts.; chiefly in Flathead and Powell cos., W Montana.

Swan River. **1.** Rivers in Australia and Canada. See SWAN.

2. Town, W Manitoba, Canada, on Swan River 30 mi. (48 km.) SW of Swan Lake; pop. (1991c) 3917.

Swans·combe \ˈswänz-kəm\. Town, Kent, SE England, on the Thames 10 mi. (16 km.) E of London; pop. (1981p) 8849; remains of prehistoric Swanscombe man discovered here mid-20th cent.

Swan·sea \ˈswän-zē, ˈswänt-sē\. **1.** Village, St. Clair co., SW Illinois, 11 mi. (18 km.) SE of East St. Louis; pop. (1990c) 8201.

2. Town, Bristol co., SE Massachusetts, 3 mi. (5 km.) NW of Fall River; pop. (1990c) 15,411; settled 1632; incorp. 1668; scene of first bloodshed in King Philip's War 1675.

3. *or Welsh* **Ab·er·tawe** \ˌa-bər-ˈtau̇-ə\ Seaport, ⊗ of West Glamorgan co., S Wales; pop. (1991p) 182,100; steelworks, oil refineries; center of tinplate industry; Univ. Coll. of Swansea (1920); medieval castle; suffered much bombing damage from German air raids in WWII. Birthplace of poet Dylan Thomas 1914.

Swans Island \ˈswänz\. Island, Atlantic Ocean, off S coast of SE Maine; part of Hancock co.

Swan·son Mountains \ˈswän-sən\. Mountain range, a subsidiary range of the Ford Ranges, Marie Byrd Land, Antarctica, ab. 77°S, 145°W; highest peak ab. 3000 ft. (915 m.).

Swan·ton \ˈswänt-ᵊn\. **1.** Village, Fulton co., NW Ohio, 19 mi. (31 km.) W of Toledo; pop. (1990c) 3557.

2. Town, Franklin co., NW Vermont, on Missisquoi River 8 mi. (13 km.) N of St. Albans; pop. (1990c) 5636.

Swan·zey \ˈswän-zē\. Town, Cheshire co., SW corner of New Hampshire, 4 mi. (6 km.) S of Keene; pop. (1990c) 6236.

Swart·ber·ge, Groot– \ˈgrōt-ˈsvärt-ˌber-gə\ *or* **Swart·berg** \ˈsvärt-ˌberg, -ˌbərg\. Mountains, S Rep. of South Africa, separating Great Karoo from Little Karoo; contains the Cango Caves; traversed by a pass at alt. 5000 ft. (1524 m.).

Swarth·more \ˈswȯrth-ˌmōr, ˈswäth-\. Borough, Delaware co., SE Pennsylvania, 11 mi. (18 km.) W of Philadelphia; pop. (1990c) 6157; residential suburb of Philadelphia; Swarthmore Coll. (1864).

Swartz Creek \ˈswȯrts\. City, Genessee co., SE cen. Michigan, 10 mi. (16 km.) WSW of Flint; pop. (1990c) 4851.

Swat \ˈswät\. River, North-West Frontier, Pakistan; flows SW and SE into Kabul River NE of Peshawar; ab. 400 mi. (645 km.) long.

Swatow. See SHANTOU.

Swa·zi·land \ˈswä-zē-ˌland\. Kingdom, S Africa, bordering on Mozambique and the Rep. of South Africa; 6705 sq. mi. (17,366 sq. km.); pop. (1986c) 676,089; ✻ Mbabane.

Physical features: W consists of high veld (elev. ranges from 4000 to 6000 ft. or 1200 to 1800 m.), cen. region consists of middle veld (max. elev. 4000 ft. or 1200 m.), and E is characterized by low veld (mean elev. 1500 ft. or 460 m.); major rivers Komati, Umbeluzi, Usutu.

Chief products: Corn, cotton, citrus fruit, sugarcane; asbestos, coal; textiles; beverages; lumber; formerly exported iron ore.

Chief towns: Mbabane and Manzini.

History: Evidence of prehistoric inhabitants include stone tools and rock paintings; region settled by emerging Swazi nation mid-19th cent.; despite guarantees of independence, came largely under British control 1880s; following Boer War (1899–1902) administered by British governor of Transvaal; governor's powers transferred to British high commissioner 1906; Union of South Africa's request for control over Swaziland rejected by British government 1949; limited self-government introduced 1963; achieved independence 1968; constitution abolished 1976 in favor of supreme authority of the king and traditional tribal form of government.

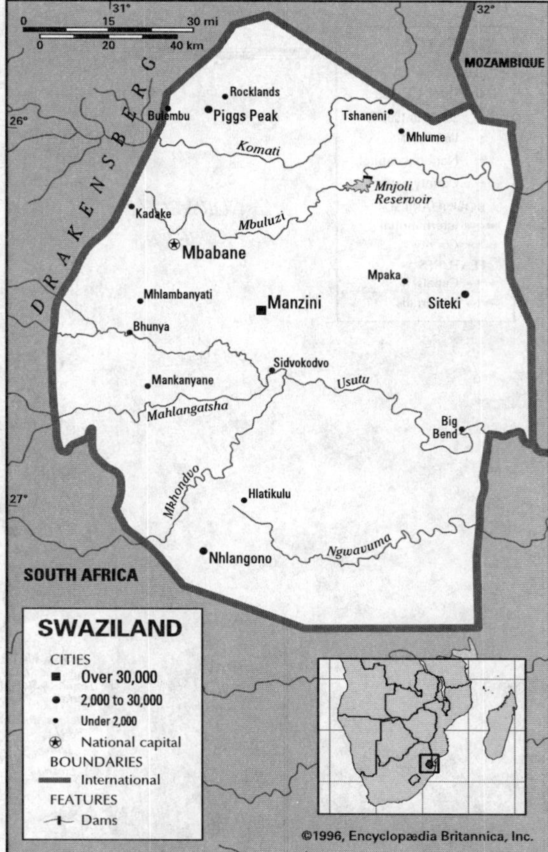

Swe·den \ˈswēd-ᵊn\ *or Swed.* **Sve·ri·ge** \ˈsvar-yə\. Kingdom, NW Europe, occupying the E and larger section of the Scandinavian Penin.; bounded on W by Norway, on NE by Finland, on E by the Gulf of Bothnia, on E and S by the Baltic Sea, and on SW by the Kattegat; 173,665 sq. mi. or 449,792 sq. km. (incl. 14,879 sq. mi. or 35,537 sq. km. of water); pop. (1993e) 8,727,000; ✻ Stockholm.

Physical features: The N part of the boundary with Norway is marked by the Kölen Mts. which include Sweden's highest peak, Kebnekaise 6965 ft. (2123 m.) and which are source of many rivers in Norrland flowing SE to Gulf of Bothnia, esp. Ljusnan, Indal, Ångerman, Luleålv, and the Torneälven on the Finnish border; abundant waterpower, and many waterfalls and lakes. In S third of country (Svealand and Götaland) is lowland, incl. Dal River and several large lakes, the largest being Vänern, Vättern, Mälaren, and Hjälmaren. Separated from Sjælland I., Denmark, on S by narrow strait of the Øresund and from Jutland Penin., Denmark, by the Kattegat; has two large islands Gotland and Öland off SE in Baltic. Extreme N forms part of Lapland.

Chief products: Wheat, oats, barley, sugar beets, potatoes; dairy products; lumbering; iron ore, copper, zinc; manufacturing: steel, electrical appliances, chemicals, paper; tourism.

Chief cities: Stockholm, Göteborg, Malmö.

Political divisions: Divided into the following 24 provinces (for pronunciation of their names, see their individual entries):

NAME	AREA (sq. mi.)	AREA (sq. km.)	POP. (1989c)	CAPITAL
Älvsborg	4,928	12,764	437,516	Vänersborg
Blekinge	1,173	3,038	149,960	Karlskrona
Gävleborg	7,615	19,723	288,223	Gävle
Göteborg and Bohus	1,986	5,144	735,672	Göteborg
Gotland	1,225	3,173	56,840	Visby
Halland	1,904	4,931	250,959	Halmstad
Jämtland	19,903	51,549	134,789	Östersund

\ə\ abut \ᵊ\ kitten, Fr table \ər\ further \a\ ash \ā\ ace \ä\ cot, cart \ȧ\ Fr bac \au̇\ out \b̶\ Span Avila \ch\ chin \e\ bet \ē\ easy \g\ go \i\ hit \ī\ ice \j\ job \k̲\ Ger ich, Buch \ⁿ\ Fr vin \ŋ\ sing \ō\ go \ȯ\ all \ȯ\ law \œ\ Fr bœuf \œ̄\ Fr feu \ȯi\ boy \th\ thin \t͟h\ this \ü\ loot \u̇\ foot \ue\ Ger füllen \ūe\ Fr rue \y\ yet \ʸ\ Fr digne \ˈdēnʸ\, nuit \ˈnwʸē\ \yü\ few \yu̇\ fury \zh\ vision

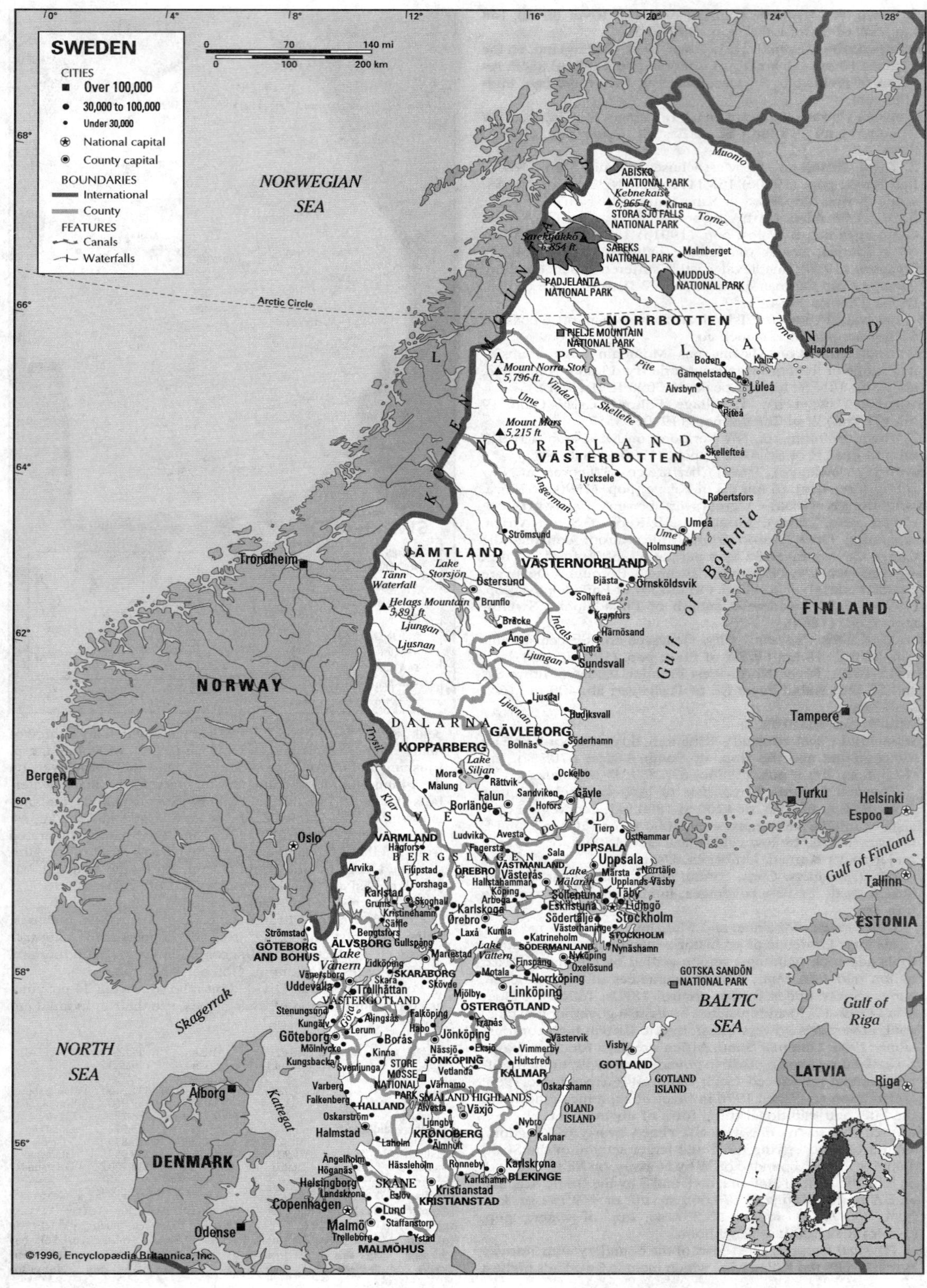
SWEDEN
CITIES
Over 100,000
30,000 to 100,000
Under 30,000
National capital
County capital
BOUNDARIES
International
County
FEATURES
Canals
Waterfalls
0 70 140 mi
0 100 200 km
NORWEGIAN SEA
Arctic Circle
NORRBOTTEN
LAPPLAND
NORRLAND
VÄSTERBOTTEN
JÄMTLAND
VÄSTERNORRLAND
GÄVLEBORG
DALARNA
KOPPARBERG
SVEALAND
VÄRMLAND
BERGSLAGEN
UPPSALA
VÄSTMANLAND
ÖREBRO
STOCKHOLM
SÖDERMANLAND
ÄLVSBORG
GÖTEBORG AND BOHUS
SKARABORG
VÄSTERGÖTLAND
ÖSTERGÖTLAND
JÖNKÖPING
KALMAR
HALLAND
KRONOBERG
SMÅLAND HIGHLANDS
BLEKINGE
SKÅNE
KRISTIANSTAD
MALMÖHUS
GOTLAND
GOTLAND ISLAND
ÖLAND ISLAND
KOLEN MOUNTAINS
ABISKO NATIONAL PARK
Kebnekaise 6,965 ft.
Kiruna
STORA SJÖ FALLS NATIONAL PARK
Sarektjåkkå 6,854 ft.
SAREKS NATIONAL PARK
Malmberget
MUDDUS NATIONAL PARK
PADJELANTA NATIONAL PARK
PIELJE MOUNTAIN NATIONAL PARK
Mount Norra Stor 5,796 ft.
Mount Mars 5,215 ft.
Helags Mountain 3,891 ft.
Tänn Waterfall
Lake Storsjön
Muonio
Torne
Pite
Vindel
Ume
Skellefte
Ångerman
Indals
Ljungan
Ljusnan
Trysil
Klar
Dal
Göta
Haparanda
Kalix
Boden
Gammelstaden
Luleå
Älvsbyn
Piteå
Skellefteå
Lycksele
Robertsfors
Umeå
Holmsund
Strömsund
Östersund
Brunflo
Bjästa
Örnsköldsvik
Sollefteå
Kramfors
Härnösand
Bräcke
Ånge
Timrå
Sundsvall
Ljusdal
Hudiksvall
Söderhamn
Bollnäs
Lake Siljan
Mora
Malung
Rättvik
Ockelbo
Falun
Sandviken
Gävle
Borlänge
Hofors
Tierp
Östhammar
Ludvika
Avesta
Hagfors
Fagersta
Sala
Uppsala
Arvika
Filipstad
Västerås
Lake Mälaren
Märsta
Norrtälje
Forshaga
Hallstahammar
Upplands-Väsby
Karlstad
Köping
Sollentuna
Täby
Grums
Skoghall
Arboga
Eskilstuna
Lidingö
Kristinehamn
Karlskoga
Södertälje
Stockholm
Säffle
Örebro
Västerhaninge
Bengtsfors
Laxå
Kumla
Strömstad
Gullspång
Katrineholm
Nynäshamn
Lake Vänern
Lidköping
Mariestad
Lake Vättern
Finspång
Nyköping
Vänersborg
Skara
Oxelösund
Motala
Norrköping
Uddevalla
Trollhättan
Skövde
Mjölby
Linköping
Stenungsund
Falköping
Kungälv
Alingsås
Tranås
Lerum
Habo
Göteborg
Jönköping
Västervik
Mölnlycke
Borås
Nässjö
Eksjö
Vimmerby
Kinna
Kungsbacka
Svenljunga
STORE MOSSE NATIONAL PARK
Vetlanda
Hultsfred
Varberg
Värnamo
Oskarshamn
Falkenberg
Alvesta
Växjö
Oskarström
Ljungby
Nybro
Halmstad
Laholm
Älmhult
Kalmar
Ängelholm
Höganäs
Hässleholm
Ronneby
Karlskrona
Helsingborg
Karlshamn
Landskrona
Eslöv
Kristianstad
Copenhagen
Lund
Malmö
Staffanstorp
Trelleborg
Ystad
Visby
GOTSKA SANDÖN NATIONAL PARK
BALTIC SEA
Gulf of Bothnia
FINLAND
Tampere
Turku
Helsinki
Espoo
Gulf of Finland
Tallinn
ESTONIA
Gulf of Riga
LATVIA
Riga
NORWAY
Trondheim
Bergen
Oslo
Skagerrak
NORTH SEA
Kattegat
Ålborg
DENMARK
Odense
©1996, Encyclopædia Britannica, Inc.

NAME	AREA (sq. mi.)	AREA (sq. km.)	POP. (1989c)	CAPITAL
Jönköping	4,436	11,489	306,590	Jönköping
Kalmar	4,487	11,621	239,564	Kalmar
Kopparberg	11,722	30,360	286,667	Falun
Kristianstad	2,478	6,418	286,654	Kristianstad
Kronoberg	3,827	9,912	176,589	Växjö
Malmöhus	1,878	4,864	771,361	Malmö
Norrbotten	40,879	105,877	262,838	Luleå
Örebro	3,493	9,047	271,523	Örebro
Östergötland	4,278	11,080	399,506	Linköping
Skaraborg	3,262	8,448	274,546	Mariestad
Södermanland	2,645	6,850	253,363	Nyköping
Stockholm	3,070	7,951	1,629,631	Stockholm
Uppsala	2,084	5,398	264,738	Uppsala
Värmland	7,497	19,417	282,375	Karlstad
Västerbotten	2,284	5,916	250,134	Umeå
Västernorrland	9,924	25,703	260,488	Härnösand
Västmanland	2,615	6,773	256,510	Västerås

History: Evidence of Stone Age inhabitants; inhabited by several independent tribes by 9th cent. A.D.; inhabitants of Sweden were among Scandinavian (Viking) adventurers of 9th–10th cents. who established domination over river trade in E Europe bet. the Baltic Sea and the Black Sea, and who also raided W European lands; loosely united and Christianized 11th–12th cents.; conquered Finns in 12th cent., united in Union of Kalmar with Denmark and Norway 1397; broke away 1523 under Gustav I Vasa, founder of Vasa dynasty of Swedish monarchs, who established the hereditary monarchy and began territorial expansion; acquired territory comprising S mainland Sweden from Denmark 1558; took Estonia 1561, E Karelia and Ingria 1617, and Livonia 1629; acquired Jämtland and islands of Gotland and Saaremaa 1645; through participation in Thirty Years' War (Swedish phase 1630–35) won territory on German mainland (briefly), Hither Pomerania, Wismar, and bishoprics of Bremen and Verden; leading Baltic power in 17th cent.; greatly weakened by defeat in Great Northern War 1700–21, as result of which Sweden lost Livonia, Estonia, Ingria, Karelia, Saaremaa I., Bremen, Verden, and part of Hither Pomerania; Finland (*q.v.*) and Åland Is. were gradually lost to Russia 1743–1809; became constitutional monarchy 1809; gave up Swedish Pomerania in return for Norway which entered personal union with Sweden (1814–1905); acknowledged independence of Norway 1905; maintained armed neutrality in both World Wars; became a member of the UN 1946, Nordic Council 1952, EFTA 1959; abstained from membership in the EC and NATO in the interest of maintaining the foreign policy stance of neutrality; replaced bicameral parliament with unicameral parliament 1971; new constitution 1975 reduced monarch's powers to ceremonial head of state; upon end of the cold war, joined NATO's "partnerships for peace" program 1994, and became member of EU 1995.

Swedish Pomerania. See POMERANIA.

Swee·ny \ˈswē-nē\. Town, Brazoria co., SE Texas, 50 mi. (81 km.) SSW of Houston; pop. (1990c) 3297.

Sweet Bri·ar \ˈswēt-ˌbrī-ər\. Village, Amherst co., cen. Virginia, ab. 12 mi. (19 km.) N of Lynchburg; Sweet Briar Coll. (1901).

Sweet Grass. County in S cen. Montana. See table at MONTANA.

Sweet Home. City, Linn co., W Oregon, 32 mi. (52 km.) NE of Eugene; pop. (1990c) 6850.

Sweet·wa·ter \ˈswēt-ˌwȯ-tər, -ˌwä-\. **1.** River, cen. Wyoming; rises in SW Fremont co., flows E to Pathfinder Reservoir, which was formed by damming the North Platte River; ab. 175 mi. (280 km.) long.

2. County in SW Wyoming. See table at WYOMING.

3. City, Miami-Dade co., SE Florida; pop. (1990c) 13,909; grew rapidly in 1970s and 1980s.

4. City, Monroe co., SE Tennessee, 41 mi. (66 km.) SW of Knoxville; pop. (1990c) 5066.

5. City, ⊗ of Nolan co., NW Texas, 40 mi. (64 km.) W of Abilene; pop. (1990c) 11,967; gypsum products; meatpacking.

Swel·len·dam *also* **Zwel·len·dam** \ˈswel-ᵊn-ˌdam\. Town, Western Cape prov., S Rep. of South Africa, 115 mi. (185 km.) E of Cape Town in Bree River valley; pop. (1985c) 8193. One of the oldest nonnative settlements in South Africa, founded c. 1745; in 1795 rebelled against Dutch East India Company but surrendered to English in same year.

Swett Peninsula \ˈswet\. Peninsula, extending W from SW coast in Chile, SSE of the Gulf of Penas.

Świd·ni·ca \shfēd-ˈnēt-sä\ *or Ger.* **Schweid·nitz** \ˈshfīt-nits\. City, N Wałbrzych prov., SW Poland, 33 mi. (53 km.) SW of Wrocław; pop. (1989e) 62,845; chemicals, textiles; 14th cent. church; 13th cent. town hall; founded c. 13th cent.; ✱ of an independent principality from late 13th cent. until it passed to Bohemia late 14th cent.; to Prussia 1742; suffered much in Hussite Wars 15th cent., Thirty Years' War 17th cent., and in Silesian Wars 18th cent.; assigned to Poland by Potsdam Conference 1945.

Świd·nik \ˈshfēd-nik\. Town, Lublin prov., E Poland, ab. 5 mi. (8 km.) ESE of the city of Lublin; pop. (1989e) 39,701.

Świe·bo·dzi·ce \ˌshfe-bȯ-ˈjēt-se\. Commune, Wałbrzych prov., SW Poland; pop. (1989e) 24,527.

Świe·bo·dzin \shfye-ˈbȯ-ˌjēn\ *or Ger.* **Schwie·bus** \ˈshvē-ˌbu̇s\. Town, Zielona Góra prov., W Poland, ab. 25 mi. (40 km.) N of the city of Zielona Góra; pop. (1989e) 21,671; formerly in Brandenburg, Germany.

Świe·cie \ˈshfye-che\. Commune, Bydgoszcze prov., N cen. Poland; on Vistula River; pop. (1989e) 25,982.

Świet·o·chlo·wi·ce \ˌshfyen-tȯ-k̲wȯ-ˈvēt-se\. Commune, Katowice prov., S Poland; pop. (1989e) 60,247.

Swift \ˈswift\. **1.** River, cen. Massachusetts; rises in Franklin co., flows S; 16 mi. (26 km.) ENE of Springfield it is joined by Quaboag River to form Chicopee River; dammed 1939 for water supply.

2. County in W Minnesota. See table at MINNESOTA.

Swift Creek Dam *and* **Swift Creek Reservoir.** See UNITED STATES, *Dams and Reservoirs.*

Swift Current. City, SW Saskatchewan, Canada, 105 mi. (169 km.) W of Moose Jaw; pop. (1991c) 14,815; railroad divisional point and trading center for large wheat-growing district.

Swift·cur·rent Mountain \ˈswift-ˌkər-ənt\. Peak, Glacier National Park, NW Montana; 8300 ft. (2530 m.).

Swift Dam. See table at UNITED STATES, *Dams and Reservoirs.*

Swil·ly, Lough \läk̲-ˈswi-lē\. Inlet of Atlantic Ocean, in N co. Donegal, N coast of Ireland; extends inland 24 mi. (39 km.).

Świ·na \ˈshfē-nä\. River, NW Poland; ab. 10 mi. (16 km.) long; main outlet of Zalew Szczeciński.

Swin·burne Island \ˈswin-bərn\. Island off E coast of Staten I., New York City, New York, in Lower New York Bay; part of Staten Island borough.

Swin·don \ˈswin-dən\. Town, Wiltshire, S England, 70 mi. (113 km.) W of London; pop. (1981c) 128,493; electronics, clothing.

Świ·no·ujś·cie \ˌshfē-nȯ-ˈü-ēsh-che\ *or Ger.* **Swi·ne·mün·de** \ˌsvē-nə-ˈmu̅e̅n-də\. Seaport city, NW Szczecin prov., NW Poland, on Baltic Sea on N coast of Usedom I. at mouth of the Świna River 37 mi. (60 km.) NNW of the seaport of Szczecin; pop. (1989e) 42,886; resort. Formerly in Prussia, Germany; bombed in WWII; captured by U.S.S.R. May 1945; following WWII assigned to Poland by Potsdam Conference 1945.

Swin·ton \ˈswint-ᵊn\. Town, South Yorkshire, N England, 10 mi. (16 km.) NE of Sheffield; pop. (1981p) 15,182; in coal-mining area.

Swinton and Pen·dle·bury \ˈpen-dᵊl-ˌber-ē\. Town, Greater Manchester, NW England, 4 mi. (6 km.) NW of Manchester; pop. (1981p) 39,621; cotton; coal mining.

Swish·er \ˈswi-shər\. County in NW Texas. See table at TEXAS.

Swiss·vale \ˈswis-ˌvāl\. Borough, Allegheny co., SW Pennsylvania, 7 mi. (11 km.) E of Pittsburgh; pop. (1990c) 10,637.

Swit·zer·land \ˈswit-sər-lənd\. **1.** *or Fr.* **Suisse** \ˈswʸēs\ *or Ger.* **Schweiz** \ˈshvīts\ *or Ital.* **Sviz·ze·ra** \ˈzvēt-tsā-rä\ *or Romansh* **Hel·ve·ti·ca** \hel-ˈvā-tē-kə\ *or Latin* **Hel·ve·tia**

\hel-ˈvē-shə\; *officially (in Eng.)* **Swiss Confederation.** Federal republic, cen. Europe, bounded on N by Germany, on E by Austria and Liechtenstein, on SE and S by Italy, and on SW, W, and NW by France; 15,941 sq. mi. (41,287 sq. km.); pop. (1993e) 6,996,000; ✻ Bern.

Physical features: Jura Mts. in the W and the Swiss Alps in S and E incl. Bernese, Lepontine, Pennine, and the Rhaetian Alps (see ALPS); highest peak Monte Rosa 15,217 ft. (4638 m.).

Chief rivers: In S part the Rhone, which has its source in E Valais canton; in E and N, forming part of the N boundary, the Rhine; in cen. and NW part the Aare, the largest river completely within Switzerland.

Lakes: In SW Lake Geneva on French border, in W Lac de Neuchâtel, on the N boundary Lake Constance, and in cen. part Brienzersee, Lake of Lucerne, Zürichsee, Lake Wallen, and Thunersee.

Chief products: Wheat, sugar beets, fruits and vegetables, potatoes, food products, dairy products, wines; salt; manufacturing: textiles, chemicals, watches and clocks, precision tools, machinery; pharmaceuticals; abundant waterpower; tourism; international finance.

Chief cities: Zürich, Basel, Geneva, Bern, Lausanne.

Political divisions: Divided into the following cantons (for pronunciation of their names, see their individual entries):

NAME	AREA (sq. mi.)	AREA (sq. km.)	POP. (1989c)	CAPITAL
Aargau	542	1,404	489,567	Aarau
Appenzell Inner Rhodes[1]	67	173	14,680[2]	Appenzell
Appenzell Outer Rhodes[1]	94	243	54,087[2]	Herisau
Basel-Land[1]	165	427	234,910[2]	Liestal
Basel-Stadt[1]	14	37	197,403[2]	Basel
Bern	2,327	6,027	942,721	Bern
Fribourg	645	1,670	203,878	Fribourg
Geneva	109	282	377,108	Geneva
Glarus	264	684	37,686	Glarus
Graubünden	2,745	7,110	177,096	Chur
Jura	322	834	65,376	Delémont
Lucerne	577	1,494	316,210	Lucerne
Neuchâtel	308	798	159,543	Neuchâtel
Nidwalden[1]	106	276	35,393[2]	Stans
Obwalden[1]	189	490	30,837[2]	Sarnen
Saint Gall	778	2,015	416,578	Saint Gall
Schaffhausen	115	298	71,210	Schaffhausen
Schwyz	351	909	108,576	Schwyz
Solothurn	305	790	223,803	Solothurn
Thurgau	389	1,008	201,773	Frauenfeld
Ticino	1,085	2,810	286,537	Bellinzona
Uri	415	1,075	34,042	Altdorf
Valais	2,020	5,232	249,473	Sion
Vaud	1,240	3,212	576,319	Lausanne
Zug	92	238	84,742	Zug
Zürich	668	1,730	1,152,769	Zürich

[1]Demicanton functioning as a canton.
[2]POP. (1994e).

History: Occupied by Helvetians who were conquered by Romans; SW invaded by Burgundians, NE by Alamanni; made part of Frankish empire; part in kingdom of Arles (*q.v.*, see also BURGUNDY); region without political unity under Holy Roman Empire; in 1291 the Forest Cantons, Uri, Schwyz, and Unterwalden, formed anti-Hapsburg league which became nucleus of Swiss Confederation; added Lucerne, Zürich, Glarus, Bern, and Zug by mid-14th cent.; Solothurn and Fribourg joined confederation 1481 and later, Basel and Appenzell; various cantons expanded their territories and won virtual independence in 15th cent. (not recognized until 1648); center of Protestant Reformation (see ZÜRICH and GENEVA 2) which divided cantons and inaugurated a period of political and religious rivalry; organized by French as Helvetic Republic 1798–1803; with new cantons added

1803 and 1815, restored as independent confederation of 22 cantons 1815; after war of Sonderbund (seven Roman Catholic cantons—Lucerne, Uri, Schwyz, Unterwalden, Zug, Fribourg, and Valais—against the Protestants) adopted new constitution 1848, present constitution 1874; perpetual neutrality guaranteed by international agreement 1815 (Congress of Vienna) and 1919 (Treaty of Versailles); remained neutral in WWI and WWII; became a member of the European Free Trade Association 1959; Jura became 23d canton 1979; UN membership rejected in national referendum March 16, 1986.

2. County in SE Indiana. See table at INDIANA.

Sworbe. See SÕRVE.

Swoy·ers·ville \ˈswȯi-ərz-ˌvil\. Borough, Luzerne co., E Pennsylvania, 4 mi. (6 km.) N of Wilkes-Barre; pop. (1990c) 5630.

Syas' *or* **Syas** \ˈsyäsʸ\. River, E St. Petersburg Oblast, NW Russia in Europe; flows NW to S end of Lake Ladoga, just E of the Volkhov River; 162 mi. (261 km.) long. With its tributary, the Tikhvinka, forms part of a canal system connecting the lake with the Volga through the Mologa to Rybinsk.

Syb·a·ris \ˈsi-bə-rəs\. Ancient city, S Italy, on N side of mouth of Crathis River on the Gulf of Tarentum; site near modern **Ter·ra·no·va di Si·ba·ri** \ˌter-ə-ˈnō-və-dē-si-ˈbä-rē\, Cosenza prov., N Calabria. Founded c. 720 B.C. by Achaeans, one of the oldest cities of Magna Graecia; became noted for its luxury; defeated in war with Crotona and was destroyed 510 B.C.; although efforts to rebuild and then to relocate were made, city never regained importance.

Sycaminum. See HAIFA 2.

Syc·a·more \ˈsi-kə-ˌmōr\. City, ⊗ of De Kalb co., N Illinois, 30 mi. (48 km.) ESE of Elgin; pop. (1990c) 9708.

Sych, Moel. See MOEL SYCH.

Sydlige Jylland. See SOUTH JUTLAND.

Syd·ney \ˈsid-nē\. **1.** City, ✱ of New South Wales, Australia, in E part on Port Jackson (*q.v.*) on Pacific Ocean; met. area pop. (1991c) 3,097,956; has one of world's finest natural harbors, with extensive port facilities (incl. container terminal); a major commercial and manufacturing center; chemicals, electronics; shipbuilding, oil refining, food processing; wool market; exports include wheat, wool; Anglican cathedral, Roman Catholic cathedral; city connected with North Sydney by Sydney Harbour Bridge (steel arch; main span 1650 ft. or 503 m.; completed 1932); Gladesville Bridge (concrete arch; main span 1000 ft. or 305 m.; completed 1964) spans Parramatta River nearby; Univ. of Sydney (1850), Univ. of New South Wales (1949), Macquarie Univ. (1964); State Parliament House (1811–17); Old Mint Building (1811); Government House (1837–45); town hall (1889); opera house (1973); several museums. First British settlement in Australia; founded 1788 by British officials in charge of group of convicts (penal settlement had been estab. on Botany Bay [*q.v.*]).

2. City, ⊗ of Cape Breton co., E Nova Scotia, Canada, on **Sydney Harbor,** an inlet of Atlantic Ocean; pop. (1991c) 26,063; steel and coal center; fisheries. First English settlement c. 1784; ✱ of Cape Breton I. 1784–1820.

3. Island of the Phoenix Is., S Pacific Ocean. See MANRA.

Sydney Mines. Town, Cape Breton co., E Nova Scotia, Canada, on Atlantic Ocean 10 mi. (16 km.) N of Sydney; pop. (1991c) 7551; coal mining formerly significant.

Syedlets. See SIEDLCE.

Syene. See ASWĀN 2.

Syk·tyv·kar *also* **Sik·tiv·kar** \sik-tif-ˈkär\; *formerly* **Ust' Sy·sol'sk** *or* **Ust Sy·solsk** \ˈüst-siʸ-ˈsȯlʸsk\. Town, ✱ of Komi Rep., NE Russia in Europe, on the Sysola River just above its junction with the Vychegda, 220 mi. (354 km.) N of Vyatka; pop. (1992e) 226,000; lumber.

Syl·a·cau·ga \ˌsi-lə-ˈkȯ-gə\. City, Talladega co., E cen. Alabama, 42 mi. (68 km.) SE of Birmingham; pop. (1990c) 12,520; marble, calcium carbonate; ice cream, textiles.

Sy·lar·na \ˈsǖ-lär-ˌnä\. Peak, W cen. Sweden, on the Norwegian border; 5781 ft. (1762 m.).

Syl·het \sil-ˈhet\. Town, E Bangladesh, on Surma River 120 mi. (193 km.) NE of Dhaka; pop. (1991p) 114,284; tea; several colleges.

Sylt \ˈzilt, ˈsilt\. Island off W coast of Schleswig-Holstein, Germany; 36 sq. mi. (93 sq. km.); pop. (1989e) 4835; chief island of North Frisian Is.; connected with mainland by causeway; summer resort.

Syl·va \ˈsil-və\. Town, ⊗ of Jackson co., SW North Carolina, 40 mi. (64 km.) WSW of Asheville; pop. (1990c) 1809.

Syl·va·nia \sil-ˈvā-nyə\. **1.** City, ⊗ of Screven co., E Georgia, 55 mi. (88 km.) NW of Savannah; pop. (1990c) 2871.

2. City, Lucas co., NW Ohio, on Michigan border; pop. (1990c) 17,301; Lourdes Coll. (1958).

Syl·ves·ter \sil-ˈves-tər\. City, ⊗ of Worth co., S Georgia, 20 mi. (32 km.) E of Albany; pop. (1990c) 5702.

Sylvia, Mount. See TZ'U-KAO.

Symē *or* **Symi.** See SÍMI.

Sym·me·try Spire \ˈsi-mə-trē-ˈspīr\. Peak, cen. Grand Teton National Park, NW Wyoming; 10,546 ft. (3214 m.).

Syra. See SYROS.

Syr·a·cuse \ˈsir-ə-ˌkyüs, -ˌkyüz\. **1.** Town, Kosciusko co., N Indiana; pop. (1990c) 2729.

2. City, ⊗ of Hamilton co., W Kansas; pop. (1990c) 1606.

3. City, ⊗ of Onondaga co., cen. New York, 12 mi. (19 km.) S of W end of Oneida Lake; pop. (1990c) 163,860; electronic equipment, pharmaceuticals, chinaware; State Univ. of New York Health Science Center at Syracuse (1834), Syracuse Univ. (1870), State Univ. of New York Coll. of Environmental Science and Forestry (1911), Le Moyne Coll. (1946), Onondaga Community Coll. (1961); Everson Museum of Art.

History: Original village ✱ of Iroquois Confederacy; territory visited by French 17th cent., subsequently by English; salt springs discovered 1654; trading post set up by pioneers c. 1786; saltworks estab. c. 1789 and flourished until after Civil War; salt settlements sprang up, incl. Salina (also called Salt Point, now N section of Syracuse) and site of present Syracuse; became important port on Erie Canal at junction with Oswego Canal (opened 1838); Syracuse incorp. 1825; became ⊗ 1827; Syracuse and Salina first incorp. as city of Syracuse 1847.

4. Town, Kosciusko co., N Indiana, on Lake Wawasee; pop. (1990c) 2729.

5. City, Davis co., N Utah, SW of Ogden; pop. (1990c) 4658.

6. *anc.* **Syr·a·cu·sae.** Seaport, SE Sicily, Italy. See SIRACUSA 2.

Syr Dar'·ya *or* **Syr Dar·ya** \sir-dər-ˈyä\. **1.** *also* **Syr Dar·ia** \dər-ˈyä\; *anc.* **Iax·ar·tes** \ˌī-ak-ˈsär-tēz\ *or* **Jax·ar·tes** \jak-\. River, W cen. Asia, in Tajikistan, Uzbekistan, and Kazakhstan; formed by two headstreams in Kazakhstan rising in the Tian Shan; flows W and NW into the Aral Sea at its NE corner; flows through the fertile Fergana Valley; ab. 1370 mi. (2204 km.) long; its lower course on E edge of Qizilkum Desert; has often changed its course.

2. Administrative subdivision of Uzbekistan; 8919 sq. mi. (23,100 sq. km.); pop. (1991e) 580,300; ✱ Gulistan; formed 1963.

Syr·ia \ˈsir-ē-ə\. **1.** *or Heb.* **Aram** \ˈā-ˌram, ˈer-əm\; *Arab.* **Ash Shām** *or* **Esh Shām** \ash-ˈshäm\. Ancient country, Asia, at E end of Mediterranean Sea, incl. modern Syria, Lebanon, Israel, and Jordan.

History: Evidence of human inhabitation for several thousand years; from mid-3d millennium B.C. under control variously of Sumerians, Akkadians, Amorites, Egyptians, Assyrians, and Babylonians; became part of Persian Empire 6th cent. B.C.; conquered by Macedonian King Alexander the Great 4th cent. B.C.; ruled by the Seleucids who carried on war against Egypt in 3d cent B.C.; made a Roman province by Pompey the Great 64 B.C. and flourished; invaded on several occasions by Persians before Khosrow II conquered it c. 611 A.D.; overrun by Muslim Arabs 635–636; seat of Umayyad dynasty with ✱ at Damascus (*q.v.*) 661–750; in hands of Seljuqs and later, of Fatimids, during early Crusades; came under Ottoman Turks 1516; European influence

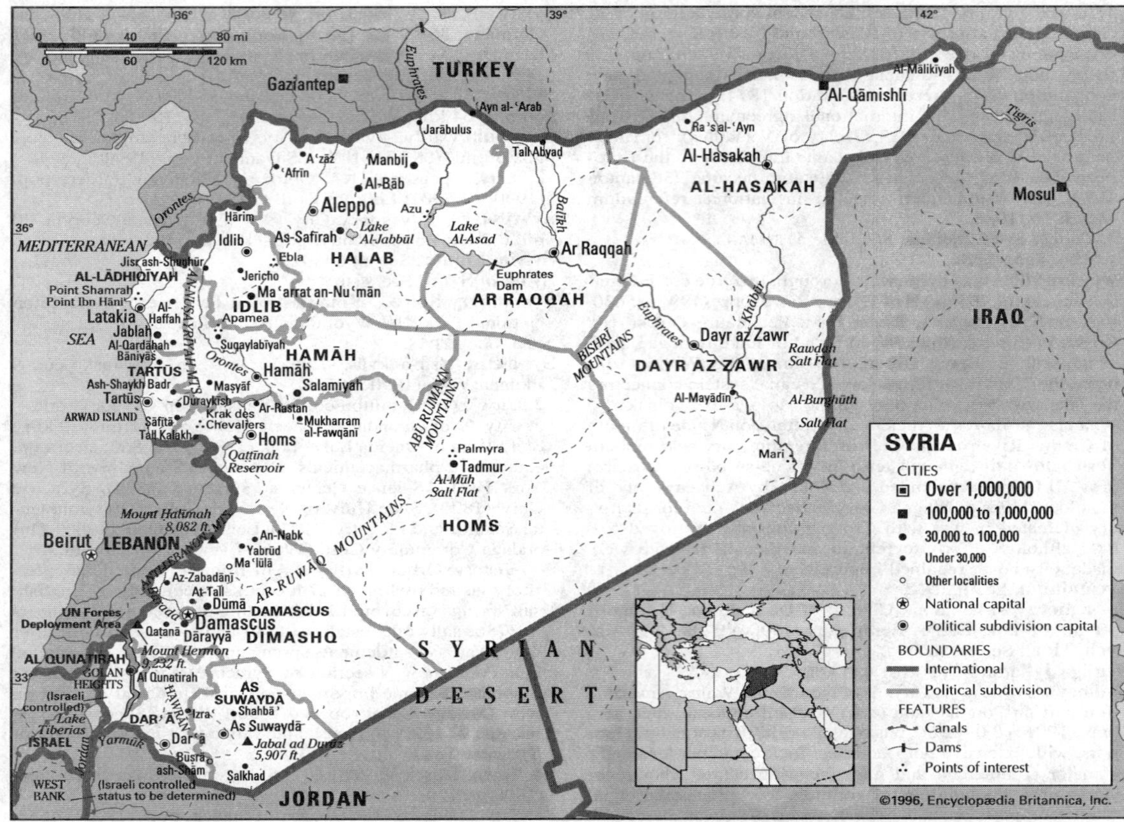

grew with increase of trade 17th–18th cents.; occupied by forces of Egyptian ruler Muḥammad 'Alī Pasha 1831; reverted to Turks mid-19th cent.; in WWI invaded by British and saw end of Turkish rule 1918; part of area to France following WWI.

2. *Fr.* **Sy·rie** \sē-'rē\ *or* **La Syrie** \lȧ-\. Former French mandate, W Asia, at E end of Mediterranean Sea; consisted of Syria (see SYRIA 3) and Lebanon (known as the **Le·vant States** \lə-'vant\).

History: Became French mandate 1920; in 1925 Damascus and Aleppo were united to form state of Syria which became republic 1930; Lebanon formed 1920; sanjak (district) of Alexandretta (*q.v.*), previously autonomous, ceded to Turkey 1939; under control of French Vichy forces 1940–41; taken over by British and Free French forces June–July 1941; ceased to be French mandate 1941 with occupation by French and British forces during remainder of WWII.

3. *officially* **Syr·i·an Arab Republic** \'sir-ē-ən\. Republic, SW Asia, at E end of Mediterranean Sea, bounded on N by Turkey, on E and SE by Iraq, on S by Jordan, on SW by Israel and Lebanon, and on W by Lebanon and the Mediterranean Sea; 71,498 sq. mi. (185,180 sq. km.); pop. (1993e) 13,398,000; ✻ Damascus.

Physical features: In the SE is the N part of the Syrian Desert; in center is a plateau region having elev. 1500 to 4500 ft. (460 to 1370 m.); in NE lies the upper part of the plain of Mesopotamia; in W are Anti-Lebanon and the N extension of the Lebanon Mts.; in SW is Jebel Druze 5907 ft. (1800 m.); in E cen. part is the Euphrates, flowing from NW to SE and receiving on the left the tributaries Balīkh and Khābūr.

Chief products: Wheat, cotton, barley, olives, grapes and other fruit, sugar beets, tobacco; oil and natural gas, gypsum, phosphates; manufacturing: textiles, cement.

Chief towns: Aleppo, Damascus, Homs.

History: For history before 1941, see SYRIA 1 and SYRIA 2. French mandate declared terminated 1941, but total independence not achieved until 1944; withdrawal of French and British troops completed 1946; united with Egypt 1958, forming United Arab Republic (union dissolved 1961); participated in Arab-Israeli War 1967 (see GOLAN HEIGHTS); formed short-lived federation with Egypt and Libya 1971; occupied part of Lebanon from 1970s but defeated by Israelis there 1982; backed opponents of Iraq in Gulf War 1991; signed treaty with Lebanon 1991.

Syriae Portae. See SYRIAN GATES.

Syr·i·am \'sir-ē-əm\. Town, Pegu div., Myanmar, on Rangoon River opp. Yangon; seaport.

Syr·i·an Desert \'sir-ē-ən\. Extensive desert region, W Asia, N Saudi Arabia, SE Syria, W Iraq, and NE Jordan, bet. lat. 30° and 34°N and long. 36° and 44°E; its W part known as **Al–Ha·mad** \ˌȧl-hə-'mȧd\, a name applied by some to the entire desert; crossed by pipelines connecting the oil fields of Kirkuk with Haifa and Tripoli.

Syrian Gates; *anc.* **Syr·i·ae Por·tae** \'sir-ē-ˌē-'pōr-tē\. Mountain pass, Hatay prov., S Turkey in Asia, S of İskenderun; cuts through the Nur Mts.; connected ancient Cilicia with Syria.

Syrie. See SYRIA 2.

Syr·mia \'sər-mē-ə\ *or Serb.* **Srem** \'srem\ *or Hung.* **Sze·rém** \'ser-'ām\. Region, S Europe; formerly the E division of Slavonia; since 1945 corresponds to E part of Croatia.

Sy·ros \'sī-ˌräs\ *or Gk.* **Sí·ros** \'sē-ˌrōs\ *also* **Sy·ra** \'sī-rə\. Island, cen. Cyclades, Greece, in Aegean Sea; 31 sq. mi. (80 sq. km.); pop. (1981c) 19,668; chief town Ermoúpolis, which is also ✻ of Cyclades dept., Greece. Haven of many Greek refugees during War of Independence; in 19th cent. of considerable commercial importance.

Syrtis Major. See SIDRA, GULF OF.

Syrtis Minor. See GABÈS.

Syv Systre. See SEVEN SISTERS.

Syz·ran' *or* **Syz·ran** \ˈsiz-rənʸ\. City, SW Samara Oblast, Russia in Europe, on right bank of the Volga 80 mi. (129 km.) W of the city of Samara; pop. (1992e) 175,000; on railroad line from Moscow to Samara and Chelyabinsk which crosses the Volga here on long bridge; river port; oil refining; founded 1683.

Szabadka. See SUBOTICA.

Sza·bolcs–Szat·már–Be·reg \ˈsö-ˌbȯlch-ˈsöt-ˌmär-ˈbe-rek\. County of NE Hungary. See table at HUNGARY.

Szalánkemén. See NOVI SLANKAMEN.

Szamos. See SOMEŞ.

Szar·vas \ˈsör-ˌvösh\. Commune, Békés co., SE Hungary, on the Körös ab. 83 mi. (134 km.) SE of Budapest; pop. (1980p) 20,598.

Szatmár–Németi. See SATU MARE 2.

Száva. See SAVA.

Szczara. See SHCHARA.

Szcze·cin \ˈshchet-ˌshēn\. **1.** *formerly* **Po·mo·rze Za·chod·nie** \pȯ-ˈmȯ-zhe-zä-ˈkȯd-nye\. Province, NW Poland; formerly in Prussia, Germany. See table at POLAND.
2. *or Ger.* **Stet·tin** \shte-ˈtēn\. Seaport, its ✱, near mouth of Oder River ab. 125 mi. (200 km.) NE of Poznán; pop. (1989e) 412,058; metallurgical industries; shipbuilding; one of Poland's chief ports; several institutions of higher education; cultural center.

History: Incorporated into Polish state by Mieszko I at end of 10th cent. A.D.; joined Hanseatic League 1360; to Sweden 1648 by Treaty of Westphalia; to Prussia 1720. In WWII frequently bombed; taken 1945 by Soviet troops after long siege and battle; after WWII assigned to Poland by Potsdam Conference 1945.

Szcze·ci·nek \shche-ˈchē-ˌnek\ *or Ger.* **Neu·stet·tin** \ˌnȯi-shte-ˈtēn\. City, Koszalin prov., N Poland, 41 mi. (66 km.) SE of the city of Koszalin; pop. (1989e) 40,444; summer resort. Founded 1310 by duke of Pomerania; in WWII occupied by Soviet troops 1945; assigned to Poland by Potsdam Conference 1945.

Szczyt·no \ˈshchit-nȯ\ *or Ger.* **Or·tels·burg** \ˈȯrt-ᵊls-ˌbu̇rk\. City, Olsztyn prov., N Poland, 27 mi. (43 km.) SE of the city of Olsztyn; pop. (1989e) 26,926; formerly in East Prussia, Germany; founded c. 13th cent.; suffered heavy damage WWI; in WWII taken by Soviets 1945; assigned to Poland by Potsdam Conference 1945.

Szechuan *or* **Szechwan.** See SICHUAN.

Sze·chwan·ese Alps \ˌsech-wə-ˈnēz-ˈalps\. Mountain ranges, NW, W, and SW borders of Sichuan prov., S cen. China, the E scarp of the Plateau of Tibet, from 10,000 to 24,900 ft. (3050 to 7590 m.); Gongga Shan is the highest peak.

Sze·ged \ˈse-ˌged\ *or Ger.* **Sze·ge·din** \ˈse-gā-ˌdēn\. City, ⊗ of Csongrád co., S Hungary, on the Yugoslav border; 43 sq. mi. (111 sq. km.); pop. (1991e) 184,000; timber, salt; university (1921); important port on the Tisza River; old town damaged by flood 1879; subsequently rebuilt on a radial plan.

Szé·kes·fe·hér·vár \ˈsā-ˌkesh-ˌfe-hār-ˌvär\ *or Ger.* **Stuhl·weis·sen·burg** \shtül-ˈvīs-ᵊn-ˌbu̇rk\. City, ⊗ of Fejér co., W cen. Hungary; pop. (1991e) 111,200; scene of crowning of kings of Hungary 1027–1527; occupied by Turks 1543; many of its buildings destroyed 1686 at end of Turkish occupation; rebuilt during Hapsburg rule; suffered heavy damage during WWII.

Szek·szárd \ˈsek-ˌsärd\; *formerly* **Szeg·szárd** \ˈseg-ˌsärd\. City, ⊗ of Tolna co., S Hungary, 85 mi. (137 km.) S of Budapest; pop. (1991e) 38,600.

Szemao. See SIMAO.

Szent. See SAINT.

Szent·en·dre \ˈsen-ten-dre\ *or Ger.* **Sankt An·drä** \zäŋkt-ˈän-drā\. City, Pest co., N Hungary, on a branch of the Danube ab. 12 mi. (19 km.) N of Budapest; pop. (1980p) 16,844.

Szent·es \ˈsen-ˌtesh\. City, Csongrád co., SE Hungary, 30 mi. (48 km.) N of Szeged; pop. (1991e) 33,500.

Szent·gott·hárd \ˈsent-gȯt-ˌhärd\ *or Eng.* **Saint Gott·hard** \sānt-ˈgä-tərd\. Commune, Vas co., W Hungary, on Rába River, on Austrian boundary; pop. (1980p) 5837; scene of battle 1664 in which Austrian imperial forces under Gen. Raimundo Montecuccoli defeated the Turks. See VASVÁR.

Szepingkai. See SIPING.

Szerém. See SYRMIA.

Szi·get·köz \ˈsē-get-ˌkœz\ *also* **Little Schütt** \ˈshu̇t\. Island in NW Hungary, formed by arms of the Danube near Győr; ab. 28 mi. (45 km.) long and 7 mi. (11 km.) wide.

Szi·get·vár \ˈsē-get-ˌvär\. Commune, Baranya co., S Hungary, W of Pécs; pop. (1980p) 12,114; object of siege 1566 in which Hungarian commander Miklós Zrīnyi with fewer than 3000 soldiers heroically defended the city against Ottoman army of Süleyman the Magnificent.

Sziszek. See SISAK.

Szol·nok \ˈsōl-ˌnōk\. City, ⊗ of Jasz-Nagykun-Szolnok co., Hungary, ab. 55 mi. (88 km.) SE of Budapest; pop. (1991e) 82,900; commercial center; Franciscan convent.

Szom·bat·hely \ˈsōm-ˌbȯt-ˌhā\ *or Ger.* **Stein·am·ang·er** \ˌshtīn-äm-ˈäŋ-ər\; *anc.* **Sa·bar·ia** \sə-ˈbar-ē-ə\ *or* **Sa·var·ia** \-ˈvar-\. City, ⊗ of Vas co., W Hungary, near Austrian frontier; pop. (1991e) 87,700; commercial center in rich wine-producing region; cathedral; episcopal palace; Roman ruins; ancient Sabaria was an important city in Roman prov. of Pannonia; in WWII suffered extensive damage, but much has been rebuilt.

Szpro·ta·wa \shprȯ-ˈtä-vä\ *or Ger.* **Sprot·tau** \ˈshprȯ-ˌtau̇\. Town, Zielona Góra prov., SW Poland, on Bóbr River ab. 25 mi. (40 km.) S of the city of Zielona Góra; pop. (1981p) 12,116; formerly in Silesia, Germany; after WWII assigned to Poland by Potsdam Conference 1945.

T

Ta·al \tä-'äl, 'täl\. **1.** Volcano on Volcano I. (14 mi. or 23 km. in circumference, 6 sq. mi. or 16 sq. km.), in center of Lake Taal, Batangas prov., Luzon, Philippines; its crater is more than 1.25 mi. (2 km.) in diameter. Has had numerous recorded eruptions from late 16th cent. into late 20th cent.
2. Municipality, Batangas prov., Luzon, Philippines, on Pansipit River near its mouth, SW of Lake Taal and near the NE coast of Balayan Bay; pop. (1980c) 29,699; named after older town destroyed by the eruption of Mt. Taal in 1754.

Taal, Lake; *formerly* **Lake Bom·bon** \bòm-'bòn\. Lake, Batangas prov., Luzon, Philippines, ab. 40 mi. (65 km.) S of Manila; 17 mi. (27 km.) long by 12 mi. (19 km.) wide; 94 sq. mi. (243 sq. km.); its outlet is the Pansipit River flowing S to Balayan Bay.

Ta·a·nach \'tā-ə-ˌnak\. Ancient city of Canaan, on S side of Plain of Esdraelon ab. 5 mi. (8 km.) SE of Megiddo. Mentioned several times in Old Testament, notably where near here Canaanite commander Sisera was defeated by Israelite commander Barak and the prophetess Deborah (*Judges* v. 19); important during Hebrew King Solomon's reign.

Taasinge. See TÅSINGE.

Tab. See ZOHREH.

Ta·ba·co \tä-'bä-kō\. Municipality, E coast of Albay prov., Luzon, Philippines, on Tabaco Bay, N of Mayon Volcano and ab. 15 mi. (24 km.) N of Legazpi; pop. (1990c) 85,697.

Tabaco Bay. Inlet of Lagonoy Gulf, E coast of Albay prov., Luzon, Philippines; ab. 12 mi. (19 km.) long; San Miguel I. and Cagraray I. enclose it on the E; it affords sheltered harbors for Tabaco and Bacacay.

Ta·bar Islands \tə-'bär\. Group of small islands, NE part of the Bismarck Archipelago, Papua New Guinea, W Pacific Ocean, off NE coast of island of New Ireland; comprise the three islands of Tabar, Tatau, and Simberi.

Ţabarīyā, Buḩayrat. See GALILEE, SEA OF.

Ta·bas \tə-'bäs\. **1.** Town, S Khorāsān prov., NE Iran, at N border of the Dasht-e-Lūt 180 mi. (290 km.) NE of Yazd.
2. Town, SE Khorāsān prov., NE Iran, ESE of Bīrjand near Afghan border.

Ta·ba·sa·rá Mountains \ˌtä-bä-sä-'rä\ *or Span.* **Ser·ra·nía de Tabasará** \ˌser-rä-'nē-ä-thā-\. Mountain range, W Panama; highest point Mt. Santiago 9269 ft. (2825 m.).

Ta·bas·co \tä-'bäs-kō, tə-'bas-kō\. **1.** State of SE Mexico. See table at MEXICO.
2. River, Mexico. See GRIJALVA.

Ta·ber \'tā-bər\. Town, Alberta, Canada, 32 mi. (51 km.) E of Lethbridge; pop. (1991c) 6660.

Ta·be·ris, La·gu·na \lä-'gü-nä-tä-'bā-rēs\ *or* **Laguna Tua·pi** \'twä-pē\. Inlet of the Caribbean Sea, NE coast of Nicaragua.

Ta·bi·te·u·ea \ˌtä-bē-ˌtā-ü-'ā-ə\. Island (atoll), near S end of Gilbert Is., Kiribati, W Pacific Ocean, ab. 80 mi. (130 km.) S of the Equator; ab. 50 mi. (80 km.) long.

Ta·blas \'tä-bläs\. Largest island of Romblon group, Romblon prov., cen. Philippines, in W marking part of W border of Sibuyan Sea; 265 sq. mi. (686 sq. km.); ab. 40 mi. (64 km.) long; chief municipality Odioñgan. Long narrow island, separated from E Mindoro by Tablas Strait, and from Romblon I. at its N end by a channel 8 mi. (13 km.) wide; has low mountain range through its center.

Tablas, Las. See LAS TABLAS.

Tablas Strait. Passage, Philippines, bet. Mindoro on the W and Tablas, Simara, and Banton islands on the E, ab. 35 mi. (55 km.) wide; connects E end of Verde Island Passage with Sulu Sea.

Ta·ble Bay \'tā-bəl\. Inlet forming the harbor of Cape Town, SW Western Cape prov., Rep. of South Africa; 6 mi. (10 km.) wide.

Table Cape. 1. Cape, E cen. coast of North I., New Zealand, at the base of Mahia Penin. at 39°06′S, 178°E.
2. Cape, NW Tasmania, Australia, N of Wynyard.
3. Town, Tasmania. See WYNYARD.

Table Mountain. 1. Peak, cen. Churchill co., W Nevada; ab. 8300 ft. (2530 m.).
2. Peak in Catskill Mts., Ulster co., SE New York; 3847 ft. (1173 m.).
3. Peak, Kittitas co., cen. Washington; 6358 ft. (1938 m.).
4. Peak in Teton Range, W Teton co., NW Wyoming; 11,101 ft. (3384 m.).
5. Peak, Yellowstone National Park, NW Wyoming; 10,063 ft. (3067 m.).
6. Mountain, Western Cape prov., Rep. of South Africa, S of Cape Town; 3563 ft. (1086 m.).

Table Rock. Peak, Scotts Bluff co., W Nebraska; 4139 ft. (1262 m.).

Ta·ble·top Mountain \'tā-bəl-ˌtäp\. Peak in the Adirondack Mts., Essex co., NE New York; 4440 ft. (1353 m.).

Ta·bo·ga \tä-'bō-gä\. Small island, Gulf of Panama, 10 mi. (16 km.) S of Panama City; part of Panama.

Ta·bo·gon \ˌtä-bä-'gòn\. Municipality, NE coast of Cebu I., Cebu prov., Philippines, 47 mi. (76 km.) N of City of Cebu; pop. (1980c) 21,840.

Tá·bor \'tä-ˌbòr\. Town, SW cen. Czech Republic, on Lužnice River 47 mi. (76 km.) S of Prague; pop. (1989c) 35,942; manufactures textiles and tobacco products; founded 1420 by Jan Žižka, a Hussite; remained Protestant stronghold (of Taborites) during Hussite Wars; 15th cent. church.

Ta·bor, Mount \'tā-bər\ *or Heb.* **Har Ta·vor** \'här-tä-'vòr\. Mountain, N Israel, 6 mi. (10 km.) ESE of Nazareth; 1929 ft. (588 m.); notable in biblical and Roman times.

Ta·bo·ra \tä-'bōr-ä\. **1.** Administrative region of W Tanzania. See table at TANZANIA.
2. Town, its ✳, on railroad line 430 mi. (692 km.) WNW of Dar es Salaam; pop. (1985e) 214,641; trade center; modern town founded by Arabs early 19th cent.; became German outpost in German East Africa late 19th cent.; in WWI taken by Belgian forces 1916.

Ta·brīz \ta-'brēz\. Commercial city, ✳ of East Azerbaijan prov., NW Iran, ab. 38 mi. (61 km.) E of Daryācheh-ye Orūmīyeh and N of Kūh-e Sahand; pop. (1986c) 971,482; alt. 4400 ft. (1341 m.); center of road and rail transportation, incl. a rail connection (80 mi. or 129 km.) to Dzhul'fa on the Araks in independent Azerbaijan; produces carpets, textiles, leather goods, soap, dried fruits and nuts; 14th cent. citadel; restored 15th cent. mosque; university (1946). Has been subject to frequent destructive earthquakes and several times destroyed by invaders—Arabs, Turks, Mongols, and esp. Turkic ruler Timur in 1392. Became Persian 1618; occupied alternately by Turks and by Russians 18th–19th cents.; object of conflict bet. Turks and Russians in WWI; suffered bombing damage during Iran-Iraq War 1980s.

Ta·bu·a·er·an \tə-ˌbü-ə-'er-ən\; *formerly* **Fan·ning** \'fa-niŋ\. One of the Line Is. (*q.v.*), Kiribati, in cen. Pacific Ocean, S of Hawaii, 3°52′N, 159°W; 15 sq. mi. (39 sq. km.); included 1916 in British colony of Gilbert and Ellice Is.; discovered 1798 by American navigator, Capt. Edward Fanning. See AMERICA ISLANDS.

Ta·buk \tä-'bük\. Municipality, ✳ of Kalinga-Apayao prov., N Luzon, Philippines; pop. (1980c) 42,768.

Ta·bwe·ma·sa·na, Mount \ˌtä-bwā-mä-'sä-nä, -sä-'nä\. Mountain, Espíritu Santo I., Vanuatu; 6167 ft. (1880 m.); highest peak on the island.

Ta·cám·bar·o \tä-'käm-bä-ˌrō\. Municipality, Michoacan state, Mexico, 45 mi. (72 km.) SE of Uruapan; pop. (1990p) 52,798.

Ta·ca·ná \ˌtä-kä-'nä\. **1.** Volcano, SW Guatemala, on the Guatemala-Mexico boundary in the Sierra Madre Range; 13,428 ft. (4093 m.).

2. Town, San Marios dept., SW Guatemala, NE of the volcano; munic. pop. (1981c) 37,466.
Tacape. See GABÈS.
Tacarigua. See VALENCIA 4.
Ta·cheng *or W.-G.* **T'a–ch'eng** *or* **T'ah–ch'eng** \'tä-'cheŋ\; *formerly* **Chu·gu·chak** \'chü-'gü-'chäk\. Town, N Xinjiang Uygur, W China, near Kazakhstan border.
Ta·chi·ka·wa \tä-'chē-kä-wä, ˌtä-chē-'kä-wä\. Town, Tokyo prefecture, SE Honshū, Japan, 19 mi. (31 km.) W of the city of Tokyo; pop. (1990p) 152,817.
Tá·chi·ra \'tä-chē-ˌrä\. State of W Venezuela. See table at VENEZUELA.
Ta·clo·ban \tä-'klō-bän\. Chartered city, ✻ of Leyte prov., NE coast of Leyte I., Philippines, at S end of San Juanico Strait and on NW shore of San Pedro Bay; pop. (1990p) 138,000; has good harbor with coastal trade; university (1946). Made ✻ by Spanish in 19th cent. and as port opened to foreign trade 1874; seized by Japanese 1942 and retaken with its airport by U.S. forces Oct. 1944.
Tac·na \'täk-nä\. **1.** Mostly arid region, extreme S Peru; enclosed on E by foothills of the Andes. Part of **Tacna–Ari·ca** \-ä-'rē-kä\ region, which was occupied by Chile from 1884 (see ANCÓN for Treaty of Ancón 1883) to 1930 when region was divided bet. Peru and Chile. See ARICA.
2. Town, Tacna region, ab. 40 mi. (64 km.) by rail N of Arica, Chile; pop. (1990e) 150,200; Peruvian and Bolivian forces defeated near here by Chileans 1880.
Ta·co·ma \tə-'kō-mə\. Seaport city, ⊗ of Pierce co., W cen. Washington, on Puget Sound 26 mi. (42 km.) S of Seattle; pop. (1990c) 176,664; lumber and wood products, aluminum; food processing; boatbuilding center; center of resort area; Univ. of Puget Sound (1888), Pacific Lutheran Univ. (1890), Pierce Coll. (1967); McChord Air Force Base, Fort Lewis. First permanent settlement 1860s.
Tacoma, Mount. See RAINIER, MOUNT.
Ta·con·ic Range \tə-'kä-nik\. Ridge, NE United States, extending along N part of New York-Connecticut boundary and entire New York-Massachusetts boundary and into Vermont; highest peak Big Equinox, 3816 ft. (1163 m.), in Bennington co., SW Vermont.
Ta·co·ra \tä-'kō-rä\. Peak, Tacna region, S Peru; 19,522 ft. (5950 m.).
Ta·cua·rem·bó \ˌtä-kwä-rem-'bō\. **1.** Department of N cen. Uruguay. See table at URUGUAY.
2. *formerly* **San Fruc·tu·o·so** \ˌsän-frük-'twō-sō\. City, its ✻, 215 mi. (346 km.) N of Montevideo; pop. (1985c) 40,513; trade center for wool and hides.
Ta·cua·rí \ˌtä-kwä-'rē\. River, E Uruguay; flows E into Lagoa Mirím; ab. 90 mi. (145 km.) long.
Tacurupucú. See HERNANDARIAS.
Tacuta Island. See TAGULA ISLAND.
Ta·cu·tu *or in Guyana* **Ta·ku·tu** \ˌtä-kü-'tü\. River, Guyana and N Brazil; flows N, forming a section of the boundary bet. SW Guyana and Brazil, curves W into N Brazil and S to unite with the Uraricoera River and form the Rio Branco; 220 mi. (354 km.) long. See IRENG.
Ta·djou·ra *also* **Ta·ju·ra** \tä-'jü-rä\. Seaport, Djibouti, on N side of the Gulf of Tadjoura.
Tadjoura, Gulf of *also* **Gulf of Tajura.** Inlet of the Gulf of Aden, E coast of Djibouti.
Tadmor. See PALMYRA 7.
Tad·mur \'täd-mu̇r\ *or* **Tud·mur** \'təd-\ *also* **Pal·my·ra** \pal-'mī-rə\. City, cen. Syria, in Syrian Desert; pop. (1985e) 20,627; located at a road junction and along an oil pipeline that extends from Iraq to Lebanon; built on site of ancient Palmyra (*q.v.*).
Tad·ous·sac \'ta-də-ˌsak, ˌtä-dü-'säk\. Village, SE Quebec, Canada, on N bank of St. Lawrence River at mouth of the Saguenay on its left bank, 117 mi. (188 km.) NE of Quebec; pop. (1991c) 832. An Indian village at time of visit by French explorer Jacques Cartier c. 1534; trading station for furs and fish; European settlement made 1600, one of the oldest in Canada.
Tadzhikistan. See TAJIKISTAN.
Tadzhik Soviet Socialist Republic. See TAJIKISTAN.
Tae·dong \ta-'dȯŋ, tī-\; *formerly* **Dai·do** \'dī-dō\. River and inlet, North Korea; river flows into Korea Bay at Namp'o; 245 mi. (394 km.) long.
Tae·gu \'ta-gü\ *or Jp.* **Tai·kyu** \'tī-ˌkyü\. Special city (province) and ✻ of North Kyŏngsang prov., South Korea, 56 mi. (90 km.) NNW of Pusan; several parks, ancient pagodas, Buddhist temple; long inhabited and important historically as far back as 8th cent. A.D.; significant economically and culturally during reign of Yi dynasty (1392–1910). See table at KOREA, SOUTH.
Tae Han. See KOREA.
Tae Han Min'guk. See KOREA, SOUTH.
Tae·jŏn \'ta-'jȯn\ *or Jp.* **Tai·den** \'tī-'den\. Special city (province) and ✻ of South Ch'ungch'ŏng prov., South Korea, on railroad line 70 mi. (113 km.) NW of Taegu; site of an international technology expo Aug.–Nov. 1994. See table at KOREA, SOUTH.
Taenarum. See TAÍNARON, ÁKRA.
Ta·en·ga \tä-'eŋ-gä\. Island, E cen. part of Tuamotu Archipelago, French Polynesia, S Pacific Ocean.
Ta·fa·hi \tä-'fä-hē\; *formerly* **Bos·caw·en** \bä-'skō-ən, -'skȯ-\. Island, N part of Tonga, SW cen. Pacific Ocean, ab. 125 mi. (200 km.) E of Niuafoo and 6 mi. (10 km.) from Niuatoputapu (*q.v.*); 7 sq. mi. (18 sq. km.).
Ta·fel Berg \'ta-fəl-ˌberg\. Hill, Curaçao I., Netherlands Antilles, West Indies; 636 ft. (194 m.).
Taff \'taf\. River, SE Wales; flows SE through Mid Glamorgan and South Glamorgan cos. into Bristol Channel at Cardiff; 40 mi. (64 km.) long.
Ta·fi·lalt \ˌta-fi-'lalt\ *also* **Ta·fi·lelt** \-'lelt\ *or* **Ta·fi·let** \-'let\ *or* **Ta·fi·la·let** \-'lä-lət\. Oasis, SE Morocco; ab. 533 sq. mi. (1380 sq. km.); dates.
Ta·fí Vie·jo \tä-'fē-'vyā-hō\. Town, Tucuman prov., N Argentina; pop. (1980p) 26,625.
Taf·na \'taf-nə\. Unnavigable river, NW Algeria, flowing N into Mediterranean Sea.
Taft \'taft\. **1.** City, Kern co., S California, 28 mi. (45 km.) SW of Bakersfield; pop. (1990c) 5902.
2. City, San Patricio co., S Texas, 15 mi. (24 km.) N of Corpus Christi; pop. (1990c) 3222.
Taf·tān, Kūh–e *or* **Kuh–i–Taf·tan** \ˌkü-hē-taf-'tän\. Volcano, SE Iran, 65 mi. (105 km.) SSE of Zāhedān; 13,261 ft. (4042 m.).
Ta·fua, Mount \tä-'fü-ä\. Peak, W Upolu I., Samoa, SW cen. Pacific; 2194 ft. (669 m.); of volcanic origin.
Ta·gāb \tə-'gäb\. Town, E Afghanistan, ab. 30 mi. (48 km.) NE of Kabul.
Ta·gan·rog \'tə-ˌgən-'rȯk\. City, SW Rostov Oblast, S Russia in Europe, on N shore of Gulf of Taganrog 45 mi. (72 km.) W of Rostov-na-Donu; pop. (1992e) 293,000; seaport, shipping grain; shipyards. Founded as naval base by Czar Peter the Great 1698; fought over by Russians and Turks during 18th cent.; annexed to Russia 1769 and further developed as naval base; in WWII occupied by Germans 1941–43. Birthplace of author Anton Chekhov 1860.
Taganrog, Gulf of *or Russ.* **Ta·gan·rog·skiy Za·liv** \tə-gən-'rȯk-skē-zə-'lēf\. NE arm of the Sea of Azov, S Russia in Europe and SE Ukraine; receives the Don River.
Tagaste. See SOUK-AHRAS.
Ta·gay·tay \tä-ˌgī-'tī\. Chartered city, S border of Cavite prov., Luzon, Philippines; pop. (1990p) 24,000; nearby is **Tagaytay Ridge,** a mountain range, highest point ab. 2000 ft. (610 m.), running E and W along N Batangas boundary NW of Lake Taal.
Tag·bi·la·ran \ˌtäg-bē-'lär-ˌän\. Chartered city, ✻ of Bohol prov., Philippines, in SW part on narrow strait opp. Panglao I.; pop. (1990p) 56,000; has shallow harbor.

Ta·gi·nae \tə-'jī-,nē\. Ancient village, cen. Italy, in the Apennines near modern Gubbio; Totila, Gothic king, defeated and killed here 552 by Byzantine Gen. Narses.

Tag·ish Lake \'ta-gish\. Lake, across boundary of S Yukon Terr. and N British Columbia, Canada, W of Atlin Lake; 130 sq. mi. (337 sq. km.); alt. 2152 ft. (656 m.); discharges into Lewes River.

Ta·glia·coz·zo \,tä-lyä-'kot-sō\. Commune, L'Aquila prov., Abruzzi, cen. Italy, 21 mi. (34 km.) SSW of commune of L'Aquila; pop. (1981p) 6339; Gothic church; 14th cent. castle; scene of battle 1268 in which German Prince Conradin was defeated by Charles of Anjou.

Ta·glia·men·to \,tä-lyä-'men-tō\. River, N Italy; flows S from the Carnic Alps into the head of the Gulf of Venice; 106 mi. (171 km.) long.

Ta·go \tä-'gō\. Municipality, Surigao del Sur prov., Mindanao, Philippines, ab 70 mi. (115 km.) SE of Surigao; pop. (1980c) 21,192.

Ta·go·lo Point \tä-'gō-lō\. N point of Zamboanga del Norte prov., Mindanao, Philippines, just NW of Dapitan; extends into W end of Mindanao Sea.

Ta·gu·din \,tä-gü-'dēn\. Municipality, Ilocos Sur prov., Luzon, Philippines, on coast highway 43 mi. (69 km.) S of Vigan and on N bank of Amburayan River; pop. (1980c) 23,432.

Ta·gu·la Island \'tä-gə-lə\ *also* **Ta·cu·ta Island** \tə-'kü-tə\; *formerly* **Sudest Island** \sü-'dest\. Island, S Louisiade Archipelago, Papua New Guinea, off SE point of New Guinea I., 50 mi. (80 km.) SE of Misima I.; ab. 50 mi. (80 km.) long and 15 mi. (24 km.) max. width; 310 sq. mi. (803 sq. km.); highest point 3000 ft. (914 m.).

Ta·gum \'tä-,güm\. Municipality, ✻ of Davao prov., Mindanao, Philippines, at head of Davao Gulf 27 mi. (43 km.) NE of City of Davao; pop. (1980c) 86,201.

Ta·gus \'tā-gəs\ *or Span.* **Ta·jo** \'tä-hō\ *or Port.* **Te·jo** \'tā-zhü\. River, Spain and Portugal; rises in E cen. Spain ab. 80 mi. (130 km.) E of Madrid, flows W across cen. Spain to Portuguese border; continues W forming a section (ab. 25 mi. or 40 km.) of Spain-Portugal boundary, then turns SW and empties into Atlantic Ocean at Lisbon; 626 mi. (1007 km.) long; longest river in Iberian Penin.; ab. 10 mi. (16 km.) above Lisbon expands into a lagoon ab. 7 mi. (11 km.) wide which narrows at Lisbon to a channel ab. 2 mi. (3 km.) wide and 8 mi. (13 km.) long; navigable ab. 100 mi. (160 km.).

Ta·haa \tä-'hä-,ä\ *also* **Ta·hao** \tä-'haù\. One of the Leeward Is., Society Is., French Polynesia, S Pacific Ocean, just N of Raiatéa; 34 sq. mi. (88 sq. km.); pop. (1988c) 4005.

Ta·han, Gu·nong \'gü-,nòŋ-'tä-,hän\. Mountain (*gunong*), N Pahang state on Kelantan boundary, Malaysia, S Malay Penin.; 7186 ft. (2190 m.); highest peak in the peninsula.

T'ah–ch'eng. See TACHENG.

Taheiho. See AIHUI.

Ta·hi·ti \tə-'hēt-ē\ *or Fr.* **Ta·ï·ti** \tà-ē-'tē\; *formerly* **Ota·hei·te** \,ō-tə-'hē-tē, -'hā-\. Island of E group (Windward Is.) of the Society Is., French Polynesia, S Pacific Ocean, 17°37′S, 149°27′W; 408 sq. mi. (1057 sq. km.); pop. (1988c) 131,309; ✻ Papeete; tourism. The largest and most important of the French islands of the S Pacific; the main part is nearly circular and very mountainous with several high peaks (highest Orohena, in the center, 7352 ft. or 2241 m.) and fertile but narrow coastal strip; to the SE connected by narrow isthmus with broad peninsula; all villages are on the coast. Political as well as commercial center of French Polynesia. Long inhabited by Polynesians; first European visitors, British 1767; French arrived 1768 and claimed the land; Polynesian rule fell into disarray 19th cent.; became a French colony 1880; during WWII in 1940 joined the Free French movement; late 20th cent. move for independence spurred by continued French testing of nuclear bombs in area.

Tahlab. See TALAB.

Tah·le·quah \'ta-lə-,kwò\. City, ⊗ of Cherokee co., E Oklahoma, 26 mi. (42 km.) ENE of Muskogee; pop. (1990c) 10,398; lumber; Northeastern State Univ. (1846). Became permanent ✻ of the Cherokee Nation 1839. Cherokee capitol; courthouse; museum.

Ta·hoe, Lake \'tä-hō\. Lake, W U.S., on N cen. California-Nevada boundary; 22 mi. (35 km.) long by 10 mi. (16 km.) wide; 192 sq. mi. (497 sq. km.); elev. 6229 ft. (1899 m.); greatest depth 1685 ft. (514 m.); outlet Truckee River; tourist resort.

Tahoelandang. See TAHULANDANG.

Tahoena. See TAHUNA.

Ta·ho·ka \tə-'hō-kə\. City, ⊗ of Lynn co., NW Texas, 32 mi. (51 km.) S of Lubbock; pop. (1990c) 2868.

Ta·houa \'taù-ä\. Town, SW Niger, ab. 225 mi. (362 km.) NE of Niamey; pop. (1988c) 49,948; airport.

Tahpanhes. See DAPHNAE.

Ta–hsing–an Ling. See DA HINGGAN LING.

Tah·tā \'tä-,ta, -,tä\. Town, Asyût governorate, Egypt, on the Nile SSE of the city of Asyût.

Ta·hua \'tä-wä\. Peak, W Bolivia, S of Lake Poopó; 17,547 ft. (5348 m.).

Ta·hua·ta *also* **Ta·ua·ta** \tä-'wä-tä\. One of the Marquesas Is., French Polynesia, S Pacific Ocean, ab. 3 mi. (5 km.) S of Hiva Oa; pop. (1988c) 633.

Ta·hu·lan·dang *or* **Ta·hoe·lan·dang** \,tä-hü-'län-,däŋ\. One of the main islands of the Sangihe Is. (*q.v.*), Indonesia.

Ta·hu·na *or* **Ta·hoe·na** \tä-'hü-nä\. Chief town, Sangihe I., Indonesia (see SANGIHE ISLANDS).

Tahura. See KAULA.

Ta·hure \tä-'ür\. Site of former village in Marne dept., NE France, 30 mi. (48 km.) ESE of Reims; devastated during WWI fighting.

Tai·'an *or* **T'ai–an** *or* **Tai·an** \'tī-'än\. Town, W cen. Shandong prov., NE China, on railroad line 37 mi. (60 km.) S of Jinan; noted as a starting point of ascent of sacred mountain Tai Shan; a very old place, dating back to at least first millennium B.C.; temple begun 3d cent. B.C.; pagodas.

T'ai–chou *or* **Tai·chow.** See TAIZHOU.

T'ai–chung *or* **Tai·chung** \'tī-'chùŋ\ *or Jp.* **Tai·chu** \'tī-,chü\; *formerly* **Tai·wan** \'tī-'wän\. City, W cen. Taiwan, on railroad line along W coast; pop. (1992e) 779,370.

Taiden. See TAEJŎN.

Tai·e·ri \'tī-ə-rē\. River, SE South I., New Zealand; flows SE into Pacific Ocean near Dunedin; 179 mi. (288 km.) long.

Ta·if \'tä-if\ *or* **Aṭ Ṭā·'if** \,ät-'tä-if\. Town, W Saudi Arabia, ab. 40 mi. (65 km.) ESE of Mecca; in mountains at over 5000 ft. (1520 m.) alt.; resort town and unofficial summer ✻ of Saudi Arabia; produces great variety of fruit. Important town in time of Muḥammad; resisted him 630 but finally capitulated; taken by Arabs from the Turks 1916 and captured by Muslim leader Ibn Sa'ūd 1924 on his way to founding Saudi Arabia; treaty signed 1934 establishing boundary bet. Saudi Arabia and Yemen.

Tai·hang Shan *or* **T'ai–hang Shan** \'tī-'häŋ-'shän\. Mountain range on boundary bet. Hebei and Shanxi and bet. Henan and Shanxi, NE China, N of the Huang.

Taihoku. See TAIPEI.

Taih·pa Ga \,tī-pə-'gä\. Village, N Myanmar, on the Chindwin River; involved in WWII fighting.

Tai Hu *or* **T'ai Hu** \'tī-'hü\. Lake, Jiangsu and Zhejiang provs., E China; 44 mi. (71 km.) long; Huangpu is one of its outlets; large city of Suzhou is near its E shore.

Taikyu. See TAEGU.

Taima. See TAYMĀ'.

Taimyr Autonomous Okrug. See TAYMYR AUTONOMOUS OKRUG.

Taimyr Peninsula. See TAYMYR PENINSULA.

T'ai–nan \'tī-'nän\; *formerly* **Dai·nan** \'dī-'nän\. City, SW coast of Taiwan; pop. (1994e) 702,237; agriculture, food processing; textiles, rubber products, plastics, aluminum, iron products, electrical appliances; salt; university (1956). One of the oldest and largest cities on Taiwan; from mid-17th cent. to late 19th cent. the ✻ and cultural center of the island.

Taí·na·ron, Ákra \'ä-krä-'te-nä-,rön\ *or* **Cape Mat·a·pan** \,ma-tə-'pan\; *anc.* **Tae·na·rum** \'tē-nə-,rəm\. Southernmost point of mainland of Greece, 36°22′N, 22°30′E, at tip of cen. peninsula of Peloponnese. WWII naval battle nearby 1941 in which British under Adm. Andrew Cunningham prevailed over several Italian ships.

Tai·o·hae *or* **Tai–o–hae** \ˌtī-ō-ˈhī\ *also* **Ha·ka·pe·hi** \ˌhä-kä-ˈpä-hē\. Town, ✱ of the Marquesas Is., on S shore of Nuku Hiva I., French Polynesia, S Pacific Ocean; huge prehistoric stone platforms of unknown origin nearby.

Tai·pa \ˈtī-pä\. See MACAO 1.

Tai·pei *or* **T'ai–pei** \ˈtī-ˈpā, -ˈbā\; *formerly* **Tai·ho·ku** \ˈtī-ˈhō-ˈkü\ *or* **Dai·ho·ku** \ˈdī-ˈhō-ˈkü\. City, ✱ of Taiwan, at N end of the island; pop. (1994e) 2,651,419; commercial, financial, industrial, and transportation center of Taiwan; produces textiles, rubber goods, electronics, machinery; National Taiwan Univ. (1928) and several other educational institutions. Founded 1708 and became important center of tea trade mid-19th cent.; under Japanese rule (1895–1945) administrative ✱ of the island; became seat of Chinese Nationalist government 1949.

Tai Peng Wan. See DAPENG WAN.

Tai·ping \ˈtī-ˈpiŋ, -ˈbiŋ\. City, Perak state, Malaysia, in NW part on railroad line 50 mi. (80 km.) SE of George Town; pop. (1980c) 146,002.

Tai Po \ˈtī-ˈpō\. Town, New Territories, Hong Kong, at head of inlet of Dapeng Wan on railroad line to Guangzhou.

Taira. See IWAKI 2.

Tai Shan *or W.-G.* **T'ai Shan** \ˈtī-ˈshän\. Mountain, Shandong prov., China, 32 mi. (51 km.) S of Jinan; 5048 ft. (1539 m.); many temples on the mountain road and on the top; has been considered as sacred for several thousand years; formerly an important place of pilgrimage, still visited by many.

Tai·tao, Cape \tī-ˈtau̇\. Cape, SW Chile, extending into Pacific Ocean on NW tip of Taitao Penin.

Taitao Peninsula. Peninsula, SW Chile, extending into Pacific Ocean, S of Chonos Archipelago and N of the Gulf of Penas.

Taïti. See TAHITI.

T'ai–tung \ˈtī-ˈdu̇ŋ\; *formerly* **Tai·to** \ˈtī-tō\. Coastal town, SE Taiwan.

Tai·vu Point \ˈtī-vü\. Cape, NE coast of Guadalcanal I., in the Solomon Is. in the W Pacific Ocean; ab. 40 mi. (64 km.) E of Cape Esperance.

Tai·wan \ˈtī-ˈwän\. **1.** *also* **For·mo·sa** \fȯr-ˈmō-sə, fər-, -zə\. Island, seat of Chinese Nationalist government, off Fujian prov., SE China; 13,807 sq. mi. (35,760 sq. km.), incl. its outlying islands 13,887 sq. mi. (35,967 sq. km.); total pop. (1993e) 20,926,000; ✱ Taipei.

Physical features: Has lofty mountain range extending through E cen. part, highest peaks Yü Shan 13,113 ft. (3997 m.), and Tz'u-kao 12,743 ft. (3884 m.); no long rivers; its S point, O-luan, on Bashi Channel, which separates it from Batan Is. of the Philippines; minor dependencies include P'eng-hu (*q.v.*).

Chief products: Rice, sugarcane, tea, citrus fruit, soybeans, sweet potatoes, bananas, pineapples; fishing; salt, sulfur, coal; manufacturing: textiles, chemicals, plastics, cement, electronics, steel.

Chief cities: Taipei, Kao-hsiung, T'ai-chung, T'ai-nan, Pan-ch'iao.

History: Known to Chinese since 7th cent. A.D.; visited by Portuguese 1590 who named it *Ilha Formosa* "beautiful island"; widely settled by Chinese early 17th cent.; forts estab. 1624 by Dutch who were driven out by Chinese invaders from Ming dynasty 1661–62; fell to Manchus 1683; not open to Europeans again until two ports opened 1858 by Treaties of Tientsin; ceded to Japan 1895 after Chinese-Japanese War; in WWII made a military center by the Japanese; frequently bombed by U.S. planes; after defeat of Japan returned to China; became seat of Chinese Nationalist government 1949; concluded mutual security pact with U.S. 1955; replaced in the UN by People's Republic of China 1971; U.S. opened talks with mainland China shortly thereafter; ties maintained with U.S. through Special Relations Act passed by U.S. Congress 1979; lifted martial law 1987; lifted travel restrictions with mainland China 1988; legalized opposition parties 1989.

2. City, Taiwan. See T'AI-CHUNG.

Taiwan Strait *or* **For·mo·sa Strait** \fȯr-ˈmō-sə, fər-, -zə\. Channel bet. Fujian prov., SE China, and Taiwan; connects East China Sea with South China Sea; ab. 115 mi. (185 km.) wide.

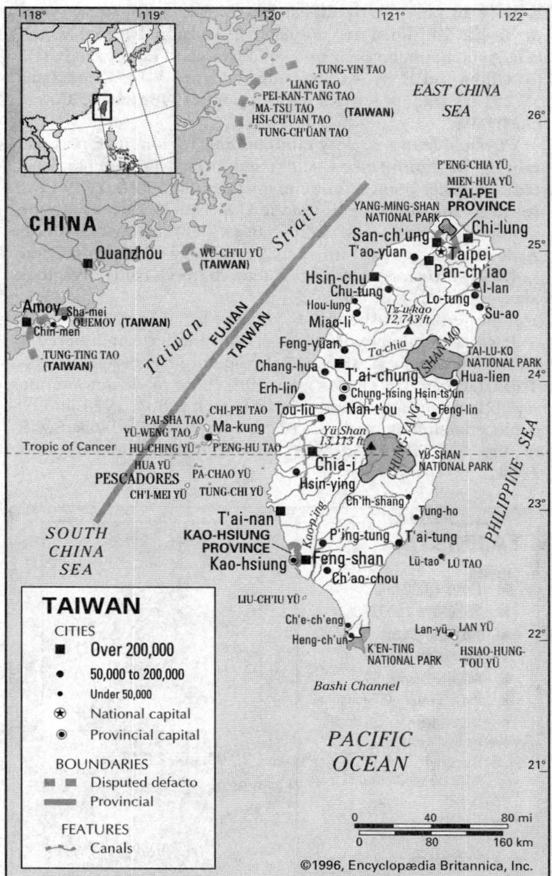

Tai·ya Inlet \ˈtī-yə\. Upper arm, Chilkoot Inlet, SE Alaska; ab. 15 mi. (24 km.) long. See LYNN CANAL.

Taí·ye·tos \ˈtī-ye-ˌtös\ *or* **Ta·yg·e·tus** \tā-ˈi-jə-təs\. Mountain range, S Peloponnese, Greece, forming border bet. Laconia and Messenia depts. and extending S in W Laconia along coast of Gulf of Messenia; highest point 7904 ft. (2409 m.).

Tai·yuan *or W.-G.* **T'ai–yüan** \ˈtī-ˈywän\; *formerly* **Yang·ku** \ˈyaŋ-ˈkü\. City, ✱ of Shanxi prov., NE China, in center of province on the Fen 265 mi. (426 km.) SW of Beijing; pop. (1990c) 1,533,884; alt. 2600 ft. (792 m.); railroad terminus; cement, steel; coal mines. Several notable ancient temples; historical museum; Shanxi Univ. Known since time of Chou dynasty (3d cent. B.C.); a strategic center and administrative ✱ of province in time of Mongols (12th–14th cents.); scene of massacre 1900 of foreign missionaries in Boxer Rebellion; one of first areas to rise up against emperor 1911; besieged by Communist forces 1948–49.

Tai·zhou *or W.-G.* **T'ai–chou** \ˈtī-ˈjō\ *also* **Tai·chow** \ˈtī-ˈchau̇\. Town, Jiangsu prov., E China, ab. 80 mi. (130 km.) ENE of Nanjing; pop. (1990c) 152,442.

Ta·'izz *also* **Ta·iz** \tä-ˈēz\. Town in highlands of SW Yemen, SW Arabian Penin., 32 mi. (51 km.) E of Mocha; pop. (1986c) 178,430; government offices; several mosques.

Ta·jik·i·stan *also* **Ta·dzhik·i·stan** \tä-ˌji-ki-ˈstan, -ˌjē-, -ˈstän\ *or* **Ta·jik To·jik·i·ston** \tä-ˈjik-tō-ˌji-ki-ˈstȯn\. Republic, SW cen. Asia, bounded on N by Uzbekistan and Kyrgyzstan, on E by China, on S by Afghanistan, and on W by Uzbekistan; 55,251 sq. mi. (143,100 sq. km.); pop. (1993e) 5,705,000; ✱ Dushanbe.

Physical features: Very mountainous region, its E part containing the Pamirs (see PAMIRS) and Trans Alai mountain systems; highest point Communism Peak 24,590 ft. (7495 m.); formerly the highest point in the U.S.S.R.; W part also mountainous, marked by several valleys of N tributaries of the Amu Dar'ya, which forms the S boundary with Afghanistan.

Chief products: Cotton, wheat, barley, fruit; livestock; lead, zinc, oil, gas, coal.

Chief cities: Dushanbe, Khudzhand.

History: Settled by Persians c. 6th cent. B.C.; conquered by Uzbek invaders c. 15th cent. A.D.; acquired as part of Russian Turkistan (see TURKESTAN) late 19th cent.; made autonomous republic under administration of Uzbek S.S.R. 1924 and became constituent republic 1929; comprised Tadzhik S.S.R. of the U.S.S.R. 1929–91; became independent republic 1991.

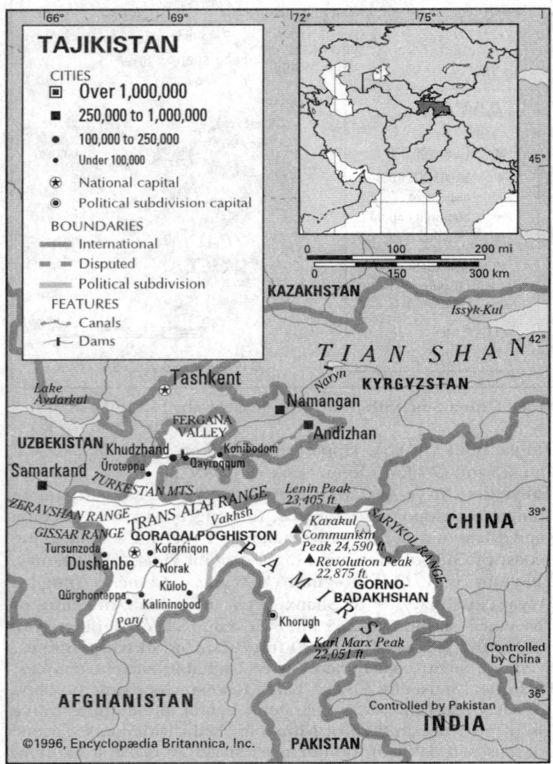

Ta·ji·mi \tä-ˈjē-mē\. City, Gifu prefecture, Honshū, Japan, 17 mi. (27 km.) NE of Nagoya; pop. (1990p) 94,036.

Tajo. See TAGUS.

Ta·ju·mul·co, Volcan \ˌtä-hü-ˈmül-kō\. Volcanic mountain, W Guatemala; 13,845 ft. (4220 m.); highest point in Central America.

Ta·ju·ña \tä-ˈhü-nyä\. River, cen. Spain; flows SW through Guadalajara prov. and on into Jarama River ab. 7 mi. (11 km.) NE of Aranjuez; ab. 150 mi. (241 km.) long.

Tā·jū·rā' \tä-ˈjü-ˌrä\. Seaport oasis, NW Libya, E of Tripoli.

Tajura. See TADJOURA.

Tajura, Gulf of. See TADJOURA, GULF OF.

Tak \ˈtäk\ *also* **Ra·haeng** \ˈrä-ˈhaŋ\. **1.** Province, W Thailand; 6027 sq. mi. (15,610 sq. km.); pop. (1991e) 358,474; ✱ Tak.

2. Town, its ✱, on left bank of Ping River 40 mi. (64 km.) from Myanmar border and 70 mi. (113 km.) W of Phitsanulok; pop. (1991e) 19,804.

Ta·ka·chi·ho·da·ke \tä-ˌkä-chē-hō-ˈdä-kä\. See KIRISHIMA.

Ta·ka·ma·tsu \ˌtä-kä-ˈmät-sü\. City, ✱ of Kagawa prefecture, NE Shikoku I., Japan; pop. (1990p) 329,695; a major seaport on the Inland Sea; pulp, paper, cotton goods; notable public gardens.

Takao. See KAO-HSIUNG.

Ta·ka·o·ka \tä-ˈkaù-kä\. City, Toyama prefecture, Honshū, Japan, 15 mi. (24 km.) W of the city of Toyama; pop. (1990p) 175,469; aluminum.

Ta·ka·pu·na \ˌtä-kə-ˈpü-nə\. City, N North I., New Zealand, N suburb of Auckland; pop. (1981c) 64,844.

Ta·ka·ra·zu·ka \tä-ˌkä-rä-ˈzü-kä\. City, Hyōgo prefecture, Honshū, Japan, ab. 13 mi. (21 km.) NW of Ōsaka; pop. (1990p) 201,863.

Ta·ka·sa·go \ˌtä-kä-ˈsä-gō, tä-ˈkä-sä-ˌgō\. City, Hyōgo prefecture, Honshū, Japan, 24 mi. (39 km.) WNW of Kōbe; pop. (1990p) 93,267.

Ta·ka·sa·ki \ˌtä-kä-ˈsä-kē\. City, Gumma prefecture, cen. Honshū, Japan, 10 mi. (16 km.) SW of Maebashi; pop. (1990p) 236,463; silk.

Ta·kat·su·ki \tä-ˈkät-skē\. City, Ōsaka prefecture, Honshū, Japan, ab. 13 mi. (21 km.) NNE of the city of Ōsaka; pop. (1990p) 359,867.

Ta·kaw \tə-ˈkȯ\. Town, Shan State, Myanmar, on right bank of the Salween.

Takht–i–Su·lai·man \ˌtäkt-ē-ˌsù-lī-ˈmän\. **1.** Twin peaks at N end of the Sulaiman Range, Pakistan; the higher peak, sometimes known as **Kai·sar·garh** \ˈkī-zər-ˌgär, -sər-\ 11,289 ft. (3441 m.).

2. Legendary rock, Kyrgyzstan. See OSH.

Tak·ka·kaw \ˈta-kə-ˌkȯ\. Waterfall, Yoho National Park, SE British Columbia, Canada; total drop 1650 ft. (503 m.), with highest single fall 1200 ft. (366 m.); source is glacier in Rocky Mts.; its waters flow into Yoho River; highest waterfall in Canada.

Takkaze. See TEKEZE.

Ta·kli·ma·kan *or* **Ta·kla Ma·kan** \ˌtä-klə-mə-ˈkän\ *or W.-G.* **T'a–k'o–la–ma–kan Shan–mo** \ˈtä-ˈkō-ˈlä-ˈmä-ˈkän-ˈshän-ˈmō\. Desert, forming greater part of Tarim basin, cen. Xinjiang Uygur, W China, bet. Tian Shan on N and Kunlun Shan on S; ab. 38° to 41°N and 78° to 88°E; ab. 600 mi. (965 km.) across, ab. 125,000 sq. mi. (323,750 sq. km.); desert marked by shifting sand dunes.

Ta·ko·ma Park \tə-ˈkō-mə\. City, Montgomery and Prince Georges cos., cen. Maryland, just N of Washington, D.C.; pop. (1990c) 16,700; Columbia Union Coll. (1904).

Ta·ko·ra·di \ˌtä-kō-ˈrä-dē\. Seaport, SW Ghana; part of the joint municipality Sekondi-Takoradi (*q.v.*).

Takow. See KAO-HSIUNG.

Ta–ku *or* **Ta·ku.** See DAGU.

Ta·ku Glacier \ˈtä-kü\. Glacier in Coast Mountains, on Alaska-British Columbia border; 33 mi. (53 km.) long, 3 mi. (5 km.) wide near its terminus.

Ta·ku·tea \ˌtä-kü-ˈtā-ä\. One of the Cook Is. in S Pacific Ocean, NE of Rarotonga.

Takutu. See TACUTU.

Ta·lab *or* **Tah·lab** \tə-ˈläb\. River, SE Iran; rises near Zāhedān and flows SE to the border, then along the Iran-Pakistan boundary to Hammun-i-Mashkel; ab. 175 mi. (282 km.) long.

Talabriga. 1. Seaport, Portugal. See AVEIRO 3.

2. Commune, Spain. See TALAVERA DE LA REINA.

Ta·la·kag \tä-ˈlä-ˌkäg\. Municipality, Mindanao, Philippines; pop. (1980c) 25,055.

Ta·lak·mau, Mount \tə-ˈläk-ˌmaù\; *formerly* **Mount Ophir** \ˈō-fər\. Peak in Barisan Mts., W Sumatra, Indonesia, NW of Bukittinggi; 9554 ft. (2912 m.).

Talamanca, Cordillera de. See CORDILLERA DE TALAMANCA.

Ta·la·na Hill \tə-ˈlä-nə\. See DUNDEE 3.

Ta·lang \ˈtä-ˌläŋ\. Volcanic peak in Barisan Mts., W Sumatra, Indonesia; 8517 ft. (2596 m.).

Ta·la·ra \tä-ˈlä-rä\. Seaport, NW Peru, ab. 40 mi. (64 km.) N of Paita and 610 mi. (981 km.) NW of Lima; pop. (1990e) 89,500; oil refinery; export center for petroleum industry.

Ta·la·sea \ˌtä-lä-ˈsā-ä\. Settlement, E side of Willaumez Penin. on N coast of New Britain, Bismarck Archipelago, Papua New Guinea, W Pacific Ocean; active trade in copra.

Talat. See MAHA SARAKHAM.

Ta·la·ta·koh \tə-ˌlä-tə-ˈkō\. See PENJU ISLANDS.

Ta·laud Islands \tə-ˈlau̇d\ *or* **Ta·laur Islands** \tə-ˈlau̇r\. Island group, Indonesia, NE of Sulawesi and SE of the island of Mindanao, Philippines; 494 sq. mi. (1279 sq. km.); chief town Beo. Comprises the main large island of Karakelong, two small islands S of it (Salebabu and Kaburuang), and the group of islets to the NE, Nanusa Is.; produces copra. First came under Dutch 17th cent.

Ta·la·ve·ra \ˌtä-lä-ˈvā-rä\. Municipality, cen. Luzon, Philippines, 8 mi. (13 km.) N of Cabanatuan; pop. (1980c) 62,225.

Talavera de la Rei·na \ˌthä-lä-ˈrā-nä\; *anc.* **Tal·a·bri·ga** \ˌta-lə-ˈbrī-gə\. Commune, Toledo prov., cen. Spain, on Tagus River 41 mi. (66 km.) WNW of Toledo; pop. (1991c) 68,700; tobacco; town walls with 18 medieval towers. Founded by Romans; conquered from Moors by King Alfonso VI of Castile late 11th cent.; important center of woolen industry 16th–18th cents.; in 1809 scene of notable victory in Peninsular War of British and Spanish forces under Gen. Arthur Wellesley and Capt. Gen. Gregario García de la Cuesta over French under Joseph Bonaparte, brother of Emperor Napoléon.

Tal·bot \ˈtȯl-bət, ˈtal-\. Name of counties in two states of the U.S. See tables at GEORGIA and MARYLAND.

Talbot, Cape. Point, N coast of Western Australia, Australia, W of Cape Londonderry; 13°48′S, 126°43′E.

Tal·bot·ton \ˈtȯl-bət-ᵊn\. City, ⊗ of Talbot co., W Georgia; pop. (1990c) 1046; agriculture.

Tal·ca \ˈtäl-kä\. City, ✱ of Maule region, cen. Chile 155 mi. (249 km.) S of Santiago on the Claro River; pop. (1982c) 128,544.

Tal·ca·hua·no \ˌtäl-kä-ˈwä-nō\. Seaport, Bío-Bío region, S cen. Chile, 9 mi. (14 km.) NW of Concepción; pop. (1982c) 202,368; good anchorage; naval base.

Tal·dy–Kur·gan \ˈtal-dē-ku̇r-ˈgän\. **1.** Subdivision of Kazakhstan; 45,753 sq. mi. (118,500 sq. km.); pop. (1991e) 731,000; ✱ Taldy-Kurgan. Lies bet. Semey on N and Alma Ata on S and borders on E on Xinjiang Uygur, China; an oblast of the U.S.S.R. before 1991.

2. *or* **Tal·dy·qor·ghan** \ˌtal-dē-ku̇r-ˈgän\. Town, its ✱, SE of Lake Balkhash and ab. 140 mi. (225 km.) NE of Alma Ata; pop. (1991e) 136,100.

Ta·lence \tȧ-ˈläⁿs\. Commune, Gironde dept., SW France, SW suburb of Bordeaux; pop. (1990c) 36,172; produces wine.

Tal·ent \ˈta-lənt\. City, Jackson co., SW Oregon, SE of Medford; pop. (1990c) 3274.

Ta–li. See DALI.

Ta·li·a·bu *or Du.* **Ta·li·a·boe** \ˌtä-lē-ˈä-bü\. Island, largest of the Sula Is., W Moluccas, Indonesia, E of Sulawesi; ab. 68 mi. (109 km.) long by 26 mi. (42 km.) at its greatest width; highest point 3796 ft. (1157 m.).

Tal·ia·ferro \ˈtä-lə-vər—*sic*\. County in NE cen. Georgia. See table at GEORGIA.

Ta·li·bon \ˌtä-lē-ˈbōn\. Municipality, Bohol prov., N coast of Bohol I., Philippines, 48 mi. (77 km.) NE of Tagbilaran; pop. (1980c) 46,110.

Ta–lien. See DALIAN.

Ta·li·ko·ta \ˌtä-lē-ˈkō-tə\ *or* **Ta·li·kot** \ˈtä-lē-ˌkōt\. Town, N Karnataka, W India; scene in 1565 of major battle in which Muslim chieftains of the Deccan united in overthrowing the Hindu kingdom of Vijayanagar.

Ta·lim Island \tä-ˈlēm\. Island in N cen. Laguna de Bay, cen. Luzon, Philippines; 10 mi. (16 km.) long, ab. 11 sq. mi. (28 sq. km.); its S point is **Talim Point,** 14°07′N, 121°14′E.

T'a–li–mu. See TARIM.

Talin. See TALLINN.

Ta·li·qan \ˌtä-li-ˈkän\ *or* **Tā·lo·qān** \ˌtä-lō-ˈkän\. Town, NE Afghanistan; pop. (1982e) 20,947.

Ta·li·say \tä-ˈlē-ˌsī\. **1.** Municipality, E coast of Cebu I., Philippines, at N end of Bohol Strait 6 mi. (10 km.) SW of City of Cebu; pop. (1980c) 69,720.

2. Municipality, NW Negros I., Philippines, on Guimaras Strait 5 mi. (8 km.) N of City of Bacolod; pop. (1980c) 53,624.

Tal·keet·na \tal-ˈkēt-nə\. Unincorporated settlement, S cen. Alaska, bet. Anchorage to the SSE and Mt. McKinley to the NW; pop. (1990c) 250; base for outdoor recreation.

Tal·la·de·ga \ˌta-lə-ˈdē-gə\. **1.** County in E cen. Alabama. See table at ALABAMA.

2. City, its ⊗, 55 mi. (88 km.) E of Birmingham; pop. (1990c) 18,175; agricultural region; marble and limestone deposits; Talladega Coll. (1867); incorp. 1835. Scene of battle 1813, in which Gen. Andrew Jackson defeated Creek Indians.

Tal·la·has·see \ˌta-lə-ˈha-sē\. City, ✱ of Florida and ⊗ of Leon co., N Florida, 25 mi. (40 km.) N of Apalachee Bay; pop. (1990c) 124,773; lumber; Florida State Univ. (1857), Florida Agricultural and Mechanical Univ. (1887), Tallahassee Community Coll. (1965). Settlement of Appalachee Indians when visited by Spanish explorer Hernando de Soto 1539; made ✱ of territory of Florida 1823; incorp. 1825; state ✱ 1845; scene of adoption of secession resolution 1861.

Tal·la·hatch·ie \ˌta-lə-ˈha-chē\. **1.** River, N Mississippi; rises in Tippah co., flows SW to unite with Yalobusha River in Leflore co. and form the Yazoo River; 230 mi. (370 km.) long; navigable for ab. 100 mi. (160 km.).

2. County in NW Mississippi. See table at MISSISSIPPI.

Tall al–Dafana. See DAPHNAE.

Tal·la·poo·sa \ˌta-lə-ˈpü-sə\. **1.** Navigable river, Alabama; rises in Paulding co., NW Georgia, flows SW across Alabama border E of Heflin, S and then W to join the Coosa River in cen. Alabama and form the Alabama River; 268 mi. (431 km.) long.

2. County in E Alabama. See table at ALABAMA.

3. City, Haralson co., W Georgia, 35 mi. (56 km.) S of Rome; pop. (1990c) 2805.

Tal·las·see \ˈta-lə-ˌsē\. City, Elmore and Tallapoosa cos., E cen. Alabama; pop. (1990c) 5112.

Tal·linn \ˈta-lən, ˈtä-\ *or Russ.* **Tal·lin** \ˈtȧ-lyin\; *formerly* **Re·vel** \ˈrā-vəl\ *or Ger.* **Re·val** \ˈrā-ˌväl\. Seaport city, ✱ of Estonia, on the Gulf of Finland opp. Helsinki, Finland, and ab. 200 mi. (322 km.) W of St. Petersburg, Russia; pop. (1989p) 482,000; extensive port facilities; industrial center, producing electrical equipment, textiles; large shipyards; naval and military installations; medieval city wall; remains of 13th cent. citadel; several churches; institutions of higher learning; museums.

History: Ancient fort settlement captured and rebuilt by Danish King Valdemar II 1219; developed as trading port and member of Hanseatic League 13th cent.; sold to Teutonic Knights 1346; on dissolution of order passed to Sweden 1561; taken by Russians 1710; ✱ of Estonia 1918–40 and of annexed Estonian S.S.R. 1940–91; in WWII occupied by Germans 1941–44 and suffered heavy damage, substantially repaired since 1945; ✱ of independent republic of Estonia since 1991.

Tall Ka·lakh \ˈtal-ka-ˈla͟k\ *or* **Tel·ka·lakh** \ˈtel-\. Town, S Latakia, Syria, on Lebanon border and on railroad line from Tripoli to Homs.

Tall·madge \ˈtal-mij\. City, Summit co., NE Ohio, 4 mi. (6 km.) E of Akron; pop. (1990c) 14,870.

Tal·lu·lah \tə-ˈlü-lə\. **1.** River, Georgia. See BURTON, LAKE.

2. City, ⊗ of Madison parish, NE Louisiana, 57 mi. (92 km.) E of Monroe; pop. (1990c) 8526.

Ta·lo·ga \tə-ˈlō-gə\. Town, ⊗ of Dewey co., W Oklahoma; pop. (1990c) 415.

\ə\ **abut** \ᵊ\ **kitten**, Fr table \ər\ **further** \a\ **ash** \ā\ **ace** \ä\ **cot, cart** \ȧ\ Fr **bac** \au̇\ **out** \b̲\ Span Avila \ch\ **chin** \e\ **bet** \ē\ **easy** \g\ **go** \i\ **hit** \ī\ **ice** \j\ **job** \k̲\ Ger **ich, Buch** \ⁿ\ Fr **vin** \ŋ\ **sing** \ō\ **go** \ȯ\ **all** \ȯ\ **law** \œ\ Fr **bœuf** \œ̄\ Fr **feu** \ȯi\ **boy** \th\ **thin** \t͟h\ **this** \ü\ **loot** \u̇\ **foot** \ue\ Ger **füllen** \ue̅\ Fr **rue** \y\ **yet** \ʸ\ Fr **digne** \ˈdēnʸ\, **nuit** \ˈnwʸē\ \yü\ **few** \yu̇\ **fury** \zh\ **vision**

Tāloqān. See TALIQAN.
Tal·tal \täl-'täl\. Seaport, Antofagasta region, N Chile.
Ta·lu·ti Bay *also* **Te·loe·ti Bay** \tə-'lü-tē\. Inlet of Banda Sea, S coast of Ceram I., Indonesia.
Ta·ma \'tā-mə\. **1.** County in E cen. Iowa. See table at IOWA.
2. City, Tama co., E cen. Iowa; pop. (1990c) 2697.
Ta·ma \'tä-mä\. **1.** Peak, N Colombia, 20 mi. (32 km.) ESE of Cúcuta; 13,126 ft. (4001 m.).
2. City, Tokyo prefecture, SE cen. Honshū, Japan; pop. (1990p) 144,490.
Ta·ma·le \tä-'mä-lā\. Town, ✻ of Northern Region, N Ghana, in plain E of the Volta, ab. 270 mi. (434 km.) N of Accra; pop. (1984c) 135,952; road junction and trade and educational center; ships agricultural products.
Tam·al·pa·is, Mount \ˌta-məl-'pī-əs\. Peak, Marin co., W California, NW of San Francisco and overlooking the Pacific Ocean and San Francisco Bay; 2572 ft. (784 m.); scenic resort area.
Ta·man \tə-'män\ *or Russ.* **Ta·man'** \tə-'mänʸ\ *or* **Ta·man·skiy** \-skē\. Peninsula E side of Kerch Strait, W Krasnodar Kray, S Russia in Europe; ab. 25 mi. (40 km.) long; oil field.
Ta·man Ne·ga·ra National Park \'tä-män-ne-'gä-rä\. National park, Malaysia; rain forest; varied wildlife; estab. 1938.
Ta·ma·no \tä-'mä-nō\. City, Okayama prefecture, Honshū, Japan, on coast of Inland Sea; pop. (1990p) 73,240.
Tam·an·ras·set \ˌta-mən-'ra-sət\. Town, S Algeria, N of the Adrar des Iforas; pop. (1987p) 38,146.
Ta·man·skiy. See TAMAN.
Ta·ma·qua \tə-'mä-kwə\. Borough, Schuylkill co., E cen. Pennsylvania, 15 mi. (24 km.) ENE of Pottsville; pop. (1990c) 7943.
Ta·mar \'tā-mər\. **1.** River, SW England; rises in NW Devon, flows SSE, forming boundary bet. Devon and Cornwall, empties into the English Channel through Plymouth Sound; 60 mi. (97 km.) long.
2. Navigable river, N Tasmania, Australia; formed by confluence at Launceston of the North Esk and South Esk rivers; flows N to Bass Strait; ab. 40 mi. (65 km.) long.
Ta·ma·ra \tə-'mär-ə\. Largest island of the Los Is. (*q.v.*), Guinea.
Tam·a·rac \'ta-mə-ˌrak\. City, Broward co., SE Florida; pop. (1990c) 44,822.
Tamarida. See TAMRIDAH.
Tamatave. See TOAMASINA.
Ta·mau·li·pas \ˌtä-ˌmau̇-'lē-päs\. State of E Mexico. See table at MEXICO.
Ta·ma·zun·cha·le \ˌtä-mä-sün-'chä-lā\. Municipality, San Luis Potosí state, Mexico, 150 mi. (241 km.) SE of the city of San Luis Potosí; pop. (1990p) 100,222.
Tam·ba·coun·da \ˌtäm-bä-'kün-dä\. Town, E cen. Senegal, on railroad line bet. Dakar and Mali; pop. (1994e) 53,401.
Tam·be·lan Islands \ˌtäm-bə-'län\. Group of 17 small islands, Indonesia, in the South China Sea bet. the S tip of Malay Penin. and W coast of Borneo; administratively a part of Riau prov.
Tam·bo \'täm-bō\. **1.** River, S Peru; flows SW into Pacific Ocean SE of Mollendo; ab. 150 mi. (240 km.) long.
2. River, Peru. See APURÍMAC 1.
Tam·bo·pa·ta \ˌtäm-bō-'pä-tä\. River, SE Peru; flows N into the Madre de Dios at Puerto Maldonado; 160 mi. (257 km.) long.
Tam·bo·ra, Gu·nung \'gü-ˌnu̇ŋ-'täm-bə-rə\. Volcano, N coast of Sumbawa, Indonesia; 9350 ft. (2850 m.); had disastrous eruption in 1815 when it lost much of its top; was formerly ab. 13,000 ft. (3960 m.) high.
Tam·bov \tȧm-'bóf, -'bóv\. City, ✻ of Tambov Oblast, S cen. Russia in Europe, on unnavigable Tsna River 260 mi. (418 km.) SE of Moscow; pop. (1992e) 311,000; railroad junction; flour mills, distilleries; chemicals. Founded 1636 as fort to defend Moscow against Crimean raiders; became ✻ of province late 18th cent.
Tambov Oblast \'ó-bləst, -ˌblast\ *or* **Tam·bov·ska·ya Oblast'** \tȧm-'bóf-skə-yə-'ó-bləstʸ\. Subdivision of S cen. Russia in Europe; 13,243 sq. mi. (34,299 sq. km.); pop. (1992e) 1,310,000; ✻ Tambov. A level black-earth region, with hills 400 to 800 ft. (122 to 244 m.) and valleys of the upper Tsna (unnavigable tributary of the Moksha) and in the S of the upper courses of Don tributaries. Economy principally agricultural: grain, sunflowers, potatoes; livestock. Chief towns: Tambov, Michurinsk, Morshansk. Part of Moscow principality from medieval period, but conflicts with Tatars limited colonization until Russian authority was consolidated in late 17th cent.; scene of fighting and famine 1917–20 during Russian Civil War.
Tame \'tām\. **1.** Small river, cen. England, flows past the city of Birmingham into the Trent in Staffordshire.
2. River, Greater Manchester co., NW England; flows SW to the Mersey at Stockport; 18 mi. (29 km.) long.
Tamed. See TAMET.
Tamesis *or* **Tamesa.** See THAMES 3.
Ta·met \'tä-mit\ *or* **Ta·med** \'tä-mid\ *or* **Thā·mit** \'tä-mit\. Short river in W Libya; flows N into Gulf of Sidra.
Ta·mia·hua, Laguna de \tä-'myä-wä\. Coastal lagoon, N Veracruz state, Mexico; ab. 60 mi. (95 km.) long; at S end has outlet to Gulf of Mexico.
Ta·mil Na·du \'ta-məl-'nä-dü\; *formerly* **Ma·dras** \mə-'dras, -'dräs\. State, SE India, on Coromandel Coast; ✻ Madras; formerly comprised a much larger area extending as far N as Orissa and incl. Laccadive Is. and part of Malabar Coast on W. Eastern Ghats extend from NE border to Nilgiri Hills in W; Kāveri River traverses the state. See table at INDIA.

Chief products: Rice, millet, peanuts, sugarcane, cotton, timber.

Chief cities: Madras, Madurai, Coimbatore.

History: By 2d cent. A.D. region occupied by Tamil kingdoms of Pāṇḍya and Cōla and in the NE by the kings of Kalinga; later in 14th cent. occupied by Muslim invaders. Hindu kingdom of Vijayanagar comprised area S of the Kistna (now Krishna) 1336–1565; Portuguese explorer Vasco da Gama reached Calicut 1498; Portuguese displaced by Dutch in 16th and early 17th cents.; English made first settlement in 1611 at Masulipatam (now Machilipatnam); after founding of Madras city 1640 English extended conquests; territory made a separate presidency 1653; captured by French 1746 but retroceded under Treaty of Aix-la-Chapelle 1748; under the British received additional territory until early in 19th cent. Made autonomous province 1937; became part of Republic of India 1947; reorganized administratively 1956.

Tamiš. See TIMIŞ.
Tam·luk *also* **Tum·luk** \təm-'lük\. Town, West Bengal, NE India, ab. 30 mi. (50 km.) SW of Calcutta; pop. (1991p) 38,656. In ancient times, as **Tam·ra·lip·ti** \ˌtəm-rə-'lip-tə\, a seaport at the mouth of the Ganges from which Chinese Buddhist pilgrims embarked; it is now 60 mi. (97 km.) from the sea with a fine temple, but most of its ancient remains are buried in the silt of the Hugli.
Tam·ma·ny, Mount \'ta-mə-nē\. Peak, New Jersey; forms the E side of Delaware Water Gap; ab. 1480 ft. (450 m.).
Tammerfors. See TAMPERE.
Tam·pa \'tam-pə\. City, ⊗ of Hillsborough co., W cen. Florida Penin., on NE end of Tampa Bay; pop. (1990c) 280,015; winter and fishing resort; ships citrus fruit and phosphates; produces cigars, chemicals; shrimp fishing; Busch Gardens amusement park; Tampa Coll. (1890), Univ. of Tampa (1931), Univ. of South Florida (1956), Hillsborough Community Coll. (1968). Fort Brooke estab. on site by U.S. Army 1824; town incorp. 1855; developed as cigar-making center after Vicente Martínez Ybor established town's first cigar factory; grew as major tourist center from turn of 20th cent.
Tampa Bay. Inlet of Gulf of Mexico, W coast of Hillsborough co., W Florida Penin.; spanned at its mouth by Sunshine Skyway (cable-stayed bridge; main span 1204 ft. or 367 m., total length 15.2 mi. or 24.5 km.); the city of Tampa is at its NE end and St. Petersburg on W shore.
Tam·pe·re \'täm-pe-re\ *or Swed.* **Tam·mer·fors** \ˌtä-mər-'fórsh\. City, Häme prov., SW Finland, on Lake Näsijärvi; pop. (1989c) 171,561; 3d largest city of Finland; industrial, cultural, and transportation center; textiles, machinery, footwear, paper; hydroelectric power plants; has many notable

public buildings in contemporary styles; technological institute (1965), university (1966); chartered 1779; developed as industrial center in 19th cent.

Tam·pi·co \täm-ˈpē-kō\. Seaport, S Tamaulipas state, E Mexico, ab. 6 mi. (10 km.) from the Gulf of Mexico on the Pánuco River; munic. pop. (1990p) 271,636; transportation center and one of the principal seaports of Mexico; modern port facilities; exports include oil, livestock, copper ore, agricultural products; boatyards, sawmills; tourist center and seaside resort. Developed around Franciscan monastery founded 1532; abandoned 1683 after destruction by pirates; resettled 1823; occupied by U.S. troops under Gen. Zachary Taylor 1846 during Mexican-American War and by French 1862 during French intervention.

Tamralipti. See TAMLUK.

Tam·ri·dah \tam-ˈrē-də\ *also* **Ta·ma·ri·da** \ˌta-mə-ˈrē-də\; *formerly* **Ha·di·bu** \ˈha-di-ˌbü\. Chief town of Socotra I., Yemen, in Indian Ocean, S of Arabia; on NE coast.

Tam·worth \ˈtam-ˌwərth\. **1.** Town, E New South Wales, SE Australia, 190 mi. (306 km.) N of Sydney; pop. (1991c) 35,205; ships eggs; flour milling; starch.
2. Town, Staffordshire, W cen. England, at confluence of Tame and Anker rivers 15 mi. (24 km.) NE of Birmingham; pop. (1991p) 68,900; textiles, paper, bricks, aluminum ware; coal deposits in area; Tamworth swine orig. bred here.

Ta·na \ˈtä-nä\. River, Kenya; rises in S cen. region, flows in a curve NE, E, and S into Indian Ocean at Ungama Bay; 440 mi. (708 km.) long; longest river in Kenya.

Ta·na \ˈtä-nə\ *or Finn.* **Te·no** \ˈte-nȯ\. River, NE Norway; flows N and NE, forming a section of boundary bet. Norway and Finland, and empties into Tana Fjord; 224 mi. (360 km.) long.

Ta·na, Lake \ˈtä-nə\ *or* **Lake Tsa·na** \ˈtsä-nə\. Lake, N Ethiopia; 47 mi. (76 km.) long and 44 mi. (71 km.) wide; ab. 1100 sq. mi. (2849 sq. km.); largest lake in the country and source of the Blue Nile.

Tan·a·cross \ˈta-nə-ˌkrȯs\; *formerly* **Tan·a·na Crossing** \ˈta-nə-ˌnȯ\. Unincorporated settlement, Alaska, on Alaska Highway and on Tanana River ab. 150 mi. (240 km.) SE of Fairbanks; pop. (1990c) 106.

Ta·na Fjord \ˈtä-nə\. Inlet of Arctic Ocean, NE coast of Norway; receives the Tana River from the S.

Ta·na·ga \tə-ˈnä-gə\. Island, W Andreanof Is., Aleutians, SW Alaska, 51°47′N, 177°57′W; 209 sq. mi. (541 sq. km.); has active volcano. **Tanaga Bay** is on W coast; **Tanaga Pass** separates it from small islands on W.

Tan·a·gra \ˈta-nə-grə, tə-ˈna-grə\. Ancient town, E Boeotia, E cen. Greece, ab. 14 mi. (23 km.) E of Thebes; scene of battle 457 B.C. in which the Spartans defeated the Athenians during Peloponnesian Wars. 19th cent. A.D. excavations revealed terra-cotta statuettes made here in 4th and 3d cents. B.C.

Ta·nah·ba·la \ˌtä-nä-ˈbä-lä\ *and* **Ta·nah·ma·sa** \ˌtä-nä-ˈmä-sä\. See BATU.

Ta·nah·me·rah Bay \tä-ˌnä-me-ˈrä\. Inlet of Pacific Ocean, NE coast of Irian Jaya, Indonesia, ab. 40 mi. (65 km.) W of Jayapura. Landings made here by Allied forces at same time as at Hollandia (now Jayapura) Apr. 1944.

Tanais. See DON 3.

Ta·nam·bo·go \ˌtä-näm-ˈbō-gō\. Small island, SE Solomon Is., W Pacific Ocean; attached to Gavutu I. by causeway; taken in WWII by U.S. marines Aug. 1942.

Tan·a·na \ˈta-nə-ˌnȯ\. **1.** River, chief S tributary of the Yukon, E and cen. Alaska; rises in glaciers of NE Wrangell Mts., flows NW to the Yukon at 65°10′N, 152°05′W; ab. 550 mi. (885 km.) long; navigable for ab. 225 mi. (360 km.) and for smaller vessels nearly to its source. Fairbanks is on it and Alaska Highway follows it for nearly its entire course.
2. City, cen. Alaska, at junction of Tanana and Yukon rivers; pop. (1990c) 345.

Tanana Crossing. See TANACROSS.

Tananarivo *and* **Tananarive.** See ANTANANARIVO.

Ta·nao Pass \tä-ˈnau̇\. Channel, extending along N coast of Camarines Norte prov., Luzon, Philippines, separating it from the Calagua Is.; ab. 10 mi. (16 km.) wide.

Ta·na·pag Harbor \ˈtä-nə-ˌpäg\. Anchorage, W coast of Saipan, Northern Mariana Is., just N of Garapan; best harbor of the island.

Tana River. See TANA.

Ta·na·ro \ˈtä-nä-rō\; *anc.* **Tan·a·rus** \ˈta-nə-rəs\. River, N Italy; rises in the Maritime Alps; flows N and NE into Po River 10 mi. (16 km.) NE of Alessandria; 171 mi. (275 km.) long.

Ta·na·shi \tä-ˈnä-shē\. City, Tokyo prefecture, SE cen. Honshū, Japan; pop. (1990p) 75,141.

Ta·na·uan \tä-ˈnä-wän\. **1.** Municipality, Leyte prov., E coast of Leyte I., Philippines, on San Pedro Bay 9 mi. (14 km.) S of Tacloban; pop. (1980c) 31,487; taken in WWII by U.S. forces Oct. 1944.
2. Municipality, Batangas prov., Luzon, Philippines, on railroad line and highway from Batangas to Calamba; NE of Lake Taal and ab. 24 mi. (39 km.) N of Batangas; pop. (1980c) 74,020; taken in WWII by U.S. Mar. 1945.

Tan–chu. See DANZHU.

Tan·cí·ta·ro \tän-ˈsē-tä-ˌrō\. Mountain, Michoacán state, SW Mexico, just W of Uruapan; 12,605 ft. (3842 m.).

Tan·da \ˈtän-də\. Town, E Uttar Pradesh, N India, on Ghāgara River 85 mi. (137 km.) NNW of Varanasi; pop. (1991p) 69,989.

Tan·dag \ˈtän-ˌdäg\. Municipality, ✻ of Surigao del Sur prov., NE coast of Mindanao, Philippines; pop. (1980c) 25,386.

Tan·dil \tän-ˈdēl\. City, Buenos Aires prov., E cen. Argentina, 190 mi. (306 km.) S of the city of Buenos Aires; pop. (1980c) 79,429; center of rich agricultural region; health and pleasure resort; university.

Tan·djoeng \ˈtän-ˌjüŋ\. Dutch transliteration of Malay word meaning "cape, point." For names containing this word, see the 2d element.

Tandjoeng Poeting. See PUTING, TANJUNG.

Tandjoeng Selatan. See SELATAN, TANJUNG.

Tandjungpinang *and* **Tandjoengpinang.** See TANJUNGPINANG.

Tandjung Rangasa. See MANDAR, GULF OF.

Ta·ne·ga–Shi·ma \tä-ˌne-gä-ˈshē-mä, tä-ˈne-gä-shē-ˌmä\ *or* **Ta·ne·ga Island.** One of the Osumi Is. (*q.v.*), off S end of Kyūshū, S Japan; ab. 25 mi. (40 km.) long; ab. 175 sq. mi. (455 sq. km.).

Ta·ney \ˈtä-nē\. County in S Missouri. See table at MISSOURI.

Ta·ney·town \ˈtä-nē-ˌtau̇n\. City, Carroll co., N Maryland, NE of Frederick; pop. (1990c) 3695.

Tan·ga \ˈtäŋ-gä\. **1.** Administrative region of NE Tanzania. See table at TANZANIA.
2. Seaport, its ✻; pop. (1988p) 187,634; rail and road transportation center.

Tan·gail \təŋ-ˈgīl\. City, cen. Bangladesh, NW of Dhaka; pop. (1991p) 111,783.

Tanga Islands. Island group, E Bismarck Archipelago, Papua New Guinea, in W Pacific Ocean ab. 55 mi. (90 km.) off the E coast of New Ireland; comprises four islands.

Tan·gan·cí·cua·ro \ˌtäŋ-gän-ˈsē-kwä-rō\. Municipality, Michoacán state, Mexico, 40 mi. (64 km.) NW of Uruapan.

Tanganyika. See TANZANIA.

Tan·gan·yi·ka, Lake \ˌtan-gən-ˈyē-kə, ˌtaŋ-\. Lake, E cen. Africa, on boundary bet. W Tanzania and E Democratic Rep. of the Congo; bet. 10 and 45 mi. (16 and 72 km.) wide and at ab. 410 mi. (660 km.), the world's longest freshwater lake; 12,700 sq. mi. (32,893 sq. km.); max. depth 4710 ft. (1436 m.).

Tang·gu·la *or W.-G.* **T'ang–ku–la** \ˈtäŋ-ˈgü-ˈlä\. **1.** *also* **Tang·la** \ˈtäŋ-ˈlä\ *or Tibetan* **Dang·la** \ˈdäŋ-ˈlä\. Mountain range, E Tibet, China, 33°N, 88° to 94°E; alt. ab. 20,000 ft. (6100 m.).
2. Pass in Himalayas, S Tibet, China, E of Sikkim; alt. ab. 15,200 ft. (4635 m.).

Tang–ho–nan Shan. See DANGHE NANSHAN.

Tan·gier \tan-ˈjir\ *also* **Tan·giers** \-ˈjirz\ *or Fr. and Ger.*

Tan·ger \ *Fr.* tän-'zhā; *Ger.* 'täŋ-ər, 'tän-jər\ *or Span.* **Tán·ger** \'täŋ-her\; *anc.* **Tin·gis** \'tin-jis\. Seaport, N Morocco, at W end of the Strait of Gibraltar; pop. (1982c) 266,346; notable Casbah, mosque, museum housed in former palace of the sultan; with surrounding territory constituted until 1956 **Tangier Zone** or **International Zone** (225 sq. mi. or 583 sq. km.).

History: A Roman city (Tingis), later taken successively by Vandals, Byzantines, and Arabs; taken 1471 by Portuguese who lost it to Spain 1580 and regained it mid-17th cent.; on marriage 1662 of Catherine of Braganza to Charles II came into possession of English who gave it up to Moroccans 1684; concern over French domination of Morocco precipitated visit of German Emperor William II 1905 in support of Moroccan sovereign, which led to conference at Algeciras (*q.v.*) 1906. Zone estab. 1923 by the Tangier Convention (revised 1928) bet. England, France, and Spain providing for permanent neutralization of the area and government by an international commission. During WWII controlled by Spain; international administration restored 1945; international status abolished 1956; became free port and royal summer residence in early 1960s. See MOROCCO.

Tangier, Bay of. Inlet of the Strait of Gibraltar, N coast of Africa. Tangier is on its W side.

Tangier Island. Island, lower Chesapeake Bay, belonging to Accomac co., E Virginia.

Tangier Sound. Inlet of Chesapeake Bay, W shore of Somerset co., SE Maryland.

Tangier Zone. See TANGIER.

Tan·gi·pa·hoa \ˌtan-jə-pə-'hō-ə, -'hō\. Parish in SE Louisiana. See table at LOUISIANA.

Tang·ku·ban·pe·ra·hu \täŋ-ˌkü-bän-pə-'rä-hü\. Mountain, E Java, Indonesia, N of Bandung; 6809 ft. (2075 m.).

T'ang–ku–la. See TANGGULA.

T'ang–ku–la–yu–mu–ts'o. See TANGRA YUMCO.

Tangla. See TANGGULA 1.

Tang·ra Yum·co \'däŋ-rä-'yüm-kō\ *or W.-G.* **T'ang–ku–la–yu–mu–ts'o** \'täŋ-'kü-'lä-'yü-'mü-'tsȯ\; *mostly formerly* **Dang·ra Yum Tso** \'däŋ-'rä-'yüm-'tsȯ\. Lake, cen. Tibet, China, 31°N, 86°22′E; ab. 45 mi. (72 km.) long.

Tang·shan *or W.-G.* **T'ang–shan** \'täŋ-'shän\. Town, Hebei prov., NE China, ab. 100 mi. (160 km.) ESE of Beijing; pop. (1990c) 1,044,194. An important industrial city when destroyed by earthquake 1976; subsequently rebuilt.

Tang·ub \täŋ-'üb\. Municipality, Misamis Occidental prov., Mindanao, Philippines, on N shore of Panguil Bay 29 mi. (47 km.) S of Oroquieta; pop. (1980c) 40,401.

Ta·nim·bar Islands \tə-'nim-ˌbär-, 'ta-nəm-\ *or* **Ke·pu·lau·an Tanimbar** \ˌke-pü-'lau̇-än\ *also* **Ti·mor·laut Islands** \'tē-ˌmȯr-ˌlau̇t\ *or* **Te·nim·bar Islands** \tə-'nim-, 'te-nəm-\. Island group of ab. 30 islands, SE Moluccas, Malay Archipelago, Indonesia, ENE of Timor I.; 2096 sq. mi. (5429 sq. km.); attached to Maluku prov. Comprises the large island of Jamdena, the islands of Larat and Selaru, and many small islands. Mostly of coralline formation, but partly volcanic; has extensive swamps and few harbors. Produces corn, rice, coconut and sago palms; fishing; discovered by Dutch 1629.

Ta·nis \'tā-nəs\; *bib.* **Zo·an** \'zō-ˌan\. Ancient city in the Nile Delta, Lower Egypt, near Lake Manzala. Explored archaeologically 19th–20th cents.; ruins include temple, royal tombs; artifacts found esp. from XXIst dynasty.

Tan·jay \täŋ-'hī\. Municipality, E Negros Oriental, Negros, Philippines, near S end of Tanon Strait 17 mi. (27 km.) NNW of Cumaguete; pop. (1980c) 57,299.

Tanjong Baram. See BARAM POINT.

Tanjong Sempang Mangayau. See SEMPANG MANGAYAU, TANJONG.

Tanjore. See THANJAVUR.

Tan·jung Ba·lai \'tän-ˌjüŋ-'bä-ˌlī\. Town, N Sumatra, Indonesia; pop. (1990c) 108,202.

Tan·jung·ka·rang \ˌtän-jüŋ-'kä-räŋ\ *or* **Ban·dar Lam·pung** \'bən-dər-'läm-püŋ\. Town, ✻ of Lampung prov., Sumatra, Indonesia; pop. (1980c) 284,275.

Tan·jung·pi·nang *also* **Tan·djung·pi·nang;** *Du.* **Tan·djoeng·pi·nang** \ˌtän-jüŋ-'pē-näŋ\. Town, Indonesia, on SW coast of Bintan I., Riau prov., E of Sumatra and ESE of Singapore; pop. (1980c) 41,894.

Tanjung Puting. See PUTING, TANJUNG.

Tanjung Selatan. See SELATAN, TANJUNG.

Tan·na \'tä-nä, tȧ-'nä\. Island, S Vanuatu, SW Pacific Ocean, ab. 25 mi. (40 km.) S of Erromango; 22 mi. (35 km.) long and 12 mi. (19 km.) wide; pop. (1991e) 19,825; highest point 3419 ft. (1042 m.); main agricultural products coconuts and copra.

Tannenberg. See STĘBARK.

Tannou Touva. See TUVA.

Tan·nu–Ola \ˌtä-nü-'ō-lə\. Mountain range, running E and W bet. NW Mongolia and S Tuva Rep., S Russia in Asia.

Tannūrah, Ra's at. See RA'S AT TANNŪRAH.

Tannu Tuva. See TUVA AUTONOMOUS SOVIET SOCIALIST REPUBLIC.

Ta·no \'tä-nō\. River, W Ghana; flows S for 250 mi. (402 km.), forming part of Ghana-Ivory Coast border before entering the Gulf of Guinea.

Ta·non Strait \tä-'nyȯn\. Strait bet. Cebu I. and Negros I., cen. Philippines; ab. 100 mi. (160 km.) long and varying in width from 3 to 27 mi. (5 to 43 km.).

Tan·qui·jo Reef \täŋ-'kē-hō\. Reef, Gulf of Mexico, N of Tuxpan Reef, off coast of N Veracruz state, Mexico.

Tan–shui \'dän-'shwā\ *also* **Tan·sui** \'dän-'shwā\. **1.** Stream, N Taiwan; ab. 50 mi. (80 km.) long. **2.** Seaport, N Taiwan, N of Taipei.

Ṭan·ṭa \'tän-tə\. City, ✻ of Gharbīya governorate, Egypt, 51 mi. (82 km.) N of Cairo; pop. (1991e) 372,000; transportation center; cotton, sugar.

Tan·ta·lus, Mount \'tant-ᵊl-əs\. See HONOLULU 2.

Tan·to·yu·ca \ˌtän-tō-'yü-kä\. Municipality, Veracruz state, Mexico, 115 mi. (185 km.) SSW of Tampico; pop. (1990p) 85,934; livestock and poultry raising; sugarcane, lemons.

Tan–tung. See DANDONG.

Tantura. See DOR.

Tanura, Ras. See R'AS AT TANNŪRAH.

Tan·za·nia \ˌtan-zə-'nē-ə\ *or officially* **United Republic of Tanzania.** Republic, E Africa, bounded on N by Uganda and Kenya, on E by the Indian Ocean, on S by Mozambique and Malawi, on SW by Zambia, on W by Democratic Rep. of the Congo, and on NW by Burundi and Rwanda; 364,900 sq. mi. (945,091 sq. km.), incl. 22,805 sq. mi. (59,065 sq. km.) of water; pop. (1993e) 26,542,000; seat of government Dar es Salaam, designated ✻ Dodoma.

Physical features: Greater part is high plateau with av. alt. 3000 to 4000 ft. (915 to 1220 m.); has many heights 7000 to 10,400 ft. (2135 to 3170 m.), esp. in S cen. part and around N end of Lake Malawi; in NE on the Kenyan border are the Kilimanjaro peaks, the highest in Africa, 19,340 ft. (5895 m.). Chief rivers are Rufiji (in S cen. part, flowing E to Indian Ocean), Ruvuma (on S border), Pangani (in NE), and the lower course of the Kagera (in NW). In W are a number of lakes and marshy regions (largest Lake Rukwa, in SW) and within its borders it includes S half of Lake Victoria, ab. one third of Lake Tanganyika, and a section of NE Lake Malawi; coastline is ab. 450 mi. (725 km.) long. Major islands: Zanzibar, Pemba, Mafia.

Chief products: Corn, sisal, cotton, coffee, sugar, tobacco, cashews, cloves, rice, coconuts; diamonds, coal, salt; textiles, cement; food processing.

Chief towns: Dar es Salaam and Arusha.

Political divisions: Divided into the following administrative regions (for pronunciation of their names, see their individual entries):

NAME	AREA (sq. mi.)	AREA (sq. km.)	POP. (1988c)	CAPITAL
Arusha	32,654	84,574	1,351,675	Arusha
Dar es Salaam	538	1,393	1,360,850	Dar es Salaam
Dodoma	15,950	41,310	1,237,819	Dodoma
Iringa	22,750	58,922	1,208,914	Iringa
Kagera	10,961	28,388	1,326,183	Bukoba
Kigoma	17,400	45,066	854,817	Kigoma
Kilimanjaro	5,100	13,209	1,108,699	Moshi
Lindi	25,500	66,046	646,550	Lindi
Mara	11,400	29,526	970,942	Musoma

NAME	AREA (sq. mi.)	AREA (sq. km.)	POP. (1988c)	CAPITAL
Mbeya	34,799	90,129	1,476,199	Mbeya
Morogoro	28,199	73,035	1,222,737	Morogoro
Mtwara	6,450	16,707	889,494	Mtwara
Mwanza	13,850	35,872	1,878,271	Mwanza
Pemba North	222	574	137,399	Wete
Pemba South	128	332	127,640	Chake Chake
Pwani	12,512	32,407	638,015	Dar es Salaam
Rukwa	26,500	68,635	694,974	Sumbawanga
Ruvuma	24,800	64,232	783,327	Songea
Shinyanga	15,599	40,401	1,772,549	Shinyanga
Singida	19,051	50,508	791,814	Singida
Tabora	29,402	76,151	1,036,293	Tabora
Tanga	10,350	26,806	1,283,636	Tanga
Zanzibar North	181	470	97,028	Mkokotoni
Zanzibar South and Central	330	854	70,184	Koani
Zanzibar West	89	230	208,327	Zanzibar

History: By 10th cent. inhabited by Arab and Indian traders and Bantu-speaking peoples; late 15th–late 18th cent. dominated in turn by Portuguese and Arabs of Oman and Zanzibar; under explorer Carl Peters, Germans made treaties with native chiefs 1884–85; German East Africa Company received charter 1887 and Germany declared region a protectorate (**German East Africa**) 1891; its boundaries with British territory (see KENYA) determined by agreements of 1886, 1890; Zanzibar declared a British protectorate 1890; put down local resistance late 19th–early 20th cent.; during WWI captured by British 1914–16; name changed to **Tan·gan·yi·ka** \ˌtan-gən-ˈyē-kə, ˌtaŋ-\ when it became a British mandate c. 1920 (Ruanda-Urundi not part of British mandate); a legislative council estab. 1926; made a UN trust territory under British administration 1946; achieved independence 1961; became a republic 1962; united with Zanzibar (*q.v.*) 1964 under new name of Tanzania; formed (1967–77) with Kenya and Uganda, the East African Community; 1977 closed border with Kenya (reopened 1983); invaded 1978 by Uganda under Idi Amin; legalized multiparty politics 1992.

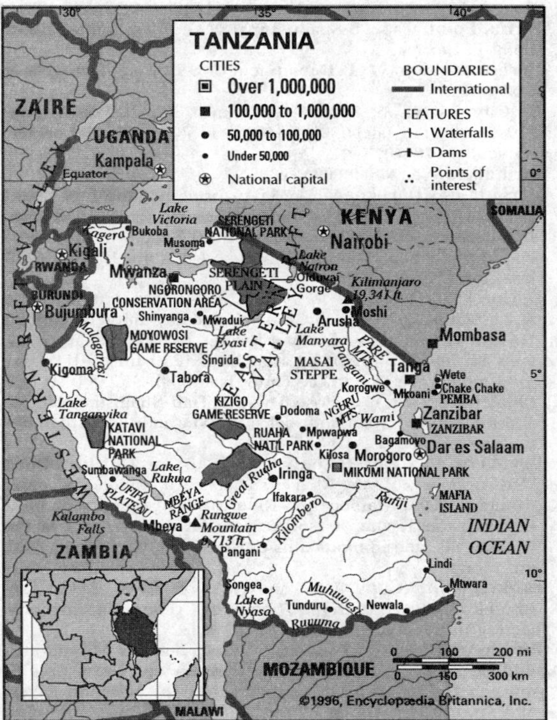

Taolanaro. See TÔLAÑARO.

Ta·or·mi·na \taůr-ˈmē-nä\; *anc.* **Tau·ro·me·ni·um** \ˌtȯr-ə-ˈmē-nē-əm\. Resort commune, Messina prov., E coast of Sicily, Italy; pop. (1991p) 9979; theater reconstructed from a Greek original; Roman remains; medieval castle. Occupied by Siculi tribe in 8th cent. B.C.; refounded by Carthaginians early 4th cent. B.C.; after defeat of Siracusan tyrant Hiero II (mid-3d cent. B.C.) became allied to Rome; destroyed by Arab invaders 902 A.D. and rebuilt by Sicilians.

Taos \ˈtaůs\. **1.** County in N New Mexico. See table at NEW MEXICO.

2. Town and resort, its ⊗, 55 mi. (88 km.) NNE of Santa Fe; pop. (1990c) 4065; legal name **Don Fer·nan·do de Taos** \ˌdän-fər-ˈnan-dō-dā-\; important commercial center in days of Santa Fe Trail; concentration of artists; outdoor recreation. Community includes also Taos Pueblo (to NE), pop. (1990c) 1187 and Ranchos de Taos (to SE), pop. (1990c) 1779.

Taos Trail. See SANTA FE TRAIL.

Taou·den·ni \ˌtaů-de-ˈnē\. Oasis, Mali, 425 mi. (684 km.) NNW of Tombouctou.

Ta·pa·chu·la \ˌtä-pä-ˈchü-lä\. Town, Chiapas state, SE Mexico, on railroad line near Guatemalan border; munic. pop. (1990p) 222,282; chief product coffee.

Ta·pa·jós *or* **Ta·pa·joz** \ˌtà-pà-ˈzhȯs\. River, N Brazil; formed by junction of Juruena (total length with Juruena ab. 1100 mi. or 1770 km.) and Teles Pires rivers on S end of the border bet. Amazonas and Pará states, flows NE into the Amazon River at Santarém; 807 mi. (1298 km.) long; important rubber plantations along its banks.

Ta–pan. See BAIRIN YOUQI.

Tapanoeli Bay. See SIBOLGA BAY.

Ta·pao Point \tē-ˈpaů\. Point, S tip of peninsula extending into Laguna de Bay, S Rizal prov., Philippines; is close to N end of Talim I.

Ta–pa Shan. See DABA SHAN.

Tā·pi \ˈtä-pē\ *also* **Tap·ti** \ˈtäp-tē\. Largely unnavigable river, W cen. India; flows W from mountains of SW Madhya Pradesh to Gulf of Khambhat near Surat in Maharashtra; 436 mi. (702 km.) long.

Taping. See DAYING.

Ta·po·tchau *or* **Ta·po·cho** \ˌtä-pō-ˈchō\. Mountain ridge, cen. Saipan I., Northern Mariana Is., W Pacific Ocean; highest point 1552 ft. (473 m.); severe fighting in WWII during U.S. conquest of island summer 1944.

Tap·pa·han·nock \ˌta-pə-ˈha-nək\. Town, ⊗ of Essex co., E Virginia; pop. (1990c) 1550.

Tap·pan \ˈta-pən\. Unincorporated settlement, Rockland co., SE New York, near Haverstraw; pop. (1990c) 6867; scene of British Major John André's execution (he was hanged as spy) 1780 during Revolutionary War.

Tappan Zee \ˈzē\. Expansion of the Hudson River, bet. Westchester and Rockland cos., SE New York; 12 mi. (19 km.) long by 2 to 3 mi. (3 to 5 km.) wide; crossed by Tappan Zee Bridge, opened 1955.

Taprobane. See SRI LANKA.

Tapti. See TĀPI.

Ta·pu·a·e·nu·ku \ˌtä-ˌpü-ī-ˈnü-kü\. Highest peak in Kaikoura Range, NE South I., New Zealand; 9463 ft. (2884 m.).

Ta·pul \tä-ˈpül\. **1.** Island group, cen. Sulu Archipelago, Philippines, bet. Jolo I. and Tawi-tawi I.; ab. 100 sq. mi. (260 sq. km.); largest is Siasi. Includes also islands of Tapul, Lapac, and Lugus and ab. 70 other small islands and islets. See SULU ARCHIPELAGO.

2. Island, Tapul group, N of Siasi I. and S of Jolo; 11 sq. mi. (28 sq. km.); forms part of Tapul municipality.

Ta·qua·ri \ˌtà-kwà-ˈrē\. River, S cen. Brazil; rises in S cen. Mato Grosso state, flows WSW into Paraguay River near Bolivian border; lower part traverses the Pantanal (marshes); ab. 350 mi. (565 km.) long.

\ə\ **abut** \ə\ matches \ᵊ\ kitten, Fr table \ər\ **further** \a\ **ash** \ā\ **ace** \ä\ **cot, cart** \à\ Fr bac \aů\ **out** \b\ Span Avila \ch\ **chin** \e\ **bet** \ē\ **easy** \g\ **go** \i\ **hit** \ī\ **ice** \j\ **job** \k\ Ger **ich, Buch** \ⁿ\ Fr vin \ŋ\ **sing** \ō\ **go** \ȯ\ **all** \ò\ **law** \œ\ Fr bœuf \œ̄\ Fr feu \ȯi\ **boy** \th\ **thin** \t͟h\ **this** \ü\ **loot** \ů\ **foot** \ue\ Ger füllen \üe\ Fr rue \y\ **yet** \ʸ\ Fr digne \ˈdēnʸ\, nuit \ˈnwʸē\ \yü\ **few** \yů\ **fury** \zh\ **vision**

Tar \ˈtär\. River, NE North Carolina; rises in Granville co., N North Carolina, flows SE into a wide estuary known as Pamlico River, Beaufort co., E North Carolina; 215 mi. (346 km.) long, incl. Pamlico River.

Tara \ˈtar-ə\. Parish, co. Meath, E Ireland, 22 mi. (35 km.) NW of Dublin; ancient ❋ (Hill of Tara) of Irish monarchs, abandoned c. 560; remains an important place in Irish legend and tradition.

Ta·ra·ba \tä-ˈrä-bä\. State of Nigeria. See table at NIGERIA.

Ṭarābulus al–Gharb. See TRIPOLI 4.

Ṭarābulus ash Sham. See TRIPOLI 3.

Taradie, Passage de. See POTERLA, COLLADO DE LA.

Taraika Bay. See TERPENIYA BAY.

Ta·ra·kan \ˌtär-ə-ˈkän\. **1.** Island, Indonesia, in E Celebes Sea, off NE coast of Borneo; 117 sq. mi. (303 sq. km.); in delta of Sesajap River; has large oil fields; taken from Dutch by Japanese in WWII after battle Jan. 1942 in which Dutch destroyed island's oil wells; retaken by Australians May 1945.
2. Town on W side of island.

Taranaki. See EGMONT, MOUNT.

Ta·ran·gi·re National Park \ˌtär-əŋ-ˈgē-rā\. National park, NE Tanzania, SE of Lake Manyara.

Tar·an·say \ˈtar-ən-ˌsā\. Island, Outer Hebrides, SW of island of Lewis with Harris, off NW coast of Scotland; ab. 4.5 mi. (7 km.) long.

Ta·ran·to \ˈtä-rän-ˌtō\. **1.** Province of Puglia, SE Italy. See table at ITALY.
2. *anc.* **Ta·ren·tum** \tə-ˈren-təm\. Seaport and naval base, its ❋, on Gulf of Taranto 156 mi. (251 km.) SE of Naples; pop. (1989c) 244,512; steel, chemicals, canned foods; shipyards, oyster and mussel fisheries; national museum; 11th cent. cathedral; castle; naval arsenal.
History: Founded by Greeks 8th cent. B.C. and a leading city of Magna Graecia; came under Rome 272 B.C. and made Roman colony but declined; bet. 5th and 11th cents. taken successively by Ostrogoths, Byzantines, Lombards, Arabs, and Normans; became part of kingdom of Naples by 15th cent. Joined kingdom of Italy 1860 and made major naval base; in WWII raided by British carrier aircraft Nov. 1940; taken by Allied troops Sept. 1943.

Taranto, Gulf of *also* **Gulf of Tarentum.** Inlet of Ionian Sea, SE coast of Italy; ab. 70 mi. (115 km.) long.

Ta·ra·pa·ća \ˌtä-rä-pä-ˈkä\. **1.** Former province of N Chile.
2. Region of N Chile. See table at CHILE.
3. Town, Amazonas commissary, SE corner of Colombia, on S bank of Putumayo River at Brazil frontier, N of Leticia.

Ta·ra·po·to \ˌtä-rä-ˈpō-tō\. Town, N Peru, on a tributary of the Huallaga River 90 mi. (145 km.) E of Chachapoyas; pop. (1990e) 70,900.

Ta·ra·rua Range \ˌtar-ə-ˈrü-ə\. Mountain range, SW North I., New Zealand; highest peak 5154 ft. (1571 m.).

Ta·ras·con \ˌtȧ-rȧ-ˈskōⁿ\. Town, Bouches-du-Rhône dept., SE France, on left bank of the Rhone N of Arles; pop. (1990c) 11,158; Romanesque-Gothic church; 15th cent. castle.

Ta·ra·wa \tə-ˈrä-wə, ˈtar-ə-ˌwä\. Island (atoll), N cen. Gilbert Is., Kiribati, ab. 90 mi. (145 km.) N of the Equator; contains the nation's ❋ and comprises chain of islets in reef around lagoon ab. 18 mi. (29 km.) long by 13 mi. (21 km.) at widest point; pop. (1990c) 28,802. Islet and village of Betio at S end; in WWII occupied by Japanese 1942; seized by U.S. marines after costly battle Nov. 1943; ❋ of Gilbert and Ellice Is. from after the war to 1975.

Ta·ra·we·ra \ˌtär-ə-ˈwer-ə\. River, N cen. North I., New Zealand; flows N out of **Lake Tarawera** (14 sq. mi. or 36 sq. km., 7 mi. or 11 km. long, max. depth 285 ft. or 87 m.) into Bay of Plenty; ab. 45 mi. (72 km.) long.

Tarawera, Mount. Volcanic peak, N cen. North I., New Zealand, ab. 90 mi. (145 km.) NNW of Napier; 3645 ft. (1111 m.); 1886 eruption destroyed the terraces of Lake Rotomahana.

Tar·bat Ness \ˈtär-bət-ˈnes\. Headland, NE coast of Scotland, S of Dornoch Firth; lighthouse.

Tar·bela Dam \tär-ˈbe-lə\. Dam across Indus River in N Pakistan, NNW of Islamabad.

Tar·bert, Loch \ˈtär-bərt\. Sea inlet, cen. Jura I., Inner Hebrides, off W Scotland; ab. 6 mi. (10 km.) long; nearly cuts the island in two.

Tarbes \ˈtärb\; *anc.* **Bi·gor·ra** \bi-ˈgȯr-ə, -ˈgär-\. City, ❋ of Hautes-Pyrénées dept., SW France, on Adour River 23 mi. (37 km.) ESE of Pau; pop. (1990c) 50,228; market town; electrical equipment; 12th–14th cent. cathedral. Ancient ❋ of prov. of Bigorre; to English during Hundred Years' War (1337–1453).

Tar·boro \ˈtär-ˌbər-ō\. Town, ⊗ of Edgecombe co., NE North Carolina, 14 mi. (23 km.) E of Rocky Mount; pop. (1990c) 11,037; historically a tobacco and cotton market; Edgecomb Community Coll. (1968).

Tar·cen·to \tär-ˈchen-tō\. Commune, Udine prov., Veneto, NE Italy, 12 mi. (19 km.) N of the commune of Udine; pop. (1981p) 8966.

Ta·ree \tə-ˈrē\. Town, New South Wales, Australia, ab. 10 mi. (16 km.) from coast, ab. 82 mi. (132 km.) NE of Newcastle; met. area pop. (1991c) 16,303; dairy products; tourism.

Ta·ren·tum \tə-ˈren-təm\. **1.** Borough, Allegheny co., SW Pennsylvania, on Allegheny River 17 mi. (27 km.) NE of Pittsburgh; pop. (1990c) 5674.
2. Seaport, Puglia, Italy. See TARANTO 2.

Tarentum, Gulf of. See TARANTO, GULF OF.

Tar·fa·ya \tär-ˈfī-yə\; *formerly* **Ca·bo Yu·bi** \ˈkä-bō-ˈyü-bē\ *or* **Cabo Ju·by** \ˈyü-bē\ *also* **Vil·la Bens** \ˈvi-lə-ˈbenz\. Town, SW Morocco, in former Spanish enclave on Cap Juby; former seat of administration of Spanish Sahara (now Western Sahara) and Ifni.

Târgovişte. See TÎRGOVIŞTE.

Târgu–Jiu. See TÎRGU JIU.

Târgu–Mureş. See TÎRGU MUREŞ.

Târgu–Neamţu *or* **Târgul–Neamţ.** See TÎRGU NEAMŢ.

Târgu–Ocna. See TÎRGU OCNA.

Ta·ri·fa \tə-ˈrē-fə\; *anc.* **Ju·lia Jo·za** \ˈjül-yə-ˈjō-zə\ *or* **Julia Tra·duc·ta** \trə-ˈdək-tə\. Seaport, Cádiz prov., SW Spain, on Strait of Gilbraltar 51 mi. (82 km.) SE of the city of Cádiz; pop. (1991c) 14,512; fisheries and fish-salting works. Roman settlement; taken 711 and fortified by Moors under Muslim Gen. Ṭāriq ibn Ziyād; reconquered by King Sancho IV of Castile 1292; besieged by French c. 1812 in Peninsular War.

Tarifa, Point. Cape, S Spain, 36°01′N, 5°36′W; southernmost point in Europe.

Ta·ri·ja \tä-ˈrē-hä\. **1.** Department of S Bolivia. See table at BOLIVIA.
2. City, its ❋, ab. 160 mi. (257 km.) SSE of Potosí; pop. (1992p) 90,115; alt. 6398 ft. (1950 m.); commercial center; university (1886).

Tarikaikea. See MAMBERAMO.

Ta·ri·ku *also* **Ta·ri·koe** \tä-ˈrē-kü\; *formerly* **Rouf·faer** \ˈrau̇-ˌfär\. W upper tributary of the Mamberamo River, Irian Jaya, Indonesia; joins the Taritatu near 3°10′S to form the Mamberamo; its sources are in W Maoke Mts.; ab. 150 mi. (240 km.) long.

Ta·rim \ˈdä-ˈrēm, ˈtä-\ *or W.-G.* **T'a–li–mu** \ˈtä-ˈlē-ˈmü\. River, Xinjiang Uygur, W China; formed by union of Yarkant He and Hotan; flows E along N edge of Taklimakan (*q.v.*), then SE into the region of Lop Nur; 1250 mi. (2011 km.) long; gives its name to the entire basin, ab. 350,000 sq. mi. (906,500 sq. km.), enclosed by the Tian Shan, the Pamirs, and the Kunlun Shan and incl. Lop Nur and the Turpan depressions in the E.

Ta·ri·ta·tu *also* **Ta·ri·ta·toe** \ˌtär-ē-ˈtä-tü\ *or Du.* **Iden·burg** \ˈēd-ᵊn-ˌbərg\. River, NE cen. Irian Jaya, Indonesia, chief tributary of the Mamberamo River; flows generally W, uniting with the Tariku; its sources are on the N slopes of the Maoke Mts. and in mountains of NE Irian Jaya; 225 mi. (362 km.) long.

Tar·khan·kut, Cape \ˌtär-kən-ˈküt\ *or Russ.* **Mys Tar·khan·kut** \ˈməs\. Extreme W point of Crimea, Ukraine, projecting into the Black Sea at 45°21′N, 32°30′E.

Tar·kio \ˈtär-kē-ˌō\. **1.** River, SW Iowa and NW Missouri; E, middle, and W forks rise in Montgomery co., Iowa, flow S, unite at Tarkio, Missouri, and flow into the Missouri River; 125 mi. (201 km.) long.

2. City, Atchison co., NW corner of Missouri, 56 mi. (90 km.) NW of St. Joseph; pop. (1990c) 2243; Tarkio Coll. (1883).

Tar·kwa \tär-ˈkwä\. Town, W Ghana, 40 mi. (64 km.) NW of Sekondi; pop. (1984c) 22,107; goldfields.

Tar·lac \ˈtär-ˌläk\. **1.** Province, N cen. Luzon, Philippines; ✻ Tarlac. W half is mountainous, comprising E slopes of Zambales Mts.; E part watered by tributaries of the Agno and Pampanga. Joined revolt against Spanish leaders 1896; civil government estab. 1901; came under control of Japanese 1941; recovered by U.S. 1945. See table at PHILIPPINES.

2. Municipality, its ✻, on a tributary of the Agno and on the Manila-Dagupan railroad line 65 mi. (105 km.) NNW of Manila; pop. (1980c) 175,691; chief trade center of the province. In WWII partly destroyed by Japanese before capture by U.S. Jan. 1945.

Tar·ma \ˈtär-mä\. Town, cen. Peru, 95 mi. (153 km.) NE of Lima; pop. (1990e) 50,000; alt. 10,000 ft. (3048 m.).

Tarn \ˈtärn\. **1.** River, S France; rises in Lozère dept. on the slopes of Lozère Mts., flows W and SW into Garonne River; 233 mi. (375 km.) long.

2. Department of S France. See table at FRANCE.

Tarn·by \ˈtärn-bē\. Town, Copenhagen co., Denmark; pop. (1989e) 39,904.

Tarn–et–Ga·ronne \ˈtärn-ā-gȧ-ˈrȯn\. Department of S France. See table at FRANCE.

Tar·nob·rzeg \tär-ˈnȯb-zhek\. **1.** Province, SE Poland. See table at POLAND.

2. City, its ✻, on Vistula River; pop. (1989e) 45,944.

Tarnopol. See TERNOPOL'.

Tar·nów \ˈtär-ˌnüf\. **1.** Province, S Poland. See table at POLAND.

2. City, its ✻, 45 mi. (72 km.) E of Kraków; pop. (1989e) 120,385; machinery, chemicals; cathedral; Gothic town hall. Founded c. 1330; by 16th cent. became cultural center; to Austria 1772; occupied by Germans in WWI and WWII; to Poland after war.

Tar·now·skie Gó·ry \tär-ˈnȯf-skye-ˈgu̇r-ē\; *unofficially* **Tar·no·wi·ce** \ˌtär-nō-ˈvēt-sə\ *or Ger.* **Tar·no·witz** \ˈtär-nō-ˌvits\. Commune, Katowice prov., S Poland, 16 mi. (26 km.) NNW of the city of Katowice; pop. (1989e) 73,743.

Ta·ro \ˈtä-rō\. River, N Italy; flows NE from the Apennines into Po River; 78 mi. (126 km.) long.

Ta·rou·dannt *also* **Ta·ru·dant** \ˌtȧr-ü-ˈdäⁿ\. Oasis, W Morocco, E of Agadir.

Tar·pe·ian Rock \tär-ˈpē-ən\. See SEVEN HILLS.

Tar·pon Springs \ˈtär-pən\. Resort city, Pinellas co., W cen. Florida Penin., on Gulf of Mexico 28 mi. (45 km.) N of St. Petersburg; pop. (1990c) 17,906; sponge fisheries historically important.

Tar·qui·nia \tär-ˈkwē-nyä\; *anc.* **Tar·quin·ii** \tär-ˈkwi-nē-ˌī\; *in medieval times* **Cor·ne·to** \kȯr-ˈnā-tō\. Town, Viterbo prov., N Lazio, cen. Italy, ab. 60 mi. (95 km.) NW of the commune of Viterbo; pop. (1991p) 13,784; medieval fortifications; government museum containing Etruscan antiquities in the 15th cent. Palazzo Vitelleschi; necropolis of archaeological interest with notable painted tombs. Chief city of Etruscan Confederation against Rome; came under Rome 4th cent. B.C. and later received Roman citizenship; population transferred to present town after Lombard and Saracen invasions (6th–8th cents. A.D.).

Tarracina. See TERRACINA.

Tarraco. See TARRAGONA 2.

Tar·ra·co·nen·sis \ˌtar-ə-kə-ˈnen-sis\ *or* **His·pa·nia Tarraconensis** \his-ˈpā-nē-ə\. Roman province comprising the greater part (N, cen., and SE) of ancient Spain (Hispania); ✻ Tarraco; other two provinces were Lusitania and Baetica.

Tar·ra·go·na \ˌtär-rä-ˈgō-nä\. **1.** Province of NE Spain. See table at SPAIN.

2. *anc.* **Tar·ra·co** \ˈtar-ə-ˌkō\. Commune, its ✻, on Mediterranean Sea 54 mi. (87 km.) WSW of Barcelona; pop. (1991p) 110,003; agricultural market town and seaport; archiepiscopal see; 12th–13th cent. cathedral; extensive Roman remains incl. walls, theater, circus, aqueduct, and triumphal arch. Captured by Romans 218 B.C. in Second Punic War and as ✻ of Roman prov. of Tarraconensis one of the leading cities of Roman Spain; razed by Moors early 8th cent.; reconquered early 12th cent. and restored under Aragonese rule; captured by British 1705 in War of Spanish Succession; sacked by French under Duke Louis-Gabriel Suchet 1811 in Peninsular War.

Tar·rant \ˈtar-ənt\. **1.** County in N Texas. See table at TEXAS.

2. *formerly* **Tarrant City.** City, Jefferson co., cen. Alabama, 10 mi. (16 km.) NNE of Birmingham; pop. (1990c) 8046.

Tar·ra·sa \tär-ˈrä-sä\ *or* **Ter·ras·sa** \ter-ˈräs-sä\. Commune, Barcelona prov., NE Spain, 14 mi. (23 km.) NNW of the city of Barcelona; pop. (1991p) 154,360; textiles, carpets, glass, machinery, electrical equipment; two 12th cent. churches; made episcopal see 5th cent.

Tar·ry·all Peak, North \ˈtar-ē-ˌȯl\. Peak in the Rocky Mts., Rio Grande co., cen. Colorado; 11,600 ft. (3536 m.).

Tar·ry·town \ˈtar-ē-ˌtau̇n\. Village, Westchester co., SE New York, on Hudson River at the Tappan Zee, 24 mi. (39 km.) N of New York City; pop. (1990c) 10,739; automobiles, clothing; Marymount Coll. (1907). Settled by Dutch 17th cent.; scene of British Maj. John André's capture 1780; home of author Washington Irving (Sunnyside) to S near Irvington and his burial place (Sleepy Hollow) in N part of village; described in Irving's *Sketch Book.*

Tar·shish \ˈtär-shish\. Ancient maritime country, often identified with Tartessus; mentioned several times in the Old Testament.

Tarso Tieroko. See TIEROKO.

Tar·sus \ˈtär-səs\. **1.** River, Turkey in Asia. See CYDNUS.

2. Commercial town, İçel prov., S Turkey in Asia, on railroad line 23 mi. (37 km.) W of Adana; pop. (1990c) 187,508. Considerable ruins of ancient city remain.

History: Settlement on site from Neolithic times; razed and rebuilt by King Sennacherib of Assyria c. 700 B.C.; annexed by Rome 67 B.C.; a leading industrial and cultural center of the Roman and early Byzantine empires and the principal city of Cilicia. Destroyed by Arabs mid-7th cent. A.D.; rebuilt by Arabs late 8th cent.; from 10th to 15th cents. held successively by Byzantines, Crusaders, Christian Kingdom of Little Armenia, Mamlūks; captured by Ottoman Turks early 16th cent. Birthplace of St. Paul (first cent. A.D.).

Tar·tes·sus *or* **Tar·tes·sos** \tär-ˈte-səs\. Ancient kingdom and its chief port, SW coast of Hispania (Spain), near the mouth of the Guadalquivir in modern Andalusia; founded c. 12th cent. B.C.; prospered in trade of silver and tin and by many identified with the biblical Tarshish. Later developed by Phoenicians and Greeks; destroyed by Carthaginians c. 500 B.C.

Tar·tu \ˈtär-ˌtü\ *or Ger.* **Dor·pat** \ˈdȯr-ˌpät\ *or Russ.* **Yur·ev** \ˈyu̇r-yif\. City, E Estonia, on Ema River W of Lake Peipus; pop. (1992e) 113,410; footwear, agricultural machinery; university (founded 1632 by Gustavus II Adolph of Sweden).

History: Founded 1030 as castle by Yaroslav I, grand prince of Kiev; member of Hanseatic League; from 16th cent. to early 18th cent. ruled alternately by Poland and Sweden; annexed to Russia 1704 by Czar Peter the Great. Scene of considerable fighting during Russian Civil War 1918–19; scene of signing of peace treaties 1920 bet. U.S.S.R. and Estonia, and bet. U.S.S.R. and Finland; occupied by Germans in WWII and suffered considerable damage.

Tar·tūs \tär-ˈtüs\; *anc.* **Tor·to·sa** \tȯr-ˈtō-sə\. Coastal town, W Syria, N of Tripoli and ab. 42 mi. (68 km.) S of Latakia; pop. (1994e) 86,000; fishing port.

Tarudant. See TAROUDANNT.

Ta·ru·mae–san \ˌtä-rü-ˌmī-ˈsän\ *or* **Ta·ru·mai** \ˈtä-rü-ˌmī\. Active volcano, S Hokkaidō, Japan, S of Sapporo; 2969 ft. (905 m.).

Ta·ru·tao, Pu·lo \ˈpü-lō-ˌtär-ə-ˈtau̇\. Island (*pulo*), SW Thailand, off W coast of Malay Penin. at N end of Strait of Malacca, just N of Langkawi I.

Tarvisium. See TREVISO 2.

Täsch·horn \ˈtesh-ˌhȯrn\. Peak, SW Switzerland, in the Pennine Alps; 14,733 ft. (4491 m.).

Tashauz. See DASHHOWUZ.

Tashi Chho Dzong. See THIMPHU.

Ta–shih–ch'iao *or* **Tashihkiao.** See YINGKOU 2.

Tash·kent \tash-ˈkent, -ˈkend\. **1.** Administrative subdivision, E Uzbekistan; 6023 sq. mi. (15,600 sq. km.); pop. (1991e) 4,298,500; ✻ Tashkent; cotton, melons, livestock; before 1991 comprised an oblast of the U.S.S.R.
2. City, ✻ of Uzbekistan, also ✻ of Tashkent subdivision; to E of the Syr Dar'ya on a small tributary; pop. (1989p) 2,073,000; industrial center, producing agricultural and textile machinery, textiles, foodstuffs; university (1920); military headquarters and important center of Uzbek culture.

History: Probably dates from first cent. B.C.; came under Arabs by 8th cent. A.D. and under empire of Turkic ruler Timur 14th–15th cents.; captured by Russians 1865 and new city built beside old one; in 1966 scene of India-Pakistan conference on Kashmir dispute; suffered heavy damage from earthquake 1966.

Tash·kur·ghān \ˌtäsh-ku̇r-ˈgän\; *anc.* **Aor·nos** \ā-ˈȯr-nəs\. Town, Afghanistan, 30 mi. (48 km.) E of Mazār-i-Sharīf; founded c. 1750 and became important trade center bet. India and Bukhara; 3 mi. (5 km.) to the N are ruins of the ancient town of Khulm. Ancient Aornos in Bactria was on the line of march of Macedonian King Alexander the Great c. 330 B.C.

Ta·sik·ma·la·ya *also* **Ta·sik·ma·la·ja** \ˌtäs-ik-mə-ˈlī-ə\. City, West Java prov., Indonesia, on railroad line 50 mi. (81 km.) SE of Bandung; pop. (1980c) 165,297; in fertile plain surrounded by high mountains.

Tå·singe *or* **Taa·singe** \ˈtȯ-ˌsiŋ-ə\. Island, Denmark, in Baltic Sea S of Fyn I.; 27 sq. mi. (70 sq. km.).

Ta·si·us·saq *or* **Ta·si·us·sak** \ˌtä-sē-ˈü-ˌsək\. Settlement on an island in Baffin Bay, W coast of Greenland.

Tas·man, Mount \ˈtaz-mən\. Peak in Southern Alps Range, W cen. South I., New Zealand, NE of Mt. Cook; 11,475 ft. (3498 m.); 2d highest mountain in New Zealand; in Mount Cook National Park.

Tasman Bay. Inlet of Tasman Sea, on N coast of South I., New Zealand; Nelson is situated on its SE shore.

Tasman Glacier. Glacier, South I., New Zealand; 18 mi. (29 km.) long, ab. 1.25 mi. (2 km.) wide; largest glacier in New Zealand.

Tas·ma·nia \taz-ˈmā-nē-ə, -nyə\; *formerly* **Van Die·men's Land** \van-ˈdē-mənz\. Island, a state of Australia, South Pacific Ocean, ab. 150 mi. (241 km.) S of state of Victoria; 26,383 sq. mi. (68,332 sq. km.); pop. (1991c) 452,834; ✻ Hobart.

Physical features: Includes Macquarie I. (89 sq. mi. or 231 sq. km.) to the SE at 54°45′S; King I. 50 mi. (81 km.) to the NW; Hunters Is. off the NW point; the Furneaux Is. off the NE point, and Bruny I. off the SE coast. Cen. part a highland incl. the Great Western Tiers and several mountains above 4000 ft. or 1220 m. (highest Mt. Ossa 5305 ft. or 1617 m.). Chief rivers: Tamar in N, to which is joined the Esk and Macquarie river systems; Derwent in cen. and SE part; Gordon and Pieman rivers in W; and Arthur River in NW. Lakes are grouped in the center: Great Lake, Lake St. Clair, Lake Echo, and Lake Sorell. More important features of the coastline: on NE, Cape Portland; on E, Freycinet Penin.; on SE, Tasman Penin., Cape Pillar, Storm Bay, South East Cape; on SW, South West Cape; on W, Cape Sorell, Macquarie Harbour; on NW Cape Grim, and Circular Head on N coast.

Chief products: Timber; copper, zinc, tin, tungsten; livestock raising; possesses ab. half of Australia's hydroelectric power potential.

Largest town: Launceston.

History: Orig. inhabited by aborigines cut off from mainland Australia when its southernmost tip became an island over 10,000 years ago. Explored and named Van Diemen's Land 1642 by Dutch navigator Abel Tasman; taken over by Great Britain after turn of 19th cent. and used as an auxiliary penal settlement until 1850s; made a colony 1825; colony granted self-government 1856 and officially renamed Tasmania; federated as state of Australian Commonwealth 1901.

Tasman Peninsula. Peninsula, SE coast of Tasmania, Australia, E of Storm Bay and Hobart; ab. 26 mi. (42 km.) long by 20 mi. (32 km.) wide; Cape Pillar is at its SE extremity. Port Arthur on its S coast was a penal settlement from 1830s to 1870s.

Tasman Sea. The part of South Pacific Ocean bet. SE Australia and W New Zealand; ab. 1200 mi. (365 km.) across.

Tas·so Island \ˈta-sō\. Small island, Sierra Leone River, Sierra Leone, ENE of Freetown; the village of **Tasso** is on its NW coast.

Ta·ta \ˈtä-tä\. Town, N Hungary; pop. (1991e) 25,600.

Ta·ta·bán·ya \ˈtö-tö-ˌbän-yö\. Town, ⊗ of Komárom-Esztergom co., NW Hungary, ab. 35 mi. (56 km.) W of Budapest; pop. (1991e) 75,300; aluminum, chemicals.

Ta·ta·ko·to \ˌtä-tä-ˈkō-tō\. Atoll, E part of the Tuamoto Archipelago, S Pacific Ocean, 17°20′S, 138°23′W.

Tatar Autonomous Soviet Socialist Republic. See TATARSTAN.

Ta·tar City \ˈtä-ˈtär\ *or* **Inner City.** Section of Beijing, China, N of Chinese (Outer) City; designated mid-16th cent. during the Ming dynasty.

Tatar Pass. See JABLONICA PASS.

Tatar Pazardzhik. See PAZARDZHIK.

Tatarskiy Proliv. See TATAR STRAIT.

Ta·tar·stan \ˌta-tər-ˈstan, -ˈstän\; *formerly* **Ta·tar Autonomous Soviet Socialist Republic** \ˈtä-ˌtär, tə-ˈtär\. Autonomous republic of E cen. Russia in Europe, at bend of the Middle Volga; 26,255 sq. mi. (68,000 sq. km.); pop. (1992e) 3,696,000; ✻ Kazan'. In level country on both sides of Volga and incl. lower course of Kama; both streams and their tributaries important for transportation and irrigation. Has a mixed economy: agriculture (fodder crops, legumes, truck crops), livestock farming; engineering, timberworking, and chemical industries; oil and natural gas fields. Crossed by two main rail lines from Moscow to Siberia; heavy freight traffic along rivers.

History: By 8th cent. A.D. colonized by Bulgars, who established an important state; conquered by Mongols of the Golden Horde 13th cent.; in 15th cent. became Tatar khanate centered on Kazan'; conquered by Moscow under Ivan IV (the Terrible) 1552; autonomous republic estab. 1920; despite declaration of statehood, made republic within Russia 1991; subsequently became member of Russian Federation.

Tatar Strait *or Russ.* **Ta·tar·skiy Pro·liv** \tə-ˈtär-skē-prə-ˈlyēf\. Wide strait, Russia in Asia, bet. W coast of Sakhalin I. and the mainland; forms the N end of the Sea of Japan.

Tate \ˈtāt\. County in NW Mississippi. See table at MISSISSIPPI.

Ta·te·ba·ya·shi \ˌtä-tā-bä-ˈyä-shē\. City, Gumma prefecture, Honshū, Japan, 41 mi. (66 km.) NNW of Tokyo; pop. (1990p) 76,223.

Ta·te·ya·ma \ˌtä-tā-ˈyä-mä\. Volcanic peak, W cen. Honshū, Japan, SE of Toyama; 9892 ft. (3015 m.).

Tatoi *or* **Tatói.** See DHEKÉLIA.

Ta·toosh Island \tə-ˈtüsh\. Small island, NW Washington, off Cape Flattery.

Ta·tra Mountains \ˈtä-trə\ *or* **High Tatra Mountains** *or Czech* **Vy·so·ké Ta·try** \ˈvē-sȯ-ˌkā-ˈtä-trē\. Chief mountain group of the cen. Carpathian Mts., bet. Slovakia and Poland; highest peak Gerlachovka 8711 ft. (2655 m.); many small lakes; resort region.

Tatra National Park. National park, S Poland; 84 sq. mi. (218 sq. km.); highest part of Carpathian Mts.; estab. 1948.

Tatsienlu. See KANGDING.

Tatt·nall \ˈtat-nəl\. County in SE cen. Georgia. See table at GEORGIA.

Ta–tu. See KHANBALIK.

Ta·tuí \tá-ˈtwē\. City, São Paulo state, SE Brazil, 75 mi. (121 km.) W of the city of São Paulo; munic. pop. (1991p) 76,372.

Ta–t'ung *or* **Tatung–fu.** See DATONG.

Tau \ˈtau̇\. Largest of the Manua Is. (*q.v.*), American Samoa, SW cen. Pacific Ocean, in E part of group; 17 sq. mi. (44 sq. km.); highest point 3056 ft. (932 m.).

Tauata. See TAHUATA.

Tau·ba·té \ˌtaù-bə-ˈtā\. City, São Paulo state, SE Brazil, 75 mi. (121 km.) ENE of the city of São Paulo on the Paraíba River; munic. pop. (1991p) 205,070.

Tau·ber \ˈtaù-bər\. River, Baden-Württemberg and Bavaria, S cen. Germany; rises W of Ansbach, flows NW to the Main at Wertheim; 75 mi. (121 km.) long.

Tau·ern \ˈtaù-ərn\. Railroad tunnel through the Hohe Tauern Range of the Alps, Austria; 5.31 mi. (8.54 km.) long; alt. 4021 ft. (1226 m.); connects the valley of the Gasteiner Ache in Salzburg with NW Carinthia.

Tauern, Hohe. See table at ALPS.

Tauern, Niedere. See NIEDERE TAUERN.

Tau·ghan·nock Falls \tə-ˈga-nək\. Waterfall in a small stream in Tompkins co., New York, 1 mi. (1.6 km.) from Cayuga Lake and 8 mi. (13 km.) NW of Ithaca; 215 ft. (66 m.) high; one of the highest in E United States.

Tau·hu·nu \ˌtaù-ˈhü-nü\. Village, W coast of island of Manihiki, Northern Cook Is., cen. Pacific Ocean.

Tau·ma·ru·nui \ˌtaù-mə-rù-ˈnü-ē\. Borough, W North I., New Zealand, on Wanganui River 170 mi. (274 km.) N of Wellington; pop. (1988e) 6400; resort and starting point for tourists to Tongariro National Park to the SE.

Taum Sauk Mountain \ˈtäm-säk\. Peak, Iron co., SE Missouri; 1772 ft. (540 m.); highest point in the state.

Taung \ˈtaùŋ\ *or* **Taungs** \ˈtaùŋz\. Village, North-West prov., Rep. of South Africa, on an affluent of Vaal River 80 mi. (129 km.) N of Kimberly. Taungs skull, a fossil skull of previously unknown hominid (*Australopithecus africanus*) found here 1924.

Taung·gyi *also* **Tawng·gyi** \ˈtaùn-ˈjē\. Town, ❋ of Shan state, cen. Myanmar, 95 mi. (153 km.) SE of Mandalay; pop. (1983c) 108,231.

Taung·myo Range \ˈtaùn-ˌmyō\. Mountain range, along the coast of Myanmar, extending S from Moulmein; highest peak 3684 ft. (1123 m.).

Taungs. See TAUNG.

Taun·ton \ˈtȯnt-ᵊn, ˈtänt-\. **1.** River, SE Massachusetts; rises in N cen. Plymouth co., flows S into Mount Hope Bay at Fall River; navigable as far as Taunton.
2. City, a ⊗ of Bristol co., SE Massachusetts, on Taunton River at head of navigation 13 mi. (21 km.) N of Fall River; pop. (1990c) 49,832; silverware, ceramic products, plastics, jewelry; founded c. 1639; industrial center since 1650s.
3. Town, ⊗ of Somerset, SW England, on the Tone 38 mi. (61 km.) SW of Bristol; pop. (1981p) 35,326; market town; cider, textiles.

Tau·nus \ˈtaù-nəs\. Mountain range, Hesse, SW cen. Germany, E of the Rhine River and N of the lower Main; highest peak Grosser Feldberg 2886 ft. (880 m.).

Tau·po \ˈtaù-pō\. Borough, North I., New Zealand; pop. (1992e) 18,500.

Taupo, Lake. Lake, cen. North I., New Zealand; 234 sq. mi. (606 sq. km.), 25 mi. (40 km.) long; max. depth 522 ft. (159 m.); largest lake on the island.

Tau·ra·ge \ˌtaù-rä-ˈgā\ *or Ger.* **Tau·rog·gen** \ˈtaù-ˌrȯ-gən\. Town, Lithuania, 65 mi. (105 km.) WNW of Kaunas and NE of Sovetsk. Meeting place of a convention 1812 resulting in neutrality agreement bet. Russia and neighboring states after invasion of Russia by France under Emperor Napoléon.

Tau·ranga \taù-ˈräŋ-ə\. City, N North I., New Zealand, on **Tauranga Harbor** (inlet of Bay of Plenty) 95 mi. (153 km.) SE of Auckland; pop. (1991c) 67,333; an important seaport of New Zealand.

Taurasia. See TURIN.

Tau·ria·no·va \ˌtaù-rē-ə-ˈnȯ-və\. Commune, Reggio di Calabria prov., Calabria, S Italy, 28 mi. (45 km.) NE of the commune of Reggio di Calabria; pop. (1981p) 15,384.

Tau·ric Cher·so·nese \ˈtȯr-ik-ˈkər-sə-ˌnēz, -ˌnēs\. Ancient name for the Crimean Penin., part of the kingdom of the Cimmerian Bosporus acquired by Rome first cent. B.C.

Tau·ri·da \ˈtȯr-ə-də\ *or Russ.* **Ta·vri·da** \təv-ˈrē-də\. Former Russian administrative subdivision, now included in Crimea, Ukraine.

Tauroggen. See TAURAGE.

Tauromenium. See TAORMINA.

Tau·rus Mountains \ˈtȯr-əs\ *or Turk.* **To·ros Dağ·la·rı** \tȯ-ˈrȯs-ˌdä-lä-ˈrē\. Mountain chain, S Turkey in Asia, running parallel to the Mediterranean coast; has many high peaks, highest above 12,000 ft. (3660 m.); crossed N of Tarsus by important pass of Cilician Gates; to the NE the extension of the range is the Anti-Taurus (*q.v.*).

Ta·var·es \tə-ˈvar-ēz\. City, ⊗ of Lake co., cen. Florida Penin., 28 mi. (45 km.) NW of Orlando; pop. (1990c) 7383.

Tavastehus. **1.** Province, Finland. See HÄME.
2. City, Finland. See HÄMEENLINNA.

Tav·da \təf-ˈdä\. **1.** River, W Russia in Asia, chiefly in NE Sverdlovsk Oblast; flows SE from Ural Mts. to Tobol River SW of Tobol'sk; 450 mi. (724 km.) long.
2. Town, E Sverdlovsk Oblast, W Russia in Asia, on lower Tavda River ab. 125 mi. (200 km.) W of Tobol'sk.

Ta·ver·ny \ˌtȧ-ver-ˈnē\. Commune, Val-d'Oise dept., France, just NNW of Paris; 12th–13th cent. church.

Ta·ve·u·ni \ˌtä-vē-ˈü-nē\. Island, Fiji, SW Pacific Ocean, 2 mi. (3 km.) SE of Vanua Levu; 28 mi. (45 km.) long; 166 sq. mi. (430 sq. km.); chief village Waiyevo; highest point 4071 ft. (1241 m.). Grows coffee; copra.

Ta·vi·gna·no \ˌtä-vē-ˈnyä-nō\. River, cen. Corsica, France, flowing ESE to Tyrrhenian Sea.

Ta·vi·ra \tȧ-ˈvir-ə\. Municipality, Faro dist., S Portugal, on Atlantic Ocean 18 mi. (29 km.) NE of the commune of Faro; pop. (1981p) 24,182; tuna fisheries.

Ta·vo·la·ra \ˌtä-vō-ˈlä-rä\. Small island off NE coast of Sardinia, Italy, E of Olbia; ab. 2.5 sq. mi. (6.5 sq. km.).

Tavor, Har. See TABOR, MOUNT.

Ta·voy \tə-ˈvȯi\. **1.** River, Myanmar; flows S into Andaman Sea E of Tavoy Penin.; ab. 90 mi. (145 km.) long. Its lower course for 30 mi. (48 km.) forms a wide estuary.
2. Town, ❋ of Tenasserim div., S Myanmar, on left bank of Tavoy River ab. 30 mi. (48 km.) from its mouth; pop. (1983c) 69,882; tin; rice.

Tavoy Island. See MALI ISLAND.

Tavoy Point. Cape at S end of **Tavoy Peninsula,** on W coast of Myanmar at mouth of the Tavoy River, 13°32′N, 98°10′E.

Tavrida. See TAURIDA.

Ta·vur·vur, Mount \tə-ˈvùr-vùr\ *also* **Mount Ma·tu·pi** \mə-ˈtü-pē\. Volcano, one of a group nearly surrounding the town of Rabaul, on Blanche Bay, E New Britain I., Papua New Guinea; eruptions in May 1937 and Sept. 1994, together with those of nearby Mt. Vulcan, caused great destruction at Rabaul and on Gazelle Penin. See MOTHER, MOUNT.

Taw \ˈtȯ\. River, Devon, SW England; flows NW into Barnstaple Bay through an estuary at Barnstaple; ab. 50 mi. (80 km.) long.

Ta·wa \ˈtä-wə\. Borough, North I., New Zealand, N of Wellington; pop. (1981c) 12,216.

Ta·was City \ˈtȯ-wəs\. City, ⊗ of Iosco co., NE Michigan; pop. (1990c) 2009.

Ta·wau \tä-ˈwaù\. Port, Sabah, Malaysia, NE Borneo I.; pop. (1980c) 43,200.

Ta·wi \ˈtə-wē\. River, Jammu and Kashmir, N India; flows SW to Chenab River on the N Punjab border, Pakistan; ab. 95 mi. (153 km.) long.

Ta·wi–ta·wi \ˌtä-wē-ˈtä-wē\. **1.** Island group, SW Sulu Archipelago, Philippines; forms a province and comprises Tawi-tawi I., Sanga Sanga I., Simunul I., several smaller islands, and a number of clusters of small islands, totaling ab. 100; 360 sq. mi. (932 sq. km.). See SULU ARCHIPELAGO and table at PHILIPPINES.
2. Large island of the group; ab. 34 mi. (55 km.) long by 6 to 14 mi. (10 to 23 km.) wide; 229 sq. mi. (593 sq. km.); of volcanic origin, with rich soil and covered with tropical vegetation. Highest point 1751 ft. (534 m.). Occupied by U.S. troops Apr. 1945 during WWII.

Tawnggyi. See TAUNGGYI.

Tax·co \ˈtäs-kō\ *or in full* **Tax·co de Alar·cón** \t͟hā-ˌä-lär-ˈkȯn\. Town, Guerrero state, S Mexico, ab. 45 mi. (72 km.) SSW of Mexico City; munic. pop. (1990p) 86,811; silver mines; silverware manufacture; tourist resort; Cacahuamilpa Caverns are nearby.

Tax·i·la \ˈtak-sə-lə\. Ruins of ancient town, Pakistan, just E of Indus River SW of Rawalpindi; under Persian rule, visited by Macedonian King Alexander the Great 326 B.C.; became an important Buddhist center under King Aśoka after his conversion to Buddhism c. 261 B.C.; destroyed by Huns 5th cent. A.D.

Tay \ˈtā\. River, Scotland; rises near NW border of Central region, flows NE through **Loch Tay** (15 mi. or 24 km. long) and then SE into the Firth of Tay; 120 mi. (193 km.) long; longest river in Scotland.

Tay, Firth of. Estuary of the Tay River, E Scotland, N of the Firth of Forth; extends inland 24.5 mi. (39.4 km.); empties into North Sea.

Ta·ya·bas \tä-ˈyä-bäs\. **1.** Province, Philippines. See QUEZON.
2. Municipality, Quezon prov., Luzon, Philippines; pop. (1980c) 42,137.

Tayabas Bay. Inlet, SW coast of Quezon prov., S Luzon, Philippines; W side borders on Batangas prov.; on SE connects with Mompog Pass; Lucena is on it.

Ta–ya Wan. See DAYA WAN.

Ta–yeh. See DAYE.

Taygetus. See TAÍYETOS.

Ta–ying. See DAYING.

Tay·lor \ˈtā-lər\. **1.** Name of counties in seven states of the U.S. See tables at FLORIDA, GEORGIA, IOWA, KENTUCKY, TEXAS, WEST VIRGINIA, WISCONSIN.
2. City, Wayne co., SE Michigan, 4 mi. (6.4 km.) WSW of Detroit; pop. (1990c) 70,811.
3. Village, ⊗ of Loup co., cen. Nebraska; pop. (1990c) 186.
4. Borough, Lackawanna co., NE Pennsylvania, 3 mi. (4.8 km.) WSW of Scranton; pop. (1990c) 6941.
5. City, Williamson co., cen. Texas, 28 mi. (45 km.) NE of Austin; pop. (1990c) 11,472.

Taylor, Mount. Peak, NE Cibola co., W New Mexico; 11,301 ft. (3444 m.).

Taylor Lake Village. City, Harris co., SE Texas, SE of Houston; pop. (1990c) 3394.

Taylor Mill. City, Kenton co., N Kentucky; pop. (1990c) 5530.

Taylor Mountain. **1.** Peak, Chaffee co., cen. Colorado; 13,600 ft. (4145 m.).
2. Peak, W cen. Lemhi co., E cen. Idaho; 9960 ft. (3036 m.).

Taylor Park Dam. Dam across **Taylor River,** tributary of Gunnison River, E Gunnison co., W cen. Colorado; height 206 ft. (63 m.); completed 1937; impounds water for irrigation, forming **Taylor Park Reservoir.**

Tay·lors·ville \ˈtā-lərz-ˌvil\. **1.** City, ⊗ of Spencer co., cen. Kentucky; pop. (1990c) 774.
2. Town, ⊗ of Alexander co., W cen. North Carolina, in Blue Ridge foothills 18 mi. (29 km.) WNW of Statesville; pop. (1990c) 1566.

Tay·lor·ville \ˈtā-lər-ˌvil\. City, ⊗ of Christian co., cen. Illinois, 25 mi. (40 km.) SE of Springfield; pop. (1990c) 11,133.

Tay·mā' \tī-ˈmä, ˈtī-ˌmä\ *or* **Tai·ma** \ˈtī-mə, ˈtā-\ *or* **Tei·ma** \ˈtā-mə\; *bib.* **Te·ma** \ˈtē-mə\. Oasis and ancient commercial town, NW Nejd, Saudi Arabia.

Taymyra River. See TAYMYR PENINSULA.

Tay·myr Autonomous Okrug \tī-ˈmir\ *or* **Tai·myr Autonomous Okrug** \tī-ˈmir ... ˈȯ-krůk\. Administrative subdivision of N Russia in Asia, incl. the Taymyr Penin.; 332,857 sq. mi. (862,100 sq. km.); pop. (1992e) 53,000; ✻ Dudinka; entirely within the Arctic Circle; reindeer herding, hunting, fishing.

Taymyr Peninsula *also* **Taimyr Peninsula.** Large peninsula, N Russia in Asia, wholly within Taymyr Autonomous Okrug, bet. the Yenisey and Khatanga rivers; includes Cape Chelyuskin, the northernmost point of Asia, 77°45′N, 104°20′E; crossed in cen. part by **Tay·my·ra River** \tī-ˈmir-ə\, 400 mi. (644 km.) long, flowing E and N through the large, irregular-shaped **Taymyr Lake** to **Taymyr Bay,** 76°15′N, 98°E. To the W of the bay is **Taymyr Island.**

Tay Ninh \ˈtī-ˈnin\. Town, SW Vietnam, NW of Ho Chi Minh City; pop. (1989c) 32,881.

Tay·ro·na National Park \tī-ˈrō-nä\. National park, N Colombia, on Caribbean coast E of Santa Marta; 58 sq. mi. (150 sq. km.); estab. 1964; beautiful beaches, tropical forests; monkeys; ruins of extinct Tairona culture.

Tay·side \ˈtā-ˌsīd\. Administrative region, E Scotland. See table at SCOTLAND.

Tay·tay \tī-ˈtī\. Town on coast at N end of Palawan I., Philippines; pop. (1980c) 22,980.

Taz \ˈtäz\. River, W cen. Russia in Asia; ab. 600 mi. (965 km.) long; rises in W Krasnoyarsk Kray, flows N and NW through E Yamalo-Nenets Autonomous Okrug into **Taz Bay,** E arm of Gulf of Ob, 230 mi. (370 km.) long, 35 mi. (56 km.) at its widest part.

Ta·za \ˈtä-zə\. Town, N Morocco, E of Fès; pop. (1982c) 77,216.

Taze·well \ˈtaz-ˌwel, -wəl\. **1.** Name of counties in two states of the U.S. See tables at ILLINOIS and VIRGINIA.
2. Town, ⊗ of Claiborne co., NE Tennessee; pop. (1990c) 2150.
3. Town, ⊗ of Tazewell co., SW Virginia; pop. (1990c) 4176.

Ta·zoult–Lam·bese \tä-ˈzült-läⁿ-ˈbez\; *formerly* **Lam·bes·sa** \lam-ˈbe-sə\ *or* **Lam·bèse** \läⁿ-ˈbez\; *anc.* **Lam·bae·sis** \lam-ˈbē-səs\. Commune, NE Algeria, SW of Batna; center of agricultural region. Ancient Lambaesis an important Roman town of S Numidia; its numerous ruins are the remains of a great Roman camp (c. 3d cent. A.D.).

Tbi·li·si \tə-bi-ˈlē-sē\ *or* **Tif·lis** \ˈti-fləs, tə-ˈflēs\. City, ✻ of Republic of Georgia, in SE part on both banks of the Kura River, 280 mi. (451 km.) WNW of Baku, Azerbaijan; pop. (1989p) 1,260,000; machine tools, electrical equipment, locomotives, textiles, plastics, leather goods, furniture, wine; hydroelectric power. Sion Cathedral (c. 6th cent., later restored), numerous parks and gardens; center of Georgian culture and education, with a university (1918), theaters, and research institutes.
History: Founded 5th cent. A.D. as ✻ of ancient Georgian kingdom; for centuries an important center on trade routes bet. Europe and Asia and frequently sacked; has been under Persian, Byzantine, Arab, Mongol, and Turkish rule; came under Russian rule c. 1801; center of rebellion against Russian government 1905; seat of new administration 1917; became ✻ of Transcaucasian Federation 1921; made ✻ of Georgian S.S.R. 1936; scene of civilian massacre 1989 by Soviet military during independence demonstration; became ✻ of independent Republic of Georgia 1991.

Tchad. See CHAD.

Tchi·ban·ga \chē-ˈbäŋ-gä\. Town, SW Gabon, NE of Mayumba; pop. (1985e) 53,500.

Tczew \ˈchef\ *or Ger.* **Dir·schau** \ˈdir-ˌshaů\. Commune, E Gdańsk prov., N Poland, on left bank of Vistula River 20 mi. (32 km.) SSE of the city of Gdańsk; pop. (1989e) 59,045; railroad junction and river port; shipyard, railroad shops; dates from c. 1200; to Poland 1282, to Prussia 1772; returned to Poland 1919.

Teague \ˈtēg\. City, Freestone co., E cen. Texas, 45 mi. (72 km.) E of Waco; pop. (1990c) 3268.

Te Anau Lake \tā-ˈä-naů\. Lake, SW South I., New Zealand; 38 mi. (61 km.) long; 133 sq. mi. (345 sq. km.); max. depth 906 ft. (276 m.); a source of the Waiau River.

Tea·neck \ˈtē-ˌnek\. Township, Bergen co., NE corner of New Jersey, 8 mi. (13 km.) E of Paterson; pop. (1990c) 37,825; residential.

Te·a·no \tā-ˈä-nō\; *anc.* **Te·a·num Sid·i·ci·num** \tē-ˈā-nəm-ˌsi-də-ˈsī-nəm\. Commune, Caserta prov., Campania, S Italy, 29 mi. (47 km.) NNW of Naples; pop. (1981p) 14,170; early 12th cent. cathedral; ruins of Roman amphitheater.

Te Aro·ha \tā-ˈär-ō-ə\. Borough, N North I., New Zealand, on Waihou River 70 mi. (113 km.) SE of Auckland; pop. (1987e) 3540; health resort with hot medicinal springs.

Teate. See CHIETI 2.

Té·bes·sa \ti-ˈbe-sə\; *anc.* **The·ves·te** \thi-ˈves-tē\. Commune, NE Algeria, near Tunisian border; pop. (1987p) 107,559; trade center; as Theveste strategic town of Roman Africa; site of extensive ruins incl. 3d cent. arch of Caracalla and 4th cent. Christian basilica.

Te·bi·cua·ry \ˌte-bi-kwä-ˈrē\. River, S Paraguay; flows W into Paraguay River; ab. 250 mi. (402 km.) long.

Te·bing·ting·gi \tə-ˌbiŋ-ˈtiŋ-gē\. **1.** *or* **Te·bing Ting·gi** \tə-ˌbiŋ-ˈtiŋ-gē\. Island, Indonesia, bet. E coast of Sumatra and W coast of Singapore.

2. Town, NE Sumatra, Indonesia, on railroad line ab. 35 mi. (56 km.) SE of Medan; pop. (1990c) 116,767.

3. Town, SE Sumatra, Indonesia, on S branch of Musi River ab. 60 mi. (95 km.) ESE of Benkulu.

Té·bour·ba \tā-ˈbu̇r-bə\. Town, N Tunisia, ab. 32 mi. (52 km.) W of city of Tunis; site of WWII battle May 1943 in which Allied forces drove out the Germans.

Tebrau, Selat. See JOHORE STRAIT.

Teche, Bayou \ˈtesh\. Navigable stream in Louisiana; flows into Atchafalaya River; ab. 175 mi. (280 km.) long; mentioned in poet Henry Wadsworth Longfellow's *Evangeline* (1847).

Te–chou. See DEZHOU.

Tecolutla. See NECAXA.

Te·co·mán \ˌtā-kō-ˈmän\. Municipality, Colima state, Mexico, 22 mi. (35 km.) S of the city of Colima; pop. (1990p) 80,842; cotton, coconuts, tropical fruits.

Tec·pan \ˈtek-ˌpän\. Municipality, Guerrero state, Mexico, 55 mi. (89 km.) NW of Acapulco; fishing, lumber; diversified agriculture.

Tec·pán Gua·te·ma·la \tek-ˈpän-ˌgwä-tā-ˈmä-lä\. Town, Chimaltenango dept., S cen. Guatemala; munic. pop. (1981c) 29,468.

Te·cuci \te-ˈküch\. City, Galaţi co., E Romania, on a tributary of the Siret ab. 30 mi. (48 km.) SSW of Bîrlad; munic. pop. (1989c) 46,686; alcoholic beverages.

Te·cum·seh \tə-ˈkəm-sə, -sē\. **1.** City, Lenawee co., S Michigan, 22 mi. (35 km.) SSW of Ann Arbor; pop. (1990c) 7462.

2. City, ⊗ of Johnson co., SE Nebraska, 31 mi. (50 km.) E of Beatrice; pop. (1990c) 1702.

3. City, Pottawatomie co., cen. Oklahoma, 5 mi. (8 km.) S of Shawnee; pop. (1990c) 5750.

4. Town, Essex co., SE Ontario, Canada, on Lake St. Clair 10 mi. (16 km.) E of Windsor; pop. (1991c) 10,495.

Te·dzhen \te-ˈjen\; *formerly* **Te·jend** \-ˈjend\. Lower course of the Harī (*q.v.*), S Turkmenistan; also the oasis near which the stream loses itself in sands of Kara-Kum Desert.

Tees \ˈtēz\. River, N England; rises in Cumbria co., flows E, empties into North Sea at Middlesbrough; 70 mi. (113 km.) long.

Tees·side \ˈtēz-ˌsīd\. Urban area, Cleveland, N England, on the Tees; 77 sq. mi. (199 sq. km.); pop. (1981p) 382,891; steel, chemicals; shipbuilding; formed 1968 by reorganization of boroughs and districts in North Riding, Yorkshire (now North Yorkshire).

Tee·wi·not, Mount \ˈtē-wə-ˌnät\. Peak, cen. Grand Teton National Park, NW Wyoming; 12,317 ft. (3754 m.).

Te·fé *or* **Tef·fé** \te-ˈfā\. River, Amazonas state, W Brazil; flows NE into Amazon River; ab. 500 mi. (805 km.) long.

Te·ga Cay \ˈtē-gə-ˈkā\. City, York co., N South Carolina, N of Rock Hill; pop. (1990c) 3016.

Te·gal \tā-ˈgäl\. Seaport, Central Java prov., Indonesia, on N coast railroad line 50 mi. (81 km.) W of Pekalongan; pop. (1990c) 229,713; processes and exports sugar.

Te·gea \ˈtē-jē-ə\. Ancient city, SE Arcadia, cen. Peloponnese, S Greece, SE of Tripolis. Under Spartan rule from mid-6th cent. B.C. until Thebes' victory over Sparta in battle of Leuctra c. 371 B.C. Site of temple of Athena Alea rebuilt 4th cent. B.C. by the sculptor Scopas. See ARCADIA 4.

Te·ge·len \ˈtā-gə-lən\. Commune, Limburg prov., SE Netherlands, just S of Venlo on German border; pop. (1992e) 19,166.

Te·gern·see \ˈtā-gərn-ˌzā\. **1.** Lake in Bavaria, S Germany, 30 mi. (48 km.) SSE of Munich, in foothills of Alps; 4 mi. (6 km.) long; elev. 2382 ft. (726 m.); popular resort.

2. Village on Tegernsee (lake); 15th cent. church; castle.

Teg·na·pa·tam \ˌteg-nə-ˈpə-təm\. See FORT SAINT DAVID.

Te·gu·ci·gal·pa \tā-ˌgü-sē-ˈgäl-pä\. **1.** Department, Honduras. See FRANCISCO MORAZÁN.

2. City, ✱ of Honduras and of Francisco Morazán dept.; area pop. (1989e) 608,100; alt. 3300 ft. (1006 m.); textiles, sugar, cigarettes; cathedral; university (1847), teacher-training college (1990). Founded as gold- and silver-mining center c. 1578; made permanent ✱ of Honduras 1880.

Te·hach·a·pi \ti-ˈha-chə-pē\. City, Kern co., SW California, ESE of Bakersfield; pop. (1990c) 5791.

Tehachapi Mountains. Mountain range, S cen. California, running E to W bet. S end of the Sierra Nevada and the Coast Ranges; highest point Double Mountain 7988 ft. (2435 m.); at E end is **Tehachapi Pass,** elev. 3793 ft. (1156 m.), leading from Mojave Desert into the San Joaquin Valley.

Te·ha·ma \ti-ˈhā-mə\. County in N California. See table at CALIFORNIA.

Tehama. See TIHAMA.

Te·hip·i·te Dome \tə-ˈhi-pə-tē\. Peak in the Sierra Nevada in E Fresno co., S cen. California; 7713 ft. (2351 m.).

Teh·ran *or* **Tehrān** *also* **Te·he·ran** \ˌtā-ə-ˈran, -ˈrän\. City, national ✱, constituting a province, NW cen. Iran, ab. 65 mi. (105 km.) S of the Caspian Sea, at foot of S slope of Elburz Mts.; met. area pop. (1986c) 6,042,584; alt. 3800 ft. (1158 m.); transportation and industrial center, producing automobiles, cement, sugar, textiles; numerous public buildings and mosques; several universities incl. Univ. of Tehran (1934).

History: Orig. a suburb of Rey, Iranian ✱ until Mongol invasion early 13th cent.; made ✱ c. 1788; underwent rapid modernization after 1925 and esp. after WWII; site of conference Nov.–Dec. 1943 bet. British Prime Minister Winston Churchill, U.S. President Franklin Delano Roosevelt, and Soviet leader Joseph Stalin; U.S. embassy seized and hostages taken by Iranian militants Nov. 1979; hostages released Jan. 1981.

Teh·ri \ˈtar-ē\. **1.** *or* **Tehri Garh·wal** \gər-ˈwäl\. Former state, N India; located entirely in the Himalayas with ranges 20,000 to 23,000 ft. (6100 to 7010 m.); contained also the sources of both the Ganges and the Yamuna and hence had many places of pilgrimage; estab. early 19th cent. as a state by the British after border war with Nepal and added to Punjab States Agency c. 1936; incorp. into Uttar Pradesh late 1940s.

2. Town, NW Uttar Pradesh, N India; in the Himalayas on the Bhagirathi River 145 mi. (233 km.) NE of Delhi.

3. Town, Madhya Pradesh, India. See TIKAMGARH.

Tehsien. See DEZHOU.

Te–hua. See DEHUA.

Te·hua·cán \ˌtā-wä-ˈkän\. Town, Puebla state, SE cen. Mexico, 65 mi. (105 km.) SE of the city of Puebla; munic. pop. (1990c) 139,450; mineral springs.

Te·huan·te·pec \tā-ˈwän-tä-ˌpek\ *or in full* **San·to Do·min·go Tehuantepec** \ˈsän-tō-t͟hō-ˈmēŋ-gō\. Town, Oaxaca state, S Mexico, on the **Tehuantepec River** which flows from the Sierra Madre to the Gulf of Tehuantepec; in oil-producing area.

Tehuantepec, Gulf of. Widemouthed inlet of the Pacific Ocean, SE Mexico, bounded by states of Oaxaca and Chiapas.

Tehuantepec, Isthmus of. Isthmus, S Mexico, bet. the Bay of Campeche on the N and the Gulf of Tehuantepec on the S; 137 mi. (220 km.) wide.

Tehuantepec River. See TEHUANTEPEC.

Tei·de, Pi·co de \ˈpē-kō-t͟hā-ˈtā-t͟hā\ *or* **Pico de Tey·de** \ˈtā-t͟hā\ *or* **Pico de Te·ne·ri·fe** \dā-ˌtān-ə-ˈrēf-ə\ *or Eng.* **Peak of Ten·er·ife** \ˌten-ə-ˈrif, -ˈrēf\. Volcanic mountain on the island of Tenerife, Canary Is. (*q.v.*), Spain; 12,198 ft. (3718 m.).

Tei·fi \ˈtī-vē\. River, W Wales; flows SW and W into S Cardigan Bay; ab. 50 mi. (80 km.) long.

\ə\ abut \ə\ matches \$^{ə}$\ kitten, Fr table \ər\ further \a\ ash \ā\ ace \ä\ cot, cart \a̍\ Fr bac \au̇\ out \b\ Span Avila \ch\ chin \e\ bet \ē\ easy \g\ go \i\ hit \ī\ ice \j\ job \k\ Ger ich, Buch \$^{n}$\ Fr vin \ŋ\ sing \ō\ go \ö\ all \ȯ\ law \œ\ Fr bœuf \œ̄\ Fr feu \ȯi\ boy \th\ thin \t͟h\ this \ü\ loot \u̇\ foot \ue\ Ger füllen \ue̅\ Fr rue \y\ yet \$^{y}$\ Fr digne \ˈdēn^{y}\, nuit \ˈnw^{y}ē\ \yü\ few \yu̇\ fury \zh\ vision

Teign \ˈtin, ˈtēn\. River, Devon, SW England; rises in Dartmoor and flows SE into the English Channel at Teignmouth; 30 mi. (48 km.) long.

Teign·mouth \ˈtin-məth, ˈtēn-\. Town, Devon, SW England, at mouth of the Teign 15 mi. (24 km.) S of Exeter; pop. (1981c) 11,913; seaside resort and yachting center.

Teil, Le. See LE TEIL.

Teima. See TAYMĀʼ.

Tei·she·bai·ni \ˌtā-shə-ˈbī-nē\. Ancient settlement of Urarty, in what is now Armenia; overcome by Assyrians c. 6th cent. B.C.; archaeological investigations have yielded many artifacts.

Tei·xei·ra Pin·to \tā-ˈshā-rə-ˈpēn-tü\; *formerly* **Can·chun·go** \kän-ˈchüŋ-gō\. Town, W Guinea-Bissau, in coastal lowlands WNW of port of Bissau.

Tejend. See TEDZHEN.

Tejo. See TAGUS.

Te·ju·pil·ca de Hi·dal·go \ˌtā-hü-ˈpēl-kä-ˌthā-ē-ˈthäl-gō\. Municipality, México state, Mexico, 70 mi. (113 km.) SW of Mexico City; numerous Indian remains of archaeological interest.

Te·ka·mah \tə-ˈkā-mə\. City, ⊗ of Burt co., E Nebraska, 28 mi. (45 km.) NE of Fremont; pop. (1990c) 1852.

Te·ka·po \tā-ˈkä-pō\. River, cen. South I., New Zealand; flows from S end of **Lake Tekapo** (32 sq. mi. or 83 sq. km.); one of the headstreams of the Waitaki River.

Te·kax \tā-ˈkäs\ *or in full* **Tekax de Ál·va·ro Obre·gón** \thā-ˈäl-bä-rō-ˌō-brā-ˈgōn\. Town, Yucatán state, on Yucatán Penin., SE Mexico, ab. 60 mi. (95 km.) SE of Mérida.

Te·kes \te-ˈkes\ *or W.-G.* **T'e–k'o–ssu** \ˌtə-ˈkə-sə\. River, E Kazakhstan and W Xinjiang Uygur, China; joins the Künes to form the Ili.

Te·ke·ze \te-ˈkā-zā\ *also* **Tak·ka·ze** \tə-ˈkā-zā\. River, E Africa; headstream of the Atbara; rises in N cen. Ethiopia and flows N and then W, forming part of border bet. Ethiopia and Eritrea, then crossing into Sudan where it is called the **Sa·tit** \ˈsä-tēt\ *or* **Se·tit** \ˈsā-tēt\; ab. 470 mi. (755 km.) long.

Te·kir·dağ \te-ˈkir-ˌdäg\. **1.** Province of Turkey in Europe. See table at TURKEY.
2. *or Ital.* **Ro·do·sto** \rō-ˈdo-stō\; *anc.* **Bi·san·the** \bə-ˈsan-thē\ *or* **Rhae·des·tus** *also* **Rai·des·tos** \ri-ˈdes-təs\. Seaport and market town, its ✻, on the Sea of Marmara 78 mi. (126 km.) W of İstanbul; pop. (1990p) 80,207; ancient Bisanthe dates from c. 7th cent. B.C.; came under Turks 1320 A.D.; served as important port for Edirne (Adrianople) until late 19th cent.

T'e–k'o–ssu. See TEKES.

Tekrit. See TIKRĪT.

Te Ku·i·ti \ˌtā-kü-ˈē-tē\. Borough, NW North I., New Zealand, on Waipa River 105 mi. (169 km.) S of Auckland; pop. (1981c) 4795; Waitomo Caves (*q.v.*) are nearby.

Te·la \ˈtā-lä\. Town, Atlántida dept., N Honduras; pop. (1989e) 23,500.

Tel Aviv \ˌtel-ə-ˈvēv\. District of W cen. Israel. See table at ISRAEL.

Tel Aviv–Jaf·fa \-ˈjä-fə, -ˈyä-\ *or* **Tel Aviv–Ya·fo** \-ˈyä-fō\. Twin cities, ✻ of Tel Aviv dist., Israel, on the Mediterranean Sea; pop. (1992e) 353,200; textiles, chemicals; food processing; banking and insurance; tourism; Habima Theater (1945), university (1953), botanical and zoological gardens; Tel Aviv founded 1909, ✻ of Israel 1948–50; Jaffa was incorp. with Tel Aviv 1950; served as a commercial seaport until 1965; damaged by Iraqi missiles 1991 during Persian Gulf War. See JAFFA.

Tel·de \ˈtel-dā\. Commune, Las Palmas prov., E Canary Is., Spain, on E Grand Canary I. 6 mi. (10 km.) S of the city of Las Palmas; pop. (1991c) 77,356.

Tel el Ke·bir \ˈtel-el-ke-ˈbir\ *or* **Tell el–Kebir** \ˈtel\ *or* **El Tell el Ke·bîr** \el-ˈtel-el-ke-ˈbir\. Village, N Egypt, near Zagazig; scene of victory of British over Egyptians 1882, subsequently leading to British rule in Egypt.

Tel·e·mark \ˈte-lə-ˌmärk\. **1.** Mountain and lake region, Telemark co., S Norway; highest peak Gausta 6178 ft. (1883 m.).
2. County of S Norway. See table at NORWAY.

Te·le·or·man \ˌtel-yor-ˈmän\. County of S Romania. See table at ROMANIA.

Tel·e·scope Peak \ˈte-lə-ˌskōp\. Mountain in Panamint Mts., SE Inyo co., E California; 11,049 ft. (3368 m.).

Te·les Pi·res \ˈte-lēs-ˈpē-rēs\; *formerly* **São Ma·nuel** \ˌsaủⁿ-mä-ˈnwel\. River, cen. Brazil; flows NW out of Mato Grosso state, forming part of boundary bet. Mato Grosso and Pará states; ab. 600 mi. (965 km.) long; joins with Juruena (*q.v.*) to form the Tapajós River.

Tel·fair \ˈtel-ˌfar\. County in S cen Georgia. See table at GEORGIA.

Tel·ford \ˈtel-fərd\. **1.** Borough, Bucks and Montgomery cos., SE Pennsylvania, 21 mi. (34 km.) S of Allentown; pop. (1990c) 4238.
2. New town, Shropshire, W England, WNW of Birmingham; pop. (1981c) 103,646.

Tel Gezer. See GEZER.

Té·li·mé·lé \ˌtā-lē-mā-ˈlā\. Town, W Guinea, NNE of Conakry; pop. (1983p) 25,951.

Telkalakh. See TALL KALAKH.

Tell Ar·pa·chi·ya \ˌtel-är-ˈpä-chē-yə\. Ancient Assyrian city; its site is just N of Mosul, N Iraq, bet. the sites of Nineveh and Dur Sharrukin (see KHORSABAD).

Tell As·mar \ˈas-mər, ˈaz-\; *anc.* **Esh·nun·na** \esh-ˈnən-ə\. Locality, E Iraq, 33 mi. (53 km.) ENE of Baghdad; archaeological site where numerous Sumerian artifacts have been found incl. stone statuettes dating from 3d millennium B.C.

Tell Atlas. See ATLAS MOUNTAINS.

Tell Basta. See BUBASTIS.

Tell City \ˈtel\. City, Perry co., S Indiana, on Ohio River 40 mi. (64 km.) E of Evansville; pop. (1990c) 8808.

Tell ed–Du·weir \ˌtel-ˌed-dủ-ˈwār\. See LACHISH.

Tell el–ʻAmâr·na \ˌtel-ˌel-ə-ˈmär-nə\. Site of ruins on the Nile River, Egypt, midway bet. Thebes and Memphis. Ancient city built 14th cent. B.C. by King Akhenaton of XVIIIth dynasty; informative artifacts discovered 19th cent. incl. hundreds of cuneiform tablets.

Tell el–Kebir. See TEL EL KEBIR.

Tel·ler \ˈte-lər\. **1.** County in cen. Colorado. See table at COLORADO.
2. City, Port Clarence Inlet, W Seward Penin., W Alaska, ab. 60 mi. (95 km.) NNW of Nome; pop. (1990c) 151.

Tel·li·cher·ry \ˌte-lə-ˈcher-ē\. Town, NW Kerala, S India, on the Malabar Coast 168 mi. (270 km.) WSW of Bangalore; pop. (1991p) 103,577; commercial seaport and distribution point; exports sandalwood, coffee, and coconuts. Factory estab. here by British East India Company 1683. Withstood attacks by Indian forces under Mysore ruler Hyder Ali in Second Anglo-Mysore War (1780–84).

Tel·li·co Dam \ˈte-lə-ˌkō\. See table at TENNESSEE VALLEY AUTHORITY.

Tel·lu·ride \ˈtel-yə-ˌrīd\. Town, ⊗ of San Miguel co., SW Colorado, 40 mi. (64 km.) S of Montrose; pop. (1990c) 1309; ski slopes.

Tel Megiddo. See MEGIDDO.

Teloeti Bay. See TALUTI BAY.

Te·lok An·son \ˈte-lōk-ˈän-sən\ *or* **Te·luk Anson** \tə-ˈlủk\. Town, Perak state, Malaysia, on the Perak River, near its mouth.

Te·lo·lo·a·pan \ˌtā-lōl-ˈwä-pän\. Municipality, Guerrero state, Mexico, 24 mi. (39 km.) W of Iguala; pop. (1990p) 55,577.

Telo Martius. See TOULON.

Te·los. See TÍLOS.

Tel'·pos–iz *or* **Tel·pos–Iz** \ˌtel-pȯ-ˈsiz\. Peak, N Ural Mts., Russia, on boundary bet. Europe and Asia, 63°54′N, 59°10′E; 5558 ft. (1694 m.).

Tel·town \ˈtel-ˌtaủn\. Village, co. Meath, Ireland, 35 mi. (56 km.) NW of Dublin; in early times scene of the great annual festival said to be instituted by the god Lug in honor of his foster mother Tailte and revived 1924 at Dublin as the Tailtean Games.

Te·luk \te-ˌlük\. Indonesian term used in place names, meaning "bay," as **Teluk Slamadatang.** For names beginning with this term, see the 2d element.

Teluk Anson. See TELOK ANSON.

Te·luk·ba·jur \te-ˌlu̇k-bä-ˈyu̇r\; *formerly* **Em·ma·ha·ven** \ˌe-mə-ˈhä-vᵊn\. Port of Padang, W Sumatra, Indonesia, on NW shore of Bajur Bay 4 mi. (6 km.) S of Padang.

Teluk Humboldt *or* **Teluk Jos Sudarso** *or* **Teluk Yos Sudarso.** See YOS SUDARSO, TELUK.

Teluk Tomini. See TOMINI, GULF OF.

Te·ma \ˈtā-mä\. Seaport, SE Ghana, 20 mi. (32 km.) ENE of Accra; pop. (1984c) 100,052; extensive harbor facilities; steel, chemicals, aluminum; automobile-assembly plants; chosen early 1950s as site for port and industrial park; officially opened harbor 1962.

Tema. See TAYMĀ'.

Te·ma·ga·mi, Lake *or* **Lake Ti·ma·ga·mi** \ti-ˈmä-gə-mē\. Lake, Ontario, Canada, N of Lake Nipissing and SW of Lake Timiskaming; 91 sq. mi. (236 sq. km.); in forest reserve.

Te·mang·gung *or Du.* **Te·mang·goeng** \tə-ˈmäŋ-gu̇ŋ\. Town, Central Java prov., Indonesia, ab. 17 mi. (27 km.) N of Mageland.

Te·ma·tangi \ˌtā-mə-ˈtäŋ-ē\. Atoll, Tuamotu Archipelago, in SW part 640 mi. (1030 km.) SE of Papeete, 21°41′S, 140°40′W.

Tem·be·ling \ˈtem-bə-ˌliŋ\. River, E headstream of the Pahang River, NE Pahang state, Malaysia; joins with the Jelai to form the Pahang.

Témbi. See TEMPE, VALE OF.

Tem·bu·land \ˈtem-bü-ˌland\. Region, Eastern Cape prov., Rep. of South Africa, bet. upper Great Kei River and the Mtata; 3339 sq. mi. (8648 sq. km.); includes Bomvanaland along the coast.

Teme \ˈtēm\. River, E Wales and W England; rises in E Wales near the English border, flows S and E across the border, and curves S to join the Severn near Worcester; 60 mi. (97 km.) long.

Te·mec·u·la \ti-ˈme-kyu̇-lə\. City, SW Riverside co., SE California; pop. (1990c) 27,099.

Tem·er·loh \ˈte-mər-ˌlō\. Village, SW Pahang state, Malaysia, on cen. peninsula railroad line and on left bank of Pahang River.

Temeš. See TIMIŞ.

Temesvár. See TIMIŞOARA.

Te·me·tiu, Mount \ˌtā-mā-ˈtē-ü\. Peak, Hiva Oa I., Marquesas Is., S Pacific Ocean; 4134 ft. (1260 m.); highest peak on Hiva Oa I.

Temir–Khan–Shura. See BUINAKSK.

Te·mir·tau \ˈtā-mir-ˌtau̇\. Town, Karaganda subdivision, Kazakhstan, ab. 20 mi. (32 km.) NW of Qaraghandy; pop. (1991e) 213,100; iron and steel works; synthetic rubber.

Té·mis·ca·ming \tə-ˈmis-kə-ˌmiŋ, ˌtā-ˌmēs-kȧ-ˈmeⁿg\. Town, SW Quebec, Canada, on left bank of Ottawa River, ab. 40 mi. (65 km.) NNE of North Bay, Ontario; pop. (1991c) 2944.

Té·mis·ca·mingue \tā-ˌmēs-kȧ-ˈmeⁿg\. County, Quebec, Canada. See table at QUEBEC.

Té·mis·coua·ta \ˌte-mi-ˈskwa-tə\. **1.** Lake, Témiscouata co., S Quebec, Canada; 24 mi. (39 km.) long; 29 sq. mi. (75 sq. km.); its outlet a tributary of St. John River.

2. County in S Quebec, Canada. See table at QUEBEC.

Te·mo·aya \ˌtā-mō-ˈī-ä\. Municipality, México state, Mexico, 25 mi. (40 km.) NW of Mexico City.

Tem·pe \tem-ˈpē, ˈtem-pē\; *formerly* **Hay·den's Ferry** \ˈhād-ᵊnz\. City, Maricopa co., SW cen. Arizona, on Salt River just E of Phoenix; pop. (1990c) 141,865; Arizona State Univ. (1885); Tempe Junior Coll. (1926). The city has experienced rapid pop. growth since 1940, having more than doubled in size in the 1940s, 1950s, 1960s and again bet. 1970 and 1990.

Tempe, Vale of \ˈtem-pē\ *or Gk.* **Tém·bi** \ˈtem-bē\. Valley, NE Thessaly, Greece; lies bet. Mt. Olympus and Mt. Ossa; ab. 5 mi. (8 km.) long; traversed by the Piniós (ancient Peneus) River in its lower course.

Tem·ple \ˈtem-pəl\. City, Bell co., cen. Texas, 34 mi. (55 km.) S of Waco; pop. (1990c) 46,109; furniture, plastics.

Temple, Mount. Mountain, Banff National Park, Alberta, Canada, near British Columbia border; 11,626 ft. (3544 m.).

Temple City. City, Los Angeles co., SW California, E suburb of Los Angeles; pop. (1990c) 31,100.

Templestowe. See DONCASTER AND TEMPLESTOWE.

Temple Terrace. City, Hillsborough co., W cen. Florida, 7 mi. (11 km.) NE of Tampa; pop. (1990c) 16,444.

Tem·ple·ton \ˈtem-pəl-tən\. Town, Worcester co., cen. Massachusetts, 14 mi. (23 km.) W of Fitchburg; pop. (1990c) 6438.

Tem·poal \tem-ˈpwäl\. Municipality, Veracruz state, Mexico, 70 mi. (113 km.) SW of Tampico.

Tem·ryuk \ˌtem-rē-ˈük\. Town, W Krasnodar Kray, S Russia in Europe, on SE shore of Sea of Azov 75 mi. (121 km.) W of the city of Krasnodar.

Te·mu·co \tā-ˈmü-kō\. City, ✱ of La Araucanía region, S cen. Chile, ab. 100 mi. (160 km.) NNE of Valdivia on the Cautín River; formerly ✱ of Cautín prov.; pop. (1982c) 157,634; trade center, esp. in grains, fruit, and timber; ceded by Araucanian Indians and founded 1881.

Te·na \ˈtā-nä\. Town, ✱ of Napo prov., E cen. Ecuador, 70 mi. (113 km.) SE of Quito; pop. (1990c) 7873.

Ten·a·fly \ˈte-nə-ˌflī\. Residential borough, Bergen co., NE corner of New Jersey, 11 mi. (18 km.) E of Paterson; pop. (1990c) 13,326.

Ten·a·kee Inlet \ˈte-nə-kē\. Inlet opening into Chatham Strait, E coast of Chichagof I., SE Alaska.

Te·na·li \tā-ˈnä-lē\. City, cen. Andhra Pradesh, E India, near Krishna River 160 mi. (257 km.) ESE of Hyderabad; pop. (1991p) 143,836.

Te·na·ru \tā-ˈnä-rü\. Small river, N coast of Guadalcanal I., SE Solomon Is., W Pacific Ocean; site of WWII battle bet. Japanese and American forces Aug. 1942.

Te·nas·ser·im \tə-ˈna-sə-rəm\. **1.** River, Tenasserim div., Myanmar; flows S and empties into Andaman Sea; ab. 250 mi. (400 km.) long.

2. Former administrative region along SW coast of Indochina Penin. See YANDABU.

3. Division of S Myanmar. See table at MYANMAR.

Ten·by \ˈten-bē\ *or Welsh* **Din·bych–y–pys·god** \ˈdin-bik̲-ə-ˈpəs-gȯd\. Seaport, Dyfed county, SW Wales, on Carmarthen Bay; pop. (1981p) 4814; seaside resort and fishing center.

Tenda. See BRIGA-TENDA.

Ten Degree Channel. See ANDAMAN ISLANDS.

Tène, La. See LA TÈNE.

Tenedos. See BOZCAADA.

Ten·er·ife \ˌte-nə-ˈrē-fē, -ˈrif, -ˈrēf\; *formerly* **Ten·er·iffe** \ˌte-nə-ˈrif, -ˈrēf\; *anc.* **Pin·tu·ar·ia** \ˌpin-chə-ˈwar-ē-ə\. Largest of the Canary Is. (*q.v.*), Santa Cruz de Tenerife prov., Spain, in Atlantic Ocean 40 mi. (64 km.) WNW of Grand Canary I.; 795 sq. mi. (2059 sq. km.); pop. (1982e) 658,884; chief city Santa Cruz de Tenerife; precipitous coast; its highest point, the volcanic Pico de Teide (called also Peak of Tenerife), 12,198 ft. (3718 m.); fertile soil; fruits; damaged by earthquake and eruption of Teide early 18th cent.

Tenerife, Peak of *or* **Tenerife, Pico de.** See TEIDE, PICO DE.

Teneriffe. See TENERIFE.

Teng River. See NAM TENG.

Teng·chong *or W.-G.* **T'eng–ch'ung** *or* **Teng·chung** \ˈtəŋ-ˈchu̇ŋ\; *formerly* **Teng·yueh** \ˈtəŋ-ˈywər\ *or* **Mo·mein** \ˈmō-ˈmān\. Town, W Yunnan prov., S China, 105 mi. (169 km.) SW of Dali; opened for trade near turn of 20th cent., esp. with Burma; during WWII taken by Chinese Sept. 1944 after being held by Japanese for two years.

Tengchow. See PENGLAI.

Ten·ge \ˈteŋ-gā\ *also* **Ten·ke** \-kā\. Town, Shaba administrative region, S Democratic Rep. of the Congo, 120 mi. (193 km.) NW of Lubumbashi; railroad junction point.

Teng·ger Mountains \ˈteŋ-gər\. Mountain group, E Java, Indonesia, S of Pasuruan; highest point 9088 ft. (2770 m.). Contains the Bromo (7848 ft. or 2392 m.); on S joined with Semeru (*q.v.*).

Teng·ger Sha·mo \ˈtəŋ-gər-ˈshä-ˌmō\ *or W.G.* **T'eng–ko–li Shamo** \ˈtəŋ-ˈkō-ˈlē\ *also* **A–la Shan** \ˈä-ˈlä-ˈshän\. Desert region of Ningxia Huizu, N China, W of Helan Shan mountain range.

Ten·giz, Lake \teŋ-ˈgēz\ *also* **Lake Ten·iz** \teŋ-ˈēz\. Lake, Kazakhstan, SW of Astana; has no outlet.

Tengri Khan. See KHAN-TENGRI.

Tengri Nor. See NAM CO.

Tengyueh. See TENGCHONG.

Tenimbar Islands. See TANIMBAR ISLANDS.

Teniz, Lake. See TENGIZ, LAKE.

Tenke. See TENGE.

Ten·ley·town \ˈten-lē-ˌtau̇n\. Neighborhood in NW part of Washington, D.C.; contains highest point (420 ft. or 128 m.) in District of Columbia.

Ten·nes·see \ˌte-nə-ˈsē, ˈte-nə-ˌ\. **1.** Navigable river, Tennessee, N Alabama, and W Kentucky; formed by confluence of Holston and French Broad rivers near Knoxville, E Tennessee, flows SW into N Alabama, W across N Alabama, then N across W Tennessee and W Kentucky and empties into Ohio River; 652 mi. (1049 km.) long. Steady flow of water and sharp descent in certain areas have made river valuable for waterpower and creation of storage reservoirs. Explored by French and English 17th and 18th cents.; used as strategic route by Union forces during Civil War; developed as power source under Tennessee Valley Authority (*q.v.*) 1933; linked to Tombigbee River by Tennessee-Tombigbee Waterway (*q.v.*).

2. Southeast central state of U.S.A., bounded on N by Kentucky and Virginia, on E by North Carolina, on S by Georgia, Alabama, and Mississippi, and on W by Arkansas and Missouri; 34th state in area, 42,144 sq. mi. (109,153 sq. km.); 17th state in population, (1990c) 4,877,185; ✻ Nashville; 16th state admitted to Union (1796). See table of states at UNITED STATES.

Nickname: Volunteer State.

State flower: Iris.

Motto: Agriculture and Commerce.

Rivers: Mississippi, forming W boundary; Tennessee (see TENNESSEE 1).

Highest point: Clingmans Dome, 6643 ft. (2025 m.), in Sevier co.

Chief products: Tobacco; soybeans, corn; livestock; coal, phosphate rock; manufacturing: chemicals, textiles, cement, electrical machinery.

Chief cities: Memphis, Nashville, Knoxville, Chattanooga.

Political divisions: Divided into the following 95 counties (for pronunciation of their names, see their individual entries):

NAME	AREA[1] (sq. mi.)	AREA[1] (sq. km.)	POP. (1990c)	CO. SEAT
Anderson	335	868	68,250	Clinton
Bedford	482	1,248	30,411	Shelbyville
Benton	392	1,015	14,524	Camden
Bledsoe	404	1,046	9,669	Pikeville
Blount[2]	576	1,492	85,969	Maryville
Bradley	334	865	73,712	Cleveland
Campbell	451	1,168	35,079	Jacksboro
Cannon	271	702	10,467	Woodbury
Carroll	596	1,544	27,514	Huntingdon
Carter	348	901	51,505	Elizabethton
Cheatham	305	790	27,140	Ashland City
Chester	285	738	12,819	Henderson
Claiborne	444	1,150	26,137	Tazewell
Clay	232	601	7,238	Celina
Cocke[2]	424	1,098	29,141	Newport
Coffee	434	1,124	40,339	Manchester
Crockett	269	697	13,378	Alamo
Cumberland	678	1,756	34,736	Crossville
Davidson	527	1,365	510,784	Nashville
Decatur	337	873	10,472	Decaturville
De Kalb	278	720	14,360	Smithville
Dickson	485	1,256	35,061	Charlotte
Dyer	529	1,370	34,854	Dyersburg
Fayette	704	1,823	25,559	Somerville
Fentress	498	1,290	14,669	Jamestown
Franklin	553	1,432	34,725	Winchester
Gibson	607	1,572	46,315	Trenton
Giles	619	1,603	25,741	Pulaski
Grainger	282	730	17,095	Rutledge
Greene	613	1,588	55,853	Greeneville
Grundy	358	927	13,362	Altamont
Hamblen	155	401	50,480	Morristown
Hamilton	550	1,425	285,536	Chattanooga
Hancock	230	596	6,739	Sneedville
Hardeman	656	1,699	23,377	Bolivar
Hardin[3]	587	1,520	22,633	Savannah
Hawkins	480	1,243	44,565	Rogersville
Haywood	519	1,344	19,437	Brownsville
Henderson	515	1,334	21,844	Lexington
Henry	567	1,469	27,888	Paris
Hickman	611	1,582	16,754	Centerville
Houston	201	521	7,018	Erin
Humphreys	530	1,373	15,795	Waverly
Jackson	323	837	9,297	Gainesboro
Jefferson	274	710	33,016	Dandridge
Johnson	293	759	13,766	Mountain City
Knox	508	1,316	335,749	Knoxville
Lake	167	433	7,129	Tiptonville
Lauderdale	477	1,235	23,491	Ripley
Lawrence	634	1,642	35,303	Lawrenceburg
Lewis	285	738	9,247	Hohenwald
Lincoln	580	1,502	28,157	Fayetteville
Loudon	237	614	31,255	Loudon
McMinn	432	1,119	42,383	Athens
McNairy	569	1,474	22,422	Selmer
Macon	304	787	15,906	Lafayette
Madison	560	1,450	77,982	Jackson
Marion	506	1,311	24,860	Jasper
Marshall	377	976	21,539	Lewisburg
Maury	614	1,590	54,812	Columbia
Meigs	191	495	8,033	Decatur
Monroe	660	1,709	30,541	Madisonville
Montgomery	539	1,396	100,498	Clarksville
Moore	124	321	4,721	Lynchburg
Morgan	539	1,396	17,300	Wartburg
Obion	556	1,440	31,717	Union City
Overton	441	1,142	17,636	Livingston
Perry	411	1,064	6,612	Linden
Pickett	158	409	4,548	Byrdstown
Polk	435	1,127	13,643	Benton
Putnam	405	1,049	51,373	Cookeville
Rhea	312	808	24,344	Dayton
Roane	350	907	47,227	Kingston
Robertson	476	1,233	41,494	Springfield
Rutherford	630	1,632	118,570	Murfreesboro
Scott	544	1,409	18,358	Huntsville
Sequatchie	273	707	8,863	Dunlap
Sevier[2]	597	1,546	51,043	Sevierville
Shelby	755	1,955	826,330	Memphis
Smith	323	837	14,143	Carthage
Stewart	470	1,217	9,479	Dover
Sullivan	413	1,070	143,596	Blountville
Sumner	534	1,383	103,281	Gallatin
Tipton	459	1,189	37,568	Covington
Trousdale	114	295	5,920	Hartsville
Unicoi	185	479	16,549	Erwin
Union	212	549	13,694	Maynardville
Van Buren	254	658	4,846	Spencer
Warren	439	1,137	32,992	McMinnville
Washington	324	839	92,315	Jonesboro
Wayne	739	1,914	13,935	Waynesboro
Weakley	576	1,492	31,972	Dresden
White	382	989	20,090	Sparta
Williamson	593	1,536	81,021	Franklin
Wilson	568	1,471	67,675	Lebanon

[1] Area = land area.
[2] Includes part of Great Smoky Mountains National Park.
[3] Shiloh National Military Park in SW part of county.

History: Original inhabitants included Chickasaw, Cherokee, and Shawnee, among others; region visited by Spanish explorer Hernando de Soto c. 1540; included in British charter of Carolina and in French Louisiana claim late 17th cent.; claim to region ceded by France to Great Britain after French and Indian War; first permanent settlements made in Watauga Valley c. 1770; acknowledged by Great Britain as a part of United States after Revolutionary War; temporary state of Franklin (*q.v.*) formed c. 1784; included in Terr. South of the Ohio River after North Carolina relinquished claims 1790; admitted to Union with present boundaries June 1, 1796; passed ordinance of secession June 8, 1861; scene of battles in Civil War, notably Shiloh, Chattanooga, Stones River, Nashville; slavery abolished and ordinance of secession declared null and void 1865; first of seceding states to be reorganized and readmitted to Union (July 24, 1866). Constitution dates from 1870.

Tennessee Pass. Mountain pass, Lake and Eagle cos., NW cen. Colorado; 10,424 ft. (3177 m.); railroad and highway; ski slopes nearby.

Tennessee–Tombigbee Waterway. Waterway, SE United

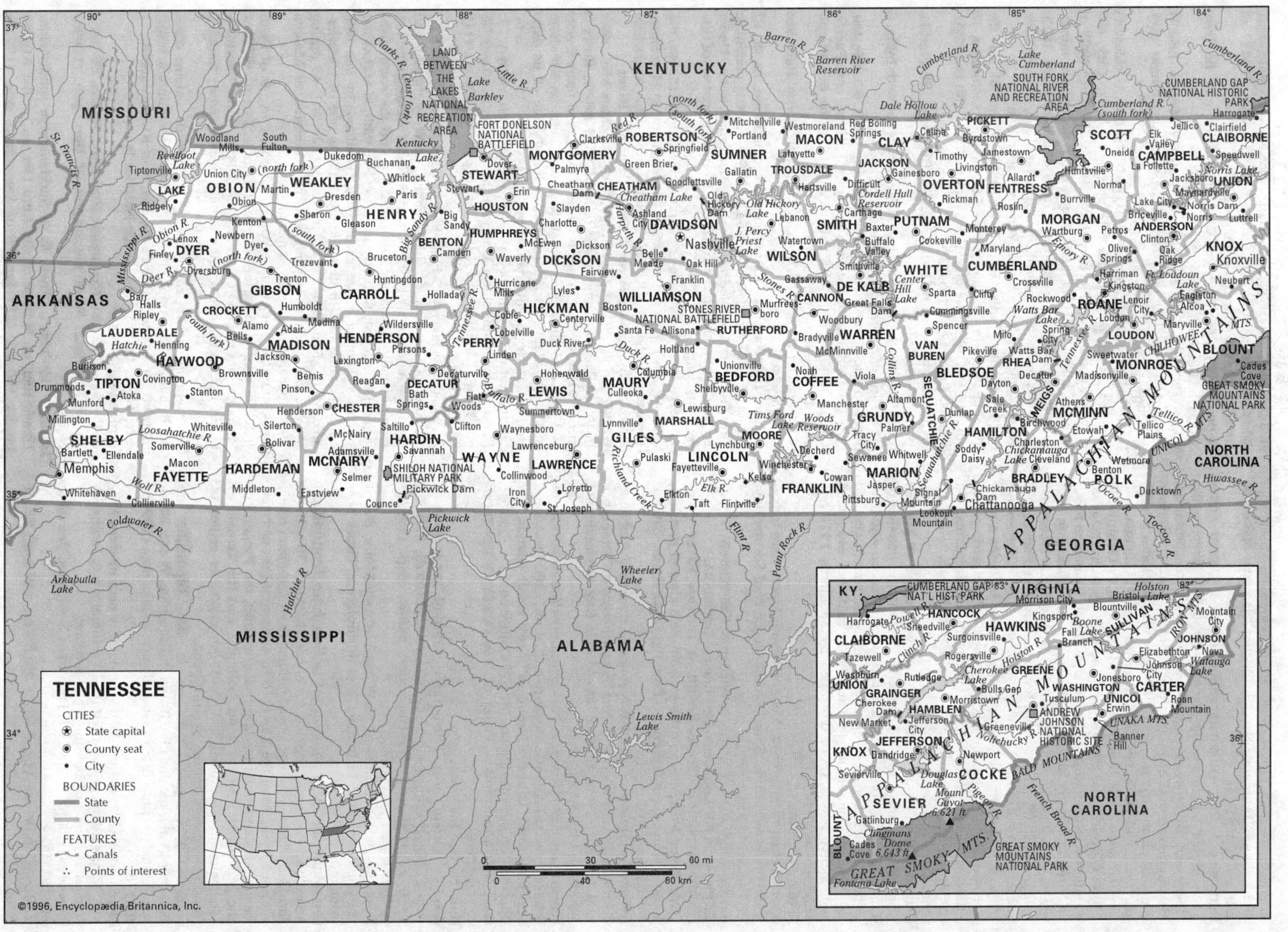
TENNESSEE
CITIES
State capital
County seat
City
BOUNDARIES
State
County
FEATURES
Canals
Points of interest
KENTUCKY
MISSOURI
ARKANSAS
MISSISSIPPI
ALABAMA
GEORGIA
NORTH CAROLINA
VIRGINIA
KY.
APPALACHIAN MOUNTAINS
GREAT SMOKY MOUNTAINS NATIONAL PARK
LAND BETWEEN THE LAKES NATIONAL RECREATION AREA
FORT DONELSON NATIONAL BATTLEFIELD
STONES RIVER NATIONAL BATTLEFIELD
SHILOH NATIONAL MILITARY PARK
SOUTH FORK NATIONAL RIVER AND RECREATION AREA
CUMBERLAND GAP NATIONAL HISTORIC PARK
ANDREW JOHNSON NATIONAL HISTORIC SITE
Nashville
Memphis
Knoxville
Chattanooga
Clarksville
Jackson
Murfreesboro
Mount Guyot 6,621 ft
Clingmans Dome 6,643 ft
0 30 60 mi
0 40 80 km
©1996, Encyclopædia Britannica, Inc.

States connecting Tennessee River on Tennessee-Mississippi border with Tombigbee River in W cen. Alabama; opened to barge traffic 1985.

Tennessee Valley Authority; *abbr.* **TVA.** A United States government administrative agency, created to develop the Tennessee River system in the interests of transportation, flood control, and economic development, and to generate and sell electricity; the region of the system includes a large part of E and W Tennessee, a large area in N Alabama, and smaller areas in W Kentucky, NE Mississippi, N Georgia, W North Carolina, and SW Virginia, and extends from Paducah, Kentucky, to the sources of tributaries of the Tennessee River in Virginia, North Carolina, and Georgia; its jurisdiction covers an area of ab. 39,000 sq. mi. (101,010 sq. km.); elevations range from 300 ft. (91 m.) above sea level at Paducah to more than 6000 ft. (1825 m.) in mountains of E Tennessee. This multiple-purpose water-control project includes a number of dams (see table on page 1171) and hydroelectric power stations; recreational facilities. Estab. by congressional act 1933; most dams constructed bet. 1933 and 1945.

Teno. See TANA.

Te·noch·ti·tlán \ˌtā-ˌnȯch-tēt-ˈlän\. Ancient name of Mexico City; ✻ of Aztec empire. Founded c. 1325 in the marshes of Lake Texcoco; formed confederacy with Texcoco and Tlacopán and became ✻ of empire by late 15th cent.; occupied by Spanish conqueror Hernán Cortés 1519 but evacuated with heavy losses 1520; destroyed by Spaniards 1521 and subsequently rebuilt.

Te·nos See TÍNOS.

Ten·ryū \ˈten-rē-ˌü\. River, S cen. Honshū, Japan; rises in Nagano prefecture, flows S into Pacific Ocean W of Suruga Bay; 134 mi. (216 km.) long.

Ten·sas \ˈten-ˌsȯ\. **1.** River in Alabama. See TENSAW.
2. Parish in NE Louisiana. See table at LOUISIANA.

Tensas River *also* **Tensas Bayou** *or* **Ten·saw River** \ˈten-ˌsȯ\. River, NE Louisiana; flows from East Carroll parish S, uniting with Ouachita River to form the Black River; 250 mi. (402 km.) long.

Ten·saw *or* **Ten·sas** \ˈten-ˌsȯ\. Navigable river, SW Alabama; formed (with the Mobile River) by confluence of Tombigbee and Alabama rivers, flows S into Mobile Bay at Mobile; ab. 40 mi. (64 km.) long.

Ten·sift \ten-ˈsift\. River, W Morocco; flows W through city of Marrakech into Atlantic Ocean; ab. 124 mi. (200 km.) long.

Ten Thousand Islands. Group of many small islands, SW Florida, in Gulf of Mexico, off SW Collier co.

Ten Thousand Smokes, Valley of. See VALLEY OF TEN THOUSAND SMOKES.

Tentyra. See DENDERA.

Te·ó·fi·lo Oto·ni *also* **The·o·phi·lo Ot·to·ni** \tē-ˈó-fē-lü-ō-ˈtōn-ē\. City, E cen. Minas Gerais state, E Brazil, 230 mi. (370 km.) NE of Belo Horizonte; munic. pop. (1991p) 140,639.

Te·os \ˈtē-ˌäs\. Ancient city, on W coast of Asia Minor, SW of Smyrna; one of the 12 Ionian Cities; birthplace of Greek poet Anacreon c. 582 B.C.

Te·o·ti·hua·cán \ˌtā-ō-ˌtē-wä-ˈkän\ *or* **San Juan Teotihuacán** \sän-ˈhwän\. Town, México state, cen. Mexico, 30 mi. (48 km.) NE of Mexico City; site of famous pre-Columbian ruins, incl. the Pyramid of the Sun (216 ft. or 66 m. high) with terraced sides and stairs leading to the summit, the Pyramid of the Moon (ab. 150 ft. or 46 m. high), and the Temple of Quetzalcoatl. Flourished c. 4th–c. 7th cents. as center of Teotihuacán civilization. See CHOLULA.

Te·pa·ti·tlán \ˌtā-pä-tēt-ˈlän\ *or in full* **Tepatitlán de Mo·re·los** \ˌthā-mō-ˈrā-lōs\. Town, Jalisco state, W cen. Mexico, 43 mi. (69 km.) ENE of Guadalajara; munic. pop. (1990p) 92,378.

Te·pe Gaw·ra \ˈte-pā-gau̇-ˈrä\. Ancient city near modern Mosul, Iraq; settlement from c. 6th–2d millennia B.C.; archaeological evidence of buildings and artifacts.

Te·pe·le·në \ˌtā-pə-ˈlā-nə\. **1.** District of S Albania. See table at ALBANIA.
2. Town, its ✻, on Vijosë River ab. 30 mi. (48 km.) SE of Vlorë.

Te·pex·pán \ˌtā-pās-ˈpän\. Village, NE México state, cen. Mexico, near Texcoco; site of discovery 1947 of 10,000–12,000-year-old human skeleton.

Te·pe Yah·ya \ˈte-pā-ˈyä-yə\. Ancient trading city, SE Iran; flourished 3d cent. B.C.

Te·pic \tā-ˈpēk\. City, ✻ of Nayarit state, W Mexico, near W coast 110 mi. (177 km.) NW of Guadalajara; munic. pop. (1990p) 238,101.

Te·pli·ce \ˈte-plēt-se\; *formerly* **Teplice–Ša·nov** \-ˈshä-nȯf\ *or Ger.* **Tep·litz–Schö·nau** \ˈte-plits-ˈshœ-ˌnau̇\. City, NW Czech Republic, in the Erzgebirge 56 mi. (90 km.) NNW of Prague; pop. (1991p) 53,039; health resort with warm mineral springs; scene of formation (Treaty of Teplitz Sept. 1813) of coalition against French Emperor Napoléon, incl. Prussia, Russia, and Austria, during Wars of Liberation.

Te·quen·da·ma Falls \ˌtā-kān-ˈdä-mä\. Waterfall in the Bogotá River (a tributary of the Magdalena), Colombia, 10 mi. (16 km.) S of the city of Bogotá; 427 ft. (130 m.) high.

Teques, Los. See LOS TEQUES.

Te·ques·ta \tē-ˈkwes-tə\. Village, Palm Beach co., SE Florida; pop. (1990c) 4499.

Te·rai \tə-ˈrī\. Region, S Nepal, along the border with India, S of the lower ranges of the Himalayas.

Te·rai·na \ter-ˈī-nə\; *formerly* **Wash·ing·ton** \ˈwȯ-shiŋ-tən, ˈwä-\. Island, one of the Line Is. (*q.v.*), Kiribati, cen. Pacific Ocean, 4°43′N, 160°24′W; included 1916 in the British colony of Gilbert and Ellice Is.

Te·ra·mo \ˈter-ä-ˌmō\. **1.** Province of Abruzzi, cen. Italy. See table at ITALY.
2. *anc.* **In·ter·am·na** \ˌin-tə-ˈram-nə\. Commune, its ✻, 82 mi. (132 km.) NE of Rome; pop. (1989c) 52,501; ceramics; 12th–14th cent. cathedral; remains of Roman town. Under Byzantines c. 6th cent.; came under Norman kingdom of Sicily 12th cent.

Ter·cei·ra \tər-ˈsir-ə, -ˈser-\. Island, cen. Azores; 153 sq. mi. (396 sq. km.); pop. (1991p) 59,248; ✻ Angra do Heroísmo.

Ter·ce·ro \ter-ˈsā-rō\. River, Córdoba prov., cen. Argentina; unites with Saladillo River to form Carcarañá River.

Te·rek \ˈter-ək\. River, SE Europe, N of Caucasus Mts.; rises in Republic of Georgia at the base of Mt. Kazbek, flows N through Daryal Pass into Russia in Europe, and turns E near Nal'chik through steppe region to a wide delta on NW shore of Caspian Sea; 373 mi. (600 km.) long; some of its delta streams are dry during part of the year.

Te·reng·ga·nu \te-reŋ-ˈgä-nü\ *also* **Treng·ga·nu** \treŋ-\. **1.** River, Terengganu state, Malaysia, Malay Penin.; flows NE into South China Sea at Kuala Terengganu; ab. 70 mi. (115 km.) long.
2. A state of Malaysia, Malay Penin., bounded on N and E by the South China Sea, on S by Pahang, on W by Pahang and Kelantan, and on NW by Kelantan; ✻ Kuala Terengganu; has several small islands ab. 20 mi. (32 km.) off the coast; fishing; rubber, copra; formerly iron ore. See table at MALAYSIA.
History: Under influence of Siam (Thailand) by late 18th cent.; became British dependency 1909 as one of Unfederated Malay States; under Japanese control 1941–45 during WWII; became part of independent Federation of Malaya 1957; became a state of Malaysia 1963.

Te·re·si·na *also* **The·re·zi·na** \ˌtā-rā-ˈzē-nə\. City, ✻ of Piauí state, NE Brazil, on Parnaíba River 170 mi. (274 km.) WSW of Parnaíba; munic. pop. (1991p) 598,449; ships livestock, hides, rice; produces textiles, lumber, soap, sugar; founded 1852.

Te·re·só·po·lis \ˌtā-rā-ˈzȯ-pü-ˌlēs\. City, Rio de Janeiro state, SE Brazil; munic. pop. (1991p) 120,701; a mountain resort (3000 ft. or 914 m.) near Petrópolis, N of Rio de Janeiro.

Te·res·sa \tə-ˈre-sə\. One of the Nicobar Is. (*q.v.*).

Terglou. See TRIGLAV.

Ter·liz·zi \ter-ˈlēt-sē\. Commune, Bari prov., Puglia, SE Italy, 16 mi. (26 km.) W of the seaport of Bari; pop. (1989c) 26,788.

Ter·mez \ter-ˈmez\. Town, ✻ of Surkhandarya subdivision, Uzbekistan, on N bank of the Amu Dar'ya, on the Afghan border 160 mi. (257 km.) S of Samarqand; pop. (1991e)

TENNESSEE VALLEY AUTHORITY—MAJOR DAMS

NAME[1]	LOCATION	YEAR OF FIRST USE	HEIGHT (feet)	HEIGHT (meters)	MAX. AREA OF RESERVOIR (acres)	MAX. AREA OF RESERVOIR (hectares)
DAMS ON TENNESSEE RIVER[2]						
Kentucky	Marshall and Livingston cos., Ky.	1944	206	63	160,300	64,922
Pickwick Landing	Hardin co., Tenn.	1938	113	34	43,100	17,456
Wilson	Lauderdale and Colbert cos., Ala.	1925	137	42	15,500	6,278
Wheeler	Lauderdale and Lawrence cos., Ala.	1936	72	22	67,100	27,176
Guntersville	Marshall co., Ala.	1939	94	29	67,900	27,500
Nickajack	Marion co., Tenn.	1968	83	25	10,900	4,414
Chickamauga	Hamilton co., Tenn.	1940	129	39	35,400	14,337
Watts Bar	Meigs and Rhea cos., Tenn.	1942	112	34	39,000	15,795
Fort Loudoun	Loudon co., Tenn.	1943	122	37	14,600	5,913
DAMS ON TRIBUTARIES OF TENNESSEE RIVER[3]						
Apalachia	Hiwassee River, Cherokee co., N.C.	1943	150	46	1,100	446
Blue Ridge	Toccoa River, Fannin co., Ga.	1931	167	51	3,290	1,332
Boone	S fork of Holston River, Sullivan and Washington cos., Tenn.	1953	160	49	4,400	1,782
Chatuge	Hiwassee River, Clay co., N.C.	1954	144	44	7,050	2,855
Cherokee	Holston River, Jefferson and Grainger cos., Tenn.	1942	175	53	30,300	12,272
Douglas	French Broad River, Sevier co., Tenn.	1943	202	62	30,400	12,312
Fontana	Little Tennessee River, Graham and Swain cos., N.C.	1945	480	146	10,640	4,309
Fort Patrick Henry	S fork of Holston River, Sullivan co., Tenn.	1953	95	29	872	353
Great Falls	Caney Fork River, Warren and White cos., Tenn.	1916	92	28	2,100	850
Hiwassee	Hiwassee River, Cherokee co., N.C.	1940	307	94	6,090	2,466
Melton Hill	Clinch River, Loudon and Roane cos., Tenn.	1964	103	31	5,690	2,304
Norris	Clinch River, Anderson and Campbell cos., Tenn.	1936	265	81	34,200	13,851
Nottely	Nottely River, Union co., Ga.	1956	184	56	4,180	1,693
Ocoee No.1	Ocoee River, Polk co., Tenn.	1912	135	41	1,890	765
Ocoee No.2	Ocoee River, Polk co., Tenn.	1913	30	9		
Ocoee No. 3	Ocoee River, Polk co., Tenn.	1943	110	34	621	252
South Holston	S fork of Holston River, Sullivan co., Tenn.	1951	285	87	7,580	3,070
Tellico	Little Tennessee River, Loudon co., Tenn.	1979	108	33	16,500	6,682
Tims Ford	Elk River, Franklin co., Tenn.	1977	170	52	10,700	4,334
Watauga	Watauga River, Carter co., Tenn.	1949	318	97	6,430	2,604

[1]The same name often applies to the reservoir or lake.
[2]Listed in the order of their location from the mouth of the Tennessee to its source near Knoxville.
[3]Listed in alphabetical order.

90,400; cotton gins; ancient city was located nearby dating from first cent. B.C.

Ter·mi·ni Ime·re·se \ˈter-mē-nē-ˌē-mā-ˈrā-sā\; *anc.* **Ther·mae Him·er·en·ses** \ˈthər-mē-ˌhi-mə-ˈren-ˌsēz\. Seaport, Palermo prov., Sicily, Italy, on N coast 22 mi. (35 km.) ESE of the seaport of Palermo; pop. (1989c) 27,033; tourism; citrus fruit, olives; mineral springs; Roman remains incl. amphitheater and baths; 17th cent. cathedral; convent; museum. Near ancient Himera (*q.v.*).

Tér·mi·nos, La·gu·na de \lä-ˈgü-nä-thā-ˈter-mē-ˌnōs\. Inlet, SE Bay of Campeche, on shore of state of Campeche, SE Mexico; enclosed by Carmen I.

Terminus. See ATLANTA 1.

Ter·mo·li \ˈter-mō-lē\. Port, Campobasso prov., S Molise, cen. Italy, on the Adriatic Sea; pop. (1989c) 26,924; 13th cent. castle; cathedral.

Termonde. See DENDERMONDE.

Ter·na·te \tər-ˈnä-tē\. **1.** Small island, Moluccas, Indonesia, off the W coast of Halmahera I.; 41 sq. mi. (106 sq. km.). Consists mainly of a conical volcano 5627 ft. (1715 m.) high, with three peaks; thickly forested; has fertile soil; produces spices, coffee, fruit. By 16th cent. became a sultanate; settled by Portuguese 1522 who were expelled 1574; made alliance with Dutch 1607; completely subjected to Dutch 1683; occupied by Japanese during WWII. See AMBON 3.
2. Port on S side of island at foot of volcano.
3. Municipality, on NW coast of Cavite prov., Luzon, Philippines, 15 mi. (24 km.) SW of City of Cavite; pop. (1980c) 9739; terminus of coastal road.

Ter·neu·zen \ter-ˈnœ-zə\ *also* **Neu·zen** \ˈnœ-zə\. Commune, Zeeland prov., SW Netherlands, on S shore of Schelde estuary ab. 25 mi. (40 km.) WNW of Antwerp; pop. (1992e) 35,176.

Ter·ni \ˈter-nē\. **1.** Province of Umbria, cen. Italy. See table at ITALY.
2. *anc.* **In·ter·am·na Na·hars** \ˌin-tər-ˈam-nə-ˈnā-ˌhärz\. Commune, its ✻, on Nera River 49 mi. (79 km.) NE of Rome; pop. (1989c) 110,020; iron and steel, machinery, textiles, firearms; cathedral (rebuilt 17th cent.) and several medieval churches; waterfalls (Cascata delle Marmore 650 ft. or 198 m.) nearby furnish hydroelectric power. Bet. 6th and 12th cents. taken successively by Ostrogoths, Byzantines, Lombards, and Germans; joined Papal States 14th cent.

Ter·no·pol' *or* **Ter·no·pol** \ter-ˈnō-pəlʸ\ *also* **Tar·no·pol'** *or* **Tar·no·pol** \tär-ˈnȯ-ˌpȯlʸ\. **1.** Administrative subdivision of Ukraine, in W part N of the Dniester River; 5328 sq. mi. (13,800 sq. km.); pop. (1991e) 1,175,100; ✻ Ternopol'. Economy heavily agricultural (grain, sugar beets, hops, sunflowers, potatoes); formed 1939 from territory annexed from Poland.
2. City, its ✻, 70 mi. (113 km.) ESE of L'viv; pop. (1991e) 218,000; concrete, food products; founded 16th cent.; passed to Austria 1772; returned to Poland 1920 and annexed by U.S.S.R. 1939.

Ter·pe·ni·ya Bay \tər-ˈpā-nē-yə\; *formerly* **Ta·rai·ka Bay** \tə-ˈrī-kə\. Large inlet, E coast of S Sakhalin I., E Russia in Asia.

Ter·ra·ci·na \ˌter-rä-ˈchē-nä\; *anc.* **Anx·ur** \ˈaŋk-sər\; *later* **Tar·ra·ci·na** \ˌtar-ə-ˈsī-nə\. Seaport, Latina prov., Lazio, cen. Italy, just SE of Agro Pontino and W of Gaeta; pop. (1989c) 39,393; ships grapes; fishing, food processing; 11th cent. cathedral; extensive Roman remains. A Volscian town which came under Rome c. 400 B.C.; flourished as royal resort town on Appian Way c. first cent. A.D.

Terranova Bracciolini. See TERRANUOVA BRACCIOLINI.

Terranova di Sibari. See SYBARIS.

Terranova di Sicilia. See GELA.

Ter·ra No·va National Park \ˌter-ə-ˈnō-və\. See CANADA, *National Parks.*

Terranova Pausania. See OLBIA 1.

Ter·ra·nuo·va Brac·cio·li·ni \ˌter-rä-ˈnwȯ-vä-ˌbrä-chō-ˈlē-nē\ *also* **Ter·ra·no·va Bracciolini** \ˌter-rä-ˈnȯ-vä\. Commune, Arezzo prov., Tuscany, W Italy, 16 mi. (26 km.) WNW of the commune of Arezzo; pop. (1981p) 9926.

Terrassa. See TARRASA.

Terre Adélie. See ADÉLIE COAST.

Terre·bonne \ˈter-ə-ˌbän\. **1.** Bayou, Terrebonne parish, SE Louisiana; flows S into Terrebonne Bay.
2. Parish in SE Louisiana. See table at LOUISIANA.
3. Town, Quebec, Canada, on left bank of the Rivière des Mille Îles 14 mi. (23 km.) N of Montreal; pop. (1991c) 39,678; incorp. 1860.

Terrebonne Bay. Inlet of Gulf of Mexico, SE coast of Terrebonne parish, SE Louisiana.

Ter·re Haute \ˌter-ə-ˈhōt, ˌter-ˈhōt, ˈter-ə-ˌhōt\. City, ⊗ of Vigo co., W Indiana, on Wabash River 67 mi. (108 km.) WSW of Indianapolis; pop. (1990c) 57,483; plastics, chemicals; Indiana State Univ. (1865), Rose-Hulman Institute of Technology (1874); city platted 1816; incorp. as city 1853. Birthplace of author Theodore Dreiser 1871.

Ter·rel, Mount \ˈter-əl\. Peak, Sevier co., cen. Utah; 11,530 ft. (3514 m.).

Ter·rell \ˈter-əl\. **1.** Name of counties in two states of the U.S. See tables at GEORGIA and TEXAS.
2. City, Kaufman co., NE Texas, 27 mi. (43 km.) E of Dallas; pop. (1990c) 12,490.

Terrell Hills. City, Bexar co., S cen. Texas, surrounded by city of San Antonio; pop. (1990c) 4592.

Terres Australes et Antarctiques françaises. See FRENCH SOUTHERN AND ANTARCTIC TERRITORIES.

Terres Mauvaises. See BADLANDS.

Ter·ri·toire de Bel·fort \ˌter-ē-ˈtwär-də-bel-ˈfȯr\. Department of E France. See table at FRANCE.

Territoire nor·dique \nȯr-ˈdēk\. County, Quebec, Canada. See table at QUEBEC.

Territory Northwest of the River Ohio. See NORTHWEST TERRITORY.

Territory of Papua. See PAPUA, TERRITORY OF.

Territory of Papua and New Guinea. See PAPUA NEW GUINEA.

Territory South of the Ohio River. Former territory, U.S.A.; comprised the region E of the Mississippi River, S of Kentucky, and W of North Carolina and Georgia; organized 1790 incl. present Tennessee and N Mississippi and Alabama, although the territory S of Tennessee was claimed by Georgia until 1802; upon Tennessee's admission to the Union 1796, territory reduced to region bet. Mississippi Terr. (*q.v.*) and Tennessee; became part of Mississippi Terr. 1804.

Ter·ror, Mount \ˈter-ər\. **1.** Peak, Skagit co., NW Washington; 8360 ft. (2548 m.).
2. Extinct volcano, Ross I. in Ross Sea, Antarctica, at 77°31′S, 168°33′E; 10,750 ft. (3277 m.).

Ter·ry \ˈter-ē\. **1.** County in NW Texas. See table at TEXAS.
2. Town, ⊗ of Prairie co., E Montana; pop. (1990c) 659.

Terry Peak. Mountain, Lawrence co., W South Dakota; 7064 ft. (2153 m.).

Ter·ry·town *or* **Terry Town** \ˈter-ē-ˌtau̇n\. Unincorporated settlement, Jefferson parish, SE Louisiana, S of New Orleans; pop. (1990c) 23,787.

Ter·schel·ling \tər-ˈske-liŋ\. Dutch island, one of the West Frisian Is., bet. Vlieland I. and Ameland I. off NW Friesland prov.; 16 mi. (26 km.) long; 41 sq. mi. (106 sq. km.); administratively part of North Holland prov.

Ter·try \ter-ˈtrē\; *formerly* **Tes·try** \tes-ˈtrē\. Village, Somme dept., N France; site of battle 687 by which Pépin II became ruler of all the Franks.

Te·ruel \tā-ˈrwel\. **1.** Province of E Spain. See table at SPAIN.
2. Commune, its ✻, 138 mi. (222 km.) E of Madrid; pop. (1991c) 28,487; manufactures leather, soap, flour, woolens; 13th cent. cathedral; 16th cent. aqueduct; notable Mudejar architecture. Conquered by Romans c. 200 B.C.; under Moorish rule 8th cent.; reconquered by Alfonso II of Aragon 1171; scene of fighting during Spanish Civil War (1936–39).

Ter·vu·ren *or* **Ter·vue·ren** \ter-ˈvu̇e-rən\. Commune, Brabant prov., cen. Belgium, 10 mi. (16 km.) E of Brussels; pop. (1991c) 19,488; park, over 500 acres (200 hectares).

Te·schen \ˈte-shən\. **1.** Former duchy, E Austrian Silesia; ab. 2820 sq. mi. (7305 sq. km.); under Polish duchy Silesia by end of 13th cent.; with Silesia passed to Bohemia 14th cent.; with Bohemia to Austrian Hapsburgs 1526; under Austria-Hungary until empire's collapse 1918 at end of WWI.

2. Region, part of former duchy; ab. 850 sq. mi. (2200 sq. km.); disputed by Poland and Czechoslovakia after WWI; part of region occupied by Czechs 1919; divided bet. the two nations along Olsa River by Conference of Ambassadors 1920; Czech section, 419 sq. mi. (1085 sq. km.), ceded to Poland during German-Czech crisis of 1938; region overrun by Germany 1939 at outset of WWII; restored to Poland and Czechoslovakia 1945 with borders estab. in 1920.
3. Former city, ✻ of Teschen duchy; divided by Olsa River into the Czech town of Český Těšín and the Polish city of Cieszyn (*qq.v.*) since Conference of Ambassadors 1920.

Te·shek·puk Lake \tə-ˈshek-ˌpük\. Lake, N Alaska, ab. 80 mi. (130 km.) SE of Point Barrow; 315 sq. mi. (816 sq. km.).

Te·shio \ˈte-shē-ˌō\. River, N Hokkaidō, Japan; flows NW into the Sea of Japan; 192 mi. (309 km.) long.

Těšín. See CIESZYN.

Těšín Český. See ČESKÝ TĚŠÍN.

Te·sis·sat Falls \ˈte-si-ˌsät\. Falls in Blue Nile, Ethiopia, ab. 20 mi. (32 km.) SE of Lake Tana; 140 ft. (43 m.) high.

Tes·lin Lake \ˈtez-lin\. Long, narrow lake, NW Canada, lying across the Yukon-British Columbia border; 142 sq. mi. (368 sq. km.); alt. 2250 ft. (686 m.); regarded as a source of the Yukon River; its outlet is **Teslin River,** ab. 100 mi. (160 km.) long, a tributary of the Lewes.

Tessin. See TICINO 2.

Test \ˈtest\. River, Hampshire, S England. See SOUTHAMPTON WATER.

Testa del Gargano. See GARGANO PROMONTORY.

Teste, La. See LA TESTE.

Testigos, Los. See LOS TESTIGOS.

Testry. See TERTRY.

Te·te \ˈtā-tə\. **1.** Province of W Mozambique. See table at MOZAMBIQUE.
2. Town, its ✻, on the Zambesi River 270 mi. (434 km.) NNW of Beira; pop. (1991e) 112,221.

Te·te·rev \ˈte-tə-ˌref, -ˌrev\. River, W Ukraine; rises W of Berdichev and flows NE to the Dnieper N of Kiev; ab. 220 mi. (355 km.) long.

Te·thys Sea \ˈtē-this\. Former sea on E coast of Pangaea; believed to have extended W upon rifting of Laurasia from Gondwana, eventually forming a nearly continuous equatorial sea; believed to have closed by mid-Cenozoic era with contact made bet. Africa and Eurasia and bet. India and Asia.

Te·ti·pa·ri \ˌtā-tē-ˈpä-rē\. Small island, New Georgia Is., cen. Solomon Is., W Pacific, SE of Rendova.

Tet·nuld \ˈtet-nəld\ *or Russ.* **Tet·nul'd** \-nəlʸd\. Mountain, W cen. Caucasus Range, on the Republic of Georgia, on border with Russia in Europe; nearby is the source of the Inguri River; 15,920 ft. (4852 m.).

Te·ton \ˈtē-ˌtän\. **1.** River, NW cen. Montana; rises in W Teton co., flows E into Missouri River; ab. 160 mi. (225 km.) long.
2. Name of counties in three states of the U.S. See tables at IDAHO, MONTANA, WYOMING.

Teton Range. Range, Teton co., NW Wyoming, extending N into Yellowstone National Park; S portion, which includes Grand Teton, highest peak (13,766 ft. or 4196 m.) in the range, is in Grand Teton National Park.

Té·touan *or* **Te·tuán** \tā-ˈtwän, tə-\. City, N Morocco, 25 mi. (40 km.) S of Ceuta; pop. (1982c) 199,615; handicrafts, textiles, soap, tiles; ships livestock and agricultural products. Founded 14th cent. by Marīnid dynasty; ✻ of former Spanish Morocco 1913–56.

Te·to·vo \ˈte-tȯ-vȯ\ *or Turk.* **Kal·kan·de·len** \ˌkäl-kän-de-ˈlen\. City, NW Republic of Macedonia, ab. 25 mi. (40 km.) W of Skopje; pop. (1991c) 180,654.

Te·trar·chy \ˈte-ˌträr-kē, ˈtē-\. The district of a subordinate ruler; literally, "the fourth part of a province"; in the Roman Empire esp.: (1) **Tetrarchy of He·rod An·ti·pas** \ˈher-əd-ˈan-tə-ˌpas\ (4 B.C.–39 A.D.), comprised of Galilee and Peraea; (2) **Tetrarchy of Phil·ip** \ˈfi-lip\ (4 B.C.–34 A.D.), incl. Ituraea, Trachonitis, Batanaea; (3) **Tetrarchy of Ly·sa·ni·as** \lī-ˈsā-nē-əs\ (c. 29 A.D.), coextensive with Abilene in SW Syria (*Luke* iii. 1); these tetrarchies united under Herod Agrippa I, king of Judea 41–44 A.D.).

Tetschen. See DĚČÍN.

Tetuán. See TÉTOUAN.

Tetulia. See GANGES DELTA.

Teu·co \ˈtā-ü-kō\. River, the middle course of the Bermejo, N Argentina; flows SE forming part of boundary bet. Formosa and Chaco provs.; ab. 350 mi. (565 km.) long.

Teu·to·burg Forest \ˈtü-tə-ˌbərg, ˈtyü-\ *or Ger.* **Teu·to·bur·ger Wald** \ˈtȯi-tə-ˌbu̇r-gər-ˌvält\. Range of hills, Lower Saxony and North Rhine-Westphalia, W Germany, S of Osnabrück; highest point ab. 1530 ft. (466 m.). Scene of battle 9 A.D. in which German tribes under Armin defeated Roman legions under Gen. Publius Quintilius Varus establishing Rhine as German-Latin border.

Tevere. See TIBER.

Teverone. See ANIENE.

Teverya. See TIBERIAS.

Te·vi·ot \ˈtē-vē-ət, ˈte-\. River, Borders region, SE Scotland; flows NE into the Tweed; 37 mi. (60 km.) long; its valley is called **Te·vi·ot·dale** \-ˌdāl\.

Te Wae·wae Bay \ta-ˈwī-wī\. Bay, S coast of South I., New Zealand; receives Waiau River.

Tewkes·bury \ˈtüks-ˌber-ē, -bə-rē, ˈtyüks-\. Town, Gloucestershire, SW cen. England, at confluence of the Avon and the Severn; pop. (1981c) 9568; scene of battle 1471, during the Wars of the Roses, in which Edward IV's Yorkists defeated the Lancastrian forces of Margaret of Anjou, queen of Henry VI. Her son Edward, last Lancastrian Prince of Wales, was killed in the battle.

Tewks·bury \ˈtüks-ˌber-ē, -bə-rē\. Town, Middlesex co., NE Massachusetts, 5 mi. (8 km.) SE of Lowell; pop. (1990c) 27,266.

Tex·ada Island \tek-ˈsa-də\. Island, cen. Strait of Georgia, bet. Vancouver I. and the British Columbia mainland, SW Canada; 30 mi. (48 km.) long, 117 sq. mi. (303 sq. km.).

Tex·ar·kana \ˌtek-sär-ˈka-nə, ˌtek-sər-\. Twin cities on Arkansas-Texas border: (1) city, ⊗ of Miller co., SW corner of Arkansas, ab. 137 mi. (220 km.) SW of Little Rock; pop. (1990c) 22,631; (2) city, Bowie co., NE Texas, 30 mi. (48 km.) SE of Oklahoma border; pop. (1990c) 31,656. Texarkana Coll. (1927), East Texas State Univ. at Texarkana (1971). Twin cities produce lumber, railroad cars; oil wells.

Tex·as \ˈtek-səs, -siz\. **1.** A southwestern state of U.S.A., bounded on N by Oklahoma, on E by Arkansas and Louisiana, on SE and S by Gulf of Mexico and Mexican state of Tamaulipas, on SW and W by Mexican states of Coahuila and Chihuahua and by New Mexico; 2d state in area, 266,807 sq. mi. (691,030 sq. km.); 3d state in population, (1990c) 16,986,510; ✻ Austin; 28th state admitted to Union (1845). See table of states at UNITED STATES.

Nickname: Lone Star State.

State flower: Bluebonnet.

Motto: Friendship.

Rivers: Red, forming N and NE boundary (with Oklahoma) and a boundary with Arkansas for a short distance; Trinity, in E region, flowing SE into Galveston Bay; Brazos, cen. region, flowing SE into Gulf of Mexico; Colorado, cen. region, flowing SE into Matagorda Bay; Rio Grande, forming S and SW boundaries.

Highest point: Guadalupe Peak, 8749 ft. (2667 m.), in Culberson co.

Chief products: Cotton, rice, sorghum grain, wheat; livestock; oil, natural gas, sulfur; chemicals, electronics; food processing.

Chief cities: Houston, Dallas, San Antonio, El Paso, Austin, Fort Worth, Arlington, Corpus Christi.

Political divisions: Divided into the following 254 counties (for pronunciation of their names, see their individual entries):

TEXAS
CITIES
State capital
County seat
City
BOUNDARIES
State
County
FEATURES
Dams
Points of interest
0 60 120 mi
0 80 160 km
COLORADO
KANSAS
OKLAHOMA
NEW MEXICO
ARKANSAS
LOUISIANA
MEXICO
Gulf of Mexico
LLANO ESTACADO
EDWARDS PLATEAU
STOCKTON PLATEAU
BALCONES ESCARPMENT
Red R.
Canadian R.
Pecos R.
Rio Grande
Colorado R.
Concho R.
Nueces R.
Lake Texoma
Toledo Bend Reservoir
Sam Rayburn Reservoir
Millwood Reservoir
Amistad Reservoir
Falcon Reservoir
Falcon Dam
El Azúcar Reservoir
Lake Meredith
Lake Kemp
Lake Travis
Prairie Dog Town Fork
Devils R.
Arroyo de la Babia
DALLAM
HARTLEY
OLDHAM
DEAF SMITH
PARMER
BAILEY
LAMB
HALE
COCHRAN
HOCKLEY
LUBBOCK
YOAKUM
TERRY
LYNN
GAINES
DAWSON
ANDREWS
MARTIN
HOWARD
ECTOR
MIDLAND
LOVING
WINKLER
WARD
CRANE
UPTON
REEVES
PECOS
BREWSTER
TERRELL
VAL VERDE
CROCKETT
SUTTON
KIMBLE
KERR
EDWARDS
REAL
KINNEY
UVALDE
MAVERICK
ZAVALA
DIMMIT
WEBB
ZAPATA
STARR
HIDALGO
CAMERON
WILLACY
KENEDY
BROOKS
JIM HOGG
DUVAL
JIM WELLS
KLEBERG
NUECES
SAN PATRICIO
ARANSAS
BEXAR
TRAVIS
HARRIS
DALLAS
TARRANT
GALVESTON
BRAZORIA
MATAGORDA
WHARTON
Amarillo
Lubbock
Abilene
Waco
Austin
San Antonio
Houston
Dallas
Fort Worth
Beaumont
Laredo
Corpus Christi
Brownsville
El Paso
Odessa
Midland
San Angelo
Texarkana
Tyler
Galveston
Del Rio
Eagle Pass
Pecos
Fort Stockton
Alpine
Santiago Pk. 6,521 ft.
Emory Peak 7,835 ft.
CHISOS MTS.
BIG BEND NATIONAL PARK
AMISTAD NATIONAL RECREATION AREA
LYNDON B. JOHNSON N.H.P.
PADRE ISLAND NATIONAL SEASHORE
PADRE I.
MATAGORDA I.
SAN JOSE I.
MATAGORDA PENINSULA
BOLIVAR PENINSULA
Cavallo Pass
Aransas Pass
Corpus Christi Pass
San Luis Pass
Sabine Lake
Laguna Madre
SEE INSET
For continuation of map, see inset below
KEY TO NUMBERED COUNTIES
1 DELTA
2 HOPKINS
3 FRANKLIN
4 TITUS
5 CAMP
6 MORRIS
7 MARION
8 GREGG
9 RAINS
10 ROCKWALL
11 HOOD
12 SOMERVELL
13 MADISON
14 WALLER
WISE
DENTON
COLLIN
ROCKWALL
KAUFMAN
ELLIS
JOHNSON
Newark
Eagle Mtn. Lake
Grapevine Reservoir
Southlake
Grapevine
Carrollton
Richardson
Plano
Forney Reservoir
Azle
N. Richland Hills
Bedford
Euless
Farmers Branch
Irving
Garland
University Park
Mesquite
Haltom City
Hurst
Richland Hills
Grand Prairie
Arlington
Balch Springs
White Settlement
Benbrook Reservoir
Everman
Duncanville
Seagoville
Crowley
Walnut Creek
Cedar Hill
Lancaster
Burleson
Mansfield
Trinity R.
NEW MEXICO
San Antonio Mtn. 7,278 ft.
Red Bluff Lake
EL PASO
Guadalupe Peak 8,749 ft.
GUADALUPE MOUNTAINS NATIONAL PARK
CHAMIZAL NATIONAL MEMORIAL
HUDSPETH
CULBERSON
REEVES
Mentone
JEFF DAVIS
Mount Livermore 8,382 ft.
Eagle Peak 7,510 ft.
Van Horn
Sierra Blanca
Fort Davis
FORT DAVIS NAT'L HIST. SITE
Marfa
PRESIDIO
Chinati Peak 7,730 ft.
Rio Conchos
BIG BEND NATIONAL PARK
MEXICO
HARRIS
CHAMBERS
Sheldon
Barrett
Mont Belvieu
Jacinto City
Channelview
Galena Park
Baytown
Deer Park
West University Place
Pasadena
South Houston
La Porte
Clear Lake City
Seabrook
Ellington Field
NASA Space Center
Galveston Bay
Trinity Bay
League City
Pearland
Friendswood
Dickinson
FORT BEND
BRAZORIA
GALVESTON
Alvin
Arcadia
Alta Loma
Texas City
La Marque
Port Bolivar
BOLIVAR PEN.
Galveston
©1996, Encyclopædia Britannica, Inc.

NAME	AREA[1] (sq. mi.)	AREA[1] (sq. km.)	POP. (1990c)	CO. SEAT
Anderson	1,072	2,776	48,024	Palestine
Andrews	1,504	3,895	14,338	Andrews
Angelina	804	2,082	69,884	Lufkin
Aransas	271	702	17,892	Rockport
Archer	913	2,365	7,973	Archer City
Armstrong	907	2,349	2,021	Claude
Atascosa	1,206	3,122	30,533	Jourdanton
Austin	663	1,717	19,832	Bellville
Bailey	835	2,163	7,064	Muleshoe
Bandera	763	1,976	10,562	Bandera
Bastrop	890	2,305	38,263	Bastrop
Baylor	875	2,266	4,385	Seymour
Bee	842	2,181	25,135	Beeville
Bell	1,066	2,761	191,088	Belton
Bexar	1,246	3,227	1,185,394	San Antonio
Blanco	719	1,862	5,972	Johnson City
Borden	907	2,349	799	Gail
Bosque	990	2,564	15,125	Meridian
Bowie	891	2,308	81,665	Boston
Brazoria	1,423	3,686	191,707	Angleton
Brazos	586	1,518	121,862	Bryan
Brewster[2]	6,204	16,068	8,681	Alpine
Briscoe	874	2,264	1,971	Silverton
Brooks	904	2,341	8,204	Falfurrias
Brown	950	2,461	34,371	Brownwood
Burleson	683	1,769	13,625	Caldwell
Burnet	996	2,580	22,677	Burnet
Caldwell	544	1,409	26,392	Lockhart
Calhoun	527	1,365	19,053	Port Lavaca
Callahan	857	2,220	11,859	Baird
Cameron	896	2,321	260,120	Brownsville
Camp	192	497	9,904	Pittsburg
Carson	900	2,331	6,576	Panhandle
Cass	941	2,437	29,982	Linden
Castro	880	2,279	9,070	Dimmitt
Chambers	616	1,595	20,088	Anahuac
Cherokee	1,049	2,717	41,049	Rusk
Childress	699	1,810	5,953	Childress
Clay	1,102	2,854	10,024	Henrietta
Cochran	783	2,028	4,377	Morton
Coke	911	2,359	3,424	Robert Lee
Coleman	1,279	3,313	9,710	Coleman
Collin	867	2,246	264,036	McKinney
Collingsworth	894	2,315	3,573	Wellington
Colorado	949	2,458	18,383	Columbus
Comal	567	1,469	51,832	New Braunfels
Comanche	966	2,502	13,381	Comanche
Concho	1,004	2,600	3,044	Paint Rock
Cooke	905	2,344	30,777	Gainesville
Coryell	1,043	2,701	64,213	Gatesville
Cottle	900	2,331	2,247	Paducah
Crane	795	2,059	4,652	Crane
Crockett	2,794	7,236	4,078	Ozona
Crosby	911	2,359	7,304	Crosbyton
Culberson[3]	3,851	9,974	3,407	Van Horn
Dallam	1,494	3,869	5,461	Dalhart
Dallas	875	2,266	1,852,810	Dallas
Dawson	902	2,336	14,349	Lamesa
Deaf Smith	1,510	3,911	19,153	Hereford
Delta	276	715	4,857	Cooper
Denton	911	2,359	273,525	Denton
De Witt	910	2,357	18,840	Cuero
Dickens	931	2,411	2,571	Dickens
Dimmit	1,344	3,481	10,433	Carrizo Springs
Donley	905	2,344	3,696	Clarendon
Duval	1,814	4,698	12,918	San Diego
Eastland	952	2,466	18,488	Eastland
Ector	907	2,349	118,934	Odessa
Edwards	2,076	5,377	2,266	Rocksprings
Ellis	950	2,461	85,167	Waxahachie
El Paso	1,058	2,740	591,610	El Paso
Erath	1,085	2,810	27,991	Stephenville
Falls	764	1,979	17,712	Marlin
Fannin	905	2,344	24,804	Bonham
Fayette	934	2,419	20,095	La Grange
Fisher	904	2,341	4,842	Roby
Floyd	993	2,572	8,497	Floydada
Foard	676	1,751	1,794	Crowell
Fort Bend	869	2,251	225,421	Richmond
Franklin	293	759	7,802	Mount Vernon
Freestone	865	2,240	15,818	Fairfield
Frio	1,116	2,890	13,472	Pearsall
Gaines	1,489	3,857	14,123	Seminole
Galveston	399	1,033	217,399	Galveston
Garza	914	2,367	5,143	Post
Gillespie	1,055	2,732	17,204	Fredericksburg
Glasscock	863	2,235	1,447	Garden City
Goliad	871	2,256	5,980	Goliad
Gonzales	1,056	2,735	17,205	Gonzales
Gray	934	2,419	23,967	Pampa
Grayson	940	2,435	95,021	Sherman
Gregg	282	730	104,948	Longview
Grimes	801	2,075	18,828	Anderson
Guadalupe	714	1,849	64,873	Seguin
Hale	979	2,536	34,671	Plainview
Hall	885	2,292	3,905	Memphis

NAME	AREA[1] (sq. mi.)	AREA[1] (sq. km.)	POP. (1990c)	CO. SEAT
Hamilton	844	2,186	7,733	Hamilton
Hansford	907	2,349	5,848	Spearman
Hardeman	687	1,779	5,283	Quanah
Hardin	895	2,318	41,320	Kountze
Harris	1,723	4,463	2,818,199	Houston
Harrison	894	2,315	57,483	Marshall
Hartley	1,488	3,854	3,634	Channing
Haskell	877	2,271	6,820	Haskell
Hays	670	1,735	65,614	San Marcos
Hemphill	904	2,341	3,720	Canadian
Henderson	943	2,442	58,543	Athens
Hidalgo	1,543	3,996	383,545	Edinburg
Hill	1,012	2,621	27,146	Hillsboro
Hockley	908	2,352	24,199	Levelland
Hood	426	1,103	28,981	Granbury
Hopkins	793	2,054	28,833	Sulphur Springs
Houston	1,237	3,204	21,375	Crockett
Howard	911	2,359	32,343	Big Spring
Hudspeth[3]	4,554	11,795	2,915	Sierra Blanca
Hunt	869	2,251	64,343	Greenville
Hutchinson	875	2,266	25,689	Stinnett
Irion	1,073	2,779	1,629	Mertzon
Jack	945	2,448	6,981	Jacksboro
Jackson	850	2,202	13,039	Edna
Jasper	927	2,401	31,102	Jasper
Jeff Davis	2,259	5,851	1,946	Fort Davis
Jefferson	951	2,463	239,397	Beaumont
Jim Hogg	1,143	2,960	5,109	Hebbronville
Jim Wells	845	2,189	37,679	Alice
Johnson	740	1,917	97,165	Cleburne
Jones	956	2,476	16,490	Anson
Karnes	758	1,963	12,455	Karnes City
Kaufman	815	2,111	52,220	Kaufman
Kendall	670	1,735	14,589	Boerne
Kenedy	1,394	3,610	460	Sarita
Kent	880	2,279	1,010	Clairemont
Kerr	1,101	2,852	36,304	Kerrville
Kimble	1,274	3,300	4,122	Junction
King	944	2,445	354	Guthrie
Kinney	1,393	3,608	3,119	Brackettville
Kleberg	853	2,209	30,274	Kingsville
Knox	845	2,188	4,837	Benjamin
Lamar	906	2,347	43,949	Paris
Lamb	1,022	2,647	15,072	Littlefield
Lampasas	726	1,880	13,521	Lampasas
La Salle	1,500	3,885	5,254	Cotulla
Lavaca	975	2,525	18,690	Hallettsville
Lee	644	1,668	12,854	Giddings
Leon	1,102	2,854	12,665	Centerville
Liberty	1,182	3,061	52,726	Liberty
Limestone	931	2,411	20,946	Groesbeck
Lipscomb	934	2,419	3,143	Lipscomb
Live Oak	1,055	2,732	9,556	George West
Llano	941	2,437	11,631	Llano
Loving	648	1,678	107	Mentone
Lubbock	893	2,313	222,636	Lubbock
Lynn	915	2,370	6,758	Tahoka
McCulloch	1,066	2,761	8,778	Brady
McLennan	1,030	2,668	189,123	Waco
McMullen	1,159	3,002	817	Tilden
Madison	480	1,243	10,931	Madisonville
Marion	380	984	9,984	Jefferson
Martin	911	2,359	4,956	Stanton
Mason	935	2,422	3,423	Mason
Matagorda	1,157	2,997	36,928	Bay City
Maverick	1,289	3,339	36,378	Eagle Pass
Medina	1,352	3,502	27,312	Hondo
Menard	914	2,367	2,252	Menard
Midland	939	2,432	106,611	Midland
Milam	1,028	2,663	22,946	Cameron
Mills	734	1,901	4,531	Goldthwaite
Mitchell	920	2,383	8,016	Colorado
Montague	934	2,419	17,274	Montague
Montgomery	1,090	2,823	182,201	Conroe
Moore	909	2,354	17,865	Dumas
Morris	260	673	13,200	Daingerfield
Motley	980	2,538	1,532	Matador
Nacogdoches	943	2,442	54,753	Nacogdoches
Navarro	1,087	2,815	39,926	Corsicana
Newton	953	2,468	13,569	Newton
Nolan	922	2,388	16,594	Sweetwater
Nueces	845	2,189	291,145	Corpus Christi
Ochiltree	907	2,349	9,128	Perryton
Oldham	1,478	3,828	2,278	Vega
Orange	359	930	80,509	Orange
Palo Pinto	948	2,455	25,055	Palo Pinto
Panola	880	2,279	22,035	Carthage

NAME	AREA[1] (sq. mi.)	AREA[1] (sq. km.)	POP. (1990c)	CO. SEAT
Parker	903	2,339	64,785	Weatherford
Parmer	859	2,225	9,863	Farwell
Pecos	4,740	12,277	14,675	Fort Stockton
Polk	1,100	2,849	30,687	Livingston
Potter	898	2,326	97,874	Amarillo
Presidio	3,892	10,080	6,637	Marfa
Rains	219	567	6,715	Emory
Randall	914	2,367	89,673	Canyon
Reagan	1,132	2,932	4,514	Big Lake
Real	622	1,611	2,412	Leakey
Red River	1,033	2,675	14,317	Clarksville
Reeves	2,608	6,755	15,852	Pecos
Refugio	774	2,005	7,976	Refugio
Roberts	899	2,328	1,025	Miami
Robertson	877	2,271	15,511	Franklin
Rockwall	147	381	25,604	Rockwall
Runnels	1,058	2,740	11,294	Ballinger
Rusk	939	2,432	43,735	Henderson
Sabine	562	1,456	9,586	Hemphill
San Augustine	545	1,412	7,999	San Augustine
San Jacinto	624	1,616	16,372	Coldspring
San Patricio	686	1,777	58,749	Sinton
San Saba	1,120	2,901	5,401	San Saba
Schleicher	1,331	3,447	2,990	Eldorado
Scurry	904	2,341	18,634	Snyder
Shackelford	887	2,297	3,316	Albany
Shelby	820	2,124	22,034	Center
Sherman	916	2,372	2,858	Stratford
Smith	934	2,419	151,309	Tyler
Somervell	197	510	5,360	Glen Rose
Starr	1,211	3,136	40,518	Rio Grande City
Stephens	923	2,391	9,010	Breckenridge
Sterling	914	2,367	1,438	Sterling City
Stonewall	926	2,398	2,013	Aspermont
Sutton	1,493	3,867	4,135	Sonora
Swisher	896	2,321	8,133	Tulia
Tarrant	868	2,248	1,170,103	Fort Worth
Taylor	913	2,365	119,655	Abilene
Terrell	2,391	6,193	1,410	Sanderson
Terry	899	2,328	13,218	Brownfield
Throckmorton	920	2,383	1,880	Throckmorton
Titus	418	1,083	24,009	Mount Pleasant
Tom Green	1,535	3,976	98,458	San Angelo
Travis	1,012	2,621	576,407	Austin
Trinity	707	1,831	11,445	Groveton
Tyler	919	2,380	16,646	Woodville
Upshur	584	1,513	31,370	Gilmer
Upton	1,312	3,398	4,447	Rankin
Uvalde	1,588	4,113	23,340	Uvalde
Val Verde	3,241	8,394	38,721	Del Rio
Van Zandt	851	2,204	37,944	Canton
Victoria	892	2,310	74,361	Victoria
Walker	790	2,046	50,917	Huntsville
Waller	508	1,316	23,390	Hempstead
Ward	827	2,142	13,115	Monahans
Washington	612	1,585	26,154	Brenham
Webb	3,306	8,563	133,239	Laredo
Wharton	1,076	2,787	39,955	Wharton
Wheeler	914	2,367	5,879	Wheeler
Wichita	611	1,582	122,378	Wichita Falls
Wilbarger	952	2,466	15,121	Vernon
Willacy	591	1,531	17,705	Raymondville
Williamson	1,126	2,916	139,551	Georgetown
Wilson	802	2,077	22,650	Floresville
Winkler	887	2,297	8,626	Kermit
Wise	922	2,388	34,679	Decatur
Wood	721	1,867	29,380	Quitman
Yoakum	830	2,150	8,786	Plains
Young	888	2,300	18,126	Graham
Zapata	1,025	2,655	9,279	Zapata
Zavala	1,291	3,344	12,162	Crystal City

[1] Area = land area.
[2] Big Bend National Park on the Rio Grande (*q.v.*), in S part.
[3] Contains part of Guadalupe Mountains National Park.

History: Orig. inhabited by Indians incl. Apaches, several tribes of the Caddo group, and others; explored by Spaniards early 16th–late 17th cents.; French explorer René-Robert Cavelier, Sieur de La Salle, attempted settlement at Matagorda Bay 1685, laying basis for French claim to region as part of Louisiana; effective Spanish occupation began c. 1700; U.S. acquired French claim in Louisiana Purchase 1803; U.S. claim to Texas relinquished by treaty with Spain 1819; became part of Mexico after Mexico gained independence from Spain 1821; Declaration of Independence from Mexico Mar. 1836; Texan army under commander Sam Houston won decisive battle against Mexican forces at San Jacinto Apr. 1836, gaining independence for the **Republic of Texas**; sought annexation to U.S. and was admitted to Union Dec. 29, 1845; boundary with Mexico along the Rio Grande fixed after Mexican War by Treaty of Guadalupe Hidalgo 1848; passed ordinance of secession Feb. 1, 1861; readmitted to Union Mar. 30, 1870; adopted constitution 1876.

2. Name of counties in two states of the U.S. See tables at MISSOURI and OKLAHOMA.

Texas City. City, Galveston co., SE Texas, on Galveston Bay 9 mi. (14 km.) NW of Galveston; pop. (1990c) 40,822; produces chemicals; oil refineries; tin smelting; Coll. of the Mainland. In Apr. 1947, explosion of shipload of ammonium nitrate in harbor resulted in over 500 deaths and destroyed much of city.

Texas Pan·han·dle \ˈpan-ˌhand-ᵊl\; *sometimes shortened to* **the Panhandle.** The NW projection of land in Texas; chief town Amarillo.

Tex·co·co \tās-ˈkō-kō\ *or in full* **Texcoco de Mo·ra** \thā-ˈmō-rä\ *also* **Tez·cu·co** \tās-ˈkü-kō\. Town, México state, cen. Mexico, on E side of Lake Texcoco. Formed confederacy with Aztec ✻ Tenochtitlán (*q.v.*) and Tlacopán early 15th cent.; used by Spanish conqueror Hernán Cortés as base for operations against Tenochtitlán 1521.

Texcoco, Lake *or* **Lake Tezcuco.** Dry lake, México state, cen. Mexico, just E of Mexico City; 12 mi. (19 km.) long; surface elev. above sea level 7340 ft. (2237 m.); on islands in its W part Aztec stronghold and ✻ Tenochtitlán was built 14th cent.

Tex·el \ˈte-səl\. Island, one of the West Frisian Is., Netherlands, in the North Sea off the N coast of North Holland prov.; 13 mi. (21 km.) long; 71 sq. mi. (184 sq. km.); pop. (1981c) 12,596; comprises a commune of North Holland prov.

Te·ya·te·ya·neng \ˌtā-yä-tā-ˈyä-neŋ\; *often shortened to* **Ty** \ˈtī\. Village, NW Lesotho, NE of Maseru; pop. (1986c) 14,251.

Teyde, Pico de. See TEIDE, PICO DE.

Tezcuco. See TEXCOCO.

Tezcuco, Lake. See TEXCOCO, LAKE.

Te·ziu·tlán \ˌtā-syüt-ˈlän\. Town, Puebla state, SE cen. Mexico, 100 mi. (161 km.) NW of Veracruz; munic. pop. (1990p) 63,196; an old town near border of Veracruz state.

Tez·pur \ˈtez-ˌpu̇r\. Town, NE India, on Brahmaputra River 90 mi. (145 km.) NE of Shillong; pop. (1991p) 54,999.

Tha·ba·na Ntlen·ya·na \tä-ˈbä-nänt-len-ˈyä-nä\. Mountain, E Lesotho; 11,425 ft. (3482 m.); highest peak in Drakensberg, also highest peak in S Africa.

Tha·ba·zim·bi \ˌtä-bä-ˈzim-bē\. Town, SW corner of Northern prov., Rep. of South Africa, ab. 96 mi. (154 km.) NW of Pretoria; pop. (1985c) 7527.

Tha·bor, Mont \ˌmōⁿ-tä-ˈbȯr\. Mountain, on France-Italy border, SW of Modane and W of Col de Fréjus; 10,453 ft. (3186 m.); small area to S transferred from Italy to France 1947.

Tha Chin \ˈtä-ˈchēn\. **1.** River, the W distributary of the main river system of W cen. Thailand, of which the Chao Phraya is E stream; flows S from Uthai Thani, where it leaves the Chao Phraya, to the Gulf of Thailand at a point ab. 21 mi. (34 km.) SW of Bangkok; ab. 135 mi. (215 km.) long.
2. Town, Thailand. See SAMUT SAKHON.

Thai·land \ˈtī-ˌland, -lənd\ *or Thai* **Mu·ang Thai** \ˈmwäŋ-ˈtī\; *formerly* **Si·am** \sī-ˈam\. Kingdom, SE Asia, lying to the N and W of the Gulf of Thailand, bounded on N by Myanmar and Laos, on E by Laos and Cambodia, on extreme S by Malaysia, on SW by the Andaman Sea, and on W by Myanmar; 198,455 sq. mi. (513,998 sq. km.); pop. (1993e) 57,829,000; ✻ Bangkok.

Physical features: The kingdom's max. length is ab. 1024 mi. (1648 km.), its max. width ab. 485 mi. (780 km.); at its narrowest point (peninsular Thailand), lying bet. the Gulf of Thailand and the Andaman Sea, width is ab. 30 mi. (48 km.); mountainous in NW with highest point Doi Inthanon 8512 ft. (2594 m.), near Myanmar border; farther S along Myanmar border are Dawna Range and Bilauktaung Range and on the SE along the Cambodia border are the Dangrek Mts. Large cen. area is a plain lying in the basins of the Chao Phraya and its tributaries and in the E the tributaries of the Mekong.

Chief products: Rice, corn, rubber, soybeans, pineapples, coconuts, sugarcane, jute; fishing; tin, iron ore, lead, gypsum, fluorite, natural gas; textiles, cement; tourism.

Chief towns: Bangkok, Nonthaburi, Nakhon Ratchasima, Chiang Mai.

History: Part of the Mon and Khmer kingdoms c. 9th cent. A.D.; migrated to by Thai peoples from cen. Asia c. 10th cent.; separate Thai state (with Ayutthaya as its ✻) formed 1350; frequently overrun by Burmese in 16th cent.; visited by Portuguese 16th cent. and by Dutch, British, and French 17th cent.; Ayutthaya destroyed by Burmese invaders 1767; lost Tenasserim to Burma late 18th cent.; recognized French claim to Cambodia 1860s and ceded territory E of Mekong to French 1893; yielded to British Malay States its rights over Kedah, Kelantan, Perlis, and Terengganu 1909; became constitutional monarchy 1932; occupied parts of French Indochina 1940; seized by Japan Dec. 1941 and declared war on Great Britain and U.S. Jan. 1942; by Japanese action received 1943 two Shan States from Burma and four of the Unfederated Malay States (ceded 1909); after defeat of Japan 1945 restored these states; participated in Korean War (1950 ff.) as member of UN force and allied with South Vietnam in Vietnam War (1965 ff.); adopted several new constitutions bet. 1940s and 1970s and another in 1991.

Thailand, Gulf of; *formerly* **Gulf of Si·am** \sī-ˈam\. Inlet of South China Sea, mostly bordered by Thailand, but its SE shore formed by Cambodia and Vietnam; ab. 385 mi. (620 km.) from NW to SE and 385 mi. (620 km.) across at its widest part (in S); Chao Phraya and Tha Chin rivers enter at NW point.

Tha·le \ˈtä-lə\. City, Saxony-Anhalt, cen. Germany, 38 mi. (61 km.) SW of Magdeburg; mineral baths.

Tha·le Lu·ang \ˌtä-lā-lu̇-ˈäŋ\ *or* **Thale Sap** \ˈsäp\. Lake on E coast of SW Thailand, near Gulf of Thailand on Malay Penin.

Thal·wil \ˈtäl-ˌvēl\. Commune, Zürich canton, NE cen. Switzerland, on Zürichsee; pop. (1980c) 15,412.

Thame \ˈtām\. Small river, Buckinghamshire and Oxfordshire, S cen. England; flows into the Thames bet. Abingdon and Wallingford; 30 mi. (48 km.) long.

Thames 1. \ˈthāmz\. River, SE Connecticut; actually a tidal estuary formed by confluence of Shetucket and Yantic rivers at Norwich, flows S into Long Island Sound 3 mi. (5 km.) below New London; 15 mi. (24 km.) long.

2. \ˈtemz\. River, SE Ontario, Canada; rises in Perth co., flows S and SW past London, St. Thomas, and Chatham to Lake St. Clair; 135 mi. (217 km.) long. In War of 1812, battle of the Thames fought on its banks just E of Thamesville Oct. 5, 1813, in which the Americans under Gen. William H. Harrison defeated British troops and American Indian confederation; Indian leader Tecumseh killed.

3. \ˈtemz\ *anc.* **Tam·e·sis** \ˈta-mə-sis\ *or* **Tam·e·sa** \-sə\. River, S England; its headstreams, the Churn and Isis (Thames), rise on the slopes of the Cotswold Hills in Gloucestershire; flows E across S cen. England into a great estuary, through which it empties into the North Sea; 210 mi. (338 km.) long; London is situated on both its sides; navigable by large vessels as far as London.

4. River, New Zealand. See WAIHOU.

5. \ˈtemz\. Borough, N North I., New Zealand, on Firth of Thames 50 mi. (80 km.) ESE of Auckland; pop. (1981c) 6456.

Thames, Firth of \ˈtemz\. Southern extension of Hauraki Gulf, N coast of North I., New Zealand; receives the Waihou River from the S.

Thames·ville \ˈtemz-ˌvil\. Village, Kent co., SE Ontario, Canada, on Thames River; pop. (1991c) 1046. See THAMES 2.

Thāmit. See TAMET.

Thamugadi *or* **Thamugadis.** See TIMGAD.

Thāne *or* **Tha·na** \ˈtä-nə\. Town, W Maharashtra, W India, on NE shore of Salsette I. 21 mi. (34 km.) NNE of Bombay; pop. (1991e) 803,389; suburb of Bombay. Settled 16th cent. by Portuguese, who were driven out early 18th cent. by the Marathas; came under British administration c. 1776.

Than·et, Isle of \ˈtha-nət\. Area, NE end of Kent, SE England; 42 sq. mi. (109 sq. km.); penetrated by arms of the Great Stour River, one of which roughly parallels course of an ancient channel once wide enough to make Thanet an island; believed to be landing site of Jute leader Hengist c. 449 A.D.

Thanh Hoa \ˈtän-ˈhwä\. Town, N Vietnam, 90 mi. (145 km.) S of Hanoi; pop. (1989c) 84,951.

Than·ja·vur \ˌtən-jə-ˈvu̇r\ *also* **Tan·jore** \tan-ˈjōr\. City, Tamil Nadu, S India, on right bank of Kāveri River 190 mi. (306 km.) SSW of Madras; pop. (1991p) 200,216; produces jewelry, textiles; 11th cent. temple to Hindu god Siva, with great tower (over 200 ft. or 60 m.); college.

History: Was ✻ from time to time of Cōla dynasty (9th–13th cents.); independent state estab. here in 16th cent. by a governor of Vijayanagar; under Madura sovereignty in 17th cent.; conquered by Marathas c. 1674; came into British possession after death of last Maratha raja 1855.

Thann \ˈtän\. Town, Haut-Rhin dept., NE France, ab. 16 mi. (26 km.) NW of Mulhouse; 14th cent. church; ruins of castle nearby.

Thap Muoi, Dong. See REEDS, PLAIN OF.

Thap·sa·cus \ˈthap-si-kəs\ *or mod.* **Dib·se** \ˈdib-sə\; *bib.* **Tiph·sah** \ˈtif-sə\ (*I Kings* iv. 24). Ancient city on the S bank

\ə\ **abut** \ᵊ\ matches \ᵊ\ kitten, Fr table \ər\ **further** \a\ ash \ā\ ace \ä\ cot, cart \á\ Fr bac \au̇\ **out** \b\ Span Avila \ch\ **chin** \e\ bet \ē\ easy \g\ go \i\ hit \ī\ ice \j\ job \k\ Ger **ich**, **Buch** \ⁿ\ Fr vin \ŋ\ sing \ō\ go \ȯ\ all \ȯ\ **law** \œ\ Fr bœuf \œ̄\ Fr **feu** \ȯi\ boy \th\ **thin** \t͟h\ **this** \ü\ **loot** \u̇\ **foot** \ue\ Ger füllen \ue̅\ Fr **rue** \y\ yet \ʸ\ Fr digne \ˈdēnʸ\, nuit \ˈnwʸē\ \yü\ **few** \yu̇\ fury \zh\ vision

of the middle Euphrates River, N Syria, ab. 60 mi. (95 km.) ESE of Alep; location of a ford, much used in ancient times.

Thap·sus \ˈthap-səs\. Ancient town, N Africa; its site is on E coast of Tunisia SE of modern town of Sousse; battle 46 B.C. in which Julius Caesar defeated the forces of Pompey the Great during Roman civil war.

Thar Desert \ˈtär, ˈtər\ *or* **Great Indian Desert.** Region of sandy desert, NW India and SE Pakistan, bet. Aravalli Range on E and Indus River on W, Sutlej River on N and Arabian Sea on S; ab. 400 mi. (645 km.) long, ab. 225 mi. (360 km.) wide; approx. 100,000 sq. mi. (259,000 sq. km.); av. alt. 250 ft. to 750 ft. (75 m. to 230 m.); max. alt. ab. 1500 ft. (455 m.), on W slope of Aravalli Range. Annual rainfall less than 15 in. (38 cm.); has continuous high temperatures. Includes portions of Rajasthan and Gujarat states, India, and Punjab and Sind in Pakistan.

Thar·ra·wad·dy \ˌthar-ə-ˈwä-dē\. Town, Myanmar, 65 mi. (105 km.) N of Yangon; pop. (1983c) 33,489.

Thá·sos \ˈthä-ˌsös\ *or* **Tha·sos** \ˈthā-ˌsäs\ *also* **Thás·sos** *or* **Thas·sos** \ˈthä-ˌsōs\. **1.** Island, N Aegean Sea, opp. the mouth of the Mesta; 146 sq. mi. (378 sq. km.); politically a part of Kavála dept., NE Macedonia, Greece; mountainous, highest point 3428 ft. (1045 m.). Colonized c. 700 B.C. by inhabitants of Paros; seized by Persians under Gen. Mardonius early 5th cent. B.C.; later came under Athens as member of Delian League, but revolted twice (465 and 411 B.C.); under Roman protection after defeat of Macedonian King Philip V 196 B.C.; ruled by Turks mid-15th cent. A.D. until ceded to Greece c. 1913.

2. Chief town of island, on N coast; now in ruins.

Thatch·er \ˈtha-chər\. Town, Graham co., SE Arizona, ab. 80 mi. (130 km.) NE of Tucson; pop. (1990c) 3763; Eastern Arizona Coll. (1888).

Tha·ton \thə-ˈtōn\. Town, Myanmar, near NE coast of Gulf of Martaban 35 mi. (56 km.) NNW of Moulmein; pop. (1983c) 23,636.

Thau, Étang de \ā-ˌtä^{n}-də-ˈtō\. Salt lagoon, S France, on coast of Hérault dept.; ab. 40 sq. mi. (105 sq. km.); separated from the Mediterranean (Gulf of Lion) by a narrow strip of sand on which Sète is located.

Thaung·gyin \ˈthau̇n-ˈjin\. River, Myanmar; flows NW into Salween River on the Myanmar-Thailand boundary; and in its own course forms a section of that boundary E of the Dawna Range; 150 mi. (241 km.) long.

Tha·yaw·tha·dang·yi Island \thä-ˌyȯ-thä-däŋ-ˈyē\; *formerly* **El·phin·stone Island** \ˈel-fin-ˌstōn, -stən\. Island, NW Mergui Archipelago (*q.v.*), Myanmar.

Thayer \ˈthar, ˈthā-ər\. County in S Nebraska. See table at NEBRASKA.

Tha·yet·myo \thə-ˈyet-ˌmyō, ˈthät-ˌmyō\. Town, Myanmar, on the Irrawaddy River opp. Allanmyo, 40 mi. (64 km.) N of Prome; pop. (1983c) 23,636.

Thebae. See THEBES 1.

The·ba·is \thē-ˈbā-is\. Roman province of Upper Egypt.

Thebes \ˈthēbz\. **1.** *bib.* **No** \ˈnō\; *classical* **The·bae** \ˈthē-ˌbē\ *or* **Di·os·po·lis** \dī-ˈäs-pə-lis\ *also* **Diospolis Mag·na** \ˈmag-nə\. Ancient ruined city, Egypt, on the W bank of the Nile, S of modern Qena; in early times included also Karnak and Luxor (*qq.v.*) on the E bank; site of remains of Great Temple of Amon at Karnak (c. 20th cent. B.C., expanded later). After brief rule of the Heracleopolitan dynasties, became ✻ of Upper Egypt under XIth dynasty (c. 22d cent. B.C.) until end of Middle Kingdom c. 18th cent. B.C. Obscured for two centuries under the rule of various foreign invaders, incl. the Hyksos dynasty (mid-17th to mid-16th cents. B.C.); rose again to great power as ✻ under the XVIIIth dynasty (16th–14th cents. B.C.); flourished as political and religious center of Egypt throughout New Kingdom period, well-known for achievements in sculpture and architecture incl. elaborate temples, statues, and tombs. Began to decline 12th cent. B.C. under King Ramses III and his successors; sacked by Assyrians mid-7th cent. B.C., later by Persians bet. 6th and 4th cents. B.C., and esp. by Romans c. 30 B.C. under Cornelius Gallus. Site of 1922 discovery by archaeologist Howard Carter of tomb of Tutankhamen, king of the XVIIIth dynasty c. 1350 B.C., in Valley of the Kings.

2. *or Gk.* **Thí·vai** \ˈthē-ve\. Commune, E Central Greece region, Greece, 33 mi. (53 km.) NNW of Athens; pop. (1991p) 18,191; market town; in low hilly country.

History: An ancient city, according to tradition founded by Cadmus, mythological brother of Europa; associated with many early legends of Greece (as Epigonus, Oedipus, and the Sphinx). Historically, inhabited before 1500 B.C. by Boeotians; began struggles against Athens 6th cent. B.C. and headed Boeotian League. Sided with Persians in Greco-Persian Wars early 5th cent. B.C. and was sacked by Greek allies after Persian defeat at Plataea 479 B.C. Under Athenian rule 457–447 B.C.; joined Sparta against Athens in Peloponnesian War (431–404 B.C.); left Sparta and joined Árgos, Athens, and Corinth in the Corinthian War (395–387 B.C.). Under Spartan rule 382 B.C. until it regained freedom 379 under Gen. Pelopidas; destroyed Spartan supremacy at Leuctra 371 B.C. under Gen. Epaminondas and held powerful position in cen. Greece until 362 B.C. Joined Athens against King Philip II of Macedon and shared defeat at Chaeronea 338 B.C.; destroyed by Macedonian King Alexander the Great 336 B.C. and rebuilt 316 B.C. under Cassander, a later Macedonian king. Home of Pindar (c. 522–c. 438 B.C.), considered the greatest Greek lyric poet.

The Bot·tom \ˈbä-təm\ *also* **Bottom.** Village, cen. Saba I., Netherlands Antilles, West Indies; the island's chief settlement.

The Camargue. See CAMARGUE.

The City. See LONDON 4.

The Col·o·ny \t͟hə-ˈkä-lə-nē\. City, Denton co., N Texas; pop. (1990c) 22,113.

The Dalles. See DALLES, THE.

Thed·ford \ˈthed-fərd\. Village, ⊗ of Thomas co., cen. Nebraska; pop. (1990c) 243.

The Hague. See HAGUE, THE.

Theiss. See TISZA.

The·o·dore Roo·se·velt Dam \ˈthē-ə-ˌdōr-ˈrō-zə-ˌvelt\. Dam across Salt River, on border bet. Maricopa and Gila cos., S cen. Arizona; height 280 ft. (85 m.); completed 1911; forms **Theodore Roosevelt Lake** 25 mi. (40 km.) long.

Theodore Roosevelt Island; *formerly* **An·a·los·tan Island** \ˌan-ᵊl-ˈȯ-stən\. Island in the Potomac River, District of Columbia; 90 acres (36 hectares); site of a memorial to President Theodore Roosevelt.

Theodore Roosevelt National Park. See UNITED STATES, *National Parks.*

Theodosia. See FEODOSIYA.

Theophilo Ottoni. See TEÓFILO OTONI.

The·ot·mal·li \ˈtā-ōt-ˌmä-lē\. See DETMOLD.

The Pas. See PAS, THE.

Thera. See THÍRA.

Thé·rèse–De Blain·ville \tā-ˈrez-də-ble^{n}-ˈvēl\. County, Quebec, Canada. See table at QUEBEC.

Therezina. See TERESINA.

Therma. See THESSALONÍKI.

Thermae Himerenses. See TERMINI IMERESE.

Thermaicus Sinus *or* **Thermaïkós Kólpos.** See SALONIKA, GULF OF.

Thermia. See KÍTHNOS.

Ther·mop·o·lis \thər-ˈmä-pə-lis\. Town, ⊗ of Hot Springs co., NW cen. Wyoming; pop. (1990c) 3247; health resort with mineral springs; founded 1897.

Ther·mop·y·lae \thər-ˈmä-pə-lē\ *or Gk.* **Ther·mo·pí·lai** \ˌther-mō-ˈpē-le\. Locality, E Greece, bet. Mt. Oeta and S shore of Gulf of Maliakós 9 mi. (14 km.) SSE of town of Lamía; in ancient times a narrow pass along the coast, now a rocky plain near the sea. Scene of several battles: (1) 480 B.C. Spartans and allies under King Leonidas defeated by Persian invaders; (2) 279 B.C. Gallic invaders under Brennus checked for several months by Greeks; (3) 191 B.C. King Antiochus III of Syria defeated by Romans; (4) Apr. 1941 German army held back by Anzacs to allow evacuation of British troops in WWII.

Thé·rou·anne \ˌtā-rü-ˈän\. Village, Pas-de-Calais dept., N France, S of St.-Omer; formerly a fortress (6th cent.); taken by the English in 1380 and 1513, and destroyed by Holy Roman Emperor Charles V in 1553.

The Snares. See SNARES ISLANDS.

Thes·pi·ae \ˈthes-pē-ˌē\. Ancient town, S cen. Boeotia, E cen. Greece, E of Mt. Helicon and ab. 10 mi. (16 km.) WSW of Thebes. Site of temples to the Muses and famous statue of Eros made by Athenian sculptor Praxiteles (fl. 370–330 B.C.). Hundreds of its citizens fought Persians with Spartan King Leonidas at Thermopylae 480 B.C. and others were at Plataea 479 B.C.; town destroyed by Thebes c. 371 B.C. and subsequently rebuilt.

Thes·pro·tia \thes-ˈprō-tē-ä\. **1.** Department of Epirus, Greece. See table at GREECE.
2. Region of ancient Epirus, NW Greece, on W coast extending S from Thyamis River to Amvrakikós Kolpos.

Thessalía. See THESSALY.

Thessalonica. See THESSALONÍKI 2.

Thes·sa·lo·ní·ki \ˌthe-sä-lō-ˈnē-kē\. **1.** Department of Central Macedonia, Greece. See table at GREECE.
2. *also* **Sa·lon·i·ka** \sə-ˈlä-ni-kə\ *or* **Sal·o·ni·ki** \ˌsa-lə-ˈnē-kē\ *or Turk.* **Se·la·nik** \ˌse-lə-ˈnēk\; *before 315 B.C. called* **Ther·ma** \ˈthər-mə\, *afterwards* **Thes·sa·lo·ni·ca** \ˌthe-sə-lə-ˈnī-kə, -ˈlä-ni-\. Seaport city, ✻ of Thessaloníki dept., W cen. Macedonia, NE Greece, at head of Gulf of Salonika; pop. (1981c) 406,413; railroad center; good harbor; exports tobacco, manganese; produces textiles, chemicals, leather goods, bricks, soap; has some Roman remains and numerous Byzantine churches (5th–14th cents.); university.

History: Founded 315 B.C. by Macedonian ruler Cassander; Roman ✻ of Macedonia 146 B.C. ff.; visited by St. Paul c. 49–50 A.D. who later addressed epistle to converts there; massacre of citizens by Roman Emperor Theodosius 390 A.D.; taken by Saracens 904 and by Sicilian Normans 1185; ✻ of Latin Empire (*q.v.*) 1204; to Epirus 1222, Nicaea 1246, before resumption of Byzantine Empire 1261; under Ottoman Empire 1430–1912; headquarters of Young Turks 1908; formally returned to Greece 1913; important base for Allied operations in WWI; in WWII occupied by Germans 1941–44.

Thes·sa·ly \ˈthe-sə-lē\ *or Gk.* **Thes·sa·lía** \ˌthā-sä-ˈlē-ä\. Administrative region, Greece; includes E cen. portion of Greek mainland; 5382 sq. mi. (13,939 sq. km.); pop. (1991p) 731,230; for subdivisions, see table at GREECE. Ancient Thessaly corresponds generally to modern region: an extensive plain almost completely hemmed in by mountains—Pindus Mts. on W, Cambunian Mts. on N, Othrys Mts. along the S border, and Mt. Olympus, Mt. Ossa, and Mt. Pelion along the coast. Drained by Piniós River with many confluents, entering Aegean Sea through Vale of Tempe.

History: Land of many migrations and cultures during the 3d and 2d millennia B.C.; by c. 1000 B.C. visited by peoples from NW Greece who established ruling families in chief cities (as the Aleuads of Larissa); dominated Amphictyonic League 6th cent. B.C.; came under King Philip II of Macedon 4th cent. B.C.; incorp. into prov. of Macedon under Roman rule 2d cent. B.C.; made a separate Roman province 4th cent. A.D.; passed to Turks late 14th cent.; ceded to modern Greece 1881; in WWII was a main area of conflict 1941 bet. Germans and forces of British and Greeks.

Thet·ford \ˈthet-fərd\. **1.** Town, Orange co., E Vermont; pop. (1990c) 2438; comprises several villages along the Connecticut River N of White River Junction.
2. Town, Norfolk, E England, 27 mi. (43 km.) SW of Norwich; pop. (1981p) 19,591; trade center; food canning.

Thetford Mines. City, S Quebec, Canada, 52 mi. (84 km.) S of Quebec City; pop. (1981c) 19,965; site of asbestos mines which have produced a large percentage of the world's supply; developed after discovery of asbestos 1876; incorp. as village 1892, as city 1912.

Theveste. See TEBESSA.

The Village. See VILLAGE, THE.

Thiais \ˈtyā\. Commune, Val-de-Marne dept., N France, S of Paris.

Thíamis. See THÝAMIS.

Thian Shan. See TIAN SHAN.

Thiau·court \tyō-ˈkür\. Village, Meurthe-et-Moselle dept., NE France, ab. 16 mi. (26 km.) ENE of St.-Mihiel; in WWI taken by U.S. troops Sept. 1918; St.-Mihiel U.S. military cemetery.

Thibet. See TIBET.

Thib·o·daux \ˈti-bə-ˌdō\. City, ⊗ of Lafourche parish, SE Louisiana, on Bayou Lafourche 49 mi. (79 km.) WSW of New Orleans; pop. (1990c) 14,035; sugar; oil and gas wells; truck farms; Nicholls State Univ. (1948).

Thick·a·net·ley Bald \ˌthi-kə-ˈnet-lē\. Peak, Gilmer co., N Georgia; 4054 ft. (1236 m.).

Thief \ˈthēf\. River, NW Minnesota; flows S out of **Thief Lake** in NE Marshall co. and empties into Red Lake River in N Pennington co.; 30 mi. (48 km.) long.

Thief River Falls. City, ⊗ of Pennington co., NW Minnesota, 50 mi. (80 km.) W of Upper Red Lake; pop. (1990c) 8010.

Thiel·sen, Mount \ˈthēl-sən, ˈtēl-\. Peak on boundary bet. Douglas and Klamath cos., S Oregon, N of Crater Lake; 9182 ft. (2799 m.).

Thielt. See TIELT.

Thie·ne \ˈtye-nā\. Commune, Vicenza prov., Veneto, NE Italy, 12 mi. (19 km.) NNW of the commune of Vicenza; pop. (1981p) 18,791.

Thienen. See TIENEN.

Thiens·ville \ˈthēnz-ˌvil\. Village, Ozaukee co., E Wisconsin, 17 mi. (27 km.) N of Milwaukee; pop. (1990c) 3301.

Thiep·val \tyep-ˈväl\. Village, Somme dept., N France, just N of Albert; heavy fighting in area during WWI.

Thiers \ˈtyer\. Commune, Puy-de-Dôme dept., S cen. France, 23 mi. (37 km.) ENE of Clermont-Ferrand; center of cutlery production.

Thiès \ˈtyes\. Town, Senegal, 40 mi. (64 km.) E of Cap Vert; pop. (1992e) 201,350.

Thi·ka \ˈtē-kä, ˈthē-\. Town, S cen. Kenya, NE of Nairobi; pop. (1983e) 45,200.

Thim·ble Islands \ˈthim-bəl\. Group of islands, Long Island Sound off the S coast of New Haven co., Connecticut.

Thim·phu \thim-ˈpü\ *also* **Thim·bu** \-ˈbü\ *or* **Ta·shi Chho Dzong** \ˈtä-shē-ˈchō-ˈjȯŋ\. Town, ✻ of Bhutan; pop. (1987e) 15,000.

Thing·val·la Lake \ˈthēŋ-ˌgvä-lä\. Lake, SW Iceland, E of Reykjavík; 32 sq. mi. (83 sq. km.); largest lake in Iceland.

Thing·vel·lir \ˈthēŋ-ˌgve-ˌlir\. Level plain with lava floor near Thingvalla Lake, SW Iceland, ab. 25 mi. (40 km.) E of Reykjavík; meeting place from 930 A.D. to 1798 of the *Althing*, parliament of Iceland.

Thinis. See THIS.

Thion·ville \tyō^{n}-ˈvēl\ *or Ger.* **Die·den·ho·fen** \ˈdēd-^{ə}n-ˌhō-fən\. Commune, ✻ of Moselle dept., NE France, on Moselle River 16 mi. (26 km.) N of Metz; pop. (1990c) 40,835; center of iron-mining district. Taken by Prussia during Franco-Prussian War after prolonged siege 1870; reverted to France 1919.

Thí·ra \ˈthē-rä\; *mostly formerly* **San·to·rin** \ˌsan-tə-ˈrēn\; *anc.* **The·ra** \ˈthir-ə\ *also* **San·to·ri·ni** \ˌsan-tə-ˈrē-nē\. Volcanic island, S Cyclades, in Aegean Sea on N side of Sea of Crete, in Cyclades dept., Greece; 29 sq. mi. (75 sq. km.); pop. (1981c) 7083. Its surface has much tufa which is exported as a cement. Has had numerous volcanic eruptions, esp. during first half of 2d millennium B.C. when eruptions nearly destroyed island; has remains of Minoan city dating back to same period; settled by Dorian invaders c. 1000 B.C.; c. 630 B.C. sent colonists to found Cyrene in North Africa.

Thirl·mere \ˈthərl-ˌmir\. Lake, Lake District, Cumbria, NW England; 3.25 mi. (5.2 km.) long; provides part of Manchester water supply.

Thiruvananthapuram. See TRIVANDRUM.

This \'this\ *or* **Thi·nis** \'thī-nəs\. City of ancient Egypt, near the great bend of the Nile NW of Abydos and near modern Girga; native city of King Menes, traditional founder of Ist dynasty (c. 3000 B.C.).

Thi·sted \'tē-steth\. Town, Viborg co., Denmark, NW Jutland Penin.; pop. (1981c) 29,974.

This·til Fjord \'this-tᵊl\. Bay, NE Iceland, bet. Cape Rifstangi and Cape Langanes; inlet of Arctic Ocean.

Thiu Khao Phanom Dongrak. See DANGREK MOUNTAINS.

Thívai. See THEBES 2.

Thjórsá \'thyōr-ˌsau̇\. River, S cen. Iceland; flows SW into Atlantic Ocean; 143 mi. (230 km.); longest river in Iceland.

Tho·hoy·an·dou \tō-'hòi-ˌän-dü\. Town, Northern prov., NE Rep. of South Africa; formerly ✻ of Venda enclave.

Tho·len \'tō-lən\. Island, Zeeland prov., SW Netherlands; 46 sq. mi. (119 sq. km.).

Thom·as \'tä-məs\. Name of counties in three states of the U.S. See tables at GEORGIA, KANSAS, NEBRASKA.

Thomas Cole Mountain \'kōl\. Peak in the Catskill Mts., Greene co., SE New York; 3940 ft. (1201 m.).

Thomas Peak. See BALDY PEAK 1.

Thom·as·ton \'tä-mə-stən\. **1.** Town, SE Litchfield co., NW Connecticut, on Naugatuck River; pop. (1990c) 6947.
2. City, ⊗ of Upson co., W cen. Georgia, 38 mi. (61 km.) W of Macon; pop. (1990c) 9127.
3. Town, Knox co., S Maine, on inlet of Atlantic Ocean 35 mi. (56 km.) ESE of Augusta; pop. (1990c) 3306.

Thom·as·ville \'tä-məs-ˌvil\. **1.** City, Clarke co., SW Alabama, 80 mi. (129 km.) NNE of Mobile Bay; pop. (1990c) 4301.
2. City, ⊗ of Thomas co., S Georgia, 40 mi. (64 km.) W of Valdosta; pop. (1990c) 17,457.
3. City, Davidson co., cen. North Carolina, 7 mi. (11 km.) SSW of High Point; pop. (1990c) 15,915.

Tho·mond \'tü-mənd\. Medieval principality in N part of Munster prov., S Ireland.

Thomp·son \'tämp-sən\. **1.** Town, NE Windham co., NE Connecticut, on Massachusetts and Rhode Island borders N of Putnam; pop. (1990c) 8668; includes Grosvenor Dale.
2. River, S British Columbia, Canada, main tributary of the Fraser River; rises among the Rocky Mts. near E boundary of British Columbia, flows S (as the **North Thompson** River, 210 mi. or 338 km. long) and turns W and SW to the Fraser River; length to head of North Thompson 304 mi. (489 km.). Joined at Kamloops by a branch (206 mi. or 331 km. long) from Shuswap Lake usually known as the **South Thompson** River.
3. City, N cen. Manitoba, Canada; pop. (1991c) 14,977; developed in late 1950s as center for nickel mining.

Thompson Falls. City, ⊗ of Sanders co., NW Montana; pop. (1990c) 1319.

Thompson Glacier. Glacier, Axel Heiberg I., Nunavut, Canada; 24 mi. (39 km.) long, ab. 1 mi. (1.6 km.) wide near its terminus.

Thompson Island. Island, S area of the harbor of Boston, Massachusetts.

Thompson Peak. Mountain, N Santa Fe co., N cen. New Mexico; ab. 10,455 ft. (3185 m.).

Thomp·son·ville \'tämp-sən-ˌvil\. Subdivision of the town of Enfield, Connecticut; pop. (1990c) 8458. See ENFIELD 1.

Thom·son \'täm-sən\. **1.** City, ⊗ of McDuffie co., E Georgia, 30 mi. (48 km.) W of Augusta; pop. (1990c) 6862.
2. Braided river, upper tributary of Cooper Creek, cen. Queensland, Australia; flows SW; 300 mi. (483 km.) long; dry bed part of the year.

Thon Bu·ri \tən-'bu̇r-ē\ *also* **Dhon·bu·ri** \tən-\. City, Thailand, just SW of Bangkok; national ✻ 1767–82.

Thong·wa \'thōŋ-'wä\. Town, Pegu div., S Myanmar, near W coast of Gulf of Martaban 23 mi. (37 km.) E of Yangon.

Tho·non–les–Bains \tō-ˌnōⁿ-lā-'beⁿ\. Commune, Haute-Savoie dept., E France, on Lake Geneva 37 mi. (60 km.) NNE of Annecy; pop. (1990c) 30,667; summer resort; mineral baths.

Thorn. See TORUŃ.

Thorn·ap·ple \'thòr-ˌna-pəl\. River, S Michigan; flows from Eaton co. to Grand River; ab. 100 mi. (160 km.) long.

Thorn·ton \'thòrn-tən\. **1.** Village, Adams co., NE cen. Colorado, N of Denver; pop. (1990c) 55,031.
2. Village, Cook co., NE Illinois, 5 mi. (8 km.) S of Chicago; pop. (1990c) 2778.
3. Village, Providence co., N Rhode Island, ab. 4 mi. (6 km.) SW of the city of Providence; administrative center of Johnston.

Thornton Cleve·leys \'klē-vlēz\. Urban area, Lancashire, NW England, on Irish Sea 7 mi. (11 km.) N of Blackpool; pop. (1981p) 26,139; resort.

Thor·o·fare Buttes \'thər-ō-ˌfar\. Mountain, SW Park co., NW Wyoming; 11,417 ft. (3480 m.).

Thor·old \'thòr-əld, 'thär-\. Town, Niagara munic. region, SE Ontario, Canada, on Welland Canal 3 mi. (5 km.) SE of St. Catharines; pop. (1991c) 17,542.

Thorshavn. See TÓRSHAVN.

Thorvald Nilsen Mountains. See NILSEN PLATEAU.

Thospitis Lacus. See VAN, LAKE.

Thou·ars \'twär\; *anc.* **To·ar·ci·um** \tō-'är-shē-əm\. Commune, Deux-Sèvres dept., W France, 49 mi. (79 km.) N of Niort. Made viscountship in 9th cent.; made duchy 1563; Protestant stronghold in Wars of Religion in 16th cent.

Thou·sand Islands \'thau̇z-ᵊnd\. **1.** Group of ab. 1500 islands, in a widening of the upper St. Lawrence River, New York state, and Ontario, Canada, just below Kingston. Summer resort, with many hotels and villas. Some of the islands are part of Canada (see *Saint Lawrence Islands* at CANADA, *National Parks*) and some the U.S. The Thousand Islands International Bridge (five spans, bet. islands; total length 8.5 mi. or 13.7 km.; opened Aug. 1938) connects Collins Landing, New York, ab. 3 mi. (5 km.) SW of Alexandria Bay, with Ivy Lea, Ontario, below Gananoque.
2. Group of about 100 small islands, SW Java Sea; part of Indonesia.

Thousand Lake Mountain. Peak, W Wayne co., S cen. Utah; 11,295 ft. (3443 m.).

Thousand Oaks \'ōks\. City, Ventura co., SW California, 30 mi. (48 km.) WNW of Los Angeles; pop. (1990c) 104,352; California Lutheran Univ. (1959).

Thousand Ships Bay. Bay, extreme SE end of Santa Isabel I., E cen. Solomon Is., W Pacific Ocean; formed partly by San Jorge I. on the W.

Thrace \'thrās\. Region, E Balkan Penin., SE Europe, varying in limits at different periods: (1) Ancient **Thra·ce** \'thrā-sē\ *or* **Thra·cia** \'thrā-shē-ə\ bordered on Pontus Euxinus (Black Sea) S of the Ister (Danube), on the Propontis (Sea of Marmara), on the N Aegean except for narrow strip of Greek settlements, and on the W on Macedonia. Drained by Hebrus (Maritsa) and included Rhodope Mts. Corresponded generally to cen. and S Bulgaria, Turkey in Europe, and NE Greece. Orig. settled by Indo-European peoples from region N of Adriatic Sea during 2d millennium B.C.; coast colonized by Greeks c. 7th cent. B.C.; c. 500 B.C. kingdom made subject to Persia; held by King Philip II of Macedon 342 B.C. Reduced to Roman province under Emperor Claudius I (41–54 A.D.) with N part annexed to Moesia; invaded by Goths, Slavs, Bulgars, and other peoples 3d–9th cents.; part of Byzantine Empire under Justinian I (527–565), but lost Adrianople to Turks 1361 and became part of Ottoman Empire 1453; N part separated 1878 as autonomous province of Eastern Rumelia (annexed to Bulgaria 1885). (2) *or Gk.* **Thrá·ki** \'thrä-kē\. Modern Thrace is S part of ancient region, now divided by the Maritsa River into Greek and Turkish parts. With E Macedonia W Thrace forms region of Eastern Macedonia and Thrace (for subdivisions, see table at GREECE); **Eastern Thrace** constitutes Turkey in Europe (see TURKEY). Ceded in great part to Bulgaria during First Balkan War (1912–13), but boundaries again rearranged after Second Balkan War (1913); after WWI S section of Bulgarian portion assigned to Greece (Treaty of Neuilly, 1919) and Eastern Thrace restored to Turkey (Treaty of Lausanne, 1923) after being lost to Greece 1920.

Thra·cian Sea \'thrā-shən\ *or Gk.* **Thrai·ki·kón Pé·la·gos** \ˌthre-ki-'kōn-'pe-lä-ˌgōs\. The NW part of the Aegean Sea, bordered on N by the peninsulas of Chalcidice, on S by the Northern Sporades, and on W by the mainland of Thessaly; its NW arm is the Gulf of Salonika.

Three Brothers. Mountain, Chelan co., cen. Washington; 7370 ft. (2246 m.).

Three Fingers. Mountain, Snohomish co., NW cen. Washington; 6854 ft. (2089 m.).

Three Forks. Town, Gallatin co., SW Montana, on Jefferson River ab. 4 mi. (6 km.) SW of the place where it joins Madison and Gallatin rivers to form the Missouri; pop. (1990c) 1203.

Three Kings Islands. Three small islands of New Zealand, S Pacific Ocean NNW of N extremity of North I., 34°09′S, 172°09′E; 3 sq. mi. (8 sq. km.).

Three Mile Island. Island, in Susquehanna River, SE cen. Pennsylvania, near Middletown; scene of 1979 accident at a nuclear power plant.

Three Pa·go·das Pass \pə-'gō-dəz\. Mountain pass, S end of Dawna Range, bet. SE Myanmar and W Thailand, at 15°18′N, 98°23′E and ab. 100 mi. (160 km.) SSE of Moulmein; for centuries used as connecting highway bet. Myanmar and the plains of the lower Chao Phraya in Thailand.

Three Points, Cape. Cape extending into the Gulf of Guinea on SW coast of Ghana, 4°45′N, 2°06′W.

Three Rivers. **1.** City, St. Joseph co., S Michigan, 24 mi. (39 km.) S of Kalamazoo; pop. (1990c) 7413.
2. City, Quebec, Canada. See TROIS-RIVIÈRES 1.

Three Sisters. Adjacent peaks, Lane co., W Oregon; 10,085 ft. (3074 m.), 10,047 ft. (3062 m.), 10,358 ft. (3157 m.).

Thrissur. See TRICHUR.

Throck·mor·ton \'thräk-ˌmȯrt-^{ə}n\. **1.** County in N Texas. See table at TEXAS.
2. Town, its ⊗; pop. (1990c) 1036.

Throgs Neck \'thrägz\. Cape projecting into Long Island Sound from the coast of Bronx co., SE New York.

Throop \'trüp\. Borough, Lackawanna co., NE Pennsylvania, 4 mi. (6 km.) NE of Scranton; pop. (1990c) 4070.

Throtmannia. See DORTMUND.

Thu·bur·bo Ma·jus \thə-'bər-bō-'mā-jəs\. Ancient city, Roman Africa, site SW of modern Tunis, Tunisia.

Thug·ga \'thə-gə\ *or mod.* **Doug·ga** \'dü-gə\. Ancient city, N Africa, SW of Carthage; ruins 68 mi. (109 km.) SW of Tunis, Tunisia; important Punic city, assimilated by Romans c. 200 A.D.; most of ruins are Roman, incl. a temple of Jupiter, Juno, and Minerva.

Thuile, La. See LA THUILE.

Thuin \'twe^{n}\. Commune, Hainaut prov., SW Belgium, just SW of Charleroi; pop. (1991c) 14,268.

Thule. See QAANAAQ.

Thumb, The \'thəm\. **1.** Peak in the Sierra Nevada, E Fresno co., S cen. California; 13,885 ft. (4232 m.).
2. Peninsula, E Michigan, bet. Lake Huron and Saginaw Bay; chiefly in Huron co.; its tip is Pointe Aux Barques.

Thun \'tün\. Commune, Bern canton, Switzerland, at head of Thunersee on Aare River 15 mi. (24 km.) SSE of the city of Bern; pop. (1991e) 37,950; machinery, pottery, dairy products; medieval castle; 16th cent. town hall; founded 12th cent.; to Bern late 14th cent.

Thun, Lake of *or* **Lake Thun.** See THUNERSEE.

Thun·der Bay \'thən-dər\. **1.** Inlet of Lake Huron, E coast of Alpena co., NE Michigan; 12 mi. (19 km.) long.
2. River, NE Michigan; flows into Thunder Bay at Alpena; ab. 50 mi. (80 km.) long.
3. Inlet of NW Lake Superior, Ontario, Canada.
4. District, Ontario, Canada. See table at ONTARIO.
5. City, ⊗ of Thunder Bay dist., SW Ontario, Canada, on NW shore of Lake Superior; pop. (1991c) 113,946; pulp and paper mills, coal docks, grain elevators; important transportation center in rich mining region; Lakehead Univ.; city formally estab. 1970 through the merging of Fort William, a French fur-trading post in 17th cent., and Port Arthur, a silver-mining town in mid-19th cent.

Thunder Cape. Headland, SE of Thunder Bay, Ontario, Canada, projecting into Lake Superior.

Thun·der·er, The \'thən-dər-ər\. Peak, NE Yellowstone National Park, NW Wyoming; 10,554 ft. (3217 m.).

Thunder Mountain. Peak in the Sierra Nevada, N Tulare co., S cen. California; 13,578 ft. (4139 m.).

Thun·er·see *or* **Thun·er See** \'tü-nər-ˌzā\ *or Eng.* **Lake of Thun** *or* **Lake Thun** \'tün\. Lake, cen. Switzerland; 10 mi. (16 km.) long, ab. 19 sq. mi. (49 sq. km.); max. depth 712 ft. (217 m.); formed by an expansion of the Aare River.

Thur \'tür\. River, NE Switzerland; rises in cen. St. Gall canton, flows N to Thurgau canton (named for this river) and turns W; joins the Rhine in N Zürich canton; 78 mi. (125 km.) long.

Thur·gau \'tür-ˌgau̇\ *or* **Thur·go·vie** \ˌtu̅e̅r-gȯ-'vē\. Canton, Switzerland. See table at SWITZERLAND.

Thu·rii \'thu̇r-ē-ˌī\. Ancient Greek city, on Gulf of Taranto, S Italy, near site of Sybaris; founded 443 B.C. by Greek colonists, among them statesman Pericles and historian Herodotus. Important city until sacked by Carthaginian Gen. Hannibal late 3d cent. B.C.

Thu·rin·gia \thu̇-'rin-je-ə\ *or Ger.* **Thü·ring·en** \'tu̅e̅-riŋ-ən\. A state of Germany comprising the land around the Thuringian Forest, approx. bet. Werra River on W and Weisse Elster on E; ✻ Weimar; crossed by the Saale; comprised former Thuringian States. See REUSS 2, SAXE, and table at GERMANY.
History: Region conquered by Franks in 6th cent. and generally under Frankish rule until early 9th cent. when Holy Roman Emperor Charlemagne founded the Thuringian Mark. To German house of Wettin 13th cent.; became part of Saxony 1485 and was divided into several states. States joined German Empire 1871 and after WWI were united as one state 1920; following partition of Germany (1945) became part of East Germany; state dissolved into districts 1952; reconstituted as state in unified Germany 1990.

Thu·rin·gi·an Forest \thu̇-'rin-jē-ən\ *or Ger.* **Thü·ring·er Wald** \'tu̅e̅-riŋ-ər-ˌvält\. Wooded mountain range in Thuringia, Germany; highest point ab. 3225 ft. (985 m.).

Thur·les \'thər-ləs\. Town, cen. co. Tipperary, S Ireland; pop. (1991p) 6683; sporting center; remains of 12th cent. castle.

Thur·rock \'thər-ək\. Town, Essex, SE England, on N bank of the Thames; pop. (1991p) 124,300; cement, soap; oil refining.

Thurs·day Island \'thərz-dā\. Small island, N Queensland, Australia, in Torres Strait 30 mi. (48 km.) NW of Cape York; pop. (1981c) 2283; administrative and service center; has excellent harbor (Port Kennedy).

Thur·so \'thər-sō\. Burgh, Highland region, N Scotland, at mouth of Thurso River; pop. (1981p) 9038; nuclear power station; in Middle Ages principal Norse town in Scotland; most northerly town on mainland of Scotland.

Thurs·ton \'thər-stən\. Name of counties in two states of the U.S. See tables at NEBRASKA and WASHINGTON.

Thurston, Mount. See NDIKEVA, MOUNT.

Thurston Island; *formerly* **Thurston Peninsula.** Island, Antarctica, bet. Bellinghausen and Amundsen seas; formerly thought to be a peninsula of Marie Byrd Land.

Thý·a·mis *or* **Thí·a·mis** \'thē-ä-ˌmēs\; *formerly* **Ka·la·mas** \'kä-lä-ˌmäs\. River, cen. Epirus, NW Greece; flows S and W to Ionian Sea opp. Corfu I.; ab. 70 mi. (115 km.) long; marked N border of ancient Thesprotia.

Thyatira. See AKHISAR.

Thyland. See VENDSYSSEL-THY.

Tia·hua·na·co \ˌtē-ä-wä-'nä-kō\ *or* **Tia·hua·na·cu** \-kü\. Site of prehistoric ruins, W Bolivia, adjacent to mountain village of Tiahuanaco, near SE end of Lake Titicaca; ruins include Akapana pyramid, Kalasasaya enclosure, and monolithic Gateway of the Sun, some dating back as far as c. 200 A.D. Believed to be ancient ✻ of pre-Incan empire (fl. c. 600 A.D.).

Ti·a·hua·tlán \ˌtē-ä-wä-ˈtlän\. Municipality, Veracruz state, Mexico, 140 mi. (225 km.) NW of the seaport of Veracruz; pop. (1970p) 53,447.

Tiananmen Square. See BEIJING.

Tian·jin *or W.-G.* **T'ien–chin** \ˈtyen-ˈjin\ *or* **Tien·tsin** \ˈtyen-ˈjin\. City and municipality (special administrative unit), NE China, ab. 80 mi. (130 km.) SE of Beijing; major seaport on Hai River, connected to the Chang by Grand Canal, and (municipality) on Bo Hai; industrial products include textiles, chemicals, iron and steel, machinery; several colleges incl. Nan-k'ai Univ. (1919). See table at CHINA.

History: Garrison town during Ming dynasty (1368–1644); occupied by British and French during Second Opium War (1856–60); treaty signed here 1858 opened 11 Chinese ports to foreign trade; became treaty port 1860 and developed rapidly with foreign concessions. In Boxer Rebellion 1900 scene of siege and heavy fighting, after which city placed under control of international commission and walls razed; in Chinese Civil War occupied by Communist forces Jan. 1949; ✻ of Hopei prov. 1957–67; treated as government-controlled municipality by 1968.

Tian Shan *or W.-G.* **Tien Shan** \ˈtyen-ˈshän\ *or Russ.* **Tyan' Shan'** \ˈtyänʸ-ˈshänʸ\. Lofty mountain chain (*shan*), Kyrgyzstan and Xinjiang Uygur, W China; highest point Pobeda Peak 24,406 ft. (7439 m.).

Tian·shui *or W.-G.* **T'ien–shui** *or* **Tien·shui** \ˈtyen-ˈshwē\; *formerly* **Tsin·chow** \ˈjin-ˈchau̇\. City, SE Gansu prov., N cen. China, SE of Lanzhou.

Tia·ong \tyä-ˈȯŋ\. Municipality, SW Quezon prov., Luzon, Philippines, 19 mi. (31 km.) W of Lucena; pop. (1980c) 48,606.

Ti·a·ret \ˌtē-ə-ˈret\. Commune, N Algeria, ab. 110 mi. (177 km.) E of Oran; pop. (1977p) 62,900; alt. 3350 ft. (1021 m.); on a pass in N Atlas Mts. Site occupied since Roman times; seat of Muslim dynasty 8th cent.; came under Turks 16th cent. and under French 1843.

Tibbermore. See TIPPERMUIR.

Ti·ber \ˈtī-bər\ *or Ital.* **Te·ve·re** \ˈtā-vā-rā\; *anc.* **Ti·ber·is** \ˈtī-bə-rəs\. River, cen. Italy; rises in the Tuscan Apennines, flows S through Umbria and Lazio; in Lazio turns SW, flows through Rome which is 16 mi. (26 km.) from its mouth at Ostia on the Tyrrhenian Sea; 252 mi. (405 km.) long.

Ti·be·ri·as \tī-ˈbir-ē-əs\ *or Heb.* **Te·ver·ya** \tə-ˈver-yə\. Town, Northern Dist., Israel, on W shore of the Sea of Galilee 30 mi. (48 km.) E of Haifa; pop. (1972p) 23,800; lake port and resort. Founded c. 20 A.D. by Herod Antipas, tetrarch of Galilee, and named after Roman Emperor Tiberius; after destruction of Jerusalem by Romans (70 A.D.) became a center of Jewish learning and later seat of Sanhedrin and rabbinical schools; Talmud edited here 3d–6th cents.; taken from Crusaders by Muslim Sultan Saladin 1187; modern town refounded under British mandate of Palestine after 1922; became part of independent Israel 1948.

Tiberias, Lake *or* **Tiberias, Sea of.** See GALILEE, SEA OF.

Ti·bes·ti Mountains \tə-ˈbes-tē\. Mountain group, NW Chad, in cen. Sahara region; highest peak Emi Koussi 11,204 ft. (3415 m.).

Ti·bet *also* **Thi·bet** \tə-ˈbet\ *or Chin.* **Xi·zang** *or W.-G.* **Hsi–tsang** \ˈshē-ˈdzäŋ\. Autonomous region, China, cen. Asia, bounded on N by Xinjiang Uygur and Qinghai, on E by Sichuan, on SE by Yunnan and Myanmar, on S by India, Nepal, Bhutan, and Sikkim, and on W by India; ✻ Lhasa; agricultural products include barley, wheat, peas, millet. See table at CHINA.

Physical features: A plateau, the highest region in the world, averaging ab. 16,000 ft. (4875 m.); its lowland regions and valleys are bet. 12,000 and 15,000 ft. (3660 and 4570 m.); its mountain ranges rise to 20,000 and 24,000 ft. (6100 and 7300 m.); the mountain passes are generally 14,000 to 18,000 ft. (4270 to 5500 m.). Bordered on N by the Kunlun Shan; the S part, comprising valley or plain of Zangbo (upper Brahmaputra) is separated from Nepal, India, and Bhutan by the Himalayas (containing highest peaks in the world); subsidiary ranges are the Gangdisê Range and the Nganglong Kangri. Its N region is broken up by mountain ranges, valleys, and lakes. The Salween River has its source in Tanggula Range in E part and flows generally SE, crossing into Yunnan; the Indus and its tributary the Sutlej rise in the SW; plateau marked by numerous lakes.

History: Emerged as powerful Buddhist kingdom 7th–8th cents. A.D. Came under Mongols 13th cent.; under Manchu dynasty 18th cent.; established trade relations with British India 1904. After Chinese Revolution (1911–12) became independent under British influence; invaded by Communist Chinese 1950; anti-Chinese rebellion 1959 suppressed by Chinese forces; made a nominally autonomous region within Communist China 1965. Buddhist culture almost destroyed during Chinese Cultural Revolution (1966 ff.); region aided in late 1970s by religious and economic reforms, but independence demonstrations increased in late 1980s.

Tibet, Little. See BALTISTAN.

Tibet, Plateau of. Vast tableland, S cen. Asia, mostly in Tibet, but extending into Xinjiang Uygur, Qinghai, and Sichuan; rises to ab. 15,000 ft. (4570 m.); approx. 850,000 sq. mi. (2,201,500 sq. km.).

Tibiscus. See TIMIŞ.

Tibur. See TIVOLI.

Tib·u·ron \ˈti-bə-ˌrän\. **1.** Peninsula, N of San Francisco, California, extending into San Francisco Bay.
2. City, Marin co., W California, on San Francisco Bay, 7 mi. (11 km.) N of San Francisco; pop. (1980c) 6685.

Ti·bu·ron \ˌtē-bü-ˈrōⁿ\. **1.** Peninsula, SW Haiti; ab. 140 mi. (225 km.) long, 18 to 36 mi. (29 to 58 km.) wide; mountainous, contains the Massif de la Hotte.
2. Cape, the SW point of Tiburon Penin., Haiti.

Ti·bu·rón \ˌtē-bü-ˈrōn\. Island, Mexico, off W cen. coast of Sonora state, in Gulf of California; 34 mi. (55 km.) long.

Tiburón, Cape. Cape on W coast of Colombia at the entrance to the Gulf of Urubá.

Ti·cao \tē-ˈkau̇\. Island, Masbate prov., Philippines, off NE coast of Masbate I. and separated from Luzon (Sorsogon prov.) by Ticao Pass; 129 sq. mi. (334 sq. km.); pop. (1969e) 41,900; coextensive with the municipalities of San Jacinto and San Fernando, both with population centers on E coast. Occupied by U.S. forces Apr. 1945 during WWII.

Ticao Pass. Strait bet. SW Sorsogon prov., SE Luzon, Philippines, and Ticao I.; ab. 37 mi. (60 km.) long by 10 or 12 mi. (16 or 19 km.) wide; sometimes considered as W part of San Bernardino Strait.

Tice \ˈtīs\. Unincorporated settlement, Lee co., SW Florida, NE of Fort Myers; pop. (1990c) 3971.

Ti·ci·no \tē-ˈchē-nō\. **1.** *anc.* **Ti·ci·nus** \ti-ˈsī-nəs\. River, Switzerland and Italy; rises on the slopes of St. Gotthard Range, flows SE and then SW in Ticino canton, traverses Lake Maggiore and continues S into Po River 3.5 mi. (5.6 km.) SSE of Pavia; 154 mi. (248 km.) long; navigable below Lake Maggiore; Carthaginian Gen. Hannibal defeated Romans on the banks of this river 218 B.C.
2. *or* **Tes·sin** \te-ˈseⁿ\. Canton, Switzerland, in Lepontine Alps, watered by Ticino River; crossed by St. Gotthard railroad; wine; tourism; formed 1803. See table at SWITZERLAND.

Ticinum. See PAVIA 2.

Ti·con·der·o·ga \ˌtī-kän-də-ˈrō-gə\. Town, Essex co., NE New York, on N outlet of Lake George and near Lake Champlain; pop. (1990c) 5149; tourist center in resort region; incorp. 1889. Old Fort Carillon (restored as museum) built at head of Lake Champlain by French 1755; defended under French commander Louis-Joseph de Montcalm-Gozon against British Gen. James Abercrombie's attack 1758 during French and Indian War; taken by English Gen. Jeffrey Amherst 1759, and renamed **Fort Ticonderoga;** captured by American soldier Ethan Allen 1775 during Revolutionary War, retaken by British Gen. John Burgoyne 1777; held by British until Burgoyne's surrender at Saratoga.

Ti·cul \tē-ˈkül\. Town, Yucatán state, SE Mexico, 40 mi. (64 km.) S of Mérida; munic. pop. (1970c) 14,341.

Tid·dim \ˈti-ˌdim\. Town, W Myanmar, in the Chin Hills, just E of Manipur River and S of Manipur border; occupied by Japanese forces in campaign against India 1944 during WWII.

Ti·do·re \tē-ˈdōr-ā\. **1.** Island of the Moluccas, Indonesia, off W coast of Halmahera I. ab. 1 mi. (1.6 km.) S of Ternate I.; ab. 45 sq. mi. (115 sq. km.); pop. (1957e) 27,753. Has several volcanic peaks, highest 5676 ft. (1730 m.); fertile soil; formerly notable producer of spice. Seat of powerful sultanate by 1500; occupied early 16th cent. by Portuguese, who built a fort 1578; occupied by Spanish early 17th cent.; conquered by Dutch mid-17th cent.; occupied by Japanese 1942–45 during WWII.
2. Town and port on E side of island; a walled town dating back to early 16th cent.

T'ieh–ling *or* **Tiehling.** See TIELING.

Tiel \ˈtēl\. Municipality, Gelderland prov., cen. Netherlands, on the Waal; pop. (1993e) 32,928.

Tie·ling *or W.-G.* **T'ieh–ling** *or* **Tieh·ling** \ˈtye-ˈliŋ\. Town, cen. Liaoning prov., NE China, on left bank of Liao River 40 mi. (64 km.) NE of Shenyang.

Tielt *also* **Thielt** \ˈtēlt\. Commune, West Flanders prov., NW Belgium, 15 mi. (24 km.) SE of Brugge; pop. (1991c) 19,339.

Tien Ch'ih *or* **Tien Chih.** See DIAN CHI.

T'ien–chin. See TIANJIN.

Tie·nen *or* **Thie·nen** \ˈtē-nən\ *or Fr.* **Tir·le·mont** \ˌtēr-lə-ˈmō^{n}\. Commune, Brabant prov., cen. Belgium; captured by the Germans 1914 during WWI.

Tien Shan. See TIAN SHAN.

T'ien–shui *or* **Tienshui.** See TIANSHUI.

Tientsin. See TIANJIN.

Tier·o·ko \ˌtye-rō-ˈkō\ *or* **Tar·so Tieroko** \ˈtär-sō\. Mountain peak, NW Chad; 9547 ft. (2910 m.); one of the highest peaks in the Tibesti Mts.

Tier·ra Am·a·ril·la \tē-ˈer-ə-ˌa-mə-ˈri-lə\. Village, ⊗ of Rio Arriba co., N New Mexico.

Tier·ra Blan·ca \ˈtyer-rä-ˈbläŋ-kä\. Town, Veracruz state, E Mexico; railroad junction point ab. 50 mi. (80 km.) SSW of the seaport of Veracruz; munic. pop. (1990c) 39,473.

Tier·ra Bom·ba \ˈtyer-rä-ˈbȯm-bä\. Small island, Caribbean Sea, off NW coast of Colombia, near city of Cartagena.

Tier·ra del Fue·go \ˈtyer-rä-thel-ˈfwā-gō\. **1.** Archipelago off S South America, comprising all islands S of Strait of Magellan; 28,434 sq. mi. (73,644 sq. km.); separated from Antarctic Archipelago on S by Drake Passage. Its main island, Tierra del Fuego, is divided bet. Chile (W half) and Argentina (E half); of its groups of smaller islands the E (incl. Isla de los Estados) belongs to Argentina, and the S (incl. Hoste I., Navarino I., Wollaston Is., and Diego Ramírez Is.) and W (incl. Desolación, Santa Inés, Clarence, and Dawson) belong to Chile; E half along with nearby Isla de los Estados comprises Tierra del Fuego prov. (✱ Ushuaia) of Argentina (see table at ARGENTINA).
2. *or* **Is·la Gran·de de Tierra del Fuego** \ˈēs-lä-ˈgrän-dā-thā-\. Chief island of Tierra del Fuego Archipelago; 18,530 sq. mi. (47,993 sq. km.); oil fields; W half belongs to Magallanes y Antártica Chilena region, Chile; **Tierra del Fuego National Territory** of Argentina (✱ Ushuaia) comprises E half and nearby Isla de los Estados; in SW corner of the Argentine section is **Tierra del Fuego National Park** (see table at ARGENTINA).

Tie·tê \tyā-ˈtā\. River, São Paulo state, SE Brazil; rises in mountains near Atlantic coast, flows NW through cen. São Paulo state and empties into Paraná River; 500 mi. (804 km.) long; city of São Paulo is on it.

Tiet·jerk·ste·ra·deel \tēt-ˈyerk-stə-rə-ˌdāl\. Commune, Friesland prov., N Netherlands; pop. (1981e) 29,675.

Ti·e·ton \ˈtī-ət-^{ə}n\. River, S Washington; a tributary of Naches River; rises in W Yakima co., flows NE; 25 mi. (40 km.) long.

Tieton Dam. Dam across Tieton River, W Yakima co., S Washington; height 235 ft. (72 m.); impounds water, **Rim·rock Lake** \ˈrim-ˌräk\, for irrigation.

Tieton Peak. Mountain, Yakima co., S Washington; 7775 ft. (2370 m.).

Tif·fa·ny Mountain \ˈti-fə-nē\. Peak, Okanogan co., N Washington; 8242 ft. (2512 m.).

Tif·fin \ˈti-fən\. City, ⊗ of Seneca co., N Ohio, 25 mi. (40 km.) ENE of Findlay; pop. (1990c) 18,604; natural gas; machinery, wire, automobile parts; Heidelberg Coll. (1850); Tiffin Univ. (1888); settled c. 1820.

Tiflis. See TBILISI.

Tift \ˈtift\. County in S Georgia. See table at GEORGIA.

Tif·ton \ˈtif-tən\. City, ⊗ of Tift co., S Georgia, 40 mi. (64 km.) ESE of Albany; pop. (1990c) 14,215; tomatoes, peanuts; Abraham Baldwin Agricultural Coll. (1933).

Tigara. See HOPE, POINT.

Ti·gard \ˈtī-gərd\. City, Washington co., NW Oregon, 7 mi. (11 km.) SSW of Portland; pop. (1990c) 29,344.

Tig·ba·uan \tēg-ˈbä-wän\. Municipality, Iloilo prov., Panay, Philippines, on Iloilo Strait 15 mi. (24 km.) W of City of Iloilo; pop. (1980c) 34,540.

Tiger. See TYGER.

Ti·ger Bay \ˈtī-gər\ *or Port.* **Ba·ia dos Ti·gres** \bə-ˈē-ə-düsh-ˈtē-grish\. Inlet of Atlantic Ocean, on SW coast of Angola.

Tiger Hill. See DARJEELING.

Ti·ghi·na \ti-ˈgē-nə\ *or* **Ben·de·ry** \ben-ˈder-ē\ *or* **Ben·der** \ben-ˈder\. Town, Moldova, near right bank of the Dniester in its lower course 30 mi. (48 km.) SE of Chişinău; pop. (1991c) 141,500; on rail line bet. Chişinău and Odessa; food products, electrical equipment, textiles.
History: Inhabited in ancient times; Genoese trading town in 12th cent.; controlled by many different peoples down to 18th cent.; site of fortress erected 16th cent. by Ottoman Sultan Süleyman the Magnificent; Swedish King Charles XII in his campaign against Russia fought a battle here 1713; became Russian early 19th cent.; became part of Bessarabia, Romania, 1918; ceded to U.S.S.R. 1940; held by Axis powers 1941–44; to U.S.S.R. after WWII; now town in independent Moldova.

Ti·gray *also* **Ti·gre** \ˈti-ˌgrā, tē-ˈgrā\. Historical region, N Ethiopia; bounded on N by Eritrea; includes part of Danakil desert region in E. Formed part of Aksum kingdom (flourished 3d cent. A.D.); disputed by Italy, Egypt, Britain, and Sudan 19th cent.; occupied by Italy 1935–41 during WWII; center of antigovernment activity after military coup 1974.

Ti·gre \ˈtē-grā\. **1.** *formerly* **Las Con·chas** \läs-ˈkȯn-chäs\. Town, Buenos Aires prov., E Argentina, 20 mi. (32 km.) N of the city of Buenos Aires; pop. (1991p) 256,005; part of Buenos Aires met. area; seaside resort.
2. River, Ecuador and Peru; rises in cen. Ecuador, flows SE across border into Peru and empties into Marañón River, headstream of Amazon River; ab. 350 mi. (565 km.) long.

Tigre. Historical region of N Ethiopia. See table at TIGRAY.

Tigre, El. See EL TIGRE.

Ti·gre Island \ˈtē-grā\. Island, Gulf of Fonseca, Honduras; chief town Amapala.

Tigres, Baia dos. See TIGER BAY.

Ti·gris \ˈtī-grəs\ *or Arab.* **Shatt Dij·la** \ˌshät-ˈdij-lə\; *bib.* (*Gen.* ii. 14; *Dan.* x. 4) **Hid·de·kel** \ˈhi-də-ˌkel\. River, SE Turkey and Iraq; rises in a lake in the mountains of Kurdistan, S of Elâziğ, Turkey in Asia; flows SSE past Diyarbakır in Turkey and Mosul and Baghdad in Iraq, and unites in SE Iraq at Al Qurnah with the Euphrates River to form the Shatt al Arab; 1180 mi. (1899 km.) long. Has many tributaries on left bank, esp. the Great Zab, Little Zab, and Diyala in Iraq. Navigable for small vessels bet. Baghdad and a point just above Al Qurnah. With Euphrates defined region of Mesopotamia; connected in its lower course with Euphrates by irrigation canals (c. 3d cent. A.D.). Sites of ruins of many ancient cities are on its banks, as Nineveh, Calah (modern Nimrud), Ashur, Ctesiphon, and Seleucia.

Tih, Al– *or* **Tih, El** *also* **Tīh, Jabal at.** See AL-TIH.

Ti·ha·ma *or* **Ti·hā·mah** *or* **Te·ha·ma** \tē-ˈhá-mə\. Low coastal plain, W Saudi Arabia and W Yemen, along the Red Sea, from S Hejaz to Bab el-Mandeb Strait.

Tihwa. See ÜRÜMQI.

Ti·jua·na \tē-ˈhwä-nä, ˌtē-ə-ˈwä-nə\. Town, Baja California, NW Mexico; pop. (1990p) 742,686; a popular tourist center and point of entry on U.S.-Mexico border.

Ti·ju·ca Peak \tē-ˈzhü-kə\. Mountain, SW side of the city of Rio de Janeiro, SE Brazil; 3350 ft. (1021 m.); main feature in one of three sectors comprising **Tijuca National Park**.

Ti·ju·cas Bay \tē-ˈzhü-kəs\. Inlet of Atlantic Ocean, E coast of Santa Catarina state, S Brazil, N of Florianópolis.

Ti·kal \tē-ˈkäl\. Ancient Mayan city, N Guatemala, NE of Petén Itza; ruins include pyramid temples and date back to 3d cent. A.D.; major excavation begun 1956; located in **Tikal National Park** (224 sq. mi. or 580 sq. km.).

Ti·kam·garh \ti-ˈkəm-ˌgär\ *or* **Teh·ri** \ˈter-ē\. Town, Madhya Pradesh, India, ab. 100 mi. (160 km.) SSE of Gwalior; pop. (1991p) 54,130; chosen as ✻ of Orchha state 1783.

Ti·kho·retsk \ˌtē-k̲ər-ˈyetsk\. Town, Krasnodar Kray, S Russia in Europe, ab. 100 mi. (160 km.) S of Rostov-na-Donu; pop. (1991e) 67,600; key railroad junction point and scene of fighting 1942–43 during WWII.

Tikh·vin \ˈtik̲-vin\. Town, E St. Petersburg Oblast, W Russia in Europe, 110 mi. (177 km.) ESE of the city of St. Petersburg; pop. (1991e) 71,800; on S bank of the **Tikh·vin·ka** \ˈtik̲-vin-kə\ tributary of the Syas', which forms part of canal system connecting Lake Ladoga with the Volga at Rybinsk via the Mologa River and Rybinsk Reservoir.

Ti·krīt *or* **Te·krit** \ti-ˈkrēt\. Town, N cen. Iraq, on the W bank of the Tigris ab. 100 mi. (160 km.) NNW of Baghdad; birthplace of Muslim Sultan Saladin (c. 1138) and Iraqi President Saddam Hussein (1937). Site of battle Nov. 1917 in WWI in which it was captured from the Turks by British forces.

Til·burg \ˈtil-ˌbœrk̲\. Commune, North Brabant prov., S Netherlands, 34 mi. (55 km.) SE of Rotterdam; pop. (1992e) 160,618; a center of Dutch textile industry.

Til·bury \ˈtil-ˌber-ē, -bə-rē\. **1.** Town, Essex, SE Ontario, Canada, 17 mi. (27 km.) SW of Chatham, near mouth of Thames River; pop. (1991c) 4362.
2. Port, Essex co., England, on the Thames downstream from London; extensive container facilities.

Til·den \ˈtil-dən\. Village, ⊗ of McMullen co., S Texas.

Tilimsen. See TLEMCEN.

Till \ˈtil\. Small river, Northumberland, N England; flows N into the Tweed on the border of Scotland; 32 mi. (52 km.) long.

Til·la·mook \ˈti-lə-ˌmək, -ˌmu̇k\. **1.** County in NW Oregon. See table at OREGON.
2. City, its ⊗, on S end of **Tillamook Bay** (inlet of Pacific Ocean) 50 mi. (81 km.) S of Astoria; pop. (1990c) 4001; resort; fisheries.

Til·leur \tē-ˈyœr\. Commune, Liège prov., E Belgium; W suburb of the city of Liège.

Till·man \ˈtil-mən\. County in SW Oklahoma. See table at OKLAHOMA.

Till·son·burg \ˈtil-sən-ˌbərg\. Town, Oxford co., SE Ontario, Canada, 28 mi. (45 km.) ESE of London; pop. (1991c) 12,019.

Til·ly \tē-ˈyē\ *or officially* **Tilly–sur–Seulles** \-sūr-ˈsœl\. Village, Calvados dept., NW France, 7 mi. (11 km.) SSE of Bayeux; in WWII retaken from German occupation forces June 1944 during Normandy campaign.

Tí·los \ˈtē-ˌlös\ *also* **Te·los** \ˈte-ləs, -ˌläs\. An island of the Dodecanese (*q.v.*), NW of Rhodes, Greece; 25 sq. mi. (65 sq. km.).

Tilsit. See SOVETSK.

Til·till Mountain \ˈtil-til\. Peak in the Sierra Nevada, in E Tuolumne co., cen. California; 8951 ft. (2728 m.).

Til·ton \ˈtilt-ᵊn\. **1.** Village, Vermilion co., E Illinois; pop. (1990c) 2729.
2. Town, Belknap co., cen. New Hampshire, 7 mi. (11 km.) SW of Laconia; pop. (1990c) 3240; united industrially, commercially, and residentially with Northfield, to the S, across Winnipesaukee River.

Timagami, Lake. See TEMAGAMI, LAKE.

Tim·a·ru \ˈti-mə-ˌrü\. Seaport, E South I., New Zealand, on Pacific Ocean 95 mi. (153 km.) SW of Christchurch; pop. (1992e) 27,100; exports grain, wool, and frozen meat; seaside resort.

Tim·ba·lier Bay \ˈtam-bəl-ˌyā\. Inlet of Gulf of Mexico, SW coast of Lafourche parish, SE Louisiana.

Timbalier Island. Island off SE Louisiana, in Lafourche parish, bet. Timbalier Bay and the Gulf of Mexico.

Tim·ba·ú·ba \ˌtim-bä-ˈü-bä\. City, Pernambuco state, E Brazil, near the coast ab. 40 mi. (64 km.) NNW of Recife; munic. pop. (1991p) 57,245.

Tim·ber Crater \ˈtim-bər\. Peak, W Klamath co., S Oregon, N of Crater Lake in Crater Lake National Park; 7403 ft. (2256 m.).

Timber Lake. City, ⊗ of Dewey co., N cen. South Dakota; pop. (1990c) 517.

Timber Mountain. Peak, S Nye co., S Nevada; 7243 ft. (2208 m.).

Tim·ber·wolf, Mount \ˈtim-bər-ˌwu̇lf\. Peak, Yakima co., S Washington; 6435 ft. (1961 m.).

Timbuktu. See TOMBOUCTOU.

Tim·gad \ˈtim-ˌgad\; *anc.* **Tham·u·ga·di** \ˌtha-mə-ˈgā-dē\ *or* **Tham·u·ga·dis** \-ˈgā-dəs\. Ruined city, NE Algeria, ESE of Batna; extensive ruins include the capitol, forum, theater, several baths, and a triumphal arch. Founded 100 A.D. by Roman Emperor Trajan, declined after 5th cent.; revived for a time by Byzantines in 7th cent., but soon destroyed by Arab invaders.

Ti·miş \ˈtē-ˌmēsh\ *or Serb.* **Ta·miš** \ˈtä-ˌmēsh\ *or Hung.* **Te·mes** \ˈte-ˌmesh\; *anc.* **Ti·bis·cus** \ti-ˈbis-kəs\. **1.** River, W Romania; flows W and S to the Danube in Yugoslavia just below Belgrade; ab. 200 mi. (320 km.) long.
2. County of W Romania. See table at ROMANIA.

Ti·mis·ka·ming \tə-ˈmis-kə-ˌmiŋ\. District, Ontario, Canada. See table at ONTARIO.

Timiskaming, Lake. Lake, SW Quebec and SE Ontario, Canada; 121 sq. mi. (313 sq. km.); discharges SE into the Ottawa River.

Ti·mi·şoa·ra \ˌtē-mē-ˈshwä-rä\ *or Hung.* **Te·mes·vár** \ˈte-ˌmesh-ˌvär\. City, ⊗ of Timiş co., W Romania, near the Timiş River and the Yugoslav border; pop. (1989c) 333,365; electrical equipment, chemicals, footwear, metal goods, food products, textiles; cultural center with four universities, state theaters, libraries; 18th cent. cathedral; 15th cent. castle. Destroyed 13th cent. by Turkic invaders; rebuilt by King Charles I of Hungary (1308–42); held by Turks 1552–1716 when it was captured by Austrians under Prince Eugene of Savoy; to Romania by Treaty of Trianon (1920). Site of demonstrations Dec. 1989 that led to execution of President Nicolae Ceauşescu and the end of Communist rule in Romania.

Tim·mins \ˈti-mənz\. Town, Cochrane dist., E Ontario, Canada, on Mattagami River 135 mi. (217 km.) N of Sudbury; pop. (1991c) 47,461; principal gold-mining center of Canada; beer; founded early 1900s.

Timms Hill \ˈtimz\. Peak, Price co., N Wisconsin; 1952 ft. (595 m.); highest point in the state.

Ti·mok \ˈtē-ˌmōk\. River, E Yugoslavia; flows NE into Danube River 18 mi. (29 km.) NNW of Vidin; ab. 100 mi. (160 km.) long; in part forms boundary bet. Yugoslavia and Romania.

Ti·mor \ˈtē-ˌmȯr, tē-ˈmȯr\. Island, S Malay Archipelago, easternmost of the Lesser Sunda Is., bet. Savu Sea on the W and Timor Sea on the E; ab. 400 mi. (645 km.) NW of Australia; ab. 300 mi. (485 km.) long by 10 to 65 mi. (16 to 105 km.) wide; 13,094 sq. mi. (33,914 sq. km.); formerly divided bet. the Dutch and the Portuguese; see TIMOR, NETHERLANDS and EAST TIMOR.

Timor, Netherlands. Former Dutch-ruled sector of Timor, now (with adjacent islands) the Indonesian prov. East Nusa Tenggara (see table at INDONESIA). Occupied by Portuguese 16th cent.; Kupang and vicinity seized by Dutch 1613 and W half of island claimed by them; occupied by Japanese Feb. 1942; transferred to Indonesia by the Dutch 1949.

Timorlaut Islands. See TANIMBAR ISLANDS.

Timor Sea. Arm of the Indian Ocean bet. Timor I. and the NW coast of Australia; ab. 300 mi. (485 km.) wide.

Timor Timur. See EAST TIMOR.

Ti·mo·ta·kem \tē-ˌmō-tä-ˈkā^{n}\. Peak, Tumuc-Humac Mts., in S French Guiana on Brazilian border.

Tim·pah·ute Range \ˌtim-pə-ˈyüt\. Small range, W Lincoln co., SE Nevada; highest peak 9380 ft. (2859 m.).

Tim·pa·no·gos, Mount \ˌtim-pə-ˈnō-gəs\. Peak, N cen. Utah; 12,008 ft. (3660 m.); highest peak in Wasatch Range.

Timpanogos Cave National Monument. See UNITED STATES, *National Monuments.*

Tim·sah \tim-ˈsä\ *or Arab.* **Bu·ḩay·rat at Tim·sāḩ** \bə-ˈhā-rət-ˌat-\. Lake, NE Egypt, at midpoint of Suez Canal; connected with the Nile by the Ismailia Canal.

Tims Ford Dam \ˈtimz-ˈfōrd\. See table at TENNESSEE VALLEY AUTHORITY.

Tin, Cape \ˈtin\. Cape, N coast of Libya, W of entrance to Gulf of Bomba.

Ti·na·ca Point \tē-ˈnä-kä\. Most southerly point of Mindanao, Philippines, in Davao del Sur prov.; 4°N, 125°20′E.

Ti·na·ga \ˌtē-nä-ˈgä\. Largest island of the Calagua group off N coast of Camarines Norte, SE Luzon, Philippines, 14 mi. (23 km.) NE of Paracale; 5 sq. mi. (13 sq. km.).

Tīnah, Khalīj aṭ–. See PELUSIUM.

Tin·che·bray *also* **Tinche·brai** \te^{n}zh-ˈbre, -ˈbrā\. Town, NW Orne dept., NW France; scene 1106 of victory of King Henry I of England over his brother Robert Courteheuse, duke of Normandy. Birthplace of surrealist André Breton 1896.

Ti·neo \tē-ˈnā-ō\. Commune, Asturias prov., NW Spain, 32 mi. (52 km.) W of Oviedo; pop. (1991c) 14,927.

Tingchou *or* **Tingchow.** See CHANGTING.

Ting–hai. See DINGHAI.

Tingis. See TANGIER.

Tin·gi·ta·na \ˌtin-jə-ˈtā-nə, -ˈta-, -ˈtä-\. Region, NW Africa; in Roman times, the W part of Mauretania; partly coextensive with Morocco.

Tingzhou. See CHANGTING.

Ti·ni·an \ˈti-nē-ən, ˌtē-nē-ˈän\. Island, Northern Mariana Is., W Pacific Ocean, 3 mi. (5 km.) SSW of Saipan; 10 mi. (16 km.) long by ab. 5 mi. (8 km.) wide; area 20 sq. mi. (52 sq. km.); chief town Tinian on SW coast. Colonized by Spain 17th cent. and acquired by Germany 1899 (see MARIANA ISLANDS); included in Japanese mandate 1919; occupied by U.S. forces July 1944 during WWII. Site of airfields from which U.S. planes were sent Aug. 1945 to drop atomic bombs on Hiroshima and Nagasaki.

Tin·i·cum \ˈti-ni-kəm\. Small island, Pennsylvania, in Delaware River just below Philadelphia; first settlement within Pennsylvania, made 1643 by Gov. Johan Printz of Swedish colony (New Sweden). See CHESTER 6.

Tin·ley Park \ˈtin-lē\. Village, Cook and Will cos., NE Illinois, SW suburb of Chicago; pop. (1990c) 37,121.

Tí·nos \ˈtē-ˌnōs\ *or* **Te·nos** \ˈtē-nəs, -ˌnäs\. **1.** Island, NE Cyclades, part of Cyclades dept., Greece; 79 sq. mi. (205 sq. km.); wine.

2. Chief town of island, on S coast.

Tin·su·kia \ˈtin-sü-kyə\. Town, NE Assam state, NE India; pop. (1991p) 73,760.

Tin·ta·gel Head \tin-ˈta-jəl\. Cape, W coast of Cornwall, SW England; site of ruins of 12th cent. Tintagel Castle, reputed birthplace of legendary King Arthur.

Tin·tern Abbey \ˈtin-tərn\. Noted ruins, Gwent co., E Wales, downstream from Monmouth, on the River Wye. Abbey founded 1131 by English nobleman Walter de Clare for Cistercian monks; most of ruins date from 13th cent. Subject of poem in William Wordsworth's *Lyrical Ballads* (1798).

Tin·to \ˈtēn-tō\. River, Huelva prov., SW Spain; flows into the Odiel River below the commune of Huelva; combined streams flow into the Mediterranean; 58 mi. (93 km.) long.

Tin·ton Falls \ˈtint-^{ə}n\; *formerly* **New Shrews·bury** \ˈshrüz-ˌber-ē, -bə-rē\. Borough, Monmouth co., E cen. New Jersey; pop. (1990c) 12,361.

Ti·o·ga \tī-ˈō-gə\. **1.** River, SW New York; rises in N Pennsylvania near W boundary of Bradford co., flows N across New York border to unite with Cohocton River near Corning and form the Chemung River; 40 mi. (64 km.) long.

2. Name of counties in two states of the U.S. See tables at NEW YORK and PENNSYLVANIA.

Tio·man \tē-ˈō-ˌmän\. Island, Malaysia, in South China Sea off SE Pahang, S Malay Penin.

Ti·o·nes·ta \ˌtī-ə-ˈnes-tə\. Borough, ⊗ of Forest co., NW Pennsylvania; pop. (1990c) 634.

Ti·o·ro Strait \tē-ˈōr-ō\. Channel bet. the islands of Sulawesi and Muna, Indonesia.

Ti·pa·sa \ˌtē-pä-ˈzä\. Village, Algeria. Orig. settled by Phoenicians, came under Roman control first cent. A.D.; large Christian settlement until invaded by Vandals 5th cent.; destroyed by 7th cent.; settlement revived 19th cent. Many Roman and early Christian ruins; resort area.

Tiphsah. See THAPSACUS.

Ti·pi·ta·pa \ˌtē-pē-ˈtä-pä\. River, W Nicaragua; flows out of Lake Managua SE into Lake Nicaragua; 23 mi. (37 km.) long.

Tip·pah \ˈti-pə\. County in N Mississippi. See table at MISSISSIPPI.

Tipp City \ˈtip\; *formerly* **Tip·pe·ca·noe City** \ˌti-pē-kə-ˈnü\. Village, Miami co., W Ohio, 14 mi. (23 km.) N of Dayton; pop. (1990c) 6027.

Tip·pe·ca·noe \ˌti-pē-kə-ˈnü\. **1.** River, N Indiana; rises in **Tippecanoe Lake** in NE cen. Kosciusko co., N Indiana, flows W and then S into Wabash River in W cen. Indiana; ab. 200 mi. (320 km.) long. See FREEMAN LAKE and SHAFER LAKE. At the junction of the Tippecanoe with the Wabash, Gen. William H. Harrison defeated the Shawnee Indians under Chief Tecumseh's brother Tenskwatawa Nov. 7, 1811.

2. County in W cen. Indiana. See table at INDIANA.

Tip·pe·rary \ˌti-pə-ˈrer-ē\. **1.** County in Munster prov., S Ireland; ⊗ Clonmel; divided into North Riding and South Riding; dairy farming, livestock raising. See table at IRELAND.

2. Town, SW co. Tipperary, S Ireland, 24 mi. (39 km.) SE of Limerick; pop. (1991p) 4783; market town; site of 13th cent. abbey.

Tip·per·muir \ˈti-pər-ˌmyu̇r\ *or* **Tib·ber·more** \ˈti-bər-ˌmōr\. Battlefield near Perth, Scotland; scene Sept. 1, 1644 of victory of Scottish Royalist James Graham, marquis of Montrose over Covenanters under David, earl of Wemyss, during English Civil War.

Tip·ton \ˈtip-tən\. **1.** Name of counties in two states of the U.S. See tables at INDIANA and TENNESSEE.

2. City, ⊗ of Tipton co., cen. Indiana, 15 mi. (24 km.) S of Kokomo; pop. (1990c) 4751.

3. City, ⊗ of Cedar co., E Iowa, 23 mi. (37 km.) ENE of Iowa City; pop. (1990c) 2998.

Tipton, Mount. Peak, cen. Mohave co., NW Arizona; 7364 ft. (2245 m.).

Tip·ton·ville \ˈtip-tən-ˌvil\. Town and resort, ⊗ of Lake co., NW Tennessee, 3 mi. (5 km.) E of Mississippi River at SW end of Reelfoot Lake; pop. (1990c) 2149.

Tira. See TIRE.

Ti·rah \ˈtē-rä\. Mountainous region, Pakistan, WSW of Khyber Pass and Peshawar; scene of campaign late 19th cent. in which British forces put down an uprising of Pashtun tribes.

Ti·rān *or* **Ti·ran** \tē-ˈrän\. Island at N end of Red Sea; with Sanafiri I. lies across entrance to Gulf of Aqaba; both belong to Saudi Arabia. Tīrān I. separated by **Strait of Tiran** from SE coast of Sinai Penin., Egypt.

Ti·ra·në *or* **Ti·ra·na** \ti-ˈrä-nə\. **1.** District of cen. Albania. See table at ALBANIA.

2. City, ✻ of Tiranë dist. and of Albania, 18 mi. (29 km.) E of Durrës; pop. (1990e) 243,000; university (1957), national library, and various government buildings. Population largely Muslim. Founded by Turks early 17th cent.; made ✻ of Albania 1920; occupied by Axis forces 1939–44.

\ə\ **abut** \ˈə\ matches \$^{ə}$\ kitten, Fr table \ər\ **further** \a\ **ash** \ā\ **ace** \ä\ **cot, cart** \a̤\ Fr bac \au̇\ **out** \b̲\ Span Avila \ch\ **chin** \e\ **bet** \ē\ **easy** \g\ **go** \i\ **hit** \ī\ **ice** \j\ **job** \k̲\ Ger **ich**, **Buch** \$^{n}$\ Fr vin \ŋ\ **sing** \ō\ **go** \ȯ\ **all** \ȯ\ **law** \œ\ Fr **bœuf** \œ̄\ Fr **feu** \ȯi\ **boy** \th\ **thin** \t̲h̲\ **this** \ü\ **loot** \u̇\ **foot** \ue\ Ger **füllen** \ue̅\ Fr **rue** \y\ **yet** \$^{y}$\ Fr digne \ˈdēn^{y}\, nuit \ˈnw^{y}ē\ \yü\ **few** \yu̇\ **fury** \zh\ **vision**

Ti·ra·no \tē-ˈrä-nō\. Commune, Sondrio prov., N Lombardy, N Italy, near the Swiss border; pop. (1981p) 8762; scene of massacre of Protestants by Catholic conspirators July 1620; church of Madonna di Tirano, object of many pilgrimages.

Ti·ras·pol \ti-ˈras-pəl\. City, Moldova, on the Dniester 55 mi. (89 km.) NW of Odessa; pop. (1991e) 186,000; wine; founded late 18th cent.; ✱ of Moldavian A.S.S.R. until 1940; heavily damaged in WWII.

Ti·re \ti-ˈre\ *also* **Ti·ra** \-ˈrä\; *anc.* **Tyr·rha** \ˈtir-ə\. Town, İzmir prov., W Turkey in Asia, on branch railroad line 38 mi. (61 km.) SE of the city of İzmir.

Ti·ree *or* **Ty·ree** \tī-ˈrē\. **1.** Island, Inner Hebrides, off W coast of Scotland; 30 sq. mi. (78 sq. km.); administratively a part of Strathclyde region.
2. Strait bet. the islands of Tiree and Mall, Inner Hebrides, off W coast of Scotland.

Tîr·go·vi·şte *or* **Târ·go·viş·te** \tər-ˈgō-vēsh-te\. City, ⊗ of Dîmboviţa co., S cen. Romania, on Ialomiţa River 45 mi. (72 km.) NW of Bucharest; pop. (1989c) 100,426; commercial center; iron, steel, oil-drilling equipment; notable 16th cent. church; ✱ of Walachia 14th–17th cents.

Tîr·gu Jiu *or* **Târ·gu–Jiu** *also* **Tur·gu–Jiu** \ˈtər-gü-ˈzhē-ü\. Town, ⊗ of Gorj co., SW Romania, on Jiu River ab. 50 mi. (80 km.) NNW of Craiova; pop. (1989c) 93,252; wood products.

Tîr·gu Mu·reş *or* **Târ·gu–Mureş** \ˈtər-gü-ˈmu̇r-esh\ *also* **Osor·hei** \ˌō-sȯr-ˈhī\ *or Hung.* **Ma·ros–Vá·sár·hely** \ˈmör-ōsh-ˌvä-shär-ˈhā\. City, ⊗ of Mureş co., N cen. Romania, ab. 50 mi. (80 km.) ESE of Cluj; pop. (1989c) 164,781; food products; 15th cent. Gothic church; palace; museum; library. In region ceded 1918 by Hungary to Romania after WWI but again, with the rest of N Transylvania, was part of Hungary 1940–45 during WWII.

Tîr·gu Neamţ \ˈtər-gü-ˈnyämts\ *or* **Târ·gu–Neam·ţu** \-ˈnyäm-tsü\ *or* **Târ·gul–Neamţ** \ˈtər-gül-ˈnyämts\. Commercial town, NE Romania, 60 mi. (96 km.) WNW of Iaşi; pop. (1989c) 21,145; fortress and ancient monastery nearby.

Tîr·gu Oc·na *or* **Târ·gu–Ocna** \ˈtər-gü-ˈōk-nä\. Town, E Romania, in E Transylvanian Alps 45 mi. (72 km.) W of Bîrlad; salt mines.

Ti·rich Mir \ˈtir-ich-ˈmir\. Mountain, Hindu Kush Range, Pakistan, N of Chitral, on border of Afghanistan; 25,260 ft. (7699 m.); highest peak in the range.

Tirlemont. See TIENEN.

Tirnova *or* **Tirnovo.** See VELIKO TŬRNOVO.

Ti·rol *or* **Ty·rol** \tə-ˈrōl, tī-; ˈtī-ˌrōl; ˈtir-əl\ *or Ital.* **Ti·ro·lo** \tē-ˈrȯ-lō\. State, W Austria, comprised of two sections separated by the state of Salzburg and the Italian region of Trentino-Alto-Adige; ✱ Innsbruck. A very mountainous region with Bavarian Alps along N border and Ötztaler Alps in S cen. part (since 1919 when South Tirol was ceded to Italy, have marked S border). Traversed W to E by the Inn and in the NW by the Lech; before 1919 by the Adige in the S; wheat, rye, corn; livestock raising; salt, copper, magnesite; winter-sports center.

History: Became part of Roman Raetia in first cent. B.C.; under various counts and bishops until it passed to Hapsburgs 1363. Scene of peasant uprising 1525 during Reformation, and after its cession to French Emperor Napoléon 1805 by Treaty of Pressburg was scene of vigorous but unsuccessful revolt against French and Bavarians 1809–10; reunited with Austria 1814 by Congress of Vienna. Its S part (called Upper Adige by Italians) transferred to Italy by Treaty of St.-Germain 1919. See table at AUSTRIA.

Tirreno, Mare. See TYRRHENIAN SEA.

Tir·so \ˈtēr-sō\. River, cen. Sardinia, Italy; flows SW into Gulf of Oristano; ab. 90 mi. (145 km.) long.

Ti·ruch·chi·rap·pal·li \ˌtir-ə-chə-ˈrä-pə-lē\ *also* **Trich·i·nop·o·ly** \ˌtri-chə-ˈnä-pə-lē\. City, cen. Tamil Nadu, S India, on right bank of the Kāveri River 200 mi. (322 km.) SSW of Madras; pop. (1991c) 711,862; railroad junction; cigars; railroad shops; 17th cent. Dravidian temple; ruins of fort surrounding large rock (273 ft. or 83 m. high). Scene of fighting bet. English and French during Carnatic Wars mid-18th cent.

Ti·ru·nel·ve·li \ˌtir-ü-ˈnel-və-lē\. Town, S Tamil Nadu state, near S tip of India; pop. (1991p) 135,762.

Ti·ru·pa·ti \ˈtir-ü-ˌpə-tē\. Town, SE Andhra Pradesh state, S India, NW of Madras; pop. (1991p) 174,393.

Ti·rup·pur \ˈtir-ə-ˌpu̇r\. Town, Tamil Nadu, India, ab. 25 mi. (40 km.) E of Coimbatore; pop. (1991p) 235,076.

Ti·ru·van·na·ma·lai \ˌtir-ə-və-ˈnä-mə-ˌlī\. Town, E Tamil Nadu, S India, 110 mi. (177 km.) SW of Madras; pop. (1991p) 108,291; temple.

Ti·ryns \ˈtir-ənz, ˈtī-rənz\. Prehistoric citadel N of Nauplia, Argolis, E Peloponnese, S Greece. In legends connected with Perseus and Hercules; historically, a Dorian city, founded 3d millennium B.C.; developed as important Mycenaean city under Minoan influence, flourished c. 1400 B.C.; declined, with Mycenae, as Árgos grew in power after 1100 B.C.; destroyed by Argives c. 468 B.C. Ruins of massive walls, palace, hall, among others, date from 15th–12th cents. B.C.

Tir·zah \ˈtər-zə\. Ancient Canaanite town, its site thought to be just NE of Nābulus, in the West Bank; during 10th–9th cents. B.C. ✱ of the Northern Kingdom of Israel (*1 Kings* xv. 21, 33); region occupied by Israel 1967.

Tisa. See TISZA.

Tis·bury \ˈtiz-ˌber-ē, -bə-rē\. Town, Dukes co., SE Massachusetts, on Martha's Vineyard; pop. (1990c) 3120.

Tis·dale \ˈtiz-ˌdāl\. Town, Saskatchewan, Canada, 75 mi. (121 km.) SE of Prince Albert; pop. (1991c) 3045.

Tish·o·min·go \ˌti-shə-ˈmiŋ-gō\. **1.** County in NE corner of Mississippi. See table at MISSISSIPPI.
2. City, ⊗ of Johnston co., S Oklahoma, 28 mi. (45 km.) E of Ardmore; pop. (1990c) 3116; ✱ of Chickasaw Nation 1856–1907; Murray State Coll. (1908).

Tisia *or* **Tissus.** See TISZA.

Tis·ta \ˈtis-tə\. River, India and Bangladesh; rises on edge of Plateau of Tibet, flows S through Sikkim and across West Bengal, India, and Bangladesh into the Brahmaputra; ab. 300 mi. (485 km.) long.

Tis·te·dals·elva \ˈtis-tə-ˌdäls-ˌel-və\. River, S Norway; flows S through several long shallow lakes connected by rapids, and empties into Oslo Fjord.

Ti·sza \ˈti-sö\ *or Ger.* **Theiss** \ˈtīs\ *or Serb.* **Ti·sa** \ˈtē-sä\; *anc.* **Tis·sus** \ˈti-səs\ *or* **Ti·sia** \ˈti-zhə, -zē-ə\. River in W Ukraine, E Hungary, and Vojvodina, Yugoslavia; rises in Carpathian Mts. in W Ukraine, flows W, forming a section of Ukraine-Romania boundary; continues SW across Hungary and into N Yugoslavia; empties into Danube River ab. 28 mi. (45 km.) N of Belgrade; 600 mi. (965 km.) long; its largest tributaries are the Someşul and the Mureşul from Transylvania on the E; navigable for light-draft boats for ab. 450 mi. (725 km.).

Tiszapolgár. See POLGÁR.

Ti·ta·garh \ti-ˈtä-gər\. Town, West Bengal, India, on Hugli River 13 mi. (21 km.) N of Calcutta; pop. (1991p) 113,831.

Ti·ta·no, Mount \tē-ˈtä-nō\. Mountain, San Marino; 2437 ft. (743 m.); city of San Marino is built on it; notable for its three peaks.

Ti·ti·ca·ca, Lake \ˌtē-tē-ˈkä-kä, ˌti-tē-\. Lake on Peru-Bolivia boundary; 122 mi. (196 km.) long, 45 mi. (72 km.) wide; 3200 sq. mi. (8288 sq. km.); max. depth 922 ft. (281 m.); alt. 12,500 ft. (3810 m.); highest large navigable lake in the world; drains S through Desaguadero River into Lake Poopó; traversed by vessels bet. Puno, Peru and Guaqui, Bolivia. The Cordillera Real of the Andes is on its E shore. Was in center of early South American civilizations (see TIAHUANACO).

Titius. See KRKA.

Titograd. See PODGORICA.

Ti·to·vo Uži·ce \ˈtē-tō-vō-ˈü-zhēt-se\ *or* **Užice.** Town, Serbia, cen. Yugoslavia, ab. 75 mi. (121 km.) SW of Belgrade; pop. (1991p) 82,700.

Ti·tov Ve·les \ˈtē-tȯv-ˈve-les\; *formerly* **Veles** *or Turk.* **Kö·pri·li** \ˈkœ-prœ-lœ\. Town, Republic of Macedonia, on the Vardar ab. 30 mi. (48 km.) SE of Skopje; commercial center.

Tit·ta·ba·was·see \ˌti-tə-bə-'wä-sē\. River, E Michigan; flows from Ogemaw co. S into the Saginaw River in Saginaw co; ab. 65 mi. (105 km.) long.

Titterstone Clee Hill. See CLEE HILLS.

Ti·tus \'tī-təs\. County in NE Texas. See table at TEXAS.

Ti·tus·ville \'tī-təs-ˌvil\. **1.** City, ⊗ of Brevard co., E Florida, on Indian River 35 mi. (56 km.) E of Orlando; pop. (1990c) 39,394; winter resort; citrus fruit.

2. City, Crawford co., NW Pennsylvania, on Oil Creek 14 mi. (23 km.) N of Oil City; pop. (1990c) 6434; tool steel, forgings, plastics; founded 1796; site of first oil well drilled in U.S. 1859.

Tium·pan Head \'tüm-ˌpän, 'tyüm-\. Cape, NE coast of island of Lewis with Harris, Outer Hebrides, off NW coast of Scotland; lighthouse.

Tiv·er·ton \'ti-vər-tən\. **1.** Town and summer resort, Newport co., SE Rhode Island, on Sakonnet River 8 mi. (13 km.) NE of the city of Newport; pop. (1990c) 14,312. Incorp. as Massachusetts town 1692; annexed to Rhode Island 1746; prominent role in the battle of Rhode Island (1778) during the American Revolution.

2. Town, Devon, SW England, at confluence of Exe and Lowman rivers 48 mi. (77 km.) NE of Plymouth; pop. (1981p) 16,539; 12th cent. castle.

Ti·vo·li \'tē-vō-lē, 'ti-və-lē\; *anc.* **Ti·bur** \'tī-bər\. Commune, Roma prov., Lazio, cen. Italy, 16 mi. (26 km.) ENE of Rome; pop. (1991p) 50,559; cathedral; Villa d'Este, with notable terraced gardens; extensive remains of ancient villas and temples, esp. villa of Roman Emperor Hadrian (76–138 A.D.). Vied for power with Rome until it came under Roman influence 4th cent. B.C.; united with Rome 90 B.C. and became a noted summer resort under the early empire.

Ti·wi \'tē-wē\. Coastal town, SE Luzon, Philippines, on Lagonoy Gulf; pop. (1980c) 28,726.

Ti·zi·mín \ˌtē-sē-'mēn\. Town, Yucatán state, SE Mexico, ab. 65 mi. (105 km.) E of Mérida; munic. pop. (1990p) 54,571; railroad terminus.

Ti·zi–Ou·zou \tē-'zē-ü-'zü\. Town, N Algeria, ab. 65 mi. (105 km.) E of Algiers; pop. (1987p) 61,163.

Tjiamis. See CIAMIS.

Tjiandjur *or Du.* **Tjiandjoer.** See CIANJUR.

Tjikuraj *or* **Tjikoeraj.** See CIKURAY.

Tjilatjap. See CILACAP.

Tjiliwong. See LIWUNG.

Tjimahi. See CIMAHI.

Tjirebon. See CIREBON.

Tjiremaj. See CIREMAY.

Tla·co·pán \ˌtlä-kō-'pän\. Ancient city which along with Texcoco and Tenochtitlán formed the confederacy of the Aztecs.

Tlá·huac \'tlä-wäk\. Municipality, Federal District, Mexico, just SE of Mexico City.

Tlal·ne·pan·tla \ˌtläl-nā-'pän-tlä\. City, México state, Mexico, just N of Mexico City; munic. pop. (1990p) 703,162.

Tlal·pán \tläl-'pän\ *or* **Tlal·pam** \-'pän\. City, Federal District, cen. Mexico; a suburb, just S of Mexico City; munic. pop. (1990p) 485,043; has church begun in 1532. Nearby, one of oldest pre-Columbian pyramids.

Tla·que·pa·que \ˌtlä-kā-'pä-kā\. Town, Jalisco state, W cen. Mexico; munic. pop. (1990p) 337,950; craft center, esp. known for glass creations.

Tlax·ca·la \tlä-'skä-lä\. **1.** State of cen. Mexico. See table at MEXICO.

2. *or in full* **Tlaxcala de Xi·coh·tén·catl** \t͟hā-ˌhē-kō-'teŋ-ˌkät-^{ə}l\ *also* **Tlas·ca·la** \tlä-'skä-lä\. Town, ✻ of Tlaxcala state, cen. Mexico; munic. pop. (1990p) 50,631; in mountainous region bet. Veracruz and Mexico City, alt. 7500 ft. (2286 m.); surrounded by hills and in sight of high peaks (Malinche, Popocatépetl, Iztaccíhuatl); has one of the oldest churches—church of San Francisco—in North America, founded early 16th cent. Home of a Nahua people, akin to Aztecs and Toltecs, who migrated from region E of Lake Texcoco c. 14th cent. Vied for power with Aztec Tenochtitlán (Mexico City) 15th–16th cents.; initially opposed Spanish explorer Hernán Cortés on his march inland but was defeated 1519 and became his ally, aiding in his conquest of Aztec Emperor Montezuma II; served as refuge for Spaniards when driven out of Tenochtitlán 1520.

Tlem·cen *or* **Tlem·sen** \tlem-'sen\ *or* **Ti·lim·sen** \ti-lim-'sen\. Town, NW Algeria, near the Moroccan border 75 mi. (121 km.) SW of Oran; pop. (1987p) 126,882; alt. 2500 ft. (762 m.); olive oil, handicrafts; numerous mosques and other medieval remains, incl. towers, walls, minarets. ✻ of Berber kingdom 13th cent.; important trading and cultural center during Moorish times; under Ottoman rule in 16th cent.; came under French 1842.

Tlemcen Mountains. Range of Little Atlas Mts., in NW Algeria.

Tmolus. See BOZ DAĞ.

tó, Fertő. See NEUSIEDLER, LAKE.

T'o. See TUO.

Toa Al·ta \ˌtō-ä-'äl-tä\. Municipality NE cen. Puerto Rico, SW of San Juan; pop. (1990c) 44,101.

Toa Ba·ja \-'bä-hä\. Municipality, NE Puerto Rico, W of San Juan; pop. (1990c) 89,454.

To·a·ma·si·na \ˌtō-ə-mə-'sē-nə\; *formerly* **Ta·ma·ta·ve** \ˌtä-mä-'täv\. Seaport, E coast of Madagascar; pop. (1990e) 145,431; principal seaport of the republic; ships coffee, vanilla, graphite, sugar; terminus of railroad from Antananarivo. Rebuilt after destruction by hurricane 1927.

To·a·no Range \'tō-ə-ˌnō\. Small range, Elko co., NE Nevada, in Great Basin, near Utah border; crossed by a pass at 6940 ft. (2115 m.).

Toarcium. See THOUARS.

To·ba, Lake \'tō-bə\. Lake in the Barisan Mts., N cen. Sumatra I., Indonesia; 45 mi. (72 km.) long; 502 sq. mi. (1300 sq. km.); elev. 2985 ft. (910 m.); thought to occupy the crater of an extinct volcano. Drains E through the Asahan River into the Strait of Malacca; contains the large island of Samosir.

To·ba·go \tə-'bā-gō\. Island, West Indies, a constituent part of Trinidad and Tobago; 32 mi. (52 km.) long; 116 sq. mi. (300 sq. km.); pop. (1990c) 50,282; ✻ Scarborough.

History: Held by Spanish after explorer Christopher Columbus' visit to Trinidad 1498; changed hands often during 17th and 18th cents.; held at various times by English, Dutch, and French; remained English after early 19th cent. United with Trinidad 1889 and made part of the colony of Trinidad and Tobago 1899; became part of independent state within British Commonwealth 1962, part of republic 1976.

To·bar·ra \tō-'bär-ə\. Commune, Albacete prov., SE Spain, 30 mi. (48 km.) SSE of the commune of Albacete; pop. (1991c) 7322.

To·ba·ta \tō-'bä-tä\. See KITAKYŪSHŪ.

To·bol \tə-'bȯl\. River, Kazakhstan and W Russia in Asia; rises in SE foothills of Ural Mts. in N Kazakhstan and flows NNE through E Chelyabinsk, Kurgan, and Tyumen' oblasts of Russia to the Irtysh River at Tobol'sk; 1042 mi. (1677 km.) long.

To·bol'sk *or* **To·bolsk** \tə-'bȯl^{y}sk\. City, N Tyumen' Oblast, W Russia in Asia, on Irtysh River where it is joined by the Tobol, 300 mi. (483 km.) NW of Omsk; pop. (1991e) 96,800; ivory carving. Founded by Cossacks 1587 and later moved to present site; frequent place of residence for political prisoners, incl. abdicated-Czar Nicholas II after Bolshevik Revolution (1917). See ISKER.

To·bruk \'tō-ˌbru̇k, tō-'\ *or Ital.* **To·bruch** \'tō-ˌbrük\ *or Arab.* **Tu·bruq** \tō-'brük\; *anc.* **An·ti·pyr·gos** \ˌan-ti-'pər-ˌgäs\. Port on coastal road, Libya; pop. (1979e) 34,200; former Italian military post. Scene of much fighting in WWII; taken by British Jan. 1941; besieged by Germans for several months in 1941; surrendered to German Field Marshal Erwin Rommel June 21, 1942; retaken by British Nov. 1942.

To·can·tins \ˌtō-kä^{n}-'tē^{n}s\. **1.** River, E cen. and NE Brazil; rises in S cen. Goiás state, flows N into Pará River; 1677 mi. (2698 km.) long.

2. State of N Brazil; ✻ Palmas; carved from Goías state 1988. See table at BRAZIL.

Toc·coa \tə-ˈkō-ə\. **1.** River, NE Georgia. See OCOEE 1. **2.** City, ⊗ of Stephens co., NE Georgia, 33 mi. (53 km.) NE of Gainesville; pop. (1990c) 8266; textiles; truck farms.

To·ce \ˈtō-chā\. River, Piedmont, N Italy; contains **Toce Falls,** 470 ft. (143 m.) high.

To·chi·gi \ˈtō-chē-gē\. **1.** Prefecture, Honshū, Japan; ✻ Utsunomiya. See table at JAPAN. **2.** Town, S Tochigi prefecture, Japan, 50 mi. (81 km.) N of Tokyo; pop. (1990p) 86,216.

To·cón Point \tō-ˈkȯn\. Cape, SW coast of Puerto Rico, E of Cape Rojo.

To·co·pil·la \ˌtō-kō-ˈpē-yä\. Seaport, Antofagasta region, N Chile, 100 mi. (161 km.) N of the seaport of Antofagasta; pop. (1990e) 20,956; iodine, copper ore.

To·cor·pu·ri, Cer·ro de \ˈser-rō-t͟hā-ˌtō-kȯr-ˈpü-rē\. Mountains, SW Bolivia, near Chilean border; highest peak 19,137 ft. (5833 m.).

To·cu·yo \tō-ˈkü-yō\. River, NW Venezuela; flows NE into Caribbean Sea ab. 50 mi. (80 km.) N of Puerto Cabrillo; ab. 200 mi. (320 km.) long.

Tocuyo, El. See EL TOCUYO.

To·da \ˈtō-dä\. City, Saitama prefecture, Honshū, Japan; pop. (1990p) 87,600.

Todd \ˈtäd\. Name of counties in three states of the U.S. See tables at KENTUCKY, MINNESOTA, SOUTH DAKOTA.

To·di \ˈtȯ-dē\; *anc.* **Tu·der** \ˈtü-dər, ˈtyü-\. Commune, Perugia prov., Umbria, cen. Italy, on Tiber River 24 mi. (39 km.) S of the commune of Perugia; pop. (1991p) 16,663; ancient and medieval walls; three 13th cent. palaces; 16th cent. church of Santa Maria della Consolazione.

Tö·di \ˈtœ-dē\ *or* **Piz Ru·sein** \ˈpēts-rü-ˈzīn\. Highest peak of the N Swiss Alps, Glarus canton, E cen. Switzerland; 11,857 ft. (3614 m.).

Tod·mor·den \ˈtäd-ˌmȯrd-ᵊn, -mərd-ᵊn\. Town, West Yorkshire, N England, on the Calder 20 mi. (32 km.) NNE of Manchester; pop. (1981c) 14,641; textiles.

To·dos los San·tos \ˈtō-t͟hōs-lōs-ˈsän-tōs\. Lake, Los Lagos region, S cen. Chile, N of Puerto Montt; in resort region.

Todos os Santos, Baía de. See ALL SAINTS BAY.

Toeban. See TUBAN.

Toe Head \ˈtō\. Cape, extending NW into Atlantic Ocean from S part of island of Lewis with Harris, Outer Hebrides, off NW coast of Scotland.

Toekangbesi Islands. See TUKANGBESI ISLANDS.

Toeloengagoeng. See TULUNGAGUNG.

To·fua \tō-ˈfü-ə\. Volcanic island, W part of Haapai group, Tonga, SW cen. Pacific Ocean; 5 mi. (8 km.) long by 4 mi. (6 km.) wide; 21 sq. mi. (54 sq. km.); large lake in crater. Events of *H.M.S. Bounty* mutiny took place to S 1789.

Togara Islands. See TOKARA ISLANDS.

Tog·gen·burg \ˈtȯ-gən-ˌbu̇rk, -ˌbərg\. District, St. Gall canton, NE Switzerland, in upper valley of the Thur. Scene of religious strife from 15th to 18th cents.; Toggenburg War 1712 ended in defeat of Catholic cantons by Protestants; to St. Gall 1803.

To·gi·an \ˈtō-gē-ˌän\. See PENJU ISLANDS.

Togliatti. See TOL'YATTI.

To·go \ˈtō-gō\. Republic, W Africa, bounded on N by Burkina Faso, on E by Benin, on S by the Bight of Benin, and on W by Ghana; 21,853 sq. mi. (56,599 sq. km.); pop. (1993e) 3,810,000; ✻ Lomé, by far the largest settlement.

Physical features: The republic consists of a strip of land (ab. 70 mi. or 113 km. wide) extending ab. 340 mi. (545 km.) inland from the Bight of Benin; coastal plain is swampy; N region characterized by savanna; in center is mountain range, with highest peak Mt. Agou 3937 ft. (1200 m.).

Chief products: Cotton, coffee, cocoa, cassava, copra; phosphates.

History: For history prior to 1914, see TOGOLAND. Territory constituted the E part of the German protectorate of Togoland, which was occupied by Anglo-French forces 1914; E part of Togoland assigned to France as mandate by League of Nations 1922; made a UN trust territory 1946; became an autonomous republic within the French Union 1956; achieved independence 1960; suspended constitution 1967–80; approved new multiparty constitution 1992.

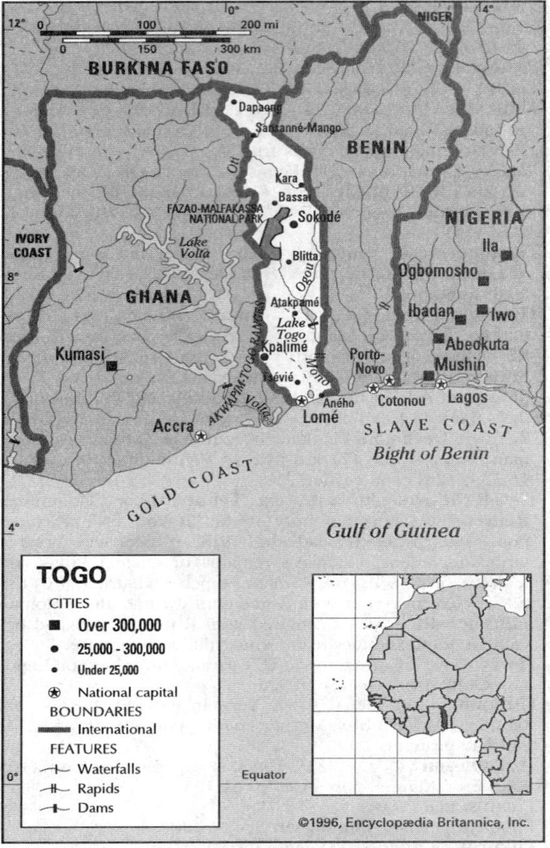

To·go·land \ˈtō-gō-ˌland\. Former German protectorate, W Africa; the W section is now part of Ghana, the remainder constituting the independent republic of Togo (*q.v.*).

History: Original inhabitants joined in S by Ewe emigrants from E after 14th cent.; German protectorate proclaimed over coastal area 1884; hinterland and frontier boundaries not estab. until c. 1900; captured by Anglo-French forces 1914 and divided into two administrative zones; British zone in W placed under control of Gold Coast (now Ghana), with which it merged 1956; French zone became independent republic of Togo 1960.

To·ho·ku \tō-ˈhō-kü\. Administrative region of Japan, in N Honshū. For subdivisions, see table at JAPAN.

To·ho·pe·kal·i·ga Lake \tə-ˌhō-pi-ˈka-li-gə\. Lake, NW Osceola co., cen. Florida Penin.

Toi·ya·be Mountains \tȯi-ˈyä-bē\. Range, extending N and S in Lander and Nye cos., cen. Nevada; highest peak 11,755 ft. (3583 m.).

To·ka·chi \tō-ˈkä-chē\. **1.** Peak, Japan. See HOKKAIDŌ. **2.** River, cen. Hokkaidō, Japan; 120 mi. (193 km.) long.

To·kai \tō-ˈkī\. City, Aichi prefecture, Honshū, Japan; pop. (1990p) 97,359.

To·ka·ra Islands \tō-ˈkä-rä\ *also* **To·ga·ra Islands** \tō-ˈgä-rä\. Group of small islands, S of Kyūshū, in Kagoshima prefecture, Japan, northernmost part of Ryukyu Is. chain. See RYUKYU ISLANDS 1.

To·ka·shi·ki \tō-ˈkä-shē-kē\. Largest of Kerama Is., Japan; 10 sq. mi. (26 sq. km.).

To·kat \tō-ˈkät\. **1.** Province of Turkey in Asia. See table at TURKEY.

2. Town, its ✻, 50 mi. (81 km.) NW of Sivas; pop. (1990p) 83,174.

To·ke·lau \ˈtō-kə-ˌlau̇\; *formerly* **Union Islands** \ˈyü-nyən\. Group of islands, cen. Pacific Ocean, N of American Samoa; 8° to 10°S and 171° to 173°W; 4 sq. mi. (10 sq. km.); pop. (1986c) 1690; includes Atafu, Fakaofo, and Nukunonu; placed under British protection late 19th cent.; part of Gilbert and Ellice Islands Colony 1916–26; administered by New Zealand 1926; made part of New Zealand 1948.

To·ke·wan·na Peak \ˌtō-kə-ˈwä-nə\. Mountain, E Summit co., NE Utah; 13,173 ft. (4015 m.).

To·ki \ˈtō-kē\. City, Gifu prefecture, Honshū, Japan, 22 mi. (35 km.) N of Nagoya; pop. (1990p) 64,946.

Tokio. See TOKYO.

Tok·mak \tȯk-ˈmäk\. Town, N Kyrgyzstan, just E of Bishkek on the Chu River; pop. (1991e) 71,200.

To·ko·na·me \tō-ˈkō-nä-mā, ˌtō-kō-ˈnä-mā\. City, Aichi prefecture, Honshū, Japan, 21 mi. (34 km.) S of Nagoya; pop. (1990p) 51,784.

To·ko·roa \ˌtō-kə-ˈrō-ə\. Borough, cen. North I., New Zealand; urban area pop. (1992e) 16,400.

To·ko·ro·za·wa \ˌtō-kō-ˈrō-zä-wä\. City, Saitama prefecture, Honshū, Japan, NE suburb of Tokyo; pop. (1990p) 303,047.

To·ku·no–Shi·ma \tō-ˈkü-nō-ˈshē-mä\. Island, cen. Amami Is., Ryukyu Is., Japan.

To·ku·shi·ma \ˌtō-kü-ˈshē-mä, tō-ˈkü-shi-mä\. **1.** Prefecture, Shikoku, Japan; ✻ Tokushima. See table at JAPAN.

2. Seaport city, its ✻, on E coast of Shikoku I. on Kii Channel; pop. (1992e) 264,503; chief city on Shikoku I.; university (1949); has close connection by water with Ōsaka and Hyōgo.

To·ku·ya·ma \ˌtō-kü-ˈyä-mä\. Town, E Yamaguchi prefecture, SW Honshū, Japan, 50 mi. (81 km.) E of Shimonoseki; pop. (1990p) 110,900; port at W end of Inland Sea.

To·kyo *also* **To·kio** \ˈtō-kē-ˌō, -ˌkyō\. **1.** Prefecture, Honshū, Japan; ✻ Tokyo. See table at JAPAN.

2. *formerly* **Edo** \ˈe-dō\ *or* **Ye·do** *also* **Yed·do** \ˈye-dō\. City, ✻ of Japan, also ✻ of Tokyo prefecture, on NW shore of Tokyo Bay, SE Honshū; pop. (1990p) 11,854,987; administrative, cultural, financial, commercial, and educational center of Japan; also center of an extensive complex of industrial suburbs producing metals, machinery, transportation and electronic equipment, chemicals, textiles, and a wide variety of consumer goods; shipbuilding; one of the principal tourist centers of Japan. Sumida River flows through it, and city has extensive network of canals; site of Imperial Palace and gardens and numerous temples and shrines; ab. 150 institutions of higher learning, incl. Univ. of Tokyo (1877); its seaport is Yokohama.

History: Village fortified with castle c. 1456; passed to Tokugawa clan 1590 and under name of Edo became ✻ of Tokugawa shogunate 1603; by 19th cent. one of the largest cities in the world, with a population exceeding 1,000,000; upon Meiji Restoration 1868 replaced Kyōto as imperial ✻ and renamed Tokyo. Developed as cultural and industrial center in late 19th cent. City largely destroyed by earthquake and subsequent fire Sept. 1, 1923 with loss of over 100,000 lives; largely rebuilt by 1930. In WWII much of city destroyed by repeated U.S. bombings 1944–45, and esp. after Mar. 1945; later reconstructed; site of Summer Olympic Games 1964.

Tokyo Bay. Inlet of W Pacific Ocean, SE coast of Honshū, Japan; ab. 30 mi. (48 km.) long by 23 mi. (37 km.) wide, providing a spacious harbor for Tokyo, Yokohama, and Yokosuka. Connects with the Pacific by Uraga Strait.

Tol \ˈtōl\. Largest island in Chuuk Is. (*q.v.*); in W part.

To·la·go Bay \tə-ˈlä-gō\. Inlet of Pacific Ocean, E coast of North I., New Zealand, ab. midway bet. East Cape and Poverty Bay.

Tô·la·ña·ro *or* **Tao·la·na·ro** \ˌtō-lä-ˈnä-rō\ *or* **Fa·ra·do·fay** \ˌfä-rə-dō-ˈfā\; *formerly* **Fort–Dau·phin** \ˌfȯr-dō-ˈfeⁿ\. Town and seaport, SE Madagascar.

To·la·ni Lakes \tō-ˈlä-nē\. Small lakes, near E boundary of Coconino co., N cen. Arizona.

Tolbiacum. See ZÜLPICH.

Tol·bu·khin \tȯl-ˈbü-kin\. See DOBRICH.

To·le·do \tə-ˈlē-dō, -də, *Span.* tō-ˈlā-thō\. **1.** Village, ⊗ of Cumberland co., SE cen. Illinois; pop. (1990c) 1199.

2. City, ⊗ of Tama co., E cen. Iowa, 17 mi. (27 km.) E of Marshalltown; pop. (1990c) 2380.

3. City and port of entry, ⊗ of Lucas co., NW Ohio, on Maumee River at SW corner of Lake Erie; pop. (1990c) 332,943; important lake port, shipping esp. coal and grain; considerable foreign commerce; Univ. of Toledo (1872), Medical Coll. of Ohio at Toledo (1964). Formed by union of two villages 1833; incorp. 1837; figured in "Toledo War" of 1835–36, bloodless dispute bet. Michigan Terr. and Ohio over location of their common boundary.

4. City, Lincoln co., W Oregon, 35 mi. (56 km.) W of Corvallis; pop. (1990c) 3174.

5. Administrative district, S Belize. See table at BELIZE.

6. Chartered city on W coast of Cebu I., Philippines, in cen. part 19 mi. (31 km.) W of City of Cebu; pop. (1990p) 120,000.

7. Province of Spain. See table at SPAIN.

8. *anc.* **To·le·tum** \tə-ˈlē-təm\. Commune, ✻ of Toledo prov. and ✻ of Castilla-La Mancha autonomous community and historical region, cen. Spain, on Tagus River 40 mi. (64 km.) SSW of Madrid; pop. (1991p) 59,563; engraved metalwork, confectionary; archiepiscopal see and seat of primate of Spain; a great wealth of notable architecture (entire urban area is a national monument); Roman remains; 13th cent. Gothic cathedral; 15th cent. Franciscan church and convent; 14th cent. synagogue; alcázar (citadel, renovated 16th cent.); city walls; bridges. Home of painter El Greco 1577–1614.

History: Stronghold of a powerful Iberian tribe (the Carpetani) when conquered by Rome 193 B.C.; became Roman colony and by 4th cent. A.D. a chief town of Roman Spain; in 6th cent. became Visigothic ✻ in Spain and center of revived conflict bet. Arianism and Roman Catholic orthodoxy; site of numerous church councils c. 400–c. 700; conquered by Moors under Gen. Ṭāriq ibn Ziyād 712; a provincial ✻ in the caliphate of Córdoba until civil war made city seat of kingdom of Toledo c. 1031; under Moors, grew commercially and industrially, becoming noted for the manufacture of swords; center of Arabic and Hebrew culture; reconquered from Moors 1085 by King Alfonso VI of León and Castile and made ✻ of New Castile; ✻ of united kingdoms of León and Castile (united 1230) until King Philip II moved seat to Madrid 1560; noted for its policy of religious tolerance toward Jews and Arabs in 11th–15th cents.; occupied by French during Peninsular War (1808–14); besieged by Nationalist forces July–Sept. 1936 in Spanish Civil War.

Toledo, Mon·tes de \ˈmȯn-tās-ˌthā-tō-ˈlā-thō\. Mountain range, cen. Spain, WSW of Toledo; highest peak 4747 ft. (1447 m.).

To·len·ti·no \ˌtō-len-ˈtē-nō\; *anc.* **Tol·en·ti·num** \ˌtä-lən-ˈtī-nəm\. Commune, Macerata prov., Marche, cen. Italy, 12 mi. (19 km.) WSW of the commune of Macerata; pop. (1981p) 17,984; cathedral; 13th cent. church of San Nicola. Treaty bet. French Emperor Napoléon and Pope Pius VI signed here 1797; French commander Joachim Murat defeated by Austrians here 1815.

Toletum. See TOLEDO 8.

To·li·ara \ˈtō-lē-ˌar-ə\ *or* **To·li·ary** \-ˌar-ē\; *formerly* **Tu·lé·ar** \ˌtü-lā-ˈär\. Seaport, SW Madagascar; pop. (1990e) 61,460.

To·li·ma \tō-ˈlē-mä\. **1.** Volcano, Cordillera Central of the Andes, W cen. Colombia; 18,425 ft. (5616 m.).

2. Department of W cen. Colombia. See table at COLOMBIA.

Tol·land \ˈtä-lənd\. **1.** County in N Connecticut. See table at CONNECTICUT.

2. Town, Tolland co., N Connecticut, on Willimantic River; pop. (1990c) 11,001.

Tol·le·son \ˈtä-lə-sən\. City, Maricopa co., SW cen. Arizona, 10 mi. (16 km.) W of Phoenix; pop. (1990c) 4434.

Tol·me·ta \täl-ˈmā-tə\ *or Arab.* **Tul·may·thah** \təl-ˈmā-tə, -ˈmī-\; *anc.* **Ptol·e·ma·ïs** \ˌta-lə-ˈmā-əs\. Town on the coast of NE Libya, 60 mi. (97 km.) NE of Benghazi; ancient ruins; ancient Ptolemaïs, port of Barka which it superseded during the time of the Ptolemies (4th–1st cents. B.C.); was one of the cities of the Pentapolis.

Tolmin \ˈtȯl-min\ *or Ital.* **Tol·mi·no** \tōl-ˈmē-nō\ *or Ger.* **Tol·mein** \ˈtȯl-ˌmīn\. Commune, Slovenia, on Isonzo River in region that belonged to Italy before 1947.

Tol·na \ˈtōl-nä\. **1.** County of S cen. Hungary. See table at HUNGARY.
2. Commune, Tolna co., S Hungary, 76 mi. (122 km.) S of Budapest; castle.

To·lo, Gulf of \ˈtō-lō\. Inlet of Banda Sea, E cen. coast of Sulawesi, Malay Archipelago; bordered on NE by the Banggai Archipelago and connected by Peleng Strait with the Molucca Sea; smallest of the three great gulfs of Sulawesi.

To·lo·no \tə-ˈlō-nō, tō-\. Village, Champaign co., E cen. Illinois, S of the city of Champaign; pop. (1990c) 2605.

To·lo·sa \tə-ˈlō-sə\. **1.** City, France. See TOULOUSE.
2. Commune, Guipúzcoa prov., N Spain, 11 mi. (18 km.) SW of San Sebastián; pop. (1991c) 18,150.

To·lu·ca \tō-ˈlü-kä\. **1.** Subdivision of the valley of Anáhuac (*q.v.*), cen. Mexico; mean elev. 8570 ft. (2612 m.).
2. *or in full* **Toluca de Ler·do** \t͟hā-ˈler-dō\. City, ✻ of México state, cen. Mexico, ab. 35 mi. (56 km.) SW of Mexico City; pop. (1990p) 487,630; alt. 8500 ft. (2590 m.); commercial center in livestock and agricultural region; textiles, beer, pottery; university (present status 1956); inhabited by Otomi Indians by 13th cent.; modern city founded 1530.

Toluca, Ne·va·do de \nā-ˈb͟ä-t͟hō-t͟hā-tō-ˈlü-kä\. Extinct volcanic peak, México state, Mexico, 27 mi. (43 km.) SW of Toluca; 15,106 ft. (4604 m.); crater partly filled with a lake formed by melting snow.

To–lun. See DUOLON.

Tol'·yat·ti *or* **Tol·yat·ti** *or* **To·gliat·ti** \tȯl-ˈyä-tē\; *formerly* **Sta·vro·pol'** *or* **Sta·vro·pol** \ˈstä-vrə-ˌpəl\. Town, Samara Oblast, Russia in Europe, on the Volga; pop. (1992e) 666,000; automobile manufacturing.

Tom' *or* **Tom** \ˈtȯmʸ, ˈtäm\. River, SE Tomsk and cen. Kemerovo oblasts, W Russia in Asia; rises in NW Altai Shan and flows NNW into the Ob' River near Tomsk; flows through the Kuznetsk Basin (*q.v.*); ab. 450 mi. (725 km.) long.

Tom, Mount \ˈtäm\. Peak in **Mt. Tom Range,** W Massachusetts; 1202 ft. (366 m.).

To·mah \ˈtō-mə\. City, Monroe co., W cen. Wisconsin, 15 mi. (24 km.) E of Sparta; pop. (1990c) 7570.

Tom·a·hawk \ˈtä-mə-ˌhȯk\. City, Lincoln co., N Wisconsin, 20 mi. (32 km.) N of Merrill; pop. (1990c) 3328; lake resort.

To·ma·hu, Mount \tō-ˈmä-hü\. Mountain, NW Buru I., Indonesia; 7969 ft. (2429 m.); highest point on island.

To·ma·ko·mai \tō-ˈmä-kō-ˌmī, ˌtō-mä-ˈkō-mī\. City, Hokkaidō prefecture, Hokkaidō, Japan, 12 mi. (19 km.) SE of Sapporo; pop. (1990p) 160,116.

To·ma·les Bay \tə-ˈmä-ləs\. Inlet of Pacific Ocean, NW coast of Marin co., W California.

To·ma·nii·vi, Mount *or* **Mount Tomanivi** \ˌtō-mä-ˈnē-vē\; *formerly* **Mount Vic·to·ria** \vik-ˈtōr-ē-ə\. Mountain on Viti Levu, Fiji; 4341 ft. (1323 m.); highest peak in Fiji.

To·ma·ri \tō-ˈmär-ē\. Town on W coast of Sakhalin I., E Russia in Asia.

To·mar·us, Mount \tō-ˈmar-əs\ *or Gk.* **Tó·ma·ros** \ˈtō-mä-ˌrȯs\. Mountain, S cen. Epirus, NW Greece; ab. 6100 ft. (1860 m.); was in ancient dist. of Thesprotia; site of legendary oracle of Dodona (*q.v.*).

Tom·a·saki, Mount \ˌtä-mə-ˈsä-kē\. Peak, S Grand co., E Utah; 12,271 ft. (3740 m.).

To·ma·szów Ma·zo·wiec·ki \tȯ-ˈmä-shüf-ˌmä-zȯ-ˈvyet-skē\; *formerly* **Tomaszów** *or Ger.* **To·ma·schow** \tō-ˈmä-shō\. Commune, NE Piotrków prov., cen. Poland, 30 mi. (48 km.) SE of Łódź; pop. (1989e) 69,836; textiles, bricks.

Tombador, Serra do. See SERRA DO TOMBADOR.

Tom·ball \ˈtäm-ˈbȯl, ˈtȯm-\. City, Harris co., SE Texas, 30 mi. (48 km.) NW of Houston; pop. (1990c) 6370.

Tom·big·bee \täm-ˈbig-bē\. River, Alabama; formed by junction of E fork and W fork near Amory, Mississippi, crosses Alabama border W of Carrollton, flows S into the Alabama River to form the Mobile and Tensaw rivers flowing into Mobile Bay at Mobile; 409 mi. (658 km.) long; navigable for 350 mi. (563 km.); linked to Tennessee River by Tennessee-Tombigbee Waterway.

Tom·bo Island \ˈtäm-bō\. Small island off the coast of Guinea; Conakry, ✻ of Guinea, is on it and is joined to the mainland by a bridge.

Tom·bouc·tou \ˌtōⁿ-bük-ˈtü\ *or traditionally* **Tim·buk·tu** \ˌtim-bək-ˈtü, tim-ˈbək-tü\. Town, Mali, E of Lake Faguibine and near the Niger River; pop. (1987p) 31,925; trades in salt; mosques; formerly an important trade center on the Saharan camel caravan routes; extensive ruins.
History: Settled by Tuaregs c. 11th cent. A.D.; became important trade center 12th cent.; came under Mali empire 13th–14th cents. and made center of Muslim culture; reached height of prosperity as commercial and cultural center under Songhai rule c. 1500; declined rapidly after passing to Morocco late 16th cent.; came under French rule 1893; became part of independent Mali 1960.

Tomb·stone \ˈtüm-ˌstōn\. City, SW cen. Cochise co., SE corner of Arizona, 20 mi. (32 km.) NNW of Bisbee; pop. (1990c) 1220; formerly (late 19th cent.) a mining center widely known for its rich mines and its lawlessness and crime; scene of gunfight at the O.K. Corral 1881.

To·mé \tō-ˈmā\. City, Bío-Bío region, S cen. Chile, ab. 20 mi. (32 km.) N of Concepción; pop. (1992c) 49,140; port for Concepción.

To·mel·lo·so \ˌtō-mel-ˈyō-sō\. Commune, Ciudad Real prov., S cen. Spain, 51 mi. (82 km.) ENE of the commune of Ciudad Real; pop. (1991c) 28,632; wine, cereals, vegetables; stock raising.

Tom Green \ˈtäm-ˈgrēn\. County in W cen. Texas. See table at TEXAS.

Tomi *or* **Tomis.** See CONSTANȚA 2.

To·mi·ni, Gulf of \tō-ˈmē-nē\ *or* **Te·luk Tomini** \ˈte-ˌlu̇k\ *also* **Gulf of Go·ron·ta·lo** \ˌgȯr-ȯn-ˈtä-lō\. Large inlet of Molucca Sea, extending deep into the coast of N Sulawesi, Malay Archipelago; ab. 240 mi. (385 km.) long; contains the Penju Is.

To·mi·ño \tō-ˈmē-nyō\. Commune, Pontevedra prov., NW Spain, 31 mi. (50 km.) SSW of the commune of Pontevedra; pop. (1991c) 10,223.

To·mo \ˈtō-mō\. River, E Colombia; flows E into the Orinoco on Venezuelan border; ab. 260 mi. (420 km.) long.

Tömös Pass. See PREDEAL PASS.

Tomp·kins \ˈtämp-kinz\. County in S cen. New York. See table at NEW YORK.

Tomp·kins·ville \ˈtämp-kinz-ˌvil\. **1.** Section of Staten I. borough, New York, New York. See STATEN ISLAND 2.
2. City, ⊗ of Monroe co., S Kentucky; pop. (1990c) 2861.

Toms \ˈtämz\. River, E New Jersey; rises in SW Monmouth co., flows SE into Barnegat Bay; ab. 25 mi. (40 km.) long.

Tomsk \ˈtȯmsk\. City, ✻ of Tomsk Oblast, Russia in Asia, on right bank of Tom' River near its junction with the Ob'; pop. (1992e) 505,000; connected with main line of Trans-Siberian R.R.; produces electrical equipment, paints and dyes; educational center, with university (1888) and several technical institutes. Founded as fort 1604 and developed as center of trade and regional administration.

Tomsk Oblast \ˈȯ-bləst, -ˌbləst\ *or* **Tom·ska·ya Oblast'** \ˈtȯm-skə-yə-ˈȯ-bləstʸ\. Subdivision of Russia in Asia; 122,355 sq. mi. (316,899 sq. km.); pop. (1992e) 1,012,000; ✻ Tomsk. Largely flat terrain in the basin of the middle course of the Ob'; agriculture limited by severe climate and numerous swamps; economy based on forestry and fur trapping.

Toms River \ˈtämz\. **1.** River, New Jersey. See TOMS.
2. Unincorporated settlement and summer resort, ⊗ of Ocean co., E New Jersey, on inlet of Barnegat Bay 22 mi. (35 km.) SSW of Asbury Park; pop. (1990c) 7524. Founded mid-18th

cent.; center for guerrilla fighting in American Revolution; burned by British 1782.

To·na·lá \ˌtō-nä-ˈlä\. **1.** River, E Veracruz state, E Mexico; flows NNW to Gulf of Mexico and in lower course forms boundary with Tabasco state; ab. 90 mi. (145 km.) long.

2. Municipality, Chiapas state, Mexico, 70 mi. (113 km.) SW of Tuxtla Gutiérrez; pop. (1990p) 67,348.

3. City, Jalisco state, W cen. Mexico; pop. (1990c) 151,190.

To·na·le Pass \tō-ˈnä-lā\. Mountain pass, Alps, NW of Trento, bet. Lombardy and Trentino-Alto Adige, NE Italy; alt. 6178 ft. (1883 m.).

Ton·a·wan·da \ˌtä-nə-ˈwän-də\. City, Erie co., W New York, 9 mi. (14 km.) N of Buffalo; pop. (1990c) 17,284; metal goods. North Tonawanda (*q.v.*), its sister city, is on opp. side of **Tonawanda Creek.**

Ton·bridge \ˈtən-brij\. Town, Kent, SE England, on the Medway 25 mi. (40 km.) SSE of London; plastics; printing.

Ton·da·ba·ya·shi \ˌtōn-dä-ˈbä-yä-shē\. City, Ōsaka prefecture, Honshū, Japan; pop. (1990p) 110,444.

Tøn·der \ˈtœn-ˌər\. Town, Sønderjylland co., SW Jutland Penin., Denmark, near German border; pop. (1988c) 12,580.

To·ne \ˈtō-nā\. River, E Honshū, Japan; flows SE and E into Pacific Ocean E of Tokyo; 200 mi. (322 km.) long.

Tong \ˈtäŋ\. Village, Shropshire, W England, 20 mi. (32 km.) E of Shrewsbury; 15th cent. church; nearby is Boscobel House where King Charles II hid after the battle of Worcester 1651.

Ton·ga \ˈtäŋ-gə, ˈtäŋ-ə\ *also* **Tonga Islands** *or* **Friend·ly Islands** \ˈfrend-lē\. Kingdom, SW Pacific Ocean; 270 sq. mi. (699 sq. km.); pop. (1986c) 94,649; ✻ Nuku'alofa.

Physical features: Comprises an archipelago of ab. 150 islands, divided into three groups, Tongatapu, Vava'u, and Haapai, together with Niuafoo and Niuatobutabu farther to the N; in the N the Vava'u group, and Tofua of the Haapai group, are high and mountainous, of volcanic origin; the other islands are low-lying, of coral formation.

Chief products: Fish, coconuts, sweet potatoes, bananas, citrus fruit, watermelons, cassava.

History: Inhabited by Polynesian peoples by 4th cent. A.D.; N islands discovered 1616 by Dutch navigator Jakob Le Maire; visited by Dutch explorer Abel Tasman 1643 and by English navigator Capt. James Cook 1773–77; modern kingdom estab. during reign (1845–93) of King George Tupou I; became British protectorate 1900; achieved independence 1970.

Ton·ga·land \ˈtäŋ-gə-ˌland\ *or* **Am·a·ton·ga·land** \ˌä-mə-\. Historical region, SE Africa, on coast S of Mozambique; ab. 600 sq. mi. (1555 sq. km.); formerly a British protectorate, ruled by Zulu hereditary dynasty. Incorp. 1898 with Ingwavuma dist., N Zululand, as part of Natal, Union (now Rep.) of South Africa.

Tongareva. See PENRHYN.

Tong·a·ri·ro \ˌtäŋ-gə-ˈrir-ō\. Volcano, cen. North I., New Zealand, in **Tongariro National Park** (260 sq. mi. or 673 sq. km.) which includes also Ruapehu and Ngauruhoe volcanoes; 6516 ft. (1986 m.).

Tong·a·ta·pu \ˌtäŋ-gä-ˈtä-pü\. **1.** Island group, S Tonga, SW cen. Pacific Ocean, incl. islands of Tongatapu and Eua; ab. 133 sq. mi. (344 sq. km.).

2. Island, S Tonga, SW cen. Pacific Ocean; ab. 100 sq. mi. (260 sq. km.); dist. pop. (1986c) 63,794; chief town Nuku'alofa, ✻ of Tonga; largest island in Tonga group.

Tonga Trench. Ocean trench, SW Pacific Ocean, E of Tonga, extending approx. from S of Samoa to NE of Kermadec Is.; subduction zone according to theory of plate tectonics.

Tong·e·ren \ˈtȯŋ-ə-rə\ *or Fr.* **Ton·gres** \ˈtō^{n}gr^{ə}\. Commune, Limburg prov., NE Belgium, 12 mi. (19 km.) NW of Liège; pop. (1991c) 29,451.

Tong·hua *or W.-G.* **T'ung–hua** *also* **Tung·hwa** \ˈtu̇ŋ-ˈhwä\. City, Jilin prov., NE China, in mountainous region 140 mi. (225 km.) E of Shenyang; ✻ of former T'ung-hua prov., S Manchukuo.

Ton·gi \ˈtȯŋ-gē\. City, cen. Bangladesh, N of Dhaka; pop. (1991p) 165,099.

Tong·jiang \ˈtu̇ŋ-ˈjyäŋ\ *or W.-G.* **T'ung–chiang** \ˈtu̇ŋ-ˈjyäŋ\. Town, E Heilongjiang prov., NE China, at juncture of the Songhua with the Amur.

Tong·jo·sŏn Man \ˈtȯŋ-ˈjō-ˈsän-ˈmän\; *formerly in Eng.* **East Cho·sen Bay** \ˈchō-ˈsen\ *or* **Brough·ton Bay** \ˈbrȯt-^{ə}n\. Inlet of the Sea of Japan, E coast of North Korea.

Tongking. See TONKIN.

Tong·ling *or W.-G.* **T'ung–ling** \ˈtu̇ŋ-ˈliŋ\. City, S cen. Anhui prov., China, on the Chang; pop. (1990c) 228,017.

Tong·quil \tȯŋ-ˈkēl\. Island, Samales group, Sulu Archipelago, Philippines; 19 sq. mi. (49 sq. km.). See SAMALES.

Tongue \ˈtəŋ\. River, Montana and Wyoming; rises in Sheridan co., N Wyoming, flows N across Montana border into Yellowstone River in Custer co., SE Montana; 246 mi. (396 km.) long.

Tongue of Arabat. See ARABAT SPIT.

Tongue of the Ocean. Strait, Bahamas, bet. Andros I. on the W and New Providence I. and Exuma Is. on the E.

Tong·xian *or W.-G.* **T'ung–hsien** *also* **Tung·hsien** \ˈtu̇ŋ-ˈshyen\; *formerly* **Tung·chow** \ˈtu̇ŋ-ˈchau̇\. City, Beijing municipality, NE China, 12 mi. (19 km.) E of Beijing on Bai River.

Tonk \ˈtȯŋk\. **1.** Former Indian state, since 1948 part of Rajasthan state, NW India; consisted of six separate regions; 2543 sq. mi. (6586 sq. km.); ruled by Afghan chieftain Amīr Khān 1806–34; under British influence after 1817.

2. Town, E Rajasthan, NW India, near right bank of Banas River 60 mi. (97 km.) S of Jaipur; pop. (1991p) 100,020; formerly ✻ of Tonk state.

Ton·ka·wa \ˈtäŋ-kə-ˌwä\. City, Kay co., N Oklahoma, 13 mi. (21 km.) W of Ponca City; pop. (1990c) 3127; Northern Oklahoma Coll. (1901).

Ton·kin \ˈtän-ˈkin, ˈtäŋ-\ *or* **Tong·king** \ˈtäŋ-ˈkiŋ\. Former French protectorate, SE Asia, now constituting the greater part of N Vietnam. Name applied to region by Europeans but not used by indigenous inhabitants.

History: Region included in ancient native kingdom by 3d cent. B.C.; part of China 2d cent. B.C. until Vietnamese won independence 10th cent. A.D.; after 1802 united to S provinces of Vietnam under Emperor Gia Long; Hanoi attacked by French 1873 and finally seized 1883; joined with other regions controlled by French to form French Indochina 1887; occupied by Japanese 1940–45 during WWII; formed part of new state of Vietnam estab. 1945–46; part of North Vietnam 1954 and of united Republic of Vietnam 1976.

Tonkin, Gulf of. Arm of the South China Sea, E of N Vietnam and N and W of Hainan I., S China; ab. 300 mi. (485 km.) long. Site of reported Vietnamese firing on American ships 1964 leading to wider American military presence in Vietnam.

Ton·le Sap \tōn-ˈlā-ˈsap\. **1.** *or Fr.* **Grand Lac** \grä^{n}-ˈlȧk\. Lake, W Cambodia; ab. 87 mi. (140 km.) long; receives floodwaters of the Mekong River; area varies from 1000 to 9500 sq. mi. (2590 to 24,605 sq. km.) according to season; abundance of fish; just N of its NW shore lie the ruins of Angkor (*q.v.*).

2. River, cen. Cambodia; flows SE to the Mekong River at Phnom Penh; ab. 75 mi. (120 km.) long; outlet of Tonle Sap (lake).

To·no·as \tō-ˈnō-əs\; *formerly* **Du·blon** \ˈdü-ˌblän\. Island, Caroline Is., main island of Chuuk (*q.v.*), in E part.

To·no·ley Harbour \ˈtō-nə-ˌlā\. Large anchorage, Bougainville Strait, S end of Bougainville I., NW Solomon Is., W Pacific; Buin and Kahili are on it.

To·no·pah \ˈtō-nə-ˌpä\. Unincorporated settlement, ⊗ of Nye co., cen. and S Nevada, 78 mi. (126 km.) ESE of S end of Walker Lake; pop. (1990c) 3616.

Tøns·berg \ˈtœns-ˌbar\. Seaport, ⊗ of Vestfold co., SE Norway, located on N end of Nøtterøy I.; pop. (1990c) 31,275;

traditionally thought to be the oldest city in Norway; formerly home port for whaling fleets; paper.

Tontio. See GORI.

Ton·to \ˈtón-tō\. River, SE cen. Mexico; flows E and NE across SE Veracruz state into the Bay of Campeche; 135 mi. (217 km.) long.

Tonto Basin. Region, N Gila co., cen. Arizona; alt. above 2000 ft. (610 m.); shut in by Mogollon Rim on the N and by mountain ranges on E and W; traversed by **Tonto Creek,** 60 mi. (97 km.) long, which flows S to the Salt River at Roosevelt Lake; fine forests and grazing land; just S of Roosevelt Lake is **Tonto National Monument** (see UNITED STATES, *National Monuments*).

Too·ele \tü-ˈe-lə\. **1.** County in NW Utah. See table at UTAH. **2.** City, its ⊗, 25 mi. (40 km.) SW of Salt Lake City; pop. (1990c) 13,887; salt and mineral extraction, gold; settled 1849.

Toole \ˈtül\. County in N Montana. See table at MONTANA.

Toombs \ˈtümz\. County in SE cen. Georgia. See table at GEORGIA.

Too·woom·ba \tə-ˈwu̇m-bə\. City, SE Queensland, Australia, 65 mi. (105 km.) W of Brisbane; pop. (1991c) 81,043; alt. 1920 ft. (585 m.); trade center for extensive agricultural and pastoral hinterland; summer resort.

Top \ˈtóp\. Large lake, N Karelia Rep., NW Russia in Europe; its outlet is Pongoma River flowing E to White Sea N of Kem.

To·pe·ka \tə-ˈpē-kə\. City, ✱ of Kansas and ⊗ of Shawnee co., NE Kansas, on Kansas River 55 mi. (88 km.) W of Kansas City; pop. (1990c) 119,883; processing center for agricultural area; tires; railroad shops; Washburn Univ. of Topeka (1865); Forbes Field (Air Force base containing Combat Air Museum). Founded by antislavery colonists 1854 and prominent in political conflict bet. pro and antislavery interests in Kansas Terr. before Civil War; became ✱ on admission of Kansas into Union 1861.

To·pol'·ča·ny *or* **To·pol·ča·ny** \ˈtó-pól-ˌchä-nē\. Town, W Slovakia; pop. (1989c) 37,630.

Topolia. See COPAIS.

To·po·lo·bam·po \tō-ˌpō-lō-ˈbäm-pō\. Village and port on coast of NW Sinaloa state, W Mexico, on Gulf of California; has good harbor.

Top·pe·nish \ˈtä-pə-ˌnish\. City, Yakima co., S Washington, 17 mi. (27 km.) SSE of the city of Yakima; pop. (1990c) 7419.

Tops·field \ˈtäps-ˌfēld\. Town, Essex co., NE Massachusetts, 20 mi. (32 km.) NE of Boston; pop. (1990c) 5754.

Tops·ham \ˈtäp-səm\. Town, Sagadahoc co., S Maine, at mouth of Androscoggin River; pop. (1990c) 8746.

To·qui·ma Range \tō-ˈkē-mə\. Range, N Nye co., cen. Nevada.

Tor·bat–e Hehy·da·rī·yeh \tór-ˈbat-i-ˈhā-də-ˈrē-yə\ *or* **Tur·bat–i–Hai·da·ri** \tu̇r-ˈbat-i-ˈhī-də-ˈrē, -ˈhā-\. Town, Khorāsān prov., NE Iran; pop. (1986c) 72,068; on trade route 75 mi. (121 km.) S of Mashhad.

Tor·bay \ˌtór-ˈbā, ˈtór-ˌbā\. Urban area, Devon, SW England, 28 mi. (45 km.) ENE of Plymouth, on Tor Bay; pop. (1991p) 122,500; seaside resort; formed 1968, incorporating Torquay and several other centers.

Tor Bay \ˈtór\. Inlet of the English Channel on the coast of Devon, SW England; landing place 1688 of Prince William of Orange, who soon after accepted British throne as William III, joint sovereign with Mary II.

Tor·cel·lo \tór-ˈchel-lō\. Island in Lagoon of Venice, NE Italy.

Torda. See TURDA.

Tor·de·sil·las \ˌtór-dā-ˈsēl-yäs\. Village, cen. Valladolid prov., N Spain, on the Duero; pop. (1991c) 7548; church; convent; residence 1509–55 of Juana la Loca (Joan the Mad), queen of Castile and Aragon. Treaty signed here June 7, 1494 bet. Spain and Portugal by which the line of demarcation bet. their respective discoveries in the New World (estab. 1493) was moved 270 leagues farther west (to ab. 48°W), thus granting to Portugal the E part of Brazil.

To·rez \tá-ˈres\; *formerly* **Chist·ya·kovo** \chist-ˈyä-kə-və\. Town, Donets'k subdivision, Ukraine, ab. 38 mi. (61 km.) E of the city of Donets'k; pop. (1991e) 88,000.

Tor·gau \ˈtór-ˌgau̇\. City, Saxony, E Germany, on Elbe River SE of Dessau; pop. (1992e) 21,772; railroad junction; agricultural machinery, glass, paper, ceramics; 13th cent. church; 15th–16th cent. castle. First mentioned 10th cent.; chartered c. 1260; scene of formation 1526 of Protestant league (Torgauer Bund) with which religious reformer Martin Luther was active; in WWII scene of first meeting bet. U.S. and Soviet troops during advance into Germany Apr. 1945.

Torg·hat·ten \ˈtórg-ˌhät-ᵊn\. Peak on a small island off W cen. coast of Norway; at a height of ab. 400 ft. (120 m.) from its base it is penetrated by a natural tunnel 553 ft. (169 m.) long, 200 to 250 ft. (60 to 75 m.) high, and 35 to 56 ft. (11 to 17 m.) wide.

To·ri·de \tō-ˈrē-dā\. City, Ibaraki prefecture, SE Honshū, Japan; pop. (1990p) 81,667.

To·ri·ña·na, Cape \ˌtō-rē-ˈnyä-nä\. Cape, NW Spain, 43°03′N, 9°18′W; westernmost point of Spanish mainland.

To·ri·no \tō-ˈrē-nō\. **1.** Province of Piedmont, Italy. See table at ITALY.
2. Commune, Italy. See TURIN.

Tor·ka·mān \ˌtór-kə-ˈmän\; *formerly* **Turk·man·chai** *also* **Turk·man·tchai** \ˌtu̇rk-män-ˈchī\. Town, East Azerbaijan prov., NW Iran, ab. 70 mi. (115 km.) SE of Tabrīz; scene of signing of treaty 1828 bet. Persia and Russia by which Russia acquired part of Armenia.

Torkeman, Bandar–e. See BANDAR-E TORKEMAN.

Tor·ko·ro, Cape \tór-ˈkōr-ō\. Point, N coast of New Britain I., Bismarck Archipelago, W Pacific Ocean, near its E end; extends into Bismarck Sea.

Tor·men·tine, Cape \ˈtór-mən-ˌtīn\. Point, SE New Brunswick, Canada, extending into Northumberland Strait; most easterly point of New Brunswick.

Tormentoso, Cabo. See GOOD HOPE, CAPE OF 2.

Tor·mes \ˈtór-ˌmās\. River, W Spain; flows N and NW into Douro River on Portuguese border; 153 mi. (246 km.) long.

Tor·na·do Mountain \tór-ˈnā-dō\. Peak in Rocky Mts., SW Canada, on border bet. SE British Columbia and Alberta; 10,167 ft. (3099 m.).

Torneå. See TORNIO 1.

Tor·ne River \ˈtór-nə\ *or Swed.* **Tor·ne·älv** \ˌtór-nē-ˈelv\ *or* **Tor·ne·äl·ven** \ˌtór-nē-ˈel-vən\ *or Finnish* **Tor·ni·o·jo·ki** \ˈtór-nē-ō-ˌyō-kē\. River, N and NE Sweden; issues from Torne Träsk in NW Sweden; flows SE and S, forming in its lower course a section of the Sweden-Finland boundary, and empties into the head of the Gulf of Bothnia; 354 mi. (570 km.) long.

Torne Träsk \ˈtór-nə-ˈtresk\. Lake (*träsk*), NW Sweden; 124 sq. mi. (321 sq. km.); source of the Torne River.

Torn·gat Mountains \ˈtórn-gat\. Mountain range, extreme N tip of Labrador, Newfoundland, Canada; extends N to Cape Chidley; highest point Cirque Mt. 5160 ft. (1573 m.), at S end.

Tor·nio \ˈtór-nē-ˌō\ *or Swed.* **Tor·neå** \ˈtór-nē-ˌō\. Seaport, Lappi prov., W Finland; built on an island in the Torne River at its mouth, opp. the Swedish town of Haparanda; pop. (1989c) 22,698; manufactures leather; chartered 1621.

Torniojoki. See TORNE RIVER.

To·ro \ˈtō-rō\. **1.** Town, Zamora prov., NW cen. Spain, on right bank of the Duero 35 mi. (56 km.) W of Valladolid; pop. (1991c) 9254; 12th cent. cathedral. Scene of battle 1476 in which Ferdinand II of Aragon and Queen Isabella I of Castile defeated the Portuguese under King Afonso V; seat of Spanish parliament 1505 convened after Queen Isabella's death to determine who would rule Castile.
2. Area, of W Uganda, near Mt. Ruwenzori; 5233 sq. mi. (13,553 sq. km.); formerly an independent kingdom; became part of Uganda under British late 19th cent.

To·ro, Cer·ro del \ˈser-rō-thel-ˈtō-rō\. Peak, cen. Chile, near border of Argentina; 20,995 ft. (6399 m.).

Tö·rök·szent·mi·klós \ˈtœr-œk-sent-ˌmē-ˌklōsh\. Commune, E Hungary, 65 mi. (105 km.) SE of Budapest; pop. (1991e) 24,300.

Tor·o·na·ic Gulf *or* **To·ro·naí·os, Kól·pos.** See KASSÁNDRA, GULF OF.

To·ron·to \tə-ˈrän-tō\. **1.** City, Jefferson co., E Ohio, on Ohio River 7 mi. (11 km.) N of Steubenville; pop. (1990c) 6127.
2. Metropolitan municipality, Ontario, Canada. See table at ONTARIO.
3. Commercial and industrial city, ✻ of Ontario and ⊗ of Toronto met. municipality, SE Ontario, Canada, at NW end of Lake Ontario; pop. (1991c) 635,395, met. area pop. 2,275,771; 3d largest city in Canada; major transportation center; lake port, shipping grain, meat, and coal; produces metal and petroleum products, clothing, machinery, automobiles; printing and publishing. Toronto Univ. (1827), Victoria Univ. (1836), Knox Coll. (1844), Univ. of St. Michael's Coll. (1852), Univ. of Trinity Coll. (1852). Notable buildings include parliament buildings and Superior Court of Ontario, City Hall (completed 1965), the Skydome, and the CN Tower, world's tallest freestanding structure at 1821 ft. (555 m.). In Exhibition Park is held annually the Canadian National Exhibition. Site of Hockey Hall of Fame.
History: Orig. inhabited by Seneca tribes; occupies the site of old French trading post, Fort Rouillé (founded c. 1750); city founded as **York** \ˈyȯrk\ by Americans loyal to the British 1793; succeeded Newark (Niagara-on-the-Lake) as ✻ of Upper Canada 1797; twice sacked by American troops during the War of 1812; received city charter 1834 and changed name to Toronto; had as first mayor William Lyon Mackenzie, leader of abortive uprising of 1837; ✻ of Canada West 1849; ✻ of Ontario 1867; damaged by fires 1849 and 1904. With adjoining towns, villages, and townships formed met. municipality 1954 (reorganized administratively 1967).

To·ron·to, Lake \tō-ˈrōn-tō\. Lake in SE cen. Chihuahua state, N Mexico, produced by damming of the Conchos River.

Toros Dağları. See TAURUS MOUNTAINS.

To·ro·to·ro National Park \ˌtō-rō-ˈtō-rō\. National park, cen. Bolivia, SSE of Cochabamba; features dinosaur tracks.

Tor·quay \ˈtȯr-ˈkē\. See TORBAY.

Tor·rá \tȯ-ˈrä\. Peak in the Cordillera Occidental of the Andes, W Colombia; 11,660 ft. (3554 m.).

Tor·rance \ˈtȯr-əns, ˈtär-\. **1.** County in cen. New Mexico. See table at NEW MEXICO.
2. City, Los Angeles co., SW California, to the S and W of the city of Los Angeles; pop. (1990c) 133,107; aircraft, electronic components, aluminum, chemicals; oil wells; El Camino Coll. (1947); city founded 1911; incorp. 1921.

Tor·re An·nun·zia·ta \ˈtȯr-rā-ˌä-ˌnün-ˈtsyä-tä\. Commune, Napoli prov., Campania, S Italy, on Bay of Naples 12 mi. (19 km.) SE of Naples; pop. (1989c) 56,471; port and seaside resort; firearms, macaroni.

Torre de Cerredo. See CERREDO, TORRE DE.

Torre del Gre·co \ˈtȯr-rā-del-ˈgre-kō\. Commune, Napoli prov., Campania, S Italy, on Bay of Naples 7 mi. (11 km.) SE of Naples; pop. (1989c) 103,577; fishing; seaside resort; damaged by volcanic eruptions several times since 17th cent.

Tor·re·don·ji·me·no \ˌtȯr-rā-ˌthōn-hē-ˈmā-nō\. Commune, Jaén prov., S Spain, 12 mi. (19 km.) W of the commune of Jaén; pop. (1991c) 13,401.

Tor·re·la·ve·ga \ˌtȯr-rā-lä-ˈvā-gä\. Commune, Cantabria prov., N Spain, 14 mi. (23 km.) SW of Santander; pop. (1991c) 60,023; chemicals, plastics.

Tor·re·mag·gio·re \ˌtȯr-rā-mä-ˈjō-rā\. Commune, Foggia prov., Puglia, SE Italy, 21 mi. (34 km.) NW of the commune of Foggia; pop. (1981p) 17,093; castle.

Tor·rens \ˈtȯr-ənz, ˈtär-\. **1.** Shallow salt lake, E South Australia, Australia, N of Spencer Gulf; 130 mi. (209 km.) long, 2230 sq. mi. (5776 sq. km.); 92 ft. (28 m.) above sea level.
2. River, South Australia, Australia; flows W to Gulf St. Vincent; 50 mi. (80 km.) long; city of Adelaide is on its banks.

Tor·rent \ˈtȯr-rent\. Commune, Valencia prov., E Spain, 8 mi. (13 km.) SW of the commune of Valencia; pop. (1991c) 56,564.

Tor·re·ón \ˌtȯr-rā-ˈōn\. City, Coahuila state, NE Mexico, 150 mi. (241 km.) W of Monterrey; munic. pop. (1990p) 459,809; railroad junction; textiles, flour, iron and steel; center of wheat- and cotton-growing district.

Tor·res del Pai·ne National Park \ˈtȯr-rās-thel-ˈpī-nā\. National park, Magallanes y Antártica Chilena region, S Chile; 95 sq. mi. (246 sq. km.); contains the Paine Towers (Torres del Paine), a group of distinctive peaks surrounded by glaciers; rare animals; estab. 1959.

Tor·res Islands \ˈtȯr-iz\. Group of four small islands at N end of Vanuatu, SW Pacific Ocean, 50 mi. (80 km.) NW of Vanua Lava; pop. (1991e) 464; largest is Hiu I.

Torres Strait. Strait bet. New Guinea and the N tip of Cape York Penin., Australia; connects Arafura Sea and Coral Sea; ab. 80 mi. (130 km.) wide; Australian boundary is ab. 3 mi. (5 km.) from New Guinea shore. Has many reefs, shoals, and islands (**Torres Strait Islands**), and is dangerous to navigation; larger islands inhabited. Strait discovered by Spanish navigator Luis Vaez de Torres in 1606; traversed by English explorer Capt. James Cook in 1770.

Tor·res Ve·dras \ˈtȯr-riz-ˈve-drəsh\. Commune, Lisboa dist., W Portugal, 26 mi. (42 km.) N of Lisbon; pop. (1990c) 11,028; noted particularly for its 25-mile (40-kilometer) stretch of fortifications (begun 1809), extending to the Tagus River, from behind which British Gen. Arthur Wellesley hindered the French march against Lisbon 1810 during the Peninsular War; sulfur baths; Moorish citadel.

Tor·reys Peak \ˈtȯr-ēz, ˈtär-\. Mountain, Clear Creek and Summit cos., cen. Colorado; 14,267 ft. (4349 m.).

Tor·ridge \ˈtȯr-ij, ˈtär-\. River, SW England; rises on Cornwall-Devon co. border, flows SE and then curves to the NW and empties into Barnstaple Bay through an estuary at Bideford in Devon co.; ab. 40 mi. (64 km.) long.

Tor·ri·don, Loch \ˈtȯr-əd-^{ə}n, ˈtär-\. Inlet, Highland region, on NW coast of Scotland; extends inland ab. 12 mi. (19 km.).

Tor·ring·ton \ˈtȯr-iŋ-tən, ˈtär-\. **1.** City, E cen. Litchfield co., NW Connecticut, on Naugatuck River 18 mi. (29 km.) NNW of Waterbury; pop. (1990c) 33,687; settled c. 1735; incorp. as city 1923. The town (incorp. 1740) is coextensive with the city.
2. Town, ⊗ of Goshen co., SE Wyoming, on North Platte River 7 mi. (11 km.) W of Nebraska border; pop. (1990c) 5651; sugar beets; livestock; Eastern Wyoming Coll. (1948).

Tórs·havn *also* **Thors·havn** \ˈtȯrs-ˌhau̇n\. Town, ✻ of Faeroe Is., Denmark, in North Atlantic Ocean; located on Strømø I.; area pop. (1993e) 16,091; occupied 1940 by the British during WWII as a defense measure against German forces in Denmark.

Tortoise Islands. See GALÁPAGOS ISLANDS.

Tor·to·la \tȯr-ˈtō-lə\. Largest of the British Virgin Is., West Indies; 21 sq. mi. (54 sq. km.); pop. (1980p) 9322; chief town Road Town; highest point Mt. Sage 1710 ft. (521 m.).

Tor·to·li·ta Mountains \ˌtȯrt-^{ə}l-ˈē-tə\. Small range, E Pinal co., S cen. Arizona.

Tor·to·na \tȯr-ˈtō-nä\; *anc.* **Der·to·na** \dər-ˈtō-nə\. Commune, Alessandria prov., Piedmont, NW Italy, 13 mi. (21 km.) E of the commune of Alessandria; pop. (1989c) 27,954; 16th cent. cathedral.

Tor·to·sa \tȯr-ˈtō-sä\. **1.** *anc.* **Der·to·sa** \dər-ˈtō-sə\. City, Tarragona prov., NE Spain, on Ebro River 40 mi. (64 km.) SW of the commune of Tarragona; pop. (1991c) 29,452; olive oil, fertilizer, hats, soap, pharmaceuticals, flour, lumber; 14th cent. cathedral. Came under Rome 3d cent. B.C.; captured by Moors early 8th cent. A.D. and ✻ of small independent Moorish kingdom; reconquered 1148 by Count Ramón Berenguer IV of Barcelona; occupied by French 1708 during War of Spanish Succession and in 1810 during Peninsular War; heavily damaged in Spanish Civil War 1936–39.
2. Town, Syria. See TARTŪS.

Tortosa, Cape. Cape, E coast of Spain, E of Tortosa.

Tortuga, La. See LA TORTUGA.

\ə\ abut \ˈə\ matches \$^{ə}$\ kitten, Fr table \ər\ further \a\ ash \ā\ ace
\ä\ cot, cart \á\ Fr bac \au̇\ out \b̲\ Span Avila \ch\ chin \e\ bet \ē\ easy
\g\ go \i\ hit \ī\ ice \j\ job \k̲\ Ger ich, Buch \$^{n}$\ Fr vin
\ŋ\ sing \ō\ go \ö\ all \ȯ\ law \œ\ Fr bœuf \œ̄\ Fr feu \ȯi\ boy
\th\ thin \th̲\ this \ü\ loot \u̇\ foot \ue\ Ger füllen \ue̅\ Fr rue
\y\ yet \$^{y}$\ Fr digne \ˈdēn^{y}\, nuit \ˈnw^{y}ē\ \yü\ few \yu̇\ fury \zh\ vision

Tor·tu·ga Island \tȯr-'tü-gə\ *or Fr.* **Île de la Tor·tue** \ˌēl-də-lä-tȯr-'tuē\. Island, West Indies, off N coast of Haiti; 25 mi. (40 km.) long; in 17th cent. a stronghold of pirates.

Torugart Pass. See TURUGART PASS.

To·ruń \'tȯr-ˌün\ *or Ger.* **Thorn** \'tȯrn\. **1.** Province, N Poland. See table at POLAND.

2. Industrial and commercial city, its ✻, on Vistula River 110 mi. (177 km.) NW of Warsaw; pop. (1989e) 200,822; railroad junction and river port; chemicals, electronics, synthetic fibers; Gothic town hall; three Gothic churches; university (1945). Birthplace of astronomer Nicolaus Copernicus 1473.

History: Founded by Teutonic Knights 1231; member of Hanseatic League 14th cent.; under protection of Poland 1454; two treaties signed here (1411 and 1466), the 2d of which assigned West Prussia (incl. Toruń) to Poland; occupied by King Charles XII of Sweden during Great Northern War (1700–21); to Prussia 1793 after Second Partition of Poland; part of Grand Duchy of Warsaw 1807–15; returned to Prussia 1815; to Poland 1919; in WWII occupied by Germans 1939–44.

To·ry \'tȯr-ē\. Small island, Atlantic Ocean, off extreme NW coast of Ireland and administratively part of co. Donegal; lighthouse. Pirate stronghold of the Fomorians of Celtic legend.

Törz·bur·ger Pass \'tœrts-ˌbu̇r-gər\. Mountain pass in the Transylvanian Alps, Romania, 25 mi. (40 km.) SW of Braşov; 4065 ft. (1239 m.).

Tor·zhok \tər-'zhȯk\. Town, Tver' Oblast, W cen. Russia in Europe, ab. 35 mi. (55 km.) WNW of the city of Tver'; pop. (1991e) 50,500.

To·sa \'tō-sä\. Old province in S Shikoku I., Japan, now Kōchi prefecture. Home of the Tosa clan, esp. influential at the time of the Meiji Restoration (1868).

Tosa Bay. Inlet of the Pacific Ocean on S coast of Shikoku I., Japan.

Toscana. See TUSCANY.

Toscanella. See TUSCANIA.

Toscano *or* **Tosco–Emiliano, Appennino.** See table at APENNINES.

Toscano, Arcipelago. See TUSCAN ARCHIPELAGO.

Tot·nes \'tät-nəs\. Town, Devon, SW England, 20 mi. (32 km.) SSW of Exeter; pop. (1981c) 5636; brewing; remains of ancient castle; an important Saxon town by 11th cent.

Totomi Sea. See ENSHŪ BIGHT.

To·to·ni·ca·pán \tō-ˌtō-nē-kä-'pän\. **1.** Department of W cen. Guatemala. See table at GUATEMALA.

2. City, its ✻, on high plateau; pop. (1993e) 14,400; flour, woolens, pottery.

To·to·wa \'tō-tə-wə\. Residential borough, Passaic co., N New Jersey, 3 mi. (5 km.) W of Paterson; pop. (1990c) 10,177; encampment of Gen. George Washington and his army during Revolutionary War.

Tot·ting·ton \'tä-tiŋ-tən\. Town, Greater Manchester co., NW England, 10 mi. (16 km.) NNW of Manchester; pop. (1981p) 10,700.

Tot·to·ri \tō-'tȯr-ē\. **1.** Prefecture, Honshū, Japan; ✻ Tottori. See table at JAPAN.

2. Seaport city, its ✻, 90 mi. (145 km.) NW of Kyōto; pop. (1990p) 142,477; textiles; sand dunes; university (1949). Formerly the castle town of a daimyo; became prosperous early 20th cent. on the opening of the railroad.

Toub·kal, Mount \'tüb-ˌkal\ *or* **Je·bel Toub·kal** \'je-bəl\. Mountain peak of the Grand Atlas, Morocco, S of Marrakech; 13,665 ft. (4165 m.); highest peak in the Atlas Mts.

Toubkal National Park. National park, Morocco; 141 sq. mi. (365 sq. km.); numerous high peaks incl. Mt. Toubkal.

Toug·gourt *or* **Tug·gurt** \tu̇-'gu̇rt\. Town and oasis, NE Algeria, 100 mi. (161 km.) S of Biskra; pop. (1987p) 70,645.

Toul \'tül\; *anc.* **Tul·lum** \'tə-ləm\. City, Meurthe-et-Moselle dept., NE France, on Moselle River 13 mi. (21 km.) WSW of Nancy; pop. (1990c) 17,702; manufactures porcelain; trades in wine and brandy; 13th–15th cent. Gothic church (former cathedral).

History: Ancient ✻ of the Leuci tribe of Belgic Gaul before coming under Romans; became episcopal see in 4th cent.; by 14th cent. an imperial city; with Metz and Verdun (*Les Trois-Évêchés,* the Three Bishoprics) occupied by France 1552 but French possession not confirmed until Treaty of Westphalia 1648; bishopric suppressed c. 1800; occupied by Germans in Franco-Prussian War 1870; heavily damaged during WWII.

Tou–liu \'dō-'lyō\. Town, W cen. Taiwan; pop. (1992e) 91,030.

Tou·lon \'tü-ˌlän\. City, ⊗ of Stark co., NW cen. Illinois; pop. (1990c) 1328.

Tou·lon \tü-'lō^{n}\; *anc.* **Te·lo Mar·ti·us** \'tē-lō-'mär-shē-əs\. Seaport, ✻ of Var dept., SE France, on the Mediterranean 30 mi. (48 km.) ESE of Marseille; pop. (1990c) 170,167; principal base of French Mediterranean fleet, with docks, naval shipyard, and arsenal; shipbuilding, fishing, wine making; episcopal see; 13th cent. cathedral; naval museum.

History: First mentioned as Roman naval station; passed, with Provence, to French crown 1481; center of conflict in wars bet. France and Holy Roman Empire 16th cent.; naval arsenal founded by King Henry IV (1589–1610); scene of victory of French artillery commander (later emperor) Napoléon Bonaparte over English, Spanish, and French royalists 1793; important port of entry and naval station in 19th cent. and during WWI; in WWII large part of French Mediterranean fleet stationed here after French armistice of 1940; majority of ships scuttled by their crews Nov. 1942, after German abrogation of armistice and occupation of Toulon; city entered by French troops Aug. 1944.

Tou·louse \tu̇-'lüz\; *anc.* **To·lo·sa** \tə-'lō-sə\. City, ✻ of Haute-Garonne dept., S France, on Garonne River 133 mi. (214 km.) SE of Bordeaux; pop. (1990c) 365,933; railroad junction and canal port; a center of the French aviation industry; produces chemicals and footwear; numerous notable buildings, incl. 11th–17th cent. Gothic cathedral, 11th–13th cent. Romanesque basilica, town hall, courthouse, museum, observatory, botanical gardens, public library; university (1229), Catholic Institute of Toulouse (1877), several professional and technical schools and academies.

History: Taken from Celtic inhabitants by Romans 106 B.C.; ✻ of Visigoths in 5th cent. A.D.; taken by Frankish King Clovis I 508; as seat of countship of Toulouse (founded 778) ✻ of a major feudal dynasty; center of resistance to Albigensian Crusade early 13th cent.; scene of massacre of Protestants during Wars of Religion 16th cent.; in 1814 scene of British victory over French in last battle of Peninsular campaign; in WWII occupied by Germans Nov. 1942–Aug. 1944.

Toun·goo \'tau̇ŋ-ˌgü\. Town, Myanmar, on Sittang River 150 mi. (241 km.) N of Yangon; pop. (1983c) 65,861; ✻ of an independent kingdom from 14th to 16th cents.; occupied by Japanese 1942–45 during WWII.

Tou·raine \tə-'rān\. Historical region of NW cen. France; bounded anciently on N by Maine, on NE by Orléanais, on SE by Berry, on SW by Poitou, and on NW by Anjou; ✻ Tours; watered by Indre, Cher, and Loire rivers; sometimes called the "Garden of France"; province until French Revolution (1789).

Tourane. See DA NANG.

Tour·coing \tür-'kwe^{n}\. City, Nord dept., N France, on Belgian frontier 8 mi. (13 km.) NE of Lille; pop. (1990c) 94,425; one of principal textile centers of France.

Tour·nai *or* **Tour·nay** \tür-'nā\ *or Flem.* **Door·nik** \'dōr-ˌnik\. Commune, Hainaut prov., SW Belgium, on the Schelde 45 mi. (72 km.) SW of Brussels; pop. (1991c) 67,732; hosiery, textiles, leather goods, cement; 11th–12th cent. cathedral; 12th cent. belfry. In 5th cent. became Merovingian ✻ of Salian Franks; made episcopal see 6th cent.; came under French rule and received charter 1188; held 16th cent. by Spanish Hapsburgs; changed hands several times bet. France and Austrian Hapsburgs during 18th cent.; incorp. into independent Belgium c. 1831; in WWI and WWII severely damaged.

Tour·non \tu̇r-'nō^{n}\. Town, Ardèche dept., SE France, on Rhone River 58 mi. (93 km.) by rail S of Lyon.

Tour·nus \tu̇r-ˈnue̅\. Town, Saône-et-Loire dept., E cen. France, on the Saône ab. 15 mi. (24 km.) N of Mâcon; site of Benedictine abbey founded 7th or 8th cent.; notable 10th–12th cent. abbey church. Birthplace of painter Jean-Baptiste Greuze 1725.

Tours \ˈtür\; *anc.* **Cae·sa·ro·du·num** \ˌsē-zər-ə-ˈdü-nəm, -ˈdyü-\; *later* **Tu·ro·ni** \ˈtu̇r-ə-ˌnī, ˈtyu̇r-\. City, ✱ of Indre-et-Loire dept., NW cen. France, 129 mi. (208 km.) SW of Paris; pop. (1990c) 133,403; chemicals; ships wine; notable Gothic cathedral (13th–16th cents.); several other Gothic churches and remains of old basilica of St. Martin of Tours.

History: Founded by Gallic tribes before Roman conquest; made episcopal see 3d cent.; near scene of victory of Frankish ruler Charles Martel over Moors from Spain 732 (also called battle of Poitiers); center of learning in time of Anglo-Saxon scholar Alcuin (c. 732–804); developed prosperous silk industry in 15th cent.; largely depopulated after revocation of Edict of Nantes 1685; seat of French government during siege of Paris 1870 in Franco-Prussian War and briefly in WWII 1940. Birthplace of novelist Honoré de Balzac 1799.

Tou·si·dé \ˌtü-sē-ˈdā\. Peak in Tibesti Mts., N Chad; 10,712 ft. (3265 m.).

Tou·tle \ˈtüt-ᵊl\. River, SW Washington; flows W in N Cowlitz co. into Cowlitz River; ab. 40 mi. (64 km.) long.

To·wa·da \tō-ˈwä-dä\. Lake, N Honshū, Japan; 25 mi. (40 km.) in circumference, elev. 1476 ft. (450 m.); resort, ab. 25 mi. (40 km.) S of Aomori.

Towada–Ha·chi·man·tai National Park \-ˌhä-chē-ˈmän-ˌtī\. National park, N Honshū, Japan; 322 sq. mi. (834 sq. km.); consists of two sections; volcanoes.

To·wan·da \tō-ˈwän-də\. Borough, ⊗ of Bradford co., N Pennsylvania, on Susquehanna River 50 mi. (80 km.) WNW of Scranton; pop. (1990c) 3242.

Tow·ces·ter \ˈtōs-tər\. Town, S Northamptonshire, cen. England; site of Roman camp on Watling Street; scene of disputes bet. Danes and Saxons 10th cent.

Tow·er Falls \ˈtau̇-ər\. Waterfall, Yellowstone National Park, NW Wyoming; 132 ft. (40 m.) high.

Tower Hamlets. Borough of Greater London, SE England. See table at LONDON 4.

Tower Island. See GENOVESA.

Tower Peak. Mountain in the Sierra Nevada, E Tuolumne co., cen. California; 11,704 ft. (3567 m.).

Town and Country. City, St. Louis co., E Missouri; pop. (1990c) 9519; pop. nearly tripled bet. 1980 and 1990.

Tow·ner \ˈtau̇-nər\. **1.** County in N North Dakota. See table at NORTH DAKOTA.

2. City, ⊗ of McHenry co., N cen. North Dakota; pop. (1990c) 669.

Towns \ˈtau̇nz\. County in N Georgia. See table at GEORGIA.

Town·send \ˈtau̇n-zənd\. **1.** Town, Middlesex co., NE Massachusetts, 7 mi. (11 km.) NE of Fitchburg; pop. (1990c) 8496.

2. City, ⊗ of Broadwater co., SW cen. Montana; pop. (1990c) 1635.

Townsend Inlet *or* **Townsend's Inlet** *or* **Townsends Inlet** \-zəndz\. Narrow strait, leading from Atlantic Ocean through barrier islands in E Cape May co., S New Jersey.

Towns·ville \ˈtau̇nz-ˌvil\. City, E Queensland, Australia, on Halifax Bay 380 mi. (611 km.) NW of Rockhampton; pop. (1991c) 101,398; major seaport exporting meat, sugar, minerals, wool; meatpacking, copper refining, sawmilling; James Cook Univ. of North Queensland (1970); city founded 1864.

Tow·son \ˈtau̇-sᵊn\. Unincorporated settlement, ⊗ of Baltimore co., N Maryland, N of the city of Baltimore; pop. (1990c) 49,445; Towson State Univ. (1866).

Tow·ton \ˈtau̇t-ᵊn\. Parish, North Yorkshire, N England; scene of battle Mar. 29, 1461 (the Wars of the Roses) in which Edward of York (soon to be King Edward IV) defeated the Lancastrians, a victory which confirmed his accession to the throne.

Towy \ˈtō-ē, ˈtau̇-ē\ *or Welsh* **Ty·wi** \ˈtə-wē\. River, SW Wales; flows SW to Carmarthen Bay; 65 mi. (105 km.) long.

To·ya·ma \tō-ˈyä-mä\. **1.** Prefecture, Honshū, Japan; ✱ Toyama; abundant hydroelectric power. See table at JAPAN.

2. Seaport city, its ✱, near S shore of Toyama Bay 110 mi. (177 km.) N of Nagoya; pop. (1990p) 321,259; textiles, pharmaceuticals, patent medicines; university (1949). An important seat of daimyos under Tokugawa shogunate (1603–1867).

Toyama Bay. Inlet of the Sea of Japan on the W cen. coast of Honshū, Japan; enclosed on W by Noto Penin.

Toyohara. See YUZHNO-SAKHALINSK.

To·yo·ha·shi \ˌtō-yō-ˈhä-shē\. City, Aichi prefecture, S Honshū, Japan, 38 mi. (61 km.) SE of Nagoya and near E shore of inlet of E Ise Bay; pop. (1990p) 337,988; textiles.

To·yo·ka·wa \ˌtō-yō-ˈkä-wä\. City, Aichi prefecture, Honshū, Japan, 41 mi. (66 km.) SE of Nagoya; pop. (1990p) 111,731.

To·yo·na·ka \ˌtō-yō-ˈnä-kä\. City, Ōsaka prefecture, Honshū, Japan; pop. (1990p) 409,843; suburb of the city of Ōsaka.

To·yo·ta \tō-ˈyō-tä, tȯi-\. City, Aichi prefecture, Honshū, Japan; pop. (1990p) 332,336.

To·zeur \tō-ˈzœr\. Town and large oasis, W Tunisia, on W shore of Chott Djerid.

Trab·zon \trab-ˈzän\ *or* **Treb·i·zond** \ˈtre-bə-ˌzänd\. **1.** Province of Turkey in Asia. See table at TURKEY.

2. *anc.* **Trap·e·zus** \ˈtra-pi-zəs\. Seaport city, its ✱, on the SE coast of the Black Sea ab. 12 mi. (19 km.) NW of Erzurum; pop. (1990c) 143,941; commercial center; 13th cent. church; technical university (1963). An ancient town, dating from 8th cent. B.C. and for many centuries terminus of a trade route to Persia and cen. Asia; held by Roman and Byzantine empires and ✱ of Greek empire of Trebizond 1204–1461.

Trach·o·ni·tis \ˌtra-kə-ˈnī-təs\. District of ancient Palestine, beyond (E of) the Jordan and S of Damascus; formed a part of the Tetrarchy of Philip 4 B.C.–34 A.D.

Tra·cy \ˈtrā-sē\. **1.** City, San Joaquin co., cen. California, 18 mi. (29 km.) SSW of Stockton; pop. (1990c) 33,558; grew rapidly in 1980s.

2. Town, S Quebec, Canada, 45 mi. (72 km.) NE of Montreal; pop. (1991c) 13,181.

Tra·fal·gar, Cape \trə-ˈfal-gər; *Span.* ˌträ-fäl-ˈḡär\. Cape, SW coast of Spain, SE of Cádiz and WNW of the Strait of Gibraltar; scene of decisive victory in Napoleonic Wars of British fleet under Adm. Horatio Nelson over French and Spanish, and of Nelson's death Oct. 21, 1805.

Traf·ford \ˈtra-fərd\. Borough, Allegheny and Westmoreland cos., SW Pennsylvania, 14 mi. (23 km.) E of Pittsburgh; pop. (1990c) 3345.

Tragurium. See TROGIR.

Trai·guén \trī-ˈgen\. Island in Chonos Archipelago, in Pacific Ocean off SW coast of Chile.

Trail \ˈtrāl\. City, SE British Columbia, Canada, on Columbia River 7 mi. (11 km.) N of U.S. border; pop. (1991c) 7919; lead and zinc refining.

Traill \ˈtrāl\. County in E North Dakota. See table at NORTH DAKOTA.

Trajani Portus. See CIVITAVECCHIA.

Tra·lee \trə-ˈlē\. Seaport, ⊗ of co. Kerry, SW Ireland, at head of **Tralee Bay** (inlet of Atlantic Ocean N of Dingle Bay); pop. (1986c) 17,109; bacon; site of Norman castle, seat of earls of Desmond.

Trälleborg. See TRELLEBORG.

Tralles. See AYDIN 2.

Tra·nent \trə-ˈnent\. Burgh, Lothian region, SE Scotland, ab. 9 mi. (14 km.) E of Edinburgh near Prestonpans (*q.v.*); pop. (1981p) 8063.

Trang \ˈträŋ\. Town, SW Thailand, on branch railroad line 15 mi. (24 km.) from the Strait of Malacca at Kantang and 85 mi. (137 km.) ESE of Phuket; pop. (1991e) 48,589.

Trang·an \träŋ-ˈgän\. Island, S cen. part of Aru Is., Indonesia; ab. 50 mi. (80 km.) long by 30 mi. (48 km.) wide.

Tra·ni \ˈträ-nē\. Commercial seaport, Bari prov., Puglia, SE Italy, on the Adriatic Sea 26 mi. (42 km.) WNW of the seaport of Bari; pop. (1989c) 49,902; ships wine and marble; furniture; notable 11th cent. cathedral; 13th cent. castle.

Tran·que·bar \ˈtraŋ-kwə-ˌbär, ˈtraŋ-kə-\. Town, Tamil Nadu, S India, 50 mi. (80 km.) NE of Tanjore. Formerly a seaport of importance; Danish settlement estab. here early 17th cent.; site of first Protestant mission in India 1706; bought by British with other Danish settlements in India in 1845.

Trans Alai \ˈtrants-ə-ˈlī, ˌtranz-\. Mountain range, NW Pamirs, W cen. Asia, extending E and W bet. Kyrgyzstan and the Gorno-Badakhshan subdivision, Tajikistan; highest point Lenin Peak 23,405 ft. (7134 m.). See ALAI.

Trans–Alas·ka Pipeline \ˈtrants-ə-ˈlas-kə, ˈtranz-\ *or* **Alaska Pipeline.** Pipeline running N to S across Alaska; carries oil from the Prudhoe Bay area to the port of Valdez.

Transalpine Gaul. See GAUL 2.

Transantarctic Mountains. See ANTARCTICA.

Trans–Ap·pa·lach·ia \ˈtrants-ˌa-pə-ˈlā-chə, ˈtranz-, -chē-ə\. Region, E cen. U.S., W of the Appalachian Mts.; used historically, esp. of period of late 18th and early 19th cents., to designate region drained by Ohio River.

Trans·bai·ka·lia \ˈtrants-bī-ˈkȯl-yə, ˈtranz-, -ˈkal-\ *or* **Trans·bai·kal** \-bī-ˈkȯl, -ˈkal\ *also* **Za·bai·kal** \ˌzä-bī-ˈkäl, -ˈkal\. Former Russian administrative subdivision, E of Lake Baikal, now included in Buryatia Rep., Chita Oblast, and Khabarovsk Kray of SE Russia in Asia.

Trans–Canada Highway. Highway, Canada, stretching from St. John's, Newfoundland (linked by ferry) to Victoria, British Columbia; 4861 mi. (7821 km.); opened 1962.

Transcarpathian Oblast. See ZAKARPATS'KA.

Trans·cas·pia \trants-ˈkas-pē-ə, tranz-\ *or* **Trans·cas·pi·an Territory** \-pē-ən\. Former Russian administrative subdivision, E of the Caspian Sea, roughly equivalent to the present Turkmenistan and a part of SW Kazakhstan.

Transcaucasia. See CAUCASIA.

Trans·cau·ca·sian Federation \ˌtrans-kȯ-ˈkā-zhən, ˌtranz-, -ˈka-\ *also* **Trans·cau·ca·sia** \-ˈkā-zhə, -zhē-ə\ *or officially* **Transcaucasian Soviet Federated Socialist Republic.** Former federated union of what are now the independent republics of Armenia, Azerbaijan, and Georgia; ✻ Tbilisi.

History: First formed 1917 after the Bolshevik Revolution (prior to Revolution region divided into various Russian governments, provinces, and districts); soon dissolved into separate republics of Georgia, Azerbaijan, and Armenia; scene of fighting in 1919–21 when Turkish Nationalists struggled with the Bolsheviks for control of the region; reformed Mar. 1922 and entered the U.S.S.R.; separated again into three autonomous republics Dec. 1936 when the U.S.S.R. adopted a new constitution.

Trans–Dnies·tria \trans-ˈnēs-trē-ə, tranz-\. Region, bet. the Dniester and Bug rivers in SW Ukraine and E Moldova; with Bessarabia was given 1941 to Romania by Germany during WWII; retaken by Soviet armies 1944; the Moldovan section was scene of conflicts bet. Moldovan forces and Trans-Dniestrian separatists 1992.

Transilvania. See TRANSYLVANIA 2.

Transjordan. See JORDAN 1.

Trans–Juba. See JUBALAND.

Trans·kei \ˈtrans-ˈkā, -ˈkī\. Region, E Eastern Cape prov., Rep. of South Africa; 16,329 sq. mi. (42,292 sq. km.); pop. (1993e) 3,664,000; ✻ Umtata. Different territories annexed to Cape Colony at various dates during late 19th cent.; internally self-governing Bantu territory formed 1963; its laws subject to the approval of the government of the Rep. of South Africa; granted independence 1976, but not internationally recognized; reincorporated into South Africa 1994.

Trans·ox·i·a·na \ˌtrans-ˌäk-sē-ˈā-nə, ˌtranz-, -ˈa-\. Region, beyond (N of) the Oxus (*mod.* Amu Dar'ya) and NE of Khorāsān, W Asia, incl. Bukhara and Samarqand. In ancient times known as Sogdiana (*q.v.*).

Transpadane Gaul. See GAUL.

Trans·pad·ane Republic \ˈtrans-pə-ˌdān, trans-ˈpā-ˌdān, tranz-\. Provisionally organized republic, N Italy; created by future French Emperor Napoléon 1796 from lands N of Po River around Milan, Bergamo, Brescia, and Cremona; incorp. into Cisalpine Republic 1797. See GAUL.

Trans·vaal \trans-ˈväl, tranz-\; *earlier, as independent state,* **South African Republic.** Former province, NE Rep. of South Africa; was located bet. Limpopo River (on N) and Vaal River (on S); 109,621 sq. mi. (283,918 sq. km.); ✻ Pretoria. Plateau land (high veld), averaging 5000 to 6400 ft. (1525 to 1950 m.), covered nearly one third of province in SE; drained by Komati, Pongolo, and other rivers flowing E to Indian Ocean. In W plateau sloped to ab. 4000-foot (1220-meter) average. Site of abundant mineral resources, esp. rich goldfield in Witwatersrand near Johannesburg, and diamonds around Pretoria; also deposits of platinum, coal, and iron. Agriculture 2d to mining in importance; livestock raising; corn, wheat, tobacco, citrus fruit. Chief towns Pretoria, Johannesburg with suburbs of Germiston, Boksburg, Springs, and Beroni.

History: About 1800 region inhabited chiefly by various Bantu-speaking peoples; immigration of Boers during Great Trek of 1830s; first settlement at Potchefstroom 1838. Independence acknowledged by British in Sand River Convention 1852. Estab. as South African Republic (*q.v.*) 1856; discovery of diamonds 1867 led to loss of Griqualand West to British 1871; annexed by British 1877–81; rebellion of Boers 1880–81 and restoration of republic 1881; discovery of gold 1886 brought in many foreigners (Uitlanders); scene of abortive attempt by physician and statesman Dr. Leander Starr Jameson to overthrow Boer government 1895 (Jameson Raid); joined Orange Free State against Great Britain in Boer War (1899–1902); as Transvaal annexed by British 1900 and later made crown colony; granted self-government 1906; joined Union (now Rep.) of South Africa 1910. Ceased to exist as an administrative entity 1994 and roughly split into Eastern Transvaal (now Mpumalanga) and Northern Transvaal (now Northern) provs.

Tran·syl·va·nia \ˌtran-səl-ˈvā-nyə, -ne-ə\. **1.** County in SW North Carolina. See table at NORTH CAROLINA.

2. *or Rom.* **Tran·sil·va·nia** \ˌträn-sēl-ˈvän-yä\ *or Hung.* **Er·dély** \er-ˈdā\ *or Ger.* **Sie·ben·bür·gen** \ˌzē-bən-ˈbu̇r-gən\. Region, NW and cen. Romania; 21,297 sq. mi. (55,159 sq. km.); comprises **Transylvanian Basin,** a plateau ranging from 1000 to 1600 ft. (305 to 490 m.) of triangular shape, shut in on N, E, and S by the Carpathian Mts. and Transylvanian Alps and drained chiefly by tributaries of the Tisza, esp. the Someşul and Mureşul; noted for its legendary association with vampires, esp. Dracula.

History: Included in the Roman prov. of Dacia 2d cent. A.D.; later overrun by various Germanic and other tribes; settled 9th cent. ff. by the Magyars, Szeklers, Vlachs, and Saxons; held by Hungarians after early 11th cent.; made a principality mid-16th cent. and came under influence of Ottoman Empire until its defeat by Austrian Hapsburgs late 17th cent.; scene of frequent religious and ethnic conflict; made a grand principality within the Austrian empire 1765; scene of severe fighting in Hungarian revolution against Austria (1848); made integral part of Hungary 1867; annexed to Romania 1918–20; its N part assigned to Hungary 1940, but returned to Romania after WWII. Scene of conflict after 1989 bet. Hungarian minorities and Romanian nationalists.

Tran·syl·va·nian Alps \ˌtran-səl-ˈvān-yən\ *also* **South Car·pa·thi·ans** \kär-ˈpā-thē-ənz\. Mountain range, a continuation of the Carpathian Mts., extending E and W in cen. Romania, along the boundary bet. N Walachia and S Transylvania; ab. 230 mi. (370 km.) long; highest point Moldoveanu 8343 ft. (2543 m.).

Tra·pa·ni \ˈträ-pä-nē\. **1.** Province of Sicily, Italy. See table at ITALY.

2. *anc.* **Drep·a·num** \ˈdre-pə-nəm\. Seaport, its ✻, on Mediterranean Sea at NW tip of the island, 48 mi. (77 km.) SW of Palermo; pop. (1991p) 69,273; salt; marble working, fish canning; commercial fisheries; 17th cent. cathedral; notable 14th and 16th cent. churches; 17th cent. town hall.

History: Founded by Carthaginians and served as important naval base during First Punic War (264–241 B.C.) after which it was ceded to Rome; taken from Arabs late 11th cent. by Normans who made it part of Kingdom of the Two Sicilies.

Trapezus. See TRABZON 2.

Trap·per Peak \ˈtra-pər\. **1.** Mountain on SW border of Ravalli co., W Montana; ab. 10,155 ft. (3095 m.).
2. Mountain, Glacier National Park, NW Montana; 7675 ft. (2339 m.).

Tra·ral·gon \trə-ˈral-gən\. Town, Victoria, Australia, 90 mi. (145 km.) SE of Melbourne; pop. (1991c) 19,699.

Tra·si·me·no \ˌträ-zē-ˈmā-nō\ *also* **Pe·ru·gia** \pə-ˈrü-jə, -jē-ə\; *anc.* **Tras·i·me·nus** \ˌtra-sə-ˈmē-nəs\. Lake, Umbria, cen. Italy, 10 mi. (16 km.) W of Perugia; scene of Carthaginian Gen. Hannibal's victory over the Romans 217 B.C. in Second Punic War; scene of severe fighting 1944 in WWII bet. British and German armies.

Tras·te·ve·re \trä-ˈstā-vā-ˌrā\. Region across the Tiber from Rome, Italy.

Trat \ˈträt\ *also* **Krat** \ˈkrät\. Town, S Thailand, on NE coast of Gulf of Thailand near Cambodian border; pop. (1991e) 9612; connected to Bangkok by highway.

Traù *or* **Trau.** See TROGIR.

Traun \ˈtraùn\. **1.** River, W cen. Austria; rises in a series of lakes in the Salzkammergut and flows N out of Styria through the Hallstätter and Traun lakes in Upper Austria into Danube River 4 mi. (6 km.) below Linz; 95 mi. (153 km.) long.
2. Town, N Austria; pop. (1991c) 22,260; paper, textiles.

Traun, Lake *or Ger.* **Traun·see** \-ˌzā\ *also* **Gmund·ner See** \gə-ˈmùnt-nər-ˌzā\. Lake, S Upper Austria, Austria, formed by Traun River; 7 mi. (11 km.) long by 2 mi. (3 km.) wide; 9.4 sq. mi. (24 sq. km.); max. depth 626 ft. (191 m.).

Trautenau. See TRUTNOV.

Trav·an·core \ˈtra-vən-ˌkōr\. Former princely state, SW India; came under British rule 18th cent.; became part of Kerala state 1956. Western Ghats reach 8000 ft. (2438 m.) here.

Travancore–Cochin. See COCHIN 1.

Trav·el·ers Rest \ˈtrav-ᵊl-ərz-ˈrest\. City, Greenville co., NW South Carolina; pop. (1990c) 3069.

Tra·ven·dal \ˈträ-vən-ˌdäl\. Village, Schleswig-Holstein, Germany, 15 mi. (24 km.) W of Lübeck; treaty signed here 1700 by which King Charles XII of Sweden forced a peace on the Danes during the Great Northern War.

Trav·erse \ˈtra-vərs\. County in W Minnesota. See table at MINNESOTA.

Traverse, Lake. Lake on boundary bet. Roberts co., NE South Dakota, and Traverse co., W Minnesota; 30 mi. (48 km.) long; outlet on N is the Bois de Sioux River, headstream of Red River of the North.

Traverse City. City, ⊗ of Grand Traverse co., NW Michigan, at S end of W arm of Grand Traverse Bay; pop. (1990c) 15,116; center of a resort region; Northwestern Michigan Coll. (1951).

Trav·is \ˈtra-vis\. County in cen. Texas. See table at TEXAS.

Trav·nik \ˈträv-nēk\. Town, cen. Bosnia and Herzegovina, 45 mi. (72 km.) NW of Sarajevo. Has a Turkish citadel; from late 17th to mid-19th cents. was ✻ of Bosnia.

Treas·ure \ˈtre-zhər\. County in SE cen. Montana. See table at MONTANA.

Treasure Island. **1.** Man-made island, San Francisco Bay, California; site of Golden Gate International Exposition 1939; naval station.
2. City, Pinellas co., W Florida Penin., Florida; pop. (1990c) 7266.

Treas·ury Islands \ˈtre-zhə-rē\. Group of small islands, off S end of Bougainville I. and SSW of Shortland Is., NW Solomon Is., W Pacific Ocean; includes Mono I. and Stirling I.; during WWII occupied by U.S. Oct. 1943.

Treb·bia \ˈtreb-byä\; *anc.* **Tre·bia** \ˈtrē-bē-ə\. River, NW Italy; rises NE of Genoa, flows N into Po River 3 mi. (5 km.) NW of Piacenza; 71 mi. (114 km.) long; scene of two battles: (1) 218 B.C. in which Carthaginian Gen. Hannibal defeated the Romans under Gen. Publius Scipio in Second Punic War; (2) June 1799 in which Russian Field Marshal Aleksandr Suvorov defeated the French under Gen. Jacques-Alexandre Macdonald.

Tře·bíč \tər-ˈzhe-bēch\ *or Ger.* **Tre·bitsch** \ˈtrā-bich\. Town, S Czech Republic, 36 mi. (58 km.) W of Brno; pop. (1989c) 39,204.

Treb·i·zond \ˈtre-bə-ˌzänd\. **1.** Greek empire, 1204–1461, W Asia; included region along SE shore of Black Sea; ✻ Trebizond (*mod.* Trabzon); founded by its first emperor, Alexius I (Grand Comnenus), as an offshoot of Byzantine Empire; one of the last Greek states to be conquered by Ottoman Turks 1461.
2. Province and city, Turkey. See TRABZON.

Tre·blin·ka \tre-ˈbliŋ-kä\. Site, E Poland, near commune of Siedlce; location of major German concentration camps in WWII.

Tre·ce Mar·ti·res \ˈtrā-sā-mär-ˈtē-rās\. Chartered city, ✻ of Cavite prov., Luzon, Philippines; pop. (1990p) 16,000.

Tre·de·gar \tri-ˈdē-gər\. Town, Gwent co., SE Wales, on the Sirhowy 33 mi. (53 km.) WNW of Bristol; pop. (1981p) 16,446; in former coal-mining area.

Trefaldwyn. See MONTGOMERY 7.

Treffynnon. See HOLYWELL.

Tre·go \ˈtrē-gō\. County in W cen. Kansas. See table at KANSAS.

Tre·grosse Islets \tri-ˈgrōs\. Group of coral islets and reefs, Coral Sea, outside Great Barrier Reef, Queensland, Australia, 17°41′S, 150°43′E.

Trein·ta y Tres \ˈtrān-tä-ē-ˈtrās\. **1.** Department of E Uruguay. See table at URUGUAY.
2. Town, its ✻, 140 mi. (225 km.) NE of Montevideo; pop. (1985c) 28,117.

Tré·la·tête, Ai·guille de \ā-ˌgwē-də-ˌtrā-lə-ˈtet\. Peak in the Alps, SE France, SW of Mont Blanc; 12,832 ft. (3911 m.).

Tre·lew \trā-ˈleù\. Commercial town, NE Chubut prov., S Argentina, W of Rawson; pop. (1980p) 52,073. Founded by Welshmen late 19th cent.

Trel·le·borg *or* **Träl·le·borg** \ˌtre-lə-ˈbòrʸ\. Seaport, Malmöhus prov., SW Sweden, on the Baltic Sea; pop. (1993e) 36,879; shipping center; sugar refineries; rubber.

Tre·mi·ti Islands \ˈtre-mē-tē\. Group of five small islands, Italy, off SE coast, in Adriatic Sea, N of Gargano Promontory; largest island **San Do·mi·no** \sän-ˈdò-mē-ˌnō\, ab. 5 mi. (8 km.) in circumference.

Tremonia. See DORTMUND.

Tre·mon·ton \ˈtrē-ˌmänt-ᵊn\. City, Box Elder co., NW Utah, 38 mi. (61 km.) NNW of Ogden; pop. (1990c) 4264.

Trem·pea·leau \ˈtrem-pə-ˌlō\. **1.** River, W Wisconsin; rises in W Jackson co., flows SW into Mississippi River on line bet. Buffalo and Trempealeau cos.; ab. 50 mi. (80 km.) long.
2. County in W Wisconsin. See table at WISCONSIN.

Tren·čín \ˈtren-ˌchēn\ *or Hung.* **Tren·csén** \ˈtren-ˌchān\ *or Ger.* **Trent·schin** \ˈtren-chin\. Town, W Slovakia, on the Váh River ab. 70 mi. (115 km.) NE of Bratislava; pop. (1991p) 56,733.

Trengganu. See TERENGGANU.

Trent \ˈtrent\. **1.** River, SE North Carolina; flows W to E across Jones and Craven cos. into Neuse River at New Bern; 40 mi. (64 km.) long.
2. River, Victoria, Peterborough, and Northumberland cos., SE Ontario, Canada; has its source in the Kawartha chain of lakes, thence flows S (here called the Otonabee) past Peterborough to Rice Lake, from which it winds generally SE to Trenton on the Bay of Quinte; ab. 150 mi. (240 km.) long. Its entire course either used or paralleled by the **Trent Canal** (also known as **Trent Waterways**); in W part canal connects Kawartha Lakes with Lake Simcoe and thence by Severn River to Georgian Bay, total length 224 mi. (360 km.) and 42 locks. Also it has S branch by way of Scugog River past Lindsay, ab. 35 mi. (56 km.).
3. River, cen. England; rises in Staffordshire, flows NNE and unites with the Ouse ab. 15 mi. (24 km.) W of Hull to form the Humber; 170 mi. (274 km.) long; navigable by barge for over half its length.
4. Commune, Italy. See TRENTO 2.

\ə\ **abut** \ᵊ\ **kitten**, F table \ər\ **further** \a\ **ash** \ā\ **ace** \ä\ **cot, cart** \à\ Fr bac \aù\ **out** \b\ Span Avila \ch\ **chin** \e\ **bet** \ē\ **easy** \g\ **go** \i\ **hit** \ī\ **ice** \j\ **job** \k\ Ger **ich, Buch** \ⁿ\ Fr vin \ŋ\ **sing** \ō\ **go** \ò\ **all** \ȯ\ **law** \œ\ Fr **bœuf** \œ̄\ Fr **feu** \òi\ **boy** \th\ **thin** \th\ **this** \ü\ **loot** \ù\ **foot** \ue\ Ger **füllen** \ue̅\ Fr **rue** \y\ **yet** \ʸ\ Fr digne \ˈdēnʸ\, nuit \ˈnwʸē\ \yü\ **few** \yù\ **fury** \zh\ **vision**

Tren·ti·no–Al·to Adi·ge \tren-ˈtē-nō-ˌäl-tō-ˈä-dē-ˌjā\; *formerly* **Ve·ne·zia Tri·den·ti·na** \ve-ˈnet-sē-ä-ˌtrē-den-ˈtē-nä\. Autonomous region, NE Italy; ✻ Trento; mountainous; corn, wheat, oats, vines; dairy farming; zinc, lead; hydroelectric power; tourism; annexed to Austria 1815; scene of much fighting throughout WWI; by Treaty of St.-Germain 1919 ceded to Italy; administratively reorganized 1948. See table at ITALY.

Tren·to \ˈtren-tō\. **1.** Province of Trentino-Alto Adige, Italy. See table at ITALY.
2. *or Eng.* **Trent** \ˈtrent\ *or Ger.* **Tri·ent** \trē-ˈent\; *anc.* **Tri·den·tum** \trī-ˈden-təm\. Commune, ✻ of Trentino-Alto Adige and of Trento prov., NE Italy, on Adige River 106 mi. (171 km.) ENE of Milan; pop. (1991p) 101,430; furniture, leather goods; printing, truck farming; 12th cent. Romanesque cathedral; 13th–16th cent. castle with palace.
History: Believed to have been founded by Raetians c. 4th cent. B.C.; later became Roman military base; in Christian era came under Ostrogoths, Lombards, and Franks; became episcopal principality 11th cent.; seat of Council of Trent 1545–63 at which was established basic doctrine of Counter-Reformation; part of Napoleonic kingdom of Italy early 19th cent. then passed to Austria 1815; to Italy by Treaty of St.-Germain 1919.

Tren·ton \ˈtrent-ᵊn\. **1.** City, ⊗ of Gilchrist co., NW Florida Penin.; pop. (1990c) 1287.
2. Town, ⊗ of Dade co., NW corner of Georgia; pop. (1990c) 1994.
3. City, Wayne co., SE Michigan, on Detroit River 15 mi. (24 km.) SSW of Detroit; pop. (1990c) 20,586; steel.
4. City, ⊗ of Grundy co., N Missouri, 22 mi. (35 km.) N of Chillicothe; pop. (1990c) 6129; North Central Missouri Coll. (1925).
5. Village, ⊗ of Hitchcock co., S Nebraska; pop. (1990c) 656.
6. City, ✻ of New Jersey and ⊗ of Mercer co., W cen. New Jersey, at head of navigation on Delaware River 28 mi. (45 km.) NE of Philadelphia; pop. (1990c) 88,675; produces steel, plastics, ceramics; Mercer County Community Coll. (1947), Thomas A. Edison State Coll. (1972). Settled c. 1679 by English Quakers; incorp. as borough and town 1745; in American Revolution scene of American victory and capture of Hessian garrison by forces under Gen. George Washington in surprise attack Dec. 26, 1776 (monument commemorating battle set up 1893); made state ✻ 1790; incorp. as city 1792.
7. Town, ⊗ of Jones co., SE North Carolina; pop. (1990c) 248.
8. Village, Butler co., SW Ohio, 25 mi. (40 km.) SW of Dayton; pop. (1990c) 6189.
9. City, ⊗ of Gibson co., NW Tennessee, 26 mi. (42 km.) NNW of Jackson; pop. (1990c) 4836.
10. Town, Pictou co., N Nova Scotia, Canada, on Pictou Harbor 3 mi. (4.8 km.) N of New Glasgow; pop. (1991c) 2957.
11. Town, Hastings co., SE Ontario, Canada, on Bay of Quinte 12 mi. (19 km.) W of Belleville; pop. (1991c) 16,908; E terminus of Trent Canal system.

Trenton Falls. Cascades in West Canada Creek, cen. New York, 15 mi. (24 km.) N of Utica; furnish waterpower for Utica; formed out of limestone which was laid down in a North American stage of the Ordovician period named the Trentonian after these formations.

Trentschin. See TRENČÍN.

Trent Waterways. See TRENT 2.

Tréport, Le. See LE TRÉPORT.

Tres Ar·ro·yos \ˈtrās-är-ˈrȯi-ōs\. City, Buenos Aires prov., E cen. Argentina, ab. 70 mi. (115 km.) NE of Bahía Blanca; pop. (1980p) 42,118; agricultural and cattle-raising center.

Tres Cru·ces \ˌtrās-ˈkrü-sās\. Mountain, N Chile, NE of Copiapó, on Argentine boundary; 20,853 ft. (6356 m.).

Tres For·cas, Cape \tras-ˈfȯr-kəs\. Cape, NE coast of Morocco; Melilla is on it.

Tres Galliae. See GAUL 2.

Tres Marias, Islas *or* **Las Tres Marias.** See MARÍAS, ISLAS.

Tres Mon·tes Gulf \ˌtrās-ˈmȯn-tās\. Inlet of Gulf of Penas, S coast of Taitao Penin., SW Chile.

Tres Montes Peninsula. Peninsula, extending from SW Taitao Penin., SW Chile.

Tres Mor·ros \ˌtrās-ˈmōr-rōs\. Peak, NW cen. Colombia, in the Cordillera Occidental; 11,155 ft. (3400 m.).

Tres Pun·tas, Cape \ˌtrās-ˈpün-täs\. **1.** Cape on NE coast of Santa Cruz prov., S Argentina, at S side of entrance to San Jorge Gulf.
2. Cape, E Guatemala, extending into the Gulf of Honduras and enclosing Amatique Bay.

Três Ri·os \trās-ˈrē-üs\. Municipality, Rio de Janeiro state, SE Brazil, 50 mi. (80 km.) N of the city of Rio de Janeiro; pop. (1991p) 81,163.

Tres Tabernae. See SAVERNE.

Tres Za·po·tes \ˌtrās-sä-ˈpō-tās\. Village in E Veracruz state, E Mexico, just W of San Andrés Tuxtla; pre-Mayan stone monuments dating back as far as the first cent. B.C.

Treut·len \ˈtrüt-lən\. County in E cen. Georgia. See table at GEORGIA.

Treves *or* **Trèves.** See TRIER.

Tre·vi·glio \trā-ˈvē-lyō\. Commune, Bergamo prov., Lombardy, N Italy, 12 mi. (19 km.) SSW of the commune of Bergamo; pop. (1989c) 25,270.

Tre·vi·ño \trā-ˈvē-nyō\. Exclave of Burgos prov., in Álava prov., Spain.

Tre·vi·so \trā-ˈvē-zō\. **1.** Province of Veneto, Italy. See table at ITALY.
2. *anc.* **Tar·vi·si·um** \tär-ˈvi-zhē-əm\. Commune, its ✻, Veneto, NE Italy, 17 mi. (27 km.) NNW of Venice; pop. (1991p) 83,222; rice refining; ceramics; surrounded by medieval ramparts; 12th cent. cathedral; 13th cent. palaces; 12th cent. Loggia dei Cavalieri.
History: Ancient Roman municipium; center of Lombard duchy after 6th cent. A.D.; taken by Frankish King (later Holy Roman Emperor) Charlemagne late 8th cent. and made center of a march; supported Lombard League against Holy Roman Emperor Frederick I 12th cent.; under the Ghibelline leader Ezzelino da Romano mid-13th cent.; passed to Venice 14th cent.; came under French Emperor Napoléon I 1797; ceded by Austria to Italy 1866; severely damaged 1944 by air raids in WWII.

Tre·vose Head \trē-ˈvōs\. Promontory, W coast of Cornwall, SW England; lighthouse.

Tré·voux \trā-ˈvü\. Commune, SW Ain dept., E France, on the Saône; ✻ of Dombes 11th cent.; noted for Jesuit press c. 18th cent. which published a newspaper and a dictionary.

TriBeCa \trī-ˈbe-kə\. Neighborhood of New York City, New York, on the lower W side of Manhattan.

Trib·une \ˈtri-ˌbyün\. City, ⊗ of Greeley co., W Kansas; pop. (1990c) 918.

Tricca. See TRÍKALA 2.

Trichinopoly. See TIRUCHCHIRAPPALLI.

Tri·chur \tri-ˈchu̇r\ *or* **Thris·sur** \tri-ˈsu̇r\. Town, N Kerala, S India, 40 mi. (64 km.) N of Cochin; met. area pop. (1991p) 274,898; commercial center; textiles; ancient Hindu temple.

Tridentine Alps. See table at ALPS.

Tridentum *and* **Trient.** See TRENTO 2.

Trier \ˈtrir\ *or Eng.* **Treves** \ˈtrēvz\ *or Fr.* **Trèves** \ˈtrev\; *anc.* **Au·gus·ta Tre·ve·ro·rum** \ȯ-ˈgəs-tə-ˌtre-və-ˈrōr-əm\. City, Rhineland-Palatinate, W Germany, on Moselle River near Luxembourg border 58 mi. (93 km.) SW of Koblenz; pop. (1992e) 98,752; vintners producing esp. Moselle. Extensive Roman remains, incl. large amphitheater, Porta Nigra (a fortified gate), baths, imperial palace; 13th cent. Gothic church; cathedral (Romanesque and Gothic additions to a Roman core); 18th cent. baroque church.
History: An ancient town, ✻ of the Treveri who were conquered by Roman Gen. Julius Caesar c. 57 B.C.; ✻ of Gaul prefecture 3d cent. A.D.; frequently an imperial residence until taken by Franks 5th cent.; seat of independent archbishops by early 9th cent.; c. 1800 fell to France and became ✻ of Sarre dept.; to Prussia 1815; in WWII suffered considerable damage and was captured by U.S. troops Mar. 1945. Birthplace of political philosopher Karl Marx 1818.

Tri·este \trē-ˈes-tā, -ˈest\. **1.** Province of Friuli-Venezia Giulia, Italy. See table at ITALY.

2. Commercial seaport, ✻ of Friuli-Venezia Giulia and of Trieste prov., NE Italy, at head of the Adriatic Sea on the **Gulf of Trieste,** on NW side of Istrian Penin.; pop. (1991p) 229,216; shipyards, steelmills, oil refineries; tourism; cathedral; 15th cent. castle; university (1924).

History: Came under Rome 2d cent. B.C.; under episcopal rule 948–1202; under Austrian rule 1382 ff.; imperial free port 1719; held by French 1809–14; made Austrian crown land mid-19th cent.; ceded to Italy by Treaty of St.-Germain 1919; in WWII occupied by Yugoslavs under Marshal Josip Tito May 1945; became center of a free territory 1947; returned to Italy 1954; made ✻ of Friuli-Venezia Giulia region 1963. See also TRIESTE 3.

3. *or in full* **Free Territory of Trieste.** Former region on W side of Istrian Penin., S Europe, surrounding and incl. city of Trieste; estab. 1947 as a free territory under the UN; divided for administrative purposes into two zones: Zone A in N, incl. city, under British and Americans; Zone B in S under Yugoslavs; in 1954 Zone B and a small part of Zone A incorp. into Yugoslavia; greater part of Zone A incorp. into Italy.

Trigarta. See JALANDHAR.

Trigg \ˈtrig\. County in SW Kentucky. See table at KENTUCKY.

Trig·gia·no \trē-ˈjä-nō\. Commune, Bari prov., Puglia, SE Italy, near the Adriatic 5 mi. (8 km.) ESE of the seaport of Bari; pop. (1989c) 24,751.

Tri·glav \ˈtrē-ˌgläv\ *or Ger.* **Ter·glou** \ˈter-ˌglü\. Mountain, NW Slovenia, near Italian border, NW of Ljubljana; 9395 ft. (2864 m.); highest in Slovenia and in Julian Alps.

Trí·ka·la *or* **Trík·ka·la** \ˈtrē-kä-lä\. **1.** Department of Thessaly, cen. Greece. See table at GREECE.

2. *anc.* **Tric·ca** \ˈtri-kə\. City, its ✻, N of Piníos River and ab. 35 mi. (56 km.) W of Larissa; pop. (1991p) 48,810; trades in grain and tobacco. Believed to be on site of ancient temple of Aesculapius, Greco-Roman god of medicine.

Tri·kho·nis, Lake \ˌtrē-k̲ō-ˈnēs\ *or Gk.* **Lím·ni Trikhonis** \ˈlēm-nē\. Lake, Greece, 125 mi. (201 km.) WNW of Athens; ab. 37 sq. mi. (96 sq. km.).

Tríkkala. See TRÍKALA.

Tri·ko·ra \trə-ˈkō-rə\; *formerly* **Wil·hel·mi·na Top** \ˌvil-hel-ˈmē-nə-ˈtäp\. Mountain, Jayawijaya Range, Irian Jaya, Indonesia; 15,585 ft. (4750 m.); highest peak in the range.

Trim \ˈtrim\. Town, ⊗ of co. Meath, E Ireland, on the Boyne; pop. (1991p) 1781; ruins of 12th cent. castle which housed several early Irish parliaments and a mint.

Trim·ble \ˈtrim-bəl\. County in N Kentucky. See table at KENTUCKY.

Trinacria. See SICILY.

Trin·che·ra Peak \trēn-ˈchā-rä\. Mountain, Las Animas, Costilla, and Huerfano cos., S Colorado; 13,540 ft. (4127 m.).

Trin·co·ma·lee *or* **Trin·ko·ma·li** \ˌtriŋ-kō-mə-ˈlē\. Seaport town, E Sri Lanka, on Bay of Bengal 110 mi. (177 km.) SE of Jaffna, on a peninsula on N side of **Bay of Trincomalee;** pop. (1990e) 50,000; excellent natural harbor, with limited export trade in dried fish, coconuts; ruins of "Temple of a Thousand Columns."

History: Early Tamil settlement in Ceylon; taken by Portuguese early 17th cent.; changed hands several times bet. Dutch and French before passing to British 1795. During WWII became principal British naval base in Far East after loss of Singapore to Japanese 1942; bombed by Japanese Apr. 1942; base ceded to Ceylon 1957.

Trindade. See TRINIDAD 4.

Tři·nec \tər-ˈzhē-nets\. Town, E Czech Republic, on border with Poland; pop. (1989c) 45,605.

Tring \ˈtriŋ\. Town, Hertfordshire, SE England, 30 mi. (48 km.) NW of London; pop. (1981p) 10,683; natural-history museum, estab. 1892 by Lionel Walter, 2d baron Rothschild.

Trin·i·dad \ˈtri-nə-ˌdad\. **1.** Commercial city, ⊗ of Las Animas co., SE Colorado, on Purgatoire River 80 mi. (129 km.) S of Pueblo; pop. (1990c) 8580; dairy products; coal mines; Trinidad State Junior Coll. (1925).

2. Island in Bahía Blanca, a bay on SE coast of Buenos Aires prov., Argentina.

3. Town, ✻ of Beni dept., N Bolivia, ab. 6 mi. (10 km.) E of the Mamoré River; pop. (1992p) 56,918; cattle market.

4. *or Port.* **Trin·da·de** \trēn-ˈdä-də\. Small rocky volcanic island, South Atlantic Ocean, 20°31′S, 29°19′W; belongs to Brazil.

5. Mountain range, S Las Villas prov., W cen. Cuba; highest peak 3724 ft. (1135 m.).

6. Municipality, Las Villas prov., W cen. Cuba; near S coast, S of Santa Clara; pop. (1981p) 65,523; founded early 16th cent.

7. Town, ✻ of Flores dept., SW Uruguay, 105 mi. (169 km.) NNW of Montevideo; pop. (1985c) 18,372.

8. Island of the West Indies, Atlantic Ocean, off NE coast of Venezuela; 1864 sq. mi. (4828 sq. km.); pop. (1990c) 1,184,106; chief town Port of Spain, ✻ of Trinidad and Tobago (*q.v.*).

Physical features: Nearly square in shape with two peninsulas extending from NW and SW corners enclosing the Gulf of Paria; the N peninsula and adjacent islands are separated by channel of Dragon's Mouth from Paria Penin. of Venezuela. Ranges of hills along N and S shores, several swamp regions on E and W.

History: Orig. inhabited chiefly by Arawak Indians among others; visited by explorer Christopher Columbus 1498; settled by Spanish late 16th cent.; occupied by British 1797 and ceded to Great Britain by Treaty of Amiens 1802; made part of colony of Trinidad and Tobago 1899; in WWII in 1941 four regions leased to U.S. for air and naval bases. Became part of independent state 1962; most military facilities relinquished by U.S. by 1971; made part of republic 1976. See TRINIDAD AND TOBAGO.

Trinidad, La. See LA TRINIDAD.

Trinidad and To·ba·go \tə-ˈbā-gō\. Independent republic, comprising the islands of Trinidad and Tobago, Atlantic Ocean, off NE coast of Venezuela; 1980 sq. mi. (5128 sq. km.); pop. (1990c) 1,234,388; ✻ Port of Spain.

Chief products: fish; oil, natural gas, asphalt; coconuts, bananas, coffee, cocoa, sugar, citrus; ammonia, methanol, fertilizer; tourism.

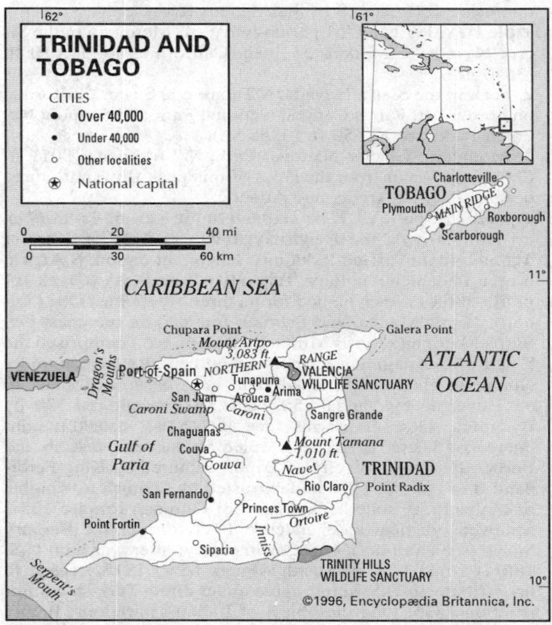

History: Union of the two islands authorized 1889 and British colony formally estab. 1899; member of the West Indies (Federation) 1958; became an independent state within the Commonwealth 1962; made a republic 1976. Scene 1990 of attempted coup against government by Muslim fundamentalists. See TRINIDAD 8 and TOBAGO.

Trinidad Gulf. Inlet of Pacific Ocean, SW of S Wellington I., off SW coast of Chile.

Tri·nil \ˈtrē-nil\. Village, S cen. Java, Indonesia, on Solo River, at base of Mt. Lawu. Site of discovery of fossil skullcap 1891 and additional parts of Java man (*Homo erectus*).

Tri·ni·ta·po·li \ˌtrē-nē-ˈtä-pō-lē\. Commune, Foggia prov., Puglia, SE Italy, on S shore of Lake Salpi 29 mi. (47 km.) ESE of the commune of Foggia; pop. (1981p) 13,170.

Trinité, La. See LA TRINITÉ.

Trin·i·ty \ˈtri-nə-tē\. **1.** River, NW California; rises in NE Trinity co., flows SW and then NW into Klamath River; ab. 130 mi. (210 km.) long.

2. River, E Texas; formed by confluence of forks just NW of Dallas; flows SE into Trinity Bay; 550 mi. (885 km.) long.

3. Name of counties in two states of the U.S. See tables at CALIFORNIA and TEXAS.

4. City, Trinity co., E Texas, on Trinity River 45 mi. (72 km.) SW of Lufkin; pop. (1990c) 2648.

Trinity, Cape. Promontory, Quebec, Canada, on S shore of Saguenay River ab. 40 mi. (64 km.) from its mouth and opp. Cape Eternity (*q.v.*); 1700 ft. (518 m.) high.

Trinity Bay. **1.** NE arm of Galveston Bay, Texas.

2. Inlet of Pacific Ocean, forming the harbor of Cairns, Queensland, NE Australia.

3. Inlet, SE Newfoundland, Canada; terminal of first transatlantic telegraph cable from Ireland 1866.

Trinity Dam. See UNITED STATES, *Dams and Reservoirs.*

Trinity Mountain. Mountain, N Elmore co., SW cen. Idaho; 9451 ft. (2881 m.).

Trinity Peaks. Mountain, San Juan co., SW Colorado; 13,752 ft. (4192 m.).

Trinkomali. See TRINCOMALEE.

Tri·phyl·ia \trī-ˈfi-lē-ə\. S district of ancient Elis (*q.v.*), W Peloponnese, S Greece, S of the Alpheus River.

Triple Di·vide Peak \ˈtri-pəl-də-ˈvīd\. **1.** Mountain in the Sierra Nevada, E Madera co., cen. California; ab. 11,610 ft. (3540 m.).

2. Peak in the Sierra Nevada, N Tulare co., S cen. California, on border bet. Kings Canyon National Park and Sequoia National Park; ab. 12,650 ft. (3855 m.).

3. Mountain, Glacier National Park, NW Montana; 8011 ft. (2442 m.). Water from the sides of this peak flows into three oceans, Pacific, Arctic, and Atlantic.

Trip·o·li \ˈtri-pə-lē\. **1.** *or* **Trip·o·li·ta·nia** \tri-ˌpä-lə-ˈtā-nē-ə, ˌtri-pə-lə-, -nyə\; *anc.* **Re·gio Syr·ti·ca** \ˈre-jē-ō-ˈsər-ti-kə\ *or* **Trip·o·li·ta·na** \ˌtri-pə-lə-ˈtā-nə\. Historical region, N Africa; orig. a Phoenician colony, **Trip·o·lis** \ˈtri-pə-ləs\ (Greek *tripolis,* "three cities") named for its three chief cities Oea (Tripoli), Leptis Magna, and Sabrata, founded on the coast bet. Syrtis Major and Syrtis Minor c. 7th cent. B.C.; comprised the E part of Carthaginian territory by 3d cent. B.C.; came under Numidian chieftains mid-2d cent. B.C.; became Roman 46 B.C.; overrun by Vandals 5th cent. A.D.; recaptured 534 by Byzantine Gen. Belisarius (see BYZANTINE EMPIRE); conquered by Islam in 7th cent.; ruled by successive Arab and Berber dynasties; the city of Tripoli captured by King Ferdinand II of Aragon 1510 and entrusted by Spanish to Knights of Malta 1530; state became part of Ottoman Empire 1551; achieved practical independence 1711; one of the Barbary States (see BARBARY), engaged in piracy; after war with U.S. 1801–05 and U.S. war with Algiers (*q.v.*) 1815, ceased to levy tribute on U.S. ships; came under direct Turkish administration 1835; long the object of Italian aspirations, finally ceded to Italy by Turkey as result of Tripolitan War (1911–12); interior not conquered until after WWI; separated from Cyrenaica as independent district of Italian Libya 1919, reunited 1929; in 1934 became administrative province (see TRIPOLI 2); part of independent Libya 1951; province dissolved 1963.

2. Former province, NW (Italian) Libya; 73,803 sq. mi. (191,150 sq. km.).

3. *or Arab.* **Ṭa·rā·bu·lus ash Sham** \tə-ˈrä-bə-ləs-esh-ˈsham\; *anc.* **Trip·o·lis** \ˈtri-pə-ləs\. Commercial town and seaport, NW Lebanon, 43 mi. (69 km.) NNE of Beirut; pop. (1985e) 500,000; ships oranges and cotton; sponge fishing, oil refining; fruit and tobacco farms; terminus of oil pipeline from Iraq.

History: Probably founded 7th cent. B.C.; ✻ of **Tripolis,** a Phoenician federation of three cities (Greek *tripolis,* "three cities"): Sidon, Tyre, and Aradus; held by Seleucids and Romans and taken by Muslims mid 7th cent. A.D.; taken by Crusaders early 12th cent.; retaken by Mamlūks 1289 and destroyed; new town on present site occupied by British 1918 and by British and Free French 1941; a center of conflict bet. Christian and Muslim factions esp. in 1958 and 1975; scene of siege by Palestinian rebels against leader Yāsir ʻArafāt 1983.

4. *or Arab.* **Ṭa·rā·bu·lus al–Gharb** \tə-ˈrä-bə-ləs-al-ˈgärb\; *anc.* **Oea** \ˈē-ə\. Coastal city, ✻ of Libya, on Mediterranean Sea 400 mi. (644 km.) W of Benghazi; pop. (1988e) 591,062; principal seaport of Libya; ships fruit, olive oil, fish; salt extraction, fishing, carpet weaving; old city largely surrounded by walls from Byzantine and later periods; 16th cent. Spanish citadel; numerous mosques; Roman triumphal arch (2d cent. A.D.). In WWII occupied by Axis forces until taken by British Jan. 1943; bombed by U.S. forces 1986 in response to terrorist activity. See also TRIPOLI 1.

5. Medieval county, Syria, N of the kingdom of Jerusalem; ✻ Tripoli.

Trip·o·lis \ˈtri-pə-ləs\. **1.** *also* **Tri·po·li·tsa** *or* **Tri·po·li·tza** \ˌtrē-pō-ˈlēt-sä\. City, ✻ of Arcadia dept., cen. Peloponnese, S Greece; pop. (1991p) 21,772. Was ✻ of Morea (Peloponnese) under Turks; taken by Greek insurgents 1821 during War of Greek Independence; retaken and destroyed by Ottoman Gen. Ibrāhīm Pasha c. 1825.

2. Ancient Phoenician colony, N Africa. See TRIPOLI 1.

3. Ancient confederacy in Phoenicia comprising Sidon, Tyre, and Aradus; ✻ Tripolis. See TRIPOLI 3.

Tripolitana *or* **Tripolitania.** See TRIPOLI 1.

Tripolitsa *or* **Tripolitza.** See TRIPOLIS 1.

Tripp \ˈtrip\. County in S South Dakota. See table at SOUTH DAKOTA.

Tri·pu·ra \ˈtri-pə-rə\; *formerly* **Hill Tip·pe·ra** \hil-ˈti-pə-rə\. State, NE India; on N, W, and S borders on Bangladesh; ✻ Agartala; area comprises parallel ranges of hills (highest ab. 3200 ft. or 975 m.); rice, jute; conquered by Moguls c. 17th cent.; after 1808 under influence of British government; became a territory 1956; estab. as a state 1972. See table at INDIA.

Tris·tan da Cu·nha \ˈtris-tən-də-ˈkü-nyə\. Island, South Atlantic Ocean, at ab. 37°15′S, 12°30′W; 38 sq. mi. (98 sq. km.); pop. (1987c) 296; highest point 6760 ft. (2060 m.). Chief of the **Tristan da Cunha Islands,** a group of five British volcanic islands incl. also Gough, Inaccessible, and Nightingale islands (total area 52 sq. mi. or 135 sq. km.); fishing; farming; collectible postage stamps. Discovered 1506 by Portuguese navigator Tristão da Cunha; annexed by Britain 1816; made a dependency of St. Helena I. 1938; in 1961 volcanic eruption forced evacuation of population, most of which returned 1963.

Tris·te, Gol·fo \ˈgȯl-fō-ˈtrēs-tā\. Bay, N coast of Venezuela, bet. Carabobo and Falcón states, W of Caracas.

Tri·sul \tri-ˈsül\. Peak in the Himalayas, N India; 23,360 ft. (7120 m.).

Tritonis, Palus. See DJERID, CHOTT.

Tri·umph, Mount \ˈtrī-əmf\. Peak, Skagit co., NW Washington; 7150 ft. (2179 m.).

Tri·van·drum \trə-ˈvan-drəm\ *or* **Thi·ru·van·an·tha·pur·am** \ˌtir-ü-və-ˌnən-tə-ˈpu̇r-əm\. Seaport city, ✻ of Kerala, SW India, on Arabian Sea 140 mi. (225 km.) SW of Madurai; pop. (1991c) 699,872; produces copra; rope, textiles, soap; 18th cent. temple; observatory; zoological garden; museum; university; made ✻ of kingdom of Travancore mid-18th cent.

Tr·na·va \ˈtər-nə-və\ *or Hung.* **Nagy·szom·bat** \ˈnäzh-sōm-ˌböt\ *or Ger.* **Tyr·nau** \ˈtuer-ˌnau̇\. Town, W Slovakia, 23 mi. (37 km.) NE of Bratislava; pop. (1991p) 71,641; market town; 14th cent. Gothic cathedral.

Trnovo. See VELIKO TŬRNOVO.

Tro·as \ˈtrō-ˌas\. **1.** *or* **The Tro·ad** \-ˌad\. Territory surrounding the ancient city of Troy in NW Mysia, Asia Minor, extending N from Cape Lectum (*mod.* Baba) to the Propontis (*mod.* Sea of Marmara) and E to include the Ida Mts. and plain of Scamander River (*mod.* Menderes).
2. *later* **Al·ex·an·dria Troas** \ˌal-ig-ˈzan-drē-ə-, ˈel-\. Seaport of Mysia, in SW part of the ancient region of Troas, and S of the site of Troy; visited by St. Paul on his 2d (*Acts* xvi. 8–11) and 3d missionary journeys.

Tro·bri·and Islands \ˈtrō-brē-ˌand\ *or* **Ki·ri·wi·na Islands** \ˌkir-ə-ˈwē-nə\. Group of small coral islands, Solomon Sea, SW Pacific Ocean, N of E end of New Guinea I. and N of D'Entrecasteaux Is.; 8°33′S, 151°05′E; total area 170 sq. mi. (440 sq. km.); largest Kiriwina I.; chief town Losuia; administratively attached to Papua New Guinea; occupied by Allies June 1943. Site of anthropological fieldwork conducted by English researcher Bronisław Malinowski (1915–18).

Troe·zen \ˈtrē-zən\. Town, SE ancient Argolis, E Peloponnese, S Greece, near the coast of the Saronic Gulf; celebrated in mythology as the home of legendary Attic hero Theseus.

Tro·gir \ˈtrō-gir\ *or Ital.* **Traù** \trä-ˈü\ *or Ger.* **Trau** \ˈtrau̇\; *anc.* **Tra·gu·ri·um** \trə-ˈgyu̇r-ē-əm\. Seaport, Croatia, near Split; pop. (1991p) 21,816; located on an island joined to mainland by a bridge; cathedral, dating in part from 13th cent.; Dominican monastery; museum. Colonized by Greeks from Siracusa in 4th cent. B.C.; since medieval times has been held by many states incl. Venice from early 15th to late 18th cents., Yugoslavia 1920–91, and independent Croatia since 1991.

Troia. See TROY 8.

Tro·i·na \trȯ-ˈē-nə\. Commune, Enna prov., cen. Sicily, Italy, 24 mi. (39 km.) NE of the commune of Enna on W slope of Mt. Etna; pop. (1981p) 10,643; Capuchin convent. In WWII scene of severe fighting bet. Germans and Allied forces July–Aug. 1943.

Trois–Évêchés, Les. See LES TROIS-ÉVÊCHÉS.

Trois Pis·toles \ˌtrwä-pi-ˈstōl\. Town, Rivière du Loup co., S Quebec, Canada, on right bank of St. Lawrence River 25 mi. (40 km.) NE of Rivière du Loup; pop. (1991c) 3886.

Trois–Ri·vières \ˌtrwä-rē-ˈvyer\. **1.** *or Eng.* **Three Rivers.** City, Francheville co., S Quebec, Canada, on N bank of St. Lawrence River at mouth of the St.-Maurice River, 75 mi. (121 km.) NE of Montreal; pop. (1991c) 49,426; paper, textiles, electrical equipment; Université du Québec á Trois-Rivières (1969). Founded by French explorer Samuel de Champlain 1634; developed as center of iron production mid-18th cent.; incorp. as city 1857.
2. Maritime village, S Basse-Terre, Guadeloupe, E West Indies.

Trois–Ri·vières–Ouest \ˌtrwä-rē-ˌvyer-ˈwest\ *or Eng.* **West Three Rivers.** Town, Francheville co., S Quebec, Canada, 4 mi. (6.4 km.) SW of Trois-Rivières; pop. (1991c) 20,076.

Tro·itsk \ˈtrȯitsk\. City, S Chelyabinsk Oblast, W Russia in Asia, on a tributary of the upper Tobol River 75 mi. (121 km.) S of the city of Chelyabinsk; pop. (1991e) 89,800; railroad junction point; supply and trading center for the S Ural mining district.

Troja. See TROY 8.

Trold·tin·der \ˈtrȯl-ˌtin-nər\. See ROMSDAL.

Troll·hät·tan \ˈtrȯl-ˌhet-tən\. Town, Älvsborg prov., SW Sweden, on Göta River near Lake Vänern; pop. (1993e) 51,673; falls in the river here which descends 108 ft. (33 m.) in ab. 1 mi. (1.6 km.) provide waterpower for the hydroelectric power plant; produces transport equipment, plastics.

Troll·tin·da·ne \ˈtrȯl-ˌtin-nä-nə\. See ROMSDAL.

Trom·be·tas \trōm-ˈbā-təs\. River, NW Pará state, N Brazil; flows S from Guyana border into Amazon River; ab. 470 mi. (755 km.) long.

Tro·me·lin \trȯm-ˈleⁿ\. Small uninhabited island, W Indian Ocean, ab. 260 mi. (420 km.) off NE Madagascar, 15°52′S, 54°25′E; administered from the French overseas dept. of Réunion; claimed also by Madagascar, Mauritius, and Seychelles.

Troms \ˈtrüms\. County of N Norway. See table at NORWAY.

Trom·sø \ˈtrüm-ˌsœ, -ˌsō\. Seaport, ⊗ of Troms co., N Norway, located on a small island bet. Kvaløy and the mainland; pop. (1990c) 50,548; chief city in N Norway; founded 13th cent.; developed late 19th cent. esp. as a center for fisheries; shipbuilding yards; exports fish; meteorological station; university.

Tro·na·dor, Mon·te \ˈmȯn-tā-ˌtrō-nä-ˈt͟hȯr\ *also* **El Tronador** \el-\. Volcano on Argentina-Chile boundary, near Lake Nahuel Huapí; 11,600 ft. (3536 m.).

Trond·heim \ˈtrȯn-ˌhām\; *formerly* **Trond·hjem** \ˈtrȯn-ˌyem, ˈtrün-\ *also* **Ni·da·ros** \ˈnē-də-ˌrōs\. Seaport, ⊗ of Sør-Trøndelag co., cen. Norway; pop. (1990c) 137,346; major seaport and 3d largest city of Norway; building materials, canned goods, soap, metal products; notable 12th cent. cathedral (restored after several fires, coronation place of Norwegian kings); 18th cent. royal palace; Technical Univ. of Norway (1900). Founded by King Olaf I Tryggvasson 997 and ✻ of Norway until 14th cent.; in WWII occupied by Germans Apr. 1940–May 1945.

Trondheim Fjord. Inlet of Norwegian Sea, lower W cen. coast of Norway; extends inland 78 mi. (126 km.).

Tron·to \ˈtrȯn-ˌtō\. River, cen. Italy; flows N and E into Adriatic; ab. 50 mi. (80 km.) long.

Troodos, Mount. See OLYMPUS, MOUNT 2.

Troon \ˈtrün\. Burgh, Strathclyde region, SW Scotland; pop. (1981p) 14,254; seaside resort; shipbuilding; shipyards.

Trop·a·co Point \ˈträ-pə-ˌkō\. Cape, N coast of St. Thomas I., Virgin Is. of the U.S., West Indies, on W side of Magens Bay.

Tropic of Can·cer \ˈkan-sər\. Parallel of latitude, approx. 23.5°N of the Equator; northernmost latitude reached by the overhead sun.

Tropic of Cap·ri·corn \ˈka-prə-ˌkȯrn\. Parallel of latitude, approx. 23.5°S of the Equator; southernmost latitude reached by the overhead sun.

Tro·po·jë \trȯ-ˈpȯ-yə\. District of N Albania. See table at ALBANIA.

Troppau. See OPAVA 2.

Tros·sachs, The *or* **Trossachs** \ˈträ-ˌsaks\. Wooded valley, Central region, cen. Scotland, bet. Loch Katrine and Loch Achray; immortalized by Scottish writer Sir Walter Scott's *Lady of the Lake* and *Rob Roy.*

Trotskoye. See GATCHINA.

Trot·wood \ˈträt-ˌwu̇d\. Village, Montgomery co., SW Ohio, 10 mi. (16 km.) NW of Dayton; pop. (1990c) 8811.

Trouée de Belfort. See BELFORT GAP.

Troup \ˈtrüp\. County in W Georgia. See table at GEORGIA.

Trous·dale \ˈtrüz-ˌdāl\. County in N Tennessee. See table at TENNESSEE.

Trout Lake \ˈtrau̇t\. Name of several lakes, Canada, incl.: (1) a source of English River, SW Ontario; 156 sq. mi. (404 sq. km.); (2) source of Mattawa River, SE Ontario.

Trouville *or in full* **Trou·ville–sur–Mer** \trü-ˌvēl-sue̅r-ˈmer\. Seaport, Calvados dept., NW France, ab. 25 mi. (40 km.) NE of Caen just NE of Deauville; pop. (1990c) 5645; popular resort; imports timber, coal, cement.

Trow·bridge \ˈtrō-ˌbrij\. Town, ⊗ of Wiltshire, S England; pop. (1981c) 23,123; woolens, dairy products, gloves, beer.

Troy \ˈtrȯi\. **1.** Commercial city, ⊗ of Pike co., SE Alabama, 48 mi. (77 km.) SSE of Montgomery; pop. (1990c) 13,051; lumber; agriculture; Troy State Univ. (1887).
2. City, ⊗ of Doniphan co., NE Kansas; pop. (1990c) 1073.
3. City, Oakland co., SE Michigan, SE of Pontiac; pop. (1990c) 72,884; residential; Walsh Coll. of Accountancy and Business Administration (1922).
4. City, ⊗ of Lincoln co., E Missouri; pop. (1990c) 3811.

5. City, ⊗ of Rensselaer co., E New York, on E bank of Hudson River 8 mi. (13 km.) NE of Albany; pop. (1990c) 54,269; at head of tidewater navigation on Hudson River and opp. mouth of Mohawk River and outlet of New York State Barge Canal; produces automobile parts; Rensselaer Polytechnic Institute (1824), Russell Sage Coll. (1916), Hudson Valley Community Coll. (1953); settled in 1780s; incorp. as city 1816; major center of steel industry until after Civil War.

6. Town, ⊗ of Montgomery co., S cen. North Carolina, 40 mi. (64 km.) S of High Point; pop. (1990c) 3404.

7. City, ⊗ of Miami co., W Ohio, 19 mi. (31 km.) N of Dayton; pop. (1990c) 19,478.

8. *or* **Il·i·um** \ˈi-lē-əm\; *anc.* **Tro·ia** \ˈtrȯi-ə, ˈtrō-yə\ *or* **Tro·ja** \ˈtrō-jə, -yə\ *or* **Il·i·on** \ˈi-lē-ˌän, -ən\. Ancient ruined city in Troas, NW Asia Minor, S of the Dardanelles; an archaeological site (*mod.* Hissarlik, Turkey in Asia) on Menderes River, said to have nine cities built each on the ruins of its predecessor, dating from Neolithic period to Roman times (c. 3000 B.C.–4th cent. A.D.). In Greek legend besieged by the confederated Greek armies during a 10-year war (Trojan War), captured, and destroyed, probably c. 1200 B.C.; its story told in the *Iliad, Odyssey,* and *Aeneid,* by the cyclic poets, and in medieval romances.

Troyes \ˈtrwä\; *anc.* **Au·gus·tob·o·na Tri·cas·si·um** \ˌȯ-gə-ˈstä-bə-nə-trī-ˈka-sē-əm\. City, ✻ of Aube dept., NE France, on Seine River 92 mi. (148 km.) SE of Paris; pop. (1990c) 60,755; center of French hosiery industry; textile machinery, tires; 13th–17th cent. cathedral; 13th cent. basilica of St. Urbain; several other notable churches.

History: In pre-Roman times a chief town of the Tricassi tribe of ancient Gaul; sacked by Normans 9th cent. A.D.; made ✻ of Champagne 11th cent.; by 12th cent. a prosperous commercial town, site of the great Champagne fairs; gave name to system of measuring (*troy weight*) first used at the fairs; treaty bet. King Charles VI of France and King Henry V of England concluded here 1420; English expelled by French national heroine Joan of Arc 1429; a center of Protestantism and declined after revocation of Edict of Nantes 1685.

Tru·an·do \trü-ˈän-dō\. River, W Colombia; a W tributary of the Atrato flowing E; ab. 60 mi. (95 km.) long.

Tru·chas Peaks \ˈtrü-chəs\. Three mountain peaks, N New Mexico, NE of Santa Fe; the highest is over 13,000 ft. (3960 m.).

Trucial Coast, Trucial Oman, Trucial States. See UNITED ARAB EMIRATES.

Truck·ee \ˈtrə-kē\. River, W Nevada; rises in Placer co., E California, flows E and NE into Pyramid Lake, S Washoe co., NW Nevada; 120 mi. (193 km.) long.

Trues·dell Heights \ˈtrüz-dᵊl\. Elevation, Garrett co., NW corner of Maryland; 2809 ft. (856 m.).

Tru·jil·lo \trü-ˈhē-yō\. **1.** Seaport, ✻ of Colón dept., Honduras, 58 mi. (93 km.) NE of Tegucigalpa; pop. (1988p) 5547; founded c. 1525. American filibuster William Walker killed nearby 1860.

2. Coastal city, NW Peru, 9 mi. (14 km.) from its port and ab. 315 mi. (505 km.) NW of Lima; pop. (1981p) 193,528; ships sugar; produces textiles, foodstuffs, soap; cathedral; university (1824); city founded c. 1534; 4 mi. (6 km.) to the W are the ruins of the pre-Incan city Chan-Chan; in area to S, ruins of temples of Moche empire (first millennium A.D.).

3. Commune, Cáceres prov., W Spain, 25 mi. (40 km.) ENE of the commune of Cáceres; pop. (1991c) 9085; birthplace of Spanish conqueror Francisco Pizarro c. 1475.

4. State of W cen. Venezuela. See table at VENEZUELA.

5. Town, ✻ of Trujillo state, W cen. Venezuela, on W slope of the Cordillera de Mérida ab. 60 mi. (95 km.) E of Lake Maracaibo; pop. (1990p) 32,683; market town.

Trujillo, Monte. See DUARTE, PICO.

Trujillo Al·to \ˈäl-tō\. Municipality, NE Puerto Rico; pop. (1990c) 61,120.

Truk. See CHUUK.

Tru·mann \ˈtrü-mən\. City, Poinsett co., NE Arkansas, 15 mi. (24 km.) S of Jonesboro; pop. (1990c) 6304.

Trum·bull \ˈtrəm-bəl\. **1.** County in NE Ohio. See table at OHIO.

2. Town, SE Fairfield co., SW Connecticut, N of Bridgeport; pop. (1990c) 32,016; residential.

Trumbull, Mount. Peak, N Mohave co., NW Arizona; 8028 ft. (2447 m.).

Tru·ro \ˈtrůr-ˌō\. **1.** Town, ⊗ of Colchester co., cen. Nova Scotia, Canada, near head (E end) of Minas Basin; pop. (1991c) 11,683; lumber, clothing; truck, dairy farms; Nova Scotia Agricultural Coll. (1905). One of the principal Acadian settlements abandoned 1755 when the inhabitants were expelled by the British; resettled chiefly by New England colonists c. 1761.

2. Town, ⊗ of Cornwall and Isles of Scilly co., SW England, at head of Falmouth Harbor 40 mi. (64 km.) W of Plymouth; pop. (1981c) 16,348; cathedral.

Truss·ville \ˈtrəs-ˌvil\. Town, Jefferson co., cen. Alabama, 10 mi. (16 km.) NNE of Birmingham; pop. (1990c) 8266.

Trust Territory of Somalia. See ITALIAN SOMALILAND.

Truth or Con·se·quen·ces \ˌtrüth-ər-ˈkän-sə-ˌkwen-səz\; *formerly* **Hot Springs.** Town, ⊗ of Sierra co., SW New Mexico, on the Rio Grande 60 mi. (96 km.) NNW of Las Cruces; pop. (1990c) 6221; hot mineral springs; renamed for a radio program 1950.

Trut·nov \ˈtrůt-ˌnȯf\ *or Ger.* **Trau·te·nau** \ˈtraůt-ᵊn-ˌaů\. Town, N Czech Republic, 83 mi. (133 km.) NE of Prague at foot of the Riesengebirge; pop. (1989c) 31,878.

Try·on \ˈtrī-ən\. Village, ⊗ of McPherson co., W cen. Nebraska.

Tsaidam. See QAIDAM.

Tsala Apop·ka Lake \tə-ˈsa-lə-ə-ˈpäp-kə\. Lake, E Citrus co., W Florida Penin.; ab. 15 mi. (24 km.) long; outlet through Withlacoochee River; has many islands.

Tsamkong. See ZHANJIANG.

Tsana, Lake. See TANA, LAKE.

Tsangpo. See ZANGBO.

Tsan·gwu. See WUZHOU.

Tsa·ra·ta·na·na Massif \ˌtsär-ə-ˈtä-nə-ˌnä\. Mountain group in N Madagascar; highest peak 9436 ft. (2876 m.), the highest point in Madagascar.

Tsaritsyn. See VOLGOGRAD.

Tsarskoye Selo. See PUSHKIN.

Tsa·vo \ˈtsä-ˌvō\. River, SE Kenya; flows from Kilimanjaro into the Galana River; ab. 80 mi. (130 km.) long.

Tsavo National Park; *formerly* **Royal Tsavo National Park.** National park, S Kenya; 8034 sq. mi. (20,808 sq. km.); semiarid region; great variety of wildlife, incl. antelope, elephant, rhinoceros, hippopotamus, lion; estab. 1948.

Tschaslau. See ČÁSLAV.

Tscheliads. See CZELADŹ.

Tschenstochau. See CZĘSTOCHOWA.

Tselinograd. See ASTANA.

Tsentral'no–Chernozemnyy Rayon. See CENTRAL BLACK EARTH REGION.

Tsernagora. See MONTENEGRO 1.

Tsesis. See CĒSIS.

Tsé·vié \ˈtsā-ˌvyā\. Town, S Togo, ab. 20 mi. (32 km.) N of Lomé; pop. (1981c) 20,247.

Tshua·pa *or* **Chua·pa** \chə-ˈwäp-ə\. River, S cen. Africa; flows W in N cen. Democratic Rep. of the Congo and empties into Busira River; ab. 420 mi. (675 km.) long.

Tsien Tang. See FUCHUN.

Tsil'ma \ˈtsilʸ-mə\. River, NW Komi Rep., NE Russia in Europe; a W tributary of the Pechora, flowing N and E to the Pechora at Ust' Tsil'ma; ab. 125 mi. (200 km.) long; navigable.

Tsinan. See JINAN.

Tsinchow. See TIANSHUI.

Tsinghai. See QINGHAI.

Tsingtao *or Ger.* **Tsingtau.** See QINGDAO.

Tsingyüan. See BAODING.

Tsinkiang. See QUANZHOU.

Tsinling Shan. See QINLING SHANDI.

Tsitsihar. See QIQIHAR.

Ts'khin·va·li *or* **Tskhin·va·li** \ˈtskin-və-lē\; *formerly* **Sta·li·nir** \ˌstä-lə-ˈnir\. Town, ✱ of South Ossetia, Republic of Georgia, 60 mi. (96 km.) NW of Tbilisi; pop. (1991e) 42,600.

Tsna \ˈtsnä\. See TAMBOV OBLAST.

Tsu \ˈtsü\. Seaport city, ✱ of Mie prefecture, on W shore of Ise Bay in S Honshū, Japan, 37 mi. (60 km.) SW of Nagoya; pop. (1992e) 161,436; bombed by U.S. planes July 1945 during WWII.

Tsu·chi·u·ra \tsü-ˈchē-ü-rä\. City, Ibaraki prefecture, Honshū, Japan, 42 mi. (68 km.) NE of Tokyo; pop. (1990p) 127,470.

Tsuen Wan \ˈtswen-ˈwen\. Industrial settlement, New Territories, Hong Kong.

Tsu·ga·ru Strait \tsü-ˈgär-ü\. Channel bet. islands of Honshū and Hokkaidō, Japan; 15 to 25 mi. (24 to 32 km.) wide.

Tsu·ku·ba \tsü-ˈkü-bä\. City, Ibaraki prefecture, SE Honshū, Japan; pop. (1990p) 143,408.

Tsu·meb \ˈtsü-ˌmeb\. Town, N Namibia, 225 mi. (362 km.) NNE of Windhoek; pop. (1988e) 13,500; chief copper-mining center in the territory; lead and silver also mined.

Tsun–i *or* **Tsunyi.** See ZUNYI.

Tsu·ru·o·ka \ˌtsü-rü-ˈō-kä\. City, Yamagata prefecture, N Honshū, Japan, near W coast S of Sakata; pop. (1990p) 99,891; produces silk fabrics.

Tsu·shi·ma \tsü-ˈshē-mä, ˈtsü-shē-ˌmä\. Island, Korea Strait, part of Nagasaki prefecture, Japan; ab. 40 mi. (64 km.) long; 271 sq. mi. (702 sq. km.).

Tsushima Strait. Channel bet. Tsushima I. and NW Kyūshū, Japan, connecting the Sea of Japan with the East China Sea and forming the SE part of Korea Strait; ab. 63 mi. (101 km.) wide. Site of battle in the Russo-Japanese War in which the Russian fleet was destroyed or captured May 1905 by Japanese fleet under Admiral Togō Heihachirō.

Tsu·ya·ma \tsü-ˈyä-mä\. Inland town, Okayama prefecture, in center of W extension of Honshū, Japan, 30 mi. (48 km.) N of the city of Okayama; pop. (1990p) 89,405.

Tu·a·la·tin \ˌtü-ˈä-lə-tən\. City, Washington co., NW Oregon; pop. (1990c) 15,013.

Tu·am \ˈtü-əm\. Town, N co. Galway, W Ireland; pop. (1986c) 4109; seat of a Catholic archbishop and of a Church of Ireland bishop.

Tu·a·mo·tu Archipelago \ˌtü-ə-ˈmō-tü\ *also* **Low Archipelago** *or* **Pa·u·mo·tu** \paù-ˈmō-tü\ *or* **Dan·ger·ous Archipelago** \ˈdān-jə-rəs\. Group of ab. 80 small islands, French Polynesia, S Pacific Ocean, E of Society Is. and S of the Marquesas; ab. 14° to 23°S and 134° to 149°W; 331 sq. mi. (857 sq. km.); pop. (1988c) 11,754; mostly low coral atolls; chief islands Makatéa, Fakarava, Rangiroa, Anaa, Hao, and Reao; administratively linked with their SE extension, the Gambier Is. Part of group visited 1606 by Portuguese navigator Pedro Fernandes de Queirós in service of Spain; occupied by France 1844 and annexed after 1880; site of nuclear testing by France since mid-1960s.

Tuapi, Laguna. See TABERIS, LAGUNA.

Tu·ap·se \ˌtü-ˌäp-ˈse\; *formerly* **Vel·ya·mi·nov·ski** *or* **Vel'·ya·mi·nov·skiy** \vel-ˌyä-mi-ˈnȯf-skē\. Seaport town, S Krasnodar Kray, S Russia in Europe, on Black Sea coast; pop. (1991e) 63,800; terminus of oil pipelines from Grozny through Armavir and Maykop; oil refineries, shipyards; food processing; founded 1838.

Tu·ban *or Du.* **Toe·ban** \ˈtü-ˌbän\. Seaport, N Java coast, East Java prov., Indonesia, 55 mi. (88 km.) NW of Surabaya; pop. (1980c) 50,977.

Tu·ba·rão \ˌtü-bə-ˈraùⁿ\. Municipality, Santa Catarina state, S Brazil, 210 mi. (338 km.) S of Curitiba; pop. (1991p) 95,057.

Tub·ber·gen \ˈtə-bər-kə\. Commune, Overijssel prov., E Netherlands, near German border; pop. (1981e) 17,633.

Tu·bi·gon \tü-ˈbē-ˌgōn\. Municipality, Bohol prov., on W coast of Bohol I., Philippines, on Bohol Strait 22 mi. (35 km.) NNE of Tagbilaran; pop. (1980c) 29,993.

Tü·bing·en \ˈtue-biŋ-ən, ˈtü-, ˈtyü-\. City, Baden-Württemberg, Germany, on Neckar River 17 mi. (27 km.) S of Stuttgart; pop. (1992e) 82,483; machinery, textiles, paper; publishing center; 16th cent. castle; 15th cent. church; 15th cent. town hall (restored); university (1477), one of the most noted German universities, with which the names of religious reformer Philipp Melanchthon, theologian Ferdinand Christian Baur, and others are associated. First mentioned 1078; sold to Württemberg 1342; captured by Swabian League 1519; changed hands several times during Thirty Years' War (1618–48).

Tubruq. See TOBRUK.

Tubuai Islands. See AUSTRAL ISLANDS.

Tubuai Manu. See MAIAO.

Tu·bu·ran \tü-ˈbür-ˌän\. Municipality, NW coast of Cebu I., Philippines; on Tanon Strait ab. 30 mi. (48 km.) NNW of City of Cebu; pop. (1980c) 42,968; has good port.

Tuck·a·hoe \ˈtə-kə-ˌhō\. **1.** River, SE New Jersey; flows from W Atlantic co. S and E into Great Egg Harbor.
2. Village, Westchester co., SE New York, 18 mi. (29 km.) NNE of New York City; pop. (1990c) 6302; residential suburb of Yonkers and New York City.

Tuck·a·se·gee *also* **Tuck·a·sei·gee** \ˌtə-kə-ˈsē-je\. River in SW North Carolina; dammed in Jackson co.

Tuck·er \ˈtə-kər\. County in NE West Virginia. See table at WEST VIRGINIA.

Tuck·er·man Ravine \ˈtə-kər-mən\. Gorge, S side of Mt. Washington, Presidential Range, White Mts., New Hampshire; trail from Pinkham Notch to the summit of Mt. Washington.

Tuck·er·nuck Island \ˈtə-kər-ˌnək\. Island in Atlantic Ocean, S of Cape Cod, Massachusetts; part of Nantucket co., Massachusetts.

Tu·co·pia \tü-ˈkō-pē-ə\. Small island, E Santa Cruz Is., SW Pacific Ocean, ESE of Vanikoro.

Tuc·son \ˈtü-ˌsän, *locally also* tü-ˈsän\. Commercial and residential city, ⊗ of Pima co., Arizona, on Santa Cruz River 103 mi. (166 km.) SE of Phoenix; pop. (1990c) 405,390; alt. 2389 ft. (728 m.); railroad junction; aircraft parts, electronic components, guided missiles, optical goods; tourist and health resort; Univ. of Arizona (1885); Davis-Monthan Air Force Base; largest U.S. city totally dependent on groundwater.
History: San Xavier del Bac Indian mission founded by Spanish near site of modern city in 1700; site of Spanish presidio by 1776; acquired by U.S. through Gadsden Purchase 1853; territorial ✱ 1867–77; incorp. as city 1883.

Tu·cu·mán \ˌtü-kü-ˈmän\. **1.** Province of N Argentina. See table at ARGENTINA.
2. City, N Argentina. See SAN MIGUEL DE TUCUMÁN.

Tu·cum·cari \ˈtü-kəm-ˌkar-ē\. City, ⊗ of Quay co., E New Mexico, 60 mi. (96 km.) NNW of Clovis; pop. (1990c) 6831; resort; ships livestock; grain farms.

Tu·cu·pi·ta \ˌtü-kü-ˈpē-tä\. Town, ✱ of Delta Amacuro terr., NE Venezuela, in delta of the Orinoco; pop. (1990p) 40,946.

Tu·de·la \tü-ˈt͟hā-lä\; *anc.* **Tu·te·la** \tü-ˈtē-lə\. Commune, Navarra prov., N Spain, on Ebro River 52 mi. (84 km.) S of Pamplona; pop. (1991c) 26,461; 12th cent. church. Conquered by Arabs 716; reconquered by Alfonso I of Aragon c. 1115; made episcopal see late 18th cent.

Tuder. See TODI.

Tudmur. See TADMUR.

Tug·a·loo *also* **Tug·a·lo** \ˈtə-gə-ˌlō\. River, NE Georgia; forms section of NE Georgia boundary with South Carolina and unites with the Seneca River in W Anderson co., NW South Carolina, to form the Savannah River. Upper course known as Chattooga River.

Tu·ge·la \tü-ˈgā-lə\. River, cen. KwaZulu-Natal prov., E Rep. of South Africa; rises in Mont aux Sources, where it plunges through a gorge forming **Tugela Falls** (total drop 3110 ft. or 948 m. in five falls, of which highest is 1350 ft. or 411 m.), and flows E to the Indian Ocean; 312 mi. (502 km.) long; not navigable; scene of battles of the Boer War 1899–1900, esp. at Colenso.

Tug Fork \ˈtəg\. River, SW West Virginia; rises in McDowell co., flows NW and forms Kentucky-West Virginia boundary until it unites with Levisa Fork to form Big Sandy River (*q.v.*).

Tuggurt. See TOUGGOURT.

Tugh·luq·a·bad *or* **Tugh·lak·a·bad** \tu̇g-ˈlə-kə-ˌbäd\. Ancient city, India, ab. 4 mi. (6 km.) to the E of the site of Old Delhi; erected c. 1321 by Ghiyās-ud-Dīn Tughluq, sultan of Delhi and founder of the Tughluq dynasty. Ruins of its walls and fort remain. See DELHI 2.

Tu·gue·ga·rao \ˌtü-gā-gä-ˈrau̇\. Municipality, ✻ of Cagayan prov., Luzon, Philippines, E side of Cagayan River, 240 mi. (386 km.) NNE of Manila; pop. (1980c) 73,507. In WWII held by Japanese Dec. 1941 to June 1945.

Tui *or* **Túy** \ˈtü-ē, ˈtwē\. Commune, Pontevedra prov., NW Spain, 30 mi. (48 km.) S of the commune of Pontevedra; pop. (1991c) 15,242; mineral baths; 12th cent. cathedral; ✻ of Visigoths c. 700.

Tui·ra \ˈtwē-rä\. River, Panama prov., E cen. Panama; rises near Colombian border, flows N and NW to Gulf of San Miguel; ab. 90 mi. (145 km.) long.

Tu·kang·be·si Islands *also* **Toe·kang·be·si Islands** \ˌtü-käŋ-ˈbā-sē\. Group of ab. 16 islands, W Banda Sea, SE of Butung Is., Sulawesi, Indonesia; largest island Wangiwangi.

Tu·kao \tü-ˈkau̇\. Village, N end of island of Manihiki, Northern Cook Is., cen. Pacific Ocean.

Tuk·uh·nik·i·vatz, Mount \ˌtə-kə-ˈni-kə-ˌväts\. Peak, N San Juan co., SE Utah; 12,004 ft. (3659 m.).

Tuk·wila \ˌtək-ˈwi-lə\. City, King co., W cen. Washington, 9 mi. (14 km.) SSE of Seattle; pop. (1990c) 11,874; pop. more than tripled bet. 1980 and 1990.

Tu·la \ˈtü-lä\. **1.** *or in full* **Tula de Al·len·de** \-thä-ä-ˈyen-dā\. Town, SW Hidalgo state, cen. Mexico, 45 mi. (72 km.) N of Mexico City; munic. pop. (1990p) 71,622. Excavations nearby have revealed ruins believed to be remains of ancient ✻ of the Toltecs, dating back probably to 10th cent. A.D.

2. City, ✻ of Tula Oblast, Russia in Europe, on a tributary of the Oka River 110 mi. (177 km.) S of Moscow; pop. (1992e) 541,000; industrial center producing armaments, chemicals, samovars; 16th cent. citadel (restored).

History: First mentioned 1146; important fortress on S approaches to Moscow in 16th cent.; center of Russian ironworking c. 17th cent.; made site of armament factory by Czar Peter the Great 1712; in WWII scene of heavy fighting in Oct. 1941 during German advance on Moscow.

Tu·la·gi \tü-ˈlä-gē\. Small island, S cen. Solomon Is., W Pacific Ocean, 22 mi. (35 km.) N of Guadalcanal I.; pop. (1986c) 1267; chief town Tulagi, on SE coast, former ✻ of British Solomon Is. protectorate, has fine harbor. Island seized from Japan by U.S. marines during WWII 1942.

Tu·la·in·yo Lake \ˌtü-lə-ˈin-yō\. Lake, Tulare and Inyo cos., California, 1.5 mi. (2.4 km.) NE of Mt. Whitney; elev. 12,865 ft. (3921 m.); highest lake in the U.S. having an area of more than one tenth of a sq. mi. or two tenths of a sq. km.

Tu·lan·cin·go \ˌtü-län-ˈsiŋ-gō\. Town, Hidalgo state, cen. Mexico, 65 mi. (105 km.) NE of Mexico City; munic. pop. (1990p) 91,831.

Tula Oblast \ˈō-bləst, -ˌblast\ *or* **Tul'·ska·ya Oblast'** \ˈtu̇lʸ-skə-yə-ˈō-bləstʸ\. Subdivision of Russia in Europe, S of Moscow; 9923 sq. mi. (25,700 sq. km.); pop. (1992e) 1,844,000; ✻ Tula; traversed by upper Don and tributaries and by the Oka; has rich soil in S part; produces rye, wheat and other grains, sugar beets, vegetables; has chemical, metallurgical, and engineering industries. Chief cities Tula, Novomoskovsk. Organized 1930s as a separate region; during WWII much of oblast briefly occupied by Germans in winter of 1941–42.

Tu·lare \tü-ˈlar-ē, -ˈlar\. **1.** County in S cen. California. See table at CALIFORNIA.

2. City, Tulare co., S cen. California, 42 mi. (68 km.) SE of Fresno; pop. (1990c) 33,249; founded 1872.

Tu·la·ro·sa \ˌtü-lə-ˈrō-sə, -zə\. Village, Otero co., S New Mexico, 65 mi. (105 km.) NNE of Las Cruces; pop. (1990c) 2615.

Tul·cán \tül-ˈkän\. Town, ✻ of Carchi prov., N Ecuador, near Colombian frontier and 90 mi. (145 km.) NE of Quito; pop. (1990c) 37,069.

Tul·cea \ˈtül-chä\. **1.** County of SE Romania. See table at ROMANIA.

2. Town, its ⊗, in delta of the Danube near border with Ukraine, ab. 60 mi. (96 km.) N of Constanta; pop. (1989c) 94,935; shipbuilding, fishing.

Tuléar. See TOLIARA.

Tu·le Lake \ˈtü-lē\. Small lake, NE corner of Siskiyou co., N California; site of Japanese-American internment camp during WWII nearby.

Tu·lia \ˈtül-yə\. City, ⊗ of Swisher co., NW Texas, in the Panhandle 25 mi. (40 km.) N of Plainview; pop. (1990c) 4699.

Tu·li·ta \ˌtü-ˈlē-tə\; *formerly* **Fort Nor·man** \ˈnȯr-mən\. Hamlet on Mackenzie River, W mainland part of Northwest Territories, Canada, at mouth of Great Bear River; pop. (1991c) 375.

Tul·la·ho·ma \ˌtə-lə-ˈhō-mə\. City and summer resort, Coffee and Franklin cos., S cen. Tennessee, 25 mi. (40 km.) ENE of Fayetteville; pop. (1990c) 16,761; leather goods, sporting equipment; tobacco.

Tul·la·more \ˌtə-lə-ˈmōr\. Town, ⊗ of co. Offaly, cen. Ireland; pop. (1991p) 8623; brewing, distilling.

Tulle \ˈtu̅e̅l\. City, ✻ of Corrèze dept., S cen. France, 47 mi. (76 km.) SSE of Limoges; pop. (1990c) 18,685; government small-arms factory; 12th cent. cathedral; 17th cent. church. Founded in 7th cent.; taken by English and devastated by Black Death mid-14th cent.; retaken by King Charles V of France c. 1370; came under Huguenots 1585. Its name was given to the fine net used in veils, ballet costumes, and other garments.

Tullum. See TOUL.

Tully \ˈtə-lē\. Short river, NE Queensland, Australia; contains **Tully Falls,** 450 ft. (137 m.) high.

Tulmaythah. See TOLMETA.

Tu·lo·ma \tu̇-ˈlō-mə\. River, NW Murmansk Oblast, NW Russia in Europe; flows E to head of Kola Bay; ab. 175 mi. (280 km.) long; its chief tributary is the Kola.

Tul·sa \ˈtəl-sə\. **1.** County in NE Oklahoma. See table at OKLAHOMA.

2. City, its ⊗, on Arkansas River; pop. (1990c) 367,302; financial, commercial, and transportation center of oil-producing region; aircraft engineering and maintenance; gas and coal deposits; Univ. of Tulsa (1894), Oral Roberts Univ. (1963). Settled in 1830s as Creek Indian village; modern town founded 1882 and incorp. 1898; developed rapidly after discovery of oil nearby in early 20th cent.

Tul'skaya Oblast'. See TULA OBLAST.

Tul·ti·tlán \ˌtül-tē-ˈtlän\. Municipality, México state, Mexico, 14 mi. (23 km.) N of Mexico City.

Tu·luá \ˌtü-lü-ˈä\. Town, Valle del Cauca dept., W Colombia, ab. 50 mi. (80 km.) NNE of Cali; pop. (1985c) 101,699.

T'ulufan. See TURPAN.

T'u–lu–ka–erh–t'e. See TURUGART PASS.

Tu·lun \tu̇-ˈlün\. Town, W Irkutsk Oblast, S Russia in Asia, on Trans-Siberian R.R. 225 mi. (362 km.) NW of the city of Irkutsk; pop. (1991e) 53,700.

Tu·lung·a·gung *or Du.* **Toe·loeng·a·goeng** \ˌtü-lu̇ŋ-ˈä-gu̇ŋ\. City, East Java prov., Indonesia, 20 mi. (32 km.) S of Malang; pop. (1980c) 61,728.

Tu·ma·ca·co·ri National Historical Park \ˌtü-mə-ˈkä-kə-rē\; *formerly* **Tumacacori National Monument.** See UNITED STATES, *National Historical Parks.*

Tu·ma·co \tü-ˈmä-kō\. Seaport, W Nariño dept., SW Colombia; munic. pop. (1985c) 49,062; located on an island; southernmost Pacific port of Colombia; exports nuts, tobacco.

Tuman–gang. See TUMEN.

Tumapel. See SINGOSARI.

Tu·ma·tu·ma·ri Falls \ˌtü-mä-tü-ˈmä-rē\. Waterfall in the Essequibo River, cen. Guyana.

Tum·ba, Lake \ˈtüm-bə\. Lake, Équateur administrative region W Democratic Rep. of the Congo, SW of Mbandaka; 23 mi. (37 km.) long, 8 to 12 mi. (13 to 19 km.) wide; the Ubangi and Congo rivers meet just NW of the lake.

Tum·bes \ˈtüm-bās\. Town, NW Peru, on Tumbes River ab. 645 mi. (1040 km.) NW of Lima, near Ecuador border; pop.

(1990e) 64,800. Spanish conqueror Francisco Pizarro landed nearby for his invasion of Peru (1532).

Tu·men *also* **T'u–men** \ˈtü-ˈmən\ *or Russ.* **Tu·myn'·tszyan** \tu̇-ˈmēn^{y}-tsyən\ *or Korean* **Tu·man–gang** \tü-ˈmän-ˈgäŋ\. River, boundary bet. NE North Korea and NE China; rises in Ch'ang-pai Shan, North Korea, flows generally N and NE but in its lower course turns sharply SE to the Sea of Japan; 324 mi. (521 km.) long; for ab. 11 mi. (18 km.) from its mouth forms boundary of North Korea with Primorskiy Kray, Russia; navigable for light craft for ab. 30 mi. (48 km.).

Tum·kur \tu̇m-ˈku̇r\. Town, E Karnataka state, S India, ab. 40 mi. (64 km.) NW of Bangalore; pop. (1991p) 138,598; soap, tools; rice mill.

Tumluk. See TAMLUK.

Tum·mo \ˈtu̇-mō\. Town and oasis, SW Libya, in the mountains on the border of Niger.

Tum·pat \ˈtu̇m-ˌpät\. Coastal town, N Kelantan state, Malaysia; pop. (1980p) 89,344; port of Kota Baharu.

Tu·muc–Hu·mac Mountains \tü-ˈmük-ü-ˈmäk, ˈtü-mük-ˈü-mäk\ *or* **Ser·ra Tu·mu·cu·ma·que** \ˈser-rä-tü-ˌmü-kü-ˈmä-kā\. Range, NE Brazil, extending W to E along the boundary bet. Suriname and French Guiana on the N, and Brazil on the S; averages 2000 to 3000 ft. (610 to 915 m.).

Tum·wa·ter \ˈtəm-ˌwȯ-tər, -ˌwä-\. Town, Thurston co., Washington, SW of Olympia; pop. (1990c) 9976; one of the first permanent settlements in the state 1845.

Tumyn'tszyan. See TUMEN.

Tu·na, Point \ˈtü-nä\. Cape, SE Puerto Rico.

Tu·na·ri \tü-ˈnä-rē\. Peak, W Cochabamba dept., cen. Bolivia; 17,060 ft. (5200 m.).

Tunas. See VICTORIA DE LAS TUNAS.

Tunb \ˈtü-nəb\. Two small islands, **Greater Tunb** and **Lesser Tunb,** Persian Gulf, ab. 68 mi. (109 km.) N of Dubayy; claimed by United Arab Emirates and Iran; occupied by Iran 1971; object of renewed dispute bet. claimants after 1992.

Tun·bridge Wells \ˈtən-brij-ˈwelz\; *officially* **Royal Tunbridge Wells.** Town, Kent, SE England; pop. (1983e) 44,821.

Tun·ce·li \ˌtün-je-ˈlē\. Province of Turkey in Asia; ✻ Kalan. See table at TURKEY.

Tun·dzha *or* **Tun·ja** \ˈtu̇n-ˌjä\. River, SE Bulgaria; rises in Balkan Mts. W of Kazanlŭk, flows E then S into the Maritsa River at Edirne, Turkey in Europe; ab. 160 mi. (255 km.) long.

Tu·ne·mah Peak \ˈtü-nə-ˌmä\. Mountain in the Sierra Nevada, E Fresno co., S cen. California; 11,873 ft. (3619 m.).

Tunes. See TUNIS 2.

Tung. See DONG.

Tun·ga·bha·dra \ˌtu̇ŋ-gə-ˈbə-drə\. River, S India; formed by confluence of Tunga and Bhadra rivers in W Karnataka; flows NE along N border of Andhra Pradesh to the Krishna River; ab. 400 mi. (645 km.) long.

T'ung–chiang. See TONGJIANG.

Tungchow. **1.** City, Jiangsu prov., China. See NANTONG.
2. Town, Shaanxi prov., China. See DALI 1.
3. City, Beijing municipality, China. See TONGXIAN.

T'ung–hsien *or* **Tunghsien.** See TONGXIAN.

T'ung–hua *or* **Tung·hwa** \ˈtu̇ŋ-ˈhwä\. **1.** Former province, S Manchukuo; 12,216 sq. mi. (31,639 sq. km.).
2. City, Jilin prov., NE China. See TONGHUA.

Tung·kil \tu̇ŋ-ˈkēl\. Town, Tongquil I., Philippines; chief town of Samales group.

T'ung–ling. See TONGLING.

T'ung–shan. See XUZHOU.

Tung–t'ing Hu *or* **Tungting Hu.** See DONGTING HU.

Tun·gu·ra·hua \ˌtu̇ŋ-gü-ˈrä-wä\. **1.** Volcano in the Andes, Ecuador; 16,684 ft. (5085 m.).
2. Province of cen. Ecuador. See table at ECUADOR.

Tun·gu·ska \tu̇n-ˈgü-skə, təŋ-\. Name of three rivers in cen. Siberia, Russia in Asia, tributaries of Yenisey River: (1) **Lower Tunguska** *or Russ.* **Nizh·nya·ya Tunguska** \ˌnish-nə-yə\, ab. 2000 mi. (3220 km.) long, rises in N cen. Irkutsk Oblast and flows N, crossing into Evenki Autonomous Okrug at ab. 63°30′N, then flowing W to the Yenisey at Turukhansk; Tura, ✻ of Evenki, is on it. (2) **Stony Tunguska** *or Russ.* **Pod·ka·men·na·ya Tunguska** \pət-ˈká-mə-nə-yə\, ab. 1000 mi. (1610 km.) long, rises in SE corner of Evenki Autonomous Okrug and flows WNW into the Yenisey at ab. 61°30′N. Region was site June 1908, of an immense airborne explosion of uncertain origin which leveled ab. 1200 sq. mi. (3108 sq. km.) of forest. (3) **Upper Tunguska.** See ANGARA 1.

Tun–huang *also* **Tunhwang.** See DUNHUANG.

Tu·ni·ca \ˈtü-nə-kə\. **1.** County in NW Mississippi. See table at MISSISSIPPI.
2. Town, its ⊗; pop. (1990c) 1175.

Tu·nis \ˈtü-nəs, ˈtyü-\. **1.** Former Barbary state, N Africa; the region S and W of the ancient city of Carthage (*q.v.*); Roman province of Africa from 2d cent. B.C. to 5th cent. A.D. when it was overrun by Vandals; reconquered by Byzantine Empire 6th cent.; taken by Muslims 7th cent.; invaded by King Louis IX of France on Eighth Crusade 1270; attacked by Holy Roman Emperor Charles V as stronghold of Barbary corsair Khayr ad-Dīn (Barbarossa), 1535; conquered by Turks 1574; engaged in piracy (see BARBARY); in late 19th cent., because of debts of its bey, accepted financial control by England, France, and Italy; after years of dispute bet. French and Italians, invaded by France and became French protectorate 1881. See TUNISIA.
2. *anc.* **Tu·nes** \ˈtü-nēz, ˈtyü-\. City, ✻ of Tunisia, in NE part SW of ancient Carthage; pop. (1989e) 620,149; produces textiles, carpets, olive oil, cement; railroad shops, lead smelter; Univ. of Tunis (1960). Situated on an isthmus bet. two lagoons; E lagoon is **Lake of Tunis,** at E end of which is Halq al-Wadi, port of the city of Tunis, with large trade. City divided into old town on the side of hills sloping down from the Kasbah (old fort) and incl. many mosques and markets, and new town on flat ground bet. old town and the lake.

History: Existed as a small town under Carthaginian empire (c. 9th cent.–2d cent. B.C.) but not important until Muslim conquest in 7th cent. A.D. Became ✻ under Abbasid dynasty (9th cent.) and under Hafsid dynasty (13th cent.) one of the leading cities of the Muslim world; captured by Spanish 1535; ceded to Turks 1574 and later history that of Tunisia (*q.v.*).

Tunis, Gulf of. Inlet of Mediterranean Sea, NE coast of Tunisia; limited on E by Cape Bon Penin.; at its head is the seaport Halq al-Wadi, the Lake of Tunis, and the city of Tunis.

Tu·ni·sia \tü-ˈnē-zhə, tyü-, -ˈni-zhē-ə\ *also* **Tu·nis** \ˈtü-nəs, ˈtyü-\ *or Fr.* **Tu·ni·sie** \tu̅e̅-nē-ˈzē\. Republic, N Africa, bounded on N and E by Mediterranean Sea, on SE by Libya, and on SW and W by Algeria; 63,378 sq. mi. (164,149 sq. km.); pop. (1993e) 8,530,000; ✻ Tunis.

Physical features: Plateau region in W and W cen. parts with highest points ab. 4500 ft. (1370 m.); coastal region low in N and esp. along E; three indentations on E coast: Gulf of Tunis at N end, shut in on E by Cape Bon; Gulf of Hammamet, S of Cape Bon; and Gulf of Gabès in S. On SE side of Gulf of Gabès, is large island of Jerba. Chief river the Medjerda in N flowing E to Gulf of Tunis; has no other sizable streams. In S is large Chott Djerid; along E coast are several marshy lakes, esp. Sīdī al-Hani, and in N is Lake Bizerte. Long S tract of country extends into the Sahara.

Chief products: Wheat, citrus fruit, dates, grapes, almonds, olives; phosphates, iron ore, oil, lead, zinc; textiles; food processing.

Chief towns: Tunis, Sfax, Ariana.

History: Became French protectorate 1881 (see TUNIS 1); government reorganized 1922; cession demanded by Italy, esp. in 1938. Occupied by Germans Nov. 1942 during WWII; captured by U.S. and British forces May 1943; recognized by France as independent 1956; abolished monarchy 1957; joined Arab League 1958; gained control over French naval facilities in Bizerte 1963; suffered major economic reverses due to severe flooding 1969; joined Arab Maghreb Union 1989.

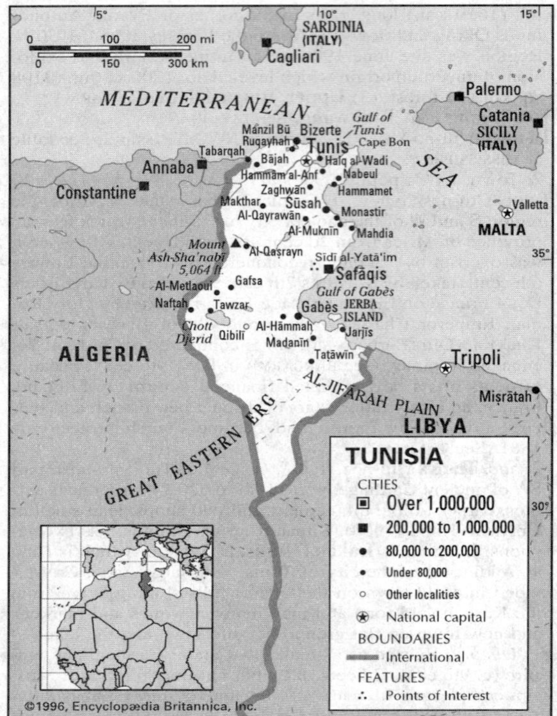

Tun·ja. **1.** \ˈtůn-ˌjä\. River, Bulgaria. See TUNDZHA.
2. \ˈtüŋ-ˌhä\. Town, ❋ of Boyacá dept., cen. Colombia, in the Cordillera Oriental of the Andes on highway 85 mi. (137 km.) NE of Bogotá; pop. (1992e) 112,400; technical university (1953).

Tunk, Mount \ˈtəŋk\. Peak, Okanogan co., N Washington; ab. 6065 ft. (1850 m.).

Tunk·han·nock \təŋk-ˈha-nək\. Borough, ⊗ of Wyoming co., NE Pennsylvania, on Susquehanna River 18 mi. (29 km.) WNW of Scranton; pop. (1990c) 2251. A short distance to the NE, at Nicholson, is **Tunkhannock Viaduct** *or* **Nich·ol·son Viaduct** \ˈni-kəl-sən\, one of the largest concrete railroad bridges in the world, 240 ft. (73 m.) high and 2375 ft. (724 m.) long, crossing **Tunkhannock Creek,** tributary of the Susquehanna.

Tun·stall \ˈtən-stəl\. See POTTERIES, THE.

Tu·nu·yán \ˌtü-nü-ˈyän\. River, W Argentina; rises in the Andes E of Santiago, Chile, flows E, chiefly in Mendoza prov., to Salado River; ab. 200 mi. (320 km.) long.

Tuo \ˈtwȯ\ *or W.-G.* **T'o** \ˈtō\; *formerly* **Lu** \ˈlü\. River, tributary of the Chang in Sichuan prov., S cen. China; flows SSE bet. the Min and the Jialing; ab. 200 mi. (320 km.) long.

Tu·ol·um·ne \tů-ˈä-lə-mē\. **1.** River, cen. California; rises in Yosemite National Park and flows W into San Joaquin River in Stanislaus co. W of Modesto; 155 mi. (249 km.) long; contains Hetch Hetchy and Don Pedro reservoirs. The **Grand Canyon of the Tuolumne** is a scenic feature of Yosemite National Park.
2. County in cen. California. See table at CALIFORNIA.

Tuolumne Peak. Mountain in Yosemite National Park in the Sierra Nevada, E Tuolumne co., cen. California; 10,845 ft. (3306 m.).

Tu·pã \tü-ˈpä^{n}\. Municipality, São Paulo state, SE Brazil, 270 mi. (434 km.) WNW of the city of São Paulo; pop. (1991p) 61,106.

Tu·par·ro \tü-ˈpär-rō\. River, NE Colombia; flows E into Orinoco River; ab. 200 mi. (320 km.) long.

Tu·pe·lo \ˈtü-pə-ˌlō\. City, ⊗ of Lee co., NE Mississippi, 57 mi. (92 km.) NNW of Columbus; pop. (1990c) 30,685; dairy products, furniture; scene of battle July 14, 1864 in Civil War in which Union forces under Gen. Andrew Jackson Smith defeated Confederate forces under Gen. Nathan Bedford Forrest. Birthplace of entertainer Elvis Presley 1935.

Tupelo National Battlefield. See UNITED STATES, *National Historical Parks.*

Tu·pi·za \tü-ˈpē-sä\. Town, Potosí dept., SW Bolivia, 125 mi. (201 km.) S of the city of Potosí; pop. (1992p) 20,195; alt. 9800 ft. (2987 m.); center of mining industries (silver, tin, bismuth, and lead); on railroad line from La Paz to Argentina.

Tup·per Lake \ˈtə-pər\. Village and resort, Franklin co., NE New York, 45 mi. (72 km.) S of Malone; pop. (1990c) 4087; alt. ab. 1560 ft. (475 m.).

Tupper Lakes. Lakes, NE New York; **Tupper Lake** *or* **Big Tupper Lake** in S Franklin co., and **Little Tupper Lake** in N Hamilton co.; Tupper Lake is ab. 7 mi. (11 km.) long; Little Tupper Lake, ab. 4 mi. (6 km.) long; both are summer resorts.

Tu·pun·ga·to, Cer·ro \ˈser-rō-ˌtü-pün-ˈgä-tō\. Peak in the Andes on the Chile-Argentina boundary ab. 40 mi. (64 km.) ENE of Santiago, Chile; 22,310 ft. (6800 m.).

Tuque, La. See LA TUQUE.

Tur, Jebel at. See GERIZIM, MOUNT.

Tu·ra \tů-ˈrä\. **1.** River, Sverdlovsk and Tyumen' oblasts, W Russia in Asia; a tributary of the Tobol; rises in the Ural Mts. and flows E past the city of Tyumen'; ab. 400 mi. (645 km.) long.
2. Town, ❋ of Evenki Autonomous Okrug, W cen. Russia in Asia, on right bank of the Lower Tunguska River in cen. part of okrug; pop. (1991e) 7300.

Tu·ran \tů-ˈrän\. Region of desert and steppe lands, cen. Asia, N of Iran; roughly equivalent to the regions around the Syr Dar'ya (Jaxartes) and Amu Dar'ya (Oxus) in modern Uzbekistan, Turkmenistan, and Kazakhstan; home of the Turanian peoples.

Tur'at al-Ismā'īlīyah. See ISMAILIA CANAL.

Tur·bat \ˈtůr-bət\. Town, Baluchistan, SW Pakistan; pop. (1981c) 52,337.

Turbat-i-Haidari. See TORBAT-E HEHYDARĪYEH.

Tur·bo \ˈtür-bō\. Municipality, Antioquia dept., NW Colombia, ab. 150 mi. (240 km.) NW of Medellín, on the Gulf of Urabá.

Turck·heim \tᵫr-ˈkem\ *or Ger.* **Türk·heim** \ˈtᵫrk-ˌhīm\. Village, Haut-Rhin dept., NE France, near Colmar; scene of battle Jan. 5, 1675 in which forces under French Marshal Turenne (Henri de La Tour d'Auvergne), defeated the forces of the Holy Roman Empire.

Tur·da \ˈtůr-də\ *or Hung.* **Tor·da** \ˈtōr-ˌdö\. City, Cluj co., NW cen. Romania, ab. 15 mi. (24 km.) SSE of the city of Cluj; munic. pop. (1989c) 64,374; chemicals, glass, bricks, cement, food products.

Tu·rek \ˈtü-rek\. Commune, Konin prov., cen. Poland; pop. (1989e) 28,618.

Turfan. See TURPAN.

Tur·gay \tůr-ˈgī\. Administrative subdivision, cen. Kazakhstan.

Tŭr·go·vish·te \tər-gə-ˈvēsh-tə\. Town, NE cen. Bulgaria, ab. 17 mi. (27 km.) W of Shumen; pop. (1988e) 71,201.

Turgu-Jiu. See TÎRGU JIU.

Tur·gut·lu \ˌtůr-gůt-ˈlü\; *formerly* **Ka·sa·ba** \kə-ˈsä-bə, ˌkä-sə-ˈbä\. City, Manisa prov., W Turkey in Asia, on railroad line 32 mi. (51 km.) E of İzmir.

Tu·ria \ˈtü-rē-ä\ *also* **Gua·da·la·vi·ar** \ˌgwä-thä-lä-ˈbyär\. River, E Spain; flows S and SE into Mediterranean Sea 3 mi. (4.8 km.) E of Valencia; 174 mi. (280 km.) long.

Tu·ria·çu Bay \ˌtur-yə-ˈsü\. Bay, NE coast of Brazil, in NW Maranhão state, at the mouth of the Turiaçu River.

Tu·rin \ˈtůr-ən, ˈtyůr-; tů-ˈrin, tyů-\ *or Ital.* **To·ri·no** \tō-ˈrē-nō\; *anc.* **Tau·ra·sia** \tȯ-ˈrā-zhə\; *later* **Au·gus·ta Tau·ri·no·rum** \ȯ-ˈgəs-tə-ˌtȯr-ə-ˈnōr-əm\. Industrial and commercial commune, ❋ of Piedmont, and of Torino prov., NW Italy, on Po River 78 mi. (125 km.) NW of Genoa; pop. (1991p) 961,916; railroad junction; center of automobile industry; produces aircraft, leather goods, rubber, paper, metal goods, plastics, chocolate, wine, clothing; an international fashion center; archiepiscopal see; military base. Notable buildings include 15th cent. Cathedral of San Giovanni Battista (which has housed the Shroud of Turin since 16th cent.), 18th cent. Basilica of Superga (royal burial chapel), 17th cent. Palazzo Reale and several other palaces, castles, libraries, and museums; university (1404), technical institute (1859).

History: Stronghold of pre-Roman Taurini, a tribe on the border bet. Gaul and Liguria; sacked by Carthaginian Gen. Hannibal late 3d cent. B.C.; made a Roman military colony under Emperor Augustus (63 B.C.–14 A.D.); became part of Lombard duchy 6th cent. A.D.; seat of government under Frankish King and Holy Roman Emperor Charlemagne (742–814); passed to house of Savoy after 11th cent.; occupied by French 1536–62 and later made ✻ of duchy; scene of victory of Prince Eugène of Savoy over French 1706; made ✻ of Kingdom of Sardinia 1720; held by French c. 1800–14 during Napoleonic Wars; center of the Risorgimento movement in 19th cent. and first ✻ of kingdom of Italy (to 1865); in WWII heavily damaged by Allied air raids.

Turiya *or* **Turja.** See TUR'YA.

Tur·ka·na, Lake \tər-ˈka-nə\ *or* **Lake Ru·dolf** \ˈrü-ˌdȯlf\. Lake, N Kenya; N tip is bet. Ethiopia and SE Sudan; 154 mi. (248 km.) long and 10 to 20 mi. (16 to 32 km.) wide; area 2473 sq. mi. (6405 sq. km.).

Tur·ke·stan \ˌtər-kə-ˈstan, -ˈstän\. **1.** Region, cen. Asia. See TURKISTAN.
2. Town, S Kazakhstan, ab. 20 mi. (32 km.) E of the Syr Dar'ya; pop. (1991e) 81,200; notable mosque.

Turkestan, Chinese. See TURKISTAN.

Turkestan, Russian. See TURKISTAN.

Tur·key \ˈtər-kē\. **1.** *or Turk.* **Tür·ki·ye** \ˌtu̇r-kē-ˈye\. Republic, SE Europe and SW Asia, bounded on N by the Black Sea, on NE by Republic of Georgia, Armenia, and Naxçıvan exclave of Azerbaijan, on E by Iran, on SE by Iraq, on S by Syria and the Mediterranean Sea, on W by the Aegean Sea, and on NW by Greece and Bulgaria; 301,380 sq. mi. (780,574 sq. km.); pop. (1985c) 50,644,458; ✻ Ankara.

Physical features: A mountainous country with extensive plateau covering cen. Asia Minor; highest ranges are in NE and E (highest peak Ararat 16,945 ft. or 5165 m.); along N coast are the Şmali Anadolu Dağları and on S coast the Taurus Range. Its rivers comprise the upper courses of Tigris and Euphrates (Frat) in the E, the Kızıl Irmak in the N, Sakarya in NW and Menderes in W with many other smaller but important streams; its lakes are numerous, esp. Lake Van in the E and several large ones in cen. and W cen. Anatolia. Its long coastline has few islands except in the Aegean and there most of them belong to Greece. About 97 percent of the republic's area lies in Asia, the remainder in Europe.

Chief products: Wheat, barley, olives, fruit, nuts, tobacco, cotton; livestock; coal, oil, chrome, iron ore; manufacturing: iron and steel, textiles, cement, chemicals; food processing.

Chief cities: İstanbul, Ankara, İzmir, Adana, Bursa, Gaziantep, Konya.

Political divisions: Divided into the following 67 provinces (for pronunciation of their names, see their individual entries):

NAME	LOCATION	AREA (sq. mi.)	AREA (sq. km.)
Adana (formerly Seyhan)	S	6,661	17,252
Adıyaman	SE	2,866	7,423
Afyonkarahisar	W cen.	5,494	14,229
Ağrı	E	4,272	11,066
Aksaray	S cen.	2,944	7,626
Amasya	N	2,105	5,452
Ankara	W cen.	9,890	25,614
Antalya	SW	7,950	20,591
Artvin	NE	2,871	7,436
Aydın	SW	3,039	7,870
Balıkesir	NW	5,518	14,292
Batman	SE	1,812	4,694
Bayburt	NE	1,410	3,652
Bilecik	NW	1,559	4,038
Bingöl	E	3,137	8,125
Bitlis	E	2,590	6,708
Bolu	NW	4,083	10,575
Burdur	SW	2,659	6,887
Bursa	NW	4,243	10,990
Çanakkale	NW	3,759	9,736
Çankırı	N cen.	3,263	8,451
Çorum	N cen.	4,915	12,729
Denizli	SW	4,582	11,867
Diyarbakır	SE	5,756	14,908
Edirne	W	2,384	6,174
Elâzığ	E cen.	3,533	9,150
Erzincan	E cen.	4,406	11,413
Erzurum	NE	9,678	25,066
Eskişehir	W cen.	5,203	13,477
Gaziantep	S	2,951	7,643
Giresun	NE	2,677	6,933
Gümüşhane	NE	2,605	6,748
Hakkâri	SE	2,749	7,121
Hatay	S	2,086	5,403
İçel	S	5,964	15,448
İsparta	SW	3,416	8,847
İstanbul	NW	2,159	5,591
İzmir	W	4,623	11,974
Kahramanmaraş	S cen.	5,532	14,328
Karaman	SW cen.	3,538	9,163
Kars	NE	7,165	18,557
Kastamonu	N	5,012	12,982
Kayseri	cen.	6,385	16,537
Kırıkkale	W cen.	1,685	4,365
Kırklareli	NE	2,462	6,378
Kırşehir	cen.	2,510	6,501
Kocaeli	NW	1,381	3,578
Konya	SW cen.	15,618	40,451
Kütahya	W	4,502	11,661
Malatya	E	4,537	11,752
Manisa	W	5,111	13,237
Mardin	SE	3,318	8,594
Muğla	SW	4,828	12,504
Muş	E	3,164	8,195
Nevşehir	cen.	2,111	5,467
Niğde	cen.	3,024	7,831
Ordu	N	2,317	6,001
Rize	NE	1,514	3,921
Sakarya	NW	1,721	4,457
Samsun	N	3,698	9,578
Siirt	SE	2,384	6,176
Sinop	N	2,184	5,657
Şirnak	SE	2,769	7,172
Sivas	E cen.	10,999	28,487
Tekirdağ	NW	2,401	6,218
Tokat	N cen.	3,810	9,869
Trabzon	NE	1,737	4,498
Tunceli	E cen.	3,002	7,775
Urfa	SE	7,175	18,583
Uşak	W	2,062	5,341
Van	E	7,363	19,070
Yozgat	cen.	5,250	13,597
Zonguldak	NW	3,305	8,560

History: For earlier history, see OTTOMAN EMPIRE; scene of Young Turk revolt 1908 against Ottoman Sultan Abdülhamid II; under Turkish statesman Mustafa Kemal, later known as Kemal Atatürk, nationalists set up government at Ankara 1920; repudiated Sèvres Treaty (1920), defeated Greece (*q.v.*) 1921–22 in Second Greco-Turkish War, adopted constitution 1921 (later amended), and formally proclaimed Turkish republic 1923; abolished caliphate 1924 and Islam as state religion 1928; joined Balkan Pact 1934 and nonaggression pact with Iraq, Iran, and Afghanistan 1937; remilitarized The Straits (see STRAITS, THE) 1936; remained neutral throughout most of WWII, sided with Allies 1945; participated in Korean War (1950–53) as part of UN force; became a member of NATO 1952; adopted new constitution 1961; relations with Greece strained (esp. 1964, 1967) due to civil unrest bet. Greeks and Turks on Cyprus; occupied N part of Cyprus 1974 after Greek coup; approved new constitution 1982; closed Bulgarian border 1989 to control influx of ethnic Turks; in 1991 restricted immigration of Kurdish refugees from Iraq after Persian Gulf War. See *Eastern Thrace* at THRACE.
2. River, NE Iowa; rises in Howard co., flows SE into Mississippi River in SE Clayton co.; 135 mi. (217 km.) long.

Türkheim. See TURCKHEIM.

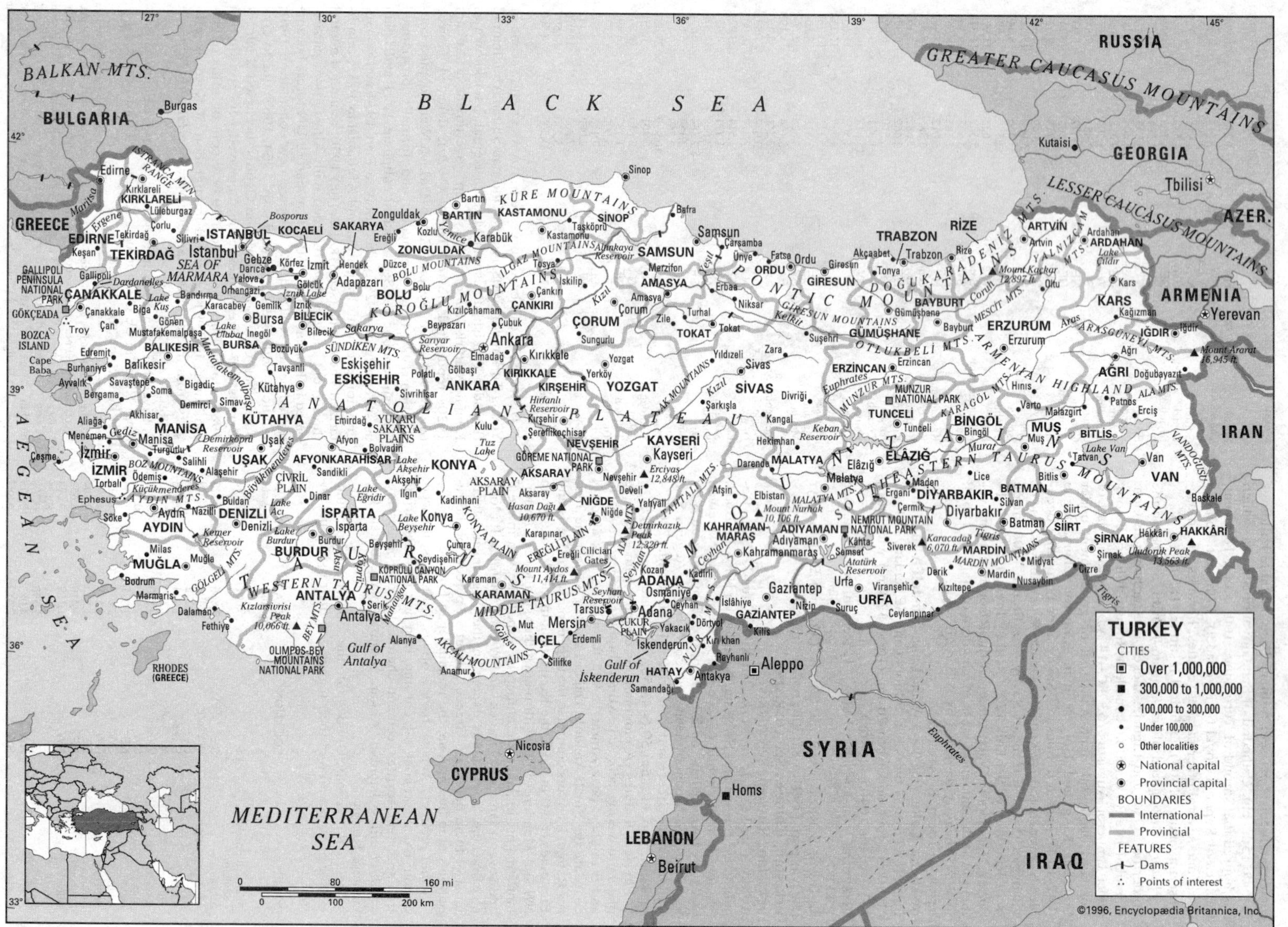
BLACK SEA
MEDITERRANEAN SEA
AEGEAN SEA
RUSSIA
GEORGIA
ARMENIA
AZER.
IRAN
IRAQ
SYRIA
LEBANON
CYPRUS
BULGARIA
GREECE
GREATER CAUCASUS MOUNTAINS
LESSER CAUCASUS MOUNTAINS
PONTIC MOUNTAINS
ANATOLIAN PLATEAU
SOUTHEASTERN TAURUS MOUNTAINS
ARMENIAN HIGHLAND
WESTERN TAURUS MTS.
MIDDLE TAURUS MTS.
Ankara
İstanbul
İzmir
Bursa
Adana
Konya
Gulf of Antalya
Gulf of İskenderun
TURKEY
CITIES
Over 1,000,000
300,000 to 1,000,000
100,000 to 300,000
Under 100,000
Other localities
National capital
Provincial capital
BOUNDARIES
International
Provincial
FEATURES
Dams
Points of interest
0 80 160 mi
0 100 200 km
©1996, Encyclopædia Britannica, Inc.

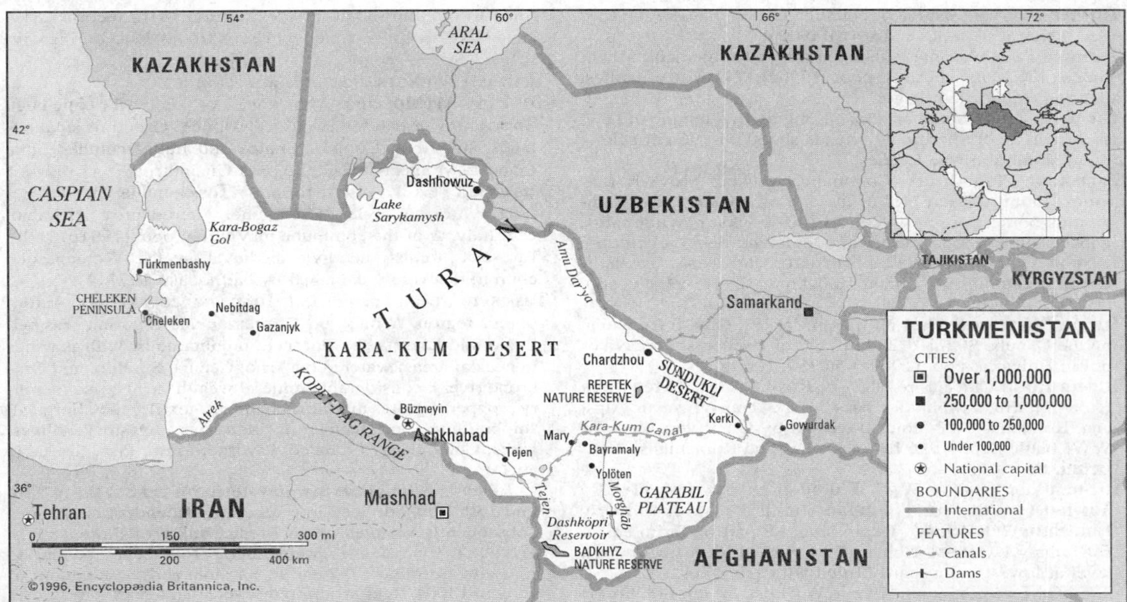

Turkish Armenia. See ARMENIA, TURKISH.

Turkish Empire. See OTTOMAN EMPIRE.

Turkish Federated State of Cyprus. See CYPRUS.

Turkish Republic of Northern Cyprus. See *History* at CYPRUS.

Tur·ki·stan *or* **Tur·ke·stan** \ˌtər-kə-ˈstan, -ˈstän\. Historical region of cen. Asia, usually thought to comprise Turkmenistan, Uzbekistan, Kyrgyzstan, Tajikistan, S Kazakhstan, W China, and NE Afghanistan. Its W part (**Russian Turkestan** *or* **West Turkistan**) was conquered by Russia mid- to late 19th cent. and later was made a government-generalship; after 1924 divided by Soviet government into the Turkmen, Uzbek, Tadzhik, and Kirgiz S.S.R.'s with remainder in S Kazakh S.S.R., U.S.S.R. For earlier history of W part, see CENTRAL ASIA, SOVIET. Its E part (**Chinese Turkestan** *or* **East Turkistan**) is now a part of China (roughly coextensive with Xinjiang Uygur). See also AFGHAN TURKISTAN.

Türkiye. See TURKEY.

Turkmanchai *also* **Turkmantchai.** See TORKAMĀN.

Turk·me·ni·stan \tərk-ˈme-nə-ˌstan\. Independent republic, W cen. Asia, bounded on NW by Kazakhstan, on N and NE by Uzbekistan, on S by Afghanistan and Iran, and on W by Caspian Sea; 188,455 sq. mi. (488,098 sq. km.); pop. (1993e) 3,958,000; ✻ Ashkhabad. W and cen. parts are level and desert (Kara-Kum); E part is plateau. Has Amu Dar'ya along E border (in part as boundary with Uzbekistan) and the Murghab in SE.

Chief products: Cotton, fruit; sheep; silk; oil.

Chief towns: Ashkhabad, Chardzhou, Dashhowuz.

History: By the 11th cent. inhabited by Turkoman tribes; by their defeat early 1880s region became part of Russian Turkestan; organized as Soviet republic 1924, and in May 1925 became a constituent republic of the U.S.S.R.; comprised **Turk·men Soviet Socialist Republic** \ˈtərk-mən\ *or* **Turk·me·nia** \tərk-ˈmē-nē-ə\ 1925–91; became independent Oct. 1991.

Turks and Cai·cos Islands \ˈtərks … ˈkā-kəs, ˈkā-ˌkōs\. A British colony, consisting of two groups of islands, N cen. West Indies, in the SE part of Bahamas and N of Hispaniola: **Turks Islands,** two islands, Grand Turk and Salt Cay, separated by Turks Island Passage from Caicos Is. to the W; **Caicos Islands,** a group of small islands comprising **South Caicos, East Caicos, Grand Caicos, North Caicos, Prov·i·den·ci·a·les** \ˌprä-vi-ˌden-chē-ˈä-lis\, **West Caicos,** and numerous small cays ENE of Great Inagua I. (see INAGUA). Total area 166 sq. mi. (430 sq. km.); pop. (1990e) 12,350; ✻ Grand Turk. Turks Is. are separated by Mouchoir Passage from Mouchoir Bank to the SE, and Caicos Is. by Caicos Passage from Mayaguana I. to the NW. Chief industries collecting sponges and tourism; chief exports sponges and shellfish. Visited by Spanish explorer Juan Ponce de León c. 1512; settled by British traders late 17th cent.; under Bahamas government late 18th cent.; a dependency of Jamaica mid-19th cent.; became crown colony 1962; shared governor with Bahamas 1965–73; adopted new constitution 1988.

Turks Island Passage. Channel, N cen. West Indies, SE of Caicos Is. and NW of Turks Is.

Turks Islands. See TURKS AND CAICOS ISLANDS.

Tur·ku \ˈtu̇r-kü\ *or Swed.* **Åbo** \ˈō-bü\. Seaport, ✻ of Turku ja Pori prov., SW Finland; pop. (1989c) 159,469; 3d largest city in Finland and one of its principal seaports; produces foodstuffs, textiles; shipbuilding and repairing; Univ. of Åbo (1918), Univ. of Turku (1920); seat of archbishop of Finland. One of Finland's oldest cities; scene of signing of Treaty of Åbo 1743 which granted to Russia a S portion of Finland; ✻ of Finland until 1812; devastated by fire 1827.

Turku ja Po·ri \yä-ˈpȯr-ē\. Province of SW Finland. See table at FINLAND.

Tur·lock \ˈtər-ˌläk\. City, Stanislaus co., cen. California, 38 mi. (61 km.) SE of Stockton; pop. (1990c) 42,198; California State Univ., Stanislaus (1957); city grew rapidly in 1970s and 1980s.

Turn·a·gain, Cape \ˈtər-nə-ˌgen, -gin\. Cape, SE coast of North I., New Zealand.

Turnagain Arm. Arm of Cook Inlet, S Alaska, SE of Anchorage and N of Kenai Penin.; ab. 50 mi. (80 km.) long.

Turnau. See TURNOV.

Turn·ber·ry Point \ˈtərn-ˌber-ē, -bə-re\. Cape, W coast of Strathclyde region, SW Scotland, on E side of entrance to Firth of Clyde; lighthouse.

Tur·neffe Islands \ˈtər-nəf\. Island group, Caribbean Sea, off coast of E cen. Belize opp. Belize City, comprising **Turneffe Island** and numerous islets.

Tur·ner \'tər-nər\. Name of counties in two states of the U.S. See tables at GEORGIA and SOUTH DAKOTA.

Tur·ners Falls \'tər-nərz\. Unincorporated settlement, Franklin co., NW Massachusetts; pop. (1990c) 4731; site of earliest dam on Connecticut River.

Tur·ner's Peninsula \'tər-nərz\. Long narrow tongue of land, W Africa, SE of Sherbro I.; extends ab. 60 mi. (96 km.) along the S shore of Sierra Leone.

Turn·hout \'tu̇rn-ˌhau̇t\. Commune, Antwerp prov., N Belgium, 26 mi. (42 km.) NE of the city of Antwerp near Netherlands border; pop. (1992e) 38,100; bricks, playing cards, paper, leather goods, electrical equipment; diamond cutting.

Tur·nov \'tu̇r-ˌnȯf\ *or Ger.* **Tur·nau** \'tu̇r-ˌnau̇\. Town, N Czech Republic, ab. 50 mi. (80 km.) NE of Prague; pop. (1980p) 13,906.

Tur·nu Mă·gu·re·le \'tu̇r-nü-mə-ˌgü-'re-le\. City, S Romania, on the Danube 80 mi. (129 km.) SW of Bucharest opp. Nikopol in Bulgaria; pop. (1989c) 36,187; furniture.

Tur·nu Ro·şu \'tu̇r-nü-'rȯ-ˌshü\ *or* **Roşu** *or Ger.* **Ro·ten·turm** \'rōt-ᵊn-ˌtu̇rm\. Mountain pass in the Transylvanian Alps, cen. Romania, S of Sibiu; traversed by Olt River; scene of WWI battle Sept. 1916 bet. Germans and Romanians.

Turoni. See TOURS.

Tur·pan \tu̇r-'pän\ *or W.-G.* **T'u–lu–p'an** \'tü-ˌlü-'pän\ *also* **Tur·fan** \tu̇r-'fän\ *or* **T'u·lu·fan** \'tü-ˌlü-'fän\. **1.** *formerly* **Luk·chun** \'lu̇k-'chu̇n\. Depression, NE part of Tarim basin, E Xinjiang Uygur, W China; ab. 426 ft. (130 m.) below sea level at lowest point; partly filled with salt lakes.
2. Town, E cen. Xinjiang Uygur, W China, 30 mi. (48 km.) N of Turpan depression and ab. 90 mi. (145 km.) SE of Ürümqi; at foot of Tian Shan Range; in vicinity are many relics of early periods. Center of earlier kingdoms under Han dynasty (206 B.C.–220 A.D.) and T'ang dynasty (618–907); ruled by the Uighurs 9th cent.; taken by Mongols 13th cent.

Tur·qui·no, Pi·co \'pē-kō-tür-'kē-nō\. Peak in the Sierra Maestra, E Cuba; 6560 ft. (2000 m.); highest mountain in Cuba.

Tur·ret Mountain \'tər-ət\. Peak, Yellowstone National Park, NW Wyoming; 10,995 ft. (3351 m.).

Turret Peak. Mountain, La Plata co., SW Colorado; 13,826 ft. (4214 m.).

Tur·ri·al·ba \ˌtür-rē-'äl-bä\. Volcano, Costa Rica, NE of Cartago; 10,650 ft. (3246 m.).

Turris Libisonis. See PORTO TORRES.

Tur·sun·za·de \ˌtu̇r-sən-'zä-de\. City, W Tajikistan, near Uzbekistan border W of Dushanbe; pop. (1991e) 40,400.

Turt·kul' *or* **Turt·kul** \tu̇rt-'külʸ\; *formerly* **Pe·tro·a·lek·san·drovsk** \ˌpi-trə-ˌȧ-lik-'sȧn-drəfsk\. Town, W Uzbekistan, just above Urganch, on right bank of lower Amu Dar'ya; formerly ❋ of Karakalpak A.S.S.R.

Tur·tle Creek \'tərt-ᵊl\. Borough, Allegheny co., SW Pennsylvania, 11 mi. (18 km.) E of Pittsburgh; pop. (1990c) 6556.

Turtle Islands. 1. Group of islands, Indonesia. See PENJU ISLANDS.
2. Group of islets, off Sabah, Borneo coast, SW Sulu Sea, ab. 25 mi. (40 km.) N of Sandakan; annexed by Philippines 1948.
3. Group of small islands off W point of Sherbo I., Sierra Leone.

Turtle Mountains. Small range, Bottineau and Rolette cos., N North Dakota.

Tur·ton \'tərt-ᵊn\. Town, Lancashire, NW England, 13 mi. (21 km.) NNW of Manchester; pop. (1981p) 25,162.

Tu·ru·gart Pass \ˌtü-rü-'gärt\ *also* **Tor·u·gart Pass** \ˌtu̇r-ə-\ *or Pinyin* **Tu·ru·gart Shan·kou** \'shäŋ-ˌkō\ *or W.-G.* **T'u–lu–ka–erh–t'e Shan–k'ou** \ˌtü-ˌlü-'gä-ər-ˌtə-'shäŋ-ˌkō\. Mountain pass through W end of the Tian Shan, cen. Asia, on highway from Kashi in W Xinjiang Uygur, China, to Kyrgyzstan; elev. 12,155 ft. (3705 m.).

Tur'·ya \'tu̇r-yə\ *or* **Tu·ri·ya** \'tu̇r-ē-yə\ *or Pol.* **Tur·ja** \'tu̇r-yä\. River, NW Ukraine; flows N into the Pripyat' River; ab. 100 mi. (160 km.) long; formerly in E Poland.

Tus·ca·loo·sa \ˌtəs-kə-'lü-sə\. **1.** County in W cen. Alabama. See table at ALABAMA.
2. City, its ⊗, on Black Warrior River 50 mi. (81 km.) SW of Birmingham; pop. (1990c) 77,759; chemicals, tires, paper; Univ. of Alabama (1831), Stillman Coll. (1876), Shelton State Community Coll. (1979). Settled 1816; incorp. 1819; state ❋ 1826–46; occupied by Union troops 1865 during Civil War.

Tuscan Apennines. See table at APENNINES.

Tus·can Archipelago \'təs-kən\ *or Ital.* **Ar·ci·pe·la·go To·sca·no** \ˌär-chē-'pe-lä-ˌgō-tō-'skä-nō\. Group of small islands, Italy, bet. Corsica, France and Italy; includes Elba, Pianosa, Montecristo, Giglio, and Giannutri.

Tus·ca·nia \təs-'kā-nē-ə\; *formerly* **Tos·ca·nel·la** \ˌtäs-kə-'ne-lə, *Ital.* ˌtȯs-kä-'ne-lä\. Commune, Viterbo prov., N Lazio, cen. Italy, W of the commune of Viterbo; pop. (1991p) 7698; Etruscan tombs nearby; medieval walls; Romanesque churches; severely damaged by earthquake 1971.

Tus·ca·ny \'təs-kə-nē\ *or Ital.* **To·sca·na** \tō-'skä-nä\. Autonomous region, W Italy; on Tyrrhenian and Ligurian seas bet. Lazio and Liguria; ❋ Florence; mountainous, with marshes in coastal areas; watered by Arno, Cecina, Serchio, and Ombrone rivers; considerable mineral wealth (lead, zinc, mercury, copper, lignite, marble); chemical, textile, metallurgical, shipbuilding, and handicraft industries; livestock, olives, vines. Chief cities: Florence, Livorno, Prato, Pisa. See table at ITALY.
History: A Frankish margravate c. 9th cent. A.D.; in 12th and 13th cents. divided into several independent city-states, subsequently reunited under Medici dukes of Florence (see FLORENCE 9); became grand duchy 16th cent.; passed to house of Lorraine 1737 and to Sardinia and the kingdom of Italy in 1860s. Region suffered severe damage in WWII, esp. during German retreat from Rome 1944, and in extensive floods 1966. Present region estab. 1948, received limited autonomy 1970.

Tus·ca·ra·was \ˌtəs-kə-'rȯ-wəs\. **1.** River, NE Ohio; rises in Summit co., flows S and joins Walhonding River in Coshocton co. to form Muskingum River; ab. 125 mi. (200 km.) long.
2. County in E Ohio. See table at OHIO.

Tus·ca·ro·ra Mountain \ˌtəs-kə-'rōr-ə\. Ridge, S Pennsylvania, extending along the boundary bet. Juniata, Huntingdon, and Fulton cos. on the NW, and Perry and Franklin cos. on the SE.

Tuscarora Mountains. Range in N Nevada, chiefly in Eureka and Elko cos.

Tus·co·la \tə-'skō-lə\. **1.** County in E Michigan. See table at MICHIGAN.
2. City, ⊗ of Douglas co., E cen. Illinois, 36 mi. (58 km.) E of Decatur; pop. (1990c) 4155.

Tus·cu·lum \'təs-kyə-ləm\. Ancient town, Latium, Italy, ab. 12 mi. (19 km.) SE of Rome and just N of Lake Albano and the Alban Hills; alt. ab. 2200 ft. (670 m.); many ruins. According to tradition a rival of Rome until made subject after battle of Lake Regillus early 5th cent. B.C.; served as resort for many prominent citizens of Rome in time of the republic; home of orator Marcus Tullius Cicero.

Tus·cum·bia \tə-'skəm-bē-ə\. **1.** City, ⊗ of Colbert co., NW Alabama, on Tennessee River 10 mi. (16 km.) from Wilson Dam; pop. (1990c) 8413; founded 1817; birthplace of author and lecturer Helen Keller 1880.
2. Town, ⊗ of Miller co., cen. Missouri; pop. (1990c) 148.

Tus·ke·gee \tə-'skē-gē\. City, ⊗ of Macon co., E Alabama, 38 mi. (61 km.) E of Montgomery; pop. (1990c) 12,257; cottonseed oil and gristmills; Tuskegee Univ. (1881); incorp. as city 1843. American educator Booker T. Washington led Tuskegee Institute (now university) from its founding; American botanist George Washington Carver conducted much of his agricultural research here.

Tus·sey Mountain \'tə-sē\. Peak, S Pennsylvania, on boundary bet. Blair, Bedford, and Huntingdon cos.; 2225 ft. (678 m.).

Tus·sum \tu̇-'süm\. Village, Egypt, on W bank of Suez Canal, near Ismailia; scene of attack by Turks 1915 during WWI.

Tus·tin \'təs-tən\. City, Orange co., SW California, 20 mi. (32 km.) E of Long Beach; pop. (1990c) 50,689; grew rapidly in 1980s.

Tutela. See TUDELA.

Tu·ti·co·rin \ˌtü-ti-kə-ˈrin\. Town, S Tamil Nadu, S India, on Gulf of Mannar 75 mi. (121 km.) S of Madurai; pop. (1991p) 284,193; seaport; manufactures salt and cotton textiles; founded by Portuguese 16th cent.; taken by Dutch 1658; acquired by British 1825.

Tut·tle \ˈtət-ᵊl\. Town, Grady co., cen. Oklahoma, SSW of Oklahoma City; pop. (1990c) 2807.

Tutt·ling·en \ˈtu̇t-liŋ-ən\. City, Baden-Württemberg, Germany, on Danube River 45 mi. (72 km.) E of Freiburg; pop. (1980c) 31,531.

Tu·tu·i·la \ˌtü-tü-ˈwē-lä\. Chief island of American Samoa, in SW cen. Pacific Ocean; 25 mi. (40 km.) long by 2 to 6 mi. (3 to 10 km.) wide; 52 sq. mi. (135 sq. km.); pop. (1990c) 45,043; chief town Pago Pago, ✻ of American Samoa, at head of deep indentation on S coast, forming Pago Pago Harbor. Has mountain range running length of island, highest point Mt. Matafao 2141 ft. (653 m.); densely wooded.

Tu·va \ˈtü-və\ *or Russ.* **Ty·va** \ˈti-və\; *formerly* **Tan·nu Tuva** *also* **Tan·nou Tou·va** \ˈtȧ-nü-ˈtü-və\ *or* **Urian·khai** \ˌu̇r-ē-äŋ-ˈk̲ī\ *also* **Uriang·hai** \-ˈhī\. Republic, S Russia in Asia, bet. Sayan and Tannu-Ola Mts.; 65,380 sq. mi. (169,334 sq. km.); pop. (1992e) 306,000; ✻ Kyzyl. Mountainous and generally well-watered; crossed from E to W by the Bei Kem and Khua Kem, headstreams of the Yenisey. Economy based on livestock raising; deposits of gold, asbestos, and cobalt, but their exploitation limited by the area's remoteness.

History: Until 1911 a part (Uriankhai) of Outer Mongolia; nominally independent 1911–14; came under Russian protection 1914; independent from 1921; signed treaty of friendship with Mongolian People's Republic 1926; annexed by U.S.S.R. 1944 as autonomous oblast; made autonomous republic 1961, comprising **Tuva A.S.S.R.** until 1991; became republic within Russia 1991; subsequently became member of Russian Federation.

Tu·va·lu \tü-ˈvä-lü\; *formerly* **El·lice Islands** \ˈe-lis\ *also* **La·goon Islands** \lə-ˈgün\. Island group, consisting of nine coral atolls, all inhabited, in W Pacific Ocean, N of Fiji and SSE of Kiribati, extending from 5° to 10°30′S and 176°E to 179°58′W (all lie W of the International Date Line); 9 sq. mi. (23 sq. km.); pop. (1994e) 9700; government headquarters and chief village on Funafuti I.; chief islands: Funafuti, Nukufetau, Nukulailai, and Nanumea. Sighted by Spanish explorer Alvaro de Mendaña de Neira 16th cent.; inhabited chiefly by Polynesian peoples when visited by European navigators late 18th–early 19th cents.; in 19th cent. visited often by blackbirders (those engaging in slave trade in South Pacific) who gradually decimated the population; made part of Gilbert and Ellice Islands Colony 1916; separated from Gilbert Is. 1976 and made a territory of the Commonwealth, with name changed to Tuvalu; achieved independence 1978; signed treaty 1979 by which U.S. relinquished claims to four islands of the group.

Tux·e·do Park \tək-ˈsē-dō\. Village, Orange co., SE New York, bet. **Tuxedo Lake** and Palisades Interstate Park, on Ramapo River; pop. (1990c) 706; the tuxedo is named for the village.

Tux·pan \ˈtüs-ˌpän\. **1.** Town, Nayarit state, W Mexico, 40 mi. (64 km.) NW of Tepic on San Pedro River.

2. Town, Veracruz state, E Mexico, on coast 145 mi. (233 km.) NW of the city of Veracruz; pop. (1980c) 56,037.

Tuxpan Reef. Reef, Gulf of Mexico, off the seaport town of Tuxpan in N Veracruz state, Mexico.

Tux·te·pec \ˌtüs-tā-ˈpek\ *or in full* **San Juan Bau·tis·ta Tux·tepec** \sän-ˈhwän-bau̇-ˈtēs-tä\. Town, NE Oaxaca state, SE Mexico, 80 mi. (129 km.) NNE of the city of Oaxaca; Plan of Tuxtepec issued 1876 as statement against policies of President Sebastián Lerdo de Tejada.

Tux·tla \ˈtüst-lä\. **1.** *or in full* **Tuxtla Gu·ti·ér·rez** \gü-ˈtyä-rās\. Town, ✻ of Chiapas state, SE Mexico; munic. pop. (1990p) 295,615; alt. 1500 ft. (457 m.); museum; university.

2. Town, Veracruz state, E Mexico. See SAN ANDRÉS TUXTLA.

Túy. See TUI.

Tuy Hoa \ˈtwē-ˈhwä\. City, E Vietnam, on South China Sea; pop. (1989c) 54,081.

Tu·zi·goot National Monument \ˈtü-zi-ˌgüt\. See UNITED STATES, *National Monuments.*

Tuz·la \ˈtüz-lä\ *or* **Dol·nja Tuzla** \dōl-nyä\. Town, Bosnia and Herzegovina, 50 mi. (81 km.) NNE of Sarajevo; pop. (1991p) 131,861. Under Turkish rule 16th–19th cents.; to Yugoslavia after WWI; became a target during 1990s Serb-Croat-Muslim fighting.

Tuz Lake \ˈtüz\ *or Turk.* **Tuz Gö·lü** \gœ̄-ˈlue̅\; *anc.* **Pa·lus Tat·tae·us** \ˈpā-ləs-ta-ˈtē-əs\. Salt lake, W cen. Turkey in Asia; 624 sq. mi. (1616 sq. km.), but greatly reduced in size during summer; alt. 2960 ft. (902 m.).

Tver' \ˈtver\. **1.** Medieval principality, E cen. Europe, NW of Moscow; ✻ Tver'; comprised city of Tver' and surrounding towns; founded 13th cent.; rivaled principality of Moscow 14th–15th cents., but annexed to it under Grand Prince Ivan III 1485.

2. *1932–90* **Ka·li·nin** \kȧ-ˈlē-nin\. City, ✻ of Tver' Oblast, W cen. Russia in Europe, 100 mi. (161 km.) NW of Moscow, on both banks of the Volga; pop. (1992e) 456,000; on Moscow-St. Petersburg railroad line; rolling stock.

History: An old city, begun 12th cent.; became part of Vladimir-Suzdal' principality early 13th cent.; ✻ of Tver' principality from mid-13th cent. until taken by Moscow 1485; in WWII briefly occupied by Germans 1941.

Tver' Oblast \ˈȯ-bləst, -ˌblast\ *or* **Tver·ska·ya Oblast'** \ˈtver-skə-yə-ˈȯ-bləstʸ\; *formerly* **Kalinin Oblast.** Subdivision of Russia in Europe, hilly country at source of the Volga; 32,471 sq. mi. (84,100 sq. km.); pop. (1992e) 1,668,000; ✻ Tver'; well drained by the upper Volga and its tributaries, esp. the Mologa; crossed by canal system connecting the Baltic Sea with the Volga; agricultural processing; textiles; light engineering.

Tver·tsa \tver-ˈtsä\. River, Tver' Oblast, Russia in Europe; flows SE to the Volga at city of Tver'; ab. 110 mi. (175 km.) long. Joined by canal with the Msta.

Tweed \ˈtwēd\. River, SE Scotland and NE England; rises in Borders region, SE Scotland, flows E, forming a section of the boundary bet. Scotland and England; crosses the extreme NE border of England and empties into North Sea at Berwick; 97 mi. (156 km.) long.

Tweeddale. See PEEBLES 1.

Twelve Apostles. See APOSTLE ISLANDS.

Twelve Bens of Bennebeola *or* **Twelve Pins, The** *or* **Twelve Pins of Bunnabeola.** See BENNEBEOLA, TWELVE BENS OF.

Twen·ty·nine Palms \ˈtwen-tē-ˌnīn\. City, San Bernardino co., SE California; pop. (1990c) 11,821; nearby to the S is Joshua Tree National Monument, to the N, a large U.S. Marine Corps base.

Twiggs \ˈtwigz\. County in cen. Georgia. See table at GEORGIA.

Twil·lin·gate \ˈtwi-liŋ-ˌgāt\. Town, E Newfoundland, Canada, on island at entrance of Notre Dame Bay; pop. (1991c) 1397; harbor.

Twin Cities \ˈtwin\. An unofficial designation for Minneapolis and St. Paul, Minnesota.

Twin Falls. **1.** County in S Idaho. See table at IDAHO.

2. City, its ⊗, 110 mi. (177 km.) W of Pocatello; pop. (1990c) 27,591; agricultural area; founded 1904 as one of the first planned communities in the West; incorp. as city 1907; Coll. of Southern Idaho (1964).

3. Falls, ab. 8 mi. (13 km.) NE of the city of Twin Falls, Idaho, in the Snake River at a place where the river divides into two channels, to reunite after drop of ab. 200 ft. (60 m.); S fall source of hydroelectric power.

Twin Lakes. **1.** Village, Kenosha co., SE corner of Wisconsin, near the Illinois border; pop. (1990c) 3989.

2. Two lakes (Washinee and Washining), extreme NW Connecticut.

Twin Lakes Reservoir. Reservoir, S Lake co., W cen. Colorado; formed from two small lakes.

Twin Mounds. Heights, Cheyenne co., W Nebraska; 4309 ft. (1313 m.) and 4349 ft. (1326 m.).

Twin Mountain. Peak in Blue Mts., NE Oregon; 8920 ft. (2719 m.).

Twin Mountains. Two peaks in the Franconia Mts., N Grafton co., New Hampshire; **North Twin Mountain** 4769 ft. (1454 m.) and **South Twin Mountain** 4926 ft. (1501 m.).

Twin Peaks. Mountain on W cen. boundary of Lemhi co., E cen. Idaho; 10,328 ft. (3148 m.).

Twins, The \ˈtwinz\. Two mountain peaks, S Jasper National Park, SW Alberta, Canada; N peak 12,085 ft. (3684 m.) and S peak 11,675 ft. (3559 m.).

Twins·burg \ˈtwinz-ˌbərg\. City, Summit co., NE Ohio, ab. 17 mi. (27 km.) NNE of Akron; pop. (1990c) 9606.

Two·fold Bay \ˈtü-ˌfōld\. Inlet of Tasman Sea, SE New South Wales, Australia; Eden on N shore has excellent harbor.

Two Harbors. City, ⊗ of Lake co., NE Minnesota, on Lake Superior 26 mi. (42 km.) NE of Duluth; pop. (1990c) 3651; ships iron ore.

Two Mountains. See DEUX-MONTAGNES.

Two Mountains, Lake of. See LAC DES DEUX-MONTAGNES.

Two Rivers. City, Manitowoc co., E Wisconsin, on Lake Michigan 7 mi. (11 km.) NE of the city of Manitowoc; pop. (1990c) 13,030.

Two Sicilies, The. See SICILIES, THE TWO.

Ty. See TEYATEYANENG.

Ty·a·na \ˈtī-ə-nə\. Ancient city, SW Cappadocia, Asia Minor, on N slope of Taurus Mts.; birthplace of Greek philosopher Apollonius of Tyana first cent. A.D.

Tyan' Shan'. See TIAN SHAN.

Ty·bee Island \ˈtī-bē\. Island, Chatham co., SE Georgia, at mouth of the Savannah River; 6 mi. (10 km.) long; pop. (1990c) 2842; contains the city of Tybee Island.

Ty·burn \ˈtī-bərn\. A former place of execution, near which is now the Marble Arch, Hyde Park, London, England; named for nearby tributary of Thames River.

Ty·chy \ˈtə-kə̇\. Town, Katowice prov., S Poland, ab. 10 mi. (16 km.) S of the city of Katowice; pop. (1989e) 189,874; breweries; motor vehicles; site of large post-WWII resettlement community (1951) **No·we Tychy** \ˈnȯ-ve\.

Ty·ee, Mount \ˈtī-ˌē\. Peak, Chelan co., cen. Washington; 6688 ft. (2039 m.).

Ty·gart \ˈtī-gərt\. River, N West Virginia; rises in Randolph co. and flows N; ab. 160 mi. (255 km.) long; a tributary source of the Monongahela.

Tygart River Dam. Dam across Tygart River, S of Grafton, Taylor co., N West Virginia; height 250 ft. (76 m.); completed 1937; impounds water for flood control.

Ty·ger *also* **Ti·ger** \ˈtī-gər\. River, South Carolina; rises in NW in Greenville co., flows SE into the Broad River; ab. 100 mi. (160 km.) long.

Tyldes·ley \ˈtildz-lē\. Town, Greater Manchester, NW England, 10 mi. (16 km.) WNW of Manchester; pop. (1981p) 23,248.

Ty·ler \ˈtī-lər\. **1.** Name of counties in two states of the U.S. See tables at TEXAS and WEST VIRGINIA.

2. City, ⊗ of Smith co., NE Texas, 85 mi. (137 km.) ESE of Dallas; pop. (1990c) 75,450; rose-bush horticulture; oil and gas wells, oil refineries; Texas Coll. (1894), Tyler Junior Coll. (1926), Univ. of Texas at Tyler (1971); estab. 1840s; incorp. as city 1907.

Ty·ler·town \ˈtī-lər-ˌtau̇n\. Town, ⊗ of Walthall co., S Mississippi; pop. (1990c) 1938.

Tý·li·sos *or* **Ty·lis·sos** \ˈtē-lē-ˌsȯs\. Archaeological site near N coast of cen. Crete, Greece, SW of Iráklion; relics of Middle to Late Minoan periods (c. 2100–c. 1100 B.C.).

Tylos. See BAHRAIN.

Tyn·dall \ˈtind-ᵊl\. City, ⊗ of Bon Homme co., SE South Dakota; pop. (1990c) 1201.

Tyndall, Mount. **1.** Peak in the Sierra Nevada, in Tulare co., S cen. California; 14,018 ft. (4273 m.).

2. Mountain in Southern Alps, South I., New Zealand, NE of Mt. Cook; 8280 ft. (2524 m.).

Tyne \ˈtīn\. **1.** River, Northumberland, N England; formed by confluence of **North Tyne** and **South Tyne;** flows E into North Sea bet. the town of Tynemouth and the seaport South Shields; 30 mi. (48 km.) long; incl. North Tyne, 80 mi. (129 km.) long.

2. River, Lothian region, SE Scotland; near Borders region border and flows NE to the North Sea near Dunbar; 28 mi. (45 km.) long.

Tyne and Wear \ˈwir\. Metropolitan county, N England, incl. areas formerly in Northumberland and Durham; lost its administrative function 1986. See table at ENGLAND.

Tyne·mouth \ˈtīn-ˌmau̇th, -məth\. Town, Tyne and Wear, N England, on North Sea at mouth of the Tyne on its N bank 9 mi. (15 km.) E of Newcastle upon Tyne; pop. (1981p) 60,022; ship-repair yards. Abbey founded on site 7th cent. A.D.

Tyngs·bor·ough \ˈtiŋz-ˌbər-ō\. Town, Middlesex co., NE Massachusetts, on Merrimack River WNW of Lowell; pop. (1990c) 8642.

Tyras. **1.** City, Ukraine. See BELGOROD-DNESTROVSKI.

2. River, S cen. Europe. See DNIESTER.

Tyre \ˈtīr\; *or* **Ṣūr** *or* **Sour** \ˈsür\; *anc.* **Ty·rus** \ˈtī-rəs\. Town, S Lebanon, on the coast of the Mediterranean Sea; pop. (1982e) 23,000; noted maritime city of antiquity; chief city of Phoenicia from ab. 11th cent. to 6th cent. B.C. In ancient times included an island with two harbors; now a peninsula formed by the widening of the causeway or mole built 4th cent. B.C. by Macedonian King Alexander the Great to gain access to the island. Was for centuries a major commercial city, center of Phoenician civilization and dominant sea power; noted for its silken garments and Tyrian purple. Probably founded before 14th cent. B.C. as a colony of Sidon. Mentioned in Bible (*1 Kings* v, *2 Sam.* v) during the reign of King Hiram (969–936 B.C.), who maintained ties with Israel under Kings David and Solomon. Withstood attacks from Assyrians but forced to pay tribute; successfully resisted in 6th cent. B.C. a siege of 13 years by Babylonian King Nebuchadrezzar II but was besieged and captured by Alexander the Great 332 B.C.; subsequently under control of Seleucids and Romans and in 7th cent. A.D. passed over to Muslims; captured by Crusaders 1124 and became a chief city of kingdom of Jerusalem; fell to Muslims 1291 and was destroyed. Modern town included in Great Lebanon 1920; occupied by Israeli forces 1982–85.

Tyree. See TIREE.

Ty·ree, Mount \tī-ˈrē\. Mountain, Sentinel Range, cen. Ellsworth Mts., Antarctica; 16,290 ft. (4965 m.); one of the highest peaks in Antarctica; first scaled 1967.

Ty·ri·fjord \ˈtūē-rē-ˌfyür\. Lake, SE Norway, 16 mi. (26 km.) W of Oslo; 16 mi. (26 km.) long by 7 mi. (11 km.) wide; on the N receives the Begna, which issues from it on the SW as the Dramselva.

Tyrnau. See TRNAVA.

Tyrol. See TIROL.

Ty·rone \tī-ˈrōn, ˈtī-ˌ\. **1.** Town, Fayette co., W Georgia, SSW of Atlanta; pop. (1990c) 2724.

2. Borough, Blair co., S cen. Pennsylvania, 15 mi. (24 km.) NE of Altoona; pop. (1990c) 5743.

Ty·rone \ti-ˈrōn\. Former county, W cen. Northern Ireland.

Tyros. See BAHRAIN.

Tyr·rell \ˈtir-əl\. County in E North Carolina. See table at NORTH CAROLINA.

Tyrrha. See TIRE.

Tyr·rhe·ni·an Sea \tə-ˈrē-nē-ən\ *or Ital.* **Ma·re Tir·re·no** \ˈmä-rā-tē-ˈre-nō\; *anc.* **Mare Tyr·rhe·num** \ˈmā-rē-tə-ˈrē-nəm, ˈmä-rā-\. The part of the Mediterranean Sea W of mainland of Italy, N of Sicily, and E of Sardinia and Corsica.

Tyrus. See TYRE.

Tys Fjord \ˈtūēs-\. Inlet, on NW coast of Norway, extending S from upper Vest Fjord.

Tytärsaari. See BOL'SHOY TYUTERS.

Tyu·men' \tyü-ˈmenʸ\. City, ✱ of Tyumen' Oblast, W Russia in Asia, in W part on Tura River 125 mi. (201 km.) SW of Tobol'sk and 190 mi. (306 km.) E of Yekaterinburg; pop.

(1992e) 496,000; sawmills, tanneries, chemicals; founded 1580s and became one of the first settled Russian towns E of the Urals.

Tyumen' Oblast \ˈȯ-bləst, -ˌblast\ *or* **Tyu·men·ska·ya Oblast'** \tyü-ˈmen-skə-yə-ˈȯ-bləstʸ\. Administrative subdivision of W Russia in Asia; in the basin of the Ob' River; 554,208 sq. mi. (1,435,399 sq. km.); pop. (1992e) 3,137,000; ✻ Tyumen'. About 80 percent of area lies in Khanty-Mansi and Yamalo-Nenets autonomous okrugs *(q.v.)*; oil fields; Tyumen' only major city.

Tyuters, Bol'shoy. See BOL'SHOY TYUTERS.

Tyva. See TUVA.

Tywi. See TOWY.

Tzeliutsing. See ZIGONG.

Tziá. See KÉA.

Tzu. See ZI.

Tz'u–kao \ˈdzü-ˈgau̇\ *also* **Mount Syl·via** \ˈsil-vē-ə\. Mountain, N cen. Taiwan; 12,743 ft. (3884 m.).

Tzu–kung. See ZIGONG.

Tzu–po. See ZIBO.

U

Ua Hu·ka \ˌü-ä-ˈhü-kä\. Small island of Marquesas Is., French Polynesia, S Pacific Ocean, ab. 30 mi. (48 km.) E of Nuku Hiva I; pop. (1988c) 539.

Ualual. See WELWEL.

Uap. See YAP.

Ua Pou *or* **Ua Pu** \ˌü-ä-ˈpü\. One of the Marquesas Is., French Polynesia, S Pacific Ocean, ab. 25 mi. (40 km.) S of Nuku Hiva; pop. (1988c) 1918; has peak 4042 ft. (1232 m.) high.

Ua·tu·mã \ˌwä-tü-ˈmä\. River, N Brazil; flows SE into the Amazon near E border of Amazonas state; 350 mi. (563 km.) long.

Uau·pés *also* **Wau·pés** \waü-ˈpes\. River, NW South America; rises in S cen. Colombia where it is called the **Vau·pés** \vaü-ˈpes\, flows ESE across Brazilian border into Río Negro; forms small section of Colombia-Brazil boundary; 500 mi. (805 km.) long.

Ua·xac·tún \ˌwä-shäk-ˈtün\. Ruins of an ancient town, N Guatemala, one of the oldest known centers of Mayan civilization, with remains that predate the Classic period (100–900 A.D.).

Ubá \ü-ˈbä\. City, SE Minas Gerais state, E Brazil, 130 mi. (209 km.) NNE of Rio de Janeiro; munic. pop. (1991p) 66,409.

Übach–Pa·len·berg \ˈue-bäk-ˈpä-lən-ˌberk\. City, North Rhine-Westphalia, Germany, 11 mi. (17 km.) N of Aachen; pop. (1980c) 22,870.

Uban·gi \ü-ˈbaŋ-gē, yü-, -ˈbäŋ-\ *or Fr.* **Ou·ban·gui** \ü-bäⁿ-ˈgē\. River, cen. Africa; formed by confluence of Bomu and Uele rivers on N cen. border of Democratic Rep. of the Congo; flows W and S, forming section of boundary bet. Democratic Rep. of the Congo and Central African Rep.; empties into Congo River W of Lake Tumba; 700 mi. (1126 km.) long, with longest headstream ab. 1400 mi. (2255 km.); sometimes called **Ma·kua** \ˈmä-kwä\ in its upper course and **Mo·ban·gi** \ˌmō-ˈbaŋ-gē, -ˈbäŋ-\ in its lower course.

Ubangi–Shari *or* **Ubangi–Shari–Chad.** See CENTRAL AFRICAN REPUBLIC.

Ubay \ˈü-ˌbī\. Municipality, NE coast of Bohol I., Philippines; pop. (1980c) 38,289.

Ubayyid, Al. See EL OBEID.

Ube \ˈü-bē, -ˌbā\. Seaport city, Yamaguchi prefecture, SW Honshū, Japan, at W end of Inland Sea 18 mi. (29 km.) E of Shimonoseki; pop. (1990p) 175,052.

Ube·da \ˈü-b̲ā-ˌt͟hä\. Commercial commune, Jaén prov., S Spain, 22 mi. (35 km.) NE of the commune of Jaén; pop. (1991p) 30,268; olives, stock raising. Many well-preserved buildings esp. from Renaissance period. Reconquered from Moors in 1234.

Ube·ra·ba \ˌü-be-ˈrä-bə\. City, W Minas Gerais state, E Brazil, ab. 260 mi. (420 km.) W of Belo Horizonte; munic. pop. (1991p) 210,803; alt. 2278 ft. (694 m.); center of extensive cattle-raising area.

Uber·lân·dia \ˌü-bər-ˈlan-dē-ə\. City, Minas Gerais state, E Brazil, on railroad line 60 mi. (97 km.) NNW of Uberaba; munic. pop. (1991p) 366,711.

Ubi·na \ü-ˈbē-nä\. Peak, Potosí dept., SW Bolivia; 16,830 ft. (5130 m.).

Ubi·nas \ü-ˈbē-näs\. Peak, S Peru; 17,390 ft. (5301 m.).

Ubon Rat·cha·tha·ni \ü-ˈbən-ˌrä-chə-ˈtä-nē\ *or* **Ubol Ra·ja·dha·ni** \ü-ˈbən-ˌrä-chə-ˈtä-nē—*sic*\. Town, SE Thailand, E terminal of railroad line from Phra Nakhon Si Ayutthaya and ab. 40 mi. (64 km.) W of the Laos border on Mun River just below its junction with the Chi; pop. (1991e) 98,950.

Ub·su–Nur *or* **Ubsu Nur** \ˌüb-sü-ˈnür\. Lake, NW Mongolia, on S border of Tuva Rep., Russia in Asia; ab. 1293 sq. mi. (3349 sq. km.).

Ubun·du \ü-ˈbün-dü\ *or* **Ubun·di** \-dē\; *formerly* **Pon·thier·ville** \ˌpōⁿ-tyā-ˈvēl\. Town, S Haut-Zaïre administrative region, NE Democratic Rep. of the Congo, on the Congo River ab. 70 mi. (115 km.) S of Kinshasa.

Uca·ya·li \ˌü-kä-ˈyä-lē\. River, cen. and N Peru; chief headstream of Amazon River; formed by confluence of Apurímac and Urubamba rivers in cen. Peru, flows N to unite with Marañón River and form Amazon River; ab. 1000 mi. (1610 km.) long; 675 mi. (1086 km.) of it are navigable by large craft.

Uccle \ˈuekᵊl\ *or* **Uk·kel** \ˈue-kəl\. Commune Brabant prov., cen. Belgium, a suburb of Brussels; pop. (1991c) 73,721.

Uchi·u·ra Bay \ü-ˈchē-ü-ˌrä\ *also* **Vol·ca·no Bay** \väl-ˈkā-nō, vȯl-\. Inlet of W Pacific Ocean, E coast of S extension of Hokkaidō, Japan.

Uda. See CHUNA.

Uda·ga·man·da·lam *or* **Udha·ga·man·da·lam** \ˌü-də-gə-mən-ˈdä-ləm\ *or* **Oo·ta·ca·mund** \ˈü-tə-kə-ˌmənd\; *mostly formerly* **Uta·ka·mand** \ˈü-tə-kə-ˌmənd\. Town and hill station, Tamil Nadu, S India, 280 mi. (451 km.) WSW of Madras; on plateau (ab. 7000 ft. or 2100 m. above sea level); pop. (1991p) 81,726; health resort.

Udai·pur \ü-ˈdī-ˌpu̇r, ˌü-dī-ˈ\ *or* **Oo·dey·pore** \ü-ˈdī-ˌpōr, ˌü-dī-ˈ\. **1.** Former Indian state, now part of Madhya Pradesh state, India; 1045 sq. mi. (2707 sq. km.).

2. *also* **Me·war** \mā-ˈwär\. Former Indian state, now part of Rajasthan state, NW India; 13,170 sq. mi. (34,110 sq. km.); offered strong resistance to Mogul emperors esp. during 16th and 17th cents.; in 18th cent. suffered from civil wars and attacks by Marathas.

3. City, ✻ of former Udaipur (Mewar) state, now in Rajasthan state, W India, 210 mi. (338 km.) SW of Jaipur; pop. (1991p) 307,682; alt. 2469 ft. (753 m.); university (1962); numerous temples and palaces, incl. 16th cent. maharajah's palace.

Udayadhani. See UTHAI THANI.

Ud·de·val·la \ˈu̇-də-ˌvä-lə\. Town, Göteborg and Bohus prov., SW Sweden, near coast 45 mi. (72 km.) N of Göteborg; pop. (1993e) 48,178; textile mills, match factories.

Udd·jaur \ˈu̇d-ˌyau̇r\. Lake, Västerbotten prov., N Sweden, connecting Hornavan and Storavan lakes, and drained by the Skellefte River; 92 sq. mi. (238 sq. km.).

Uden \ˈue-də\. Commune, North Brabant prov., Netherlands; pop. (1992e) 36,329.

Udhagamandalam. See UDAGAMANDALAM.

Udi·ne \ˈü-dē-ˌnā\. **1.** Province of Friuli-Venezia Giulia, NE Italy. See table at ITALY.

2. *anc.* **Uti·na** \ˈyüt-ᵊn-ə\. Commune, its ✻, Friuli-Venezia Giulia, NE Italy, 61 mi. (98 km.) NE of Venice; pop. (1991p) 99,157; railroad junction; iron goods, leather, textiles; 16th cent. castle; 15th cent. town hall. Ruled by Venice 15th–18th cents.; in WWI headquarters of the Italian Army 1915–17.

Ud·mur·tia \u̇d-ˈmu̇r-shə, -shē-ə\ *or* **Ud·mur·ti·ya** \-tē-yə\ *or Russ.* **Ud·murt·ska·ya Res·pu·bli·ca** \ˈu̇d-ˌmu̇rt-skə-yə-res-ˈpu̇-bli-kə\. Republic, E Russia in Europe; 16,255 sq. mi. (42,101 sq. km.); pop. (1992e) 1,637,000; ✻ Izhevsk, which is by far the largest city. Economy based on metallurgical and engineering industries, exploitation of extensive forests, and agriculture (rye and flax, livestock). Crossed at the N and S by main E and W trunk railroads, with a branch to Izhevsk.

History: Orig. inhabited by ancestors of the Udmurts, also known as Votyaks, an E branch of Finno-Ugrian peoples; region came under Russian rule after fall of Kazan khanate 1552; made autonomous oblast 1920; elevated to autonomous republic 1934; underwent substantial industrial development as part of the industrialization of the Ural Mts. area during WWII. Until 1991 comprised **Udmurt A.S.S.R.** \ˈu̇d-ˌmu̇rt\ *or earlier* **Vot·ska·ya A.S.S.R.** \ˈvȯt-skə-yə\; became republic within Russia 1991; subsequently became member of Russian Federation.

Udon Tha·ni *or* **Udorn·dha·ni** \ü-ˈdön-ˈtä-nē\ *also* **Ban Mak Khaeng** \ˈbän-ˈmäk-ˈkaŋ\. Town, NE Thailand, 40 mi. (64 km.) S of Laos border, and terminus of railroad line from Nakhon Ratchasima; pop. (1991e) 78,489.

Udot \ˈü-ˌdöt\. Island, cen. part of Chuuk (*q.v.*), Caroline Is., W Pacific Ocean.

Uea \ü-ˈwä-ä\. **1.** Island of the Loyalty Is. See OUVÉA. **2.** Main island of Wallis Is. See UVÉA.

Ue·da \ü-ˈe-dä, -ˈä-\ *or* **Uye·da** \-ˈye-, -ˈyä-\. Town, Nagano prefecture, cen. Honshū, Japan; pop. (1990p) 119,435; former center of silkworm culture.

Ue·le *or* **Wel·le** \ˈwel-ē\. River, cen. Africa; flows W across N Democratic Rep. of the Congo to unite with Bomu River and form Ubangi River; ab. 700 mi. (1125 km.) long.

Uel·zen *or* **Ül·zen** \ˈœlts-ᵊn\. City, Lower Saxony, Germany, 21 mi. (34 km.) SSE of Lüneburg; pop. (1980c) 36,261; became city c. 1270.

Ue·no \ˈwä-ˌnō\. City, Mie prefecture, Honshū, Japan, 36 mi. (58 km.) E of Ōsaka; pop. (1990p) 60,239; museums.

Ueyuk. See ALACAHÖYÜK.

Ufa \ü-ˈfä\. **1.** River, Bashkortostan, E Russia in Europe; rises in W Chelyabinsk Oblast and flows NW and SW through the Southern Ural Mts. to join the Belaya River at Ufa; 580 mi. (933 km.) long; partly navigable.
2. City, ✻ of Bashkortostan, E Russia in Europe, at junction of Belaya and Ufa rivers 250 mi. (402 km.) NE of Samara; pop. (1992e) 1,097,000; electrical equipment, lumber and veneer, typewriters; oil refining; Bashkir State Univ. (1957). Founded as fortress 1574; made a town 1586; developed as industrial center from late 19th cent. and esp. after WWII.

Ugan·da \yü-ˈgän-dä, ü-, -ˈgan-\. Republic, E Africa; bounded on N by Sudan, on E by Kenya, on S by Tanzania, on SW by Rwanda, and on W by Democratic Rep. of the Congo; 91,134 sq. mi. (236,037 sq. km.); pop. (1993e) 17,741,000; ✻ Kampala, which is by far the largest city.

Physical features: On E are high mountains along Kenyan boundary, highest Mt. Elgon 14,178 ft. (4322 m.); high Ruwenzori Mts. on W, highest 16,763 ft. (5109 m.); plateau region (Ankole) in SW, dense forests in W part, and marshes on N shore of Lake Victoria and around Lake Kyoga in S cen. part. Traversed by the Nile which issues from Lake Victoria at Ripon Falls, flows through Lake Kyoga and Lake Albert on the W and then N in NW corner of Uganda into Sudan; Lake Edward and Lake George are in the SW.

Chief products: Cotton, coffee, tea, sugar, tobacco; livestock raising, fishing; copper; manufacturing: cement, textiles.

History: By 19th cent. region comprised several separate kingdoms inhabited by various peoples incl. Bantu- and Nilotic-speaking tribes; settled by Arab traders mid-19th cent.; native kingdom of Buganda visited by British explorers James Grant and John Speke 1862; soon after arrival of first Protestant and Catholic missionaries 1870s, religious factions developed which led to religious persecution and civil strife; in 1890 Buganda visited by agent of British East Africa Company; formally proclaimed British protectorate 1894 and later extended to include other kingdoms; borders of Uganda protectorate fixed by 1914; achieved independence 1962; abolished federal system of government 1966; adopted republican constitution 1967 and formed, with Kenya and Tanzania, the East African Community; civilian government overthrown in coup 1971 and replaced by military regime under President Idi Amin; subsequently expelled much of its Asian population; fought war with Tanzania 1978–79 which resulted in collapse of Amin's regime; military government overthrown Jan. 1986 by resistance army under former defense minister Yoweri Museveni.

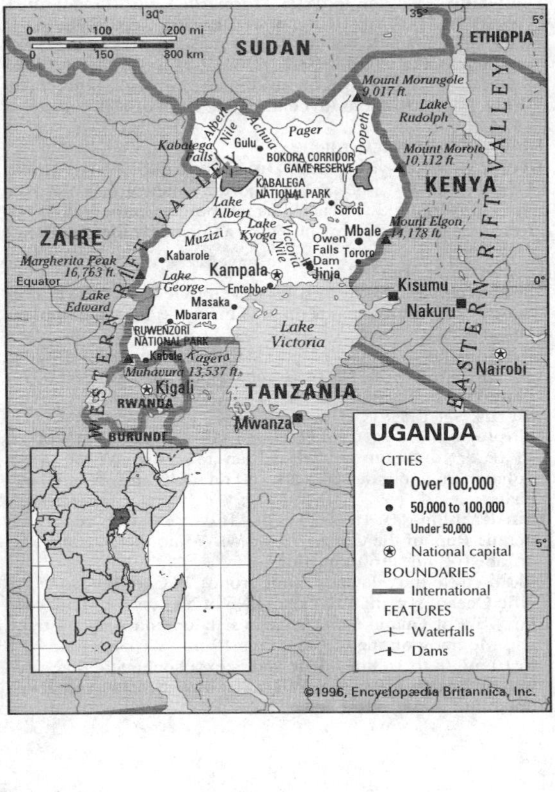

Uga·rit \yü-ˈgär-it, ˈyü-gə-rit\. Ancient city on site of modern Ras Shamra (*q.v.*), on E coast of the Mediterranean Sea N of Latakia, Syria; fl. 15th–12th cents. B.C. Its remains have contributed much to our knowledge of Western Semitic religion and language. Destroyed c. 1200 B.C.

Ugernum. See BEAUCAIRE.

Ug·le·gorsk \ˌüg-lə-ˈgörsk\ *or Jp.* **Esu·to·ru** \ˌe-sü-ˈtō-rü\. Seaport town, NW coast of Sakhalin I., Russia in Asia, on Tatar Strait; formerly Japanese.

Ugljan *or* **Uljan** \ˈül-yən\ *or Ital.* **Uglia·no** \ül-ˈyä-nō\. Island, Croatia, in Adriatic Sea off coast opp. Zadar; 18 sq. mi. (47 sq. km.).

Uhar·ie \yü-ˈhar-ē\ *or* **Uwhar·rie** \-ˈhwar-\. River, cen. North Carolina; rises in NW Randolph co., flows S into Montgomery co., and joins Yadkin River 10 mi. (16 km.) W of Troy to form Pee Dee River (*q.v.*).

Uher·ske Hra·dis·te \ˈü-ˌher-ske-ˈhräd-yēsh-te\. Town, SE Czech Republic; pop. (1989c) 38,932.

Uh·richs·ville \ˈyür-iks-ˌvil\. City, Tuscarawas co., E Ohio, 28 mi. (45 km.) S of Canton; pop. (1990c) 5604; closely linked with Dennison to the E.

Uí·ge \ˈwē-zhā\. **1.** Province of NW Angola. See table at ANGOLA.
2. Town, its ✻; pop. (1985e) 69,484.

Ui·ha \ü-ˈē-ä\. Island in E Haapai group, Tonga, SW cen. Pacific Ocean.

Ui·jong·bu \ˈwē-ˌjəŋ-ˈbü\. City, NW South Korea; pop. (1985c) 162,700.

Uil·pa·ta \ü-ēl-ˈpä-tə\ *also* **Adai Khokh** \ə-ˈdī-ˈkök\. Mountain, cen. Caucasus Mts., Alania Rep., S Russia in Europe, near border with Republic of Georgia, 42°46′N, 43°48′E; 15,239 ft. (4645 m.).

Uin·ka·ret Plateau \ü-ˈwiŋ-kə-ˌret\. Tableland, N Mohave co., NW Arizona, N of Colorado River; 5400 to 6100 ft. (1645 to 1859 m.).

Uin·ta \yü-ˈin-tə\. **1.** River, NE Utah; rises in Uinta Mts., flows SE into Duchesne River in W Uintah co.; 50 mi. (81 km.) long.
2. County in SW corner of Wyoming. See table at WYOMING.

Uin·tah \yü-ˈin-tə\. County in E Utah. See table at UTAH.

\ə\ **abut** \ᵊ\ matches \ᵊ\ kitten, Fr table \ər\ **further** \a\ **ash** \ā\ **ace** \ä\ cot, cart \å\ Fr bac \au̇\ **out** \b\ Span Avila \ch\ **chin** \e\ **bet** \ē\ **easy** \g\ **go** \i\ **hit** \ī\ **ice** \j\ **job** \k\ Ger **ich**, **Buch** \ⁿ\ Fr vin \ŋ\ **sing** \ō\ **go** \ȯ\ **all** \ō\ **law** \œ\ Fr **bœuf** \œ̄\ Fr **feu** \ȯi\ **boy** \th\ **thin** \t͟h\ **this** \ü\ **loot** \u̇\ **foot** \ue\ Ger füllen \ue̅\ Fr **rue** \y\ **yet** \ʸ\ Fr digne \ˈdēnʸ\, nuit \ˈnwʸē\ \yü\ **few** \yu̇\ **fury** \zh\ **vision**

Uinta Mountains. Range, chiefly in NE Utah, extending along the boundary bet. Summit and Daggett cos. on the N and Duchesne and Uintah cos. on the S; highest point Kings Peak 13,528 ft. or 4123 m. (highest peak in Utah).

Uist \ˈyü-ist, ˈü-ist\. Two islands, Outer Hebrides off W coast of Scotland. See NORTH UIST and SOUTH UIST.

Ui·ten·hage \ˈȯit-ᵊn-ˌhä-kə, ˈyü-tən-ˌhāg\. Town, Eastern Cape prov., S Rep. of South Africa, 20 mi. (32 km.) NW of Port Elizabeth; pop. (1985c) 54,987; textiles, tires.

Ujae \ü-ˈjä-ā\. Atoll, Marshall Is., W Pacific Ocean, in the Ralik Chain W of Kwajalein.

Ujain. See UJJAIN.

Ujda. See OUJDA.

Uji \ˈü-jē\. **1.** *or Jp.* **Uji·ga·wa** \ˌü-jē-ˈgä-wä\. River, W cen. Honshū, Japan, immediate outlet of Lake Biwa; joins the Hozu to form the Yodo. **2.** City, Kyōto prefecture, Honshū, Japan, 10 mi. (16 km.) S of the city of Kyōto; pop. (1990p) 177,018.

Uji·ji \ü-ˈjē-jē\. Town, Kigoma region, Tanzania, on E shore of Lake Tanganyika 4 mi. (6 km.) SE of the port of Kigoma; formerly an important trading town; place where British journalist Henry Morton Stanley found Scottish explorer David Livingstone 1871.

Uji–yamada. See ISE 2.

Uj·jain *or* **Ujain** \ˈü-ˌjīn\. City, W Madhya Pradesh, W cen. India, ab. 200 mi. (320 km.) E of Ahmadabad; pop. (1991c) 362,633; trades in grain; university (1957). One of the oldest cities of India and ranked as one of its seven holy cities; ancient ✻ of Avanti kingdom (6th–4th cents. B.C.) and later of Malwa; a center of Sanskrit learning by 2d cent. A.D.; ✻ of Hindu Emperor Candra Gupta II (ruled c. 380–c. 415). Fell to Muslims 1235; seat of the Maratha dynasty of Sindhia in 18th cent. Possesses notable examples of Muslim and Hindu architecture incl. temples, mosques, palaces, mausoleums, and an 18th cent. observatory.

Ujung Pan·dang \ˈü-ˌjüŋ-ˈpän-ˌdäŋ\; *formerly* **Ma·cas·sar** *or* **Ma·kas·ar** *or* **Ma·kas·sar** \mə-ˈka-sər\. Seaport, ✻ of South Sulawesi prov., SW Sulawesi, Indonesia; pop. (1990c) 944,685; harbor improved by extensive construction since 1925; exports include copra, gums and resins, rubber, coffee, spices; university (1956).

History: A thriving port when first visited by Portuguese 16th cent.; settled by Dutch 1607; town seized by the Dutch 1667 and developed by them as important trading center; made free port 1848; in WWII occupied by the Japanese 1942–45; in 1946 made ✻ of Dutch-sponsored state of East Indonesia; to Republic of Indonesia 1949.

Újvidék. See NOVI SAD.

Ukhrul \ü-ˈkrủl\. Town, NE Manipur, NE India, ab. 38 mi. (61 km.) NNE of Imphal near Myanmar border; in WWII used by Japanese as base in their invasion of India 1944.

Ukh·ta \ủk-ˈtä\; *formerly* **Chib·yu** \chi-ˈbyü\. Town, Komi Rep., NE Russia in Europe, ab. 160 mi. (255 km.) NE of Syktyvkar; pop. (1992e) 112,000.

Uki·ah \yü-ˈkī-ə\. City, ⊗ of Mendocino co., W California, on Russian River 54 mi. (87 km.) NNW of Santa Rosa; pop. (1990c) 14,599; wine; Mendocino Coll. (1973).

Ukkel. See UCCLE.

Uk·mer·gė \ˌủk-mer-ˈgā\ *or Russ.* **Vil·ko·mir** \ˌvil-kə-ˈmir\ *or Ger.* **Wil·ko·mir** \ˈvil-kə-ˌmir\. Town, E Lithuania, on tributary of Neman River 43 mi. (69 km.) NE of Kaunas.

Ukraine \yü-ˈkrān, -ˈkrīn, ˈyü-ˌ\ *also* **the Ukraine.** Republic, E cen. Europe, bounded on N by Belarus and Russia, on E by Russia, on S by the Sea of Azov and the Black Sea, on SW by Moldova, and on W by Hungary, Slovakia, and Poland; 233,089 sq. mi. (603,701 sq. km.); pop. (1993e) 52,344,000; ✻ Kiev.

Physical features: Chiefly a wide extent of steppe land covered with fertile black earth (*chernozem*); its S border is a less fertile stretch of clayey soil and marshland along the Black Sea; in E and W are low hills. Traversed by three great rivers, Dnieper, Bug, and Donets, and is bordered on the SW by a 4th, the Dniester; in the S are two smaller streams, the Ingul and Ingulets (tributaries of the Bug and Dnieper); all others except the Donets (a tributary of the Don) flow into the Black Sea.

Chief products: Wheat, corn, rye, sugar beets, potatoes, sunflowers; livestock; coal, iron ore, manganese, natural gas; manufacturing: iron and steel, chemicals, machinery, transportation equipment; hydroelectric power plants.

Chief towns: Kiev, Kharkiv, Dnipropetrovs'k, Donets'k, Odessa.

History: Settled by Slavic tribes after 4th cent.; Kiev (*q.v.*), its chief town, fl. 10th–11th cents. as ✻ of a powerful Varangian state; conquered by Tatars 13th cent.; in 14th cent. most of region taken by Lithuania (see *History* at LITHUANIA); in 1667 by Treaty of Andrusovo, Russia acquired region E of middle Dnieper; the rest acquired in partitions of Poland 1790s; Ukrainian National Republic, estab. 1917, declared its independence from Soviet Russia 1918; NW part held by Poland 1919–39; remainder reconquered by Soviets 1919 and made a republic; entered U.S.S.R. 1922; suffered severe famine in 1930s under Soviet leader Joseph Stalin; overrun by Axis armies 1941 in WWII; gradually rewon by Soviets by end of 1944; comprised **Ukrai·ni·an Soviet Socialist Republic** \yü-ˌkrā-nē-ən\ of the U.S.S.R. 1923–91; declared sovereignty within Soviet system 1990; declared independence 1991.

Uku \ˈü-ˌkü\. Island, Gotō Is. (*q.v.*), Japan.

Ulaan·baa·tar *or* **Ulan Ba·tor** \ˌü-ˌlän-ˈbä-ˌtȯr\; *formerly* **Ur·ga** \ˈủr-gə\. City, ✻ of Mongolia, in N cen. part ab. 720 mi. (1160 km.) NW of Beijing, China; pop. (1989p) 548,400; textiles; university (1942); junction point of principal Mongolian transportation routes and on branch of Trans-Siberian R.R. from Russia to China.

History: Founded mid-17th cent. as residency of the Living Buddha (*bogdo-gegen*); in mid-18th cent. a trading center on caravan routes bet. Russia and China; center of Mongolian revolt 1911; occupied by U.S.S.R. 1921; made ✻ of Mongolian People's Republic 1924 and renamed Ulaanbaatar ("Red Hero"); subsequently rebuilt and developed; heavily damaged by floods 1966.

Ulala. See GORNO-ALTAYSK.

Ulan Hot. See HORQIN YOUYI QIANQI.

Ulan–Ude \ˌü-ˌlän-ủ-ˈdā\; *formerly* **Verkh·ne·u·dinsk** \ˌvyerk-nə-ˈü-ˌdinsk\. City, ✻ of Buryatia Rep., S Russia in Asia, on Selenga River ab. 70 mi. (115 km.) SE of the S end of Lake Baikal; pop. (1992e) 366,000; junction on Trans-Siberian R.R.; glass, processed food; railroad shops, boatyards. Founded mid-17th cent.; made town c. 1780; renamed 1934.

Ulawun. See FATHER, THE.

Ul·cinj \ˈült-ˌsēn-yə\ *or Ital.* **Dul·ci·gno** \dül-ˈchē-nyō\; *anc.* **Ol·cin·i·um** \äl-ˈsi-nē-əm\. Seaport, Montenegro, S Yugoslavia, on Adriatic Sea near Albanian border; cathedral. Taken from Venetians 1571 by the Turks and held by them until late 19th cent.

Uleåborg. See OULU 2.

Ule·el·heue \ü-ˌlā-ə-ˈlü-ā, ˌü-lə-ˈlü-ā\ *or* **Oe·le·ë·heuë** \ü-ˌlā-ə-ˈhü-ə\. Seaport town at N tip of Sumatra, Indonesia, opp. the island of We.

Ul·has·na·gar \ˌül-həs-ˈnä-gər\. Town, Maharashtra, India, ab. 25 mi. (40 km.) NE of Bombay; pop. (1991c) 369,077.

Ulianovsk. See SIMBIRSK.

Uliarus. See OLÉRON, ÎLE D'.

Ulias·tay \ˈül-yä-ˌstī\ *also* **Ulias·su·tai** *or* **Ulya·su·tai** \ˈül-yä-sä-ˌtī\ *or* **Jib·ha·lan·ta** \ˈjēb-ˌkä-län-ˌtä\. Town, W cen. Mongolia, in mountainous area ab. 460 mi. (740 km.) W of Ulaanbaatar.

Ulin·di \ü-ˈlin-dē\. River, S cen. Africa; rises in E cen. Democratic Rep. of the Congo, flows WNW into the Lualaba River; ab. 100 mi. (160 km.) long.

Uli·thi \ü-ˈlē-thē\. Islands (atoll group), W Caroline Is., W Pacific Ocean, 108 mi. (174 km.) ENE of Yap, and 400 mi. (644 km.) SW of Guam. Chief islands Falalop and Asor on the E and Mogmog on the N. Lagoon is 19 mi. (31 km.) long by 5 to 10 mi. (8 to 16 km.) wide and is excellent anchorage. Visited by British 1791; in WWII taken by U.S. 1944 and developed into major naval base.

UKRAINE
CITIES
Over 1,000,000
400,000 to 1,000,000
100,000 to 400,000
Under 100,000
Other localities
National capital
Political subdivision capital
BOUNDARIES
International
Political subdivision
FEATURES
Canals
Dams
0 50 100 mi
0 80 160 km
©1996, Encyclopædia Britannica, Inc.
RUSSIA
BELARUS
POLAND
SLOVAKIA
HUNGARY
ROMANIA
MOLDOVA
Chişinău
CENTRAL RUSSIAN UPLAND
Kursk
Krasnodar
Rostov-na-Donu
Don
Gulf of Taganrog
SEA OF AZOV
BLACK SEA
CRIMEA
CRIMEAN PENINSULA
KERCH PENINSULA
ARABAT SPIT
Sivash Lagoon
Salhyr
Crimean Canal
CRIMEAN MOUNTAINS
Mount Roman-Kosh 5,068 ft.
TARKHANKUT HILLS
Karkinit Bay
Kalamit Bay
Cape Tarkhankut
Cape Sarych
CRIMEAN HUNTING RESERVE
ASKANIYA-NOVA NATURE RESERVE
AZOV-SYVASH HUNTING RESERVE
BLACK SEA NATURE RESERVE
DANUBE WATER MEADOWS NATURE RESERVE
POLISSYA NATURE RESERVE
CARPATHIAN NATIONAL PARK
CARPATHIAN MOUNTAINS
Mount Hoverlya 6,760 ft.
Mount Kamula 1,545 ft.
Mount Mohyla Belmak 1,063 ft.
VOLHYNIAN HILLS
VOLHYNIA
DNIEPER UPLAND
DNIEPER LOWLAND
BLACK SEA LOWLAND
AZOV UPLAND
DONETS BASIN
DONETS HILLS
Polesye
Pripet
Lake Svityaz
Bug
Southern Bug
Dniester
Dniester Reservoir
Zbruch
Sluch
Teterev
Desna
Dnieper
Kiev Reservoir
Kaniv Reservoir
Kremenchuk Reservoir
Dniprodzerzhynsk Reservoir
Dnieper Reservoir
Kakhovka Reservoir
Lake Lenin
Vorskla
Donets
Ingul
Tisza
Stryy
Kiev
Kharkiv
Dnipropetrovs'k
Odessa
Donetsk
Zaporizhzhya
Lviv
Kryvyy Rih
Mariupol
Luhansk
Mykolayiv
Makiyivka
Vinnytsya
Sevastopol
Simferopol
Kherson
Poltava
Chernihiv
Cherkassy
Sumy
Gorlavka
Zhytomyr
Dniprodzerzhyns'k
Kirovohrad
Khmelnitski
Rivne
Chernivtsi
Kremenchuk
Ternopil
Ivano-Frankivs'k
Lutsk
Bila Tserkva
Kramatorsk
Melitopol
Kerch
Uzhhorod
Yevpatoriya
Kam'yanets' Podil's'kyy
Berdyansk
Alchevsk
Nikopol
Slavyans'k
Severodonets'k
Lysychansk
Pavlograd
Konotop
Feodosiya
Yalta
Izmail

Uljan. See UGLJAN.

Ulloa. See ULÚA.

Ulls·wa·ter \ˈəlz-ˌwȯ-tər, -ˌwä-\. Lake, Lake District, Cumbria, NW England; 3.5 sq. mi. (9 sq. km.); 7.5 mi. (12 km.) long; max. depth 205 ft. (63 m.).

Ulm \ˈu̇lm\. City, Baden-Württemburg, W Germany, on Danube River near mouth of Iller 45 mi. (72 km.) SE of Stuttgart; pop. (1992e) 112,173; motor vehicles, electrical equipment, leather goods; notable 14th cent. cathedral with 528-foot (161-meter) tower; 14th cent. town hall; university (1967).

History: First mentioned 854; imperial city by 14th cent.; accepted Reformation 1530 and was member of Protestant League of Schmalkalden; scene of battle October 1805 in which French under Emperor Napoléon defeated the Austrians; to Württemburg 1810; in WWII occupied by French Apr. 1945. Birthplace of physicist Albert Einstein 1879.

Ul·san \ˈül-ˈsän\. Town, South Kyŏngsang prov., South Korea, 33 mi. (53 km.) NNE of Pusan; pop. (1985c) 551,014; automobile assembly.

Ul·ster \ˈəl-stər\. **1.** County in SE New York. See table at NEW YORK.

2. Historical province, N Ireland; 8567 sq. mi. (22,189 sq. km.); now forms Northern Ireland (26 districts) and Ulster prov. of Ireland (3 counties).

History: Ancient Irish kingdom; home of O'Neills (earls of Tyrone) who rebelled against English rule c. 1600; most of land subsequently confiscated by British King James I and settled with Protestant Scots, Welsh, and English; further colonized after Cromwellian settlement mid-17th cent.; in early 20th cent. its opposition to Irish home rule led to formation of Northern Ireland (*q.v.*). See also IRELAND.

3. Province, N Ireland (republic), comprising counties of Cavan, Donegal, and Monaghan; 3093 sq. mi. (8011 sq. km.).

Ulúa \ü-ˈlü-ä\ *also* **Ulloa** \ü-ˈyō-ä\. River, NW Honduras; flows NE into the Gulf of Honduras; ab. 200 mi. (320 km.) long. See YOJOA, LAKE.

Ulu Dağ \ˌü-lə-ˈdä\; *anc.* **Olym·pus** \ō-ˈlim-pəs\. Mountain, Bursa prov., NW Turkey in Asia, SE of the city of Bursa; 8343 ft. (2543 m.).

Ulugh Muztagh. See MUZTAG.

Ulun·di \ü-ˈlün-dē\. Village, KwaZulu-Natal prov., E Rep. of South Africa, ab. 115 mi. (185 km.) NNE of Durban; made ✻ of Zululand 1873; scene of battle in which British defeated the Zulus July 1879; ✻ of KwaZulu 1980–94.

Uluru. See AYERS ROCK.

Ul·ver·ston \ˈəl-vər-stən\. Town, Cumbria, NW England, on Morecambe Bay 55 mi. (89 km.) N of Liverpool; pop. (1981p) 11,963; pharmaceuticals.

Ul·ver·stone \ˈəl-vər-stən\. Town, N Tasmania, Australia, on Bass Strait; pop. (1991c) 9923.

Ul'yanovsk *or* **Ulyanovsk.** See SIMBIRSK.

Ul'·ya·novsk Oblast \u̇l-ˈyä-nəfsk-ˈȯ-bləst, -ˌblast\ *or* **Ul'·ya·nov·ska·ya Oblast'** \u̇l-ˈyä-nəf-skə-yə-ˈȯ-bləstʸ\. Administrative subdivision of SE cen. Russia in Europe, on both sides of the middle Volga; 14,402 sq. mi. (37,301 sq. km.); pop. (1992e) 1,444,000; ✻ and only major city Simbirsk. Formerly part of Kuibyshev (now Samara) Oblast; estab. as separate oblast 1943.

Ulyasutai. See ULIASTAY.

Ulys·ses \yu̇-ˈli-sēz\. **1.** City, ⊗ of Grant co., SW Kansas; pop. (1990c) 5474.

2. Town, Tompkins co., S cen. New York; pop. (1990c) 4906.

Ülzen. See UELZEN.

Uman' *or* **Uman** \ü-ˈmänʸ\. City, S Kiev subdivision, Ukraine, 125 mi. (201 km.) S of the city of Kiev; pop. (1991e) 93,000. Formerly a Polish town; long fought over by Cossacks and Poles esp. in 17th–18th cents.; in WWII held by Germans 1941–44.

Uman \ˈü-ˌmän\. Island, SE part of Chuuk (*q.v.*), Caroline Is., W Pacific Ocean.

Uma·nan·da \ˌu̇-mə-ˈnən-də\. See GAUHATI.

Umar·kot \ˈü-mär-ˌkōt\. Town, E Sind, Pakistan, in SW Thar Desert; birthplace 1542 of Akbar, Mogul emperor of India.

Uma·til·la \ˌyü-mə-ˈti-lə\. **1.** River, NE Oregon; rises in N Union co., flows W and N into Columbia River in NW Umatilla co.; ab. 80 mi. (115 km.) long.

2. County in NE Oregon. See table at OREGON.

Um·ba \ˈəm-bə\. River, E Africa, in Tanzania and Kenya; flows E into the Indian Ocean in Kenya just N of Tanzanian boundary.

Um·ba·gog Lake \əm-ˈbā-ˌgäg\. Lake, part in Coos co., New Hampshire, and part in Oxford co., Maine; 10 mi. (16 km.) long; source of the Androscoggin River.

Umbeluzi. See MBULUZI.

Um·boi \ˈüm-ˌbȯi\ *also* **Rooke** \ˈru̇k\. Island, Papua New Guinea, bet. W end of New Britain I., Bismarck Archipelago, and Huon Penin., E New Guinea; separated from New Britain by Dampier Strait and from New Guinea by Vitiaz Strait; ab. 25 mi. (40 km.) long by 15 mi. (24 km.) wide; highest point 5430 ft. (1655 m.).

Um·brel·la Point \ˌəm-ˈbre-lə\. Cape, NW coast of Jamaica, West Indies, NE of Montego Bay.

Um·bria \ˈəm-brē-ə\. Autonomous region, cen. Italy; surrounded by Tuscany, Lazio, and Marche; ✻ Perugia in Apennines; grain, sugar beets, grapes; livestock; chemical and textile industries. See table at ITALY.

History: Inhabited by ancient Italic Umbrian tribe, known through the Iguvine tables found at Gubbio 1444 A.D.; came under Rome c. 300 B.C.; during Christian era became part of Papal States (*q.v.*); seat of Umbrian school of painting 15th–16th cents.; home of St. Francis of Assisi and poet Jacopone da Todi.

Umbrian Apennines. See table at APENNINES.

Umbro. See OMBRONE.

Umbro, Appennino *or* **Umbro–Marchigiano, Appennino.** See table at APENNINES.

Ume \ˈü-mə\. River, Västerbotten prov., N Sweden; flows SE into upper Gulf of Bothnia; 286 mi. (460 km.) long.

Umeå \ˈü-mā-ˌō\. Seaport, ⊗ of Västerbotten prov., N Sweden, on the Gulf of Bothnia at the mouth of Ume River; pop. (1993e) 94,912; manufactures machinery, furniture; university (1963); incorp. 1622.

Umgeni. See MGENI.

Umin·gan \ü-ˈmēŋ-ˌgän\. Municipality, Pangasinan prov., Luzon, Philippines, 40 mi. (64 km.) ESE of Lingayen; pop. (1980c) 41,364.

Um·la·zi \üm-ˈlä-zē\. Town, KwaZulu-Natal prov., E Rep. of South Africa, just SSW of Durban; pop. (1985c) 194,933.

Um·ma \ˈə-mə\. Important city of ancient Sumer, flourishing in the 3d millennium B.C.; its site is in S Mesopotamia, WNW of Lagash.

Umm al Qay·wayn *or* **Umm al–Qai·wain** \ˈu̇m-ȧl-kī-ˈwīn\. **1.** Emirate. See table at UNITED ARAB EMIRATES.

2. Coastal town, its ✻; pop. (1980c) 9652.

Umm Durmān. See OMDURMAN.

Um·nak \ˈüm-ˌnak\. Large island, W part of Fox Is. group, Aleutian Is., SW Alaska, separated from Unalaska I. on the NE by **Umnak Pass;** 70 mi. (113 km.) long by 12 mi. (19 km.) wide; 675 sq. mi. (1748 sq. km.); highest point 7050 ft. (2149 m.).

Ump·qua \ˈəmp-ˌkwȯ\. River, SW Oregon; formed by union of North Umpqua and South Umpqua rivers in W cen. Douglas co., flows N and W into Pacific Ocean; ab. 200 mi. (320 km.) long; navigable for 20 mi. (32 km.).

Umtali. See MUTARE.

Umtamvuna. See MTAMVUNA.

Um·ta·ta \üm-ˈtä-tä\. **1.** River, E Rep. of South Africa. See MTATA.

2. Town, NE Eastern Cape prov., S Rep. of South Africa, on Mtata River 114 mi. (183 km.) NNE of East London; pop. (1984e) 80,000; formerly served as ✻ of Transkei.

Umuahia. City, S Nigeria; ✻ of Abia state.

Umua·ra·ma \ˌu̇-mwə-ˈrä-mə\. Municipality, Paraná state, S Brazil, 280 mi. (451 km.) WNW of Curitiba; pop. (1991p) 100,246.

Umur·bro·gol \ˌü-mər-ˈbrō-ˌgȯl\. Mountain, Peleliu I., Belau. See BLOODY NOSE RIDGE.

Umzimkulu. See MZIMKULU.

Um·zim·vu·bu \ˌu̇m-zim-ˈvü-bü\. **1.** River, S Rep. of South Africa. See MZIMVUBU.
2. Seaport town, Eastern Cape prov., Rep. of South Africa. See PORT SAINT JOHNS.

UN. See UNITED NATIONS.

Una \ˈü-nä\. River, S Europe; flows NW past Bihać, Bosnia and Herzegovina, then turns NE and flows into Sava River; 159 mi. (256 km.) long; forms NW boundary of Bosnia and Herzegovina, separating it from Croatia.

Una, Mount \ˈü-nə\. Peak, N South I., New Zealand; 7540 ft. (2298 m.).

Una·ka Mountains \yu̇-ˈnā-kə\. Range of the Appalachian Mts., Unicoi and Carter cos., NE Tennessee, along the Tennessee-North Carolina boundary; includes **Mount Unaka** 5258 ft. (1603 m.) in Unicoi co.

Un·a·las·ka \ˌə-nə-ˈlas-kə\. **1.** Large island, Fox Is. group of Aleutian Is., SW Alaska, 75 mi. (121 km.) long, greatest width ab. 25 mi. (40 km.); 1064 sq. mi. (2756 sq. km.). On it is Makushin volcano 6678 ft. (2035 m.).
2. City on Unalaska Bay, Alaska, at E end of island opp. Dutch Harbor; pop. (1990c) 3089; oldest Russian settlement of Aleutian Is., estab. 1760s; annexed Dutch Harbor 1965.

Unalaska Bay. Inlet, N coast at E end of Unalaska I., E Aleutian Is., Alaska; ab. 12 mi. (19 km.) long and 9 mi. (14 km.) wide at its mouth; Amaknak I. is in S cen. part.

Unci. See ALMERÍA 2.

Un·com·pah·gre Peak \ˌən-kəm-ˈpä-grē, -grā\. Mountain, Hinsdale co., SW Colorado; 14,309 ft. (4361 m.); highest in the San Juan Mts.

Uncompahgre Plateau. Tableland, W Colorado, SW of the Gunnison River.

Undavalle. See VIJAYAWADA.

Un·der·hill \ˈən-dər-ˌhil\. Town, Chittenden co., NW Vermont; pop. (1990c) 2799.

Unfederated Malay States. Former grouping of states, SE Asia; total area 22,276 sq. mi. (57,695 sq. km.); those of British Malaya on the Malay Penin. not federated: Johore (Johor), Kedah, Kelantan, Perlis, Trengganu (Terengganu). See MALAYSIA and names of individual states.

Un·ga \ˈu̇ŋ-gə\. **1.** Island, Shumagin Is. group off S end of Alaska Penin.; ab. 20 mi. (32 km.) long.
2. Village on island.

Un·ga·ma Bay \u̇ŋ-ˈgä-mä\ *or* **For·mo·sa Bay** \fȯr-ˈmō-sə\. Inlet of Indian Ocean on SE coast of Kenya; receives Tana River.

Ungarn. See HUNGARY.

Un·ga·va \ən-ˈgā-və, -ˈgä-\. Region, Canada, E of Hudson Bay and N of Eastmain River, separated from Labrador on the E by the height of land. Organized 1895 as a district of Northwest Territories; transferred 1912 as New Quebec to prov. of Quebec; divided 1927 with larger part remaining as New Quebec (*q.v.*) and E part assigned to Newfoundland as part of Labrador. Covered with hills, lakes, and rivers; sparsely inhabited. Has mineral deposits.

Ungava Bay. Large inlet of S Hudson Strait, NE Quebec, E Canada; receives several large rivers, incl. the Koksoak, Leaf, and Payne.

Ungava Peninsula. The N part of New Quebec dist., Quebec, Canada.

Ung·gi \ˈüŋ-gē\; *formerly* **Yu·ki** \ˈyü-kē\. Seaport, NE North Korea, close to borders with Russia and China; held by Japanese 1910–45; occupied by Soviets Aug. 1945 in WWII.

Ungvár. See UZHGOROD.

Uni·ão dos Pal·ma·res \ü-ˈnyau̇ⁿ-düs-pȧl-ˈmä-rēs\. City, Alagoas state, E Brazil, 40 mi. (64 km.) NW of Maceió; munic. pop. (1991p) 57,496.

Uni·coi \ˈyü-nə-ˌkȯi\. County in NE Tennessee. See table at TENNESSEE.

Unicoi Mountains. Range of the Appalachian Mts., chiefly in Monroe co., SE Tennessee, along the Tennessee-North Carolina boundary.

Uni·je \ˈü-nē-ˌyā\ *or Ital.* **Unie** \ˈü-nē-ˌā\. Small island, Croatia, W of the island of Lošinj; formerly Italian.

Uni·mak \ˈyü-nə-ˌmak\. Largest island of the Aleutian Is., in Fox Is. group SW of tip of Alaska Penin.; 65 mi. (105 km.) long by 25 mi. (40 km.) wide; 1600 sq. mi. (4144 sq. km.); on it is Shishaldin volcano 9978 ft. (3041 m.).

Unimak Pass. Wide passage bet. Bering Sea and North Pacific Ocean, SW of Unimak I., Alaska.

Un·ion \ˈyü-nyən\. **1.** River, Hancock co., SE Maine; flows S into Bluehill Bay; ab. 50 mi. (80 km.) long.
2. Name of a parish in N Louisiana and of counties in 17 states of the U.S. See tables at ARKANSAS, FLORIDA, GEORGIA, ILLINOIS, INDIANA, IOWA, KENTUCKY, LOUISIANA, MISSISSIPPI, NEW JERSEY, NEW MEXICO, NORTH CAROLINA, OHIO, OREGON, PENNSYLVANIA, SOUTH CAROLINA, SOUTH DAKOTA, TENNESSEE.
3. City, ⊗ of Franklin co., E Missouri, 50 mi. (80 km.) WSW of St. Louis; pop. (1990c) 5909.
4. Former town, Hudson co., New Jersey. See UNION CITY 4.
5. Township, Union co., NE New Jersey, 5 mi. (8 km.) WNW of Elizabeth; pop. (1990c) 50,024; Kean Univ. (1855). Settled c. 1749 by colonists from Connecticut, hence its original name **Connecticut Farms**.
6. Village, Montgomery co., SW Ohio, NW of Dayton; pop. (1990c) 5501.
7. City, ⊗ of Union co., NW South Carolina; pop. (1990c) 9836.
8. Town, ⊗ of Monroe co., SE West Virginia; pop. (1990c) 566.
9. Islands, cen. Pacific Ocean. See TOKELAU.

Union, La. See LA UNION.

Unión, La. See LA UNIÓN.

Union, Mount. Peak in cen. Yavapai co., cen. Arizona; 7973 ft. (2430 m.).

Union Beach. Borough, Monmouth co., E cen. New Jersey, on Raritan Bay 7 mi. (11 km.) SE of Perth Amboy; pop. (1990c) 6156.

Union City. **1.** City, Alameda co., W California, S of Oakland; pop. (1990c) 53,762; pop. more than doubled in 1960s and again in 1970s.
2. City, Fulton co., NW cen. Georgia, 15 mi. (24 km.) SW of Atlanta; pop. (1990c) 8375.
3. City, Randolph co., E Indiana, 30 mi. (48 km.) E of Muncie on the Ohio border; pop. (1990c) 3612.
4. City, Hudson co., NE New Jersey, on Hudson River 3 mi. (5 km.) N of and adjoining Jersey City; pop. (1990c) 58,012; toiletries, lamps; formed 1925 by merger of West Hoboken and Union.
5. Borough, Erie co., NW corner of Pennsylvania, 20 mi. (32 km.) SE of the city of Erie; pop. (1990c) 3537.
6. Town, ⊗ of Obion co., NW Tennessee, 34 mi. (55 km.) NNE of Dyersburg; pop. (1990c) 10,513.

Union·dale \ˈyün-yən-ˌdāl\. Unincorporated settlement, Nassau co., SE New York, on Long Island; pop. (1990c) 20,328.

Unión de Re·yes \ü-ˈnyȯn-t͟hā-ˈrā-yes\. Town, Matanzas prov., W cen. Cuba; pop. (1981p) 41,455; junction point on railroad line 17 mi. (27 km.) S of the city of Matanzas.

Union Gap. City, Yakima co., S Washington; pop. (1990c) 3120.

Union Grove. Village, Racine co., SE Wisconsin, 15 mi. (24 km.) W of the city of Racine; pop. (1990c) 3669.

Union Island. Island, St. Vincent and the Grenadines, West Indies; 4 sq. mi. (10 sq. km.); one of the Grenadines.

Union Islands. See TOKELAU.

Union Lake. Lake, cen. Cumberland co., SW New Jersey; ab. 3.5 mi. (6 km.) long; a widening of the Maurice River.

Union of India. See INDIA 2.

Union of South Africa. See SOUTH AFRICA, REPUBLIC OF.

Union of So·vi·et Socialist Republics \ˈsō-vē-ət, -ˌet, *chiefly Brit* ˈsä-\; *commonly shortened to* **Soviet Union** *or* **U.S.S.R.;** *often popularly* **Rus·sia** \ˈrə-shə\. Former republic, E Europe and N and cen. Asia; 8,649,512 sq. mi. or 22,402,236 sq. km. (exclusive of the Sea of Azov and the White Sea); ✻ Moscow.

Physical features: Comprised the largest country on the globe, having a max. E to W extent of ab. 6800 mi. (10,940 km.) and a max. N to S extent of ab. 2800 mi. (4505 km.) extending across 11 time zones; in Europe had common boundaries with: Norway, Finland, Poland, Czechoslovakia, Hungary, and Romania; in Asia had common boundaries with: Turkey, Iran, Afghanistan, China, Mongolia, and North Korea; wide variety of physical features, incl. the fertile black-earth lands of the Ukrainian S.S.R., the deserts of W cen. Asia, the tundra of the N, and the high mountains of the Pamirs, Caucasus, Urals, and Kamchatka; contained some of the world's largest rivers: Volga, Ob', Yenisey, Lena, and many smaller but important streams, as the Dnieper, Don, Ural, and Amur. In the SW in Europe bordered on the Black Sea and in the NW on the Baltic; its N coastline extended ab. 3000 mi. (4825 km.) on the Arctic Ocean and for more than 1000 mi. (1610 km.) along the Pacific. Most of the Caspian Sea lay within its borders; other large inland waters included the Aral Sea, Lake Baikal, and Lake Balkhash. Islands included: Novaya Zemlya, Franz Josef Land, Severnaya Zemlya, New Siberian Is., Wrangel I. (*qq.v.*). For further details, see entries for the countries which comprised its constituent republics. An agricultural, mining, and industrial power producing esp. cereal grains, abundant minerals, and a wide range of manufactured goods.

Chief cities: Moscow, Leningrad (now St. Petersburg), Kiev (in Ukraine), Tashkent (in Uzbekistan), Kharkiv, Gorki (now Nizhniy Novgorod), Novosibirsk, Minsk (in Belarus), Sverdlovsk (now Yekaterinberg), and Dnepropetrovsk (Dnipropetrovs'k, Ukraine).

Political divisions: Comprised the following 15 constituent (Union) republics:

NAME	AREA[1] (sq. mi.)	AREA[1] (sq. km.)	CAPITAL
Armenian S.S.R.	11,506	29,800	Yerevan
Azerbaijan S.S.R.	33,436	86,599	Baku
Belorussian S.S.R.	80,154	207,599	Minsk
Estonian S.S.R.	17,413	45,100	Tallinn
Georgian S.S.R.	26,911	69,699	Tbilisi
Kazakh S.S.R.	1,048,300	2,715,097	Alma-Ata
Kirgiz S.S.R.	76,641	198,500	Frunze
Latvian S.S.R.	24,595	63,701	Riga
Lithuanian S.S.R.	25,174	65,201	Vilnius
Moldavian S.S.R.	13,012	33,701	Kishinev
Russian S.F.S.R.[2]	6,592,812	17,075,383	Moscow
Tadzhik S.S.R.	55,251	143,100	Dushanbe
Turkmen S.S.R.	188,455	488,098	Ashkhabad
Ukrainian S.S.R.[3]	233,089	603,700	Kiev
Uzbek S.S.R.	173,591	449,601	Tashkent

[1]Exclusive of the Sea of Azov and the White Sea.
[2]Most populous republic with roughly 52% in 1979.
[3]2d most populous republic with roughly 19% in 1979.

History: For earlier history, see RUSSIA. Union of Soviet Socialist Republics organized 1922 from soviet republics of Russian S.F.S.R., Ukrainian S.S.R., Belorussian S.S.R., and Transcaucasian Federation; with death of Communist leader Vladimir Ilich Lenin 1924 began struggle for power among party leaders which ended with victory of Joseph Stalin by 1927 and expulsion of his opponent Leon Trotsky from the country 1929; implemented First Five-Year Plan 1928 to stimulate economic development by centralizing industry and collectivizing agriculture; peasant population suffered severe famine in early 1930s esp. in Ukraine; adopted new constitution 1936; scene of widespread purge late 1930s in which millions of persons considered dangerous to the state were imprisoned or executed. At outset of WWII signed nonaggression pact with Germany Aug. 1939; occupied E Poland 1939; took from Finland (*q.v.*) Karelian Isthmus and other territories after Russo-Finnish War 1939–40; in 1940 secured Bessarabia and N Bukovina and the Baltic States; invaded June 22, 1941 by Germany, whose armies approached but did not take Moscow and Leningrad (St. Petersburg); subsequently Kuibyshev, Russia in Europe, became temporary ✻; Ukrainian S.S.R. and Crimea overrun by June 1942; Stalingrad (now Volgograd) entered by Germans Sept. 1942; recaptured Stalingrad Feb. 1943 and drove Germans from Soviet territory by summer of 1944; reached Berlin Apr. 1945 and became one of the four powers occupying Germany after the end of the war; invaded Manchuria Aug. 1945; annexed S part of Sakhalin I. 1945 (see KARAFUTO). Founding member of the UN 1945; established the Communist Information Bureau (Cominform) 1947; brought about the establishment of Communist regimes throughout most of E Europe in late 1940s; exploded its first atomic bomb 1949; signed treaty of alliance with China 1950 and supported North Korea and China during Korean War (1950–53) with military aid; after death of Stalin Mar. 1953 experienced limited degree of political and cultural liberalization under Communist leader Nikita Khrushchev; exploded its first hydrogen bomb 1953; restored relations with Yugoslavia (severed 1948) and withdrew its forces from Austria 1955; established the Warsaw Treaty Organization 1955; intervened militarily in Hungary 1956, suppressing liberal revolt; deterioration of Sino-Soviet relations began late 1950s; launched first manned orbital space flight 1961; installed ballistic missiles in Cuba but forced to withdraw these under U.S. pressure 1962; signed Nuclear Test-Ban Treaty 1963; deposed Khrushchev Oct. 1964, and under political leader Leonid Brezhnev began partial reversal of move towards liberalization; invaded Czechoslovakia 1968, suppressing that country's liberalization program; series of border clashes with China mid- to late 1960s; sent troops to Afghanistan Dec. 1979. In mid-1980s instituted Soviet leader Mikhail Gorbachev's liberal policy of economic and political restructuring (*perestroika*); by end of 1990 abolished Communist monopoly on power and approved program to create a market economy; scene of abortive coup by conservative officials against reformist government Aug. 1991; dissolved Dec. 1991 and replaced by 15 independent states formerly comprising the S.S.R.'s and the Russian S.F.S.R.

Union Pass. Mountain pass, W Wyoming, crossing the Wind River Range; used 1807 by American explorer John Colter on his expedition into Yellowstone region.

Union Springs. City, ⊗ of Bullock co., SE Alabama, SE of Montgomery, near source of Conecuh River; pop. (1990c) 3975.

Un·ion·town \ˈyü-nyən-ˌtau̇n\. City, ⊗ of Fayette co., SW Pennsylvania, SSE of Pittsburgh; pop. (1990c) 12,034. Founded 1760s.

Union Valley Dam. See UNITED STATES, *Dams and Reservoirs.*

Un·ion·ville \ˈyü-nyən-ˌvil\. **1.** Section of the town of Farmington, Connecticut. See FARMINGTON 2.
2. City, ⊗ of Putnam co., N Missouri, 30 mi. (48 km.) NW of Kirksville; pop. (1990c) 1989.

United Arab Emir·ates \ˈe-mə-rəts, -ˌrāts\; *formerly known as* **Tru·cial States** \ˈtrü-shəl\ *or* **Trucial Oman** \ō-ˈmän, -ˈman\ *also* **Trucial Coast.** Federation of seven states, E Arabian Penin., extending from Qatar to Gulf of Oman; total length of coast ab. 400 mi. (645 km.); pop. (1993e) 1,986,000; oil production (Abu Dhabi, Dubayy), fishing, herding; dates, vegetables, limes.

Political divisions: The member states are listed in the following table (for pronunciation of their names, see their individual entries):

NAME	AREA (sq. mi.)	AREA (sq. km.)	POP. (1985p)	CAPITAL
Abu Dhabi	26,000	67,340	670,125	Abu Dhabi
ʻAjmān	100	259	64,318	ʻAjmān
Al Fujayrah	450	1,166	54,425	Al Fujayrah
Ash Shāriqah	1,000	2,590	268,722	Ash Shāriqah
Dubayy	1,500	3,885	419,104	Dubayy
Ra's al Khaymah	650	1,684	116,470	Ra's al Khaymah
Umm al Qaywayn	300	777	29,229	Umm al Qaywayn

History: Treaty of peace concluded bet. Great Britain and native rulers 1820; in treaty of 1892 rulers agreed to restrict foreign relations to Great Britain; struck great quantities of oil c. 1960 in Abu Dhabi; sheikhs terminated defense treaties with Great Britain and established independent (six-

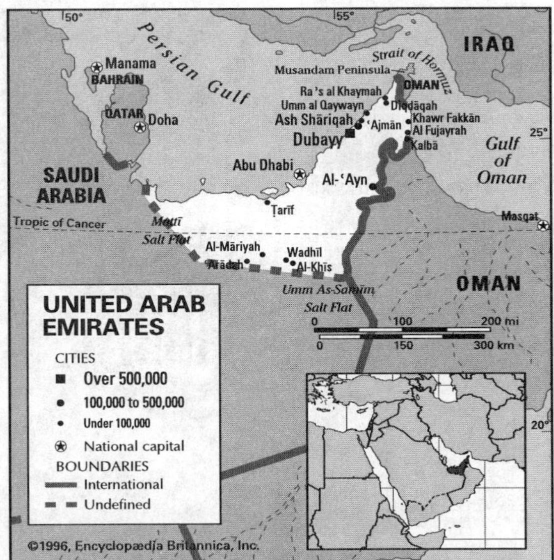

member) federation 1971; added Ra's al Khaymah to federation 1972; aided coalition forces against Iraq in Persian Gulf War 1991.

United Arab Republic. 1. Union of Egypt and Syria; formed 1958, dissolved 1961.
2. Former name of Egypt (*q.v.*).

United Dec·can State \ˈde-kən, -ˌkan\. Former state, W India; formed 1947 by the union of several Deccan states incl. Aundh, Bhor, Miraj (Junior), Phaltan, Ramdurg, and Sangli; merged with Bombay 1948.

United Kingdom of Great Britain and Northern Ireland *commonly shortened to* **United Kingdom.** Kingdom, W Europe, comprising Great Britain (England, Scotland, and Wales) and Northern Ireland; 94,251 sq. mi. (244,110 sq. km.); pop. (1994e) 58,421,700; ✻ London.

Chief products: Cereal grains; fish; coal, offshore petroleum; motor vehicles, published materials.

Chief cities: London, Birmingham, Glasgow, Leeds, Sheffield, Liverpool, Edinburgh, Manchester. For physical features and additional data, see ENGLAND; IRELAND, NORTHERN; SCOTLAND; WALES.

History: Archaeological evidence from pre-Roman times includes Neolithic mound-tombs and henge monuments, as well as Bronze Age Beaker culture tools, graves, and the famous Stonehenge monument. Brythonic-speaking Celtic peoples arrived during migrations of the first millennium B.C.; invaded by Roman Gen. Julius Caesar 55 and 54 B.C.; subjugated and became Roman province in first cent. A.D. (first attack by Emperor Claudius 43 A.D., last serious opposition the revolt of 60 A.D. under Boudicca, queen of the Iceni); Hadrian's Wall begun c. 122, extending from Solway Firth to mouth of the Tyne; Britain divided into two provinces, Britannia Superior and Britannia Inferior, 3d cent.; saw building of roads (see ERMINE STREET; FOSSE WAY; ICKNIELD STREET; WATLING STREET), establishment of cities, and introduction of Christianity; attacked by various barbarian tribes; gradually abandoned by Romans during first half of 5th cent., garrisons being withdrawn 410; invaded by Germanic tribes of Angles, Saxons, and Jutes beginning mid-5th cent.; S Britain (except Wales and Strathclyde) divided into a number of petty kingdoms incl. the so-called Heptarchy (*q.v.*); efforts to Christianize renewed late 6th cent.; Viking invasions began 8th cent.; by late 8th cent., Wessex emerged as dominant kingdom and gained much territory under King Egbert, early 9th cent.; Wessex King Alfred the Great defeated the Danes under Guthrum 878; the Danelaw reconquered c. 954; part of empire of Canute of Denmark 1016–35; conquered by William of Normandy 1066 and became a centralized feudal state; acquired holdings in France and conquered Ireland (1169–71) under Henry II; lost Normandy under John 1204; Magna Carta signed June 15, 1215 by John; Wales made principality 1284 and parliamentary system estab. 1295 under Edward I; Hundred Years' War (1337–1453) with France began under Edward III and resulted in loss of more continental holdings; torn by Wars of the Roses 1455–85 bet. houses of Lancaster and York which terminated in accession of Henry VII, first of the Tudor sovereigns; under Henry VIII broke with Roman Catholic Church; Church of England estab. with acts passed 1534 providing for English monarch to be head of Church, and Wales united with England 1536; lost last continental holding, Calais, under Mary I, 1558; under Elizabeth I entered period of maritime and colonial expansion; defeated Spanish Armada 1588; Stuart line began with James I, 1603; experienced civil wars mid–17th cent.; governed 1649–60 as Commonwealth estab. by Oliver Cromwell; Stuart line restored to throne with Charles II; Scotland formally united with England and Wales, 1707, together officially known as **Great Britain**. In 18th cent. saw evolution toward modern party system and cabinet government, Horace Walpole considered first prime minister, serving 1741–68; first Hanoverian ruler George I assumed the throne 1714; engaged in series of wars with Spain and France (incl. the War of Jenkins's Ear 1739–c. 1741 and the Seven Years' War 1756–63) which resulted in imperial gains (esp. Canada and India); led in developments of Industrial Revolution; lost American colonies 1783. In 19th cent. enacted legislative union with Ireland 1801, thus forming the **United Kingdom of Great Britain and Ireland;** participated in wars to liberate the Continent from French control 1793–1815 (see PENINSULA, THE 2 and WATERLOO 5); slave-trade abolished 1807; fought War of 1812 with United States 1812–1814; passed 1832 first of series of Reform Bills (others 1867, 1884–85, 1918) leading to universal suffrage; repealed Corn Laws 1846, removing last barrier to free trade; as an ally of Ottoman Empire fought in Crimean War 1854–56; put down Indian mutiny 1857–58 in India; defeated and annexed Transvaal and Orange Free State in Boer War 1899–1902. Participated as one of the Allies in WWI 1914–18. Granted dominion status to Ireland 1922, establishing Irish Free State, and forming with Northern Ireland the United Kingdom of Great Britain and Northern Ireland; as result of Imperial Conferences, esp. of 1926 and 1930, agreed 1931 to the Statute of Westminster granting to the self-governing dominions equality of status within the British Commonwealth of Nations (now the Commonwealth) [see COMMONWEALTH, THE]; abandoned policy of free trade 1932. Participated as one of the Allies in WWII 1939–45; after the fall of France 1940, threatened with invasion by the Germans until German defeat in air war ("Battle of Britain") 1940–41; base for the Allied invasion of Normandy, NW France, June 1944; member of UN 1945; gave up rule over India 1947; joined NATO 1949; participated with other UN forces in Korean War 1950–53; coronation of Queen Elizabeth II 1953; intervened militarily in Egypt (Suez Crises) 1956; relinquished control over most of its overseas dependencies 1940s–1970s although many remained in the Commonwealth; signed treaty of accession to European Economic Community 1972; retained sovereignty of Falkland Is. (*q.v.*) in war with Argentina 1982; as a result of continuing social strife in Northern Ireland, joined with Ireland in several peace initiatives during the 1970s, 1980s, and 1990s.

United Nations *or abbr.* **UN.** Political organization, consisting (1996) of 185 members; headquarters New York City; purpose is to promote international peace and security and advance solutions to international social and economic problems; concerned with many specialized matters incl. nuclear

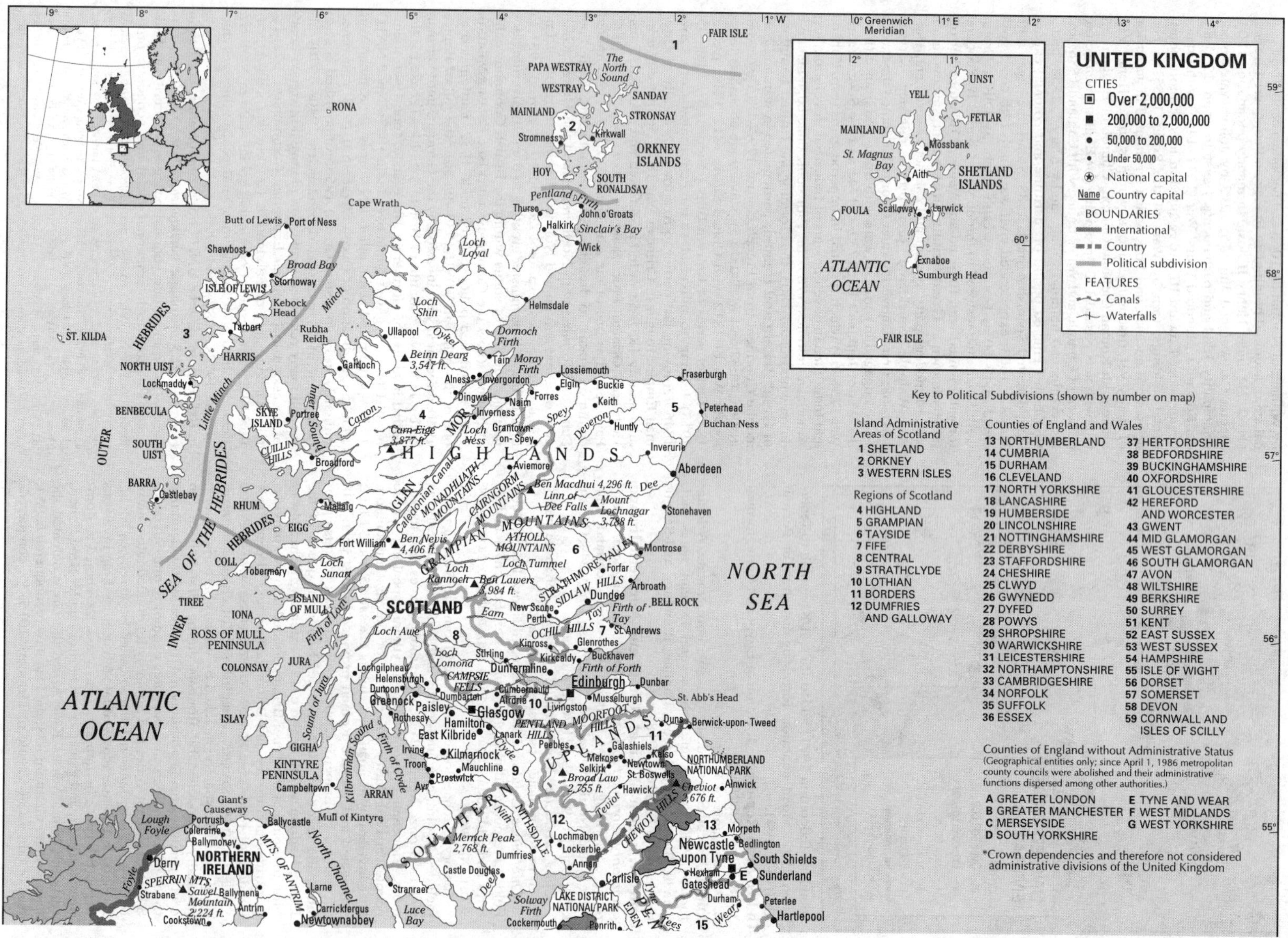
UNITED KINGDOM
CITIES
Over 2,000,000
200,000 to 2,000,000
50,000 to 200,000
Under 50,000
National capital
Name Country capital
BOUNDARIES
International
Country
Political subdivision
FEATURES
Canals
Waterfalls
Key to Political Subdivisions (shown by number on map)
Island Administrative Areas of Scotland
1 SHETLAND
2 ORKNEY
3 WESTERN ISLES
Regions of Scotland
4 HIGHLAND
5 GRAMPIAN
6 TAYSIDE
7 FIFE
8 CENTRAL
9 STRATHCLYDE
10 LOTHIAN
11 BORDERS
12 DUMFRIES AND GALLOWAY
Counties of England and Wales
13 NORTHUMBERLAND
14 CUMBRIA
15 DURHAM
16 CLEVELAND
17 NORTH YORKSHIRE
18 LANCASHIRE
19 HUMBERSIDE
20 LINCOLNSHIRE
21 NOTTINGHAMSHIRE
22 DERBYSHIRE
23 STAFFORDSHIRE
24 CHESHIRE
25 CLWYD
26 GWYNEDD
27 DYFED
28 POWYS
29 SHROPSHIRE
30 WARWICKSHIRE
31 LEICESTERSHIRE
32 NORTHAMPTONSHIRE
33 CAMBRIDGESHIRE
34 NORFOLK
35 SUFFOLK
36 ESSEX
37 HERTFORDSHIRE
38 BEDFORDSHIRE
39 BUCKINGHAMSHIRE
40 OXFORDSHIRE
41 GLOUCESTERSHIRE
42 HEREFORD AND WORCESTER
43 GWENT
44 MID GLAMORGAN
45 WEST GLAMORGAN
46 SOUTH GLAMORGAN
47 AVON
48 WILTSHIRE
49 BERKSHIRE
50 SURREY
51 KENT
52 EAST SUSSEX
53 WEST SUSSEX
54 HAMPSHIRE
55 ISLE OF WIGHT
56 DORSET
57 SOMERSET
58 DEVON
59 CORNWALL AND ISLES OF SCILLY
Counties of England without Administrative Status
(Geographical entities only; since April 1, 1986 metropolitan county councils were abolished and their administrative functions dispersed among other authorities.)
A GREATER LONDON
B GREATER MANCHESTER
C MERSEYSIDE
D SOUTH YORKSHIRE
E TYNE AND WEAR
F WEST MIDLANDS
G WEST YORKSHIRE
*Crown dependencies and therefore not considered administrative divisions of the United Kingdom
NORTH SEA
ATLANTIC OCEAN
SCOTLAND
NORTHERN IRELAND
ORKNEY ISLANDS
SHETLAND ISLANDS
H I G H L A N D S
SOUTHERN UPLANDS
GRAMPIAN MOUNTAINS
Edinburgh
Glasgow
Aberdeen
Dundee
Inverness
Newcastle upon Tyne
Ben Nevis 4,406 ft.
Ben Macdhui 4,296 ft.
SEA OF THE HEBRIDES
OUTER HEBRIDES
INNER HEBRIDES
FAIR ISLE
0° Greenwich Meridian

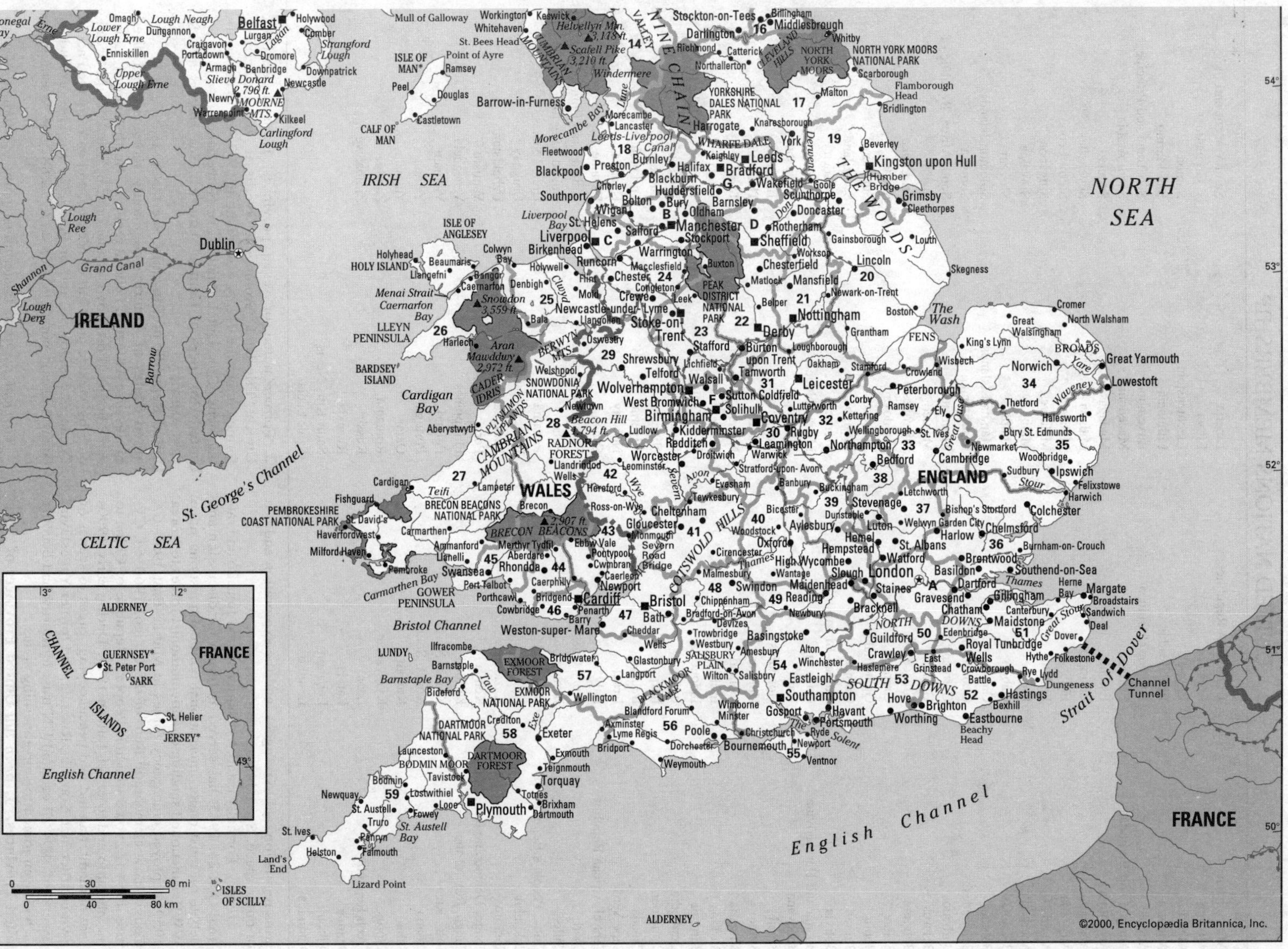
NORTH SEA
IRISH SEA
CELTIC SEA
St. George's Channel
English Channel
Bristol Channel
Cardigan Bay
Strait of Dover
Channel Tunnel
IRELAND
WALES
ENGLAND
FRANCE
ISLE OF MAN*
ISLE OF ANGLESEY
CHANNEL ISLANDS
ISLES OF SCILLY
THE WOLDS
COTSWOLD HILLS
PENNINE CHAIN
CAMBRIAN MOUNTAINS
BRECON BEACONS NATIONAL PARK
SNOWDONIA NATIONAL PARK
EXMOOR NATIONAL PARK
DARTMOOR NATIONAL PARK
PEMBROKESHIRE COAST NATIONAL PARK
NORTH YORK MOORS NATIONAL PARK
YORKSHIRE DALES NATIONAL PARK
PEAK DISTRICT NATIONAL PARK
London
Birmingham
Manchester
Liverpool
Leeds
Sheffield
Bristol
Cardiff
Dublin
Belfast
Plymouth
Southampton
Nottingham
Leicester
Coventry
Kingston upon Hull
0 30 60 mi
0 40 80 km
©2000, Encyclopædia Britannica, Inc.

UNITED NATIONS MEMBERSHIP

Afghanistan
Albania
Algeria
Andorra
Angola
Antigua and Barbuda
Argentina
Armenia
Australia
Austria
Azerbaijan
Bahamas
Bahrain
Bangladesh
Barbados
Belarus
Belgium
Belize
Benin
Bhutan
Bolivia
Bosnia and Herzegovina
Botswana
Brazil
Brunei
Bulgaria
Burkina Faso
Burundi
Cambodia
Cameroon
Canada
Cape Verde
Central African Republic
Chad
Chile
China, People's Republic of
Colombia
Comoros
Congo, Democratic Rep. of the
Congo, Rep. of the
Costa Rica
Croatia
Cuba
Cyprus
Czech Republic
Denmark
Djibouti
Dominica
Dominican Republic
Equador
Egypt
El Salvador
Equatorial Guinea
Eritrea
Estonia
Ethiopia
Fiji
Finland
France
Gabon
Gambia
Georgia, Republic of
Germany
Ghana
Greece
Grenada
Guatemala
Guinea
Guinea-Bissau
Guyana
Haiti
Honduras
Hungary
Iceland
India
Indonesia
Iran
Iraq
Ireland
Israel
Italy
Ivory Coast
Jamaica
Japan
Jordan
Kazakhstan
Kenya
Kiribati
Korea, North
Korea, South
Kuwait
Kyrgyzstan
Laos
Latvia
Lebanon
Lesotho
Liberia
Libya
Liechtenstein
Lithuania
Luxembourg
Macedonia
Madagascar
Malawi
Malaysia
Maldives
Mali
Malta
Marshall Islands
Mauritania
Mauritius
Mexico
Micronesia
Moldova
Monaco
Mongolia
Morocco
Mozambique
Myanmar
Namibia
Nauru
Nepal
Netherlands
New Zealand
Nicaragua
Niger
Nigeria
Norway
Oman
Pakistan
Palau
Panama
Papua New Guinea
Paraguay
Peru
Philippines
Poland
Portugal
Qatar
Romania
Russia
Rwanda
Saint Kitts-Nevis
Saint Lucia
Saint Vincent and the Grenadines
Samoa
San Marino
São Tomé and Príncipe
Saudi Arabia
Senegal
Seychelles
Sierra Leone
Singapore
Slovakia
Slovenia
Solomon Islands
Somalia
South Africa, Republic of
Spain
Sri Lanka
Sudan
Suriname
Swaziland
Sweden
Syria
Tajikistan
Tanzania
Thailand
Togo
Tonga
Trinidad and Tobago
Tunisia
Turkey
Turkmenistan
Uganda
Ukraine
United Arab Emirates
United Kingdom
United States
Uruguay
Uzbekistan
Vanuatu
Venezuela
Vietnam
Yemen
Yugoslavia
Zambia
Zimbabwe

arms regulation, aid to refugees, and the exploration and use of outer space. See table of members.

History: Formally estab. by charter signed June 26 and ratified Oct. 24, 1945; has served as forum for discussion and debate on most major international political questions since WWII; sanctioned sending of anticommunist forces to Korea 1950; deployed emergency forces in Middle East 1957–67, Congo (now Democratic Rep. of the Congo) 1960–64, Cyprus 1964 ff.; voted to admit People's Republic of China to membership and to expel Taiwan 1971. During early 1990s sent humanitarian aid and peacekeeping forces to scenes of civil conflict incl. Somalia, Rwanda, and former Yugoslavia. By end of 1994 all original UN trust territories had become or had been joined to self-governing states.

United Provinces. 1. *or in full* **United Provinces of Agra and Oudh.** State, India. See UTTAR PRADESH. **2.** Former union of seven provinces, Holland, Zeeland, Utrecht, Friesland, Groningen, Overijssel, and Gelderland; formed under the Treaty of Utrecht in 1579; led to the establishment of the Dutch republic, or Netherlands (*q.v.*).

United Provinces of Central America. See *History* at CENTRAL AMERICA.

United Republic of Tanzania. See TANZANIA.

United States of America *commonly shortened to* **United States** *also* **America.** Federal republic, North America; Lower 48 bounded on N by Canada, on E by the Atlantic Ocean, on S by Mexico and Gulf of Mexico, and on W by the Pacific Ocean; 3,619,969 sq. mi. or 9,375,720 sq. km. (excluding Great Lakes); pop. (1990c) 247,712,882; ✻ Washington, D.C.

Physical features: Easternmost point (excluding Alaska) West Quoddy Head, Maine, 66°57′W; westernmost point (excluding Alaska and Hawaii) Cape Alava, Washington, 124°44′W; northernmost point (excluding Alaska) Northwest Angle, Minnesota, ab. 49°23′N; southernmost mainland point (excluding Hawaii) East Cape, Florida, 25°07′N.

Chief rivers: Mississippi system (incl. Missouri, Ohio, Platte, Red, Arkansas), Colorado, Columbia, Rio Grande.

Largest lakes: Great Lakes in N (U.S.-Canada boundary runs through Ontario, Erie, Huron, and Superior; Michigan is wholly within boundary); Great Salt in Utah and Okeechobee in Florida.

Mountains: Appalachian system (incl. White Mts. and Green Mts. in New England, Adirondacks and Catskills in New York, Blue Ridge and Great Smoky Mts. in SE), Ozark Plateau in Missouri, Arkansas, and Oklahoma, Rocky Mts. across (N to S) the W (incl. Bitterroot Range in N, Wasatch, Uinta, and Front ranges in cen. part), and ranges along Pacific coast (Cascade Range, the Sierra Nevada, and Coast Ranges); highest point Mt. McKinley, Alaska, 20,320 ft. (6194 m.); lowest point Death Valley, California, 282 ft. (86 m.) below sea level; highest point (excluding Alaska) Mt. Whitney, California, 14,495 ft. (4418 m.); highest point E of Mississippi River Mt. Mitchell, North Carolina, 6684 ft. (2037 m.).

Chief islands: Hawaii, Kodiak, Prince of Wales, Chichagof, St. Lawrence, Admiralty, Nunivak, Unimak.

Chief products: Corn, wheat, soybeans, cotton, tobacco, oats, barley, rice, sugar beets, fruit; dairy products; livestock raising, fishing, lumbering; iron ore, coal, oil, natural gas, copper, zinc, sand and gravel, phosphate rock, gold; manufacturing: iron and steel, transportation equipment, machinery, chemicals, electronic equipment, textiles, paper; food products.

Largest cities: New York, Los Angeles, Chicago, Houston, Philadelphia, San Diego, Detroit, Dallas, Phoenix, San Antonio.

Principal ports: Houston, New Orleans, Corpus Christi on Gulf of Mexico; New York, Norfolk, Philadelphia on the Atlantic; Valdez, Long Beach, Los Angeles on the Pacific; Baton Rouge, Pittsburgh, St. Louis on rivers.

Political divisions: Divided into 50 states and Washington, D.C. (listed in the table *States, Territories, and Possessions;* for further details, see their individual entries).

History: Area orig. inhabited for several thousand years by numerous Indian peoples who had probably emigrated from Asia; European exploration and settlement from 16th cent. A.D. began displacement of Indians who also suffered severely from exposure to European diseases; first permanent European settlement, Spanish, at St. Augustine, Florida, 1565; English settlements in Virginia 1607, Massachusetts 1620, Maryland 1634, Pennsylvania 1681; English defeat of French in French and Indian War (1754–63) assured British political control over 13 colonies. Political unrest caused by English colonial policy culminated in American Revolution 1775–83 and Declaration of Independence 1776. U.S. organized first under the Articles of Confederation 1781 and finally under the Constitution 1787 as a federal republic. Purchased Louisiana region from France 1803; fought War of 1812 with Great Britain; acquired Florida from Spain 1819; established U.S. foreign policy with announcement of Monroe Doctrine 1823. In 1830 legalized removal of American Indians to lands W of Mississippi River, extended settlement into Far West mid-19th cent., esp. after discovery of gold in California 1848; annexed Texas 1845; established NW boundary by treaty with Great Britain 1846; secured New Mexico and California regions from Mexico 1848 by Treaty of Guadalupe Hidalgo ending Mexican War; acquired S Arizona from Mexico by Gadsden Purchase 1853. Disunified by conflict bet. slavery-based plantation economy in South and free industrial and agricultural economy in North, culminating in Civil War 1861–65 and abolition of slavery under Thirteenth Amendment. After reconstruction of union (1865–77), experienced rapid growth, urbanization, industrial development, and European immigration; in 1887 authorized allotment of Indian reservation land to individual tribesmen, resulting in widespread loss of land to whites; upheld racial segregation 1896 by declaring "separate but equal" facilities consitutional. By end of 19th cent. entered period of internationalism marked by development of foreign trade, participation in foreign wars, and acquisition of outlying territories, incl. Alaska, Midway Is., Hawaiian Is., Philippines, Puerto Rico, Guam, Wake I., American Samoa, Panama Canal Zone, and Virgin Is. of the U.S. (*qq.v.*). Participated in WWI 1917–18; granted suffrage to women 1920 and citizenship to American Indians 1924; suffered Great Depression 1929 ff.; entered WWII after Japanese invasion of Pearl Harbor Dec. 7, 1941; exploded first atomic bomb over Hiroshima, Japan, Aug. 1945, bringing about end of war; founding member of the UN 1945; granted independence to Philippines 1946; provided economic and military assistance to many European nations 1947 ff. under Truman Doctrine and Marshall Plan; founding member of NATO 1949; participated in Korean War (1950–53), U.S. troops constituting major component of UN forces; exploded first thermonuclear device 1952 and granted autonomous commonwealth status to Puerto Rico; declared racial segregation in public schools unconstitutional 1954; intervened militarily in Lebanon 1958; made Alaska and Hawaii states 1959; signed Nuclear Test-Ban Treaty 1963; President John F. Kennedy assassinated Nov. 22, 1963; passed Civil Rights Act of 1964; authorized full-scale intervention in Vietnam War 1964 (see *History* at VIETNAM); sent forces to Dominican Republic 1965; mid- to late 1960s marked by widespread civil disorders, incl. race riots and antiwar demonstrations; accomplished first manned lunar landing 1969; invaded Cambodia 1970; returned S Ryukyu Is. (occupied 1945) to Japan 1972; agreed to withdraw all U.S. forces from Vietnam Jan. 1973; sponsored peace negotiations bet. Egypt and Israel 1978–79 through mediation of President James E. Carter, Jr.; abolished Panama Canal Zone 1979; U.S. embassy in Tehran seized by Islamic militants Nov. 1979, its occupants held hostage until Jan. 1981; led coalition forces against Iraq in Persian Gulf War 1991; sent troops to Somalia 1992 to aid starving population; participated in NATO air strikes against Bosnian Serb forces in former Yugoslavia 1995.

☞ See tables containing additional United States information on pages 1228–39.

United States of Brazil. See BRAZIL.

United States of Colombia. See *History* at COLOMBIA.

United States of Indonesia. See INDONESIA 2.

United States of Venezuela. See VENEZUELA.

United States Range. Mountain range, N Ellesmere I., NE Nunavut, N Canada; highest point 9000 ft. (2743 m.).

Uni·ver·sal City \ˈyü-nə-ˌvər-səl\. **1.** Section of Los Angeles, California; motion-picture studios.

2. City, Bexar co., S cen. Texas, 17 mi. (27 km.) NE of San Antonio; pop. (1990c) 13,057.

Uni·ver·si·ty City \ˌyü-nə-ˈvər-sə-tē\. City, St. Louis co., E Missouri, WNW of the city of St. Louis; pop. (1990c) 40,087.

University Heights. Residential city, Cuyahoga co., N Ohio, 8 mi. (13 km.) E of Cleveland; pop. (1990c) 14,790; John Carroll Univ. (1886).

University Park. **1.** Village, Will co., NE Illinois; pop. (1990c) 6204; Governors State Univ. (1969).

2. City, Dallas co., NE Texas, entirely within city of Dallas; pop. (1990c) 22,259.

University Peak. Mountain in the Sierra Nevada, on NE boundary of Tulare co., S cen. California; 13,588 ft. (4142 m.).

Un·ley \ˈən-lē\. City, SE South Australia, Australia, a S suburb of Adelaide; pop. (1991c) 35,692.

Un·na \ˈu̇-nə\. City, North Rhine-Westphalia, Germany, 10 mi. (16 km.) E of Dortmund; pop. (1992e) 63,536; in coal-mining area.

\ə\ **abut** \ə̇\ match**es** \ᵊ\ kitten, Fr ta**ble** \ər\ f**ur**ther \a\ **a**sh \ā\ **a**ce
\ä\ c**o**t, c**a**rt \ȧ\ Fr b**a**c \au̇\ **ou**t \b̲\ Span A**v**ila \ch\ **ch**in \e\ b**e**t \ē\ **ea**sy
\g\ **g**o \i\ h**i**t \ī\ **i**ce \j\ **j**ob \k̲\ Ger i**ch**, Bu**ch** \ⁿ\ Fr v**in**
\ŋ\ si**ng** \ō\ g**o** \ö\ **a**ll \ȯ\ l**aw** \œ\ Fr b**œu**f \œ̄\ Fr f**eu** \ȯi\ b**oy**
\th\ **th**in \t̲h̲\ **th**is \ü\ l**oo**t \u̇\ f**oo**t \ue\ Ger f**ü**llen \ue̅\ Fr r**ue**
\y\ **y**et \ʸ\ Fr digne \ˈdēnʸ\, nuit \ˈnwʸē\ \yü\ f**ew** \yu̇\ f**u**ry \zh\ vi**si**on

PACIFIC OCEAN
Strait of Juan de Fuca
Victoria
Bellingham
Port Angeles
Mount Vernon
OLYMPIC MTS.
Everett
Bremerton
Seattle
Aberdeen
Olympia
Tacoma
Franklin D. Roosevelt Lake
Grand Coulee Dam
Lake Pend Oreille
Kalispell
Cape Disappointment
Astoria
Mount Rainier 14,410 ft.
Spokane
Coeur d'Alene
Moses Lake
Yakima
Mount St. Helens 8,366 ft.
WASHINGTON
Pullman
Moscow
Clarkston
Lewiston
Columbia
Walla Walla
Portland
Newport
Mount Hood 11,235 ft.
Salem
Pendleton
Corvallis
Eugene
Enterprise
John Day
BLUE MTS.
Baker
HELLS CANYON
Salmon
Coos Bay
Cape Blanco
Roseburg
Bend
OREGON
McCall
Weiser
Borah Peak 12,662 ft.
Caldwell
Burns
HARNEY BASIN
Crescent City
Medford
Klamath Falls
Klamath
Trinidad Head
Boise
Sun Valley
IDAHO
Snake
Owyhee
American Falls Reservoir
Twin Falls
Pocatello
Idaho Falls
Mount Shasta 14,162 ft.
Alturas
Arcata
Eureka
Redding
CALIFORNIA
Red Bluff
Fort Bragg
Ukiah
Chico
Winnemucca
Humboldt
Elko
Reno
Sparks
Carson Sink
Santa Rosa
Yuba City
Marysville
Carson City
Sacramento
Lake Tahoe
SIERRA NEVADA
GREAT NEVADA BASIN
Berkeley
Oakland
San Francisco
Modesto
San Jose
Santa Cruz
Monterey
Salinas
Los Banos
Fresno
Boundary Peak 13,140 ft.
Tonopah
Wheeler Peak 13,065 ft.
Ely
Lowest point in North America 282 ft. below sea level
WHITE MTS.
DEATH VALLEY
King City
Mount Whitney 14,495 ft.
California Aqueduct
San Luis Obispo
Bakersfield
Santa Maria
Lompoc
Santa Barbara
MOJAVE DESERT
Las Vegas
Henderson
Boulder City
Overton
Lake Mead
Hoover Dam
St. George
Los Angeles
Burbank
Pasadena
San Bernardino
Riverside
Long Beach
Santa Ana
Oceanside
Palm Springs
Escondido
San Diego
El Cajon
Chula Vista
Blythe
Needles
Kingman
Lake Havasu City
COLORADO DESERT
Yuma
PACIFIC OCEAN
SONORAN DESERT
MONTANA
Havre
Milk
Great Falls
Missouri
Glasgow
Fort Peck Lake
Missoula
Helena
Lewistown
Musselshell
Flathead Lake
Clark Fork
Anaconda
Butte
Dillon
Bozeman
Yellowstone
Billings
Glendive
Miles City
Baker
Tongue
Powder
Broadus
ROCKY MOUNTAINS
LEWIS RANGE
BITTERROOT RANGE
ABSAROKA RANGE
BIGHORN MTS.
Madison
Grand Teton 13,770 ft.
TETON RANGE
Cody
Sheridan
Gillette
WYOMING
Thermopolis
Riverton
Gannett Peak 13,804 ft.
WIND RIVER RANGE
Casper
Glendo Reservoir
GREAT DIVIDE BASIN
Rawlins
Rock Springs
Green River
Flaming Gorge Reservoir
Evanston
Laramie
Cheyenne
LARAMIE MTS.
MEDICINE BOW MTS.
GREAT SALT LAKE DESERT
Logan
Brigham City
Ogden
Great Salt Lake
Salt Lake City
Orem
Provo
WASATCH RANGE
UINTA MTS.
Vernal
Steamboat Springs
Fort Collins
Greeley
Boulder
Aurora
Denver
Meeker
Glenwood Springs
FRONT RANGE
Richfield
UTAH
Grand Jct.
Aspen
Mount Elbert 14,433 ft.
Colorado Springs
Moab
Montrose
COLORADO
Pueblo
Cedar City
Lake Powell
Glen Canyon Dam
San Juan
COLORADO PLATEAU
Durango
Alamosa
SANGRE DE CRISTO MOUNTAINS
Trinidad
Farmington
GRAND CANYON
Flagstaff
Gallup
Los Alamos
Santa Fe
Las Vegas
Prescott
Winslow
ARIZONA
Show Low
Albuquerque
Phoenix
Scottsdale
Tempe
Mesa
Gila
Casa Grande
Tucson
NEW MEXICO
Socorro
Rio Grande
Elephant Butte Reservoir
Silver City
Alamogordo
Las Cruces
SACRAMENTO MTS.
Nogales
Sierra Vista
El Paso
Ciudad Juárez
MEXICO
Winnipeg
Williston
Rugby
Minot
Devils Lake
Lake Sakakawea
Grand Forks
Beulah
NORTH DAKOTA
Dickinson
Mandan
Bismarck
Fargo
Jamestown
White Butte 3,506 ft.
Grand
Wahpeton
Mobridge
Lake Oahe
Aberdeen
Big Stone Lake
SOUTH DAKOTA
Redfield
Spearfish
Pierre
BLACK HILLS
Rapid City
Brookings
Newcastle
Hot Springs
Mitchell
Lake Francis Case
Sioux Falls
Chadron
Niobrara
Yankton
Valentine
O'Neill
Alliance
North Loup
Scottsbluff
Middle Loup
Wayne
North Platte
NEBRASKA
Fremont
North Platte
Columbus
Ogallala
Grand Island
Sterling
Kearney
Lincoln
McCook
Republican
GREAT PLAINS
Goodland
Mount Sunflower 4,039 ft.
Beloit
Junction City
Saline
Hays
Salina
Abilene
Scott City
Smoky Hill
KANSAS
Garden City
Hutchinson
La Junta
Dodge City
Wichita
Black Mesa 4,973 ft.
Liberal
Guymon
Winfield
Cimarron
Clayton
Dalhart
North Canadian
Enid
OKLAHOMA
Canadian
Oklahoma City
Conchas Lake
Amarillo
Elk City
Clinton
Norman
Pecos
Altus
Lawton
Ada
Clovis
LLANO ESTACADO
Red
Duncan
Lake Texoma
Roswell
Lubbock
Wichita Falls
Garland
Plano
Hobbs
Snyder
Fort Worth
Arlington
Dallas
Carlsbad
Midland
Abilene
Guadalupe Peak 8,749 ft.
Odessa
TEXAS
Pecos
San Angelo
Waco
DAVIS MTS.
Brady
Temple
EDWARDS PLATEAU
Sanderson
Amistad Reservoir
Austin
Bryan
San Antonio
Seguin
Uvalde
Victoria
Crystal City
Goliad
Port Lavaca
Nuevo Laredo
Laredo
Kingsville
Corpus Christi
Baffin Bay
Falcon Reservoir
Rio Grande City
McAllen
Harlingen
Monterrey
Brownsville
Mount Waialeale 5,200 ft.
KAUAI
Kapaa
NIIHAU
Lihue
OAHU
Kaneohe
MOLOKAI
Honolulu
Wailuku
LANAI
MAUI
PACIFIC OCEAN
HAWAII
Waimea
Honokaa
Mauna Kea 13,796 ft.
Hilo
HAWAII
Mauna Loa 13,680 ft.
Pahala
0 50 100 mi
0 80 160 km
Arctic Circle
Point Hope
Barrow
ARCTIC OCEAN
Kaktovik
BROOKS RANGE
RUSSIA
Bering Strait
Kotzebue
SEWARD PENINSULA
ALASKA
Porcupine
Nome
Galena
Fairbanks
ST. LAWRENCE ISLAND
Yukon
ALASKA RANGE
Mount McKinley 20,320 ft.
CANADA
Bethel
Valdez
Anchorage
Cordova
BERING SEA
Homer
Mount St. Elias 18,008 ft.
Dillingham
Bristol Bay
Skagway
Gulf of Alaska
Juneau
Stikine
Kodiak
KODIAK ISLAND
ALEXANDER ARCHIPELAGO
Sitka
Wrangell
Ketchikan
Dixon Entrance
ATTU ISLAND
ALEUTIAN ISLANDS
KISKA ISLAND
Shishaldin Volcano 9,372 ft.
0 200 400 mi
0 300 600 km
ADAK ISLAND
ATKA ISLAND
Dutch Harbor
UMNAK ISLAND
UNIMAK ISLAND

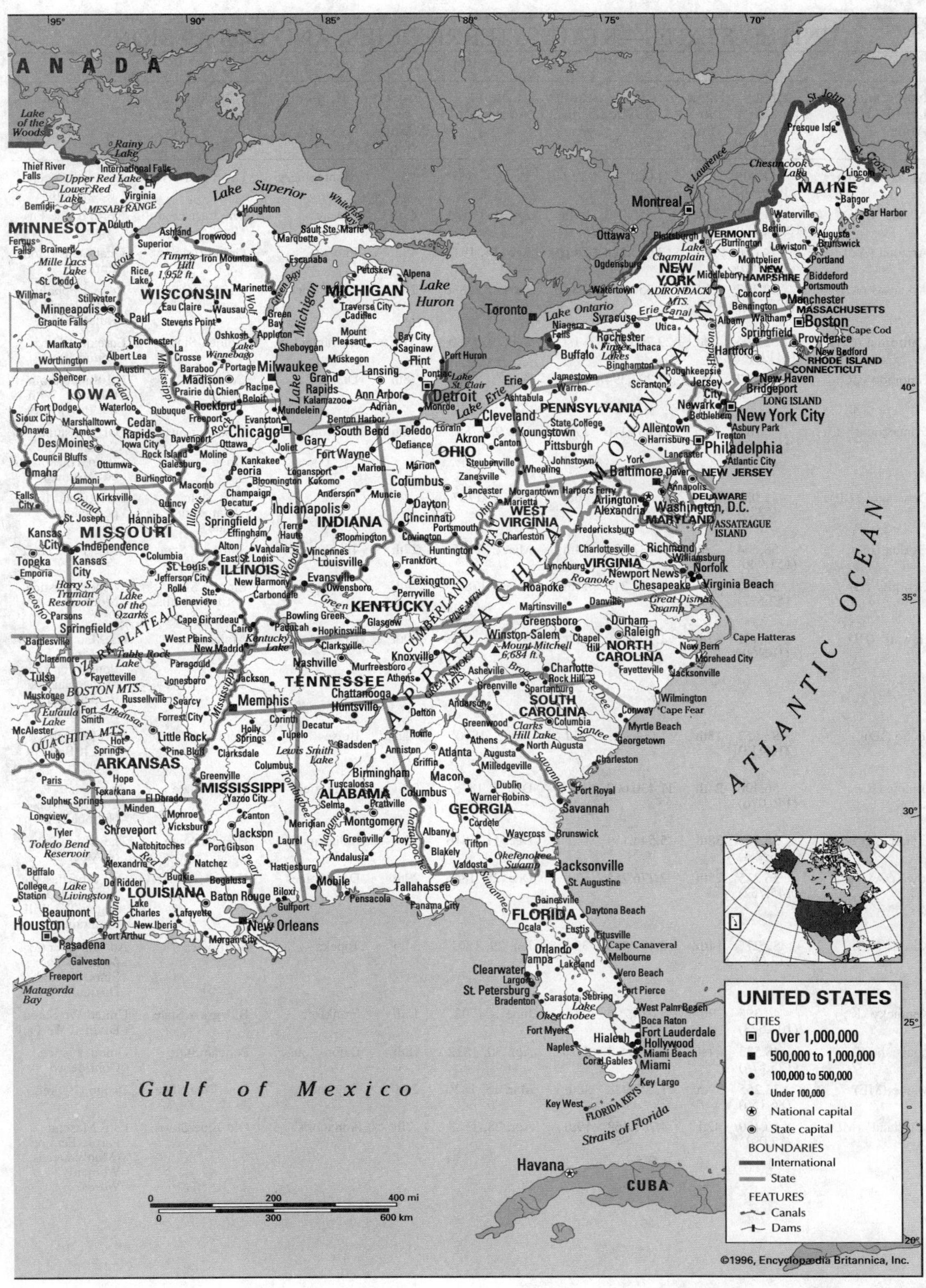

95°
90°
85°
80°
75°
70°
45°
40°
35°
30°
25°
20°
ANADA
Lake of the Woods
Rainy Lake
Thief River Falls
International Falls
Upper Red Lake
Lower Red Lake
Bemidji
Virginia
MESABI RANGE
Lake Superior
Whitefish Bay
Houghton
MINNESOTA
Duluth
Superior
Ashland
Ironwood
Marquette
Sault Ste. Marie
Fergus Falls
Brainerd
Mille Lacs Lake
St. Cloud
Timms Hill 1,952 ft.
Iron Mountain
Escanaba
Rice Lake
St. Croix
Green Bay
Petoskey
Alpena
Willmar
Stillwater
WISCONSIN
Marinette
MICHIGAN
Lake Huron
Minneapolis
St. Paul
Eau Claire
Wausau
Wolf
Green Bay
Lake Michigan
Traverse City
Cadillac
Granite Falls
Stevens Point
Oshkosh
Appleton
Mount Pleasant
Bay City
Saginaw
Mankato
Rochester
La Crosse
Lake Winnebago
Sheboygan
Flint
Port Huron
Worthington
Albert Lea
Austin
Baraboo
Portage
Milwaukee
Muskegon
Lansing
Grand Rapids
Pontiac
Lake St. Clair
Spencer
Madison
Racine
Kalamazoo
Ann Arbor
Detroit
IOWA
Prairie du Chien
Beloit
Adrian
Monroe
Fort Dodge
Waterloo
Cedar
Dubuque
Rockford
Mundelein
Sioux City
Marshalltown
Cedar Rapids
Freeport
Evanston
Benton Harbor
Lake Erie
Onawa
Ames
Rock
Chicago
South Bend
Toledo
Des Moines
Iowa City
Davenport
Gary
Defiance
Council Bluffs
Rock Island
Moline
Ottawa
Joliet
Fort Wayne
Omaha
Ottumwa
Galesburg
Kankakee
Peoria
Logansport
Marion
Kokomo
Burlington
Bloomington
Lamoni
Macomb
Champaign
Anderson
Muncie
Falls City
Kirksville
Decatur
Quincy
Illinois
Indianapolis
Grand
Hannibal
Springfield
INDIANA
St. Joseph
MISSOURI
Effingham
Terre Haute
Bloomington
Kansas City
Independence
Alton
Vandalia
Wabash
Vincennes
Topeka
Kansas City
Columbia
East St. Louis
St. Louis
ILLINOIS
Louisville
Emporia
Jefferson City
New Harmony
Evansville
Owensboro
Harry S. Truman Reservoir
Rolla
Carbondale
Neosho
Lake of the Ozarks
Ste. Genevieve
Green
Parsons
Springfield
OZARK PLATEAU
Cape Girardeau
Cairo
Paducah
Kentucky Lake
Bowling Green
Hopkinsville
Glasgow
KENTUCKY
Bartlesville
West Plains
New Madrid
Claremore
Table Rock Lake
Clarksville
Nashville
Tulsa
Paragould
Fayetteville
Jonesboro
Jackson
Murfreesboro
TENNESSEE
Muskogee
BOSTON MTS.
Russellville
Searcy
Mississippi
Memphis
Eufaula Lake
Fort Smith
Arkansas
Forrest City
Corinth
Chattanooga
Huntsville
McAlester
OUACHITA MTS.
Little Rock
Holly Springs
Tupelo
Decatur
Hot Springs
Pine Bluff
Hugo
ARKANSAS
Clarksdale
Lewis Smith Lake
Gadsden
Anniston
Columbus
Birmingham
Paris
Hope
Greenville
MISSISSIPPI
Tombigbee
Tuscaloosa
ALABAMA
Texarkana
El Dorado
Yazoo City
Selma
Prattville
Sulphur Springs
Minden
Canton
Montgomery
Longview
Monroe
Vicksburg
Jackson
Meridian
Tyler
Shreveport
Port Gibson
Laurel
Greenville
Troy
Toledo Bend Reservoir
Natchitoches
Red
Natchez
Pearl
Hattiesburg
Alabama
Andalusia
Lufkin
Alexandria
Buffalo
Bunkie
Bogalusa
College Station
Lake Livingston
De Ridder
LOUISIANA
Baton Rouge
Biloxi
Mobile
Gulfport
Pensacola
Beaumont
Lake Charles
Lafayette
Sabine
Houston
New Iberia
New Orleans
Port Arthur
Pasadena
Morgan City
Galveston
Freeport
Matagorda Bay
Gulf of Mexico
Montreal
Ottawa
St. Lawrence
St. John
Presque Isle
Chesuncook Lake
St. Croix
Lincoln
MAINE
Bangor
Bar Harbor
Waterville
Berlin
Augusta
Brunswick
Lewiston
Portland
Plattsburgh
VERMONT
Burlington
Lake Champlain
Montpelier
Ogdensburg
NEW YORK
Middlebury
NEW HAMPSHIRE
Biddeford
Portsmouth
Watertown
ADIRONDACK MTS.
Concord
Manchester
Toronto
Lake Ontario
Erie Canal
Bennington
MASSACHUSETTS
Syracuse
Utica
Albany
Waltham
Boston
Cape Cod
Niagara Falls
Rochester
Finger Lakes
Ithaca
Springfield
Providence
Buffalo
Binghamton
Hartford
New Bedford
RHODE ISLAND
CONNECTICUT
Jamestown
Warren
Poughkeepsie
New Haven
Erie
Scranton
Jersey City
Bridgeport
LONG ISLAND
Ashtabula
PENNSYLVANIA
Newark
Bethlehem
New York City
Cleveland
State College
Allentown
Asbury Park
Lorain
Akron
Youngstown
Harrisburg
Trenton
OHIO
Canton
Pittsburgh
Philadelphia
Johnstown
York
Lancaster
Atlantic City
Marion
Steubenville
Wheeling
Baltimore
Dover
NEW JERSEY
Columbus
Zanesville
Lancaster
Morgantown
Harpers Ferry
Annapolis
DELAWARE
Dayton
Marietta
Arlington
Washington, D.C.
Cincinnati
Ohio
WEST VIRGINIA
Alexandria
MARYLAND
Portsmouth
Charleston
ASSATEAGUE ISLAND
Covington
Huntington
Fredericksburg
Frankfort
Charlottesville
Richmond
Williamsburg
Lexington
CUMBERLAND PLATEAU
Lynchburg
VIRGINIA
Norfolk
Perryville
Newport News
Roanoke
Chesapeake
Virginia Beach
PINE MTN.
Martinsville
Danville
Great Dismal Swamp
APPALACHIAN MOUNTAINS
Greensboro
Durham
Raleigh
Winston-Salem
Chapel Hill
Cape Hatteras
Mount Mitchell 6,684 ft.
NORTH CAROLINA
New Bern
Knoxville
Morehead City
GREAT SMOKY MTS.
Asheville
Broad
Charlotte
Athens
Rock Hill
Pee Dee
Fayetteville
Jacksonville
Spartanburg
Greenville
Wilmington
Cape Fear
Dalton
Anderson
SOUTH CAROLINA
Conway
Greenwood
Columbia
Myrtle Beach
Rome
Clarks Hill Lake
Santee
Athens
Georgetown
Atlanta
Augusta
North Augusta
Griffin
Milledgeville
Charleston
Savannah
Macon
Dublin
Port Royal
Columbus
Warner Robins
GEORGIA
Savannah
Cordele
Chattahoochee
Albany
Waycross
Brunswick
Tifton
Blakely
Okefenokee Swamp
Valdosta
Suwannee
Jacksonville
Tallahassee
St. Augustine
Panama City
Gainesville
Daytona Beach
FLORIDA
Ocala
Eustis
Titusville
Orlando
Cape Canaveral
Tampa
Melbourne
Lakeland
Clearwater
Vero Beach
Largo
St. Petersburg
Fort Pierce
Bradenton
Sarasota
Sebring
Lake Okeechobee
West Palm Beach
Boca Raton
Fort Myers
Fort Lauderdale
Hialeah
Hollywood
Naples
Miami Beach
Coral Gables
Miami
Key Largo
Key West
FLORIDA KEYS
Straits of Florida
Havana
CUBA
ATLANTIC OCEAN
0
200
400 mi
0
300
600 km
UNITED STATES
CITIES
Over 1,000,000
500,000 to 1,000,000
100,000 to 500,000
Under 100,000
National capital
State capital
BOUNDARIES
International
State
FEATURES
Canals
Dams
©1996, Encyclopædia Britannica, Inc.

UNITED STATES—STATES, TERRITORIES, AND POSSESSIONS

STATES

Name and U.S. P.O. Abbr.	Area [sq. mi. and (sq. km.)]	Rank in Area	Pop. (1990c)	Rank in Pop.	Date of Admission[1]	Rank of Admission	Capital	Nickname	Motto
Alabama (AL)	51,705 (133,916)	29th	4,040,587	22d	Dec. 14, 1819	22d	Montgomery	Heart of Dixie	We Dare Defend Our Rights
Alaska[2] (AK)	591,004 (1,530,700)	1st	550,043	49th	Jan. 3, 1959	49th	Juneau	The Last Frontier	North to the Future
Arizona (AZ)	114,000 (295,260)	6th	3,665,228	24th	Feb. 14, 1912	48th	Phoenix	Grand Canyon State	Ditat Deus (God Enriches)
Arkansas (AR)	53,187 (137,754)	27th	2,350,725	33d	June 15, 1836	25th	Little Rock	Land of Opportunity	Regnat Populus (The People Rule)
California (CA)	158,706 (411,048)	3d	29,760,020	1st	Sept. 9, 1850	31st	Sacramento	Golden State	Eureka (I Have Found It)
Colorado (CO)	104,247 (270,000)	8th	3,294,394	26th	Aug. 1, 1876	38th	Denver	Centennial State	Nil Sine Numine (Nothing Without Providence)
Connecticut[1] (CT)	5,018 (12,997)	48th	3,287,116	27th	Jan. 9, 1788	5th	Hartford	Constitution State, Nutmeg State	Qui Transtulit Sustinet (He Who Transplanted Sustains)
Delaware[1] (DE)	2,057 (5328)	49th	666,168	46th	Dec. 7, 1787	1st	Dover	First State, Diamond State	Liberty and Independence
Florida (FL)	58,664 (151,940)	22d	12,937,926	4th	Mar. 3, 1845	27th	Tallahassee	Sunshine State	In God We Trust
Georgia[1] (GA)	58,910 (152,577)	21st	6,478,216	11th	Jan. 2, 1788	4th	Atlanta	Empire State of the South, Peach State	Wisdom, Justice, Moderation
Hawaii[3] (HI)	6,471 (16,760)	47th	1,108,229	41st	Aug. 21, 1959	50th	Honolulu	Aloha State	Ua Mau Ke Ea O Ka Aina I Ka Pono (The Life of the Land Is Perpetuated In Righteousness)
Idaho (ID)	83,557 (216,413)	13th	1,006,749	42d	July 3, 1890	43d	Boise	Gem State	Esto Perpetua (Let It Be Perpetual)
Illinois (IL)	56,400 (146,076)	24th	11,430,602	6th	Dec. 3, 1818	21st	Springfield	Prairie State	State Sovereignty—National Union
Indiana (IN)	36,291 (93,994)	38th	5,544,159	14th	Dec. 11, 1816	19th	Indianapolis	Hoosier State	The Crossroads of America
Iowa (IA)	56,275 (145,752)	25th	2,776,755	30th	Dec. 28, 1846	29th	Des Moines	Hawkeye State	Our Liberties We Prize and Our Rights We Will Maintain
Kansas (KS)	82,277 (213,097)	14th	2,477,574	32d	Jan. 29, 1861	34th	Topeka	Sunflower State	Ad Astra per Aspera (To The Stars Through Difficulties)
Kentucky (KY)	40,395 (104,623)	37th	3,685,296	23d	June 1, 1792	15th	Frankfort	Bluegrass State	United We Stand, Divided We Fall
Louisiana (LA)	48,523 (125,674)	31st	4,219,973	21st	Apr. 30, 1812	18th	Baton Rouge	Pelican State	Union, Justice, Confidence
Maine (ME)	33,265 (86,156)	39th	1,227,928	38th	Mar. 15, 1820	23d	Augusta	Pine Tree State	Dirigo (I Direct)
Maryland[1] (MD)	10,460 (27,091)	42d	4,781,468	19th	Apr. 28, 1788	7th	Annapolis	Old Line State	Fatti Maschii, Parole Femine (Manly Deeds, Womanly Words)

Name and U.S. P.O. Abbr.	Area [sq. mi. and (sq. km.)]	Rank in Area	Pop. (1990c)	Rank in Pop.	Date of Admission	Rank of Admission	Capital	Nickname	Motto
Massachusetts[1] (MA)	8,284 (21,456)	45th	6,016,425	13th	Feb. 6, 1788	6th	Boston	Bay State	Ense Petit Placidam Sub Libertate Quietem (By the Sword We Seek Peace, but Peace Only under Liberty)
Michigan (MI)	58,527 (151,585)	23d	9,295,297	8th	Jan. 26, 1837	26th	Lansing	Wolverine State, Great Lakes State	Si Quaeris Peninsulam Amoenam Circumspice (If You Seek a Beautiful Peninsula, Look Around You)
Minnesota (MN)	84,068 (217,736)	12th	4,375,099	20th	May 11, 1858	32d	St. Paul	Gopher State, North Star State	L'étoile du Nord (Star of the North)
Mississippi (MS)	47,689 (123,514)	32d	2,573,216	31st	Dec. 10, 1817	20th	Jackson	Magnolia State	Virtute et Armis (By Valor and Arms)
Missouri (MO)	69,697 (180,515)	19th	5,117,073	15th	Aug. 10, 1821	24th	Jefferson City	Show Me State	Salus Populi Suprema Lex Esto (Let the Welfare of the People Be the Supreme Law)
Montana (MT)	147,046 (380,849)	4th	799,065	44th	Nov. 8, 1889	41st	Helena	Treasure State	Oro y Plata (Gold and Silver)
Nebraska (NE)	77,355 (200,349)	15th	1,578,385	36th	Mar. 1, 1867	37th	Lincoln	Cornhusker State	Equality Before the Law
Nevada (NV)	110,561 (286,353)	7th	1,201,833	39th	Oct. 31, 1864	36th	Carson City	Silver State	All For Our Country
New Hampshire[1] (NH)	9,279 (24,033)	44th	1,109,252	40th	June 21, 1788	9th	Concord	Granite State	Live Free Or Die
New Jersey[1] (NJ)	7,787 (20,168)	46th	7,730,188	9th	Dec. 18, 1787	3d	Trenton	Garden State	Liberty and Prosperity
New Mexico (NM)	121,593 (314,926)	5th	1,515,069	37th	Jan. 6, 1912	47th	Santa Fe	Land of Enchantment	Crescit Eundo (It Grows As It Goes)
New York[1] (NY)	49,576 (128,402)	30th	17,990,456	2d	July 26, 1788	11th	Albany	Empire State	Excelsior (Ever Upward)
North Carolina[1] (NC)	52,669 (136,413)	28th	6,628,637	10th	Nov. 21, 1789	12th	Raleigh	Tar Heel State, Old North State	To Be Rather Than To Seem
North Dakota (ND)	70,665 (183,022)	17th	638,800	47th	Nov. 2, 1889	39th	Bismarck	Flickertail State	Liberty and Union, Now And Forever, One and Inseparable
Ohio (OH)	41,222 (106,765)	35th	10,847,115	7th	Feb. 19, 1803	17th	Columbus	Buckeye State	
Oklahoma (OK)	69,956 (181,186)	18th	3,145,585	28th	Nov. 16, 1907	46th	Oklahoma City	Sooner State	Labor Omnia Vincit (Labor Conquers All)
Oregon (OR)	97,073 (251,419)	10th	2,842,321	29th	Feb. 14, 1859	33d	Salem	Beaver State	Alis Volat Propriis (She Flies With Her Own Wings)
Pennsylvania[1] (PA)	45,333 (117,412)	33d	11,881,643	5th	Dec. 12, 1787	2d	Harrisburg	Keystone State	Virtue, Liberty, and Independence
Rhode Island[1] (RI)	1,212 (3,139)	50th	1,003,464	43d	May 29, 1790	13th	Providence	Ocean State, Little Rhody	Hope

Name and U.S. P.O. Abbr.	Area [sq. mi. and (sq. km.)]	Rank in Area	Pop. (1990c)	Rank in Pop.	Date of Admission	Rank of Admission	Capital	Nickname	Motto
South Carolina[1] (SC)	31,113 (80,583)	40th	3,486,703	25th	May 23, 1788	8th	Columbia	Palmetto State	Dum Spiro, Spero (While I Breathe, I Hope)
South Dakota (SD)	77,116 (199,730)	16th	696,004	45th	Nov. 2, 1889	40th	Pierre	Mount Rushmore State	Under God the People Rule
Tennessee (TN)	42,144 (109,153)	34th	4,877,185	17th	June 1, 1796	16th	Nashville	Volunteer State	Agriculture and Commerce
Texas (TX)	266,807 (691,030)	2d	16,986,510	3d	Dec. 29, 1845	28th	Austin	Lone Star State	Friendship
Utah (UT)	84,899 (219,888)	11th	1,722,850	35th	Jan. 4, 1896	45th	Salt Lake City	Beehive State	Industry
Vermont (VT)	9,609 (24,887)	43d	562,758	48th	Mar. 4, 1791	14th	Montpelier	Green Mountain State	Freedom and Unity
Virginia[1] (VA)	40,767 (105,586)	36th	6,187,358	12th	June 25, 1788	10th	Richmond	Old Dominion	Sic Semper Tyrannis (Ever Thus to Tyrants)
Washington (WA)	68,192 (176,617)	20th	4,866,692	18th	Nov. 11, 1889	42d	Olympia	Evergreen State	Alki (By and By)
West Virginia (WV)	24,181 (62,629)	41st	1,793,477	34th	June 20, 1863	35th	Charleston	Mountain State	Montani Semper Liberi (Mountaineers Are Always Free)
Wisconsin (WI)	56,154 (145,439)	26th	4,891,769	16th	May 29, 1848	30th	Madison	Badger State	Forward
Wyoming (WY)	97,914 (253,597)	9th	453,588	50th	July 10, 1890	44th	Cheyenne	Equality State, Cowboy State	Equal Rights
District of Columbia[4] (DC)	69 (179)		609,909				Washington		E Pluribus Unum (One Out of Many)
	3,619,969 (9,375,720)		247,712,882						

TERRITORIES AND POSSESSIONS

Name and U.S. P.O. Abbr.	Area (sq. mi.)	Area (sq. km.)	Pop. (1992e)	Capital
American Samoa[5] (AS)	76	197	43,000	Pago Pago
Guam (GU)	209	541	145,000	Agana
Puerto Rico[6] (PR)	3,435	8,897	3,295,000	San Juan
Virgin Islands of the U.S. (VI)	133	345	99,000	Charlotte Amalie
Other[7]	190	492	24,648	
	4,043	10,472	3,606,648	

[1]Date of admission of the 13 original colonies is that of ratification of the Constitution.
[2]The Alaska Statehood Act was signed by the President July 7, 1958.
[3]The Hawaii Statehood Act was signed by the President Mar. 18, 1959.
[4]Coextensive with the city of Washington.
[5]Includes Swains Island.
[6]Adopted constitution 1952 establishing it as a commonwealth with autonomy in internal affairs.
[7]Includes Johnston, Midway, Northern Mariana Islands, and Wake Island.

UNITED STATES—DAMS AND RESERVOIRS[1]

Shown in this table are the names of 45 major dams, with their location, year of completion, maximum height, and other important facts. Dams of the TENNESSEE VALLEY AUTHORITY are treated in a table at that entry.

Name of Dam	Year of Completion	Max. Height (feet)	Max. Height (meters)	Location	Purpose for which Water Impounded	Type[2]
Anderson Ranch	1950	456	139	S fork of Boise River, Elmore co., SW Idaho	flood control, irrigation, and power	earth
Blue Mesa	1966	390	119	Gunnison River, Gunnison co., W cen. Colorado	irrigation, power, and flood control	earth
Boulder	See Hoover, below					
Brownlee	1959	395	120	Snake River, Washington co., Idaho & Baker co., Oregon	flood control, recreation, and public water supply	earth (rock fill)
Carters	1974	464	141	Coosawattee River, NW Georgia	irrigation, power, and river regulation	earth (rock fill)
Detroit	1953	463	141	N branch of Santiam River, bet. Linn & Marion cos., W Oregon	flood control, navigation, power, and irrigation	gravity
Donnells	1957	484	148	Middle fork of Stanislaus River, Tuolumne co., cen. California	irrigation and public water supply	arch
Don Pedro	1971[3]	585	178	Tuolumne River, SW Tuolumne co., cen. California	irrigation, power	earth (rock fill)
Dworshak	1973	717	218	N fork of Clearwater River, near Orofino, NW Idaho	flood control, power, and navigation	gravity
Flaming Gorge	1964	502	153	Green River, Daggett co., NE Utah	irrigation and power	arch
Fort Peck	1940	242	74	Missouri River, Valley & McCone cos., NE Montana	flood control, power, and navigation	earth
Fort Randall	1954	160	49	Missouri River, Gregory & Charles Mix cos., S South Dakota	flood control, irrigation, and power	earth
Garrison	1956	210	64	Missouri River, Mercer & McLean cos., cen. North Dakota	flood control, irrigation, and power	earth
Glen Canyon	1966	708	216	Colorado River, Coconino co., N Arizona	power and river regulation	arch
Grand Coulee	1942	550	168	Columbia River, at junction of Douglas, Okanogan, & Lincoln cos., NE cen. Washington	flood control, irrigation, power, and river regulation	gravity
Green Peter	1967	365	111	Middle branch of Santiam River, Linn co., W Oregon	irrigation, power, flood control, and navigation	gravity
Hoover (formerly Boulder)	1936	726	221	Colorado River, bet. Clark co., Nevada & Mohave co., Arizona	flood control, irrigation, power, and river regulation	arch
Hungry Horse	1953	564	172	S fork of Flathead River, Flathead co., NW Montana	irrigation, power, and navigation	arch
Libby	1973	422	129	Kootenai River, Lincoln co., NW Montana	flood control, power, and recreation	gravity
Merriman	1949	370	113	Rondout Creek, Ulster co., SE New York	power	earth
Morris	1935	375	114	San Gabriel River, Los Angeles co., S California	water supply for Pasadena	buttress
Morrow Point	1968	468	143	Gunnison River, Montrose co., W Colorado	power	arch
Mossyrock	1968	606	185	Cowlitz River, Lewis co., SW Washington	power	arch

Name of Dam	Year of Completion	Max. Height (feet)	Max. Height (meters)	Location	Purpose for which Water Impounded	Type[2]
Mud Mountain	1948	425	130	White River, bet. Pierce & King cos., W cen. Washington	flood control	earth (rock fill)
Navajo	1963	402	122	San Juan River, on boundary bet. San Juan & Rio Arriba cos., N New Mexico	irrigation and flood control	earth
New Bullards Bar (or Bullards Bar)	1970	635	194	N Yuba River, Yuba co., N cen. California	irrigation, power, and water supply	arch
New Croton	1906	294	90	Croton River, Westchester co., SE New York	water supply for New York City	
New Exchequer	1926	479	146	Merced River, Mariposa co., cen. California	irrigation, flood control, and power	earth (rock fill)
Oahe	1959	242	74	Missouri River, cen. South Dakota, near Pierre	flood control, irrigation, navigation, and power	earth
Oroville	1968	754	230	Feather River, Butte co., N cen. California	flood control, recreation, and power	earth
O'Shaughnessy	1923	430	131	Tuolumne River, in Yosemite National Park, E cen. California	power and public water supply	gravity
Owyhee	1932	417	127	Owyhee River, Malheur co., SE Oregon	irrigation	arch
Pacoima	1929	420	128	Pacoima River, Los Angeles co., S California, NW of Los Angeles	flood control	arch
Pine Flat	1954	440	134	Kings River, Fresno co., S cen. California	irrigation, flood control, power, and recreation	gravity
Robert Moses	1962	389	118	Niagara River, (off stream), Niagara co., W New York	power	gravity
Ross	1949	540	164	Skagit River, NW Washington	power and flood control	arch
Round Butte	1964	440	134	Deschutes River, Jefferson co., N cen. Oregon	power and flood control	earth
San Gabriel No. 1	1939	405	123	San Gabriel River, Los Angeles co., S California	irrigation and flood control	earth (rock fill)
San Luis	1967	382	116	San Luis Creek, Merced co., cen. California	irrigation and power	earth
Shasta	1945	602	183	Sacramento River, Shasta co., N California	irrigation, power, navigation, and river regulation	gravity
Summersville	1966	398	121	Gauley River, Nicholas co., cen. West Virginia	flood control and river navigation	earth (rock fill)
Swift (or Swift Creek)	1958	610	186	Lewis River, Skamania co., S Washington	irrigation	earth
Trinity	1962	537	164	Trinity River, Trinity co., NW California	irrigation and power	earth
Union Valley	1963	453	138	Silver Creek, El Dorado co., E California	power	earth
Yellowtail	1966	525	160	Bighorn River, Big Horn co., S Montana	power, irrigation, and flood control	arch

[1]Dams arranged in alphabetical order. A dam and the lake or reservoir it creates have the same name except for the following: Fort Randall Dam (Lake Francis Case), Garrison Dam (Lake Sakakawea), Glen Canyon Dam (Lake Powell), Grand Coulee Dam (Franklin D. Roosevelt Lake), Hoover Dam (Lake Mead), Libby Dam (Lake Koocanusa), Merriman Dam (Rondout Reservoir), Morrow Point Dam (Blue Mesa Reservoir), Mossyrock Dam (Riffe Lake), New Exchequer Dam (Lake McClure), O'Shaughnessy Dam (Hetch Hetchy Reservoir), Round Butte Dam (Lake Chinook), San Gabriel No. 1 Dam (San Gabriel Reservoir), Trinity Dam (Clair Engle Lake), and Yellowtail Dam (Bighorn Lake).

[2]Modern dams fall essentially into two broad categories based on the dams' primary construction material. Earth dams (also known as embankment dams) are constructed of earth materials: rock, gravel, sand, silt, or clay. They have a broadly triangular cross section and include an impermeable core. Where the primary construction material is rock fill, that fact is noted in parentheses. Concrete dams are classified as arch dams, gravity dams, and buttress dams. Arch dams span narrow canyons and have the form of an arch with its apex pointed upstream when viewed from overhead. Gravity dams are generally linear in construction; they function by using the mass of their concrete to resist the pressure of the water they constrain. Buttress dams consist of thin walls of concrete supported by buttresses or piers; the buttresses may appear as multiple arches. Concrete dams are listed in this table according to whether they are of the arch, gravity, or buttress variety.

[3]Replaced one built in 1923.

UNITED STATES—NATIONAL PARKS

Name	Established	Area (acres)	Area (hectares)	Location	Features and Facts of Interest
Acadia	1919[1]	41,933	16,983	Maine coast	Granite peaks on Mount Desert I. and promontory on mainland across Frenchman Bay
American Samoa	1988[2]	9,000	3,645	at three locations in American Samoa	Rain forest, coral reef, white sand beach; tropical wildlife
Arches	1929[3]	73,379	29,718	Grand co., E Utah	Wind-eroded natural arch formations
Badlands	1929[3]	242,756	98,316	SW South Dakota	Eroded formations; fossils
Big Bend	1944[4]	708,221	286,830	on big bend of Rio Grande, W Texas, on Mexico border	Mountain and desert scenery
Biscayne	1968[3]	172,925	70,035	S Florida	Coral reef; wide variety of sea life
Black Canyon of the Gunnison	1933[3]	30,766	12,460	W Colorado	Deep gorge formed by Gunnison River; see BLACK CANYON 2
Bryce Canyon	1928[5]	35,835	14,513	S Utah	Canyon with curiously eroded pinnacles of various colors
Canyonlands	1964	337,570	136,716	SE Utah	Area of great geological interest
Capitol Reef	1937[3]	241,904	97,971	S cen. Utah	Petroglyphs, strange geologic formations
Carlsbad Caverns	1930[5]	46,766	18,940	SE New Mexico	Huge natural caves; see CARLSBAD CAVERNS
Channel Islands	1938[3]	249,354	100,988	five islands off S California	Fossils; examples of volcanic activity; marine birds and mammals
Crater Lake	1902	183,224	74,206	S Oregon	Lake, maximum depth 1932 ft. (589 m.), in crater of extinct volcano in Cascade Range
Death Valley	1933[3]	3,336,000	1,351,080	E California	Curious geological formations; see DEATH VALLEY
Denali	1917[6]	5,000,000	2,025,000	S cen. Alaska	Mount McKinley 20,320 ft. (6194 m.), highest peak in North America; wildlife esp. caribou and white Alaska mountain sheep
Dry Tortugas	1935[7]	64,700	26,204	Dry Tortugas (islands), W of Key West, Florida	Marine exhibit, remains of fortifications built in 1846
Everglades	1934	1,506,499	610,132	S Florida Peninsula	See EVERGLADES, THE
Gates of the Arctic	1980	7,523,888	3,047,175	N cen. Alaska	Vast wilderness
Glacier	1910	1,013,572	410,497	NW Montana; U.S. part of Waterton-Glacier International Peace Park (*q.v.*)	Mountain region with many lakes and small glaciers
Glacier Bay	1925[3]	3,225,284	1,306,240	SE Alaska, at S end of St. Elias Mts.	Large tidewater glaciers
Grand Canyon	1919	1,217,158	492,949	NW Arizona	Canyon of the Colorado River; see GRAND CANYON
Grand Teton	1929	309,994	125,548	NW Wyoming	Most spectacular part of Teton Range incl. Grand Teton 13,766 ft. (4196 m.)
Great Basin	1986	77,100	31,226	E Nevada	Centered on Wheeler Peak; has alpine lakes, meadows, caves, bristlecone pine groves; includes former Lehman Caves National Monument
Great Smoky Mountains	1930	520,269	210,709	along S section of Tennessee-North Carolina boundary	Great Smoky Mts. (*q.v.*); dense forests, flowering shrubs and many varieties of flowers
Guadalupe Mountains	1972	86,416	34,998	100 mi. (161 km.) E of El Paso, Texas	Area of great geological interest; contains major Permian limestone fossil reef
Haleakala	1961	28,099	11,380	Maui I., Hawaii	Large extinct volcanic crater
Hawaii Volcanoes	1916	229,177	92,817	Hawaii I., Hawaii	Volcanic area incl. active volcanoes Kilauea and Mauna Loa
Hot Springs	1921	5,839	2,365	W cen. Arkansas, in Ouachita Mts.	Forty-seven hot springs (143°F or 62°C)
Isle Royale	1931[2]	571,790	231,575	Michigan, NW Lake Superior	Isle Royale (*q.v.*) and surrounding islands; forested wilderness, cascades, inland lakes; old Indian copper pits
Joshua Tree	1936	559,954	226,781	S California	Desert flora and fauna

Name	Estab- lished	Area (acres)	Area (hectares)	Location	Features and Facts of Interest
Katmai	1918[3]	3,716,000	1,504,980	S Alaska, on N end of Alaska Penin.	Mount Katmai volcano (6715 ft. or 2047 m.) and Valley of Ten Thousand Smokes
Kenai Fjords	1980[8]	669,541	271,164	Kenai Penin., S Alaska	Fjords, jagged cliffs, one of the world's largest ice fields
Kings Canyon	1940	461,901	187,070	S cen. California, in the Sierra Nevada	Canyons of middle and S branches of Kings River; snow-covered mountains, giant sequoias in General Grant Grove Section and Redwood Mountain
Kobuk Valley	1980[8]	1,750,421	708,920	NW Alaska	Timberline transition zone containing the Kobuk River, the Baird Mountains and unusual landscapes; important archaeological sites
Lake Clark	1980[8]	2,636,839	1,067,920	across Cook Inlet from Anchorage, Alaska	Scenic wilderness with abundant fish and wildlife
Lassen Volcanic	1916[9]	106,372	43,081	N California, at S end of Cascade Range	Lassen Peak, active (1914–21) volcano; hot springs, mud geysers
Mammoth Cave	1941[10]	52,708	21,347	SW cen. Kentucky	Series of huge caves; see MAMMOTH CAVE
Mesa Verde	1906	52,122	21,109	SW Colorado	Prehistoric cliff dwellings
Mount Rainier	1899	235,612	95,423	W cen. Washington	Mount Rainier with extensive glacier systems; wild flowers in parks at its base
North Cascades	1968	504,781	204,436	NW Washington	Numerous glaciers and mountain lakes
Olympic	1938[11]	922,651	373,674	NW Washington	Olympic Mts., virgin forests incl. temperate rain forests; glaciers
Petrified Forest	1962[12]	93,532	37,880	E Arizona	Petrified wood; Indian ruins and petroglyphs
Redwood	1968	110,232	44,644	NW California, along the coast	Groves of ancient trees, some of which are the world's tallest
Rocky Mountain	1915	265,727	107,619	N cen. Colorado	Heart of the Rockies; Longs Peak 14,255 ft. (4345 m.) dominates region; interesting records of glacial period
Sequoia	1890	402,482	163,005	S cen. California S of Kings Canyon National Park	Fine stands of sequoias; over 300 lakes; high mountains, Sierra Nevada, incl. Mount Whitney 14,494 ft. (4418 m.)
Shenandoah	1935[10]	196,466	79,569	N Virginia	Section of Blue Ridge; Hawksbill Mt. ab. 4050 ft. (1234 m.); Skyline Drive part of Appalachian Trail
Theodore Roosevelt	1978[13]	70,446	28,531	at three locations near the Little Missouri River, W North Dakota	Memorial to Theodore Roosevelt in Badlands where he did some cattle ranching
Virgin Islands	1956[2]	14,689	5,949	St. John, Virgin Is.	Interesting fauna and flora; prehistoric Caribbean Indian relics
Voyageurs	1975[14]	218,035	88,304	N Minnesota	Lakes, forests; area of geological interest
Wind Cave	1903	28,295	11,459	SW South Dakota	Cavern with intermittent air current; boxwork formations
Wrangell-Saint Elias	1980[8]	8,331,604	3,374,300	E of Anchorage, Alaska	Mountains; abundant wildlife
Yellowstone	1872	2,219,791	899,015	NW Wyoming, S Montana, and E Idaho	Geysers, hot springs; lakes and waterfalls; Grand Canyon of the Yellowstone; see MAMMOTH HOT SPRINGS, YELLOWSTONE 1
Yosemite	1890	761,236	308,300	cen. California	Lofty cliffs; high waterfalls; groves of giant sequoias
Zion	1919	146,598	59,372	SW Utah	Zion Canyon cut by Virgin River, sandstone cliffs, remarkable for colors; fossils; abundant wildlife

[1] Estab. as Lafayette National Park; name changed 1929.
[2] Authorized.
[3] Proclaimed as a national monument.
[4] Authorized 1935.
[5] Proclaimed as a national monument 1923.
[6] Estab. as Mount McKinley National Park; name changed 1980.
[7] Proclaimed as Fort Jefferson National Monument; name and designation changed 1992.
[8] Proclaimed as a national monument 1978.
[9] Proclaimed as a national monument 1907.
[10] Authorized 1926.
[11] Proclaimed as Mount Olympus National Monument 1909.
[12] Proclaimed as a national monument 1906.
[13] Estab. as a national memorial park 1947.
[14] Authorized 1971.

UNITED STATES—NATIONAL MONUMENTS

Name	Established	Area (acres)	Area (hectares)	Location	Features and Facts of Interest
Agate Fossil Beds	1965[1]	3,055	1,237	Sioux co., W Nebraska	Miocene mammal fossils
Alibates Flint Quarries	1965[2]	1,371	555	Potter co., NW Texas	Quarries worked by prehistoric Indians
Aniakchak	1980	137,176	55,556	Alaska Peninsula, Alaska	Volcanic features including Aniakchak crater; tundra; lakes; rivers; wildlife
Aztec Ruins	1923	319	129	San Juan co., NW New Mexico	Prehistoric pueblo
Bandelier	1916	32,737	13,258	N cen. New Mexico	Cliff-dweller ruins
Booker T. Washington	1957	224	91	Franklin co., SW cen. Virginia	Booker T. Washington's birthplace and childhood home
Buck Island Reef	1961	880	356	St. Croix, Virgin Is.	Marine gardens
Cabrillo	1913	137	55	San Diego Bay, SW California	Land first sighted 1542 by Juan Rodriguez Cabrillo (d. 1543)
Canyon de Chelly	1931	83,840	33,955	NE Arizona	Cliff-dweller ruins
Cape Krusenstern	1978	659,807	267,222	NW Alaska	Arctic coastal features; offshore animals, migratory birds during summer; archaeological sites
Capulin Volcano	1916[3]	793	321	Union co., NE New Mexico	Site of ancient volcano, 8368 ft. (2550 m.)
Casa Grande Ruins	1918	472	191	Coolidge, Pinal co., S Arizona	Prehistoric ruins
Castillo de San Marcos	1924	21	8	St. Augustine, Florida	Old Spanish fort dating from 1672; see SAINT AUGUSTINE
Castle Clinton	1946	1	0.4	New York City, New York	Structure built 1808–11; used for defense, later served as immigrant landing depot
Cedar Breaks	1933	6,155	2,493	SW Utah, N of Zion National Park	Canyons and cliffs, vast natural highly colored amphitheater
Chiricahua	1924	11,985	4,854	Cochise co., SE Arizona	Curious natural rock formations
Colorado	1911	20,454	8,284	Mesa co., W Colorado	Monoliths and eroded formations; fossils, prehistoric Indian ruins
Congaree Swamp	1976	22,200	8,991	SE of Columbia, South Carolina	Forested stretch of Congaree River floodplain
Craters of the Moon	1924	53,545	21,686	Butte and Blaine cos., S Idaho	Lava flows in strange landscape effects
Devils Postpile	1911	798	323	Madera co., cen. California	Peculiar polygonal columns, like a pile of fence posts
Devils Tower	1906	1,347	546	on Belle Fourche River, Wyoming	Rock tower 865 ft. (264 m.) high, of volcanic origin
Dinosaur	1915	210,844	85,392	NE Utah and NW Colorado	Fossil remains of prehistoric animals
Effigy Mounds	1949	1,481	600	NE Iowa	Indian mounds
El Malpais	1987	114,272	46,280	Cibola co., W New Mexico	Volcanic features; diverse ecosystems
El Morro	1906	1,279	518	Cibola co., W New Mexico	Ruins of ancient pueblos; castellated sandstone with 17th–18th cent. inscriptions
Florissant Fossil Beds	1969	5,998	2,429	Teller co., Colorado	Oligocene fossils
Fort Frederica	1945	216	87	W coast of Saint Simons I., Georgia	Site of fort built by Oglethorpe (1736–48) to protect against Spaniards from Florida
Fort McHenry	1925	43	17	Baltimore, Maryland	Bombardment by British 1814, occasion of writing of *Star-Spangled Banner*
Fort Matanzas	1924	228	92	NE Florida, S of Saint Augustine	Relics of Spanish occupation; see MATANZAS INLET
Fort Pulaski	1924	5,623	2,277	island in mouth of Savannah River, Georgia	Fort built 1829–47 to replace Fort Greene. Fort bombarded 1862 by Union rifle cannon

Name	Established	Area (acres)	Area (hectares)	Location	Features and Facts of Interest
Fort Stanwix	1935	16	6	Rome, upstate New York	Reconstruction of fort built by the British c. 1758. Scene (1768) of the Indian treaty of Fort Stanwix
Fort Sumter	1948	195	79	Charleston, South Carolina	Object of attack April 12–13, 1861, which began Civil War
Fort Union	1954	721	292	Mora co., NE New Mexico	Ruins of Fort Union; ruts from Santa Fe Trail
Fossil Butte	1972	8,198	3,320	SW Wyoming	Fish fossils of the Paleocene and Eocene epochs; floodplain deposits
George Washington Birthplace	1930	538	218	Frederick co., NE Virginia	Part of family plantation and site of house where George Washington was born
George Washington Carver	1951	210	85	Newton co., SW Missouri	Carver's birthplace and childhood home
Gila Cliff Dwellings	1907	533	216	30 mi. (48 km.) N of Silver City, New Mexico	Cliff dwellings
Grand Canyon-Parashant	2000	1,000,000	405,000	NW Arizona, N of Grand Canyon National Park	Canyons, plateaus, and desert; archaeological remains
Grand Portage	1958	710	288	NE Minnesota	Portage on route used by early settlers and explorers
Grand Staircase-Escalante	1996	1,870,000	757,350	Kane & Garfield cos., S Utah	Erosion features; areas of fragile relief vegetation
Great Sand Dunes	1932	38,662	15,658	S cen. Colorado	Sand dunes of San Luis Park
Hagerman Fossil Beds	1988[1]	4,280	1,733	Twin Falls co., S Idaho	Exposed fossil beds along the Snake River
Hohokam Pima[4]	1972[1]	1,690	684	SE of Phoenix, Arizona	Archaeological remains of a prehistoric desert culture
Homestead	1936[1]	195	79	Gage co., SE Nebraska	Site of first homestead entered under General Homestead Act of 1862
Hovenweep	1923	785	318	SE Utah and SW Colorado	Prehistoric towers, pueblos, cliff dwellings
Jewel Cave	1908	1,274	516	SW South Dakota	Cave of limestone formations
John Day Fossil Beds	1975	14,014	5,676	N cen. Oregon	Fossils providing a paleontological record of 5 epochs of the Cenozoic era
Lava Beds	1925	46,560	18,857	N California	Volcanic landscape features; battleground of Modoc Wars 1873
Little Bighorn Battlefield[5]	1879[6]	765	310	Big Horn co., S Montana, on Little Bighorn River	Site where Gen. George A. Custer and his command were slain by Indians June 25–26, 1876; made national cemetery 1886
Montezuma Castle	1906	858	347	cen. Arizona	Prehistoric cliff dwellings
Mount Saint Helens[7]	1982	110,000	44,550	Skamania co., S Washington	Mount Saint Helens volcano
Muir Woods	1908	554	224	San Francisco, California	Fine redwood grove
Natural Bridges	1908	7,636	3,092	SE Utah	Three large natural bridges, largest 222 ft. (68 m.) high with span of 261 ft. (80 m.)
Navajo	1909	360	146	Navajo co., N Arizona	Cliff-dweller ruins
Ocmulgee	1934	702	284	Bibb co., cen. Georgia	Indian mounds
Oregon Caves	1909	488	198	Josephine co., SW Oregon	Caves of limestone formation
Organ Pipe Cactus	1937	330,689	133,929	S Arizona	Specimens of organ-pipe cactus; plants and animals not found elsewhere in the U.S.
Pinnacles	1908	16,265	6,587	W cen. California	Spirelike rock formations
Pipe Spring	1923	40	16	Mohave co., NW Arizona	Old stone fort in a desert region
Pipestone	1937	282	114	SW Minnesota	Quarry from which Indians obtained material for ceremonial peace pipes

Name	Established	Area (acres)	Area (hectares)	Location	Features and Facts of Interest
Poverty Point	1988[1]	911	369	West Carroll co., NE Louisiana	Prehistoric earthworks
Rainbow Bridge	1910	160	65	San Juan co., S Utah	Natural bridge 290 ft. (88 m.) above creek, span 278 ft. (85 m.)
Russell Cave	1961	310	126	NE Alabama	Cave containing valuable archaeological record of human habitation
Saguaro	1933	87,687	35,513	S Arizona	Giant cacti, or saguaro
Salinas Pueblo Missions	1980[8]	1,080	437	Torrance co., cen. New Mexico	Pueblo ruins and ruins of an early Spanish mission
Scotts Bluff	1919	3,003	1,216	W Nebraska	Landmark on old Oregon Trail
Statue of Liberty	1924	58	23	Liberty I., New York harbor, New York	Bartholdi's statue, Liberty Enlightening the World (unveiled 1886); Ellis Island immigration museum
Sunset Crater Volcano	1930	3,040	1,231	N Arizona	Volcanic crater; lava flows
Timpanagos Cave	1922	250	101	cen. Utah	Limestone cavern
Tonto	1907	1,120	454	Gila co., E cen. Arizona	Cliff-dweller ruins
Tuzigoot	1939	801	324	Yavapai co., cen. Arizona	Ruins of prehistoric pueblo
Walnut Canyon	1915	2,249	911	Coconino co., N cen. Arizona	Cliff dwellings in canyon
White Sands	1933	143,733	58,212	S cen. New Mexico	Dunes of gypsum sands
Wupatki	1924	35,253	14,277	Coconino co., N cen. Arizona	Prehistoric Indian dwellings
Yucca House[4]	1919	10	4	Montezuma co., SW Colorado	Prehistoric ruins

[1] Year authorized.
[2] Estab. as Alibates Flint Quarries and Texas Panhandle Pueblo Culture National Monument.
[3] Estab. as Capulin Mountain National Monument.
[4] Not open to the public.
[5] Formerly Custer Battlefield National Monument.
[6] Estab. as a national cemetery.
[7] Also known as Mount Saint Helens National Volcanic Monument.
[8] Estab. as Gran Quivira National Monument; later named Salinas National Monument.

UNITED STATES—NATIONAL HISTORICAL PARKS, NATIONAL BATTLEFIELDS, NATIONAL MILITARY PARKS

Name	Established	Area (acres)	Area (hectares)	Location	Features and Facts of Interest
Antietam National Battlefield	1890	3,244	1,314	Sharpsburg, Maryland	Site of battle Sept. 16-17, 1862, where Union army checked Lee's first invasion of the North in the Civil War; see SHARPSBURG 1
Appomattox Court House National Historical Park	1954	1,325	537	Appomattox, S cen. Virginia	Scene of surrender of Confederate army, April 9, 1865
Big Hole National Battlefield	1910[1]	656	266	SW Montana	Site of battle Aug. 9, 1877, bet. U.S. troops and Nez Perce Indians under Chief Joseph
Boston National Historical Park	1974	41	17	eight different sites in Boston, Massachusetts	Includes the historical sites of Bunker Hill, the Charlestown Navy Yard, Dorchester Heights, Faneuil Hall, the Old North Church, the Old South Meeting House, the Old State House, and the Paul Revere House
Chaco Culture National Historical Park	1907[2]	33,974	13,759	NW New Mexico	Cliff-dweller ruins
Chesapeake and Ohio Canal National Historical Park	1961	19,237	7,791	District of Columbia, Maryland, and West Virginia	Historic canal along the Potomac upstream from Washington, D.C.
Chickamauga and Chattanooga National Military Park	1890	8,106	3,283	NW Georgia and SE Tennessee	Includes battlefields of Chickamauga and Missionary Ridge in the Civil War
Colonial National Historical Park	1930[3]	9,327	3,777	SE Virginia	Includes sites of Jamestown, Williamsburg, and Yorktown
Cowpens National Battlefield	1929	842	341	Spartanburg co., NW South Carolina	Site of battle Jan. 17, 1781, of American Revolution; see COWPENS
Cumberland Gap National Historical Park	1940	20,312	8,226	Kentucky, Tennessee, and Virginia	Mountain pass explored by Daniel Boone; of strategic importance during Civil War
Dayton Aviation Heritage National Historical Park	1992[4]	undetermined	undetermined	Dayton, Ohio	Sites associated with the Wright brothers and poet Paul Laurence Dunbar
Fort Donelson National Battlefield	1928[5]	536	217	NW Tennessee	Includes site of a Civil War fort, captured by Gen. Grant 1862
Fort Necessity National Battlefield	1931	903	366	50 mi. (80 km.) SE of Pittsburgh, Pennsylvania	Site of entrenchments thrown up by Major George Washington in the French and Indian War, finally surrendered by Washington July 3, 1754
Fredericksburg and Spotsylvania County Battlefields Memorial National Military Park	1927	7,774	3,148	Spotsylvania co., NE Virginia	Includes battlefields of Fredericksburg, Chancellorsville, Spotsylvania Court House, and the Wilderness
George Rogers Clark National Historical Park	1966	26	10.5	Knox co., SW Indiana	Memorial near site of Fort Sackville, captured from British Feb. 25, 1779
Gettysburg National Military Park	1895	5,733	2,322	S Pennsylvania	Battlefield of Gettysburg
Guilford Courthouse National Military Park	1917	220	89	N cen. North Carolina	Site of battle Mar. 15, 1781, in which Americans defeated British and ended British control of the Carolinas
Harpers Ferry National Historical Park	1944[3]	2,262	916	West Virginia, Maryland, and Virginia	Scene of John Brown raid 1859; changed hands many times during Civil War
Hopewell Culture National Historical Park	1923[6]	1,032	418	Ross co., S Ohio	Prehistoric mounds; Hopewell cultural artifacts
Horseshoe Bend National Military Park	1959	2,040	826	Tallapoosa co., E Alabama	Site of battle bet. Gen. Andrew Jackson's forces and Creek Indian Confederacy, Mar. 27, 1814
Independence National Historical Park	1956	45	18	Philadelphia, Pennsylvania	Several structures closely associated with the American Revolution and founding of the United States
Jean Laffite National Historical Park	1978	20,020	8,108	on Mississippi River delta in and near New Orleans, Louisiana	Historic and cultural exhibits; site of the last major battle of the War of 1812
Kalaupapa National Historical Park	1980[4]	10,779	4,365	Molokai I., Hawaii	Commemorates early Hawaiian settlement; contains the site of a former leper colony; endangered species habitat
Kaloko-Honokohau National Historical Park	1978[4]	1,161	470	coastal area of W Hawaii I.	Exhibits of native Hawaiian culture
Keweenaw National Historical Park	1992	undetermined	undetermined	Keweenaw Penin., NW Michigan	Site of early copper mining activity
Kings Mountain National Military Park	1931	3,945	1,598	York co., N South Carolina	Includes site of battle Oct. 7, 1780, in which Americans defeated British in important battle of American Revolution
Klondike Gold Rush National Historical Park	1980	13,191	5,342	in and near Skagway, Alaska, and in Seattle, Washington	Commemorates the gold rush of 1898
Lowell National Historical Park	1978	137	55	several locations in Lowell, Massachusetts	Commemorates the beginnings of the industrial revolution in the United States
Lyndon B. Johnson National Historical Park	1969[7]	1,572	637	locations in and near Johnson City, Texas	Reconstructed birthplace and boyhood home of Lyndon B. Johnson

Name	Established	Area (acres)	Area (hectares)	Location	Features and Facts of Interest
Marsh-Billings National Historical Park	1992[4]	643	260	Woodstock, Vermont	Home of diplomat and linguist George Perkins Marsh
Minute Man National Historical Park	1959	772	313	Concord, Massachusetts	Scene of first fighting of American Revolution, April 19, 1775
Monocacy National Battlefield	1934[5]	1,647	667	NW of Washington, D.C. on Monocacy River	Site of battle July 9, 1864, in Civil War defense of Washington, D.C.
Moores Creek National Battlefield	1926[5]	86	35	Pender co., SE North Carolina	Site of battle Feb. 27, 1776, of the American Revolution; the "Lexington and Concord" of the South
Morristown National Historical Park	1933	1,684	682	Morristown, New Jersey	Main campsite of American armies during winters of 1776–77 and 1779–80
Natchez National Historical Park	1988[4]	108	44	Natchez, Mississippi	Historical houses
Nez Perce National Historical Park	1965	2,110	854	Idaho, Montana, Oregon, Washington	Commemorates culture and history of the Nez Perce Indian country
Pea Ridge National Military Park	1960	4,300	1,742	29 mi. (47 km.) N of Fayetteville, Arkansas	Scene of major engagement of the Civil War W of the Mississippi, March 7–8, 1862
Pecos National Historical Park	1965[3]	6,577	2,664	N cen. New Mexico	Sites of historical and archaeological importance incl. ruins of a pueblo and two Spanish missions
Petersburg National Battlefield	1926[5]	2,735	1,108	SE Virginia	Site of Civil War battles 1864–65; see PETERSBURG 4
Pu'uhonua o Honaunau National Historical Park	1955[8]	182	74	on W coast of Hawaii I., Hawaii	Site which until 1819 served as a refuge for Hawaiians defeated in battle or found guilty of crimes
Salt River Bay National Historical Park	1992[4]	912	369	St. Croix, Virgin Is.	Sites of cultural and historic interest incl. a prehistoric ceremonial ball court and a Dutch fort
San Antonio Missions National Historical Park	1978	613	248	four different sites in San Antonio, Texas	Includes four missions through which the Spanish extended their influence on American Indians in the 1700s
San Francisco Maritime National Historical Park	1988	50	20	San Francisco, California	Preserved vessels and maritime museum
San Juan Island National Historical Park	1966	1,752	710	San Juan I., NW Washington	Commemorates the harmonious relations existing bet. the U.S., United Kingdom, and Canada since 1872 border dispute in the region
Saratoga National Historical Park	1948	3,393	1,374	Saratoga co., E New York	Scene of victory of Americans over British Oct. 1777; turning point of the American Revolution
Shiloh National Military Park	1894	3,963	1,605	Hardin co., SW Tennessee	Site of battle of Shiloh Apr. 1862 in Civil War; see PITTSBURG LANDING
Sitka National Historical Park	1910	107	43	Baranof I., SE Alaska	Scene of last stand of Tlingit Indians against the Russians
Stones River National Battlefield	1927[5]	702	284	cen. Tennessee, near Murfreesboro	Site of battle 1862–63 of Civil War; see MURFREESBORO
Tumacacori National Historical Park	1908[3]	46	19	Santa Cruz co., S Arizona	Ruins of Spanish mission
Tupelo National Battlefield	1929	1	0.4	Lee co., NE Mississippi	Site of battle July 13–14, 1864, during Civil War; see TUPELO
Valley Forge National Historical Park	1976	3,468	1,404	Valley Forge, SE Pennsylvania	Site where the Continental Army camped during the winter of 1777–78
Vicksburg National Military Park	1899	1,625	658	W Mississippi	Includes site of siege of Vicksburg 1862–63 in Civil War
War In The Pacific National Historical Park	1978	1,960	794	Guam I., W Pacific Ocean	Scenic park memorializing WWII combatants in the Pacific
Wilson's Creek National Battlefield	1960	1,750	709	5 mi. (8 km.) WSW of Springfield, Missouri	Site of battle in Civil War, Aug. 10, 1861
Women's Rights National Historical Park	1980[4]	6	2	Seneca Falls, New York	Site where the women's rights movement was started by Susan B. Anthony and Elizabeth C. Stanton in 1848
Zuni-Cibola National Historical Park	1988[9]	800	324	Zuni, New Mexico	Zuni Indian cultural and archaeological sites

[1]Estab. as Big Hole Battlefield National Monument.
[2]Access restricted to guided tours.
[3]Estab. as a national monument.
[4]Year authorized.
[5]Authorized/estab. as a national military park.
[6]Estab. as Mound City Group National Monument.
[7]Authorized as a national historic site.
[8]Authorized as City of Refuge National Historical Park.
[9]Authorized, but not estab.

Unst \ˈənst\. One of the Shetland Is., NE of N Scotland; 38 sq. mi. (98 sq. km.).

Unterelsass. See *History* at ALSACE-LORRAINE.

Un·ter·wal·den \ˈu̇n-tər-ˌväl-dən\. Former canton, Switzerland; now divided into two demicantons: **Nid·wal·den** \ˈnēd-ˌväl-dən\; ✱ Stans and **Ob·wal·den** \ˈȯp-ˌväl-dən\; ✱ Sarnen. See *History* and table at SWITZERLAND.

Unyam·we·zi \ˌü-ˌnyäm-ˈwā-zē\. Plateau region, W Tanzania, around Tabora.

Un·zen \ˈu̇n-ˌzen\. Active volcano, Nagasaki prefecture, NW Kyūshū, Japan, on peninsula at S end of Shimabara Bay and opp. Kumamoto; 4462 ft. (1360 m.).

Un·zha \ˈün-zhə\. River, cen. Russia in Europe; rises in Vologda Oblast, flows S through Kostroma and Ivanovo oblasts to the Volga below Kineshma; 342 mi. (550 km.) long; navigable for ab. 250 mi. (400 km.).

Upem·ba National Park \ü-ˈpem-bä\. National park, Shaba administrative region, Democratic Rep. of the Congo; 4580 sq. mi. (11,862 sq. km.); variety of wildlife; estab. 1939.

Uper·na·vik *or* **Uper·ni·vik** \ü-ˈper-nä-ˌvēk\. Settlement, W coast of Greenland, N of Qeqertarsuaq I., 72°47′N, 56°10′W; pop. (1991e) 964.

Up·ing·ton \ˈə-piŋ-tən\. Town, Northern Cape prov., S Rep. of South Africa, on N bank of Orange River ab. 405 mi. (650 km.) NNE of Cape Town.

Up·land \ˈəp-lənd\. **1.** City, San Bernardino co., SE California, 30 mi. (48 km.) E of Los Angeles; pop. (1990c) 63,374; pop. doubled in 1960s and has continued to grow rapidly since.
2. Town, Grant co., Indiana; pop. (1990c) 3295; Taylor Univ. (1846).
3. Borough, Delaware co., SE Pennsylvania, 15 mi. (24 km.) WSW of Philadelphia; pop. (1990c) 3334.

Upo·lu \ü-ˈpō-lü\. Volcanic island, Samoa, in SW cen. Pacific Ocean, ab. 38 mi. (61 km.) WNW of Tutuila; 46 mi. (74 km.) long by ab. 16 mi. (26 km.) wide; 403 sq. mi. (1044 sq. km.); chief town Apia on N coast. Has many mountains, highest peak Mt. Fito 3608 ft. (1100 m.). Has fertile soil; copra, cocoa, bananas, rubber. Apia and Saluafata are chief harbors.

Upolu Point. Cape, N tip of Hawaii I., Hawaii, 20°16′N, 155°51′W; airport.

Upper Alsace. See *History* at ALSACE-LORRAINE.

Upper Andalusia. See ANDALUSIA 2.

Upper Angara. See ANGARA 2.

Upper Ar·ling·ton \ˈär-liŋ-tən\. City, Franklin co., cen. Ohio, 8 mi. (13 km.) NNW of Columbus; pop. (1990c) 34,128.

Upper Arrow Lake. See ARROW LAKE.

Upper Austria *or Ger.* **Ober·ö·ster·reich** \ˌō-bər-ˈœ-stər-ˌrīk\; *from 1938 to 1945* **Upper Danube** *or Ger.* **Ober·do·nau** \ˌō-bər-ˈdȯ-nau̇\. State, Austria, bet. Lower Austria and Germany and mostly W of the Enns River; ✱ Linz; crossed by the Danube; chiefly agricultural. In 12th cent. divided bet. duchies of Styria and Bavaria; later part of the duchy of Austria, then of the archduchy and empire. See table at AUSTRIA.

Upper Avon. See AVON 9.

Upper Bann. See BANN.

Upper Burma. See MYANMAR.

Upper California. See ALTA CALIFORNIA.

Upper Canada. Former British province, North America, N of the Great Lakes and S of the watershed bet. the Great Lakes and Hudson Bay, equivalent to S part of modern prov. of Ontario, Canada. Settled largely by American Loyalists after Revolutionary War (1775–83); estab. as separate province by act of 1791; after rebellion of 1837, reunited with Lower Canada (*q.v.*) 1841.

Upper Chateaugay Lake. See CHATEAUGAY LAKES.

Upper Danube. See UPPER AUSTRIA.

Upper Dar·by \ˈdär-bē\. Township, Delaware co., SE Pennsylvania; pop. (1990c) 81,177.

Upper East Region. Administrative region of NE Ghana. See table at GHANA.

Upper Egypt. See EGYPT.

Upper Engadine. See ENGADINE.

Upper Gastein. See GASTEINER ACHE.

Upper Guinea. See GUINEA 1.

Upper Hutt \ˈhət\. City, S North I., New Zealand; pop. (1991c) 37,092.

Upper Io·wa \ˈī-ə-wə\. River, NE Iowa; rises in S Mower co., S Minnesota, flows E into Mississippi River in NE Allamakee co., NE Iowa; 135 mi. (217 km.) long.

Upper Ka·pu·as Mountains \ˈkä-pü-ˌäs\. Mountain range in W cen. Borneo, extending E and W along the boundary bet. the Malaysian state of Sarawak and the Indonesian prov. of West Kalimantan; highest point ab. 2650 ft. (810 m.).

Upper Klamath Lake. See KLAMATH LAKES.

Upper Lorraine. See LORRAINE 2.

Upper Lough Erne. See ERNE.

Upper Marl·boro \ˈmärl-ˌbər-ō\. Town, ⊗ of Prince Georges co., S cen. Maryland; pop. (1990c) 745.

Upper Mat·e·cum·be Key \ˌma-tə-ˈkəm-bē\. See FLORIDA KEYS.

Upper More·land \ˈmōr-lənd\. Urban township, Montgomery co., SE Pennsylvania, N of Philadelphia; pop. (1990c) 25,313.

Upper New York Bay. See NEW YORK BAY.

Upper Palatinate. See PALATINATE.

Upper Peninsula. N part of Michigan, bet. Lake Superior and Lake Michigan.

Upper Peoria Lake. See PEORIA LAKE.

Upper Peru. Early name for region of South America corresponding approx. to Bolivia; orig. the audiencia of Charcas, a part (16th–18th cents.) of the Spanish viceroyalty of Peru, ✱ Chuquisaca (modern Sucre); subsequently became N part of new viceroyalty of La Plata; estab. as the independent state of Bolivia 1825.

Upper Red Lake. See RED LAKE 1.

Upper Region. Former administrative region of N Ghana; divided 1984 into Upper East Region and Upper West Region.

Upper Rhine *or Ger.* **Ober·rhein** \ˈō-bər-ˌrīn\. The section of the Rhine River, Europe, bet. Basel, Switzerland and Mainz, Germany.

Upper Richardson Lake. See RICHARDSON LAKES.

Upper Sad·dle River \ˈsad-ᵊl\. Borough, Bergen co., NE New Jersey, 10 mi. (16 km.) NNE of Paterson; pop. (1990c) 7198.

Upper San·dus·ky \sən-ˈdəs-kē, san-\. Village, ⊗ of Wyandot co., NW cen. Ohio, 18 mi. (29 km.) NNW of Marion; pop. (1990c) 5906.

Upper Saranac Lake. See SARANAC LAKES.

Upper Senegal–Niger. See *History* at MALI.

Upper Silesia. See SILESIA.

Upper Sind Frontier. See JACOBABAD 1.

Upper Suncook Lake. See SUNCOOK.

Upper Tunguska. See ANGARA 1.

Upper Volta. See BURKINA FASO.

Upper West Region. Administrative region of NW Ghana. See table at GHANA.

Upper Yukon. See LEWES 2.

Upp·sa·la \ˈu̇p-ˌsä-ˌlä\. **1.** Province of E Sweden. See table at SWEDEN.
2. City, its ⊗, 40 mi. (64 km.) NNW of Stockholm; pop. (1993e) 174,554; railroad junction; produces machinery, printed matter; military and air base; educational center, with university (1477) and many other academic institutions; 13th–15th cent. cathedral; episcopal palace (now a museum); 16th cent. castle. Near a small village which was orig. ✱ of ancient pre-Christian kingdom of Svea and original site of archiepiscopal see 1164; see transferred to site of city 1270.

Up·sa·la Glacier \üp-ˈsä-lä\. Glacier in the Andes, Argentina; ab. 35 mi. (55 km.) long, ab. 2 mi. (3 km.) wide near its terminus.

Up·shur \ˈəp-shər\. Name of counties in two states of the U.S. See tables at TEXAS and WEST VIRGINIA.

Up·son \ˈəp-sən\. County in W cen. Georgia. See table at GEORGIA.

Up·ton \ˈəp-tən\. **1.** County in W Texas. See table at TEXAS.
2. Town, Worcester co., cen. Massachusetts, 10 mi. (16 km.) ESE of the city of Worcester; pop. (1990c) 4677.

3. *earlier* **Camp Upton.** Former army camp, on Long Island, Suffolk co., New York, ab. 10 mi. (16 km.) WSW of Riverhead; estab. in WWI (1914–18); site since 1947 of Brookhaven National Laboratory for nuclear research.

'Uqaylah, Al. See AL 'UQAYLAH.

'Uqayr, Al–. See OQAIR.

Uqsor, Al–. See LUXOR.

Ur \ˈər, ˈu̇r\; *bib.* **Ur of the Chal·dees** \ˈkal-ˌdēz\. City and district, ancient Sumer, S Babylonia, the modern **Mu·qai·yir** \mu̇-ˈkī-yir, -ˈkā-\, ab. 12 mi. (19 km.) SW of An Nāsirīyah, S Iraq, on a former channel of the Euphrates River and near the Baghdad-Basra railroad line. One of the oldest cities of Mesopotamia, probably settled in 4th millennium B.C.; its first dynasty ruled c. 2500 B.C.; seat of worship of Nanna (Sin), the moon-god. Declined, but again important under a new dynasty, the third, founded c. 2100 by Sumerian King Ur-Nammu. Mentioned in Bible as early home of Hebrew patriarch Abraham in early 2d millennium (*Gen.* xi. 28, 31). In subsequent centuries captured and destroyed by Elamites, Babylonians, and others; restored by Chaldean king of Babylon Nebuchadrezzar II in 6th cent. B.C.; known in records as late as 4th cent. B.C. Excavations, esp. in 1920s and 1930s, have uncovered remains of great archaeological value incl. predynastic tombs, a first-dynasty temple, and a massive ziggurat of the third dynasty.

Ura·bá, Gulf of \ˌü-rä-ˈbä\ *or Span.* **Golfo de Urabá** \ˈgȯl-fō-ˌthä-\. Bay, NW coast of Colombia, at the inner end of the Gulf of Darien (*q.v.*).

Ura·ga \ü-ˈrä-gä\. Seaport, Kanagawa prefecture, SE Honshū, Japan, 5 mi. (8 km.) SE of Yokosuka on **Uraga Strait.** Port where first U.S. emissaries attempted 1846 to establish relations with the Japanese; their repulse led to American Commodore Matthew Perry's successful 1853 expedition.

Ural \ˈyu̇r-əl\ *or Kazakh* **Zhayyq** \ˈzhīk\. River, E Europe and W Asia; rises at the S end of the Ural Mts. on the E border of Bashkortostan Rep., E Russia in Europe, flows S, then W through Orenburg Oblast, crossing its SW border to flow S through W Kazakhstan to the Caspian Sea at Atyraū; 1575 mi. (2534 km.) long; Magnitogorsk, Orsk, Orenburg, and Oral are on its banks; navigable in lower course.

Ural Mountains. Mountain range, Russia and Kazakhstan, constituting the boundary bet. Europe and Asia; ab. 1640 mi. (2640 km.) long; extends S from Kara Sea to the W Kirgiz Steppe region of Kazakhstan, averaging 3000 to 4000 ft. (915 to 1220 m.); highest peak Mt. Narodnaya 6214 ft. (1894 m.). Cen. part (**Middle Urals** \ˈyu̇r-əlz\) is ab. 80 mi. (130 km.) broad and lower in alt., actually a plateau region 1000 to 2000 ft. (305 to 610 m.); densely forested and very rich in minerals incl. deposits of iron, copper, chromium, platinum, potassium, asbestos, and oil; comprises one of the largest industrial regions of the Commonwealth of Independent States, producing metal goods, chemicals, machinery, and wood products; during WWII this region developed rapidly with movement of many industrial plants from western U.S.S.R. to prevent their destruction by Germans. **Southern Urals** have three parallel ranges, with rich pasture grounds.

Uralsk *or* **Ural'sk.** see ORAL.

Ura·ri·coe·ra *or* **Ura·ri·cue·ra** \u̇-ˌrä-rē-ˈkwā-rə\. River, N Brazil; rises in Serra Parima near S Venezuelan border, flows E to unite with Tacutu River in N Amazonas and form Rio Branco; ab. 300 mi. (485 km.) long.

Urar·tu \u̇-ˈrär-ˌtü\ *or* **Van** \ˈvan\ *or Heb.* **Ar·a·rat** \ˈar-ə-ˌrat\. The Assyrian name for ancient kingdom around Lake Van (ancient Thospitis Lacus), N of Assyria. Kingdom lasted from c. 13th to 7th cents. B.C.; first inscriptions date from time of King Shalmaneser I (c. 1274–1245) of Assyria; repeatedly attacked by Assyrian kings and declined late 8th cent. B.C.; in 7th cent. B.C. ceased to exist after invasions by Cimmerians, Scythians, and Medes. See ARMENIA 1.

Ura·soe \ü-ˌrä-ˈsō-wā\. City, Okinawa prefecture, on Okinawa I., Japan; pop. (1990p) 89,993.

Ura–Tyu·be. See ŬROTEPPA.

Ura·wa \ü-ˈrä-wä\. Town, ✻ of Saitama prefecture, SE cen. Honshū, Japan, 13 mi. (21 km.) N of Tokyo; pop. (1992e) 434,976; university (1949); has an ancient Shinto shrine.

Ura·ya·su \ü-ˌrä-ˈyä-sü\. City, Chiba prefecture, SE Honshū, Japan; pop. (1990p) 115,675.

Ur·bana \ər-ˈba-nə\. **1.** City, ⊗ of Champaign co., E cen. Illinois, 47 mi. (76 km.) ENE of Decatur; pop. (1990c) 36,344; commercial center in agricultural region; Univ. of Illinois at Urbana-Champaign (1867); settled 1820s; incorp. as town 1833, as city 1855. Adjoins city of Champaign (combination often known as **Cham·paign–Urbana** \sham-ˈpān-\ *or* **Urbana–Champaign**).

2. City, ⊗ of Champaign co., W Ohio, 13 mi. (21 km.) N of Springfield; pop. (1990c) 11,353; Urbana Univ. (1850).

Ur·ban·dale \ˈər-bən-ˌdāl\. Town, Polk co., S cen. Iowa, NW suburb of Des Moines; pop. (1990c) 23,500.

Ur·bi·no \u̇r-ˈbē-nō\; *anc.* **Ur·bi·num Hor·ten·se** \ər-ˈbī-nəm-hȯr-ˈten-sē\ *or* **Ur·vi·num Met·au·ren·se** \ər-ˈvī-nəm-ˌme-tȯ-ˈren-ˈsē\. Commune, Pesaro e Urbino prov., Marche, cen. Italy, 19 mi. (31 km.) SW of Pesaro; pop. (1991p) 15,125; tourism; cathedral (rebuilt after earthquake 1789); 15th cent. ducal palace; university (1506). An Umbrian town which came under Rome 3d cent. B.C.; ruled by Church 9th–12th cents. A.D.; in 15th cent. a major political and cultural center; came under Papacy 1626; to kingdom of Italy 1860. Birthplace of painter Raphael 1483.

Urbino, Pesaro e. See PESARO E URBINO.

Urbinum Hortense. See URBINO.

Urbs Vetus. See ORVIETO.

Ur·cos \ˈu̇r-kōs\. Town, SE Peru, SE of Cuzco on railroad line in upper valley of the Urubamba; pop. (1981p) 8935.

Ur·da·ne·ta \ˌu̇r-dä-ˈnā-tä\. Municipality, Pangasinan prov., Luzon, Philippines, 20 mi. (32 km.) ESE of Lingayen; pop. (1980c) 71,796.

Ure \ˈyu̇r\. River, North Yorkshire, N England; ab. 50 mi. (80 km.) long; unites with the Swale River to form the Ouse.

Ure·we·ra National Park \ˌu̇-rə-ˈwer-ə\. National park, North I., New Zealand; 821 sq. mi. (2126 sq. km.); waterfalls, hiking trails; estab. 1954.

Ur·fa \ˈu̇r-fä\. **1.** Province of Turkey in Asia. See table at TURKEY.

2. *or* **Şan·lı·ur·fa** \ˌshän-lə-ˈu̇r-fä\; *anc.* **Edes·sa** \i-ˈde-sə\. City, its ✻, 75 mi. (121 km.) E of Gaziantep; pop. (1990c) 276,528; trading town with remains of ancient walls and citadel.

History: Ancient Edessa had independent dynasty, but its history is little known; an early center of Syriac-speaking Christianity until conquered by Arabs c. 639 A.D.; conquered from Seljuq Turks during First Crusade by Baldwin I of Boulogne who erected Christian county of Edessa 1098; reconquered by Muslims 1144; under Turkish rule by 1637; modern Urfa scene of massacres of Armenians late 19th cent. Home of Christian poet and theologian Bardesanes (154–c. 222).

Urga. See ULAANBAATAR.

Ur·ganch *or* **Ur·gench** \u̇r-ˈgyench\; *formerly* **No·vo Ur·gench** \ˌnȯ-və\ *or Eng.* **New Urgench.** Town, ✻ of Khorezm subdivision, W Uzbekistan, on left bank of the Amu Dar'ya (ancient Oxus); pop. (1991e) 130,400.

Urgel, Seo de. See LA SEU D'URGELL.

Ur·genj \u̇r-ˈgenj\. Ancient town, Uzbekistan, ab. 85 mi. (135 km.) NW of Urganch; once dominated trade in the lower Oxus region.

Uri \ˈu̇-rē\. Canton, Switzerland. See *History* and table at SWITZERLAND.

Uri, Bay of *or* **Uri, Lake of.** See URNER SEE.

Urianghai *or* **Uriankhai.** See TUVA.

Uriburu, General J. F. See ZÁRATE.

Uriconium. See WROXETER.

Urmia. See ORŪMĪYEH.

Urmia, Lake. See ORŪMĪYEH, DARYĀCHEH-YE.

\ə\ abut \ə\ matches \ᵊ\ kitten, Fr table \ər\ further \a\ ash \ā\ ace \ä\ cot, cart \à\ Fr bac \au̇\ out \b\ Span Avila \ch\ chin \e\ bet \ē\ easy \g\ go \i\ hit \ī\ ice \j\ job \k\ Ger ich, Buch \ⁿ\ Fr vin \ŋ\ sing \ō\ go \ȯ\ all \ȯ\ law \œ\ Fr bœuf \œ̄\ Fr feu \ȯi\ boy \th\ thin \th\ this \ü\ loot \u̇\ foot \ue\ Ger füllen \ue̅\ Fr rue \y\ yet \ʸ\ Fr digne \ˈdēnʸ\, nuit \ˈnwʸē\ \yü\ few \yu̇\ fury \zh\ vision

Ur·ner See \'u̇r-nər-ˌzā\ *also* **Bay of Uri** \'ü-rē, 'yu̇r-ē\ *or* **Lake of Uri.** Extension of Lake of Lucerne, cen. Switzerland; receives Reuss River at its S end.

Ur of the Chaldees. See UR.

Ŭro·tep·pa \ˌu̇r-ə-'te-pə\ *or* **Ura–Tyu·be** \ü-'rä-tyü-'be\. Town, NW Tajikistan, 40 mi. (64 km.) SW of Khudzhand; pop. (1991e) 47,700.

Ur·re Lau·quen \ˌür-rā-lau̇-'kān\. Lake, S La Pampa prov., S cen. Argentina.

Urseren. See ANDERMATT.

Urso. See OSUNA.

Ur·sus \'u̇r-süs\. Town, Warszawa prov., Poland, ab. 7 mi. (11 km.) WSW of Warsaw.

Urua·pan \ür-'wä-ˌpän\ *or in full* **Uruapan del Pro·gre·so** \ˌthel-prō-'grā-sō\. City, Michoacán state, SW Mexico, 60 mi. (97 km.) SW of Morelia; munic. pop. (1990p) 217,142; noted for production of lacquerwork; in center of rich agricultural region and just E of Paricutín volcano. One of the chief towns of the Tarascan Indians; founded 1530s.

Uru·bam·ba \ˌü-rü-'bäm-bä\. **1.** River, cen. Peru; rises in Andes and flows NNW bet. parallel ranges of the Andes to unite with Apurímac River and form Ucayali River; 451 mi. (726 km.) long; Cuzco is on it.
2. Town, cen. S Peru, 20 mi. (32 km.) NE of the city of Cuzco; pop. (1981p) 9519.

Uru·gua·ia·na \ˌü-rü-gwə-'yä-nə\. City, W Rio Grande do Sul state, S Brazil, on Argentine border; munic. pop. (1991p) 117,457; meatpacking plants.

Uru·guay \ˌü-rü-'gwī; 'yu̇r-ə-ˌgwā, 'u̇r-, -ˌgwī\. **1.** *officially* **Re·pú·bli·ca Ori·en·tal del Uruguay** \rā-'pü-blē-ˌkä-ˌōr-yen-'täl-thel-ˌü-rü-'gwī\. Republic, SE cen. South America, E of the lower Uruguay River, bounded on N by Brazil, on E by Brazil and the Atlantic Ocean, on S by the La Plata River, and on W by Argentina; 68,039 sq. mi. (176,221 sq. km.); pop. (1993e) 3,149,000; ✻ Montevideo, which is the nation's only large city.

Physical features: Generally flat country (pampas region) with low range of highlands in NE, less than 2000 ft. (610 m.). Traversed from NE to SW by the Río Negro.

Chief products: Cattle; fish; corn, oats, barley, rice; manufacturing: textiles, chemicals, leather products, cement; meatpacking.

Political divisions: Divided into the following 19 departments (for pronunciation of their names, see their individual entries):

NAME	AREA (sq. mi.)	AREA (sq. km.)	POP. (1985c)	CAPITAL
Artigas	4,689	12,144	69,145	Artigas
Canelones	1,750	4,532	364,248	Canelones
Cerro Largo	5,348	13,851	78,416	Melo
Colonia	2,372	6,143	112,717	Colonia
Durazno	4,713	12,207	55,077	Durazno
Flores	1,982	5,133	24,739	Trinidad
Florida	4,009	10,383	66,474	Florida
Lavalleja	3,918	10,148	61,466	Minas
Maldonado	1,817	4,706	94,314	Maldonado
Montevideo	198	513	1,311,976	Montevideo
Paysandú	5,446	14,105	103,763	Paysandú
Río Negro	3,721	9,637	48,644	Fray Bentos
Rivera	3,513	9,099	89,475	Rivera
Rocha	4,244	10,992	66,601	Rocha
Salto	5,544	14,359	108,487	Salto
San José	1,928	4,994	89,893	San José
Soriano	3,442	8,915	79,439	Mercedes
Tacuarembó	6,166	15,970	83,498	Tacuarembó
Treinta y Tres	3,736	9,676	46,869	Treinta y Tres

History: Orig. inhabited chiefly by Charrúa Indians. Río de la Plata visited by Spanish explorer Juan Díaz de Solís 1516; Colonia founded by Portuguese 1680 and Montevideo (*q.v.*) in 1726; region (called Banda Oriental by the Spaniards) long in dispute bet. Portuguese and Spanish; included in Spanish viceroyalty of La Plata 1776; with Buenos Aires, gained independence from Spain 1811 ff.; incorp. in Brazil as a province c. 1821; revolted against Brazil 1825 and was recognized as independent state 1828; in war against Paraguay (*q.v.*) 1865–70; broke off relations with Germany 1917; declared war on Germany and Japan Feb. 1945; abolished presidential office 1951, replacing it with a nine-member council; adopted new constitution and restored presidential system 1966; scene of military coup 1973; returned to civilian rule 1985.
2. River, SE South America; flows W in Santa Catarina state, S Brazil, forming section of boundary bet. Santa Catarina and Rio Grande do Sul states; turns SW and forms boundary bet. S Brazil and Argentina, and bet. Uruguay and Argentina; empties into Río de la Plata; 1000 mi. (1609 km.) long.

Uruk. See ERECH.

Uruk·tha·pel \ˌü-ru̇k-'tä-pel\. Island, W Pacific Ocean, S of Babelthuap I.; 2d largest of Palau.

Urumiyah, Lake. See ORŪMĪYEH, DARYĀCHEH–YE.

Ürüm·qi \œ-'rœm-'chē\ *or* **Urum·chi** *or* **Urum·tsi** \u̇-'ru̇m-'chē\ *or* *W.-G.* **Wu–lu–mu–ch'i** \'wü-'lü-'mü-'chē\ *also* **Ti·hwa** \'dē-'hwä\. City, ✻ of Xinjiang Uygur, W China, in cen. part; pop. (1990c) 1,046,898; industrial center in coal-mining area; on N side of Tian Shan at ab. 3000 ft. (915 m.) alt. Long a center of Muslim influence.

Urundi. See BURUNDI.

Urup \ü-'rüp\. One of the Kuril Is. (*q.v.*), Russia in Asia, NE of Iturup.

Urville, Cape d'. See PERKAM, CAPE.

Urvinum Metaurense. See URBINO.

Usa \ü-'sä, 'ü-ˌsä\. City, Ōita prefecture, Kyūshū, Japan, 25 mi. (40 km.) NW of the city of Ōita; pop. (1990p) 50,830.

Usa \ü-'sä\. River, NE Komi Rep., NE Russia in Europe, an E tributary of the Pechora; rises at N end of Ural Mts. and flows SW into the Pechora; 351 mi. (565 km.) long; navigable.

Usa·ga·ra \ˌü-sä-'gä-rä\. Hill region, Tanzania, at E edge of the cen. plateau; traversed by the Great Ruaha River.

Uşak \'ü-shäk\ *or* **Ushak** \'ü-shäk\. **1.** Province of Turkey in Asia. See table at TURKEY.
2. Town, its ✻, on railroad line 55 mi. (89 km.) W of Afyon; pop. (1990c) 105,270; carpets; sugar refining.

Usam·ba·ra Mountains \ˌü-säm-'bä-rä\. Highlands, E Africa, in NE Tanzania and SE Kenya; highest peak 8428 ft. (2569 m.).

Us·borne \'əz-bərn\. Peak, East Falkland I., Falkland Is. (*q.v.*), South Atlantic Ocean; 2312 ft. (705 m.); highest peak in the Falkland Is.

Use·dom \'ü-zə-ˌdōm\ *or Pol.* **Uz·nam** \'üz-ˌnäm\. Island, Poland and Germany, bet. Zalew Szczeciński and the Pomeranian Bay; 170 sq. mi. (440 sq. km.); in 1945 divided bet. Poland and East Germany; chief town is port of Świnioujście in Polish section.

Useless Bay. See INÚTIL BAY.

U. S. Grant Peak \ˌyü-ˌes-'grant\. Mountain, San Juan and San Miguel cos., SW Colorado; 13,692 ft. (4173 m.).

Ushak. See UŞAK.

Ushant. See OUESSANT, ÎLE D'.

Ush·ba \'u̇sh-ˌbä\. Peak, W cen. Caucasus Mts. in Republic of Georgia, SE of Mt. Elbrus; 15,453 ft. (4710 m.) high; glaciers.

Us·hua·ia \ü-'swä-yä\. Town, ✻ of Tierra del Fuego prov., S Argentina, on S Tierra del Fuego I. on Beagle Channel; pop. (1980c) 11,029; southernmost city in the world, at 54°47′S, 68°20′W.

Usk \'əsk\. River, S Great Britain, in S Wales and W England; rises in S cen. Wales, flows E and S into the estuary of the Severn just below Newport in Gwent co.; ab. 70 mi. (115 km.) long.

Üsküb. See SKOPJE.

Üs·kü·dar \ˌœs-kœ-'där\; *formerly* **Scu·ta·ri** \'skü-tə-rē\; *anc.* **Chry·sop·o·lis** \krə-'sä-pə-ləs, krī-\. Town, İstanbul prov., Turkey in Asia, across the Bosporus from the city of İstanbul; munic. pop. (1990p) 401,398; residential suburb of İstanbul. Base of British Army in Crimean War (1853–56) and site of hospital under charge of English nurse and philanthropist Florence Nightingale. Ancient Chrysopolis was port of Chalcedon (modern Kodıköy).

Üsküp. See SKOPJE.

Usol'·ye–Si·bir·sko·ye *or* **Usol·ye–Si·bir·sko·ye** \ü-'sȯl-ye-sē-'bir-skə-yə\; *formerly* **Usol'ye** *or* **Usolye.** Town, Irkutsk

Oblast, S Russia in Asia, ab. 50 mi. (80 km.) NW of the city of Irkutsk; pop. (1992e) 107,000.

Us·pal·la·ta Pass \ˌü-spä-'yä-tä, -'zhä-tä\ *or* **La Cum·bre** \lä-'küm-brā\. Pass in the Andes. See ANDES.

Us·su·ri *also* **Usu·ri** \u̇-'su̇r-ē\. River, W Asia; rises in mountains at extreme S end of Primorskiy Kray, Russia, flows N forming part of boundary bet. Russia and China, and joins the Amur near Khabarovsk; 365 mi. (587 km.) long; a W tributary of upper course is outlet for Lake Khanka. Chief Russian town on its bank is Dal'nerechensk. Scene of border clashes bet. Soviet and Chinese forces esp. in 1969.

Ussuri Bay. NE extension of Peter the Great Bay, Primorskiy Kray, SE Russia in Asia, just E of Vladivostok.

Us·su·riysk *also* **Us·su·risk** \ˌü-su̇-'rēsk\; *before 1957* **Vo·ro·shi·lov** \ˌvȯr-ə-'shē-ləf\; *before 1935* **Ni·kolsk–Us·su·rii·ski** *or* **Ni·kol'sk–Us·su·riy·skiy** \ni-'kȯlʸsk-ˌü-su̇-'rēs-kē\. City, SW Primorskiy Kray, SE Russia in Asia, 50 mi. (81 km.) N of Vladivostok; pop. (1992e) 161,000; founded 1860s.

Ust Dvinsk. See DAUGAVGRĪVA.

Uster \'u̇s-tər\. Commune, Zürich canton, Switzerland, 8 mi. (13 km.) ESE of the city of Zürich; pop. (1980c) 23,702.

Ústí. See ÚSTÍ NAD LABEM.

Usti·ca \'ü-stē-ˌkä\. Small island, Tyrrhenian Sea, Italy, NW of Sicily.

Ust'–Ilimsk \ˌüstʸ-i-'lēmsk\. City, Irkutsk Oblast, S Russia in Asia; pop. (1992e) 114,000

Ústí nad La·bem \'ü-styē-'näd-lä-ˌbem\ *or* **Ústí** *or Ger.* **Aus·sig** \'au̇-sik\. City, NW Czech Republic, on Elbe River; pop. (1991p) 99,739; dates from 10th cent.

Ustinov. See IZHEVSK.

Ust'–Kamenogorsk *or* **Ust–Kamenogorsk.** See ÖSKEMEN.

Ust'–Kut \üstʸ-'küt\. Town, N cen. Irkutsk Oblast, S Russia in Asia, ab. 310 mi. (500 km.) N of the city of Irkutsk.

Ust'–Orda. See UST'-ORDYNSKIY.

Ust'–Or·dyn–Bur·yat Autonomous Okrug \ˌü-styər-'din-bu̇r-'yät ... 'ȯ-ˌkrük\. Administrative district, SE Irkutsk Oblast, S Russia in Asia, W of Lake Baikal; 8494 sq. mi. (22,000 sq. km.); pop. (1992e) 140,000; ✻ Ust'-Ordynskiy; has coalfield and important timber resources nearby.

Ust'–Or·dyn·skiy *or* **Ust–Ordynskiy** \ˌüst^{y}-ər-'din-skē\; *formerly* **Ust' Or·da** *or* **Ust Or·da** \ˌüst^{y}-ər-'dä\. Town, ✻ of Ust'-Ordyn-Buryat Autonomous Okrug, S Russia in Asia, 40 mi. (64 km.) N of Irkutsk, W of Lake Baikal.

Ust' Sysol'sk *or* **Ust Sysolsk.** See SYKTYVKAR.

Ust' Tsil'·ma *or* **Ust Tsil·ma** \ˌüst^{y}-'tsil^{y}-mə\. Settlement, Komi Rep., N Russia in Europe, where the Tsil'ma feeds into the Pechora.

Ust·yurt *or* **Ust' Urt** *or* **Ust Urt** \ü-'styu̇rt\. Plateau, SW Kazakhstan, extending bet. the Caspian Sea and Aral Sea; 77,220 sq. mi. (200,000 sq. km.).

Usu·ki \ü-'sü-kē\. Town, Ōita prefecture, NE Kyūshū, Japan, ab. 12 mi. (19 km.) SE of the city of Ōita; pop. (1990p) 37,870; has harbor in Bungo Strait.

Usu·lu·tán \ˌü-sü-lü-'tän\. **1.** Department of SE El Salvador. See table at EL SALVADOR.
2. Town, its ✻, near coast 55 mi. (89 km.) ESE of San Salvador; pop. (1987e) 75,283.

Usu·ma·cin·ta \ˌü-sü-mä-'sēn-tä\. River, N Guatemala and SE Mexico; rises in W Guatemala, flows NW forming section of Guatemala-Mexico (Chiapas state) boundary, empties into Grijalva River near its mouth in N Tabasco state, Mexico; ab. 270 mi. (435 km.) long; navigable for a short distance; known as the **Chi·xoy** \chē-'hȯi\ *or* **Sa·li·nas** \sə-'lē-nəs\ River in its upper course.

Usumbura. See BUJUMBURA.

Usuri. See USSURI.

Usu·tu \ü-'sü-tü\ *also* **Lu·sut·fu** \lü-'su̇t-fü\. River, S Africa; flows E in E Mpumalanga prov., Rep. of South Africa, and in Swaziland and unites with Pongolo River in Mozambique to form the Maputo River; 135 mi. (217 km.) long.

Utah \'yü-ˌtȯ, -ˌtä\. **1.** A western state of U.S.A., bounded on N by Idaho and Wyoming, on E by Colorado, on S by Arizona, and on W by Nevada; 11th state in area, 84,899 sq. mi. (219,888 sq. km.); 35th state in population, (1990c) 1,722,850; ✻ Salt Lake City; 45th state admitted to Union (1896). See table of states at UNITED STATES.

Nickname: Beehive State.

State flower: Sego lily.

Motto: Industry.

Rivers: Colorado flowing SW across SE region; Green in E region flowing S to join the Colorado; Sevier in SW cen. region, flowing N and SW to empty into Sevier Lake.

Highest point: Kings Peak, 13,528 ft. (4123 m.), in Duchesne co.

Chief products: Wheat, hay; livestock, turkeys; dairy products; copper, gold, silver, molybdenum; manufacturing: high-tech products, food products; tourism.

Chief cities: Salt Lake City, West Valley City, Provo, Sandy, Orem, Ogden.

Political divisions: Divided into the following 29 counties (for pronunciation of their names, see their individual entries):

NAME	AREA[1] (sq. mi.)	AREA[1] (sq. km.)	POP. (1990c)	CO. SEAT
Beaver	2,584	6,693	4,765	Beaver
Box Elder[2]	5,627	14,574	36,485	Brigham
Cache	1,174	3,041	70,183	Logan
Carbon	1,476	3,823	20,228	Price
Daggett	706	1,829	690	Manila
Davis[2]	297	769	187,941	Farmington
Duchesne	3,355	8,689	12,645	Duchesne
Emery	4,439	11,497	10,332	Castle Dale
Garfield[3,4]	5,185	13,429	3,980	Panguitch
Grand	3,697	9,575	6,620	Moab
Iron[5]	3,300	8,547	20,789	Parowan
Juab	3,412	8,837	5,817	Nephi
Kane[3,5]	4,016	10,401	5,169	Kanab
Millard[6]	6,793	17,594	11,333	Fillmore
Morgan	610	1,580	5,528	Morgan City
Piute	754	1,953	1,277	Junction
Rich	1,023	2,650	1,725	Randolph
Salt Lake[2]	764	1,979	725,956	Salt Lake City
San Juan[4,7]	7,799	20,199	12,621	Monticello
Sanpete	1,597	4,136	16,259	Manti
Sevier	1,929	4,996	15,431	Richfield
Summit	1,848	4,786	15,518	Coalville
Tooele[2]	6,923	17,931	26,601	Tooele
Uintah	4,472	11,582	22,211	Vernal
Utah[8]	2,014	5,216	263,590	Provo
Wasatch	1,191	3,085	10,089	Heber
Washington[5]	2,427	6,286	48,560	St. George
Wayne[4]	2,486	6,439	2,177	Loa
Weber[2]	581	1,505	158,330	Ogden

[1] Area = land area.
[2] Upper part of Great Salt Lake in cen. and SE Box Elder co.; lower part in Weber, Davis, Salt Lake, and Tooele cos.
[3] Bryce Canyon National Park in SW Garfield co. and NW Kane co.
[4] Canyonlands National Park in NE Garfield co., NW San Juan co., and E Wayne co.
[5] Zion National Park in NE and E Washington co., with small regions in abutting S part of Iron co. and W part of Kane co.
[6] Includes Sevier Lake and several smaller lakes.
[7] SE point of county the only point in U.S. common to four states (Utah, Colorado, New Mexico, Arizona).
[8] Utah Lake in W cen. part.

History: Orig. inhabited by American Indian peoples incl. the Shoshoni, Ute, and Paiute. Possibly explored by Spaniards sent out by explorer Francisco Vásquez de Coronado 1540; visited by Spanish missionaries 1776; Great Salt Lake discovered by American pioneer James Bridger 1824; acquired by U.S. from Mexico in Treaty of Guadalupe Hidalgo 1848; first permanent settlers were Mormons, led to valley of Great Salt Lake by Brigham Young, head of Mormon Church, in 1847; part of Utah Terr. (*q.v.*) organized 1850 (see DESERET); territory reduced to area of present state by 1868; conflict bet. Mormon authorities and U.S. government, known as Utah War (1857–58); admitted to Union Jan. 4, 1896.

2. County in N cen. Utah. See table at UTAH.

Utah Lake. Lake, Utah co., N cen. Utah; 150 sq. mi. (389 sq. km.); 23 mi. (37 km.) long by 8 mi. (13 km.) wide; has outlet, Jordan River.

Utah Territory. Former territory, U.S.A.; comprised the portion of lands ceded to U.S. by Mexico 1848 and bounded by Oregon Terr. in the N, California in the W, and New Mexico Terr. in the S; territory organized 1850 incl. most of what is now Nevada, all of Utah, W Colorado, and SW Wyoming; reduced 1861 upon formation of territories of Colorado and Nevada (*qq.v.*), and to the area of the present state 1868 upon formation of territory of Wyoming; Utah admitted to the Union 1896.

Utaidhani. See UTHAI THANI.

Utakamand. See UDAGAMANDALAM.

Ute Pass \'yüt\. Mountain pass, Teller co., cen. Colorado, near Pikes Peak; 9165 ft. (2793 m.); named for American Indian tribe; traversed by road.

Ute Peak. **1.** Mountain, Grand and Summit cos., Colorado, S of Middle Park; 12,298 ft. (3748 m.).
2. Mountain, Taos co., N New Mexico, on Colorado boundary; 10,093 ft. (3076 m.).

Uthai Tha·ni *or* **Utai·dha·ni** *or* **Uda·ya·dha·ni** \ˌu̇-ˌtī-'tä-nē\. Town, W cen. Thailand, on the Chao Phraya where the Tha Chin distributary leaves it, 25 mi. (40 km.) S of Nakhon Sawan; pop. (1991e) 17,257.

Uti·ca \'yü-ti-kə\. **1.** City, Macomb co., SE Michigan, ab. 12 mi. (19 km.) N of Detroit; pop. (1990c) 5081.
2. City and port of entry, a ⊗ of Oneida co., cen. New York, on Mohawk River and New York State Barge Canal, ab. 50 mi. (80 km.) E of Syracuse; pop. (1990c) 68,637; Munson-Williams-Proctor Art Institute; Mohawk Valley Community Coll. (1946), Utica Coll. of Syracuse Univ. (1946), State Univ. of New York Institute of Technology at Utica/Rome (1966). Part of tract granted to New York Colony by King George II of England in 1730s; settlement of region increased after Revolutionary War; industrial development followed opening of Erie Canal 1825; incorp. as village 1798, as city 1832.

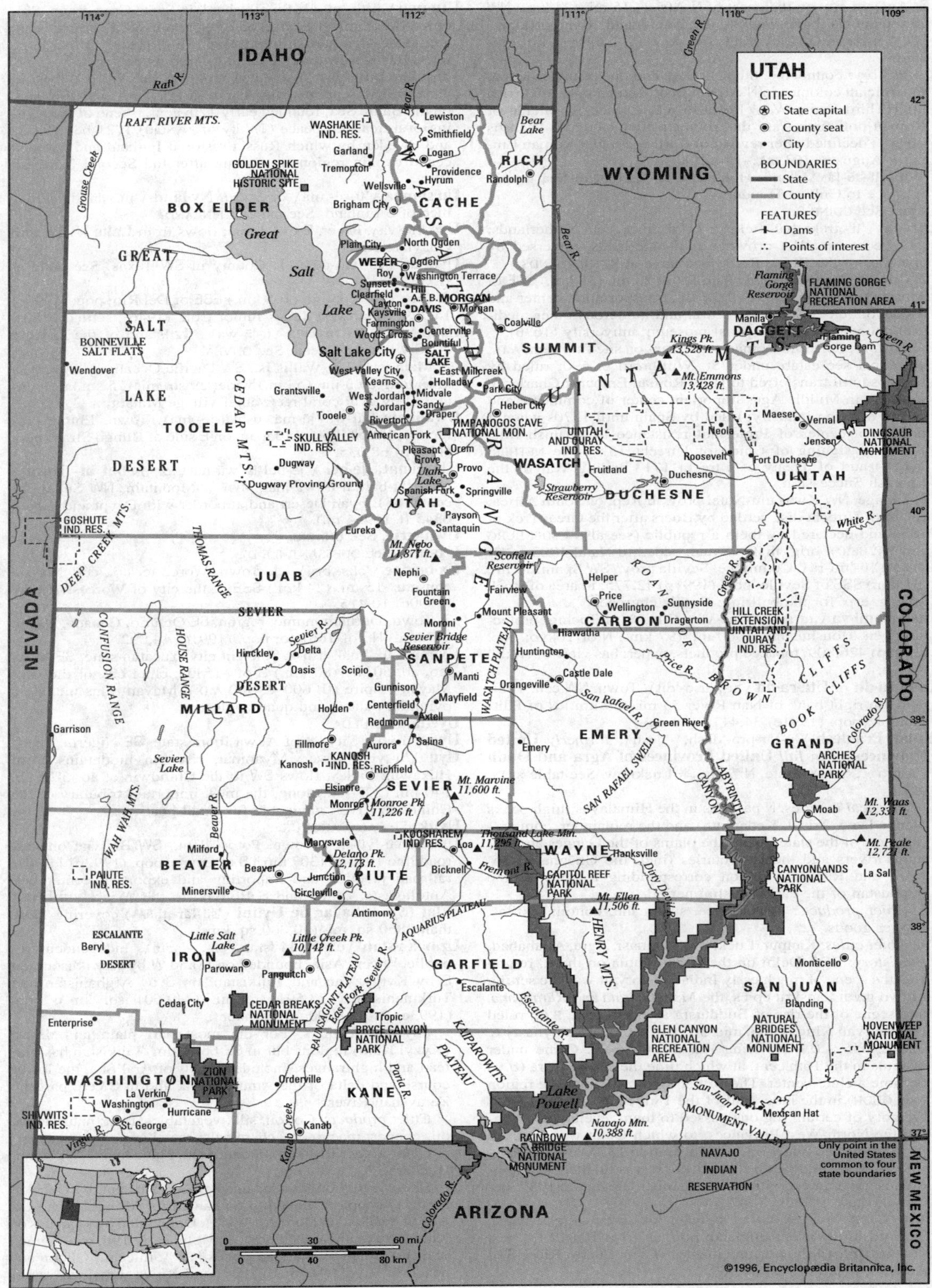
UTAH
CITIES
State capital
County seat
City
BOUNDARIES
State
County
FEATURES
Dams
Points of interest
IDAHO
WYOMING
NEVADA
COLORADO
ARIZONA
NEW MEXICO
BOX ELDER
CACHE
RICH
WEBER
MORGAN
DAVIS
SALT LAKE
SUMMIT
DAGGETT
TOOELE
UTAH
WASATCH
DUCHESNE
UINTAH
JUAB
SANPETE
CARBON
MILLARD
EMERY
GRAND
SEVIER
BEAVER
PIUTE
WAYNE
IRON
GARFIELD
SAN JUAN
WASHINGTON
KANE
GREAT SALT LAKE DESERT
SEVIER DESERT
ESCALANTE DESERT
Great Salt Lake
RAFT RIVER MTS.
WASHAKIE IND. RES.
GOLDEN SPIKE NATIONAL HISTORIC SITE
BONNEVILLE SALT FLATS
SKULL VALLEY IND. RES.
GOSHUTE IND. RES.
TIMPANOGOS CAVE NATIONAL MON.
UINTAH AND OURAY IND. RES.
FLAMING GORGE NATIONAL RECREATION AREA
DINOSAUR NATIONAL MONUMENT
HILL CREEK EXTENSION UINTAH AND OURAY IND. RES.
KANOSH IND. RES.
KOOSHAREM IND. RES.
PAIUTE IND. RES.
ARCHES NATIONAL PARK
CANYONLANDS NATIONAL PARK
CAPITOL REEF NATIONAL PARK
CEDAR BREAKS NATIONAL MONUMENT
BRYCE CANYON NATIONAL PARK
ZION NATIONAL PARK
SHIVWITS IND. RES.
GLEN CANYON NATIONAL RECREATION AREA
NATURAL BRIDGES NATIONAL MONUMENT
HOVENWEEP NATIONAL MONUMENT
RAINBOW BRIDGE NATIONAL MONUMENT
NAVAJO INDIAN RESERVATION
Only point in the United States common to four state boundaries
WASATCH RANGE
UINTA MTS.
CEDAR MTS.
DEEP CREEK MTS.
THOMAS RANGE
HOUSE RANGE
CONFUSION RANGE
WAH WAH MTS.
WASATCH PLATEAU
ROAN OR BROWN CLIFFS
BOOK CLIFFS
SAN RAFAEL SWELL
LABYRINTH CANYON
HENRY MTS.
AQUARIUS PLATEAU
PAUNSAUGUNT PLATEAU
KAIPAROWITS PLATEAU
MONUMENT VALLEY
Kings Pk. 13,528 ft.
Mt. Emmons 13,428 ft.
Mt. Nebo 11,877 ft.
Mt. Marvine 11,600 ft.
Monroe Pk. 11,226 ft.
Thousand Lake Mtn. 11,295 ft.
Delano Pk. 12,173 ft.
Mt. Ellen 11,506 ft.
Little Creek Pk. 10,142 ft.
Mt. Waas 12,331 ft.
Mt. Peale 12,721 ft.
Navajo Mtn. 10,388 ft.
Raft R.
Grouse Creek
Bear R.
Bear Lake
Green R.
Flaming Gorge Reservoir
Flaming Gorge Dam
White R.
Strawberry Reservoir
Utah Lake
Scofield Reservoir
Price R.
San Rafael R.
Colorado R.
Sevier R.
Sevier Bridge Reservoir
Sevier Lake
Beaver R.
Fremont R.
Dirty Devil R.
Escalante R.
Little Salt Lake
East Fork Sevier R.
Paria R.
Kanab Creek
Virgin R.
Lake Powell
San Juan R.
Lewiston
Smithfield
Logan
Garland
Tremonton
Providence
Hyrum
Wellsville
Randolph
Brigham City
Plain City
North Ogden
Ogden
Roy
Washington Terrace
Sunset
Clearfield
Hill A.F.B.
Layton
Kaysville
Morgan
Farmington
Centerville
Woods Cross
Bountiful
Coalville
Salt Lake City
West Valley City
East Millcreek
Kearns
Holladay
Wendover
Grantsville
West Jordan
Midvale
S. Jordan
Sandy
Tooele
Draper
Riverton
Park City
Heber City
American Fork
Pleasant Grove
Orem
Provo
Dugway
Dugway Proving Ground
Spanish Fork
Springville
Payson
Santaquin
Eureka
Manila
Maeser
Vernal
Jensen
Neola
Roosevelt
Fort Duchesne
Fruitland
Duchesne
Nephi
Fountain Green
Fairview
Moroni
Mount Pleasant
Helper
Price
Wellington
Sunnyside
Dragerton
Hiawatha
Hinckley
Delta
Oasis
Scipio
Manti
Huntington
Castle Dale
Orangeville
Gunnison
Mayfield
Centerfield
Holden
Axtell
Redmond
Salina
Green River
Garrison
Fillmore
Aurora
Emery
Kanosh
Richfield
Elsinore
Monroe
Moab
Marysvale
Loa
Hanksville
Milford
Beaver
Bicknell
Junction
Minersville
Circleville
Antimony
La Sal
Beryl
Parowan
Panguitch
Escalante
Monticello
Cedar City
Tropic
Blanding
Enterprise
Orderville
La Verkin
Washington
Hurricane
St. George
Kanab
Mexican Hat
114°
113°
112°
111°
110°
109°
42°
41°
40°
39°
38°
37°
0 30 60 mi
0 40 80 km

3. Ancient city on the coast of N Africa, 15 mi. (24 km.) NW of ancient Carthage (and modern Tunis) and 10 mi. (16 km.) SE of modern Ghār al-Milḩ; site now ab. 7 mi. (11 km.) inland.

History: Founded c. 8th cent. B.C. and one of the principal Phoenician colonies in N Africa; ✻ of Roman prov. of Africa after Third Punic War (149–146 B.C.); scene of suicide of Roman politician Cato the Younger after battle of Thapsus 46 B.C.; declined after revival of Carthage under Roman Emperor Augustus (63 B.C.–14 A.D.).

Uti·la \ü-ˈtē-lä\. Island, Honduras, in Caribbean Sea near S entrance to Gulf of Honduras.

Utina. See UDINE 2.

Utrecht \ˈüe-ˌtrekt, ˈyü-ˌtrekt\. **1.** Province, cen. Netherlands; ✻ Utrecht; smallest province of Netherlands, traversed by branches of the Rhine River. See table at NETHERLANDS.

2. City, its ✻, on the Oude Rijn River 20 mi. (32 km.) SSE of Amsterdam; pop. (1992e) 232,705; transportation center and residential city; Gothic cathedral and numerous other medieval churches, archiepiscopal museum; university (1636).

History: Fortified Roman settlement on site first cent. A.D.; episcopal see estab. under St. Willibrord c. 690; ruled by bishops until transferred to Holy Roman Emperor Charles V in 1527; in Middle Ages important center of commerce and of the weaving industry; ruled by Spain until 1570s when it became a center of Protestant resistance to Spanish rule. Scene of signing of Union of Utrecht 1579 (see NETHERLANDS) and of Treaty of Utrecht 1713 ending War of the Spanish Succession.

3. Village, NW KwaZulu-Natal prov., E Rep. of South Africa; center of Utrecht dist. settled by Boers after the Great Trek of 1836 and declared by them a republic (see also LYDENBURG and VRYHEID); orig. in Transvaal, ceded to Natal 1903.

Utre·ra \ü-ˈtrā-rä\. Commune, Sevilla prov., SW Spain, 19 mi. (31 km.) SSE of Seville; pop. (1991p) 42,775; in area of stock raising, esp. for the bullring; Gothic churches.

Utsu·no·mi·ya \ˌüt-sü-ˈnō-mē-yä\. City, ✻ of Tochigi prefecture, cen. Honshū, Japan, 60 mi. (97 km.) N of Tokyo; pop. (1990p) 426,809; tobacco products, paper; has view of Nikkō Range.

Ut·ta·ra·dit *or* **Uta·ra·dit** \ˌü-ˌtär-ə-ˈdit\. Town, NW cen. Thailand, on right bank of Nan River 55 mi. (89 km.) N of Phitsanulok; pop. (1991e) 34,417.

Ut·tar Pra·desh \ˈü-tər-prə-ˈdāsh, -ˈdesh\; *formerly* **United Provinces** *or in full* **United Provinces of Agra and Oudh** \ˈä-grə ... ˈaud\. State, N India; ✻ Lucknow. See table at INDIA.

Physical features: N part lies in the Himalayas (high peaks Nanda Devi, Trisul, Kedarnath) and the remainder, comprising most of the state, forms the plains of the Ganges and Yamuna rivers and their tributaries (incl. the Ghāghara, Gomati, and Rapti); a region corresponding roughly to the Hindustan of the early Muslim period.

Chief products: Wheat, rice, sugarcane, cotton; textiles, leather goods.

Chief cities: Kanpur, Lucknow, Varanasi, Agra, Allahabad.

History: With Delhi on the W and Patna on the E, region was the scene of much early Indian history. It was the setting of two great Sanskrit epics, the *Mahābhārata* and *Rāmāyaṇa*, and scene of the rise of Buddhism after 6th cent. B.C.; ruled by Mauryan King Aśoka mid-3d cent. B.C., Gupta dynasty c. 320–c. 415 A.D., and King Harṣa (606–647). Came under Moguls in the 16th cent. at which time the city of Agra (*q.v.*) became a chief center. The British first came into the region (see OUDH) in the latter half of the 18th cent.; by 1830s sovereignty of certain regions passed to them, eventually forming the North-West Provinces, to which Oudh was annexed in 1856; placed under one administration 1877. United Provinces of Agra and Oudh formed 1902; was granted an autonomous government with a two-chamber legislature 1937; became a state of India 1947.

Ut·tox·e·ter \yü-ˈtäk-sə-tər, ə-ˈtäk-; ˈək-sə-tər—*sic*\. Town, Staffordshire, W cen. England; pop. (1981p) 10,012.

Utua·do \ü-ˈtwä-thō\. Municipality, W cen. Puerto Rico, S of Arecibo; pop. (1990c) 34,980.

Utu·pua \ˌü-tü-ˈpü-ä\. Small island, in Santa Cruz group, Solomon Is., 62 mi. (100 km.) SE of Nendo I., SW Pacific Ocean; a circular island ab. 8 mi. (13 km.) in diameter, with a large inlet, Basilisk Harbour, extending into its center.

Uu·si·kau·pun·ki \ˈü-sē-ˌkaù-ˌpùŋ-kē\ *or Swed.* **Ny·stad** \ˈnüe-ˌstäd\. Seaport town, Turku ja Pori prov., SW Finland, on the Baltic Sea; founded early 17th cent.; scene of the signing of a treaty of peace (Treaty of Nystad) 1721 bet. Russia and Sweden by which Russia restored Finland and Sweden ceded certain regions to Russia after the Second Northern War.

Uu·si·maa \ˈü-sē-ˌmä\ *or Swed.* **Ny·land** \ˈnüe-ˌländ\. Province of S Finland. See table at FINLAND.

Uvá \ü-ˈvä\. River, E Colombia; flows from **Lake Uvá** E into Guaviare River.

Uval·de \yü-ˈval-dē\. **1.** County in SW Texas. See table at TEXAS.

2. City, its ⊗, 65 mi. (105 km.) ESE of Del Rio; pop. (1990c) 14,729; Southwest Texas Junior Coll. (1946); settled 1850s.

Uvéa \ü-ˈvā-ä\ *or* **Uea** \ü-ˈā-wä\. **1.** Island of the Loyalty Is., SW Pacific Ocean. See OUVÉA.

2. Main island of Wallis Is., SW Pacific Ocean; ab. 8 mi. (13 km.) long by 3 mi. (5 km.) wide; 29 sq. mi. (75 sq. km.); enclosed by oval coral reef; chief village Matautu.

Uwa·ji·ma \ˌü-wä-ˈjē-mä, ù-ˈwä-jē-ˌmä\. Town, Ehime prefecture, NW Shikoku I., Japan, on E side of Bungo Strait; pop. (1990p) 68,035.

ʻU·wei·nat, Je·bel \ˈje-bel-ü-ˈwā-nàt\ *or* **Ja·bal al–ʻU·way·nāt** \ˈjà-bəl-ˌàl-ü-ˈwā-ˌnàt, -ˈwī-\. Mountain, NW Sudan, in center of Libyan Desert and at border with Egypt and Libya; 6345 ft. (1934 m.).

Uwharrie. See UHARIE.

Uxantis. See OUESSANT, ÎLE D'.

Ux·bridge \ˈəks-ˌbrij\. **1.** Town, Worcester co., cen. Massachusetts, 15 mi. (24 km.) SSE of the city of Worcester; pop. (1990c) 10,415.

2. Town, Durham munic. region, SE Ontario, Canada, 29 mi. (47 km.) NE of Toronto; pop. (1991c) 14,092.

Ux·mal \üz-ˈmäl, üsh-\. Ancient city, Yucatán state, SE Mexico, ab. 50 mi. (80 km.) S of Mérida; chief city of the later Mayan empire (fl. 600–c. 900 A.D.); Mayan ruins include a pyramid, palace, and quadrangle.

Uyeda. See UEDA.

Uyo \ˈü-yō\. City, ✻ of Akwa Ibom state, SE Nigeria.

Uyu \ˈü-ˌyü\. River, Myanmar, rises in mountains S of Hukawng Valley, flows SW to the Chindwin at ab. 5°N; ab. 140 mi. (225 km.) long; the most important tributary of the Chindwin River; navigable for small boats.

Uyuk. See ALACAHÖYÜK.

Uyu·ni \ü-ˈyü-nē\. Town, Potosí dept., SW Bolivia; on railroad line 191 mi. (307 km.) S of Oruro; pop. (1992p) 11,301; railroad junction and importing and exporting center bet. Antofagasta, Chile, and S Bolivia; to the W is **Uyuni Salt Flat** (*Span.* **Sa·lar de Uyuni** \ˈsä-lär-ˌthā-\) covering more than 3860 sq. mi. (10,000 sq. km.).

Uz·bek·i·stan \ùz-ˌbe-ki-ˈstan, əz-, -ˈstän\. Independent republic, W cen. Asia, bounded on N and W by Kazakhstan, on E by Kyrgyzstan and Tajikistan, on S by Afghanistan and Turkmenistan; 173,591 sq. mi. (449,601 sq. km.); pop. (1993e) 21,179,000; ✻ Tashkent.

Physical features: For the most part plain and desert (Kyzyl Kum) regions but in SE bordering Tajikistan has plateau and high ranges. Includes S half of Aral Sea, the lower course and delta of the Amu Dar'ya, and in S cen. part the Zeravshan River.

Chief products: Cotton, silk, vegetables, fruit; natural gas, oil, copper; machinery, chemicals; metallurgical industries.

Chief cities: Tashkent, Samarqand, Namangan, Andizhan, Bukhara.

History: Region invaded and settled 15th cent. by Uzbeks, a Turkic people believed to be named for Mongol Khan Öz Beg of the Golden Horde (d. 1341). Dominated by khanates of Khiva, Bukhara, and Qŭqon (*qq.v.*) by early 19th cent.; gradually occupied by Russian forces late 19th cent.; Qŭqon annexed to Russia 1876; Bukhara and Khiva remained vassal

states of Russian empire until 1917; after the Bolshevik Revolution, soviet governments set up but conditions unstable until organization 1924 of Uzbek Soviet Socialist Republic; scene of ethnic violence June 1989 bet. Uzbeks and Meskhet minority; movement toward self-rule intensified 1990; gained independence 1991.

Uzès \ᵫ-'zes\. Manufacturing town, Gard dept., S France, ab. 15 mi. (24 km.) N of Nîmes; cathedral; ducal castle.

Uzh·go·rod \'üzh-gə-rət\ *or Hung.* **Ung·vár** \'u̇ŋ-ˌvär\ *or Slovak* **Už·ho·rod** \'u̇zh-hȯ-ˌrȯt\. City, ✱ of Zakarpats'ka subdivision, SW Ukraine, on a headstream of the Tisza; pop. (1991e) 123,000. Formerly a Hungarian city; from 1919 to 1938 chief town of Carpathian Ruthenia in Czechoslovakia; taken over by U.S.S.R. 1945.

Uzhok *or Czech* **Užok** \'u̇-ˌzhȯk\. Mountain pass, Zakarpats'ka subdivision, Ukraine, E Carpathian Mts., 36 mi. (58 km.) NE of Uzhgorod; 2197 ft. (670 m.).

Užice. See TITOVO UŽICE.

Uz·lo·va·ya \ˌüz-lə-'vī-yə\. Town, Tula Oblast, Russia in Europe, ab. 30 mi. (48 km.) SE of the city of Tula; pop. (1991e) 64,000.

Uznam. See USEDOM.

\ə\ **abut** \ə\ **matches** \ᵊ\ **kitten, Fr table** \ər\ **further** \a\ **ash** \ā\ **ace**
\ä\ **cot, cart** \á\ **Fr bac** \au̇\ **out** \b̶\ **Span Avila** \ch\ **chin** \e\ **bet** \ē\ **easy**
\g\ **go** \i\ **hit** \ī\ **ice** \j\ **job** \k̲\ **Ger ich, Buch** \$^n$\ **Fr vin**
\ŋ\ **sing** \ō\ **go** \ȯ\ **all** \ó\ **law** \œ\ **Fr bœuf** \œ̄\ **Fr feu** \ȯi\ **boy**
\th\ **thin** \t͟h\ **this** \ü\ **loot** \u̇\ **foot** \ue\ **Ger füllen** \ᵫ\ **Fr rue**
\y\ **yet** \$^y$\ **Fr digne** \'dēn^y\, **nuit** \'nw^{y}ē\ \yü\ **few** \yu̇\ **fury** \zh\ **vision**

V

Vaagö. See VÅGØ.
Vaal \ˈväl\. River, Rep. of South Africa; rises in Mpumalanga prov., flows W, forming part of boundary bet. Mpumalanga and Free State; empties into Orange River in Northern Cape prov.; 720 mi. (1158 km.) long.
Vaals \ˈväls\. Commune, Limburg prov., Netherlands, at the place where boundaries of Netherlands, Belgium, and Germany meet, just W of Aachen; pop. (1981e) 10,589.
Vaa·sa \ˈvä-sä\ *or Swed.* **Va·sa** \ˈvä-sä\. **1.** Province of W Finland. See table at FINLAND.
2. *formerly* **Ni·ko·lain·kau·pun·ki** \ˈnē-kō-līn-ˌkaù-pùŋ-kē\. Seaport city, its ✻, on the Gulf of Bothnia ab. 220 mi. (355 km.) NW of Helsinki; pop. (1989c) 53,364; founded 1606; destroyed by fire 1852 but rebuilt on present site c. 1860.
Vác \ˈväts\ *or Ger.* **Wait·zen** \ˈvīt-sən\. City, N Hungary, on left bank of the Danube ab. 20 mi. (32 km.) N of Budapest; pop. (1991e) 35,400; cathedral and episcopal palace.
Vaca Key. See FLORIDA KEYS.
Va·ca·ria \ˌvȧ-kȧ-ˈrē-ə\. Municipality, Rio Grande do Sul state, S Brazil, ab. 100 mi. (160 km.) NNE of Pôrto Alegre; munic. pop. (1991p) 58,571.
Vac·a·ville \ˈva-kə-ˌvil\. City, Solano co., cen. California, 33 mi. (53 km.) WSW of Sacramento; pop. (1990c) 71,479; maximum security medical facility; founded 1850; has experienced steady rapid growth since 1950.
Vacca. See BÉJA.
Vache, Île à \ˌēl-ȧ-ˈvȧsh\ *or Eng.* **Vache Island** \ˈväsh\. Island, Haiti, in Caribbean Sea, off S coast of W Hispaniola.
Va·co·as–Phoe·nix \və-ˈkō-əs-ˈfē-niks\. Town, W Mauritius, ab. 10 mi. (16 km.) S of Port Louis; pop. (1991e) 57,227.
Väddö \ˈve-ˌdœ\. Island off SE coast of Sweden, opp. Åland in W entrance to the Gulf of Bothnia.
Vad·nais Heights \ˈvad-ˌnes\. City, Ramsey co., E Minnesota; pop. (1990c) 11,041; pop. doubled bet. 1980 and 1990.
Va·do·dara \və-ˈdō-də-ˌrä\ *or* **Ba·ro·da** \bə-ˈrō-də\. City, SE Gujarat, India, 244 mi. (392 km.) N of Bombay; pop. (1991c) 1,061,598; chemicals, textiles; university (1949); ✻ of former Baroda state.
Vadsø \ˈväd-sœ\. Seaport, ⊗ of Finnmark co., N Norway, on N shore of Varanger Fjord; pop. (1990c) 5967; ice-free harbor; fishing.
Vad·ste·na \ˈväd-ˌstā-nə\. Town, Östergötland prov., SE Sweden, on E shore of Vättern Lake 25 mi. (40 km.) W of Linköping; pop. (1989c) 7423; site of convent estab. by St. Bridget, founder of the Bridgettine order 14th cent.
Va·duz \fä-ˈdüts\. Commune, ✻ of Liechtenstein, on right bank of the Upper Rhine ab. 50 mi. (80 km.) SE of Zürich, Switzerland; pop. (1991e) 4870; tourism. Greatly damaged in 1499 in war bet. the Swiss and Holy Roman Emperor Maximilian I, but subsequently rebuilt; came into possession of Liechtenstein family early 18th cent.
Vær·øy \ˈver-ȯi\. Island of the Lofoten group, Norway, in Norwegian Sea, off NW coast.
Vág. See VÁH.
Va·ga \ˈvä-gə\. **1.** River, SW Arkhangel'sk Oblast, Russia in Europe; flows N to the Northern Dvina River; 357 mi. (574 km.) long.
2. Town, Tunisia. See BÉJA.
Vagarshapat. See ECHMIADZIN.
Va·ghe·na \və-ˈgē-nə\ *or* **Wa·gi·na** \və-ˈgē-\. Small island, E Solomon Is., W Pacific Ocean, W of Manning Strait and off SE end of Choiseul I.
Vågø *also* **Vaagö** \ˈvȯ-gœ\. One of the Faeroe Is. (*q.v.*), Denmark; 69 sq. mi. (179 sq. km.).
Váh \ˈväk\ *or Hung.* **Vág** \ˈväg\ *or Ger.* **Waag** \ˈväk\. River, W Slovakia; rises in the Tatra Mts., flows W and S into the Danube at Komárno; 245 mi. (394 km.) long.
Vahalis. See WAAL.
Vai·den \ˈvā-dᵊn\. Town, a ⊗ of Carroll co., cen. Mississippi; pop. (1990c) 789.
Vaigach. See VAYGACH.
Vai·gai \ˈvī-gī\. River, SE India; rises in the Cardamom Hills, flows NE and ESE in SE Tamil Nadu into Palk Strait; ab. 180 mi. (290 km.) long.
Vail \ˈvāl\. Town, Eagle co., NW cen. Colorado, in the Rocky Mts., W of Denver; pop. (1990c) 3659; resort.
Vakh \ˈväk\. River, mostly in SE Khanty-Mansi Autonomous Okrug, W Russia in Asia; rises in W Krasnoyarsk Kray and flows W into Ob' River; 599 mi. (964 km.) long.
Vā·khān \vä-kän\. **1.** Valley, NE Afghanistan, See WAKHAN. **2.** *or mostly formerly* **Wa·khan** \wä-ˈkän\. River, NE Afghanistan, an upper tributary of the Panj.
Vakhsh *or* **Vaksh** \ˈväksh\. River, a N tributary of the Amu Dar'ya, SW Tajikistan; flows W and SW; 497 mi. (800 km.) long.
Va·la·am \ˈvä-lä-ˌäm\ *or Finnish* **Va·la·mo** \ˈvä-lä-ˌmȯ\. Island group, N Lake Ladoga, Karelia Rep., NW Russia in Europe; formerly belonged to Finland; site of medieval Greek Orthodox monastery.
Va·lais \vȧ-ˈlā\ *or Ger.* **Wal·lis** \ˈvä-lis\. Canton, Switzerland. See *History* and table at SWITZERLAND.
Va·las·ske Me·zi·ri·ci \ˈvä-ˌläs-ke-ˈme-zi-ˌrē-chē\. Town, E Czech Republic; pop. (1989c) 26,821.
Val·cour Island \ˈval-ˌkùr\. Island, Lake Champlain, 5 mi. (8 km.) SE of Plattsburgh, New York; near scene of British naval victory Oct. 1776 in Revolutionary War.
Val·da·gno \väl-ˈdä-ˌnyō\. Commune, Vicenza prov., Veneto, NE Italy, in Alps 15 mi. (24 km.) NW of the commune of Vicenza; pop. (1989c) 27,519.
Val·dai Hills \väl-ˈdī\. Hills and plateau, N Tver' and S Novgorod oblasts, W Russia in Europe; av. height 600 to 1000 ft. (185 to 305 m.); highest point 1053 ft. (321 m.). Source of the Volga, Western Dvina, and Dnieper, and rivers flowing into Lake Il'men'; many lakes and marshes. In WWII overrun by Germans 1941.
Val d'Ajol, Le. See LE VAL D'AJOL.
Val–de–Marne \ˌvȧl-də-ˈmȧrn\. Department of N France. See table at FRANCE.
Val·de·pe·ñas \ˌväl-dā-ˈpā-nyäs\. Commune, Ciudad Real prov., S cen. Spain, 33 mi. (53 km.) SE of the commune of Ciudad Real; pop. (1991p) 25,421; red wines.
Valderaduey. See ARADUEY.
Val·dese \ˈval-ˌdēz\. Town, Burke co., W North Carolina, in foothills of the Blue Ridge 12 mi. (19 km.) S of Lenoir; pop. (1990c) 3914.
Val·dés *also* **Val·déz** \väl-ˈdes\. Peninsula, extending into Atlantic Ocean from NE coast of Chubut prov., S Argentina, S of the Gulf of San Matías; encloses Gulf of San José on N.
Val·dez \val-ˈdēz\. City and port at head of inlet on NE shore of Prince William Sound, S Alaska; pop. (1990c) 4068; S terminus of Trans-Alaska Pipeline; moved 4 mi. (6 km.) to SW from original site after destruction by earthquake 1964.
Val·dez–Cor·do·va \val-ˈdēz-kȯr-ˈdō-və\. Division in Alaska. See table at ALASKA.
Valdéz. See VALDÉS.
Val di Gardena. See GARDENA, VAL DI.
Val·di·via \väl-ˈdē-byä\. **1.** River, Los Lagos region, S cen. Chile; rises in Andes, flows W into Pacific Ocean; ab. 100 mi. (160 km.) long.
2. Former province of S cen. Chile.
3. City, Los Lagos region, S cen. Chile, on the Valdivia River 16 mi. (26 km.) from its mouth; pop. (1982c) 100,046; formerly ✻ of Valdivia prov.; lumber, metal goods, boats, foodstuffs; railroad shops; tourist base in lake region; university (1954). Founded 1552; developed after mid-19th cent. influx of German settlers; severely damaged by earthquake 1960.

Val·dob·bia·de·ne \ˌväl-dȯb-ˈbyä-de-ˌnā\. Commune, Treviso prov., Veneto, NE Italy, 22 mi. (35 km.) NW of the commune of Treviso; pop. (1981p) 11,024; ferruginous springs.

Val–d'Oise \väl-ˈdwäz\. Department of N France. See table at FRANCE.

Val–d'Or \väl-ˈdȯr\. Town, Abitibi co., SW Quebec, Canada; pop. (1991c) 23,842; has historically been a gold-mining center.

Val·dos·ta \val-ˈdäs-tə\. City, ⊗ of Lowndes co., S Georgia, 57 mi. (92 km.) WSW of Waycross; pop. (1990c) 39,806; transportation center; tobacco; Valdosta State Coll. (1906); Moody Air Force Base is nearby to the N; settled c. 1859.

Vale \ˈvāl\. City, ⊗ of Malheur co., SE Oregon, on Malheur River 62 mi. (100 km.) SSE of Baker City; pop. (1990c) 1491.

Va·len·ça \və-ˈlān-sə\. **1.** City, Bahia state, E Brazil, on coast 50 mi. (81 km.) SW of Salvador; munic. pop. (1991p) 66,786.

2. City, Rio de Janeiro state, SE Brazil, 40 mi. (64 km.) NNW of the city of Rio de Janeiro; munic. pop. (1991p) 62,035.

Va·lence \vä-ˈlä^{n}s\; *anc.* **Ven·tia** \ˈven-chē-ə\; *later* **Va·len·tia** \və-ˈlen-chē-ə\. Commune, ✱ of Drôme dept., SE France, on left bank of Rhone River 116 mi. (187 km.) NNW of Marseille; pop. (1990c) 65,026; 11th cent. Romanesque cathedral; site of university from mid-15th cent. until late 18th cent.

Va·len·cia \və-ˈlen-chē-ə\. County in W New Mexico. See table at NEW MEXICO.

Va·len·cia \bä-ˈlen-thē-ä, və-ˈlen-chē-ə, -ˈlen-sē-ə\. **1.** Autonomous community and ancient kingdom, E Spain, bounded on N by Aragon and Catalonia, on E by the Mediterranean, on S by Murcia, and on W by Murcia, Castilla-La Mancha, and Aragon; comprises modern provs. of Alicante, Castellón, and Valencia; 8886 sq. mi. (23,015 sq. km.); ✱ Valencia; watered by the Segura, Turia, Júcar, and Mijares rivers; generally mountainous, broken by coastal and inland plains; numerous salt lagoons on coast; wide variety of agricultural produce owing to wide variations in temperature and rainfall. See table at SPAIN.

History: Conquered successively by Romans, Visigoths, and Moors; part of Caliphate of Córdoba until its decline in early 11th cent.; subsequently became independent Moorish kingdom; held by Spanish commander Rodrigo Díaz de Vivar (El Cid) 1094–99, but after his death again lost to Moors; reconquered 1238 by King James I of Aragon. Became autonomous community 1982.

2. Province of E Spain. See table at SPAIN.

3. *anc.* **Va·len·tia** \və-ˈlen-chē-ə\. Commune, ✱ of Valencia prov. and ✱ of Valencia autonomous community and ancient kingdom, E Spain, on Mediterranean at mouth of the Turia 188 mi. (303 km.) ESE of Madrid; pop. (1991p) 752,909; ships fruit, wine, textiles, ironwork; produces metal goods; 13th–15th cent. cathedral, 15th cent. Gothic silk exchange, and several other notable buildings; university (1500).

History: First mentioned as Roman settlement c. 138 B.C.; taken by Visigoths 413 A.D. and Moors 714; made ✱ of independent Moorish kingdom of Valencia early 11th cent. (see *History* at VALENCIA 1). Believed to be site of first Spanish printing press 1474; severely damaged in Peninsular War (early 19th cent.), Spanish Civil War (1936–39), and by flood 1957.

4. *formerly* **Ta·ca·ri·gua** \ˌtä-kä-ˈrē-gwä\. Lake, N Venezuela, SW of Caracas and ab. 20 mi. (30 km.) S of coast of Caribbean Sea; 125 sq. mi. (324 sq. km.).

5. Commercial city, ✱ of Carabobo state, N Venezuela, 80 mi. (129 km.) W of Caracas and near W end of Lake Valencia; pop. (1990p) 903,706; 3d largest city in Venezuela and one of its principal industrial and transportation centers; produces textiles, paper, cement, furniture, dairy products, soap, vegetable oils, pharmaceuticals, feed, fertilizer; automobile-assembly plants; founded 1555.

Va·len·cia \və-ˈlen-chē-ə, -sē-ə\. Island off SW coast of Ireland. See VALENTIA 2.

Va·len·cia, Gol·fo de \bä-ˈlen-thē-ä, və-ˈlen-chē-ə, -ˈlen-sē-ə\ *or Eng.* **Gulf of Va·len·cia** \və-ˈlen-chē-ə, -sē-ə\. Wide-mouthed inlet of Mediterranean Sea, E coast of Spain bet. Cape Tortosa and Cape Nao.

Va·len·cia de Al·cán·ta·ra \bä-ˈlen-thē-ä-ˌthā-äl-ˈkän-tä-rä\. Commune, Cáceres prov., W Spain, near Portuguese border 47 mi. (76 km.) W of the commune of Cáceres; pop. (1991c) 6577.

Va·len·ci·ennes \ˌvä-lä^n-ˈsyen, və-ˌlen-sē-ˈenz\. Town, Nord dept., N France, on the Schelde 29 mi. (47 km.) SE of Lille; pop. (1990c) 39,276; museum; library; several notable churches; 17th cent. town hall.

History: Held by Holy Roman Emperor Charlemagne early 9th cent.; later became a chief city of Hainaut; conquered by King Louis XIV 1677 and ceded to France 1678; in WWI captured and occupied by Germans 1914–18; severely damaged 1918 and during WWII.

Va·len·tia \vä-len-ˈtyä\. **1.** Commune, France. See VALENCE.

2. \və-ˈlen-chē-ə\ *also* **Va·len·cia** \və-ˈlen-chē-ə, -sē-ə\. Island, co. Kerry, Ireland, off SW coast, S of entrance to Dingle Bay; 7 mi. (11 km.) long and 2 mi. (3.2 km.) wide; 10 sq. mi. (26 sq. km.); E terminus of the first transatlantic cable (to Newfoundland), laid in 1866.

3. Commune, Spain. See VALENCIA 3.

Val·en·tine \ˈva-lən-ˌtīn\. City, ⊗ of Cherry co., N Nebraska, on Niobrara River 10 mi. (16 km.) S of South Dakota border; pop. (1990c) 2826.

Va·le·ra \bä-ˈlā-rä\. Town, Trujillo state, W cen. Venezuela, 25 mi. (40 km.) WSW of the town of Trujillo; munic. pop. (1990p) 111,114; trading center.

Va·le·ri·an Way \və-ˈlir-ē-ən\ *or Lat.* **Via Va·le·ria** \ˌvī-ə-və-ˈlir-ē-ə\. Ancient Roman road, cen. Italy, from Tibur (Tivoli) along the N bank of the Anio (Aniene) E and NE through the Apennines to Aternum (Pescara) on the Adriatic.

Va·lé·rien, Mont \ˌmō^n-ˌvä-ler-ˈye^n\. Hill, W of Paris, France, near Suresnes; 531 ft. (162 m.); site of a fort, important defensively in siege of Paris during Franco-Prussian War 1870–71.

Valetta. See VALLETTA.

Val·ga \ˈväl-gä\. Town, S Estonia, at boundary with Latvia.

Valgrund. See VALLGRUND.

Va·lien·te, Cape \bäl-ˈyen-tā\. Cape, NW coast of Panama, enclosing Chiriquí Lagoon.

Va·li·ra \vä-ˈlē-rä\ *or* **Gran Valira** \ˌgrän\. River, SW Europe; flows through Andorra into the Segre River at La Seu d'Urgell in Spain.

Va·lje·vo \ˈväl-yā-ˌvō\ *also* **Val·ye·vo** \ˈväl-yā-ˌvō\. Town, Serbia, Yugoslavia, ab. 45 mi. (70 km.) SW of Belgrade; seized by Serbs 1804 during first open revolt against Turkish rule.

Val·ke·a·ko·ski \ˈväl-kā-ä-ˌkȯs-kē\. City, SW Finland, SE of Tampere; pop. (1993e) 21,435.

Val·kens·waard \ˈväl-kəns-ˌvärt\. Commune, North Brabant prov., Netherlands; pop. (1992e) 30,495.

Val·la·do·lid \ˌbäl-yä-thō-ˈlēth, ˌbä-yä-; ˌva-lə-də-ˈlid\. **1.** Town, E Yucatán state, SE Mexico, E of the ruins of Chichén Itzá.

2. Municipality, Negros Occidental, Negros, Philippines, on Guimaras Strait 16 mi. (26 km.) SSW of City of Bacolod; pop. (1980c) 21,728.

3. Province of NW cen. Spain. See table at SPAIN.

4. Commune, ✱ of Valladolid prov. and ✱ of Castilla y León autonomous community and historical region, NW cen. Spain, on Pisuerga River 98 mi. (158 km.) NNW of Madrid; pop. (1991p) 328,365; produces leather goods, textiles, chemicals, flour; 16th cent. cathedral; 12th cent. church; 17th cent. palace; university (13th cent.). First mentioned 1074; seat of Castilian court until c. 1600; site of marriage of Isabella of Castile and Ferdinand of Aragon 1469; heavily damaged by fire 1561 and by French in Peninsular War (1808–14). Explorer Christopher Columbus died here 1506.

Val·lau·ris \ˌvȧ-lȯ-ˈrēs\. Commune, Alpes-Maritimes dept., SE France, 13 mi. (21 km.) SW of Nice; site of a Picasso museum.

Val·le \ˈvä-yā\. Department of S Honduras. See table at HONDURAS.

Val·le·ci·to Reservoir \ˌvī-ˈsē-tə, ˌvī-ə-\. Reservoir in Pine (or Los Pinos) River, tributary of San Juan River, E La Plata co., SW Colorado; impounds water for irrigation.

Val·le d'Aos·ta \ˈvä-lā-dä-ˈȯ-stä\. Autonomous region, NW Italy; ✱ Aosta. See table at ITALY.

Val·le de la Pas·cua \ˈbä-yā-ˌthā-lä-ˈpäs-kwä\. Town, Guárico, N cen. Venezuela, ab. 100 mi. (160 km.) SE of San Juan de los Morros; pop. (1990e) 72,703.

Val·le del Cau·ca \ˈvä-yā-thel-ˈkau̇-kä\; *often shortened to* **Valle.** Department of Colombia. See table at COLOMBIA.

Val·le de San·tia·go \ˈbä-yā-ˌthā-ˌsän-tē-ˈä-gō\. Town, Guanajuato state, cen. Mexico, 40 mi. (64 km.) S of the city of Guanajuato; munic. pop. (1990p) 129,227.

Valle di Pompei. See POMPEI.

Val·le·du·par \ˌbä-yā-dü-ˈpär\. Town, ✱ of César dept., N Colombia; munic. pop. (1992e) 251,600.

Val·lée–de–l'Or \vȧ-ˌlā-də-ˈlōr\. County, Quebec, Canada. See table at QUEBEC.

Val·le·her·mo·so \ˌvä-yā-er-ˈmō-sä\. Municipality, Negros Oriental prov., Negros, Philippines, on Tanon Strait 34 mi. (55 km.) SE of City of Bacolod; pop. (1980c) 25,043.

Val·le Her·mo·so \ˈbä-yā-er-ˈmō-so\. Municipality, Tamaulipas state, Mexico, 20 mi. (32 km.) SW of Matamoros; pop. (1990p) 51,311.

Val·le·jo \və-ˈlā-ō, -ˈlā-ˌhō\. Commercial city, Solano co., cen. California, on San Pablo Bay 20 mi. (32 km.) N of Oakland; pop. (1990c) 109,199; ships agricultural products; California Maritime Academy (1929). Settled c. 1850; served briefly as state ✱ in early 1850s; incorp. late 1860s.

Val·le·nar \ˌbä-yā-ˈnär\. City, Atacama region, N cen. Chile, ab. 80 mi. (130 km.) SSW of Copiapó; pop. (1992c) 47,094.

Val·les \ˈbä-yās\. **1.** River, E cen. Mexico, a tributary of the Pánuco River.

2. *or officially* **Ciu·dad de Valles** \ˌsyü-ˈthäth-thā-\. Town, San Luis Potosí state, cen. Mexico, ab. 125 mi. (200 km.) E of the city of San Luis Potosí.

Val·let·ta *also* **Va·let·ta** \və-ˈle-tə\. Seaport city, ✱ of Malta, on the NE coast of island of Malta; pop. (1988c) 9210; commercial center of the country; tourism. Located on a rocky promontory with harbors on either side; library; museum; 16th cent. cathedral; governor-general's residence; Univ. of Malta (1769).

History: Built after Ottoman siege of 1565; named for Jean Parisot de La Valette, grand master of the Knights of Malta, and made ✱ 1570; made principal base of British Mediterranean fleet after 1814 and remained important until after WWII, during which it suffered heavy damage from bombing raids.

Val·ley \ˈva-lē\. **1.** Name of counties in three states of the U.S. See tables at IDAHO, MONTANA, NEBRASKA.

2. City, Lee co., E Alabama; pop. (1990c) 8173.

Valley Center. City, Sedgwick co., S cen. Kansas, 10 mi. (16 km.) N of Wichita; pop. (1990c) 3624.

Valley City. City, ⊗ of Barnes co., E North Dakota, 60 mi. (97 km.) W of Fargo; pop. (1990c) 7163; Valley City State Univ. (1890); city settled 1872.

Valley East. Town, Ontario, Canada, N of Sudbury; pop. (1991c) 21,939.

Valley Falls. Unincorporated settlement, Providence co., N Rhode Island, 2 mi. (3 km.) N of Central Falls; pop. (1990c) 11,175; governmental center for Cumberland.

Valleyfield. See SALABERRY DE VALLEYFIELD.

Valley Forge \ˈfōrj\. Locality, Chester co., SE Pennsylvania, on Schuylkill River ab. 4 mi. (6 km.) SE of Phoenixville; winter headquarters of Gen. George Washington and his army 1777–78 during Revolutionary War; **Valley Forge National Historical Park** estab. 1976 (see UNITED STATES, *National Historical Parks*).

Valley Junction. See WEST DES MOINES.

Valley of Ten Thousand Smokes. Volcanic region, SW Alaska, in Katmai National Monument W of Mt. Katmai; formed June 1912 when the valley—17 mi. (27 km.) long by 4 mi. (6 km.) wide—was covered by a flow of lava; later (1915), when discovered by an expedition of the National Geographic Society, its floor was found to have not 10,000, but possibly millions of steam jets (largest 150 ft. or 46 m. in diameter), some of which had a temperature as high as 1200°F.

Valley of the Kings. See KINGS, VALLEY OF THE.

Valley Park. City, St. Louis co., E Missouri, 16 mi. (26 km.) W of the city of St. Louis; pop. (1990c) 4165.

Valley Station. Unincorporated settlement, Jefferson co., N cen. Kentucky, S of Louisville; pop. (1990c) 22,840.

Valley Stream. Residential village, Nassau co., SE New York, on Long Island 16 mi. (26 km.) ESE of New York City; pop. (1990c) 33,946; incorp. 1925.

Vall·grund *or* **Val·grund** \ˈväl-gru̇nd\. Island, Gulf of Bothnia, Vaasa prov., Finland, opp. city of Vaasa.

Val·mi·era \ˈväl-ˌmyer-ä\ *or Ger.* **Wol·mar** \ˈvȯl-ˌmär\. Town, N Latvia, 65 mi. (105 km.) NE of Riga.

Val·my \vȧl-ˈmē, ˈval-mē\. Village, Marne dept., NE France; scene of victory of French Revolutionary army under Gen. Charles-François Dumouriez and Gen. François-Christophe Kellermann over combined Austrian-Prussian force Sept. 1792.

Va·lognes \vȧ-ˈlōnʸ\. Commercial town, Manche dept., NW France, SSE of Cherbourg; 14th cent. church; a few Roman remains in vicinity.

Va·lois \ˈvȧl-ˌwä\. Medieval county and duchy, NE Île-de-France, N France, now included in modern depts. of Aisne and Oise; ✱ Crépy-en-Valois. County united to crown by King Philip Augustus 1214, but soon detached; granted 1285 by Philip III to his son Charles (count of Valois), whose son Philip VI became first ruler of the house of Valois 1328; its last representative, Henry III, was succeeded 1589 by the house of Bourbon.

Valona. See VLORË.

Val·pa·rai \ˌväl-pə-ˈrī\. Town, Tamil Nadu, India, ab. 50 mi. (80 km.) NW of Madurai; pop. (1981e) 115,662.

Val·pa·rai·so 1. \ˌval-pə-ˈrī-zō\. City, Okaloosa co., NW Florida, on Choctawhatchee Bay; pop. (1990c) 4672; Eglin Air Force Base.

2. \ˌval-pə-ˈrā-zō\. Residential city, ⊗ of Porter co., NW Indiana, 12 mi. (19 km.) S of Lake Michigan; pop. (1990c) 24,414; popping corn grown in area; Valparaiso Univ. (1859).

Val·pa·ra·í·so \ˌbäl-pä-rä-ˈē-sō\; *Eng.* **Val·pa·rai·so** \ˌval-pə-ˈrā-zō, -ˈrī-\. **1.** Former province of cen. Chile.

2. *formerly* **Acon·ca·gua** \ˌak-ən-ˈkäg-wə, ˌäk-\. Region of cen. Chile. See table at CHILE.

3. Seaport, its ✱, 75 mi. (121 km.) WNW of Santiago on the **Bay of Valparaíso;** pop. (1982e) 265,718; formerly ✱ of Valparaíso prov. and later ✱ of Aconcagua region; principal seaport of Chile, handling the bulk of the country's imports; extensive modern dock facilities; produces chemicals, textiles, paint, leather goods, vegetable oils; foundries, naval facilities; Univ. of Valparaíso (1912), Catholic university (1928), technical university (1932), teacher-training university (1985), naval academy. Viña del Mar (*q.v.*) to NE is residential suburb. Founded 1536; bombarded by Spanish fleet 1866; treaty signed here 1884 by which Bolivia ceded to Chile coastal region containing principal nitrate deposits. Seaport has been subject to frequent severe earthquakes, esp. in 1906–07 after which modern development began, and in 1971.

4. Municipality, Zacatecas state, Mexico, 65 mi. (105 km.) W of city of Zacatecas.

Vals, Tan·jung \ˈtän-ˌju̇ŋ-ˈväls\ *or Du.* **Kaap Valsch** \käp-ˈväls\ *or Eng.* **False Cape.** Cape, SW tip of Dolak I., off S coast of Irian Jaya, Indonesia.

Val·sad \ˈvəl-ˌsəd\ *also* **Bal·sad** \ˈbəl-ˌsəd\; *formerly* **Bul·sar** \ˈbəl-ˌsər\. Seaport town, S Gujarat, W India, 115 mi. (185 km.) N of Bombay; pop. (1991p) 57,903.

Valua. See MOTA LAVA.

Val·ver·de \bäl-ˈber-thā, val-ˈver-dē\. **1.** Province, Dominican Republic. See table at DOMINICAN REPUBLIC.
2. Chief town, Hierro I., Canary Is., Spain; pop. (1991c) 3550.

Val Ver·de \val-ˈvər-dē\. County in SW Texas. See table at TEXAS.

Valyevo. See VALJEVO.

Vam·sa·dha·ra \ˌvəm-shə-ˈdär-ə\. River, SW Orissa and NE Andhra Pradesh, India; rises in Eastern Ghats and flows S to Bay of Bengal; 170 mi. (274 km.) long.

Van \ˈvan\. **1.** Ancient kingdom, W Asia, N of Assyria. See URARTU and ARMENIA 1.
2. Province of Turkey in Asia. See table at TURKEY.
3. Town, its ✻, on SE shore of Lake Van; pop. (1990c) 153,111; ships hides, fruit, grain; ancient citadel.
History: Nearby archaeological site of old city dates back to kingdom of Urartu (see ARMENIA 1 and URARTU) of which it was ✻ c. 8th cent. B.C.; fell to Seljuq Turks after 1071 A.D. and to Ottoman Turks 1543.

Van, Lake *or Turk.* **Van Gö·lü** \ˈvän-ˈgœ-ˌlue\; *anc.* **Thos·pi·tis La·cus** \thäs-ˈpī-təs-ˈlā-kəs\. Salt lake, E Turkey in Asia; 1419 sq. mi. (3675 sq. km.); 80 mi. (129 km.) long; max. depth 82 ft. (25 m.); alt. 5643 ft. (1720 m.); largest lake in Turkey; has no apparent outlet; earthquake in area Nov. 1976 resulted in ab. 4000 deaths.

Va·nad·zor \və-ˈnäd-ˌzōr\ *or* **Ki·ro·va·kan** \ˌkē-rə-və-ˈkän\ *or* **Ka·ra·klis** \kə-ˈrä-ˌklis\. Town, Armenia, ab. 40 mi. (65 km.) N of Yerevan; pop. (1989c) 159,000; suffered severe earthquake damage Dec. 7, 1988.

Van Bu·ren \van-ˈbyu̇r-ən\. **1.** Name of counties in four states of the U.S. See tables at ARKANSAS, IOWA, MICHIGAN, TENNESSEE.
2. City, ⊗ of Crawford co., NW Arkansas, on Arkansas River 6 mi. (10 km.) NE of Fort Smith; pop. (1990c) 14,979.
3. Town, Aroostook co., N Maine, on St. John River 34 mi. (55 km.) N of Presque Isle; pop. (1990c) 3045; lumber; potatoes.
4. Town, ⊗ of Carter co., SE Missouri; pop. (1990c) 893.

Vance \ˈvans\. County in N North Carolina. See table at NORTH CAROLINA.

Vance·burg \ˈvans-ˌbərg\. City, ⊗ of Lewis co., NE Kentucky; pop. (1990c) 1713.

Van·cou·ver \van-ˈkü-vər\. **1.** City, ⊗ of Clark co., SW Washington, on Columbia River ab. 8 mi. (13 km.) N of Portland, Oregon; pop. (1990c) 46,380; ships grain; produces aluminum, chemicals, wood and paper products; in farming region; Clark Coll. (1933). Founded as Hudson's Bay Company Post 1824; taken over by U.S. government 1846 and made military reservation 1848; incorp. as city 1857.
2. City, S British Columbia, Canada, at mouth of Burrard Inlet on S side; pop. (1991c) 471,844; met. area pop. 1,602,502; principal Pacific seaport of Canada and the industrial and commercial center of British Columbia; ships forest products and grain; produces lumber, plywood, pulp and paper; oil refining, food processing; commercial fisheries, shipyards, grain elevators; W terminus for transcontinental railroad. Many museums; parks, incl. Stanley Park with notable aquarium; Univ. of British Columbia (1908, at Point Gray), site of Museum of Anthropology, Simon Fraser Univ. (1963, at Burnaby). Orig. inhabited by native coastal Indians, perhaps as early as late first millennium B.C.; first nonnative settlement in area estab. by 1865; founded 1881 and incorp. as city 1886; suffered major fire 1886 but rebuilt; development aided by completion of transcontinental railroad 1887 and of Panama Canal 1914; increasingly important as port servicing Pacific Rim countries in late 20th cent.

Vancouver, Mount. Peak in St. Elias Mts., SW Yukon Terr., Canada, near Alaskan boundary SE of Mt. Logan; 15,700 ft. (4785 m.).

Vancouver Island. Island off SW British Columbia, Canada; on the S separated from Washington, U.S.A., by Strait of Juan de Fuca and on E from Canadian mainland by Strait of Georgia, Johnstone Strait, and Queen Charlotte Sound; 12,408 sq. mi. (32,137 sq. km.); largest island off W coast of Canada; chief city Victoria. Has several fine harbors incl. Esquimalt in the S, Ladysmith and Nanaimo on the Strait of Georgia, and Port Alberni at the head of Alberni Canal. Mountainous, averaging 2000 to 3000 ft. (610 to 915 m.); highest peak Golden Hinde 7219 ft. (2200 m.). Contains Pacific Rim National Park; coal, iron ore, copper; lumbering, fishing; tourism. Inhabited by coastal Indians for several millennia; visited by early Spanish and English explorers and at Nootka Sound by Capt. James Cook 1778; made a British crown colony 1849 and united with British Columbia 1866.

Van·da·lia \van-ˈdāl-yə\. **1.** City, ⊗ of Fayette co., S cen. Illinois, 30 mi. (48 km.) N of Centralia; pop. (1990c) 6114; ✻ of Illinois 1820–39; Vandalia Correctional Center.
2. City, Audrain co., NE cen. Missouri, 29 mi. (47 km.) SSW of Hannibal; pop. (1990c) 2683.
3. City, Montgomery co., SW Ohio, N of Dayton; pop. (1990c) 13,882.

Van·der·bijl·park \ˈvan-dər-ˌbīl-ˌpärk\. Town, Gauteng prov., Rep. of South Africa, SW of Johannesburg; pop. (1985c) 59,865; steel.

Van·der·burgh \ˈvan-dər-ˌbərg\. County in SW Indiana. See table at INDIANA.

Van·der·grift \ˈvan-dər-ˌgrift\. Borough, Westmoreland co., SW Pennsylvania, on Kiskiminetas River 25 mi. (40 km.) ENE of Pittsburgh; pop. (1990c) 5904.

Van Die·men, Cape \van-ˈdē-mən\. NW point of Melville I., Northern Terr., Australia.

Van Diemen Gulf. Inlet of Arafura Sea, N Northern Terr., Australia, shut in by Melville I. and Cobourg Penin.; connected on the N by Dundas Strait with Arafura Sea and on the W by Clarence Strait with Timor Sea.

Van Diemen's Land. See TASMANIA.

Van Diemen Strait. See OSUMI ISLANDS.

Vä·nern \ˈva-nərn\ *also* **Ven·ern** \ˈve-\ *or* **Vä·ner** \-nər\. Lake, SW Sweden; 2156 sq. mi. (5584 sq. km.); 91 mi. (146 km.) long; 328 ft. (100 m.) max. depth; largest lake in Sweden; W section called **Dal·bo** \ˈdäl-ˌbü\.

Vä·ners·borg \ˌva-nərs-ˈbȯrg, -ˈbȯr-yə\. Town, ⊗ of Älvsborg prov., SW Sweden, at S end of Lake Vänern; pop. (1980p) 34,574.

Van Gölü. See VAN, LAKE.

Vang·u·nu \ˈväŋ-ü-ˌnü\. One of the New Georgia Is., cen. Solomon Is., W Pacific Ocean, off SE end of New Georgia I. Mountainous, its highest point 3686 ft. (1123 m.); its N coast encloses Marovo lagoon (see NEW GEORGIA).

Van Horn \van-ˈhȯrn\. Village, ⊗ of Culberson co., W Texas; pop. (1990c) 2930.

Van Horn Mountains. Range, SW Culberson co., W Texas; highest peak 5786 ft. (1764 m.).

Va·nier \vȧ-ˈnyā, və-ˈnir\. **1.** *formerly* **East·view** \ˈēst-ˌvyü\. City, SE Ontario, Canada, on Ottawa River; pop. (1991c) 18,150.
2. *formerly* **Que·bec West** \kwi-ˈbek-ˈwest\ *or Fr.* **Québec-Ouest** \kā-ˌbek-ˈwest\. Town, Quebec co., S Quebec prov., Canada, W suburb of Quebec City; pop. (1991c) 10,833.

Va·ni·ko·lo \ˌvä-ni-ˈkō-lō\ *or* **Va·ni·ko·ro** \-rō\. Island, S Santa Cruz group, Solomon Is., SW Pacific Ocean, 20 mi. (32 km.) SE of Utupua I.; 11°37′S, 166°58′E; scene of the wreck of French navigator Jean-François de Galaup, comte de La Pérouse's fleet 1788; fate of expedition's members never fully determined.

Va·ni·yam·ba·di \ˌva-ni-yəm-ˈbä-dē\. Town, N Tamil Nadu, S India, on two islands in Palar River 118 mi. (190 km.) WSW of Madras; pop. (1991p) 72,282.

Vannes \ˈvȧn\. Town, ✻ of Morbihan dept., NW France, 67 mi. (108 km.) WNW of Nantes; pop. (1990c) 48,454; tires, metal goods, feed; poultry farming, tourism; 14th–17th cent. fortifications; cathedral with 16th cent. chapel; museum of Celtic and Roman antiquities; public gardens. Ancient ✻ of the Veneti, for whom it is named; came under Brittany late 10th cent.

Vann·øy \ˈvä-ˌnȯi\. Island, Norway, in Arctic Ocean, off NW coast.

Va·noise National Park \vä-ˈnwäz\. National park, E France; 208 sq. mi. (539 sq. km.); alpine fauna and flora; estab. 1963.

Van·taa \ˈvän-ˌtä\. City, S Finland, just NNE of Helsinki; pop. (1993e) 159,462.

Vanua Balavu. See VANUA MBALAVU.

Va·nua La·va \ˌvän-ˌwä-ˈlä-vä\. Largest of the Banks Is., N Vanuatu, SW Pacific Ocean; ab. 15 mi. (24 km.) long and 12 mi. (19 km.) wide. Of volcanic origin; highest point 3120 ft. (951 m.); has excellent harbor, Port Patteson, on SE coast.

Va·nua Le·vu \ˌvän-ˌwä-ˈlā-ˌvü\. Island, Fiji, 38 mi. (61 km.) NE of Viti Levu; 2137 sq. mi. (5535 sq. km.). Covered with mountains, highest Mt. Ndikeva 3134 ft. (955 m.). Its coastline irregular, esp. on E end where Natewa Bay makes deep indentation bet. mainland and Natewa Penin. (40 mi. or 64 km. long). Chief river is the Ndreketi. Has many small coastal villages; long reef and islets along its N shore.

Va·nua Mba·la·vu \ˌvän-ˌwäm-bä-ˈlä-ˌvü\ *or* **Vanua Ba·la·vu** \-ˌwä-bä-\. Island, Fiji, largest of the Exploring Isles; 14 mi. (23 km.) long and from 0.5 to 2.5 mi. (0.8 to 4 km.) wide; chief town Lomaloma.

Va·nu·atu \ˌvan-ˌwä-ˈtü, ˌvän-, -ˈwä-tü\; *before independence* **New Heb·ri·des** \ˈhe-brə-ˌdēz\. Republic, a group of islands in SW Pacific Ocean NE of New Caledonia and W of Fiji; 5700 sq. mi. (14,763 sq. km.); pop. (1991e) 142,419; ✻ Port-Vila; an independent country, formerly under joint British and French administration. Principal islands are Espíritu Santo, Malekula, Efate, Ambrim, Erromango, Tanna, Epi, Aneityum, Maéwo, and Pentecost. Larger islands volcanic in origin and mountainous; three active volcanoes; some of the islands, esp. Efate and Malekula, have good harbors.

Chief products: Copra, cocoa, beef, timber, coffee; tourism.

History: Inhabited for thousands of years by Melanesians before discovered 1606 by Portuguese navigator Pedro Fernandes de Queirós; forgotten for 160 years, then visited by French navigator Louis-Antoine de Bougainville 1768, explored by English mariner Capt. James Cook 1774, and named New Hebrides; control of group sought by both French and British who finally signed a convention Oct. 20, 1906 by which a condominium was set up, superseded by a 2d protocol 1914, ratified 1922; in WWII major Allied naval base on Espíritu Santo I., 1942–45; became independent as Republic of Vanuatu July 30, 1980.

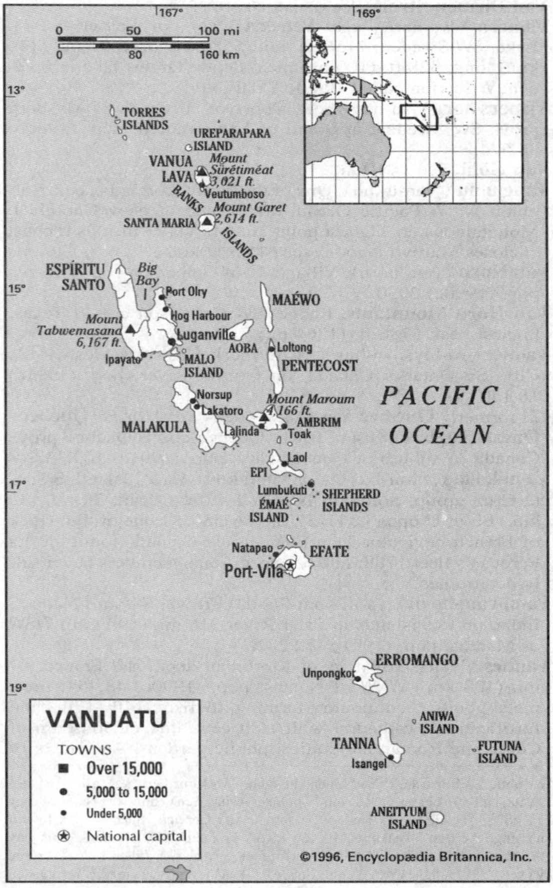

Vanves \ˈvänv\. Commune, Hauts-de-Seine dept., N France, SW suburb of Paris.

Van Wert \van-ˈwərt\. **1.** County in NW Ohio. See table at OHIO.
2. City, its ⊗, 26 mi. (42 km.) WNW of Lima; pop. (1990c) 10,891; settled 1835.

Van Zandt \van-ˈzant\. County in NE Texas. See table at TEXAS.

Vaph·io \vä-ˈfyȯ, ˈva-fē-ˌō\. Site, Laconia dept., SE Peloponnese, S Greece, on Eurotas River 5 mi. (8 km.) S of Sparta; beehive tomb excavated late 19th cent.; among other discoveries were two finely ornamented gold cups (the Vaphio cups), dating from c. 1500 B.C. (Late Minoan).

Vapincum. See GAP.

Var \ˈvär\. **1.** *or Ital.* **Va·ro** \ˈvä-rō\; *anc.* **Va·rus** \ˈvar-əs\. River, extreme SE France; rises in the Alps, in Alpes-Maritimes dept., flows SE and S into Mediterranean Sea 4 mi. (6 km.) SW of Nice; 75 mi. (121 km.) long.
2. Department of SE France. See table at FRANCE.

Va·ra·na·si \və-ˈrä-nə-ˌsē\ *also* **Be·na·res** \bə-ˈnär-əs, -ēz\ *or* **Ba·na·ras** \-əs\ *or* **Ka·si** \ˈkä-sē\. City, SE Uttar Pradesh, India, on Ganges River 400 mi. (644 km.) WNW of Calcutta; pop. (1991c) 932,399; silk fabrics, brass vessels, lacquered toys; Banaras Hindu Univ. (1916), Sanskrit Univ. (1958); one of India's most ancient cities, inhabited for millennia. Holy city of the Hindus and the object of constant pilgrimages; also sacred to Jains, Sikhs, and Buddhists, and it is said that Buddha preached his first sermon near here. Has great number of temples and large mosques; among its most famous structures are the Viśvanātha, the Mosque of Aurangzeb, and a Maratha temple of the goddess Durga; ghats line the river for religious bathing rituals.

Va·rang·er Fjord \vä-ˈräŋ-ər\. Inlet of the Arctic Ocean, extreme NE coast of Norway, NW of Pechenga, Russia; ab. 42 mi. (70 km.) long.

Va·ra·no, Lake \vä-ˈrä-nō\. Lagoon of Adriatic Sea, SE Italy, on N side of Gargano Promontory.

Va·raž·din \vä-ˈräzh-ˌdēn\ *or Hung.* **Va·rasd** \ˈvör-ˌösht\ *or Ger.* **Wa·ras·din** \ˈvär-äs-ˌdēn\. Town, Croatia, on Drava River ab. 38 mi. (61 km.) NE of Zagreb; pop. (1991c) 48,834; industrial and commercial center.

Var·berg \ˈvär-ˌber-ē\. Town, Halland prov., SW Sweden, on the Kattegat ab. 45 mi. (70 km.) S of Göteborg; pop. (1993e) 50,465; museum; port; fishing.

Var·dar \ˈvär-ˌdär\ *or* **Ax·i·ós** \ˌäk-sē-ˈȯs\; *anc.* **Ax·i·us** \ˈak-sē-əs\. River, S Europe, in Republic of Macedonia and N Greece; rises in W Republic of Macedonia and flows NNE then SSE through Greece into the Gulf of Salonika; 241 mi. (388 km.) long. Chief tributary the Crna.

Var·dar·ska \ˈvär-där-ˌskä\. Former county, SE Yugoslavia, now mostly in Republic of Macedonia, with N section in Serbia, Yugoslavia; 15,007 sq. mi. (38,868 sq. km.); ⊗ Skopje.

Var·de \ˈvär-də\. River, cen. Jutland, Denmark; flows SW into North Sea NW of Esbjerg; ab. 45 mi. (70 km.) long.

Vardø \ˈvär-ˌdœ\. Port on **Vard·øya Island** \-ˌdȯi-yə\ off NE tip of Norway, N of entrance to Varanger Fjord.

Va·rennes \vå-ˈren\; *officially* **Varennes–en–Ar·gonne** \-ä-når-ˈgän\. Commune, Meuse dept., NE France; pop. (1991c)

14,758; place where Louis XVI was arrested 1791 in his flight from Paris.

Va·re·se \vä-'rā-sē\. **1.** Province of Lombardy, N Italy. See table at ITALY.

2. Commune, its ✻, near **Lake Varese** 30 mi. (48 km.) NW of Milan; pop. (1991p) 85,461; leather goods and footwear, textiles; 18th cent. palace with public gardens; 16th cent. basilica; 12th cent. baptistery.

Var·gi·nha \vȧr-'zhē-nyə\. City, Minas Gerais state, E Brazil, 170 mi. (274 km.) NW of Rio de Janeiro; munic. pop. (1991p) 88,034.

Var·kaus \'vär-ˌkau̇s\. City, SE Finland, S of Kuopio; pop. (1993e) 24,554; wood products incl. boats.

Värm·land \'varm-ˌländ\. Province of SW Sweden. See table at SWEDEN.

Varna \'vär-nə\. **1.** Region of E Bulgaria. See table at BULGARIA.

2. *1949–57* **Sta·lin** \'stä-ˌlēn\; *anc.* **Odes·sus** \ō-'de-səs\. Seaport, its ✻, on Black Sea ab. 182 mi. (293 km.) NE of Plovdiv; pop. (1991e) 314,913; transportation center and principal seaport of Bulgaria; flour; shipbuilding and repair facilities; naval base; university, naval school.

History: Founded 6th cent. B.C.; came under Turks 1391; scene of battle Nov. 10, 1444, in which Turks under Murad II defeated Hungarians under János Hunyadi and killed Władysław III, king of Poland and Hungary; ceded to Bulgaria by Treaty of Berlin 1878; harbor opened 1906.

Varns·dorf \'värns-ˌdȯrf\ *or Ger.* **Warns·dorf** \'värns-\. City, N Czech Republic, 58 mi. (93 km.) N of Prague near German border; pop. (1980p) 16,356.

Varo. See VAR 1.

Vár·pa·lo·ta \'vär-pö-ˌlō-tö\. Town, W Hungary, ab. 50 mi. (80 km.) SW of Budapest; pop. (1991e) 27,400.

Varus. See VAR 1.

Vary Karlovy. See KARLOVY VARY.

Vas \'väsh\. County of W Hungary. See table at HUNGARY.

Vasa. See VAASA.

Vasai. See BASSEIN.

Vasconia. See GASCONY.

Vash·on Island \'va-ˌshän\. Island, Puget Sound, Washington, midway bet. Seattle and Tacoma; 14 mi. (23 km.) long; belongs to King co.

Va·sil·kov \və-sil-'kȯf\ *or* **Va·syl·kiv** \və-sil-'kē-ü\. Town, Kiev subdivision, NW Ukraine, 19 mi. (31 km.) S of city of Kiev.

Vas·lui \väs-'lü-ē\. **1.** County of E Romania. See table at ROMANIA.

2. City, its ⊗, 35 mi. (56 km.) S of Iaşi; pop. (1989c) 73,666. Moldavian Prince Stephen IV (the Great) defeated Ottoman Turks nearby 1475.

Vas·quez Peak \'vas-ˌkez\. Mountain, Clear Creek and Grand cos., N Colorado; 12,800 ft. (3901 m.).

Vas·sal·boro \'vas-əl-ˌbər-ō\. Town, Kennebec co., SW Maine, on Kennebec River 6 mi. (10 km.) S of Waterville; pop. (1990c) 3679; dairy farms.

Vas·sar \'va-sər\. City, Tuscola co., E Michigan, 19 mi. (31 km.) ESE of Saginaw; pop. (1990c) 2559.

Vassarí Mountains. See SERRA UAÇARI.

Vas·sou·ras \və-'sōr-əs\. City, Rio de Janeiro state, SE Brazil, 45 mi. (72 km.) NW of the city of Rio de Janeiro; munic. pop. (1980c) 44,398.

Väs·ter·ås \ˌves-tə-'rōs\. City, ⊗ of Västmanland prov., E Sweden, at mouth of Svart River on Lake Mälaren; pop. (1993e) 120,889; major inland port; a center of the Swedish electrical industry; Gothic cathedral; 12th cent. castle; scene of parliament 1527 which formally introduced Reformation into Sweden.

Väs·ter·bot·ten \'ves-tər-ˌbȯ-tən\. Province of N Sweden. See table at SWEDEN.

Väster Dal. See DAL.

Väs·ter·norr·land \'ves-tər-ˌnȯr-lȧnd\. Province of E Sweden. See table at SWEDEN.

Väs·ter·vik \'ves-tər-ˌvēk\. Seaport, Kalmar prov., SE Sweden, on Baltic Sea 73 mi. (117 km.) N of the seaport of Kalmar; pop. (1980p) 41,263; manufactures machinery.

Väst·man·land \'vest-mȧn-ˌlȧnd\. Province of E Sweden. See table at SWEDEN.

Va·sto \'väs-tō\; *anc.* **His·to·ni·um** \hi-'stō-nē-əm\. Commune, Chieti prov., Abruzzi, cen. Italy, on the Adriatic 32 mi. (51 km.) ESE of the commune of Chieti; pop. (1991p) 32,810; 13th cent. castle; 11th cent. church; cathedral.

Vas·vár \'vösh-ˌvär\ *or Ger.* **Ei·sen·burg** \'ī-zən-ˌbu̇rk\. Commune, Vas co., W Hungary, ab. 15 mi. (24 km.) SE of Szombathely; pop. (1980p) 4275; treaty signed here Aug. 10, 1664 after battle of St. Gotthard (see SZENT-GOTTHÁRD) concluding, by 20-year truce, war bet. Holy Roman Emperor Leopold I and the Turks.

Vasylkiv. See VASILKOV.

Vaté. See EFATE.

Va·ter·nish Point \'wȯ-tər-nish\. Cape, NW coast of the island of Skye, Inner Hebrides, off NW coast of Scotland; bet. Loch Dunvegan and Loch Snizort.

Va·ter·say \'vä-tər-ˌsā\. See BARRA.

Va·thy *or Gk.* **Va·thí** \vä-'thē\. Seaport city, ✻ of Sámos dept., Aegean Is., Greece, on NE coast of Sámos I.

Vat·i·can City \'va-ti-kən\ *or Ital.* **Cit·tà del Va·ti·ca·no** \chēt-'tä-del-ˌvä-tē-'kä-nō\. Independent papal state, S Europe, within commune of Rome, Italy, on right bank of Tiber River; 108.7 acres (44 hectares); pop. (1991c) 771; created 1929 by the Lateran Pact as a settlement of question bet. Roman Catholic Church's and Italian state's ruling powers; extraterritoriality of the state extends to Castel Gandolfo and to several churches and palaces in Rome proper; under jurisdiction of the Vatican are the Basilica of St. John Lateran (the cathedral church of Rome and highest ranking of all Roman Catholic churches), the Basilica of St. Peter (founded by Roman Emperor Constantine the Great on site of Circus of Caligula where St. Peter is said by tradition to have suffered martyrdom), the Vatican (collection of papal palaces, incl. the Sistine Chapel), churches of Santa Maria Maggiore, San Paolo Fuori le Mura, San Lorenzo, and San Sebastiano; several educational institutions incl. Pontifical Gregorian Univ. (1551); railroad station; radio station, newspaper; independent postal and monetary systems; diplomatic missions; publishing. Concordat of 1929 amended and signed 1984. Holy See, or Apostolic See, designates Rome as the official seat of the pope. For history of temporal domain of the popes 755–1870, see PAPAL STATES.

Va·ti·ca·no, Cape \ˌvä-tē-'kä-nō\. Cape, SW coast of Calabria, the "toe" of Italy, extending into Tyrrhenian Sea S of Gulf of Sant'Eufemia.

Va·ti·lau \ˌvä-ti-'lau̇\. Small island, SE Solomon Is., in W Pacific Ocean, off NW coast of Florida I. beyond Olevuga I.

Vatiu. See ATIU.

Vat·na·jö·kull \'vät-nä-ˌyœ̄-küt-ᵊl\ *also* **Klo·fa Jö·kull** \'klō-vä-'yœ̄-ˌküt-ᵊl\. Snowfield, SE Iceland; 3247 sq. mi. (8410 sq. km.); contains several mountains incl. a couple of active volcanoes.

Va·toa Island \vä-'tō-ä\. Small island, Fiji, S end of Lau group, 19°50′S, 178°13′W.

Vät·tern \'ve-tərn\ *also* **Vat·ter** \'va-tər\ *or* **Vet·tern** \'ve-tərn\. Lake, S Sweden, E of Vänern Lake; 738 sq. mi. (1911 sq. km.); connected with the Baltic by the Göta Canal; Jönköping is at its S end.

Vau·clin \vō-'klaⁿ\ *or* **Le Vauclin** \lə-\. Seaport commune, SE Martinique, West Indies.

Vau·cluse \vō-'klu̅e̅z\. Department of SE France. See table at FRANCE.

Vaud \'vō\ *or Ger.* **Waadt** \'vät\. Canton, Switzerland; ✻ Lausanne; includes part of Lake Geneva and Lac de Neuchâtel; watered by Rhone River; wine; tourism. Conquered by Romans 58 B.C.; taken by Franks; passed to Bern 1536 and forced to accept Reformation; former canton of Leman (1798–1803). See table at SWITZERLAND.

Vau–de–Vire. See VIRE 2.

Vau·dreuil \vō-ˈdrœ̄-ē, vō-ˈdrōl\. Town, Quebec, Canada, on Ottawa River near its mouth ab. 24 mi. (39 km.) WSW of Montreal; pop. (1991c) 11,187.

Vau·dreuil–Sou·langes \vō-ˌdrœ̄-ē-sü-ˈläⁿzh\. County, Quebec, Canada. See table at QUEBEC.

Vaughan \ˈvȯn\. City, York munic. region, Ontario, Canada, NW of Toronto; pop. (1991c) 111,359; grew rapidly in 1980s.

Vaught, Mount \ˈvȯt\. Peak, Glacier National Park, NW Montana; 8840 ft. (2694 m.).

Vau·pés \vau̇-ˈpās\. **1.** River, South America. See UAUPÉS. **2.** Department of SE Colombia. See table at COLOMBIA.

Vaux \ˈvō\. Village, Meuse dept., NE France, 3 mi. (5 km.) NE of Verdun; scene of severe fighting in WWI 1916.

Va·va·'u \vä-ˈvä-ü\. **1.** Island group, N Tonga, SW cen. Pacific Ocean; includes island of Vava'u and ab. 30 islets; ab. 60 sq. mi. (155 sq. km.); mountainous, of volcanic origin. **2.** Chief island of the Vava'u group; 10 mi. (16 km.) long; 44 sq. mi. (114 sq. km.); pop. (1986c) 15,175; island noted for its caves.

Va·vu·ni·ya \ˈvə-vü-ˌnē-yə, ˈvä-\. Town, N cen. Sri Lanka; pop. (1989e) 21,000.

Väx·jö \ˈvek-ˌshœ̄\. Town, ⊗ of Kronoberg prov., S Sweden, 60 mi. (97 km.) WNW of Kalmar; pop. (1993e) 70,704; manufactures matches; cathedral.

Vayenga. See SEVEROMORSK.

Vay·gach *also* **Vai·gach** \vī-ˈgäch\. Island, NE Nenets Autonomous Okrug, NE Russia in Europe, bet. the mainland and Novaya Zemlya, SE of Kara Strait; 1306 sq. mi. (3382 sq. km.); 68 mi. (109 km.) long.

Vecchia, Città. See MDINA.

Vech·te \ˈfek-tə\ *or Du.* **Vecht** \ˈvekt\. River, Germany and the Netherlands; flows NW through North Rhine-Westphalia, Germany, and W through prov. of Overijssel, Netherlands, into IJsselmeer; ab. 125 mi. (200 km.) long.

Vectis. See ISLE OF WIGHT 3.

Ve·dea \ˈvā-ˌdyä\. River, S Romania, E of the Olt; flows SE into the Danube near Giurgiu; ab. 130 mi. (210 km.) long.

Veen·dam \vān-ˈdäm, ˈvān-ˌ\. Commune, Groningen prov., NE Netherlands, 14 mi. (23 km.) SE of the city of Groningen; pop. (1981e) 28,487.

Vee·nen·daal \ˈvā-nən-ˌdäl\. Commune, Utrecht prov., cen. Netherlands, just N of the Neder Rijn SE of the city of Utrecht; pop. (1992e) 50,791.

Ve·ga \ˈvā-gə\. Town, ⊗ of Oldham co., NW Texas; pop. (1990c) 840.

Vega, La. See LA VEGA.

Ve·ga Al·ta \ˌbā-gä-ˈäl-tä\. Municipality, N Puerto Rico, SW of San Juan; pop. (1990c) 34,559.

Ve·ga Ba·ja \ˈbā-gä-ˈbä-hä\. Municipality, N Puerto Rico, WSW of San Juan; pop. (1990c) 55,997.

Ve·ga Re·al \ˈbā-gä-rā-ˈäl\. Valley, N Dominican Republic; formed by two streams flowing in opposite directions.

Vegas. See LAS VEGAS 1.

Veglia. See KRK.

Ve·go·ri·tis, Lake \ˌve-gə-ˈrē-təs\ *or Gk.* **Lím·ni Ve·gor·rí·tis** \ˈlēm-nē-ˌve-gö-ˈrē-tēs\. Lake, N Greece, near border with Republic of Macedonia; ab. 25 sq. mi. (65 sq. km.).

Veg·re·ville \ˈve-gər-ˌvil\. Town, E Alberta, Canada, on a tributary of the North Saskatchewan River 57 mi. (92 km.) E of Edmonton; pop. (1991c) 5138.

Ve·ii \ˈvē-yī, ˈvā-yē\; *mod.* **Veio** \ˈvā-ō\. Ancient city of Etruria, ab. 12 mi. (19 km.) N of Rome, Italy; an Etruscan stronghold, one of the important cities of the Etruscan Confederation; for 350 years almost continually at war with Rome; captured by Roman soldier Camillus 396 B.C. after a 10-year siege.

Vej·le \ˈvī-lə\. **1.** County of SE Jutland, Denmark. See table at DENMARK. **2.** Seaport, its ⊗, at the head of **Vejle Fjord** (inlet 15 mi. or 24 km. long); pop. (1989e) 50,879; ships dairy products; textile mills, ironworks; St. Nicholas church, dating from 13th cent.

Ve·la·de·ro \ˌbā-lä-ˈthā-rō\ *or* **Ve·la·de·res** \-rās\. Peak, NW La Rioja prov., NW Argentina, near border of Chile; 20,735 ft. (6320 m.).

Vé·lan \vā-ˈläⁿ\. Mountain in the Pennine Alps, on the Switzerland-Italy border; 12,353 ft. (3765 m.).

Ve·la·nai Island \ˈvā-lə-ˌnī\. Island, N Palk Bay, off N tip of Sri Lanka.

Ve·las, Cape \ˈbā-läs\. Cape, NW coast of Costa Rica, extending into the Pacific Ocean.

Vel·bert \ˈfel-bərt\. City, North Rhine-Westphalia, Germany, in the Ruhr Valley 14 mi. (23 km.) NE of Düsseldorf; pop. (1992e) 89,347; manufactures locks.

Velch. See VULCI.

Veld·ho·ven \ˈvelt-ˌhō-və\. Commune, North Brabant prov., Netherlands; pop. (1981e) 35,191.

Ve·le·bit \ve-ˈle-bit\. Mountain range, W Croatia, extending from NW to SE along the Adriatic coast from ab. 44° to 45°N; greatest height 5768 ft. (1758 m.).

Ve·leb·it·ski Ka·nal \ve-ˈle-bit-skē-kə-ˈnäl\; *formerly* **Mor·lac·ca** \mȯr-ˈlä-kə, -ˈla-\. Channel along the coast of Croatia, bet. Krk I. and the mainland.

Ve·len·je \ˈve-ˌlen-ye\. Town, N Slovenia; pop. (1992e) 27,665.

Veles. See TITOV VELES.

Ve·le·ta, Pi·ca·cho de \pē-ˈkä-chō-thā-bā-ˈlā-tä\. Peak in the Sierra Nevada, Granada prov., S Spain, just WNW of Mulhacén; 11,125 ft. (3391 m.).

Vé·lez–Má·la·ga \ˈbā-lās-ˈmä-lä-ˌgä\. Commune, Málaga prov., S Spain, on the Mediterranean 16 mi. (26 km.) ENE of the city of Málaga; pop. (1991c) 50,999; sugarcane; remains of ancient Moorish castle.

Velho. See PÔRTO VELHO.

Ve·lia \ˈvē-lē-ə\ *or* **Elea** \ˈē-lē-ə\. Ancient town of Lucania, S Italy, its ruins near coast ab. halfway bet. Gulf of Salerno and Gulf of Policastro; includes remains of walls; founded c. 530 B.C. by Phocaean Greeks; home of Parmenides and Zeno of the Eleatic school of philosophers.

Velika Morava. See MORAVA 3.

Ve·li·ka·ya \vi-ˈlē-kə-yə\. River, Pskov Oblast, W Russia in Europe; flows N into Lake Pskov; 252 mi. (405 km.) long.

Veliki Bečkerek. See ZRENJANIN.

Ve·li·ki Ustyug *or* **Ve·li·kiy Ustyug** \vi-ˈlē-kē-ˈü-ˌstyu̇k\. Town, NE Vologda Oblast, N cen. Russia in Europe, on the left bank of the Northern Dvina River just below the junction of the Sukhona and the Yug; pop. (1991e) 36,200.

Ve·li·ki·ye Lu·ki \vi-ˈlē-kē-yə-ˈlü-kē\. Town, Pskov Oblast, W Russia in Europe, on right bank of upper Lovat' River 200 mi. (322 km.) W of Tver'; pop. (1992e) 116,000; railroad junction; railroad shops; first mentioned 1166; scene of heavy fighting in WWII.

Velikiy Ustyug. See VELIKI USTYUG.

Ve·li·ko Tŭr·no·vo \ˈvel-i-ˌkȯ-ˈtər-nə-ˌvō\ *or* **Tir·no·vo** \ˈtir-\ *or* **Tir·no·va** \ˈtir-nə-və\ *also* **Trno·vo** \ˈtər-nə-ˌvō\. City, N Bulgaria, on the Yantra River 55 mi. (88 km.) ESE of Pleven; pop. (1991e) 72,600; furniture, textiles; university; cultural center. Situated on a deep gorge with two high promontories and a connecting ridge. Served as ✻ of 2d Bulgarian empire 1186–1393; under Turkish rule 1394–1877; independent kingdom of Bulgaria proclaimed here Oct. 5, 1908; destructive earthquake 1911; much of medieval city has been restored.

Ve·lin·grad \ˈve-liŋ-ˌgrät\. Town, SW Bulgaria.

Ve·li·no \vā-ˈlē-nō\. River, cen. Italy; flows out of the Apennines into Nera River; 54 mi. (87 km.) long; contains noted waterfall, **Cas·ca·ta del·le Mar·mo·re** \kä-ˈskä-tä-ˌdel-lē-ˈmär-mō-ˌrā\, in three separate cascades.

Vel'ký Žitný. See GREAT SCHÜTT.

Vel·la Gulf \ˈve-lə\. Open water area in Solomon Is., W Pacific Ocean, SE of Vella Lavella I. and NW of Kolombangara I.; partly closed on the W by Ganongga I.

Vel·la La·vel·la \ˈve-lə-lə-ˈvel-ə\. Island in the New Georgia Is., cen. Solomon Is., W Pacific Ocean, NW of Kolombangara I. and separated from it by Vella Gulf; ab. 200 sq. mi. (520 sq. km.); surrounded by coral reefs which prevent use of its many bays. Highest point 3000 ft. (914 m.).

Vel·le·tri \ve-ˈlā-trē\. Commune, Roma prov., W Lazio, cen. Italy, 20 mi. (32 km.) SE of Rome; pop. (1989c) 45,245; 17th cent. cathedral (probably on site of 4th cent. cathedral); 16th cent. town hall.

Vel·lore \və-ˈlōr\. City, Tamil Nadu, S India, on Palar River 80 mi. (129 km.) WSW of Madras; pop. (1991p) 172,467; notable hospital; has temple to Siva, and a strong fortress (c. 14th cent.). Occupied by British in 1760; withstood two-year siege by Indian ruler Hyder Ali, 1780–82; after 1799 became residence of sons of Tipu Sultan who instigated Indian mutiny here in 1806.

Vel·sen \ˈvel-sə\. Commune, North Holland prov., W Netherlands, at the mouth of the North Sea Canal; pop. (1992e) 61,506; has port facilities serving Amsterdam; iron and steel, chemical fertilizers, cement.

Ve·luwe \ˈvā-lue-wə\. Range of hills, Gelderland prov., E Netherlands, N of Arnhem; highest point 361 ft. (110 m.).

Velyaminovski *or* **Vel'yaminovskiy.** See TUAPSE.

Ven *also* **Hveen** *or* **Hven** \ˈvān\. Island, Sweden, in Øresund, off SW coast; home of Danish astronomer Tycho Brahe and his influential observatory.

Ve·na·do Tuer·to \bā-ˈnä-thō-ˈtwer-tō\. Town, Santa Fe prov., Argentina; pop. (1980p) 46,775.

Venaissin *or* **Venaissin, Comtat.** See COMTAT VENAISSIN.

Ve·nan·go \vi-ˈnaŋ-gō\. County in NW Pennsylvania. See table at PENNSYLVANIA.

Ve·na·ria \ˌve-nä-ˈrē-ä\. Commune, Torino prov., Piedmont, NW Italy, 5 mi. (8 km.) NNW of Turin; pop. (1989c) 30,860.

Vence \ˈvä^{n}s\. Commune, Alpes-Maritimes dept., SE France, W of Nice; medieval walls; Romanesque cathedral; chapel (c. 1950) decorated by artist Henri Matisse.

Ven·da \ˈven-dä\. Former black enclave, NE Rep. of South Africa, near Zimbabwe border, in what is now Northern prov.; ✻ Thohoyandou; granted independence 1979, but never internationally recognized; began reincorporation into South Africa 1994.

Ven·dée \vä^{n}-ˈdā\. **1.** River, Vendée dept., France; flows to the Sèvre Niortaise; ab. 45 mi. (72 km.) long.
2. Department of W France. Formed (c. 1790) at the time of the French Revolution out of part of the ancient region of Poitou (*q.v.*); became, with adjoining regions of Poitou, Anjou, and Brittany, the scene of the Wars of the Vendée, a series of peasant insurrections against the Revolutionary government 1793–96. See table at FRANCE.

Ven·dôme \vä^{n}-ˈdōm\. Town, Loir-et-Cher dept., N cen. France; pop. (1990c) 18,359; ancient countship, in 1515 made duchy whose dukes included César de Bourbon, illegitimate son of Henry IV, and noted soldier Louis-Joseph de Bourbon, marshal of France during time of Louis XIV; ruins of 11th cent. castle and 11th cent. abbey of the Trinity.

Vend·sys·sel–Thy \ˈven-ˌsue-səl-ˈtue\. Island, N of Limfjorden, forming the N end of the peninsula of Jutland, Denmark; 1792 sq. mi. (4641 sq. km.); pop. (1989e) 308,403; chief town Hjørring. The E section is called **Vendsyssel,** the W section **Thy·land** \ˈtue-ˌlan\.

Venedig. See VENICE 4.

Venern. See VÄNERN.

Veneta, Laguna. See VENICE, LAGOON OF.

Venetae, Alpes. See table at ALPS.

Ve·ne·tia \vi-ˈnē-shē-ə\. **1.** Ancient Roman division of NE Italy, incl. the territory bet. the Po River and the Alps and incl. the Istrian Penin.; named for its ancient inhabitants, the Veneti; principal towns among others included Aquileia, Patavium, Atria, Vicentia, Verona, Mantua, Brixia; prosperous under Roman rule; overrun by N invaders in early Christian era.
2. *or Ital.* **Ve·ne·zia** \vā-ˈnet-syä\. Region, N Italy, E of Lombardy; approx. coextensive with ancient region (see VENETIA 1); administratively divided into Friuli-Venezia Giulia, Trentino-Alto Adige, and Veneto (*qq.v.*); part of its territory ceded by Italy to Croatian part of Yugoslavia 1947.
3. Seaport, Italy. See VENICE 4.

Venetian Republic. See *History* at VENICE 4.

Ve·ne·to \ˈve-nā-ˌtō\ *also* **Ve·ne·zia Eu·ga·nea** \vā-ˈnet-syä-eu̇-ˈgä-nē-ä\. Autonomous region, N Italy; ✻ Venice; wheat, sugar beets, hemp, corn. See table at ITALY.

Ve·ne·zia \vā-ˈnet-syä\. **1.** Region, Italy. See VENETIA 2.
2. Province of Veneto, Italy. See table at ITALY.
3. Seaport, Italy. See VENICE 4.

Venezia, Golfo di. See VENICE, GULF OF.

Venezia Euganea. See VENETO.

Venezia Giu·lia \ˈjül-yä\. Narrow strip of territory, along the Isonzo River, Friuli-Venezia Giulia, Italy; left to Italy after the formation of the Free Terr. of Trieste and cession of the greater part of Istrian Penin. and the city of Zara (Zadar) to Croatian part of Yugoslavia by treaty following WWII.

Venezia Tridentina. See TRENTINO-ALTO ADIGE.

Ven·e·zu·e·la \ˌve-nə-ˈzwā-lə, -zə-ˈwā-; ˌbā-nā-ˈswā-lä\; *formerly* **United States of Venezuela** *or Span.* **Es·ta·dos Uni·dos de Venezuela** \es-ˌtäd-əs-ü-ˈnēd-əs-dā-\. Republic, N South America, bounded on the N by the Caribbean Sea, on the E by Guyana, on the S by Brazil, and on the W by Colombia; 352,143 sq. mi. (912,050 sq. km.); pop. (1993e) 20,609,000; ✻ Caracas.

Physical features: In the W are the highest ranges, the Cordillera de Mérida, a NE spur of the Andes E of Lake Maracaibo; highest point Pico Bolívar, 16,427 ft. (5007 m.); along Caribbean coast extends the Cordillera de Venezuela, ranging from 5000 to 8530 ft. (1525 to 2600 m.). Lower ranges are in the S, esp. along the Brazilian border (Serra Parima, Pacaraima Mts.). In cen. part are the great plains (*llanos*) watered by the Orinoco and its many tributaries, a rich agricultural region.

Rivers: The Orinoco system covers practically the entire country and has an extensive and thickly-wooded delta; its main tributaries the Apure, Arauca, Meta, Guaviare, and Ventuari, some of which drain E Colombia; in the S the Casiquiare unites the Orinoco with the Amazon system through the Rio Negro.

Lakes: In the W is the large Lake Maracaibo, noted for its wealth in petroleum products, and in N is Lake Valencia.

Coastline: Coastline is long and irregular extending from the large Gulf of Venezuela and Paraguaná Penin. on the W to the Gulf of Paria and mouths of the Orinoco on the E. Chief Venezuelan island is Margarita.

Chief products: Oil, iron ore, natural gas, bauxite, gold; sugar, coffee, corn, rice, bananas, cacao; livestock raising; steel, chemicals, textiles; oil refining.

Chief cities: Caracas, Maracaibo, Valencia, Barquisimeto, Ciudad Guayana.

Political divisions: Divided into the following administrative units (for pronunciation of their names, see their individual entries):

NAME	AREA (sq. mi.)	AREA (sq. km.)	POP. (1990c)	CAPITAL
Federal District	745	1,930	2,103,661	Caracas
States				
Anzoátegui	16,718	43,300	859,758	Barcelona
Apure	29,537	76,501	285,412	San Fernando
Aragua	2,708	7,014	1,120,132	Maracay
Barinas	13,591	35,201	424,491	Barinas
Bolívar	91,892	238,000	900,310	Ciudad Bolívar
Carabobo	1,795	4,649	1,453,232	Valencia
Cojedes	5,714	14,799	182,066	San Carlos
Falcón	9,575	24,799	599,185	Coro
Guárico	25,091	64,986	488,623	San Juan de los Morros
Lara	7,645	19,800	1,193,161	Barquisimeto
Mérida	4,363	11,300	570,215	Mérida
Miranda	3,069	7,949	1,871,093	Los Teques
Monagas	11,158	28,899	470,157	Maturín
Nueva Esparta[1]	444	1,150	263,748	La Asunción
Portuguesa	5,869	15,200	576,435	Guanare
Sucre	4,556	11,800	679,595	Cumaná
Táchira	4,286	11,101	807,712	San Cristóbal
Trujillo	2,857	7,400	493,912	Trujillo

\ə\ **abut** \ə̇\ matches \$^{ə}$\ kitten, Fr table \ər\ **further** \a\ **ash** \ā\ **ace** \ä\ **cot, cart** \ȧ\ Fr bac \au̇\ **out** \b̲\ Span Avila \ch\ **chin** \e\ bet \ē\ **easy** \g\ **go** \i\ hit \ī\ **ice** \j\ **job** \k̲\ Ger **ich**, Buch \$^{n}$\ Fr vin \ŋ\ **sing** \ō\ **go** \ö\ **all** \ȯ\ **law** \œ\ Fr bœuf \œ̄\ Fr **feu** \ȯi\ **boy** \th\ **thin** \th̲\ **this** \ü\ **loot** \u̇\ **foot** \ue\ Ger **fü**llen \ue̅\ Fr **rue** \y\ **yet** \$^{y}$\ Fr digne \ˈdē$n^{y}$\, nuit \ˈn$w^{y}$ē\ \yü\ **few** \yu̇\ **fury** \zh\ **vision**

NAME	AREA (sq. mi.)	AREA (sq. km.)	POP. (1990c)	CAPITAL
Yaracuy	2,741	7,099	384,536	San Felipe
Zulia	24,363	63,100	2,235,305	Maracaibo
Territories				
Amazonas	67,857	175,750	55,717	Puerto Ayacucho
Delta Amacuro	15,521	40,199	84,564	Tucupita
federal dependencies	46	119	2,245	

[1]Comprises island group in the Caribbean Sea; chief island Margarita.

History: Inhabited by indigenous peoples perhaps as early as 2d millennium B.C.; sighted by explorer Christopher Columbus 1498; coast traced by navigators Alonso de Ojeda, Amerigo Vespucci, and Juan de la Cosa 1499; first European settlement by Spanish missionary Bartolomé Las Casas at Cumaná c. 1520; granted to Augsburg banking firm of the Welsers 1528–46; Caracas founded 1567; included in viceroyalty of New Granada (see COLOMBIA) 1718; was made a captaincy general 1731; Venezuelan independence from Spain, proclaimed 1811, not assured until battle of Carabobo 1821; part of Greater Colombia 1819–29; formally separated from Colombia 1830; in boundary dispute late 19th cent. with Great Britain over territory in British Guiana (now Guyana); neutral in WWI; oil deposits discovered before the war began to be heavily exploited; in WWII severed relations with Axis powers 1941; overthrew dictatorship of Pérez Jiménez 1958; adopted new constitution 1961; as a founding member of OPEC, enjoyed relative economic prosperity from oil production during 1970s, but suffered economic decline with fluctuating oil prices 1980s; unrest continued into 1990s.

Venezuela, Cordillera de. See CORDILLERA DE VENEZUELA.

Venezuela, Gulf of *also* **Gulf of Mar·a·cai·bo** \ˌmar-ə-ˈkī-bō, ˌmä-rä-ˈkī-bō\. Inlet of Caribbean Sea, NW Venezuela, bet. La Guajira Penin., Colombia, and Paraguana Penin., Venezuela; extends S as Lake Maracaibo (*q.v.*).

Veng·e·tind·er \ˈveŋ-ə-ˌti-nər\. See ROMSDAL.

Ven·ice \ˈve-nəs\. **1.** Coastal community, SW California; part of the city of Los Angeles; developed 1904 with a series of canals patterned after Venice, Italy.

2. City, Sarasota co., W cen. Florida, 18 mi. (29 km.) S of the city of Sarasota; pop. (1990c) 16,922; resort; pop. grew rapidly bet. 1970 and 1980.

3. City, Madison co., SW Illinois, on Mississippi River 5 mi. (8 km.) N of East St. Louis; pop. (1990c) 3571.

4. *or Ital.* **Ve·ne·zia** \vā-ˈnet-syä\ *or Ger.* **Ve·ne·dig** \vā-ˈnā-dik\ *or Lat.* **Ve·ne·tia** \vi-ˈnē-shē-ə\. Seaport, ✻ of Veneto, also ✻ of Venezia prov., NE Italy, on 118 islands in Lagoon of

Venice 162 mi. (261 km.) E of Milan; pop. (1991p) 308,717; glass, textiles; tourism; university (1968); site of several international festivals, incl. annual film festival and Biennale (arts festival). Majority of islands separated only by narrow canals (Ital. *rio;* pl. *rii*) crossed by ab. 400 bridges; main part of city traversed by S-shaped Grand Canal crossed by famous Rialto Bridge (built 1588–91) connecting Rialto I. (site of the exchange and center of commercial activity) and San Marco I.; intracity transportation facilities include gondolas, ferries, motorboats; islands not forming part of main mass of city include Giudecca, San Giorgio Maggiore, Murano (group), Burano, Torcello, and San Lazzaro; sand banks and reefs (Ital. *lido;* pl. *lidi*) popular as resorts; Cathedral of St. Mark (begun in Romanesque style 830, with additions representing Byzantine, Gothic, Greek, and Oriental architecture; the separate campanile rebuilt after its fall 1902); secular buildings include the Procuratie Vecchie group (built 1496–1520) and opposite them the Procuratie Nuove group (begun 1584 which together with the fine 16th cent. library form the royal palace), the Palace of the Doges (Palazzo Ducale; first built c. 800 and subsequently rebuilt; contains Porta della Carta, Scala dei Giganti, and library of St. Mark), the Bridge of Sighs (Ponte dei Sospiri; connects Palace of the Doges and the prisons), and numerous palaces, chiefly along the Grand Canal; art museums (among them the Accademia di Belle Arti), and public gardens.

History: Grew from settlements on lagoons founded by refugees from N invasions (begun by Goths) of mainland (see AQUILEIA) 5th cent. A.D.; elected first doge 697; vassal of Byzantine Empire until 10th cent.; spread onto coastal mainland E of Adige River, and acquired Istria and islands along Dalmatian coast; beginning with control of trading route to Levant, Venice emerged from Fourth Crusade (1202–04) as ruler of colonial empire which included Crete, Euboea, Cyclades, Ionian Is., and footholds in Morea and Epirus; ruled by Council of Ten 1310–1797; defeated Genoa (*q.v.*) 1381 after century-long struggle for commercial supremacy in the Levant and E Mediterranean; in 15th cent., with acquisition of Friuli, Padua, Vicenza, Verona, Polesine, Brescia, Bergamo, and Crema, Venetian Republic became an extensive Italian state; gradually lost Eastern possessions to Ottoman Turks with whom Venice fought intermittently 15th–18th cents.; driven from Cyprus (ceded to Turks 1573), Crete 1669, and Tínos, its last hold in Aegean, 1715; republic dissolved and territory ceded to Austria 1797; incorp. in French Emperor Napoléon's kingdom of Italy 1805; restored to Austria 1815; revolted against Austria (Italian politician Daniele Manin's Republic of St. Mark) 1848–49; ceded to Italy 1866. Suffered little damage during WWII; suffered severe damage caused by flooding 1966; in last part of 20th cent. widespread efforts made to control inundation of city.

Venice, Gulf of *or Ital.* **Gol·fo di Ve·ne·zia** \ˈgōl-fō-ˌdē-vā-ˈnet-syä\. N section of the Adriatic Sea.

Venice, Lagoon of *or Ital.* **La·gu·na Ve·ne·ta** \lä-ˈgü-nä-ˈve-ne-ˌtä\. Inlet of the Gulf of Venice, NE Italy, separated from the Gulf of Venice by a bar, the Lido; area 95 to 210 sq. mi. (245 to 545 sq. km.), according to season; forms a shallow bay with more than 100 small islands on which the city of Venice is built.

Vé·nis·sieux \ˌvā-nē-ˈsyœ\. Commune, Rhône dept., E cen. France, 3 mi. (5 km.) SSE of Lyon.

Ven·lo *or* **Ven·loo** \ˈven-ˌlō\. Commune, Limburg prov., SE Netherlands, on Maas (Meuse) River on German border; pop. (1992e) 64,890; medieval town hall; 15th cent. Gothic church of St. Martin.

Ven·na·char, Loch \ˈve-nə-k̲ər\. Lake, Central region, Scotland; max. depth 111 ft. (34 m.).

Ve·no·sa \vā-ˈnō-sä\; *anc.* **Ve·nu·sia** \vi-ˈnü-zhē-ə, -ˈnyü-\. Commune, Potenza prov., Basilicata, S Italy, 22 mi. (35 km.) N of the commune of Potenza; pop. (1991p) 12,008; 15th cent. castle; 11th cent. abbey (containing tomb of Norman military leader Robert Guiscard); 15th cent. cathedral; Jewish catacombs nearby. Roman colony 291 B.C.; important as base of Roman operations against Pyrrhus, king of Epirus, and Carthaginian Gen. Hannibal. Birthplace of Roman poet and satirist Horace 65 B.C.

Venosti, Alpi. See ÖTZTALER ALPS.

Ven·ray *or* **Ven·raij** \ˈven-ˌrī\. Commune, Limburg prov., SE Netherlands, 21 mi. (34 km.) S of Nijmegen; pop. (1992e) 34,486.

Ven·ta \ˈven-tä\ *or Ger.* **Win·dau** \ˈvin-ˌdau̇\; *formerly* **Vin·da·va** \vin-ˈdä-vä\. River, Lithuania and Latvia; rises in W Lithuania and flows NNW into Baltic Sea at Ventspils, Latvia; 217 mi. (349 km.) long.

Venta, La. See LA VENTA.

Venta Belgarum. See WINCHESTER 9.

Ventana, Sierra de la. See SIERRA DE LA VENTANA.

Ventia. See VALENCE.

Ven·ti·mi·glia \ˌven-tē-ˈmēl-yä\ *or Fr.* **Vin·ti·mille** \ˌveⁿ-tē-ˈmēl\. Commune, Imperia prov., W Liguria, NW Italy, on Ligurian Sea 21 mi. (34 km.) WSW of the seaport of Imperia and just across the border from Menton, France; pop. (1991p) 25,221; in flower-growing region; resort; 11th cent. cathedral. See GRIMALDI.

Vent·nor \ˈvent-nər\. Town, S Isle of Wight, S England, on English Channel 15 mi. (24 km.) SSW of Portsmouth; pop. (1981c) 6450; health resort. Burial place of English poet Algernon Charles Swinburne is nearby.

Ventnor City *or mostly formerly* **Ventnor.** City, Atlantic co., SE New Jersey, on Atlantic Ocean 3 mi. (5 km.) WSW of Atlantic City; pop. (1990c) 11,005.

Ven·to·te·ne \ˌven-tȯ-ˈtā-nē\. Italian island, Tyrrhenian Sea, W of Naples, Italy, SW of Ponza Is., and S of the Gulf of Gaeta.

Vents·pils \ˈvent-ˌspils\ *or Ger.* **Win·dau** *or* **Vin·dau** \ˈvin-ˌdau̇\. Seaport city, Latvia, on the Baltic Sea at mouth of Venta River N of Liepāja and 100 mi. (161 km.) WNW of Riga; pop. (1991e) 50,400; has castle dating from 13th cent. Founded 14th cent.; an important Russian port before WWI; in WWII occupied by Germans.

Ven·tua·ri \ven-ˈtwä-rē\. River, S Venezuela; flows W into Orinoco River near Colombian boundary; ab. 350 mi. (565 km.) long.

Ven·tu·ra \ven-ˈtu̇r-ə, -ˈtyu̇r-\. **1.** County in SW California. See table at CALIFORNIA.

2. *officially* **San Bue·na·ven·tu·ra** \san-ˌbwe-nə-ven-ˈtu̇r-ə, -ˈtyu̇r-\. Seaport city, its ⊗, on Santa Barbara Channel 23 mi. (37 km.) SE of Santa Barbara; pop. (1990c) 92,575; oil-producing center; citrus fruit; Ventura Coll. (1925); city founded 1782 as Spanish mission; incorp. 1866; pop. size nearly doubled bet. 1960 and 1970.

Venue, Ben. See BEN VENUE.

Venusberg. See HÖRSELBERGE.

Venusia. See VENOSA.

Ve·ra·cruz \ˌver-ə-ˈkrüz, ˌbā-rä-ˈkrüs\. **1.** State of E Mexico. See table at MEXICO.

2. *or in full* **Veracruz Lla·ve** \ˈyä-bā\. Seaport, Veracruz state, E Mexico, on the Gulf of Mexico 264 mi. (425 km.) from Mexico City; munic. pop. (1990p) 327,522; one of the chief Mexican ports; terminus of two railroads and a commercial center for the Gulf coast.

History: Area inhabited by pre-Columbian cultures; original settlement (**Vil·la Ri·ca de la Ve·ra Cruz** \ˈbē-yä-ˈrē-kä-t̲h̲ā-ˌb̲ā-rä-ˈkrüs\) founded by Spanish explorer Hernán Cortés 1519; present city and port date from 1599; principal Mexican port for Spanish trade fleets 16th–18th cents. and frequently sacked by pirates, esp. 1653 and 1712; captured by French 1838 and 1861 and by U.S. troops under Winfield Scott 1847; scene of revolt against Mexican President Francisco Madero 1912; occupied Apr.–Nov. 1914 by U.S. forces in dispute with President Victoriano Huerta; port facilities expanded and modernized after 1946.

Ve·ra·gua \bā-'rä-gwä\. Region, W part of Isthmus of Panama; discovered and named by explorer Christopher Columbus 1502; later included Nombre de Dios, Portobelo, and Panama City. In 1537 Luis Columbus, grandson of Christopher, granted title of duke of Veragua by Spanish King Charles I.

Ve·ra·guas \bā-'rä-gwäs\. Province of SW cen. Panama. See table at PANAMA.

Ve·ra·val \vā-'rä-vəl\. Town, SW Gujarat, W India, in S Kathiawar Penin., on Arabian Sea 210 mi. (338 km.) NW of Bombay; pop. (1991p) 93,826; seaport since ancient times; nearby is the old port of Somnath (*q.v.*).

Ver·ba·nia \ver-'bä-nyä\. Commune, Novara prov., Piedmont, NW Italy, on W shore of Lake Maggiore 34 mi. (55 km.) N of the commune of Novara; pop. (1991p) 30,525; summer resort; museum; two 16th cent. churches.

Verbanus Lacus. See MAGGIORE, LAKE.

Ver·cel·li \ver-'chel-lē\. **1.** Province of Piedmont, NW Italy. See table at ITALY.

2. *anc.* **Ver·cel·lae** \vər-'se-lē\. Commune, its ✻, on Sesia River 39 mi. (63 km.) WSW of Milan; pop. (1991p) 48,597; rice market; machinery, textiles, flour; cathedral (remodeled 1572); 13th cent. castle; 13th cent. basilica. The Cimbri defeated by Roman Gen. Marius 101 B.C. nearby; city-state in Middle Ages; under Visconti family of Milan 1335 ff. and dukes of Piedmont-Savoy 1427 ff.

Ver·chères \ver-'sher\. Village, S Quebec, Canada, on S bank of St. Lawrence River 22 mi. (35 km.) NE of Montreal; pop. (1991c) 4781.

Ver·de. **1.** \'vər-dē, 'ver-\. River, cen. Arizona; formed by confluence of forks in N cen. Yavapai co., flows SE into Salt River ab. 20 mi. (32 km.) E of Phoenix; ab. 190 mi. (305 km.) long.

2. \'ver-də\. River, S Mato Grosso state, SW Brazil; flows SE into Paraná River; ab. 200 mi. (320 km.) long.

Verde, Cape. **1.** Promontory, Senegal. See VERT, CAPE.

2. Independent island group in Atlantic Ocean. See CAPE VERDE.

Verde Island \'ver-dā\. Island, center of Verde Island Passage S of Batangas, Luzon, Philippines, ab. 3 mi. (5 km.) from mainland; 7 sq. mi. (18 sq. km.); 5 mi. (8 km.) long; part of Batangas municipality.

Verde Island Passage. Channel bet. SW Luzon and N Mindoro, Philippines, connecting waters S of Luzon with South China Sea; ab. 80 mi. (130 km.) long and 9 to 22 mi. (14 to 35 km.) wide; the W end of main interisland passage for oceangoing vessels to Manila. See SAN BERNARDINO STRAIT.

Verde Islands, Cape. See CAPE VERDE

Ver·den \'ferd-ᵊn\ *or in full* **Verden an der Al·ler** \än-dər-'ä-lər\. City, Lower Saxony, Germany, on Aller River 57 mi. (92 km.) SW of Hamburg; pop. (1980c) 24,261. A bishopric founded c. 800; later became a duchy and was ceded 1648 to Sweden; passed to Hannover 1719.

Ver·di·gris \'vər-də-grəs\. River, SE Kansas and NE Oklahoma; rises in SE Chase co., E cen. Kansas, flows S across Oklahoma border and into Arkansas River in N Muskogee co., E Oklahoma; 351 mi. (565 km.) long.

Ver·don \ver-'dōⁿ\. River, Alpes-de-Haute Provence dept., SE France; flows into Durance River; 110 mi. (177 km.) long.

Ver·dun \vər-'dən\. **1.** City, Montreal I., S Quebec, Canada, on St. Lawrence River SE of the city of Montreal; pop. (1991c) 61,307; residential suburb of Montreal; Jean-Jacques Olier Coll. (1951).

2. *or* **Verdun–sur–Meuse** \-sūr-'mœ̄z\; *anc.* **Ver·o·du·num** \,ver-ə-'dü-nəm, -'dyü-\. City, Meuse dept., NE France, on Meuse River 29 mi. (47 km.) NNE of Bar-le-Duc; pop. (1990c) 23,427; furniture; foundries; restored Romanesque cathedral; 14th cent. castle; episcopal palace; citadel.

History: Treaty partitioning Holy Roman Emperor Charlemagne's empire among his three grandsons signed here 843 A.D.; with Metz and Toul (*Les Trois-Évêchés,* the three bishoprics) taken by Henry II of France 1552, and French possession confirmed by Treaty of Westphalia 1648; taken by Prussians 1792 and 1871. In WWI scene of one of the major battles on the Western Front, Feb.–Dec. 1916, in which French repelled a large-scale German offensive at great cost; total casualties ab. 750,000 and city practically destroyed. In WWII occupied by Germans. Has numerous monuments and museums commemorating WWI battle; for further references, see DOUAUMONT, FLEURY, LE MORT HOMME, VAUX, and WOËVRE.

Ve·ree·ni·ging \və-'rā-nə-kiŋ\. Town, S Gauteng prov., NE Rep. of South Africa, on Vaal River 35 mi. (56 km.) S of Johannesburg; pop. (1985c) 60,584; industrial community in coal-bearing district. Founded 1892; negotiations here resulted in treaty ending Boer War signed May 31, 1902.

Ver·en·drye National Monument \'ver-ən-,drī\. Former national monument, South Dakota; abolished 1956; site now partly a state historical area, partly inundated by Garrison Reservoir.

Ver·ga, Cape \'vər-gə\. Cape, extending into Atlantic Ocean on W coast of Guinea, 10°12′N, 14°27′W.

Ver·ga·ra \ber-'gä-rä\ *or* **Ber·ga·ra** \ber-\. Commune, Guipúzcoa prov., N Spain; pop. (1991c) 15,567; Convention of Vergara Aug. 31, 1839 concluded First Carlist War.

Ver·gennes \vər-'jenz\. City, Addison co., W Vermont, on Otter Creek near Lake Champlain; pop. (1990c) 2578; in War of 1812 U.S. fleet on Lake Champlain built here.

Ver·ghi·na *or* **Ver·gi·na** \ver-'gē-nä\. Archaeological site, Macedonia, Greece; widely considered to have been ✻ (known then as Aigai) of ancient Macedonia; royal tomb of Philip II of Macedon; remains of theater.

Verkhne–Saldinski Zavod. See VERKHNYAYA SALDA.

Verkhneudinsk. See ULAN-UDE.

Verkh·niy Ufa·ley *or* **Verkh·ni Ufa·lei** \'vyerk-nē-,ü-fäl-'yā\; *formerly* **Verkh·ne·ufa·lei·ski Za·vod** \,vyerk-nə-,ü-fəl-'yās-kē-zə-'vȯd\. Town, Chelyabinsk Oblast, W Russia in Asia, ab. 80 mi. (130 km.) NW of city of Chelyabinsk.

Verkhnyaya Angara. See ANGARA 2.

Verkh·nya·ya Sal·da \'vyerk-nə-yə-'säl-də\; *formerly* **Verkh·ne–Sal·din·ski Za·vod** \'vyerk-nə-säl-'din-skē-zə-'vȯd\. Town, Sverdlovsk Oblast, cen. W Russia in Asia, ab. 80 mi. (130 km.) N of Yekaterinburg; pop. (1991e) 55,100.

Ver·kho·yansk \,vyer-kə-'yänsk\. Town, N cen. Sakha Rep., Russia in Asia, on right bank of Yana River 385 mi. (619 km.) NNE of Yakutsk, 67°35′N, 133°27′E; mining, fur trading; formerly a place of political exile. Has January mean temperature of below –55°F (–48°C), absolute minimum of –89.9°F (–67.7°C), and a range bet. Jan. and July means of 119°F (66°C). See OIMYAKON and FORT CONGER.

Ver·kho·yan·skiy Khre·bet \,vyer-kə-'yän-skē-kri-'byet\ *or Eng.* **Verkhoyanski Mountains.** Mountain range, N cen. Sakha Rep., Russia in Asia; extends for ab. 950 mi. (1530 km.) in a semicircle along right banks of the Lena and lower Aldan rivers; highest peak 7838 ft. (2389 m.). Source of the headstreams of the Indigirka, Yana, and Omoloi rivers and of many short (E) tributaries of the Lena and Aldan.

Ver·man·dois \,ver-mäⁿ-'dwä\. Ancient district, N France, in E Picardy; now included in the depts. of Aisne, Somme, and Oise.

Vermejo. See BERMEJO.

Ver·mil·ion \vər-'mil-yən\. **1.** River, N cen. Illinois; formed by the junction of two forks in Livingston co., flows NW into Illinois River in La Salle co.; 50 mi. (80 km.) long.

2. River, N Minnesota. See VERMILION LAKE.

3. River, SE South Dakota; rises in Lake co., flows S into Missouri River on S boundary of Clay co.; ab. 100 mi. (160 km.) long.

4. Name of a parish in S Louisiana and of a county in E Illinois. See tables at ILLINOIS and LOUISIANA.

5. City, Erie and Lorain cos., N Ohio, on Lake Erie E of Sandusky; pop. (1990c) 11,127; summer resort.

6. Town, Alberta, Canada, 100 mi. (161 km.) E of Edmonton; pop. (1991c) 3891.

Vermilion Bay. Inlet of Gulf of Mexico, SW Iberia parish and SE Vermilion parish, S Louisiana.

Vermilion Lake. Lake, N St. Louis co., NE Minnesota; ab. 35 mi. (55 km.) long; 59 sq. mi. (153 sq. km.); outlet, **Vermilion**

River (ab. 50 mi. or 80 km. long) flowing N into Crane Lake, at SE end of Rainy Lake.

Vermilion Peak. Mountain, San Juan and San Miguel cos., SW Colorado; 13,870 ft. (4228 m.).

Vermilion Sea. See CALIFORNIA, GULF OF.

Ver·mil·lion \vər-ˈmil-yən\. **1.** County in W Indiana. See table at INDIANA.

2. City, ⊗ of Clay co., SE South Dakota, on Missouri River where the Vermilion unites with it, 27 mi. (43 km.) ESE of Yankton; pop. (1990c) 10,034; Univ. of South Dakota (1862). Founded 1859 W of Fort Vermillion, a trading post (estab. 1835).

Ver·mont \vər-ˈmänt\. A northeastern state of U.S.A., bounded on N by Canadian prov. of Quebec, on E by New Hampshire (boundary line is W bank of Connecticut River), on S by Massachusetts, and on W by New York (boundary line goes through Lake Champlain); 43d state in area, 9609 sq. mi. 24,887 sq. km.); 48th state in population, (1990c) 562,758; ✻ Montpelier; 14th state admitted to Union (1791). See table of states at UNITED STATES.

Nickname: Green Mountain State.

State flower: Red clover.

Motto: Freedom and Unity.

Rivers: Flowing into Lake Champlain on W boundary are the Lamoille and Winooski rivers, Otter Creek, and the Poultney River, which forms for a short distance the state boundary with New York; chief Vermont tributary of the Connecticut River is the White River in cen. part.

Highest point: Mt. Mansfield, 4393 ft. (1339 m.), in Lamoille co. in N Green Mts.

Chief products: Dairy products, maple syrup, apples, food products; marble, talc; manufacturing: metalworking; textiles, furniture, electronics, paper goods; tourism.

Chief cities: Burlington, Rutland, South Burlington.

Political divisions: Divided into the following 14 counties (for pronunciation of their names, see their individual entries):

NAME	AREA[1] (sq. mi.)	AREA[1] (sq. km.)	POP. (1990c)	CO. SEAT(S)
Addison	784	2,031	32,953	Middlebury
Bennington	672	1,740	35,845	Bennington and Manchester
Caledonia	612	1,585	27,846	St. Johnsbury
Chittenden	533	1,380	131,761	Burlington
Essex	663	1,717	6,405	Guildhall
Franklin	660	1,709	39,980	St. Albans
Grand Isle	83	215	5,318	North Hero
Lamoille	474	1,228	19,735	Hyde Park
Orange	690	1,787	26,149	Chelsea
Orleans	715	1,852	24,053	Newport
Rutland	927	2,401	62,142	Rutland
Washington	707	1,831	54,928	Montpelier
Windham	787	2,038	41,588	Newfane
Windsor	965	2,499	54,055	Woodstock

[1] Area = land area.

History: Inhabited orig. by American Indians, the Abnaki; explored 1609 by French expedition led by Samuel de Champlain, who discovered the lake now bearing his name; temporary settlement by French at Fort Ste. Anne on Isle La Motte 1666; English established Fort Dummer near site of present Brattleboro 1724; disputes arose bet. New Hampshire and New York concerning jurisdiction of area, New Hampshire having awarded grants to settlers; Green Mountain Boys organized by Ethan Allen 1770 to repel encroachers from W, New York having won its appeal to crown for rights to settle; when Revolutionary War intervened, Allen and Green Mountain Boys fighting for colonies captured Fort Ticonderoga from British 1775; Vermont declared itself independent republic 1777; claims to the region later dropped by New Hampshire and New York; admitted to Union Mar. 4, 1791; present constitution adopted 1793 (since amended).

Ver·nal \ˈvərn-^{ə}l\. City, ⊗ of Uintah co., E Utah, ab. 25 mi. (40 km.) W of Colorado border; pop. (1990c) 6644; tourism.

Vernal Fall. Waterfall, Yosemite National Park, E cen. California; 317 ft. (97 m.).

Ver·neuil \ver-ˈnœ^{y}\. Town, S Eure dept., N France, ab. 25 mi. (40 km.) SW of Évreux; 11th–17th cent. church; 12th cent. keep built by Henry I of England; scene of battle 1424 in which John of Lancaster, duke of Bedford, defeated the French and Scots.

Ver·nier \ver-ˈnyā\. Commune, Geneva canton, Switzerland; pop. (1989c) 28,857.

Vernoleninsk. See MYKOLAYIV 2.

Ver·non \ˈvər-nən\. **1.** Name of a parish in W Louisiana and of counties in two states of the U.S. See tables at LOUISIANA, MISSOURI, WISCONSIN.

2. City, ⊗ of Lamar co., NW Alabama; pop. (1990c) 2247.

3. Town, W Tolland co., N Connecticut, NE of Manchester; pop. (1990c) 29,841; incorp. 1808; includes city of Rockville (*q.v.*).

4. Town, ⊗ of Jennings co., SE Indiana; pop. (1990c) 370.

5. City, ⊗ of Wilbarger co., N Texas, 45 mi. (72 km.) WNW of Wichita Falls; pop. (1990c) 12,001.

6. City, S British Columbia, Canada, 5 mi. (8 km.) E of N end of Okanagan Lake; pop. (1991c) 23,514; in area of outdoor recreation.

Ver·non \ver-ˈnō^{n}\. Commune, Eure dept., N France, on Seine River 17 mi. (27 km.) ENE of Évreux. Changed hands bet. French and English in wars during medieval times; suffered heavy damage in WWII, since rebuilt.

Vernon Hills. Village, Lake co., NE Illinois, N of Chicago; pop. (1990c) 15,319.

Vernyi. See ALMA-ATA 2.

Ve·ro Beach \ˈvir-ō\. City, ⊗ of Indian River co., E Florida, on Indian River 70 mi. (113 km.) NNW of West Palm Beach; pop. (1990c) 17,350.

Verőcze. See VIROVITICA.

Verodunum. See VERDUN 2.

Ve·roia *or Gk.* **Vé·roia** \ˈver-yä\; *anc.* **Be·roea** *or* **Be·rea** \bə-ˈrē-ə\; *Turk.* **Ka·ra·fe·ri·eh** \ˌkär-ə-ˈfer-ē-ˌye\. Town, ✻ of Hematheia dept., Central Macedonia, Greece, 40 mi. (64 km.) WSW of Thessaloníki. An ancient city, flourished from 4th cent. B.C.; came under the Romans; according to the Bible (*Acts* xvii. 10), St. Paul and his companion Silas preached here; under Turkish rule 14th cent.

Ve·ro·li \ˈver-ō-lē\. Commune, Frosinone prov., Lazio, cen. Italy, 4 mi. (6 km.) NE of the commune of Frosinone; pop. (1981p) 18,253.

Ve·ro·na \və-ˈrō-nə\. **1.** Borough, Allegheny co., SW Pennsylvania, on Allegheny River 10 mi. (16 km.) ENE of Pittsburgh; pop. (1990c) 3260.

2. City, Dane co., Wisconsin; pop. (1990c) 5374.

3. Province of Veneto, NE Italy. See table at ITALY.

4. Commune, ✻ of Verona prov., NE Italy, on Adige River 92 mi. (148 km.) E of Milan; pop. (1991p) 252,689; railroad junction; chemicals, paper, furniture, wine; city walls flanked by bastions and towers; city gates; notable buildings include the ancient Roman amphitheater (first cent. A.D.) known as the Arena, now used for opera, and many churches, incl. the 15th cent. Gothic cathedral with 12th cent. Romanesque facade and the 5th cent. St. Zeno Maggiore (rebuilt 12th cent.); 15th cent. Loggia del Consiglio; 12th cent. town hall; 14th cent. Gothic tombs of the Scaligeri (or della Scala) family; 14th cent. Castelvecchio (now a museum). Birthplace of artist Paolo Veronese 1528.

History: Came under Roman rule 89 B.C.; after fall of Roman Empire, captured by Goths; here Odoacer, first barbarian king of Italy, defeated by Ostrogothic King Theodoric 489 A.D.; captured 774 by Holy Roman Emperor Charlemagne (then king of the Franks); became independent republic 1107; under della Scala family 1260–1387, during which time the story of fated lovers Romeo and Juliet occurred, providing basis for English writer William Shakespeare's later play; to the Visconti family of Milan 1387–1405, Venice

---

\ə\ **abut** \ə̇\ matches \$^{ə}$\ kitten, Fr table \ər\ **further** \a\ **ash** \ā\ **ace**
\ä\ **cot**, **cart** \ȧ\ Fr **bac** \au̇\ **out** \b̲\ Span A**v**ila \ch\ **chin** \e\ **bet** \ē\ **easy**
\g\ **go** \i\ **hit** \ī\ **ice** \j\ **job** \k̲\ Ger **ich**, Bu**ch** \$^{n}$\ Fr v**in**
\ŋ\ si**ng** \ō\ **go** \ȯ\ **all** \ȯ\ **law** \œ\ Fr b**œu**f \œ̄\ Fr f**eu** \ȯi\ **boy**
\th\ **thin** \t͟h\ **this** \ü\ **loot** \u̇\ **foot** \ue\ Ger f**ü**llen \ue̅\ Fr **rue**
\y\ **yet** \$^{y}$\ Fr digne \ˈdēn^{y}\, nuit \ˈnw^{y}ē\ \yü\ **few** \yu̇\ **fury** \zh\ **vision**

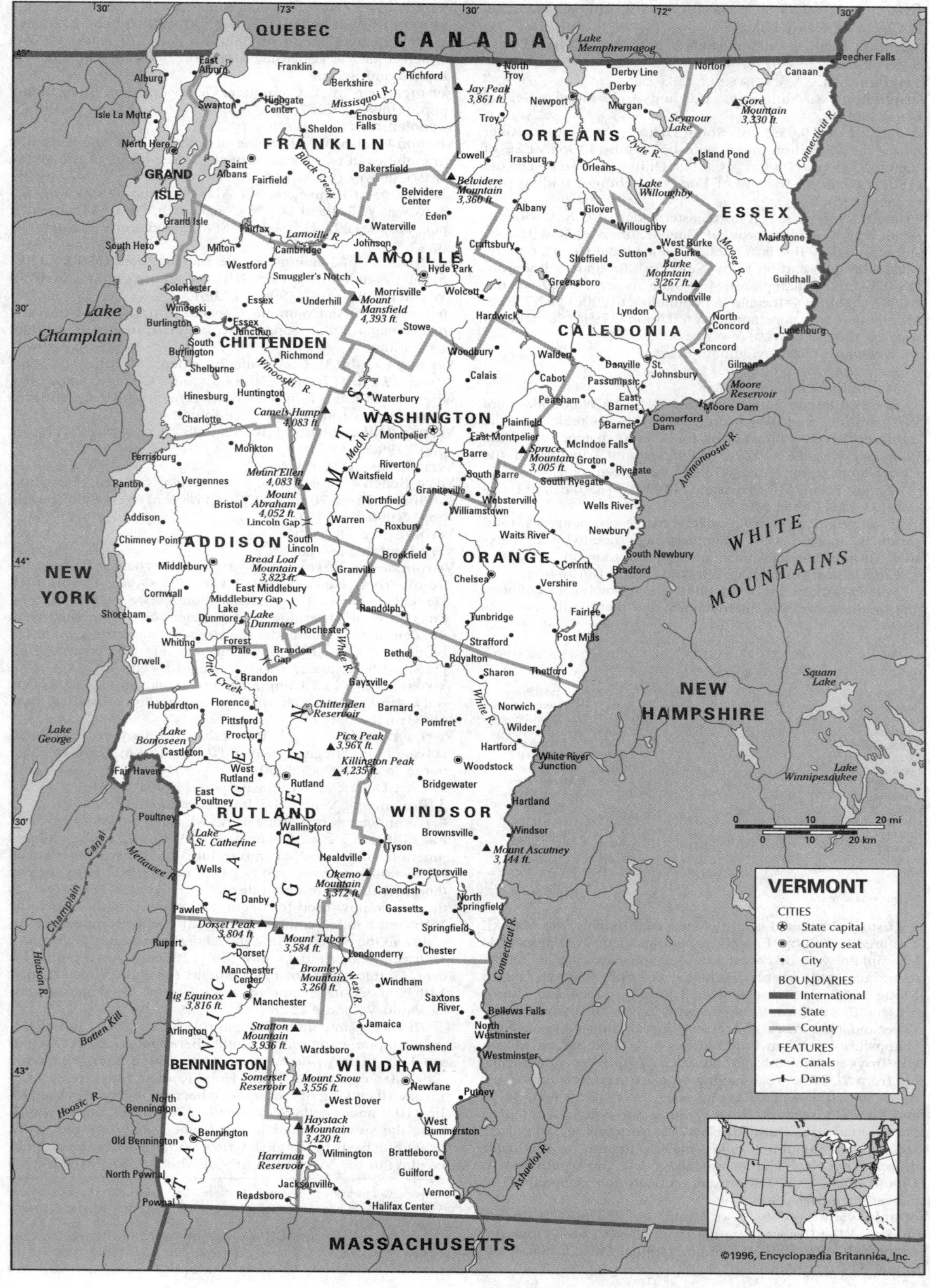

QUEBEC
CANADA
Lake Memphremagog
East Alburg
Alburg
Franklin
Berkshire
Richford
North Troy
Jay Peak 3,861 ft.
Derby Line
Derby
Norton
Canaan
Beecher Falls
Swanton
Highgate Center
Missisquoi R.
Newport
Troy
Morgan
Gore Mountain 3,330 ft.
Isle La Motte
Sheldon
Enosburg Falls
Seymour Lake
North Hero
FRANKLIN
ORLEANS
Clyde R.
Island Pond
Saint Albans
Black Creek
Lowell
Irasburg
Orleans
GRAND ISLE
Fairfield
Bakersfield
Belvidere Mountain 3,360 ft.
Belvidere Center
Lake Willoughby
Connecticut R.
Albany
Glover
Eden
ESSEX
Grand Isle
Waterville
Willoughby
Fairfax
South Hero
Milton
Lamoille R.
Johnson
Craftsbury
West Burke
Burke
Maidstone
Cambridge
LAMOILLE
Sutton
Sheffield
Moose R.
Westford
Smuggler's Notch
Hyde Park
Burke Mountain 3,267 ft.
Guildhall
Greensboro
Colchester
Morrisville
Wolcott
Lyndonville
Winooski
Essex
Underhill
Mount Mansfield 4,393 ft.
Lake Champlain
Burlington
Essex Junction
Hardwick
Lyndon
North Concord
Lunenburg
Stowe
CALEDONIA
South Burlington
CHITTENDEN
Richmond
Woodbury
Walden
Concord
Danville
St. Johnsbury
Gilman
Shelburne
Winooski R.
Calais
Cabot
Passumpsic
Moore Reservoir
Hinesburg
Huntington
Waterbury
Peacham
East Barnet
Moore Dam
Camels Hump 4,083 ft.
WASHINGTON
Charlotte
Plainfield
Barnet
Comerford Dam
Montpelier
East Montpelier
Monkton
Spruce Mountain 3,005 ft.
McIndoe Falls
Mad R.
Barre
Groton
Ammonoosuc R.
Ferrisburg
Riverton
Ryegate
Mount Ellen 4,083 ft.
Waitsfield
South Barre
South Ryegate
Panton
Vergennes
Graniteville
Mount Abraham 4,052 ft.
Northfield
Websterville
Bristol
Williamstown
Wells River
Lincoln Gap
Warren
Addison
Roxbury
Waits River
Newbury
WHITE MOUNTAINS
Chimney Point
ADDISON
South Lincoln
Brookfield
Bread Loaf Mountain 3,823 ft.
ORANGE
Corinth
South Newbury
Middlebury
Granville
Bradford
NEW YORK
Chelsea
East Middlebury
Vershire
Cornwall
Middlebury Gap
Lake Dunmore
Dunmore
Randolph
Fairlee
Shoreham
Tunbridge
Rochester
Post Mills
Whiting
Forest Dale
Brandon Gap
White R.
Strafford
Bethel
Royalton
Orwell
Otter Creek
Brandon
Sharon
Thetford
Gaysville
Squam Lake
Hubbardton
Florence
Chittenden Reservoir
NEW HAMPSHIRE
Barnard
Norwich
Pittsford
Pomfret
White R.
Lake George
Lake Bomoseen
Proctor
Pico Peak 3,967 ft.
Wilder
Castleton
Killington Peak 4,235 ft.
Hartford
White River Junction
Fair Haven
West Rutland
Woodstock
Lake Winnipesaukee
Rutland
Bridgewater
East Poultney
Hartland
RUTLAND
WINDSOR
Poultney
Canal
Wallingford
Brownsville
Windsor
Lake St. Catherine
Tyson
Mount Ascutney 3,144 ft.
0 10 20 mi
0 10 20 km
Mettawee R.
Wells
Healdville
Okemo Mountain 3,372 ft.
Proctorsville
VERMONT
Pawlet
Danby
Cavendish
North Springfield
CITIES
State capital
County seat
City
Champlain
TACONIC RANGE
GREEN MTS
Gassetts
Springfield
Dorset Peak 3,804 ft.
Rupert
Mount Tabor 3,584 ft.
Chester
Dorset
Londonderry
Connecticut R.
BOUNDARIES
International
State
County
Hudson R.
Manchester Center
Bromley Mountain 3,260 ft.
Windham
Big Equinox 3,816 ft.
West R.
Saxtons River
Manchester
Bellows Falls
FEATURES
Canals
Dams
Batten Kill
Arlington
Stratton Mountain 3,936 ft.
Jamaica
North Westminster
Wardsboro
Townshend
Westminster
BENNINGTON
WINDHAM
Somerset Reservoir
Mount Snow 3,556 ft.
Newfane
Putney
Hoosic R.
North Bennington
West Dover
Haystack Mountain 3,420 ft.
West Dummerston
Old Bennington
Bennington
Wilmington
Brattleboro
Harriman Reservoir
Ashuelot R.
North Pownal
Guilford
Jacksonville
Readsboro
Vernon
Pownal
Halifax Center
MASSACHUSETTS
30′
73°
72°
45°
44°
43°

1405–1797; passed to Austria and gained great strategic importance as a member of the Mantua-Verona-Peschiera-Legnago Quadrilateral; Congress of Verona held here 1822; became part of kingdom of Italy 1866.

Ve·ró·ni·ca \bā-'rō-nē-kä, və-'rä-ni-kə\. Peak in Andes, Peru, 30 mi. (48 km.) NW of Cuzco; 19,342 ft. (5895 m.).

Ver·sailles \vər-'sālz\. **1.** Town, ⊗ of Ripley co., SE Indiana; pop. (1990c) 1791.
2. City, ⊗ of Woodford co., E cen. Kentucky, 13 mi. (21 km.) W of Lexington; pop. (1990c) 7269.
3. City, ⊗ of Morgan co., cen. Missouri; pop. (1990c) 2365.

Versailles \ver-'sī, vər-\. City, ✻ of Yvelines dept., N France, 10 mi. (16 km.) WSW of Paris; pop. (1990c) 91,029; episcopal see and garrison town; tourist center; cathedral and 17th cent. church; large palace built by Louis XIV served as royal palace until 1793, converted into national historical museum by Louis Philippe 1830s; fountains, parks, and extensive gardens; Grand Trianon and Petit Trianon châteaux; hippodrome; military hospital; public library.
History: Built by French kings around site of hunting lodge of Louis XIII; principal royal residence; seat of court of Louis XIV; palace, as symbol of royal lavishness became target during French Revolution; negotiations for peace treaty bet. U.S. and Great Britain ending American Revolution concluded here 1782 (final treaty signed at Paris 1783); German headquarters during Franco-Prussian War 1870–71; place where Wilhelm I was declared emperor of Germany and where treaty bet. France and Germany ending Franco-Prussian War was signed 1871; seat of French government 1871–79; at end of WWI scene of signing of treaty bet. Allies and Germany 1919.

Versecz. See VRŠAC.

Vert, Cap \,käp-'ver\ *or* **Vert, Cape** \'ver\ *also* **Cape Verde** \'vərd, 'vər-dē\. Promontory on the coast of Senegal, bet. the Senegal and Gambia rivers; site of the port of Dakar; its W tip known as Cape Almadies (*q.v.*).

Verulamium. See SAINT ALBANS 3.

Ver·viers \ver-'vyā\. Commune, Liège prov., E Belgium, on the Vesdre River 13 mi. (21 km.) E of the city of Liège; pop. (1992e) 53,700.

Ver·vins \ver-'vaⁿ\. Town, Aisne dept., N France; treaty signed here 1598 bet. Philip II of Spain and Henry IV of France, ending Wars of Religion.

Ves·dre \'vādrᵊ, 'vedrᵊ\ *or Ger.* **We·ser** \'vā-zər\. River, Liège prov., E Belgium; flows W out of Germany into the Ourthe River S of Liège; ab. 45 mi. (70 km.) long.

Vésinet, Le. See LE VÉSINET.

Vesle \'vāl, 'vel\. River, France; flows from NE of Châlons-sur-Marne past Reims into the Aisne River; 89 mi. (143 km.) long.

Vesontio. See BESANÇON.

Ve·soul \və-'zül\; *Lat.* **Ves·u·lum** \'ves-yu̇-ləm\ *or* **Ve·su·li·um** \ve-'sü-lē-əm\. Commune, ✻ of Haute-Saône dept., E France, 58 mi. (93 km.) ENE of Dijon; pop. (1990c) 19,404. Suffered during Wars of Religion; annexed to France 1678.

Ves·per Peak \'ves-pər\. Mountain, Snohomish co., NW cen. Washington; 6190 ft. (1887 m.).

Ves Spišská Nová. See SPIŠSKÁ NOVÁ VES.

Vest–Ag·der \'vest-'äg-dər\; *formerly* **Lis·ter og Man·dals** \'lis-tər-ȯ-'män-,däls\. County of S Norway. See table at NORWAY.

Ves·tal Peak \'vest-ᵊl\. Mountain, San Juan co., SW Colorado; 13,846 ft. (4220 m.).

Ves·ta·via Hills \ves-'tā-vē-ə\. City, Jefferson co., cen. Alabama, 4 mi. (6 km.) S of Birmingham; pop. (1990c) 19,749.

Ves·ter·å·len \'ves-tə-,rō-lən\. Island group in Norwegian Sea, off NW Norway, N of the Lofoten; includes islands of Hinnøy, Langøy, and Andøya.

Vest Fjord \'vest-,fyȯrd\ *or* **Vest·fjord·en** \-,fyȯr-dən\. Inlet of Norwegian Sea extending NNE for 95 mi. (153 km.) bet. the Lofoten island group and the Norwegian mainland.

Vest·fold \'vest-,fōl\; *formerly* **Jarls·berg** \'yärls-,bar\. County of SE Norway. See table at NORWAY.

Vest·man·na·ey·jar \'vest-,män-nä-'ā-,yär\ *or* **West·man Islands** \'west-mən\. Small island group, Iceland, S of the main island.

Vests·jæl·land \'vests-,ē-län\. County, W Sjælland I., Denmark. See table at DENMARK.

Vest·våg·øy \'vest-,vȯ-,gȯi\. Island in the Lofoten group, NE of Moskenes, Norway, in the Norwegian Sea off NW coast; 159 sq. mi. (412 sq. km.).

Vesulium *or* **Vesulum.** See VESOUL.

Vesuna. See PÉRIGUEUX.

Ve·su·vi·us \və-'sü-vē-əs\ *or Ital.* **Ve·su·vio** \vā-'zü-vyō\. Volcano, E side of Bay of Naples, Italy; current height of 4190 ft. (1277 m.) has varied with eruptions (1900: 4275 ft. or 1303 m.; 1906: 3668 ft. or 1118 m.; 1960s: 4203 ft. or 1281 m.); the cone is half encircled on N side by **Mon·te Som·ma** \,mȯnt-ē-'sō-mə\, part of the wall of a large crater in which the present cone has formed; numerous destructive eruptions, esp. Aug. 24, 79 A.D. when Pompeii and Herculaneum were destroyed, Dec. 16, 1631, in 1906 when height was greatly reduced, and in 1944.

Vesz·prém \'ves-,prām\. **1.** County of W Hungary. See table at HUNGARY.
2. City, its ⊗, N of Lake Balaton; pop. (1991e) 65,000; cathedral; university (1949).

Vet \'fet\. River, N Free State, Rep. of South Africa; flows NW into Vaal River; 130 mi. (209 km.) long.

Veta Pass, La. See LA VETA PASS.

Vet·lu·ga \vit-'lü-gə\. River, cen. Russia in Europe; rises in E Vologda Oblast, flows S through Kostroma and Nizhegorod oblasts to join the Volga in SW Mari El Rep.; 528 mi. (850 km.) long. Important channel for lumber floated down it; navigable to Vetluga, town in N Nizhegorod Oblast.

Vettern. See VÄTTERN.

Vet·tis·foss \'ve-tis-,fōs\. Waterfall in the Mörkedola River, a small stream in the Sogne Fjord region of W Norway; total drop 1214 ft. (370 m.), with highest single fall 889 ft. (271 m.).

Vet·to·re, Mon·te \'mȯn-tā-ve-'tō-rā\. Mountain in cen. Italy; highest peak in Roman Apennines. See table at APENNINES.

Vet·u·lo·nia \,ve-chə-'lō-nē-ə\. Ancient city of Etruria, ab. 10 mi. (16 km.) NW of the commune of Grosseto, Grosseto prov., Tuscany, W Italy; one of 12 in the Etruscan Confederation; remains, esp. of tombs.

Veur·ne \'vœr-nə\ *or Fr.* **Furnes** \'fu̅e̅rn\. Commune, West Flanders prov., NW Belgium; pop. (1991c) 11,175; Belgian headquarters in WWI, 6 mi. (10 km.) behind the Yser front.

Ve·vay \'vē-vē\. Town, ⊗ of Switzerland co., SE Indiana; pop. (1990c) 1393.

Ve·vey \və-'vā\ *or Ger.* **Vi·vis** \'vē-vis\; *anc.* **Vi·bis·cum** \və-'bis-kəm, vī-\. Commune, Vaud canton, W Switzerland, on NE shore of Lake Geneva 11 mi. (18 km.) ESE of Lausanne; pop. (1980c) 16,139; chocolate, wine; tourist resort.

Vex·in \vek-'seⁿ\. Ancient district of France, N of the Seine and the Oise, bounded on NW by Normandy; ✻ Gisors; divided in 911, part (incl. Gisors) going to Normandy, and part remaining French as a dependency of Île-de-France.

Vé·zère \vā-'zer\. River, SW cen. France; rises in Corrèze dept., flows SW into Dordogne River; ab. 120 mi. (195 km.) long.

Via Appia. See APPIAN WAY.

Via Aurelia. See AURELIAN WAY.

Via Cassia. See CASSIAN WAY.

Via·da·na \,vē-ä-'dä-nä, vyä-\. Commune, Mantova prov., Lombardy, N Italy, on Po River 22 mi. (35 km.) SW of Mantua; pop. (1981p) 15,941.

Viadua. See ODER.

Via Flaminia. See FLAMINIAN WAY.

Via Latina. See LATIN WAY.

Via·na do Cas·te·lo \ˈvyȧ-nə-ˌdü-kȧsh-ˈte-lü\. **1.** District of NW Portugal. See table at PORTUGAL.
2. Commercial seaport, its ✻, near Atlantic Ocean; pop. (1987e) 83,800.

Viangchan. See VIENTIANE.

Via Ostiensis. See OSTIAN WAY.

Via·reg·gio \ˌvē-ä-ˈre-jō, vyä-\. Seaport, Lucca prov., Tuscany, cen. Italy, on Ligurian Sea 12 mi. (19 km.) WNW of the commune of Lucca; pop. (1991p) 57,099; seaside resort; monument to English poet Percy Bysshe Shelley, whose body was washed ashore here; burial place nearby of operatic composer Giacomo Puccini.

Via Salaria. See SALARIAN WAY.

Viatka. See VYATKA.

Via Valeria. See VALERIAN WAY.

Vibiscum. See VEVEY.

Vibo, Gulf of. See SANT'EUFEMIA, GULF OF.

Vi·borg \ˈvē-ˌbȯrg, -bȯr\. **1.** County of N cen. Jutland, Denmark. See table at DENMARK.
2. City, its ⊗; pop. (1989e) 39,507; machinery, textiles; beer; Gothic cathedral c. 1130. Important in the early history of Denmark, its kings being crowned here from 11th cent.
3. City, Russia. See VYBORG.

Vi·bo Va·len·tia \ˈvē-bō-vä-ˈlen-tē-ä\; *formerly* **Mon·te·le·o·ne di Ca·la·bria** \ˌmȯn-tā-lā-ˈō-nā-ˌdē-kä-ˈlä-brē-ä\; *anc.* **Hip·po·ni·um** \hi-ˈpō-nē-əm\. Commune, Catanzaro prov., Calabria, S Italy, 30 mi. (48 km.) SW of the city of Catanzaro; pop. (1991p) 31,204; Greek and Roman ruins; earthquakes 1783 and 1905. An ancient city inhabited by Greeks, then Romans; conquered by Arabs 9th cent.

Vic. See VICH.

Vi·cen·te, Point \və-ˈsen-tē\. Point, SW coast of Los Angeles co., SW California.

Vi·cen·te Ló·pez \bē-ˈsen-tā-ˈlō-pes\. City, Buenos Aires prov., E cen. Argentina, just NW of the city of Buenos Aires; pop. (1991p) 289,142; incorp. 1905.

Vi·cen·te Pe·rez Ro·sa·les National Park \bē-ˈsen-tā-ˈpā-res-rō-ˈsä-lās\. National park, S cen. Chile; 522 sq. mi. (1352 sq. km.); volcanic activity; estab. 1926.

Vi·cen·za \vē-ˈchen-sä\. **1.** Province of Veneto, NE Italy. See table at ITALY.
2. *anc.* **Vi·cen·tia** \vī-ˈsen-chē-ə\. Commune, its ✻, 40 mi. (64 km.) W of Venice; pop. (1991p) 107,076; chemicals; food processing; 12th cent. cathedral with 15th cent. façade (restored after WWII); 13th cent. churches of Santa Corona and San Lorenzo; numerous buildings designed by Italian architect Andrea Palladio, among them, 16th cent. Basilica Palladiana, Loggia del Capitanio, and Teatro Olimpico; many palaces of 14th, 15th, and 16th cents.; campanile in Piazza dei Signori; nearby is noted pilgrimage church, the Basilica di Monte Berico.
History: Founded c. first cent. B.C. by Ligurians; ✻ of Lombard duchy in early Middle Ages; gained independence 1164 and joined Lombard League; destroyed by Holy Roman Emperor Frederick II 1236; ruled by della Scala family of Verona 1311 ff., Visconti of Milan 1384 ff., and Venetian Republic 1404 ff.; to Austria 1797 ff.; became part of kingdom of Italy 1866. Suffered extensive damage in WWII. Home of Italian artist Bartolomeo Montagna (c. 1450–1523), founder of school of Vicenza.

Vich *or* **Vic** \ˈvēk\; *anc.* **Au·sa** \ˈȯ-sə\ *or later* **Vi·cus Au·so·nen·sis** \ˈvī-kəs-ˌȯ-sə-ˈnen-sis\. Commune, Barcelona prov., NE Spain, 38 mi. (61 km.) NE of city of Barcelona; pop. (1991p) 28,289; manufactures textiles; museum; 11th cent. cathedral with many later alterations, contains murals by Spanish painter José Sert.

Vi·cha·da \bē-ˈchä-thä\. **1.** River, cen. and E Colombia; flows ENE into Orinoco River on Venezuelan border; ab. 400 mi. (645 km.) long.
2. Department of E Colombia. See table at COLOMBIA.

Vichegda. See VYCHEGDA.

Vi·chu·ga \vi-ˈchü-gə, ˈvē-chu̇-gə\. Town, Ivanovo Oblast, cen. Russia in Europe, ab. 40 mi. (65 km.) NE of the city of Ivanovo; pop. (1991e) 49,700.

Vi·chy \ˈvi-shē, ˈvē-\. Commune, Allier dept., cen. France, on Allier River 200 mi. (322 km.) SSE of Paris; pop. (1990c) 28,048; noted spa; many thermal alkaline springs used since Roman times; Vichy water exported. Rediscovered and made popular esp. after Emperor Napoléon III's many visits 19th cent.; as result of French armistice with Germany 1940, made ✻ of unoccupied France; seat of French collaborationist government led by Marshal Philippe Pétain during WWII.

Vicks·burg \ˈviks-ˌbərg\. City, ⊗ of Warren co., W Mississippi, on Mississippi River 40 mi. (64 km.) W of Jackson; pop. (1990c) 20,908; river port and railroad center; tourism; many antebellum homes; U.S. Army Corps of Engineers experiment station. Settled first by the French 1719, later c. 1790 by the Spanish; American settlement began early 19th cent.; during Civil War besieged 1862–63; final siege operations Apr.–June 1863, captured July 4 by Union forces under Gen. Ulysses S. Grant, securing Union control of the Mississippi River. See CHICKASAW BAYOU.

Vicksburg National Military Park. See UNITED STATES, *National Historical Parks.*

Vi·co Equen·se \ˈvē-kō-ā-ˈkwen-sā\. Commune, Napoli prov., Campania, S Italy, on Bay of Naples 15 mi. (24 km.) SSE of Naples; pop. (1981p) 17,359; seaside resort.

Vi·ço·sa \vi-ˈsó-zə\. City, SE Minas Gerais state, E Brazil, 85 mi. (137 km.) SE of Belo Horizonte; munic. pop. (1980c) 38,686; university (1948).

Vic·to·ria \vik-ˈtōr-ē-ə, *Span.* bēk-ˈtōr-yä\. **1.** County in S Texas. See table at TEXAS.
2. City, ⊗ of Victoria co., S Texas, 20 mi. (32 km.) WNW of Matagorda Bay; pop. (1990c) 55,076; oil and gas, petrochemicals; Victoria Coll. (1925), Univ. of Houston–Victoria (1973); settled 1824 by Spanish and named for Mexico's first president, Guadalupe Victoria.
3. City, Entre Ríos prov., E Argentina, ab. 40 mi. (65 km.) NE of Rosario; pop. (1980p) 18,883.
4. River, NW Northern Terr., Australia; flows N and NW to Queens Channel; 350 mi. (563 km.) long; navigable for ab. 100 mi. (160 km.).
5. State, SE Australia; ✻ Melbourne. See table at AUSTRALIA.
Physical features: Separated on N from New South Wales by Murray River which forms almost entire boundary from its source in Australian Alps to point at 34°S where it crosses into South Australia. W and NW parts sandy desert and lowland; cen. and E parts are highlands forming S end of Great Dividing Range (here known as Australian Alps). Highest part is Darg Plateau with Mt. Bogong 6516 ft. (1986 m.). SW coastal region known as Gippsland. In cen. part of S coast is spacious Port Phillip Bay, harbor of Melbourne; on coast SE of it is Wilson's Promontory, most S point of Australian mainland. Separated on S from Tasmania by Bass Strait.
Chief products: Wheat, oats, barley, wool, dairy products, wine grapes; coal; food processing.
Chief cities: Melbourne, Geelong, Ballarat, Bendigo.
History: Inhabited for thousands of years by aborigines; European discovery led by English navigator Capt. James Cook 1770, a few days before his arrival at Botany Bay to the N; Port Phillip Bay discovered 1802; first settled by immigrants from Tasmania; much of aboriginal population decimated by diseases spread by settlers; set off 1851 from New South Wales as separate colony; received many new settlers as result of discovery of gold in Ballarat region 1851; self-government estab. 1855; became a state of Commonwealth of Australia 1901.
6. Seaport town, SW Cameroon. See LIMBE 1.
7. Name of counties in three provinces of Canada. See tables at NEW BRUNSWICK, NOVA SCOTIA, ONTARIO.
8. City, ✻ of British Columbia, Canada, on SE Vancouver I. and at E end of Strait of Juan de Fuca; pop. (1991c) 71,228; seaport; lumber; fishing; tourism; museum; parks; Univ. of Victoria (university status 1963); Pacific headquarters of Canadian Navy. Founded 1843; selected as ✻ 1866 when Vancouver I. united with British Columbia.
9. *or* **Hong Kong** \ˈhäŋ-ˌkäŋ, -ˈkäŋ, ˈhȯŋ-ˌkȯŋ, -ˈkȯŋ\. Seaport city, Hong Kong, China, NW Hong Kong I.; pop.

(1981c) 590,771; has extensive wharves; Univ. of Hong Kong (1911); city served as ✻ of Hong Kong colony.

10. Town, ✻ of Labuan Federal Terr., on Labuan I., off NW coast of Borneo, Sabah, Malaysia.

11. Town, Malta. See RABAT.

12. Seaport, ✻ of Seychelles, Indian Ocean; chief town on Mahé I.

13. Town, Zimbabwe. See MASVINGO.

Victoria, La. See LA VICTORIA.

Victoria, Lake 1. *or* **Victoria Ny·an·za** \nē-'an-zə, nī-\. Lake, E cen. Africa, S half in Tanzania and N half in Uganda, borders on Kenya in NE; 26,828 sq. mi. (69,485 sq. km.); 2d largest freshwater body (after Lake Superior in North America) in the world; ab. 250 mi. (400 km.) long (N to S) and 200 mi. (320 km.) wide; max. depth 265 ft. (81 m.); alt. ab. 3720 ft. (1135 m.); has indented coastline with deep gulfs, numerous islands; many tributaries (largest, Kagera) draining nearby uplands of E Africa, but chief source of water supply is rainfall; only outlet is the Nile (*q.v.*).

History: First European discovery 1858 by English explorer John Hanning Speke in search of source of Nile; circumnavigated by British explorer Henry Morton Stanley 1875; became a reservoir with raised water level by completion of Owen Falls Dam 1954.

2. Lake, Tajikistan. See ZORKUL, LAKE.

Victoria, Mount. 1. Peak on the boundary bet. Alberta and British Columbia, SW Canada, behind Lake Louise; 11,365 ft. (3464 m.).

2. Peak, Fiji. See TOMANIIVI, MOUNT.

3. Peak, W cen. Myanmar at N end of Arakan Yoma and NE of Sittwe; 10,016 ft. (3053 m.).

4. Peak, highest in the Owen Stanley Range, New Guinea I., Papua New Guinea, NE of Port Moresby; 13,363 ft. (4073 m.).

Victoria de Durango. See DURANGO 3.

Vic·to·ria de las Tu·nas \bēk-'tōr-yä-ˌthā-läs-'tü-näs\ *also* **Tunas.** Municipality, ✻ of Las Tunas prov., E Cuba, 100 mi. (161 km.) NW of Santiago de Cuba; pop. (1990e) 119,400.

Victoria Falls. 1. Falls, Brazil. See IGUAÇU.

2. *or native* **Mo·si–oa–Tu·nya** \'mō-sē-ˌō-ä-'tü-nyä\. Falls in the Zambezi River, at a place where river is 5580 ft. (1701 m.) wide, on the boundary bet. Zambia and Zimbabwe, S Africa, near the town of Livingstone; broken by islands on precipice edge into four parts; height 355 ft. (108 m.); volume varies with the seasons; water of falls drops into narrow chasm, hitting opp. wall 80 to 240 ft. (24 to 73 m.) above chasm floor. Railroad bridge (657 ft. or 200 m. long) crosses Zambezi just below falls. Zimbabwean side is preserved as **Victoria Falls National Park.** First European sighting of falls by Scottish explorer and missionary David Livingstone 1855 who named them after Queen Victoria.

Victoria Fjord. Fjord, N coast of Greenland, W of Peary Land; 140 mi. (225 km.) long.

Victoria Island. 1. Third largest island of Arctic Archipelago, N of W mainland part of Nunavut, Canada; now split bet. Northwest Territories and Nunavut; 81,930 sq. mi. (212,199 sq. km.); separated from mainland by Dolphin and Union Strait, Coronation Gulf, and Dease Strait.

2. Island, Chonos Archipelago, Chile, in Pacific Ocean off SW coast.

Victoria Land *formerly* **South Victoria Land.** Section of Antarctica, on W shore of Ross Sea and Ross Ice Shelf, 70°–78°S and 164°E; largely included in Ross Dependency (*q.v.*); has mountain ranges, with highest peak ab. 13,000 ft. (3960 m.).

Victoria Nile. See NILE.

Victoria Nyanza. See VICTORIA, LAKE 1.

Victoria Peak. 1. Mountain, N cen. Vancouver I., British Columbia, Canada; 7096 ft. (2163 m.).

2. Hill above Victoria city, NW Hong Kong I., Hong Kong colony; highest point on island, 1805 ft. (550 m.); has view of Hong Kong harbor; in WWII last point surrendered to Japanese by British in fall of Hong Kong Dec. 25, 1941.

Victoria Quadrant. Former division of Antarctica; the quarter section bet. 90°E and 180°E; now chiefly Wilkes Land and Victoria Land (W part of Ross Dependency).

Victoria River. See VICTORIA 4.

Victoria Strait. Channel bet. SE Victoria I. and King William I., off N Canada mainland in Nunavut.

Vic·to·ri·a·ville \vik-'tōr-ē-ə-ˌvil\. Town, Arthabaska co., S Quebec, Canada, 36 mi. (58 km.) SE of Trois Rivières; pop. (1991c) 21,495; furniture; incorp. 1890.

Vic·tor·ville \'vik-tər-ˌvil\. City, San Bernardino co., SE California, N of the city of San Bernardino; pop. (1990c) 40,674; Victor Valley Coll. (1961); former site of U.S. Air Force base. The pop. nearly tripled bet. 1980 and 1990.

Vicus Ausonensis. See VICH.

Vicus Elbii. See VITERBO 2.

Vicus Julii. Commune, France. See AIRE 3.

Vid \'vit\. River, NW cen. Bulgaria; flows from the Balkan Mts. NE into Danube River 8 mi. (13 km.) W of Nikopol; 117 mi. (188 km.) long.

Vi·da·lia \və-'dāl-yə\. **1.** City, Toombs and Montgomery cos., SE cen. Georgia, 76 mi. (122 km.) W of Savannah; pop. (1990c) 11,078; noted for onions grown there.

2. Town, ⊗ of Concordia parish, E cen. Louisiana; pop. (1990c) 4953.

Vi·din \'vē-din\; *anc.* **Bo·no·nia** \bə-'nō-nē-ə, -'nōn-yə\. City, NW Bulgaria, on Danube River near Yugoslav border; pop. (1991e) 67,992; river port in agricultural region producing esp. wine; Celtic settlement on site 3d cent. B.C., later important Roman fortress; seat of independent state in 14th cent.; under Turks 1396–1878.

Vi·dor \'vī-ˌdȯr\. City, Orange co., E Texas, 7 mi. (11 km.) NE of Beaumont; pop. (1990c) 10,935.

Vied·ma \'byād-mä\. Town, ✻ of Río Negro prov., S cen. Argentina, on the Río Negro ab. 19 mi. (31 km.) above its mouth; pop. (1980c) 24,346.

Viedma, Lake. Lake, W Santa Cruz prov., S Argentina, S of Lake San Martín and N of Lake Argentino; 420 sq. mi. (1088 sq. km.); 53 mi. (85 km.) long.

Viedma Glacier. Glacier in the Andes, Argentina; 27 mi. (43 km.) long, ab. 3 mi. (5 km.) wide near its terminus.

Viejo, El. See EL VIEJO.

Vieng Chan. See VIENTIANE.

Vi·en·na \vī-'e-nə\. **1.** City, ⊗ of Dooly co., SW cen. Georgia, 40 mi. (64 km.) NE of Albany; pop. (1990c) 2708.

2. City, ⊗ of Johnson co., S Illinois; pop. (1990c) 1446.

Vi·en·na \vē-'e-nə\. **1.** City, ⊗ of Maries co., S cen. Missouri; pop. (1990c) 611.

2. Town, Fairfax co., NE Virginia, NW of Alexandria; pop. (1990c) 14,852.

3. City, Wood co., W West Virginia, on Ohio River 5 mi. (8 km.) N of Parkersburg; pop. (1990c) 10,862.

4. State of Austria. See table at AUSTRIA.

5. *or Ger.* **Wien** \'vēn\; *anc.* **Vin·dob·o·na** \vin-'dä-bə-nə\ *or* **Vin·dob·na** \-'däb-nə\. City, ✻ of Austria, on Danube River; 160 sq. mi. (414 sq. km.); pop. (1991c) 1,539,848; commercial and industrial center of Austria; railroad junction and river port; produces machine tools, electrical equipment, clothing, tourism. An important cultural center, with the Univ. of Vienna (1365), Vienna Technical Univ. (1815), several other higher educational institutions, opera, library, several museums, major theaters; headquarters of the International Atomic Energy Agency (IAEA) and of the Organization of the Petroleum Exporting Countries (OPEC). Notable buildings include 14th–15th cent. Gothic St. Stephen's Cathedral, several churches, Hofburg (former seat of the Hapsburgs), archiepiscopal palace, Rathaus, Schönbrunn Palace, Belvedere (now museum); extensive system of public parks (incl. amusement

---

\ə\ **abut** \ə̇\ matches \$^{ə}$\ kitten, Fr table \ər\ **further** \a\ **ash** \ā\ **ace** \ä\ cot, cart \ȧ\ Fr bac \au̇\ **out** \b̲\ Span Avila \ch\ **chin** \e\ bet \ē\ **easy** \g\ **go** \i\ hit \ī\ **ice** \j\ **job** \k̲\ Ger **ich**, Bu**ch** \$^{n}$\ Fr vin \ŋ\ sing \ō\ **go** \ö\ **all** \ȯ\ **law** \œ\ Fr bœuf \œ̄\ Fr **feu** \ȯi\ **boy** \th\ **thin** \th̲\ **this** \ü\ **loot** \u̇\ **foot** \ue\ Ger füllen \ue̅\ Fr **rue** \y\ **yet** \$^{y}$\ Fr digne \'dēn^{y}\, nuit \'nw^{y}ē\ \yü\ **few** \yu̇\ **fury** \zh\ vision

park, the Prater) and gardens. Home of composers Joseph Haydn and Wolfgang Amadeus Mozart 18th cent.; Johannes Brahms and Gustav Mahler 19th cent.; birthplace of Arnold Schoenberg and Anton Friedrich von Webern 20th cent.; home of psychoanalysis founder Sigmund Freud.

History: Founded by Celts; made Roman military station first cent. B.C.; came under Avars and in 6th cent. A.D. under Franks; to Magyars 10th cent.; to Margrave Leopold I of Babenberg 976; became seat of dukes of Babenberg; important trade center during Crusades; taken and fortified by King Otakar II of Bohemia 1251; taken by Holy Roman Emperor Rudolf I of Hapsburg 1278 and remained seat of Hapsburgs until 1918; besieged by Turks 1529 and 1683; under Empress Maria Theresa (reigned 1740–80) became one of leading cultural centers of Europe; under Francis I became seat of Austrian empire; occupied by French 1805–09; seat of Congress of Vienna 1814–15 which organized Europe following French Emperor Napoléon's reign; scene of revolution 1848. Became ✻ of Austrian republic 1918; administrative center of German Austria 1938–45; in WWII frequently bombed by Allies and taken by Soviet troops Apr. 1945; suffered heavy damage. Under joint Soviet-Western Allied occupation 1945–55; has undergone considerable rebuilding since WWII. Site of Strategic Arms Limitations Talks bet. U.S. and U.S.S.R. 1970 ff.

6. City, France. See VIENNE 3.

Vienne \ 'vyen\. **1.** Navigable river, SW cen. France; rises in Corrèze dept., flows NW through Limoges and Chinon into Loire River; 217 mi. (349 km.) long.

2. Department of W cen. France. See table at FRANCE.

3. *anc.* **Vi·en·na** \ vē-'e-nə\. Manufacturing city, Isère dept., SE France, on the Rhone River 47 mi. (76 km.) NW of Grenoble; pop. (1990c) 30,386; river port; footwear; 12th cent. Romanesque-Gothic cathedral; several churches, incl. one begun 5th cent.; Roman remains include a Corinthian temple of Emperor Augustus and his wife Livia, water conduits, theater, and obelisk.

History: In ancient times chief town of Allobroges and rival of Lyon; taken by Romans and became important city in Roman Gaul; formerly ✻ of Viennois; church council held here 1311–12 resulting in suppression of Knights Templars, a powerful Crusading order.

Vien·nois \ vyen-'wä\. Ancient county of SE France, in Dauphiné; now in Drôme and Isère depts.; ✻ Vienne.

Vien·tiane \ vyen-'tyän\ *or Laotian* **Viang·chan** \ ˌvyeŋ-'chän\ *or* **Vieng Chan** \ ˌvyeŋ-'chän\. City, administrative ✻ of Laos, near Thai border ab. 5 mi. (8 km.) N of Mekong River; pop. (1985c) 178,203; commercial center of the region; temple, begun c. 12th cent.; museum. Administrative center of early Laotian kingdom 16th cent.; taken by Siamese c. 1827; made ✻ of French colony 1890s; remained ✻ at Laotian independence 1953.

Vie·ques \ 'byā-kās\. **1.** *also* **Crab Island** \ 'krab\. Fertile island, forming a municipality off E coast of Puerto Rico, 21 mi. (34 km.) long by 6 mi. (10 km.) wide; pop. (1990c) 8602; administratively a part of Puerto Rico.

2. Chief town on Vieques I., Puerto Rico. See ISABEL SEGUNDA.

Viern·heim \ 'firn-ˌhīm\. Agricultural commune, Hesse, Germany, NE suburb of Mannheim; pop. (1980c) 29,590.

Vier·sen \ 'firz-ᵊn\. City, North Rhine-Westphalia, Germany, 18 mi. (29 km.) W of Düsseldorf; pop. (1992e) 77,658.

Vier Waldstätter, Die. See FOREST CANTONS, THE FOUR.

Vierwaldstätter See. See LUCERNE, LAKE OF.

Vier·zon \ vyer-'zōⁿ\. Town, Cher dept., cen. France, on the Cher River 18 mi. (29 km.) NW of Bourges; pop. (1990c) 32,900.

Vie·ste \ 'vyes-tā\. Commune, Foggia prov., Puglia, SE Italy, 43 mi. (69 km.) NE of the commune of Foggia; pop. (1981p) 12,729; castle.

Vi·et·nam *also* **Vi·et Nam;** *officially since 1976* **Socialist Republic of Vietnam** \ vē-'et-'näm, vyet-, ˌvē-ət-, vēt-, -'nam\. Republic, SE Asia, bounded on N by China, on E by Gulf of Tonkin and South China Sea, on SW by Gulf of Thailand, and on W by Cambodia and Laos; pop. (1993e) 70,454,000; ✻ Hanoi; divided 1954–75 into North Vietnam and South Vietnam (see VIETNAM, NORTH and VIETNAM, SOUTH).

Chief products: Rice, corn, coffee, sugarcane; fish; textiles; rubber, coal, steel, fertilizer, phosphates, cement.

Chief towns: Ho Chi Minh City and Hanoi.

History: Region came under Chinese influence and N part made a province of Chinese Empire first cent. B.C.; Vietnamese under continuous Chinese control until 10th cent. A.D.; reimposition of Chinese rule 1407–28; S region gradually overrun by Vietnamese from N late 15th cent.; Cambodia conquered by Vietnamese 1698–1757; area divided into two parts early 17th cent. (N part later known as Tonkin, S part as Cochin China); Vietnamese ports visited by Spanish and Portuguese traders early 16th cent., by Dutch and English traders 17th cent.; N and S parts of Vietnam unified under single dynasty 1802; Saigon captured by Franco-Spanish naval force (following several years of attempted French colonial expansion in the region) 1859; three provinces of Cochin China ceded to France 1862; whole of Cochin China occupied by French 1867; appeal by emperor for Chinese support immediate cause of French military actions in N (Hanoi captured 1883); French protectorate estab. over Tonkin 1884; Vietnam occupied by Japanese (who declared it independent 1945) 1940–45; number of French troops in Vietnam increased following WWII and period 1946–54 marked by war bet. French (supported by Nationalists under Emperor Bao Dai) and Viet Minh (Communist forces under Ho Chi Minh); French forces (with U.S. financial backing) were defeated at Dien Bien Phu 1954 and evacuation of French troops ensued; following international conference at Geneva (Switzerland) 1954, Vietnam partitioned along 17th parallel, with N part under Ho Chi Minh, and S part under Bao Dai (partition was to be temporary, and for purposes of reunification elections were to be held 1956—elections never held); Bao Dai declared independence of S region (see VIETNAM, SOUTH); Communist republic established N region (see VIETNAM, NORTH). After Apr. 1975, when South Vietnamese government fell, the North Vietnamese government reunified the country with Hanoi as ✻; invaded and occupied Cambodia 1978–89; suffered from trade embargo imposed by U.S. and other W countries; embargo lifted by U.S. 1994 and move to normalization in relations begun.

Vietnam, North; *officially* **Democratic Republic of Vietnam.** Former republic, SE Asia, in N part of Vietnam; 63,360 sq. mi. (164,102 sq. km.); ✻ Hanoi.

Physical features: Mountainous in N and NW (highest peak Fan-si-pan 10,306 ft. or 3141 m.); E part consists of coastal plain; Red River delta is an important agricultural region.

Chief towns: Hanoi, Haiphong, Vinh, Thanh Hoa, Nam Dinh.

History: Communist republic set up in N part of Vietnam (*q.v.*) 1954, opposed to the existence of an anticommunist government in S; suppressed peasant revolts 1956; intensified aid to Communist groups in South Vietnam; adopted new constitution 1960; initiated large-scale troop infiltration into South Vietnam 1960s; intensified fighting in S led to military targets in North Vietnam being bombed by U.S. 1964 ff.; during latter part of 1960s expanded its military activities into Laos and Cambodia, all the while gaining ground in S; defeat of South Vietnamese and U.S. forces led to U.S. withdrawal 1973 and ultimately to complete takeover of South Vietnam Apr. 1975.

Vietnam, South; *officially* **Republic of Vietnam.** Former republic, SE Asia, in S part of Vietnam; 67,108 sq. mi. (173,810 sq. km.); ✻ Saigon.

Physical features: S part of country characterized by Mekong Delta, a flat, frequently marshy region with rich soils suited esp. for rice production; N and cen. regions hilly (highest peak Ngoo Linh 8521 ft. or 2597 m.) with narrow coastal plain.

Chief towns: Saigon, Da Nang, Hue, Gia Dinh, Qui Nhon.

History: Nationalist government under Emperor Bao Dai estab. in S part of Vietnam (*q.v.*) 1954; government offered economic aid and military aid by U.S.; abolished monarchy (1955) and rejected Geneva formula (which called for reunification of Vietnam); latter part of 1950s characterized by increase in antigovernment activity (initiated by South Vietnamese Communists and soon supported by infiltrators from North Vietnam); North Vietnam charged with complicity in attempts to overthrow the South Vietnam government in majority report of International Control Commission 1962; 1960s marked by massive U.S. military and economic assistance program in support of anticommunist South Vietnam government; first U.S. ground combat troops deployed in South Vietnam 1965 (U.S. forces reached over 500,000 in 1969); gradual withdrawal of U.S. forces begun July 1969 with intention of South Vietnamese forces carrying on independently; protracted peace negotiations resulted in peace agreement and cease-fire Jan. 1973; last U.S. forces left Mar. 1973; fighting continued; South Vietnam capitulated to North Vietnam and the Vietcong Apr. 1975; reintegrated with North Vietnam to form Vietnam.

Vieux Car·ré \ˌvü-kä-ˈrā, ˌvyü-, ˌvyœ-\. Neighborhood of New Orleans, Louisiana, bordering on the Mississippi River; a popular tourist area noted for its nightclubs, restaurants, and Creole architecture.

Vieux Fort \ˌvyœ-ˈfȯr\. **1.** Point, S tip of Basse-Terre I., French overseas dept. of Guadeloupe, West Indies.
2. Town and former ✻ of St. Lucia I., Windward Is., West Indies, on **Vieux Fort Bay**, at S tip of the island; administrative area pop. (1989e) 14,226.

Vi·ga \ˈvē-gä\. Municipality, Catanduanes prov., Philippines, ab. 3 mi. (5 km.) from coast; pop. (1980c) 15,863.

Vi·gan \ˈvē-ˌgän\. Municipality, ✻ of Ilocos Sur prov., Luzon, Philippines, just N of the mouth of the Abra; pop. (1980c) 33,483.

Vi·ge·va·no \vē-ˈje-vä-ˌnō\. Commune, Pavia prov., Lombardy, N Italy, near Ticino River 18 mi. (29 km.) NW of the commune of Pavia; pop. (1989c) 61,731; 15th cent. castle; 16th cent. cathedral.

Vi·gia \vi-ˈzhē-ə\. City, E Pará state, N Brazil, at the mouth of Pará River on E bank; munic. pop. (1991p) 63,166.

Vigne·male, Pic de \ˌpēk-də-ˌvēnʸ-ˈmȧl\. Peak in the Pyrenees Mts., S France; 10,820 ft. (3298 m.); highest peak in the French Pyrenees.

Vi·go **1.** \ˈvē-ˌgō, ˈvī-\. County in W Indiana. See table at INDIANA.
2. \ˈbē-ḡō\. Seaport, Pontevedra prov., NW Spain, on the **Estuary of Vigo,** an inlet of Atlantic Ocean 17 mi. (27 km.) SSW of the commune of Pontevedra; pop. (1991c) 276,109; leather, paper, brandy; fisheries. Under attack by English Adm. Sir Francis Drake 1585, 1589; scene of French and Spanish naval defeat by English and Dutch 1702.

Vi·gon·za \vē-ˈgōn-tsä\. Commune, Padova prov., Veneto, NE Italy, NE of Padua; pop. (1981p) 15,076.

Vi·ha·ri \vi-ˈhär-ē\. Town, Punjab prov., Pakistan, ESE of Multan; pop. (1981c) 53,799.

Viipuri. See VYBORG.

Viipuri Bay. See VYBORG BAY.

Vi·ja·ya·na·gar \ˌvi-jə-yə-ˈnə-gər\ *also* **Bi·ja·na·gar** \ˌbi-jə-ˈnə-gər\. **1.** Former Hindu kingdom, S India, S of the Krishna; estab. 1336 by two brothers of the Kanarese people; for more than two centuries formed defense of Hindu peoples against Muslim raiders from the N; was an important center of Brahman culture and Dravidian art. Downfall of empire began with defeat at Talikota 1565 by confederacy (Bijapur, Ahmadnagar, and Golconda) of Deccan Muslim sultans; empire dissolved early 17th cent.
2. City, its ✻ (destroyed 1565); its ruins, incl. several temples, now at modern Hampi on S bank of the Tungabhadra, Karnataka, India, ab. 30 mi. (48 km.) WNW of Bellary.

Vi·ja·ya·pu·ri \ˌvi-jə-yə-ˈpu̇r-ē\. Town, Andhra Pradesh, India, ab. 80 mi. (130 km.) SE of Hyderabad.

Vi·ja·ya·wa·da \ˌvi-jə-yə-ˈwä-də\; *formerly* **Bez·wa·da** \bez-ˈwä-də\. Town, Andhra Pradesh, SE India, on Krishna River at the head of its delta 155 mi. (250 km.) ESE of Hyderabad; pop. (1991c) 701,827; manufactures toys. Headquarters of Krishna irrigation canal system; active trade center and rail junction. Inhabited for at least 2000 years; several temples; museum. Village of **Un·da·val·le** \ˈu̇n-də-ˌvə-lā\ nearby has interesting rock temples and ruins.

Vi·jo·së \vē-ˈō-sə\ *also* **Vi·o·sa** \vē-ˈō-sə\ *or* **Vo·yu·tsa** \vō-ˈyüt-sə\ *or Gk.* **Aó·ös** \ˈau̇-ös\. River, NW Greece and S Albania; rises in Pindus Mts., Greece, flows NW across Albania into Adriatic Sea 14 mi. (23 km.) N of Vlorë; 148 mi. (238 km.) long.

Vík \ˈvēk\. Village, on most southerly point of Iceland, 63°25′N, 19°01′W.

Vik·na \'vik-nə\. Small island, Norway, in Norwegian Sea, off W cen. coast; 74°54′N, 11°E.

Vila. See PORT–VILA.

Vi·la da Ma·nhi·ça \'vē-lə-də-mə-'nyē-sə\ *often shortened to* **Ma·nhi·ça** *or* **Manica** \mə-'nyē-sə\; *formerly* **Ma·ce·que·ce** *or* **Ma·si·ke·si** \,mä-sə-'kā-sē\. Town, W cen. Mozambique; pop. (1991e) 54,052.

Vila de João Belo. See XAI-XAI.

Vi·la do Con·de \'vē-lə-dü-'kōn-dē\. Town, NW Portugal, NNW of Porto; pop. (1991p) 21,800.

Vilafro, Lake. See VILLAFRO, LAKE.

Vilagarcía de Arousa. See VILLAGARCÍA DE AROSA.

Vi·laine \vi-'lān, -'len\. Navigable river, NW France; rises in Mayenne dept., flows W to Rennes, and turns SW through Morbihan dept. into the Bay of Biscay; 140 mi. (225 km.) long.

Vi·la No·va de Ga·ia \'vē-lə-'nò-və-dē-'gī-ə\. Town, Pôrto dist., NW Portugal, just S of the city of Porto; pop. (1987e) 240,200; port wine.

Vila Nova de Portimão. See PORTIMÃO.

Vilanova i la Geltrú. See VILLANUEVA Y GETTRÚ.

Vila–real. See VILLARREAL.

Vi·la Re·al \'vē-lə-'rē-əl\. **1.** District of N Portugal. See table at PORTUGAL.
2. *also* **Vila Ri·al** \'rē-əl\. Commune, its ✻; munic. pop. (1987e) 47,000; episcopal see.

Vi·las \'vī-ləs\. County in N Wisconsin. See table at WISCONSIN.

Vila Salazar. See NDALATANDO.

Vi·la Ve·lha \'vē-lə-'vel-yə\. Coastal city, Espirito Santo state, E Brazil, just SSW of Vitória; pop. (1991p) 263,897.

Vil·ca·no·ta Knot \,bēl-kä-'nō-tä\. Mountain mass in the Andes, S Peru, NW of Lake Titicaca; highest point 17,988 ft. (5483 m.); junction point of ranges entering Peru from Bolivia and Chile.

Vîl·cea \vil-'chā-ə\. County of S cen. Romania. See table at ROMANIA.

Vildmose. See LILLE VILDMOSE.

Vilich. See BEUEL.

Viliya. See NERIS.

Vil·jan·di *or* **Vil·yan·di** \'vil-,yän-dē\ *also* **Wil·jan·di** \-,yän-\; *Ger.* **Fel·lin** \fe-'lēn\. Town, S cen. Estonia, 42 mi. (68 km.) E of Pärnu.

Vil·kits·ki Strait \vil-'kit-skē\ *or Russ.* **Pro·liv Vil'·kit·sko·go** \,prə-'lyēf-vilʸ-'kit-skə-və\. Channel, N coast of Taymyr Penin., Taymyr Autonomous Okrug, N Russia in Asia; separates Bol'shevik I. of the Severnaya Zemlya Is. from mainland and connects Laptev and Kara seas.

Vilkomir. See UKMERGĖ.

Villa Acuña. See CIUDAD ACUÑA.

Vil·la Ale·ma·na \'bē-yä-,ä-le-'mä-nä\. City, Valparaíso region, cen. Chile, E of the seaport of Valparaíso; pop. (1992c) 70,664.

Vil·la Al·ta \'bē-yä-'äl-tä\. Municipality, Oaxaca state, Mexico, 45 mi. (72 km.) NE of the city Oaxaca.

Vil·la Bel·la \'bē-yä-'bā-yä\. Frontier town on border with Brazil at N tip of El Beni dept., N Bolivia, at confluence of the Beni and Mamoré rivers; trading center.

Villa Bens. See TARFAYA.

Vil·la·car·ril·lo \,vēl-yä-kär-'rēl-yō\. Commune, Jaén prov., S Spain, 41 mi. (66 km.) NE of the commune of Jaén; pop. (1991c) 11,672.

Villa Cecilia. See CIUDAD MADERO.

Vil·lach \'fi-,läk\ *or Slovenian* **Be·ljak** \'bel-,yäk\. City, Carinthia, Austria, on Drava River 21 mi. (34 km.) W of Klagenfurt; pop. (1991c) 54,640; railroad junction; tourist resort; manufactures paper, beer; mineral springs nearby.

Villa Cisneros. See DAKHLA 2.

Vil·la Cla·ra \'bē-yä-'klä-rä\. Province of W cen. Cuba. See table at CUBA.

Villa Concepción. See CONCEPCIÓN 5.

Vil·la Con·sti·tu·ción \'bē-yä-,kòn-stē-,tü-'syòn\ *also* **Constitución.** Port, Santa Fe prov., E cen. Argentina, on Paraná River 23 mi. (37 km.) SE of Rosario; pop. (1980p) 36,157.

Vil·la de Cu·ra \'bē-yä-thā-'kü-rä\ *or* **Cura.** Town, Aragua state, N Venezuela, 50 mi. (81 km.) SW of Caracas.

Villa del Pilar. See PILAR 2.

Vil·la Do·lo·res \'bē-yä-thō-'lō-rās\. Town, W Córdoba prov., N cen. Argentina, 75 mi. (121 km.) SW of the city of Córdoba; pop. (1980p) 21,508.

Vil·la Flo·res \'bē-yä-'flō-rās\. Municipality, Chiapas state, Mexico, 50 mi. (81 km.) S of Tuxtla Gutiérrez; pop. (1990p) 73,113.

Vil·la·fran·ca de los Bar·ros \,bēl-yä-'fräŋ-kä-,thā-lōs-'bär-,rōs\. Commune, Badajoz prov., SW Spain, 37 mi. (60 km.) SE of the city of Badajoz; pop. (1991c) 12,443.

Vil·la·fran·ca di Ve·ro·na \,vē-lä-'fräŋ-kä-,dē-ve-'rō-nä\. Commune, Verona prov., Veneto, NE Italy, 10 mi. (16 km.) SW of the commune of Verona; pop. (1989c) 26,547; treaty bet. Austria and France signed here 1859.

Vil·la·fro, Lake \bē-'yä-frō\ *or* **Lake Vi·la·fro** \bē-'lä-\. Lake, S Peru; regarded by some as remotest source of Amazon River through the Apurímac.

Vil·la Fron·te·ra \'bē-yä-frón-'tā-rä\. Town, Coahuila state, NE Mexico in outliers of Sierra Madre Oriental.

Vil·la·gar·cía de Aro·sa \,bēl-yä-gär-'sē-ä-,thā-ä-'rō-sä\ *or* **Villagarcía de Arou·sa** \-ä-'raù-sä\ *or* **Vi·la·gar·cía de Arousa** \,bē-lä-\. Seaport, Pontevedra prov., NW Spain, on Atlantic Ocean 13 mi. (21 km.) NNW of the commune of Pontevedra; pop. (1991c) 32,170.

Village, The. City, Oklahoma co., cen. Oklahoma, N suburb of Oklahoma City; pop. (1990c) 10,353.

Vil·la Giu·sti \,vē-lä-'jüs-tē\. Villa, near Padua, Padova prov., Veneto, NE Italy, where during WWI armistice bet. Italy and Austria-Hungary was signed Nov. 1918.

Vil·la Grove \'vi-lə\. City, Douglas co., E cen. Illinois, 20 mi. (32 km.) S of Champaign; pop. (1990c) 2734.

Vil·la·guay \,bē-yä-'gwī\. Town, Entre Ríos prov., E Argentina, 90 mi. (145 km.) E of Paraná; pop. (1980p) 18,699.

Villa Gustavo A. Madero. See GUSTAVO A. MADERO, VILLA.

Vil·la Hayes \,bē-yä-'īs, -yä-'hāz\. Town, W cen. Paraguay, on right bank of the Paraguay River 9 mi. (15 km.) N of Asunción; pop. (1992p) 11,843; former ✻ of Presidente Hayes dept.; named for Rutherford B. Hayes, president of the U.S. who arbitrated Argentina-Paraguay boundary.

Vil·la·her·mo·sa \,bē-yä-er-'mō-sä\; *formerly* **San Juan Bau·tis·ta** \sän-'hwän-baù-'tēs-tä\. City, ✻ of Tabasco state, SE Mexico, on the Grijalva River; pop. (1980c) 158,216; ships sugar; 17th cent. cathedral; anthropological and archaeological museums containing artifacts from excavations at La Venta (*q.v.*); university (1958).

Vil·la Hills \'vi-lə\. City, Kenton co., N Kentucky, S of Cincinnati, Ohio; pop. (1990c) 7739.

Vil·la·jo·yo·sa \,bēl-yä-hō-'yō-sä\. Seaport town and commune, Alicante prov., SE Spain, 20 mi. (32 km.) NE of the commune of Alicante; pop. (1991c) 21,982.

Vil·lal·ba 1. \bē-'yäl-bä\. Municipality, S cen. Puerto Rico, in hilly region NE of Ponce; pop. (1990c) 23,559.
2. \bēl-'yäl-bə\. Commune, Lugo prov., NW Spain, 16 mi. (26 km.) NNW of the commune of Lugo; pop. (1991c) 16,110.

Vil·la Ma·ría \,bē-yä-mä-'rē-ä\. City, cen. Córdoba prov., N cen. Argentina, ab. 90 mi. (145 km.) SE of the city of Córdoba; pop. (1980c) 67,560.

Vil·la·no·va \,vi-lə-'nō-və\. Locality, Delaware co., SE Pennsylvania, ab. 6 mi. (10 km.) W of Philadelphia; Villanova Univ. (1842), Northeastern Christian Junior Coll. (1956).

Vil·la·nue·va de Cór·do·ba \,bēl-yä-'nwā-bä-thā-'kōr-thō-bä\. Commune, Córdoba prov., S Spain, 31 mi. (50 km.) NNE of the city of Córdoba; pop. (1991c) 10,402.

Vil·la·nue·va del Ar·zo·bis·po \,bēl-yä-'nwā-bä-thā-thel-,är-sō-'bēs-pō\. Commune, Jaén prov., S Spain, 47 mi. (76 km.) NE of the commune of Jaén; pop. (1991c) 8555.

Vil·la·nue·va y Gel·trú \,bē-lä-'nwā-bä-ē-hel-'trü\ *or* **Vi·la·no·va i la Gel·trú** \,bē-lä-'nō-bä-,ē-lä-\. Commune, Barcelona prov., NE Spain, on Mediterranean 26 mi. (42 km.) WSW of the city of Barcelona; pop. (1991p) 45,864; textiles.

Vil·lány \'vē-,län\. Town, Baranya co., S Hungary, near Croatian border, ab. 18 mi. (29 km.) SSE of Pécs; pop. (1980p) 2764.

Vil·la Oli·va \ˈbē-yä-ō-ˈlē-bä\. Town, Neembucú dept., SW corner of Paraguay, on the Paraguay River 55 mi. (89 km.) S of Asunción.

Villa Orotava. See LA OROTAVA.

Vil·la Park \ˈvi-lə\. **1.** City, Orange co., SW California, NE of Santa Ana; pop. (1990c) 6299.
2. Village, Du Page co., NE Illinois, 10 mi. (16 km.) W of Chicago; pop. (1990c) 22,253.

Vil·la Rica \ˌvi-lə-ˈri-kə\. City, Carroll and Douglas cos., W Georgia, 30 mi. (48 km.) W of Atlanta; pop. (1990c) 6542; gold-mining center in early 19th cent.

Villa Rica de la Vera Cruz. See VERACRUZ 2.

Vil·lar·re·al \ˌbēl-yär-rā-ˈäl\ *or in full* **Villarreal de los In·fan·tes** \thā-ˌlōs-in-ˈfän-tās\ *also shortened to* **Vi·la–re·al** \ˌbē-lä-rā-ˈäl\. Commune, Castellón de la Plana prov., E Spain, 7 mi. (11 km.) SSW of the city of Castellón de la Plana; pop. (1991p) 37,845; manufactures paper.

Vil·lar·ri·ca \ˌbē-yä-ˈrē-kä\. **1.** Volcanic peak, S cen. Chile, near Argentine border and bet. regions of La Araucanía and Los Lagos; 9318 ft. (2840 m.).
2. City, ✻ of Guairá dept., S cen. Paraguay, 70 mi. (113 km.) SE of Asunción; pop. (1992p) 27,673; sugar refineries, distilleries, sawmills, flour mills; founded 1570s.

Vil·lar·ro·ble·do \ˌbēl-yär-rō-ˈblā-thō\. Commune, Albacete prov., SE Spain, 42 mi. (68 km.) WNW of the commune of Albacete; pop. (1991c) 20,705.

Villas, Las. See LAS VILLAS.

Vil·la·sis \vē-ˈyä-sēs\. Municipality, SE Pangasinan prov., Luzon, Philippines, near right bank of Agno River 25 mi. (40 km.) ESE of Lingayen; pop. (1980c) 39,126.

Vil·la·vi·cen·cio \ˌbē-yä-bē-ˈsen-ˌsyō\. Town, ✻ of Meta dept., cen. Colombia, on Meta River ab. 45 mi. (70 km.) SE of Bogotá; munic. pop. (1992e) 233,000.

Vil·la·vi·cio·sa \ˌbē-yä-bē-ˈsyō-sä\. Commune, Asturias prov., NW Spain, on inlet of Bay of Biscay 21 mi. (34 km.) ENE of Oviedo; pop. (1991p) 15,041.

Ville de Laval. See LAVAL 2.

Ville–de–Pa·ris \ˌvēl-də-pä-ˈrē\. Department of France. See table at FRANCE.

Ville·franche \ˌvēl-ˈfrä^{n}sh\. **1.** *or in full* **Villefranche–sur–Mer** \-sǖr-ˈmer\. Seaport, Alpes-Maritimes dept., SE France, on coast E of Nice; pop. (1990c) 8123; resort. Restored medieval chapel decorated by artist Jean Cocteau.
2. *also* **Villefranche–sur–Saône** \-sǖr-ˈsōn\. Commune, Rhône dept., E cen. France, on Saône River 16 mi. (26 km.) NNW of Lyon; pop. (1990c) 29,889; textiles; trades in wine.

Villefranche–de–Rou·ergue \-də-rü-ˈerg\. Commune, Aveyron dept., S France, ab. 26 mi. (42 km.) W of Rodez; 13th–16th cent. church; 15th–16th cent. Carthusian monastery; commune founded c. 1252.

Villefranche–sur–Mer. See VILLEFRANCHE 1.

Villefranche–sur–Saône. See VILLEFRANCHE 2.

Ville·juif \ˌvēl-ˈzhwēf\. Commune, Val-de-Marne dept., N France, S suburb of Paris; pop. (1990c) 48,671.

Ville–Ma·rie \ˌvēl-mə-ˈrē\. Town, SW Quebec, Canada, on E shore of Lake Timiskaming ab. 72 mi. (116 km.) N of North Bay, Ontario; pop. (1991c) 2581.

Ville–Marie de Montréal. See MONTREAL 3.

Ville·mom·ble \vēl-ˈmō^{n}bl^{ə}\. Commune, Seine-St.-Denis dept., N France, ENE suburb of Paris.

Vil·le·na \bēl-ˈyā-nä\. Commune, Alicante prov., SE Spain, 26 mi. (42 km.) NW of the city of Alicante; pop. (1991p) 31,206; soap.

Ville·nave–d'Or·non \vēl-ˌnäv-dȯr-ˈnō^{n}\. Commune, Gironde dept., SW France, just S of Bordeaux in the Graves dist.

Villeneuve–d'Agen. See VILLENEUVE-SUR-LOT.

Ville·neuve–la–Ga·renne \vēl-ˌnœv-lä-gä-ˈren\. Commune, Hauts-de-Seine dept., N France, ab. 5 mi. (8 km.) NNW of Paris.

Villeneuve–le–Roi \-lər-ˈwä\. Commune, Val-de-Marne dept., N France, SSE suburb of Paris.

Villeneuve–Saint–Georges \-se^{n}-ˈzhȯrzh\. Commune, Val-de-Marne dept., N France, on the Seine 7 mi. (11 km.) SSE of Paris.

Villeneuve–sur–Lot \-sǖr-ˈlȯt\ *or sometimes* **Villeneuve–d'Agen** \-dä-ˈzhe^{n}\. Commune, Lot-et-Garonne dept., SW France, on Lot River 13 mi. (21 km.) N of Agen.

Ville Platte \vēl-ˈplat\. Town, ⊗ of Evangeline parish, S cen. Louisiana, 35 mi. (56 km.) NNW of Lafayette; pop. (1990c) 9037.

Vil·lers–Cot·te·rêts \ˌvē-ˌler-kȯ-ˈtre\. Town, Aisne dept., N France, 14 mi. (23 km.) SW of Soissons; birthplace of author Alexandre Dumas père 1802; forest in vicinity was a battlefield in WWI; severe fighting 1918 when it was the scene of the opening action of Allied offensive.

Ville·rupt \vēl-ˈrǖ\. Commune, Meurthe-et-Moselle dept., NE France, on Alzette River on Luxembourg border 36 mi. (58 km.) N of Metz.

Ville·ur·banne \ˌvē-lœr-ˈbän\. Industrial commune, Rhône dept., E cen. France, E suburb of Lyon; pop. (1990c) 119,848; metal goods, textiles, chemicals.

Vil·ling·en–Schwen·ning·en \ˈfi-liŋ-ən-ˈshve-niŋ-ən\. Twin cities, Baden-Würtemberg, Germany, ab. 30 mi. (48 km.) E of Freiburg; combined pop. (1992e) 80,121.

Villmanstrand. See LAPPEENRANTA.

Vil·lu·pu·ram \ˌvi-lə-ˈpu̇r-əm\. Town, NE Tamil Nadu, SE India, 92 mi. (148 km.) SSW of Madras; pop. (1991p) 88,916.

Vil·ni·us \ˈvil-nē-əs\ *or Pol.* **Wil·no** \ˈvil-nō\ *or Russ.* **Vil·na** \ˈvil-nə\ *or* **Vil·no** \-nō\; *Ger.* **Wil·na** \ˈvil-nə\. Commercial city, ✻ of Lithuania, 57 mi. (92 km.) ESE of Kaunas; pop. (1989p) 582,000; railroad junction; agricultural machinery, electrical equipment, foodstuffs, machine tools; seat of Roman Catholic and Orthodox archbishops; cathedral; numerous 17th cent. churches; ruins of castle; university (1579, abolished 1832, reestablished 1919).
History: Founded in 10th cent.; made ✻ of Lithuania 1323; destroyed by Teutonic Knights 1377; suffered frequently from plagues, fires, and invasions 15th–18th cents.; passed to Russia 1795; noted European center for Jewish learning for several centuries. Occupied by Germans 1915–19; made ✻ of independent Lithuania 1918; occupied by Polish 1920–39; restored to Lithuania 1939, but in WWII occupied by Soviet troops 1939 and by Germans 1941–44; Jewish population exterminated; made ✻ of Lithuanian S.S.R. 1944; became ✻ of independent Lithuania 1991.

Vilp·pu·la \ˈvil-pu̇-ˌlä\. Town, Häme prov., SW Finland, on railroad line 45 mi. (72 km.) NNE of Tampere; pop. (1980c) 6895.

Vil·voor·de \ˈvil-ˌvȯr-də\ *or* **Vil·vorde** \vēl-ˈvȯrd\. Commune, Brabant prov., cen. Belgium, on Senne River just N of Brussels; pop. (1992e) 33,000.

Vilyandi. See VILJANDI.

Vi·lyui *or* **Vi·lyuy** \vil-ˈyü-ē\. River, W Sakha Rep., Russia in Asia; rises in E Evenki Autonomous Okrug, flows E into Lena River; as chief tributary on the W, it enters the Lena ab. 200 mi. (320 km.) NW of Yakutsk; over 1510 mi. (2425 km.) long; navigable for 900 mi. (1448 km.).

Vi·lyu·isk Mountains \vil-ˈyü-isk\. Mountain range, W Sakha Rep., Russia in Asia, W of Lena River and serving as watershed bet. Olenek and tributaries and the Vilyui tributaries; highest point ab. 3500 ft. (1065 m.).

Vilyuy. See VILYUI.

Vi·mei·ro \vē-ˈmā-rü\. Village, Lisboa dist., W Portugal, near Atlantic Ocean 32 mi. (52 km.) NW of Lisbon; important victory 1808 (Peninsular War) of British Gen. Sir Arthur Wellesley (later duke of Wellington) over French under Gen. Andoche Junot.

Vi·mer·ca·te \ˌvē-mer-ˈkä-tā\. Commune, Milano prov., Lombardy, N Italy, 14 mi. (23 km.) NE of Milan; pop. (1989c) 25,473.

Vim·i·nal \ˈvim-ən-^{ə}l\. One of the Seven Hills of Rome, Italy. See SEVEN HILLS.

\ə\ abut \ə\ matches \$^{ə}$\ kitten, Fr table \ər\ further \a\ ash \ā\ ace \ä\ cot, cart \å\ Fr bac \au̇\ out \b\ Span Avila \ch\ chin \e\ bet \ē\ easy \g\ go \i\ hit \ī\ ice \j\ job \k\ Ger ich, Buch \$^{n}$\ Fr vin \ŋ\ sing \ō\ go \ȯ\ all \ȯ\ law \œ\ Fr bœuf \œ̄\ Fr feu \ȯi\ boy \th\ thin \th\ this \ü\ loot \u̇\ foot \ue\ Ger füllen \ǖ\ Fr rue \y\ yet \$^{y}$\ Fr digne \ˈdēn^{y}\, nuit \ˈnw^{y}ē\ \yü\ few \yu̇\ fury \zh\ vision

Vi·mou·tiers \ˌvē-mü-ˈtyā\. Town, Orne dept., NW France, NE of Argentan; center for Camembert cheese, first made in village 3 mi. (5 km.) SW (see CAMEMBERT).

Vi·my Ridge \ˈvi-mē, vē-ˈmē\. Ridge, Pas-de-Calais dept., N France, near **Vimy** commune, 10 mi. (16 km.) N of Arras; during WWI captured by Canadians with heavy casualties 1917. Many WWI cemeteries in area.

Vi·ña del Mar \ˈbē-nyä-thel-ˈmär\. City, Chile; a residential suburb 6 mi. (10 km.) E of Valparaíso; pop. (1982c) 249,977; important seaside resort; textiles, paint.

Vi·nai·gre, Mont \ˌmōⁿ-vē-ˈnāgrᵊ, -ˈnegrᵊ\. Mountain, Var dept., S France; highest point 2020 ft. (616 m.) in the Estérel.

Vi·nal·ha·ven \ˈvīn-ᵊl-ˌhā-vən\. **1.** Island at mouth of Penobscot Bay off S cen. Maine coast, part of Knox co.

2. Town on S end of Vinalhaven I., Maine; pop. (1990c) 1072; summer resort and fishing center; settled 1789; incorp. 1803.

Vin·cennes **1.** \vin-ˈsenz\. City, ⊗ of Knox co., SW Indiana, on Wabash River 55 mi. (89 km.) S of Terre Haute; pop. (1990c) 19,859; paper products, glass; in agricultural region; Vincennes Univ. (1801); site of George Rogers Clark National Historical Park (see UNITED STATES, *National Historical Parks*).

History: Oldest town in Indiana. On site of a former Indian village, settled by Europeans early 18th cent.; fortified 1732 by French commandant François Marie Bissot, Sieur de Vincennes and renamed after him 1736; ceded to Great Britain 1763 and received English settlers; during American Revolution seized by American soldier George Rogers Clark 1779; ✱ of Indiana Terr. 1800–13 (see NORTHWEST TERRITORY); incorp. 1856.

2. *Fr.* veⁿ-ˈsen\. Commune, Val-de-Marne dept., N France, 5 mi. (8 km.) E of Paris; pop. (1990c) 42,651; 14th cent. castle, the residence of French kings until court moved to Versailles; later a state prison, now restored; extensive park (**Bois de Vin·cennes** \ˌbwäd-veⁿ-ˈsen\) with zoo and racetrack.

Vindau. See VENTSPILS.

Vindava. See VENTA.

Vin·del \ˈvin-dᵊl\. River, Västerbotten prov., N Sweden; flows SE into Ume River; ab. 280 mi. (450 km.) long.

Vin·de·li·cia \ˌvin-də-ˈli-shē-ə\. Ancient Roman province, cen. Europe, S of the Danube River, incl. modern Bavaria, Germany; later called **Rae·tia Se·cun·da** \ˈrē-shē-ə-si-ˈkən-də\.

Vindhyachal. See MIRZAPUR.

Vin·dhya Range \ˈvin-dyə, -dē-ə\. Mountain range, cen. India, extending ENE from Gujarat to the Ganges Valley, dividing the Ganges Basin from the Deccan; greatest elev. 3651 ft. (1113 m.) N of and parallel with the Narmada River.

Vindhya Pra·desh \prə-ˈdäsh, -ˈdesh\. Former state, NE cen. India bet. Uttar Pradesh and Madhya Pradesh; created 1948; merged 1956 in reorganized Madhya Pradesh.

Vindobona *or* **Vindobna.** See VIENNA 5.

Vin·e·gar Hill \ˈvi-ni-gər\. Hill, co. Wexford, SE Ireland, E of Enniscorthy on the Slaney River; 398 ft. (121 m.); scene of defeat of Irish rebels by English Gen. Gerard Lake 1798.

Vine Grove \ˈvīn\. City, Hardin co., cen. Kentucky, 29 mi. (47 km.) SW of Louisville; pop. (1990c) 3586.

Vine·land \ˈvīn-lənd\. **1.** City, Cumberland co., SW New Jersey, 11 mi. (18 km.) ENE of Bridgeton; pop. (1990c) 54,780; glassware, clothing; in area of diversified agriculture; Cumberland County Coll. (1964).

2. Coast, North America. See VINLAND.

Vineta. See JULIN.

Vine·yard Haven \ˈvin-yərd\. Unincorporated settlement, N Martha's Vineyard, SE Massachusetts, on W shore of **Vineyard Haven Harbor,** inlet of Nantucket Sound; pop. (1990c) 1762; summer resort. See TISBURY.

Vineyard Sound. Body of water, SE of Elizabeth Is. and NW of Martha's Vineyard, SE Massachusetts; connects with Nantucket Sound on the NE and Atlantic Ocean on the SW.

Vinh \ˈvin, ˈvi-nyə\. Town, near coast of N Vietnam, ab. 160 mi. (255 km.) S of Hanoi.

Vinh Cam Ranh. See CAM RANH, VINH.

Vinh Long *or* **Vinh·long** \ˈvin-ˈlȯŋ, ˈvi-nyə-\. Town, S Vietnam, on right bank of the Mekong in the delta 65 mi. (105 km.) SW of Ho Chi Minh City (Saigon); pop. (1989c) 81,620.

Vi·ni·ta \vi-ˈnē-tə\. City, ⊗ of Craig co., NE Oklahoma; pop. (1990c) 5804.

Vin·ja·tin·da·ne \ˈvin-yə-ˌtin-də-nə\. See ROMSDAL.

Vin·kov·ci \ˈviŋ-ˌkȯft-sē\. Town, E Croatia, ab. 85 mi. (135 km.) NW of Belgrade; pop. (1991c) 38,580.

Vin·land \ˈvin-lənd\ *also* **Wine·land** \ˈwīn-\ *or* **Vine·land** \ˈvīn-\. A portion of the coast of North America visited and so-called by Norse voyagers, c. 1000 A.D., according to whose accounts it was well-wooded and produced fruit, esp. grapes; has been variously located from E or NE Canada, to New Jersey. See L'ANSE AU MEADOWS.

Vin·ny·tsya *or Russ.* **Vin·ni·tsa** \ˈvi-nit-syə\. **1.** Administrative subdivision of Ukraine; 10,232 sq. mi. (26,501 sq. km.); pop. (1991e) 1,914,400; ✱ Vinnytsya.

2. City, its ✱, on left bank of the upper Bug and on main railroad line 130 mi. (209 km.) SW of Kiev; pop. (1991e) 381,000; fertilizer, footwear; founded in 14th cent.; to Russia 1793.

Vin·son Massif \ˈvin-sən\. Mountain, Sentinel Range, cen. Ellsworth Mts., Antarctica; 16,066 ft. (4897 m.); highest peak in Antarctica.

Vintimille. See VENTIMIGLIA.

Vin·ton \ˈvint-ᵊn\. **1.** County in S Ohio. See table at OHIO.

2. City, ⊗ of Benton co., E cen. Iowa, 19 mi. (31 km.) NW of Cedar Rapids; pop. (1990c) 5103.

3. Town, Calcasieu parish, SW Louisiana, 23 mi. (37 km.) W of Lake Charles; pop. (1990c) 3154.

4. Town, Roanoke co., W cen. Virginia, 4 mi. (6 km.) NE of the city of Roanoke; pop. (1990c) 7665.

Vion·ville \vyōⁿ-ˈvēl\. Village, Moselle dept., NE France, near Metz and near Mars-la-Tour (*q.v.*).

Viosa. See VIJOSË.

Vi·pi·te·no \ˌvē-pē-ˈtā-nō\ *or Ger.* **Ster·zing** \ˈshtert-siŋ\. Town, Bolzano prov., Trentino-Alto Adige, NE Italy, just S of the Brenner Pass; pop. (1981p) 5293; 15th cent. church; several medieval houses; hospital founded by Teutonic Knights 14th cent.

Vipuri. See VYBORG.

Vi·rac \vē-ˈräk\. Port city, ✱ of Catanduanes prov., Catanduanes I., Philippines; pop. (1980c) 40,102.

Vir·den \ˈvərd-ᵊn\. **1.** City, Macoupin co., SW cen. Illinois, 23 mi. (37 km.) SSW of Springfield; pop. (1990c) 3635.

2. Market town, SW Manitoba, Canada, 47 mi. (76 km.) W of Brandon; pop. (1991c) 2894.

Vire \ˈvēr\. **1.** River, Normandy, NW France; flows N past Vire and St.-Lô to the Bay of the Seine near Isigny; ab. 75 mi. (120 km.) long; during WWII featured in Allied D-Day invasion June 1944.

2. Town, Calvados dept., NW France, on Vire River 32 mi. (52 km.) SW of Caen. Important Norman stronghold in Middle Ages. Nearby is the valley **Vau–de–Vire** \ˌvō-də-\ where Olivier Basselin lived in 15th cent. and supposedly composed the lively drinking songs by which the name of the valley became the source of the word *vaudeville.* In WWII suffered heavy damage in Allied Normandy invasion 1944.

Vír·ge·nes \ˈbēr-he-ˌnās\ *or angl.* **Vir·gins** \ˈvər-jənz\ *also* **Cape of the Eleven Thousand Virgins.** Headland, S Argentina, on the N side of the E entrance to the Strait of Magellan; adjoins Point Dungeness.

Vir·gi·lio \vēr-ˈjēl-yō\; *formerly* **Pie·to·la** \ˈpyā-tō-lä\. Commune, Mantova prov., Lombardy, N Italy, ab. 3 mi. (5 km.) S of the commune of Mantova; pop. (1981p) 7,544; on site of ancient **An·des** \ˈan-ˌdēz\, birthplace of poet Virgil 70 B.C.

Vir·gin \ˈvər-jən\. River, SW Utah and SE Nevada; rises in W Kane co., S Utah, flows SW across NW corner of Arizona and across border of Nevada, then S into Lake Mead; 200 mi. (322 km.) long. In Utah portion is Zion Canyon, now included in Zion National Park (see UNITED STATES, *National Parks*).

Virgin Gor·da \ˈgȯr-də\. **1.** One of the British Virgin Is., West Indies; 8 sq. mi. (21 sq. km.); pop. (1980c) 1412.

2. Peak on Virgin Gorda, West Indies; 1370 ft. (418 m.).

Vir·gin·ia \vər-ˈji-nyə, -nē-ə\. **1.** Eastern state of U.S.A., bounded on N by West Virginia and Maryland, on E by Maryland, Chesapeake Bay, and Atlantic Ocean, on S by North Carolina and Tennessee, on W by Kentucky and West Virginia; 36th state in area, 40,767 sq. mi. (105,586 sq. km.); 12th state in population, (1990c) 6,187,358; ✻ Richmond; an original state of the Union, the 10th to ratify the U.S. Constitution (June 25, 1788). See table of states at UNITED STATES.

Nickname: Old Dominion.

State flower: American dogwood.

Motto: Sic Semper Tyrannis (Ever Thus to Tyrants).

Rivers: Potomac, forming N cen., NE, and upper E boundary; Shenandoah, flowing NE to the Potomac in West Virginia; James, flowing from W cen. area E into Atlantic Ocean; Roanoke flowing from W area SE across North Carolina border.

Highest point: Mt. Rogers, 5729 ft. (1746 m.), in Grayson and Smyth cos.

Chief products: Dairy products, tobacco, vegetables; livestock; coal; manufacturing: chemicals, food products, transportation equipment, electrical equipment, textiles; federal-government employment.

Chief cities: Virginia Beach, Norfolk, Richmond.

Political divisions: Divided into the following 95 counties and 41 independent cities (for pronunciation of their names, see their individual entries):

NAME	AREA[1] (sq. mi.)	AREA[1] (sq. km.)	POP. (1990c)	CO. SEAT
Accomac	470	1,217	31,703	Accomac
Albemarle	739	1,914	68,040	Charlottesville
Alleghany	446	1,155	13,176	Covington
Amelia	366	948	8,787	Amelia Courthouse
Amherst	467	1,210	28,578	Amherst
Appomattox	343	888	12,298	Appomattox
Arlington[2]	24	62	170,936	Arlington
Augusta	986	2,554	54,677	Staunton
Bath	540	1,399	4,799	Warm Springs
Bedford	770	1,994	45,656	Bedford
Bland	369	956	6,514	Bland
Botetourt	548	1,419	24,992	Fincastle
Brunswick	579	1,500	15,987	Lawrenceville
Buchanan	508	1,316	31,333	Grundy
Buckingham	576	1,492	12,873	Buckingham
Campbell	524	1,357	47,572	Rustburg
Caroline	544	1,409	19,217	Bowling Green
Carroll	494	1,279	26,594	Hillsville
Charles City	184	477	6,282	Charles City
Charlotte	467	1,210	11,688	Charlotte Courthouse
Chesterfield	460	1,191	209,274	Chesterfield
Clarke	174	451	12,101	Berryville
Craig	336	870	4,372	New Castle
Culpeper	389	1,008	27,791	Culpeper
Cumberland	288	746	7,825	Cumberland
Dickenson	335	868	17,620	Clintwood
Dinwiddie	507	1,313	20,960	Dinwiddie
Essex	250	648	8,689	Tappahannock
Fairfax	399	1,033	818,584	Fairfax
Fauquier	660	1,709	48,741	Warrenton
Floyd	383	992	12,005	Floyd
Fluvanna	282	730	12,429	Palmyra
Franklin	718	1,860	39,549	Rocky Mount
Frederick	433	1,121	45,723	Winchester
Giles	356	922	16,366	Pearisburg
Gloucester	225	583	30,131	Gloucester
Goochland	289	749	14,163	Goochland
Grayson	450	1,166	16,278	Independence
Greene	153	396	10,297	Standardsville
Greensville	301	780	8,853	Emporia
Halifax	800	2,072	29,033	Halifax
Hanover	466	1,207	63,306	Hanover
Henrico	232	601	217,881	Richmond
Henry	384	995	56,942	Martinsville
Highland	416	1,077	2,635	Monterey
Isle of Wight	319	826	25,053	Isle of Wight
James City	148	383	34,859	Williamsburg
King and Queen	318	824	6,289	King and Queen Courthouse
King George	178	461	13,527	King George
King William	278	720	10,913	King William
Lancaster	142	368	10,896	Lancaster
Lee	434	1,124	24,496	Jonesville
Loudoun	517	1,339	86,129	Leesburg
Louisa	514	1,331	20,325	Louisa
Lunenburg	443	1,147	11,419	Lunenburg
Madison	327	847	11,949	Madison
Mathews	87	225	8,348	Mathews
Mecklenburg	626	1,621	29,241	Boydton
Middlesex	132	342	8,653	Saluda
Montgomery	395	1,023	73,913	Christiansburg
Nelson	468	1,212	12,778	Lovingston
New Kent	212	549	10,445	New Kent
Northampton	226	585	13,061	Eastville
Northumberland	200	518	10,524	Heathsville
Nottoway	308	798	14,993	Nottoway
Orange	354	917	21,421	Orange
Page	316	818	21,690	Luray
Patrick	469	1,215	17,473	Stuart
Pittsylvania	1,012	2,621	55,655	Chatham
Powhatan	268	694	15,328	Powhatan
Prince Edward	357	925	17,320	Farmville
Prince George	281	728	27,394	Prince George
Prince William	345	894	215,686	Manassas
Pulaski	327	847	34,496	Pulaski
Rappahannock	267	692	6,622	Washington
Richmond	192	497	7,273	Warsaw
Roanoke	277	717	79,332	Salem
Rockbridge	604	1,564	18,350	Lexington
Rockingham	868	2,248	57,482	Harrisonburg
Russell	483	1,251	28,667	Lebanon
Scott	539	1,396	23,204	Gate City
Shenandoah	507	1,313	31,636	Woodstock
Smyth	435	1,127	32,370	Marion
Southampton	607	1,572	17,550	Courtland
Spotsylvania	409	1,059	57,403	Spotsylvania
Stafford	271	702	61,236	Stafford
Surry	280	725	6,145	Surry
Sussex	496	1,285	10,248	Sussex
Tazewell	522	1,352	45,960	Tazewell
Warren	219	567	26,142	Front Royal
Washington	579	1,500	45,887	Abingdon
Westmoreland	236	611	15,480	Montross
Wise	411	1,064	39,573	Wise
Wythe	460	1,191	25,466	Wytheville
York	123	319	42,422	Yorktown

INDEPENDENT CITIES[3]

NAME	COUNTY	AREA[1] (sq. mi.)	AREA[1] (sq. km.)	POP. (1990c)
Alexandria	Arlington	15	39	111,183
Bedford	Bedford	7	18	6,073
Bristol	Washington	4	10	18,426
Buena Vista	Rockbridge	3	8	6,406
Charlottesville	Albemarle	6	16	40,341
Chesapeake		344	891	151,976
Clifton Forge	Alleghany	2	5	4,679
Colonial Heights	Chesterfield	8	21	16,064
Covington	Alleghany	4	10	6,991
Danville	Pittsylvania	14	36	53,056
Emporia	Greensville	2	5	5,306
Fairfax	Fairfax	6	16	19,622
Falls Church	Fairfax	2	5	9,578
Franklin	Southampton	4	10	7,864
Fredericksburg	Spotsylvania	6	16	19,027
Galax	Carroll and Grayson	3	8	6,670
Hampton		57	148	133,793
Harrisonburg	Rockingham	3	8	30,707
Hopewell	Prince George	7	18	23,101
Lexington	Rockbridge	2	5	6,959
Lynchburg	Campbell	23	60	66,049
Manassas	Prince William			27,957
Manassas Park	Prince William			6,734
Martinsville	Henry	10	26	16,162
Newport News		75	194	170,045
Norfolk		50	130	261,229
Norton	Wise	3	8	4,247
Petersburg	Dinwiddie	8	21	38,386
Poquoson	York			11,005
Portsmouth		18	47	103,907
Radford	Montgomery	5	13	15,940
Richmond	Henrico	37	96	203,056
Roanoke	Roanoke	26	67	96,397
Salem	Roanoke	8	21	23,756
South Boston	Halifax	2	5	6,997
Staunton	Augusta	9	23	24,461
Suffolk[4]		404	1,046	52,141
Virginia Beach		259	671	393,069
Waynesboro	Augusta	7	18	18,549
Williamsburg	James City and York	3	8	11,530
Winchester	Frederick	3	8	21,947

[1]Area = land area.

[2]Governed as a unit, without districts or other subdivisions and classified as urban with no incorp. places. The city of Alexandria is located in but independent of the county.

[3]These 41 cities have the status of counties. They are located geographically in the counties named, which do not include their area and population figures. Counties are not given for cities which have annexed their parent county.

[4]The former Nansemond co. was consolidated with the independent city of Suffolk, Jan. 1, 1974.

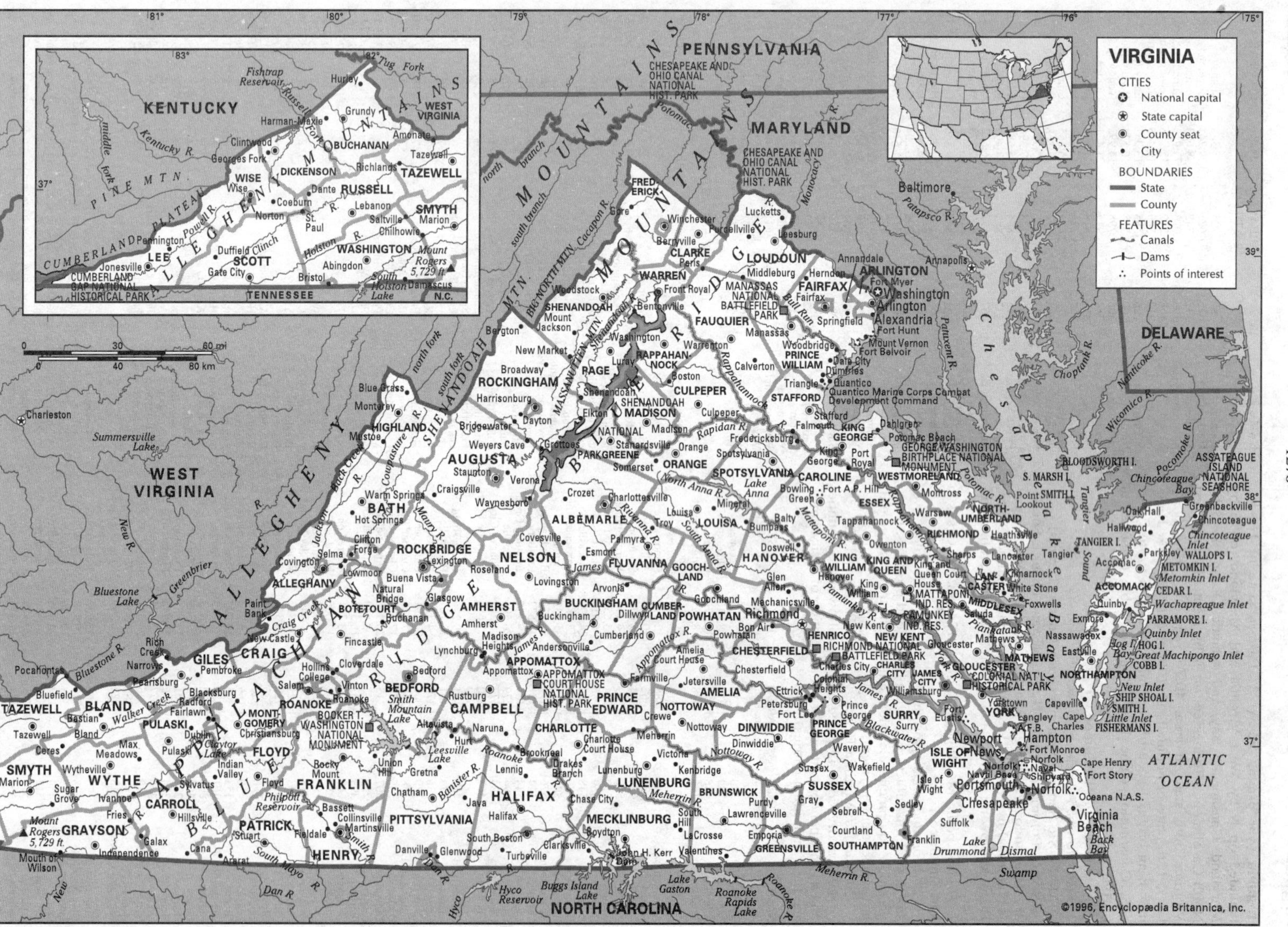
VIRGINIA
CITIES
National capital
State capital
County seat
City
BOUNDARIES
State
County
FEATURES
Canals
Dams
Points of interest
PENNSYLVANIA
MARYLAND
DELAWARE
WEST VIRGINIA
KENTUCKY
TENNESSEE
NORTH CAROLINA
ATLANTIC OCEAN
Chesapeake Bay
BLUE RIDGE
ALLEGHENY MOUNTAINS
APPALACHIAN RIDGE
Washington
Richmond
Baltimore
Annapolis
Norfolk
Virginia Beach
Chesapeake
Portsmouth
Newport News
Hampton
Alexandria
Arlington
Roanoke
Lynchburg
Charlottesville
Fredericksburg
Petersburg
Danville
Charleston
CHESAPEAKE AND OHIO CANAL NATIONAL HIST. PARK
ASSATEAGUE ISLAND NATIONAL SEASHORE
SHENANDOAH NATIONAL PARK
MANASSAS NATIONAL BATTLEFIELD PARK
RICHMOND NATIONAL BATTLEFIELD PARK
APPOMATTOX COURT HOUSE NATIONAL HIST. PARK
COLONIAL NAT'L HISTORICAL PARK
BOOKER T. WASHINGTON NATIONAL MONUMENT
GEORGE WASHINGTON BIRTHPLACE NATIONAL MONUMENT
CUMBERLAND GAP NATIONAL HISTORICAL PARK
Mount Rogers 5,729 ft.
0 30 60 mi
0 40 80 km
©1996, Encyclopædia Britannica, Inc.

History: Orig. inhabited by American Indians when futile attempts were made by English navigator Sir Walter Raleigh to found settlements 1584–87; first royal charter to London (Virginia) Company followed by first permanent settlement, made by colonists sent out by this company, at Jamestown 1607; first popular assembly in America convened 1619; colony finally thrived primarily on successful tobacco cultivation introduced to settlers by Indians; one of the first colonies to express resistance to the Stamp Act and other British taxes 1765; active in movement for independence during the Revolution; scene of surrender of British Lord Charles Cornwallis at Yorktown 1781; NW part of W lands ceded to U.S. 1784, S part admitted to the Union as the state of Kentucky 1792; ratified the U.S. Constitution June 25, 1788; although slavery had been outlawed, it continued to be important part of economy; tensions heightened bet. slaveholders and abolitionists during first half of 19th cent.; passed ordinance of secession 1861; W counties remained loyal to the Union, separated from Virginia 1861 and admitted to the Union as the state of West Virginia 1863; scene of many battles of the Civil War, among them Bull Run (first and second), Fair Oaks, Chancellorsville, Fredericksburg, the Wilderness, Cold Harbor, and many engagements in Shenandoah Valley; readmitted to Union Jan. 26, 1870. New constitution promulgated 1902, revised 1971.

2. City, ⊗ of Cass co., W cen. Illinois, 30 mi. (48 km.) NW of Springfield; pop. (1990c) 1767.

3. City, St. Louis co., NE Minnesota, 20 mi. (32 km.) E of Hibbing; pop. (1990c) 9410; lake resort; iron mines; Mesabi Community Coll. (1918).

4. Town, Free State, Rep. of South Africa, ab. 80 mi. (130 km.) NE of Bloemfontein.

Virginia Beach. Independent city, SE Virginia, on Atlantic Ocean, bordering Norfolk on E and S; 259 sq. mi. (671 sq. km.); pop. (1990c) 393,069; naval facilities; summer resort; marine science museum. The pop. increased more than twentyfold bet. 1960 and 1970 and grew by about 50 percent in the 1970s and again in the 1980s.

Virginia City. 1. Town, ⊗ of Madison co., SW Montana; pop. (1990c) 142; a tourist center with many restored buildings; founded 1863, after discovery of gold in Alder Gulch nearby; became Montana's first incorporated town 1864; territorial ✱ 1865–75.

2. Village, ⊗ of Storey co., W Nevada, 16 mi. (26 km.) SSE of Reno; settled 1859 at time of discovery on this site of the Comstock Lode, a gold and silver lode which until 1880s yielded half the silver output of the U.S. Samuel Clemens (Mark Twain) worked for its newspaper; town now restored as tourist attraction.

Virginia Mountains *also* **Virginia Range.** Small range W Nevada, S of Pyramid Lake; highest point **Virginia Peak** ab. 8365 ft. (2550 m.).

Virginia Pass. Mountain pass, Tuolumne co., cen. California, at N end of Yosemite National Park; 10,500 ft. (3200 m.); one of passes most used by emigrants and explorers in crossing the Sierra Nevada Mts.

Vir·gin Islands \ˈvər-jən\. Group of islands, NE West Indies, westernmost of the Lesser Antilles, ab. 60 mi. (95 km.) E of Puerto Rico. Divided bet. Great Britain and U.S.A.: (1) The **British Virgin Islands,** a British dependent territory; 59 sq. mi. (153 sq. km.); pop. (1990e) 14,786; ✱ Road Town (on Tortola I.); chief islands: Tortola, Virgin Gorda, Anegada, Jost Van Dyke, Peter, and Norman; includes also ab. 24 other small islands; tourism; fruit. (2) *Officially,* the **Virgin Islands of the United States;** *before 1917* **Danish West Indies,** an unincorporated territory, consisting of the islands St. Thomas, St. Croix, and St. John, and ab. 50 islets; 133 sq. mi. (345 sq. km.); pop. (1990c) 101,809; ✱ Charlotte Amalie. **Virgin Islands National Park** is situated on St. John I. (see UNITED STATES, *National Parks*); tourism; sugar, cattle.

History: Inhabited by Carib natives when discovered and named by explorer Christopher Columbus 1493; St. Croix occupied by Dutch, English, French, and Spanish and at one time owned by Knights of Malta; St. Thomas occupied by Denmark 1666, St. John in 1684 and St. Croix in 1733 (the three islands estab. as a Danish colony 1754); British group, part of Leeward Is. colony until formation of West Indies (Federation), of which the British Virgin Is. were not a member, acquired by England 1666. Danish group, known as Danish West Indies, purchased by U.S. 1917 (partly because of its strategic location to Panama Canal) and name changed to Virgin Is.; until 1931 administered by U.S. Navy Department; Organic Act 1936 (later revised) established governmental system; governor first elected by popular vote 1970; area suffered extensive damage by hurricane 1995.

Virgin Mountains. Range, NW Arizona, extending along E bank of Virgin River into SE Nevada.

Virgin Passage. Channel bet. W St. Thomas I., Virgin Is. of the U.S. and Culebra I., Puerto Rico; ab. 9 mi. (15 km.) wide.

Virgins. See VÍRGENES.

Viroconium. See WROXETER.

Vi·ro·qua \vī-ˈrōk-wə\. City, ⊗ of Vernon co., SW Wisconsin, 25 mi. (40 km.) SE of La Crosse; pop. (1990c) 3922.

Vi·ro·vi·ti·ca \vē-ˈrȯ-vē-ˌtēt-sä, ˌvē-rȯ-ˈvē-\ *or Hung.* **Ve·rö·cze** \ˈver-œt-ˌsā\. Town, Croatia, 65 mi. (105 km.) E of Zagreb; pop. (1991c) 22,931.

Vir·rat \ˈvir-rät\. Town, Häme prov., SW cen. Finland, at N end of Näsijärvi.

Virtsjärv. See VÕRTS-JÄRV.

Vi·ru·du·na·gar *or* **Vi·ru·dhu·na·gar** \ˈvir-ə-ˌdə-nə-ˌgər\. Town, Tamil Nadu, India, ab. 25 mi. (40 km.) SW of Madurai; pop. (1991p) 70,951.

Vi·ru Harbour \ˈvir-ü\. Harbor, W side of S end of New Georgia I., cen. Solomon Is., W Pacific Ocean.

Vi·run·ga \vē-ˈrüŋ-gä\ *also* **Mfum·bi·ro** \əm-ˈfüm-bē-ˌrō, -füm-ˈbē-\ *or* **Mu·fum·bi·ro** \mə-ˈfüm-bē-ˌrō, -füm-ˈbē-\. Range of volcanic mountains, E Africa, in E Democratic Rep. of the Congo, SW Uganda, and Rwanda, N of Lake Kivu; highest peak Karisimbi 14,187 ft. (4324 m.) on border bet. Rwanda and Democratic Rep. of the Congo.

Virunga National Park. Extensive park, E Democratic Rep. of the Congo, bet. Lake Kivu and Lake Edward; 3088 sq. mi. (8000 sq. km.); a game preserve and gorilla sanctuary estab. 1925, subsequently enlarged.

Vi·ry–Cha·til·lon \vē-ˌrē-ˌshä-tē-ˈyō^{n}\. Commune, Essone dept., N France, S of Paris.

Vis \ˈvēs\ *or Ital.* **Lis·sa** \ˈli-sə, ˈlē-\; *anc.* **Is·sa** \ˈi-sə\. **1.** Island, Croatia, in Adriatic Sea, SSW of Split; 33 sq. mi. (86 sq. km.); pop. (1991p) 4169; has fertile central plain; highest point 1926 ft. (587 m.) in SW; wine, citrus fruit; fishing.

History: Ruled by Venice from 996; held by French during Napoleonic Wars until British victory over Franco-Venetian squadron 1811 in nearby waters; ceded to Austria 1815; nearby waters again scene of naval battle 1866 in which Austrians defeated Italians; island became Yugoslav after WWI; occupied by Axis forces in WWII; when Croatia declared independence 1991, Vis became a part of it.

2. Chief town on the island of Vis, Croatia; palace of Venetian counts; ruins of ancient Greek, then Roman city of Issa.

Visakhapatnam. See VISHAKHAPATNAM.

Vi·sa·lia \vi-ˈsāl-yə\. City, ⊗ of Tulare co., S cen. California, 38 mi. (61 km.) SE of Fresno; pop. (1990c) 75,636; Coll. of the Sequoias (1926); settled 1852; the pop. has increased by more than 50 percent every 10 years since 1960.

Vi·sa·yan Islands \vi-ˈsī-ən\ *also* **Vi·sa·yas** \-yəz\ *or* **Bi·sa·yas** \bi-ˈsī-əz\. Large group of islands, cen. Philippines; 23,944 sq. mi. (62,015 sq. km.); inhabited chiefly by the Bisayan peoples; chief islands Panay, Samar, Leyte, Cebu, Negros, Bohol, Masbate, and the Romblon group; adjacent are many smaller islands.

Visayan Sea. Open body of interisland water, cen. Philippines, bordered on N by Masbate, on E by Leyte and Cebu, on

S by Negros, and on W by Panay; connects with Sibuyan Sea by Jintotolo Channel, with Mindanao Sea by Tanon Strait, and with Sulu Sea by Guimaras Strait.

Visayas. See VISAYAN ISLANDS.

Vis·by \ˈviz-bē\ *or Ger.* **Wis·by** \ˈviz-bē\. Seaport, ⊗ of Gotland prov., Sweden; on Gotland I., in Baltic Sea; remains of medieval walls; seaside resort; inhabited long before it became a major commercial center of N Europe 10th–14th cents.; member of Hanseatic League.

Vis·count Mel·ville Sound \ˈvī-kau̇nt-ˈmel-ˌvil, -vəl\; *formerly* **Melville Sound.** Body of water, Northwest Territories and Nunavut, N Canada, in Arctic Archipelago, bet. Melville I. on the N and Victoria I. on the S.

Vi·sé \vē-ˈzā\. Commune, Liège prov., Belgium, NE of the city of Liège; pop. (1991c) 17,019.

Vi·seu *also* **Vi·zeu** \vi-ˈzā-ü\. **1.** District of N cen. Portugal. See table at PORTUGAL.
2. Commune, its ✻, 41 mi. (66 km.) NE of Coimbra; pop. (1991p) 83,016; wine; 12th and 16th cent. cathedral; Roman and Moorish ruins; train collision nearby Sept. 11, 1985 resulted in 100 deaths.

Vi·sha·kha·pat·nam *or* **Vi·sa·kha·pat·nam** \vi-ˌshä-kə-ˈpət-nəm\ *also* **Vi·za·ga·pa·tam** \vi-ˌzä-gə-ˈpə-təm\. City, NE Andhra Pradesh, E India, on Bay of Bengal 380 mi. (611 km.) NE of Madras; pop. (1991p) 752,037; a major port; only protected harbor on the Coromandel Coast; exports sugar; shipyard; university (1926; at N end of bay). Trading station estab. by English 17th cent.

Visla. See VISTULA.

Vis·lin·ski Za·liv *or* **Vis·lin·skiy Zaliv** \vis-ˈlin-skē-zä-ˈlyif\ *or Pol.* **Za·lew Wiś·la·ny** \ˈzä-lef-vēsh-ˈlä-nē\ *or Ger.* **Fri·sches Haff** \ˈfri-shəs-ˌhäf\ *or Eng.* **Vis·tu·la Lagoon** \ˈvish-chə-lə, ˈvis-tə-\. Lagoon on SW coast of Baltic Sea; bet. Poland and Russia's Kaliningrad Oblast, 56 mi. (90 km.) long, 4 to 12 mi. (6 to 19 km.) wide; separated from Gulf of Danzig by long, narrow spit of land (**Vistula Spit** *or Russ.* **Bal·tiy·ska·ya Ko·sa** \bäl-ˈtē-skə-yə-kə-ˈsä\ *or Pol.* **Mie·rze·ja Wiś·la·na** \mye-ˈzhe-yä-vēsh-ˈlä-nə\ *or Ger.* **Fri·sche Neh·rung** \ˈfri-shə-ˈnā-ru̇ŋ\) which has an opening at N end; receives the Pregolya at NE; formerly in East Prussia; divided 1945 bet. Poland and U.S.S.R.

Vi·so, Mount \-ˈvē-zō\ *or* **Mon·vi·so** \mōm-\. Peak, Torino prov., Piedmont, Italy, 40 mi. (64 km.) SW of Turin near the French border; highest peak in Cottian Alps. See table at ALPS.

Vis·ta \ˈvis-tə\. City, San Diego co., SW California, N of the city of San Diego; pop. (1990c) 71,872; pop. doubled bet. 1980 and 1990.

Vistritsa. See ALIÁKMON.

Vis·tu·la \ˈvish-chə-lə, ˈvis-tə-\ *or Pol.* **Wis·ła** \ˈvē-swä\ *or Russ.* **Vis·la** \ˈvē-slə\ *or Ger.* **Weich·sel** \ˈvīk-səl\. River, Poland; rises on N slope of the Carpathian Mts. in SW Poland; flows in a great curve NE, N, and NW through Warsaw and Toruń, then N into the Baltic Sea at Gdańsk; 675 mi. (1086 km.) long; navigable for most of its course; its chief tributaries on left are Bzura and Pilica; on right the Bug, San, Wisłoka, and Dunajec.

Vistula Lagoon *and* **Vistula Spit.** See VISLINSKI ZALIV.

Visurgis. See WESER 2.

Vitebsk. See VITSYEBSK.

Vi·ter·bo \vē-ˈter-bō\. **1.** Province of Lazio, cen. Italy. See table at ITALY.
2. *anc.* **Vi·cus El·bii** \ˈvī-kəs-ˈel-bē-ˌī\. Commune, its ✻, 42 mi. (68 km.) NNW of Rome; pop. (1991p) 58,353; center of an agricultural region; 12th cent. Gothic cathedral; 13th cent. episcopal palace; 13th cent. town hall; 15th cent. Farnese palace; churches of 9th, 11th, and 12th cents.; medieval walls, gates, and fountains. Orig. an Etruscan town; to Romans early 3d cent. B.C.; in medieval times long a rival of Rome; home to several popes; lost some importance after Papacy was transferred to Avignon (1309).

Vi·ti·az Strait \ˈvē-tē-ˌaz\. Channel, W Pacific Ocean, separating island of New Guinea from Long I. and Umboi I. and connecting Bismarck Sea with Solomon Sea; ab. 150 mi. (240 km.) long by 35 mi. (56 km.) wide.

Vi·ti Le·vu \ˈvē-tē-ˈlā-vü\. Island, Fiji, SW Pacific Ocean; 90 mi. (145 km.) from E to W and 50 mi. (81 km.) from N to S; 4010 sq. mi. (10,386 sq. km.); largest island in Fiji group; chief town Suva, ✻ of Fiji. Most of it mountainous; highest point Mt. Tomaniivi 4341 ft. (1323 m.). Has several sizable streams; largest is the Rewa in the E. Most of its villages on the coast on a highway that encircles the island. Produces sugar.

Vi·tim \və-ˈtēm\. River, S Russia in Asia; rises in cen. Buryatia, flows NE and N draining the **Vitim Plateau** and forming in part the NE boundary of the republic, then across NE Irkutsk Oblast to join the Lena on SW border of Sakha; 1133 mi. (1823 km.) long.

Vi·to·ria \vē-ˈtōr-ē-ä\ *or Basque* **Gas·teiz** \ˈgäsh-ˌtās\. City, ✻ of Basque Country autonomous community and of Álava prov., N Spain, 50 mi. (81 km.) W of Pamplona; pop. (1991p) 204,961; furniture; 12th–14th cent. cathedral; several medieval churches; museums; scene of battle 1813 in which allied forces under English Gen. Sir Arthur Wellesley (later duke of Wellington) defeated the French, driving them from Spain, leading to the end of the Peninsular War.

Vi·tó·ria \vē-ˈtōr-yə\. Seaport, ✻ of Espírito Santo state, E Brazil, on Espírito Santo River ab. 250 mi. (402 km.) NE of Rio de Janeiro; munic. pop. (1991p) 258,243; ships coffee; sugar refineries; founded 1535; until 1960s leading iron-ore port of Brazil.

Vi·tó·ria da Con·qui·sta \vē-ˈtōr-yə-dȧ-kōn-ˈkē-stə\. City, Bahia state, E Brazil; pop. (1991p) 179,868.

Vi·tó·ria de San·to An·tão \vē-ˈtōr-yə-dē-ˌsȧn-tü-ȧn-ˈtau̇ⁿ\. City, E Pernambuco state, E Brazil, on railroad line just W of Recife; munic. pop. (1991p) 106,644.

Vi·to·ri·no Frei·re \ˌvē-tȯ-ˈrē-nō-ˈfrā-rə\. Municipality, Maranhão state, NE Brazil; pop. (1980c) 88,215.

Vi·tré \vē-ˈtrā\. Town, Ille-et-Vilaine dept., NW France, 22 mi. (35 km.) E of Rennes; several 15th–16th cent. buildings; 14th cent. castle; 15th cent. cathedral; once a Huguenot stronghold.

Vi·try–le–Fran·çois \vē-ˌtrē-lə-fräⁿ-ˈswä\. Town, Marne dept., NE France, on the Marne 20 mi. (32 km.) SE of Châlons-sur-Marne; built 1545 by Francis I; in WWI scene of fighting during battle of the Marne 1914; suffered heavy damage WWII.

Vitry–sur–Seine \-ˌsu̇r-ˈsān, -ˈsen\. Commune, Val-de-Marne dept., N France, SSE suburb of Paris; pop. (1990c) 82,820.

Vit·syebsk \ˈvēt-syipsk\ *or* **Vi·tebsk** \ˈvē-tipsk\. **1.** Administrative subdivision of Belarus; 15,483 sq. mi. (40,101 sq. km.); pop. (1991e) 1,434,200; ✻ Vitsyebsk; in basin of the Western Dvina with extensive forests and many swamp regions. Economy primarily agricultural (rye, flax, livestock, dairying).
2. City, its ✻, in NE part of the country, on both banks of the Western Dvina 140 mi. (225 km.) NE of Minsk; pop. (1991e) 361,500; on the Riga-Moscow railroad line; important industrial center, producing machine tools; several medieval churches.
History: First mentioned 1021; trade center and chief town of an independent principality for ab. 200 years; long in an area of contention; came under Lithuania 1320 and under Poland in 16th cent.; came under Russia after First Partition of Poland 1772; in WWII occupied by Germans 1941–1944 and heavily damaged.

Vit·tel \vē-ˈtel\. Town, Vosges dept., NE France, ab. 30 mi. (48 km.) W of Épinal; mineral waters; resort.

Vit·to·ria \vē-ˈtōr-ē-ä\. Commune, Ragusa prov., SE Sicily, Italy, 11 mi. (18 km.) W of the commune of Ragusa; pop. (1991p) 54,015; wine, olive oil; 18th cent. churches.

Vittoriosa. See BORMLA.

Vit·to·rio Ve·ne·to \vē-ˈtōr-ē-ō-ˈve-nā-ˌtō\. Commune, Treviso prov., Veneto, NE Italy, 23 mi. (37 km.) N of the commune of Treviso; pop. (1991p) 29,002; mineral baths; summer resort; cathedral; scene of a decisive battle in WWI Oct.–Nov. 1918, culminating in an armistice bet. Italians and Austrians.

Vitu. See WITU.

Vitz·nau \ˈfits-ˌnaủ\. Village in Lucerne canton, cen. Switzerland, on Lake of Lucerne near Rigi Mt.; pop. (1980c) 897; resort.

Vi·va·rais \ˌvē-vȧ-ˈre\. Ancient district, SE France, now mostly in dept. of Ardèche; ✻ Viviers.

Vi·ve·ro *or* **Vi·vei·ro** \bē-ˈb̲ā-rō\. Commune, Lugo prov., NW Spain, on Bay of Biscay 42 mi. (68 km.) N of the commune of Lugo; pop. (1991c) 15,098.

Viv·i·an \ˈvi-vē-ən\. Town, Caddo parish, NW corner of Louisiana, 28 mi. (45 km.) NNW of Shreveport; pop. (1990c) 4156.

Vi·viers \vē-ˈvyā\. Town, Ardèche dept., SE France, on the Rhone SSE of Privas; cathedral with Gobelin tapestries; ✻ of ancient Vivarais.

Vivis. See VEVEY.

Vi·vo·ril·lo, Cayos \ˈkä-yōs-ˌbē-b̲ä-ˈrē-yō\ *or* **Vivorillo Cays.** Group of small islands, Carribean Sea, E of NE coast of Honduras.

Vizagapatam. See VISHAKHAPATNAM.

Viz·ca·ya \vēs-ˈkī-ä, vēth-\ *or* **Bis·ca·ya** \bēs-\ *or Eng.* **Bis·cay** \ˈbis-ˌkā, -kē\. Province of Spain. See table at SPAIN.

Vizcaya, Golfo de. See BISCAY, BAY OF.

Vizeu. See VISEU.

Viz·i·a·na·ga·ram \ˌvi-zē-ə-ˈnə-gə-rəm\ *also* **Viz·i·a·nag·ram** \-ˈnə-grəm\. Town, NE Andhra Pradesh, E India, 410 mi. (660 km.) NNE of Madras and just NNE of Vishakhapatnam; pop. (1991p) 159,461; 18th cent. fort.

Vi·zille \vē-ˈzēl\. Town, Isère dept., SE France, S of Grenoble; Roman military post; château where the estates of Dauphiné met 1788 to protest against the government, an act which foreshadowed the 1789 French Revolution.

Vlaanderen. See FLANDERS.

Vlaar·ding·en \ˈvlär-diŋ-ən\. Commune, South Holland prov., SW Netherlands, on the Nieuwe Maas River 6 mi. (10 km.) W of Rotterdam; pop. (1992e) 73,893; an important port; metal goods, chemicals, dairy products; commercial fisheries.

Vla·di·kav·kaz \ˌvlə-di-ˌkəf-ˈkȧs\; *1932–43 and 1955–90* **Or·dzho·ni·kid·ze** \ˌär-jə-ni-ˈkid-zi\; *1944–54* **Dzau·dzhi·kau** \dzaủ-ˈjē-kaủ\. City, ✻ of Alania, S Russia in Europe; pop. (1992e) 325,000; auto parts; metalworking, food processing; university (1970); during WWII marked the farthest advance of German armies into Caucasus Mts. Nov. 1942; founded 1784 as a fort.

Vlad·i·mir \ˈvla-də-ˌmir, vlə-ˈdē-\. **1.** Former principality, cen. Russia; ✻ Vladimir; founded by Andrew Bogolyubsky from Kiev 12th cent.; later, with Suzdal' and Rostov, a part of joint principality of **Vladimir–Suz·dal'** \-ˈsüz-dəlʸ\ under princes of Vladimir; its last ruler, Ivan I (Kalita) removed court to Moscow; absorbed by Moscow in 15th cent.
2. City, ✻ of Vladimir Oblast, cen. Russia in Europe, on N bank of Klyaz'ma River 110 mi. (177 km.) E of Moscow; pop. (1992e) 356,000; textiles; two 12th cent. cathedrals (restored).

History: An old town, founded possibly as early as 991; ✻ of Vladimir principality from c. 1157; sacked by Mongols 13th cent.; seat of Orthodox metropolitan 1300; court transferred to Moscow c. 1330 and city brought under authority of Moscow 15th cent.; made provincial ✻ 1796; developed industrially during 20th cent.

Vladimir Oblast \ˈȯ-bləst, -ˌblast\ *or* **Vla·di·mir·ska·ya Oblast'** \vlə-ˈdē-mir-skə-yə-ˈȯ-bləstʸ\. Administrative subdivision of cen. Russia in Europe; 11,197 sq. mi. (29,000 sq. km.); pop. (1992e) 1,656,000; ✻ Vladimir; textiles, engineering goods.

Vladimir–Suzdal'. See VLADIMIR 1.

Vladimir–Volynski. See VOLODYMYR–VOLYNS'KYY.

Vla·di·vos·tok \ˌvla-də-və-ˈstäk, -ˈväs-ˌtäk\. Seaport city, ✻ of Primorskiy Kray, SE Russia in Asia, at the S tip of a peninsula extending into Peter the Great Bay; pop. (1992e) 648,000; its harbor, the Golden Horn, is an inlet of Amur Bay; E terminus of Trans-Siberian R.R., principal Russian Pacific seaport, and main base of the Russian Pacific fleet; dock and storage facilities; flour; base for fishing fleets; a cultural center for Russian Far East, with several institutions of higher learning and museums. Harbor freezes in winter but can be kept open with icebreakers.

History: Founded 1860; made naval base 1872; connected with Europe by Chinese Eastern Railway c. 1900, and later, Trans-Siberian R.R.; became free commercial port 1904; major development as commercial center and military and naval base following Bolshevik Revolution; port for Allied supplies during WWII; site 1970s of Strategic Arms Limitation Talks (SALT) dealing with disarmament bet. U.S. and U.S.S.R.

Vlagt·wed·de \ˈflakt-ˌved-ə\. Commune, Groningen prov., NE Netherlands, 25 mi. (40 km.) SE of the city of Groningen near German border; pop. (1981e) 16,427.

Vlie·land \ˈvlē-ˌlänt\. Island in the West Frisian Is., Netherlands, N of Texel I.; 10 mi. (16 km.) long; administratively a part of North Holland prov.

Vlie Stroom *or* **Vlie·stroom** \ˈvlē-ˌstrōm\. Strait bet. Vlieland I. and Terschelling I. in the West Frisian Is., Netherlands, connecting the North Sea with Waddenzee.

Vlis·sing·en \ˈvli-siŋ-ə\ *or Eng.* **Flush·ing** \ˈflə-shiŋ\. Commune and seaport, Walcheren I., Zeeland prov., SW Netherlands; pop. (1992e) 43,913; chief town on the island, on its S shore and on Schelde Estuary; commercial and naval port and seaside resort; ferry connections to England. Because of its strategic location, long an area of contention; one of first Dutch cities to revolt against Spanish rule 16th cent. Birthplace of Adm. Michiel Adriaanszoon de Ruyter 1607.

Vlo·rë \ˈvlȯr-ə\. **1.** District of SW Albania. See table at ALBANIA.
2. *or Ital.* **Va·lo·na** \vä-ˈlō-nä\; *formerly* **Av·lo·na** \av-ˈlō-nə\; *anc.* **Au·lon** \ˈȯ-ˌlän\. Seaport town, its ✻, on Bay of Vlorë; pop. (1990e) 73,800; olive oil, canned fish; commercial fisheries; harbor protected by island of Sazan on W.

History: In ancient times a Greek colony; consequential during Roman era; important in wars bet. Normans and Byzantines 11th–12th cents.; under Turkish rule 1464–1912; independence of Albania proclaimed here Nov. 28, 1912; occupied by Italians during WWI and WWII.

Vlorë, Bay of *or Alb.* **Gji–i–Vlo·rës** \ˌgyē-ē-ˈvlȯr-əs\. Inlet of SE Adriatic Sea on SW coast of Albania; harbor for the city of Vlorë.

Vlotslavsk. See WŁOCŁAWEK.

Vl·ta·va \ˈvəl-tə-və\ *or Ger.* **Mol·dau** \ˈmōl-ˌdaủ, ˈmȯl-\. River, Czech Republic; flows SE, then N through České Budějovice and Prague into the Elbe River 20 mi. (32 km.) N of Prague; 267 mi. (430 km.) long.

Vluck Point \ˈvlək\. Cape, NW coast of St. Thomas I., Virgin Is. of the U.S., West Indies, on E side of entrance to Santa Maria Bay.

Vly, Mount \ˈvlī, ˈflī\. Peak in the Catskill Mts., Greene co., SE New York; 3476 ft. (1060 m.).

Vodena. See EDESSA 1.

Vod·njan \ˈvȯd-ˌnyän\ *or Ital.* **Di·gna·no d'Is·tria** \dē-ˈnyä-nō-ˈdēs-trē-ä\; *anc.* **At·tin·i·a·num** \ə-ˌti-nē-ˈā-nəm\. Commune, Istrian Penin., W Croatia, 8 mi. (13 km.) N of Pula; before WWI belonged to Austria; in Italy after 1918; to Yugoslavia following WWII; part of independent Croatia since 1991.

Voer·de \ˈfœr-də, ˈvȯr-\. City, North Rhine-Westphalia, Germany, 15 mi. (24 km.) NW of Essen; pop. (1980c) 31,588.

Vogelkop. See DOBERAI.

Vo·gels·berg \ˈfō-gəls-ˌberk\. Mountain range, Hesse, Germany; highest point 2539 ft. (774 m.).

Vogesus. See VOSGES 1.

Vo·ghe·ra \vō-ˈgā-rä\. Commune, Pavia prov., Lombardy, N Italy, 15 mi. (24 km.) SSW of the commune of Pavia; pop. (1991p) 40,504; 14th cent. castle; churches of San Lorenzo (17th cent.) and Sant'Ilario (12th cent.).

Vogt·land \ˈfōkt-ˌlänt\. Old district of Germany, later included in SW Saxony and SE Thuringia.

Voi \ˈvȯi\. Town, Coast prov., SE Kenya, 90 mi. (145 km.) NW of Mombasa; railroad junction on the Mombasa-Nairobi line.

Voiotia. See BOEOTIA 2.

Voi·ron \vwä-ˈrōⁿ\. Commune, Isère dept., SE France, 15 mi. (24 km.) NNW of Grenoble; Chartreuse liqueur.

Voj·vo·dina *also* **Voi·vo·di·na** *or* **Voy·vo·di·na** \ˈvȯi-vȯ-ˌdē-nä, -dē-ˌnä\. Province, N Serbia, Yugoslavia; pop. (1991p) 2,012,605; ✻ Novi Sad; formerly part of Hungary.

Volaterrae. See VOLTERRA.

Vol·cán \bȯl-ˈkän\. Peak, E Coquimbo region, cen. Chile, near Argentine border; 18,077 ft. (5510 m.).

Volcano Bay. See UCHIURA BAY.

Vol·ca·no Island \väl-ˈkā-nō, vȯl-\. Island in Lake Taal, Batangas, Philippines. See TAAL 1.

Volcano Islands; *Jp.* **Ka·zan Ret·tō** \ˈkä-zän-ˈret-ˌtō\ *also* **Iwo Rettō** \ˈē-wō\. Group of three small islands, W Pacific Ocean S of Bonin Is., 25°N, 141°E; comprise Iwo Jima (*q.v.*), Kita Iwo, and Minami Iwo; administered by U.S. following WWII; returned to Japan 1968.

Vol·chans'k *or Russ.* **Vol·chansk** \vəl-ˈchänsk\. Town, Kharkiv subdivision, Ukraine, ab. 40 mi. (64 km.) NE of the city of Kharkiv.

Vol·ga \ˈväl-gə, ˈvȯl-, ˈvōl-\; *anc.* **Rha** \ˈrā\. River, Russia in Europe; rises W of Lake Seliger in the Valdai Hills in N Kalinin Oblast, flows with greatly winding course E and SE to Kazan' in Tatarstan, then S in great bend at Samara, SW to Volgograd and SE to the Caspian Sea near Astrakhan; 2293 mi. (3689 km.) long; longest river in Europe; area of drainage basin 532,818 sq. mi. (1,379,999 sq. km.); navigable for almost its entire course but in some sections too shallow for large vessels; subject to great floods. Has extensive delta ab. 75 mi. (121 km.) wide. Fed by many tributaries; on left bank: Tvertsa, Mologa, Kostroma, Unzha, Vetluga, Kama, and Samara; on right bank: Oka, Sura. Chief cities on its banks are Kalinin, Rybinsk, Yaroslavl', Kostroma, Nizhniy Novgorod, Kazan', Samara, Saratov, Volgograd, and Astrakhan. Fishing is important on its lower course; connects by canals in several places with Baltic rivers (see VOLGA-BALTIC WATERWAY) and in lower course near Volgograd with the Don. Long important in Russian history, also very important for power production, irrigation, flood control (see RYBINSK RESERVOIR), and transportation.

Volga–Bal·tic Waterway \-ˈbȯl-tik\; *formerly* **Ma·ri·insk Waterway** \mə-ri-ˈēnsk\. A series of navigable rivers and canals, Russia in Europe; system links Volga River with the Baltic Sea. Its course is: (a) the Neva, (b) canal along S shore of Lake Ladoga, (c) the Svir' (canalized in part), (d) canal along S shore of Lake Onega to Vytegra, (e) the Vytegra, a connecting canal (the **Bel·o·ye** \ˈbye-lə-yə\), and the Kovzha, (f) canal along W and S shores of Beloye Ozero, and (g) the Sheksna past Cherepovets through the Rybinsk Reservoir on the Volga; total length ab. 701 mi. (1128 km.) Beloye canal constructed 1799–1810; system expanded and improved at various intervals, incl. major reconstruction during early 1960s.

Volga–Don Canal \-ˈdän\. Shipping canal, S Russia in Europe, linking the Volga and Don rivers; completed 1952.

Volga German Autonomous Soviet Socialist Republic *also* **German Volga Republic.** Former autonomous republic, Russian S.F.S.R., U.S.S.R., on E bank of Volga River except for a small area which was on W bank; 10,888 sq. mi. (28,200 sq. km.); ✻ Engel's. Region settled 18th cent. by Germans invited by special decree of Empress Catherine the Great. At first granted special privileges, lost all autonomy by 1870; Bolshevik Revolution of 1917 prevented transfer of colonists to Siberia which had been ordered 1915. Organized in 1924 as an autonomous republic; suffered greatly in famine of 1921–22; republic abolished 1941, its territory divided bet. Saratov and Volgograd oblasts.

Vol·go·grad \ˈväl-gə-ˌgrad, ˈvȯl-, ˈvōl-; ˌvəl-gə-ˈgrȧt\; *formerly* **Sta·lin·grad** \ˈstä-lən-ˌgrad, ˈsta-; stə-ˌlēn-ˈgrȧt\; *earlier* **Tsa·ri·tsyn** \tsə-ˈrēt-sən\. City, ✻ of Volgograd Oblast, S Russia in Europe, in S part of oblast on the Volga ab. 280 mi. (450 km.) from its mouth; pop. (1992e) 1,006,000; major river port and railroad junction; E terminus of Volga-Don Canal; produces chemicals, building materials, food products; important hydroelectric power station.

History: Originated as a Russian fort 1589 as defense against Kalmuck, Cossack, and other raiders; captured by Cossack Stenka Razin 1670; importance increased rapidly with building of railroads; held by Bolsheviks 1917; a point of conflict during civil war 1919–20, for a time held by White Russian forces of Anton Denikin; renamed 1925 (in honor of Josef Stalin) and again in 1961. Suffered great destruction in WWII when it was the scene of severe fighting; German attack begun Aug. 1942; entered, but not completely occupied, by German army during siege of 66 days from Sept. to Nov., 1942; German forces cut off by Soviet counteroffensive begun in Nov.; finally recaptured, together with large German force, on surrender of Gen. Friedrich Paulus Feb. 1943, the decisive German defeat on the Eastern Front.

Volgograd Oblast *or* **Vol·go·grad·ska·ya Oblast'** \ˌvəl-gə-ˈgrȧt-skə-yə-ˈȯ-bləstʸ\; *formerly* **Stalingrad Oblast** \ˈȯ-bləst, -ˌblast\. Administrative subdivision of S Russia in Europe, on the lower Volga; 44,054 sq. mi. (114,100 sq. km.); pop. (1992e) 2,643,000; ✻ Volgograd. On the SE a long arm of the region extends along the Volga to the Caspian Sea; flat steppe land E of the Volga, fairly good brown soil bet. Volga and Don rivers, and rich black earth W of the Don. Besides the two main rivers, region is crossed by Don tributaries—Khoper and Medveditsa; also contains the Volga-Don Canal. In E are Elton and other lakes. Economy predominantly agricultural (wheat, millet, sunflowers, truck crops, dairy farming) with some heavy industry largely concentrated in Volgograd, the only major urban center.

History: Region occupied long ago by Bulgars, later by Khazars; after Mongol invasion of Europe, Batu Khan fixed upon lands of the lower Volga as home of the Golden Horde and established Sarai (*q.v.*) as his ✻; conquest of this Tatar territory begun in 15th cent. by Russians, who established Astrakhan 1557 and Tsaritsyn 1589 and in 17th and 18th cents. were in continual conflict with Nogai, Kirghiz, and Kalmuck tribesmen; in latter part of 18th cent. scene of Cossack Yemelyan Ivanovich Pugachov's rebellion; after Bolshevik Revolution of 1917 there was much disorder for several years; suffered great famine 1921; in WWII its S part reached in farthest E advance of German armies 1942.

Vol·hyn·ia \väl-ˈhi-nē-ə, vä-ˈli-nē-ə\; *or* **Vo·ly·nia** \və-ˈlin-yə\; *Russ.* **Vo·lyn'** \və-ˈlinʸ\; *Pol.* **Wo·łyń** \ˈvȯ-win\. Historical region, E cen. Europe, around the headstreams of the Pripyat' and Bug rivers; well forested, with marshlands and many lakes; orig. a Russian medieval principality, SW of Polotsk and W of Pinsk and Kiev; in 14th cent. in Lithuania; in 1569 to Poland; in 1790s became part of Russia. Divided 1921 by Treaty of Riga bet. Poland (Wołyń) and U.S.S.R. (Volyn'). Polish section taken by U.S.S.R. in 1939 and retained as Volyn' Oblast after 1945.

Vol·khov \ˈvȯl-k̲əf\. **1.** Navigable river, St. Petersburg Oblast, W Russia in Europe; outlet of Lake Il'men'; flows N to Lake Ladoga; 142 mi. (228 km.) long; area of drainage basin 30,977 sq. mi. (80,230 sq. km.); bisects Novgorod and, at Volkhov near Lake Ladoga, forms rapids (fall nearly 30 ft. or 9m.) that produce power at a hydroelectric station, opened 1926 (first one in U.S.S.R.).

2. *formerly* **Vol·khov·stroi** *or* **Vol·khov·stroy** \ˈvȯl-k̲əf-ˌstrȯi\. Town, St. Petersburg Oblast, W Russia in Europe, ab. 70 mi. (115 km.) E of the city of St. Petersburg.

Völk·ling·en \ˈfœlk-liŋ-ən\. Commune, Saarland, Germany, on the Saar just W of Saarbrücken; pop. (1980c) 44,800.

Vol·ko·vysk \vəl-ˈkȯ-visk\ *or Pol.* **Woł·ko·wysk** \vō-ˈkȯ-visk\. Town, Hrodna subdivision, Belarus, 55 mi. (88 km.) E of Białystok; pop. (1991e) 42,000; formerly in Poland.

Volks·rust \ˈvōlks-ˌrəst\. Town, S Mpumalanga prov., NE Rep. of South Africa, 134 mi. (216 km.) SE of Johannesburg on KwaZulu Natal border in Drakensberg; center of pastoral region.

Volo, Gulf of. See PAGASITIKÓS KÓLPOS.

Vo·lo·dy·myr–Vo·lyn·s'kyy \ˌvə-lə-ˈdi-mir-və-ˈlin^{y}-skē\ *or Russ.* **Vla·di·mir–Vo·lyn·ski** \vlə-ˈdē-mir-və-ˈlin-skē\ *or Pol.* **Wło·dzi·mierz** \vwȯ-ˈjē-ˌmyesh\. City Volyn' subdivision, Ukraine, 45 mi. (72 km.) WNW of Luts'k; pop. (1988e) 40,900; food processing; 12th cent. cathedral; city founded in 10th cent.; ✻ of Volhynia, a principality known in the 12th and 13th cents. as Vladimir in Volhynia. Its name was Latinized as Lodomeria (*q.v.*). City alternately under Polish or Russian rule; to Russia 1795; to Poland following WWI; to Russia after WWII.

Vo·log·da \ˈvȯ-ləg-də\. City, ✻ of Vologda Oblast, N cen. Russia in Europe, in S part of oblast on the **Vologda River** (tributary of upper Sukhona River) and SE of Lake Kubenskoye, ab. 330 mi. (530 km.) E of St. Petersburg; pop. (1992e) 290,000; railroad junction and river port; lumber. First mentioned 1147; disputed during 14th cent. bet. Moscow and Novgorod; came under Moscow 1478; important trading town until early 18th cent.; revived late 19th cent. as center of timber industry.

Vologda Oblast \ˈȯ-bləst, -ˌblast\ *or* **Vo·log·od·ska·ya Oblast'** \ˈvȯ-lə-ˌgət-skə-yə-ˈȯ-bləst^{y}\. Administrative subdivision of Russia in Europe; 56,255 sq. mi. (145,700 sq. km.); pop. (1992e) 1,362,000; ✻ Vologda. Level area with marshes, many lakes, and extensive forests. Beloye and Kubenskoye are largest lakes and chief rivers are the Sukhona and Sheksna; includes part of Volga-Baltic Waterway. Economy dominated by timber industry (lumbering, sawmilling, pulp and papermaking); some agriculture (flax, dairying). In medieval times part of the Novgorod principality; came under Moscow 15th cent.; made separate oblast 1937.

Vo·los \ˈvō-ˌläs\; *Gk.* **Vó·los** \ˈvö-ˌlös\ *or* **Bo·los** \ˈvö-\. Seaport city, ✻ of Magnesia dept., E Thessaly, NE Greece, on Pagasitikós Kolpós; pop. (1981c) 71,378. Many ancient ruins found in vicinity; sites of ancient Iolcus and Demetrias nearby.

Volos, Gulf of. See PAGASITIKÓS KÓLPOS.

Volscian Mountains \ˈvȯl-shən\. See LEPINI MOUNTAINS.

Vol·sin·ii \väl-ˈsi-nē-ˌī\. **1.** Commune, Lazio, cen. Italy. See BOLSENA.

2. Commune, Umbria, cen. Italy. See ORVIETO.

Vol'sk *or* **Volsk** \ˈvȯl^{y}sk\. Town, cen. Saratov Oblast, Russia in Europe, on W bank of the Volga 70 mi. (113 km.) NE of the city of Saratov; pop. (1991e) 65,500; important river port; made town 1780.

Vol·ta \ˈväl-tə, ˈvōl-, ˈvȯl-\. **1.** River, Ghana; flows S into Bight of Benin; includes Lake Volta ab. 300 mi. (485 km.) long, and Black Volta ab. 1000 mi. (1610 km.) long.

2. Administrative region of E Ghana. See table at GHANA.

Volta, Black *or Fr.* **Volta Noire** \ˌvȯl-tȧ-ˈnwär\. Chief headstream of Volta River, Burkina Faso and Ghana, W Africa; rises in Burkina Faso (where it is known as the **Mou·houn** \mü-ˈhün\), flows S, forming section of W boundary of Ghana, turns E and flows into Lake Volta, Ghana.

Volta, Lake. Reservoir, Ghana; 3275 sq. mi. (8482 sq. km.); has inundated point of confluence of White Volta and Black Volta; hydroelectric power production.

Volta, Red *or Fr.* **Volta Rouge** \ˈvȯl-tȧ-ˈrüzh\. Tributary of the White Volta, N Ghana and Burkina Faso (where it is known as the **Na·zi·non** \ˌnä-zē-ˈnōn\).

Volta, White *or Fr.* **Volta Blanche** \ˌvȯl-tȧ-ˈblä^{n}sh\. River, Burkina Faso and Ghana, W Africa; rises in Burkina Faso (where it is known as the **Na·kan·be** \nä-ˈkän-bē\), flows SW and S into Lake Volta, Ghana; ab. 550 mi. (885 km.) long.

Voltaic Republic. See BURKINA FASO.

Volta Noire. See VOLTA, BLACK.

Volta Re·don·da \ˈväl-tə-ri-ˈdän-də, ˈvōl-, ˈvȯl-\. City, Rio de Janeiro state, E Brazil, on the Paraíba River ab. 50 mi. (80 km.) NNW of the city of Rio de Janeiro; munic. pop. (1991p) 220,086; center of steel industry; founded 1941; steel plants constructed 1942–46.

Volta Rouge. See VOLTA, RED.

Vol·ter·ra \väl-ˈter-ə, vōl-, vȯl-\; *anc.* **Vol·a·ter·rae** \ˌvō-lə-ˈter-ˌī, -ē\. Commune, Pisa prov., Tuscany, W Italy, 29 mi. (47 km.) SE of the commune of Pisa; pop. (1991p) 12,885; alabaster goods; tourism; notable buildings include the citadel, several palaces (13th–17th cents.), cathedral (13th–16th cents.), churches of 13th and 14th cents., and an old abbey; Etruscan antiquities, incl. city walls; home of ancient Roman poet Persius; birthplace of artist Daniele da Volterra 1509. Orig. an Etruscan city; became Roman first cent. B.C.; to the ruling Medici family 14th cent.

Vol·tur·no \väl-ˈtu̇r-nō, vōl-, vȯl-\. River, S cen. Italy; flows S and SE out of the Apennines, then turns W through Capua into the Gulf of Gaeta 20 mi. (32 km.) SE of the seaport of Gaeta; 109 mi. (175 km.) long; German line of defense in WWII; after severe fighting crossed by Allies Oct. 1943.

Vo·lu·bi·lis \və-ˈlü-bi-ləs\. Ancient Roman town, W Mauretania; now ruins in N Morocco E of Rabat and ab. 19 mi. (31 km.) N of Meknès; ruins extensive, with remains of many buildings and of city walls; most notable Roman remains in Morocco.

Vo·lu·sia \və-ˈlü-shə\. Coastal county in E Florida. See table at FLORIDA.

Vólvi, Límni. See BOLBĒ, LAKE.

Vo·lyn' \və-ˈlin^{y}\. **1.** *or* **Volynia.** Historical region, E cen. Europe. See VOLHYNIA.

2. Administrative subdivision of Ukraine; 7799 sq. mi. (20,199 sq. km.); pop. (1991e) 1,069,000; ✻ Luts'k; economy predominantly agricultural (grain, sugar beets, livestock); coal. Formerly part of Volhynia (*q.v.*) and a province of Poland; formed **Volyn' Oblast** \ˈȯ-bləst, -ˌblast\ of U.S.S.R. 1939.

Volzhsk \ˈvȯlshsk\; *formerly* **Lo·pa·ti·no** \lə-ˈpä-tə-nə\. Town, Mari El Rep., cen. Russia in Europe, ab. 55 mi. (88 km.) SSE of Yoshkar-Ola; pop. (1991e) 62,500.

Volzh·skiy *also* **Volzh·ski** \ˈvȯlsh-shkē\. Town, Volgograd Oblast, S Russia in Europe, ab. 10 mi. (16 km.) E of the city of Volgograd; pop. (1992e) 281,000.

Voor·burg \ˈvōr-ˌbu̇rk\. Commune, South Holland prov., SW Netherlands; E suburb of The Hague; pop. (1981e) 42,577.

Voor·ne \ˈvōr-nə\. Island, South Holland prov., SW Netherlands, bet. the estuary of the Nieuwe Maas and the Haringvliet; chief town Brielle (*q.v.*).

Voorst \ˈvōrst\. Commune, Gelderland prov., E Netherlands, just NW of Zutphen; pop. (1981e) 23,189.

Vop·na Fjord \ˈvȯp-nə\. Inlet of Norwegian Sea, NE Iceland, SE of Thistil Fjord.

Vor·arl·berg \ˈfōr-ˌärl-ˌbərg\. State, Austria, in extreme W part; ✻ Bregenz; a mountainous region, incl. source of the Lech and several upper tributaries of the Rhine, and noted for its alpine scenery and glaciers; textile industry. See table at AUSTRIA.

Vor·der·rhein *also* **Vor·der Rhein** \ˈfȯr-dər-ˌrīn\. River, SE Switzerland; flows E to unite with the Hinterrhein and form the Rhine River.

Vor·ding·borg \ˌvȯr-diŋ-ˈbȯr^{y}\. Town, Storstrøm co., SE Sjælland, Denmark, on coast opp. Falster I.; pop. (1989c) 19,969.

Voríai Sporádhes. See SPORADES.

Vø·ring·foss \ˈvœr-iŋ-ˌfȯs\. Waterfall, Bjoreia River, a small stream in SW Norway E of Hardanger Fjord; total drop 597 ft. (182 m.).

Vor·ku·ta \vȯr-ˈkü-tə\. Town, Komi Rep., NE Russia in Europe, at N end of the Ural Mts. on the **Vorkuta River;** pop. (1992e) 116,000; coal mines; formerly site of one of largest forced labor camps in U.S.S.R.

Vorlich, Ben. See BEN VORLICH.

Vorm·si \ˈvȯrm-sē\ *or Ger.* **Worms** \ˈvȯrms\. Small island, Baltic Sea, off W coast of Estonia, bet. Hiiumaa and the mainland; 36 sq. mi. (93 sq. km.).

Vo·ro·na \və-ˈrō-nə\. River, S cen. Russia in Europe; flows S through Penza and Tambov oblasts, to the Khoper near Borisoglebsk in E Voronezh Oblast; 282 mi. (454 km.) long.

Vo·ro·nezh \və-ˈrò-nish\ **1.** Navigable river, Russia in Europe; rises in S Ryazan' Oblast, flows S to the Don just S of the city of Voronezh; 291 mi. (468 km.) long.
2. City, ✻ of Voronezh Oblast, Russia in Europe, in W part of the oblast, on right bank of Voronezh River near its junction with the Don, 165 mi. (265 km.) NE of Kharkiv, Ukraine; pop. (1992e) 902,000; railroad junction; produces chemicals, food products; university (1919). Founded as fortress 1586; base for naval operations of Czar Peter the Great against Turkish fortress of Azov late 17th cent.; in WWII occupied by Germans 1942–43; largely destroyed but rebuilt since 1945.

Voronezh Oblast \ˈò-bləst, -ˌblast\ *or* **Vo·ro·nezh·ska·ya Oblast'** \və-ˈrò-nish-skə-yə-ˈò-bləstʸ\. Administrative subdivision of Russia in Europe; 20,232 sq. mi. (52,401 sq. km.); pop. (1992e) 2,475,000; ✻ Voronezh. Chiefly in the valley of the Don bet. two plateau areas, but W part is hilly; wheat, corn, sunflowers, potatoes; livestock raising. In early times on the S border of Moscow principality; came entirely under Russian czars in 16th cent.

Voroshilov. See USSURIYSK.

Voroshilovgrad. See LUHANS'K.

Voroshilovsk. 1. City, Russia. See STAVROPOL' 1.
2. City, Ukraine. See ALCHEVSK.

Vorpommern. See POMERANIA.

Vor·skla \ˈvòr-sklə\. River, Russia and Ukraine; rises in S Kursk Oblast, Russia, and flows S into Ukraine past Poltava to the Dnieper above Dnipropetrovs'k.

Vorst. See FOREST.

Võrts–Järv *also* **Virtsjärv** \ˈvərts-ˌyarv\. Lake, S cen. Estonia; 95 sq. mi. (246 sq. km.); largest lake in Estonia; its outlet is the Ema, flowing E to Lake Peipus.

Vosges \ˈvōzh\. **1.** *anc.* **Vos·e·gus** \ˈvä-si-gəs\ *or* **Vog·e·sus** \ˈvä-ji-səs\. Mountain range, extending bet. Haut-Rhin and Vosges depts., NE France; separated on S from Jura Mts. by Belfort Gap; highest point Mt. Guebwiller 4672 ft. (1424 m.); has many rounded summits.
2. Department of NE France. See table at FRANCE.

Vos·kre·sensk \ˌvəs-kri-ˈshensk\. Town, Moscow Oblast, W cen. Russia in Europe, ab. 50 mi. (80 km.) SE of the city of Moscow; pop. (1991e) 81,400.

Voss \ˈvòs\. Resort town, Hordaland co., SW Norway, ab. 44 mi. (71 km.) ENE of Bergen; pop. (1992e) 13,979.

Vos·tok *also* **Vos·tock** \vä-ˈstäk\. Small uninhabited island, Line Is., Kiribati, cen. Pacific Ocean, ab. 100 mi. (160 km.) SW of Caroline I.; discovered 1820; U.S. claim dropped 1983.

Vos·tok \vä-ˈstòk\. Russian research station, Antarctica, near the S geomagnetic pole; site of world's lowest recorded temperature (−128°F or −89°C on July 21, 1983).

Vot·kinsk \ˈvòt-ˌkinsk\. Town, E Udmurtia Rep., E Russia in Europe, on right bank of Kama River; pop. (1992e) 105,000; terminus of branch railroad line 35 mi. (56 km.) E of Ustinov. Birthplace of composer Pyotr Ilich Tchaikovsky 1840.

Votskaya Autonomous Soviet Socialist Republic. See UDMURTIA.

Voúxa, Ákra. See BUSA, CAPE.

Vou·ziers \vü-ˈzhā\. Commune, Ardennes dept., NE France, on Aisne River. Birthplace of French historian and philosopher Hippolyte Taine 1828.

Voya·geurs National Park \ˌvwä-ˌyä-ˈzhər, ˌvòi-ˌä-\. See UNITED STATES, *National Parks.*

Voyutsa. See VIJOSË.

Voyvodina. See VOJVODINA.

Voz·ne·sens'k *or Russ.* **Voz·ne·sensk** \ˌväz-nə-ˈsensk\. Town, Mykolayiv subdivision, S Ukraine, at head of navigation of the Bug River 80 mi. (129 km.) NNE of Odessa.

Vraca. See VRATSA.

Vran·cea \vrän-ˈchā-ä\. County of E Romania. See table at ROMANIA.

Vrangelya, Ostrov. See WRANGEL ISLAND.

Vra·nje *also* **Vra·nja** \ˈvrän-yə\. Town, Serbia, SE Yugoslavia, ab. 45 mi. (72 km.) NE of Skopje, Republic of Macedonia.

Vra·tsa \ˈvrät-sə\ *also* **Vra·ca** \ˈvrät-sə\. City, N Bulgaria, 35 mi. (56 km.) NNE of Sofia; pop. (1991e) 85,272; railroad junction; textiles, chemicals, ceramics; estab. on present site 15th cent.

Vr·bas \ˈvər-ˌbäs\. **1.** River, Bosnia and Herzegovina; flows N into Sava River; 149 mi. (240 km.) long.
2. Town, Serbia, NW Yugoslavia, ab. 67 mi. (108 km.) NW of Belgrade.

Vr·bas·ka \ˈvər-bəs-kə\. Former county, NW cen. Yugoslavia; 7888 sq. mi. (20,430 sq. km.); ⊗ Banja Luka; now forms NW part of Bosnia and Herzegovina.

Vries Island. See Ō-SHIMA.

Vriesland. See FRIESLAND.

Vrie·zen·veen \ˈvrē-zən-ˌvān\. Commune, Overijssel prov., Netherlands, just N of Almelo; pop. (1981e) 17,716.

Vrin·da·van \ˈvrin-də-vən\; *formerly* **Brin·da·ban** \ˈbrin-\ *also* **Bind·ra·ban** \ˈbin-drə-bən\. Town, Uttar Pradesh, N India, on Yamuna River ab. 80 mi. (130 km.) S of Delhi; Hindu holy city with numerous temples. Many stories told of Krishna are associated with the area.

Vr·šac \ˈvər-ˌshäts\ *or Hung.* **Ver·secz** \ˈver-ˌshets\ *or Ger.* **Wer·schetz** \ˈver-ˌshets\. City, Serbia, NE Yugoslavia, ab. 45 mi. (70 km.) NW of Belgrade near Romanian border; trade center.

Vry·burg \ˈfrī-ˌbərg, ˈfrā-\. Town, North West prov., S Rep. of South Africa, on a tributary of Vaal River 125 mi. (201 km.) N of Kimberly; center of pastoral and grazing region. See STELLALAND.

Vry·heid \ˈfrī-ˌhāt, ˈfrā-, -ˌhīt\. Town, N KwaZulu Natal prov., E Rep. of South Africa, 140 mi. (225 km.) N of Durban; coal mined nearby. Chief town of a district ceded to Boers by a Zulu chief 1884 and declared by them a republic (New Republic); in 1888 incorp. in Transvaal and after Boer War 1899–1902 transferred to Natal.

Vrystaat. See FREE STATE.

Vse·tín \ˈfset-ˌyēn\. Town, E Czech Republic; pop. (1980p) 29,927.

Vught \ˈvœkt\. Commune, North Brabant prov., S Netherlands; pop. (1981e) 23,130; S suburb of 's Hertogenbosch.

Vui·ma·sia \ˌvü-ē-ˈmä-sē-ə\ *or* **Na·mo·si Peak** \nä-ˈmō-sē\. Mountain, SE Viti Levu I., Fiji, SW Pacific Ocean; 3947 ft. (1203 m.).

Vu·ko·var \vü-ˈkō-ˌvär\. Town, E Croatia, on the Danube ab. 83 mi. (133 km.) NW of Belgrade, Yugoslavia; pop. (1991c) 45,963; an industrial area before it suffered heavy damage in Yugoslav civil war 1991.

Vul·can \ˈvəl-kən\. Town, Hunedoara co., W cen. Romania, ab. 40 mi. (64 km.) SE of Deva; pop. (1989c) 35,931; coal.

Vulcan, Mount. Volcano, Blanche Bay, E New Britain I., Bismarck Archipelago, Papua New Guinea, SSW of Rabaul and Mt. Tavurvur (volcano); formed 1937, at time of eruption of Mt. Tavurvur, by crater being built up on **Ma·nam Island** \mä-ˈnäm\ in the bay (island formed by eruption of Mt. Mother 1878).

Vulcan Crest. Peak, Mineral and Saguache cos., S Colorado; 13,722 ft. (4182 m.).

Vul·ca·no \vül-ˈkä-nō\; *anc.* **Hi·era** \ˈhī-ə-rə\. Southernmost island of the Lipari Is., Italy; contains three volcanoes, one of which is still active; most recent major eruption 1890.

Vul·can Pass \ˈvəl-kən\. Mountain pass, W Transylvanian Alps, Romania; 5000 ft. (1524 m.).

Vul·ci \ˈvəl-ˌsī\ *or Etruscan* **Velch** \ˈvelch\. Ancient Etruscan city, the ruins of which are in Viterbo prov., Italy; trading center mid-first millennium B.C.; excavated 1950s; noted for its bronze and pottery, of which many artifacts have been found in huge necropolis; later, under Romans; Roman ruins.

Vul·ture Peak \ˈvəl-chər\. Mountain, Glacier National Park, NW Montana; 9638 ft. (2938 m.).

Vung Tau \ˈvu̇ŋ-ˈtau̇\. **1.** *formerly known in Eng. as* **Cape Saint Jacques** \seⁿ-ˈzhäk\. Point on SE coast of Vietnam, N of entrance to Ho Chi Minh City at 10°19′N, 107°05′E.
2. Seaport, S Vietnam, on South China Sea SE of Ho Chi Minh City; pop. (1989c) 123,528.

Vuok·si \ˈvü-ˌȯk-sē\ *or Russ.* **Vuok·sa** \ˈvü-ək-sə\. River, SE Finland and W Russia in Europe; flows out of Lake Saimaa E into Lake Ladoga.

Vyat·ka *also* **Viat·ka** \ˈvyät-kə\. **1.** River, E Russia in Europe; rises in N Udmurtia Rep. and flows W, S, and SE into Kama River in N Tatarstan; 775 mi. (1247 km.) long. **2.** *or* **Ki·rov** \ˈkē-rəf\. City, ✻ of Vyatka Oblast, E Russia in Europe; on left bank of Vyatka River 265 mi. (426 km.) NE of Nizhniy Novgorod; pop. (1992e) 493,000; a cultural center with research and technical institutes. Founded 12th cent. as a colony of Novgorod; ✻ of a medieval principality; plundered twice by Tatars in 14th and 15th cents.; came under Moscow 1489.

Vyatka Oblast \ˈȯ-bləst, -ˌblast\ *or* **Ki·rov Oblast** \ˈkē-rəf\. Administrative subdivision of E cen. Russia in Europe, plateau country W of the Ural Mts.; 46,641 sq. mi. (120,800 sq. km.); pop. (1992e) 1,700,000; ✻ Vyatka; occupies large part of Vyatka River basin; thickly forested, extensive peat beds.

Vyaz'·ma \ˈvyäzʸ-mə\. Town, E Smolensk Oblast, W Russia in Europe, 125 mi. (201 km.) WSW of Moscow on a tributary of the Desna; pop. (1991e) 59,900; railroad junction. In 11th cent. a trading town; held alternately by Lithuania, Russia, and Poland, from 15th cent.; finally ceded to Russia 17th cent. In WWII occupied by Germans 1941–43 and suffered heavy destruction.

Vyaz·ni·ki \ˈvyäz-nē-kē\. Town, Vladimir Oblast, W cen. Russia in Europe, ab. 70 mi. (115 km.) E of the city of Vladimir.

Vy·borg \ˈvē-ˌbȯrg\ *or Swed.* **Vi·borg** \ˈvē-ˌbȯr\ *or Finn.* **Vii·pu·ri** *also* **Vi·pu·ri** \ˈvē-pü-rē\. Seaport city, NW St. Petersburg Oblast, W Russia in Europe, on Vyborg Bay 70 mi. (113 km.) NW of the city of St. Petersburg; pop. (1991e) 81,100. Founded as fortification by Swedes 1293; captured by Russians 1710; to Finland 1918; ceded back to U.S.S.R. 1940; occupied by Finnish and German forces 1941–44; returned to U.S.S.R. 1944.

Vyborg Bay *formerly* **Viipuri Bay.** Inlet of NE Gulf of Finland, St. Petersburg Oblast, W Russia in Europe; at its head is the city of Vyborg.

Vy·cheg·da *or* **Vi·cheg·da** \ˈvi-chəg-də\. River, chiefly in Komi Rep., N Russia in Europe; flows W to the Northern Dvina River near Kotlas; 702 mi. (1129 km.) long.

Vyernyi. See ALMA-ATA.

Vyk·sa \ˈvik-sə\. Town, Nizhegorod Oblast, cen. Russia in Europe, ab. 100 mi. (160 km.) SW of Nizhniy Novgorod; pop. (1991e) 62,200.

Vyr·nwy \ˈvər-nü-ē\. River, N cen. and E Wales; flows E into the Severn; 35 mi. (56 km.) long; **Lake Vyrnwy,** a reservoir ab. 5 mi. (8 km.) long in N Powys co., was created 1880–90 by damming up the river, and is the largest lake in Wales. See BALA LAKE.

Vysh·niy Vo·lo·chek *or* **Vysh·ni Vo·lo·chek** \ˈvish-nyē-ˌvə-lə-ˈchək\. Town, N Tver' Oblast, W Russia in Europe, 70 mi. (113 km.) NW of the city of Tver'; pop. (1991e) 64,600.

Vy·so·ké Mý·to \ˈvi-sȯ-kā-ˈmē-tō\ *or Ger.* **Ho·hen·mauth** \ˈhō-ən-ˌmau̇t\. Town, cen. Czech Republic, on the upper Elbe River 75 mi. (121 km.) E of Prague.

Vysoké Tatry. See TATRA MOUNTAINS.

Vy·te·gra \ˈvi-ti-grə\. Town, NW Vologda Oblast, Russia in Europe, near SE shore of Lake Onega on the **Vytegra River,** a short stream flowing into Lake Onega and forming part of the Volga-Baltic Waterway.

Wa \ˈwäl\. **1.** Group of states, Myanmar. See WA STATES.
2. Town, ✻ of Upper West Region, Ghana, 120 mi. (193 km.) NW of Tamale near Ivory Coast border.

Waadt. See VAUD.

Waag. See VÁH.

Waal \ˈväl\; *anc.* **Va·ha·lis** \ˈvā-ə-lis, -hə-\. River, Netherlands, the S branch of the Lower Rhine; unites with estuaries of the Meuse River at Gorinchem. Its course to the North Sea continues as the Merwede and its two branches, the Nieuwe Maas and the Oude Maas.

Waal·wijk \ˈväl-ˌvīk\. Commune, North Brabant prov., S Netherlands, N of Tilburg; pop. (1981e) 28,961.

Waas, Mount \ˈwäs\. Peak, S Grand co., E Utah; 12,331 ft. (3758 m.).

Wa·bana \wȯ-ˈba-nə\. Town, Newfoundland, Canada, on Bell I., ab. 11 mi. (18 km.) WNW of St. John's; pop. (1991c) 3608.

Wa·bash \ˈwȯ-ˌbash\. **1.** River, Indiana and Illinois; rises in Darke co., W Ohio, flows W and SW across Indiana to form S section of Indiana-Illinois boundary, and empties into Ohio River at SW extremity of Indiana; 475 mi. (764 km.) long.
2. Name of counties in two states of the U.S. See tables at ILLINOIS and INDIANA.
3. City, ⊗ of Wabash co., N Indiana, 20 mi. (32 km.) NNW of Marion; pop. (1990c) 12,127.

Wa·ba·sha \ˈwȯ-bə-ˌshȯ\. **1.** County in SE Minnesota. See table at MINNESOTA.
2. City, its ⊗, on Mississippi River 30 mi. (48 km.) NW of Winona; pop. (1990c) 2384; summer resort; settled 1838.

Wa·baun·see \wä-ˈbȯn-sē\. County in E Kansas. See table at KANSAS.

Wa·bē Ges·tro \ˈwä-bē-ˈges-trō\ *or* **Weyib** \ˈwā-yib\ *also* **Web** \ˈweb\. River, SE Ethiopia; flows S to join the Genale and Dawa rivers, forming the Jubba; ab. 280 mi. (450 km.) long.

Wac·ca·maw \ˈwä-kə-ˌmȯ\. River, S North Carolina and NE South Carolina; flows through **Lake Waccamaw,** in Columbus co., North Carolina, SW across South Carolina border into Pee Dee River near its mouth; ab. 130 mi. (210 km.) long.

Wac·ca·sas·sa Bay \ˌwȯk-ə-ˈsa-sə\. Inlet of Gulf of Mexico, SW coast of Levy co., NW Florida Penin.

Wa·cho·via \wä-ˈchō-vē-ə\. Historical region, W cen. North Carolina, E of Yadkin River; settled and named by Moravians from Bethlehem, Pennsylvania, in c. 1752; Bethabara (now a small village) was the first settlement, followed by Salem (now part of Winston-Salem) nearby.

Wa·chu·sett Mountain \wä-ˈchü-sət\. Isolated peak, Worcester co., cen. Massachusetts; 2006 ft. (611 m.).

Wachusett Reservoir. Reservoir, E cen. Worcester co., cen. Massachusetts; ab. 6 mi. (10 km.) long; formed by **Wachusett Dam.** A rock tunnel 24.5 mi. (39.4 km.) long connected with Quabbin Reservoir furnishes water supply for Boston.

Wa·co \ˈwā-kō\. City, ⊗ of McLennan co., cen. Texas, on Brazos River 82 mi. (132 km.) S of Fort Worth; pop. (1990c) 103,590; diversified industry; ships livestock and cotton; Baylor Univ. (1845), McLennan Community Coll. (1966); city settled on site of former Indian village 1849; incorp. 1856; suffered devastating tornado 1953; scene 1993 of standoff bet. militant cult members and federal law enforcement members, resulting in extensive loss of life.

Wa·co·nia \wə-ˈkō-nyə, ˌwä-\. City, Carver co., SE cen. Minnesota; pop. (1990c) 3498.

Wa·dai *or Fr.* **Oua·daï** *or* **Ouad·daï** \wä-ˈdī\. Former Muslim sultanate, cen. Africa; ✻ Abéché; came under French influence 1899; Muslim population fought fiercely; French control estab. after 1912; area now largely in E Chad.

Wadan. See OUADANE.

Wad·denzee \ˈväd-ᵊn-ˌzā\. Outer section of the former Zuider Zee, bet. the outer islands and the dike enclosing IJsselmeer, Netherlands.

Wad·ding·ton, Mount \ˈwä-diŋ-tən\. Peak, SW British Columbia, Canada, near head of Knight Inlet; 13,104 ft. (3994 m.); a peak of the Coast Ranges and highest point in British Columbia.

Wad Dra. See DRÂA.

Wade, Mount \ˈwād\. Mountain, Antarctica, 84°51′S, 174°15′W; 13,399 ft. (4084 m.).

Wade Hamp·ton \ˈwād-ˈhamp-tən\. Division in Alaska. See table at ALASKA.

Wa·de·na \wȯ-ˈdē-nə\. **1.** County in cen. Minnesota. See table at MINNESOTA.
2. Village, its ⊗, 43 mi. (69 km.) WNW of Brainerd; pop. (1990c) 4131.

Wä·dens·wil \ˈväd-ᵊns-ˌvēl\. Commune, Zürich canton, NE cen. Switzerland, on S shore of Zürichsee 12 mi. (19 km.) SSE of the city of Zürich; pop. (1980c) 18,485.

Wades·boro \ˈwādz-ˌbər-ō\. Town, ⊗ of Anson co., S North Carolina, 46 mi. (74 km.) ESE of Charlotte; pop. (1990c) 3645.

Wadh·wan \wə-ˈdwän\. **1.** Former state, W India, now part of Gujarat state; 242 sq. mi. (627 sq. km.).
2. Town, its ✻. See SURENDRANAGAR.

Wa·di \ˈwä-dē\. In the Near East and North Africa Arabic word used in place names, meaning "valley, river, dry river bed." For names beginning with this term, see the 2d element (e.g., for Wadi al-Mawjib, see MAWJIB, WADI AL-).

Wadi al–Kebir. See GUADALQUIVIR.

Wā·dī as Sir·ḥān \ˈwä-ˌdē-ˌás-sir-ˈkän\ *or* **Wa·di Sir·han** \ˈwä-dē-sir-ˈhän\. Region, NW Saudi Arabia; extends NW to SE just E of Jordan; alt. ab. 1850 ft. (565 m.); contains pools of brackish water.

Wadi Hal·fa \ˈhal-fə\ *or* **Halfa.** Town, N Sudan, on E shore of Lake Nubia; N terminus of Khartoum railroad line; site of old town of Wadi Halfa (just below 2d of several cataracts) flooded as a result of Aswan Dam projects.

Wādī Mūsā. See PETRA.

Wad Me·da·ni \wäd-ˈmed-ᵊn-ē\ *also* **Wad Ma·da·nī** \mə-ˈdä-nē\. City, E Sudan, ab. 100 mi. (160 km.) SSE of Khartoum; pop. (1983c) 141,065; center of irrigated agricultural region.

Wads·worth \ˈwädz-ˌwərth\. City, Medina co., N Ohio, 11 mi. (18 km.) WSW of Akron; pop. (1990c) 15,718.

Waereghem. See WAREGEM.

Waes \ˈvas\ *or* **Pays de Waes** \ˌpā-ˌē-də-ˈvas\. Ancient district, comprising part of the modern provinces of East Flanders in Belgium and Zeeland in the Netherlands.

Wagadugu. See OUAGADOUGOU.

Wa·ge·ning·en \ˈvä-kə-ˌniŋ-ən\. Commune, Gelderland prov., E Netherlands, on N bank of Neder Rijn 11 mi. (18 km.) W of Arnhem; pop. (1992e) 32,854.

Wa·ger Bay \ˈwā-jər\. Inlet, E mainland part of Nunavut, Canada, opening into Roes Welcome Sound; 160 mi. (257 km.) long, max. width 38 mi. (62 km.).

Wag·ga Wag·ga \ˌwä-gə-ˈwä-gə\. Town, S New South Wales, SE Australia, in Riverina area, on Murrumbidgee River 100 mi. (161 km.) W of Canberra; pop. (1991c) 53,447.

Wagina. See VAGHENA.

Wag·on·er \ˈwa-gə-nər\. **1.** County in NE Oklahoma. See table at OKLAHOMA.
2. City, its ⊗, 14 mi. (23 km.) N of Muskogee; pop. (1990c) 6894.

Wa·gram \ˈvä-ˌgräm\. Village, Lower Austria, Austria, in the Marchfeld 11 mi. (18 km.) NE of Vienna; battle July 5 and 6, 1809 in which French forces under Napoléon defeated the

Austrians under Archduke Charles Louis with heavy loss of life on both sides.

Wah \ˈwä, ˈvä\. Town, Punjab, NE Pakistan, NW of Islamabad; pop. (1981c) 122,335.

Wa·ha Lake \ˈwȯ-ˌhȯ\. Lake, Nez Perce co., W Idaho, 18 mi. (29 km.) SE of Lewiston; noted for its trout.

Wa·hi·a·wa \ˌwä-hē-ə-ˈwä\. City, Honolulu co., cen. Oahu I., Hawaii, on cen. plateau; pop. (1990c) 17,386; U.S. Army post of Schofield Barracks adjoins it.

Wahiawa Bay. Bay, S coast of Kauai I., Hawaii, bet. Lawai Bay and Hanapepe Bay.

Wa·hi·ba Sands \wə-ˈhē-bə\ *or Arab.* **Ram·lat āl Wa·hī·bah** \ˈräm-lət-ˌäl-wä-ˈhē-bə\. Region of sand dunes, E Oman, stretching along the Arabian Sea coast.

Wa·hie Point \wä-ˈhē-ˌā\. Cape, NE coast of Lanai I., Hawaii.

Wah·ki·a·kum \wȯ-ˈkī-ə-kəm\. County in SW Washington. See table at WASHINGTON.

Wahlstatt. See LEGNICKIE POLE.

Wa·hoo \ˈwä-ˌhü\. City, ⊗ of Saunders co., E Nebraska, 17 mi. (27 km.) SSW of Fremont; pop. (1990c) 3681.

Wah·pe·ton \ˈwȯ-pə-tən\. City, ⊗ of Richland co., SE corner of North Dakota, on Red River 44 mi. (71 km.) S of Fargo; pop. (1990c) 8751; North Dakota State Coll. of Science (1903).

Wah Wah Mountains \ˈwä-wä\. Range, S Millard and N Beaver cos., W Utah.

Wai·a·le·a·le, Mount \wī-ˌä-lā-ˈä-lā\. Mountain, cen. Kauai I., Hawaii; ab. 5200 ft. (1585 m.).

Wai·a·lua \ˌwī-ä-ˈlü-ä\. *or* **Waialua Mill.** City, Honolulu co., N Oahu I., Hawaii, near N coast; pop. (1990c) 3943.

Waialua Bay. Bay, N coast of Oahu I., Hawaii, bet. Kaiaka Bay and Waimea Bay.

Wai·a·nae \ˌwī-ä-ˈnī\. City, Honolulu co., W Oahu I., Hawaii, on W coast; pop. (1990c) 8758.

Waianae Range *also* **Waianae Mountains.** Mountain range, extending along SW side of Oahu I., Hawaii; highest peak Kaala ab. 4040 ft. (1230 m.).

Wai·au \ˈwī-ˌau̇\. **1.** River, S South I., New Zealand; flows S from Te Anau Lake and Manapouri Lake into Te Waewae Bay on Foveaux Strait; 135 mi. (217 km.) long from head of Clinton River.

2. *also* **Wai·au–uha** \ˌwī-au̇-ˈü-hə\. River, South I., New Zealand; flows S and SE into Pacific Ocean N of Pegasus Bay; 105 mi. (169 km.) long.

Wai·bling·en \ˈvī-bliŋ-ən\. City, Baden-Württemberg, Germany, 9 mi. (14 km.) NE of Stuttgart; pop. (1980c) 45,114.

Wai·geo \wī-ˈgā-ō\. Island, NE Moluccas, Indonesia, off NW end of Irian Jaya; 80 mi. (129 km.) long by 28 mi. (45 km.) wide; highest point 3281 ft. (1000 m.); nearly divided in two parts by long inlet; covered with dense forests.

Wai·he·ke \ˈwī-ˌhā-kē\. Island, Hauraki Gulf, N coast of North I., New Zealand; pop. (1986c) 4662.

Wai·hi \wī-ˈhē\. Borough, N North I., New Zealand, 75 mi. (121 km.) ESE of Auckland; pop. (1987e) 3680.

Wai·hou \ˈwī-ˌhō-ü\ *or* **Thames** \ˈtemz\. River, North I., New Zealand; flows N into Firth of Thames; 109 mi. (175 km.) long.

Wai·ka·to \wī-ˈkä-tō\. River, NW North I., New Zealand; flows N and W into Pacific Ocean S of Manukau Harbor; source of hydroelectric power; 264 mi. (425 km.) long.

Wai·ki·ki Beach \ˌwī-kə-ˈkē\. Seaside resort, SE Oahu I., Hawaii, SE section of Honolulu, near Diamond Head; noted for its beach and boating.

Wailangi Lala. See WELANGILALA.

Wailing Wall. See WESTERN WALL.

Wai·lua Bay \wī-ˈlü-ä\. Bay, E coast of Maui I., Hawaii.

Wai·lu·ku \wī-ˈlü-kü\. City, ⊗ of Maui co., on N coast of Maui I., Hawaii; pop. (1990c) 10,688; sugar mill set up early 19th cent., before arrival of missionaries.

Wailuku Valley. See IAO VALLEY.

Wai·ma·ka·ri·ri \wī-ˌmä-kə-ˈrir-ē\. River, NE cen. South I., New Zealand; flows SE into Pegasus Bay ab. 12 mi. (19 km.) N of Port Lyttelton; ab. 100 mi. (160 km.) long.

Wai·mea \wī-ˈmā-ä\. **1.** *or* **Ka·mu·e·la** \ˌkä-mü-ˈā-lä\. Village, Hawaii co., Hawaii, in N part of Hawaii I.; pop. (1990c) 1840; a place of importance in early wars of the Hawaiian kingdom.

2. Town, SW coast of Kauai I., Hawaii; pop. (1990c) 5972; canyon nearby 3000 ft. (914 m.) deep. A chief settlement of the Hawaiian kingdom; important in supplying ships 19th cent.

Waimea Bay. **1.** Harbor of Waimea town, SW coast of Kauai I., Hawaii; first anchorage of English mariner Capt. James Cook Jan. 1778; visited by English explorer George Vancouver 1792.

2. Bay, N coast of Oahu I., Hawaii.

Wain·gan·ga \wīn-ˈgəŋ-gə\ *or* **Wain River** \ˈwīn\. River (*ganga*), Madhya Pradesh and Maharashtra, cen. India; rises S of Seoni, flows S to unite with Wardha and form the Pranhita River; 360 mi. (579 km.) long.

Wain·ga·pu *or Du.* **Wain·ga·poe** \wīn-ˈgä-pü\. Seaport and chief town of Sumba I., Lesser Sunda Is., Indonesia, on N coast.

Wai·ni \ˈwī-nē\. River, NW Guyana; flows NE, then curves to NW and empties into Atlantic Ocean near border of Venezuela; ab. 140 mi. (225 km.) long.

Wain River. See WAINGANGA.

Wain·wright \ˈwān-ˌrīt\. Town, Alberta, Canada, 120 mi. (193 km.) SE of Edmonton; pop. (1991c) 4732.

Wai·pa \wī-ˈpä\. River, S tributary of Waikato River in SW North I., New Zealand; ab. 60 mi. (95 km.) long.

Wai·pa·hu \wī-ˈpä-ˌhü\. City, Honolulu co., S Oahu I., Hawaii, on NW shore of Pearl Harbor just W of Pearl City; pop. (1990c) 31,435; suffered damage in Japanese attack on Pearl Harbor Dec. 7, 1941.

Wai·pa·pa Point \ˌwī-ˈpä-pə\. Cape, NE coast of South I., New Zealand, at mouth of Clarence River.

Wai·rau \ˈwī-ˌrau̇\. River, N South I., New Zealand; flows ENE into Cloudy Bay; ab. 105 mi. (170 km.) long.

Wai·roa \wī-ˈrō-ə\. **1.** River, E cen. North I., New Zealand; flows S into N Hawke Bay; 85 mi. (137 km.) long.

2. River in N extension of North I., New Zealand; flows S into Kaipara Harbour on W coast; 82 mi. (132 km.) long.

3. Seaport borough, E North I., New Zealand, on Hawke Bay at mouth of Wairoa River; pop. (1981c) 5439.

Wai·ta·ki \ˈwī-ˌtä-kē\. River, SE cen. South I., New Zealand; flows ESE into Pacific Ocean N of Oamaru; source of hydroelectric power; 130 mi. (209 km.) long.

Wai·tan·gi \ˈwī-ˌtäŋ-gē\. Village, N North I., New Zealand, on Bay of Islands 115 mi. (185 km.) NNW of Auckland. In 1840 treaty signed here bet. Maori chiefs and Great Britain; inequities resulting from application of treaty provisions led to tensions bet. Maori tribes and European settlers and conflict followed; attempts to resolve problems came later in 19th cent.

Wai·ta·ra \ˈwī-tə-rə\. Borough on North Taranaki Bight, W North I., New Zealand, NE of New Plymouth; pop. (1981c) 6012.

Wai·te·ma·ta Harbor \ˌwī-tə-ˌmä-tə\. Inlet, SW corner of Hauraki Gulf, on N coast of North I., New Zealand; harbor for Auckland.

Wai·to·mo Caves \wī-ˈtō-mō\. Underground caverns, W North I., New Zealand, near Te Kuiti; their Glowworm Grotto is illuminated by large numbers of glowworms.

Waitzen. See VÁC.

Waiyeung. See HUIZHOU.

Wajh, Al. See AL WAJH.

Wa·ka·mat·su \ˌwä-kə-ˈmät-sü\. See KITAKYŪSHŪ.

Wa·ka·sa Bay \wä-ˈkä-sä\. Inlet of the Sea of Japan, W coast of Honshū, Japan, in Fukui prefecture.

Wa·ka·ti·pu Lake \ˌwä-kə-ˈtē-pü, -ˈti-\. Lake, SW South I., New Zealand; 48 mi. (77 km.) long; 113 sq. mi. (293 sq. km.); max. depth 1239 ft. (378 m.).

\ə\ **abut** \ᵊ\ **matches** \ᵊ\ **kitten,** Fr **table** \ər\ **further** \a\ **ash** \ā\ **ace** \ä\ **cot, cart** \á\ Fr **bac** \au̇\ **out** \b̶\ Span **Avila** \ch\ **chin** \e\ **bet** \ē\ **easy** \g\ **go** \i\ **hit** \ī\ **ice** \j\ **job** \k̲\ Ger **ich, Buch** \ⁿ\ Fr **vin** \ŋ\ **sing** \ō\ **go** \ȯ\ **all** \ō̇\ **law** \œ\ Fr **bœuf** \œ̄\ Fr **feu** \ȯi\ **boy** \th\ **thin** \t̲h̲\ **this** \ü\ **loot** \u̇\ **foot** \ue\ Ger **füllen** \ue̅\ Fr **rue** \y\ **yet** \ʸ\ Fr **digne** \ˈdēnʸ\, **nuit** \ˈnwʸē\ \yü\ **few** \yu̇\ **fury** \zh\ **vision**

Wa·ka·ya·ma \ˌwä-kä-ˈyä-mä\. **1.** Prefecture, SW Honshū, Japan; ✻ Wakayama. See table at JAPAN.

2. Seaport city, its ✻, 35 mi. (56 km.) SSW of Ōsaka on Kii Channel; pop. (1990p) 396,554. Was seat of one of the Tokugawa branches; has large castle built in 16th cent. by warrior and statesman Hideyoshi Toyotomi.

Wak·de \ˈwäk-də\. Group of small islands off NE coast of Irian Jaya, Indonesia, halfway bet. Tanahmerah Bay and the mouth of the Mamberamo River; 1°57′S, 139°01′E.

Wake \ˈwāk\. County in E cen. North Carolina. See table at NORTH CAROLINA.

WaKee·ney \ˈwo-ˌkē-nē\. City, ⊗ of Trego co., W cen. Kansas, 78 mi. (125 km.) NW of Great Bend; pop. (1990c) 2585.

Wake·field \ˈwāk-ˌfēld\. **1.** Town, Middlesex co., NE Massachusetts, 10 mi. (16 km.) N of Boston; pop. (1990c) 24,825.

2. Village and summer resort, Washington co., S Rhode Island, ab. 3 mi. (5 km.) SSE of Kingston; administrative center of South Kingstown.

3. *or* **Bridg·es Creek** \ˈbri-jəz\. Estate, Westmoreland co., Virginia, S bank of Potomac River and near mouth of Popes Creek; birthplace of George Washington 1732, first president of U.S.; estate acquired by George's father Augustine Washington 1718; house burned 1779; area became property 1923 of Wakefield National Memorial Association which later conveyed its acres and reconstructed colonial house (c. 1930) to the U.S. as the George Washington Birthplace National Monument (see UNITED STATES, *National Monuments*).

4. City, ⊗ of West Yorkshire, N England, on the Calder 10 mi. (16 km.) S of Leeds; pop. (1981c) 75,838; textiles; former coal-mining center; brewing. Scene of battle (Wars of the Roses) at which Richard, duke of York, was captured and beheaded by Lancastrians; scene 15th cent. of presentation of the Towneley Mysteries or Wakefield Plays, one of the four collections of English miracle plays (see CHESTER 11, COVENTRY 3, and YORK 13).

Wake Forest. Town, Wake co., E cen. North Carolina, 16 mi. (26 km.) NNE of Raleigh; pop. (1990c) 5769.

Wake Island. Small sandy island, N Pacific Ocean, 480 mi. (772 km.) N of N Marshall Is., 1180 mi. (1899 km.) W of Midway and 1500 mi. (2414 km.) ENE of Guam, 19°17′N, 166°36′E; total area 3 sq. mi. (7.7 sq. km.); pop. (1980c) 302; highest point 21 ft. (6.4 m.); actually three islets around a lagoon: Wake, the largest, on the E, Peale on the N, and Wilkes on the SW. Acquired by U.S. 1898; building of naval and air station by U.S. begun 1939. Captured by Japan Dec. 1941, after resistance of 15 days by small contingent of U.S. marines; occupied by Japan 1942–45; now a stopover for aircraft.

Wake·ly, Mount \ˈwā-klē\. Peak in the Adirondack Mts., Hamilton co., NE cen. New York; 3617 ft. (1102 m.).

Wa·ke·naam \ˌwä-kə-ˈnäm\. Island at mouth of Essequibo River, off NE coast of Guyana.

Wa·khan \wä-ˈkän\ *or* **Vā·khān** \vä-ˈkän\. **1.** High narrow valley in the Pamirs, NE Afghanistan, bet. Tajikistan and Pakistan.

2. River, NE Afghanistan. See VĀKHĀN 2.

Wak·ka·nai \ˌwä-kä-ˈnī\. Seaport town, Hokkaidō prefecture, N extremity of Hokkaidō, Japan, on S side of Sōya Strait; pop. (1990p) 48,232.

Wakrah, Al–. See AL-WAKRAH.

Wa·kul·la \wä-ˈkə-lə\. **1.** County in NW coastal Florida. See table at FLORIDA.

2. Village, N Wakulla co., NW Florida, S of Tallahassee; nearby is **Wakulla Springs,** a pool (ab. 4 acres or 1.6 hectares) out of which flows the **Wakulla River.**

Wa·la·chia *or* **Wal·la·chia** \wä-ˈlā-kē-ə\. Former principality S cen. Europe, bet. Danube River and Transylvanian Alps, now part of Romania; 29,575 sq. mi. (76,599 sq. km.).

History: Inhabited by a people, the Vlach, who possibly are partially descended from Roman colonists of Dacia (*q.v.*); estab. as principality by Radu Negru (d. 1310), a vassal of Hungary; Târgovişte (Tîrgovişte) its ✻ 14th–17th cents.; made tributary to Turks in 15th cent. although resistance to Turks provided notably by Vlad Dracul (1436–47) and Vlad Ţepeş (1456–62, 1476–77), often cited as historical basis for the vampire tales of Dracula; under Prince Michael the Brave (1593–1601) annexed Moldavia and Transylvania (*qq.v.*); from 1716 ruled by Greek Phanariots appointed from Constantinople instead of by dependent native princes; Russian interests in area grew 18th cent.; occupied by Russia 1774, but remained nominally under Turkish control; for history after 1774, see DANUBIAN PRINCIPALITIES and ROMANIA.

Wał·brzych \ˈvälb-ˌzhik\; *Ger.* **Wal·den·burg** \ˈväl-dən-ˌbu̇rk\ *also* **Waldenburg in Schle·si·en** \in-ˈshlā-zē-ən\. **1.** Province, SW Poland. See table at POLAND.

2. City, its ✻, on the Bóbr 42 mi. (68 km.) SW of Wrocław; pop. (1989e) 141,139; chemicals; coal mines in area; assigned to Poland by Potsdam Conference 1945 following WWII.

Wal·che·ren \ˈväl-kə-rən\. Former island of the Netherlands, in Zeeland prov., in the North Sea off the SW coast; 11 mi. (18 km.) in diameter; area 82 sq. mi. (212 sq. km.); now part of South Beveland.

Wałcz \ˈvau̇ch\. Commune, Piła prov., W cen. Poland; pop. (1989e) 26,420.

Wal·deck \ˈväl-ˌdek\. Former German state, now part of Hesse, Germany; 407 sq. mi. (1054 sq. km.); ✻ Arolsen. In Middle Ages a county; in 1712 raised to a principality; became part of Prussia 1867 and 1918–29 was a republic, forming a constituent state of the Weimar Republic; part of Hesse-Nassau prov., Prussia, 1929–45.

Wal·den \ˈwȯl-dən\. **1.** Town, ⊗ of Jackson co., N Colorado; pop. (1990c) 890.

2. Village, Orange co., SE New York, 10 mi. (16 km.) WNW of Newburgh; pop. (1990c) 5836.

3. Town, Sudbury munic. region, Ontario, Canada; pop. (1991c) 9805.

Waldenburg *or* **Waldenburg in Schlesien.** See WAŁBRZYCH.

Walden Pond. Pond, Middlesex co., NE Massachusetts, near Concord; on its shore author Henry Thoreau lived 1845–47 and drew inspiration for *Walden, or Life in the Woods.*

Walden Ridge. Ridge extending from NE to SW in E cen. Tennessee.

Wal·do \ˈwȯl-dō, ˈwäl-\. County in S coastal Maine. See table at MAINE.

Wal·do·boro \ˈwȯl-dō-ˌbər-ō, ˈwäl-\. Town, Lincoln co., S Maine, 26 mi. (42 km.) ESE of Augusta; pop. (1990c) 4601.

Wal·dron \ˈwȯl-drən\. City, ⊗ of Scott co., W Arkansas; pop. (1990c) 3024.

Waldstätter, Die Vier. See FOREST CANTONS, THE FOUR.

Wald·wick \ˈwȯl-ˌdwik\. Residential borough, Bergen co., NE New Jersey, 7 mi. (11 km.) N of Paterson; pop. (1990c) 9757.

Walensee. See WALLEN, LAKE.

Wales \ˈwālz\. **1.** *or Welsh* **Cym·ru** \ˈkəm-rē\. Principality, forming wide peninsula on W of island of Great Britain; constitutes an integral part of the United Kingdom of Great Britain and Northern Ireland; 8016 sq. mi. (20,761 sq. km.); pop. (1991p) 2,799,000; ✻ Cardiff.

Physical features: Bounded on N by Irish Sea, on E by England, on S by Bristol Channel, and on W by St. George's Channel; St. David's Head, Dyfed, its westernmost point, 5°19′W. Almost entirely an upland region, known generally as the Cambrian Mts.; highest mountains Snowdon Massif in NW 3560 ft. (1085 m.), highest point in England and Wales; Berwyn Mts. in NE and Brecon Beacons in SE. Its chief streams are the Dee in N, upper course of Severn in E, and Conwy in N; numerous small lakes. Coastline irregular, indented by wide bays, esp. Cardigan Bay on W, enclosed on N by Lleyn Penin. and bounded on S by the large peninsula formed by Dyfed county. Only large island is Anglesey off NW coast, separated from mainland by narrow Menai Strait.

Chief products: Dairy products; coal, slate, lead; oil refining; sheep farming, engineering, forestry, fishing; tourism.

Chief settlements: Cardiff, Swansea, Newport.

Political divisions: Divided into the following administrative counties (for pronunciation of their names, see their individual entries):

NAME	AREA (sq. mi.)	AREA (sq. km.)	POP. (1991p)	CO. SEAT
Clwyd	937	2,426	401,900	Mold
Dyfed	2,227	5,768	341,600	Carmarthen
Gwent	531	1,376	432,300	Cwmbran
Gwynedd	1,494	3,869	238,600	Caernarvon
Mid Glamorgan	393	1,018	526,500	Cardiff
Powys	1,960	5,077	116,500	Llandrindod Wells
South Glamorgan	161	416	383,300	Cardiff
West Glamorgan	317	820	357,800	Swansea

Prior to 1974 divided into the following 13 counties (for pronunciation of their names, see their individual entries): Anglesey, Brecknockshire, Caernarvonshire, Cardiganshire, Carmarthenshire, Denbighshire, Flintshire, Glamorganshire, Merionethshire, Monmouthshire, Montgomeryshire, Pembrokeshire, Radnorshire.

History: Inhabited in prehistoric times by tribal divisions of the British Celtic speakers who dominated all of Britain S of the Firth of Forth and the Firth of Clyde; inhabited by Romans in their occupation of Britain (see *History* at UNITED KINGDOM); remained Celtic with small powerful fiefdoms repelling Anglo-Saxon invasions; in 12th cent. Normans established marches on Welsh border and in S Wales to defend their boundaries; N Wales conquered by English King Edward I 1277–84 and Wales made an English principality by Statute of Wales 1284; since 1301 the heir to the English throne has carried the title Prince of Wales; incorp. with England by series of statutes drawn up in reign of Henry VIII; became a leading international coal-mining center during 19th cent.; a national political party formed 1920s with view to gaining more representation in parliament, but candidates unsuccessful until 1960s; secretary of state for Wales, having seat in British cabinet, appointed 1964; Welsh nationalist aspirations continued late 20th cent.

2. City on Cape Prince of Wales, W Alaska; westernmost point of mainland of North America, 168°05′W; pop. (1990c) 161.

Walfischbai. See WALVIS BAY 2.

Walfish Bay. See WALVIS BAY 1.

Wal·green Coast \ˌwȯl-grēn\. Region on coast of Antarctica, W of Thurston I. (*q.v.*) and bordering on Amundsen Sea.

Wal·hal·la \wȯl-ˈha-lə\. Town, ⊗ of Oconee co., NW South Carolina, near the Blue Ridge 31 mi. (50 km.) WNW of Anderson; pop. (1990c) 3755.

Wal·hon·ding \wȯl-ˈhän-diŋ\. River, Coshocton co., cen. Ohio, formed by junction of forks 16 mi. (26 km.) NW of the city of Coshocton; flows SE and joins Tuscarawas River to form Muskingum River.

Walk·er \ˈwȯ-kər\. **1.** River, W cen. Nevada; formed in Lyon co. by branches which rise in California, flows N and then SE through Walker River Indian Reservation into **Walker Lake** (ab. 28 mi. or 45 km. long with no outlet); river is ab. 50 mi. (80 km.) long.

2. Name of counties in three states of the U.S. See tables at ALABAMA, GEORGIA, TEXAS.

3. Town, Livingston parish, SE Louisiana, W of the village of Livingston; pop. (1990c) 3727.

4. City, Kent co., W Michigan, a suburb of Grand Rapids, adjoining it on the W and NW; pop. (1990c) 17,279; the Grand River forms its SW boundary.

5. Village, ⊗ of Cass co., N cen. Minnesota; pop. (1990c) 950.

Walker Pass. Mountain pass, Kern co., S California, in S end of the Sierra Nevada; ab. 5245 ft. (1600 m.); named for the American trapper and guide, Joseph Walker, who explored this region 1834 ff.

Walk·er·ton \ˈwȯ-kər-tən\. Town, ⊗ of Bruce co., SE Ontario, Canada, on Saugeen River 33 mi. (53 km.) S of Owen Sound; pop. (1991c) 4939.

Wall·a·bout Bay \ˈwȯ-lə-ˌbau̇t\. Inlet of the East River, N shore of W end of Long Island, New York, and opp. SE corner of Manhattan I.

Wal·lace \ˈwä-ləs\. **1.** County in W Kansas. See table at KANSAS.

2. City, ⊗ of Shoshone co., NE Idaho, 45 mi. (72 km.) ESE of Coeur d'Alene; pop. (1990c) 1010; formerly a center for the mining of lead, silver, and zinc.

Wal·lace·burg \ˈwä-ləs-ˌbərg\. Town, Kent co., SE Ontario, Canada, 17 mi. (27 km.) NW of Chatham; pop. (1991c) 11,846; glass, plastics.

Wal·lace's line \ˈwä-lə-səz\. Hypothetical boundary that separates the highly distinctive floras and faunas of the Asian and Australian biogeographic regions and passes bet. the islands of Bali and Lombok, bet. Borneo and Sulawesi, and bet. the Philippines and the Moluccas.

Wallachia. See WALACHIA.

Wal·la·roo \ˈwä-lə-ˌrü\. Seaport town, SE South Australia, Australia, on E shore of Spencer Gulf 90 mi. (145 km.) NW of Adelaide; pop. (1991c) 2272.

Wal·la·sey \ˈwä-lə-sē\. Town, Merseyside, NW England, on Irish Sea 9 mi. (14 km.) W of Liverpool. pop. (1981p) 90,057; residential suburb of Liverpool.

Wal·la Wal·la \ˌwä-lə-ˈwä-lə, ˈwä-lə-ˌ\. **1.** County in SE Washington. See table at WASHINGTON.

2. City, its ⊗, ab. 118 mi. (190 km.) SW of Spokane near **Walla Walla River;** pop. (1990c) 26,478; agricultural processing; Whitman Coll. (1859), Walla Walla Community Coll. (1967). Nearby, mission estab. 1836 by Marcus Whitman; relations bet. settlers and Indians deteriorated leading to "Whitman Massacre" (1847) with several people killed (incl. Whitman) and more kidnapped by Indians; later, U.S. Army fort built and attracted settlers; founded 1856; incorp. 1862.

Walled Lake \ˈwȯld\. City, Oakland co., SE Michigan, 10 mi. (16 km.) NW of Detroit; pop. (1990c) 6278.

Wal·len, Lake \ˈvä-lən\; *Ger.* **Wa·len·see** *or* **Wal·len·see** \ˈvä-lən-ˌzā\. Lake, St. Gall canton, NE Switzerland; 9 sq. mi. (23 sq. km.); receives the Linth River from the S; linked by Linth Canal with the Zürichsee to the W.

Wal·len·pau·pack, Lake \ˌwä-lən-ˈpȯ-ˌpak\. Lake on boundary bet. Wayne and Pike cos., NE Pennsylvania; 9 sq. mi. (23 sq. km.); formed by dam in **Wallenpaupack Creek.**

Wal·ler \ˈwä-lər\. County in SE Texas. See table at TEXAS.

Wall·face Mountain \ˈwȯl-ˌfās\. Peak in the Adirondack Mts., Essex co., NE New York; 3860 ft. (1177 m.).

Wal·ling·ford \ˈwä-liŋ-fərd, -ˌfōrd\. **1.** Town, NE New Haven co., S Connecticut, S of Meriden; pop. (1990c) 40,822; includes borough of Wallingford on Quinnipiac River 12 mi. (19 km.) NE of New Haven; Choate Rosemary Hall coeducational preparatory school formed 1971 by merger of Rosemary Hall (1890) and Choate School (1896).

2. Town, Oxfordshire, S England; pop. (1981p) 6328; treaty negotiated here 1153 bet. English King Stephen and Prince Henry of Anjou, by which Stephen kept throne for his lifetime, and Henry succeeded him, which he did as King Henry II 1154.

Wal·ling·ton \ˈwȯ-liŋ-tən\. Borough, Bergen co., NE corner of New Jersey, on Passaic River 6 mi. (10 km.) SSE of Paterson; pop. (1990c) 10,828.

Wallis. See VALAIS.

Wal·lis and Fu·tu·na Islands \ˈwä-ləs … fə-ˈtü-nə\. French overseas territory, SW Pacific Ocean; 106 sq. mi. (275 sq. km.); pop. (1993e) 14,000; comprises the two groups of Wallis Is. (*q.v.*) and Futuna Is. (*q.v.*); until 1961 a protectorate under French authority attached to New Caledonia.

Wallis Islands. Island group, SW Pacific Ocean, a part of Wallis and Futuna Is. (*q.v.*); 35 sq. mi. (91 sq. km.); pop. (1990c) 8973; comprises the main island of Uvéa and eight islets, all enclosed in one coral reef. Named for English navigator Samuel Wallis, who visited 1767; occupied by French 1842; joined with Futuna Is. 1887 and administratively attached to New Caledonia colony until 1961 when it became part of French overseas territory of Wallis and Futuna Is.

Wal·lo·nia \wä-ˈlō-nē-ə\ *or* **Wal·loo·nia** \-ˈlü-\ *or Fr.* **Wal·lo·nie** \ˌwä-lȯ-ˈnē\. Region of Belgium, comprising the French-speaking provinces of Hainaut, Liège, Luxembourg, Namur, and S part of Brabant; limited autonomy granted 1980; became one of three regions in new federation of Belgium 1993. See table at BELGIUM.

Wal·lops Island \ˈwä-ləps\. Island, Accomac co., E Virginia, in Atlantic Ocean NE of Assawaman Inlet; 6 sq. mi. (16 sq. km.); NASA facility.

Wal·lowa \wä-ˈlau̇-ə\. **1.** River, NE Oregon; rises in Wallowa Lake, S Wallowa co., flows NW into Grande Ronde River on Wallowa co. boundary; ab. 50 mi. (80 km.) long.

2. County in NE corner of Oregon. See table at OREGON.

Wallowa Lake. Lake, S Wallowa co., NE corner of Oregon.

Wallowa Mountains. Range, S Wallowa, N Baker, and E Union cos., NE Oregon; highest peak 9838 ft. (2999 m.).

Walls·end \ˈwȯl-ˌzend\. Town, Tyne and Wear, N England, on the Tyne 4 mi. (6 km.) ENE of Newcastle upon Tyne; pop. (1981c) 44,622; shipyards. At E end of Hadrian's Wall (built by Romans), hence the name.

Wal·ney \ˈwȯl-nē\. Island off NW coast of England, N of entrance to Morecambe Bay; 8 mi. (13 km.) long; bridge connects with Barrow in Furness, Cumbria.

Wal·nut \ˈwȯl-ˌnət\. **1.** River, SE Kansas; rises in N Butler co., flows S into Arkansas River at Arkansas City, S Cowley co., S Kansas; ab. 90 mi. (145 km.) long.

2. City, Los Angeles co., SW California, 18 mi. (29 km.) E of the city of Los Angeles; pop. (1990c) 29,105; pop. more than doubled bet. 1980 and 1990.

Walnut Canyon National Monument. See UNITED STATES, *National Monuments.*

Walnut Creek. City, Contra Costa co., W California, 10 mi. (16 km.) S of Suisun Bay; pop. (1990c) 60,569.

Walnut Ridge. City, ⊗ of Lawrence co., NE Arkansas; pop. (1990c) 4388; Williams Baptist Coll. (1941).

Wal·pole \ˈwȯl-ˌpōl, ˈwäl-\. **1.** Town, Norfolk co., E Massachusetts, 18 mi. (29 km.) SW of Boston; pop. (1990c) 20,212; state prison.

2. Town, Cheshire co., SW New Hampshire, on Connecticut River 13 mi. (21 km.) NW of Keene; pop. (1990c) 3210; settled 1749.

Walpole Island. Island, New Caledonia, SW Pacific Ocean, ab. 154 mi. (248 km.) SSE of Nouméa; ab. 310 acres (125 hectares).

Wal·sall \ˈwȯl-ˌsȯl\. Town, West Midlands, W cen. England, 10 mi. (16 km.) NNW of Birmingham; pop. (1991p) 255,600; diversified industries include leather goods, electrical and electronic equipment, machine tools, aircraft parts, chemicals.

Wal·sen·burg \ˈwȯl-sən-ˌbərg\. City, ⊗ of Huerfano co., S Colorado, 45 mi. (72 km.) S of Pueblo; pop. (1990c) 3300.

Walsh \ˈwȯlsh\. County in NE North Dakota. See table at NORTH DAKOTA.

Wal·sing·ham, Cape \ˈwȯl-siŋ-ˌham\. Cape, E Baffin I., Arctic Archipelago, Nunavut, Canada, extending into Davis Strait.

Wal·sum \ˈväl-ˌzu̇m\. Commune, North Rhine-Westphalia, Germany, ab. 8 mi. (13 km.) NNW of Duisburg, on the Rhine River.

Wal·ter·boro \ˈwȯl-tər-ˌbər-ō\. Town, ⊗ of Colleton co., S South Carolina, 45 mi. (72 km.) W of Charleston; pop. (1990c) 5492; winter resort; lumber.

Wal·ters \ˈwȯl-tərz\. City, ⊗ of Cotton co., SW Oklahoma, 17 mi. (27 km.) S of Lawton; pop. (1990c) 2519.

Wal·thall \ˈwȯl-ˌthȯl\. **1.** County in S Mississippi. See table at MISSISSIPPI.

2. Village, ⊗ of Webster co., N cen. Mississippi; pop. (1990c) 167.

Wal·tham \ˈwȯl-ˌtham, *chiefly by outsiders* -thəm\. City, Middlesex co., NE Massachusetts, 9 mi. (14 km.) W of Boston; pop. (1990c) 57,878; Bentley Coll. (1917), Brandeis Univ. (1948). Settled c. 1636; incorp. as town 1738; first power loom for manufacture of cotton textiles set up here 1814; incorp. as city 1884.

Waltham Abbey *also* **Waltham Holy Cross.** Town, Essex, SE England, NE suburb of London; pop. (1981p) 19,432; plastics; remains of 11th cent. abbey church.

Waltham Forest \ˈwȯl-thəm, -təm\. A borough of Greater London, SE England. See table at LONDON 4.

Wal·ton \ˈwȯlt-ᵊn\. **1.** Name of counties in two states of the U.S. See tables at FLORIDA and GEORGIA.

2. Village, Delaware co., S New York, on Delaware River 42 mi. (68 km.) E of Binghamton; pop. (1990c) 3326.

Walton–le–Dale \-lə-ˈdāl\. Town, Lancashire, NW England, on the Ribble 26 mi. (42 km.) NW of Manchester; pop. (1981p) 29,009.

Walton Mountain. Peak, Glacier National Park, NW Montana; ab. 8930 ft. (2720 m.).

Walton–on–Thames \-ˈtemz\. Town, Surrey, S England, just W of Greater London; pop. (1981p) 49,237.

Walton–on–the–Naze \-ˈnāz\. Resort, Essex, SE England, on North Sea coast.

Wal·trop \ˈväl-ˌtrȯp\. Commune, North Rhine-Westphalia, Germany, NNW suburb of Dortmund; pop. (1980c) 27,045.

Wal·vis Bay \ˈwȯl-vəs\. **1.** *also* **Wal·fish Bay** \ˈwȯl-fish\. Inlet of Atlantic Ocean, W cen. coast of Namibia, 22°59′S, 14°31′E.

2. *or Ger.* **Wal·fisch·bai** \ˈväl-fish-ˌbī\. Town, W Namibia, on Atlantic Ocean 170 mi. (274 km.) W of Windhoek and by sea 710 mi. (1142 km.) N of Cape Town, Rep. of South Africa; town, harbor, and immediate vicinity (434 sq. mi. or 1124 sq. km.; pop. [1985c] 16,652) a former exclave of Cape Province, South Africa; transferred to Namibia 1994; good harbor and railroad terminus; fishing.

Walwal. See WELWEL.

Wal·worth \ˈwȯl-ˌwərth\. Name of counties in two states of the U.S. See tables at SOUTH DAKOTA and WISCONSIN.

Wa·me·go \wä-ˈmē-gō\. City, Pottawatomie co., NE Kansas, on Kansas River E of Manhattan; pop. (1990c) 3706.

Wamps·ville \ˈwämps-ˌvil\. Village, ⊗ of Madison co., cen. New York, 25 mi. (40 km.) E of Syracuse; pop. (1990c) 501.

Wa·na \ˈwä-nə\. Village and frontier post, Pakistan, 85 mi. (137 km.) WNW of Dera Ismail Khan, beyond Gumal Pass and near Afghanistan border; occupied 19th cent. by British.

Wa·na·ka, Lake \ˈwä-nə-kə\. Lake, SW cen. South I., New Zealand; 74 sq. mi. (192 sq. km.); 28 mi. (45 km.) long.

Wan·a·pi·tei Lake \ˌwä-nə-pə-ˈtā\. Lake, S cen. Sudbury dist., SE Ontario, Canada; drains S through the **Wanapitei River** (ab. 60 mi. or 95 km. long) into Georgian Bay.

Wan·a·que \wə-ˈnä-kē, -kwē; ˈwä-nə-ˌkyü, -kē\. Borough, Passaic co., N New Jersey, 10 mi. (16 km.) NW of Paterson; pop. (1990c) 9711; just NW is **Wanaque Reservoir.**

Wa·na·wa·na \ˌwä-nə-ˈwä-nə\. Small island off NW coast of New Georgia I., cen. Solomon Is., W Pacific Ocean, S of Arundel I.

Wan–ch'uan. See ZHANGJIAKOU.

Wan·damm·en Bay \wän-ˈdä-mən\. Inlet, W Teluk Cenderawasih, NW coast of Irian Jaya, Indonesia, nearly opp. Berau Bay.

Wan·ding·zhen \ˈwän-ˈdiŋ-ˈjən\ *or W.-G.* **Wan–ting–chen** \-ˈdiŋ-ˈjən\ *or* **Wan·t'ing** \ˈwän-ˈtiŋ\. Border town on E bank of Longchuan River, W Yunnan, China, N of Namhkam, Myanmar; alt. 3200 ft. (975 m.); held by Japanese during WWII.

Wan·di·wash *or* **Wan·de·wash** \ˈwən-di-ˌwäsh\. Town, Tamil Nadu, S India, 60 mi. (97 km.) SW of Madras; scene of several conflicts bet. French and British 18th cent. and esp. of victory 1760 of British under Col. (later Sir) Eyre Coote over the French under Thomas-Arthur de Lally.

Wan·dle \ˈwȯn-dᵊl\. River, Greater London, S England; flows NW into the Thames at Wandsworth; 9 mi. (14 km.) long.

Wands·worth \ˈwändz-ˌwərth\. A borough of Greater London, SE England. See table at LONDON 4.

Wang \ˈwäŋ\. River, N tributary of the Ping River, NW Thailand; flows S from hills S of Chiang Rai to the Ping above Tak; ab. 150 mi. (240 km.) long.

Wan·ga·nui \ˌwäŋ-gə-ˈnü-ē\. **1.** River, SW cen. North I., New Zealand; rises in Tongariro National Park, flows W and

S into N part of Cook Strait; ab. 180 mi. (290 km.) long; flows through region which was original home of Maoris.
2. Seaport city, W North I., New Zealand, at mouth of Wanganui River 95 mi. (153 km.) N of Wellington; pop. (1992e) 41,400; has export trade. Settled by Europeans 1842; Maoris and British engaged in conflicts in this locality in 1847 and 1860s.

Wan·ga·rat·ta \ˌwaŋ-gə-ˈra-tə\. Town, N Victoria, SE Australia, 130 mi. (209 km.) NE of Melbourne; pop. (1991c) 15,984.

Wang·er·oo·ge \ˌväŋ-ə-ˈrō-gə\. Island, most easterly of the East Frisian Is., in North Sea off NW coast of Germany; 6 mi. (10 km.) long.

Wang·i·wangi \ˌwäŋ-ē-ˈwäŋ-ē\. Island, Banda Sea, 25 mi. (40 km.) off E coast of Butung I., and in NW part of the Tukangbesi Is.

Wangyehmiao. See HORQIN YOUYI QIANQI.

Wanhsien. See WANXIAN.

Wan·ka·ner \wäŋ-ˈkä-nər\. Former state, W India, S of Morvi; now part of Gujarat state.

Wankie. See HWANGE.

Wan·ne–Eick·el \ˈvä-nə-ˈī-kəl\. City, North Rhine-Westphalia, Germany, in Ruhr Valley 8 mi. (13 km.) NE of Essen; railroad center; chemicals; coal mines; formed 1926.

Wanping *or* **Wan–p'ing.** See LUGOUQIAO.

Wan·shan *or* **Wan–shan** \ˈwän-ˈshän\; *formerly* **La·drone** \lə-ˈdrōn\. Island group, China Sea, opp. entrance to the Zhu River.

Wan·shou·shan *or* **Wan–shou–shan** \ˈwän-ˈshō-ˈshän\. Park, Beijing municipality, NE China; nearby was the Summer Palace, resort of imperial family, built by Emperor Qianlong in 18th cent.; original palaces destroyed 1860 by British under orders from James Bruce, 8th earl of Elgin; rebuilt by Chinese Dowager Empress Cixi (Tz'u-hsi).

Wan·tage \ˈwän-tij\. Town, Oxfordshire, England, in the Vale of the White Horse (*q.v.*); pop. (1981c) 8899; birthplace of king of England, Alfred the Great 849.

Want'ing *or* **Wan–ting–chen.** See WANDINGZHEN.

Wan·xian *or W.-G.* **Wan·hsien** \ˈwän-ˈshyen\. City, E Sichuan prov., S cen. China, on left bank of the Chang 130 mi. (209 km.) below Chongqing in mountainous district at upper end of Chang Gorges; pop. (1990c) 156,823; important river port, opened to foreign trade 1917.

Waoekara. See WAUKARA.

Wa·pa·ko·neta \ˌwȯ-pə-kə-ˈne-tə\. City, ⊗ of Auglaize co., W Ohio, 13 mi. (21 km.) S of Lima; pop. (1990c) 9214.

Wa·pa·to \ˈwȯ-pə-tō, ˈwä-\. City, Yakima co., S Washington, S of the city of Yakima; pop. (1990c) 3795.

Wap·el·lo \ˈwä-pə-ˌlō\. **1.** County in SE Iowa. See table at IOWA.
2. City, ⊗ of Louisa co., SE Iowa, 19 mi. (31 km.) SSW of Muscatine; pop. (1990c) 2013; prehistoric Indian mounds nearby.

Wap·pin·gers Falls \ˈwä-pin-jərz\. Village, Dutchess co., SE New York, near Hudson River 8 mi. (13 km.) S of Poughkeepsie; pop. (1990c) 4605; name comes from 75-foot (23-meter) cascade in **Wap·pin·ger Creek** \ˈwä-pin-jər\.

Wap·si·pin·i·con \ˌwäp-sə-ˈpi-nə-kən\. River, E Iowa and S Minnesota; rises in S Mower co., S Minnesota, flows SE into Mississippi River forming most of boundary bet. Clinton and Scott cos., E Iowa; 255 mi. (410 km.) long.

Wa·quoit Bay \ˈwȯ-ˌkwȯit\. Inlet of Nantucket Sound, S coast of W Barnstable co., SE Massachusetts.

Wa·ra·bi \wä-ˈrä-bē\. City, Saitama prefecture, Honshū, Japan, 12 mi. (19 km.) NW of Tokyo; pop. (1990p) 73,620.

Wa·ra·maug, Lake \ˈwȯr-ə-ˌmȯg\. Lake, W cen. Litchfield co., NW Connecticut; resort region.

Wa·ran·gal \ˈwȯr-əŋ-gəl\. City, N Andhra Pradesh, S cen. India, 86 mi. (138 km.) ENE of Hyderabad; pop. (1991c) 447,653; silk, carpets; 12th cent. ✻ of Kakatíya kingdom.

Warasdin. See VARAŽDIN.

War·bur·ton, The \ˈwȯr-ˌbərt-ᵊn\. River, NE South Australia; flows SW into Lake Eyre; 275 mi. (442 km.) long.

Ward \ˈwȯrd\. Name of counties in two states of the U.S. See tables at NORTH DAKOTA and TEXAS.

Wardastalla. See GUASTALLA.

War·dha \ˈwȯr-də\. **1.** River, E Maharashtra, cen. India; rises in NW, flows SE to unite on the S border with Wainganga River and form the Pranhita River; receives the Penganga from the W; ab. 290 mi. (465 km.) long.
2. Town, E Maharashtra, cen. India, 45 mi. (72 km.) SW of Nagpur; pop. (1991p) 102,974; nearby, Indian nationalist and spiritual leader Mohandas Gandhi established an ashram 1933.

Ward Hunt, Cape \ˈwȯrd-ˈhənt\. Cape, New Guinea I., in Papua New Guinea, on Solomon Sea, 8°05′S, 149°55′E.

Ward Hunt Strait. Passage bet. D'Entrecasteaux Is. and New Guinea I., connecting Collingwood Bay and Solomon Sea on the NW with Goschen Strait on SE; 75 mi. (121 km.) long, ab. 20 mi. (32 km.) wide.

Wards Island \ˈwȯrdz\. Island in East River, New York, part of Manhattan borough, just S of Randalls I.; 255 acres (103 hectares). Crossed by Triborough Bridge.

Ware \ˈwar\. **1.** River, cen. Massachusetts; rises in Worcester co., flows SW into Swift River near N border of Hampden co.; ab. 40 mi. (64 km.) long.
2. County in SE Georgia. See table at GEORGIA.
3. Town, Hampshire co., W Massachusetts, 21 mi. (34 km.) ENE of Springfield; pop. (1990c) 9808.
4. Town, Hertfordshire, SE England, on the Lea 23 mi. (37 km.) N of London; pop. (1981c) 14,334; railroad cars.

Wa·re·gem *or* **Wae·re·ghem** \ˈvär-ə-gəm\. Commune, West Flanders prov., NW Belgium, 43 mi. (69 km.) W of Brussels; pop. (1991c) 34,902; site of Flanders Field Cemetery, the only U.S. military cemetery in Belgium for soldiers of WWI.

Ware·ham \ˈwar-əm, ˈwar-ˌham\. **1.** Town, Plymouth co., SE Massachusetts, 13 mi. (21 km.) ENE of New Bedford; pop. (1990c) 19,232.
2. Town, Dorset, S England, on NW edge of the Isle of Purbeck; pop. (1981p) 4577.

Wa·ren \ˈvär-ən\. City, Mecklenburg-West Pomerania, NE Germany, 60 mi. (97 km.) E of Schwerin; pop. (1981c) 23,353.

Wargla. See OUARGLA.

War In The Pacific National Historical Park. See UNITED STATES, *National Historical Parks.*

Wark·worth \ˈwȯrk-ˌwərth\. Town, Northumberland, N England, ab. 1.5 mi. (2.4 km.) from the North Sea coast; pop. (1981c) 1308; remains of Norman castle; 12th cent. church.

War·ley \ˈwȯr-lē\. Town, West Midlands, W cen. England, WSW of Birmingham; pop. (1981p) 152,455.

Warmia. See ERMELAND.

War·min·ster \ˈwȯr-ˌmin-stər\. **1.** Urban township, Bucks co., SE Pennsylvania; pop. (1990c) 32,832.
2. Town, Wiltshire, S England; pop. (1981p) 15,065.

Warm Springs \ˈwȯrm\. **1.** City, S Meriwether co., W Georgia; pop. (1990c) 407; health resort; site of Warm Springs Foundation, estab. 1927 by Franklin D. Roosevelt for treatment of infantile-paralysis patients, and of Roosevelt's Little White House, now a museum.
2. Village, ⊗ of Bath co., W Virginia, 23 mi. (37 km.) NNE of Covington; warm sulfur springs.

Warm Springs Reservoir. Irrigation reservoir in middle fork of Malheur River, bet. Harney and Malheur cos., E Oregon; formed by **Warm Springs Dam.**

War·ner \ˈwȯr-nər\. Town, Muskogee co., E Oklahoma, ab. 18 mi. (29 km.) S of the city of Muskogee; pop. (1990c) 1479; Connors State Coll. (1908).

Warner Mountains. Range, E Modoc co., NE California, and S Lake co., S Oregon.

Warner Rob·ins \ˈrä-bənz\. City, Houston co., cen. Georgia, S of Macon; pop. (1990c) 43,726; Robins Air Force Base.

War·now \ˈvär-ˌnō\. Stream, NE Germany; flows N to Gulf of Mecklenburg; 80 mi. (129 km.) long; navigable for seagoing vessels to Rostock.

Warnsdorf. See VARNSDORF.

Warqla. See OUARGLA.

Warr Acres \ˈwȯr\. City, Oklahoma co., cen. Oklahoma, W suburb of Oklahoma City; pop. (1990c) 9288.

War·ra·gul \ˈwȯr-ə-gəl\. Town, SE Victoria, Australia, ESE of Melbourne; pop. (1991c) 8910.

War·re·go \ˈwär-i-ˌgō\. River, Australia; flows SSW from S cen. Queensland to the Darling in N New South Wales; 495 mi. (796 km.) long.

War·ren \ˈwȯr-ən\. **1.** Name of counties in 14 states of the U.S. See tables at GEORGIA, ILLINOIS, INDIANA, IOWA, KENTUCKY, MISSISSIPPI, MISSOURI, NEW JERSEY, NEW YORK, NORTH CAROLINA, OHIO, PENNSYLVANIA, TENNESSEE, VIRGINIA.

2. City, ⊗ of Bradley co., S Arkansas, 46 mi. (74 km.) E of Camden; pop. (1990c) 6455.

3. Town, Lincoln co., Maine, 30 mi. (48 km.) SE of Augusta; pop. (1990c) 3192.

4. Town, Worcester co., cen. Massachusetts, 20 mi. (32 km.) W of the city of Worcester; pop. (1990c) 4437.

5. City, Macomb co., SE Michigan, NNE of Detroit; pop. (1990c) 144,864; suburb of Detroit; Macomb County Community Coll. (1953); pop. doubled bet. 1960 and 1970 and has fallen since.

6. City, ⊗ of Marshall co., NW Minnesota, 27 mi. (43 km.) WNW of Thief River Falls; pop. (1990c) 1813.

7. City, ⊗ of Trumbull co., NE Ohio, 13 mi. (21 km.) NW of Youngstown; pop. (1990c) 50,793; steel; incorp. as city 1905.

8. Borough, ⊗ of Warren co., NW Pennsylvania, 30 mi. (48 km.) WSW of Bradford; pop. (1990c) 11,122.

9. Town, Bristol co., E Rhode Island, on Narragansett Bay 10 mi. (16 km.) SE of Providence; pop. (1990c) 11,385; summer resort. Settled 1632; orig. part of Massachusetts; annexed by Rhode Island and incorp. as town 1747; seat of Rhode Island Coll. (now Brown Univ.) beginning 1764; pillaged and burned by British during American Revolution 1778.

War·rens·burg \ˈwȯr-ənz-ˌbərg\. City, ⊗ of Johnson co., W Missouri, 30 mi. (48 km.) W of Sedalia; pop. (1990c) 15,244; Central Missouri State Univ. (1871).

War·rens·ville Heights \ˈwȯr-ənz-ˌvil\. City, Cuyahoga co., N Ohio, SE of Cleveland; pop. (1990c) 15,745.

War·ren·ton \ˈwȯr-ən-tən\. **1.** City, ⊗ of Warren co., E cen. Georgia; pop. (1990c) 2056.

2. City, ⊗ of Warren co., E Missouri; pop. (1990c) 3564.

3. Town, ⊗ of Warren co., N North Carolina; pop. (1990c) 949.

4. City, Clatsop co., NW Oregon; pop. (1990c) 2681.

5. Town, ⊗ of Fauquier co., N Virginia, in foothills of Blue Ridge 35 mi. (56 km.) NNW of Fredericksburg; pop. (1990c) 4830.

War·ren·ville \ˈwȯr-ən-ˌvil\. City, Du Page co., NE Illinois, 8 mi. (13 km.) NE of Aurora; pop. (1990c) 11,333.

War·ri \ˈwȯr-ē\. Town, S Nigeria, 190 mi. (306 km.) ESE of Lagos in Niger Delta; pop. (1991e) 111,300.

War·rick \ˈwȯr-ik\. County in SW Indiana. See table at INDIANA.

War·ring·ton \ˈwȯr-iŋ-tən\. Town, Cheshire, NW England, on the Mersey 14 mi. (23 km.) E of Liverpool; pop. (1981p) 57,389; breweries.

War·ri·or \ˈwȯr-ē-ər, ˈwär-\. City, Jefferson co., Alabama, 20 mi. (32 km.) N of Birmingham; pop. (1990c) 3280.

Warr·nam·bool \ˈwȯr-nəm-ˌbül\. Seaport town, SW Victoria, SE Australia, 140 mi. (225 km.) WSW of Melbourne; pop. (1991p) 23,950.

War·saw \ˈwȯr-ˌsȯ\. **1.** City, ⊗ of Kosciusko co., N Indiana, 36 mi. (58 km.) SE of South Bend; pop. (1990c) 10,968.

2. City, ⊗ of Gallatin co., N Kentucky; pop. (1990c) 1202.

3. City, ⊗ of Benton co., W cen. Missouri; pop. (1990c) 1696.

4. Village, ⊗ of Wyoming co., W New York, 39 mi. (63 km.) SW of Rochester; pop. (1990c) 3830.

5. Town, Duplin co., SE North Carolina; pop. (1990c) 2859.

6. Town, ⊗ of Richmond co., E Virginia; pop. (1990c) 961.

Warsaw *or Pol.* **War·sza·wa** \vär-ˈshä-vä\. **1.** Province of Poland. See WARSZAWA.

2. *or Ger.* **War·schau** \ˈvär-ˌshau̇\. City, ✻ of Poland, also ✻ of Warszawa prov., E cen. Poland, on both banks of Vistula River; pop. (1989e) 1,655,063; railroad junction; diversified industries incl. textiles. Location of Polish parliament (Sejm); archiepiscopal see (seat of Roman Catholic primate of Poland) and cultural and educational center; technical university (1826), Univ. of Warsaw, Polish Academy of Sciences, and other institutions; notable buildings (largely rebuilt since WWII) include 14th cent. Gothic cathedral, medieval royal castle, numerous 17th and 18th cent. palaces (most now housing various government agencies), national theater and museum, monuments, parks, zoological gardens; 17th cent. castle of King John III Sobieski to S.

History: First settlement on site in 11th cent.; city founded c. 1300 and important trade center 14th–16th cents.; came under Poland 1526; made ✻ of Poland 1596; destroyed by Charles X Gustav of Sweden 1656; expanded rapidly during late 18th cent.; city partly burned and ab. one half of population massacred by Russians 1794; lost status after Third Partition of Poland 1790s; made ✻ of Grand Duchy of Warsaw by French Emperor Napoléon 1807; taken by Russians 1813 and made ✻ of kingdom under Russian rule 1815; center of Polish insurrection 1830–31 and in 1860s; in WWI occupied by Germans 1916–18; became ✻ of Polish republic 1918; in WWII occupied by Germans after severe bombing Sept. 27, 1939; large Jewish population segregated in ghetto revolted 1943 with great loss of life; city's population revolted in Warsaw Uprising 1944 but put down by Germans who then destroyed nearly whole city; taken by U.S.S.R. 1945. Since WWII, city has been largely rebuilt. Treaty establishing Warsaw Treaty Organization signed here 1955.

Warsaw, Grand Duchy of. Former grand duchy, E Europe. See *History* at POLAND.

Warsaw Treaty Organization *or commonly* **Warsaw Pact.** Former military alliance, consisting of Bulgaria, Czechoslovakia, Hungary, Poland, Romania, U.S.S.R.; headquarters Moscow, U.S.S.R.; purpose was to promote joint defense of the Soviet bloc nations; represented the Communist counterpart of NATO; estab. 1955; Albania withdrew 1968; forces of the Organization carried out invasion of Czechoslovakia 1968; Romania resisted integration of its forces with those of other members of the alliance, and refused to participate in the invasion of Czechoslovakia; withdrawal of East Germany effective Sept. 24, 1990 (with signing of protocol); Organization dissolved 1991 with breakup of E European Communist governments.

Warschau. See WARSAW 2.

War·sop \ˈwȯr-səp\. Town, Nottinghamshire, N cen. England, on the Meden 18 mi. (29 km.) N of Nottingham; pop. (1981p) 13,675.

War·sza·wa \vär-ˈshä-vä\ *or Eng.* **War·saw** \ˈwȯr-ˌsȯ\. Province of NE cen. Poland. See table at POLAND.

War·ta \ˈvär-tä\ *or Ger.* **War·the** \ˈvär-tə\. River, Poland; rises 35 mi. (56 km.) NW of Kraków, flows NW and W into the Odra (Oder) at Kostrzyn; 502 mi. (808 km.) long; navigable for 250 mi. (402 km.). Its lower course formerly in Germany, now in region assigned to Poland by Potsdam Conference 1945. Its chief tributaries are the Prosna and Notec.

Wart·burg \ˈwȯrt-ˌbərg\. Town, ⊗ of Morgan co., NE cen. Tennessee; pop. (1990c) 932.

War·wick \ˈwär-ik; *U.S. also* ˈwȯr-ik, ˈwȯr-ˌwik, ˈwär-ˌwik\. **1.** Former county in Virginia, incorp. 1952 as independent city of Warwick and consolidated 1958 with city of Newport News.

2. Village, Orange co., SE New York, 40 mi. (64 km.) NNW of New York City; pop. (1990c) 5984.

3. City and summer resort, Kent co., cen. Rhode Island, on Narragansett Bay 10 mi. (16 km.) S of Providence; pop. (1990c) 85,427; site of state's major airport; amusement park; New England Institute of Technology (1940), Community Coll. of Rhode Island (1964). Settled c. 1643; incorp. as town 1647.

4. Former city, Virginia. See WARWICK 1.

5. Town, SE Queensland, Australia, 80 mi. (129 km.) WSW of Brisbane; pop. (1991c) 10,393.

6. County, England. See WARWICKSHIRE.

7. Town, ⊗ of Warwickshire, cen. England, on the Avon 20 mi. (32 km.) SSE of Birmingham; pop. (1981p) 21,936; 14th cent. castle.

War·wick·shire \ˈwär-ik-ˌshir, -shər\ *or* **War·wick** \ˈwär-ik\. **1.** Former county, cen. England; major settlements Birmingham, Coventry, Solihull.

2. Administrative county, cen. England, incl. most of the former county except area now in West Midlands (*q.v.*); agriculture. See table at ENGLAND.

Wa·satch \ˈwȯ-ˌsach\. County in N cen. Utah. See table at UTAH.

Wasatch Mountain. Peak, San Miguel co., SW Colorado; 13,335 ft. (4065 m.).

Wasatch Range. Range in Idaho and Utah, extending from Bannock co., SE Idaho, S along the E boundary of the Great Basin to Sanpete co., cen. Utah; highest peak Mt. Timpanogos 12,008 ft. (3660 m.).

Was·co \ˈwäs-kō\. **1.** County in N Oregon. See table at OREGON.

2. City, Kern co., S California, NW of Bakersfield; pop. (1990c) 12,412.

Wa·se·ca \wä-ˈsē-kə\. **1.** County in S Minnesota. See table at MINNESOTA.

2. City, its ⊗, 23 mi. (37 km.) ESE of Mankato; pop. (1990c) 8385.

Wash, The \ˈwȯsh, ˈwäsh\. Shallow bay, an inlet of the North Sea, on the NW coast of Norfolk co. and the SE coast of Lincolnshire, E England; 22 mi. (35 km.) long, 15 mi. (24 km.) wide; includes the estuaries of several rivers, incl. the Witham, Welland, Nene, and Ouse.

Wash·a·baugh \ˈwä-shə-ˌbȯ\. Former unorganized county, SW South Dakota; now part of Jackson co.

Wash·a·kie \ˈwä-shə-kē\. County in N cen. Wyoming. See table at WYOMING.

Wash·burn \ˈwȯsh-bərn\. **1.** County in NW Wisconsin. See table at WISCONSIN.

2. City, ⊗ of McLean co., W cen. North Dakota, on Missouri River 35 mi. (56 km.) N of Bismarck; pop. (1990c) 1506.

3. City, ⊗ of Bayfield co., NW Wisconsin, on Lake Superior 7 mi. (11 km.) N of Ashland; pop. (1990c) 2285.

Washburn, Mount. Peak, N part of Yellowstone National Park, NW Wyoming, W of the Grand Canyon of the Yellowstone; 10,243 ft. (3122 m.).

Wash·ing·ton \ˈwȯsh-iŋ-tən, ˈwäsh-\. **1.** A northwestern state of U.S.A., bounded on N by Canadian prov. of British Columbia, on E by Idaho, on S by Oregon, and on W by the Pacific Ocean, Juan de Fuca Strait, and Strait of Georgia; 20th state in area, 68,192 sq. mi. (176,617 sq. km.); 18th state in population, (1990c) 4,866,692; ✻ Olympia; 42d state admitted to Union (1889). See table of states at UNITED STATES.

Nickname: Evergreen State.

State flower: Rhododendron.

Motto: Alki (By and By).

Rivers: Columbia, flowing from NE to cen. region, then S to the border and W to form boundary bet. Washington and Oregon; its tributaries, Pend Oreille in NE, Snake in SE, and Yakima in S cen. region.

Highest point: Mt. Rainier, 14,410 ft. (4392 m.), Pierce co.

Chief products: Wheat, apples and other fruit; dairy products; fishing; zinc, lead, gravel; manufacturing: aircraft and other transportation equipment, lumber, chemicals.

Chief cities: Seattle, Spokane, Tacoma.

Political divisions: Divided into the following 39 counties (for pronunciation of their names, see their individual entries):

NAME	AREA[1] (sq. mi.)	AREA[1] (sq. km.)	POP. (1990c)	CO. SEAT
Adams	1,894	4,905	13,603	Ritzville
Asotin	633	1,639	17,605	Asotin
Benton	1,722	4,460	112,560	Prosser
Chelan	2,926	7,578	52,250	Wenatchee
Clallam[2]	1,753	4,540	56,464	Port Angeles
Clark	627	1,624	238,053	Vancouver
Columbia	860	2,227	4,024	Dayton
Cowlitz	1,144	2,963	82,119	Kelso
Douglas	1,839	4,763	26,205	Waterville
Ferry	2,202	5,703	6,295	Republic
Franklin	1,260	3,263	37,473	Pasco
Garfield	713	1,847	2,248	Pomeroy
Grant[3]	2,681	6,944	54,758	Ephrata
Grays Harbor	1,910	4,947	64,175	Montesano
Island[4]	212	549	60,195	Coupeville
Jefferson[2]	1,805	4,675	20,146	Port Townsend
King	2,131	5,519	1,507,319	Seattle
Kitsap	393	1,018	189,731	Port Orchard
Kittitas	2,320	6,009	26,725	Ellensburg
Klickitat	1,908	4,942	16,616	Goldendale
Lewis[5]	2,449	6,343	59,358	Chehalis
Lincoln	2,306	5,973	8,864	Davenport
Mason[2]	960	2,486	38,341	Shelton
Okanogan	5,301	13,730	33,350	Okanogan
Pacific	908	2,352	18,882	South Bend
Pend Oreille	1,402	3,631	8,915	Newport
Pierce[5]	1,676	4,341	586,203	Tacoma
San Juan[6]	179	464	10,035	Friday Harbor
Skagit[7]	1,735	4,494	79,555	Mount Vernon
Skamania	1,672	4,330	8,289	Stevenson
Snohomish	2,098	5,434	465,642	Everett
Spokane	1,758	4,553	361,364	Spokane
Stevens	2,481	6,426	30,948	Colville
Thurston	714	1,849	161,238	Olympia
Wahkiakum	261	676	3,327	Cathlamet
Walla Walla	1,267	3,282	48,439	Walla Walla
Whatcom	2,126	5,506	127,780	Bellingham
Whitman	2,166	5,610	38,775	Colfax
Yakima	4,271	11,062	188,823	Yakima

[1] Area = land area.
[2] Olympic National Park occupies adjoining areas in S Clallam co., cen. Jefferson co., and NW corner of Mason co.
[3] Grand Coulee Dam at NE corner.
[4] Composed of islands lying N of Puget Sound and E of Admiralty Inlet.
[5] Mount Rainier National Park occupies SE corner of Pierce co. and adjoining smaller area in NE Lewis co.
[6] Composed of islands lying NE of Juan de Fuca Strait and S of Strait of Georgia.
[7] Includes islands separated from San Juan co. by Rosario Strait.

History: Area inhabited by Pacific coast Indians when region visited by Spanish, Russian, British, and French explorers 1543–1792 (short-lived settlement 1791 at Neah Bay (*q.v.*); explored by Americans Meriwether Lewis and William Clark, who sailed down Columbia River 1805; part of Oregon Country; occupied jointly by Great Britain and U.S. 1818–46; first permanent settlement at Tumwater 1845; by treaty with Great Britain 1846 N boundary set at 49th parallel; part of Oregon Terr. 1848; settlement at Seattle 1851, at Tacoma 1852; became part of Washington Terr. (*q.v.*) 1853; territory reduced to area of present state 1863; admitted to Union as state Nov. 11, 1889.

2. Name of a parish of E Louisiana and of counties in 30 states of the U.S. See tables at ALABAMA, ARKANSAS, COLORADO, FLORIDA, GEORGIA, IDAHO, ILLINOIS, INDIANA, IOWA, KANSAS, KENTUCKY, LOUISIANA, MAINE, MARYLAND, MINNESOTA, MISSISSIPPI, MISSOURI, NEBRASKA, NEW YORK, NORTH CAROLINA, OHIO, OKLAHOMA, OREGON, PENNSYLVANIA, RHODE ISLAND, TENNESSEE, TEXAS, UTAH, VERMONT, VIRGINIA, WISCONSIN.

3. City, Hempstead co., SW Arkansas, 33 mi. (53 km.) NE of Texarkana; pop. (1990c) 148; state ✻ 1863–65; ⊗ to 1939.

4. Residential town, S cen. Litchfield co., NW Connecticut, NE of New Milford; pop. (1990c) 3905; incorp. 1779.

5. Capital city of U.S.A., coextensive with the District of Columbia, bet. Maryland and Virginia, on the E bank of the Potomac River at the head of navigation and at its confluence with the Anacostia River ab. 40 mi. (64 km.) SW of Baltimore, Maryland; area 69 sq. mi. (179 sq. km.); pop. (1990c) 606,900; a leading international political center; educational center; tourism and convention trade; scientific research.

Public buildings, monuments, institutions, and parks: Capitol (located on Capitol Hill, 88 ft. or 27 m. above the Potomac; begun 1793), White House (the oldest government

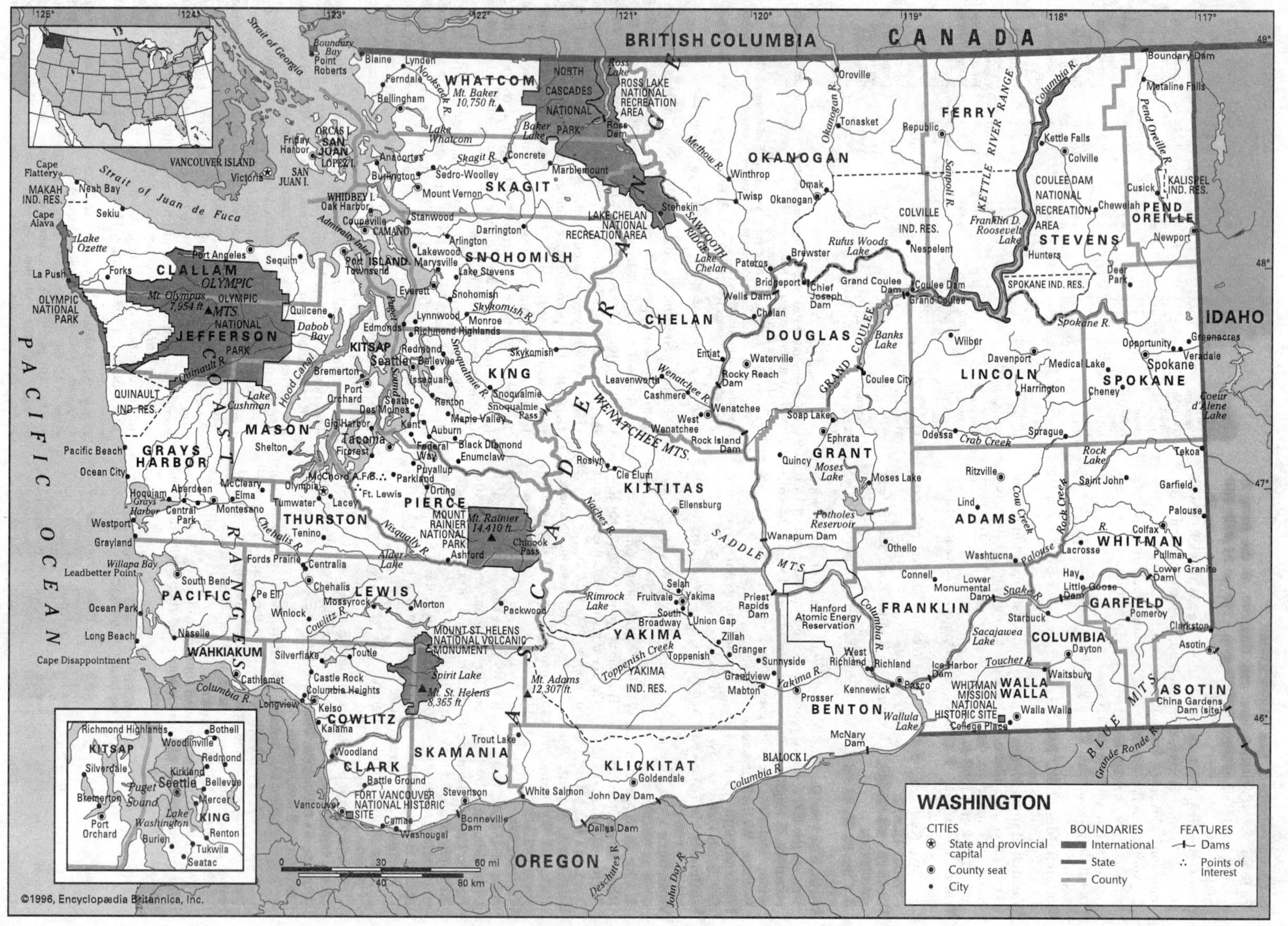

WASHINGTON
CITIES
State and provincial capital
County seat
City
BOUNDARIES
International
State
County
FEATURES
Dams
Points of interest
0 30 60 mi
0 40 80 km
©1996, Encyclopædia Britannica, Inc.
BRITISH COLUMBIA
CANADA
IDAHO
OREGON
PACIFIC OCEAN
Strait of Juan de Fuca
Strait of Georgia
VANCOUVER ISLAND
Victoria
WHATCOM
SKAGIT
OKANOGAN
FERRY
STEVENS
PEND OREILLE
SPOKANE
LINCOLN
DOUGLAS
CHELAN
SNOHOMISH
KING
KITSAP
ISLAND
SAN JUAN
CLALLAM
JEFFERSON
MASON
GRAYS HARBOR
THURSTON
PIERCE
KITTITAS
GRANT
ADAMS
WHITMAN
GARFIELD
ASOTIN
COLUMBIA
WALLA WALLA
FRANKLIN
BENTON
YAKIMA
KLICKITAT
SKAMANIA
LEWIS
PACIFIC
WAHKIAKUM
COWLITZ
CLARK
CASCADE RANGE
COAST RANGES
BLUE MTS.
KETTLE RIVER RANGE
SAWTOOTH RIDGE
WENATCHEE MTS.
SADDLE MTS.
OLYMPIC MTS.
Mt. Olympus 7,954 ft.
Mt. Baker 10,750 ft.
Mt. Rainier 14,410 ft.
Mt. Adams 12,307 ft.
Mt. St. Helens 8,365 ft.
OLYMPIC NATIONAL PARK
NORTH CASCADES NATIONAL PARK
MOUNT RAINIER NATIONAL PARK
ROSS LAKE NATIONAL RECREATION AREA
LAKE CHELAN NATIONAL RECREATION AREA
COULEE DAM NATIONAL RECREATION AREA
MOUNT ST. HELENS NATIONAL VOLCANIC MONUMENT
WHITMAN MISSION NATIONAL HISTORIC SITE
FORT VANCOUVER NATIONAL HISTORIC SITE
HANFORD ATOMIC ENERGY RESERVATION
COLVILLE IND. RES.
SPOKANE IND. RES.
YAKIMA IND. RES.
QUINAULT IND. RES.
MAKAH IND. RES.
KALISPEL IND. RES.
Franklin D. Roosevelt Lake
Banks Lake
Moses Lake
Potholes Reservoir
Lake Chelan
Ross Lake
Columbia R.
Snake R.
Yakima R.
Spokane R.
Okanogan R.
Puget Sound
Hood Canal
Seattle
Spokane
Tacoma
Olympia
Bellingham
Everett
Yakima
Vancouver
Walla Walla
Wenatchee
Richland
Kennewick
Pasco
Ellensburg
Port Angeles
Aberdeen
Longview
Pullman
Moses Lake
Grand Coulee Dam
Chief Joseph Dam
Bonneville Dam
John Day Dam
McNary Dam
Cape Flattery
Cape Disappointment
Richmond Highlands
Bothell
Woodinville
Redmond
Kirkland
Bellevue
Mercer I.
Renton
Tukwila
Seatac
Burien
Bremerton
Port Orchard
Silverdale
Lake Washington

building in Washington; cornerstone laid 1792), Library of Congress (one of largest libraries in world), Senate Office Buildings, House Office Buildings, Treasury Building, State Dept. Building, Lincoln Memorial, Washington Monument (555 ft. 5.125 in. or 169.29 m. high), Jefferson Memorial, National Bureau of Standards, National Archives, Supreme Court, Federal Reserve Board, Dept. of Justice, Post Office Dept., Dept. of Interior, Dept. of Agriculture, Dept. of Commerce, Bureau of Engraving and Printing, Government Printing Office, and the Pentagon Building (in Virginia 3 mi. or 5 km. from White House), National Science Foundation, National Aeronautics and Space Administration, Taft Memorial, Vietnam Veterans Memorial, U.S. Holocaust Memorial Museum; among the outstanding nongovernment buildings are: Constitution Hall, Washington National Cathedral (Episcopal Cathedral of St. Peter and St. Paul), National Shrine of the Immaculate Conception, John F. Kennedy Center for the Performing Arts; institutions include Walter Reed Army Medical Center and U.S. Soldiers' Home. Parks include the Mall (oldest park in city), Potomac Park, Rock Creek Park, National Zoological Park, Anacostia Park (containing the National Arboretum), and a large number of other public open spaces.

Educational and cultural institutions: Georgetown Univ. (1789), George Washington Univ. (1821), Gallaudet Univ. (1864, for those with special needs), Howard Univ. (1867), Mount Vernon Coll. (1875), Southeastern Univ. (1879), Catholic Univ. of America (1887), American Univ. (1893), Trinity Coll. (1897), Oblate Coll. (1904), Univ. of the District of Columbia (1976); cultural agencies include the Smithsonian Institution (incl. the Sackler Gallery, Arts and Industries Building, Freer Gallery of Art, Hirshhorn Museum and Sculpture Garden, the National Air and Space Museum, National Museum of African Art, National Museum of American History, and National Museum of Natural History), Washington Public Library, Folger Shakespeare Library, departmental government libraries, Corcoran Gallery of Art, National Gallery of Art; among the many institutes and societies with headquarters in Washington are: Carnegie Institution of Washington (physical sciences), Brookings Institution (social sciences), American Association for the Advancement of Science, National Geographic Society, American Political Science Association, American Historical Association, American Institute of Architects, Daughters of the American Revolution.

History: Site chosen by first U.S. President George Washington in 1790 as compromise to other competing locations; planned by French-born American soldier and engineer Major Pierre Charles L'Enfant; occupied by Federal government 1800; occupied by British troops and burned 1814 during War of 1812; part of N Virginia (what is now Alexandria and Arlington) orig. within capital district, returned to Virginia mid-1800s; with annexation of Georgetown, became coterminous with District of Columbia (*q.v.*).

6. City, ⊗ of Wilkes co., NE Georgia, 40 mi. (64 km.) ESE of Athens; pop. (1990c) 4279; founded 1780.

7. City, Tazewell co., cen. Illinois, 10 mi. (16 km.) E of Peoria; pop. (1990c) 10,099.

8. City, ⊗ of Daviess co., SW Indiana, 18 mi. (29 km.) E of Vincennes; pop. (1990c) 10,838.

9. City, ⊗ of Washington co., SE Iowa, 25 mi. (40 km.) SSW of Iowa City; pop. (1990c) 7074.

10. City, ⊗ of Washington co., N Kansas, 52 mi. (84 km.) NNW of Manhattan; pop. (1990c) 1304.

11. City, Franklin co., E Missouri, on Missouri River 50 mi. (80 km.) E of St. Louis; pop. (1990c) 10,704.

12. Borough, Warren co., NW New Jersey, 12 mi. (19 km.) ENE of Phillipsburg; pop. (1990c) 6474.

13. City, ⊗ of Beaufort co., E North Carolina, on Pamlico River at head of navigation 30 mi. (48 km.) N of New Bern; pop. (1990c) 9075.

14. City, Ohio. See WASHINGTON COURT HOUSE.

15. City, ⊗ of Washington co., SW Pennsylvania, 25 mi. (40 km.) SW of Pittsburgh; pop. (1990c) 15,864; Washington and Jefferson Coll. (1781).

16. Village, Kent co., cen. Rhode Island; governmental seat of Coventry; settled c. 1750.

17. City, Washington co., SW Utah, near Virgin River; pop. (1990c) 4198.

18. Town, ⊗ of Rappahannock co., N Virginia; pop. (1990c) 198.

19. Island, Kiribati. See TERAINA.

20. Town, Tyne and Wear, N England, 6.25 mi. (10 km.) SSE of Newcastle upon Tyne; pop. (1981p) 42,666; electronic and electrical equipment, motor vehicles, chemicals, textiles.

Washington, Lake. Lake, King co., W cen. Washington; ab. 20 mi. (32 km.) long, 4 mi. (6 km.) wide; max. depth 225 ft. (69 m.); forms E boundary of city of Seattle; completion 1916 of ship canal 8 mi. (13 km.) long, 100 ft. (30 m.) wide, and 30 ft. (9 m.) deep bet. the lake and Puget Sound gave Seattle a waterfront 140 mi. (225 km.) long and a freshwater, nontidal harbor; crossed by two of the longest floating pontoon bridges in the U.S.

Washington, Mount. Peak in the Presidential Range of the White Mts., in S Coos co., N New Hampshire; 6288 ft. (1917 m.); highest point in NE United States.

Washington Court House *or* **Washington.** City, ⊗ of Fayette co., SW Ohio, 27 mi. (43 km.) WNW of Chillicothe; pop. (1990c) 12,983.

Washington Crossing. 1. Recreational area comprising twin parks in Pennsylvania (440 acres or 178 hectares) and New Jersey (292 acres or 118 hectares) on both sides of the Delaware River ab. 8 mi. (13 km.) NNW of Trenton, New Jersey; estab. to commemorate the crossing of the river by Gen. George Washington and his army Dec. 25–26, 1776, prior to the battle of Trenton.

2. Hamlet and post office, Bucks co., SE Pennsylvania, within the state park.

Washington Island. Island in Door co., NE Wisconsin, NW Lake Michigan S of entrance to Green Bay; 20 sq. mi. (52 sq. km.).

Washington Land. Section of NW Greenland along E shore of Kennedy Channel.

Washington Park. Village, St. Clair co., SW Illinois, near St. Louis, Missouri; pop. (1990c) 7431.

Washington Sound. Body of water bet. Strait of Juan de Fuca and the Strait of Georgia, off SE Vancouver I. and NW Washington; has many islands, most of them forming San Juan co., Washington.

Washington Terrace. City, Weber co., N Utah; pop. (1990c) 8189.

Washington Territory. Former territory, U.S.A.; comprised a region of varying extent within the bounds of Oregon Country (*q.v.*); territory organized 1853 incl. what is now Washington, N Idaho, and W Montana; expanded to include the rest of Idaho and SW Wyoming 1859 (upon admission of Oregon to the Union); reduced to area of present state 1863 upon formation of Idaho Terr. (*q.v.*); Washington admitted to the Union 1889.

Wash·i·ta \ˈwä-shə-ˌtȯ, ˈwȯ-\. **1.** River, Arkansas and Louisiana. See OUACHITA 1.

2. River, W and S cen. Oklahoma; rises in Hemphill co., NW Texas, flows E across Oklahoma boundary, then SE to S cen. Oklahoma, and S into Red River; 500 mi. (805 km.) long.

3. County in Arkansas and parish in Louisiana. See *Ouachita* in tables at ARKANSAS and LOUISIANA.

4. County in W Oklahoma. See table at OKLAHOMA.

Wash·oe \ˈwä-shō\. County in NW corner of Nevada. See table at NEVADA.

Wash·te·naw \ˈwäsh-tə-ˌnȯ\. County in SE Michigan. See table at MICHIGAN.

Wa·sil·la \wä-ˈsi-lə\. City, S Alaska, N of Anchorage; pop. (1990c) 4028.

\ə\ **abut** \ə̇\ **matches** \ᵊ\ **kitten, Fr table** \ər\ **further** \a\ **ash** \ā\ **ace** \ä\ **cot, cart** \à\ **Fr bac** \au̇\ **out** \b\ **Span Avila** \ch\ **chin** \e\ **bet** \ē\ **easy** \g\ **go** \i\ **hit** \ī\ **ice** \j\ **job** \k\ **Ger ich, Buch** \ⁿ\ **Fr vin** \ŋ\ **sing** \ō\ **go** \ö\ **all** \ȯ\ **law** \œ\ **Fr bœuf** \œ̄\ **Fr feu** \ȯi\ **boy** \th\ **thin** \t͟h\ **this** \ü\ **loot** \u̇\ **foot** \ue\ **Ger füllen** \ue̅\ **Fr rue** \y\ **yet** \ʸ\ **Fr digne** \ˈdēnʸ\, **nuit** \ˈnwʸē\ \yü\ **few** \yu̇\ **fury** \zh\ **vision**

Was·se·naar \ˈvä-sə-ˌnär\. Commune, South Holland prov., SW Netherlands, just SSW of Leiden; pop. (1981e) 27,025.

Was·ser·kup·pe \ˈvä-sər-ˌku̇-pə\. Mountain in SE Hesse, Germany; 3116 ft. (950 m.); highest peak in the Rhön Range.

Was·suk Range \ˈwä-sək\. Range, Mineral co., SW Nevada; highest point Mt. Grant 11,245 ft. (3427 m.).

Wa States \wä\. Region of Myanmar, E of the Salween, a part of Shan State; 3332 sq. mi. (8630 sq. km.); inhabited by the Wa.

Wast Water \ˈwäst\. Lake, Lake District, NW England, in Cumbria co. 14 mi. (23 km.) SW of Keswick; 3 mi. (5 km.) long; max. depth 258 ft. (79 m.).

Wa·tau·ga \wä-ˈtȯ-gə\. **1.** River, NE Tennessee; rises in NW North Carolina, flows NW into S fork of Holston River SE of Kingsport, S Sullivan co., Tennessee; ab. 60 mi. (95 km.) long. It contains **Watauga Dam,** one of the dams in the Tennessee Valley Authority (see table at TENNESSEE VALLEY AUTHORITY). In its valley were estab. 1769–75 the Watauga settlements of early settlers crossing the mountains by Boone's Gap from North Carolina and Virginia; they formed the Watauga Association 1772 to band together for protection and they were the nucleus and starting point of further settlements in Tennessee and other states.

2. County in NW North Carolina. See table at NORTH CAROLINA.

3. City, Tarrant co., N Texas, N and E of Fort Worth; pop. (1990c) 20,009; pop. nearly doubled bet. 1980 and 1990.

Watch Hill \ˈwäch\. Village, Westerly town, Washington co., S Rhode Island, on Block Island Sound ab. 3 mi. (5 km.) SE of Stonington, Connecticut; summer resort since 1840.

Watch Hill Point. Promontory, SW extremity of Washington co., S Rhode Island, ab. 1 mi. (2 km.) E of Napatree Point.

Watch·ung \wä-ˈchu̇ŋ, ˈwä-ˌ\. Borough, Somerset co., N cen. New Jersey, W of Plainfield; pop. (1990c) 5110.

Watenstedt–Salzgitter. See SALZGITTER.

Wa·ter·bury \ˈwȯ-tər-ˌber-ē, ˈwä-\. **1.** City, New Haven co., S Connecticut, at confluence of Naugatuck and Mad rivers 19 mi. (30.5 km.) NNW of New Haven; pop. (1990c) 108,961; financial and commercial center of W Connecticut; historically a major brass center; Teikyo Post Coll. (1890), Waterbury State Technical Coll. (1964), Mattatuck Community Coll. (1964). Founded 1674 and incorp. as town 1686, and as city 1853; town and city consolidated 1902.

2. Village in Waterbury town, Washington co., N cen. Vermont, on Winooski River 10 mi. (16 km.) WNW of Montpelier; pop. (1990c) 1702 (village), 4589 (town); Community Coll. of Vermont (1970).

Wa·ter·ee \ˈwȯ-tə-ˌrē, ˈwä-\. River, cen. South Carolina; enters state from North Carolina as Catawba River (*q.v.*) but known as Wateree River in South Carolina and joins the Congaree to form Santee River; length of Wateree-Catawba River 395 mi. (636 km.).

Wateree Lake. Long narrow lake, N cen. South Carolina, formed by a dam in the Wateree River; extends along boundary bet. Kershaw and Fairfield cos.

Wa·ter·ford \ˈwȯ-tər-fərd, ˈwä-\. **1.** City, Stanislas co., cen. California; pop. (1990c) 4771.

2. Town, S New London co., SE Connecticut, on Thames River and Long Island Sound adjoining New London on E; pop. (1990c) 17,930; nuclear power plant; incorp. 1801.

3. Town, Saratoga co., E New York, on Hudson River 10 mi. (16 km.) N of Albany; pop. (1990c) 8695. See CHAMPLAIN CANAL.

4. County, in Munster prov., S Ireland; ⊗ Waterford; rivers Suir, Blackwater. See table at IRELAND.

5. Seaport city, ⊗ of co. Waterford, S Ireland, on Suir River; pop. (1991p) 40,345; one of the principal ports of S Ireland; internationally known Waterford crystal; two 18th cent. cathedrals. A historic seaport at which many English sovereigns landed; James II left from here for France after his defeat at the Boyne; revolted against government 17th cent. and successfully resisted siege by Parliamentarian commander Oliver Cromwell 1649 but fell to his second in command Henry Ireton 1650.

Waterford Harbour. Inlet of St. George's Channel, SE coast of Ireland, in co. Waterford; the city of Waterford is at the head of the inlet.

Wa·ter·loo \ˌwȯ-tər-ˈlü, ˈwȯ-tər-ˌ; ˌwä-tər-ˈlü, ˈwä-tər-ˌ\. **1.** City, ⊗ of Monroe co., SW Illinois, 22 mi. (35 km.) S of East St. Louis; pop. (1990c) 5072.

2. City, ⊗ of Black Hawk co., NE cen. Iowa, on Cedar River 52 mi. (84 km.) NW of Cedar Rapids; pop. (1990c) 66,467; agricultural equipment. Settled 1845; incorp. 1868.

3. Village, a ⊗ of Seneca co., W cen. New York, 15 mi. (24 km.) W of Auburn; pop. (1990c) 5116; in lake-resort region.

4. City, Jefferson co., SE Wisconsin, NE of Madison; pop. (1990c) 2712.

5. *Flem.* ˈvä-tər-ˌlō\. Commune, Brabant prov., cen. Belgium, ab. 12 mi. (19 km.) S of Brussels; pop. (1991c) 27,860; battle called Waterloo nearby (at La Belle Alliance, 3 mi. or 4.8 km. to SE) June 18, 1815 in which the British under Arthur Wellesley, duke of Wellington and the Prussians under Field Marshal Gebhard Leberecht von Blücher decisively defeated French Emperor Napoléon and ended his power.

6. Municipal region in SE Ontario, Canada. See table at ONTARIO.

7. Town, Waterloo munic. region, SE Ontario, Canada; adjoins Kitchener; pop. (1991c) 71,181; Univ. of Waterloo (1957), incl. four formerly separate institutions.

8. Town, S Quebec, Canada, 30 mi. (48 km.) W of Sherbrooke; pop. (1991c) 3964.

9. Town on railroad line in N cen. part of Sierra Leone Penin., Sierra Leone, 14 mi. (23 km.) SE of Freetown.

Wa·ter·mael–Boits·fort \ˈvä-tər-ˌmäl-bwä-ˈfȯr\. Commune, Brabant prov., cen. Belgium, a suburb of Brussels; pop. (1991c) 24,567.

Wat·er·man, Mount \ˈwȯ-tər-mən, ˈwä-\. Mountain, Antarctica, 84°27′S, 175°24′E; 12,730 ft. (3880 m.).

Wat·er·rock Knob \ˈwȯ-tər-ˌräk, ˈwä-\. Peak, Haywood co., W North Carolina; 6399 ft. (1950 m.).

Wa·ter·ton–Gla·cier International Peace Park \ˈwȯ-tərt-ᵊn-ˈglā-shər, ˈwä-\. International park, comprising Waterton Lakes National Park in S Alberta, Canada, and Glacier National Park in NW Montana; estab. 1932. See CANADA, *National Parks* and UNITED STATES, *National Parks.*

Waterton Lakes National Park. See CANADA, *National Parks.*

Wa·ter·town \ˈwȯ-tər-ˌtau̇n, ˈwä-\. **1.** Town, SE Litchfield co., NW Connecticut, on W bank of branch of Naugatuck River NW of Waterbury; pop. (1990c) 20,456; incorp. 1780.

2. Town, Middlesex co., NE Massachusetts, 7 mi. (11 km.) W of Boston; pop. (1990c) 33,284; settled 1630.

3. City, ⊗ of Jefferson co., N New York, 10 mi. (16 km.) E of Lake Ontario; pop. (1990c) 29,429; to the NE is Fort Drum; Jefferson Community Coll. (1963); settled c. 1800. Bisected by Black River, with 112 ft. (34 m.) falls within city.

4. City, ⊗ of Codington co., NE South Dakota, 70 mi. (113 km.) ENE of Huron; pop. (1990c) 17,592; incorp. 1885.

5. City, Dodge and Jefferson cos., SE Wisconsin, 32 mi. (52 km.) E of Madison; pop. (1990c) 19,142; Northwestern Coll. (1865); home of soldier and reformer Carl Schurz 1855–61; site of what is considered to be first kindergarten in America, estab. by Schurz's wife, Margarethe 1856.

Water Valley. City, a ⊗ of Yalobusha co., N Mississippi, 53 mi. (85 km.) E of Clarksdale; pop. (1990c) 3610.

Wa·ter·ville \ˈwȯ-tər-ˌvil, ˈwä-\. **1.** City, Kennebec co., SW Maine, on Kennebec River 18 mi. (28 km.) N of Augusta; pop. (1990c) 17,173; Colby Coll. (1813), Thomas Coll. (1894).

2. Village, Oneida co., cen. New York, 13 mi. (21 km.) SW of Utica; pop. (1990c) 1664; birthplace of inventor George Eastman 1854.

3. Village, Lucas co., NW Ohio, on Maumee River, SW of Toledo; pop. (1990c) 4517.

4. Town, ⊗ of Douglas co., cen. Washington; pop. (1990c) 995.

Wa·ter·vliet \ˈwȯ-tər-ˌvlēt, ˈwä-\. City, Albany co., E New York, on Hudson River opp. Troy near terminus of New York State Barge Canal, 6 mi. (10 km.) N of Albany; pop. (1990c)

11,061. Seat of U.S. Arsenal, estab. 1813, producing arms for War of 1812 and subsequent wars.

Wat·ford \ˈwät-fərd\. Town, Hertfordshire, SE England, on the Colne 17 mi. (27 km.) NW of London; pop. (1991p) 72,100; a small part lies within Greater London.

Watford City. City, ⊗ of McKenzie co., W North Dakota, 28 mi. (45 km.) SE of Williston; pop. (1990c) 1784.

Wath upon Dearne \ˈwäth ... ˈdərn\. Town, South Yorkshire, N England, 8 mi. (13 km.) SE of Barnsley; pop. (1981p) 14,480.

Wat·kins Glen \ˈwät-kinz\. Village, ⊗ of Schuyler co., SW cen. New York, at S end of Seneca Lake 18 mi. (28 km.) N of Elmira; pop. (1990c) 2207; summer resort; auto racing; **Watkins Glen** nearby, a gorge 2 mi. (3 km.) long, 100 to 300 ft. (30 to 90 m.) deep, the stream falling in many cascades.

Wat·kins·ville \ˈwät-kinz-ˌvil\. Town, ⊗ of Oconee co., NE cen. Georgia; pop. (1990c) 1600.

Watling *or* **Watlings** *or* **Watling's.** See SAN SALVADOR 1.

Wat·ling Street \ˈwät-liŋ\. Orig. an ancient Roman road in Britain, extending from London to Wroxeter (near Shrewsbury) in a general northwesterly direction; later applied to other roads, such as one that began at Richborough, or Dover, ran through Canterbury to London, and continued from Wroxeter to Chester. SW of Leicester it was intersected by Fosse Way. In 9th cent. divided Mercia (*q.v.*); one of the four great Roman roads of Britain (see ERMINE STREET, FOSSE WAY, and ICKNIELD STREET).

Watling Town. See WELLINGTON 6.

Wa·ton·ga \wə-ˈtäŋ-gə\. City, ⊗ of Blaine co., W cen. Oklahoma, 50 mi. (81 km.) SW of Enid; pop. (1990c) 3408.

Wat·on·wan \ˈwät-ᵊn-ˌwän\. County in S Minnesota. See table at MINNESOTA.

Wa·trous \ˈwȯ-trəs, ˈwä-\. Village, S Mora co., NE New Mexico; ruins of Fort Union nearby (see FORT UNION NATIONAL MONUMENT).

Wat·se·ka \wät-ˈsē-kə\. City, ⊗ of Iroquois co., E Illinois, 27 mi. (43 km.) SSE of Kankakee; pop. (1990c) 5424.

Wat·son, Mount \ˈwät-sən\. Peak, S Summit co., NE Utah; 11,473 ft. (3497 m.).

Watson Lake. Town, left bank of Liard River, S Yukon, Canada, 12 mi. (19 km.) N of British Columbia border, on the Alaska Highway; pop. (1991c) 912; nearby is a collection of thousands of signposts showing hometowns of visitors.

Wat·son·ville \ˈwät-sən-ˌvil\. City, Santa Cruz co., W California, near Monterey Bay 30 mi. (48 km.) S of San Jose; pop. (1990c) 31,099; founded 1852.

Wat·ten·scheid \ˈvät-ᵊn-ˌshīt\. City, North Rhine-Westphalia, Germany, in Ruhr Valley; E suburb of Essen.

Wat·ti·gnies \ˌvä-tē-ˈnyē\ *or in full* **Wattignies–la–Vic·toire** \-lä-vēk-ˈtwär\. Village, Nord dept., N France; scene of battle 1793 in which the French under Gen. Jean-Baptiste Jourdan defeated the Austrians.

Wat·tre·los \ˌvä-trə-ˈlō\. Commune, Nord dept., N France, 9 mi. (15 km.) NE of Lille; pop. (1990c) 43,874; suburb of Roubaix.

Watts \ˈwäts\. Neighborhood of Los Angeles, California; scene of severe racial violence 1965.

Watts Bar Dam. See table at TENNESSEE VALLEY AUTHORITY.

Watts Island. Island, lower Chesapeake Bay, W cen. coast of Accomac co., Virginia.

Wau \ˈwau̇\. **1.** Settlement, Papua New Guinea, E New Guinea I., 32 mi. (52 km.) SW of Salamaua; alt. 3500 ft. (1067 m.); gold mining; settlement begun c. 1925; in WWII fighting occurred bet. Japanese and Australians and Americans.

2. *or* **Wāw** \ˈwȯ\. Town, S Sudan, on the Jur River; pop. (1980e) 116,000.

Wau·bay Lake \wȯ-ˈbā\. Lake, Day co., NE South Dakota; wildlife refuge nearby.

Wau·be·sa, Lake \wȯ-ˈbē-sə\. See FOUR LAKES.

Wau·chu·la \wȯ-ˈchü-lə\. City, ⊗ of Hardee co., cen. Florida Penin., 37 mi. (60 km.) S of Lakeland; pop. (1990c) 3253.

Wau·con·da \wȯ-ˈkän-də\. Village, Lake co., NE Illinois, 18 mi. (28 km.) WSW of Waukegan; pop. (1990c) 6294; summer resort.

Waugh Mountain \ˈwȯ\. Peak, SE Idaho co., N cen. Idaho; 8882 ft. (2707 m.).

Wau·ka·ra *or Du.* **Waoe·ka·ra** \wau̇-ˈkär-ə\. Mountain, NW cen. Sulawesi, Indonesia; 10,259 ft. (3127 m.).

Wau·kee \ˈwȯ-kē\. City, Dallas co., S cen. Iowa, W of Des Moines; pop. (1990c) 2512.

Wau·ke·gan \wȯ-ˈkē-gən\. Residential city, ⊗ of Lake co., NE corner of Illinois, on Lake Michigan 40 mi. (64 km.) N of Chicago; pop. (1990c) 69,392; lake port; Shimer Coll. (1853); visited by French 18th cent. when area was inhabited by Indians who continued to live there until nonnative settlement 1835; incorp. as town 1849, as city 1859; Great Lakes Naval Training Center to S.

Wau·ke·sha \ˈwȯ-ki-ˌshȯ\. **1.** County in SE Wisconsin. See table at WISCONSIN.

2. City, its ⊗, 15 mi. (24 km.) W of Milwaukee; pop. (1990c) 56,958; trade center for agricultural area; bottles mineral water; Carroll Coll. (1846), Univ. of Wisconsin–Waukesha (1966); Underground Railroad stop for slaves before Civil War; settled 1835; incorp. as city 1896.

Wau·kon \wȯ-ˈkän\. City, ⊗ of Allamakee co., NE corner of Iowa, 17 mi. (27 km.) E of Decorah; pop. (1990c) 4019.

Waum·bek, Mount *also* **Waumbek Mountain** \ˈwȯm-ˌbek\. Peak, S Coos co., N New Hampshire; 4020 ft. (1225 m.).

Wau·na·kee \ˌwȯ-nə-ˈkē\. Village, Dane co., S Wisconsin, N of Madison; pop. (1990c) 5897.

Wau·paca \wȯ-ˈpa-kə\. **1.** County in E cen. Wisconsin. See table at WISCONSIN.

2. City, its ⊗, 32 mi. (52 km.) WNW of Appleton; pop. (1990c) 4957; outdoor recreation.

Waupés. See UAUPÉS.

Wau·pun \wȯ-ˈpän—*sic*\. City, Dodge and Fond du Lac cos., SE cen. Wisconsin, 17 mi. (27 km.) SW of the city of Fond du Lac; pop. (1990c) 8207.

Wau·ri·ka \wȯ-ˈrē-kə\. City, ⊗ of Jefferson co., S Oklahoma, 38 mi. (61 km.) SSE of Lawton; pop. (1990c) 2088.

Wau·sau \ˈwȯ-ˌsȯ\. City, ⊗ of Marathon co., cen. Wisconsin, on Wisconsin River 84 mi. (135 km.) WNW of Green Bay (city); pop. (1990c) 37,060; dairy products; art museum; North Central Technical Coll. (1912); incorp. 1872.

Wau·se·on \ˈwȯ-sē-ˌȯn\. City, ⊗ of Fulton co., NW Ohio, 32 mi. (52 km.) W of Toledo; pop. (1990c) 6322.

Wau·shara \wȯ-ˈshar-ə\. County in cen. Wisconsin. See table at WISCONSIN.

Wau·to·ma \wȯ-ˈtō-mə\. City, ⊗ of Waushara co., cen. Wisconsin; pop. (1990c) 1784.

Wau·wa·to·sa \ˌwȯ-wə-ˈtō-sə\. City, Milwaukee co., SE Wisconsin, 5 mi. (8 km.) W of the city of Milwaukee; pop. (1990c) 49,366; suburb of Milwaukee.

Wave·land \ˈwāv-lənd\. City, Hancock co., S Mississippi, on Mississippi Sound, SW of Gulfport; pop. (1990c) 5369.

Waveney. See BROADS, THE.

Wa·ver·ley \ˈwā-vər-lē\. **1.** Municipality, E New South Wales, SE Australia, E suburb of Sydney, on Pacific Ocean; pop. (1991c) 59,095.

2. City, Victoria, Australia, a SE suburb of Melbourne; pop. (1991c) 118,265.

Wa·ver·ly \ˈwā-vər-lē\. **1.** City, ⊗ of Bremer co., NE Iowa, 15 mi. (24 km.) NNW of Waterloo; pop. (1990c) 8539; Wartburg Coll. (1852).

2. Village, Tioga co., S New York, on Pennsylvania border 15 mi. (24 km.) ESE of Elmira; pop. (1990c) 4787.

3. Village, ⊗ of Pike co., S Ohio, 15 mi. (24 km.) S of Chillicothe; pop. (1990c) 4477.

4. City, ⊗ of Humphreys co., W Tennessee; pop. (1990c) 3925.

Wa·vre \ˈvävrᵊ\. Commune, Brabant prov., cen. Belgium, 14 mi. (23 km.) SE of Brussels; pop. (1991c) 28,565. Battle here 1815, a phase of battle of Waterloo, in which French Gen.

Emmanuel Grouchy drove back part of Prussian Field Marshal Gebhard Leberecht von Blücher's force but failed to aid French Emperor Napoléon.

Wavre–Sainte–Catherine. See SINT-KATELIJNE-WAVER.

Wāw. See WAU 2.

Wa·wa \ˈwä-wä\. Village, Rizal prov., Luzon, Philippines, NE of Manila; **Wawa Dam,** E of Montalban, in the Manila water system; scene of fighting bet. Japanese and U.S. forces 1945.

Wa·wa·see, Lake *also* **Wawasee Lake** \ˌwä-wə-ˈsē\. Lake, NE Kosciusko co., N Indiana; 4 sq. mi. (10 sq. km.).

Wax·a·hach·ie \ˌwȯk-sə-ˈha-chē\. City, ⊗ of Ellis co., NE cen. Texas, 30 mi. (48 km.) S of Dallas; pop. (1990c) 18,168; Southwestern Assemblies of God Coll. (1927).

Wax·haw \ˈwaks-ˌhȯ\. Village, Lancaster co., N South Carolina; in the region, on border of North and South Carolina, Andrew Jackson, 7th president of the U.S., was born 1767; both states claim him.

Way·ah Bald \ˈwī-ə\. Peak, N Macon co., SW North Carolina; 5336 ft. (1626 m.).

Way·cross \ˈwā-ˌkrȯs\. City, ⊗ of Ware co., SE Georgia, 50 mi. (81 km.) W of Brunswick; pop. (1990c) 16,410; honey, pecans; Okefenokee Swamp is nearby to the S; incorp. 1874.

Way·land \ˈwā-lənd\. **1.** Town, Middlesex co., NE Massachusetts, 15 mi. (24 km.) W of Boston; pop. (1990c) 11,874. **2.** City, Allegan co., SW Michigan, S of Grand Rapids; pop. (1990c) 2751.

Wayne \ˈwān\. **1.** Name of counties in 16 states of the U.S. See tables at GEORGIA, ILLINOIS, INDIANA, IOWA, KENTUCKY, MICHIGAN, MISSISSIPPI, MISSOURI, NEBRASKA, NEW YORK, NORTH CAROLINA, OHIO, PENNSYLVANIA, TENNESSEE, UTAH, WEST VIRGINIA.
2. City, Wayne co., SE Michigan, 13 mi. (21 km.) WSW of Detroit; pop. (1990c) 19,899.
3. City, ⊗ of Wayne co., NE Nebraska, 26 mi. (42 km.) ENE of Norfolk; pop. (1990c) 5142; Wayne State Coll. (1910).
4. Urban township, Passaic co., N New Jersey, 6 mi. (10 km.) W of Paterson; pop. (1990c) 47,025; William Paterson Coll. of New Jersey (1855).
5. Locality, Delaware co., SE Pennsylvania, ab. 6 mi. (10 km.) SSW of Norristown; Valley Forge Military Junior Coll. (1928).
6. Town, ⊗ of Wayne co., SW West Virginia; pop. (1990c) 1128.

Waynes·boro \ˈwānz-ˌbər-ō\. **1.** City, ⊗ of Burke co., E Georgia, 28 mi. (45 km.) S of Augusta; pop. (1990c) 5701.
2. City, ⊗ of Wayne co., SE Mississippi; pop. (1990c) 5143.
3. Borough, Franklin co., S Pennsylvania, 14 mi. (23 km.) S of Chambersburg; pop. (1990c) 9578; ships fruit.
4. City, ⊗ of Wayne co., S Tennessee; pop. (1990c) 1824.
5. Independent city, Augusta co., N cen. Virginia, in Shenandoah Valley at foot of Blue Ridge 12 mi. (19 km.) ESE of Staunton; 7 sq. mi. (18 sq. km.); pop. (1990c) 18,549. Site first settled c. mid-18th cent.; scene of battle Mar. 2, 1865 in which Confederate forces under Gen. Jubel Early were defeated by Union forces of Gen. Philip Sheridan.

Waynes·burg \ˈwānz-ˌbərg\. Borough, ⊗ of Greene co., SW corner of Pennsylvania, 26 mi. (42 km.) W of Uniontown; pop. (1990c) 4270; Waynesburg Coll. (1850).

Waynes·ville \ˈwānz-ˌvil\. **1.** City, ⊗ of Pulaski co., S cen. Missouri; pop. (1990c) 3207.
2. Town, ⊗ of Haywood co., W North Carolina, 26 mi. (42 km.) WSW of Asheville; pop. (1990c) 6758.

Way·zata \wī-ˈze-tə\. City, Hennepin co., SE cen. Minnesota, on Lake Minnetonka, W of Minneapolis; pop. (1990c) 3806.

Wazan. See OUEZZANE.

Wa·ziers \vä-ˈzhā\. Commune, Nord dept., N France; ENE suburb of Douai.

Wa·zir·ā·bād \wə-ˈzir-ə-ˌbäd\. Ancient city, Bactria. See BALKH 2.

Wa·zir·a·bad \wə-ˈzir-ə-ˌbäd\. Town, Punjab, Pakistan, on Chenab River 60 mi. (97 km.) N of Lahore; munic. pop. (1981c) 62,725; railroad junction with bridge over the Chenab.

Wa·zir·i·stan \wə-ˌzir-i-ˈstan, -ˈstän\. Mountainous region, NW Pakistan; 4373 sq. mi. (11,326 sq. km.); pop. (1981p) 235,000; divided into **North Waziristan** and **South Waziristan;** lies along border of Afghanistan; inhabited by members of Pashtun tribes, Wazirs and Mahsuds. When British occupied the area 19th–20th cents., Pashtuns rebelled against them several times.

Wazzan. See OUEZZANE.

We *or* **Weh** \ˈwā\. Island, ab. 14 mi. (23 km.) off extreme NW tip of Sumatra, Indonesia, directly N of Banda Atjeh; 65 sq. mi. (168 sq. km.); has irregular coastline with large bay on N coast, on which is Sabang, an important fueling port until WWII.

Weak·ley \ˈwēk-lē\. County in NW Tennessee. See table at TENNESSEE.

Weald, The \ˈwēld\. Wooded area, Kent, Surrey, East Sussex, and West Sussex cos., SE England, lying bet. the North Downs and South Downs; formerly heavily forested.

Wear \ˈwir\. River, Durham, N England; flows E and NE into North Sea at Sunderland; 67 mi. (108 km.) long.

Wearmouth. See SUNDERLAND 2.

Weath·er·ford \ˈwe-t͟hər-fərd\. **1.** City, Custer co., W Oklahoma, 11 mi. (18 km.) E of Clinton; pop. (1990c) 10,124; Southwestern Oklahoma State Univ. (1901).
2. City, ⊗ of Parker co., N cen. Texas, 25 mi. (40 km.) W of Fort Worth; pop. (1990c) 14,804; Weatherford Coll. (1869).

Weath·er·ly \ˈwe-t͟hər-lē\. Borough, Carbon co., E Pennsylvania, 21 mi. (34 km.) S of Wilkes-Barre; pop. (1990c) 2640.

Wea·ver \ˈwē-vər\. **1.** River, Cheshire, NW England; rises in SW, flows NE, and then NW into the Mersey; ab. 45 mi. (70 km.) long; navigable as far as Winsford.
2. City, Calhoun co., NE Alabama, N of Anniston; pop. (1990c) 2715.

Wea·ver·ville \ˈwē-vər-ˌvil\. Unincorporated settlement, ⊗ of Trinity co., NW California; pop. (1990c) 3370.

Web. See WABĒ GESTRO.

Webb \ˈweb\. County in S Texas. See table at TEXAS.

Webb City. City, Jasper co., SW Missouri, 6 mi. (10 km.) N of Joplin; pop. (1990c) 7449.

Webbe Mana. See MANA, WEBBE.

We·ber \ˈwē-bər\. **1.** River, N Utah; rises in S Summit co., flows NW into Great Salt Lake; ab. 100 mi. (160 km.) long.
2. County in N Utah. See table at UTAH.

Web·ster \ˈweb-stər\. **1.** Name of a parish in NW Louisiana and of counties in seven states of the U.S. See tables at GEORGIA, IOWA, KENTUCKY, LOUISIANA, MISSISSIPPI, MISSOURI, NEBRASKA, WEST VIRGINIA.
2. Town, Worcester co., cen. Massachusetts, 15 mi. (24 km.) S of the city of Worcester, on Lake Chargoggagoggmanchauggauggagoggchaubunagungamaugg; pop. (1990c) 16,196.
3. Village, Monroe co., W New York, 10 mi. (16 km.) ENE of Rochester; pop. (1990c) 5464.
4. City, ⊗ of Day co., NE South Dakota, 37 mi. (60 km.) NNW of Watertown; pop. (1990c) 2017.
5. City, Harris co., SE Texas, just SE of Houston; pop. (1990c) 4678.

Webster, Lake. See CHARGOGGAGOGGMANCHAUGGAUGGAGOGGCHAUBUNAGUNGAMAUGG, LAKE.

Webster, Mount. Peak, S Coos co., N New Hampshire; 3876 ft. (1181 m.).

Webster City. City, ⊗ of Hamilton co., N cen. Iowa, 20 mi. (32 km.) E of Fort Dodge; pop. (1990c) 7894.

Webster Groves. City, St. Louis co., E Missouri, 8 mi. (13 km.) W of the city of St. Louis; pop. (1990c) 22,987.

Webster Springs. Town, ⊗ of Webster co., E cen. West Virginia, 43 mi. (69 km.) SW of Elkins; pop. (1990c) 674; incorp. 1892.

Wed·dell Island \wə-ˈdel, ˈwed-ᵊl\. One of the Falkland Is. (*q.v.*), South Atlantic Ocean; W of West Falkland.

Weddell Quadrant. Former name of the quarter section of Antarctica bet. the Prime Meridian and 90°W; now chiefly W Queen Maud Land, Weddell Sea and Coats Land, and Palmer Archipelago and Antarctic Penin.

Weddell Sea. Arm of S Atlantic Ocean in Antarctica, SE of Antarctic Penin.; its W shore is along 60th meridian, W long.; its E shore is Coats Land (*q.v.*); Filchner Ice Shelf is at its S end; largely covered by ice; discovered 1823 by British navigator Capt. James Weddell.

Wed·ding·ton \ˈwe-diŋ-tən\. Town, Union co., S North Carolina, S of Charlotte; pop. (1990c) 3803.

We·del \ˈvād-ᵊl\. City, Schleswig-Holstein, Germany, 12 mi. (19 km.) W of Hamburg; pop. (1980c) 30,493.

Wed·more \ˈwed-ˌmōr\. Village, N cen. Somerset, SW England; in 878 scene of signing of peace treaty bet. King Alfred the Great and Guthrum, Danish king of East Anglia, by which Danes were restricted to territory (the Danelaw) in NE England, N of Watling Street.

Wednes·bury \ˈwenz-bə-rē, ˈwej-bə-rē\. Town, West Midlands, W cen. England, on the Tame 8 mi. (13 km.) NW of Birmingham.

We·dow·ee \wē-ˈdau̇-ē, wi-\. Town, ⊗ of Randolph co., E Alabama; pop. (1990c) 796.

Weed \ˈwēd\. City, Siskiyou co., N California, 55 mi. (88 km.) N of Redding; pop. (1990c) 3062; Coll. of the Siskiyous (1957).

Wee·haw·ken \wē-ˈhȯ-kən\. Township, Hudson co., NE New Jersey, on Hudson River opp. New York City (connected by Lincoln Tunnel), 5 mi. (8 km.) N of Jersey City; pop. (1990c) 12,385; scene of duel 1804 in which Vice President Aaron Burr fatally wounded politician Alexander Hamilton.

Wee·nen \ˈvē-nən\. Town, cen. KwaZulu-Natal prov., E Rep. of South Africa, 85 mi. (137 km.) NW of Durban; founded 1838; scene of massacre of Boer Voortrekkers by Zulus under Dingane 1838—hence its name, literally "place of weeping."

Weert \ˈvert\. Commune, Limburg prov., SE Netherlands, near Belgian border 16 mi. (26 km.) SE of Eindhoven; pop. (1992e) 40,695.

Weesp \ˈvāsp\. Commune, North Holland prov., W Netherlands, 7 mi. (11 km.) SE of Amsterdam; pop. (1981e) 17,812.

We·go·ra·pa \ˌve-gȯ-ˈrä-pä\ *or Russ.* **An·gra·pa** \əŋ-ˈgrä-pə\ *or Ger.* **Ang·e·rapp** \ˈäŋ-ə-ˌräp\. River in N Poland and E Kaliningrad Oblast, Russia; flows N from Masurian Lakes into Pregolya River at Chernyakhovsk, Russia; ab. 106 mi. (170 km.) long.

Wę·go·rze·wo \ˌveⁿ-gȯ-ˈzhe-vȯ\ *or Ger.* **Ang·er·burg** \ˈäŋ-ər-ˌbu̇rk\. Town, NW Suwałki prov., N Poland, 60 mi. (97 km.) N of Olsztyn; pop. (1981p) 9753; terminus on Wegorapa River at N end of Lake Mamry for boat service and recreation on Masurian Lakes. Received city rights 1571, having been settled earlier; in WWI scene of heavy fighting 1914; after WWII assigned to Poland by Potsdam Conference 1945.

Weh. See WE.

Wehlau. See ZNAMENSK.

Wei \ˈwā\. **1.** River, N cen. China; rises in mountains of SE Gansu prov., and flows E across Shaanxi to join the Huang at the point where it turns E; 537 mi. (864 km.) long; on its S bank in Shaanxi is Xi'an.

2. Ancient kingdom, NE China, estab. 220 A.D.; with Shu and Wu, formed the Three Kingdoms and was strongest of the three; overthrown c. 265 A.D.

3. Town, China. See WEIFANG.

Wei–chou *or* **Weichow.** See WEIZHOU.

Weichsel. See VISTULA.

Weiden. See WEIDEN IN DER OBERPFALZ.

Wei·de·nau \ˈvīd-ᵊn-ˌau̇\ *or* **Weidenau an der Sieg** \ˌän-dər-ˈzēk\. Commune, North Rhine-Westphalia, Germany, on Sieg River 48 mi. (77 km.) E of Cologne.

Wei·den in der Ober·pfalz \ˈvīd-ᵊn-ˌin-dər-ˈō-bər-ˌpfälts\; *often shortened to* **Weiden.** City, Bavaria, Germany, on Naab River 31 mi. (50 km.) SE of Bayreuth; pop. (1992e) 42,552; 16th cent. town hall; 15th cent. church.

Wei·fang *or W.-G.* **Wei–fang** \ˈwā-ˈfäŋ\ *also* **Wei·hsien** \ˈwā-ˈshyen\ *or* **Wei** \ˈwā\. Commercial town, E cen. Shandong prov., NE China, on railroad line 85 mi. (137 km.) NW of Qingdao; pop. (1990c) 428,522.

Wei·hai *or W.-G.* **Wei–hai** \ˈwā-ˈhī\ *also* **Wei·hai·wei** \ˈwā-ˈhī-ˈwā\. Seaport, NE Shandong prov., NE China, at E end of peninsula on N coast 40 mi. (64 km.) E of Yantai; pop. (1990c) 128,888; naval base, fishing port; good harbor protected by Liugong I.

History: Chinese fleet destroyed here by Japanese 1895 and port occupied by Japanese 1895–98; leased to Great Britain 1898 and used as a naval base; returned to China 1930; occupied by Japanese 1938–45; occupied by Communist naval forces 1949.

Weihsien. See WEIFANG.

Wei·mar \ˈvī-ˌmär, ˈwī-\. City, Thuringia, E cen. Germany, 13 mi. (23 km.) E of Erfurt; pop. (1981c) 64,000; railroad junction; Goethe National Museum, composer Franz Liszt's house, archives containing writings of poets Johann Wolfgang von Goethe and Friedrich von Schiller.

History: First mentioned 975; chartered 1348; ❋ of duchy of Saxe-Weimar 1547–1918; long a cultural center; in 16th cent. home of artists Lucas Cranach the Elder and the Younger; in 18th cent. court musician was Johann Sebastian Bach and town was residence of poets Johann Wolfgang von Goethe, Johann Herder, and Friedrich von Schiller; in 19th cent. composers Franz Liszt and Richard Wagner worked here; architect Walter Gropius founded Bauhaus school here (later moved to Dessau) 1919. In 1919 German National Assembly met here and ratified Treaty of Versailles and established republican regime (often referred to as the "Weimar Republic") which lasted until 1933; ❋ of Thuringia 1920–48; Buchenwald concentration camp was located nearby during WWII and memorial begun there 1950s.

Wein·heim \ˈvīn-ˌhīm\. City, Baden-Württemberg, Germany, 10 mi. (16 km.) NE of Mannheim; pop. (1992e) 42,675; 16th cent. Gothic town hall.

Weins·berg \ˈvīns-ˌberk\. Commune, Baden-Württemberg, Germany, on a tributary of the Neckar just E of the Heilbronn; scene of defeat 1140 of Welf VI by Conrad III, first Hohenstaufen king of Germany; free imperial city, in league of Swabian cities 14th cent.

Wei·pa \ˈwā-pə\. Town, N Queensland, Australia, on W coast of Cape York Penin.; pop. (1991c) 2510; major bauxite-mining center.

Weir·ton \ˈwirt-ᵊn\. City, Brooke and Hancock cos., N West Virginia, on Ohio River ab. 26 mi. (42 km.) NNE of Wheeling; pop. (1990c) 22,124; coal mines; steel mills estab. c. 1909; city incorp. 1947.

Wei·ser \ˈwē-sər\. City, ⊗ of Washington co., W Idaho, on Snake River 62 mi. (100 km.) NW of Boise; pop. (1990c) 4571.

Weissbad. See APPENZELL 2.

Weisse Elster. See ELSTER.

Weis·sen·burg \ˈvīs-ᵊn-ˌbu̇rk\. **1.** Town, NE France. See WISSEMBOURG.

2. *or in full* **Weissenburg in Bay·ren** \in-ˈbī-ərn\; *formerly* **Weissenburg–am–Sand** \-äm-ˈzänt\. Town, Bavaria, Germany, ab. 30 mi. (48 km.) SW of Nürnberg; built on remains of former Roman site; has Gothic town hall, remains of fortifications.

Weis·sen·fels \ˈvīs-ᵊn-ˌfels\. Commune, Saxony-Anhalt, E Germany; pop. (1992e) 35,664; railroad junction; footwear; 17th cent. castle; first mentioned 12th cent.; to Prussia 1815.

Weisser Berg. See WHITE MOUNTAIN 3.

Weiss·horn \ˈvīs-ˌhȯrn\. Peak, Valais canton, SW cen. Switzerland, in Pennine Alps; 14,782 ft. (4506 m.).

Weisskirchen. See BELA CRKVA.

Weiss·ku·gel \ˈvīs-ˌkü-gəl\ *or Ital.* **Pa·la Bian·ca** \ˈpä-lä-bē-ˈäŋ-kä\. Peak in the Ötztaler Alps, on the border bet. Tirol, Austria and Veneto, NE Italy; 12,257 ft. (3736 m.).

Weiss·mies \ˈvīs-ˌmēs\. Mountain, SW cen. Switzerland, in E part of the Pennine Alps; 13,199 ft. (4023 m.).

Weiss·was·ser \ˈvīs-ˌvä-sər\. Commune, Saxony, E Germany, 25 mi. (40 km.) NNE of Bautzen and near Polish border.

Wei·zhou \ˈwā-ˈjō\ *or W.-G.* **Wei–chou** \-ˈjō\ *also* **Wei·chow** \-ˈjō\. Island in NE Gulf of Tonkin, Guangxi Zhuangzu, SE China, S of Beihai.

Wejh. See AL WAJH.

Wej·he·ro·wo \ˌvā-he-ˈrȯ-vȯ\. Commune, Gdańsk prov., N Poland, 23 mi. (37 km.) NW of the city of Gdańsk; pop. (1989e) 46,546; on railroad line from Gdynia to Szczecin.

We·lan·gi·la·la \wā-ˌläŋ-gē-ˈlä-lə\ *or* **Wai·lan·gi La·la** \wī-\. Small island, NE Fiji, SW Pacific Ocean; site of lighthouse for ships passing through Nanuku Passage.

Welch \ˈwelch, ˈwelsh\. City, ⊗ of McDowell co., S West Virginia, 24 mi. (39 km.) WNW of Bluefield; pop. (1990c) 3028.

Welcome Bay. See SLAMADATANG, TELUK.

Weld \ˈweld\. County in N Colorado. See table at COLORADO.

Wel·don \ˈwel-dən\. Town, Halifax co., NE North Carolina, on Roanoke River at head of navigation 34 mi. (55 km.) NNE of Rocky Mount; pop. (1990c) 1392.

Welfare Island. See ROOSEVELT ISLAND 2.

Wel·kom \ˈvel-kəm\. Town, Free State, Rep. of South Africa, ab. 85 mi. (135 km.) NE of Bloemfontein; pop. (1985c) 54,488; center of mining area.

Welkomst Baai. See SLAMADATANG, TELUK.

Wel·land \ˈwel-ᵊnd\. **1.** City, Niagara munic. region, Ontario, Canada, on Welland Canal 14 mi. (23 km.) S of St. Catharines; pop. (1991c) 47,914; founded c. 1830; incorp. as city 1917.

2. River, E cen. England; rises in Leicestershire and flows NE into the Wash; 70 mi. (113 km.) long.

Welland Canal *or* **Welland Ship Canal.** Government-owned ship waterway, SE Ontario, Canada, connecting Lake Erie with Lake Ontario in Welland and Lincoln cos.; 27 mi. (43.5 km.) long and having 8 locks and minimum depth of 30 ft. (9 m.); extends from Port Colborne on Lake Erie to Port Weller on Lake Ontario, with a rise of 326 ft. (99 m.) bet. the two. Old canal had 25 locks, was first built 1824–33; reconstructed 1872–87, and entirely rebuilt as a ship canal 1912–32.

Welle. See UELE.

Welles·ley \ˈwelz-lē\. Residential town, Norfolk co., E Massachusetts, 12 mi. (19 km.) WSW of Boston; pop. (1990c) 26,615; Wellesley Coll. (1870), Babson Coll. (1919), Massachusetts Bay Community Coll. (1961).

Wellesley, Province. See PROVINCE WELLESLEY.

Wellesley Islands. Group of islands off N coast of Queensland, Australia, at head of Gulf of Carpentaria.

Well·fleet \ˈwel-ˌflēt\. Town, Barnstable co., SE Massachusetts, on Cape Cod Bay ab. 15 mi. (24 km.) from Provincetown; pop. (1990c) 2493; summer resort; inlet of the bay here called **Wellfleet Harbor**.

Well·ford \ˈwel-fərd\. City, Spartanburg co., NW South Carolina, W of the city of Spartanburg; pop. (1990c) 2511.

Wel·ling·bor·ough \ˈwe-liŋ-bə-rə\. Town, Northamptonshire, cen. England, on the Nene 60 mi. (97 km.) NNW of London; pop. (1991p) 71,100; footwear.

Wel·ling·ton \ˈwe-liŋ-tən\. **1.** City, ⊗ of Sumner co., S Kansas, 30 mi. (48 km.) S of Wichita; pop. (1990c) 8411.

2. Village, Lorain co., N Ohio, 35 mi. (56 km.) SW of Cleveland; pop. (1990c) 4140.

3. City, ⊗ of Collingsworth co., NW Texas, in Texas Panhandle 87 mi. (140 km.) ESE of Amarillo; pop. (1990c) 2456.

4. County in SE Ontario, Canada. See table at ONTARIO.

5. Island, Chile, in S Pacific Ocean, W of SW part of the country and N of Madre de Dios Archipelago; 100 mi. (161 km.) long by 15 to 25 mi. (24 to 40 km.) wide.

6. *formerly* **Wat·ling Town** \ˈwät-liŋ\. Town, Shropshire, W England, 30 mi. (48 km.) WNW of Birmingham; pop. (1981p) 15,699.

7. Town, Somerset, SW England, 44 mi. (71 km.) SW of Bristol; pop. (1981c) 10,623; manufactures bedding.

8. City, ❋ of New Zealand, in S part of North I. on Port Nicholson, an inlet of Cook Strait; pop. (1992e) 149,400; financial, commercial, and transportation center of New Zealand; produces motor vehicles, footwear, machinery, metal goods, chemicals. Site of the major government buildings and headquarters of many cultural, scientific, and agricultural organizations; museums, public parks; Victoria Univ. of Wellington (1962). Founded 1840; ❋ transferred from Auckland 1865.

9. Town, Western Cape prov., S Rep. of South Africa, 38 mi. (61 km.) NE of Cape Town.

Wellington, Mount. Mountain, S Tasmania, Australia, 4 mi. (6 km.) WSW of Hobart; 4166 ft. (1270 m.).

Wellington Harbour. See PORT NICHOLSON.

Wells \ˈwelz\. **1.** Name of counties in two states of the U.S. See tables at INDIANA and NORTH DAKOTA.

2. Town, York co., SW Maine, 12 mi. (19 km.) SSW of Biddeford; pop. (1990c) 7778; seaside resort.

3. City, Somerset, SW England, at foot of Mendip Hills 17 mi. (27 km.) S of Bristol; pop. (1981c) 8435; notable 12th cent. cathedral; 15th cent. deanery; 15th cent. church; an old town, important in ancient Wessex; its origin and development have been chiefly ecclesiastical; received first charter 1201.

Wells·boro \ˈwelz-ˌbər-ō\. Borough, ⊗ of Tioga co., N Pennsylvania, 38 mi. (61 km.) NNW of Williamsport; pop. (1990c) 3430; mountain resort.

Wells·burg \ˈwelz-ˌbərg\. City, ⊗ of Brooke co., N West Virginia, in N Panhandle on Ohio River 15 mi. (24 km.) NNE of Wheeling; pop. (1990c) 3385.

Wells River. Village, Orange co., E Vermont, at junction of Wells and Connecticut rivers; pop. (1990c) 424; gateway bet. White Mts. and Green Mts.

Wells·ton \ˈwel-stən\. **1.** City, St. Louis co., E Missouri, NW suburb of St. Louis; pop. (1990c) 3612.

2. City, Jackson co., S Ohio, 26 mi. (42 km.) ESE of Chillicothe; pop. (1990c) 6049.

Wells·ville \ˈwelz-ˌvil\. **1.** Village, Allegany co., SW New York, 20 mi. (32 km.) SW of Hornell; pop. (1990c) 5241.

2. City, Columbiana co., E Ohio, on Ohio River 16 mi. (26 km.) N of Steubenville; pop. (1990c) 4532; settled 1797.

Wels \ˈvels\; *anc.* **Ovi·la·va** \ˌō-və-ˈlā-və\. City, Upper Austria, Austria, on Traun River 26 mi. (42 km.) SW of Linz; pop. (1991c) 52,594; Gothic church; medieval imperial palace; site occupied since prehistoric times; later settlement grew up around ancient Roman settlement.

Welsh \ˈwelsh\. Town, Jefferson Davis parish, SW Louisiana, 25 mi. (40 km.) E of Lake Charles; pop. (1990c) 3299.

Welsh·pool \ˈwelsh-ˌpül\. Town, NE Powys co., E Wales; pop. (1981c) 7326; medieval castle, residence of the earls of Powis (or Powys).

Wel·wel \ˈwel-ˌwel\ *or* **Wal·wal** \ˈwal-ˌwal\ *or* **Ual·ual** \ˈwal-ˌwal\. Settlement, SE Ethiopia; scene of clash bet. Italian and Ethiopian forces Dec. 5, 1934. See *History* at ETHIOPIA.

Wel·wyn Garden City \ˈwe-lən\. Town, Hertfordshire, SE England, on tributary of the Lea 24 mi. (39 km.) N of London; pop. (1981c) 41,102; pharmaceuticals, plastics, food products; estab. as the 2d English garden city in 1920.

Wembley. See BRENT.

We·natch·ee \wə-ˈna-chē\. **1.** River, cen. Washington; flows SE in Chelan co. into Columbia River at city of Wenatchee; ab. 60 mi. (95 km.) long.

2. City, ⊗ of Chelan co., cen. Washington, at confluence of Columbia and Wenatchee rivers 30 mi. (48 km.) S of Lake Chelan; pop. (1990c) 21,756; packs and ships apples; outdoor recreation; large national forest nearby; Wenatchee Valley Coll. (1939).

Wenatchee, Lake *also* **Wenatchee Lake.** Lake, cen. Chelan co., cen. Washington.

Wenatchee Mountains. Range, cen. Washington, extending along boundary bet. Chelan and Kittitas cos.

Wen–chou *also* **Wenchow.** See WENZHOU.

Wen·dell \ˈwend-ᵊl\. Town, Wake co., E cen. North Carolina, E of Raleigh; pop. (1990c) 2822.

Wenden. See CĒSIS.

Wen·ham \ˈwe-nəm\. Town, Essex co., NE Massachusetts, N of Salem; pop. (1990c) 4212; Gordon Coll. (1889).

We·no \ˈwā-nō\; *formerly* **Mo·en** \ˈmō-ən\. Island in NE part of Chuuk (*q.v.*), W Pacific Ocean; ab. 5 mi. (8 km.) long by 4 mi. (6 km.) wide.

Wensu *or W.-G.* **Wen–su.** See AKSU 2.

Went·worth \ˈwent-wərth\. Village, ⊗ of Rockingham co., N North Carolina; Rockingham Community Coll. (1964).

Wentworth, Lake. Lake, S Carroll co., E New Hampshire, E of Lake Winnipesaukee; 4 mi. (6 km.) long.

Wentz·ville \ˈwents-ˌvil, -vəl\. City, St. Charles co., E Missouri, W of the city of St. Charles; pop. (1990c) 5088.

Wen·zhou or *W.-G.* **Wen–chou** *also* **Wen·chow** \ˈwen-ˈjō\; *formerly* **Yung·kia** \ˈyu̇ŋ-ˈjyä\. City, SE Zhejiang prov., E China, at mouth of Ou; pop. (1990c) 401,871; former treaty port. An old city, possibly founded in 4th cent. A.D.; has many old buildings; opened to foreign trade 1876; in WWII occupied by Japanese; grew in importance from 1950s.

Wer·dau \ˈver-ˌdau̇\. City, Saxony, E Germany, on Pleisse River 5 mi. (8 km.) WNW of Zwickau; pop. (1981c) 20,418; 18th cent. church; city chartered 1304.

Wer·dohl \ver-ˈdōl\. Commune, North Rhine-Westphalia, Germany, 41 mi. (66 km.) E of Düsseldorf; pop. (1980c) 21,666.

Wer·mels·kir·chen \ˈver-məls-ˌkirk-ᵊn\. City, North Rhine-Westphalia, Germany, 19 mi. (31 km.) ESE of Düsseldorf; pop. (1980c) 34,737.

Werne an der Lip·pe \ˈver-nə-ˌän-dər-ˈli-pə\. City, North Rhine-Westphalia, Germany, on Lippe River 22 mi. (35 km.) S of Münster.

Wer·ner Peak \ˈwər-nər\. Mountain, W Flathead co., NW Montana; 7000 ft. (2134 m.).

Wer·ni·ge·ro·de \ˌver-ni-gə-ˈrō-də\. City, Saxony-Anhalt, cen. Germany, 30 mi. (48 km.) SSE of Brunswick; pop. (1992e) 35,167; 15th cent. town hall; replica (built 19th cent.) of medieval castle. Became city 1229; member of Hanseatic League from 1267.

Wer·ra \ˈver-ə\. River, cen. Germany; rises in Thuringian Forest, Thuringia, flows NW, N, and NE to unite with Fulda River at Münden, Lower Saxony, and form the Weser River; 181 mi. (291 km.) long.

Wer·ri·bee \ˈwer-ə-bē\. City, Victoria, Australia, SW of Melbourne; pop. (1991c) 72,230.

Werschetz. See VRŠAC.

Wert·heim \ˈvert-ˌhīm\. Town, Baden-Württemberg, Germany, at the confluence of the Tauber and the Main; Wertheim Bible published 1735.

Wer·wik or **Wer·vicq** \ver-ˈvēk\. Commune, West Flanders prov., W Belgium, 8 mi. (13 km.) SE of Ieper (Ypres); pop. (1991c) 17,986.

We·sel \ˈvā-zəl\. City, North Rhine-Westphalia, Germany, on the Rhine at mouth of Lippe River 49 mi. (79 km.) WSW of Münster; pop. (1992e) 60,260; seaport and railroad junction; chartered 1241; member of Hanseatic League 1407; to Brandenburg 17th cent.; occupied by French 1808–14; almost completely destroyed in air raids during WWII and since rebuilt in modern style.

We·ser \ˈvā-zər, ˈwē-\. **1.** River, Belgium. See VESDRE.
2. *anc.* **Vi·sur·gis** \vī-ˈsər-jəs\. Navigable river, Germany; formed by confluence of Fulda and Werra rivers at Münden in SE Lower Saxony, flows NW into the North Sea through a large estuary; 273 mi. (439 km.) long; its chief tributary is the Aller from the E, joining it near Verden.

Wesermünde. See BREMERHAVEN.

Wes·la·co \ˈwes-lə-ˌkō\. City, Hidalgo co., S Texas, 17 mi. (27 km.) E of McAllen; pop. (1990c) 21,877.

Wes·ley Hills \ˈwes-lē\. Village, Rockland co., SE New York; pop. (1990c) 4305.

Wes·ley·ville \ˈwes-lē-ˌvil\. Borough, Erie co., NW corner of Pennsylvania, on Lake Erie 5 mi. (8 km.) E of city of Erie; pop. (1990c) 3655.

Wes·se·ling \ˈve-sə-liŋ\. Town, North Rhine-Westphalia, Germany, on left bank of Rhine just S of Cologne; pop. (1980c) 29,005.

Wes·sel Islands \ˈwe-səl\. Island group, off coast of N Northern Terr., Australia, NW of Gulf of Carpentaria.

Wes·sex \ˈwe-siks\. Ancient Anglo-Saxon kingdom, S Britain; ❋ Winchester; also, the corresponding section of modern England, used esp. with reference to the novels of Thomas Hardy; approx. the counties of Avon, Berkshire, Dorset, Hampshire, Somerset, and Wiltshire.
History: Kingdom traditionally thought to have been founded by Saxon invaders of Britain; conquered Kent and Sussex (see KENT 7 and SUSSEX 5) and, in 9th cent., leader of the Anglo-Saxon Heptarchy (*q.v.*); under King Alfred the Great 871–899, successfully kept Danes from conquest of England S of Danelaw; by c. 927 Wessex had reconquered the Danelaw and become ruler of all England; important Anglo-Saxon earldom.

Wes·sing·ton Springs \ˈwe-siŋ-tən\. City, ⊗ of Jerauld co., SE cen. South Dakota; pop. (1990c) 1083.

West \ˈwest\. **1.** River, Windham co., SE corner of Vermont; formed by confluence of forks in NW part of the county, flows SE into Connecticut River above Brattleboro; ab. 50 mi. (80 km.) long.
2. City, McLennan co., cen. Texas, 19 mi. (31 km.) N of Waco; pop. (1990c) 2515.
3. River, China. See XI.

West Al·lis \ˈa-ləs\. City, Milwaukee co., SE Wisconsin, 6 mi. (10 km.) WSW of the city of Milwaukee; pop. (1990c) 63,221; suburb of Milwaukee; incorp. 1906.

West Antarctica. See ANTARCTICA.

West Azerbaijan. Province of Iran. See AZERBAIJAN 1.

West Bank. Area, Palestine, W of the Jordan River. Includes the settlements of Nābulus, Hebron, Jenin, Rām Allāh, Bethlehem, and Jericho. Under UN agreement 1947 area was to become Palestinian at formation of State of Israel; Arabs denouncing agreement attacked Israel; Israel responded by occupying an area larger than was called for in 1947 agreement; following a truce Jordan annexed West Bank 1950; Israel occupied West Bank 1967; Israel began establishing settlements in area 1970s and 1980s provoking Arab resentment; Arab uprisings began 1987 in Gaza and spread to West Bank; Jordan relinquished claim to area 1988; peace talks among powers in region begun 1991; Israeli-Palestinian self-rule agreement reached with view to gradually returning parts of area to Palestinians, but terrorist attacks continued.

West Bat·on Rouge \ˈbat-ᵊn-ˈrüzh\. Parish in SE cen. Louisiana. See table at LOUISIANA.

West Bend. City, ⊗ of Washington co., SE Wisconsin, 29 mi. (47 km.) NNW of Milwaukee; pop. (1990c) 23,916; appliances and other kitchenware.

West Ben·gal \ben-ˈgȯl, beŋ-\. State, NE India; ❋ Calcutta; rice, jute, cereals, oilseeds; coal; aluminum, steel, fertilizer; chief cities: Calcutta, Howrah, Durgapur; estab. 1947; grew with incorporation of former Indian state of Cooch-Behar 1950, former French possession Chandernagagore 1954, and part of Bihar 1956. See table at INDIA; for history, see BENGAL.

West Berlin. See BERLIN, WEST.

West Beskids. See BESKIDS, EAST.

West·bor·ough or **West·boro** \ˈwest-ˌbər-ō\. Town, Worcester co., cen. Massachusetts, 9 mi. (14 km.) E of the city of Worcester; pop. (1990c) 14,133.

West Boun·ti·ful \ˈbau̇n-ti-fəl\. City, Davis co., N Utah, N of Salt Lake City; pop. (1990c) 4477.

West Boyls·ton \ˈbȯil-stən\. Residential town, Worcester co., cen. Massachusetts, 7 mi. (11 km.) N of the city of Worcester; pop. (1990c) 6611.

West Branch. **1.** Town, Cedar co., E Iowa, just E of Iowa City; pop. (1990c) 1908; birthplace 1874 of Herbert C. Hoover, 31st president of the U.S.
2. City, ⊗ of Ogemaw co., NE Michigan, 50 mi. (80 km.) N of Bay City; pop. (1990c) 1914.

West Bridge·water \ˈbrij-ˌwȯ-tər, -ˌwä-\. **1.** Town, Plymouth co., SE Massachusetts, 4 mi. (6 km.) S of Brockton; pop. (1990c) 6389.
2. Residential borough, Pennsylvania. See BRIDGEWATER 2.

West Bridg·ford \ˈbrij-fərd\. Town, Nottinghamshire, N cen. England, SE suburb of Nottingham; pop. (1981p) 28,073; residential.

West Brom·wich \ˈbrə-mij, ˈbrä-, -mich\. Town, West Midlands, W cen. England, 5 mi. (8 km.) NW of Birmingham; pop. (1981c) 154,531; coal mines.

West·brook \ˈwest-ˌbru̇k\. **1.** Town, Middlesex co., S Connecticut, on Long Island Sound 4 mi. (6 km.) W of mouth of Connecticut River; pop. (1990c) 5414; seasonal recreation. **2.** City, Cumberland co., SW Maine, 7 mi. (11 km.) W of Portland; pop. (1990c) 16,121.

West Brook·field \ˈbru̇k-ˌfēld\. Town, Worcester co., cen. Massachusetts, 18 mi. (29 km.) W of the city of Worcester; pop. (1990c) 3532.

West Bur·ling·ton \ˈbər-liŋ-tən\. Town, Des Moines co., SE Iowa, W of Burlington; pop. (1990c) 3083.

West·bury \ˈwest-ˌber-ē, -bə-rē\. Residential village, Nassau co., SE New York, on Long Island 23 mi. (37 km.) E of New York City; pop. (1990c) 13,060.

Westbury Down. See SALISBURY PLAIN.

West Caicos. See TURKS AND CAICOS ISLANDS.

West Cald·well \ˈkäld-ˌwel, -wəl\. Borough, Essex co., NE New Jersey, 9 mi. (14 km.) SW of Paterson; pop. (1990c) 10,422.

West Canada Creek. Stream, cen. New York; flows S into Mohawk River at Herkimer; ab. 55 mi. (88 km.) long; contains Trenton Falls (*q.v.*).

West Cape. Cape, W coast of Guadalcanal I., SE Solomon Is., W Pacific Ocean.

West Car·roll \ˈkar-əl\. Parish in NE Louisiana. See table at LOUISIANA.

West Car·roll·ton City \ˈkar-əl-tən\. City, Montgomery co., SW Ohio, on Miami River 8 mi. (13 km.) S of Dayton; pop. (1990c) 14,403.

West·ches·ter \ˈwest-ˌches-tər\. **1.** County in SE New York. See table at NEW YORK. **2.** Village, Cook co., NE Illinois, W suburb of Chicago; pop. (1990c) 17,301.

West Chester. Borough, ⊗ of Chester co., SE Pennsylvania, 26 mi. (42 km.) W of Philadelphia; pop. (1990c) 18,041; West Chester Univ. (1871).

West Chicago. City, Du Page co., NE Illinois, 20 mi. (32 km.) W of Chicago; pop. (1990c) 14,796.

West·cliffe \ˈwest-ˌklif\. Town, ⊗ of Custer co., S cen. Colorado; pop. (1990c) 312.

West Columbia. **1.** City, Lexington co., cen. South Carolina, on Congaree River W of Columbia; pop. (1990c) 10,588. **2.** City, Brazoria co., SE Texas, 19 mi. (31 km.) ENE of Bay City; pop. (1990c) 4372; temporary ✻ of Republic of Texas in 1836.

West Cote Blanche Bay. See COTE BLANCHE BAY.

West Co·vi·na \kō-ˈvē-nə\. City, Los Angeles co., SW California, W of the city of Los Angeles; pop. (1990c) 96,086; residential; incorp. 1923.

West Des Moines. City, Polk co., S cen. Iowa, 7 mi. (11 km.) W of Des Moines; pop. (1990c) 31,702; name changed from **Valley Junction** in 1938.

West Dinajpur. See DINAJPUR.

West Dun·dee \dən-ˈdē\. Village, Kane co., Illinois, ab. 25 mi. (40 km.) NW of Chicago; pop. (1990c) 3728.

West Ems. See EMS.

West End. Town, W tip of Grand Bahama I., Bahamas, 64 mi. (103 km.) directly E of Palm Beach, Florida.

We·ster·land \ˈves-tər-ˌlänt\. Town, NW Germany, on the island of Sylt; resort.

Wes·ter·ly \ˈwes-tər-lē\. Town, Washington co., S Rhode Island, on Pawcatuck River and Connecticut state boundary 27 mi. (43 km.) WSW of Newport; pop. (1990c) 21,605; trade center in resort area; comprises Westerly village and several others; area orig. inhabited by American Indians; settlement by Europeans 1648; involved in the boundary dispute bet. Rhode Island and Connecticut until 1728.

Western Australia. State, W Australia, W of 129°E; ✻ Perth. See table at AUSTRALIA.

Physical features: Extensive interior region covered by three deserts, Great Sandy, Gibson, and Great Victoria; in W part is plateau and semidesert with numerous salt lakes. Coast along Timor Sea and Indian Ocean generally rugged with promontories, islands, and coral reefs with only a few good harbors; notable inlets are Joseph Bonaparte Gulf, King Sound, Exmouth Gulf, and Shark Bay.

Rivers: Swan (with estuary forming excellent natural harbor of Fremantle), Murchison, Fortescue, and Fitzroy.

Mountains: Highest point Mt. Bruce in NW, 4024 ft. (1227 m.); Darling Range along SW coast. Its great extent from N to S affords several distinct climatic regions.

Chief products: Wheat, wool; gold, iron ore, coal, nickel.

Chief settlements: Perth, Rockingham, Mandurah, Bunbury, Kalgoorlie-Boulder, Fremantle.

History: Inhabited by aborigines for several thousands years before Europeans arrived 17th cent.; W coast first visited 1616 by Dutch navigator Dirck Hartog; explored by English explorer William Dampier 1688, 1699; New South Wales formed small settlement there in 1826 but permanent colonization began in 1829; was penal settlement 1850–88; became part of colonial government 1886; granted responsible government 1890; last state to ratify the federation 1900. Important mineral discoveries made during the 1960s.

Western Bug. See BUG 1.

Western Cape. Province of SW Rep. of South Africa. See table at SOUTH AFRICA, REPUBLIC OF.

Western Channel; *formerly* **Cho·sen Strait** \ˈchō-ˈsen\. Channel bet. South Korea and island of Tsushima, Japan, connecting Sea of Japan with Yellow Sea and East China Sea; ab. 35 mi. (56 km.) wide; NW part of Korea Strait (*q.v.*).

Western Desert. Desert, W cen. Egypt, approx. 25° to 30°N and 26° to 30°E; includes Siwa, Baharīya, and Farafa oases; actually a part of the greater Libyan Desert.

Western Dvina. See DVINA, WESTERN.

Western Empire *or* **Western Roman Empire.** The W part of the Roman Empire; first set apart 286 A.D. by Emperor Diocletian with the establishment of joint emperors of the East and West; later in 395 after the death of Theodosius I (the Great) and the actual division of the Empire (see BYZANTINE EMPIRE) the W part comprising Italy, Spain, Gaul, Britain, Illyricum, and Africa; it ceased to exist 476 on the death of Romulus Augustulus. By some considered to have been revived by Charlemagne in 800 (see HOLY ROMAN EMPIRE).

Western Euphrates. See KARASU.

Western Ghats. See GHATS, EASTERN.

Western Greece. Region of Greece; 4382 sq. mi. (11,349 sq. km.); pop. (1991c) 702,027. For subdivisions, see table at GREECE.

Western Hemisphere. The part of the Earth comprising North and South America and surrounding waters; longitudes 20°W and 160°E often considered as its boundaries.

Western India States. Formerly an agency, W India, comprising a group of states in Kathiawar and Gujarat; 37,894 sq. mi. (98,145 sq. km.); ✻ Rajkot; formed 1924; comprised several states; among the more important were Kutch, Junagadh, Navanagar, Bhaunagar, Porbandar; incorp. into Gujarat state 1944, which in turn joined Republic of India 1947.

Western Isles. **1.** *also* **Western Islands.** See HEBRIDES. **2.** Administrative area, NW Scotland, comprising the Outer Hebrides. See table at SCOTLAND.

Western Ka·thi·a·war \ˌkä-tē-ə-ˈwär\. Former agency, India, forming a part of Western India States agency; 2552 sq. mi. (6610 sq. km.); chief town Jetpur.

Western Locris. See LOCRIS.

Western Mac·e·do·nia \ˌma-sə-ˈdō-nē-ə\. Region of Greece; 3649 sq. mi. (9451 sq. km.); pop. (1991c) 292,751. For subdivisions, see table at GREECE.

Western Manych. See MANYCH 3.

Western Min·da·nao \ˌmin-dä-ˈnau̇\. Region of the Philippines. See table at PHILIPPINES.

West·ern·port \ˈwes-tərn-ˌpōrt\. Town, Allegany co., NW Maryland, on Potomac River 20 mi. (32 km.) SW of Cumberland; pop. (1990c) 2454.

Western Province. Province of W Kenya. See table at KENYA.

Western Punjab. See PUNJAB 4.

Western Raj·pu·ta·na States \ˌräj-pə-ˈtä-nə\. W part of former Rajputana Agency, NW India, comprising Danta, Jaisalmer, Jodhpur, Palanpur, and Sirohi states.

Western Region. Administrative region of SW Ghana. See table at GHANA.

Western Reserve *also* **Connecticut Reserve.** Tract of land, NE corner of Ohio, on S shore of Lake Erie, forming the part of the W lands of Connecticut not included in region surrendered to Congress in 1786; extended southward to ab. 41°N and westward as far as Willard and Port Clinton; ab. 3,500,000 acres (1,417,500 hectares); sold in part to immigrants from Connecticut 1786–1800; ceded 1800 to Ohio to form Trumbull co., later divided into many counties. See NORTHWEST TERRITORY.

Western Roman Empire. See WESTERN EMPIRE.

Western Sa·hara \sə-'har-ə, -'här-\; *formerly* **Span·ish Sa·hara** \'spa-nish\. Territory, NW Africa, bounded on N by Morocco, touching Algeria on NE, bounded on E and S by Mauritania, and on W by the Atlantic Ocean; 102,703 sq. mi. (266,001 sq. km.); pop. (1993e) 213,000; ✻ El Aaiún.

Chief products: Livestock, fish; vast phosphate deposits.

History: Little European contact until 19th cent.; Spanish protectorate over region extending from Cape Bojadar to Cape Blanc proclaimed 1884; boundary agreements concluded with France 1900 and 1912; status changed from colony to overseas province 1958; relinquished by Spain 1976 and divided bet. Mauritania which gave up its claim 1979 and Morocco which subsequently occupied the entire territory; armed resistance of separatists erupted and continued until 1988 cease-fire; fighting later resumed.

Western Sa·mar \'sä-ˌmär\. Province, W Samar, Philippines; ✻ Catbalogan. See table at PHILIPPINES.

Western Sa·moa *or since 1997* **Samoa** \sə-'mō-ə\. Independent state, a group of islands of Samoa (*q.v.*), SW cen. Pacific Ocean, 172°W; ab. 1100 sq. mi. (2850 sq. km.); pop. (1981c) 156,349; ✻ Apia; copra, cocoa, pineapples; fishing; chief islands Savai'i and Upolu. See AMERICAN SAMOA.

History: Long inhabited by Polynesians before the coming of Europeans 18th cent.; Apia granted to Germany by treaty with native ruler 1879; after period of joint administration of Samoan Is. (see SAMOA) by Great Britain, U.S., and Germany (1889–99), Savai'i and Upolu recognized as German 1899–1900; occupied by New Zealand expeditionary force 1914–20; surrendered by Germany; became mandate of New Zealand 1920; resentment against ruling outsiders caused rebellions for several years; became UN trust territory (administered by New Zealand) 1947; achieved independence 1962; has often suffered severe hurricane damage, esp. 1990.

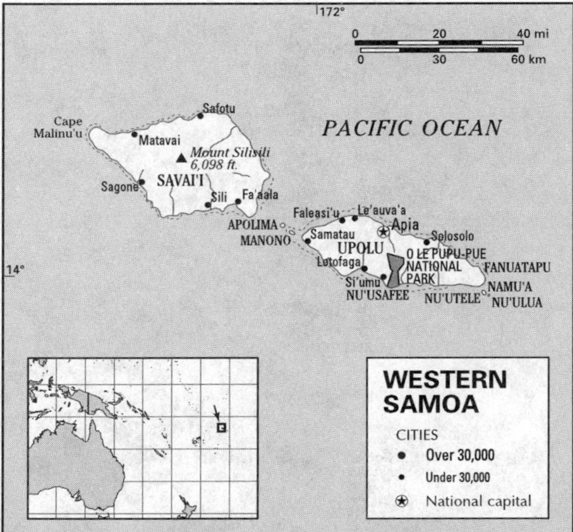

Western Sierra Madre. See SIERRA MADRE OCCIDENTAL.

Western Springs. Village, Cook co., NE Illinois, 8 mi. (13 km.) W of Chicago; pop. (1990c) 11,984.

Western Ukrai·nia \yü-'krā-nē-ə, -'krī-\. Republic, E Galicia, cen. Europe, 1918–19; soon taken over by Poland; to Ukrainian S.S.R. 1939; now in W Ukraine.

Western Vi·sa·yas \vē-'sä-yäs\. Region of the Philippines. See table at PHILIPPINES.

Western Wall *or chiefly by outsiders* **Wail·ing Wall** \'wā-liŋ\. Wall, Jerusalem, Israel; remains of the Second Temple which was otherwise destroyed by the Romans in 70 A.D.; more than 150 ft. (45 m.) long, ab. 60 ft. (18 m.) high, and extending a considerable distance underground; a sacred place of Jewish prayer; recovered by Israel in 1967 war.

Wes·ter·schel·de \'ves-tər-ˌskel-də\ *or* **West Schel·de** \'skel-də\ *or* **De Hon·te** \də-'hon-tə\. Inlet of the North Sea, SW coast of Netherlands, at mouth of the Schelde River, extending S of Walcheren I. and South Beveland I.

Wes·ter·ville \'wes-tər-ˌvil\. City, Franklin and Delaware cos., cen. Ohio, 12 mi. (19 km.) N of Columbus; pop. (1990c) 30,269; Otterbein Coll. (1847); city grew rapidly in 1960s and esp. in 1970s.

We·ster·wald \ˌves-tər-'vält\. Mountainous region in W Germany, stretching NE from near Koblenz for ab. 70 mi. (115 km.) bet. the rivers Rhine, Sieg, and Lahn; highest peak 2156 ft. (657 m.).

West Falkland. See FALKLAND ISLANDS.

West Fargo. See FARGO.

West Fe·li·ci·ana \fə-ˌli-shē-'a-nə\. Parish in E cen. Louisiana. See table at LOUISIANA.

West·field \'west-ˌfēld\. **1.** Unnavigable river, W Massachusetts; rises in NE Berkshire co., NW Massachusetts, flows SE into Connecticut River opp. Springfield; ab. 50 mi. (80 km.) long.

2. City, Hampden co., SW Massachusetts, on Westfield River 8 mi. (13 km.) W of Springfield; pop. (1990c) 38,372; Westfield State Coll. (1838). Founded 1660 as trading post and estab. as town 1669; in 19th cent. important whip-manufacturing center; chartered as city 1920.

3. Residential town, Union co., NE New Jersey, 7 mi. (11 km.) W of Elizabeth; pop. (1990c) 28,870; incorp. 1903.

4. Village, Chautauqua co., SW corner of New York, on Lake Erie 23 mi. (37 km.) WNW of Jamestown; pop. (1990c) 3451.

West Flanders *or Flem.* **West Vlaan·der·en** \'vlän-dər-ən\. Province, NW Belgium; ✻ Brugge (Bruges). See table at BELGIUM.

West Florida. See *History* at FLORIDA.

West·ford \'west-fərd\. Town, Middlesex co., NE Massachusetts, 8 mi. (13 km.) SW of Lowell; pop. (1990c) 16,392.

West Fork \'fork\. River, N cen. West Virginia; joins the Tygart to form the Monongahela.

West Frank·fort \'fraŋk-fərt\. City, Franklin co., S Illinois, 33 mi. (53 km.) S of Mount Vernon; pop. (1990c) 8526.

West Frisian Islands. See FRISIAN ISLANDS.

West Germany. See GERMANY, WEST.

West Glacier; *formerly* **Bel·ton** \'belt-^{ə}n\. Village, Flathead co., NW Montana; W entrance to Glacier National Park.

West Glamorgan. County, S Wales. See table at WALES.

West Grand Lake; *formerly* **Grand Lake.** Lake, E Maine, near W boundary of Washington co.

West Greenwich. Town, Kent co., W cen. Rhode Island; pop. (1990c) 3492.

West Hartford. Town, cen. Hartford co., N Connecticut, W of Hartford; pop. (1990c) 60,110; Univ. of Hartford (1877), St. Joseph Coll. (1932); settled 1679; incorp. 1854; birthplace 1758 of lexicographer Noah Webster.

West Haven. Suburban residential town, SW New Haven co., S Connecticut, separated from New Haven by West River; pop. (1990c) 54,021; Univ. of New Haven (1920).

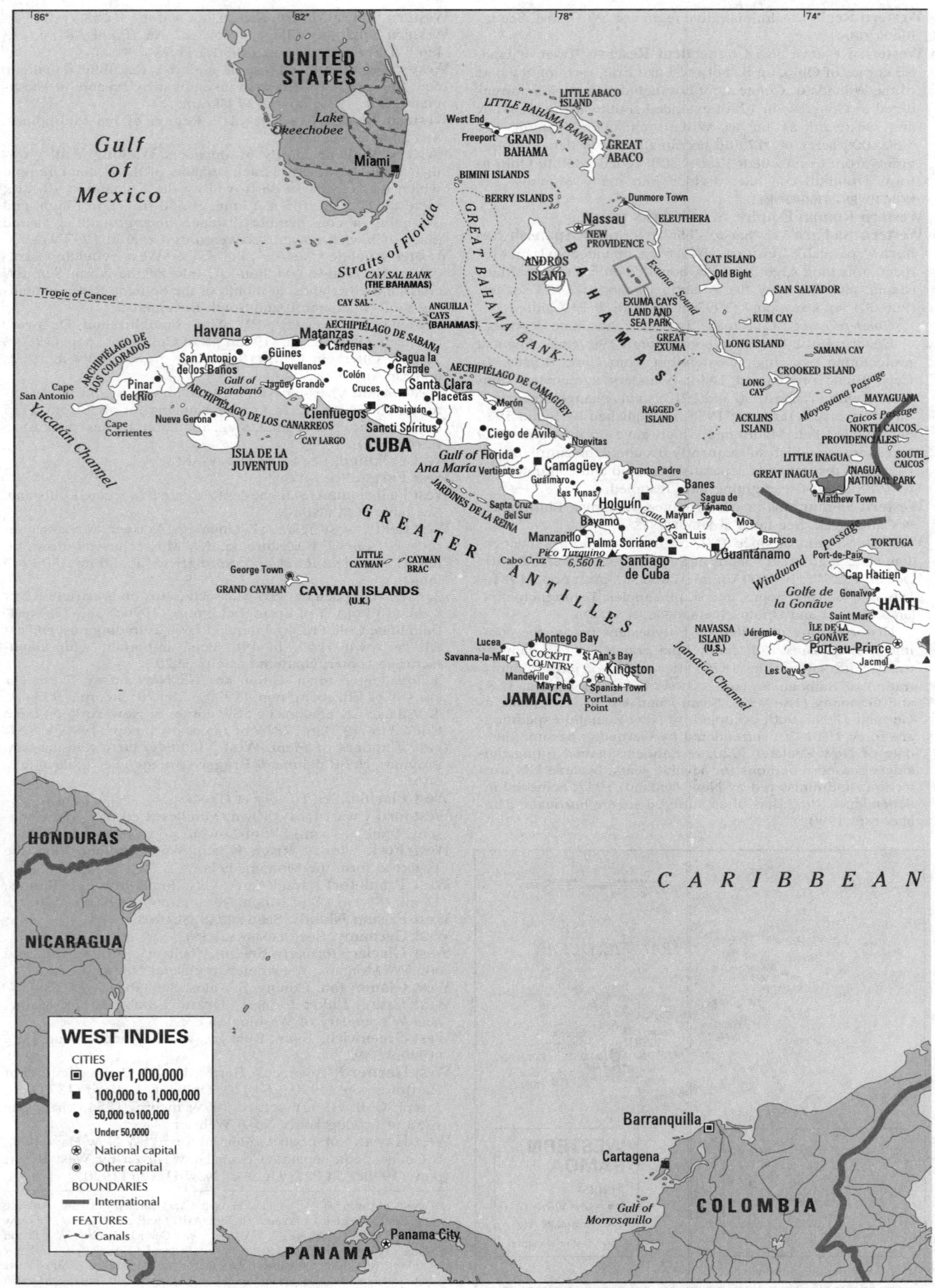

UNITED STATES
Lake Okeechobee
Miami
Gulf of Mexico
Straits of Florida
Tropic of Cancer
LITTLE ABACO ISLAND
LITTLE BAHAMA BANK
West End
Freeport
GRAND BAHAMA
GREAT ABACO
BIMINI ISLANDS
BERRY ISLANDS
Dunmore Town
Nassau
NEW PROVIDENCE
ELEUTHERA
ANDROS ISLAND
BAHAMAS
GREAT BAHAMA BANK
Exuma Sound
CAT ISLAND
Old Bight
SAN SALVADOR
EXUMA CAYS LAND AND SEA PARK
RUM CAY
GREAT EXUMA
LONG ISLAND
SAMANA CAY
CROOKED ISLAND
LONG CAY
RAGGED ISLAND
ACKLINS ISLAND
Mayaguana Passage
MAYAGUANA
Caicos Passage
NORTH CAICOS
PROVIDENCIALES
SOUTH CAICOS
LITTLE INAGUA
GREAT INAGUA
INAGUA NATIONAL PARK
Matthew Town
CAY SAL BANK (THE BAHAMAS)
CAY SAL
ANGUILLA CAYS (BAHAMAS)
ARCHIPIÉLAGO DE LOS COLORADOS
Havana
Matanzas
AECHIPIÉLAGO DE SABANA
Cárdenas
Güines
San Antonio de los Baños
Jovellanos
Sagua la Grande
Colón
Gulf of Batabanó
Jagüey Grande
Cruces
Santa Clara
Placetas
Cape San Antonio
Pinar del Río
ARCHIPIÉLAGO DE LOS CANARREOS
Cienfuegos
Cabaiguán
Sancti Spíritus
AECHIPIÉLAGO DE CAMAGÜEY
Morón
Cape Corrientes
Nueva Gerona
CAY LARGO
CUBA
Ciego de Avila
Nuevitas
Yucatán Channel
ISLA DE LA JUVENTUD
Gulf of Florida
Ana María
Vertientes
Camagüey
Puerto Padre
Guáimaro
Las Tunas
Banes
JARDINES DE LA REINA
Santa Cruz del Sur
Holguín
Sagua de Tánamo
Cauto R.
Mayarí
Moa
Bayamo
San Luis
Baracoa
GREATER ANTILLES
Manzanillo
Palma Soriano
Guantánamo
Cabo Cruz
Pico Turquino 6,560 ft.
Santiago de Cuba
Windward Passage
TORTUGA
Port-de-Paix
Cap Haïtien
LITTLE CAYMAN
CAYMAN BRAC
George Town
GRAND CAYMAN
CAYMAN ISLANDS (U.K.)
Golfe de la Gonâve
Gonaïves
HAITI
Saint Marc
NAVASSA ISLAND (U.S.)
Jérémie
ÎLE DE LA GONÂVE
Port-au-Prince
Jacmel
Les Cayes
Lucea
Montego Bay
Savanna-la-Mar
COCKPIT COUNTRY
St Ann's Bay
Mandeville
Kingston
May Pen
Spanish Town
JAMAICA
Portland Point
Jamaica Channel
HONDURAS
CARIBBEAN
NICARAGUA
WEST INDIES
CITIES
Over 1,000,000
100,000 to 1,000,000
50,000 to100,000
Under 50,0000
National capital
Other capital
BOUNDARIES
International
FEATURES
Canals
Barranquilla
Cartagena
COLOMBIA
Gulf of Morrosquillo
Panama City
PANAMA
86°
82°
78°
74°

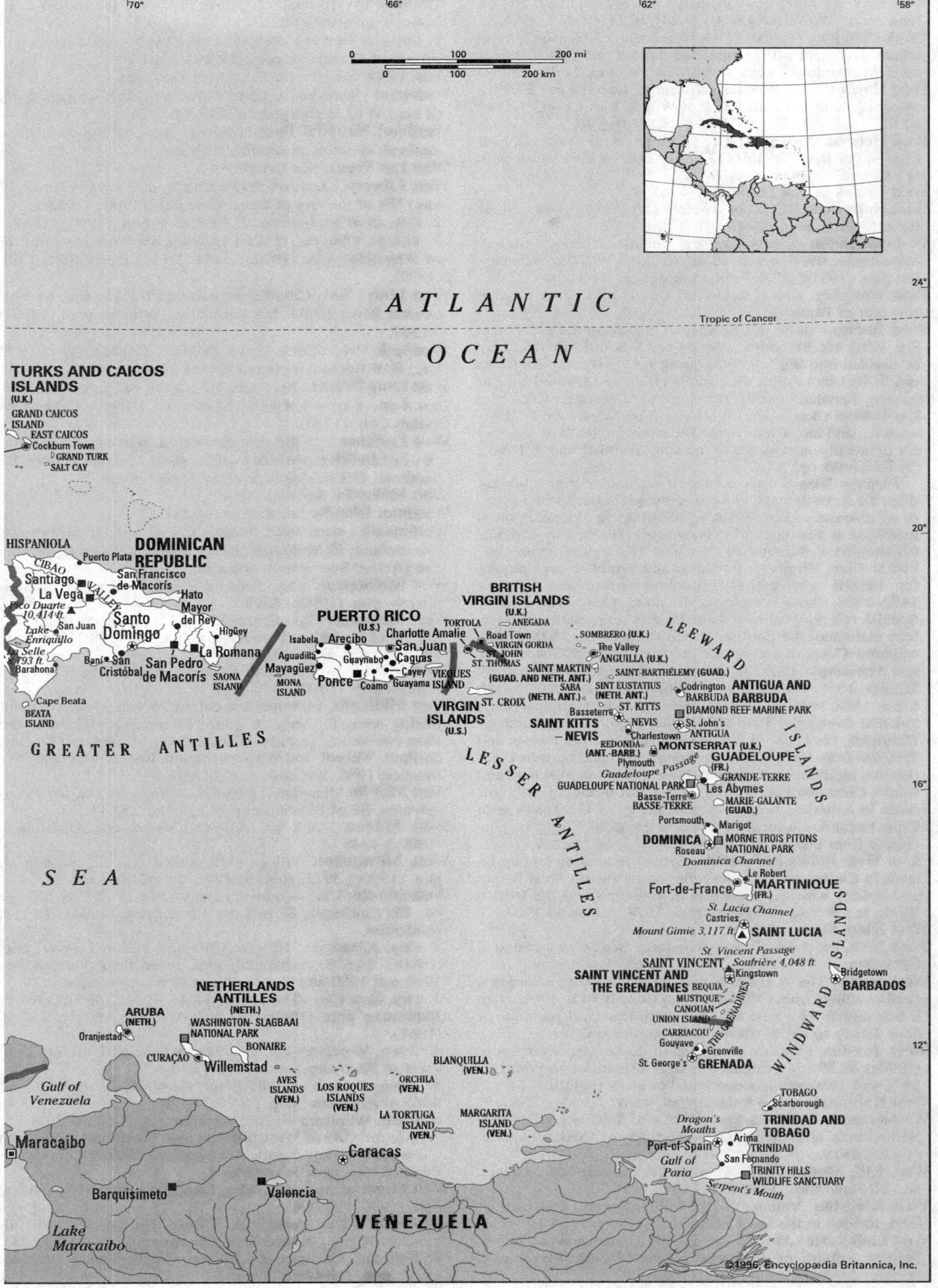

70°
66°
62°
58°
0 100 200 mi
0 100 200 km
24°
20°
16°
12°
ATLANTIC
OCEAN
Tropic of Cancer
TURKS AND CAICOS ISLANDS
(U.K.)
GRAND CAICOS ISLAND
EAST CAICOS
Cockburn Town
GRAND TURK
SALT CAY
HISPANIOLA
DOMINICAN REPUBLIC
Puerto Plata
CIBAO VALLEY
Santiago
San Francisco de Macorís
La Vega
Pico Duarte 10,414 ft.
Hato Mayor del Rey
Santo Domingo
San Juan
Lake Enriquillo
Higüey
La Selle 8,793 ft.
Barahona
Baní
San Cristóbal
San Pedro de Macorís
La Romana
SAONA ISLAND
Cape Beata
BEATA ISLAND
GREATER ANTILLES
PUERTO RICO
(U.S.)
Isabela
Arecibo
Aguadilla
Mayagüez
Guaynabo
San Juan
Caguas
Cayey
Ponce
Coamo
Guayama
MONA ISLAND
VIEQUES ISLAND
Charlotte Amalie
BRITISH VIRGIN ISLANDS
(U.K.)
TORTOLA
ANEGADA
Road Town
VIRGIN GORDA
ST. JOHN
ST. THOMAS
ST. CROIX
VIRGIN ISLANDS
(U.S.)
LEEWARD ISLANDS
SOMBRERO (U.K.)
The Valley
ANGUILLA (U.K.)
SAINT MARTIN
(GUAD. AND NETH. ANT.)
SAINT-BARTHÉLEMY (GUAD.)
SABA
(NETH. ANT.)
SINT EUSTATIUS
(NETH. ANT.)
Codrington
BARBUDA
ANTIGUA AND BARBUDA
DIAMOND REEF MARINE PARK
ST. KITTS
Basseterre
NEVIS
Charlestown
St. John's
ANTIGUA
SAINT KITTS – NEVIS
REDONDA
(ANT.-BARB.)
MONTSERRAT (U.K.)
Plymouth
Guadeloupe Passage
GUADELOUPE
(FR.)
GRANDE-TERRE
Les Abymes
GUADELOUPE NATIONAL PARK
Basse-Terre
BASSE-TERRE
MARIE-GALANTE
(GUAD.)
LESSER ANTILLES
Portsmouth
Marigot
DOMINICA
Roseau
MORNE TROIS PITONS NATIONAL PARK
Dominica Channel
Le Robert
Fort-de-France
MARTINIQUE
(FR.)
St. Lucia Channel
Castries
Mount Gimie 3,117 ft.
SAINT LUCIA
St. Vincent Passage
SAINT VINCENT
Soufrière 4,048 ft.
Kingstown
SAINT VINCENT AND THE GRENADINES
BEQUIA
MUSTIQUE
CANOUAN
UNION ISLAND
THE GRENADINES
CARRIACOU
Gouyave
Grenville
St. George's
GRENADA
Bridgetown
BARBADOS
WINDWARD ISLANDS
SEA
NETHERLANDS ANTILLES
(NETH.)
ARUBA
(NETH.)
Oranjestad
WASHINGTON- SLAGBAAI NATIONAL PARK
BONAIRE
CURAÇAO
Willemstad
AVES ISLANDS
(VEN.)
LOS ROQUES ISLANDS
(VEN.)
BLANQUILLA
(VEN.)
ORCHILA
(VEN.)
LA TORTUGA ISLAND
(VEN.)
MARGARITA ISLAND
(VEN.)
TOBAGO
Scarborough
TRINIDAD AND TOBAGO
Dragon's Mouths
Port-of-Spain
Arima
TRINIDAD
Gulf of Paria
San Fernando
TRINITY HILLS WILDLIFE SANCTUARY
Serpent's Mouth
Gulf of Venezuela
Maracaibo
Caracas
Barquisimeto
Valencia
VENEZUELA
Lake Maracaibo
©1996, Encyclopædia Britannica, Inc.

West Hav·er·straw \ˈha-vər-ˌstrȯ\. Village, Rockland co., SE New York, W of Hudson River 34 mi. (55 km.) N of New York City; pop. (1990c) 9183; former site of Treason House, where American officer Benedict Arnold and British Major John André plotted betrayal of West Point to the British.

West Ha·zle·ton \ˈhā-zəl-tən\. Borough, Luzerne co., E Pennsylvania, 20 mi. (32 km.) SSW of Wilkes-Barre; pop. (1990c) 4136.

West Hel·e·na \ˈhe-lə-nə\. City, Phillips co., E Arkansas, near Mississippi River 85 mi. (137 km.) ENE of Pine Bluff; pop. (1990c) 9695; founded 1909.

West Hoboken. See UNION CITY 4.

West Hollywood. City, Los Angeles co., SW California, NE of Beverly Hills; pop. (1990c) 36,118.

West·hough·ton \ˈwest-ˈhȯt-ᵊn, -ˈhau̇t-\. Town, Greater Manchester, NW England, 13 mi. (21 km.) WNW of Manchester; pop. (1981p) 20,627; pharmaceutical products.

West Hungary. Name applied to Burgenland (*q.v.*) when it was part of Hungary.

West In·dies \ˈin-dēz\. **1.** Islands, enclosing the Caribbean Sea, lying bet. SE North America and N South America; may be divided into the following groups: (1) **Greater An·til·les** \an-ˈti-lēz\ incl. Cuba, Hispaniola (Haiti and Dominican Republic), Jamaica, and Puerto Rico; (2) **Lesser Antilles** *also* **Car·ib·bees** \ˈkar-ə-ˌbēz\ incl. Virgin Is., Windward Is., Leeward Is., and the islands in the S Caribbean Sea N of Venezuela (generally considered to include Trinidad and Tobago); (3) **Bahamas** (*q.v.*).

History: Islands first inhabited by native tribes, among them the Arawak and Caribs; in subsequent European voyages of discovery, San Salvador (Watling) in Bahamas often identified as first landfall in New World reached by explorer Christopher Columbus 1492; Cuba, Hispaniola, Dominica, Puerto Rico, Virgin Is., Jamaica, and Trinidad were among the islands visited by Columbus during his voyages 1492–1504; Santo Domingo, founded 1496, was seat of Spanish rule in West Indies and base for expansion to American mainland; the English settled Barbados c. 1625, Dutch captured Curaçao 1634, and French occupied Guadeloupe and Martinique 1635; Jamaica was taken from Spanish by English 1655; St. Thomas in Virgin Is. came into Danish hands 1666; became a central theater of bitter Anglo-French colonial rivalry; by 1814 British had acquired the islands of Dominica, Grenada, St. Lucia, and Tobago from France and Trinidad from Spain; Santo Domingo and Haiti became independent republics in 19th cent. (see DOMINICAN REPUBLIC and HAITI); Cuba and Puerto Rico (*qq.v.*), last of the Spanish colonies in America, became dependencies of U.S. 1898 with Cuba becoming a republic 1902; S group of Virgin Is. purchased from Denmark by U.S. 1916–17. See INDIES.

2. *or* **West Indies Federation.** Former federation among islands in Caribbean Sea, consisting of the British West Indian possessions with the exception of Bahamas and the British Virgin Is.; ✱ Port-of-Spain; estab. 1958, dissolved 1962.

West Irian. See IRIAN JAYA.

West Java. Province of Java, Indonesia. See JAVA and table at INDONESIA.

West Jersey. The W and S part of New Jersey, constituting a Quaker colony under William Penn from 1676 to 1702 when it was united with East Jersey to form the royal province of New Jersey (*q.v.*); ✱ (from 1681) Burlington.

West Jor·dan \ˈjȯrd-ᵊn\. City, Salt Lake co., Utah; pop. (1990c) 42,892; experienced a sixfold increase in pop. bet. 1970 and 1980 and has continued to grow rapidly.

West Kalimantan. See KALIMANTAN, WEST.

West·ka·pel·le \ˌvest-kə-ˈpe-lə\. Town, Zeeland prov., SW Netherlands, at W tip of Walcheren I. NW of Vlissingen; pop. (1981e) 2619.

West Kill, Mount \ˈkil\. Peak in the Catskill Mts., Greene co., SE New York; 3880 ft. (1183 m.).

West Kingston. Village, ⊗ of Washington co., S Rhode Island; located in the town of South Kingstown (*q.v.*).

West La·fay·ette \ˌlä-fē-ˈet, ˌla-\. City, Tippecanoe co., W cen. Indiana, suburb of Lafayette across Wabash River; pop. (1990c) 25,907; Purdue Univ. (1869).

West·lake \ˈwest-ˌlāk\. **1.** Town, Calcasieu parish, SW Louisiana; pop. (1990c) 5007.

2. *formerly* **Do·ver** \ˈdō-vər\. City, Cuyahoga co., N Ohio, W suburb of Cleveland; pop. (1990c) 27,018.

West Lake. See *Kagera* in table at TANZANIA.

West·land \ˈwest-lənd\. City, Wayne co., SE Michigan, 5 mi. (8 km.) W of Detroit; pop. (1990c) 84,724.

Westland National Park. National park, W South I., New Zealand; contains mountains with glaciers.

West Las Vegas. See LAS VEGAS 2.

West Liberty. 1. Town, Muscatine co., E Iowa, 17 mi. (27 km.) NW of the city of Muscatine; pop. (1990c) 2935.

2. City, ⊗ of Morgan co., E Kentucky; pop. (1990c) 1887.

3. Village, Ohio co., N West Virginia, ab. 9 mi. (14 km.) NE of Wheeling; pop. (1990c) 1434; West Liberty State Coll. (1837).

West Linn \ˈlin\. City, Clackamas co., NW Oregon, on Willamette River 10 mi. (16 km.) S of Portland; pop. (1990c) 16,367.

West·lock \ˈwest-ˌläk\. Town, Alberta, Canada, 45 mi. (72 km.) N of Edmonton; pop. (1991c) 4719.

West Long Branch. Borough, Monmouth co., E cen. New Jersey, 4 mi. (6 km.) N of Asbury Park; pop. (1990c) 7690; Monmouth Coll. (1933).

West Lo·thi·an \ˈlō-t͟hē-ən\; *formerly* **Lin·lith·gow** \lin-ˈlith-gō\ *or* **Lin·lith·gow·shire** \-ˌshir, -shər\. Former county, SE Scotland; ⊗ Linlithgow; rivers Almond, Avon.

West Malaysia. See MALAYSIA.

Westman Islands. See VESTMANNAEYJAR.

West·meath \west-ˈmēt͟h, ˈwest-\. County in Leinster prov., N cen. Ireland; ⊗ Mullingar; rivers Shannon, Brosna; farming and fishing. See table at IRELAND.

West Melbourne. City, Brevard co., E Florida, W of Melbourne; pop. (1990c) 8399.

West Memphis. City, Crittenden co., E Arkansas, 8 mi. (13 km.) W of Memphis, Tennessee; pop. (1990c) 28,259; incorp. under present name 1927.

West Miami. Town, Miami-Dade co., SE Florida, N of Coral Gables; pop. (1990c) 5727.

West Midlands. Metropolitan county, W cen. England, comprising areas formerly in Staffordshire, Warwickshire, and Worcestershire; includes Birmingham, Coventry, Dudley, Solihull, Walsall, and Wolverhampton; lost its administrative function 1986. See table at ENGLAND.

West Miff·lin \ˈmi-flən\. Borough, Allegheny co., SW Pennsylvania, SE of Pittsburgh; pop. (1990c) 23,644.

West Mil·ton \ˈmilt-ᵊn\. Village, Miami co., Ohio; pop. (1990c) 4348.

West Milwaukee. Village, Milwaukee co., SE Wisconsin; pop. (1990c) 3973; suburb of the city of Milwaukee.

West·min·ster \ˈwest-ˌmin-stər, ˌwest-ˈmin-\. **1.** City, Orange co., SW California, SE of Long Beach; pop. (1990c) 78,118; residential.

2. City, Adams co., NE cen. Colorado, NW of Denver; pop. (1990c) 74,625; residential; pop. more than doubled bet. 1970 and 1980 and has continued to increase rapidly.

3. City, ⊗ of Carroll co., N Maryland, 30 mi. (48 km.) NW of Baltimore; pop. (1990c) 13,068; Western Maryland Coll. (1867).

4. Town, Worcester co., cen. Massachusetts, 7 mi. (11 km.) WSW of Fitchburg; pop. (1990c) 6191.

5. Town, Oconee co., NW South Carolina, 29 mi. (47 km.) WNW of Anderson; pop. (1990c) 3120.

6. Town, Windham co., SE Vermont; pop. (1990c) 3026.

7. *or in full* **City of Westminster;** *anc.* **West·mon·as·te·ri·um** \ˈwest-ˌmä-nə-ˈstir-ē-əm\. A borough of Greater London, SE England. See table at LONDON 4.

West Mon·roe \mən-ˈrō\. City, Ouachita parish, N Louisiana; pop. (1990c) 14,096.

West·mont \ˈwest-ˌmänt\. **1.** Village, Du Page co., NE Illinois, ab. 10 mi. (16 km.) W of Chicago; pop. (1990c) 21,228.

2. Borough, Cambria co., SW cen. Pennsylvania, near Altoona; pop. (1990c) 5789.

West·more·land \ *Kans. and Pa.* west-ˈmōr-lənd, *Va.* ˈwest-mər-lənd\. **1.** Name of counties in two states of the U.S. See tables at PENNSYLVANIA and VIRGINIA.
2. City, ⊗ of Pottawatomie co., NE Kansas; pop. (1990c) 541.

West·mor·land \ˈwest-mər-lənd; *U.S. also* west-ˈmōr-\. **1.** County in SE New Brunswick, Canada. See table at NEW BRUNSWICK.
2. Former county, NW England; lakes include Windermere, Hawes Water, Rydal Water; rivers include Eden and Kent. See CUMBRIA.

West·mount \ˈwest-ˌmau̇nt\. Residential city, Montreal I., S Quebec, Canada, adjacent to the city of Montreal; pop. (1991c) 20,239.

West New Brigh·ton \ˈbrīt-ᵊn\. See STATEN ISLAND 2.

West New Britain. See NEW BRITAIN 2.

West New·bury \ˈnü-ˌber-ē, ˈnyü-\. Town, Essex co., NE corner of Massachusetts, 19 mi. (31 km.) NE of Lowell; pop. (1990c) 3421.

West New Guinea. See IRIAN JAYA.

West Newton. **1.** Village, Massachusetts. See NEWTON 6.
2. Borough, Westmoreland co., SW Pennsylvania, on Youghiogheny River 20 mi. (32 km.) SE of Pittsburgh; pop. (1990c) 3152.

West New York. Town, Hudson co., NE New Jersey, on Hudson River 4 mi. (6 km.) N of Jersey City; pop. (1990c) 38,125; made separate town 1898.

West Nishnabotna. See NISHNABOTNA.

West Nor·ri·ton \ˈnȯr-ət-ᵊn, ˈnär-\. Urban township, Montgomery co., SE Pennsylvania, W of Philadelphia; pop. (1990c) 15,209.

West Nusa Tenggara. Province of Indonesia, in Lesser Sunda Is. See table at INDONESIA.

West Okoboji. See OKOBOJI.

Wes·ton \ˈwes-tən\. **1.** County in NE Wyoming. See table at WYOMING.
2. Town, Fairfield co., SW Connecticut, 8 mi. (13 km.) WNW of Bridgeport; pop. (1990c) 8648.
3. Residential town, Middlesex co., NE Massachusetts, 12 mi. (19 km.) W of Boston; pop. (1990c) 10,200; Regis Coll. (1927).
4. City, ⊗ of Lewis co., N cen. West Virginia, on West Fork River 18 mi. (29 km.) SSW of Clarksburg; pop. (1990c) 4994.
5. Town, Marathon co., cen. Wisconsin; pop. (1990c) 11,450.
6. Town, W Sabah, Malaysia; port at head of Brunei Bay ab. 15 mi. (24 km.) SW of Beaufort.

Weston Peak. Mountain, Park co., cen. Colorado; 13,500 ft. (4115 m.).

Weston–su·per–Mare \-ˌsü-pər-ˈmar\. Seaside resort, Avon, SW England, on Bristol Channel at mouth of the Severn 20 mi. (32 km.) WSW of Bristol; pop. (1981c) 62,261.

West Orange. **1.** Town, Essex co., NE New Jersey, 5 mi. (8 km.) NW of Newark; pop. (1990c) 39,103; separated from Orange 1862; incorp. 1900; "Glenmont," home of inventor Thomas A. Edison after 1887, now set aside as an historic site.
2. City, Orange co., E Texas, 4 mi. (6 km.) SW of the city of Orange; pop. (1990c) 4187.

West·o·ver \ˈwes-ˌtō-vər\. City, Monongalia co., N West Virginia, on Monongahela River 3 mi. (5 km.) SW of Morgantown; pop. (1990c) 4201.

West Pakistan. See PAKISTAN.

West Palm Beach. City, ⊗ of Palm Beach co., SE Florida, on Lake Worth 64 mi. (103 km.) N of Miami and 40 mi. (64 km.) E of Lake Okeechobee; pop. (1990c) 67,643; winter resort; Palm Beach Atlantic Coll. (1968); incorp. 1894.

West Pat·er·son \ˈpa-tər-sən\. Borough, Passaic co., N New Jersey, SW suburb of Paterson; pop. (1990c) 10,982; Berkeley Coll. of Business (1931).

West·pha·lia \vest-ˈfāl-yə, west-, -ˈfā-lē-ə\. Former province of Prussia, now part of Germany.
History: Duchy created in 12th cent.; for several centuries administered for the archbishop of Cologne. Peace of Westphalia, terminating Thirty Years' War and in large measure determining political status of modern Europe, signed at Münster Oct. 24, 1648. In 1803 divided bet. Prussia and Hesse-Darmstadt; created a kingdom 1807 by French Emperor Napoléon for his brother, Jérôme Bonaparte, with boundaries extended eastward and with ✻ at Kassel; reorganized by Congress of Vienna 1815; became province of Prussia 1816. Its cities suffered many and severe bombings in WWII. In 1946 divided among North Rhine-Westphalia, Lower Saxony, and Hesse states of West Germany.

West Pitts·ton \ˈpits-tən\. Residential borough, Luzerne co., E Pennsylvania, on Susquehanna River 8 mi. (13 km.) NNE of Wilkes-Barre; pop. (1990c) 5590.

West Plains. City, ⊗ of Howell co., S Missouri, 90 mi. (145 km.) ESE of Springfield; pop. (1990c) 8913.

West Point. **1.** City, Harris and Troup cos., W Georgia, 14 mi. (23 km.) SW of La Grange; pop. (1990c) 3571; scene nearby of a battle fought Apr. 16, 1865, at end of Civil War, troops not knowing truce had been declared a week earlier.
2. City, ⊗ of Clay co., E Mississippi, 16 mi. (26 km.) NW of Columbus; pop. (1990c) 8489; Mary Holmes Coll. (1892).
3. City, ⊗ of Cuming co., NE Nebraska, 30 mi. (48 km.) NNW of Fremont; pop. (1990c) 3250.
4. Unincorporated settlement, Orange co., SE New York, on W bank of Hudson River just SE of Storm King and Crow's Nest mountains; ab. 35 mi. (55 km.) by railroad N of New York City; pop. (1990c) 8024; site of United States Military Academy (founded by act of Congress 1802), 3500-acre (1418-hectare) reservation on W bank of Hudson River and (since 1908) Constitution I. in river; occupied as military post and fortified by Americans 1778, and has served as military post since American Revolution; center of American officer Benedict Arnold's treason plot in 1780.
5. Town, King William co., E Virginia, on York River at junction of Pamunkey and Mattaponi rivers 38 mi. (61 km.) E of Richmond; pop. (1990c) 2938.
6. W tip of Anticosti I., at the mouth of the St. Lawrence River, E Canada.

West·port \ˈwest-ˌpōrt\. **1.** Residential town, S Fairfield co., SW Connecticut, on Long Island Sound at mouth of Saugatuck River; pop. (1990c) 24,410; settled 1648; incorp. 1835.
2. Town, Bristol co., SE Massachusetts, 8 mi. (13 km.) W of New Bedford; pop. (1990c) 13,852.
3. Former town, W Missouri, on Missouri River, now residential district of Kansas City (*q.v.*); scene of battle during Civil War 1864 in which Union forces defeated Confederates under Gen. Sterling Price.
4. Town and seaport, SW co. Mayo, on shore of Clew Bay, NW Ireland; pop. (1986c) 3456.
5. Seaport, NW South I., New Zealand, at mouth of Buller River 90 mi. (145 km.) WSW of Nelson; pop. (1988e) 4640; coal shipping.

West Prussia *or Ger.* **West·preus·sen** \ˈvest-ˌprȯis-ᵊn\. **1.** Coastal region of Pomerania, W cen. Europe; of varying boundaries and ownership, 13th–18th cents.; after 1772 part of Prussia (see WEST PRUSSIA 2).
2. Former province, Prussia, Germany, on Baltic coast; by Treaty of Versailles 1919 divided subsequently bet. Poland and Germany into Pomorze prov., Poland, Free City of Danzig, West Prussia government dist. in East Prussia prov. of Germany, and part of Grenzmark Posen-Westpreussen; entire region assigned to Poland after WWII.

West Punjab. See PUNJAB 4.

West Quod·dy Head \ˈkwä-dē\. Cape, NE Maine, S of Eastport at S entrance to Passamaquoddy Bay; lighthouse; easternmost point of the Lower 48; 66°57′W, 44°49′N.

Wes·tray \ˈwes-ˌtrā\. One of the Orkney Is., off N coast of Scotland; ab. 10 mi. (16 km.) long.

Westray Firth. Channel, off N coast of Scotland, bet. islands of Westray on the N and Rousay on the S in the N Orkney Is.

West Read·ing \ˈre-diŋ\. Borough, Berks co., SE Pennsylvania, on the Schuylkill River; pop. (1990c) 4142.

West Rich·land \ˈrich-lənd\. City, Benton co., S Washington; pop. (1990c) 3962.

West Riding. See YORKSHIRE.

West River. See WEST 1.

West Rox·bury \ˈräks-ˌber-ē\. Former town, E Massachusetts, became part of Boston 1874; site of Brook Farm where a communal living experiment was tried 1841–47 by a group of noted Americans, incl. reformer George Ripley (the leader) and writers Nathaniel Hawthorne, George W. Curtis, Charles A. Dana, and Margaret Fuller; figures in Hawthorne's novel *Blithedale Romance* (1852).

West Sacramento. City, Yolo co., N cen. California; pop. (1990c) 28,898.

West Saint Paul. City, Dakota co., SE Minnesota, 5 mi. (8 km.) S of St. Paul; pop. (1990c) 19,248.

West Salem. Village, La Crosse co., W Wisconsin, 7 mi. (11 km.) E of the city of La Crosse; pop. (1990c) 3611.

West Sen·e·ca \ˈse-nə-kə\. Unincorporated settlement, Erie co., NW New York, SE of Buffalo; pop. (1990c) 47,866.

West Side. The W part of Manhattan borough, New York City, New York; includes stretch along Hudson River.

West Smithfield. See SMITHFIELD 5.

West Spanish Peak. Mountain, Huerfano and Las Animas cos., S Colorado; 13,623 ft. (4152 m.).

West Spitsbergen. See SPITSBERGEN.

West Springfield. **1.** Town, Hampden co., SW Massachusetts, on Connecticut River across from Springfield; pop. (1990c) 27,537; site of annual Eastern States Exposition. **2.** Unincorporated settlement, Fairfax co., NE Virginia, SW of Washington, D.C.; pop. (1990c) 28,126.

West·stel·ling·werf \ˌvest-ˌste-liŋ-ˈverf\. Commune, Friesland prov., N Netherlands; pop. (1981e) 24,381.

West Suffolk. See SUFFOLK 3.

West Su·ma·tra \sü-ˈmä-trə\. Province of Indonesia. See table at INDONESIA.

West Sussex. **1.** Former county, SE England. See SUSSEX 6. **2.** Administrative county, SE England, approx. equivalent to the former county. See table at ENGLAND.

West Three Rivers. See TROIS-RIVIÈRES–OUEST.

West Turkistan. See TURKISTAN.

West Union. **1.** City, ⊗ of Fayette co., NE Iowa, 25 mi. (40 km.) S of Decorah; pop. (1990c) 2490. **2.** Village, ⊗ of Adams co., S Ohio; pop. (1990c) 3096. **3.** Town, ⊗ of Doddridge co., N West Virginia; pop. (1990c) 830.

West University Place. City, Harris co., SE Texas, entirely within city of Houston; pop. (1990c) 12,920.

West Valley City. City, Salt Lake co., N Utah, just S and SW of Salt Lake City; pop. (1990c) 86,976.

West View. Borough, Allegheny co., SW Pennsylvania, a suburb N of Pittsburgh; pop. (1990c) 7734.

West·ville \ˈwest-ˌvil\. **1.** Village, Vermilion co., E Illinois, 6 mi. (10 km.) S of Danville; pop. (1990c) 3387. **2.** Town, La Porte co., N Indiana; pop. (1990c) 5255. **3.** Borough, Gloucester co., SW New Jersey, 5 mi. (8 km.) S of Camden; pop. (1990c) 4573. **4.** Town, Pictou co., N Nova Scotia, Canada, ab. 5 mi. (8 km.) W of New Glasgow; pop. (1991c) 4228.

West Virginia. An east central state of U.S.A., bounded on N by Ohio, Pennsylvania, and Maryland, on E and S by Virginia, and on W by Kentucky and Ohio; 41st state in area, 24,181 sq. mi. (62,629 sq. km.); 34th state in population, (1990c) 1,793,477; ✻ Charleston; 35th state admitted to Union (1863). See table of states at UNITED STATES.

Nickname: Mountain State.

State flower: Rhododendron.

Motto: Montani Semper Liberi (Mountaineers Are Always Free).

Rivers: Ohio, forming large section of upper W boundary, and its tributaries Big Sandy, Guyandotte, Great Kanawha, Little Kanawha, Monongahela; Potomac, forming section of N boundary.

Highest point: Spruce Knob, 4861 ft. (1482 m.), in Pendleton co.

Chief products: Corn, tobacco, apples and other fruit; dairy products, cattle; coal, stone; primary metals, chemicals; recreation.

Chief cities: Charleston and Huntington.

Political divisions: Divided into the following 55 counties (for pronunciation of their names, see their individual entries):

NAME	AREA[1] (sq. mi.)	AREA[1] (sq. km.)	POP. (1990c)	CO. SEAT
Barbour	341	883	15,699	Philippi
Berkeley	316	818	59,253	Martinsburg
Boone	501	1,298	25,870	Madison
Braxton	517	1,339	12,998	Sutton
Brooke	88	228	26,992	Wellsburg
Cabell	279	723	96,827	Huntington
Calhoun	281	728	7,885	Grantsville
Clay	343	888	9,983	Clay
Doddridge	319	826	6,994	West Union
Fayette	663	1,717	47,952	Fayetteville
Gilmer	339	878	7,669	Glenville
Grant	478	1,238	10,428	Petersburg
Greenbrier	1,026	2,657	34,693	Lewisburg
Hampshire	639	1,655	16,498	Romney
Hancock	83	215	35,233	New Cumberland
Hardy	585	1,515	10,977	Moorefield
Harrison	418	1,083	69,371	Clarksburg
Jackson	461	1,194	25,938	Ripley
Jefferson	211	546	35,926	Charles Town
Kanawha	907	2,349	207,619	Charleston
Lewis	392	1,015	17,223	Weston
Lincoln	438	1,134	21,382	Hamlin
Logan	456	1,181	43,032	Logan
McDowell	533	1,380	35,233	Welch
Marion	311	805	57,249	Fairmont
Marshall	304	787	37,356	Moundsville
Mason	433	1,121	25,178	Point Pleasant
Mercer	417	1,080	64,980	Princeton
Mineral	330	855	26,697	Keyser
Mingo	423	1,096	33,739	Williamson
Monongalia	365	945	75,509	Morgantown
Monroe	473	1,225	12,406	Union
Morgan	233	603	12,128	Berkeley Springs
Nicholas	650	1,684	26,775	Summersville
Ohio	106	275	50,871	Wheeling
Pendleton	695	1,800	8,054	Franklin
Pleasants	129	334	7,546	St. Marys
Pocahontas	943	2,442	9,008	Marlinton
Preston	645	1,671	29,037	Kingwood
Putnam	348	901	42,835	Winfield
Raleigh	605	1,567	76,819	Beckley
Randolph	1,036	2,683	27,803	Elkins
Ritchie	452	1,171	10,233	Harrisville
Roane	486	1,259	15,120	Spencer
Summers	350	907	14,204	Hinton
Taylor	174	451	15,144	Grafton
Tucker	421	1,090	7,728	Parsons
Tyler	256	663	9,796	Middlebourne
Upshur	352	912	22,867	Buckhannon
Wayne	513	1,329	41,636	Wayne
Webster	551	1,427	10,729	Webster Springs
Wetzel	363	940	19,258	New Martinsville
Wirt	235	609	5,192	Elizabeth
Wood	368	953	86,915	Parkersburg
Wyoming	504	1,305	28,990	Pineville

[1] Area = land area.

History: Inhabited orig. by Mound Builders and later by other American Indian peoples; European arrival 17th–18th cents. brought conflicts among French, British, and Indians; although part of Virginia, rugged terrain restricted settlement; after American Revolution, concerns of inhabitants who were less likely to have slaves differed from those in E Virginia; dissatisfaction with Virginia government grew, as did sentiment for separation from E part of state; with outbreak of Civil War, residents from W Virginia voted against ordinance of secession May 1861; government loyal to U.S. federal government organized at Wheeling June 1861; population voted to create new state 1861 and a state constitution ratified 1862; admitted to Union June 20, 1863; state constitution adopted 1872 (since amended).

West Vlaanderen. See WEST FLANDERS.

Westwall. See SIEGFRIED LINE.

West Warwick. Town, Kent co., cen. Rhode Island; pop. (1990c) 29,268; governmental center River Point village; separated from Warwick and incorp. 1913.

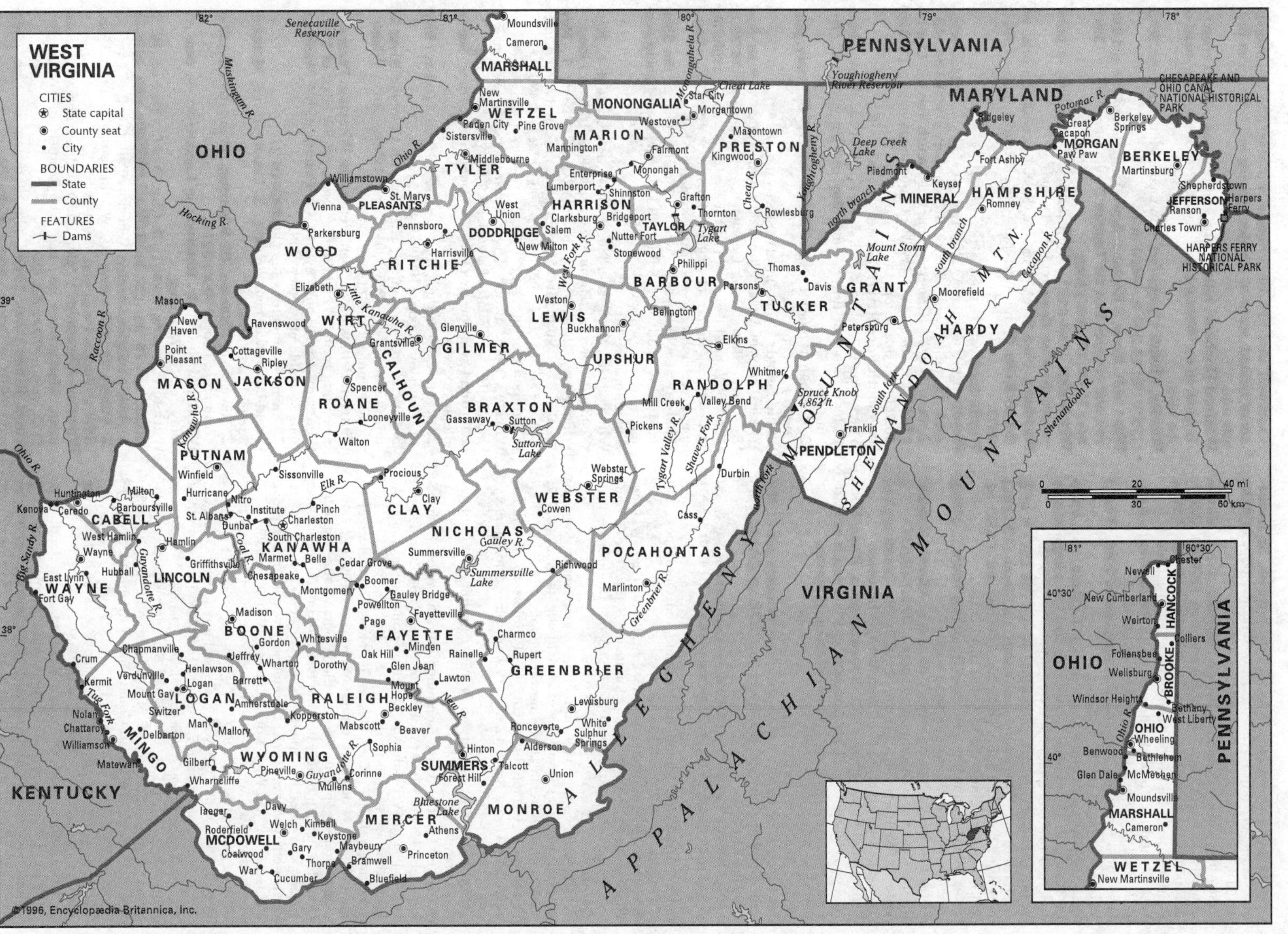
WEST VIRGINIA
CITIES
State capital
County seat
City
BOUNDARIES
State
County
FEATURES
Dams
OHIO
PENNSYLVANIA
MARYLAND
VIRGINIA
KENTUCKY
APPALACHIAN MOUNTAINS
ALLEGHENY MOUNTAINS
SHENANDOAH MTN.
SHENANDOAH MOUNTAINS
CHESAPEAKE AND OHIO CANAL NATIONAL HISTORICAL PARK
HARPERS FERRY NATIONAL HISTORICAL PARK
Spruce Knob 4,862 ft.
MARSHALL
WETZEL
MONONGALIA
MARION
PRESTON
TYLER
PLEASANTS
HARRISON
DODDRIDGE
TAYLOR
WOOD
RITCHIE
BARBOUR
TUCKER
GRANT
MINERAL
HAMPSHIRE
MORGAN
BERKELEY
JEFFERSON
HARDY
WIRT
LEWIS
GILMER
CALHOUN
UPSHUR
RANDOLPH
MASON
JACKSON
ROANE
BRAXTON
PENDLETON
PUTNAM
WEBSTER
CLAY
CABELL
NICHOLAS
KANAWHA
POCAHONTAS
LINCOLN
WAYNE
BOONE
FAYETTE
GREENBRIER
LOGAN
RALEIGH
MINGO
WYOMING
SUMMERS
MONROE
MERCER
MCDOWELL
Moundsville
Cameron
New Martinsville
Paden City
Pine Grove
Sistersville
Middlebourne
Williamstown
St. Marys
Vienna
Parkersburg
Pennsboro
Harrisville
West Union
Salem
New Milton
Mannington
Fairmont
Monongah
Enterprise
Lumberport
Shinnston
Clarksburg
Bridgeport
Nutter Fort
Stonewood
Westover
Star City
Morgantown
Masontown
Kingwood
Grafton
Thornton
Rowlesburg
Philippi
Belington
Thomas
Davis
Parsons
Elkins
Ridgeley
Piedmont
Keyser
Fort Ashby
Romney
Great Cacapon
Paw Paw
Berkeley Springs
Martinsburg
Shepherdstown
Harpers Ferry
Ranson
Charles Town
Moorefield
Petersburg
Whitmer
Franklin
Elizabeth
Ravenswood
Grantsville
Glenville
Weston
Buckhannon
Mason
New Haven
Point Pleasant
Cottageville
Ripley
Spencer
Looneyville
Walton
Gassaway
Sutton
Mill Creek
Valley Bend
Pickens
Winfield
Hurricane
Nitro
Sissonville
Procious
Clay
Institute
Pinch
Charleston
St. Albans
Dunbar
South Charleston
Huntington
Kenova
Ceredo
Milton
Barboursville
West Hamlin
Hamlin
Wayne
Griffithsville
Hubball
East Lynn
Fort Gay
Marmet
Belle
Chesapeake
Cedar Grove
Montgomery
Boomer
Summersville
Richwood
Webster Springs
Cowen
Durbin
Cass
Marlinton
Gauley Bridge
Powellton
Fayetteville
Page
Madison
Gordon
Whitesville
Jeffrey
Wharton
Dorothy
Oak Hill
Minden
Glen Jean
Rainelle
Charmco
Rupert
Lawton
Mount Hope
Beckley
Chapmanville
Crum
Verdunville
Henlawson
Logan
Barrett
Mount Gay
Amherstdale
Kermit
Switzer
Kopperston
Mabscott
Beaver
Man
Mallory
Nolan
Chattaroy
Delbarton
Williamson
Matewan
Gilbert
Wharncliffe
Pineville
Corinne
Mullens
Sophia
Hinton
Talcott
Forest Hill
Alderson
Ronceverte
Lewisburg
White Sulphur Springs
Union
Iaeger
Davy
Roderfield
Welch
Kimball
Keystone
Gary
Coalwood
Thorpe
War
Cucumber
Maybeury
Bramwell
Bluefield
Athens
Princeton
Senecaville Reservoir
Muskingum R.
Ohio R.
Hocking R.
Raccoon R.
Big Sandy R.
Tug Fork
Kanawha R.
Little Kanawha R.
Guyandotte R.
Coal R.
Elk R.
Gauley R.
Summersville Lake
Sutton Lake
Bluestone Lake
New R.
Greenbrier R.
Tygart Valley R.
Shavers Fork
West Fork R.
Tygart Lake
Cheat R.
Cheat Lake
Monongahela R.
Youghiogheny R.
Youghiogheny River Reservoir
Deep Creek Lake
Mount Storm Lake
north branch
south branch
south fork
north fork
Potomac R.
Cacapon R.
Shenandoah R.
0 20 40 mi
0 30 60 km
82°
81°
80°
79°
78°
39°
38°
OHIO
PENNSYLVANIA
HANCOCK
BROOKE
OHIO
MARSHALL
WETZEL
Chester
Newell
New Cumberland
Weirton
Colliers
Follansbee
Wellsburg
Windsor Heights
Bethany
West Liberty
Wheeling
Benwood
Bethlehem
Glen Dale
McMechen
Moundsville
Cameron
New Martinsville
81°
80°30′
40°30′
40°
©1996, Encyclopædia Britannica, Inc.

West·we·go \west-ˈwē-gō\. City, Jefferson parish, SE Louisiana, 8 mi. (13 km.) WSW of New Orleans; pop. (1990c) 11,218.

West·wood \ˈwest-ˌwu̇d\. **1.** Town, Norfolk co., E Massachusetts, 12 mi. (19 km.) SW of Boston; pop. (1990c) 12,557.
2. Residential borough, Bergen co., NE corner of New Jersey, 9 mi. (14 km.) NE of Paterson; pop. (1990c) 10,446.

West Wyoming. Borough, Luzerne co., E Pennsylvania, 5 mi. (8 km.) N of Wilkes-Barre; pop. (1990c) 3117.

West York. Borough, York co., S Pennsylvania, 2 mi. (3 km.) W of York; pop. (1990c) 4283.

West Yorkshire. Metropolitan county, N England, incl. cities of Bradford, Leeds, and Wakefield; lost its administrative function 1986. See table at ENGLAND.

We·tar \ˈwe-ˌtär\. Island, Indonesia, 30 mi. (48 km.) N of E East Timor and WNW of the Leti group; ab. 80 mi. (130 km.) long by 23 mi. (37 km.) wide; ab. 1400 sq. mi. (3625 sq. km.); highest point 4633 ft. (1412 m.).

Wetar Strait. Channel bet. NE East Timor and Wetar I., Malay Archipelago; ab. 30 mi. (48 km.) wide.

We·tas·ki·win \wi-ˈtas-kə-ˌwin\. City, S cen. Alberta, Canada, 40 mi. (64 km.) S of Edmonton; pop. (1991c) 10,634.

We·te *or* **We·ti** \ˈwā-tē\. Town, ✻ of Pemba North region, Tanzania, on Pemba I., N of Zanzibar, off NE coast.

Weth·ers·field \ˈwe-t͟hərz-ˌfēld\. Suburban town, S cen. Hartford co., N Connecticut, on Connecticut River just S of Hartford; pop. (1990c) 25,651; restored colonial houses.

Weti. See WETE.

Wetter. See VÄTTERN.

Wet·te·ren \ˈve-tə-rə\. Commune, East Flanders prov., NW cen. Belgium, on Schelde River just ESE of Ghent; pop. (1991c) 22,655.

Wet·ter·horn \ˈve-tər-ˌhȯrn\. Peak in the Bernese Alps, SW cen. Switzerland, N of the Finsteraarhorn; 12,142 ft. (3701 m.).

Wetterhorn Peak. Mountain, Hinsdale and Ouray cos., SW Colorado; 14,017 ft. (4272 m.).

Wet·ter·stein Mountains \ˈve-tər-ˌshtīn\ *or Ger.* **Wet·ter·stein·ge·bir·ge** \-gə-ˈbir-gə\. Mountains, S Bavaria, Germany; include Zugspitze, 9720 ft. (2963 m.), highest peak in Germany.

Wet·ting·en \ˈve-tiŋ-ən\. Commune, Aargau canton, Switzerland, ab. 10 mi. (16 km.) NW of Zürich; pop. (1980c) 18,377; 13th cent. Cistercian abbey, now a school.

We·tump·ka \wi-ˈtəmp-kə\. City, ⊗ of Elmore co., E cen. Alabama, on Coosa River 12 mi. (19 km.) NE of Montgomery; pop. (1990c) 4670.

Wet·zel \ˈwet-səl\. County in N West Virginia. See table at WEST VIRGINIA.

Wet·zi·kon \ˈvet-si-ˌkȯn\. Commune, Zürich canton, Switzerland, ab. 12 mi. (19 km.) ESE of the city of Zürich; pop. (1980c) 15,859; railroad junction point near Lake of Pfäffikon (see PFÄFFIKON).

Wetz·lar \ˈvet-ˌslär\. City, Hesse, Germany, on Lahn River 30 mi. (48 km.) N of Frankfurt am Main; pop. (1992e) 52,403; manufactures optical goods; old Romanesque cathedral (founded in 12th cent.); became free city in 12th cent.; poet Johann von Goethe worked as a lawyer here.

We·vel·gem \ˈvā-vəl-k͟əm\. Commune, West Flanders prov., NW Belgium, just W of Kortrijk; pop. (1991c) 30,566.

We·wa·hitch·ka \ˌwē-wə-ˈhich-kə\. Town, ⊗ of Gulf co., NW Florida; pop. (1990c) 1779.

We·wak \ˈwā-ˌwäk, ˈwē-ˌwak\. Coastal town, New Guinea I., Papua New Guinea, ab. 75 mi. (120 km.) W of the mouth of the Sepik River; pop. (1990c) 23,224.

We·wo·ka \wē-ˈwō-kə\. City, ⊗ of Seminole co., cen. Oklahoma, 28 mi. (45 km.) ESE of Shawnee; pop. (1990c) 4050.

Wex·ford \ˈweks-fərd\. **1.** County in NW Michigan. See table at MICHIGAN.
2. County, Leinster prov., SE Ireland; ⊗ Wexford; chief river Slaney; agriculture. See table at IRELAND.
3. Town and seaport, ⊗ of co. Wexford, SE Ireland; pop. (1991p) 9537; agricultural implements. Remains of 12th cent. abbey. An early settlement of Norse and later of Anglo-Normans; sacked and garrison massacred 1649 by Oliver Cromwell, then English commander in chief and lord lieutenant of Ireland; scene of a major uprising in 1798 against British rule.

Wexford Harbour. Inlet of St. George's Channel, SE coast of Ireland, in co. Wexford; the city of Wexford is at the head of the inlet.

Wex·ler, Mount \ˈweks-lər\. Mountain, Antarctica, 84°30′S, 175°01′E; 13,202 ft. (4024 m.).

Wey \ˈwā\. River, S England; flows NE in Hampshire and Surrey, and empties into the Thames 2 mi. (3 km.) SE of Chertsey; 35 mi. (56 km.) long.

Wey·bridge \ˈwā-ˌbrij\. Town, Surrey, S England, at point where the Wey flows into the Thames.

Wey·burn \ˈwā-bərn\. City, SE Saskatchewan, Canada, on Souris River 65 mi. (105 km.) SE of Regina; pop. (1991c) 9673.

Weyib. See WABĒ GESTRO.

Wey·mouth \ˈwā-məth\. **1.** Town, Norfolk co., E Massachusetts, 11 mi. (18 km.) SSE of Boston; pop. (1990c) 54,063.
2. Port, Dorset, S England, on **Weymouth Bay** of English Channel 53 mi. (85 km.) WSW of Southampton; pop. (1981p) 46,260; seaside resort.

Weymouth Fore River. See FORE RIVER.

Wha·ka·ta·ne \ˌwä-kə-ˈtä-nē, ˌhwä-\. **1.** River, N cen. North I., New Zealand; flows N into Bay of Plenty; 65 mi. (105 km.) long.
2. Borough, N North I., New Zealand, on Bay of Plenty; pop. (1981c) 12,286.

Whale Islands \ˈwāl, ˈhwāl\. See HVALER.

Whales, Bay of \ˈwālz, ˈhwālz\. Former inlet of Ross Sea, Ross Ice Shelf, Ross Dependency, Antarctica, 78°30′S, 164°20′W; used from 1911 as a base for Antarctic exploring expeditions (see LITTLE AMERICA). Disappeared 1987 when a massive chunk broke off from Ross Ice Shelf.

Whal·say *also* **Whal·sey** \ˈwȯl-sē, ˈhwȯl-\. One of the Shetland Is., N Scotland; 5.5 mi. (8.9 km.) long; sea-fishing center.

Whampoa. See HUANGPU 2.

Whang·a·ehu \ˌwäŋ-gə-ā-ˈhü, ˌhwäŋ-\. River, North I., New Zealand; flows into Tasman Sea; 100 mi. (161 km.) long.

Whang·a·rei \ˌwäŋ-gə-ˈrā, ˌhwäŋ-\. City, N North I., New Zealand, on **Whangarei Harbor,** deep inlet of the Pacific, 85 mi. (137 km.) N of Auckland; pop. (1992e) 44,300.

Whangpoo. See HUANGPU 1.

Wharfe \ˈwȯrf, ˈhwȯrf\. River, North Yorkshire, N cen. England; flows ESE into the Ouse; 7.5 mi. (12 km.) long.

Whar·ton \ˈwȯrt-ᵊn, ˈhwȯrt-\. **1.** County in SE Texas. See table at TEXAS.
2. Borough, Morris co., N New Jersey, 10 mi. (16 km.) NNW of Morristown; pop. (1990c) 5405.
3. City, ⊗ of Wharton co., SE Texas, on Colorado River 28 mi. (45 km.) N of Bay City; pop. (1990c) 9011; Wharton County Junior Coll. (1946).

Wharton Peninsula *or Span.* **Península Wharton.** Peninsula extending from SW cen. Wellington I., off SW coast of Chile.

What·com \ˈwät-kəm, ˈhwät-\. **1.** County in NW Washington. See table at WASHINGTON.
2. Town, Washington. See BELLINGHAM 2.

Wheat·land \ˈwēt-lənd, ˈhwēt-\. **1.** County in cen. Montana. See table at MONTANA.
2. Town, ⊗ of Platte co., SE Wyoming, 43 mi. (69 km.) W of Torrington; pop. (1990c) 3271.

Wheatland Reservoir. Reservoir in Laramie River, cen. Albany co., SE Wyoming.

Whea·ton \ˈwēt-ᵊn, ˈhwēt-\. **1.** City, ⊗ of Du Page co., NE Illinois, ab. 18 mi. (29 km.) W of Chicago; pop. (1990c) 51,464; a religious center; Wheaton Coll. (1860).
2. Village, ⊗ of Traverse co., W Minnesota, 39 mi. (63 km.) SSW of Fergus Falls; pop. (1990c) 1615.

Wheaton–Glen·mont \-ˈglen-ˌmänt\. Unincorporated settlement, Montgomery co., cen. Maryland, N of Washington, D.C.; pop. (1990c) 53,720.

Wheat Ridge \ˈwēt, ˈhwēt\. City, Jefferson co., cen. Colorado, WNW of Denver; pop. (1990c) 29,419.

Whee·ler \ˈwē-lər, ˈhwē-\. **1.** Name of counties in four states of the U.S. See tables at GEORGIA, NEBRASKA, OREGON, TEXAS.
2. Town, ⊗ of Wheeler co., NW Texas; pop. (1990c) 1393.

Wheeler Dam. Dam across Tennessee River, NW Alabama, at head of Lake Wilson, forming **Wheeler Lake,** 74 mi. (119 km.) long. See table at TENNESSEE VALLEY AUTHORITY.

Wheeler Peak. 1. Mountain in Snake Range, SE White Pine co., E Nevada; ab. 13,065 ft. (3980 m.).
2. Mountain, Taos co., N New Mexico; ab. 13,160 ft. (4010 m.); highest point in the state.

Whee·ling \ˈwē-liŋ, ˈhwē-\. **1.** Village, Cook co., NE Illinois, SW of Highland Park; pop. (1990c) 29,911; Forest Institute of Professional Psychology (1979).
2. City, ⊗ of Ohio co., N West Virginia, on Ohio River in N Panhandle ab. 40 mi. (64 km.) SW of Pittsburgh, Pennsylvania; pop. (1990c) 34,882; Wheeling Jesuit Coll. (1954), West Virginia Northern Community Coll. (1972). Settled 1769; Fort Henry (built 1774) scene of one of last battles in American Revolution 1782; incorp. as city 1836; important trading post on Cumberland Road until 1850s; center of Unionist activity in W Virginia 1861 which lead to creation of state of West Virginia; ✻ of state of West Virginia 1863–70 and 1875–85; has continually lost pop. since 1940.

Whern·side \ˈwərn-ˌsīd, ˈhwərn-\. Mountain, N England; 2414 ft. (736 m.); a peak in the Pennine Chain.

Whetstone Buttes. Isolated peaks, NW Adams co., SW North Dakota.

Whick·ham \ˈwi-kəm, ˈhwik-\. Town, Tyne and Wear, N England, 6 mi. (10 km.) SW of Newcastle upon Tyne; pop. (1981p) 31,543.

Whid·bey Island \ˈwid-bē, ˈhwid-\. Island, Island co., Washington, in upper Puget Sound, E of Admiralty Inlet; ab. 45 mi. (70 km.) long. Oak Harbor is by far the island's largest settlement.

Whid·dy Island \ˈwi-dē, ˈhwi-\. Island, Bantry Bay, SW coast of Ireland; ruins of old castle.

Whip·snade \ˈwip-ˌsnād, ˈhwip-\. Village, SE cen. England, NW of Hemel Hempstead; site of zoological park.

Whirl·wind Peak \ˈwərl-ˌwind, ˈhwərl-\. Mountain, W Park co., NW Wyoming; 10,981 ft. (3347 m.).

Whis·tler \ˈwis-lər, -ᵊl-ər\. Settlement, S British Columbia, Canada, in Coast Ranges; pop. (1991c) 4459; resort featuring skiing and other forms of outdoor recreation.

Whit·by \ˈwit-bē, ˈhwit-\. **1.** Town, ⊗ of Durham munic. region, SE Ontario, Canada, a port of entry on Lake Ontario 5 mi. (8 km.) W of Oshawa; pop. (1991c) 61,281; grew rapidly in 1980s.
2. Port, North Yorkshire, N England, on the seacoast at mouth of the Esk River; pop. (1981p) 13,763; seaside resort; fishing, boatbuilding; plastics; site of an abbey founded by St. Hilda (c. 657); meeting place of the Synod of Whitby c. 663, at which the English church allied itself to Rome in preference to Ireland; Anglo-Saxon poet Caedmon was a monk of Whitby; navigator Capt. James Cook sailed from here to Pacific 1768. See NORTHUMBRIA.

White \ˈwīt, ˈhwīt\. **1.** River, Arkansas; rises in Boston Mts., Madison co., NW Arkansas, bends N into Missouri, then SE across Arkansas to empty into the Mississippi on E boundary of Desha co., SE Arkansas; 690 mi. (1110 km.) long; navigable for 260 mi. (418 km.).
2. River, NW Colorado and E Utah; rises in NE Garfield co., Colorado, flows W across Utah border into Green River in cen. Uintah co., E Utah; 250 mi. (402 km.) long.
3. River, SW Indiana; formed by confluence of W fork 255 mi. (410 km.) long rising in Randolph co., E Indiana, and E fork 282 mi. (454 km.) long rising in Henry co., E cen. Indiana; flows W into Wabash River in NW corner of Gibson co., SW Indiana; 52 mi. (84 km.) long. See BLUE 2.
4. River, SW and S cen. South Dakota; rises in NW Nebraska, flows NE across South Dakota border, then E into Missouri River on SE boundary of Lyman co.; ab. 325 mi. (525 km.) long.
5. River, NW Texas; formed by confluence of Callahan Draw and Running Water Draw in N Hale co., flows SE into Salt Fork in Kent co.; 130 mi. (209 km.) long.
6. River, E cen. Vermont; rises in E Addison co., flows S, then E and SE into Connecticut River at White River Junction; ab. 50 mi. (80 km.) long.
7. River, W cen. Washington; rises in Mt. Rainier National Park, flows NW and unites with Green River in SW King co. to form Duwamish River; ab. 60 mi. (95 km.) long.
8. Name of counties in five states of the U.S. See tables at ARKANSAS, GEORGIA, ILLINOIS, INDIANA, TENNESSEE.
9. River, SW Yukon Territory, Canada; rises in Wrangell Mts. in Alaska, flows E, then N in Yukon to the Yukon River above Dawson; 161 mi. (259 km.) long. Its upper course crossed by Alaska Highway.
10. River, Iceland. See HVÍTÁ RIVER.

White Bay. Inlet of Atlantic Ocean, N coast of Newfoundland, Canada; ab. 60 mi. (95 km.) long.

White Bear Lake. City, Ramsey and Washington cos., E Minnesota, on White Bear Lake 11 mi. (18 km.) NNE of St. Paul; pop. (1990c) 24,704; Lakewood Community Coll. (1967).

White Butte. Peak, Slope co., SW North Dakota; 3506 ft. (1069 m.); highest peak in the state.

White Car·pa·thi·an Mountains \kär-ˈpā-thē-ən\ *also* **White Car·pa·thi·ans** \-ənz\ *or Czech* **Bí·le Kar·pa·ty** \ˈbē-le-ˈkär-pä-tē\. Mountain range, W cen. Europe, a SW spur of the Carpathian Mts. running NE and SW and forming boundary bet. Czech Republic and Slovakia; highest point 3514 ft. (1071 m.).

White·chap·el \ˈwīt-ˌcha-pəl, ˈhwīt-\. Parish, Tower Hamlets, London, England, E of the City of London and N of the Thames; art gallery, London Hospital.

White Cloud. City, ⊗ of Newaygo co., W Michigan; pop. (1990c) 1147.

White·cross Mountain \ˈwīt-ˌkrȯs, ˈhwīt-\. Peak, Hinsdale co., SW Colorado; 13,550 ft. (4130 m.).

White Dome. Peak, San Juan co., SW Colorado; 13,607 ft. (4147 m.).

White Earth. River, NW North Dakota; rises in NE Williams co., flows S into Missouri River on SW boundary of Mountrail co.; ab. 60 mi. (95 km.) long.

White·face \ˈwīt-ˌfās, ˈhwīt-\. River, NE Minnesota; rises in E cen. St. Louis co., flows SW into St. Louis River, SW St. Louis co.; ab. 60 mi. (95 km.) long.

Whiteface Mountain. Peak in the Adirondack Mts., Essex co., NE New York; 4867 ft. (1484 m.).

White·field \ˈwīt-ˌfēld, ˈhwīt-\. Town, Greater Manchester co., NW England, 5 mi. (8 km.) N of Manchester; pop. (1981p) 22,235.

White·fish \ˈwīt-ˌfish, ˈhwīt-\. City, Flathead co., NW Montana, 15 mi. (24 km.) N of Kalispell; pop. (1990c) 4368; lake resort.

Whitefish Bay. 1. Inlet of Lake Superior, N coast of Chippewa co., E part of Michigan's Upper Penin.
2. Village, Milwaukee co., SE Wisconsin, on Lake Michigan 5 mi. (8 km.) N of the city of Milwaukee; pop. (1990c) 14,272; residential.

Whitefish Lake. Lake, N Crow Wing co., cen. Minnesota.

Whitefish Mountain. Peak, Glacier National Park, NW Montana; 8000 ft. (2438 m.).

Whitefish Point. Point on extreme N coast of Chippewa co., E part of Michigan's Upper Penin., at W entrance to Whitefish Bay.

Whitefish Range. A range of the Rocky Mts., NW Montana, extending along N section of boundary bet. Lincoln and Flathead cos.; highest peak 8107 ft. (2471 m.).

White·fri·ars \ˈwīt-ˌfrī-ərz, ˈhwīt-\. Section of London, England, in cen. part; named for a Carmelite monastery (built during Middle Ages) in Fleet Street, part of which housed a theater during Renaissance times.

White·hall \ˈwīt-ˌhȯl, ˈhwīt-\. **1.** City, Muskegon co., W Michigan, 13 mi. (21 km.) NNW of the city of Muskegon; pop. (1990c) 3027.
2. Village, Washington co., E New York, on Vermont border at S end of Lake Champlain and N terminus of Champlain Canal, 10 mi. (16 km.) E of Lake George; pop. (1990c) 3071; settled 1759.
3. City, Franklin co., cen. Ohio, E suburb of Columbus; pop. (1990c) 20,572.
4. Borough, Allegheny co., SW Pennsylvania, S suburb of Pittsburgh; pop. (1990c) 14,451.
5. City, ⊗ of Trempealeau co., W Wisconsin; pop. (1990c) 1494.
6. Wide thoroughfare, Westminster borough, London, England, running N and S bet. Trafalgar Square and the Houses of Parliament; lined with the chief government offices and hence frequently used figuratively for the British Government or its policies. Orig. site of Whitehall Palace (from 1529 to 1698 when most of it was destroyed by fire), a royal residence that included a famous banquetting hall designed by Inigo Jones. Charles I was executed there 1649 on an outdoor scaffold.
White Hall \ˈwīt-ˌhȯl, ˈhwīt-\. **1.** City, Jefferson co., SE cen. Arkansas, just NW of Pine Bluff; pop. (1990c) 3849.
2. City, Greene co., W Illinois, 48 mi. (77 km.) WSW of Springfield; pop. (1990c) 2814.
White·ha·ven \ˈwīt-ˌhā-ven, ˈhwīt-\. Town, Cumbria, NW England, on Irish Sea SW of Carlisle; pop. (1981c) 27,925; chemicals.
White Haven. Borough, Luzerne co., E Pennsylvania, on Lehigh River 14 mi. (22 km.) S of Wilkes-Barre; pop. (1990c) 1132; resort.
White·horse \ˈwīt-ˌhȯrs, ˈhwīt-\. City, ✻ of Yukon, Canada, on left bank of Yukon River ab. 52 mi. (84 km.) N of British Columbia border; pop. (1991c) 17,925; terminus of railroad line from Skagway, Alaska, and one of most important stations on Alaska Highway; active trading town in Klondike gold-rush days; head of navigation on Yukon River.
White Horse, Vale of the. Valley, Oxfordshire, S England; named from the *White Horse*, a prehistoric figure of a horse 374 ft. (114 m.) long, formed by cutting away the turf on the side of a chalk hill; many ancient earthworks in the valley which contains the town of Wantage (*q.v.*).
Whitehorse Rapids. Former rapids on the Yukon River at the city of Whitehorse, Yukon, Canada; now submerged in a dam-created lake.
White·house \ˈwīt-ˌhau̇s, ˈhwīt-\. **1.** City, Smith co., NE Texas, SE of Tyler; pop. (1990c) 4032.
2. Village, Lucas co., NW Ohio, SW of Toledo; pop. (1990c) 2528.
White House \ˈwīt-ˌhau̇s, ˈhwīt-\. City, Robertson and Sumner cos., N Tennessee, bet. Nashville and Kentucky border; pop. (1990c) 2987.
Whitehouse Mountain. Peak, Ouray co., SW Colorado; 13,493 ft. (4113 m.).
White Island. 1. Small island, Bay of Plenty, New Zealand, off NE cen. coast of North I.
2. Island, Spitzbergen Archipelago, Norway. See KVITØYA.
White Lake. Lake, SW Vermilion parish, S Louisiana; connected by intracoastal canal with Vermilion Bay.
White·man Range \ˈwīt-mən, ˈhwīt-\. Mountain range, New Britain I., Papua New Guinea, W Pacific Ocean; highest peak 6650 ft. (2027 m.).
White·marsh \ˈwīt-ˌmärsh, ˈhwīt-\. Township, Montgomery co., SE Pennsylvania, on Wissahickon Creek 14 mi. (23 km.) N of Philadelphia; pop. (1990c) 14,863; in American Revolution site of Gen. George Washington's encampment 1777 during battle of Germantown and before retirement to Valley Forge.
White Mountain. 1. Peak in the Sierra Nevada, on boundary bet. Alpine and Mono cos., E cen. California; 14,246 ft. (4342 m.).
2. Mountain, New Mexico. See SIERRA BLANCA PEAK.
3. *or* **White Hill** *or Ger.* **Weis·ser Berg** \ˈvī-sər-ˈberk\ *or Czech* **Bí·lá Ho·ra** \ˈbē-lä-ˈhȯr-ä\. Hill, W Czech Republic, W of Prague; 1243 ft. (379 m.); scene of battle 1620 at beginning of Thirty Years' War in which the Catholic forces of Maximilian I, duke of Bavaria, defeated the Bohemian Protestants under Frederick V, by which Bohemia lost its independence.
White Mountains. 1. Mountains, E California and SW Nevada, on boundary bet. Esmeralda co., Nevada, and Mono co., California; contain Boundary Peak 13,140 ft. (4005 m.), highest peak in Nevada.
2. Mountains of the Appalachian Range, N New Hampshire; highest point Mt. Washington 6288 ft. (1917 m.) in Presidential Range (*q.v.*).
Whit·en Head \ˈwit-ᵊn, ˈhwit-\. Cape, N coast of Scotland, in Highland region, 15 mi. (24 km.) E of Cape Wrath.
White Nile. See NILE.
White Oak. 1. Borough, Allegheny co., SW Pennsylvania, SSE suburb of Pittsburgh; pop. (1990c) 8761.
2. City, Gregg co., NE Texas; pop. (1990c) 5136.
White Pass. Pass in mountains N of Skagway, SE Alaska; highest point 2890 ft. (881 m.); superseded Chilkoot Pass ab. 1900 as easier route to Klondike goldfields; now traversed by railroad.
White Peak. Mountain in Saguache co., S Colorado; 13,600 ft. (4145 m.).
White Pine. County in E Nevada. See table at NEVADA.
White Pine Mountains. Range in SW White Pine co., E Nevada; highest point is **Duck·water Peak** \ˈdək-ˌwȯ-tər, -ˌwä-\ 11,188 ft. (3410 m.).
White Plains. City, ⊗ of Westchester co., SE New York, 25 mi. (40 km.) NNE of New York City; pop. (1990c) 48,718; residential suburb of New York City. Settled by Europeans end of 17th cent.; meeting place of New York Provincial Congress 1776, which ratified Declaration of Independence; scene of Gen. George Washington's retreat from Manhattan and of British attack under Gen. Sir William Howe and battle at Chatterton Hill Oct. 28, 1776; incorp. as village 1866, as city 1916.
White River. 1. Name of several rivers of the U.S. and one of Canada. See WHITE.
2. City, ⊗ of Mellette co., S South Dakota; pop. (1990c) 595.
3. River, Iceland. See HVÍTÁ RIVER.
White River Junction. Unincorporated settlement, Windsor co., E Vermont, at junction of Connecticut and White rivers ab. 9 mi. (15 km.) NNE of Woodstock; pop. (1990c) 2521.
White Rock. City, British Columbia, Canada, 25 mi. (40 km.) S of Vancouver; pop. (1991c) 16,314.
White Rock Mountain. Peak, Gunnison co., W cen. Colorado; 13,532 ft. (4125 m.).
White Russian Soviet Socialist Republic. See BYELORUSSIAN SOVIET SOCIALIST REPUBLIC.
White Sands Missile Range. Region of white (gypsum) sand dunes, Dona Ana co., S New Mexico, SE of San Andres Mts. and SW of the White Sands National Monument; ab. 125 mi. (200 km.) long; U.S. testing site; Holloman Air Force Base adjacent, 11 mi. (18 km.) SW of Alamogordo.
White Sands National Monument. See UNITED STATES, *National Monuments.*
Whites·boro \ˈwīts-ˌbər-ō, ˈhwīts-\. **1.** Village, Oneida co., cen. New York, on Mohawk River 5 mi. (8 km.) WNW of Utica; pop. (1990c) 4195; settled c. 1784.
2. Town, Grayson co., NE Texas, 18 mi. (29 km.) W of Sherman; pop. (1990c) 3209.
Whites·burg \ˈwīts-ˌbərg, ˈhwīts-\. City, ⊗ of Letcher co., SE Kentucky, 30 mi. (48 km.) SW of Pikeville; pop. (1990c) 1636.
White Sea *or Russ.* **Be·lo·ye Mo·re** \ˈbye-lə-yə-ˈmȯr-i\. Large inlet of the Barents Sea, N coast of Russia in Europe; ab. 34,700 sq. mi. (89,875 sq. km.); enclosed on the N by Kola Penin.; chief port Arkhangel'sk, on Dvina Gulf; on S borders on Arkhangel'sk Oblast and on W on Karelia Rep.; receives the Northern Dvina and Onega rivers.
White Settlement. City, Tarrant co., N Texas, W suburb of Fort Worth; pop. (1990c) 15,472.
White·side \ˈwīt-ˌsīd, ˈhwīt-\. County in NW Illinois. See table at ILLINOIS.

White·stone \ˈwīt-ˌstōn, ˈhwīt-\. Neighborhood, N Queens co., New York City, New York, at W end of Long Island N of Flushing; terminus of Bronx Whitestone Bridge across East River to the Bronx; settled by Dutch farmers c. 1645.

White Sulphur Springs. **1.** City, ⊗ of Meagher co., cen. Montana; pop. (1990c) 963.

2. Residential city, Greenbrier co., SE West Virginia, near Virginia border 36 mi. (58 km.) ENE of Hinton; pop. (1990c) 2779; in area of outdoor recreation; mineral springs; served as summer White House for U.S. presidents, among them Martin Van Buren, John Tyler, and Millard Fillmore.

White Top Mountain. Peak, Smyth co., SW Virginia; 5520 ft. (1683 m.).

White·ville \ˈwīt-ˌvil, ˈhwīt-\. City, ⊗ of Columbus co., S North Carolina, 44 mi. (71 km.) W of Wilmington; pop. (1990c) 5078; Southeastern Community Coll. (1964).

White Volta. See VOLTA, WHITE.

White·wa·ter \ˈwīt-ˌwȯ-tər, ˈhwīt-, -ˌwä-\. **1.** River, E Indiana; rises in E cen. Indiana, flows S, then E across Ohio border to empty into the Miami River just above its junction with the Ohio River, SW Ohio; 100 mi. (161 km.) long.

2. City, Walworth and Jefferson cos., S Wisconsin, 18 mi. (29 km.) NE of Janesville; pop. (1990c) 12,636; Univ. of Wisconsin–Whitewater (1868).

Whitewater Baldy \ˈbȯl-dē\. Mountain, S Catron co., W New Mexico; 10,892 ft. (3320 m.).

Whitewater Bay. Inlet of Gulf of Mexico, Monroe co., SW Florida, bet. the mainland and Cape Sable.

Whitewater Lake. Lake, SW Manitoba, Canada, 42 mi. (68 km.) SSW of Brandon; ab. 10 mi. (16 km.) long.

White·wood Peak \ˈwīt-ˌwu̇d, ˈhwīt-\. Mountain in Lawrence co., W South Dakota; 5140 ft. (1567 m.).

Whit·field \ˈwit-ˌfēld, ˈhwit-\. County in NW Georgia. See table at GEORGIA.

Whit·horn \ˈwit-ˌhȯrn, ˈhwit-\. Burgh, Dumfries and Galloway region, SW Scotland, in S part near Burrow Head; pop. (1981c) 983; an old town, with first stone church in Scotland built 397 by St. Ninian; ruins of 12th cent. priory.

Whit·ing \ˈwī-tiŋ, ˈhwī-\. City, Lake co., NW corner of Indiana, on Lake Michigan 17 mi. (27 km.) SE of Chicago; pop. (1990c) 5155; oil refinery; Calumet Coll. of St. Joseph (1951).

Whit·ley \ˈwit-lē, ˈhwit-\. Name of counties in two states of the U.S. See tables at INDIANA and KENTUCKY.

Whitley Bay; *formerly* **Whitley and Monks·ea·ton** \ˈməŋk-ˌsēt-ᵊn\. Resort town, Tyne and Wear, N England, on North Sea 9 mi. (15 km.) ENE of Newcastle upon Tyne; pop. (1981p) 37,079.

Whitley City. Unincorporated settlement, ⊗ of McCreary co., SE Kentucky; pop. (1990c) 1133.

Whit·man \ˈwit-mən, ˈhwit-\. **1.** County in SE Washington. See table at WASHINGTON.

2. Town, Plymouth co., SE Massachusetts, 4 mi. (6 km.) E of Brockton; pop. (1990c) 13,240.

Whit·ney, Mount \ˈwit-nē, ˈhwit-\. Peak in the Sierra Nevada, on boundary bet. Tulare and Inyo cos., SE cen. California, in Sequoia National Park; 14,495 ft. (4418 m.); highest point in the state, and in continental U.S. outside of Alaska. See DEATH VALLEY.

Whit·sta·ble \ˈwit-stə-bəl, ˈhwit-\. Resort town, Kent, SE England, on North Sea 50 mi. (81 km.) E of London; pop. (1981c) 26,451; oyster fisheries.

Whit·sun·day Island \ˈwit-ˌsən-dē, ˈhwit-, -ˌdā\. Island, N of Cumberland Is. off E coast of Queensland, Australia, SE of Townsville, 20°17′S, 148°59′E; 38 sq. mi. (98 sq. km.).

Whit·ti·er \ˈwi-tē-ər, ˈhwi-\. **1.** Seaport city on W shore of Prince William Sound, S Alaska; connected by rail with Fairbanks; pop. (1990c) 243.

2. Suburban residential city, Los Angeles co., SW California, 12 mi. (19 km.) E of Los Angeles; pop. (1990c) 77,671; Whittier Coll. (1887), Los Angeles Coll. of Chiropractic (1911), Rio Hondo Coll. (1963); founded 1887; incorp. as city 1898.

Whit·tle·sea \ˈwit-ᵊl-sē, ˈhwit-\. City, S cen. Victoria, Australia, NNE of Melbourne; pop. (1991c) 95,672.

Whit·tle·sey; *formerly* **Whit·tle·sea** \ˈwit-ᵊl-sē, ˈhwit-\. Town, Cambridgeshire, E England, 43 mi. (69 km.) E of Leicester; bricks.

Whit·worth \ˈwit-ˌwərth, ˈhwit-\. Town, Lancashire, NW England, N of Manchester; pop. (1981p) 7696.

Why·al·la \wī-ˈa-lə, hwī-\. Port city, South Australia, Australia, on Spencer Gulf; pop. (1993e) 24,997; blast furnaces.

Whydah. See OUIDAH.

Wiak. See BIAK.

Wi·ar·ton \ˈwī-ərt-ᵊn\. Town, Bruce co., SE Ontario, Canada, at head of an inlet of Georgian Bay 15 mi. (24 km.) NW of Owen Sound; pop. (1991c) 2313.

Wi·baux \ˈwē-ˌbō\. **1.** County in E Montana. See table at MONTANA.

2. Town, its ⊗; pop. (1990c) 628.

Wich·i·ta \ˈwi-chə-ˌtȯ\. **1.** River, N Texas; flows ENE into Red River; 250 mi. (402 km.) long.

2. Name of counties in two states of the U.S. See tables at KANSAS and TEXAS.

3. City, ⊗ of Sedgwick co., S cen. Kansas, on Arkansas River 177 mi. (458 km.) SW of Kansas City; pop. (1990c) 304,011; important aircraft-manufacturing center; precision tools, castings, chemicals, pharmaceuticals; flour mills, stockyards, printing plants, grain elevators; Wichita State Univ. (1895), Friends Univ. (1898), Kansas Newman Coll. (1933). Founded on former Indian village 1864; incorp. 1871; major cattle-shipping center in early 1870s; developed as center of aircraft industry 1920 ff.

Wichita Falls. City, ⊗ of Wichita co., N Texas, 105 mi. (169 km.) NNW of Fort Worth; pop. (1990c) 96,259; oil refineries, oil wells; Midwestern State Univ. (1922); founded 1876; incorp. 1889.

Wichita Falls Dam. See BIG WICHITA DAM.

Wichita Mountains. Range, SW Oklahoma, chiefly in Comanche and Kiowa cos.; highest peak Mt. Scott 2464 ft. (751 m.).

Wick \ˈwik\. Burgh, NE Highland region, N Scotland, at mouth of the Wick River; pop. (1981c) 7902; fisheries, distillery; glass.

Wick·en·burg \ˈwik-ᵊn-ˌbərg\. Town, Maricopa co., SW cen. Arizona; pop. (1990c) 4515.

Wick·ford \ˈwik-fərd\. Village, Washington co., S Rhode Island, on Narragansett Bay ab. 8 mi. (13 km.) NE of Kingston; administrative center of North Kingstown.

Wick·liffe \ˈwi-kləf, -ˌklif\. **1.** City, ⊗ of Ballard co., W Kentucky; pop. (1990c) 851.

2. City, Lake co., NE Ohio, on Lake Erie 13 mi. (21 km.) NE of Cleveland; pop. (1990c) 14,558.

Wick·low \ˈwik-ˌlō\. **1.** County, E Ireland, in Leinster prov.; ⊗ Wicklow. See table at IRELAND.

2. Town and seaport, its ⊗; pop. (1991p) 5847; ruins of Franciscan abbey and 12th cent. castle.

Wicklow Head. Cape, E coast of Ireland, E of Wicklow; lighthouse.

Wicklow Mountains. Range extending along E coast of co. Wicklow, E Ireland; highest point **Lug·na·quil·lia** \ˌləg-nə-ˈkil-yə\ 3039 ft. (926 m.).

Wi·com·i·co \wī-ˈkä-mə-ˌkō\. County in SE Maryland. See table at MARYLAND.

Wida. See OUIDAH.

Wid·nes \ˈwid-nəs\. Town, Cheshire, NW England, on the Mersey 10 mi. (16 km.) E of Liverpool; pop. (1981c) 55,926; chemicals.

Wid·ows' Tears \ˈwi-dōz-ˌtirz\. Waterfall, Yosemite National Park, E cen. California; 1170 ft. (357 m.).

Wie·licz·ka \vye-ˈlēch-kä\. Commune, Kraków prov., S Poland, 8 mi. (13 km.) SE of the city of Kraków; pop. (1981p) 17,082; ancient rock-salt mines have been worked for 700 years; rooms, incl. a chapel, have been carved from the salt.

Wie·luń \'vye-lün^y\. Commune, S Sieradz prov., cen. Poland, 61 mi. (98 km.) SW of Łódź; pop. (1989e) 24,106.

Wien. See VIENNA 5.

Wie·ner Neu·stadt \'vē-nər-'nȯi-ˌshtät\. City, Lower Austria, Austria, 24 mi. (39 km.) SSW of Vienna; pop. (1991c) 35,134; 13th cent. cathedral; 13th cent. castle and three towers of medieval fortifications; 18th cent. Jesuit college (now museum). Burial place of Emperor Maximilian I. First mentioned c. 1194; at height of prosperity during 15th cent.; in WWII suffered heavy destruction and extensive rebuilding has occurred.

Wie·ner·wald \'vē-nər-ˌvält\. A spur of the Eastern Alps, Lower Austria, Austria, W and NW of Vienna and S of the Danube, covered with forests; in N part is the Kahlenberg.

Wieprz \'vyepsh\. River, cen. Poland; rises in S Zamość prov., flows NW and W into the Vistula River; 194 mi. (312 km.) long.

Wier·den \'vēr-də\. Commune, Overijssel prov., E Netherlands, just W of Almelo; pop. (1981e) 21,570.

Wie·ring·en \'vēr-iŋ-ə\. Commune, North Holland prov., W Netherlands; pop. (1981e) 8183; formerly an island in Zuider Zee, now constitutes N section of Wieringermeer.

Wie·ring·er·meer \'vē-riŋ-ər-ˌmer\. Polder, Netherlands; 77 sq. mi. (199 sq. km.); NW part of former Zuider Zee; completed 1930.

Wies·ba·den \'vēs-ˌbäd-ᵊn\. City, ✻ of Hesse, Germany, on the Rhine 20 mi. (32 km.) W of Frankfurt am Main; pop. (1992e) 264,022; health resort, noted for numerous hot springs known since Roman times; 17th cent. town hall; castle; remains of 4th cent. Roman wall. Fortified by Romans first cent. A.D.; first mentioned under present name 829 A.D.; free imperial city c. 1242; ✻ of duchy of Nassau 1806–66; after WWI seat of Rhineland Commission under French and British occupation 1918–29; after WWII became ✻ of Hesse.

Wig·an \'wi-gən\. Town, Greater Manchester, NW England, on the Douglas 18 mi. (29 km.) W of Manchester; munic. area pop. (1991p) 301,900; textiles, canned goods; engineering; coal mining began 14th cent.

Wig·gins \'wi-gənz\. City, ⊗ of Stone co., SE Mississippi; pop. (1990c) 3185.

Wight, Isle of. **1.** Island, England. See ISLE OF WIGHT 3.
2. Administrative county of England. See ISLE OF WIGHT 4.

Wig·ston \'wig-stən\ *also* **Wigston Mag·na** \'mag-nə\. Town, Leicestershire, cen. England, 4 mi. (6 km.) S of Leicester; textiles; engineering.

Wig·town \'wig-tən, -ˌtau̇n\. **1.** *or* **Wig·town·shire** \-ˌshir, -shər\. Former county, SW Scotland; ⊗ Wigtown; hilly region; rivers Cree, Bladenoch.
2. Burgh, SW Dumfries and Galloway region, Scotland, on Wigtown Bay.

Wigtown Bay. Inlet of Irish Sea, S coast of Scotland; extends 15 mi. (24 km.) inland in Dumfries and Galloway region.

Wij·de·fjord·en \'vē-də-ˌfyȯr-dən, 'vī-\ *or* **Wij·de Bay** \'vē-də, 'vī-\. Fjord, N coast of the island of Spitsbergen, Svalbard, Norway; 70 mi. (113 km.) long.

Wijm·brit·se·ra·deel *or* **Wym·brit·se·ra·deel** \vīm-'brit-sər-ə-ˌdāl\. Commune, Friesland prov., N Netherlands; pop. (1981e) 12,163.

Wijnkoops–Baai. See PELABUHANRATU BAY.

Wijt·scha·te *or* **Wyt·schae·te** \'vīt-ˌskä-tə, 'vāt-\. Village in West Flanders prov., NW Belgium, S of Ieper (Ypres); scene of fighting WWI, esp. during the battle of Messines Ridge 1917.

Wil \'vēl\. Commune, NW St. Gall canton, NE Switzerland; pop. (1980c) 16,245.

Wil·bar·ger \'wil-ˌbär-gər\. County in N Texas. See table at TEXAS.

Wil·ber \'wil-bər\. City, ⊗ of Saline co., SE Nebraska; pop. (1990c) 1527.

Wil·ber·force \'wil-bər-ˌfōrs\. Unincorporated settlement, Greene co., SW Ohio, ab. 3 mi. (5 km.) NE of Xenia; pop. (1990c) 2639; Wilberforce Univ. (1856); Central State Univ. (1887).

Wilberforce, Cape. Point, Northern Terr., N coast of Australia, just NW of Cape Arnhem, 11°54′S, 136°35′E.

Wil·bra·ham \'wil-brə-ˌham\. Town, Hampden co., SW Massachusetts, 8 mi. (13 km.) E of Springfield; pop. (1990c) 12,635; Wilbraham and Monson Academy formed 1971 by merger of Monson Academy (1804) and Wilbraham Academy (1817).

Wil·bur, Mount \'wil-bər\. Peak, Glacier National Park, NW Montana; 9293 ft. (2833 m.).

Wil·bur·ton \'wil-bərt-ᵊn\. City, ⊗ of Latimer co., E Oklahoma, 28 mi. (45 km.) E of McAlester; pop. (1990c) 3029; Eastern Oklahoma State Coll. (1909).

Wil·cox \'wil-ˌkäks\. Name of counties in two states of the U.S. See tables at ALABAMA and GEORGIA.

Wil·czek Land \'vil-ˌchek\. See FRANZ JOSEF LAND.

Wild·bad \'vilt-ˌbät\. Commune, Baden-Württemberg, Germany; mineral springs; resort.

Wild·cat Mountain \'wīld-ˌkat\. Peak, Iron co., SE Missouri; 1757 ft. (536 m.); connected with Taum Sauk by a saddle.

Wild Coast \'wīld\. Coast of the Indian Ocean, along shore of Eastern Cape prov., Rep. of South Africa —so called from its danger to mariners.

Wil·der·ness, the \'wil-dər-nəs\. Region, Orange and Spotsylvania cos., N Virginia, S of Rapidan River; battle (Chancellorsville) 1863 during Civil War; battle May 5–7, 1864 bet. Union forces under Gen. Ulysses S. Grant and Confederates under Gen. Robert E. Lee, one of the bloodiest of the Civil War.

Wild·spit·ze \'vilt-ˌshpit-sə\. Highest peak in Ötztaler Alps, Tirol, Austria; 12,382 ft. (3774 m.).

Wild·wood \'wīld-ˌwu̇d\. **1.** City, Sumter co., cen. Florida, SSE of Ocala; pop. (1990c) 3421.
2. City and seaside resort, Cape May co., S New Jersey, on Atlantic Ocean 33 mi. (53 km.) SW of Atlantic City; pop. (1990c) 4484; boardwalk, amusements.

Wildwood Crest. Borough, Cape May co., S New Jersey, on a barrier island; pop. (1990c) 3631; resort.

Wild·woods, the \t͟hə-'wīld-ˌwu̇dz\. The resort communities occupying the southernmost barrier island of New Jersey —North Wildwood, Wildwood, and Wildwood Crest (*qq.v.*).

Wil·helm, Mount \'vil-ˌhelm\. Mountain, Bismarck Range, E New Guinea I., Papua New Guinea; 14,762 ft. (4500 m.); highest peak in Papua New Guinea.

Wil·hel·mi·na Ge·berg·te \ˌwil-hel-'mē-nə-gə-'berk-tə, ˌwi-lə-'mē-nə, ˌvi-lə-\ *or* **Wilhelmina Mountains.** Mountain range, cen. Suriname; highest peak 4200 ft. (1280 m.).

Wilhelmina Top. See TRIKORA.

Wilhelm–Pieck–Stadt Guben. See GUBEN 2.

Wil·helms·ha·ven \ˌvil-helmz-'häf-ᵊn\. Seaport city, Lower Saxony, NW Germany, on W shore of Jade Bay 19 mi. (31 km.) W of Bremerhaven; pop. (1992e) 91,149; textiles; important North Sea naval base; seaside resort; oil storage facilities. Founded 1853; current name from 1869; principal base of German Navy in WWI; major naval base in WWII, during which it was heavily damaged by Allied bombing; largely rebuilt since the war.

Wilhelm II Coast \'vil-helm-t͟hə-'se-kənd\; *formerly* **Kai·ser Wilhelm II Land** \'kī-zər\. Section of coast of Antarctica ab. 67°S, 90°E; formerly claimed by Germany; now lies within region claimed by Great Britain.

Wi·lis \'vē-lis\. Mountain group, E cen. Java, Indonesia; highest point Mt. Liman 8409 ft. (2563 m.).

Wilja. See NERIS.

Wiljandi. See VILJANDI.

Wilkes \'wilks\. Name of counties in two states of the U.S. See tables at GEORGIA and NORTH CAROLINA.

Wilkes–Bar·re \'wilks-ˌbar-ə, -ˌbar-ē, -ˌbar\. City, ⊗ of Luzerne co., E Pennsylvania, on Susquehanna River 18 mi. (29 km.) SW of Scranton; pop. (1990c) 47,523; formerly an important coal-mining center; Wilkes Univ. (1933), King's Coll. (1946), Luzerne County Community Coll. (1966). Settled by colonists from Connecticut 1769; burned by British and Indians 1778 and 1784; competing claims bet. settlers resolved early 19th cent. when Connecticut dropped claim of ownership; has steadily lost pop. since 1940; suffered extensive damage from flooding 1972, but much of city rebuilt.

Wilkes·boro \ˈwilks-ˌbər-ə, -ˌbər-ō\. Town, ⊗ of Wilkes co., NW cen. North Carolina; pop. (1990c) 2573; Wilkes Community Coll. (1965).

Wilkes Land. Coastal region of Antarctica, extending approx. through 66° to 70°S and 102° to 142°E along the Indian Ocean from Queen Mary Coast to George V Coast; max. ice thickness ab. 15,670 ft. (4776 m.); includes French claim of Adélie Coast (*q.v.*).

History: Discovered 1839 by Charles Wilkes, U.S. naval officer, who coasted along this part of Antarctic barrier from ab. 150°E to 108°E. As result of explorations of British explorers T.W.E. David and Douglas Mawson, region claimed 1908 by Great Britain. Except for Adélie Coast, became part of the Australian claim as estab. 1933 and 1936, with concurrence of Great Britain.

Wil·kin \ˈwil-kən\. County in W Minnesota. See table at MINNESOTA.

Wil·kins \ˈwil-kənz\. Township, Allegheny co., SW Pennsylvania, E suburb of Pittsburgh; pop. (1990c) 7585.

Wil·kins·burg \ˈwil-kənz-ˌbərg\. Residential borough, Allegheny co., SW Pennsylvania, 7 mi. (11 km.) E of Pittsburgh; pop. (1990c) 21,080; residential suburb of Pittsburgh.

Wil·kin·son \ˈwil-kən-sən\. Name of counties in two states of the U.S. See tables at GEORGIA and MISSISSIPPI.

Wilkomir. See UKMERGĖ.

Will \ˈwil\. County in NE Illinois. See table at ILLINOIS.

Wil·la·cy \ˈwi-lə-sē\. Coastal co., S Texas. See table at TEXAS.

Wil·lam·ette \wə-ˈla-mət\. River, NW Oregon; formed by junction of forks in cen. Lane co., flows N into Columbia River near Portland; ab. 300 mi. (485 km.) long; spanned by Fremont Bridge (steel arch; main span 1255 ft. or 366 m.; completed 1973) at Portland, Oregon.

Wil·la·pa Bay \ˈwi-lə-ˌpȯ, -ˌpä\. Inlet of Pacific Ocean, W coast of Pacific co., SW Washington.

Wil·lard \ˈwi-lərd\. City, Huron co., N Ohio, 26 mi. (42 km.) S of Sandusky; pop. (1990c) 6210.

Wil·lau·mez Peninsula \ˌvē-yō-ˈmez\. Long point of land, N coast of New Britain I., Papua New Guinea, extending into Bismarck Sea, Bismarck Archipelago, W Pacific Ocean; Cape Hollman is at N extremity, Kimbe Bay to the E, and Talasea on its E shore.

Will·cox \ˈwil-ˌkäks\. City, Cochise co., SE corner of Arizona, 81 mi. (130 km.) E of Tucson; pop. (1990c) 3122.

Wil·le·broeck \ˈvi-lə-ˌbrůk\. Commune, Antwerp prov., N Belgium, halfway bet. Antwerp and Brussels; pop. (1991c) 22,146.

Wil·lem·stad \ˈvi-ləm-ˌstät\. City, ✻ of the Netherlands Antilles, West Indies, on Curaçao, at S end; pop. (1985e) 125,000; oil refineries; tourism. Many Dutch-Colonial style buildings; oldest (1732) synagogue in Western Hemisphere; handles crude oil from the Lake Maracaibo area of Venezuela. Founded 1634; became major oil-refining center after 1918.

Wil·len·dorf \ˈvi-lən-ˌdȯrf\. Village, Lower Austria, Austria, on the Danube near Krems; site of Paleolithic station where the Venus of Willendorf (a limestone statuette ab. 4.5 inches or 11.4 centimeters tall representing a female, assigned to the Aurignacian period) was discovered.

Willes·den \ˈwilz-dən\. See BRENT.

Wil·ley, Mount \ˈwi-lē\. Peak on W side of Crawford Notch, White Mts., New Hampshire, in NE Grafton co.; 4261 ft. (1299 m.).

Wil·liam, Mount \ˈwil-yəm\. See GRAMPIANS, THE.

Wil·liams \ˈwil-yəmz\. **1.** River, W cen. Arizona; formed by confluence of Big Sandy and Santa Maria rivers on SE boundary of Mohave co., flows W into Colorado River; ab. 50 mi. (80 km.) long.

2. Name of counties in two states of the U.S. See tables at NORTH DAKOTA and OHIO.

Williams Bay. Village, Walworth co., S Wisconsin, 24 mi. (39 km.) ESE of Janesville; pop. (1990c) 2108; site of Yerkes Observatory (founded 1892; belongs to Univ. of Chicago).

Wil·liams·burg \ˈwil-yəmz-ˌbərg\. **1.** County in E South Carolina. See table at SOUTH CAROLINA.

2. City, ⊗ of Whitley co., SE Kentucky, 28 mi. (45 km.) WNW of Middlesborough; pop. (1990c) 5493; Cumberland Coll. (1889).

3. Neighborhood, Brooklyn borough, New York City, New York. See *History* at BROOKLYN 3.

4. Independent city, ⊗ of James City co., SE Virginia; on peninsula bet. James and York rivers 27 mi. (43 km.) NNW of Newport News; 3 sq. mi. (8 sq. km.); pop. (1990c) 11,530; Coll. of William and Mary (1693). Site of a large-scale restoration project, Colonial Williamsburg (financed by Rockefeller Foundation), in which several hundred modern buildings were removed, many original colonial-era existing buildings renovated, and other buildings reconstructed on original sites, 1926 ff.; made part of Colonial National Historical Park 1936.

History: Settled 1633; made new ✻ of Virginia 1699; incorp. as city 1722 (first incorp. municipality in Virginia); political and social center of Virginia during 18th cent. until ✻ removed to Richmond 1780; in Civil War scene of battle 1862 in which Union troops took the city.

Williams Lake. Town, British Columbia, Canada, 125 mi. (201 km.) NW of Kamloops; pop. (1991c) 10,385; sawmills.

Wil·liam·son \ˈwil-yəm-sən\. **1.** River, Klamath co., S Oregon; flows NW then S to N end of Upper Klamath Lake; ab. 70 mi. (115 km.) long; receives the Sprague near its mouth.

2. Name of counties in three states of the U.S. See tables at ILLINOIS, TENNESSEE, TEXAS.

3. Town, Wayne co., W New York; pop. (1990c) 6540.

4. City, ⊗ of Mingo co., SW West Virginia, on Tug Fork opposite Pike co., Kentucky, 52 mi. (84 km.) S of Huntington; pop. (1990c) 4154.

Williamson, Mount. Peak in the Sierra Nevada, W Inyo co., SE cen. California; 14,375 ft. (4382 m.).

Williamson Head. Headland on Oates Coast, Antarctica, W of Ross Sea, 69°11′S, 157°57′E.

Wil·liams·port \ˈwil-yəmz-ˌpōrt\. **1.** Town, ⊗ of Warren co., W Indiana; pop. (1990c) 1798.

2. City, ⊗ of Lycoming co., N cen. Pennsylvania, on W branch of Susquehanna River 70 mi. (113 km.) N of Harrisburg; pop. (1990c) 31,933; Lycoming Coll. (1812), Pennsylvania Coll. of Technology (1965). Home of Annual Little League World Series. Founded 1795; incorp. as city 1866; in 1860s a major lumbering center.

Wil·liams·ton \ˈwil-yəm-stən\. **1.** City, Ingham co., S Michigan, 13 mi. (21 km.) E of Lansing; pop. (1990c) 2922.

2. Town, ⊗ of Martin co., E North Carolina, on Roanoke River 42 mi. (68 km.) E of Rocky Mount; pop. (1990c) 5503.

3. Town, Anderson co., NW South Carolina, 13 mi. (21 km.) NE of the city of Anderson; pop. (1990c) 3876.

Wil·liams·town \ˈwil-yəmz-ˌtau̇n\. **1.** City, ⊗ of Grant co., N Kentucky; pop. (1990c) 3023.

2. Town, Berkshire co., W Massachusetts, 19 mi. (31 km.) N of Pittsfield; pop. (1990c) 8220; Williams Coll. (1793); city incorp. 1765.

3. City, Wood co., W West Virginia, on Ohio River across from Marietta, Ohio; pop. (1990c) 2774.

4. City, E Victoria, SE Australia, SW suburb of Melbourne on Port Phillip Bay; pop. (1991c) 22,100; seaport.

Wil·liams·ville \ˈwil-yəmz-ˌvil\. Residential village, Erie co., W New York, 10 mi. (16 km.) NE of Buffalo; pop. (1990c) 5583; Erie Community Coll. (1946).

Willimansett. See CHICOPEE 2.

Wil·li·man·tic \ˌwi-lə-ˈman-tik\. **1.** River, NE Connecticut; rises in S Massachusetts, flows S across cen. Tolland co. and unites with the Natchaug River at Willimantic to form the Shetucket River; ab. 30 mi. (50 km.) long.

2. Unincorporated settlement, Windham co., NE Connecticut, at junction of Natchaug and Willimantic rivers; pop. (1990c) 14,746; formerly an industrial city with important textile mills; Eastern Connecticut State Univ. (1889); textile museum; incorp. as borough 1833, as city 1893; merged into town of Windham 1983.

Wil·ling·bo·ro \ˈwi-liŋ-ˌbər-ə, -ˌbər-ō\; *formerly* **Lev·it·town** \ˈle-vət-ˌtau̇n\. Urban township, Burlington co., S cen. New Jersey, NE of Camden; pop. (1990c) 36,291.

Wil·ling·ton \ˈwi-liŋ-tən\. **1.** Town, NW cen. Tolland co., N Connecticut, on E bank of Willimantic River opp. town of Tolland; pop. (1990c) 5979; incorp. 1727.
2. See WILMINGTON 1.

Wil·lis \ˈwi-ləs\. **1.** City, Montgomery co., E Texas, N of Houston; pop. (1990c) 2764.
2. Group of coral islets and reefs, Coral Sea, outside Great Barrier Reef, Queensland, Australia, 16°18′S, 150°E.

Wil·lis·ton \ˈwi-lə-stən\. **1.** City, ⊗ of Williams co., NW North Dakota, on Missouri River 20 mi. (32 km.) E of Montana border; pop. (1990c) 13,131.
2. Town, Barnwell co., W South Carolina, WSW of Orangeburg; pop. (1990c) 3099.
3. Town, Chittenden co., NW Vermont, on the Winooski River E of Burlington; pop. (1990c) 4887.

Williston Park. Residential village, Nassau co., SE New York, on Long Island 18 mi. (29 km.) E of New York City; pop. (1990c) 7516.

Wil·lits \ˈwi-ləts\. City, Mendocino co., N California, 73 mi. (118 km.) NNW of Santa Rosa; pop. (1990c) 5027.

Will·mar \ˈwil-ˌmär, -mər\. City, ⊗ of Kandiyohi co., SW cen. Minnesota, 52 mi. (84 km.) SW of St. Cloud; pop. (1990c) 17,531; Willmar Community Coll. (1961).

Wil·lough·by \ˈwi-lə-bē\. **1.** City, Lake co., NE Ohio, on Lake Erie 18 mi. (29 km.) NE of Cleveland; pop. (1990c) 20,510.
2. City, E New South Wales, Australia, a N suburb of Sydney; pop. (1991c) 51,503.

Willoughby Hills. City, Lake co., NE Ohio, ENE of Cleveland; pop. (1990c) 8427.

Willoughby, Lake. Lake, E Orleans co., N Vermont, 20 mi. (32 km.) N of St. Johnsbury; ab. 6 mi. (10 km.) long by 2 mi. (3 km.) wide; outdoor recreation.

Wil·low·brook \ˈwi-lō-ˌbru̇k\. Village, DuPage co., NE Illinois, W of Chicago; pop. (1990c) 8598.

Wil·lo·wick \ˈwi-lə-ˌwik\. City, Lake co., NE Ohio, E suburb of Cleveland; pop. (1990c) 15,269.

Wil·low Mountain \ˈwi-lō\. Peak, SW Brewster co., W Texas; 3080 ft. (939 m.).

Wil·lows \ˈwi-lōz\. City, ⊗ of Glenn co., N California, 42 mi. (68 km.) NE of Clear Lake; pop. (1990c) 5988.

Willow Springs. Village, Cook co., NE Illinois, 8 mi. (13 km.) W of the S part of Chicago; pop. (1990c) 4509.

Wills·boro \ˈwilz-ˌbər-ə, -ˌbər-ō\. Village in town of Willsboro, Essex co., NE New York, ab. 25 mi. (40 km.) S of Plattsburg; town pop. (1990c) 1736; settled 1765; during Revolutionary War scene of British Gen. John Burgoyne's encampment 1777.

Wills Point \ˈwilz\. City, Van Zandt co., NE Texas, 40 mi. (64 km.) E of Dallas; pop. (1990c) 2986.

Willyama. See BROKEN HILL 1.

Wil·mette \wil-ˈmet\. Residential village, Cook co., NE Illinois, on Lake Michigan, 5 mi. (8 km.) N of Chicago; pop. (1990c) 26,690; site of a nine-sided Baha'i house of worship.

Wil·ming·ton \ˈwil-miŋ-tən\. **1.** City, ⊗ of New Castle co., N Delaware, at junction of Delaware and Christina rivers and Brandywine Creek; pop. (1990c) 71,529; seaport; Goldey-Beacom Coll. (1886); 17th cent. church; several museums.
History: Fort Christina (*q.v.*) founded by Swedes 1638; a chief city of New Sweden; held by Dutch 1655–64 and then captured by English; renamed **Wil·ling·ton** \ˈwi-liŋ-tən\ 1731; chartered as borough and renamed Wilmington 1739; during American Revolution battle of Brandywine fought just N of city 1777 and city captured by British; Du Pont powder mills (predecessor to modern Dupont corporation) estab. 1802; chartered as city 1832.
2. City, Will co., NE Illinois, 15 mi. (24 km.) S of Joliet; pop. (1990c) 4743.
3. Town, Middlesex co., NE Massachusetts, 9 mi. (15 km.) SE of Lowell; pop. (1990c) 17,651.
4. City, ⊗ of New Hanover co., SE North Carolina, on Cape Fear River 30 mi. (48 km.) N of its mouth; pop. (1990c) 55,530; principal seaport of the state; shipments include wood pulp; products include fertilizer; Univ. of North Carolina at Wilmington (1947), Cape Fear Community Coll. (1959).
History: Settled c. 1730; incorp. as town 1740; scene of armed resistance to Stamp Act 1765–66; during American Revolution occupied by British under Lord Charles Cornwallis 1781; a major port of entry for Confederate blockade-runners during the Civil War until closed by capture of Fort Fisher by Union forces Jan. 15, 1865; incorp. as city 1866.
5. City, ⊗ of Clinton co., SW Ohio, 29 mi. (47 km.) SE of Dayton; pop. (1990c) 11,199; Wilmington Coll. (1870); founded 1810.

Wil·more \ˈwil-ˌmōr\. City, Jessamine co., E cen. Kentucky, 17 mi. (27 km.) SW of Lexington; pop. (1990c) 4215; Asbury Coll. (1890), Asbury Theological Seminary (1923).

Wilms·low \ˈwilmz-ˌlō\. Town, Cheshire, NW England, on the Bollin 12 mi. (19 km.) S of Manchester; pop. (1981p) 30,207; textiles, garments.

Wilna. See VILNIUS.

Wil·no \ˈvil-ˌnō\. **1.** Former Polish department, now split bet. Lithuania and Belarus; 11,196 sq. mi. (28,998 sq. km.); area for several centuries scene of conflict bet. neighboring peoples; in 1922 in region ceded to Poland; part ceded to Lithuania by U.S.S.R. 1939; to U.S.S.R. 1940 when it seized all of Lithuania.
2. City, Lithuania. See VILNIUS.

Wil·ryck \ˈvil-ˌrīk\. Former commune N Belgium; a S suburb that became part of Antwerp 1983.

Wil·son \ˈwil-sən\. **1.** Name of counties in four states of the U.S. See tables at KANSAS, NORTH CAROLINA, TENNESSEE, TEXAS.
2. Subdivision of town of Windsor, Connecticut. See WINDSOR 3.
3. City, ⊗ of Wilson co., E North Carolina, 18 mi. (29 km.) SSW of Rocky Mount; pop. (1990c) 36,930; tobacco market; Barton Coll. (1902), Wilson Technical Community Coll. (1958); incorp. 1849.
4. Borough, Northampton co., E Pennsylvania, 14 mi. (23 km.) ENE of Allentown; pop. (1990c) 7830.

Wilson, Mount. **1.** Peak in San Gabriel Mts., Los Angeles co., SW California, just NE of Pasadena; 5710 ft. (1740 m.); site of Mount Wilson Observatory.
2. Peak in San Juan Mts., Dolores co., SW Colorado; 14,246 ft. (4342 m.).

Wilson Dam. Dam across Tennessee River, NW Alabama, forming **Wilson Lake** 15.5 mi. (25 km.) long submerging Muscle Shoals. See TENNESSEE 1 and table at TENNESSEE VALLEY AUTHORITY.

Wilson Peak. **1.** Peak in San Miguel co., SW Colorado; 14,017 ft. (4272 m.).
2. Mountain in E Summit co., NE Utah; 13,095 ft. (3991 m.).

Wil·son's Creek \ˈwil-sənz\. Small stream near Springfield, Greene co., SW Missouri; battle Aug. 10, 1861 in which Confederates under Gen. Sterling Price defeated Union forces under Gen. Nathaniel Lyon who was killed in the battle.

Wilson's Creek National Battlefield. See UNITED STATES, *National Historical Parks.*

Wilson's Promontory. Cape, S Victoria, Australia, 38°55′S, 146°20′E; set aside as **Wilson's Promontory National Park**.

Wil·ton \ˈwilt-ᵊn\. **1.** Town, W Fairfield co., SW Connecticut, on New York border N of Norwalk; pop. (1990c) 15,989; settled c. 1701.
2. City, Cedar and Muscatine cos., Iowa; pop. (1990c) 2577.
3. Town, Franklin co., W Maine, 29 mi. (47 km.) NW of Augusta; pop. (1990c) 4242.
4. Town, Hillsborough co., S New Hampshire, 15 mi. (24 km.) WNW of Nashua; pop. (1990c) 3122.
5. Town, Saratoga co., E New York; pop. (1990c) 9623.

6. Town, Wiltshire, S England; pop. (1981p) 4005; historically noted for rug manufacture; former seat of kings of Wessex; site of battle 871 bet. Alfred the Great and the invading Danes.

Wilton Manors. City, Broward co., SE Florida, N of Fort Lauderdale; pop. (1990c) 11,804.

Wilt·shire \ˈwilt-ˌshir, -shər\. **1.** *or* **Wilts** \ˈwilts\. Former county, S England.

2. Administrative county, S England, approx. equivalent to the former county; rivers Avon, Kennet; agriculture; carpets; largest settlements Swindon, Salisbury. See table at ENGLAND.

Wi·lu·na \wi-ˈlü-nə\. Town, cen. Western Australia, Australia; the S terminus of Canning Stock Route.

Wim·ble·don \ˈwim-bəl-dən\. Former municipal borough, S England, now part of Merton, Greater London; known for its sports facilities, esp. for lawn tennis where the "All-England" championships are played annually.

Wim·borne Minster; *often shortened to* **Wimborne** \ˈwim-bərn\. Town, Dorset, S England, ab. 7 mi. (11 km.) NNW of Bournemouth; pop. (1981c) 5554; 12th cent. church.

Wim·mera \ˈwi-mə-rə\. River, W Victoria, SE Australia; flows N into Lake Hindmarsh; 228 mi. (367 km.) long.

Win·a·mac \ˈwi-nə-ˌmak\. Town, ⊗ of Pulaski co., NW Indiana, 23 mi. (37 km.) NW of Logansport; pop. (1990c) 2262.

Win·chell, Mount \ˈwin-chəl\. Peak in the Sierra Nevada, California, on boundary bet. Fresno and Inyo cos.; 13,479 ft. (4108 m.).

Win·chel·sea \ˈwin-chəl-sē\. Village, East Sussex, S England, near coast just SW of Rye and ab. 8 mi. (13 km.) NE of Hastings; major seaport 13th–15th cents., one of the Cinque Ports (*q.v.*); church of St. Thomas Becket (c. 1300) with chancel and aisles in Decorated style.

Win·chen·don \ˈwin-chən-dən\. Town, Worcester co., cen. Massachusetts, 14 mi. (23 km.) WNW of Fitchburg; pop. (1990c) 8805.

Win·ches·ter \ˈwin-ˌches-tər, -chə-stər\. **1.** Town, NE Litchfield co., NW Connecticut, N of Torrington; pop. (1990c) 11,524; incorp. 1771; includes city of Winsted (*q.v.*).

2. City, ⊗ of Scott co., W Illinois, 45 mi. (72 km.) WSW of Springfield; pop. (1990c) 1769.

3. City, ⊗ of Randolph co., E Indiana, 20 mi. (32 km.) E of Muncie; pop. (1990c) 5095.

4. City, ⊗ of Clark co., E cen. Kentucky, 20 mi. (32 km.) E of Lexington; pop. (1990c) 15,799.

5. Residential town, Middlesex co., NE Massachusetts, 5 mi. (8 km.) NW of Boston; pop. (1990c) 20,267.

6. Town, Cheshire co., SW corner of New Hampshire, on Ashuelot River 12 mi. (19 km.) SSW of Keene; pop. (1990c) 4038.

7. City, ⊗ of Franklin co., S Tennessee, 25 mi. (40 km.) E of Fayetteville; pop. (1990c) 6305.

8. City, ⊗ of Frederick co., N Virginia, in Shenandoah Valley 70 mi. (113 km.) WNW of Alexandria; 3 sq. mi. (8 sq. km.); pop. (1990c) 21,947; politically independent; ships apples; cider, plastics, rubber goods, tin cans, woolens; Shenandoah Coll. and Conservatory of Music (1875).

History: Founded 1744; George Washington began career as surveyor here 1748; Fort Loudoun built here by Washington after defeat of English Gen. Edward Braddock 1755 during French and Indian War; incorp. as town 1779; military base and headquarters during Civil War and scene of several battles with town changing hands many times; incorp. as city 1874. Birthplace of author Willa Cather (1873) and of polar explorer Richard Byrd (1888).

9. *anc.* **Ven·ta Bel·ga·rum** \ˈven-tə-bel-ˈgar-əm\. City, ⊗ of Hampshire, S England, on Itchin River, 21 mi. (34 km.) NNW of Portsmouth; pop. (1981p) 30,642; notable 11th–14th cent. cathedral (the longest in Britain); 12th cent. hospital; 13th cent. gate; ruins of castle and episcopal palace; Winchester Coll. (founded 1382 by William of Wykeham, who had become bishop in 1367).

History: Initially inhabited by Celtic peoples; became important under Roman rule; a center for trade and cloth making in Saxon times; ✻ of Wessex and seat of government under Alfred the Great; remained important under Norman kings until emergence of London as sole ✻ of England late 12th cent.

Wind \ˈwind\. River, W cen. Wyoming; rises in NW Fremont co., flows SE along E slopes of Wind River Range and unites with Popo Agie River in cen. Fremont co. to form Bighorn River; ab. 120 mi. (195 km.) long.

Windau. 1. River, Lithuania and Latvia. See VENTA.

2. City, Latvia. See VENTSPILS.

Wind·ber \ˈwind-bər\. Borough, Somerset co., S Pennsylvania, 8 mi. (13 km.) SE of Johnstown; pop. (1990c) 4756.

Wind Cave National Park \ˈwind\. See UNITED STATES, *National Parks.*

Wind·crest \ˈwind-ˌkrest\. City, Bexar co., S cen. Texas; pop. (1990c) 5331.

Win·der \ˈwīn-dər\. City, ⊗ of Barrow co., N Georgia, 20 mi. (32 km.) W of Athens; pop. (1990c) 7373.

Win·der·mere \ˈwin-dər-ˌmir\. **1.** Lake in the Lake District, Cumbria, NW England; 10.5 mi. (17 km.) long; max. depth 219 ft. (67 m.); largest lake in England.

2. Resort, Cumbria, NW England, on Lake Windermere 33 mi. (53 km.) S of Carlisle; pop. (1981p) 8575.

Wind Gap. Borough, Northampton co., E Pennsylvania; pop. (1990c) 2741.

Wind·ham \ˈwin-dəm\. **1.** Name of counties in two states of the U.S. See tables at CONNECTICUT and VERMONT.

2. Town, SW Windham co., NE Connecticut; pop. (1990c) 22,039; incorp. 1692; includes former industrial city of Willimantic. See WILLIMANTIC 2.

3. Town, Cumberland co., SW Maine, 15 mi. (24 km.) NW of Portland; pop. (1990c) 13,020; St. Joseph's Coll. (1912).

4. Town, Rockingham co., SE New Hampshire, 20 mi. (32 km.) SSE of Manchester; pop. (1990c) 9000; has grown steadily since 1970.

5. Village, Portage co., NE Ohio; pop. (1990c) 2943.

Wind·hoek \ˈvint-ˌhu̇k\. Town, ✻ of Namibia, in cen. part 400 mi. (644 km.) N of mouth of Orange River; pop. (1991c) 144,558; commercial and transportation center; sheep processing, clothing manufacture. Orig. settled by native African peoples; occupied and further settled by Germans 1880s; captured and annexed by South African troops 1915. Became ✻ of Namibia on its independence 1990.

Win·dom \ˈwin-dəm\. City, ⊗ of Cottonwood co., SW Minnesota, 30 mi. (48 km.) NE of Worthington; pop. (1990c) 4283.

Windom Peak. Mountain in La Plata co., SW Colorado; 14,082 ft. (4292 m.).

Win·dow Rock \ˈwin-ˌdō\. Unincorporated settlement, Apache Co., NE Arizona, on New Mexico border; pop. (1990c) 3306; headquarters of Navajo Indian Reservation.

Wind River. See WIND.

Wind River Range \ˈwind\. Range of the Rocky Mts., W cen. Wyoming, extending along the boundary bet. Sublette and Fremont cos.; highest point Gannett Peak 13,804 ft. (4207 m.).

Wind·sor \ˈwin-zər\. **1.** County in E Vermont. See table at VERMONT.

2. Town, Weld co., N Colorado; pop. (1990c) 5062.

3. Town, N cen. Hartford co., N Connecticut, on Connecticut River N of the city of Hartford; pop. (1990c) 27,817. One of the oldest towns in the state, settled c. 1635 by colonists from Massachusetts Bay Colony; named in 1637.

4. City, Henry co., W Missouri; pop. (1990c) 3044.

5. Town, ⊗ of Bertie co., NE North Carolina, 15 mi. (24 km.) W of Albemarle Sound; pop. (1990c) 2056.

6. Town, Windsor co., E Vermont, on Connecticut River 13 mi. (21 km.) N of Springfield; pop. (1990c) 3714; settled c. 1764.

7. Town, ⊗ of Hants co., cen. Nova Scotia, Canada, on inlet of Minas Basin 37 mi. (60 km.) NW of Halifax; pop. (1991c)

\ə\ **abut** \ə̇\ matches \ᵊ\ kitten, Fr table \ər\ **further** \a\ **ash** \ā\ **ace** \ä\ cot, cart \å\ Fr bac \au̇\ **out** \b̲\ Span Avila \ch\ **chin** \e\ bet \ē\ **easy** \g\ **go** \i\ hit \ī\ **ice** \j\ **job** \k̲\ Ger **ich**, Bu**ch** \ⁿ\ Fr vin \ŋ\ si**ng** \ō\ **go** \ȯ\ **all** \ȯ\ **law** \œ\ Fr bœuf \œ̄\ Fr **feu** \ȯi\ **boy** \th\ **thin** \t̲h̲\ **this** \ü\ **loot** \u̇\ **foot** \ue\ Ger f**ü**llen \ue̅\ Fr **rue** \y\ **yet** \ʸ\ Fr digne \ˈdēnʸ\, nuit \ˈnwʸē\ \yü\ **few** \yu̇\ **fury** \zh\ vision

3625. Former site of King's Coll., oldest (1789) English college in Canada, now part of Dalhousie Univ. in Halifax. Founded by French at turn of 18th cent.; came under English 1750; received present name 1764.

8. Industrial city, ⊗ of Essex co., SE Ontario, Canada, on Detroit River opp. Detroit, Michigan; pop. (1991c) 191,435; transportation center; automobiles, automobile parts; distilling; Univ. of Windsor (1857). Connected with Detroit by Ambassador Bridge and by vehicular and railroad tunnels. French settlement of region begun after founding of Detroit 1701; American Loyalist settlers arrived subsequently; occupied by U.S. forces during War of 1812; incorp. as village 1854, as city 1892.

9. Town, S Quebec, Canada, on St. Francis River 12 mi. (19 km.) N of Sherbrooke; pop. (1991c) 4813.

10. *officially* **New Windsor.** Town, Berkshire, S England, on the Thames 20 mi. (32 km.) W of London; pop. (1981p) 28,330; seat of Windsor Castle, principal residence of England's sovereigns since the time of William the Conqueror (11th cent.); St. George's Chapel and Albert Memorial Chapel, burial places of many English kings and queens; expansive parklands adjacent.

Windsor Heights. City, Polk co., S cen. Iowa, W of Des Moines; pop. (1990c) 5190.

Windsor Locks. Town, NE Hartford co., N Connecticut, on Connecticut River S of Suffield; pop. (1990c) 12,358; international airport; settled c. 1663; incorp. 1854. Named for locks in canal (1828) to bypass rapids in Connecticut River and provide waterpower. Birthplace of Ella Grasso 1919, first woman to hold U.S. state governorship in her own right.

Wind·ward Islands \ˈwin-dwərd\. **1.** Island group, forming the S chain of the Lesser Antilles, West Indies, extending from Martinique S to 12°N; they do not include Barbados, Trinidad, and Tobago. See LEEWARD ISLANDS.

2. *or Fr.* **Îles du Vent** \ˌēl-dʉ̄-ˈvän\. E group in the Society Is., French Polynesia, S Pacific Ocean; chief islands Tahiti and Mooréa; 467 sq. mi. (1210 sq. km.); pop. (1988c) 140,341.

3. Former British colony in the West Indies comprising the territories of St. Lucia, St. Vincent, Grenada, and Dominica.

Windward Passage. Channel bet. the E end of Cuba and the NW tip of Hispaniola.

Windy Butte \ˈwin-dē\. Isolated peak, Fall River co., SW corner of South Dakota; 3563 ft. (1086 m.).

Windy·gate Hill \ˌwin-dē-ˌgāt\. Peak in the Cheviot Hills along border bet. England and Scotland; 2034 ft. (620 m.).

Wineland. See VINLAND.

Win·field \ˈwin-ˌfēld\. **1.** City, Marion co., NW Alabama; pop. (1990c) 3689.

2. Village, Du Page co., NE Illinois, 20 mi. (32 km.) W of Chicago; pop. (1990c) 7096.

3. City, ⊗ of Cowley co., S Kansas, 13 mi. (21 km.) N of Arkansas City; pop. (1990c) 11,931; Southwestern Coll. (1885).

4. Town, ⊗ of Putnam co., W West Virginia; pop. (1990c) 1164.

Win·gate \ˈwin-ˌgāt\. Town, Union co., S North Carolina, SE of Charlotte; pop. (1990c) 2821; Wingate Coll. (1896).

Win·isk \ˈwi-nisk\. River, N cen. Ontario, Canada; flows N and NW into Hudson Bay; 295 mi. (475 km.) long.

Wink·ler \ˈwiŋ-klər\. **1.** County in W Texas. See table at TEXAS.

2. Town, Manitoba, Canada, 58 mi. (93 km.) SW of Winnipeg; pop. (1991c) 6397.

Winn \ˈwin\. Parish in N cen. Louisiana. See table at LOUISIANA.

Win·ne·ba \wi-ˈnā-bə\. Coastal town, S Ghana, ab. 35 mi. (55 km.) WSW of Accra; pop. (1984c) 27,105.

Win·ne·ba·go \ˌwi-nə-ˈbā-gō\. Name of counties in three states of the U.S. See tables at ILLINOIS, IOWA, WISCONSIN.

Winnebago, Lake. Lake, E Wisconsin, bounded by Winnebago, Calumet, and Fond du Lac cos.; ab. 30 mi. (50 km.) long and 10 mi. (16 km.) wide at its greatest extent; 215 sq. mi. (557 sq. km.); the Fox River enters from the W and flows out in the N; the cities of Menasha, Oshkosh, Fond du Lac, and Neenah are on its shores.

Win·ne·muc·ca \ˌwi-nə-ˈmə-kə\. City, ⊗ of Humboldt co., NW Nevada, on Humboldt River 77 mi. (124 km.) NE of Humboldt Lake; pop. (1990c) 6134.

Winnemucca Lake. Intermittent lake, NW Nevada, ab. 6 mi. (10 km.) E of Pyramid Lake; ab. 20 mi. (32 km.) long; usually dry.

Winnepesaukee. See WINNIPESAUKEE.

Winnepesaukee, Lake. See WINNIPESAUKEE, LAKE.

Win·ner \ˈwi-nər\. City, ⊗ of Tripp co., S South Dakota, 33 mi. (53 km.) SW of confluence of White and Missouri rivers; pop. (1990c) 3354.

Win·ne·shiek \ˈwi-nə-ˌshēk\. County in NE Iowa. See table at IOWA.

Win·net·ka \wə-ˈnet-kə\. Residential village, Cook co., NE Illinois, 6 mi. (10 km.) N of Chicago; pop. (1990c) 12,174.

Win·nett \ˈwi-nət\. Town, ⊗ of Petroleum co., cen. Montana; pop. (1990c) 188.

Winn·field \ˈwin-ˌfēld\. City, ⊗ of Winn parish, N cen. Louisiana, 45 mi. (72 km.) N of Alexandria; pop. (1990c) 6138.

Win·ni·bi·go·shish, Lake \ˌwi-nə-bə-ˈgō-shish\. Lake in Mississippi River on boundary of Itasca and Cass cos., N cen. Minnesota; ab. 14 mi. (23 km.) long; dam built in late 19th cent. more than doubled the lake's area.

Win·ni·peg \ˈwi-nə-ˌpeg\. **1.** River, SW Ontario and SE Manitoba, Canada; outlet of Lake of the Woods flowing NW to SE part of Lake Winnipeg; 475 mi. (764 km.) long; near Ontario border receives tributary, English River, outlet of a number of large lakes in SW Ontario.

2. City, ✻ of Manitoba, Canada, at confluence of Assiniboine and Red rivers and 45 mi. (72 km.) S of Lake Winnipeg; pop. (1991c) 616,790; 4th largest city in Canada; cultural center; railroad junction; financial and government center; Univ. of Winnipeg (1871), Univ. of Manitoba (1877). Fur-trading post estab. by French on site 1738; Scottish colony founded by Thomas Douglas, earl of Selkirk early 19th cent. with ensuing conflicts bet. original settlers and new colonists; incorp. 1873; development ensued with coming of railroad 1880s. Devastating flood 1950 resulted in much of city being rebuilt.

Winnipeg, Lake. Lake, S cen. Manitoba, Canada; 9465 sq. mi. (24,514 sq. km.); 266 mi. (428 km.) long; max. depth 60 ft. (18 m.); receives the Red and Winnipeg rivers in the S and the Saskatchewan in the N; outlet is the Nelson; remnant of Lake Agassiz, ancient Pleistocene lake. Summer recreation area; visited by Canadian explorer Pierre de la Vérendrye in 1733.

Win·ni·peg·o·sis, Lake \ˌwi-nə-pə-ˈgō-səs\. Lake, W Manitoba, Canada, W of Lake Winnipeg; 2075 sq. mi. (5374 sq. km.); 141 mi. (227 km.) long; max. depth 38 ft. (12 m.); connects with Lake Manitoba.

Win·ni·pe·sau·kee; *mostly formerly* **Win·ne·pe·sau·kee** \ˌwi-nə-pə-ˈsȯ-kē\. Short River, cen. New Hampshire; flows SW out of Lake Winnipesaukee to unite with the Pemigewasset River at Franklin and form the Merrimack River.

Winnipesaukee, Lake; *mostly formerly* **Lake Winnepesaukee.** Lake, Carroll and Belknap cos., cen. New Hampshire; 71 sq. mi. (184 sq. km.); 25 mi. (40 km.) long; largest lake in New Hampshire; summer resort.

Win·nis·quam Lake \ˈwi-nə-ˌskwäm\. Lake, Belknap co., cen. New Hampshire, W of Lake Winnipesaukee; summer resort.

Winns·boro \ˈwinz-ˌbər-ō\. **1.** Town, ⊗ of Franklin parish, NE Louisiana, 33 mi. (53 km.) SE of Monroe; pop. (1990c) 5755.

2. Town, ⊗ of Fairfield co., N cen. South Carolina, 27 mi. (43 km.) N of Columbia; pop. (1990c) 3475.

3. City, Franklin and Wood cos., NE Texas, 40 mi. (64 km.) N of Tyler; pop. (1990c) 2904.

Wi·no·na \wə-ˈnō-nə\. **1.** County in SE Minnesota. See table at MINNESOTA.

2. City, its ⊗, on Mississippi River 40 mi. (64 km.) E of Rochester; pop. (1990c) 25,399; river port; limestone; Winona State Univ. (1858), St. Mary's Coll. of Minnesota (1912); city settled 1851; incorp. 1857; formerly a major wheat- and lumber-shipping center.

3. City, ⊗ of Montgomery co., N cen. Mississippi, 25 mi. (40 km.) E of Greenwood; pop. (1990c) 5705.

Winona Lake. Town, Kosciusko co., N Indiana; pop. (1990c) 4053; Grace Coll. (1948).

Wi·noos·ki \wə-ˈnü-skē\. **1.** *also* **On·ion** \ˈən-yən\. River, N cen. Vermont; rises in NE Vermont, flows S to Montpelier, turns NW into Lake Champlain in W Chittenden co.; ab. 100 mi. (160 km.) long.

2. City, Chittenden co., NW Vermont, on Winooski River 3 mi. (5 km.) NE of Burlington; pop. (1990c) 6649; settled 1787.

Win·scho·ten \ˈvin-ˌskō-tə\. Commune, Groningen prov., NE Netherlands, 19 mi. (31 km.) ESE of the city of Groningen, near German border; pop. (1981e) 20,795.

Winschoten Canal. Canal, NE Netherlands; 18 mi. (29 km.) long; joins the city of Groningen with the Dollart.

Wins·ford \ˈwinz-fərd\. Town, Cheshire, NW England, on the Weaver River 23 mi. (37 km.) SE of Liverpool; pop. (1981p) 26,915; salt; chemicals; engineering.

Wins·low \ˈwinz-lō\. **1.** City, Navajo co., NE Arizona, near Little Colorado River 58 mi. (93 km.) E of Flagstaff; pop. (1990c) 8190; settled as railroad terminal 1882.

2. Town, Kennebec co., SW Maine, SE suburb of Waterville; pop. (1990c) 7997.

Win·sted \ˈwin-stəd\. City in town of Winchester, Connecticut (see WINCHESTER 1); pop. (1990c) 8254; lake recreation; settled mid-18th cent.; incorp. as city 1917; Northwestern Connecticut Community Coll. (1965).

Win·ston \ˈwin-stən\. **1.** Name of counties in two states of the U.S. See tables at ALABAMA and MISSISSIPPI.

2. City, Douglas co., SW Oregon; pop. (1990c) 3773.

Winston–Sa·lem \-ˈsā-ləm\. City, ⊗ of Forsyth co., N cen. North Carolina, 68 mi. (109 km.) NNE of Charlotte; pop. (1990c) 143,485. Cultural and educational center; cigarettes; restoration of several buildings from 18th cent. Salem. Salem Coll. (1772), Wake Forest Univ. (1834), Winston-Salem State Univ. (1892), Piedmont Bible Coll. (1945), Forsyth Technical Community Coll. (1960). Salem founded 1766; incorp. 1856; Winston founded 1849; incorp. 1859; two towns consolidated as Winston-Salem 1913.

Win·ter·ber·ge \ˈwin-tər-ˌbər-gə\. Mountain range, cen. Eastern Cape prov., Rep. of South Africa; highest peak 7772 ft. (2369 m.).

Winter Garden. **1.** Agricultural region, S Texas. See CRYSTAL CITY 2.

2. City, Orange co., cen. Florida Penin., 12 mi. (19 km.) W of Orlando; pop. (1990c) 9745.

Winter Haven. City, Polk co., cen. Florida Penin., 15 mi. (24 km.) E of Lakeland; pop. (1990c) 24,725; packs and ships citrus fruit; recreation; Cypress Gardens; Polk Community Coll. (1964).

Winter Park. Resort city, Orange co., cen. Florida Penin., 5 mi. (8 km.) NE of Orlando; pop. (1990c) 22,242; art museum; Rollins Coll. (1885); city founded 1858.

Win·ter·port \ˈwint-ər-ˌpōrt\. Town, Waldo co., S Maine, on Penobscot River 12 mi. (19 km.) S of Bangor; pop. (1990c) 3175.

Win·ters \ˈwin-tərz\. City, Runnels co., W cen. Texas, 37 mi. (60 km.) S of Abilene; pop. (1990c) 2905.

Win·ter·set \ˈwin-tər-ˌset\. City, ⊗ of Madison co., S cen. Iowa, 30 mi. (48 km.) SW of Des Moines; pop. (1990c) 4196.

Winter Springs. City, Seminole co., cen. Florida Penin., NE of Orlando; pop. (1990c) 22,151; pop. doubled in 1980s.

Win·ters·ville \ˈwin-tərz-ˌvil\. Village, Jefferson co., E Ohio, just W of Steubenville; pop. (1990c) 4102.

Win·ters·wijk \ˈvin-tərs-ˌvīk\. Commune, Gelderland prov., E Netherlands, ab. 33 mi. (53 km.) E of Arnhem near German border; pop. (1981e) 27,658.

Win·ter·thur \ˈvin-tər-ˌtür\. Commune, Zürich canton, NE cen. Switzerland, 12 mi. (19 km.) NE of the city of Zürich; pop. (1993e) 86,600; important railroad junction; 16th cent. late Gothic church; 18th cent. town hall; commune founded c. 1175; passed to Hapsburg family 1264; made imperial city 1415; to Zürich 1467.

Win·throp \ˈwin-thrəp\. **1.** Town, Kennebec co., SW Maine, 10 mi. (16 km.) W of Augusta; pop. (1990c) 5968.

2. Town, Suffolk co., E Massachusetts, separated from Boston's Logan International Airport by an inlet of Boston Harbor; pop. (1990c) 18,127.

Winthrop Harbor. Village, Lake co., NE Illinois, on Lake Michigan 9 mi. (15 km.) N of Waukegan; pop. (1990c) 6240.

Win·ton \ˈwint-^{ə}n\. Town, ⊗ of Hertford co., NE North Carolina, 43 mi. (69 km.) W of Elizabeth City; pop. (1990c) 796.

Win·yah Bay \ˈwin-yȯ\. Inlet of Atlantic Ocean, SE coast of Georgetown co., E South Carolina, receiving the Black River on the NW and the Pee Dee River on the N.

Wir·ral \ˈwər-əl\. Peninsula, NW England, bet. the estuaries of the Dee and the Mersey.

Wirt \ˈwərt\. County in W West Virginia. See table at WEST VIRGINIA.

Wis·bech \ˈwiz-ˌbēch\. Town, Cambridgeshire, E England, on the Nene 83 mi. (134 km.) N of London; pop. (1981c) 17,294; seaport; center of an agricultural area.

Wisby. See VISBY.

Wis·cas·set \wis-ˈka-sət\. Seaport town, ⊗ of Lincoln co., S Maine; pop. (1990c) 3339.

Wisch \ˈvis\. Commune, Gelderland prov., E Netherlands, E of Arnhem near German border; pop. (1981e) 20,029.

Wis·con·sin \wi-ˈskän-sən\. **1.** River, cen. and SW Wisconsin; rises in Lac Vieux Desert in N Vilas co., flows S through cen. Wisconsin, turns W and enters Mississippi River on boundary line bet. Crawford and Grant cos.; 430 mi. (692 km.) long; navigation, difficult because of shifting sandbars, is possible for small craft for ab. 200 mi. (320 km.).

2. A northern state of U.S.A., bounded on N by Lake Superior and Lake Michigan, on E by Lake Michigan, on S by Illinois, and on W by Iowa and Minnesota; 26th state in area, 56,154 sq. mi. (145,439 sq. km.), in addition to this Wisconsin has 10,062 sq. mi. (26,062 sq. km.) of water of Lake Michigan; 16th state in population, (1990c) 4,891,769; ✻ Madison; 30th state admitted to Union (1848). See table of states at UNITED STATES.

Nickname: Badger State.

State flower: Violet.

Motto: Forward.

Rivers: Mississippi, forming lower W boundary; St. Croix (forming section of upper W boundary), Wisconsin (see WISCONSIN 1), Black, and Chippewa rivers flowing into the Mississippi; Menominee, forming NE boundary.

Lakes: Winnebago in E; Mendota in S.

Highest point: Timms Hill, 1952 ft. (595 m.), Price co.

Chief products: Dairy products; corn, cranberries, potatoes; livestock; manufacturing: machinery, paper products, metal products; recreation.

Chief cities: Milwaukee, Madison, Green Bay, Racine, Kenosha.

Political divisions: Divided into the following 72 counties (for their pronunciations, see individual entries):

NAME	AREA[1] (sq. mi.)	AREA[1] (sq. km.)	POP. (1990c)	CO. SEAT
Adams	645	1,671	15,682	Friendship
Ashland[2]	1,038	2,688	16,307	Ashland
Barron	864	2,238	40,750	Barron
Bayfield[2]	1,460	3,781	14,008	Washburn
Brown	524	1,357	194,594	Green Bay
Buffalo	711	1,841	13,584	Alma
Burnett	840	2,176	13,084	Grantsburg
Calumet	322	834	34,291	Chilton
Chippewa	1,018	2,637	52,360	Chippewa Falls
Clark	1,221	3,162	31,647	Neillsville
Columbia	776	2,010	45,088	Portage
Crawford	568	1,471	15,940	Prairie du Chien
Dane	1,199	3,105	367,085	Madison
Dodge	889	2,303	76,559	Juneau
Door	492	1,274	25,690	Sturgeon Bay

\ə\ **abut** \ə\ matches \$^{ə}$\ kitten, Fr table \ər\ **further** \a\ **ash** \ā\ **ace** \ä\ **cot, cart** \á\ Fr bac \au̇\ **out** \b\ Span Avila \ch\ **chin** \e\ **bet** \ē\ **easy** \g\ **go** \i\ **hit** \ī\ **ice** \j\ **job** \k\ Ger **ich, Buch** \$^{n}$\ Fr vin \ŋ\ **sing** \ō\ **go** \ö\ **all** \ȯ\ **law** \œ\ Fr **bœuf** \œ̄\ Fr **feu** \ȯi\ **boy** \th\ **thin** \t͟h\ **this** \ü\ **loot** \u̇\ **foot** \ue\ Ger **füllen** \u̅e\ Fr **rue** \y\ **yet** \$^{y}$\ Fr digne \ˈdēn^{y}\, nuit \ˈnw^{y}ē\ \yü\ **few** \yu̇\ **fury** \zh\ **vision**

93°
92°
91°
90° CANADA
89°
88°
87°
47°
46°
45°
44°
43°
42°
Lake Superior
MINNESOTA
APOSTLE ISLANDS NATIONAL LAKESHORE
OUTER I.
APOSTLE ISLANDS
RED CLIFF IND. RES.
STOCKTON I.
BAD RIVER IND. RES.
MADELINE I.
St. Louis R.
Cornucopia
Bayfield
Washburn
Chequamegon Bay
Superior
Iron River
Ashland
BAD RIVER IND. RES.
Hurley
Montreal
Lake Gogebic
MICHIGAN
DOUGLAS
BAYFIELD
Solon Springs
St. Croix Flowage
Mellen
IRON
Namekagon Lake
Clam Lake
Flambeau Flowage
Mercer
VILAS
Land O'Lakes
WASHBURN
Namekagon R.
Glidden
LAC DU FLAMBEAU IND. RES.
Phelps
Hayward
ASHLAND
LAC COURT OREILLES IND. RES.
Chippewa Lake
Park Falls
Eagle River
Florence
St. Croix R.
BURNETT
Spooner
Winter
Minocqua
FLORENCE
Menominee R.
Grantsburg
Shell Lake
SAWYER
Willow Reservoir
Three Lakes
Niagara
Frederic
Birchwood
Phillips
ONEIDA
FOREST
POLK
Chippewa R.
Flambeau R.
PRICE
Rhinelander
Crandon
Goodman
Luck
Balsam Lake
Cumberland
Rice Lake
Prentice
Laona
MARINETTE
WASHINGTON I.
BARRON
Bruce
Ladysmith
Timms Hill 1,953 ft.
Tomahawk
Wabeno
St. Croix Falls
Barron
Cameron
RUSK
Irma
Wolf R.
Peshtigo R.
Osceola
Amery
Chetek
Rib Lake
LINCOLN
LANGLADE
CHAMBERS I.
New Richmond
Holcombe Flowage
Cornell
TAYLOR
Medford
Merrill
Antigo
Oconto R.
Marinette
Wisconsin R.
Peshtigo
Egg Harbor
Glenwood City
Bloomer
MENOMINEE IND. RES.
MENOMINEE
Hudson
DUNN
CHIPPEWA
Thorp
Abbotsford
Marathon
Wausau
Neopit
OCONTO
ST. CROIX
Red Cedar R.
Owen
Keshena
Oconto Falls
Oconto
Baldwin
Colfax
Chippewa Falls
Colby
Rib Mtn. 1,941 ft.
Rothschild
STOCKBRIDGE IND. RES.
Green Bay
DOOR
Sturgeon Bay
River Falls
Spring Valley
Menomonie
Eau Claire
Stratford
Mosinee
Shawano
Shawano Lake
Prescott
Ellsworth
Altoona
Greenwood
Loyal
Big Eau Pleine Reservoir
MARATHON
Wittenberg
SHAWANO
Bonduel
Mississippi R.
Chippewa R.
Augusta
CLARK
Marshfield
Lake Du Bay
Marion
Clintonville
Embarrass
Pulaski
Howard
Algoma
PIERCE
Arkansaw
PEPIN
EAU CLAIRE
Stevens Point
PORTAGE
WAUPACA
ONEIDA IND. RES.
Green Bay
Durand
Mondovi
Osseo
Neillsville
WOOD
Whiting
Manawa
Seymour
Ashwaubenon
KEWAUNEE
Pepin
Wisconsin Rapids
Iola
De Pere
Kewaunee
BUFFALO
TREMPEALEAU
Whitehall
JACKSON
Yellow R.
Plover
New London
OUTAGAMIE
BROWN
Alma
Independence
Port Edwards
Waupaca
Little Chute
Kaukauna
Denmark
Arcadia
Blair
Black River Falls
Nekoosa
Weyauwega
Appleton
Black R.
Menasha
Kimberly
Brillion
Petenwell Flowage
Lake Poygan
Neenah
MANITOWOC
Two Rivers
Fountain City
Wautoma
Winneconne
WINNEBAGO
CALUMET
Manitowoc
Galesville
MONROE
Tomah
JUNEAU
ADAMS
Friendship
Adams
WAUSHARA
Omro
Oshkosh
Lake Winnebago
Chilton
New Holstein
MINNESOTA
Onalaska
LA CROSSE
West Salem
Sparta
New Lisbon
Castle Rock Flowage
Berlin
GREEN LAKE
North Fond du Lac
Kiel
SHEBOYGAN
La Crosse
Mauston
MARQUETTE
Green Lake
Ripon
Fond du Lac
Sheboygan
Elroy
Montello
FOND DU LAC
Kohler
Plymouth
Sheboygan Falls
Westby
Hillsboro
Wonewoc
Wisconsin Dells
Lake Puckaway
Waupun
Oostburg
VERNON
La Farge
Portage
Pardeeville
Randolph
Campbellsport
Cedar Grove
Viroqua
Kewaskum
Reedsburg
Baraboo
COLUMBIA
Beaver Dam
Mayville
West Bend
OZAUKEE
Port Washington
Kickapoo R.
RICHLAND
SAUK
Poynette
Columbus
Juneau
Horicon
WASHINGTON
Grafton
Mount Sterling
Richland Center
Prairie du Sac
Lodi
DODGE
Hartford
Cedarburg
SEE INSET
CRAWFORD
Spring Green
Sauk City
De Forest
Sun Prairie
Watertown
Menomonee Falls
Mequon
Wisconsin R.
Muscoda
Lake Mendota
Madison
JEFFERSON
Oconomowoc
Whitefish Bay
Prairie du Chien
Boscobel
Middleton
Monona
Rock R.
Jefferson
West Allis
Milwaukee
MILWAUKEE
Lake Michigan
Fennimore
IOWA
Mount Horeb
Verona
DANE
McFarland
Fort Atkinson
Waukesha
WAUKESHA
South Milwaukee
Dodgeville
Oregon
Stoughton
Mukwonago
GRANT
Mineral Point
New Glarus
Edgerton
Lake Koshkonong
Whitewater
Waterford
RACINE
Beetown
Lancaster
Darlington
Albany
Evansville
Elkhorn
Burlington
Racine
Cassville
Platteville
LAFAYETTE
Argyle
GREEN
Janesville
WALWORTH
Union Grove
Mississippi R.
Cuba City
Shullsburg
Monroe
Sugar R.
ROCK
Delavan
Silver Lake
KENOSHA
Kenosha
Hazel Green
Benton
Beloit
Lake Geneva
Twin Lakes
IOWA
Pecatonica R.
Rock R.
Fox R.
ILLINOIS
Chicago
0 40 80 mi
0 50 100 km
WASHINGTON
DODGE
Germantown
Thiensville
Mequon
Menomonee Falls
OZAUKEE
Sussex
Lannon
Brown Deer
Bayside
Fox Point
Okauchee
Hartland
Butler
Glendale
Whitefish Bay
Oconomowoc
Pewaukee
Brookfield
Shorewood
Delafield
Elm Grove
Wauwatosa
Milwaukee
Waukesha
West Allis
West Milwaukee
WAUKESHA
Greenfield
St. Francis
MILWAUKEE
Cudahy
Hales Corners
Greendale
South Milwaukee
Muskego
Mukwonago
Franklin
Oak Creek
WALWORTH
East Troy
RACINE
Wind Point
0 10 20 mi
0 10 20 km
WISCONSIN
CITIES
State capital
County seat
City
BOUNDARIES
International
State
County
FEATURES
Dams

NAME	AREA[1] (sq. mi.)	AREA[1] (sq. km.)	POP. (1990c)	CO. SEAT
Douglas	1,313	3,401	41,758	Superior
Dunn	853	2,209	35,909	Menomonie
Eau Claire	647	1,676	85,183	Eau Claire
Florence	487	1,261	4,590	Florence
Fond du Lac	725	1,878	90,083	Fond du Lac
Forest	1,007	2,608	8,776	Crandon
Grant	1,147	2,971	49,264	Lancaster
Green	585	1,515	30,339	Monroe
Green Lake	354	917	18,651	Green Lake
Iowa	762	1,974	20,150	Dodgeville
Iron	747	1,935	6,153	Hurley
Jackson	999	2,587	16,588	Black River Falls
Jefferson	564	1,461	67,783	Jefferson
Juneau	774	2,005	21,650	Mauston
Kenosha	272	704	128,181	Kenosha
Kewaunee	330	855	18,878	Kewaunee
La Crosse	451	1,168	97,904	La Crosse
Lafayette	643	1,665	16,076	Darlington
Langlade	856	2,217	19,505	Antigo
Lincoln	892	2,310	26,993	Merrill
Manitowoc	590	1,528	80,421	Manitowoc
Marathon	1,586	4,108	115,400	Wausau
Marinette	1,378	3,569	40,548	Marinette
Marquette	455	1,178	12,321	Montello
Menominee	256	663	3,890	Keshena
Milwaukee	237	614	959,275	Milwaukee
Monroe	915	2,370	36,633	Sparta
Oconto	1,106	2,865	30,226	Oconto
Oneida	1,097	2,841	31,679	Rhinelander
Outagamie	634	1,642	140,510	Appleton
Ozaukee	236	611	72,831	Port Washington
Pepin	235	609	7,107	Durand
Pierce	590	1,528	32,765	Ellsworth
Polk	931	2,411	34,773	Balsam Lake
Portage	806	2,088	61,405	Stevens Point
Price	1,261	3,266	15,600	Phillips
Racine	337	873	175,034	Racine
Richland	583	1,510	17,521	Richland Center
Rock	721	1,867	139,510	Janesville
Rusk	906	2,347	15,079	Ladysmith
Saint Croix	735	1,904	50,251	Hudson
Sauk	841	2,178	46,975	Baraboo
Sawyer	1,259	3,261	14,181	Hayward
Shawano	919	2,380	37,157	Shawano
Sheboygan	505	1,308	103,877	Sheboygan
Taylor	975	2,525	18,901	Medford
Trempealeau	735	1,904	25,263	Whitehall
Vernon	802	2,077	25,617	Viroqua
Vilas	867	2,246	17,707	Eagle River
Walworth	557	1,443	75,000	Elkhorn
Washburn	817	2,116	13,772	Shell Lake
Washington	428	1,109	95,328	West Bend
Waukesha	555	1,437	304,715	Waukesha
Waupaca	751	1,945	46,104	Waupaca
Waushara	627	1,624	19,385	Wautoma
Winnebago	448	1,160	140,320	Oshkosh
Wood	807	2,090	73,605	Wisconsin Rapids

[1]Area = land area.
[2]Most of Apostle Is. in Ashland co., rest in Bayfield co.

History: Orig. inhabited by prehistoric Mound Builders; by time of European arrival, several different Indian tribes were inhabiting the region; area visited by French explorer Jean Nicolet 1634; first permanent European settlement 1717; French settlement at Green Bay 1745; throughout 18th cent. some Indian tribes sided with French while others sided with English, provoking general unrest; French claim ceded to Great Britain 1763 after French and Indian War; recognized by Great Britain as part of U.S. 1783; claims relinquished during 1780s by Virginia, Massachusetts, and Connecticut; part of Northwest Terr. 1787, Indiana Terr. 1800, Illinois Terr. 1809, and Michigan Terr. 1818; conflicts bet. Indians and settlers continued into 19th cent. culminating in Black Hawk War 1832, in which Indians suffered massacre; included in Wisconsin Terr. (*q.v.*) 1836; admitted to Union May 29, 1848; constitution ratified 1848, since amended.

Wisconsin Rapids. City, ⊗ of Wood co., cen. Wisconsin, on Wisconsin River 40 mi. (64 km.) S of Wausau; pop. (1990c) 18,245; manufactures paper; ships cranberries; Mid-State Technical Coll. (1917).

Wisconsin Territory. Former territory, U.S.A.; comprised region of varying size W of Lake Michigan and E of the Missouri River; region acquired by U.S. from British 1783, in Louisiana Purchase (*q.v.*) 1803, and by treaty with British 1818; parts included in Louisiana Terr., Missouri Terr., Northwest Terr., Indiana Terr., Illinois Terr., and Michigan Terr. (*qq.v.*) 1787-1836; Wisconsin Terr. organized 1836 incl. present states of Wisconsin, Minnesota, Iowa, and the parts of North and South Dakota E of the Missouri River; also laid some claim to Michigan's Upper Peninsula until it was awarded to Michigan by Congress 1837; reduced to area of Wisconsin and part of Minnesota (E of the Mississippi) upon creation of Iowa Terr. 1838; Wisconsin admitted to the Union with present boundaries 1848.

Wise \ˈwīz\. **1.** Name of counties in two states of the U.S. See tables at TEXAS and VIRGINIA.
2. Town, ⊗ of Wise co., SW Virginia; pop. (1990c) 3193.

Wish·kah \ˈwish-kə\. River, W Washington; flows S in Grays Harbor co. into Chehalis River near its mouth; 40 mi. (64 km.) long.

Wisła. See VISTULA.

Wis·ło·ka \vē-ˈswȯ-kä\. River, Rzeszów, Tarnów, and Krosno provs., SE Poland; flows N from Carpathian Mts. to the Vistula; ab. 125 mi. (200 km.) long.

Wis·mar \ˈvis-ˌmär\. Seaport and industrial city, Mecklenburg-West Pomerania, Germany, on **Wismar Bay** (arm of Mecklenburg Bay) 19 mi. (31 km.) N of Schwerin; pop. (1992e) 54,471; shipbuilding. Chartered during 13th cent. and became member of Hanseatic League; to Sweden 1649; governed by Mecklenberg-Schwerin from 1803; Sweden renounced claim 1903; in WWII suffered considerable damage but medieval center survived.

Wis·sa·hick·on Creek \ˌwi-sə-ˈhi-kən\. Short stream, SE Pennsylvania; flows SE through Whitemarsh to Schuylkill River in Philadelphia; furnished power for mills before the American Revolution, esp. first paper mill in America 1690.

Wis·sem·bourg \ˌvē-sän-ˈbür\ *or* **Weis·sen·burg** \ˈvīs-ᵊn-ˌbu̇rk, -ˌbərg\. Town, Bas-Rhin dept., NE France, ab. 40 mi. (64 km.) NE of Strasbourg; 13th cent. church of Benedictine abbey founded 7th cent.; place where German monk Otfrid completed his Old High German poetical version of the Gospels 9th cent. and in the process introduced end line rhyme to the German language; scene of battles during French Revolution (1793) and during Franco-Prussian War (1870); suffered damage in WWII.

Wis·so·ta, Lake \wi-ˈsō-tə\. Lake, S Chippewa co., W Wisconsin.

Wis·ter, Mount \ˈwis-tər\. Peak, cen. Grand Teton National Park, NW Wyoming; 11,480 ft. (3499 m.).

Wit·bank \ˈwit-ˌbaŋk\. Town, Mpumalanga prov., NE Rep. of South Africa, 60 mi. (97 km.) E of Pretoria; pop. (1985c) 41,784; carbide; coal mines.

With·am \ˈwi-t͟həm\. **1.** River, E England; rises in Leicestershire, flows N into Lincolnshire, passing Grantham and Lincoln, turns SE and continues past Boston into the Wash; 80 mi. (129 km.) long.
2. Town, Essex, SE England; pop. (1981p) 25,373.

With·la·coo·chee \ˌwith-lə-ˈkü-chē\. **1.** River, W Florida Penin.; forms boundary bet. Levy and Citrus cos. and empties into Gulf of Mexico; ab. 120 mi. (195 km.) long; outlet for Tsala Apopka Lake in Citrus co.
2. River, SE United States; rises in S Georgia, flows S across Florida border forming Madison-Hamilton co. boundary and empties into Suwannee River; ab. 110 mi. (175 km.) long.

Wit·ney \ˈwit-nē\. Town, Oxfordshire, cen. England, ab. 60 mi. (95 km.) WNW of London; pop. (1981p) 14,109; blankets.

Wit·ten \ˈvit-ᵊn\. City, North Rhine-Westphalia, Germany, on Ruhr River 9 mi. (15 km.) SW of Dortmund; pop. (1992e) 105,242; steel, glass, chemicals; chartered 1825; heavily damaged in WWII but since rebuilt.

Wit·ten·berg \ˈvit-ᵊn-ˌberk, -ˌbərg\. City, Saxony-Anhalt, E Germany, on the right bank of the Elbe River 19 mi. (31 km.) E of Dessau; pop. (1992e) 48,718; railroad junction; chemicals, cellulose, machinery, soap. Starting point of the Reformation (1517) and residence of religious reformers Martin

Luther and Philipp Melanchthon; has several historical structures associated with the Reformation: 15th cent. Schlosskirche (restored 19th cent.) to the doors of which Luther nailed his 95 theses; Stadtkirche in which Luther preached; homes of Luther and Melanchthon; university (merged with Univ. of Halle 1817) at which Luther taught. German painter Lucas Cranach lived and worked here 16th cent. First mentioned 1180; chartered 1293; residence of dukes and electors of Saxe-Wittenberg to 1547; to Prussia 1814.

Wittenberg, Mount \ˈwit-ᵊn-ˌbərg\. Peak in the Catskill Mts., Ulster co., SE New York; 3802 ft. (1159 m.).

Wit·ten·ber·ge \ˌvit-ᵊn-ˈber-gə\. City, NW Brandenburg, NE Germany, on Elbe River 80 mi. (129 km.) SE of Hamburg and 78 mi. (126 km.) NW of Berlin; pop. (1981c) 32,104; river port.

Witt·stock \ˈvit-ˌshtȯk, ˈwit-ˌstäk\. Town, Brandenburg, NE Germany, 58 mi. (93 km.) NW of Berlin; scene of battle Oct. 4, 1636 during Thirty Years' War in which Swedes under Johan Banér decisively defeated imperial and Saxon forces.

Wi·tu \ˈwē-ˌtü\. **1.** Former sultanate, E Africa; now part of Kenya; ab. 1200 sq. mi. (3110 sq. km.); proclaimed German protectorate 1885, but given up to British in agreement of 1890.
2. Town, its ✱, near the mouth of the Tana River.

Wi·tu \ˈvē-ˌtü\ *or* **Vi·tu** \ˈvē-\. Group of small islands, Papua New Guinea, in S Bismarck Sea, off the N coast of W end of New Britain I., Bismarck Archipelago; largest is Garove I.

Wit·wa·ters·rand \ˈwit-ˌwȯ-tərz-ˌränd, -ˌwä-, -ˌrand\ *or popularly* **The Rand** \ˈrand\. Ridge of auriferous rock, NE Rep. of South Africa, in North West and Gauteng provs.; ab. 62 mi. (100 km.) long, 23 mi. (35 km.) wide; Johannesburg located nearly at its center. Watershed for streams on N to Olifants River and on S to Vaal; exceptionally rich goldfields; gold first discovered 1886.

Wix·om \ˈwik-səm\. City, Oakland co., SE Michigan, 13 mi. (21 km.) NW of Detroit; pop. (1990c) 8550.

Wło·cła·wek \vwȯt-ˈswä-vek\ *or Russ.* **Vlo·tslavsk** \vlət-ˈsläfsk\. **1.** Province, N cen. Poland. See table at POLAND.
2. Commune, its ✱, on Vistula River 87 mi. (140 km.) WNW of Warsaw; pop. (1989e) 120,823; machinery; 14th cent. cathedral; founded 11th cent.; Russians defeated here during WWI 1914; held by Germans during WWII.

Włodzimierz. See VLODYMYR-VOLYNS'KYY.

Wo·burn. **1.** \ˈwü-bərn, ˈwō-\. City, Middlesex co., NE Massachusetts, 10 mi. (16 km.) NNW of Boston; pop. (1990c) 35,943; chemicals, leather goods, pharmaceuticals; incorp. as town 1642, as city 1888.
2. \ˈwü-bərn\. Parish, Bedfordshire, SE cen. England; noted for Woburn Abbey, estate of duke of Bedford.

Wo·dzi·sławŚlą·ski \vȯ-ˈjē-swäf-ˈshlȯⁿ-skē\. City, Katowice prov., S Poland, ab. 30 mi. (48 km.) SW of the city of Katowice; pop. (1989e) 111,329.

Woer·den \ˈvür-də\. Commune, South Holland prov., SW Netherlands, on a branch of the Rhine, just W of Utrecht; pop. (1993e) 35,361.

Woëvre \ˈvwävrᵊ\. Plateau, E of Verdun, NE France, extending N and S parallel with the Meuse for 15 to 20 mi. (24 to 32 km.).

Woh·len \ˈvō-lən\. Commune, Aargau canton, Switzerland; pop. (1980c) 11,704.

Wo·kam \ˈwō-ˌkäm\. Island, N cen. Aru Is., Indonesia; ab. 35 mi. (55 km.) long by 30 mi. (48 km.) wide.

Wo·king \ˈwō-kiŋ\. Town, Surrey, S England, on the Wey 22 mi. (35 km.) WSW of London; pop. (1991p) 84,000; residential suburb and commercial center; printing.

Wo·king·ham \ˈwō-kiŋ-əm\. Town, Berkshire, S England, 32 mi. (52 km.) WSW of London; pop. (1991p) 136,300; electronics.

Wol·cott \ˈwu̇l-kət\. Town, N New Haven co., S Connecticut, NE of Waterbury; pop. (1990c) 13,700; incorp. 1796.

Wolds, The \ˈwōldz\. Highland plain district, NE England; comprises **York·shire Wolds** \ˈyȯrk-ˌshir, -shər\ in North Yorkshire and Humberside and **Lin·coln Wolds** \ˈliŋ-kən\ in Lincoln.

Wo·le·ai \ˌwō-lē-ˈī\. Island (atoll), Federated States of Micronesia, in W Caroline Is., W Pacific Ocean, 7°21′N, 143°52′E.

Wolf \ˈwu̇lf\. **1.** River, Mississippi and Tennessee; flows WNW from Benton co., Mississippi, to Mississippi River just above Memphis, Tennessee; 100 mi. (161 km.) long.
2. River, E Wisconsin; rises in N Langlade co., flows S into Lake Poygan, and then E into Fox River near Oshkosh; ab. 200 mi. (320 km.) long.

Wolf Creek. River, N Texas and NW Oklahoma; rises in N Texas, flows E and NE into Oklahoma, joining Beaver River to form the North Canadian River; ab. 110 mi. (180 km.) long.

Wolfe \ˈwu̇lf\. County in Kentucky. See table at KENTUCKY.

Wolfe·boro \ˈwu̇lf-ˌbər-ō\. Town, Carroll co., E New Hampshire, on Lake Winnipesaukee 13 mi. (21 km.) ENE of Laconia; pop. (1990c) 4807; summer resort.

Wolfe Island. Island, NE end of Lake Ontario, Ontario, Canada; 18 mi. (29 km.) long; divides head of St. Lawrence River, S of Kingston, but channel most used is on S or U.S. side.

Wol·fen \ˈvȯl-fən\. Town, Halle dist., Germany, 17 mi. (27 km.) NE of the city of Halle; pop. (1981c) 38,329.

Wol·fen·büt·tel \ˈvȯl-fən-ˌbœt-ᵊl\. Manufacturing city, Lower Saxony, Germany, on Oker River S of Brunswick; pop. (1992e) 52,490; canned goods, chemicals, musical instruments; late 16th cent. town hall; 17th cent. castle; 17th cent. armory; several churches; notable library; first mentioned 1118.

Wolf Jaws \ˈwu̇lf-ˌjȯz\. Mountain in the Adirondack Mts., Essex co., NE New York; 4225 ft. (1288 m.).

Wolf·pin Ridge \ˈwu̇lf-ˌpin\. Ridge, Towns co., N Georgia; 4251 ft. (1296 m.).

Wolf Point. City, ⊗ of Roosevelt co., NE Montana, on Missouri River 48 mi. (77 km.) E of Glasgow; pop. (1990c) 2880.

Wolf River. Two rivers in the U.S. See WOLF.

Wolf Rock. Elevation, Allegany co., NW corner of Maryland; 2976 ft. (907 m.).

Wolfs·berg \ˈvȯlfs-ˌberk, ˈwu̇lfs-ˌbərg\. Manufacturing commune, Carinthia, S Austria; pop. (1991c) 27,791; summer resort.

Wolfs·burg \ˈvȯlfs-ˌbu̇rk, ˈwu̇lfs-ˌbərg\. City, Lower Saxony, Germany, 15 mi. (24 km.) NE of Brunswick; pop. (1992e) 128,995; automobiles (site of Volkswagen plant); founded 1938.

Wolf·ville \ˈwu̇lf-ˌvil\. Town, Kings co., W Nova Scotia, Canada, on Minas Basin 15 mi. (24 km.) NW of Windsor; pop. (1991c) 3475; Acadia Univ. (1838). Center of land of Henry Wadsworth Longfellow's poem *Evangeline* near the original settlement of Grand Pré (*q.v.*); founded by the English in mid-18th cent.

Wo·lin \ˈvȯ-ˌlēn\ *or Ger.* **Wol·lin** \vȯ-ˈlēn\. **1.** Island off the NW coast of Szczecin prov., NW Poland, bet. Zalew Szezeciński and the Baltic Sea; 95 sq. mi. (246 sq. km.); contains **Wolin National Park** (18 sq. mi. or 47 sq. km.; estab. 1960); island assigned to Poland following WWII.
2. Commune, SE point of Wolin I., Poland; pop. (1988e) 4413. See JULIN.

Wołkowysk. See VOLKOVYSK.

Wollaston Islands. Island group Chile, in S Tierra del Fuego Archipelago (*q.v.*); largest islands are Wollaston, Hermite, Grévy; includes also, at S extremity, Horn I. on which is Cape Horn.

Wollaston Lake. Lake, NE Saskatchewan, Canada; 796 sq. mi. (2062 sq. km.); connected through its outlet with Reindeer Lake and Churchill River.

Wollaston Peninsula. Peninsula, SW part of Victoria I., Northwest Territories & Nunavut, N Canada; bet. Prince Albert Sound, and Dolphin and Union Strait.

Wollin. See WOLIN.

Wol·lon·dil·ly \ˈwu̇-lən-ˌdi-lē\. City, E New South Wales, Australia; pop. (1991c) 30,267.

Wol·lon·gong \ˈwu̇-lən-ˌgän, -ˌgȯŋ\. City, E New South Wales, SE Australia, on Pacific Ocean 40 mi. (64 km.) S of Sydney; pop. (1991c) 211,417; coal; university (1961).

Wolmar. See VALMIERA.

Wo·ło·min \vȯ-ˈwȯ-ˌmēn\. Commune, Warszawa prov., NE cen. Poland, 15 mi. (24 km.) ENE of Warsaw; pop. (1989e) 36,587.

Wo·lu·we–Saint–Lam·bert \ˌvȯ-lə-ˈvā-seⁿ-läⁿ-ˈber\ *or Flemish* **Sint–Lam·brechts–Wo·lu·we** \sint-ˈläm-ˌbrekts-ˈvō-lə-və\. Commune, Brabant prov., cen. Belgium, a suburb of Brussels; pop. (1991c) 47,963.

Wo·lu·we–Saint–Pierre \ˌvȯ-lə-ˌvā-seⁿ-ˈpyer\ *or Flemish* **Sint–Pie·ters–Woluwe** \sint-ˌpē-tərs-ˈvō-lü-və\. Commune, Brabant prov., cen. Belgium; pop. (1991c) 38,160.

Wol·ver·hamp·ton \ˈwu̇l-vər-ˌhamp-tən\. Town, West Midlands, W cen. England, 12 mi. (19 km.) NW of Birmingham; pop. (1991p) 239,800; metal goods; engineering.

Wol·ver·ine Lake \ˌwu̇l-və-ˈrēn\. Village, Oakland co., SE Michigan, 26 mi. (42 km.) NW of Detroit; pop. (1990c) 4727.

Wol·ver·ton \ˈwu̇l-vər-tən\. Town, Buckinghamshire, SE cen. England, on the Ouse 48 mi. (77 km.) NW of London; pop. (1981p) 22,249.

Wo·łyń \ˈvȯ-ˌwin\. See VOLHYNIA.

Wom·an Bay \ˈwu̇-mən\. Inlet of Gulf of Alaska, E coast of Kodiak I., S Alaska, ab. 8 mi. (13 km.) SW of the city of Kodiak.

Womb·well \ˈwu̇m-bəl, ˈwu̇m-wəl\. Town, South Yorkshire, N England; pop. (1981p) 16,628; coal.

Women's Rights National Historical Park. See UNITED STATES, *National Historical Parks.*

Wŏn·ju \ˈwən-ˈjü\. Town, Kangwŏn prov., South Korea, ab. 53 mi. (85 km.) ESE of Seoul; pop. (1985c) 151,165.

Wo·no·so·bo \ˌwō-nō-ˈsō-bō\. Town, Central Java prov., Indonesia, 45 mi. (72 km.) WNW of Magelang.

Wŏn·san \ˈwən-ˌsän\ *or Jp.* **Gen·zan** \ˈgen-ˌzän\. City, North Korea, on Sea of Japan; pop. (1987e) 274,000; engineering industries; cultural center.

Won·se·ra·deel \ˈvȯn-sər-ə-ˌdāl\. Commune, Friesland prov., N Netherlands, on NE coast of IJsselmeer S of Harlingen; pop. (1981e) 11,807.

Won·thag·gi \wän-ˈtha-gē\. Town on coast of S Victoria, SE Australia, 65 mi. (105 km.) SE of Melbourne; pop. (1993e) 6990.

Wood \ˈwu̇d\. Name of counties in four states of the U.S. See tables at OHIO, TEXAS, WEST VIRGINIA, WISCONSIN.

Wood, Mount. Peak in St. Elias Mts., SW Yukon Terr., Canada, N of Mt. Logan; 15,885 ft. (4842 m.).

Wood·all Mountain \ˈwu̇-ˌdȯl\. Peak, Tishomingo co., NE Mississippi; 806 ft. (246 m.); highest peak in the state.

Wood·bine \ˈwu̇d-ˌbīn\. **1.** City, ⊗ of Camden co., SE corner of Georgia; pop. (1990c) 1212.

2. Borough, Cape May co., S New Jersey, 22 mi. (35 km.) WSW of Atlantic City; pop. (1990c) 2678.

Wood·bridge \ˈwu̇d-ˌbrij\. **1.** Suburban residential town, SW New Haven co., S Connecticut, NW of the city of New Haven; pop. (1990c) 7924; incorp. 1784.

2. Township, Middlesex co., cen. New Jersey, 4 mi. (6 km.) N of Perth Amboy; pop. (1990c) 93,086; chemicals; settled 1665.

3. Unincorporated settlement, Prince William co., NE Virginia, SW of Washington, D.C.; pop. (1990c) 26,401.

4. Town, Suffolk, SE England, just ENE of Ipswich at head of wide inlet; pop. (1981c) 7263; was residence of writers Edward FitzGerald and Bernard Barton.

Wood Buffalo National Park. See CANADA, *National Parks.*

Wood·burn \ˈwu̇d-bərn\. City, Marion co., NW Oregon, SSW of Portland; pop. (1990c) 13,404.

Wood·bury \ˈwu̇d-ˌber-ē, -bə-rē\. **1.** County in W Iowa. See table at IOWA.

2. Town, S Litchfield co., NW Connecticut; pop. (1990c) 8131; settled 1672; Samuel Seabury elected first Episcopal bishop in America here 1783.

3. City, Washington co., E Minnesota, an E suburb of St. Paul; pop. (1990c) 20,075; grew rapidly in 1980s.

4. Residential city, ⊗ of Gloucester co., SW New Jersey, 8 mi. (13 km.) S of Camden; pop. (1990c) 10,904; settled 17th cent.

5. Town, ⊗ of Cannon co., cen. Tennessee; pop. (1990c) 2287.

Woodbury Heights. Borough, Gloucester co., SW New Jersey, S of Philadelphia; pop. (1990c) 3392.

Wood·cliff Lake \ˈwu̇d-ˌklif\. Borough, Bergen co., NE corner of New Jersey, NW of New York City; pop. (1990c) 5303.

Wood Dale. City, Du Page co., NE Illinois, 2 mi. (3.2 km.) W of Chicago's O'Hare International Airport; pop. (1990c) 12,425.

Wood·fin \ˈwu̇d-ˌfin\. Town, Buncombe co., W North Carolina, just NNW of Asheville; pop. (1990c) 2736.

Wood·ford \ˈwu̇d-fərd\. Name of counties in two states of the U.S. See tables at ILLINOIS and KENTUCKY.

Wood·haven \ˈwu̇d-ˌhā-vən\. City, Wayne co., SE Michigan, 15 mi. (23 km.) S of Detroit; pop. (1990c) 11,631.

Wood·lake \ˈwu̇d-ˌlāk\. City, Tulare co., S cen. California, 38 mi. (61 km.) SE of Fresno; pop. (1990c) 5678.

Wood·land \ˈwu̇d-lənd\. City, ⊗ of Yolo co., N cen. California, 15 mi. (24 km.) WNW of Sacramento; pop. (1990c) 39,802; processing and shipment of agricultural products incl. olive oil, rice, and sugar beets; founded c. 1853.

Woodland Park. City, Teller co., cen. Colorado, NW of Colorado Springs; pop. (1990c) 4610.

Wood·lark \ˈwu̇d-ˌlärk\ *also* **Mu·rua** \ˈmü-rü-wä\. Island, Papua New Guinea, in Solomon Sea, NE of SE end of New Guinea I.; ab. 38 mi. (61 km.) long, 12 mi. (19 km.) wide; ab. 400 sq. mi. (1036 sq. km.). Together with small island groups surrounding it, known as **Woodlark Islands** group and sometimes considered a part of the Trobriand Is. Low and hilly with good harbor; gold mining 1934–38. During WWII used as airbase, first by Japanese, then by Allied forces.

Wood·lawn \ˈwu̇d-ˌlȯn\. Village, Hamilton co., SW corner of Ohio, N of Cincinnati; pop. (1990c) 2674.

Wood·lynne \ˈwu̇d-ˌlin\. Borough, Camden co., SW New Jersey, 2 mi. (3 km.) SSE of the city of Camden; pop. (1990c) 2547.

Wood Mountain. Peak, Hinsdale and San Juan cos., SW Colorado; 13,640 ft. (4158 m.).

Wood·ridge \ˈwu̇d-ˌrij\. Village, Du Page co., NE Illinois, 15 mi. (24 km.) W of Chicago; pop. (1990c) 26,256.

Wood–Ridge \ˈwu̇d-ˌrij\. Borough, Bergen co., NE New Jersey, 7 mi. (11 km.) SSE of Paterson; pop. (1990c) 7506.

Wood River. City, Madison co., SW Illinois, 15 mi. (24 km.) N of East St. Louis; pop. (1990c) 11,490.

Wood·roffe, Mount \ˈwu̇-drəf\. Mountain in Musgrave Range, South Australia, Australia; at 4724 ft. (1440 m.), highest point in South Australia.

Wood·ruff \ˈwu̇-drəf\. **1.** County in NE cen. Arkansas. See table at ARKANSAS.

2. Town, Spartanburg co., NW South Carolina, 17 mi. (27 km.) SSW of the city of Spartanburg; pop. (1990c) 4365.

Woods \ˈwu̇dz\. County in NW Oklahoma. See table at OKLAHOMA.

Woods, Lake. Salt lake, cen. Northern Terr., Australia.

Woods, Lake of the. See LAKE OF THE WOODS.

Woods Cross. City, Davis co., N Utah, N of Salt Lake City; pop. (1990c) 5384.

Woods·field \ˈwu̇dz-ˌfēld\. Village, ⊗ of Monroe co., SE Ohio, 30 mi. (48 km.) NE of Marietta; pop. (1990c) 2832.

Woods Hole. See FALMOUTH 3.

Wood·side \ˈwu̇d-ˌsīd\. Town, San Mateo co., W California, 27 mi. (43 km.) S of San Francisco; pop. (1990c) 5035.

Wood·son \ˈwu̇d-sən\. County in SE Kansas. See table at KANSAS.

Woodson Terrace. City, St. Louis co., E Missouri, NW of the city of St. Louis; pop. (1990c) 4362.

Wood·stock \ˈwu̇d-ˌstäk\. **1.** Town, NE Windham co., NE Connecticut, NW of Putnam; pop. (1990c) 6008.

2. City, Cherokee co., Georgia; pop. (1990c) 4361.

3. City, ⊗ of McHenry co., N Illinois, 33 mi. (53 km.) W of Waukegan; pop. (1990c) 14,353.

4. Town, Ulster co., SE New York; pop. (1990c) 6290.
5. Town, ⊗ of Windsor co. E Vermont, 23 mi. (37 km.) E of Rutland; pop. (1990c) 3212.
6. Town, ⊗ of Shenandoah co., N Virginia, 30 mi. (48 km.) SW of Winchester; pop. (1990c) 3182.
7. Market town, ⊗ of Carleton co., W New Brunswick, Canada, on St. John River 48 mi. (77 km.) WNW of Fredericton; pop. (1991c) 4631.
8. City, ⊗ of Oxford co., SE Ontario, Canada, on Thames River 26 mi. (42 km.) ENE of London; pop. (1991c) 30,075; diversified industry.
9. Town, Oxfordshire, cen. England, 8 mi. (13 km.) NW of Oxford; pop. (1981p) 2036; nearby is Blenheim Palace (18th cent.) built for John Churchill, first duke of Marlborough; birthplace of statesman Winston Churchill 1874.

Woods·town \ˈwu̇dz-ˌtau̇n\. Borough, Salem co., SW New Jersey, 16 mi. (26 km.) NNW of Bridgeton; pop. (1990c) 3154; began as Quaker center early 1700s.

Woods·ville \ˈwu̇dz-ˌvil\. Unincorporated settlement, ⊗ of Grafton co., W New Hampshire, on Connecticut River 17 mi. (27 km.) SW of Littleton; pop. (1990c) 1122.

Wood·ville \ˈwu̇d-ˌvil, -vəl\. **1.** Town, ⊗ of Wilkinson co., SW corner of Mississippi; pop. (1990c) 1393.
2. Town, ⊗ of Tyler co., E Texas; pop. (1990c) 2636.

Wood·ward \ˈwu̇d-wərd, ˈwu̇-dərd\. **1.** County in NW Oklahoma. See table at OKLAHOMA.
2. City, its ⊗, 35 mi. (56 km.) E of Oklahoma Panhandle; pop. (1990c) 12,340; U.S. agricultural research station.

Wood·way \ˈwu̇d-ˌwā\. City, McLennan co., cen. Texas, 5 mi. (8 km.) SW of Waco; pop. (1990c) 8695.

Woody Mountain \ˈwu̇-dē\. Peak, S cen. Coconino co., Arizona, near Flagstaff; 8064 ft. (2458 m.).

Wool·lah·ra \wu̇-ˈlär-ə\. City, E New South Wales, SE Australia, E suburb of Sydney on S shore of Port Jackson; pop. (1993e) 51,150.

Woo·me·ra Prohibited Area \ˈwü-mə-rə\. Semiarid area, cen. South Australia, Australia, 100 mi. (161 km.) NW of Port Augusta; restricted government rocket range and test site.

Woon·sock·et \wün-ˈsä-kət, ˈwün-ˌ\. **1.** City, Providence co., N Rhode Island, 13 mi. (21 km.) NNW of the city of Providence; pop. (1990c) 43,877; textiles, electronic components, plastics, machine tools, clothing; settled 1666; made separate town 1871; incorp. as city 1888.
2. City, ⊗ of Sanborn co., South Dakota; pop. (1990c) 766.

Woos·ter \ˈwu̇s-tər\. City, ⊗ of Wayne co., NE cen. Ohio, 27 mi. (43 km.) W of Canton; pop. (1990c) 22,191; rubber products, pumps; Coll. of Wooster (1866); settled c. 1807.

Worces·ter \ˈwu̇s-tər\. **1.** Name of counties in two states of the U.S. See tables at MARYLAND and MASSACHUSETTS.
2. City, a ⊗ of Worcester co., cen. Massachusetts, 37 mi. (60 km.) W of Boston; pop. (1990c) 169,759; diversified industry; Coll. of the Holy Cross (1843), Worcester Polytechnic Institute (1865), Worcester State Coll. (1874), Clark Univ. (1887), Becker Junior Coll.–Worcester campus (1887), Assumption Coll. (1904), Quinsigamond Community Coll. (1963). First permanent settlement made 1713; industrial development begun after opening of Blackstone Canal 1828; incorp. as city 1848.
3. Former county, England. See WORCESTERSHIRE.
4. Town, ⊗ of Hereford and Worcester, W cen. England, on the Severn 25 mi. (40 km.) SSW of Birmingham; pop. (1991p) 81,000; Worcestershire sauce; 11th–14th cent. cathedral. Site of battle 1651 in which Charles II and his Scottish army were routed by Oliver Cromwell and Parliamentarian army, a decisive battle ending English Civil War.
5. Town, Western Cape prov., S Rep. of South Africa, on Bree River 60 mi. (97 km.) ENE of Cape Town; pop. (1985c) 46,043.

Worces·ter·shire \ˈwu̇s-tər-ˌshir, -shər\ *or* **Worcester.** Former county, W cen. England; rivers: Severn, Avon, Stour, Teme. See HEREFORD AND WORCESTER and WEST MIDLANDS.

Wor·den Pond \ˈwər-dən\; *mostly formerly* **Wor·dens Pond** \-dənz\. Small lake, S cen. Washington co., S Rhode Island.

Wor·king·ton \ˈwər-kiŋ-tən\. Port town, Cumbria, NW England, on Irish Sea at mouth of the Derwent 32 mi. (52 km.) SW of Carlisle; pop. (1981c) 26,123; engineering; packaging products.

Work·sop \ˈwərk-səp\. Town, Nottinghamshire, N cen. England, 17 mi. (27 km.) ESE of Sheffield; pop. (1981c) 34,993; coal mines; glass.

Wor·land \ˈwər-lənd\. City, ⊗ of Washakie co., N cen. Wyoming, on Bighorn River 78 mi. (126 km.) SW of Sheridan; pop. (1990c) 5742.

World's View. Height, in the Matopo Hills, S Zimbabwe, 23 mi. (37 km.) SW of Bulawayo; burial place of British administrator and financier Cecil Rhodes.

Wormatia. See WORMS 2.

Wor·mer·veer \ˌvȯr-mər-ˈver\. Commune, North Holland prov., W Netherlands, just N of Amsterdam; pop. (1981e) 11,042.

Worm·leys·burg \ˈwərm-lēz-ˌbərg\. Borough, Cumberland co., S Pennsylvania; pop. (1990c) 2847.

Worms **1.** \ˈvōrms\. Island, Baltic Sea. See VORMSI.
2. \ˈwərmz, ˈvȯrms\; *anc.* **Bor·be·tom·a·gus** \ˌbȯr-bə-ˈtä-mə-gəs\; *later* **Au·gus·ta Van·gi·o·num** \ȯ-ˈgəs-tə-ˌvan-jē-ˈō-nəm\ *also* **Wor·ma·tia** \wȯr-ˈmā-shē-ə\. City, Rhineland-Palatinate, Germany, on the Rhine 10 mi. (16 km.) NNW of Mannheim; pop. (1992e) 77,429; trades in wine; river port; diversified industry; notable 11th–14th cent. cathedral; 13th cent. synagogue destroyed 1938, since rebuilt; several notable churches.
History: Its destruction by Huns 436 provided source for later German epic poem *Nibelungenlied*; city rebuilt 6th cent.; episcopal see to 1803; Concordat of Worms, ending investiture controversy bet. pope and Holy Roman emperor over who would control church offices concluded here 1122; free imperial city from 12th cent.; seat of numerous imperial diets, incl. esp. the Diet of Worms 1521 convoked by Holy Roman Emperor Charles V at which religious reformer Martin Luther made his defense; destroyed by French 1689; to France by Peace of Lunéville 1801, to Hesse-Darmstadt 1816; occupied by French 1918–30; in WWII suffered severe damage that since has largely been repaired.

Worms Head \ˈwərmz\. Cape, SW Gower Penin., off S coast of Wales.

Wors·bor·ough \ˈwərz-ˌbər-ō, -bə-rə\. Locality, South Yorkshire, N England; pop. (1981p) 14,702.

Wors·ley \ˈwər-slē\. Town, Greater Manchester, NW England, 6 mi. (10 km.) WNW of the city of Manchester; pop. (1981p) 49,021; coal mines.

Wor·stead \ˈwu̇s-təd\. Parish and village, Norfolk, E England; 14th cent. church; settled 12th cent. by Flemish weavers who manufactured wool fabric.

Worth \ˈwərth\. **1.** Name of counties in three states of the U.S. See tables at GEORGIA, IOWA, MISSOURI.
2. Village, Cook co., NE Illinois, SW of Chicago; pop. (1990c) 11,208.

Wörth \ˈvœrt\. Commune, Bas-Rhin dept., NE France; scene of battle Aug. 1870 in which French under Marshal MacMahon were defeated by Crown Prince Frederick of Prussia.

Worth, Lake \ˈwərth\. Lagoon, SE Florida, in Palm Beach co. bet. mainland and coastal island; 22 mi. (35 km.) long.

Wör·ther See \ˈvœr-tər-ˌzā\. Lake, largest in Carinthia, S Austria, in valley of the Drava just W of Klagenfurt; 7.5 sq. mi. (19.4 sq. km.); 11 mi. (18 km.) long; max. depth 279 ft. (85 m.).

Wor·thing \wər-t͟hiŋ\. Town, West Sussex, S England, on English Channel 47 mi. (76 km.) S of London; pop. (1991p) 94,100; seaside resort and residential suburb.

Wor·thing·ton \ˈwər-t͟hiŋ-tən\. **1.** City, ⊗ of Nobles co., SW Minnesota, 55 mi. (88 km.) W of Fairmont; pop. (1990c) 9977; Worthington Community Coll. (1936).
2. City, Franklin co., cen. Ohio, 9 mi. (14 km.) N of Columbus; pop. (1990c) 14,869.

Worthington Peak. Mountain, NW Lincoln co., E Nevada; ab. 8850 ft. (2700 m.).

Wot·ho \ˈwät-hō\. Island (atoll), N cen. part of Ralik Chain, W Marshall Is., W Pacific Ocean, 10°06′N, 165°59′E.

Wot·je \ˈwät-jə\. Island (atoll), cen. part of Ratak Chain, E Marshall Is., W Pacific, 9°27′N, 170°02′E; has 65 islets; a Japanese base in WWII.

Wound·ed Knee \ˌwün-dəd-ˈnē\. Unincorporated settlement, Shannon co., SW South Dakota; pop. (1990c) 18; site Dec. 1890 where U.S. troops massacred more than 200 Sioux people.

Wo·wo·ni \wō-ˈwō-nē\. Island, Indonesia, in W Banda Sea, off SE coast of Sulawesi, N of Butung I., at 4°08′S, 123°06′E.

Wran·gel Island \ˈraŋ-gəl\ *or Russ.* **Ostrov Vran·ge·lya** \ˈȯ-strəf-ˈvrȧŋ-gəl-yə\. Island, NE Russia in Asia, in Arctic Ocean, ab. 100 mi. (160 km.) off N coast of Chukchi Autonomous Okrug; ab. 2000 sq. mi. (5180 sq. km.); crossed by the 180th meridian; sought early 1820s by Russian explorer Baron Ferdinand von Wrangel (who heard about the island from native Siberians) but not found; discovered 1867 by a U.S. whaler, and named for Wrangel by him.

Wran·gell \ˈraŋ-gəl\. **1.** Island, SE Alaska, NE of Prince of Wales I.; 217 sq. mi. (562 sq. km.).

2. City, N tip of Wrangell I., SE Alaska, just S of mouth of Stikine River; pop. (1990c) 2479; estab. as a Russian stockade 1834; became a U.S. military post 1867.

Wrangell, Mount. Mountain in cen. part of Wrangell Mts., S Alaska; 14,163 ft. (4317 m.).

Wrangell Mountains. Range, S Alaska, near Canadian border; highest peaks Mt. Bona 16,500 ft. (5029 m.), Mt. Blackburn 16,390 ft. (4996 m.), and Mt. Sanford 16,237 ft. (4949 m.).

Wran·gell–Pe·ters·burg \-ˈpē-tərz-ˌbərg\. Division in Alaska. See table at ALASKA.

Wrangell–Saint Elias National Park \-sānt-i-ˈlī-əs\. See UNITED STATES, *National Parks*.

Wrath, Cape \ˈrath\. Extreme NW point of Scotland, 58°37′N, 5°01′W; lighthouse.

Wray \ˈrā\. Town, ⊗ of Yuma co., NE Colorado, 65 mi. (105 km.) SE of Sterling; pop. (1990c) 1998.

Wreake \ˈrēk\. River, Leicestershire, cen. England; flows SW to the Soar; 18 mi. (29 km.) long.

Wreck Island \ˈrek\. Island, Northampton co., Virginia, in Atlantic Ocean, off SE coast of Delmarva Penin.

Wreck Point. Cape, extreme NW coast of Northern Cape prov., Rep. of South Africa, S of Alexander Bay.

Wreck Reef. Coral reef, South Pacific Ocean, 300 mi. (483 km.) off E coast of Queensland, Australia, 22°13′S, 155°17′E.

Wrecsam. See WREXHAM.

Wre·kin, The \ˈrē-kən\. A sugarloaf hill, an extinct volcano, in Shropshire, W England; 1335 ft. (407 m.).

Wren·tham \ˈren-thəm\. Town, Norfolk co., E Massachusetts, 15 mi. (24 km.) W of Brockton; pop. (1990c) 9006; settled 1669; burned during King Philip's War 1675.

Wrex·ham *or Welsh* **Wrec·sam** \ˈrek-səm\. Borough, Clwyd co., N Wales; pop. (1981c) 40,479; burial place of Elihu Yale, the English colonial administrator for whom Yale Univ. is named.

Wright \ˈrīt\. **1.** Name of counties in three states of the U.S. See tables at IOWA, MINNESOTA, MISSOURI.

2. Municipality, Western Samar prov., W Samar I., Philippines, at head of an inlet of Villareal Bay ab. 9 mi. (14 km.) E of Catbalogan; pop. (1980c) 21,556.

Wrights·town \ˈrīts-ˌtau̇n\. Borough, Burlington co., S cen. New Jersey, ab. 10 mi. (16 km.) NNE of Mount Holly; pop. (1990c) 3843.

Wrights·ville \ˈrīts-ˌvil\. City, ⊗ of Johnson co., cen. Georgia, 53 mi. (85 km.) E of Macon; pop. (1990c) 2331.

Wrig·ley Gulf \ˈri-glē\. Inlet, South Pacific Ocean, E of Hobbs Coast in Marie Byrd Land, Antarctica, 74°S, 129°W; separated from Amundsen Sea by Mt. Siple.

Wro·cław \ˈvrȯt-ˌswäf\. **1.** Province of SW Poland. Formed after 1945 from former German Lower Silesia and part of Brandenburg and at first called **Śląsk Dol·ny** \ˈshlōⁿsk-ˈdȯl-nē\. See table at POLAND.

2. *or Ger.* **Bres·lau** \ˈbres-ˌlau̇\. Commercial city, its ✱, on Oder (Odra) River ab. 190 mi. (305 km.) SW of Warsaw; pop. (1989e) 642,334; railroad junction; major industrial center, producing machinery, electrical equipment, chemicals, textiles, food products; cathedral; several notable churches; old town hall; museums; public parks; university (1702, university status 1811), technical university (1945).

History: Settlement dates from at least 10th cent.; became bishopric c. 1000; became ✱ of Silesia 12th cent.; destroyed by Tatars 1241; new town merged with old town 1327; passed to Bohemia 1335 and with Bohemia to Hapsburgs 1526; passed to Prussia 1741; in WWII besieged by U.S.S.R. 1945 and suffered heavy damage; assigned to Poland by Potsdam Conference 1945; largely rebuilt since the war.

Wrox·e·ter \ˈräk-sət-ər\. Village on the Severn River, Shropshire, W England, just below Shrewsbury, on the site of an ancient Roman town **Uri·co·ni·um** \ˌyu̇r-ə-ˈkō-nē-əm\ *or* **Vir·o·co·ni·um** \ˌvir-ə-\ of which parts have been excavated.

Wrzes·nia \ˈvzhesh-nyä\. Commune, Poznań prov., W cen. Poland; pop. (1989e) 27,492.

Wu \ˈwü\. **1.** River, cen. China; rises in cen. Guizhou, flows NE, N, and NW forming part of Guizhou-Sichuan boundary, and continuing through Sichuan into the Chang ab. 50 mi. (80 km.) below Chongqing; 700 mi. (1126 km.) long; navigable for much of its course.

2. River, Hunan prov., SE cen. China. See LI 1.

3. River, Zhejiang prov., E China. See OU.

4. Ancient kingdom, SE China; formed at the breakup of the Chinese Empire with the fall of the Eastern Han dynasty 220 A.D.; with Shu and Wei formed the Three Kingdoms; overrun by Chin dynasty 280 A.D.

Wu·chang *or W.-G.* **Wu–ch'ang** \ˈwü-ˈchäŋ\. City, Hubei prov., E cen. China, part of the conurbation of Wuhan on S bank of the Chang, 425 mi. (684 km.) W of Shanghai; university (1913). See WUHAN.

History: Oldest of the Wuhan cities, probably dating from the Han dynasty (206 B.C.–200 A.D.); ✱ of kingdom of Wu 3d cent. A.D.; ✱ of an administrative district under Yüan dynasty (1279–1368), later becoming ✱ of Hupeh (Hubei) prov.; in 1911 was starting point of revolution against Imperial regime; occupied by Japanese 1938–45; fell to Communists 1949.

Wu–chou. See WUZHOU.

Wu·han *or W.-G.* **Wu–han** \ˈwü-ˈhän\. Tri-city conurbation, SE Hubei prov., E cen. China, at the junction of the Han River with the Chang; pop. (1990c) 3,284,229; the principal industrial, commercial, and transportation center of cen. China; produces iron and steel. Formed 1950 by the consolidation under a single administration of Hankow, Han-yang, and Wu-ch'ang (see HANKOU, HANYANG, and WUCHANG for historical data).

Wu–hsi. See WUXI.

Wuhsien. See SUZHOU 2.

Wu–hsing. See WUXING.

Wu·hu *or W.-G.* **Wu–hu** \ˈwü-ˈhü\. City, E Anhui, E China, on right bank of the Chang 50 mi. (80 km.) SSW of Nanjing and 260 mi. (418 km.) by river above Shanghai; pop. (1990c) 425,740; connected by canals with neighboring towns; area inhabited as early as first millennium B.C.; since 14th cent. A.D. has been important commerical center; opened to foreign trade 1877.

Wu–lan–hao–t'e. See HORQIN YOUYI QIANQI.

Wu·lar Lake \ˈwu̇-lər, ˈvu̇-\. Lake in course of the Jhelum, Jammu and Kashmir, N India, 25 mi. (40 km.) NW of Srinagar; ab. 10 mi. (16 km.) long by 12 mi. (19 km.) wide; largest in the state.

Wülf·rath \ˈvuel-ˌfrät\. City, North Rhine-Westphalia, Germany, NE suburb of Düsseldorf; pop. (1980c) 20,912.

Wul·sten Peak \ˈwu̇l-stən\. Mountain, Custer co., S cen. Colorado; 13,659 ft. (4163 m.).

Wu–lu–mu–ch'i. See ÜRÜMQI.

Wu·pat·ki National Monument \wu̇-ˈpat-kē\. See UNITED STATES, *National Monuments.*

Wup·per \ˈvu̇-pər\. River, S edge of the Ruhrgebiet (Ruhr Valley), Germany; with many windings flows generally W and SW past Wuppertal to the Rhine just N of Cologne; ab. 65 mi. (105 km.) long.

Wup·per·tal \ˈvu̇-pər-ˌtäl\. Industrial city, North Rhine-Westphalia, Germany, on Wupper River in the Ruhrgebiet (Ruhr Valley) 16 mi. (26 km.) ENE of Düsseldorf; pop. (1992e) 385,463; products include rubber, tools, and textiles.

Würmer See *or* **Würmsee.** See STARNBERGER SEE.

Wür·se·len \ˈvu̇er-zə-lən\. City, North Rhine-Westphalia, Germany, N suburb of Aachen; pop. (1980c) 34,847.

Würt·tem·berg \ˈvu̇er-təm-ˌberk; ˈwər-təm-ˌbərg, ˈwu̇r-\. Former German state, now part of Baden-Württemberg, Germany; 7530 sq. mi. (19,503 sq. km.); ✻ Stuttgart.

History: Orig. inhabited by Celts; later occupied successively by Suevi, Romans, Alamanni, and Franks; became part of duchy of Swabia; from c. 11th cent. ruled by counts who gradually extended the territory; became duchy 1495; suffered in wars of 17th and 18th cents.; became electorate 1803, kingdom 1806; constitutional monarchy 1819–1918; became independent republic 1918, but joined Weimer Republic 1919; became part of Third Reich 1934; in WWII overrun by Allies 1945; made part of Baden-Württemberg 1952. See BADEN-WÜRTTEMBERG.

Würz·burg \ˈvu̇erts-ˌbu̇rk; ˈwərts-ˌbərg, ˈwu̇rts-\. City, Bavaria, Germany, on Main River 60 mi. (96 km.) ESE of Frankfurt am Main; pop. (1992e) 128,512; ships wine. Romanesque cathedral (begun 11th cent.); fortress (residence of bishops 13th–18th cents.) with early 8th cent. church; 14th–15th cent. chapel; old bridge; 18th cent. baroque episcopal palace; university (1582). Bishopric estab. here c. 742 A.D.; bishops gained secular authority as dukes by 12th cent.; bishopric secularized 1801 (later revived); belonged to Bavaria c. 1803–05 and again from c. 1815; heavily damaged in WWII but subsequently largely restored.

Wur·zen \ˈvu̇rt-sən\. City, Saxony, E Germany, on Mulde River 16 mi. (26 km.) E of Leipzig; pop. (1981c) 19,282; 12th cent. cathedral; 15th cent. episcopal palace. First mentioned 961 A.D.

Wusih. See WUXI.

Wu·song \ˈwü-ˈsu̇ŋ\ *or W.-G.* **Wu–sung** \-ˈsu̇ŋ\. Town, Shanghai munic., E China, N of the city of Shanghai at the point where the Huangpu flows into the Chang.

Wu–sung. See WUSONG.

Wu·tai Shan *or W.-G.* **Wu–t'ai Shan** \ˈwü-ˈtī-ˈshän\. Mountain, NE Shanxi prov., NE China, ab. 100 mi. (160 km.) N of Taiyuan; 10,033 ft. (3058 m.); a place sacred to Buddhism; popular pilgrimage site. Its top and slopes covered with temples, monasteries, and lamaseries.

Wu·ti·vi, Mount \wü-ˈtē-vē\. Mountain, N Liberia; 4528 ft. (1380 m.); highest peak in the country.

Wutsin. See CHANGZHOU.

Wu·xi \ˈwü-ˈshē, -ˈshə\ *or W.-G.* **Wu–hsi** \-ˈshē, -ˈshə\; *mostly formerly* **Wu·sih** \-ˈshi\. City, S Jiangsu prov., E China, on Grand Canal (Da Yunhe) 70 mi. (113 km.) WNW of Shanghai; pop. (1990c) 826,833; intersected by many canals; an old city, area having been inhabited since at least 3d cent. B.C.; after the building of Grand Canal 7th cent. A.D. became important shipping center for agricultural goods.

Wu·xing \ˈwü-ˈshiŋ\ *or W.-G.* **Wu–hsing** \-ˈshiŋ\; *locally* **Hu·zhou** \ˈhü-ˈjō\ *or W.-G.* **Hu–chou** \-ˈjō\. City, N Zhejiang prov., E China, WSW of Shanghai; pop. (1990c) 218,071.

Wu·zhou \ˈwü-ˈjō\ *or W.-G.* **Wu–chou** \-ˈjō\; *formerly* **Tsang·wu** \ˈdzäŋ-ˈwü\. City, E Guangxi Zhuangzu, SE China, on N bank of the Xi at its confluence with the Gui, 130 mi. (209 km.) W of Guangzhou (220 mi. or 354 km. by river); pop. (1990c) 210,452; distribution center. Made treaty port 1897; important U.S. air base in WWII.

Wy·a·lu·sing \ˌwī-ə-ˈlü-siŋ\. Town, NW Grant co., SW Wisconsin, on the Mississippi River; pop. (1990c) 364; nearby is Elephant Mound (*q.v.*).

Wy·an·dot \ˈwī-ən-ˌdät, ˈwīn-ˌdät\. County in NW cen. Ohio. See table at OHIO.

Wy·an·dotte \ˈwī-ən-ˌdät, ˈwīn-ˌdät\. **1.** County in NE Kansas. See table at KANSAS.

2. City, Wayne co., SE Michigan, on Detroit River 4 mi. (6 km.) S of Detroit; pop. (1990c) 30,938; settled c. 1820 on the site of a Wyandot Indian village; first Bessemer steel plant in U.S. estab. here 1864; incorp. as city 1867.

Wyck·off \ˈwī-ˌko̊f\. Town, Bergen co., NE corner of New Jersey, 7 mi. (11 km.) N of Paterson; pop. (1990c) 15,372.

Wye \ˈwī\. **1.** *or Welsh* **Gwy** \ˈgü-ē\. River, E Wales and W England; rises in Powys co., cen. Wales, flows SE across English border W of Hereford, and continues S into the estuary of the Severn; 130 mi. (209 km.) long; the ruins of Tintern Abbey (the inspiration for William Wordsworth's poem) are on its banks.

2. Small stream, tributary of the Thames, Buckinghamshire, SE cen. England.

3. River, Derbyshire, N cen. England; flows E to the Derwent; 20 mi. (32 km.) long.

Wy·lie \ˈwī-lē\. City, Collin co., NE Texas, SE of McKinney; pop. (1990c) 8716.

Wy·man Dam \ˈwī-mən\. Dam across upper part of Kennebec River, W cen. Maine, NW of Bingham; height 263 ft. (80 m.); completed 1931; impounds water for waterpower, forming **Wyman Lake.**

Wymbritseradeel. See WIJMBRITSERADEEL.

Wynd·ham \ˈwin-dəm\. Town, NE Western Australia, Australia, near mouth of the Ord River; northernmost point in the state; ships cattle, lead, and zinc.

Wynkoops Bay. See PELABUHANRATU BAY.

Wynne \ˈwin\. City, ⊗ of Cross co., E Arkansas, 46 mi. (74 km.) W of Memphis, Tennessee; pop. (1990c) 8187.

Wy·noo·chee *also* **Wy·noo·che** \wī-ˈnü-chē\. River, W Washington; flows S in Grays Harbor co. into Chehalis River W of Montesano; 60 mi. (96 km.) long.

Wyn·yard \ˈwin-yərd\; *formerly* **Ta·ble Cape** \ˈtā-bəl\. Town, NW coast of Tasmania, Australia, 12 mi. (19 km.) W of Burnie; munic. pop. (1991c) 12,918.

Wy·o·ming \wī-ˈō-miŋ\. **1.** A western state of U.S.A., bounded on N by Montana, on E by South Dakota and Nebraska, on S by Colorado and Utah, and on W by Utah and Idaho; 9th state in area, 97,914 sq. mi. (253,597 sq. km.); 50th state in population, (1990c) 453,588; ✻ Cheyenne; 44th state admitted to Union (1890). See table of states at UNITED STATES.

Nicknames: Equality State, Cowboy State.

State flower: Indian paintbrush.

Motto: Equal Rights.

Rivers: Green, with its tributaries, draining SW corner of state and flowing S across border into Utah; Bighorn, flowing from cen. region N into Montana; Yellowstone, rising in NW region and flowing N into Montana; Powder, flowing from cen. region E of the Bighorn, N into Montana; North Platte, flowing from S section N and then SW across border into Nebraska, receiving waters of the Laramie near the border; Snake, rising in NW corner of state and flowing S then NW across border into Idaho.

Highest point: Gannett Peak, 13,804 ft. (4207 m.), Fremont co.

Chief products: Sugar beets, beans, barley, hay, wheat; livestock; oil, natural gas, uranium, coal; oil refining; tourism.

Chief cities: Cheyenne, Casper, Laramie.

Political divisions: Divided into the following 23 counties (for pronunciation of their names, see their individual entries):

NAME	AREA[1] (sq. mi.)	AREA[1] (sq. km.)	POP. (1990c)	CO. SEAT
Albany	4,248	11,002	30,797	Laramie
Big Horn	3,177	8,228	10,525	Basin
Campbell	4,756	12,318	29,370	Gillette
Carbon	7,905	20,474	16,659	Rawlins
Converse	4,282	11,090	11,128	Douglas
Crook	2,882	7,464	5,294	Sundance

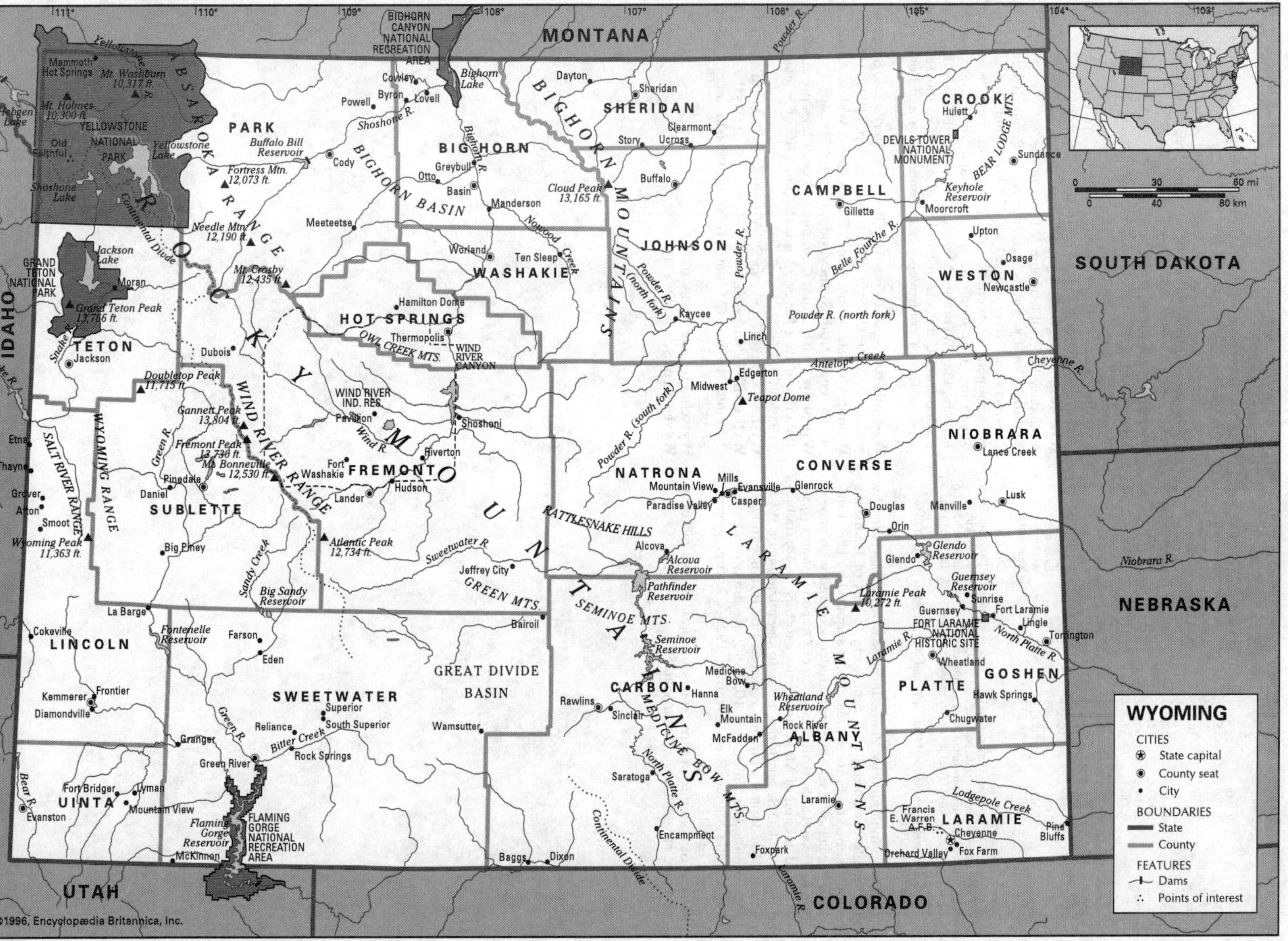
WYOMING
CITIES
State capital
County seat
City
BOUNDARIES
State
County
FEATURES
Dams
Points of interest
MONTANA
SOUTH DAKOTA
NEBRASKA
COLORADO
UTAH
IDAHO
ROCKY MOUNTAINS
BIGHORN MOUNTAINS
LARAMIE MOUNTAINS
MEDICINE BOW MTS.
WIND RIVER RANGE
WYOMING RANGE
SALT RIVER RANGE
ABSAROKA RANGE
BIGHORN BASIN
GREAT DIVIDE BASIN
RATTLESNAKE HILLS
SEMINOE MTS.
GREEN MTS.
OWL CREEK MTS.
BEAR LODGE MTS.
PARK
BIGHORN
SHERIDAN
JOHNSON
CAMPBELL
CROOK
WESTON
NIOBRARA
CONVERSE
NATRONA
WASHAKIE
HOT SPRINGS
FREMONT
TETON
SUBLETTE
LINCOLN
UINTA
SWEETWATER
CARBON
ALBANY
PLATTE
GOSHEN
LARAMIE
YELLOWSTONE NATIONAL PARK
GRAND TETON NATIONAL PARK
DEVILS TOWER NATIONAL MONUMENT
FORT LARAMIE NATIONAL HISTORIC SITE
BIGHORN CANYON NATIONAL RECREATION AREA
FLAMING GORGE NATIONAL RECREATION AREA
WIND RIVER IND. RES.
WIND RIVER CANYON
Cheyenne
Casper
Laramie
Rock Springs
Gillette
Sheridan
Cody
Jackson
Rawlins
Riverton
Lander
Evanston
Green River
Torrington
Douglas
Buffalo
Worland
Thermopolis
Kemmerer
Pinedale
Newcastle
Sundance
Lusk
Wheatland
Basin
Rock River
Continental Divide
Grand Teton Peak 13,766 ft.
Gannett Peak 13,804 ft.
Cloud Peak 13,165 ft.
Laramie Peak 10,272 ft.
Yellowstone Lake
Jackson Lake
Pathfinder Reservoir
Seminoe Reservoir
Flaming Gorge Reservoir
Keyhole Reservoir
Buffalo Bill Reservoir
Bighorn Lake
North Platte R.
Green R.
Powder R.
Snake R.
Bighorn R.
Wind R.
Sweetwater R.
Laramie R.
Cheyenne R.
Belle Fourche R.
Shoshone R.
Bear R.
Niobrara R.
104°
105°
106°
107°
108°
109°
110°
111°
45°
44°
43°
42°
41°
0
30
60 mi
0
40
80 km
©1996, Encyclopædia Britannica, Inc.

NAME	AREA[1] (sq. mi.)	AREA[1] (sq. km.)	POP. (1990c)	CO. SEAT
Fremont	9,196	23,818	33,662	Lander
Goshen	2,228	5,771	12,373	Torrington
Hot Springs	2,122	5,496	4,809	Thermopolis
Johnson	4,175	10,813	6,145	Buffalo
Laramie	2,703	7,001	73,142	Cheyenne
Lincoln	4,098	10,614	12,625	Kemmerer
Natrona	5,342	13,836	61,226	Casper
Niobrara	2,614	6,770	2,499	Lusk
Park[2]	6,958	18,021	23,178	Cody
Platte	2,086	5,403	8,145	Wheatland
Sheridan	2,532	6,558	23,562	Sheridan
Sublette	4,851	12,564	4,843	Pinedale
Sweetwater	10,473	27,125	38,823	Green River
Teton[3]	3,999	10,357	11,172	Jackson
Uinta	2,086	5,403	18,705	Evanston
Washakie	2,262	5,859	8,388	Worland
Weston	2,407	6,234	6,518	Newcastle

[1]Area = land area.
[2]Main part of Yellowstone National Park (its area is included in Park and Teton cos.) is within Wyoming state boundaries (2930.8 sq. mi. or 7591 sq. km.), with adjacent strips in Montana (268.9 sq. mi. or 696 sq. km.) and Idaho (57.6 sq. mi. or 149 sq. km.). Total area with inland waters 3419 sq. mi. (8855 sq. km.).
[3]Contains Grand Teton National Park in W and NW part, also part of Yellowstone National Park.

History: Inhabited by Plains Indians when first visited by white explorers during 18th cent.; orig. a part of Louisiana region claimed by France; greater part acquired by U.S. Louisiana Purchase (*q.v.*) 1803; remainder acquired with annexation of Texas 1845, British cession of Oregon Country (*q.v.*) 1846, and cession of Mexican territory to U.S. 1848; included in several U.S. territories prior to organization of Wyoming 1868; adopted women's suffrage, first instance in U.S., 1869; admitted to Union July 10, 1890; constitution adopted 1890; Nellie Tayloe Ross governor 1925–27, first woman governor of a U.S. state.
2. Name of counties in three states of the U.S. See tables at NEW YORK, PENNSYLVANIA, WEST VIRGINIA.
3. City, Kent co., W Michigan, SW of Grand Rapids; pop. (1990c) 63,891.
4. City, Hamilton co., SW corner of Ohio, 8 mi. (13 km.) N of Cincinnati; pop. (1990c) 8128.
5. Borough, Luzerne co., E Pennsylvania, in Wyoming Valley on Susquehanna River 6 mi. (10 km.) NNE of Wilkes-Barre; pop. (1990c) 3255. See WYOMING VALLEY.

Wyoming Mountain. Ridge, Luzerne co., E Pennsylvania, extending along SE bank of Susquehanna River and bordering Wyoming Valley; ab. 18 mi. (29 km.) long.

Wyoming Peak. Mountain, N Lincoln co., W Wyoming, at S end of Wyoming Range; 11,418 ft. (3480 m.).

Wyoming Range. Range, W Wyoming, extending along boundary bet. Sublette and N Lincoln cos.

Wyoming Valley. Valley, Luzerne co., E Pennsylvania, along Susquehanna River; ab. 20 mi. (32 km.) long, 3 mi. (5 km.) wide; noted for scenery; old Forty Fort, near borough of Wyoming, was scene of an Indian and Tory attack on the settlers, the "Wyoming Massacre," July 3, 1778. Valley was settled from Connecticut and in the 2d half of the 18th cent. was subject of controversy bet. Connecticut and Pennsylvania.

Wy·o·mis·sing \ˌwī-ō-ˈmi-siŋ\. Borough, Berks co., SE Pennsylvania, 3 mi. (5 km.) W of Reading; pop. (1990c) 7332.

Wy·ong \ˈwī-ˌäŋ, -ˌȯŋ\. Shire, E New South Wales, Australia, up the coast from Sydney; pop. (1991c) 100,468.

Wysz·ków \ˈvish-ˌküf\. Commune, S Ostrołeka prov., NE cen. Poland, on Bug River 33 mi. (53 km.) NE of Warsaw; pop. (1989e) 23,453.

Wythe \ˈwith\. County in SW Virginia. See table at VIRGINIA.

Wythe·ville \ˈwith-ˌvil, -vəl\. Town, ⊗ of Wythe co., SW Virginia, 19 mi. (31 km.) WSW of Pulaski; pop. (1990c) 8038.

Wytschaete. See WIJTSCHATE.

Wyvis, Ben. See BEN WYVIS.

X

Xaafuun, Raas. See HAFUN, RAS.

Xai–Xai \ˈshī-ˈshī\; *formerly* **Vila de João Be·lo** \ˈvē-lə-dē-ˈzhwau̇^{n}-ˈbā-ˌlü\. Seaport town, ❋ of Gaza prov., S Mozambique, at mouth of Limpopo River; pop. (1991e) 93,519.

Xalapa. See JALAPA 3.

Xal·to·cán \ˌsäl-tō-ˈkän\. Lake in the Valley of Mexico, cen. Mexico, NNE of Mexico City and N of Lake Texcoco.

Xan·kän·dı \zän-ˈkan-dē\; *formerly* **Ste·pa·na·kert** \ˌstye-ˌpə-nə-ˈkyert\. Town, ❋ of Nagorno-Karabakh Rep., Azerbaijan, in mountains 62 mi. (100 km.) SSE of Gäncä; pop. (1991e) 55,200.

Xan·ten \ˈksänt-^{ə}n\. Town, W North Rhine-Westphalia, Germany, on left bank of the Rhine 7 mi. (11 km.) W of Wesel; cathedral; treaty signed here 1614 settling inheritance dispute over possession of the duchies of Jülich and Kleve. In WWII scene of severe fighting Mar. 1945.

Xán·thi *or* **Xan·the** \ˈzan-thē; *mod. Gk.* ˈksän-thē\. **1.** Department of Greece. See table at GREECE.
2. *or Turk.* **Es·ki·je** \es-kē-ˈjā\. City, its ❋, 30 mi. (48 km.) W of Komotiní, near E bank of Mesta River; pop. (1991p) 37,462.

Xan·thus \ˈzan-thəs\. **1.** *or mod.* **Ko·ca** \kō-ˈjä\. River, Muğla and Antalya provs., SW Turkey in Asia; flows SW and S to the Mediterranean; 78 mi. (125 km.) long.
2. Ancient city of Lycia, Asia Minor, near mouth of Xanthus River; its ruins (theater, pillar, temples, tombs, and other remains), from which a number of pieces now in the British Museum were taken, are in SE Muğla prov., SW Turkey in Asia. The ancient city was twice besieged and destroyed: first in c. 540 B.C. by the Persians under Gen. Harpagus; later in 42 B.C. by Romans under Marcus Junius Brutus.

Xàtiva. See JÁTIVA.

Xe·nia \ˈzē-nyə, -nē-ə\. City, ⊗ of Greene co., SW Ohio, 15 mi. (24 km.) ESE of Dayton; pop. (1990c) 24,664.

Xera *or* **Xeres.** See JEREZ.

Xi *or W.-G.* **Hsi** \ˈshē, ˈshi\ *also* **Si** \ˈshē, ˈshi\; *Eng.* **West** \ˈwest\. River, SE China; known in its upper course as the Hongshui (*q.v.*); the Xi proper begins in E Guangxi Zhuangzu, then flows E ab. 300 mi. (485 km.) through Guangdong prov. into China Sea near Macao and W of the island of Hong Kong; 1200 mi. (1930 km.) long; important commercial waterway; the city of Guangzhou (Canton) is in its delta; navigable for large vessels to Wuzhou and for smaller vessels beyond; receives the Gui from the N.

Xia·men \ˈshyä-ˈmən\ *or W.-G.* **Hsia–men** \ˈshyä-\ *or* **Amoy** \ä-ˈmȯi, a-\. Seaport, Fujian prov., SE China, on two islands in Taiwan Strait; 140 mi. (225 km.) W of Taiwan; food processing and canning; university (1921); good natural harbor.
History: One of the first ports through which Europeans traded with China, beginning with the Portuguese 16th cent., followed by the Dutch and the English; occupied by British 1841; opened as treaty port by Treaty of Nanking at close of first British war against China 1842; gradually declined as center of tea export; captured by Japanese in 1938 campaign against China and held till end of WWII; designated a center for trade and foreign investment c. 1980.

Xi·'an \ˈshē-ˈän, -ˈan\ *or W.-G.* **Hsi–an** \ˈshē-ˈän, -ˈan\ *also* **Si·an** \ˈshē-ˈän, -ˈan\ *or* **Si·an·fu** \-ˈfü\ *or* **Si–ngan** \ˈshē-ˈän\ *or* **Si·ngan–fu** \ˈshē-ˈän-ˈfü\; *formerly* **Si·king** \ˈshē-ˈjiŋ\ *or earlier* **Ch'ang-an** \ˈchäŋ-ˈän\. City, ❋ of Shaanxi prov., E cen. China, in S cen. part of province, on S bank of the Wei ab. 80 mi. (130 km.) above its junction with the Huang; pop. (1990c) 1,959,044; textiles, chemicals; several educational institutions; 14th cent. walls; numerous temples and pagodas; ancient tombs in nearby hills, incl. tomb of Emperor Shih Huang Ti (d. 210 B.C.) with its nearby army of 6,000 life-size terracotta warriors, excavated beginning 1974; museum containing over 1,000 inscribed stelae dating from Han period (3d cent. B.C.) to T'ang period, incl. one from 8th cent. recording foundation of Nestorian Christianity in Xi'an.
History: Site has served as ❋ of 11 dynasties, beginning with Chou (founded 1111 B.C.); ❋ centered at Xianyang near present city under Emperor Shih Huang Ti, who unified China 221 B.C., and at Ch'ang-an just to NW under Han dynasty (206 B.C.–220 A.D.); as ❋ of T'ang dynasty (618–907) Ch'ang-an (which by then encompassed a larger area) reached zenith; due to location on inland trade route a thriving commercial center; declined after fall of T'ang dynasty but still important in trade when Venetian traveler Marco Polo visited 13th cent.; revived somewhat during Ming period (1368–1644) and given present name. In modern times, scene of kidnapping of Chinese Nationalist President Chiang Kai-shek by one of his generals 1936 which resulted in a united Communist-Nationalist front against Japanese invaders; 20th cent. decline reversed by industrial development under Communists after 1949.

Xiang \ˈshyäŋ\ *or W.-G.* **Hsiang** \ˈshyäŋ\ *or* **Siang** \ˈshyäŋ\. Navigable river, cen. Hunan prov., SE cen. China; rises in NE Guangxi Zhuangzu and flows N into Dongting Hu (lake); its valley is highly developed agriculturally and for centuries has been a N to S trade route.

Xiang·fan \ˈshyäŋ-ˈfan, -ˈfän\ *or W.-G.* **Hsiang–fan** \ˈshyäŋ-\. City, N Hubei prov., E cen. China, on Han River, NW of Wuhan; pop. (1990c) 410,407; textiles.

Xiang·shan \ˈshyäŋ-ˈshan, -ˈshän\ *or W.-G.* **Hsiang–shan** \ˈshyäŋ-\ *or* **Siang·shan** \ˈshyäŋ-\. Town, E Zhejiang prov., E China, 120 mi. (193 km.) S of Shanghai on S shore of **Xiangshan Bay,** long narrow inlet of East China Sea S of Ningbo.

Xiang·tan \ˈshyäŋ-ˈtän\ *or W.-G.* **Hsiang–t'an** \ˈshyäŋ-ˈtän\ *or* **Siang·tan** \ˈshyäŋ-\. Town, E cen. Hunan prov., SE China, on Xiang River ab. 20 mi. (32 km.) SSW of Changsha; pop. (1990c) 441,968.

Xiang·yun \ˈshyäŋ-ˈyœ̄n, -ˈyün\ *or W.-G.* **Hsiang–yün** \ˈshyäŋ-\ *or* **Siang·yun** \ˈshyäŋ-\. Town, NW cen. Yunnan prov., S China, 30 mi. (48 km.) SE of Dali; junction point.

Xian·yang \ˈshyen-ˈyäŋ\ *or W.-G.* **Hsien–yang** \ˈshyen-\ *or* **Sien·yang** \ˈshyen-\. Town, Shaanxi prov., NE cen. China, ab. 15 mi. (24 km.) NW of Xi'an; pop. (1990c) 352,125.

Xiao Hing·gan Ling \ˈshyau̇-ˈhiŋ-ˈgän-ˈliŋ\ *or W.-G.* **Hsiao–hsing–an Ling** \ˈshyau̇-ˈshiŋ-ˈän-ˈliŋ\ *or Eng.* **Lesser Khin·gan Mountains** \ˌkiŋ-ˈgän, ˌki̱ŋ-\. Mountain range, Heilongjiang prov., NE China, W of Amur River, separating it from the Songhua Valley; highest point ab. 3600 ft. (1095 m.); together with Da Hinggan Ling sometimes referred to as the Khingan.

Xiaojinmen. See QUEMOY.

Xi·ga·zê \ˈshē-ˈgä-ˈdzə\ *or W.-G.* **Jih–k'a–tse** \ˈjē-ˈkä-ˈdzə\ *or* **Shi·ga·tse** \ˈshē-ˈgä-ˈdzə\. Town, S Tibet, W China, on S bank of Zangbo (Brahmaputra) River, ab. 140 mi. (225 km.) W of Lhasa; ab. 1 mi. (1.6 km.) SW is a walled and fortified monastery in which more than 3000 priests lived prior to the Chinese occupation of Tibet (1950).

Xi·li·tla \sē-ˈlēt-lä, shē-\. Municipality, San Luis Potosí state, Mexico, 135 mi. (217 km.) SE of the city of San Luis Potosí.

Xinchu. See HSIN-CHU.

Xin·feng \ˈshin-ˈfəŋ\ *or W.-G.* **Hsin–feng** \ˈshin-\ *or* **Sin·feng** \ˈshin-\. Town, S Jiangxi prov., SE China, ab. 33 mi. (53 km.) S of Ganzhou.

Xingkai. See KHANKA.

\ə\ **abut** \ə̇\ matches \$^{ə}$\ kitten, Fr table \ər\ **fur**ther \a\ **a**sh \ā\ **a**ce
\ä\ cot, cart \ȧ\ Fr bac \au̇\ **ou**t \b̲\ Span Avila \ch\ **ch**in \e\ bet \ē\ **ea**sy
\g\ **g**o \i\ h**i**t \ī\ **i**ce \j\ **j**ob \k̲\ Ger i**ch**, Bu**ch** \$^{n}$\ Fr v**in**
\ŋ\ si**ng** \ō\ g**o** \ö\ **a**ll \ȯ\ l**aw** \œ\ Fr b**œu**f \œ̄\ Fr f**eu** \ȯi\ b**oy**
\th\ **th**in \th̲\ **th**is \ü\ l**oo**t \u̇\ f**oo**t \ue\ Ger f**ü**llen \ue̅\ Fr r**ue**
\y\ **y**et \$^{y}$\ Fr digne \ˈdēn^{y}\, nuit \ˈnw^{y}ē\ \yü\ **few** \yu̇\ f**ur**y \zh\ vi**si**on

Xing·tai \ˈshiŋ-ˈtī\ *or W.-G.* **Hsing–t'ai** \ˈshiŋ-\. City, SW Hebei prov., NE cen. China, SW of Beijing; pop. (1990c) 302,789.

Xin·gu \shēŋ-ˈgü\. River, cen. and N Brazil; rises in several headstreams in N part of the Planalto do Mato Grosso and flows N through NE Mato Grosso state and cen. Pará state into the Amazon River near its mouth; 1230 mi. (1979 km.) long; in its cen. part goes through a series of rapids 400 mi. (644 km.) long; explored by a German ethnologist 1884–87.

Xi·ning \ˈshē-ˈniŋ\ *or W.-G.* **Hsi–ning** \ˈshē-\ *or* **Hsi·ning** \ˈshē-\ *or* **Si·ning** \ˈshē-\. City, ✻ of Qinghai prov., W cen. China; pop. (1990c) 551,776.

Xin·jiang Uy·gur \ˈshin-ˈjyäŋ-ˈwē-ˈgu̇r\ *or W.-G.* **Sin·kiang Ui·ghur** \ˈshin-ˈjyäŋ-ˈwē-ˈgu̇r\; *often shortened to* **Xinjiang** *or W.-G.* **Sinkiang.** Autonomous region, W China, bounded on NE by Mongolia, on E by Gansu prov., on SE by Qinghai, on S by Xizang (Tibet), on SW by Jammu and Kashmir (disputed bet. India and Pakistan), and Afghanistan, on W by Tajikistan and Kyrgyzstan, on W and N by Kazakhstan, and on N just touching Russia; ✻ Ürümqi.

Physical features: Tableland above 2000 ft. (610 m.) surrounded on three sides by high mountain ranges: on S by the Kunlun Shan, on SW by the Pamirs, on W by the Tian Shan (which extends E as N boundary of Taklimakan Desert), on NW by the Ala Tau, and on the N and NE by the Altay Shan; cen. part is extensive Taklimakan Desert, which includes the Tarim basin (in places less than 1000 ft. or 305 m. in alt.), watered seasonally by the Tarim River and its branches, incl. the Yarkant He and the Hotan; in the S are other desert streams incl. the Keriya and the Qarqan; in the N are the headstreams of the Irtysh. Has many salt lakes, incl. Turpan Depression (below sea level) in center, Lop Nur in SE, and Ebinur Lake in NW. Inhabitants include various peoples speaking Turkic languages. Products include wheat, corn; oil, molybdenum, tungsten. W and cen. parts correspond to Chinese Turkestan; Junggar and Tacheng are regions in N. Ürümqi is by far the largest city.

History: Inhabited since earliest times by nomad tribes; important in Chinese history as the region traversed by the Silk Road (*q.v.*) by which China traded with the West. Area fell under control of local leaders with fall of Han dynasty 3d cent. A.D.; regained by China under T'ang dynasty in 7th cent.; subject to Tibetans 8th cent. and Uighurs c. 9th cent.; invaded 10th cent. by Arabs; conquered by Mongol leader Genghis Khan 13th cent.; again came under Chinese control during Manchu dynasty (1644–1912); estab. as a Chinese province, **Sinkiang,** c. 1884; came under Chinese Communists 1949; reconstituted as an autonomous region 1955. See table at CHINA.

Xin·min \ˈshin-ˈmin\ *or W.-G.* **Hsin–min** \ˈshin-\ *or* **Sin·min** \ˈshin-\. Town, E cen. Liaoning prov., NE China, 35 mi. (56 km.) WNW of Shenyang.

Xinpu. See LIANYUNGANG.

Xin·xiang \ˈshin-ˈshyäŋ\ *or W.-G.* **Hsin–hsiang** \ˈshin-ˈshyäŋ\ *or* **Sin·siang** \ˈshin-ˈshyäŋ\. Town, N Henan prov., E cen. China, ab. 35 mi. (56 km.) N of Zhengzhou; pop. (1990c) 473,762.

Xin·yang \ˈshin-ˈyäŋ\ *or W.-G.* **Hsin–yang** \ˈshin-\ *or* **Sin·yang** \ˈshin-\. Town, S Henan prov., E cen. China, ab. 180 mi. (290 km.) SSE of Zhengzhou; pop. (1990c) 192,509.

Xi·pho·nia \zi-ˈfō-nē-ə, zī-\. Commune, Sicily. See AUGUSTA.

Xisha Qundao. See PARACEL ISLANDS.

Xi·xa·bang·ma Feng \ˈshē-ˌshä-ˈbäŋ-ˌmä-ˈfəŋ\; *mostly formerly* **Go·sain·than** \ˌgō-ˌsīn-ˈtän\ *or* **Go·sai·than** \-ˌsī-\. Peak in the Himalayas, in S Tibet, China, near border of Nepal, ab. 55 mi. (88 km.) NE of Kathmandu; 26,291 ft. (8013 m.); first scaled 1964.

Xi·zang \ˈshē-ˈzäŋ\. Autonomous region of China. See TIBET and table at CHINA.

Xo·chi·cal·co \ˌsō-chē-ˈkäl-kō\. Ruins, Morelos state, Mexico, of ancient Toltec city which was a trading center in 8th cent.; an elaborately carved pyramid is chief remaining structure.

Xo·chi·mil·co \ˌsō-chē-ˈmēl-kō\. **1.** Shallow lake in Valley of Mexico, cen. Mexico, 7 mi. (11 km.) SE of Mexico City. **2.** Town, Federal District, cen. Mexico, 10 mi. (16 km.) S of Mexico City on W shore of Lake Xochimilco; area pop. (1990p) 271,020; site of chinampas or "floating gardens," actually gardens on reclaimed land that is interlaced by canals. The chinampas of pre-colonial times were formed by piling mud onto rafts which were composed of interlacing twigs and floated in the water until the roots of the plants that were grown on them finally anchored the rafts to the bottom of the lake, the number of these artificial islands being multiplied until they formed a meadow interlaced by waterways.

Xo·is \ˈzō-is\. City of ancient Egypt, in the middle of the Nile Delta ab. 20 mi. (32 km.) NW of Busiris; according to one ancient source, ✻ of the XIVth (Xoite) dynasty c. 17th cent. B.C.

Xuan·cheng \ˈshwän-ˈchəŋ\ *or W.-G.* **Hsüan–ch'eng** \ˈshwän-ˈchəŋ\. City, SE Anhui prov., E cen. China, SE of Wuhu; pop. (1990c) 112,673.

Xuan·hua \ˈshwän-ˈhwä\ *or W.-G.* **Hsüan–hua** \ˈshwän-\. City, NW Hebei prov., NE China, WNW of Beijing.

Xu·chang \ˈshü̅-ˈchäŋ\ *or W.-G.* **Hsü–ch'ang** \ˈshü̅-ˈchäŋ\; *formerly* **Hsu·chow** \ˈshü-ˈjō, -ˈchau̇\. Town, cen. Henan prov., E cen. China, S of Zhengzhou.

Xulla Islands. See SULA ISLANDS.

Xu·zhou \ˈshü̅-ˈjō\ *or W.-G.* **Hsü–chou** \ˈshü̅-ˈjō\ *also* **Su·chou** *or* **Su·chow** \ˈsü-ˈjō\ *or* **Sü·chow·fu** \ˈsü̅-ˈjō-ˈfü\; *formerly* **T'ung–shan** \ˈtu̇ŋ-ˈshän\. Town, Jiangsu prov., E China, ab. 180 mi. (290 km.) NW of Nanjing; pop. (1990c) 805,695; in mining area; engineering, textiles. Long a transportation center; scene of important Communist victory 1948 in which Nationalists were routed.

Y

Y. See IJ.

Ya·'an *or W.-G.* **Ya–an** *or* **Ya·an** \'yä-'än\; *formerly* **Ya·chow** \'yä-'jō\. Town, Sichuan, S China, on tributary of Min River 70 mi. (113 km.) SW of Chengdu; pop. (1985e) 86,000; center for tea trade.

Yablonitsa Pass. See JABLONICA PASS.

Ya·blo·no·vyy *or* **Ya·blo·no·vy** \'yä-,blə-nə-vē\ *also* **Ya·blo·noi** \,yä-blə-'nȯi\. Mountain range, S Russia in Asia, along border bet. W Chita Oblast and E Buryatia Rep.; highest peak Sokhondo 7188 ft. (2191 m.), at its S end near border with Mongolia; forms watershed for rivers flowing to Arctic and Pacific oceans.

Ya·bu·coa \,yä-b̲ü-'kō-ä\. Municipality, SE Puerto Rico, ENE of Guayama; pop. (1990c) 36,483.

Ya·chi·yo \yä-'chē-yō, 'yä-chē-,yō\. City, Chiba prefecture, SE Honshū, Japan; pop. (1990p) 148,615.

Yachow. See YA'AN.

Ya·cui·ba \yä-'kwē-b̲ä\. Town, Tarija dept., S Bolivia, on Argentine frontier; pop. (1992p) 31,049; port of entry and trading center for Gran Chaco region.

Ya·cu·ma \yä-'kü-mä\. River, NW Bolivia; flows NE into Mamoré River; ab. 200 mi. (320 km.) long.

Yad·kin \'yad-kən\. **1.** River, cen. North Carolina; rises in Watauga co., flows E, then S, and joins Uharie River to form Pee Dee River (*q.v.*); 202 mi. (325 km.) long. See NARROWS DAM and HIGH ROCK LAKE.

2. County in NW cen. North Carolina. See table at NORTH CAROLINA.

Yadkin Dam. See NARROWS DAM.

Yad·kin·ville \'yad-kən-,vil\. Town, ⊗ of Yadkin co., NW cen. North Carolina; pop. (1990c) 2525.

Ya·e·ya·ma Ret·tō \yī-'yä-mä-'ret-tō\ *or Eng.* **Yaeyama Islands.** Group of islands, S Ryukyu Is., Japan; part of Sakishima Is.; 247 sq. mi. (640 sq. km.); chief islands Iriomote and Ishigaki.

Yafa *or* **Yafo.** See JAFFA.

Ya·gua·jay \,yä-gwä-'hī\. Municipality, Las Villas prov., W cen. Cuba, 45 mi. (72 km.) E of Santa Clara.

Ya·gua·rón \,yä-gwä-'rȯn\. **1.** River, South America. See JAGUARÃO 1.

2. Town, E Central dept., S Paraguay, 20 mi. (32 km.) SE of Asunción; noted for its old church.

Yaila Range. See YALTINSKAYA YAYLA.

Yai·nax Butte \'yī-,naks\. Mountain, SE Klamath co., S Oregon; 7226 ft. (2202 m.).

Yai·zu \'yī-zü\. City, Shizuoka prefecture, Honshū, Japan, 9 mi. (14 km.) SW of the city of Shizuoka; pop. (1990p) 112,188.

Yakapınar. See MOPSUESTIA.

Yak·i·ma \'ya-kə-,mȯ, -mə\. **1.** River, S cen. Washington; flows SE through Kittitas and Yakima cos. into Columbia River in Benton co.; 203 mi. (327 km.) long.

2. County in S Washington. See table at WASHINGTON.

3. City, its ⊗, on Yakima River 5 mi. (8 km.) N of **Yakima Indian Reservation;** pop. (1990c) 54,827; in irrigated agricultural region; Yakima Valley Community Coll. (1928); city made ⊗ 1886.

Ya·ku Shi·ma \,yä-kü-'shē-mä, 'yä-kü-shē-,mä\ *or Eng.* **Ya·ku Island** \'yä-kü\. One of the Osumi Is. (*q.v.*), Japan, off S tip of Kyūshū; with adjacent small island, 208 sq. mi. (539 sq. km.).

Yak·u·tat \'ya-kə-,tat\. City on Ocean Cape, S shore of Yakutat Bay, SE Alaska; pop. (1990c) 534.

Yakutat Bay. Inlet of Gulf of Alaska, SE Alaska, 59°45′N, 140°45′W.

Yakut Autonomous Soviet Socialist Republic *or* **Yakutia.** See SAKHA.

Ya·kutsk \yə-'kütsk\. Town, ✻ of Sakha Rep., E Russia in Asia, on Lena River; pop. (1992e) 198,000; river port; university (1956).

Yakutsk Autonomous Soviet Socialist Republic. See SAKHA.

Ya·la \'yä-lə\. Town, SW Thailand, 22 mi. (35 km.) S of Pattani; pop. (1991e) 68,834.

Yale, Mount \'yāl\. Peak in Sawatch Range, Chaffee co., cen. Colorado; 14,196 ft. (4327 m.).

Yales·ville \'yālz-,vil\. Subdivision of town of Wallingford, Connecticut. See WALLINGFORD 1.

Ya·lias \yäl-'yäs\. River, Cyprus; flows E into Famagusta Bay; 45 mi. (72 km.) long.

Yal·o·busha \,ya-lə-'bu̇-shə\. **1.** River, N cen. Mississippi; rises in Chickasaw co., flows W and SW to unite with Tallahatchie River in Leflore co. and form the Yazoo River; ab. 80 mi. (130 km.) long.

2. County in N Mississippi. See table at MISSISSIPPI.

Ya·long \'yä-'lu̇ŋ\ *or W.-G.* **Ya–lung** *or* **Ya·lung** \-'lu̇ŋ\. River, Sichuan prov., S China; rises in A'Nyêmaqên Shan in Qinghai prov. and flows S into the Chang on the Yunnan border W of Huili; 822 mi. (1323 km.) long; unnavigable.

Yal·puh \'yäl-,pu̇k̲\ *or* **Yal·pukh** \-,pu̇k̲\ *or Rom.* **Ial·pug** \'yäl-,püg\. Lake, Odessa subdivision, SW Ukraine; 58 sq. mi. (150 sq. km.); outlet is into Danube River near the delta.

Yal·ta \'yȯl-tə\. Town, S Crimea, Ukraine, 30 mi. (48 km.) E of Sevastopol'; pop. (1991e) 89,000; resort. The suburb of Livadia (*q.v.*) was scene of "Big Three Conference" (U.S. President Franklin Delano Roosevelt, British Prime Minister Sir Winston Churchill and Soviet Premier Joseph Stalin) Feb. 4–11, 1945.

Yal·tins·ka·ya Yay·la \yəl-'tin-skə-yə-'yī-lə\ *or* **Yaila Range** \'yī-lə\. Mountain range along SE coast of Crimean Penin., Crimea, Ukraine, highest peak ab. 5000 ft. (1525 m.).

Ya·lu *or W.-G.* **Ya–lü** \'yä-'lü\ *or Korean* **Am·nok** \'äm-,nək\ *or Jp.* **Oryok·ko** \ȯr-'yō-kō\. River, bet. NE China and North Korea; rises in Changbai Shan on N border of North Korea, flows N, W, and SW to Korea Bay; 501 mi. (806 km.) long. Near its mouth is Dandong, important city of Liaoning prov., China; crossed here by railroad bridge 3000 ft. (910 m.) long. Has many tributaries, esp. in NE China; navigable for most of its course for smaller vessels. As UN-sponsored troops battled toward it 1950, Chinese troops crossed river to meet the threat, thus entering Korean War.

Ya–lung *or* **Yalung.** See YALONG.

Ya·lu·to·rovsk \yə-'lü-tə-,rəfsk\. Town, SW Tyumen' Oblast, W Russia in Asia, on left bank of the Tobol River 50 mi. (80 km.) SE of the city of Tyumen'.

Yal·vaç \yäl-'väch\. Town, N İsparta prov., SW Turkey in Asia, 48 mi. (77 km.) NE of the town of İsparta. Ruins of ancient city of Pisidian Antioch lie nearby; founded c. 290 B.C. by Macedonian general and ruler Seleucus Nicator and made free city by the Romans 189 B.C.; estab. as a Roman colony by Emperor Augustus and became important Roman administrative center in S Galatia; visited by St. Paul on first missionary journey c. 46 A.D.

Yama. See KINGISEPP 2.

Ya·ma·chiche \,ya-mə-'shēsh\. Village, S Quebec, Canada, on N shore of Lake St. Peter; pop. (1991c) 2784.

Ya·ma·ga·ta \'yä-mä-gä-,tä, yä-'mä-gä-\. **1.** Prefecture, N Honshū, Japan; rice, fruit; fishing; oil, natural gas. See table at JAPAN.

---

2. City, its ✻, on Mogami River 30 mi. (48 km.) W of Sendai; pop. (1992e) 250,620; ships rice; large metal-casting industry; university (1949). Former residence of daimyos.

Ya·ma·gu·chi \yä-'mä-gü-chē, ˌyä-mä-'gü-chē\. **1.** Prefecture, W Honshū, Japan; ✻ Yamaguchi; rice; fishing; coal, limestone. See table at JAPAN.

2. City, its ✻, 35 mi. (56 km.) NE of Shimonoseki; pop. (1990p) 129,467. From 14th to 16th cents. under the Ouchi family one of the leading cities of feudal Japan; visited c. 1550 by the Jesuit missionary Francis Xavier; important during Meigi Restoration period 19th cent.

Ya·mal \yə-'mäl\. Peninsula bet. Kara Sea and Gulf of Ob, N Yamalo-Nenets Autonomous Okrug, NW Russia in Asia; 434 mi. (698 km.) long by 93 to 149 mi. (150 to 240 km.) wide.

Ya·ma·lo–Ne·nets Autonomous Okrug \yə-'mä-lə-nə-'nets ... 'ō-ˌkrük\. Administrative subdivision, Tyumen' Oblast, SW Russia in Asia; 289,691 sq. mi. (750,300 sq. km.); pop. (1992e) 479,000; ✻ Salekhard; includes Yamal Penin., region on E coast of Gulf of Ob, and the tundra along the lower Ob' River and to the E of it; estab. 1930.

Ya·ma·na·ka Ko \ˌyä-mä-'nä-kä-'kō\. Lake (ko), S Honshū, Japan; highest of lakes on slopes of Fuji; alt. 3270 ft. (997 m.).

Ya·ma·na·shi \ˌyä-mä-'nä-shē\. Prefecture, Honshū, Japan; ✻ Kōfu; fruit. See table at JAPAN.

Ya·mas·ka \yə-'mas-kə\. River, S Quebec, Canada; flows N to Lake St. Peter; ab. 75 mi. (120 km.) long.

Ya·ma·to \yä-'mä-tō\. **1.** Old province, W cen. Honshū, Japan, now Nara prefecture; in Japanese tradition, the region of the original settlement of the imperial clan; here Jimmu Tennō, considered first emperor of legendary period, began rule 660 B.C.

2. City, Kanagawa prefecture, Honshū, Japan, SW of Tokyo; pop. (1990p) 194,870.

Ya·ma·to–kō·ri·ya·ma \yä-'mä-tō-ˌkō-rē-'yä-mä\. Town, Nara prefecture, Honshū, Japan; pop. (1990p) 92,948.

Yam·bol *also* **Jam·bol** \'yäm-ˌbōl\ *or Turk.* **Yan·bo·li** \ˌyän-bə-'lē\. City, SE Bulgaria, on Tundzha River, 45 mi. (72 km.) E of Stara Zagora; pop. (1991e) 99,225; wine; Roman ruins nearby. At one time under Byzantine rule.

Yamburg. See KINGISEPP 2.

Yamdena. See JAMDENA.

Yamdok Tso *or* **Yamdrok Tso.** See YAMZHO YUMCO.

Ya·me·thin \yə-'mā-t͟hən\. Town, Mandalay division, Myanmar, on Yangon-Mandalay railroad line 105 mi. (169 km.) S of the city of Mandalay; pop. (1983c) 23,055.

Yam·hill \'yam-ˌhil\. County in NW Oregon. See table at OREGON.

Y'A·mi \'yä-mē\. Islet, N Batan Is., N Philippines, 21°07′N, 121°57′E; 1 sq. mi. (2.6 sq. km.); the northernmost point in Philippines.

Ya·mous·sou·kro \ˌyä-mü-'sü-krō\. Town, S cen. Ivory Coast; pop. (1984e) 120,000; site of world's largest Christian church; designated official ✻ 1983; presently shares some of Abidjan's functions.

Yam·pa \'yam-pə\. River, NW Colorado; rises in S Routt co., flows N then W into the Green River near Utah boundary; ab. 250 mi. (400 km.) long.

Yam·say \'yam-zē\. Mountain, E Klamath co., S Oregon; 8196 ft. (2498 m.).

Ya·mu·na \'yə-mə-nə\ *also* **Jum·na** \'jəm-nə\; *anc.* **Jom·a·nes** \'jä-mə-ˌnēz\. River, N cen. India; rises in the Himalayas, flows S and SE into the Ganges at Allahabad, in its upper course forming long section of W boundary of Uttar Pradesh; flows just E of Delhi and past Mathura and Agra; ab. 860 mi. (1385 km.) long; connects with numerous canals; navigable for most of its course for barges and small vessels; chief tributaries, all from S, the Chambal, Sind, Betwa, and Ken.

Yamundá. See NHAMUNDÁ.

Yam·zho Yum·co \'yäm-'jō-'yu̇m-'kō\ *or W.-G.* **Yang–cho–yung Hu** \'yäŋ-'jō-'yu̇ŋ-'hü\; *mostly formerly* **Yamdok Tso** \'yäm-'dȯk-'tsȯ\ *or* **Yam·drok Tso** \-'drȯk-\; *Eng.* **Lake Pal·ti** \'päl-tē\. Lake (*hu, tso, yumco*), SE Tibet, China, ab. 45 mi. (70 km.) S of Lhasa; alt. 13,800 ft. (4206 m.).

Ya·na \'yä-nə\. River, N cen. Sakha Rep., Russia in Asia; rises in Verkhoyansk Mts. and flows N into Laptev Sea; 546 mi. (878 km.) long.

Ya·nam \yə-'näm\ *or* **Ya·naon** \yə-'nau̇n\. Town and seaport, Pondicherry terr., E India, on the N mouth of delta of the Godavari 290 mi. (467 km.) NNE of Madras; pop. (1991p) 20,297; founded by French 1750; captured by British and returned to French in 1817; voted to join India 1954.

Yan·'an \'yan-'än\ *or W.-G.* **Yen–an** *or* **Yen·an** \'yen-'än\; *formerly* **Fu·shih** \'fü-'shir\. Town, cen. N Shaanxi prov., NE cen. China, on S bank of a tributary of the Huang; pop. 1990c 113,277; museum (honoring Mao Tse-tung and Communist Party's years of refuge in Yan'an); famous pagoda. Terminus of the Long March across China (1934–35) and headquarters of the Chinese Communists during the Sino-Japanese War (1937–45) and the subsequent civil war (1945–49).

Yanboli. See YAMBOL.

Yan·bu' al Baḩr \'yan-bu̇k̲-ˌal-'bä-k̲ər\; *often shortened to* **Yan·bu** \'yan-bü\ *or* **Yen·bo** \'yen-ˌbȯ\. Port on the Red Sea, Hejaz, W Saudi Arabia, 185 mi. (298 km.) NNW of Jidda; seaport of Medina; oil pipeline terminus; petrochemicals.

Yan·cey \'yan-sē\. County in W North Carolina. See table at NORTH CAROLINA.

Yan·cey·ville \'yan-sē-ˌvil\. Town, ⊗ of Caswell co., N North Carolina; pop. (1990c) 1973.

Yan·cheng \'yan-'chəŋ\ *or W.-G.* **Yen–ch'eng** *or* **Yen·cheng** \'yen-'chəŋ\. City, N cen. Jiangsu prov., E China, 125 mi. (201 km.) NE of Nanjing; pop. (1990c) 296,831.

Yan·da·bu \ˌyän-də-'bü\ *also* **Yan·da·bo** \-'bō\. Town on the Irrawaddy River, cen. Myanmar, 40 mi. (64 km.) W of Mandalay, in Upper Burma; treaty signed here 1826, by which the king of Ava abandoned his claim to Assam and ceded to the British, Arakan (now Rakhine) and Tenasserim.

Yang·bi \'yäŋ-'bē\ *or W.-G.* **Yang–pi** \-'bē\. River, W Yunnan, S China, flowing S to the Mekong and outlet of Er Hai (lake); 170 mi. (273 km.) long.

Yang–chou. See YANGZHOU.

Yang–cho–yung Hu. See YAMZHO YUMCO.

Yang–ch'üan. See YANGQUAN.

Yan·gi·yul' *or* **Yan·gi·yul** \yəŋ-ˌgē-'yu̇lʸ\. Town, Tashkent subdivision, Uzbekistan, ab. 20 mi. (32 km.) SW of the city of Tashkent; pop. (1991e) 56,900.

Yangku. See TAIYUAN.

Yan·gon \ˌyäŋ-'gōn\ *or* **Yan·gôn** \-'gōn\ *or* **Ran·goon** \ˌraŋ-'gün\. **1.** River, S Myanmar; ab. 25 mi. (40 km.) long; E outlet of the Irrawaddy in the Irrawaddy Delta.

2. Administrative division of Myanmar. See table at MYANMAR.

3. City, ✻ of Myanmar, also ✻ of Yangon div., on Yangon River 21 mi. (34 km.) from its mouth; commercial center and principal seaport of Myanmar; has an extensive network of parks and gardens, notable gold-covered pagoda; several educational institutions.

History: Until 18th cent. site of fishing village around ancient Shwe Dagon Pagoda; present city founded c. 1755 by Burmese King Alaungpaya and developed into port; occupied by British 1824–26 in First Anglo-Burmese War and taken by them 1852 in Second Anglo-Burmese War; became important city under British; severely damaged by earthquake and tidal wave 1930; in WWII occupied by Japanese 1942–45 and suffered very heavy damage; scene of severe repression by military of unarmed antigovernment demonstrators 1988.

Yang–pi. See YANGBI.

Yang·quan \'yäŋ-'chwen\ *or W.-G.* **Yang–ch'üan** \-'chwen\. City, Shaanxi, cen. China, SSW of Yan'an; pop. (1990c) 362,268.

Yangtze. Principal river of China. See CHANG.

Yangtze Gorges. See CHANG GORGES.

Yang·zhou \'yäŋ-'jō\ *or W.-G.* **Yang–chou** \-'jō\; *formerly* **Kiang·tu** \'jyäŋ-'dü\. City, Jiangsu, E China, on Grand Canal (Da Yunhe) 15 mi. (24 km.) N of Zhenjiang and the Chang River; pop. (1990c) 312,892; old walled city, a ✻ under Sui dynasty (581–618 A.D.); long noted as a flourishing commercial and cultural center; Venetian traveler Marco Polo is believed to have been appointed as an official of town 1282–85 by Kublai Khan.

Ya·nis·yar·vi *or Finnish* **Jä·nis·jär·vi** \ˈya-nis-ˌyar-vē\. Lake, SW Karelia Rep., NW Russia in Europe, near Finnish border; formerly in Finland.

Yan·ji \ˈyan-ˈjē\ *or W.-G.* **Yen–chi** \ˈyen-ˈjē\ *or* **Yen·ki** \ˈyen-ˈjē\. Town, SE Jilin prov., NE China, ab. 225 mi. (360 km.) ESE of Changchun; pop. (1990c) 230,892; ✻ of a former province of SE Manchukuo.

Yank·ton \ˈyaŋk-tən\. **1.** County in SE South Dakota. See table at SOUTH DAKOTA.

2. City, its ⊗, on Missouri River 60 mi. (96 km.) SW of Sioux Falls; pop. (1990c) 12,703; Mount Marty Coll. (1936). Settled 1858; was ✻ of Dakota Terr. 1861–83.

Yannina. See IOÁNNINA 2.

Yan·qi \ˈyan-ˈchē\ *or W.-G.* **Yen–ch'i** \ˈyen-ˈchē\ *or* **Yen·ki** \ˈyen-ˈjē\; *formerly* **Ka·ra·shar** \ˌkä-rä-ˈshär\. Town, cen. Xinjiang Uygur, W China, SSW of Ürümqi; a notable oasis in Chinese Turkestan.

Yan·tai \ˈyan-ˈtī\ *or W.-G.* **Yen–t'ai** \ˈyen-ˈtī\ *or* **Che·foo** \ˈjə-ˈfü\. Commercial city, Shandong, NE China, on N coast of E end of Shandong Penin., 112 mi. (180 km.) NE of Qingdao, at E end of Bo Hai (strait); pop. (1990c) 452,127; fishing; fruit; wine and brandy. Made open port 1863; Chefoo Convention, signed 1876, forced China to open additional ports and to improve status of foreigners in China.

Yan·tic \ˈyan-tik\. River, SE Connecticut; formed by confluence of forks in W cen. New London co., flows E to join the Shetucket River at Norwich and form the Thames River; ab. 20 mi. (32 km.) long.

Yan·tra \ˈyän-trä\. River, NE cen. Bulgaria; flows N into Danube River E of Nikopol; 178 mi. (286 km.) long.

Yao \ˈyau̇, ˈyä-ō\. City, Ōsaka prefecture, Honshū, Japan; pop. (1990p) 277,724.

Ya·oun·dé \yau̇n-ˈdā\ *or* **Yaun·de** \yau̇n-ˈdā\. City, ✻ of Cameroon, 125 mi. (201 km.) E of coast of the Gulf of Guinea; pop. (1987e) 649,000; university (1962).

Yap \ˈyap, ˈyäp\ *or* **Uap** \ˈwäp\. Island group, Federated States of Micronesia, in W Caroline Is., W Pacific Ocean ab. 225 mi. (360 km.) NE of Palau; 9°31′N, 138°06′E; 85 sq. mi. (220 sq. km.); pop. (1987c) 6650; comprises four islands close together, of which Yap is largest. One of most fertile of the Carolines; covered with hills and notable for its numerous remains of an early people and for its large pieces of circular stone money.

History: Sold to Germany by Spain 1899; after WWI became subject of dispute bet. Japan and U.S., settled by inclusion in Japanese mandate but with cable rights secured to U.S.; site of Japanese air and naval base WWII; became part of U.S. Trust Terr. of the Pacific Islands 1947; became part of Federated States of Micronesia 1986.

Ya·pen \ˈyä-pən\ *or* **Ja·pen** \ˈyä-\ *or* **Jap·pen** \ˈyä-\. Island in Teluk Cenderawasih, on coast of Irian Jaya, Indonesia, S of Schouten Is.; 936 sq. mi. (2424 sq. km.); has elevated cen. ridge; highest point 4907 ft. (1496 m.).

Yap·hank \ˈyap-ˌhaŋk\. Unincorporated settlement, Suffolk co., SE New York, on Long Island ab. 7 mi. (11 km.) NE of Patchogue; pop. (1990c) 4637. Camp Upton was located nearby (see UPTON 3).

Yapurá. See JAPURÁ.

Ya·qui \yä-ˈkē\. River, Sonora, NW Mexico; rises near U.S. border, flows S and SW into the Gulf of California; ab. 420 mi. (675 km.) long.

Ya·ra·cuy \ˌyä-rä-ˈkwē\. State of Venezuela. See table at VENEZUELA.

Yare. See BROADS, THE.

Ya·ren \ˈyä-ˌren\. District, SW Nauru; seat of government offices.

Ya·ri \ˈyä-rē\ *or* **Ya·ri·ga·ta·ke** \ˌyä-rē-gä-ˈtä-kä\. Peak, cen. Honshū, Japan, on W border of Nagano prefecture; 10,433 ft. (3180 m.).

Yarkand *or Pinyin* **Yarkant.** See SHACHE.

Yar·kant He \ˌyär-ˈkänt-ˈhə\; *traditionally in Eng.* **Yar·kand River** \yär-ˈkand\; *W.-G.* **Yeh–erh–ch'iang Ho** \ˈyə-ˈər-ˈchyäŋ-ˈhə\. River, W Xinjiang Uygur, W China; rises on N slopes of Karakoram Range; flows N and W forming small part of border bet. Jammu and Kashmir, India, and Xinjiang Uygur, China; then N around W end of Kunlun Shan, then N and NE to join the Hotan at ab. 41°N, 81°E and form the Tarim River; ab. 600 mi. (965 km.) long.

Yarlung. See DIHANG.

Yar·mouth \ˈyär-məth\. **1.** Seaport town, Cumberland co., SW Maine, on Casco Bay 10 mi. (16 km.) N of Portland; pop. (1990c) 7862.

2. Town, Barnstable co., SE Massachusetts, 4 mi. (6 km.) E of the town of Barnstable; pop. (1990c) 21,174.

3. County in SW Nova Scotia, Canada. See table at NOVA SCOTIA.

4. Town, ⊗ of Yarmouth co., SW Nova Scotia, Canada, on Atlantic Ocean; pop. (1991c) 7781; dairy products; fish curing; has ferry and cruise-boat connections with Maine; founded 1761.

5. Town, Norfolk, England. See GREAT YARMOUTH.

Yar·mūk \yär-ˈmük\. River, NW Jordan; flows W into the Jordan River just S of the Sea of Galilee and in its course forms a section of the boundary bet. Syria and Jordan; ab. 50 mi. (80 km.) long; a major battle won by Arabs over Byzantines 636 A.D. estab. Arabic dominance in area; scene of fighting 1967 during Arab-Israeli War in which Israel seized some of the area.

Yaroslav. See JAROSŁAW.

Ya·ro·slavl' *or* **Ya·ro·slavl** \ˌyär-ə-ˈsläv-ᵊlʸ\. Industrial city, ✻ of Yaroslavl' Oblast, cen. Russia in Europe, on the Volga ab. 160 mi. (255 km.) NE of Moscow; pop. (1992e) 637,000; 12th cent. monastery (its cathedral built early 16th cent.); many notable churches; 18th cent. theater; university (1970). According to tradition founded 1010 by Yaroslav the Wise; ✻ of independent principality for more than two centuries before passing to Moscow's control 15th cent.; burned by Tatars 1238 and 1332; important textile manufacturing center from early 18th cent.

Yaroslavl' Oblast *or* **Yaroslavl Oblast** \ˈō-bləst, -ˌblast\ *or* **Ya·ro·slav·ska·ya Oblast'** \ˌyär-ə-ˈsläf-skə-yə-ˈō-bləstʸ\. Administrative subdivision of cen. Russia in Europe, part of level plain traversed by the upper Volga; 14,015 sq. mi. (36,299 sq. km.); pop. (1992e) 1,472,000; ✻ Yaroslavl'. In NW is Rybinsk Reservoir (*q.v.*); in S part is Lake Pleshcheyevo. Extensive marshes and considerable forest areas. Produces potatoes and dairy products. In early 15th cent. came under Moscow principality; made separate oblast 1936.

Yaroslavski, Rostov–. See ROSTOV 2.

Yar·ra \ˈyar-ə\; *formerly* **Yarra Yarra** \ˌyar-ə-ˈyar-ə\. River, Victoria, SE Australia; flows W to Port Phillip Bay at Melbourne; 115 mi. (185 km.) long.

Yar·row \ˈyar-ō\ *or* **Yarrow Water.** Small river, Borders region, SE Scotland; flows into the Ettrick and on into the Tweed; celebrated by English poet William Wordsworth in his verse.

Yar·tse·vo \ˈyärt-sə-və\. Town, W cen. Smolensk Oblast, W Russia in Europe, on Moscow-Smolensk R.R. ab. 35 mi. (55 km.) ENE of the city of Smolensk; pop. (1991e) 54,000.

Ya·ru·mal \ˌyä-rü-ˈmäl\. Town, Antioquia dept., NW Colombia, 50 mi. (80 km.) N of Medellín.

Yar·vi·co·ya \ˌyär-vē-ˈkō-yä\. Peak, E Tarapacá region, N Chile; 16,994 ft. (5180 m.).

Ya·sa·wa Group \yä-ˈsä-wä\. Chain of islands and rocky islets extending NNE and SSW for 45 mi. (72 km.) NW of Viti Levu I., W Fiji, SW Pacific Ocean.

Ya·sel·da \ˈyȧ-sil-də\ *or Pol.* **Ja·sioł·da** \yä-ˈsyȯl-də\. River, SW Belarus; flows SE into the Pripyat' River; 134 mi. (216 km.) long.

\ə\ **abut** \ə\ **matches** \ᵊ\ **kitten, Fr table** \ər\ **further** \a\ **ash** \ā\ **easy** \ä\ **cot, cart** \ȧ\ **Fr bac** \au̇\ **out** \b\ **Span Avila** \ch\ **chin** \e\ **bet** \ē\ **easy** \g\ **go** \i\ **hit** \ī\ **ice** \j\ **job** \k\ **Ger ich, Buch** \ⁿ\ **Fr vin** \ŋ\ **sing** \ō\ **go** \ȯ\ **all** \ȯ\ **law** \œ\ **Fr bœuf** \œ̄\ **Fr feu** \ȯi\ **boy** \th\ **thin** \th\ **this** \ü\ **loot** \u̇\ **foot** \ue\ **Ger füllen** \ue\ **Fr rue** \y\ **yet** \ʸ\ **Fr digne** \ˈdēnʸ\, **nuit** \ˈnwʸē\ \yü\ **few** \yu̇\ **fury** \zh\ **vision**

Yas·na·ya Po·lya·na \ˈyäs-nə-yə-pəl-ˈyä-nə\. Village, cen. Tula Oblast, Russia in Europe, ab. 13 mi. (21 km.) S of the city of Tula; birthplace and residence of novelist Count Leo Tolstoy. Tolstoy's home, a museum and national shrine, was plundered by Germans in WWII but subsequently restored.

Yasoof. See YĀSŪJ.

Yass \ˈyas\. Town, SE New South Wales, SE Australia, on tributary of Murrumbidgee River 32 mi. (51 km.) N of Canberra; pop. (1991c) 8780.

Yassy. See IAŞI.

Yā·sūj \yō-ˈsüj\ *also* **Ya·soof** \yə-ˈsüf\. Town, ✱ of Kohkīlūyeh va Boyer Ahmadī-ye Sardīr prov., W cen. Iran; pop. (1986c) 29,991.

Ya·sun, Cape \yä-ˈsün\ *or Turk.* **Yasun Bur·nu** \bu̇r-ˈnü\. Cape on Black Sea, N coast of Turkey in Asia, bet. Samsun and Giresun.

Ya·te·ras \yä-ˈtā-räs\. Municipality, E Cuba, just N of Guantánamo; pop. (1981p) 21,393.

Yates \ˈyāts\. County in W New York. See table at NEW YORK.

Yates Center. City, ⊗ of Woodson co., SE Kansas, NW of Chanute; pop. (1990c) 1815.

Yath·ky·ed Lake \ˌyath-ˈkī-ed\. Lake, S cen. mainland part of Nunavut, Canada; 860 sq. mi. (2227 sq. km.); in course of Kazan River.

Yathrib. See MEDINA 7.

Ya·tsu·shi·ro \yät-ˈsü-shē-ˌrō\. Town, Kumamoto prefecture, W cen. Kyūshū, Japan, on NE coast of Yatsushiro Bay 25 mi. (40 km.) S of the city of Kumamoto; pop. (1990p) 108,135.

Yatsushiro Bay. Inlet of East China Sea, W coast of Kyūshū, Japan; ab. 50 mi. (80 km.) long by 5 to 15 mi. (8 to 24 km.) wide; shut in on W by Amakusa Is.

Yauapery. See JAUAPERI.

Yau·co \ˈyau̇-ˌkō\. Municipality, SW Puerto Rico, W of Ponce; pop. (1990c) 42,058; in sugar-growing area.

Yaunde. See YAOUNDÉ.

Yau·te·pec \ˌyau̇-tā-ˈpek\. Municipality, Morelos state, Mexico, 35 mi. (56 km.) S of Mexico City; munic. pop. (1990p) 60,328.

Yav·a·pai \ˈya-və-ˌpī\. County in cen. Arizona. See table at ARIZONA.

Yavari. See JAVARI.

Ya·vat·mal \ˈyä-vät-ˌmäl, -wät-\ *also* **Ye·ot·mal** \ˈyā-ōt-ˌmäl\. Town, E Maharashtra, E cen. India, 85 mi. (137 km.) SW of Nagpur; pop. (1991p) 108,591; trade center.

Yavero River. See PAUCARTAMBO.

Ya·wa·ta \yä-ˈwä-tä, ˈyä-wä-ˌtä\. **1.** Former settlement, Fukuoka prefecture, Japan. See KITAKYŪSHŪ.
2. City, Kyoto prefecture, Honshū, Japan; pop. (1990p) 75,761.

Ya·wa·ta·ha·ma \yä-ˌwä-tä-ˈhä-mä\. Seaport town, Ehime prefecture, NW Shikoku I., Japan, on Bungo Strait; pop. (1990c) 38,550.

Yawng·hwe \ˈyau̇ŋ-ˈhwā\. **1.** Former state, Myanmar, now part of Shan State; 1389 sq. mi. (3598 sq. km.).
2. Town, its ✱, 110 mi. (177 km.) SE of Mandalay.

Yazd \ˈyazd\ *or* **Yezd** \ˈyezd\. **1.** Province (formerly a governorship) of cen. Iran. See table at IRAN.
2. City, its ✱, 170 mi. (274 km.) SE of Eşfahān; pop. (1986c) 230,483; on main highway from Tehran and Qom to Kermān; distribution point for agricultural products from the area; numerous mosques; city dates from 5th cent.

Yaz·oo \ya-ˈzü\. **1.** Navigable river, W cen. Mississippi; formed by confluence of Tallahatchie and Yalobusha rivers in Leflore co., flows SW into Mississippi River above Vicksburg; 189 mi. (304 km.) long.
2. County in W cen. Mississippi. See table at MISSISSIPPI.

Yazoo City. City, ⊗ of Yazoo co., W cen. Mississippi, 42 mi. (68 km.) N of Jackson; pop. (1990c) 12,427.

Ybbs \ˈips\. River in W Lower Austria, Austria; flows N into Danube River 25 mi. (40 km.) W of Sankt Pölten; 83 mi. (134 km.) long.

Yea·don \ˈyād-ᵊn\. Borough, Delaware co., SE Pennsylvania, just W of Philadelphia; pop. (1990c) 11,980.

Ye·cheng \ˈye-ˈchəŋ\ *or W.-G.* **Yeh–ch'eng** \ˈye-ˈchəŋ\ *or* **Kar·gi·lik** *or* **Kar·gha·lik** \ˌkär-gə-ˈlik\. Town, SW Xinjiang Uygur, W China, SE of Kashi.

Ye·cla \ˈyā-klä\. Commune, Murcia prov., SE Spain, 43 mi. (69 km.) N of the commune of Murcia; pop. (1991c) 27,362; produces wines.

Yeddo *or* **Yedo.** See TOKYO 2.

Ye·fre·mov \yi-ˈfre-məf\. Town, Tula Oblast, SW cen. Russia in Europe, ab. 75 mi. (120 km.) SSE of the city of Tula; pop. (1991e) 56,600.

Ye·gor'·yevsk \yi-ˈgȯrʸ-yifsk\ *or* **Egor·evsk** \yi-\. City, Moscow Oblast, W cen. Russia in Europe, on branch railroad line 60 mi. (97 km.) SE of the city of Moscow; pop. (1991e) 74,200.

Ye·guas, Point \ˈyā-ˌgwäs\. Cape, SE Puerto Rico.

Yeh–ch'eng. See YECHENG.

Yeh–erh–ch'iang Ho. See YARKANT HE.

Yehhsien. See YE XIAN.

Yeisk. See YEYSK.

Yejmiadzin. See ECHMIADZIN.

Ye·ka·te·rin·burg \yi-ˌkä-ti-rən-ˈbu̇rk\; *or* **Eka·te·rin·burg** \yi-ˌkä-\; *1924–91* **Sverd·lovsk** \sfyird-ˈlȯfsk, ˈsverd-ˌ\. City, ✱ of Sverdlovsk Oblast, W Russia in Asia; pop. (1992e) 1,371,000; has long been a mining center; ball bearings; university (1920); railroad junction and a W terminus of the Trans-Siberian R.R.
History: Founded as fortress c. 1721 and named after Empress Catherine I (Russ. *Yekaterina*); place where Czar Nicholas II and his family were held as prisoners by the Bolsheviks after the Revolution of 1917 and executed July 16, 1918; renamed 1924 after Bolshevik leader Yakov Sverdlov; grew during WWII with evacuation of industries to this region; renamed Yekaterinburg 1991 after breakup of U.S.S.R.

Yekaterinenshtadt. See MARKS 2.

Yekaterinodar. See KRASNODAR.

Ye·ke·pa \ye-ˈkā-pə\. City, N Liberia, near the point where Liberia, Guinea, and Ivory Coast borders come together.

Ye·la·bu·ga \yi-ˈlä-bü-gə\ *or* **Ela·bu·ga** \yi-\. Town, N Tatarstan, E cen. Russia in Europe, on Kama River 100 mi. (161 km.) E of Kazan'; pop. (1991e) 60,500; on the Kama 3 mi. (5 km.) above the town, ancient burial mound in which were found artifacts of Stone, Bronze, and Iron ages.

Ye·lets \yi-ˈlyets\ *or* **Elets** \yi-\. City, Lipetsk Oblast, SW cen. Russia in Europe, on the Sosna River ab. 100 mi. (160 km.) E of Orel; pop. (1992e) 121,000; railroad junction bet. Tula and Voronezh. Mentioned in 12th cent. when it was an outlying fort of Ryazan' principality; taken by Turkic ruler Timur 1395 and by Mongols 1414; passed to Moscow 15th cent.; its modern prosperity dates from 17th cent.

Yelgava. See JELGAVA.

Yelizavetgrad. See KIROVOHRAD 2.

Yelizavetpol. See GÄNCÄ.

Ye·li·za·ve·ty, Mys \ˈmis-ˌyi-li-zə-ˈvye-tē\ *or Eng.* **Cape Eliz·a·beth** \i-ˈli-zə-bəth\. N point of Sakhalin I., E Russia in Asia, 54°26′N.

Yell \ˈyel\. **1.** County in W cen. Arkansas. See table at ARKANSAS.
2. One of the Shetland Is., Scotland; 55 sq. mi. (142 sq. km.).

Yel·low \ˈye-lō\. **1.** River, Alabama and Florida; flows SW across border from S Alabama into NW Florida; empties into NE Pensacola Bay; ab. 90 mi. (145 km.) long.
2. River, cen. Wisconsin; rises in E Clark co., flows S into Wisconsin River in E cen. Juneau co.; ab. 75 mi. (120 km.) long.
3. River, NW cen. Wisconsin; rises in cen. Taylor co., flows SW into Lake Wissota near Chippewa Falls; ab. 70 mi. (115 km.) long.
4. River, China. See HUANG.

Yel·low·head Pass \ˈye-lō-ˌhed\. Mountain pass, Canadian Rocky Mts., Canada, on border bet. Jasper National Park, Alberta, and British Columbia; 3717 ft. (1133 m.); traversed by railroad and highway.

Yel·low·knife \ˈye-lō-ˌnīf\. Town, ✱ of Northwest Territories, Canada, in S cen. mainland part and on NW shore of Great Slave Lake at mouth of **Yellowknife River;** pop. (1991c)

15,179; largest town in Northwest Territories; gold mining; became ⁕ 1967.

Yellow Med·i·cine \ˈme-də-sən\. County in SW Minnesota. See table at MINNESOTA.

Yellow Mountain. Peak, Glacier National Park, NW Montana; 8900 ft. (2713 m.).

Yellow River. **1.** Name of several rivers in the U.S. See YELLOW.
2. Name of river in China. See HUANG.

Yellow Sea *or Chin.* **Huang Hai** \ˈhwäŋ-ˈhī\; *mostly formerly* **Hwang Hai** \ˈhwäŋ\. Large inlet of Pacific Ocean, bet. NE China and Korean Penin.; ab. 180,000 sq. mi. (466,200 sq. km.); av. depth 121 ft. (37 m.), max. depth 250 ft. (76 m.); N inlets are Bo Hai and Korea Bay; connects with East China Sea on the S; Shandong Penin. extends into it from W.

Yellow Springs. Village, Greene co., SW Ohio, 8 mi. (13 km.) S of Springfield; pop. (1990c) 3973; Antioch Univ. (1852).

Yel·low·stone \ˈye-lō-ˌstōn\. **1.** River, NW Wyoming and S and E Montana; rises in Park co., Wyoming, flows N through Yellowstone Lake and Yellowstone National Park, continues N across Montana border, then flows E and NE into Missouri River on boundary bet. Montana and North Dakota; 671 mi. (1080 km.) long; navigable for 300 mi. (483 km.) during high water; the Grand Canyon of the Yellowstone is the valley, 2000 ft. (610 m.) wide and 1200 ft. (365 m.) deep, of this river in Yellowstone National Park; the park also includes **Yellowstone Falls,** upper fall 109 ft. (33 m.), lower fall 308 ft. (94 m.).
2. County in S cen. Montana. See table at MONTANA.

Yellowstone Lake. Lake, Yellowstone National Park, NW Wyoming; 137 sq. mi. (355 sq. km.); ab. 20 mi. (32 km.) long; alt. 7735 ft. (2358 m.); largest body of water in North America at so great an altitude. Yellowstone River flows through the lake from S to N.

Yellowstone National Park. See UNITED STATES, *National Parks.*

Yel·low·tail Dam \ˈye-lō-ˌtāl\. Dam in Bighorn River, S Montana; 525 ft. (160 m.) high; completed 1966; forms **Bighorn Lake** (*formerly* **Yellowtail Reservoir**); 71 mi. (114 km.) long in Montana and Wyoming. See UNITED STATES, *Dams and Reservoirs.*

Yellowtail Reservoir. See BIGHORN LAKE.

Yell·ville \ˈyel-ˌvil\. City, ⊗ of Marion co., N Arkansas; pop. (1990c) 1181.

Yel·mo \ˈyel-mō\. Highest peak in Sierra de Segura, SE Spain; 5935 ft. (1809 m.).

Yem·en \ˈye-mən\ *or officially* **Republic of Yemen.** Republic, S Arabian Penin., SW Asia, bounded on N by Saudi Arabia, on E by Oman, on S by the Gulf of Aden, and on W by the Red Sea; 203,849 sq. mi. (527,969 sq. km.); pop. (1994e) 12,961,000; ⁕ Sanaa.

Physical features: From the Gulf of Aden and Red Sea, a narrow coastal plain leads to highlands that cover most of the country; to the N is desert, the S and SW parts of the Rub'al-Khali.

Chief products: Oil, salt; livestock, chickens; fruit; oil products.

Chief settlements: Sanaa, Aden, Ta'izz, Al Ḥudaydah.

History: Home of ancient Minaean, Sabaean, and Himyarite kingdoms; region invaded by Romans first cent. A.D.; in 6th cent. conquered first by Ethiopians and then by Persians; following conversion to Islam 7th cent., ruled at least nominally under caliphate; from 16th cent. through 1918 Ottoman Turks maintained varying degrees of control esp. in the NW section (later Yemen Arab Republic [*q.v.*]); boundary agreement reached 1934 bet. the NW imam-controlled territory, which subsequently evolved into Yemen Arab Republic, and the SE British-controlled territory, which subsequently evolved into People's Democratic Republic of Yemen (*q.v.*); relations bet. two areas were volatile with frequent fighting erupting; regimes within two areas constantly changed hands, but sporadic talks of unification occurred; united as Republic of Yemen May 22, 1990, but country remained unstable; suffered two-month civil war 1994.

Yemen, People's Democratic Republic of *or* **South Yemen** *also* **Southern Yemen.** Former republic, S Arabian Penin., SW Asia, bounded on W by Yemen Arab Republic; ⁕ Aden. Declared independence Nov. 30, 1967 under leadership of the National Liberation Front following collapse of Federation of South Arabia (*q.v.*) and withdrawal of British (in region since 1839 occupation of Aden [*q.v.*]); brief civil war Jan. 1986; united with Yemen Arab Republic 1990 to form Yemen (*q.v.*).

Yemen Arab Republic *or* **North Yemen.** Former republic, SW Arabian Penin., SW Asia, bounded on E by People's Democratic Republic of Yemen; ⁕ Sanaa. Republic formed 1962 bringing to an end religious and political rule of imams of the Zaidi sect (important in region since the 9th cent.); period 1962–70 marked by civil war bet. royalist and republican forces; united with People's Democratic Republic of Yemen 1990 to form Yemen (*q.v.*).

Yen \'yen\. Feudal state of early China under the Chou dynasty (11th–3d cents. B.C.), in the extreme NE. Also so called during the Five Dynasties and Ten Kingdoms period (10th cent. A.D.).

Ye·na·ki·ye·ve *or* **Ye·na·ki·ye·vo** \yi-'nä-kē-yi-və\; *formerly* **Or·dzho·ni·kid·ze** \,är-jə-nē-'kēd-zi\. City, Donets'k subdivision, E Ukraine; pop. (1991e) 120,000; suburb of the city of Donets'k.

Yen–an *or* **Yenan.** See YAN'AN.

Ye·nan·gyaung \'ye-nän-'jaùŋ\. Town, W cen. Myanmar, on the Irrawaddy River 130 mi. (209 km.) SW of Mandalay; extensive oil fields, the most important in Myanmar; in WWII destroyed when abandoned to the Japanese 1942; retaken 1945.

Yenbo. See YANBU' AL BAḪR.

Yen–ch'eng *or* **Yencheng.** See YANCHENG.

Yen–chi. See YANJI.

Yen–ch'i. See YANQI.

Yen·di \'yen-dē\. Town, NE Ghana, ab. 60 mi. (95 km.) E of Tamale; pop. (1984c) 31,633.

Ye·ni·ce \,yə-nē-'je\ *also* **Sa·man·ti** \,sä-män-'tē\. River, the W headstream of the Seyhan River in E cen. Turkey in Asia; rises at N end of Anti-Taurus Mts. and flows S into the Seyhan at ab. 37°30'N; ab. 100 mi. (160 km.) long.

Yenifoça. See FOÇA 1.

Yenikale Strait. See KERCH STRAIT.

Ye·ni·şe·hir \,ye-nē-she-'hir\; *anc.* **Si·ge·um** \sī-'jē-əm\. Village and promontory, Çanakkale prov., NW Turkey in Asia, on coast S of the entrance to the Dardanelles; near the site of ancient Troy.

Ye·ni·sey *or* **Ye·ni·sei** \,yi-ni-'sā\. River, W Russia in Asia; formed by confluence of the Bol'shoy Yenisei (Bei Kem) and the Malyy Yenisey (Khua Kem), with many tributaries rising in the mountains of E Tuva Rep.; flows W, then N through the Sayan Mts. past Minusinsk and Krasnoyarsk through Krasnoyarsk Kray into Yeniseyskiy Zaliv at 71°45'N; 2566 mi. (4129 km.) long. Receives Angara, Stony Tunguska, and Lower Tunguska rivers from the plateau region to the E; its basin has an area of 1,003,474 sq. mi. (2,598,998 sq. km.). At the delta frozen over generally from Oct. to June, at Minusinsk frozen over from Nov. to May.

Ye·ni·seysk *also* **Ye·ni·seisk** \,yi-ni-'sāsk\. Town, W Krasnoyarsk Kray, NW Russia in Asia, on left bank of the Yenisey just below the point where it receives the Angara, ab. 150 mi. (240 km.) N of the town of Krasnoyarsk; has vessel connection with Krasnoyarsk. Founded c. 1618.

Ye·ni·sey·skiy Za·liv \,yi-ni-'sā-skē-zə-'lyēf\ *or* **Ye·ni·sey Bay** \,yi-ni-'sā\. Inlet of Kara Sea, Krasnoyarsk Kray, NW Russia in Asia, on coast of NW Siberia W of Taymyr Penin., 72°30'N, 80°E.

Yenki. 1. Town, Jilin prov., China. See YANJI.
2. Town, Xinjiang Uygur, China. See YANQI.

Yenping. See NANPING.

Yen–t'ai. See YANTAI.

Yeotmal. See YAVATMAL.

Yeo·vil \'yō-,vil\. Town, Somerset, SW England, on the Yeo 36 mi. (58 km.) S of Bristol; pop. (1981p) 27,265; helicopters, leather products, electronics.

Yer·ba Bue·na Island \,yər-bə-'bwā-nə\; *formerly* **Goat Island** \'gōt\. Island, San Francisco Bay, California.

Ye·re·van \,yer-ə-'vän, ,yir-i-\; *mostly formerly* **Eri·van** \,yer-ə-'vän, ,yir-i-\. City, ✻ of Armenia, in W part on Hrazdan River, 110 mi. (177 km.) S of Tbilisi, Republic of Georgia; pop. (1989p) 1,199,000; chemicals, plastics, machinery, textiles. Ruins of 16th cent. Turkish fort; Armenian state museum and theaters, state university (1919) and various cultural institutions.

History: Site fortified since 8th cent. B.C. and part of Armenian kingdom since 6th cent. B.C.; a center of caravan trade across Transcaucasia since ancient times; variously under Romans, Parthians, Arabs, Mongols, Turks, Persians, Georgians, and Russians; fell to Russians 1827; made ✻ of Armenia 1920.

Yer·ing·ton \'yer-iŋ-tən\. City, ⊗ of Lyon co., W Nevada, 30 mi. (48 km.) ESE of Carson City; pop. (1990c) 2367.

Yerushalayim. See JERUSALEM 3.

Ye·şil·ir·mak \yə-'shē-lir-'mäk\; *anc.* **Iris** \'ī-rəs\. River, chiefly in Tokat and Amasya provs., N Turkey in Asia; rises in Akdağ range W of Sivas, flows generally N into Black Sea, with wide delta just E of Samsun; receives the Kelkit from the E; 291 mi. (468 km.) long.

Ye·şil·köy \,ye-shēl-'kòi\ *or Ital.* **San Ste·fa·no** \sän-'ste-fä-,nō\. Village, İstanbul prov., Turkey in Europe, on the Sea of Marmara ab. 7 mi. (11 km.) W of İstanbul. Treaty signed here Mar. 3, 1878 ending the Russo-Turkish War; its terms were: Romania, Serbia, and Montenegro recognized as independent; Bulgaria made a principality; part of Armenia ceded to Russia by the Ottomans, an indemnity paid, and reforms promised; modified by Treaty of Berlin July 13, 1878.

Yeso. See HOKKAIDŌ.

Yes·sen·tu·ki \,yə-sən-tù-'kē\ *also* **Es·sen·tu·ki** \,yə-\. Town, Stavropol' Kray, S Russia in Europe, on N slopes of Caucasus Mts. 10 mi. (16 km.) W of Pyatigorsk; pop. (1991e) 95,500.

Yetorofu. See ITURUP.

Yeu, Île d' \ēl-'dyœ\. Island in Bay of Biscay off coast of Vendée dept., W France; 6 mi. (10 km.) long by 2 mi. (3 km.) wide; Philippe Pétain, premier of Fascist-dominated Vichy government during WWII, imprisoned here until his death 1951.

Yev·pa·to·ri·ya \,yef-pə-'tōr-ē-yə\ *or* **Ev·pa·to·ria** \,yef-\ *or* **Eu·pa·to·ria** \,ef-\. Town and seaport, W coast of Crimea, Ukraine, ab. 45 mi. (70 km.) NW of Simferopol'; pop. (1991e) 111,000; fishing port and resort; taken from Turks by Russians 1783; landing place for Allied armies in Crimean War 1854.

Yevreyskaya Autonomous Oblast. See JEWISH AUTONOMOUS OBLAST.

Ye Xian \'yə-'shyen\ *or W.-G.* **Yeh·hsien** \'yə-'shyen\ *or* **I–hsien** \'ē-\; *formerly* **Lai·chow** \'lī-'jō\. City, N Shandong prov., NE China, near Bo Hai 80 mi. (129 km.) NNW of Qingdao.

Yeysk *also* **Yeisk** \'yāsk\. City, Krasnodar Kray, S Russia in Europe, on S side of Gulf of Taganrog; pop. (1991e) 86,300.

Yezd. See YAZD.

Yezhovo–Cherkessk. See CHERKESSK.

Yezo. See HOKKAIDŌ.

Yi \'yē\. River, cen. Uruguay; flows W into Río Negro; 120 mi. (193 km.) long.

Yi·bin \'ē-'bin\ *or W.-G.* **I–pin** \'ē-'bin\; *formerly* **Su·chow** \'sü-'jō\ *or* **Hsü–chau** \'shü-'jaù\ *or* **Sui·fu** \'swē-'fü\. Commercial city, S Sichuan prov., S cen. China, on the Chang at its junction with the Min, 140 mi. (225 km.) SW of Chongqing; pop. (1990c) 805,695.

Yi·chang \'ē-'chäŋ\ *or W.-G.* **I–ch'ang** \'ē-'chäŋ\. Walled city, S Hubei prov., E cen. China, at head of navigation of the Chang 1000 mi. (1610 km.) from the East China Sea; pop. (1990c) 371,601; food products; made treaty port by Chefoo Convention 1876; transshipment point for goods to and from Sichuan through Chang Gorges (*q.v.*).

Yi·chun \'ē-'chùn\ *or W.-G.* **I–ch'un** \'ē-'chùn\. Town, Heilongjiang prov., NE China, ab. 90 mi. (145 km.) NW of Jiamusi; pop. (1990c) 795,789.

Yi·lan \'ē-'len\ *or W.-G.* **I–lan** \'ē-'len\; *formerly* **San·hsing** \'sän-'shiŋ\ *or* **San·sing** \-'siŋ\. City, Heilongjiang prov., NE China, on right bank of Songhua River where it is joined by the Mudan, ab. 190 mi. (305 km.) NE of Harbin; wood products.

Yıldız. See ISTRANCA.

Yi·le·hu·li Shan \'ē-'lə-'hü-'lē-'shän\ *or W.-G.* **I–le–hu–li Shan** \'ē-\; *mostly formerly* **Il·khu·ri Alin** \,ēl-k̲ù-'rē-ä-'lēn\. Mountain range, Heilongjiang prov., NE China, connecting N ends of Da Hinggan Ling and Xiao Hinggan Ling; forms a watershed bet. Nen and Huma rivers.

Yin·chuan *or W.-G.* **Yin–ch'uan** \'yin-'chwän\. Town, ✻ of Ningxia Huizu, N cen. China; pop. (1990c) 356,652.

Ying·kou *or W.-G.* **Ying–k'ou** \ˈyiŋ-ˈkō\. **1.** *also* **Ying·kow** \ˈyiŋ-ˈkō\; *formerly* **New·chwang** *or* **Niu·chwang** \ˈnyü-ˈchwäŋ\. City, S Liaoning prov., NE China, on left bank of Liao ab. 13 mi. (21 km.) from its mouth, 120 mi. (193 km.) N of Dalian; pop. (1990c) 421,589. Became open treaty port mid-19th cent. instead of older inland Newchwang (by which name Yingkou was also known) because of its superior location; chief port of Manchuria until early 20th cent., was main export town for various goods; in 20th cent. lost trade in competition with Dalian.

2. *or locally* **Da·shi·qiao;** *W.-G.* **Ta–shih–ch'iao** *or* **Ta·shih·kiao** *all* ˈdä-ˈshir-ˈchyau̇\. Town, S Liaoning prov., NE China, ab. 95 mi. (153 km.) SSW of Shenyang; railroad junction point for city of Yingkou, 14 mi. (23 km.) distant.

Yingkow. See YINGKOU 1.

Yi·ning \ˈē-ˈniŋ\ *or* **Gul·ja** \ˈgu̇l-jə\; *W.-G.* **I–ning** \ˈē-ˈniŋ\ *or* **Kul·dja** *or* **Kul·ja** \ˈku̇l-jə\; *formerly* **Ning·yuan** \ˈniŋ-ˈywen\. Town, NW Xinjiang Uygur, W China, 320 mi. (515 km.) W of Ürümqi; in mountain region bet. ranges of the Tian Shan; pop. (1990c) 177,193; formerly an important trade center and still connected by routes to Issyk-Kul, Kyrgyzstan and Alma-Ata, Kazakhstan. Seized by Russia in 1871, but restored by treaty 1881.

Yioúra. See GYAROS.

Yí·thi·on \ˈyē-thē-ˌȯn\ *or angl.* **Gyth·i·um** \ˈji-thē-əm\. Seaport town, S Laconia department, SE Peloponnese, Greece, near head of Gulf of Laconia; important ancient port and arsenal of Sparta.

Yi·xing \ˈē-ˈshiŋ\ *or W.-G.* **I–hsing** \ˈē-ˈshiŋ\ *also* **Ihing** \ˈē-ˈhiŋ\. Town, S Jiangsu prov., E China, near W shore of Tai Hu (lake) 28 mi. (45 km.) S of Changzhou; noted for a usu. dark red stoneware (boccaro) introduced into Europe in 17th cent.

Yizréel. See JEZREEL.

Yizre'el, 'Emeq. See ESDRAELON, PLAIN OF.

Y Mynydd Du. See BLACK MOUNTAINS 3.

Yngavi. See INGAVÍ.

Yoa·kum \ˈyō-kəm\. **1.** County in NW Texas. See table at TEXAS.

2. City, De Witt and Lavaca cos., S Texas, 36 mi. (58 km.) N of Victoria; pop. (1990c) 5611.

Yo·be \ˈyō-bā\. **1.** River, NE Nigeria; formed by confluence of Hadejia and another headstream; flows E to NW Lake Chad; ab. 100 mi. (160 km.) long.

2. State of Nigeria. See table at NIGERIA.

Yochow. See YUEYANG.

Yo·do \ˈyō-dō\. **1.** Lake, Kyōto prefecture, W cen. Honshū, Japan, just S of the city of Kyōto, near junction of Uji and Hozu rivers which form the Yodo River.

2. *or Jp.* **Yo·do·ga·wa** \ˌyō-dō-ˈgä-wä\. River (*gawa*), W cen. Honshū, Japan; formed by the Uji and Hozu in S Kyōto prefecture S of Kyōto, flows S into Ōsaka Bay at Ōsaka through two mouths, the Ajikawa and the Kizugawa. See UJI 1.

Yog Point \ˈyōg\. Point at N tip of Catanduanes I., E Philippines, 14°06′N, 124°12′E.

Yog·ya·kar·ta \ˌyä-gyə-ˈkär-tə\ *or* **Jog·ja·kar·ta** \ˌjä-gyə-, ˌjäg-jə-\ *also* **Jok·ja·kar·ta** \ˌjä-kyə-, ˌjäk-jə-\ *or* **Djok·ja·kar·ta** \ˌjä-kyə-, ˌjäk-jə-\. **1.** Special autonomous district, Java, Indonesia; 1193 sq. mi. (3090 sq. km.). See table at INDONESIA. Part of a Buddhist kingdom 7th cent. A.D.; ruled by Hindus 13th cent.; a sultanate in 17th cent., area resisted Dutch incursions; after falling successively to French, then British early 19th cent., area came under Dutch control; after Japanese occupation during WWII, area became center of Indonesian independence movement.

2. City, its ✻, at foot of Gunung Merapi 175 mi. (282 km.) WSW of Surabaya; pop. (1990c) 412,392; palace built by sultans 17th–18th cent. (part of which now houses university); colleges; museums; nearby are Buddhist shrine of Borobudur (*q.v.*) and Hindu Prambanan (*q.v.*). Political center during Indonesians' move for independence 1946–50.

Yo·ho \ˈyō-hō\. River through scenic valley, Yoho National Park, SE British Columbia, Canada; joins Kicking Horse River to flow into the Columbia; contains Takkakaw waterfall.

Yoho National Park. See CANADA, *National Parks.*

Yo·joa, Lake \yō-ˈhō-ä\. Lake, W cen. Honduras; 25 mi. (40 km.) long, ab. 6 mi. (10 km.) wide (largest lake in Honduras); affords water communication via the Blanco River and the Ulúa River with the seaport town of Puerto Cortés.

Yok·kai·chi \yō-ˈkī-chē\. City, Mie prefecture, S Honshū, Japan, on NW shore of Ise Bay 25 mi. (40 km.) SW of Nagoya; pop. (1990p) 274,184; textiles; in WWII bombed by U.S. 1945.

Yo·ko·ha·ma \ˌyō-kō-ˈhä-mä\. Seaport city, ✻ of Kanagawa prefecture, SE Honshū, Japan, on W shore of Tokyo Bay, 18 mi. (29 km.) S of Tokyo; pop. (1990p) 3,220,350; one of the principal Japanese seaports and part of the Tokyo urban-industrial region, producing textiles (incl. silk) and chemicals; shipyards, oil refineries; Yokohama City Univ. (1928), Yokohama National Univ. (1949).

History: A fishing village when visited by American naval officer Matthew Perry 1854 to negotiate American-Japanese trading possibilities; opened for foreign settlement and trade 1859; almost entirely destroyed by earthquake and fire 1923; rebuilt and modernized. Largely destroyed by U.S. bombing during WWII 1945 but since rebuilt.

Yo·ko·su·ka \yō-ˈkō-sə̇-kä\. Seaport city, Kanagawa prefecture, SE Honshū, Japan, on Tokyo Bay, 12 mi. (19 km.) S of Yokohama; pop. (1990p) 433,361; shipbuilding. A fishing village until the establishment in the 2d half of the 19th cent. of one of the principal Japanese naval bases and shipyards; largely destroyed by U.S. bombing during WWII 1945 but since rebuilt.

Yo·la \ˈyō-lä\. Town, ✻ of Adamawa state, E Nigeria, on the upper Benue River near Cameroon border; ab. 480 mi. (770 km.) by river above Lokoja and reached by vessels of light draft in flood season; a former Fulani ✻.

Yo·lo \ˈyō-lō\. County in N cen. California. See table at CALIFORNIA.

Yom \ˈyəm, ˈyäm\. River, NW Thailand; flows S from mountains on N border to join the Nan just above its confluence with the Ping; 345 mi. (555 km.).

Yo·me–Ji·ma \ˌyō-mā-ˈjē-mä, ˈyō-mā-jē-ˌmä\. One of the Bonin Is., Japan.

Yo·na·ba·ru \ˌyō-nä-ˈbä-rü\. Locality on E coast of Okinawa I., Ryukyu Is., Japan, at S end across from Naha on S shore of Nakagusuku Bay.

Yo·na·go \yō-ˈnä-gō\. City, Tottori prefecture, W Honshū, Japan; pop. (1990p) 131,453; a rail center N of Okayama on Sea of Japan.

Yo·ne·za·wa \yō-ˈnā-zä-ˌwä, ˌyō-nā-ˈzä-wä\. City, Yamagata prefecture, N Honshū, Japan, 55 mi. (88 km.) E of Niigata; pop. (1990p) 94,763; long noted for weaving of silken fabrics.

Yong·ding \ˈyu̇ŋ-ˈdiŋ\ *or W.-G.* **Yung–ting** \ˈyu̇ŋ-ˈdiŋ\; *formerly* **Hun** \ˈhən, ˈhu̇n\. River, China; rises in N Shanxi prov. and flows generally E and SE through Hebei prov. and Beijing municipality and into the Bai at Tianjin; ab. 300 mi. (485 km.) long.

Yon·kers \ˈyäŋ-kərz\. City, Westchester co., SE New York, on Hudson River just N of Greater New York; center of city is ab. 15 mi. (24 km.) N of S end of Manhattan I.; pop. (1990c) 188,082; suburb of New York City; diversified industry; St. Joseph's Seminary (1839). Formerly the site of an American Indian village, was part of purchase made by Dutch West India Company from Indians 1639; included in grant of land made 1646 to "Jonker" or "Jonkheer" Adriaen Van der Donck; acquired in the 2d half of the 17th cent. by Frederick Philipse, whose great-grandson lost the manor in 1779 for being a Loyalist sympathizer in the Revolutionary War; incorp. as village 1855, chartered as city 1872.

Yonne \ˈyȯn\. **1.** River, cen. France; flows N out of Nièvre dept. into Seine River at Montereau-faut-Yonne; 182 mi. (293 km.) long.

2. Department of NE cen. France. See table at FRANCE.

Yo·no \ˈyō-ˌnō\. City, Saitama prefecture, Honshū, Japan, 17 mi. (27 km.) NNW of Tokyo; pop. (1990p) 79,058.

Yo·pal \yō-ˈpäl\. Town, ✻ of Casanare dept., cen. Colombia.

Yor·ba Lin·da \ˌyōr-bə-ˈlin-də\. City, Orange co., SW California, E of Fullerton; pop. (1990c) 52,422. Birthplace and burial place of Richard M. Nixon, 37th president of the U.S. City has more than quadrupled in size since 1970.

York \ˈyȯrk\. **1.** *or* **York River.** Estuary of Chesapeake Bay, E Virginia; formed by confluence of Pamunkey and Mattaponi rivers at West Point; ab. 40 mi. (64 km.) long.

2. Name of counties in five states of the U.S. See tables at MAINE, NEBRASKA, PENNSYLVANIA, SOUTH CAROLINA, VIRGINIA.

3. City, Sumter co., W Alabama, 5 mi. (8 km.) E of Mississippi border and 18 mi. (29 km.) W of Tombigbee River; pop. (1990c) 3160.

4. Town, York co., SW Maine, on Atlantic Ocean 25 mi. (40 km.) SSW of Biddeford; pop. (1990c) 9818. One of first English cities in North America to receive a charter (1641), later reduced to town status. Includes the fashionable summer resort of **York Harbor.**

5. City, ⊗ of York co., SE Nebraska, 41 mi. (66 km.) E of Grand Island; pop. (1990c) 7884; York Coll. (1890).

6. City, ⊗ of York co., S Pennsylvania, 23 mi. (37 km.) S of Harrisburg; pop. (1990c) 42,192; historical society museum; York Coll. of Pennsylvania (1787). Laid out 1741; ✻ of American colonies during British occupation of Philadelphia 1777–78; chartered as borough 1787; during Civil War briefly occupied June 1863 by Confederate forces; incorp. as city 1887.

7. City, ⊗ of York co., N South Carolina, 13 mi. (21 km.) WNW of Rock Hill; pop. (1990c) 6709.

8. County in SW New Brunswick, Canada. See table at NEW BRUNSWICK.

9. Municipal region in SE Ontario, Canada. See table at ONTARIO.

10. Former name of Toronto, Ontario, Canada. See TORONTO 3.

11. City, Toronto metropolitan municipality, SE Ontario, Canada; pop. (1991c) 140,525.

12. Former county in England. See YORKSHIRE.

13. *anc.* **Ebo·ra·cum** \i-ˈbȯr-ə-kəm, -ˈbär-\ *or* **Ebu·ra·cum** \i-ˈbyu̇r-ə-kəm\. City, North Yorkshire, N England, at confluence of Foss and Ouse rivers 20 mi. (32 km.) ENE of Leeds; pop. (1991p) 100,600; railroad center; produces chocolate products, scientific instruments, railway cars; 13th–15th cent. cathedral (York Minster) with notable stained glass; 14th cent. walls; National Railway Museum; Univ. of York (1963).

History: Successively a Celtic, Roman, Anglo-Saxon, Danish, and Norman settlement; Constantine I proclaimed Roman emperor here 306 A.D.; prosperous wool-trading town in Middle Ages; scene of presentation of the 48 plays of the York Cycle, one of four collections of English mystery plays (see CHESTER 10, COVENTRY 3, WAKEFIELD 4).

York, Cape. **1.** N point of Cape York Penin., Queensland, Australia, on E side of Gulf of Carpentaria, 10°42′S, 142°31′E; extends into Torres Strait.

2. *or* **Kap York** \ˈkäp-ˈyȯrk\. Point, SW Hayes Penin., NW Greenland, on N shore of Baffin Bay, 75°55′N, 66°27′W. Station here used by polar explorers Robert Peary and Robert Bartlett. Noted for its large iron meteorites, one of which (weighing 100 tons or 91 metric tons) was brought by Peary to American Natural History Museum in New York. Monument erected here 1932 to Peary.

Yorke Peninsula \ˈyȯrk\ *also* **Yorke's Peninsula** \ˈyȯrks\. Peninsula, SE South Australia, Australia, bet. Spencer Gulf on W and Gulf St. Vincent on E; ab. 100 mi. (160 km.) long.

York·shire \ˈyȯrk-ˌshir, -shər\ *or* **York.** Former county, N England; included three administrative counties, North Riding (⊗ Northallerton), East Riding (⊗ Beverley), West Riding (⊗ Wakefield), and the City of York, which was a county of itself, outside the ridings. Rivers included Ouse, Swale, Wharfe, Aire, Derwent; agriculture, fishing, and manufacturing. Chief settlements included Leeds, Sheffield, Hull, Bradford, Wakefield, Middlesbrough, Rotherham.

Yorkshire Dales National Park. Park, North Yorkshire and Cumbria, N England, in the Pennines.

Yorkshire Wolds. See WOLDS, THE.

York·ton \ˈyȯrk-tən\. City, SE Saskatchewan, Canada, 110 mi. (177 km.) ENE of Regina; pop. (1991c) 15,315.

York·town \ˈyȯrk-ˌtau̇n\. **1.** Town, Delaware co., Indiana; pop. (1990c) 4106.

2. Town, ⊗ of York co., SE Virginia, on York River 20 mi. (32 km.) N of Newport News; in Colonial National Historical Park; scene in 1781 of siege of British forces under Gen. Charles Cornwallis by Gen. George Washington and Comte de Rochambeau in Revolution and of surrender of Cornwallis; besieged by Union forces under Gen. George McClellan in Civil War and evacuated 1862.

York·ville \ˈyȯrk-ˌvil\. **1.** City, ⊗ of Kendall co., NE Illinois; pop. (1990c) 3925.

2. Village, Oneida co., cen. New York, on Mohawk River 3 mi. (5 km.) WNW of Utica; pop. (1990c) 2972.

Yo·ro \ˈyō-rō\. **1.** Department of N Honduras. See table at HONDURAS.

2. Town, its ✻; pop. (1988p) 9231.

Yor·tan Te·pe \ˈyȯr-ˌtän-te-ˈpā\. Archaeological site, W Turkey in Asia; contains ruins of an ancient city of W Lydia, ESE of Pergamum.

Yor·u·ba·land \ˈyȯr-u̇-bə-ˌland\. Name for area of W Africa, in present-day Nigeria; once comprised several kingdoms headed by individual Yoruba kings; flourished esp. before 18th cent.; among cities with historical Yoruba background are Cyo, Ife, and Oshogbo.

Yo·sem·i·te Falls \yō-ˈse-mə-tē\. Two falls, Yosemite National Park, E cen. California; upper 1430 ft. (436 m.), lower 320 ft. (98 m.), total drop incl. a series of cascades 2425 ft. (739 m.).

Yosemite National Park. See UNITED STATES, *National Parks.*

Yosemite Valley. Valley of the upper Merced River, cen. California, in S Yosemite National Park; ab. 7 mi. (11 km.) long; valley floor ab. 4000 ft. (1220 m.) above sea level, walls 3000 to 4000 ft. (910 to 1220 m.) high; many waterfalls.

Yo·shi·no \ˈyō-shē-ˌnō\. River, NE Shikoku, Japan; flows E into Kii Channel at Tokushima; 146 mi. (235 km.) long.

Yosh·kar–Ola *also* **Iosh·kar Ola** \yəsh-ˈkär-ə-ˈlä\. Town, ✻ of Mari El Rep., E Russia in Europe, ab. 80 mi. (130 km.) NW of Kazan'; pop. (1992e) 249,000.

Yos Su·dar·so, Te·luk *or* **Teluk Jos Sudarso** \tə-ˈlu̇k-ˈyōs-sü-ˈdär-sō\; *mostly formerly* **Teluk Hum·boldt** *or Eng.* **Humboldt Bay** \ˈhəm-ˌbōlt\. Bay, NE coast of Irian Jaya, New Guinea, Indonesia.

Yŏ·su \ˈyə-ˈsü\. Town, South Chŏlla prov., South Korea, ab. 50 mi. (80 km.) SE of Kwangju; pop. (1985c) 171,933.

Youghal \ˈyȯl\. Commercial seaport, E co. Cork, SW Ireland, on **Youghal Bay,** estuary of Blackwater River; pop. (1986c) 5706; resort. Granted charter by King John of England early 13th cent.; Sir Walter Raleigh was mayor briefly 16th cent. and is said to have planted the first potato here.

Yough·io·ghe·ny \ˌyä-kə-ˈgā-nē\. River, NW Maryland and SW Pennsylvania; flows N through NW Maryland into Pennsylvania, and NW into Monongahela River at McKeesport; ab. 150 mi. (240 km.) long; navigable for 9 mi. (14 km.).

Young \ˈyəŋ\. County in N Texas. See table at TEXAS.

Young Island. One of the Balleny Is., Antarctica; ab. 19 mi. (31 km.) long by 5 mi. (8 km.) wide; rises to a plateau ab. 4000 ft. (1220 m.).

Youngs·town \ˈyəŋz-ˌtau̇n\. **1.** Town, Maricopa co., SW cen. Arizona, W of Phoenix; pop. (1990c) 2542.

2. City, ⊗ of Mahoning co., Mahoning and Trumbull cos., NE Ohio, on Mahoning River 43 mi. (69 km.) E of Akron; pop. (1990c) 95,732; historically a major center of the steel industry; now has diversified industry; Youngstown State Univ. (1908). Town dates from 1797; iron manufacturing began early 19th cent. and progressively expanded throughout 19th and early 20th cents.

Young·wood \ˈyəŋ-ˌwu̇d\. Borough, Westmoreland co., SW Pennsylvania; pop. (1990c) 3372.

Yount·ville \ˈyau̇nt-ˌvil\. Town, Napa co., W California, NNW of the city of Napa; pop. (1990c) 3259.

Yous·sou·fia \yu̇-ˈsü-fē-ə\; *formerly* **Lou·is Gen·til** \ˌlwē-zhäⁿ-ˈtē\. Town, W cen. Morocco, ENE of Safi; junction point on railroad line connecting the port of Safi with Casablanca and Marrakech; phosphate mines in region.

Youth, Isle of. See ISLA DE LA JUVENTUD 1.

Yoz·gat \yȯz-ˈgät\. **1.** Province of Turkey in Asia. See table at TURKEY.

2. Town, its ✱, 100 mi. (161 km.) E of Ankara; pop. (1990p) 51,360.

Ypa·ca·raí \ˌē-pä-ˈkä-rī\. Town, Central dept., S Paraguay, ab. 160 mi. (255 km.) ESE of Asunción; pop. (1992p) 7098.

Ypacaraí, Lake. Lake, S cen. Paraguay, near Asunción; pleasure resort.

Ypi·ran·ga *or* **Ipi·ran·ga** \ˌē-pē-ˈrȧŋ-gə\. Plain, São Paulo state, SE Brazil, near the city of São Paulo; site where independence of Brazil from Portugal was declared Sept. 7, 1822 by regent Dom Pedro, who was crowned emperor of Brazil as Pedro I the following month.

Ypoá, Lake \ˌē-pō-ˈwä\. Lake, S Paraguay; ab. 100 sq. mi.; (260 sq. km.); navigable for small boats.

Ypres. See IEPER.

Yp·si·lan·ti \ˌip-sə-ˈlan-tē\. City, Washtenaw co., SE Michigan, 8 mi. (13 km.) SE of Ann Arbor; pop. (1990c) 24,846; diversified industry; Eastern Michigan Univ. (1849), Cleary Coll. (1883).

Yp·si·lon Mountain \ˈip-sə-ˌlän\. Peak, Larimer co., N Colorado; 13,507 ft. (4117 m.).

Yre·ka \wī-ˈrē-kə\ *also* **Yreka City.** City, ⊗ of Siskiyou co., N California; pop. (1990c) 6948.

Yr Wyddfa. See SNOWDON.

Ysabel. See SANTA ISABEL 4.

Ysa·bel Channel \ˈi-zə-ˌbel\. Passage, N Bismarck Archipelago, Papua New Guinea, bet. New Hanover I. and the St. Matthias Group, connecting Pacific Ocean with Bismarck Sea.

Yser \ē-ˈzer\. River, N France and Belgium; flows into North Sea near Nieuwpoort, Belgium; 48 mi. (77 km.) long. During WWI German advance was halted at the Yser Oct. 1914.

Ys·le·ta \ēs-ˈle-tə\. Neighborhood of El Paso, Texas; preceded the city of El Paso and is thought to be the oldest settlement in present-day Texas; founded 1682.

Yssel. See IJSSEL.

Yssel, Lake. See IJSSELMEER.

Ystad \ˈᵫ-ˌstäd\. Seaport, Malmöhus prov., SW Sweden, on the Baltic Sea; pop. (1989c) 24,761.

Ystrad Fflur. See STRATA FLORIDA.

Ystradyfodwg. See RHONDDA.

Yst·wyth \ˈist-with, ˈəst-\. Small river, cen. Wales; flows W into cen. Cardigan Bay at Aberystwyth.

Ysyk Köl. See ISSYK-KUL.

Ythan \ˈī-thən\. River, NE Scotland; flows SE in Grampian region and empties into North Sea ab. 12 mi. (19 km.) N of Aberdeen; 35 mi. (56 km.) long.

Yuan *or W.-G.* **Yüan** \ˈywen, ˈywän\. **1.** River, China. See RED 4.

2. River, SE cen. China; rises in Guizhou, flows NE in Hunan prov. to Dongting Hu (lake); 537 mi. (864 km.) long; navigable for most of its course.

Yuanchow. See ZHIJIANG.

Yu·ba \ˈyü-bə\. **1.** River, N cen. California; its branches from Sierra and Nevada cos. join in Yuba co., then flow SW into Sacramento River N of Sacramento.

2. County in N cen. California. See table at CALIFORNIA.

Yuba City. City, ⊗ of Sutter co., N cen. California, on Feather River 42 mi. (68 km.) N of Sacramento; pop. (1990c) 27,437; packs and ships agricultural products.

Yu·cai·pa \yü-ˈkī-pə\. City, San Bernardino co., California, 20 mi. (32 km.) E of Riverside; pop. (1990c) 32,824.

Yu·ca·ma·ni \ˌyü-kä-ˈmä-nē\. Peak in the Andes in S Peru; 17,860 ft. (5444 m.).

Yu·ca·tán \ˌyü-kä-ˈtän, -ˈtan\. **1.** Peninsula, comprising the states of Campeche, Yucatán, and Quintana Roo in SE Mexico, and Belize and the N section of Guatemala in Central America; separates Gulf of Mexico from Caribbean Sea; its NE point, Cape Catoche, extends into Yucatán Channel; Bay of Campeche to the W and Cozumel I. off NE coast. Rich in historical associations; seat of Mayan civilization (pre-Classic period through c. 250 A.D., Classic period c. 250–900, post-Classic period 900 through Spanish conquest 16th cent.); came under Toltec influence c. 1000. Many notable ruins of cities, temples, pyramids, esp. Chichén Itzá, Uaxactún, and Uxmal (*qq.v.*).

2. State, N Yucatán Penin., SE Mexico. See table at MEXICO.

Yucatán Channel. Channel off coast of Mexico, bet. W end of Cuba and Yucatán Penin., connecting the Caribbean Sea with the Gulf of Mexico.

Yuc·ca House National Monument \ˈyə-kə\. See UNITED STATES, *National Monuments.*

Yüeh \ˈywā\. Ancient state, modern Zhejiang prov., China; flourished mid-first millennium B.C.

Yue·yang \ˈywā-ˈyäŋ\ *or W.-G.* **Yüeh–yang** \ˈywā-\; *formerly* **Yo·chow** \ˈyō-ˈjō\. City, NE Hunan, SE China, on Dongting Hu (lake) SW of Wuhan; pop. (1990c) 302,800; exports cotton and timber; the site has been settled for more than 2000 years.

Yug \ˈyük\. River, E Vologda Oblast, cen. Russia in Europe; flows N to unite with the Sukhona and form the Northern Dvina just above Veliki Ustyug; 305 mi. (491 km.) long.

Yu·gor·skiy *or* **Yo·gor·ski** \yu̇-ˈgȯr-skē\; *formerly* **Pai Khoi** \ˈpī-ˈkȯi\. Peninsula, E Nenets Autonomous Okrug, N Russia in Europe, bet. Kara Sea and Barents Sea.

Yu·go·sla·via \ˌyü-gō-ˈslä-ve-ə\ *also* **Ju·go·sla·via** \ˌyü-gō-\ *or Serb.* **Ju·go·sla·vi·ja** \yü-ˈgō-ˌslä-vē-ä\; *officially* **Sa·vez·na Re·pu·bli·ka Jugoslavija** \ˈsä-vez-nä-rā-ˈpü-blē-kä\ *or Eng.* **Federal Republic of Yugoslavia;** *formerly* **Kingdom of the Serbs, Cro·ats, and Slo·venes** \ˈsərbz, ˈkrō-ˌats … ˈslō-ˌvēnz; ˈkrōts\. Republic, SE Europe, bounded on N by Hungary and Romania, on E by Romania and Bulgaria, on S by Republic of Macedonia and Albania, on SW by the Adriatic Sea, and on W by Bosnia and Herzegovina and Croatia; 39,449 sq. mi. (102,173 sq. km.); pop. (1993e) 10,561,000; ✱ Belgrade.

Physical features: Vojvodina autonomous prov. lies in an extensive plain watered by the Danube, Timiş, and Tisza rivers; the S two thirds of the country is mountainous, with the Dinaric Alps in the W and the Balkan Mts. in the E, and is watered by the Morava and its chief tributary the Ibar.

Chief products: Corn, wheat, potatoes, fruit; livestock; steel.

Chief settlements: Belgrade, Novi Sad, Niš, Kragujevac, Subotica.

Political divisions: Consists of the republics of Montenegro and Serbia (*qq.v.*). Prior to 1991 divided into the following six republics (for pronunciation of their names, see their individual entries): Bosnia and Herzegovina, Croatia, Macedonia, Montenegro, Serbia, and Slovenia.

History: At collapse of Austria-Hungary at end of WWI proclaimed Kingdom of Serbs, Croats, and Slovenes, 1918 (see AUSTRIA-HUNGARY, SERBIA, CROATIA, BOSNIA, MONTENEGRO, DALMATIA, and SLOVENIA for earlier history of component parts); engaged in dispute with Italy over Fiume (now Rijeka [*q.v.*]) 1919–24; signed treaties with Czechoslovakia and Romania 1920–21, the beginning of Little Entente; constitution of 1921 abandoned in favor of absolute monarchy 1929, at which time name was changed officially to Yugoslavia and the country was divided without regard to racial boundaries; tried to end struggle bet. Croats and the predominantly Serbian government by providing for greater autonomy of Croatia 1939; overthrew the government which had

signed Axis pact Mar. 1941; invaded by German forces Apr. 6, 1941 and during rest of war was occupied by German, Italian, Hungarian, and Bulgarian troops; established a Communist republic 1945; its insistence on developing a national form of Communism precipitated friction with the U.S.S.R. and led to Yugoslavia's expulsion from the Cominform 1948; settled Trieste dispute with Italy 1954 and again in 1975; partial reconciliation with U.S.S.R. 1955; internal ethnic tensions again flared up in the 1980s and in 1991–92 independence was declared by Croatia, Slovenia, Macedonia, and Bosnia and Herzegovina (*qq.v.*), and a new Federal Republic of Yugoslavia was proclaimed by Serbia and Montenegro; still fueled by long-standing ethnic tensions, hostilities continued into 1990s resulting in much destruction and accusations of ethnic cleansing; Dayton peace accord approved 1995 among Bosnia, Croatia, and Serbia, but sporadic fighting continued.

Yuki. See UNGGI.

Yu·kon \ˈyü-ˌkän\. **1.** City, Canadian co., cen. Oklahoma, 13 mi. (21 km.) W of Oklahoma City; pop. (1990c) 20,935. **2.** River, NW North America; formed by confluence of Lewes and Pelly rivers in SW Yukon Terr., Canada; flows NW across Yukon border into Alaska, then SW from its junction with the Porcupine across cen. Alaska to Bering Sea S of Norton Sound. Receives Stewart and Klondike tributaries from the E in Yukon Terr., the Porcupine (*q.v.*) from the NE, the Koyukuk from the N, and the Tanana from the S, in Alaska; 1979 mi. (3184 km.) long from the headwaters of the Lewes; has delta 80 to 90 mi. (129 to 145 km.) wide with only one mouth navigable. Third longest river highway in North America; its entire course of 1265 mi. (2035 km.) in Alaska is navigable, also as far as Dawson and to Whitehorse for smaller vessels. Frozen over Oct. to June. Its lower course is broad and muddy flowing through a marshy plain. At its bend

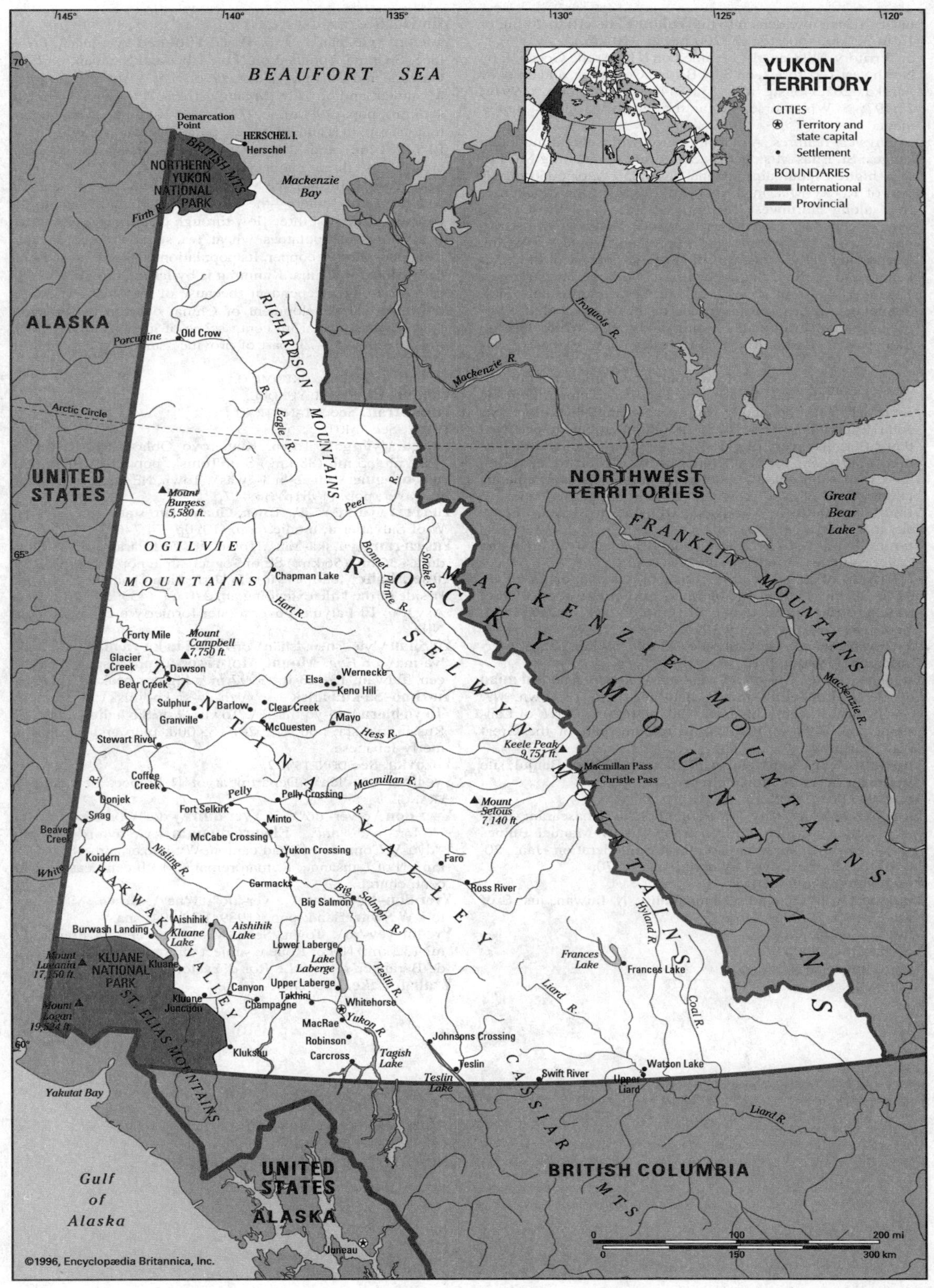
YUKON TERRITORY
CITIES
Territory and state capital
Settlement
BOUNDARIES
International
Provincial
BEAUFORT SEA
Demarcation Point
HERSCHEL I.
Herschel
BRITISH MTS
NORTHERN YUKON NATIONAL PARK
Firth R.
Mackenzie Bay
ALASKA
Porcupine
Old Crow
RICHARDSON MOUNTAINS
Eagle R.
Arctic Circle
UNITED STATES
Mount Burgess 5,580 ft.
Peel
OGILVIE MOUNTAINS
Chapman Lake
Bonnet Plume
Snake R.
Hart R.
ROCKY
MACKENZIE MOUNTAINS
SELWYN MOUNTAINS
Forty Mile
Mount Campbell 7,750 ft.
Glacier Creek
Dawson
Bear Creek
Elsa
Wernecke
Keno Hill
Sulphur
Barlow
Clear Creek
Granville
Mayo
McQuesten
Hess R.
Stewart River
Keele Peak 9,751 ft.
Macmillan Pass
Christle Pass
TINTINA VALLEY
Coffee Creek
Pelly
Pelly Crossing
Macmillan R.
Donjek
Fort Selkirk
Mount Selous 7,140 ft.
Snag
Minto
Beaver Creek
McCabe Crossing
Koidern
Nisling R.
Yukon Crossing
Faro
White
Carmacks
Ross River
SHAKWAK VALLEY
Big Salmon
Big Salmon R.
Aishihik
Burwash Landing
Kluane Lake
Aishihik Lake
Hyland R.
Mount Lucania 17,150 ft.
KLUANE NATIONAL PARK
Kluane
Lower Laberge
Lake Laberge
Teslin R.
Frances Lake
Frances Lake
Canyon
Upper Laberge
Liard R.
Coal R.
Kluane Junction
Takhini
Champagne
Whitehorse
Mount Logan 19,524 ft.
ST. ELIAS MOUNTAINS
Yukon R.
MacRae
Robinson
Johnsons Crossing
Klukshu
Carcross
Tagish Lake
Teslin
Swift River
Watson Lake
Teslin Lake
Upper Liard
CASSIAR MTS
Yakutat Bay
Liard R.
Iroquois R.
Mackenzie R.
NORTHWEST TERRITORIES
Great Bear Lake
FRANKLIN MOUNTAINS
Mackenzie R.
BRITISH COLUMBIA
UNITED STATES
ALASKA
Gulf of Alaska
Juneau
0 100 200 mi
0 150 300 km
145° 140° 135° 130° 125° 120°
70° 65° 60°

in NE Alaska it widens into the **Yukon Flats** (10 to 20 mi. or 16 to 32 km. wide for ab. 200 mi. or 320 km.).

3. Territory, NW Canada, bounded on N by Arctic Ocean, E by Northwest Territories, on S by British Columbia, and on W by Alaska; 205,345 sq. mi. (531,844 sq. km.); pop. (1991c) 27,797; ✻ Whitehorse, by far the territory's largest settlement.

Physical features: A plateau region with several mountain ranges: St. Elias Mts., across SW corner (containing Mt. Logan, highest mountain in Canada, 19,850 ft. or 6050 m.); N end of Rocky Mts. in S, incl. Stikine Mts.; the Mackenzie Mts. along Northwest Territories border; and the Ogilvie Mts. in cen. part. Chief river the upper Yukon, with its tributaries and headstreams, the Porcupine, Klondike, White, Lewes, and Pelly; in the N is the Peel, a tributary of the Mackenzie and in the S the upper Liard. No large lakes (largest Kluane 184 sq. mi. or 477 sq. km.), but many small ones. Whitehorse is head of navigation of the Yukon and also terminus of only railroad, running S through White Pass to Skagway in Alaska. Many river valleys have extensive forests.

Chief products: Silver, lead, gold; wood products; tourism.

History: Inhabited by American Indians, among them the Inuit, when first visited by Europeans; English explorer Sir John Franklin arrived 1825; sporadic settlement occurred thereafter; discovery of gold late 19th cent. resulted in Klondike gold rush; formed from Northwest Territories 1898; gold rush soon abated, with exploitation of other minerals taking over.

Yukon–Koy·u·kuk \ -ˈkī-ə-ˌkək \. Division in Alaska. See table at ALASKA.

Yu·ma \ ˈyü-mə \. **1.** Name of counties in two states of the U.S. See tables at ARIZONA and COLORADO.

2. City, ⊗ of Yuma co., SW corner of Arizona, on Colorado River 20 mi. (32 km.) N of Mexican border; pop. (1990c) 54,923; Arizona Western Coll. (1963); city platted 1854; incorp. as town 1871, city 1914.

3. City, Yuma co., NE Colorado, 43 mi. (69 km.) SE of Sterling; pop. (1990c) 2719.

Yu·men *or W.-G.* **Yü–men** \ ˈyu̅e̅-ˈmən \; *locally* **Lao·jun·miao** *or W.-G.* **Lao–chün–miao** \ ˈlau̇-ˈjuẹn-ˈmyau̇ \. Town, NW Gansu prov., N cen. China, ab. 430 mi. (690 km.) NW of Lanzhou; pop. (1990c) 109,234; petroleum; part of the Great Wall is nearby.

Yun·dum \ ˈyün-ˌdüm \. Town, W Gambia, SSW of Banjul; site of Gambia's international airport.

Yungang. See DATONG.

Yun·gay \ yüŋ-ˈgī \. City, NW Peru, W of Mt. Huascarán; scene of a battle in which Chilean troops under Manuel Bulnes overthrew the Peruvian-Bolivian Confederation Jan. 20, 1839; largely destroyed by earthquake 1970.

Yungchang. See BAOSHAN.

Yung·ho \ ˈyəŋ-ˈhə, -ˈhō \. Municipality, N Taiwan, just S of Taipei; pop. (1993e) 246,355.

Yungki. See JILIN 2.

Yungkia. See WENZHOU.

Yung–ning. See NANNING.

Yung–ting. See YONGDING.

Yün Ho. See GRAND CANAL 1.

Yun·nan \ yu̅e̅-ˈnän \. **1.** *or W.-G.* **Yün–nan** \ yu̅e̅-ˈnän \. Province, S China, bounded on N by Tibet and Sichuan, on E by Guizhou and Guangxi Zhuangzu, on S by Vietnam, Laos, and Myanmar, and on W by Myanmar; 168,417 sq. mi. (436,200 sq. km.); pop. (1990c) 36,972,610; ✻ Kunming. Very mountainous esp. in N and W; its cen. part a plateau averaging 6500 ft. (1981 m.) and sloping to SE. Has many small lakes; crossed by three major river systems—the Chang (here known as the Jinsha), the Mekong, and the Salween—and the source of two others—the Hongshui and the Yuan; the N courses of the first three flow through great gorges; produces rice, corn, sweet potatoes, wheat, tea, sugar, coffee; tin, coal, iron, phosphorus, copper. Its population is one of most ethnically mixed of China. Kunming is by far the province's largest city. Long independent (because of its isolation) during the historical development of China; overrun by Mongols (Yüan dynasty) in 13th cent.; scene of great Panthay (Muslim) revolt 1855–73; part of province seized by Japanese in WWII.

2. City, China. See KUNMING.

Yunque, El. See EL YUNQUE.

Yura Strait. See KITAN STRAIT.

Yurev. See TARTU.

Yur·ga \ ˈyu̇r-gə \. Town, Kemerovo Oblast, SW Russia in Asia, ab. 55 mi. (88 km.) S of Tomsk; pop. (1991e) 94,000.

Yu·ri·ma·guas \ ˌyü-rē-ˈmä-gwäs \. Town, NE Peru, on Huallaga River; pop. (1981p) 36,417.

Yu·ri·ria \ yü-ˈrē-rē-ä \. Town, Guanajuato state, cen. Mexico, W of Salvatierra; munic. pop. (1990p) 74,746.

Yus·ca·rán \ ˌyü-skä-ˈrän \. Town, ✻ of El Paraíso dept., Honduras, 35 mi. (56 km.) SE of Tegucigalpa; pop. (1988p) 2155.

Yûsef, Bahr \ ˌbȧ-hər-ˈyü-səf \. Irrigation channel, Egypt, on W side of the Nile extending ab. 270 mi. (435 km.) from near Asyūt to El Faiyūm governorate; formerly a channel of the Nile.

Yü Shan \ ˈyu̅e̅-ˈshen, ˈshän \ *or Jp.* **Nii·ta·ka·ya·ma** \ ˌnē-ˌtä-kä-ˈyä-mä \ *or Eng.* **Mount Mor·ri·son** \ ˈmo̊r-ə-sən \. Peak, S cen. Taiwan; 13,113 ft. (3997 m.); highest peak in Taiwan.

Yu·zhno–Sa·kha·linsk \ ˈyüzh-nə-sə-k̲ə-ˈlinsk \; *formerly* **To·yo·ha·ra** \ ˌtō-yō-ˈhä-rä \. Town, ✻ of Sakhalin Oblast, SE Russia in Asia; pop. (1992e) 165,000; pulp and paper; formerly Japanese.

Yuzovka. See DONETS'K 2.

Yve·lines \ ēv-ˈlēn \. Department of N France. See table at FRANCE.

Yver·don \ ē-ver-ˈdōⁿ \ *or* **Yver·dun** \ -ˈdœⁿ \ *or Ger.* **Ifer·ten** \ ˈē-fərt-ᵊn \; *anc.* **Eb·u·ro·du·num** \ ˌe-byə-rō-ˈdü-nəm, -ˈdyü- \. Commune, Vaud canton, W Switzerland, 18 mi. (29 km.) N of Lausanne; Roman remains; 13th cent. castle; 18th cent. church.

Yver·don–les–Bains \ ˌē-ver-ˈdōⁿ-lā-ˈbeⁿ \. Town, Vaud canton, W Switzerland; pop. (1989c) 22,004; spa.

Yve·tot \ ēv-ˈtō \. Town, Seine-Maritime dept., N France, 20 mi. (32 km.) NW of Rouen; subject of French poet Pierre-Jean de Béranger's song, *Le Roi d'Yvetot* (c. 1813).

Yzabal, Lake. See IZABAL, LAKE.

Z

Zaan·dam \zän-ˈdäm, -ˈdam\. Former commune, North Holland prov., W Netherlands; place where Czar Peter the Great of Russia lived while he studied shipbuilding 1697; merged with surrounding communes to form Zaanstad 1974.

Zaan·stad \ˈzän-ˌstät\. Commune, North Holland prov., W Netherlands; pop. (1993e) 131,785; many windmills; formed 1974 by merger of Zaandam with surrounding communes.

Zab, Great \ˈzäb\ *or Arab.* **Zab al–Ka·bir** \ˈzȧb-ˌȧl-kȧ-ˈbir\. River, SE Turkey in Asia and N Iraq; rises in mountains of Kurdistan and flows S and SW into the Tigris River below Mosul; ab. 260 mi. (420 km.) long.

Zab, Little *or Arab.* **Zab al–As·fal** \ˈzȧb-ˌȧl-ˈȧs-ˌfȧl\. River, NW Iran and N Iraq; flows SW into the Tigris River ab. 50 mi. (80 km.) below the Great Zab; ab. 230 mi. (370 km.) long.

Zabaikal. See TRANSBAIKALIA.

Zab·bar \zä-ˈbär\. Town, E Malta; pop. (1988c) 13,338.

Zabern. See SAVERNE.

Ząb·ko·wi·ce \ˌzȯmp-kȯ-ˈvēt-se\ *or in full* **Ząbkowice Śląs·kie** \ˈshlō^{n}s-kye\; *Ger.* **Fran·ken·stein** \ˈfräŋ-kən-ˌshtīn\ *or in full* **Frankenstein in Schle·si·en** \in-ˈshlā-zē-ən\. City, E cen. Wałbrzych prov., SW Poland, 39 mi. (63 km.) SSW of Wrocław; pop. (1981p) 16,384; formerly in Prussia, Germany; late Gothic church. Founded 13th cent.; assigned to Poland 1945.

Zab Mountains \ˈzäb\. Range of the Atlas Mts., N Algeria; highest peak ab. 4300 ft. (1310 m.).

Zā·bol \zä-ˈbōl\ *or* **Shahr–i–Za·bul** \ˈshär-ē-zä-ˈbōl\; *formerly* **Nas·rat·a·bad** \nas-ˈra-tə-ˌbad\. Town, E Iran, 275 mi. (443 km.) ENE of Kermān, in cen. part of Lake Helmand depression; pop. (1986c) 75,105.

Zab·rze \ˈzäb-zhe\; *Ger.* **Hin·den·burg** \ˈhin-dən-ˌbu̇rk, -ˌbərg\ *or in full* **Hindenburg in Ober·schle·si·en** \in-ˌō-bər-ˈshlā-zē-ən\. City, Katowice prov., S Poland, WNW of the city of Katowice; pop. (1989e) 203,367; coal mining; chemicals. Founded c. 1300; passed to Prussia 1742; significantly damaged during WWII; assigned to Poland 1945.

Za·ca·pa \sä-ˈkä-pä\. **1.** Department of E Guatemala. See table at GUATEMALA.
2. Town, its ✱; pop. (1993e) 18,809; sulfur springs; cigars, cheese.

Za·ca·pu \sä-ˈkä-pü\. Municipality, Michoacán state, Mexico, 40 mi. (64 km.) W of Morelia; pop. (1990p) 63,150; diversified agriculture.

Za·ca·te·cas \ˌsä-kä-ˈtā-käs\. **1.** State of cen. Mexico. See table at MEXICO.
2. City, its ✱, 65 mi. (105 km.) NNW of Aguascalientes; munic. pop. (1990c) 100,051; alt. 8075 ft. (2461 m.); cathedral; mines and smelters. Ruins of Chicomóztoc, pre-Columbian city, to the S.

Za·ca·te·co·lu·ca \ˌsä-kä-ˌtā-kō-ˈlü-kä\. City, ✱ of La Paz dept., S El Salvador; pop. (1992p) 57,032; commercial center for surrounding agricultural area.

Za·ca·tlán \ˌsä-kät-ˈlän\. Municipality, Puebla state, Mexico, 65 mi. (105 km.) NNE of the city of Puebla; pop. (1990p) 58,894.

Zach·a·ry \ˈza-kə-rē\. City, East Baton Rouge parish, Louisiana, N of Baton Rouge; pop. (1990c) 9036.

Zacynthus. See ZÁKINTHOS 1.

Za·dar \ˈzä-ˌdär\ *or Ital.* **Za·ra** \ˈzär-ä\; *anc.* **Iad·era** \ī-ˈa-də-rə\. Port on the Adriatic, Croatia, 72 mi. (116 km.) NW of Split; pop. (1991c) 80,355; seaside resort; produces maraschino liqueur; fortified until 19th cent.; ancient Roman remains; 13th cent. cathedral; several medieval churches. Became a colony under Romans; long disputed by Hungary and Venice, finally being purchsed by Venice 1409; passed to Austria 1797, Italy 1920, and Yugoslavia 1947. Rebuilt after being severely damaged in WWII.

Za·det·skyi Island \zä-ˈdet-skyē\; *formerly* **Saint Mat·thew Island** \ˈmath-ˌyü\. Island in Mergui Archipelago (*q.v.*), Myanmar.

Zafarin Islands. See CHAFARINAS ISLANDS.

Ża·gań *also* **Że·gań** \ˈzhä-ˌgän^{y}\ *or Ger.* **Sa·gan** \ˈzä-ˌgän\. City, Zielona Góra prov., SW Poland, on Bóbr River ab. 25 mi. (40 km.) SSW of the city of Zielona Góra; pop. (1989e) 27,454; formerly in Prussia, Germany.

Za·ga·zig \zə-ˈgä-zig\ *or Arab.* **Az–Za·qā·zīq** \ˌaz-zȧ-ˌkä-ˈzēk\. City, ✱ of Sharqīya governorate, Lower Egypt; pop. (1991e) 279,000; trades in cotton and grain.

Zagh·wān \zäg-ˈwän\ *or* **Zagh·ouan** \zȧ-ˈgwe^{n}\. Town, N Tunisia, ab. 25 mi. (40 km.) W of Hammamet; pop. (1989e) 12,161; railroad terminus and road junction.

Zagorsk. See SERGIYEV POSAD.

Za·greb \ˈzä-ˌgreb\ *or Hung.* **Zá·gráb** \ˈzä-ˌgräb\ *or Ger.* **Agram** \ˈä-ˌgräm\; *anc.* **Za·gra·bia** \zə-ˈgrā-bē-ə\. City, ✱ of Croatia, on Sava River; pop. (1991c) 867,865; was 2d largest city in Yugoslavia; machinery, chemicals, textiles; university (1669), botanical gardens; nuclear energy institute; cathedral; museums; several churches; Krk Bridge, world's longest concrete-arch bridge (main span 1280 ft. or 390 m.; completed 1980) is nearby; first mentioned 1093; long an important center for Croats.

Zag·ros Mountains \ˈza-grəs\. Mountain system in many parallel ranges, S and SW Iran, extending along and across the Iran-Iraq border; many peaks above 9000 ft. (2743 m.), highest Zard Kuh 14,921 ft. (4548 m.).

Zagy·va \ˈzöj-ˌvö\. River, E cen. Hungary; flows S into Tisza River at Szolnok; ab. 100 mi. (160 km.) long.

Zā·he·dān *or* **Za·hi·dan** \ˌzä-hi-ˈdän\; *formerly* **Duz·dab** \du̇z-ˈdäb\. Town, ✱ of Sīstān va Balūchestān prov., E Iran; pop. (1986c) 281,923; transportation center.

Zah·lé \zä-ˈlā\ *or* **Zah·lah** \ˈzä-lə\. Town, cen. Lebanon, 23 mi. (37 km.) E of Beirut in Bekáa Valley.

Ẓahrān, Aẓ. See DHAHRAN.

Żairam Nor. See SAYRAM HU.

Za·ire *or* **Za·ïre** \zä-ˈir *also* ˈzīr\. **1.** *or since 1997* **Democractic Republic of the Con·go** \ˈkäŋ-gō\; *from 1960 to 1971* **Congo**; *from 1908 to 1960* **Bel·gian Congo** \ˈbel-jən\; *from 1885 to 1908* **Congo Free State.** Republic, equatorial part of Africa, bounded on NW and N by Central African Rep., on NE by Sudan and Uganda, on E by Rwanda, Burundi, and Tanzania, on SE by Zambia, on S by Zambia and Angola, on SW by Angola, and on W by Rep. of the Congo; its W extremity forms narrow corridor along lower Congo River with less than 25 mi. (40 km.) of coastline on the Atlantic Ocean; 905,356 sq. mi. (2,344,872 sq. km.); pop. (1994e) 43,775,000; ✱ Kinshasa.

Physical features: A tropical country, crossed by the Equator in N cen. part; occupies greater part of Congo River basin. Chief tributaries of the Congo (upper course known as the Lualaba): Ubangi (on NW and N border), Aruwimi, Lindi, Lomami, Lukuga (outlet of Lake Tanganyika), Lulonga, Ruki, and Kasai.

Lakes: Tanganyika and Mweru on E and SE borders, Kivu in E, Edward and Albert on NE border, Mai-Ndomde in W and Pool Malebo. Mostly low plateau, with marshes along Congo in NW.

Mountains: Ranges in SE with several peaks ab. 6000 ft. (1830 m.), higher ranges along W shore of Lake Tanganyika, and high mountains on E (highest point of Virunga group 14,786 ft. or 4507 m., of Ruwenzori 16,791 ft. or 5118 m.).

\ə\ **abut** \ə\ **matches** \ᵊ\ **kitten, Fr table** \ər\ **further** \a\ **ash** \ā\ **ace** \ä\ **cot, cart** \ȧ\ **Fr bac** \au̇\ **out** \b\ **Span Avila** \ch\ **chin** \e\ **bet** \ē\ **easy** \g\ **go** \i\ **hit** \ī\ **ice** \j\ **job** \k\ **Ger ich, Buch** \$^{n}$\ **Fr vin** \ŋ\ **sing** \ō\ **go** \ȯ\ **all** \ȯi\ **law** \œ\ **Fr bœuf** \œ̄\ **Fr feu** \ȯi\ **boy** \th\ **thin** \th\ **this** \ü\ **loot** \u̇\ **foot** \ue\ **Ger füllen** \ue̅\ **Fr rue** \y\ **yet** \$^{y}$\ **Fr digne** \ˈdēn^{y}\, **nuit** \ˈnw^{y}ē\ \yü\ **few** \yu̇\ **fury** \zh\ **vision**

Chief products: Corn, palm oil, cassava, bananas, coffee, rubber; copper, gold, cobalt, industrial diamonds, tin, zinc, manganese.

Chief settlements: Kinshasa, Lubumbashi, Mbuji-Mayi, Kolwezi.

Political divisions: Divided into the following 11 administrative regions (for pronunciation of their names, see their individual entries):

NAME	AREA (sq. mi.)	AREA (sq. km.)	POP. (1994e)	CAPITAL
Bandundu	114,154	295,659	4,907,000	Bandundu
Bas-Zaïre	20,819	53,921	2,578,000	Matadi
Équateur (formerly Coquilhatville)	155,712	403,294	4,789,000	Mbandaka
Haut-Zaïre	194,302	503,242	5,432,000	Kisangani
Kasai-Occidental	59,746	154,742	3,117,000	Kananga
Kasai-Oriental	65,754	170,303	3,778,000	Mbuji-Mayi
Kinshasa	3,848	9,966	4,655,000	
Maniema	51,062	132,250	1,048,000	Kindu
Nord-Kivu	22,967	59,484	3,546,000	Goma
Shaba	191,845	496,878	5,602,000	Lubumbashi
Sud-Kivu	25,147	65,131	3,093,000	Bukavu

History: Prior to European colonization, several native kingdoms had emerged in region; territory subsequently developed by Leopold II of Belgium who sponsored British journalist Sir Henry Morton Stanley's explorations in the area (1879–84); Congo Free State, with Leopold autonomous sovereign, estab. and recognized by Berlin Conference 1884–85; after international criticism of treatment of natives, annexed to Belgium 1908; achieved independence June 30, 1960; immediate post-independence period marked by internal unrest, incl. the secession of Katanga (now Shaba) 1960–63; military coup 1965; name changed to Zaire 1971; Katanga rebels based in Angola invaded the country in 1977 and 1978 but were defeated with foreign help; resistance to presidential power increased early 1990s; named changed to Democratic Rep. of the Congo 1997.

2. *formerly* **Congo.** Province of NW Angola; site of native kingdom (Kongo) 15th–18th cents. See table at ANGOLA.

3. River, Africa. See CONGO 4.

Zaisan. See ZAYSAN.

Zaiton *or* **Zai·tun** \zī-ˈtün\. See QUANZHOU.

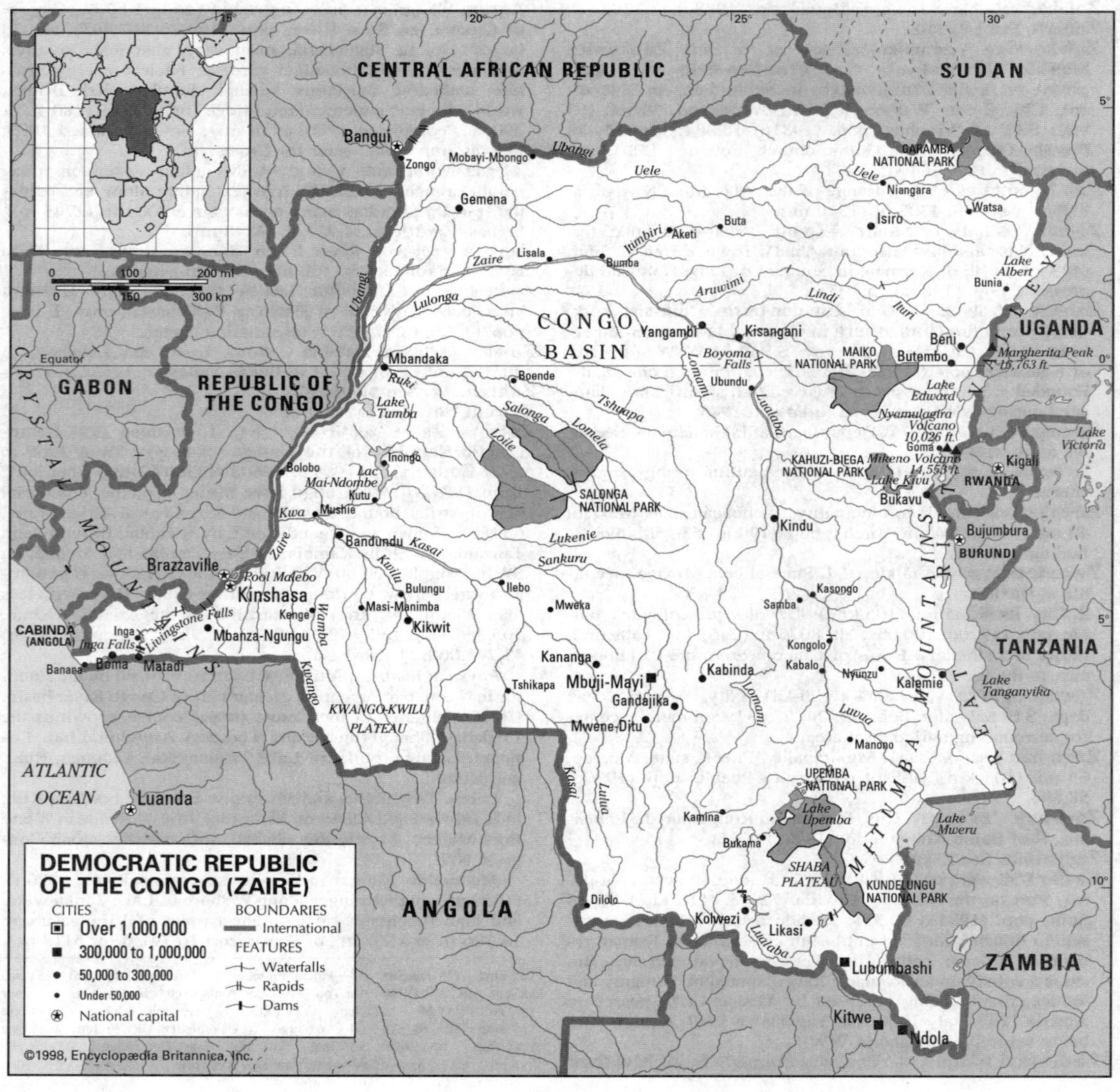

Zakak, Bab al–. See GIBRALTAR, STRAIT OF.

Za·kar·pat·s'ka \ˌzä-kər-ˈpät-skə\ *or Russ.* **Za·kar·pat·ska·ya** \-skə-yə\; *formerly* **Trans·car·pa·thi·an Oblast** \ˌtranz-kär-ˈpā-thē-ən-ˈó-bləst, ˌtrans-, -ˌblast\ *or* **Car·pa·tho–Ukraine** \kär-ˈpā-thō-yü-ˈkrān, -ˈkrīn, -ˈyü-ˌ\; *earlier* **Car·pa·thi·an Ru·the·nia** \kär-ˈpā-thē-ən-rü-ˈthē-nē-ə, -nyə\ *or Czech* **Pod·kar·pat·ská Rus** \ˈpòt-kär-ˌpät-skä-ˈrùs\. The extreme W administrative subdivision of Ukraine; 4942 sq. mi. (12,800 sq. km.); pop. (1991e) 1,265,900; ✻ Uzhgorod. Economy largely based on timber, wheat, rye, oats, tobacco. Organized from territory ceded to U.S.S.R. by Czechoslovakia 1945.

Zá·kin·thos \ˈzä-ken-ˌthös\ *also* **Zan·te** \ˈdzän-tā, ˈzan-tē\. **1.** *or* **Za·cyn·thus** \zə-ˈsin-thəs\ *or* **Zá·kyn·thos** \ˈzä-kēn-ˌthös\. One of the Ionian Is., Ionian Sea, off W coast of Greece, 8 mi. (13 km.) S of Cephalonia; 25 mi. (40 km.) long by 12 mi. (19 km.) wide; 157 sq. mi. (407 sq. km.); constitutes a department of Greece. Has wide fertile plain in cen. part with low hills on W; produces currants for export. Subject to frequent earthquakes. According to tradition belonged to Odysseus, king of Ithaca; historically, in classical period, belonged to various states—Athens, Macedon, Rome—often as a military base; ravaged by Vandals and Saracens; in 11th cent. held by Norman kings of Sicily; from c. 1485 to 1797 belonged to Venice. (For later history, see IONIAN ISLANDS.) **2.** Department, Greece. See ZÁKINTHOS 1 and table at GREECE. **3.** *or* **Zákynthos.** Town, ✻ of Zákinthos dept., Ionian Is., Greece, on E coast of Zante I.; pop. (1981p) 9742; traditionally said to have been founded by Zacynthus, son of the Arcadian chief Dardanus.

Za·ko·pa·ne \ˌzä-kò-ˈpä-ne\. Commune, SW Nowy Sącz prov., S Poland, in Tatra Mts. 52 mi. (84 km.) S of Kraków; pop. (1989e) 28,669; summer resort and winter-sports center; alt. ab. 3300 ft. (1005 m.); founded in 16th cent.

Zákynthos. See ZÁKINTHOS.

Za·la \ˈzö-lö\. County of W Hungary. See table at HUNGARY.

Zalaca. See ZALLAKA.

Za·la·e·ger·szeg \ˈzö-lö-ˌe-ger-ˌseg\. City, ⊗ of Zala co., W Hungary, W of Lake Balaton; pop. (1991e) 64,200.

Za·lău \zə-ˈlə-ü, -ˈlaů\ *or Hung.* **Zi·lah** \ˈzē-ˌlö\. Commune, ✻ of Sălaj co., Romania, ab. 55 mi. (89 km.) ENE of Oradea; pop. (1989c) 65,190.

Zalew Szczeciński. See STETTINER HAFF.

Zalew Wiślany. See VISLINSKI ZALIV.

Zaliv Petra Velikogo. See PETER THE GREAT BAY.

Zaliv Shelikhova. see SHELIKHOVA, ZALIV.

Zal·la·ka *or* **Za·la·ca** \zə-ˈlä-kə\ *or Arab.* **Al–Zal·lā·qah** \ˌal-zȧ-ˈlä-kə\ *or Span.* **Sa·cra·lias** \sä-ˈkräl-yäs\. Ancient town, SW Spain, N of Badajoz; scene of battle 1086 in which Yūsef ibn Tāshufīn, king of the Almoravids, defeated Alfonso VI, king of León and of Castile.

Za·ma \ˈzā-mə\. Ancient town, N Africa, SW of Carthage; scene of decisive defeat of the Carthaginians under Hannibal by the Romans under Scipio Africanus 202 B.C.

Za·ma \ˈzä-mä\. City, Kanagawa prefecture, Honshū, Japan; pop. (1990p) 112,100.

Zam·ba·les \zäm-ˈbä-lās\. Province, W Luzon, Philippines; ✻ Iba. In NE are the Zambales Mts., consisting of more or less isolated volcanic cones; highest point High Peak 6683 ft. (2037 m.) in N cen. part. Coast irregular with sheltered anchorage of Subic Bay in S. Rice is chief product. See table at PHILIPPINES.

Zambales Mountains. Mountain range, W Luzon, Philippines, running from Lingayen Gulf in N to entrance to Manila Bay in S; many peaks from 2500 to 5000 ft. (762 to 1524 m.); highest point High Peak 6683 ft. (2037 m.) in N cen. Zambales; Mt. Mariveles 4444 ft. (1355 m.) is highest in Bataan.

Zam·be·zi *or* **Zam·be·si** \zam-ˈbē-zē\ *or Port.* **Zam·be·ze** \zȧm-ˈbā-zə\. River, S cen. and SE Africa; rises in NW Zambia, flows S across E Angola and W Zambia to the border of Botswana; turns E and forms boundary bet. Zambia and Zimbabwe; crosses cen. Mozambique and empties into Mozambique Channel at Chinde; ab. 1700 mi. (2735 km.) long; navigable in three long stretches, separated by rapids and by Victoria Falls (*q.v.*). Has many headstreams in the marshlands of SE Angola and W Zambia; chief tributaries on the N are the Kafue and Luangwa in Zambia and the Shire, outlet of Lake Malawi; on the S the Chobe bet. Caprivi Strip and Botswana and the Sanyati in Zimbabwe. Explored by Scottish missionary David Livingstone 1850s.

Zam·bé·zia \zam-ˈbē-zē-ə\. Province of cen. Mozambique. See table at MOZAMBIQUE.

Zam·bia \ˈzam-bē-ə\; *formerly* **Northern Rho·de·sia** \rō-ˈdē-zhə\. Republic, S cen. Africa, bounded on N by Democratic Rep. of the Congo and Tanzania, on E by Malawi, on SE by Mozambique, on S by Zimbabwe and Namibia, and on the W by Angola; 290,585 sq. mi. (752,615 sq. km.); pop. (1994e) 9,132,000; ✻ Lusaka.

Physical features: Consists of tableland (3000 to 4500 ft. or 914 to 1372 m.) through which flow three main streams, Zambezi (also forming boundary with Zimbabwe), Kafue, and Luangwa. Victoria Falls (*q.v.*) are in the Zambezi near Livingstone in SW; Lake Bangweulu is in N and Lake Mweru in N on boundary with Democratic Rep. of the Congo; S end of Lake Tanganyika touches N boundary.

Chief product: Copper.

Other products: Corn, tobacco, peanuts, cotton, sugarcane; livestock; lead, zinc, cobalt, coal, gold.

Chief towns: Lusaka, Ndola, Kitwe.

History: Inhabited since earliest times although most of the ancestors of today's primarily Bantu-speaking population did not settle in the area until c. 17th–18th cents.; under jurisdiction of British South Africa Company 1889 to 1924; became a British protectorate 1924; part of Federation of Rhodesia and Nyasaland 1953–63; achieved independence Oct. 24, 1964; completion of Chinese-built railroad (1975) following sanctions against Rhodesia enabled rerouting of exports through Tanzania; constitutional amendment allowing opposition parties approved 1990.

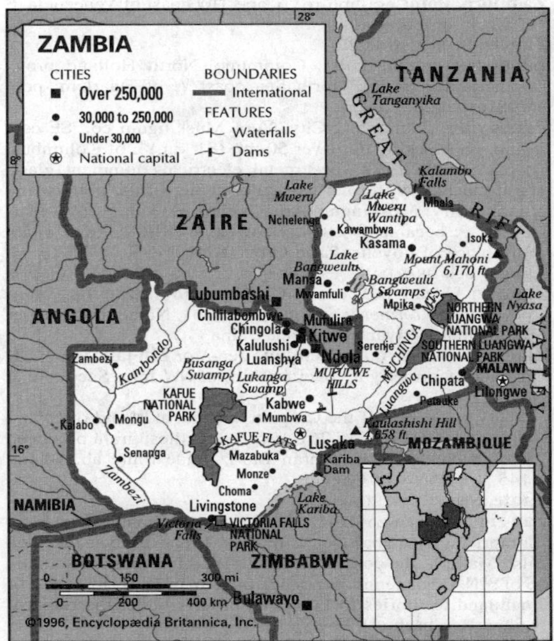

Zam·bo·an·ga \ˌzäm-bō-ˈwäŋ-gä\. **1.** Former province, W Mindanao, Philippines, now divided into **Zamboanga del**

\ə\ abut \ᵊ\ matches \ᵊ\ kitten, Fr table \ər\ further \a\ ash \ā\ ace \ä\ cot, cart \ȧ\ Fr bac \aů\ out \b\ Span Avila \ch\ chin \e\ bet \ē\ easy \g\ go \i\ hit \ī\ ice \j\ job \k\ Ger ich, Buch \ⁿ\ Fr vin \ŋ\ sing \ō\ go \ȯ\ all \ò\ law \œ\ Fr bœuf \œ̄\ Fr feu \ȯi\ boy \th\ thin \t͟h\ this \ü\ loot \ů\ foot \ue\ Ger füllen \ue̅\ Fr rue \y\ yet \ʸ\ Fr digne \ˈdēnʸ\, nuit \ˈnwʸē\ \yü\ few \yů\ fury \zh\ vision

Nor·te \del-ˈnȯr-tā\ (✱ Dipolog) and **Zamboanga del Sur** \del-ˈsür\ (✱ Pagadian). Mountainous region, with range through cen. part; highest is Mt. Dapiak in NE Zamboanga del Sur, 8416 ft. (2565 m.). Coastline has many bays, largest being Sindangan on N and Sibuguey on S; forest resources, rice. See table at PHILIPPINES.

2. *officially* **City of Zamboanga.** Chartered city, Zamboanga del Sur prov., Mindanao, Philippines; pop. (1990c) 442,000; exports copra and timber; port 600 mi. (965 km.) S of Manila; has good roadstead but not a safe anchorage in SW monsoon. Founded 1635 as a fort by Spanish; later became the chief market of S Philippines. The City of Zamboanga was created c. 1940; in WWII a Japanese defense headquarters, taken by U.S. troops Mar. 1945.

Zámky Nové. See NOVÉ ZÁMKY.

Za·mo·ra \sä-ˈmō-rä\. **1.** River, S and SE Ecuador; flows E and N to join Paute River and form Santiago River, a tributary of the Marañón; 190 mi. (306 km.) long.

2. Town, ✱ of Zamora-Chinchipe prov., S Ecuador; pop. (1990c) 8048.

3. *or in full* **Zamora de Hi·dal·go** \thā-ē-ˈthäl-gō\. Town, Michoacán state, SW Mexico, 80 mi. (129 km.) SE of Guadalajara; in center of rich agricultural region; founded 1540.

4. Province of NW Spain. See table at SPAIN.

5. City, ✱ of Zamora prov., NW Spain, on Duero River 129 mi. (208 km.) NW of Madrid; pop. (1992e) 64,631; 12th cent. Romanesque cathedral; contested by Moors and Christians 10th cent. A.D.

6. State, Venezuela. See *Barinas* in table at VENEZUELA.

Zamora–Chin·chi·pe \-chēn-ˈchē-pä\. Province of E Ecuador. See table at ECUADOR.

Za·mość \ˈzä-ˌmȯshch\ *or Russ.* **Za·moste** \zə-ˈmȯs-tyə\. **1.** Province, E Poland. See table at POLAND.

2. Commune, its ✱, 48 mi. (77 km.) SE of Lublin; pop. (1989e) 60,682. Founded 16th cent.

Za·mu·ro, Point \sä-ˈmü-rō\. Cape, NW coast of Venezuela, S of island of Curaçao.

Zancle. See MESSINA 2.

Zand·voort \ˈzänt-ˌvōrt\. Commune, North Holland prov., Netherlands, on the North Sea coast W of Haarlem; pop. (1981e) 16,067; resort.

Zanes·ville \ˈzānz-ˌvil\. City, ⊗ of Muskingum co., SE cen. Ohio, on Muskingum River 50 mi. (81 km.) E of Columbus; pop. (1990c) 26,778; sheet metal, electrical equipment, glass, farm machinery; formerly a major center of the pottery and tile industry; Muskingum Area Technical Coll. (1969). Platted 1799; became ⊗ 1804, ✱ of Ohio 1810–12, city 1850. Birthplace of novelist Zane Grey 1875.

Zanga. See HRAZDAN.

Zang·bo \ˈdzäŋ-ˈbō\ *or W.-G.* **Tsang·po** \ˈdzäŋ-ˈbō, ˈtsäŋ-ˈpō\; *mostly formerly* **San·po** \ˈsän-ˈpō\. Name of the upper Brahmaputra River in S Tibet, China.

Zan·jān \zan-ˈjän\ *also* **Zen·jan** \zen-\ *or* **Zin·jan** \zin-\. **1.** Province (formerly a governorship) of NW Iran. See table at IRAN.

2. City, its ✱, SW of the Caspian Sea and at W end of Elburz Mts.; pop. (1986c) 215,261; carpets, textiles; grain produced nearby; on the main Tehran-Tabrīz trade route ab. 90 mi. (145 km.) WNW of Qazvīn.

Zante. See ZÁKINTHOS.

Zan·zi·bar \ˈzan-zə-ˌbär\. **1.** Former sultanate, E Africa, comprising Zanzibar (see ZANZIBAR 2) and Kenya; included also Mafia I., the coast of Tanzania, and the coast of Somalia S of 3°N. Became independent from Oman 1861; lost most of mainland territories to European powers under the reign of Sultan Barghash (1870–88).

2. Former British protectorate, E Africa, comprising Zanzibar I., Pemba I., and adjacent small islands; 1020 sq. mi. (2642 sq. km.); ✱ Zanzibar; created as protectorate 1890; became an independent sultanate Dec. 10, 1963 and a republic Jan. 12, 1964; united with Tanganyika later in 1964 to form Tanzania. See TANZANIA.

3. Chief island of Tanzania, in the Indian Ocean off E coast of Africa; administratively divided into **Zanzibar North, Zanzibar South and Central,** and **Zanzibar West** regions; a major source of cloves; also produces coconuts. See table at TANZANIA.

History: Settled by Africans from mainland East Africa, followed by Persians and Arabs; became dominated by Portuguese early 16th cent.; came under control of Arabs of Oman (*q.v.*) late 17th cent.; with adjacent territory became independent sultanate (see ZANZIBAR 1) 1861; with Pemba became British protectorate (see ZANZIBAR 2) 1890; became part of Tanzania 1964.

4. Commercial seaport, ✱ of Zanzibar West region, Tanzania, on W coast of the island of Zanzibar; pop. (1988p) 157,634; was ✱ of Muscat and Oman mid-19th cent. and ✱ of former British protectorate (see ZANZIBAR 2); in 19th cent. a base for slave and ivory traders in E Africa.

Zapadnaya Dvina. See DVINA, WESTERN.

Za·pa·ta \zə-ˈpä-tə\. **1.** County in S Texas. See table at TEXAS.

2. Unincorporated settlement, its ⊗, 130 mi. (209 km.) SW of Corpus Christi; pop. (1990c) 7119.

3. Swamp, SW Las Villas prov., Cuba; ab. 600 sq. mi. (1555 sq. km.).

Zapata Peninsula. Peninsula extending from SW coast of Las Villas prov., W cen. Cuba; encloses Broa Bay from the S.

Za·po·pan \ˌsä-pō-ˈpän\. City, Jalisco state, Mexico, 10 mi. (16 km.) W of Guadalajara; munic. pop. (1990c) 668,323; commercial center for area of livestock raising and diversified agriculture; 17th cent. church.

Za·po·rizh·zhya *or Russ.* **Za·po·ro·zh'ye** \ˌzäp-ə-ˈrȯ-zhə\. **1.** Administrative subdivision of Ukraine; 10,502 sq. mi. (27,200 sq. km.); pop. (1991e) 2,099,600; ✱ Zaporizhzhya; winter wheat, corn, potatoes, melons.

2. *formerly* **Ale·ksan·drovsk** \ˌal-ik-ˈsan-drəfsk\. City, its ✱, on the left bank of the Dnieper 45 mi. (72 km.) S of Dnipropetrovs'k; pop. (1991e) 897,000; metallurgical industries. In 16th cent. and later the surrounding country was the home of the Zaporozhye Cossacks.

Za·po·tla·ne·jo \zä-ˌpȯt-lä-ˈnā-hō\. Municipality, Jalisco state, Mexico, 18 mi. (29 km.) E of Guadalajara.

Zaqāzīq, Az–. See ZAGAZIG.

Zara. See ZADAR.

Za·ra·go·za \ˌsä-rä-ˈgō-sä\. **1.** Province of NE Spain. See table at SPAIN.

2. City, Spain. See SARAGOSSA.

Zaraka. See STYMPHALIS.

Za·ranj \zə-ˈränj\. Town, SW Afghanistan.

Zá·ra·te \ˈzä-rä-ˌtā\; *formerly* **Ge·ne·ral J. F. Uri·bu·ru** \ˌhā-nā-ˈräl-ˈhō-tä-ˈā-fā-ˌü-rē-ˈbü-rü\. Town, N Buenos Aires prov., E Argentina, on Paraná River 56 mi. (90 km.) NW of the city of Buenos Aires; pop. (1980c) 67,143.

Zard Kūh \ˌzärd-ˈkü\ *also* **Zar·deh Kuh** \ˌzär-də-ˈkü\. Peak, W Iran, W of Eşfahān; 14,921 ft. (4548 m.); highest point in the Zagros Mts.

Zarephath. See SAREPTA.

Za·ria \ˈzär-ē-ə\. **1.** *formerly* **Zaz·zau** \ˌza-ˈzau̇\. Historic kingdom, Ethiopia, traditionally dating from 11th cent.

2. Traditional emirate, Ethiopia, dating from early 19th cent., encompassing some lands of historic kingdom.

3. Town, N cen. Nigeria, on railroad line ab. 87 mi. (140 km.) SW of Kano; pop. (1993e) 351,800; in region producing cotton and peanuts; university (1962).

Zar·qa \ˈzär-kə\. **1.** *also* **Jab·bok** \ˈja-ˌbäk\. River, NW Jordan, flowing W into the Jordan River ab. 25 mi. (40 km.) N of Dead Sea; ab. 100 mi. (160 km.) long; in ancient Palestine it was in Gilead and formed N boundary of the Amorites (*Josh.* xii. 2).

2. *or* **Az–Zar·qā'** \àz-ˈzàr-ˌkä\. Town, Jordan, ab. 12 mi. (19 km.) NNE of Amman; pop. (1993e) 605,000; 2d largest town in Jordan.

Ża·ry \ˈzhär-ē\; *Ger.* **So·rau** \ˈzō-ˌrau̇\ *or in full* **Sorau in der Nie·der·lau·sitz** \in-dər-ˌnē-dər-ˈlau̇-ˌzits\. City, Zielona Góra prov., SW Poland, ab. 25 mi. (40 km.) SW of city of Zielona Góra; pop. (1989e) 39,308; formerly in Brandenburg, Germany; assigned to Poland by Potsdam Conference 1945.

Zatishye. see ELEKTROSTAL.

Za·va·la \zə-ˈvä-lə\. County in S Texas. See table at TEXAS.

Zāwia See AZ-ZĀWIYAH.

Za·wier·cie \zä-ˈvyer-che\. Commune, Katowice prov., S Poland, ab. 25 mi. (40 km.) NW of the city of Katowice; pop. (1989e) 56,212.

Zay·san *or* **Zai·san** \zī-ˈsän\. Lake, NE Kazakhstan, in the Ala Tau; 695 sq. mi. (1800 sq. km.); traversed by the Irtysh River.

Zay·tūn *or* **Zay·ton** \zā-ˈtün\. See QUANZHOU.

Zazzau. See ZARIA 1.

Zba·razh \zə-ˈbär-əsh\ *or Pol.* **Zba·raż** \zə-ˈbär-ˌäsh\. Town, W Ukraine, just NE of Ternopol'; formerly in Poland; involved in Polish wars in 17th cent.

Zbruch \zə-ˈbrüch\ *or Pol.* **Zbrucz** \zə-ˈbrüch\. River, bet. Ternopol' and Khmel'nyts'kyy subdivisions, W Ukraine; flows S into the Dniester; 152 mi. (245 km.) long.

Zdar nad Sa·za·vou \ˈzhdär-näd-ˈsä-zä-ˌvō\. Town, Czech Republic, on Sázava River; pop. (1989c) 26,924.

Zduńska Wo·la \zə-ˈdün-skä-ˈvȯ-lä\. Commune, cen. Sieradz prov., cen. Poland, 28 mi. (45 km.) WSW of Łódź; pop. (1989e) 44,928.

Zealand. See SJÆLLAND.

Zeb·u·lon \ˈze-byə-lən\. **1.** City, ⊗ of Pike co., W Georgia; pop. (1990c) 1035.
2. Town, Wake co., E cen. North Carolina, E of Raleigh; pop. (1990c) 3173.

Zee·brug·ge \ˈzā-ˌbrœ-kə\. Seaport, West Flanders prov., NW Belgium, port of the city of Brugge (Bruges) with which it is connected by canal; occupied by the Germans WWI and used as a submarine base; raided Apr. 1918 by British naval contingents who succeeded in blocking the canal by sinking vessels at its mouth. Port again blocked during WWII; destroyed by Germans; subsequently rebuilt.

Zee·land **1.** \ˈzē-lənd\. City, Ottawa co., W Michigan, 21 mi. (34 km.) WSW of Grand Rapids; pop. (1990c) 5417.
2. \ˈzā-ˌlänt, ˈzē-lənd\. Province, SW Netherlands, composed of several islands (esp. Walcheren, North Beveland, South Beveland, Schouwen, and Tholen) on the North Sea coast, and a part of the mainland S of the estuary of Schelde; ✻ Middelburg, on Walcheren I.; largely below sea level, protected by dikes; wheat, oats, potatoes, flax. United with Holland 14th cent. and with other provinces during 16th cent.; Damaged by severe flooding 1953. See table at NETHERLANDS.

Zee·rust \ˈzā-ˌrəst\. Town, Northern prov., NE Rep. of South Africa, 135 mi. (217 km.) W of Pretoria; center of fertile Marico Valley.

Ze·fat \ˈtse-ˌfät\ *also* **Sa·fad** \ˈsä-ˌfäd\ *or* **Sa·fed** \ˈsä-ˌfed\. City, N Israel, 7 mi. (11 km.) NNW of the Sea of Galilee; tourism. One of the four Jewish holy cities of Palestine; fortified first cent. by Jewish general and historian Flavius Josephus and in Middle Ages by Crusaders; seat of important school of medieval Jewish mysticism (Kabbala); taken from Arabs by Jewish forces 1948.

Żegań. See ŻAGAŃ.

Zeil, Mount \ˈzēl\. Mountain, S Northern Terr., Australia; 5023 ft. (1531 m.); highest in the state.

Zeist \ˈzīst\. Commune, Utrecht prov., cen. Netherlands, 6 mi. (10 km.) E of the city of Utrecht; pop. (1993e) 59,096.

Zeitz \ˈtsīts, ˈzīts\. City, Saxony-Anhalt, E Germany, on Weisse Elster River 21 mi. (34 km.) SSW of Leipzig; pop. (1981c) 44,200.

Zela. See ZILE.

Ze·la·ya \sä-ˈlä-yä\. Department of E Nicaragua. See table at NICARAGUA.

Ze·le \ˈzā-lə\. Commune, East Flanders prov., NW cen. Belgium, E of Ghent; pop. (1991c) 20,097.

Ze·lee, Cape \zā-ˈlā\. Cape, S end of Maramasike I., SE Solomon Is., W Pacific Ocean.

Ze·le·no·dol'sk \zə-ˈlyȯ-nə-ˌdȯlʸsk\; *formerly* **Ze·le·ny Dol** \zə-ˈlyȯ-nē-ˈdȯl\. Town, Tatarstan, E cen. Russia in Europe, ab. 25 mi. (40 km.) E of Kazan'; pop. (1991e) 97,000.

Ze·li·e·no·ple \ˌzēl-yə-ˈnō-pəl\. Borough, Butler co., W Pennsylvania, 18 mi. (29 km.) SE of New Castle; pop. (1990c) 4158.

Zel·za·te \zel-ˈzä-tə\ *or* **Sel·zae·te** \sel-ˈzä-tə\. Commune, East Flanders prov., NW cen. Belgium, ab. 27 mi. (43 km.) W of Antwerp near the Netherlands boundary; pop. (1991c) 12,373.

Žemaitija. See SAMOGITIA.

Zemlya Frantsa Iosifa. See FRANZ JOSEF LAND.

Zem·po·al·te·pec \ˌzem-pō-ˈwäl-tā-ˌpek\ *or* **Zem·po·al·te·petl** \-ˌwäl-ˈtā-ˌpet-ᵊl\. Mountain, SE Mexico, 55 mi. (89 km.) E of the city of Oaxaca; 11,138 ft. (3395 m.); stands at the convergence of the Sierra Madre Occidental and the Sierra Madre Oriental.

Ze·mun \ˈze-ˌmün\ *or Ger.* **Sem·lin** \zem-ˈlēn\. City, S Vojvodina autonomous region, Serbia, N Yugoslavia, on Danube River WNW of Belgrade.

Zengg. See SENJ.

Ze·ni·ca \ˈze-nēt-sä\. Town, cen. Bosnia and Herzegovina, ab. 35 mi. (55 km.) NW of Sarajevo; pop. (1991c) 145,577.

Zenj \ˈzenj\ *or* **Zinj** \ˈzinj\. Name used for E Africa.

Zenjan. See ZANJĀN.

Zenta. See SENTA.

Zen·tsu·ji \zent-ˈsü-jē, ˈzent-sü-ˌjē\. Town, Kagawa prefecture, NE Shikoku I., Japan, SW of Takamatsu; pop. (1990p) 38,425; birthplace 774 A.D. of Kūkai, the founder of the Buddhist sect Shingon; has temple.

Zeph·yr·hills \ˌze-fər-ˈhilz\. City, Pasco co., Florida, NE of Tampa; pop. (1990c) 8220.

Ze·rav·shan \ˌzer-əf-ˈshän\. River, W cen. Asia; rises at W end of Alai Mts., flows W through NW Tajikistan and the oasis region of Samarqand in SE Uzbekistan to the desert near Bukhara; 460 mi. (740 km.) long.

Zerbst \ˈtserpst, ˈzerpst\. City, Saxony-Anhalt, E cen. Germany, NW of Dessau; pop. (1981c) 19,283; 13th cent. church (now a museum); medieval walls.

Zer·matt \tser-ˈmät\. Village in Valais canton, SW cen. Switzerland; pop. (1990c) 4225; elev. 5315 ft. (1620 m.), in the Pennine Alps; tourism; surrounded by meadows (*Matten*) forming a valley from which can be seen the Matterhorn to the SW.

Zet·land \ˈzet-lənd\ *or* **Shet·land** \ˈshet-\. **1.** Former county, Scotland, comprising the Shetland Is. (*q.v.*); ⊗ Lerwick.
2. Administrative region, N Scotland. See SHETLAND 3.

Ze·ven \ˈtsā-fən, ˈzā-\. Town, Lower Saxony, Germany, 24 mi. (39 km.) NE of Bremen; scene Sept. 8, 1757 during the Seven Years' War of William Augustus, duke of Cumberland's, capitulation to the French (the Convention of Kloster-Zeven) by which Hannover was abandoned.

Ze·ve·naar \ˌzā-və-ˈnär\. Town, Gelderland prov., Netherlands, SE of Arnhem near the German border on the Rhine; pop. (1981e) 26,814.

Ze·ya \ˈzā-yə\. River, S Russia in Asia; rises in Stanovoy Mts. in E Chita Oblast and flows S and SE into the Amur River in Khabarovsk Kray; 751 mi. (1208 km.) long; joined by the Selemdzha in its lower course.

Zê·ze·re \ˈzā-zə-rə\. River, cen. Portugal; rises near Spanish border and flows SW to the Tagus below Abrantes; ab. 130 mi. (210 km.) long; waterpower development.

Zgierz \zə-ˈgyesh\ *or Russ.* **Zgerzh** \zə-ˈgersh\. Town, Łódź prov., cen. Poland, 4 mi. (6 km.) N of the city of Łódź; pop. (1989e) 58,900.

Zgorzelec \zgȯ-ˈzhe-lets\. City, W Poland, across the Neisse River from Dresden, Germany; pop. (1989e) 35,881. See GÖRLITZ.

Zham·byl \jäm-ˈbil\ *also* **Dzham·bul** \jäm-ˈbül\. **1.** Administrative subdivision of Kazakhstan; 55,830 sq. mi. (144,600 sq. km.); ✻ Zhambyl; mostly steppe and desert; traversed by Chu River; cereals, tobacco, livestock; formed as **Dzhambul Oblast** \ˈȯ-bləst, ˈō-ˌblast\ of Kazakh S.S.R., U.S.S.R. 1939.

2. *or* **Au·lie Ata** \ˈau̇-lē-ˌā-ə-ˈtä\. Town, its ✻, on Turkistan-Siberian railroad line, 130 mi. (209 km.) NE of Tashkent; pop. (1991e) 312,300; food products.

Zhan·ga·qa·za·ly \ˌzhäŋ-gə-kə-ˈzä-lē\; *formerly* **No·vo·ka·za·linsk** \ˌnō-və-ˌkə-zəl-ˈyinsk\. Town, S Kazakhstan, on the lower Syr Dar'ya near its mouth, NE of the Aral Sea.

Zhang·guang·cai Ling \ˈjäŋ-ˈgwäŋ-ˈchī-ˈliŋ\ *or W.-G.* **Chang–kuang–tsai Ling** \ˈjäŋ-ˈgwäŋ-ˈdzī-ˈliŋ\. Mountain range extending NE and SW in cen. Jilin prov., NE China, E of Harbin; highest peak ab. 4400 ft. (1220 m.).

Zhang·jia·kou \ˈjäŋ-ˈjyä-ˈkō\ *or W.-G.* **Chang–chia–k'ou** \ˈjäŋ-ˈjyä-ˈkō\; *formerly* **Wan–ch'uan** \ˈwen-ˈchwen\; *Eng.* **Kal·gan** \ˈkal-ˈgan\. City, Hebei prov., N China; pop. (1990c) 529,136; under Ming and Manchu dynasties was a city of military and commercial importance; occupied by Japanese 1937–45; taken over by Communist forces Dec. 1948.

Zhang·zhou \ˈjäŋ-ˈjō\ *or W.-G.* **Ch'ang–chou** \ˈchäŋ-ˈjō\; *formerly* **Lung·ki** \ˈlu̇ŋ-ˈchē\. City, S Fujian prov., SE China, 30 mi. (48 km.) W of Xiamen; an important trading center 12th–16th cents.; residence of Chu Hsi (1130–1200), philosopher and expounder of Confucianism, under the Southern Sung dynasty.

Zhan·jiang \ˈjän-ˈjyäŋ\ *or W.-G.* **Chan–chiang** \ˈjän-ˈjyäŋ\; *formerly* **Tsam·kong** \ˈjäm-ˈgu̇ŋ\. Town, Guangdong prov., China, ab. 210 mi. (340 km.) SW of Guangzhou; pop. (1990c) 400,997.

Zhan·jiang Gang \ˈjän-ˈjyäŋ-ˈgäŋ\ *or W.-G.* **Chan–chiang Kang** \ˈjän-ˈjyäŋ-ˈgäŋ\; *or Eng.* **Kwang·cho·wan Bay** \ˈgwäŋ-ˈjō-ˈwen\. Bay on E side of Leizhou Penin., SW mainland part of Guangdong prov., S China.

Zhao·qing *or W.-G.* **Chao–ch'ing** \ˈjau̇-ˈchiŋ\. City, W cen. Guangdong prov., S China, W of Guangzhou; pop. (1990c) 194,784.

Zhao·tong *or W.-G.* **Chao–t'ung** \ˈjau̇-ˈtu̇ŋ\. City, NE Yunnan prov., S China, near the Chang ab. 175 mi. (280 km.) NNE of Kunming.

Zhayyq. See URAL.

Zhdanov. See MARIUPOL'.

Zhe·fang *or W.-G.* **Che–fang** \ˈjə-ˈfäŋ\. Town, SW Yunnan prov., S China, near Wandingzhen; alt. ab. 3200 ft. (975 m.); held by Japanese during WWII.

Zhe·jiang *or W.-G.* **Che·kiang** \ˈjə-ˈjyäŋ\. Coast province, E China, bounded on N by Jiangsu, on E by East China Sea, on S by Fujian, and on W by Jiangxi and Anhui; ✻ Hangzhou. The smallest province of China but one of the most densely populated; N part lies just S of the delta of the Chang; cen. part drained by the Fuchun, flowing into Hangzhou Bay; the S part drained by the Ou; many hills and low mountain ranges. The Zhoushan Archipelago is off NE coast. A cultural center of early China; during 12th and 13th cents. A.D. its chief city, Hangzhou (*q.v.*), was ✻ of China under Sung dynasty. See table at CHINA.

Chief products: Wheat, rice, cotton, tea, silk, sweet potatoes, rapeseed; fishing and aquaculture.

Chief cities: Hangzhou and Ningbo.

Zhe·lez·no·do·ro·zhnyy *or* **Zhe·lez·no·do·ro·zhny** \zhə-ˌliz-nə-də-ˈrȯzh-nē\; *formerly* **Obi·ra·lov·ka** \ˌə-bər-ə-ˈləf-kə\. Town, Moscow Oblast, W cen. Russia in Europe, 16 mi. (26 km.) E of the city of Moscow; pop. (1991e) 99,300.

Zhe·lez·no·gorsk \zhə-ˌliz-nə-ˈgȯrsk\. City, Kursk Oblast, W Russia in Europe, NW of city of Kursk; pop. (1991e) 88,200.

Zhengjiatun. See SHUANGLIAO.

Zheng·zhou \ˈjəŋ-ˈjō\ *or W.-G.* **Cheng–chou** \ˈjəŋ-ˈjō\ *or* **Cheng·chow** \ˈjəŋ-ˈjō\; *1913–49* **Cheng·hsien** \ˈjəŋ-ˈshyen\. City, ✻ of Henan prov., on right bank of the Huang, E cen. China, 40 mi. (64 km.) W of Kaifeng; pop. (1990c) 1,159,679; textiles, heavy machinery; thermal power plant; important railroad junction. Considerable fighting in 1944 for adjacent sections of the railroad. Important archaeological remains (believed to be of a Shang ✻ which flourished 2d millennium B.C.) nearby.

Zhen·hai \ˈjən-ˈhī\ *or W.-G.* **Chen–hai** \ˈjən-\ *or* **Chin·hai** \ˈjən-\. City and port, NE Zhejiang prov., E China, ab. 12 mi. (19 km.) ENE of Ningbo on SE shore of Hangzhou Bay.

Zhen·jiang \ˈjən-ˈjyäŋ\ *or W.-G.* **Chen–chiang** \ˈjən-ˈjyäŋ\ *also* **Chin·kiang** \ˈjən-ˈjyäŋ\. City, Jiangsu prov., E China, on S bank of the Chang 43 mi. (69 km.) below Nanjing at the junction of the Grand Canal (Da Yunhe) with the river; pop. (1990c) 368,316; food products; lumber and paper products. About 2500 years old; long an important city; known to Venetian traveler Marco Polo; flourished esp. under Ming and Manchu dynasties.

Zhen·yuan \ˈjən-ˈywen\ *or W.-G.* **Chen–yüan** \ˈjən-ˈywen\. Town, E Guizhou prov., S China, 110 mi. (177 km.) ENE of Guiyang.

Zhi·gu·levsk \ˌzhə-gəl-ˈyȯfsk\; *formerly* **Ot·vazh·ny** \ət-ˈväzh-nē\. Town, Samara Oblast, Russia in Europe, ab. 30 mi. (48 km.) WNW of the city of Samara.

Zhi·jiang \ˈjə-ˈjyäŋ\ *or W.-G.* **Chih–chiang** \ˈjə-ˈjyäŋ, ˈjir-\ *or* **Chih·kiang** \ˈjir-ˈjyäŋ\; *formerly* **Yuan·chow** \ˈywen-ˈjō\. City, W Hunan prov., SE China, on railroad line 210 mi. (338 km.) WSW of Changsha near border of Guizhou prov.

Zhitomir 1. Administrative subdivision of Ukraine. See ZHYTOMYR 1.

2. City, Ukraine. See ZHYTOMYR 2.

Zhlo·bin \zhlō-ˈbyin\. Town, Homyel' subdivision, Belarus, on right bank of the Dnieper ab. 75 mi. (120 km.) S of Mahilyow; pop. (1991e) 60,800; in WWII a bitterly contested point in Soviet campaign of 1944; retaken by Soviets in June.

Zhme·ryn·ka *or Russ.* **Zhme·rin·ka** \zhmə-ˈriŋ-kə\. Town, W Vinnytsya subdivision, W cen. Ukraine, 20 mi. (32 km.) SW of the city of Vinnytsya; railroad junction, a key point in WWII campaigns of 1944.

Zhob \ˈzhōb\. River, cen. Pakistan; a tributary of the Gumal which is direct route bet. North-West Frontier prov. and Quetta in Pakistan. Its valley was scene of frontier disturbances late 19th cent.; under British rule from 1890 to Pakistani independence 1947.

Zho·di·no \ˈzhȯ-ji-nȧ, -dʸi-nə\. City, cen. Belarus, NE of Minsk; pop. (1991e) 56,000.

Zhong·tiao Shan \ˈju̇ŋ-ˈtyau̇-ˈshän\ *or W.-G.* **Chung–t'io Shan** \ˈju̇ŋ-ˈtyȯ-\. Mountain range along border bet. Henan and Shanxi provs., NE cen. China; in bend of the Huang.

Zhong Xian *or* **Zhong·xian** \ˈju̇ŋ-ˈshyen\; *or W.-G.* **Chung–hsien** \ˈju̇ŋ-ˈshyen\; *formerly* **Chung·chow** \ˈju̇ŋ-ˈjō\. City, E cen. Sichuan prov., S cen. China, on the Chang ab. 100 mi. (160 km.) below Chongqing.

Zhou·kou·dian·zhen *or W.-G.* **Chou–k'ou–tien–chen** \ˈjō-ˈkō-ˈdyen-ˈjən\; *often shortened to* **Chou·kou·tien** \ˈjō-ˈkō-ˈtyen\. Village, Beijing municipality, NE China, 37 mi. (60 km.) SW of the city of Beijing; site of discovery late 1920s of remains of extinct Peking Man (*Homo erectus pekinensis*).

Zhou·shan *or W.-G.* **Chou–shan** \ˈjō-ˈshän\ *or* **Chu Shan** \ˈjü-\ *or* **Chu·san** \ˈchü-ˈsän\.**1.** Archipelago in East China Sea off NE coast of Zhejiang prov., E China, at entrance to Hangzhou Bay, consisting of ab. 100 islands; ✻ Dinghai, on Zhoushan I.; for several centuries a base for trade with foreign governments, esp. Japan and Great Britain. See PUTUO SHAN.

2. Island, largest of the Zhoushan Archipelago, East China Sea, ab. 50 mi. (80 km.) E of Ningbo; 20 mi. (32 km.) long, 10 mi. (16 km.) wide; on its S shore is Dinghai.

Zhu \ˈjü\ *or W.-G.* **Chu** \ˈjü\ *or* **Pearl** \ˈpərl\. River, SE China, forming part of the delta of the Xi and flowing from the city of Guangzhou to the South China Sea; divided by a narrow channel into upper and lower rivers, the lower one constituting the bay (ab. 20 mi. or 32 km. wide) bet. Hong Kong and Macao; below Guangzhou the upper river is joined by the Dong from the E.

Zhu·kov·skiy *or* **Zhu·kov·ski** \zhü-ˈkȯf-skē\; *formerly* **Ot·dykh** \ȯt-ˈdik\ *or* **Sta·kha·no·vo** \stə-ˈkȯ-nə-və\. Town, Moscow Oblast, W cen. Russia in Europe, 23 mi. (37 km.) SE of the city of Moscow; pop. (1992e) 101,000.

Zhu·zhou \ˈjü-ˈjō\ *or W.-G.* **Chu–chou** \ˈjü-ˈjō\ *or* **Chu·chow** \-ˈjō\. Town, Hunan prov., China, ab. 25 mi. (40 km.) SSE of Changsha; pop. (1990c) 409,924; transportation and industrial center.

Zhy·to·myr *or* **Zhi·to·mir** \zhi-ˈtȯ-ˌmir\. **1.** Administrative subdivision of Ukraine; 11,544 sq. mi. (29,899 sq. km.); pop. (1991e) 1,510,700; ✻ Zhytomyr; winter wheat, hops, sugar beets, flax.

2. *also* **Ji·to·mir** \zhi-\.City, its ✻, on the Teterev River 85 mi. (137 km.) W of Kiev; pop. (1991e) 298,000; furniture; flax processing.

History: An old town on the early trade route from Scandinavia to Constantinople and on the direct route W from Kiev; plundered by Tatars in medieval times; belonged to Lithuania from 14th cent., then passed to Poland 16th cent.; incorp. in Russia late 18th cent.; occupied by Axis forces 1941 in WWII; retaken by Soviets 1943.

Zi \ˈdzə\ *or W.-G.* **Tzu** \ˈdzə, ˈdzü\. River, cen. Hunan prov., SE cen. China; flows into Dongting Hu just W of mouth of the Xiang; ab. 375 mi. (605 km.) long.

Zi·bo \ˈdzə-ˈbwȯ, -ˈbō\ *or W.-G.* **Tzu–po** \ˈdzə-ˈbō\. City, cen. Shandong prov., China, ENE of Jinan; pop. (1990c) 1,138,074.

Zidon. See SIDON.

Zie·bach \ˈzē-bäk, -ˈbä, -ˈbȯ\. County in NW cen. South Dakota. See table at SOUTH DAKOTA.

Zie·lo·na Gó·ra \zhe-ˈlȯ-nä-ˈgü-rä\. **1.** Province of W cen. Poland. See table at POLAND.

2. *or Ger.* **Grün·berg** \ˈgrœn-ˌberk\ *also* **Grünberg in Schle·si·en** \in-ˈshlā-zē-ən\. City, its ✻; pop. (1989e) 113,322; wine, textiles; metal foundries; formerly in Germany; assigned to Poland by Potsdam Conference 1945.

Zie·rik·zee \ˈzē-rik-ˌzā\. Commune, Zeeland prov., SW Netherlands, on S shore of Schouwen I.; pop. (1981e) 9658.

Zi·gong *or W.-G.* **Tzu–kung** \ˈdzə-ˈgůŋ\ *also* **Tze·liu·tsing** \ˈdzə-ˈlyů-ˈdziŋ\. City, S Sichuan prov., S cen. China, 110 mi. (177 km.) W of Chongqing; pop. (1990c) 393,184.

Zi·guin·chor \ˌzē-ˌge^{n}-ˈshȯr\. River port, SW Senegal, on Casamance River 45 mi. (72 km.) from its mouth; pop. (1992e) 148,831; ships peanuts.

Zilah. See ZALĂU.

Zi·le \zi-ˈlā\; *anc.* **Ze·la** \ˈzē-lə\. Town, Tokat prov., N cen. Turkey in Asia, on tributary of Yeşilirmak; pop. (1990p) 46,323. In a battle here 47 B.C. Pharnaces II, king of Pontus, was defeated by Roman Gen. Julius Caesar who announced his victory to the senate at Rome by his famous laconic message: *Veni, Vidi, Vici* ("I came, I saw, I conquered").

Ži·li·na \ˈzhē-lē-ˌnä\ *or Hung.* **Zsol·na** \ˈzhōl-ˌnö\ *or Ger.* **Sil·lein** \zi-ˈlīn\. Town, NW Slovakia, on Váh River ab. 45 mi. (70 km.) SE of Ostrava; pop. (1991p) 83,853.

Zil·le·be·ke \ˈzi-lə-ˌbā-kə\. Commune, West Flanders prov., NW Belgium, near Ieper (Ypres); involved in battles of WWI.

Zil·ler·ta·ler Alps \ˈtsi-lər-ˌtä-lər\. Subsidiary range of the E Alps, SW cen. Europe, along boundary bet. NE Italy and the Tirol, Austria, at W end of the Hohe Tauern; highest peak Hochfeiler 11,513 ft. (3509 m.).

Zilling Tso. See SILING CO.

Zi·ma \zi-ˈmä, ˈzē-mə\. Town, Irkutsk Oblast, S Russia in Asia, ab. 150 mi. (240 km.) NW of the city of Irkutsk.

Zim·ba·bwe \zim-ˈbä-bwā, -bwē\. **1.** Site of ruins, Zimbabwe (republic), 17 mi. (27 km.) SE of Masvingo. Distinguished as **Great Zimbabwe** from a smaller and more recent group of ruins 8 mi. (13 km.) distant (**Little Zimbabwe**). Ruins comprise a hilltop fortress and an elliptical enclosure formed by huge walls of stone monoliths fitted without mortar, as well as a number of smaller buildings. Discovered c. 1870; excavations have yielded a variety of artifacts; radiocarbon dates indicate initial settlement by Iron Age people c. 3d cent. A.D.; fl. esp. 11th–15th cents. Similar ruins found in other parts of S Africa.

2. *before 1979* **Rho·de·sia** \rō-ˈdē-zhə\ *also* **Southern Rhodesia.** Republic, S cen. Africa. bounded on NW by Zambia, on N by Zambia and Mozambique, on E and SE by Mozambique, on S by the Rep. of South Africa, and on SW and W by Botswana; 150,820 sq. mi. (390,624 sq. km.); pop. (1982c) 7,540,000; ✻ Harare.

Physical features: Forms part of a vast plateau sloping from SW to NE; cen. part at av. elev. of 4000 to 5000 ft. (1200

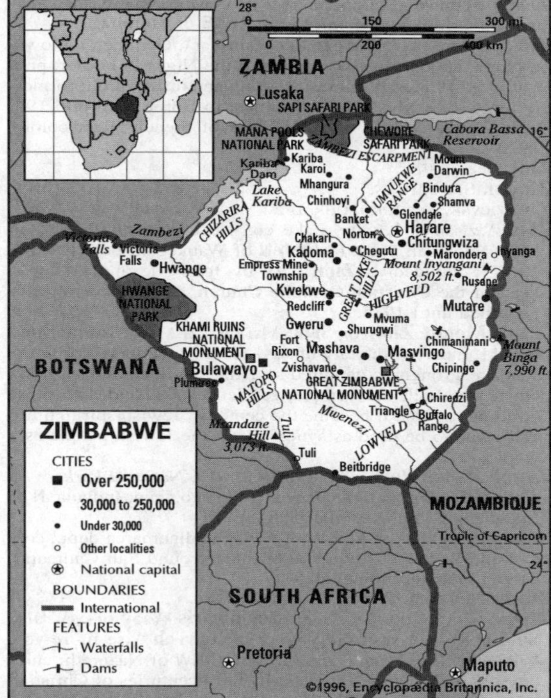

to 1500 m.) is broad watershed bet. Zambezi (boundary with Zambia) and Limpopo and Sabi systems on SE. These large streams have many tributaries, esp. Sanyati flowing to Zambezi in NW and Lundi to Sabi in SE. In NW is Victoria Falls (*q.v.*) in the Zambezi.

Chief products: Wheat, corn, tobacco, barley, sugar; livestock; gold, chrome, coal, copper, nickel; manufacturing: textiles, iron and steel, chemicals.

Chief cities: Harare, Bulawayo, Chitungwiza, Gweru, Mutare, Kwekwe, Masvingo.

History: Early inhabitants displaced by migrations of Bantu-speaking peoples from c. 5th cent. A.D.; remnants of early settlements (see ZIMBABWE 1) scattered throughout area; region under administration of British South Africa Company 1889–1923; became a self-governing British colony 1923; member of the Federation of Rhodesia and Nyasaland 1953–63; issued a unilateral declaration of independence 1965 (considered illegal by the British government); proclaimed itself a republic 1970; instituted limited majority rule 1979; formally granted independence by United Kingdom April 1980 and became Zimbabwe.

Zimbabwe Rhodesia. Name used for Rhodesia during its transition to majority rule 1979–80.

Zim·ni·cea \ˈzēm-ni-ˌchä\. Town, Teleorman co., S Romania, on the Danube ab. 27 mi. (43 km.) SW of Bucharest.

Zin, Wilderness of \ˈzin\ *or Heb.* **Mid·bar Zin** \ˌmid-ˈbär\. Desert region, SW of the Dead Sea, S Israel; in biblical times the region bet. W Edom and SE Judaea, traversed by the Israelites on their journey to Canaan (*Num.* xx. 1).

Zi·nal Rot·horn \tsē-ˈnäl-ˈrōt-ˌhȯrn, zi-\ *also* **Mo·ming** \ˈmō-miŋ\. Peak, SW cen. Switzerland, in the Pennine Alps near Zermatt; 13,849 ft. (4221 m.).

\ə\ abut \ə\ matches \ᵊ\ kitten, Fr table \ər\ further \a\ ash \ā\ ace \ä\ cot, cart \à\ Fr bac \au̇\ out \b\ Span Avila \ch\ chin \e\ bet \ē\ easy \g\ go \i\ hit \ī\ ice \j\ job \k\ Ger ich, Buch \$^{n}$\ Fr vin \ŋ\ sing \ō\ go \ȯ\ all \ȯ\ law \œ\ Fr bœuf \œ̄\ Fr feu \ȯi\ boy \th\ thin \th\ this \ü\ loot \u̇\ foot \ue\ Ger füllen \üe\ Fr rue \y\ yet \$^{y}$\ Fr digne \ˈdēn^{y}\, nuit \ˈnw^{y}ē\ \yü\ few \yu̇\ fury \zh\ vision

Zi·na·pé·cua·ro \ˌzē-nä-ˈpā-kwä-ˌrō\. Municipality, Michoacán state, Mexico, 32 mi. (52 km.) NE of Morelia.

Zin·der \ˈzin-dər\ *also* **Sin·der** \ˈsin-dər\. Commercial town, S Niger, ab. 65 mi. (105 km.) N of the Nigerian border; pop. (1988c) 119,838; peanut processing and distribution; formerly the ✻ of a Muslim state, subject to Bornu until mid-19th cent.; occupied by French 1899; ✻ of French Niger colony 1922–26.

Zinj. See ZENJ.

Zinjan. See ZANJĀN.

Zinovievsk. See KIROVOHRAD 2.

Zi·on \ˈzī-ən\. **1.** City, Lake co., NE corner of Illinois, on Lake Michigan 5 mi. (8 km.) N of Waukegan; pop. (1990c) 19,775; founded as **Zion City** by John Alexander Dowie, head of the Christian Catholic Church, 1901; theocratically governed until 1935.

2. *or* **Mount Zion** *or* **Si·on** \ˈsī-ən, ˈzī-\ *or* **Mount Sion.** Height, E part of the city of Jerusalem (*q.v.*), Israel; orig. the Jebusite stronghold captured by King David (*2 Sam.* v. 6–9). On it was built the Temple, residence of David, and other buildings so that it became the center of Jewish spiritual life and came to be used as synonym for the Jewish people as a whole.

Zion National Park. See UNITED STATES, *National Parks.*

Zi·ons·ville \ˈzī-ənz-ˌvil\ Town, Boone co., cen. Indiana, N of Indianapolis; pop. (1990c) 5281.

Zi·pa·qui·rá \ˌzē-pä-kē-ˈrä\. Town, Cundinamarca dept., cen. Colombia, N of Bogotá; site of underground Salt Cathedral, carved in a salt mountain.

Zipfer Neudorf. See SPIŠSKÁ NOVÁ VES.

Zip·po·ri \zə-ˈpȯr-ē\; *anc.* **Sep·pho·ris** \sə-ˈfȯr-əs\ *also* **Saf·fu·ri·yah** \ˌsa-fu̇-ˈrē-yə\ *or* **Sef·u·ri·eh** \ˌse-fu̇-ˈrē-yə\. Village, N Israel, ab. 3 mi. (53 km.) NNW of Nazareth; chief city of Galilee first cent. A.D.; in early centuries of Christian era a rival of Tiberias.

Ziria. See CYLLENE.

Zi·ro \ˈzir-ō\. Town, former ✻ of Arunachal Pradesh, NE India, ab. 185 mi. (300 km.) NE of Shillong.

Zi·sters·dorf \ˈtsis-tərz-ˌdȯrf, ˈzis-\. Town, Lower Austria, Austria, ab. 27 mi. (43 km.) NE of Vienna; once extensive oil fields.

Zi·tá·cua·ro \zä-ˈtä-kwä-ˌrō\. City, Michoacán state, Mexico, 60 mi. (97 km.) SE of Morelia; munic. pop. (1990p) 107,658; early center of Mexican War of Independence, 1811 ff.; Junta of Zitácuaro the first central directing body of the independence movement; burned 1865.

Zit·tau \ˈtsi-ˌtau̇, ˈzi-\. City, Saxony, E Germany, on left bank of Neisse River 46 mi. (74 km.) ESE of Dresden; pop. (1992e) 33,092; textiles, chemicals. Became city 1255; to Saxony early 17th cent.

Zituni. See LAMÍA.

Ziwa Magharibi. See KAGERA.

Zi·way Hāyk' \zi-ˈwī-ˈhīk\ *or* **Lake Zwai** \ˈzwī\. Lake, cen. Ethiopia, ab. 65 mi. (105 km.) S of Addis Ababa.

Zla·to·ust \ˌzlä-tə-ˈüst\. City, W Chelyabinsk Oblast, W Russia in Asia, in S part of Ural Mts. 75 mi. (121 km.) W of the city of Chelyabinsk; pop. (1992e) 208,000; from its establishment mid-18th cent. a center of the iron and steel industry; became city 1865.

Zlín *or 1948–91* **Gott·wal·dov** \ˈgȯt-ˌväl-ˌdȯf\. Town, E Czech Republic; pop. (1989c) 87,082.

Znaim. See ZNOJMO.

Zna·men·ka *or* **Zna·myan·ka** \ˈznä-myən-kə\. Town, cen. Kirovohrad subdivision, Ukraine, 20 mi. (32 km.) NNE of the city of Kirovohrad.

Zna·mensk \ˈznä-mənsk\; *formerly* **Weh·lau** \ˈvā-lau̇\. Town, Kaliningrad Oblast, Russian enclave in cen. Europe, on S bank of the Pregolya at the mouth of the Lava; in part of Prussia assigned to the U.S.S.R. 1945. Treaty signed here 1657 bet. Brandenburg and Poland by which Poland renounced sovereignty over duchy of Prussia.

Znoj·mo \ˈznȯi-ˌmȯ, ˈsnȯi-\ *or Ger.* **Zna·im** \ˈtsnīm\. City, S Czech Republic; pop. (1991p) 39,910; food processing; armistice signed here 1809 bet. Austria and France following the battle of Wagram.

Zoan. See TANIS.

Zoar \ˈzōr, ˈzō-ər\. Village, Tuscarawas co., E Ohio; pop. (1990c) 177; site of separatist community founded 1817 by group of German Protestants, disbanded 1898.

Zoe·ter·meer \ˌzü-tər-ˈmār\. Municipality, South Holland prov., W Netherlands, N of Rotterdam; pop. (1993e) 102,937.

Zo·fing·en \ˈtsō-fiŋ-ən, ˈzō-\. Commune, Aargau canton, Switzerland; pop. (1980c) 8643.

Zoh·reh *or* **Zuh·reh** \zə-ˈrā\; *formerly* **Tab** \ˈtäb\. River, SW Iran; flows W and SW into the head of the Persian Gulf along the boundary bet. Khūzestān and Fārs provs.; 200 mi. (322 km.) long.

Zol·lern \ˈtsȯl-ərn, ˈzȯ-\. Mountain, Baden-Württemberg, Germany, near Hechingen; 2805 ft. (855 m.).

Zolotoy Rog. See GOLDEN HORN 3.

Zólyom. See ZVOLEN.

Zom·ba \ˈzōm-bä\. Town, S Malawi, in Shire Highlands, ab. 70 mi. (115 km.) S of Lake Malawi; pop. (1993e) 51,838; tobacco; dairy products. Developed by British late 19th cent.; ✻ of Malawi from independence 1966 to 1975.

Zombor. See SOMBOR.

Zone of the Straits. Demilitarized zone Europe and Asia, around the Bosporus, the Dardanelles, and the Sea of Marmara, administered 1920–22 by the League of Nations; mostly returned to Turkey 1923. See STRAITS, THE 2.

Zon·gul·dak \ˌzȯŋ-gu̇l-ˈdäk\. **1.** Province of Turkey in Asia. See table at TURKEY.

2. Seaport city, its ✻, on the Black Sea 140 mi. (225 km.) E of the Bosporus; pop. (1990c) 116,725.

Zon·ne·be·ke \ˈzȯ-nə-ˌbā-kə\. Commune, West Flanders prov., NW Belgium; pop. (1991c) 11,001; battlefield in WWI.

Zoppot. See SOPOT.

Zor \ˈzȯr\. Former region, W Asia, extending on both sides of Euphrates River; ✻ Dayr az Zawr; now divided bet. Turkey and Syria.

Zor·kul, Lake \zȯr-ˈkül\ *or in Afghanistan* **Sa·rī Qūl** \ˌsär-ē-ˈkül\ *or Eng.* **Lake Vic·to·ria** \vik-ˈtōr-ē-ə\. Small lake in high Pamirs, Tajikistan, on NE border of Afghanistan; alt. 13,400 ft. (4084 m.).

Zorndorf. See SARBINOWO.

Zo·ry \ˈzhȯ-rē\. Commune, Katowice prov., S Poland; pop. (1989e) 66,123.

Zoui·rat \zwē-ˈrät\. Town, Mauritania, near Western Sahara; pop. (1988c) 25,892; one of Mauritania's largest settlements.

Zoutpans Berg. See SOUTPANSBERG.

Zren·ja·nin \ˈzren-yə-nin, zə-ˈren-\; *formerly* **Pe·trov·grad** \ˈpe-trȯv-ˌgräd\ *or* **Ve·li·ki Beč·ke·rek** \ˈve-lē-kē-bech-ˈker-ək\ *or Hung.* **Nagy·becs·ke·rek** \ˈnöj-ˈbech-kə-ˌrek\. City, Vojvodina autonomous prov., N Yugoslavia, ab. 30 mi. (48 km.) NE of Novi Sad; pop. (1991c) 81,382; commercial center.

Zsolna. See ŽILINA.

Zsombolya. See JIMBOLIA.

Zuetina, Ez. See QARYAT AZ ZUWAYTĪNAH.

Zufār. See DHOFAR.

Zug \ˈtsük, ˈzüg\. **1.** Canton, Switzerland; ✻ Zug; fruit growing; victory of Swiss Confederation over Hapsburgs 1315; joined Catholic Sonderbund 1845; constitution dates from 1894. See table at SWITZERLAND.

2. Commune, its ✻, N cen. Switzerland, on Lake of Zug 15 mi. (24 km.) S of Zürich; pop. (1989c) 21,752; electrical equipment, textiles; cattle market; tourism; clock tower (1480); town hall (1505); 15th–16th cent. Gothic church; commune purchased by Holy Roman Emperor Rudolf I 1273; entered Swiss Confederation mid-14th cent.

Zug, Lake of *or Ger.* **Zu·ger See** \ˈtsü-gər-ˌzā, ˈzü-\. Lake, N cen. Switzerland, N of Lake of Lucerne; ab. 15 sq. mi. (39 sq. km.); max. depth 650 ft. (198 m.); alt. 1368 ft. (417 m.).

Zug·spit·ze \ˈtsük-ˌshpit-sə\. Peak in Wetterstein Mts. of the Bavarian Alps, S Bavaria, Germany, on border of the Tirol 54 mi. (87 km.) SSW of Munich; 9720 ft. (2963 m.); highest peak in Germany.

Zuhreh. See ZOHREH.

Zui·der Zee *also* **Zuy·der Zee** \ˌzī-dər-ˈzā, -ˈzē\; *anc.* **Fle·vo La·cus** \ˈflē-vō-ˈlā-kəs\. Former inlet of the North Sea, N coast of Netherlands; extended inland ab. 80 mi. (130 km.); orig. a lake, but was joined to the North Sea by inundations; now divided into Waddenzee (*q.v.*) and IJsselmeer (*q.v.*) by a dike (completed 1932); partly drained, four polders having been created, the Wieringermeer (*q.v.*), the Northeast Polder (completed 1942), the Eastern Flevoland (completed 1957), and the Southern Flevoland (completed 1969), of the five which were orig. planned.

Zuid–Holland. See SOUTH HOLLAND.

Zú·jar \ˈzü-ˌhär\. River, Badajoz prov., SW Spain; flows into Guadiana River; 100 mi. (161 km.) long.

Zukur. See ZUQAR.

Zu·la \ˈzü-lə\. Seaport town, Eritrea, on Gulf of Zula; ancient ruins nearby.

Zula, Gulf of; *formerly* **Annes·ley Bay** \ˈanz-lē\. Inlet of the Red Sea, Eritrea.

Zu·lia \ˈzül-yä\. State of Venezuela. See table at VENEZUELA.

Zül·pich \ˈtsœl-pik̲, ˈzül-\; *anc.* **Tol·bi·a·cum** \tȯl-ˈbī-ə-kəm\. Commune, North Rhine-Westphalia, Germany, SW of Cologne; site where the Franks defeated the Alamanni c. 496.

Zu·lu·land \ˈzü-lü-ˌland\. Region, NE KwaZulu-Natal prov., E Rep. of South Africa; 10,362 sq. mi. (26,838 sq. km.). Historically, the home of Zulus, a Bantu nation that first came into prominence in early part of 19th cent. Chief Shaka established dominance over neighboring peoples and was noted for his cruelty and for the fighting efficiency of his *impis* (regiments); his successor Dingaan fought against the Boers and was replaced by his brother Mpande 1840 as a result of Boer intervention; Cetewayo, Mpande's successor, resisted British rule 1878, but was defeated in battle 1879; land of Zulus taken under British control 1887 and annexed to Natal 1897.

Zu·mar·ra·ga \zü-ˈmär-ä-gä\. Municipality, W coast of Buad I. off W Samar, Philippines, 9 mi. (15 km.) S of Catbalogan; pop. (1980c) 12,821; includes barrios on Daram I.

Zum·bo \ˈzüm-bō, ˈzəm-\. Westernmost town of Mozambique, 600 mi. (965 km.) up the Zambezi River.

Zum·pan·go \züm-ˈpäŋ-gō\. Lake in the Valley of Mexico, cen. Mexico, ab. 30 mi. (48 km.) N of Mexico City.

Zu·ni \ˈzü-nē, -nyē\. **1.** River, New Mexico and Arizona; rises in W New Mexico and flows W into the Little Colorado River in Arizona; ab. 90 mi. (145 km.) long.

2. *or* **Zu·ñi** \ˈzü-nyē\. Indian pueblo, McKinley co., NW New Mexico, in Zuni Indian Reservation, on Zuni River ab. 32 mi. (52 km.) S of Gallup; pop. (1990c) 5857; inhabited by descendants of people of Cíbola (*q.v.*), reported in 1539 by the Spaniards; agriculture, weaving, pottery.

Zu·ni–Ci·bo·la National Historical Park \ˈzü-nē-ˈsē-bə-lə, -nyē-\. See UNITED STATES, *National Historical Parks.*

Zuni Mountains. Range, McKinley and Cibola cos., W New Mexico; highest peak 8110 ft. (2472 m.).

Zun·yi \ˈdzün-ˈē\ *or W.-G.* **Tsun–i** \ˈdzün-ˈē\ *or* **Tsun·yi** \ˈdzün-ˈē\. Town, N cen. Guizhou prov., S China; on highway ab. 75 mi. (120 km.) NNE of Guiyang; pop. (1990c) 261,862.

Zu·po, Piz \pēts-ˈtsü-pō\. Mountain, 2d highest of the Bernina Mts. of the Rhaetian Alps, on the border between Switzerland and Italy; 13,120 ft. (3999 m.); its peak is hidden (*zupò*).

Zu·qar \ˈzü-ˌkär\ *or* **Az Zu·qar** \ˌäz-\ *also* **Zu·kur** \ˈzü-kər\. Island at S end of Red Sea, bet. Yemen and Eritrea. Belongs to Yemen.

Zü·rich \ˈtsue̅-rik̲\. **1.** Canton, Switzerland. See table at SWITZERLAND.

2. City, its ✻, at foot of Alps on Limmat River at NW end of Zürichsee 60 mi. (97 km.) NE of Bern; pop. (1989c) 347,021; center of finance and manufacturing; tourism; railway center; among its buildings are three medieval churches (Grossmünster, Fraumünster, and St. Peter's), numerous restored houses, and a town hall; university (founded 1833), and the Swiss Federal Institute of Technology (founded mid-19th cent.); museums; botanical and zoological gardens.

History: Occupied first by prehistoric lake dwellers and later by the Helvetii before Roman occupation c. 58 B.C.; subsequently held by the Alamanni, followed by the Franks; became free imperial city 1218; joined Swiss Confederation 1351; became center of Swiss Reformation under leadership of Huldrych Zwingli 16th cent.; scene of Austrian victory over French, and later of French victory over Russians 1799; place where treaty ending Franco-Italian war against Austria was concluded 1859.

Zü·rich·see \ˈtsue̅-rik̲-ˌzā\ *or* **Lake of Zürich** *or* **Lake Zürich.** Lake, N cen. Switzerland, for the most part in Zürich canton; 34 sq. mi. (88 sq. km.); 25 mi. (40 km.) long; max. depth 469 ft. (143 m.).

Zu·shi \ˈzü-shē\. Town, Kanagawa prefecture, SE Honshū, Japan, ab. 30 mi. (48 km.) SW of Tokyo near Kamakura; pop. (1990p) 56,705.

Zus·mars·hau·sen \ˌtsu̇s-ˌmärs-ˈhau̇z-^{ə}n, ˌzu̇s-\. Village, Bavaria, Germany, ab. 14 mi. (23 km.) W of Augsburg; battle 1648 in which the Swedes under Count Karl Gustav Wrangel and the French under Henri de LaTour d'Auvergne, vicomte de Turenne defeated the Imperialists and Bavarians.

Zut·phen \ˈzœt-fə\. Commune, Gelderland prov., E Netherlands, on IJssel River; pop. (1993e) 31,117; formerly a fortified town; church of St. Walpurgis, 12th cent. Gothic structure; battlefield on which English poet and soldier Sir Philip Sidney was mortally wounded 1586 while fighting in support of the Dutch against Spain.

Zuwaytīnah, Az. See QARYAT AZ ZUWAYTĪNAH.

Zuyder Zee. See ZUIDER ZEE.

Zvi·sha·va·ne \ˌzvē-shä-ˈvä-nā\; *formerly* **Sha·ba·ni** \shä-ˈbä-nē\. Town, S cen. Zimbabwe, 90 mi. (145 km.) SW of Harare; pop. (1982c) 26,597; nearby are asbestos mines.

Zvo·len \ˈzvȯ-ˌlen, ˈsfȯ-\ *or Hung.* **Zó·lyom** \ˈzō-ˌlyōm\ *or Ger.* **Alt·sohl** \ˈält-ˌzōl\. Town, cen. Slovakia, on the Hron River 100 mi. (161 km.) NE of Bratislava; pop. (1980p) 36,538.

Zwai, Lake. See ZIWAY HĀYK'.

Zwei·brück·en \tsfī-ˈbrue-kən\ *or Fr.* **Deux·ponts** \ˌdœ-ˈpō^{n}\ *or Lat.* **Bi·pon·ti·um** \bī-ˈpän-chē-əm\. City, Rhineland-Palatinate, Germany, 53 mi. (85 km.) WSW of Mannheim; pop. (1992e) 34,645; textiles, machinery, footwear; received charter 1352; known to scholars for its early editions of Greek and Latin classics; under Swedish crown 1697–1718; most of city destroyed in WWII, since largely rebuilt.

Zwe·lit·sha \ˈzwā-lit-ˌshä\. Town, Eastern Cape prov., Rep. of South Africa, just SSE of King William's Town in former Ciskei enclave; pop. (1987e) 55,000.

Zwellendam. See SWELLENDAM.

Zwick·au \ˈtsfi-kau̇, ˈzwi-\. City, Saxony, E Germany, on the Mulde River 42 mi. (68 km.) S of Leipzig; pop. (1992e) 112,565; coal mines in area; 14th and 15th cent. churches; 15th cent. town hall; 16th cent. castle. Birthplace of composer Robert Schumann 1810; Schumann Museum (1956). First mentioned 1118; became city early 13th cent.; free imperial city 1290–1323; prominent in rise of Anabaptists 16th cent.

Zwijn·drecht \ˈzvīn-ˌdrek̲t, ˈsfīn-\. **1.** Commune, Belgium. See ZWYNDRECHT.

2. Commune, South Holland prov., Netherlands; pop. (1993e) 42,684; suburb of Dordrecht.

Zwil·linge \ˈtsvi-liŋ-ə, ˈzvi-\. Twin peaks in Pennine Alps on the border bet. Switzerland and Italy; the E peak is **Cas·tor** \ˈkas-tər\ 13,865 ft. (4226 m.); the W peak is **Pol·lux** \ˈpä-ləks\ 13,422 ft. (4091 m.).

Zwol·le \ˈzvȯ-lə, ˈsfȯ-\. Commune, ✻ of Overijssel prov., E Netherlands, on IJssel River; pop. (1993e) 98,318; shipbuilding; iron; railroad junction; church of St. Michael, church of our Lady, and town hall, all dating from 15th cent. Ecclesiastic and writer Thomas à Kempis lived for most of his life in a monastery 3 mi. (5 km.) from Zwolle.

Zwyn·drecht *or* **Zwijn·drecht** \ˈzvīn-ˌdrek̲t, ˈsfīn-\. Commune, Antwerp prov., Belgium; pop. (1991c) 18,239; W suburb of Antwerp.

\ə\ **abut** \ə̇\ matches \$^{ə}$\ kitten, Fr table \ər\ **further** \a\ **ash** \ā\ **ace**
\ä\ cot, cart \ȧ\ Fr bac \au̇\ **out** \b̲\ Span Avila \ch\ **chin** \e\ bet \ē\ **easy**
\g\ **go** \i\ hit \ī\ **ice** \j\ **job** \k̲\ Ger **ich**, Buch \$^{n}$\ Fr vin
\ŋ\ sing \ō\ **go** \ȯ\ **all** \ȯ\ **law** \œ\ Fr **bœuf** \œ̄\ Fr **feu** \ȯi\ **boy**
\th\ **thin** \th̲\ **this** \ü\ **loot** \u̇\ **foot** \ue\ Ger **fü**llen \ue̅\ Fr **rue**
\y\ **yet** \$^{y}$\ Fr digne \ˈdēn^{y}\, nuit \ˈnw^{y}ē\ \yü\ **few** \yu̇\ **fury** \zh\ vision

Ży·rar·dów \zhi-'rär-ˌdüf\. Commune, Skierniewice prov., cen. Poland, 25 mi. (40 km.) WSW of Warsaw; pop. (1989e) 42,196.

Zyrian Autonomous Area. See KOMI.

Zyr·ya·novsk \zər-'yä-nəfsk\. Town, East Kazakhstan subdivision, Kazakhstan, ab. 80 mi. (130 km.) ESE of Öskemen; pop. (1991e) 53,800.

Ży·wiec \'zhi-vets\. Town, S cen. Bielsko Bidała prov., S Poland, ab. 40 mi. (64 km.) SW of Kraków; pop. (1989e) 30,608.

Glossary

This glossary is intended to provide brief definitions of geographical terms used in this dictionary. It does not include names of peoples, languages, religions, and geologic eras. For definitions of such terms, and for more comprehensive treatment of geographical terms, please refer to a standard dictionary such as *Merriam-Webster's Collegiate Dictionary*.

Small capitals in the entries below indicate cross-references to other entries within this glossary. A boldface colon followed by a term in small capitals indicates that the entry word has the same meaning as the word in small capitals, which is entered and defined in this glossary. A dash followed by the word "see" and a term in small capitals indicates that information about the entry word can be found at the entry whose name is shown in small capitals.

acropolis : the upper fortified part of an ancient Greek city
agency : the headquarters of a British government agent
alpine : of or relating to mountains
amphitheater 1 : an oval or circular building with rising tiers of seats ranged about an open space and used in ancient Rome esp. for contests and spectacles **2 :** a flat or gently sloping area surrounded by abrupt slopes
aqueduct 1 : a conduit for carrying a large quantity of flowing water **2 :** a structure for conveying a canal over a river or hollow
archiepiscopal see : the seat of an archbishop
archipelago : a group of islands
arrondissement : the largest division of a French department
atoll : a coral island consisting of a reef surrounding a lagoon
audiencia 1 : a high court of justice in a Spanish colony frequently exercising military power as well as judicial and political functions **2 :** the jurisdiction of an audiencia
autonomous community : an administrative subdivision of Spain
bank 1 : an undersea elevation rising esp. from the continental shelf **2 :** the rising ground bordering a lake, river, or sea or forming the edge of a cut or hollow **3 :** SANDBANK
basin 1 a : a large or small depression in the surface of the land or in the ocean floor **b :** the entire tract of country drained by a river and its tributaries **c :** a great depression in the surface of Earth occupied by an ocean **2 :** a broad area of Earth beneath which the strata dip usu. from the sides toward the center
bay — see INLET
beehive tomb : an ancient Greek tomb shaped like a beehive, cut in a hillside, and usu. approached by a horizontal passage
bight : a bay formed by a bend in a coast
borough 1 : an urban area in Great Britain incorporated for purposes of self-government **2 a :** a municipal corporation proper in some states (as New Jersey and Minnesota) corresponding to the incorporated town or village of the other states **b :** one of the five constituent political divisions of New York City **c :** a political division of Greater London
burgh : an incorporated town in Scotland having local jurisdiction of certain services
canton : one of the states of Switzerland
cantonment : a military station in south Asia
cape : a point or extension of land jutting out into water as a peninsula or as a projecting point
captaincy general : the territory of a captain general (the military governor of a Spanish colony)
cascade : one of a series of steep usu. small falls of water
cataract : steep rapids in a river
causeway : a raised way across wet ground or water
cay : a low island or reef of sand or coral
channel : a strait or narrow sea between two close land areas
circumscription : an area or district having a definite boundary
citadel : a fortress that commands a city
city — see SETTLEMENT
collectivity — see TERRITORIAL COLLECTIVITY
comandancia : a province or district under military control
commune : the smallest administrative district (as one governed by a mayor and municipal council) of many countries
continent : one of the six or seven great divisions of land on Earth
country 1 : an indefinite usu. extended expanse of land **2 :** a state or nation or its territory
county 1 : the domain of a count **2 :** one of the territorial divisions of England and Wales and formerly also of Scotland and Northern Ireland constituting the chief units for administrative, judicial, and political purposes **3 :** the largest territorial division for local government within a state of the U.S. **4 :** a primary administrative subdivision of a country
county borough : a borough that is administratively separate from the county in which it is located
county seat : a town that is the seat of county administration
county town : COUNTY SEAT
crown land : land belonging to a monarchy and yielding revenues that the reigning sovereign is entitled to
crust : the outer part of Earth composed essentially of crystalline rocks
defile : a narrow passage or gorge
demicanton : one of the two divisions into which each of the former Swiss cantons of Appenzell, Basel, and Unterwalden are separated
department : a primary or secondary administrative subdivision of a country
dependency : a territorial unit under the jurisdiction of a nation but not formally annexed by it
depression : an area of land in which the central part lies lower than the margin
division : a portion of a territorial unit marked off for a particular purpose (as administrative or judicial functions)
duchy : the territory of a duke or duchess
elevation 1 : the height above sea level **2 :** a place that rises above its surroundings

eminence : a natural elevation
emirate : the state or juridiction of an emir (a ruler in an Islamic country)
enclave : a foreign territorial unit enclosed within a larger territory ◇ The difference between an enclave and an exclave is one of perspective. An enclosed territorial unit is an enclave with respect to the territory that surrounds it, but it is an exclave of the country to which it belongs.
episcopal see : the seat of a bishop
escarpment : a long cliff or steep slope separating two comparatively level or more gently sloping surfaces and resulting from erosion or faulting
estuary : an arm of the sea at the lower end of a river
exclave : a portion of a country separated from the main part and surrounded by foreign territory — compare ENCLAVE
factory : a trading station where agents reside and transact business for their employers
fjord : a narrow inlet of the sea between cliffs or steep slopes
fortress : a fortified place
free association : a relationship affording sovereignty with independent control of internal affairs and foreign policy except defense
garden city : a planned residential community with park and planted areas
geyser : a spring that throws forth intermittent jets of heated water and steam
gorge : a narrow steep-walled canyon or part of a canyon
governorate : an administrative subdivision of Egypt that is ruled by a governor
governorship : a former administrative subdivision of Iran
gulf — see INLET
hamlet — see SETTLEMENT
harbor : a protected part of a body of water that is deep enough to furnish anchorage; *esp* : one with port facilities
headland : a point of usu. high land jutting out into a body of water
headstream : a stream that is the source of a river
highland : elevated or mountainous land
hill — see MOUNTAIN
hill station : a village or government post (as in India) situated in the hills or low mountain ranges and serving usu. as a health resort in the hot season
ice field : a glacier flowing outward from the center of an extensive area of relatively level land
independent city : a city in the state of Virginia having a status equivalent to that of a county
inlet **1 :** a recess in the shore of a larger body of water ◇ In this sense, *inlet* is a general term for *bay* or *gulf*. The chief difference between a bay and a gulf is one of size. A bay is usu. smaller than a gulf. **2 :** a narrow water passage between peninsulas or through a barrier island leading to a bay or lagoon
intermittent lake : a lake that is sometimes dry
intermittent stream : a stream that is sometimes dry
intermontane : situated between mountains
islet : a little island
isthmus : a narrow strip of land connecting two larger land areas
key : any of the coral islets off the southern coast of Florida
kill : CHANNEL ◇ used chiefly in place-names in Delaware, Pennsylvania, and New York
kingdom : a major territorial unit headed by a king or queen
lagoon : a shallow sound, channel, or pond near or connected with a larger body of water
lake : a considerable inland body of standing water
landmass : a large area of land
locality : a specific location
loch : a lake in Scotland
lough : a lake in Ireland
mandate : a former German colony or other conquered territory granted by an international body to another nation for the establishment of a responsible government
market town : a usu. small town that holds a public market
marsh : a tract of soft wet land
massif : a principal mountain mass
mesa : an isolated relatively flat-topped natural elevation usu. less extensive than a plateau
monarchy : a nation or state having a government headed by a hereditary chief of state with life tenure
mountain **1 :** an elevated mass of land that projects above its surroundings ◇ Among the many types of natural land elevations, a distinction needs to be made between *hill, mountain,* and *peak*. A hill is likely to be lower than a mountain or peak and typically has a rounded summit. A mountain is larger and projects more conspicuously than a hill, while a peak is usu. a prominent type of mountain having a well-defined summit. **2 :** an elongated ridge
municipality : a primarily urban political unit
narrows : a strait connecting two bodies of water
national battlefield — see NATIONAL PARK
national historical park — see NATIONAL PARK
national military park — see NATIONAL PARK
national monument — see NATIONAL PARK
national park ◇ Units of the U.S. National Park System have various designations. *National battlefield* and *national military park* denote areas having special significance in America's military history. Areas designated "military park" tend to be larger than those designated "battlefield." The designation *national historical park* denotes an area commemorating an event or site of historical interest that may or may not be of a military nature. Most "historical parks" are much more recently established than military parks and, though there is a wide variation in their size, they tend to be larger as well. Units in all three of these park types usually contain period displays or re-creations of historical events. ◇ The designation *national monument* is widely and variously used. National monuments can be natural or man-made, large or small, and of historical, scenic, or scientific interest. Areas given the designation *national park* are fewer in number than national monuments and are generally larger, more diverse, and more widely recognized. In almost all instances they were primarily established to preserve scenic natural features.
new town : an urban development comprising a small to medium-sized city with a broad range of housing and planned industrial, commercial, and recreational facilities
notch : a deep close pass
ocean : any of the large bodies of water into which the whole body of salt water that covers much of Earth is divided
parish **1 :** a subdivision of a British county constituting the unit of local government **2 :** a civil division of the state of Louisiana corresponding to a county in other states
pass : a low place in a mountain range
passage : a place through which it is possible to pass
peak — see MOUNTAIN
plain **1 :** an extensive area of level or rolling treeless country **2 :** a broad unbroken expanse
plate : any of the large movable segments into which Earth's crust is divided

plateau : a usu. extensive land area having a relatively level surface raised sharply above adjacent land on at least one side ◊ sometimes used synonymously with *tableland*
point : a place having a precisely indicated position
polder : a tract of lowland reclaimed from a body of water
pole : either extremity of Earth's axis
pool **1 :** a small and rather deep body of water **2 :** a quiet place in a stream **3 :** a body of water forming above a dam
prefecture **1 :** the district governed by a prefect (any of various high officials of ancient Rome) **2 :** an administrative subdivision of Japan
presidio : a military post or fortified settlement in an area currently or originally under Spanish control
primary administrative subdivision : any of the largest units into which an independent country is divided for administrative purposes
princely state : a state governed by a prince in preindependent India
principality : the territory of a prince
promontory **1 :** a high point of land or rock projecting into a body of water **2 :** a prominent mass of land overlooking or projecting into a lowland
protectorate : a political unit dependent on the authority of another
race : a narrow channel through which a strong or rapid current of water flows
reef : a chain of rocks or coral or a ridge of sand at or near the surface of water
region **1 :** a primary administrative subdivision of a country **2 :** an indefinite area of Earth **3 :** a broad geographical area distinguished by similar features
republic **1 :** a political unit having a form of government headed by a chief of state who is not a monarch **2 :** a political unit having a form of government in which supreme power resides in a body of citizens entitled to vote and is exercised by elected officers and representatives responsible to them and governing according to law **3 :** a constituent political and territorial unit of a country
residency : a territory in a protected state in which the powers of the protecting state are executed by a resident agent
ridge **1 :** a range of hills or mountains **2 :** an elongate elevation on an ocean bottom
river : a natural stream of water of usu. considerable volume
roadstead : a place less enclosed than a harbor where ships may ride at anchor
sandbank : a large deposit of sand forming a shoal
sanjak : a Turkish district or secondary administrative subdivision
sea **1 :** a more or less landlocked body of salt water **2 :** OCEAN **3 :** an inland body of water
secondary administrative subdivision : any of the units into which the primary administrative subdivisions of a country are divided
semidesert : an arid area that has some of the characteristics of a desert but has greater annual precipitation
settlement ◊ In this book *settlement* is used for an unspecified type of populated place, esp. where populated places are referred to collectively. Although several terms meaning "populated place" are sometimes used interchangeably, there are some usual distinctions that can be made. *City, town, village,* and *hamlet* are general terms listed in descending order of size and/or importance, though complex patterns of usage esp. within particular states account for many exceptions to this order. Use of *township* and *urban township* is restricted to certain states; *commune* and *parish* are used in foreign countries. The designations *garden city* and *new town* are used for planned settlements. ◊ Most of the U.S. settlements defined in this dictionary are incorporated, meaning that they have a charter legalizing them as populated entities. In general, places without such legal status have been exempted from the 2500 population cutoff and are omitted from this book. Those having notably large populations or some particular significance have been included with the designation *unincorporated settlement.*
shire **1 :** a county in England **2 :** a rural government area in some states of Australia
shoal : a ridge or large deposit of sand that makes the water shallow
site : the location of some particular thing
sound **1 :** a long broad inlet of the ocean generally parallel to the coast **2 :** a long passage of water connecting two larger bodies of water or separating a mainland and an island
spa : a town or resort with mineral springs
special city : a Korean city having a status equivalent to that of a province
spring : a source of water issuing from the ground
state **1 :** a sovereign politically organized body of people usu. occupying a definite territory **2 :** one of the constituent units of a nation having a federal government
steppe **1 :** one of the vast usu. level and treeless tracts in southeastern Europe or Asia **2 :** arid land found usu. in regions of extreme temperature range
strait : a comparatively narrow passageway connecting two large bodies of water
subcontinent : a major subdivision of a continent
subduction zone : an area in which the edge of one of Earth's plates descends below the edge of another
sultanate : a state or nation governed by a sultan
supercontinent : a former large continent from which other continents are held to have broken off and drifted away
swamp : a tract of wetland often partially or intermittently covered with water
tableland : a broad level elevated area ◊ sometimes used synonymously with *plateau*
territorial collectivity : a French overseas territorial unit enjoying some degree of local authority and having a status lesser than an overseas department but greater than an overseas territory
territory **1 a :** a geographical area belonging to or under the jurisdiction of a governmental authority **b :** an administrative subdivision of a country **c :** a part of the U.S. not included within any state but organized with a separate legislature **d :** a geographical area dependent on an external government but having some degree of autonomy **2 :** an indeterminate geographical area
town **1** — see SETTLEMENT **2 :** a New England territorial and political unit usually containing both rural and unincorporated urban areas under a single town government
township **1 a :** TOWN 2 **b :** a unit of local government in some northeastern and north central states usu. having a chief administrative officer or board **c :** an electoral and administrative district of a county in the southern U.S. **2 :** an area in the Republic of South Africa established to segregate persons of non-European descent
trading post : a station of a trader or trading company established in a sparsely settled region where trade in products of local origin is carried on
trench : a long, narrow, and usu. steep-sided depression in the ocean floor

tributary : a stream feeding a larger stream or a lake
unincorporated settlement — see SETTLEMENT
union territory : a centrally administered subdivision of India consisting of an island group, the area surrounding a city, or an area containing a linguistic minority
valley **1 :** an elongate depression of Earth's surface usu. between ranges of hills or mountains **2 :** an area drained by a river and its tributaries
village — see SETTLEMENT
waterway : a navigable body or course of water

Geographical Terms in Other Languages

A selection of geographical terms in various languages and their equivalents in English is provided in the following lists for the convenience of users of the dictionary. The terms have been selected on the basis of their appearance as elements of boldface entries in the dictionary or their general usefulness to the average consultant. In addition to the names of physical features and of political subdivisions, the list contains a number of words (such as *old* and *new; eastern, western,* and *central; upper* and *lower*) that are often used in compound proper names. Styling of some terms varies with regard to spelling and use of diacritics. Although this list is not exhaustive, we have included more than one styling for many terms that have commonly used variant forms.

List I is a single alphabetical list of foreign-language terms showing their equivalents in English; list II groups terms in different languages under the alphabetical listing of their equivalents in English.

List I

ab	Persian	water, river
-abad	Hindi, Persian	city, town
abajo	Spanish	lower
aber	Welsh	confluence, river mouth
Ache	German	stream
acqua	Italian	water
ada, adası	Turkish	island
afon	Welsh	river
agua	Portuguese, Spanish	water
aiguille	French	peak
ain	Arabic	spring, well
ákra, akrotírion	Greek	cape, point
alt	German	old
altipiano	Italian	plateau
altiplano	Spanish	plateau
alto	Italian, Portuguese, Spanish	high, upper
älv, älven	Swedish	river
angra	Spanish	bay
anse	French	bay, inlet
ao	Thai	bay
archipel	Dutch, French	archipelago
archipiélago	Spanish	archipelago
arkhipelag	Russian	archipelago
arquipélago	Portuguese	archipelago
arroyo	Spanish	brook, creek
austral	Spanish	southern
ayer	Malay	water
baai	Dutch	bay
bab	Arabic	strait, gate
Bach	German	brook
Bad	German	spa
bælt	Danish	strait
bahía	Spanish	bay
bahr	Arabic	sea, river
Bai	German	bay
baía	Portuguese	bay
baie	French	gulf, bay
baixo	Portuguese	low, lower
bajo	Spanish	low, lower
banco	Spanish	shoal
band	Persian	mountain range
bandao	Chinese	peninsula
bandar	Persian	port, harbor
barat	Indonesian, Malay	west
baru	Indonesian, Malay	new
bas, basse	French	low
basseyn	Russian	basin
basso	Italian	low
batang	Malay	river
batu	Indonesian, Malay	rock
bei	Chinese	north
beinn	Scottish Gaelic	mountain
bel	Turkish	pass
ben	Scots	mountain
bereg	Russian	shore, coast
berg	Dutch	mountain
Berg	German	mountain
besar	Indonesian, Malay	great, big
bir	Arabic	spring, well
birkat, birket	Arabic	lake
boca	Spanish	mouth, estuary
bogaz, boğaz, boğazı, boghaz	Turkish	strait, pass
bois	French	forest, wood
bol'shaya, bolshoi, bol'shoy	Russian	big, great
bolsón	Spanish	basin
bosque	Portuguese, Spanish	forest
bryn	Welsh	hill
Bucht	German	bay, bight
bugt	Danish	bay, bight
buḩayrat, buheirat	Arabic	lake
bukhta	Russian	bay, bight

Term	Language	Meaning
bukit	Indonesian, Malay	hill, mountain
burnu, burun	Turkish	cape
cabo	Portuguese, Spanish	cape
campo	Portuguese, Spanish	plain
cañada	Spanish	ravine
canal	French, Spanish	channel, canal
canale	Italian	channel, canal
cañon	Spanish	canyon
cap	French	cape
capo	Italian	cape
cascada	Spanish	waterfall
cascata	Portuguese	waterfall
cascata d'acqua	Italian	waterfall
cataracta	Portuguese	waterfall
catarata	Portuguese, Spanish	waterfall
cataratta	Italian	waterfall
cayo	Spanish	islet
central	French, Spanish	middle, central
centrale	Italian	middle, central
cerro	Spanish	hill
chaîne	French	mountain range
champ	French	plain, field
chhung	Khmer	bay, gulf
chico	Spanish	little, small
chiisai	Japanese	little, small
chott	Arabic (French transliteration)	river, (salt) lake, swamp
chute d'eau	French	waterfall
cidade	Portuguese	city, town
ciénaga	Spanish	swamp
cima	Italian	peak
cime	French	peak
cité	French	city, town
città	Italian	city, town
ciudad	Spanish	city, town
co	Tibetan	lake
col	French	pass
colline	French	hill
cordillera	Spanish	mountain range
corne	French	peak
corno	Italian	peak
costa	Italian, Portuguese, Spanish	coast
côte	French	coast
cuenca	Spanish	valley
cuesta	Spanish	mesa, upland
cumbre	Spanish	peak
cwm	Welsh	valley
dağ, dagh, dağı	Turkish	mountain
dağlar, dağları	Turkish	mountain range
dake	Japanese	mount
dal	Dutch	valley
dan	Korean	point
dao	Chinese	island
daryācheh	Persian	lake
dasht	Persian	plain, desert
deniz	Turkish	sea, lake
derbent	Turkish	pass, defile
dere	Turkish	valley
désert	French	desert
deserto	Italian	desert
desht	Persian	plain, desert
desierto	Spanish	desert
détroit	French	strait
djebel	Arabic (French transliteration)	mountain
doi	Thai	mountain
dolina	Russian	valley
dong	Chinese	east
dong	Vietnamese	plain
eau	French	water
eiland	Dutch	island
'emeq	Hebrew	valley, plain
ensenada	Spanish	cove
erg	Arabic	desert
est	French, Italian	east
este	Portuguese, Spanish	east
estero	Spanish	estuary
estrecho	Spanish	strait
estreito	Portuguese	strait
estuaire	French	estuary
estuario	Spanish	estuary
étang	French	lagoon, pond
falaise	French	cliff
Feld	German	field, plain
Fels	German	cliff
fiume	Italian	river
fleuve	French	river
Fluss	German	river
fonn	Norwegian	snowfield
forêt	French	forest
Forst	German	forest
foz	Portuguese	estuary
fretum	Latin	strait
-gawa	Japanese	river
gebel	Arabic	mountain
gebergte	Dutch	mountain range
Gebirge	German	mountain range
Gegend	German	region
ghat	Hindi	bank, pass, steps
gherb	Arabic	west
ghubbat	Arabic	bay
Gipfel	German	peak
gji	Albanian	bay
glacier	French	glacier
Gletscher	German	glacier
glyn	Welsh	glen
gobi	Mongolian	arid steppe
goenoeng	Malay (Dutch transliteration)	mount, mountain
göl	Turkish	lake
golf	Danish, Dutch	gulf
Golf	German	gulf
golfe	French	gulf
golfo	Italian, Portuguese, Spanish	gulf
gölü	Turkish	lake
gora	Russian	mountain
gorod	Russian	city
gory	Russian	mountain range
grand	French	big
grande	Spanish	big
groot	Dutch	big
gross	German	big
grosso	Italian, Portuguese	big
guba	Russian	gulf, bay

Term	Language	Meaning
gunong	Malay	mountain
guntō	Japanese	archipelago
gunung	Indonesian	mountain
Hafen	German	port
Haff	German	lagoon
hai	Chinese	sea
Halbinsel	German	peninsula
ḩamādah	Arabic	desert
hāmūn	Persian	plain, marsh
hantō	Japanese	peninsula
har	Hebrew	mountain
hara	Japanese	plain, field
haut	French	high
hawr	Arabic	lake
hāyk'	Amharic	lake
he	Chinese	river
Heide	German	heath, moor
higashi	Japanese	east
ho	Chinese	river
hoch	German	high
Hochebene	German	plateau
hoek	Dutch	cape
hoku-	Japanese	north
hoog	Dutch	high
hor	Arabic	marsh
hsiao	Chinese	little, small
hu	Chinese	lake
île	French	island
ilha	Portuguese	island
ilhéu	Portuguese	island
inférieur	French	lower
inferiore	Italian	lower
Insel	German	island
ırmak	Turkish	river
isla	Spanish	island
isola	Italian	island
itadaki	Japanese	peak
jabal	Arabic	mountain
janub	Arabic	south
järv	Estonian	lake
järvi	Finnish	lake
jazā'ir	Arabic	islands
jebel	Arabic	mountain
jezira, jeziret	Arabic	island
jiang	Chinese	river
jiao	Chinese	cape, point
jima	Japanese	island
jøkel	Norwegian	glacier
joki	Finnish	river
jökull	Icelandic	glacier
kaap	Dutch	cape
kai	Japanese	sea
kaikyō	Japanese	channel, strait
kali	Indonesian, Malay	river
kam	Korean	cape
kap	Danish, German, Norwegian, Swedish	cape
kawa	Japanese	river
kebir	Arabic	big
kechil	Malay	small
kep	Albanian	cape
kepulauan	Indonesian, Malay	archipelago
khalīj	Arabic	bay
khao	Thai	mountain
khrebet	Russian	mountain range
kiang	Chinese	river
kiao	Chinese	cape, point
kidul	Indonesian, Malay	south
kita	Japanese	north
klein	Dutch, German	small
ko	Japanese	lake
ko	Thai	island
koh	Persian	mountain, mountain range
koh	Thai	island
köl	Turkic	lake
kólpos	Greek	gulf
kong	Chinese (southeastern dialects)	river
kop	Afrikaans	hill
körfez, körfezi	Turkish	gulf, bay
kosa	Russian	spit
kosui	Japanese	lake
krai, kray	Russian	territory
kuala	Indonesian, Malay	estuary
kūh	Persian	mountain
kul	Turkic	lake
kulon	Indonesian, Malay	west
kum	Turkic	desert
kyst	Danish	coast
kyun	Burmese	island
laag	Dutch	low
lac	French	lake
lacus	Latin	lake
lago	Italian, Portuguese, Spanish	lake
lagoa	Portuguese	lagoon
laguna	Spanish	lagoon, lake
Land	German	country, state
lang	Dutch, German	long
largo	Spanish	long
laut	Indonesian, Malay	sea, ocean
lembah	Indonesian, Malay	valley
les	Russian	forest
levante	Italian	east
lido	Italian	beach
límni	Greek	lake
litoral	Portuguese	coast
llano	Spanish	plain
llyn	Welsh	lake
loma	Spanish	hill
long	French	long
longo	Portuguese	long
lungo	Italian	long
mā'	Arabic	water
maha	Hindi	big, great
maidan	Hindi, Persian	plain, field
malo-, malyy	Russian	little, small
man	Korean	bay
mar	Portuguese, Spanish	sea
mare	Italian	sea
marina	Italian	coast
massif	French	mountain group

medio	Spanish	middle
meer	Dutch	lake
Meer	German	sea
meio	Portuguese	middle
mer	French	sea
meridional	Spanish	southern
méridional	French	southern
middel-, midden-	Dutch	middle
midi	French	south
minami	Japanese	south
misaki	Japanese	cape
Mittel	German	middle
mizu	Japanese	water
moel	Welsh	hilltop
mont	French	mountain
montagna	Italian	mountain
montagnes	French	mountain range
montaña	Spanish	mountain, mountain range
montanha	Portuguese	mountain, mountain range
monte	Italian, Portuguese, Spanish	mountain
monti	Italian	mountain range
more	Russian	sea
morro	Portuguese	hill
morro	Spanish	headland
moyen	French	middle
mui	Vietnamese	cape
Mündung	German	river mouth, estuary
mynydd	Welsh	mountain
mys	Russian	cape
nada	Japanese	gulf, sea
nagai	Japanese	long
nagor'ye	Russian	mountain range
nahr	Arabic	river
naka	Japanese	middle
nan	Chinese	south
nant	Welsh	brook, stream
negri	Malay	country
neu	German	new
nevado	Spanish	snow-covered mountain
nieder	German	lower
niedrig	German	low
nieuw	Dutch	new
nishi	Japanese	west
nizhni, nizhniy, nizyny, nizhnyaya	Russian	lower
noord	Dutch	north, northern
nor	Mongolian	lake
nord	French	north
nord-	German	north
nördlich	German	northern
norte	Italian, Portuguese, Spanish	north
nos	Russian	cape
nosy	Malagasy	island
nouveau, nouvelle	French	new
novaya	Russian	new
novo	Portuguese	new
novo-, novyy	Russian	new
nuevo	Spanish	new
nuovo	Italian	new
nuruu	Mongolian	mountain range
nuur	Mongolian	lake
ö	Swedish	island
ø (ö)	Danish, Norwegian	island
ō-	Japanese	big
ober-	German	upper
oblast'	Russian	region
occidental	French, Spanish	western
occidentale	Italian	western
occidente	Italian	west
oceaan	Dutch	ocean
océan	French	ocean
oceano	Italian, Portuguese	ocean
océano	Spanish	ocean
odde	Danish	cape
oedjoeng	Malay (Dutch transliteration)	cape
oeste	Portuguese, Spanish	west
ojo	Spanish	spring
okrug	Russian	district
oost	Dutch	east
oosters	Dutch	eastern
opper-	Dutch	upper
oriental	French, Spanish	eastern
orientale	Italian	eastern
oriente	Spanish	east
órmos	Greek	bay
orta	Turkish	middle
ost-	German	east
östlich	German	east, eastern
ostrov	Russian	island
otok	Serbo-Croatian	island
oud	Dutch	old
oued	Arabic (French transliteration)	valley (dry watercourse)
ouest	French	west
over-	Dutch	upper
øy	Norwegian	island
oya	Sinhalese	stream, river
Ozean	German	ocean
ozero	Russian	lake
padang	Indonesian, Malay	plain
paese	Italian	country
país	Portuguese, Spanish	country
paiz	Portuguese	country
pan-tao	Chinese	peninsula
paso	Spanish	pass
Pass	German	pass
passo	Italian, Portuguese	pass
pays	French	country
pegunungan	Indonesian	mountain range
peh, pei	Chinese	north
pélagos	Greek	sea
pen	Welsh	hilltop
península	Spanish	peninsula
penisola	Italian	peninsula
pequeno	Portuguese	small
pequeño	Spanish	small

pereval	Russian	pass
pervo-, pervyy	Russian	first
petit	French	small
pi	Chinese	cape
pic	French	peak
picco	Italian	peak
piccolo	Italian	small
pico	Portuguese, Spanish	peak
pik	Russian	peak
pinhal	Portuguese	pine forest
piz	Romansh	peak
pizzo	Italian	peak
plage	French	beach
plaine	French	plain, field
planalto	Portuguese	plateau
planina	Bulgarian	mountain, mountain range
plateau	French	plateau
playa	Spanish	beach
ploskogor'ye	Russian	plateau
poelau	Malay (Dutch transliteration)	island
pointe	French	point
poluostrov	Russian	peninsula
ponta	Portuguese	point
port	French	port
porthmós	Greek	strait
porto	Italian, Portuguese	port
poulo	Malay	island
praia	Portuguese	beach
presqu'île	French	peninsula
prokhod	Russian	pass
proliv	Russian	strait
promontorio	Italian	promontory
pueblo	Spanish	town, village
puerto	Spanish	port
pulau	Indonesian, Malay	island
puncak	Indonesian	peak, mount
punta	Italian, Spanish	point
pustynya	Russian	desert
puy	French	peak
quan dao	Vietnamese	archipelago
qum	Turkic	desert
qundao	Chinese	archipelago
ramlat	Arabic	sandy area
ran, rān (Anglicized rann)	Hindi, Gujarati	wilderness
ras, ra's	Arabic	cape
ravnina	Russian	plain, field
rayon	Russian	district, region
região	Portuguese	region
région	French	region
región	Spanish	region
regione	Italian	region
reka	Russian	river
respublika	Russian	republic
rettō	Japanese	archipelago
rio	Portuguese	river
río	Spanish	river
riva	Italian	beach
rivier	Dutch	river
rivière	French	river
rūd	Persian	river
sabaku	Japanese	desert
sabchat, sebcha, sebkret	Arabic	salt flat, salt marsh
ṣaghīr	Arabic	little, small
sahra (*pl.* sahara)	Arabic	desert
saki	Japanese	cape, point
salar	Spanish	salt flat
salto	Spanish	waterfall
sammyaku	Japanese	mountain range
-san	Japanese, Korean	hill, mountain
saut	French	waterfall
schiereiland	Dutch	peninsula
See	German	sea, lake
selat	Indonesian, Malay	channel, strait
selva	Portuguese, Spanish	wood, forest
septentrional	French, Portuguese, Spanish	northern
serra	Portuguese	mountain range
serranía	Spanish	mountain range
seto	Japanese	strait
settentrionale	Italian	northern
sever	Russian	north
severnaya, severo-	Russian	northern
shan	Chinese	hill, mountain, mountain range
shang	Chinese	upper
shankou, shan-k'ou	Chinese	pass
sharq	Arabic	east
shat, shatt	Arabic	river, (salt) lake, swamp
shemal	Arabic	north
shi	Japanese	city
shima	Japanese	island
shimo	Japanese	lower
shotō	Japanese	archipelago
shott	Arabic	river, (salt) lake, swamp
shui	Chinese	water
si	Chinese	west
sierra	Spanish	mountain range
sinus	Latin	gulf
song	Vietnamese	river
sopka	Russian	volcano
souterrain	French	tunnel
Spitze	German	peak
spruit	Afrikaans	brook, stream
sredinnyy	Russian	middle
stad	Dutch	city, town
Stadt	German	city, town
-stan	Hindi, Persian	country
staraya, stary, staryy	Russian	old
step'	Russian	plain
stor, store	Danish	big, great
straat	Dutch	strait
Strand	German	beach
Strasse	German	strait
strelka	Russian	spit
stretto	Italian	strait
Strom	German	river
stroom	Afrikaans	river

Term	Language	Meaning
su	Turkic	water, river
sud	French, Italian, Spanish	south
süd-	German	south
südlich	German	southern
suid	Afrikaans	south
suidō	Japanese	channel
sul	Portuguese	south
supérieur	French	upper
superior	Portuguese, Spanish	upper
superiore	Italian	upper
sur	Spanish	south
suyu	Turkish	water, river
sziget	Hungarian	island
tafelland	Dutch	plateau
tagh	Turkic	mountain, mountain range
takai	Japanese	high
take	Japanese	peak
Tal	German	valley
tandjoeng	Malay (Dutch transliteration)	cape, point
tani	Japanese	valley
tanjong	Malay	cape, point
tanjung	Indonesian	cape, point
tao	Chinese	island
tau	Turkic	mountain
taung	Burmese	hill, mountain
tel, tell	Arabic	hill
telok	Malay	cape, point
teluk	Indonesian, Malay	bay, gulf
tengiz	Turkic	lake, sea
tepe	Turkish	hill
terara	Amharic	mountain
terra	Italian, Portuguese	land
terre	French	land
-thal	German	valley
thiu kao	Thai	mountain range
tian	Chinese	plain
t'ien	Chinese	plain, field
tierra	Spanish	land
timur	Indonesian, Malay	east
tind	Norwegian	mountain
tinggi	Indonesian, Malay	high
tó	Hungarian	lake
-tō	Japanese	island
tōge	Japanese	pass
tonle	Khmer	river
trouée	French	gap
tso	Tibetan	lake
tua	Indonesian, Malay	old
tung	Chinese	east
tunturi	Finnish	treeless mountain
tur'at	Arabic	canal
ue-no-	Japanese	upper
ujung	Indonesian	cape
ulu, ulugh	Turkic	big, great
umi	Japanese	sea

Term	Language	Meaning
unter	German	lower
ura	Japanese	bay
ust'-, ust'ye	Russian	estuary
utan	Malay	forest, woods
utara	Indonesian, Malay	north
val	Italian	valley
valle	Italian, Portuguese, Spanish	valley
vallée	French	valley
vecchio	Italian	old
veld	Afrikaans	plain (grassland)
velho	Portuguese	old
velikaya, veliki	Russian	big, great
veliki, velika	Serbo-Croatian	big
velikiy, velikiye	Russian	big, great
verkhni, verkhniy, verkhnyaya	Russian	upper
vershina	Russian	peak
vidda, vidde	Norwegian	plateau
viejo	Spanish	old
vieux, vieille	French	old
vik	Swedish	bay
ville	French	city, town
vlei	Afrikaans	pond, marsh
voda	Russian	water
volcán	Spanish	volcano
vostok	Russian	east
wadi	Arabic	valley (dry watercourse)
Wald	German	forest, woods
wan	Chinese, Japanese	gulf, bay
Wasser	German	water
Wasserfall	German	waterfall
water	Dutch	water
waterval	Dutch	waterfall
wenz	Amharic	river
west	Dutch, German	west
westlich	German	western
wetan, wétan	Indonesian, Malay	east
woud	Dutch	forest
Wüste	German	desert
xi	Chinese	south
xiao	Chinese	little, small
yama	Japanese	mountain
yarımada, yarımadası	Turkish	peninsula
ynys	Welsh	island
yoma	Burmese	mountain range
yug	Russian	south
yuzhno-	Russian	southern
zaki	Japanese	cape, point
zalew	Polish	bay, lagoon
zaliv	Russian	bay, gulf
zapad	Russian	west
zapadnaya	Russian	western
zee	Dutch	sea
zemlya	Russian	country, land
zizhiqu	Chinese	autonomous region
zuid	Dutch	south

List II

archipelago:
- Chinese: qundao
- Dutch: archipel
- French: archipel
- Indonesian: kepulauan
- Japanese: guntō, rettō, shotō
- Malay: kepulauan
- Portuguese: arquipélago
- Russian: arkhipelag
- Spanish: archipiélago
- Vietnamese: quan dao

arid steppe:
- Mongolian: gobi

autonomous region:
- Chinese: zizhiqu

bank:
- Hindi: ghat

basin:
- Russian: basseyn
- Spanish: bolsón

bay:
- Albanian: gji
- Arabic: ghubbat, khalīj
- Chinese: wan
- Danish: bugt
- Dutch: baai
- French: anse, baie
- German: Bai, Bucht
- Greek: órmos
- Indonesian: teluk
- Japanese: ura, wan
- Khmer: chhung
- Korean: man
- Malay: teluk
- Polish: zalew
- Portuguese: baía
- Russian: bukhta, guba, zaliv
- Spanish: angra, bahía
- Swedish: vik
- Thai: ao
- Turkish: körfez, körfezi

beach:
- French: plage
- German: Strand
- Italian: lido, riva
- Portuguese: praia
- Spanish: playa

big:
- Arabic: kebir
- Danish: stor, store
- Dutch: groot
- French: grand
- German: gross
- Hindi: maha
- Indonesian: besar
- Italian: grosso
- Japanese: ō-
- Malay: besar
- Portuguese: grosso
- Russian: bol'shaya, bolshoi, bol'shoy, velikaya, veliki, velikiy, velikiye
- Serbo-Croatian: veliki, velika
- Spanish: grande
- Turkic: ulu, ulugh

bight:
- Danish: bugt
- German: Bucht
- Russian: bukhta

brook:
- Afrikaans: spruit
- German: Bach
- Spanish: arroyo
- Welsh: nant

canal:
- Arabic: tur'at
- French: canal
- Italian: canale
- Spanish: canal

canyon:
- Spanish: cañon

cape:
- Albanian: kep
- Arabic: ras, ra's
- Chinese: jiao, kiao, pi
- Danish: kap, odde
- Dutch: hoek, kaap
- French: cap
- German: Kap
- Greek: ákra, akrotírion
- Indonesian: tanjung, ujung
- Italian: capo
- Japanese: misaki, saki, zaki
- Korean: kam
- Malay: tanjong, telok
- Malay (Dutch transliteration): oedjoeng, tandjoeng
- Norwegian: kap
- Portuguese: cabo
- Russian: mys, nos
- Spanish: cabo
- Swedish: kap
- Turkish: burnu, burun
- Vietnamese: mui

central:
- French: central
- Italian: centrale
- Spanish: central

channel:
- French: canal
- Indonesian: selat
- Italian: canale
- Japanese: kaikyō, suidō
- Malay: selat
- Spanish: canal

city:
- Dutch: stad
- French: cité, ville
- German: Stadt

Hindi -abad
Italian città
Japanese shi
Persian -abad
Portuguese cidade
Russian gorod
Spanish ciudad

cliff:
French falaise
German Fels

coast, shore:
Danish kyst
French côte
Italian costa, marina
Portuguese costa, litoral
Russian bereg
Spanish costa

confluence:
Welsh aber

country:
French pays
German land
Hindi -stan
Italian paese
Malay negri
Persian -stan
Portuguese país, paiz
Russian zemlya
Spanish país

cove:
Spanish ensenada

creek:
Spanish arroyo

defile:
Turkish derbent

desert:
Arabic erg, ḩamādah, sahra (*pl.* sahara)
French désert
German Wüste
Italian deserto
Japanese sabaku
Persian dasht, desht
Russian pustynya
Spanish desierto
Turkic kum, qum

district:
Russian okrug, rayon

east:
Arabic sharq
Chinese dong, tung
Dutch oost
French est
German ost-
Indonesian timur, wetan, wétan
Italian est, levante
Japanese higashi
Malay timur, wetan, wétan
Portuguese este
Russian vostok
Spanish este, oriente

eastern:
Dutch oosters
French oriental
German östlich
Italian orientale
Spanish oriental

estuary:
French estuaire
German Mündung
Indonesian kuala
Malay kuala
Portuguese foz
Russian ust'-, ust'ye
Spanish boca, estero, estuario

field:
Chinese t'ien
French champ, plaine
German Feld
Hindi maidan
Japanese hara
Persian maidan
Russian ravnina

first:
Russian pervo-, pervyy

forest:
Dutch woud
French bois, forêt
German Forst, Wald
Malay utan
Portuguese bosque, pinhal, selva
Russian les
Spanish bosque, selva

gap:
French trouée

gate:
Arabic bab

glacier:
French glacier
German Gletscher
Icelandic jökull
Norwegian jøkel

glen:
Welsh glyn

great:
Danish stor, store
Hindi maha
Indonesian besar
Malay besar
Russian bol'shaya, bolshoi, bol'shoy, velikaya, veliki, velikiy, velikiye
Turkic ulu, ulugh

gulf:
Danish golf
Dutch golf
French golfe
German Golf
Greek kólpos
Indonesian teluk
Italian golfo
Japanese nada
Khmer chhung
Latin sinus
Malay teluk
Portuguese golfo
Russian guba, zaliv
Spanish golfo
Turkish körfez, körfezi

harbor:
Persian bandar

headland:
Spanish morro

heath, moor:
German Heide
high:
Dutch hoog
French haut
German hoch
Indonesian tinggi
Italian alto
Japanese takai
Malay tinggi
Portuguese alto
Spanish alto
hill:
Afrikaans kop
Arabic tel, tell
Burmese taung
Chinese shan
French colline
Indonesian bukit
Japanese -san
Korean -san
Malay bukit
Portuguese morro
Spanish cerro, loma
Turkish tepe
Welsh bryn
hilltop:
Welsh moel, pen
island:
Arabic jazā'ir, jezira, jeziret
Burmese kyun
Chinese dao, tao
Danish ø (ö)
Dutch eiland
French île
German Insel
Hungarian sziget
Indonesian pulau
Italian isola
Japanese jima, shima, -tō
Malagasy nosy
Malay poulo, pulau
Malay (Dutch transliteration) poelau
Norwegian ø (ö), øy
Portuguese ilha, ilhéu
Russian ostrov
Serbo-Croatian otok
Spanish isla
Swedish ö
Thai ko, koh
Turkish ada, adası
Welsh ynys
islet:
Spanish cayo
lagoon:
French étang
German Haff
Polish zalew
Portuguese lagoa
Spanish laguna
lake:
Amharic hāyk'
Arabic birkat, birket, buḩayrat, buheirat, hawr
Chinese hu
Dutch meer
Estonian järv
Finnish järvi
French lac
German See
Greek límni
Hungarian tó
Italian lago
Japanese ko, kosui
Latin lacus
Mongolian nor, nuur
Persian daryācheh
Portuguese lago
Russian ozero
Spanish lago, laguna
Tibetan co, tso
Turkic köl, kul, tengiz
Turkish deniz, göl, gölü
Welsh llyn
lake (salt):
Arabic shat, shatt, shott
Arabic (French transliteration) chott
land:
Italian terra
French terre
Portuguese terra
Russian zemlya
Spanish tierra
little: see SMALL
long:
Dutch lang
French long
German lang
Italian lungo
Japanese nagai
Portuguese longo
Spanish largo
low:
Dutch laag
French bas, basse
German niedrig
Italian basso
Portuguese baixo
Spanish bajo
lower:
French inférieur
German nieder, unter
Italian inferiore
Japanese shimo
Portuguese baixo
Russian nizhni, nizhniy, nizhny, nizhnyaya
Spanish abajo, bajo
marsh:
Afrikaans vlei
Arabic hor
Persian hāmūn
mesa, upland:
Spanish cuesta
middle:
Dutch middel-, midden-
French central, moyen
German Mittel
Italian centrale
Japanese naka
Portuguese meio
Russian sredinnyy

Spanish central, medio
Turkish orta

moor: see HEATH

mount:
Japanese dake
Indonesian puncak
Malay (Dutch transliteration) goenoeng

mountain:
Amharic terara
Arabic gebel, jabal, jebel
Arabic (French transliteration) djebel
Bulgarian planina
Burmese taung
Chinese shan
Dutch berg
French mont
German Berg
Hebrew har
Indonesian bukit, gunung
Italian montagna, monte
Japanese -san, yama
Korean -san
Malay bukit, gunong
Malay (Dutch transliteration) goenoeng
Norwegian tind
Persian koh, kūh
Portuguese montanha, monte
Russian gora
Scots ben
Scottish Gaelic beinn
Spanish montaña, monte
Thai doi, khao
Turkic tagh, tau
Turkish dağ, dagh, dağı
Welsh mynydd

mountain group:
French massif

mountain range:
Bulgarian planina
Burmese yoma
Chinese shan
Dutch gebergte
French chaîne, montagnes
German Gebirge
Indonesian pegunungan
Italian monti
Japanese sammyaku
Mongolian nuruu
Persian band, koh
Portuguese montanha, serra
Russian gory, khrebet, nagor'ye
Spanish cordillera, montaña, serranía, sierra
Thai thiu kao
Turkic tagh
Turkish dağları

mouth:
Spanish boca

new:
Dutch nieuw
French nouveau, nouvelle
German neu
Indonesian baru
Italian nuovo
Malay baru
Portuguese novo
Russian novaya, novo-, novyy
Spanish nuevo

north:
Arabic shemal
Chinese bei, peh, pei
Dutch noord
French nord
German nord-
Indonesian utara
Italian norte
Japanese hoku-, kita
Malay utara
Russian sever
Spanish norte

northern:
Dutch noord
French septentrional
German nördlich
Italian settentrionale
Portuguese septentrional
Russian severnaya, severo-
Spanish septentrional

ocean:
Dutch oceaan
French océan
German Ozean
Indonesian laut
Italian oceano
Malay laut
Portuguese oceano
Spanish océano

old:
Dutch oud
French vieux, vieille
German alt
Indonesian tua
Italian vecchio
Malay tua
Portuguese velho
Russian staraya, stary, staryy
Spanish viejo

pass:
Chinese shankou, shan-k'ou
French col
German Pass
Hindi ghat
Italian passo
Japanese tōge
Portuguese passo
Russian pereval, prokhod
Spanish paso
Turkish bel, bogaz, boğaz, boğazı, boghaz, derbent

peak:
French aiguille, cime, corne, pic, puy
German Gipfel, Spitze
Indonesian puncak
Italian cima, corno, picco, pizzo
Japanese itadaki, take
Portuguese pico
Romansh piz
Russian pik, vershina
Spanish cumbre, pico

peninsula:
Chinese bandao, pan-tao
Dutch schiereiland
French presqu'île
German Halbinsel
Italian penisola
Japanese hantō
Russian poluostrov
Spanish península
Turkish yarımada, yarımadası

pine forest:
Portuguese pinhal

plain:
Afrikaans veld
Chinese t'ien, tian
French champ, plaine
German Feld
Hebrew 'emeq
Hindi maidan
Indonesian padang
Japanese hara
Malay padang
Persian dasht, desht, hāmūn, maidan
Portuguese campo
Russian ravnina, step'
Spanish campo, llano
Vietnamese dong

plateau:
Dutch tafelland
French plateau
German Hochebene
Italian altipiano
Norwegian vidda, vidde
Portuguese planalto
Russian ploskogor'ye
Spanish altiplano

point:
Chinese jiao, kiao
French pointe
Greek ákra, akrotírion
Indonesian tanjung
Italian punta
Japanese saki, zaki
Korean dan
Malay (Dutch transliteration) tandjoeng
Portuguese ponta
Spanish punta

pond:
Afrikaans vlei
French étang

port:
French port
German Hafen
Italian porto
Persian bandar
Portuguese porto
Spanish puerto
Persian bandar

promontory:
Italian promontorio

ravine:
Spanish cañada

region:
French région
German Gegend
Italian regione
Portuguese região
Russian oblast', rayon
Spanish región

republic:
Russian respublika

river:
Afrikaans stroom
Amharic wenz
Arabic bahr, nahr, shat, shatt, shott
Arabic (French transliteration) chott
Chinese he, ho, jiang, kiang
Chinese (southeastern dialects) kong
Dutch rivier
Finnish joki
French fleuve, rivière
German Fluss, Strom
Indonesian kali
Italian fiume
Japanese -gawa, kawa
Khmer tonle
Malay batang, kali
Persian ab, rūd
Portuguese rio
Russian reka
Sinhalese oya
Spanish río
Swedish älv, älven
Turkic su
Turkish ırmak, suyu
Vietnamese song
Welsh afon

river mouth:
German Mündung
Welsh aber

rock:
Indonesian batu
Malay batu

salt flat:
Arabic sabchat, sebcha, sebkret
Spanish salar

salt marsh:
Arabic sabchat, sebcha, sebkret

sandy area:
Arabic ramlat

sea:
Chinese hai
Dutch zee
French mer
German Meer, See
Greek pélagos
Indonesian laut
Italian mare
Japanese kai, nada, umi
Malay laut
Portuguese mar
Russian more
Spanish mar
Turkic tengiz
Turkish deniz

shoal:
Spanish banco

shore: see COAST

small, little:
Arabic ṣaghīr

Chinese hsiao, xiao
Dutch klein
French petit
German klein
Italian piccolo
Japanese chiisai
Malay kechil
Portuguese pequeno
Russian malo-, malyy
Spanish chico, pequeño

snow-covered mountain:
Spanish nevado

snowfield:
Norwegian fonn

south:
Afrikaans suid
Arabic janub
Chinese nan, xi
Dutch zuid
French midi, sud
German süd-
Indonesian kidul
Italian sud
Japanese minami
Malay kidul
Portuguese sul
Russian yug
Spanish sud, sur

southern:
French méridional
German südlich
Russian yuzhno-
Spanish austral, meridional

spa:
German Bad

spit:
Russian kosa, strelka

spring:
Arabic ain, bir
Spanish ojo

steps:
Hindi ghat

strait:
Arabic bab
Danish bælt
Dutch straat
French détroit
German Strasse
Greek porthmós
Indonesian selat
Italian stretto
Japanese kaikyō, seto
Latin fretum
Malay selat
Portuguese estreito
Russian proliv
Spanish estrecho
Turkish bogaz, boğaz, boğazı, boghaz

stream:
Afrikaans spruit
German Ache
Sinhalese oya
Welsh nant

swamp:
Arabic shat, shatt, shott
Arabic (French transliteration) chott
Spanish ciénaga

territory:
Russian krai, kray

town:
Dutch stad
French cité, ville
German Stadt
Hindi -abad
Italian città
Persian -abad
Portuguese cidade
Spanish ciudad, pueblo

treeless mountain:
Finnish tunturi

tunnel:
French souterrain

upland: see MESA

upper:
Chinese shang
Dutch opper-, over-
French supérieur
German ober-
Italian alto, superiore
Japanese ue-no-
Portuguese alto, superior
Russian verkhni, verkhniy, verkhnyaya
Spanish alto, superior

valley:
Dutch dağlar, dal
French vallée
German Tal, -thal
Hebrew ‘emeq
Indonesian lembah
Italian val, valle
Japanese tani
Malay lembah
Portuguese valle
Russian dolina
Spanish cuenca, valle
Turkish dere
Welsh cwm

valley (dry watercourse):
Arabic wadi
Arabic (French transliteration) oued

village:
Spanish pueblo

volcano:
Russian sopka
Spanish volcán

water:
Arabic mā’, wadi
Chinese shui
Dutch water
French eau
German Wasser
Italian acqua
Japanese mizu
Malay ayer
Persian ab
Portuguese agua
Russian voda
Spanish agua
Turkic su

Turkish suyu

waterfall:

Dutch waterval

French chute d'eau, saut

German Wasserfall

Italian cascata d'acqua, cataratta

Portuguese cascata, cataracta, catarata

Spanish cascada, catarata, salto

well:

Arabic ain, bir

west:

Arabic gherb

Chinese si

Dutch west

French ouest

German west

Indonesian barat, kulon

Italian occidente

Japanese nishi

Malay barat, kulon

Portuguese oeste

Russian zapad

Spanish oeste

western:

French occidental

German westlich

Italian occidentale

Russian zapadnaya

Spanish occidental

wilderness:

Gujarati, Hindi ran, rān (Anglicized rann)

wood, woods:

French bois

German Wald

Malay utan

Portuguese selva

Spanish selva

Other Fine Reference Works from Merriam-Webster